DIRECT MARKETING MARKET PLACE®

The Networking Source of the Direct Marketing Industry

DMMP 2019

DIRECT
MARKETING
MARKET PLACE®

The Networking Source of the Direct Marketing Industry

DMMP
2019

NRP Direct

A division of Treasured Works, LLC

New Providence, New Jersey

NRP Direct
A divison of Treasured Works, LLC.

President	R. Brett Grayson
Publisher	Robert J. Docherty

EDITORIAL

Managing Editor	Eileen Fanning
Content Manager	Ian Sidney O'Blenis
Content Editor	Linda Hummer

MARKETING

Creative Services Manager	Kathleen F. Stein

SALES

Sales Manager	Christopher Sharp

Published by NRP Direct, a divison of Treasured Works, LLC.

For information, contact:
NRP Direct
430 Mountain Avenue, Suite 403
New Providence, New Jersey 07974
1-844-592-4197
www.nrpdirect.com

DIRECT MARKETING MARKET PLACE is a trademark of Treasured Works, LLC.

Library of Congress Catalog Card Number 79-649244
International Standard Book Number 978-0-87217-071-1

Manufactured in the United States of America.

CONTENTS

PREFACE

Since 1980, NRP Direct's Direct Marketing Market Place (DMMP) has been the one-stop source for all of your direct marketing needs. DMMP encompasses each segment of the industry, from companies who use direct marketing to the companies that supply them.

CONTENT AND COVERAGE

At your fingertips are more than 8,500 organizations in the direct marketing industry, with more than 15,000 key personnel listed. To keep pace with the changing industry, we enhanced this directory to include e-mail and web site addresses when provided by the entrant. A company's listing will note whether a catalog is available online and if its products and services are available online.

Entries generally include the company name, address, phone and fax numbers, and at least one key executive. Some companies provide gross sales or billings, number of employees, countries in which they conduct business, whether they market primarily to consumers or businesses, and information about their direct marketing budget.

ARRANGEMENT AND INDEXES

DMMP is comprised of 43 sections divided into five chapters representing key segments of the direct marketing industry: Direct Marketers (1-19); Service Firms & Suppliers (20-34); Creative Services (35-39); Associations, Courses & Events (40-42); Bibliography (43).

DMMP features a cumulative Alphabetical Index to Companies & Individuals, which references all companies and personnel by section number. The company entries in this index feature the name, city and state or province, telephone and fax numbers, as well as e-mail and website addresses. The individual entries in this index reference each company's name, city and state or province, telephone and fax numbers. Companies and individuals are listed together in an alphabetical format.

The Direct Marketers chapter includes a geographic index listing all companies contained in the chapter by state or province. Two additional indexes identify direct marketers by their market: business or consumer. Geographic indexes precede each section in both the Service Firms and Suppliers and Creative Services chapters. These indexes allow the user to easily locate a company providing a particular service in his or her local area.

COMPILATION METHOD

The Direct Marketing Market Place is compiled and updated from information supplied by the organizations themselves. Wherever possible, entrants are verified by our research department.

RELATED SERVICES

Mailing lists or database licenses for data contained in the Direct Marketing Market Place may be ordered from Agnes Orlowska, 430 Mountain Avenue, Suite 403, New Providence, NJ 07974; Tel: 908-517-1116.

ACKNOWLEDGEMENTS

Thanks to the thousands of organizations throughout the United States and Canada who took the time to provide us with the information necessary to compile an accurate, comprehensive Direct Marketing Market Place.

In addition to keeping information in our directory as up to date as possible, we are constantly trying to improve the design and add features, which our subscribers will find useful. If you have a question about your company's listing or would like to offer any comments or suggestions, please call the NRP Direct Editorial Staff at 844-592-4197, or write to us at: NRP Direct, DMMP Editorial, 430 Mountain Avenue, Suite 403, New Providence, NJ 07974.

Association, Membership & Fundraising Organizations (1)

Listed in this section are associations, membership and fundraising organizations that use direct marketing. These may include, but are not limited to non-profit, religious, service or professional organizations. Direct marketing related organizations can be found in the section on Direct Marketing Associations, Clubs & Organizations (40).

AAA AUTO CLUB SOUTH
Subs. of American Automobile Association
1515 N Westshore Blvd
Tampa, FL 33607-4599
Telephone: (813) 289-5800, FAX:
(813) 289-1475, Web Site: www.aaa.com
Chmn Bd: Robert "Bob" R. Sharp
Pres & CEO: Thomas E. O'Brien
VP Mktg: Phil Malcolm
Conducts Business: U.S.
Employees: 2,000
Primary Market Served: Business & Consumer
Direct Marketing ad budget: $200,000
Founded: 1938

Offers roadside assistance, travel, insurance, & membership services.

AAA-CHICAGO MOTOR CLUB
Affiliate of American Automobile Association
975 Meridian Lake Dr
Aurora, IL 60504-4904
Telephone: (630) 328-7000, FAX:
(630) 499-8200, Web Site: www.aaa.com
Pres: Brad Roeber
Conducts Business: U.S.
Employees: 525
Primary Market Served: Business & Consumer
Catalog available online
Indirect online sales
Advertising/Marketing Budget Related to Direct Marketing: 26-50%
Direct Marketing ad budget: $6,000,000
Founded: 1905

Membership, travel, insurance & financial services.

AAA SOUTHERN NEW ENGLAND
Div. of American Automobile Association
110 Royal Little Dr
Providence, RI 02904-1860
Telephone: (401) 868-2045, FAX:
(401) 868-2088, Web Site: www.aaa.com
CEO & Pres: Mark A. Shaw
VP, Mktg: Mary Wyatt
Mng Dir Branch & Travel Opers: Mark Pelletuer
Car Doctor: John Paul
Conducts Business: U.S.
Employees: 1,900
Primary Market Served: Consumer
Catalog available online
Advertising/Marketing Budget Related to Direct Marketing: 26-50%
Direct Marketing ad budget:
Direct Mail: 74%
Magazines: 2%
TV/Radio: 24%
Founded: 1900

Tax-paying, not-for-profit organization offering a wide range of member services: automotive, travel agency, insurance & financial.

AAAS/SCIENCE
1200 New York Ave NW
Washington, DC 20005-3928
Telephone: (202) 326-6400, FAX:
(202) 371-9526, E-Mail:
membership@aaas.org, Web Site:
www.aaas.org
CEO & Dir: Alan I. Leshner Dr.
Pres: Phillip A. Sharp
Treas: David Evans Shaw
Conducts Business: U.S.
Employees: 210
Catalog available online
Direct online sales
Founded: 1848

Membership organization with some 137,000 individual members who are scientists, engineers & others interested in science. Publish Science, a weekly journal; Science Books & Films, a critical review of books, films, video cassettes & filmstrips & numerous other books. Also conduct various meetings each year.

AARP
601 E St NW
Washington, DC 20049-0003
Telephone: (202) 434-2277, FAX:
(202) 434-2525, Web Site: www.aarp.org
Sr VP Membership Devel & Member Experience: Lynn Mento
CEO: Jo Ann Jenkins
Pres & Dir: Jeannine English
Mng Editor & Dir: Carolyn Hall
Editor-in-Chief: Robert Love
CFO: Jocelyn Davis
Founded: 1958

Non-profit organization for the senior community offering automobile & homeowners insurance, as well as producing magazines. AARP serves members throughout the U.S.

ACBL
6575 Windchase Dr
Horn Lake, MS 38637-1523
Telephone: (662) 253-3100, FAX:
(662) 253-3187, E-Mail: service@acbl.org, Web Site: www.acbl.org
CEO: Robert Hartman
Dir. Fin: Joe Jones
Dir Mktg & Communs: Alexandra Turner
Human Resources Dir: Barbara Varner
Acctg: Stan Katz
Conducts Business: U.S., Canada, Mexico, Bermuda
Employees: 85
Primary Market Served: Business & Consumer
Founded: 1937

Membership service organization for bridge players in North America.

ACN USA
725 Leonard St
Brooklyn, NY 11222-2350
Telephone: (718) 609-0939, Toll Free:
(800) 628-6333, FAX: (718) 609-0938, Web Site: www.churchinneed.org
Exec Dir: Sarkis Boghjalian

Founded: 1947

Gift store selling religious items in support of the Church in Need

ADRA INTERNATIONAL
12501 Old Columbia Pike
Silver Spring, MD 20904-6601
Telephone: (301) 680-6373, Toll Free: (800) 424-2372, Web Site: www. adra.org
Bureau Chief, Mktg & Devel: Julio Munoz

Agency that helps those in need

ADRFCO
1612 K St NW (Suite 1102)
Washington, DC 20006-2849
Telephone: (202) 293-9640, FAX: (202) 463-7980, E-Mail: adrfco@ msn.com, Web Site: www.adrfco.org
Gen Counsel: Robert S. Tigner
Member: Kaitlin Barry
Primary Market Served: Business & Consumer

AFL-CIO
815 16th St NW
Washington, DC 20006
Telephone: (202) 637-5000, FAX: (202) 637-5323, (202) 637-5058, Web Site: www.aflcio.org
Pres: Richard Trumka
Sec & Treas: Elizabeth Shuler
Exec VP: Tefere Gebre
Employees: 380
Primary Market Served: Business & Consumer
Founded: 1955

Association federation of approximately 80 international unions.

AIIM INTERNATIONAL
1100 Wayne Ave (Suite 1100)
Silver Spring, MD 20910-5616
Telephone: (301) 587-8202, Toll Free: (800) 477-2446, FAX: (301) 587-2711, E-Mail: aiim@aiim.org, Web Site: www.aiim.org
CEO & Pres: John F. Mancini
Vice Chmn & Treas: Paul Engel
Dir. Fin & Admin: Felicia Dillard
VP: Atle Skjekkeland
Dir Systems of Engagement: Jesse Wilkins
Conducts Business: Worldwide
Employees: 27
Primary Market Served: Business
Catalog available online
Direct online sales
Founded: 1943

Global industry association that connects the users and suppliers of information management technologies; focuses on the technologies that are enablers of e-business; and produces events, provides industry research, education & information.

ALSAC - ST JUDE
262 Danny Thomas Pl
Memphis, TN 38105-1905
Telephone: (901) 495-3300, Toll Free: (800) 278-5833, FAX: (901) 495-3966, Web Site: www.stjude.org
Pres & CEO: Richard C. Shadyac
Chief Mktg. Officer: Emily Callahan
Chief Admin Officer: Emily S. Greer
Employees: 3,000
Primary Market Served: Consumer
Catalog available online
Indirect online sales
Founded: 1962

An international resource in the battle against childhood cancers. Conducts basic & clinical research into catastrophic childhood diseases, primarily childhood cancer & provides the necessary medical care for patients admitted to its research programs. Admission is based solely on medical criteria: children must be under 18 years of age with a physician referral, an illness relevant to studies at St Jude & have had no extensive treatment elsewhere. No family is turned away because of inability to pay. The hospital relies on donations from fund-raising throughout the U.S. The family & patient's domiciliary care is fully paid by St Jude.

AMVETS NATIONAL SERVICE FOUNDATION
Div. of AMVETS
4647 Forbes Blvd
Lanham, MD 20706
Telephone: (301) 459-6181, Toll Free: (800) 810-7148, FAX: (301) 459-5578, Web Site: www.amvetsnsf.org
Exec Dir: Kent A.D. Clark
Chair: Jimmy T. Smith
Conducts Business: U.S.
Employees: 2,000
Primary Market Served: Consumer
Direct Marketing ad budget:
Direct Mail: $10,000,000
Gross sales or billing: $23,000,000

Fundraising through direct mail for parent organization.

ARE PRESS
Div. of Association for Research & Enlightenment
215 67th St
Virginia Beach, VA 23451-2061
Telephone: (757) 428-3588, Toll Free: (800) 333-4499, FAX: (757) 491-0689, Web Site: www.arepress.com

Dir. Production, Customer Svc, Rights & Permissions ARE: Cassie McQuagge
Conducts Business: Worldwide
Primary Market Served: Business & Consumer
Advertising/Marketing Budget Related to Direct Marketing: 51-75%
Direct Marketing ad budget:
Direct Mail: $300,000
Founded: 1931

Non-profit open membership organization interested in spiritual growth, holistic healing & parapsychology through the Edgar Cayce readings.

ASM INTERNATIONAL
9639 Kinsman Rd
Materials Park, OH 44073-0002
Telephone: (440) 338-5151, Toll Free: (800) 336-5152, FAX: (440) 338-4634, E-Mail: customerservice@ asminternational.org, Web Site: www.asminternational.org
Interim Mng Dir: Tom Dudley
Conducts Business: Worldwide
Employees: 125
Primary Market Served: Consumer
Catalog available online
Direct online sales
Advertising/Marketing Budget Related to Direct Marketing: 76-100%
Direct Marketing ad budget:
Direct Mail: $2,000,000
Magazines: $10,000
Founded: 1913
Gross sales or billing: $16,000,000

Society of professionals in applications & research of metals & materials, supplying technical publications & educators.

ASPCA
424 E 92nd St
New York, NY 10028-6804
Telephone: (212) 876-7700, Web Site: www.aspca.org
Sr VP, Devel: Todd Hendricks

National animal welfare organization.

ASTM INTERNATIONAL
100 Barr Harbor Dr
West Conshohocken, PA 19428-2959
Telephone: (610) 832-9500, FAX: (610) 832-9555, E-Mail: service@ astm.org, Web Site: www.astm.org
Pres: James Thomas
Exec. VP: Katherine E. Morgan
VP: Teresa Cendrowska
Dir: Jim Olshefsky
Dir: Robert Morgan
Conducts Business: Worldwide
Employees: 200
Primary Market Served: Business
Catalog available online

Indirect online sales
Founded: 1898

Developer of voluntary consensus standards for materials, products, systems & services. Branch offices in Washington, DC & Hertfordshire, England.

ABBEY OF GETHSEMANI

3642 Monks Rd
Trappist, KY 40051
Telephone: (502) 549-4133, FAX: (502) 549-4124, E-Mail: reservations@monks.org, Web Site: www.monks.org
Mgr: Brother Anselm Brown
Friar: Peter Tong
Friar: Anton Rusnak
Conducts Business: U.S.
Employees: 85
Primary Market Served: Business & Consumer
Advertising/Marketing Budget Related to Direct Marketing: 76-100%
Founded: 1848

Monastery of Cistercian monks. Markets cheese, fruitcakes & fudge.

ACCURACY IN MEDIA INC

4350 E West Hwy (Suite 555)
Bethesda, MD 20814
Telephone: (202) 364-4401, FAX: (202) 364-4098, E-Mail: info@aim.org, Web Site: www.aim.org
Chmn: Donald Irvine
Dir: Cliff Kincaid
Conducts Business: U.S.
Employees: 16
Primary Market Served: Business & Consumer
Catalog available online
Direct online sales
Founded: 1969

Newsletter about news media bias, error & distortion - target audience is news media consumers.

ACTIONAID

1420 K St NW (Suite 900)
Washington, DC 20005-2507
Telephone: (202) 835-1240, E-Mail: info@actionaid.org, Web Site: www.actionaidusa.org
Exec Dir: Marie Clarke
Dir Devel: Scotti Hutton

International organization for a world free from poverty & injustice.

THE ADVERTISING COUNCIL INC

815 2nd Ave (fl 9)
New York, NY 10017-4511

Telephone: (212) 922-1500, FAX: (212) 922-1676, E-Mail: info@adcouncil.org, Web Site: www.adcouncil.org
Pres & CEO: Lisa Sherman
CFO & Exec VP: Jon Fish
Conducts Business: U.S.
Employees: 45
Primary Market Served: Business & Consumer
Catalog available online
Advertising/Marketing Budget Related to Direct Marketing: 51-75%
Founded: 1942
Gross sales or billing: $1,000,000,000

Non-profit organization that works to create, produce, & distribute public service announcements to the media, to increase public awareness of critical issues in education, environment, substance abuse, community service, health & public safety.

AFFINITY FEDERAL CREDIT UNION

73 Mountainview Blvd
Basking Ridge, NJ 07920
Telephone: (908) 860-7300, FAX: (908) 860-3883, Web Site: www.affinityfcu.org
Pres & CEO: John Fenton
Primary Market Served: Consumer

Member owned not-for-profit full service financial institution.

AFRICAN WILDLIFE FOUNDATION

1400 16th St NW (Suite 120)
Washington, DC 20036-2249
Telephone: (202) 939-3333, Toll Free: (888) 494-5354, FAX: (202) 939-3332, Web Site: www.awf.org
VP Philanthropy & Mktg: Craig Sholley

International organization that benefits wildlife & people alike.

AIR FORCE SERGEANTS ASSOCIATION

5211 Auth Rd
Suitland, MD 20746-4339
Telephone: (301) 899-3500, Toll Free: (800) 638-0594, FAX: (301) 899-8136, E-Mail: staff@hqafsa.org, Web Site: www.hqafsa.org
CEO: Robert L. Frank
Dir Member, Field Rels & Communs: Keith A. Reid
Conducts Business: U.S. & Europe
Primary Market Served: Consumer
Catalog available online
Direct online sales
Advertising/Marketing Budget Related to Direct Marketing: 76-100%

Founded: 1961

Non-profit association for Air Force Active Duty, Air National Guard, Air Force Reserve & personnel in active retired and veteran status. Legislation & lobbying for Air Force enlisted personnel. Also group insurance & service policies for members.

AIRCRAFT OWNERS & PILOTS ASSOCIATION

421 Aviation Way
Frederick, MD 21701-4756
Telephone: (301) 695-2000, Toll Free: (800) 872-2672, FAX: (301) 695-2375, E-Mail: aopahq@aopa.org, Web Site: www.aopa.org
Pres CEO: Craig Fuller
VP, New Prod Devel & Interactive Mktg: Chris Ward
Conducts Business: U.S.
Employees: 180
Primary Market Served: Consumer
Direct Marketing ad budget:
Direct Mail: 90%
Magazines: 3%
Telephone: 7%
Founded: 1939

Membership solicitation, aviation safety seminars & courses promoted by mail. Also offer merchandise & special services to members.

ALEXIAN BROTHERS BONAVENTURE HOUSE

825 W Wellington Ave
Chicago, IL 60657
Telephone: (773) 327-9921, FAX: (773) 327-9113, E-Mail: info@abam.org, Web Site: www.bonaventurehouse.org
Exec Dir: Cheryl Potts
Dir Community Housing: Nora Johnson
Bus Mgr: Adrian Cerda
Primary Market Served: Consumer

Non-profit housing project for men & women living with AIDS.

ALLIANCE DEFENSE FUND

15100 N 90th St
Scottsdale, AZ 85260-2901
Telephone: (480) 444-0020, Web Site: www.telladf.org
Direct Mktg Analyst: Candace Duncan
Primary Market Served: Consumer

ALLIANCE OF AREA BUSINESS PUBLICATIONS

c/o American Academy of Medical Acupuncture, 4929 Wilshire Blvd, Ste 428, Los Angeles, Ca 90010-3817
1970 E Grand Ave (Suite 300)

Redondo Beach, CA 90245-5038
Telephone: (310) 379-8261, FAX: (310) 379-8283, E-Mail: info@ bizpubs.org, Web Site: www. bizpubs.org
Pres: Jeff Nuttall
VP: Lisa Jones
Sec & Treas: Joe Zwiebel
Exec Dir: C. James Dowden
Dir: Shelly Elmore
Conducts Business: U.S., Canada
Employees: 3
Primary Market Served: Business
Founded: 1979
Gross sales or billing: $500,000

Products include a database of 2500 privately held companies & "The Newsmaker's Guide to Local Business Publications."

ALPHA DOG MARKETING INC

9060 Andermatt Dr Ste 101
Lincoln, NE 68526-9644
Telephone: (402) 486-0668, Web Site: www.alphadogmktg.com
CEO: Mike Monk

Full service direct marketing agency serving non-profit organizations

ALZHEIMER SOCIETY OF CANADA

20 Eglinton Ave W (Suite 1600)
Toronto, ON, Canada M4R 1K8
Telephone: (416) 488-8772, Toll Free: (800) 616-8816, FAX: (416) 488-3778, E-Mail: gpage@alzheimer.ca, Web Site: www.alzheimer.ca
Chief Commun & Devel: Graeme Page
Conducts Business: Canada
Employees: 25
Primary Market Served: Business & Consumer
Founded: 1977

Not-for-profit health organization working nationwide to improve the quality of life for Canadians affected by Alzheimer's disease & other dementias & advance the research for the cause & cure.

ALZHEIMER'S ASSOCIATION

225 N Michigan Ave, Fl 17
Chicago, IL 60601-7757
Telephone: (312) 335-8700, Toll Free: (800) 272-3900, Web Site: www.alz. org
VP Mktg & Brand Engagement: Michael Carson
Primary Market Served: Consumer

AMERGENT

9 Centennial Dr Unit 201
Peabody, MA 01960-7940
Toll Free: (800) 370-7500, FAX: (978) 531-0400, Web Site: www.amergent. com
Pres: Jack Doyle

AMERICAN ACADEMY OF NEUROLOGY

201 Chicago Ave
Minneapolis, MN 55415-1126
Telephone: (651) 695-2793, Toll Free: 800 (879)-1960, FAX: (612) 454-2746, E-Mail: memberservices@aan. com, Web Site: www.aan.com
Dir. & CEO: Catherine M. Rydell
Chief Membership, Communs & Publications Officer: Jason Kopinski

AMERICAN ARBITRATION ASSOCIATION

120 Broadway (fl 15)
New York, NY 10271-0016
Telephone: (212) 716-5800, Toll Free: (800) 778-7879, FAX: (212) 716-5905, E-Mail: kesslerw@adr.org, Web Site: www.adr.org
VP Corp Communs: Wayne Kessler
Conducts Business: U.S., Europe, Asia
Employees: 65
Primary Market Served: Business & Consumer
Catalog available online
Direct online sales
Gross sales or billing: $125,000,000

The American Arbitration Association (AAA) is available to resolve a wide range of disputes through mediation, arbitration, elections and other out-of-court settlement procedures. AAA offers ADR (alternative dispute resolution), systems design, educational seminars and publications.

AMERICAN ASSOCIATION FOR JUSTICE

777 6th St NW (Suite 200), The Leonard M Ring Law Center
Washington, DC 20001-3707
Telephone: (202) 965-3500, Toll Free: (800) 424-2725, FAX: (202) 625-7313, E-Mail: membership@justice. org, Web Site: www.justice.org
CEO: Linda Lipsen
Treas: Bruce H. Stern
VP: Kathleen Nastri
Conducts Business: U.S., Canada
Employees: 160
Primary Market Served: Business
Direct Marketing ad budget: $40,000
Direct Mail: 60%
Magazines: 40%

Founded: 2006
Membership association for trial lawyers. Market membership lists of trial attorneys.

AMERICAN ASSOCIATION OF CRITICAL-CARE NURSES

101 Columbia
Aliso Viejo, CA 92656-4109
Telephone: (949) 362-2000, Toll Free: (800) 809-CARE, FAX: (949) 362-2020, E-Mail: info@aacn.com, Web Site: www.aacn.org
Pres: Karen McQuillan
CEO: Dana Woods
Sec & Dir: Debra Klein
Conducts Business: Worldwide
Employees: 110
Primary Market Served: Consumer
Catalog available online
Direct online sales
Advertising/Marketing Budget Related to Direct Marketing: 51-75%
Direct Marketing ad budget:
Direct Mail: 50%
Magazines: 50%
Founded: 1969

Specialty nursing organization with over 76,000 members. The Association now has more than 270 chapters worldwide & is working toward a healthcare system driven by patients' needs where critical care nurses make their optimal contribution.

AMERICAN ASSOCIATION OF INDIVIDUAL INVESTORS

625 N Michigan Ave
Chicago, IL 60611-3110
Telephone: (312) 280-0170, FAX: (312) 280-9883, E-Mail: adam@aaii. com, Web Site: www.aaii.com
Chmn: James B. Cloonan
VP Mktg: Adam B. Pfeffer
Pres: John D. Markese
VP, Opers: Harry Madorin
Conducts Business: U.S.
Employees: 21
Primary Market Served: Consumer
Catalog available online
Direct online sales
Direct Marketing ad budget: $2,000,000
Direct Mail: 96%
Online: 4%
Founded: 1978
Gross sales or billing: $5,000,000

Membership organization for serious individuals managing own assets. Publish journal & other educational materials.

AMERICAN ASSOCIATION OF UNIVERSITY WOMEN

1111 16th St NW
Washington, DC 20036-4809
Telephone: (202) 785-7700, FAX:
(202) 872-1425, E-Mail: connect@
aauw.org, Web Site: www.aauw.org
VP Direct Mktg: Christy Jones
VP Editorial & Media: Rebecca Lanning

AMERICAN BANKERS ASSOCIATION

1120 Connecticut Ave NW
Washington, DC 20036-3959
Telephone: (202) 663-5000, Toll Free:
(800) 226-5377, FAX: (202) 663-
7543, Web Site: www.aba.com
Pres & CEO: Rob Nichols
Conducts Business: U.S.
Employees: 400
Primary Market Served: Business
Catalog available online
Direct online sales
Advertising/Marketing Budget Related
to Direct Marketing: 51-75%
Direct Marketing ad budget:
Direct Mail: 70%
Magazines: 5%
Newspapers: 20%
TV/Radio: 5%
Founded: 1875
Gross sales or billing: $83,700,000
Non-profit organization of American
Bankers.

AMERICAN BAR ASSOCIATION

321 N Clark St
Chicago, IL 60654-5000
Telephone: (312) 988-5000, Toll Free:
(800) 285-2221, FAX: (312) 988-
5177, Web Site: www.abanet.org
Pres: Paulette Brown
Primary Market Served: Business &
Consumer

Professional organization with over
380,000 members. All lists available
for rental. Provides law school accreditation, legal education, & lawyers &
judges assistance programs to lawyers,
law students & legal professionals.

AMERICAN BASEBALL COACHES ASSOCIATION

4101 Piedmont Pkwy (Suite C)
Greensboro, NC 27410
Telephone: (336) 821-3140, FAX:
(336) 886-0000, E-Mail: abca@abca.
org, Web Site: www.abca.org
Exec Dir: Craig Keilitz
Membership/Convention Coord: Zack
Haile
Admin Asst: Juahn Clark

Conducts Business: U.S.
Employees: 4
Catalog available online
Advertising/Marketing Budget Related
to Direct Marketing: 0-25%
Founded: 1945
National organization of amateur baseball coaches.

AMERICAN BIBLE SOCIETY

1865 Broadway
New York, NY 10023-7505
Telephone: (212) 408-1200, FAX:
(212) 408-1264, Web Site: www.
americanbible.org
Pres & CEO: Roy L. Peterson
Sr VP & CFO: Julia A. Oliver
Sr VP Devel: Laura Dabkowski
Sr VP Ministry: Dr. Geof Morin
Conducts Business: Worldwide
Employees: 300
Primary Market Served: Consumer
Advertising/Marketing Budget Related
to Direct Marketing: 76-100%
Founded: 1816

Translate, publish & distribute scriptures.

AMERICAN BREAST CANCER FOUNDATION

10400 Little Patuxent Pkwy (Suite 480)
Columbia, MD 21044
Telephone: (410) 730-5105, E-Mail:
info@abcf.org, Web Site: www.abcf.
org
CEO: Paul "Jacky" Loube
Dir Devel: Katherine Mele
Primary Market Served: Consumer

AMERICAN CANCER SOCIETY

1599 Clifton Rd NE
Atlanta, GA 30329-4251
Telephone: (404) 320-3333, Toll Free:
(800) ACS-2345, FAX: (404) 329-
5787, Web Site: www.cancer.org
CEO & Dir: Gary M. Reedy
Sr VP Prevention & Early Detection:
Ralph DeVitto
Chief Devel Officer: Sharon Byers
Founded: 1913
Gross sales or billing: $1,000,000,000

Nationwide volunteer health organization dedicated to eliminating cancer as
a major health problem through research, education & service.

AMERICAN CATALOG MAILERS ASSOCIATION

PO Box 41211
Providence, RI 02940-1211
Toll Free: (800) 509-9514, E-Mail:
info@catalogmailers.org, Web Site:
www.catalogmailers.org

Pres & Exec Dir: Hamilton Davison
VP & Deputy Dir: Paul Miller
Primary Market Served: Consumer

Furnishing services for direct mail advertising.

AMERICAN CHEMICAL SOCIETY

1155 16th St NW
Washington, DC 20036-4839
Telephone: (202) 872-4600, Toll Free:
(800) 227-5558, FAX: (202) 452-
8913, E-Mail: service@acs.org, Web
Site: www.acs.org
CEO & Exec Dir: Thomas M. Connelly
Jr
Pres: Donna J. Nelson
Conducts Business: Worldwide
Employees: 1,800
Founded: 1876

Scientific society providing chemical
knowledge for chemists & chemical engineers, through journals, books, professional development courses &
national meetings.

AMERICAN CIVIL LIBERTIES UNION FOUNDATION

125 Broad St (fl 18)
New York, NY 10004-2454
Telephone: (212) 549-2500, Web Site:
www.aclu.org
CEO: Anthony Romero
Pres: Susan N. Herman
Chief Devel Officer: Mark Wier
Primary Market Served: Consumer
Founded: 1920

Works to preserve the individual rights
& liberties guaranteed by the Constitution & the laws of the US to everyone
in this country.

AMERICAN COLLEGE OF CARDIOLOGY

2400 N St NW
Washington, DC 20037-1153
Telephone: (202) 375-6000, FAX:
(202) 375-7000, E-Mail: resource@
acc.org, Web Site: www.acc.org
CEO: Shalom Jacobovitz
Assoc VP Mktg: Catherine Ort-Mabry
Primary Market Served: Consumer

Strives to achieve its purpose to improve cardiovascular health through education, research, quality care &
policy.

AMERICAN COLLEGE OF EMERGENCY PHYSICIANS

1125 Executive Cir
Irving, TX 75038-2522

Telephone: (972) 550-0911, Toll Free:
(800) 798-1822, FAX: (972) 580-
2816, Web Site: www.acep.org
Dir: Marjorie Geist
Primary Market Served: Consumer

AMERICAN COLLEGE OF PHYSICIAN EXECUTIVES
400 N Ashley Dr (Suite 400)
Tampa, FL 33602-4322
Telephone: (813) 287-2000, Toll Free:
(800) 562-8088, FAX: (813) 287-
8993, E-Mail: acpe@acpe.org, Web
Site: www.acpe.org
CEO: Peter Angood
Sr Mgr Mktg: Debra Sher
Sr Mgr, Membership & Community:
Charisse Jimenez
Graphic Designer: Jill Howell Fasnacht
Conducts Business: U.S.
Employees: 20
Primary Market Served: Consumer
Founded: 1974

Provide medical business management
education to physician executives.

AMERICAN COUNCIL ON EXERCISE
4851 Paramount Dr
San Diego, CA 92123
Telephone: (858) 576-6500, Toll Free:
(888) 825-3636, FAX: (858) 576-
6564, Web Site: www.acefitness.org
Pres CEO: Scott Goudeseune
Exec VP Product & Bus Devel: Kerri
O'Brien
Primary Market Served: Consumer
Catalog available online
Direct online sales

Non-profit fitness education & certification organization.

AMERICAN COUNSELING ASSOCIATION
305 N Beech Cir
Broken Arrow, OK 74012-2293
Telephone: (918) 994-4413, FAX:
(918) 663-7058, E-Mail:
webmaster@counseling.org, Web
Site: www.counseling.org
Pres: Susan Meyerle
Exec Dir: Mary Alice Olsan
Conducts Business: U.S.
Employees: 60
Primary Market Served: Business &
Consumer
Catalog available online
Direct online sales
Advertising/Marketing Budget Related
to Direct Marketing: 51-75%
Founded: 1942

Gross sales or billing: $9,000,000
Non-profit membership organization
with a growing membership of over
52,000 counselors & human development specialists.

AMERICAN DIABETES ASSOCIATION
1701 N Beauregard St
Alexandria, VA 22311-1733
Telephone: (703) 549-1500, Toll Free:
(800) 342-2383, Web Site: www.
diabetes.org
CEO: Larry Hausner
Natl Dir Govt Affairs: Megan Gordon
Exec VP & CFO: Debbie Johnson
Primary Market Served: Consumer
Founded: 1940

Provides research based advisory services focusing on diabetes & its treatment as well as conducting programs &
publishing its findings.

AMERICAN FEDERATION OF ASTROLOGERS
6535 S Rural Rd
Tempe, AZ 85283-3746
Telephone: (480) 838-1751, Toll Free:
(888) 301-7630, FAX: (480) 838-
8293, E-Mail: afa@msn.com, Web
Site: www.astrologers.com
Exec Dir: Kris Brandt Riske
Opers Mgr: Jack Cipolla
Conducts Business: Worldwide
Employees: 3
Primary Market Served: Business &
Consumer
Catalog available online
Direct online sales
Direct Marketing ad budget:
Online: 100%
Founded: 1938

Membership, educational, astrology.

THE AMERICAN FILM INSTITUTE
2021 N Western Ave
Los Angeles, CA 90027-1657
Telephone: (323) 856-7600, FAX:
(323) 467-4578, Web Site: www.afi.
com
Dir & CEO: Jean Firstenberg
Chief Devel Officer: John Campbell
Conducts Business: U.S.
Employees: 115
Primary Market Served: Consumer
Catalog available online

A national trust dedicated to preserving
the heritage of film & television; to
identifying, developing & training creative individuals; and to presenting the
moving image as an art form. Offices
in Los Angeles.

AMERICAN FORESTS
1220 L St NW (Suite 750)
Washington, DC 20005-4079
Telephone: (202) 737-1944, FAX:
(202) 737-2457, E-Mail: info@
amfor.org, Web Site: www.
americanforests.org
Pres. & CEO: Scott Steen
COO: Peter Hutchins
VP Corp & Member Engagement: Mat-
thew Boyer
Conducts Business: U.S., Canada
Employees: 20
Primary Market Served: Business &
Consumer
Direct Marketing ad budget: $250,000
Direct Mail: 98%
Magazines: 2%
Founded: 1875
Gross sales or billing: $4,000,000

All members, 30,000+, receive a quarterly highlighting our Global ReLeaf
projects, involving tree planting and re-
forestation projects aimed at repairing
damaged ecosystems.

AMERICAN FOUNDATION FOR THE BLIND INC
2 Penn Plaza (Suite 1102)
New York, NY 10121-1100
Telephone: (212) 502-7600, FAX:
(212) 502-7777, E-Mail: afbinfo@
afb.org, Web Site: www.afb.org
Pres & CEO: Carl Augusto
Mktg & Communs Mgr: Amanda Kol-
ling
Press & Professional Devel: George
Abbott
Conducts Business: U.S.
Employees: 125
Primary Market Served: Business &
Consumer
Catalog available online
Direct online sales
Gross sales or billing: $20,500,000

Individual and family services for people who are blind or visually impaired.
Taking a national leadership role in
public policy & legislation, information
& education programs, and diversified
products & services.

AMERICAN HEALTH INFORMATION MANAGEMENT ASSOCIATION
233 N Michigan Ave (21st fl)
Chicago, IL 60601-5519
Telephone: (312) 233-1100, Toll Free:
(800) 335-5535, FAX: (312) 233-
1090, E-Mail: info@ahima.org, Web
Site: www.ahima.org
CEO & Dir: Alan F. Dowling
Dir Pub Rels: Craig G. May
Conducts Business: Worldwide

Primary Market Served: Business & Consumer
Catalog available online
Direct online sales
Advertising/Marketing Budget Related to Direct Marketing: 76-100%
Founded: 1928
Gross sales or billing: $7,500,000

AMERICAN HEART ASSOCIATION

7272 Greenville Ave
Dallas, TX 75231-5129
Telephone: (214) 373-6300, Toll Free: (800) AHA-USA-1, FAX: (214) 373-3406, Web Site: www.americanheart.org
CEO: Nancy Brown
Chief Devel Officer: Suzie Upton
Pres: Mark A. Creager
Chmn: Alvin L. Royse
Conducts Business: Worldwide
Employees: 550
Primary Market Served: Consumer

Association dedicated to the reduction of death & disability due to cardiovascular disease & stroke. Affiliates nationwide.

AMERICAN HUMANE ASSOCIATION

1400 16th St NW Ste 360
Washington, DC 20036-2215
Telephone: (303) 925-9497, Web Site: www.americanhumane.org
CEO, Pres & Dir: Robin R. Ganzert

AMERICAN INDIAN COLLEGE FUND

8333 Greenwood Blvd
Denver, CO 80221
Telephone: (303) 426-8900, Toll Free: (800) 776-3863, FAX: (303) 426-1200, Web Site: www.collegefund.org
Exec Dir: Richard B. Williams
Primary Market Served: Consumer
Founded: 1989

AMERICAN INSTITUTE FOR CANCER RESEARCH

1759 R St NW
Washington, DC 20009-2570
Telephone: (202) 328-7744, Toll Free: (800) 843-8114, FAX: (202) 328-7226, E-Mail: aicrweb@aicr.org, Web Site: www.aicr.org
Pres: Marilyn Gentry
CEO: Kelly B. Browning
Conducts Business: U.S.
Catalog available online
Direct online sales

Founded: 1982
Funding support for research into prevention of cancer through nutrition & diet.

AMERICAN INSTITUTE FOR ECONOMIC RESEARCH

250 Division St
Great Barrington, MA 01230-1198
Telephone: (413) 528-1216, Toll Free: (888) 528-1216, FAX: (413) 528-0103, E-Mail: info@aier.org, Web Site: www.aier.org
Pres: Stephen Adams
Dir, Member Svcs, Production & Fulfillment: Kelly Fox
Communs & Pub Affairs Mgr: Aaron Nathans
Employees: 22
Founded: 1933

AMERICAN INSTITUTE OF CHEMICAL ENGINEERS

120 Wall St (fl 23)
New York, NY 10005-4020
Telephone: (203) 702-7660, Toll Free: (800) 242-4363, FAX: (203) 775-5177, E-Mail: xpress@aiche.org, Web Site: www.aiche.org
Exec Dir: June C. Wispelwey
Dir Opers: Bette Lawler
Primary Market Served: Business & Consumer
Catalog available online
Indirect online sales
Advertising/Marketing Budget Related to Direct Marketing: 76-100%
Direct Marketing ad budget: $200,000
Founded: 1908

Individual professional organization of chemical engineers, dedicated to continually improving service to members, employees, the chemical engineering profession & society.

AMERICAN INSTITUTE OF CPAS

RP-NFOA
1211 Avenue of the Americas (Suite 1900)
New York, NY 10036-8775
Telephone: (212) 596-6200, Toll Free: (888) 777-7077, FAX: (212) 596-6213, Web Site: www.aicpa.org
Pres & CEO: Barry C. Melancon
Sr VP Commun, Media, News & Prof Pathways: Janice Maiman
Sr VP Mngmt Acctg & Global Markets: Arleen R. Thomas
Conducts Business: U.S.
Employees: 400
Primary Market Served: Business & Consumer

Advertising/Marketing Budget Related to Direct Marketing: 76-100%
Founded: 1887
Non-profit membership organization for CPAs.

AMERICAN KIDNEY FUND

6110 Executive Blvd (Suite 1010)
Rockville, MD 20852
Telephone: (301) 881-3052, Toll Free: (800) 638-8299, FAX: (301) 881-0898, Web Site: www.kidneyfund.org
Dir Communs: Tamara Ruggiero
Mng Dir Devel: Tracy Hart
Founded: 1971

Not for profit organization that provides clinical research & financial assistance services focusing on kidney related diseases.

THE AMERICAN LEGION NATIONAL HEADQUARTERS

5745 Lee Rd, John H. Geiger Operations Ctr
Indianapolis, IN 46216
Telephone: (317) 860-3100, Toll Free: (800) 433-2700, FAX: (317) 860-3001, Web Site: www.legion.org
Exec Dir: Jeffrey Brown
Membership Dir: Billy R. Johnson
Mktg Dir: Ronald E. Brooks
Conducts Business: U.S., Canada
Primary Market Served: Consumer
Direct Marketing ad budget:
Direct Mail: 90%
TV/Radio: 10%

Non-profit service organization serving the needs of wartime veterans.

AMERICAN LIBRARY ASSOCIATION-PUBLISHING SERVICES

50 E Huron St
Chicago, IL 60611
Telephone: (312) 944-6780, Toll Free: (800) 545-2433, FAX: (312) 440-9374, Web Site: www.ala.org
Dir: Rachel Johnson
Assoc Exec Dir: Donald Chatham
Conducts Business: Worldwide
Employees: 0
Primary Market Served: Business & Consumer
Direct online sales
Advertising/Marketing Budget Related to Direct Marketing: 26-50%
Direct Marketing ad budget:
Direct Mail: 90%
Magazines: 10%

Founded: 1894

Publish & market books & periodicals (advertising & subscriptions) for librarians, information specialists & educators.

AMERICAN LUNG ASSOCIATION

55 W Wacker Dr (Suite 1150)
Chicago, IL 60601
Telephone: (212) 889-3370, Toll Free: (800) 548-8252, FAX: (212) 889-3375, E-Mail: info@alany.org, Web Site: www.lungusa.org
Natl Pres & CEO: Harold P. Wimmer
VP Mktg & Communs: Kim Lacina
Conducts Business: U.S.
Primary Market Served: Consumer
Founded: 1904

Non-profit health organization whose mission is to prevent lung disease and promote lung health. Uses direct mail to raise funds from the general public.

AMERICAN MANAGEMENT ASSOCIATION

1601 Broadway
New York, NY 10019-7434
Telephone: (212) 586-8100, FAX: (212) 903-8186, Web Site: www.amanet.org
Pres & CEO: Edward T. Reilly
Sr VP Mktg & Membership: Robert Smith
VP Sales & Mktg: Rosemary Carlough
Conducts Business: U.S., Canada, Mexico, Japan, Belgium
Employees: 800
Primary Market Served: Business
Advertising/Marketing Budget Related to Direct Marketing: 76-100%
Direct Marketing ad budget:
Direct Mail: 90%
Telephone: 10%
Founded: 1923
Gross sales or billing: $200,000,000

Business management seminars and publishing to business professionals.

AMERICAN MEDICAL ASSOCIATION

Div. of Data Base Products & Licensing
515 N State St
Chicago, IL 60610
Telephone: (312) 464-5000, Toll Free: (800) 621-8335, FAX: (312) 464-4184, Web Site: www.ama-assn.org
CEO & Exec VP: James L. Madara
COO: Bernard L. Hengesbaugh
Sr VP & Chief Communs & Mktg Officer: Rodrigo A. Sierra
Conducts Business: Worldwide
Employees: 1,000

Primary Market Served: Business
Advertising/Marketing Budget Related to Direct Marketing: 26-50%
Gross sales or billing: $260,000,000

Non-profit organization promoting the science & art of medicine.

AMERICAN NATIONAL STANDARDS INSTITUTE

25 W 43rd St (fl 4)
New York, NY 10036
Telephone: (212) 642-4900, FAX: (212) 398-0023, Web Site: www.ansi.org
Sr Mgr Membership & Devel: Susan Bose

AMERICAN NICARAGUAN FOUNDATION

1000 NW 57th Ct Ste 770
Miami, FL 33126-3288
Telephone: (305) 374-3391, FAX: (305) 374-5993, Web Site: www.aidnicaragua.org
Pres: F. Alfredo Pellas Jr
Exec Dir: Rafael Sanchez
Primary Market Served: Consumer

AMERICAN NUMISMATIC ASSOCIATION

818 N Cascade Ave
Colorado Springs, CO 80903-3279
Telephone: (719) 632-2646, Web Site: www.money.org
Exec Dir: Kim Kiick

AMERICAN NURSES' ASSOCIATION

8515 Georgia Ave (Suite 400)
Silver Spring, MD 20006-3492
Telephone: (301) 628-5000, Toll Free: (800) 274-4262, (800) 284-2378, FAX: (301) 628-5001, Web Site: www.nursingworld.org
CEO: Marla J. Weston
Conducts Business: U.S.
Employees: 150
Primary Market Served: Consumer

National, professional association for registered nurses.

THE AMERICAN PHYTOPATHOLOGICAL SOCIETY

3340 Pilot Knob Rd
Saint Paul, MN 55121-2055
Telephone: (651) 454-7250, FAX: (651) 454-0766, E-Mail: apsheadquarters@scisoc.org, Web Site: www.apsnet.org
Exec VP: Amy Hope
Publications: Greg Grahek

AMERICAN PSYCHOLOGICAL ASSOCIATION

750 First St NE
Washington, DC 20002-4242
Telephone: (202) 336-5500, Toll Free: (800) 374-2721, FAX: (202) 336-5568, E-Mail: order@apa.org, Web Site: www.apa.org
Pres: Ronald Levant
Publr & Exec Dir Pubns & Databases: Gary R. VandenBos
Conducts Business: Worldwide
Employees: 650
Primary Market Served: Business & Consumer
Catalog available online
Direct online sales
Direct Marketing ad budget: $600,000
Direct Mail: $400,000
Magazines: $200,000
Founded: 1892
Gross sales or billing: $5,500,000

Publish scientific, scholarly journals, psychology books, computer tapes & CD-ROMs. Focuses on diagnosis, treatment & prevention of mental illnesses including mental retardation & substance-related disorders serving communities in the US.

AMERICAN RADIO RELAY LEAGUE

225 Main St
Newington, CT 06111-1494
Telephone: (860) 594-0200, FAX: (860) 594-0259, Web Site: www.arrl.org
CEO: Thomas "Tom" J. Gallagher
Primary Market Served: Consumer

Provides entertainment related services and broadcasts aural programs by radio to local public in the state of Connecticut.

AMERICAN RED CROSS

2025 East St NW (Suite 100), National HQ
Washington, DC 20006-5009
Telephone: (202) 303-5214, Toll Free: (800) RED-CROSS, FAX: (202) 303-6604, Web Site: www.redcross.org
Pres, CEO & Dir: Gail J. McGovern
Chief Mktg Officer: Peggy Dyer
Chief Devel Officer: Neal Litvack
Chief Information Officer: John Crary
Conducts Business: U.S.
Employees: 25,000
Primary Market Served: Business & Consumer

Founded: 1881

Non-profit organization providing disaster relief, blood collection & health & safety education.

AMERICAN RUNNING ASSOCIATION

dba American Medical Athletic Association
4405 East-West Hwy (Suite 405)
Bethesda, MD 20814-4522
Telephone: (301) 913-9517, Toll Free: (800) 776-2732, FAX: (301) 913-9520, E-Mail: run@americanrunning.org, Web Site: www.americanrunning.org
Exec Dir: David Watt
Editor Running & FitNews: Jeffrey Venables
Proj Cons: Barbara Baldwin
Conducts Business: U.S.
Employees: 3
Primary Market Served: Business & Consumer
Catalog available online
Direct online sales
Advertising/Marketing Budget Related to Direct Marketing: 51-75%
Direct Marketing ad budget: $10,000
Direct Mail: 70%
Magazines: 10%
Online: 20%
Founded: 1968
Gross sales or billing: $400,000

Non-profit educational association of athletes & sports medicine professionals, dedicated to enhancing the physical & mental well-being of runners from youth to adult through the promotion of exercise.

AMERICAN SOCIETY FOR QUALITY

600 N Plankinton Ave
Milwaukee, WI 53203
Telephone: (414) 272-8575, Toll Free: (800) 248-1946, FAX: (414) 272-1734, E-Mail: help@asq.org, Web Site: www.asq.org
CEO: William Troy
Pres: Ron Atkinson
Employees: 220
Primary Market Served: Business & Consumer
Catalog available online
Direct online sales
Founded: 1946
Gross sales or billing: $10,000,000

Identify, communicate & promote the use of quality principles, concepts & technologies through membership in a professional society; also has a substantial book publishing operation; offers training, conferences & a series of professional certifications in the field of quality.

AMERICAN SOCIETY OF CIVIL ENGINEERS

1801 Alexander Bell Dr
Reston, VA 20191-4382
Telephone: (703) 295-6000, Toll Free: (800) 548-2723, FAX: (703) 295-6343, Web Site: www.asce.org
Exec Dir & Chief of Staff & Sec: Mark W. Woodson
Deputy Exec Dir: Lawrence H. Roth
Catalog available online

Non-profit professional association for civil engineers.

AMERICAN SOCIETY OF INTERIOR DESIGNERS

718 7th St NW (Floor 4)
Washington, DC 20001
Telephone: (202) 546-3480, FAX: (202) 546-3240, E-Mail: membership@asid.org, Web Site: www.asid.org
CEO: Randy W. Fiser
VP Strategic Mktg & Commun: Kevin Mulvaney
Conducts Business: U.S., Canada, U.K.
Employees: 45
Primary Market Served: Business & Consumer
Catalog available online
Indirect online sales
Founded: 1931

Mailing list rentals to firms that promote products or services to the interior design profession.

AMERICAN SOCIETY OF RADIOLOGIC TECHNOLOGISTS

15000 Central Ave SE
Albuquerque, NM 87123-3909
Telephone: (505) 298-4500, FAX: (505) 298-5063, Web Site: www.asrt.org
Pres: William J. Brennan
Primary Market Served: Consumer

Operates as a non-profit organization advocating advancement in the imaging & radiation therapy profession.

AMERICAN SOCIETY ON AGING

575 Market St (Suite 2100)
San Francisco, CA 94105-2869
Telephone: (415) 974-9600, Toll Free: (800) 537-9728, FAX: (415) 974-0300, E-Mail: info@asaging.org, Web Site: www.asaging.org
Pres & CEO: Robert G. Stein

VP Education: Carole A Anderson
Sr Dir Opers & IT: Robert R Lowe
Dir Mktg: Linda Jones
Conducts Business: U.S., Canada
Employees: 30
Primary Market Served: Business & Consumer
Catalog available online
Direct online sales
Advertising/Marketing Budget Related to Direct Marketing: 76-100%
Direct Marketing ad budget: $750,000
Direct Mail: 100%
Founded: 1954
Gross sales or billing: $2,500,000

Market membership, subscriptions, conferences, advertising & mailing lists, trade shows & videos to professionals in the field of aging & those who want to reach it.

AMERICAN SPEECH-LANGUAGE-HEARING ASSOCIATION

2200 Research Blvd
Rockville, MD 20850-3289
Telephone: (301) 897-5700, Toll Free: (800) 638-8255, FAX: (301) 296-8580, E-Mail: productsales@asha.org, Web Site: www.asha.org
CEO: Arlene Pietranton
Dir Assets & Corp Alliances: Barb Lecker
Mktg Dir: Rick Henderson
Dir Brand Mktg: Leslie Katz
List Mktg Mgr: Leah Byndon
Conducts Business: Worldwide
Employees: 250
Primary Market Served: Business & Consumer
Catalog available online
Indirect online sales
Advertising/Marketing Budget Related to Direct Marketing: 0-25%
Direct Marketing ad budget: $4,000,000
Founded: 1925
Gross sales or billing: $46,000,000

National professional & scientific association for speech-language pathologists, audiologists & speech, language & hearing scientists concerned with communication behavior & disorders. Market products, mailing list, journals, advertising & conferences to membership & interested parties.

AMERICAN STUDENT ASSISTANCE

100 Cambridge St (Suite 1600)
Boston, MA 02114-2567
Toll Free: (800) 999-9080, Web Site: www.asa.com
Pres & CEO: Paul C. Combe

Primary Market Served: Business & Consumer

Non-profit organization focusing on federal student loans. Services include grants, scholarships, fellowships & federal loans.

AMERICAN TRUCKING ASSOCIATION

950 N Glebe Rd (Suite 210)
Arlington, VA 22203-4181
Telephone: (703) 838-1700, FAX: (800) 254-2571, E-Mail: atamembership@trucking.org, Web Site: www.trucking.org
Pres & CEO: Bill Graves
VP, Commun: Jeffery "Jeff" Mason
Conducts Business: Worldwide
Employees: 300
Primary Market Served: Business
Catalog available online
Indirect online sales

Trade association offering publications & services to the trucking industry.

AMERICANS FOR PEACE NOW

2100 M St NW (Suite 619)
Washington, DC 20037-1269
Telephone: (202) 408-9898, FAX: (202) 408-9899, E-Mail: apndc@peacenow.org, Web Site: www.peacenow.org
Pres & CEO: Debra DeLee
Asst Exec Dir, Planning & Devel: Mark Bilisky
Conducts Business: U.S.
Primary Market Served: Business & Consumer

Raise funds in support of Middle East peace.

AMERICARES

88 Hamilton Ave
Stamford, CT 06902-3100
Telephone: (203) 658-9500, Toll Free: (800) 486-4357, E-Mail: info@americares.org, Web Site: www.americares.org
U.S. Programs: Linsay O'Brien

An emergency response & global health organization committed to saving lives & building healthier futures for people in crisis in the U.S. & around the world.

AMNESTY INTERNATIONAL USA

Five Penn Plaza (fl 16)
New York, NY 10001-1823
Telephone: (212) 807-8400, FAX: (212) 627-1451, Web Site: www.amnestyusa.org

Exec Dir Devel: Danny McGregor

Membership organization engaging in monitoring, reporting, & acting on grave abuses of the rights to physical & mental integrity, freedom of conscience and expression, & freedom from discrimination worldwide.

AMPLIFY FEDERAL CREDIT UNION

607 Congress Ave
Austin, TX 78758
Telephone: (512) 836-5901, Web Site: www.goamplify.com
Bus Intelligence Analyst: Sheryl Williams
Primary Market Served: Consumer

AMREF HEALTH AFRICA IN THE USA

4 W 43rd St (Floor 2)
New York, NY 10036-7408
Telephone: (212) 768-2440, FAX: (212) 768-4230, Web Site: www.amrefusa.org
Exec Dir: Robert Kelty

Nonprofit health services provider.

MD ANDERSON CANCER CENTER - CHILDREN'S ART PROJECT

6900 Fannin St (Suite FHB 1 1000)
Houston, TX 77030-3800
Telephone: (713) 745-2575, Toll Free: (800) 231-1580, FAX: (713) 794-1950, E-Mail: krenner@mdanderson.org, Web Site: www.childrensart.org
Mgr Sls & Mktg - Direct Mail: Kelly Renner
Exec Dir: Shannon Murray
Assoc Dir Mktg: Angela Cheves
Conducts Business: USA
Employees: 26
Primary Market Served: Consumer
Catalog available online
Direct online sales
Advertising/Marketing Budget Related to Direct Marketing: 0-25%
Direct Marketing ad budget: $400,000
Founded: 1973
Gross sales or billing: $2,500,000

Offers merchandise inspired by the artwork of Children's Cancer patients at the University of Texas MD Anderson Cancer Center.

ANGLICANS UNITED & LATIMER PRESS

904 Forest Hill Ct
Cedar Hill, TX 75104-5712
Telephone: (972) 293-7443, Toll Free: (800) 553-3645, FAX: (972) 293-7559, E-Mail: anglicansunited@

sbcglobal.net, Web Site: www.anglicansunited.com, www.latimerpress.com
Exec Dir: Rev Todd H. Wetzel
Admin: Cheryl M. Wetzel
Conducts Business: U.S. & Canada
Employees: 2
Primary Market Served: Business & Consumer
Catalog available online
Indirect online sales
Advertising/Marketing Budget Related to Direct Marketing: 0-25%
Direct Marketing ad budget: $1,400
Magazines: $1,000
Online: $400
Founded: 1986

Provide bi-monthly newspaper & resources for church members & prospective members to educate the laity to fight liberal trends to keep the Episcopal church orthodox.

ANSAR INC

6651 Bethesda Arno Rd
Thompsons Station, TN 37179-9216
Telephone: (615) 368-2025, Web Site: www.ansarinc.com
Pres: Patricia Hinton

Provides print & mail services to non-profit organizations, universities & corporations

ANTI-DEFAMATION LEAGUE

605 3rd Ave (fl 9)
New York, NY 10158-0102
Telephone: (212) 885-7700, Web Site: www.adl.org
CEO & Natl Dir: Jonathan Greenblatt
Dir Mktg & Commun: Todd M. Gutnick
Deputy Natl Dir: Kenneth Jacobson

Civil rights/human relations agency.

ANTIQUARIAN BOOKSELLERS ASSOCIATION OF AMERICA INC

20 W 44th St
New York, NY 10036
Telephone: (212) 944-8291, FAX: (212) 944-8293, E-Mail: sbenne@abaa.org, Web Site: www.abaa.org
Exec Dir: Susan Benne
Primary Market Served: Business & Consumer
Catalog available online
Founded: 1949

Non-profit trade organization for antiquarian book dealers.

APPALACHIAN MOUNTAIN CLUB
5 Joy St
Boston, MA 02108-1490
Telephone: (617) 523-0655, FAX:
(617) 523-0722, Web Site: www.
outdoors.com
VP Communs & Mktg: Kevin Breunig

Offers backcountry leadership & skills training in conservation and outdoor recreation.

APPRAISAL INSTITUTE
200 W Madison St Ste 1500
Chicago, IL 60606-3515
Telephone: (312) 335-4100, Toll Free:
(888) 756-4624, FAX: (312) 335-
4400, E-Mail: aiservice@
appraisalinstitute.org, Web Site:
www.appraisalinstitute.org
Pres: Jim Amorin
VP: James L. Murrett
Conducts Business: U.S.
Employees: 100
Primary Market Served: Business &
Consumer
Catalog available online
Indirect online sales
Advertising/Marketing Budget Related
to Direct Marketing: 0-25%
Direct Marketing ad budget:
Direct Mail: 40%
Magazines: 50%
Newspapers: 5%
TV/Radio: 5%
Founded: 1991

Professional association of real estate appraisers, engaged in marketing books, videotapes, periodicals & educational functions.

ARBOR DAY FOUNDATION
100 Arbor Ave
Nebraska City, NE 68410
Telephone: (402) 474-5655, Toll Free:
(888) 448-7337, Web Site: www.
arborday.org
CEO: Matt Harris
Primary Market Served: Consumer
Founded: 1972

ARTHRITIS FOUNDATION
1355 W Peachtree St NW (fl 6)
Atlanta, GA 30309-2922
Telephone: (404) 872-7100, FAX:
(404) 872-0457, Web Site: www.
arthritis.org
Program & Svcs Dir: Ayana Charleston
Devel Dir: Kelly Maliska
Conducts Business: U.S.
Employees: 160
Primary Market Served: Business &
Consumer
Founded: 1948

Gross sales or billing: $748,000,000
Voluntary health agency using direct marketing to raise funds to distribute educational information about the prevention, control & cure of arthritis.

ASSOCIATION FOR COMPUTING MACHINERY
2 Penn Plaza (Suite 701)
New York, NY 10121-0701
Telephone: (212) 626-0500, Toll Free:
(800) 342-6626, FAX: (212) 944-
1318, Web Site: www.acm.org
Exec Dir & CEO: Bobby Schnabel
Pres: Alexander L. Wolf
Conducts Business: Worldwide
Employees: 94
Primary Market Served: Business &
Consumer

Non-profit international educational & scientific society serving the computing community.

ASSOCIATION FOR FACILITIES ENGINEERING
8200 Greensboro Dr (Suite 400)
McLean, VA 22102
Telephone: (571) 203-7171, FAX:
(571) 766-2142, E-Mail: info@afe.
org, Web Site: www.afe.org
Exec. Dir: Wayne P. Saya Sr.
Conducts Business: U.S.
Employees: 8
Primary Market Served: Business &
Consumer
Catalog available online
Indirect online sales
Direct Marketing ad budget:
Direct Mail: 10%
Online: 90%
Founded: 1954

Membership organization.

ASSOCIATION FOR TALENT DEVELOPMENT
1640 King St
Alexandria, VA 22314
Telephone: (703) 683-8100, Toll Free:
(800) 628-2783, FAX: (703) 683-
8103, E-Mail: customercare@td.org
CEO: Tony Bringham
Primary Market Served: Business &
Consumer
Catalog available online
Direct online sales
Founded: 1944

A professional society in the field of workplace learning & performance offering membership, conferences & publications.

ASSOCIATION OF AMERICAN PUBLISHERS
455 Massachusetts Ave NW (Suite
700)
Washington, DC 20001-2777
Telephone: (202) 347-3375, FAX:
(202) 347-3690, E-Mail: info@
publishers.org, Web Site: www.
publishers.org
Pres & CEO: Tom Allen
Gen Counsel & VP, Govt Affairs: Allan Adler
Dir, Membership Mktg: Gail Kump
Conducts Business: Worldwide
Employees: 25
Primary Market Served: Business &
Consumer
Catalog available online
Indirect online sales
Founded: 1970

Trade association of publishing companies.

ASSOCIATION OF BRIDAL CONSULTANTS
56 Danbury Rd (Suite 11)
New Milford, CT 06776-2521
Telephone: (860) 355-0464, FAX:
(860) 354-1404, E-Mail: office@
bridalassn.com, Web Site: www.
bridalassn.com
Dir Mktg: Dena Davey
Pres: David Wood III
Conducts Business: Worldwide
Primary Market Served: Business &
Consumer
Catalog available online
Indirect online sales
Advertising/Marketing Budget Related
to Direct Marketing: 0-25%
Founded: 1955

Professional services for Wedding Planner worldwide.

ASSOCIATION OF FUNDRAISING PROFESSIONALS
4300 Wilson Blvd (Suite 300)
Arlington, VA 22203-4179
Telephone: (703) 684-0410, Toll Free:
(800) 666-3863, FAX: (703) 684-
0540, Web Site: www.afpnet.org
Pres & CEO: Andrew Watt
Dir Mktg: Todd McLaughlin

ASSOCIATION OF MARIAN HELPERS
Eden Hill
Stockbridge, MA 01263
Telephone: (413) 298-3931, Toll Free:
(800) 462-7426, Web Site: www.
marian.org
Prog Planner: James G. Morrison
Gen Mgr: Fran Borden

Conducts Business: U.S., Canada
Employees: 90
Primary Market Served: Business &
  Consumer
Advertising/Marketing Budget Related
  to Direct Marketing: 0-25%
Catholic fund raising organization.

ASSOCIATION OF THE MIRACULOUS MEDAL

Subs. of Congregation of the Mission
  Province
1811 W Saint Joseph St
Perryville, MO 63775-1598
Telephone: (573) 547-8343, Toll Free:
  (800) 264-6279, FAX: (573) 547-
  1389, E-Mail: amm1@amm.org,
  Web Site: www.amm.org
Finance Dir: Wesley Sparkman
Opers Dir: Renee Brueckner
Conducts Business: U.S.
Primary Market Served: Consumer
Catalog available online
Direct online sales
Advertising/Marketing Budget Related
  to Direct Marketing: 76-100%
Direct Marketing ad budget:
Direct Mail: 99%
Online: 1%
Founded: 1918

Non-profit direct mail evangelization
& fund-raising organization to national
Catholic mailing lists.

ASTRONOMICAL SOCIETY OF THE PACIFIC

390 Ashton Ave
San Francisco, CA 94112-1722
Telephone: (415) 337-1100, Toll Free:
  (800) 335-2624, FAX: (415) 337-
  5205, E-Mail: service@astrosociety.
  org, Web Site: www.astrosociety.org
Mng Editor: Joseph Jensen
Exec Dir: Linda Shore
Publication Mgr: J. Ward Moody
Conducts Business: Worldwide
Primary Market Served: Business &
  Consumer
Catalog available online
Direct online sales
Advertising/Marketing Budget Related
  to Direct Marketing: 0-25%
Direct Marketing ad budget:
Direct Mail: 90%
Magazines: 10%
Founded: 1889

Non-profit society. Online store sells
materials in astronomy including slides,
CD-ROMS, prints, posters, video &
audio tapes, books, maps, globes &
charts. Wholesale products also available.

AUDIO-DIGEST FOUNDATION

Affiliate of Calif Medical Assn
450 N Brand Blvd (Suite 900)
Glendale, CA 91203-2397
Telephone: (818) 240-7500, Toll Free:
  (800) 423-2308, FAX: (818) 240-
  7379, Web Site: www.audio-digest.
  org
VP, Mktg: George Groveman
Pres: Allen Stamey
Conducts Business: Worldwide
Employees: 135
Primary Market Served: Business &
  Consumer
Direct Marketing ad budget:
Direct Mail: 80%
Magazines: 20%
Founded: 1953

Involved in continuing postgraduate
medical education. Publish medical education on audio & video cassette recordings sold to health care profession
via direct mail.

AVMED HEALTH PLAN INC

9400 S Dadeland Blvd (Suite 120)
Miami, FL 33156-2823
Telephone: (305) 671-5437, FAX:
  (305) 671-4782, Web Site: www.
  avmed.org
CFO & Sr VP: Randall L. Stuart
CIO & Sr VP: Anthony F. Tardugno
Sr VP: Steve DeMontmollin
Founded: 1969

Provides health coverage solutions to
individuals & businesses in Florida &
offers various health care options that
include commercial, individual, Medicare, & ASO/self funded plans.

THE AYN RAND INSTITUTE

2121 Alton Pkwy (Suite 250)
Irvine, CA 92606-4926
Telephone: (949) 222-6550, FAX:
  (949) 222-6558, E-Mail: archives@
  aynrand.org, Web Site: www.
  aynrand.org
Pres & Exec Dir: Yaron Brook
Employees: 33
Primary Market Served: Business
Catalog available online
Advertising/Marketing Budget Related
  to Direct Marketing: 76-100%
Founded: 1985
Gross sales or billing: $5,900,000

Non-profit fundraiser for academia &
publishers.

BBS & ASSOCIATES

130 Springside Dr (Suite 200)
Akron, OH 44333-4553

Telephone: (330) 665-5227, E-Mail:
  contactus@servantheart.com, Web
  Site: www.servantheart.com
Project Asst: Suzanne Ludwick
Primary Market Served: Consumer
Consulting firm serving ministries

BMI

10 Music Sq E
Nashville, TN 37203-4321
Telephone: (615) 401-2000, Toll Free:
  (800) 925-8451, FAX: (615) 401-
  2812, E-Mail: nashville@bmi.com,
  Web Site: www.bmi.com
Chmn Bd: Susan Davenport Austin
Pres & CEO: Michael O'Neill
Exec Dir, Strategic Partnerships & Bus
  Devel: Mason Hunter
Primary Market Served: Business
Catalog available online
Direct online sales
Founded: 1939

Performing rights organization. Market
music property rights of songwriters.

BATON ROUGE CONVENTIONS & VISITORS BUREAU

359 3rd St Ste A
Baton Rouge, LA 70801-1310
Telephone: (225) 383-1825, Toll Free:
  (800) LA-ROUGE, FAX: (225) 346-
  1253, E-Mail: karron@
  visitbatonrouge.com, Web Site:
  www.bracvb.com
Pres & CEO: Paul J. Arrigo
Dir Mktg & Tech: Karron Alford
Destination Svcs Mgr: Courtney Hunt
Conducts Business: U.S.
Employees: 15
Primary Market Served: Business &
  Consumer
Catalog available online

Promote Baton Rouge to tourists &
conventions.

BENET ACADEMY

2200 Maple Ave
Lisle, IL 60532-2393
Telephone: (630) 719-2794, Web Site:
  www.benet.org

BENEVILLA

16752 Greenwood St, 16752 N.
  Greasewood St.
Surprise, AZ 85378
Telephone: (623) 584-4999, FAX:
  (623) 546-1589, Web Site: www.
  interfaithcommunitycare.org
Pres & CEO: Michelle Dionisio
Primary Market Served: Consumer

BEST FRIENDS ANIMAL SOCIETY
5001 Angel Canyon Rd
Kanab, UT 84741-5000
Telephone: (435) 644-2001, E-Mail:
info@bestfriends.org, Web Site:
www.bestfriends.org

Animal society for abused & abandoned animals

BETHESDA HOSPITAL FOUNDATION
2815 S Seacrest Blvd
Boynton Beach, FL 33435-7934
Telephone: (561) 737-7733, FAX:
(561) 735-7942
Exec Dir: Kay Harvey
Dir Special Events & Communs: Paula
Henerson

Non-profit organization established for
the benefit & support of Bethesda Memorial Hospital.

BIG BROTHERS BIG SISTERS OF GREATER KANSAS CITY
1709 Walnut St
Kansas City, MO 64108
Telephone: (816) 561-5269, FAX:
(816) 561-5273, Web Site: www.
bigbrothersbigsisterskc.org
Chief Mktg Officer: Kristi Hutchison

Provides children facing adversity in
one-to-one life-changing friendships
with adult mentors.

B'NAI B'RITH INTERNATIONAL
1120 20th St NW (Suite 300 N)
Washington, DC 20036
Telephone: (202) 857-6600, Toll Free:
(888) 388-4224, FAX: (202) 857-
6609, E-Mail: info@bnaibrith.org,
Web Site: www.bnaibrith.org
Pres: Gary P. Saltzman
Primary Market Served: Business
Founded: 1843

Jewish non-profit organization.

BORN FREE USA
United with Animal Protection Institute
PO Box 32160
Washington, DC 20007
Telephone: (202) 450-3168, Toll Free:
(800) 348-7387, FAX: (202) 450-
3581, E-Mail: info@bornfreeusa.org,
Web Site: www.bornfreeusa.org
CEO: Adam Roberts
Devel Dir: Angela Grimes
Creative Dir: Sharie Lesniak
Online Store & Campaign Matls: Steve
Wyckoff
Conducts Business: U.S.

Employees: 21
Primary Market Served: Consumer
Catalog available online
Direct online sales
Advertising/Marketing Budget Related
to Direct Marketing: 76-100%
Direct Marketing ad budget:
Direct Mail: 100%
Founded: 1968
Gross sales or billing: $1,500,000

National non-profit organization for the
protection & welfare of animals.

THE BOWERY MISSION
432 Park Ave S (fl 3)
New York, NY 10016
Telephone: (212) 684-2800, Web Site:
www.bowery.org
Pres & CEO: David P. Jones
CFO: Robert Depue
Chief Devel Officer: James Winans
Primary Market Served: Consumer
Founded: 1879

Gospel mission

BOY SCOUTS OF AMERICA/ NATIONAL SUPPLY GROUP
2109 Westinghouse Blvd
Charlotte, NC 28273-6310
Toll Free: (800) 323-0736, FAX: (704)
588-5822, E-Mail: customerservice@
scoutstuff.org, Web Site: www.
scoutstuff.org
Chief Scout Exec: Wayne Brock
Asst Chief Scout Exec, CFO: Alf Tuggles
Asst Chief Scout Exec, Devel: Bradley
D. Farmer
Asst Chief Scout Exec, Council Opers:
Gary P. Butler
Primary Market Served: Consumer
Catalog available online
Direct online sales

Provide uniforms, equipment & literature for the Boy Scouts of America.

BOYS & GIRLS CLUBS OF AMERICA NATIONAL HEADQUARTERS
1275 Peachtree St NE
Atlanta, GA 30309-3506
Telephone: (404) 487-5700, FAX:
(404) 815-5757, (404) 487-5757,
E-Mail: info@bgca.org, Web Site:
www.bgca.org
Pres & CEO: Jim Clark
SVP Mktg & Commun: Evan McElroy
Conducts Business: U.S.
Primary Market Served: Consumer

Non-profit organization with over 2000
Boys & Girls Clubs facilities nationwide. Solicit funds through direct mail.

BRIGHTFOCUS FOUNDATION
22512 Gateway Ctr Dr
Clarksburg, MD 20871-2005
Telephone: (301) 948-3224, Toll Free:
(800) 437-2423, FAX: (301) 358-
9454, E-Mail: info@brightfocus.org,
Web Site: www.brightfocus.org
CEO & Pres: Stacy Pagos Haller
Founded: 1973

Supports research & provides public
education on brain & eye diseases, including Alzheimer's disease, macular
degeneration & glaucoma.

BRONX COUNCIL ON THE ARTS
1738 Hone Ave
Bronx, NY 10461-1486
Telephone: (718) 931-9500, FAX:
(718) 409-6445, E-Mail: info@
bronxarts.org, Web Site: www.
bronxarts.org
Exec Dir: Deirdre Scott
Mktg & Communs: Tony Holmes
Employees: 21
Primary Market Served: Business &
Consumer
Founded: 1962

Non-profit organization. Official cultural agency of Bronx county.

BROOKFIELD ZOO
Chicago Zoological Society
3300 Golf Rd
Brookfield, IL 60513-1060
Telephone: (708) 485-0263, Toll Free:
(800) 201-0784, FAX: (708) 485-
3532, Web Site: www.brookfieldzoo.
org
Pres & CEO: Dr. Stuart D. Strahl
Sr VP Opers: Richard G. Gamble
Sr VP Devel: Chris Jabin
Employees: 500
Primary Market Served: Consumer
Founded: 1934
Gross sales or billing: $64,100,000

Uses direct mail to recruit members &
animal adoption parents.

CAA AUTO CLUB & TRAVEL AGENCY INC
60 Commerce Valley Dr E
Thornhill, ON, Canada L3T 7P9
Telephone: (905) 371-3000, Toll Free:
(866) 988-, FAX: (905) 371-3101,
E-Mail: membership@caasco.ca,
Web Site: www.central.on.caa.ca
Chmn: Bill Graham
Conducts Business: Canada
Employees: 200
Primary Market Served: Business &
Consumer

Advertising/Marketing Budget Related to Direct Marketing: 51-75%
Founded: 1903

Auto club services.

CCIM INSTITUTE
Div. of National Association of Realtors
430 N Michigan Ave (Suite 800)
Chicago, IL 60611-4011
Telephone: (312) 321-4460, Toll Free: (800) 621-7027, FAX: (312) 321-4530, Web Site: www.ccim.com
CEO: Jonathan Salk
Pres: Tim Hatlestad
Pres-Elect: Charles McClure
First VP: Richard E. Juge
Treas: Stephen Perfit
Conducts Business: U.S., Canada, China, Mexico, U.K.
Employees: 40
Primary Market Served: Business
Catalog available online
Direct online sales
Advertising/Marketing Budget Related to Direct Marketing: 51-75%
Direct Marketing ad budget:
Direct Mail: 85%
Magazines: 5%
Newspapers: 5%
Telephone: 5%
Founded: 1969

National trade association specializing in education & business development programs for commercial investment real estate practitioners.

CDMI INC
711 Pacific Coast Hwy (Unit 118)
Huntington Beach, CA 92648-5051
Telephone: (714) 969-4064
Pres: Phillip F. Sheats
Primary Market Served: Consumer

CDR FUNDRAISING GROUP
16900 Science Dr (Suite 210)
Bowie, MD 20715-4412
Telephone: (301) 858-1500, FAX: (301) 858-0107, Web Site: www.cdr-nfl.com
Pres & CEO: Geoffrey Peters

CMS LLC
1900 Campus Commons Dr (Suite 450)
Reston, VA 20191-1559
Telephone: (703) 258-0000, Web Site: www.craveronline.com
Principal & CEO: Ellen Church

Direct response fundraising

COSE
Council of Smaller Enterprises
240 Huron Rd E (Suite 200)
Cleveland, OH 44115-1722
Telephone: (216) 592-2222, Toll Free: (866) 553-5427, E-Mail: memberservices@cose.org, Web Site: www.cose.org
Pres & Exec Dir: Steve Millard
Mng VP, Membership Devel & Mktg: Megan Kim

Small business advocacy organization.

CALENDAR MARKETING ASSOCIATION
214 N Hale St
Wheaton, IL 60187-5115
Telephone: (630) 510-4564, FAX: (630) 510-4501, E-Mail: info@calendarassociation.org, Web Site: www.calendarassociation.org
Exec Dir: Michael Hansen
Employees: 6
Primary Market Served: Business & Consumer
Advertising/Marketing Budget Related to Direct Marketing: 26-50%
Founded: 1989

Involved in all aspects of the calendar industry including publishing, printing & manufacturing.

CALIFORNIA CHAMBER OF COMMERCE
1215 K St (Suite 1400)
Sacramento, CA 95814
Toll Free: (800) 649-4921, FAX: (916) 325-1272, E-Mail: techsupport@calchamber.com, Web Site: www.calbizcentral.com
VP Mktg: Karen Olson
Primary Market Served: Business

CALIFORNIA SOCIETY OF CPA'S
1800 Gateway Dr (Suite 200)
San Mateo, CA 94404-4072
Toll Free: (800) 922-5272, FAX: (650) 522-3009, E-Mail: info@culcpa.org, Web Site: www.calcpa.org
Chair: Jennifer E. Ziegler
CEO: Loretta Doon
Conducts Business: U.S.
Employees: 120
Primary Market Served: Business & Consumer
Catalog available online
Direct online sales

Association representing 30,000 California CPA's.

CANADIAN BLOOD SERVICES
1800 Alta Vista Dr
Ottawa, ON, Canada K1G 4J5
Telephone: (613) 739-2300, Web Site: www.blood.ca
Natl Dir, Sls & Mktg: Jeff Moat

Primary Market Served: Consumer

CANADIAN INSTITUTE OF CHARTERED ACCOUNTANTS
277 Wellington St W
Toronto, ON, Canada M5V 3H2
Telephone: (416) 977-3222, FAX: (416) 977-8585, Web Site: www.cica.ca
VP, Member Svcs: Cairine Wilson
Primary Market Served: Business

CANCER RESEARCH SOCIETY
625 President Kennedy Ave (Suite 402)
Montreal, QC, Canada H3A 3S5
Telephone: (514) 861-9227, Toll Free: (888) 766-2262, FAX: (514) 861-9220, E-Mail: info@crs-src.ca, Web Site: www.cancerresearchsociety.ca
Pres & CEO: Andy Chabot
VP & COO: Nathalie Giroux
Conducts Business: Canada
Employees: 23
Primary Market Served: Business & Consumer
Founded: 1945
Gross sales or billing: $18,500,000

CARE2
1100 15th S NW (Suite 600)
Washington, DC 20005-1759
Telephone: (650) 622-0860, Web Site: www.care2.com
VP, Bus Devel: Eric Rardin
Primary Market Served: Business & Consumer
Founded: 1998

Online community focusing on green living. Connects individuals with non-profit organizations

CARE USA
151 Ellis St NE
Atlanta, GA 30303-2420
Telephone: (404) 681-2552, Toll Free: (800) 422-7385, FAX: (404) 589-2600, E-Mail: info@care.org, Web Site: www.careusa.org
CFO & VP Fin & IT: Peter Buijs
Pres & CEO: Michelle Nunn
Sec Bd: Carol Hudson
Conducts Business: Worldwide
Employees: 7,000
Primary Market Served: Business & Consumer
Catalog available online
Founded: 1945
Gross sales or billing: $646,000,000

International development & relief organization.

CAREER EDUCATION CORP

231 N Martingale Rd Ste 100
Schaumburg, IL 60173-2007
Telephone: (847) 781-3600, E-Mail:
    inquiries@careered.com, Web Site:
    www.careered.com
Pres & CEO: Todd Nelson
Primary Market Served: Consumer
Founded: 1999

Educational services company

CATHOLIC CHARITIES - BROOKLYN & QUEENS

191 Joralemon St
Brooklyn, NY 11201-4306
Telephone: (718) 722-6001, Web Site:
    www.ccbq.org
Primary Market Served: Consumer

Social services for struggling New
Yorkers.

CATHOLIC CHURCH EXTENSION SOCIETY

150 S Wacker Dr (Suite 2000)
Chicago, IL 60606-4103
Telephone: (312) 795-5109, Toll Free:
    (800) 842-7804, FAX: (312) 236-
    5276, E-Mail: info@
    catholicextension.org, Web Site:
    www.catholicextension.org
Pres & CEO: Reverend John J. Wall
VP Mktg & Broadcast Media: Angela
    D'Antonio

CATHOLIC RELIEF SERVICES

228 Lexington St
Baltimore, MD 21201-3443
Telephone: (877) 435-7277, Toll Free:
    (888) 277-7575, Web Site: www.
    catholicrelief.org
Dir, Direct Response Fundraising: Jean
    Simmons
Primary Market Served: Consumer

BRAD CECIL & ASSOCIATES

2115 Arlington Downs Rd
Arlington, TX 76011-8210
Telephone: (817) 795-8808, FAX:
    (817) 795-8898
Pres: Brad Cecil

Direct response fundraising

CENTER FOR EBUSINESS & ADVANCED IT

5340 Fryling Rd (Suite 201)
Erie, PA 16510-4672
Telephone: (814) 898-6500, FAX:
    (814) 898-6534, Web Site: www.
    ebizitpa.org
Dir E-Mktg: Catherine Von Birgelen

Gen Mgr: Marty Barclay
Offers a variety of training programs &
resources for electronic business environment.

CENTER FOR SCIENCE IN THE PUBLIC INTEREST

dba Nutrition Action Healthletter
1220 L St NW Ste 300
Washington, DC 20005-4053
Telephone: (202) 332-9110, FAX:
    (202) 265-4954, E-Mail: circ@
    cspinet.org, Web Site: www.cspinet.
    org
Dir Fin: Don Allen
Conducts Business: U.S., Canada
Employees: 65
Primary Market Served: Consumer
Catalog available online
Direct online sales
Direct Marketing ad budget:
Direct Mail: 98%
Newspapers: 2%
Founded: 1971
Gross sales or billing: $17,052,338

Also publishes the Nutrition Action
Healthletter.

CHARITY DYNAMICS

3721 Executive Center Dr (Suite 100)
Austin, TX 78731-1615
Telephone: (512) 241-0561, FAX:
    (512) 532-6037, Web Site: www.
    charitydynamics.com
Pres: Donna Wilkins
VP Sales & Mktg: Mike Peloquin
VP Strategic Svcs: Jett Winders

Online marketing agency for nonprofits.

CHARLOTTE CHAMBER OF COMMERCE

330 S Tryon St (Ste 200)
Charlotte, NC 28202-1923
Telephone: (704) 378-1300, Web Site:
    www.boomcharlotte.com
Primary Market Served: Consumer

CHERRY BROTHERS LLC/ CHERRYDALE

707 N Valley Forge Rd
Lansdale, PA 19446
Toll Free: (800) 333-4525, Web Site:
    www.cherrydale.com
Exec Asst: Kim Snyder

Fundraising ideas & products for
school fundraising

CHESAPEAKE BAY FOUNDATION

6 Herndon Ave
Annapolis, MD 21403-4503

Telephone: (410) 268-8816, Web Site:
    www.savethebay.cbf.org
Pres: William C. Baker
VP Devel: Katharene Snavely
VP Commns: Elizabeth Buckman

CHICAGO CONVENTION & TOURISM BUREAU

2301 S Lakeshore Dr
Chicago, IL 60616-1490
Telephone: (312) 791-7000, FAX:
    (312) 567-8599, Web Site: www.
    choosechicago.com
Mktg Dir: Harvey Morris
Primary Market Served: Consumer

CHILDFUND INTERNATIONAL

2821 Emerywood Pkwy
Richmond, VA 23294
Telephone: (804) 756-2700, Toll Free:
    (800) 776-6767, FAX: (804) 756-
    2718, Web Site: www.
    christianchildrensfund.org
Pres & CEO: Anne Lynam Goddard
Dir, Mktg: Mary Arnold
Employees: 130
Primary Market Served: Consumer
Direct Marketing ad budget:
    $9,000,000
Founded: 1938

International non-profit & non-sectar-
ian humanitarian organization dedicated to serving the needs of children
worldwide, primarily through person-
to-person assistance programs.

CHILDFUND INTERNATIONAL

2821 Emerywood Pkwy
Richmond, VA 23294-3726
Telephone: (804) 756-2700, Web Site:
    www.ChildFund.org
Dir Mktg: Mary Arnold
Primary Market Served: Consumer

CHILDREN INTERNATIONAL

2000 E Red Bridge Rd
Kansas City, MO 64131-3694
Telephone: (816) 942-2000, Toll Free:
    (800) 888-3089, FAX: (816) 942-
    3714, E-Mail: RobS@cikc.org, Web
    Site: www.children.org
VP Mktg: Robert Saint Thomas
Dir, Mktg Children Intl: Carole
    Spencer

CHILDREN OF THE NIGHT

14530 Sylvan St
Van Nuys, CA 91411

Telephone: (818) 908-4474, Toll Free: (800) 551-1300, FAX: (818) 908-1468, E-Mail: llee@ childrenofthenight.com, Web Site: www.childrenofthenight.org
Exec Dir: Dr. Lois Lee
Primary Market Served: Business & Consumer
Catalog available online
Advertising/Marketing Budget Related to Direct Marketing: 0-25%
Founded: 1979

Children's shelter dealing with youths ages 11-17 involved in prostitution and/or pornography. A 24-bed licensed shelter.

CHILDREN'S AID SOCIETY
711 3rd Ave (Suite 700)
New York, NY 10017
Telephone: (212) 949-4800, Web Site: www.childrensaidsociety.org
Pres & CEO: Phoebe Bohyer
VP Child Welfare & Family Svcs: Georgia Boothe
VP Mktg & Communs: Anthony Ramos
Employees: 1,000
Primary Market Served: Consumer
Founded: 1853

Serves New York's neediest children & their families at more than 40 locations.

CHILDREN'S BETTER HEALTH INSTITUTE
1100 Waterway Blvd
Indianapolis, IN 46202
Telephone: (317) 634-1100, FAX: (317) 684-8094, E-Mail: a. mcdowell@cbhi.org, Web Site: www.cbhi.org
Pres: Joan Servaas
Contact: Amanda . McDowell
Conducts Business: Worldwide
Primary Market Served: Consumer
Catalog available online
Direct online sales
Founded: 1976

A non-profit organization providing information & encouragement to parents, teachers & health professionals to educate on the fundamentals of good health.

CHILDREN'S HOSPITAL FOUNDATION
801 Roeder Rd ·
Silver Spring, MD 20910
Telephone: (202) 476-3000, Toll Free: (800) 884-LIFE, FAX: (202) 884-5999, Web Site: www.dcchildrens.com
Exec VP: Pam King Sams
Communs: Mark Miller

Conducts Business: U.S.
Primary Market Served: Business & Consumer
Catalog available online
Founded: 1870

Pediatric hospital.

CHILDREN'S HOSPITAL OF PITTSBURGH
4401 Penn Ave
Pittsburgh, PA 15224
Telephone: (412) 692-5325, FAX: (412) 692-7140, Web Site: www.chp.edu
Devel Dir Giving: Carol Ashby
Primary Market Served: Consumer

Various fund-raising projects.

CHRISTIAN APPALACHIAN PROJECT
485 Ponderosa Dr
Paintsville, KY 41240
Telephone: (866) 270-4227, Toll Free: (866) 270-4CAP, FAX: (859) 792-6560, E-Mail: capinfo@chrisapp.org, Web Site: www.christianapp.org
Pres & CEO: Guy Adams
Controller & Corp Treas: Sharon Adams
Conducts Business: U.S.
Employees: 40
Primary Market Served: Consumer

Charitable, non-profit fund-raising organization. Also, catalog sales of Christmas season wreaths.

CHRISTIAN BROADCASTING NETWORK INC
977 Centerville Tpke
Virginia Beach, VA 23463-1001
Telephone: (757) 226-7000, FAX: (757) 226-2017, Web Site: www.cbn.com
Pres, COO & Dir: Michael D. Little
Chmn: M. G. Robertson
VP Devel Integration: Edie Wasserberg
Controller: Jim Barr
DM Dir: Kathy Pollack
Primary Market Served: Business & Consumer

Christian services.

CHRISTIAN HERALD ASSOCIATION
432 Park Ave S (fl 3)
New York, NY 10016
Telephone: (212) 684-2800, Toll Free: (800) BOWERY-1, FAX: (212) 684-3740, E-Mail: info@chaonline.org, Web Site: www.bowery.org
Chmn Bd: Jan Nagel
Pres & CEO: Edward H. Morgan
Exec Dir: Bruce Terrrell

Dir: Donald Kolowsky
Dir: Miguel Sanchez
Conducts Business: U.S.
Employees: 75
Primary Market Served: Consumer
Founded: 1879
Gross sales or billing: $12,000,000

Ministry encompassing Bowery mission, women's mission & summer camp for kids.

CHRISTIAN RELIEF SERVICES CHARITIES INC
8301 Richmond Hwy
Alexandria, VA 22309
Telephone: (703) 317-9086, E-Mail: info@christianrelief.org, Web Site: www.christianrelief.org
Gen Counsel: Paul Krizek
Pres & CEO: Bryan Krizek
Primary Market Served: Consumer

CHURCH PENSION FUND
19 E 34th St
New York, NY 10016
Telephone: (866) 802-6333, Toll Free: (800) 223-6602, Web Site: www.cpg.org
CEO & Pres: Mary Kate Wold
Primary Market Served: Business

CITIZENS AGAINST GOVERNMENT WASTE
1301 Pennsylvania Ave NW Ste 1075
Washington, DC 20004-1707
Telephone: (202) 467-5300, Toll Free: (800) USA-DEBT, FAX: (202) 467-4253, E-Mail: membership@cagw.org, Web Site: www.cagw.org
Pres: Thomas A. Schatz
VP, Devel: Ariane E. Sweeney
Pres & CFO: Robert J. Tedeschi
Employees: 16
Primary Market Served: Business & Consumer
Founded: 1984
Gross sales or billing: $5,501,194

Non-profit, non-partisan taxpayer watchdog.

CITY OF CERRITOS
18125 Bloomfield Ave
Cerritos, CA 90703
Telephone: (562) 916-1319, Web Site: www.ci.cerritos.ca.us
City & Theatre Mktg Mgr: Annie Hylton
Primary Market Served: Consumer

CITY OF HOPE NATIONAL MEDICAL CENTER
1500 E Duarte Rd
Duarte, CA 91010

Telephone: (626) 256-4673, FAX:
(626) 301-8468, Web Site: www.
cityofhope.org
Pres & CEO: Robert W. Stone
Primary Market Served: Consumer

CITY OF LAGRANGE
200 Ridley Ave, PO Box 430
LaGrange, GA 30240
Telephone: (706) 883-2010, FAX:
(706) 883-2020, Web Site: www.
lagrange-ga.org
Interim City Mgr: Meg Kelsey
Exec Asst: Sue Olson
Primary Market Served: Business &
Consumer

Municipal government.

CIVIL WAR PRESERVATION
TRUST
1156 15th St NW (Suite 900)
Washington, DC 20005-4761
Telephone: (202) 367-1861, Toll Free:
(800) 298-7878, E-Mail: info@
civilwar.org, Web Site: www.
civilwar.org
Pres: O. James Lighthizer
Founded: 1987

CLEVELAND CLINIC
FOUNDATION
dba Cleveland Clinic Health System
9500 Euclid Ave (AC311)
Cleveland, OH 44195-0001
Telephone: (216) 444-2200, Web Site:
www.clevelandclinic.org
Coo: William M. Peacock III
Founded: 1921

Owns & operates hospitals & healthcare centers & provides clinical and
hospital care, research and educational
services.

THE CLEVELAND
ORCHESTRA
The Musical Arts Association
11001 Euclid Ave
Cleveland, OH 44106-1796
Telephone: (216) 231-7300, FAX:
(216) 231-4038, Web Site: www.
clevelandorchestra.com
Exec Dir: Andre Gremillet
Mktg Dir: Ross Binnie
Conducts Business: U.S.
Primary Market Served: Consumer
Direct Marketing ad budget:
Direct Mail: 25%
Newspapers: 25%
TV/Radio: 25%
Telephone: 25%

Perform 26 concert weekends per year
at Severance Hall & ten weekends at
Blossom Music Center.

COAST TO COAST INC
Div. of Affinity Group AGI
PO Box 6574
Englewood, CO 80155-6574
Telephone: (303) 728-2267, Web Site:
www.coastresorts.com
Chmn Bd: Kenneth R. Jensen
Pres, CEO & Dir: Michael A.
Schneider
Sr VP & CFO: Thomas F. Wolfe
Primary Market Served: Consumer
Catalog available online
Direct online sales

Membership camping.

COASTAL HOTEL GROUP
15375 SE 30th Pl (Suite 290)
Bellevue, WA 98007-6500
Telephone: (206) 388-0400, FAX:
(206) 388-0401, E-Mail: info@
coastalhotel.com, Web Site: www.
coastalhotels.com
Pres & CEO: Yogi Hutsen
CFO: Peter LaFemina
Sr VP & Mktg: Bradley K. Walker
Primary Market Served: Business
Catalog available online
Direct online sales

Hotel management company.

COIN LAUNDRY
ASSOCIATION
1S660 Midwest Rd (Suite 205)
Oakbrook Terrace, IL 60181-4738
Telephone: (630) 963-7920, Toll Free:
(800) 570-5629, FAX: (630) 963-
7925, Web Site: www.coinlaundry.
org
Pres & CEO: Brian Wallace
COO: Michael Sokolowski
Mgr Mktg & Online Devel: April
Smith-Miller
Conducts Business: U.S., Canada
Employees: 8
Primary Market Served: Business
Catalog available online
Direct online sales
Advertising/Marketing Budget Related
to Direct Marketing: 51-75%
Direct Marketing ad budget: $75,000
Direct Mail: 75%
Magazines: 10%
Telephone: 15%
Founded: 1960

National trade association to coin laun-
dry/dry cleaning industry offering
membership to qualified business owners, manufacturers & distributors.

THE COLLEGE BOARD
250 Vesey St
New York, NY 10281

Telephone: (212) 713-8000, FAX:
(212) 713-8143, Web Site: www.
collegeboard.com
CEO: David Coleman
Conducts Business: U.S., Canada, Eu-
rope
Primary Market Served: Consumer
Founded: 1899

Non-profit education association. Offer
services & programs for the transition
between high school & college.

COLLEGEAMERICA
4021 S 700 E (Suite 300)
Salt Lake City, UT 84107-2184
Toll Free: (801) 284-7553
Primary Market Served: Consumer
Founded: 1964

College programs

THE COLONIAL
WILLIAMSBURG
FOUNDATION
PO Box 1776
Williamsburg, VA 23187-1776
Telephone: (757) 229-1000, (757) 220-
7275, Toll Free: (800) 761-8331,
Web Site: www.
williamsburgmarketplace.com
Chmn, Pres & CEO: Michael B. Reiss
Conducts Business: U.S.
Primary Market Served: Consumer
Catalog available online
Indirect online sales

Non-profit educational foundation.

COMMUNITY FOOD BANK
3003 S Country Club Rd (Ste 221)
Tucson, AZ 85713-4084
Telephone: (520) 622-0525, FAX:
(520) 624-6349, Web Site: www.
communityfoodbank.org
CEO: Michael McDonald
Chief HR Officer: Laura Bird

COMPASSION
INTERNATIONAL
12290 Voyager Pkwy
Colorado Springs, CO 80921-3694
Toll Free: (800) 336-7676, Web Site:
www.compassion.com
Pres & CEO: Santiago Mellado
Global Mktg & Engagement: Mark
Hanlon

Child charity organization.

CONCERN WORLDWIDE
355 Lexington Ave Fl 19
New York, NY 10017-6603
Telephone: (212) 557-8000, FAX:
(212) 557-8004, Web Site: /www.
concernusa.org
Devel Officer: Aine Doddy

CEO: Dominic MacSorley

International humanitarian organization dedicated to tackling poverty & suffering in the world's poorest countries.

CM CONNOLLY
7220 Greenhaven Dr (Suite 7)
Sacramento, CA 95831-3592
Telephone: (916) 897-8095, Web Site: www.cmconnolly.com
Proprietor: Catherine Connolly

Direct marketing for non-profit organizations

CONSERVATION INTERNATIONAL
2011 Crystal Dr (Suite 500)
Arlington, VA 22202
Telephone: (703) 341-2400, E-Mail: community@conservation.org
Chmn Bd & CEO: Peter Seligmann
COO: Jennifer Morris
Primary Market Served: Consumer

CONTINUING EDUCATION OF THE BAR (CEB)
2100 Franklin St Ste 500
Oakland, CA 94612-3098
Telephone: (510) 302-2000, Toll Free: (800) 232-3444, FAX: (510) 302-2001, Web Site: www.ceb.com
Dir Mktg: Michael Taylor
Consultant: Diane Kretschmer
Employees: 210
Primary Market Served: Business
Catalog available online
Direct online sales
Advertising/Marketing Budget Related to Direct Marketing: 76-100%
Founded: 1947
Gross sales or billing: $22,375,068

Provide tools for legal continuing education. Also publish legal publications & CD ROM's in print and online.

CORNELL LAB OF ORNITHOLOGY
Div. of Cornell University
159 Sapsucker Woods Rd
Ithaca, NY 14850-1923
Telephone: (607) 254-2157, Toll Free: (800) 843-2473, FAX: (607) 254-2415, E-Mail: birdslides@cornell.edu, Web Site: www.birds.cornell.edu
Exec Dir: John W. Fitzpatrick
Mktg Mgr: Barry Bermudez
Dir Prog Devel & Evaluation: Rick Bonney
Conducts Business: U.S., Canada
Primary Market Served: Business & Consumer
Catalog available online
Direct online sales

Advertising/Marketing Budget Related to Direct Marketing: 76-100%
Direct Marketing ad budget:
Direct Mail: 90%
Magazines: 10%
Founded: 1954

All supplies for birding. Books, binoculars, bird song recordings, etc.

CORPUS CHRISTI MUSEUM OF SCIENCE & HISTORY
1900 N Chaparral St
Corpus Christi, TX 78401-1114
Telephone: (361) 826-4667, FAX: (361) 884-7392, Web Site: www.ccmuseum.com
Opers & Pub Rels: Bonnie Laya
Dir: Richard Stryker
Dev Dir: Patricia Drolet
Conducts Business: U.S.
Employees: 30
Primary Market Served: Business & Consumer
Advertising/Marketing Budget Related to Direct Marketing: 0-25%
Founded: 1957

Sell membership in the Corpus Christi Museum of Science & History.

COUNCIL FOR ADVANCEMENT AND SUPPORT OF EDUCATION
1307 New York Ave NW (Suite 1000)
Washington, DC 20005-4701
Telephone: (202) 328-2273, Web Site: www.case.org
Primary Market Served: Business & Consumer

COUNCIL OF BETTER BUSINESS BUREAUS - BBBONLINE
3033 Wilson Blvd Ste 600
Arlington, VA 22201-3863
Telephone: (703) 276-0100, FAX: (703) 525-8277, Web Site: www.bbb.org
Pres & CEO: Mary E. Power
Conducts Business: U.S., Canada
Employees: 113
Primary Market Served: Business & Consumer
Catalog available online
Advertising/Marketing Budget Related to Direct Marketing: 26-50%
Direct Marketing ad budget:
Direct Mail: $25,000
Founded: 1975
Gross sales or billing: $21,900,000

Supported by 350 companies & 138 local Better Business Bureaus operated autonomously in the United States, which are in turn supported by 230,000 local business members. Seeks to pro-

mote & foster the highest ethical relationship between businesses & the public through voluntary self-regulation, consumer & business education and service excellence.

COUNTRY DANCE AND SONG SOCIETY
116 Pleasant St (Suite 345)
Easthampton, MA 01027-2759
Telephone: (413) 203-5467, FAX: (413) 203-5471, E-Mail: office@cdss.org, Web Site: www.cdss.org
Exec Dir: Rima Dael
Database & Membership Asst: Loretta Stober
Dir Devel: Robin Hayden
Conducts Business: U.S., Canada, Western Europe
Employees: 8
Primary Market Served: Business & Consumer
Catalog available online
Advertising/Marketing Budget Related to Direct Marketing: 0-25%
Founded: 1915
Gross sales or billing: $110,000

Non-profit organization dedicated to the preservation, study, teaching & enjoyment of our English & American dance, music & song heritage.

COURAGE CARDS & GIFTS
3915 Golden Valley Rd Courage Ctr
Golden Valley, MN 55422-4249
Toll Free: (800) 992-6872, Web Site: www.couragecards.org
Dir Mktg: Wayne Mikos
Primary Market Served: Business & Consumer

COVENANT HOUSE INTERNATIONAL HEADQUARTERS
460 W 41st St
New York, NY 10036
Telephone: (212) 613-0300, Toll Free: (800) 388-3888, FAX: (212) 727-4992, Web Site: www.covenanthouse.org
Pres: Kevin M. Ryan
Sr VP, Devel: Jill Rottman
Sr VP, Direct Mktg: Joan H. Smyth Dengler
Conducts Business: U.S., Canada, Guatemala, Honduras, Mexico
Employees: 180
Primary Market Served: Consumer
Founded: 1972
Gross sales or billing: $34,000,000

Crisis intervention for runaway & homeless children who are under 21.

THE BEN CRAIG CENTER
8701 Mallard Creek Rd # 106
Charlotte, NC 28262-6007
Telephone: (704) 548-9113, Web Site:
   www.bencraigcenter.com
Primary Market Served: Business

CRAIG/VARTORELLA INTERNATIONAL MARKETING & ADVERTISING INC
277 Peckwood Rd
Camden, SC 29020
Telephone: (803) 432-4353, FAX:
   (803) 432-4353, E-Mail: globebiz@
   juno.com, Web Site: www.colasc.
   com/Marketing_&_Fundraising
Pres: Joanna B. Craig
Exec VP: William F. Vartorella
Conducts Business: Worldwide
Primary Market Served: Business &
   Consumer
Catalog available online
Indirect online sales
Advertising/Marketing Budget Related
   to Direct Marketing: 26-50%
Direct Marketing ad budget:
Direct Mail: 25%
Magazines: 50%
Online: 25%
Founded: 1985

CRAVER MATHEWS SMITH & CO
1900 Campus Commons Dr (Suite 450)
Reston, VA 20191-1559
Telephone: (703) 258-0000, FAX:
   (703) 258-0001, E-Mail: ellenc@
   cms1.com, Web Site: www.
   craveronline.com
Principal & CEO: Ellen Cobb
Conducts Business: U.S.
Employees: 100
Primary Market Served: Business
Gross sales or billing: $4,000,000

Represent 40 non-profit organizations
engaged in direct mail fund-raising &
membership development efforts. Provide a full range of services from creative to production to management.
Services include telephone marketing.

CREDIT UNION EXECUTIVES SOCIETY
5510 Research Park Dr
Fitchburg, WI 53711-5377
Telephone: (608) 271-2664, FAX:
   (608) 271-2303, E-Mail: cues@cues.
   org, Web Site: www.cues.org
CEO: Charles E. Fagan III
VP Mktg & Prof Devel: Christopher
   Stevenson
Primary Market Served: Consumer

CROHN'S & COLITIS FOUNDATION OF AMERICA
733 3rd Ave (Suite 510)
New York, NY 10017-3210
Telephone: (212) 685-3440, Toll Free:
   (800) 932-2423, E-Mail: info@ccfa.
   org, Web Site: www.ccfa.org
Mgr Donor Svcs: Alicia Kozma
Pres & CEO: Michael Osso
Chief Scientific Officer: Caren Heller
Exec VP, Chapter Growth & Devel:
   Mike Elkow
Primary Market Served: Consumer
Founded: 1967

Non-profit, volunteer-driven organization dedicated to finding the cures for
Crohn's disease & ulcerative colitis.

CUNA - TRADE ASSOCIATION
5710 Mineral Point Rd
Madison, WI 53705-4454
Telephone: (608) 231-4215, Toll Free:
   (800) 356-9655, FAX: (608) 231-
   4333, Web Site: www.cuna.org
Chief Mktg & Tech Officer: Amy Nigrelli
Primary Market Served: Consumer

CYSTIC FIBROSIS FOUNDATION
6931 Arlington Rd (fl 2)
Bethesda, MD 20814-5231
Telephone: (301) 951-4422, FAX:
   (301) 951-6378, E-Mail: info@cff.
   org, Web Site: www.cff.org
Dir, Direct Mail Opers: Keith Hinnant
Primary Market Served: Consumer

D/FW GROCERS ASSOCIATION
Associated with Texas Grocery & Con-
   venience Association
3044 Old Denton Rd (Suite 111)
Carrollton, TX 75007-5074
Telephone: (972) 353-5885, FAX:
   (469) 574-5252, Web Site: www.
   dfwga.net
Conducts Business: U.S.
Primary Market Served: Business
Advertising/Marketing Budget Related
   to Direct Marketing: 0-25%
Direct Marketing ad budget:
Direct Mail: 60%
Telephone: 40%
Founded: 1906

Trade association & trade journal representing grocers, convenience store
owners & suppliers in 50 counties of
the Dallas/Fort Worth metroplex area,
north central Texas and east Texas.

DAIRY COUNCIL OF CALIFORNIA
2151 Michelson Dr (Suite 235)
Irvine, CA 92612-1339
Telephone: (949) 756-7892, Web Site:
   www.dairycouncilofca.org
Dir Mktg & Communs: LeAnne Ruzza-
   menti
Primary Market Served: Business &
   Consumer

DAIRY MANAGEMENT INC
dba National Dairy Council
10255 W Higgins Rd (Suite 900)
Rosemont, IL 60018
Telephone: (847) 803-2000, FAX:
   (847) 803-2077, Web Site: www.
   nationaldairycouncil.org
CEO: Thomas P. Gallagher
Chief Communs Officer: Mollie Waller
Employees: 80
Primary Market Served: Business &
   Consumer
Founded: 1970
Gross sales or billing: $5,200,000

Educational material on health.

DANA-FARBER CANCER INSTITUTE
450 Brookline Ave
Boston, MA 02215-5450
Telephone: (617) 632-3000, Toll Free:
   (866) 408-3324, FAX: (617) 632-
   4070, E-Mail: suzanne_fountain@
   dfci.harvard.edu, Web Site: www.
   dana-farber.org
Pres & CEO: Edward J. Benz, Jr MD
Sr VP Devel: Susan S. Paresky
Employees: 3,000
Primary Market Served: Consumer
Direct online sales
Founded: 1947
Gross sales or billing: $616,000,000

Comprehensive cancer center.

DARDEN SCHOOL FOUNDATION EXECUTIVE FOUNDATION
100 Darden Blvd
Charlottesville, VA 22903
Telephone: (434) 924-3900, Web Site:
   www.darden.virginia.edu/execed
Sr Exec Dir: Michael Woodfolk
Primary Market Served: Consumer

DARTMOUTH-HITCHCOCK
Hinman Box 7070, One Medical Center
   Dr
Lebanon, NH 03756-1000
Telephone: (603) 650-5000, Web Site:
   www.dmsnet.org
CEO & Pres: James N. Weinstein
Primary Market Served: Consumer

DAVINCI DIRECT
36 Cordage Park Cir (Suite 339)
Plymouth, MA 02360-7320
Telephone: (508) 746-2555, FAX:
(815) 301-9884, E-Mail: steve@
davinci-direct.com, Web Site: www.
davinci-direct.com
Pres & CCO: Steven J. Maggio
Conducts Business: U.S.
Employees: 5
Primary Market Served: Consumer
Advertising/Marketing Budget Related
to Direct Marketing: 76-100%
Direct Marketing ad budget: $20,000
Direct Mail: 10%
Magazines: 90%
Founded: 2005
Gross sales or billing: $2,000,000

Strategy: Creative production and analysis for non-profit and consumer direct marketing campaigns.

DEFENDERS OF WILDLIFE
1130 17th St NW
Washington, DC 20036-4604
Telephone: (202) 682-9400, Toll Free:
(800) 385-9712, E-Mail: defenders@
mail.defenders.org, Web Site: www.
defenders.org
Pres & CEO: Jamie Rappaport Clark
VP Communs: Cindy Hoffman

**DEMOCRATIC
CONGRESSIONAL
CAMPAIGN COMMITTEE**
430 S Capitol St SE
Washington, DC 20003
Telephone: (202) 863-1500, FAX:
(202) 485-3436, Web Site: www.
dccc.com
Deputy, Exec Dir Outreach & Voter
Contact: Dan Sena
Conducts Business: U.S.
Employees: 65
Primary Market Served: Business &
Consumer
Direct Marketing ad budget:
Direct Mail: 75%
Telephone: 25%

National political party committee.

**DENVER METRO
CONVENTION & VISITORS
BUREAU**
1555 California St (Suite 300)
Denver, CO 80202
Telephone: (303) 892-1112, Toll Free:
(800) 233-6837, FAX: (303) 892-
1636, Web Site: www.denver.org
Dir: Cathy Ritter
Dir Visitor Svcs: Kelly Barbello
Dir US Mktg: Amber Kollman
Conducts Business: U.S.
Employees: 43

Primary Market Served: Business &
Consumer
Catalog available online
Indirect online sales
Advertising/Marketing Budget Related
to Direct Marketing: 51-75%
Direct Marketing ad budget:
Magazines: 30%
Newspapers: 70%
Founded: 1944
Gross sales or billing: $900,000

A private non-profit corporation organized in 1908 to promote Denver as a convention & leisure travel destination.

**DIAKON LUTHERAN SOCIAL
MINISTRIES**
798 Hausman Rd (Suite 300)
Allentown, PA 18104-9108
Toll Free: (877) 342-5667, FAX: (610)
682-1559, E-Mail: swangerb@
diakon.org, Web Site: www.diakon.
org
Sr Exec Dir: Rev. Cynthia Bonney
Exec Dir Family Life Svcs: Rita Rousseau
Employees: 3,100
Primary Market Served: Consumer
Founded: 1868

Adoption, foster care, retirement communities, and social sciences.

**DIRECT GARDENING
ASSOCIATION**
PO Box 429
La Grange, GA 30241
Telephone: (706) 298-0022, FAX:
(706) 883-8215, Web Site: www.
directgardeningassociation.com
Exec Dir: Caitlin Hyatt
Primary Market Served: Business &
Consumer
Founded: 1933

Trade association representing mail order gardening industry.

**THE DIRECT MARKETING
ASSOCIATION**
1333 Broadway (Suite 301)
New York, NY 10018
Telephone: (212) 768-7277, E-Mail:
info@the-dma.org, Web Site:
thedma.org
CEO: Thomas J. Benton
Gen Counsel & Sr VP Compliance &
Ethics: Xenia Boone
Sr VP Commun: Lindsay Hunter
Sr VP CRM & Member Engagement:
Neil O'Keefe
Primary Market Served: Business

Founded: 1917

A national association of direct marketing advertising agencies dedicated to education & service to direct marketing agencies. Membership roster is available.

**THE DIRECT MARKETING
CLUB OF NEW YORK INC**
54 Adams St
Garden City, NY 11530-3918
Telephone: (516) 746-6700, FAX:
(516) 294-8141, E-Mail: info@
dmcny.org, Web Site: www.dmcny.
org
Pres: Paulette Oliva
First VP: Tim Kennon
Treas: Arthur Blumenfield
Sec: Ray Schneeberger
Past Pres: Pam Haas
Conducts Business: U.S.
Employees: 1
Primary Market Served: Business
Indirect online sales
Advertising/Marketing Budget Related
to Direct Marketing: 76-100%
Direct Marketing ad budget:
Direct Mail: 20%
Online: 80%
Founded: 1926

Non-profit association serving the direct marketing interests of its members who are primarily located in the New York City metropolitan area. Membership is available to individuals and or companies who use direct marketing in their business or who create, manage or provide services to such businesses. Holds monthly meetings.

DIRECTBUY INC
Subs. of United Consumers Club Franchising Corp
8450 Broadway
Merrillville, IN 46410
Telephone: (219) 736-1100, FAX:
(219) 755-6279, Web Site: www.
ucctotalhome.com
CEO: Mike Bornhorst
Mktg Dir: Kristy Hughes
CIO: Armin Roeseler
Chief Mktg Officer & Exec VP Sales:
Curt Hilliard
Conducts Business: U.S.
Primary Market Served: Consumer
Catalog available online
Founded: 1971

Private buying service offering furniture, furnishings, carpeting, electronics & appliances to members.

**DISABLED AMERICAN
VETERANS**
PO Box 14301

Cincinnati, OH 45250-0301
Telephone: (859) 441-7300, FAX:
(859) 442-2084, E-Mail: feedback@
davmail.org, Web Site: www.dav.org
Exec Dir: Barry A. Jesinoski
Mgr Planned Giving: Judy Sweeney
Dir, Fundraising: Susan M. Loth
Direct Mktg Mgr: Tracey Burgoon
Asst Dir, Fundraising: Jim Walding
Conducts Business: U.S.
Primary Market Served: Consumer
Catalog available online
Direct online sales
Advertising/Marketing Budget Related
to Direct Marketing: 0-25%
Founded: 1921

Veterans' membership service organization with approximately one million
disabled veterans. Funds are raised
from the general public to support service programs for disabled veterans &
their dependents.

DIVINE WORD
MISSIONARIES

1835 Waukegan Rd
Techny, IL 60082-6099
Telephone: (847) 412-7233, Toll Free:
(800) 275-0626, Web Site: www.
svdmissions.org
Devel Officer: Carmelita Linden
Primary Market Served: Business &
Consumer

DOCTORS WITHOUT
BORDERS

333 7th Ave (fl 2)
New York, NY 10001-5004
Telephone: (212) 679-6800, FAX:
(212) 679-7016, Web Site: www.
doctorswithoutborders.org
Exec Dir: Jason Cone
Primary Market Served: Consumer

DONOR SERVICES GROUP

6715 W Sunset Blvd
Los Angeles, CA 90028-7107
Telephone: (310) 788-9000, Toll Free:
(888) 474-1900, Web Site: www.
donorservicesgroup.com
Dir of Bus Devel: Colin Bickley

DOUGLAS SHAW &
ASSOCIATES

1717 Park St Ste 300
Naperville, IL 60563-4864
Telephone: (630) 562-1321, Web Site:
www.douglasshaw.com
Chmn Bd & CEO: Douglas Shaw
Founded: 1994

Full service fundraising counsel for
non-profit organizations

DRUG INFORMATION
ASSOCIATION

800 Enterprise Rd (Suite 200)
Horsham, PA 19044-3595
Telephone: (215) 442-6100, FAX:
(215) 442-6199, Web Site: www.
diahome.org
Pres: Tatsuo Kurokawa
Primary Market Served: Consumer

DRUG POLICY ALLIANCE

131 W 33 St (fl 15)
New York, NY 10001-2938
Telephone: (212) 613-8020, FAX:
(212) 613-8021, E-Mail: nyc@
drugpolicy.org, Web Site: www.
drugpolicy.org
Exec Dir: Ethan Nadelmann
Mng Dir Fin & Admin: Ryan Chavez
Mng Dir Communs: Sharda Sekaran
Primary Market Served: Business &
Consumer
Founded: 1986

Non-profit organization.

DUCKS UNLIMITED

1 Waterfowl Way
Memphis, TN 38120-2351
Telephone: (901) 758-3825, Toll Free:
(800) 45DUCKS, FAX: (901) 758-
3850, Web Site: www.ducks.org
Pres: Paul R. Bonderson Jr.
Mktg & Communs: Doug Schoenrock
Conducts Business: U.S., Canada,
Mexico
Employees: 500
Primary Market Served: Business &
Consumer
Catalog available online
Direct online sales
Advertising/Marketing Budget Related
to Direct Marketing: 0-25%
Direct Marketing ad budget:
$1,100,000
Direct Mail: 20%
Magazines: 60%
Newspapers: 5%
Online: 15%
Founded: 1937
Gross sales or billing: $198,400,000

Sportsman & environmentalist supported non-profit organization, dedicated to preserving & restoring North
America's wetland wildlife habitat.

DUNHAM & CO

6111 W Plano Pkwy (Suite 2700)
Plano, TX 75093
Telephone: (469) 454-0100
Pres & CEO: Rick Dunham
Global Dir Mktg & Brand Strategy:
Elizabeth West

Strategic consulting company working
with non-profit organizations

EASTER SEALS

233 S Wacker Dr (Suite 2400)
Chicago, IL 60606-6410
Telephone: (312) 726-6200, Toll Free:
(800) 221-6827, FAX: (312) 726-
1494, Web Site: www.easter-seals.
org
Sr VP, Devel Svcs: Maureen Haller
Conducts Business: U.S., Canada
Employees: 80
Primary Market Served: Consumer
Advertising/Marketing Budget Related
to Direct Marketing: 51-75%
Founded: 1919

National agency serving the needs of
people with disabilities.

EBERLE & ASSOCIATES INC

Subs. of Eberle Communications
Group Inc
1420 Spring Hill Rd (Suite 490)
McLean, VA 22102-3006
Telephone: (703) 821-1550, FAX:
(703) 821-0920, E-Mail: info@
eberle1.com, Web Site: www.
eberleassociates.com
Chmn: Bruce W. Eberle
Pres: M. Declan Bransfield
CFO: William D. Griffiths
Conducts Business: U.S.
Employees: 33
Primary Market Served: Consumer
Founded: 1974
Gross sales or billing: $3,000,000

Create, consult & implement direct
mail fundraising campaigns for conservative political organizations, candidates & charitable organizations.

EDISON ELECTRIC
INSTITUTE

701 Pennsylvania Ave NW
Washington, DC 20004-2696
Telephone: (202) 508-5000, FAX:
(202) 508-5096, Web Site: www.eei.
org
Exec VP Public Policy & External Af-
fairs: Brian Wolff
Chief Admin Officer: Mary Miller
Conducts Business: Worldwide
Employees: 197
Primary Market Served: Business
Catalog available online
Founded: 1933

Trade association for shareholder-
owned electric utilities.

EDUCATION MANAGEMENT
CORP

210 6th Ave (fl 33)
Pittsburgh, PA 15222-2603
Telephone: (412) 562-0900, FAX:
(412) 562-0598, Web Site: www.
edmc.edu

Sr VP & CFO: Frank Jalufka

EDUCATIONAL FIRST STEPS
2815 Gaston Ave
Dallas, TX 75226
Telephone: (214) 824-7940), FAX:
(214) 824-7428, Web Site:
educationalfirststeps.org
Exec Dir: John R. Breitfeller

Non-profit organization dedicated to
improving the quality and availability
of early childhood education for eco-
nomically disadvantaged children between the ages of birth to five.

ELDERHOSTEL INC
650 Suffolk St (#300)
Lowell, MA 01854-3694
Telephone: (978) 323-4291, Toll Free:
(800) 454-5678, FAX: (617) 426-
2166, Web Site: www.elderhostel.org
Pres & CEO: James Moses
Contact: Paula Burke
Conducts Business: Worldwide
Employees: 100
Primary Market Served: Consumer
Catalog available online
Direct online sales
Founded: 1975
Gross sales or billing: $190,000,000

Provide educational programs for
adults over 55.

ENVELOPE MANUFACTURERS ASSOCIATION
500 Montgomery St (Suite 550)
Alexandria, VA 22314-1581
Telephone: (703) 739-2200, FAX:
(703) 739-2209, Web Site: www.
envelope.org
Pres & CEO: Maynard H. Benjamin
Dir Member Svcs & GEA Administra-
tor: Jacqueline E. Jordan
Office Manager: Margie Benjamin
Conducts Business: Worldwide
Employees: 7
Primary Market Served: Business &
Consumer
Indirect online sales
Founded: 1933

Trade association of commercial envelope manufacturers.

ENVIRONMENTAL DEFENSE FUND
1875 Connecticut Ave NW (# 600)
Washington, DC 20009-5739
Telephone: (202) 387-3500, Toll Free:
(800) 684-
Dir Membership Analytics & Opers:
Bill Bond

EPILEPSY FOUNDATION
8301 Professional Pl E (Suite 200)
Landover, MD 20785-2353
Toll Free: (800) 332-1000, E-Mail:
contactus@efa.org, Web Site: www.
efa.org
Pres & CEO: Phil Gattone
Chief Devel Officer: M. Vaneeda Ben-
nett
VP Research & New Therapies:
Brandy Fureman
Conducts Business: U.S.
Employees: 80
Primary Market Served: Consumer
Catalog available online
Direct online sales
Advertising/Marketing Budget Related
to Direct Marketing: 76-100%
Direct Marketing ad budget:
$2,700,000
Direct Mail: 100%
Founded: 1988
Gross sales or billing: $16,000,000

Non-profit health organization dedicated to the welfare of people with epilepsy.

EPISCOPAL RELIEF & DEVELOPMENT
815 2nd Ave (fl 7)
New York, NY 10017-4503
Toll Free: (855) 312-4325, FAX: (212)
687-5302, Web Site: www.er-d.org
Primary Market Served: Consumer

EVENT 360 INC
55 E Jackson Blvd (Suite 1010)
Chicago, IL 60604
Telephone: (773) 247-5360, Web Site:
www.event360.com
Exec VP: Michael Murphy
Pres: Tim Brockman

FIU ONLINE
11200 SW 8th St (Marc 210)
Miami, FL 33199
Telephone: (305) 348-2000
Primary Market Served: Business &
Consumer

FALLON COMMUNITY HEALTH PLAN
10 Chestnut St
Worcester, MA 01608-2898
Telephone: (508) 799-2100, Toll Free:
(800) 333-2535, Web Site: www.
fchp.org
Dir Sls & Svc Commun: Melissa Cor-
dial
Primary Market Served: Business &
Consumer

FASHION INSTITUTE OF TECHNOLOGY LIBRARY
7th Ave at 27th St
New York, NY 10001-5992
Telephone: (212) 217-7999, FAX:
(212) 217-4371, Web Site: www.
fitnyc.edu
Head Acquisitions, Library: Leslie
Preston

Supports the academic & research
needs of the FIT community.

FATHER FLANAGAN'S BOY'S HOME
14100 Crawford St
Boys Town, NE 68010-7520
Telephone: (402) 498-1111, FAX:
(402) 498-1969, Web Site: www.
boystown.org
Pres & Natl Exec Dir: Rev. Steven E.
Boes
Exec VP Healthcare Dir: John Arch
Sr VP Mktg & Communs: Laura Tatten
Conducts Business: U.S.
Primary Market Served: Business &
Consumer
Founded: 1921

Non-profit children's home.

FATHERS OF ST EDMUND SOUTHERN MISSIONS INC
1428 Broad St
Selma, AL 36701-4300
Telephone: (334) 872-2359, FAX:
(334) 875-8189, E-Mail: jm1428@
aol.com, Web Site: www.
edmunditemissions.org
Exec Dir: Father Chad McEachern
Conducts Business: U.S.
Employees: 21
Primary Market Served: Consumer
Gross sales or billing: $3,400,000

Direct fund-raising for Fathers of St.
Edmund's mission, a sponsor for the
Edmundite missions in Alabama &
New Orleans.

FEED THE CHILDREN
333 N Meridian
Oklahoma City, OK 73107
Toll Free: (800) 627-4556, Web Site:
www.feedthechildren.org
Pres & CEO: J. C. Watts Jr.
Chief Opers Officer: Travis Arnold
Primary Market Served: Consumer

FEEDING AMERICA
35 E Wacker Dr (Suite 2000)
Chicago, IL 60601-2200
Telephone: (312) 263-2303, FAX:
(312) 263-5626, Web Site: www.
secondharvest.org
CEO: Diana Aviv

Chief Mktg Officer: Johanna Vetter

Hunger organization with nationwide network of food banks feeding the hungry.

THE FIELD MUSEUM

1400 S Lake Shore Dr
Chicago, IL 60605-2827
Telephone: (312) 665-7600, FAX: (312) 665-7601, E-Mail: events@ fieldmuseum.org, Web Site: www. fieldmuseum.org
Pres & CEO: Richard Lariviere
Chief Mktg Officer: Raymond De-Thorne
Employees: 400
Primary Market Served: Business & Consumer
Catalog available online
Direct online sales
Advertising/Marketing Budget Related to Direct Marketing: 76-100%
Direct Marketing ad budget: $600,000
Gross sales or billing: $30,000,000

Non-profit membership organization using direct response for marketing, development & fund-raising.

FIFTH AVENUE COMMITTEE

621 DeGraw St
Brooklyn, NY 11217
Telephone: (718) 237-2017, FAX: (718) 237-5366, Web Site: www. fifthave.org
Exec Dir: Michelle de la Uz
Conducts Business: U.S.
Employees: 3
Primary Market Served: Business & Consumer
Catalog available online
Founded: 1977

Commercial revitalization & community support organization.

FINANCIAL EXECUTIVES INTERNATIONAL

1250 Headquarters Plaza (fl 7)
Morristown, NJ 07960
Telephone: (973) 765-1000, FAX: (973) 765-1018, Web Site: www. financialexecutives.org
Pres & CEO: Andrej Suskavcevic
CFO: Asa Beck
Sr Mgr, Mktg & Communs: Tish Ysambart
Conducts Business: Worldwide
Employees: 40
Primary Market Served: Business
Direct online sales
Founded: 1931

Publisher of Financial Executive Magazine.

FITTER INTERNATIONAL INC

dba Fitter First
3050 - 2600 Portland St SE
Calgary, AB, Canada T2G 4M6
Telephone: (403) 243-6830, Toll Free: (800) 348-8371, FAX: (403) 229-1230, E-Mail: sales2@fitter1.com, Web Site: www.fitter1.com
Pres: Louis Stack
Controller: Margaret Stack
Conducts Business: U.S., Canada, Europe
Employees: 21
Primary Market Served: Business & Consumer
Catalog available online
Direct online sales
Founded: 1985

We promote "Balance and Fitness for Life", globally, through education and the use of functional products. We sell retail & wholesale - quality products.

FLORIDA GIFT FRUIT SHIPPERS ASSOCIATION

5500 W Concord Ave
Orlando, FL 32808-7700
Telephone: (407) 295-1491, FAX: (407) 290-0918, E-Mail: info@fgfsa. com, Web Site: www.fgfsa.com
Exec VP: Donna Garren
Conducts Business: U.S., Canada, Europe
Employees: 18
Primary Market Served: Business & Consumer
Founded: 1946
Gross sales or billing: $9,600,000

Members use direct mail to obtain orders for gift fruit packages. Packages are packed at members' packing houses & picked up by association trucks where they are brought to the association terminal for routing & shipping.

FLORIDA INSTITUTE OF CPA'S

325 W College Ave
Tallahassee, FL 32301
Telephone: (850) 224-2727, Toll Free: (800) 342-3197 (FL), FAX: (850) 222-8190, E-Mail: msc@ficpa.org, Web Site: www.ficpa.org
Pres & CEO: Deborah L. Curry
Conducts Business: U.S.
Employees: 56
Primary Market Served: Business
Catalog available online
Founded: 1905

Dedicated to the advancement of public accounting.

FOOD & WATER WATCH

1616 P St NW
Washington, DC 20036-1408
Telephone: (202) 683-2500, E-Mail: info@fwwatch.org, Web Site: www. foodandwaterwatch.org
COO: Lane Brooks

FOOD FOR THE HUNGRY INC

1224 E Washington St
Phoenix, AZ 85034-1102
Telephone: (480) 998-3100, Toll Free: (800) 248-6437, FAX: (480) 998-4806, E-Mail: hunger@fh.org, Web Site: www.fh.org
Pres & CEO: Gary Edmonds
CFO & COO: Barry Gardner
Conducts Business: Worldwide
Employees: 50
Primary Market Served: Consumer
Catalog available online
Direct online sales
Advertising/Marketing Budget Related to Direct Marketing: 76-100%
Direct Marketing ad budget: $1,851,045
Direct Mail: 95%
Online: 2%
Telephone: 3%
Founded: 1971
Gross sales or billing: $10,000,000

Non-profit, charitable organization offering both disaster & long range self-help assistance.

FOOD FOR THE POOR INC

6401 Lyons Rd
Coconut Creek, FL 33073-3602
Telephone: (954) 427-2222, Web Site: www.foodforthepoor.com
Pres & CEO: Robin Mahfood
Primary Market Served: Consumer

FOOTE, FRANCISCO & CO

19 Beverly Rd
West Caldwell, NJ 07006-6501
Telephone: (973) 226-1212, FAX: (973) 226-3409
Founder & CEO: Willy Foote
Conducts Business: U.S.
Employees: 15
Primary Market Served: Business

Full-service direct mail fund-raising consultants. Work with all production & data preparation configurations including in-house programs.

FOUNDATION FIGHTING BLINDNESS

7168 Columbia Gateway Dr Ste 100
Columbia, MD 21046-3256

Telephone: (410) 423-0600, Toll Free: (800) 683-5555, Web Site: www. fightblindness.org
CEO: William T. Schmidt
Sr Dir, Communs & Mktg: Rhea K. Faberman APR
Founded: 1971

Foundation leading the fight against blindness by advancing retinal disease research, education & public awareness.

FOUNDATION FOR CHIROPRACTIC EDUCATION & RESEARCH

380 Wright Rd
Norwalk, IA 50211-1661
Telephone: (515) 981-9888
Exec Dir: Robin Merrifield
Conducts Business: U.S.
Primary Market Served: Business & Consumer

Foundation that promotes research and education to further the chiropractic profession.

FOUNDATION OF FIRSTHEALTH

150 Applecross Rd
Pinehurst, NC 28374-8520
Telephone: (910) 695-7500, Web Site: www.firsthealth.org/foundation
Dir Program Devel: Carrie Driver
Primary Market Served: Consumer

FOX CHASE CANCER CENTER

333 Cottman Ave
Philadelphia, PA 19111-2497
Telephone: (215) 728-6900, Toll Free: (888) 369-2427, FAX: (215) 728-2594, Web Site: www.fccc.edu
Pres & CEO: Richard I. Fisher MD
Conducts Business: U.S.
Employees: 1,800
Primary Market Served: Business & Consumer
Catalog available online
Indirect online sales
Advertising/Marketing Budget Related to Direct Marketing: 0-25%
Direct Marketing ad budget:
Direct Mail: 10%
Magazines: 15%
Newspapers: 15%
TV/Radio: 60%
Founded: 1974

Hospital & institute for cancer research.

RICH FOX & ASSOCIATES INC

175 Chaparral Rd
Carmel Valley, CA 93924-9634
Telephone: (831) 659-1123
Chmn & CEO: Rich Fox

Firm that consults with & trains nonprofit fundraisers in North America, Europe & South America.

FRANCISCAN FRIARS OF THE ATONEMENT - GRAYMOOR

Rte Nine
Garrison, NY 10524
Telephone: (845) 424-3671, Toll Free: (800) 338-2620, FAX: (845) 424-2168, E-Mail: info@atonementfriars. org, Web Site: www.atonementfriars. org
Dir: Rev. James Loughran
Conducts Business: U.S., Canada, England, Italy & Japan
Employees: 300
Primary Market Served: Consumer
Founded: 1898

Ecumenical & missionary religious order.

FRANCISCAN MISSION ASSOCIATES

274-280 W Lincoln Ave
Mount Vernon, NY 10550-2509
Telephone: (914) 664-5604, FAX: (914) 664-3017, E-Mail: admin@ franciscanmissionassoc.org, Web Site: www.franciscanmissionassoc. org
Exec Dir: Kim Smolik
Assoc Dir Programs & Opers: Meghan Meros
Conducts Business: U.S., Canada
Employees: 34
Primary Market Served: Consumer
Indirect online sales
Advertising/Marketing Budget Related to Direct Marketing: 0-25%
Direct Marketing ad budget: $100,000
Direct Mail: 95%
Magazines: 1%
Newspapers: 4%
Founded: 1961

Religious non-profit organization.

FRENCH TRADE OFFICE EMBASSY OF FRANCE

1700 Broadway Ste 3201
New York, NY 10019-5925
Telephone: (212) 400-2167, Web Site: www.missioneco.org
Trade Counselor: Cecile Delettre

FUND FOR PUBLIC INTEREST RESEARCH

218 D St SE Fl 2
Washington, DC 20003-1900
Telephone: (202) 546-3965, Web Site: www.ffpir.org
Assoc Dir Partnership Prog: David Wyman
Primary Market Served: Consumer

FUNDAMENTALS CO INC

411 Euclid Ave
Bristol, VA 24201
Toll Free: (800) 303-8861, (800) 303-8861 (Fax)
Pres: Bud Cooper
Conducts Business: U.S., Canada, Mexico
Employees: 8
Primary Market Served: Business & Consumer
Advertising/Marketing Budget Related to Direct Marketing: 26-50%
Direct Marketing ad budget:
Direct Mail: 30%
Telephone: 70%
Founded: 1983

Fund-raising products - candy, cookies, citrus fruits, first aid kits, flower bulbs, fire extinguishers, greeting cards & gift wrap to schools, leagues, churches, businesses (executive gifts) & groups.

GALLUP INTER-TRIBAL INDIAN CEREMONIAL

206 W Coal Ave
Gallup, NM 87301-6306
Telephone: (505) 863-3896, E-Mail: cermonial@qwestoffice.net, Web Site: www.theceremonial.com
Pres: John Beeman
Conducts Business: U.S.
Employees: 4
Primary Market Served: Business & Consumer
Catalog available online
Direct online sales
Advertising/Marketing Budget Related to Direct Marketing: 0-25%
Founded: 1922

Nonprofit organization presenting Indian culture to tourists in the form of tribal dances, rodeos, arts & crafts displays, food & performing arts. Year-round wholesale & retail of posters, prints & stationery of American Indian design.

GALVESTON BAY FOUNDATION

17330 Hwy 3 (TX-3)
Webster, TX 77598-4133
Telephone: (281) 332-3381, Web Site: www.galvbay.org
Mktg & Membership Dir: Vicki Conley

GAY MEN'S HEALTH CRISIS
446 W 33rd St
New York, NY 10001-2601
Telephone: (212) 367-1000, FAX:
   (212) 367-1220, E-Mail:
   webmaster@gmhc.org, Web Site:
   www.gmhc.org
CEO: Kelsey Louie
VP Devel: Felecia Webb
Primary Market Served: Consumer
Non-profit AIDS service organization.

GEORGETOWN UNIVERSITY MCDONOUGH SCHOOL OF BUSINESS
37th & O Streets, NW
Washington, DC 20057
Telephone: (202) 687-3883, Web Site:
   www.msb.edu
Dean: David A. Thomas
Primary Market Served: Business &
   Consumer

GEORGIA INSTITUTE OF TECHNOLOGY
North Ave
Atlanta, GA 30332
Telephone: (404) 894-2000, Web Site:
   www.dlpe.gatech.edu

GILLETTE CHILDREN'S SPECIALTY HEALTHCARE
200 University Ave E
Saint Paul, MN 55101-2507
Telephone: (651) 291-2848, Web Site:
   www.gillettechildrens.org
Pres & CEO: Barbara Joers
Chief of Staff: Michael Healy
Primary Market Served: Business &
   Consumer
Founded: 1897

GIRL SCOUTS OF THE USA
420 Fifth Ave
New York, NY 10018-2729
Telephone: (212) 852-8000, Toll Free:
   (800) 478-7248, Web Site: www.
   girlscouts.org
CEO: Anna Maria Chavez
CFO: Angela Olden
Chief Mktg & Communs Officer: Lynn
   Godfrey
Primary Market Served: Consumer

GLENS FALLS HOSPITAL FOUNDATION
126 South St
Glens Falls, NY 12801-4321
Telephone: (518) 926-5960, FAX:
   (518) 926-7012, Web Site: www.
   glensfallshospital.org
Chair: Carl Cedrone
VP Devel: Cindy Sherwood

Primary Market Served: Consumer
Non-profit healthcare organization.

GOLDEN KEY INTERNATIONAL HONOUR SOCIETY
1040 Crown Pointe Pkwy (Suite 900)
Atlanta, GA 30338-4724
Telephone: (678) 689-2200, Toll Free:
   (800) 377-2401, FAX: (678) 689-
   2297, E-Mail: memberservices@
   goldenkey.org, Web Site: www.
   goldenkey.org
Exec Dir: Brad Rainey
VP, Commun: Melissa Leitzell
Mgr Opers & Membership: Chris Yar-
   brough

GOLF CARD INTERNATIONAL
Subs. of Affinity Group Inc
64 Inverness Dr E
Englewood, CO 80112
Telephone: (303) 792-7284, Toll Free:
   (800) 321-8269, Web Site: www.
   golfcard.com
CEO: Steve Mona
Primary Market Served: Consumer
Catalog available online
Direct online sales
Founded: 1974

Golf memberships providing savings at over 3500 courses.

THE JANE GOODALL INSTITUTE
1595 Spring Hill Rd (Suite 550)
Vienna, VA 22182-4100
Telephone: (703) 682-9220, Web Site:
   www.janegoodall.org
Founder: Jane Goodall Dr.
Chair: Brian Graff

Non profit institute whose goal is to improve the global understanding & treatment of great apes through research, public education & advocacy

GOODWILL INDUSTRIES OF SAN FRANCISCO
Subs. Goodwill Industries International
1580 Mission St
San Francisco, CA 94103-2513
Telephone: (415) 575-2240, FAX:
   (415) 575-2170, Web Site: www.
   sfgoodwill.org
CEO: Maureen Sedonaen
Conducts Business: U.S.
Employees: 450
Primary Market Served: Consumer
Advertising/Marketing Budget Related
   to Direct Marketing: 76-100%
Direct Marketing ad budget: $30,000
Direct Mail: 100%

Gross sales or billing: $60,000
Raise money for successful vocational rehabilitation & job training for adults with disabling or disadvantaging conditions.

GOVERNMENT OF INDIA TOURIST OFFICE
1270 Ave of the Americas (Suite 1808)
New York, NY 10020-1700
Telephone: (212) 586-4901, Toll Free:
   (800) 953-9399, FAX: (212) 582-
   3274, Web Site: www.
   incredibleindia.org
Contact: Kalyan Sengupta
Conducts Business: U.S., Canada, S.
   America
Employees: 8
Primary Market Served: Business &
   Consumer
Advertising/Marketing Budget Related
   to Direct Marketing: 76-100%
Founded: 1952

Publicity & promotion of tourism.

GRADUATE SCHOOL USA
US Dept. of Agriculture
600 Maryland Ave SW
Washington, DC 20024
Telephone: (202) 314-3300, FAX:
   (202) 690-6577, E-Mail: pubaffairs@
   grad.usda.gov, Web Site: www.grad.
   usda.gov
Interim Pres: Jack Maykoski
Conducts Business: Worldwide
Employees: 235
Primary Market Served: Consumer
Catalog available online
Indirect online sales
Advertising/Marketing Budget Related
   to Direct Marketing: 0-25%
Direct Marketing ad budget:
Direct Mail: $200,000
Magazines: $10,000
Newspapers: $20,000
TV/Radio: $5,000
Telephone: $20,000
Founded: 1921
Gross sales or billing: $45,000,000

Provide continuing education for adults with focus on government job skills.

BILLY GRAHAM EVANGELISTIC ASSOCIATION
1 Billy Graham Pkwy
Charlotte, NC 28201-0001
Telephone: (704) 401-2432, Toll Free:
   (877) 247-2426, Web Site: www.
   billygraham.org
Chmn: Billy Graham
CEO: Franklin Graham
Program Dir: Cliff Barrows

Conducts Business: U.S., Canada, U. K., France, Australia, Germany
Employees: 500
Primary Market Served: Consumer
Catalog available online
Direct online sales

Religious evangelistic organization.

GRAND CANYON ASSOCIATION

PO Box 399
Grand Canyon, AZ 86023
Telephone: (928) 638-2481, Toll Free: (800) 858-2808, FAX: (928-638-2484, E-Mail: gcassociation@ grandcanyon.org, Web Site: www. grandcanyon.org
CEO: Susan Schroeder
Mktg Dir: Miriam Robbins

THE GREAT BOOKS FOUNDATION

35 E Wacker Dr (Suite 400)
Chicago, IL 60601-2298
Telephone: (312) 332-5870, Toll Free: (800) 222-5870, FAX: (312) 407-0224, Web Site: www.greatbooks.org
VP: Mary Kent Sweeton

GREATER FORT WORTH BUILDERS ASSOCIATION

100 E 15th St Ste 600
Fort Worth, TX 76102-6569
Telephone: (817) 284-3566, FAX: (817) 284-6465, E-Mail: info@ fortworthbuilders.org, Web Site: www.forthworthbuilders.org
Exec VP: Kimberly Eaton-Pregler
Dir Opers: Sharon Liles Love
Conducts Business: U.S.
Employees: 6
Primary Market Served: Business & Consumer
Advertising/Marketing Budget Related to Direct Marketing: 0-25%
Direct Marketing ad budget: $150,000
Direct Mail: 5%
Newspapers: 45%
TV/Radio: 45%
Telephone: 5%
Founded: 1945
Gross sales or billing: $1,000,000

Trade association promoting housing. Sell memberships to builder, supplier & subcontractor companies.

GREATER PUBLIC

401 N 3rd St (Suite 370)
Minneapolis, MN 55401-1350
Telephone: (612) 677-1505, Toll Free: (888) 454-2314, Web Site: www. deiworksite.org
Pres: Doug Eichten

Sr Mktg Mgr: Brooke Fuchs
Assists local public radio stations with fundraising activities

GUIDEPOSTS

39 Old Ridgebury Rd Ste 2AB
Danbury, CT 06810-5122
Toll Free: (800) 932-2154, Web Site: www.guideposts.org
Sr VP: Rocco Martino
Pres & CEO: Richard V. Hopple
CFO & Sr VP: David Teitler
Conducts Business: U.S., Canada
Employees: 300
Primary Market Served: Consumer
Direct online sales
Advertising/Marketing Budget Related to Direct Marketing: 76-100%
Founded: 1945

A non-profit organization & publisher of inspirational magazines, books, audio/video & related products. Guideposts magazine circulation 4,000,000.

HIMSS

33 W Monroe St Ste 1700
Chicago, IL 60603-5616
Telephone: (312) 664-4467, FAX: (312) 664-6143, Web Site: www. himss.org

US not-for-profit organization dedicated to promoting a better understanding of health care information & management systems

HSP DIRECT

20130 Lakeview Center Plaza
Ashburn, VA 20147
Telephone: (703) 793-3220, FAX: (703) 723-5405, E-Mail: info@ hspdirect.com, Web Site: www. hspdirect.com
CEO: Jamie Hogan
Partner: Amy Paul
Partner: Matthew Schenk
Conducts Business: U.S.
Employees: 30
Primary Market Served: Business
Founded: 2001

Direct mail fundraising.

HABITAT FOR HUMANITY INTERNATIONAL

121 Habitat St
Americus, GA 31709-3499
Telephone: (229) 924-6935, Toll Free: (800) HABITAT, FAX: (229) 924-6541, Web Site: www.habitat.org
CEO: Jonathan Reckford
Exec VP, Intl Field Opers: Mike Carscaddon
VP, Govt Rels & Advocacy: Chris Vincent
Sr VP, Mktg & Commun: Chris Clarke

Primary Market Served: Business & Consumer
Gross sales or billing: $19,500,000

Non-profit ecumenical Christian housing ministry which works in partnership with families in need of housing.

HARPER COLLEGE

1200 W Algonquin Rd
Palatine, IL 60067-7373
Telephone: (847) 925-6000, Web Site: www.harpercollege.com
Pres.: Kenneth L. Ender Ph.D.

HARRIS CONNECT LLC

1400 Crossways Blvd
Chesapeake, VA 23320
Toll Free: (800) 877-6554, Web Site: www.harrisconnect.com
CEO: Robert Gluck

Directory publishers serving non-profit organizations including educational institutions, associations & organizations

HARRIS DIRECT

21250 Califa St (Suite 114)
Woodland Hills, CA 91367-5023
Telephone: (818) 222-3470 x102, Web Site: www.harris-direct.org

Telefundraising

HARVARD BUSINESS SCHOOL - EXECUTIVE EDUCATION

Soldiers Field, Teele Hall
Boston, MA 02163-1000
Telephone: (617) 496-2193, Toll Free: (800) 427-5577, E-Mail: executive_education@hbs.edu, Web Site: www.exed.hbs.edu
Porfolio Dir: Vicki Good
Primary Market Served: Consumer

HEALTHRIGHT INTERNATIONAL

240 Greene St
New York, NY 10012
Telephone: (212) 226-9890, Web Site: www.healthright.org
Exec Dir: Peter Navario
Primary Market Served: Consumer

HEBRON ACADEMY

309 Paris Rd
Hebron, ME 04238-0309
Telephone: (207) 966-2100, Toll Free: (888) 432-7664, Web Site: www. habronacademy.org
Head of School: John J. King

JAMES J HILL REFERENCE LIBRARY

80 4th St W
Saint Paul, MN 55102-1605
Telephone: (651) 265-5500, Web Site: www.jjhill.org
VP: Liz Sanborn
Devel: Danielle Parish
Primary Market Served: Consumer

Private non-profit business library

CONRAD N HILTON COLLEGE OF HOTEL & RESTAURANT MANAGEMENT UNIVERSITY OF HOUSTON

229 CN Hilton Hotel College
Houston, TX 77204-3028
Telephone: (713) 743-2255
Pres: Renu Khator
Primary Market Served: Consumer

THE HUMANE SOCIETY OF THE US

2100 L St NW
Washington, DC 20037
Telephone: (202) 452-1100, Toll Free: (866) 720-2676, Web Site: www. hsus.org
Pres & CEO: Wayne Pacelle
Primary Market Served: Consumer

IDC, LTD

2500 Paseo Verde Pkwy
Henderson, NV 89074-7117
Telephone: (702) 450-1000, FAX: (702) 450-1020, E-Mail: info@goidc.com, Web Site: www.goidc.com
Partner: Bradley S. Carlson
VP Client Svcs & Sr Consultant: Bruce Wenger
Conducts Business: U.S., Canada, Australia, U.K.
Employees: 300
Primary Market Served: Consumer
Founded: 1974

Fund-raising consultants. Specialists in mail & phone solicitation.

IHFRA

209 S Main
High Point, NC 27260
Telephone: (336) 889-3920, FAX: (336) 464-2125, E-Mail: ihfra@ihfra.org, Web Site: www.ihfra.org
Exec Dir: Kathy Parks

ISA-THE INTERNATIONAL SOCIETY OF AUTOMATION

67 T W Alexander Dr
Research Triangle Park, NC 27709
Telephone: (919) 549-8411, FAX: (919) 549-8288, E-Mail: info@isa.org, Web Site: www.isa.org
Pres: James Keaveney
Conducts Business: Worldwide
Employees: 120
Primary Market Served: Business & Consumer
Catalog available online
Direct online sales
Advertising/Marketing Budget Related to Direct Marketing: 26-50%
Direct Marketing ad budget:
Direct Mail: 70%
Magazines: 20%
Telephone: 10%
Founded: 1945
Gross sales or billing: $20,000,000

Technical magazines, books, trade shows & training centers.

IN TOUCH MINISTRIES

PO Box 7900
Atlanta, GA 30357
Toll Free: (800) 789-1473, Web Site: www.intouch.org
Dir, Strategy: Andy Maddocks
Primary Market Served: Consumer

INDEPENDENT INSURANCE AGENTS & BROKERS OF AMERICA

127 S Peyton St
Alexandria, VA 22314
Telephone: (703) 683-4422, Toll Free: (800) 221-7917, FAX: (703) 683-7556, E-Mail: info@iiaba.org, Web Site: www.iiaba.org
Exec Dir: Ron Berg
Conducts Business: U.S.
Employees: 65
Primary Market Served: Business
Catalog available online
Direct online sales
Founded: 1896
Gross sales or billing: $20,000,000

Trade association of insurance agents.

INDIAN ARTS & CRAFTS ASSOCIATION

4010 Carlisle NE (Suite C)
Albuquerque, NM 87107
Telephone: (505) 265-9149, FAX: (505) 265-8251, E-Mail: info@iaca.com, Web Site: www.iaca.com
Membership Dir: Beth Hale
Conducts Business: U.S., U.K., Australia, Canada, Germany, Italy, Japan, New Zealand
Employees: 3
Primary Market Served: Business
Catalog available online
Indirect online sales
Advertising/Marketing Budget Related to Direct Marketing: 0-25%
Direct Marketing ad budget:
Direct Mail: $10,000
Magazines: $63,000
Founded: 1974

Trade association promoting, protecting & preserving handmade Native American arts & crafts.

THE INNOVATION MACHINE

30 S Wacker Dr (Suite 2200), Chicago Mercantile Exchange
Chicago, IL 60606-7452
Telephone: (312) 238-9362, E-Mail: contact@theinnovationmachine.com, Web Site: www. theinnovationmachine.com
Pres: Scott Miller

Help companies market products

THE INSPIRATION NETWORKS

PO Box 7750
Charlotte, NC 28241
Telephone: (704) 561-7872, Toll Free: (803) 578-1000, FAX: (803) 578-1735, Web Site: www.insptoday.com
Chmn & CEO: David Cerullo

INSTITUTE FOR STUDENT ACHIEVEMENT

1 Old Country Rd Ste 250
Carle Place, NY 11514-1818
Telephone: (516) 812-6700, Web Site: www.studentachievement.org
Pres: Gerry House

INSTITUTE OF BUSINESS FORECASTING

350 Northern Blvd
Great Neck, NY 11021-4809
Telephone: (516) 504-7576, E-Mail: info@ibf.org, Web Site: www.ibf.org
Mktg Coord: Jonathan Tafarella

INSTITUTE OF MANAGEMENT ACCOUNTANTS INC

Ten Paragon Dr (Suite 1)
Montvale, NJ 07645-1718
Telephone: (201) 573-9000, Toll Free: (800) 638-4427, FAX: (201) 474-1600, E-Mail: ima@imanet.org, Web Site: www.imanet.org
Pres & CEO: Jeffrey C. Thomson
Conducts Business: U.S.
Employees: 60
Primary Market Served: Business & Consumer
Catalog available online
Direct online sales

Advertising/Marketing Budget Related
to Direct Marketing: 0-25%
Direct Marketing ad budget:
Direct Mail: 20%
Magazines: 70%
Online: 10%
Founded: 1919
Gross sales or billing: $2,500,000

A non-profit membership organization.
Develop practices for measurement,
control & reporting of accounting &
business financial results. List rental
available on conditional basis. Provide
educational programs for member continuing education needs. Publish magazines & books.

INSTITUTE OF READING DEVELOPMENT

Five Commercial Blvd
Novato, CA 94949
Telephone: (415) 884-8100, Toll Free:
(800) 964-2030, FAX: (415) 382-
0760, E-Mail: contactus@
readingprograms.org, Web Site:
www.readingprograms.org
Pres: Paul Copperman
Dir Mktg: Ryan O'Leary
Primary Market Served: Business &
Consumer

Private reading enrichment school.

INSTITUTE OF REAL ESTATE MANAGEMENT

430 N Michigan Ave
Chicago, IL 60611-4090
Telephone: (312) 329-6000, Toll Free:
(800) 837-0706, FAX: (800) 338-
4736, E-Mail: custserv@irem.org,
Web Site: www.irem.org
CEO: Russ Salzman
Conducts Business: U.S.
Employees: 80
Primary Market Served: Business
Catalog available online
Direct online sales
Advertising/Marketing Budget Related
to Direct Marketing: 76-100%
Direct Marketing ad budget:
Direct Mail: 90%
Magazines: 10%
Founded: 1933
Gross sales or billing: $11,000,000

Real estate management education,
designations & public policy advocacy.

INSTITUTIONAL ADVANCEMENT PROGRAMS INC

65 Main St (#208)
Tuckahoe, NY 10707
Telephone: (914) 779-4092, FAX:
(914) 961-4202
Pres: Bernard Brecher

Conducts Business: Worldwide
Employees: 3
Primary Market Served: Business &
Consumer
Founded: 1979
Gross sales or billing: $240,000

Strategic planners for not for profit organizations, board retreats, governance
consulting, feasibility studies & institutional managers.

THE INTERFAITH ALLIANCE

1250 24th NW (Suite 300)
Washington, DC 20037
Telephone: (202) 466-0567, Web Site:
www.interfaithalliance.org
Dir Devel: Mary Semeta
Primary Market Served: Consumer

INTERNATIONAL ACADEMY - COMPOUNDING PHARMACISTS

4638 Riverstone Blvd Ste 100
Missouri City, TX 77459-6157
Telephone: (281) 933-8400, Web Site:
www.iacprx.org
Mktg & Communs: Dagmar Anderson
Primary Market Served: Business

INTERNATIONAL ADVERTISING ASSOCIATION

747 3rd Ave (fl 2)
New York, NY 10017-2878
Telephone: (646) 722-2612, FAX:
(646) 722-2501, E-Mail: iaa@
iaaglobal.com, Web Site: www.
iaaglobal.org
Dir Membership Svcs: Marie Scotti
Mng Dir: Michael Lee
Education Coord: Nubia Martinez
Conducts Business: Worldwide
Employees: 5
Primary Market Served: Business &
Consumer
Founded: 1938

International trade association for marketing communications/advertising industry.

INTERNATIONAL CITY/ COUNTY MANAGEMENT ASSOCIATION

777 N Capitol St NE (Suite 500)
Washington, DC 20002-4201
Telephone: (202) 289-4262, FAX:
(202) 962-3500, E-Mail:
customerservice@icma.org, Web
Site: www.icma.org
Exec Dir: Robert J. O'Neil
Sr Mgr Membership Recruitment &
Benefits: Alison Miller Richards

Conducts Business: Worldwide
Employees: 123
Primary Market Served: Business
Catalog available online
Indirect online sales
Advertising/Marketing Budget Related
to Direct Marketing: 51-75%
Founded: 1914

Professional & educational organization for over 7500 appointed local government administrators.

INTERNATIONAL FELLOWSHIP OF CHRISTIANS AND JEWS

PO Box 96105
Washington, DC 20090-6105
Telephone: (312) 641-7200, Toll Free:
(800) 486-8844, Web Site: www.ifcj.
org
Pres & CEO: Yechiel Eckstein

INTERNATIONAL FOUNDATION OF EMPLOYEE BENEFIT PLANS

18700 W Bluemound Rd
Brookfield, WI 53045-2936
Telephone: (262) 373-7758, FAX:
(262) 786-8670, Web Site: www.
ifebp.org
CEO: Michael Wilson
Pres: Nicholas Counter
Sr Dir Mktg, Membership & Pub Rels:
Terry Davidson
Conducts Business: U.S. & Canada
Employees: 130
Primary Market Served: Business &
Consumer
Catalog available online
Direct online sales
Advertising/Marketing Budget Related
to Direct Marketing: 51-75%
Gross sales or billing: $25,800,000

Nonprofit educational association providing information to the employee
benefits and compensation industry
through seminars and conferences,
books, an information center, online resources, distance learning, a job and re-
sume posting service. Certified
Employee Benefits Specialist (CEBS)
and Certificate Series courses. Visit
www.ifebp.org for more information.

INTERNATIONAL FUND FOR ANIMAL WELFARE

290 Summer St
Yarmouth Port, MA 02675-1734
Telephone: (508) 744-2000, Toll Free:
(800) 932-4329, FAX: (508) 744-
2099, E-Mail: info-int@ifaw.org,
Web Site: www.ifaw.org
Mktg Mgr: Samantha Ferrigno

Primary Market Served: Consumer

INTERNATIONAL PLANNED PARENTHOOD FEDERATION WESTERN HEMISPHERE REGION INC

125 Maiden Ln (9th Fl)
New York, NY 10038-5063
Telephone: (212) 248-6400, Toll Free: (866) IPPFWHR, FAX: (212) 248-4221, E-Mail: info@ippfwhr.org, Web Site: www.ippfwhr.org
Reg Dir: Giselle Carino
Conducts Business: U.S.
Employees: 62
Primary Market Served: Consumer
Advertising/Marketing Budget Related to Direct Marketing: 76-100%
Direct Marketing ad budget: $580,000
Direct Mail: 100%
Founded: 1954
Gross sales or billing: $21,000,000

Global service provider & a leading advocate of sexual & reproductive health and rights for all

INTERNATIONAL SIGN ASSOCIATION

1001 N Fairfax St (Suite 301)
Alexandria, VA 22314-1587
Telephone: (703) 836-4012, FAX: (703) 836-8353, E-Mail: info@signs.org, Web Site: www.signs.org
Pres & CEO: Lori Anderson
Primary Market Served: Business
Founded: 1944

INTERNATIONAL SOCIETY FOR TECHNOLOGY IN EDUCATION

180 W 8th Ave (Suite 300)
Eugene, OR 97401-2916
Toll Free: (800) 336-5191, FAX: (541) 302-3778, Web Site: www.iste.org
CEO: Brian Lewis
Primary Market Served: Consumer

INVESTORS ALLIANCE INC

4710 N Federal Hwy, #381C-2, Pompano Beach, FL 33064-6553
300 Bowie St (Suite 100A)
Austin, TX 78703
Telephone: (512) 480-8100, FAX: (512) 480-9100, E-Mail: info@powerinvestor.com, Web Site: www.powerinvestor.com
Pres & Owner: Diana G. Zuniga
Conducts Business: U.S.
Employees: 10
Primary Market Served: Business & Consumer
Catalog available online
Direct online sales

Advertising/Marketing Budget Related to Direct Marketing: 76-100%
Direct Marketing ad budget:
Direct Mail: 95%
Online: 5%
Founded: 1987
Gross sales or billing: $2,000,000

Investment education & research publications. Computer software, investment models & research databases for individual investors.

INVOLVE SOCIAL

44288 Fremont Blvd
Fremont, CA 94538-6000
Telephone: (510) 396-3941, Web Site: www.involvesocial.com
Opers Mgr: Mush Ahmad

IOWA MEDICAL SOCIETY

aka IMS
515 E Locust St (#400)
Des Moines, IA 50309
Telephone: (515) 223-1401, Toll Free: (800) 747-3070, FAX: (515) 223-0590, Web Site: www.iowamedical.org
Exec Dir: Mike Abrams
VP Communs: Lucinda Stephenson APR
Conducts Business: U.S., Canada
Employees: 22
Primary Market Served: Business & Consumer
Founded: 1850

Raises money through private donations for political action.

IOWA STUDENT LOAN LIQUIDITY CORP

6805 Vista Dr, Ashford I Bldg
West Des Moines, IA 50266-9362
Telephone: (515) 243-5626, Web Site: www.studentloan.org
Mktg Dir: Suzanne Lowman
Primary Market Served: Consumer

JDRF

26 Broadway (fl 15)
New York, NY 10004-1838
Telephone: (212) 689-2860, Toll Free: (800) 533-CURE, FAX: (212) 785-9595, E-Mail: newyorkchapter@jdrf.org, Web Site: www.jdrf.org
Exec Dir: Kristin DiFoglio
Devel Dir: Kyler Hale
Primary Market Served: Business & Consumer
Founded: 1970
Gross sales or billing: $196,727,000

Raises money to fund research in the search for a cure for diabetes & its complications.

THE JACKSON LABORATORY JAX RESEARCH SYSTEMS

600 Main St
Bar Harbor, ME 04609-1523
Toll Free: (800) 422-6423, Web Site: www.jax.org/jaxmice
Database Mktg: Christian Gilbert

Non-profit organization focusing on mammalian genetics research to advance human health

THE JEWISH FEDERATION OF GREATER WASHINGTON

6101 Montrose Rd (Suite 100)
North Bethesda, MD 20852-4816
Telephone: (301) 230-7200, Web Site: www.shalomdc.org
Chief Mktg Officer: Stacye Zeisler
Primary Market Served: Consumer

JOINT COMMISSION

1 Renaissance Blvd
Oakbrook Terrace, IL 60181-4805
Telephone: (630) 792-5000, Web Site: www.jcaho.org
Assoc Dir: Donna Rutkowski
Primary Market Served: Consumer

KCEOC COMMUNITY ACTION PARTNERSHIP INC

PO Box 490
Barbourville, KY 40906-0490
Telephone: (606) 546-3152, Web Site: kceoc.com
Pres & CEO: Paul Dole

KCET

2900 W Alameda Ave #600)
Burbank, CA 91505-4268
Telephone: (747) 201-5000, FAX: (747) 201-5877, E-Mail: contact@kcet.org, Web Site: www.kcet.org
Exec Dir: Amy Nance
Chair: Scott A. Edelman
VP, Membership Mktg: Renee Williams
Vice Chmn: Ann Ehringer
Sr VP, Devel & Mktg: Nancy Rishagen
Treas: W. Scott Sanford
Sec: Vicki Reynolds
Conducts Business: U.S.
Employees: 260
Primary Market Served: Business & Consumer
Catalog available online
Advertising/Marketing Budget Related to Direct Marketing: 51-75%

Gross sales or billing: $52,400,000

Viewer-supported public television station broadcasting alternative entertainment & educational programs for southern & central California.

KMA DIRECT COMMUNICATIONS

10334 Brockwood Rd
Dallas, TX 75238
Telephone: (214) 866-7700, E-Mail: info@pursuant.com, Web Site: www.pursuant.com/kma
Pres: Tom McCabe
Conducts Business: Worldwide
Employees: 60
Primary Market Served: Business & Consumer
Advertising/Marketing Budget Related to Direct Marketing: 76-100%
Founded: 1980
Gross sales or billing: $19,000,000

Full service agency specializing in direct response communications fundraising for non-profit organizations.

KPBS FM/TV

5200 Campanile Dr San Diego State Univ
San Diego, CA 92182-1901
Telephone: (619) 594-1515, Web Site: www.kpbs.org
Dir Mktg & Corp Support: Charlotte Albergetis
Commun Mgr: Julie Schauble
Employees: 100
Primary Market Served: Consumer
Advertising/Marketing Budget Related to Direct Marketing: 0-25%
Founded: 1960

KAISER FOUNDATION HEALTH PLAN OF THE MID-ATLANTIC STATES INC

2101 E Jefferson St
Rockville, MD 20852-4908
Telephone: (301) 816-5641, Web Site: kp.org
Dir Mktg: Keith Montgomery

KANSAS STATE UNIVERSITY DIVISION OF CONTINUING EDUCATION

13 College Ct Bldg
Manhattan, KS 66506-6005
Telephone: (785) 532-5888, Web Site: www.dce.ksu.edu
Pub Info Coord: Melinda Sinn
Primary Market Served: Business & Consumer

KAPLAN TEST PREP

395 Hudson St
New York, NY 10014
Telephone: (212) 997-5800, Web Site: www.kaptest.com
CEO: John Polstein
Sr Commun Mgr: Russell Schaffer
Primary Market Served: Consumer

KENTUCKY BANKERS ASSOCIATION

600 W Main St (Suite 400)
Louisville, KY 40202-2998
Telephone: (502) 582-2453, FAX: (502) 584-6390, Web Site: www.kybanks.com
Pres: Luther Deaton
VP Spec Projects, Opers & Member Svcs Dir: Selina Parrish
Conducts Business: U.S.
Primary Market Served: Business

Vendors, banking & financial institution products.

THE KIDNEY FOUNDATION OF CANADA/GREATER ONTARIO BRANCH

1599 Hurontario St (Suite 201)
Hamilton, ON, Canada L5G 4S1
Toll Free: (800) 414-3484, FAX: (905) 318-8491, E-Mail: kidneyfoundation@bellnet.ca, Web Site: www.kidney.on.ca
Exec Dir: Jim O'Brien
Dir Mktg & Communs: Wendy Kudeba
Conducts Business: Canada
Primary Market Served: Business & Consumer
Founded: 1964
Gross sales or billing: $13,000,000

National non-profit health organization dedicated to the eradication of kidney diseases & related disorders.

SUSAN G KOMEN FOR THE CURE

5005 LBJ Fwy (Suite 250)
Dallas, TX 75244-6125
Toll Free: (877) 465-6636, Web Site: www.komen.org
Dir, Direct Mktg: Tabetha Leinweber
Primary Market Served: Business & Consumer

LIM COLLEGE

12 E 53rd St
New York, NY 10022-5268
Telephone: (212) 752-1530, Web Site: www.limcollege.edu
Professor Mktg Dept: Sally Shapiro

LIMRA INTERNATIONAL

300 Day Hill Rd
Windsor, CT 06095-1783
Toll Free: (860) 688-3358, Web Site: www.limra.com
Primary Market Served: Consumer

LAHEY CLINIC

41 Mall Rd
Burlington, MA 01805-0002
Telephone: (781) 744-5100, Web Site: www.lahey.org
Annual Fund Prog Dir: David Pearson
Primary Market Served: Consumer

Physician-led non-profit group medical practice

LARKWOOD GROUP LLC

4096 Piedmont Ave (Suite 214)
Oakland, CA 94611-5221
Telephone: (510) 444-7766
Principal: Ann Thompson-Hass

LAUTMAN MASKA NEILL & CO

1730 Rhode Island Ave NW (Suite 301)
Washington, DC 20036-3120
Telephone: (202) 296-9660, Web Site: www.lautmandc.com
Partner: Tiffany Neill
Partner: Lisa Maska
VP: Amy Sukol
Primary Market Served: Business

Consulting firm specializing in direct response fundraising for non-profit organizations

LEAGUE OF AMERICAN ORCHESTRAS

33 W 60th St (5th fl)
New York, NY 10023-7905
Telephone: (212) 262-5161, FAX: (212) 262-5198, Web Site: www.symphony.org; www.americanorchestras.org
Pres & CEO: Jesse Rosen
COO: Stephen Lisner
Conducts Business: U.S.
Employees: 38
Primary Market Served: Business
Founded: 1973
Gross sales or billing: $5,600,000

National service association chartered by Congress to ensure artistic excellence & administrative effectiveness of symphony orchestras in North America.

THE LEGAL STUDIES FORUM

101 Law School Dr
Morgantown, WV 26505

Telephone: (304) 293-5301, FAX:
(304) 293-6891, E-Mail: wvulaw@
mail.wvu.edu
Ed: James Elkins
Conducts Business: U.S., Canada
Employees: 4
Primary Market Served: Business
Advertising/Marketing Budget Related
to Direct Marketing: 76-100%
Direct Marketing ad budget: $1,500
Direct Mail: 90%
Telephone: 10%
Gross sales or billing: $14,000

Professional quarterly journal for professionals & scholars in legal studies.

THE LEUKEMIA & LYMPHOMA SOCIETY
3 International Dr (Suite 200)
Rye Brook, NY 10573
Telephone: (914) 949-5213, FAX:
(914) 949-6691, Web Site: www.lls.
org
Pres & CEO: Louis J. Degennaro
Primary Market Served: Consumer

LIBERTY FUND INC
8335 Allison Pointe Trail (Suite 300)
Indianapolis, IN 46250-1684
Telephone: (317) 842-0880, Web Site:
www.libertyfund.org
VP Publishing: Patricia Gallagher
Primary Market Served: Consumer

LIFEWAY CHRISTIAN RESOURCES
1 Lifeway Plaza
Nashville, TN 37234-1002
Telephone: (615) 251-5822, Web Site:
www.lifeway.com
Mktg Mgr: Ben Harbin

LIFT OUTREACH
7370 Dogwood Pk
Richland Hills, TX 76118-6403
Telephone: (817) 658-2980
Principal: Gary Lawrence

LINCOLN PARK ZOO
2001 N Clark St
Chicago, IL 60614
Telephone: (312) 742-2000, FAX:
(312) 742-2137, E-Mail:
webmaster@lpzoo.com, Web Site:
www.lpzoo.com
Pres, CEO & Dir: Kevin Bell
Mktg Dir: Ann Carson
Membership Dir: Michelle Clayton
Conducts Business: U.S.
Employees: 240
Primary Market Served: Consumer
Catalog available online
Direct online sales

Advertising/Marketing Budget Related
to Direct Marketing: 0-25%
Direct Marketing ad budget: $150,000
Direct Mail: 70%
Telephone: 30%
Founded: 1868
Gross sales or billing: $8,000,000

Regional fund-raisers through direct
mail & telemarketing.

LOCAL SEARCH ASSOCIATION
820 Kirts Blvd (Suite 100)
Troy, MI 48084-4836
Telephone: (248) 244-6200, FAX:
(248) 244-0700, Web Site: www.
localsearchassociation.org
Pres: Negley Norton
Creative Mktg Specialist: Matthew
Fisher
Conducts Business: Worldwide
Employees: 50
Primary Market Served: Business &
Consumer
Catalog available online
Direct online sales
Founded: 1988

Trade association representing the Yellow Pages industry.

LORMAN EDUCATION SERVICES
2510 Alpine Rd
Eau Claire, WI 54703-9560
Telephone: (715) 833-3940
CEO: John Busch

LOUISIANA STATE MUSEUM
Div. of Dept of Culture Recreation &
Tourism State of Louisiana
701 Chartres St
New Orleans, LA 70116-3205
Telephone: (504) 568-6968, Toll Free:
(800) 568-6968, FAX: (504) 568-
4995, Web Site: www.lsm.crt.state.
la.us
Dir: Mark A. Tullos Jr.
Conducts Business: U.S.
Employees: 100
Primary Market Served: Consumer
Catalog available online
Advertising/Marketing Budget Related
to Direct Marketing: 0-25%
Founded: 1912

State museum system comprised of
nine landmarks & permanent collections of artifacts, documents & works
of art.

LOYOLA UNIVERSITY CHICAGO
820 N Michigan Ave
Chicago, IL 60611-2147

Telephone: (312) 915-8900, Web Site:
www.luc.edu

LUTHERAN CHURCH EXTENSION FUND - MISSOURI SYNOD
10733 Sunset Office Dr (Suite 300),
Sunset Corporate Center
Saint Louis, MO 63127-1020
Toll Free: (800) 843-5233, FAX: (314)
996-1131, Web Site: www.lcef.org
Pres & CEO: Rev. Robert C. Robertson
VP Mktg & Customer Support: Becca
Jones
Conducts Business: U.S.
Employees: 50
Primary Market Served: Business &
Consumer

Provides funds for church construction.

MGMA-ACMPE
104 Inverness Terr Dr E
Englewood, CO 80112-5306
Telephone: (303) 799-1111, Toll Free:
(877) 275-6462, E-Mail: infocenter@
mgma.com, Web Site: www.mgma.
com
CEO: Mickey Smith
COO & Staff Contact: Kevin Spencer
Primary Market Served: Business

Medical group administration professional association.

MSU FEDERAL CREDIT UNION
3777 West Rd
East Lansing, MI 48823-8029
Telephone: (517) 333-2254, Web Site:
www.msufcu.org
VP, Mktg Ecommerce: April Clobes

MAINE POTATO BOARD
744 Main St (Rm 1)
Presque Isle, ME 04769
Telephone: (207) 769-5061, FAX:
(207) 764-4148, E-Mail:
mainepotatoes@mainepotatoes.com,
Web Site: www.mainepotatoes.com
Pres: Thomas Qualey
Exec Dir: Michael P. Corey
Asst Exec Dir: Donald Flannery
Employees: 4
Primary Market Served: Business &
Consumer

State agency promoting Maine potatoes.

MAKE-A-WISH FOUNDATION OF AMERICA
4742 N 24th St (Suite 400)
Phoenix, AZ 85016-4862

Telephone: (602) 279-9474, FAX: (602) 279-0855, Web Site: www.wish.org
Pres & CEO: David Williams
Primary Market Served: Consumer
Founded: 1980

Fund-raising organization that grants wishes for children with life-threatening illnesses.

MANHATTAN COLLEGE
Manhattan College Pkwy
Bronx, NY 10471-3915
Telephone: (718) 862-7285, Web Site: www.manhattan.edu
Primary Market Served: Consumer

MAP INTERNATIONAL
2200 Glynco Pkwy
Brunswick, GA 31521
Telephone: (912) 265-6010, Toll Free: (800) 225-8550, FAX: (912) 265-6170, Web Site: www.map.org
Pres: Michael Nyenauis
Primary Market Served: Business & Consumer
Founded: 1954

Non-profit Christian global organization.

MARCH OF DIMES FOUNDATION
1275 Mamaroneck Ave
White Plains, NY 10605
Telephone: (914) 997-4488, Web Site: www.marchofdimes.org
Pres: Jennifer Howse
Sr VP: Lisa Bellsey
Conducts Business: Worldwide
Primary Market Served: Business & Consumer

Not-for-profit health agency.

MARIAN HELPERS CENTER
Subs. of Congregation of Marians
2 Prospect Hill Rd
Stockbridge, MA 01262
Telephone: (413) 298-3691, Toll Free: (800) 462-7426, FAX: (413) 298-3583, Web Site: www.marian.org
Dir: Father Chris Alar MIC
Conducts Business: Worldwide
Employees: 95
Primary Market Served: Consumer
Advertising/Marketing Budget Related to Direct Marketing: 0-25%
Direct Marketing ad budget:
Direct Mail: $400,000
Founded: 1945

Non-profit Catholic religious fund-raising & publishing organization.

MARKET DEVELOPMENT GROUP INC
1832 Connecticut Ave N, 1832 Connecticut Avenue, NW
Washington, DC 20009
Telephone: (202) 298-8030, FAX: (202) 244-4999, Web Site: www.mdginc.org
Pres: W. Michael Gretschel
Employees: 50
Founded: 1978

MARYKNOLL FATHERS & BROTHERS
55 Ryder Rd, 55 Ryder Rd, Ossining
Ossining, NY 10562
Telephone: (914) 941-7590, Toll Free: (888) 627-9566, FAX: (914) 944-3613, E-Mail: mkweb@maryknoll.org, Web Site: www.maryknoll.org
Reg Dir: Deacon Paul Bork
Conducts Business: Worldwide
Employees: 429
Primary Market Served: Consumer
Catalog available online
Indirect online sales
Advertising/Marketing Budget Related to Direct Marketing: 76-100%
Founded: 1911

Recruit, train, send & support American missionaries working in 38 foreign countries.

GEORGE MASON UNIVERSITY SCHOOL OF MANAGEMENT
4400 University Dr (MS 1B1)
Fairfax, VA 22030-4422
Telephone: (703) 993-1871
Primary Market Served: Consumer

Business school

MASSACHUSETTS HORTICULTURAL SOCIETY
900 Washington St
Wellesley, MA 02482
Telephone: (617) 933-4900, (617) 933-4929, FAX: (617) 933-4901, E-Mail: hort_line@masshort.org, Web Site: www.masshort.org
Pres: Kathy Macdonald
Dir Mktg & Commun: Jeanne O'Rourke
Dir Horticulture Education & Outreach: Trish Wesley Umbrell
Dir Flower Show & Special Events: Carolyn H. Weston
Gardens Curator: David Fiske
Conducts Business: U.S.
Employees: 26
Primary Market Served: Business & Consumer
Catalog available online

Direct online sales
Advertising/Marketing Budget Related to Direct Marketing: 0-25%
Direct Marketing ad budget:
Direct Mail: $20,000
Founded: 1829

Non-profit educational organization specializing in horticultural books, prints, shows & instructional classes.

MASTERWORKS
19462 Powder Hill Pl NE Ste 100
Poulsbo, WA 98370-7472
Telephone: (360) 394-4300, Web Site: www.masterworks.com
Sr VP Fin & Admin: Thomas Behrens
Pres: Stephen Woodworth

Marketing firm for non-profit fundraising Christian ministries

MATT & KUMPANY KUZINS
1512 14th St
Sacramento, CA 95814
Telephone: (916) 446-2008, FAX: (916) 446-5302, E-Mail: matt@kuzins.com
Pres: Matt Kuzins
Conducts Business: U.S.
Employees: 5
Primary Market Served: Consumer
Catalog available online
Advertising/Marketing Budget Related to Direct Marketing: 76-100%
Direct Marketing ad budget:
Direct Mail: 100%
Founded: 1983
Gross sales or billing: $400,000

Direct mail fund-raising consultants.

MCPHERSON ASSOCIATES INC
1235 Westlakes Dr (Suite 130)
Berwyn, PA 19312-2412
Telephone: (610) 640-1555, Web Site: www.mcphersonassociates.com
Pres & Creative Dir: Richard McPherson

Fundraising consulting

MEDIC ALERT FOUNDATION
5226 Pirrone Court
Salida, CA 95368
Telephone: (209) 668-3333, Toll Free: (800) 432-5378, FAX: (209) 669-2495, Web Site: www.medicalert.org
Pres & CEO: David Leslie
Primary Market Served: Consumer

Founded: 1956

Provides medical emergency information to emergency responders via a body-worn emblem (bracelet or necklace) with critical information tied to a medical hotline.

MEDICAL LETTER INC

145 Huguenot St (Suite 312)
New Rochelle, NY 10801-7537
Telephone: (914) 235-0500, Web Site: www.medicalletter.org
Dir Mktg: Joanne Valentino
Primary Market Served: Business
Direct online sales
Advertising/Marketing Budget Related to Direct Marketing: 76-100%
Founded: 1959

MEDILL IMC/ NORTHWESTERN UNIVERSITY

1870 Campus Dr
Evanston, IL 60208-0885
Telephone: (847) 467-3433
Assoc Dean: Tom Collinger
Primary Market Served: Consumer

MEMORIAL SLOAN KETTERING CANCER CENTER

1275 York Ave
New York, NY 10065
Telephone: (212) 639-2000, Web Site: www.mskcc.org
Dir: Joan Massague
Primary Market Served: Consumer

THE MENNINGER FOUNDATION

2801 Gessner Dr, Menninger Clinic
Houston, TX 77280
Telephone: (713) 275-5000, Toll Free: (800) 351-9058, FAX: (713) 275-5107, Web Site: www.menningerclinic.com
Pres, CEO & Chief of Staff: C. Edward Coffey
Conducts Business: U.S.
Employees: 1,100
Primary Market Served: Business & Consumer
Catalog available online
Advertising/Marketing Budget Related to Direct Marketing: 26-50%
Direct Marketing ad budget:
Direct Mail: $400,000
Newspapers: $200,000
Telephone: $50,000
Founded: 1926

Gross sales or billing: $60,000,000

Psychiatric institute providing care & treatment. Also involved in research, education & the promotion of mental health.

MERCY HOME FOR BOYS & GIRLS

1140 W Jackson Blvd
Chicago, IL 60607-2906
Telephone: (312) 738-7560, Toll Free: (888) 981-4682, Web Site: www.mercyhome.org
Dir: Dee Atkins

THE METROPOLITAN OPERA

30 Lincoln Center
New York, NY 10023
Telephone: (212) 362-6000, (212) 799-3100, FAX: (212) 870-7695, Web Site: www.metoperafamily.org
Gen Mgr: Peter Gelb
Music Dir: James Levine
Asst Mgr, Mktg & Commun: Lisa Mallory
Dir, Patron & Individual Giving: Lisa Hayward
Primary Market Served: Consumer
Catalog available online
Direct online sales
Founded: 1883

Performing arts association.

JOYCE MEYER MINISTRIES

700 Grace Pkwy
Fenton, MO 63026-5390
Telephone: (636) 349-0303, Web Site: www.joycemeyer.org
Division Mgr, Mktg Dir: Paul Huse

MEYER PARTNERS

1701 E Woodfield Rd (Suite 425)
Schaumburg, IL 60173-5313
Telephone: (630) 339-3930, Toll Free: (800) 676-4176, FAX: (630) 339-3939, E-Mail: info@meyerpartners.com, Web Site: www.meyerpartners.com
Pres: Dennis L. Meyer

Full service integrated fundraising & marketing communications agency serving non-profit organizations

MICHIGAN APPLE COMMITTEE

13750 S Sedona Pkwy (Suite 3)
Lansing, MI 48906-8101
Telephone: (517) 669-8353, Toll Free: (800) 456-2753, FAX: (517) 669-9506, E-Mail: staff@michiganapples.com, Web Site: www.michiganapples.com

Dir, Fin: Diane Smith
Mktg & Communs: Gretchen Mensing
Conducts Business: U.S., Europe
Employees: 6
Primary Market Served: Business & Consumer

Management of marketing & promotional programs for apple growers located in Michigan.

MILITARY OFFICERS ASSOCIATION OF AMERICA

201 N Washington St
Alexandria, VA 22314-2539
Telephone: (703) 549-2311, Toll Free: (800) 234-6622, E-Mail: msc@moaa.org, Web Site: www.moaa.org
Dir Membership & Mktg: Kathy Partain
Primary Market Served: Business & Consumer

MILITARY ORDER OF THE PURPLE HEART SVC

PO Box 49
Annandale, VA 22003-0049
Telephone: (703) 256-6139
Primary Market Served: Business & Consumer

MINDSET DIRECT

1700 N Jefferson St
Arlington, VA 22205-2817
Telephone: (703) 538-6463, Web Site: www.mindsetdirect.com
Principal: Kristin McCurry

MINNESOTA MULTI HOUSING ASSOCIATION

1600 W 82nd St (Suite 110)
Bloomington, MN 55431-1411
Telephone: (952) 854-8500, FAX: (952) 854-3810, E-Mail: mha@mmha.com, Web Site: www.mmha.com
Pres: Mary Rippe
Dir Membership & Mktg: Connie Anderson
Conducts Business: U.S.
Employees: 11
Primary Market Served: Business
Catalog available online
Direct online sales
Advertising/Marketing Budget Related to Direct Marketing: 26-50%
Direct Marketing ad budget:
Direct Mail: 75%
Newspapers: 15%
Telephone: 10%
Founded: 1967

Gross sales or billing: $450,000

Membership - apartment owners association, owners & vendors. Forms, leases, legal handbooks. Exhibit space in one trade show.

MINNESOTA PUBLIC RADIO

480 Cedar St
Saint Paul, MN 55101-2230
Telephone: (651) 290-1500, Toll Free: (800) 228-7123, FAX: (651) 290-1260, E-Mail: mail@mpr.org, Web Site: www.mpr.org
VP, Devel: Jon Gossett
Dir, Membership Mktg: Al Anderson
Employees: 450
Primary Market Served: Business & Consumer
Catalog available online
Direct online sales
Advertising/Marketing Budget Related to Direct Marketing: 0-25%
Founded: 1967
Gross sales or billing: $46,000,000

Public Radio.

MISSIONARY SOCIETY OF ST COLUMBAN

PO Box 10
Saint Columbans, NE 68056-0010
Telephone: (402) 291-1920, Web Site: www.columban.org
COO: Jeff Norton

MISSOURI LANDSCAPE & NURSERY ASSOCIATION

16072 Pike 9292
Bowling Green, MO 63334
Telephone: (636) 542-1234, E-Mail: admin@mlng.org, Web Site: www.mlna.org
Pres: Aaron Jung
Conducts Business: U.S.
Employees: 250
Primary Market Served: Business
Catalog available online
Direct Marketing ad budget: $10,000
Direct Mail: 90%
Magazines: 10%
Gross sales or billing: $40,000

Professional trade association representing the nursery, landscape & garden center industry in the state of MO.

MITSUBISHI MOTORS NORTH AMERICA INC

6400 Katella Ave
Cypress, CA 90630
Telephone: (714) 372-6000, Toll Free: (888) 648-7820, Web Site: www.mitsubishicars.com
CEO: Yoichi Yokozawa
Conducts Business: U.S.
Primary Market Served: Consumer

Catalog available online
Indirect online sales
Advertising/Marketing Budget Related to Direct Marketing: 0-25%
Direct Marketing ad budget: $500,000
Direct Mail: 1%
Magazines: 8%
Newspapers: 5%
TV/Radio: 85%
Telephone: 1%
Founded: 1981

Automobile distributor to franchisees.

THE MORTON ARBORETUM

4100 Illinois (Route 53)
Lisle, IL 60532-1293
Telephone: (630) 968-0074, Web Site: www.mortonarb.org
Asst Dir, Membership: Karin Jaros

MOTION PICTURE & TELEVISION FUND

23388 Mulholland Dr
Woodland Hills, CA 91364-2733
Toll Free: (855) 760-6783, E-Mail: info@mptf.com, Web Site: www.mptf.com
CEO: Bob Beitcher
Primary Market Served: Business & Consumer
Founded: 1921

Fund-raising for hospital & health-care for anyone in motion picture & television industry.

MULTI-LEVEL MARKETING INTERNATIONAL ASSOCIATION (MLMIA)

119 Stanford CT, Irvine, CA 92612-1671-POST
119 Stanford Ct
Irvine, CA 92612-1671
Telephone: (949) 257-0931, FAX: (949) 281-2114, E-Mail: info@mlmia.com, Web Site: www.mlmia.com
Chmn: Doris Wood
Co-Founder: Michael L. Sheffield
Conducts Business: U.S., Canada, Malaysia, U.K., Australia, Hong Kong
Employees: 2
Primary Market Served: Business & Consumer
Indirect online sales
Advertising/Marketing Budget Related to Direct Marketing: 51-75%
Direct Marketing ad budget:
Newspapers: 100%
Founded: 1985

MLMIA is a non-profit association representing the Network Marketing Industry. The three major categories of membership are: Network Marketing Companies, Independent Network Mar-

keting Distributors or Representatives & Support Companies - those companies who provide products or services to MLM companies or distributors.

MULTIPLE SCLEROSIS ASSOCIATION OF AMERICA

375 Kings Hwy N
Cherry Hill, NJ 08034
Telephone: (856) 488-4500, Toll Free: (800) 532-7667, FAX: (856) 661-9797, Web Site: www.mymsaa.com
Pres & CEO: Gina Ross Murdoch

MULTIVIEW

7701 Las Colinas Ridge (Suite 800)
Irving, TX 75063-7555
Telephone: (972) 402-7056
VP Sls: Michael Scheevel
Catalog available online

MURDER BY MAIL

PO Box 789
West Tisbury, MA 02575
Telephone: (508) 693-5205, (617) 670-9400, FAX: (508) 693-7997, E-Mail: info@murderbymail.com, Web Site: www.murderbymail.com
Pres: Janice Sparks
Conducts Business: U.S., U.K., S. America, Canada
Employees: 3
Primary Market Served: Business & Consumer
Catalog available online
Indirect online sales
Advertising/Marketing Budget Related to Direct Marketing: 51-75%
Direct Marketing ad budget:
Magazines: 75%
Newspapers: 25%
Founded: 1980
Gross sales or billing: $125,000

Interactive murder mystery parties & events. Used for social events, incentive groups, fund raisers, private parties, T & E, used professionally by restaurants, hotels, inns & event planners. Package includes: custom materials, complete scenario, props, storyline & assistance in planning. Done on a reasonable per person fee. Package is customized by size & theme.

MUSCULAR DYSTROPHY ASSOCIATION

222 S Riverside Plaza (Suite 1500)
Chicago, IL 60606
Toll Free: (800) 572-1717, Web Site: www.mda.org
Pres & CEO: Steven M. Derks
Exec VP, Chief Communs & Mktg Officer: Steven G. Ford

Conducts Business: U.S.
Employees: 1,500
Primary Market Served: Business &
   Consumer
Advertising/Marketing Budget Related
   to Direct Marketing: 0-25%
Direct Marketing ad budget:
Direct Mail: $10,000,000
Online: $10,000
TV/Radio: $6,000,000
Founded: 1950
Gross sales or billing: $187,000,000

Voluntary national health agency dedicated to conquering neuromuscular diseases.

NAACP

4805 Mount Hope Dr
Baltimore, MD 21215-3206
Telephone: (410) 580-5777, Web Site:
   www.naacp.org
COO: Claudia Withers
Exec VP, Devel: Virgil Ecton
Primary Market Served: Consumer

The National Association for the Advancement of Colored People is a civil
rights organization with a core mission
to ensure the political, educational, social & economic equality of all persons.

NARAL PRO-CHOICE
AMERICA

1156 15th St NW (Suite 700)
Washington, DC 20005-1704
Telephone: (202) 973-3000, FAX:
   (202) 973-3096, Web Site: www.
   naral.com
Pres: Ilyse Hogue

NASA FEDERAL CREDIT
UNION

500 Prince Georges Blvd
Upper Marlboro, MD 20774-8732
Telephone: (301) 249-1800, Web Site:
   www.nasafcu.com

NASW ASSURANCE
SERVICES INC

Subs. of National Association of Social
   Workers Inc
50 Citizens Way (Suite 304)
Frederick, MD 21701
Toll Free: (800) 668-4274, E-Mail:
   zxi@naswasi.org, Web Site: www.
   naswinsurancetrust.org
CEO: Tony Benedetto
Conducts Business: U.S.
Employees: 6
Primary Market Served: Consumer
Catalog available online
Indirect online sales
Direct Marketing ad budget:
   $3,000,000

Direct Mail: 85%
Magazines: 5%
Online: 5%
Telephone: 5%
Founded: 2007
Gross sales or billing: $6,000,000

Sell group and professional liability insurance to National Association of Social Workers members.

NBI INC

PO Box 3067
Eau Claire, WI 54702-3067
Telephone: (715) 835-8525, Web Site:
   www.nbi-sems.com
Dir Mktg: Tia Embke
Primary Market Served: Consumer

Provides continuing legal education

NEA'S MEMBER BENEFITS
CORP

900 Clopper Rd
Gaithersburg, MD 20878-1360
Telephone: (301) 251-9600, FAX:
   (301) 527-8210, Web Site: www.
   neamb.com
VP Mktg: Steve Levy
Primary Market Served: Consumer
Founded: 1941

Market to NEA members & family.

NNE MARKETING

105 Paul Revere Rd
Concord, MA 01742-4817
Telephone: (617) 429-7999, Web Site:
   www.nnemarketing.com
Principal: Craig Zelstar

Direct marketing agency focusing on
fundraising & membership programs

NTL INSTITUTE

8380 Colesville Rd (Suite 560)
Silver Spring, MD 20910-6262
Telephone: (301) 565-3200, E-Mail:
   info@ntl.org, Web Site: www.ntl.org
COO: Scott McVicker
Conducts Business: Worldwide
Employees: 20
Primary Market Served: Business &
   Consumer
Catalog available online
Indirect online sales
Advertising/Marketing Budget Related
   to Direct Marketing: 0-25%
Direct Marketing ad budget: $139,000
Founded: 1947
Gross sales or billing: $5,000,000

Conducts programs in the areas of human relations training, diversity, management development, organizational
development & training of facilitators
& consultants; also run a joint Masters

program with The American University
in OD & with Cleveland State University in Diversity.

NYSARC, INC

393 Delaware Ave
Delmar, NY 12054
Telephone: (518) 439-8311, FAX:
   (518) 439-1893, E-Mail: info@
   nysarc.org, Web Site: www.nysarc.
   org
Primary Market Served: Consumer

Family-based organization working
with and for people with intellectual &
other developmental disabilities

NATIONAL ACTIVE &
RETIRED FEDERAL
EMPLOYEES
ASSOCIATION

606 N Washington St
Alexandria, VA 22314-1914
Telephone: (703) 838-7760, Toll Free:
   (800) 456-8410, FAX: (703) 838-
   7785, Web Site: www.narfe.org
Natl Pres: Joseph A. Beaudoin
Natl VP: Paul H. Carew
Natl Sec: Elaine Hughes
Natl Treas: Richard Thissen
Primary Market Served: Business &
   Consumer
Direct online sales
Founded: 1921

Association for retired federal employees.

NATIONAL ASSOCIATION
FOR FEMALE
EXECUTIVES

Div. of Working Mother Media
2 Park Ave (fl 10)
New York, NY 10016-5604
Toll Free: (800) 927-6233, E-Mail:
   info@nafe.com, Web Site: www.
   nafe.com
Pres: Betty Spence
Newsletter Editor: Paula Damiano
Commun Mgr & Producer: Roxanne
   Natale
Conducts Business: U.S.
Employees: 32
Primary Market Served: Business &
   Consumer
Catalog available online
Direct online sales
Advertising/Marketing Budget Related
   to Direct Marketing: 76-100%
Founded: 1972
Gross sales or billing: $9,000

Woman's organization & publisher of a
magazine for career-oriented women.

NATIONAL ASSOCIATION FOR PRINTING LEADERSHIP

75 W Century Rd (Suite 100)
Paramus, NJ 07652-1461
Telephone: (201) 634-9600, Toll Free:
    (800) 642-6275, FAX: (201) 634-
    0324, E-Mail: webwaster@napl.org,
    Web Site: www.napl.org
Sr Dir: Dawn Lospaluto
Employees: 36
Primary Market Served: Business
Founded: 1933
Gross sales or billing: $2,700,000

Non-profit printing association.

NATIONAL ASSOCIATION OF HOME BUILDERS

1201 15th St NW
Washington, DC 20005-2800
Telephone: (202) 266-8200, Toll Free:
    (800) 368-5242, FAX: (202) 266-
    8400, Web Site: www.nahb.org
VP & CEO: Jerry Howard
Sls & Bus Mgr: Stephanie Thomas
Founded: 1942

National trade association of the American housing industry.

NATIONAL ASSOCIATION OF PROFESSIONAL INSURANCE AGENTS

400 N Washington St
Alexandria, VA 22314-2353
Telephone: (703) 836-9340, FAX:
    (703) 836-1279, E-Mail: web@
    pianet.org, Web Site: www.pianet.
    com
Exec VP & CEO: Mike Becker
Primary Market Served: Consumer
Catalog available online
Founded: 1931

Consumer not-for-profit association.

NATIONAL ASSOCIATION OF PUBLISHERS REPRESENTATIVES

2800 W Higgins Rd (Suite 440)
Hoffman Estates, IL 60169
Telephone: (877) 263-9640, FAX:
    (847) 885-8393, E-Mail: info@
    napronline.com, Web Site: www.
    napronline.com
Pres: Darren Dunay
VP: Craig Pitcher
Sec & Treas: Tom Brun
Primary Market Served: Business
Catalog available online
Founded: 1952

Over 300 independent ad space representatives handling consumer, trade, business, international print & electronic media. Regional meetings.

NATIONAL ASSOCIATION OF REALTORS

430 N Michigan Ave
Chicago, IL 60611-4087
Telephone: (312) 329-8526, Toll Free:
    (800) 874-6500, Web Site: www.
    realtors.org
Mgr Mktg Res: Lisa Herceg
Primary Market Served: Business & Consumer

NATIONAL AUTOMATED CLEARING HOUSE ASSOCIATION

RP-NFOA
13450 Sunrise Valley Dr (Suite 100)
Herndon, VA 20171
Telephone: (703) 561-1100, FAX:
    (703) 787-0996, Web Site: www.
    nacha.org
Pres: Elliott C. McEntee
Membership Mktg & Commun Dir:
    Robin Reeder
Conducts Business: U.S.
Employees: 21
Primary Market Served: Business & Consumer
Founded: 1974

Electronic payments network association.

NATIONAL BASKETBALL ASSOCIATION

645 Fifth Ave
New York, NY 10022
Telephone: (212) 407-8000, FAX:
    (212) 826-0579, Web Site: www.nba.
    com
Commissioner: Adam Silver
Exec VP Team Mktg & Bus Opers:
    Amy Brooks
Exec VP Global Mktg Partnerships:
    Emilio Collins
Sr VP Mktg: Kelly Flatow
Sr VP Sls Devel & Retail Mktg: Chris
    Brennan
Sr VP Team Mktg & Bus Opers: Brendan Donohue
Sr VP Entertainment & Player Mktg:
    Charles Rosenzweig
Conducts Business: U.S., Italy, Germany, Australia, Mexico
Employees: 400
Primary Market Served: Consumer
Advertising/Marketing Budget Related
    to Direct Marketing: 0-25%
Direct Marketing ad budget:
Magazines: 90%
TV/Radio: 10%
Gross sales or billing: $500,000

Promotes the association and catalog.

NATIONAL COMMITTEE TO PRESERVE SOCIAL SECURITY & MEDICARE

10 "G" St NE (Suite 600)
Washington, DC 20002-4215
Telephone: (202) 216-0420, Toll Free:
    (800) 966-1935, FAX: (202) 216-
    0446, E-Mail: kreard@ncpssm.org,
    Web Site: www.ncpssm.org
Chair: Carroll L. Estes Ph.D.
Exec VP: Max Richtman
Dir Mktg: J. David Krear
Sec: Sandra J. Wagenfeld
Conducts Business: U.S.
Employees: 43
Primary Market Served: Consumer
Catalog available online
Direct online sales
Advertising/Marketing Budget Related
    to Direct Marketing: 76-100%
Direct Marketing ad budget:
    $18,000,000
Direct Mail: 100%
Founded: 1982
Gross sales or billing: $25,000,000

Non-profit organization.

NATIONAL COMMUNITY PHARMACISTS ASSOCIATION

100 Daingerfield Rd
Alexandria, VA 22314
Telephone: (703) 683-8200, Toll Free:
    (800) 544-7447, FAX: (703) 683-
    3619, E-Mail: info@ncpanet.org,
    Web Site: www.ncpanet.org
CEO: B. Douglas Hoey
Sr VP & COO: Patrick Berryman
Conducts Business: U.S.
Employees: 40
Primary Market Served: Business & Consumer
Catalog available online
Direct online sales
Advertising/Marketing Budget Related
    to Direct Marketing: 51-75%
Direct Marketing ad budget:
Direct Mail: 35%
Magazines: 30%
Telephone: 35%
Founded: 1898

Provide professional services, co-sponsored continuing education & promotional programs to the owners of over 30,000 pharmacies.

NATIONAL CONTRACT MANAGEMENT ASSOCIATION

21740 Beaumeade Cir (Suite 125)
Ashburn, VA 20147-6237

Telephone: (571) 382-0082, Toll Free: (800) 344-8096, FAX: (703) 448-0939, E-Mail: memberservices@ ncmghq.org, Web Site: www. ncmahq.org
Exec Dir: Michael Fischetti
Dir Member Membership & Natl Sec: Karen Secker
Primary Market Served: Business & Consumer

NATIONAL COUNCIL ON COMPENSATION INSURANCE INC

901 Peninsula Corp Cir
Boca Raton, FL 33487
Telephone: (561) 893-1000, Toll Free: (800) 622-4123, FAX: (561) 893-1191, Web Site: www.ncci.com
Pres & CEO: Stephen J. Klingel
Mktg: Diane Clifton
Primary Market Served: Business
Founded: 1919

Data products for insurance companies.

NATIONAL COURT REPORTERS ASSOCIATION

12030 Sunrise Valley Dr (Suite 400)
Reston, VA 20191
Telephone: (703) 556-6272, Toll Free: (800) 272-6272, FAX: (703) 391-0629, E-Mail: msic@ncrahg.org, Web Site: www.ncraonline.org
Exec Dir & CEO: Michael S. Nelson
Conducts Business: U.S., Canada
Primary Market Served: Business & Consumer
Catalog available online
Direct online sales
Founded: 1899

Memberships, programs & services to court reporters, court reporting students, and other members of the legal system.

NATIONAL DEFENSE INDUSTRIAL ASSOCIATION

2111 Wilson Blvd (Suite 400)
Arlington, VA 22201-3061
Telephone: (703) 522-1820, FAX: (703) 522-1885, Web Site: www. ndia.org
Mktg: Rekdal Scott
Conducts Business: U.S.
Employees: 60
Primary Market Served: Consumer
Direct online sales
Advertising/Marketing Budget Related to Direct Marketing: 26-50%
Founded: 1919

Non-profit membership association that represents the concerns & business interests of nearly 1,000 companies &

their one million employees, & over 28,000 individual members from both government & industry. Members come from a broad range of commercial, research & development, legal & educational entities & individuals from the United States & countries that have reciprocal procurement agreements with the U.S. Department of Defense & educational entities from U.S. Department of Defense. Our basic mission is to foster awareness of and support for a technological/industrial infrastructure that is capable of responding to any global challenge. Sponsors more than fifty technical symposia & exhibitions annually. The journal, National Defense, is published twelve times a year.

NATIONAL FEDERATION OF INDEPENDENT BUSINESS

53 Century Blvd (Suite 250)
Nashville, TN 37214-4618
Telephone: (615) 872-5800, Web Site: www.nfib.com
Mktg Res Mgr: Deidre Popovich

NATIONAL FIRE PROTECTION ASSOCIATION

1 Batterymarch Park Bsmt
Quincy, MA 02169-7484
Telephone: (617) 770-3000, FAX: (617) 770-0700, Web Site: www. nfpa.org
Pres: Jim Pauley
Division Dir Mktg & Sales: Kimberly A. Fontes
VP DM: Paul G. Crossman
Conducts Business: Worldwide
Employees: 300
Primary Market Served: Business
Catalog available online
Advertising/Marketing Budget Related to Direct Marketing: 76-100%
Direct Marketing ad budget:
Direct Mail: 95%
Magazines: 2%
Telephone: 3%
Founded: 1896

Non-profit membership association. Produce & distribute a variety of publications, films, A/V, seminar/training material for both members & non-members. Markets served include: fire service, government, health care, schools, architects, engineers & industry.

NATIONAL FOUNDATION FOR CANCER RESEARCH

4600 E West Hwy (Suite 525)
Bethesda, MD 20814-6900

Telephone: (301) 654-1250, Toll Free: (800) 321-CURE, FAX: (301) 654-5824, E-Mail: info@nfcr.org, Web Site: www.nfcr.org
Pres & CEO: Franklin C. Salisbury
Conducts Business: U.S.
Employees: 21
Primary Market Served: Business & Consumer
Direct online sales
Advertising/Marketing Budget Related to Direct Marketing: 26-50%
Direct Marketing ad budget: $1,500,000
Direct Mail: $8,400,000
Telephone: $100,000
Founded: 1973
Gross sales or billing: $7,090,000

Not-for-profit organization conducting basic cancer research.

NATIONAL GOLF FOUNDATION

501 N Hwy A1A
Jupiter, FL 33477-4577
Telephone: (561) 744-6006, FAX: (561) 744-6107, E-Mail: ngf@ngf. org, Web Site: www.ngf.org
Pres & CEO: David Abeles
Conducts Business: Worldwide
Employees: 47
Primary Market Served: Business
Catalog available online
Indirect online sales
Founded: 1936

Unparalleled clearinghouse of industry information, provided in the form of research, reports, seminars, consulting services & more

NATIONAL HUMANE EDUCATION SOCIETY

3731 Berryville Pike
Charles Town, WV 25415
Telephone: (304) 725-0506, FAX: (304) 725-1523, E-Mail: information@nhes.org, Web Site: www.nhes.org
Pres: James D. Taylor
Founder & VP: Anna C. Briggs
VP: Cynthia L. Taylor
Sec: Christina B. Fernandez
Treas: Virginia B Dungan
Employees: 38
Primary Market Served: Consumer
Founded: 1948
Gross sales or billing: $4,188,634

Non-profit humane education service on rescue services for animals.

NATIONAL INSTITUTE FOR TRIAL ADVOCACY

1685 38th St
Boulder, CO 80301-2735

Toll Free: (800) 225-6482, Web Site:
www.nita.org
Dir Programs Sls & Mktg: Daniel
McHugh

NATIONAL JEWISH HEALTH

1400 Jackson St
Denver, CO 80206-2761
Telephone: (303) 398-1070, Toll Free:
(800) 222-LUNG, (800) 423, FAX:
(303) 398-1663, E-Mail: trubeyp@
njhealth.org, Web Site: www.
njhealth.org
Pres & CEO: Michael Salem
Conducts Business: Worldwide
Employees: 1,200
Primary Market Served: Consumer
Direct Marketing ad budget:
Direct Mail: $1,500,000
Telephone: $35,000
Founded: 1899

National direct mail fund-raising program for medical research center.

NATIONAL LAW
ENFORCEMENT OFFICERS
MEMORIAL FUND

901 E St NW Ste 100
Washington, DC 20004-2025
Telephone: (202) 737-3400, Web Site:
www.nleomf.com
Chairman & CEO: Craig Floyd
Primary Market Served: Business &
Consumer

NATIONAL LEAGUE FOR
NURSING

RP-NFOA
2600 Virginia Ave NW (#8)
Washington, DC 20037-1905
Telephone: (212) 363-5555, Toll Free:
(800) 669-1656, FAX: (212) 812-
0391, E-Mail: generalinfo@nln.org,
Web Site: www.nln.org
Dir: Dr Virginia Adams
Conducts Business: U.S.
Employees: 50
Primary Market Served: Business &
Consumer
Founded: 1893
Gross sales or billing: $9,500,000

As the voice for nursing education, the
National League for Nursing is the premier organization for nurse faculty and
leaders in nursing education offering
faculty development, networking opportunities, testing services, nursing research grants, and public policy
initiatives to more than 30,000 individual and 1,100 education and associate
members.

NATIONAL LUGGAGE
DEALERS ASSOCIATION

Div. of NLDA Associates Inc
1817 Elmdale Ave
Glenview, IL 60625-1355
Telephone: (847) 998-6869, FAX:
(847) 998-6884, E-Mail: inquiry@
nlda.com, Web Site: www.nlda.com
CEO: John Mori
Conducts Business: U.S.
Employees: 10
Primary Market Served: Business &
Consumer
Catalog available online
Advertising/Marketing Budget Related
to Direct Marketing: 0-25%
Founded: 1925
Gross sales or billing: $10,000,000

National Association of 300 stores selling luggage, small leather goods, gifts
& handbags. Produce various consumer
catalogs & import merchandise for
stores.

NATIONAL MEDICAL
FELLOWSHIPS

347 5th Ave (Suite 510)
New York, NY 10016-5007
Telephone: (212) 483-8880, FAX:
(212) 483-8897, E-Mail: info@nmf-
online.org, Web Site: www.nmf-
online.org
Pres & CEO: Dr. Esther R. Dyer
Exec VP: Paula Madison
Sec & Treas: Stephen N. Keith MD
Primary Market Served: Business &
Consumer
Advertising/Marketing Budget Related
to Direct Marketing: 0-25%
Founded: 1946

Non-profit organization that provides
financial & other assistance to under
represented minority medical students.

NATIONAL MOTOR CLUB
OF AMERICA INC

130 E John Carpenter Fwy
Irving, TX 75062-2708
Telephone: (972) 999-4400, Toll Free:
(800) 523-4582, FAX: (972) 999-
4405, Web Site: www.nmca.com
Pres: Jeffrey J. Jensen
VP, Corp Sls: Brian Joseph
Conducts Business: U.S., Canada,
Mexico
Employees: 400
Primary Market Served: Business &
Consumer
Catalog available online
Founded: 1956

Motor club membership organization.

NATIONAL MULTIPLE
SCLEROSIS SOCIETY

900 S Broadway (Suite) 210
Denver, CO 80209-4269
Telephone: (303) 813-1052, Web Site:
www.nmss.org
Pres & CEO: Cyndi Zagieboylo
Chief Mktg & Devel Officer: Graham
McReynolds
Exec VP, Mktg: Sherri Giger

NATIONAL OSTEOPOROSIS
FOUNDATION

1150 17th St NW (Suite 850)
Washington, DC 20037-1216
Telephone: (202) 721-6346, Web Site:
www.nof.org
Exec Dir/CEO: Amy Porter
Primary Market Served: Consumer

NATIONAL PARKINSON
FOUNDATION

200 SE 1st St (Suite 800)
Miami, FL 33131-1909
Telephone: (305) 243-6666, Toll Free:
(800) 937-4545, FAX: (305) 243-
6073, E-Mail: contact@parkinson.
org, Web Site: www.parkinson.org
Pres & CEO: Joyce Oberdorf
VP Mktg & Commun: Leilani Pearl
Dir Mktg: Nerissa Balland

NATIONAL RELIEF
CHARITIES

13318 Airport Dr
Elkwood, VA 22718-1760
Telephone: (540) 825-5950
Dir Fundraising: Chuck Smith

NATIONAL RESEARCH
CENTER FOR COLLEGE &
UNIVERSITY ADMISSIONS

3651 NE Ralph Powell Rd
Lees Summit, MO 64064-2357
Telephone: (816) 525-2201, Web Site:
www.nrccua.org
Pres: Don Munce

THE NATIONAL
RESTAURANT
ASSOCIATION
EDUCATIONAL
FOUNDATION

2055 L St NW
Washington, DC 20036
Toll Free: (800) 424-5156
Pres & CEO: Dawn Sweeney
Primary Market Served: Business &
Consumer

Educational arm of the national restaurant association.

NATIONAL RETAIL FEDERATION INC

1101 New York Ave
Washington, DC 20005
Telephone: (202) 783-7971, Toll Free:
(800) 673-4692, FAX: (202) 737-
2849, E-Mail: webmaster@nrf.com,
Web Site: www.nrf.com
Pres & CEO: Matthew Shay
Employees: 96
Primary Market Served: Business &
Consumer
Direct online sales
Gross sales or billing: $30,600,000

Industry services.

NATIONAL RIFLE ASSOCIATION OF AMERICA

11250 Waples Mill Rd
Fairfax, VA 22030-7400
Telephone: (703) 267-1000, Toll Free:
(800) 672-3888, FAX: (703) 267-
3957, E-Mail: nra.contact@nra.org,
Web Site: www.nra.org
Exec VP: Wayne R. LaPierre Jr.
Exec Dir Legislative Action: Chris W.
Cox
Exec Dir: Chris Cox
Conducts Business: U.S.
Employees: 360
Primary Market Served: Consumer
Founded: 1871

National membership association. Publish The American Rifleman, The American Hunter, InSights & The American Guardian.

NATIONAL RIGHT TO WORK LEGAL DEFENSE FOUNDATION

8001 Braddock Rd
Springfield, VA 22160-2115
Telephone: (703) 321-8510, Toll Free:
(800) 336-3600, FAX: (703) 321-
9613, E-Mail: info@nrtw.org, Web
Site: www.nrtw.org
VP & Legal Dir: Jr Raymond J. LaJeunesse
Conducts Business: U.S.
Employees: 50
Primary Market Served: Business &
Consumer
Catalog available online
Direct Marketing ad budget:
Direct Mail: $3,500,000
Gross sales or billing: $6,500,000

Organization of citizens dedicated to the principle of the right to work. Conducts nationwide educational & lobbying activities in Congress & state legislatures.

NATIONAL RURAL ELECTRIC COOPERATIVE ASSOCIATION

4301 Wilson Blvd
Arlington, VA 22203-1860
Telephone: (703) 907-5500, FAX:
(703) 907-5528, Web Site: www.
nreca.org
CEO: Glenn English
Media & PR Dir: Patrick Levigne
Assoc Membership Mgr: Nancy
McMahen
Conducts Business: U.S.
Employees: 900
Primary Market Served: Business
Founded: 1942
Gross sales or billing: $139,400,000

A service organization that represents the nation's 1000 non-profit, consumer-owned electric cooperatives which provide service to more than 25 million people in 46 states.

NATIONAL SCHOOL BOARDS ASSOCIATION INC

1680 Duke St (fl 2)
Alexandria, VA 22314-3493
Telephone: (703) 838-6722, FAX:
(703) 683-7590, E-Mail: info@nsba.
org, Web Site: www.nsba.org
Exec Dir: Thomas J. Gentzel
Conducts Business: United States
Employees: 150
Primary Market Served: Business
Indirect online sales
Advertising/Marketing Budget Related
to Direct Marketing: 0-25%
Founded: 1940
Gross sales or billing: $23,500,000

Non-profit organization aiming to advance the quality of education in public schools, providing up-to-date information & training for educators & strengthening local support for schools.

NATIONAL SOCIETY OF COLLEGIATE SCHOLARS

2000 M St NW Ste 600
Washington, DC 20036-3328
Telephone: (202) 265-9000, Web Site:
www.nscs.org
Exec Dir & Founder: Stephen Loflin
Primary Market Served: Business &
Consumer

NATIONAL TRUST FOR HISTORIC PRESERVATION

2600 Virginia Ave NW (Suite 1000)
Washington, DC 20037-1922
Telephone: (202) 588-6000, Toll Free:
(800) 944-6847, E-Mail: info@
savingplaces.org, Web Site: www.
preservationnation.org
Pres & CEO: Stephanie K. Meeks
Exec VP, Chief Preservation Officer:
David J. Brown
Chief Devel Officer: Debra Neuman
Chief Mktg Officer: Terry Richey

NATIONAL UNIVERSITY

11355 N Torrey Pines Rd
La Jolla, CA 92037-1013
Toll Free: (800) 628-8648, Web Site:
www.nu.edu
Dir Media & Markets: Kendra Losee
Primary Market Served: Consumer

NATIONAL WILDLIFE FEDERATION

11100 Wildlife Center Dr
Reston, VA 20190-5362
Telephone: (703) 438-6000, Web Site:
www.nwf.org
Sr Dir Membership: Anne Senft
Primary Market Served: Consumer

NATIVE AMERICAN HERITAGE ASSOCIATION

12085 Quaal Rd
Black Hawk, SD 57718
Telephone: (605) 341-9110, FAX:
(605) 341-91413, E-Mail: info@
naha-inc.org, Web Site: www.naha-
inc.org
Pres: David G. Meyers
VP & Treas: Pamela J. Myers
Sec: Erin Hibbs

NATIVE AMERICAN RIGHTS FUND

1506 Broadway
Boulder, CO 80302-6217
Telephone: (303) 447-8760, FAX:
(303) 443-7776, Web Site: www.
narf.org
Exec Dir: John E. Echohawk
Dir Devel: Morgan O'Brien
Devel Projects Mgr: Mereille Martinez

THE NATURE CONSERVANCY

RP-NFOA
4245 N Fairfax Dr (Suite 100)
Arlington, VA 22203-1606
Telephone: (703) 841-5300, Toll Free:
(800) 628-6860, FAX: (703) 841-
1283, Web Site: www.nature.org
Pres & CEO: Mark Tercek
Chief Fin & Administrative Officer:
Stephen Howell
Chief Mktg Officer: Geof Rochester
Principal Devel Officer: Rebecca Bowen
Dir Membership Fundraising: Begona
Vazquez Santos
Conducts Business: Worldwide
Employees: 230

Primary Market Served: Business & Consumer
Founded: 1951

A non-profit organization that preserves plants, animals & natural communities that represent the diversity of life on earth by protecting the lands & water they need to survive in.

NAVEEN JINDAL SCHOOL OF MANAGEMENT

The University of Texas at Dallas
800 W Campbell Rd (SM 42)
Richardson, TX 75080-3021
Telephone: (972) 883-2705, (972) 883-2750, (972) 883-2275, Web Site: www.utdallas.edu
Dean: Dr. Hasan Pirkul
Primary Market Served: Consumer

College

NEIGHBORHOOD CLEANERS ASSOCIATION INTERNATIONAL

252 W 29th St
New York, NY 10001
Telephone: (212) 967-3002, Toll Free: (800) 888-1622, FAX: (212) 967-2240, E-Mail: info@nca-i.com, Web Site: www.nca-i.com
Exec Dir: Nora Nealis
Conducts Business: Worldwide
Employees: 12
Primary Market Served: Business
Advertising/Marketing Budget Related to Direct Marketing: 0-25%
Direct Marketing ad budget: $85,000
Founded: 1946
Gross sales or billing: $900,000

Advertising & promotional services, educational material & customer relations insurance to members. A cleaning industry trade association.

NETWORK FOR GOOD

1140 Connecticut Ave NW (Suite 700)
Washington, DC 20036-4011
Telephone: (240) 482-3211, Web Site: www.networkforgood.org
Mktg Assoc: Rebecca Higman

NEVADA COMMISSION ON TOURISM

401 N Carson St
Carson City, NV 89701-4221
Telephone: (775) 687-4322, Toll Free: (800) NEVADA 8, FAX: (775) 687-6779, Web Site: www.travelnevada.com
Dir: Tim Maland
Chair: Lorraine Hunt
Exec Dir: Bruce C. Bommarito
Conducts Business: U.S.
Employees: 35

Primary Market Served: Consumer
Direct Marketing ad budget: $2,000,000

State tourism promotion agency.

NEW JERSEY INSTITUTE FOR CONTINUING LEGAL EDUCATION

1 Constitution Sq
New Brunswick, NJ 08901-1587
Telephone: (732) 249-5100, Web Site: www.njicle.com
Exec Dir: Lawrence Maron Esq.
Primary Market Served: Business & Consumer

NEW YORK BLOOD CENTER INC

310 E 67th St
New York, NY 10021
Telephone: (212) 570-3000, Toll Free: (800) 933-2566, FAX: (212) 570-3195, Web Site: www.nybloodcenter.org
Pres & CEO: MD Christopher D. Hillyer
Sr VP & CFO: Beth Gibson
VP, Strategic Svcs & Facilities Admin: Jeffrey Jacob
Conducts Business: U.S.
Employees: 1,500
Primary Market Served: Business & Consumer
Catalog available online
Advertising/Marketing Budget Related to Direct Marketing: 0-25%
Direct Marketing ad budget: $2,000,000
Direct Mail: 50%
Newspapers: 25%
Telephone: 25%
Founded: 1964
Gross sales or billing: $327,600,000

Blood products and services: Rely on volunteer blood donations & financial contributions.

NEW YORK EASTER SEAL SOCIETY

40th W 37th St (Suite 503), Development Office
New York, NY 10018-7345
Telephone: (212) 220-2290, FAX: (212) 695-4807, Web Site: ny.easterseals.com
Exec Dir: John W. McGrath
Sr VP Devel: Beth Weber
VP Devel: Hayrim Byun
Conducts Business: U.S.
Employees: 70
Primary Market Served: Business & Consumer
Indirect online sales

Advertising/Marketing Budget Related to Direct Marketing: 76-100%
Founded: 1923
Gross sales or billing: $20,200,000

Fund-raising, and other health and human services.

NEW YORK FOUNDATION FOR THE ARTS

20 Jay St (fl 7)
Brooklyn, NY 11201-8352
Telephone: (212) 366-6900, FAX: (212) 366-1778, Web Site: www.nyfa.org
Exec Dir: Michael L. Royce
Deputy Dir: Mark Rossier
Conducts Business: U.S.
Employees: 20
Primary Market Served: Business
Advertising/Marketing Budget Related to Direct Marketing: 0-25%

Foundation working with New York State artists.

NEW YORK LANDMARKS CONSERVANCY

One Whitehall St
New York, NY 10004
Telephone: (212) 995-5260, FAX: (212) 995-5268, Web Site: www.nylandmarks.org
Pres: Peg Breen
Treas: Lloyd P. Zuckerberg
Dir Devel: Scott Leurquin
Dir: Justin Abelow
Conducts Business: U.S.
Employees: 17
Primary Market Served: Business & Consumer
Advertising/Marketing Budget Related to Direct Marketing: 0-25%

Non-profit organization preserving historic buildings.

NEW YORK PHILHARMONIC

10 Lincoln Ctr Plaza, Avery Fisher Hall
New York, NY 10023-6970
Telephone: (212) 875-5691, Web Site: www.nyphil.org
Exec Dir: Matthew VanBesien
VP, Mktg & Commun: David Snead
Dir Individual Giving: Elizabeth McColgan
Primary Market Served: Consumer

NEW YORK UNIVERSITY

11 W 42nd St (Rm 431)
New York, NY 10036-8083
Telephone: (212) 992-3221, Web Site: www.scps.nyu.edu
Academic Dir, Professor: Dr. Marjorie Kalter

NEW YORK UNIVERSITY MEDICAL CENTER

550 First Ave
New York, NY 10016
Telephone: (212) 263-7800, FAX: (212) 263-8426, Web Site: www.med.nyu.edu
Dean & CEO, NYU Medical Ctr: Robert I. Grossman M.D.
Exec VP, Vice Dean & Chief of Staff: Andrew W. Litt M.D.
Conducts Business: U.S., Canada
Primary Market Served: Business & Consumer

Non-profit medical organization.

NEWPORT CREATIVE COMMUNICATIONS

33 Railroad Ave
Duxbury, MA 02332-3884
Telephone: (781) 934-1414, Web Site: www.newportcreative.com
Acct Mgr: Allie Moore

Direct marketing fundraising agency that assists non-profit charitable organizations

NEWSPAPER ASSOCIATION OF AMERICA

4401 Wilson Blvd (Suite 900)
Arlington, VA 22203-4195
Telephone: (571) 366-1000, FAX: (571) 366-1195, Web Site: www.naa.org
Pres & CEO: Donna Barrett
Primary Market Served: Business & Consumer
Catalog available online
Direct online sales
Founded: 1992
Gross sales or billing: $31,100,000
Provide help for member newspapers.

NORTH POINT RESOURCES

4400 North Point Pkwy (Suite 152)
Alpharetta, GA 30022-2429
Telephone: (678) 892-5000, Web Site: www.northpointstore.org
Assoc Dir Ministry: Daniel Stonaker
Provide Christian resources

NORTH SHORE ANIMAL LEAGUE AMERICA INC

25 Davis Ave
Port Washington, NY 11050
Telephone: (516) 883-7575, Web Site: www.animalleague.org
Pres: J. John Stevenson
Sr VP Opers: Joanne Yohannan
Sr VP & CFO: Valerie Fields
Sr VP Commun: Devera Lynn
Sr VP Devel: Jill Burkhardt
Conducts Business: U.S.

Employees: 250
Primary Market Served: Consumer
Catalog available online
Direct online sales
Advertising/Marketing Budget Related to Direct Marketing: 0-25%
Founded: 1944
Direct mail sweepstakes for fund-raising purposes.

NOVA SOUTHEASTERN UNIVERSITY FISCHLER COLLEGE OF EDUCATION

1750 NE 167th St
North Miami Beach, FL 33162-3017
Telephone: (954) 262-8651, Web Site: www.schoolofed.nova.edu
Exec Dir Creative Devel & Innovation: Brian Croswhite
Primary Market Served: Consumer

OMP

1133 19th St NW (Suite 300)
Washington, DC 20036-3610
Telephone: (202) 467-0048, Web Site: www.ompdirect.com
COO: Anita Pearson

Full service fundraising & communications agency

OMSI INC

9480 N Demazenod Dr
Belleville, IL 62223-1159
Telephone: (618) 398-7640, Web Site: www.oblatesusa.org

Missionaries

OBLATE MISSIONS

323 Oblate Dr, PO Box 659432
San Antonio, TX 78265-9432
Telephone: (210) 736-1685, FAX: (210) 736-1314, E-Mail: contact@oblatemissions.org, Web Site: www.oblatemissions.org
Dir: Fr. Saturnino Lajo
Assoc Dir: Ken Amerson

OCEAN CONSERVANCY

1300 19th St NW
Washington, DC 20036
Telephone: (202) 429-5609, Web Site: www.oceanconservancy.org
Primary Market Served: Business & Consumer

OKLAHOMA DEPT OF COMMERCE

900 N Stiles Ave
Oklahoma City, OK 73104-3234
Telephone: (405) 815-6552, Toll Free: (800) 879-6552, FAX: (405) 815-5344, Web Site: www.okcommerce.com

Sr Economic Devel Fin Specialist: Karen Adair
Mktg Project Mgr: Stefanie Appleton
Employees: 1,007
Primary Market Served: Business

An economic developer in Oklahoma.

OPERATION SMILE INC

3641 Faculty Blvd
Virginia Beach, VA 23453-8000
Telephone: (757) 321-7645, Web Site: www.operationsmile.org
Co-founder & Exec Chmn: William P. Magee
Co-founder & Pres: Kathleen S. Magee
Sr VP Response Mktg & Devel: Kyla Shawyer

An international children's medical charity that provides free life-changing surgeries for children with cleft lip, cleft palate & other facial deformities.

ORAL ROBERTS UNIVERSITY

Graduate Ctr (7th fl), 7777 S Lewis Ave
Tulsa, OK 74171
Telephone: (918) 495-6161, FAX: (918) 495-6222, E-Mail: admissions@oru.edu, Web Site: www.oru.edu
Pres: Richard Roberts
Dean: Dr. Debbie Sowell
VP, Devel: George Fisher
Conducts Business: Worldwide
Primary Market Served: Consumer
Catalog available online
Non-profit religious organization.

ORANGE LEAP

13800 Montfort Dr (Suite 220)
Dallas, TX 75240-4347
Telephone: (972) 220-0341, Web Site: www.orangeleap.com
CEO: Randy McCabe
Office Mgr: Leslie McCabe

Provides software-based solutions to non-profit organizations

ORION

33926 9th Ave S
Federal Way, WA 98003-6708
Telephone: (253) 661-7805, Web Site: www.orionworks.org
Dir, Teleservices: Mathew Van De Voorde

Orion provides job assessment, training, placement and support services to individuals with disabilities & barriers to employment

OUR LADY OF VICTORY HOMES OF CHARITY

780 Ridge Rd
Lackawanna, NY 14218-1682
Telephone: (716) 828-9648, FAX: (716) 828-9643, E-Mail: rheist@olv-bvs.org, Web Site: www. ourladyofvictory.org
Exec VP & Treas: Rev. Msgr Paul J.E. Burkarel
Exec Dir: Richard L. Heist
Conducts Business: U.S., Canada
Employees: 65
Primary Market Served: Consumer
Advertising/Marketing Budget Related to Direct Marketing: 0-25%
Direct Marketing ad budget:
Direct Mail: 100%
Founded: 1854

Raise funds to subsidize the programs of Baker Victory Services, a therapeutic program for children with emotional disturbances & mental illnesses, children with physical & mental disabilities & unwed mothers.

OXFAM AMERICA

226 Causeway St (5th fl)
Boston, MA 02114-2206
Telephone: (617) 482-1211, Toll Free: (800) 776-9326, FAX: (617) 728-2594, E-Mail: info@oxfamamerica. org, Web Site: www.oxfamamerica. org
Dir Annual Fund: Ken Mallette
International relief & development organization

PC ONTARIO FUND

401-19 Duncan St
Toronto, ON, Canada M5H 3H1
Telephone: (416) 861-0020, (416) 861-3085, Toll Free: (800) 903-6453, FAX: (416) 861-9593, (416) 861-1760, E-Mail: comments@ontariopc. net, Web Site: www.ontariopc.com
Party Leader: Tim Hudak
Conducts Business: Canada
Primary Market Served: Business & Consumer
Advertising/Marketing Budget Related to Direct Marketing: 51-75%
Political fund-raising.

PALLOTTINE CENTER FOR APOSTOLIC CAUSES INC/ ST JUDE SHRINE

Div. of Catholic Church of the US
308 N Paca St
Baltimore, MD 21201
Telephone: (410) 685-6026, Toll Free: (877) 278-5833, FAX: (410) 234-1459, E-Mail: info@stjudeshrine.org, Web Site: www.stjudeshrine.org

Pastoral Dir: Father Louis Micca
Asst Pastoral Dir: Father Joseph Kochar
Pastor: Father Frank Donio
Pastor: Father Peter Sticco
Conducts Business: U.S.
Employees: 19
Primary Market Served: Consumer
Catalog available online
Indirect online sales
Direct Marketing ad budget:
Direct Mail: 100%
Founded: 1953
Gross sales or billing: $600,000

Social services religious fund-raising organization promoting devotions to St. Jude.

PARALYZED VETERANS OF AMERICA

801 18th St NW
Washington, DC 20006-3517
Telephone: (212) 255-9078, Toll Free: (800) 424-8200, FAX: (202) 416-7643, E-Mail: info@pva.org, Web Site: www.pva.org
Natl Pres: Al Kovach
Conducts Business: U.S.
Employees: 300
Primary Market Served: Consumer
Catalog available online
Direct online sales
Advertising/Marketing Budget Related to Direct Marketing: 76-100%
Direct Marketing ad budget:
Direct Mail: $20,000,000
Founded: 1946
Gross sales or billing: $111,000,000

Advocate for appropriate health care & benefits for veterans. Promotes medical research to cure spinal cord dysfunction & educates society about the abilities of the disabled.

PARKINSON'S DISEASE FOUNDATION

1359 Broadway (Suite 1509)
New York, NY 10018
Telephone: (212) 923-4700, Toll Free: (800) 457-6676, FAX: (212) 923-4778, E-Mail: info@pdf.org, Web Site: www.pdf.org
Exec Dir: Robin Elliot

PENN STATE HAZLETON

76 University Dr
Hazleton, PA 18202-8025
Telephone: (570) 450-3175, Web Site: www.hn.psu.edu
Dir Institutional Advancement: Kevin Salaway
Primary Market Served: Consumer

PEOPLE FOR THE AMERICAN WAY

1101 15th St NW (Suite 600)
Washington, DC 20005-5023
Telephone: (202) 467-4999, Web Site: www.pfaw.org
Dir Membership & Online Strategy: Kristin Smith

PHARMACEUTICAL CARE MANAGEMENT ASSOCIATION

325 7th St NW
Washington, DC 20004
Telephone: (202) 756-7210, FAX: (202) 207-3623, E-Mail: info@pcmanet.org, Web Site: www. pcmanet.org
Pres & CEO: Mark Merritt
Asst VP, Pub Affairs & Policy: Timothy Brogan
Dir, Indus Rels & Policy: Kristen Pumphrey
Mgr, Indus Rels & Policy: John Stelmachowicz
Employees: 16
Primary Market Served: Business
Founded: 1975

Represents managed care pharmacy & healthcare partners in pharmaceutical care: managed healthcare organizations, PBMs, HMOs, PPOs, third party administrators & community pharmacy networks. Serves its members & America's healthcare system by promoting education, legislation, practice standards & research that foster quality, & affordable pharmaceutical care. Members serve more than 150 million.

PHILADELPHIA MUSEUM OF ART

PO Box 7646
Philadelphia, PA 19101-7646
Telephone: (215) 684-7840, FAX: (215) 235-0042, E-Mail: memberservices@philamuseum.org, Web Site: www.philamuseum.org
Exec Dir Mktg: Jennifer Francis

PHONE BANK SYSTEMS INC

4990 Northwind Dr (Suite 235)
East Lansing, MI 48823-5091
Telephone: (517) 332-1500, FAX: (517) 332-1514, E-Mail: rusha@phonebanks.com, Web Site: www.phonebanks.com
Pres: Sarah Shaw

PITTSBURGH PARKS CONSERVANCY

2000 Technology Dr (Suite 300)
Pittsburgh, PA 15219-3137

Telephone: (412) 682-7275, Web Site:
www.pittsburghparks.org
Pres & CEO: Meg Cheever

PLAN INTERNATIONAL USA

US Member of Plan International
155 Plan Way
Warwick, RI 02886-1099
Telephone: (401) 562-8400, Toll Free:
(800) 556-7918, FAX: (401) 738-
5608, Web Site: www.planusa.org
Pres & CEO: Paul Dwyer
Pres & CEO Mktg: Vincent Jackson
Conducts Business: Worldwide
Employees: 80
Primary Market Served: Consumer
Advertising/Marketing Budget Related
to Direct Marketing: 76-100%
Direct Marketing ad budget:
Direct Mail: $1,600,000
Newspapers: $50,000
TV/Radio: $1,000,000
Telephone: $100,000
Founded: 1937
Gross sales or billing: $30,000,000

Recruit sponsors for needy children
overseas. The cost to the sponsor is $22
per month.

PLANNED PARENTHOOD FEDERATION OF AMERICA

434 W 33rd St
New York, NY 10001-2600
Telephone: (212) 541-7800, FAX:
(212) 245-1845, Web Site: www.
plannedparenthood.org
Assoc Dir, Direct Response Fundrais-
ing: Paul Vogel
Primary Market Served: Consumer

PLANNED PARENTHOOD MAR MONTE

Affiliate of Planned Parenthood Feder-
ation
1691 The Alameda
San Jose, CA 95126-2203
Telephone: (408) 287-7532, FAX:
(408) 971-6935, Web Site: www.
plannedparenthood.org
CEO: Linda Williams
CFO: John Giambruno
VP, Clinic Svcs: Lynn Fielder
Conducts Business: U.S.
Employees: 250
Primary Market Served: Consumer
Advertising/Marketing Budget Related
to Direct Marketing: 0-25%
Direct Marketing ad budget: $40,000
Founded: 1916

Reproductive health care provider in
Santa Clara, San Benito, Santa Cruz,
Sacramento Valley, San Joaquin Val-
ley, the Central Valley including Fres-

no & Bakersfield, Reno & Monterey
counties, including all of northern Nevada with 35 clinic sites. Extensive
community education, training programs & family planning services provided to women, teens & men.

PONTIFICAL MISSION SOCIETIES IN THE US

70 W 36th St (fl 8)
New York, NY 10018-1256
Telephone: (212) 563-8700, Web Site:
www.onefamilyinmission.org
Dir Devel & Programs, Editor, Mis-
sion: Monica Yehle

POPULATION CONNECTION

2120 L St NW (Suite 500)
Washington, DC 20037-1534
Telephone: (202) 332-2200, Web Site:
www.populationconnection.net
Dir Mktg & Info Svcs: Ray Huber
Primary Market Served: Consumer

Grassroots population organization.
Educate grades K-12 about unsustain-
able population growth

RICHARD M PORDES LLC

99 Dolphin Cove Quay
Stamford, CT 06902-7716
Telephone: (203) 316-9190
Pres: Richard Pordes

PORTLAND CEMENT ASSOCIATION

1150 Connecticut Ave NW
Washington, DC 20036
Telephone: (202) 408-9494, Web Site:
www.cement.org
Pres & CEO: James G. Toscas
Primary Market Served: Business &
Consumer
Founded: 1917

Trade association.

PORTLAND RESCUE MISSION

PO Box 3713
Portland, OR 97208-3713
Telephone: (503) 906-7605, Web Site:
www.portlandrescuemission.org
Dir Devel: Bill Miller

PREVENT BLINDNESS AMERICA

211 W Wacker Dr (Suite 1700)
Chicago, IL 60606-1375
Toll Free: (800) 331-2020, Web Site:
www.preventblindness.org

PRIESTS OF THE SACRED HEART

6889 S Lovers Ln Rd
Hales Corners, WI 53130-0900
Telephone: (414) 425-3383, FAX:
(414) 425-5719, Web Site: www.
poshusa.org
Exec Dir: William B. Rondeau
Assoc Dir: John Cain
Primary Market Served: Consumer

Solicit donations for the education of
priests.

PRINT SERVICES DISTRIBUTION ASSOCIATION

330 N Wabash Ave (Suite 2000)
Chicago, IL 60611
Toll Free: (800) 230-0175, FAX: (312)
673-6880, Web Site: www.psda.org
Exec VP: Matt Sanderson
Mktg Mgr: Carli Franks
Conducts Business: Worldwide
Employees: 48
Primary Market Served: Business
Catalog available online
Indirect online sales
Advertising/Marketing Budget Related
to Direct Marketing: 0-25%
Founded: 1946

Trade association organized for promoting & encouraging the independent
concept of business printed products
distribution.

THE PROFESSIONAL GOLFERS' ASSOCIATION OF AMERICA

100 Avenue of the Champions
Palm Beach Gardens, FL 33410-9601
Telephone: (561) 624-8400, Web Site:
www.pga.com
Sr Dir, Mktg & Indus Rels: Paul Met-
zler
Primary Market Served: Consumer

THE PROFESSIONAL PUTTERS ASSOCIATION

Subs. of Putt-Putt Golf Courses of
America Inc
300 S Liberty St (Suite 100)
Winston Salem, NC 27101-5279
Toll Free: (866) 788-8788, Web Site:
www.proputters.com
Commissioner: Joe Aboid
Conducts Business: U.S., Canada, Ja-
pan, Lebanon, Indonesia, Australia
Employees: 300
Primary Market Served: Business &
Consumer
Catalog available online
Indirect online sales
Advertising/Marketing Budget Related
to Direct Marketing: 26-50%

Direct Marketing ad budget:
Direct Mail: 40%
Newspapers: 10%
TV/Radio: 40%
Telephone: 10%
Founded: 1960

Sports organization that rewards the nation's best putters cash prizes & awards through local, state, regional & national tournament competition on Putt-Putt Golf Courses.

PROFIT POTENTIALS INC
Div. of The Foreign Candy Co. Inc
1 Foreign Candy Dr
Hull, IA 51239-7719
Telephone: (712) 439-1496, Toll Free: (800) 543-5480, FAX: (712) 439-1434, Web Site: www. profitpotentials.com
Pres: Peter W. De Yager
Mktg Mgr Fundraising: Barb Bentele
Conducts Business: U.S.
Employees: 50
Primary Market Served: Business & Consumer
Advertising/Marketing Budget Related to Direct Marketing: 26-50%
Direct Marketing ad budget: $400,000
Direct Mail: 20%
Magazines: 60%
Newspapers: 10%
Telephone: 10%
Gross sales or billing: $18,000,000

Sell fund-raising products to community groups, schools, churches, scouts & all other groups involved in fund-raising activities.

PROJECT HOPE
255 Carter Hall Ln
Millwood, VA 22646-0255
Telephone: (540) 837-2100, Web Site: www.projecthope.org
Mgr Direct Mail: Dorothy Combs
Primary Market Served: Consumer

PROMOTION MARKETING ASSOCIATION (PMA) INC
650 1st Ave (Suite 2-SW)
New York, NY 10016-3207
Telephone: (212) 420-1100, FAX: (212) 533-7622, E-Mail: pma@ pmalink.org, Web Site: www. pmalink.org
Pres: Bonnie J. Carlson
VP Mktg: Mike Kaufman
Conducts Business: Worldwide
Primary Market Served: Business & Consumer
Catalog available online
Direct online sales

Founded: 1911

A not-for-profit organization and resource for research, education and collaboration for marketing professionals.

PROMOTIONAL PRODUCT PROFESSIONALS OF CANADA
455 Fenelon Blvd (Suite 202)
Dorval, QC, Canada H9S 5T8
Telephone: (514) 489-5359, FAX: (800) 489-8741, (514) 489-7760, E-Mail: gladys@pppc.ca, Web Site: www.pppc.ca
Pres & CEO: Edward Ahad
Dir Membership: Debbie Pinkerton
Dir Professional Devel: Chantal Fontaine
Dir, Info Tech: Marc C. Phillips
Dir Communs: Carol Phillips
Mktg Mgr: Gladys Kasp
Employees: 10
Primary Market Served: Business
Catalog available online
Indirect online sales
Founded: 1956

A major show & exposition of the Promotional Products Association of Canada, of interest to promotional products distributors & open only to members of the association.

RMA-THE RISK MANAGEMENT ASSOCIATION
1801 Market St (Suite 300)
Philadelphia, PA 19103-1628
Telephone: (215) 446-4000, FAX: (215) 446-4101, E-Mail: customers@ rmahq.org, Web Site: www.rmahq. org
CEO: William F. Githens
Conducts Business: U.S., Canada, Puerto Rico
Employees: 80
Primary Market Served: Business
Direct Marketing ad budget:
Direct Mail: $350,000
Magazines: $5,000
Newspapers: $5,000
Founded: 1914

Association of bank loan & credit officers.

RAPPAHANNOCK ELECTRIC COOPERATIVE
247 Industrial Ct
Fredericksburg, VA 22408-2443
Telephone: (540) 898-8500, Toll Free: (800) 552-3904, E-Mail: office@ myrec.coop, Web Site: www.myrec. coop
Dir Mktg Devel: Todd Jordan

READING FOR EDUCATION
180 Freedom Ave
Murfreesboro, TN 37129-6926
Telephone: (615) 494-4000, FAX: (615) 895-9041, Web Site: www. readingforeducation.com
CEO: Tom Crook
Conducts Business: U.S.
Primary Market Served: Business & Consumer
Advertising/Marketing Budget Related to Direct Marketing: 0-25%
Direct Marketing ad budget:
Direct Mail: 20%
Telephone: 80%
Founded: 1981

School fund-raising.

REDSTONE FEDERAL CREDIT UNION
220 Wynn Dr NW
Huntsville, AL 35893-0001
Telephone: (256) 837-6110, Web Site: www.redfcu.org
Adv VP Mktg: Kenneth Jost

REFEREE ENTERPRISES
2017 Lathrop Ave
Racine, WI 53405
Toll Free: (800) 733-6100, FAX: (262) 632-5460, E-Mail: questions@ referee.com, Web Site: www.referee. com
Pres: Barry Mano
Mktg & Mngmt Dir: Tom Herre
Conducts Business: U.S., Canada
Employees: 21
Primary Market Served: Business & Consumer
Catalog available online
Direct online sales
Advertising/Marketing Budget Related to Direct Marketing: 76-100%
Direct Marketing ad budget:
Direct Mail: 100%

Manage the National Association of Sports Officials. Publish Referee magazine & two monthly newsletters.

RESEARCH TO PREVENT BLINDNESS INC
360 Lexington Ave (fl 22)
New York, NY 10017
Telephone: (212) 752-4333, Toll Free: (800) 621-0026, FAX: (212) 688-6231, E-Mail: inforequest@rpbusa. org, Web Site: www.rpbusa.org
Pres: Brian Hofland
Dir, Commun & Mktg: Matthew Levine
Conducts Business: U.S.
Employees: 10
Primary Market Served: Business & Consumer

Founded: 1960

Non-profit voluntary health agency funding research into the causes & treatment of blinding diseases.

ROSE RESNICK LIGHTHOUSE FOR THE BLIND & VISUALLY IMPAIRED

214 Van Ness Ave
San Francisco, CA 94102
Telephone: (415) 431-1481, FAX: (415) 863-7568, E-Mail: executive@lighthouse-sf.org, Web Site: www.lighthouse-sf.org
Exec Dir: Anita S. Baldwin
Chief Devel Officer: George L. Clark
CFO: Howard Maull
Sr Dir Svcs: Kathy Abrahamson
Devel & Mktg Assoc: Andrea Ogarrio
Conducts Business: U.S.
Employees: 12
Primary Market Served: Business & Consumer
Founded: 1993

Develop & deliver services to people who are blind or visually impaired.

LW ROBBINS ASSOCIATES

201 Summer St
Holliston, MA 01746-2258
Telephone: (508) 893-0210, Toll Free: (800) 229-5972, FAX: (508) 893-0212, E-Mail: ppapsador@lwra.com, Web Site: www.lwra.com
Pres: Lynn S. Edmonds
Dir Mktg: Polly Papsadore
Primary Market Served: Consumer
Advertising/Marketing Budget Related to Direct Marketing: 76-100%
Founded: 1970

Strategic fundraising specialists serving non-profit organizations.

ROBBINSKERSTEN DIRECT

855 E Collins Blvd
Richardson, TX 75081-2251
Toll Free: (800) 222-6070, E-Mail: connect@robbinskersten.com, Web Site: www.robbinskersten.com
CEO: Tim Kersten
Sr VP Client Svcs: Max Bunch
Dir Mktg: Polly Papsadore

Direct marketing & non-profit fund-raising agency.

ROCHESTER INSTITUTE OF TECHNOLOGY

55 Lomb Memorial Dr
Rochester, NY 14623-5602
Telephone: (585) 475-7436, Web Site: www.rit.edu
Mng Editor, Print in the Mix: Liz Dopp

ROSICRUCIAN ORDER AMORC

1342 Naglee Ave
San Jose, CA 95191
Telephone: (408) 947-3600, FAX: (408) 947-3677, E-Mail: membership@rosicrucian.org, Web Site: www.rosicrucian.org
Pres: Julie Scott
Conducts Business: U.S., Canada, Europe, Central America, S. America, Africa, Asia, Australia, Mexico.
Employees: 65
Primary Market Served: Business & Consumer
Advertising/Marketing Budget Related to Direct Marketing: 0-25%
Founded: 1915
Gross sales or billing: $10,000,000

Books, audio & video cassettes, miscellaneous, to members & the public. Study course to members.

RURAL ALASKA COMMUNITY ACTION PROGRAM INC

aka RurAL CAP
731 E 8th Ave
Anchorage, AK 99501-3772
Telephone: (907) 279-2511, FAX: (907) 278-2309, Web Site: www.ruralcap.com
Exec Dir: David Hardenbergh
Employees: 500
Primary Market Served: Business & Consumer
Gross sales or billing: $20,000,000

Non-profit community action program.

SCA DIRECT

11200 Waples Mill Rd (Suite 150)
Fairfax, VA 22030-7418
Telephone: (703) 293-6339, Web Site: www.scadirect.com
VP Mktg: Katie Oakes

Provides marketing to non-profit organizations.

SIFMA

120 Broadway (fl 35)
New York, NY 10271-0080
Telephone: (212) 313-1200, FAX: (212) 313-1301, E-Mail: inquiry@sifma.org, Web Site: www.sifma.org
Pres & CEO: T. Timothy Ryan Jr
Employees: 70
Primary Market Served: Business
Catalog available online
Founded: 1976

Trade association.

SOS CHILDREN'S VILLAGES - USA

1001 Connecticut Ave NW Ste 1250
Washington, DC 20036-5520
Telephone: (202) 347-7920, Web Site: www.sos-usa.org
Comptroller: David Stinson

THE SAINT FRANCIS COMMUNITY SERVICES

509 E Elm St
Salina, KS 67401
Telephone: (785) 825-0541, Toll Free: (800) 423-1342, FAX: (785) 825-2940, Web Site: www.st-francis.org
Dir Mktg: Vickee Spicer
Conducts Business: U.S.
Employees: 400
Primary Market Served: Business & Consumer
Catalog available online
Advertising/Marketing Budget Related to Direct Marketing: 0-25%
Direct Marketing ad budget:
Direct Mail: 60%
Magazines: 20%
Newspapers: 20%
Founded: 1945

Fund-raising for community-based treatment programs for boys & girls. A system of behavioral, healthcare, non-profit hospitals & programs treating at-risk youth ages 10-18. Located in Indianapolis, IN; Salina, Ellsworth, & Atchison, KS; Picayune & Pascaguola, MS; Santa Fe, Espanola, NM; Lake Placid, NY; Philadelphia, PA & Cincinnati, OH.

ST JOSEPH'S COLLEGE

245 Clinton Ave
Brooklyn, NY 11205-3602
Telephone: (718) 399-1223, Web Site: www.sjcny.edu
Coord Recruitment & Mktg: Robert Napolitano
Primary Market Served: Consumer

ST JOSEPH'S INDIAN SCHOOL

1301 N Main St
Chamberlain, SD 57325-1656
Telephone: (605) 734-3300, Web Site: www.stjo.org
Exec Dir Devel: Kory Christianson

ST LABRE INDIAN SCHOOL

PO Box 77
Ashland, MT 59003-0077
Telephone: (406) 784-4500, Web Site: www.stlabre.org
Devel Assoc: Rachel Earl
Advertising/Marketing Budget Related to Direct Marketing: 26-50%

Direct Marketing ad budget:
Direct Mail: 97%
Online: 2%
Telephone: 1%
Founded: 1884

ST PETERSBURG/ CLEARWATER AREA CVB

13805 58th St N (Suite 2-200)
Clearwater, FL 33760-3716
Telephone: (727) 464-7200, Web Site:
www.floridasbeach.com
Internet Mktg Mgr: Deborah Holland
Primary Market Served: Business &
Consumer

SALESIAN MISSIONS

2 Le Fevres Ln
New Rochelle, NY 10801-5710
Telephone: (914) 633-8344, FAX:
(914) 633-7404, E-Mail: info@
salesianmissions.org, Web Site:
www.salesianmissions.org.
Production Coord: Jennifer Blum
Conducts Business: U.S.
Employees: 80
Primary Market Served: Business &
Consumer
Catalog available online
Direct online sales
Advertising/Marketing Budget Related
to Direct Marketing: 0-25%
Founded: 1962
Gross sales or billing: $40,000,000

Fundraising association supporting
seminaries and missionaries at home
and abroad who provide services to
poor youth.

THE SALVATION ARMY NATIONAL HEADQUARTERS

615 Slaters Ln
Alexandria, VA 22314-1112
Telephone: (703) 684-5500, Web Site:
www.salvationarmyusa.org
National Community Rels & Devel
Sec: George Hood

SANKY COMMUNICATIONS INC

599 11th Ave (fl 6)
New York, NY 10036-2110
Telephone: (212) 868-4300, Web Site:
www.sankyinc.com
Pres: Judy Maneval

Direct mail & website fundraising for
non-profits

SAVE THE CHILDREN FEDERATION INC

501 Kingss Hwy E (Suite 400)
Fairfield, CT 06825

Telephone: (203) 221-4000, Toll Free:
(800) 728-3843, FAX: (203) 222-
1067, E-Mail: majorgivng@
savethechildren.org, Web Site: www.
savethechildren.org
Pres & CEO: Carolyn Miles
VP, Mktg & Commun: Susan Ridge
VP, Intl Program Leadership: Diana
Myers
Conducts Business: Worldwide
Employees: 276
Primary Market Served: Business &
Consumer
Advertising/Marketing Budget Related
to Direct Marketing: 0-25%
Founded: 1932
Gross sales or billing: $332,400,000

Child assistance agency.

SCHOOLCRAFT COLLEGE

18600 Haggerty Rd
Livonia, MI 48152-2696
Telephone: (734) 462-4400, Web Site:
www.schoolcraft.edu
Dir Mktg: Marty Heator
Pres: Dr. Conway A. Jeffress

SCHULTZ & WILLIAMS INC

325 Chestnut St (Suite 700)
Philadelphia, PA 19106-2616
Telephone: (215) 625-9955, FAX:
(215) 625-2701, E-Mail: mail@
schultzwilliams.com, Web Site: www.
www.sw-inc.com
Pres: L. Scott Schultz
Principal: M. Jane Williams
VP Direct Response: Jessica Harring-
ton
VP: Rick Biddle
VP: Cathy Card Sterling
Conducts Business: U.S.
Employees: 9
Primary Market Served: Business
Founded: 1987

Consulting services to non-profit organizations in marketing & fund-raising. Creative through production,
fulfillment & analysis of direct-mail.

SESAME WORKSHOP

1 Lincoln Plaza
New York, NY 10023-7163
Telephone: (212) 875-6677, Web Site:
www.sesameworkshop.org
CEO & Pres: Jeffrey D. Dunn
Primary Market Served: Consumer

SETON HALL UNIVERSITY

400 South Orange Ave
South Orange, NJ 07079-2646
Telephone: (973) 761-9000, Web Site:
www.shu.edu
Primary Market Served: Consumer

SICKKIDS FOUNDATION

525 University Ave (fl 14)
Toronto, ON, Canada M5G 2L3
Toll Free: (800) 661-1083, FAX: (416)
813-5024, Web Site: www.
sickkidsfoundation.com
Pres & CEO: Ted Garrard

SIMMONS COLLEGE

300 The Fenway
Boston, MA 02115-5898
Telephone: (617) 521-2000, Web Site:
www.simmons.edu
Dir Online Mktg: Jake Berry
Pres: Helen G. Drinan

SMALL BUSINESS SERVICE BUREAU INC

554 Main St, PO Box 15014
Worcester, MA 01615-2014
Telephone: (508) 756-3513, Toll Free:
(800) 343-0939, FAX: (508) 770-
0528, E-Mail: info@sbsb.com, Web
Site: www.sbsb.com
CEO: Francis R. Carroll
Conducts Business: U.S., China
Employees: 140
Primary Market Served: Business
Founded: 1968
Gross sales or billing: $12,500,000

National membership organization for
small businesses.

THE SMILE TRAIN

41 Madison Ave (fl 28)
New York, NY 10010-2325
Telephone: (212) 689-9199, Toll Free:
(800) 932-9541, E-Mail: info@
smiletrain.org, Web Site: www.
smiletrain.org
VP Mktg & Commun: Shari Mason
Exec Vice Chair & CEO: Susannah
Schaeffer
Primary Market Served: Consumer

SOCIETY FOR HUMAN RESOURCE MANAGEMENT

1800 Duke St (Suite 100)
Alexandria, VA 22314-3499
Telephone: (703) 548-3440, Toll Free:
(800) 283-7476, FAX: (703) 535-
6490, E-Mail: shrmstore@shrm.org,
Web Site: www.shrm.org
Pres & CEO: Henry G. Jackson
Sr VP Membership, Mktg & External
Affairs: J. Robert Carr
Sr VP, Publishing and E-Media: Gary
K. Rubin
Primary Market Served: Business &
Consumer
Catalog available online
Direct online sales
Founded: 1948

Gross sales or billing: $88,000,000

S.H.R.M. is the voice of the human resource professionals, representing the interest of more than 77,000 professionals & student members from around the world.

SOCIETY FOR NEUROSCIENCE

1121 14th St NW (Suite 1010)
Washington, DC 20005-5642
Telephone: (202) 962-4000, Web Site: www.sfn.org
Dir, Membership & Mktg: Wendy Sturley
Pres: Hollis Cline
Pres-Elect: Eric Nestler

SOCIETY OF AMERICAN MAGICIANS INC

4927 S Oak Ct
Littleton, CO 80127
Telephone: (303) 362-0575, E-Mail: samadministrator@magicsam.com, Web Site: www.magicsam.com
Pres: David Bowers
Natl Administrator: Manon Rodriquez
Conducts Business: Worldwide
Employees: 6,000
Primary Market Served: Consumer
Catalog available online
Direct online sales
Direct Marketing ad budget:
Direct Mail: 30%
Magazines: 70%
Gross sales or billing: $150,000

Non-profit association of amateur & professional magicians & magic hobbyists. More than 200 local "Assemblies" throughout U.S. & foreign countries. Publish monthly magazine, M-U-M.

SOCIETY OF FINANCIAL SERVICE PROFESSIONALS

19 Campus Blvd (Suite 225)
Newtown Square, PA 19073-3239
Telephone: (610) 526-2500, FAX: (610) 359-8115, E-Mail: info@financialpro.org, Web Site: www.financialpro.org
Pres: Michael P. Dow
Conducts Business: U.S.
Employees: 53
Primary Market Served: Business
Advertising/Marketing Budget Related to Direct Marketing: 0-25%
Founded: 1928
Gross sales or billing: $7,000,000

Professional membership association. Services include continuing education programs & public relations tools sold to members & others in life insurance & financial services.

SOCIETY OF MANUFACTURING ENGINEERS

One SME Dr, PO Box 930
Dearborn, MI 48121
Telephone: (313) 425-3000, Toll Free: (800) 733-4763, FAX: (313) 425-3400, E-Mail: communications@sme.org, Web Site: www.sme.org
Exec Dir: Mark C. Tomlinson
Business Devel Mgr: Gary Mikola
Pres: Dean L. Bartles
CEO: Jeffrey Krause
Dir, HR: Jim Spilos
Conducts Business: Worldwide
Employees: 300
Primary Market Served: Business
Catalog available online
Direct online sales
Founded: 1932

Technical training, technical books & videotapes. Also rent mailing lists from 570,000 name database.

SOCIETY OF PETROLEUM ENGINEERS

222 Palisades Creek Dr
Richardson, TX 75080-2040
Telephone: (972) 952-9393, Toll Free: (800) 456-6863, FAX: (972) 952-9435, E-Mail: spedal@spe.org, Web Site: www.spe.org
Exec Dir: Mark A. Rubin
Dir Commun: Georgeann Bilich
Dir Member Programs & Svcs: Jane Boyce
Primary Market Served: Consumer

SOCIETY OF THE DIVINE SAVIOR

1303 Milwaukee Dr
New Holstein, WI 53062
Telephone: (920) 898-4201, Web Site: www.salvatoriancenter.com
Production Svcs Mgr: Jean Keuler
Primary Market Served: Consumer

SOUTHERN CALIFORNIA GAS CO

1919 S State College Blvd
Anaheim, CA 92806-6114
Telephone: (714) 634-3054, Toll Free: (877) 238-0092, FAX: (714) 937-7712, E-Mail: Tjavid@socalgas.com, Web Site: www.socalgas.com
CEO: Dennis Arriola
Primary Market Served: Business & Consumer
Catalog available online
Indirect online sales
Advertising/Marketing Budget Related to Direct Marketing: 26-50%
Direct Marketing ad budget:

Direct Mail: $1,000,000
Public utilities company.

SOUTHERN POVERTY LAW CENTER

400 Washington Ave
Montgomery, AL 36104-4344
Telephone: (334) 956-8200, Toll Free: (888) 414-7752, FAX: (334) 956-8483, Web Site: www.splcenter.org
Chmn Bd: Alan B. Howard
Employees: 113
Primary Market Served: Consumer
Advertising/Marketing Budget Related to Direct Marketing: 76-100%
Direct Marketing ad budget:
Direct Mail: 80%
Telephone: 20%
Founded: 1971

Non profit organizations that combats hate, intolerance and discrimination through education and litigation.

SPECIAL OLYMPICS INTERNATIONAL

1133 19th St NW Ste 1200
Washington, DC 20036-3604
Telephone: (202) 628-3630, Toll Free: (800) 700-8585, FAX: (202) 824-0200, E-Mail: info@specialolympics.org, Web Site: www.specialolympics.org
Chmn Bd: Timothy Shrivers
CEO: Mary Davis
Chief Mktg Officer: Kirsten Suto Seckler

Consumer/non-profit organization.

SPECIALIZED ASSOCIATION SERVICES

130 E John Carpenter Fwy
Irving, TX 75062-2708
Telephone: (469) 524-5000, E-Mail: hvincent@1sas.com, Web Site: www.1sas.com
Pres: Jeff Jensen
Mktg Dir: Heidi Vincent
Conducts Business: U.S.
Employees: 100
Primary Market Served: Business
Catalog available online
Founded: 1986
Gross sales or billing: $3,500,000

Association management company, membership marketing and retention.

SPECIALIZED INFORMATION PUBLISHERS ASSOCIATION

8229 Boone Blvd (Suite 260)
Vienna, VA 22182

Telephone: (781) 754-4771, FAX: (703) 992-7512, E-Mail: nbrand@ sia.net, Web Site: www.siia.net
Exec Dir: Janine Hergesell
Mng Editor: Ronn Levine
Conducts Business: Worldwide
Primary Market Served: Business & Consumer
Catalog available online
Indirect online sales
Direct Marketing ad budget:
Direct Mail: 100%
Founded: 1977

International trade association of subscription newsletter publishers & information services.

SPECIALTY EQUIPMENT MARKET ASSOCIATION

1575 S Valley Vista Dr
Diamond Bar, CA 91765-3914
Telephone: (909) 396-0289, Web Site: www.sema.org
Pres & CEO: Christopher J. Kersting
VP Commun & Events: Peter MacGillivray
VP Mktg & Market Res: Tom Myroniak
Primary Market Served: Consumer

DON STEWART ASSOCIATION

PO Box 21004
Tulsa, OK 74121-1004
Telephone: (602) 326-2267, FAX: (602) 678-3288, Web Site: www.donstewartassociation.com
Pres: Don Stewart
Conducts Business: Worldwide
Employees: 30
Primary Market Served: Consumer
Catalog available online
Direct online sales

Non-profit religious organization involved in humanitarian causes.

STUDENT UNION AT SJSU

1 Washington Sq (Suite 1400)
San Jose, CA 95192-0038
Telephone: (408) 924-5950, FAX: (408) 924-5953, E-Mail: getinvolved@sjsu.edu, Web Site: www.union.sjsu.edu
Mktg & Info Svcs: Gloria Robertson

SUSTAINABLE FORESTRY INITIATIVE INC

2121 K St NW (Suite 750)
Washington, DC 20037
Telephone: (202) 596-3450, FAX: (202) 596-3451, E-Mail: info@sfiprogram.org, Web Site: www.sfiprogram.org
Office Mgr: Julia Hershberger

CEO & Pres: Kathy Abusow

JIMMY SWAGGART MINISTRIES

8919 World Ministry Ave Ste B
Baton Rouge, LA 70810-9007
Telephone: (225) 768-8300, Toll Free: (800) 288-8350, FAX: (225) 769-2244, E-Mail: swaggart@cogeco.net, Web Site: www.jsm.org
Owner: Rev Jimmy Swaggart
Conducts Business: Worldwide
Primary Market Served: Consumer
Catalog available online
Direct online sales

Spread the gospel.

SYRACUSE UNIVERSITY

900 S Crouse Ave
Syracuse, NY 13244-0001
Telephone: (315) 443-1870, Toll Free: (315) 443-4226, E-Mail: orange@syr.edu, Web Site: syr.edu
Exec Dir, Devel Communs: Veronica Hotaling

TECHBA - FUMEC

1737 1st St (Suite 110)
San Jose, CA 95112-4522
Telephone: (408) 821-6297, Web Site: www.techba.com
CEO: Luis Medina

THD INC

80 Hayden Ave (Suite 300)
Lexington, MA 02421-7962
Telephone: (781) 859-1400, FAX: (781) 859-1500, E-Mail: info@thdinc.com, Web Site: www.thdinc.com
Co-Founder & EVP: Jay Denison

Full service non-profit agency

TAYMARK INC

dba M&N International; Parent is Taylor Corp
4875 White Bear Pkwy
White Bear Lake, MN 55110
Telephone: (651) 426-1667, Toll Free: (800) 479-2043, FAX: (651) 426-0275, Web Site: www.taymarkinc.com
Pres: Troy Ethen
Mktg Mgr: David Larson
Employees: 350
Primary Market Served: Business & Consumer
Catalog available online
Indirect online sales
Founded: 1970
Gross sales or billing: $59,200,000

Sell goods for holidays & theme parties, as well as novelty promotional items to businesses & consumers.

TEACHERS CREDIT UNION

110 S Main St
South Bend, IN 46601-1833
Telephone: (574) 284-6247, Toll Free: (800) 552-4745, Web Site: www.tcunet.com
Res Analyst: Julie Sisco
Pres: Paul Marsh

TECHNICAL ASSOCIATION OF THE PULP & PAPER INDUSTRY

15 Technology Pkwy S (Suite 115)
Norcross, GA 30092-2923
Telephone: (770) 446-1400, Toll Free: (800) 332-8686, FAX: (770) 446-6947, E-Mail: memberconnection@tappi.org, Web Site: www.tappi.org
Pres & CEO: Larry N. Montague
Conducts Business: Worldwide
Employees: 91
Primary Market Served: Business
Catalog available online
Direct online sales
Advertising/Marketing Budget Related to Direct Marketing: 51-75%
Direct Marketing ad budget:
Direct Mail: $400,000

Association serving the pulp & paper, packaging & converting, non-wovens & allied industries. Membership includes over 30,000 industry professionals from over 80 countries.

TEXAS CHILDREN'S HOSPITAL

6621 Fannin St
Houston, TX 77030
Telephone: (832) 824-1000, Web Site: www.texaschildrenshospital.org
Pres & CEO: Mark A. Wallace
Primary Market Served: Consumer

TEXAS PARKS & WILDLIFE DEPT

4200 Smith School Rd
Austin, TX 78744
Telephone: (512) 389-4800, Toll Free: (800) 792-1112, FAX: (512) 389-8029, Web Site: www.tpwd.state.tx.us
Dir: Peter P. Flores
Project Mgr: Walter Moldenhauer
Division Attorney: Boyd Kennedy
Budget/Purchasing: Brenda Braune
Primary Market Served: Business & Consumer

State agency.

THEATRE DEVELOPMENT FUND INC

520 8th Ave (Suite 801)
New York, NY 10018-6507

Telephone: (212) 912-9770, E-Mail:
   info@tdf.org, Web Site: www.tdf.org
Chmn Bd: Earl D. Weiner
Mng Dir: Michael Naumann
Exec Dir: Victoria Bailey
Conducts Business: U.S.
Employees: 77
Primary Market Served: Business &
   Consumer
Founded: 1968

Promote marketing services for commercial & non-profit theatre, dance &
music. Mailing list owner of TKTS
Times Square ticket booth purchasers
list.

THIRTEEN/WNET

825 Eighth Ave
New York, NY 10019
Telephone: (212) 560-1313, FAX:
   (212) 560-1314, E-Mail:
   programming@thirteen.org, Web
   Site: www.thirteen.org
Pres & CEO: Neal Shapiro
Conducts Business: U.S.
Primary Market Served: Business &
   Consumer

Public television station soliciting
membership contributions by direct
mail.

STEPHEN THOMAS

184 Front St E (Suite 501)
Toronto, ON, Canada M5A 4N3
Telephone: (416) 690-8801, FAX:
   (416) 690-7256, E-Mail: mail@
   stephenthomas.ca, Web Site: www.
   stephenthomas.ca
Pres: Marie Sauve Lloyd
Pres & CEO: Neal Gallaiford
VP, Client Svcs: Mary Attfield
Conducts Business: U.S., Canada, Aus-
   tralia, W. Europe
Employees: 30
Primary Market Served: Business &
   Consumer
Founded: 1980
Gross sales or billing: $2,000,000

Direct marketing consultant specializing in fund-raising. Clients include
charities, causes, political campaigns,
educational institutions, PBS stations,
universities & hospitals.

TORONTO HYDRO-
ELECTRIC SYSTEM

14 Carlton St
Toronto, ON, Canada M5B 1K5
Telephone: (416) 542-8000, Web Site:
   www.torontohydro.com
Mktg & Communs: Marina Tomasone
CEO & Pres: Anthony Haines

Primary Market Served: Business
Provides municipal electric distribution
utility service

TRANSITCENTER INC

1 Whitehall St (fl 17)
New York, NY 10004
Telephone: (646) 395-9555, E-Mail:
   info@transitcenter.org, Web Site:
   www.transitcenter.org
VP Mktg: Susan Ginsberg O'Sullivan
Exec Dir: David Bragdon
Primary Market Served: Consumer

TROUT UNLIMITED

1777 N Kent St (Suite 100)
Arlington, VA 22209-3800
Telephone: (703) 522-0200, Toll Free:
   (800) 834-2419, FAX: (703) 284-
   9400, E-Mail: trout@tu.org, Web
   Site: www.tu.org
Membership Mktg Dir: Lori Held
Pres & CEO: Chris Wood
Primary Market Served: Business

UCEA

PO Box 1168
New York, NY 10040-0815
FAX: (212) 781-6500, Web Site: www.
   revike.org
DM Project Mgr: Carolyn Jackson
Project Coord: Linda Norman
Conducts Business: U.S., Canada
Primary Market Served: Consumer
Fund-raising organization.

UNICEF

3 United Nations Plaza
New York, NY 10017
Telephone: (212) 326-7000, FAX:
   (212) 887-7465, Web Site: www.
   unicef.org
CEO: Anthony Lake
Primary Market Served: Business &
   Consumer

UNICEF CANADA

2200 Yonge St (#1100)
Toronto, ON, Canada M4S 2C6
Telephone: (416) 482-4444, Toll Free:
   (800) 567-4483, FAX: (416) 487-
   8875, E-Mail: on.secretary@unicef.
   ca, Web Site: www.unicef.ca
Pres & CEO: David Morley
Chief Devel Officer: Sharon Avery
COO: Dave Spedding
Conducts Business: Canada
Employees: 60
Primary Market Served: Business &
   Consumer
Catalog available online
Advertising/Marketing Budget Related
   to Direct Marketing: 26-50%
Direct Marketing ad budget:

Direct Mail: 10%
Magazines: 75%
Online: 15%
Founded: 1955
Gross sales or billing: $6,500,000

Use direct marketing techniques to solicit donations & sell UNICEF greeting
cards to individuals & corporations.

UPMC HEALTH PLAN

600 Grant St
Pittsburgh, PA 15219
Telephone: (888) 876-2756, Toll Free:
   (800) 361-2629, Web Site: www.
   upmchealthplan.com
Mgr Medicare Mktg: Alicia McVey
CEO & Pres: Diane Holder

USC VITERBI SCHOOL OF
ENGINEERING

3650 McClintock Ave, Olin Hall (Suite
   5)
Los Angeles, CA 90089-1451
Telephone: (213) 740-7832, Web Site:
   viterbi.usc.edu
Dean: Yannis C Yortsos
Exec Dir Mktg & Communs: Leslie
   DaCruz

USO INC

PO Box 96860
Washington, DC 20077-7677
Telephone: (703) 908-6400, Toll Free:
   (888) 484-3876, Web Site: www.uso.
   org
Primary Market Served: Consumer

Private, non-profit & non-political organization that aids troops & their families

UMASS DARTMOUTH

285 Old Westport Rd
North Dartmouth, MA 02747-2356
Telephone: (508) 999-8000, Toll Free:
   (508) 999-9250, Web Site: www.
   umassd.edu
Chancellor: Peyton Randolph Helm
Primary Market Served: Business &
   Consumer

UNION PRIVILEGE, AFL-CIO

1100 1st St NW (Suite 850)
Washington, DC 20002
Telephone: (202) 293-5311, Toll Free:
   (800) 472-2005, FAX: (202) 293-
   5311, E-Mail: info@unionprivilege.
   org, Web Site: www.unionplus.org
VP Direct Mktg: Karol Olson
Pres: Ed Grebow
VP Mktg: Eleanor Trice
Primary Market Served: Consumer
Catalog available online
Indirect online sales
Founded: 1986

Gross sales or billing: $4,500,000

Labor union organization.

UNITED CHURCH HOMES
170 E Center St
Marion, OH 43301-1806
Telephone: (740) 382-4885, Toll Free: (800) 837-2211, FAX: (740) 382-4884, Web Site: www. unitedchurchhomes.org
CEO: James L. Henry
Primary Market Served: Business & Consumer
Catalog available online
Provides older adults with Christian caring and quality services

UNITED FARM WORKERS OF AMERICA, AFL-CIO
29700 Woodford-Tehachapi Rd
Keene, CA 93531
Telephone: (661) 823-6151, FAX: (661) 823-6177, E-Mail: execoffice@ufw.org, Web Site: www.ufw.org
Pres: Arturo Rodriguez
Sec & Treas: Sergio Guzman
Conducts Business: U.S.
Employees: 75
Primary Market Served: Consumer
Catalog available online
Direct online sales
Advertising/Marketing Budget Related to Direct Marketing: 51-75%
Founded: 1962

Labor Union supported through donations.

UNITED JEWISH APPEAL FEDERATION OF NEW YORK
RP-NFOA
130 E 59th St
New York, NY 10022-1302
Telephone: (212) 980-1000, FAX: (212) 785-9321, E-Mail: contact@ujafedny.org, Web Site: www. ujafedny.org
Pres: Alisa Robbins Doctoroff
Chmn Bd: Linda Mirels
Conducts Business: Worldwide
Primary Market Served: Consumer

Raise funds for social & human services programs for 130 agencies in New York, Long Island, Westchester, Israel & worldwide.

UNITED JEWISH COMMUNITIES
25 Broadway (fl 17)
New York, NY 10004-1015

Telephone: (212) 284-6500, E-Mail: info@jewishfederations.org, Web Site: www.jewishfederations.org
Mgr Direct Mktg Analysis: David Semler
Primary Market Served: Consumer

UNITED NATIONS FEDERAL CREDIT UNION
2401 44th Rd (fl 7) Ct Sq Pl
Long Island City, NY 11101-4605
Telephone: (347) 686-6000, E-Mail: email@unfcu.org, Web Site: www. unfcu.org
VP Mktg: Debra I. Da Costa
Pres & CEO: William Predmore
Primary Market Served: Consumer

UNITED NATIONS FOUNDATION
1750 Pennsylvania Ave NW (#300)
Washington, DC 20006-4502
Telephone: (202) 887-9040, FAX: (202) 887-9021, Web Site: www. unfoundation.org
Pres & CEO: Kathy Calvin
Exec Dir, Global Partnerships & Mktg: Jennifer Kim Field
Exec Dir, Commun & Pub Affairs: Caleb Tiller

UNITED SPINAL ASSOCIATION
120-34 Queens Blvd (#320)
Kew Gardens, NY 11415
Telephone: (718) 803-3782, Toll Free: (800) 404-2898, FAX: (718) 803-0414, E-Mail: info@unitedspinal.org, Web Site: www.unitedspinal.org
Pres & CEO: Paul Tobin
Sr VP Devel & Commun: Cary Castle
Pres: James Weisman
Primary Market Served: Business & Consumer

UNITED STATES BRONZE SIGN CO INC
811 Second Ave
New Hyde Park, NY 11040
Telephone: (516) 352-5155, Toll Free: (800) 872-5155, FAX: (516) 253-2328, E-Mail: peter@usbronze.com, Web Site: www.usbronze.com
Pres: George T. Barbeosch
VP NY: Alan Kasten
Gen Mgr NY: Peter Kasten
Conducts Business: U.S.
Employees: 30
Primary Market Served: Business & Consumer
Advertising/Marketing Budget Related to Direct Marketing: 0-25%
Founded: 1933

Gross sales or billing: $2,000,000

Sell to churches, temples, organizations & commercial accounts. Trees of life, donor tablets, honor rolls, dedicatory tablets, memorial plaques & metal letters.

US CHAMBER OF COMMERCE
1615 "H" St NW
Washington, DC 20062-2000
Telephone: (202) 659-6000, Toll Free: (800) 638-6582, FAX: (202) 887-3430, Web Site: www.uschamber. com
Pres & CEO: Thomas J. Donohue
Conducts Business: Worldwide
Employees: 1,200
Primary Market Served: Business
Catalog available online
Direct online sales
Advertising/Marketing Budget Related to Direct Marketing: 76-100%
Founded: 1912
Gross sales or billing: $70,000,000

Publisher of Nation's Business & The Business Advocate. Produce TV programs. Lobbyist for business on economic legislative issues. Regional Offices: San Mateo, CA; Alpharetta, GA; Oak Brook, IL; Rockville, MD & Dallas, TX.

US DEPARTMENT OF COMMERCE
1401 Constitution Ave NW
Washington, DC 20230
Telephone: (202) 482-2000, E-Mail: thesec@doc.gov, Web Site: www. commerce.gov
Sec of Commerce: Penny Pritzker
Primary Market Served: Business & Consumer

US PHARMACOPEIA
12601 Twinbrook Pkwy
Rockville, MD 20852-1790
Telephone: (301) 881-0666, Toll Free: (800) 227-8772, FAX: (301) 816-8236, Web Site: www.usp.org
Sls & Mktg: Maureen Rawson
CEO: Ronald T. Piervincenzi
Primary Market Served: Business
Sets the drug standard for the U.S.

UNITED STATES TENNIS ASSOCIATION
70 W Red Oak Ln
White Plains, NY 10604-3610
Telephone: (914) 696-7000, Toll Free: (800) 990-8782, E-Mail: memberservices@usta.com, Web Site: www.usta.com
Mng Dir Mktg: Sherry Elinsky

CEO: Gordon Smith

US TRAVEL ASSOCIATION
1100 New York Ave NW (Suite 450)
Washington, DC 20005-6130
Telephone: (202) 408-8422, FAX:
   (202) 408-1255, E-Mail: feedback@
   ustravel.org, Web Site: www.
   ustravel.org
Pres & CEO: Roger Dow
Sr VP, Member Svcs: Gary Oster
Sr VP, Opers: Adam Vance
Sr Dir, Program & Mktg Svcs: Laura
   Holmberg
Conducts Business: U.S., Canada,
   Mexico, Europe
Employees: 54
Primary Market Served: Business &
   Consumer
Advertising/Marketing Budget Related
   to Direct Marketing: 76-100%
Founded: 1973

National non-profit center for travel &
tourism research. Produce reports on
demographics & trip characteristics of
U.S. travelers.

UNITED WAY TORONTO & YORK REGION
26 Wellington St E (fl 12)
Toronto, ON, Canada M5E 1S2
Telephone: (416) 777-2001, Toll Free:
   (866) 620-2993, FAX: (416) 777-
   0962, Web Site: www.unitedwaytyr.
   com
Pres & CEO: Susan McIsaac
Conducts Business: Canada
Primary Market Served: Business &
   Consumer
Direct Marketing ad budget:
Direct Mail: 80%
Telephone: 20%
Gross sales or billing: $61,000,000

Help over 1.2 million people in Toronto through 205 agencies. The direct
marketing arm is responsible for soliciting donations outside of the traditional employee campaigns.

UNITED WAY WORLDWIDE
701 N Fairfax St
Alexandria, VA 22314-2058
Telephone: (703) 836-7112, Web Site:
   www.unitedway.org
Pres & CEO: Brian Gallagher
Exec VP & Chief Mktg Officer: Lisa
   Bowman

UNIVERSITY OF AKRON
302 E Butchel Ln
Akron, OH 44325-0001
Telephone: (330) 972-7111
Pres: Scott L. Scarborough

Primary Market Served: Business &
Consumer

UNIVERSITY OF CALIFORNIA IRVINE EXTENSION
Pereira Dr W (Bldg 234)
Irvine, CA 92697-5700
Telephone: (949) 824-5414, E-Mail:
   unex-services@uci.edu, Web Site:
   extension.uci.edu
Strategic Mktg Mgr: Michelle Mador-
sky
Dean: Gary W. Matkins
Primary Market Served: Consumer

UNIVERSITY OF CHICAGO GSB
450 N Cityfront Plaza Dr (Suite 514)
Chicago, IL 60611-4316
Telephone: (312) 464-8733, E-Mail:
   exec.ed@chicagobooth.edu, Web
   Site: www.chicagobooth.edu
Assoc Dean: Steven LaCivita
Pres & CEO: Susan Lucia Annunzio
Primary Market Served: Consumer

UNIVERSITY OF ILLINOIS COLLEGE OF LAS, OFFICE OF ADVANCEMENT
702 S Wright St MC-446, 2090 Lincoln
Hall
Urbana, IL 61801
Telephone: (217) 333-1705, E-Mail:
   las-studentoffice@illinois.edu, Web
   Site: www.las.illinois.edu
Sr Dir Commun: Holly Korab
Dean: Barbara Wilson

UNIVERSITY OF ILLINOIS FOUNDATION
1305 W Green St (MC-386)
Urbana, IL 61801-2962
Telephone: (217) 333-0810, FAX:
   (217) 333-5577, E-Mail: uif@
   uillinois.edu, Web Site: www.uif.
   uillinois.edu
Pres & CEO: Jim Moore
Conducts Business: U.S.
Employees: 125
Primary Market Served: Business &
   Consumer
Advertising/Marketing Budget Related
   to Direct Marketing: 51-75%
Direct Marketing ad budget:
Direct Mail: 50%
Telephone: 50%
Founded: 1935

Fund-raising arm of the University of
Illinois campuses at Chicago, Springfield & Urbana-Champaign.

UNIVERSITY OF MINNESOTA
100 Church St SE (3 Morrill Hal)l
Minneapolis, MN 55455
Telephone: (612) 625-0256, Web Site:
   www.twin-cities.umn.edu
Mktg Mgr: Sheila Flatz
Pres: Eric W. Kaler
Primary Market Served: Consumer

UNIVERSITY OF MINNESOTA ALUMNI ASSOCIATION
Div. of University of Minnesota
200 Oak St SE (Suite 200)
Minneapolis, MN 55455-2040
Telephone: (612) 624-2323, Toll Free:
   (800) 862-5867, FAX: (612) 626-
   8167, E-Mail: umalumni@umn.edu,
   Web Site: www.minnesotaalumni.org
Chair: Anthony R. Baraga
Vice Chair: Patricia S. Simmons
Pres: Robert H. Pruiniks
Sr VP, Academic Affairs & Provost: E.
   Thomas Sullivan
Vice Provost & Dean: Craig Swan
Employees: 35
Primary Market Served: Consumer
Catalog available online
Direct online sales
Founded: 1904
Gross sales or billing: $1,500,000,000

Membership organization for alumni &
friends of the University of Minnesota.

UNIVERSITY OF NORTH TEXAS
1155 Union Cir #311277
Denton, TX 76203-5017
Telephone: (940) 565-2000, Web Site:
   www.unt.edu
Regents Professor: Roy Busby

UNIVERSITY OF PENNSYLVANIA
3451 Walnut St, 601 Franklin Bldg
Philadelphia, PA 19104-6285
Telephone: (215) 898-5000, FAX:
   (215) 898-9659, Web Site: www.
   upenn.edu
Pres: Amy Gutman
VP Devel & Alumni Rels: John H. Zel-
ler
Provost: Ronald J. Daniels
Dept Chair: Chuck Snow
Dept Chair: Lee A. Fleischer
DM Dir: Jean Findley
Conducts Business: U.S.
Primary Market Served: Consumer
Catalog available online
Founded: 1751

UNIVERSITY OF PENNSYLVANIA - VETERINARY MEDICINE (DEVELOPMENT)

3800 Spruce St (Suite 172E)
Philadelphia, PA 19104-4192
Telephone: (215) 898-8841, E-Mail:
vetdean@vet.upenn.edu, Web Site:
www.vet.upenn.edu
Dir Annual Giving: Mary Berger

UNIVERSITY OF SOUTHERN MISSISSIPPI

118 College Dr (Box 5016)
Hattiesburg, MS 39406-0001
Telephone: (601) 266-1000, Web Site:
www.usm.edu
Mktg Mgr: Melanie Gardner
Pres: Rodney D. Bennett
Primary Market Served: Consumer

UNIVERSITY OF TEXAS SCHOOL OF LAW

727 E Dean Keeton St, Continuing Legal Education
Austin, TX 78705-3224
Telephone: (512) 475-6700, FAX:
(512) 475-6876, E-Mail: services@
utcle.org, Web Site: www.utcle.org
Asst Dean: Gregory J. Smith
Primary Market Served: Consumer

UNIVERSITY OF WASHINGTON EDUCATIONAL OUTREACH

2012 Skagit Ln (Miller Hall Box 353600)
Seattle, WA 98195-3600
Telephone: (206) 685-6566, E-Mail:
edinfo@u.washington.edu, Web Site:
www.pce.uw.edu
Dean: Mia Tuan

Professional & continuing education

UNIVERSITY OF WISCONSIN-MADISON SCHOOL OF BUSINESS

975 University Ave
Madison, WI 53706
Telephone: (608) 262-1550, E-Mail:
info@bus.wisc.edu, Web Site: bus.
wisc.edu
Dir Exec Mktg Education: Linda Gorchels
Primary Market Served: Consumer

THE URBAN LAND INSTITUTE

1025 Thomas Jefferson St NW (Suite 500W)
Washington, DC 20007-5201
Telephone: (202) 624-7000, FAX:
(202) 624-7140, E-Mail:
customerservice@uli.org, Web Site:
www.uli.org
CEO: Patrick L. Phillips
Conducts Business: Worldwide
Primary Market Served: Business
Advertising/Marketing Budget Related
to Direct Marketing: 76-100%
Direct Marketing ad budget:
Direct Mail: $800,000
Telephone: $100,000
Founded: 1936

Non-profit real estate development research & educational organization. Publish & sell books through direct mail.

VAN GROESBECK & CO

2124 Hanover Ave
Richmond, VA 23220
Telephone: (804) 285-3176, FAX:
(804) 359-7271, E-Mail: info@
vangroesbeckco.com, Web Site:
www.vangroesbeckco.com
Pres: Stefani Fisher

VERIDIAN CREDIT UNION

PO Box 6000 1827 Ansborough Ave
Waterloo, IA 50704
Telephone: (319) 236-5692, Toll Free:
(800) 235-3228, FAX: (319) 833-
1185, E-Mail: sarahma@veridiancu.
org, Web Site: www.veridiancu.org
VP Commun: Ann Longseth
Mgr Commun: Eric Kinman
Project Specialist: Amela Cejvanovic
Res Specialist: Sarah Austin
Conducts Business: U.S.
Employees: 400
Primary Market Served: Business & Consumer
Indirect online sales
Advertising/Marketing Budget Related
to Direct Marketing: 0-25%
Direct Marketing ad budget: $40,000
Direct Mail: 100%
Founded: 1924

Financial services, members and non-members.

VERMONT SKI AREAS ASSOCIATION

26 State St, PO Box 368
Montpelier, VT 05601
Telephone: (802) 223-2439, FAX:
(802) 229-6917, E-Mail: info@
skivermont.com, Web Site: www.
skivermont.com
Pres: Parker Riehle
Dir, Mktg: Kyle Opuszynski
Mktg Mgr: Adam Rowe
Conducts Business: U.S.
Primary Market Served: Consumer

Advertising/Marketing Budget Related
to Direct Marketing: 0-25%
Founded: 1960

Trade association promoting skiing in the state of Vermont.

VETERANS OF FOREIGN WARS OF THE US

406 W 34th St
Kansas City, MO 64111-2736
Telephone: (816) 756-3390, FAX:
(816) 968-1149, E-Mail: info@vfw.
org, Web Site: www.vfw.org
Commander-in-Chief: John A. Biedrzycki
Primary Market Served: Business & Consumer
Catalog available online
Founded: 1899

The VFW is a nonprofit service organization helping to meet the needs of veterans & their families.

VIETNAM VETERANS OF AMERICA

8719 Colesville Rd (Suite 100)
Silver Spring, MD 20910-3710
Telephone: (301) 585-4000, Toll Free:
(800) 882-1316, FAX: (301) 585-
0519, Web Site: www.vva.org
Bus Mgr: Quentin Butcher
Primary Market Served: Consumer

VIRGINIA HOME FOR BOYS & GIRLS

8716 W Broad St
Richmond, VA 23294
Telephone: (804) 270-6566, FAX:
(804) 270-6574, E-Mail: info@vhbg.
org, Web Site: www.vhbg.org
Exec Dir: Tod Balsbaugh
Pres: Claiborne Mason
Conducts Business: U.S.
Employees: 50
Primary Market Served: Business & Consumer

Non-profit children's home providing residential care & services to disadvantaged young people.

VOLUNTEERS OF AMERICA

1660 Duke St
Alexandria, VA 22314
Telephone: (703) 341-5000, Toll Free:
(800) 899-0089, FAX: (703) 341-
7000, E-Mail: info@voa.org, Web
Site: www.voa.org
Pres & CEO: Michael King
COO: Thomas Turnbull
Commun Dir: David Burch
Exec VP, External Affairs: Jatrice Martel Gaiter
Primary Market Served: Consumer

WGBH EDUCATIONAL FOUNDATION

1 Guest St
Brighton, MA 02135-2016
Telephone: (617) 300-2000, FAX: (617) 300-1026, Web Site: www. wgbh.org
Pres & CEO: Jonathan C. Abbot
Exec VP & COO: Benjamin Godley
VP, Mktg & Commun: Jamie Parker
Employees: 1,100
Primary Market Served: Consumer
Catalog available online
Gross sales or billing: $198,000,000

Commercial activities including selling books, videos & gifts.

WAKE FOREST UNIVERSITY BAPTIST MEDICAL CENTER

Medical Center Blvd
Winston Salem, NC 27157-0001
Telephone: (336) 716-2011, Web Site: www.wakehealth.edu
Dir PR & Mktg: Susan McBurney
CEO: John D. McConnell
Primary Market Served: Consumer

WALK THRU THE BIBLE MINISTRIES INC

555 Triangle Pkwy (Suite 250)
Norcross, GA 30092
Telephone: (770) 458-9300, Toll Free: (800) 361-6131, Web Site: www. walkthru.org
CEO: Chip Ingram
Primary Market Served: Consumer

MAL WARWICK ASSOCIATES

2550 9th St (Suite 103)
Berkeley, CA 94710-2551
Telephone: (510) 843-8888, FAX: (510) 843-0142, E-Mail: info@ malwarwick.com, Web Site: www. malwarwick.com
Pres & CEO: Daniel S. Doyle

Develops direct marketing programs for non-profit causes

WASHINGTON MARKETING GROUP

5155 N 37th St
Arlington, VA 22207
Telephone: (703) 534-9331, FAX: (703) 534-0242, E-Mail: william. shaker@twmg.com, Web Site: www. twmg.com
CEO & Creative Dir: William Shaker
Conducts Business: U.S.
Employees: 4
Primary Market Served: Business & Consumer

Catalog available online
Indirect online sales
Advertising/Marketing Budget Related to Direct Marketing: 76-100%
Direct Marketing ad budget:
Direct Mail: 100%
Founded: 1987
Gross sales or billing: $3,000,000

Full-service production, printing & creative organization, serving both non-profit & commercial clients.

WASHINGTON UNIVERSITY

1 Brookings Dr
Saint Louis, MO 63130-4899
Telephone: (314) 935-5000, Web Site: www.wustl.edu
Chmn: David W. Kemper
Chancellor: Mark S. Wrighton
Exec VP Chancellor, Alumni & Devel Programs: David T. Blasingame
Mktg & Strategic Planning: Annette Unsur
Conducts Business: United States
Employees: 9,600
Primary Market Served: Consumer
Catalog available online
Gross sales or billing: $1,700,000,000

Fund-raising, development, alumnae resources.

WELLNESS COUNCILS OF AMERICA

17002 Marcy St (Suite 140)
Omaha, NE 68118-2933
Telephone: (402) 827-3590, FAX: (402) 827-3594, E-Mail: wellworkplace@welcoa.org, Web Site: www.welcoa.org
VP, Opers: Brittanie Leffelman
Pres: Ryan Picarella
Dir Mktg: William Kizer Jr.
Conducts Business: U.S.
Employees: 8
Primary Market Served: Business
Advertising/Marketing Budget Related to Direct Marketing: 51-75%
Direct Marketing ad budget:
Direct Mail: 75%
Telephone: 25%
Founded: 1987

Books, manuals & videotapes for business owners & health promotion planners in companies on corporate health promotion. Mailing list for rent. Also, newsletters & brochures.

WESTERN PENNSYLVANIA CONSERVANCY

800 Waterfront Dr Fl 2
Pittsburgh, PA 15222-4718

Telephone: (412) 288-2777, Toll Free: (866) 564-6972, FAX: (412) 231-1414, E-Mail: info@paconserve.org, Web Site: www.paconserve.org
Pres: Thomas Saunders
Primary Market Served: Business & Consumer

Non-profit conservation organization

SIMON WIESENTHAL CENTER

1399 S Roxbury Dr Ste 100
Los Angeles, CA 90035-4709
Telephone: (310) 553-9036, Toll Free: (800) 900-9036, FAX: (310) 553-4521, E-Mail: information@ wiesenthal.com, Web Site: wiesenthal.com
Dean & Founder: Rabbi Marvin Hier

WINNIPEG ART GALLERY

300 Memorial Blvd
Winnipeg, MB, Canada R3C 1V1
Telephone: (204) 786-6641, FAX: (204) 788-4998, E-Mail: inquiries@ wag.mb.ca, Web Site: www.wag.ca
Adv: Heather Mousseau
Exec Asst: Sandra Udell
Mgr: Crystal Hiebert
Deputy Dir: Claire Whelan
Graphic Design: Lisa Frisen
Conducts Business: U.S., Canada
Employees: 60
Primary Market Served: Consumer
Founded: 1912

Public art gallery using direct mail for fund-raising & to sell art books, exhibition catalogs, reproductions & gift items.

WISCONSIN HISTORICAL FOUNDATION

816 State St
Madison, WI 53706
Telephone: (608) 318-1044
Chmn: Michael L. Youngman

WOMEN'S SPORTS FOUNDATION

1899 Hempstead Turnpike, Eisenhower Park
East Meadow, NY 11554-1099
Telephone: (516) 542-4700, Toll Free: (800) 227-3988, FAX: (516) 542-0095, Web Site: www. womenssportsfoundation.org
CEO: Kathryn Olson
VP, Devel: Michael Rodgers
Dir, Sponsorship & Mktg: Aleia Naylor

WORLD FUTURE SOCIETY

333 N LaSalle St
Chicago, IL 60654

Telephone: (301) 656-8274, Toll Free: (800) 989-8274, FAX: (301) 951-0394, E-Mail: info@wfs.org, Web Site: www.wfs.org
Pres: Timothy C. Mack
Bus Mgr: Jefferson Cornish
Dir Commun: Patrick Tucker
Founder: Edward Cornish
Chair & Interim Exec Dir: Julie Friedman-Steele
Conducts Business: U.S., Canada, Australia, Western Europe
Employees: 13
Primary Market Served: Business & Consumer
Catalog available online
Indirect online sales
Advertising/Marketing Budget Related to Direct Marketing: 76-100%
Direct Marketing ad budget:
Direct Mail: $300,000
Founded: 1966
Gross sales or billing: $900,000

Membership association & publisher of periodicals & books dealing with social & technological change.

WORLD VISION CANADA
1 World Dr
Mississauga, ON, Canada L5T 2Y4
Telephone: (905) 565-6100, Toll Free: (866) 595-5550, FAX: (866) 219-8620, Web Site: www.worldvision.ca
Pres & CEO: Michael Messenger

WORLD VISION INC
PO Box 9716, Dept W
Federal Way, WA 98063-9716
Telephone: (253) 815-1000, Toll Free: (888) 511-6548, FAX: (253) 815-3140, E-Mail: info@worldvision.org, Web Site: www.worldvision.org
Pres & CEO: Richard Stearns
Sr VP, Mobilization: Joan Mussa
VP & Mktg Dir: Marty Lonsdale
Employees: 1,500
Primary Market Served: Consumer
Catalog available online
Direct online sales
Founded: 1953
Gross sales or billing: $274,600,000

Christian world relief and non-profit community development organization.

WORLD WILDLIFE FUND
1250 24th St NW PO Box 97180
Washington, DC 20090-7180
Telephone: (202) 293-4800, Web Site: www.worldwildlife.org
Pres & CEO: Carter Roberts
Sr VP, Commun & Mktg: Terry Macko

YWCA OF THE USA
2025 M St NW (Suite 550)
Washington, DC 20036-3320
Telephone: (202) 467-0801, FAX: (202) 467-0802, E-Mail: info@ywca.org, Web Site: www.ywca.org
CEO: Dara Richardson-Heron
Dir, Advocacy & Policy: Desiree Hoffman
Employees: 53
Primary Market Served: Consumer
Founded: 1855
Gross sales or billing: $7,944,131

YOUNG AMERICA'S FOUNDATION
11480 Commerce Park Dr (fl 6)
Reston, VA 20191-1556
Toll Free: (800) USA-1776, FAX: (703) 318-9122, Web Site: www.yaf.org
Primary Market Served: Consumer

Principal outreach program of the conservative movement

ZOOLOGICAL SOCIETY OF SAN DIEGO
2920 Zoo Dr, PO Box 120551
San Diego, CA 92112
Telephone: (619) 231-1515, FAX: (619) 557-3937, Web Site: www.sandiegozoo.org
Pres & CEO: Douglas G. Myers
Chief Devel & Membership Officer: Mark Stuart
Corp Dir, Mktg: Ted Molter
Primary Market Served: Business & Consumer
Catalog available online
Founded: 1916

A-T SURGICAL MANUFACTURING CO
115 Clemente St
Holyoke, MA 01040-5644
Telephone: (413) 532-4551, Toll Free: (800) 225-2023, FAX: (413) 532-0826, Web Site: www.atsurgical.com
Pres & CEO: Mark Shoham
Conducts Business: U.S.
Employees: 38
Primary Market Served: Business
Catalog available online
Direct online sales
Advertising/Marketing Budget Related to Direct Marketing: 0-25%
Founded: 1969
Gross sales or billing: $3,100,000
Health products & elastic supports.

AMC INC
Div. of The Portman Cos
240 Peachtree St NW (Suite 2200)
Atlanta, GA 30303-1327
Telephone: (404) 220-2000, FAX: (404) 220-3030
Pres & COO: Jeff Portman
Exec VP Mktg: Douglas Broward
Conducts Business: Worldwide
Employees: 300
Primary Market Served: Business
Home accents & furnishings, holiday & floral, decorative garden accessories & area rugs. General gifts - table top, linens, fashion accessories, jewelry & gourmet.

AEROSOLES
PO Box 1916
Edison, NJ 08818-1916
Telephone: 732-985-6900, Toll Free: (800)798-9478, FAX: (732) 985-3697, Web Site: www.aerosoles.com
VP Dir Mktg: Jeff Barney

AMAZON DRYGOODS
3788 Wilson St
Osgood, IN 47037
FAX: (812)852-1780, Web Site: www.amazondrygoods.com
Owner: Samantha Hickle
Owner: Kevin Hickle
Conducts Business: Worldwide
Employees: 10
Primary Market Served: Business & Consumer
Indirect online sales
Advertising/Marketing Budget Related to Direct Marketing: 76-100%
Direct Marketing ad budget:
Magazines: 100%
Founded: 1982

Gross sales or billing: $1,000,000
Historic reproductions of 3,300 items in four catalogs. Clothing, shoes, hats, sewing patterns, books & much more.

AMERICAN EAGLE OUTFITTERS
77 Hot Metal St
Pittsburgh, PA 15203-2382
Telephone: (412) 432-3382, Web Site: www.ae.com
Exec Chairman & CFO: Jay L Schottenstein

AMERIMARK DIRECT LLC
6864 Engle Rd
Middleburg Heights, OH 44130
Telephone: (440) 325-2000, FAX: (440) 234-8925, E-Mail: affiliate@amerimark.com, Web Site: www.amerimark.com
Pres: Louis Giesler
Founded: 1969
Mail order, direct marketer of women's apparel, shoes, cosmetics, fragrance & jewelry.

HANNA ANDERSSON CORP
608 NE 19th Ave
Portland, OR 97232
Telephone: (503) 242-0920, Toll Free: (800) 222-0544, FAX: (503) 321-5289, Web Site: www.hannaandersson.com
Pres & CEO: Adam Stone
Conducts Business: U.S., Canada
Employees: 270
Primary Market Served: Business & Consumer
Gross sales or billing: $45,200,000
Mail order catalog of 100% cotton children's clothing.

ANN INC
7 Times Square Tower (Fl 14)
New York, NY 10036
Telephone: (212) 541-3300, Toll Free: (800) 342-5266, FAX: (866) 232-9266, Web Site: www.anninc.com
Pres & CEO: Gary Muto
Conducts Business: U.S.
Employees: 2,000
Primary Market Served: Business & Consumer
Catalog available online
Direct online sales
Marketer of contemporary women's fashions under the Ann Taylor & LOFT brands.

ARAMARK UNIFORM SERVICES
115 N First St
Burbank, CA 91502-1856
Toll Free: (800) 272-6275, Web Site: www.aramark-uniform.com
Chairman, Pres & CEO: Eric Foss

BACHRACH CLOTHING INC
Div. of Sun Capital
323 W 39th St (Fl 11)
New York, NY 10018
Web Site: www.bachrach.com
Conducts Business: U.S.
Employees: 300
Primary Market Served: Consumer
Catalog available online
Direct online sales
Retail chain. Produce & mail catalogs featuring clothing for men.

MAURICE BADLER FINE JEWELRY LTD
485 Park Ave
New York, NY 10022-1228
Telephone: (212) 575-9632, Toll Free: (800) M-BADLER, FAX: (212) 575-9205, E-Mail: info@badler.com, Web Site: www.badler.com
Pres: Jeffrey P. Badler
Primary Market Served: Consumer
Catalog available online
Indirect online sales
Advertising/Marketing Budget Related to Direct Marketing: 76-100%
Retailing & cataloging fine jewelry.

BANANA REPUBLIC
Div. of The Gap Inc
2 Folsom St
San Francisco, CA 94105
Telephone: (650) 952-4400, Toll Free: (888) 277-8953, Web Site: www.bananarepublic.com
Conducts Business: U.S.
Primary Market Served: Consumer
Authentic, classic, travel & safari clothing in natural fabrics for men & women sold in retail stores.

JOSEPH A BANK CLOTHIERS INC
500 Hanover Pike
Hampstead, MD 21074-2002
Telephone: (410) 239-2700, Toll Free: (800) 285-2265, FAX: (410) 239-5911, E-Mail: service@jos-a-bank.com, Web Site: www.josbank.com
Pres & CEO: Doug Ewert
Exec VP Mktg: Matt Stringer
Conducts Business: U.S.

Employees: 2,000
Primary Market Served: Consumer
Catalog available online
Founded: 1905
Gross sales or billing: $500,000,000

Manufacturers & merchants of fine traditional clothing for men through own retail stores & catalog. Stores located throughout U.S.

BARELY NOTHINGS LINGERIE

530 W Tefft St
Nipomo, CA 93444
Telephone: (805) 489-5591, Toll Free: (800) 422-7359, FAX: (888) 489-5987, E-Mail: lingerie@barelynothings.com, Web Site: www.getpassionhere.com
Co-Owner: Sandi Spinelli
Co-Owner: Ozzie Spinelli
Conducts Business: U.S.
Primary Market Served: Consumer
Catalog available online
Direct online sales
Advertising/Marketing Budget Related to Direct Marketing: 0-25%
Founded: 1991
Gross sales or billing: $600,000

Lingerie for sizes 4 to 14 & another catalog for sizes 16 to 26.

RG BARRY CORP

13405 Yarmouth Rd NW
Pickerington, OH 43147-8493
Telephone: (614) 864-6400, Toll Free: (800) 848-7560, FAX: (614) 866-9787, E-Mail: sales@rgbarry.com, Web Site: www.rgbarry.com
Pres & CEO: Greg A. Tunney
Sr VP & CFO: Jose Ibarra
Sr VP, Sls: Pam Gentile
Sr VP: Glenn Evans
Conducts Business: U.S.
Employees: 2,500
Primary Market Served: Business & Consumer
Catalog available online
Direct online sales
Gross sales or billing: $108,900,000

Footwear manufacturer.

EDDIE BAUER GROVEPORT SERVICE CENTER

6600 Alum Creek Dr
Groveport, OH 43125
Telephone: (614) 497-1083, E-Mail: gpscrecruiting@eddiebauer.com, Web Site: www.eddiebauer.com
Conducts Business: U.S., Canada
Primary Market Served: Consumer
Direct Marketing ad budget: $25,000

Merchandise distribution & customer service center.

LL BEAN INC

15 Casco St
Freeport, ME 04033-0001
Telephone: (207) 865-4761, Toll Free: (800) 441-5713, FAX: (207) 552-3080, Web Site: www.llbean.com
Pres & CEO: Christopher McCormick
Conducts Business: U.S.
Employees: 5,300
Primary Market Served: Business & Consumer
Catalog available online
Direct online sales
Advertising/Marketing Budget Related to Direct Marketing: 76-100%
Founded: 1912
Gross sales or billing: $1,400,000,000

Direct mail catalog featuring active & casual apparel for men, women & children, footwear, sporting equipment, luggage, furnishings & accessories for home & camp.

BENCONE UNIFORM CONNECTION

1855 Runnymede Rd
Winston Salem, NC 27104-3109
Toll Free: (800) 326-3261, FAX: (866) 311-8254, E-Mail: bencone1@bellsouth.net, Web Site: www.bencone.com
Conducts Business: U.S.
Employees: 15
Primary Market Served: Business & Consumer
Catalog available online
Direct online sales

Sell professional uniforms & accessories to nurses, doctors, dentists, hospitals, restaurants & hotels. Also sell white professional shoes, hosiery, maternity uniforms, watches & novelty tops.

BENETTON USA

601 Fifth Ave
New York, NY 10017-1024
Telephone: (212) 593-0290, Toll Free: (800) 274-7192, FAX: (212) 371-1438, E-Mail: mtaylor@bennettonusa.com, Web Site: www.benetton.com
CEO: Carlo Tunioli
Conducts Business: Worldwide
Employees: 3,700
Primary Market Served: Business
Advertising/Marketing Budget Related to Direct Marketing: 0-25%
Gross sales or billing: $2,000,000,000

Marketer of men's, women's & children's clothing, including Nautica and Prince clothing.

BERGDORF GOODMAN

625 Madison Ave (fl 14)
New York, NY 10022
Telephone: (646) 735-5200, Toll Free: (800) 967-3788, (800) 218-4918, FAX: (212) 872-8677, E-Mail: clientservices@bergdorfgoodman.com, Web Site: www.bergdorfgoodman.com
Pres: Joshua Shulman
Conducts Business: U.S.
Primary Market Served: Consumer
Founded: 1901

Retail ladies' & men's apparel & decorative housewares.

THE BLACK DOG TAVERN CO INC

PO Box 2219, 20 Beach St Extension
Vineyard Haven, MA 02568
Toll Free: (800) 626-1991, E-Mail: contactus@theblackdog.com, Web Site: www.theblackdog.com; www.theblackdogtshirt.com
CEO: Robert S. Douglas
Dir Retail Opers: Jaime Douglas
Primary Market Served: Consumer
Founded: 1971

Restaurant-bakery, general store, & catalog on Martha's Vineyard for 25 years. Catalog features casual clothing & outerwear with Black Dog logo. Packaged foods prepared by the bakery: cookies, scotties, bread & jellies.

BLAIR CORP

220 Hickory St
Warren, PA 16366-0001
Telephone: (814) 723-3600, Toll Free: (800) 458-6057, FAX: (814) 726-6123, E-Mail: blair@blair.com, Web Site: www.blair.com
Pres & CEO: Jim Metscher
Conducts Business: U.S.
Employees: 900
Primary Market Served: Consumer
Direct Marketing ad budget:
Direct Mail: $67,300,000
Founded: 1910
Gross sales or billing: $433,000,000

Sell low to medium-priced men's and women's apparel and home furnishings, primarily by mail.

BLUBLOCKER CORP

3350 Palm Ctr Dr
Las Vegas, NV 89103-5668
Telephone: (702) 597-2000, Toll Free: (800) BLUBLOCKER, FAX: (702) 597-2002, Web Site: www.blublocker.com
Treas: Joseph Sugarman

VERA BRADLEY
12420 Stonebridge Rd
Roanoke, IN 46783
Toll Free: (800) 823-8372, Web Site:
    www.verabradley.com
Pres & CEO: Robert Wallstrom
Chief Mktg Officer: Theresa Palerno
Primary Market Served: Business &
    Consumer

BROOKS BROTHERS
346 Madison Ave (fl 10)
New York, NY 10017-3788
Telephone: (212) 682-8800, Toll Free:
    (800) 274-1815, FAX: (212) 309-
    7273, Web Site: www.
    brooksbrothers.com
Pres: Claudio Del Vecchio
Sr VP: Debra Del Vecchio
Dir, Adv & Pub Rels: Arthur Wayne
Dir CRM: Jan Cantler
Conducts Business: United States, Ja-
    pan, China, Italy, United Kingdom
Employees: 3,500
Primary Market Served: Consumer
Catalog available online
Direct online sales
Founded: 1818
Gross sales or billing: $260,000,000

Men's, women's & boys' retail & mail
order clothing.

BRYLANE
Subs. of Pinault Printemps Redoute
Div. of Redcats
PO Box 8320
Taunton, MA 02780
Toll Free: (800) 544-3793, Web Site:
    www.brylanehome.com
Conducts Business: U.S.
Employees: 8,000
Primary Market Served: Consumer
Catalog available online
Advertising/Marketing Budget Related
    to Direct Marketing: 0-25%
Direct Marketing ad budget:
Direct Mail: 100%
Founded: 1924
Gross sales or billing: $2,000,000,000

Publish Lane Bryant, Roaman's, Lerner, Chadwicks, Jessica London, King
Size, BrylaneHome

BURBERRY
444 Madison Ave
New York, NY 10022-6903
Telephone: (877) 217-4085, E-Mail:
    us.customerservice@burberry.com,
    Web Site: www.burberry.com
Chmn: Sir John Peace
CEO & CCO: Christopher Bailey
Primary Market Served: Business &
    Consumer

CABLE CAR CLOTHIERS/ ROBERT KIRK LTD
110 Sutter St (Suite 108)
San Francisco, CA 94104
Telephone: (415) 397-4740, FAX:
    (415) 616-8998, E-Mail: info@
    cablecarclothiers.com, Web Site:
    www.cablecarclothiers.com
Pres: Jonathan Levin
Conducts Business: Worldwide
Employees: 7
Primary Market Served: Consumer
Catalog available online
Direct online sales
Advertising/Marketing Budget Related
    to Direct Marketing: 76-100%
Direct Marketing ad budget:
Direct Mail: 80%
Magazines: 15%
Newspapers: 5%
Founded: 1939

Mail order & retail clothing store specializing in traditional clothing for
men.

CARABELLA COLLECTION
Div. of Carabella Corp
17662 Armstrong Ave
Irvine, CA 92614
Telephone: (949) 263-2300, Toll Free:
    (800) 227-2235, FAX: (949) 263-
    2323, Web Site: www.carabella.com
Pres: Houshang Jalili
VP: Monir Jalili
Conducts Business: U.S.
Employees: 150
Primary Market Served: Consumer
Catalog available online
Direct online sales
Advertising/Marketing Budget Related
    to Direct Marketing: 76-100%
Direct Marketing ad budget: $500,000
Magazines: $100,000
Online: $400,000
Founded: 1983
Gross sales or billing: $20,000,000

Women's swim, sports & evening wear
& accessories.

CASUAL MALE RETAIL GROUP
555 Turnpike St
Canton, MA 02021-2724
Telephone: (781) 828-9300, Toll Free:
    (800) 767-0319, E-Mail: info@
    casualmale.com, Web Site: www.
    casualmale.com
CEO & Pres: David A Levin
Sr VP: Sahal Laher
Conducts Business: U.S.
Employees: 4,000
Primary Market Served: Business &
    Consumer
Catalog available online
Direct online sales

Advertising/Marketing Budget Related
    to Direct Marketing: 0-25%
Gross sales or billing: $700,000,000
Men's apparel. Retail clothing.

CATTLE KATE
6701 W State St
Boise, ID 83714-7412
Telephone: (208) 377-5283, Toll Free:
    (800) 332-5283, FAX: (208) 375-
    3827, E-Mail: cattlekate@rmisp.
    com, Web Site: www.cattlekate.com
Owner & Pres: Michelle Oster
Conducts Business: U.S., Canada, Ja-
    pan, Germany, France, Switzerland
Employees: 10
Primary Market Served: Business &
    Consumer
Catalog available online
Indirect online sales
Advertising/Marketing Budget Related
    to Direct Marketing: 76-100%
Direct Marketing ad budget:
Direct Mail: 50%
Magazines: 50%
Founded: 1981

Manufacture and design Old West style
clothing for men & women. High quality specialty line.

CHADWICK'S OF BOSTON INC
Owned by Redcats USA; part of PPR
500 Bic Dr (Bldg 4)
Milford, CT 06461
Toll Free: (877) 330-3393, E-Mail:
    service@cs.chadwicks.com, Web
    Site: www.chadwicks.com
CEO: Aldus Chapin
Conducts Business: U.S.
Employees: 805
Primary Market Served: Consumer
Founded: 1983
Gross sales or billing: $139,200,000

Consumer catalog offering women's
name brand off-price fashions & casual
apparel.

CHARMING SHOPPES INC.
3750 State Rd
Bensalem, PA 19020-5903
Telephone: (215) 245-9100, Web Site:
    www.charmingshoppers.com
Pres: Bill Bass
CEO & Pres: David Jaffe
Primary Market Served: Consumer

CHICO'S FAS INC
11215 Metro Pkwy
Fort Myers, FL 33966-1206
Telephone: (239) 277-6200, Web Site:
    www.chicos.com
VP, CRM: Charlie White
CFO & EVP: Todd Vogenson

Primary Market Served: Business & Consumer

COACH
516 W 34th St
New York, NY 10001-1394
Telephone: (212) 594-1850, Toll Free: (800) 444-3611, FAX: (212) 594-1682, Web Site: www.coach.com
Pres & CEO: Victor Louis
Conducts Business: Worldwide
Employees: 7,500
Primary Market Served: Consumer
Catalog available online
Direct online sales
Advertising/Marketing Budget Related to Direct Marketing: 51-75%

Marketer of quality leather goods & accessories.

COLDWATER CREEK
5389 E Provident Dr
Cincinnati, OH 45246
Toll Free: (800) 787-9196, FAX: (800) 262-0080, Web Site: www.coldwatercreek.com
Pres & CEO: Jill Brown Dean
Conducts Business: U.S.
Primary Market Served: Business & Consumer

Sells nature related items.

COLUMBIA SPORTSWEAR
14375 NW Science Park Dr
Portland, OR 97229
Telephone: (503) 985-4203, Toll Free: (800) 622-6953, Web Site: www.columbia.com
Chmn Bd: Gert Boyle
Pres & CEO: Tim Boyle
Exec VP & COO: Bryan L. Timm
Sr VP & CFO: Thomas B. Cusick
VP Global Mktg: Daniel G. Hanson

CROSSTOWN TRADERS INC
3740 E 34th St
Tucson, AZ 85710
Telephone: (520) 745-4500
Pres: Steve Lightman
Primary Market Served: Consumer

Swaps clothing & footwear across the country through catalogs & e-commerce sites

DESTINATION MATERNITY CORP
456 N Fifth St
Philadelphia, PA 19123-4007
Telephone: (215) 873-2200, Web Site: www.motherswork.com
Pres: Rebecca Mathias

DHARMA TRADING CO
1805 S McDowell Blvd Ext (Suite D)
Petaluma, CA 94954-6945
Telephone: (415) 456-1211, Toll Free: (800) 542-5227, FAX: (415) 456-8747, E-Mail: service@dharmatrading.com, Web Site: www.dharmatrading.com
Owner & Pres: Isaac Goff
Gen Mgr: Sharon Lang
Conducts Business: Worldwide
Employees: 50
Primary Market Served: Business & Consumer
Catalog available online
Direct online sales
Direct Marketing ad budget:
Magazines: 5%
Online: 95%
Founded: 1969

Catalog marketer of natural cotton & silk clothing & fabric, dyes, paints & related supplies.

DIAMOND ESSENCE
1115 Innman Ave (Suite 333)
Edison, NJ 08820
Toll Free: (800) 909-2525, E-Mail: info@diamondessence.com, Web Site: www.diamond-essence.com
Pres: Ranjit Singh
VP: Shri Singh
Conducts Business: U.S.
Primary Market Served: Consumer
Advertising/Marketing Budget Related to Direct Marketing: 76-100%
Direct Marketing ad budget:
Direct Mail: 100%
Founded: 1978

A leading designer and marketer of the high-quality 14 karat solid gold cubic zirconia and other simulated gem jewelry. Sold through catalog (70%), retail stores (10%) & department & jewelry stores (10%).

DRS FOSTER & SMITH INC
2253 Airpark Rd, PO Box 100
Rhinelander, WI 54501-0100
Telephone: (715) 369-3305, Web Site: www.drsfostersmith.com
Mktg: Ann Mapes
Pres: Spencer Insolia
Primary Market Served: Consumer

Pet supplies & pet medications

DONNA SALYERS' FABULOUS-BRIDAL INC
25 W Robbins St
Covington, KY 41011-3005
Telephone: (859) 291-3300, Toll Free: (800) 848-4650, E-Mail: abell@fabulousfurs.com, Web Site: fabulousfurs.com

CEO: Guy van Rooyen
Pres: Ms. Donna Salyers
Dir Opers: Diane Combs
Mktg Dir: John D. Engel
Sr Mktg Mgr: Allison Bell
Conducts Business: U.S., Canada
Employees: 16
Primary Market Served: Consumer
Catalog available online
Direct online sales
Advertising/Marketing Budget Related to Direct Marketing: 76-100%
Founded: 1989
Gross sales or billing: $5,800,000

High quality faux fur fashion.

DR JAYS
7720 Kenamar Ct (Suite C)
San Diego, CA 92121-2425
Telephone: (212) 334-7999, Web Site: drjays.com
Pres: Elliot Betesh
Primary Market Served: Consumer

Sells apparel & accessories

DRAPER'S & DAMON'S
PO Box 57088, Irvine, CA 92619-7088
Subs. of Orchard Brands
9 Pasteur (Suite 200)
Irvine, CA 92618-3804
Telephone: (949) 784-3000, Toll Free: (800) 843-1174, FAX: (949) 784-3400, E-Mail: jilld@drapers.com, Web Site: www.drapers.com
Co-Pres: Brent Bostwick
CEO: Brad Farmer
Conducts Business: U.S.
Employees: 200
Primary Market Served: Consumer
Catalog available online
Direct online sales
Advertising/Marketing Budget Related to Direct Marketing: 0-25%
Direct Marketing ad budget:
Direct Mail: 90%
Magazines: 2%
Newspapers: 8%
Founded: 1927

Ready-to-wear clothing for women.

EASTBAY RUNNING STORE INC
Div. of Woolworth's Corp
111 S First Ave
Wausau, WI 54401
Telephone: (715) 845-5538, Toll Free: (800) 826-2205, FAX: (715) 261-9500, Web Site: www.eastbay.com
Pres & CEO: Tilema Dowe
Conducts Business: U.S.
Primary Market Served: Business & Consumer

Catalog & retail sales for athletic footwear & sportswear.

EBBETS FIELD FLANNELS INC

dba Stall & Dean
562 First Ave S (Suite 200)
Seattle, WA 98104
Telephone: (206) 382-7249, FAX: (206) 382-4411, E-Mail: clubhouse@ebbets.com, Web Site: www.ebbets.com
Pres & CEO: Jerry P. Cohen
VP: Lisa Cooper
Primary Market Served: Business & Consumer
Founded: 1987

Vintage athletic apparel sold through mail order catalogs & retail store.

ELITE SPORTSWEAR LP

2136 N 13th St (Suite A)
Reading, PA 19604-1213
Telephone: (610) 921-1469, Toll Free: (800) 345-4087, FAX: (610) 921-0208, E-Mail: gkelite@gkelite.com, Web Site: www.gk-elitesportswear.com
CEO: Dan Casciano
Chief Mktg Officer: Mark Cowan
Conducts Business: Worldwide
Primary Market Served: Business & Consumer
Catalog available online
Direct online sales
Founded: 1981

Sells men's & women's gymnastics apparel (workout wear & competitive wear) direct to individuals, gyms, dance schools, YMCAs, public schools, colleges, universities & specialty stores.

ELKHART CASES

dba Sprunger Engineering, Sprunger Parts Company Inc
3605 Cooper Dr
Elkhart, IN 46514
Telephone: (574) 295-7700, Toll Free: (800) 582-0319, FAX: (574) 295-7761, E-Mail: elkcases@aol.com
Pres: Dale D. Fahlbeck
Conducts Business: U.S.
Employees: 30
Primary Market Served: Business & Consumer
Advertising/Marketing Budget Related to Direct Marketing: 26-50%
Direct Marketing ad budget: $260,000
Direct Mail: 60%
Magazines: 20%
Newspapers: 5%
Telephone: 15%
Founded: 1964
Gross sales or billing: $2,000,000

Manufactures briefcases, attache cases, catalog cases, all types of custom carrying cases & musical instrument cases.

EXPRESS LLC

1 Express Dr
Columbus, OH 43230
Telephone: (614) 474-7000, Web Site: www.expressfashion.com
Pres & CEO: David Kornberg

EYEGLASS SERVICE INDUSTRIES

dba Vision World
481 Sunrise Hwy
Lynbrook, NY 11563
Telephone: (516) 599-1135, FAX: (516) 599-4825
Pres & CEO: Bruce Topol
VP: Leonard Baritz
Conducts Business: U.S.
Employees: 75
Primary Market Served: Consumer
Advertising/Marketing Budget Related to Direct Marketing: 76-100%
Direct Marketing ad budget:
Direct Mail: 80%
Newspapers: 20%
Founded: 1958
Gross sales or billing: $4,900,000

Sells Ray-Ban sunglasses at low prices.

FAIR INDIGO

579 Donofrio Dr (Suite 104)
Madison, WI 53719-2838
Telephone: (608) 824-8974, Toll Free: (800) 520-1806, E-Mail: service@fairindigo.com, Web Site: www.fairindigo.com
Pres & CEO: Bill Bass
Pres: Rob Behnke

FORMAL APPROACH

281 W Old Andrew Johnson Hwy
Jefferson City, TN 37760-1805
Telephone: (865) 475-8641, Web Site: www.formalapproach.com
Owner: Mike Denton
Primary Market Served: Consumer

FOSSIL

901 S Central Expy
Richardson, TX 75080
Telephone: (469) 587-2628, Web Site: www.fossil.com
CEO & Chmn Bd: Kosta N. Kartsotis
Primary Market Served: Consumer

FREDERICK'S OF HOLLYWOOD GROUP INC

6255 Sunset Blvd (fl 6)
Los Angeles, CA 90028-7403
Telephone: (323) 466-5151, Toll Free: (855) 655-2514, FAX: (323) 464-5149, E-Mail: support@fredericks.com, Web Site: www.fredericks.com
CEO: Linda LoRe
Sr VP, Mktg: Yolanda Dunbar

Sr VP: Denise Marsicano
Sr VP: John Schulman
VP Direct Mktg: Tracy Rhyan
PR Mgr: Jennifer Lowitz
Conducts Business: U.S., Canada
Employees: 1,000
Primary Market Served: Consumer
Catalog available online
Direct online sales
Direct Marketing ad budget: $8,800,000
Direct Mail: $7,000,000
Magazines: $1,000,000
Newspapers: $800,000
Founded: 1946
Gross sales or billing: $57,000,000

Mail order company specializing in ladies' & men's apparel & accessories. Sells direct to the public through catalogs & approximately 206 retail stores.

PAUL FREDRICK MENSTYLE

223 W Poplar St
Fleetwood, PA 19522
Telephone: (610) 944-0909, Toll Free: (800) 247-1417, FAX: (610) 944-6452, E-Mail: custserv@menstyle.com, Web Site: www.paulfredricks.com
Pres: Paul Sacher
VP: Ross Alaimo
Treas: Leonard Abrams
Conducts Business: U.S., Japan
Employees: 85
Primary Market Served: Business & Consumer
Catalog available online
Direct online sales
Gross sales or billing: $32,000,000

Design & manufacture men's shirts, sell through catalog & retail sales. Catalog co. for men's clothing.

FRENCH CREEK SHEEP & WOOL CO INC

600 Pine Swamp Rd
Elverson, PA 19520
Telephone: (610) 286-5700, Toll Free: (800) 977-4337, FAX: (610) 286-0324, E-Mail: info@frenchcreeksw.com, Web Site: www.frenchcreeksw.com
Pres: Jean Flaxenburg
Co Owner: Eric Flaxenburg
Conducts Business: Worldwide
Employees: 50
Primary Market Served: Consumer
Catalog available online
Direct online sales

Mail order catalog company specializing in the manufacture & retailing of sheepskin coats, leather & suede fashions & sweaters.

ALAN FURMAN & CO

RP-NFOA
12250 Rockville Pike (Suite 270)
Rockville, MD 20852
Telephone: (202) 397-8463, Toll Free:
(800) 654-7184, FAX: (301) 881-
0810, E-Mail: watches@alanfurman.
com, Web Site: www.alanfurman.
com
Pres & CEO: Alan Furman
Conducts Business: U.S.
Employees: 8
Primary Market Served: Consumer
Catalog available online
Indirect online sales
Advertising/Marketing Budget Related
to Direct Marketing: 76-100%
Founded: 1985
Gross sales or billing: $9,000,000

Direct marketing of jewelry & watches.
85% mail order.

GTM SPORTSWEAR

PO Box 8
Manhattan, KS 66505-0008
Toll Free: (877) 569-3095, Web Site:
www.gtmsportswear.com
VP Mktg: Nikki Miller

GARNET HILL INC

231 Main St
Franconia, NH 03580
Telephone: (603) 823-5545, Toll Free:
(800) 870-3513, FAX: (888) 842-
9696, Web Site: www.garnethill.com
Pres: Claire Spofford
Conducts Business: U.S.
Employees: 85
Primary Market Served: Consumer
Advertising/Marketing Budget Related
to Direct Marketing: 76-100%

All natural fiber apparel, beddings &
furnishings.

GENESCO INC

1415 Murfreesboro Rd (Suite 190)
Nashville, TN 37217-2895
Telephone: (615) 367-7000, Toll Free:
(888) 324-6189, FAX: (615) 367-
8278, Web Site: www.genesco.com
CEO Pres & Chmn Bd: Robert J. Den-
nis
Sr VP, Fin & CFO: James S. Gulmi
Employees: 12,450
Primary Market Served: Business &
Consumer
Catalog available online
Direct online sales
Gross sales or billing: $1,400,000,000

Retail & wholesale men's footwear.
High-end or up-scale.

WL GORE & ASSOCIATES INC

555 Paper Mill Rd
Newark, DE 19711
Telephone: (410) 506-7787, Toll Free:
(888) 914-4673, E-Mail: info@
wlgore.com, Web Site: www.wlgore.
com
Pres & CEO: Torri Kelly
Conducts Business: U.S.
Primary Market Served: Business &
Consumer

Manufacture fabrics for catalog & retail
sales.

GORSUCH LTD

263 E Gore Creek Dr
Vail, CO 81657
Telephone: (970) 476-2294, Toll Free:
(800) 525-9808, FAX: (970) 476-
4323, Web Site: www.gorsuchltd.
com
Pres: David Gorsuch
Owner: Renie Gorsuch
Catalog Consultant: Jane Imber
Conducts Business: U.S.
Employees: 100
Primary Market Served: Consumer
Catalog available online
Direct online sales
Advertising/Marketing Budget Related
to Direct Marketing: 51-75%
Direct Marketing ad budget:
Direct Mail: $2,500,000
Founded: 1966
Gross sales or billing: $20,000,000

Retail and catalog marketer. Offer
products from designer casual wear to
furnishings & gifts. Specialize in ski
wear. Eight locations.

GOULD & GOODRICH

709 E McNeil St
Lillington, NC 27546
Telephone: (910) 893-2071, Toll Free:
(800) 277-0732, FAX: (910) 893-
4742, E-Mail: service@gouldusa.
com, Web Site: www.gouldusa.com
Pres: Scott G. Nelson
Conducts Business: Worldwide
Primary Market Served: Business
Catalog available online
Indirect online sales

Holsters, belts & accessories of leather
& nylon. Full line for law enforcement
& sporting.

THE GYMBOREE CORP

500 Howard St
San Francisco, CA 94105-3000
Telephone: (877) 449-6932, Web Site:
www.gymboree.com
Dir Mktg: Marc Laven

HABAND CO INC

110 Bauer Dr, Oakland, NJ 07436-
3105-POST
110 Bauer Dr
Oakland, NJ 07436-3105
Telephone: (201) 651-1000, FAX:
(201) 405-7777, Web Site: www.
haband.blair.com
Dir Mktg: Steve Schlumpf
Conducts Business: U.S.
Employees: 349
Primary Market Served: Consumer
Catalog available online
Direct online sales
Founded: 1925
Gross sales or billing: $59,100,000

Retail mail order catalog for men's &
women's clothing.

HANESBRANDS INC

1000 E Hanes Mill Rd
Winston Salem, NC 27105-1384
Telephone: (336) 519-8080, Web Site:
www.hanesbrands.com
CEO & Chmn Bd: Richard Noll
Primary Market Served: Consumer

HERMES OF PARIS

55 E 59th St (#3)
New York, NY 10022
Telephone: (212) 759-7585, Toll Free:
(800) 441-4488, FAX: (212) 644-
2132
Exec Chmn Bd: Axel Dumas
Conducts Business: U.S.
Employees: 140
Primary Market Served: Business
Catalog available online
Direct online sales

Manufacturer & retailer of leather
goods, perfume, ready-to-wear & porcelain.

TOMMY HILFIGER

601 W 26th St (#500)
New York, NY 10001-1142
Telephone: (212) 548-1368, Web Site:
www.tommy.com
CEO: Daniel Grieder

HITCHCOCK SHOES INC

225 Beal St
Hingham, MA 02043-1543
Telephone: (781) 749-3571, Toll Free:
(888) 599-9433, FAX: (781) 749-
3576, E-Mail: hitchcock@wideshoes.
com, Web Site: www.wideshoes.com
Pres & CEO: Thomas R. Bright
Gen Mgr: Shirley A. Mortland
Conducts Business: U.S.
Employees: 20
Primary Market Served: Consumer
Catalog available online
Direct online sales

Founded: 1951
Gross sales or billing: $7,000,000
Catalog marketer of men's shoes in widths EEE to EEEEEE only.

HOOVER'S MFG CO
4133 Progress Blvd, PO Box 547
Peru, IL 61354-1125
Telephone: (815) 223-1159, FAX: (815) 333-1499, Web Site: www. hmchonors.com
Pres & CFO: David R. Hoover
Conducts Business: U.S., Europe, Asia
Employees: 18
Primary Market Served: Business & Consumer
Catalog available online
Direct online sales
Advertising/Marketing Budget Related to Direct Marketing: 0-25%
Founded: 1963
Gross sales or billing: $2,000,000

Advertising specialties such as hats, military & political pins & belt buckles.

HOT TOPIC INC
18305 E San Jose Ave
City of Industry, CA 91748
Telephone: (626) 839-4681, Toll Free: (800) 275-9169, FAX: (626) 839-4686, Web Site: www.hottopic.com
CEO & Chmn Bd: Lisa M. Harper
Employees: 9,794
Primary Market Served: Consumer
Catalog available online
Direct online sales
Founded: 1989
Gross sales or billing: $751,000,000

Specialty retail company selling apparel & accessories through mall-based stores.

HOUSE OF EYES
2222 A Patterson St (Ste A)
Greensboro, NC 27407-2539
Telephone: (336) 852-7107, FAX: (336) 854-0311
Pres: Clay Hoff
VP: Jeff Hoff
Sec & Treas: Tammy Hoff
Mktg Mgr: Ricky Sheldon
Conducts Business: U.S.
Employees: 10
Primary Market Served: Business & Consumer
Advertising/Marketing Budget Related to Direct Marketing: 0-25%
Direct Marketing ad budget: $20,000
Newspapers: 30%
TV/Radio: 30%
Telephone: 40%
Founded: 1980

Gross sales or billing: $1,000,000
Repair shop for sunglasses, frames & accessories.

HOUSE OF ORANGE
PO Box 444
Brentwood Bay, BC, Canada V8M 1R3
Toll Free: (866) 401-9174, FAX: (250) 652-8673, E-Mail: houseoforange@ shaw.ca, Web Site: www. houseoforangeltd.com
Mgr: Ed Johnson
Conducts Business: U.S., Canada
Employees: 3
Primary Market Served: Business & Consumer
Advertising/Marketing Budget Related to Direct Marketing: 0-25%
Direct Marketing ad budget: $20,000
Magazines: 50%
Telephone: 50%
Founded: 1968
Gross sales or billing: $500,000

Beads & findings for costume jewelry manufacturers & bead stores. Also wholesales hobby supplies.

HYMAN'S
5809 N Rhett Ave
Hanahan, SC 29410-2510
Telephone: (843) 571-7870, Toll Free: (800) 354-9626, FAX: (843) 571-7575, E-Mail: support@hymans.com, Web Site: www.hymans.com
Owner, Pres & CEO: David Odle
VP: Mier Hyme
Conducts Business: U.S., Canada
Primary Market Served: Business & Consumer
Catalog available online
Direct online sales
Advertising/Marketing Budget Related to Direct Marketing: 0-25%
Direct Marketing ad budget:
Direct Mail: 50%
Magazines: 25%
Telephone: 25%
Founded: 1890

Uniforms & corporate apparel.

ICIS INC
1908 Ringing Rock Rd
Upper Black Eddy, PA 18912
Telephone: (610) 982-0429, E-Mail: icis@ptdprolog.net, Web Site: www. icisjewelry.com
Pres: Lisa Schwartz
Primary Market Served: Business & Consumer
Catalog available online
Indirect online sales

Manufactures fashion accessories. Market through wholesale & catalogs.

INDUSTRIAL UNIFORM CO INC
902 E Indianapolis St
Wichita, KS 67211-2407
Telephone: (316) 264-2871, Toll Free: (800) 333-3666, FAX: (316) 264-2708, E-Mail: info@logodepotweb. com, Web Site: www. industrialuniform.com
Pres: Tony Taravella
Pur Dir: Elaine Stull
Conducts Business: U.S.
Employees: 21
Primary Market Served: Business & Consumer
Advertising/Marketing Budget Related to Direct Marketing: 76-100%
Direct Marketing ad budget: $45,000
Founded: 1938
Gross sales or billing: $2,500,000

Working apparel to industrial customers & franchisers. Corporate embroidered apparel & accessories.

INSTRUCTOR'S CHOICE DANCEWEAR
5020 Sunrise Hwy
Massapequa Park, NY 11762-2913
Telephone: (516) 799-6000, FAX: (516) 799-7993, E-Mail: customerservice@instructorschoice. com, Web Site: www. instructorschoice.net
Owner: Felicia Marino
Conducts Business: Worldwide
Employees: 1
Primary Market Served: Business & Consumer
Catalog available online
Direct online sales
Advertising/Marketing Budget Related to Direct Marketing: 76-100%
Direct Marketing ad budget: $20,000
Direct Mail: 80%
Magazines: 20%
Founded: 1980
Gross sales or billing: $200,000

Ladies' & girls' dancewear & shoes.

JOS A BANK CLOTHIERS INC
500 Hanover Pike
Hampstead, MD 21074-2002
Telephone: (410) 239-2700, Web Site: www.josbank.com
CEO: R. Neal Black

JAZZERCISE INC
2460 Impala Dr, Carlsbad, CA 92008-7226
2460 Impala Dr
Carlsbad, CA 92008

Telephone: (760) 476-1750, FAX: (760) 602-7180, E-Mail: customercare@jazzercise.com, Web Site: www.jazzercise.com
CEO: Judi Shepphard Missett
COO & CFO: Sally Baldridge
Exec VP: Shanna Missett Nelson
VP, Mktg: Kathy Missett
VP, Tech: Brad Jones
Conducts Business: Worldwide
Employees: 80
Primary Market Served: Consumer
Catalog available online
Direct online sales
Advertising/Marketing Budget Related to Direct Marketing: 0-25%
Direct Marketing ad budget:
Direct Mail: 80%
Magazines: 5%
Newspapers: 5%
TV/Radio: 5%
Telephone: 5%
Founded: 1982
Gross sales or billing: $5,000,000

Fitness related products. Fitness wear & accessories, fitness videos, exercise mats, weights, etc.

J JILL GROUP, INC
Subs. of Talbots
4 Batterymarch Park
Quincy, MA 02169
Telephone: (617) 376-4300, Toll Free: (800) 642-9989, FAX: (617) 769-0177, Web Site: www.jjillgroup.com
CEO: Paula Bennett
CFO: David Biese
Conducts Business: U.S.
Employees: 3,041
Primary Market Served: Consumer
Catalog available online
Direct online sales
Gross sales or billing: $532,000,000

Publisher of the "J. Jill Catalog," a catalog featuring apparel in the 4-20 size range.

JOCKEY INTERNATIONAL GLOBAL INC
2300 60th St
Kenosha, WI 53140-3822
Telephone: (262) 658-8111
VP, E-Commerce & Catalog: Christopher Smith
Primary Market Served: Business & Consumer

JOHNNY APPLESEED'S INC
35 Village Rd (Suite 500)
Middleton, MA 01949-1236
Telephone: (978) 922-2040, Toll Free: (800) 546-4554, FAX: (978) 922-7001, Web Site: www.appleseeds.blair.com
Pres & CEO: Steve Nave

Exec VP & CMO: Chidam Chidambaram
Conducts Business: U.S.
Employees: 450
Primary Market Served: Consumer
Catalog available online
Direct online sales
Direct Marketing ad budget:
Direct Mail: 100%
Founded: 1946
Gross sales or billing: $50,000,000

Women's ready-to-wear & gifts. Catalog sales to consumers.

JOURNEYS
Div. of Genesco Inc
1415 Murfreesboro Pike Ste 181, Genesco Park
Nashville, TN 37217-2829
Telephone: (615) 367-7000, Toll Free: (888) 324-6356, FAX: (615) 367-8123, Web Site: www.journeys.com
Pres, Journeys: Jim Estepa
Conducts Business: U.S., Puerto Rico, US Virgin Islands
Employees: 360
Primary Market Served: Consumer
Catalog available online
Direct online sales
Advertising/Marketing Budget Related to Direct Marketing: 0-25%
Direct Marketing ad budget:
Direct Mail: 33%
Magazines: 33%
Online: 34%
Founded: 1925
Gross sales or billing: $593,516

Marketer of cutting edge footwear products & accessories for young men & women, ages 12-24, and shoes for women early 20's to mid-30 years old. Retailer & wholesaler of shoes.

KAPPLER PROTECTIVE APPAREL & FABRICS
55 Grimes Dr, PO Box 490
Guntersville, AL 35976
Telephone: (256) 505-4005, Toll Free: (800) 600-4019, FAX: (256) 505-4151, E-Mail: customerservice@kappler.com, Web Site: www.kappler.com
Pres: George Kappler
Sr VP, Sls & Mktg: Craig Woodward
Sr VP & Dir: Jerry Jones
VP & CFO: Chuck Strader
VP: Mike Willis
Conducts Business: U.S., Canada
Employees: 1,400
Primary Market Served: Business & Consumer
Catalog available online
Indirect online sales
Advertising/Marketing Budget Related to Direct Marketing: 0-25%

Direct Marketing ad budget: $200,000
Direct Mail: 40%
Magazines: 50%
Telephone: 10%
Founded: 1976
Gross sales or billing: $85,000,000

Manufacturer of protective clothing, selling everything from coveralls to fully encapsulated suits through distributors.

KAYSER-ROTH CORP INC
Div. of Kayser Roth Corp
102 Corporate Center Blvd
Greensboro, NC 27408
Toll Free: (800) 575-3497, Web Site: www.nononsense.com
Exec VP & Gen Mgr: Julia Townsend
Conducts Business: U.S.
Employees: 85
Primary Market Served: Consumer
Advertising/Marketing Budget Related to Direct Marketing: 76-100%
Direct Marketing ad budget:
Direct Mail: 100%
Founded: 1985
Gross sales or billing: $10,000,000

Manufacture & market men's & women's hosiery & leg wear.

KELLY'S KIDS
391 Liberty Rd
Natchez, MS 39120
Telephone: (601) 442-5332, Toll Free: (800) 837-2066, FAX: (601) 442-4399, E-Mail: hello@kellyskids.com, Web Site: www.kellyskids.com
Dir & Pres: Lynn James
Treas: Ashton James
Conducts Business: U.S.
Employees: 50
Primary Market Served: Consumer
Catalog available online
Direct online sales
Advertising/Marketing Budget Related to Direct Marketing: 51-75%
Direct Marketing ad budget:
Direct Mail: 80%
Newspapers: 2%
Online: 18%
Founded: 1983

High quality, classic clothing for girls, boys & the entire family.

LEATHER UNLIMITED CORP
7155 Co Rd B, PO Box L
Belgium, WI 53004
Telephone: (920) 994-9464, FAX: (920) 994-4099, E-Mail: leatherunltd@yahoo.com, Web Site: www.leatherunltd.com
Pres: Joseph M. O'Connell
Treas: Patricia C. O'Connell
Conducts Business: U.S.
Employees: 12

Primary Market Served: Business &
  Consumer
Catalog available online
Indirect online sales
Advertising/Marketing Budget Related
  to Direct Marketing: 51-75%
Direct Marketing ad budget:
Direct Mail: 80%
Online: 20%
Founded: 1970
Gross sales or billing: $1,000,000
Manufacturer & distributor of leather
accessories & leathercraft supplies.
Also, steel cutting dies & centrifugally
cast buckles & other small accessories.

LESLIE JORDAN
1930 NW 24th Ave
Portland, OR 97210
Telephone: (503) 295-1987, Toll Free:
  (800) 935-3343, FAX: (503) 295-
  0939, E-Mail: ljsales@lesliejordan.
  com, Web Site: www.lesliejordan.
  com
Pres & Owner: Leslie Jordan
Mktg & Sls: Vicky Hartwig
Mktg & Sls: Dickie Christensen
Mktg & Sls: Craig Lamar
Conducts Business: U.S.
Employees: 50
Primary Market Served: Business
Advertising/Marketing Budget Related
  to Direct Marketing: 26-50%
Manufacture jackets, bags, aprons &
apparel out of Dupont Tyvek.

LESLIE SHOE CO INC
dba sexyshoes.com
480 N Second St
Rogers City, MI 49779-1367
Telephone: (989) 734-4030, Toll Free:
  (800) 716-8617, E-Mail: info@
  sexyshoes.com, Web Site: www.
  sexyshoes.com
CEO: Jeffrey Hopp
COO: Sandra Ruttan
Conducts Business: U.S., Canada
Employees: 10
Primary Market Served: Consumer
Catalog available online
Direct online sales
Advertising/Marketing Budget Related
  to Direct Marketing: 76-100%
Direct Marketing ad budget:
Direct Mail: 100%
Founded: 1984
Gross sales or billing: $1,400,000
Catalog marketer of ladies' tall-heeled
shoes.

LION APPAREL
7200 Poe Ave (# 400)
Dayton, OH 45414-2547

Telephone: (937) 898-1949, Toll Free:
  (800) 548-6614, FAX: (937) 913-
  5667, Web Site: www.lionprotects.
  com
Chmn Bd: Richard Lapedes
CEO: Steve Schwartz
VP, Sls & Mktg Mgr: Steve Allison
Dir Sls: Cliff Gallarneau
Conducts Business: U.S.
Employees: 700
Primary Market Served: Business &
  Consumer
Gross sales or billing: $25,700,000
Uniforms, identity apparel, protective
fire & safety clothing.

LOEHMANN'S
2500 Halsey St
Bronx, NY 10461-3637
Telephone: (718) 409-2000, Web Site:
  www.loehmanns.com
CEO: Steven M. Newman
Primary Market Served: Consumer

LOTIONS & LACE
3960 Garner Rd
Riverside, CA 92501
Telephone: (951) 686-5223, FAX:
  (951) 686-5765, E-Mail: linda@ez-
  access.com, Web Site: www.
  sexyvideos.com
Pres: Ray Hargreaves
VP & Treas: Linda Hargreaves
Conducts Business: U.S., Australia,
  Canada, Europe, Japan, S. America
Employees: 30
Primary Market Served: Business &
  Consumer
Catalog available online
Direct online sales
Advertising/Marketing Budget Related
  to Direct Marketing: 51-75%
Direct Marketing ad budget: $100,000
Direct Mail: 50%
Magazines: 45%
Newspapers: 5%
Founded: 1981
Gross sales or billing: $2,000,000
Ladies & men's exotic lingerie, swim-
wear, costumes, hosiery, day/evening
wear, massage lotions, adult games,
books, videos & novelties.

LUXOTTICA RETAIL
4000 Luxottica Pl
Mason, OH 45040-8114
Telephone: (513) 765-6956, Web Site:
  www.luxottica.com
Exec Pres: Leonardo Del Vecchio
Dir CRM - Database/Analytics: Greg
  Branch

M&M HEALTH CARE APPAREL CO
1541 60th St
Brooklyn, NY 11219-5023
E-Mail: info@fashionease.com
CEO: Abraham M Klein
Conducts Business: U.S.
Employees: 17
Primary Market Served: Business &
  Consumer
Catalog available online
Direct online sales
Advertising/Marketing Budget Related
  to Direct Marketing: 0-25%
Founded: 1973
Specialized clothing & footwear for the
disabled.

MAKING IT BIG
525 Portal St
Cotati, CA 94931-3023
Telephone: (707) 795-1997, Toll Free:
  (877) 644-1995, FAX: (707) 795-
  4874, E-Mail: mib@makingitbig.
  com, Web Site: www.makingitbig.
  com
Pres: Tracy Amiral
Mktg Mgr: Leila Van Meter
Conducts Business: U.S., Canada, Eu-
  rope, Asia, Australia, Russia
Employees: 20
Primary Market Served: Consumer
Direct online sales
Advertising/Marketing Budget Related
  to Direct Marketing: 51-75%
Founded: 1984
Gross sales or billing: $5,000,000
Retail and Mail order clothing for plus
size women sizes 1X - 8X.

THE MARK GROUP
1155 Broken Sound Pkwy NW
Boca Raton, FL 33487
Telephone: (561) 241-1700, Toll Free:
  (800) 637-0152, FAX: (561) 241-
  1055, Web Site: www.bostonproper.
  com
Pres & CEO: Michael W. Tiernan
Conducts Business: U.S.
Primary Market Served: Consumer
Catalog available online
Direct online sales
Founded: 1951
A multi-brand, multi-channel, direct-
to-consumer marketer of apparel and
home accessories, The Mark Group
consists of three dynamic brands: Boston Proper, Charles Keath, and Mark,
Fore & Strike. The company, founded
in 1951, is headquartered in Boca Raton, Fla., and mails more than 60 million catalogs annually. Additionally,
the company operates 18 retail and outlet stores along the eastern seaboard of
the United States in coastal, resort com-

munities and three e-commerce Web sites. The company's annual sales for the year 2000 exceeded $118 million.

MASON COMPANIES INC

1251 First Ave
Chippewa Falls, WI 54729-1408
Telephone: (715) 723-1871, Toll Free: (800) 826-7030, FAX: (715) 720-4247, Web Site: www. masoncompaniesinc.com
Pres & CEO: Dan Hunt
Conducts Business: U.S.
Employees: 550
Primary Market Served: Business & Consumer
Advertising/Marketing Budget Related to Direct Marketing: 51-75%
Direct Marketing ad budget:
Direct Mail: $5,000,000
Magazines: $50,000
Newspapers: $5,000
Founded: 1904

Manufacturer & marketer of men's & women's shoes through independent representatives.

MAUS & HOFFMAN INC

225 SE 6th Ave
Fort Lauderdale, FL 33301
Toll Free: (800) 628-6287, FAX: (954) 463-8735, E-Mail: info@ mausandhoffman.com, Web Site: www.mausandhoffman.com
Catalog Dir: Greg Goodwin
Pres: William H. Maus Jr.

MERCURY INTERNATIONAL TRADING

20 Alice Agnew Dr
North Attleboro, MA 02763-1036
Telephone: (508) 699-9000, FAX: (508) 699-9088, Web Site: www. mercuryfootwear.com
Chmn & Founder: Irwin Wiseman
Pres & CEO: Howard Wisemen
Pres: Gary Gorsuch
Primary Market Served: Business
Founded: 1979
Gross sales or billing: $15,000,000

Athletic & men's casual footwear for the mass market.

METROPOLIS MAGAZINE

Part of Bellerophon Publications, Inc
205 Lexington Ave (fl 17)
New York, NY 10016
Telephone: (212) 627-9977, Toll Free: (800) 334-3046, FAX: (212) 627-9988, E-Mail: edit@metropolismag. com, Web Site: www.metropolismag. com
Publr: Susan S. Szenasy
Adv Mgr: Tamara Stout

Conducts Business: U.S., Canada
Employees: 35
Primary Market Served: Consumer
Advertising/Marketing Budget Related to Direct Marketing: 76-100%
Gross sales or billing: $3,600,000

Examines contemporary life through design architecture, interior design, product design, graphic design, crafts, planning, and preservation.

MILLER STOCKMAN

Div. of Rocky Mountain Clothing Co
8500 Zuni St
Denver, CO 80260-5007
Telephone: (303) 428-5696, FAX: (303) 430-1130
Pres: Les Ball
CFO & VP: Larry Hagen
MO Dir: Joyce Hunter
Primary Market Served: Consumer

Western apparel.

MOBY WRAP INC

PO Box 1066
Chico, CA 95927-1066
Telephone: (530) 898-8201, E-Mail: info@mobywrap.com
CEO: David Beerman

NATIONAL WHOLESALE CO INC

400 National Blvd
Lexington, NC 27292-2631
Telephone: (336) 248-5904, Toll Free: (800) 480-4673, FAX: (336) 248-2880, E-Mail: customerservice@ shopnational.com, Web Site: www. shopnational.com
Pres: Lynda Smith Swann
CFO: Mike Tate
VP, Adv & DM: Betty Allred
Mktg Mgr: Ian Silverdides
Admin Sec: Cathy Reich
Primary Market Served: Consumer
Catalog available online
Direct online sales
Founded: 1952
Gross sales or billing: $32,355,890

Catalog apparel, lingerie & hosiery sales.

NEW YORK & CO

33 W 34th St
New York, NY 10001
Telephone: (212) 884-2169, Toll Free: (800) 961-9906, Web Site: www. nyandcompany.com
Dir CRM: Evan Rubin

NIKE INC

1 SW Bowerman Dr
Beaverton, OR 97005-0979

Telephone: (503) 671-4565, Toll Free: (800) 344-6543, FAX: (503) 671-6300, Web Site: www.nike.com
Co-Founder & Chmn: Phil Knight
CEO: Mark Parker
Consultant: P.J. Santoro
Pres: Charles D. Denson
Pres Global Opers: Gary M. DeStefano
VP & CFO: Donald W. Blair
Employees: 30,000
Primary Market Served: Consumer
Catalog available online
Direct online sales
Gross sales or billing: $16,300,000,000

Manufacturer & retailer of athletic footwear & apparel.

NORDSTROM INC

1617 6th Ave
Seattle, WA 98101
Toll Free: (888) 282-6060, FAX: (206) 373-3198
Co-Pres: Peter Nordstrom
Co-Pres: Eric Nordstrom
Co-Pres: Blake Nordstrom
Primary Market Served: Consumer

Retail children's, men's & women's apparel, accessories & shoes. Also, catalog sales.

NU-PARR SWIMWEAR

929 E Indian School Rd
Phoenix, AZ 85014-4745
Telephone: (602) 279-4044, Toll Free: (800) 230-7277, FAX: (602) 212-2636, E-Mail: info@nu-parr.com, Web Site: www.nu-parr.com
Owner: Kim Dye
Conducts Business: U.S., Canada
Primary Market Served: Business & Consumer
Advertising/Marketing Budget Related to Direct Marketing: 0-25%

European men's bikinis, underbriefs & low-rise shorts; tights, short tights & tank tops. Women's custom bikinis & activewear.

OAKLEY INC

1 Icon
Foothill Ranch, CA 92610-3000
Toll Free: (800) 403-7449, Web Site: www.oakley.com
Direct Mktg Coord: Cale Thompson
Primary Market Served: Business & Consumer

Sunglasses, goggles & apparel

OKUN BROTHERS SHOES INC

179 Portage Rd
Kalamazoo, MI 49007-4801

Telephone: (269) 342-1536, Toll Free: (800) 433-6344, FAX: (269) 383-3401
Owner: Marvin Okun
Conducts Business: U.S., Canada
Primary Market Served: Consumer

Catalog mail order company offering famous brand footwear at discount prices.

ONE HANES PLACE CATALOG

Div. of HanesBrands
450 W Hanes Mill Rd
Winston Salem, NC 27105
Telephone: (336) 519-8080, Toll Free: (800) 300-2600, FAX: (336) 519-0655, Web Site: www.onehanesplace.com
VP & Gen Mgr: John Craig
Customer & Electronic Mktg Dir: Carol Davis
Conducts Business: U.S.
Primary Market Served: Consumer
Catalog available online
Direct online sales
Advertising/Marketing Budget Related to Direct Marketing: 76-100%

Apparel.

ORIENT EXPRESSED IMPORTS INC

3446 Magazine St
New Orleans, LA 70115
Toll Free: (888) 856-3948, FAX: (504) 899-5566, E-Mail: orient@orientexpressed.com, Web Site: www.orientexpressed.com
Owner: Dabney Jacob
Owner: Bee Fitzpatrick
Catalogue Dir: Mary Malone
Employees: 22
Primary Market Served: Consumer
Catalog available online
Direct online sales
Founded: 1978
Gross sales or billing: $4,000,000

Catalogue company specializing in children's clothes and antiques.

PFI WESTERN STORES INC

2816 S Ingram Mill Rd
Springfield, MO 65804
Telephone: (417) 889-2668, Toll Free: (800) 222-4734, FAX: (417) 889-7204, E-Mail: pfi.@pfiwestern.com, Web Site: www.pfiwestern.com
Owner & Mgr: Randy Little
Employees: 250
Primary Market Served: Business & Consumer
Catalog available online
Direct online sales

Advertising/Marketing Budget Related to Direct Marketing: 51-75%
Direct Marketing ad budget:
Direct Mail: 20%
Magazines: 15%
Newspapers: 5%
TV/Radio: 50%
Telephone: 10%
Founded: 1974

Retail seller of western clothes, boots & gifts.

PANGO PANGO SWIMWEAR CORP

1909 E Atlantic Blvd
Pompano Beach, FL 33060-6562
Telephone: (954) 786-0255, Toll Free: (800) 858-9431, FAX: (954) 786-7745, E-Mail: pango_swimwear@bellsouth.net, Web Site: www.pango-pangoswimwear.com
Pres & CEO: Joan Ashby
Mgr: Meere Sahadeo
Conducts Business: U.S.
Employees: 6
Primary Market Served: Business & Consumer
Catalog available online
Direct online sales
Advertising/Marketing Budget Related to Direct Marketing: 26-50%
Direct Marketing ad budget:
Direct Mail: 45%
Magazines: 5%
Newspapers: 5%
Online: 35%
TV/Radio: 5%
Telephone: 5%
Gross sales or billing: $300,000

Sell mix & match swimwear separates in all sizes from XS to XXL.

PATAGONIA

259 W Santa Clara St
Ventura, CA 93001-2545
Telephone: (805) 643-8616, Toll Free: (800) 638-6464, E-Mail: customer_service@patagonia.com, Web Site: www.patagonia.com
Pres: Rose Marcario
Primary Market Served: Consumer

PATAGONIA MAIL ORDER INC

Subs. of Patagonia Inc
8550 White Fir St
Reno, NV 89523-2050
Telephone: (775) 747-1992, Toll Free: (800) 638-6464, FAX: (775) 747-6159, Web Site: www.patagonia.com
CEO: Rose Marcario
CFO: Dave Abeloe
Mktg Dir Patagonia Inc: Bill Kulczycki
Mktg Mgr: Marlee Griswald
Circ Mgr Catalog Div: Jeff Wogoman

Conducts Business: Worldwide
Employees: 50
Primary Market Served: Consumer
Catalog available online
Direct online sales
Advertising/Marketing Budget Related to Direct Marketing: 0-25%
Direct Marketing ad budget:
Magazines: 90%
Newspapers: 10%
Founded: 1982

Mail order retail & wholesale distributor of outdoor clothing.

PAYLESS SHOESOURCE INC

3231 SE 6th Ave
Topeka, KS 66607-2260
Telephone: (785) 233-5171, Toll Free: (877) 474-6379, E-Mail: customerservice@csr.payless.com, Web Site: www.payless.com
Dir CRM: Brent Cooke
CEO: W. Paul Jones
Chief Mktg Officer: Vincent DeSantis

PERUVIAN CONNECTION LTD

24535 McLouth Rd
Tonganoxie, KS 66086-3132
Telephone: (913) 845-2450, Toll Free: (800) 221-8520, E-Mail: sales@peruvianconnection.com, Web Site: www.peruvianconnection.com
CFO: Lori Green
CEO: Annie Hurlbut

Men's & women's luxury alpaca sweaters. Peruvian pima knitwear & jewelry

PHILLIPS-VAN HEUSEN CORP

200 Madison Ave
New York, NY 10016
Telephone: (212) 381-3500, Toll Free: (800) 388-9122, FAX: (212) 381-3950, Web Site: www.pvh.com
Chmn & CEO: Emanuel Chirico
Chief Mktg Officer: Melissa Goldie
Exec VP: Michael Shaffer
VP: Lynn Spindell
Primary Market Served: Business & Consumer
Catalog available online
Indirect online sales

Manufacturers of men's & women's apparel & footwear, mainly shirts.

PILANI'S LIVE IN STYLE

Div. of Overseas Manufacturing Inc
284 Steelmanville Rd
Egg Harbor Township, NJ 08234-7806
Telephone: (609) 927-4686, Toll Free: (800) 537-1832, FAX: (609) 927-5686, E-Mail: sihart@aol.com
Dir: Sanjay Aggarwal

Dir: Bharat Aggarwal
Conducts Business: U.S.
Employees: 6
Primary Market Served: Business &
   Consumer
Advertising/Marketing Budget Related
   to Direct Marketing: 76-100%
Direct Marketing ad budget:
Direct Mail: 75%
Magazines: 25%
Founded: 1985
Gross sales or billing: $700,000

Fashion jewelry & accessories. Sell
mainly to wholesalers.

PLANET COTTON

8001 Cessna Ave
Gaithersburg, MD 20879-4116
Telephone: (301) 948-0400, FAX:
   (301) 948-9031, Web Site: www.
   planetcotton.com
Sr Mng Partner: Phil Garfinkle
Conducts Business: U.S.
Employees: 18
Primary Market Served: Business &
   Consumer
Catalog available online
Indirect online sales
Direct Marketing ad budget: $300,000
Direct Mail: 80%
Magazines: 20%
Gross sales or billing: $10,000,000

Custom printing of T-shirts, sweat
shirts & other accessories.

POLO RALPH LAUREN

625 Madison Ave
New York, NY 10022
Telephone: (212) 813-7868, Toll Free:
   (800) 377-7656, Web Site: www.
   ralphlauren.com
Chmn Bd & CCO: Ralph Lauren
Pres & CEO: Stefan Larsson
Sr Dir, Database Mktg Sys: Eli Cohen
Conducts Business: Worldwide
Employees: 14,000
Primary Market Served: Business &
   Consumer
Catalog available online
Direct online sales
Advertising/Marketing Budget Related
   to Direct Marketing: 0-25%
Direct Marketing ad budget:
Direct Mail: 3%
Magazines: 90%
Newspapers: 5%
TV/Radio: 1%
Telephone: 1%
Founded: 1967
Gross sales or billing: $4,200,000,000

Designer & manufacturer of men's,
women's & children's apparel, footwear, accessories & home furnishings.

QUARTERMASTER UNIFORM & EQUIPMENT CO

PO Box 4147
Cerritos, CA 90703-4147
Toll Free: (866) 673-7645, FAX: (562)
   304-7335, E-Mail: help@
   qmuniforms.com, Web Site: www.
   qmuniforms.com
Pres: James R. DiRosa
Conducts Business: Worldwide
Primary Market Served: Business &
   Consumer
Catalog available online
Direct online sales

Sells military clothing–flight jackets,
wearing apparel, insignias, security
uniforms & equipment. Law enforcement uniforms & equipment.

RANGER JOE'S INTERNATIONAL MILITARY SUPPLY

325 Farr Rd
Columbus, GA 31907
Telephone: (706) 689-0082, Toll Free:
   (800) 247-4541, FAX: (706) 682-
   8840, E-Mail: customerservice@
   rangerjoes.com, Web Site: www.
   rangerjoes.com
Owner & CEO: Janice Voorhees
Owner: Paul Voorhees
Employees: 85
Primary Market Served: Business &
   Consumer
Catalog available online
Advertising/Marketing Budget Related
   to Direct Marketing: 26-50%
Founded: 1963

Military and law enforcement gear.

REDCATS USA

463 Fashion Ave (#1603)
New York, NY 10018-7421
Telephone: (212) 613-9500, Web Site:
   www.brylane.com
VP: Milton Pappas
CEO: Paul Tarvin
Primary Market Served: Consumer

REEBOK INTERNATIONAL LTD

1895 JW Foster Blvd
Canton, MA 02021
Telephone: (781) 401-5000, Toll Free:
   (800) 843-4444, FAX: (781) 401-
   4402, Web Site: www.reebok.com
CEO: Matthew O'Toole
Employees: 400
Primary Market Served: Consumer
Gross sales or billing: $310,800,000

Retail sales manufacturer of athletic
footwear & apparel.

ROCKETWEAR

Div. of the P'nena Group Inc
101 W 57th St (#15 D)
New York, NY 10019
Telephone: (212) 977-9227, E-Mail:
   info@rocketwear.com, Web Site:
   www.rocketwear.net
CEO: P.J. Frishman
Conducts Business: U.S.
Primary Market Served: Business &
   Consumer
Catalog available online
Indirect online sales
Founded: 1994

Mail order business offering sleepwear
and loungewear in conversational
prints.

ROD'S WESTERN PALACE

3099 Silver Dr D
Columbus, OH 43224-3945
Telephone: (614) 268-8200, Toll Free:
   (800) 325-8508, FAX: (800) 330-
   7637, E-Mail: rods@rods.com, Web
   Site: www.rods.com
Pres: Scott Hartle
VP: Charles Hartle
Employees: 100
Primary Market Served: Business &
   Consumer
Founded: 1976
Gross sales or billing: $14,000,000

Western clothing store.

ROMAN RESEARCH INC/ SIMPLY WHISPERS EARRING

800 Franklin St
Hanson, MA 02341
Toll Free: (800) 225-8652, FAX: (781)
   447-0995, E-Mail: earpiercingstore@
   romanresearch.com, Web Site: www.
   simplywhispers.com
Pres: Dale Southworth
Mktg Dir: Bill Russell
Conducts Business: U.S.
Employees: 100
Primary Market Served: Business &
   Consumer
Catalog available online
Direct online sales
Advertising/Marketing Budget Related
   to Direct Marketing: 76-100%
Direct Marketing ad budget: $400,000
Magazines: 100%
Founded: 1970
Gross sales or billing: $5,000,000

Fashion earrings.

SC DIRECT

Div. of Specialty Catalog
400 Manley St Ste 1
West Bridgewater, MA 02379-1085

Toll Free: (800) 343-9695, Web Site:
www.scdirect.com
CFO: Peter Tulp
CEO: Michael Ippolito
VP Adv & E Commerce: Scott Moore
Employees: 359
Primary Market Served: Business &
Consumer
Catalog available online
Direct online sales
Advertising/Marketing Budget Related
to Direct Marketing: 51-75%
Founded: 1978
Gross sales or billing: $60,800,000

Sell women's wigs & fashion apparel to
the Caucasian & African American
market.

SARA LEE DIRECT HOME SHOPPING

Div. of Sara Lee Corp
1000 E Hanes Mill Rd
Winston-Salem, NC 27105-1384
Telephone: (336) 519-4400, Toll Free:
(800) 671-5056, E-Mail: ohp.
manager@onehanesplace.com, Web
Site: www.onehanesplace.com
CEO: Charles Chambers
VP, One Hanes Place: John Craig
Dir, Just My Size: Jennifer Akers
Dir, New Ventures: Cindy Sutton
Conducts Business: U.S.
Employees: 3,000
Primary Market Served: Consumer
Catalog available online
Direct online sales
Advertising/Marketing Budget Related
to Direct Marketing: 76-100%
Direct Marketing ad budget:
Direct Mail: $40,000,000
Founded: 1978
Gross sales or billing: $200,000,000

Direct sales of Sara Lee apparel.

SCULPTZ

1150 Northbrook Dr (Suite 200)
Feasterville Trevose, PA 19053-8409
Telephone: (215) 494-2900, E-Mail:
sdudek@sculptz.com, Web Site:
www.silkies.com
Pres: Deirdre J. Mistri
Sr Dir Mktg: Sue Dudek
Natl Sls Rep: Amanda Bird
Conducts Business: United States, Can-
ada, United Kingdom, Germany
Primary Market Served: Consumer
Founded: 1974

SICKAFUS SHEEPSKINS

8373 Rte 183
Strausstown, PA 19559
Telephone: (610) 488-1782, Toll Free:
(888) 751-1300, FAX: (610) 488-
1576, E-Mail: pat@patgarrett.com,
Web Site: www.sheepcoat.com

Pres: Patrick Garrett
Conducts Business: U.S., Canada
Primary Market Served: Consumer
Catalog available online
Indirect online sales
Founded: 1966

Sell sheepskin coats, vests, slippers &
car, truck, airplane & motorcycle seat
covers both wholesale & retail.

SIERRA TRADING POST

5025 Campstool Rd
Cheyenne, WY 82007-1816
Toll Free: (800) 713-4534, FAX: (800)
378-8946, E-Mail: customerservice@
sierratradingpost.com, Web Site:
www.sierratradingpost.com
CEO: Keith Richardson
Pres: Gary Imig
Employees: 500
Primary Market Served: Consumer
Catalog available online
Direct online sales
Founded: 1986

Sell name brand clothing, footwear,
and outdoor gear.

SIGNATURE STYLES LLC

2711 Centerville Rd (Suite 400)
Wilmington, DE 19808
Telephone: (302) 636-5401
VP Acctg: Patty Lyon
Primary Market Served: Consumer

SOFT SURROUNDINGS

1100 N Lindbergh Blvd
Saint Louis, MO 63132-2914
Telephone: (314) 812-5200, Web Site:
www.softsurroundings.com
CEO: Thomas Wilcher
Vice Chmn: Robin Sheldon
Primary Market Served: Consumer

SPIEGEL BRANDS INC

Div. of Signature Styles LLC.
110 William St (11th Fl)
New York, NY 10038-3945
Toll Free: (800) 222-5680, E-Mail:
customerservice@spiegel.com, Web
Site: www.spiegel.com
Chmn & CEO: Lynn Tinton
Primary Market Served: Consumer

SPORTIF MAIL ORDER INC

Div. of Sportif USA Inc
1415 Greg St (Suite 101)
Sparks, NV 89431
Telephone: (888) 260-7676, FAX:
(775) 356-3567, Web Site: www.
sportif.com
Pres: John E. Kirsch
Controller: Doug Moir
Inventory Mgr & Buyer: Kim Radzik
MIS Mgr: Mike Youngblood

Circ Mgr: Matt Glerum
Conducts Business: Worldwide
Employees: 29
Primary Market Served: Business &
Consumer
Catalog available online
Advertising/Marketing Budget Related
to Direct Marketing: 76-100%
Direct Marketing ad budget:
$2,500,000
Direct Mail: 100%
Founded: 1965
Gross sales or billing: $4,500,000

Specialty active apparel for the outdoor
enthusiast & comfortable casual wear
for business & pleasure.

STAR SILKSCREEN DESIGN INC

2281 Hubbard Ave
Decatur, IL 62526-2149
Telephone: (217) 877-0804, FAX:
(217) 877-0843, Web Site: www.
starsilkscreendesign.com
Pres: Jon Kozeliski
VP: Karen Rajee
Employees: 5
Primary Market Served: Consumer
Gross sales or billing: $600,000

Silk screen & embroidery on fabric articles.

PAUL STUART

Madison Ave & 45th St
New York, NY 10017
Toll Free: (800) 678-8278, E-Mail:
info@paulstuart.com, Web Site:
www.paulstuart.com
CEO: Michael Ostrove
Conducts Business: U.S.
Employees: 250
Primary Market Served: Consumer
Direct online sales
Advertising/Marketing Budget Related
to Direct Marketing: 51-75%
Direct Marketing ad budget:
Direct Mail: 60%
Newspapers: 35%
Online: 5%

Retail & catalog sales of men's & wom-
en's apparel.

STULLER INC

302 Rue Louis XIV
Lafayette, LA 70508
Toll Free: (800) 877-7777, FAX: (800)
444-4741, E-Mail: info@stuller.com,
Web Site: www.stuller.com
Chmn & CEO: Matthew G. Stuller
Pres & COO: Chuck Lein
Exec VP & CFO: Linus Cortez
VP, Mktg: Ray Stroup Jr.
Primary Market Served: Consumer
Catalog available online

Direct online sales
Advertising/Marketing Budget Related
to Direct Marketing: 26-50%
Founded: 1970
Jewelry items.

TAFFORD UNIFORMS

PO Box 481912
Charlotte, NC 28269
Telephone: (215) 643-9666, E-Mail:
customerservice@tafford.com, Web
Site: www.tafford.com
VP Mktg: David Kaplan
Conducts Business: U.S., Canada
Primary Market Served: Consumer
Catalog available online
Direct online sales
Advertising/Marketing Budget Related
to Direct Marketing: 76-100%

Nursing uniforms, scrubs, stethoscopes,
nursing shoes and medical accessories
sold to nurses, doctors, dentists, hy-
gienists and veterinarians.

TALBOTS

Div. of Jusco Co Ltd/AEON Group
1 Talbots Dr
Hingham, MA 02043-1583
Telephone: (781) 749-7600, Toll Free:
(800) 825-2687, FAX: (781) 741-
4369, Web Site: www.talbots.com
CFO: Edward Larsen
CEO: Lizanne Kindler
Exec VP & Chief Mktg Officer: Lori
Wagner
Sr VP Dir Mktg & Customer Svc:
Bruce Prescott
Conducts Business: Worldwide
Employees: 10,000
Primary Market Served: Consumer
Catalog available online

Specialty retailer, cataloger and e-tailer
of women's classic apparel, shoes and
accessories. Also offers children's and
men's clothing.

TAMRAC INC

154 E 21st St
Ogden, UT 84401
Telephone: (385) 405-2700, E-Mail:
info@tamrac.com, Web Site: www.
tamrac.com
CEO: Gregory Schern
Primary Market Served: Business &
Consumer

Camera carrying systems, such as camera bags, camera cases, photo daypacks
& photo backpacks

TEAM CHEER

131 Main St (Ste 2)
Geneseo, NY 14454-1242
Telephone: (800) 350-1562, Toll Free:
(877) 243-5268, E-Mail: custserv@
teamcheer.com, Web Site: www.
teamcheer.com
Pres & CEO: Randy Cofield
VP Creative Svcs: Linda Cofield
Dir Sls & Mktg: Cindy Sobieraj
Fulfillment Mgr: Dan Johnson
Mktg Mgr: Sherry Paddon
Conducts Business: U.S.
Employees: 25
Primary Market Served: Business &
Consumer
Catalog available online
Direct online sales
Advertising/Marketing Budget Related
to Direct Marketing: 76-100%
Founded: 1991
Gross sales or billing: $2,800,000

Provides cheer and dance apparel and
accessories.

NORM THOMPSON OUTFITTERS INC

3188 NW Aloclek Dr
Hillsboro, OR 97124
Toll Free: (800) 547-1160, (877) 718-
7899, FAX: (503) 614-4599, Web
Site: www.normthompson.com
Pres & CEO: Martin McClanan
Conducts Business: U.S.
Employees: 500
Primary Market Served: Consumer
Advertising/Marketing Budget Related
to Direct Marketing: 0-25%
Founded: 1949
Gross sales or billing: $200,000,000

Mail order firm selling high quality
clothing by direct mail to the general
public. Also, footwear, foods & gifts.

THE TOG SHOP INC

Subsidiary of Appleseed's
30 Tozer Rd
Beverly, MA 01915
Toll Free: (800) 262-8888, FAX: (800)
755-7557, Web Site: www.togshop.
com
CEO & Pres: Paula Bennett
CIO: Jane Pendergast
Dir: Margaret Donohue
Conducts Business: U.S.
Employees: 350
Primary Market Served: Consumer
Catalog available online
Direct online sales
Advertising/Marketing Budget Related
to Direct Marketing: 76-100%
Direct Marketing ad budget:
Direct Mail: 100%

Retail & mail order sales of ladies
clothing & footwear.

TUTTLE

23 Village Ln
Wallingford, CT 06492
Telephone: (203) 949-4290, Toll Free:
(800) 882-7511, FAX: (203) 949-
4288, Web Site: www.tuttlecatalog.
com
Pres: Adam Mosher
Conducts Business: Worldwide
Primary Market Served: Business &
Consumer
Catalog available online
Direct online sales
Advertising/Marketing Budget Related
to Direct Marketing: 76-100%
Founded: 1990

Consumer mail order products. Sports
apparel for golf & tennis.

UNDERCOVERWEAR INC

30 Commerce Way (Unit 2)
Tewksbury, MA 01876
Telephone: (978) 851-8580, Toll Free:
(800) 733-0007, FAX: (978) 640-
2882, E-Mail: service@
undercoverwear.com, Web Site:
www.undercoverwear.com
Pres: Walter James
CEO: Tiffany James
VP: Adrian Canto
VP: Jamie Jamitkowski
Sls Dir: Nancy Cosimini
Conducts Business: U.S., Canada
Employees: 140
Primary Market Served: Consumer
Catalog available online
Direct online sales
Advertising/Marketing Budget Related
to Direct Marketing: 26-50%
Founded: 1977
Gross sales or billing: $100,000,000

Distributes Lingerie - Home Party
Planning.

UNIFIRST CORP

68 Jonspin Rd
Wilmington, MA 01887
Telephone: (270) 683-5250 X523, Web
Site: www.unifirst.com
Pres: Ronald Croatti
Primary Market Served: Consumer

UNITED RETAIL INC

365 W Passaic St (Suite 230)
Rochelle Park, NJ 07662-3017
Telephone: (201) 845-0880, Web Site:
www.avenue.com
VP Mktg: Brad Orloff
Primary Market Served: Consumer

VF IMAGEWEAR

Div. of VF Workwear
105 Corporate Center Blvd
Greensboro, NC 27408

Telephone: (336) 424-6000, Toll Free: (800) 733-5271, Web Site: www.vfimagewear.com
COO: Robert Gates
VP, Direct Sls: Ronald O. Pate Sr
VP, Indirect Sls: Jim Tewmey
Mdsg & Prod Devel Dir: Dave Neimer
Mktg Svcs Dir: Elaine Wilber
Conducts Business: Worldwide
Employees: 1,500
Primary Market Served: Business
Catalog available online
Advertising/Marketing Budget Related to Direct Marketing: 26-50%
Founded: 1972
Gross sales or billing: $218,400,000

Complete uniform & accessory programs for government & law enforcement agencies & private industry. Apparel manufacturing company.

VENUS FASHION, INC
11711 Marco Beach Dr
Jacksonville, FL 32224
Telephone: (904) 645-6000, Web Site: www.venus.com
CEO: James Brewster
Primary Market Served: Business & Consumer

WASSERMAN UNIFORM CO
700 NW 57th Pl
Fort Lauderdale, FL 33309
Telephone: (614) 279-7000, (614) 279-8888, Toll Free: (800) 848-3576, FAX: (614) 464-0416, (800) 204-0416, E-Mail: custserv@wassermanuniform.com, Web Site: www.wassermanuniform.com
CEO, CFO & Gen Mgr: Joel Luck
Postal Sls Mgr: Ted McCord
Conducts Business: U.S.
Employees: 105
Primary Market Served: Business & Consumer
Founded: 1971
Gross sales or billing: $5,500,000

Uniform apparel & shoes: postal, fire & industrial.

WATHNE LTD
156 W 56 St
New York, NY 10019
Telephone: (212) 757-3001, FAX: (212) 757-2448
CEO: Bergljot Wathne
Primary Market Served: Business & Consumer

Handbag manufacturer.

WEARGUARD CORP
141 Longwater Dr
Norwell, MA 02061-1683

Telephone: (781) 871-4100, Toll Free: (800) 388-3300, FAX: (781) 871-2639, Web Site: www.wearguard.com
Pres: Richard M. Salem
Conducts Business: U.S.
Employees: 1,200
Primary Market Served: Business & Consumer
Catalog available online
Direct online sales

Catalog & mail order house selling work clothing, footwear & accessories.

THE WEXNER COMPANIES INC
418 S Grove Park Rd
Memphis, TN 38117-3518
Telephone: (901) 763-3925, Toll Free: (800) 890-5470, FAX: (901) 763-3736, E-Mail: info@JosephStores.com, Web Site: www.josephstores.com
Pres: Alfred B. Wexner
Adv Coord: Nancy Sewell
Asst Adv Coord: Lee Thompson
Conducts Business: U.S.
Employees: 60
Primary Market Served: Consumer
Catalog available online
Direct online sales
Gross sales or billing: $12,800,000

Retailer of high fashion ladies shoes & related products, apparel & accessories. Manufacturer, wholesale & retail shoe stores.

THE WIG CO
Div. of Vincent James Co Inc
1391 McLaughlin Run Rd
Pittsburgh, PA 15241
Toll Free: (800) 568-3499, E-Mail: custserv@twcwigs.com, Web Site: www.thewigcompany.com
Owner & Pres: Vincent James DeCarlucci
Co-Owner: Karen DeCarlucci
Controller: Jim McCassney
Conducts Business: U.S., Canada
Employees: 40
Primary Market Served: Consumer

Catalog shopping service featuring Eva Gabor brand of ladies' synthetic wigs & hairpieces. Mail or Customer Service available for wigs.

WILLIAMSON-DICKIE MANUFACTURING CO
509 W Vickery Blvd
Fort Worth, TX 76104
Toll Free: (800) 336-7201, FAX: (817) 877-5027, E-Mail: customerservice@dickies.com, Web Site: www.dickies.com

Chmn, CEO & Pres: Phillip C. Williamson
CFO: Britt Ingebritson
VP, Mktg Svcs: John Ragsdale
Primary Market Served: Business
Catalog available online
Direct online sales

A garment manufacturing company.

WILSONS LEATHER
7401 Boone Ave N
Brooklyn Park, MN 55428
Telephone: (763) 391-4000, Toll Free: (866) 305-4704, FAX: (763) 391-4906, E-Mail: customercare@wilsonsleather.com, Web Site: www.wilsonsleather.com
CEO: Michael M. Searles
VP Store Sls & Real Estate: M. Adam Boucher
Mktg Mgr: Lisa Kummer
Employees: 3,461
Primary Market Served: Consumer
Founded: 1899
Gross sales or billing: $321,300,000

Sells leather goods.

WINTERSILKS LLC
100 Murray Dr
Warren, PA 16368-0001
Telephone: (904) 645-6000, Web Site: www.wintersilks.com
Pres: Chris Vig
VP, Mdsg: Jay Saftchick
Mgr: Kimberly During
Conducts Business: U.S., Canada
Employees: 10
Primary Market Served: Consumer
Catalog available online
Direct online sales
Advertising/Marketing Budget Related to Direct Marketing: 76-100%

Catalog marketer of silk clothing for winter warmth. Mail order catalog company.

WOOLRICH INC
2 Mill St
Woolrich, PA 17779
Telephone: (570) 769-6464, Toll Free: (800) 966-5372, Web Site: www.woolrich.com
Special Projects Mgr: Lisa Smith
Primary Market Served: Consumer

ZAPPOS.COM
400 Stewart Ave (Suite A)
Las Vegas, NV 89101-2914
Toll Free: (800) 927-7671, Web Site: www.zappos.com
Brand Mktg Mgr: Michelle Thomas

Electronics, Audio, Computer & Video Catalogs (3)

APC BY SCHNEIDER ELECTRIC

Subs. of Schneider Electric
132 Fairgrounds Rd
West Kingston, RI 02889
Toll Free: (800) 555-7927, FAX: (401) 789-3710, E-Mail: public.relations@apcc.com, Web Site: www.apcc.com
CEO & Pres: Laurent Vernerey
Pres Opers: Rob McKernan
CFO: Karen Miranda
Conducts Business: Worldwide
Primary Market Served: Business & Consumer
Catalog available online
Advertising/Marketing Budget Related to Direct Marketing: 0-25%
Direct Marketing ad budget: $1,500,000
Direct Mail: 100%
Founded: 1981

Designs, develops, manufactures & markets a line of uninterruptible power supply products (UPS) for use with computers & other sensitive electronic devices. Markets its products worldwide through computer distributor & dealers, mass merchandisers, catalog merchandisers & private label accounts.

AMERICAN MEGATRENDS INC

5555 Oakbrook Pkwy (Suite 200)
Norcross, GA 30093-2286
Telephone: (770) 246-8600, Toll Free: (800) 828-9264, FAX: (770) 246-8790, Web Site: www.ami.com
Pres & CEO: Subromanian Shankar
Sec: Pat Sarma
Treas: Victor Kannan
Sls Dir: Howard Johnston
Dir Engrng: Carl Sheadoker
Conducts Business: U.S., Germany, India, Japan, Taiwan, U.K.
Employees: 500
Primary Market Served: Business & Consumer
Catalog available online
Direct online sales
Advertising/Marketing Budget Related to Direct Marketing: 0-25%
Founded: 1985

Core technology provider of RAID, BIOS, motherboard and utilities.

ANTIQUE ELECTRONIC SUPPLY

6221 S Maple Ave
Tempe, AZ 85283
Telephone: (480) 820-5411, Toll Free: (800) 706-6789, FAX: (480) 820-4643, E-Mail: info@tubesandmore.com, Web Site: www.tubesandmore.com
Pres, Opers: Noreen Cravener
VP, Tech Svcs: Greg Cravener
Conducts Business: Worldwide
Employees: 24
Primary Market Served: Business & Consumer
Catalog available online
Indirect online sales
Founded: 1982

Electron tubes (vacuum tubes) & other electronic parts, supplies & books.

ARROW ELECTRONICS INC

76459 S Lima St
Englewood, CO 80112
Telephone: (952) 828-5350, Toll Free: (800) 833-3557, FAX: (952) 828-5399, Web Site: www.arrow.com
Chmn, Pres & CEO: Michael J. Long
Conducts Business: U.S.
Employees: 26
Primary Market Served: Business & Consumer
Advertising/Marketing Budget Related to Direct Marketing: 0-25%

Distributor of electronic components.

AUDIO CLASSICS LTD

3501 Vestal Rd
Vestal, NY 13850-2244
Telephone: (607) 766-3501, FAX: (607) 766-3502, E-Mail: steve@audioclassics.com, Web Site: www.audioclassics.com
Pres: Steve Rowell
VP: Mike Sastra
Retail Sls Mgr: Brian Smith
Sls Rep: Frank Gow
Sls Rep: Ernie Schleider
Conducts Business: Worldwide
Primary Market Served: Business & Consumer
Catalog available online
Indirect online sales
Advertising/Marketing Budget Related to Direct Marketing: 51-75%
Direct Marketing ad budget: $90,000
Direct Mail: 65%
Magazines: 25%
Newspapers: 10%
Founded: 1979
Gross sales or billing: $2,600,000

High-end stereo equipment.

AUDIO EDITIONS BOOKS-ON-CASSETTE & CD

Div. of The Audio Partners Inc
PO Box 6930
Auburn, CA 95604-6930
Toll Free: (800) 231-4261, FAX: (800) 882-1840, E-Mail: info@audioeditions.com, Web Site: www.audioeditions.com
VP: Chris Benson
Dir Sls & Mktg: Janet Benson
Conducts Business: U.S.
Employees: 35
Primary Market Served: Consumer
Catalog available online
Direct online sales
Advertising/Marketing Budget Related to Direct Marketing: 76-100%
Direct Marketing ad budget:
Direct Mail: 80%
Online: 20%
Founded: 1987

Complete AudioBook source. Over 19,000 titles including bestsellers, mysteries and more.

BBC WORLDWIDE AMERICAS INC

1120 Ave of the Americas (Fl 5)
New York, NY 10036-6700
Telephone: (212) 705-9300, Toll Free: (800) 898-4921, FAX: (212) 888-0576, Web Site: www.bbcamerica.com
Pres: Herb Scannell
COO: Ann Sarnoff
CFO: Andrew Bott
Conducts Business: U.S.
Primary Market Served: Consumer
Catalog available online
Direct online sales

Offers the U.S. British programming through its website & catalog. Markets DVDs, books, audiobooks, music, home decor & collectibles developed for BBC & British brands.

BELTONE CORP

2601 Patriot Blvd
Glenview, IL 60026-8023
Toll Free: (800) 235-8663, FAX: (847) 832-3300, E-Mail: info@beltone.com, Web Site: www.beltone.com
Pres: Richard Swanson
Conducts Business: Worldwide
Employees: 1,000
Primary Market Served: Business & Consumer
Advertising/Marketing Budget Related to Direct Marketing: 76-100%
Direct Marketing ad budget: $10,000,000

In-house agency for Beltone Electronics Corp, manufacturer of hearing aids & hearing test instruments distributed through 3,000 authorized dispenser offices in the U.S., Canada & 47 countries worldwide.

BENNETT MARINE VIDEO

RP-NFOA
2321 Abbot Kinney Blvd (Suite 101)
Venice, CA 90291-4876
Telephone: (310) 827-8064, Toll Free:
   (800) 733-8862, FAX: (310) 827-
   8074, E-Mail: questions@
   bennettmarine.com, Web Site: www.
   bennettmarine.com
Pres: Michael Bennett
Catalog available online
Direct online sales
Gross sales or billing: $100,000

BERKSHIRE RECORD
OUTLET INC

Rte 102 Pleasant St
Lee, MA 01238-9804
Telephone: (413) 243-4080, FAX:
   (413) 243-4340, E-Mail: broinc@
   berkshirerecordoutlet.com, Web Site:
   www2.broinc.com
Mgr: Steve Nikitas
CEO: Joseph Eckstein
Conducts Business: U.S., Japan
Employees: 15
Primary Market Served: Business &
   Consumer
Catalog available online
Direct online sales
Advertising/Marketing Budget Related
   to Direct Marketing: 0-25%
Founded: 1974

Deleted & overstocked classical compact discs, tapes, LPs & videos, as well as books on classical music.

BERWAY VISUAL
PRODUCTS INC

668 Main St (Suite 10)
Wilmington, MA 01887
Telephone: (978) 694-9195, Toll Free:
   (800) 452-0410, FAX: (978) 694-
   9212, E-Mail: sales@berway.com,
   Web Site: www.berway.com
Pres: Bernadette Gerald
VP: Wayne E. Gerald
Conducts Business: U.S.
Employees: 7
Primary Market Served: Business &
   Consumer
Catalog available online
Indirect online sales
Advertising/Marketing Budget Related
   to Direct Marketing: 0-25%
Direct Marketing ad budget: $10,000
Direct Mail: 60%
Magazines: 15%
Telephone: 25%
Founded: 1996

Gross sales or billing: $1,300,000
AV sales, design & installation.

BEST BUY

7601 Penn Ave S
Richfield, MN 55423-3683
Telephone: (612) 291-1000, Web Site:
   www.bestbuy.com
Dir Customer Loyalty Mktg: Mark
   Juba
CEO: Hubert Joly
Primary Market Served: Consumer

BIGELOW ELECTRONICS

186 E Jefferson St
Bluffton, OH 45817-0125
Telephone: (419) 358-7851
Owner: Clarence Bigelow
Conducts Business: U.S.
Primary Market Served: Business &
   Consumer
Advertising/Marketing Budget Related
   to Direct Marketing: 76-100%
Founded: 1954

Sell electronic parts, tools & kits to factories, schools, repair shops & hobbyists.

BLACK BOX CORP

1000 Park Dr
Lawrence, PA 15055-1018
Telephone: (724) 746-5500, Toll Free:
   (877) 877-2269, FAX: (800) 321-
   0746, E-Mail: brian.kutchma@
   blackbox.com, Web Site: www.
   blackbox.com
Pres & CEO: E.C. Sykes
Conducts Business: Worldwide
Employees: 4,384
Primary Market Served: Business
Catalog available online
Direct online sales
Founded: 1976
Gross sales or billing: $999,458,000

Providers of voice communications, data infrastructure & 118,000 networking products, dedicated to designing & building & maintaining today's integrated voice & data communications systems.

BLUE RAVEN TECHNOLOGY

110 Fordham Rd
Wilmington, MA 01887-2165
Telephone: ((978) 658-4676, Toll Free:
   (800) 274-5343, (800) 20RAVEN,
   FAX: (781) 778-4848, E-Mail:
   sales@blueraven.com, Web Site:
   www.blueraven.com
Pres & CEO: Glen A. Kashgegian
VP: Charles H. Kouyoumjian
Conducts Business: United States
Employees: 200

Primary Market Served: Business &
   Consumer
Catalog available online
Direct online sales
Advertising/Marketing Budget Related
   to Direct Marketing: 0-25%
Direct Marketing ad budget:
Online: 25%
Telephone: 75%
Founded: 1985
Gross sales or billing: $100,000

Remanufacturer of brand personal computers (Compaq, H-P, IBM, Apple) and repair parts. Sell through catalogs.

BOSE CORP

100 The Mountain Rd
Framingham, MA 01701-9168
Telephone: (508) 879-7330, Toll Free:
   (800) 379-2703, FAX: (508) 766-
   7543, Web Site: www.bose.com
Pres & CEO: Bob Maresca
Conducts Business: Worldwide
Primary Market Served: Consumer
Stereo equipment.

BRIM ELECTRONICS INC

120 Home Pl
Lodi, NJ 07644
Telephone: (201) 796-2886, FAX:
   (973) 778-2792, E-Mail: info@
   brimelectronics.com, Web Site:
   www.brimelectronics.com
Pres: B. Danziger
Gen Mgr: B. Brown
Sls: M. Aaron
Conducts Business: U.S., Canada, Europe, Asia, Africa
Employees: 45
Primary Market Served: Business
Catalog available online
Indirect online sales
Advertising/Marketing Budget Related
   to Direct Marketing: 0-25%
Direct Marketing ad budget:
Direct Mail: 25%
Magazines: 60%
Telephone: 15%
Founded: 1975

Sell electronic wires & cables, tubings & sleevings, fastening devices & ceramic insulators to OEMs, government, institutions, distributors & supply houses.

BROADCAST ELECTRONICS
INC

4100 N 24th St
Quincy, IL 62305
Telephone: (217) 224-9600, FAX:
   (217) 224-9607, E-Mail: bdcast@
   bdcast.com, Web Site: www.bdcast.
   com
Pres & CEO: Timothy Bealor

Conducts Business: Worldwide
Employees: 150
Primary Market Served: Business
Catalog available online
Advertising/Marketing Budget Related
   to Direct Marketing: 0-25%
Direct Marketing ad budget: $35,000
Direct Mail: 7%
Magazines: 93%
Founded: 1959
Gross sales or billing: $20,000

Radio broadcast equipment.

BROOKE DISTRIBUTORS INC

16250 NW 52nd Ave
Miami, FL 33014
Telephone: (305) 624-9752, Toll Free:
   (800) 275-8792, FAX: (305) 620-
   3988, E-Mail: sales@brookedms.
   com, Web Site: www.brookedist.com
Pres: David Rutter
VP Opers Mdsg Sls: Mark Cohen
Conducts Business: U.S., Caribbean
   Basin, Latin America
Employees: 30
Primary Market Served: Business
Indirect online sales
Advertising/Marketing Budget Related
   to Direct Marketing: 26-50%
Direct Marketing ad budget:
Direct Mail: 50%
Magazines: 15%
Newspapers: 5%
Telephone: 30%
Founded: 1949
Gross sales or billing: $7,700,000

Wholesale distributor of consumer
electronics, specialty gift items, computers & computer peripherals.

BROOKSTONE CO

1 Innovation Way
Merrimack, NH 03054-4873
Telephone: (603) 880-9500, Toll Free:
   (800) 846-3000, FAX: (603) 577-
   8005, E-Mail: customerservice@
   brookstone.com, Web Site: www.
   brookstone.com
Pres & CEO: Thomas Via
Conducts Business: U.S.
Employees: 3,278
Primary Market Served: Consumer
Catalog available online
Direct online sales
Advertising/Marketing Budget Related
   to Direct Marketing: 76-100%
Founded: 1965
Gross sales or billing: $511,900,000

Sell hard-to-find products to consumers
& business firms through catalog mailings & retail stores.

BUENA VISTA HOME ENTERTAINMENT

Div. of Walt Disney Co
500 S Buena Vista St
Burbank, CA 91521
Telephone: (818) 560-1000, FAX:
   (818) 845-8728, Web Site: www.
   bvhe.com
CEO & Pres: Janice Marinelli
Conducts Business: Worldwide
Employees: 100
Primary Market Served: Business &
   Consumer
Catalog available online
Direct online sales
Founded: 1982
Gross sales or billing: $20,000,000

Marketer of Disney, Touchstone, Hollywood Pictures, Buena Vista, Jim
Henson & Miramax home video products.

BUTLER DISTRIBUTING CO

Subs. of B&W Printing Co Inc
730 Fairfield Ave
Kenilworth, NJ 07033-2012
Telephone: (908) 241-3060, FAX:
   (908) 298-9248, E-Mail:
   bwprinting@worldnet.att.net, Web
   Site: www.bwprinting.com
Pres: Gary L. Butler
Conducts Business: U.S.
Employees: 4
Primary Market Served: Business &
   Consumer
Catalog available online
Direct online sales
Advertising/Marketing Budget Related
   to Direct Marketing: 0-25%
Direct Marketing ad budget:
Direct Mail: 70%
Magazines: 10%
Telephone: 20%
Founded: 1979
Gross sales or billing: $500,000

Manufacturer of ideal self inking and
handle rubber stamps. Order on-line at
bwprinting.com.

C2G

Subs of Legrand, Inc
3555 Kettering Blvd
Moraine, OH 45439
Telephone: (937) 224-8646, Toll Free:
   (800) 506-9607, FAX: (937) 496-
   2666, (800) 331-2841, Web Site:
   www.cablestogo.com
Pres & CEO: John Selldorff
Employees: 217
Primary Market Served: Business
Catalog available online
Direct online sales
Gross sales or billing: $68,400,000

Connectivity products distributor.

CABLE CONNECTION

1035 Mission Ct
Fremont, CA 94539
Telephone: (510) 249-9000, E-Mail:
   cables4u@cable-connection.com,
   Web Site: www.cable-connection.
   com
Chmn: Jim Johnson
Pres: Greg Gaches
Employees: 100
Primary Market Served: Business &
   Consumer
Founded: 1985
Gross sales or billing: $14,000,000

Manufacturer of cable products and accessories serving the electronics, communications and medical industries.

CATALOG MUSIC CORP

4301 Hillsboro Rd (Suite 320), PO Box
   159297
Nashville, TN 37215
Telephone: (615) 298-4338, Toll Free:
   (800) 744-8204, FAX: (615) 298-
   4628, Web Site: www.catalogmusic.
   com
Mng Dir: Martin D. Davis
Conducts Business: U.S., Canada
Primary Market Served: Consumer
Advertising/Marketing Budget Related
   to Direct Marketing: 76-100%
Founded: 1988

Old time country music greats on cassette, CD & video.

CHAMPS SOFTWARE INC

1255 N Vantage Point Dr
Crystal River, FL 34429
Telephone: (352) 795-2362, FAX:
   (352) 795-9100, E-Mail: champs@
   champsinc.com, Web Site: www.
   champsinc.com
Pres & CEO: Brian Gay
Conducts Business: Worldwide
Employees: 50
Primary Market Served: Business
Catalog available online
Direct online sales
Advertising/Marketing Budget Related
   to Direct Marketing: 0-25%
Founded: 1979
Gross sales or billing: $5,000,000

Business solutions.

COMPUTER DYNAMICS INC

Div of CIMTEC Automation, LLC
3030 Whitehall Park Dr
Charlotte, NC 28273
Telephone: (866) 599-6512, FAX:
   (704) 586-9671, E-Mail: CDIsales@
   gefanuc.com, Web Site: www.
   cdynamics.com
Catalog available online
Founded: 1981

COMPUTER STATION CORP
6611 Bissonnet St (Suite 107)
Houston, TX 77074
Telephone: (713) 777-6860, FAX:
(713) 777-3431, E-Mail: csc@
computerstationcorp.com, Web Site:
www.computerstationcorp.com
Pres: Jeff T. Jow
Gen Mgr: Annie Jow
Employees: 15
Primary Market Served: Business &
Consumer
Catalog available online
Founded: 1983

Computer hardware, software, sales &
service.

THE COMPUTER SUPPLY PEOPLE
N93 W14636 Whitaker Way
Menomonee Falls, WI 53051
Telephone: (262) 251-5511, Toll Free:
(800) 242-2090, FAX: (262) 251-
4737, E-Mail: medmgt@
computersupplypeople.com, Web
Site: www.computersupplypeople.
com
Pres: John Schimberg
Sls Mgr: Jim Noonan
Conducts Business: U.S., Canada, Eu-
rope, S. America
Employees: 9
Primary Market Served: Business &
Consumer
Founded: 1974

Sell complete line of computer supplies
& accessories.

CONCURRENT COMPUTER CORP
4375 River Green Pkwy
Duluth, GA 30096-2572
Telephone: (678) 228-4000, Toll Free:
(877) 978-7363, FAX: (954) 977-
5580, Web Site: www.ccur.com
Pres & CEO: Derek Elder
CFO & Exec VP Opers: Emory Berry
Conducts Business: U.S., Canada
Primary Market Served: Business

Sales of computer supplies & accessories, spare parts for Concurrent Computer Corporation OS/32 & RT Series
Computer Systems.

CONSOLIDATED ELECTRONICS INC
705 Watervliet Ave
Dayton, OH 45420
Telephone: (937) 252-5662, Toll Free:
(800) 543-3568, FAX: (937) 252-
4066, E-Mail: scoy@ceitron.com,
Web Site: www.ceitron.com
Pres: Steven S. Coy
Conducts Business: Worldwide

Employees: 1
Primary Market Served: Business &
Consumer
Catalog available online
Indirect online sales
Advertising/Marketing Budget Related
to Direct Marketing: 51-75%
Direct Marketing ad budget: $5,000
Online: 40%
Telephone: 60%
Founded: 1979
Gross sales or billing: $500,000

Electronic parts & equipment.

CRUTCHFIELD CORP
1 Crutchfield Pk
Charlottesville, VA 22911-9097
Telephone: (434) 817-1000, Toll Free:
(800) 955-9091, FAX: (804) 817-
1010, E-Mail: administration@
crutchfield.com, Web Site: www.
crutchfield.com
Pres: William G. Crutchfield
Exec VP, Mdsg: Rick Sounder
Sr VP, Mdsg: Daniel Hodgson
Sr VP, Mktg & Creative Svcs: John
Haydock
Sr VP, Fin: Richard L. Stavitski
VP, HR: Mark Maynard
VP, Direct Mktg: Brendan Edgerton
Conducts Business: U.S.
Employees: 500
Primary Market Served: Consumer
Catalog available online
Direct online sales
Founded: 1974

Mail order catalog of consumer electronics.

CRYSTAL RECORDS INC
28818 NE Hancock Rd
Camas, WA 98607
Telephone: (360) 834-7022, FAX:
(360) 834-9680, E-Mail: info@
crystalrecords.com, Web Site: www.
crystalrecords.com
Pres: Peter Christ
Conducts Business: U.S., Asia, Austral-
ia, Canada, Europe, New Zealand
Employees: 4
Primary Market Served: Business &
Consumer
Catalog available online
Indirect online sales
Advertising/Marketing Budget Related
to Direct Marketing: 0-25%
Direct Marketing ad budget:
Direct Mail: 20%
Magazines: 80%
Founded: 1966
Gross sales or billing: $140,000

Sell compact discs, classical only.

DALCO ELECTRONICS
425 S Pioneer Blvd

Springboro, OH 45066-1180
Telephone: (937) 743-8042, Toll Free:
(800) 445-5342, FAX: (937) 743-
9251, Web Site: www.dalco.com
Owner: Dale Ditmer
Conducts Business: Worldwide
Employees: 20
Primary Market Served: Business &
Consumer
Catalog available online
Indirect online sales
Advertising/Marketing Budget Related
to Direct Marketing: 51-75%
Direct Marketing ad budget: $250,000
Direct Mail: 25%
Online: 75%
Founded: 1986

IBM compatible computer components
& accessories sold to end users & re-
sellers, corporate & individual consumers.

DATA DIRECT NETWORKS
9351 Deering Ave
Chatsworth, CA 91311
Telephone: (818) 700-7607, Toll Free:
(800) 837-2298, FAX: (818) 700-
7601, E-Mail: info@ddn.com, Web
Site: www.datadirectnet.com
CEO: Alex Bouzari
Pres: Paul Bloch
Sr VP Sls & Support: Scott Genereaux
VP Prod Mktg: Josh Goldstein
Primary Market Served: Business
Founded: 1988

Catalogs & brochures of computer related items.

DELORME MAPPING
2 DeLorme Dr
Yarmouth, ME 04096
Telephone: (207) 846-7100, Toll Free:
(800) 642-0970, FAX: (207) 846-
7051, E-Mail: caleb.mason@
delorme.com, Web Site: www.
delorme.com
Chmn & CEO: David Delorme
Pres: Gordon Pow
VP, Sls & Mktg: David Eshelman
VP Sls: Jim Skillings
Mktg Dir: Caleb Mason
Conducts Business: U.S.
Primary Market Served: Consumer
Catalog available online
Indirect online sales

Maps, atlases & mapping software for
consumers.

DIGI INTERNATIONAL
11001 Bren Rd E
Minnetonka, MN 55343-4410
Telephone: (952) 912-3444, Toll Free:
(877) 912-3444, FAX: (952) 912-
4952, Web Site: www.digi.com
Pres & CEO: Ron Konezny

VP Sales & Mktg Asia & EMEA: Frederic Luu
Sr VP Mktg: Larry Kraft
Sr VP Sales: Kevin Riley
Sr VP & CFO: Steve Snyder
Conducts Business: Worldwide
Employees: 50
Primary Market Served: Business & Consumer
Catalog available online
Indirect online sales
Advertising/Marketing Budget Related to Direct Marketing: 0-25%
Direct Marketing ad budget: $200,000
Direct Mail: 40%
Magazines: 30%
Telephone: 30%
Founded: 1983

PC connectivity products.

DIGI-KEY CORP
701 Brooks Ave S
Thief River Falls, MN 56701
Telephone: (218) 681-6674, Toll Free: (800) 344-4539, FAX: (218) 681-3380, E-Mail: sales@digikey.com, Web Site: www.digikey.com
Pres & CEO: Dave Doherty
VP, Mktg: Steven G. Tsukichi
Conducts Business: U.S., Canada
Employees: 1,900
Primary Market Served: Business & Consumer
Catalog available online
Advertising/Marketing Budget Related to Direct Marketing: 76-100%
Founded: 1972
Gross sales or billing: $236,000,000

Catalog marketer of electronic parts.

DIGITAL SPEECH SYSTEMS
1241 N Glenville Dr
Richardson, TX 75081-2412
Telephone: (972) 235-2999, FAX: (972) 235-3036, E-Mail: sales@digitalspeech.com, Web Site: www.digitalspeech.com
Pres: Lev Frenkel
Primary Market Served: Business
Catalog available online
Founded: 1983

Voice mail systems.

DIRECT SAT TV LLC
1930 N Poplar St (Ste 21)
Southern Pines, NC 28387-7092
Telephone: (910) 693-3042, Toll Free: (800) 595-4101, FAX: (866) 935-4097, Web Site: www.directsattv.com
Mgr: Steven Baldelli
Primary Market Served: Business & Consumer

DISC MAKERS
150 W 25th St (#402)
New York, NY 10001
Toll Free: (800) 468-9353, Web Site: www.discmakers.com
Pres: Tony Van Veen

DYNAMIC ENGINEERING
150 Dubois St (Suite C)
Santa Cruz, CA 95060-2114
Telephone: (831) 457-8891, FAX: (831) 457-4793, E-Mail: sales@dyneng.com, Web Site: www.dyneng.com
Sls Mgr: Joyce Boncato
Office Mgr, Sls & Mktg Mgr: Dedra Lakely
Conducts Business: Worldwide
Employees: 6
Primary Market Served: Business & Consumer
Catalog available online
Direct online sales
Advertising/Marketing Budget Related to Direct Marketing: 0-25%
Direct Marketing ad budget:
Direct Mail: 20%
Magazines: 60%
Newspapers: 5%
Telephone: 15%
Founded: 1988

Full service engineering & computer company & embedded hardware specialist.

EFSTONSCIENCE INC
1 High Meadow Pl (Unit 5)
Toronto, ON, Canada M9L 0A3
Telephone: (416) 787-4581, Toll Free: (888) 777-5255, FAX: (416) 787-5140, E-Mail: info@escience.ca, Web Site: www.e-sci.com
Pres: Nick Efston
VP, Mktg: Irene Efston
Conducts Business: Canada
Employees: 12
Primary Market Served: Business & Consumer
Catalog available online
Direct online sales
Advertising/Marketing Budget Related to Direct Marketing: 26-50%
Direct Marketing ad budget: $250,000
Direct Mail: 70%
Magazines: 10%
Newspapers: 5%
TV/Radio: 10%
Telephone: 5%
Founded: 1970

Sell today's technology products: optics, specialty tools, electronic instruments, telescopes, microscopes & consumer electronics.

ELECTRONIC ARTS INC
209 Redwood Shores Pkwy
Redwood City, CA 94065-1175
Telephone: (650) 628-1500, Web Site: www.ea.com
Pres & CEO: Andrew Wilson
Primary Market Served: Consumer

Video game maker.

FILMS MEDIA GROUP
An Infobase Learning Company
132 W 31st St (Fl 17)
New York, NY 10001-3406
Toll Free: (800) 322-8755, FAX: (800) 678-3633, E-Mail: custserv@films.com, Web Site: www.films.com
Pres & CEO: Mark McDonnell
Conducts Business: Worldwide
Employees: 50
Primary Market Served: Business
Catalog available online
Direct online sales
Founded: 1981

Educational software, videos, books, posters, CD-ROMs to junior high through college age markets, libraries, prisons, DOD schools, etc.

GBH COMMUNICATIONS
1309 S Myrtle Ave
Monrovia, CA 91016-4150
Telephone: (818) 246-9900, Toll Free: (800) 222-5424, FAX: (818) 246-5850, E-Mail: customerservice@gbh.com, Web Site: www.gbh.com
Pres & CEO: Von Bedikian
Mktg Mgr: Hans Matthes
Mgr: Randy Lee
Primary Market Served: Business
Catalog available online
Direct online sales
Founded: 1986

Wireless headsets, teleconferencing & video conferencing products.

GMG PRODUCTIONS INC
346 Baltustrol Cr
Roslyn, NY 11021
Telephone: (516) 482-0093, FAX: (516) 482-0097, Web Site: www.gmgproductions.com
VP, Sls & Mktg: Arthur Gurtman
Pres: Bernard Gurtman
Employees: 5
Primary Market Served: Business & Consumer
Catalog available online
Indirect online sales
Founded: 1987

Video marketing firm.

GATEWAY INC
7565 Irvine Center Dr
Irvine, CA 92618

Telephone: (949) 471-7000, Toll Free: (800) 369-1409, FAX: (949) 471-7041, Web Site: www.gateway.com
Chmn: Richard D. Snyder
CEO: James E. Coleman
Sr VP & CFO: John P. Goldsberry
Sr VP, Mktg: Bart R. Brown
Sr VP: James R. Burdick
Conducts Business: Worldwide
Employees: 1,700
Primary Market Served: Business & Consumer
Catalog available online
Direct online sales
Advertising/Marketing Budget Related to Direct Marketing: 76-100%
Direct Marketing ad budget:
Magazines: 100%
Gross sales or billing: $3,900,000,000

One of the largest manufacturers of PC's for home & office. Sell a full line of PC's in the U.S. & abroad to large corporations & home users.

GLOBAL COMPUTER CORP

Div. of Systemax
100 Oakland Ave
Port Jefferson, NY 11777
Telephone: (516) 625-4300, Toll Free: (888) 845-6225, FAX: (516) 625-4072, Web Site: www.globalcomputer.com
CEO: Alan Paulus
Conducts Business: U.S., Canada, U.K., France
Employees: 1,000
Primary Market Served: Business
Catalog available online
Direct online sales
Direct Marketing ad budget:
Direct Mail: 90%
Magazines: 5%
Telephone: 5%
Gross sales or billing: $500,000,000

Sell industrial, office & computer products to business & institutional firms. Branch offices in Compton, CA; Suwanee, GA; Addison, IL; France & Scotland

GULF COAST DATA SUPPLY INC

5455 Rowe Trl
Milton, FL 32571-9556
Telephone: (850) 994-7042, Toll Free: (800) 226-DISK, FAX: (850) 479-4441, Web Site: www.gulfdata.com
Pres: Alan Johnson
Primary Market Served: Business & Consumer
Founded: 2003

Authorized media distributor of computer supplies, video & audio supplies, custom forms & 3M media supplies.

HARVARD SQUARE RECORDS

dba LPNOW
PO Box 19517
Austin, TX 78760-9517
Toll Free: (877) 465-7669, E-Mail: LPnow@yahoo.com, Web Site: www.lpnow.com
Pres: Barry D. Mayer
Conducts Business: U.S.
Employees: 1
Primary Market Served: Consumer
Catalog available online
Direct online sales
Advertising/Marketing Budget Related to Direct Marketing: 76-100%
Direct Marketing ad budget:
Online: 100%
Founded: 1985

Sell in print & out-of-print rare LP's to people worldwide. All products are new & unplayed.

HAVE INC

350 Power Ave
Hudson, NY 12534-2448
Telephone: (518) 828-2000, Toll Free: (800) 999-HAVE (4283), FAX: (518) 828-2008, E-Mail: kstein@haveinc.com, Web Site: www.haveinc.com
Pres: Nancy Gordon
Mktg Mgr: Kevin Stein
Conducts Business: Worldwide
Employees: 35
Primary Market Served: Business
Catalog available online
Direct online sales
Advertising/Marketing Budget Related to Direct Marketing: 26-50%
Direct Marketing ad budget:
Direct Mail: 25%
Magazines: 10%
Online: 25%
TV/Radio: 5%
Telephone: 35%
Founded: 1977

Complete Multimedia duplication & replication services including CD-Rom & DVD presentation development, authoring & mastering, CD, DVD & Video Duplication & Replication, packaging and graphic design services, and web-based order fulfillment services. Manufacture of professional audio, video & data cable assemblies & distribution of cable-connected products & blank professional media.

HEAR MUSIC

Subs. of Concord Music Group
100 N Crescent Dr
Beverly Hills, CA 90210
Telephone: (425) 452-5534, E-Mail: gail@hearmusic.com, Web Site: www.hearmusic.com

CEO: Glenn Barros
Conducts Business: U.S.
Primary Market Served: Consumer
Catalog available online
Direct online sales
Founded: 1990

Retail CD & tape store.

HEARTLAND AMERICA

8085 Century Blvd
Chaska, MN 55318
Telephone: (952) 361-3640, Toll Free: (800) 229-2901, FAX: (952) 368-3452, E-Mail: info@heartlandamerica.com, Web Site: www.heartlandamerica.com
CEO: Bruce Brekke
Pres: Mark Platt
VP, Opers & Mfg: Thomas Bulver
Conducts Business: U.S.
Employees: 100
Primary Market Served: Business & Consumer
Catalog available online
Direct online sales
Advertising/Marketing Budget Related to Direct Marketing: 100%
Direct Marketing ad budget: $8,000,000
Direct Mail: 75%
Newspapers: 25%
Founded: 1985
Gross sales or billing: $40,000,000

Auto, cameras, electronics, furniture, tools, housewares, lighting, luggage, phones, sporting goods, TV/VCR, video & stereo.

HOMESPUN TAPES MUSIC INSTRUCTION

dba Homespun Video
PO Box 340
Woodstock, NY 12498-0340
Telephone: (845) 246-2550, Toll Free: (800) 338-2737, FAX: (845) 246-5282, E-Mail: info@homespuntapes.com, Web Site: www.homespuntapes.com
Pres: Harry Traum
VP: Jane Traum
Office Mgr: Susan Robinson
Adv Dept: Scott Steyer
Conducts Business: Worldwide
Employees: 12
Primary Market Served: Business & Consumer
Catalog available online
Direct online sales
Founded: 1967
Gross sales or billing: $1,300,000

Retail Mail order musical instruments. Video & audio tapes to teach people to play musical instruments. Hundreds of tapes of all levels & styles. Wide variety of instruments.

HOOLEON CORP
304 W Denby Ave, PO Box 589
Melrose, NM 88124
Telephone: (575) 253-4503, Toll Free:
(800) 937-1337, E-Mail: sales@
hooleon.com, Web Site: www.
hooleon.com
Pres: Joan Crozier
VP: Robert F. Crozier
Opers: Bill Whitney
Gen Mgr: Barry Green
Conducts Business: Canada, Europe,
Middle East, Far East, S. America,
Mexico
Employees: 14
Primary Market Served: Business &
Consumer
Catalog available online
Direct online sales
Advertising/Marketing Budget Related
to Direct Marketing: 0-25%
Direct Marketing ad budget: $30,000
Direct Mail: 10%
Telephone: 90%
Founded: 1982
Gross sales or billing: $55,000,000

Customized computer keyboard keys,
keyboard covers, labels, templates &
keyboard accessories.

INDIAN HOUSE RECORDS & TAPES
27 Valencia Rd
Taos, NM 87571
Telephone: (575) 776-2953, Toll Free:
(800) 748-0522, FAX: (575) 776-
2804, E-Mail: music@indianhouse.
com, Web Site: www.indianhouse.
com
Owner: Tony Isaacs
Conducts Business: Worldwide
Employees: 1
Primary Market Served: Business &
Consumer
Catalog available online
Direct online sales
Advertising/Marketing Budget Related
to Direct Marketing: 0-25%
Founded: 1966

Catalog marketer of high fidelity recordings of traditional American Indian
music.

INFOSOURCE INC
1300 City View Ctr
Oviedo, FL 32755-5530
Telephone: (407) 796-5200, Toll Free:
(800) 393-4636, FAX: (407) 796-
5190, E-Mail: isisale@howtomaster.
com, Web Site: www.
infosourcelearning.com
CEO: Michael Werner
Pres: Thomas Warrner
Acct Exec Fin & Insurance: Lisa Mc-
Govern

Acct Exec: Chris Niemir
Acct Exec: Dylan Punter
Conducts Business: U.S., United King-
dom
Employees: 105
Primary Market Served: Business
Catalog available online
Direct online sales
Advertising/Marketing Budget Related
to Direct Marketing: 0-25%
Founded: 1983

Training company that develops & sells
computer-based training tutorials, in-
structor-led training materials & skills
assessment software on all of today's
popular PC applications, MCSE certification & A+ certification.

INTER7 INTERNET TECHNOLOGIES INC
219 S Prospect St
Galena, IL 61036-2119
Telephone: (815) 776-9465, Web Site:
www.inter7.com
CFO: Catherine Kouzmanoff
Pres: Ken Jones
Primary Market Served: Business

JDR MICRODEVICES
4101 Dublin Blvd (Suite F120)
Dublin, CA 94568
Telephone: (650) 625-1400, Toll Free:
(800) 538-5000, FAX: (800) 538-
5005, E-Mail: sales@jdr.com, Web
Site: www.jdr.com
Pres & CEO: Jeffrey D. Rose
VP, MIS: Matthew Smith
Mktg Mgr: George Zenos
Conducts Business: Worldwide
Employees: 150
Primary Market Served: Business &
Consumer
Catalog available online
Direct online sales
Advertising/Marketing Budget Related
to Direct Marketing: 76-100%
Direct Marketing ad budget:
Direct Mail: 70%
Newspapers: 10%
TV/Radio: 20%
Founded: 1979
Gross sales or billing: $10,000,000

Manufactures & sells PC related products, including systems, components,
peripherals & software nationally & internationally via direct market & web
advertising.

JAMECO ELECTRONICS
1355 Shoreway Rd
Belmont, CA 94002

Telephone: (650) 592-8097, Toll Free:
(800) 831-4242, FAX: (650) 592-
2503, (800) 237-6948, E-Mail:
domestic@jameco.com, Web Site:
www.jameco.com
CEO: James Farrey
VP Mktg & Sales: Greg Harris
Employees: 100
Primary Market Served: Business &
Consumer
Catalog available online
Direct online sales
Advertising/Marketing Budget Related
to Direct Marketing: 26-50%
Founded: 1974
Gross sales or billing: $14,800,000

Mail order electronic & computer parts
& components.

MARLIN P JONES & ASSOCIATES INC
8380 Resource Rd
West Palm Beach, FL 33404
Telephone: (561) 848-1414, Toll Free:
(800) 652-6733, FAX: (561) 844-
8764, E-Mail: mpja@mpja.com,
Web Site: www.mpja.com
Pres: Marlin P. Jones
VP: David A. Jones
VP: Marlin L. Jones
Conducts Business: U.S.
Employees: 17
Primary Market Served: Business &
Consumer
Catalog available online
Direct online sales
Advertising/Marketing Budget Related
to Direct Marketing: 0-25%
Direct Marketing ad budget:
Direct Mail: 90%
Magazines: 10%
Founded: 1973

Sell electronic parts for industrial, commercial & educational electronics.

LAPLINK SOFTWARE INC
610 108th Ave NE (Suite 610)
Bellevue, WA 98004-5125
Telephone: (425) 952-6000, Toll Free:
(800) 527-5465, FAX: (425) 952-
6002, E-Mail: marketing@laplink.
com, Web Site: www.laplink.com
Sr VP Corp Sls & Bus Devel: Mark
Chestnut
Mktg Mgr: Neil Minetto
Pres: Mark Eppley
CEO: Thomas Koll
Conducts Business: Worldwide
Employees: 90
Primary Market Served: Business &
Consumer
Founded: 1982

Developer of communications & remote access software.

LEARNING SEED

641 W Lake St (#301)
Chicago, IL 60661
Telephone: (847) 540-8855, Toll Free: (800) 634-4941, FAX: (800) 998-0854, E-Mail: info@learningseed.com, Web Site: www.learningseed.com
VP: Kari McCarthy
Primary Market Served: Consumer

Publishes educational videotapes & CD-ROMS

LENOVO

1009 Think Pl
Morrisville, NC 27560-9002
Telephone: (919) 257-6315, Toll Free: (855) 253-6686, Web Site: www.uslenovo.com
Dir Mktg: Ajay Kaul
CEO: Yang Yuanqing

Maker of personal computers

LISTENING LIBRARY INC, RANDOM HOUSE AUDIO

Div. of Random House Audio Publishing Group
1745 Broadway
New York, NY 10019
Telephone: (212) 782-8482, Toll Free: (800) 726-0600, FAX: (212) 940-7381, E-Mail: rhacademic@penguinrandomhouse.com, Web Site: www.randomhouse.com/audio
Pres: Peter Olsen
Conducts Business: U.S., Canada
Employees: 20
Primary Market Served: Consumer
Catalog available online
Indirect online sales
Advertising/Marketing Budget Related to Direct Marketing: 26-50%
Direct Marketing ad budget:
Direct Mail: 100%
Founded: 1956

Audio books - literature based media for children & adults. Sell to schools, libraries, individuals & distributors.

LOCATION SOUND CORP

10639 Riverside Dr
North Hollywood, CA 91602-2355
Telephone: (818) 980-9891, Toll Free: (800) 228-4429, FAX: (818) 980-9911, E-Mail: information@locationsound.com, Web Site: www.locationsound.com
Pres & CEO: David Panfili
Conducts Business: Worldwide
Employees: 50
Primary Market Served: Business
Catalog available online
Indirect online sales
Direct Marketing ad budget:

Direct Mail: 10%
Magazines: 90%
Founded: 1977

Professional audio equipment for film & video production, broadcast & live sound. Consulting, sales, service & rental.

LONG'S ELECTRONICS INC

2630 S Fifth Ave
Irondale, AL 35210-1209
Telephone: (205) 956-6767, Toll Free: (800) 633-3410, FAX: (800) 633-2530, E-Mail: info@longselectronics.com, Web Site: www.longselectronics.com
E-Commerce Dept Mgr: Blanche Beardon
Pres: Roy Long
Conducts Business: U.S.
Employees: 126
Primary Market Served: Business
Catalog available online
Direct online sales
Advertising/Marketing Budget Related to Direct Marketing: 76-100%
Direct Marketing ad budget: $960,000
Direct Mail: 100%
Founded: 1969
Gross sales or billing: $27,500,000

Sell audio-visual equipment & accessories to churches & schools. Major manufacturers: Sony, Panasonic, 3M, Magnavox, Sharp, JVC, Elmo, TEAC, Tascam, Bogen, Shure & Telex.

MRV COMMUNICATIONS

RP-NFOA
20415 Nordhoff St
Chatsworth, CA 91311
Telephone: (818) 773-0900, FAX: (818) 773-0906, Web Site: www.mrv.com
Pres & CEO: Mark J. Bonney
Chmn Bd: Ken Traub
CFO: Stephen Krulik
Employees: 1,450
Primary Market Served: Business & Consumer
Gross sales or billing: $356,000,000

Manufacture computer networking devices.

MARKERTEK VIDEO SUPPLY

Div. of Tower Products Inc
1 Tower Dr, PO Box 397
Saugerties, NY 12477-4386
Telephone: (845) 246-3036, Toll Free: (800) 522-2025, FAX: (845) 246-1757, E-Mail: sales@markertek.com, Web Site: www.markertek.com
VP, Gen Mgr: Erick Krein
Head Mktg Coord: Vince Morano

Pres & CEO: Max Braunstein
Conducts Business: Worldwide
Employees: 110
Primary Market Served: Consumer
Catalog available online
Direct online sales
Gross sales or billing: $18,400,000

Pro Audio-IAV Supplies & Accessories.

MICRO CENTER

4119 Leap Rd
Hilliard, OH 43026
Telephone: (614) 850-3675, Toll Free: (800) 634-3478, FAX: (614) 777-2620, E-Mail: csrs@microcenterorder.com, Web Site: www.microcenter.com
Chmn, Pres & CEO: Richard M. Mershad
COO: Peggy Wolfe
CFO: James Koehler
CIO: Misty Kuamoo
VP, Retail Sls: Robert Demme
Conducts Business: U.S.
Primary Market Served: Business & Consumer
Catalog available online
Direct online sales
Advertising/Marketing Budget Related to Direct Marketing: 0-25%
Direct Marketing ad budget:
Direct Mail: 95%
Magazines: 5%
Founded: 1986

Computers & computer related supplies sold to businesses & consumers.

MICROBIZ CORP

655 Oak Grove Ave (#493)
Menlo Park, CA 94026-0493
Telephone: (702) 749-5353, Toll Free: (800) 726-3282, FAX: (650) 440-4870, E-Mail: info@microbiz.com, Web Site: www.microbiz.com
VP: Dina Puccio
Owner: Craig Aberle
Pres: Kevin Kogler
CFO: Sheri McMillan
Conducts Business: International
Employees: 24
Primary Market Served: Business
Catalog available online
Direct online sales
Advertising/Marketing Budget Related to Direct Marketing: 0-25%
Founded: 1987

MITSUBISHI DIGITAL ELECTRONICS AMERICA INC

RP-NFOA
10833 Valley View St (Suite 300)
Cypress, CA 90630

Telephone: (949) 465-6000, FAX: (949) 859-4770, Web Site: www. mitsubishi-tv.com
Pres & CEO: Masaki Sukuyama
Primary Market Served: Consumer
Catalog available online
Indirect online sales

Manufacture of audio & video equipment.

MOTO FRANCHISE CORP

dba Moto Photo and Portrait Avenue
444 Lake Center Dr
Dayton, OH 45459
Telephone: (937) 291-1900, Toll Free: (800) 733-6686, FAX: (937) 291-2005, E-Mail: expert@motophoto. com, Web Site: www.motophoto. com; www.portraitavenue.com
Pres & CEO: Harry D. Loyle
VP Opers: Ron A. Mohney
Chief Mktg Officer: Jim Brown
VP Franchise Sls: Joseph M. O'Hara
Employees: 52
Primary Market Served: Consumer
Gross sales or billing: $4,600,000

Franchises about 90 photo development stores in nearly 20 US states and the District of Columbia offering one-hour processing and other services such as enlargements and digital reproductions.

MOUNTAIN WEST SUPPLY CO

5116 E Charter Oak
Scottsdale, AZ 85254
Telephone: (602) 971-1200, Toll Free: (800) 528-6169, FAX: (602) 996-5077
Pres: Faye Towns
Intl Opers Mgr: Erlene Lan
Conducts Business: Worldwide
Employees: 10
Primary Market Served: Business & Consumer
Advertising/Marketing Budget Related to Direct Marketing: 76-100%
Direct Marketing ad budget:
Direct Mail: $100,000
Magazines: $10,000
Telephone: $25,000
Gross sales or billing: $1,700,000

One-hundred page direct mail catalog, representing 200 manufacturers & offering security products. Includes burglar & fire alarm systems & supplies, as well as closed circuit television, personal protection products, access control devices, bugging & debugging equipment, intercoms, vacuum systems (built in) & voice stress analysis.

MUSTEK INC

3002 Dow Ave (Suite 210)

Tustin, CA 92780-7234
Telephone: (949) 790-3800, FAX: (949) 788-3670, Web Site: www. mustek.com
CEO: David Kan
Prod & Mktg Mgr: Michael Todd
Acct Mgr: Mel Fouse
Primary Market Served: Business & Consumer
Catalog available online
Indirect online sales
Advertising/Marketing Budget Related to Direct Marketing: 0-25%
Founded: 1988

Scanners & digital cameras.

NESTFAMILY.COM

PO Box 293446
Lewisville, TX 75029
Toll Free: (800) 596-7386, FAX: (972) 629-7181, Web Site: www. nestfamily.com
Pres & CEO: Ernie Frausto
VP: Charles Len
VP: Donna McManus
Primary Market Served: Consumer
Catalog available online
Direct online sales

Family video distribution.

NEW & UNIQUE VIDEOS

Subs. of Crystal Pyramid Inc.
7323 Rondel Ct
San Diego, CA 92119
Telephone: (619) 644-3000, FAX: (619) 644-3001, E-Mail: info@ newuniquevideos.com, Web Site: www.newuniquevideos.com
CEO: Mark Schulze
COO: Patricia Mooney
Conducts Business: U.S., Europe
Employees: 5
Primary Market Served: Business & Consumer
Catalog available online
Indirect online sales
Advertising/Marketing Budget Related to Direct Marketing: 0-25%
Founded: 1981
Gross sales or billing: $500,000

Television shows & home video titles to the general public (via distributors & mail-order marketing). Extensive stock footage, library & custom shots. One-stop video production house.

THE NEWMAN GROUP COMPUTER SERVICES CORP

2577 Newport Rd
Ann Arbor, MI 48103-2274
Telephone: (734) 426-3200, FAX: (734) 426-0777, E-Mail: anewman@ newman.com

Pres: Allan Newman
VP, Mktg: Mark Morton
VP, Messaging Svcs: Anthony J. Comazzi
Treas: Rob Havens
Acct Mgr: Andy Hood
Conducts Business: Worldwide
Employees: 95
Primary Market Served: Business & Consumer
Catalog available online
Indirect online sales
Direct Marketing ad budget: $100,000
Direct Mail: 15%
Telephone: 85%
Founded: 1971

Sell used DEC, HP, Sun and Cisco minicomputers & peripherals.

PBS DISTRIBUTION

2100 Crystal Dr
Arlington, VA 22202
Telephone: (617) 208-0720, Web Site: shoppbs.org
Managing Dir: John Domaschko
Pres & CEO: Paula Kerger
Primary Market Served: Consumer

Online shopping that supports PBS public television

PARTS EXPRESS

725 Pleasant Valley Dr
Springboro, OH 45066-1158
Telephone: (937) 743-3000, Toll Free: (800) 338-0531, FAX: (937) 743-1677, E-Mail: sales@parts-express. com, Web Site: www.partsexpress. com
Pres: Jeffrey Stahl
Primary Market Served: Business & Consumer
Catalog available online
Direct online sales
Founded: 1986

Electronics distributor catalog.

POLYLINE LLC

845 N Church St
Elmhurst, IL 60126
Toll Free: (800) 701-7689, FAX: (630) 834-6800, E-Mail: customerservice@ polylinecorp.com, Web Site: www. polylinecorp.com
Pres: Ed Kaiser
Mktg: Ray Kaiser
Employees: 40
Primary Market Served: Business
Catalog available online
Direct online sales
Advertising/Marketing Budget Related to Direct Marketing: 76-100%
Direct Marketing ad budget:
Direct Mail: 95%
Magazines: 5%
Founded: 1972

Gross sales or billing: $4,700,000

Catalog audio, video & CD production packaging & mailing supply.

PREFERRED COMMUNICATIONS

410 Central Ave
Butner, NC 27509-1916
Telephone: (919) 575-4600, Toll Free: (877) 589-9800, E-Mail: bob. meeker@satstar.com, Web Site: www.satstar.com
Pres & CEO: Bob Meeker
Conducts Business: U.S.
Primary Market Served: Business & Consumer
Founded: 1994

Satellite & GPS communications products and services.

PSION TEKLOGIX INC

2100 Meadowvale Blvd
Mississauga, ON, Canada L5N 719
Telephone: (905) 813-9900, Toll Free: (800) 322-3437, E-Mail: ptinfo@ psion.com, Web Site: www. psionteklogix.com
VP HR: Louise Martin
Pres & CEO: I.D. McElroy
CFO: Bill Jessup
COO: Michael Homer
Conducts Business: Worldwide
Employees: 1,100
Primary Market Served: Business
Catalog available online
Indirect online sales
Founded: 1967
Gross sales or billing: $190,000,000

Manufacturer of hand-held computing products.

RECYCLED SOFTWARE INC

3764 Serenity Trl
Palm Springs, CA 92262-9774
Telephone: (760) 655-5666, Toll Free: (760) 534-5338, FAX: (702) 323-5333, E-Mail: support@ recycledsoftware.com, Web Site: www.recycledsoftware.com
Pres: Diane M. Hathaway
Conducts Business: Worldwide
Employees: 2
Primary Market Served: Business & Consumer
Catalog available online
Direct online sales
Advertising/Marketing Budget Related to Direct Marketing: 0-25%
Direct Marketing ad budget: $6,000
Direct Mail: 50%
Magazines: 50%
Founded: 1992
Gross sales or billing: $170,000

Mail order computer software.

RESUMATE INC

2500 Packard St (Suite 200)
Ann Arbor, MI 48104
Telephone: (734) 429-8510, E-Mail: info@resumate.com, Web Site: www.resumate.com
Pres: C.L. Schaldenbrand
Conducts Business: U.S., Canada
Employees: 5
Primary Market Served: Business
Catalog available online
Direct online sales
Advertising/Marketing Budget Related to Direct Marketing: 76-100%
Direct Marketing ad budget:
Telephone: 100%
Gross sales or billing: $500,000

Sell software for human resource professionals. Several versions include a candidate search & match program; an integrated multiple database for candidate, client & job order searching & matching - both available for networks or single users.

ROSE ELECTRONICS

10707 Stancliff Rd
Houston, TX 77099
Telephone: (281) 933-7673, Toll Free: (800) 333-9343, FAX: (281) 933-0044, E-Mail: sales@rose.com, Web Site: www.rose.com
Partner: Peter Macourek
Partner: David Rahvar
VP, Mktg: Sande Olson
VP, Mktg: Brenda Munson
Primary Market Served: Business & Consumer
Catalog available online
Indirect online sales

Computer peripherals, printers and data switches.

SF GLOBAL SOURCING INC

3626 Geary Blvd
San Francisco, CA 94118
Telephone: (415) 288-9400, Toll Free: (800) 545-5865, FAX: (415) 288-9410, E-Mail: selfservice@sfvideo. com, Web Site: www.sfvideo.com
CEO: Dawn Tognoli
Pres: Steven Feinberg
Exec VP: Michael Brandon
VP: Stan Feinberg
Conducts Business: Canada, Israel
Employees: 10
Primary Market Served: Business
Catalog available online
Direct online sales
Founded: 1990

SEASTROM MANUFACTURING CO INC

456 Seastrom St
Twin Falls, ID 83301

Telephone: (208) 737-4300, Toll Free: (800) 634-2356, FAX: (208) 734-7222, E-Mail: info@seastrom-mfg. com, Web Site: www.seastrom-mfg. com
Pres: Robert A. Seastrom
Dir: Diane Mueke
Catalog available online
Direct online sales
Gross sales or billing: $7,000,000

Manufacture electronic parts & brackets.

SHAPE LLC

2105 Corporate Dr
Addison, IL 60101
Telephone: (630) 620-8394, Toll Free: (800) 367-5811, FAX: (630) 620-0784, E-Mail: sales@shapellc.com, Web Site: www.shapellc.com
Pres: Ted Maka
Sls: Scott Wood
Primary Market Served: Business & Consumer

Manufacture OEM electrical transformers.

SOFTWARE AG USA

Div. of Software AG
11700 Plaza America Dr (Suite 700)
Reston, VA 20190
Telephone: (703) 860-5050, Toll Free: (877) 724-4965, FAX: (703) 391-6975, E-Mail: sales@softwareagusa. com, Web Site: www.softwareagusa. com
CEO: Karl-Heinz Streibich
Primary Market Served: Business

Enterprise software company.

SOFTWARE ASSISTANCE INTERNATIONAL LTD

85 Moraine Rd
Morris Plains, NJ 07950
Telephone: (973) 285-1400, FAX: (201) 539-3253
Mgr: John Smith
Primary Market Served: Business & Consumer

Market electronic commerce hybrid solutions that run on CD ROM & the Internet.

SONY CREATIVE SOFTWARE

8215 Greenway Blvd (Suite 400)
Middleton, WI 53562-3685
Telephone: (608) 256-3133
VP Mktg: David Chaimson

SONY DADC

1800 N Fruitridge Ave
Terre Haute, IN 47804

Telephone: (812) 462-8100, Web Site:
www.sonydadc.com
Dir Bus Devel: John MacDonald

SPRINT CORP

6391 Sprint Pkwy
Overland Park, KS 66251-4300
Telephone: (703) 433-4000, Web Site:
www.sprint.com
CEO: Marcelo Claure
Primary Market Served: Business

Wireless communication products.

THE SUPPLIES GUYS

268 Greenwood Ave
Midland Park, NJ 07432-1445
Telephone: (201) 493-8433, Web Site:
www.suppliesguys.com
Primary Market Served: Consumer

Sells computer ink, toner & printers

TWL KNOWLEDGE GROUP

Div. of Trinity Workplace Learning
4101 International Pkwy
Carrollton, TX 75007
Telephone: (972) 309-4000, Toll Free:
(800) 624-2272, FAX: (972) 309-
5105, Web Site: www.twlk.com
CEO: Dennis J. Cagan
CFO & COO: Pat Quinn
VP & CIO: Andrew Lechner
Sr VP & CMO: Thomas E. Morris
Exec VP: Douglas D. Cole
Primary Market Served: Business
Catalog available online
Advertising/Marketing Budget Related
to Direct Marketing: 0-25%
Founded: 1986
Gross sales or billing: $43,000,000

TIGERDIRECT.CA

Div. of Systemax
55 E Beaver Creek Rd (Unit G)
Richmond Hill, ON, Canada L4B 1E5
Toll Free: (800) 800-8300, (888) 771-
9999, FAX: (905) 482-3134, Web
Site: www.tigerdirect.ca
VP & Gen Mgr: Frank Pacione
Conducts Business: Canada
Employees: 23
Primary Market Served: Business &
Consumer
Catalog available online
Direct online sales
Advertising/Marketing Budget Related
to Direct Marketing: 76-100%
Direct Marketing ad budget: $950,000
Direct Mail: 95%
Magazines: 5%
Gross sales or billing: $11,000,000

Trade in computer supplies & accessories, networking & data communications products.

TIGERDIRECT INC

Subs. of Systemax Inc
1940 E Mariposa Ave
El Segundo, CA 90245
Telephone: (305) 415-2199, Toll Free:
(800) 800-8300, FAX: (305) 415-
2202, Web Site: biz.tigerdirect.com
Chmn & CEO: Richard Leeds
Vice Chmn: Bruce Leeds
Vice Chmn: Robert Leeds
Conducts Business: Worldwide
Employees: 140
Primary Market Served: Business
Catalog available online
Direct online sales
Advertising/Marketing Budget Related
to Direct Marketing: 0-25%
Direct Marketing ad budget:
Direct Mail: 20%
Online: 15%
Telephone: 65%
Founded: 1978

Catalog marketer of computer supplies
& accessories.

TUCKER ELECTRONICS CO

1717 Reserve St
Garland, TX 75042
Telephone: (214) 348-8800, Toll Free:
(887) 667-6044, FAX: (214) 348-
0367, E-Mail: sales@tucker.com,
Web Site: www.tucker.com
Pres: James Tucker
Dir: Duanne Harvey
Adv Mgr: Lynn Cage
Conducts Business: Worldwide
Employees: 65
Primary Market Served: Business &
Consumer
Catalog available online
Direct online sales
Advertising/Marketing Budget Related
to Direct Marketing: 76-100%
Direct Marketing ad budget:
$1,000,000
Direct Mail: 100%
Founded: 1967
Gross sales or billing: $13,000,000

Sells new & re-conditioned electronic
test equipment to businesses, schools &
individuals. Authorized Tektronics distributor.

UNIVERSAL STUDIOS INC

Subs. of NBCUniversal
100 Universal City (Plz #3)
Universal City, CA 91608-1138
Telephone: (818) 777-1000, FAX:
(818) 866-3330, Web Site: www.
universalstudios.com
CEO: Stephen B. Burke
Primary Market Served: Business &
Consumer

Film studio.

VCOM INTERNATIONAL MULTI-MEDIA CORP

55 Ruta Ct, PO Box 3171
South Hackensack, NJ 07606
Telephone: (201) 229-9800, Toll Free:
(800) 572-6373, FAX: (973) 439-
1522, E-Mail: info@vcomimc.com,
Web Site: www.vcomimc.com
Pres: Sheldon Goldstein
Branch Mgr: Brian Gluck
VP: Vincent Bruno
Conducts Business: U.S., Canada
Employees: 30
Primary Market Served: Business &
Consumer
Founded: 1963

Video, audio & audio/visual presentation equipment.

VERIZON COMMUNICATIONS INC

140 West St LBBY 1
New York, NY 10013
Telephone: (212) 395-1000, Toll Free:
(800) 621-9900, FAX: (212) 571-
1897, Web Site: www.verizon.com
Chmn Bd & CEO: Lowell C. McAdam
Employees: 242,000
Primary Market Served: Business &
Consumer
Catalog available online
Direct online sales
Founded: 1983
Gross sales or billing: $6,100,000,000

VIDEO ARTISTS INTERNATIONAL

109 Wheeler Ave
Pleasantville, NY 10570
Telephone: (914) 769-3691, Toll Free:
(800) 477-7146, FAX: (914) 769-
5407, E-Mail: orders@vaimusic.com,
Web Site: www.vaimusic.com
Pres: Ernest Gilbert
Gen Mgr: Edward Cardona
Prod Devel Mgr: Allan Altman
Mgr, Sls: Foster Grimm
Conducts Business: Worldwide
Employees: 8
Primary Market Served: Business &
Consumer
Catalog available online
Direct online sales
Advertising/Marketing Budget Related
to Direct Marketing: 0-25%
Direct Marketing ad budget: $10,000
Magazines: 100%
Founded: 1983

Video Artists produces, manufactures
and distributes DVDs for the home video market focusing on classical music
performances of orchestral, instrumen-
tal, opera and dance. VAI also produces
and distributes compact discs of classical music.

VILLAGE SOFTWARE INC

76 Summer St (Suite 600)
Boston, MA 02110-1267
Telephone: (617) 695-9332, Toll Free:
    (800) 724-9332, FAX: (617) 695-
    1935, E-Mail: requests@villagesoft.
    com, Web Site: www.villagesoft.com
Mktg Mgr: Eric Talbot
Pres: Keith Mackay
Conducts Business: U.S., Canada, Eu-
    rope, Far East
Primary Market Served: Business &
    Consumer
Catalog available online
Direct online sales
Advertising/Marketing Budget Related
    to Direct Marketing: 76-100%
Direct Marketing ad budget:
Direct Mail: 65%
Magazines: 20%
Telephone: 15%
Founded: 1991

Microsoft Excel, Lotus 1-2-3 & Quatro
Pro spreadsheet add-ons as well as Microsoft Office, Lotus Smart-Suite &
Perfect Office add-ons, solving most
common business problems for small
businesses & individuals.

WARNER BROS

Div. of Time-Warner
4000 Warner Blvd
Burbank, CA 91522-0001
Telephone: (818) 954-6000, Web Site:
    www.warnerbros.com
Chmn Bd & CEO: Kevin Tsujihara
Conducts Business: U.S.
Primary Market Served: Consumer
Advertising/Marketing Budget Related
    to Direct Marketing: 0-25%
Founded: 1923
Gross sales or billing: $11,850,000,000

Distributes videos, DVDs, apparel &
gifts.

ZONES INC

1102 15th St SW (Suite 102)
Auburn, WA 98001-6509
Telephone: (253) 205-3000, Toll Free:
    (800) 408-9663, FAX: (425) 430-
    3626, E-Mail: corpsales@zones.com,
    Web Site: www.zones.com
Pres & CEO: Firoz Lalji
Pres & COO: Christina Corley
Exec VP Sls: Sean Hobday
Exec VP Bus Devel: Tom Ducatelli
Sr VP & CFO: Ronald McFadden
Primary Market Served: Business
Catalog available online
Direct online sales

Hardware, software & services provider for small to medium businesses.

ATLANTIC SPICE CO

2 Shore Rd
North Truro, MA 02652
Telephone: (508) 487-6100, Toll Free:
(800) 316-7965, FAX: (508) 487-
2550, E-Mail: weborders@
atlanticspice.com, Web Site: www.
atlanticspice.com
Owner & Pres: Mark Irving
Conducts Business: U.S.
Employees: 8
Primary Market Served: Business &
Consumer
Catalog available online
Direct online sales
Advertising/Marketing Budget Related
to Direct Marketing: 0-25%
Founded: 1994
Gross sales or billing: $1,000,000

Bulk herbs, spices, teas & potpourri ingredients.

BELUGA BAR BY
CAVIARTERIA

75 Murray St
New York, NY 10007
Telephone: (212) 759-7410, Toll Free:
(800) 422-8427, FAX: (212) 750-
0358, E-Mail: info@caviarteria.com,
Web Site: www.caviarteria.com
Owner: Walter Drobenko
Conducts Business: U.S., S. America,
Asia, EEC
Primary Market Served: Business &
Consumer
Catalog available online
Indirect online sales
Advertising/Marketing Budget Related
to Direct Marketing: 26-50%
Direct Marketing ad budget:
Direct Mail: 40%
Magazines: 25%
Newspapers: 25%
TV/Radio: 10%
Founded: 1950

Russian & American Caviar, smoked
Scottish salmon, French Foie Gras -
gourmet specialty foods & accessories.

RC BIGELOW INC

201 Black Rock Tpke
Fairfield, CT 06825-5512
Telephone: (203) 334-1212, Web Site:
www.bigelowtea.com
Direct Mktg Mgr: Renee Walker
Employees: 330
Primary Market Served: Consumer
Catalog available online
Direct online sales
Advertising/Marketing Budget Related
to Direct Marketing: 26-50%
Founded: 1945

BISSINGER FRENCH
CONFECTIONS

1600 N Broadway
Saint Louis, MO 63102
Telephone: (314) 615-2436, Toll Free:
(800) 325-8881, Web Site: www.
bissingers.com
CEO & Pres: Tim Fogerty
Conducts Business: U.S.
Employees: 55
Primary Market Served: Business &
Consumer
Catalog available online
Direct online sales
Advertising/Marketing Budget Related
to Direct Marketing: 51-75%
Founded: 1668

Manufacture & sell gourmet confections through direct mail catalog, retail
stores & website.

BLAND FARMS

1126 Raymond Bland Rd
Glennville, GA 30427
Telephone: (912) 654-1300, Web Site:
www.blandfarms.com
CFO & Gen Mgr: Michael Hively
Dir Sls & Mktg: Richard Pazderski
Conducts Business: U.S.
Primary Market Served: Business &
Consumer
Catalog available online
Indirect online sales
Founded: 1982

Vidalia sweet onions, by-products,
cakes, pies, candies, meats, frozen Vidalia bits & southern produce.

BOCA JAVA

200 S Biscayne Blvd Ste 1818
Miami, FL 33131-2329
Telephone: (954) 949-2010, Toll Free:
(888) 262-2528, Web Site: www.
bocajava.com
Pres: Kevin Holbrook

BRAND NEW PRODUCTS
LLC

2503 N Clark St (#280)
Chicago, IL 60614
Telephone: (773) 486-8813, Web Site:
www.brandnewllc.com
Owner: Steven Faso
Primary Market Served: Business &
Consumer

Confections

BROWN & JENKINS
TRADING CO

3929 Vermont Rt 15
Jeffersonville, VT 05464

Telephone: (802) 644-8300, Toll Free:
(800) 456-JAVA, Web Site: www.
brownjenkins.com
Pres: Jay Michaud
Conducts Business: U.S.
Employees: 4
Primary Market Served: Consumer
Catalog available online
Direct online sales
Advertising/Marketing Budget Related
to Direct Marketing: 76-100%
Direct Marketing ad budget:
Direct Mail: 100%
Founded: 1984
Gross sales or billing: $5,000,000

Gourmet coffees.

BURGER'S OZARK
COUNTRY CURED HAMS
INC

32819 Hwy 87
California, MO 65018
Telephone: (573) 796-4111, Toll Free:
(800) 345-5185, FAX: (573) 796-
3137, E-Mail: burgers@smokehouse.
com, Web Site: www.smokehouse.
com
Pres: Steve Burger
Conducts Business: U.S.
Employees: 250
Primary Market Served: Business &
Consumer
Catalog available online
Direct online sales
Advertising/Marketing Budget Related
to Direct Marketing: 51-75%
Direct Marketing ad budget:
Direct Mail: 95%
Magazines: 3%
TV/Radio: 2%
Founded: 1952

Smoked meats, primarily country cured
hams via direct mail, food services, distributors & warehouses.

BYRON PLANTATION

Div. of Holland Investments Inc
500 Atlantic Ave
Vidalia, GA 30474-3705
Toll Free: (800) 356-0171, FAX: (912)
538-8043, E-Mail: greenlinebyron@
bellsouth.net, Web Site: www.
byronplantation.com
Pres, Owner: Mike Holland
Conducts Business: U.S., Europe, Can-
ada
Employees: 4
Primary Market Served: Business &
Consumer
Catalog available online
Direct online sales
Advertising/Marketing Budget Related
to Direct Marketing: 76-100%

Direct Marketing ad budget:
Direct Mail: $50,000
Magazines: $30,000
Gross sales or billing: $500,000

Specializes in Southern gourmet foods, both fresh & processed, packaged for gifts & home use.

CARVEL CORP

5620 Glenridge Dr NE
Atlanta, GA 30342
Telephone: (404) 255-3250, Toll Free: (800) 227-8353, FAX: (404) 255-4978, Web Site: www.carvel.com
Pres: Scott Colwell
Conducts Business: U.S.
Employees: 599
Primary Market Served: Business & Consumer
Advertising/Marketing Budget Related to Direct Marketing: 0-25%
Direct Marketing ad budget: $7,000,000
Direct Mail: 20%
TV/Radio: 80%
Founded: 1936
Gross sales or billing: $181,200,000

Ice cream - both soft-serve ice cream fountain & bakery style desserts, (ice cream cakes & novelties). Sold through retail outlets & via direct response.

CHECKMARK COMMUNICATIONS

Div. of Nestle Purina
1111 Chouteau Ave
Saint Louis, MO 63102-1025
Telephone: (314) 982-1000, FAX: (314) 982-3580, Web Site: www.purina.com
VP & Gen Mgr: Gordon Wade

In-house creative content communications agency of Nestle Purina PetCare.

COLLIN STREET BAKERY

401 W Seventh Ave
Corsicana, TX 75110-6362
Toll Free: (800) 292-7400, Web Site: www.collinstreetbakery.com
Pres: Bob McNutt
Conducts Business: Worldwide
Employees: 60
Primary Market Served: Business & Consumer
Catalog available online
Direct online sales
Advertising/Marketing Budget Related to Direct Marketing: 76-100%
Direct Marketing ad budget: $300,000
Founded: 1896
Gross sales or billing: $30,000,000

Sells the Deluxe Fruitcake through catalog sales.

COMMUNITY COFFEE CO

3332 Partridge Ln (Bldg A)
Baton Rouge, LA 70809-2413
Telephone: (225) 291-3900, Toll Free: (800) 884-5282, FAX: (800) 643-8199, E-Mail: customerservice@communitycoffee.com, Web Site: www.communitycoffee.com
Pres & CEO: David Belanger
Conducts Business: U.S.
Employees: 30
Primary Market Served: Business & Consumer
Catalog available online
Direct online sales

Sell coffees, teas & other gourmet food items.

CORONA-LOTUS INC

Subs. of Gourmet Center
50 Francisco St
San Francisco, CA 94133-2107
Telephone: (415) 956-8956, Toll Free: (800) 422-2924, FAX: (415) 956-4922, E-Mail: customerservice@biscoff.com, Web Site: www.biscoff.com
Pres: Michael McGuire
Conducts Business: U.S.
Employees: 20
Primary Market Served: Business & Consumer
Catalog available online
Direct online sales
Advertising/Marketing Budget Related to Direct Marketing: 76-100%
Direct Marketing ad budget: $100,000
Direct Mail: 100%
Founded: 1990
Gross sales or billing: $3,000,000

Sell imported gourmet cookies - individually wrapped in tins & gift boxes - via catalog.

CRABTREE & EVELYN LTD

777 Post Rd E
Westport, CT 06880
Telephone: (860) 928-2761, Toll Free: (800) CRABTREE, FAX: (860) 928-1296, Web Site: www.crabtree-evelyn.com
Pres: Robert E. Crabtree
Conducts Business: U.S.
Employees: 150
Primary Market Served: Consumer
Catalog available online
Direct online sales
Founded: 1972
Gross sales or billing: $100,000,000

Sell imported toiletries & gourmet foods from England, France & Switzerland.

CUBA CHEESE SHOPPE

53 Genesee St
Cuba, NY 14727-1199
Telephone: (585) 968-3949, FAX: (716) 968-1746, Web Site: www.cubacheese.com
Pres & Owner: Jeff Bradley
Primary Market Served: Business & Consumer
Catalog available online
Direct online sales
Gross sales or billing: $1,000,000

Retail & wholesale cheese products; NY state cheddar cheese.

CUSHMAN FRUIT CO INC

1884 Indian Rd W
West Palm Beach, FL 33406
Telephone: (561) 965-3535, Toll Free: (800) 776-2295, FAX: (800) 776-4329, E-Mail: info@honeybell.com, Web Site: www.honeybell.com
Pres: Michael Cushman
Conducts Business: U.S. & Canada
Employees: 50
Primary Market Served: Business & Consumer
Catalog available online
Direct online sales
Advertising/Marketing Budget Related to Direct Marketing: 76-100%
Direct Marketing ad budget: $500,000
Direct Mail: 75%
Newspapers: 24%
Online: 1%
Founded: 1945

Citrus gifts.

CUVAISON INC

1221 Duhig Rd
Napa, CA 94559
Telephone: (707) 942-2455, E-Mail: info@cuvaison.com, Web Site: www.cuvaison.com
Pres: Jay Schuppert
CFO: Bonnie Britton Schoch
Dir Retail Opers: Mary Pencek
Mgr Tasting Room: Jean Varner
Assoc Winemaker: Todd Heth
Primary Market Served: Business & Consumer
Catalog available online
Direct online sales

Winery.

DS SERVICES OF NORTH AMERICA LP

200 Eagles Blvd
Lakeland, FL 33810
Telephone: (770) 933-1400, Toll Free: (800) 669-3402, FAX: (770) 956-9495, E-Mail: customerservice@water.com, Web Site: www.water.com

VP, Mktg: Joseph Silva
CEO: Jerry Fowden
Primary Market Served: Business &
Consumer
Founded: 1985

Manufacturer & distributor of bottled water.

DAKIN FARM

5797 Rte 7
Ferrisburgh, VT 05456-9798
Telephone: (802) 425-3971, Toll Free:
(800) 993-2546, FAX: (802) 425-
2765, E-Mail: scutting@dakinfarm.
com, Web Site: www.dakinfarm.com
Pres: Sam Cutting IV
Mktg Exec: Sue Downing
Conducts Business: U.S.
Employees: 50
Primary Market Served: Business &
Consumer
Catalog available online
Indirect online sales
Advertising/Marketing Budget Related
to Direct Marketing: 76-100%
Direct Marketing ad budget: $340,000
Direct Mail: $225,000
Magazines: $10,000
Newspapers: $30,000
Online: $65,000
TV/Radio: $20,000
Founded: 1960
Gross sales or billing: $5,000,000

Vermont specialty foods: cob-smoked meats, aged Vermont cheddar cheese & pure Vermont maple syrup.

DEAN & DELUCA BRANDS INC

2526 E 36th Cir N
Wichita, KS 67219-2300
Telephone: (316) 683-1255, Web Site:
www.deandeluca.com
CEO: Mark Daley
Primary Market Served: Consumer

DECKO PRODUCTS INC

2105 Superior St
Sandusky, OH 44870
Telephone: (419) 626-5757, FAX:
(419) 626-3135, Web Site: www.
decko.com
Owner: W.F. Niggemeyer
Conducts Business: U.S., Canada
Employees: 70
Primary Market Served: Business &
Consumer
Gross sales or billing: $5,000,000

Manufacturer of candy cake decorations & lay-ons for candy manufacturing.

DELICIOUS ORCHARDS

320 Rte 34

Colts Neck, NJ 07722-2430
Telephone: (732) 462-1989, FAX:
(732) 409-4993, E-Mail: info@
deliciousorchardsnj.com, Web Site:
www.deliciousorchardsnjonline.com
Owner: Chris McDonald
Pres: William McDonald
Conducts Business: U.S.
Employees: 300
Primary Market Served: Consumer
Founded: 1911
Gross sales or billing: $16,500,000

Catalog marketer of quality fruit baskets & bakery products.

DINEWISE

500 Bi-County Blvd (Suite 400)
Farmingdale, NY 11735-3996
Telephone: (631) 694-1111, Toll Free:
(800) 749-1170, FAX: (631) 694-
4064, E-Mail: info@dinewise.com,
Web Site: www.dinewise.com
Chmn, Pres & CEO: Paul Roman
VP & CFO: Thomas McNeil
Conducts Business: U.S.
Primary Market Served: Business &
Consumer
Catalog available online
Founded: 1959

Marketer & distributor of fully prepared gourmet & nutritional meals.

DUCKTRAP RIVER FISH FARM

57 Little River Dr
Belfast, ME 04915
Telephone: (207) 338-6280, Toll Free:
(800) 828-3825, FAX: (207) 338-
6288, E-Mail: smoked@ducktrap.
com, Web Site: www.ducktrap.com
CEO: Rafaeo Puga
Employees: 150
Primary Market Served: Business &
Consumer
Catalog available online
Direct online sales
Advertising/Marketing Budget Related
to Direct Marketing: 76-100%
Founded: 1979

Gourmet smoked seafood.

S WALLACE EDWARDS & SONS INC

PO Box 25
Surry, VA 23883-0025
Telephone: (757) 294-3121, Toll Free:
(800) 290-9213, FAX: (757) 294-
5378, E-Mail: info@
virginiatraditions.com, Web Site:
www.virginiatraditions.com
Pres: Samuel W. Edwards III
Primary Market Served: Consumer

Founded: 1926

Sell specialty meats, Virginia seafood, smoked poultry & desserts.

EICHTEN'S HIDDEN ACRES

16809 310th St, PO Box 216
Center City, MN 55012
Telephone: (651) 257-4752, FAX:
(651) 257-6286, E-Mail: eichtens@
frontiernet.net, Web Site: www.
specialtycheese.com
Mng: Tammy Stephens
Conducts Business: U.S.
Employees: 7
Primary Market Served: Business &
Consumer
Catalog available online
Direct online sales
Advertising/Marketing Budget Related
to Direct Marketing: 0-25%
Founded: 1976

Producers of European style cheeses & American Bison. Retail & wholesale gift packages containing cheese & bison to the general public, grocery stores, co-ops & farm markets.

EILENBERGER'S BAKERY INC

512 N John St
Palestine, TX 75801-2725
Telephone: (903) 729-2176, Toll Free:
(800) 831-2544, FAX: (903) 723-
2915, Web Site: www.
eilenbergerbakery.com
Pres: Terresa Smith
Co-Owner: Stephen Smith
Conducts Business: Worldwide
Employees: 70
Primary Market Served: Business &
Consumer
Catalog available online
Direct online sales
Advertising/Marketing Budget Related
to Direct Marketing: 26-50%
Founded: 1898
Gross sales or billing: $4,000,000

Mail order of fruit cake, pecan apple cake, pecan apricot cake & Texas fudge pecan pie.

EMPIRE COFFEE & TEA CO

568 9th Ave Frnt 1
New York, NY 10036-3726
Telephone: (212) 268-1220, Toll Free:
(800) 262-5908, E-Mail: owners@
empirecoffeetea.com, Web Site:
www.empirecoffeetea.com
Owner: Paul Shaytin
Conducts Business: U.S.
Primary Market Served: Business &
Consumer
Catalog available online
Direct online sales

Founded: 1908

Retailer of gourmet coffee & tea. Appliances & accessories available.

ETHEL M CHOCOLATES INC

Div. of M&M/Mars
1 Sunset Way
Henderson, NV 89014
Telephone: (702) 435-2655, Toll Free: (800) 471-0352, FAX: (702) 451-8379, E-Mail: chocolatier@ethelm.com, Web Site: www.ethelm.com
Pres: Dagner Musilova
Conducts Business: U.S.
Employees: 450
Primary Market Served: Business & Consumer
Catalog available online
Direct online sales
Founded: 1981

Fine boxed chocolate confections.

THE FX MATT BREWING CO

830 Varick St
Utica, NY 13502-4001
Telephone: (315) 624-2400, Toll Free: (800) 765-6288, FAX: (315) 624-2401, E-Mail: info@saranac.com, Web Site: www.saranac.com
CEO: Nicolas O. Matt
Conducts Business: U.S.
Employees: 150
Primary Market Served: Business
Founded: 1888

Brewers.

FAIRYTALE BROWNIES

4610 E Cotton Center Blvd (Suite 100)
Phoenix, AZ 85040-8898
Toll Free: (800) 324-7982, FAX: (602) 489-5133, E-Mail: service@brownies.com, Web Site: www.brownies.com
Co-Owner, Sls & Mktg Team Leader: Eileen Spitalny
Corp Sls: Brandie Davenport
VP: David Kravetz
Conducts Business: Worldwide
Employees: 26
Primary Market Served: Business & Consumer
Catalog available online
Direct online sales
Advertising/Marketing Budget Related to Direct Marketing: 51-75%
Direct Marketing ad budget: $13,000
Direct Mail: 80%
Online: 20%
Founded: 1992
Gross sales or billing: $7,800,000

Mail order gourmet Belgian chocolate brownie gifts.

FERRARA BAKERY & CAFE INC

195 Grand St
New York, NY 10013
Telephone: (212) 226-6150, FAX: (212) 226-0667, E-Mail: information@ferraracafe.com, Web Site: www.ferraracafe.com
Pres & CEO: Peter Lepore
Conducts Business: U.S., Canada, Italy
Employees: 110
Primary Market Served: Business & Consumer
Catalog available online
Direct online sales
Founded: 1892

Mail order & retail outlets for Italian specialty foods & confections.

FIGI'S INC

Subs. of Fingerhut Corp
3200 S Central Ave
Marshfield, WI 54404-2000
Telephone: (715) 387-1771, Toll Free: (800) 422-3444, FAX: (715) 384-1129, Web Site: www.figis.com
Pres: Jim Krueger
Conducts Business: U.S.
Employees: 150
Primary Market Served: Business & Consumer
Catalog available online
Direct online sales
Founded: 2005
Gross sales or billing: $24,800,000

Produce seasonal mail order catalogs featuring decorative gift packages of aged cheeses, sausages, smoked meats, nuts, cookies, jams & other gift ideas.

FIORELLA'S JACK STACK BARBECUE

13441 Holmes Rd
Kansas City, MO 64145
Telephone: (816) 942-9141, Web Site: www.jackstackbbq.com
Gen Mgr: Storme Blakenship
Conducts Business: U.S.
Primary Market Served: Consumer
Founded: 1957

Restaurateur & caterer of Kansas City barbecue.

FOWLER'S CHOCOLATES INC

100 River Rock Dr (Suite 102)
Buffalo, NY 14207-2163
Telephone: (716) 877-9983, Toll Free: (800) 824-2263, FAX: (716) 877-9959, E-Mail: customerservice@fowlerschocolates.com, Web Site: www.fowlerschocolates.com
Pres & Owner: Ted Marks
Conducts Business: U.S.

Employees: 19
Primary Market Served: Business
Catalog available online
Direct online sales
Founded: 1910

Manufacturer & distributor of chocolates & related products.

GODIVA CHOCOLATIER

333 W 34th St Fl 6
New York, NY 10001-2566
Telephone: (212) 984-5900, Toll Free: (800) 946-3482, Web Site: www.godiva.com
Sr VP: Ed Jankowski
CEO: Mohamed Elsarky
Primary Market Served: Consumer

GOLDEN BISON LLC

dba Highplains Bison
1395 S Platte River Dr
Denver, CO 80223-3467
Telephone: (303) 962-0018, Web Site: www.highplainsbison.com
Pres: Jonathan Harding
Primary Market Served: Consumer
Founded: 1987

GOLDEN TROPHY

Div. of The Bruss Co
3548 N Kostner Ave
Chicago, IL 60641
Telephone: (773) 282-2900, Toll Free: (800) 821-3882, FAX: (800) 835-6601, E-Mail: goldentrophy@bruss.com, Web Site: www.giftsteaksonline.com
Sr VP, Beef Production Opers: Dan Brook
Mng: Mona Manning
Sr VP, Beef Margin Mngmt: Chris Daniel
Conducts Business: U.S.
Primary Market Served: Business & Consumer
Catalog available online
Direct online sales
Advertising/Marketing Budget Related to Direct Marketing: 51-75%
Direct Marketing ad budget:
Direct Mail: 80%
Magazines: 10%
Telephone: 10%
Founded: 1975

Supplier of gourmet cuisine for gifts & incentives.

GRANDMA BROWN'S BEANS INC

5837 Scenic Ave
Mexico, NY 13114
Telephone: (315) 963-7221, FAX: (315) 963-4072
Pres: Sandra L. Brown

Conducts Business: U.S.
Employees: 15
Primary Market Served: Business &
   Consumer
Advertising/Marketing Budget Related
   to Direct Marketing: 0-25%
Founded: 1938

Canned food specialties, including
baked beans & soups, sold to wholesale
& retail accounts as well as to individual consumers.

GREEN MOUNTAIN COFFEE ROASTERS, INC
33 Coffee Ln
Waterbury, VT 05676
Telephone: (802) 244-5621, Toll Free:
   (800) 545-2326, FAX: (802) 244-
   5436, Web Site: www.gmcr.com
CEO: Brian P. Kelley
Conducts Business: U.S.
Employees: 849
Primary Market Served: Business &
   Consumer
Catalog available online
Direct online sales
Advertising/Marketing Budget Related
   to Direct Marketing: 0-25%
Founded: 1981
Gross sales or billing: $342,000,000

Manufacture & sell gourmet coffees.

HADLEY FRUIT ORCHARDS INC
47993 Seminole Dr
Cabazon, CA 92230
Telephone: (951) 849-5255, FAX:
   (951) 849-5255, Web Site: www.
   hadleys.com
Pres: Gerald Bench
Conducts Business: Worldwide
Employees: 86
Primary Market Served: Business &
   Consumer
Catalog available online
Direct online sales
Advertising/Marketing Budget Related
   to Direct Marketing: 26-50%
Founded: 1931
Gross sales or billing: $16,800,000

Sell dried fruit, nuts, dates, honey, vitamins, natural foods & gifts. Offer a
complete mail order catalog featuring a
wide range of products. Also operate
retail stores. 800 # available Mon.-Fri.
8:00 AM - 4:40 PM.

HARMAN'S CHEESE & COUNTRY STORE INC
1400 Rte 117
Sugar Hill, NH 03586
Telephone: (603) 823-8000, E-Mail:
   cheese@harmanscheese.com, Web
   Site: www.HarmansCheese.com

Owner & Pres: Maxine Aldrich
Mgr & Owner: Brenda Aldrich
Conducts Business: U.S.
Employees: 5
Primary Market Served: Business &
   Consumer
Catalog available online
Advertising/Marketing Budget Related
   to Direct Marketing: 0-25%
Direct Marketing ad budget: $20,000
Direct Mail: 30%
Magazines: 10%
Newspapers: 20%
Founded: 1955
Gross sales or billing: $300,000

Retail mail order of aged cheddar (over
2 years), maple products, preserves,
condiments & gourmet food items.

HARRINGTON'S OF VERMONT INC
210 E Main St
Richmond, VT 05477-7721
Telephone: (802) 434-4444, E-Mail:
   info@harringtonham.com, Web Site:
   www.harringtonham.com
COO: R.B. Klinkenberg
DM Mgr: Carol Wisley
Conducts Business: U.S.
Employees: 50
Primary Market Served: Consumer
Catalog available online
Direct online sales
Founded: 1873
Gross sales or billing: $16,600,000

Sell specialty foods & smoked meats
through direct mail & retail shops.

HARRY & DAVID HOLDINGS INC
A subs of 1-800-FLOWERS
2500 S Pacific Hwy
Medford, OR 97501-8724
Telephone: (541) 864-2362, Toll Free:
   (877) 322-1200, FAX: (800) 648-
   6640, Web Site: www.hndcorp.com
CEO: Steven Lightman
Conducts Business: U.S., Canada
Employees: 900
Primary Market Served: Business &
   Consumer
Catalog available online
Direct online sales
Advertising/Marketing Budget Related
   to Direct Marketing: 76-100%
Direct Marketing ad budget:
   $12,000,000
Founded: 1934

Grower, processor & marketer of fine
fruit, gift baskets, bakery delicacies &
gourmet foods; specialize in mail-order
distribution.

HAWAIIAN HOST INC
500 Alakawa St (Suite 111)
Honolulu, HI 96817-4576
Telephone: (808) 848-0500, Toll Free:
   (866) 972-6879, E-Mail: info@
   hawaiianhost.com, Web Site: www.
   hawaiianhost.com
Direct Sls Mgr: Carolyn Hara

THE HERSHEY CO
100 Crystal A Dr
Hershey, PA 17033-9524
Telephone: (717) 534-4200, Toll Free:
   (800) 454-7737, FAX: (717) 534-
   5204, Web Site: www.hersheygifts.
   com
Chmn: James Nevels
Pres, CEO: John P. Bilbrey
Sr VP & CIO: George Davis
Conducts Business: U.S.
Employees: 250
Primary Market Served: Business &
   Consumer
Catalog available online
Direct online sales
Advertising/Marketing Budget Related
   to Direct Marketing: 0-25%
Founded: 1894

Provides unique and personalized chocolate gifts for the holidays and special
occasions.

HICKORY FARMS
1505 Holland Rd, PO Box 219
Maumee, OH 43537-0219
Telephone: (419) 893-7611, Toll Free:
   (800) 776-4111, (800) 442-5671,
   FAX: (419) 893-0164, Web Site:
   www.hickoryfarms.com
Pres & CEO: Mark Rodriguez
VP: Michael Holton
VP: Joe Loch
VP: James O'Neill
Conducts Business: U.S.
Employees: 250
Primary Market Served: Business &
   Consumer
Catalog available online
Direct online sales
Advertising/Marketing Budget Related
   to Direct Marketing: 76-100%
Gross sales or billing: $16,300,000

Specialty foods.

THE HONEYBAKED HAM CO
aka The Original HoneyBaked Ham Co
   of Georgia, Inc
6145 Merger Dr
Holland, OH 43528-8430
Telephone: (419) 724-4267, Toll Free:
   (866) 492-4267, E-Mail: info@
   honeybaked.com, Web Site: www.
   honeybaked.com
Chmn Bd: Linda F. Van Rees
Pres: George J. Kurz

Mktg Mgr: Kathleen Regan
Conducts Business: U.S., Canada
Employees: 650
Primary Market Served: Business &
  Consumer
Catalog available online
Direct online sales
Founded: 1957
Gross sales or billing: $58,000,000

Full line gourmet food catalog, featuring the authentic honeybaked ham & gift packages.

HOT SAUCE HARRY'S

1077 Innovation Ave Unit 109
North Port, FL 34289-9345
Telephone: (214) 902-8552, Toll Free:
  (800) 588-8979, FAX: (214) 956-
  9885, E-Mail: info@hotsauceharrys.
  com, Web Site: www.hotsauceharrys.
  com
VP: Bob Harris
CEO: Kevin Harris

HYATT FRUIT CO

PO Box 639
Vero Beach, FL 32961-0639
Telephone: (772) 567-3766, Toll Free:
  (866) 991-8889, FAX: (772) 567-
  0973, Web Site: www.hyattfruitco.
  com
Pres: Tom R. Jones
Adv Mgr: Jennifer Jones
Conducts Business: U.S. Canada
Employees: 25
Primary Market Served: Business &
  Consumer
Catalog available online
Advertising/Marketing Budget Related
  to Direct Marketing: 76-100%
Direct Marketing ad budget:
Direct Mail: 70%
Online: 25%
TV/Radio: 5%
Founded: 1946
Gross sales or billing: $5,200,000

Catalog & retail sales of Indian River citrus gift cartons & baskets for individuals, businesses & fund-raising. Also, tropical jellies & candy. Packing & retail located in Vero Beach, FL.

ILLY CAFFE NORTH
AMERICA

800 Westchester Ave (Suite S440)
Rye Brook, NY 10573-1329
Telephone: (914) 253-4500, Toll Free:
  (877) 469-4559, E-Mail: info@
  illyusa.com, Web Site: www.illyusa.
  com
VP Mktg: Beverly Stotz
CEO: Andrea Illy
Primary Market Served: Business &
  Consumer

INTERNATIONAL WINE
ACCESSORIES INC

Subs. of Dean & DeLuca
1445 N McDowell Blvd
Petaluma, CA 94954
Telephone: (214) 349-6097, Toll Free:
  (800) 527-4072, FAX: (214) 349-
  8712, E-Mail: customerservice@
  iwawine.com, Web Site: www.
  iwawine.com
Pres: Robert Orenstein
Conducts Business: U.S., Canada,
  Spain, Mexico, Japan
Employees: 17
Primary Market Served: Business &
  Consumer
Catalog available online
Direct online sales
Advertising/Marketing Budget Related
  to Direct Marketing: 76-100%
Direct Marketing ad budget: $885,000
Founded: 1983
Gross sales or billing: $9,000,000

Cataloger of wine accessory products. Everything for the wine lover, including wine storage systems, racking systems, stemware, corkscrews, books & videos.

JAFFE BROTHERS NATURAL
FOODS

28560 Lilac Rd
Valley Center, CA 92082
Telephone: (760) 749-1133, Toll Free:
  (877) 975-2333, FAX: (760) 749-
  1282, E-Mail: jaffebros@att.net,
  Web Site: www.organicfruitsandnuts.
  com
CEO: Lawrence Jaffe
Exec Sec: S. Wentz
Conducts Business: U.S., Canada, Japan, Hong Kong, Singapore, Germany
Employees: 9
Primary Market Served: Business &
  Consumer
Catalog available online
Direct online sales
Advertising/Marketing Budget Related
  to Direct Marketing: 0-25%
Founded: 1948

Mail order dried fruits, nuts, seeds, grains, beans, oils, nut butters, & other natural foods. Specialize in organically grown foods. Sell to stores, co-ops & individuals.

KNOTT'S BERRY FARM
FOODS

Div. of ConAgra Foods
1 Strawberry Ln
Orrville, OH 44667-0280

Telephone: (714) 220-5200, Toll Free:
  (866) 828-5502, FAX: (714) 220-
  5148, Web Site: www.
  knottsberryfarmfoods.com
Gen Mgr: Raffi Kaprelyan
Conducts Business: U.S.
Employees: 200
Primary Market Served: Business &
  Consumer
Founded: 1928

Manufacturer & marketer of jams, jellies, preserves, salad dressings, fruit syrups and cookies.

THE KRAFT HEINZ CO

One PPG Pl
Pittsburgh, PA 15222
Telephone: (412) 456-5700, Web Site:
  www.kraftheinzcompany.com
Chmn: Alexandre Behring
COO: George Zoghbi
Head US Sls: Sergio Nahuz
Conducts Business: U.S.
Primary Market Served: Business &
  Consumer
Catalog available online
Gross sales or billing: $27,000,000,000

Food & beverage company.

EC KRAUS HOME WINE &
BEER MAKING SUPPLIES

733 S Northern Blvd, PO Box 7850
Independence, MO 64054
Telephone: (816) 254-7448, Toll Free:
  (800) 353-1906, FAX: (816) 254-
  7051, E-Mail: customerservice@
  eckraus.com, Web Site: www.
  eckraus.com
Owner: Ed Kraus
Conducts Business: U.S.
Primary Market Served: Consumer
Catalog available online
Direct online sales
Founded: 1966

Sell home wine & beer making supplies.

THE KROGER CO

1014 Vine St (Suite 1000)
Cincinnati, OH 45202-1100
Telephone: (513) 762-4000, Toll Free:
  (866) 221-4141, FAX: (513) 762-
  1575, Web Site: www.kroger.com
CEO & Chmn Bd: W. Rodney
  McMullen
Primary Market Served: Business &
  Consumer

LAPREFERIDA INC

3400 W 35th St
Chicago, IL 60632

Telephone: (773) 254-7200, Toll Free: (800) 621-5422, FAX: (773) 254-8546, Web Site: www.lapreferida.com
Sls Mgr: Juan Badillo
Conducts Business: U.S., Canada
Primary Market Served: Business & Consumer
Catalog available online
Direct online sales
Founded: 1898

Manufacturers & distributors of Mexican food.

LEGAL SEA FOODS INC
1 Seafood Way
Boston, MA 02210-2702
Telephone: (617) 530-9000, Toll Free: (800) 343-5804, FAX: (617) 530-9649, Web Site: www.legalseafoods.com
Pres & CEO: Roger Berkowitz
Exec VP Restaurants & Exec Chef: Richard Vellante
Conducts Business: Worldwide
Employees: 3,000
Primary Market Served: Business & Consumer
Catalog available online
Direct online sales
Founded: 1950
Gross sales or billing: $65,100,000

Catalog marketer of fresh seafood products for personal gifts, corporate premiums & incentives.

MAISON GLASS DELICACIES
3180 US 9
Cold Spring, NY 10516
Telephone: (212) 755-3316, Toll Free: (800) 822-5564, E-Mail: info@maisonglass.com, Web Site: www.maisonglass.com
Consultant: Vincent Lampariello
Conducts Business: Worldwide
Employees: 10
Primary Market Served: Business & Consumer
Advertising/Marketing Budget Related to Direct Marketing: 51-75%
Direct Marketing ad budget: $75,000
Direct Mail: 80%
Magazines: 5%
Newspapers: 5%
Telephone: 10%
Founded: 1902

Selling & worldwide shipping of imported & domestic delicacies: caviar, foie gras, truffles, smoked salmon, cheeses, chocolates, freshly-roasted nuts, oils, vinegars, coffees, teas, candies, Smithfield Hams, mustards, honeys, preserves, Spanish, French & Italian specialties & gift baskets.

MANCHESTER FARMS INC
8126 Garners Ferry Rd
Columbia, SC 29209-9402
Toll Free: (803) 845-0421, FAX: (803) 227-3103, E-Mail: customerservice@manchesterfarms.com, Web Site: www.manchesterfarms.com
Mktg Mgr: Matt Miller
Dir Opers: Michael Davis
Plant Mgr: Jennifer Alexander
Primary Market Served: Business & Consumer
Catalog available online
Gross sales or billing: $5,500,000

MAPLE GROVE FARMS OF VERMONT INC
1052 Portland St
Saint Johnsbury, VT 05819-2815
Telephone: (802) 748-5141, FAX: (802) 748-9647, E-Mail: maple@maplegrove.com, Web Site: www.maplegrove.com
Pres: Dave Wenner
Conducts Business: U.S., Canada, Europe
Employees: 75
Primary Market Served: Business & Consumer
Founded: 1915

Catalog featuring pure maple syrup, meat, cheese, candy, preserves & other gifts.

T MARZETTI CO INC
1105 Schrock Rd (Suite 300)
Columbus, OH 43229-1146
Telephone: (614) 846-2232, FAX: (614) 848-8330, Web Site: www.marzetti.com
Chmn & CEO: John B. Gerlach
Employees: 8
Primary Market Served: Business & Consumer
Direct Marketing ad budget:
Direct Mail: 40%
Magazines: 20%
Newspapers: 20%
Telephone: 20%
Founded: 1896

Importers & packers of all varieties of caviar, both fresh & pasteurized.

MATTHEWS 1812 HOUSE INC
250 Kent Rd S
Cornwall Bridge, CT 06754
Telephone: (860) 672-0230, Toll Free: (800) 662-1812, FAX: (860) 672-1812, E-Mail: info@matthews1812house.com, Web Site: www.matthews1812house.com
Pres: Deanna Matthews
Sec: Blaine Matthews

Conducts Business: U.S.
Employees: 14
Primary Market Served: Consumer
Catalog available online
Direct online sales
Advertising/Marketing Budget Related to Direct Marketing: 76-100%
Direct Marketing ad budget:
Direct Mail: 100%
Founded: 1979

Mail-order gourmet foods to consumers.

MCCORMICK & CO INC
18 Loveton Cir
Sparks, MD 21152-9202
Telephone: (410) 771-7301, Toll Free: (800) 474-7742, FAX: (410) 527-6337, Web Site: www.mccormick.com
Dir Corp Communs: Jim Lynn
CEO: Alan D. Wilson
Conducts Business: Worldwide
Employees: 8,000
Primary Market Served: Business & Consumer
Catalog available online
Direct online sales
Founded: 1889

Manufacture specialty food products, spices, seasonings, flavorings & decorations for cakes.

MEDIFAST INC
11445 Cronhill Dr Ste 200
Owings Mills, MD 21117-2270
Telephone: (410) 581-8042, Toll Free: (800) 209-0878, FAX: 410 581-8070, Web Site: www.medifastdiet.com
Exec VP Info Tech: Donald Gould
Primary Market Served: Consumer

MELITTA USA
13925 58th St N
Clearwater, FL 33760-3721
Telephone: (727) 535-2111, Web Site: www.melitta.com
Dir E-Commerce: Donna Gray
Pres & CEO: Marty Miller

MILLERCOORS LLC
250 S Wacker Dr Ste 800
Chicago, IL 60606-5888
Telephone: (312) 496-2700, Toll Free: (800) 645-5376, Web Site: www.millercoors.com
Pres & CEO: Tom Long
Chief Mktg Officer: Andrew J. England
Primary Market Served: Consumer
Founded: 2008

MOON SHINE TRADING CO
Div. of Z Specialty Food Co LLC

1250-A Harter Ave
Woodland, CA 95776-6134
Telephone: (530) 668-0660, Toll Free: (800) 678-1226, FAX: (530) 668-6061, E-Mail: store@moonshinetrading.com, Web Site: www.moonshinetrading.com
Owner: Amina Harris
Owner: Ishai Zeldner
Conducts Business: U.S.
Employees: 6
Primary Market Served: Business & Consumer
Catalog available online
Direct online sales
Advertising/Marketing Budget Related to Direct Marketing: 0-25%
Direct Marketing ad budget:
Direct Mail: 95%
Magazines: 5%
Founded: 1979
Gross sales or billing: $1,000,000

Varietal honeys, comb honey, nut butters, honey fruit spreads, gift boxes, honey straws, all items Kosher, Judaica Goodies (food gifts).

MORKES CHOCOLATES

aka Morkes Inc
1890 N Rand Rd
Palatine, IL 60074
Telephone: (847) 359-3454, FAX: (847) 359-3553, E-Mail: yummy@morkeschocolates.com, Web Site: www.morkeschocolates.com
Pres: Rhonda Morkes
Conducts Business: U.S.
Employees: 10
Primary Market Served: Business & Consumer
Catalog available online
Direct online sales
Advertising/Marketing Budget Related to Direct Marketing: 0-25%
Direct Marketing ad budget: $14,000
Direct Mail: 30%
Newspapers: 10%
TV/Radio: 40%
Telephone: 20%
Founded: 1920

Marketer of gourmet chocolates, caramel apples & specialty items.

NATIONAL PECAN CO

Subs. of King Ranch, Inc
5757 Main St (Suite 205)
Frisco, TX 75034
Telephone: (469) 353-2993, E-Mail: info@nationalpecan.com, Web Site: www.nationalpecan.com
CEO: David Lawrence
Conducts Business: U.S.
Employees: 183
Primary Market Served: Business & Consumer

Advertising/Marketing Budget Related to Direct Marketing: 26-50%
Direct Marketing ad budget:
Direct Mail: 100%
Founded: 1923
Gross sales or billing: $98,800,000

Sell fresh pecans & pecan gift items.

NELSON CRAB INC

3088 Kindred Ave
Tokeland, WA 98590
Telephone: (360) 267-2911, Toll Free: (800) 262-0069, FAX: (360) 267-2921, E-Mail: seatreats@techline.com, Web Site: www.nelsoncrab.com
Pres: Kristi Nelson
Conducts Business: U.S.
Employees: 30
Primary Market Served: Business & Consumer
Catalog available online
Indirect online sales
Advertising/Marketing Budget Related to Direct Marketing: 0-25%
Direct Marketing ad budget: $5,000
Direct Mail: 50%
Magazines: 10%
Newspapers: 5%
TV/Radio: 10%
Telephone: 25%
Founded: 1934
Gross sales or billing: $2,700,000

Retail & mail order wholesale seafood: fresh, frozen & canned.

NESTLE USA

800 N Brand Blvd
Glendale, CA 91203-1216
Telephone: (818) 549-6000, Toll Free: (800) 225-2270, FAX: (818) 553-3547, Web Site: www.nestleusa.com
Chmn: Paul Grimwood
CFO: Peter Argentine
Pres Nestle Bus Svcs: Steve Presley
Primary Market Served: Business
Catalog available online
Indirect online sales
Founded: 1990

Food service manufacturer.

NEW ENGLAND CHEESEMAKING SUPPLY CO

54B Whately Rd Ste B
South Deerfield, MA 01373-9608
Telephone: (413) 397-2012, FAX: (413) 397-2014, E-Mail: info@cheesemaking.com, Web Site: www.cheesemaking.com
Owner: Ricki Carroll
Conducts Business: Worldwide
Employees: 4

Primary Market Served: Business & Consumer
Catalog available online
Direct online sales
Advertising/Marketing Budget Related to Direct Marketing: 0-25%
Founded: 1978
Gross sales or billing: $425,000

Cheese making & dairy supplies to individuals & businesses.

NODINE'S SMOKEHOUSE

65 Fowler Ave
Torrington, CT 06790-6529
Telephone: (860) 489-3213, Toll Free: (800) 222-2059, FAX: (860) 496-9787, E-Mail: nodinesmoke@optonline.net, Web Site: www.nodinesmokehouse.com
Pres: Ronald Nodine
Primary Market Served: Business & Consumer
Founded: 1969

Smoked foods such as hams, bacon, poultry, whole birds, cheese, fish & sausage.

OMAHA CREATIVE GROUP INC

11030 O St
Omaha, NE 68137-2346
Telephone: (402) 597-3000, Toll Free: (800) 228-9872, FAX: (800) 428-1593, Web Site: www.omahasteaks.com
VP Gen Mgr: Vickie Hagen
Primary Market Served: Consumer

OMAHA STEAKS INC

11030 "O" St
Omaha, NE 68137-2346
Telephone: (402) 597-8370, FAX: (402) 597-8125, E-Mail: info@omahasteaks.com, Web Site: www.omahasteaks.com
Pres & COO: Bruce A. Simon
Chmn Bd & CEO: Alan D. Simon
Exec VP: Frederick J. Simon
Owner & Sr VP: Todd D. Simon
CFO & VP: Dave Hersheiser
Conducts Business: U.S.
Employees: 1,800
Primary Market Served: Business & Consumer
Catalog available online
Direct online sales
Advertising/Marketing Budget Related to Direct Marketing: 76-100%
Direct Marketing ad budget:
Direct Mail: 60%
Magazines: 10%
Newspapers: 10%
Online: 13%
TV/Radio: 2%
Telephone: 5%

Founded: 1917
Gross sales or billing: $457,000,000

Sell steaks & frozen gourmet foods to businesses & consumers for gifts and/ or personal use. Sales are made through direct mail, space ads online, telephone marketing & retail stores.

OREGON FREEZE DRY INC

525 25th Ave SW
Albany, OR 97321-3900
Telephone: (541) 926-6001, FAX: (541) 967-6527, Web Site: www.ofd.com
Pres & COO: James Merryman
Sr VP Sls & Bus Devel: Larry Von Deylen
Employees: 250
Primary Market Served: Business
Advertising/Marketing Budget Related to Direct Marketing: 0-25%
Founded: 1963
Gross sales or billing: $106,000,000

Sell freeze-dried products.

PAPA JOHN'S INTERNATIONAL

2002 Papa John's Blvd
Louisville, KY 40299-2333
Telephone: (502) 261-7272, Web Site: www.papajohns.com
Dir Database Mktg: Susan Poulsen
Chmn Bd & CEO: John H. Schnatter
Primary Market Served: Business & Consumer

PECAN PRODUCERS INTERNATIONAL

2131 E State Hwy 31
Corsicana, TX 75151-1301
Telephone: (903) 872-1337, Toll Free: (800) 732-2648, FAX: (903) 874-7143
Mgr: Linda Garza
Primary Market Served: Business & Consumer

Mail order pecans & candy.

PEET'S COFFEE & TEA INC

1776 4th St
Berkeley, CA 94710-1711
Telephone: (510) 525-3207, Toll Free: (800) 999-2132, FAX: (510) 594-2180, E-Mail: mailorder@peets.com, Web Site: www.peets.com
Mgr: Milette Duque
Employees: 3,000
Primary Market Served: Business & Consumer
Catalog available online
Direct online sales
Advertising/Marketing Budget Related to Direct Marketing: 0-25%
Founded: 1966

Gross sales or billing: $210,000,000

PIONEER HI-BRED INTERNATIONAL INC

7100 NW 62nd Ave, PO Box 1000
Johnston, IA 50131-1000
Telephone: (515) 535-3200, FAX: (515) 535-4415, E-Mail: web.editor@pioneer.com, Web Site: www.pioneer.com
Chmn Bd & CEO: Edward D. Breen
VP Fin: Laurie Conslato
Conducts Business: Worldwide
Employees: 5,025
Primary Market Served: Business & Consumer
Founded: 1926

Distribute catalog sales of corn, soybean, wheat & alfalfa seeds.

PITTMAN & DAVIS INC

801 N Expressway 77
Harlingen, TX 78552
Telephone: (956) 423-2154, Toll Free: (800) 289-7829, FAX: (866) 329-7829, E-Mail: fruit@pittmandavis.com, Web Site: www.pittmandavis.com
CEO: Ned Davis
VP: Dee Davis
Conducts Business: U.S.
Employees: 50
Primary Market Served: Business & Consumer
Catalog available online
Direct online sales
Advertising/Marketing Budget Related to Direct Marketing: 76-100%
Direct Marketing ad budget:
Direct Mail: 95%
Magazines: 5%
Founded: 1926
Gross sales or billing: $18,000,000

Specializes in the sale of gift packages of fresh fruit, smoked meat, cheese, pastries, candy & nuts.

THE POPCORN FACTORY

13970 W Laurel Dr
Lake Forest, IL 60045-4533
Telephone: (847) 247-3342, Toll Free: (888) 238-8107, FAX: (888) 333-4595, E-Mail: service@ thepopcornfactory.com, Web Site: www.thepopcornfactory.com
Pres: Nancy P. Hensel
Conducts Business: Worldwide
Employees: 80
Primary Market Served: Business & Consumer
Catalog available online
Indirect online sales
Advertising/Marketing Budget Related to Direct Marketing: 76-100%
Direct Marketing ad budget:

Direct Mail: 99%
Magazines: 1%
Founded: 1979

Specialty gift catalog featuring exclusively designed baskets, gift assortments & popcorn cans, fresh-packed & shipped for gift giving. Also features other confectionery, snack & non-food gift items. Offers both consumer & corporate catalogs.

PRESQUE ISLE WINE CELLARS INC

9440 W Main Rd
North East, PA 16428
Telephone: (814) 725-1314, Toll Free: (800) 488-7492, FAX: (814) 725-2092, E-Mail: info@piwine.com, Web Site: www.piwine.com
Pres & Chmn Bd: Erik Moorhead
VP & Dir: Douglas P. Moorhead
Conducts Business: U.S., Canada
Employees: 11
Primary Market Served: Business & Consumer
Catalog available online
Direct online sales
Advertising/Marketing Budget Related to Direct Marketing: 51-75%
Direct Marketing ad budget:
Direct Mail: $16,000
Magazines: $3,000
Newspapers: $1,500
Founded: 1964
Gross sales or billing: $3,600,000

Sell supplies to amateur winemakers & small commercial wineries.

PRIESTER PECAN CO INC

208 E Old Fort Rd
Fort Deposit, AL 36032-4012
Telephone: (334) 227-4301, Toll Free: (800) 277-3226, FAX: (334) 227-4294, E-Mail: customerservice@ priester.com, Web Site: www.priesters.com
Pres: Thomas Ellis
Primary Market Served: Consumer

QUEEN BEE GARDENS

262 E Main St
Lovell, WY 82431-2102
Telephone: (307) 548-2818, Toll Free: (800) 225-7553, FAX: (307) 548-7994, E-Mail: queenbee@ queenbeegardens.com, Web Site: queenbeegardens.com
Mktg: Bessie Zeller
Mgr: Gene Zeller
Mktg Dir: Ben Zeller
Conducts Business: U.S.
Employees: 12
Primary Market Served: Business & Consumer
Catalog available online

Indirect online sales
Advertising/Marketing Budget Related
   to Direct Marketing: 0-25%
Direct Marketing ad budget:
Direct Mail: 50%
Magazines: 20%
Newspapers: 20%
Telephone: 10%
Founded: 1976
Gross sales or billing: $350,000

Sell honey candy, truffles, turtles, English toffee & pralines to health food stores, gourmet shops & consumers.

RANCH HOUSE MEAT CO

1313 Grand Ave (Suite 1)
Billings, MT 59102
Toll Free: (800) 749-6329, FAX: (888)
   917-6328, E-Mail: sales@brisket.net,
   Web Site: www.brisket.net
Owner: Max Stabel
Mail Order Mgr: Marsha Stabel
Conducts Business: U.S.
Employees: 15
Primary Market Served: Business &
   Consumer
Catalog available online
Direct online sales
Advertising/Marketing Budget Related
   to Direct Marketing: 0-25%
Direct Marketing ad budget: $75,000
Direct Mail: 60%
Online: 40%
Founded: 1978
Gross sales or billing: $2,173,708

Mail order marketer of meat products including smoked brisket, turkey, ham & bacon.

RENT MOTHER NATURE

RP-NFOA
PO Box 380193
Cambridge, MA 02238
Telephone: (617) 868-5059, Toll Free:
   (800) 232-4048, FAX: (617) 868-
   5861, Web Site: www.
   rentmothernature.com
Pres: Richard Hill
Conducts Business: U.S.
Primary Market Served: Business &
   Consumer
Advertising/Marketing Budget Related
   to Direct Marketing: 76-100%
Direct Marketing ad budget: $600,000
Founded: 1979
Gross sales or billing: $2,000,000

Foods & gifts.

RIVER STREET SWEETS

13 E River St
Savannah, GA 31401
Telephone: (912) 234-4608, Toll Free:
   (800) 793-3876, Web Site: www.
   riverstreetsweets.com
Owner: Tim Strickland

Pres: Pamela Strickland
Conducts Business: U.S.
Primary Market Served: Business &
   Consumer
Catalog available online
Direct online sales
Advertising/Marketing Budget Related
   to Direct Marketing: 76-100%
Direct Marketing ad budget:
Direct Mail: 97%
Magazines: 1%
Newspapers: 1%
TV/Radio: 1%
Founded: 1973

Gourmet Southern candies and gifts.

ROCKY MOUNTAIN CHOCOLATE FACTORY

265 Turner Dr
Durango, CO 81303-7941
Telephone: (970) 259-0554, Toll Free:
   (888) 525-2462, FAX: (970) 259-
   5895, E-Mail: customerservice@
   rmcfusa.com, Web Site: www.rmcf.
   com
Pres: Frank Crail
Conducts Business: U.S., Canada, Taiwan, UAE
Employees: 450
Primary Market Served: Business &
   Consumer
Catalog available online
Direct online sales
Advertising/Marketing Budget Related
   to Direct Marketing: 0-25%
Founded: 1981
Gross sales or billing: $27,000,000

Retail candy manufacturer.

SAN FRANCISCO HERB & NATURAL FOOD CO

240 Stockton St (#400)
San Francisco, CA 94108
Telephone: (510) 770-1215, Toll Free:
   (800) 227-2830, FAX: (510) 770-
   9021, E-Mail: customerservice@
   herbspicetea.com, Web Site: www.
   herbspicetea.com
CEO & Owner: Neil Hanscomb
Conducts Business: U.S.
Employees: 80
Primary Market Served: Business &
   Consumer
Catalog available online
Direct online sales
Advertising/Marketing Budget Related
   to Direct Marketing: 0-25%
Direct Marketing ad budget:
Direct Mail: 75%
Magazines: 25%
Founded: 1969
Gross sales or billing: $16,000,000

Sell herbal teas, bulk herbs & spices to pharmaceutical companies, retailers & herbal tea manufacturers.

SANTA FE SCHOOL OF COOKING

125 N Guadalupe St
Santa Fe, NM 87501
Telephone: (505) 983-4511, Toll Free:
   (800) 982-4688, FAX: (505) 983-
   7540, Web Site: www.
   santafeschoolofcooking.com
Owner & Dir: Susan Curtis
Conducts Business: U.S.
Employees: 7
Primary Market Served: Consumer
Catalog available online
Direct online sales
Founded: 1989

Regional cooking ingredients and products.

THE SAUSAGE MAKER INC

1500 Clinton St (Bldg 7)
Buffalo, NY 14206-3099
Telephone: (716) 824-5814, Toll Free:
   (888) 490-8525, FAX: (716) 824-
   6465, E-Mail: customerservice@
   sausagemaker.com, Web Site: www.
   sausagemaker.com
Pres: Kris Stanuscek
Conducts Business: U.S., Canada
Employees: 24
Primary Market Served: Business &
   Consumer
Catalog available online
Direct online sales
Advertising/Marketing Budget Related
   to Direct Marketing: 76-100%
Direct Marketing ad budget:
Direct Mail: $115,000
Magazines: $28,000
Founded: 1976
Gross sales or billing: $4,000,000

Equipment & supply catalog for sausage-making, meat-curing & food smoking.

SCHERMER PECANS

819 S Veterans Blvd
Glennville, GA 30427-8000
Telephone: (912) 654-2230, Toll Free:
   (800) 841-3403, E-Mail:
   information@schermerpecans.com,
   Web Site: www.pecantreats.com
Mgr: Melita Humphries
Pres: Kenny Tarver
Conducts Business: U.S.
Employees: 50
Primary Market Served: Business &
   Consumer
Advertising/Marketing Budget Related
   to Direct Marketing: 76-100%
Founded: 1946

Processor & marketer of pecans for fund-raising purposes.

SEE'S CANDIES INC
20600 S Alameda St
Carson, CA 90810-1105
Toll Free: (800) 347-7337, Web Site:
www.sees.com
Sr Admin Asst: Carol Lowe
CEO: Brad Kinstler
Primary Market Served: Consumer

THE JM SMUCKER CO
1 Strawberry Ln
Orrville, OH 44667-0280
Telephone: (888) 550-9555, Web Site:
www.smucker.com
CEO: Richard K. Smucker
Primary Market Served: Business &
Consumer

STARBUCKS CORP
2401 Utah Ave S, PO Box 34067
Seattle, WA 98134
Telephone: (206) 447-1575, Toll Free:
(800) 344-1575, FAX: (206) 447-
0828, Web Site: www.starbucks.com
Chmn Bd & Pres: Kevin Johnson
Conducts Business: U.S., Canada
Employees: 145,000
Primary Market Served: Business &
Consumer
Catalog available online
Direct online sales
Founded: 1985
Gross sales or billing: $7,700,000,000
Coffee roaster & retail distributor.

STEW LEONARD'S
100 Westport Ave
Norwalk, CT 06851
Telephone: (203) 847-7214, FAX:
(203) 846-3472, Web Site: www.
stewleonards.com
CEO & Pres: Stew Leonards Jr.
Employees: 30
Primary Market Served: Business &
Consumer
Advertising/Marketing Budget Related
to Direct Marketing: 0-25%
Founded: 1990
Gross sales or billing: $5,000,000
Grocery store, dairy & gifts catalog.

**STOCK YARDS PACKING CO
INC**
2500 S Pacific Hwy
Medford, OR 97501
Telephone: (312) 733-6050, Toll Free:
(888) 842-6111, FAX: (888) 700-
9919, E-Mail: customerservice@
stockyards.com, Web Site: www.
stockyards.com
CEO: Daniel Pollack
Pres: Mark Saviski
VP, Fin: Ross Bridge
Conducts Business: U.S.

Primary Market Served: Business &
Consumer
Catalog available online
Direct online sales
Advertising/Marketing Budget Related
to Direct Marketing: 76-100%
Founded: 1893
Marketers of U.S. prime meats & gour-
met foods to consumers & businesses
via catalogs, direct mail & space ads.

SUGARBUSH FARM INC
591 Sugarbush Farm Rd
Woodstock, VT 05091
Telephone: (802) 457-1757, Toll Free:
(800) 281-1757, FAX: (802) 457-
3269, E-Mail: contact@
sugarbushfarm.com, Web Site: www.
sugarbushfarm.com
Pres: Elizabeth Luce
Conducts Business: U.S.
Employees: 20
Primary Market Served: Business &
Consumer
Catalog available online
Direct online sales
Advertising/Marketing Budget Related
to Direct Marketing: 51-75%
Direct Marketing ad budget:
Direct Mail: 90%
Magazines: 10%
Founded: 1945
Sell natural & aged Vermont cheeses in
waxed cracker sized sticks & maple
syrup.

**SULLIVAN-VICTORY
GROVES**
990 US-1
Rockledge, FL 32955
Toll Free: (800) 672-6431, (866) 676-
4311, E-Mail: sales@sullivancitrus.
com, Web Site: www.sullivancitrus.
com
Mgr: Norma Thomas
Conducts Business: U.S., Canada, Eu-
rope
Employees: 6
Primary Market Served: Business &
Consumer
Indirect online sales
Direct Marketing ad budget: $50,000
Direct Mail: 80%
Newspapers: 20%
Founded: 1952
Gift order citrus. Sell citrus fruit gifts.

SUNNYLAND FARMS INC
PO Box 8200
Albany, GA 31706-8200
Toll Free: (800) 999-2488, Web Site:
www.sunnylandfarms.com
Pres: Jane Willson
VP: Larry Willson

VP: Frankye Lemay
Conducts Business: U.S.
Employees: 100
Primary Market Served: Business &
Consumer
Catalog available online
Direct online sales
Advertising/Marketing Budget Related
to Direct Marketing: 76-100%
Founded: 1948
Sell pecans, nuts, candies, cakes &
dried fruits through catalogs to the gen-
eral public.

**SWANSON HEALTH
PRODUCTS**
4075 40th Ave SW
Fargo, ND 58104-3912
Telephone: (701) 356-2700, Toll Free:
(800) 824-4491, FAX: (701) 356-
2708, E-Mail: customercare@
swansonvitamins.com, Web Site:
www.swansonvitamins.com
CEO: Kenneth Harris
Catalog available online
Founded: 1969
Natural health catalog & Internet mar-
keting company.

SWEET TOOTH CANDIES
1020 Saratoga St
Newport, KY 41071-2129
Telephone: (859) 581-4663, Toll Free:
(877) 581-5132, FAX: (859) 581-
1979
Pres: Robert Schneider
Office Mgr: Judy Bedwell
Conducts Business: U.S.
Primary Market Served: Consumer
Sell boxed chocolates.

THE SWISS COLONY INC
112 7th Ave
Monroe, WI 53566-1364
Telephone: (608) 324-4603, FAX:
(608) 328-8735, Web Site: www.
swisscolony.com
Pres CEO: John Baumann
CFO: Don Hughes
Chmn Bd: Pat Kubly
Conducts Business: U.S.
Employees: 4,000
Primary Market Served: Business &
Consumer
Founded: 1926
Mail order company specializing in
corporate & individual food gifts.

**TILLAMOOK COUNTY
CREAMERY ASSOCIATION**
4185 Hwy 101 N
Tillamook, OR 97141-7770
Telephone: (503) 842-4481, Web Site:
www.tillamook.com

Pres & CEO: Patrick G. Criteser
VP Opers: William Tennant
Conducts Business: U.S.
Employees: 650
Primary Market Served: Business &
 Consumer
Direct Marketing ad budget: $900,000
Direct Mail: $50,000
Magazines: $100,000
Newspapers: $650,000
TV/Radio: $100,000
Founded: 1909
Gross sales or billing: $326,000,000

Sell natural cheddar cheese in gift
packs. Gift packs may also contain
canned seafood, smoked meats, local
jams & jellies.

TODARO BROTHERS MAIL
ORDER CO

Div. of Todaro Brothers
555 Second Ave (Front A)
New York, NY 10016-6346
Telephone: (212) 679-7766, Toll Free:
 (877) 472-2767, FAX: (212) 689-
 1679, E-Mail: eat@todarobros.com,
 Web Site: www.todarobros.com
Pres & Treas: Luciano Todaro
Store Mgr: Michael Spano
Conducts Business: U.S.
Employees: 50
Primary Market Served: Business &
 Consumer
Catalog available online
Direct online sales
Advertising/Marketing Budget Related
 to Direct Marketing: 0-25%
Direct Marketing ad budget:
Online: 100%
Founded: 1917
Gross sales or billing: $5,000,000

Catalog marketer of imported & domestic gourmet specialty foods.

UNCLE BEN'S INC

Div. of Mars Food US, LLC
1098 N Broadway St
Greenville, MS 38701-2004
Telephone: (601) 335-8000, Toll Free:
 (800) 54-UNCLE, (800) 548-6253,
 FAX: (601) 378-4370, E-Mail:
 info@unclebens.com, Web Site:
 www.unclebens.com
Opers Exec: Anthony Fox
Mgr: Zelma Johnson
Conducts Business: Worldwide.
Employees: 150
Primary Market Served: Business
Catalog available online
Indirect online sales
Founded: 1977
Gross sales or billing: $500,000

Manufacture & sell rice products.

US FOODSERVICE

9399 W Higgins Rd Ste 500
Rosemont, IL 60018-4992
Toll Free: (847) 720-8000, FAX: (847)
 720-8099, Web Site: www.
 usfoodservice.com
Pres & CEO: Pietro Satriano
Employees: 27,630
Primary Market Served: Business
Founded: 1989
Gross sales or billing: $25,356,900,000

Food service distributor.

UNIVERSAL TEA CO INC

dba as Stash Tea Co
16655 SW 72nd Ave (Ste 200)
Tigard, OR 97224
Telephone: (503) 684-4482, Toll Free:
 (800) 547-1514, FAX: (503) 684-
 4424, E-Mail: stash@stashtea.com,
 Web Site: www.stashtea.com
VP Mktg: Dorothy Arnold
Conducts Business: U.S.
Employees: 49
Primary Market Served: Consumer
Catalog available online
Indirect online sales
Founded: 1972
Gross sales or billing: $9,900,000

A full line of premium specialty teas.

URBANI TRUFFLES USA
CORP

Div. of Urbani-Italy
10 West End Ave
New York, NY 10023
Telephone: (212) 247-8800, FAX:
 (212) 247-8900, E-Mail: info@
 urbani.com, Web Site: www.urbani.
 com
VP: Vittorio Giordano
VP: Olga Urbani
Conducts Business: Worldwide
Employees: 3
Primary Market Served: Business &
 Consumer
Advertising/Marketing Budget Related
 to Direct Marketing: 0-25%

Market white & black truffles packed
in tins, jars & tubes. Also fresh truffles
in season & flash frozen truffles.

THE VIRGINIA DINER INC

322 W Main St
Wakefield, VA 23888-2940
Toll Free: (888) 823-4637, E-Mail:
 vadiner@vadiner.com, Web Site:
 www.vadiner.com
Pres: Christine Epperson
Owner: Maryann Galloway
VP & CEO: William B. Jones
Conducts Business: Worldwide
Employees: 100

Primary Market Served: Business &
 Consumer
Catalog available online
Indirect online sales
Advertising/Marketing Budget Related
 to Direct Marketing: 51-75%
Direct Marketing ad budget:
Direct Mail: 77%
Newspapers: 8%
TV/Radio: 15%
Founded: 1929

Restaurant, gift shop & mail order business.

WAKEFIELD PEANUT CO

Subs. of Wakefield Peanut Co LLC
11253 General Mahone Hwy (Rte 460)
Wakefield, VA 23888
Telephone: (757) 899-5481, Toll Free:
 (800) 803-1309, FAX: (757) 899-
 7604, Web Site: www.
 wakefieldpeanutco.com
Gen Mgr & Owner: Jimmy Laine
Conducts Business: U.S., Worldwide
Employees: 20
Primary Market Served: Consumer
Catalog available online
Direct online sales
Founded: 1965

Sell peanuts wholesale & retail to customers, other peanut businesses, to
farmers, mail order, and fundraising activities.

WHOLE FOODS MARKET
INC

550 Bowie St (Ste 99)
Austin, TX 78703-4644
Telephone: (512) 477-4455, FAX:
 (512) 482-7000, Web Site: www.
 wholefoodsmarket.com
CEO: Walter E. Robb IV
Founded: 1994

WILD FLAVORS INC

1261 Pacific Ave
Erlanger, KY 41018-1260
Telephone: (859) 342-3600, FAX:
 (859) 342-3610, Web Site: www.
 wildflavors.com
Sr Dir Mktg: Donna Hansee
Chmn Bd & CEO: Patricia Woertz
Primary Market Served: Business &
 Consumer

WIMMER'S MEAT
PRODUCTS INC

126 W Grant St, PO Box 286
West Point, NE 68788-0286
Toll Free: (800) 762-9865, E-Mail:
 consumer.affairs@landofrost.com,
 Web Site: www.wimmersmeats.com
Chmn, CEO & Pres: Dave Wimmer
VP, Sls & Mktg: Terry Maul

Pres & COO: Ron Gross
Conducts Business: U.S.
Primary Market Served: Business &
  Consumer
Catalog available online
Indirect online sales
Founded: 1934

Ethnic & European-style sausage &
cured meat products.

WINE ENTHUSIAST COS

333 N Bedford Rd
Mount Kisco, NY 10549-1158
Telephone: (914) 345-9463, Toll Free:
  (800) 356-8466, FAX: (914) 345-
  3129, Web Site: www.
  wineenthusiast.com
Pres & Chmn: Adam M. Strum
COO: Sybil N. Strum
Conducts Business: Worldwide
Primary Market Served: Business &
  Consumer
Catalog available online
Direct online sales
Founded: 1979

Source for wine accessories, storage,
information, education, events and
travel.

WINETASTING.COM

578 Gateway Dr
Napa, CA 94558-7517
Toll Free: (800) 435-2225, FAX: (707)
  257-7470, Web Site: www.
  winetasting.com
Gen Mgr: Chris Edwards
Conducts Business: U.S.
Employees: 105
Primary Market Served: Consumer
Catalog available online
Direct online sales
Advertising/Marketing Budget Related
  to Direct Marketing: 0-25%
Founded: 1986
Gross sales or billing: $30,000,000

Wine & wine accessories.

General Catalogs (5)

AAFES
3911 S Walton Walker Blvd
Dallas, TX 75236-1598
Telephone: (214) 312-2011, Toll Free:
(800) 527-2345, FAX: (800) 446-
0163, Web Site: www.aafes.com
CEO: Tom Schull
Employees: 45,000
Primary Market Served: Consumer
Gross sales or billing: $8,921,400,000

Produce exchange mail order catalog
for Army, Navy, Air Force, Marine &
Coast Guard.

CM ALMY & SON INC
28 Kaysal Ct
Armonk, NY 10504
Toll Free: (800) 225-2569, FAX: (800)
426-2569, E-Mail: almyaccess@
almy.com, Web Site: www.almy.com
Pres: Stephen Fendler
Conducts Business: U.S., Canada
Employees: 160
Primary Market Served: Business &
Consumer
Advertising/Marketing Budget Related
to Direct Marketing: 76-100%
Direct Marketing ad budget:
Direct Mail: $700,000
Magazines: $70,000
Founded: 1892
Gross sales or billing: $13,000,000

Outfitters to the church & clergy, including furnishings (vestments, hangings & metalware), clergy clothing &
choir robes.

AMSTERDAM PRINTING
166 Wallins Corners Rd
Amsterdam, NY 12010
Toll Free: (800) 846-6600, FAX: (518)
770-7018, Web Site: www.
amsterdamprinting.com
Pres: Tim Broadhead
Conducts Business: U.S., Canada, U.
K., Germany
Employees: 165
Primary Market Served: Business
Catalog available online
Direct online sales
Advertising/Marketing Budget Related
to Direct Marketing: 76-100%
Direct Marketing ad budget:
$5,000,000
Direct Mail: 75%
Magazines: 5%
Telephone: 20%
Founded: 1904
Gross sales or billing: $22,000,000

Imprinted promotional products, advertising specialties, office products &
business gifts.

**ANIMAL HEALTH EXPRESS,
INC**
aka Reprotec, Inc & Vaquero Feed &
Livestock
3301 N Freeway Rd
Tucson, AZ 85705-5015
Telephone: (520) 888-0294, Toll Free:
(800) 533-8115, FAX: (520) 888-
0297, (800) 437-9898, E-Mail: info@
animalhealthexpress.com, Web Site:
www.animalhealthexpress.com
Owner: Barbara Jackson
Owner: Tim Jackson
Employees: 14
Primary Market Served: Consumer
Catalog available online
Direct online sales
Founded: 1990

A catalog of livestock, equine and pet
equipment and animal health supplier,
including tack and supplements.

ARMENTO INC
1011 Military Rd, PO Box 39
Buffalo, NY 14217-0039
Telephone: (716) 875-2423, Toll Free:
(866) 276-3686, FAX: (716) 875-
8011, E-Mail: info@armento.com,
Web Site: www.armento-
columbarium.com
CEO: Douglas D. Knox
Conducts Business: U.S.
Employees: 22
Primary Market Served: Business &
Consumer
Catalog available online
Direct online sales
Advertising/Marketing Budget Related
to Direct Marketing: 0-25%
Direct Marketing ad budget:
Direct Mail: 25%
Magazines: 25%
Online: 50%
Founded: 1947
Gross sales or billing: $1,000,000

Specialty items, including bronze plaques, columbariums (repository of cre-
mated remains) & church designs.

BACK TO THE BIBLE
6400 Cornhusker Hwy
Lincoln, NE 68507-3123
Telephone: (402) 464-7200, Toll Free:
(800) 759-2425, FAX: (402) 464-
7474, E-Mail: info@backtothebible.
org, Web Site: www.backtothebible.
org
CEO: Dr. Arnie Kroll
Pres Foundation & Editor: Byron
Swanson
Conducts Business: U.S., Canada
Employees: 130

Primary Market Served: Business &
Consumer
Catalog available online
Direct online sales
Advertising/Marketing Budget Related
to Direct Marketing: 51-75%
Direct Marketing ad budget: $120,000
Direct Mail: 65%
Magazines: 10%
TV/Radio: 25%
Founded: 1939
Gross sales or billing: $850,000

Produce religious products in the form
of books, cassette messages, cassette &
CD music & videos. All products are
mainly targeted at adults.

BOB BARKER CO INC
134 N Main St
Fuquay Varina, NC 27526-0429
Toll Free: (800) 334-9880, FAX: (800)
322-7537, Web Site: www.
bobbarker.com
Dir Mktg: Mike Reed
Dir Fin: Jack Frakenfield
Pres: Robert Barker
Primary Market Served: Business &
Consumer

Detention supplier. Correctional clothing & supplies

**THE BELL GROUP RIO
GRANDE**
7500 Bluewater Rd NW
Albuquerque, NM 87121-1962
Telephone: (505) 839-3000, Web Site:
www.riogrande.com
Dir: Alan Bell
Pres: Dave Meleski
Primary Market Served: Business

Worldwide supplier to the jewelry industry

BENCHMARK BRANDS INC
1375 Peachtree St NE (Suite 600)
Norcross, GA 30309-3170
Telephone: (770) 242-1254, FAX:
(770) 242-1962, Web Site: www.
footsmart.com
CEO: Alan Beychok
Registered Agent: Earle J. Schwarz
CFO: David Rogalski

Direct-to-consumer retailer & product
development company

BIRTHDAY EXPRESS INC
11220-120th Ave NE
Kirkland, WA 98033
Telephone: (425) 250-1064, Toll Free:
(800) 247-8432, FAX: (425) 641-
2028, Web Site: www.
birthdayexpress.com

Co CEO: Jan Jewell
VP Mktg: Michael Eisenberg
Co CEO: Michael Jewell
Employees: 332
Primary Market Served: Consumer
Gross sales or billing: $85,000,000

Children's party supplies.

BLISS WORLD LLC

200 Vesey St (fl 25)
New York, NY 10281
Telephone: (212) 931-6383, Toll Free:
(888) 243-8825, Web Site: www.
blissworld.com
Dir Consumer Insights: Christopher
McGrath
Primary Market Served: Consumer

Operates spa centers in the United
States & United Kingdom. It also re-
tails its bath, body & skincare products
through its catalogs & website

BOBLEY-HARMANN CORP

GiftValues.com
200 Tradezone Ave
Ronkonkoma, NY 11779
Telephone: (516) 364-1800, Toll Free:
(800) 323-1692, FAX: (516) 364-
1899, E-Mail: info.giftvalues@gmail.
com, Web Site: www.giftvalues.com
Owner, Pres & CEO: Mark Bobley
VP Mktg: John Traola
Opers Mgr: Janice Tuerberg
Primary Market Served: Business &
Consumer
Founded: 1975

BROWNCOR
INTERNATIONAL

Div. of C & H Distributors Inc
500 W Oklahoma Ave
Milwaukee, WI 53207
Toll Free: (800) 327-2278, Web Site:
www.bcadvantage.com
Pres: Phil Arredia
Conducts Business: U.S.
Employees: 65
Primary Market Served: Business &
Consumer

Catalog business-to-business marketing
for shipping, packing & warehouse
supplies.

BUYFILTERS.COM LLC

PO Box 581
Silverhill, AL 36576
Telephone: (866) 863-1262, E-Mail:
customerservice@buyfilters.com,
Web Site: www.buyfilters.com
Partner: Jim Gates
President: Jennifer Minto

Standard & custom sized filters for air
conditioning or furnace systems

BUYSEASONS INC

5915 S Moorland Rd
New Berlin, WI 53151
Telephone: (262) 901-2000, FAX:
(262) 901-2315, Web Site: www.
buyseasons.com
Dir, Database Mktg: Matthew Sand
CEO: Rick Barton
Primary Market Served: Business &
Consumer

Party supplies & themes

CNY AWARDS & APPAREL
INC

106 New Hartford Shopping Center
New Hartford, NY 13413
Telephone: (315) 733-0931, FAX:
(800) 732-3617, Web Site: www.
cnyapprel.com
Partner & Pres: Michael Forsythe
Partner: Kevin Neejer
Conducts Business: U.S.
Employees: 2
Primary Market Served: Business &
Consumer
Advertising/Marketing Budget Related
to Direct Marketing: 0-25%
Direct Marketing ad budget:
Direct Mail: 40%
Newspapers: 5%
TV/Radio: 5%
Telephone: 50%
Founded: 1993
Gross sales or billing: $500,000

Retail & wholesale awards, imprintable
products, engraving, rubber stamps.

CTA INC

1625 Larkin Williams Rd
Fenton, MO 63026-1205
Telephone: (636) 305-3100, Toll Free:
(800) 999-1874, FAX: (800) 315-
8713, Web Site: www.ctainc.com
CEO: Terry Knoploh
Primary Market Served: Consumer

Christian gifts

CHANNEL 13 WNET
CATALOG DIVISION

825 8th Ave
New York, NY 10019
Telephone: (212) 560-1313, FAX:
(212) 560-1314, E-Mail:
programming@thirteen.org, Web
Site: www.thirteen.org
CEO: William F. Baker
Pres: Neal B. Shapiro
VP Natl Mktg & Content Devel: Don
Rogosin
Dir Mktg Commun: Barbara Bantivo-
glio
Dir Online Fund Raising: Ben Smith
Conducts Business: US
Employees: 500

Primary Market Served: Business &
Consumer
Catalog available online
Direct online sales
Founded: 1962
Gross sales or billing: $167,900,000

Premiums offered to Channel 13 members and online donations.

CLARIN BY HUSSEY
SEATING

Div. of Greenwich Industries
38 Dyer St Ext
North Berwick, ME 03906-6763
Toll Free: (800) 341-0401, FAX: (207)
676-2222, Web Site: www.
husseyseating.com
VP, Adv: Wilson Troup
Pre & CEO: Tim Hussey
Employees: 100
Primary Market Served: Business &
Consumer
Advertising/Marketing Budget Related
to Direct Marketing: 0-25%
Founded: 1925
Gross sales or billing: $7,000,000

Manufacture & distribute portable seating products.

CLARKSON EYECARE

217 Clarkson Rd
Ellisville, MO 63011-2219
Telephone: (636) 227-2600, Toll Free:
(888) 393-2273, E-Mail: info@
clarksoneyecare.com, Web Site:
clarksoneyecare.com
Primary Market Served: Consumer

COLUMBIA UNIVERSITY,
ANNUAL FUND
PROGRAMS

622 W 113th St (MC4520)
New York, NY 10025-7982
E-Mail: donorrelations@columbia.edu,
Web Site: http://giving.columbia.edu
Exec VP Univ Devel & Alumni Rels:
Fred Van Sickle
Exec VP for Univ Devel & Alumni
Rel: Amelia J. Alverson
Primary Market Served: Consumer

CORNERSTONE BRANDS INC

5568 W Chester Rd
West Chester, OH 45069
Telephone: (513) 603-1400, Web Site:
www.cornerstonebrands.com
CFO: Jim Pekarek
Pres: Jeffrey Kuster
Primary Market Served: Consumer

Comprised of home & apparel lifestyle
brands, such as Frontgate, Ballard Designs & Garnet Hill

CORONA CIGAR CO
7792 W Sand Lake Rd
Orlando, FL 32819
Telephone: (407) 248-1212, Toll Free: (888) 702-4427, FAX: (407) 248-1211, E-Mail: info@coronacigar.com, Web Site: www.coronacigar.com
Pres & Founder: Jeff Borysiewicz
Conducts Business: U.S.
Employees: 42
Primary Market Served: Consumer
Catalog available online
Direct online sales
Founded: 1996
Gross sales or billing: $4,000,000

Cigars, humidors & cigar accessories.

CORTZ INC
320 Industrial Dr
West Chicago, IL 60185-1817
Telephone: (630) 876-1080, Toll Free: (800) 288-7946, Web Site: www.intheswim.com
Pres: Barry Pace
Primary Market Served: Business & Consumer
Founded: 1982

Pool supplies

CUSTOM TOLL FREE
10940 Wilshire Blvd (fl 17)
Los Angeles, CA 90024
Toll Free: (800) 933-3030, E-Mail: service@customtollfree.com, Web Site: www.customtollfree.com
VP Sls & Mktg: Christy Brugger

Provides customized toll free numbers for businesses

DFS GROUP LIMITED
Subs. of LVMH Moet Hennessy Louis Vuitton
525 Market St, First Market Tower
San Francisco, CA 94105-2708
Telephone: (415) 977-2700, FAX: (415) 977-2970, Web Site: www.dfsgalleria.com
Dir of Strategy & Devel: Sossina Shenkute

Operates more than 180 duty free & general merchandise stores throughout the Pacific Rim. DFS Direct manages the company's database of international customers and all direct marketing initiatives.

DAEDALUS BOOKS INC
PO Box 6000
Columbia, MD 21046-6000
Telephone: (410) 309-2706, Toll Free: (800) 944-8879, E-Mail: custserv@daedalusbooks.com, Web Site: www.salebooks.com
Pres & Founder: Robin Moody
VP: Helaine Harris
Conducts Business: Worldwide
Employees: 100
Primary Market Served: Business & Consumer
Catalog available online
Direct online sales
Advertising/Marketing Budget Related to Direct Marketing: 26-50%
Direct Marketing ad budget:
Direct Mail: 100%
Founded: 1980

Literary sale books & classical, jazz & world compact discs to direct consumers & wholesale customers.

DAVE'S SODA & PET CITY
151 Springfield St
Agawam, MA 01001-1553
Telephone: (413) 786-3339, Web Site: www.daveratner.com
Pres: Dave Ratner

Pet supplies

DECK THE WALLS INC
221 First Executive Ave
Saint Peters, MO 63376-1697
Telephone: (314) 719-8200, Toll Free: (866) 719-8200, FAX: (314) 719-8290, E-Mail: dtwcontact@fcibiz.com, Web Site: www.deckthewalls.com
Pres & CEO: John W. Jones
COO & Exec VP: Connie Williams
Spokeswoman: Jane Seymour
Primary Market Served: Consumer
Catalog available online

Franchisor of antique & custom framing specialty store.

DIAPERS.COM
PO Box 483
Jersey City, NJ 07303
Toll Free: (800) 342-7377, E-Mail: customercare@diapers.com, Web Site: www.diapers.com
CEO & Chmn: Marc Lore
COO & Bd Dir: Vinit Bharara
EVP Opers: Scott Hilton
CIO: Prasad Pola

Online baby care specialty site

DREAM PRODUCTS INC
412 Dream Ln
Van Nuys, CA 91496-0001
Telephone: (818) 773-4233, Toll Free: (800) 410-2153, FAX: (816) 206-8061, Web Site: www.dreamproducts.net
Pres: Rick Goldman
Primary Market Served: Consumer

Sells a variety of products through direct mail

EOS INTERNATIONAL INC
1902 Wright Pl (fl 2)
Carlsbad, CA 92008
Telephone: (760) 431-8400, Toll Free: (800) 876-5484, FAX: (760) 431-8448, Web Site: www.eosintl.com
Pres & CEO: Scot Cheatham
VP Global Sls & Mktg: Salvatore Provenza
VP Product Devel: Jeff Goodwin
Conducts Business: U.S., Canada
Employees: 125
Primary Market Served: Business & Consumer
Advertising/Marketing Budget Related to Direct Marketing: 26-50%
Direct Marketing ad budget: $10,000,000
Gross sales or billing: $25,000,000

Personal development, seminars & tape programs.

ESPN
ESPN Plaza
Bristol, CT 06010
Telephone: (212) 456-4995
Pres & CEO: John Skipper
Primary Market Served: Consumer

Provides comprehensive sports coverage

ELDERLY INSTRUMENTS
1100 N Washington
Lansing, MI 48906
Telephone: (517) 372-7890, Toll Free: (888) 473-5810, FAX: (517) 372-5155, E-Mail: web@elderly.com, Web Site: www.elderly.com
Pres: Stanley R. Werbin
Mktg Dir: Steve Szilagyi
Conducts Business: U.S.
Employees: 86
Primary Market Served: Consumer
Catalog available online
Direct online sales
Founded: 1972
Gross sales or billing: $16,700,000

Sell vintage & new musical instruments, compact discs, instruction books & accessories.

EXCELLIGENCE LEARNING CORP
2 Lower Ragsdale Dr (Suite 125)
Monterey, CA 93940-7810
Telephone: (831) 333-2000, E-Mail: contactus@excelligence.com, Web Site: www.excelligencelearning.com
Dir, Direct Mktg: Kevin Kiper
Pres: Kelly Crampton

Primary Market Served: Business &
Consumer

Developer, manufacturer & retailer of
educational products, which are sold to
child care programs, preschools, elementary schools & consumers

FAIRE HARBOUR LIMITED
44 Captain Pierce Rd
Scituate, MA 02066-2644
Telephone: (781) 545-2465, FAX:
    (781) 545-2465
Pres: Irving R. Versoy Jr.
VP: Mary J. Versoy
Conducts Business: U.S., Canada
Employees: 6
Primary Market Served: Business &
    Consumer
Catalog available online
Indirect online sales
Advertising/Marketing Budget Related
    to Direct Marketing: 51-75%
Founded: 1960
Gross sales or billing: $200,000

Catalog sales of kerosene lamps, cooking devices & marine supplies.

FAMILY CHRISTIAN STORES
5300 Patterson Ave SE
Grand Rapids, MI 49530
Toll Free: (888) 887-6555, E-Mail:
    customerservice@familychristian.
    com, Web Site: www.
    familychristian.com
Sr VP, HR: Hal Bailey
Conducts Business: U.S., Canada, Ko-
    rea, Taiwan
Employees: 5,000
Primary Market Served: Business &
    Consumer
Catalog available online
Direct online sales
Founded: 1999
Gross sales or billing: $360,300,000

Sell Christian products to the public &
to the CBA market.

FEDERAL CITIZEN
INFORMATION CENTER
Consumer Information Catalog
Pueblo, CO 81009
Telephone: (719) 295-2675, Toll Free:
    (888) 8-PUEBLO, FAX: (719) 948-
    9724, E-Mail: pueblo@gpo.gov,
    Web Site: www.pueblo.gsa.gov
Exec VP: Mark Simon
Dir: Teresa S. Nasif
Dir, Publications & Media: Mark Levy
Consumer Education Specialist: Sa-
    mantha Donaldson
Consumer Education Specialist: Shan-
    tae Goodloe
Conducts Business: U.S.
Employees: 48

Primary Market Served: Consumer
Catalog available online
Direct online sales
Advertising/Marketing Budget Related
    to Direct Marketing: 0-25%
Founded: 1970

Consumer information catalog listing
200+ free & low cost federal publications.

FINCK CIGAR CO
6100 West Ave, PO Box 831007
San Antonio, TX 78283-1007
Telephone: (210) 341-8888, Toll Free:
    (800) 221-0638, FAX: (210) 341-
    8890, E-Mail: custser@
    finckcigarcompany.com, Web Site:
    www.finckcigar.com
Pres: Bill Finck Jr
Chief Mktg Officer: Lynn Rangel
Conducts Business: U.S.
Employees: 80
Primary Market Served: Consumer
Catalog available online
Direct online sales
Advertising/Marketing Budget Related
    to Direct Marketing: 76-100%
Direct Marketing ad budget:
Direct Mail: 85%
Magazines: 5%
Online: 10%
Founded: 1893

Sell cigars, pipes, pipe tobacco, ciga-
rette tobacco & accessories direct to
consumers.

FLAGHOUSE INC
601 Flaghouse Dr
Hasbrouck Heights, NJ 07604
Telephone: (201) 288-7600, Toll Free:
    (800) 793-7900, FAX: (800) 793-
    7922, E-Mail: sales@flaghouse.com,
    Web Site: www.flaghouse.com
CEO & Pres: George Carmel
COO: Douglas Carmel
Mgr Athletic Catalog Products: Keith
    Gold
Conducts Business: Worldwide
Employees: 100
Primary Market Served: Business
Catalog available online
Direct online sales
Advertising/Marketing Budget Related
    to Direct Marketing: 76-100%
Direct Marketing ad budget:
    $3,000,000
Direct Mail: 99%
Magazines: 1%
Founded: 1954
Gross sales or billing: $29,000,000

Mail order & catalog firm selling furniture, athletic equipment, recreational,
special needs & rehabilitation supplies
to schools & institutions.

FORD FOUNDATION OFFICE
OF COMMUNICATIONS
320 E 43rd St
New York, NY 10017-4816
Telephone: (212) 573-5000, E-Mail:
    office-of-communications@
    fordfound.org, Web Site: www.
    fordfound.org
Dissemination & Admin Mgr: Carolee
    E. Iltis
Conducts Business: Worldwide
Primary Market Served: Business &
    Consumer
Catalog available online
Founded: 1936

Publishes and distributes free publications covering Foundation programs.

FREESTYLE
PHOTOGRAPHIC SUPPLIES
5124 Sunset Blvd
Los Angeles, CA 90027-9897
Telephone: (323) 660-3640, Toll Free:
    (800) 292-6137, FAX: (323) 284-
    0050, Web Site: www.freestylephoto.
    biz
Pres & COO: Gerald Karmele
Primary Market Served: Consumer
Founded: 1946

Photographic supplies

FRESHDIRECT
23-30 Borden Ave
Long Island City, NY 11101-4515
Telephone: (212) 796-8002
CEO: Jason Ackerman
Primary Market Served: Consumer

Online grocer

THE FULLER BRUSH CO
One Fuller Way
Great Bend, KS 67530
Toll Free: (800) 522-0499, FAX: (620)
    792-1906, E-Mail: custom@fuller.
    com, Web Site: www.fuller.com
CEO: David Sabin
Conducts Business: U.S.
Primary Market Served: Business
Catalog available online
Direct online sales
Advertising/Marketing Budget Related
    to Direct Marketing: 26-50%
Direct Marketing ad budget:
Direct Mail: 100%
Founded: 1991

Cleaning products, including cleaning
brushes & boar bristle hair brushes, for
consumers & businesses.

GENERAL GROWTH
PROPERTIES
110 N Wacker Dr
Chicago, IL 60606-1511

Telephone: (312) 960-5000, Web Site:
www.generalgrowth.com
Chmn: J. Bruce Flatt
CEO: Sandeep Mathrani
Exec VP & CFO: Michael Berman
COO: Shobi Khan

Real estate investment trust that owns,
develops & operates regional shopping
malls

GO PROMOS
Div. of EGI
PO Box 698
Amsterdam, NY 12010-0698
Toll Free: (800) 523-9909, FAX: (800)
523-3292, E-Mail: customerservice@
gopromos.com, Web Site: www.
gopromos.com
Pres: Kevin Kirby
Primary Market Served: Business &
Consumer
Catalog available online
Indirect online sales

Print promotional products, logos &
slogans & provide samples as needed.

GOHN BROTHERS
105 S Main St
Middlebury, IN 46540
Telephone: (574) 825-2400, Toll Free:
(800) 595-0031, E-Mail:
gohnbrothers@gmail.com, Web Site:
www.gohnbrothers.com
Pres: John S. Swartzentruber
Conducts Business: U.S.
Employees: 10
Primary Market Served: Business &
Consumer

Sell Amish work clothing: hats, hosiery
& underwear. Also, quilting supplies,
yard goods, notions & Red Wing shoes.

W W GRAINGER INC
4514 19th St Ct E
Bradenton, FL 34203-3709
Telephone: (941) 747-5566, Toll Free:
(800) 472-4643, E-Mail: info@
grainger.com, Web Site: www.
grainger.com
CEO & Chmn Bd: James T. Ryan
Founded: 1914

Industrial supply company,

HSN INC
Subs. of IAC
1 HSN Dr
Saint Petersburg, FL 33729
Telephone: (727) 872-1000, Toll Free:
(800) 284-5757, Web Site: www.hsn.
com
Chmn Bd: Barry Diller
CEO: Mindy Grossman
Exec VP Mdsg: Lynne Ronon
Conducts Business: U.S.

Employees: 4,000
Primary Market Served: Consumer
Catalog available online
Direct online sales
Founded: 1977
Gross sales or billing: $3,290,000,000

Mail order shoes, clothing & hard
goods sold through catalogs, package
inserts, solo direct mail & space advertising offers.

HALLELUJAH ACRES
916 Cox Rd (Ste 210)
Gastonia, NC 28054-3434
Telephone: (704) 481-1700, Toll Free:
(800) 915-9355, Web Site: www.
myhdiet.com
CEO & Pres: Paul Malkmus
Primary Market Served: Consumer

Vegan raw food diet

HAMAKOR JUDAICA INC
4150 Dempster Dt
Skokie, IL 60076
Telephone: (847) 966-4040, Toll Free:
(800) 677-4150, FAX: (847) 966-
4033, E-Mail: service@ewishource.
com, Web Site: www.jewishsource.
com
Pres: Herschel Strauss
VP & List Mgr: Naomi Strauss
Conducts Business: U.S.
Employees: 25
Primary Market Served: Consumer
Catalog available online
Direct online sales
Advertising/Marketing Budget Related
to Direct Marketing: 76-100%
Founded: 1975

Producers of several catalogs including
the Source for Everything Jewish
which contains collectibles, fine art,
festival & ritual products, books, cassettes, videos, jewelry & children's
items.

HANOVER DIRECT INC
1200 Harbor Blvd
Weehawken, NJ 07086
Telephone: (201) 863-7300, FAX:
(201) 272-3465, Web Site: www.
hanoverdirect.com
CEO: Don Kelley
Corp Legal Administrator: Sherran
Turner
Conducts Business: U.S.
Employees: 2,500
Primary Market Served: Consumer
Advertising/Marketing Budget Related
to Direct Marketing: 76-100%
Direct Marketing ad budget:
Direct Mail: 80%
Magazines: 10%
Telephone: 10%
Founded: 1952

Gross sales or billing: $550,000,000

Sell ladies ready-to-wear, shoes, gifts,
household items, home furnishings,
electronics & garden products through
catalogs & space ads.

HEAVEN & EARTH
1255 Fordham Dr (Suite 120)
Virginia Beach, VA 23464
Telephone: (757) 420-3576, E-Mail:
heavenandearthkr8@gmail.com,
Web Site: www.heavenandearth.com
Owner & Mgr: Nathan Quade
Primary Market Served: Consumer

Specialty Christian store.

HERSCHEND FAMILY ENTERTAINMENT
5445 Triangle Pkwy (Ste 200)
Norcross, GA 30092
Telephone: (417) 338-3810, FAX:
(417) 338-8144, Web Site: www.
hfecorp.com
CEO: Andrew Wexler
Conducts Business: U.S.
Employees: 2,500
Primary Market Served: Business &
Consumer
Direct online sales
Direct Marketing ad budget: $250,000
Direct Mail: 75%
TV/Radio: 15%
Telephone: 10%
Founded: 1960
Gross sales or billing: $50,000,000

Theme park/crafts marketer. Sell season passes, crafts products & classes directly to consumers & tickets through
companies, associations, etc.

INTELISPEND PREPAID SOLUTIONS
1400 S Highway Dr
Fenton, MO 63099
Toll Free: (888) 234-7725, E-Mail:
saleads@intellispend.com, Web Site:
www.my.intelispend.com
Pres: Jim Menadier
CEO: Daryl Hutson
Primary Market Served: Consumer

JC PENNEY INC
6501 Legacy Dr
Plano, TX 75024-3612
Telephone: (972) 431-1000, FAX:
(972) 431-1977, Web Site: www.
jcpenney.com
Chmn: Mike Ullman
CEO: Marvin R. Ellison
Conducts Business: Brazil & Mexico
Employees: 155,000
Primary Market Served: Consumer
Catalog available online
Direct online sales

Founded: 1902
Gross sales or billing: $19,000,000,000
Retail department store.

JR CIGAR

800-JR Cigar Inc
2589 Eric Ln
Burlington, NC 27215
Toll Free: (800) 572-4427, FAX: (800)
457-3299, E-Mail: manager@
jrburlington.com, Web Site: www.
jrcigars.com
Pres & CEO: Lew Rothman
Mgr: Linda Thompson
CFO: Michael E. Colleton
VP: LaVonda Rothman
CEO: Jane Vargas
Employees: 1,100
Primary Market Served: Business &
Consumer
Advertising/Marketing Budget Related
to Direct Marketing: 76-100%
Direct Marketing ad budget: $250,000
Direct Mail: 100%
Founded: 1970
Gross sales or billing: $285,000,000

Sell cigars & related products mail order, retail & wholesale.

JEFFERS & CO

Subs. of Jeffers Inc
310 W Saunders Rd
Dothan, AL 36301
Telephone: (334) 793-6257, Toll Free:
(800) 533-3377, FAX: (334) 793-
5179, E-Mail: customerservice@
jefferspet.com, Web Site: www.
jefferspet.com
Pres & Owner: Dorothy Jeffers
Mktg Svcs Mgr: Ruth Jeffers
Primary Market Served: Business &
Consumer
Founded: 1975

Livestock, veterinary & pet care products.

JEFFREY LANT ASSOCIATES
INC

50 Follen St (Suite 507)
Cambridge, MA 02138
Telephone: (617) 547-6372, FAX:
(617) 547-0061, E-Mail: drjlant@
worldprofit.com, Web Site: www.
thejeffreylanttrust.org
Pres: Jeffrey Lant
Conducts Business: Worldwide
Employees: 5
Primary Market Served: Business &
Consumer
Catalog available online
Direct online sales

Founded: 1979

Extensive product line focused on assisting businesses prosper on and offline.

KV VET SUPPLY CO, INC

3190 N Rd (#245)
David City, NE 68632-5142
Telephone: (402) 367-6047, Web Site:
www.kvvet.com
Founder, Pres & CEO: Raymond Metz-
ner
Gen Mgr: Tracie Lloyd
Mktg: Deb Lensch
Conducts Business: U.S.
Employees: 100
Primary Market Served: Business &
Consumer
Catalog available online
Direct online sales
Advertising/Marketing Budget Related
to Direct Marketing: 76-100%
Founded: 1979

Pet & equine animal health supplies &
equipment to pet owners and retailers.

KARAOKE USA

1185 Gooden Xing
Largo, FL 33778
Telephone: (727) 209-1313, Toll Free:
(800) 776-7464, FAX: (702) 209-
1312, Web Site: www.karaokeusa.
com
Pres: Jack Strauser
Primary Market Served: Business

Distributor of karaoke catalogs.

LAB SAFETY SUPPLY INC

Subs. of W W Grainger Inc
401 S Wright Rd, Box 1368
Janesville, WI 53547-1368
Telephone: (608) 754-2345, Toll Free:
(800) 356-2855, FAX: (800) 543-
9910, Web Site: www.labsafety.com
Pres: Larry Loizzo
VP, Fin: Tom Drury
Conducts Business: Worldwide
Employees: 800
Primary Market Served: Business
Catalog available online
Direct online sales
Advertising/Marketing Budget Related
to Direct Marketing: 76-100%
Direct Marketing ad budget:
Direct Mail: 90%
Magazines: 10%
Founded: 1978

Catalog distributor of safety & industrial products.

LARK IN THE MORNING

PO Box 1176
Mendocino, CA 95460

Telephone: (707) 964-5569, FAX:
(707) 964-1979, E-Mail: info@
larkinam.com, Web Site: www.
larkinthemorning.com
Owner & Co Dir: Mickie Zekley
Owner & Co Dir: Elizabeth Zekley
Conducts Business: Worldwide
Employees: 35
Primary Market Served: Business &
Consumer
Catalog available online
Indirect online sales
Advertising/Marketing Budget Related
to Direct Marketing: 76-100%
Direct Marketing ad budget: $200,000
Founded: 1974
Gross sales or billing: $3,100,000

Sell world musical instruments, recordings, instructional videos & books to
individuals, music stores & book
stores. From over 60 cultures.

LEVENGER

420 S Congress Ave Ste 101
Delray Beach, FL 33445-4696
Telephone: (561) 276-2436, Toll Free:
(800) 544-0880, FAX: (800) 544-
6910, E-Mail: corpsales@levenger.
com, Web Site: www.levenger.com
CEO: Steven Hansen
Employees: 350
Primary Market Served: Business &
Consumer
Catalog available online
Direct online sales
Advertising/Marketing Budget Related
to Direct Marketing: 76-100%
Founded: 1987
Gross sales or billing: $59,200,000

Mail order catalog & retail store.

LIBERTYTREE PRESS

The Independent Institute
100 Swan Way
Oakland, CA 94621-1428
Telephone: (510) 632-1366, Toll Free:
(800) 927-8733, FAX: (510) 568-
6040, E-Mail: info@liberty-tree.com,
Web Site: www.independent.org
Pres: David J. Theroux
Customer Svc Dir: Nichelle Beardsley
Conducts Business: U.S.
Employees: 12
Primary Market Served: Business &
Consumer
Catalog available online
Direct online sales
Advertising/Marketing Budget Related
to Direct Marketing: 76-100%
Direct Marketing ad budget:
Direct Mail: 90%
Magazines: 10%

Founded: 1986

Mail order catalog featuring books, tapes & collectibles on the history & pursuit of liberty.

LIFEWAY CHRISTIAN STORES
RP-NFOA
Div. of Standard Publishing Co
1 LifeWay Plaza
Nashville, TN 37234
Telephone: (615) 251-2000, Toll Free: (800) 458-2772, FAX: (513) 728-6975, E-Mail: customerservice@berean.com, Web Site: www.berean.com
Store Mgr: Laura Stephenson
Primary Market Served: Consumer

Christian religious products.

LIGONIER MINISTRIES
421 Ligonier Ct
Sanford, FL 32771-8608
Telephone: (407) 333-4244, Toll Free: (800) 435-4343, FAX: (407) 333-4377, Web Site: www.ligonier.org
Founder & Owner: Dr. R. C. Sproul
Dir: Vesta Sproul
Mktg Dir: Alan Yardis
Dir Devel: John Peterson
Pres & CEO: Chris Larson
Primary Market Served: Business & Consumer
Catalog available online
Direct online sales
Founded: 1971
Gross sales or billing: $12,500,000

Christian education materials.

LOVE TO LEARN INC
741 N State Rd 198
Salem, UT 84653
Telephone: (801) 423-2009, Toll Free: (888) 771-1034, FAX: (801) 423-9188, E-Mail: customerservice@lovetolearn.net, Web Site: www.lovetolearn.net
Pres: Rick Hopkins
Primary Market Served: Consumer
Catalog available online
Direct online sales

Educational products for parents with children under five years old.

LOVES TRAVEL STOPS & COUNTRY STORES
10601 N Pennsylvania
Oklahoma City, OK 73120-4198
Telephone: (405) 242-2490, Toll Free: (800) 655-6837, E-Mail: comments@loves.com, Web Site: www.loves.com
CEO: Tom Love

Primary Market Served: Consumer

Chain of travel stops & country stores located across the USA

MMS EDUCATION
105 Terry Dr (Suite 120)
Newtown, PA 18940-1872
Telephone: (215) 579-8590, Toll Free: (800) 523-5948, FAX: (215) 579-8589, Web Site: www.mmseducation.com
CEO: Susan Meell
Primary Market Served: Consumer

Education data, marketing & consulting

MACY'S INC
7 W Seventh St
Cincinnati, OH 45202
Telephone: (513) 579-7912, Toll Free: (800) 289-6229, Web Site: www.macysinc.com
Chmn, Pres & CEO: Terry J. Lundgren
Primary Market Served: Business & Consumer

Retail department stores-complete clothing & home store products catalogs.

MAGELLAN'S CATALOG
PO Box 3390
Chelmsford, MA 01824-0990
Toll Free: (800) 450-7715, FAX: (800) 866-3235, E-Mail: sales@magellans.com, Web Site: www.magellans.com
Pres & CEO: Mark Gallo
Mktg Dir: Lynn Staneff
Conducts Business: U.S., Canada, Japan, Europe
Employees: 100
Primary Market Served: Business & Consumer
Catalog available online
Direct online sales
Advertising/Marketing Budget Related to Direct Marketing: 76-100%
Direct Marketing ad budget:
Direct Mail: 75%
Online: 25%
Founded: 1989
Gross sales or billing: $35,000,000

Travel gear including security wallets, electrical converters, water purifiers, packing aids, luggage, etc.

MAGNA-TEL INC
775 S Kingshighway St
Cape Girardeau, MO 63703
Telephone: (573) 334-3096, Toll Free: (800) 467-2537, FAX: (573) 335-1715, Web Site: www.magna.tel.com
Pres: Lionel K. Hastings
Mktg Dir: Donna Rosanswank
Conducts Business: U.S.

Primary Market Served: Business
Catalog available online
Indirect online sales
Advertising/Marketing Budget Related to Direct Marketing: 26-50%

Advertising specialty firm specializing in custom magnetic products.

MARSHALL FIELDS DEPT STORES
Subs. of Target Corp
7235 France Ave S
Minneapolis, MN 55435-4337
Telephone: (612) 375-3004, Web Site: www.fields.com
Print Buying Mgr: Barbara DiBlasi
Project Mngmt Mgr: Linda Stokes
Sr Analyst Mktg Effectiveness: Jill Hungsberg
Conducts Business: U.S.
Primary Market Served: Consumer
Direct online sales
Advertising/Marketing Budget Related to Direct Marketing: 26-50%
Gross sales or billing: $3,000,000,000

Department store retailer with 64 stores.

MAVERICK VENTURES PRODUCT LINE
Maverick Ventures Inc
15698 Ferncreek Dr
Chesterfield, MO 63017-0702
Telephone: (636) 537-4656, Toll Free: (800) 467-4656, FAX: (636) 537-4657, E-Mail: hang10cd@aol.com, Web Site: www.hang10cd.com
Pres: Ronald Kuczer
Conducts Business: U.S., Australia, Canada
Employees: 3
Primary Market Served: Business
Catalog available online
Direct online sales
Advertising/Marketing Budget Related to Direct Marketing: 0-25%
Founded: 1984
Gross sales or billing: $1,000,000
Innovative gadgets.

MEDIBADGE INC
PO Box 12307
Omaha, NE 68112-0307
Telephone: (402) 571-1800, Toll Free: (800) 228-0040, FAX: (800) 546-1072, E-Mail: stan@medibadge.com, Web Site: www.medibadge.com
CEO: Stanley Teutsch
Pres: Teri A. Teutsch
Conducts Business: Ireland, Japan, Australia
Employees: 46
Primary Market Served: Business & Consumer

Catalog available online
Direct online sales
Advertising/Marketing Budget Related
    to Direct Marketing: 51-75%
Direct Marketing ad budget:
Direct Mail: 100%
Founded: 1980
Gross sales or billing: $8,500,000

Motivational stickers, character licensed stickers and awards catalog.

THE MILLER GROUP
1610 Design Way
Dupo, IL 62239-1820
Toll Free: (800) 325-3350, FAX: (618) 286-6202, E-Mail: info@millergroup.com, Web Site: www. multiplexdisplays.com
Pres: Randy Castle
Mktg Dir: Kathy Webster
VP Sls & Mktg: Tom Grzywa
Conducts Business: Worldwide
Employees: 100
Primary Market Served: Business
Catalog available online
Direct online sales
Founded: 1903

Display systems for schools, libraries, hotels, real estate, printers, gift & retail stores, etc. Assortment of swinging panels, freestanding & portable panels, plus book displays & art displays. Catalogs available for floor-covering products, fabric, wallpaper, trim & custom production.

THE MUSEUM OF MODERN ART
11 W 53rd St
New York, NY 10019-5497
Telephone: (212) 708-9400, FAX: (212) 333-1123, E-Mail: info@ moma.org, Web Site: www.moma. org
Chmn Bd: Jerry I. Speyer
Pres: Marie Josee Kravis
Dir: Glen D. Lowry
Conducts Business: U.S.
Primary Market Served: Business & Consumer
Catalog available online

Mail order catalog of books & objects of industrial design.

MUSICIAN'S FRIEND
PO Box 5111
Westlake Village, CA 91359-5111
Telephone: (541) 772-5173, Toll Free: (800) 449-9128, Web Site: www. musiciansfriend.com
Co Founder: Rob Eastman
Co Founder: Deanna Eastman
Founded: 1983

Direct marketer of music gear

NETC
215 Knob Hill
Hamden, CT 06518
Telephone: (617) 851-8535, Toll Free: (203) 288-5938, E-Mail: mail@ netconline.org
Pres: Sabine Klein

NASCO
Div. of Nasco International Inc
901 Janesville Ave
Fort Atkinson, WI 53538-2497
Telephone: (920) 563-2446, Toll Free: (800) 558-9595, FAX: (920) 563-8296, E-Mail: info@nasco.com, Web Site: www.enasco.com
Pres: W. Phil Niemeyer
Dir Mktg & Commun: Bob Meier
Adv Dir: Kent Parks
Conducts Business: Worldwide
Employees: 400
Primary Market Served: Business & Consumer
Catalog available online
Gross sales or billing: $200,000,000

Mail order supplier of products for education, agriculture & industry.

NATURAL ESSENTIALS INC
1800 Miller Pkwy
Streetsboro, OH 44241-5067
Telephone: (330) 562-8022, Toll Free: (888) 968-7220, FAX: (330) 562-8022, E-Mail: questions@ naturalessentials.com, Web Site: www.naturalessentials.com
CEO: Gary Pellegrino
Conducts Business: Worldwide
Employees: 50
Primary Market Served: Business & Consumer
Catalog available online
Indirect online sales
Advertising/Marketing Budget Related to Direct Marketing: 51-75%
Direct Marketing ad budget:
Direct Mail: 65%
Magazines: 5%
Newspapers: 10%
TV/Radio: 10%
Telephone: 10%
Founded: 1992

Consumer products to retail cosmetic products via catalog & in home demos.

NEW WAVE MEDIA INC
dba Exponential
5858 Horton St (Ste 300)
Emeryville, CA 94608
Telephone: (510) 250-5500, FAX: (510) 250-5700, Web Site: www. exponential.com
CEO: Dilip Da Silva
Primary Market Served: Consumer

NORSCOT GROUP
1000 W Donges Bay Rd
Mequon, WI 53092
Telephone: (262) 241-3313, Toll Free: (800) 653-3313, FAX: (262) 241-4904, Web Site: www.norscot.com
Pres & CEO: Scott Stern
Chmn Bd: Norm Stern
Conducts Business: Worldwide
Employees: 80
Primary Market Served: Business & Consumer
Founded: 1970
Gross sales or billing: $35,000,000

Develops turn-key marketing, promotional product and brand identity programs for Fortune 500 companies.

ORIENTAL TRADING CO INC
5455 S 90th St
Omaha, NE 68127-3501
Toll Free: (800) 348-6483, FAX: (800) 327-8904, Web Site: www.oriental. com
CEO: Sam Taylor
Employees: 4,000
Primary Market Served: Business & Consumer
Catalog available online
Direct online sales
Advertising/Marketing Budget Related to Direct Marketing: 76-100%
Direct Marketing ad budget:
Direct Mail: 97%
Magazines: 2.5%
Telephone: 0.5%
Founded: 1932
Gross sales or billing: $166,400,000

Mail order catalog.

PHE INC
PO Box 8200
Hillsborough, NC 27278-8200
Telephone: (919) 644-8100, Toll Free: (800) 293-4654, FAX: (919) 644-8150, E-Mail: custserv@adameve. com
VP: David Groves
Conducts Business: U.S.
Employees: 325
Primary Market Served: Consumer
Catalog available online
Advertising/Marketing Budget Related to Direct Marketing: 76-100%
Founded: 1970
Gross sales or billing: $88,000,000

Books, condoms, lingerie, adult videos & marital aids.

PACIFIC SPORTSWEAR CO INC
dba Pacific Sportswear & Emblem Co
6160 Fairmount Ave (Suite F)

San Diego, CA 92120-3427
Telephone: (619) 281-6688, Toll Free:
(800) USA-8778, FAX: (619) 281-
6687, E-Mail: info@pacsport.com,
Web Site: www.pacsport.com
Pres: Rich C. Soergel
Controller: Cathy Cain
Conducts Business: U.S., Japan, Eu-
rope
Employees: 12
Primary Market Served: Business
Catalog available online
Advertising/Marketing Budget Related
to Direct Marketing: 0-25%
Founded: 1984
Gross sales or billing: $3,000,000

Licensee & founder of Class of 2000
(TM) brand caps, jackets, countdown
clocks, pins & keychains. Custom, private label headwear, patches & rubber
products.

PAPYRUS
500 Chadbourne Rd
Fairfield, CA 94534-9656
Telephone: (707) 428-0200, Web Site:
www.papyrusonline.com
VP Info Svcs: Bob Jellison
Primary Market Served: Business &
Consumer

Stationery, greeting cards, gifts, wrap
& ribbons

PETCO ANIMAL SUPPLIES
9125 Rehco Rd
San Diego, CA 92121-2270
Telephone: (858) 453-7845, Toll Free:
(877) 738-6742, FAX: (858) 453-
6585, Web Site: www.petco.com
CEO & Dir: James M. Myers
Conducts Business: U.S.
Employees: 17,900
Primary Market Served: Consumer
Gross sales or billing: $1,161,000,000

Retail pet supplies stores.

J PETERMAN CO
Subs. of Paul Harris Stores Inc
400 Old Vine St Ste 200
Lexington, KY 40507-1910
Toll Free: (888) 647-2555, FAX: (859)
254-0869, Web Site: www.
jpeterman.com
VP, Fin, Controller & Corp Sec: Keith
L. Himmel Jr.
VP, Mdsg Accessories: Terri L. Erick-
son
Primary Market Served: Business &
Consumer

Catalog sales.

PETSMART INC
Div. of Pet's Mart Direct
19601 N 27th Ave

Phoenix, AZ 85027-4010
Telephone: (623) 587-2009, Toll Free:
(888) 839-9638, FAX: (623) 580-
6183, Web Site: www.petsmart.com
CEO & Pres: Michael J. Massey
Employees: 38,400
Primary Market Served: Consumer
Catalog available online
Direct online sales
Founded: 1986
Gross sales or billing: $4,233,900,000

Complete line of pet supplies & services (engraving, tags, etc).

PHOTOSTAMPS.COM
1990 E Grand Ave
El Segundo, CA 90245-5013
Telephone: (310) 482-5800, Web Site:
www.photostamps.com
Chmn & CEO: Ken McBride
Chief Technology Officer: Michael
Biswas
Co Pres: James M. Bortnak
Co Pres & CFO: Kyle Huebner
Primary Market Served: Business

Personalized stamps

PROFESSIONAL CREATIONS
1220 Church St
New Castle, IN 47362
Telephone: (765) 529-1590, Toll Free:
(800) 428-8855, E-Mail: sales@
professionaldesignllc.com, Web Site:
www.professionaldesignllc.com
Pres & CEO: Pam Brake
Conducts Business: U.S.
Primary Market Served: Business
Catalog available online

Market a wide variety of promotional
products to professionals - orthodont-
ists, dentists, chiropractors, medical
doctors, optometrists, veterinarians,
teachers & podiatrists. The focus of the
product line is practice promotion. Also
carry a line of office apparel & sportswear geared to each individual profession.

PROGRESSIVE ENERGY CORP
650 Corte Raquel
San Marcos, CA 92069-7320
Telephone: (760) 727-2906, Toll Free:
(800) 525-8624, FAX: (760) 727-
0947, E-Mail: patrickkilleen@cox.
net
Pres: Patrick Killeen
Catalog Prod Mgr: Judith Trevaskis
Conducts Business: Worldwide
Employees: 3
Primary Market Served: Business &
Consumer
Advertising/Marketing Budget Related
to Direct Marketing: 51-75%

Direct Marketing ad budget:
Direct Mail: 40%
Magazines: 60%
Founded: 1980

Market automotive aftermarket products & home security products through
catalogs, space ads & export.

PUTNAM ROLLING LADDER CO INC
32 Howard St
New York, NY 10013-3112
Telephone: (212) 226-5147, FAX:
(212) 941-1836, E-Mail:
putnam1905@aol.com, Web Site:
www.putnamrollingladder.com
Owner Pres: Gregg Peters Monsees
Conducts Business: Worldwide
Employees: 16
Primary Market Served: Business &
Consumer
Catalog available online
Direct online sales
Advertising/Marketing Budget Related
to Direct Marketing: 26-50%
Direct Marketing ad budget:
Magazines: 75%
Online: 25%
Founded: 1905
Gross sales or billing: $3,500,000

Sell custom-made solid hardwood rolling ladders for homes, home libraries,
businesses, lofts & stores; step stools &
library carts; step & extension ladders
in wood, aluminum & fiberglass; steel
warehouse ladders, oak telephone ladders.

REAL GOODS TRADING CORP
Subs. of Gaiam Inc
13771 S Hwy 101
Hopland, CA 95449
Telephone: (707) 472-2403, Toll Free:
(888) 919-2400, FAX: (707) 472-
2430, Web Site: www.realgoods.com
Pres & CEO: John Schaeffer
Employees: 102
Primary Market Served: Consumer
Catalog available online
Direct online sales
Advertising/Marketing Budget Related
to Direct Marketing: 0-25%
Founded: 1978

Renewable energy & conservation
products.

RENAISSANCE GREETING CARDS INC
Subs. of FTD Inc
3113 Woodcreek Dr
Downers Grove, IL 60515
Toll Free: (800) 736-3383, Web Site:
www.ftd.com

Pres: Randy Kleinrock
VP: Bill Grabin
Mktg Commun Dir: Ken Caitlin
Mktg Dir: Margaret Kleinrock
Natl Sls Mgr: Scott Lovejoy
Conducts Business: Worldwide
Employees: 65
Primary Market Served: Business
Indirect online sales
Advertising/Marketing Budget Related to Direct Marketing: 0-25%
Direct Marketing ad budget:
Direct Mail: $100,000
Magazines: $50,000
Telephone: $100,000
Founded: 1977

Greeting cards for all occasions to small businesses for resale to consumers. Customers are primarily card & gift shops, grocery stores, drug stores, hospital gift shops & florists.

RENAISSANCE LEARNING
2911 Peach St
Wisconsin Rapids, WI 54494
Telephone: (715) 424-3636, Toll Free: (800) 338-4204, FAX: (877) 280-7642, E-Mail: electronicorders@renaissance.com, Web Site: www.renlearn.com
CEO: John J. Lynch Jr
Chief Mktg Officer: Tracy Hansen
Conducts Business: Worldwide
Employees: 893
Primary Market Served: Business & Consumer
Catalog available online
Direct online sales
Advertising/Marketing Budget Related to Direct Marketing: 51-75%
Founded: 1986
Gross sales or billing: $130,094,000

Publish & market Accelerated Reader, STAR Reading, STAR Math & NEO laptops. School improvement & student assessment programs for K-12 schools.

THE RIGHT START INC
3000 E Third Ave (#15)
Denver, CO 80206
Telephone: (303) 320-8312, Toll Free: (888) 856-8004, E-Mail: customerservice@rightstart.org, Web Site: www.rightstart.com
VP Opers & HR: Gigi Healy
Conducts Business: U.S.
Primary Market Served: Consumer
Advertising/Marketing Budget Related to Direct Marketing: 76-100%
Direct Marketing ad budget:
Direct Mail: 100%
Founded: 1985

Sell quality juvenile & preschool products to upscale families through catalogs & retail stores.

ROBERT MARKETING INC
17 The Court of Island Point
Northbrook, IL 60062-3210
Telephone: (847) 564-3550, FAX: (847) 564-3551
Pres: Lewis Robert
VP: Jeff Robert
Conducts Business: U.S., Mexico, S. America, Caribbean
Employees: 5
Primary Market Served: Business
Catalog available online
Direct online sales
Advertising/Marketing Budget Related to Direct Marketing: 0-25%
Direct Marketing ad budget:
Direct Mail: 100%
Founded: 1987
Gross sales or billing: $5,000,000

Find new products for introduction to direct mail catalogs & export items.

RONELL CLOCK CO
Div. of Roland V Tapp Imports
PO Box 5510
Grants Pass, OR 97527
Toll Free: (800) 334-0135, FAX: (541) 471-0099, E-Mail: info@ronellclock.com, Web Site: www.ronellclock.com
Owner: Roland V. Tapp
Bus Mgr: Lucia M. Foxx
Office Mgr: Lynell L. Tapp
Conducts Business: U.S., Australia, U.K.
Employees: 3
Primary Market Served: Business & Consumer
Catalog available online
Direct online sales
Advertising/Marketing Budget Related to Direct Marketing: 76-100%
Direct Marketing ad budget: $250,000
Direct Mail: 50%
Magazines: 20%
Newspapers: 5%
Telephone: 25%
Founded: 1972
Gross sales or billing: $1,000,000

Clock-related supplies, parts & tools to the clock, watch & jewelry industry. Also, cleaning solutions & ultrasonic tanks.

SAM ASH MUSIC DIRECT
Subs. of Sam Ash Music Group
PO Box 9047
Hicksville, NY 11802
Toll Free: (800) 472-6274, E-Mail: sales@samash.com, Web Site: www.samash.com
Pres: Paul J. Ash
Conducts Business: Worldwide
Employees: 77

Primary Market Served: Business & Consumer
Catalog available online
Direct online sales
Advertising/Marketing Budget Related to Direct Marketing: 0-25%
Founded: 1924

Discount sales of musical instruments, digital pianos, electronic keyboards, sound & recording equipment & computer software for musicians.

JACQUES C SCHIFF JR INC
195 Main St
Ridgefield Park, NJ 07660
Telephone: (201) 641-5566, FAX: (201) 641-5705
Pres: Jacques C. Schiff Jr
Conducts Business: Worldwide
Employees: 7
Primary Market Served: Business & Consumer
Advertising/Marketing Budget Related to Direct Marketing: 76-100%
Direct Marketing ad budget:
Direct Mail: 50%
Magazines: 20%
Newspapers: 20%
Telephone: 10%
Founded: 1947
Gross sales or billing: $600,000

Philatelic auctioneers selling U.S. & worldwide postage stamps & postal history to collectors, dealers & investors throughout the world.

THE SCHWAN FOOD CO
115 W College Dr
Marshall, MN 56258-1747
Telephone: (507) 532-3274, Web Site: www.theschwanfoodcompany.com
CEO: Dimitrios Smyrnios

SEARS CANADA INC
290 Yonge St (Suite 700)
Toronto, ON, Canada M5B 2C3
Telephone: (416) 362-1711, Toll Free: (888) 473-2772, FAX: (613) 391-3047, E-Mail: home@sears.ca, Web Site: www.sears.ca
Exec Chmn: Brandon Stranzl
Pres & Chief Merchant: Carrie Kirkman
Conducts Business: Canada
Employees: 41,000
Primary Market Served: Consumer
Catalog available online
Direct online sales
Founded: 1953
Gross sales or billing: $6,000,000,000

Mass merchandiser selling to consumers through retail stores & catalogs.

SETA CORP OF BOCA INC

6400 E Rogers Cir
Boca Raton, FL 33499-0002
Telephone: (561) 994-2660, Toll Free:
(800) 497-7209, FAX: (561) 994-
2660, Web Site: www.setacorporatin.
com
Pres: Joe D. Seta
VP: Angie Seta
Conducts Business: U.S.
Primary Market Served: Consumer
Catalog available online
Indirect online sales
Advertising/Marketing Budget Related
to Direct Marketing: 76-100%
Gross sales or billing: $14,800,000

Mail order marketer of costume jewelry, cosmetics, health care products &
general merchandise.

SHORTAGE CONTROL INC & SC VIDEO

22643 Ascoa Ct
Strongsville, OH 44149-4700
Telephone: (440) 238-5432, Toll Free:
(800) 332-2288, FAX: (440) 238-
8687, E-Mail: sales@
shortagecontrol.com, Web Site:
www.shortagecontrol.com
Pres: Joseph Young
Dir Mktg Adv: Mark Young
Employees: 16
Primary Market Served: Business
Catalog available online
Direct online sales
Gross sales or billing: $1,800,000

Sell closed circuit television equipment
& accessories through dealer division
to resellers in NA & WW. CCTV systems, consulting services to major retailers, manufacturers & entertainment
users in the US.

SIPCAMADVAN

dba Advan LLC
2525 Meridian Pkwy (Suite 350)
Durham, NC 27713-2261
Toll Free: (800) 295-0733, FAX: (919)
226-1196, Web Site: www.
sipcamadvan.com
CEO: Stefano Della Torre
Primary Market Served: Consumer

SOLAR CINE PRODUCTS INC

4247 S Kedzie Ave
Chicago, IL 60632
Telephone: (773) 254-8310, Toll Free:
(800) 621-8796, FAX: (773) 254-
4124
Conducts Business: U.S.
Primary Market Served: Business &
Consumer
Advertising/Marketing Budget Related
to Direct Marketing: 51-75%
Founded: 1940

SPORTY'S PREFERRED LIVING

Div. of Sportsman's Market Inc
2001 Sportys Dr, Clermont County Airport
Batavia, OH 45103-9719
Telephone: (513) 735-9000, Toll Free:
(800) 776-7897, FAX: (800) 543-
8633, E-Mail: csmgr@sportys.com,
Web Site: www.sportys.com
Chmn: Hal Shevers Jr.
VP, Mktg: Howard W. Law
Primary Market Served: Consumer
Catalog available online
Direct online sales
Advertising/Marketing Budget Related
to Direct Marketing: 76-100%
Founded: 1962

Consumer catalog.

STAGESTEP INC

4701 Bath St (# 46)
Philadelphia, PA 19137
Telephone: (215) 636-9000, Toll Free:
(800) 523-0960, FAX: (267) 672-
2912, E-Mail: stagestep@stagestep.
com, Web Site: www.stagestep.com
Pres: Randy Swartz
VP, Opers: David Bock
Acctg: Christina Crozzoli
Conducts Business: Worldwide
Employees: 20
Primary Market Served: Business &
Consumer
Catalog available online
Direct online sales
Advertising/Marketing Budget Related
to Direct Marketing: 51-75%
Direct Marketing ad budget: $400,000
Direct Mail: 45%
Magazines: 45%
Online: 10%
Founded: 1969

Catalog of performing arts merchandise
including books, CDs, video tapes &
services directed to universities, professionals, libraries, schools & individuals
& health & fitness including books,
CDs, videos, CD-ROMs & equipment.
Sell a complete line of dance & theatrical stage flooring, plus aerobic &
weight room floors. Carry tapes, adhesives & other floor care products.

STOCK DRIVE PRODUCTS

2101 Jericho Tpke
New Hyde Park, NY 11040
Telephone: (516) 328-3300, Toll Free:
(800) 819-8900, FAX: (516) 326-
8827, E-Mail: sdp-sisupport@sdp-si.
com, Web Site: www.sdp.si.com
CEO & Pres: Robert Kufner
Mktg Mgr: Herbert R. Arum
Gen Mgr: Robert E. Lindemann
Conducts Business: U.S.

Employees: 180
Primary Market Served: Business
Catalog available online
Advertising/Marketing Budget Related
to Direct Marketing: 26-50%
Direct Marketing ad budget: $220,000
Direct Mail: 50%
Magazines: 50%
Founded: 1969
Gross sales or billing: $12,000,000

Publish a 2,400-page catalog for machinists, mechanics, inventors & hobbyists. Feature over 53,000 electromechanical components.

SUMMIT INDUSTRIES INC

839 Pickens Industrial Dr
Marietta, GA 30062
Telephone: (770) 590-0600, Toll Free:
(800) 241-6996, FAX: (770) 590-
0714, E-Mail: info@summitinds.
com, Web Site: www.summitinds.
com
CEO: Kenneth Evans
Conducts Business: U.S. & 40 other
countries
Employees: 30
Primary Market Served: Business &
Consumer
Catalog available online
Direct online sales
Advertising/Marketing Budget Related
to Direct Marketing: 0-25%
Direct Marketing ad budget:
Direct Mail: 25%
Magazines: 75%
Founded: 1920

Sell leather care products to owners of
high-end cars with leather seats. Sell
skincare products to nursing homes,
home health care & hospitals. Also sell
over-the-counter cough/cold & animal
health products.

SVOBODA COLLINS LLC

dba Svoboda Capital Partners
1 North Franklin (Suite 1500)
Chicago, IL 60606
Telephone: (312) 267-8750, FAX:
(312) 267-6025, E-Mail: info@
svoco.com, Web Site: www.svoco.
com
Sr Mng Dir: John A. Svoboda
Mng Dir: Alex R. Miller
Mng Dir & Oper Partner: Andrew B.
Albert
Conducts Business: U.S.
Employees: 180
Primary Market Served: Business &
Consumer
Catalog available online
Direct online sales
Advertising/Marketing Budget Related
to Direct Marketing: 0-25%
Founded: 1998

Gross sales or billing: $80,000,000

Pool supplies & used printer parts.

TABCOM

dba 1800PetSupplies
1 Maplewood Dr
Hazleton, PA 18202-9790
Telephone: (570) 384-5555, Toll Free: (800) 738-7877, FAX: (570) 384-2500, E-Mail: customerservice@petsupplies.com, Web Site: www.petsupplies.com
VP, Mdsg: Judith Patterson
Conducts Business: Worldwide
Employees: 96
Primary Market Served: Business & Consumer
Indirect online sales
Advertising/Marketing Budget Related to Direct Marketing: 76-100%
Founded: 1969

International mail order company that publishes four titles-The Dog Outfitters (business to business pet supply catalog). Discount Master Animal Care (consumer pet product catalog). Maplewood Crafts (institutional & consumer craft catalog). Home Pet Shop (consumer pet product catalog).

TEACHERS' DISCOVERY

Div. of American Eagle Co Inc
2741 Paldan Dr
Auburn Hills, MI 48326-1827
Toll Free: (800) 832-2437, FAX: (800) 287-4509, E-Mail: orders@teachersdiscovery.com, Web Site: teachersdiscovery.com
Chmn: Bruce McWilliams
Opers Mgr: Julie Hart
Conducts Business: U.S.
Primary Market Served: Business

Direct mail marketer to schools & hospitals including supplies to aid teachers in English, social studies & foreign languages.

TERUMO CARDIOVASCULAR SYSTEMS CORP

6200 Jackson Rd
Ann Arbor, MI 48103-9586
Telephone: (734) 663-4145, Toll Free: (800) 521-2818, Web Site: www.terumo-cvs.com
Dir, Corp Communs: Barbara Schmid
CEO: Mark Sutter

Develop, manufacture & distribute medical devices for cardiac & vascular surgery

3D MAIL RESULTS

6205 S 231st St
Kent, WA 98032-3208

Toll Free: (888) 250-1834, FAX: (253) 398-1551, E-Mail: info@3dmailresults.com, Web Site: www.3dmailresults.com
Owner & Pres: Travis Lee
VP, Mktg: Gerri Norris
Conducts Business: U.S.
Employees: 32
Primary Market Served: Business
Advertising/Marketing Budget Related to Direct Marketing: 51-75%
Direct Marketing ad budget: $500,000
Direct Mail: 30%
Telephone: 70%
Founded: 1970
Gross sales or billing: $6,000,000

Supplies & fixtures for retail stores. Marking, packaging display products & computer systems.

TORAH UMESORAH PUBLICATIONS

Div. of Torah Umesorah-National Society for Hebrew Day Schools
620 Foster Ave
Brooklyn, NY 11230
Telephone: (212) 227-1000, FAX: (212) 406-6934, E-Mail: umesorah@aol.com, Web Site: torahumesorah.com
Natl Dir: Rabbi Dovid Nojowitz
Conducts Business: Worldwide
Employees: 6
Primary Market Served: Business & Consumer
Catalog available online
Advertising/Marketing Budget Related to Direct Marketing: 0-25%
Founded: 1945

Learning material to be used by Hebrew teachers & Hebrew day schools students & parents.

TOTAL TRAINING SOLUTIONS LLC

PO Box 310
Waunakee, WI 53597-0310
Telephone: (608) 849-5563, Toll Free: (800) 831-0678, FAX: (608) 849-5605, (800) 831-3776, E-Mail: kbennett@ttstrain.com, Web Site: www.ttstrain.com
Pres: Mark D. Bennett
Conducts Business: U.S.
Employees: 5
Primary Market Served: Business
Catalog available online
Indirect online sales
Advertising/Marketing Budget Related to Direct Marketing: 51-75%

Provide quality videos, software, furniture displays, & coin handling materials to financial organizations. Fax line for orders: (800) 845-2262.

TRACTOR SUPPLY CO

5401 Virginia Way
Brentwood, TN 37027
Telephone: (615) 366-4600, Toll Free: (877) 718-6750, FAX: (615) 227-4608, Web Site: www.mytscstore.com
Pres & CEO: Gregory A. Sandfort
Conducts Business: U.S.
Employees: 1,400
Primary Market Served: Consumer
Direct Marketing ad budget:
Direct Mail: $800,000
Newspapers: $3,900,000
TV/Radio: $100,000
Gross sales or billing: $216,000,000

Retail chain of 206 farm supply stores.

TROPHYLAND USA INC

7001 W 20th Ave
Hialeah, FL 33014
Telephone: (305) 823-4830, Toll Free: (800) 327-5820, FAX: (305) 823-4836, E-Mail: info@trophyland.com, Web Site: www.trophyland.com
Pres: Anthony Mendez
Mgr: Jackie Moran
Conducts Business: Worldwide
Employees: 75
Primary Market Served: Business & Consumer
Catalog available online
Indirect online sales
Advertising/Marketing Budget Related to Direct Marketing: 51-75%
Direct Marketing ad budget: $40,000
Direct Mail: 45%
Magazines: 15%
Telephone: 40%
Founded: 1969
Gross sales or billing: $3,000,000

Sell trophies, plaques, medals, desk sets, display cases & laminations.

ULINE

12575 Uline Dr
Pleasant Prairie, WI 53158-3686
Telephone: (847) 473-3000, Toll Free: (800) 295-5510, FAX: (800) 295-5571, E-Mail: customer.service@uline.com, Web Site: www.uline.com
Chmn: Richard Uihlein
Pres: Elizabeth Uihlein
Govt Cust Svcs: Trish Schultz
Conducts Business: U.S., Canada, Puerto Rico, Mexico
Employees: 2,000
Primary Market Served: Business
Catalog available online
Direct online sales
Advertising/Marketing Budget Related to Direct Marketing: 76-100%
Direct Marketing ad budget:
Direct Mail: 100%

Founded: 1980

Industrial mail order firm selling shipping & packaging supplies.

UNIVERSITY AT BUFFALO CENTER FOR ENTREPRENEURIAL LEADERSHIP

77 Goodell St (Ste 201)
Buffalo, NY 14203
Telephone: (716) 885-5715, FAX: (716) 845-6999, E-Mail: mgt-cel@ buffalo.edu, Web Site: http://mgt. buffalo.edu/entrepreneurship/cel
Exec Dir & Asst Dean: Tom Ulbrich
Primary Market Served: Consumer

VECTOR MARKETING CORP

Subs. of Atlas Corp
1116 E State St
Olean, NY 14760-3814
Telephone: (716) 373-6141, (267) 880-1750, FAX: (716) 373-6145, Web Site: www.cutco.com
Production Coord: Michele Oakley
Mktg Mgr: Steve Pokrzyk
Pres - Vector East: Albert DiLeonardo
Pres - Vector West: Bruce Goodman
Mktg Web Coord: Charles LaBorde
Pres & COO: John Whelpley
Conducts Business: U.S., Canada, Korea
Primary Market Served: Consumer
Founded: 1985

Marketer of consumer products including cutlery & sporting knives.

VEHICLE ASSURANCE

3902 S Old Hwy 94
Saint Charles, MO 63304
Telephone: (636) 925-7800, Toll Free: (866) 522-5581
Primary Market Served: Consumer

THE VERMONT COUNTRY STORE

5650 Main St
Manchester Center, VT 05255-9711
Telephone: (802) 362-8200, Web Site: www.vermontcountrystore.com
Dir Mktg: Lori Vilbrin

General store.

WHAT ON EARTH

Div. of Universal Direct Fulfillment Corp
5581 Hudson Industrial Pkwy
Hudson, OH 44236-5019
Telephone: (330) 963-6554, Toll Free: (800) 945-2552, FAX: (800) 950-9569, Web Site: www. whatonearthcatalog.com
Pres & CEO: Jared Florian

Primary Market Served: Consumer
Catalog available online
Direct online sales
Mail order catalog.

WHIRLEY DRINK WORKS

618 Fourth Ave
Warren, PA 16365
Telephone: (814) 723-7600, Toll Free: (800) 825-5575, FAX: (814) 723-3245, E-Mail: info@ whirleydrinkworks.com, Web Site: www.whirleydrinkworks.com
Pres: Lincoln Sokolski
VP: Andrew Sokolski
VP, Mktg & Natl Accts Sls Mgr: Bill Turner
HR Mgr: Rita Bevevino
Employees: 300
Primary Market Served: Business
Catalog available online
Direct online sales
Advertising/Marketing Budget Related to Direct Marketing: 0-25%

Custom decorated plastic beverage containers including Thermo Mugs and sports bottles.

WIN CRAFT INC

1124 W Fifth St, PO Box 888
Winona, MN 55987
Telephone: (507) 454-5510, Toll Free: (800) 533-8100, FAX: (507) 454-6403, E-Mail: inquiries@ wincraftschool.com, Web Site: www. wincraftschool.com
Pres: Richard Pope
Sr VP: Robert Flom
VP, Sls: Don Trandem
VP, Mktg: Eric Johnson
VP: John Killen
Conducts Business: U.S.
Employees: 300
Primary Market Served: Consumer
Catalog available online
Direct online sales
Direct Marketing ad budget: $300,000
Direct Mail: 100%

Sell school related novelty items (personalized with school colors) & cheerleader related products by mail order catalog. Used for fund-raising purposes.

WOODWIND & BRASSWIND INC

4004 Technology Dr, South Bend, IN 46628-9745-POST
PO Box 7479
Westlake Village, CA 91359
Telephone: (574) 251-3500, Toll Free: (800) 348-5003, FAX: (800) 266-5962, Web Site: www.wwbw.com
Pres: Dennis Bamber

Gen Mgr: Joe Hickner
Adv: Rona Palmer
Conducts Business: Worldwide
Employees: 170
Primary Market Served: Business & Consumer
Catalog available online
Indirect online sales
Advertising/Marketing Budget Related to Direct Marketing: 76-100%
Direct Marketing ad budget:
Direct Mail: 90%
Newspapers: 10%
Founded: 1978

Sell musical instruments & supplies.

XCEL ENERGY

414 Nicollet Mall (GO 6)
Minneapolis, MN 55401-1927
Telephone: (612) 330-6783, Web Site: xcelenergy.com
Pres, CEO & Chmn Bd: Ben Fowke
Primary Market Served: Consumer

DAVID YURMAN ENTERPRISES LLC

24 Vestry St
New York, NY 10013-1903
Telephone: (212) 896-1550, Toll Free: (888) 398-7626, Web Site: davidyurman.com
CEO: David Yurman
Primary Market Served: Consumer

Jewelry, timepieces & gift items

Gifts & Collectibles Catalogs (6)

ABBEY PRESS
Subs. of St Meinrad Archabbey
One Hill Dr
Saint Meinrad, IN 47577-1004
Telephone: (812) 357-8368, FAX: (812) 357-8388, Web Site: www.abbeypress.com
CEO: Gerald Wilhite
Mgr: Norma Schipp
Sr Customer Svc Rep: Tracy Schaefer
Conducts Business: U.S.
Employees: 280
Primary Market Served: Business & Consumer
Advertising/Marketing Budget Related to Direct Marketing: 76-100%

Direct mail marketing company specializing in publishing The Abbey Press Christian Family Gift Catalog. Seventeen catalogs are mailed each year to over 25 million families.

AMERICAN GIRL BRANDS LLC
8400 Fairway Pl
Middleton, WI 53562-2548
Telephone: (608) 836-4848, Web Site: www.americangirl.com
Exec VP: Jean McKenzie
Primary Market Served: Consumer

AMERICAN MINT LLC
5051 Louise Dr
Mechanicsburg, PA 17055-4927
Telephone: (717) 458-9200, Toll Free: (877) 807-MINT, FAX: (717) 458-9211, E-Mail: contact@americanmint.com, Web Site: www.americanmint.com
Pres: Kevin Sacher
Conducts Business: U.S.
Primary Market Served: Consumer
Catalog available online
Direct online sales
Advertising/Marketing Budget Related to Direct Marketing: 76-100%
Direct Marketing ad budget: $5,000,000
Direct Mail: 70%
Magazines: 5%
Newspapers: 10%
Online: 5%
TV/Radio: 5%
Telephone: 5%
Founded: 1999
Gross sales or billing: $10,000,000

Consumer mail order products and continuity offers.

ANCIENT CIRCLES
Div. of Open Circle Distributors
190 North St
Willits, CA 95490-3420
Toll Free: (800) 726-8032, FAX: (707) 459-0261, E-Mail: ancient@pacific.net, Web Site: www.ancientcircles.com
Owner & Adv: Ann Weller
Conducts Business: U.S., U.K., Germany, Canada
Employees: 5
Primary Market Served: Business & Consumer
Catalog available online
Indirect online sales
Advertising/Marketing Budget Related to Direct Marketing: 26-50%
Direct Marketing ad budget: $4,000
Magazines: 90%
Telephone: 10%
Founded: 1986

Celtic & symbolic jewelry, scarves, masks, textiles & drums to the pagan, Celtic & metaphysical market.

ANHEUSER-BUSCH INC PROMOTIONAL PRODUCTS GROUP
Anheuser-Busch Co Inc
20 Constitution Blvd S
Shelton, CT 06484
Toll Free: (800) 742-5283, Web Site: www.budshop.com
Prod Promos Dir: Mary Houlihan
Mdsg Mgr: Ann Gast
Web Project Mgr: Karen Garrett
Category Mgr: Regina Garofalo
Category Mgr: Tami Bafaro
Category Mgr: Beth Schlegel
Category Mgr: Melissa Toennies
Conducts Business: U.S.
Employees: 200
Primary Market Served: Business & Consumer
Advertising/Marketing Budget Related to Direct Marketing: 0-25%

Direct to consumer & business-to-business catalog marketers of Anheuser-Busch Inc logo merchandise.

ANYTHING GOES
dba Heavenly Treasures
321 Main St
Allenhurst, NJ 07711-1037
Telephone: (732) 531-8040, Web Site: www.heavenlytreasures.com
Pres: Abraham Ades
Sec: Michael Ades
Primary Market Served: Consumer

ARCTIC TRADING CO INC
Kelsey & Bernier Sts, Box 910
Churchill, MB, Canada R0B 0E0
Telephone: (204) 675-8804, Toll Free: (800) 665-0431, FAX: (204) 675-2164, E-Mail: atcpenny@mts.net, Web Site: www.arctictradingco.com
Owner: Penny Rawlings
Sls Assoc Computer Skills: Susie Bunka
Conducts Business: U.S., Canada, Japan, France, U.K.
Employees: 9
Primary Market Served: Business & Consumer
Catalog available online
Direct online sales
Advertising/Marketing Budget Related to Direct Marketing: 0-25%
Direct Marketing ad budget: $50,000
Direct Mail: 66%
Magazines: 5%
Newspapers: 3%
TV/Radio: 2%
Telephone: 24%
Founded: 1978
Gross sales or billing: $850,000

Native arts & crafts. Manufacturing mittens, moccasins, mukluks, gauntlets, caribou hair sculptures, tuftings & jewelry. Native Inuit & Indian carvings, tools & other handcrafts. Sell to tourists, businesses on the wholesale level & mail order catalog sales.

WENDELL AUGUST FORGE INC
390 Lincoln Ave
Grove City, PA 16127
Telephone: (724) 458-8360, Toll Free: (800) 923-1390, FAX: (724) 458-0906, E-Mail: info@wendell.com, Web Site: www.wendellaugust.com
Mgr: Karl Hart
Artisan: David Bruck
Artisan: Leonard Youngo
Owner: Will Knecht
Primary Market Served: Business & Consumer
Catalog available online
Direct online sales
Advertising/Marketing Budget Related to Direct Marketing: 76-100%
Direct Marketing ad budget: $425,000
Direct Mail: 94%
Magazines: 6%
Founded: 1923

Creators & merchandisers of artistic hand wrought metal gifts.

AWARD CO OF AMERICA
Div. of Randall Publishing Co Inc
3200 Rice Mine Rd
Tuscaloosa, AL 35406-1510

Telephone: (205) 349-2990, Toll Free: (800) 633-5953, FAX: (205) 752-0930, Web Site: www.randallpub.com

Pres: Michael Reilly
Conducts Business: U.S.
Primary Market Served: Business & Consumer
Founded: 1975

Sell laminated & do-it-yourself award plaques & advertising specialties through direct mail.

BABYSHOE.COM

306 Hebron St
Hendersonville, NC 28739-5210
Telephone: (828) 697-5811, Toll Free: (800) 543-8566, FAX: (828) 697-5815, E-Mail: info@babyshoe.com, Web Site: www.babyshoe.com

Pres: Michael Schwartz
Opers Dir: Joy Keifer
Sr Baby Gift Specialist: Connie Medlin
Employees: 6
Primary Market Served: Business & Consumer
Catalog available online
Advertising/Marketing Budget Related to Direct Marketing: 76-100%
Direct Marketing ad budget:
Direct Mail: 90%
Magazines: 10%
Founded: 1950

Infant products.

BATTLEGROUND ANTIQUES INC

3910 US Hwy 70 E
New Bern, NC 28560
Telephone: (252) 636-3039, FAX: (252) 637-1862, E-Mail: tarheelrebel2000@aol.com, Web Site: www.civilwarantiques.com

Sec: William D. Gorges
Textiles Specialist: Lynn Gorges
Conducts Business: Worldwide
Employees: 6
Primary Market Served: Business & Consumer
Catalog available online
Indirect online sales
Advertising/Marketing Budget Related to Direct Marketing: 51-75%
Direct Marketing ad budget: $30,000
Direct Mail: 10%
Magazines: 70%
Newspapers: 10%
Telephone: 10%
Founded: 1983
Gross sales or billing: $600,000

Antique militaria, primarily Civil War era, sports collectibles, gold & silver coins, quilts & fine art.

BICK INTERNATIONAL

dba "International Coin & Stamp Collectors Society"
PO Box 854
Van Nuys, CA 91408-0854
Telephone: (818) 997-6496, FAX: (818) 988-4337, E-Mail: iibick@sbcglobal.net, Web Site: www.bickinternational.com

Pres: Israel Bick
Conducts Business: Worldwide
Employees: 6
Primary Market Served: Business & Consumer
Catalog available online
Direct online sales
Advertising/Marketing Budget Related to Direct Marketing: 0-25%
Direct Marketing ad budget: $100,000
Founded: 1952

Wholesale & retail collectibles.

BIRTHDAY KEEPSAKES

1323 S Garfield Ave
Loveland, CO 80537-6334
Telephone: (970) 669-5506, Web Site: www.bkeepsakes.com

Gen Mgr: Karin Delaney

BIZZARO RUBBER STAMPS

PO Box 292
Greenville, RI 02828-0292
Telephone: (401) 231-8777, FAX: (401) 231-4770, E-Mail: bizzaroinc@earthlink.net, Web Site: www.bizzaro.com

Pres: Doreen Tirocchi
Mktg Mgr: Bob Tirocchi
Conducts Business: U.S., Canada
Employees: 5
Primary Market Served: Business & Consumer
Catalog available online
Indirect online sales
Advertising/Marketing Budget Related to Direct Marketing: 0-25%
Direct Marketing ad budget: $5,000
Direct Mail: 20%
Magazines: 40%
Online: 40%
Founded: 1971
Gross sales or billing: $80,000

Artistic rubber stamps & supplies sold retail & wholesale.

BEVERLY BREMER SILVER SHOP

3164 Peachtree Rd NE
Atlanta, GA 30305-1853
Telephone: (404) 261-4009, Toll Free: (800) 270-4009, E-Mail: sterlingsilver@worldnet.att.net, Web Site: www.beverlybremer.com

Pres: Beverly H. Bremer
Employees: 22

Primary Market Served: Consumer
Founded: 1975

Retailer of sterling silver products, flatware, hollowware & gifts.

BRONNER'S CHRISTMAS WONDERLAND

25 Christmas Ln
Frankenmuth, MI 48734-1807
Telephone: (989) 652-9931, Web Site: www.bronners.com

Pres & CEO: Wayne Bronner
Primary Market Served: Consumer
Founded: 1945

Retailer of Christmas ornaments, Christmas trees, Christmas decorations, collectibles & more.

BROWNELL HOLLY FARMS

17251 S Clackamas River Dr, Oregon City, OR 97045-9493
17251 S Clackamas River Dr
Oregon City, OR 97045-9493
Telephone: (503) 631-7475, FAX: (503) 631-7481, E-Mail: sales@brownellhollyfarms.com, Web Site: www.brownellhollyfarms.com

Owner: Granville R. Lee
Assoc: Lauren Lee
Assoc: Jenny Lee
Conducts Business: U.S.
Employees: 10
Primary Market Served: Business & Consumer
Catalog available online
Advertising/Marketing Budget Related to Direct Marketing: 76-100%
Direct Marketing ad budget:
Direct Mail: 80%
Magazines: 10%
Newspapers: 5%
Telephone: 5%
Founded: 1918
Gross sales or billing: $200,000

Grower & shipper of Christmas holly & wreaths directly to the consumer or as gifts. Supplier to florists, fund raisers & businesses.

BUNKER HILL AUCTIONS

21 Foxhurst Ln
Millbrook, IL 60536
Telephone: (630) 553-8968, E-Mail: bunkerhillauctions@joimail.com, Web Site: www.bunkerhillauctions.com

Owner: Kaye Kerekes-Bruscato
Co-Owner & Sls: Nick Bruscato
Conducts Business: U.S.
Employees: 2
Primary Market Served: Business & Consumer
Catalog available online
Indirect online sales

Advertising/Marketing Budget Related to Direct Marketing: 0-25%
Founded: 1985
Gross sales or billing: $35,000

Close-out & discounted name brand holiday decorations & collectibles.

CARIBE DIRECT INC
107 Calle Tres Hermanos
San Juan, PR 00907-2306
Telephone: (787) 722-5188, FAX: (787) 723-6165, E-Mail: islaonline@prw.net, Web Site: www.islaonline.com
Pres: Elizabeth Parker
VP, Opers: Gerardo Cumpiano
Conducts Business: U.S.
Employees: 8
Primary Market Served: Business & Consumer
Catalog available online
Indirect online sales
Advertising/Marketing Budget Related to Direct Marketing: 76-100%
Direct Marketing ad budget:
Direct Mail: 100%
Founded: 1994
Gross sales or billing: $1,000,000

Mail order catalog of products from Puerto Rico.

HARRIET CARTER GIFTS INC
PO Box 427
Montgomeryville, PA 18936-0427
Telephone: (215) 361-5100, FAX: (215) 361-1127, Web Site: www.harrietcarter.com
Pres: Ronald P. Lassin
VP: Gary Lassin
Dir Circulation: Linda Mallory
Conducts Business: U.S.
Primary Market Served: Consumer
Catalog available online
Direct online sales

Sell gifts & decorative accessories direct to the consumer.

CARTOUCHE LTD
100 S Early St
Alexandria, VA 22304
Telephone: (703) 823-7904, Toll Free: (800) AT-EGYPT, FAX: (888) 283-4978, E-Mail: sales@egyptianimports.com, Web Site: www.egyptianimports.com
Co-Owner: Steve Collins
Co-Owner: David Brayer
Employees: 5
Primary Market Served: Business & Consumer
Catalog available online
Direct online sales

Advertising/Marketing Budget Related to Direct Marketing: 76-100%
Direct Marketing ad budget:
Direct Mail: 40%
Magazines: 60%
Founded: 1980

Gold importers; personalized hieroglyphic jewelry.

CHARISMA BRANDS LLC
23482 Peralta Dr Ste A
Laguna Hills, CA 92653-1733
Telephone: (949) 788-8803, Toll Free: (800) 779-5335, Web Site: www.charismabrands.com
Pres & CEO: Anthony Shutts
Primary Market Served: Business & Consumer

CHARTIFACTS
3221 Marlboro Ct
Richmond, VA 23225-0654
Telephone: (804) 272-7120
VP: Susan Auburn
Conducts Business: U.S.
Employees: 1
Primary Market Served: Business & Consumer
Indirect online sales
Advertising/Marketing Budget Related to Direct Marketing: 76-100%
Direct Marketing ad budget: $2,000
Direct Mail: 20%
Magazines: 80%
Founded: 1987
Gross sales or billing: $50,000

Antique nautical maps & reproductions to general public.

CHELSEA CLOCK CO INC
284 Everett Ave
Chelsea, MA 02150-1598
Telephone: (617) 884-0250, Toll Free: (866) 899-2805, FAX: (617) 830-0599, Web Site: www.chelseaclock.com
Pres: J. K. Nicholas
Mktg Commun Mgr: Rosanne Spinali
Conducts Business: Worldwide
Employees: 41
Primary Market Served: Business
Advertising/Marketing Budget Related to Direct Marketing: 0-25%
Direct Marketing ad budget:
Online: 100%
Founded: 1897

Sell wall clocks: marine, striking & non-striking, 8 day spring wound, quartz crystal, tide & time & barometers. Also carry an assortment of jeweler's clocks.

CLUBS OF AMERICA
484 W Wagner Rd

Lakemoor, IL 60051
Telephone: (815) 363-4000, Toll Free: (800) CLUB-USA, FAX: (815) 363-4677, E-Mail: info@greatclubs.com, Web Site: www.clubsofamerica.com
Pres: Douglas M. Doretti
VP: Dirk J. Doretti
Conducts Business: U.S.
Employees: 30
Primary Market Served: Business & Consumer
Catalog available online
Direct online sales
Founded: 1994

Continuity mail order company. Eight gift-of-the-month clubs in beer, wine, flowers, coffee, cigars, pizza, fruit & chocolate. Customers have the option to join any or all clubs. Different selections are delivered each month. No minimum membership time. Corporate discount plans available.

COLLECTOR'S ARMOURY LTD
PO Box 2948
McDonough, GA 30253-1743
Telephone: (678) 593-2660, Toll Free: (877) 276-6879, FAX: (678) 593-2660, E-Mail: sales@collectorsarmoury.com, Web Site: www.collectorsarmoury.com
VP: Scott Nelson
CEO: Tom Nelson
Pres: Jim Kemp
Conducts Business: U.S., Canada, Australia, Belgium, France, U.K., Germany, S. America, Scandinavia
Employees: 15
Primary Market Served: Business & Consumer
Catalog available online
Advertising/Marketing Budget Related to Direct Marketing: 0-25%
Direct Marketing ad budget:
Direct Mail: 55%
Magazines: 45%
Founded: 1968
Gross sales or billing: $4,000,000

Provide non-firing replicas of famous guns & other military memorabilia to the general public through mail order catalogs, retail store & wholesale operations.

COLLECTOR'S TEAPOT
Subs. of Bailey Pottery Corp
10 Broeck Ave
Kingston, NY 12401
Telephone: (845) 339-1109, Toll Free: (800) 724-3306, FAX: (845) 339-5530, Web Site: www.collectorsteapot.com
CEO: Anne Bailey
CEO: Jim Bailey

Conducts Business: U.S.
Employees: 20
Primary Market Served: Business &
   Consumer
Advertising/Marketing Budget Related
   to Direct Marketing: 0-25%
Direct Marketing ad budget:
Direct Mail: 75%
Magazines: 25%
Founded: 1978

Full-color catalog direct mail to retail
consumers selling food & collectible
giftware.

THE COUNTRY HOUSE INC

805 E Main St
Salisbury, MD 21804-5024
Telephone: (410) 749-1959, Toll Free:
   (800) 331-3602, FAX: (410) 548-
   3224, E-Mail: web@
   thecountryhouse.com, Web Site:
   www.thecountryhouse.com
Pres: Michael Delano
Employees: 30
Primary Market Served: Consumer
Catalog available online
Direct online sales
Advertising/Marketing Budget Related
   to Direct Marketing: 51-75%
Founded: 1985

Gifts, accessories & mail order catalogs.

CREATIVE CATALOGS
CORP

1005 101st St
Lemont, IL 60439-9642
Telephone: (630) 783-2400, Web Site:
   www.personalcreations.com
Dir Mktg: Judy Nelson
CEO: John Semmelhack
Primary Market Served: Consumer
Founded: 1997

Operates a catalog and internet direct
marketing company.

CREATIVE IRISH GIFTS

3801 Woodland Heights Rd Ste 100
Little Rock, AR 72212-2410
Telephone: (330) 954-1200, FAX:
   (330) 650-8888, E-Mail: gifts@
   shopirish.com, Web Site: www.
   shopirish.com
Pres: Diane O'Connor
COO: Robert O'Connor
Conducts Business: Worldwide
Employees: 50
Primary Market Served: Consumer
Catalog available online
Direct online sales
Advertising/Marketing Budget Related
   to Direct Marketing: 0-25%
Founded: 1982

Gross sales or billing: $8,000,000
Irish items & gifts.

CURRENT USA INC

Subs. of Deluxe Corp
1025 E Woodmen Rd
Colorado Springs, CO 80920-3181
Telephone: (719) 594-4100, Toll Free:
   (877) 665-4458, FAX: (719) 531-
   2283, Web Site: www.currentinc.
   com
Pres: Wendy Huxta
Sales Exec: Kirby Heck
Dir, IT: Mickey Gardner
Dir, HR: Paul Andersen
Conducts Business: U.S.
Employees: 1,600
Primary Market Served: Consumer
Catalog available online
Direct online sales
Advertising/Marketing Budget Related
   to Direct Marketing: 76-100%
Founded: 1950
Gross sales or billing: $208,000,000

Sell greeting cards, stationery, calendars, gift wrapping paper, gift items,
personal & business checks via catalog.

CUSTOM MINIATURES

19 Winnhaven Dr
Hudson, NH 03051-4748
Telephone: (603) 882-6392
Owner: Al Chandronnait
Conducts Business: U.S.
Employees: 1
Primary Market Served: Business &
   Consumer
Advertising/Marketing Budget Related
   to Direct Marketing: 0-25%
Direct Marketing ad budget: $3,000
Direct Mail: 80%
Magazines: 20%
Gross sales or billing: $50,000

Custom dollhouse miniatures sold to
miniature shops & retail customers
throughout the country.

DAVIDOFF OF GENEVA INC

Subs. of Davidoff of Geneva of Swit-
   zerland
3001 Gateway Centre Pkwy N
Pinellas Park, FL 33782-6124
Telephone: (727) 828-5400, Toll Free:
   (800) 328-4365, FAX: (203) 975-
   0090
Pres, US Division: Peter Banninger
VP, Opers: Eva Baurenfeind
Sr Mktg Mgr: Samuel Russell
Gen Mgr: Michael Herklots
Conducts Business: Worldwide
Employees: 90
Primary Market Served: Business &
   Consumer
Catalog available online

Advertising/Marketing Budget Related
   to Direct Marketing: 0-25%
Founded: 1906

Catalog marketer of cigars, smoker's &
men's accessories.

DESIGN TOSCANO, INC

1400 Morse Ave
Elk Grove Village, IL 60007-5722
Telephone: (847) 952-0100, Toll Free:
   (800) 525-5141, FAX: (847) 952-
   8992, Web Site: www.designtoscano.
   com
Pres: Michael Stopka
Primary Market Served: Consumer
Founded: 1989
Gross sales or billing: $17,000,000

Sells classic European reproductions &
French tapestry. Catalog & mail-order
houses.

DIAMONDS BY RENNIE
ELLEN

15 W 47th St (Rm 503)
New York, NY 10036
Telephone: (212) 869-5525, FAX:
   (212) 869-5526, Web Site: www.
   rennieellen.com
Owner: Rennie Ellen
Conducts Business: U.S.
Primary Market Served: Business &
   Consumer
Catalog available online
Founded: 1965

Diamonds sold direct to the public.

DRUMBEAT INDIAN ARTS
INC

4143 N 16th St (Suite 1)
Phoenix, AZ 85016-5351
Telephone: (602) 266-4823, Toll Free:
   (800) 895-4859, FAX: (602) 265-
   2402, E-Mail: info@
   drumbeatindianarts.com, Web Site:
   www.drumbeatindianarts.com
Pres: Robert L. Nuss
Conducts Business: Worldwide
Primary Market Served: Business &
   Consumer
Catalog available online
Advertising/Marketing Budget Related
   to Direct Marketing: 51-75%
Direct Marketing ad budget:
Direct Mail: 40%
Magazines: 35%
Newspapers: 20%
TV/Radio: 5%
Founded: 1984

Wholesale & retail seller of American
Indian music recordings, cassettes,
compact discs, DVDs, books & craft
supplies.

EMBLEM & BADGE INC
16 Sunnyside Ave
Johnston, RI 02919-5318
Telephone: (401) 365-1265, Toll Free:
 (800) 875-5444, FAX: (401) 365-
 1263, E-Mail: sales@recognition.
 com, Web Site: www.recognition.
 com
Pres: David A. Resnik
Conducts Business: U.S.
Employees: 35
Primary Market Served: Business &
 Consumer
Catalog available online
Indirect online sales
Advertising/Marketing Budget Related
 to Direct Marketing: 26-50%
Founded: 1932

Awards & recognition products.

FAMILY ALBUM
4887 Newport Rd
Kinzers, PA 17535-9793
Telephone: (717) 442-0220, FAX:
 (717) 442-7904, E-Mail: rarebooks@
 pobox.com
Dir: Ron Lieberman
Conducts Business: U.S., Canada, Eu-
 rope
Employees: 2
Primary Market Served: Business &
 Consumer
Catalog available online
Indirect online sales
Advertising/Marketing Budget Related
 to Direct Marketing: 26-50%
Direct Marketing ad budget:
Direct Mail: 60%
Magazines: 30%
Telephone: 10%
Founded: 1969
Gross sales or billing: $250,000

Antiquarian books & library supplies.

MICHAEL C FINA
500 Park Ave (Frnt A)
New York, NY 10022-1606
Telephone: (212) 557-2500, Web Site:
 www.michaelcfina.com
Pres: George Fina

Designer of fine jewelry.

GAELSONG
PO Box 15356
Seattle, WA 98115-0356
Telephone: (206) 526-8350, Web Site:
 www.gaelsong.com
Pres: Colleen Connell

GALLERY OF CATS
26136 Galvez Ct
Valencia, CA 91355-3349
Telephone: (818) 782-6264, E-Mail:
 helpdesk@galleryofcats.com, Web
 Site: www.galleryofcats.com
Pres: Neil L. Kleeger
Conducts Business: U.S., Canada,
 Hong Kong
Primary Market Served: Consumer
Catalog available online
Indirect online sales
Advertising/Marketing Budget Related
 to Direct Marketing: 0-25%
Founded: 1987

Sell gifts & collectibles of cats to
wholesale & consumer outlets.

THE GALLERY SHOP
1285 Elmwood Ave, Albright-Knox
 Art Gallery
Buffalo, NY 14222-1096
Telephone: (716) 882-8700 X258,
 FAX: (716) 882-1958, E-Mail:
 gallshop@albrightknox.org, Web
 Site: www.albrightknox.org
Dir: Louis Granchos
Dir Advancement: Elaine Pyne
Dep Dir: Karen Lee Spaulding
CFO: Patrick Kilcullen
Sr Curator: Douglas Dreishpoon Ph.D.
Conducts Business: U.S., Canada, Eu-
 rope, Asia
Employees: 8
Primary Market Served: Business &
 Consumer
Catalog available online
Advertising/Marketing Budget Related
 to Direct Marketing: 0-25%

Sell publications & reproductions from
the permanent collection of the Albright-Knox Art Gallery. Art objects,
educational toys & stationery designed
& created by contemporary artists com-
missioned by the Gallery Shop.

**GEARY'S OF BEVERLY
 HILLS**
aka Tjb Geary's LLC
351 N Beverly Dr
Beverly Hills, CA 90210-4794
Telephone: (310) 273-4741, Toll Free:
 (800) 793-6670, FAX: (310) 858-
 7555, Web Site: www.gearys.com
Pres: Tom Blumental
Conducts Business: U.S.
Employees: 65
Primary Market Served: Consumer
Advertising/Marketing Budget Related
 to Direct Marketing: 26-50%
Founded: 1930
Gross sales or billing: $5,000,000

Catalog & retail sales of fine china,
crystal, silver, gifts, table linens, tabletop items & accessories.

GERSTNER WOODWORKS
Div of H. Gerstner & Sons, Inc.
20 Gerstner Way
Dayton, OH 45402-8408
Telephone: (937) 228-1662, FAX:
 (937) 228-8557, E-Mail: info@
 gerstnerusa.com, Web Site: www.
 gerstnerusa.com
Pres: Jack Campbell
Conducts Business: U.S.
Employees: 10
Primary Market Served: Business &
 Consumer
Catalog available online
Indirect online sales
Advertising/Marketing Budget Related
 to Direct Marketing: 0-25%
Founded: 1906
Gross sales or billing: $1,500,000

Manufacturer of wooden tool chests,
jewelry chests & other fine wood products to industrial & retail markets.

GIFT SERVICES INC
Div. of Gifttree
1800 W Fourth Plain Blvd (Suite
 120B)
Vancouver, WA 98660-1367
Toll Free: (800) 379-4065, FAX: (360)
 699-0597, E-Mail: corpsales@
 gifttree.com, Web Site: www.
 gifttree.com
Mktg Dir: Bonny Elder
Pres & CEO: Craig Bowen
Dir Customer Svc: Shawna Fuller
Reg VP Sls: David Kresser
Conducts Business: U.S.
Employees: 40
Primary Market Served: Business &
 Consumer
Catalog available online
Direct online sales
Direct Marketing ad budget:
Direct Mail: 95%
Telephone: 5%
Founded: 1997
Gross sales or billing: $11,000,000

Retail ecommerce website. Hand
crafted gift baskets, fresh flowers, balloons, fruit baskets, corporate & unique
gifts.

GIFTS CORP
130 Bell Farm Rd (Unit 2)
Barrie, ON, Canada L4M 6J4
Telephone: (905) 670-1126, Toll Free:
 (800) 565-3130, FAX: (905) 670-
 1127, E-Mail: customerservice@
 regal.ca, Web Site: www.
 regalgreetings.com
CEO & Sr VP Fin: Kevin Watkinson
Pres: Greg Neanth
Exec VP & COO: Gregory W. Dunn
Dir Mktg: Brian Lucas
Conducts Business: Canada

Employees: 1,100
Primary Market Served: Consumer
Catalog available online
Direct online sales
Advertising/Marketing Budget Related
   to Direct Marketing: 26-50%
Founded: 1928
Gross sales or billing: $100,000,000

Manufacturer of greeting cards, gift
wrap & novelties sold via seasonal catalogs.

GIMBELS OF MAINE INC
14 Commercial St
Boothbay Harbor, ME 04538-1821
Telephone: (207) 633-5088, FAX:
   (207) 633-5128, Web Site: www.
   gimbelscollectibles.com
Pres: Mark S. Gimbel
CEO: Diane Gimbel
Conducts Business: U.S.
Employees: 28
Primary Market Served: Consumer
Advertising/Marketing Budget Related
   to Direct Marketing: 76-100%
Direct Marketing ad budget:
Direct Mail: 100%
Gross sales or billing: $2,500,000

By mail-collectors thimbles, dolls &
figurines.

GRACELAND
Div. of Elvis Presley Entertainment
3734 Elvis Presley Blvd
Memphis, TN 38116-4106
Telephone: (901) 332-3322, Toll Free:
   (800) 238-2010, FAX: (901) 344-
   3120, Web Site: www.elvis.com
Dir Mdsg: Danny Hiltenbrand
Conducts Business: U.S., Canada
Employees: 250
Primary Market Served: Consumer
Catalog available online
Direct online sales
Founded: 1981
Gross sales or billing: $12,600,000

Print two catalogs per year, offering Elvis Presley memorabilia.

GREAT CHEFS TELEVISION
PUBLISHING
Div. of GCI Inc
747 Magazine St
New Orleans, LA 70130
Telephone: (504) 581-5000, Toll Free:
   (800) 321-1499, FAX: (504) 581-
   1188, E-Mail: info@greatchefs.com,
   Web Site: www.greatchefs.com
COO & Exec Producer: John Shoup
Admin Asst: Cybil Curtis
Conducts Business: U.S., Europe, Far
   East, South America
Employees: 10

Primary Market Served: Business &
   Consumer
Catalog available online
Direct online sales
Advertising/Marketing Budget Related
   to Direct Marketing: 0-25%
Direct Marketing ad budget:
Direct Mail: $100,000
Magazines: $25,000
TV/Radio: $200,000
Telephone: $25,000
Founded: 1979
Gross sales or billing: $1,000,000

Publisher & marketer of cookbooks,
video & audio cassettes & CD's.

GUMP'S BY MAIL INC
Subs. of Hanover Direct
135 Post St
San Francisco, CA 94108
Telephone: (415) 982-1616, Toll Free:
   (800) 882-8055, FAX: (800) 984-
   9361, Web Site: www.gumpsbymail.
   com
Pres: John Di Francesco
VP: Farley Nachemin
Media Mgr: Shirley Wilson
Conducts Business: U.S.
Employees: 150
Primary Market Served: Consumer
Catalog available online
Direct online sales
Advertising/Marketing Budget Related
   to Direct Marketing: 76-100%
Gross sales or billing: $5,500,000

Retail store & mail order operation
selling jewelry, jade, silver, china, crystal, interior design, Asian & contemporary gifts & stationery. Store is located
in San Francisco.

THE HAMILTON
COLLECTION
Div of The Bradford Exchange
7018 A C Skinner Pkwy (Suite 300)
Jacksonville, FL 32256-6975
Telephone: (904) 279-1300, Toll Free:
   (866) 323-5577, FAX: (904) 279-
   1495, Web Site: www.
   hamiltoncollection.com
Mktg Dir: Marianne Graham
Conducts Business: Worldwide
Employees: 400
Primary Market Served: Consumer
Advertising/Marketing Budget Related
   to Direct Marketing: 76-100%
Founded: 1982

Direct mail marketer of collectible
products.

HAMPSHIRE PEWTER CO
Route 108 Box 350 (#201)
Somersworth, NH 03878-1564

Telephone: (603) 569-4944, Toll Free:
   (800) 639-7704, FAX: (603) 569-
   4524, E-Mail: gifts@
   hampshirepewter.com, Web Site:
   www.hampshirepewter.com
Pres & Owner: Robert S. Steele
Co-Owner: Jenine Steele
Conducts Business: U.S., Canada
Employees: 15
Primary Market Served: Business &
   Consumer
Catalog available online
Direct online sales
Advertising/Marketing Budget Related
   to Direct Marketing: 0-25%
Direct Marketing ad budget: $25,000
Founded: 1974
Gross sales or billing: $750,000

Handcast pewter tableware & ornaments.

HARRIET CARTER GIFTS,
INC
dba Harriet Carter
425 Stump Rd
Montgomeryville, PA 18936-9631

HOFFMAN MINT
1400 NW 65th Pl
Fort Lauderdale, FL 33309-1902
Telephone: (954) 971-5451, Toll Free:
   (800) 227-5813, (800) 441-0292,
   FAX: (954) 917-3079, E-Mail:
   sales@hoffmanmint.com, Web Site:
   www.hoffmanmint.com
Pres & CEO: Michael Hoffman
VP: Terry Spaight
Conducts Business: Worldwide
Primary Market Served: Business &
   Consumer
Catalog available online
Indirect online sales
Founded: 1980

Manufacturer of medals, tokens, name-
plates & special coins.

HOUSE OF OLDIES
35 Carmine St Frnt 1
New York, NY 10014-4429
Telephone: (212) 243-0500, FAX:
   (212) 989-1697, E-Mail:
   rabramson@houseofoldies.com, Web
   Site: www.houseofoldies.com
Pres: Robert Abramson
Conducts Business: Worldwide
Primary Market Served: Business &
   Consumer
Founded: 1968

Sell 45s & LPs. Feature collectors'
items & out-of-print records.

HOUSE OF ONYX, INC
120 N Main St, The Aaron Bldg
Greenville, KY 42345-1504

Telephone: (270) 338-2363, Toll Free: (800) 844-3100, FAX: (270) 338-9605, E-Mail: sales@houseofonyx.com, Web Site: www.houseofonyx.com
VP & Mgr: Charlotte Lewis
Gemologist: Jeff Curry
Owner: Shirley Rowe
Conducts Business: U.S.
Employees: 20
Primary Market Served: Business & Consumer
Catalog available online
Direct online sales
Advertising/Marketing Budget Related to Direct Marketing: 76-100%
Direct Marketing ad budget: $500,000
Direct Mail: 90%
Magazines: 10%
Founded: 1967
Gross sales or billing: $2,000,000

Fine gemstones, gold jewelry & GIA diamonds.

THE IEI CORP
Subs. of Imperial Enterprises Inc
29 Emmons Dr Ste A30
Princeton, NJ 08540-5994
Telephone: (609) 987-2700, FAX: (609) 987-2703
Pres: Yuko Shaub
Conducts Business: Japan
Primary Market Served: Consumer
Founded: 1985

Sell collectibles & luxury merchandise through catalogs to consumers in Japan.

INTERNATIONAL COINS & CURRENCY INC
62 Ridge St
Montpelier, VT 05602
Telephone: (802) 223-6331, Toll Free: (800) 451-4463, FAX: (800) 229-3239, E-Mail: info@iccoin.org, Web Site: www.iccoin.com
Pres: Michael Boardman
VP, Mktg: John Devitt
Conducts Business: Worldwide
Employees: 20
Primary Market Served: Consumer
Catalog available online
Direct online sales
Advertising/Marketing Budget Related to Direct Marketing: 76-100%
Direct Marketing ad budget:
Direct Mail: 60%
Magazines: 20%
Newspapers: 5%
Telephone: 15%
Founded: 1974
Gross sales or billing: $3,500,000

Offer U.S. & world coins & other fine collectibles.

ISLANDS TROPICALS
PO Box 1989
Keaau, HI 96749-1989
Telephone: (808) 961-0606, Toll Free: (800) 367-5155, FAX: (808) 966-7684, Web Site: www.islandtropicals.com
Pres & Treas: Michael Goldstein
Conducts Business: U.S.
Employees: 4
Primary Market Served: Business & Consumer
Catalog available online
Direct online sales
Advertising/Marketing Budget Related to Direct Marketing: 76-100%
Direct Marketing ad budget: $100,000
Direct Mail: 70%
Magazines: 30%
Founded: 1967
Gross sales or billing: $750,000

Flowers by mail order.

MICHAEL JAFFE STAMPS INC/BROOKMAN STAMP CO
6300 NE St James Rd
Vancouver, WA 98663
Telephone: (360) 695-6161, Toll Free: (800) 782-6770, FAX: (360) 695-1616, E-Mail: mjaffe@brookmanstamps.com, Web Site: www.brookmanstamps.com
Pres: Michael Jaffe
Conducts Business: U.S., Canada
Employees: 5
Primary Market Served: Consumer
Catalog available online
Direct online sales
Advertising/Marketing Budget Related to Direct Marketing: 26-50%
Direct Marketing ad budget: $30,000
Direct Mail: 40%
Magazines: 5%
Newspapers: 47%
Telephone: 8%
Founded: 1975
Gross sales or billing: $1,000,000

Federal, state & foreign duck stamps by subscription at $1.75 over issue price.

BRIAN JENNER INC
2810 W Kennewick Ave #E
Pasco, WA 99302-2466
Telephone: (509) 735-2172, FAX: (509) 783-8042
Pres: Brian Jenner
Conducts Business: U.S., Canada
Primary Market Served: Consumer

Mail order marketer of rare coins & precious metals.

JONES SCHOOL SUPPLY CO INC
PO Box 2909
Irmo, SC 29063-4009
Telephone: (803) 772-3796, FAX: (800) 942-5921, Web Site: www.jonesawards.com
Pres: Sarah Jones
Mktg Dir: Shelly O'Quinn-Humphries
Conducts Business: U.S.
Employees: 8
Primary Market Served: Business
Advertising/Marketing Budget Related to Direct Marketing: 76-100%
Direct Marketing ad budget:
Direct Mail: 100%
Gross sales or billing: $1,500,000

Academic awards, certificates, medals & pins.

KENMORE STAMP CO
119 West St, PO Box 331
Milford, NH 03055-4855
Telephone: (603) 673-1745, Toll Free: (800) 225-5059, FAX: (603) 673-3222, Web Site: www.kenmorestamp.com
Owner: Henry E. Harris Jr.
Conducts Business: United States
Employees: 40
Primary Market Served: Consumer
Catalog available online
Direct online sales
Advertising/Marketing Budget Related to Direct Marketing: 76-100%
Direct Marketing ad budget:
Direct Mail: 15%
Magazines: 10%
Newspapers: 50%
Online: 25%
Founded: 1952
Gross sales or billing: $4,800,000

Deals in all aspects of stamp collecting.

KING'S CHANDELIER CO
dba Chandelier.com
729 S Van Buren Rd (Hwy 14 S)
Eden, NC 27288-5321
Telephone: (336) 623-6188, FAX: (336) 627-9935, E-Mail: crystal@chandelier.com, Web Site: www.chandelier.com
Pres: Franklin K. Ricks
Asst Mgr & Mktg Dir: Nancy Talbert
Conducts Business: Worldwide
Employees: 10
Primary Market Served: Business & Consumer
Catalog available online
Direct online sales
Advertising/Marketing Budget Related to Direct Marketing: 0-25%

Founded: 1933

Sell chandeliers of imported crystal in original designs. Also wired Victorian gas reproductions of hand polished brass with Victorian crystals. Publish a yearly illustrated catalog of showline chandeliers & sconces.

WILL KIRKPATRICK SHOREBIRD DECOYS INC

124 Forest Ave
Hudson, MA 01749-2840
Telephone: (978) 562-7841, FAX: (978) 562-3514, E-Mail: wekdecoys@aol.com, Web Site: www.kirkpatrickdecoys.com
Owner: Will Kirkpatrick
Conducts Business: U.S., Canada
Employees: 19
Primary Market Served: Business & Consumer
Catalog available online
Direct online sales
Founded: 1979

Handmade reproductions of antique decoys & folk art carvings of other whimsical animals - songbirds, cows, fish, frogs, chickens & more. Sell to museum shops, fine galleries & direct mail (retail).

KLITZNER INDUSTRIES

530 Wellington Ave (Suite 4)
Cranston, RI 02910-2950
Telephone: (401) 751-7500, Toll Free: (800) 556-6860, FAX: (800) 556-3199, E-Mail: info@klitzner.com, Web Site: www.klitzner.com; www.providenceline.com
Chmn: Alan Klitzner
COO: Dean Klitzner
Pres: Hank Riccitelli
Conducts Business: U.S., Canada
Employees: 200
Primary Market Served: Consumer
Catalog available online
Direct online sales
Founded: 1907
Gross sales or billing: $10,000,000

Manufacturing emblematic jewelry through direct mail.

KLOCKIT

Div. of Primex
PO Box 636, N3211 Country Rd H
Lake Geneva, WI 53147-0636
Telephone: (262) 248-7000, Toll Free: (800) 556-2548, FAX: (262) 248-9899, E-Mail: klockit@klockit.com, Web Site: www.klockit.com
Mktg Coord: Tammy Roath
Mktg Dir: Barb Heath
Conducts Business: U.S., Canada
Employees: 120

Primary Market Served: Business & Consumer
Founded: 1971

Sell clock movements, dials, hands & accessories. Also, clock & toy kits, wood & lamp parts & tools. Books, weather instruments, mini-fit-ups. Retail outlet store in Lake Geneva, WI. Free catalog. Quantity discounts.

LEANIN' TREE INC

6055 Longbow Dr, Box 9800
Boulder, CO 80301
Telephone: (303) 530-7768, Toll Free: (800) 525-0656, FAX: (303) 530-5124, E-Mail: info@leanintree.com, Web Site: www.leanintree.com
Founder & Chmn Bd: Ed Trumble
Pres & CEO: Tom Trumble
Sr VP: Jane Trumble
Mktg Mgr: Pat Wallace
Conducts Business: U.S., Canada
Employees: 200
Primary Market Served: Business & Consumer
Catalog available online
Indirect online sales
Gross sales or billing: $20,000,000

Manufacture & sell Christmas cards, all occasion cards, poster prints & related products through direct mail to consumers & wholesale through dealers.

LEFTY'S CORNER

601 Nichols St, PO Box 615
Clarks Summit, PA 18411-1487
Telephone: (570) 586-5338, (570) 586-LEFT, FAX: (570) 585-2906, E-Mail: info@leftyscorner.com, Web Site: www.leftyscorner.com
Owner: Dale Hersh
Co-Owner: Bob Hersh
Conducts Business: U.S.
Employees: 1
Primary Market Served: Business & Consumer
Catalog available online
Direct online sales
Advertising/Marketing Budget Related to Direct Marketing: 0-25%
Direct Marketing ad budget:
Direct Mail: 25%
Magazines: 25%
Newspapers: 25%
Online: 25%
Founded: 1988
Gross sales or billing: $100,000

Products for lefthanders. Retail & wholesale.

LENOX GROUP INC

1414 Radcliffe St
Bristol, PA 19007-5413

Telephone: (267) 525-7800, Toll Free: (800) 223-4311, Web Site: www.lenox.com
Primary Market Served: Business

LILLIAN VERNON CORP

800 E Woodman Rd
Colorado Springs, CO 80920
Telephone: (757) 427-7923, Toll Free: (800) 545-5426, FAX: (757) 427-7819, E-Mail: publicrelations@lillianvernon.com, Web Site: www.lillianvernon.com
Chief Mktg Officer: Kevin Green
Pres & CEO: Michael Muoio
Chief Mktg Officer: Alyce Goodman
VP Fin: Jane Lee
Pub Rels: Phillip Read
Conducts Business: U.S.
Employees: 3,500
Primary Market Served: Consumer
Catalog available online
Direct online sales
Advertising/Marketing Budget Related to Direct Marketing: 76-100%
Direct Marketing ad budget:
Direct Mail: 90%
Newspapers: 5%
TV/Radio: 5%
Founded: 1951

Gift catalogs & website for customers. Publish catalog titles selling 6,000 products.

LIN TERRY

185 6th Ave Ste 4
Paterson, NJ 07524-1247
Telephone: (973) 345-6677, FAX: (973) 345-5551, E-Mail: linterry@aol.com, Web Site: www.linterry.com
Pres: Dan Neufeld
Sec: Heidi Neufeld
Conducts Business: U.S.
Employees: 5
Primary Market Served: Business & Consumer
Catalog available online
Direct online sales
Advertising/Marketing Budget Related to Direct Marketing: 51-75%
Founded: 1984
Gross sales or billing: $1,000,000

Sports card supplies, acrylic cases for collectibles, custom cases & point of purchases cases, mail order to consumers as well as businesses. Others include, restaurant table tents, acrylic wall mountable menu holders, sign holders, and custom acrylic displays.

LITTLETON COIN CO INC

1309 Mt Eustis Rd
Littleton, NH 03561

Telephone: (603) 444-5386, Toll Free: (800) 645-3122, FAX: (603) 444-0121, E-Mail: jhennessey@ littletoncoin.com, Web Site: www. littletoncoin.com
Pres: David Sundman
CFO: Edward Hennessey
COO: Michael Morelli
Mktg Dir: Jeffrey Marsh
Employees: 350
Primary Market Served: Consumer
Catalog available online
Direct online sales
Advertising/Marketing Budget Related to Direct Marketing: 76-100%
Founded: 1945

Sell coins, paper money & ancient coins & supplies to collectors by mail.

MADISONAVEGIFTS.COM

325 Barben Ave
Watertown, NY 13601-4503
Telephone: (315) 779-9228, Toll Free: (866) 421-1744, E-Mail: magsales@ madisonavegifts.com, Web Site: www.madisonavegifts.com
Owner: Joan A. Smith
Conducts Business: U.S.
Employees: 5
Primary Market Served: Consumer
Catalog available online
Direct online sales
Advertising/Marketing Budget Related to Direct Marketing: 26-50%
Direct Marketing ad budget: $5,000
Direct Mail: 15%
Magazines: 5%
Newspapers: 5%
Online: 75%
Founded: 2000
Gross sales or billing: $200,000

Upscale online gift store featuring latest products in the gift market today; offering corporate gifts, bridal registry and home decor.

MCGAW GRAPHICS

6378 Route 7A
Manchester Center, VT 05250
Telephone: (845) 353-8600, Toll Free: (888) 4BMCGAW, FAX: (845) 353-3155, E-Mail: sales@bmcgaw.com, Web Site: www.bmcgaw.com
Pres: Nancy McGaw
CEO: Gyr King
Mgr, Mktg: Alissa Passoff
VP, Sls & Design: Amy Wessan
Supvr Cust Svc: Ursula Carioscia
Conducts Business: U.S., Australia, Canada, Europe, Japan, South Africa, South America
Employees: 100
Primary Market Served: Business
Catalog available online
Direct online sales

Advertising/Marketing Budget Related to Direct Marketing: 51-75%
Direct Marketing ad budget:
Direct Mail: 50%
Magazines: 50%
Founded: 1978

Publisher & distributor of American & European fine art posters.

MEDALS OF AMERICA

114 Southchase Blvd
Fountain Inn, SC 29644-9019
Telephone: (864) 862-0635, Toll Free: (800) 308-0849, FAX: (800) 407-8640, E-Mail: medals@usmedals.com, Web Site: www.usmedals.com
Pres: Linda Foster
Dir: Frank Foster
Conducts Business: U.S.
Employees: 30
Primary Market Served: Consumer
Catalog available online
Direct online sales
Advertising/Marketing Budget Related to Direct Marketing: 76-100%
Direct Marketing ad budget:
Direct Mail: 20%
Magazines: 80%
Founded: 1976

U.S. military medals, display cases & all military insignia.

MUSIC BARN INC

PO Box 1083
Niagara Falls, NY 14304-0383
Toll Free: (800) 984-0047, FAX: (905) 513-6918, E-Mail: info@ themusicbarn.com, Web Site: www.themusicbarn.com
Pres: Robert Bell
Conducts Business: U.S., Canada
Primary Market Served: Consumer
Catalog available online
Direct online sales
Advertising/Marketing Budget Related to Direct Marketing: 26-50%
Founded: 1985

MUSIC TREASURES CO

Div. of Technical Marketing Inc
PO Box 9138
Richmond, VA 23227-0138
Telephone: (804) 730-8800, Toll Free: (800) 666-7565, FAX: (888) MU-SIC-TC, E-Mail: musict@ musictreasures.com, Web Site: www.musictreasures.com
Pres & CEO: Daniel J. Tuszynski Jr.
VP Opers: Leslie Radock
Conducts Business: U.S., Canada
Employees: 10
Primary Market Served: Business & Consumer
Catalog available online
Indirect online sales

Advertising/Marketing Budget Related to Direct Marketing: 51-75%
Direct Marketing ad budget: $480,000
Direct Mail: 90%
Magazines: 10%
Founded: 1985
Gross sales or billing: $2,000,000

Music & dance gift and educational resource items, fund-raising to qualified groups. Over 9000 custom imprinted products, such as totes, mugs, stationery, T's & candy, teaching resources, awards, trophies, certificates, stationery, videos & CDs.

MYSTIC SEAPORT MUSEUM STORES

75 Greenmanville Ave
Mystic, CT 06355-0990
Telephone: (860) 572-5315, Toll Free: (860) 572-0711, FAX: (860) 572-5324, Web Site: www.mysticseaport.org
Mdsg Dir: Jane Wilkins
Conducts Business: Worldwide
Employees: 75
Primary Market Served: Business & Consumer
Direct Marketing ad budget:
Direct Mail: 90%
Magazines: 8%
Newspapers: 2%
Sells nautical merchandise.

NARROW WAY

712 Moraga Rd
Lafayette, CA 94549-4916
Telephone: (925) 283-4074
Mgr: Olajire Idowu
Conducts Business: U.S.
Employees: 2
Primary Market Served: Consumer
Advertising/Marketing Budget Related to Direct Marketing: 26-50%
Founded: 2005
Gross sales or billing: $110,000

Egg yolk separator, skirt printing, bumper stickers, mugs, flyers & logos.

NATIONAL PEN CORP

12121 Scripps Summit Dr (Suite 200)
San Diego, CA 92131-4609
Telephone: (858) 675-3000, FAX: (858) 675-3030, E-Mail: info@ nationalpen.com, Web Site: www.pens.com
Pres: Tom Liguory
Sr VP, Direct Mktg: Ron Childs
VP Mktg: Mike Delaney
Conducts Business: Worldwide
Employees: 1,000
Primary Market Served: Business
Catalog available online
Direct online sales

Advertising/Marketing Budget Related to Direct Marketing: 76-100%
Founded: 1966
Gross sales or billing: $100,000,000

Manufacturer & distributor of imprinted products, ball point pens, key tags & calendars.

NEW YORK FINDINGS
72 Bowery
New York, NY 10013
Telephone: (212) 925-5745, Toll Free: (888) 925-5745, FAX: (212) 925-5870, E-Mail: nyfindings@aol.com, Web Site: www.newyorkfindings.com
Pres: Cheryl Kerber
Conducts Business: U.S., Canada
Primary Market Served: Business
Advertising/Marketing Budget Related to Direct Marketing: 76-100%
Founded: 1953

Sells precious metal jewelry parts.

NOWETAH'S AMERICAN INDIAN STORE & MUSEUM
2 Colegrove Rd
New Portland, ME 04961-3821
Telephone: (207) 628-4981, Web Site: www.nowetahs.webs.com
Pres, Owner & Purchaser: Mrs. Nowetah Cyr
Purchaser: Mr. Tom Cyr
Artist: Wahleyah Black
Conducts Business: U.S., Canada, U.K., Japan, Italy, Germany, France
Employees: 2
Primary Market Served: Consumer
Advertising/Marketing Budget Related to Direct Marketing: 0-25%
Direct Marketing ad budget:
Magazines: 10%
Newspapers: 85%
TV/Radio: 5%
Founded: 1969
Gross sales or billing: $60,000

American Indian art, gifts, and collectibles. Mail order & retail store selling & manufacturing hand-woven Indian rugs, baskets, pottery, bead jewelry, leather goods & gifts. Receive a free brochure listing the 12 different catalogs available by sending a S.A.S.E. Educational classes on history, wild plants and herbs as food and medicines are also conducted for schools and scouts.

ONE WORLD PROJECTS
43 Ellicott Ave
Batavia, NY 14020-2010

Telephone: (585) 343-4490, FAX: (585) 344-3551, E-Mail: sales@oneworldprojects.com, Web Site: www.oneworldprojects.com
Owner, Pres: Phil Smith
Employees: 7
Primary Market Served: Business
Catalog available online
Direct online sales
Founded: 1992
Gross sales or billing: $800,000

Wholesale distribution of forest harvest material products & forest preservation products.

OOMINGMAK MUSK OX PRODUCERS COOPERATIVE
604 "H" St
Anchorage, AK 99501
Telephone: (907) 272-9225, Toll Free: (888) 360-9665, FAX: (907) 258-4225, E-Mail: oomingmak@qiviut.com, Web Site: www.qiviut.com
Pres: Mesonga Atkinson
Exec Dir: Ms. Sigrun C. Robertson
Conducts Business: U.S.
Employees: 7
Primary Market Served: Consumer
Catalog available online
Indirect online sales
Founded: 1969
Gross sales or billing: $1,000,000

Hand-knitted hats & scarves from the underwool of the Musk Ox. Made by cooperative members & Eskimo women from remote Alaskan villages.

PACIFIC SPIRIT CORP
1334 Pacific Ave
Forest Grove, OR 97116-2315
Telephone: (503) 357-1566, Toll Free: (800) 634-9057, FAX: (503) 357-1699, Web Site: www.pacificspiritcatalogs.com
Pres: Mark Kenzer
Conducts Business: U.S.
Employees: 15
Primary Market Served: Consumer
Direct online sales
Advertising/Marketing Budget Related to Direct Marketing: 76-100%
Direct Marketing ad budget:
Direct Mail: 98%
Magazines: 2%
Founded: 1984

Mail order gifts & collectibles.

PARADISE GALLERIES
23482 Peralta Dr
Laguna Hills, CA 92653

Telephone: (858) 793-4050, Toll Free: (800) 67-DOLLS, FAX: (949) 743-8974, E-Mail: omancinelli@paradisegalleries.com, Web Site: www.paradisegalleries.com
Pres: David Brownlee
VP New Mkts & Wholesale: Ozzie Mancinelli
Primary Market Served: Consumer

Porcelain dolls.

PARMER BOOKS
7644 Forrestal Rd
San Diego, CA 92120-2203
Telephone: (619) 287-0693, E-Mail: parmerbook@aol.com, Web Site: www.parmerbook.com
Owner: Jean Marie Parmer
Conducts Business: Worldwide
Employees: 3
Primary Market Served: Consumer
Catalog available online
Direct online sales
Advertising/Marketing Budget Related to Direct Marketing: 76-100%
Direct Marketing ad budget:
Direct Mail: 15%
Online: 85%
Founded: 1983

Rare & out of print books to collectors & libraries.

PARTY KITS & EQUESTRIAN GIFTS
10920 Plantside Dr Ste C
Louisville, KY 40299-6113
Telephone: (502) 425-2126, Toll Free: (800) 99-DERBY, FAX: (502) 425-5230, E-Mail: info@partykits.com, Web Site: www.derbygifts.com
Pres & CEO: Becky Biesel
Conducts Business: Worldwide
Employees: 10
Primary Market Served: Business & Consumer
Catalog available online
Direct online sales
Advertising/Marketing Budget Related to Direct Marketing: 76-100%
Direct Marketing ad budget:
Direct Mail: 90%
Magazines: 5%
Newspapers: 3%
TV/Radio: 2%
Founded: 1979
Gross sales or billing: $1,000,000

Equestrian party supplies, fine equine gifts & Kentucky delicacies for horse lovers, party supply stores & tack shops.

PERSONAL CREATIONS
1005 101st St Ste A
Lemont, IL 60439-9628

Telephone: (630) 783-2400, Toll Free: (866) 834-7695, Web Site: www.personalcreations.com
VP: Judy Nelson
CEO: John Semmelhack
VP: Brian Hyzy
Primary Market Served: Consumer

Mail order personalized gifts.

PHARMART
Div. of Healthcare Logistics
450 Town St
Circleville, OH 43113
Telephone: (860) 932-8588, Toll Free: (800) 848-1633, FAX: (800) 477-2923, Web Site: www.healthcarelogistics.com/Pharmart
Owner: Gary Sharp
Owner: Bethany Reid
Conducts Business: U.S., Canada
Employees: 3
Primary Market Served: Business & Consumer
Catalog available online
Direct online sales
Advertising/Marketing Budget Related to Direct Marketing: 76-100%
Direct Marketing ad budget: $150,000
Direct Mail: 90%
Telephone: 10%
Founded: 1990
Gross sales or billing: $700,000

Gifts & collectibles to the pharmacy profession.

BUD PLANT ILLUSTRATED BOOKS
3809 Laguna Ave
Palo Alto, CA 94306-2629
Telephone: (650) 493-1191, FAX: (650) 493-1145, E-Mail: jim@bpib.com, Web Site: www.bpib.com
Owner: Jim Vadeboncoeur Jr.
Conducts Business: Worldwide
Employees: 3
Primary Market Served: Business & Consumer
Catalog available online
Indirect online sales
Advertising/Marketing Budget Related to Direct Marketing: 0-25%
Founded: 1987

Out-of-print illustrated books to collectors, artists & libraries.

POSH PAPERS
73 Terrace Ave
Riverside, RI 02915-4726
Telephone: (401) 331-9873, FAX: (401) 331-2229, E-Mail: info@poshpapersonline.com, Web Site: www.poshpapersonline.com
Owner: Judi Boren
Conducts Business: U.S.

Employees: 2
Primary Market Served: Business & Consumer
Catalog available online
Direct online sales
Advertising/Marketing Budget Related to Direct Marketing: 0-25%
Direct Marketing ad budget:
Direct Mail: 75%
Magazines: 25%
Founded: 1983
Gross sales or billing: $100,000

Personalized handcrafted note cards by mail order - over 50 gift boxed assortments.

POTPOURRI GROUP INC
101 Billerica Ave - Bldg 2
North Billerica, MA 01862
Telephone: (978) 256-4100, FAX: (978) 256-1961/0344, Web Site: www.potpourrigroup.com
Buyer (Nature's Jewelry): Gwen House
Buyer (The Stitchery): Donna Saiia
Buyer (Potpourri): Peter Maloney
Buyer (Expressions): Doug Star
Sr VP Mktg: Bob Webb
Buyer (Back In The Saddle): Mikako Fukagawa
Buyer (In The Company of Dogs): Kim Kavanagh
Buyer (Serengeti): Peri Siegel
Buyer (The Pyramid Collection): Terry Renwick
Circulation Dir: David Wilson
Buyer (Catalog Favorites): Kathy Harvey
Buyer (NorthStyle): Caitlin Palange
Buyer (Whatever Works): Mark Fairman
Buyer (Young Explorers): Clarisse Cowdery
Buyer (Country Store): Katy Halligan
CEO: John Fleischmann
Employees: 700
Primary Market Served: Consumer
Direct online sales
Advertising/Marketing Budget Related to Direct Marketing: 76-100%
Founded: 1963

Nature, wildlife and gift catalogs. Spiritual, ethnic & self-help. Affiliates: Nature's Jewelry; The Stitchery; Potpourri; Expressions: Back in the Saddle; In The Company of Dogs; Serengeti; The Pyramid Collection; Catalog Favorites; NorthStyle; Whatever Works; Young Explorers; Country Store.

REDENVELOPE INC
4840 Eastgate Mall
San Diego, CA 92121-1977

Telephone: (619) 528-4888, Toll Free: (877) 733-3683, Web Site: www.redenvelope.com
Pres & CEO: Alison May
Mktg Dir: Steve Fleming
Conducts Business: U.S.
Primary Market Served: Business & Consumer
Catalog available online
Advertising/Marketing Budget Related to Direct Marketing: 76-100%
Founded: 1999

Gifts for major gift giving and everyday occasions, decorative items for the home, jewelry, plants and flowers, and baby gifts.

ROSS-SIMONS
9 Ross Simons Dr
Cranston, RI 02920-4475
Telephone: (401) 463-3100, Toll Free: (800) 835-0919, FAX: (401) 463-8599, Web Site: www.ross-simons.com
Pres & CEO: Darrell S. Ross
VP Mktg: Larry Davis
Exec VP & COO: Robert Simone
Internet Mktg Dir: Mario Protano
VP HR: Tom Gibson
Conducts Business: U.S., Japan
Employees: 500
Primary Market Served: Business & Consumer
Catalog available online
Direct online sales
Advertising/Marketing Budget Related to Direct Marketing: 76-100%
Founded: 1952
Gross sales or billing: $166,000,000

Sells fine jewelry, china, silver, crystal, giftware & home decor.

RUBBER STAMPS OF AMERICA
1110 Main St
Dublin, NH 03444
Toll Free: (800) 553-5031, FAX: (603) 563-8102, E-Mail: stampusa@verizon.net, Web Site: www.stampusa.com
Partner: Laurie Indenbaum
Partner: Andy Toepfer
Conducts Business: Worldwide
Employees: 4
Primary Market Served: Business & Consumer
Advertising/Marketing Budget Related to Direct Marketing: 76-100%

Manufactures & sells pictorial rubber stamps used to make artwork out of stationery, invitations & to decorate paperwork.

SAE INTERNATIONAL

400 Commonwealth Dr
Warrendale, PA 15086-7511
Telephone: (724) 776-4841, Web Site:
 www.sae.org
Mktg Mgr: Marcy Estok

ST LAWRENCE ISLAND ORIGINAL IVORY COOPERATIVE

PO Box 189
Gambell, AK 99742
Telephone: (907) 985-5707, FAX:
 (907) 985-5927
Mgr: William Soonagrook Jr.
Conducts Business: U.S.
Employees: 1
Primary Market Served: Business &
 Consumer
Founded: 1982

Original Ivory carvings made from
walrus & whale bone.

ST LOUIS SLOT MACHINE CO

9617 Dielman Rock Island Industrial
 Dr
Saint Louis, MO 63132-2149
Telephone: (314) 432-1699, E-Mail:
 stlslot@earthlink.net, Web Site:
 www.stlouisslot.com
Pres: Tom Kolbrener
Mgr: Marty Wilke
Conducts Business: U.S.
Employees: 4
Primary Market Served: Business &
 Consumer
Advertising/Marketing Budget Related
 to Direct Marketing: 0-25%
Founded: 1979

Antique slot machines, neon signs &
decoratives, old soda machines & juke-
boxes.

SAUNDERS MILITARY INSIGNIA

PO Box 1831
Naples, FL 34106-1831
Telephone: (239) 298-8228, Toll Free:
 (800) 442-3133, FAX: (239) 774-
 3323, E-Mail: info@
 saundersinsignia.com, Web Site:
 www.saundersinsignia.com
Pres: Earl Keaton
Owner: Dan Bannister
Customer Svc Supvr: Ana Labra
Conducts Business: U.S.
Primary Market Served: Business &
 Consumer
Catalog available online
Direct online sales
Advertising/Marketing Budget Related
 to Direct Marketing: 0-25%

Founded: 1968

A large retail insignia company with
over 14,000 different patches, badges,
wings, ribbons & medals plus 100 different publications on insignia. Sell to
veterans & collectors.

SCHWARTZ & CO

12 Cook Ln
Verona, NJ 07044-2002
Telephone: (973) 571-2160, Toll Free:
 (800) 526-1440, FAX: (973) 571-
 2165, E-Mail: swartzandcompany@
 gmail.com, Web Site: www.
 natschwartz.com
VP: Larry Schwartz
Gen Mgr: Marilyn Schwartz
Conducts Business: U.S.
Employees: 25
Primary Market Served: Consumer
Direct online sales
Advertising/Marketing Budget Related
 to Direct Marketing: 76-100%
Direct Marketing ad budget:
Direct Mail: 75%
Magazines: 20%
Newspapers: 5%
Founded: 1979

China, crystal, flatware, gifts, collectibles & housewares (most major manufacturers). Also maintains a national
bridal registry service.

LH SELMAN LTD

410 S Michigan Ave Ste 207
Chicago, IL 60605-1448
Telephone: (831) 427-1177, Toll Free:
 (800) 538-0766, FAX: (831) 427-
 0111
Pres: L.H. Selman
Owner: Ben Clark
Owner: Mitch Clark
Conducts Business: Worldwide
Employees: 13
Primary Market Served: Business &
 Consumer
Direct Marketing ad budget: $100,000
Founded: 2009

Catalog marketer of paperweights and
art glass sold mainly to collectors & retail gift shops.

B SHACKMAN & CO INC

9964 W Miller Dr
Galesburg, MI 49053
Telephone: (269) 484-1000, Toll Free:
 (800) 221-7656, FAX: (269) 484-
 1010, Web Site: www.shackman.com
Mgr: Johanna Durrett
Mgr: Jason Durrett
Conducts Business: U.S., Canada, Eng-
 land, Germany
Employees: 35
Primary Market Served: Business &
 Consumer

Catalog available online
Direct online sales
Direct Marketing ad budget:
Direct Mail: 85%
TV/Radio: 5%
Telephone: 10%
Founded: 2001
Gross sales or billing: $5,000,000

Turn of the century paper novelties:
greeting cards, children's picture books,
stickers, favors, toys, tree trims, etc.
Sells to gift shops, boutiques & stationery shops.

SILVER STAR BRANDS

250 City Center
Oshkosh, WI 54901
Telephone: (920) 231-3800, FAX:
 (920) 231-1247, Web Site: www.
 silverstarbrands.com
Pres: Vicki Updike
Employees: 500
Primary Market Served: Business &
 Consumer
Founded: 1935

Giftwares, housewares, toys & greeting
cards.

ALBERT S SMYTH CO INC

Smyth Jewelers
2020 York Rd
Timonium, MD 21093
Telephone: (410) 252-6666, Toll Free:
 (800) 638-3333, FAX: (410) 252-
 2355, E-Mail: smyth@albertsmyth.
 com, Web Site: www.albertsmyth.
 com
Mktg Pres: Tom Smyth
Mktg Dir: Ruth Ann Carroll
Conducts Business: U.S.
Employees: 180
Primary Market Served: Consumer
Catalog available online
Direct online sales
Founded: 1914

Retail store marketing nationally
through catalogs. Products include china, crystal, silver, watches, clocks, jewelry & diamonds at discounted prices.
Showroom located at company address.

SOITENLY STOOGES

Subs. of C3 Entertainment Inc
1415 Gardena Ave
Glendale, CA 91204-2709
Telephone: (818) 543-0778, Toll Free:
 (800) 543-0778, FAX: (818) 543-
 0779, E-Mail: custserv@
 threestooges.com, Web Site: www.
 soitenlystooges.com
Pres: Earl Benjamin
Dir, Mktg: Eric Lamond
VP, Licensing: Ani Khachoian
Conducts Business: U.S.
Primary Market Served: Consumer

Catalog available online
Direct online sales
Founded: 1989

Soitenly Stooges is licensed by Comedy III Productions to sell and market official "Three Stooges" products nationally through the mail order operation.

SOTHEBY'S
1334 York Ave at 72nd St
New York, NY 10021-4806
Telephone: (212) 606-7000, FAX: (212) 606-7107, Web Site: www.sothebys.com
Chmn: Michael I. Sovern
Pres & CEO: William F. Ruprecht
Pres Sotheby's Fin Svcs & Sotheby's Ventures Intl: Mitchell Zuckerman
Exec VP & CEO Sotheby's Intl: Robin G. Woodhead
CFO: Patrick McClymont
Conducts Business: Worldwide
Employees: 1,497
Primary Market Served: Business & Consumer
Catalog available online
Indirect online sales
Founded: 1967
Gross sales or billing: $664,800,000

Provides auction catalogs & art books, covering a complete range of art & collectibles to galleries, dealers & individual collectors.

SOUNDPRINTS
Div. of Trudy Corp
353 Main Ave
Norwalk, CT 06851-1552
Telephone: (203) 846-2274, Toll Free: (800) 228-7839, FAX: (203) 846-1776, E-Mail: soundprints@soundprints.com, Web Site: www.soundprints.com
Pres: William Burnham
Conducts Business: U.S., Canada
Employees: 16
Primary Market Served: Business & Consumer
Catalog available online
Indirect online sales
Founded: 1947
Gross sales or billing: $6,000,000

Children's storybooks, audio cassettes, dolls & stuffed animals sold to retailers, wholesalers & direct mail consumers.

THE SPERRY & HUTCHINSON CO INC
S&H Green Points
1625 S Congress Ave
Delray Beach, FL 33445

Telephone: (561) 454-7621, FAX: (561) 265-2493, E-Mail: mediarelations@shsolutions.com, Web Site: www.greenpoints.com
Sr Mgr: Dianne Morris
Conducts Business: U.S.
Employees: 1,300
Primary Market Served: Business

Electronic incentive promotions.

STICKERS 'N' STUFF INC
245 W Sycamore Ln
Louisville, CO 80027-2235
Telephone: (303) 661-0200, E-Mail: sales@stickersnstuff.com, Web Site: www.stickersnstuff.biz
Pres: Marilyn McVoy
Conducts Business: U.S., Belgium, Japan
Employees: 1
Primary Market Served: Consumer
Catalog available online
Direct online sales
Advertising/Marketing Budget Related to Direct Marketing: 0-25%
Direct Marketing ad budget: $20,000
Direct Mail: 50%
Magazines: 50%
Founded: 1980
Gross sales or billing: $50,000

Prism, glitter, holographic, fuzzy, flowers, butterflies, hummingbirds, teddy bears, unicorn & other assorted stickers. Send $2 for samples & catalog.

SUN HARVEST CITRUS
14601 Six Mile Cypress Pkwy
Fort Myers, FL 33912-4307
Telephone: (239) 768-2686, Toll Free: (800) 743-1480, FAX: (239) 768-9255, E-Mail: info@sunharvestcitrus.com, Web Site: www.SunHarvestCitrus.com
Pres: David McKenzie
Co-Owner & Mgr: Sandy McKenzie
VP: Jr. Robert Edsall
Mktg Mgr: Tina Giufre
Primary Market Served: Business & Consumer
Catalog available online
Direct online sales
Founded: 1940

Mail order gifts & fruit.

SUNDANCE CATALOG CO
3865 W 2400 S
Salt Lake City, UT 84120-7212
Telephone: (801) 973-2711, Toll Free: (800) 422-2770, FAX: (801) 973-4989, E-Mail: jessica.bassin@sundance.net, Web Site: www.sundancecatalog.com
Pres & CEO: Bruce Willard
Primary Market Served: Consumer
Catalog available online

Direct online sales
Founded: 1969

Gift items, jewelry, clothing & home furnishings.

TVC ENTERPRISES AND THE TV COLLECTOR MAGAZINE
6704 Fruit Flower Ave
Las Vegas, NV 89130
Telephone: (760) 495-7956, E-Mail: tvcinquiries@happyretrogirl.com, Web Site: www.angelfire.com/ma/tvcollector/home.html
Owner: Diane Albert
Conducts Business: U.S., Canada
Employees: 2
Primary Market Served: Business & Consumer
Catalog available online
Indirect online sales
Advertising/Marketing Budget Related to Direct Marketing: 0-25%
Founded: 1980

TV, movie & rock 'n roll memorabilia catalog. Memorabilia catalog is online only; no hard copies available. TV nostalgia magazine "The TV Collector" no longer published, but all back issues still available.

TAILWINDS INC
775 E Blithedale (#166)
Mill Valley, CA 94941-1554
Telephone: (415) 380-8181, Toll Free: (800) TAILWIND, FAX: (415) 927-0199, E-Mail: service@tailwinds.com, Web Site: www.tailwinds.com
Pres & CEO: Nancy Palozola
Conducts Business: U.S.
Primary Market Served: Business & Consumer
Catalog available online
Direct online sales
Founded: 1986

Aviation gifts & software.

THINGS DECO
130 E 18th St (Suite 8F)
New York, NY 10003-2416
Telephone: (212) 362-8961, E-Mail: thingsdeco@hotmail.com, Web Site: www.thingsdeco.com
Owner, Pres: Harriet Seltzer
Creative: Bob Josen
Conducts Business: U.S., Canada, U.K., Australia, New Zealand, Europe
Employees: 2
Primary Market Served: Business & Consumer
Catalog available online
Indirect online sales
Advertising/Marketing Budget Related to Direct Marketing: 76-100%

Direct Marketing ad budget:
Direct Mail: 90%
Magazines: 5%
Newspapers: 2%
Online: 3%
Founded: 1994

Consumer gift catalog with products of Art Deco and early 20th century design.

THINGS REMEMBERED

Subs. of Cole National Corp
5500 Avion Park Dr
Highland Heights, OH 44143-1992
Telephone: (440) 473-2000, Toll Free: (866) 902-4438, FAX: (440) 473-2018, E-Mail: customerservice@ thingsremembered.com, Web Site: www.thingsremembered.com
Chmn, Pres & CEO: Michael F. Anthony
Sr VP Store Sls & Opers: Ron Batts
VP HR: Alice Guiney
Mktg Dir: Michael Bargas
Sr VP Mktg: Tony Chivari
Dir Customer Svc: Diane McCarty
Employees: 4,000
Primary Market Served: Business & Consumer
Advertising/Marketing Budget Related to Direct Marketing: 0-25%
Direct Marketing ad budget:
Direct Mail: 100%
Founded: 1945
Gross sales or billing: $300,000,000

Retailer of personalized gifts.

THOMPSON CIGAR CO

5401 Hangar Ct
Tampa, FL 33634
Telephone: (813) 884-6344, Toll Free: (800) 216-7107, FAX: (813) 882-4605, Web Site: www. thompsoncigar.com
Pres: R.M. Franzblau
Conducts Business: U.S.
Employees: 400
Primary Market Served: Consumer
Catalog available online
Indirect online sales
Advertising/Marketing Budget Related to Direct Marketing: 76-100%

Sells cigars, pipes, tobacco & gift items through direct mail.

TIFFANY & CO

600 Madison Ave (fl 4)
New York, NY 10022-1689
Telephone: (212) 755-8000, FAX: (212) 320-7550, Web Site: www. tiffany.com
Chmn Bd & CEO: Michael J Kowolaski
Exec VP & CFO: James N Fernandez
Sr VP Mktg: Caroline Naggiar

VP Direct Mktg: Kevin O'Halloran
Pres: Frederic Cumenal
Primary Market Served: Consumer
Retail jeweler.

TRUMBLE GREETINGS

Sub-org of Leanin Tree
6055 Longbow Dr
Boulder, CO 80301-3203
Toll Free: (800) 525-0656, FAX: (303) 530-5124, E-Mail: info@leanintree. com, Web Site: www.leanintree.com
Dir Consumer Svcs: Dana Pauley
Direct Mktg Analyst: Jean-Marie Peirce
Mgr Order Entry & Customer Svc: Marcia Soderberg
Pres & CEO: Tom Trumble
Mktg Mgr: Kate Frohlich
Conducts Business: U.S., Canada
Primary Market Served: Business & Consumer
Catalog available online
Direct online sales
Advertising/Marketing Budget Related to Direct Marketing: 76-100%
Direct Marketing ad budget:
Direct Mail: 80%
Online: 20%
Founded: 1949

Fine-art greeting cards and gifts for consumers and businesses.

TURNCRAFT CLOCKS INC

4310 Shoreline Dr
Spring Park, MN 55384-9722
Telephone: (952) 471-9573, Toll Free: (800) 544-1711, FAX: (952) 471-8579, E-Mail: office@ meiselwoodhobby.com, Web Site: www.meiselwoodhobby.com
Owner & Mgr: Eric Meisel
Owner: Greg Meisel
Pres: Paul Meisel
Conducts Business: U.S.
Primary Market Served: Business & Consumer
Catalog available online
Direct online sales
Advertising/Marketing Budget Related to Direct Marketing: 26-50%
Direct Marketing ad budget:
Direct Mail: 100%
Founded: 1972

Clock plans, kits, movements, dials, hardware & fit-ups (inserts).

UNICOVER CORP

1 Unicover Ctr
Cheyenne, WY 82008-0001
Telephone: (307) 771-3000, Toll Free: (800) 443-3232, FAX: (307) 771-3134, E-Mail: qands@unicover.com, Web Site: www.unicover.com
Pres & CEO: James A. Willms

VP, Client Svcs: Larry Schoeler
Conducts Business: U.S., Canada
Primary Market Served: Business & Consumer
Catalog available online
Direct online sales
Advertising/Marketing Budget Related to Direct Marketing: 76-100%
Founded: 1968

Marketer of postage stamps and original art. Supplier of services including advertising agency and packaging.

US CAVALRY

2855 Centennial Ave
Radcliff, KY 40160-9000
Telephone: (270) 351-1164, Toll Free: (800) 777-7172, FAX: (270) 352-0266, E-Mail: hq@uscavalry.com, Web Site: www.uscavalry.com
Pres & CEO: Randy Acton
Opers Dir: Ron Miller
Conducts Business: Worldwide
Employees: 300
Primary Market Served: Consumer
Indirect online sales
Advertising/Marketing Budget Related to Direct Marketing: 51-75%
Direct Marketing ad budget: $7,000,000
Direct Mail: $6,880,000
Magazines: $100,000
Newspapers: $20,000
Founded: 1973
Gross sales or billing: $45,000,000

Sells to civilian, military & law enforcement markets: gifts, jewelry, books, boots, shoes, military equipment, uniforms, police equipment, martial arts & adventure equipment. Stores located in Radcliff, Louisville & Oak Grove, KY, Fayetteville, NC, Columbus, GA & Kileen, TX.

US FUND FOR UNICEF

125 Maiden Ln
New York, NY 10038-4912
Telephone: (212) 686-5522, FAX: (212) 779-1679, Web Site: www. unicefusa.org
Dir Product Mktg: Wendy Miller
Mng Dir: Christine Squires
VP Direct Mktg: Helene Vallone-Raffaele
Conducts Business: U.S.
Employees: 200
Primary Market Served: Business & Consumer
Catalog available online
Founded: 1947

Sells UNICEF cards & gifts to consumers & businesses through catalogs.

VERMONT TEDDY BEAR CO

6655 Shelburne Rd

Shelburne, VT 05482
Telephone: (802) 985-3001, Toll Free:
(800) 829-BEAR, (800) 282-3131,
FAX: (802) 985-1304, E-Mail:
info@vtbear.com, Web Site: www.
vermontteddybear.com
Pres & CEO: Elisabeth Robert
Conducts Business: U.S.
Employees: 289
Primary Market Served: Business &
Consumer
Catalog available online
Advertising/Marketing Budget Related
to Direct Marketing: 76-100%
Direct Marketing ad budget:
$5,000,000
Direct Mail: 36%
Magazines: 2%
Newspapers: 2%
TV/Radio: 60%
Founded: 1984
Gross sales or billing: $7,200,000

Manufactures custom teddy bears and
sells them as gifts & collectibles. Sells
other merchandise with the teddy bear
theme.

VILLAGE COIN SHOP
Div. of USG Inc
51C Plaistow Rd
Plaistow, NH 03865
Telephone: (603) 382-5492/7151,
FAX: (603) 382-5682, E-Mail: don@
villagecoin.com, Web Site: www.
villagecoin.com
Owner & Pres: Domenic J. Mangano
Conducts Business: U.S., Canada
Employees: 5
Primary Market Served: Business &
Consumer
Catalog available online
Indirect online sales
Advertising/Marketing Budget Related
to Direct Marketing: 76-100%
Direct Marketing ad budget: $110,000
Direct Mail: 40%
Magazines: 5%
Newspapers: 10%
TV/Radio: 5%
Telephone: 40%
Founded: 1959
Gross sales or billing: $2,000,000

Sell coin and coin supplies to the individual collector.

WINTERTHUR MUSEUM &
COUNTRY ESTATE
5105 Kennett Pike
Wilmington, DE 19735
Telephone: (302) 888-4600, Toll Free:
(800) 448-3883, FAX: (302) 888-
4730, E-Mail: tourinfo@winterthur.
org, Web Site: www.winterthur.org
DM Gen Mgr: Bonnie Maradonna

Dir of Mktg Commun: Lynn Davis-Tri-
er
Media Rels Mgr: Hillary K. Holland
Sr Mgr Adv & Mktg: Lynne Boyle
Conducts Business: U.S.
Employees: 200
Direct online sales
Gross sales or billing: $60,000,000

Collection of American decorative arts
- 175 display rooms; galleries & changing exhibitions; naturalistic garden. Direct mail catalog sells reproductions,
gifts, home accessories & plants.

ZALE CORP
901 W Walnut Hill Ln
Irving, TX 75038-1001
Telephone: (972) 580-4376, Toll Free:
(800) 311-5393, Web Site: www.
zalecorp.com
VP E-Commerce: Vicki Spencer
E-Commerce Mgr: Johnnie R Mercer
Primary Market Served: Business &
Consumer

ABBOTT
100 Abbott Park Rd
Abbott Park, IL 60064-3502
Telephone: (224) 667-6100, FAX:
(847) 937-9555, Web Site: www.
abbott.com
Chmn Bd & CEO: Miles White
Dir Corp Mktg: Mitchell West
Exec VP, Corp Devel: Richard W. Ashley
Conducts Business: Worldwide
Employees: 90,000
Primary Market Served: Business &
Consumer
Founded: 1888
Gross sales or billing: $22,500,000,000
Healthcare company.

ACURIAN
2 Walnut Grove (Suite 375)
Horsham, PA 19044-2286
Telephone: (215) 323-9000, Toll Free:
(866) 566-5966, FAX: (215) 323-
9001, Web Site: www.acurian.com
VP Mktg: Scott Connor
CEO: Richard (Rick) Malcolm
Primary Market Served: Consumer

ADVANCED MEDICAL
NUTRITION INC
Subs. of HVL, LLC
600 Boyce Rd
Pittsburgh, PA 15205-9742
Telephone: (412) 494-0100, Toll Free:
(800) 437-8888, (800) 879-2664,
FAX: (888) 245-4440, Web Site:
www.douglaslabs.com
Pres: Douglas L. Lioon
Conducts Business: Worldwide
Employees: 275
Primary Market Served: Business &
Consumer
Catalog available online
Direct online sales
Advertising/Marketing Budget Related
to Direct Marketing: 76-100%
Direct Marketing ad budget:
Direct Mail: 85%
Telephone: 15%
Gross sales or billing: $500,000
Manufacturer & wholesale distributor
of vitamins & nutritional supplements
to Gaines Nutrition & Vitamin Shoppe
Inc.

ALIMED INC
297 High St
Dedham, MA 02026-2898
Telephone: (781) 329-2900, Toll Free:
(800) 225-2610, FAX: (800) 437-
2966, (781) 329-8392, E-Mail: info@
alimed.com, Web Site: www.alimed.
com
Chmn Bd: Julian Cherubini
CEO: Scott Lewis
Sr VP Mktg: Rob Brown
Conducts Business: U.S.
Employees: 150
Primary Market Served: Business &
Consumer
Catalog available online
Direct online sales
Founded: 1972
Orthopedic, occupational & physical
therapy products. Products for Alz-
heimer's, wound management, speech
therapy & ergonomics.

ALMORE INTERNATIONAL
INC
10950 SW 5th St #270
Beaverton, OR 97005
Telephone: (503) 643-6633, Toll Free:
(800) 547-1511, FAX: (503) 643-
9748, E-Mail: info@almore.com,
Web Site: www.almore.com
Pres: Chuck Hastings
Employees: 15
Primary Market Served: Business &
Consumer
Catalog available online
Direct online sales
Advertising/Marketing Budget Related
to Direct Marketing: 76-100%
Direct Marketing ad budget:
Direct Mail: 90%
Magazines: 10%
Founded: 1946
Gross sales or billing: $2,000,000
Dental manufacturer & distributor
(hand instruments, optical aids, regis-
tration wax & waxing units).

AMBIENT SHAPES INC
856 21st Street Dr SE
Hickory, NC 28602-8376
Toll Free: (800) 438-2244, FAX: (800)
872-2005, E-Mail: sales@
ambientshapes.com, Web Site: www.
ambientshapes.com
Pres: Christoph Klingspor
VP: Rosemarie Klingspor
Conducts Business: U.S., Germany
Employees: 4
Primary Market Served: Business &
Consumer
Catalog available online
Direct online sales
Direct Marketing ad budget:
Direct Mail: $250,000

Magazines: $250,000
Sells health aids, tinnitus maskers &
white noise generators.

AMERICAN PRINTING
HOUSE FOR THE BLIND
1839 Frankfort Ave
Louisville, KY 40206-0085
Telephone: (502) 895-2405, Toll Free:
(800) 223-1839, FAX: (502) 899-
2274, E-Mail: info@aph.org, Web
Site: www.aph.org
Pres: Tuck Tinsley III
VP: William Beavin
VP, Production: Jack Decker
VP, Devel: Donald J. Keefe
VP, Prods & Svcs: Robert P. Brasher
Conducts Business: Worldwide
Employees: 320
Primary Market Served: Business &
Consumer
Catalog available online
Indirect online sales
Advertising/Marketing Budget Related
to Direct Marketing: 76-100%
Founded: 1858
Gross sales or billing: $17,000,000
A not-for-profit manufacturer of prod-
ucts for blind people. Offers books in
large type, Braille, recorded & com-
puter disk form. Also offers instruction-
al aids, tools, supplies, computer
products & on-line database accessible
books.

AMERISOURCEBERGEN
1300 Morris Ave
Chesterbrook, PA 19087-5559
Telephone: (610) 727-7000, Toll Free:
(800) 829-3132, E-Mail: solutions@
amerisourcebergan.com, Web Site:
www.amerisourcebergan.com
VP Mktg: David New
CEO: Steven H. Collis
Media Rels Mgr: Barbara Proni
Conducts Business: U.S.
Employees: 4,000
Primary Market Served: Consumer
Founded: 2001
Distributor of pharmaceuticals, health
& beauty aids, over-the-counter medi-
cine, consumer electronics & video
software.

AMMED DIRECT
Subs of ArrivaMedical
1971 Tennessee Ave N
Parsons, TN 38363-5049
Telephone: (615) 941-3900, Toll Free:
(800) 282-3524, Web Site: www.
arrivamedical.com
VP Mktg: John Mills

CEO: Dennis Berry
Exec VP & Chief Mktg Officer: Gina Clark
Pres: Jim Smith
Primary Market Served: Business & Consumer

ANATOMICAL CHART CO

Div. of Wolters Kluwer Health
2700 Lake Cook Rd
Riverwoods, IL 60015
Telephone: (847) 580-5000, Toll Free: (800) 621-7500, FAX: (847) 674-0211, E-Mail: service@anatomical.com, Web Site: www.anatomical.com
CEO & Chmn Bd: Nancy McKinstry
Conducts Business: Worldwide
Primary Market Served: Business & Consumer
Catalog available online
Direct online sales
Founded: 1971

Anatomical charts & models, medical & nursing training aids, medical books & pamphlets.

ANDA INC

400 Interpace Pkwy (Corporate Ctr 3)
Parsippany, NJ 07054
Telephone: (954) 217-4500, Toll Free: (800) 331-2632, FAX: (866) 600-3860, Web Site: www.andanet.com
Sr Mktg Mgr: Pamela Ossa
Pres: A. Robert Bailey
Primary Market Served: Business & Consumer

ANTHEM INC

120 Monument Cir
Indianapolis, IN 46204
Telephone: (317) 488-6000, Web Site: www.antheminc.com
Chmn, Pres & CEO: Joseph R. Swedish

APOTHECARY PRODUCTS INC

11750 12th Ave S
Burnsville, MN 55337-1297
Telephone: (952) 890-1940, Toll Free: (800) 328-2742, FAX: (800) 328-1584, E-Mail: info@apothecaryproducts.com, Web Site: www.apothecaryproducts.com
CEO & Pres: Nathan Hanson
Conducts Business: Worldwide
Employees: 240
Primary Market Served: Business & Consumer
Catalog available online
Direct online sales
Advertising/Marketing Budget Related to Direct Marketing: 76-100%
Founded: 1975

Gross sales or billing: $29,500,000

Manufacture & distribute health related products sold in any pharmacy. Sales are made via telemarketing, personal sales force, key representatives & by catalog.

ARNET PHARMACEUTICAL

2525 Davie Rd
Davie, FL 33317
Telephone: (954) 236-9053, Toll Free: (800) 968-6673, FAX: (954) 370-2508, E-Mail: arnet@arnetusa.com, Web Site: www.arnetusa.com
Pres: Jose Tabacinic
VP Sls: Mark Tabacinic
VP Opers: Manuel Tabacinic
Conducts Business: Worldwide
Employees: 270
Primary Market Served: Business
Catalog available online
Advertising/Marketing Budget Related to Direct Marketing: 76-100%
Direct Marketing ad budget:
Direct Mail: 10%
TV/Radio: 90%
Founded: 1972

Manufacturer of nutritional supplements.

AS WE CHANGE

250 City Center
Oshkosh, WI 54901
Telephone: (619) 213-2200, Toll Free: (855) 202-7392, (800) 699-6993, FAX: (888) 534-8469, E-Mail: help@aswechange.com, Web Site: www.aswechange.com
Pres & CEO: John Dullea
Employees: 45
Primary Market Served: Consumer
Catalog available online
Direct online sales
Advertising/Marketing Budget Related to Direct Marketing: 76-100%
Direct Marketing ad budget: $5,000,000
Direct Mail: 80%
Online: 20%
Founded: 1996

Main Demographics: Perimenopause/Menopausal Women, Sell Vitamins/Supplements, Activewear/Activegear, Pampering Items (Body/Hair Care).

ASTRAL BRANDS LLC

3715 Northside Pkwy (Suite 200)
Atlanta, GA 30327
Telephone: (678) 303-3088, Web Site: www.astralbrands.com
Exec VP Mktg Astral Direct: David Brown
Primary Market Served: Business & Consumer
Founded: 1978

ASTRAZENECA

1800 Concord Pike A3C-122
Wilmington, DE 19850
Telephone: (302) 866-1482, Web Site: www.astrazeneca-us.com
Sr Dir Comml Info Systems: Doug Caldwell
CEO: Pascal Soriot
Primary Market Served: Consumer

AT LAST NATURALS

PO Box 338
North Salem, NY 10560-0338
Telephone: (914) 747-3599, Toll Free: (800) 527-8123, FAX: (914) 747-3791, E-Mail: info@atlastnaturals.com, Web Site: www.atlastnaturals.com
Sr VP: Zane Last
Pres: Stacey M Rosen
Gen Mgr VP: Ray Last
Conducts Business: Worldwide
Employees: 60
Primary Market Served: Business & Consumer
Catalog available online
Direct online sales
Advertising/Marketing Budget Related to Direct Marketing: 0-25%
Founded: 1967
Gross sales or billing: $6,000,000

Health & beauty aids to wholesalers, retailers, catalogs, consumers & private labels.

AVEDA CORP

Subsidiary of Estee Lauder
4000 Pheasant Ridge Dr
Blaine, MN 55449
Telephone: (763) 951-4201, Toll Free: (800) 644-4831, Web Site: www.aveda.com
Dir Consumer Mktg: Rachael Ostrom
Pres: Dominique Conseil

AVON PRODUCTS INC

777 Third Ave
New York, NY 10017
Telephone: (212) 282-7000, Toll Free: (800) 367-2866, FAX: (212) 282-6225, Web Site: www.avon.com
Sr VP, Gen Counsel: Jeff Benjamin
CEO: Sheri McCoy
Sr VP & Chief Mktg Officer: Patricia Perez-Ayala
Exec VP & CFO: Kimberly A. Ross
Conducts Business: Worldwide
Employees: 30,000
Primary Market Served: Consumer
Advertising/Marketing Budget Related to Direct Marketing: 0-25%
Gross sales or billing: $3,500,000,000

Sells cosmetics, fragrances, toiletries, jewelry & gift items to consumers via direct marketing.

BACK DESIGNS INC
PO Box 2810
Novato, CA 94948-2810
Telephone: (415) 883-4683, Toll Free:
    (800) 466-1341, FAX: (707) 557-
    2225, E-Mail: info@backdesigns.
    com, Web Site: www.backdesigns.
    com
Pres & Founder: Eileen Vollowitz
Conducts Business: U.S.
Employees: 20
Primary Market Served: Business &
    Consumer
Catalog available online
Direct online sales
Advertising/Marketing Budget Related
    to Direct Marketing: 0-25%
Direct Marketing ad budget:
Direct Mail: 50%
Magazines: 25%
Newspapers: 25%
Founded: 1984
Gross sales or billing: $2,000,000

Ergonomic & orthopedic products &
furniture for office, home & travel.
Marketed to clinics, businesses & individuals.

BASIC RESEARCH
5742 Harold Gatty Dr
Salt Lake City, UT 84116-3762
Telephone: (801) 530-2911, Toll Free:
    (888) 865-5326, E-Mail:
    customerservice@basicresearch.com,
    Web Site: www.silversage.com
Dir Mktg & Adv: Gina Daines
Dir Opers: Jessica Crow
Employees: 50

BAXTER HEALTHCARE,
    RENAL DIVISION
One Baxter Pkwy
Deerfield, IL 60015-4625
Toll Free: (800) 284-4060, Web Site:
    www.baxter.com
CEO & Chmn Bd: Jose Alameida

BEAUTICONTROL
    COSMETICS INC
2121 Midway Rd
Carrollton, TX 75006-5039
Telephone: (972) 458-0601, Toll Free:
    (800) BEAUTI-1, FAX: (972) 458-
    6904, E-Mail: clientservices@
    beauticontrol.com, Web Site: www.
    beauticontrol.com
CEO & Co-Founder: Jinger L. Heath
Pres: Kristi Hubbard
COO & Exec VP: J. Robert Ward-
    Burns
Sr VP, Mktg: Jo-Anne C. Jaeger
Conducts Business: U.S., Canada, Tai-
    wan, Hong Kong
Employees: 275
Primary Market Served: Consumer

Catalog available online
Indirect online sales
Founded: 1981
Gross sales or billing: $120,000,000
Direct sales cosmetics company.

BEAUTY NATURALLY
PO Box 4005
Burlingame, CA 94011-4005
Telephone: (650) 596-5742, Toll Free:
    (800) 432-4323, FAX: (650) 596-
    5742, E-Mail: sales@
    beautynaturally.com, Web Site:
    www.beautynaturally.com
Pres: Frederick K. Wong
Co Owner: Janet Wong
Co Owner: Karen Barnes
Conducts Business: U.S., Canada,
    Mexico, New Zealand
Employees: 4
Primary Market Served: Business &
    Consumer
Catalog available online
Direct online sales
Founded: 1981
Gross sales or billing: $200,000

Catalog marketer of unique cosmetics.
Also, hair & skin products.

J&H BERGE/THE LAB MART
4111 S Clinton Ave
South Plainfield, NJ 07080
Telephone: (908) 561-3002, Toll Free:
    (800) 684-1234, FAX: (908) 561-
    3002, E-Mail: info@jhberge.com,
    Web Site: www.jhberge.com
Pres: Steven Krupp
VP, Sls & Mktg: Robert Gardner
Mktg Coord: Nicole Hartman
Mktg Mgr: James Thomson
Graphic Designer: Mark Chua
Conducts Business: U.S.
Employees: 30
Primary Market Served: Business
Catalog available online
Direct online sales
Advertising/Marketing Budget Related
    to Direct Marketing: 51-75%
Founded: 1850

Marketer of laboratory equipment to research scientists.

BIOMERICA INC
17571 Von Karman Ave
Irvine, CA 92614-6207
Telephone: (949) 645-2111, Toll Free:
    (800) 854-3002, FAX: (949) 553-
    1231, E-Mail: info@biomerica.com,
    Web Site: www.biomerica.com
Pres: Francis Capitanio
CEO: Zackary Irani
Quality Control: Joe Rink
Cust Svc: Dar Barber
CFO: Janet Moore
Cust Svc: Connie Trahan

Dir Mktg: Patrick Garcia
Conducts Business: Worldwide
Employees: 150
Primary Market Served: Business &
    Consumer
Catalog available online
Direct online sales
Advertising/Marketing Budget Related
    to Direct Marketing: 0-25%
Direct Marketing ad budget:
Direct Mail: $30,000
Magazines: $25,000
Newspapers: $20,000
TV/Radio: $10,000
Telephone: $15,000
Founded: 1971

Medical home test kits, such as preg-
nancy, stool, blood, urine, etc, sold in
AARP, pharmacies & catalogs.

THE BODY SHOP INC
A Subs the L'Oreal Group
575 5th Ave
New York, NY 10017
Telephone: (919) 554-4900, Toll Free:
    (800) 263-9746, FAX: (919) 554-
    4361, Web Site: www.thebodyshop.
    com
CEO: Jeremy Schwartz
Employees: 15,000
Primary Market Served: Consumer
Catalog available online
Direct online sales
Advertising/Marketing Budget Related
    to Direct Marketing: 76-100%
Gross sales or billing: $849,000,000

Naturally based skin & hair care preparations.

CAROL BOND HEALTH
    FOODS
334 Main St
Liberty, TX 77575-4806
Toll Free: (800) 833-8282, E-Mail:
    customerservice@carolbond.com,
    Web Site: www.carolbond.com
CEO: Carol Bond
Conducts Business: U.S.
Employees: 8
Primary Market Served: Consumer
Catalog available online
Direct online sales
Advertising/Marketing Budget Related
    to Direct Marketing: 76-100%
Direct Marketing ad budget:
Direct Mail: $60,000
Magazines: $135,000
Newspapers: $7,000
TV/Radio: $250,000
Founded: 1978
Gross sales or billing: $2,000,000

Mail-order marketer of vitamin supplements.

BOSOM BUDDY BREAST FORMS

aka B & B Lingerie Co, Inc
2417 Bank Dr (Suite 201)
Boise, ID 83705-0731
Telephone: (208) 343-9696, Toll Free: (800) 262-2789, FAX: (208) 343-9266, E-Mail: custserv@bosombuddy.com, Web Site: www.bosombuddy.com
Pres: Stacie Neely
Mktg Dir: Daniel Neely
Conducts Business: Worldwide
Employees: 10
Primary Market Served: Business & Consumer
Catalog available online
Indirect online sales
Advertising/Marketing Budget Related to Direct Marketing: 76-100%
Founded: 1976

Manufacture & distribute internationally an all-fabric, weight-adjustable external breast prosthesis for women who have had mastectomies.

BRONSON NUTRITIONALS LLC

70 Commerce St
Hauppauge, NY 11788-3962
Telephone: (631) 750-0000, Web Site: www.bronsonnutritionals.com
Mktg Dir: Sheri Taubes
Primary Market Served: Business & Consumer

BRUCE MEDICAL SUPPLY

411 Waverly Oaks Rd (Suite 154)
Waltham, MA 02452
Telephone: (781) 894-6262, Toll Free: (800) 225-8446, FAX: (781) 894-9519, E-Mail: sales@brucemedical.com, Web Site: www.brucemedical.com
Pres: Richard A Najarian
Conducts Business: U.S., Canada
Primary Market Served: Business & Consumer
Catalog available online
Direct online sales

Sells medical supplies by mail.

CHG

6440 S Millrock Dr (Suite 175)
Salt Lake City, UT 84121
Telephone: (866) 615-5536, Toll Free: (800) 453-3030, Web Site: www.comphealth.com
Pres: Melissa Byington
Primary Market Served: Business & Consumer

CVS CAREMARK

1 CVS Dr
Woonsocket, RI 02895-6146
Telephone: (401) 765-1500, FAX: (401) 769-4488, Web Site: www.cvs.com
Exec VP & Chief Health Care Strategy & Mktg Officer: Helena B Foulkes
Pres & CEO: Larry J. Merlo
Conducts Business: U.S.
Primary Market Served: Consumer
Catalog available online
Direct online sales
Advertising/Marketing Budget Related to Direct Marketing: 0-25%
Direct Marketing ad budget: $5,000,000
Direct Mail: 100%
Founded: 1963
Gross sales or billing: $43,800,000,000

Prescriptions, health & beauty aids.

CALIFORNIA PACIFIC RESEARCH & NEW GENERATION

300 Brinkby Ave (Suite 200)
Reno, NV 89509-4359
Telephone: (775) 829-5600, Toll Free: (800) 745-5642, FAX: (775) 829-5619, E-Mail: sales@newgen2000.com, Web Site: www.newgen2000.com
Pres: Robert E. Murphy
Conducts Business: Worldwide
Primary Market Served: Consumer
Catalog available online
Direct online sales

Sells hair preparations for male pattern baldness. Also, health care products.

CANYON MARKETING

920 S Oyster Bay Rd
Hicksville, NY 11801
CEO: Jonathan Greenhut
Primary Market Served: Consumer

CAREINGTON INTERNATIONAL

7400 Gaylord Pkwy (fl 3)
Frisco, TX 75034-9463
Telephone: (972) 335-6970, Toll Free: (800) 441-0380, Web Site: www.careington.com
CEO: Barbara Williams
Chief Sales & Mktg Officer: Stewart Sweda
Primary Market Served: Consumer

CARESTREAM HEALTH INC

150 Verona St
Rochester, NY 14608
Telephone: (585) 627-1800, Toll Free: (888) 777-2072, E-Mail: corporatesecurity@carestream.com, Web Site: www.carestreamhealth.com
CEO: Kevin J Hobert
Chmn Bd: Robert E Le Blanc
Primary Market Served: Business & Consumer

CASWELL-MASSEY CO LTD

29 Northfield Ave
Edison, NJ 08837
Telephone: (732) 225-2181, Toll Free: (800) 326-0500, FAX: (800) 868-4407, E-Mail: info@caswellmasseyltd.com, Web Site: www.caswellmassey.com
Pres & CEO: Anne E. Robinson
COO: Anthony Nichtawitz
Dir, Consumer Bus: Sally Rue
Conducts Business: U.S., Canada, Hong Kong, Philippines
Employees: 71
Primary Market Served: Consumer
Catalog available online
Direct online sales
Founded: 1752
Gross sales or billing: $22,500,000

Fine personal care products for men & women.

CLAIROL INC

Div. of P&G
One Blachley Rd
Stamford, CT 06922-0003
Telephone: (203) 357-5000, Toll Free: (800) 252-4765, FAX: (203) 357-5003, Web Site: www.clairol.com
Global Mktg Officer: Jim Stengel
Primary Market Served: Consumer

Hair care company.

COASTAL TRAINING TECHNOLOGIES CORP

Subs of Dupont Sustainable Solutions
500 Studio Dr
Virginia Beach, VA 23452-1175
Telephone: (877) 262-7825, FAX: (757) 498-3657, E-Mail: info@training.dupont.com, Web Site: www.coastalhealth.com
Dir Mktg: Lori Stanley

COLLIS CURVE CATALOG SALES

Subs. of Collis Curve Inc
6110 California Rd
Brownsville, TX 78521
Telephone: (956) 546-4818, Toll Free: (800) 298-4818, FAX: (956) 546-4818, E-Mail: brushteeth@aol.com, Web Site: www.colliscurve.com
Pres: David Collis
VP: Jane Gonzalez
Conducts Business: U.S.
Employees: 3
Primary Market Served: Business & Consumer

Catalog available online
Indirect online sales
Advertising/Marketing Budget Related
   to Direct Marketing: 51-75%
Direct Marketing ad budget: $5,000
Online: 60%
Founded: 1981

Toothbrushes with curved bristles &
dental home care products to consumers, handicapped individuals & institutions.

CONNEY SAFETY
PRODUCTS LLC
Owned by Caxton-Iseman Capital
3202 Latham Dr
Madison, WI 53744-4190
Toll Free: (888) 356-9100, FAX: (800)
   845-9095, E-Mail: safety@conney.
   com, Web Site: www.conney.com
VP Mktg: Chuck Moyer
CEO: Mike Wessner
VP Sls: Joe Scime
Conducts Business: U.S.
Employees: 175
Primary Market Served: Business &
   Consumer
Catalog available online
Direct online sales
Advertising/Marketing Budget Related
   to Direct Marketing: 76-100%
Direct Marketing ad budget:
Direct Mail: 90%
Telephone: 10%
Founded: 1946
Gross sales or billing: $30,300,000

Sells first-aid & personal safety supplies directly to industry, schools, utilities, contractors & government.

COOPER SURGICAL INC
75 Corporate Dr
Trumbull, CT 06611
Telephone: (203) 601-5202, Toll Free:
   (800) 243-2974, FAX: (203) 601-
   1007, E-Mail: orders@
   coopersurgical.com, Web Site: www.
   coopersurgical.com
Pres & CEO: Paul L. Reummell
Exec VP & Chief Medical Officer:
   Robert D Auerbach
Employees: 500
Primary Market Served: Business
Catalog available online
Indirect online sales
Gross sales or billing: $125,000,000
Manufacturer of Ob-Gyn products.

COOPER VISION
370 Woodcliff Dr (Suite 200)
Fairport, NY 14450
Telephone: (855) 526-6737, Toll Free:
   (800) 341-2020, Web Site: www.
   coopervision.com

Pres: Daniel G McBride
Exec VP, Global Sales & Mktg: Dennis
   Murphy
Primary Market Served: Business

Manufactures soft contact lenses, Preference & PreferenceToric Planned Replacement lenses, Hydrasoft & Custom
Toric lenses.

DR HO'S
150 Stewart Pkwy
Greensboro, GA L6E 1A4-30642
Telephone: (905) 471-4735, Toll Free:
   (877) 374-6669, FAX: (877) 836-
   7466, Web Site: www.drhonow.com
Pres: Vincent Ho
Primary Market Served: Consumer

DENTSPLY INTERNATIONAL
221 West Philadelphia St
York, PA 17401
Telephone: (844) 848-0137, Toll Free:
   (800) 877-0020, E-Mail: contact@
   dentsplysirona.com, Web Site: www.
   dentsply.com
Corp Commun: Michele Mummert
CEO: Jeffrey T. Slovin
Primary Market Served: Consumer

CHRISTIAN DIOR
PERFUMES
151 W 34th St
New York, NY 10001
Telephone: (877) 903-4671, Toll Free:
   (800) 929-3467, FAX: (212) 931-
   2954, Web Site: www.dior.com
Pres: Bernard Potier
Sr VP Mktg, Sls & Edn: Terry Darland
Chmn Bd: Bernard Armault
CEO: Sidney Toledano
Conducts Business: Worldwide
Primary Market Served: Consumer

Retail cosmetic, fragrance & skin care
products to consumers.

DNE NUTRACEUTICALS INC
700 Central Ave
Farmingdale, NJ 07727
Telephone: (212) 235-5200, Toll Free:
   (800) 221-1833, FAX: (212) 235-
   5243, E-Mail: info@dnenutra.com,
   Web Site: www.dnenutra.com
Pres: Eric Organ
CEO: Denise Organ
Dir Opers: Richard Quine
Sls Mgr: Todd Weller
Pur Mgr: Ted Weller
Conducts Business: U.S.
Primary Market Served: Business &
   Consumer
Catalog available online
Direct online sales
Founded: 1979

Mail order pharmaceuticals.

DR LEONARD'S
HEALTHCARE CORP
100 Nixon Ln
Edison, NJ 08837-3804
Telephone: (732) 225-0100, Toll Free:
   (800) 455-1918, FAX: (732) 225-
   0302, Web Site: www.doctorleonard.
   com
Exec VP, Mdse & Mktg: Susan Met-
   calfe
Mktg Dir: Susan Pizzano
Mdse Dir: Gina Van Der Veer
Primary Market Served: Consumer

Healthcare catalog-Dr. Leonard's product buyers are active, mature individuals who purchase high quality
attractively priced products to enhance
their lifestyles.

E-Z-EM INC
1111 Marcus Ave (Suite M-60)
Lake Success, NY 11042
Telephone: (516) 333-8230, Toll Free:
   (800) 544-4624, FAX: (516) 333-
   8278, E-Mail: webmaster@ezem.
   com, Web Site: www.ezem.com
Pres, CEO & Dir: Anthony A. Lombar-
   do
Sr VP, Global Sls Mktg Engrng: Brad
   S. Schreck
VP NA Imaging Sls: Tom McLaughlin
Dir Corp & Mktg Commun: Tom John-
   son
Conducts Business: Worldwide
Employees: 611
Primary Market Served: Business
Catalog available online
Founded: 1962
Gross sales or billing: $137,800,000

CT Imaging, virtual colonoscopy,
speech pathology, gastrointestinal devices & accessories & Healthcare decon-
taminants. Leading manufacturer of
contrast agents for gastrointestinal radiology.

ETR ASSOCIATES
100 Enterprise Way (Suite G300)
Scotts Valley, CA 95066
Toll Free: (800) 321-4407, E-Mail:
   customerservice@etr.org, Web Site:
   www.etr.org
Dir: Vignetta Charles
DM Mgr: Coleen Cantwell
Dir Mktg: Matt McDowell
Primary Market Served: Consumer
Founded: 1981

Behavioral health nonprofit devoted to
providing science-based programs &
services to advance health & opportunities for youth & families.

EMERSON ECOLOGICS
1230 Elm St (Suite 301)

Manchester, NH 03101-1336
Telephone: (603) 656-9778, Toll Free:
(800) 654-4432, FAX: (603) 656-
9797, (800) 718-7238, E-Mail: cs@
emersonecologics.com
Pres & CEO: Adam Carr
Primary Market Served: Consumer

Distributor of natural & herbal health
care products to healthcare professionals

ESSENTIAL PRODUCTS CO INC

90 Water St
New York, NY 10005-3511
Telephone: (212) 344-4288
Pres: Barry Striem
Conducts Business: U.S.
Primary Market Served: Business &
Consumer
Founded: 1895

Offer discount versions of designer fragrances. Offer 68-72 perfumes & men's
colognes as recommended on TV, radio
& shopping guides. Request free scent
cards & list.

FIRST TO THE FINISH INC

1325 N Broad St
Carlinville, IL 62626-9770
Toll Free: (800) 747-9013, FAX: (877)
631-9687, E-Mail:
customer_service@fttf.com, Web
Site: www.firsttothefinish.com
Gen Mgr: John Costello
Primary Market Served: Consumer

FITNESS SYSTEMS MANUFACTURING CORP

1745 Portland Ave
Wyomissing, PA 19609
Toll Free: (800) 822-9995, FAX: (610)
670-0135, E-Mail: vitaminout@aol.
com, Web Site: www.fitness-
systems.net
Pres: David Hoffman
Conducts Business: Worldwide
Primary Market Served: Business &
Consumer
Catalog available online
Direct online sales
Advertising/Marketing Budget Related
to Direct Marketing: 0-25%
Founded: 1985

Athletic, body building & weight loss
vitamin supplements such as human
growth hormones, creatine, andros,
proteins & vitamin packs at wholesale
prices.

FRONTIER NATURAL PRODUCTS CO-OP

Div. of Frontier Cooperative Herbs
3021 78th St, PO Box 299

Norway, IA 52318
Toll Free: (800) 669-3275, FAX: (800)
717-4372, E-Mail: info@
frontiercoop.com, Web Site: www.
frontiercoop.com
CEO: Tony Bedard
Chief Mktg Officer: Clint Landis
VP Sls: Dan Lloyd
Conducts Business: U.S.
Employees: 225
Primary Market Served: Business &
Consumer
Advertising/Marketing Budget Related
to Direct Marketing: 0-25%
Founded: 1976
Gross sales or billing: $48,000,000

Bulk herbs, spices, teas, bottled spices,
baking flavors; essential oils, fragrances, soaps, shampoos, homeopathics,
extracts, encapsulated herbs, salves &
cough syrups, bulk & packaged coffee
& teas.

GARDEN BOTANIKA INC

Div. of Schroeder & Tremayne
8500 Valcour Ave
Saint Louis, MO 63123
Telephone: (425) 881-9603, Toll Free:
(800) 724-7227, FAX: (314) 633-
4804, E-Mail: customercare@zidle.
com, Web Site: www.zidle.com
Dir Mktg: Mary Holmes
Pres: Jamie Wilmsen
Employees: 250
Primary Market Served: Consumer
Founded: 1989

Retail & catalog selling botanically
based skin care products & cosmetics.

GENERAL NUTRITION CORP

300 6th Ave Fl 2
Pittsburgh, PA 15222-2511
Telephone: (412) 288-4600, Toll Free:
(877) 462-4700, FAX: (412) 402-
7218, Web Site: www.gnc.com
Pres & CEO: Joseph Fortunato
VP Mktg: Rich Oprison
CEO: Michael Arnold
Conducts Business: U.S.
Employees: 12,707
Primary Market Served: Consumer
Direct Marketing ad budget:
Direct Mail: 5%
Magazines: 10%
Newspapers: 3%
TV/Radio: 80%
Telephone: 2%
Founded: 1935
Gross sales or billing: $1,490,000,000

A national retail chain of vitamins,
health foods & cosmetics which direct
markets to an internal mail file with
various promotions.

GIBSON AUER LLC

dba Spiral Energetics & GA Labs
PO Box 228
Victor, ID 83455-0228
Telephone: (208) 201-3143, Toll Free:
(888) 425-2250, E-Mail: helpdesk@
galabs.com, Web Site: www.
spiralenergetics.com
Owner: Rebecca Franklin
Conducts Business: U.S., Canada
Primary Market Served: Business &
Consumer
Catalog available online
Indirect online sales
Advertising/Marketing Budget Related
to Direct Marketing: 0-25%
Direct Marketing ad budget:
Direct Mail: 90%
Magazines: 10%
Founded: 2003
Gross sales or billing: $80,000

Mail order company selling proprietary
medicines & cosmetics.

GOLD MEDAL HAIR PRODUCTS INC

330 Conklin St
Farmingdale, NY 11735-2609
Telephone: (631) 465-0202, FAX:
(631) 465-0207, E-Mail:
customerservice@goldmedalhair.
com, Web Site: www.goldmedalhair.
com
Pres: Rick Laban
Art Dir: Ray Wallace
Conducts Business: U.S., U.K.
Employees: 6
Primary Market Served: Business &
Consumer
Catalog available online
Direct online sales
Advertising/Marketing Budget Related
to Direct Marketing: 76-100%
Direct Marketing ad budget: $50,000
Direct Mail: 100%
Founded: 1942
Gross sales or billing: $1,000,000

Mail order company specializing in
sales to black clientele.

GRAHAM FIELD HEALTH PRODUCTS INC

2935 Northeast Pkwy
Atlanta, GA 30360-2808
Telephone: (770) 368-4700, Toll Free:
(800) 347-5678, FAX: (800) 726-
0601, E-Mail: cs@grahamfield.com,
Web Site: www.grahamfield.com
Pres & CEO: Kenneth Spett
VP, Natl Sls: Harvey Cohen
Export Dir: Ed Roark
Conducts Business: U.S., Canada, Eu-
rope, S. America, Asia
Employees: 100

Primary Market Served: Business & Consumer

Advertising/Marketing Budget Related to Direct Marketing: 0-25%

Health care products, fitness & personal care products & medical instruments. Sells to professional, retail & premium markets.

HANDI-RAMP INC

510 North Ave
Libertyville, IL 60048-2025
Telephone: (847) 680-7700, Toll Free: (800) 876-RAMP, FAX: (847) 816-7689, E-Mail: info@handiramp.com, Web Site: www.handiramp.com
Pres: Thomas R. Disch
Conducts Business: U.S., Canada
Employees: 8
Primary Market Served: Business & Consumer
Catalog available online
Direct online sales
Advertising/Marketing Budget Related to Direct Marketing: 26-50%
Direct Marketing ad budget:
Direct Mail: 25%
Magazines: 75%
Founded: 1958

Ramps for the handicapped & for hotels etc.

HARVARD PILGRIM HEALTH CARE

93 Worcester St
Wellesley, MA 02481-3609
Telephone: (617) 509-1000, Toll Free: (888) 888-4742, FAX: (617) 509-7590, Web Site: www. harvardpilgrim.org
CFO: Joseph C. Capezza
CEO: Eric H. Schultz
COO: Bruce M. Bullen
VP HR: Deborah A. Hicks
VP Customer Svc: Lynn A. Bowman
Sr Mktg Mgr: Tim Walsh
Conducts Business: U.S.
Employees: 1,350
Primary Market Served: Business & Consumer
Catalog available online
Advertising/Marketing Budget Related to Direct Marketing: 0-25%
Direct Marketing ad budget:
Direct Mail: 15%
Newspapers: 40%
TV/Radio: 45%
Founded: 1969

Healthcare/Insurance.

HAVEL'S INC

3726 Lonsdale St
Cincinnati, OH 45227-3651

Telephone: (513) 271-2117, Toll Free: (800) 638-4770, FAX: (800) 628-3458, E-Mail: customercare@havels. com, Web Site: www.havels.com
Primary Market Served: Consumer

Specialty medical supplies distributor

HAZELDEN

Div. of Hazelden Foundation
PO Box 11
Center City, MN 55012-0011
Telephone: (651) 213-4200, Toll Free: (800) 257-7810, FAX: (651) 213-4411, E-Mail: info@ hazeldenbettyford.org, Web Site: www.hazelden.org
VP, Publr: Nick Moto
Pres: Mark Mishek
Conducts Business: Worldwide
Employees: 140
Primary Market Served: Business & Consumer
Catalog available online
Direct online sales
Advertising/Marketing Budget Related to Direct Marketing: 76-100%
Direct Marketing ad budget:
Direct Mail: 80%
Magazines: 5%
Newspapers: 5%
TV/Radio: 10%
Founded: 1954
Gross sales or billing: $24,000,000

Educational programs of videos, workbooks, pamphlets & other media for substance abuse treatment.

HERBALIFE INTERNATIONAL OF AMERICA INC

PO Box 80210
Los Angeles, CA 90080
Telephone: (310) 216-9661, Toll Free: (866) 866-4744, FAX: (310) 258-7019, Web Site: www.herbalife.com
Chmn & CEO: Michael O. Johnson
Pres & COO: Gregory Probert
CFO: Richard Goudis
VP, Corp Mktg: Doug Braun
Employees: 3,600
Primary Market Served: Business
Catalog available online
Gross sales or billing: $1,885,500,000

Health & nutrition company & personal care products.

HOPKINS MEDICAL PRODUCTS

Div. of Hopkins Uniform Co Inc.
5 Greenwood Pl
Baltimore, MD 21208-2763

Telephone: (410) 484-2036, Toll Free: (800) 835-1995, FAX: (410) 484-4036, E-Mail: customerservice@ hopkinsmedical.net, Web Site: www. hopkinsmedicalproducts.com
Chmn Bd: Kurt Hilzinger
Conducts Business: U.S.
Employees: 11
Primary Market Served: Business & Consumer
Catalog available online
Direct online sales
Founded: 1945
Gross sales or billing: $1,800,000

Medical supplies, devices and hospital equipment for the medical profession.

HUMANA INC

500 W Main St
Louisville, KY 40202
Telephone: (502) 580-5005, Toll Free: (800) 486-2620, FAX: (502) 580-3141, Web Site: www.humana.com
CEO: Bruce D. Broussard
Conducts Business: U.S., England, Switzerland
Employees: 30,000
Primary Market Served: Business & Consumer

Provides health coverage through Humana Health Care Plans.

INDEPENDENT LIVING AIDS

137 Rano Rd
Buffalo, NY 14207
Telephone: (516) 450-3829, Toll Free: (800) 537-2118, FAX: (516) 937-3906, E-Mail: techsupport@ independentliving.com, Web Site: www.independentliving.com
Pres: Marvin Sandler
Sales Dir: Fran Hennelly
VP & Owner: Mimi Berman
Conducts Business: U.S., Europe, Asia
Employees: 25
Primary Market Served: Business & Consumer
Catalog available online
Direct online sales
Advertising/Marketing Budget Related to Direct Marketing: 0-25%
Founded: 1977
Gross sales or billing: $2,200,000

Catalog of aids for visually, audibly & physically disabled.

JAFRA COSMETICS INTERNATIONAL INC

Subs of Vorwerk & Co KG
2451 Townsgate Rd
Westlake Village, CA 91361
Telephone: (260) 423-9571, Toll Free: (888) 848-4077, FAX: (960) 423-6742, Web Site: www.jafra.com

CEO & Pres: Mauro Schnaidman
Sr VP & Chief Mktg Officer: Matt Petersen
Conducts Business: Worldwide
Employees: 1,016
Primary Market Served: Consumer
Founded: 1956
Gross sales or billing: $90,500,000

Direct selling & marketing company specializing in cosmetics, toiletries, fragrances & related products & skincare.

JAMES MEDICAL RENTS & SALES INC
7821 Coldwater Rd Ste A
Fort Wayne, IN 46825-8412
Telephone: (260) 739-0874, E-Mail: sales@jamesmedical.com, Web Site: www.jamesmedical.net
Pres & Owner: Doug James
VP & Owner: Jeff Castator
Sls Mgr: Mark Church
Consultant: Dave Ponder
Primary Market Served: Business
Catalog available online

Healthcare.

JASON NATURAL PERSONAL CARE PRODUCTS
Part of Hain Celestial Group
4600 Sleepytime Dr
Boulder, CO 80301-3284
Toll Free: (88) 659-7730, Web Site: www.jason-natural.com
Chmn, Pres & CEO: Irwin David Simon
Exec VP, CFO & Sec: Ira J. Lamel
Exec VP: John Carroll
Sr VP, Sls & Mktg: James R. Lemsky
Dir: Melanie Brown
Conducts Business: U.S., Canada, Mexico, Europe, Korea
Employees: 39
Primary Market Served: Business & Consumer
Catalog available online
Direct online sales
Advertising/Marketing Budget Related to Direct Marketing: 0-25%
Founded: 1959

Manufactures & sells private label natural cosmetics.

KALMED DENTAL PRODUCTS INC
3048 Alberta Dr
Marietta, GA 30062-1513
Telephone: (770) 971-8815, Toll Free: (800) 322-8815, FAX: (770) 509-8823, E-Mail: sales@kalmed.com, Web Site: www.kalmed.com
Pres: Leonard Jacobs
Conducts Business: U.S.
Employees: 2

Primary Market Served: Business
Catalog available online
Direct online sales
Advertising/Marketing Budget Related to Direct Marketing: 76-100%
Direct Marketing ad budget:
Direct Mail: 100%
Founded: 1984
Gross sales or billing: $500,000

Dental consumables & small instruments to general & some specialty dentists.

KING PHARMACEUTICALS, INC
Part of Pfizer
132 Windsor Rd
Tenafly, NJ 07670
Telephone: (972) 885-0929, Toll Free: (888) 840-5370, E-Mail: igal@navehpharma.com, Web Site: www.kingpharma.com
Chmn, Pres & CEO: Brian A. Markinson
CFO: Joseph Squicciarino
CCO: Steve Andrzejewski
Primary Market Served: Consumer
Catalog available online
Gross sales or billing: $2,000,000,000

Specializes in critical care pharmaceuticals.

CALVIN KLEIN COSMETICS CO
Subs. of Calvin Klein Inc
205 W 39th St
New York, NY 10018
Telephone: (212) 719-2600, E-Mail: customerservice@calvinklein.com, Web Site: www.calvinklein.com
CEO, Calvin Klein: Gaetano Sallorenzo
Pres: Paulanne Mancuso
VP, Mktg: Lori Singer
Primary Market Served: Consumer

Fragrances.

LATEST PRODUCTS CORP
36 Orchard Dr
Woodbury, NY 11797-2830
Telephone: (516) 367-4700, Toll Free: (800) 288-3547, FAX: (516) 367-4714, E-Mail: lpcorp@aol.com, Web Site: www.latestproducts.net
Pres: Steven E. Spaeth
Sr VP: Aaron M. Herman
Conducts Business: U.S.
Employees: 4
Primary Market Served: Business
Catalog available online
Indirect online sales
Advertising/Marketing Budget Related to Direct Marketing: 76-100%
Direct Marketing ad budget:

Direct Mail: 80%
Online: 20%
Founded: 1972
Gross sales or billing: $2,000,000

Distributor & direct marketer of specialty items to hospitals & nursing homes, government agencies, VAMC's, prisons, correctional facilities & other institutions.

LIFE EXTENSION FOUNDATION
3600 W Commercial Blvd Ste 100
Fort Lauderdale, FL 33309-3324
Telephone: (954) 766-8144, Toll Free: (800) 678-8989, FAX: (954) 771-2827, E-Mail: info@lef.org, Web Site: www.lef.org
CEO: Paul Gilner
Dir Mktg & Sls: Rey Searles
Conducts Business: U.S.
Employees: 100
Primary Market Served: Business & Consumer
Catalog available online
Direct online sales
Advertising/Marketing Budget Related to Direct Marketing: 76-100%
Founded: 1980
Gross sales or billing: $55,000,000

Sells top quality dietary supplements to consumers and re-sellers. Also funds anti-aging research.

LIFE LINE SCREENING
901 S Mopac Expressway
Austin, TX 78746
Telephone: (216) 581-6556, Toll Free: (800) 449-2350, Web Site: www.lifelinescreening.com
VP Mktg: Eric Greenburg
Primary Market Served: Consumer

LIFESCRIPT
4000 MacArthur Blvd
Newport Beach, CA 92660
Telephone: (949) 454-0422, Toll Free: (800) 637-9382, Web Site: www.lifescript.com
COO: Jack Hogan
CEO: Ronald L. Caporale

LONGEVITY NETWORK LTD
2764 N Green Valley Pkwy (Suite 401)
Henderson, NV 89014-2121
Telephone: (702) 454-7000, Toll Free: (800) 242-1000, FAX: (702) 434-8259, E-Mail: info@longevity.com, Web Site: www.longevity.com
Pres: Adi Song
CEO: Jim Song
Chmn Bd: Yoan Kim
CIO: Kirk Johnsong
Conducts Business: U.S.

Employees: 55
Primary Market Served: Consumer
Founded: 1993

Makes over 45 nutritional supplements, weight loss, skin, hair & body-care products.

LONGEVITY PURE MEDICINE

Subs. of Lacausa Inc
10415 Ravenwood Ct
Los Angeles, CA 90077-2517
Toll Free: (800) 919-2090, FAX: (760) 329-3651, E-Mail: info@
longetivtypuremedicine.com, Web Site: www.longevitypuremedicine. com
Mng Dir: Reni Chase
Conducts Business: U.S., S. America, Central America, Asia, Europe
Employees: 11
Primary Market Served: Business & Consumer
Catalog available online
Direct online sales
Advertising/Marketing Budget Related to Direct Marketing: 26-50%
Direct Marketing ad budget: $150,000
Direct Mail: 45%
Magazines: 5%
Newspapers: 5%
TV/Radio: 20%
Telephone: 25%
Founded: 1984
Gross sales or billing: $1,000,000

14 natural homeopathic medicines for colds & flu, PMS, stress, sinus, hay fever, insomnia, cough & sore throat.

LUCKY HEART COSMETICS INC

390 Mulberry St
Memphis, TN 38103-4212
Telephone: (901) 526-7658, Toll Free: (800) 283-1014, FAX: (901) 526-7660, Web Site: www.luckyheart. com
Pres: Tom Colturi
VP: Chandra Miller
Conducts Business: U.S.
Employees: 20
Primary Market Served: Consumer
Catalog available online
Indirect online sales
Advertising/Marketing Budget Related to Direct Marketing: 76-100%
Direct Marketing ad budget:
Direct Mail: 35%
Magazines: 65%
Founded: 1935
Gross sales or billing: $2,000,000

Manufactures & sells cosmetics to independent sales representatives. Also carries an ethnic line which includes hair & skin products.

LUZIER PERSONALIZED COSMETICS

5601 E 135th St
Grandview, MO 64030
Telephone: (816) 531-8338, Toll Free: (800) 821-6632, FAX: (816) 531-6979, E-Mail: customerservice@
luzier.com, Web Site: www.luzier. com
CEO: Kathleen Grissom
Pres: Kari Johnson
Primary Market Served: Consumer
Catalog available online
Indirect online sales

Cosmetics.

MDR

14101 NW Fourth St
Sunrise, FL 33325-6209
Telephone: (954) 845-9500, Toll Free: (800) 637-8227, FAX: (954) 845-9505, E-Mail: info@mdr.org, Web Site: www.mdr.org
Pres & CEO: Patricia Riley
Conducts Business: U.S.
Employees: 60
Primary Market Served: Consumer
Catalog available online
Direct online sales
Advertising/Marketing Budget Related to Direct Marketing: 0-25%
Direct Marketing ad budget:
Direct Mail: $100,000
Magazines: $1,000,000
TV/Radio: $1,000,000

Catalog marketer of cosmetics & skin care products.

MJA INTERNATIONAL

31 Stonywell Ct
Dix Hills, NY 11746-5424
Telephone: (516) 676-5990, FAX: (516) 674-3309
VP: Jay Berliner
Conducts Business: U.S.
Primary Market Served: Business
Advertising/Marketing Budget Related to Direct Marketing: 0-25%
Founded: 1988

Medical equipment.

MYLAN NV

Subs. of Mylan Laboratories, Inc
1000 Mylan Blvd
Canonsburg, PA 15317
Telephone: (724) 514-1800, Toll Free: (800) 231-3052, FAX: (281) 240-0002, E-Mail: communications@
mylan.com, Web Site: www.mylan. com
Exec Chmn: Robert J. Coury
CEO: Heather Bresch
Conducts Business: U.S.
Employees: 230

Primary Market Served: Business
Catalog available online
Direct Marketing ad budget: $70,000
Direct Mail: 20%
Magazines: 70%
Telephone: 10%
Gross sales or billing: $30,000,000

Manufacturer & marketer of wound care products for chronic & burn related wounds.

ROBERT J MATTHEWS CO

dba PBS Animal Health
2780 Richville Dr SE
Massillon, OH 44646-8396
Telephone: (330) 834-3000, Toll Free: (800) 578-9234, FAX: (330) 830-2762, E-Mail: email@rjmatthews. com, Web Site: www. pbsanimalhealth.com
Pres: J. Daniel Matthews
Mktg Production Supvr: Bridget Gillogly
Conducts Business: U.S.
Primary Market Served: Business & Consumer
Catalog available online
Indirect online sales
Advertising/Marketing Budget Related to Direct Marketing: 76-100%
Founded: 1941

Distributor of animal health products & livestock pharmaceuticals.

MCKESSON CORP

Div. of Red Line Medical Supply
1 Post St
San Francisco, CA 94104-5203
Telephone: (415) 983-8300, FAX: (415) 983-7160, Web Site: www. mckesson.com
Chmn, Pres & CEO: John H. Hammergren
Exec VP & Grp Pres: Paul C. Julian
Exec VP & CFO: Jeffrey C. Campbell
Conducts Business: U.S.
Employees: 31,800
Primary Market Served: Business & Consumer
Advertising/Marketing Budget Related to Direct Marketing: 0-25%
Gross sales or billing: $93,000,000,000

National distributor of medical supplies.

MEAD JOHNSON CO

2400 W Lloyd Expwy
Evansville, IN 47721-0001
Telephone: (812) 429-5204, Web Site: www.MeadJohnson.com
Dir: Andrew Mosier
CEO & Pres: Kasper Jakobsen
Primary Market Served: Business & Consumer

MEDCO HEALTH SOLUTIONS INC
100 Parsons Pond Dr
Franklin Lakes, NJ 07417-2604
Telephone: (201) 269-3400, Toll Free:
(800) 556-3326, FAX: (800) 222-1934, E-Mail: customersupport@
medcosupply.com, Web Site: www.
medco-athletics.com
VP Prod & Channel Generics Strategy:
Kenneth Malley
Pres & CEO: David Snow
Chmn: Richard Clark
Dir: Boris Fainstein
Primary Market Served: Business
Catalog available online
Direct online sales
Gross sales or billing: $42,000,000,000

Leading pharmacy benefit management
company providing benefits to more
than 53 million Americans, including
more than 14 million retirees. Merck-
Medco subsidiary National Rx Services
Inc serves patients through 12 state of
the art mail service facilities, and its
paid prescription subsidiary manages
prescriptions dispensed at 52,000 community pharmacies worldwide.

MEDCO SUPPLY CO INC
500 Fillmore Ave
Tonawanda, NY 14150
Telephone: (716) 743-8400, Toll Free:
(800) 556-3326, FAX: (800) 222-1934, E-Mail: sales@medcosupply.
com, Web Site: www.medcosupply.
com
Sr Prod Mgr: Karen Blaha
Pres: Mark Ladouceur
VP, Sls: Paul DeMartins
Dir, Mktg: Don Laux
Conducts Business: United States
Employees: 120
Primary Market Served: Business
Catalog available online
Direct online sales
Advertising/Marketing Budget Related
to Direct Marketing: 76-100%
Direct Marketing ad budget:
Direct Mail: 90%
Magazines: 10%
Founded: 1955

National distributor of first aid, safety
sports medicine and podiatry products
for athletic physical therapy, chiropractic, school nurse and podiatry markets.

MEDTRONIC
710 Medtronic Pkwy
Minneapolis, MN 55432-5604
Telephone: (763) 514-4000, Toll Free:
(800) 633-8766, Web Site: www.
covidien.com
Chmn Bd & CEO: Omar Ishrak
Conducts Business: Worldwide

Employees: 43,000
Primary Market Served: Business &
Consumer
Catalog available online
Indirect online sales
Advertising/Marketing Budget Related
to Direct Marketing: 0-25%
Gross sales or billing: $9,600,000,000

Manufactures, markets, and distributes
disposable medical supplies and devices.

MIDWEST CENTER FOR STRESS & ANXIETY INC
106 N Church St (Suite 200), PO Box
205
Oak Harbor, OH 43449
Telephone: (419) 898-4357, Toll Free:
(877) 989-8229, FAX: (419) 898-0669, Web Site: www.stresscenter.
com
Pres & CEO: Lucinda Bassett
VP: David Bassett
Conducts Business: U.S., Canada
Primary Market Served: Business &
Consumer
Indirect online sales
Advertising/Marketing Budget Related
to Direct Marketing: 51-75%
Direct Marketing ad budget:
$5,000,000
Direct Mail: 1%
TV/Radio: 99%

Self help program for anxiety & panic
disorder to professionals & lay individuals.

MIRACLE OF ALOE
4401 Diplomacy Ave
Dallas, TX 75261-2688
Toll Free: (800) 966-2563, FAX: (800)
859-9881, E-Mail: LJohnson@
miracleofaloe.com, Web Site: www.
miracleofaloe.com
Founder: Jess F. Clarke Jr.
Pres: Jess F. Clarke III
Creative Dir: Chris Sykes
New Products Mgr: Chris Clarke
CFO: Jennifer Babiak
Conducts Business: U.S., Nigeria, Tai-
wan, U.K., Finland, Argentina, Chi-
na, Canada, Japan
Employees: 20
Primary Market Served: Business &
Consumer
Catalog available online
Direct online sales
Advertising/Marketing Budget Related
to Direct Marketing: 76-100%
Direct Marketing ad budget:
$1,000,000
Direct Mail: 70%
Magazines: 20%
Newspapers: 10%
Founded: 1986

Gross sales or billing: $7,000,000

Mail order catalog specializing in
health & beauty aids made with pure
aloe vera gel.

MOORE MEDICAL LLC
Subs. of McKesson Corp
1690 New Britain Ave Ste A
Farmington, CT 06032-3361
Telephone: (860) 826-3600, FAX:
(860) 223-2382, E-Mail: e-support@
mooremedical.com, Web Site: www.
mooremedical.com
VP, Mktg: Lori Steinberg
VP, Direct Mktg & Market Mgr: Tim
Bidwell
Conducts Business: U.S.
Employees: 305
Primary Market Served: Business
Catalog available online
Direct online sales
Advertising/Marketing Budget Related
to Direct Marketing: 76-100%
Direct Marketing ad budget:
Direct Mail: 90%
Magazines: 2%
Telephone: 8%
Founded: 1965
Gross sales or billing: $46,000,000

Medical supply distributor to alternate
care facilities.

MURAD INC
2121 Rosecrans Ave (Floor 5)
El Segundo, CA 90245-4744
Telephone: (310) 726-0600, Toll Free:
(888) 996-8723, Web Site: www.
murad.com
Exec VP Direct to Consumer: Carey
Grange
Primary Market Served: Consumer

MYLAN ENTERPRISES
dba Silkskin
18563 Ventura Blvd (#272)
Tarzana, CA 91356
Telephone: (818) 538-8080, Toll Free:
(888) 528-3928, FAX: (818) 538-7646, E-Mail: calcos@silkskin.com,
Web Site: www.silkskin.com
Pres: Bob Sidell
Conducts Business: U.S., Canada
Employees: 19
Primary Market Served: Consumer
Founded: 1985
Gross sales or billing: $2,600,000

Skin care & cosmetics via mail order &
catalog sales.

NBTY INC
2100 Smithtown Ave
Ronkonkoma, NY 11779-7347

Telephone: (631) 200-2000, FAX: (631) 567-7148, Web Site: www.nbty.com
Pres & CEO: Steve Cahiliane
Conducts Business: Worldwide
Employees: 10,900
Primary Market Served: Business & Consumer
Catalog available online
Direct online sales
Advertising/Marketing Budget Related to Direct Marketing: 26-50%
Direct Marketing ad budget: $103,614,000
Founded: 1971
Gross sales or billing: $1,880,222,000

Manufacturer, marketer & distributor of nutritional supplements including vitamins, minerals, herbs & sports drinks to pharmacies, wholesalers, supermarkets, health food stores & consumers via mail order and online.

NATURMED

dba Institute for Vibrant Living
661 E Howards Rd
Camp Verde, AZ 86322
Telephone: (928) 567-5175, Toll Free: (800) 720-1245, Web Site: www.ivlproducts.com
VP Sales & Mktg: Gina Lascano
Pres: Bill Ruble

NOVARTIS PHARMACEUTICALS CORP

1 Health Plaza (Bldg 701 Rm 060)
East Hanover, NJ 07936-1016
Telephone: (862) 778-2100, Toll Free: (800) 669-6682, FAX: (973) 781-8119, Web Site: www.novartis.com
COO & VP Mktg: David Epstein
Dir Head Relationship Mktg: Marc Schwartz
CEO: Joseph Jimenez
Primary Market Served: Business & Consumer

Ethical & over-the-counter pharmaceuticals.

NUMARK BRANDS

164 Northfield Ave
Edison, NJ 08837
Telephone: (732) 417-1870, Toll Free: (800) 338-8079, FAX: (732) 225-0066, E-Mail: newmark@injersey.com
Pres: Moaiz F. Daya
Chmn Bd: Robert Stites
Primary Market Served: Consumer

Sells over-the-counter pharmaceuticals, health & beauty aids.

NUTRISYSTEM INC

600 Office Center Dr

Fort Washington, PA 19034-3232
Telephone: (215) 706-5300, Toll Free: (800) 435-4074, FAX: (215) 706-5388, E-Mail: customerservice@nutrisystem.com, Web Site: www.nutrisystem.com
Pres & CEO: Dawn M. Zier
Chief Mktg Officer: Keira Krausz
Conducts Business: Worldwide
Primary Market Served: Consumer
Catalog available online
Direct online sales
Advertising/Marketing Budget Related to Direct Marketing: 51-75%
Direct Marketing ad budget:
Direct Mail: 25%
Newspapers: 25%
TV/Radio: 50%
Founded: 1971
Gross sales or billing: $568,000,000

National weight loss company.

1-800-CONTACTS

261 Data Dr
Draper, UT 84020
Toll Free: (800) 266-8228, FAX: (801) 924-9000, Web Site: www.1800contacts.com
Chief Mktg Officer: Tim Roush
CEO: Brian W. Bethers
Primary Market Served: Business & Consumer

PACIFIC BOTANICALS LLC

4840 Fish Hatchery Rd
Grants Pass, OR 97527-9547
Telephone: (541) 479-7777, FAX: (541) 479-7780, E-Mail: pacbot1@earthlink.net, Web Site: www.pacificbotanicals.com
Founder: Mark Wheeler
COO: Toni Corrente-Evans
Farm Mgr: Dave Metzger
Mill Mgr: Bruce Fain
QC Mgr: Dori Moran
Conducts Business: Worldwide
Employees: 15
Primary Market Served: Consumer
Catalog available online
Advertising/Marketing Budget Related to Direct Marketing: 0-25%
Founded: 1979

Certified organic bulk herbs & spices.

PARIS PRESENTS INC

3800 Swanson Ct
Gurnee, IL 60031-1226
Telephone: (847) 263-5500, Toll Free: (800) 431-5723, FAX: (847) 263-5191, E-Mail: support@parispresents.com, Web Site: www.parispresents.com
CEO: Patrick O'Brien
VP Mktg: Eva Oreskovich

Conducts Business: U.S., Canada, Mexico, Sweden, Europe, Far East
Employees: 75
Primary Market Served: Business
Direct online sales
Founded: 1947
Gross sales or billing: $9,800,000

Distributor of cosmetics, bath, beauty & travel accessories.

PENN HERB CO LTD

dba Nature's Wonderland
10601 Decatur Rd (Suite 2)
Philadelphia, PA 19154-3293
Telephone: (215) 632-6100, Toll Free: (800) 523-9971, FAX: (215) 632-7945, E-Mail: information@pennherb.com, Web Site: www.pennherb.com
Pres & CEO: Ronald Betz
VP: William P. Betz Jr
Gen Mgr: Jerome Hannah
Conducts Business: U.S.
Employees: 26
Primary Market Served: Business & Consumer
Founded: 1924
Gross sales or billing: $3,500,000

Sell dried herbs, herbal products, capsules, books, essential oils, homeopathic remedies, vitamins, health food items, herbal extracts & Olbas products.

PHILIPS LIFELINE

111 Lawrence St
Framingham, MA 01702-8156
Telephone: (855) 332-7799, Toll Free: (800) 635-6156, Web Site: www.lifeline.philips.com
Dir Direct Mktg: Brenda Vere
Primary Market Served: Consumer

POCKET NURSE ENTERPRISES INC

610 Frankfort Rd
Monaca, PA 15061-2218
Telephone: (720) 480-3777, Toll Free: (800) 225-1600, FAX: (720) 480-3778, E-Mail: sales@pocketnurse.com, Web Site: www.pocketnurse.com
Primary Market Served: Consumer
Founded: 1992

Medical supplies & equipment for health care educators

PURITAN'S PRIDE

2100 Smithtown Ave
Ronkonkoma, NY 11779-7347
Telephone: (631) 567-9500, Toll Free: (800) 645-1030, FAX: (631) 471-5693, E-Mail: info@puritan.com, Web Site: www.puritan.com

CEO: Peter Shapiro
Conducts Business: Worldwide
Employees: 100
Primary Market Served: Consumer
Catalog available online
Direct online sales
Advertising/Marketing Budget Related to Direct Marketing: 76-100%
Gross sales or billing: $1,900,000

Manufactures & distributes top quality natural vitamins, minerals, herbs & other nutritional supplements by mail order & online.

RAVEN'S NEST HERBALS, LLC

PO Box 370
Duluth, GA 30096
Telephone: (678) 642-6691, (678) 584-0830, E-Mail: info@ravensnestherbals.com, Web Site: www.ravensnestherbals.com
Owner, Master Herbalist & Sls: Terry Cochran
Seasonal Mgr: Mark Gravitt
Conducts Business: U.S., Canada, Caribbean, Japan, U.K., S. Africa
Employees: 1
Primary Market Served: Consumer
Catalog available online
Direct online sales
Advertising/Marketing Budget Related to Direct Marketing: 0-25%
Direct Marketing ad budget: $1,500
Direct Mail: 50%
Magazines: 5%
Newspapers: 45%
Founded: 1985
Gross sales or billing: $30,000

Herbs, spices, teas, essential oils, fragrances, potpourri, dried flowers & incense to health food/vitamin stores, herb shops, crafters & individuals.

RELAXO-BAK INC

4956 W 300 N
Anderson, IN 46011
Telephone: (765) 643-2934, Toll Free: (866) 369-6914, FAX: (765) 641-7448, Web Site: www.relaxobak.com
Pres: Diane Cameron
Conducts Business: U.S.
Employees: 3
Primary Market Served: Business & Consumer
Catalog available online
Direct online sales
Direct Marketing ad budget: $10,000
Direct Mail: 25%
Magazines: 75%
Founded: 1963
Gross sales or billing: $200,000

Thin form-fitting plastic auxiliary seat. Used on any over-soft seat to give it firmness. Contoured for better weight

distribution & greater comfort. Recessed at the spine's end to shield the tailbone. Used in office chairs, autos, trucks, buses & airplanes.

ROCHE DIAGNOSTICS CORP

9115 Hague Rd
Indianapolis, IN 46256-1045
Telephone: (317) 521-2000, Web Site: www.usdiagnostics.roche.com
Group Mgr Prof Mktg: Angie Nelis
Pres: Jack J. Phillips
Primary Market Served: Consumer

SALLY BEAUTY SUPPLY LLC

3001 Colorado Blvd
Denton, TX 76210
Telephone: (940) 898-7500, Toll Free: (866) 234-9442, Web Site: www.sallybeauty.com
Pres & CEO: Christian A. Brickman
Pres: Sharon M. Leite
Conducts Business: U.S., Canada, UK, Germany, Japan, Ireland, Spain, Mexico
Employees: 5,500
Primary Market Served: Business & Consumer
Catalog available online
Direct online sales
Advertising/Marketing Budget Related to Direct Marketing: 76-100%
Direct Marketing ad budget: $10,000,000
Direct Mail: 86%
Magazines: 5%
Newspapers: 7%
TV/Radio: 2%
Founded: 1969
Gross sales or billing: $1,300,000,000

Professional beauty products to salons, hairdressers & consumers. Over 2700 store locations.

SEDONA LABS

260 Justin Dr
Cottonwood, AZ 86326
Telephone: (928) 340-5400, Toll Free: (888) 816-8804, FAX: (928) 634-0657, E-Mail: info@sedonalabs.com, Web Site: www.sedonalabs.com
Customer Svcs Mgr: Jennifer McTurk

SHIELD HEALTHCARE

Div. of Kobayashi Pharmaceuticals Inc (Japan)
27911 Franklin Pkwy
Valencia, CA 91355-4110
Telephone: (661) 294-4200, Toll Free: (800) 765-8775, FAX: (661) 294-1043, (800) 748-0713, Web Site: www.shieldhealthcare.com
Pres: Jim Snell
Info Sys Mgr: Tillman Lindsay

Mktg Mgr: Todd Smith
Catalog Mgr: Tim Baker
Conducts Business: U.S.
Employees: 187
Primary Market Served: Business & Consumer
Advertising/Marketing Budget Related to Direct Marketing: 76-100%
Direct Marketing ad budget:
Direct Mail: 60%
Magazines: 5%
Telephone: 35%
Founded: 1955
Gross sales or billing: $30,000,000

National wholesaler of disposable medical products. Ostomy, Diabetes, incontinence, urology, airway & internal. Retailer with reimbursement capabilities in California, Colorado & Illinois. Managed Care Division, Retail Catalog Division.

SHISEIDO COSMETICS AMERICA

366 Princeton-Hightstown Rd
East Windsor, NJ 08520
Telephone: (212) 805-2300, FAX: (212) 688-0109, Web Site: www.sca.shiseido.com
CEO: Yoichi Shimatani
VP, Mktg: Anne Marino
VP, Mktg: Tomoko Yamagishi
VP: Seiji Nishimori
Primary Market Served: Consumer
Catalog available online
Founded: 1965

Market cosmetics & skincare.

SIMPLY BATTERIES INC

105 N 1st St
De Kalb, IL 60115
Telephone: (815) 758-8332, Web Site: www.simplybatteries.com
Pres: Laura Stuebing
Primary Market Served: Consumer

SONGBIRD HEARING INC

210 N Center Dr
North Brunswick, NJ 08902
Telephone: (732) 422-7203, Toll Free: (800) 647-5560, Web Site: www.songbirdhearing.com
VP Mktg: Jennifer Haus
Primary Market Served: Consumer
Founded: 2007

SPA-FINDER INC

333 SE 2nd Ave (Suite 3750)
New York, NY 33131
Telephone: (305) 307-5852, Toll Free: (800) ALL-SPAS, Web Site: www.spafinder.com
Chmn Bd & CEO: Pete Ellis
VP Grp Publr: Sara Greenwood

Mktg Dir: Patricia Steele
Pres: Susie Ellis
VP: Milana Knowles
COO: Sallie Fraenkel
Conducts Business: U.S., Canada, Europe, Japan
Employees: 25
Primary Market Served: Business & Consumer
Catalog available online
Direct online sales
Direct Marketing ad budget: $875,000
Direct Mail: $500,000
Magazines: $300,000
Newspapers: $75,000
Gross sales or billing: $10,000,000

Marketer of spa vacations worldwide through 140-page catalog.

SPADET
178 Columbus Ave (#230119)
New York, NY 10023
Telephone: (781) 275-8363, E-Mail: soapfac@verizon.net, Web Site: www.alcasoft.com/soapfact/
Pres & Owner: Marietta Ellis
VP: Arthur Ellis
Conducts Business: U.S.
Employees: 2
Primary Market Served: Business & Consumer
Catalog available online
Indirect online sales
Advertising/Marketing Budget Related to Direct Marketing: 76-100%
Direct Marketing ad budget:
Direct Mail: 80%
Magazines: 10%
Newspapers: 10%
Founded: 1989
Gross sales or billing: $25,000

Handcrafted castile toilet soap. Sell our handmade soaps direct to the retail consumer at craft shows & direct mail to our customer lists. Sell to owners of herb & gift shops.

SPALDING LABORATORIES INC
PO Box 10000
Reno, NV 89510-9928
Telephone: (888) 562-5696, Toll Free: (888) 880-1579, FAX: (866) 738-9632, Web Site: www.spalding-labs.com
Pres & Owner: Tom Spalding
VP: Jake Blehm
Sec: Lee Ann Merrill
Treas: Glen Scriven
Conducts Business: U.S.
Primary Market Served: Business & Consumer
Catalog available online
Indirect online sales

Advertising/Marketing Budget Related to Direct Marketing: 26-50%
Direct Marketing ad budget:
Direct Mail: 70%
Magazines: 25%
Newspapers: 5%
Founded: 1976

Beneficial insects called fly predators. Sell to dairies, chicken farms, horse ranches & anyone who has a pest fly problem.

THE STAYWELL CO
780 Township Line Rd
Yardley, PA 19067-4200
Telephone: (267) 685-2800, Web Site: www.staywell.com
CEO: Bill Goldberg

SUPPORT PLUS
Div. of Surgical Products
5581 Hudson Industrial Pkwy, PO Box 2599
Hudson, OH 44236-5019
Telephone: (866) 553-8875, Toll Free: (800) 229-2910, FAX: (800) 950-9569, E-Mail: cs@supportplus.com, Web Site: www.supportplus.com
Pres: Edward H. Janos
VP: Eloise Janos
Conducts Business: U.S., Canada, Asia, Europe
Employees: 47
Primary Market Served: Consumer
Catalog available online
Indirect online sales
Advertising/Marketing Budget Related to Direct Marketing: 76-100%
Direct Marketing ad budget:
Direct Mail: 99%
Magazines: 1%
Founded: 1972

Sells home health care products directly to consumer.

SYMRISE
300 North St
Teterboro, NJ 07608-1204
Telephone: (201) 288-3200, FAX: (201) 462-2200, Web Site: www.symrise.com
VP, Mktg & Sensory Consumer Science: Emmanuel Laroche
CEO: Heinz-Jurgen Bertram
Primary Market Served: Business

TEVA PHARMACEUTICALS USA
1090 Horsham Rd
North Wales, PA 19454-1090
Telephone: (215) 591-3000, Toll Free: (888) 838-2872, FAX: (215) 591-8600, Web Site: www.tevausa.com
VP, Generic Sls: Larry Rosenthal

Pres & CEO: Erez Vigoodman
CFO: Dan Suesskind
Dir Investor Rels: Dorit Meltzer
COO: George Barnett
Conducts Business: Worldwide
Employees: 1,025
Primary Market Served: Business
Catalog available online
Indirect online sales
Advertising/Marketing Budget Related to Direct Marketing: 0-25%
Direct Marketing ad budget:
Direct Mail: 35%
Magazines: 30%
Telephone: 35%
Founded: 1945
Gross sales or billing: $2,100,000,000

Sell generic pharmaceutical products through direct mail, personal & general sales.

TOOLS FOR WELLNESS
2900 N Quinlan Rd (Suite B240-217)
Austin, TX 78732
Toll Free: (800) 456-9887, FAX: (818) 532-1775, E-Mail: info@toolsforwellness.com, Web Site: www.toolsforwellness.com
VP: Andrew Chane
Pres: Michael Roth
Conducts Business: Worldwide
Employees: 13
Primary Market Served: Consumer
Catalog available online
Direct online sales
Advertising/Marketing Budget Related to Direct Marketing: 0-25%
Direct Marketing ad budget: $300,000
Direct Mail: 40%
Online: 60%
Founded: 1989
Gross sales or billing: $5,000,000

Consciousness technologies, peak performance, optimum wellness & cognitive enhancement products.

TOVA CORP
1200 Wilson Dr, Studio Park
West Chester, PA 19380
Toll Free: (800) 852-9999, Web Site: www.beautybytova.com
Chmn: Tova Borgnine
Mktg Dir: David Johnson
Conducts Business: U.S.
Employees: 50
Primary Market Served: Consumer

Market skin care, bath & fragrance products for men & women through mail order.

TROY BIOLOGICALS INC
1238 Rankin Dr
Troy, MI 48083

Telephone: (248) 585-9720, Toll Free: (800) 521-0445, FAX: (248) 585-2490, E-Mail: info@troybio.com, Web Site: www.troybio.com
Pres: Robert Ricketts
Supvr: Lynn Michaud
Opers Mgr: Tom Ricketts
Mktg Dir: Janine Deighan
Conducts Business: U.S.
Employees: 25
Primary Market Served: Business
Catalog available online
Direct online sales
Advertising/Marketing Budget Related to Direct Marketing: 76-100%
Direct Marketing ad budget:
Direct Mail: 100%
Founded: 1976
Gross sales or billing: $10,000,000

Distribute microbiology supplies & rapid diagnostic kits to surgical supply houses nationwide.

ULTA SALON COSMETICS FRAGRANCE
1000 Remington Blvd
Bolingbrook, IL 60440
Telephone: (630) 410-4800, Toll Free: (866) 983-8582
Dir CRM: Andrew McGarry
CEO: Mary Dillon

ULTRADENT PRODUCTS INC
505 W 10200 S
South Jordan, UT 84095-3935
Telephone: (801) 572-4200, FAX: (801) 553-4600, E-Mail: onlineordersupport@ultradent.com, Web Site: www.ultradent.com
CRM Dir: Mary Lou Lettig
Pres: Dirk Jeffs
Primary Market Served: Consumer

UNIFORMS & SCRUBS.COM
910 Kehrs Mill Rd (Suite 106)
Ballwin, MO 63011-2404
Telephone: (636) 391-9200, Toll Free: (855) 391-9200, FAX: (636) 391-9205, E-Mail: questions@uniformsandscrubs.com, Web Site: www.uniformsandscrubs.com
Pres: David Huelsbeck
VP, Mktg: Bob Fogel
Conducts Business: U.S.
Employees: 450
Primary Market Served: Business
Advertising/Marketing Budget Related to Direct Marketing: 51-75%
Direct Marketing ad budget: $2,000,000
Founded: 1896
Gross sales or billing: $30,000,000

Identity & image apparel for healthcare (nursing) industry.

UNITED SYSTEMS C/O BIOMED
2354 Stanwell Dr
Concord, CA 94520-4822
Telephone: (925) 609-2820
Pres: Richard Colman
VP: Deborah Cheung
Primary Market Served: Business & Consumer

VAXSERVE
54 Glenmaura Ntl Blvd (Suite 301)
Moosic, PA 18507-2101
Toll Free: (800) 752-9338, FAX: (800) 553-9908, Web Site: www.vaxserve.com
Pres: Albert Thomas
E-Commerce/Mktg Mgr: Edward Russo
Primary Market Served: Business

VEMMA NUTRITION CO
1621 W Rio Salado Pkwy
Tempe, AZ 85012
Telephone: (480) 927-8999, Toll Free: (800) 577-0777, FAX: (888) 314-9827, E-Mail: ms@vemma.com, Web Site: www.vemma.com
Founder: Glen Halverson
Pres & CEO: B.K. Boreyko
Co-CEO: Jason Boreyko
Sls & Mktg Dir: Laurie Prondzinski
Primary Market Served: Business & Consumer
Catalog available online
Indirect online sales

Nutritional liquid antioxidants

VISIONWORKS OF AMERICA INC
Subs. of HVHC, Inc.
175 E Houston St (Floor 6)
San Antonio, TX 78205-2210
Telephone: (210) 340-3531, Toll Free: (800) 669-1183, FAX: (210) 201-8445, E-Mail: websupport@visionworks.com, Web Site: www.visionworks.com
Pres: James Eisen
Conducts Business: U.S.
Employees: 4,800
Primary Market Served: Consumer
Advertising/Marketing Budget Related to Direct Marketing: 26-50%
Direct Marketing ad budget:
Direct Mail: $100,000
Newspapers: $110,000
Gross sales or billing: $301,900,000

Operates or manages over 550 optical retail stores in 39 states and the District of Columbia through 12 store names that are leaders in eye care service in each of their respective markets. Vision insurance & contact lenses by mail.

VITAMIN POWER INC
75 Commerce Dr
Hauppauge, NY 11788
Telephone: (516) 378-0900, Toll Free: (800) 645-6567, FAX: (631) 273-4394, E-Mail: contactus@vitaminpower.com, Web Site: www.vitaminpower.com
Chmn: Edward Friedlander
Pres: David H. Friedlander
Conducts Business: Worldwide
Employees: 42
Primary Market Served: Business & Consumer
Catalog available online
Direct online sales
Advertising/Marketing Budget Related to Direct Marketing: 76-100%
Direct Marketing ad budget: $300,000
Direct Mail: $230,000
Magazines: $60,000
Newspapers: $10,000
Founded: 1975
Gross sales or billing: $6,000,000

Manufacturer & marketer of health & fitness products including nutritional supplements & skin care products.

VITAMIN RESEARCH PRODUCTS
260 Justin Dr
Cottonwood, AZ 86326
Toll Free: (888) 362-1699, FAX: (775) 884-1331, E-Mail: customerservice@vrp.com, Web Site: www.vrp.com
VP Mktg: Staci Glovsky
Primary Market Served: Business & Consumer

VITAMIN SPECIALTIES CO
IVC Industries
500 Halls Mill Rd
Freehold, NJ 07728
Telephone: (732) 308-3000, FAX: (855) 482-3291, Web Site: www.ivcinc.com
VP, Mktg: Rich Meyers
Conducts Business: U.S.
Primary Market Served: Consumer

Mail order sales of vitamins & other health items. Operate retail outlets in PA & NJ.

WRS GROUP LTD
5045 Franklin Ave
Waco, TX 76710-6919
Telephone: (254) 776-6461, Toll Free: (800) 299-3366, FAX: (888) 977-7653, E-Mail: custom@wrsgroup.com, Web Site: www.wrsgroup.com
CEO: Scott J. Salmans
Primary Market Served: Business & Consumer
Catalog available online
Direct online sales

Founded: 1969
Gross sales or billing: $18,949,955

Provider of health education materials.
Available online or via catalog.

WALGREENS CO
200 Wilmont Rd
Deerfield, IL 60015
Toll Free: (800) 925-4733, Web Site:
   www.walgreens.com
Exec Chmn: James Skinner
Exec VP & Pres Customer Experience
   & Daily Living: Alex Gourlay
Exec Vice Chmn & CEO: Stefano Pes-
   sina
Employees: 200,000
Primary Market Served: Consumer
Catalog available online
Direct online sales
Gross sales or billing: $53,000,000,000

Drug store chain.

WYSONG CORP
7550 Eastman Ave
Midland, MI 48642-7779
Telephone: (989) 631-0009, Toll Free:
   (800) 748-0188, FAX: (989) 631-
   9280, E-Mail: wysong@wysong.net,
   Web Site: www.wysong.net
Pres: Randy L. Wysong
Mktg Dir: Christine Johnsten
Conducts Business: Worldwide
Employees: 30
Primary Market Served: Business &
   Consumer
Catalog available online
Direct online sales
Advertising/Marketing Budget Related
   to Direct Marketing: 0-25%
Founded: 1979

Full line of nutritional foods, natural vitamins, pet foods, pet supplements, cat
litter to veterinarians, consumers, etc.

YVES ROCHER NORTH
   AMERICA INC
102 Pickering Way (Suite 300)
Exton, PA J4G2V7-19341-1330
Telephone: (450) 442-9555, Toll Free:
   (888) 909-0771, E-Mail:
   customer_services@yrnet.com, Web
   Site: www.yvesrocherusa.com
Dir Sls: Philippe Hervieu
Primary Market Served: Business &
   Consumer

Home & Garden Catalogs (8)

ABC CARPET & HOME
888 Broadway at E 19th St
New York, NY 10003-1280
Toll Free: (212) 473-3000, Web Site:
  www.abccarpet.com
CEO: Paulette Cole
Conducts Business: Worldwide
Employees: 300
Primary Market Served: Business &
  Consumer
Founded: 1897

Direct marketer & retailer of broad-
loom rugs, antique & fine reproduction
furniture, handmade oriental rugs, bed,
bath & linen, gifts & accessories.

ACME TOOLS
1705 13th Ave N
Grand Forks, ND 58203-2304
Telephone: (701) 746-6481, Toll Free:
  (800) 732-4287, FAX: (701) 746-
  2857, Web Site: www.acmetools.
  com
VP: Paul Kuhlman
Primary Market Served: Consumer

AMARYLLIS INC
4350 Pine Ridge Rd.
Baton Rouge, LA 70809
Telephone: (225) 924-5560
Owner: Ed Beckham
Conducts Business: Worldwide
Employees: 1
Primary Market Served: Business &
  Consumer

Amaryllis bulbs wholesale & retail.

**AMERICAN MEADOWS INC
  & VERMONT WILD
  FLOWERS FARM**
Subs. of Foster & Gallagher Inc
2438 Shelburne Rd., Ste. 1
Shelburne, VT 05482
Toll Free: (877) 309-7333, FAX: (802)
  951-9089, E-Mail: customerservice@
  americanmeadows.com, Web Site:
  www.americanmeadows.com
Founder: Chy Allen
Pres & Founder: Ray Allen
VP: Ethan Platt
Mng Partner: Mike Lizotte
Conducts Business: U.S., Canada
Employees: 15
Primary Market Served: Business &
  Consumer
Catalog available online
Advertising/Marketing Budget Related
  to Direct Marketing: 76-100%
Direct Marketing ad budget:
Direct Mail: 90%
Magazines: 10%

Founded: 1981
Sell wildflower seed mixes & individual species of wildflower seeds to consumer home gardeners & landscapers,
states, municipalities & commercial accounts.

**AMERICAN PERIOD
  LIGHTING INC**
3004 Columbia Ave
Lancaster, PA 17603-4001
Telephone: (717) 392-5649, FAX:
  (717) 509-3127, E-Mail: info@
  americanperiodlighting.com, Web
  Site: www.americanperiodlighting.
  com
Pres: Jack Cunningham
Conducts Business: U.S., Canada
Employees: 3
Primary Market Served: Business &
  Consumer
Catalog available online
Indirect online sales
Advertising/Marketing Budget Related
  to Direct Marketing: 51-75%
Direct Marketing ad budget: $40,000
Magazines: 50%
Online: 50%
Founded: 1969
Gross sales or billing: $300,000

Manufactures retail & wholesale traditional, period & historical hand crafted
lighting fixtures for home & garden.

AMES-TRU-TEMPER
465 Railroad Ave
Camp Hill, PA 17011-5611
Telephone: (800) 393-1846, Web Site:
  ames.com
Pres: Mark H. Traylor
Conducts Business: U.S., Canada
Employees: 1,452
Primary Market Served: Consumer
Advertising/Marketing Budget Related
  to Direct Marketing: 0-25%
Direct Marketing ad budget:
Direct Mail: 15%
Telephone: 85%
Founded: 1808
Gross sales or billing: $300,000,000

Manufacturer of lawn & garden products.

AMVAC CHEMICAL CORP
Div. of American Vanguard Corp
4100 E Washington Blvd
Los Angeles, CA 90023-4406
Telephone: (323) 264-3910, Toll Free:
  (888) 462-6822, Web Site: www.
  amvac-chemical.com
Chmn & CEO: Eric Wintermute
VP, DM: Bob Trogele

Dir Mktg: Timothy J. Donnelly
CFO: David T. Johnson
Conducts Business: Worldwide
Employees: 126
Primary Market Served: Business
Advertising/Marketing Budget Related
  to Direct Marketing: 0-25%
Direct Marketing ad budget:
Direct Mail: 20%
Magazines: 80%
Founded: 1945
Gross sales or billing: $50,000,000

Agricultural chemical manufacturer
selling insecticides, molluscicides,
pheromones, herbicides, plant growth
regulators & fungicides to licensed pes-
ticide distributors.

ANTIQUE ROSE EMPORIUM
9300 Lueckemeyer Rd
Brenham, TX 77833-6453
Telephone: (979) 836-9051, Toll Free:
  (800) 441-0002, FAX: (979) 836-
  0928, E-Mail: roses@weareroses.
  com, Web Site:
  antiqueroseemporium .com
Pres: Mike Shoup
Conducts Business: U.S.
Primary Market Served: Consumer
Catalog available online
Direct online sales
Advertising/Marketing Budget Related
  to Direct Marketing: 51-75%
Direct Marketing ad budget:
Direct Mail: 75%
Magazines: 10%
Newspapers: 2%
TV/Radio: 3%
Telephone: 10%
Founded: 1982

ART.COM
2100 Powell St 13th Fl
Emeryville, CA 94608-1893
Telephone: (510) 879-4700, Toll Free:
  (800) 952-5592, FAX: (510) 588-
  3915, E-Mail: support@art.com,
  Web Site: www.art.com
CEO & Bd Member: Kira Wampler
Sr VP Opers: Chuck Kurth
Primary Market Served: Consumer
Founded: 1998

ASSOCIATED MATERIALS
3773 State Rd
Cuyahoga Falls, OH 44223-2603
Telephone: (330) 922-2182, Web Site:
  www.alside.com
Dir Mktg, Siding: Mike Kemper

AUTHENTIC DESIGNS
154 Mill Rd

West Rupert, VT 05776-9716
Telephone: (802) 394-7713, Toll Free:
(800) 844-9416, E-Mail: lighting@
authenticdesigns.com, Web Site:
www.authenticdesigns.com
Pres: Michael Krauss
Conducts Business: U.S., Canada
Employees: 10
Primary Market Served: Business &
Consumer
Catalog available online
Indirect online sales
Advertising/Marketing Budget Related
to Direct Marketing: 26-50%
Founded: 1971
Gross sales or billing: $1,000,000

Makers of colonial & early American
reproduction chandeliers, sconces, lanterns. Custom work. 64 page catalog
available for $3.

BALLARD DESIGNS
1670 Defoor Ave
Atlanta, GA 30318-7528
Telephone: (404) 603-7033, Toll Free:
(800) 536-7551, FAX: (800) 989-
4510, Web Site: www.
ballarddesigns.com
Pres: Ryan McKelvey
Conducts Business: U.S.
Employees: 70
Primary Market Served: Business &
Consumer

Unique direct mail catalog of decorative furnishings & accessories for the
home; garden statuary, plaques, pedes-
tals, glass tops & gifts.

BAMBOO SOURCERY
666 Wagnon Rd
Sebastopol, CA 95472-9546
Telephone: (707) 823-5866, FAX:
(707) 829-8106, Web Site: www.
bamboosourcery.com
Owner: Jennifer York
Employees: 4
Primary Market Served: Business &
Consumer
Catalog available online
Direct online sales
Advertising/Marketing Budget Related
to Direct Marketing: 0-25%
Founded: 1980

Specialty nursery with nearly 300 species of bamboo from around the world.
Offer expert consultation services &
extensive demonstration gardens as
well as rhizome barriers, books & bamboo poles.

BATHROOM MACHINERIES
495 Main St
Murphys, CA 95247

Telephone: (209) 728-2031, Toll Free:
(800) 255-4426, FAX: (209) 728-
2320, Web Site: www.deabath.com
Pres & Owner: Tom Scheller
Conducts Business: U.S., Canada, Ja-
pan
Employees: 11
Primary Market Served: Business &
Consumer
Catalog available online
Direct online sales
Advertising/Marketing Budget Related
to Direct Marketing: 76-100%
Direct Marketing ad budget:
Direct Mail: $20,000
Magazines: $5,000
Founded: 1976
Gross sales or billing: $700,000

Antique or reproduction plumbing,
hardware & lighting.

BED BATH & BEYOND
650 Liberty Ave
Union, NJ 07083-8107
Telephone: (631) 420-7050, Toll Free:
(800) 462-3966, Web Site:
bedbathandbeyond.com
VP Mktg: Rita Little
Primary Market Served: Consumer

BELLACOR
251 1st Ave, N (Suite 900)
Minneapolis, MN 55401
Toll Free: (877) 723-5522, FAX: (651)
294-2595, E-Mail: customerservice@
bellacor.com, Web Site: www.
bellacor.com
Pres & Owner: Brenda Boehler
Conducts Business: Worldwide
Primary Market Served: Business &
Consumer
Catalog available online
Direct online sales
Founded: 2000

Sell lighting fixtures, ceiling fans &
lamps online at Bellacor.com

BERGER'S TABLE PAD CO
1501 W Market St
Indianapolis, IN 46222
Toll Free: (800) 305-7237, Web Site:
tablepads.com
Pres & Owner: Dave Berger
Conducts Business: Worldwide
Employees: 27
Primary Market Served: Business &
Consumer
Catalog available online
Direct online sales
Advertising/Marketing Budget Related
to Direct Marketing: 26-50%
Direct Marketing ad budget:
$1,000,000
Direct Mail: 50%
Magazines: 25%

Newspapers: 25%
Founded: 1981

Manufacture custom made table pads
as well as custom made tablecloths.

BERRY HILL LTD
75 Burwell Rd
Saint Thomas, ON, Canada N5P 3R5
Telephone: (519) 631-0480, Toll Free:
(800) 668-3072, FAX: (519) 631-
8935, E-Mail: customerservice@
berryhill.ca, Web Site: www.
berryhilllimited.com
Gen Mgr: Ken Fox
Conducts Business: Canada
Employees: 10
Primary Market Served: Business &
Consumer
Advertising/Marketing Budget Related
to Direct Marketing: 76-100%
Direct Marketing ad budget: $50,000
Direct Mail: 50%
Magazines: 30%
Newspapers: 10%
TV/Radio: 10%
Founded: 1946
Gross sales or billing: $1,160,000

Mail order company selling hobby
farm equipment, country living products & hobby garden equipment.

BLISSLIVING HOME
5515 Security Ln (Suite 1100)
Rockville, MD 20852-5009
Telephone: (240) 485-3492, Web Site:
www.blisslivinghome.com
CEO: Mei Xu
Employees: 10
Founded: 2007

Interior decorating brand

BLUESTONE PERENNIALS
INC
7211 Middle Ridge Rd
Madison, OH 44057-3050
Toll Free: (800) 852-5243, FAX: (800)
852-5243, E-Mail: service@
bluestoneperennials.com, Web Site:
www.bluestoneperennials.com
Pres: William N. Boonstra
Corp Sec & Treas: Sarah Boonstra
Conducts Business: U.S.
Primary Market Served: Business &
Consumer
Catalog available online
Direct online sales
Advertising/Marketing Budget Related
to Direct Marketing: 76-100%
Founded: 1972

Retailer if perennials & ornamental
shrubs

THE BOMBAY CO
98 Orfus Rd.

Toronto, ON, Canada M6A 1L9
Telephone: (514) 428-9399, Toll Free:
(877) 326-6229, E-Mail:
customerservice@bombay.ca, Web
Site: bombay.ca
Conducts Business: U.S., Canada
Primary Market Served: Consumer
furnishings & accessories for the home

BOUNTIFUL GARDENS

Div. of Ecology Action Inc
1712 S Main St (Suite D)
Willits, CA 95490-4400
Telephone: (707) 459-6410, FAX:
(707) 459-1925, E-Mail: bountiful@
sonic.net, Web Site: www.
bountifulgardens.org
Mktg Mgr: Bill Bruneau
Conducts Business: Worldwide
Employees: 7
Primary Market Served: Business &
Consumer
Catalog available online
Advertising/Marketing Budget Related
to Direct Marketing: 0-25%
Founded: 1983

Training materials for sustainable high-yield organic gardening & untreated heirloom seeds. Specializes in unusual vegetables, herbs, grains, compost crops & organic controls & supplies.

BRECK'S BULBS

Subs. of Foster & Gallagher
PO Box 65
Guilford, IN 47022
Telephone: (513) 354-1512, FAX:
(513) 354-1505, E-Mail: service@
brecks.com, Web Site: brecks.com
President: Ben van der Veldt
Conducts Business: U.S.
Primary Market Served: Consumer
Founded: 1818

Market European flower bulbs, roses & domestically grown garden plants.

BROWN & CO

8527 Semiahmoo Dr
Blaine, WA 98230
Telephone: (360) 371-2489
Owner: Ed Brown
Owner: Barbara Brown
Conducts Business: U.S.
Employees: 2
Primary Market Served: Business &
Consumer
Advertising/Marketing Budget Related
to Direct Marketing: 0-25%
Founded: 1985

Plants wholesale & retail.

BROWN'S OMAHA PLANT FARMS

110 McLean Ave

Omaha, TX 75571
Telephone: (903) 884-2421, FAX:
(903) 884-2423, E-Mail: mail@bopf.
com, Web Site: www.bopf.com
President: Jim D Brown
Conducts Business: U.S.
Employees: 2
Primary Market Served: Business &
Consumer
Catalog available online
Direct online sales
Advertising/Marketing Budget Related
to Direct Marketing: 0-25%
Direct Marketing ad budget: $10,000
Direct Mail: 100%
Founded: 1938
Gross sales or billing: $350,000

Vegetable plants for the home garden-er.

W ATLEE BURPEE CO

300 Park Ave
Warminster, PA 18974-4860
Telephone: (215) 674-4900, Toll Free:
(800) 888-1447, FAX: (215) 674-4170, Web Site: www.burpee.com
Pres & Owner: George Ball
Conducts Business: U.S.
Primary Market Served: Consumer
Catalog available online
Direct online sales
Advertising/Marketing Budget Related
to Direct Marketing: 51-75%
Founded: 1876

Sell garden products, flower & vegetable seeds, nursery stock, bulbs & roots, plus general garden aids to the home gardener. Commercial seed sales & retail seed distribution. Catalogs mailed to homeowners.

DV BURRELL SEED GROWERS CO

405 N Main St
Rocky Ford, CO 81067
Telephone: (719) 254-3318, Toll Free:
(844) 254-7333, FAX: (719) 254-3319, E-Mail: burrellseeds@gmail.
com, Web Site: www.burrellseeds.us
Pres: Bill Burrell
Conducts Business: U.S., Canada
Employees: 8
Primary Market Served: Business &
Consumer
Catalog available online
Advertising/Marketing Budget Related
to Direct Marketing: 0-25%
Founded: 1898

Sell vegetable, flower & herb seed, both wholesale & retail.

CAMELLIA FOREST NURSERY

620 Hwy 54 W

Chapel Hill, NC 27516-7955
Telephone: (919) 968-0504, FAX:
(919) 929-8971, E-Mail:
camelliaforest@gmail.com, Web
Site: www.camforest.com
Pres: Kai-Mei Parks
Pres: David Parks
Conducts Business: U.S.
Employees: 4
Primary Market Served: Consumer
Catalog available online
Indirect online sales
Advertising/Marketing Budget Related
to Direct Marketing: 0-25%
Direct Marketing ad budget:
Direct Mail: 90%
Magazines: 10%
Founded: 1979

Mail order nursery

CANE & BASKET SUPPLY CO

1283 S Cochran Ave
Los Angeles, CA 90019-2846
Telephone: (323) 939-9644, FAX:
(323) 939-7237, E-Mail: info@
caneandbasket.com, Web Site: www.
caneandbasket.com
Pres: William L. Fimpler
VP: William Fimpler Jr.
Conducts Business: U.S.
Employees: 10
Primary Market Served: Business &
Consumer
Catalog available online
Indirect online sales
Advertising/Marketing Budget Related
to Direct Marketing: 0-25%
Founded: 1934

Catalog marketer of caning & basketry supplies.

CAPE COD CUPOLA CO INC

78 State Rd
North Dartmouth, MA 02747-2994
Telephone: (508) 994-2119, FAX:
(508) 997-2511, E-Mail:
capecodcupola@gmail.com, Web
Site: www.capcodcupola.com
Pres: John E. Bernier
Mgr: Brian Chabot
Conducts Business: U.S., Canada
Employees: 5
Primary Market Served: Business &
Consumer
Founded: 1939

Specialize in custom cupolas & weathervanes.

CARTER & HOLMES INC

629 Mendenhall Rd
Newberry, SC 29108-6351

Telephone: (803) 276-0579, FAX: (803) 276-0588, E-Mail: orchids@ carterandholmes.com, Web Site: www.carterandholmes.com
Owner: Mac Holmes
Conducts Business: Worldwide
Employees: 35
Primary Market Served: Business & Consumer
Catalog available online
Direct online sales
Advertising/Marketing Budget Related to Direct Marketing: 76-100%
Founded: 1945
Gross sales or billing: $1,000,000

Orchid plants, house plants.

CHADSWORTH'S 1-800-COLUMNS

277 N Front St
Wilmington, NC 28401-3907
Telephone: (910) 763-7600, Toll Free: (800) 265-8667, FAX: (910) 763-3191, E-Mail: sales@columns.com, Web Site: shop.columns.com
Chmn: Jeffrey L Davis
Conducts Business: Worldwide
Employees: 15
Primary Market Served: Business & Consumer
Catalog available online
Advertising/Marketing Budget Related to Direct Marketing: 0-25%
Direct Marketing ad budget:
Direct Mail: 25%
Magazines: 75%
Founded: 1987

Columns to consumers, builders, architects & designers.

CHAR-BROIL GRILL LOVER'S CATALOG

Div. of Char-Broil/WC Bradley Co
1442 Belfast Ave
Columbus, GA 31904
Toll Free: (866) 241-7548, Web Site: charbroil.com
Pres & CEO: Christine M Robins
Conducts Business: U.S.
Employees: 250
Primary Market Served: Consumer
Catalog available online
Direct online sales
Advertising/Marketing Budget Related to Direct Marketing: 76-100%
Founded: 1885
Gross sales or billing: $20,000,000

Offer barbecue grills & accessories to gas, charcoal & electric grill owners.

CHARMASTER

2307 Hwy 2 W
Grand Rapids, MN 55744-2152

Telephone: (218) 326-6786, FAX: (218) 326-1065, E-Mail: info@ charmaster.com, Web Site: www.charmaster.com
Pres: Larry Lessin
Conducts Business: U.S. and Canada
Primary Market Served: Business & Consumer
Catalog available online
Indirect online sales
Advertising/Marketing Budget Related to Direct Marketing: 76-100%
Founded: 1964

Manufacture wood central heating systems.

CINMAR LP

dba Frontgate; Parent Cornerstone Brands, Inc (CBI)
5566 West Chester Rd
West Chester, OH 45069-2914
Toll Free: (888) 263-9850, Web Site: www.frontgate.com
Pres Founder: Paul Tarvin
Conducts Business: U.S.
Employees: 130
Primary Market Served: Consumer
Founded: 1991
Gross sales or billing: $20,200,000

General merchandise for the homeowner.

COHASSET COLONIALS

14 S Pleasant St
Ashburnham, MA 01430-1649
Telephone: (978) 827-3001, Toll Free: (800) 288-2389, FAX: (978) 827-3227, E-Mail: cohassetcolonials. custservice@gmail.com, Web Site: www.cohassetcolonials.com
Pres & Treas: Richard Dabrowski
Conducts Business: U.S., Canada
Employees: 10
Primary Market Served: Consumer
Catalog available online
Direct online sales
Advertising/Marketing Budget Related to Direct Marketing: 76-100%
Founded: 1949
Gross sales or billing: $4,800,000

Reproduction of American Colonial furniture, lighting, and decorative accessories.

COLD STREAM FARM

8585 N Stephens Rd
Free Soil, MI 49411
Telephone: (231) 464-5809, E-Mail: info@coldstreamfarm.net, Web Site: www.coldstreamfarm.net
Owner: Craig Hradel
Conducts Business: US & Canada
Employees: 40
Primary Market Served: Business & Consumer

Catalog available online
Direct online sales
Direct Marketing ad budget:
Direct Mail: 10%
Online: 90%
Founded: 1978
Gross sales or billing: $240,000

Bare root tree & shrub nursery.

COLE'S APPLIANCE & FURNITURE CO

4026 Lincoln Ave
Chicago, IL 60618-3097
Telephone: (773) 525-1797, Web Site: shopcoles.com, Social: Facebook; Instagram; Twitter; Pinterest
Owner: Kevin Krasney
Conducts Business: U.S.
Employees: 11
Primary Market Served: Consumer
Advertising/Marketing Budget Related to Direct Marketing: 0-25%
Direct Marketing ad budget: $20,000
Founded: 1946
Gross sales or billing: $1,500,000

Sell appliances & furniture.

COMPANION PLANTS

7247 N Coolville Ridge Rd
Athens, OH 45701
Telephone: (740) 592-4643, FAX: (740) 593-3092, E-Mail: peter@ companionplants.com, Web Site: www.companionplants.com
Pres: Peter Borchard
Conducts Business: U.S.
Employees: 10
Primary Market Served: Business & Consumer
Catalog available online
Direct online sales
Advertising/Marketing Budget Related to Direct Marketing: 76-100%
Direct Marketing ad budget:
Direct Mail: 80%
Magazines: 20%
Founded: 1982
Gross sales or billing: $120,000

Sell herb plants & seeds to the industry & the consumer.

THE CONTAINER STORE

500 Freeport Pkwy Ste 100
Coppell, TX 75019-3998
Toll Free: (888) 266-8246, Web Site: www.containerstore.com
Dir Direct Mktg: Catherine Davis

Sell containers & organizers.

COPPA WOODWORKING, INC

1231 Paraiso Ave
San Pedro, CA 90731

Telephone: (310) 548-4142, FAX: (310) 548-6740, E-Mail: info@ coppawoodworking.com, Web Site: www.coppawoodworking.com
Pres: Ciro C. Coppa
Conducts Business: U.S.
Employees: 10
Primary Market Served: Business & Consumer
Catalog available online
Direct online sales
Advertising/Marketing Budget Related to Direct Marketing: 0-25%
Direct Marketing ad budget: $25,000
Magazines: 75%
Newspapers: 25%
Founded: 1980
Gross sales or billing: $800,000

Wood screen & storm doors & lawn chairs.

JOSIAH R COPPERSMYTHE

10 Mill Pond Rd
Harwich, MA 02645-1205
Telephone: (508) 432-8590, Toll Free: (800) 426-8249, FAX: (508) 432-8587, E-Mail: kethompson@ jrcoppersmythe.com, Web Site: www.jrcoppersmythe.com
Conducts Business: U.S.
Employees: 1
Primary Market Served: Business & Consumer
Catalog available online
Indirect online sales
Advertising/Marketing Budget Related to Direct Marketing: 76-100%
Direct Marketing ad budget: $15,000
Founded: 1984
Gross sales or billing: $100,000

Handcrafted lighting.

COUNTRY CURTAINS INC

P.O. Box 955
Stockbridge, MA 01262
Toll Free: (800) 937-1237, Web Site: www.countrycurtains.com
Owner: Nancy Fitzpatrick
Conducts Business: U.S., Canada, U. K., Japan
Primary Market Served: Consumer
Catalog available online
Founded: 1956

Sell curtains, bedding & home decorating accessories.

CRATE & BARREL

1250 Techny Rd
Northbrook, IL 60062-5419
Telephone: (847) 272-2888, Toll Free: (800) 967-6696, FAX: (630) 369-4497, Web Site: www.crateandbarrel.com
CEO: Doug Diemoz

Catalog available online

Sell housewares, furniture & accessories.

CUDDLEDOWN INC

Subs of Bush Equities, Inc
14 Yarmouth Junction
Yarmouth, ME 04096
Toll Free: (800) 323-6793, FAX: (207) 761-1948, Web Site: www.cuddledown.com
CEO: Christopher W. Bradley
Natl Sales Mgr: Charles Cilley
Conducts Business: U.S.
Employees: 70
Primary Market Served: Consumer
Founded: 1973
Gross sales or billing: $13,400,000

Marketer of down comforters, pillows, flannel sheets, fine linens & bath products.

D'LIGHTS

2107 Chico Ave
South El Monte, CA 91733-1606
Telephone: (626) 246-1094, Toll Free: (800) 414-5109, FAX: (626) 433-0267, E-Mail: lizzy@spjlighting.com, Web Site: www.dlights.com
Owner: Paul Lestz
Conducts Business: U.S., Canada
Employees: 14
Primary Market Served: Business
Advertising/Marketing Budget Related to Direct Marketing: 0-25%
Direct Marketing ad budget:
Direct Mail: 40%
Magazines: 20%
Telephone: 40%
Founded: 1974
Gross sales or billing: $1,500,000

Custom light manufacturing.

DAVIS INSTRUMENTS CORP

3465 Diablo Ave
Hayward, CA 94545-2746
Telephone: (510) 732-9229, (510) 670-0589, Toll Free: (800) 678-3669, FAX: (510) 732-9188, E-Mail: info@davisnet.com, Web Site: www.davisnet.com
CEO: Bob Selig
Conducts Business: Worldwide
Primary Market Served: Business & Consumer
Catalog available online
Indirect online sales
Advertising/Marketing Budget Related to Direct Marketing: 51-75%
Founded: 1963
Gross sales or billing: $7,700,000

Distributes marine products, weather instruments & driving monitors.

DOROTHY BIDDLE SERVICE

348 Greeley Lake Rd
Greeley, PA 18425-9749
Telephone: (570) 226-3239, FAX: (570) 226-0349, E-Mail: info@ dorothybiddle.com, Web Site: www.dorothybiddle.com
Owner: Lynne Dodson
Owner: Larry Dodson
Conducts Business: U.S., Canada
Employees: 6
Primary Market Served: Business & Consumer
Catalog available online
Indirect online sales
Advertising/Marketing Budget Related to Direct Marketing: 0-25%
Direct Marketing ad budget:
Magazines: 100%
Founded: 1936
Gross sales or billing: $900,000

Sell flower arranging equipment & gardening accessories to garden centers, gift shops & florists.

DOROTHY'S RUFFLED ORIGINALS INC

6721 Market St
Wilmington, NC 28405-3703
Toll Free: (800) 367-6849, FAX: (910) 791-0729, E-Mail: curtains@ dorothysoriginals.com, Web Site: www.dorothysoriginals.com
Pres: Dorothy C. Noe
Conducts Business: U.S., Canada
Employees: 40
Primary Market Served: Business & Consumer
Catalog available online
Indirect online sales
Advertising/Marketing Budget Related to Direct Marketing: 0-25%
Founded: 1978
Gross sales or billing: $1,200,000

Sells window treatments.

DOWN HOME COMFORTS

126 County Rte 3
Putnam Station, NY 12861
Telephone: (518) 547-8966, (518) 223-2193, Web Site: downhomecomforts.com
Owner: Elizabeth Eisenhauer
Conducts Business: U.S.
Employees: 1
Primary Market Served: Consumer
Catalog available online
Indirect online sales
Advertising/Marketing Budget Related to Direct Marketing: 0-25%
Direct Marketing ad budget:
Online: 100%
Founded: 1981

New & remade to order comforters, covers & pillows.

DROLL YANKEES INC
55 Lathrop Rd Ext
Plainfield, CT 06374-1965
Telephone: (860) 799-8980, Toll Free:
(800) 352-9164, FAX: (860) 564-
8031, E-Mail: drollbird@
drollyankees.com, Web Site: www.
drollyankees.com
Pres: Betsy Puckett
Conducts Business: U.S., Canada
Employees: 30
Primary Market Served: Business &
Consumer
Catalog available online
Advertising/Marketing Budget Related
to Direct Marketing: 0-25%
Founded: 1960

Sell bird feeders & accessories.

DULUTH TRADING CO INC
Div. of Kempler
170 Countryside Dr, PO Box 200
Belleville, WI 53508-0200
Toll Free: (800) 300-9719, FAX: (888)
950-3199, E-Mail: customerservice@
duluthtrading.com, Web Site: www.
duluthtrading.com
Pres & Chief Mdse Officer: Stephanie
Pugliese
Primary Market Served: Consumer
Catalog available online
Direct online sales

Sell, clothing, tool carriers, parts, organizers & accessories.

DURIO NURSERY
5853 Hwy 182
Opelousas, LA 70570
Telephone: (337) 948-3696, FAX:
(337) 942-6404, E-Mail: dalton@
durionursery.biz, Web Site: www.
durionursery.com
VP: Dalton Durio
Sec: Belle Durio
Conducts Business: Worldwide
Employees: 10
Primary Market Served: Consumer
Catalog available online
Advertising/Marketing Budget Related
to Direct Marketing: 76-100%
Founded: 1950

Sell plants.

DUTCH GARDENS USA INC
PO Box 2999
Bloomington, IL 61702-2999
Toll Free: (800) 944-2250, E-Mail:
customerservice@dutchgardens.com,
Web Site: www.dutchgardens.com
Pres: Leo Vandervlugt
Primary Market Served: Consumer

Catalog available online
Mail order company selling perennials
& flower bulbs at close to wholesale
prices shipped directly from Holland.

EDIBLE LANDSCAPING
361 Spirit Ridge Ln
Afton, VA 22920
Telephone: (434) 361-9134, Toll Free:
(800) 524-4156, FAX: (434) 361-
1916, E-Mail: info@
ediblelandscaping.com, Web Site:
www.eat-it.com
Owner: Mike McConkey
Conducts Business: Worldwide
Employees: 5
Primary Market Served: Business &
Consumer
Catalog available online
Direct online sales
Advertising/Marketing Budget Related
to Direct Marketing: 0-25%
Founded: 1983
Gross sales or billing: $360,000

Mail order potted plants, shipped
throughout the year.

ELECTROWARMTH
PRODUCTS LLC
513 Market St
Danville, OH 43014
Toll Free: (800) 990-4622, E-Mail:
sales@electrowarmth.com, Web Site:
www.electrowarmth.com
Owner/Pres: Dan Grindle
Conducts Business: U.S., Canada
Employees: 6
Primary Market Served: Business &
Consumer
Indirect online sales
Advertising/Marketing Budget Related
to Direct Marketing: 51-75%
Direct Marketing ad budget:
Direct Mail: 25%
Magazines: 75%
Founded: 1939
Gross sales or billing: $750,000

Manufacturers of heated mattress pads
& massage table warmers.

EVERFAST INC
dba Calico Corners
203 Gale Ln
Kennett Square, PA 19348-1735
Toll Free: (800) 213-6366, Web Site:
www.calicocorners.com
Pres: Bert G. Kerstetter
Catalog available online
Direct online sales
Founded: 1936

Sells fabrics.

EVERGREEN ENTERPRISES INC
5915 Midlothian Tpke
Richmond, VA 23225-5917
Toll Free: (800) 774-3837, E-Mail:
customerservice@myevergreen.com,
Web Site: www.myevergreen.com
Pres: Ting Xu
CEO: Frank Qiu
Pres: John Toler
CFO: Leslie Newton
Primary Market Served: Business
Founded: 1993

FANCY FRONDS
40830 172nd St SE
Gold Bar, WA 98251-9453
Telephone: (360) 793-1472, E-Mail:
fancyfronts@gmail.com, Web Site:
www.fancyfronds.com
Pres: Judith Jones
Conducts Business: U.S.
Employees: 1
Primary Market Served: Consumer
Catalog available online
Direct online sales
Advertising/Marketing Budget Related
to Direct Marketing: 0-25%
Direct Marketing ad budget: $7,000
Direct Mail: $2,000
Founded: 1977
Gross sales or billing: $45,000

Mail order sales of temperate, tree &
desert ferns.

FIELDER'S CHOICE DIRECT
Subs. of Monsanto
306 N Main St
Monticello, IN 47960-2133
Telephone: (812) 492-1700, FAX:
(812) 492-1799, Web Site: monsanto,
com
Pres: Hugh Grant
Conducts Business: U.S. & Canada
Employees: 100
Catalog available online
Direct online sales
Founded: 1983

Agricultural products to farmers.

FIELDSTONE GARDENS INC
55 Quaker Ln
Vassalboro, ME 04989-3816
Telephone: (207) 923-3836, FAX:
(207) 923-3836, Web Site: www.
fieldstonegardens.com
Owner: Steven D. Jones
Conducts Business: U.S.
Employees: 6
Primary Market Served: Business &
Consumer
Catalog available online
Indirect online sales
Advertising/Marketing Budget Related
to Direct Marketing: 26-50%

Direct Marketing ad budget:
Direct Mail: 50%
Magazines: 20%
Newspapers: 30%
Founded: 1985

Variety of hardy northern grown perennials.

FLICKINGER'S NURSERY

Rte 85
Beyer, PA 16211
Toll Free: (800) 368-7381, FAX: (724) 783-6528, Web Site: www. flicknursery.com
Owner & Pres: Richard Flickinger
Conducts Business: U.S.
Employees: 20
Primary Market Served: Business & Consumer
Catalog available online
Indirect online sales
Advertising/Marketing Budget Related to Direct Marketing: 0-25%
Direct Marketing ad budget: $20,000
Founded: 1947

Nursery specializing in pine, spruce, fir, hemlock & myrtle.

FLORIAN TOOLS

157 Water St
Southington, CT 06489-3018
Telephone: (860) 628-9643, Toll Free: (800) 275-3618, E-Mail: info@ floriantools.com, Web Site: www. floriantools.com
Pres & COO: Sean E. Florian
Conducts Business: U.S., Europe, S. America
Employees: 20
Primary Market Served: Business & Consumer
Catalog available online
Direct online sales
Advertising/Marketing Budget Related to Direct Marketing: 0-25%
Founded: 1937
Gross sales or billing: $4,000,000

FOUR SEASONS SOLAR PRODUCTS LLC

Div. of Latium USA
5005 Veterans Memorial Hwy
Holbrook, NY 11741
Telephone: (631) 563-4000, Toll Free: (800) 368-7732, FAX: (631) 563-4010, E-Mail: info@ fourseasonssunrooms.com, Web Site: www.fourseasonssunrooms.com
Owner: Barb Homar
Conducts Business: U.S., Canada, U. K., Germany, France, Switzerland
Employees: 250
Primary Market Served: Business & Consumer

Direct Marketing ad budget:
$2,000,000
Founded: 1975

Manufacturer & distributor of greenhouses & sunrooms.

FRAN'S BASKET HOUSE, INC

295 Rte 10 E
Succasunna, NJ 07876-1380
Telephone: (973) 584-2230, Toll Free: (800) 372-6799, E-Mail: sales@ franswicker.com, Web Site: www. franswicker.com
Jeff Gruber
Conducts Business: U.S.
Employees: 50
Primary Market Served: Consumer
Founded: 1967
Gross sales or billing: $3,200,000

Wicker furniture & accessories.

GALLOWAY FARMS

7790 SW 87th Ave
Miami, FL 33173-3506
Telephone: (305) 274-7472, FAX: (305) 274-3233, E-Mail: galloway_inc@bellsouth.net, Web Site: www.gallowayfarm.com
Owner: Pat Lawrence
Conducts Business: U.S.
Employees: 20
Primary Market Served: Consumer
Advertising/Marketing Budget Related to Direct Marketing: 0-25%
Direct Marketing ad budget:
Direct Mail: 15%
Magazines: 10%
Newspapers: 70%
Telephone: 5%
Founded: 1888
Gross sales or billing: $500,000

Market range of annuals & perennials.

GARDEN PERENNIALS

85261 Hwy 15
Wayne, NE 68787-7097
Telephone: (402) 375-3615, Toll Free: (888) 375-3615, Web Site: www. gardenperennials.net
Owner: Gail Korn
Conducts Business: U.S.
Employees: 4
Primary Market Served: Consumer
Advertising/Marketing Budget Related to Direct Marketing: 76-100%
Direct Marketing ad budget:
Direct Mail: 75%
Magazines: 10%
Newspapers: 5%
TV/Radio: 10%
Founded: 1981
Gross sales or billing: $50,000
Specialize in flowering perennials.

GARDENER'S SUPPLY CO

128 Intervale Rd
Burlington, VT 05401-2804
Toll Free: (888) 833-1412, FAX: (800) 551-6712, E-Mail: info@gardeners. com, Web Site: www.gardeners.com
Pres: Jim Feinson
Employees: 220
Primary Market Served: Consumer
Founded: 1983
Gross sales or billing: $36,400,000

Gardening mail order company.

GARDENS ALIVE! INC

PO Box 4028
Lawrenceburg, IN 47025
Telephone: (513) 354-1483, FAX: (513) 354-1484, E-Mail: service@ gardensalive.com, Web Site: www. gardensalive.com
Chmn: Niles Kinerk
Conducts Business: U.S.
Employees: 150
Primary Market Served: Consumer
Founded: 1991

Sell seeds & natural garden supplies.

GARDENS OF THE BLUE RIDGE INC

Subs. of Fletcher Enterprises
PO Box 10
Pineola, NC 28662
Telephone: (828) 733-2417, FAX: (828) 733-8894, E-Mail: contact@ gardensoftheblueridge.com, Web Site: www.gardensoftheblueridge. com
Sec & Treas: Robyn P. Fletcher
Conducts Business: Worldwide
Employees: 7
Primary Market Served: Business & Consumer
Catalog available online
Direct online sales
Advertising/Marketing Budget Related to Direct Marketing: 0-25%
Direct Marketing ad budget: $3,000
Direct Mail: 30%
Magazines: 50%
Newspapers: 10%
Telephone: 10%
Founded: 1892
Gross sales or billing: $260,000

Wildflowers, ferns & native plants.

GARY'S PERENNIALS, LLC

Subs. of perennialmarket.com
1122 E Welsh Rd
Maple Glen, PA 19002-2224
Telephone: (215) 628-4070, Toll Free: (800) 898-6653, FAX: (215) 628-0216, E-Mail: roots@

garysperennials.com, Web Site:
www.garysperennials.com; www.
perennialmarket.com
Partner: Gary Steinberg
Gen Mgr: Andrea Steinberg
Conducts Business: U.S., Canada
Employees: 4
Primary Market Served: Business
Catalog available online
Indirect online sales
Advertising/Marketing Budget Related
  to Direct Marketing: 76-100%
Direct Marketing ad budget: $35,000
Direct Mail: 55%
Magazines: 10%
Online: 15%
Telephone: 20%
Founded: 1984
Gross sales or billing: $800,000

Sell perennial roots & large plugs.

GENERAL MILLS INC
One General Mills Blvd
Minneapolis, MN 55426
Toll Free: (800) 248-7310, FAX: (763)
  764-8330, Web Site: www.
  generalmills.com
Chmn & CEO: Kendall J. Powell
Pres & COO: Jeffrey L. Harmening
Conducts Business: U.S.
Primary Market Served: Consumer
Catalog available online
Indirect online sales
Advertising/Marketing Budget Related
  to Direct Marketing: 76-100%
Gross sales or billing: $12,400,000,000

Marketer of housewares & food-related
merchandise available from the Betty
Crocker catalog.

GODDARD
  MANUFACTURING CO
109 S Mill St
Logan, KS 67646-5112
Telephone: (785) 689-4341, Toll Free:
  (800) 536-4341, Web Site: www.
  spiral-staircases.com
Pres: Jerry Goddard
Conducts Business: U.S.
Employees: 9
Primary Market Served: Business &
  Consumer
Catalog available online
Advertising/Marketing Budget Related
  to Direct Marketing: 76-100%
Founded: 1978

Custom-built spiral steel & wood stairs.
Extra railings, balusters & newels.
Wholesale prices.

GOOD DIRECTIONS CO INC
20 Commerce Dr
Danbury, CT 06810-4131

Telephone: (203) 743-3775, FAX:
  (203) 743-5226, E-Mail: contact@
  gooddirections.com, Web Site: www.
  gooddirections.com
Owner: Michael Lodato
Primary Market Served: Business &
  Consumer

Sell weathervanes & other outdoor
products.

GOSSLER FARMS NURSERY
1200 Weaver Rd
Springfield, OR 97478-9663
Telephone: (541) 746-3922, FAX:
  (541) 744-7924, Web Site: www.
  gosslerfarms.com
Owner: Marjory Gossler
Partner: Roger Gossler
Partner: Eric Gossler
Conducts Business: U.S.
Primary Market Served: Business &
  Consumer
Catalog available online
Advertising/Marketing Budget Related
  to Direct Marketing: 0-25%
Founded: 1969

Sell ornamental trees & shrubs wholesale & retail.

GOTHIC ARCH
  GREENHOUSES INC
309 Glenwood St
Mobile, AL 36606-1741
Telephone: (251) 471-5238, Toll Free:
  (800) 531-4769, FAX: (251) 471-
  5465, E-Mail: info@
  gothicarchgreenhouses.net, Web Site:
  www.GothicArchGreenhouses.com
Owner: William H. Sierke
Conducts Business: Worldwide
Employees: 5
Primary Market Served: Business &
  Consumer
Catalog available online
Direct online sales
Advertising/Marketing Budget Related
  to Direct Marketing: 76-100%
Direct Marketing ad budget:
Direct Mail: 20%
Magazines: 80%
Founded: 1946
Gross sales or billing: $500,000

Sell greenhouse kits & supplies.

GRIMES HORTICULTURE
  INC
11335 Concord Hambden Rd
Concord, OH 44077-0640
Toll Free: (800) 241-7333, FAX: (440)
  352-1800, E-Mail: sales@grimes-
  hort.com, Web Site: www.
  grimesseeds.com
Pres: Rod LeDrew
Conducts Business: Worldwide

Employees: 40
Primary Market Served: Business
Catalog available online
Indirect online sales
Advertising/Marketing Budget Related
  to Direct Marketing: 0-25%
Direct Marketing ad budget:
Direct Mail: 10%
Telephone: 90%
Founded: 1925

Sell seeds and plants.

GROWER'S SUPPLY CO
2326 Bishop Circle E
Dexter, MI 48130-1566
Telephone: (734) 426-5852, FAX:
  (734) 426-5750, E-Mail: growers@
  grower-supply.com, Web Site: www.
  growerssupplycompany.com
Pres: Donald Plasterer
Conducts Business: U.S.
Employees: 8
Primary Market Served: Business
Catalog available online
Advertising/Marketing Budget Related
  to Direct Marketing: 0-25%
Direct Marketing ad budget:
Direct Mail: 100%
Founded: 1954
Gross sales or billing: $1,000,000

Indoor gardening supplies.

HANDY STORE FIXTURES
  INC
337 Sherman Ave
Newark, NJ 07114-1592
Telephone: (973) 242-1600, Toll Free:
  (800) 631-4280, FAX: (973) 642-
  6222, Web Site: www.
  handystorefixtures.com
Mktg Mgr: Steven DiOrio
Conducts Business: U.S., Canada
Employees: 200
Direct Marketing ad budget:
Direct Mail: 60%
Magazines: 20%
Newspapers: 20%
Founded: 1952
Gross sales or billing: $21,000,000

Wall units, display cases, gondolas &
counters.

HISTORICAL REPLICATIONS
  INC
3908 N State St
Jackson, MS 39206-5752
Toll Free: (800) 426-5628, FAX: (601)
  981-8185, E-Mail: info@
  historicaldesigns.com, Web Site:
  www.historicaldesigns.com
Co-Owner: Cecilia Reese Bullock
Pres: Mike Stephens
Conducts Business: U.S.
Employees: 2

Primary Market Served: Consumer
Catalog available online
Direct online sales
Advertising/Marketing Budget Related
  to Direct Marketing: 76-100%
Direct Marketing ad budget: $30,000
Online: 100%
Founded: 1977
Gross sales or billing: $200,000

House plans that specialize in historic
facades with updated interiors.

HOLLAND WILDFLOWER FARM

290 O'Neil Ln
Elkins, AR 72727
Telephone: (479) 643-2622, Toll Free:
  (800) 684-3734, E-Mail: info@
  hollandwildflowerfarm.com, Web
  Site: www.hollandwildflowerfarm.
  com
Pres & Owner: Julie Holland
Conducts Business: U.S.
Employees: 5
Primary Market Served: Business &
  Consumer
Catalog available online
Direct online sales
Advertising/Marketing Budget Related
  to Direct Marketing: 26-50%
Direct Marketing ad budget: $4,000
Direct Mail: 50%
Magazines: 30%
Newspapers: 10%
TV/Radio: 10%
Founded: 1985
Gross sales or billing: $40,000

Sell wildflower seeds.

HOME DECORATORS COLLECTION INC

3074 Chastain Meadows Pkwy
Marietta, GA 30066-3356
Toll Free: (800) 245-2217, Web Site:
  www.homedecoratorscom
Founder: Gil Kemp
Conducts Business: U.S.
Employees: 180
Primary Market Served: Consumer
Catalog available online
Direct online sales
Direct Marketing ad budget:
Direct Mail: $8,500,000
Founded: 1991
Gross sales or billing: $44,000,000

Direct seller of home decor.

HOMECRAFT VENEER & WOODWORKER SUPPLY

1102 Manor Ave
Latrobe, PA 15650-4506
Telephone: (724) 537-8435, Toll Free:
  (800) 796-6348, FAX: (724) 537-
  0543, E-Mail: woodman@
  homecraftveneer.com, Web Site:
  www.homecraftveneer.com
Owner: Alan J. McCullough
Conducts Business: U.S., Canada
Primary Market Served: Business &
  Consumer
Advertising/Marketing Budget Related
  to Direct Marketing: 0-25%

Sell domestic & imported veneers.
Also veneering tools, woodworking
supplies, flexible veneers, lumber &
plywood.

HOUSE OF WESLEY INC

1704 Morrissey Dr
Bloomington, IL 61704-7107
Telephone: (309) 664-7334, E-Mail:
  customercare@houseofwesley.com,
  Web Site: www.houseofwesley.com
Conducts Business: U.S.
Employees: 100
Primary Market Served: Consumer
Founded: 1954

Sell horticultural products through mail
order space advertising.

IMPROVEMENTS

Subs. of Home Shopping Network
8879 West Chester Rd
West Chester, OH 45069-2914
Toll Free: (800) 634-9484, Web Site:
  www.improvementscatalog.com
Pres & CEO, HSN: Mindy F. Gross-
  man
Pres: Geoff Brownrigg
Conducts Business: U.S.
Employees: 150
Primary Market Served: Business &
  Consumer
Catalog available online
Direct online sales
Advertising/Marketing Budget Related
  to Direct Marketing: 76-100%
Direct Marketing ad budget:
Direct Mail: 95%
Magazines: 5%

Marketer of home repair & improvement items.

INDOOR GARDENING SUPPLIES

PO Box 527
Dexter, MI 48130
Toll Free: (800) 823-5740, Web Site:
  www.indoorgardensupplies.com
Pres: Tina Havro
Conducts Business: U.S.
Employees: 3
Primary Market Served: Consumer
Catalog available online
Direct online sales
Marketer of indoor gardening equip-
ment. & accessories.

INTERNATIONAL IRRIGATION SYSTEMS

RP-NFOA
Div. of Regional Leasing Corp Ltd
291 Riverview Blvd
St. Catherines, ON, Canada L2T 3N3
Telephone: (905) 688-4090, Toll Free:
  (877) 477-4476, FAX: (905) 688-
  4093, Web Site: www.irrigro.com
Pres: R.L. Neff
Conducts Business: Worldwide
Employees: 5
Primary Market Served: Business &
  Consumer
Catalog available online
Direct online sales
Advertising/Marketing Budget Related
  to Direct Marketing: 76-100%
Direct Marketing ad budget:
Direct Mail: 10%
Magazines: 90%
Founded: 1975
Gross sales or billing: $300,000

Manufacture & market micro-porous
drip irrigation systems.

INTERNATIONAL MANUFACTURING CO

Div. of Textile Enterprises Inc
216 Main St
Whitesburg, GA 30185-3203
Telephone: (770) 834-2094, FAX:
  (770) 834-2096, E-Mail:
  textilenterprise@aol.net
Pres: Martha G. Arnold
Conducts Business: U.S.
Primary Market Served: Business &
  Consumer
Catalog available online
Direct online sales
Founded: 1973

Sell dried floral items & accessories.

JANICE'S LLC

30 Arbor St (#3)
Hartford, CT 06106-1215
Telephone: (860) 523-4479, Toll Free:
  (800) 526-4237, FAX: (860) 523-
  4178, E-Mail: dlerner@janices.com,
  Web Site: www.janices.com
Owner & Pres: David Lerner
Conducts Business: U.S., Europe, Ja-
  pan, Canada, Mexico
Employees: 20
Primary Market Served: Consumer
Catalog available online
Direct online sales
Advertising/Marketing Budget Related
  to Direct Marketing: 76-100%
Founded: 1980

Gross sales or billing: $1,000,000

Manufacturer & catalog marketer of bedding, linens, clothing & organic cleaning products.

JW JUNG SEED CO
335 S High St
Randolph, WI 53957-0001
Toll Free: (800) 297-3123, Web Site: www.jungseed.com
Pres: Richard Zondag
Conducts Business: U.S.
Employees: 150
Primary Market Served: Consumer
Catalog available online
Direct online sales
Founded: 1907

Seed & nursery company supplying complete line of vegetable & flower seeds, nursery stock & gardening accessories for the home gardener.

K-LOG
1224 27th St
Zion, IL 60099-2673
Toll Free: (800) 872-6611, FAX: (847) 872-3728, E-Mail: info@k-log.com, Web Site: www.k-log.com
Pres: Tim Klebe
Catalog available online
Direct online sales

Sell furniture.

KAR GRAPHICS
PO Box 2430
Mashpee, MA 02649
Toll Free: (800) 760-5192, FAX: (508) 539-1108, E-Mail: hoop@cape.com, Web Site: www.hoophouse.com
Conducts Business: U.S., Canada, Bermuda, Argentina
Employees: 4
Primary Market Served: Business & Consumer
Catalog available online
Direct online sales
Advertising/Marketing Budget Related to Direct Marketing: 76-100%
Direct Marketing ad budget: $20,000
Magazines: 100%
Founded: 1985
Gross sales or billing: $500,000

Hoop house, green house kits sold to commercial & hobby garden growers.

KAYNE & SON CUSTOM HARDWARE INC
100 Daniel Ridge Rd
Candler, NC 28715-9434
Telephone: (828) 667-8868, FAX: (828) 665-8303, Web Site: www.customforgedhardware.com
VP: David Kayne

Conducts Business: U.S., Canada, Japan
Employees: 4
Primary Market Served: Business & Consumer
Founded: 1971

Custom-forged hardware. Repairs, restorations & reproductions.

KESTER'S WILD GAME FOOD NURSERIES INC
4582 Hwy 116 E
Omro, WI 54963
Telephone: (920) 685-2929, Toll Free: (800) 558-8815, FAX: (920) 685-6727, E-Mail: pkester@vbe.com, Web Site: www.kestersnursery.com
Pres: Paul Kester
Conducts Business: U.S., Canada
Employees: 4
Primary Market Served: Business & Consumer
Advertising/Marketing Budget Related to Direct Marketing: 0-25%
Founded: 1903

Sell aquatic plants & various seeds for planting to attract & provide food for wildlife.

KING RANCH SADDLE SHOP
Subs. of King Ranch Inc
120 S 6th St
Kingsville, TX 78363
Toll Free: (800) 282-KING, E-Mail: krsaddleshop@king-ranch.com, Web Site: www.krsaddleshop.com
Gen Mgr: Rose Morales
Conducts Business: U.S.
Primary Market Served: Business & Consumer
Catalog available online
Direct online sales
Founded: 1926

Leather goods and home furnishings.

KITCHEN KOMPACT INC
911 E 11th St
Jeffersonville, IN 47130-4142
Telephone: (812) 282-6681, FAX: (812) 282-7880, E-Mail: webmaster@kitchenkompact.com, Web Site: www.kitchenkompact.com
CEO: Dwight Gahm
Conducts Business: U.S., Canada, Mexico
Employees: 260
Primary Market Served: Business
Catalog available online
Advertising/Marketing Budget Related to Direct Marketing: 0-25%
Direct Marketing ad budget: $400,000
Magazines: 100%
Founded: 1937

Gross sales or billing: $87,000,000
Kitchen & bath cabinets.

THE LADYBUG CO
12857 Oroville Quincy Hwy
Berry Creek, CA 95916
Telephone: (530) 589-5227
Owner: Julie Steele
Conducts Business: U.S., Canada
Primary Market Served: Business & Consumer
Direct Marketing ad budget:
Magazines: 75%
Newspapers: 25%

Sell beneficial insects.

LE JARDIN DU GOURMET
1354 Memorial Dr
Saint Johnsbury Center, VT 05863
Telephone: (802) 748-1446, FAX: (802) 748-1446, E-Mail: orderdesk@artisticgardens.com, Web Site: www.artisticgardens.com
Owner: Paul Taylor
Conducts Business: U.S.
Employees: 3
Primary Market Served: Consumer
Catalog available online
Direct online sales
Advertising/Marketing Budget Related to Direct Marketing: 26-50%
Direct Marketing ad budget:
Direct Mail: 50%
Magazines: 50%
Founded: 1954
Gross sales or billing: $320,000

Florist & mail order seed & Christmas wreath.

LEE'S NURSERY
233 Lee's Dr
McMinnville, TN 37110-6939
Telephone: (931) 668-4870
Owner: Malinda L. Brown
Conducts Business: U.S.
Employees: 2
Advertising/Marketing Budget Related to Direct Marketing: 76-100%
Direct Marketing ad budget:
Direct Mail: 40%
Online: 60%
Founded: 1968
Gross sales or billing: $100,000

Sell over plants to home gardeners & businesses.

LEHMAN'S
aka Lehman Hardware & Appliances, Inc
4779 Kidron Rd
Dalton, OH 44618
Toll Free: (800) 438-5346, Web Site: www.lehmans.com
Founder: Jay Lehman

Conducts Business: Worldwide
Employees: 8
Primary Market Served: Business &
 Consumer
Catalog available online
Direct online sales
Founded: 1955

Sell non-electric appliances, tools, kitchenware & wood stoves & health & wellness items.

LEMEE'S INC

Subs. of Lemee's Fireplace Equipment
138 Robinson St
Hanson, MA 02341
Telephone: (781) 294-8209, E-Mail:
 slemeephot@aol.com, Web Site:
 www.lemeesfireplace.com
VP: Susan Lemee
Conducts Business: U.S.
Employees: 4
Primary Market Served: Consumer
Catalog available online
Direct online sales
Founded: 1954

Sell fireplace screens, toolsets, irons, grates, wood baskets & other fireplace accessories.

AM LEONARD INC

241 Fox Dr
Piqua, OH 45356
Toll Free: (800) 543-8955, FAX: (800)
 433-0633, E-Mail: info@amleo.com,
 Web Site: www.amleo.com
Owner & Pres: Gregory Stephens
Conducts Business: U.S.
Employees: 90
Primary Market Served: Business &
 Consumer
Catalog available online
Founded: 1885
Sell horticulture supplies and hardware.

LIFETIME BRANDS INC

1000 Stewart Ave
Garden City, NY 11530
Telephone: (516) 683-6000, FAX:
 (516) 555-0101, E-Mail: questions@
 lifetimebrands.com, Web Site: www.
 lifetimebrands.com
Pres & CEO: Jeffrey Siegel
Vice Chmn & COO: Ronald Shiftan
Pres: Daniel Siegel
Conducts Business: U.S., Eastern Eu-
 rope, S. America, Mexico, Canada
Employees: 1,199
Primary Market Served: Business
Catalog available online
Advertising/Marketing Budget Related
 to Direct Marketing: 0-25%
Direct Marketing ad budget:
Magazines: 100%
Founded: 1945

Gross sales or billing: $457,400,000
Sell products for kitchen, tableware, home decor & lifestyle.

LILYPONS WATER GARDENS

6800 Lilypons Rd
Adamstown, MD 21710-8606
Toll Free: (800) 999-5459, FAX: (800)
 879-5459, E-Mail: info@lilypons.
 com, Web Site: www.lilypons.com
Pres: Margaret Koogle
Conducts Business: U.S.
Primary Market Served: Business &
 Consumer
Catalog available online
Direct online sales
Founded: 1917

Aquatic plants, water lilies & water garden supplies.

LOWE'S COMPANIES INC

1000 Lowes Blvd
Mooresville, NC 28117-8520
Telephone: (704) 758-1000, Toll Free:
 (800) 445-6937, Web Site: www.
 lowes.com
Chmn: Robert A. Niblock
Chief Customer Officer: Gregory M.
 Bridgeford
CFO: Marshall A Croom
Conducts Business: U.S.
Employees: 160,000
Primary Market Served: Business &
 Consumer
Direct online sales
Founded: 1946
Gross sales or billing: $6,117,814
Home center chain.

MAGNOLIA HALL

49 Bryant St
Jasper, GA 30143
Telephone: (404) 351-1910, Toll Free:
 (866) 410-2755, FAX: (404) 692-
 4068, E-Mail: belvedere@
 magnoliahall.com, Web Site: www.
 magnoliahall.com
Pres: Barry Nerli
Conducts Business: U.S., Canada,
 Mexico, Puerto Rico, Caribbean Is-
 lands
Employees: 4
Primary Market Served: Consumer
Catalog available online
Direct online sales
Founded: 1962

Sell yesteryear furniture & accessories.

MARIMAC INC

6395 Cote deLiesse
Montreal, QC, Canada H4T 1E5

Telephone: (514) 376-7882, FAX:
 (514) 376-0801, E-Mail: sales@
 marimacgroup.com, Web Site: www.
 marimac.com
Pres: Paul Nassar
Conducts Business: Worldwide
Employees: 200
Primary Market Served: Business &
 Consumer

Sell bedding.

MARY'S PLANT FARM & LANDSCAPING

2410 Lanes Mill Rd
Hamilton, OH 45013-9181
Telephone: (513) 894-0022, FAX:
 (513) 892-2053, E-Mail:
 marysplantfarm@zoomtown.com,
 Web Site: www.marysplantfarm.com
Pres & Owner: Mary E. Harrison
Conducts Business: U.S.
Employees: 4
Primary Market Served: Business &
 Consumer
Catalog available online
Direct online sales
Advertising/Marketing Budget Related
 to Direct Marketing: 26-50%
Direct Marketing ad budget:
Direct Mail: 50%
Newspapers: 25%
Online: 25%
Founded: 1976

Nursery stock.

MCCLURE & ZIMMERMAN

Subs of J. W. Jung Seed Co
335 S High St
Randolph, WI 53956-1425
Toll Free: (800) 883-6998, FAX: (800)
 374-6120, Web Site: www.mzbulb.
 com
Pres: Richard Zondag
Conducts Business: U.S.
Primary Market Served: Business &
 Consumer
Catalog available online
Indirect online sales

Flower bulbs, corns & rootstocks for the bulb enthusiast.

MELANIPHY & ASSOCIATES, INC

RP-NFOA
6348 N Milwaukee Ave (Suite 198)
Chicago, IL 60646
Telephone: (773) 467-1212, FAX:
 (773) 775-7584, Web Site: www.
 melaniphy.com
Pres: John Melaniphy Sr
VP: John Melaniphy III
Primary Market Served: Business &
 Consumer

Catalog available online
Consultants for various industries.

METROPOLITAN MUSEUM OF ART

1000 Fifth Ave
New York, NY 10028
Telephone: (212) 570-3894, Toll Free: (800) 468-7386, FAX: (718) 628-5485, Web Site: www.metmuseum.org/store
Gen Mgr, Mktg & Publicity: Jody Malordy
Conducts Business: Worldwide
Primary Market Served: Business & Consumer
Catalog available online
Direct online sales

Sell museum reproductions, adaptations, jewelry, apparel & books.

METROPOLITAN WINDOW FASHIONS AT FABRICLAND

855 Rte 22
North Plainfield, NJ 07060-3619
Telephone: (908) 755-4700, Toll Free: (877) 722-1100, FAX: (908) 755-6368
Member: Bruce Heyman

Ready-made designer curtains, drapes, shades & window treatments

MOULTRIE MANUFACTURING CO

1403 Hwy 133 S
Moultrie, GA 31788
Telephone: (229) 985-1312, Toll Free: (800) 841-8674, FAX: (229) 890-7245, Web Site: www.moultriemanufacturing.com
Owner: William Smith
Conducts Business: U.S., Canada
Employees: 75
Primary Market Served: Consumer
Catalog available online
Direct online sales
Direct Marketing ad budget:
Magazines: 90%
Newspapers: 5%
TV/Radio: 5%
Founded: 1952

Sell rail systems.

NEIMAN-MARCUS GROUP

4121 Pinnacle Point Drive # 100
Dallas, TX 75211-1570
Telephone: (214) 339-0396, Toll Free: (888) 888-4757, Web Site: www.neimanmarcus.com
CEO: Karen Katz
CEO,: James J Gold
Employees: 15,800

Primary Market Served: Consumer
Catalog available online
Direct online sales

Sell hard goods, soft goods & apparel.

NORTHERN GREENHOUSE SALES

PO Box 42
Neche, ND 58265-0042
Telephone: (204) 327-5540, FAX: (204) 327-5527, E-Mail: info@northerngreenhouse.com, Web Site: www.northerngreenhouse.com
Partner: Bob Davis
Partner: Margaret Davis
Conducts Business: U.S., Canada
Primary Market Served: Business & Consumer
Catalog available online
Indirect online sales
Advertising/Marketing Budget Related to Direct Marketing: 76-100%
Founded: 1979

Manufacture & sell Superstrong Woven Poly.

NORTHERN RESPONSE INTERNATIONAL

50 Staples Ave - Richmond Hill
Toronto, ON, Canada L4B O47
Telephone: (905) 737-6698, Toll Free: (866) 584-1694, FAX: (905) 737-0099, E-Mail: general@nresponse.com, Web Site: northernresponse.com
Web Mgr: Allyson Woodrooffe
Conducts Business: Worldwide
Employees: 60
Primary Market Served: Consumer
Advertising/Marketing Budget Related to Direct Marketing: 76-100%

Full service distributor.

NOURSE FARMS

41 River Rd
South Deerfield, MA 01373
Telephone: (413) 665-2658, FAX: (413) 665-7888, E-Mail: info@noursefarms.com, Web Site: www.noursefarms.com
Owner: Tim Nourse
Conducts Business: U.S.
Employees: 100
Primary Market Served: Business & Consumer
Catalog available online
Direct online sales
Advertising/Marketing Budget Related to Direct Marketing: 76-100%
Direct Marketing ad budget: $35,000
Direct Mail: 75%
Magazines: 24%
Newspapers: 1%

Founded: 1932
Sell berry plants & accessories.

NOWELL'S INC

615 Irwin St
San Rafael, CA 94901-3940
Telephone: (415) 332-4933, E-Mail: contact@nowellslighting.com, Web Site: www.nowellslighting.com
VP: Lennart Sandin
Conducts Business: U.S., Canada, U.K., Australia, Hong Kong, Taiwan
Employees: 10
Primary Market Served: Business & Consumer
Catalog available online
Indirect online sales
Advertising/Marketing Budget Related to Direct Marketing: 0-25%
Founded: 1954

Manufacturer & marketer of antique & traditional-style light fixtures & custom lighting; restorations of Victorian fixtures.

OFFICEFURNITURE.COM

A National Bus Furniture, Inc company. Subs of K&K America, LLC
80 S 70th St
West Allis, WI 53214
Telephone: (414) 272-6080, Toll Free: (800) 933-0053, FAX: (800) 468-1526, Web Site: www.officefurniture.com
Gen Mgr: Jeff Riddick
Conducts Business: U.S.
Employees: 70
Primary Market Served: Business
Catalog available online
Direct online sales
Gross sales or billing: $24,800,000

Sell office furniture through catalogs & showroom.

OMAHA FIXTURE INTERNATIONAL

10320 "J" St
Omaha, NE 68127-1092
Telephone: (402) 592-3720, Toll Free: (800) 637-2257, FAX: (402) 593-5716, (800) 531-6627, E-Mail: sales@omahafixture.com, Web Site: www.omahafixture.com
Pres: Joel Alperson
Primary Market Served: Business

Sell retail store fixtures.

GEORGE W PARK SEED CO INC

3507 Cokesbury Rd
Hodges, SC 29653

Telephone: (864) 330-2003, Toll Free:
(800) 845-3369, E-Mail: info@
parkseed.com, Web Site: www.
parkseed.com
Pres: Paul Ambrose
Conducts Business: U.S., Canada
Employees: 600
Primary Market Served: Business &
Consumer
Catalog available online
Direct online sales
Founded: 1868

Sell flower, garden & vegetable seeds,
bulbs, plants & gardening accessories
to consumers by mail order.

PARTYLITE GIFTS INC
600 Cordwainer Dr
Norwell, MA 02061
Telephone: (508) 830-3100, Toll Free:
(888)999-5706, FAX: (508) 830-
0026, E-Mail: infona@partylite.com,
Web Site: www.partylite.com
Pres: Martin Kohler
Mgr Mktg Commun: Paul Katz

PENNSYLVANIA FIREBACKS
Div. of Pennsylvania Firebacks Inc
50 Levick St
Philadelphia, PA 19111
Telephone: (215) 722-1221, E-Mail:
info@fireback.com, Web Site: www.
fireback.com
Owner & Pres: Jay Del Conner
Conducts Business: U.S.
Employees: 2
Primary Market Served: Consumer
Advertising/Marketing Budget Related
to Direct Marketing: 0-25%
Direct Marketing ad budget:
Magazines: $1,500
Gross sales or billing: $250,000

Sell firebacks & accessories.

PERENNIAL PLEASURES
NURSERY
63 Brickhouse Rd
East Hardwick, VT 05836
Telephone: (802) 472-5104, FAX:
(802) 472-6572, E-Mail: annex@
perennialpleasures.net, Web Site:
www.perennialpleasures.net
Owner: Rachel Kane
Conducts Business: U.S.
Employees: 4
Primary Market Served: Consumer
Catalog available online
Indirect online sales
Advertising/Marketing Budget Related
to Direct Marketing: 0-25%
Direct Marketing ad budget:
Direct Mail: 70%
Magazines: 30%
Founded: 1981

Gross sales or billing: $120,000
Nursery & tea garden.

PFALTZGRAFF CO
Subs. of Susquehanna Pf
140 E Market St
York, PA 17401-1219
Toll Free: (800) 999-2811, FAX: (800)
757-6872, E-Mail: service@
pfaltzgraff.com, Web Site: www.
pfaltzgraff.com
Chmn: Louis J. Appell
Conducts Business: Worldwide
Employees: 2,000
Primary Market Served: Business &
Consumer
Catalog available online
Founded: 1811
Gross sales or billing: $23,700,000

Manufacturer & marketer of tabletop
products.

PIER 1 IMPORTS INC
100 Pier 1 Pl
Fort Worth, TX 76102-2600
Telephone: (817) 252-6300, Toll Free:
(800) 245-4595, E-Mail:
customervice@pier1.com, Web
Site: www.pier1.com
CEO: Terry E. London
Catalog available online
Direct online sales

Sell tableware, furniture, lighting & decor.

THE PLOW & HEARTH INC
Subs. of 1-800-FLOWERS
7021 Wolftown-Hood Rd
Madison, VA 22727-2200
Toll Free: (800) 494-7544, Web Site:
www.plowhearth.com
Pres: John Haydock
Conducts Business: U.S., Canada, Ja-
pan
Employees: 150
Primary Market Served: Consumer
Catalog available online
Direct online sales
Direct Marketing ad budget:
Direct Mail: 100%
Founded: 1980
Gross sales or billing: $100,000,000

Sell home & lifestyle products.

PRAIRIE NURSERY
W5875 Dyke Ave
Westfield, WI 53964-8579
Toll Free: (800) 476-9453, FAX: (608)
296-2741, Web Site: www.
prairienursery.com
Owner & Pres: Neil Diboll
Conducts Business: U.S., Canada
Employees: 26

Primary Market Served: Business &
Consumer
Catalog available online
Direct online sales
Founded: 1972

Sell native grasses & wild flowers,
plants & seeds.

ST PRESTON & SON INC
102 Main St Wharf
Greenport, NY 11944-1422
Telephone: (631) 477-1990, E-Mail:
catalog@prestons.com, Web Site:
www.prestons.com
Mktg Mgr: Andrew Rowsom
Conducts Business: U.S., Canada, Eu-
rope
Employees: 16
Primary Market Served: Business &
Consumer
Catalog available online
Direct online sales
Advertising/Marketing Budget Related
to Direct Marketing: 51-75%
Direct Marketing ad budget:
Direct Mail: 60%
Magazines: 5%
Online: 35%

Publisher of catalogs featuring ships
models, decor, apparel & nautical gifts.

QUALCO, INC
225 Passaic St
Passaic, NJ 07055-6414
Telephone: (973) 473-1222, Social:
Facebook
Conducts Business: Worldwide
Employees: 30
Primary Market Served: Business
Direct Marketing ad budget:
Direct Mail: $25,000
Magazines: $25,000
Newspapers: $100,000
TV/Radio: $50,000
Telephone: $50,000
Founded: 1986
Gross sales or billing: $5,000,000

Sales of swimming pool chemicals &
accessories.

REDWOOD CITY SEED CO
PO Box 361
Redwood City, CA 94064-0361
Telephone: (650) 325-7333, FAX:
(650) 325-4056, Web Site: www.
ecoseeds.com
Co-Owner, Sales & Res: Craig C. Dre-
mann
Co-Owner & Mgr: Sue Dremann
Conducts Business: Worldwide
Primary Market Served: Business &
Consumer
Catalog available online
Indirect online sales

Advertising/Marketing Budget Related
to Direct Marketing: 100%
Direct Marketing ad budget:
Direct Mail: 90%
Magazines: 5%
Online: 5%
Founded: 1971

Sell seeds.

THE REGGIO REGISTER CO INC

31 Jytek Rd
Leominster, MA 01453-5934
Telephone: (978) 870-1020, Toll Free:
(800) 880-3090, FAX: (978) 870-
1030, E-Mail: reggio@
reggioregister.com, Web Site: www.
reggioregister.com
Pres: Michael Reggio
Conducts Business: U.S., Canada, U.K.
Employees: 13
Primary Market Served: Business &
Consumer
Catalog available online
Direct online sales
Advertising/Marketing Budget Related
to Direct Marketing: 0-25%
Direct Marketing ad budget:
Direct Mail: 67%
Magazines: 33%
Founded: 1978

Manufacturer of register grilles.

REPLACEMENTS LTD

1089 Knox Rd
Greensboro, NC 27420-6029
Toll Free: (800) REPLACE, E-Mail:
inquire@replacements.com, Web
Site: www.replacements.com
CEO & Pres: Bob Page
Conducts Business: U.S.
Employees: 450
Primary Market Served: Business &
Consumer
Catalog available online
Direct online sales
Advertising/Marketing Budget Related
to Direct Marketing: 51-75%
Direct Marketing ad budget:
Direct Mail: 40%
Magazines: 55%
Newspapers: 5%
Founded: 1981
Gross sales or billing: $75,000,000

Discontinued & active china, crystal,
silver & collectibles.

RINFRET LTD

354 Greenwich Ave
Greenwich, CT 06830-6522
Telephone: (203) 622-0000, E-Mail:
jmz@rinfretltd.com, Web Site: www.
rinfretltd.com
Principal Designer: Cindy Rinfret

Primary Market Served: Consumer

ROCKLER WOODWORKING & HARDWARE

Div. of Rockler Cos Inc
4365 Willow Dr
Medina, MN 55340
Telephone: (763) 478-8200, Toll Free:
(800) 279-4441, FAX: (800) 865-
1229, E-Mail: info@rockler.com,
Web Site: www.rockler.com
CEO: Ann Rockler Jackson
CEO: Ron Hornbaker
Sr VP, Prod Devt: Steve Krohmer
Conducts Business: Worldwide
Employees: 300
Primary Market Served: Business &
Consumer
Catalog available online
Direct online sales
Advertising/Marketing Budget Related
to Direct Marketing: 0-25%
Direct Marketing ad budget:
Direct Mail: 75%
Magazines: 25%
Founded: 1954

Retailer of hardware & woodworking
supplies.

SANDY MUSH HERB NURSERY

316 Surrett Cove Rd
Leicester, NC 28748
Telephone: (828) 683-2014, E-Mail:
info@sandymushherbs.com, Web
Site: www.sandymushherbs.com
Owner: Fairman Jayne
Owner: Kate Jayne
Conducts Business: U.S.
Primary Market Served: Consumer
Catalog available online
Founded: 1976

Catalog featuring over 1700 items: tea,
culinary, decorative & fragrant herbs
plus books, seeds, garden plants &
growing instructions. Catalog $5.

SANTA BARBARA GREENHOUSES

721 Richmond Ave
Oxnard, CA 93030-7229
Toll Free: (800) 544-5276, E-Mail:
robsbg@aol.com, Web Site: www.
sbgreenhouse.com
Founder: Robert West
Conducts Business: U.S.
Employees: 6
Primary Market Served: Business &
Consumer
Catalog available online
Advertising/Marketing Budget Related
to Direct Marketing: 76-100%
Founded: 1972

Sell greenhouse kits.

THE SCOTTS CO LLC

Scotts Miracle-Gro Products
14111 Scottslawn Rd
Marysville, OH 43041
Toll Free: (888) 270-3714, Web Site:
www.scotts.com
Pres & CEO: James Hagedorn
Conducts Business: U.S., Canada, Ger-
many
Employees: 850
Primary Market Served: Business &
Consumer
Advertising/Marketing Budget Related
to Direct Marketing: 0-25%
Gross sales or billing: $390,000,000

Manufacturer of lawn fertilizers & control products, grass seed & mechanical
lawn & garden equipment.

SEEDBURO EQUIPMENT CO

2293 S Mount Prospect Rd
Des Plaines, IL 60018-1810
Telephone: (312) 738-3700, Toll Free:
(800) 284-5779, E-Mail: sales@
seedburo.com, Web Site: www.
seedburo.com
Pres: Thomas E. Runyon
Conducts Business: Worldwide
Employees: 17
Primary Market Served: Business &
Consumer
Catalog available online
Indirect online sales
Advertising/Marketing Budget Related
to Direct Marketing: 51-75%
Direct Marketing ad budget:
Direct Mail: 2%
Magazines: 80%
Online: 10%
Telephone: 8%
Founded: 1912

Worldwide sales & distribution of handling, testing & inspection equipment
for the agricultural (grain, feed & seed)
industry.

SERVICEMASTER CO

860 Ridge Lake Blvd
Memphis, TN 38120-9434
Telephone: (901) 766-1400, Toll Free:
(866) 782-6787, Web Site: www.
servicemaster.com
Chmn Bd: Mark E Tomkins
Robert J Gillette
CIO: Dan Marks
Sr VP & CFO: Anthony DiLucente
Chief Mktg Officer: Marvin Davis
Employees: 32,000
Primary Market Served: Consumer
Catalog available online
Direct online sales
Founded: 2007

Gross sales or billing: $3,429,100,000

Lawn care & landscape maintenance, termite & pest control, home warranties, home inspection, house cleaning & furniture repair, disaster response & reconstruction, cleaning & disaster restoration.

SHADES OF LIGHT

4924 W Broad St
Richmond, VA 23230-3122
Telephone: (804) 288-6515, Toll Free: (877) 288-5029, E-Mail: customercare@shadesoflight.com, Web Site: www.shadesoflight.com
Owner & Pres: Ashton Harrison
Primary Market Served: Business & Consumer
Gross sales or billing: $14,500,000

Sell lighting & home decor.

SHAKER WORKSHOPS

14 S Pleasant St
Ashburnham, MA 01430-1649
Telephone: (978) 827-9900, Toll Free: (800) 849-9121, FAX: (978) 827-6554, E-Mail: shakerworkshops.customerservice@gmail.com, Web Site: www.shakerworkshops.com
Owner & Pres: Richard C. Dabrowski
Conducts Business: U.S., Canada, Denmark, Germany, Japan, U.K., Ireland, Italy
Primary Market Served: Consumer
Catalog available online
Direct online sales
Advertising/Marketing Budget Related to Direct Marketing: 76-100%
Direct Marketing ad budget:
Direct Mail: 85%
Magazines: 10%
Online: 5%
Founded: 1970

Manufacture Shaker furniture & furniture kits.

SILO-HUNT HILL FARM

44 Upland Rd
New Milford, CT 06776-2199
Telephone: (860) 355-0300, Web Site: thesiloct.org
Cooking School Dir: Dawn Leahy
Conducts Business: U.S.
Employees: 7
Primary Market Served: Consumer
Direct online sales
Advertising/Marketing Budget Related to Direct Marketing: 0-25%
Founded: 1972

A country kitchen store, gallery & cooking school.

SIMPLICITY PATTERN CO INC/STYLE PATTERNS LTD/NEW LOOK ENGLISH PATTERN CO LTD

Subs. Conso Products Co
261 Madison Ave (fl 4)
New York, NY 10016-3906
Telephone: (212) 372-0500, Toll Free: (800) 653-7301, Web Site: www.simplicitypatt.com
CFO: Richard Zonin
Conducts Business: U.S., Australia, New Zealand, Canada, U.K.
Employees: 200
Primary Market Served: Business & Consumer
Catalog available online
Advertising/Marketing Budget Related to Direct Marketing: 0-25%
Founded: 1927

Publisher of home sewing, fashion, home decorating, craft patterns, catalogs & instruction booklets for quilters & crafters.

SMITH & NOBLE

1181 California Ave
Corona, CA 92881
Toll Free: (888) 241-2134, E-Mail: contactus@smithnoble.com, Web Site: www.smithandnoble.com
Pres: Ken Constable
VP Mktg: Tari Huddleston
Conducts Business: U.S.
Employees: 150
Primary Market Served: Consumer
Catalog available online
Direct online sales
Founded: 1987

Sell custom window treatments.

SPATES THE FLORIST

PO Box 407
Newport, VT 05855-5729
Telephone: (802) 334-8330, Toll Free: (800) 473-3688, E-Mail: sales@spatestheflorist.com, Web Site: www.spatestheflorist.com
Partner: Douglas Spates
Conducts Business: U.S., Canada
Employees: 30
Primary Market Served: Business & Consumer
Catalog available online
Direct online sales
Founded: 1945

Flower shop, greenhouse & landscaping service plus mail order division.

STANLEY HOME PRODUCTS

Fuller Brush Co
1 Fuller Way
Great Bend, KS 67530-2466

Toll Free: (800) 732-1118, E-Mail: customer@fuller.com, Web Site: www.fullerdirect.com
CEO: David Sabin
Conducts Business: U.S.
Primary Market Served: Consumer
Founded: 1931

Sell household & personal brushes, mops, cleaners, polishes, cosmetics & giftware.

STARK BROTHERS NURSERIES & ORCHARDS

PO Box 1800
Louisiana, MO 63353
Telephone: (573) 754-8800, Toll Free: (800) 325-4180, E-Mail: info@starkbros.com, Web Site: www.starkbros.com
Pres: Cameron Brown
Primary Market Served: Business & Consumer

Sell fruit & nut trees, bushes, supplies & tools.

STEPTOE & WIFE ANTIQUES LTD

225 Nugget Ave, Unit 2
Scarborough, ON, Canada M1S 3L2
Telephone: (416) 780-1707, Toll Free: (800) 461-0060, FAX: (416) 780-1814, E-Mail: info@steptoewife.com, Web Site: www.steptoewife.com
Conducts Business: Worldwide
Employees: 35
Primary Market Served: Business & Consumer
Catalog available online
Advertising/Marketing Budget Related to Direct Marketing: 76-100%
Direct Marketing ad budget:
Direct Mail: 25%
Magazines: 75%
Founded: 1972
Gross sales or billing: $5,000,000

Manufacture & sell staircases.

STOKES SEEDS INC

2495 Walden Ave (# 800)
Buffalo, NY 14225-4767
Toll Free: (800) 396-9238, FAX: (800) 272-5560, E-Mail: stokes@stokeseeds.com, Web Site: www.stokeseeds.com
Pres: Wayne Gale
Conducts Business: U.S., Canada
Employees: 200
Primary Market Served: Consumer
Catalog available online
Direct online sales
Advertising/Marketing Budget Related to Direct Marketing: 76-100%

Founded: 1886

Sell flower & vegetable seed & gardening accessories.

SUNBILT SOLAR PRODUCTS

Div. of J Sussman Inc
109-10 180th St
Jamaica, NY 11433-2622
Telephone: (718) 297-0228, FAX: (718) 297-3090, E-Mail: robin@jsussmaninc.com, Web Site: jsussmaninc.com/sunbilt-solar-products
Pres: Steve Sussman
VP: David Sussman
Mktg Dir: Mel Wachsstock
Conducts Business: U.S., Europe
Employees: 55
Primary Market Served: Business & Consumer
Catalog available online
Indirect online sales
Advertising/Marketing Budget Related to Direct Marketing: 0-25%
Direct Marketing ad budget:
Direct Mail: 25%
Magazines: 75%
Founded: 1984
Gross sales or billing: $1,000,000

Sell solar products.

SUNBURST FARMS INC

Subs. of Dole Food Co
2200 NW 70th Ave
Miami, FL 33122-1816
Telephone: (305) 594-4300, Toll Free: (800) 333-1223, E-Mail: moreinfo@sunburstfarms.com, Web Site: www.sunburstfarms.com
Primary Market Served: Business & Consumer
Founded: 1988

Sell floral products.

SUNSHINE FARM & GARDENS

HC 67 Box 539B
Renick, WV 24966
Telephone: (304) 497-2208, E-Mail: barry@sunfarm.com, Web Site: www.sunfarm.com
Pres: Barry Glick
Sec & Treas: Angie Glick
Mgr: Zak Glick
Conducts Business: Worldwide
Employees: 27
Primary Market Served: Business & Consumer
Catalog available online
Direct online sales
Advertising/Marketing Budget Related to Direct Marketing: 26-50%
Direct Marketing ad budget:
Direct Mail: 25%

Magazines: 50%
Newspapers: 10%
Telephone: 15%
Founded: 1972
Gross sales or billing: $400,000

Grower of rare and unusual perennial plants. Sells retail & wholesale worldwide.

SUR LA TABLE

PO Box 840
Brownsburg, IN 46112
Toll Free: (800) 243-0852, FAX: (317) 858-5521, E-Mail: customerservice@surlatable.com
CEO: Diane L Neal
Employees: 250
Primary Market Served: Business & Consumer
Advertising/Marketing Budget Related to Direct Marketing: 76-100%
Founded: 1972

Equipment for domestic & professional kitchens.

SURE FIT INC

8000 Quarry Rd (Suite C)
Alburtis, PA 18011-9599
Toll Free: (888) 796-0500, FAX: (610) 336-8995, Web Site: www.surefit.net
CEO: Hugh R Rovit
Catalog available online
Direct online sales

Sell furniture covers, home & pet items.

TIDEWATER WORKSHOP

Div. of Modern Boatworks Inc
1 No New York Rd (Suite 15)
Galloway, NJ 08205
Toll Free: (800) 666-8433, E-Mail: help@tidewaterworkshop.com, Web Site: www.tidewaterworkshop.net
CEO: Peter Caporilli
Employees: 35
Primary Market Served: Consumer
Catalog available online
Direct online sales
Advertising/Marketing Budget Related to Direct Marketing: 76-100%
Founded: 1991

Garden furniture catalog.

TIMBERLINE GEODESICS

2015 Blake St
Berkeley, CA 94704
Telephone: (510) 849-4481, Toll Free: (800) 366-3466, FAX: (510) 849-3265, E-Mail: info@domehome.com, Web Site: www.domehome.com
Pres: Robert M. Singer
Conducts Business: U.S., Canada, Pacific Rim
Employees: 5

Primary Market Served: Business & Consumer
Direct online sales
Advertising/Marketing Budget Related to Direct Marketing: 0-25%
Direct Marketing ad budget:
Direct Mail: 25%
Magazines: 75%
Founded: 1969

Sell geodesic dome houses in kit form.

TOUCH OF CLASS CATALOG

Div. of Parke-Bell Ltd Inc
709 W 12th St
Huntingburg, IN 47542-8915
Toll Free: (800) 457-7456, FAX: (812) 683-5921, E-Mail: customerservice@touchofclass.com, Web Site: www.touchofclass.com
Chmn: Carla Parke-Bell
Pres & CEO: Frederick Bell
Admin Asst: Chris Schlachter
Conducts Business: Worldwide
Employees: 225
Primary Market Served: Consumer
Catalog available online
Direct online sales

Mail-order catalog house featuring bed linens, down comforters & custom monogramming.

TURNER GREENHOUSES

Div. of Turner Equipment Co Inc
US Hwy 117 S, PO Box 1260
Goldsboro, NC 27533
Toll Free: (800) 672-4770, E-Mail: customerservice@turnergreenhouses.com, Web Site: www.turnergreenhouses.com
Pres: Gary Smithwick
Conducts Business: U.S.
Employees: 9
Primary Market Served: Consumer
Catalog available online
Direct online sales
Advertising/Marketing Budget Related to Direct Marketing: 76-100%
Founded: 1957
Gross sales or billing: $900,000

Manufacture & sell greenhouses & related equipment & accessories.

U-BILD

Div. of U-Build Inc
821B S Tremont St Ste B
Oceanside, CA 92054-4158
Toll Free: (800) 828-2453, FAX: (760) 754-2356, Web Site: www.ubild.com
Pres: Kevin Taylor
Conducts Business: U.S.
Employees: 7
Primary Market Served: Business & Consumer

Catalog available online
Indirect online sales
Advertising/Marketing Budget Related
to Direct Marketing: 0-25%
Direct Marketing ad budget:
Direct Mail: 20%
Newspapers: 80%
Founded: 1948

Sell woodworking plans.

K VAN BOURGONDIEN & SONS INC

Div. of K. Van Bourgondien of VA,
Inc.
Toll Free: (800) 552-9916, E-Mail:
blooms@dutchbulbs.com, Web Site:
www.dutchbulbs.com
VP Mktg: Fred Van Bourgondien
Conducts Business: U.S.
Employees: 300
Primary Market Served: Business &
Consumer
Catalog available online
Direct online sales
Advertising/Marketing Budget Related
to Direct Marketing: 76-100%
Direct Marketing ad budget:
Direct Mail: 75%
Magazines: 25%
Founded: 1919
Gross sales or billing: $5,000,000

Wholesale & retail catalog of Dutch
bulbs & perennials.

VENEER FACTORY OUTLET

6521 Jacob Dr
Westport, KY 40077
E-Mail: bob@veneerfactoryoutlet.com,
Web Site: veneer-factory-outlet.com
Owner: Bob Morgan
Conducts Business: U.S.
Primary Market Served: Business &
Consumer
Catalog available online
Direct online sales
Advertising/Marketing Budget Related
to Direct Marketing: 0-25%
Direct Marketing ad budget:
Direct Mail: 100%
Founded: 1974

Sell hardwood veneers, raised panel
cabinet doors, inlays, exotic hard-
woods, cane, dowels, carving blocks.

VESEY'S SEEDS LTD

PO Box 9000
Charlottetown, PE, Canada C1A 8K6
Telephone: (902) 368-7333, Toll Free:
(800) 363-7333, FAX: (800) 686-
0329, E-Mail: customerservice@
veseys.com, Web Site: www.veseys.
com
VP: Gerry Simpson
Conducts Business: U.S., Canada

Employees: 60
Primary Market Served: Consumer
Catalog available online
Direct online sales
Advertising/Marketing Budget Related
to Direct Marketing: 51-75%
Direct Marketing ad budget:
Direct Mail: 75%
Magazines: 10%
Newspapers: 5%
TV/Radio: 10%
Founded: 1939
Gross sales or billing: $4,400,000

Mail order seed company offering vegetable & flower seeds.

VILLAGE INTERIORS CARPET ONE

3203 Hwy 70 SE
Newton, NC 28658
Telephone: (704) 325-2304, E-Mail:
sales@carpet-one.net, Web Site:
villlageinteriorshickory.com
VP: Patsy Norris
Conducts Business: U.S.
Employees: 10
Primary Market Served: Business &
Consumer
Advertising/Marketing Budget Related
to Direct Marketing: 0-25%
Founded: 1989
Gross sales or billing: $1,000,000

Retail carpet, vinyl, ceramic, wood &
laminate flooring.

VINTAGE WOOD WORKS

9195 Hwy 34 S
Quinlan, TX 75474
Telephone: (903) 356-2158, FAX:
(903) 356-3023, E-Mail: mail@
vintagewoodworks.com, Web Site:
www.vintagewoodworks.com
Owner: Roland Tatsch
Conducts Business: U.S., Canada
Employees: 50
Primary Market Served: Business &
Consumer
Catalog available online
Direct online sales
Advertising/Marketing Budget Related
to Direct Marketing: 76-100%
Direct Marketing ad budget: $400,000
Direct Mail: 5%
Magazines: 95%
Gross sales or billing: $2,500,000

Handcrafted millwork.

WEST SHORE DISTRIBUTORS

Div. of Curatolo Enterprises Inc
31060 Clemens Rd
Westlake, OH 44145-1005

Telephone: (440) 835-5600, Toll Free:
(800) 344-8141, FAX: (440) 835-
8654, E-Mail: westshore@ameritech.
net, Web Site: www.
westshoreframes.com
Conducts Business: U.S.
Employees: 5
Primary Market Served: Business
Catalog available online
Direct online sales
Advertising/Marketing Budget Related
to Direct Marketing: 76-100%
Founded: 1985

Wholesale picture framing supplies,
commercial framing services, and fine
art giclee printing.

WHITE FLOWER FARM

PO Box 50
Litchfield, CT 06759
Telephone: (860) 496-9624, Toll Free:
(800) 503-9624, FAX: (860) 496-
1418, Web Site: www.
whiteflowerfarm.com
Owner: Eliot Wadsworth II
Conducts Business: U.S.
Employees: 250
Primary Market Served: Business &
Consumer
Catalog available online
Direct online sales
Advertising/Marketing Budget Related
to Direct Marketing: 0-25%
Founded: 1950

Nursery marketer of perennials, shrubs,
annuals, tools & garden supplies.

GILBERT H WILD & SON INC

2944 State Hwy 37
Reeds, MO 64859
Telephone: (417) 548-3514, Toll Free:
(888) 449-4537, FAX: (417) 548-
6831, E-Mail: gregj@gilberthwild.
com, Web Site: www.gilberthwild.
com
Pres: Gregory P. Jones
Conducts Business: U.S.
Primary Market Served: Consumer
Catalog available online
Direct online sales
Advertising/Marketing Budget Related
to Direct Marketing: 76-100%
Founded: 1885

Plants: daylilies, iris & peonies.

WILDSEED FARMS

100 Legacy Dr, PO Box 3000
Fredericksburg, TX 78624
Toll Free: (800) 848-0078, FAX: (830)
990-8090, E-Mail: orders1@
wildseedfarms.com, Web Site: www.
wildseedfarms.com
Pres: John Thomas

Primary Market Served: Business &
   Consumer
Catalog available online
Advertising/Marketing Budget Related
   to Direct Marketing: 26-50%
Founded: 1983
Gross sales or billing: $5,718,407

Seed company.

WILLIAMS-SONOMA INC

3250 Van Ness Ave
San Francisco, CA 94109-1012
Telephone: (415) 421-7900, Toll Free:
   (800) 840-2591, Web Site: www.
   williams-sonomainc.com
Pres: Laura J Alber
CFO & Exec VP: Julie P Whalen
Exec VP, Chief Mktg Officer: Patrick
   J. Connolly
Conducts Business: U.S.
Employees: 38,800
Primary Market Served: Consumer
Catalog available online
Direct online sales
Advertising/Marketing Budget Related
   to Direct Marketing: 0-25%
Founded: 1956
Gross sales or billing: $3,727,500,000

Retail & mail order sales of cooking &
serving equipment, tabletop accessories
& bed/bath products.

WILLIAMSBURG
BLACKSMITHS INC

26 Williams St
Williamsburg, MA 01096
Telephone: (413) 268-7341, Toll Free:
   (800) 248-1776, FAX: (413) 268-
   9317, E-Mail:
   williamsburgblacksmiths@gmail.
   com, Web Site: www.
   williamsburgblacksmiths.com
Conducts Business: U.S., Canada
Primary Market Served: Business &
   Consumer
Founded: 1840

Reproductions of early American
wrought iron hardware.

WINSTON MARKETING
GROUP

PO Box 7985
Elk Grove Village, IL 60009-7985
Telephone: (620) 584-8000, FAX:
   (847) 350-5701, Web Site: www.
   collectionset.com
Pres: Todd Lustbader
Primary Market Served: Consumer
Catalog available online
Direct online sales

Multichannel merchandising company.

WRISCO INDUSTRIES INC

355 Hiatt Dr (Suite B)

Palm Beach Gardens, FL 33418-7106
Telephone: (561) 626-5700, Toll Free:
   (800) 627-2646, FAX: (561) 627-
   3574, Web Site: www.wrisco.com
Owner: Jim Monastra
Pres: Mark Davidson
Division Mgr: Roman Bender
Conducts Business: Worldwide
Employees: 95
Primary Market Served: Business &
   Consumer
Catalog available online
Indirect online sales
Advertising/Marketing Budget Related
   to Direct Marketing: 0-25%
Direct Marketing ad budget: $100,000
Direct Mail: $70,000
Magazines: $10,000
Telephone: $20,000
Founded: 1916

Manufacture & sell aluminum products.

AGCO INC

2782 Simpson Cir
Norcross, GA 30071
Telephone: (770) 447-6990, FAX:
(770) 446-2102, Web Site: www.
agcomarble.com
Pres: Larry Pulliam
VP: Gary Pulliam
HR Exec: Paula Wedding
Primary Market Served: Business &
Consumer
Catalog available online

Manufacturer of bath tiles.

ABBEON CAL INC

123 Gray Ave
Santa Barbara, CA 93101-1809
Telephone: (805) 966-0810, Toll Free:
(800) 922-0977, FAX: (805) 966-
7659, E-Mail: abbeoncal@abbeon.
com, Web Site: www.abbeon.com
Pres: A.J. Wertheim
Conducts Business: U.S.
Employees: 11
Primary Market Served: Business
Catalog available online
Direct online sales
Advertising/Marketing Budget Related
to Direct Marketing: 76-100%
Direct Marketing ad budget:
$1,000,000
Direct Mail: 100%
Founded: 1970
Gross sales or billing: $2,000,000

Marketer of industrial products through
350 page catalog.

ACTIVE WEB GROUP

Subs. of Lab Safety Supply
30 Oser Ave (Suite 500)
Hauppauge, NY 11788
Toll Free: (800) 978-3417, FAX: (800)
719-4402, E-Mail: info@
activewebgroup.com, Web Site:
www.activewebgroup.com
Pres: Pat Norton
Sr SEO & Dir Bus Devel: David Mon-
talvo
Conducts Business: U.S., Canada
Primary Market Served: Business
Catalog available online
Direct online sales

Full-service web marketing agency
specializing in website design and development, search engine optimization,
pay per click management, e-commerce solutions, and email marketing.

ADAMS MANUFACTURING CO

RP-NFOA
9790 Midwest Ave
Cleveland, OH 44125-2497
Telephone: (216) 587-6801, FAX:
(216) 587-6807, E-Mail: adamsx@
att.net, Web Site: www.
adamsmanufacturing.com
Pres: Marty Schonberger Sr.
VP: Ruth Schonberger
VP Pur: M. Schonberger Jr.
Sls Mgr: J. Dubasek
Primary Market Served: Business
Founded: 1945

Manufacture heating equipment & sell
to wholesale distributors. Gas & oil residential & commercial warm air furna-
ces, gas & oil burners, air cleaners &
gas conversion heaters.

ADVANCED MACHINERY

2 McCullough Dr
New Castle, DE 19720
Telephone: (302) 322-2226, Toll Free:
(800) 727-6553, FAX: (866) 686-
1615, E-Mail: jean@advmachinery.
com, Web Site: www.advmachinery.
com
Pres: Wolfgang Derke
VP, Sls & Mktg: Hanns Derke
Conducts Business: U.S., Canada
Employees: 10
Primary Market Served: Business &
Consumer
Catalog available online
Direct online sales
Advertising/Marketing Budget Related
to Direct Marketing: 76-100%
Direct Marketing ad budget:
Direct Mail: 45%
Magazines: 40%
Telephone: 15%
Founded: 1975
Gross sales or billing: $1,600,000

Specialty woodcrafting & woodworking equipment for upscale hobbyists &
professionals.

AGRI DRAIN CORP

1462 340th St
Adair, IA 50002
Telephone: (641) 742-5211, Toll Free:
(800) 232-4742, FAX: (800) 282-
3353, (641) 742-5222, E-Mail: info@
agridrain.com, Web Site: www.
agridrain.com
Pres: Charlie Schafer
Sls & Mktg Mgr: Lisa Newby
Employees: 54
Primary Market Served: Business
Gross sales or billing: $4,600,000

Manufacturer of water management
products.

AIR CHEK INC

RP-NFOA
PO Box 2000
Naples, NC 28760-5000
Telephone: (828) 684-0893, Toll Free:
(800) AIR-CHEK, FAX: (828) 684-
8498, Web Site: www.radon.com
Cust Svc Mgr: Nancy Fairchild
Conducts Business: U.S.
Employees: 12
Primary Market Served: Business &
Consumer
Advertising/Marketing Budget Related
to Direct Marketing: 0-25%
Direct Marketing ad budget:
Direct Mail: 30%
Magazines: 15%
Newspapers: 15%
Telephone: 40%
Founded: 1985

Manufactures & analyzes radon test
kits. Sell to the National Safety Council, State & Federal agencies, as well as
private citizens & major corporations.
Radon kits are used to determine the radon levels in schools, workplaces &
homes all over the U.S.

ALFA AESAR-A JOHNSON MATTHEY CO

Div. of Johnson Matthey
26 Partridge Rd
Ward Hill, MA 01835-8099
Toll Free: (800) 343-0660, FAX: (800)
322-4757, E-Mail: info@alfa.com,
Web Site: www.alfa.com
Controller: Kimberly Keniston
VP Bus Devel: Barry Singelais
Mktg Mgr: Anthony Pietrantoni
Bulk & Specialty Sls Dir: Gwilym
Clarke
Mktg Mgr & Catalog Sls Mgr: John
Shirley
Prod Mgr: Aaron Frederick
Acctg Supv: Rosalie Berard
Mktg Specialist: Pamela Poulin
Credit Analyst: Allison Corcoran
Conducts Business: Worldwide
Employees: 79
Primary Market Served: Business
Catalog available online
Indirect online sales
Advertising/Marketing Budget Related
to Direct Marketing: 26-50%
Direct Marketing ad budget:
Direct Mail: $250,000
Magazines: $30,000
Telephone: $20,000
Founded: 1991

Catalog sales operation featuring research chemicals & materials for the
worldwide research community.

AMERICAN SCIENCE & SURPLUS

7410 N Lehigh Ave
Niles, IL 60714-4024
Telephone: (847) 647-0020, Toll Free: (888) SCI-PLUS, FAX: (847) 647-5010, E-Mail: info@sciplus.com, Web Site: www.sciplus.com
Pres: Philip E. Cable
Conducts Business: U.S.
Employees: 70
Primary Market Served: Business & Consumer
Catalog available online
Direct online sales
Advertising/Marketing Budget Related to Direct Marketing: 76-100%
Direct Marketing ad budget:
Direct Mail: 90%
Magazines: 10%
Founded: 1937

Unusual surplus items at 50-90% discount from original price.

AMERICAN TRIM

Div. of American Trim
1005 W Grand Ave
Lima, OH 45801
Telephone: (419) 228-1145, FAX: (419) 996-4850, E-Mail: sales@amtrim.com, Web Site: www.amtrim.com
CEO: Jeffrey A. Hawk
VP & Chief Technical Officer: Rick Pfeifer
Pres & COO: Bob Stead
Conducts Business: U.S. & Mexico
Employees: 90
Primary Market Served: Business
Catalog available online
Founded: 1970
Gross sales or billing: $230,000,000

Plastic injected molded parts.

AMES TAPING TOOL SYSTEM INC

Subs. of AXIA Enterprise Inc
1380 Beverage Dr Ste W
Stone Mountain, GA 30083-2133
Telephone: (770) 243-2647, Toll Free: (800) 303-1827, FAX: (770) 243-2658, Web Site: www.amestools.com
Pres: Robert G. Zdravecky
Mktg Mgr: Ford Owen
VP Sales: James T Mathers
Conducts Business: U.S., Canada
Primary Market Served: Business
Advertising/Marketing Budget Related to Direct Marketing: 76-100%

Feature quality tools & accessories in 22 page catalog to meet the needs of both worker & contractor in the drywall field.

ANALYTICAL MEASUREMENTS

22 Mountain View Dr
Chester, NJ 07930-3104
Toll Free: (800) 635-5580, FAX: (973) 399-1446, E-Mail: phmeter@bellatlantic.net, Web Site: www.analyticalmeasurements.com
Pres: W. Richard Adey
Conducts Business: U.S., Canada, S. America, Singapore
Employees: 7
Primary Market Served: Business
Catalog available online
Indirect online sales
Advertising/Marketing Budget Related to Direct Marketing: 76-100%
Direct Marketing ad budget: $100,000
Direct Mail: 40%
Magazines: 40%
Online: 20%
Founded: 1948
Gross sales or billing: $1,000,000

Manufacture Ph & ORP meters, recorders & controllers which are then sold to plants, schools & laboratories.

ARBILL SAFETY PRODUCTS

aka Arbill Industries, Inc
10450 Drummond Rd
Philadelphia, PA 19154
Telephone: (215) 632-2000, Toll Free: (800) 523-5367, FAX: (800) 426-5808, E-Mail: orders@arbill.com, Web Site: www.arbill.com
Chmn Bd: Barry Bickman
Pres & CEO: Julie Bickman Copeland
CFO: Sharon Miller
Conducts Business: U.S.
Employees: 75
Primary Market Served: Business
Catalog available online
Direct online sales
Advertising/Marketing Budget Related to Direct Marketing: 0-25%
Direct Marketing ad budget:
Direct Mail: 40%
Magazines: 10%
Telephone: 50%
Founded: 1945
Gross sales or billing: $4,000,000

Safety products to businesses: gloves, respirators, hearing, head, eye & face protection & clothing, safety compliance, training & services.

ARENT FOX LLP

1050 Connecticut Ave NW
Washington, DC 20036
Telephone: (202) 715-8582, Web Site: www.arentfox.com
Primary Market Served: Business & Consumer

ASTRO AIR, LP

1653 N Bolton St, Jacksonville, TX 75766-5103
Subs. of Luvata
1653 N Bolton
Jacksonville, TX 75766
Telephone: (903) 586-3691, FAX: (903) 589-8094, E-Mail: sales@astroair.com, Web Site: www.astroair.com
Pres & CEO (Luvata): John-Peter Leesi
VP: Eric Tate
Conducts Business: U.S., Canada
Employees: 195
Primary Market Served: Business & Consumer
Catalog available online
Advertising/Marketing Budget Related to Direct Marketing: 0-25%
Direct Marketing ad budget: $20,000
Direct Mail: 20%
Magazines: 80%
Founded: 1972
Gross sales or billing: $20,000,000

Manufacturer of condensers, heating and cooling coils (tube & finishing) for HVACR industry.

BAILEY'S INC

1210 Commerce Ave (Suite 8)
Woodland, CA 95776
Toll Free: (800) 322-4539, FAX: (530) 406-0895, E-Mail: baileys@bbaileys.com, Web Site: www.baileys-online.com
Pres: Nik Bailey

Supplier of chainsaws & accessories, work clothing, arborist supplies & small scale forestry equipment.

BASIC ADHESIVES INC

Also dba Dritac
60 Webro Rd
Clifton, NJ 07012
Toll Free: (800) 394-9310, FAX: (973) 614-9099, E-Mail: info@basicadhesives.com, Web Site: www.basicadhesives.com
Pres: Yale Block
Exec VP: Myrna Block
Conducts Business: Worldwide
Employees: 60
Primary Market Served: Business
Catalog available online
Founded: 1960
Gross sales or billing: $11,000,000

Industrial, water-based & solvent adhesives: laminating, pressure sensitive, cohesive, heat activated, remoistenable, etc.

BATTERY PROS INC

dba Pro Battery
161 1st St

Horseshoe Beach, FL 32648-0054
Telephone: (352) 498-2662, Toll Free:
(800) 451-7171, FAX: (352) 498-
2482, E-Mail: sales@probattery.com,
Web Site: www.probattery.com
Pres & CEO: Patty Novak
VP: Maria Arce
Conducts Business: U.S., Canada
Employees: 25
Primary Market Served: Business
Advertising/Marketing Budget Related
to Direct Marketing: 76-100%
Direct Marketing ad budget:
Magazines: 100%
Founded: 1980
Gross sales or billing: $3,500,000
Batteries & battery assemblies.

BELL & HOWELL LTD

Subs. of Bell & Howell Co
5650 Yonge St (Suite 1802)
North York, ON, Canada M2M 4G3
Telephone: (416) 746-2200, FAX:
(416) 228-2439, Web Site: www.
bellhowell.com
CFO: Leader Wong
Sls Dir & Mktg Mgr: Eric Pascoe
Conducts Business: U.S.
Primary Market Served: Business &
Consumer

Business equipment manufacturer of
Phillipsburg inserters & Documail sorting systems.

BELL PERFORMANCE INC

1340 Bennett Dr
Longwood, FL 32750-7623
Telephone: (407) 834-3690, Toll Free:
(800) 659-2355, FAX: (407) 767-
8685, E-Mail: info@
bellperformance.net, Web Site:
www.bellperformance.net
Pres: Glenn Williams
CEO: Ola Williams-Milam
Exec Sales Admin: Rhonda Stutes
Technical Sales Dir: Erik Bjornstad
Conducts Business: U.S., Canada, Eu-
rope, Asia, Pacific Rim
Primary Market Served: Business &
Consumer
Catalog available online
Direct online sales
Advertising/Marketing Budget Related
to Direct Marketing: 0-25%
Direct Marketing ad budget:
Direct Mail: 25%
Magazines: 15%
Telephone: 60%
Founded: 1909

Fuel conditioners for gasoline, diesel &
fuel oil. All purpose grease, oil en-
hancer for motors, gearboxes, transmis-
sions, bearings & compressors.

BETTER TOOLS FOR INDUSTRY

9525 Pathway St
Santee, CA 92071
Telephone: (619) 562-3071, FAX:
(619) 562-0592, Web Site: www.bti-
tool.com
Pres: Jim Barnhill
VP, Sls & Mktg: Chris Barnhill
Conducts Business: U.S.
Employees: 32
Primary Market Served: Business &
Consumer
Catalog available online
Direct online sales
Founded: 1967

Manufacturer of specialty & contract
tooling & hand tools & pneumatic shop
vacuums & stainless hex wrenches.

BLAINE WINDOW HARDWARE INC

17319 Blaine Dr
Hagerstown, MD 21740
Telephone: (301) 797-6500, Toll Free:
(800) 678-1919, FAX: (888) 250-
3960, E-Mail: info@blainewindow.
com, Web Site: www.blainewindow.
com
Pres: Margaret Blaine
Adv & Mktg Mgr: Elaine Swartz
Conducts Business: U.S.
Employees: 55
Primary Market Served: Business &
Consumer
Catalog available online
Founded: 1954

Obsolete, hard-to-find & current replacement hardware for windows,
doors, patio doors, lockers. Also custom made screens, toilet partitions &
components.

BRIDGE CITY TOOL WORKS INC

5820 NE Hassalo St, Portland, OR
97213-3644
Div. of Fine Tools, LLC
2545 SW Spring Garden St (Suite 120)
Portland, OR 97219-3942
Telephone: (503) 282-6997, Toll Free:
(800) 253-3332, FAX: (503) 287-
1085, E-Mail: jjeconomaki@
comcast.net, Web Site: www.
bridgecitytools.com
Pres: John Economaki
Mktg Mgr: Ming Sok
Conducts Business: Worldwide
Employees: 25
Primary Market Served: Consumer
Catalog available online
Indirect online sales
Advertising/Marketing Budget Related
to Direct Marketing: 26-50%

Founded: 1983
Manufacturer of precision layout tools
& distributor of high quality woodworking layout tools.

BROOKS EQUIPMENT CO

10926 David Taylor Dr (Ste 300)
Charlotte, NC 28262
Telephone: (704) 596-9438, Toll Free:
(800) 826-3473, FAX: (704) 596-
1096, Web Site: www.
brooksequipment.com
VP, Commun: Kathryn Mahan
Mktg Coord: Carole Seagle
Conducts Business: U.S.
Employees: 400
Primary Market Served: Business &
Consumer
Catalog available online
Direct online sales
Advertising/Marketing Budget Related
to Direct Marketing: 51-75%
Direct Marketing ad budget: $50,000
Founded: 1941
Gross sales or billing: $90,000,000

Wholesaler in the fire equipment district market, supply chain management
in fire and police equipment to municipalities and individuals.

BURDEN SALES CO

dba Surplus Center.
1015 W O St
Lincoln, NE 68528-1322
Telephone: (402) 474-4055, Toll Free:
(800) 488-3407, FAX: (402) 474-
5198, Web Site: www.burdensales.
com
Pres: David Burden
VP, Sls & Mktg: Chris Cole
Sls Mgr: Jeff Atkinson
Conducts Business: U.S.
Employees: 40
Primary Market Served: Business &
Consumer
Catalog available online
Indirect online sales
Advertising/Marketing Budget Related
to Direct Marketing: 76-100%
Founded: 1933

Mail order sales of hydraulics, air compressors, winches, chemical spraying
equipment & alarm systems.

C&H DISTRIBUTORS LLC

770 S 70th St, PO Box 14770
Milwaukee, WI 53214-0770
Telephone: (414) 443-1700, Toll Free:
(888) 316-2223, FAX: (414) 443-
9213, E-Mail: customerservice@
chdist.com, Web Site: www.chdist.
com
Pres & CEO: David McKeon
CFO: Dan Paruzynski

VP, Catalog & Creative: Marvin D. Mason
VP, Mdsg: Steve J. Preiss
VP, Customer Svc: Anita Kowalski
Conducts Business: U.S., Canada
Employees: 175
Primary Market Served: Business & Consumer
Catalog available online
Direct online sales
Gross sales or billing: $158,000,000

Mail order distributor of industrial products to warehouses, offices, stores, factories, institutions. Products include storage shelving, shop furniture, parts bins, dock equipment, hoists, winches, iron handlers, hand trucks, office equipment & safety aids. Branches in Reno, NV; Dallas, TX; Atlanta, GA; Dayton, NJ; Milwaukee, WI.

C&S SALES INC
150 Carpenter Ave
Wheeling, IL 60090
Telephone: (847) 541-0710, Toll Free: (800) 292-7711, FAX: (847) 541-9904, E-Mail: sales@cs-sales.com, Web Site: www.cs_sales.com
Pres: James Cecchin
Gen Mgr: David Jonesi
Asst Gen Mgr: Paula Asher
Conducts Business: U.S., Canada
Employees: 5
Primary Market Served: Business & Consumer
Catalog available online
Advertising/Marketing Budget Related to Direct Marketing: 0-25%
Founded: 1985
Gross sales or billing: $2,000,000

Electronic testing equipment & educational material.

CAIG LABORATORIES INC
12200 Thatcher Ct
Poway, CA 92064
Telephone: (858) 486-8388, FAX: (858) 486-8398, E-Mail: caig123@caig.com, Web Site: www.caig.com
Pres: Mark Lohkemper
Corp Sls: Diane James
Mktg Mgr: Susan Prenatt
Conducts Business: Worldwide
Employees: 12
Primary Market Served: Business & Consumer
Catalog available online
Direct online sales
Advertising/Marketing Budget Related to Direct Marketing: 26-50%
Direct Marketing ad budget:
Direct Mail: 10%
Magazines: 90%

Founded: 1956
Manufacturer of high quality, environmentally-safe, electronic chemicals & soldering apparatus. Products include: gold conditioners, lubricants, preservatives, deoxidizers, anti-static sprays, degreasers, solder pots & controls. Products sold to a variety of industries requiring clean electrical connections.

CALBIOCHEM-NOVABIOCHEM CORP
Div. of EM Industrial & Subs. of Merck
10394 Pacific Ctr Ct
San Diego, CA 92121-4340
Telephone: (858) 450-9600, Toll Free: (800) 854-3417, FAX: (858) 453-3552, E-Mail: customerservice@emdbioscience.com, Web Site: www.calbiochem.com
Pres, CEO & Chmn: Richard T. Clark
Sr VP: Willie A. Deese
Sr VP, HR: Mirian Graddick Weir
Dir: Douglas Brown
Conducts Business: U.S., Germany, U.K., Switzerland, Australia, Japan
Employees: 260
Primary Market Served: Business & Consumer
Catalog available online
Direct online sales
Advertising/Marketing Budget Related to Direct Marketing: 0-25%
Direct Marketing ad budget:
Direct Mail: 80%
Magazines: 15%
Telephone: 5%
Founded: 1952
Gross sales or billing: $50,000,000

Four brands (CALBIOCHEM, NOVA-BIOCHEM, Oncogene Research Products & Novagen) encompass over 10,000 reagents & tools for the life sciences academic research, biotechnology, pharmaceutical & industrial markets. Niche catalogs with in-depth technical information, reviews, structures & references are offered in Signal Transduction, Apoptosis, Neuroscience/Drug Discovery, Glycobiology, Combinatorial Chemistry & Molecular Biology.

CAMELOT ENTERPRISES
8234 199th Ave
Bristol, WI 53104-9701
Telephone: (262) 857-2695
Pres: James R. Zinkel
VP: Sandra L. Zinkel
Conducts Business: U.S.
Employees: 4
Primary Market Served: Business & Consumer

Advertising/Marketing Budget Related to Direct Marketing: 76-100%
Direct Marketing ad budget: $4,000
Direct Mail: 10%
Magazines: 80%
Newspapers: 5%
Telephone: 5%
Founded: 1983

Industrial & automotive fasteners & tools.

CAMPBELL TOOLS CO
125 N Tecumseh Rd
Springfield, OH 45504-3404
Telephone: (937) 882-6716, FAX: (937) 882-6648, E-Mail: campbell@campbelltools.com, Web Site: www.campbelltools.com
Pres: Leo Foster
Member: Renee Morningstar
Conducts Business: U.S., Canada
Employees: 6
Primary Market Served: Business & Consumer
Catalog available online
Indirect online sales

Sell machinery, precision tools & shop supplies.

CAROLINA BIOLOGICAL SUPPLY CO
2700 York Rd
Burlington, NC 27215-3387
Toll Free: (800) 334-5551, (800) 222-7112, E-Mail: carolina@carolina.com, Web Site: www.carolina.com
VP, Operations: Ray Gladden
VP Bus Devel: Daniel E. James
VP, Fin: Leon Joyce
Adv Dir: Harry L. Shoffner
Conducts Business: Worldwide
Employees: 450
Primary Market Served: Business
Catalog available online
Direct online sales
Advertising/Marketing Budget Related to Direct Marketing: 76-100%
Direct Marketing ad budget:
Direct Mail: 90%
Magazines: 5%
Online: 5%
Founded: 1927

Direct marketer of science teaching materials & supplies to schools.

CENTAUR FORGE LLC
117 N Spring St
Burlington, WI 53105-1532
Telephone: (262) 763-9175, Toll Free: (800) 666-9175, FAX: (262) 763-8350, E-Mail: info@centaurforge.com, Web Site: www.centaurforge.com
Pres: Maj Ernest Lifynski

Gen Mgr: Tom Riddle
Conducts Business: Worldwide
Employees: 9
Primary Market Served: Business
Founded: 1960

Blacksmith's & horseshoer's equipment & supplies, including books & videos.

CHEM-TAINER INDUSTRIES INC

361 Neptune Ave
North Babylon, NY 11704
Telephone: (631) 661-8300, Toll Free: (800) 275-2436, (800) ASK-CHEM, FAX: (631) 661-8209, E-Mail: sales@chemtainer.com, Web Site: www.chemtainer.com
Pres: Robert Devine
VP: Anthony Lamb
Conducts Business: U.S., Europe, South America
Employees: 256
Primary Market Served: Business & Consumer
Catalog available online
Indirect online sales
Advertising/Marketing Budget Related to Direct Marketing: 26-50%
Direct Marketing ad budget: $150,000
Direct Mail: 5%
Magazines: 70%
Online: 15%
TV/Radio: 10%
Founded: 1958
Gross sales or billing: $32,000,000

Manufacturer of wholesale roto-molded plastic industrial containers and products.

CLINGZ INC

541 Laser Dr NE
Rio Rancho, NM 87124-4518
Telephone: (505) 892-2500, Toll Free: (800) 795-1415, FAX: (505) 892-2510, Web Site: www.clingz.com
Primary Market Served: Consumer

COLLIDER MEDIA

619 Congress Ave Ste B
Austin, TX 78701-3024
Telephone: (512) 745-8070, Web Site: collidermedia.com
Primary Market Served: Consumer
Founded: 2009

WM F COMLY & SON INC

1825 E Boston St
Philadelphia, PA 19125-1201
Telephone: (215) 634-2500, Web Site: www.comly.com
VP & Treasurer: Daniel F Comly
Primary Market Served: Consumer

Auctioneers & appraisers.

COMPASS ELECTRONICS

47920 NW Waldheim Way, Forest Grove, OR 97116-7414-POST
397 SW Stringtown Rd
Forest Grove, OR 97116
Telephone: (503) 357-2111, FAX: (503) 357-2111
Pres: Steve Garriss
Primary Market Served: Business & Consumer

Manufacture & repair electronic metal detectors.

CONSOLIDATED PLASTICS CO INC

4700 Prosper Rd
Stow, OH 44224-1068
Telephone: (330) 425-3900, Toll Free: (800) 362-1000, FAX: (330) 425-3333, Web Site: www.consolidatedplastics.com
Pres: Brent Harland
Sr VP, Mktg: Gregg Gilkey
Conducts Business: U.S.
Employees: 100
Primary Market Served: Business & Consumer
Catalog available online
Direct online sales
Advertising/Marketing Budget Related to Direct Marketing: 76-100%

Business-to-business catalog marketer of plastic products for industry & laboratories including bottles, containers, bags & commercial matting & carpeting.

CONTINENTAL SUPPLY INC

7505 James Dr
Cleveland, OH 44133
Telephone: (440) 864-6231, Toll Free: (800) 672-0321, FAX: (888) 672-9808
Pres: Bruce Abbott
Primary Market Served: Business & Consumer
Advertising/Marketing Budget Related to Direct Marketing: 76-100%
Direct Marketing ad budget:
Direct Mail: 95%
Magazines: 5%

Janitorial & safety supply company.

CORONIS BUILDING SYSTEMS INC

92 Columbus Jobstown Rd, PO Box 200
Columbus, NJ 08022
Telephone: (609) 723-2600, FAX: (609) 723-6700, E-Mail: coronis@trussframe.com, Web Site: www.trussframe.com
Pres: Emanuel A. Coronis Jr
Conducts Business: Worldwide

Employees: 21
Primary Market Served: Business & Consumer
Direct Marketing ad budget:
Magazines: 50%
Telephone: 50%
Founded: 1956
Gross sales or billing: $2,000,000

Trussframes pre-engineered structural steel building framing for commercial, industrial, agricultural & recreational projects.

CREATIVE BANNER ASSEMBLIES

2730 Nevada Ave
Minneapolis, MN 55427-2807
Telephone: (763) 566-1118, Web Site: www.creativebanner.com
Primary Market Served: Consumer

CREATIVE LEARNING SYSTEMS INC

1140 Boston Ave (Unit A)
Longmont, CO 80501-5890
Telephone: (303) 772-6400, Toll Free: (800) 458-2880, FAX: (303) 772-6422, Web Site: www.clsinc.com
CEO: Robert McIntosh
Pres: Brick Kani
VP, Opers: Bret Vedder
Mktg Dir: Kyle Hudson
Primary Market Served: Business

Cutting edge technology products, especially for schools.

CRYSTEK CORP

12730 Commonwealth Dr
Fort Myers, FL 33913
Telephone: (239) 561-3311, Toll Free: (800) 237-3061, FAX: (239) 561-1025, E-Mail: sales@crystek.com, Web Site: www.crystek.com
Pres & CEO: Anthony Mastropole
Dir: Mark S. Stearns
Dir Sls, West Coast: Daniel Loomis
Dir Sls, Miami: Maria Guerra
Sls Mgr: Jim Carrasco
Conducts Business: U.S.
Employees: 25
Primary Market Served: Business
Catalog available online
Direct online sales
Advertising/Marketing Budget Related to Direct Marketing: 76-100%
Direct Marketing ad budget: $150,000
Founded: 1958
Gross sales or billing: $5,000,000

Manufacture crystals & crystal oscillators.

DARCO INTERNATIONAL INC

810 Memorial Blvd

Huntington, WV 25701-7002
Telephone: (304) 522-4883, Toll Free: (800) 999-8866, FAX: (304) 522-0037, Web Site: www.darcointernational.com

Provide post-op, trauma & wound care solutions to the global foot & ankle community.

DATUM TIMING, TEST & MEASUREMENT

34 Tozer Rd
Beverly, MA 01915
Telephone: (978) 927-8220, FAX: (978) 927-4099, E-Mail: wriley@datum.com, Web Site: www.datum.com
Pres: Paul E. Baia
VP Sls & Mktg: David Briggs
Prod Mgr Instruments: Karl Reuning
Prod Mgr Instruments: Fred Zwart
Mktg Mgr: Doug Lowrie
Conducts Business: Worldwide
Employees: 100
Primary Market Served: Business
Catalog available online
Indirect online sales
Advertising/Marketing Budget Related to Direct Marketing: 51-75%
Direct Marketing ad budget:
Direct Mail: 40%
Magazines: 50%
Telephone: 10%
Founded: 1970
Gross sales or billing: $33,000,000

Electronic instruments-precision clocks (atomic, space & hi-rel), frequency sources, quartz oscillators & military electronics. Active hydrogen masers & atomic clocks (cesium-subidium).

DIAMOND MACHINING TECHNOLOGY

85 Hayes Memorial Dr
Marlborough, MA 01752-1831
Telephone: (508) 481-5944, Toll Free: (800) 666-4368, FAX: (508) 485-3924, Web Site: www.dmtsharp.com
VP, Mktg & Sls: William E. Fletcher
VP Sls: Daniel Ekberg
Pres: Mark Brandon
Conducts Business: Worldwide
Employees: 45
Primary Market Served: Consumer
Catalog available online
Direct online sales
Advertising/Marketing Budget Related to Direct Marketing: 0-25%
Founded: 1976
Gross sales or billing: $4,000,000

Manufacturer of handheld diamond and unbreakable ceramic sharpeners sold to distributors & retailers in gourmet, hardware, skiing, hunting, fishing, woodworking, industrial & commercial markets.

DINYARI INC

500 Phelan Ave
San Jose, CA 95112-2506
Telephone: (408) 289-5400, Toll Free: (888) 997-0400, Web Site: www.dinyari.com
Pres: Farbod Dinyari
Founded: 1989

DISCOVERY

12 Christopher Way Ste 202
Eatontown, NJ 07724-3331
Telephone: (732) 933-1899, Web Site: www.discoveryco.com
Primary Market Served: Consumer

DO-IT CORP

1201 Blue Star Hwy, PO Box 592
South Haven, MI 49090-0592
Telephone: (269) 637-1121, Toll Free: (800) 426-4822, FAX: (269) 637-7223, E-Mail: sales@do-it.com, Web Site: www.do-it.com
Pres: Mark McClendon
Sls Mgr: Ron MacIntyre
Fin Mgr: Mary Colvin
Conducts Business: U.S., Canada, UK, Mexico, Hong Kong
Employees: 70
Primary Market Served: Business & Consumer
Catalog available online
Direct online sales
Advertising/Marketing Budget Related to Direct Marketing: 0-25%
Founded: 1973
Gross sales or billing: $10,000,000

Manufacturer of plastic hang tabs.

DOUBLEVERIFY

575 8th Ave (fl 7)
New York, NY 10018-3186
Telephone: (212) 631-2111, Web Site: www.doubleverify.com
CEO & Pres: Wayne Gattinella
Founder & Chmn: Oren Netzer
COO: Matt McLaughlin
CFO: Jack McClunn
Sr VP Sales & Mktg: Mark Pearlstein
Sr VP Sales Opers: Karen Gross
Primary Market Served: Consumer

DOZIER EQUIPMENT INTERNATIONAL

770 S 70th St, PO Box 88031
Milwaukee, WI 53288
Toll Free: (800) 251-1234, FAX: (800) 336-6608, Web Site: www.dozierequip.com
Pres: David Stark

Mktg Mgr: Amy Tartarsky
Conducts Business: Worldwide
Primary Market Served: Business & Consumer
Advertising/Marketing Budget Related to Direct Marketing: 76-100%
Direct Marketing ad budget:
Direct Mail: 80%
Magazines: 10%
Telephone: 10%
Founded: 1952

Headquartered in Nashville, TN with over 1800 distributors selling dumpers, drum handlers, hoist & crane attachments & all material handling products.

E-PIPECONNECTION

Div. of PVC Plastics Co Inc
4406 E Morgan Ave
Evansville, IN 47715-2254
Telephone: (812) 474-4529, Toll Free: (800) 262-4300, FAX: (812) 474-4531, E-Mail: sales@e-pipeconnection.com, Web Site: www.e-pipeconnection.com
Pres & CEO: William D. Smith
VP: Jeff Eckels
Catalog Mgr: Mark Moore
Conducts Business: U.S.
Employees: 50
Primary Market Served: Business & Consumer
Catalog available online
Indirect online sales
Advertising/Marketing Budget Related to Direct Marketing: 51-75%
Direct Marketing ad budget:
Direct Mail: 90%
Telephone: 10%
Founded: 1990
Gross sales or billing: $12,000,000

Industrial plastic distribution, such as plastic pipe valves, fittings & related products.

EDMUND OPTICS INC

101 E Gloucester Pike
Barrington, NJ 08007-1331
Telephone: (856) 573-6250, Toll Free: (800) 363-1992, FAX: (856) 573-6295, E-Mail: sales@edmundoptic.com, Web Site: www.edmundoptics.com
Pres: John Stack
CEO: Robert M. Edmund
Dir Sls: Wallace Latimer
Chief Scientist: Jim Michalski
Exec VP Mktg & Commun: Marisa Edmund
Conducts Business: Worldwide
Employees: 300
Primary Market Served: Business & Consumer
Catalog available online
Direct online sales

Advertising/Marketing Budget Related
to Direct Marketing: 51-75%
Founded: 1942

Optics & optical instruments for industry & research.

89 DEGREES
25 Burlington Mall Rd (Suite 610)
Burlington, MA 01803-4100
Telephone: (781) 221-5400, Web Site:
www.89degrees.com
Pres: Phil Hussey
VP Strategic Mktg Svcs: Laura Saati
VP Sales & Mktg: Bill Carino
VP Creative Svcs: Tim Ryan
Primary Market Served: Business &
Consumer

ELEMENTAL SCIENTIFIC LLC
PO Box 754, Manitowoc, WI 54221-0754
Storefront is Galaxy Science & Hobby
Center, Inc
1607 N Richmond St
Appleton, WI 54911-3553
Telephone: (920) 882-1277, E-Mail:
info@elementalscientific.net, Web
Site: www.elementalscientific.net
Pres: Wade Van Ryzin
Conducts Business: U.S.
Employees: 3
Primary Market Served: Business &
Consumer
Indirect online sales
Gross sales or billing: $500,000
Scientific chemicals & apparatus.

ELLERBUSCH INSTRUMENT CO
4505 Vine St
Cincinnati, OH 45217-1617
Telephone: (513) 641-1800, Toll Free:
(800) 582-2644, FAX: (513) 641-4360, E-Mail: info@ellerbusch.com,
Web Site: www.ellerbusch.com
Pres: Michael Ellerbusch
Conducts Business: U.S.
Employees: 5
Primary Market Served: Business
Advertising/Marketing Budget Related
to Direct Marketing: 51-75%
Direct Marketing ad budget: $10,000
Direct Mail: 90%
Magazines: 5%
Telephone: 5%
Founded: 1955
Gross sales or billing: $1,000,000

Sales & service of surveying equipment
to builders, contractors, surveyors &
engineers.

ELLIS SYSTEMS CORP
28457 N Ballard Dr Ste F

Lake Forest, IL 60045-4545
Telephone: (847) 371-0200, Toll Free:
(800) 253-5547, FAX: (847) 371-0202, E-Mail: tom@ellisfiling.com,
Web Site: www.ellismh.com
CEO & Sls mgr: Tom Hynes
Primary Market Served: Business
Founded: 1962

Distributor of high density storage systems including high density shelving,
vertical carousels, rotary files & vertical lift modules.

ENCO MANUFACTURING CO
RP-NFOA
400 Nevada Pacific Hwy
Fernley, NV 89408
Telephone: (775) 788-7175, Toll Free:
(800) 873-3626, FAX: (800) 965-5857, E-Mail: milanesp@use-enco.
com, Web Site: www.use-enco.com
Catalog Mgr: Jack Rayher
Gen Mgr Mktg & Mdse: Perry Milane-si
Opers Mgr: Doug Styes
Conducts Business: U.S., Canada,
Mexico
Employees: 100
Primary Market Served: Business &
Consumer
Catalog available online
Indirect online sales
Advertising/Marketing Budget Related
to Direct Marketing: 76-100%
Direct Marketing ad budget:
Direct Mail: 95%
Magazines: 2%
Online: 3%
Founded: 1940
Gross sales or billing: $45,000,000

Machinery and industrial tools.

ENGINEERING SERVICES & PRODUCTS CO
FarmTek & TekSupply
1395 John Fitch Blvd
South Windsor, CT 06074-1029
Telephone: (860) 528-1119, Toll Free:
(800) 835-7877, FAX: (800) 457-8887, Web Site: www.teksupply.com
Pres: Barry Goldsher
Sr VP: Matt Niaura
Pur Mgr: Jack Jordan
Employees: 199
Primary Market Served: Business &
Consumer
Catalog available online
Direct online sales
Direct Marketing ad budget: $30,000
Founded: 1979
Gross sales or billing: $87,200,000

Supplier of industrial, construction,
maintenance, lighting and plumbing
products.

ENMAX CORP
141 - 50 Ave SE
Calgary, AB, Canada T2G 4S7
Telephone: (403) 514-3122, Web Site:
www.enmax.com
Primary Market Served: Business &
Consumer

FLIGHT FORM CASES INC
Div A W Enterprises Inc
6543 S Laramie Ave
Bedford Park, IL 60638
Telephone: (708) 458-8989, Toll Free:
(800) 657-1199, FAX: (708) 458-9023, E-Mail: info@caseguys.net,
Web Site: www.flightform.com
Pres: Edward Ostrusina
Conducts Business: U.S.
Employees: 40
Primary Market Served: Business &
Consumer
Catalog available online
Advertising/Marketing Budget Related
to Direct Marketing: 0-25%
Direct Marketing ad budget: $3,000
Founded: 1966
Gross sales or billing: $2,000,000

Carrying & reusable shipping cases.
Also a major guitar case company serving the music products industry through
distributors.

FORESTRY SUPPLIERS INC
205 W Rankin St, PO Box 8397
Jackson, MS 39284-6126
Telephone: (601) 354-3565, Toll Free:
(800) 647-5368, FAX: (601) 292-0165, E-Mail: fsi@forestry-suppliers.
com, Web Site: www.forestry-suppliers.com
Sr VP Mktg: Ray Hansen
VP Mktg: Ken Peacock
Admin Asst: Deborah Barlow
Prod & Mktg Mgr: Clay Walker
Pres: John Gwaltney
Conducts Business: Worldwide
Employees: 100
Primary Market Served: Business
Catalog available online
Direct online sales
Founded: 1949

Mail order catalog featuring forestry,
engineering & environmental equipment.

FOSTORIA INDUSTRIES INC
Div. of TPI
114 Roscoe Fitz Rd
Johnson City, TN 37615
Telephone: (419) 435-9201, Toll Free:
(800) 495-4525, FAX: (419) 435-0842, E-Mail: email@
fostoriaindustries.com, Web Site:
www.fostoriaindustries.com
Pres & CEO: Larry E. Dunlap

CFO: Jerry L. Donaldson
VP & Mktg Mgr: Steve Fruth
Conducts Business: U.S., Canada, Japan, England, Korea, China, Brazil, Peru, Poland
Employees: 120
Primary Market Served: Business & Consumer
Catalog available online
Founded: 1917
Gross sales or billing: $9,400,000

Manufacturer of electric & gas process infrared equipment. Comfort heating & machine tool lighting. Products include gas & electric infrared and convection process heating systems, gas & electric infrared comfort heating systems, electric infrared snow & ice control systems, maritime tool lighting, portable industrial lighting, loading area lighting, and critical work area lighting.

FOX LITE, INC
8300 Dayton Springfield Rd
Fairborn, OH 45324
Telephone: (937) 864-1966, FAX: (937) 864-7010, E-Mail: doug@foxlite.com, Web Site: www.foxlite.com
Pres: Douglas Hoy
VP Res & Devel: Walt Hoy
VP, Sls: Mark Hopkins
Conducts Business: Worldwide
Employees: 30
Primary Market Served: Business & Consumer
Advertising/Marketing Budget Related to Direct Marketing: 0-25%
Gross sales or billing: $4,000,000

Manufacture vacuum & thermal formed plastic parts; in particular, skylights, plastic & glass, to wholesalers of building products.

FOX VALLEY SYSTEMS INC
5A Production Dr
Brookfield, CT 06804
Toll Free: (844) 627-5255, E-Mail: info@foxvalleypaint.com, Web Site: www.foxvalleypaint.com
Conducts Business: U.S.
Primary Market Served: Business
Catalog available online
Direct online sales

Manufacturer & direct mail marketer of aerosol paints, striping & marking equipment.

FRESNO OXYGEN
Div. of RRAM Sales
2825 S Elm Ave (#101)
Fresno, CA 93706-5460

Telephone: (559) 233-6684, Toll Free: (800) 404-9353, FAX: (559) 233-4206, E-Mail: info@fresnooxygen.com, Web Site: www.fresnooxygen.com
Chmn Bd: Red Barnes
Pres: Mike Barnes
CFO: Todd Rayburn
VP, Opers & Mktg Dir: David Barnes
Primary Market Served: Business & Consumer
Catalog available online
Direct online sales
Founded: 1949
Gross sales or billing: $20,000,000

Welding & industrial distributor.

GE CANADA
Subs. of General Electric Co
2300 Meadowvale Blvd
Mississauga, ON, Canada L5N 5P9
Telephone: (905) 858-5100, Web Site: www.ge.com/canada
Pres & CEO: Elyse Allan
Conducts Business: Canada
Primary Market Served: Business & Consumer

Industrial manufacturer & service organization. Manufacture & service electrical appliances

GAIAM INC
PO Box 3095
Boulder, CO 80307-3095
Toll Free: (877) 989-6321, Web Site: life.gaiam.com
Pres & Founder: John Schaeffer
Conducts Business: U.S., Canada, Mexico, Africa, Papua-New Guinea
Employees: 4
Primary Market Served: Business & Consumer
Catalog available online
Direct online sales
Advertising/Marketing Budget Related to Direct Marketing: 76-100%
Direct Marketing ad budget: $15,000
Direct Mail: 95%
Magazines: 3%
Newspapers: 2%
Founded: 2006
Gross sales or billing: $500,000

Appropriate technology products sold mail-order worldwide.

GATES CORP
1551 Wewatta St
Denver, CO 80202
Telephone: (303) 744-1911, FAX: (303) 744-4000, Web Site: www.gates.com
Chmn Bd & CEO: James Nicol
CFO: John Zimmerman
Exec VP Comml & Corp Devel: David Carroll

Pres, Americas: Ken Friedman
Pres, Europe, Middle East & Africa: Giorgio Brusco
Pres, Asia Pacific: Paul Lee
Sr VP HR: Heather Dumas
VP Research & Devel: Ken Parks
Conducts Business: Worldwide
Primary Market Served: Business & Consumer
Catalog available online
Indirect online sales

Manufacturer of industrial rubber products: automotive & industrial v-belts & hoses & power transmission belting.

GEMS SENSORS & CONTROLS
Div. of Danaker Corp
One Cowles Rd
Plainville, CT 06062-1198
Telephone: (860) 747-3000, Toll Free: (800) 378-1600, FAX: (860) 747-4244, E-Mail: info@gemssensors.com, Web Site: www.gemssensors.com
Pres: Muriel Bras-Jorge
VP Opers: Bill Vincelette
Dir Sls: John Mauer
Dir Opers: Patrick Murphy
VP Worldwide Mktg: David Allen
Conducts Business: Worldwide
Employees: 299
Primary Market Served: Business
Catalog available online
Direct online sales
Advertising/Marketing Budget Related to Direct Marketing: 0-25%
Direct Marketing ad budget:
Direct Mail: 10%
Magazines: 60%
Online: 30%
Founded: 1955
Gross sales or billing: $21,400,000

Manufacturer & marketer of fluid sensors & controls.

GILSON CO INC
7975 N Central Dr
Lewis Center, OH 43035
Telephone: (740) 548-7298, Toll Free: (800) 444-1508, FAX: (740) 548-5314, E-Mail: sales@gilsonco.com, Web Site: www.globalgilson.com
Mktg Mgr: Carl Kramer
Technical Support Specialist: Todd Gertler
Conducts Business: Worldwide
Employees: 40
Primary Market Served: Business & Consumer
Catalog available online
Direct online sales
Advertising/Marketing Budget Related to Direct Marketing: 26-50%
Direct Marketing ad budget: $350,000

Direct Mail: 25%
Magazines: 65%
Telephone: 10%
Founded: 1939
Gross sales or billing: $12,000,000

Laboratory equipment for materials testing asphalt, concrete, soils & general laboratory equipment for particle sizing, sampling, etc.

GLOBAL EQUIPMENT CO INC

Div. of Systemax
11 Harbor Park Dr
Port Washington, NY 11050
Telephone: (516) 484-3100, Toll Free: (888) 381-2861, FAX: (516) 608-7111, E-Mail: sales@ globalindustrial.com, Web Site: www.globalindustrial.com
Chmn & CEO: Richard Leeds
Vice Chmn: Bob Leeds
Vice Chmn: Bruce Leeds
VP, Controller: Thomas Axmacher
Dir Mktg: Sean Aryai
Conducts Business: U.S.
Employees: 400
Primary Market Served: Business & Consumer
Catalog available online
Direct online sales
Advertising/Marketing Budget Related to Direct Marketing: 76-100%
Direct Marketing ad budget: $2,000,000
Direct Mail: 75%
Magazines: 5%
Telephone: 20%
Founded: 1949
Gross sales or billing: $15,000,000

Material handling equipment, office furniture & products, computer furniture, safety products, shop equipment.

WW GRAINGER INC

100 Grainger Pkwy
Lake Forest, IL 60045
Telephone: (847) 535-1000, Toll Free: (800) 472-4643, FAX: (847) 535-9122, Web Site: www.grainger.com
Chmn, Pres & CEO: James T. Ryan
Sr VP & Grp Pres Americas: Court Carruthers
Sr VP & CFO: Ronald L. Jadin
Sr VP & Grp Pres Global Supply Chain & Intl: D.G. Macpherson
Conducts Business: U.S.
Employees: 17,074
Primary Market Served: Business
Founded: 1927
Gross sales or billing: $9,400,000,000

Supplier of maintenance, repair and operating products.

GRAVES LAPIDARY CO

Subs. of Vee Enterprises Inc.
1800 N Andrews Ave
Pompano Beach, FL 33069-1421
Telephone: (954) 960-0300, Toll Free: (800) 327-9103, FAX: (954) 960-0301, E-Mail: sales@ gravescompany.com, Web Site: www.gravescompany.com
Pres: Peter Erdo
Mktg Mgr: Victoria Erdo
Conducts Business: U.S., Europe, Asia, Australia
Employees: 10
Primary Market Served: Business & Consumer
Catalog available online
Direct online sales
Direct Marketing ad budget: $30,000
Direct Mail: $15,000
Magazines: $15,000
Founded: 1946
Gross sales or billing: $800,000

Manufacture machines & supplies used to cut gemstones. Also, optical machinery & deburring equipment. Supplier of loose, natural & rough gemstones.

GRIZZLY INDUSTRIAL INC

1821 Valencia St
Bellingham, WA 98229-4746
Telephone: (360) 647-0801, Toll Free: (800) 523-4777, FAX: (360) 671-8375, E-Mail: csr@grizzly.com, Web Site: www.grizzly.com
VP & CFO: Don Osterloh
Primary Market Served: Consumer
Catalog available online
Direct online sales
Advertising/Marketing Budget Related to Direct Marketing: 76-100%
Founded: 1983

Mail order company for woodworking & metalworking tools.

HAGIE MANUFACTURING CO

721 Central Ave W, PO Box 273
Clarion, IA 50525
Telephone: (515) 532-2861, Toll Free: (800) 247-4885, FAX: (515) 532-3553, E-Mail: info@hagie.com, Web Site: www.hagie.com
Pres: John Hagie
COO: Alan Hagie
Mktg Mgr: Jim Williams
Conducts Business: Worldwide
Employees: 120
Primary Market Served: Business & Consumer
Catalog available online
Direct online sales
Advertising/Marketing Budget Related to Direct Marketing: 0-25%
Founded: 1947

Gross sales or billing: $8,900,000

Manufacturer of high clearance self-propelled sprayers & detasseler equipment. Factory direct sales.

HARBOR FREIGHT TOOLS

3491 Mission Oaks Blvd
Camarillo, CA 93012-5034
Telephone: (805) 445-4791, Toll Free: (800) 423-2567, FAX: (800) 445-4925, Web Site: www.harborfreight.com
Chmn: Alan Smidt
CEO & Pres: Eric Smidt
CFO: Bob Glickman
VP Mktg: David Martel
Conducts Business: U.S.
Employees: 1,600
Primary Market Served: Business & Consumer
Catalog available online
Direct online sales
Advertising/Marketing Budget Related to Direct Marketing: 0-25%
Founded: 1968
Gross sales or billing: $278,000,000

Mail order sales of tools & equipment.

HARWIL CORP

541 Kinetic Dr
Oxnard, CA 93030
Telephone: (805) 988-6800, Toll Free: (800) 562-2447, FAX: (805) 988-6804, E-Mail: harwil@harwil.com, Web Site: www.harwil.com
VP & Gen Mgr: Bruce Bowman
Pres: Geoffrey Strand
Founded: 1956

Designer, manufacturer & marketer of fluid flow and liquid level switches.

HERBACH & RADEMAN CO

353 Crider Ave
Moorestown, NJ 08057
Telephone: (856) 802-0422, Toll Free: (800) 848-8001, FAX: (856) 802-0465, E-Mail: sales@herbach.com, Web Site: www.herbach.com
Pres: Frank Lobascio
Conducts Business: Worldwide
Employees: 20
Primary Market Served: Business & Consumer
Catalog available online
Indirect online sales
Direct Marketing ad budget:
Direct Mail: $250,000
Founded: 1936
Gross sales or billing: $1,000,000

Electronic, electro-mechanical & optical mail order catalog to industry, universities, labs, institutions & hobbyists.

HILLSIDE WIRE CLOTH CO

109 Roosevelt Ave
Belleville, NJ 07109
Telephone: (973) 751-3131, Toll Free:
(800) 826-7395, FAX: (973) 470-
8183, E-Mail: info@
hillsidewirecloth.com, Web Site:
www.hillsidewirecloth.com
Pres: William Messinger
Conducts Business: Worldwide
Employees: 12
Primary Market Served: Business
Catalog available online
Indirect online sales
Advertising/Marketing Budget Related
to Direct Marketing: 0-25%
Direct Marketing ad budget:
Direct Mail: 35%
Magazines: 50%
Telephone: 15%
Founded: 1986
Gross sales or billing: $3,000,000

Wire cloth & wire cloth fabrications.

HOME SAFEGUARD INDUSTRIES

29706 Baden Pl
Malibu, CA 90265
Telephone: (310) 457-5813, FAX:
(310) 457-4862, E-Mail: expert@
homesafeguard.com, Web Site:
www.homesafeguard.com
Pres: Leon Cooper
Conducts Business: Worldwide
Employees: 4
Primary Market Served: Business
Catalog available online
Indirect online sales
Advertising/Marketing Budget Related
to Direct Marketing: 0-25%
Direct Marketing ad budget: $60,000
Direct Mail: 15%
Magazines: 85%
Founded: 1979
Gross sales or billing: $1,500,000

Fire safety devices allowing user to test
smoke & heat & carbon monoxide detectors.

HYDRA GROUP LLC

10940 Wilshire Blvd (Fl 11)
Los Angeles, CA 90024
Telephone: (310) 526-6680, FAX:
(310) 526-6682, Web Site: www.
hydragroup.com
Sr VP Mktg: Mason Wiley

IDEAL INDUSTRIES (CANADA) CORP

33 Fuller Rd
Ajax, ON, Canada L1S 2E1
Telephone: (905) 683-3400, Toll Free:
(800) 824-3325, FAX: (905) 683-
0209, E-Mail: nick.shkordoff@
idealindustries.com, Web Site: www.
idealindustries.com
Gen Mgr: Nick Shkordoff
Fin Dir: Rob Ackford
Sr Assoc Deputy Minister: Paul Boothe
Conducts Business: Canada
Primary Market Served: Business
Catalog available online
Direct Marketing ad budget: $100,000

Annual catalog of industrial & institutional items (18,000) mailed directly to
national accounts throughout Canada.

INDUSTRIAL INSTRUMENTS & SUPPLIES INC

125 James Way
Southampton, PA 18966
Telephone: (215) 396-0822, Toll Free:
(800) 523-6079, FAX: (215) 396-
0833, E-Mail: customerservice@
iisusa.com, Web Site: www.iisusa.
com
Pres: Charles Walter
Mktg Mgr: Christine Walter
Conducts Business: Worldwide
Employees: 15
Primary Market Served: Business
Catalog available online
Direct online sales
Advertising/Marketing Budget Related
to Direct Marketing: 76-100%
Direct Marketing ad budget:
Direct Mail: 70%
Magazines: 20%
Telephone: 10%
Founded: 1989
Gross sales or billing: $1,000,000

Tools & test equipment, industrial instrumentation & safety supplies to government & industrial manufacturers.

INTELLIGENT DIRECT

10 1st St
Wellsboro, PA 16901-8167
Telephone: (570) 724-7355, Web Site:
www.marketmaps.com
Natl Client Svcs Mgr: Theresa Bordas

Sells mapping software & databases.

J&L INDUSTRIAL SUPPLY

20921 Lahser Rd
Southfield, MI 48034-4432
Telephone: (734) 458-7000, Toll Free:
(800) 521-9520, FAX: (734) 261-
0352, Web Site: www.jlindustrial.
com
Adv Mgr: Therese Snow
Conducts Business: U.S., Europe & U.
K.
Employees: 300

Primary Market Served: Business &
Consumer
Founded: 1941

Distributors of tools & machinery. Mail
order industrial supply company specializing in high speed cutting tools &
machine shop accessories.

JANTZ SUPPLY KOVAL KNIVES

309 W Main, PO Box 584
Davis, OK 73030
Telephone: (580) 369-2316, Toll Free:
(800) 351-8900, FAX: (580) 369-
3082, Web Site: www.knifemaking.
com
Pres: Mick Koval
VP: Judy Koval
Primary Market Served: Business &
Consumer
Catalog available online
Direct online sales

Catalogs for knife making & knife accessories. Knifemaking supplies and
equipment.

KAO BRANDS

2535 Spring Grove Ave
Cincinnati, OH 45214
Telephone: (512) 421-1400, Web Site:
www.kaobrands.com
Primary Market Served: Business

Global manufacturer of beauty care
brands.

KETT TOOL CO

5055 Madison Rd
Cincinnati, OH 45227
Telephone: (513) 271-0333, FAX:
(513) 271-5318, E-Mail: info@kett-
tool.com, Web Site: www.kett-tool.
com
CEO: Rowe Hoffman
Pres: Kathy Conlon
VP Sls: Rick Fowkes
Conducts Business: Worldwide
Employees: 31
Primary Market Served: Business &
Consumer
Catalog available online
Advertising/Marketing Budget Related
to Direct Marketing: 51-75%
Direct Marketing ad budget:
Direct Mail: 5%
Magazines: 95%
Founded: 1940

Portable power saws, shears & nib-
blers.

KLINGSPOR'S WOODWORKING SHOP

Div. of Klingspor Corp
856 21st St Dr SE
Hickory, NC 28602

Telephone: (828) 326-WOOD, Toll Free: (800) 228-0000, FAX: (828) 327-4634, E-Mail: sales@ woodworkingshop.com, Web Site: www.woodworkingshop.com
Pres: Christoph Klingspor
VP, Mktg: Peter Spuller
Gen Mgr: Coleman Fourshee
Conducts Business: U.S., Canada, Mexico
Employees: 25
Primary Market Served: Business & Consumer
Catalog available online
Direct online sales
Advertising/Marketing Budget Related to Direct Marketing: 76-100%
Direct Marketing ad budget: $1,500,000
Direct Mail: 96%
Magazines: 1%
TV/Radio: 3%
Founded: 1989
Gross sales or billing: $4,000,000

Sanding & finishing equipment, abrasives & power tools for home hobbyists, small to medium sized woodworking shops & custom woodworkers.

LAFFERTY EQUIPMENT MANUFACTURING INC
5614 Oak Grove Rd
North Little Rock, AR 72118
Telephone: (501) 851-2820, Toll Free: (800) 999-2820, FAX: (501) 851-3719, (800) 699-3719, E-Mail: webmaster@laffertyequipment.com, Web Site: www.laffertyequipment.com
Pres: Drew Lafferty
VP: Alex Lafferty
Primary Market Served: Business
Catalog available online

Manufacture chemical applicators.

LESMAN INSTRUMENT CO
135 Bernice Dr
Bensenville, IL 60106-3366
Telephone: (630) 595-8400, Toll Free: (800) 953-7626, FAX: (630) 595-2386, E-Mail: sales@lesman.com, Web Site: www.lesman.com
Pres: Mike De Lacluyse
Mktg Mgr: Beth Rose
VP Sls: George Maumee
Conducts Business: U.S.
Employees: 33
Primary Market Served: Business
Direct Marketing ad budget: $200,000
Direct Mail: 95%
Telephone: 5%
Founded: 1962

Gross sales or billing: $12,500,000
Catalog sales of process control instrumentation to industry. Distributor for instrumentation.

LIFE TECHNOLOGIES
Subs. of Thermo Fisher Scientific
3175 Staley Rd
Grand Island, NY 14072-2028
Telephone: (716) 774-6700, Toll Free: (800) 955-6288, FAX: (800) 331-2286, E-Mail: catalog@lifetech.com, Web Site: www.lifetechnologies.com
Conducts Business: Worldwide
Primary Market Served: Business
Catalog available online
Direct online sales
Founded: 1982
Gross sales or billing: $500,000,000

Sell biotechnical products for research.

LOCKHART INDUSTRIES INC
9610 Skillman St
Dallas, TX 75243-8202
Telephone: (214) 348-1422, Web Site: www.lockhartadvantage.com
VP: Donald Bacon
VP: Doris L Lockhart

MFE INSTRUMENTS
Div. of Stocker & Yale Inc
32 Hampshire Rd
Salem, NH 03079
Telephone: (603) 893-8778, Toll Free: (800) 843-8011, FAX: (603) 893-8851, Web Site: www.stockeryale.com
Chmn: M.W. Blodgett
Pres: Alain Beauregard
VP, Fin: Gary Godin
Sls & Mktg Mgr: Joe Diruzza
Mfg Mgr: Jim Sullivan
Conducts Business: Worldwide
Primary Market Served: Business

Manufacturer of oscillographic strip chart recorders, thermal printers & galvanometers for OEM & End User medical & industrial test & measurement applications.

MI-T-M CORP
8650 Enterprise Dr
Peosta, IA 52068-9433
Telephone: (563) 556-7484, Web Site: www.mitm.com
Founder & CEO: AJ Spiegel
Pres: Sam Humphrey
VP: Dana Schrack
Mktg Mgr: Karen Anderson
Primary Market Served: Business & Consumer
Founded: 1971

Pressure washer equipment.

THE MR GROUP INC
2042 Dogwood Rd
Charleston, SC 29414
Telephone: (843) 402-0566, FAX: (843) 852-9051, E-Mail: mgm@ themrgroup.com, Web Site: www.themrgroup.com
Pres: Mike Murray
Conducts Business: U.S.
Employees: 5
Primary Market Served: Business
Catalog available online
Indirect online sales
Founded: 1995

Consultant marketing, direct mail/interact/telemarketing. Mostly industrial, also consumer startups.

MSC INDUSTRIAL SUPPLY CO
75 Maxess Rd
Melville, NY 11747-3151
Telephone: (516) 812-2000, Toll Free: (800) 645-7270, FAX: (800) 255-5067, E-Mail: executive@mscdirect.com, Web Site: www.mscdirect.com
Chmn: Mitchell Jacobson
Pres & CEO: David Sandler
VP: Steve Armstrong
Conducts Business: Worldwide
Employees: 4,500
Primary Market Served: Business
Catalog available online
Indirect online sales
Advertising/Marketing Budget Related to Direct Marketing: 51-75%
Direct Marketing ad budget:
Direct Mail: 80%
Magazines: 5%
Telephone: 15%
Founded: 1941
Gross sales or billing: $1,700,000,000

International distributor of industrial supplies.

MAGNA VISUAL INC
9400 Watson Rd
Saint Louis, MO 63126
Telephone: (314) 843-9000, Toll Free: (800) 843-3399, FAX: (314) 843-0000, E-Mail: magna@magnavisual.com, Web Site: www.magnavisual.com
Chmn Bd: Phillip Cady
COO & Technology Mgr: William R. Cady
HR Dir: Linda Todaro
Pres: Diane L. Crews
Dir, Sls & Mktg: Frank J. Venturella
Conducts Business: U.S.
Employees: 50
Primary Market Served: Business
Catalog available online
Advertising/Marketing Budget Related to Direct Marketing: 0-25%

Direct Marketing ad budget: $200,000
Direct Mail: 70%
Magazines: 10%
Online: 10%
Telephone: 10%
Founded: 1961
Gross sales or billing: $5,500,000

Sell magnetic dry erase white boards & accessories through dealers. Custom boards available.

MARKSON SCIENTIFIC LLC

dba Markson LabSales
336 E Montgomery St
Henderson, NC 27536-4618
Telephone: (808) 791-0490, Toll Free: (800) 528-5114, FAX: (800) 858-2243, E-Mail: sales@markson.com, Web Site: www.markson.com
Gen Mgr: John W. Marlowe
Customer Svc Rep: Trevor Barnes
Conducts Business: Worldwide
Employees: 7
Primary Market Served: Business
Catalog available online
Indirect online sales
Advertising/Marketing Budget Related to Direct Marketing: 76-100%
Direct Marketing ad budget:
Direct Mail: 80%
Magazines: 5%
Newspapers: 5%
Telephone: 10%
Founded: 1968

Catalog marketer of laboratory equipment, sell to food industry, universities & labs.

MCMASTER-CARR SUPPLY CO (HQ)

600 County Line Rd
Elmhurst, IL 60126-2081
Telephone: (630) 834-9600, FAX: (630) 834-9427, E-Mail: chi.sales@mcmaster.com, Web Site: www.mcmaster.com
Pres & CEO: Jay Delaney
Dir Sls & Mktg: Jim Friedland
Employees: 800
Primary Market Served: Business
Catalog available online
Direct online sales
Founded: 1901

Sell industrial equipment via catalog.

METHODE ELECTRONICS INC

7401 W Wilson Ave
Chicago, IL 60706
Telephone: (708) 867-6777, FAX: (708) 867-6999, E-Mail: info@methode.com, Web Site: www.methode.com
Chmn: William T. Jensen

Pres & CEO Stratos Lightware, Inc: James W. McGinley
Pres: Donald Duda
CFO & EVP: Dale W. Phillips
Dir: Kevin Hayes
Mktg Mgr: Ken Mitsui
Conducts Business: Worldwide
Employees: 3,400
Primary Market Served: Business & Consumer
Advertising/Marketing Budget Related to Direct Marketing: 26-50%
Founded: 1946
Gross sales or billing: $422,000,000

Interconnection devices including one & two piece printed circuit board connectors, chip carrier sockets, emulator cables & adapters, P.C. boards, fiber optic products, computer I/O terminators, automotive connectors/controls/switches & sensors, power wiring harnesses, battery cables, electronic chemicals, electronic & related materials testing, & testing & fixturing services. Sell to OEM's & distributors.

MEYLAN CORP

543 Valley Rd (Suite 1)
Montclair, NJ 07043-1844
Telephone: (973) 744-6400, Toll Free: (888) 769-9667, FAX: (973) 744-1011, E-Mail: meylan1@aol.com, Web Site: www.meylan.com/home.html
Sls Mgr: Alex Prinaris
Pres: Celia Prinaris
Conducts Business: U.S., Canada, S. America
Employees: 6
Primary Market Served: Business & Consumer
Catalog available online
Indirect online sales
Advertising/Marketing Budget Related to Direct Marketing: 76-100%
Direct Marketing ad budget:
Direct Mail: 90%
Magazines: 5%
Online: 5%
Founded: 1921
Gross sales or billing: $1,000,000

Serve industry, labs & schools with all types of measuring and timing devices. Digital & mechanical stopwatches, counters, loggers & timers.

MIDWEST TECHNOLOGY PRODUCTS & SERVICES

aka Midwest Shop Supplies, Inc
2600 Bridgeport Dr
Sioux City, IA 51111

Telephone: (712) 252-3601, Toll Free: (800) 831-5904, FAX: (800) 258-7054, E-Mail: web@midwesttechnology.com, Web Site: www.midwesttechnology.com
CEO: Linda Karlstad Flom
Pres: Robin Peterson
Gen Mgr: Rick Oldenkamp
Conducts Business: U.S., Guam, China, Germany, West Africa, Saudi Arabia
Employees: 26
Primary Market Served: Business & Consumer
Catalog available online
Direct online sales
Gross sales or billing: $7,900,000

Industrial arts supplier & technology education.

MILLIPORE CORP

75 Wiggins Ave
Bedford, MA 01730-2337
Telephone: (781) 869-5141, FAX: (781) 533-3110, Web Site: www.millipore.com
CFO & Corp VP: Kathleen Allen
VP Mktg: Edward Graham Brown
Conducts Business: Worldwide
Employees: 6,100
Primary Market Served: Business
Catalog available online
Direct online sales
Advertising/Marketing Budget Related to Direct Marketing: 0-25%
Founded: 1954
Gross sales or billing: $1,260,000,000

Filtration products for lab researchers, biopharmaceutical & microelectronics manufacturers.

MOHAWK LIFTS

Div. of Mohawk Resources
65 Vrooman Ave, PO Box 110
Amsterdam, NY 12010
Telephone: (518) 842-1431, Toll Free: (800) 833-2006, FAX: (518) 842-1289, E-Mail: rwells@mohawklifts.com, Web Site: www.mohawklifts.com
Pres: Rick Wells
Mgr, Sls & Mktg: Steve Perlstein
GSA Sales Mgr: Sherri Abell
Mgr, Govt Sls: Ray Pedrick
Asst Sls Mgr: Tim Malone
Conducts Business: U.S., Canada
Employees: 70
Primary Market Served: Business
Catalog available online
Advertising/Marketing Budget Related to Direct Marketing: 76-100%
Direct Marketing ad budget:
Direct Mail: 20%
Magazines: 60%
Telephone: 20%
Founded: 1981

Gross sales or billing: $7,400,000

Vehicle service lifts sold to public or private sector businesses/agencies with fleet of cars and/or trucks.

MORCON INDUSTRIAL SPECIALTY INC

658 Hardy Way (Suite 2)
Mesquite, NV 89027-3914
Telephone: (702) 346-3447, Toll Free: (888) 842-7953, Web Site: www.morcon-ind.com
Pres: Scott Siemers
Mgr: John Collom
Employees: 15
Primary Market Served: Business & Consumer
Catalog available online
Indirect online sales
Advertising/Marketing Budget Related to Direct Marketing: 0-25%
Founded: 1987
Gross sales or billing: $2,700,000

Big industry supplies & equipment, power tools, hand tools, pipe fitting hoses, generators & water pumps.

NELSON-JAMESON INC

2400 E Fifth St, PO Box 647
Marshfield, WI 54449-0647
Telephone: (715) 387-1151, Toll Free: (800) 826-8302, FAX: (715) 387-8746, (800) 472-0840, E-Mail: sales@nelsonjameson.com, Web Site: www.nelsonjameson.com
Dir Sls & Mktg: Murray Smith
Chmn Bd: John Nelson
Pres: Jerry Lippert
Conducts Business: U.S., Canada
Employees: 83
Primary Market Served: Business
Catalog available online
Indirect online sales
Founded: 1947
Gross sales or billing: $11,300,000

Products, equipment & supplies used in food processing.

NEW PIG CORP

1 Pork Ave
Tipton, PA 16684
Telephone: (814) 684-0101, Toll Free: (800) 468-4647, FAX: (814) 684-0961, E-Mail: hothogs@newpig.com, Web Site: www.newpig.com
Chmn & CEO: Ben Stapelfeld
Pres: Nino Vella
Dir Pub Rels: Carl DeCaspers
CFO: Rebecca Cowan
Exec VP: Douglas Hershey
VP, Mktg: Mark DeYulis
Conducts Business: Worldwide
Employees: 320

Primary Market Served: Business & Consumer
Catalog available online
Direct online sales
Advertising/Marketing Budget Related to Direct Marketing: 0-25%
Founded: 1985

Industrial maintenance industry provider of innovative solutions & technical expertise to customers to help maintain a cleaner, safer workplace.

NORTHEAST HINGE DISTRIBUTORS INC

261 Proctor Hill Rd
Hollis, NH 03049
Telephone: (603) 465-3244, Toll Free: (800) 882-0120, FAX: (603) 465-3313, E-Mail: nehinge@nehinge.com, Web Site: www.nehinge.com
Pres: Martha Myers
Conducts Business: U.S.
Employees: 5
Primary Market Served: Business & Consumer
Catalog available online
Advertising/Marketing Budget Related to Direct Marketing: 0-25%
Founded: 1983
Gross sales or billing: $1,000,000

We sell all types of hinges and their related products.

NORTHWEST LABORATORIES

241 S Holden St
Seattle, WA 98108
Telephone: (206) 763-6252, FAX: (206) 763-3949, Web Site: www.nwlabs.net
Pres & CEO: Patrick Tessier
Primary Market Served: Business

Full-service testing & research laboratory

O'BRIEN MANUFACTURING

PO Box 7, Letters Ford, IN 46945-9999-POST
Subs. of Hi-Vac
117 Industry Rd
Marietta, OH 45750-9355
Telephone: (740) 374-2306, Toll Free: (800) 638-1901, FAX: (740) 374-5447, Web Site: www.obrienmfg.com
Pres: Tom Bonnell
Primary Market Served: Business & Consumer
Catalog available online
Direct online sales
Founded: 1950

Sewer Equipment: Sewer cleaning tools and accessories.

OLD WORLD MOULDINGS INC

821 Lincoln Ave
Bohemia, NY 11716
Telephone: (631) 563-8660, FAX: (631) 563-8815, E-Mail: mouldings@optonline.com, Web Site: www.oldworldmouldings.com
Pres: Alan D. Havranek
Mgr: Michael Diers
Conducts Business: U.S., Canada
Employees: 5
Primary Market Served: Business & Consumer
Indirect online sales
Advertising/Marketing Budget Related to Direct Marketing: 51-75%
Direct Marketing ad budget:
Direct Mail: 10%
Magazines: 20%
Telephone: 70%
Founded: 1975
Gross sales or billing: $700,000

Sell interior wood moulding, both wholesale & retail.

ORBIT MANUFACTURING CO

1507 W Park Ave
Perkasie, PA 18944
Telephone: (215) 257-0727, Toll Free: (888) 895-0958, FAX: (215) 257-7399, Web Site: www.orbitmfg.com
CEO: Norman Shriver
VP, Sls & Mktg Mgr: Terry Allen
Pres: Ronald Herd
Conducts Business: U.S.
Employees: 26
Primary Market Served: Business
Catalog available online
Direct Marketing ad budget:
Magazines: 100%
Founded: 1961

Electric in-floor heating cables, gutter ice & snow melting cables & commercial electric heating products.

PPC

aka PPC BEST
PO Box 246
Johnston, IA 50131
Telephone: (515) 986-5070, E-Mail: sales@ppcbest.com, Web Site: www.ppcbest.com
Pres: Dean Bibler
Primary Market Served: Business & Consumer
Catalog available online
Indirect online sales
Founded: 1981

Surface care products for exterior & interior. Whenever feasible, incorporates ag-based chemistry into formulations, avoiding the use of hazardous or questionable ingredients that potentially could damage the environment.

PARKER HANNIFIN CORP
6035 Parkland Blvd
Cleveland, OH 44124-4186
Telephone: (216) 896-2490, Web Site: www.parker.com
Primary Market Served: Consumer
Manufacture components & systems that facilitate motion & the controlled flow of liquids & gasses for a variety of global markets to increase the productivity & profitability of its customers.

PHOTOGRAPHER'S FORMULARY INC
7079 Hwy 83 N
Condon, MT 59826
Telephone: (406) 754-2891, Toll Free: (800) 922-5255, FAX: (406) 754-2896, E-Mail: formulary@blackfoot.net, Web Site: www.photoformulary.com
Pres: Bud Wilson
VP: Lynn Wilson
Conducts Business: Worldwide
Employees: 4
Primary Market Served: Business & Consumer
Catalog available online
Direct online sales
Advertising/Marketing Budget Related to Direct Marketing: 26-50%
Direct Marketing ad budget:
Direct Mail: 20%
Magazines: 80%
Founded: 1977
Sell photographic chemicals for the amateur & professional darkroom enthusiast.

PLAS-TANKS INDUSTRIES INC
39 Standen Dr
Hamilton, OH 45015
Telephone: (513) 942-3800, FAX: (513) 942-3993, E-Mail: info@plastanks.com, Web Site: www.plastanks.com
Pres: J. Kent Covey
Mktg Mgr: Dave Alarie
CFO: Connie Royse
Conducts Business: U.S., Canada
Employees: 39
Primary Market Served: Business
Founded: 1976
Gross sales or billing: $6,500,000
Fiberglass reinforced plastic vessels to business & government.

PLASTIC VIEW ATC
4585 Runway (Suite B)

Simi Valley, CA 93063
Telephone: (805) 520-9390, Toll Free: (800) 468-6301, FAX: (805) 520-0260, E-Mail: info@pvatc.com, Web Site: www.pvatc.com
Pres: Sonny Voges
Gen Mgr: Ryan Voges
VP: Chris Voges
Conducts Business: Worldwide
Employees: 8
Primary Market Served: Business & Consumer
Indirect online sales
Advertising/Marketing Budget Related to Direct Marketing: 51-75%
Direct Marketing ad budget:
Direct Mail: 80%
Magazines: 5%
Online: 15%
Founded: 1947
Gross sales or billing: $700,000
Manufacture & distribute "See Thru" (transparent) window shades.

POLYAIR PACKAGING
808 E 113th St
Chicago, IL 60628
Telephone: (773) 995-1818, Toll Free: (888) POLYAIR X444, FAX: (773) 995-7725, E-Mail: marketing@polyair.com, Web Site: www.polyair.com
Pres: Alan Castle
Interim CEO: Victor D'Souza
Mktg Mgr: John Crowe
VP, Opers: Lew C. Coffin
VP Sales: David Swart
Dir, Fin: Michael Freel
Sec: Louis Manetti
Conducts Business: U.S., Canada
Employees: 400
Primary Market Served: Business & Consumer
Catalog available online
Advertising/Marketing Budget Related to Direct Marketing: 0-25%
Founded: 1987
Sell protective packaging products such as bubble wrap, courier envelopes, foam & foam-in-place systems through distributors.

POWR-FLITE, A TACONY CO
3101 Wichita Ct
Fort Worth, TX 76140-1755
Toll Free: (800) 880-2913, FAX: (817) 551-0719, Web Site: www.powrflite.com
VP Mktg: Rob Godlewski
Founded: 1967
Manufactures commercial floor care equipment.

PRINT PRODUCTS INTERNATIONAL
9893 Brewers Ct, Laurel, MD 20723-1905
Subs. of Pace Inc
9030 Junction Dr
Annapolis Junction, MD 20701
Telephone: (910) 695-7223, FAX: (910) 944-1724, Web Site: www.paceworldwide.com
Opers Mgr: Keith Rice
Mktg Mgr: Tracey Stanley
Sls Mgr: Scott MacDonald
Conducts Business: Worldwide
Employees: 9
Primary Market Served: Business & Consumer
Indirect online sales
Advertising/Marketing Budget Related to Direct Marketing: 51-75%
Direct Marketing ad budget:
Direct Mail: 75%
Magazines: 25%
Founded: 1978
Gross sales or billing: $5,000,000
Distributor of electronic test equipment.

QUICK DRAW CLIP SYSTEMS INC
4869 McGrath St (Suite 130)
Ventura, CA 93003-7767
Telephone: (805) 644-6888, Toll Free: (888) 254-7797, FAX: (805) 644-7320, E-Mail: ron@clipsystems.com, Web Site: www.clipsystems.com
Pres: Terry Ward-Llewellyn
Dir Opers: Ron Boyd
Mktg Mgr: Linda Luce
Conducts Business: Worldwide
Employees: 15
Primary Market Served: Business & Consumer
Catalog available online
Direct online sales
Advertising/Marketing Budget Related to Direct Marketing: 51-75%
Direct Marketing ad budget: $30,000
Direct Mail: $5,000
Online: $25,000
Founded: 1953
Gross sales or billing: $2,000,000
The clip system is designed for anyone who carries a cellular phone, pager, tools or any of the portable music systems. Most cameras can also be carried by any of the stainless units with the simple addition of the camera bolt.

REB STORAGE SYSTEMS INTERNATIONAL
4556 W Grand Ave
Chicago, IL 60639-4734

Telephone: (773) 252-0400, Toll Free: (800) 252-5955, FAX: (773) 252-0303, E-Mail: sales@rebsteel.com, Web Site: www.industrialebuy.com
Pres: Tom Lesko
Co-Founder: Edward Lesko
Sr VP: Mike Bailey
Conducts Business: U.S.
Employees: 10
Primary Market Served: Business & Consumer
Catalog available online
Direct online sales
Direct Marketing ad budget: $1,200,000
Direct Mail: 100%
Gross sales or billing: $12,000,000

Wholesale catalog of material handling industrial products.

REGITAR USA INC

Subs. of Mobiletron Electronics Co Ltd
2575 Container Dr
Montgomery, AL 36109
Telephone: (334) 244-1885, Toll Free: (877) 734-4827, FAX: (334) 244-1901, E-Mail: info@regitar.com, Web Site: www.regitar.com
Pres & CEO: Y.T. Tsai
VP: Chau Lee
Conducts Business: U.S., Canada, South America
Primary Market Served: Business
Catalog available online
Indirect online sales
Advertising/Marketing Budget Related to Direct Marketing: 0-25%
Direct Marketing ad budget:
Direct Mail: 5%
Magazines: 10%
Newspapers: 10%
Telephone: 75%
Founded: 1987
Gross sales or billing: $21,000,000

Auto parts & ignition components for domestic & import autos, power tools, fastening systems, tackers & cordless tools.

RELIANCE ELECTRIC

Div. of Rockwell Automation
RP-NFOA
5711 RS Boreham Jr St
Fort Smith, AR 72901-8301
Telephone: (479) 646-4711, FAX: (479) 648-5792, E-Mail: smtraylor@powersystems.rockwell.com, Web Site: www.reliance.com
Pres: Joseph Swann
Exec VP: Tom Mascari
Corp Commun Mgr: Shawn Traylor
Info Technologist: Elaine Durrah
Conducts Business: U.S., Europe, Asia, Latin America
Primary Market Served: Business

Catalog available online
Advertising/Marketing Budget Related to Direct Marketing: 0-25%

Industrial electrical motors, variable speed drives, motor controls, mechanical power transmission products & telecommunications equipment.

THE RENOVATOR'S SUPPLY INC

Renovator's Old Mill
Millers Falls, MA 01349
Telephone: (413) 423-3300, Toll Free: (800) 659-2211, FAX: (413) 423-3800, E-Mail: customercare@rensup.com, Web Site: www.rensup.com
Pres: Claude Jenloz
Conducts Business: Worldwide
Primary Market Served: Business & Consumer
Catalog available online
Direct online sales
Gross sales or billing: $5,000,000

Manufacture & sell hardware, lighting & plumbing supplies for residential & commercial applications. 2000 item catalog available.

RETAWMATIC CORP

14911 41st Ave
Flushing, NY 11355-1025
Telephone: (718) 886-0502
Pres: Charles J. Hsu
Conducts Business: U.S.
Primary Market Served: Business & Consumer

Sell surface water & oil detectors, water-in-oil detectors & water separators.

ROCK-TRED CORP

405 N Oakwood Ave
Waukegan, IL 60085
Telephone: (847) 673-8200, Toll Free: (800) 762-8733, FAX: (847) 679-6665, Web Site: www.rocktred.com
Sales Exec: Dan Moran
Mktg Exec: Jim Selcke
Controller: Rosie Galler
Conducts Business: Worldwide
Employees: 35
Primary Market Served: Business
Advertising/Marketing Budget Related to Direct Marketing: 0-25%
Founded: 1939
Gross sales or billing: $3,100,000

Floor coatings marketed to qualified applicators.

RUUD LIGHTING INC

Div of Cree Inc
9201 Washington Ave
Racine, WI 53406-3772

Telephone: (262) 886-1900, Toll Free: (800) 236-7000, FAX: (800) 236-7500, E-Mail: sales@ruudlighting.com, Web Site: www.ruudlighting.com
Pres: Alan Ruud
VP, Mktg: Stephen Morelli
Direct Mktg Mgr: Gianna O'Keefe
Dev: Troy Rosengarten
VP Mfg: Wayne Gillien
Conducts Business: Worldwide
Employees: 475
Primary Market Served: Business
Catalog available online
Indirect online sales
Advertising/Marketing Budget Related to Direct Marketing: 76-100%
Direct Marketing ad budget:
Direct Mail: 90%
Magazines: 10%
Founded: 1982

Lighting fixtures directly marketed to electrical contractors.

SSHC INC/RADIANT HEATING COMMERCIAL APPLICATIONS

Four Custom Dr
Old Saybrook, CT 06475-4008
Telephone: (860) 399-5434, Toll Free: (800) 544-5182, FAX: (860) 399-6460, (877) 675-4968, E-Mail: info@sshcinc.com, Web Site: www.sshcinc.com
Pres, CEO & CFO: Richard Watson
Conducts Business: U.S., Canada
Employees: 10
Primary Market Served: Business & Consumer
Catalog available online
Advertising/Marketing Budget Related to Direct Marketing: 26-50%
Founded: 1989
Gross sales or billing: $5,000,000

Manufacturer of energy efficient electric radiant heat modules.

SAN FRANCISCO VICTORIANA INC

2070 Newcomb Ave
San Francisco, CA 94124
Telephone: (415) 648-0313, FAX: (415) 648-2812, Web Site: www.sfvictoriana.com
Pres: Gary Root
Conducts Business: U.S.
Employees: 12
Primary Market Served: Business & Consumer
Catalog available online
Indirect online sales
Gross sales or billing: $500,000

Manufacture & supply architectural moldings & castings for restoration & new construction.

SEDGWICK MORAN DETERT & ARNOLD LLP

1 N Wacker Dr (Suite 4200)
Chicago, IL 60606-2862
Telephone: (312) 849-1985, Web Site:
www.michaelbest.com

SIERRA SCIENTIFIC INC

dba Value-Tek
1005 N 50th St (Suite 150)
Phoenix, AZ 85008-0117
Telephone: (602) 256-0540, FAX:
(602) 252-1972, Web Site: www.
value-tek.com
Pres: George Heiland
Dir Sls: Chris Heiland
Employees: 25
Primary Market Served: Business
Catalog available online
Direct online sales
Advertising/Marketing Budget Related
to Direct Marketing: 0-25%
Direct Marketing ad budget:
Online: 100%
Founded: 1988
Gross sales or billing: $8,000,000

Clean room products. Distributor of
critical environment products.

SNAP-ON INC

2801 80th St
Kenosha, WI 53141-1410
Telephone: (262) 656-5200, Toll Free:
(800) 866-5748, (800) 786-6600,
FAX: (262) 656-5577, Web Site:
www.snapon.com
Pres & CEO: Nicholas T. Pinchuk
VP, Chief Mktg Officer: Andrew R.
Ginger
Conducts Business: Worldwide
Employees: 12,400
Primary Market Served: Business &
Consumer
Gross sales or billing: $2,840,000,000

Direct marketer of hand tools & related
equipment for professional mechanics.

SOLAR COMPONENTS CORP

121 Valley St
Manchester, NH 03103-0237
Telephone: (603) 668-8186, FAX:
(603) 668-1783, Web Site: www.
solar-components.com
Mktg Mgr: Mark Miville
Pres: Scott Keller
Conducts Business: Worldwide
Employees: 5
Primary Market Served: Business &
Consumer
Catalog available online
Direct online sales
Advertising/Marketing Budget Related
to Direct Marketing: 0-25%
Direct Marketing ad budget:
Direct Mail: 10%

Magazines: 75%
Telephone: 15%
Founded: 1972
Gross sales or billing: $500,000

Energy saving, energy producing pho-
tovoltaics, aquaculture tanks & greenhouse kits. Complete catalog available,
also check our website.

SPECTRONICS CORP

956 Brush Hollow Rd
Westbury, NY 11590-1731
Telephone: (516) 333-4840, Toll Free:
(800) 274-8888, FAX: (800) 491-
6868, E-Mail: vscherer@spectroline.
com, Web Site: www.spectroline.
com
Pres: Jonathan Cooper
VP, Sls & Mktg: Gary Fixel
VP Opers: John Duerr
Mktg Commun Mgr: Bob Savasta
Customer Svc Mgr: Gloria Blusk
Publicist: Valerie Scherer
Conducts Business: U.S., Canada
Employees: 200
Primary Market Served: Business
Catalog available online
Advertising/Marketing Budget Related
to Direct Marketing: 0-25%
Direct Marketing ad budget:
Direct Mail: 75%
Magazines: 20%
Online: 5%
Founded: 1955
Gross sales or billing: $25,000,000

Wide variety of products based on ul-
tra-violet technology: laboratory equipment, security, banking, forensics,
NDT, air conditioning & refrigeration
& vehicle leak detectors.

STANDARD TOOLS & EQUIPMENT CO

4810 Clover Rd
Greensboro, NC 27405-9607
Telephone: (336) 697-7177, Toll Free:
(800) 336-2776, Web Site: www.
toolsusa.com
Pres & CEO: Bob Shepley
Founded: 1959

Sells automotive shop equipment.

STAR SPRINKLER INC

Subs. of Tyco International Ltd
1400 Pennbrook Pkwy
Lansdale, PA 19446-3840
Telephone: (414) 570-5000, Toll Free:
(800) 558-5236, FAX: (414) 570-
5010, Web Site: www.starsprinkler.
com
Mktg Mgr: John Corcorah
Conducts Business: Worldwide
Employees: 150

Primary Market Served: Business &
Consumer
Catalog available online
Advertising/Marketing Budget Related
to Direct Marketing: 26-50%
Direct Marketing ad budget: $20,000
Direct Mail: 70%
Magazines: 30%
Founded: 1894

Fire sprinklers & accessories. Branches
in West Springfield, MA; Nashville,
TN; Dardanelle, AR & Oakland, CA.

START INTERNATIONAL

4270 Airborn Dr
Addison, TX 75001-5182
Telephone: (972) 248-1999, Toll Free:
(800) 259-1986, FAX: (972) 248-
1991, E-Mail: info@
startinternational.com, Web Site:
www.startinternational.com
Pres: Todd Sternbert
Conducts Business: U.S., Canada, Eu-
rope, Asia
Employees: 15
Primary Market Served: Business
Catalog available online
Advertising/Marketing Budget Related
to Direct Marketing: 51-75%
Founded: 1981

Industrial tape and label dispensers.
Optical inspection devices and magnifiers.

STATSOFT INC

2300 E 14th St
Tulsa, OK 74104
Telephone: (918) 749-1119, FAX:
(918) 749-2217, E-Mail: info@
statsoft.com, Web Site: www.
statsoft.com
CFO: Elizabeth Paszkiewic
Mgr: John Hillis
Sls: Gary Miner
Mktg Coord: Sarah Beaumont
Conducts Business: Worldwide
Primary Market Served: Business &
Consumer
Catalog available online
Indirect online sales
Founded: 1984

Statistical software called STATISTI-
CA, sells worldwide.

STELLAR TECHNOLOGY INC

Div of LORD Corp
237 Commerce Dr
Amherst, NY 14228-2302
Telephone: (716) 250-1900, Toll Free:
(800) 274-1846, FAX: (716) 250-
1909, E-Mail: info@stellartech.com,
Web Site: www.stellartech.com
Pres: Bob Haefner

Sls Mgr: James Borkowski
Employees: 35
Primary Market Served: Business
Catalog available online
Founded: 1991

Manufacture pressure transducers.

STILE-TILE LIKE METAL ROOFING
Metal Sales Manufacturing Corp
7800 State Rd (#60)
Sellersburg, IN 47172
Telephone: (812) 246-1866, Toll Free:
(800) 999-7777, FAX: (800) 477-
9318, (800) 944-6884, Web Site:
www.mtsales.com
Mktg Dir: Don Durs
Pres & CEO: Tom Morris
Primary Market Served: Business &
Consumer
Founded: 1963

Manufacture metal roofing products.

STRONGWELL
400 Commonwealth Ave
Bristol, VA 24201-3800
Telephone: (276) 645-8000, FAX:
(276) 645-8132, E-Mail: gbarefoot@
strongwell.com, Web Site: www.
strongwell.com
Pres & CEO: G David Oakley Jr
Treas & CFO: John E Delaney
VP Bus Develop & Mktg: Glenn P
Barefoot
Natl Sales Mgr: Mike Carr
VP Sales & Engrng: David Gibbs
Conducts Business: Worldwide
Employees: 800
Primary Market Served: Business &
Consumer
Catalog available online
Advertising/Marketing Budget Related
to Direct Marketing: 0-25%
Direct Marketing ad budget: $150,000
Direct Mail: 45%
Magazines: 50%
Online: 5%
Founded: 1971
Gross sales or billing: $120,000,000

Fiberglass structural shapes & grating.
Precast polymer concrete.

SUNSHINE UNLIMITED INC
303 W Normal Dr
Lindsborg, KS 67456-1519
Telephone: (785) 227-3880, FAX:
(785) 227-3880, E-Mail: cpeterjr@
aol.com, Web Site: www.sunshine-
unlimited.com
Pres: Chester Peterson Jr.
Conducts Business: Worldwide
Primary Market Served: Business &
Consumer
Catalog available online

Indirect online sales
Advertising/Marketing Budget Related
to Direct Marketing: 76-100%
Founded: 1976
Computer software.

SURPLUS CENTER
Div. of Burden Sales Co
1015 W "O" St
Lincoln, NE 68528-1322
Telephone: (402) 474-4055, Toll Free:
(800) 488-3407, FAX: (402) 474-
5198, E-Mail: customerservice@
surpluscenter.com, Web Site: www.
surpluscenter.com
Pres: David Burden
VP, Sls: Chris Cole
Sls Mgr: Jeff Atkinson
Conducts Business: U.S.
Employees: 40
Primary Market Served: Business &
Consumer
Catalog available online
Direct online sales
Advertising/Marketing Budget Related
to Direct Marketing: 76-100%
Direct Marketing ad budget: $350,000
Direct Mail: 67%
Magazines: 33%
Founded: 1933
Gross sales or billing: $16,000,000

Hydraulic equipment, motors, pumps,
etc. Customer base of farmers, contractors & small fabrication shops.

TECRA TOOLS INC
2925 S Umatilla St
Englewood, CO 80110-1217
Telephone: (303) 338-9224, Toll Free:
(800) 284-0808, FAX: (303) 338-
9289, E-Mail: info@tecratools.com,
Web Site: www.tecratools.com
Pres: Terry Tautz
VP: Nicole Tautz
Catalog available online
Direct online sales

TELPRO INC
7251 S 42nd St
Grand Forks, ND 58201
Telephone: (701) 775-0551, FAX:
(701) 775-0629
Pres: Rolland Young
Fin Exec: Dana Young
Sls Mgr Mktg: Mark Haaland
Primary Market Served: Business

Manufacturer of construction equipment.

TEMPCO ELECTRIC HEATER CORP
607 N Central Ave
Wood Dale, IL 60191-1452

Telephone: (630) 350-2252, Toll Free:
(800) 323-6859, FAX: (630) 350-
0232, E-Mail: dpadlo@tempco.com,
Web Site: www.tempco.com
Pres: Fermin Adames
VP Sls: William Kilberry
Dept Mgr: Dennis C. Padlo
Conducts Business: U.S., Canada,
Mexico, Japan, Netherlands
Employees: 325
Primary Market Served: Business
Catalog available online
Indirect online sales
Advertising/Marketing Budget Related
to Direct Marketing: 0-25%
Founded: 1972
Gross sales or billing: $15,000,000

Manufacturer of electric heating ele-
ments for commercial & industrial
heating of liquids, solids & process air.
From stock or made to specifications.

TEXAS REFINERY CORP
840 N Main St
Fort Worth, TX 76106-9419
Telephone: (817) 332-1161, FAX:
(817) 336-8441, E-Mail: jhopkins@
texasrefinery.com, Web Site: www.
texasrefinery.com
Owner & Chmn Bd: A Mac Pate
Dir HR: Jim Peel
CEO & Pres: Chris Pate
VP, Pur: Barbara Main
Exec VP: Dennis Parks
Exec VP: Patrick M Walsh
Conducts Business: U.S., Canada, Eu-
rope, Mexico
Employees: 125
Primary Market Served: Business
Catalog available online
Indirect online sales
Founded: 1922

Marketer of building maintenance
products & heavy duty lubricants to
business & industry.

THERMO FISHER SCIENTIFIC INC
81 Wyman St
Waltham, MA 02451-1223
Telephone: (781) 622-1000, Toll Free:
(800) 678-5599, FAX: (781) 622-
1207, Web Site: www.thermofisher.
com
Chmn: Jim P. Manzi
Pres & CEO: Marc C Casper
Sr VP & CFO: Peter M. Wilver
Conducts Business: Worldwide
Primary Market Served: Business &
Consumer
Catalog available online
Direct online sales
Founded: 1950
Gross sales or billing: $3,700,000,000
Manufacturing of lab equipment.

THOMAS SCIENTIFIC
1654 High Hill Rd
Swedesboro, NJ 08085
Telephone: (856) 467-2000, Toll Free: (800) 345-2100, FAX: (856) 467-3087, E-Mail: value@thomassci.com, Web Site: www.thomassci.com
Chm Bd: R. Patterson
Pres: Gerald Wesner
VP, Mktg & Sls: Ed Pierzynski
Conducts Business: U.S., Canada, Europe, S. America, Asia
Employees: 100
Primary Market Served: Business
Catalog available online
Indirect online sales
Advertising/Marketing Budget Related to Direct Marketing: 51-75%
Direct Marketing ad budget:
Direct Mail: 75%
Magazines: 20%
Telephone: 5%
Founded: 1900

Lab & scientific equipment & supplies.

THREEFOLD
5151 N Shadeland Ave
Indianapolis, IN 46226-2603
Telephone: (317) 607-1995, Web Site: www.certaindy.com
Primary Market Served: Consumer

TIME MOTION TOOLS
Div. of WASSCO
12778 Brookprinter Pl
Poway, CA 92064
Toll Free: (800) 779-8170, FAX: (800) 779-8171, Web Site: www.timemotion.com
CEO: Ward Leber
VP: Al Rios
Conducts Business: U.S., Canada
Employees: 50
Primary Market Served: Business
Catalog available online
Direct online sales
Advertising/Marketing Budget Related to Direct Marketing: 76-100%
Direct Marketing ad budget:
Direct Mail: 100%
Founded: 1985

Service tools to the service & repair industry.

TINSLEY TOOL SUPPLY INC
8038 Canter Ln
Powell, TN 37849-3143
Telephone: (865) 681-9633, FAX: (865) 982-1655, E-Mail: gene@tinsleytool.com, Web Site: www.tinsleytool.com
Pres & Owner: Ellen Sapp
Inside Sls Mgr: Paula Snyder
Office Mgr: Gene Sapp
Sls Mgr: Michael Sapp

Sls: Charlie Pepper
Primary Market Served: Business
Catalog available online
Founded: 1986

Distributor of metal cutting tools & cutting tool machinery.

TORQMASTER INTERNATIONAL
200 Harvard Ave
Stamford, CT 06902-6230
Telephone: (203) 326-5945, Toll Free: (888) 414-4643, FAX: (203) 326-5944, E-Mail: info@torqmaster.com, Web Site: www.torqmaster.com
Pres: Garrett Bebell
Exec VP: Steven Rubin
Fin Controller & HR Dir: Nisley Montes
Dir Sls: Douglas Collins
Dir Mktg: Van Valkenburgh
Conducts Business: Worldwide
Employees: 70
Primary Market Served: Business
Catalog available online
Indirect online sales
Advertising/Marketing Budget Related to Direct Marketing: 0-25%
Founded: 1979
Gross sales or billing: $6,000,000

Friction hinges & torque producing devices.

TRICOR DIRECT INC
dba Seton Identification Products
20 Thompson Rd
Branford, CT 06405-2842
Telephone: (203) 488-8059, Toll Free: (800) 243-6624, FAX: (800) 571-2596, E-Mail: custsvc_setonus@seton.com, Web Site: www.seton.com
Database Mktg Assoc: Donna J. Canestri
Employees: 250
Primary Market Served: Business
Catalog available online
Direct online sales
Founded: 1956

Manufacturer of all types of identification products including signs, tags, labels, pipe & valve markers & much more.

TRIDIUM INC
3951 Westerre Pkwy
Richmond, VA 23233-1317
Telephone: (804) 525-1648, Web Site: www.tridium.com
Pres & Gen Mgr: Nino A Dicosmo
Founder & Chief Tech Officer: Gerald Frank
VP Fin: Laura B Bacon

Pres Tricium Europe: Terry Casey
A global software & services company.

UNITRON LTD
73 Mall Dr
Commack, NY 11725-5703
Telephone: (631) 589-6666, FAX: (631) 589-6795, E-Mail: johnc@unitronusa.com, Web Site: www.unitronusa.com
Pres: Jay Berliner
Exec VP & COO: Brian Taub
Sr VP: Peter I. Indrigo
Consultant: John D. Coyle
Conducts Business: U.S., Canada
Employees: 20
Primary Market Served: Business & Consumer
Catalog available online
Indirect online sales
Advertising/Marketing Budget Related to Direct Marketing: 51-75%
Direct Marketing ad budget: $120,000
Founded: 1952
Gross sales or billing: $4,000,000

Service & market a full line of microscopes, telescopes, & binoculars to the industrial, medical, educational & retail markets.

UPBEAT INC
211 N Lindbergh Blvd (fl 2)
Saint Louis, MO 63141-7838
Telephone: (314) 535-5005, Toll Free: (800) 325-3047, FAX: (314) 535-4419, E-Mail: custservice@upbeat.com, Web Site: www.upbeat.com
Pres: Terry Knoplol
Dir Mktg: Eric Gilbert
Dir Mdsg: Nancy Mills
Natl Sales: Carl van der Horst
Conducts Business: U.S.
Employees: 70
Primary Market Served: Business & Consumer
Catalog available online
Direct online sales
Advertising/Marketing Budget Related to Direct Marketing: 76-100%
Founded: 1982

Institutional catalog company.

VARIAN MEDICAL SYSTEMS
RP-NFOA
3100 Hansen Way
Palo Alto, CA 94304
Telephone: (650) 493-4000, FAX: (650) 842-5196, Web Site: www.varian.com
CFO & Exec VP: Elisha W Finney
Sr VP & Pres of Oncology: Kolleen T Kennedy
Sr VP Gen Counsel & Sec: John W. Kuo
CEO & Pres: Dow R Wilson

Employees: 3,900
Primary Market Served: Business
Catalog available online
Founded: 1948
Gross sales or billing: $1,600,000,000
Medical equipment.

VICTOR MACHINERY EXCHANGE

56 Bogart St
Brooklyn, NY 11206-3817
Toll Free: (800) 723-5359, FAX: (718) 366-7026, E-Mail: sales@victornet. com, Web Site: www.victornet.com
Pres: Marc Freidus
Conducts Business: U.S.
Employees: 10
Primary Market Served: Business & Consumer
Catalog available online
Indirect online sales
Advertising/Marketing Budget Related to Direct Marketing: 76-100%
Direct Marketing ad budget:
Direct Mail: 50%
Magazines: 10%
Online: 40%
Founded: 1918

Industrial & metalworking supplies to machine shops, manufacturers & hobbyists.

WATTS RADIANT

Subs. of DBA
4500 E Progress Pl
Springfield, MO 65803
Telephone: (417) 864-6108, Toll Free: (800) 276-2419, FAX: (417) 864-8161, Web Site: www.wattsheatway. com
Pres & CEO: Mike Chiles
VP: Dan Chiles
VP, Sls: Russ Rose
Engr Design Asst: Tony Ledford
Conducts Business: U.S., Canada, New Zealand
Employees: 51
Primary Market Served: Business & Consumer
Catalog available online
Indirect online sales
Advertising/Marketing Budget Related to Direct Marketing: 0-25%
Founded: 1980
Gross sales or billing: $7,900,000
Radiant floor heating & snow melting.

WELCH ALLYN, INC

4341 State Street Rd
Skaneateles Falls, NY 13153-5300
Telephone: (315) 685-4100, Web Site: www.welchallyn.com
CEO: Stephen F Meyer
Owner & Dir: David Allyn

CFO & Exec VP Fin: Joseph Hennigan
Ex VP Global Opers & Supply Chain Mgmt: Darrell Clapper
Chief Global Customer Experience Officer: Eric Hunt
Primary Market Served: Consumer
Founded: 1915

Manufacturers medical devices, products & solutions for caregivers in doctors' offices, hospitals & emergency response settings worldwide.

WELCOMEMAT SERVICES INC

3348 Peachtree Rd (Suite 1095)
Atlanta, GA 30326-1400
Telephone: (404) 841-2226, E-Mail: info@welcomematservices.com, Web Site: www. welcomematservices.com
Founder & Pres: Brian Mattingly
Primary Market Served: Business & Consumer
Founded: 2003

Marketing strategies & technology company providing monthly direct mail packages to individuals & families who have recently changed their address.

WESTHOFF MACHINE CO

9462 Watson Industrial Park
Saint Louis, MO 63126
Telephone: (314) 963-7130, Toll Free: (800) 364-0280, FAX: (800) 324-1942, E-Mail: mail@westhoffinc. com, Web Site: www.westhoffinc. com
CEO: Allen Johnson
Pres: Janice Westhoff Johnson
Conducts Business: U.S.
Employees: 12
Primary Market Served: Business & Consumer
Catalog available online
Direct online sales
Advertising/Marketing Budget Related to Direct Marketing: 76-100%
Direct Marketing ad budget:
Direct Mail: 85%
Magazines: 10%
Telephone: 5%
Founded: 1967
Gross sales or billing: $2,750

Sell small industrial magnetic products, hand tools & die casting supplies through direct mail to the metal working industries.

WHOLESALE TOOL CO

12155 Stephens Dr
Warren, MI 48089

Toll Free: (800) 521-3420, FAX: (800) 521-3661, E-Mail: wtmich@aol.com, Web Site: www.wttool.com
Pres: Mark Dowdy
Adv Dir: Matthew Decker
Fin Exec: Chuck Lowen
Conducts Business: U.S., Canada, Mexico
Employees: 45
Primary Market Served: Business & Consumer
Catalog available online
Direct online sales
Direct Marketing ad budget: $1,600,000
Direct Mail: 75%
Magazines: 8%
Newspapers: 2%
Telephone: 15%
Founded: 1960
Gross sales or billing: $20,000,000

Industrial tooling, hand, power, & cutting tools, precision, machinery, abrasives, material handling equipment.

WIRE WORKS

200 Keystone Rd (Suite 1)
Chester, PA 19013
Telephone: (610) 485-1981, Toll Free: (800) 292-1940, Web Site: www. wire-works.com
Pres & Chmn Bd: Ron Francis
Conducts Business: Worldwide
Employees: 14
Primary Market Served: Business & Consumer
Catalog available online
Direct online sales
Founded: 1974

Sell wiring harnesses for auto, marine & industrial use.

WOOD CARVERS SUPPLY INC

3031 Placida Rd (Ste 7)
Englewood, FL 34224-8547
Telephone: (941) 698-0123, Toll Free: (800) 284-6229, FAX: (941) 698-0329, E-Mail: info@ woodcarverssupply.com, Web Site: www.woodcarverssupply.com
Pres: Timothy Effrem
VP: Deborah Effrem
Primary Market Served: Business & Consumer
Founded: 1955

Complete line of tools, equipment & supplies for woodcarving.

WOODCRAFT SUPPLY CORP LLC

Subs. of SBR Inc
1177 Rosemar Rd
Parkersburg, WV 26105-8272

Telephone: (304) 422-5412, Toll Free: (800) 344-3348, FAX: (304) 422-5417, Web Site: www.woodcraft.com
Pres: Jody Garrett
Editor-in-Chief Woodcraft Magazine: Jim Harrold
VP Internet Devel & Strategic Projects: Nancy Miller
Project Admin - Freedom Pens Project: Keith Outtan
VP Multi-Channel Sales: Gary Lombard
Conducts Business: U.S., Canada
Employees: 300
Primary Market Served: Business & Consumer
Advertising/Marketing Budget Related to Direct Marketing: 76-100%
Founded: 1928

Sells woodworking hand tools, books & related equipment & supplies to industrial, vocational & consumer markets. Retail locations in 29 major cities from coast to coast.

WOODCRAFTERS LUMBER SALES INC

212 NE Sixth Ave
Portland, OR 97232-2976
Telephone: (503) 231-0226, Toll Free: (800) 777-3709, FAX: (503) 232-0511, E-Mail: spen@worldnet.att.net, Web Site: www.woodcrafters.us
Pres: Stephen Penberthy
Sls Mgr: Carl Paasche
Conducts Business: U.S.
Employees: 25
Primary Market Served: Business & Consumer
Advertising/Marketing Budget Related to Direct Marketing: 51-75%
Direct Marketing ad budget: $114,000
Direct Mail: 10%
Magazines: 10%
Newspapers: 10%
TV/Radio: 70%
Founded: 1973
Gross sales or billing: $5,000,000

Sell hardware, tools, books & stair cast woodwork. Catalogs for carving, tools, millwork & books related to woodworking.

ZORO TOOLS INC

sub of W W Grainger Inc
1000 Asbury Dr (Suite 1)
Buffalo Grove, IL 60089-4551
Toll Free: (855) 289-9676, E-Mail: askzoro@zorotools.com, Web Site: www.zorotools.com
CEO: Gloria Ysasi-Diaz

Industrial equipment & supplies.

Office, Printing & Graphic Arts Supplies Catalogs (10)

ACCOUNTANTS EDUCATION GROUP

8111 Lyndon B Johnson Fwy Ste 1345
Dallas, TX 75251-1354
Telephone: (214) 373-3486, Toll Free:
(800) 627-7310, FAX: (800) 627-
7310, E-Mail: customerservice@
accountantsed.com, Web Site: www.
accountantsed.com
Pres: Marc C. Pinelli
Primary Market Served: Business &
Consumer
Catalog available online
Direct online sales

Business/industrial mail order & books:
catalogs, printed & recorded materials.

ACCOUNTANTS' SUPPLY HOUSE

Div. of Histacount Corp
PO Box 1186
Lancaster, CA 93584-1186
Telephone: (856) 384-1144, Toll Free:
(800) 342-5274, FAX: (800) 468-
4446, Web Site: www.rapidforms.
com
Pres: John Fairbanks
VP, Mktg: Tom Jule
VP, Fin: Tim Broadhead
Mktg Mgr: Kent Fegley
Mgr, Circulation Svcs: Christopher
Gordon
Conducts Business: Worldwide
Employees: 300
Primary Market Served: Business &
Consumer
Advertising/Marketing Budget Related
to Direct Marketing: 76-100%
Direct Marketing ad budget:
Direct Mail: 98%
Magazines: 2%
Founded: 1952
Gross sales or billing: $3,000,000

Manufacture & sell office, accounting
supplies, printers, medical & dental sta-
tioneries.

AD-LIB ADVERTISING INC

109 White Oak Ln (Suite 72A)
Old Bridge, NJ 08857
Telephone: (732) 679-9226, Toll Free:
(800) 622-3542, FAX: (732) 679-
9511, E-Mail: info@adlibadvertising.
com, Web Site: www.
adlibadvertising.com
Pres: Don Cogland
Customer Svc: Victoria DeLuca
Conducts Business: U.S.
Employees: 4
Primary Market Served: Business
Advertising/Marketing Budget Related
to Direct Marketing: 0-25%

Founded: 1968
Gross sales or billing: $1,000,000

Custom printed post-it note pads, calendars & specialty advertising products.

ADIRONDACK DIRECT

Div. of Adirondack Chair Co Inc
3040 48th Ave
Long Island City, NY 11101
Telephone: (718) 932-4003, Toll Free:
(800) 221-2444, FAX: (800) 477-
1330, E-Mail: info@
adirondackdirect.com, Web Site:
www.adirondackdirect.com
Pres: Syl Cangero
Adv Dir: Marianna Lokis
Conducts Business: Worldwide
Employees: 100
Primary Market Served: Business
Catalog available online
Direct online sales
Founded: 1926

Catalog offering business & institutional furniture distributed to business
firms, churches, schools, clubs & organizations.

ADMORE INC

Subs. of Ennis Business Forms
24707 Wood Ct
Macomb, MI 48042-5378
Telephone: (810) 949-8200, Toll Free:
(800) 523-6673, FAX: (800) 215-
2664, Web Site: www.admoreonline.
com
Gen Mgr: Bill Tignanelli
Natl Acct Rep: John Andersen
Dir Customer Svc: Brenda Barozzini
Primary Market Served: Business
Catalog available online
Indirect online sales
Founded: 1947

Manufacture paper presentation products through distributors.

ALFA CTP SYSTEMS

554 Clark Rd # 2
Tewksbury, MA 01876-1631
Telephone: (603) 689-1101, FAX:
(603) 689-1197, Web Site: www.
alfactp.com
Gen Mgr: Tony Ford
Primary Market Served: Business &
Consumer

Provider of innovative & leading edge
publishing systems.

AMERICAN STATIONERY CO INC

100 N Park Ave, Box 207
Peru, IN 46970

Telephone: (765) 473-4438, Toll Free:
(800) 822-2577, FAX: (800) 253-
9054, Web Site: www.
americanstationery.com
VP Mktg: Kathy Calderbank
Pres: Michael Bakehorn
Controller: Joyce McCarty
Conducts Business: U.S.
Employees: 250
Primary Market Served: Consumer
Catalog available online
Direct online sales
Advertising/Marketing Budget Related
to Direct Marketing: 26-50%
Founded: 1919

Quality personalized paper products &
accessories for home or office. Complete line of wedding stationery & accessories.

ARMBRUST PAPER TUBES INC

6255 S Harlem Ave
Chicago, IL 60638-3990
Telephone: (773) 586-3232, FAX:
(773) 586-8997, E-Mail: tubesrus@
corecomm.net, Web Site: www.
tubesrus.com
Pres: Bernerd Armbrust
CFO: Jack Slattery
Fin Exec: Alberta Pantoja
VP: Marc Armbrust
Chmn Bd: Chris Armbrust
Sales Exec: Bill Constable
Conducts Business: U.S., Canada
Employees: 30
Primary Market Served: Business &
Consumer
Catalog available online
Direct online sales
Advertising/Marketing Budget Related
to Direct Marketing: 51-75%
Direct Marketing ad budget: $50,000
Telephone: $25,000
Founded: 1938
Gross sales or billing: $3,200,000

Manufacturer of paper tubes, cores &
cans for packaging & shipping.

ASSOCIATED BAG CO

400 W Boden St
Milwaukee, WI 53207-7120
Telephone: (414) 769-1000, Toll Free:
(800) 926-6100, FAX: (800) 926-
4610, E-Mail: customerservice@
associatedbag.com, Web Site: www.
associatedbag.com
Pres: Herb Rubenstein
Founded: 1938

AVERY DENNISON CORP

50 Pointe Dr

Brea, CA 92821-3699
Telephone: (714) 674-8500, Toll Free: (800) 462-8379, FAX: (714) 674-6929, Web Site: www.avery.com
Pres & CEO: Dean A. Scarborough
Sr VP Corp Commun & Adv: Diane B. Dixon
Conducts Business: U.S., Canada
Employees: 22,700
Primary Market Served: Business & Consumer
Catalog available online
Advertising/Marketing Budget Related to Direct Marketing: 0-25%
Direct Marketing ad budget:
Direct Mail: 70%
Online: 30%
Founded: 1935
Gross sales or billing: $5,575,900,000

Company specializing in office products.

BROOKHOLLOW CARDS

Div. of Taylor Corp
1 Stationary Pl
Rexburg, ID 83440-3567
Toll Free: (800) 822-0256, FAX: (800) 443-8847, E-Mail: service@ brookhollowcards.com, Web Site: www.brookhollowcards.com
Mktg Rep: Jamie Eckman
Conducts Business: U.S.
Primary Market Served: Business & Consumer
Direct Marketing ad budget:
Direct Mail: 100%

Sell imprinted greeting cards & calendars for business-to-business use.

ARTHUR BROWN & BRO INC

2 W 45th St Frnt 1
New York, NY 10036-4214
Telephone: (212) 575-5555, Toll Free: (800) 772-PENS, FAX: (212) 575-5825, E-Mail: penshop@artbrown.com, Web Site: www.artbrown.com
Owner: B. Warren Brown
Pres: J. Powell Brown
Mgr: Marilyn Brown
Conducts Business: U.S.
Employees: 30
Primary Market Served: Business & Consumer
Catalog available online
Direct online sales
Founded: 1924

Fine art, commercial art & drafting supplies, fine writing instruments - wholesale & retail. Publishers of pen catalogs & dealer imprint programs.

CABLEXPRESS TECHNOLOGIES

5404 S Bay Rd
Syracuse, NY 13212-3801
Telephone: (315) 476-3000, Toll Free: (800) 913-9467, FAX: (315) 455-1800, E-Mail: info@cablexpress.com, Web Site: www.CXTec.com
Founder & CEO: William G. Pomeroy
CFO & VP: Barbara S Ashkin
VP Acctg: Al Gough
CIO: Ray Oliver
Presl: Peter Belyea
Conducts Business: U.S., Canada, Europe, Pacific Rim
Employees: 160
Primary Market Served: Business & Consumer
Catalog available online
Indirect online sales
Advertising/Marketing Budget Related to Direct Marketing: 51-75%
Founded: 1978
Gross sales or billing: $116,000,000

Reseller of connectivity solutions for IBM & compatible mainframe, mid-range & LAN environments. Free catalog.

CENTURY PHOTO

Div. of Centis Inc
PO Box 308
Newtown, CT 06470-0308
Toll Free: (800) 767-0777, FAX: (714) 441-4550, Web Site: www.centuryphoto.com
Circ Dir: Bill Martin
Conducts Business: U.S.
Employees: 480
Primary Market Served: Business & Consumer
Catalog available online
Direct online sales
Advertising/Marketing Budget Related to Direct Marketing: 51-75%
Direct Marketing ad budget: $5,000,000
Direct Mail: 75%
Telephone: 25%
Founded: 1950

Manufacture & sell via mail order business products that protect, organize & display office paper work & photographic materials.

CHAMPION AMERICA INC

A Tricor Direct Co
28 Flax Mill Rd
Branford, CT 06405-2803
Telephone: (203) 315-1181, Toll Free: (877) 242-6709, FAX: (800) 336-3707, E-Mail: teamca@champion-america.com, Web Site: www.champion-america.com
Dir, Mktg Admin: Donna J. Canestri

Mktg Exec: Cynthia Czyz
Conducts Business: U.S.
Employees: 250
Primary Market Served: Business
Catalog available online
Direct online sales
Advertising/Marketing Budget Related to Direct Marketing: 76-100%
Direct Marketing ad budget:
Direct Mail: 100%
Founded: 1989

Safety signs & identification products.

CLASSIC THERMOGRAPHERS

1680 Roe Crest Dr
North Mankato, MN 56003-2658
Telephone: (623) 582-0002, Toll Free: (800) 727-4200, FAX: (800) 727-4202
Mktg Mgr: Tiffany Bennett
Conducts Business: U.S.
Primary Market Served: Business & Consumer
Founded: 1976

Printer of wedding invitations.

COLONIAL REDI-RECORD CORP

1225 36th St
Brooklyn, NY 11218-2023
Telephone: (718) 972-7433, Toll Free: (800) 637-0040, FAX: (718) 972-7438, Web Site: www.asisupplier.com/81110
Pres: Joe Berkobits
Conducts Business: U.S.
Employees: 8
Primary Market Served: Business
Catalog available online
Direct online sales
Founded: 1948

Sell business forms to stationers.

COMMUNICATION INDUSTRIES CORP

117 J L H Memorial Dr
Grafton, VT 05146-0116
Telephone: (802) 869-6500, FAX: (802) 869-6565, E-Mail: info@ cicmail.com, Web Site: www.careersatcic.com
Pres: Scott Heller
VP & Gen Mgr: Bob Singleton
Mktg Supvr: Paula Ryan
Web Mktg Coord: Nathan Schmidt
Employees: 36
Primary Market Served: Business
Catalog available online
Direct online sales
Advertising/Marketing Budget Related to Direct Marketing: 76-100%
Direct Marketing ad budget: $2,000,000

Direct Mail: $2,000,000
Founded: 1976

Product distributor of audio visual equipment to schools, hospitals & government agencies & corporations.

DSP INC USA

Subs. of delfortgroup AG, Austria
216 3rd St NE (Suite C)
Charlottesville, VA 22902
Telephone: (434) 202-7870, E-Mail: iorder@delfortgroup.com, Web Site: www.delfortgroup.com
Pres: Joe Kofler
VP: Terry Griffis
Mktg Supvr: Lee Culler

Service an array of ultra lightweight paper specialties.

DATABAZAAR.COM

12070 Miramar Pkwy
Miramar, FL 33025
Telephone: (954) 843-0483, Toll Free: (888) 335-3282, FAX: (954) 843-0429, E-Mail: rudy@databazaar.com, Web Site: www.databazaar.com
VP Mktg: David L. Cohen
CEO: Oney Seal
Conducts Business: U.S.
Employees: 55
Primary Market Served: Business & Consumer
Catalog available online
Direct online sales
Advertising/Marketing Budget Related to Direct Marketing: 0-25%
Direct Marketing ad budget:
Direct Mail: 1%
Magazines: 1%
Newspapers: 1%
Online: 95%
TV/Radio: 1%
Telephone: 1%
Founded: 1999
Gross sales or billing: $50,000,000

Discount original & value priced compatible ink and toner, specialty paper, backup tapes, flash memory & cables.

DAY RUNNER DIRECT

Subs. of Day Runner Inc
101 Oneil Rd
Sidney, NY 13838-1055
Toll Free: (800) 643-9923, FAX: (800) 643-9927, Web Site: www.dayrunner.com
Mgr: Nancy Lloyd
Primary Market Served: Business & Consumer

Personal organizers, planners, calendars, refills & accessories.

DECAL SHOP

1849 Foster Dr

Jacksonville, FL 32216
Toll Free: (800) 634-1889, FAX: (253) 276-3467, E-Mail: decalshop@decalshop.com
Pres: Jerry Walsh
Conducts Business: U.S.
Employees: 6
Primary Market Served: Business & Consumer

Manufacture decals & bumper strips.

DEMCO INC

4810 Forest Run Rd
Madison, WI 53704-7338
Telephone: (608) 241-1201, Toll Free: (800) 356-1200, FAX: (608) 241-1799, E-Mail: custserv@demco.com, Web Site: www.demco.com
Chmn: John Wall
VP, Mktg: Michael Snapper
Pres: Mike Grasee
VP, Fin: Donald Rogers
Dir Customer Mktg: Stephanie Mueller
VP, Opers: Mike Goethel
VP, IS: Mark Anderson
Conducts Business: U.S.
Employees: 250
Primary Market Served: Business
Advertising/Marketing Budget Related to Direct Marketing: 76-100%
Direct Marketing ad budget:
Direct Mail: 95%
Magazines: 5%
Founded: 1905
Gross sales or billing: $50,000,000

Supplies & equipment for libraries, schools, business & professional offices.

DIVERSIFIED PHOTO SUPPLY CORP

333 W Alondra Blvd (Suite C)
Gardena, CA 90248-2428
Telephone: (310) 328-8577, Toll Free: (800) 544-1609, FAX: (310) 328-8518, Web Site: www.diversifiedphoto.com
Pres: Darrell Benton
Conducts Business: U.S.
Employees: 32
Primary Market Served: Business & Consumer
Catalog available online
Indirect online sales
Advertising/Marketing Budget Related to Direct Marketing: 51-75%
Direct Marketing ad budget:
Direct Mail: 20%
Magazines: 5%
Telephone: 75%

Founded: 1989

Distributor of all major brands of photographic amateur & professional film, papers, chemicals, lab supplies, equipment & graphic arts. Sales are conducted via telemarketing & direct mail.

EGGS BY BYRD

HC 3 Box 3653
Wappapello, MO 63966-9727
Telephone: (573) 222-7999, Toll Free: (800) 235-EGGS, FAX: (573) 222-8009, E-Mail: eggsbybyrd@dishmail.net
Owner: Kim Allen
Conducts Business: Worldwide
Employees: 3
Primary Market Served: Consumer
Catalog available online
Indirect online sales
Advertising/Marketing Budget Related to Direct Marketing: 0-25%
Founded: 1979

Sell complete line of egg art supplies, ten varieties of eggshells, instruction books & miniatures. 80 page catalog $4.50.

EPSON AMERICA

3840 Kilroy Airport Way
Long Beach, CA 90806-2469
Telephone: (562) 981-3840, Toll Free: (800) 873-7766, FAX: (562) 290-5220, Web Site: www.epson.com
Pres & CEO: John Lang
Sr VP & CFO: Alan Pound Sr.
VP: Tadaaki Hagata
Sr VP: James Marshall Sr.
VP, Legal Affairs: Judith S. Bain
VP, Mktg: Keith Krutzberg
Conducts Business: U.S.
Primary Market Served: Business & Consumer
Catalog available online
Direct online sales
Advertising/Marketing Budget Related to Direct Marketing: 0-25%
Direct Marketing ad budget:
Direct Mail: $1,000,000
Founded: 1988

Provide accessories & supplies for Epson imaging products.

FARM HOME OFFICES

Div. of Sylvette Corp
6739 12th Ave S
Richfield, MN 55423
Telephone: (612) 920-0907, Toll Free: (800) 788-7218, FAX: (866) 404-0257, Web Site: www.sylvette.com
Pres: Jim Halbur
Conducts Business: U.S.
Employees: 3
Primary Market Served: Business & Consumer

Advertising/Marketing Budget Related
to Direct Marketing: 76-100%
Direct Marketing ad budget: $40,000
Direct Mail: 75%
Magazines: 25%
Founded: 1980
Gross sales or billing: $250,000

Farm & agricultural business forms &
business management products.

A I FRIEDMAN INC

44 W 18th St
New York, NY 10011
Telephone: (212) 243-9000, Toll Free:
(800) 204-6352, FAX: (212) 929-
7320, Web Site: www.aifriedman.
com
VP: Jeff Goldfarb
Partner: Peter Brandeis
Conducts Business: U.S.
Employees: 150
Primary Market Served: Business &
Consumer
Catalog available online
Direct online sales
Advertising/Marketing Budget Related
to Direct Marketing: 0-25%
Founded: 1929

Art supplies.

G-NEIL DIRECT MAIL

Subs. of Taylor Corp.
720 International Pkwy, PO Box
450939
Sunrise, FL 33345-0939
Toll Free: (800) 999-9111, FAX: (954)
851-1264, E-Mail: tcs@gneil.com,
Web Site: www.gneil.com
Pres: Joe Hilger
Former Pres: Terry Tukes
VP: Steve Singer
Conducts Business: U.S., U.K.
Employees: 275
Primary Market Served: Business
Catalog available online
Direct online sales
Advertising/Marketing Budget Related
to Direct Marketing: 51-75%
Founded: 1987

Provide human resource products to
over 800,000 business professionals.
Also, labor law forms, software quality
tools, manuals, videos, testing & motivational products. Free catalog.

GCC PRINTERS

209 Burlington Rd
Bedford, MA 01730
Telephone: (781) 275-5800, Toll Free:
(800) 422-7777, FAX: (781) 275-
1115, (800) 442-2329, E-Mail:
sales@gccprinters.com, Web Site:
www.gcctech.com
Pres, CEO: Kevin Curran
Conducts Business: Worldwide

Employees: 7
Primary Market Served: Business &
Consumer
Catalog available online
Direct online sales
Direct Marketing ad budget:
Direct Mail: 40%
Magazines: 60%
Founded: 1981

Printer consumables.

GENERAL BINDING CORP

Subs AACO Brands Corp.
One GBC Plaza
Northbrook, IL 60062
Toll Free: (800) 723-4000, FAX: (847)
272-1389, (800) 952-1166, Web Site:
www.gbc.com
Pres, Europe Group: Thomas Stenebr-
ing
VP: Steven Rubin
VP HR: Perry Zukowski
Conducts Business: Worldwide
Employees: 1,000
Primary Market Served: Business &
Consumer
Advertising/Marketing Budget Related
to Direct Marketing: 0-25%
Direct Marketing ad budget: $300,000
Direct Mail: 40%
Magazines: 60%
Founded: 1947
Gross sales or billing: $600,000,000

Specializing in document finishing systems including binding & laminating,
paper shredders & visual communications products.

GHENT MANUFACTURING INC

US Partner - The Millennium Group
2999 Henkle Dr
Lebanon, OH 45036-9260
Telephone: (513) 932-3445, Toll Free:
(800) 543-0550, FAX: (513) 932-
9252, E-Mail: customer_service@
ghent.com, Web Site: www.ghent.
com
Pres: George Leasure
Sr VP Sales & Mktg: John Rouse
Exec VP: G. Mark Leasure
Dir Prod Management: Scott Bowers
Conducts Business: U.S.
Employees: 160
Primary Market Served: Business &
Consumer
Catalog available online
Founded: 1977
Gross sales or billing: $10,200,000

Sell visual communication aids such as
markerboards, chalkboards, bulletin
boards, directory boards, easels & glass
enclosed boards to dealers, distributors
& wholesalers.

HR DIRECT

Div. of Executive Greetings Inc
PO Box 452049
Sunrise, FL 33345-2049
Toll Free: (800) 346-1231, FAX: (800)
350-7760, Web Site: www.hrdirect.
com
Pres: Lee Bracken
Conducts Business: U.S.
Employees: 12
Primary Market Served: Business &
Consumer
Advertising/Marketing Budget Related
to Direct Marketing: 76-100%

Direct marketer of personal & career
development products.

INTUIT

2632 Marine Way
Mountain View, CA 94043
Telephone: (650) 944-6000, Web Site:
www.inuit.com
Chmn & CEO: Brad Smith
Exec VP & Chief Mktg & Sls Officer:
Caroline Donahue
Exec VP & Chief Tech Officer: H Tay-
loe Stansbury
Employees: 8,500
Primary Market Served: Business &
Consumer
Founded: 1983

Develop, manufacture & market financial software.

IROQUOIS PRODUCTS

Div. of Iroquois Industries Corp
2220 W 56th St
Chicago, IL 60636-3900
Telephone: (773) 436-3900, Toll Free:
(800) 453-3355, FAX: (773) 436-
4908, E-Mail: sales@
iroquoisproducts.com, Web Site:
www.iroquoisproducts.com
Pres: Alan R. Gordon
Conducts Business: U.S.
Primary Market Served: Business
Advertising/Marketing Budget Related
to Direct Marketing: 76-100%
Founded: 1957

Direct mail marketer of discount-priced
office, information processing, shipping supplies & disposable wipers.
Printer of business forms, envelopes,
stationery, shipping & mailing labels.

ROBERT JAMES CO INC

930 Marketta Spur Rd
Moody, AL 35004
Telephone: (205) 640-7081, Toll Free:
(800) 633-8296, FAX: (205) 640-
7087
Chmn: James A. Abele Jr.
Conducts Business: U.S.
Primary Market Served: Business

Founded: 1935

Printing, graphic arts & receipt books to businesses & dealers.

JERRY'S ARTARAMA

3060 Wake Forest Rd
Raleigh, NC 27609
Telephone: (919) 878-8478, Toll Free: (800) U-ARTIST, FAX: (919) 873-9565, E-Mail: micah@ jerrysartarama.com, Web Site: www. jerrysartarama.com
Pres: Ira Goldstein
CEO: David Goldstein
Mktg: Micah Mullen
Conducts Business: U.S., Canada
Employees: 200
Primary Market Served: Business & Consumer
Catalog available online
Direct online sales
Advertising/Marketing Budget Related to Direct Marketing: 76-100%
Direct Marketing ad budget:
Direct Mail: 70%
Magazines: 30%
Founded: 1968
Gross sales or billing: $50,000,000

Artist supplies & picture frames at near wholesale prices. Market to artists, schools, students & advertising agencies.

KRAFTBILT

Div. of Corporate Express DPM
6504 E 44th St
Tulsa, OK 74145-4614
Telephone: (918) 628-1260, Toll Free: (800) 331-7290, FAX: (918) 632-7371, Web Site: www.kraftbilt.com
Asst Mktg Mgr: Carolyn Hartman
Conducts Business: U.S., Canada
Employees: 12
Primary Market Served: Business & Consumer
Catalog available online
Direct online sales
Advertising/Marketing Budget Related to Direct Marketing: 76-100%
Direct Marketing ad budget: $300,000
Direct Mail: $295,000
Telephone: $5,000
Founded: 1951
Gross sales or billing: $1,400,000

Catalog marketer of office products, stationery, analysis & writing pads & all-weather marking tags.

LASER LABEL TECHNOLOGIES INC

Div. of Bemis Co
4560 Darrow Rd
Stow, OH 44224-1888

Toll Free: (800) 882-4050, FAX: (800) 395-4721, E-Mail: sales@lltproducts. com, Web Site: www.lltproducts.com
Mgr: Kathy Altenpohl
Conducts Business: U.S., Canada
Employees: 33
Primary Market Served: Business
Catalog available online
Direct online sales
Advertising/Marketing Budget Related to Direct Marketing: 0-25%
Direct Marketing ad budget:
Direct Mail: 90%
Newspapers: 5%
Telephone: 5%
Founded: 1991
Gross sales or billing: $6,300,000

Labels, ribbons, equipment & supplies for bar code systems.

MAGNAPLAN CORP

dba Visual Planning Group
1320 State Rte 9 (#3314)
Champlain, NY 12919-5412
Telephone: (518) 298-8404, Toll Free: (800) 361-1192, FAX: (518) 298-2368, E-Mail: info@visualplanning. com, Web Site: www.visualplanning. com
Mng Dir: Joseph P. Josephson
Sls Mgr: Carl Maurice
Conducts Business: U.S., Canada
Employees: 20
Primary Market Served: Business & Consumer
Catalog available online
Indirect online sales
Founded: 1958

Magnetic & perforated scheduling boards, t-cards & accessories. Graphic Arts materials: lettering, precision knives, etc. Audio-Visual equipment & supplies: easels & pads, lecterns, bulletin boards, projectors, screens, markers & signs.

MAXON FURNITURE INC

505 Ford Ave
Muscatine, IA 52761-5662
Telephone: (253) 395-4139, Toll Free: (800) 876-4274, FAX: (800) 257-2635, Web Site: www. maxonfurniture.com
Bus Devel: Bill Duncan
Primary Market Served: Business & Consumer

Manufactures office furniture

MEAD WESTVACO CONSUMER & OFFICE PRODUCTS

Div. of Mead Corp
501 S 5th St
Richmond, VA 23219-0501

Telephone: (937) 222-6323, Toll Free: (804) 444-1000, FAX: (937) 495-3192, Web Site: www. meadwestvaco.com
Chmn & CEO: John A Luke Jr
Exec VP Global Opers: Robert A Feeser
VP: Donna O Cox
Exec VP Global Commercial: Robert K Beckler
VP & Controller: Brent A Harwood
Primary Market Served: Business & Consumer
Founded: 1846

Make paper products. Sell office & school supplies.

MERRIMADE STATIONERY CO LLC

Sub. of American Stationery Co.
275 Billerca Rd
Chelmsford, MA 01824-4113
Toll Free: (800) 344-4256, FAX: (800) 883-6515, E-Mail: custserv@ merrimadestationery.com, Web Site: www.merrimade.com
Conducts Business: U.S.
Employees: 15
Primary Market Served: Consumer
Catalog available online
Direct online sales
Advertising/Marketing Budget Related to Direct Marketing: 76-100%
Founded: 1934

Sell personalized stationery, paper goods & gifts primarily through catalog.

MODERN POSTCARD

1675 Faraday Ave
Carlsbad, CA 92008-7314
Toll Free: (800) 959-8365, Web Site: www.modernpostcard.com
Founder & CEO: Steve Hoffman
VP Corp Solutions: Keith Goodman
CFO: John P Mei
Dir Manufacturing: Jason Anderson
Primary Market Served: Business
Founded: 1976

Postcard printing & direct marketing solutions.

NEBS

Acquired by Deluxe Corp. in 2004.
500 Main St
Groton, MA 01471-0001
Telephone: (978) 448-6111, Toll Free: (800) 225-6380, (888) 823-6327, FAX: (978) 448-3653, (800) 234-4324, E-Mail: customerservice@ nebs.com, Web Site: www.nebs.com
Sr VP & Pres, Chiswick Div: John F. Fairbanks

Sr VP & Pres Diversified Opers:
George P Allman
Sr VP & Pres NEBS Direct Mktg: Robert D Warren
Sr VP & Pres PremiumWear: David E Berg
Sr VP Mfg & Tech Opers: Steven G Schlerf
Conducts Business: U.S., Canada, U. K., France
Employees: 3,800
Primary Market Served: Business
Catalog available online
Indirect online sales
Advertising/Marketing Budget Related to Direct Marketing: 76-100%
Founded: 1952

Supplier of personalized business products for small businesses.

NATIONAL BUSINESS FURNITURE INC

735 N Water St Ste 440
Milwaukee, WI 53202-4103
Telephone: (414) 276-8511, Toll Free: (800) 558-1010, FAX: (414) 276-8371, Web Site: www. nationalbusinessfurniture.com
Pres: George A Mosher
Gen Mgr: Rick Wachowiak
Dir Ecommerce: Eric Nebbia
VP Multi-Channel Mktg: Dean Stoer
Comml Interiors Consultant: Lucy Eastabrook
Conducts Business: U.S.
Employees: 150
Primary Market Served: Business & Consumer
Catalog available online
Direct online sales
Advertising/Marketing Budget Related to Direct Marketing: 76-100%
Direct Marketing ad budget: $10,000,000
Direct Mail: 100%
Founded: 1975
Gross sales or billing: $24,800,000

Sells office furniture by catalog throughout the U.S. Branches in Atlanta, Dallas, Los Angeles, New York & Chicago.

OFFICEMAX INC

Subs. of Office Depot Inc
6600 N Military Trail
Boca Raton, FL 33496
Toll Free: (877) 633-4236, Web Site: www.officemax.com
Chmn & CEO: Roland C. Smith
Exec VP & CFO: Stephen E. Hare
Exec VP Mktg: Tim Rea
Exec VP E-Commerce: Mike Kirschner
Dir Direct Mktg: Maureen E Gilroy
Primary Market Served: Business & Consumer

Catalog available online
Direct online sales
Founded: 1913

Office supplies & furniture.

ONE POINT

101 Poplar St Unit 2
Scranton, PA 18509-2745
Telephone: (570) 342-0737, Toll Free: (800) 526-4460, FAX: (570) 343-6361, Web Site: www.opoffice.com
Owner: Pat McMahon
Dir Bus Devel: Wayne Whipple
Conducts Business: U.S.
Primary Market Served: Business
Founded: 1980

Sell examination & office forms, pegboard systems, office desk accessories to physicians, dentists & other health professionals.

PTI PYRAMID TECHNOLOGIES LLC

45 Gracey Ave
Meriden, CT 06451-2284
Telephone: (203) 238-0550, Toll Free: (888) 479-7264, FAX: (203) 634-1696, Web Site: www.pyramid-technologies.com
Sls & Mktg Mgr: Bob Cooper
Pres: John Augustyn
VP Sales & Mktg: Bob Lennon
Primary Market Served: Business

Manufacturer of time clocks, ribbons and inks.

PAASCHE AIRBRUSH CO

4311 N Normandy Ave
Chicago, IL 60634-1395
Telephone: (773) 867-9191, FAX: (773) 867-9198, E-Mail: info@paascheairbrush.com, Web Site: www.paascheairbrush.com
VP: Brian Pettersen
VP & Sls Mgr: John Lagerlof
CFO: Steven Petterson
Asst Sls Mgr: Patricia Lagerlof
Employees: 95
Primary Market Served: Business & Consumer
Catalog available online
Direct online sales
Advertising/Marketing Budget Related to Direct Marketing: 0-25%
Founded: 1904

Manufacturer of the most complete line of artist's airbrushes, industrial, manual & automatic spray guns, paint spray booths & special coating equipment.

PATTERSON DENTAL

1031 Mendota Heights Rd
Saint Paul, MN 55120-1419

Telephone: (651) 686-1600, Toll Free: (800) 328-5536, FAX: (651) 686-9331, Web Site: www.pattersondental.com
Chmn, Pres & CEO: Scott P Anderson
Exec VP & CFO: Ann Gugino
VP, Opers: Sean Muniz
Conducts Business: U.S.
Primary Market Served: Business
Catalog available online
Direct online sales
Direct Marketing ad budget:
Direct Mail: 90%
Magazines: 3%
Telephone: 7%

Sell practice management supplies (bookkeeping systems, appointment logs, stationery, filing supplies) to the medical & dental industry. Also, business forms, stationery & computer supplies for small businesses & attorneys.

PENNY WISE OFFICE PRODUCTS

6911 Laurel Bowie Rd (Suite 209)
Bowie, MD 20715-1712
Telephone: (301) 805-7733, Toll Free: (800) 942-3311, FAX: (800) 622-4411, Web Site: www.penny-wise.com
VP, Mktg: Kathryn Peffers
Pres: Kathryn Morley
Primary Market Served: Business
Catalog available online
Direct online sales
Advertising/Marketing Budget Related to Direct Marketing: 76-100%

Sell office products via catalog & the internet.

PITNEY BOWES

Div. of Pitney Bowes Americas
1 Elmcroft Rd
Stamford, CT 06926-0700
Telephone: (203) 356-5000, Toll Free: (800) MR-BOWES, Web Site: www.pitneybowes.com
Exec VP & Pres, Mailing Solutions Mngmt: Leslie Abi-Karam
Pres & CEO: Marc B Lautenbach
VP & Pres Bitney Bowes Mailing North America: Patrick Brand
Exec VP & CFO: Michael Monahan
Exec VP & Chief Mktg Officer: Abbey F Kohnstamm
Conducts Business: Worldwide
Employees: 34,454
Primary Market Served: Business
Advertising/Marketing Budget Related to Direct Marketing: 51-75%
Gross sales or billing: $4,213,000

Manufacture mailing systems, including addressing, inserting, weighing, and postage.

PRO CHEMICAL & DYE INC
126 Shove St
Fall River, MA 02724-2039
Telephone: (508) 676-3838, FAX:
(508) 676-3980, Web Site: www.
prochemicalanddye.com
Pres: Adelle S. Wiener
VP: Donald Wiener
Conducts Business: Worldwide
Primary Market Served: Consumer
Catalog available online
Direct online sales
Advertising/Marketing Budget Related
to Direct Marketing: 51-75%
Founded: 1970

Sell dyes, chemicals & supplies for batik, silkscreen & dyeing. Suppliers of
Pebeo products & PROfab Textile Inks
for painting, stenciling & silkscreening,
marbling colors & supplies.

QUALITY PRODUCTS INC
2415 Hwy 45 N, PO Box 564
Columbus, MS 39703
Telephone: (662) 328-1477, Toll Free:
(800) 647-1057, FAX: (800) 824-
8510, E-Mail: kshep@
classroomsupply.com, Web Site:
www.classroomsupply.com
Pres: Fred Jones
VP: Bethea Jones
Conducts Business: U.S.
Employees: 14
Primary Market Served: Business
Catalog available online
Direct online sales
Advertising/Marketing Budget Related
to Direct Marketing: 76-100%
Direct Marketing ad budget:
Direct Mail: 90%
Online: 10%
Founded: 1964

Sell school items.

QUILL LINCOLNSHIRE INC
A Staples Inc company
100 Schelter Rd
Lincolnshire, IL 60069
Toll Free: (800) 982-3400, FAX: (800)
789-8955, Web Site: www.quill.com
Pres: Sergio Pereira
VP Mktg: Kayrle Sieber
Conducts Business: U.S.
Primary Market Served: Business
Founded: 1956

Distributor of technology, cleaning &
breakroom supplies, business furniture,
safety products and general office supplies to small & medium sized businesses.

RENTON'S INC
10107 Quarry Hill Pl
Parker, CO 80134-3748

Telephone: (303) 865-7025, Toll Free:
(800) 365-6644, E-Mail: info@
rentons.com, Web Site: www.
rentons.com
Owner: Dawn Goldwasser
Employees: 4
Primary Market Served: Business
Catalog available online
Direct online sales
Founded: 1989

Mail order business-to-business labels.

THE RYTEX CO
CD Bakehorn Inc/The Rytex Co
100 N Park Ave
Peru, IN 46970-1701
Telephone: (317) 872-8553, Toll Free:
(800) 277-5458, FAX: (317) 872-
8535, (800) 329-1669, Web Site:
www.rytex.com
Pres & Owner: Mike Bakehorn
Gen Mgr: Bob Ellett
Primary Market Served: Consumer
Advertising/Marketing Budget Related
to Direct Marketing: 76-100%
Direct Marketing ad budget:
Direct Mail: 100%
Founded: 1929

Catalog & retail sales of personalized
stationery.

SAX ARTS & CRAFTS
Div. of School Specialty, Inc
PO Box 1579
Appleton, WI 54912-1579
Toll Free: (800) 558-6696, FAX: (800)
328-4729, E-Mail: info@saxarts.
com, Web Site: www.saxarts.com
Exec VP: John Thoreson
Conducts Business: U.S.
Employees: 160
Primary Market Served: Business
Advertising/Marketing Budget Related
to Direct Marketing: 0-25%
Founded: 1945

Full line of art supplies to schools.

DANIEL SMITH INC
4150 1st Ave S
Seattle, WA 98134
Telephone: (206) 223-9599, Toll Free:
(800) 426-6740, FAX: (800) 238-
4065, E-Mail: sales@danielsmith.
com, Web Site: www.danielsmith.
com
Owner: Daniel Smith
CEO: John Cogley
VP, Mktg & Sls: Debra Kehoe
Conducts Business: Worldwide
Employees: 150
Primary Market Served: Consumer
Catalog available online
Direct online sales

Founded: 1976
Cataloger/retailer of fine artists' materials.

STAPLES INC
500 Staples Dr
Framingham, MA 01702-4474
Telephone: (508) 253-5000, FAX:
(508) 253-7803, Web Site: www.
staples.com
Sr VP: Peter Howard
CEO: Ronald L Sargent
CFO: Christine T Komola
COO: Joseph G Doody
Conducts Business: U.S., Canada
Primary Market Served: Business &
Consumer
Founded: 1986

Sell discount office supplies to small &
mid-sized businesses & to home offices.

STRATFORD HALL
1680 Roe Crest Dr
North Mankato, MN 56003-2658
Telephone: (708) 496-4908, Toll Free:
(800) 628-9028, FAX: (708) 496-
8058, E-Mail: stratfordhall@
myprinter.com, Web Site: www.
stratfordhall.com
VP, Opers: Tom Kleen
Conducts Business: U.S.
Employees: 300
Primary Market Served: Business &
Consumer

Sell personalized Christmas cards.

SUNRISE BUSINESS PRODUCTS
99 Mark Tree Rd Ste 202, Centereach,
NY 11720-2276
69 E Jericho Tpke
Mineola, NY 11501
Toll Free: (800) 222-7367, FAX: (631)
588-3900
Pres: Joseph Caldwell
Conducts Business: U.S., Canada
Employees: 21
Primary Market Served: Business
Catalog available online
Indirect online sales
Advertising/Marketing Budget Related
to Direct Marketing: 0-25%
Direct Marketing ad budget: $300,000
Direct Mail: $200,000
Magazines: $50,000
Telephone: $50,000
Founded: 1945
Gross sales or billing: $4,500,000

Supplier of office products, industrial
products and restaurant supplies.

TALAS
330 Morgan Ave

Brooklyn, NY 11211
Telephone: (212) 219-0770, FAX:
(212) 219-0735, E-Mail: info@
talasonline.com, Web Site: www.
talasonline.com
CEO: Jacob Salic
Employees: 25
Primary Market Served: Business &
Consumer
Catalog available online
Founded: 2006

Serves the museum & library community with hand bookbinding & conservation supplies.

THINK INK

9709 Riverbend Dr
Bothell, WA 98011-4030
Telephone: (425) 778-1935, Toll Free:
(800) 778-1935, E-Mail: jean.
lewis1@comcast.net, Web Site:
www.thinkink.net
Owner: Jean Lewis
Primary Market Served: Business &
Consumer
Catalog available online
Direct online sales
Founded: 1981

Hand-operated printers & embossing powder.

TUTTLE PRINTING & ENGRAVING

414 Quality Ln
Rutland, VT 05702
Telephone: (802) 773-9171, Toll Free:
(800) 776-7682, FAX: (802) 773-
5785, E-Mail: info@tuttleprinting.
com, Web Site: www.tuttleprinting.
com
Chmn: Deva M. Bolgioni
Pres & CEO: Joanne Cillo
Reg Sales Mgr: Joel Perry
VP, Plant Opers: Paul Bishop
VP Sales & Mktg: Eugenia Cooke
Reg Sales Mgr: Don Goodman
Dir, Mktg: Patrick J. McMorrow
Customer Svc Mgr: Diane Haggerty
Conducts Business: U.S.
Employees: 61
Primary Market Served: Business
Catalog available online
Direct online sales
Advertising/Marketing Budget Related
to Direct Marketing: 76-100%
Direct Marketing ad budget:
Direct Mail: 80%
Magazines: 15%
Online: 5%
Founded: 1912

Professional stationery and professional office supplies & services.

UTRETCH ART SUPPLIES

6 Corporate Dr Ste 1
Cranbury, NJ 08512-3616
Telephone: (609) 409-8001, Toll Free:
(800) 223-9132, FAX: (800) 382-
1979, Web Site: www.utrechtart.com
Web Content Mgr: Don Rodriguez
Primary Market Served: Business &
Consumer

Manufactures & supplies fine art materials & supplies to artists, teachers & students.

VAGABOND CREATIONS INC

2560 Lance Dr
Dayton, OH 45409-1581
Telephone: (937) 298-1124, Toll Free:
(800) 738-7237, FAX: (937) 298-
1124, E-Mail: sales@
vagabondcreations.net, Web Site:
www.vagabondcreations.net
Pres: George F. Stanley Jr.
Conducts Business: U.S., Canada, Japan
Employees: 5
Primary Market Served: Business
Catalog available online
Direct online sales
Advertising/Marketing Budget Related
to Direct Marketing: 76-100%
Direct Marketing ad budget: $2,000
Direct Mail: 20%
Online: 60%
Telephone: 20%
Founded: 1955
Gross sales or billing: $110,000

Illustrated stationery tablets with assorted pages. Sell to all types of retail outlets.

APSCO

7994 CR Ten
Davenport Center, NY 13751
Telephone: (607) 278-6218, FAX:
(607) 278-6218, E-Mail:
webmaster@antiquephono.com, Web
Site: www.antiquephono.com
Owner: Dennis J. Valente
Owner: Patricia F. Valente
Conducts Business: Worldwide
Employees: 2
Primary Market Served: Business &
Consumer
Catalog available online
Indirect online sales
Direct Marketing ad budget: $800
Magazines: 5%
Newspapers: 95%
Founded: 1976
Gross sales or billing: $125,000

Repairs, parts & service for antique &
wind-up phonographs. Steel needles,
record sleeves, steel mainsprings &
decals. Sell to dealers, hobbyists & collectors. Supply catalog is $3.

ACTION DIRECT INC

14285 SW 142nd St
Miami, FL 33186
Telephone: (305) 969-0056, E-Mail:
info@action-direct.com, Web Site:
www.action-direct.com
Pres: J.O. Flores
VP: Eliezer Flores
Treas: Omar Flores
Conducts Business: US
Employees: 9
Primary Market Served: Business &
Consumer
Catalog available online
Direct online sales
Advertising/Marketing Budget Related
to Direct Marketing: 76-100%
Direct Marketing ad budget: $500,000
Direct Mail: 35%
Magazines: 5%
Online: 60%
Founded: 1981

Publisher of camping, hunting, self defense & outdoor merchandise catalogs.

ACUSPORT CORP

1 Hunter Pl
Bellefontaine, OH 43311-3001
Telephone: (937) 593-7010, FAX:
(937) 592-5625, E-Mail: mwsales@
acusport.com, Web Site: www.
acusport.com
Chmn & CEO: William L. Fraim
Pres & COO: James A. Broering
Dir, IT: Deb Ward
Prod Mgr: Rick Robinson
Conducts Business: U.S.

Employees: 150
Primary Market Served: Business
Direct online sales
Advertising/Marketing Budget Related
to Direct Marketing: 76-100%
Founded: 1965
Gross sales or billing: $142,000,000

Distributor of hunting & shooting
sports products.

AKERS SKI INC

51 Akers Way
Andover, ME 04216
Telephone: (207) 392-4582, FAX:
(207) 392-1225, E-Mail: sales@
akers-ski.com, Web Site: www.
akers-ski.com
Pres: Leon Akers
Conducts Business: U.S.
Employees: 5
Primary Market Served: Consumer
Catalog available online
Direct online sales
Advertising/Marketing Budget Related
to Direct Marketing: 76-100%
Founded: 1958

Sell cross-country ski equipment & accessories via mail order.

ALLBRANDS.COM SEWING
MACHINE SUPERSTORE

20415 Highland Rd
Baton Rouge, LA 70817-7348
Telephone: (225) 923-1285, Toll Free:
(866) 255-2726, FAX: (225) 923-
1261, E-Mail: info@allbrands.com,
Web Site: www.allbrands.com
Owner & Teacher: Annette Douthat
Owner & Technician: John M. Douthat
VP, Opers: Warren Sagen
Conducts Business: Worldwide
Employees: 20
Primary Market Served: Business &
Consumer
Catalog available online
Direct online sales
Advertising/Marketing Budget Related
to Direct Marketing: 0-25%
Direct Marketing ad budget: $250,000
Magazines: $50,000
Newspapers: $50,000
Online: $100,000
Telephone: $50,000
Founded: 1976
Gross sales or billing: $12,000,000

Sewing, embroidery, serger, knitting, &
industrial machines for home & industry. Also, vacuum cleaners and small
appliances.

AMERICAN HORSE
PRODUCTS

Div. of Interfab Corp
31896 Plaza Dr (Suite C4)
San Juan Capistrano, CA 92675
Telephone: (949) 248-5300, Toll Free:
(800) 500-0799, FAX: (949) 248-
5305, E-Mail: zjim@sbcglobal.net,
Web Site: www.
americanhorseproducts.com
Pres: James Carter
Mktg: Diane Carter
Office Mgr: Mary Weinik
Sls: Lori Melville
Buyer: Lorinda Engelhorn
Conducts Business: U.S.
Employees: 12
Primary Market Served: Consumer
Catalog available online
Direct online sales
Advertising/Marketing Budget Related
to Direct Marketing: 51-75%
Direct Marketing ad budget: $200,000
Direct Mail: 75%
Magazines: 15%
Online: 10%
Founded: 1998
Gross sales or billing: $2,500,000

Products for horses including saddles,
boots, supplements, topicals, hoof care,
grooming & leather care products,
books, music & trail accessories.

AMERICAN RECREATION
PRODUCTS INC

Div. of Kellwood Corp
1224 Fern Ridge Pkwy
Saint Louis, MO 63141-4404
Telephone: (314) 576-8000, FAX:
(314) 576-8072
Chmn: Hal Upbin
VP Fin: Len Klonowski
VP, Opers: Tim Hinds
Mktg & Sls Mgr: Eric Reinsfelder
Conducts Business: U.S., Canada
Employees: 750
Primary Market Served: Business

Manufacturer of outdoor recreational
gear: tents, sleeping bags, backpacks &
sleep systems. Retail stores & catalogs.

AMPERSAND PRESS

750 Lake St
Port Townsend, WA 98368-2216
Telephone: (360) 379-5187, Toll Free:
(800) 624-4263, FAX: (360) 379-
0324, E-Mail: info@ampersandpress.
com, Web Site: www.
ampersandpress.com
Pres: Lou Haller
Conducts Business: U.S., Canada, Australia

Employees: 6
Primary Market Served: Business
Catalog available online
Direct online sales
Advertising/Marketing Budget Related
to Direct Marketing: 0-25%
Direct Marketing ad budget: $500
Magazines: 100%
Founded: 1973
Gross sales or billing: $1,000,000

Nature & science games, rubber stamps
& educational materials & supplies.

ANGLER'S CATALOG CO
3551 W Deerfield Dr
Eagle, ID 83616
Telephone: (208) 378-9536, Toll Free:
(800) 657-8040, FAX: (208) 735-
8758, E-Mail: sales@anglers-catalog.
com, Web Site: www.anglers-
catalog.com
Owner: John Meyer
Conducts Business: Worldwide
Employees: 4
Primary Market Served: Business &
Consumer
Catalog available online
Direct online sales
Founded: 1976
Gross sales or billing: $600,000

Unique gift ideas for the fly fisherman.

THE ANGLER'S DEN
11 W Main St (Suite 4)
Pawling, NY 12564-1341
Telephone: (845) 855-5182, E-Mail:
flyfish@anglersden.net, Web Site:
www.anglersden.net
Partner: Rob O'Neill
Conducts Business: U.S., Canada
Employees: 2
Primary Market Served: Consumer
Catalog available online
Indirect online sales
Advertising/Marketing Budget Related
to Direct Marketing: 51-75%
Direct Marketing ad budget: $15,000
Direct Mail: 30%
Magazines: 70%
Founded: 1984
Gross sales or billing: $100,000

High quality fly tying materials. Specialize in natural & hard-to-find. Catalogs upon request ($2.50 a piece).

ANNIE'S ATTIC LLC
1 Annie Ln
Big Sandy, TX 75755-9400
Telephone: (903) 636-4303, Toll Free:
(800) 282-6643, FAX: (903) 636-
4088, Web Site: www.anniesattic.
com
CEO & Pres: David McKee
Partner: Arthur K. Muselman
VP, Sls & Mktg: Marge Evans

VP: Dan Kennedy
Conducts Business: U.S., Canada
Employees: 150
Primary Market Served: Business &
Consumer
Catalog available online
Direct online sales
Advertising/Marketing Budget Related
to Direct Marketing: 76-100%

Mail order needlecraft company specializing in crochet & needlecraft patterns.

**ANTIQUE & COLLECTIBLE
TOOLS INC**
27 Fickett Rd
Pownal, ME 04069
Telephone: (207) 688-4962, FAX:
(207) 688-4831, E-Mail: ceb@
finetoolj.com, Web Site: www.
finetoolj.com
Pres: Clarence Blanchard
Conducts Business: Worldwide
Employees: 4
Primary Market Served: Business &
Consumer
Catalog available online
Direct online sales
Advertising/Marketing Budget Related
to Direct Marketing: 76-100%
Direct Marketing ad budget:
Direct Mail: $10,000
Magazines: $4,000
Founded: 1970

Market antique, obsolete & vintage
hand tools through "The Fine Tool
Journal" for collectors & craftsmen.
Also market books on antique tools and
sell advertising in "Fine Tool Journal."
Direct sales of vintage, high quality
hand tools. Quarterly absentee auction
of antique tools.

ATLANTA CUTLERY CORP
2147 Gees Mill Rd NE
Conyers, GA 30013-1333
Telephone: (770) 922-3700, Toll Free:
(800) 833-8838, FAX: (770) 760-
8993, E-Mail: webmaster@
atlantacutlery.com, Web Site: www.
atlantacutlery.com
CEO: Pradeep Windlass
Pres: Sudhir Windlass
VP: Robin Chauduri
VP: Dave DiPietro
VP: Bruce Brookhurt
Conducts Business: Worldwide
Employees: 45
Primary Market Served: Business &
Consumer
Catalog available online
Direct online sales
Advertising/Marketing Budget Related
to Direct Marketing: 76-100%

Direct Marketing ad budget:
$1,200,000
Direct Mail: 60%
Magazines: 10%
Online: 30%
Founded: 1971
Gross sales or billing: $9,000,000

Hunting, survival & military issue knives plus finished blades, handle materials & books for knifemakers.

**BARON/BARCLAY BRIDGE
SUPPLIES**
Div. of Devyn Press
3600 Chamberlain Ln (Suite 206)
Louisville, KY 40241
Telephone: (502) 426-0410, Toll Free:
(800) 274-2221, FAX: (502) 426-
2044, E-Mail: baronbarclay@
baronbarclay.com, Web Site: www.
baronbarclay.com
Founder: Randall Baron
Pres: Jim Maier
VP: Mary Baron
Conducts Business: Worldwide
Employees: 12
Primary Market Served: Business &
Consumer
Catalog available online
Direct online sales
Advertising/Marketing Budget Related
to Direct Marketing: 51-75%
Founded: 1942

Everything on the game of bridge.

BART'S WATERSPORTS
7581 E 800th N
North Webster, IN 46555-9604
Telephone: (574) 834-7666, Toll Free:
(800) 348-5016, FAX: (574) 834-
4246, E-Mail: info@barts.com, Web
Site: www.bartswatersports.com
Pres: J. Bart Culver
CEO: Bringier McConnell
Art Dir: Judy Wagner
Mgr: Michael Wilson
Conducts Business: Worldwide
Employees: 45
Primary Market Served: Business &
Consumer
Catalog available online
Direct online sales
Advertising/Marketing Budget Related
to Direct Marketing: 76-100%
Founded: 1971

Discount marketer of water sports
equipment & accessories.

BASS PRO SHOPS
1935 S Campbell Ave
Springfield, MO 65807
Telephone: (417) 887-7334, FAX:
(417) 873-5882, Web Site: www.
basspro.com

Founder: John Morris
COO: Jim Hagale
Dir, Corp Database Mktg: Carl Kendrick
Dir, Database Mktg: Timothy Scott
Conducts Business: Worldwide
Employees: 4,000
Primary Market Served: Business & Consumer
Catalog available online
Direct online sales
Founded: 1969

Catalog & retail marketer of fishing, hunting & outdoor recreational products.

BEAR WOODS SUPPLY CO INC

PO Box 275
Cornwallis, NS, Canada B0S 1H0
Telephone: (902) 638-8622, Toll Free: (800) 565-5066, FAX: (902) 638-8637, Web Site: www.bearwood.com, www.woodparts.ca
Pres: Victor Schneweiss
VP Mktg: Shela Breau
Conducts Business: Canada, U.S., U.K., Hong Kong, Iceland, New Zealand
Employees: 10
Primary Market Served: Business & Consumer
Catalog available online
Direct online sales
Advertising/Marketing Budget Related to Direct Marketing: 76-100%
Direct Marketing ad budget:
Magazines: 100%
Founded: 1987

Mail order wood turnings, hardware & craft supplies.

BEEMAN PRECISION AIRGUNS

SR Industries Inc
10652 Bloomfield Ave
Santa Fe Springs, CA 90670-3912
Telephone: (562) 968-5891, Toll Free: (800) 227-2744, FAX: (562) 968-5823, E-Mail: sales@beeman.com, Web Site: www.beeman.com
Pres: Robert Eck
Conducts Business: Worldwide
Employees: 20
Primary Market Served: Business & Consumer
Founded: 1971

Importer & distributor of precision adult air rifles, pistols, pellets & related accessories. Sell through jobbers, dealers, mail-order & export.

BETTER HEALTH FITNESS

5302 New Utrecht Ave

Brooklyn, NY 11219-4139
Telephone: (718) 436-4693, FAX: (718) 854-3381, Web Site: www.betterhealthfitness.com
Pres & Owner: Rita Gottehrer
Gen Mgr: Marvin Friedman
Conducts Business: U.S.
Employees: 9
Primary Market Served: Business & Consumer
Catalog available online
Direct online sales
Advertising/Marketing Budget Related to Direct Marketing: 0-25%
Direct Marketing ad budget:
Direct Mail: 10%
Magazines: 70%
Newspapers: 10%
Telephone: 10%
Founded: 1977
Gross sales or billing: $180,000

Fitness & recreation equipment.

BIKE NASHBAR

Div. of Nashbar & Associates Inc
PO Box 1455
Crab Orchard, WV 25827-1455
Toll Free: (800) NAS-HBAR, FAX: (877) 778-9456, E-Mail: custserv@nashbar.com, Web Site: www.bikenashbar.com
Pres: Gary Snook
CFO: David Prvitt
VP: Bob Martin
VP, Mktg: Stewart Westland
Conducts Business: U.S., Canada
Employees: 240
Primary Market Served: Consumer
Catalog available online
Direct online sales
Advertising/Marketing Budget Related to Direct Marketing: 76-100%
Direct Marketing ad budget:
Direct Mail: 80%
Magazines: 20%
Founded: 1974
Gross sales or billing: $30,000,000

Catalog sales of high-tech bicycles, parts, accessories & apparel.

BITS & PIECES INC

PO Box 4150
Lawrenceburg, IN 47025
Toll Free: (866) 503-6395, FAX: (513) 354-1290, Web Site: www.bitsandpieces.com
Pres: Alan Segal
Conducts Business: Worldwide
Primary Market Served: Consumer
Catalog available online
Direct online sales
Advertising/Marketing Budget Related to Direct Marketing: 26-50%
Founded: 1983

Mail order marketer of jigsaw puzzles.

BRIGADE QUARTERMASTERS LTD

177 Georgia Ave
Providence, RI 02905-4422
Telephone: (770) 428-1248, Toll Free: (800) 338-4327, FAX: (800) 892-2992, Web Site: www.actiongear.com
Pres: Mitchell L. WerBell IV
CFO: Geoffrey WerBell
Mktg Dir: Wendy Abney
Conducts Business: Worldwide
Employees: 80
Primary Market Served: Business & Consumer
Advertising/Marketing Budget Related to Direct Marketing: 76-100%
Founded: 1978
Gross sales or billing: $40,500,000

Sell products for camping, hunting, survival, military & police use.

BUSHNELL CORPORATION

Owned by Worldwide Sports & Recreation
9200 Cody St
Overland Park, KS 66214-1734
Telephone: (913) 752-3400, Toll Free: (800) 423-3537, FAX: (913) 752-3561, Web Site: www.bushnell.com
VP, Sls: Mark Welch
Conducts Business: Worldwide
Employees: 150
Primary Market Served: Business & Consumer
Founded: 1947

Sell Bushnell, Bausch & Lomb & Jason binoculars, telescopes, riflescopes & rangefinders.

C&T BRIDGE SUPPLIES

3532 Katella Ave (Suite 103)
Los Alamitos, CA 90720-3138
Telephone: (562) 598-7010, Toll Free: (800) 525-4718, FAX: (562) 430-8309, E-Mail: tedinlosal@aol.com
VP: Chris Brown
Conducts Business: Worldwide
Employees: 2
Primary Market Served: Business & Consumer
Catalog available online
Direct online sales
Advertising/Marketing Budget Related to Direct Marketing: 51-75%
Direct Marketing ad budget: $10,000
Newspapers: 70%
Telephone: 30%
Founded: 1982
Gross sales or billing: $200,000

Books & supplies about the game of bridge distributed to individuals & bridge clubs.

CJ HUMMUL CO
PO Box 522, 422 Third St
Nescopeck, PA 18635-0522
Telephone: (570) 752-0936, Toll Free:
(800) 762-0235, FAX: (570) 752-
0938, E-Mail: mail@hummul.com,
Web Site: www.hummul.com
Pres: Raymond Zajac
Conducts Business: U.S., Canada, Ja-
pan, U.K.
Employees: 3
Primary Market Served: Consumer
Catalog available online
Direct online sales
Advertising/Marketing Budget Related
to Direct Marketing: 76-100%
Direct Marketing ad budget:
Direct Mail: 98%
Magazines: 2%
Founded: 1977

Woodcarving supplies.

CPM DELTA 1, INC
10830 Sanden Dr
Dallas, TX 75238
Telephone: (214) 349-6886, Toll Free:
(800) 627-0252, FAX: (214) 503-
1557, Web Site: www.cpmdelta1.
com
Adv Mgr & Sls: Teresa Dingus
Dir: Larry Long
Technical Support & Sales: Brad Evans
Sls: Rick Wait
Conducts Business: Worldwide
Employees: 30
Primary Market Served: Business &
Consumer
Advertising/Marketing Budget Related
to Direct Marketing: 26-50%
Direct Marketing ad budget: $100,000
Magazines: 100%
Founded: 1972
Gross sales or billing: $2,000,000

Manufacture photographic, darkroom
& studio equipment. Sell direct through
catalogs to distributors.

CABELA'S INC
1 Cabela Dr
Sidney, NE 69160-1001
Telephone: (308) 254-5505, Toll Free:
(800) 237-4444, FAX: (308) 254-
4800, Web Site: www.cabelas.com
Chmn & Dir: Richard Cabela
Vice Chmn & Dir: James Cabela
CEO: Tommy Millner
Sr VP of Bus Devel & Intl Opers: Mi-
chael Callahan
Dir, Direct Mktg: Ryan Watchorn
Conducts Business: Worldwide
Employees: 12,000
Primary Market Served: Business &
Consumer
Catalog available online
Direct online sales

Founded: 1961
Gross sales or billing: $2,000,000,000
Catalog marketer of outdoor products
for fishing, camping, hunting, archery
& gift items for the outdoor enthusiasts.

CAMPING WORLD INC
Box 90018
Bowling Green, KY 42102-9018
Telephone: (270) 781-2718, Toll Free:
(800) 626-6189, FAX: (270) 796-
8991, Web Site: www.
campingworld.com
Pres & CEO: Marcus Lemonis
Chief Mktg Officer: Tamara Ward
Exec Dir, Good Sam Club: Mike Sie-
mens
Conducts Business: U.S., Canada
Employees: 675
Primary Market Served: Consumer
Catalog available online
Direct online sales
Direct Marketing ad budget:
$7,500,000
Direct Mail: $7,250,000
Magazines: $200,000
Newspapers: $30,000
TV/Radio: $20,000
Gross sales or billing: $250,000,000

Mass merchandiser & mail order catalog house for recreational vehicle accessories.

THE CANING SHOP
926 Gilman St
Berkeley, CA 94710
Telephone: (510) 527-5010, Toll Free:
(800) 544-3373, FAX: (510) 527-
7718, Web Site: www.caning.com
Owner: Jim Widess
Conducts Business: Worldwide
Primary Market Served: Business &
Consumer
Catalog available online
Direct online sales
Advertising/Marketing Budget Related
to Direct Marketing: 51-75%
Direct Marketing ad budget:
Direct Mail: 100%
Founded: 1969

Complete selection of basketry, chair
caning & gourd embellishment supplies, books & tools.

CASCADE OUTFITTERS
604 E 45th St
Boise, ID 83714-4848
Telephone: (208) 322-4411, Toll Free:
(800) 223-7328, FAX: (208) 322-
5016, E-Mail: mail@
cascadeoutfitters.com, Web Site:
www.cascadeoutfitters.com
VP: Gary Scott

Conducts Business: U.S., Canada, Ja-
pan, Chile, Mexico, Israel, Australia,
New Zealand
Employees: 7
Primary Market Served: Consumer
Direct Marketing ad budget: $15,000
Magazines: 100%
Gross sales or billing: $950,000

Sell quality whitewater & outdoor
equipment through 80 page catalog.

CATCH THE WIND KITE SHOP
266 SE Hwy 101
Lincoln City, OR 97367-2749
Telephone: (541) 994-9500, Toll Free:
(800) 227-7878, FAX: (541) 994-
4766, E-Mail: catchthewindkites@
yahoo.com, Web Site: www.
catchthewind.com
Mgr: Keith McNeil
Sls Mgr: Lisa M. Herndon
Employees: 5
Primary Market Served: Consumer
Founded: 1979

Sells kites, windsocks, banners & fun
wind-related items through catalogs &
stores.

CHAMPS CORP
311 Manatee Ave W
Bradenton, FL 34205
Telephone: (941) 748-0577, Toll Free:
(800) 991-6813, E-Mail:
customer_service@champssports.
com, Web Site: www.champssports.
com
Chmn, Pres & CEO: Matthew D. Serra
Sr VP: Gary M. Bahler
Sr VP: Peter D. Brown
Sr VP: Lauren B. Peters
CFO & Sr VP: Robert W. Mc Hugh
Primary Market Served: Consumer

All types sporting goods. Corp Headquarters (212) 720-3700.

CHARLOTTE FORD TRUNKS
PO Box 495
Dumas, TX 79029
Telephone: (806) 934-8477, Toll Free:
(800) 659-5614, FAX: (806) 372-
3061, E-Mail: charolette@
charolettefordtrunks.com, Web Site:
www.charolettefordtrunks.com
Pres: Charolette Ford
Conducts Business: U.S., Canada
Primary Market Served: Business &
Consumer
Catalog available online
Direct online sales
Advertising/Marketing Budget Related
to Direct Marketing: 51-75%
Direct Marketing ad budget:
Magazines: $30,000

Founded: 1977
Publish trunk parts catalog, how-to-restore trunks & trunk talk.

CHERRY TREE TOYS INC
12446 W State Rd 81
Beloit, WI 53511-8049
Telephone: (608) 314-3090, Toll Free: (800) 848-4363, FAX: (608) 314-3097, E-Mail: sales@cherrytreetoys.com, Web Site: www.cherrytreetoys.com
Pres: Matt Simon
CEO: Cynthia Stewart
Conducts Business: Worldwide
Primary Market Served: Business & Consumer
Catalog available online
Direct online sales

Supply plans, parts, kits, tools, books, supplies & accessories for making wooden toys, whirligigs, doll houses, door harps, clocks & weather instruments.

CHICK HARNESS & SUPPLY INC
dba Chick's Discount Saddlery & Equine Wholesalers
18011 S Dupont Hwy
Harrington, DE 19952-2135
Telephone: (302) 398-4630, Toll Free: (800) 444-2441, FAX: (302) 398-3920, E-Mail: saddles@chicksaddlery.com, Web Site: www.chicksaddlery.com
Pres: Robert L. Fleming
Conducts Business: U.S., Canada, Middle East, Europe
Employees: 55
Primary Market Served: Business & Consumer
Catalog available online
Direct online sales
Advertising/Marketing Budget Related to Direct Marketing: 76-100%
Founded: 1975
Gross sales or billing: $4,100,000

Retailer & wholesaler of products for horse owners.

CON-COR INTERNATIONAL
8101 E Research Ct, Tucson, AZ 85710-6758
Div. of James M Conway Corp
8101 E Research Ct Ste 101
Tucson, AZ 85710-6758
Telephone: (520) 721-8939, Toll Free: (888) 255-7688, FAX: (520) 721-8940, E-Mail: concor@con-cor.com, Web Site: www.con-cor.com
Pres: James Conway
Conducts Business: U.S., Canada
Employees: 15

Primary Market Served: Consumer
Catalog available online
Direct online sales
Founded: 1959
Sell a large selection of model trains & railroad books & videos.

CRAZY CROW TRADING POST
1801 Airport Rd, PO Box 847
Pottsboro, TX 75076-3094
Telephone: (903) 786-2287, Toll Free: (800) 786-6210, FAX: (903) 786-9059, E-Mail: info@crazycrow.com, Web Site: www.crazycrow.com
Owner: J. Rex Reddick
Mktg Dir: Jessica Reddick
Conducts Business: U.S., Canada, Europe
Employees: 35
Primary Market Served: Business & Consumer
Catalog available online
Direct online sales
Advertising/Marketing Budget Related to Direct Marketing: 26-50%
Direct Marketing ad budget: $100,000
Direct Mail: 85%
Magazines: 10%
Telephone: 5%
Founded: 1970
Gross sales or billing: $5,000,000

American Indian craft supplies & muzzleloading supplies to Indians, hobbyists, crafts people, muzzleloaders & buckskinners.

CUSTOM ACCESSORIES
5900 Ami Dr
Richmond, IL 60071-8968
Telephone: (847) 966-6900, Toll Free: (800) 962-6676, FAX: (847) 966-9650, Web Site: www.causa.com
Chmn Bd: Abe Matthew
Pres: Ken Matthew
Sr Exec VP: Norman Matthew
Conducts Business: U.S.
Employees: 30
Primary Market Served: Business
Catalog available online
Indirect online sales
Advertising/Marketing Budget Related to Direct Marketing: 0-25%

Auto compasses, Sherrill compasses, private labels & automotive accessories.

DIMMOCK HILL GOLF COURSE PRO SHOP
638 Dimmock Hill Rd
Binghamton, NY 13905-9801

Telephone: (607) 729-5511, Toll Free: (800) 727-5511, FAX: (607) 797-7434, Web Site: www.dimmockhill.com
Owner: Michael Senio
Conducts Business: U.S.
Employees: 8
Primary Market Served: Business & Consumer
Catalog available online
Indirect online sales
Advertising/Marketing Budget Related to Direct Marketing: 51-75%
Direct Marketing ad budget: $50,000
Direct Mail: 10%
Magazines: 40%
Newspapers: 40%
TV/Radio: 10%
Founded: 1970
Gross sales or billing: $1,500,000

Professional golf equipment to golfers.

DIRECT SPORTS SUPPLY
Eastern Gun & Supply Co Inc
1720 Curve Rd
Pearisburg, VA 24134
Telephone: (540) 921-1243, Toll Free: (800) 456-0072, FAX: (540) 921-1475, Web Site: www.directsports.com
VP & CEO: Mike Lively
Pres: Paul V. Wagner
Sec & Treas: Charlotte Wagner
Conducts Business: U.S., England, Germany
Employees: 10
Primary Market Served: Consumer
Advertising/Marketing Budget Related to Direct Marketing: 76-100%
Direct Marketing ad budget:
Direct Mail: $15,000
Newspapers: $6,000
Gross sales or billing: $2,000,000

Sell softball & baseball supplies to consumers.

DOVER SADDLERY
525 Great Rd
Littleton, MA 01460-6221
Telephone: (978) 952-8062, Toll Free: (800) 406-8204, Web Site: www.doversaddlery.com
VP: Lorelle Carpenter
Founded: 1975

Saddlery shop.

EWA & MINIATURE CARS USA INC
369 Springfield Ave, PO Box 188
Berkeley Heights, NJ 07922-0188
Telephone: (732) 424-7811, Toll Free: (800) 392-4454, FAX: (732) 424-7814, E-Mail: ewa@ewacars.com
Pres: Eric Waiter

VP: Carl Pflanzer
Conducts Business: U.S., Canada
Employees: 12
Primary Market Served: Business &
   Consumer
Founded: 1981

Sell model cars, auto books, auto videos & magazines to consumers & businesses.

EAGLE CLAW FISHING
TACKLE

Privately owned by Wright/McGill Co
4245 E 46th Ave
Denver, CO 80216-3219
Telephone: (720) 941-8700, FAX:
   (303) 321-4750, E-Mail: info@
   eagleclaw.com, Web Site: www.
   eagleclaw.com
Owner & Chmn: Lee McGill
Vice Chmn: Bill Miller
Pres: John Jilling
Sr VP, Sls: Tenny Mount
Programmer: Jackie Hock
Conducts Business: Worldwide
Primary Market Served: Business &
   Consumer
Catalog available online
Direct online sales
Advertising/Marketing Budget Related
   to Direct Marketing: 0-25%
Founded: 1925

Manufacturer of Eagle Claw fish
hooks, rods, reels & fishing apparel.

EBERSOLE LAPIDARY
SUPPLY INC

5830 W Hendryx St
Wichita, KS 67209-1234
Telephone: (316) 945-4771, Toll Free:
   (877) EBERSOLE, FAX: (316) 945-
   4773, E-Mail: ebersolerocks@
   sbcglobal.net, Web Site: www.
   ebersolelapidary.com
Pres: Del Ebersole
VP: Len Ebersole
Treas: Carolyn Hendryx
Conducts Business: U.S.
Employees: 4
Primary Market Served: Business &
   Consumer
Catalog available online
Direct online sales
Direct Marketing ad budget: $35,000
TV/Radio: 100%

Complete lapidary line: jewelry mountings, equipment, tools & supplies for
the hobbyist. Shells, rough rock cabs &
books. Arts & crafts, casting & silversmithing supplies & equipment. Complete art supplies: brushes, paints,
canvas, paper, pens, inks, solvents, mediums, books & pastels. Wood forms &
plaques.

EDWIN WATTS GOLF

20 Hill Ave
Fort Walton Beach, FL 32548
Telephone: (850) 244-2066, Toll Free:
   (800) 874-0146, FAX: (850) 244-
   5217, Web Site: www.edwinwatts.
   com
CEO & Pres: Edwin Watts
VP Catalog & Online: John Watts
VP Mktg & Adv: Lincoln Cox
Conducts Business: Worldwide
Primary Market Served: Consumer
Catalog available online
Direct online sales
Founded: 1968

Retailer of golf equipment: clubs, bags,
balls & shoes.

ESTES INDUSTRIES

aka Estes-Cox Corp
1295 "H" St
Penrose, CO 81240
Telephone: (719) 372-6565, FAX:
   (719) 372-3419, Web Site: www.
   estesrockets.com
Pres: Barry Tunick
CFO: James Mauss
Mktg Dir: Mike Fritz
Conducts Business: U.S.
Employees: 200
Primary Market Served: Business &
   Consumer
Advertising/Marketing Budget Related
   to Direct Marketing: 0-25%
Founded: 1958
Gross sales or billing: $17,000,000

Manufacturer of flying model rockets
& airplanes, engines & accessory products sold to the public through retail
distribution throughout the U.S.

ETCHWORLD

176-180 Fifth Ave
Hawthorne, NJ 07506
Telephone: (973) 423-4002, Toll Free:
   (800) 872-3458, FAX: (973) 427-
   8823, Web Site: www.etchworld.com
Pres: Terrence Picone
VP: Sydney St James
Primary Market Served: Consumer
Catalog available online
Direct online sales
Advertising/Marketing Budget Related
   to Direct Marketing: 0-25%
Founded: 1975

Glass etching & mirror decorating supplies.

FAUNTLEROY SUPPLY CO/
WING SUPPLY

820 N Main St
Greenville, KY 42345

Telephone: (270) 338-5866, Toll Free:
   (800) 388-9464, FAX: (270) 338-
   0057, Web Site: www.wingsupply.
   com
Pres: Walter Fauntleroy
Gen Mgr: Joey Steele
Conducts Business: U.S.
Employees: 75
Primary Market Served: Consumer
Catalog available online
Direct online sales
Direct Marketing ad budget:
Direct Mail: 5%
Online: 95%
Founded: 1975

Sell hunting & sports clothing.

FREEPORT MUSIC INC

65 Clove Ave
Farmingville, NY 11738-1630
Telephone: (631) 549-4108, Toll Free:
   (888) 549-4108, E-Mail: sales@
   musicalinstruments.com; sales@
   freeportmusic.com, Web Site: www.
   musicalinstruments.com
Pres: Steve Interrante
Conducts Business: Worldwide
Primary Market Served: Business &
   Consumer
Catalog available online
Direct online sales
Advertising/Marketing Budget Related
   to Direct Marketing: 76-100%
Founded: 1921

Sell name brand & hard-to-find musical
instruments & accessories at discount
prices.

FROG TOOL CO LTD

2169 IL Rte 26
Dixon, IL 61021-9217
Telephone: (815) 288-3811, E-Mail:
   info@frogwoodtools.com, Web Site:
   www.frogwoodtools.com
Pres: Richard Watkins
Conducts Business: Worldwide
Employees: 4
Primary Market Served: Business &
   Consumer
Catalog available online
Indirect online sales
Advertising/Marketing Budget Related
   to Direct Marketing: 76-100%
Direct Marketing ad budget:
Direct Mail: $10,000
Magazines: $11,000
Online: $1,000
Founded: 1961
Gross sales or billing: $1,900,000

Catalog sales of hand woodworking
tools, books on woodworking & wood
finishing materials.

GAMETIME INC

Subs. of Playcore Wisconsin

150 Playcore Dr
Fort Payne, AL 35967
Telephone: (256) 845-5610, Toll Free:
 (800) 235-2440, FAX: (256) 845-
 9361/2649, Web Site: www.
 gametime.com
Pres & CEO: Bob Fansworth
Sr VP Opers: Spencer Cheak
Mktg Coord: Matt Meeks
VP, Sls & Mktg: Tom Norquist
VP HR: David H. Hammelman
Conducts Business: Worldwide
Employees: 1,000
Primary Market Served: Business &
 Consumer
Catalog available online
Indirect online sales
Advertising/Marketing Budget Related
 to Direct Marketing: 0-25%
Direct Marketing ad budget: $500,000
Gross sales or billing: $30,000,000

Park, playground, site furnishings &
sports equipment.

GILMAN'S LAPIDARY
SUPPLY
726 Durham St
Hellertown, PA 18055-1926
Telephone: (610) 838-8767, FAX:
 (610) 838-2961, E-Mail: info@
 lostcave.com, Web Site: www.
 lostcave.com
Partner: Robert Gilman
Conducts Business: Worldwide
Employees: 15
Primary Market Served: Business &
 Consumer
Advertising/Marketing Budget Related
 to Direct Marketing: 0-25%
Direct Marketing ad budget: $10,000
Gross sales or billing: $500,000

Products for all aspects of jewelry making including findings, cut & rough
gem stones, metals, small tools, saws,
grinders & polishers, lapidary & lapidary equipment & metal detectors

GOLF HAUS
700 N Pennsylvania Ave
Lansing, MI 48906-5319
Telephone: (517) 482-8842, FAX:
 (517) 482-8843
Owner: Jim Hornberger
Employees: 3
Primary Market Served: Consumer
Advertising/Marketing Budget Related
 to Direct Marketing: 0-25%
Founded: 1973

Pro-Line golf clubs, bags & balls.

GOLFSMITH
INTERNATIONAL INC
11000 Middle Fiskville Rd
Austin, TX 78753-3152

Telephone: (512) 821-4050, Toll Free:
 (800) 813-6897, FAX: (512) 837-
 9347, E-Mail: comments@golfsmith.
 com, Web Site: www.golfsmith.com
Pres & Co-Owner: Carl F. Paul
VP & Co-Owner: Frank C. Paul
VP & Gen Mgr: Ken Brugh
VP Mktg: Barry Rinke
VP Opers: Curt Young
VP DM: Steve Jones
Conducts Business: Worldwide
Employees: 1,400
Primary Market Served: Consumer
Catalog available online
Direct online sales
Advertising/Marketing Budget Related
 to Direct Marketing: 76-100%
Direct Marketing ad budget:
Direct Mail: 75%
Magazines: 10%
Newspapers: 15%
Founded: 1967

Golf club components, tools, supplies
& accessories.

GUN VIDEO CATALOG/LMP
4585 Murphy Canyon Rd
San Diego, CA 92123-4318
Telephone: (858) 569-4000, Toll Free:
 (800) 942-8273, FAX: (858) 569-
 0505, Web Site: www.gunvideo.com;
 www.glockstore.com
Owner & Pres: Lenny Magill
Exec Asst: Stacy Eckstein
Bus Mgr: Chad Casper
Conducts Business: Worldwide
Employees: 40
Primary Market Served: Business &
 Consumer
Catalog available online
Direct online sales
Advertising/Marketing Budget Related
 to Direct Marketing: 0-25%
Direct Marketing ad budget:
Direct Mail: 80%
Magazines: 20%
Founded: 1983

Sell self-defense/firearms instructional
videos to consumers, dealers, gun
stores, sporting goods stores & the military.

HAPPY JACK INC
2122 US 258
Snow Hill, NC 28580
Telephone: (252) 747-2911, Toll Free:
 (800) 326-5225, FAX: (252) 747-
 4111, E-Mail: happyjack@
 happyjackinc.com, Web Site: www.
 happyjackinc.com
Co-Owner: Ashe B. Exum
Co-Owner: Joe Exum
Conducts Business: U.S.
Employees: 10

Advertising/Marketing Budget Related
 to Direct Marketing: 0-25%
Direct Marketing ad budget: $250,000
Founded: 1946
Gross sales or billing: $3,900,000

Sell animal health products for dogs,
cats & horses. Also, sportswear & gifts
for the outdoorsman.

HASBRO INC
1027 Newport Ave
Pawtucket, RI 02861-2500
Telephone: (401) 431-8697, Toll Free:
 (800) 242-7276, FAX: (401) 727-
 5121, Web Site: www.hasbro.com
Chmn Bd: Alfred Verrecchia
Pres & CEO: Brian D Goldner
Sr VP Mktg Svcs: Edward Kriete
Conducts Business: Worldwide
Primary Market Served: Consumer

Manufacturer of toys for U.S. & international sales. Utilize direct marketing
via package inserts & direct mail.

HEARTHSIDE QUILTS &
SUPPLIES
90 Mechanicsville Rd, PO Box 610
Hinesburg, VT 05461
Telephone: (802) 482-7800, Toll Free:
 (800) 451-3533, FAX: (802) 482-
 7803, E-Mail: hearthsidequilts@att.
 net, Web Site: www.hearthsidequilts.
 com
Pres: George Wachob
Conducts Business: U.S., Canada, Eu-
 rope, Australia, Japan, New Zealand
Employees: 14
Primary Market Served: Business &
 Consumer
Catalog available online
Direct online sales
Direct Marketing ad budget: $120,000
Direct Mail: 20%
Magazines: 60%
Telephone: 20%
Founded: 1981
Gross sales or billing: $950,000

Sell full line of pre-cut quilt kits &
sewing supplies. Also, custom die-cut-
ting of fabric shapes.

HERRSCHNERS INC
2800 Hoover Rd
Stevens Point, WI 54492-0001
Telephone: (715) 341-8686, Toll Free:
 (800) 441-0838, FAX: (715) 341-
 2250, E-Mail: customerservice@
 herrschners.com, Web Site: www.
 herrschners.com
Pres: Ted Hesemann
VP Mktg: John Gritzmacher
Conducts Business: U.S., Canada
Employees: 200
Primary Market Served: Consumer

Advertising/Marketing Budget Related
to Direct Marketing: 76-100%
Gross sales or billing: $33,700,000

Catalog sales operation selling needlecraft kits & supplies to the consumer.

HIREKO GOLF

16185 Stephens St
City of Industry, CA 91745
Telephone: (626) 330-5525, Toll Free:
(800) 367-8912, FAX: (888) 367-
8912, E-Mail: support@hirekogolf.
com, Web Site: www.hireko.com
Primary Market Served: Business &
Consumer

HOBBY BUILDERS SUPPLY

2388 Pleasantdale Rd
Atlanta, GA 30340
Telephone: (770) 242-1498, Toll Free:
(800) 223-7171, FAX: (770) 242-
1497, (800) 926-6464, E-Mail: hbs@
miniatures.com, Web Site: www.
miniatures.com
Mktg Mgr: Sue Johnson
Primary Market Served: Consumer

World supplier of doll houses & miniature supplies.

HOBBY SURPLUS SALES

Sub. of Amato's Enterprises, LLC
287 Main St
New Britain, CT 06050-2202
Telephone: (860) 223-0600, Toll Free:
(800) 233-0872, FAX: (860) 225-
5316, E-Mail: amatohobby@
sbcglobal.net, Web Site: www.
hobbysurplus.com
Owner: Vincent Amato
Owner & Principal: Sheri L. Amato
Owner: Steven Amato
Conducts Business: U.S., Canada
Employees: 18
Primary Market Served: Consumer
Catalog available online
Direct online sales
Advertising/Marketing Budget Related
to Direct Marketing: 76-100%
Direct Marketing ad budget:
Direct Mail: 75%
Magazines: 25%
Founded: 1940
Gross sales or billing: $260,000

Sell hobby items: model trains, airplanes, cars, tools, books & miniatures.

HOME-SEW INC

1825 W Market St, PO Box 4099
Bethlehem, PA 18018-0099
Telephone: (610) 867-3833, Toll Free:
(800) 344-4739, FAX: (610) 867-
9717, E-Mail: customerservice@
homesew.com, Web Site: www.
homesew.com

Pres: Edward Perusse
Principal & Treas: Lucy Perusse
Dir: Rebecca Lentz
Conducts Business: Worldwide
Employees: 25
Primary Market Served: Consumer
Catalog available online
Direct online sales
Advertising/Marketing Budget Related
to Direct Marketing: 76-100%
Direct Marketing ad budget:
Direct Mail: 90%
Magazines: 1%
Online: 9%
Founded: 1960
Gross sales or billing: $3,000,000

Mail order sewing supplies.

HOOK & HACKLE CO INC

607 Ann St Rear
Homestead, PA 15120
Telephone: (412) 476-8620, Toll Free:
(800) 652-8342, FAX: (412) 476-
8639, E-Mail: ron@hookhack.com,
Web Site: www.hookhack.com
Pres: Robert K. Ellsworth
Conducts Business: Worldwide
Employees: 13
Primary Market Served: Business &
Consumer
Catalog available online
Direct online sales
Advertising/Marketing Budget Related
to Direct Marketing: 0-25%
Founded: 1975

Mail order marketer of fly fishing
equipment/supplies.

WILLIAM B HUGG
ENTERPRISE INC SWIM
WEAR & ACCESSORIES

44 W Butler Ave
Ambler, PA 19002-4517
Telephone: (215) 646-5544, Toll Free:
(800) 255-7946, FAX: (215) 646-
1280, E-Mail: wbhswim@aol.com,
Web Site: www.800allswim.com
Pres: Bill Hugg
Conducts Business: Worldwide
Primary Market Served: Business &
Consumer
Catalog available online
Direct online sales
Advertising/Marketing Budget Related
to Direct Marketing: 51-75%
Founded: 1975

Racing swimwear, accessories & swimwear for mature people.

INFORMAL EDUCATION
PRODUCTS

dba Museum Tour Catalog
2517 SE Mailwell Dr
Milwaukie, OR 97222-7329

Telephone: (503) 794-7045, Toll Free:
(888) 444-5500, FAX: (503) 794-
7111, E-Mail: sales@museumtour.
com, Web Site: www.museumtour.
com
Pres: Marilynne Eichinger
Mktg: Barbara Lund
Operations Mgr: Linda Woytcke
Design Dir: Macia Mantz
Conducts Business: U.S.
Primary Market Served: Consumer
Catalog available online
Direct online sales
Advertising/Marketing Budget Related
to Direct Marketing: 51-75%
Direct Marketing ad budget:
$1,800,000
Direct Mail: 80%
Online: 20%
Founded: 1995

Children's educational products.

INFORMATION UNLIMITED
INC

19 Brook Rd
Mont Vernon, NH 03057
Telephone: (603) 673-4730, Toll Free:
(800) 221-1705, FAX: (603) 672-
5406, E-Mail: wako2@xtdl.com,
Web Site: www.amazing1.com
Pres & Owner: Robert E. Iannini
Conducts Business: Worldwide
Employees: 15
Primary Market Served: Business &
Consumer
Direct online sales
Direct Marketing ad budget: $120,000
Magazines: 100%
Founded: 1974
Gross sales or billing: $1,750,000

Marketer of scientific products & kits
for the home hobbyist, school education & laboratory.

INTERNATIONAL
CURRENCY LLC

8725 Eastex Fwy
Beaumont, TX 77708-1307
Telephone: (409) 866-0588
Partner: Jeff Knight

Coin collections, jewelry & paper currency

JAYPRO SPORTS

976 Hartford Tpke
Waterford, CT 06385-4044
Telephone: (860) 447-3001, Toll Free:
(800) 243-0533, FAX: (800) 988-
3363, E-Mail: info@jaypro.com,
Web Site: www.jaypro.com
Graphic Designer & Mktg Asst: Doreen
Fratoni
Exec VP: Bill Wild
VP Sls & Mktg: Michael Gullickson

Conducts Business: U.S.
Employees: 40
Primary Market Served: Business &
  Consumer
Catalog available online
Direct online sales
Advertising/Marketing Budget Related
  to Direct Marketing: 51-75%
Direct Marketing ad budget:
Direct Mail: 50%
Magazines: 50%
Founded: 1953
Gross sales or billing: $3,500,000

Manufacturer & distributor of athletic,
physical education, recreation & special education equipment.

KELLYCO METAL
DETECTOR DISTRIBUTORS

1085 Belle Ave
Winter Springs, FL 32708
Telephone: (407) 699-8700, Toll Free:
  (800) 327-9697, FAX: (407) 695-
  6671, E-Mail: customerservice@
  kellycodetectors.com, Web Site:
  www.kellycodetectors.com
CEO: Stuart Auerbach
VP: Carolyn Auerbach
VP: John Fetner
Conducts Business: Worldwide
Employees: 50
Primary Market Served: Business &
  Consumer
Catalog available online
Direct online sales
Advertising/Marketing Budget Related
  to Direct Marketing: 26-50%
Direct Marketing ad budget: $500,000
Direct Mail: 5%
Magazines: 2%
Online: 90%
Telephone: 3%
Founded: 1953
Gross sales or billing: $26,000,000

Wholesale & retail sales of all major
lines of metal detecting equipment, including gold detector, d.p. radar & security detectors.

KENNEL VET

28424 Seaford Rd
Laurel, DE 19956
Telephone: (302) 875-7111, Toll Free:
  (800) 782-0627, FAX: (302) 269-
  3986, E-Mail: info@petmarket.com,
  Web Site: www.kennelvet.com
CEO: Fred Kretschmann
Pres: Meryl Kretschmann
Sls & Mktg Dir: Nancy Lynn
Conducts Business: Worldwide
Employees: 14
Primary Market Served: Business &
  Consumer
Catalog available online
Direct online sales

Advertising/Marketing Budget Related
  to Direct Marketing: 26-50%
Direct Marketing ad budget:
Direct Mail: 80%
Magazines: 10%
Newspapers: 5%
Telephone: 5%
Founded: 1971

Dog & cat supplies at discount prices,
such as cages, vaccines, flea & tick
products, show needs, health needs, vitamins, grooming supplies, toys, &
bones shipped worldwide.

KINGSLEY NORTH INC

910 Brown St, PO Box 216
Norway, MI 49870
Telephone: (906) 563-9228, Toll Free:
  (800) 338-9280, FAX: (906) 563-
  7143, E-Mail: sales@kingsleynorth.
  com, Web Site: www.kingsleynorth.
  com
Pres, Sec & Treas: Daniel Paupore
VP: Mark Paupore
Conducts Business: Worldwide
Employees: 8
Primary Market Served: Business &
  Consumer
Advertising/Marketing Budget Related
  to Direct Marketing: 0-25%
Founded: 1939

Sell tools, supplies, equipment, gemstones & accessories for the jewelry-
lapidary trade, hobbyist & craftsman.

LAKEWOOD PRODUCTS LLC

Div of Midwest Textile Mfg Corp
3188 Bowling Green Ln
Suamico, WI 54173
Telephone: (920) 361-7717, Toll Free:
  (800) 872-8458, FAX: (920) 361-
  7719, E-Mail: info@
  lakewoodproducts.com, Web Site:
  www.lakewoodproducts.com
Pres: Steve Wagnitz
Conducts Business: Worldwide
Primary Market Served: Business
Catalog available online
Advertising/Marketing Budget Related
  to Direct Marketing: 0-25%
Founded: 1992

Manufacture sporting goods & specialty cases, such as gun/bow, tackle
boxes & convenience cases.

LAMKIN CORP

6530 Gateway Park Dr
San Diego, CA 92154-7510
Telephone: (619) 661-7090, Toll Free:
  (800) 642-7755, FAX: (619) 661-
  0014, E-Mail: info@lamkingrips.
  com, Web Site: www.lamkingrips.
  com
Pres & CEO: Bob Lamkin
VP Mktg: Kerri Kauffman

VP Sales: Peter Brown
Sell golf grips.

LEGO DIRECT MARKETING

555 Taylor Rd
Enfield, CT 06082-2372
Telephone: (860) 749-2291, Toll Free:
  (800) 838-4386, FAX: (860) FAX-
  LEGO, Web Site: www.lego.com
VP, Direct-to-Consumer: Skip Kodak
DM Mgr: Steven Hawco
Conducts Business: Worldwide
Employees: 250
Primary Market Served: Consumer

Mail order catalog services.

LIFE FITNESS

Div. of Brunswick Corp
5100 N River Rd
Schiller Park, IL 60176
Telephone: (847) 288-3300, Toll Free:
  (800) 735-3867, FAX: (847) 288-
  3703, E-Mail: webmaster@
  lifefitness.com, Web Site: www.
  lifefitness.com
Exec VP Global Sls: Jay Megna
Pres: John E. Stransky
Sr Dir Prod Mngmt: Bob Quast
Conducts Business: Worldwide
Employees: 1,400
Primary Market Served: Business &
  Consumer
Catalog available online
Founded: 1977
Gross sales or billing: $145,700,000

Fitness products manufacturer & marketer.

THE LOS ANGELES LAKERS
INC

555 N Nash St
El Segundo, CA 90245
Telephone: (310) 426-6000, FAX:
  (310) 426-6110, E-Mail: vlawlor@
  la-lakers.com, Web Site: www.nba.
  com/lakers
Pres & Gen Mgr: Mitchell Kupchak
VP Mktg: Keith Harris
Conducts Business: U.S.
Primary Market Served: Business &
  Consumer
Catalog available online
Founded: 1946

LOWRANCE ELECTRONICS

Subs. of Navico Holdings AS
12000 E Skelly Dr
Tulsa, OK 74128
Telephone: (918) 437-6881, FAX:
  (918) 234-1707, Web Site: www.
  lowrance.com
Dir: Darrell Lowrance
CIO & CTO: Ronald Weber
Mfg: David Craig

Conducts Business: U.S., Canada
Employees: 5
Primary Market Served: Consumer
Catalog available online
Indirect online sales
Direct Marketing ad budget: $80,000
Gross sales or billing: $1,000,000

Sell accessory parts for Lowrance &
Eagle Fish Locators to the consumer.

LURE CRAFT
513 W Central Ave
Lagrange, IN 46761
Telephone: (260) 463-2687, Toll Free:
(800) 925-9088, FAX: (260) 463-
8383, E-Mail: lurcraft@clickanerd.
com, Web Site: www.lurecraft.com
Owner: Shawn Straley
Mgr: Kim Straley
Conducts Business: U.S.
Employees: 3
Primary Market Served: Business &
Consumer
Catalog available online
Direct online sales
Advertising/Marketing Budget Related
to Direct Marketing: 76-100%
Direct Mail: 80%
Magazines: 20%
Founded: 1970
Gross sales or billing: $500,000

Manufacturing & sales of fishing lure
components, especially plastics & coloring for plastic worm production. Specialize in production & custom molds.

MARDIRON OPTICS
Dept DMP
Four Spartan Cir
Stoneham, MA 02180
Telephone: (781) 938-8339, FAX:
(781) 938-8339, Web Site: www.
mardironooptics.com
Proprietor: K. Greg Mardirosian
Conducts Business: U.S.
Employees: 2
Primary Market Served: Business &
Consumer
Catalog available online
Indirect online sales
Advertising/Marketing Budget Related
to Direct Marketing: 0-25%
Direct Marketing ad budget:
Direct Mail: 5%
Magazines: 95%
Founded: 1983
Gross sales or billing: $300,000

Provides binoculars, telescopes, opera-
glasses, range finders, nightvision &
microscopes to consumers.

THE MARYLAND SADDLERY INC
14924 Falls Rd
Butler, MD 21023
Telephone: (410) 771-4135, Toll Free:
(800) 428-5077, FAX: (410) 472-
9722, E-Mail: mdsaddle@aol.com,
Web Site: www.marylandsaddlery.
com
Pres & Natl Sls Dir: Hope Birsh
Conducts Business: U.S.
Primary Market Served: Business &
Consumer
Catalog available online
Direct online sales
Founded: 1989

Specialize in children's riding apparel
& ponies.

MASTERGRIP INC
3410 Century Cir
Irving, TX 75062-4904
Telephone: (972) 554-4450, Toll Free:
(800) 275-1100, FAX: (972) 554-
1109, Web Site: www.mastergrip.
com
Pres: Richard Card
Gen Mgr: Don Dowdle
Conducts Business: U.S.
Employees: 60
Primary Market Served: Consumer
Catalog available online
Direct online sales
Direct Marketing ad budget: $100
Direct Mail: 100%
Founded: 1979
Gross sales or billing: $7,500,000

Mail order sales of golf equipment,
clubs, shirts, sweaters & gloves.

MARY MAXIM INC
2001 Holland Ave
Port Huron, MI 48061-5019
Telephone: (810) 987-2000, Toll Free:
(800) 962-9504, FAX: (810) 987-
5056, E-Mail: info@marymaxim.
com, Web Site: www.marymaxim.
com
Pres: Rusty McPhedrain
VP, Mktg: Brian Harris
VP, Opers: Chuck Cowley
Comptroller: Donna Hietikko
Conducts Business: U.S., Canada
Employees: 225
Primary Market Served: Consumer
Catalog available online
Direct online sales
Advertising/Marketing Budget Related
to Direct Marketing: 51-75%
Founded: 1956
Gross sales or billing: $20,000,000

Sell needlecraft kits to make sweaters,
afghans, baby items, needlepoint,
counted cross-stitch & Christmas ornaments.

MEMPHIS NET & TWINE CO INC
2481 Matthews Ave
Memphis, TN 38108
Telephone: (901) 458-2656, Toll Free:
(888) 674-7638, FAX: (901) 458-
1601, E-Mail: fishinfo@memphisnet.
net, Web Site: www.memphisnet.net
Pres: Albert Carruthers
Mktg Exec: Bryan Denley
Gen Mgr: Frank A. Gibson
Conducts Business: Worldwide
Employees: 36
Primary Market Served: Business &
Consumer
Catalog available online
Direct online sales
Advertising/Marketing Budget Related
to Direct Marketing: 76-100%
Direct Marketing ad budget: $213,000
Direct Mail: $150,000
Magazines: $3,000
Telephone: $60,000
Founded: 1962
Gross sales or billing: $5,000,000

Catalog sales of commercial fishing
supplies, netting, nets, seines, twine &
rope to commercial fishermen, fish
farmers, hatcheries, state & federal institutions. Also, baseball & other sport
nets.

METRO SPEEDGEAR
Div. of F1 Marketing
70 Okner Pkwy (Suite A)
Livingston, NJ 07039
Telephone: (973) 251-2814, Toll Free:
(800) 777-4453, FAX: (908) 286-
0002, E-Mail: info@speedgear.com,
Web Site: www.speedgear.com
Pres: Gary M. Low
Mktg Dir: Fred Ritter
Conducts Business: Worldwide
Employees: 50
Primary Market Served: Business &
Consumer
Catalog available online
Direct online sales
Advertising/Marketing Budget Related
to Direct Marketing: 76-100%
Direct Marketing ad budget:
Direct Mail: 25%
Magazines: 25%
TV/Radio: 50%
Founded: 1987
Gross sales or billing: $7,000,000

Car racing apparel.

MICHAEL'S
8000 Bent Branch
Irving, TX 75063-6023
Telephone: (972) 409-1300, FAX:
(972) 409-1551, Web Site: www.
michaels.com
Sr VP, Mktg: Stuart Aitken

Conducts Business: U.S.
Employees: 2,000
Primary Market Served: Consumer
Catalog available online
Direct online sales
Founded: 1976

Specialty retailing chain selling arts, crafts, needlework, framing & floral supplies.

FRANK MITTERMEIER INC

3577 E Tremont Ave
Bronx, NY 10455-2008
Telephone: (718) 828-3843, Toll Free: (800) 360-3843, FAX: (718) 518-7233, E-Mail: info@dastrausa.com, Web Site: www.dastrausa.com
Owner: Angelo Morales
Primary Market Served: Business & Consumer
Advertising/Marketing Budget Related to Direct Marketing: 0-25%
Founded: 1936

Sell wood carving tools to consumers, businesses, clubs, schools that sell or teach woodcarving.

MOUNTAIN CRAFT SHOP CO

7901 Proctor Creek Rd, RR1 Box 122
Proctor, WV 26055
Toll Free: (877) 365-5869, FAX: (304) 455-1740, E-Mail: info@folktoys.com, Web Site: www.folktoys.com
Owner: Steve A. Conlon
Pres: E.T. Conlon
Conducts Business: U.S.
Employees: 3
Primary Market Served: Business & Consumer
Catalog available online
Indirect online sales
Advertising/Marketing Budget Related to Direct Marketing: 0-25%
Direct Marketing ad budget: $10
Founded: 1963
Gross sales or billing: $100,000

American folk toys, including games, puzzles, dolls & curios. Most made of hardwood, all authentic reproductions.

NRS

1410 S Fm 51
Decatur, TX 76234-2416
Telephone: (940) 627-3949, Web Site: www.nrsworld.com
Dir: Jim Lamirand
Owner: David Isham
Opers Exec: Brad Davis

Specializing in products for ropers, including tack for barrel racing, calf & ranch roping. Western clothing, cowboy boots, cowboy hats, gifts & home decor.

NANCY'S NOTIONS LLC

A Tacony Co
333 Beichl Ave
Beaver Dam, WI 53916-0683
Telephone: (920) 887-0321, Toll Free: (800) 833-0690, FAX: (800) 255-8119, E-Mail: comments@nancysnotions.com, Web Site: www.nancysnotions.com
Pres & Gen Mgr: Mike Schuster
VP, Mdsg: Chris Stam
VP, Info Sys: Scott Stanton
VP Creative Svcs: Kathleen Gittus
VP HR & Fulfillment: Lori Bartruff
Conducts Business: U.S., Canada, Australia
Employees: 110
Primary Market Served: Business & Consumer
Catalog available online
Indirect online sales
Advertising/Marketing Budget Related to Direct Marketing: 76-100%
Direct Marketing ad budget: $2,800,000
Direct Mail: 75%
Magazines: 1%
Online: 20%
TV/Radio: 4%
Founded: 1979
Gross sales or billing: $14,000,000

Multi-channel direct marketer of sewing supplies.

NAUTILUS INC

17750 SE 6th Way
Vancouver, WA 98683-5535
Telephone: (360) 859-2900, Toll Free: (800) 675-0171, FAX: (360) 694-2755, Web Site: www.nautilus.com
COO: Bill McMahon
CEO & Pres: Robert S. Falcone
CFO, VP & Treas: William D. Meadowcroft
Pres Intl Equipment Bus: Darryl K. Thomas
Pres Fitness Apparel: Juergen Eckmann
Employees: 1,500
Primary Market Served: Business & Consumer
Catalog available online
Direct online sales
Gross sales or billing: $680,000,000

Manufacture exercise equipment marketed by infomercial & catalogs.

NO FAULT SPORTS PRODUCTS

2101 Briarglen Dr
Houston, TX 77027-3711
Telephone: (713) 683-7101, Toll Free: (800) 462-7766, FAX: (713) 683-7103, E-Mail: nofaultsports@comcast.net, Web Site: www.nofaultsports.com

Pres: Alfredo Trullenque
Conducts Business: U.S., Canada
Employees: 4
Primary Market Served: Business
Catalog available online
Indirect online sales
Advertising/Marketing Budget Related to Direct Marketing: 0-25%
Founded: 1982

Tennis court equipment & accessories.

NOMADICS TIPI MAKERS

17671 Snow Creek Rd
Bend, OR 97701-9149
Telephone: (541) 389-3980, FAX: (541) 389-3980, Web Site: www.tipi.com
Pres & Owner: John Barton
Bus Mgr: Harry Janicki
Conducts Business: Worldwide
Employees: 2
Primary Market Served: Business & Consumer
Catalog available online
Advertising/Marketing Budget Related to Direct Marketing: 0-25%
Founded: 1970

Market authentic Native American Indian tipis for adults & children.

NYLON NET CO

1340 Farmville Rd
Memphis, TN 38122
Telephone: (901) 526-6500, Toll Free: (800) 238-7529, (877) 893-6535, FAX: (901) 526-6538, E-Mail: nylonnet@nylonnet.com, Web Site: www.nylonnet.com
Pres: Stephen Christides
Conducts Business: U.S., Canada, Mexico
Employees: 100
Primary Market Served: Business & Consumer
Catalog available online
Direct online sales
Founded: 1953

Mail order catalog marketer of sports related items such as nets.

OPTRONICS INC

401 S 41st St E
Muskogee, OK 74403
Telephone: (918) 683-9514, Toll Free: (800) 364-5483, FAX: (918) 683-9517, E-Mail: sales@optronicsinc.com, Web Site: www.optronicsinc.com
CEO: Greg G. Bland
VP OEM Sls & Mktg: Brett Johnson
Purchasing Mgr: Richard Tracy
Conducts Business: Worldwide
Employees: 40
Primary Market Served: Business & Consumer

Catalog available online
Indirect online sales
Advertising/Marketing Budget Related
　to Direct Marketing: 0-25%
Direct Marketing ad budget: $200,000
Direct Mail: 10%
Magazines: 45%
Newspapers: 40%
Telephone: 5%
Founded: 1972
Gross sales or billing: $16,000,000

Twelve-volt vehicular & recreational lighting equipment & accessories sold to consumers & specialized end-users via direct mail, mail order, telephone, distributors, warehouse clubs, mass merchandisers & specialty chains.

ORION TELESCOPES & BINOCULARS

Owned by Imaginova.
89 Hangar Way
Watsonville, CA 95076
Telephone: (831) 763-7000, Toll Free:
　(800) 447-1001, FAX: (408) 763-
　7017, E-Mail: sales@telescope.com,
　Web Site: www.telescope.com
CEO: Tim J. Gieseler
Mktg VP: Terry D'Auray
Conducts Business: U.S., Canada
Employees: 50
Primary Market Served: Business &
　Consumer
Catalog available online
Direct online sales
Advertising/Marketing Budget Related
　to Direct Marketing: 76-100%
Founded: 1975

Manufacturer & distributor of recreational telescopes, binoculars & other optical products.

THE ORVIS CO INC

4180 Main St
Manchester, VT 05254
Telephone: (802) 362-3622, FAX:
　(802) 362-3525, Web Site: www.
　orvis.com
Chmn: Leigh H. Perkins
Pres & CEO: Perk Perkins
VP, Fin: Thomas Vaccaro
VP, Internet Sls & Mktg: Joseph Cassidy
Catalog Mktg Dir: Eric Johnson
Fishing & Hunting Catalog Mgr: Tom
　Rosenbauer
Conducts Business: Worldwide
Employees: 400
Primary Market Served: Consumer
Founded: 1856

Offer seasonal catalogs displaying hunting & fishing items, as well as country clothes & gifts for the sporting family.

OUTDOOR RESEARCH

2203 First Ave S (Suite 700)
Seattle, WA 98134-1424
Telephone: (206) 467-1496, Toll Free:
　(888) 467-4327, FAX: (206) 467-
　0374, Web Site: www.
　outdoorresearch.com
Pres & CEO: Daniel J. Nordstrom
VP: Dan Gulden
Mktg Mgr: Candace Springstead
Copywriter, Mktg Assoc: Teresa Bruffey
Conducts Business: U.S.
Primary Market Served: Business
Catalog available online
Direct online sales
Advertising/Marketing Budget Related
　to Direct Marketing: 0-25%
Gross sales or billing: $11,000,000

Manufacturers of innovative accessories for the outdoors.

OVERTON'S INC

111 Red Banks Rd
Greenville, NC 27858-5702
Telephone: (252) 355-5783, Toll Free:
　(800) 334-6541, FAX: (252) 355-
　2923, E-Mail: service@overtons.
　com, Web Site: www.overtons.com
CFO: John Daigle
Mgr: Richard Finlaysonitsj
Mfg: Mark Metcalfe
Conducts Business: U.S.
Employees: 231
Primary Market Served: Consumer
Catalog available online
Direct online sales
Advertising/Marketing Budget Related
　to Direct Marketing: 76-100%
Direct Marketing ad budget:
　$5,000,000
Founded: 1976
Gross sales or billing: $38,300,000

Watersports & marine equipment & accessories dealer featuring ten catalogs yearly.

PACHMAYR LTD

Subs. of Lyman Products Corp
475 Smith St
Middletown, CT 06457-1529
Toll Free: (800) 225-9626, FAX: (860)
　632-1699, Web Site: www.
　lymanproducts.com
Pres: Mace Thompson
Conducts Business: Worldwide
Employees: 80
Primary Market Served: Business &
　Consumer

Manufacturer & catalog marketer of gun accessories.

PARTNERS VILLAGE STORE

865 Main Rd

Westport, MA 02790-4315
Telephone: (508) 636-2572, FAX:
　(508) 636-2529, E-Mail: info@
　partnersvillagestore.com, Web Site:
　www.partnersvillagestore.com
Partner: Nancy C. Crosby
Partner: Jan Hall
Store Opers: Dorri Legge
Conducts Business: U.S.
Employees: 9
Primary Market Served: Business &
　Consumer
Catalog available online
Direct online sales
Founded: 1979

Sell books, gifts, cards, toys, gourmet foods & garden supplies.

PLAYER PIANO CO INC

704 E Douglas Ave
Wichita, KS 67202-2745
Telephone: (316) 263-3241, FAX:
　(316) 263-5480, Web Site: www.
　playerpianocompany.com
Pres: Durrell Armstrong
Conducts Business: Worldwide
Employees: 6
Primary Market Served: Business &
　Consumer
Catalog available online
Advertising/Marketing Budget Related
　to Direct Marketing: 0-25%
Founded: 1951
Gross sales or billing: $700,000

Player piano restoration supplies, rolls & accessories.

PLEASANT COMPANY

Subs. of Mattel Inc
8400 Fairway Pl
Middleton, WI 53562
Telephone: (608) 831-4116, Toll Free:
　(800) 845-0005, FAX: (608) 836-
　1999, Web Site: www.americangirl.
　com
Exec VP & Pres: Jean McKenzie
VP Mktg: Kathy Monetti
Conducts Business: U.S.
Employees: 1,500
Primary Market Served: Consumer
Catalog available online
Direct online sales
Advertising/Marketing Budget Related
　to Direct Marketing: 76-100%
Founded: 1986

Direct mail marketer of books, dolls & toys to girls 7-12. Products include The American Girls Collection, American Girl Magazine, American Girl Today, American Girl Library, American Girl Gear & Bitty Baby.

PORTA-BOTE INTERNATIONAL

Div. of Sandy Kaye Enterprises
1074 Independence Ave
Mountain View, CA 94043-1602
Telephone: (650) 961-5334, Toll Free:
(800) 227-8882, Web Site: www.
porta-bote.com
Pres: Sandy Kaye
Sales Exec: Paul Mintz
Conducts Business: Worldwide
Primary Market Served: Business &
Consumer
Catalog available online
Direct online sales
Advertising/Marketing Budget Related
to Direct Marketing: 51-75%
Founded: 1973

Sell portable folding boats, accessories,
jewelry & gifts to dealers & end users.

REI-RECREATIONAL EQUIPMENT INC

6750 S 228th St
Kent, WA 98032
Telephone: (253) 891-2500, Toll Free:
(800) 426-4840, FAX: (253) 891-
2523, Web Site: www.rei.com
Mktg Mgr: Cindy Huffman
Conducts Business: Worldwide
Employees: 6,000
Primary Market Served: Consumer
Catalog available online
Direct online sales
Advertising/Marketing Budget Related
to Direct Marketing: 26-50%
Founded: 1938
Gross sales or billing: $460,000,000

Outdoor gear & clothing for muscle-
power activities.

RAINBOW GROUP LLC

dba Beacon Athletics
8233 Forsythia St Ste 120
Middleton, WI 53562-1496
Telephone: (608) 824-0068, Web Site:
www.beaconathletics.com
Owner: Michael Hoesly
Owner: Brian Myrland
Primary Market Served: Business &
Consumer

RECREATIONAL EQUIPMENT INC

6750 S 228th St
Kent, WA 98032-4803
Telephone: (253) 395-4803, Web Site:
www.rei.com
Dir, Direct Mktg & Analysis: Michael
Bowcut
Primary Market Served: Consumer

RELIABLE RACING SUPPLY

643 Upper Glen St (Suite B)
Queensbury, NY 12804-2014
Telephone: (518) 793-5677, FAX:
(518) 793-6491, Web Site: www.
reliableracing.com
Pres: Tom Jacobs
Commun Dir: Mike Sylvia
Conducts Business: U.S., Canada
Employees: 40
Primary Market Served: Business &
Consumer
Catalog available online
Indirect online sales
Advertising/Marketing Budget Related
to Direct Marketing: 51-75%
Direct Marketing ad budget: $350,000
Direct Mail: 70%
Magazines: 30%
Founded: 1965
Gross sales or billing: $6,000,000

Snow skiing products, golf course &
event supplies & timing equipment.

RHYTHM BAND INC

1316 E Lancaster Ave
Fort Worth, TX 76102-6634
Telephone: (817) 335-2561, Toll Free:
(800) 424-4724, FAX: (800) 784-
9401, E-Mail: sales@rhythmband.
com, Web Site: www.rhythmband.
com
Pres: Brad Kirkpatrick
Dir Sales: Bob Fogle
VP, Sls: Laura Bergin
VP, Opers: Flora Brewer
Conducts Business: U.S.
Employees: 25
Primary Market Served: Business &
Consumer
Catalog available online
Direct online sales
Advertising/Marketing Budget Related
to Direct Marketing: 51-75%
Direct Marketing ad budget:
Direct Mail: 95%
Newspapers: 5%
Founded: 1961

Musical instruments geared to the early
childhood & elementary school market.

PETE RICKARD INC

115 Roy Walsh Rd
Cobleskill, NY 12043-4422
Telephone: (518) 234-2731, Toll Free:
(800) 282-5663, FAX: (518) 234-
2454, E-Mail: info@peterickard.com,
Web Site: www.peterickard.com
Staff Shooter: John Johnston Jr.
Staff Shooter: Scott Alkinburgh
Staff Shooter: John Haynes
Conducts Business: Worldwide
Employees: 8
Primary Market Served: Business &
Consumer
Catalog available online
Direct online sales
Advertising/Marketing Budget Related
to Direct Marketing: 0-25%
Direct Marketing ad budget:
Direct Mail: 1%
Magazines: 20%
Newspapers: 1%
Online: 25%
TV/Radio: 30%
Telephone: 23%
Founded: 1934

Deer hunting scents & lures, accessories, gun dog training scents & trapping
lures. Scotch game calls & gear.

ROAD RUNNER SPORTS INC

5553 Copley Dr
San Diego, CA 92111-7904
Telephone: (858) 974-4455, Toll Free:
(800) 636-3560, FAX: (800) 453-
5443, Web Site: www.
roadrunnersports.com
Pres & CEO: Mike Gotfredson
Dir E-Commerce: Peter Taylor
Conducts Business: U.S., Canada
Employees: 280
Primary Market Served: Consumer
Direct online sales
Founded: 1983
Gross sales or billing: $105,000,000

Sell athletic shoes, fitness apparel &
accessories to sports enthusiasts ranging from the triathlete, marathoner &
team sport player to the weekend fitness enthusiast.

AG RUSSELL KNIVES INC

2900 S 26th St
Rogers, AR 72758-8571
Telephone: (479) 631-0055, Toll Free:
(800) 255-9034, FAX: (479) 631-
8493, E-Mail: ag@agrussell.com,
Web Site: www.agrussell.com
Pres: Goldie Russell
Co-Owner: A.G. Russell
Conducts Business: Worldwide
Employees: 13
Primary Market Served: Consumer
Catalog available online
Direct online sales
Advertising/Marketing Budget Related
to Direct Marketing: 76-100%
Direct Marketing ad budget:
Direct Mail: $1,000,000
Magazines: $100,000
Founded: 1964

Sell high quality & handmade knives.

S&S WORLDWIDE

75 Mill St
Colchester, CT 06415-0513
Telephone: (860) 537-3451, Toll Free:
(800) 288-9941, FAX: (860) 537-
2866, E-Mail: cservice@ssww.com,
Web Site: www.ssww.com
Co-Pres: Hy Schwartz

Co-Pres: Adam Schwartz
Dir Mktg: Greg Hilbert
Database Dir: Kathy Knapp
Conducts Business: U.S., Canada, International
Employees: 300
Primary Market Served: Business & Consumer
Catalog available online
Direct online sales
Advertising/Marketing Budget Related to Direct Marketing: 26-50%
Direct Marketing ad budget:
Direct Mail: 80%
Online: 10%
Telephone: 10%
Founded: 1906
Gross sales or billing: $40,000,000
Catalog sales of arts, crafts, games & adaptive equipment. Manufacturers of arts, crafts & small wood products.

SAFE PUBLICATIONS INC
PO Box 74
Doylestown, PA 18901-0074
Telephone: (215) 357-9049, FAX: (215) 357-5202, E-Mail: sales@safepub.com, Web Site: www.safepub.com
Pres: Axel J. Braun
Conducts Business: U.S., Canada
Employees: 4
Primary Market Served: Business & Consumer
Catalog available online
Indirect online sales
Advertising/Marketing Budget Related to Direct Marketing: 0-25%
Direct Marketing ad budget:
Direct Mail: 30%
Newspapers: 70%
Founded: 1974
Gross sales or billing: $500,000
Catalog marketer of German made stamp & coin albums & supplies.

SAILRITE ENTERPRISES, INC
2390 E 100 S
Columbia City, IN 46725-8751
Telephone: (260) 693-2242, Toll Free: (800) 348-2769, FAX: (260) 693-2246, E-Mail: sailrite@sailrite.com, Web Site: www.sailrite.com
VP: Matthew Grant
VP: Hallie Grant
Conducts Business: Worldwide
Employees: 13
Primary Market Served: Consumer
Catalog available online
Direct online sales
Direct Marketing ad budget:
Direct Mail: 20%
Magazines: 80%
Founded: 1969

Gross sales or billing: $1,500,000
Sell sailmaking supplies & instructions & offer a home study program in sailmaking. Also, sewing machines for sailmaking.

SCHNEIDER SADDLERY
8255 E Washington St
Chagrin Falls, OH 44023
Telephone: (440) 543-2700, Toll Free: (800) 365-1311, FAX: (440) 543-2710, Web Site: www.sstack.com
Pres: Donald Schneider
VP: Stan Schneider
Conducts Business: U.S., Canada, Europe, Australia, S. America, Middle East, Japan
Employees: 35
Primary Market Served: Business & Consumer
Catalog available online
Direct online sales
Advertising/Marketing Budget Related to Direct Marketing: 76-100%
Direct Marketing ad budget:
Direct Mail: 75%
Magazines: 20%
Newspapers: 5%
Equestrian riding equipment, apparel & supplies-private label lines.

SCOTT'S DOG SUPPLY INC
2619 Cressmoor Cir
Indianapolis, IN 46234-7020
Telephone: (317) 222-5382, Toll Free: (800) 966-3647, FAX: (317) 298-7284, E-Mail: cmurphy154@aol.com, Web Site: www.scottsdog.com
Pres: C. Joe Murphy
Conducts Business: U.S., Canada
Primary Market Served: Business & Consumer
Catalog available online
Direct online sales
Advertising/Marketing Budget Related to Direct Marketing: 0-25%
Direct Marketing ad budget:
Direct Mail: 20%
Magazines: 80%
Founded: 1982
Gross sales or billing: $500,000
Hunter & hunting dog supplies.

SHAKESPEARE CO
Div. of K/2 Inc
6111 Shakespeare Rd
Columbia, SC 29223
Telephone: (803) 754-7000, Toll Free: (800) 347-3759, FAX: (803) 754-7342, Web Site: www.shakespeare-fishing.com
Pres, K/2: Rich Rodstein
VP, Sls & Gen Mgr: Scott Hogsett
Conducts Business: U.S., Canada

Primary Market Served: Business & Consumer
Fishing rods, reels, kits, combos & lines.

SIMS STOVES
7452 Burlington Ave
Billings, MT 59106
Telephone: (406) 259-5644, Toll Free: (800) 736-5259, Web Site: www.simsstoves.com
Owner: Wyatt Sims
Conducts Business: U.S., Canada
Employees: 4
Primary Market Served: Business & Consumer
Catalog available online
Indirect online sales
Advertising/Marketing Budget Related to Direct Marketing: 51-75%
Direct Marketing ad budget:
Magazines: 80%
Telephone: 20%
Founded: 1946
Gross sales or billing: $50,000
Manufacturer & catalog marketer of folding, wood burning camp stoves & related sporting goods such as packsaddles & tents.

SMART DOG PRODUCTS
1009 S College St
Winchester, TN 37398
Telephone: (931) 967-7482, Toll Free: (800) 264-3647, FAX: (931) 967-7483, E-Mail: sales@shopsmartdog.com
Pres & Treas: Michael Rudder
Conducts Business: U.S.
Employees: 10
Primary Market Served: Business & Consumer
Quality accessories for house pets.

SOAR INFLATABLES
20 Healdsburg Ave
Healdsburg, CA 95448
Telephone: (707) 433-5599, FAX: (707) 433-4499, E-Mail: sales@soar1.com, Web Site: www.soar1.com
Pres: Larry Laba
Conducts Business: Worldwide
Employees: 3
Primary Market Served: Business & Consumer
Catalog available online
Indirect online sales
Direct Marketing ad budget:
Direct Mail: 38%
Magazines: 40%
Newspapers: 2%
Telephone: 20%
Founded: 1993

SPILSBURY PUZZLE CO
70 W Madison St (Suite 2300)
Chicago, IL 60602-4250
Toll Free: (800) 722-1760, FAX: (630)
  575-0857, E-Mail: service@
  spilsbury.com, Web Site: www.
  spilsbury.com
Pres: Herbert Laney
Conducts Business: U.S.
Employees: 5
Primary Market Served: Consumer
Catalog available online
Direct online sales
Advertising/Marketing Budget Related
  to Direct Marketing: 76-100%
Direct Marketing ad budget:
Direct Mail: 100%
Founded: 1995

Puzzles, games & gifts.

SPORT SUPPLY GROUP
1901 Diplomat Dr
Dallas, TX 75234
Telephone: (972) 484-9484, FAX:
  (972) 247-0650, Web Site: www.
  sportsupplygroup.com
Pres: John Walker
VP, Opers: Douglas Pryor
Mktg Dir: Bob Parks
Investor Rels: Peggy Rozelle
Primary Market Served: Business
Catalog available online
Indirect online sales

Manufacturer of sports gear & equipment. Sell via catalog.

SPORTIME INTERNATIONAL
Subs. of School Specialty Inc
3155 Northwoods Pkwy
Norcross, GA 30071
Telephone: (770) 449-5700, Toll Free:
  (800) 283-5700, FAX: (770) 510-
  7290, E-Mail: orders@sportime.com,
  Web Site: www.sportime.com
VP, Sls: Duane Puckett
Mktg Info Mgr: Greg Bayer
Mktg Dir: Tom Jones
Sportime Catalog Dir: Mark Dresser
Conducts Business: U.S., Japan, New
  Zealand, Australia
Employees: 120
Primary Market Served: Business
Indirect online sales
Advertising/Marketing Budget Related
  to Direct Marketing: 76-100%
Direct Marketing ad budget:
Direct Mail: 98%
Magazines: 2%
Founded: 1967

Two mail order catalogs featuring
movement & physical education equipment for elementary grade, secondary
& therapy markets.

THE SPORTSMAN'S GUIDE INC
411 Farwell Ave
South Saint Paul, MN 55075-2428
Telephone: (651) 451-3030, Toll Free:
  (800) 882-2962, FAX: (651) 450-
  6130, E-Mail: custserv@
  sportsmansguide.com, Web Site:
  www.sportsmansguide.com
Pres & CEO: Gregory R. Binkley
Exec VP Mdsg, Mktg & Creative Svcs:
  John M. Casler
Conducts Business: U.S., Canada
Employees: 754
Primary Market Served: Consumer
Catalog available online
Direct online sales
Founded: 1970
Gross sales or billing: $130,200,000

Sporting goods, accessories & clothing
sold primarily to hunters, wild life enthusiasts, fishermen, campers & RV
owners.

SPORTSMITH LLC
5925 S 118th Ave
Tulsa, OK 74146-6827
Telephone: (918) 307-2446, Toll Free:
  (800) 713-2880, Web Site: www.
  sportsmith.net
Mktg Mgr: Troy Mosley
Pres: Brad Schupp
Primary Market Served: Consumer

SUNSHINE DISCOUNT CRAFTS
12335 62nd St N
Largo, FL 33773
Telephone: (727) 538-2878, Toll Free:
  (800) 729-2878, FAX: (727) 531-
  2739, E-Mail: webmaster@
  sunshinecrafts.com, Web Site: www.
  sunshinecrafts.com
Pres: David Rothschild
Conducts Business: U.S.
Employees: 12
Primary Market Served: Business &
  Consumer
Catalog available online
Direct online sales
Advertising/Marketing Budget Related
  to Direct Marketing: 76-100%
Direct Marketing ad budget:
Direct Mail: 90%
Magazines: 10%
Founded: 1980
Gross sales or billing: $1,000,000

Offer discounts on 14,000 craft supply
items. Doll making, jewelry, muslin animals, wood, paints, glass painting &
etching.

SUNSHINE GLASSWORKS LTD
111 Industrial Pkwy
Buffalo, NY 14227-2712
Telephone: (716) 668-2918, Toll Free:
  (800) 828-7159, FAX: (716) 668-
  2932, E-Mail: info23@sunshineglass.
  com, Web Site: www.sunshineglass.
  com
Pres: Scott G. Emslie
Conducts Business: U.S.
Employees: 10
Primary Market Served: Business &
  Consumer
Catalog available online
Direct online sales
Advertising/Marketing Budget Related
  to Direct Marketing: 76-100%
Direct Marketing ad budget: $35,000
Direct Mail: 90%
Magazines: 10%
Founded: 1979
Gross sales or billing: $1,250,000

Sell stained glass supplies: sheet glass,
lead, foil, tools, solder & accessories.

TACKLE CRAFT
W5043 480th Ave
Ellsworth, WI 54011-5209
Telephone: (715) 273-5300, FAX:
  (715) 273-5320, E-Mail: customer
  service@tackle-craft.com
Pres: Alan M. Woll
Partner: Linda J. Woll
Conducts Business: Worldwide
Primary Market Served: Business &
  Consumer
Advertising/Marketing Budget Related
  to Direct Marketing: 76-100%
Direct Marketing ad budget:
Magazines: 100%
Founded: 1970

Fly & lure making materials.

TANDY LEATHER CO
1900 SE Loop 820
Fort Worth, TX 76140-1003
Telephone: (817) 872-3200, FAX:
  (817) 496-7859, E-Mail: tlfhelp@
  tandyleather.com, Web Site: www.
  tandyleatherfactory.com
Mktg Mgr: Dana Jones
Exec VP: Mark A Angus
Conducts Business: U.S., Canada, Aus-
  tralia, U.K., Japan
Employees: 125
Primary Market Served: Business &
  Consumer
Indirect online sales
Advertising/Marketing Budget Related
  to Direct Marketing: 76-100%
Founded: 1919

Gross sales or billing: $7,500,000

Retail & mail-order sales with over 25 company-owned leathercraft stores nationwide.

TOWER HOBBIES/HOBBICO

2904 Research Rd
Champaign, IL 61822
Telephone: (217) 398-3636, Toll Free: (800) 637-6050, FAX: (217) 398-1104, Web Site: www.towerhobbies.com
Pres: Clint Atkins
CFO: Willard Muirheid
VP, Admin: Sue Ciolli
VP, Sls: Ken Cutler
VP, Mktg: Rick Priester
Conducts Business: Worldwide
Primary Market Served: Consumer
Catalog available online
Direct online sales
Advertising/Marketing Budget Related to Direct Marketing: 76-100%

Supplier of radio controlled model cars, planes, boats, parts & accessories.

TOYS "R" US

1 Geoffrey Way
Wayne, NJ 07470-2066
Telephone: (973) 617-5879, FAX: (973) 617-4006, Web Site: www.toysrus.com
Chmn & CEO: Gerald L. Storch
Exec VP & CFO: F. Clay Creasey Jr.
Exec VP HR: Daniel Caspersen
Sr VP, Adv & Mktg: Ernest V. Speranza
Dir CRM & Loyalty: Barbara Canning Brown
Conducts Business: Worldwide
Employees: 59,000
Primary Market Served: Consumer
Catalog available online
Direct online sales
Gross sales or billing: $13,000,000,000

Toy specialty retailing chain.

TOYS TO GROW ON

Div. of Lakeshore Learning Materials
2695 E Dominguez St
Carson, CA 90895
Telephone: (310) 537-8600, Toll Free: (800) 874-4242, FAX: (800) 537-5403, E-Mail: toyinfo@toystogrowon.com, Web Site: www.ttgo.com
Pres: Bo Kaplan
CEO: Michael Kaplan
VP, Mdsg: Charles Kaplan
Conducts Business: U.S.
Employees: 78
Primary Market Served: Consumer
Catalog available online

Direct online sales

Produce & distribute catalogs of quality, educator-approved toys for children aged one month to 12 years.

US GAMES SYSTEMS INC

179 Ludlow St
Stamford, CT 06902
Telephone: (203) 353-8400, Toll Free: (800) 544-2637, FAX: (203) 353-8431, Web Site: www.usgamesinc.com
Chmn: Stuart R. Kaplan
Owner: Rhianna Mirabello
Conducts Business: Worldwide
Employees: 40
Primary Market Served: Business & Consumer
Catalog available online
Direct online sales
Advertising/Marketing Budget Related to Direct Marketing: 0-25%
Founded: 1968

Publish playing cards, tarot cards & new age books from around the world. Also, reproductions of antique & museum playing cards, historical cards, plus adult card games & award winning children's card games.

UNIVERSAL HOVERCRAFT

1204 Third St S
Cordova, IL 61242
Telephone: (309) 654-2588, FAX: (309) 654-2588, Web Site: www.hovercraft.com
Owner: R.J. Windt
Pres: Bill Zang
Conducts Business: Worldwide
Employees: 3
Primary Market Served: Business & Consumer
Catalog available online
Direct online sales
Advertising/Marketing Budget Related to Direct Marketing: 0-25%
Founded: 1971

Sell Hovercraft plans, props & fans.

UNIVERSAL VINTAGE TIRE CO

2994 Elizabethtown Rd
Hershey, PA 17033
Telephone: (717) 534-0175, Toll Free: (800) 233-3827, FAX: (717) 534-0719, E-Mail: sales@universaltire.com, Web Site: www.universaltire.com
Pres: Joseph Coker
Mgr: John Northeimer
Conducts Business: U.S.
Employees: 3
Primary Market Served: Business & Consumer

Catalog available online
Direct online sales
Advertising/Marketing Budget Related to Direct Marketing: 26-50%
Direct Marketing ad budget:
Direct Mail: 5%
Magazines: 95%
Founded: 1968
Gross sales or billing: $1,500,000

Classic automobile tires for vehicles made between 1900-1970.

VET VAX

1203 E Hwy 24-40
Tonganoxie, KS 66086-9507
Telephone: (913) 845-3760, Toll Free: (800) 369-8297, FAX: (913) 845-9472, E-Mail: sales@vetvax.com
Pres: Bud Moomau
Conducts Business: U.S.
Employees: 8
Primary Market Served: Business & Consumer
Catalog available online
Advertising/Marketing Budget Related to Direct Marketing: 26-50%
Direct Marketing ad budget: $50,000
Direct Mail: 70%
Magazines: 20%
Newspapers: 10%
Founded: 1969
Gross sales or billing: $1,800,000

Animal health & hunting supplies for dogs, horses & cats.

VOYAGEUR INC

Div. of Mad River Canoe Co
111 Kayaker Way
Easley, SC 29642-2433
Telephone: (802) 496-3127, Toll Free: (800) 311-7245, FAX: (802) 496-6247
VP, Mfg & Prodn Mgr: Ken Beauchemin
Paddle Sport Equip Dir: Gordon Colby
Foreman: Scott Griffith
Conducts Business: U.S., Canada, Germany, Japan, England, Finland, The Netherlands, Norway, France
Employees: 7
Primary Market Served: Business & Consumer
Direct Marketing ad budget:
Direct Mail: 15%
Magazines: 85%
Gross sales or billing: $350,000

Manufacturer of waterproof gear storage bags, flotation, & accessories for canoeing & kayaking.

WM K WALTHERS INC

5601 W Florist Ave
Milwaukee, WI 53218

Telephone: (414) 527-0770, Toll Free: (800) 487-2467, FAX: (414) 527-4423, Web Site: www.walthers.com
Pres: Phil Walthers
VP Mktg & Sls: John Sanheim
Dir: Chris Schaenzer
Conducts Business: U.S.
Employees: 187
Primary Market Served: Business & Consumer
Catalog available online
Direct online sales

Catalog marketer of model railroad kits & accessories.

WARRIOR CUSTOM GOLF INC

15 Mason (Suite A)
Irvine, CA 92618-2707
Telephone: (949) 699-2499, Toll Free: (800) 600-5113, Web Site: www.warriorcustomgolf.com
Pres: Brendan Flaherty

WE-NO-NAH CANOE INC

1252 Bundy Blvd, Box 247
Winona, MN 55987-4872
Telephone: (507) 454-5430, FAX: (507) 454-5448, E-Mail: info@wenonah.com, Web Site: www.wenonah.com
Pres: Mike Cichanowski
Conducts Business: U.S., Canada, Germany
Employees: 50
Primary Market Served: Business & Consumer
Catalog available online
Indirect online sales
Advertising/Marketing Budget Related to Direct Marketing: 0-25%
Founded: 1966
Gross sales or billing: $5,000,000

Manufacturer of canoes, kayaks and accessories.

WEST MARINE INC

500 Westridge Dr
Watsonville, CA 95076-4171
Telephone: (831) 728-2700, Toll Free: (800) 262-8464, (800) BOATING, FAX: (831) 768-5000, E-Mail: customercare@westmarine.com, Web Site: www.westmarine.com
Pres, CEO & Dir: Geoffrey A. Eisenberg
Sr VP & CFO: Thomas Moran
Exec VP Mdsg: Ronald Japinga
Dir Database & Loyalty: Craig Ajeska
Conducts Business: US, Puerto Rico & Canada
Employees: 5,026
Primary Market Served: Business & Consumer
Catalog available online

Direct online sales
Advertising/Marketing Budget Related to Direct Marketing: 76-100%
Direct Marketing ad budget:
Direct Mail: 80%
Newspapers: 10%
TV/Radio: 10%
Founded: 1968
Gross sales or billing: $716,600,000

Sell retail boating equipment to pleasure boaters. Produce 12 catalogs yearly. 4.5 million total pieces mailed.

WHITEHORSE GEAR

107 E Conway Rd
Center Conway, NH 03813-4012
Telephone: (603) 356-6556, FAX: (603) 356-6590, E-Mail: customerservice@whitehorsepress.com, Web Site: www.whitehorsepress.com
Pres: Daniel W. Kennedy
Co-Owner: Judith M. Kennedy
Primary Market Served: Business & Consumer
Catalog available online
Direct online sales
Advertising/Marketing Budget Related to Direct Marketing: 76-100%
Founded: 1989

Publishers of books & a catalog for motorcycle enthusiasts.

WIND IN THE RIGGING

Div. of Port Publications, Inc
123 E Main St, PO Box 249
Port Washington, WI 53074-0249
Telephone: (262) 284-3494, Toll Free: (800) 236-7444, FAX: (262) 284-0067, E-Mail: info@windintherigging.com, Web Site: www.windintherigging.com
Pres: William F. Schanen III
Mgr: Jean Schanen
Conducts Business: U.S., Canada, Europe, Australia, Japan, Puerto Rico
Employees: 50
Primary Market Served: Consumer
Catalog available online
Direct online sales
Advertising/Marketing Budget Related to Direct Marketing: 76-100%
Founded: 1970
Gross sales or billing: $3,500,000

Sell nautical gifts, clothing, personalized products & specialty items relating to sailing & cruising.

SYLVIA WOODS HARP CENTER

Div. of Woods Music & Books Inc
PO Box 816
Montrose, CA 91021

Toll Free: (800) 272-4277, FAX: (818) 247-5212, E-Mail: info@harpcenter.com, Web Site: www.harpcenter.com
Pres: Sylvia Woods
Conducts Business: U.S.
Primary Market Served: Consumer
Catalog available online
Direct online sales
Advertising/Marketing Budget Related to Direct Marketing: 76-100%

Sell harps, harp music books & accessories.

WOODWORKER'S SUPPLY INC

1108 N Glenn Rd
Casper, WY 82601
Telephone: (307) 237-5528, Toll Free: (800) 321-9841, FAX: (307) 57-5272, E-Mail: kenp@woodworker.com, Web Site: www.woodworker.com
Pres: John Wirth Jr
Dept Mgr: Ken Pollitt
Conducts Business: U.S.
Employees: 150
Primary Market Served: Business & Consumer
Advertising/Marketing Budget Related to Direct Marketing: 76-100%
Founded: 1972

Market woodworking machinery, tools, accessories, & supplies to advanced amateur & professional woodworkers.

YOUR MOVE CHESS & GAMES

Div. of ICD Corp
832 N Broadway
North Massapequa, NY 11758
Telephone: (516) 882-9800, Toll Free: (800) 645-4710, FAX: (631) 424-3405, E-Mail: icd@icdchess.com, Web Site: www.icdchess.com
Gen Mgr: Steven A. Schwartz
Conducts Business: Worldwide
Employees: 18
Primary Market Served: Business & Consumer
Catalog available online
Direct online sales
Advertising/Marketing Budget Related to Direct Marketing: 0-25%
Founded: 1978
Gross sales or billing: $5,000,000

Sell chess & other games.

Transportation Catalogs (12)

AW DIRECT INC
Subs. of Ariens Co.
1125 Deming Way
Madison, WI 53717-1953
Telephone: (860) 828-7800, Toll Free:
(800) 243-3194, FAX: (800) 828-
9678, E-Mail: contactus@awdirect.
com, Web Site: www.awdirect.com
VP: Richard Thibadeau
Pres: Patrick Thibadeau
Conducts Business: Worldwide
Employees: 85
Primary Market Served: Consumer
Founded: 2005
Gross sales or billing: $28,000,000
Sell accessories for tow trucks, recovery and service vehicles.

ACCELLOS INC
90 S Cascade Ave (Suite 1200)
Colorado Springs, CO 80903-1678
Telephone: (719) 433-7000, Web Site:
www.accellos.com
Chmn & CEO: Michael Cornell
Exec VP & Chief Tech Officer: Ross
Elliott
CFO: Flint Seaton
Gen Mgr & Chief Mktg Officer: Chad
Collins
Sr VP & Gen Mgr: Joe Cuoto
Sr VP & Gen Mgr: Bill Ashburn
Supply chain execution software provider.

AIR POWER USA
Div. of Multitech Industries Ltd
8366 Isis Ave
Los Angeles, CA 90045
Telephone: (310) 641-0830, Toll Free:
(888) 888-8231, FAX: (310) 641-
8515, Web Site: www.airpowerusa.
com
Pres: Robert Go
Asst Controller & Import Mgr: Amanda Yee
Export Mgr: Samuel Moon
Controller: Sheila Liao
Export Mgr: Leila Valderrama
Conducts Business: U.S.
Employees: 30
Primary Market Served: Business &
Consumer
Catalog available online
Advertising/Marketing Budget Related
to Direct Marketing: 25-50%
Founded: 1995
Gross sales or billing: $3,000,000
Global air & ocean freight, logistics,
transportation, insurance warehousing,
distribution & customs.

**AIRCRAFT SPRUCE &
SPECIALTY CO**
Div. of Irwin International
225 Airport Cir
Corona, CA 92880-2527
Telephone: (909) 372-9555, Toll Free:
(877) 4-Spruce, FAX: (909) 372-
0555, E-Mail: info@aircraft-spruce.
com, Web Site: www.aircraft-spruce.
com
Pres: Jim Irwin
VP, Fin: Nanci Irwin
Dir Opers West: Tom Marrachi
Dir Opers East: Don Arrington
Mktg Mgr: Desiree Czaplinski
Conducts Business: Worldwide
Employees: 100
Primary Market Served: Business &
Consumer
Catalog available online
Direct online sales
Founded: 1965
Gross sales or billing: $25,000,000
Distributor of aircraft supplies for
home-built & certified aircraft. Over
30,000 parts sold through a 600 page
catalog.

AMERICAN AIRLINES
AMR Corp
4333 Amon Carter Blvd
Fort Worth, TX 76155-2605
Telephone: (817) 963-1234
CEO: W Douglas Parker
Pres: J Scott Kirby
Exec VP People & Commun: Elise R
Eberwein
Exec VP & CFO: Derek J Kerr
Primary Market Served: Consumer

AUTOBYTEL INC
18872 MacArthur Blvd (Suite 200)
Irvine, CA 92612-1448
Telephone: (949) 225-4500, E-Mail:
consumercareabtl@autobytel.com,
Web Site: www.autobytel.com
Direct Mktg Analyst: Jeffrey Coats
Exec VP & CFO: Kimberly Boren
Exec VP & COO: William Ferriolo
Conducts Business: U.S.
Primary Market Served: Consumer
Founded: 1995
Online marketplace for the automotive
industry.

AUTOMOD
3353 W Hospital Ave
Atlanta, GA 30341-3419
Telephone: (770) 457-9663, Toll Free:
(800) 241-1832, FAX: (770) 457-
6089, E-Mail: info@automod.fdn.
com, Web Site: www.automod.net

Pres: Earl Rogers
Conducts Business: U.S.
Employees: 5
Primary Market Served: Business &
Consumer
Founded: 1972
Distributor & retailer of high-end automotive accessories, racing & restoration products.

BUGGIES UNLIMITED
3510 Port Jacksonville Pkwy
Jacksonville, FL 32226
Toll Free: (888) 444-6364, E-Mail:
support@buggiesunlimited.com,
Web Site: www.buggiesunlimited.
com
Founder & CEO: Bart Mahan
Primary Market Served: Consumer
Golf cart parts & accessories.

CAMBRIDGE EDUCATIONAL
Imprint of Films Media Group - a div.
of Primedia, Inc
132 W 31st St Fl 17
New York, NY 10001-3406
Toll Free: (800) 257-5126, FAX: (917)
339-0325, Web Site: www.
filmsmediagroup.com
CFO: James Housley
Conducts Business: U.S., Canada, U.
K., Australia, New Zealand, Hong
Kong
Primary Market Served: Business &
Consumer
Catalog available online
Indirect online sales
Founded: 1985
Market videocassettes, CD-Rom books
& posters to guidance counselors,
home economists, coaches, business,
social studies, vocational, science, art
& music & physical education teachers,
librarians, corporations & government
programs.

CARFAX INC
5860 Trinity Pkwy (Suite 600)
Centreville, VA 20120-1998
Telephone: (703) 934-2664, Web Site:
www.carfax.com
Pres: Richard Raines
Commun Dir: Larry Gamache
VP, Dealer Bus: Bill Eager
VP: Joe Koenig
Primary Market Served: Business &
Consumer

**CLARK'S CORVAIR PARTS,
INC**
400 Mohawk Trl
Shelburne Falls, MA 01370-8503

Telephone: (413) 625-9776, FAX: (413) 625-8498, E-Mail: clarks@corvair.com, Web Site: www.corvair.com
Pres: Calvin Clark Jr.
VP: Joan Clark
Conducts Business: U.S., Canada
Employees: 25
Primary Market Served: Consumer
Catalog available online
Direct online sales
Advertising/Marketing Budget Related to Direct Marketing: 76-100%
Direct Marketing ad budget:
Direct Mail: 10%
Magazines: 80%
Newspapers: 10%
Founded: 1973

Over 14,000 restoration parts for the Chevy Corvair automobile.

CON-WAY FREIGHT
2211 Old Earhart Rd Ste 100
Ann Arbor, MI 48105-2963
Telephone: (734) 994-6600, FAX: (734) 757-1153
Direct Mktg Mgr: Tanya Koziara
Pres: W Gregory Lehmkuhl
Sr VP Opers: Thomas W Clark
Sr VP Sales: Stephen F Dearn

CON-WAY TRUCKLOAD
4701 E 32nd St
Joplin, MO 64804
Telephone: (417) 623-5229, Toll Free: (800) CFI-DRIVE, FAX: (417) 623-8939, E-Mail: gnichols@cfi-us.com, Web Site: www.cfi-us.com
Pres & CEO: Herbert Schmidt
VP Sales: Pete Montano
Pres: Saul Gonzalez
VP, IT: Mark Swab
Conducts Business: U.S., Canada, Mexico
Employees: 2,400
Primary Market Served: Business
Catalog available online
Indirect online sales
Advertising/Marketing Budget Related to Direct Marketing: 0-25%
Founded: 1951
Gross sales or billing: $272,400,000

Trucking, specializing in transportation of high value & time sensitive equipment & products throughout North America.

DAIMLERCHRYSLER CORP
1000 Chrysler Dr (CIMS 485-06-73)
Auburn Hills, MI 48326-2766
Telephone: (248) 512-1879, Web Site: www.daimlerchrysler.com
Co-Chmn: Jurgen E Schrempp
Co-Chmn: Robert J Eaton

Primary Market Served: Business & Consumer

DAKOTA DIGITAL
4510 W 61st St N
Sioux Falls, SD 57107-0639
Telephone: (605) 332-6513, Toll Free: (800) 593-4160, FAX: (605) 339-4106, E-Mail: sales@dakotadigital.com, Web Site: www.dakotadigital.com
Pres: Ross Ortman
Sls Exec: Scott Johnson
Conducts Business: U.S.
Employees: 30
Primary Market Served: Business & Consumer
Catalog available online
Direct online sales
Advertising/Marketing Budget Related to Direct Marketing: 51-75%
Direct Marketing ad budget: $250,000
Direct Mail: 20%
Magazines: 70%
Telephone: 10%
Founded: 1985
Gross sales or billing: $3,000,000

Electronic automotive instrumentation & remote vehicle entry systems sold directly to auto enthusiasts & through dealer network.

DELTA TECH INDUSTRIES
1901 S Vineyard Ave # 7
Ontario, CA 91761-7747
Telephone: (714) 577-8028, FAX: (714) 577-0140, E-Mail: sales@deltatechindustries.com, Web Site: www.deltatechindustries.com
Pres & CEO: Bogdan Durian
Natl Sales Mgr: Paul Barnaby
Conducts Business: U.S., U.K., S. Africa, Australia, Canada, Germany, Italy, Korea, Poland, Taiwan, China, Indonesia, Russia
Employees: 15
Primary Market Served: Business & Consumer
Catalog available online
Indirect online sales
Advertising/Marketing Budget Related to Direct Marketing: 0-25%
Direct Marketing ad budget:
Direct Mail: 40%
Magazines: 30%
Telephone: 30%
Founded: 1978

Manufacturing of auxiliary automobile lighting to distributors & consumers.

DESERT RAT TRUCK CENTERS
3705 S Palo Verde St
Tucson, AZ 85713-5401

Telephone: (520) 790-8502, Toll Free: (866) 444-5337, FAX: (520) 750-1918, Web Site: www.desertrat.com
Chmn: Jack Furrier
Pres: Mike Furrier
Conducts Business: Worldwide
Employees: 15
Primary Market Served: Consumer
Advertising/Marketing Budget Related to Direct Marketing: 0-25%
Gross sales or billing: $4,200,000

Sell tires & accessories for RV & 4-wheel drive pick-ups.

DYNAMIC DEVELOPMENT CO
25512 Pampero Cir
Mission Viejo, CA 92691-5436
Telephone: (949) 768-5798, E-Mail: antiwear@dynamicdevelopment.com, Web Site: www.dynamicdevelopment.com
Pres: Eugene F. Lally
Conducts Business: U.S., Canada, Europe
Employees: 2
Primary Market Served: Business & Consumer
Catalog available online
Indirect online sales
Advertising/Marketing Budget Related to Direct Marketing: 26-50%
Founded: 1962

Chemical oil additive that reduces metal parts wear 90% & increases auto engine compression, performance, and fuel mileage. The additive is also used in industrial and aerospace mechanical equipment to reduce maintenance costs and improve equipment efficiency.

EASTHILL GROUP INC
dba The Eastwood Co
263 Shoemaker Rd
Pottstown, PA 19464-6433
Telephone: (610) 323-9063, (610) 323-9099, (610) 323-2200, Toll Free: (800) 345-1178, (888) 869-4433, FAX: (610) 323-6268, Web Site: www.eastwoodcompany.com
Founder & Chmn: Curt Strohacker
Circulation Coord: Diane Short
Affiliate Mktg: John Schell
Conducts Business: Worldwide
Employees: 40
Primary Market Served: Business & Consumer
Catalog available online
Direct online sales
Advertising/Marketing Budget Related to Direct Marketing: 51-75%
Direct Marketing ad budget: $500,000
Magazines: 100%
Founded: 1978

Automotive tools.

ECKLERS

5200 S Washington Ave
Titusville, FL 32780-7316
Toll Free: (888) 787-3626, (800) 284-3906, E-Mail: custsvc@ecklers.net,
Web Site: www.ecklers.com
CEO: Matt Jordan
Primary Market Served: Business &
Consumer

Sell automotive parts & accessories.

FARRINGTON TRANSPORTATION

553 S Joliet Rd (Suite B)
Bolingbrook, IL 60440-3631
Telephone: (630) 783-9200
CEO: Victor Warren
Pres: Greg Rocque
CFO: Sheryl Cox
VP Operations: Jim Slattery
Exec VP: Phillip C Warren
Primary Market Served: Business
Founded: 1981

Freight broker.

FIRSTGROUP AMERICA

600 Vine St (Suite 1400)
Cincinnati, OH 45202-2426
Telephone: (513) 241-2200, FAX:
(513) 419-3242, Web Site: www.
firstgroup.com/north_america
Sr Dir Mktg & Sales Support: Bobbie
Hartman
CEO & Pres: Michael Murray
Exec VP Engrng for North American
Opers: Kevin Middleton
Employees: 95,000
Primary Market Served: Business
Advertising/Marketing Budget Related
to Direct Marketing: 0-25%
Founded: 1993

Provider of surface transportation services.

FOUR WHEEL DRIVE HARDWARE LLC

44488 State Rte 14
Columbiana, OH 44408-9540
Telephone: (330) 482-4924, FAX:
(330) 482-5035, E-Mail: info@4wd.
com, Web Site: www.4wd.com
CEO & Pres: George Adler
Conducts Business: Worldwide
Employees: 155
Primary Market Served: Business &
Consumer
Catalog available online
Indirect online sales
Advertising/Marketing Budget Related
to Direct Marketing: 76-100%
Founded: 1977
Gross sales or billing: $14,900,000

Automotive retail catalogs specializing
in Jeep products.

HARLEY-DAVIDSON INC

3700 W Juneau Ave
Milwaukee, WI 53208-2865
Telephone: (414) 343-7286, FAX:
(414) 343-4806, Web Site: www.
harley-davidson.com
Exec VP Corp Prod Plng: James A
McCaslin
Pres & COO: Matthew S Levatich
Sr VP - Manufacturing: Karl M Eberle
VP & Gen Mgr of Matls Mngmt: Michelle Kumbier
Employees: 9,704
Primary Market Served: Business
Advertising/Marketing Budget Related
to Direct Marketing: 26-50%
Founded: 1903

Manufacture motorcycles, recreational
vehicles, specialized commercial vehicles, motorcycle fashions & clothing
& liquid fueled target drone rocket engines for the military.

HISTORIC AVIATION

Div. of Sky Media LLC
640 Taft St NE
Minneapolis, MN 55413-2815
Telephone: (651) 635-0100, Toll Free:
(800) 225-5575, FAX: (651) 635-0700, E-Mail: info@historicaviation.
com, Web Site: www.
historicaviation.com
Pres & CEO: Gregory Herrick
Conducts Business: Worldwide
Employees: 9
Primary Market Served: Consumer
Catalog available online
Direct online sales
Direct Marketing ad budget: $250,000
Magazines: $20,000
Founded: 1970

Catalog marketer of aviation books,
video cassettes & art.

IPD CO INC

11744 NE Ainsworth Cir
Portland, OR 97220
Telephone: (503) 257-7500, Toll Free:
(800) 444-6473, FAX: (503) 257-7596, E-Mail: info@ipdusa.com,
Web Site: www.ipdusa.com
CEO: Sue Hart
COO: David Precechtil
Conducts Business: U.S., Canada, Japan
Employees: 24
Primary Market Served: Business &
Consumer
Catalog available online
Indirect online sales
Advertising/Marketing Budget Related
to Direct Marketing: 26-50%
Direct Marketing ad budget: $150,000
Direct Mail: $80,000
Magazines: $39,000

Telephone: $31,000
Founded: 1963

Sell parts & accessories for Volvo and
Subaru to both retail & wholesale markets.

INDUS-TOOL

Div. of Bird-X Inc
300 N Oakley Blvd
Chicago, IL 60612
Telephone: (312) 226-2473, Toll Free:
(800) 662-5021, FAX: (312) 226-2480, E-Mail: sales@indus-tool.com,
Web Site: www.indus-tool.com
Pres: Ronald Schwarcz
Export Sls: Luisa Ramirez
Conducts Business: Worldwide
Employees: 28
Primary Market Served: Business &
Consumer
Catalog available online
Direct online sales
Founded: 1962

Vehicle warning lights & backup
alarms, dock loading lights & electric
footwarmers.

INTERNATIONAL AUTO PARTS

4351 Seminole Trail
Charlottesville, VA 22911
Telephone: (434) 973-0550, Toll Free:
(800) 953-0813, FAX: (434) 973-2368, E-Mail: iap1@international-auto.com, Web Site: www.
international-auto.com
Pres: Paul Opiela
Conducts Business: U.S.
Employees: 45
Primary Market Served: Consumer
Advertising/Marketing Budget Related
to Direct Marketing: 76-100%
Direct Marketing ad budget:
Direct Mail: 100%
Founded: 1971

Auto accessories & travel products.

J&P CYCLES

13225 Circle Dr
Anamosa, IA 52205-7321
Telephone: (319) 462-4819, Toll Free:
(800) 318-4817, Web Site: www.j-pcycles.com
Pres: John Parham

Motorcycle parts & accessories.

JC WHITNEY

225 N Michigan Ave (Suite 9)
Chicago, IL 60601-7757
Telephone: (312) 431-6000, FAX:
(312) 431-5650, (800) 537-2700,
Web Site: www.jcwhitney.com
Mktg Dir: Bob Sebastian
CEO & Pres: Thomas M West

VP Mdsg: Joe Risch
VP E-Commerce: Geoff Robertson
Conducts Business: U.S., Canada
Primary Market Served: Business &
  Consumer
Catalog available online
Direct online sales
Advertising/Marketing Budget Related
  to Direct Marketing: 76-100%
Direct Marketing ad budget:
Direct Mail: 95%
Magazines: 5%
Founded: 1915

Sell auto parts & accessories direct to
consumers.

K-D LAMP CO
Div. of Advanced Technology Corp
101 Parker Dr
Andover, OH 44003-9456
Telephone: (440) 293-4064, FAX:
  (440) 293-4591, E-Mail: admin@atc-
  lighting-plastics.com, Web Site:
  www.k-dlamp.com
Pres & CEO: Seymour S. Stein
Dir Opers: Kevin Kirby
Conducts Business: Worldwide
Employees: 261
Primary Market Served: Business
Catalog available online
Direct online sales
Advertising/Marketing Budget Related
  to Direct Marketing: 51-75%
Direct Marketing ad budget:
Direct Mail: 60%
Magazines: 40%
Founded: 1914

O.E.M. vehicle lighting includes but
not limited to: heavy duty truck,
school/transit/coach buses, emergency,
automobile, military, motorcycle, and
agricultural applications. Products provided are headlights, in H.I.D., halogen
and composite. Other light products in
L.E.D. and incandescent are: interior,
tail, marker, clearance, back-up, license, and signal lights. Mirrors and
custom wiring harnesses also available.

LAZYDAYS RV CENTER
6131 Lazydays Blvd
Seffner, FL 33584-2968
Telephone: (813) 246-4333, FAX:
  (813) 246-4408, Web Site: www.
  lazydays.com
Chief Mktg Officer: Stewart Schaffer
CEO: Timothy R Sheehan
VP & CFO: Randall R Lay
VP Svcs: David Witty
Primary Market Served: Consumer

Motorhomes

LEXUS DIVISION OF TOYOTA
19001 S Western Ave (Suite L100)
Torrance, CA 90501-1106
Telephone: (213) 328-2075
Customer Info Mgr: Paul Nieberding
Primary Market Served: Business &
  Consumer

LITHIA MOTORS INC
360 E Jackson St
Medford, OR 97501-5892
Telephone: (541) 774-7602
Direct Mktg Coord: Sandy Stack
CEO & Pres: Bryan B DeBoer
Primary Market Served: Business &
  Consumer

MID AMERICA DESIGNS INC
Div. of Mid America Direct
17082 N US Hwy 45
Effingham, IL 62401-6764
Telephone: (217) 540-4200, Toll Free:
  (800) 350-4543, FAX: (217) 540-
  4800, E-Mail: mail@mamotorworks.
  com, Web Site: www.
  mamotorworks.com
Pres: Michael Yager
Treas: Stephen Wiedman
VP, Opers: Lori Worman
VP: Perrie Richards
Dir Mktg: Cheryl Habing
Dir: Ed Baumgarten
Conducts Business: Worldwide
Employees: 130
Primary Market Served: Business &
  Consumer
Catalog available online
Indirect online sales
Advertising/Marketing Budget Related
  to Direct Marketing: 76-100%
Direct Marketing ad budget:
  $1,500,000
Direct Mail: $13,000
Magazines: $500,000
Newspapers: $1,000
Online: $5,000
TV/Radio: $150,000
Founded: 1972
Gross sales or billing: $13,900,000

Parts & accessories for the Chevrolet
Corvette, Porsche & air-cooled Volkswagen.

MID AMERICA MOTORWORKS
RP-NFOA
Subs. of Mid America Direct
17082 N US Hwy 45
Effingham, IL 62401-7107
Telephone: (217) 347-5591, Toll Free:
  (800) 500-1500, FAX: (217) 347-
  2952, E-Mail: mail@mamotorworks.
  com, Web Site: www.
  mamotorworks.com

Pres: Mike Yager
Dir Procurement: Tim Curtis
Treas: Steve Wiedman
VP Mktg: Henk vanDongen
VP Events: Lori Worman
Conducts Business: Worldwide
Employees: 100
Primary Market Served: Business &
  Consumer
Catalog available online
Direct online sales
Advertising/Marketing Budget Related
  to Direct Marketing: 51-75%
Direct Marketing ad budget:
  $10,000,000
Direct Mail: 70%
Magazines: 15%
Newspapers: 5%
Online: 5%
TV/Radio: 5%
Founded: 1974
Gross sales or billing: $35,000,000

Mail order catalog for restoration, accessories & performance parts for Corvette & Air-Cooled Volkswagen.

MINI CITY LTD
799 Holt Rd Ste 170
Webster, NY 14580-9188
Telephone: (585) 872-6560, FAX:
  (716) 872-4094, E-Mail:
  minicityus@aol.com, Web Site:
  www.minicityltd.com
Mgr: Laurie Blue
Conducts Business: Worldwide
Employees: 9
Primary Market Served: Business &
  Consumer
Catalog available online
Indirect online sales
Advertising/Marketing Budget Related
  to Direct Marketing: 51-75%
Direct Marketing ad budget:
Direct Mail: 75%
Magazines: 25%
Founded: 1967

Parts & accessories for British automo-
biles including Austin & Morris Minis,
Morris Minors, MG 1100s & 1300s, &
Austin Americas

OMEGA RESEARCH & DEVELOPMENT
981 N Burnt Hickory Rd
Douglasville, GA 30134
Telephone: (770) 942-9876, Toll Free:
  (800) 554-4053, Web Site: www.
  caralarm.com
Pres: Kenneth E. Flick
Employees: 30
Founded: 1971
Gross sales or billing: $3,300,000

Keyless vehicle entry & security.

PARTS PLACE INC

5510 E 10 Mile Rd
Warren, MI 48091-3899
Telephone: (248) 373-2300, Toll Free: (888) 432-3548, FAX: (248) 373-5950, Web Site: www.partsplaceinc.com
Primary Market Served: Business & Consumer
Catalog available online
Founded: 2013

Mail order Volkswagen parts.

PEGASUS AUTO RACING SUPPLIES INC

2475 S 179th St
New Berlin, WI 53146-2150
Telephone: (262) 317-1234, Toll Free: (800) 688-6946, FAX: (262) 317-1201, E-Mail: info@pegasusautoracing.com, Web Site: www.pegasusautoracing.com
Co-Owner: Christopher J. Heitman
Conducts Business: Worldwide
Employees: 15
Primary Market Served: Business & Consumer
Catalog available online
Direct online sales
Advertising/Marketing Budget Related to Direct Marketing: 26-50%
Direct Marketing ad budget: $100,000
Direct Mail: 40%
Magazines: 5%
Online: 55%
Founded: 1980
Gross sales or billing: $5,800,000

Auto racing parts, components & accessories.

RACER WALSH CO

1849 Foster Dr
Jacksonville, FL 32216-3104
Telephone: (904) 721-2289, FAX: (904) 721-2935, Web Site: www.racerwalsh.com
Pres: Jerry Walsh
Conducts Business: U.S., Canada, Europe, South America, Australia
Employees: 5
Primary Market Served: Business & Consumer
Direct Marketing ad budget:
Magazines: 100%

Sell auto parts. Specialize in Ford performance cars.

RAYBUCK AUTOBODY PARTS

2829 Saint John Rd
Punxsutawney, PA 15767-8501
Telephone: (814) 938-5248, FAX: (814) 938-4250, E-Mail: service@raybuck.com, Web Site: www.raybuck.com
Owner: Randy Raybuck
Office Mgr: Lisa Raybuck
Sls Mgr: Deb Macko
Employees: 6
Primary Market Served: Business & Consumer
Catalog available online
Indirect online sales
Direct Marketing ad budget: $65,000
Direct Mail: 10%
Magazines: 70%
Newspapers: 10%
TV/Radio: 10%
Founded: 1985

Post market truck & car body parts and accessories to shops and do-it-yourselfers.

SPEEDWAY

Speedway Motors Inc
PO Box 81906
Lincoln, NE 68501-1906
Telephone: (402) 323-3100, FAX: (402) 477-7476
Gen Partner: Clay Smith
CFO: Mike Tavlin
Leasing Agent: Brett C Harris
Founded: 1952

STORAGE BATTERY SYSTEMS INC

dba SBS
N 56 W 16665 Ridgewood Dr
Menomonee Falls, WI 53051
Telephone: (262) 703-5800, Toll Free: (800) 554-2243, FAX: (262) 703-3073, E-Mail: sbs@sbsbattery.com, Web Site: www.sbsbattery.com
Pres: Scott Rubenzer
VP: Robert Rubenzer
VP Sls & Mktg: Bill Rubenzer
Employees: 46
Founded: 1915
Gross sales or billing: $22,900,000

Batteries.

SUMMIT RACING EQUIPMENT

1200 Southeast Ave
Tallmadge, OH 44278-3161
Telephone: (330) 630-0250, Toll Free: (800) 230-3030, FAX: (330) 630-5571, Web Site: www.summitracing.com
Pres: Raymond J. Tatko
Mgr Motorsports & Events: Kirk Heinbuch
Chief Mktg Officer: Jeff Winters
Pur Mgr: Frank Kremer
Opers Mgr: Scott Peterson
Conducts Business: Worldwide
Primary Market Served: Business & Consumer
Catalog available online
Direct online sales
Advertising/Marketing Budget Related to Direct Marketing: 76-100%
Founded: 1968

Sell specialty automotive performance equipment & truck accessories by direct mail.

TIME LOGISTICS INC

1406 Nashville Hwy
Columbia, TN 38401
Toll Free: (866) 293-8463, FAX: (866) 591-5697, E-Mail: quote@timelogisticsinc.com, Web Site: www.timelogisticsinc.com
Owner & Pres: Laura Shorette
COO & VP Opers: Scott Coble
CFO & VP Bus Devel & Fin: Ken Shorette
CIO & Dir Planning & Devel: Michael Shorette

Freight management.

TRANSIT TREASURE INC

311 E 38th St (Suite 19B)
New York, NY 10016-0748
Telephone: (646) 706-1001, Web Site: www.transittreasure.com
Founder & CEO: Dan Miller
Primary Market Served: Business & Consumer
Founded: 2008

This section contains listings for clubs, continuities and correspondence schools that utilize direct marketing and direct response services.

ALLSTATE MOTOR CLUB INC

Subs. of Allstate Insurance
PO Box 3094
Arlington Heights, IL 60006-3094
Telephone: (847) 551-2300, Toll Free: (800) 998-8697
Pres: Patrick M. O'Brien
Conducts Business: U.S.
Primary Market Served: Consumer
Founded: 1961

National motor club.

ART INSTRUCTION SCHOOLS

3400 Technology Dr
Minneapolis, MN 55418-6000
Telephone: (612) 362-5075, Toll Free: (800) 801-6940, FAX: (612) 362-5260, Web Site: www.artinstructionschools.edu
Pres: Patrick Stuart
Conducts Business: U.S., Canada, Puerto Rico
Employees: 30
Primary Market Served: Consumer
Advertising/Marketing Budget Related to Direct Marketing: 76-100%
Direct Marketing ad budget:
Magazines: 5%
Online: 85%
TV/Radio: 10%
Founded: 1914

Distance education art instruction.

ASHEVILLE COMPASSIONATE COMMUNICATION CENTER

150 E Chestnut St (#1)
Asheville, NC 28801-2337
Telephone: (828) 252-0538, E-Mail: jerry@ashevilleccc.com, Web Site: ashevilleccc.com
Pres: Jerry Donoghue
Primary Market Served: Business

Video training.

ASHWORTH COLLEGE

430 Technology Pkwy, Norcross, GA 30092-3406-POST
6625 The Corner Pkwy
Norcross, GA 30092
Telephone: (770) 729-8400, Toll Free: (800) 957-5412, FAX: (770) 729-9294, Web Site: www.ashworthcollege.edu

Chief Academic Officer & Dean Degree Programs: Leslie Gargiulo PhD
Academic Opers Mgr: Kelsha Abraham
Dir Education Opers: John Riser
Registrar: Eric Ryall
Dir Product Devel: Deepa Chadha
Bus Svcs Mgr: Melissa Maddox
Primary Market Served: Business & Consumer
Catalog available online
Direct online sales
Founded: 1987

Accredited online career courses & degree programs.

BJ'S WHOLESALE CLUB INC

dba BJ's
25 Research Dr
Westborough, MA 01582
Telephone: (508) 651-7400, FAX: (508) 651-6167, Web Site: www.bjs.com
Pres & CEO: Laura Sen
Exec VP & CFO: Bob Eddy
VP Mktg Opers: Steven Germain
Conducts Business: U.S.
Employees: 25,000
Primary Market Served: Business & Consumer
Founded: 1984

Membership-only warehouse club offering name brand & general merchandise.

BMG COLUMBIA HOUSE

1 Penn Plaza
New York, NY 10119-0002
Telephone: (212) 287-0081, E-Mail: cs1@bmgmusicservice.com
Sr VP, Commun: Paula Batson
Conducts Business: U.S.
Primary Market Served: Consumer
Advertising/Marketing Budget Related to Direct Marketing: 26-50%

Direct marketers of music, CDs & other entertainment products.

BENTLEY UNIVERSITY

Center for Executive Education
175 Forest St
Waltham, MA 02452-4705
Telephone: (781) 891-2473, E-Mail: execed@bentley.edu, Web Site: www.bentley.edu
Pres: Gloria Cordes Larson Esq.
Conducts Business: U.S.
Primary Market Served: Business & Consumer
Catalog available online

Indirect online sales
Advertising/Marketing Budget Related to Direct Marketing: 51-75%
Founded: 1917

BERKELEY COLLEGE

44 Rifle Camp Rd
West Paterson, NJ 07424
Telephone: (973) 278-5400, Toll Free: (800) 446-5400, FAX: (973) 278-6243, E-Mail: info@berkeleycollege.edu, Web Site: www.berkeleycollege.edu
Pres: Dario A. Cortes PhD
Provost: Marianne Vakalis
Sr VP Govt Rels, NJ: Teri Duda
Sr VP Fin & Admin: Robert F. Herzog
Sr VP Enrollment Mgmt: Diane Recinos
Primary Market Served: Business & Consumer

For-profit, accredited business education college offering associate's and bachelor's degree programs across eight campuses in NY and NJ.

BOOKSPAN

2 Park Ave (fl 10)
New York, NY 10016-5604
Telephone: (516) 490-4561, FAX: (516) 490-4856, E-Mail: info@directbrands.com, Web Site: bookspan.com
Pres & CEO: Deborah Fine
Conducts Business: U.S., Canada
Employees: 1,200
Primary Market Served: Consumer
Catalog available online
Direct online sales
Advertising/Marketing Budget Related to Direct Marketing: 76-100%
Founded: 1928

Operate 20 book clubs including Book of the Month and Doubleday Book Club. Sell to the general public through a combination of print, direct mail & other advertising vehicles.

CENTER FOR PROFESSIONAL ADVANCEMENT

190 Route 18 (Suite 203)
East Brunswick, NJ 08816-1407
Telephone: (732) 238-1600, FAX: (732) 238-9113, E-Mail: info@cfpa.com, Web Site: www.cfpa.com
Pres: Charles W. Bendel Jr
Conducts Business: U.S., Amsterdam, Holland

Employees: 41
Primary Market Served: Business
Catalog available online
Direct online sales
Founded: 1967
Gross sales or billing: $8,685,000

Sell technical short courses to professional engineers in chemical processing, pharmaceutical technology & mechanical engineering.

CLEVELAND INSTITUTE OF ELECTRONICS

1776 E 17th St
Cleveland, OH 44114-3636
Telephone: (216) 781-9400, Toll Free: (800) 243-6446, FAX: (216) 781-0331, E-Mail: instruct@cie-wc.edu, Web Site: www.cie-wc.edu
Pres: J. Randall Drinko
Conducts Business: Worldwide
Employees: 65
Primary Market Served: Business & Consumer
Catalog available online
Direct online sales
Advertising/Marketing Budget Related to Direct Marketing: 26-50%
Direct Marketing ad budget:
Direct Mail: $250,000
Magazines: $100,000
Newspapers: $200,000
TV/Radio: $360,000
Founded: 1934

Correspondence school in electronic technology & engineering.

COSMETIQUE, INC

dba Cosmetique Beauty Club Inc
859 West End Ct
Vernon Hills, IL 60061
Telephone: (847) 913-9099, Toll Free: (800) 621-8822, E-Mail: customerservice@cosmetique.com, Web Site: www.cosmetique.com
Pres: June Giugni
Conducts Business: U.S.
Primary Market Served: Consumer
Advertising/Marketing Budget Related to Direct Marketing: 0-25%
Founded: 1974
Gross sales or billing: $13,000,000

Marketer of name-brand cosmetics via continuity club. Distribute over 3 million kits annually. Direct marketing programs include: lists rental, package inserts & statement stuffers.

THE CROSS COUNTRY GROUP LLC

1 Cabot Rd
Medford, MA 02155-5117

Telephone: (781) 396-3700, FAX: (781) 391-7504, E-Mail: info@crosscountrygroup.com, Web Site: www.ccgroup.com
Chmn & CEO: Sidney D. Wolk
Co-Pres: Howard L. Wolk
Co-Pres: Jeffrey Wolk
CFO: Thomas P. Graham
Conducts Business: U.S., Canada, Mexico
Employees: 1,500
Primary Market Served: Business
Advertising/Marketing Budget Related to Direct Marketing: 76-100%
Founded: 1972
Gross sales or billing: $250,000,000

Specialty marketing organization.

DAY-TIMER

Div. of Acco Brands Corp
1 Willow Ln
East Texas, PA 18046
Telephone: (610) 398-1151, Toll Free: (800) 457-5702, (800) 225-5005, FAX: (800) 452-7398, E-Mail: connie@lomottastrategic.com, Web Site: www.daytimer.com
Exec VP & Pres US Office & Consumer Products: Thomas W. Tedford
Conducts Business: Worldwide
Employees: 510
Primary Market Served: Business & Consumer
Catalog available online
Direct online sales
Founded: 1947
Gross sales or billing: $49,900,000

Time management planners & organizers and business accessories.

DIRECT BRANDS INC

W 34th St (fl 5), 1 Penn Plaza
New York, NY 10119-0002
Telephone: (212) 930-4949, Web Site: www.columbiahouse.com
Pres & CEO: Deborah Fine
Chief Mktg Officer: David Gitow

Direct-to-consumer distributor of media products. Operates Columbia House, Book-of-the-Month Club and other special interest and lifestyle book clubs.

GEORGETOWN UNIVERSITY LAW CENTER

RP-NFOA
Academic Conferences & Continuing Legal Education
600 New Jersey Ave NW
Washington, DC 20001
Telephone: (202) 662-9890, FAX: (202) 662-9891, E-Mail: cle@law.georgetown.edu, Web Site: www.law.georgetown.edu

Asst Dean: Lawrence J. Center
Dir: Jill C. Castleman
Dir Bus Opers: Marc A. Dizon
Program Mgr: Alisha Avril
Mktg Mgr: Brittany Cain
Conducts Business: U.S.
Primary Market Served: Business & Consumer

Legal educational programs for attorneys.

GRAND CANYON UNIVERSITY

3300 W Camelback Rd
Phoenix, AZ 85017-1097
Telephone: (602) 639-7500, Toll Free: (877) 860-3951, Web Site: www.gcu.edu
Pres & CEO: Brian Mueller
COO: Dr. Stan Meyer
CFO: Dan Bachus
Primary Market Served: Business & Consumer

Private, Christian university offering bachelor's, master's and doctoral programs.

THE HISTORY BOOK CLUB INC

1225 S Market St
Mechanicsburg, PA 17055
Telephone: (718) 918-2665, E-Mail: paula.batson@dgna.com, Web Site: www.historybookclub.com
Pres & CEO: Deborah Fine
Conducts Business: U.S., Canada
Primary Market Served: Consumer
Catalog available online
Direct online sales
Advertising/Marketing Budget Related to Direct Marketing: 76-100%
Direct Marketing ad budget:
Direct Mail: 40%
Magazines: 40%
Newspapers: 20%
Founded: 1947

Offer club memberships to history buffs, sell history & children's books at discounts.

IVY TECH COMMUNITY COLLEGE OF INDIANA

50 W Fall Creek Pkwy N Dr
Indianapolis, IN 46208-5752
Telephone: (317) 921-4800, Toll Free: (888) IVY-LINE, FAX: (317) 921-4753, Web Site: www.ivytech.edu
Pres: Thomas J. Snyder
Exec VP & COO: Jeff Terp
Sr VP, CFO & Gen Counsel: Christopher Ruhl
VP Student Experience, Commun/Mktg: Jeff Fanter

VP Corp College Sls & Mktg: Tim Harris
Dir Mktg & Commun: Lauren Rochefort
Primary Market Served: Consumer
Catalog available online

Public postsecondary institution offering affordable, open-access education and training programs.

THE LIBRARY OF AMERICA

14 E 60th St
New York, NY 10022-1006
Telephone: (212) 308-3360, Toll Free: (800) 964-5778, FAX: (212) 750-8352, E-Mail: info@loa.org, Web Site: www.loa.org
Pres & CEO: Cheryl Hurley
VP & CFO: Daniel Baker
VP & Publr: Max Rudin
Editor in Chief: Geoffrey O'Brien
Dir Prodn & Online Mktg: David Cloyce Smith
Conducts Business: U.S.
Employees: 15
Primary Market Served: Business & Consumer
Founded: 1979

Publish deluxe hardcover collections of America's greatest writers.

LINCOLN EDUCATIONAL SERVICES CORP

dba Lincoln Group of Schools
200 Executive Dr (Suite 340)
West Orange, NJ 07052-3303
Telephone: (973) 736-9340, Web Site: www.lincolnedu.com
CEO: Shaun E. McAlmont
Pres & Chief Administrative Officer: Scott M. Shaw
Exec VP, CFO & Treas: Cesar Ribeiro
Exec VP & Chief Mktg Officer: Piper Jameson
Primary Market Served: Business & Consumer
Founded: 1946

Provider of career-orientated post-secondary education.

NEW YORK ROAD RUNNERS

Nine E 89th St
New York, NY 10128
Toll Free: (855) 5MY-NYRR, E-Mail: mynyrr@nyrr.org, Web Site: www.nyrr.org
Pres & CEO: Mary Wittenberg
Exec VP Opers, Admin & Strategy: Michael Capiraso
Exec VP Event, Devel & Broadcast Production: Peter Ciaccia
VP Fin & Admin: Linda A. Franken
VP Mktg & Digital: Ronnie Tucker
Primary Market Served: Consumer

Founded: 1958
Running organization.

PROFESSIONAL EDUCATION INSTITUTE

7020 High Grove Blvd
Chicago, IL 60527-7637
Telephone: (312) 521-8002, Toll Free: (800) 320-7517, Web Site: www.thepei.com
Pres: Michael E. Hussey
Conducts Business: U.S.
Primary Market Served: Business & Consumer
Advertising/Marketing Budget Related to Direct Marketing: 76-100%

Interactive education & training programs that focus on self improvement.

RANDOM HOUSE CHILDREN'S BOOKS

RP-NFOA
Div. of Random House, Inc.
1745 Broadway (fl 10)
New York, NY 10019
Telephone: (212) 782-9000, Toll Free: (800) 726-0600, E-Mail: rhkidspublicity@randomhouse.com, Web Site: www.randomhousekids.com
Pres & Publr: Barbara Marcus
Sr VP & Assoc Publr: Judith Haut
Sr VP Mktg: John Adamo
Conducts Business: U.S., Canada
Primary Market Served: Consumer

One of the largest English-language children's trade book publishers. Creates books for preschool children through young adult readers, in all formats from board books to activity books to picture books and novels. Brings together award-winning authors and illustrators, world-famous franchise characters, and multimillion-copy series.

REMINGTON COLLEGE

500 International Pkwy (Suite 200)
Heathrow, FL 32746-5627
Telephone: (407) 562-5691, Toll Free: (800) 560-6192, Web Site: www.remingtoncollege.edu
Pres & CEO: Jack W. Forrest
CFO: A. Reid Allison
VP Bus Opers: Jonathan Baker

Non-profit institution offering diploma and degree programs designed for non-traditional students.

TOONUP COACH

11 West Ave (Suite 220)
Wayne, PA 19087-3224

Telephone: (610) 902-0430, Toll Free: (866) 866-6877, E-Mail: info@toonupcoach.com, Web Site: www.toonupcoach.com
Chmn & CEO: Raymond Hansell
Pres & COO: Marysue Lucci
Conducts Business: U.S.
Catalog available online
Direct online sales
Advertising/Marketing Budget Related to Direct Marketing: 0-25%
Founded: 1998

Production of animated training & communications cartoons.

UNIVERSITY OF ALABAMA

College of Continuing Studies
624 Paul W Bryant Dr
Tuscaloosa, AL 35487
Telephone: (205) 348-6330, Toll Free: (866) 307-3917, FAX: (205) 348-9246, Web Site: continuingstudies.ua.edu
Dean: Rebecca Pow
Dir Bus Devel: Bill Elrod
Asst Dean Academic Outreach, Program Devel & Mktg: Dixie MacNeil
Conducts Business: U.S.
Primary Market Served: Business & Consumer
Founded: 1831

Provides correspondence school, weekend seminars & workshops. Evening & weekend programs in credit course.

UNIVERSITY OF PHOENIX

Subs. of Apollo Education Group Inc
1625 W Fountainhead Pkwy
Tempe, AZ 85282-2371
Telephone: (480) 557-1662, Toll Free: (866) 766-0766, Web Site: www.phoenix.edu
University Pres: Dr. William J. Pepicello
Founded: 1976

Offers campus & online degree programs, certificate courses and individual online courses.

WESTON DISTANCE LEARNING INC

2001 Lowe St
Fort Collins, CO 80525-3474
Telephone: (970) 282-6322, Web Site: www.westondistancelearning.com
Pres: Ann Rohr
VP Opers: Joyce Lindquist
Primary Market Served: Business & Consumer

Distance-learning education institution.

WORKFORCE ADVANTAGE USA

66 Elmora Ave

Elizabeth, NJ 07202-1630
Telephone: (908) 355-2299, FAX:
   (908) 352-2931, Web Site: www.
   workforceadvantageusa.com
Pres & CEO: Julio Sabater
CFO: Laura Garza
Conducts Business: U.S.
Primary Market Served: Business &
   Consumer
Founded: 1988

Job coaching and supported work services.

ACADEMIC MANAGEMENT SERVICES

Sub of: SLM Corp
463 Swansea Mall Dr
Swansea, MA 02777-4119
Telephone: (508) 235-2870, Toll Free: (800) 891-4203, FAX: (508) 235-2991, E-Mail: info@amsweb.com, Web Site: www.amsweb.com
Pres: Judith Grassi
Sr VP, Sls Midwest: Tom Quinn
VP, Sls North: Amy Miranda
VP, Sls South: Nanette White
VP, Sls West: Pia Labos
Conducts Business: U.S.
Employees: 125
Primary Market Served: Business & Consumer
Advertising/Marketing Budget Related to Direct Marketing: 51-75%
Founded: 1970

Tuition payment plans, loans & credit lines for education. Sell to colleges & prep schools, direct mail to parents.

ACCOUNTING WITH DEBITS AND CREDITS WITH COATES & HUTCHINSON PC

PO Box 561
Odenton, MD 21113
Telephone: (410) 672-6339, Toll Free: (800) 833-5933, FAX: (301) 912-3364, E-Mail: info@awdc.org
VP: Theresa Hutchinson
Pres: Doreen Coates
Conducts Business: U.S.
Employees: 4
Primary Market Served: Business
Advertising/Marketing Budget Related to Direct Marketing: 0-25%
Founded: 1989
Gross sales or billing: $290,000

Charitable solicitation filings. Tax & bookkeeping services.

ACCUTRADE INC

Sub. of Ameritrade Holding Corp
1005 Ameritrade Pl
Bellevue, NE 68005
Telephone: (402) 970-7400, Toll Free: (800) 882-4887, FAX: (816) 243-3762, E-Mail: info@accutrade.com
Pres: Mark Gibson
Conducts Business: U.S.
Primary Market Served: Business & Consumer
Founded: 1975

Discount stock brokerage firm.

ADVANCED FINANCIAL SERVICES

25 Enterprise Dr
Middletown, RI 02842-7233
Telephone: (401) 849-0892, Toll Free: (800) 620-6292, FAX: (401) 851-5621, Web Site: www.embracehomeloans.com
CEO: Dennis Hardiman
Sr VP & CFO: Bob Barber
Pres: Kurt Noyce
VP: Gil Almeida
VP: Peter Mircroulis
Primary Market Served: Consumer

ADVANCEME INC

2015 Vaughn Rd NW (Suite 500)
Kennesaw, GA 30144-7831
Telephone: (888) 700-8181, Web Site: www.advanceme.com
VP, Direct Mktg: Christopher Rabbu

ADVANTA CORP

625 West Ridge Pike
Conshohocken, PA 19428
Telephone: (215) 657-4000, Toll Free: (800) 255-0022, Web Site: www.advanta.com
CEO & Chmn: Dennis Alter
VP Mktg & Acquisition: Meredith Hein
CFO: Philip M. Browne
Employees: 841
Founded: 1951

AEGON USA INVESTMENT MANAGEMENT, INC

4333 Edgewood Rd NE
Cedar Rapids, IA 52499-3830
Telephone: (502) 560-2000, FAX: (502) 560-2030, Web Site: www.aegonins.com
Dir Mezzanine Investments: John Skaggs
Head US Fixed Income: William Frank Koster
Dir: J. Staley Stewart
Conducts Business: U.S.
Employees: 60
Primary Market Served: Consumer

Reverse mortgages to over 2,000 homeowners whose homes are worth at least $75,000.

AETNA - MARKETING PRODUCT & COMMUNICATION

RP-NFOA
151 Farmington Ave
Hartford, CT 06156
Telephone: (860) 273-0123, Toll Free: (800) 872-3862, FAX: (860) 273-3971, Web Site: www.aetna.com
Chmn & CEO: Ronald A. Williams
Pres: Mark T. Bertolini
Sr VP & CIO: Margaret McCarthy
Sr VP Strategic Mktg & Communs: Robert M Mead
VP Mktg: Frank McCauley
Conducts Business: U.S.
Employees: 34,024
Primary Market Served: Business & Consumer
Catalog available online
Gross sales or billing: $25,100,000,000

Direct marketing of mutual funds to business & consumer.

AGILIS CO

2380 Crossroads Blvd
Albert Lea, MN 56007-4001
Telephone: (507) 377-5028
Pres: Patty Tewes
Primary Market Served: Business & Consumer

ALERUS FINANCIAL NATIONAL ASSOC

401 Demers Ave Ste 100
Grand Forks, ND 58201-4574
Telephone: (701) 795-3200, Toll Free: (800) 279-3200, Web Site: www2.alerusfinancial.com
CEO & Pres: Randy Louis Newman
CFO: Eric Anthony Carlson
COO: Kris Ellen Compton
Chief Info Officer & Sr VP Consumer Segment: Jon H. Hendry
Sr VP: James B. Faircloth
Primary Market Served: Consumer
Founded: 1879

ALLIANCE BERNSTEIN

1345 Ave of the Americas
New York, NY 10105-0302
Telephone: (212) 969-1000, Toll Free: (800) 962-2134, FAX: (212) 969-2293, Web Site: www.alliancebernstein.com
CEO & Chmn: Peter Steven Kraus
Sr VP & CFO: John C. Weisenseel
Exec VP & CTO: Lawrence H. Cohen
Sr VP & CFO: Robert H. Joseph Jr.
COO: James A. Gingrich
CIO: Sharon E. Fay
Employees: 5,580
Primary Market Served: Business & Consumer
Founded: 1971
Gross sales or billing: $4,700,000,000

AMERICAN APPRAISAL ASSOCIATES

411 E Wisconsin Ave (Suite 1900)
Milwaukee, WI 53202-4466
Telephone: (414) 271-7240, Toll Free:
(800) 558-8650, FAX: (414) 221-
7065, Web Site: www.american-
appraisal.com
Chm & CEO: Joseph Zvesper
Mng Dir: Roberto Palma
Mng Dir Bus Devel: David G. Easterly
Mktg Specialist: Paul Perez
Conducts Business: U.S., Canada, Europe, Asia
Employees: 850
Primary Market Served: Business
Advertising/Marketing Budget Related
to Direct Marketing: 51-75%
Founded: 1896

Valuation consulting services.

AMERICAN CENTURY INVESTMENTS

4500 Main St, Box 418210
Kansas City, MO 64111
Telephone: (816) 531-5575, Toll Free:
(800) 345-2021, FAX: (816) 340-
4964, Web Site: www.
americancentury.com
Founder & Dir: James Evans Stowers
III
Pres: Jonathan Stuart Thomas
COO: Patrick Thomas Bannigan
Sr VP: Glen Foggle
Conducts Business: U.S.
Employees: 1,837
Primary Market Served: Business &
Consumer
Catalog available online
Indirect online sales
Founded: 1958
Gross sales or billing: $249,000,000

Mutual fund company serving retail &
institutional markets.

AMERICAN EXPRESS CO

Div. of American Express Co
200 Vesey St (fl 47
New York, NY 10285-0002
Telephone: (212) 640-2000, FAX:
(212) 619-9802, Web Site: www.
americanexpress.com
CEO: Kenneth I. Chenault
Grp VP: Edward Gilligan
VP Mktg, Consumer Tvl: Audrey
Hendley
Dir, Brand Mngmt: Lisa Drapkin
Conducts Business: Worldwide
Employees: 58,400
Primary Market Served: Business &
Consumer

Gross sales or billing: $24,300,000

Promotes traveler's cheques & card
products. Engaged in acquisition of
new cardmembers & cross-selling of
various services.

AMERIPRISE FINANCIAL SERVICES INC

70100 Ameriprise Financial Center
Minneapolis, MN 55474-0023
Telephone: (612) 671-3131, (651) 671-
3434, Toll Free: (800) 386-2042,
FAX: (612) 547-2736, Web Site:
www.ameriprise.com
Client Acquisition Direct Mktg Mgr:
Cid Rode
Fin Officer Roseville Office: Douglas
Emitte
Founded: 1971

ARBOR CAPITAL 1

1414 Harney St (Suite 400)
Omaha, NE 68102-2255
Telephone: (402) 991-4962
Mng Partner: Susan Henricks
Primary Market Served: Consumer

ARBOR COMMERCIAL MORTGAGE

333 Earle Ovington Blvd
Uniondale, NY 11553-3610
Telephone: (516) 229-6615, Web Site:
www.thearbornet.com
Sr VP Mktg: Bonnie Habyan

ASSOCIATION FOR FINANCIAL PROFESSIONALS

4520 East West Hwy (Suite 750)
Bethesda, MD 20814-3574
Telephone: (301) 907-2862, FAX:
(301) 907-2864, Web Site: www.
afponline.org
Pres & CEO: James A. Kaitz
Primary Market Served: Business

Serves financial professionals with
products, education and training for
treasury and corporate finance.

ASTORIA FEDERAL SAVINGS

1 Astoria Federal Plaza
Lake Success, NY 11042-1076
Telephone: (516) 327-7000, Web Site:
www.astoriafederal.com

AVIVA USA CORP

611 Fifth Ave
Des Moines, IA 50309
Telephone: (515) 362-3600, FAX:
(800) 531-0038, Web Site: www.
avivausa.com
Sr VP Corp Communs: Jonna LaToure

Pres & CEO: Thomas C. Godlasky
Primary Market Served: Consumer
Advertising/Marketing Budget Related
to Direct Marketing: 0-25%
Founded: 1896
Gross sales or billing: $101,400,000

Holding company for banks, realty, investment & mortgage companies.

AXIS CAPITAL

430 Park Ave (fl 2)
New York, NY 10022-3539
Telephone: (212) 500-7743
Primary Market Served: Consumer

BNY MELLON

1 Wall St
New York, NY 10286
Telephone: (412) 234-5000, (212) 495-
1784, FAX: (412) 635-1799, Web
Site: www.bnymellon.com
Chmn: Gerald L. Hassell
CFO: Thomas P. Gibbons
Conducts Business: Worldwide
Employees: 16,000
Primary Market Served: Business &
Consumer
Founded: 1784

Retail bank.

BANK BOSTON

100 Federal St
Boston, MA 02110
Telephone: (617) 434-2200, FAX:
(617) 434-7547, Web Site: www.
bankboston.com
Conducts Business: U.S.
Employees: 2,000
Primary Market Served: Business &
Consumer
Founded: 1784

Full-service bank.

BANK OF AMERICA

100 N Tryon St
Charlotte, NC 28255
Telephone: (704) 386-5681, Toll Free:
(800) 841-4000, FAX: (704) 386-
6699, Web Site: www.
bankofamerica.com
Sr VP: Timothy N. Tobin
Mktg Exec: Peter Dontas
Sr VP: Aaron Eichler
Conducts Business: U.S.
Employees: 203,000
Primary Market Served: Business &
Consumer
Catalog available online
Founded: 1904
Gross sales or billing:
$117,000,000,000

Full-service bank.

BANK OF HAWAII

Subs. of Bank of Hawaii Corporate
PO Box 2900
Honolulu, HI 96846-0001
Telephone: (808) 537-8398, FAX:
(808) 536-9433, Web Site: www.boh.
com
Exec VP & Mgr Mktg & Commun
Grp: Laurie McCarney
CEO: Michael O'Neil
VP & Mgr: Margaret Dang
VP, DM & Collateral: June Kaneshiro
Sr VP: Cindy Thomas
Conducts Business: U.S.
Employees: 4,000
Primary Market Served: Business &
Consumer
Advertising/Marketing Budget Related
to Direct Marketing: 0-25%

Full-service bank.

THE BANK OF NEW YORK/ DELAWARE

Subs. of The Bank of New York Corp
100 White Clay Center Dr (102)
Newark, DE 19711-5478
Telephone: (302) 451-2500, Toll Free:
(800) 942-1977, FAX: (302) 451-
2537, Web Site: www.bankofny.com
Conducts Business: U.S.
Employees: 850
Primary Market Served: Business &
Consumer

Lending company.

BANK OF THE WEST

300 S Grand Ave
Los Angeles, CA 90071-3109
Telephone: (509) 736-0131, Web Site:
www.bankofthewest.com
Sr VP: David Covert

BANK ONE

One Bank One Plaza
Chicago, IL 60670
Toll Free: (888) 963-4000, (800) 452-
3141, (866) 265-1727, FAX: (614)
248-5624, Web Site: www.bankone.
com
Primary Market Served: Business &
Consumer

User of direct marketing to sell financial services.

THE BAUMAN GROUP

50 Main St
Ashland, MA 01721-3113
Telephone: (508) 879-3009, Toll Free:
(800) 876-3009, FAX: (508) 875-
3751, E-Mail: info@bauman.com,
Web Site: www.bauman.com
Pres & Owner: Marcia Bauman
Primary Market Served: Business &
Consumer

Founded: 1987
Credit card marketing firm.

BEARINGPOINT INC

100 Crescent Court (Suite 700)
Dallas, TX 75201-2112
Telephone: (703) 747-3000, FAX:
(703) 747-3215, Web Site: www.
bearingpoint.com
Mng Partner: Peter Mockler
Exec VP & CIO: Eric Goldfarb
Sr VP: Sarah Beardsley
Conducts Business: Worldwide
Employees: 15,200
Primary Market Served: Business
Advertising/Marketing Budget Related
to Direct Marketing: 0-25%
Founded: 1999

Accounting, audit & tax consulting
firm.

BILL ME LATER INC

9690 Deereco Rd (fl 7)
Timonium, MD 21093-6936
Telephone: (443) 921-1900, FAX:
(443) 921-1985, Web Site: www.
billmelater.com
Head Consumer Strategy: Carolyn
Groobey
Founded: 2000

WILLIAM BLAIR & CO LLC

222 W Adams St
Chicago, IL 60606-5312
Telephone: (312) 236-1600, Toll Free:
(800) 621-0687, FAX: (312) 368-
9418, E-Mail: info@williamblair.
com, Web Site: www.williamblair.
com
Pres & CEO: John R. Ettelson
CFO: Jon Walter Zindel
Dir Opers: Thomas Pace
Primary Market Served: Business &
Consumer
Catalog available online
Founded: 1935

Investment banking firm.

THE BOSTON CO ASSET MANAGEMENT LLC

Subs. of Mellon Corp
1 Boston Pl
Boston, MA 02108-4407
Telephone: (617) 722-7029, FAX:
(617) 722-3928, Web Site: www.
thebostoncompany.com
CIO: Bart A. Grenier
Pres: Joseph P. Gennaco
CFO & Treas: Marie Stewart
Conducts Business: U.S., England
Primary Market Served: Business &
Consumer

Founded: 1970
Multi-faceted investment management
& banking organization.

BRAINTREE PAYMENT SOLUTIONS LLC

833 W Jackson Blvd (Suite 500)
Chicago, IL 60607-5400
Telephone: (773) 489-9539, Web Site:
www.braintreepaymentsolutions.com

BRANCH BANKING & TRUST CO

RP-NFOA
Subs. of BB&T Financial Corp
200 W 2nd St
Winston-Salem, NC 27101
Telephone: (336) 733-2000, FAX:
(336) 733-2189, Web Site: www.bbt.
com
Pres: Robert E. Greene
Chmn: Kelly S. King
Exec VP: Donna C. Goodrich
Conducts Business: U.S.
Employees: 3,000
Primary Market Served: Business &
Consumer
Founded: 1872
Gross sales or billing: $6,500,000,000

Financial institution.

CIT

Change of control 2002
1 CIT Dr
Livingston, NJ 07039-5703
Telephone: (973) 740-5000, FAX:
(973) 740-5383, Web Site: www.cit.
com
Exec VP: Omar Farooq
Dir Mktg Communs: Gia Porto-Lenza
Conducts Business: U.S.
Employees: 5,620
Primary Market Served: Business
Direct Marketing ad budget:
Direct Mail: 50%
Magazines: 25%
Newspapers: 25%
Founded: 2002
Gross sales or billing: $3,036,400

Financial service corporation specializing in equipment financing & leasing
for business firms. Financing of office
products, manufactured housing & recreational vehicles.

CMS INC

2650 Pilgrim Ct
Winston Salem, NC 27106-5238
Telephone: (336) 631-2500, FAX:
(336) 631-2903, Web Site: www.
promotionslogistics.com
Dir Mktg: Matthew Tilley
Mgr: Sheila Templeton
Employees: 499

Primary Market Served: Consumer

CARDFLEX FINANCIAL SERVICES
2900 Bristol Ave (bldg F)
Costa Mesa, CA 92626-5981
Telephone: (714) 361-1900, E-Mail:
aphillips@cliq.com, Web Site: www.
flex1.com
Owner: Andy Phillips
VP Bus Devel: Jaime Gonzalez
Employees: 49

CASHNETUSA II LLC
200 W Jackson Blvd (Suite 1400)
Chicago, IL 60606-6941
Telephone: (312) 568-4200, Toll Free:
(888) 801-9075, FAX: (866) 326-
5265, Web Site: www.cashnetusa.
com
Owner: J. Linscott

CENTRAL PACIFIC BANK
220 S King St
Honolulu, HI 96813-4530
Telephone: (808) 544-0500, Toll Free:
(800) 544-0500, (800) 342-8422,
FAX: (808) 531-2875, Web Site:
www.centralpacificbank.com
CEO: John C. Dean
CFO & Exec VP: Lawrence D. Rodri-
guez
Employees: 850
Primary Market Served: Business &
Consumer
Founded: 1954
Gross sales or billing: $320,400,000

Operates 40 branch locations in the Hawaiian Islands. Targets individuals &
local businesses. Checking, savings,
money market accounts & CDs, commercial real-estate loans including residential mortgages, business,
construction, & consumer loans.

CHARTER ONE BANK
Subs. of Citizens Financial Group
1215 Superior Ave
Cleveland, OH 44114-3299
Telephone: (216) 566-5300, Toll Free:
(877) CHARTER, (877) 242-7837,
FAX: (216) 664-1481, Web Site:
www.charterone.com
CEO & Pres: Edward O'Handy III
Mktg: Gayle Hanisko
Primary Market Served: Business &
Consumer
Catalog available online
Indirect online sales
Founded: 1934
Gross sales or billing: $8,255,000,000
Full service bank.

CHECKS BY PHONE/CHECKS BY WEB
9770 S Military Trail (Suite 380)
Boynton Beach, FL 33436
Telephone: (561) 737-8700, FAX:
(561) 737-5800, E-Mail:
LarrySchwartz@checksbyphone.
com, Web Site: www.
checksbyphone.com
Pres, CEO & Founder: Larry Schwartz
Founder & Dir: Pearl Sax
Natl Sls Mgr: Leslie Adams
Conducts Business: Worldwide
Employees: 20
Primary Market Served: Business
Catalog available online
Direct online sales
Advertising/Marketing Budget Related
to Direct Marketing: 76-100%
Direct Marketing ad budget: $100,000
Direct Mail: 25%
Magazines: 25%
Online: 25%
Telephone: 25%
Founded: 1982
Gross sales or billing: $20,000,000

Worldwide processor of check transactions received by merchants via phone,
fax, modem, e-mail & the internet.

CHECKVANTAGE
26 Long Creek Rd
Austin, TX 78737-9303
Telephone: (512) 970-4958, Toll Free:
(877) 243-2501, FAX: (512) 442-
5515, E-Mail: marya@checkvantage.
com, Web Site: www.checkvantage.
com
Mgr: Nann Orina
Conducts Business: U.S.
Employees: 3
Primary Market Served: Business
Catalog available online
Advertising/Marketing Budget Related
to Direct Marketing: 0-25%
Founded: 1999

Electronic check processing.

CHURCH EXTENSION PLAN
4070 27th Ct SE (Suite 210)
Salem, OR 97302-1359
Toll Free: (800) 821-1112, Web Site:
www.cepnet.com
Pres: Patrick L. Clements Rev.
Primary Market Served: Consumer
Founded: 1950

Ministry providing financial & administrative services to the churches & dis-
tricts to the Assemblies of God

CITI CARDS / CITICORP CREDIT SERVICES
1 Court Sq
Long Island City, NY 11120-0001

Telephone: (718) 248-5400
Sr VP Dir of Adv: Jennifer Lindauer
Primary Market Served: Business

CITIBANK
Subs. of Citigroup Inc
399 Park Ave
New York, NY 10022-4699
Telephone: (212) 559-9425, Toll Free:
(800) 285-3000, FAX: (212) 527-
2318, Web Site: www.citibank.com
Pres: Vikram Pandit
Conducts Business: U.S.
Primary Market Served: Business &
Consumer
Advertising/Marketing Budget Related
to Direct Marketing: 51-75%

Personal & credit card banking.

CITIFINANCIAL CREDIT CO
Subs. of Citigroup Inc
300 Saint Paul Pl
Baltimore, MD 21202-2120
Telephone: (410) 332-3000, Toll Free:
(800) 922-6235, (800) 995-2274,
FAX: (410) 332-3489, Web Site:
www.citifinancial.com
CEO: Mary McDowell
Exec VP & CFO: David Neaves
Conducts Business: U.S., CA
Employees: 18,500
Primary Market Served: Consumer
Founded: 1912
Gross sales or billing: $2,147,500,000

Consumer lending subsidiary of Citigroup offering bill consolidation, debt
refinancing, home equity, home improvement, auto and other personal
loans.

CITIGROUP INC
399 Park Ave
New York, NY 10043-0001
Telephone: (212) 559-1000, Toll Free:
(800) 285-3000, FAX: (212) 793-
3946, Web Site: www.citigroup.com
Chmn: Michael O'Neill
CEO,: Michael Corbat
CFO: John C. Gerspach
Conducts Business: U.S., Canada, Aus-
tralia, U.K.
Employees: 6,000
Primary Market Served: Consumer
Catalog available online
Advertising/Marketing Budget Related
to Direct Marketing: 76-100%
Founded: 1988

Financial services company specializing in consumer loans.

CITIZENS BANK
28 State St
Boston, MA 02109

Telephone: (617) 725-5900, FAX: (617) 725-5921, Web Site: www.citizensbank.com
Chmn: Robert E. Smyth
Exec VP: Robert C. Rubino
Conducts Business: U.S.
Employees: 400
Primary Market Served: Business & Consumer
Gross sales or billing: $529,100,000

A full-service state commercial bank.

CITIZENS REPUBLIC BANK

328 S Saginaw St
Flint, MI 48502-1923
Toll Free: (810) 766-7500, Web Site: www.citizensbanking.com
CEO: Cathy Nash
Exec VP: Charles Christy
Exec VP: Clinton Sampson
Exec VP: John Schwab

CLEARONE ADVANTAGE

1501 S Clinton St (320)
Baltimore, MD 21224
Toll Free: (888) 785-5376, FAX: (888) 785-5365, Web Site: www.clearoneadvantage.com
CEO: Tomas Gordon
VP: Joseph A. Campanella
Founded: 2006

CLIENTS & PROFITS WORLDWIDE

4755 Oceanside Blvd (#200)
Oceanside, CA 92056-3056
Telephone: (760) 945-4334, Web Site: www.clientsandprofits.com
Owner: Mark Robillard
Sls Exec: Mary Peczeli
Opers: Rhonda Brazelton
Primary Market Served: Business

COMDATA CORP

5301 Maryland Way
Brentwood, TN 37027
Telephone: (615) 370-7000, Toll Free: (800) 266-3282, FAX: (615) 370-7614, Web Site: www.comdata.com
Pres: Steve Stevenson
Exec VP Strategy & Opers: Joseph P. Daly
Primary Market Served: Business & Consumer
Founded: 1969

Provider of transaction and information services offering information management, credit and debit transaction, processing and reporting, telecommunications, fuel management & travel plaza products and services.

COMERICA INC

1717 Main St
Dallas, TX 75201-4612
Toll Free: (800) 521-1190, FAX: (925) 941-1999, Web Site: www.comerica.com
Chmn, Pres & CEO: Ralph W. Babb Jr.
Vice-Chmn: Lars C. Anderson
Vice Chmn & CFO: Karen L. Parkhill
Exec VP: Jon W. Bilstrom
Exec VP & Chief HR Resources Officer: Megan D. Burkhart
Conducts Business: U.S.
Employees: 11,200
Primary Market Served: Business & Consumer
Catalog available online
Gross sales or billing: $4,200,000,000

Bank holding company. Comerica Banks in Michigan, California, Florida, & Texas.

COMMERCE BANCSHARES INC

8000 Forsyth Blvd (CBIR-1)
Saint Louis, MO 63105-1707
Toll Free: (800) 453-2265, Web Site: www.commercebank.com
Corp Mktg Dir: Eric Steinhouse
Primary Market Served: Business

COMMERCIAL FEDERAL BANK

Commercial Federal Corp
13220 California St (Suite 100)
Omaha, NE 68154-5228
Telephone: (402) 554-9200, FAX: (402) 390-3592
Pres & COO: Frederick R Kulikowski
Conducts Business: U.S.
Employees: 2,827
Primary Market Served: Business & Consumer
Founded: 1887

Full-service financial institution.

COMPASS BANK

15 20th St S
Birmingham, AL 35233-2011
Telephone: (205) 297-4900, Toll Free: (800) 239-4357, FAX: (205) 933-3702, Web Site: www.compassbank.com
CEO: Manuel Sanchez
CFO: Angel Reglero
Conducts Business: U.S.
Primary Market Served: Business & Consumer
Founded: 1964

Sell retail, commercial & correspondent banking services to individuals, corporations & financial institutions.

COPILEVITZ & CANTER, LLC

310 W 20th St (Suite 300)
Kansas City, MO 64108-2025
Telephone: (816) 472-9000, FAX: (816) 472-5000, Web Site: www.copilevitz-canter.com
Sr Partner: Errol Copilevitz

CORNERSTONE BUSINESS SERVICES INC

200 S Washington St (Suite 205)
Green Bay, WI 54301
Telephone: (920) 436-9890, FAX: (920) 436-9894, E-Mail: sbushkie@cornerstone-business.com, Web Site: www.cornerstone-business.com
Pres: Scott Bushkie
Conducts Business: U.S.
Primary Market Served: Business & Consumer

National full-service mergers & acquisitions firm.

COSGROVE ASSOCIATES

747 Third Ave (fl 16l)
New York, NY 10017-2803
Telephone: (212) 888-7202, FAX: (212) 888-7201, Web Site: www.cosgrovejuro.com
Pres: Jerry Cosgrove
Conducts Business: U.S.
Employees: 35
Primary Market Served: Business & Consumer
Advertising/Marketing Budget Related to Direct Marketing: 76-100%

Direct response & marketing communications firm for financial institutions & health-related firms.

COUGAR MOUNTAIN SOFTWARE

7180 Potomac Dr
Boise, ID 83704
Telephone: (208) 375-4455, Toll Free: (800) 388-3038, FAX: (208) 375-4460, E-Mail: sales@cougarmtn.com, Web Site: www.cougarmtn.com
CEO: Chuck Gossett
Chief Sls Officer: Dave Haworth
Conducts Business: U.S., Canada
Employees: 40
Primary Market Served: Business
Catalog available online
Direct online sales
Advertising/Marketing Budget Related to Direct Marketing: 0-25%
Direct Marketing ad budget: $500,000
Direct Mail: 50%
Magazines: 45%
Newspapers: 5%
Founded: 1982
Gross sales or billing: $5,000,000

Full featured accounting, fund accounting & point of sale software for small to mid-sized businesses.

COUNTRYWIDE FINANCIAL CORP
45 Park Granada
Calabasas, CA 91302
Telephone: (818) 225-3000, FAX:
(818) 225-4051, Web Site: www.
countrywide.com
Chmn Bd & CEO: Angelo R. Mozillo
CFO & Exec Mng Dir: Eric P. Sieracki
Employees: 50,386
Primary Market Served: Business &
Consumer
Founded: 1969
Gross sales or billing: $2,675,000,000
Mortgage bankers.

DB ALEX BROWN INC
Subs. of Bankers Trust NY Corp
100 International Dr (fl 22)
Baltimore, MD 21202-3298
Telephone: (410) 727-1700, Toll Free:
(800) 638-2956, Web Site: www.
dbalexbrown.com
Pres: Douglas Brent
Mng Dir: Jeffrey Ott
Sr Mng Dir: Joseph Wood
Conducts Business: Worldwide
Employees: 2,575
Primary Market Served: Business &
Consumer
Founded: 1800

Investment banking subsidiary providing financial services.

DMB FINANCIAL
500 Cummings Center (Suite 5450)
Beverly, MA 01915-6519
Telephone: (866) 810-3210, FAX:
(978) 338-2347, E-Mail: help@
dmbfinancial.com, Web Site: www.
dmbfinancial.com
Owner: Matthew Guthrie
HR Exec: Trish Carolan
Fin Exec: Derek Valley

Private company not affiliated with the
credit bureaus or the credit industry,
providing clients with sound debt settlement products.

DWS INVESTMENTS SERVICE CO
Division of Deutsche Bank
210 W 10th St
Kansas City, MO 64105-1614
Toll Free: (800) 543-5776, Web Site:
www.dws-investments.com
COO DWS Investments America:
Chris Burns
Head Mktg America: Kristen Peters
Pres DWS Funds & Head Product
Mngmt America: W Douglas Beck
Conducts Business: U.S.
Primary Market Served: Business &
Consumer

Catalog available online
Direct online sales
Direct marketing of mutual funds &
other financial products to the public &
to AARP members.

DALRADA FINANCIAL CORP
11956 Bernardo Plaza Dr (Suite 516)
San Diego, CA 92128-2538
Telephone: (858) 791-6200, Toll Free:
(877) 325-7232, FAX: (858) 277-
3448, E-Mail: inquiries@dalrada.
com, Web Site: www.dalrada.com
Principal: Brian Bonner
Exec VP: Stanley Costello
Chief Acctg Officer: Robert Dietrich
Primary Market Served: Business &
Consumer
Catalog available online
Founded: 1982
Gross sales or billing: $70,400,000
Manufacture computer printers.

DEALERTRACK
1111 Marcus Ave (fl 3)
New Hyde Park, NY 11042-2039
Telephone: (516) 734-3600, Web Site:
www.dealertract.com
Chmn: Mark O'Neil
Primary Market Served: Business
Founded: 2000

DELAWARE INVESTMENTS
Subs. of Lincoln National Corp
2005 Market St
Philadelphia, PA 19103-7042
Telephone: (215) 255-1200, E-Mail:
service@delinvest.com, Web Site:
www.delawareinvestments.com
Pres: Patrick Coyne
Exec VP: J. Scott Coleman
Exec VP: Michael Hogan
Conducts Business: U.S., U.K.
Employees: 550
Primary Market Served: Business
Advertising/Marketing Budget Related
to Direct Marketing: 0-25%
Founded: 1929

Investment advisory company & provider of mutual funds to individual &
institutional investors.

DELOITTE & TOUCHE
200 Berkeley St (#820)
Boston, MA 02116
Telephone: (617) 437-2000, FAX:
(617) 437-2111, Web Site: www.
deloitte.com
Global CEO: James H. Quigley
Partner, CPA, Mng: Bill Bacic
Sr Partner: William G. Parrett
Global Svc Line Leader Intl Tax: Peter
N. Corcoran

European Leader Intl Tax Svc Line:
Jan Roels
Primary Market Served: Business
Catalog available online
Founded: 1891

Accounting firm offering auditing &
tax services.

DEUTSCHE BANK ALEX BROWN INC
60 Wall St
New York, NY 10005
Telephone: (212) 250-2500, FAX:
(212) 797-4664, Web Site: www.db.
com
Primary Market Served: Business
Merchant/retail investment.

THE DIME SAVINGS BANK OF NEW YORK FSB
589 5th Ave
New York, NY 10017
Telephone: (212) 326-6170, FAX:
(212) 326-6194, Web Site: www.
dimewill.com
Conducts Business: U.S.
Primary Market Served: Business &
Consumer
Founded: 1859

Full-service savings bank.

DISCOVER FINANCIAL SERVICES
2500 Lake Cook Rd
Riverwoods, IL 60015-1838
Telephone: (224) 405-0900
VP: Gerald Wagner
Primary Market Served: Business

DIVERSIFIED INVESTMENT ADVISORS
440 Mamaroneck Ave
Harrison, NY 10528-2421
Telephone: (914) 627-3000, FAX:
(914) 627-3280, Web Site: www.
divinvest.com
Pres & Treas: Gregory Kunkel
CFO & Sr VP: Colette F. Vargas
COO: Alice Hocking
VP West Coast Client Relationship De-
vel Team: Lisa Steinberg
Employees: 900
Primary Market Served: Business
Catalog available online
Founded: 1992

Pension investment firm.

DOMESTIC BANK
15 Park Row W
Providence, RI 02903-1104

Telephone: (401) 943-1600, Toll Free: (800) 566-6600, FAX: (401) 943-6708, Web Site: www.domesticbank.com
Pres: Nathaniel Baker
CFO: Walter H. Braillard II
Exec VP: Craig A. Baker
Sr VP: Joseph LaPlume
VP: Jeff Baker
Primary Market Served: Business & Consumer
Catalog available online

Full service banking institution for businesses & consumers, specializing in loans & long term investments.

THE DREYFUS CORP
Subs. of Mellon Bank NA
200 Park Ave
New York, NY 10166
Telephone: (212) 922-6000, FAX: (212) 922-6880, Web Site: www.dreyfus.com
Chmn: Jonathan Russell Baum
Pres & Dir: John Charles Cardona
Vice Chmn & COO: John David Officer
Conducts Business: U.S.
Employees: 1,864
Primary Market Served: Business & Consumer
Founded: 1951

Investment advisor & manager of mutual funds.

ESL FEDERAL CREDIT UNION
225 Chestnut St
Rochester, NY 14604
Telephone: (585) 336-1000, Toll Free: (800) 848-2265, FAX: (585) 336-1138, Web Site: www.esl.org
Pres, CEO, Dir: David L. Fieldler
Pres & COO: Faheem Masood
CFO: Thomas J. Rogers
VP & Dir Systems & Technology: Joseph S. Buscaglia
Conducts Business: Canada
Employees: 560
Primary Market Served: Business & Consumer
Catalog available online
Gross sales or billing: $189,900,000

EAGLE ASSET MANAGEMENT INC
Subs. of Raymond James Financial Corp
880 Carillon Pkwy
Saint Petersburg, FL 33716
Telephone: (727) 573-2453, FAX: (727) 573-8655, Web Site: www.eagleasset.com
Co-CEO: James Cooper Abbott
Pres & Co-COO: Richard Rossi

Conducts Business: Worldwide
Employees: 85
Primary Market Served: Consumer

Professionally managed investment portfolios including individual retirement plans, endowments & trusts with assets exceeding $100M.

EASTERN BANK
265 Franklin St
Boston, MA 02110
Telephone: (617) 897-1008, Toll Free: (800) EASTERN, FAX: (617) 897-1105, Web Site: www.easternbank.com
Pub Rels Dir: Joe Bartolotta
Primary Market Served: Business

ELITE DEBIT
11450 Sheldon St
Sun Valley, CA 91352-1121
Telephone: (435) 688-0634 X302, Web Site: www.elitedebit.com

EMBRACE HOME LOANS
25 Enterprise Ctr
Middletown, RI 02842-7233
Telephone: (401) 846-3100, Web Site: www.afsfitfinance.com
Mktg Dir: Dana Fortin
Primary Market Served: Business & Consumer

EMIGRANT SAVINGS BANK
5 E 42nd St
New York, NY 10017-6904
Telephone: (212) 850-4521, Toll Free: (800) EMIGRANT, FAX: (212) 850-4372, Web Site: www.emigrant.com
Chmn & CEO: Howard P. Milstein
Sr VP & Mktg Dir: Ted Morehouse
Sr VP, Chief Credit Officer: Patricia Goldstein
Mng Dir: David Feingold
Mng Dir: Chris Grey
Conducts Business: U.S.
Employees: 1,600
Primary Market Served: Consumer
Catalog available online
Gross sales or billing: $639,000,000
Retail bank.

ENCIRCLE
1691 NW 107th Ave
Miami, FL 33172
Telephone: (305) 592-7800, FAX: (305) 470-2662, E-Mail: merchantservices@encirclepayments.com, Web Site: www.insta-check.com
Conducts Business: U.S.
Primary Market Served: Business

Provide financial/cash payment systems services to retailers.

ENTREPRENEUR PARTNERS
2000 Market St Ste 720
Philadelphia, PA 19103-3214
Telephone: (267) 322-7000, FAX: (267) 322-7001, E-Mail: info@epfunds.com, Web Site: www.epfunds.com
Mng Partner: Salem Shuchman
Primary Market Served: Business & Consumer

ESIGNAL
3955 Point Eden Way
Hayward, CA 94545-3720
Telephone: (510) 266-6000, Web Site: www.esignal.com
VP Mktg: Julie Craig
Primary Market Served: Business

FNC INC
1214 Office Park Dr
Oxford, MS 38655-3597
Telephone: (662) 236-8254, Web Site: www.fncinc.com
CEO, Chmn Bd & Co-Founder: William Rayburn
Primary Market Served: Business & Consumer
Founded: 1994

FATWALLET
100 E Grand Ave
Beloit, WI 53511-6255
Toll Free: (888) 634-0098, Web Site: www.fatwallet.com
Dir Mktg: Brent Shelton
Primary Market Served: Business & Consumer

FEDERATED INVESTORS CO
RP-NFOA
Corporate Communications
1001 Liberty Ave, Federated Investors Tower
Pittsburgh, PA 15222-3779
Telephone: (412) 288-1900, Toll Free: (800) 341-7400, FAX: (412) 288-1171, Web Site: www.federatedinvestors.com
Pres & CEO: J. Christopher Donahue
Conducts Business: U.S.
Employees: 1,243
Primary Market Served: Business & Consumer
Catalog available online
Direct online sales
Founded: 1955
Gross sales or billing: $978,900,000

Mutual fund investment company dealing with institutions & individuals.

FIDELITY INVESTMENTS
Subs. of FMR Corp
82 Devonshire St

Boston, MA 02109-3605
Telephone: (617) 563-7000, Toll Free: (800) 343-3548, FAX: (617) 476-6150, Web Site: www.fidelity.com
Chmn & CEO: Edward C. Johnson
Pres: Roger Allan Lawson
Pres, Fidelity Strategic New Bus Devel: Roger T. Servison
VP, Customer Programs: Henry Wellott
Pres, Fidelity Shared Svcs: Marvin Adams
Exec VP & CFO: Claire S. Richer
Conducts Business: Worldwide
Employees: 30,000
Primary Market Served: Business & Consumer
Direct online sales
Founded: 1946
Gross sales or billing: $12,800,000,000

Mutual fund manager serving as an investment advisor to the Fidelity Group of Funds.

FIFTH THIRD BANK
38 Fountain Square Plz
Cincinnati, OH 45202-3102
Toll Free: (800) 972-3030, FAX: (231) 922-4060, Web Site: www.53.com
Chmn: George A. Schaefer Jr
Pres & CEO: Kevin T. Kabat
EVP & COO: Greg D. Carmichael
EVP: Charles Drucker
EVP: Bruce K. Lee
Conducts Business: U.S.
Employees: 4,000
Primary Market Served: Business & Consumer
Advertising/Marketing Budget Related to Direct Marketing: 26-50%
Direct Marketing ad budget: $1,000,000
Direct Mail: 30%
Magazines: 10%
Newspapers: 20%
TV/Radio: 30%
Telephone: 10%

Financial services & banking.

FINANCIAL SERVICES INTERNATIONAL CORP
701 Fifth Ave (#4200)
Seattle, WA 98104
Telephone: (206) 386-5475, FAX: (206) 654-0499
Pres: Candy Lee
Conducts Business: U.S., Canada, Brazil
Employees: 7
Primary Market Served: Business & Consumer
Advertising/Marketing Budget Related to Direct Marketing: 76-100%
Direct Marketing ad budget:
Direct Mail: $10,000

Magazines: $10,000
Newspapers: $10,000
TV/Radio: $20,000
Telephone: $100,000
Founded: 1992
Gross sales or billing: $2,000,000

Brokerage firm.

FIREMAN'S FUND INSURANCE CO
Subs. of Allianz A G
777 San Marin Dr
Novato, CA 94998-0002
Telephone: (415) 899-2000, FAX: (415) 899-3600, Web Site: www.firemansfund.com
Chmn Bd: John Carendi
Pres & COO: Joseph J. Beneducci
Pres Comml Bus: Gary C. Bhojwani
Bd Member: Charles Kravitsky
Pres Specialty Insurance: Art Moosmann
Conducts Business: U.S., Canada
Employees: 8,000
Primary Market Served: Business & Consumer
Advertising/Marketing Budget Related to Direct Marketing: 0-25%
Founded: 1991

Insurance - property, casualty, workers' compensation & homeowners.

FIRST ADVANTAGE MEMBERSHIP SERVICES
12395 First American Way
Poway, CA 92064-6897
Toll Free: (866) 424-3223, FAX: (619) 938-7017, Web Site: www.fmembershipservices.com
Sr VP, FAMS: Scott Hermann
Primary Market Served: Consumer

FIRST BANKS INC
135 N Meramec Ave
Clayton, MO 63105
Telephone: (314) 854-4600, FAX: (314) 592-6840, Web Site: www.firstbanks.com
CFO: Lisa K. Vansickle
CEO: Terrance M. McCarthy
Employees: 1,177
Primary Market Served: Business & Consumer
Catalog available online
Founded: 1910

Credit card processing.

FIRST DATA MERCHANT SERVICES
5565 Glenridge (Suite 2000), Connector NE
Atlanta, GA 30342

Telephone: (404) 890-2000, FAX: (303) 967-5188, Web Site: www.firstdata.com
Chmn: Charlie T. Fote
CFO & Exec VP: Kimberly S. Patmore
Chief Admin Officer: Michael T. Whealy
Conducts Business: Worldwide
Employees: 900
Primary Market Served: Business & Consumer
Catalog available online
Gross sales or billing: $7,000,000,000

Full service card processing featuring Direct Solutions to maximize card approvals & Citi Profiles, targeted marketing information to increase sales.

FIRST HAWAIIAN BANK
Div. of BancWest Corp
999 Bishop St Ste 3200
Honolulu, HI 96813-4424
Telephone: (808) 525-6273, Toll Free: (888) 844-4444, FAX: (808) 525-5798, E-Mail: bfarias@fhb.com, Web Site: www.fhb.com
EVP, Corp Commun: Gerald J. Keir
VP: Susan Soken
Conducts Business: HI, Guam, Saipan, British W Indies, Japan
Employees: 2,100
Primary Market Served: Business & Consumer
Founded: 1974
Gross sales or billing: $596,300,000

Traditional deposit and lending services, commercial equipment and vehicle leasing, money management for individual and institutional investors.

FIRST MERIT BANK (HQ)
aka First Merit Corp
III Cascade Plaza (7 fl)
Akron, OH 44308-1124
Telephone: (330) 996-6300, Toll Free: (888) 554-4362, Web Site: www.firstmerit.com
Chmn, Pres & CEO: Paul G. Greig
Conducts Business: U.S.
Employees: 2,755
Primary Market Served: Business & Consumer
Founded: 1981
Gross sales or billing: $799,000,000

A diversified financial services company that provides a complete range of banking & financial services. Serves individuals & businesses through approx 160 branches in 25 northeastern & central OH counties & PA's Lawrence County.

FIRST TENNESSEE BANK
165 Madison Ave
Memphis, TN 38103-2725

Telephone: (901) 523-4883, FAX:
(901) 523-4030, Web Site: www.
firsttennessee.com
CFO & VP: Elbert L. Thomas
COO: David T. Popwell
Primary Market Served: Business
Founded: 1864

FISERV
4411 E Jones Bridge Rd
Norcross, GA 30092-1615
Telephone: (678) 375-3000, Web Site:
www.checkfreecorp.com
Dir, Channel Mktg: Kim Sergent
Primary Market Served: Business

FISHER INVESTMENTS
13100 Skyline Blvd
Woodside, CA 94062-4542
Telephone: (650) 851-3334, Toll Free:
(800) 587-5512, FAX: (650) 350-
1436, E-Mail: info@fi.com, Web
Site: www.fi.com
CEO: Ken Fisher
Primary Market Served: Business &
Consumer

CAIMIN FLANNERY & ASSOCIATES
4275 Stableford Ln
Naperville, IL 60564-9768
Telephone: (630) 236-1955
Partner: Caimin Flannery
Pres: Marlene Flannery
Primary Market Served: Consumer

FLEET ONE LLC
613 Bakertown Rd
Antioch, TN 37013-2657
Telephone: (615) 523-6465, Web Site:
www.fleetone.com
VP Mktg: Stacey Bright
Primary Market Served: Business

FLORIDA CREDIT UNION
PO Box 5549
Gainesville, FL 32627
Telephone: (352) 377-4141, Web Site:
www.flcu.org
Primary Market Served: Business &
Consumer

FORECASTER PUBLISHING CO INC
19623 Ventura Blvd
Tarzana, CA 91356
Telephone: (818) 345-4421
Pres & Owner: John V. Kamin
Conducts Business: Worldwide
Employees: 4
Primary Market Served: Business &
Consumer
Advertising/Marketing Budget Related
to Direct Marketing: 0-25%

Founded: 1962
Publish a speculator's weekly money
letter that predicts economic trends,
money movements, gold, silver & rare
coin trends, interest rates & distressed
property speculation. Also business
forecasts & management consulting.

FREDDIE MAC
Federal Home Loan Mortgage Corp
8200 Jones Branch Dr
McLean, VA 22102-3110
Telephone: (703) 903-2000, Toll Free:
(800) 424-5401, Web Site: www.
freddiemac.com
Chmn & CEO: Richard F. Syron
Pres, COO & Dir: Eugene M.
McQuade
Exec VP & CFO: Anthony S. Piszel
Sr VP & COO: Michael C. May
Mktg Commun Dir: Sara E. Leonard
Sr VP & CIO: Robert Lux
Conducts Business: Worldwide
Employees: 5,500
Primary Market Served: Business
Catalog available online
Indirect online sales
Gross sales or billing: $14,260,000,000
Purchase pools of home loans & pack-
age into securities for resale to invest-
ors.

FROST BANK
100 W Houston St (Ste 100)
San Antonio, TX 78205-1400
Telephone: (210) 220-4011, Web Site:
www.frostbank.com
Sr VP: Ericka Pullin
Primary Market Served: Business

GE MONEY
4125 Windward Plaza Dr
Alpharetta, GA 30005-8738
Telephone: (678) 518-2403
Direct Mktg Opers Execution Leader:
Patrick Blankman
Primary Market Served: Business

GE PARTNERSHIP MARKETING GROUP
200 N Martingale Rd
Schaumburg, IL 60173
Telephone: (847) 605-3000, FAX:
(847) 605-3044, Web Site: www.
gepmg.com
Chmn & CEO: Jeffrey R. Immelt
Vice Chmn: Michael A. Neal
Vice Chmn: John G. Rice
Conducts Business: Worldwide
Employees: 300
Primary Market Served: Business &
Consumer
Catalog available online

Advertising/Marketing Budget Related
to Direct Marketing: 76-100%
Provider of credit card enhancement
services & fee-generating continuity
programs.

GRP FUNDING LLC
1350 Main St (fl 4)
Springfield, MA 01103-1664
Telephone: (877) 571-7999, E-Mail:
info@grpfunding.com, Web Site:
www.grpfunding.com
Dir Opers: Gary Emond
Primary Market Served: Business &
Consumer

GWR WEALTH MANAGEMENT
900 S 74th Plaza (Suite 400)
Omaha, NE 68114
Telephone: (402) 452-3737, FAX:
(402) 452-3676, Web Site: www.
gwrwealth.com
Dir: Gail Werner-Robinson
Primary Market Served: Business
Investment bankers.

GATEWAY BANK AND TRUST
2235 Gateway Access Point (Ste 200)
Raleigh, NC 27607-3076
Telephone: (919) 789-2799, Web Site:
www.gatewaybankandtrust.com
Primary Market Served: Consumer

GENWORTH FINANCIAL INC
6620 W Broad St
Richmond, VA 23230
Telephone: (804) 281-6000, Toll Free:
(888) 436-9678, FAX: (804) 662-
2414, Web Site: www.genworth.com
Chmn, Pres & CEO: Michael D. Fra-
izer
Sr VP & CFO: Patrick Kelleher
Sr VP & CIO: Scott J. McKay
Conducts Business: U.S.
Employees: 7,200
Primary Market Served: Business &
Consumer
Catalog available online
Gross sales or billing: $11,000,000,000
Securities & annuities.

GLENVIEW CAPITAL MANAGEMENT
767 Fifth Ave (fl 44)
New York, NY 10153-0023
Telephone: (212) 812-4700
Primary Market Served: Consumer

GLENVIEW STATE BANK
800 Waukegan Rd
Glenview, IL 60025-4300

Telephone: (847) 729-1900, FAX: (847) 729-5847, E-Mail: info@gsb.com, Web Site: www.glenviewstatebank.com
VP & Dir HR: Joan Cantrell
Exec VP & Dir: William A. Campbell
Conducts Business: U.S.
Employees: 210
Primary Market Served: Business & Consumer
Catalog available online
Indirect online sales
Advertising/Marketing Budget Related to Direct Marketing: 0-25%
Direct Marketing ad budget:
Direct Mail: 15%
Magazines: 10%
Newspapers: 70%
Online: 2%
Telephone: 3%
Founded: 1920
Gross sales or billing: $42,800,000

State commercial bank & user of direct marketing for financial services.

THE GRAPH CO

PO Box 961
Vineland, NJ 08362-0961
Telephone: (856) 825-9199, FAX: (856) 825-5573, E-Mail: graphco2@verizon.net
Mng Dir: Reginald Johnston
Primary Market Served: Consumer
Indirect online sales
Founded: 1986

GREAT WESTERN BANK

100 N Phillips Ave
Sioux Falls, SD 57104-6715
Telephone: (605) 334-2545, Web Site: greatwesternbank.com
Primary Market Served: Consumer

GRIDLEY & CO LLC

10 E 53rd St (fl 24)
New York, NY 10022-5070
Telephone: (212) 400-9720, Web Site: www.gridleyco.com
Pres & CEO: Linda Gridley
Primary Market Served: Consumer

GRUPPO LEVEY & CO

122 E 42nd St (fl 46)
New York, NY 10168-0002
Telephone: (212) 867-, FAX: (212) 949-7294, E-Mail: info@glconline.com, Web Site: www.glconline.com
Pres & Mng Dir: Claire Gruppo
Chmn & Mng Dir: Hugh Levey
VP: Antonia Ness
Sr VP: Edward McCabe
Primary Market Served: Business
Catalog available online
Indirect online sales

Founded: 1992
Investment banking for the direct marketing industry.

GUARANTY BANK

4000 W Brown Deer Rd
Brown Deer, WI 53209
Telephone: (414) 362-4000, Toll Free: (800) 235-4636, Web Site: www.guarantybank.com
Chmn, Pres & CEO: Kenneth Debuque
Sr VP Mktg: Bruce McCall
Primary Market Served: Business & Consumer
Advertising/Marketing Budget Related to Direct Marketing: 26-50%

Full-service financial institution.

H&R BLOCK INC

1 H&R Block Way
Kansas City, MO 64105-1905
Telephone: (816) 854-3000, Toll Free: (800) 472-5625, FAX: (816) 854-8500, Web Site: www.hrblock.com
Chmn Bd: Henry W. Bloch
Interim CEO: Alan Bennett
VP & Corp Controller: Colby R. Brown
Employees: 136,000
Primary Market Served: Business & Consumer
Advertising/Marketing Budget Related to Direct Marketing: 0-25%
Founded: 2007
Gross sales or billing: $4,000,000,000

Nationwide tax, financial and mortgage service.

HSBC BANK USA, NA

452 5th Ave
New York, NY 10018
Telephone: (716) 841-2424, FAX: (716) 841-5391, Web Site: www.banking.us.hsbc.com
Exec Officer HSBC Retail Svcs Inc: Joseph W. Hoff
CEO HSBC North American Holdings Inc: Brendan Paul McDonagh
Primary Market Served: Business & Consumer
Founded: 1999

Full service financial institution.

HAMPSHIRE AGENCY

Hampshire Planning Inc
33 Great Neck Rd (#7)
Great Neck, NY 11021-3335
Telephone: (516) 466-3814, FAX: (516) 466-0910
Pres: Stanley R. Goldberg
Owner & Mgr: Pat Giordano
Conducts Business: U.S.
Employees: 11

Primary Market Served: Business & Consumer
Advertising/Marketing Budget Related to Direct Marketing: 51-75%
Direct Marketing ad budget:
Direct Mail: 60%
Magazines: 20%
Newspapers: 10%
Telephone: 10%
Founded: 1954

Financial management & turn-around services for failing companies, as well as tax, financial planning, insurance & estate planning for small businesses & individuals. Elder-plan meets needs of seniors with long term care insurance. General agents for life insurance and annuities, qualified retail agents are welcome.

HARRIS BANCORP INC

111 W Monroe St (fl 21W)
Chicago, IL 60603-4096
Telephone: (312) 461-2121, Toll Free: (888) 340-BANK, FAX: (312) 461-7869, E-Mail: onlineservices@harrisbank.com, Web Site: www.harrisbank.com
Vice-Chmn & Head Bus Banking: Peter B. McNitt
CEO & Pres: Franklin J. Techar
CFO & Sr VP: Pamela C. Piarowski
Conducts Business: U.S.
Employees: 6,015
Primary Market Served: Business & Consumer
Catalog available online
Advertising/Marketing Budget Related to Direct Marketing: 51-75%
Direct Marketing ad budget:
Direct Mail: 75%
Telephone: 25%
Founded: 1875

Provide all phases of consumer banking services to consumers.

HELLER FINANCIAL

Div. of Heller Financial
500 W Monroe St (fl 44)
Chicago, IL 60661-3671
Telephone: (312) 441-7000, FAX: (312) 441-7499, Web Site: www.hellerfin.com
Pres: Scott Miller
VP, Mktg: Paul Puryear
Employees: 2,514
Primary Market Served: Business
Founded: 1919

Provide asset based financing to middle market companies.

HOME LOAN INVESTMENT BANK

One Home Loan Plaza (Suite 3)

Warwick, RI 02886
Telephone: (401) 739-8800, Toll Free: (800) 223-1700 X278, FAX: (401) 739-9675, E-Mail: contactus@ homeloanbank.com, Web Site: www. homeloanbankfsb.com
CEO & Pres: John J. Murphy
CFO & Exec VP: Randy A. Wyrofsky
COO & Exec VP: Eric B. Rose
Conducts Business: U.S.
Primary Market Served: Consumer
Catalog available online
Indirect online sales
Advertising/Marketing Budget Related to Direct Marketing: 76-100%
Founded: 1959

Mortgage banking company soliciting loans & mortgages through the mail.

HOME 123 MORTGAGE

2033 Milwaukee Ave (Suite 237)
Riverwoods, IL 60015
Toll Free: (888) 215-0080, E-Mail: info@home123.com, Web Site: www.home123.com

HOULIHAN LOKEY HOWARD & ZUKIN

10250 Constellation Blvd (fl 5)
Los Angeles, CA 90067
Telephone: (310) 553-8871, Toll Free: (800) 788-5300, FAX: (310) 553-2173, Web Site: www.hlhz.com
Co-CEO: Scott L. Beiser
Co-Chmn & Sr Mng Dir: Jeffrey Werbalowsky
Co-Pres: David A. Preiser
Co-Pres: Scott J. Adelson
Conducts Business: Worldwide
Primary Market Served: Business
Catalog available online
Founded: 1972

Investment banking services.

HOWARD RICE NEMEROVSKI CANADY FALK & RABKIN

3 Embarcadero Ctr (fl 7)
San Francisco, CA 94111-4078
Telephone: (415) 464-1600, FAX: (415) 217-5910, Web Site: www.howardrice.com
CEO: Michelle Johnson
Chmn & Mng Dir: Douglas A. Winthrop
Primary Market Served: Business & Consumer

HUNTINGTON BANCSHARES

41 S High St Fl 1
Columbus, OH 43215-6167

Telephone: (614) 480-5160, Toll Free: (800) 480-BANK, FAX: (614) 480-5284, Web Site: www.huntington.com
CEO: Stephen Steinour
Exec VP: Zahid Afzal
Primary Market Served: Business
Catalog available online
Indirect online sales
Gross sales or billing: $338,000,000
Financial institution.

ICMA RETIREMENT CORP

777 N Capitol St NE (Suite 600)
Washington, DC 20002
Telephone: (202) 962-4600, Toll Free: (800) 669-7400, FAX: (202) 962-4601, E-Mail: investorservices@ icmarc.org, Web Site: www.icmarc.org
Pres: Joan McCallen
Sr VP & CFO: Elizabeth Stephenson Glista
Sr VP & Chief Investment Officer: John Tobey
Employees: 600
Catalog available online
Indirect online sales
Founded: 1914
Gross sales or billing: $132,500,000
Offers pension funds for city government employees.

IPS - SENDERO CORP

Subs. of Fiserv Inc
230 Scientific Dr (Suite 800)
Norcross, GA 30092-2909
Telephone: (480) 941-8112, Toll Free: (800) 879-1996, FAX: (770) 409-1735, E-Mail: sales@ips-sendero.com, Web Site: www.ips-sendero.com
Pres: Dave Ulrich
VP: Dennis Lindsey
Conducts Business: Worldwide
Employees: 200
Primary Market Served: Business
Founded: 1997

Provides a suite of integrated products which comprise "Sendero Vision," a comprehensive strategic management solution for financial institutions. These products include a centralized data management system, asset/liability management systems, funds transfer pricing & profitability measurement systems.

INMAR

635 Vine St
Winston-Salem, NC 27101-4185
Telephone: (336) 631-2500, FAX: (336) 631-2888, E-Mail: ibizdev@ inmar.com, Web Site: www.promotionslogistics.com

CEO: L. David Mounts
CFO & Exec VP: Drew Dixon
Chief Mktg Officer & Pres Digital Solutions: Travis Lewis
Conducts Business: U.S.
Catalog available online
Direct online sales
Founded: 1980

Clearing house for retailers.

INTERSECTIONS

3901 Stonecroft Blvd
Chantilly, VA 20151-1032
Telephone: (703) 488-6100, Web Site: www.charteredmarketing.com
Exec VP: Steven Schwartz
Primary Market Served: Business & Consumer

INVESTORS MARKETING SERVICES

168 Centre St
Danvers, MA 01923-1321
Telephone: (978) 774-2990, Toll Free: (800) 462-2551, FAX: (978) 774-4249, Web Site: www.investorsmarketing.com
CEO: Jan Charles
Dir Mktg: Carol Rugeiro
Conducts Business: U.S.
Employees: 15
Primary Market Served: Business
Advertising/Marketing Budget Related to Direct Marketing: 51-75%
Founded: 1987

Provides insurance products & fixed annuities to financial planners & insurance agents.

JP MORGAN CHASE & CO

345 Park Ave Fl 10, New York, NY 10154-0004
270 Park Ave (10th fl)
New York, NY 10017-2070
Telephone: (212) 270-6000, E-Mail: jpmcinvestorrelations@jpmchase.com, Web Site: www.jpmorgan.com
Chmn, Pres & CEO: James Dimon
CFO: Marianne Lake
Chief Admin Officer: Paul H. Compton
CIO: Guy Chiarello
HR Dir: John F. Bradley
Conducts Business: Worldwide
Primary Market Served: Consumer
Catalog available online

Investment services.

JEFFERSON NATIONAL

10350 Ormsby Park Pl (Suite 600)
Louisville, KY 40223-6175
Telephone: (502) 587-3853, Web Site: www.jeffnat.com
Mktg Mgr: Amber Mullaney

Primary Market Served: Business &
Consumer

JOHN DEERE FINANCIAL
Div. of Deere & Co
6400 NW 86th St, PO Box 6600
Johnston, IA 50131-6600
Telephone: (515) 267-3000, Toll Free:
  (800) 275-5322, FAX: (515) 267-
  3292, Web Site: www.deere.com
Pres: James A. Israel
Sr VP Sls & Mktg: Daniel C. McCabe
Sr VP Credit & Opers: Lawrence W.
  Sidwell
Primary Market Served: Business &
  Consumer

Provides retail, wholesale & lease financing, and offers revolving credit &
operating loans for John Deere equipment.

**JOHN HANCOCK
RETIREMENT PLAN
SERVICES**
200 Bloor St W - ET6
Toronto, ON, Canada M4W1E5
Telephone: (416) 852-1035, Web Site:
  www.jhancock.com
Primary Market Served: Business

EDWARD JONES
12555 Manchester Rd
Des Peres, MO 63131-3710
Telephone: (314) 515-2000, FAX:
  (314) 515-3269, Web Site: www.
  edwardjones.com
CFO: Steve Novik
Primary Market Served: Business

**THE JORDAN EDMISTON
GROUP INC**
150 E 52nd St (18th fl)
New York, NY 10022-6260
Telephone: (212) 754-0710, FAX:
  (212) 754-0337, Web Site: www.jegi.
  com
Chief Mktg Officer: Adam Gross
Primary Market Served: Consumer

KEY BANK
127 Public Sq
Cleveland, OH 44114
Toll Free: (800) 539-2968, FAX: (216)
  689-5115, Web Site: www.key.com
Pres: Michael McNamara
Conducts Business: Worldwide
Employees: 1,110
Primary Market Served: Business &
  Consumer
Catalog available online
Founded: 1825
Gross sales or billing: $4,800,000

Full-service commercial bank with 96
branch offices statewide.

**KEY BANK NATIONAL
ASSOCIATION**
Affiliate of KeyCorp
19 Corporate Woods Blvd
Albany, NY 12211-2345
Telephone: (518) 434-4871, Toll Free:
  (800) 539-2968, Web Site: www.
  keybank.com
Chmn, Pres & CEO: Henry L. Miller
  III
Vice Chmn: Beth E. Mooney
Vice Chmn: Thomas W. Bunn
Sr Exec VP & CFO: Jeffrey B. Weeden
Sr VP: Charles Miller
Conducts Business: U.S.
Employees: 3,900
Primary Market Served: Business &
  Consumer
Catalog available online
Indirect online sales
Founded: 1825

State commercial bank. Consumer
banking & finance, investment management & trust, corporate & investment banking, securities brokerage,
private banking & customized financial
services within 38 states & more than
1300 branch & affiliates offices.

L6 HOLDINGS CORP
6555 Sugarloaf Pkwy (Suite 307)
Duluth, GA 30097-4934
Telephone: (678) 957-0511, FAX:
  (678) 957-0551
Founder & Mng Partner: Daniel Lone-
  rgan
Primary Market Served: Business &
  Consumer
Founded: 2007

**THE LAW OFFICES OF
JAMES SOKOLOVE**
93 Worcester St # 101
Wellesley Hills, MA 02481-3609
Telephone: (617) 742-0696, Web Site:
  www.jimsokolove.com
Exec Asst: Randi Donovan

**LAZARD MIDDLE MARKET
LLC**
Subs. of Lazard Ltd.
80 S 8th St
Minneapolis, MN 55402
Telephone: (612) 339-0500, FAX:
  (612) 339-0507, Web Site: www.
  lazardmm.com
Chmn: Jack P. Helms
Conducts Business: U.S., Canada, Eu-
  rope, Pacific Rim
Primary Market Served: Business
Direct online sales

Founded: 1979
Provides financial advisory services to
middle market businesses. Services include mergers and acquisitions, distressed advisory and restructuring,
valuations and fairness opinions, and
private placements of debt and equity.

LEADFLASH
6700 Broken Sound Pkwy NW
Boca Raton, FL 33487-5701
Telephone: (561) 997-5759, Web Site:
  www.leadflash.com
Dir Bus Devel: John Dalton
Primary Market Served: Business &
  Consumer

**LENDING TREE/HOME
LOAN CENTER**
11115 Rushmore Dr
Charlotte, NC 28277-3442
Telephone: (704) 541-5351, Toll Free:
  (800) 555-8733, FAX: (704) 541-
  1824, Web Site: www.lendingtree.
  com
Dir Direct Mktg: Tracy Jenkins
Primary Market Served: Consumer

LEUCADIA NATIONAL CORP
315 Park Ave S (fl 20)
New York, NY 10010-3649
Telephone: (212) 460-1900, FAX:
  (212) 598-4869, Web Site: www.
  leucadia.com
Exec VP: Thomas Mara
VP: Barbara Lowenthol
Pres: Joseph S. Steinberg
VP: Rocco Nittoli
Conducts Business: U.S.
Employees: 1,300
Primary Market Served: Business &
  Consumer
Gross sales or billing: $862,000,000

Investment holding company for businesses & consumers.

LIBERTY TAX SERVICE
1716 Corporate Landing Pkwy
Virginia Beach, VA 53454-5681
Telephone: (757) 493-8855 X8115,
  Toll Free: (800) 790-3863, FAX:
  (800) 880-6432
Primary Market Served: Consumer
Income Tax Preparation

**LIFE INVESTORS
INSURANCE CO OF
AMERICA**
Member of Aegon Insurance Group
4333 Edgewood Rd NE
Cedar Rapids, IA 52499-0001

Telephone: (319) 398-8511, Toll Free: (800) 231-7220, FAX: (319) 369-2188, Web Site: www.lifeinvestors. com
Pres: Pat Baird
HR Exec: Mitchell Levin
Pres: K. J. Storm
Employees: 1,953
Primary Market Served: Consumer
Gross sales or billing: $1,123,800,000

Provides financial services, life insurance, annuities & mutual funds.

LITLE & CO
900 Chelmsford St
Lowell, MA 01851-8100
Telephone: (978) 275-6500, Toll Free: (800) 548-5326, FAX: (978) 937-7250, Web Site: www.litle.com
Chmn: Tim Litle
Exec VP Sls & Mktg: Jason Pavona
Primary Market Served: Consumer

LOCAL GOVERNMENT FEDERAL CREDIT UNION
323 W Jones St (Ste 600)
Raleigh, NC 27603-1369
Telephone: (919) 755-0534, Web Site: www.lgfcu.org
Dir Mktg Mgr: Karen Mantica
Primary Market Served: Consumer

LOTSOLUTIONS
10151 Deerwood Park Blvd (Suite 200-330)
Jacksonville, FL 32256-0564
Toll Free: (888) 784-3539, Web Site: www.lotsolutions.com
Pres: Robert Fullington
Primary Market Served: Business & Consumer

MCCS
Div. of Macy's Inc.
9111 Duke Blvd
Mason, OH 45040-8999
Telephone: (513) 573-2284, FAX: (513) 573-2197, Web Site: www.federated.com
VP, Opers & Credit Mktg: Jan Rosenbaum
Credit Mktg Dir: Maya Wadleigh
Dir Mktg: Robyn Wentzel
Conducts Business: U.S.
Primary Market Served: Consumer
Advertising/Marketing Budget Related to Direct Marketing: 76-100%

New credit accounts of Macy's Inc.

MFS INVESTMENT MANAGEMENT
500 Boylston St
Boston, MA 02116-3740

Telephone: (617) 954-5000, FAX: (617) 350-2163, Web Site: www.mfs. com
Chmn & CEO: Robert James Manning
Primary Market Served: Consumer
Founded: 1969

MXT CARD SERVICES, LLC
2 Penns Way (Suite 201)
New Castle, DE 19720-2407
Telephone: (302) 323-6203, FAX: (302) 323-6219, Web Site: www.mxtcs.com
Chief Mktg Officer: Mark Chronister
Dir Sls: Steve Cochran
Primary Market Served: Consumer

MASTERCARD WORLDWIDE
2000 Purchase St
Purchase, NY 10577-2509
Telephone: (914) 249-2000, Toll Free: (800) 622-7747, FAX: (914) 249-4220, Web Site: www.mastercard. com
Pres & CEO: Ajay Banga
Conducts Business: Worldwide
Employees: 5,000
Primary Market Served: Business & Consumer
Founded: 1966
Gross sales or billing: $3,000,000,000

Credit-debit products for consumers; transaction processing & settlement services, as well as business-building cooperative marketing programs for businesses.

MAX FEDERAL CREDIT UNION
2785 Zelda Rd
Montgomery, AL 36106-2698
Telephone: (334) 260-2600, Toll Free: (800) 776-6776, FAX: (334) 270-0921, Web Site: www.mymax.com
Own: Kenneth Nesbitt
Owner: Brandon Davis
Conducts Business: U.S.
Employees: 235
Primary Market Served: Consumer
Catalog available online
Indirect online sales
Advertising/Marketing Budget Related to Direct Marketing: 26-50%
Founded: 1955
Gross sales or billing: $3,500,000

Financial services including: savings, investments & loans.

MECHANICAL BREAKDOWN ADMINISTRATORS INC
Subs. of MBA Holdings Inc
9419 E San Salvador (Suite 105)
Scottsdale, AZ 85258-5510

Telephone: (480) 860-2288, FAX: (480) 860-0867, E-Mail: gaylenb@mbadirect.com, Web Site: www.mbadirect.com
Chmn: Gaylen M. Brotherson
VP: Judy K. Brotherson
Conducts Business: U.S.
Employees: 60
Primary Market Served: Business & Consumer
Catalog available online
Indirect online sales
Advertising/Marketing Budget Related to Direct Marketing: 26-50%
Direct Marketing ad budget:
Direct Mail: $3,500,000
Magazines: $20,000
Newspapers: $10,000
TV/Radio: $250,000
Telephone: $500,000
Founded: 1984
Gross sales or billing: $30,000,000

General financial & marketing services.

MERCHANT E-SOLUTIONS
3600 Bridge Pkwy (Suite 102)
Redwood City, CA 94065
Telephone: (509) 232-5639, Toll Free: (866) 663-6132, FAX: (509) 232-5625, E-Mail: help@merchante-solutions.com, Web Site: www.merchante-solutions.com
Pres & CEO: Paulo Guzzo
CFO & Corp Devel: Marcelo F. Perez
Exec VP Sls & Bus Devel: Bob Butler
Chief Product Officer: Leo Rocco
Chief Tech Officer: Kiril Bilitardo
Founded: 1999

MERGENT INC
Div. of Financial Information Corp
580 Kingslet Park Dr
Fort Mill, SC 29715-6403
Toll Free: (800) 342-5647, Web Site: www.mergent.com
CEO: Jonathan Worra
Conducts Business: U.S.
Primary Market Served: Business
Catalog available online
Direct online sales
Advertising/Marketing Budget Related to Direct Marketing: 0-25%
Founded: 1900

Offer business & financial information on public domestic & foreign companies.

MERRICK BANK
10705 S Jordan Gtwy (Suite 200)
South Jordan, UT 84095-3977
Toll Free: (801) 545-6647, Web Site: www.merrickbank.com
Sr VP: Kellie Harper

Primary Market Served: Business & Consumer

MERRILL LYNCH INTERNATIONAL INC

250 Vesey St (fl 12), Four World Financial Center
New York, NY 10281-1023
Telephone: (212) 449-1000, Toll Free: (800) 637-7455, FAX: (212) 449-9418, Web Site: www.ml.com
CEO: James B. Quigley
Conducts Business: U.S.
Employees: 56,000
Primary Market Served: Business & Consumer
Catalog available online
Founded: 1820
Gross sales or billing: $62,000,000,000

Financial service & investment firm dealing in stocks, investments & other financial services. Sell to the public & to institutions.

MIDCONTINENT FINANCIAL CENTER INC

3401 W Broadway Bus Park Ct (Suite 205)
Columbia, MO 65203-0393
Telephone: (573) 443-6002, Web Site: www.americanmutualloans.com
Pres: J. Schulte
Primary Market Served: Business & Consumer

MONEX DEPOSIT CO

4910 Birch St Ste 103
Newport Beach, CA 92660-2188
Telephone: (949) 752-1400, Toll Free: (800) 444-8317, FAX: (949) 752-7214, E-Mail: info@monex.com, Web Site: www.monex.com
Founder: Louis E. Carabini
Pres: Michael Carabini
Dir: Christina Carabini
VP, Sls: William A. Nelles
Conducts Business: U.S., Canada, Mexico
Employees: 250
Primary Market Served: Consumer
Catalog available online
Indirect online sales
Direct Marketing ad budget: $3,000,000
Founded: 1967
Gross sales or billing: $9,600,000

Brokerage firm specializing in marketing precious metals for investment purposes to the general public.

MONEYGRAM INTERNATIONAL

2828 N Harwood (fl 15)
Dallas, TX 75201

Toll Free: (800) 666-3947, Web Site: www.moneygram.com
Dir Loyalty & Database Mktg: Brent Carter
Primary Market Served: Consumer

MONTAG & CALDWELL INC

Alleghany Corp
3455 Peachtree Rd NE (Suite 1200)
Atlanta, GA 30326-3248
Telephone: (404) 836-7100, Toll Free: (800) 458-5868, FAX: (404) 836-7168, Web Site: www.montag.com
CEO: William Alan Vogel
Exec VP: Janet Boutin Bunch
Conducts Business: U.S.
Employees: 35
Primary Market Served: Business & Consumer
Founded: 1945

Investment counseling firm.

MORGAN STANLEY

1585 Broadway
New York, NY 10036
Telephone: (212) 761-4000, FAX: (212) 761-0096
COO: Jim Rosenthal
Pres: Timothy A. Hultquist
Conducts Business: Worldwide
Primary Market Served: Business & Consumer
Catalog available online
Gross sales or billing: $76,500,000,000

Provide managed commodity trading programs for corporate & individual clients.

MORNINGSTAR INC

22 W Washington St
Chicago, IL 60602
Telephone: (312) 696-6000, Web Site: www.morningstar.com
Chmn & CEO: Joe Mansueto
Pres Software Div: Chris Boruff
Pres Global Investment: Peng Chen
Pres Intl Opers & Global HR: Bevin Desmond
CFO: Scott Cooley
Pres Equity Research: Catherine Gillis Odelbo
Pres Data Div: Elizabeth Kirscher
Pres Fund Research: Don Phillips
Primary Market Served: Consumer

THE MOTLEY FOOL

123 N Pitt St
Alexandria, VA 22314-3128
Telephone: (703) 838-3665, FAX: (703) 254-1999, E-Mail: cs@fool.com, Web Site: www.Fool.com
Partner: David Gardner
Partner: Tom Gardner
Conducts Business: U.S., UK

Employees: 200
Primary Market Served: Business & Consumer
Founded: 1993

Provider of investment advice and financial information.

MUTUAL OF AMERICA LIFE INSURANCE CO

320 Park Ave
New York, NY 10022-6839
Telephone: (212) 224-1600, Toll Free: (800) 468-3785, FAX: (212) 207-3001, Web Site: www.mutualofamerica.com
Chmn Bd: William J. Flynn
Pres & CEO: Thomas J. Moran
Sr VP, Corp Commun: Thomas A. Harwood
Exec VP: Manfred Altstadt
Exec VP, Mktg & Corp Commun: William S. Conway
Conducts Business: U.S.
Employees: 1,100
Primary Market Served: Business
Catalog available online
Advertising/Marketing Budget Related to Direct Marketing: 76-100%
Founded: 1945
Gross sales or billing: $1,700,000,000

Employee retirement plans.

NATIONAL ASSOCIATION OF FEDERAL CREDIT UNIONS

3138 10th St N
Arlington, VA 22201-2160
Toll Free: (800) 336-4644, Web Site: www.nafcu.org
Sr VP Mktg & Communs: Karen Tyson

NATIONAL CITY BANK

Subs. of National City Corp
1900 E Ninth St
Cleveland, OH 44114
Telephone: (216) 222-2000, Toll Free: (800) 622-8100, FAX: (216) 575-, Web Site: www.nationalcity.com
Sr VP, Corp Mktg: Karin Stone
Conducts Business: U.S.
Employees: 29,828
Primary Market Served: Business & Consumer
Direct online sales
Founded: 1845

Commercial bank.

NATIONAL PENSION SERVICE INC

40 Main St (Suite 300)
Burlington, VT 05401-8433

Telephone: (802) 862-3994, FAX: (802) 865-2861, E-Mail: retirementservices@people.com, Web Site: www.peoples.com/retirementservices/
Pres: S. Tracy Braun
Conducts Business: U.S.
Employees: 140
Primary Market Served: Business & Consumer
Founded: 1976

Design & administer pension plans for corporations.

NAVY FEDERAL CREDIT UNION
820 Follin Ln SE
Vienna, VA 22180-4907
Telephone: (703) 206-4245, Web Site: www.navyfederal.org
Primary Market Served: Business

NETSPEND
1825 S Grant St (Suite 800)
San Mateo, CA 94402-2663
Toll Free: (866) 387-7363, Web Site: www.netspend.com
Dir Bus Devel: Preet Chhokar
Primary Market Served: Consumer

NEUBERGER & BERMAN MANAGEMENT
605 3rd Ave (fl 21)
New York, NY 10158-3698
Telephone: (212) 476-9000, Toll Free: (800) 877-9700, FAX: (212) 476-8937, Web Site: www.nb.com
CEO & Pres: Robert John Conti
CFO: James J. Dempsey
Mng Dir & COO: John Alexander Dorogoff
Sr VP & Chief Admin: Brian Kerrane
Conducts Business: U.S.
Employees: 1,247
Primary Market Served: Business & Consumer
Catalog available online
Founded: 1970

Mutual fund management firm.

NISSAN MOTOR ACCEPTANCE CORP
8900 Freeport Pkwy
Irving, TX 75063
Telephone: (972) 929-7214, Toll Free: (800) 647-7261, Web Site: www.nissanusa.com
Pres: Jeff Edwards
Mng: Jess Edwards
Employees: 670
Primary Market Served: Business
Founded: 1982
Gross sales or billing: $2,000,000,000

Financial products.

NO LOAD FUND INVESTOR
PO Box 3029
Brentwood, TN 37024-3029
Toll Free: (800) 706-6364, FAX: (800) 785-9212, E-Mail: NoLoad@mleesmith.com, Web Site: www.noloadfundinvestor.com
Editor: Sheldon Jacobs
Publr: Mark Salzinger
Assoc Ed: Layne Aurand
Conducts Business: U.S.
Employees: 5
Primary Market Served: Consumer
Catalog available online
Direct online sales
Advertising/Marketing Budget Related to Direct Marketing: 76-100%
Direct Marketing ad budget:
Direct Mail: 80%
Online: 20%
Founded: 1979

Mutual fund & exchange traded fund investment newsletter & book.

NO LOAD FUNDX
235 Montgomery St (Suite 1049)
San Francisco, CA 94104-2994
Telephone: (415) 986-7979, Toll Free: (800) 763-8639, FAX: (415) 986-1595, Web Site: www.noloadfundx.com
Pres Fundx Investment Grp & Mng Ed: Janet Brown
Conducts Business: U.S.
Employees: 12
Primary Market Served: Business & Consumer
Catalog available online
Direct online sales
Advertising/Marketing Budget Related to Direct Marketing: 0-25%
Direct Marketing ad budget: $400,000
Direct Mail: 92%
Magazines: 2%
Newspapers: 2%
TV/Radio: 4%
Founded: 1976
Gross sales or billing: $1,000,000

A monthly newsletter that monitors the performance of over 730 no-load mutual funds for sophisticated fund investors. Also, CAP - Mid-month report & shorter version of newsletter & update of monthly report.

THE NORTHERN TRUST CO
50 S LaSalle St
Chicago, IL 60603-1003
Telephone: (312) 630-6000, Toll Free: (888) 289-6542, FAX: (312) 444-5244, Web Site: www.ntrs.com
Chmn & CEO: Frederick H. Waddell
CFO: Perry R. Perro
Pres & COO: Barry G. Hastings
Primary Market Served: Business

Catalog available online
Founded: 1889

Full service financial institution.

NORTHWESTERN MUTUAL
720 E Wisconsin Ave
Milwaukee, WI 53202-4703
Telephone: (414) 271-1444, FAX: (414) 299-7022, Web Site: www.northwesternmutual.com
Primary Market Served: Business & Consumer

NUVEEN INVESTMENTS
333 W Wacker Dr
Chicago, IL 60606
Telephone: (312) 917-7700, Toll Free: (800) 257-8787, FAX: (312) 917-8049, Web Site: www.nuveen.com
CEO & Dir: John P. Amboian
Exec VP: Glenn R. Richter
Exec VP: John L. MacCarthy
Primary Market Served: Business & Consumer
Catalog available online
Gross sales or billing: $709,000,000

Investment services.

OLESUK FINANCIAL SERVICES
Affiliated with SagePoint Financial Inc
5206 W Elm St (#100)
McHenry, IL 60050-4000
Telephone: (815) 363-0808, FAX: (815) 363-0843, E-Mail: folesuk@sagepointadvisor.com, Web Site: www.olesukfinancialservices.com
Pres & Owner: Frank D. Olesuk
Admin Asst: Patricia S. Olesuk
Admin Asst: Karlene M. Olesuk
Conducts Business: U.S.
Employees: 3
Primary Market Served: Business & Consumer
Direct Marketing ad budget:
Direct Mail: 20%
Online: 5%
Telephone: 75%
Founded: 1985
Gross sales or billing: $4,500,000

Mutual funds, insurance products, tax preparation, investment products & services, stocks & bonds, Investment Management.

OLIVER WYMAN
1166 Avenue of the Americas
New York, NY 10036-2726
Telephone: (212) 345-8000, (212) 541-8100, Web Site: www.oliverwyman.com
Pres: Scott McDonald
Chmn: John Drzik
COO: Jeremy Badman

Mktg: Pertha Bose

OPPENHEIMER FUNDS
225 Liberty St (fl 11), 2 World Financial Ctr
New York, NY 10281-1005
Telephone: (212) 323-0200, FAX: (212) 323-4070, Web Site: www.oppenheimerfunds.com
Sr VP & CFO: David Matthew Pfeffer
Exec VP & COO: Michael Baldwin
Primary Market Served: Business
Founded: 1960

Market & sell mutual funds.

OVERSEAS PRIVATE INVESTMENT CORP (OPIC)
1100 New York Ave NW
Washington, DC 20527
Telephone: (202) 336-8799, FAX: (202) 336-7949, E-Mail: info@opic.gov, Web Site: www.opic.gov
Pres & CEO: Elizabeth Littlefield
Chief of Staff: John E. Morton
Employees: 140
Primary Market Served: Business
Catalog available online
Indirect online sales
Founded: 1971

Self-sustaining U.S. government agency. Developing countries & emerging economies.

PNC BANK CORP
249 5th Ave Ste 1200, One PNC Plaza
Pittsburgh, PA 15222-2707
Telephone: (412) 762-2000/3514, Toll Free: (800) 422-6537, FAX: (412) 762-4482
Chmn: Tom O'Brien
VP, Mktg Svc: Tim Doering
Direct Mktg Mgr: Gregg Fink
Primary Market Served: Business & Consumer

Provide a variety of financial services for consumers & commercial corporation.

PNC GLOBAL INVESTMENT SERVICING
66 Broadway Ste 3
Lynnfield, MA 01940-2369
Telephone: (781) 477-4124, Web Site: www.pnc.com
VP: Mark Stranberg
Primary Market Served: Business & Consumer

PACNET SERVICES LTD
595 Howe St (fl 4)
Vancouver, BC, Canada V6C 2T5

Telephone: (604) 689-0399, FAX: (604) 689-0313, E-Mail: info@pacnetservices.com, Web Site: www.pacnetservices.com
Mng Dir: Rosanne Day
Commun Specialist: Joy Wood
Dir Mktg: Renee Frappier
Bus Devel Mgr: Brendan Mahar
Mktg Asst: Melody Buchwitz
Conducts Business: U.S., Canada
Primary Market Served: Business
Indirect online sales
Founded: 1994

Offering a wide range of international payment processing services including multi currency cheque cashing, cheque issuing, electronic cheque conversion, credit card processing, direct debit & transfer collection.

PAYMENTECH
Four Northeastern Blvd
Salem, NH 03079-5916
Telephone: (603) 896-6000, FAX: (603) 896-8717, Web Site: www.paymentech.com
Pres: Michael Duffy
Opers Exec: Gerry Gilbert
Dir: Steve Martin
Employees: 300
Primary Market Served: Business
Indirect online sales

Payment processing service provider dedicated to the direct response industry - process merchant payment transactions covering a broad range of marketing channels. Support authorization & settlement for all major credit cards, consumer bank account (electronic check) debit processing, private-label & purchasing cards & international currencies.

PAYPAL INC
2211 N First St
San Jose, CA 95131
Telephone: (402) 935-2050, Web Site: www.paypal.com
Pres & CEO: Dan Schulman
VP Global Brand Mktg: Greg Fisher
Primary Market Served: Consumer
Founded: 1998
Gross sales or billing: $9,240,000,000

Online payments system company,

PEAK IMPACT INC
Meriline RPO Box 78029
Ottawa, ON, Canada K2E 1B1
Telephone: (613) 592-3100, E-Mail: customerservice@peakimpact.com, Web Site: www.peakimpact.com
Mktg Dir: David Lipson
Primary Market Served: Business & Consumer

PEOPLE'S UNITED BANK
850 Main St
Bridgeport, CT 06604-4917
Telephone: (203) 338-7171, Web Site: www.peoples.com
VP: Jeff Lee
Primary Market Served: Consumer

PETSKY PRUNIER LLC
60 Broad St (Ste 3810)
New York, NY 10004-2329
Telephone: (212) 842-6001, FAX: (212) 842-6039, Web Site: www.petskyprunier.com
Partner: Michael Petsky
Pres: John Prunier
Mng Dir: Sanjay Chadda
Mktg Mgr: Elizabeth Ehmann
Conducts Business: U.S.
Primary Market Served: Business
Advertising/Marketing Budget Related to Direct Marketing: 76-100%

An investment bank providing merger and acquisition and private placement advisory services for clients in direct marketing, marketing services & technology, advertising & promotion and information industries.

PIPER JAFFRAY
800 Nicollet Mall (Suite 1000)
Minneapolis, MN 55402-7036
Telephone: (612) 303-0000, Web Site: www.pjc.com

POWERPAY
320 Cumberland Ave
Portland, ME 04101
Telephone: (207) 775-6900, Toll Free: (877) 877-3737, FAX: (888) 204-4040, Web Site: www.powerpay.biz
Founder & CEO: Stephen Goodrich
Pres & COO: Jim Raftice

PRICEWATERHOUSECOOPERS LLP
300 Madison Ave (fl 24)
New York, NY 10017
Telephone: (646) 471-4000, FAX: (813) 286-6000, Web Site: www.pwc.com
Chmn & Sr Partner: Robert E. Moritz
Employees: 146,000
Primary Market Served: Business
Founded: 1849
Gross sales or billing: $21,900,000,000

Professional services, including accounting, taxes, management & human resources consulting & outsourcing.

PROPAY USA INC
3400 N Ashton Blvd (Suite 200)
Lehi, UT 84043-5310

Telephone: (801) 766-3758, Web Site:
www.propay.com
CEO: Garry Goodrich
Pres: Greg Pesci

PRUDENTIAL FINANCIAL

751 Broad St
Newark, NJ 07102-2195
Telephone: (973) 802-2195, Web Site:
www.prudential.com
VP eBusiness Devel Group: James
Brett
Primary Market Served: Business

PUTNAM INVESTMENTS

Div. of Marsh & McLennan Cos Inc
1 Post Office Sq
Boston, MA 02109-2106
Telephone: (617) 292-1400, Toll Free:
(800) 225-1581, FAX: (617) 292-
1683, Web Site: www.putnam.com
Sr VP: Patricia C. Flaherty
Conducts Business: U.S., Japan, U.K.
Employees: 2,000
Primary Market Served: Business &
Consumer

Investment firm managing assets for individual shareholders & institutional
clients.

RBC DAIN RAUSCHER INC

60 S Sixth St
Minneapolis, MN 55402-4422
Telephone: (612) 371-2711, FAX:
(612) 373-1627, Web Site: www.
rbcdain.com
Head RBC Wealth Mngmt US: John
Taft
Primary Market Served: Business &
Consumer
Founded: 1909

Brokerage firm.

RBC FUNDS

Div. of RBC Global Asset Management
(US) Inc
PO Box 702
Milwaukee, WI 53201-0701
Toll Free: (800) 422-2766, Web Site:
us.rbcgam.com
Pres: Jennifer Lammers
VP & Dir: David P. Lux
Mng Dir & Chief Compliance Officer:
Kathleen A. Gorman
Sec & Chief Legal Officer: Monica V.
Ballard
Mgr, Mutual Fund Admin: Martin A.
Cramer
Conducts Business: U.S., Canada, Eu-
rope
Employees: 3
Primary Market Served: Consumer
Catalog available online
Indirect online sales

Gross sales or billing: $100,000
Direct marketing of 100%, no load mutual funds.

RBS CITIZENS FINANCIAL GROUP INC

770 Legacy Pl (MLP 250)
Dedham, MA 02026-6837
Telephone: (781) 471-1565, Web Site:
www.citizensbank.com
Sr VP: Pete Constant
Primary Market Served: Business &
Consumer

REGIONS

1900 5th Ave N Ste 300
Birmingham, AL 35203-2669
Telephone: (205) 944-1300, FAX:
(205) 326-4072, Web Site: www.
regions.com
Pres & CEO: O. B. Grayson Hall Jr
Employees: 35,900
Primary Market Served: Consumer
Gross sales or billing: $7,756,400,000

Commercial bank.

ROLLYSON FINANCIAL GROUP

150 Oak Dr
Pasadena, MD 21122-4421
Telephone: (410) 437-5596
Dir & CEO: Richard V. Rollyson
Conducts Business: U.S.
Employees: 3
Primary Market Served: Business &
Consumer
Advertising/Marketing Budget Related
to Direct Marketing: 76-100%
Direct Marketing ad budget: $150,000
Direct Mail: 10%
Newspapers: 10%
Telephone: 80%
Gross sales or billing: $400,000

Investment, annuities & retirement
services & college funding to small
businesses & individuals.

ROSLAND CAPITAL LLC

429 Santa Monica Blvd (Suite 450)
Santa Monica, CA 90401-3401
Toll Free: (800) 891-2341, Web Site:
www.roslandcapital.com
CEO & Mgr: Marin Aleksov
Primary Market Served: Business &
Consumer

ROYAL BANK OF CANADA

200 Bay St, Royal Bank Plaza
Toronto, ON, Canada M5J 2J5
Telephone: (416) 974-5151, FAX:
(416) 955-7800, Web Site: www.
royalbank.com
Pres & CEO: Gordon M. Nixon

Conducts Business: U.S., Canada
Primary Market Served: Business &
Consumer

Markets financial data to promote investment opportunities.

RUSSELL INVESTMENTS

1301 Second Ave (18th Fl)
Seattle, WA 98101
Telephone: (206) 505-7877, Toll Free:
(800) 426-7969, Web Site: www.
russell.com

SDI MARKETING

65 International Blvd (Suite 200)
Toronto, ON, Canada M9W 6L9
Telephone: (416) 674-9010, Toll Free:
(877) SDI-TEAM, FAX: (416) 674-
9011, E-Mail: info@sdicapital.com,
Web Site: www.sdimarketing.com
Founder & CEO: Roy Roger
Sr VP: Andy Harkness
Sr VP: Jeff Conant
Conducts Business: U.S.
Employees: 70
Primary Market Served: Business
Direct online sales
Advertising/Marketing Budget Related
to Direct Marketing: 26-50%
Direct Marketing ad budget: $800,000
Direct Mail: 28%
Magazines: 10%
Newspapers: 8%
Telephone: 54%
Founded: 1993
Gross sales or billing: $45,000,000

Commercial financing source offering
programs for equipment leasing, working capital, acquisition, expansion &
sale & lease back transactions.

SEI

One Freedom Valley Dr
Oaks, PA 19456-9989
Telephone: (610) 676-1000, FAX:
(610) 676-1406, E-Mail:
webmaster@seic.com, Web Site:
www.seic.com
Mng Dir: David Schug
CEO: Alfred West
Primary Market Served: Business &
Consumer
Founded: 1968

SW CAGING CORP

5342 NW 25th St
Topeka, KS 66618-3738
Telephone: (785) 232-0061, Web Site:
www.swcaging.com
Pres: Thomas Bender
Primary Market Served: Consumer

SWBC

9311 San Pedro Ave (Suite 600)

San Antonio, TX 78216-4459
Telephone: (210) 525-1241, Web Site:
www.swbc.com
VP Mktg: Julie Ring
Primary Market Served: Business &
Consumer

SAGE FINANCIAL GROUP
300 Barr Harbor Dr (Suite 200), Five
Tower Bridge
West Conshohocken, PA 19428
Telephone: (484) 342-4400, FAX:
(484) 537-0550, E-Mail: sage@
sagefinancial.com, Web Site: www.
sagefinancial.com
CEO: David Cohn
Co-Pres & VP Mktg: Stephen Cohn
Co-Pres & VP Mktg: Alan J. Cohn
VP Principal: Mitchell E. Bednoff
VP Principal: John J. Sion
Conducts Business: U.S.
Employees: 10
Primary Market Served: Business &
Consumer
Catalog available online
Advertising/Marketing Budget Related
to Direct Marketing: 76-100%
Direct Marketing ad budget: $80,000
Direct Mail: 100%
Gross sales or billing: $1,000,000
Financial planning for individuals.

CHARLES SCHWAB & CO INC
211 Main St
San Francisco, CA 94105-1905
Telephone: (415) 627-7000, Toll Free:
(800) 648-5300, FAX: (415) 627-
8538, Web Site: www.schwab.com
Investment Specialist: William E. Martin
Pres & CEO: Walter W. Bettinger II
Conducts Business: U.S.
Employees: 5,000
Primary Market Served: Consumer
Direct Marketing ad budget:
$15,000,000
Founded: 1971
Gross sales or billing: $1,000,000,000
Provide discount securities brokerage
& related financial services to individual investors.

SKINDER-STRAUSS ASSOCIATES
890 Mountain Ave (Suite 300)
New Providence, NJ 07974
Telephone: (973) 642-1440, FAX:
(973) 242-1905, Web Site: www.
elaw.com
CEO: Andrew W. Strauss
Primary Market Served: Business &
Consumer

PETER J SOLOMON CO
1345 Avenue of the Americas
New York, NY 10105
Telephone: (212) 508-1600, FAX:
(212) 508-1633, Web Site: www.
pjsc.com
Founder & Chmn: Peter J. Solomon

SOVEREIGN BANK NEW ENGLAND
140 Hebron Ave
Glastonbury, CT 06033-4239
Toll Free: (860) 633-3688, FAX: (860)
727-6517
Conducts Business: U.S.
Employees: 1,100
Primary Market Served: Business &
Consumer
Catalog available online
Regional banking institution.

SPOKANE TEACHERS CREDIT UNION
1620 N Signal Dr
Liberty Lake, WA 99019-9517
Telephone: (509) 326-1954, Web Site:
www.stcu.org
CEO & Pres: Thomas A. Johnson
Primary Market Served: Business &
Consumer
Founded: 1934

ROBERT A STANGER & CO INC
1129 Broad St
Shrewsbury, NJ 07702
Telephone: (732) 389-3600, FAX:
(732) 389-1751, E-Mail: info@
rastanger.com, Web Site: www.
rastranger.com
Mng Dir: Kevin T. Gannon
Conducts Business: U.S., Canada, Europe
Employees: 25
Primary Market Served: Business
Advertising/Marketing Budget Related
to Direct Marketing: 0-25%
Direct Marketing ad budget:
Direct Mail: 15%
Magazines: 25%
Telephone: 60%
Founded: 1978
Gross sales or billing: $1,400,000
Investment banking, research & publishing firm serving real estate industry
& financial intermediaries.

STATE STREET GLOBAL ADVISORS
1 Lincoln St (fl 33)
Boston, MA 02111-2901
Telephone: (617) 786-3000, FAX:
(617) 664-2950, Web Site: www.
ssga.com

Pres & CEO: Scott Francis Powers
Primary Market Served: Consumer
Founded: 1978

STERLING BUSINESS SERVICES
202 Dunhagan Pl
Cary, NC 27511-5049
Telephone: (919) 467-5062
Pres: Edward B. Rickless
Accounting services except auditing

THE SUBURBAN CHAMBER OF COMMERCE
71 Summit Ave Ste 1
Summit, NJ 07901-3690
Telephone: (908) 522-1700, FAX:
(908) 522-9252, E-Mail: info@
suburbanchambers.org, Web Site:
www.suburbanchambers.org
Pres: Maureen C. Kelly
Conducts Business: U.S.
Employees: 31
Primary Market Served: Consumer
Catalog available online
Founded: 1917
Gross sales or billing: $1,200
NJ Chamber of Commerce representing
Summit, New Providence & Berkeley
Heights

SUNSHINE MINTING INC
7600 N Mineral Dr (Suite 700)
Coeur D'Alene, ID 83815-9170
Telephone: (208) 772-9592, Toll Free:
(800) 274-5837, FAX: (208) 772-
9739, E-Mail: sunshine@
sunshinemint.com, Web Site: www.
sunshinemint.com
Owner: Tom Powers
Dir Bus Devel: Tony Williams
Conducts Business: U.S., U.K., Asia
Employees: 95
Primary Market Served: Business &
Consumer
Advertising/Marketing Budget Related
to Direct Marketing: 0-25%
Founded: 1983
Gross sales or billing: $51,500,000
Provide investment grade silver & gold
bullion to the dealer market & handle
custom minting.

SUNTRUST BANKS INC
303 Peachtree Center Ave NE (Suite
320)
Atlanta, GA 30303-1280
Telephone: (404) 588-7914, Toll Free:
(800) 786-8787, FAX: (404) 532-
0550, E-Mail: emmett.harmon@
suntrust.com, Web Site: www.
suntrust.com
Grp VP DM: Emmett Harmon
VP DM: Angela Holland

VP Direct Mktg: Christine Farrell
VP DM: Terri Hawkins
Asst VP DM: Allyson Barrington
Asst VP DM: Tracy Kennedy
Asst VP DM: Kathleen Tucker
Employees: 28,000
Primary Market Served: Business & Consumer
Catalog available online
Indirect online sales
Advertising/Marketing Budget Related to Direct Marketing: 0-25%
Direct Marketing ad budget: $10,000,000
Direct Mail: $8,000,000
Online: $2,000,000
Founded: 1891

Financial services.

T ROWE PRICE ASSOCIATES INC

Subs. of T. Rowe Price Group Inc.
100 E Pratt St (fl 4)
Baltimore, MD 21202-1081
Telephone: (410) 345-2000, Toll Free: (800) 638-7890, FAX: (410) 986-3618, E-Mail: info@troweprice.com, Web Site: www.troweprice.com
Vice Chmn: Edward C. Bernard
CEO, Dir & Pres: James A.C. Kennedy
Pres: George J. Collins
Conducts Business: U.S.
Employees: 4,100
Primary Market Served: Business & Consumer
Founded: 1937
Gross sales or billing: $462,100,000

Investment research & counsel firm with $36 billion in assets under management. Direct marketer of mutual funds.

TAB BOARDS INTERNATIONAL INC

11031 Sheridan Blvd
Westminster, CO 80020-3201
Telephone: (303) 839-1200, FAX: (303) 839-0012, Web Site: www.tabboards.com
Sr Mktg Dir: Jeffrey Pederson
Primary Market Served: Business
Founded: 1990

TD BANK NA

70 Gray Rd
Falmouth, ME 04105-2019
Telephone: (207) 770-2196, Web Site: www.tdbanknorth.com
VP Direct Mktg: Maria Michaud
Primary Market Served: Consumer

TAX REDUCTION INSTITUTE

13200 Executive Park Ter
Germantown, MD 20874-5313
Telephone: (301) 972-3600, Toll Free: (800) TRI-0-TAX, FAX: (301) 972-0819, E-Mail: info@taxreductioninstitute.com, Web Site: www.taxreductioninstitute.com
Pres: Sanford Botkin
Conducts Business: U.S.
Employees: 5
Primary Market Served: Business & Consumer
Catalog available online
Direct online sales
Founded: 1989

Provide speakers to lecture on tax strategies.

TAYLOR CAPITAL GROUP, INC

dba Cole Taylor Bank
9550 W Higgins Rd
Rosemont, IL 60018-4906
Telephone: (847) 653-7978, FAX: (847) 653-7890, E-Mail: investor.relations@coletaylor.com, Web Site: www.taylorcapitalgroup.com
Chmn Bd, Pres & CEO: Bruce W. Taylor
CFO: Robin Van Castle
Exec Mng Dir, Mktg Devel & New Ventures: Jeffrey W. Taylor
Mktg Dir: Kathy Kaporis
Employees: 421
Primary Market Served: Business & Consumer
Gross sales or billing: $46,200,000

User of direct marketing for financial services.

TEXADA CAPITAL CORP

62 Greenwood Shoals
Grasonville, MD 21638-9659
Toll Free: (866) 595-6224, Web Site: www.texada.com

THOMA CRESSEY BRAVO

300 N La Salle Dr (Suite 4300)
Chicago, IL 60654-3422
Telephone: (312) 777-4444, FAX: (312) 777-4445, Web Site: www.tcb.com
Partner: Lee Mitchell
Partner: Carl Thoma
CFO: Scott A. Maskalunas
VP: Seth J. Boro
IT Mgr: Damian McIntosh
Conducts Business: U.S.
Primary Market Served: Business

Private equity investor. Capital source for direct marketing & other service businesses. Existing or past investments in direct mail, telemarketing, newspaper, trade magazines & trade show businesses. Provider of growth & acquisition equity & recapitalization financing.

THOMSON RESEARCH

Div. of Thomson Reuters
22 Thompson Pl
Boston, MA 02210
Telephone: (617) 856-2000, Web Site: research.thomsonib.com
Conducts Business: Worldwide
Employees: 9,300
Primary Market Served: Business
Catalog available online
Direct online sales
Gross sales or billing: $2,000,000,000

Provides businesses with an electronic collection of company, industry & product research & analysis.

THOMSON REUTERS LPC

Subs. of Reuters
3 Times Sq
New York, NY 10036
Telephone: (646) 223-6890, E-Mail: lpc.americas@reuters.com, Web Site: www.loanpricing.com
Pres: Jim Davis
Conducts Business: Worldwide
Employees: 105
Primary Market Served: Business
Catalog available online
Direct online sales
Advertising/Marketing Budget Related to Direct Marketing: 26-50%

Business & industrial financial services.

THRIVENT FINANCIAL FOR LUTHERANS

4321 N Ballard Rd
Appleton, WI 54919-0001
Telephone: (920) 734-5721, Toll Free: (800) 847-4836, FAX: (920) 730-4781, E-Mail: mail@thrivent.com, Web Site: www.thrivent.com
Exec VP, Mktg & Prods: Pam Moret
Strategic Mktg: Beth Larsen
Sr VP Mktg: Timothy J. Lehman
Sr VP Communs: Marie A. Uhrich
Conducts Business: U.S.
Employees: 2,676
Primary Market Served: Consumer
Founded: 1902
Gross sales or billing: $6,086,200,000

Fortune 500 national fraternal benefit society. Provides insurance and financial products as well as educational and volunteer opportunities.

TRANS UNION CORP

555 W Adams St
Chicago, IL 60661-3614

Telephone: (312) 985-2000, Web Site: www.transunion.com
CEO & Pres: James M. Peck
CFO & Exec VP: Samuel Allen Hamood
Conducts Business: U.S.
Employees: 3,400
Primary Market Served: Business
Founded: 1968
Gross sales or billing: $1,200,000,000

Sell credit & non-credit promotional listings to various industries.

TRANSFIRST EPAYMENT SERVICES
13220 Birch Dr (Suite 110)
Omaha, NE 68164-5434
Toll Free: (888) 541-9800, Web Site: epay.transfirst.com
Pres: Mike Phelan
Primary Market Served: Consumer

TRANSFIRST HOLDINGS INC
5400 Lyndon B Johnson Fwy (Suite 900)
Dallas, TX 75240-1054
Telephone: (214) 453-7700, Toll Free: (888) 254-4137, FAX: (214) 453-7739, Web Site: www.transfirst.com
Sr VP & CFO: Mark Travis
Sr VP & CIO: John Peterson
Sr VP, Corp Devel: Andrew Rueff
VP, Client Svcs: Alea Brim
Conducts Business: U.S.
Employees: 20
Primary Market Served: Business
Catalog available online
Indirect online sales
Founded: 1991
Gross sales or billing: $10,000,000

Provide payment processing solutions designed for the direct marketing/electronic retailing industry. Offer credit card processing, electronic check drafting & ACH payment services. Complete data management facilities accommodate monthly management needs such as installment and/or continuity billing. Offer seamless interface between the order taking & fulfillment facilities and/or new payment methods.

TRAVELEX AMERICA INC
Subs. of Travelex
1152 15th St NW (fl 7)
Washington, DC 20005
Telephone: (202) 408-1200, FAX: (202) 513-5215, Web Site: business.travelex.com/us
Conducts Business: U.S., Canada
Employees: 428
Primary Market Served: Consumer
Gross sales or billing: $112,000,000

TULLY & HOLLAND INC
20 William St Ste 135
Wellesley, MA 02481-4133
Telephone: (781) 239-2900, FAX: (781) 239-2901, E-Mail: info@tullyandholland.com, Web Site: www.tullyandholland.com
Pres: Timothy Tully
Sr VP: Elizabeth Richards Tulley
Mng Dir: Chris Kaupe
Mng Dir: Andrew Crain
Mng Dir: Russ Robb
Mng Dir: Elizabeth Napier
Mng Dir: Donald O'Connor
Mng Dir: Stuart Rose
Mng Dir: Alfred Rossou
Employees: 10
Primary Market Served: Business
Founded: 1992

Investment banking.

UBS WEALTH MANAGEMENT US
1200 Harbor Blvd
Weehawken, NJ 07086-6728
Telephone: (201) 352-3000, Toll Free: (888) 279-3343, FAX: (201) 617-8589, Web Site: www.ubs.com/financialservicesinc
Chmn & CEO: Joseph Grano
Conducts Business: U.S.
Primary Market Served: Business & Consumer

Brokerage firm using direct marketing techniques to gain qualified prospects for investment brokers.

USAA ALLIANCE SERVICES MARKETING
Subs. of United Services Automobile Association (USAA)
9800 Fredericksburg Rd
San Antonio, TX 78288-0141
Telephone: (210) 456-9857, FAX: (210) 498-4542, Web Site: www.usaa.com
Pres: Donna Bhatia
Conducts Business: Worldwide
Employees: 200
Primary Market Served: Consumer
Catalog available online
Direct online sales
Advertising/Marketing Budget Related to Direct Marketing: 76-100%
Direct Marketing ad budget: $6,600,000
Direct Mail: 100%
Founded: 1922
Gross sales or billing: $65,200,000

Member merchandise buying & cruise travel services. Alliance services include long distance telephone service, home security, internet service pro-

vider, rental cars, the USAA/Sprint program, USAA Choice Ride & USAA Floral Service.

UNION FEDERAL SAVINGS BANK
1565 Mineral Spring Ave
North Providence, RI 02904
Telephone: (401) 353-8900, Toll Free: (800) 992-0278, FAX: (401) 353-8938, Web Site: www.unionfsb.com
Chmn: Peter Tarr
Pres: William F. Sullivan
Telecomm Exec: Richard Shaw
Fin: Patricia North
Primary Market Served: Business & Consumer
Catalog available online
Gross sales or billing: $4,800,000,000

Financial services.

UNITED COMMUNITY BANK
63 Hwy 51 S
Blairsville, GA 30512
Telephone: (706) 745-0911, Web Site: www.ucbi.com
VP Direct Mktg: Tricia Stoeckig
Primary Market Served: Business & Consumer

US BANCORP
Div. of US Bancorp Minneapolis
800 Nicollet Mall
Minneapolis, MN 55402-7014
Telephone: (651) 466-3000, Toll Free: (800) 872-2657, FAX: (612) 303-0782, Web Site: www.usbank.com
Chmn, Pres & CEO: Richard K. Davis
Vice Chmn: Richard C. Hartnack
Vice Chmn: Joseph M. Otting
Sr VP Mktg: Jenny Powell
Conducts Business: U.S.
Employees: 50,000
Primary Market Served: Business & Consumer
Catalog available online
Indirect online sales
Advertising/Marketing Budget Related to Direct Marketing: 0-25%
Gross sales or billing: $19,109,000,000

Full-service commercial & retail bank serving the Colorado market.

US BANK
200 S 6th St
Minneapolis, MN 55402-1403
Telephone: (612) 973-1111, Web Site: www.usbank.com
Direct Mktg Mgr, Co-branded Credit Cards: Joan Forde
Primary Market Served: Business & Consumer

US DIGITAL TRANSACTIONS CORPORATION

228 Park Ave S
New York, NY 10003-1502
Toll Free: (800) 728-1190, FAX: (800) 729-6530, Web Site: www.usdtcorp.com
Primary Market Served: Consumer

US TAX SHIELD

17328 Ventura Blvd
Encino, CA 91316-3904
Toll Free: (877) 929-3535, Web Site: www.ustaxshield.com
Mktg Mgr: Andy Klein
Conducts Business: USA
Primary Market Served: Consumer
Advertising/Marketing Budget Related to Direct Marketing: 51-75%

UNIVERSAL FIDELITY CORP

16325 Westheimer Rd
Houston, TX 77082-1233
Telephone: (281) 647-4100, Toll Free: (800) 580-8887, FAX: (281) 647-4207, Web Site: www.ufccorp.com
Pres & CEO: Terry Simonds
Primary Market Served: Business
Advertising/Marketing Budget Related to Direct Marketing: 0-25%
Founded: 1991

Collection agency.

UNIVERSITY BANK

2015 Washtenaw Ave
Ann Arbor, MI 48104
Telephone: (734) 741-5858, FAX: (734) 741-5859, E-Mail: ranzini@university-bank.com, Web Site: www.university-bank.com
CEO: Nicholas Fortson
Employees: 4
Primary Market Served: Business
Founded: 1993

Business investment development for corporations & financing.

UWHARRIE CAPITAL CORP

PO Box 338
Albemarle, NC 28002-0338
Telephone: (704) 991-1181, Web Site: www.uwharriecapitalcorp.com
Primary Market Served: Consumer

VW CREDIT

2200 Ferdinand Porsche Dr
Herndon, VA 20171-5884
Telephone: (248) 340-5000
Pres: R. Andrew Steward
Primary Market Served: Consumer

VANDERBILT ADVERTISING

Div. of Value Line Publishing Inc

220 E 42nd St (fl 6)
New York, NY 10017-5806
Telephone: (212) 907-1500, FAX: (212) 907-1914, Web Site: www.valueline.com
CEO: Jean Bernhard
Chief Mktg Officer: Donald Ross
Conducts Business: U.S., Canada
Employees: 6
Primary Market Served: Business & Consumer
Catalog available online
Advertising/Marketing Budget Related to Direct Marketing: 26-50%

Value Line Investment Survey (weekly advisory service) & related financial investment information to individual investors.

VANGUARD

100 Vanguard Blvd
Malvern, PA 19355
Telephone: (610) 669-1000, FAX: (610) 669-6600, Web Site: www.vanguard.com
Chmn: John J. Brennan
Primary Market Served: Business & Consumer
Founded: 1975

THE VANTAGE GROUP INC

90 Canal St
Boston, MA 02114
Telephone: (617) 878-6000, FAX: (617) 878-6154, Web Site: www.vantagetravel.com
Exec VP: Harry Melikian
Conducts Business: Worldwide
Primary Market Served: Consumer
Catalog available online
Founded: 1983
Gross sales or billing: $140,000,000

Consumer financial services & mail order products.

VERONIS SUHLER STEVENSON LLC

55 E 52nd St (fl 33)
New York, NY 10055-0007
Telephone: (212) 935-4990, FAX: (212) 381-8168, E-Mail: stevensonj@vss.com, Web Site: www.vss.com
Chmn: John J. Veronis
Pres & Founding Gen Partner: John S. Suhler
Partner: Marco Sodi
Partner: Jeffrey T. Stevenson
Exec VP: James P. Rutherford
Conducts Business: Worldwide
Employees: 114
Primary Market Served: Business
Catalog available online
Indirect online sales
Founded: 1981

Gross sales or billing: $203,000,000
Investment bankers to the direct marketing, media, communications & information industries.

VISA USA

900 Metro Center Blvd
Foster City, CA 94404-2173
Telephone: (650) 432-3200, FAX: (650) 432-2875, Web Site: www.visa.com
Primary Market Served: Business & Consumer

WASHINGTON MUTUAL HOME LOAN, INC

75 N Fairway Dr
Vernon Hills, IL 60061-1846
Telephone: (847) 918-5549, FAX: (847) 549-2975
Pres: Kerry Killinger
Conducts Business: U.S.
Employees: 2,500
Primary Market Served: Business
Catalog available online
Indirect online sales
Direct Marketing ad budget:
Direct Mail: 45%
Magazines: 5%
Newspapers: 5%
Telephone: 45%
Founded: 1932

Direct marketing of mortgage loan products through mail & telemarketing.

WEBSTER BANK

Subs. of Webster Financial Corp
145 Bank St Fl 1
Waterbury, CT 06702-2211
Telephone: (203) 578-2230, FAX: (203) 578-2507, Web Site: www.websterbank.com
Chmn & CEO: James C. Smith
CFO & Chief Fin Officer: Glenn I MacInnes
Primary Market Served: Business & Consumer
Founded: 1870

Savings & loan bank.

WEICHERT CO

1625 State Route 10
Morris Plains, NJ 07950-2905
Telephone: (973) 397-8516, Web Site: www.weichert.com
VP Info Svcs: George La Penta
Primary Market Served: Business & Consumer

RICHARD WEINER CONSULTANT

1814 NE Miami Gardens Dr (Suite 904)

North Miami Beach, FL 33179-5043
Telephone: (305) 441-6470
Consultant: Richard Weiner
Primary Market Served: Consumer

WELLS FARGO
420 Montgomery St
San Francisco, CA 94163
Toll Free: (800) 869-3557, (866) 249-
   3302, FAX: (626) 312-3015, Web
   Site: www.wellsfargo.com
Pres & CEO: John Stumpf
Sr Exec VP & CFO: Timothy J Sloan
Conducts Business: U.S.
Employees: 160,000
Primary Market Served: Business &
   Consumer
Catalog available online
Direct online sales
Founded: 1872
Gross sales or billing: $31,000,000,000

Financial services & bank holding
company.

WINMILL & CO
11 Hanover Sq
New York, NY 10005-2818
Telephone: (212) 785-0900, Toll Free:
   (800) 400-MIDAS 6432, FAX: (212)
   363-1100, E-Mail: info@midasfunds.
   com, Web Site: www.midasfunds.
   com
Pres: Thomas Winmill
Chmn: Bassett S. Winmill
VP, CFO & Chief Acctg Officer: Tho-
   mas O'Malley
Vice Chair: Robert D. Anderson
Conducts Business: Worldwide
Employees: 33
Primary Market Served: Business &
   Consumer
Catalog available online
Indirect online sales
Founded: 1985
Gross sales or billing: $17,000,000

No-load mutual fund & discount brokerage service.

WOLTERS KLUWER
FINANCIAL SERVICES
100 S 5th St (Suite 700)
Minneapolis, MN 55402-1219
Telephone: (612) 656-7700, Toll Free:
   (800) 552-9408, Web Site: www.
   wolterskluwerfs.com
CEO: Richard Flynn
Exec VP & CFO: Paul Kuhn
VP Strategy & Commun: Rochelle
   Blease

National provider of forms and compliance software to the financial industry.

XCELERATED
INVESTMENTS INC
2940 Hebron Park Dr (Suite 307)
Hebron, KY 41048-9573
Toll Free: (877) 489-3347, Web Site:
   www.xcelerated.com

Insurance (15)

A-MARK INC
715 Twining Rd (Suite 118)
Dresher, PA 19025-1832
Telephone: (215) 886-4740, FAX:
 (215) 886-4749
Pres & CEO: John Myers
Conducts Business: U.S.
Employees: 2

Financial Services

**AAA MID-ATLANTIC
 INSURANCE GROUPS**
Div. of AAA Midatlantic
1 River Pl
Wilmington, DE 19801-5125
Telephone: (302) 299-4700, Toll Free:
 (800) 451-5921, FAX: (215) 864-
 5486, Web Site: www.
 aaamidatlantic.com
CEO: Donald Gagnon
Chief Mktg Officer & Sr VP Brand:
 Marke Dickinson
Sr VP Sls: Nick Eppinger
Primary Market Served: Consumer

Property, casualty, accident & health
insurance.

AFLAC
1932 Wynnton Rd
Columbus, GA 31999
Telephone: (706) 243-5428, Web Site:
 www.aflac.com

AGIA INSURANCE SERVICES
1155 Eugenia Pl
Carpinteria, CA 93013-2061
Telephone: (805) 566-9191, FAX:
 (805) 566-1887, Web Site: www.
 agia.com
VP Mktg: Susan Roe
Conducts Business: U.S.
Employees: 200
Primary Market Served: Consumer
Founded: 1964

Broker/administrator of group insurance programs.

AIG ACCIDENT & HEALTH
Div. of AIG
70 Pine St (50th fl)
New York, NY 10270
Telephone: (212) 770-7000, Toll Free:
 (877) 638-4244, FAX: (212) 509-
 9705, Web Site: www.aig.com
VP, Accident Health Div: Jeff Kesten-
baum
Chmn: Rob B. Willumstad
Pres: Jim Mallon
Exec VP & CFO: Steven J. Bensinger
Primary Market Served: Business &
 Consumer
Catalog available online

Indirect online sales
Founded: 1919

Provide insurance products worldwide.

AIG MARKETING
Div. of American International Group
70 Pine St (40th fl)
New York, NY 10270-0002
Telephone: (212) 770-7000, (212) 770-
 2237, Web Site: www.agac.com
Sr VP, New Bus: John G. Colona
VP, Sls: Mark Duchene
EVP & Chief Direct Mktg Officer: Eu-
gene Raitt
Conducts Business: International
Employees: 400
Primary Market Served: Consumer

Marketer of property, casualty, health
& life insurance products to affinity
groups.

**AMA INSURANCE AGENCY
 INC**
Subs. of American Medical Associa-
tion
515 N State St
Chicago, IL 60654
Telephone: (312) 464-2425, Toll Free:
 (800) 458-5736, FAX: (312) 419-
 5096, Web Site: www.amainsure.
 com
Direct Tech Mktg: Cynthia K. Warden
VP, Sls: Denise S. Friday
Conducts Business: U.S.
Employees: 135
Primary Market Served: Business &
 Consumer
Catalog available online
Indirect online sales
Advertising/Marketing Budget Related
 to Direct Marketing: 76-100%
Direct Marketing ad budget:
 $6,000,000
Founded: 1988

Provide insurance for medical students,
physicians, other health care professionals & other professional associations.

AON CENTER
200 E Randolph St
Chicago, IL 60601-6436
Telephone: (312) 381-1000, FAX:
 (312) 381-6032, Web Site: www.aon.
 com
Pres & CEO: Greg Case
Sr Exec VP: Michael O'Halleran
Chief Diversity Officer: Corbette
 Doyle
Conducts Business: U.S., Canada
Employees: 43,000
Primary Market Served: Business &
 Consumer

Catalog available online
Direct Marketing ad budget:
 $1,800,000
Direct Mail: 90%
Magazines: 4%
Newspapers: 4%
Telephone: 2%
Founded: 1982
Gross sales or billing: $9,000,000,000

Sell group life & health insurance by
mail through sponsoring organizations
& through an agency sales force. Also,
sell life & health products through mail
on a broad market basis.

**AON CONSULTING NEW
 YORK**
Aon Corp
199 Water St (fl 12)
New York, NY 10038-3551
Telephone: (212) 792-9700, (212) 792-
 9759, (212) 441-2000, FAX: (212)
 792-9720, E-Mail: garry_sullivan@
 aoncons.com
Sr VP, Mktg: Frank J. Fimmano
Conducts Business: Worldwide
Employees: 50,000
Primary Market Served: Business &
 Consumer
Advertising/Marketing Budget Related
 to Direct Marketing: 0-25%

Provide sales, service & administration
of insurance services to associations, financial institutions & other membership organizations.

ARAG
400 Locust St (Suite 480)
Des Moines, IA 50309
Toll Free: (800) 247-4184, FAX: (515)
 246-8710, E-Mail: service@
 ARAGgroup.com, Web Site: www.
 araggroup.com
Chief Mktg Officer: Ann Dieleman
Primary Market Served: Business &
 Consumer

AXA EQUITABLE
1290 Ave of the Americas (fl 7)
New York, NY 10104-0101
Telephone: (212) 554-1234, (212) 314-
 2956, Web Site: www.axaonline.com
AVP: Lisa Mahaffey
AVP Mktg: Santo Loporto

**AEGON DIRECT
 MARKETING SERVICES
 INC**
Aegon USA Inc
100 Light St Fl B1
Baltimore, MD 21202-1098

Telephone: (410) 209-5617, FAX: (410) 209-5932, Web Site: www. aegondms.com
Dir, Mktg: Dien Sapp
Pub Rels Mgr: Veronica Mouring
Primary Market Served: Consumer
Advertising/Marketing Budget Related to Direct Marketing: 76-100%

Insurance.

JOHN ALDEN LIFE INSURANCE CO/NORTH STAR MARKETING
Div. of Fortis Health
11465 Johns Creek Pkwy (Suite 160)
Duluth, GA 30097-1573
Telephone: (678) 473-1211, Toll Free: (800) 768-6288, FAX: (678) 473-9573, Web Site: www. nstarmarketing.com
CEO: Kae Groshong Wagner
Exec VP: Bowen Smith
VP: Bob Bartlett
VP: Amy Neary
Mgr: Joe McLaughlin
Conducts Business: U.S., Canada
Primary Market Served: Business & Consumer
Catalog available online

Sell life, accident & health insurance.

ALFA INSURANCE
PO Box 11000
Montgomery, AL 36191-0001
Telephone: (334) 288-3900, Web Site: www.alfains.com
VP Mktg Communs: Christy Cantrell
Primary Market Served: Consumer

ALLIANZ LIFE INSURANCE CO OF NORTH AMERICA
5701 Golden Hills Dr, PO Box 1344
Minneapolis, MN 55416-1297
Telephone: (763) 765-6500, Toll Free: (800) 950-5872, Web Site: www. allianzlife.com
CEO: Gary C. Bhojwani
Exec VP: Jill Paterson
Sr VP: Tom Burns
Sr VP, HR: Cary Brinkley
CFO: Giulio Terzariol
Conducts Business: U.S.
Employees: 1,800
Primary Market Served: Business & Consumer
Catalog available online
Founded: 1896

Sell life insurance.

AMERICAN CAPITAL
aka American Capital Strategies Ltd
2 Bethesda Metro Ctr 14th Fl
Bethesda, MD 20814-5390

Telephone: (301) 951-6122, FAX: (301) 654-6714, E-Mail: info@ americancapital.com, Web Site: www.americancapital.com
Chmn & CEO: Malon Wilkus
Exec VP & COO: Ira J. Wagner
Exec VP & CFO: John R. Erikson
Conducts Business: U.S.
Employees: 484
Primary Market Served: Business & Consumer
Advertising/Marketing Budget Related to Direct Marketing: 26-50%
Direct Marketing ad budget: $10,000
Direct Mail: 75%
Telephone: 25%
Gross sales or billing: $1,330,000,000

AMERICAN FAMILY INSURANCE GROUP
6000 American Pkwy
Madison, WI 53783-0001
Telephone: (608) 249-2111, FAX: (608) 243-6525, E-Mail: akin1@ amfam.com, Web Site: www.amfam. com
DM Mgr: Andy King
DM Specialist: Christina Parrott
DM Specialist: Justin Miller
DM Specialist: Erik Busse
DM Specialist: Cynthia Mochalski
Conducts Business: U.S.
Employees: 7,000
Primary Market Served: Business & Consumer
Indirect online sales
Direct Marketing ad budget:
Direct Mail: 70%
Online: 10%
Telephone: 20%
Founded: 1927
Gross sales or billing: $4,000,000,000

Multi-line captive agent insurance company.

AMERICAN FAMILY LIFE ASSURANCE CO OF COLUMBUS (AFLAC)
1932 Wynnton Rd
Columbus, GA 31999-0001
Telephone: (706) 323-3431, Toll Free: (800) 992-3522, FAX: (706) 660-7446, Web Site: www.aflac.com
CEO, AFLAC Inc: Daniel P. Amos
CFO & Pres: Kriss Cloninger III
Dir: Sheryl Manville
Mgr Investor Rels: Delia Moore
Conducts Business: U.S. & Japan
Employees: 7,400
Primary Market Served: Business & Consumer
Catalog available online
Indirect online sales
Founded: 1955

Gross sales or billing: $14,600,000,000
Market supplemental health insurance to consumers & businesses.

AMERICAN FIDELITY ASSURANCE CO
2000 N Classen Blvd, PO Box 25523
Oklahoma City, OK 73125
Telephone: (405) 525-6900, FAX: (405) 523-5215, Web Site: www. afadvantage.com
Asst VP Mktg: Mike Carroll
Chmn & CEO: Bill Cameron
Team Leader Direct Mktg: Kim Hood
Conducts Business: Worldwide
Employees: 1,400
Primary Market Served: Business & Consumer
Catalog available online
Advertising/Marketing Budget Related to Direct Marketing: 0-25%
Founded: 1960

Insurance for trade associations, groups, employers & educators.

AMERICAN GENERAL CO
Subs. of American International Group Inc
AIG Benefit Solutions
3600 State Rte 66
Neptune, NJ 07753
Telephone: (732) 922-7000, FAX: (732) 922-7595
CEO: Ken Griesemer
CFO: Frank Kophamal
Conducts Business: U.S.
Employees: 700
Primary Market Served: Business
Advertising/Marketing Budget Related to Direct Marketing: 0-25%
Direct Marketing ad budget: $125,000
Magazines: 100%

Designs, develops, and manufactures a variety of group insurance products and services for the Employer-Paid, Voluntary, Worksite, Association and Financial Institution markets. Products include life, disability, dental, vision, mortgage, credit account protector, traditional loan, debt protection, voluntary and worksite products which are distributed nationwide through multiple channels including general agents, brokers and independent agents, third party administrators, benefit consultants or financial institutions. Product flexibility exists to accommodate all size groups on a national or international basis.

AMERICAN GENERAL LIFE & ACCIDENT INSURANCE
Div. of American International Group, Inc

American General Ctr
Nashville, TN 37250
Telephone: (615) 749-1000, Toll Free:
(800) 888-2452, Web Site: www.
agla.com
Pres & CEO: Jim Mallon
DM Mgr: Steven Doster
Employees: 5,000
Primary Market Served: Consumer
Catalog available online
Gross sales or billing: $2,100,000,000

Provider of life & health insurance.

AMERICAN GENERAL LIFE INSURANCE CO
2929 Allen Pkwy
Houston, TX 77019-2155
Telephone: (713) 522-1111, FAX:
(713) 522-8531, Web Site: www.
aglife.com
Sr VP, Strategic Mktg & Bus Devel:
Erik Baden
VP, Branding & Media Svcs: Susan
Howard
Employees: 11,000
Primary Market Served: Business &
Consumer
Catalog available online

Life insurance.

AMERICAN HEALTH & LIFE INSURANCE CO
Div. of Citigroup
3001 Meacham Blvd (Suite 200)
Fort Worth, TX 76137
Telephone: (817) 348-7500, Toll Free:
(800) 995-2274, FAX: (817) 348-
7553, Web Site: www.citifinancial.
com
CEO: Dava Carson
Pres.: Peter Dahlberg
Sr VP, Corp Citizenship: Pamela M.
Flaherty
Conducts Business: U.S.
Employees: 75
Primary Market Served: Business &
Consumer

Health & life insurance company.

AMERICAN INSURANCE ADMINISTRATORS INC
3070 Riverside Dr
Columbus, OH 43221
Telephone: (614) 486-5388, FAX:
(614) 486-2728
Pres & COO: Philip Super
VP, Direct Mktg: Jeff Roedel
Conducts Business: U.S.
Employees: 32
Primary Market Served: Business &
Consumer
Advertising/Marketing Budget Related
to Direct Marketing: 76-100%

Founded: 1967
Marketer & administrator of life &
health insurance products to constituents of affinity associations.

AMERICAN INTERNATIONAL GROUP
Div. of AIG
70 Pine St (fl 50)
New York, NY 10270
Telephone: (212) 770-7000, Toll Free:
(877) 638-4244, FAX: (212) 742-
8692, Web Site: www.aig.com
CEO & Pres: Bob Benmosche
Conducts Business: 138 Countries
worldwide
Employees: 5,700
Primary Market Served: Business &
Consumer
Founded: 1919

International division handles life, accident, and health insurance direct marketing outside the USA in 138
countries worldwide.

AMERICAN MODERN INSURANCE GROUP
Subs. of The Midland Co
7000 Midland Blvd
Amelia, OH 45102-2607
Telephone: (513) 943-7200, Toll Free:
(800) 759-9008, FAX: (513) 947-
4779, (800) 217-5150, E-Mail:
customer_care@amig.com, Web
Site: www.amig.com
Pres & CEO: Manuel Z. Rios
Sr. VP & Dir, Natl Life Sls: Larry
Compton
Employees: 1,170
Primary Market Served: Business

Property & casualty insurance.

AMERICAN SECURITIES CAPITAL PARTNERS
666 3rd Ave (fl 29)
New York, NY 10017-4030
Telephone: (212) 476-8000, Web Site:
www.american-securities.com
Dir of Strategic Initiatives: Lee Dranik-
off
Primary Market Served: Consumer

AMERISURE INSURANCE COS
26777 Halsted Rd
Farmington Hills, MI 48331-3586
Telephone: (248) 615-9000, Toll Free:
(800) 257-1900, FAX: (248) 615-
8224, Web Site: www.amerisure.com
Chmn: James B. Nicholson
Pres & CEO: Richard F. Russell
Mgr Corp Commun & Adv: Linda S.
DeSimone

Sr VP, CFO & Treas: R. Douglas
Kinnan
Conducts Business: U.S.
Employees: 685
Primary Market Served: Business
Advertising/Marketing Budget Related
to Direct Marketing: 0-25%
Founded: 1912
Gross sales or billing: $430,000,000

Commercial property casualty insurance.

AMICA INSURANCE
100 Amica Way
Lincoln, RI 02865-1158
Telephone: (401) 334-6000, Toll Free:
(800) 652-6422, FAX: (401) 334-
4241, Web Site: www.amica.com
Exec VP & Gen Mgr: Carl R. Neal
Sr Asst VP: Bruce Maynard
VP: James E. McDermott Jr.
Sr Asst VP: Craig Phelps
Pres & CEO: Robert A. DiMuccio
Sr VP HR: Patricia A. Talin
Primary Market Served: Business &
Consumer
Catalog available online
Indirect online sales
Founded: 1907

Life insurance.

ANTHEM BLUE CROSS
Formerly Blue Cross of California
1 Wellpoint Way
Westlake Village, CA 91362-3893
Telephone: (805) 557-6655, Toll Free:
(800) 333-0912, FAX: (800) 557-
6872, Web Site: www.bluecrossca.
com
VP Mktg & Brand Strategy: Kate
Quinn
Sr VP Individual & Grp Svcs: Deborah
F. Lachman
VP Cust Svc: Bob Novelli
Employees: 7,000
Primary Market Served: Business &
Consumer
Founded: 1937

Insurance sales.

ANTHEM BLUE CROSS BLUE SHIELD
370 Bassett Rd
North Haven, CT 06473
Telephone: (203) 239-8381, Toll Free:
(800) 545-0948, FAX: (203) 985-
7918, Web Site: www.anthem.com
Pres: Marjorie Dorr
Primary Market Served: Consumer

Provide health insurance to Connecticut, Maine & New Hampshire residents.

ANTHEM BLUE CROSS BLUE SHIELD

1831 Chestnut St (#1)
Saint Louis, MO 63103-2275
Telephone: (314) 923-4444, Toll Free: (888) 877-9125, FAX: (314) 923-5151, E-Mail: moreinfo@bcbsmo. com, Web Site: www.bcbsmo.com
Exec VP & CIO: Mark Boxer
Dir, HR: Morry Berger
Employees: 2,300
Primary Market Served: Business & Consumer
Catalog available online

Healthcare insurance.

ANTHEM CORPORATE COMMUNICATIONS

Div. of Anthem Inc
120 Monument Cir
Indianapolis, IN 46204
Telephone: (207) 822-7000, FAX: (207) 822-7741, Web Site: www. anthem.com
Primary Market Served: Business & Consumer
Founded: 1938

A managed-care insurance company.

AON'S AFFINITY INSURANCE SERVICES INC

159 E County Line Rd
Hatboro, PA 19040-1218
Telephone: (215) 773-4600, Web Site: www.aon.com
Sr VP Corp Mktg & Commun: Sharon Cohen
Primary Market Served: Business & Consumer

ASSURANT GROUP

Parent Co of Fortis Inc
1 Chase Manhattan Plaza
New York, NY 10005-1401
Telephone: (305) 253-2244, FAX: (305) 252-6987, Web Site: www. assurant.com
Pres & CEO: Rob Pollock
Exec VP Sls & Mktg: Kevin Clotz
Conducts Business: U.S., Canada, U.K.
Primary Market Served: Business & Consumer
Founded: 1999

Insurance services for financial institutions & business. Provide specialty insurance, membership and extended services program. Typically serving segments of the population underserved by other mainstream insurance agencies.

ASSURANT HEALTH

Bus seg of Assurant, Inc.
501 W Michigan St
Milwaukee, WI 53203-2706
Telephone: (414) 244-0658, Toll Free: (800) 800-1212, FAX: (414) 224-0472, Web Site: www.assuranthealth. com
Pres & CEO: Don Hamm
Dir Online Mktg & Ecommerce: Steven Keller
VP Sls Strategy: Mike Norderhaug
Sr VP Strategic Devel: Mike Kellen
Conducts Business: Worldwide
Employees: 3,000
Primary Market Served: Business & Consumer
Founded: 1892
Gross sales or billing: $634,500,000

Health insurance.

ASSURANT SOLUTIONS PRENEED DIVISION

260 Interstate North Cir SE
Atlanta, GA 30339-2110
Telephone: (770) 763-1000, Toll Free: (800) PRE NEED, FAX: (770) 859-4325, Web Site: www. assurantpreneed.com
Pres & CEO: S Craig Lemasters
Exec VP & CFO: Ivan C. Lopez
Sr VP: Christopher Reznyk
Employees: 13,400
Primary Market Served: Business
Catalog available online

Preneed insurance.

BALBOA LIFE & CASUALTY

3349 Michelson (Suite 200)
Irvine, CA 92623-9702
Telephone: (949) 222-8000, Toll Free: (800) 854-6115, FAX: (949) 222-8777, Web Site: www. balboainsurance.com
Pres, CEO & Sr Mng Dir: Robert James
Exec VP & COO: Doreen DeLaney
Exec VP & CFO: Kenneth Mertzel
Exec VP: Ron Closser
Conducts Business: U.S., U.K., Canada, Australia
Employees: 1,980
Primary Market Served: Business & Consumer
Advertising/Marketing Budget Related to Direct Marketing: 51-75%
Direct Marketing ad budget:
Direct Mail: $50,000
Telephone: $100,000
Gross sales or billing: $1,710,000,000

Creditor & lender related insurance programs & services for financial institutions & their customers.

BANKERS LIFE & CASUALTY CO

Subs. of Conseco
600 W Chicago Ave
Chicago, IL 60654-2800
Telephone: (312) 396-6000, Toll Free: (800) 231-9150, Web Site: www. bankerslife.com
Pres: Scott Perry
Sr VP Mktg & Commun: Chris Campbell
Sr VP, Sls & Distr: Michael J. Buckley
VP, Strategy & Planning: Scott L. Goldberg
Sr VP, Underwriting & New Bus: David Vega
VP, Bankers Long Term Care: Gerardo Monroy
Conducts Business: U.S.
Primary Market Served: Consumer
Catalog available online
Indirect online sales
Direct Marketing ad budget:
Direct Mail: 100%
Founded: 1880
Gross sales or billing: $2,800,000,000

Sell life & health insurance through agents who are provided with leads obtained through direct response promotions.

BENEFITMALL

485 Lyndon B Johnson Fwy (Suite 1100)
Dallas, TX 75244-6025
Telephone: (469) 791-3355, Web Site: www.benefitmall.com
VP Mktg: Laura Clenney
Primary Market Served: Business & Consumer

BLUE CROSS BLUE SHIELD OF FLORIDA

4800 Deerwood Corporate Campus Pkwy
Jacksonville, FL 32246
Telephone: (904) 791-6111, Toll Free: (800) 477-3736, FAX: (904) 905-6638, E-Mail: katie.magee@bcbsfl. com, Web Site: www.bcbsfl.com
CEO: Patrick Geraghty
Exec VP, CAO, & CFO: R. Chris Doerr
Exec VP & COO: Arnold Livermore
Sr VP: Fred Ryder
Conducts Business: U.S.
Employees: 9,500
Primary Market Served: Business & Consumer
Indirect online sales
Direct Marketing ad budget:
Direct Mail: 80%
Newspapers: 20%
Founded: 1944
Gross sales or billing: $2,147,500,000

Marketer of individual & group healthcare insurance coverage.

BLUE CROSS BLUE SHIELD OF ILLINOIS
300 E Randolph St
Chicago, IL 60601
Telephone: (312) 938-6000, FAX: (312) 938-5722, Web Site: www.bcbsil.com
Sr VP, Mktg: Paula Steiner
Acct Exec: Cary Goldstein
Acct Exec: Dan MacKenzie
Acct Exec: Dave Gieselman
Primary Market Served: Business & Consumer
Catalog available online
Healthcare insurance.

BLUE CROSS BLUE SHIELD OF LOUISIANA
5525 Reitz Ave
Baton Rouge, LA 70809-3802
Telephone: (225) 295-3307, Toll Free: (800) 599-2583, FAX: (225) 295-2054, E-Mail: help@bcbsla.com, Web Site: www.bcbsla.com
VP, Corp Commun: John Maginnis
Reg Dir: Larry Blackman
Reg Dir: James Bustillo
Reg Dir: Dan Wagner
Reg Mgr: Merle Francis
Conducts Business: U.S.
Employees: 1,500
Primary Market Served: Business & Consumer
Catalog available online
Advertising/Marketing Budget Related to Direct Marketing: 76-100%
Direct Marketing ad budget: $2,000,000
Direct Mail: 90%
Newspapers: 5%
TV/Radio: 5%
Founded: 1934
Gross sales or billing: $500,000,000
Health insurance.

BLUE CROSS BLUE SHIELD OF NORTH CAROLINA
PO Box 2291
Durham, NC 27702-2291
Toll Free: (800) 250-3630, Web Site: www.bcbsnc.com
SEM Mgr: Marc Moore

BLUE CROSS BLUE SHIELD OF OKLAHOMA
1400 S Boston Ave
Tulsa, OK 74119-3612
Telephone: (918) 560-3500, Toll Free: (800) 942-5837, E-Mail: info@bcbsok.com, Web Site: www.bcbsok.com
Dir: Dr. Joseph Cunningham
CIO & VP: Jerry D. Scherer
VP, Plng: Jon Polcha

Conducts Business: U.S.
Employees: 1,000
Primary Market Served: Business & Consumer
Catalog available online
Marketer of health & life insurance products.

BLUE CROSS BLUE SHIELD OF SOUTH CAROLINA
I-20 E at Alpine Rd
Columbia, SC 29219
Telephone: (803) 788-0222, Toll Free: (800) 288-2227, FAX: (803) 736-4516, Web Site: www.bcbssc.com
Pres: Jim Deyling
Sr VP Info: Wayne Roberts
VP: Fred Rowell
Employees: 7,000
Primary Market Served: Business & Consumer
Catalog available online
Indirect online sales
Advertising/Marketing Budget Related to Direct Marketing: 0-25%
Direct Marketing ad budget: $3,000,000
Founded: 1946
Gross sales or billing: $4,000,000,000
Health insurance marketer.

BLUE SHIELD LIFE
Subs. of Blue Shield of California
50 Beale St
San Francisco, CA 94105-1813
Toll Free: (888) 800-2742, FAX: (800) 329-2742, Web Site: www.blueshieldca.com
Pres: Paul Markovich
Exec VP & CFO: Heidi Kunz
Exec VP Customer Svcs & Corp Mktg: Bob Novelli
Sr VP Chief Actuary: Ed Cymerys
Sr VP HR: Marianne Jackson
Conducts Business: U.S.
Employees: 40
Primary Market Served: Business & Consumer
Catalog available online
Advertising/Marketing Budget Related to Direct Marketing: 0-25%
Founded: 1953
Gross sales or billing: $39,000,000
Life & health insurance.

BLUE SHIELD OF CALIFORNIA
50 Beale St
San Francisco, CA 94105-1808
Telephone: (415) 229-5000, FAX: (415) 229-5056, Web Site: www.blueshieldca.com
Pres & CEO: Paul Markovich
VP Corp Mktg: Doug Biehn

Conducts Business: U.S.
Employees: 750
Primary Market Served: Business & Consumer
Founded: 1939
Gross sales or billing: $8,150,000,000
Healthcare insurance.

BRITISH COLUMBIA AUTOMOBILE ASSOCIATION
dba BCAA
4567 Canada Way
Burnaby, BC, Canada V5G 4T1
Telephone: (604) 268-5000, Toll Free: (800) 564-6222, FAX: (604) 268-5585, Web Site: www.bcaa.com
Pres & CEO: William Bullis
VP HR & Corp Communs: John Evans
Dir, Customer Mngmt: Liliana Daminato
Conducts Business: Canada
Primary Market Served: Business & Consumer
Gross sales or billing: $115,000,000
Full service agency providing auto, travel & insurance services.

BROKERS/CONSULTANTS INC
1332 Dartmouth Rd
Flossmoor, IL 60422-1905
Telephone: (708) 957-2900, FAX: (708) 957-4155
Pres: James S. Tiernan
Conducts Business: U.S.
Employees: 4
Primary Market Served: Business & Consumer
Advertising/Marketing Budget Related to Direct Marketing: 0-25%
Direct Marketing ad budget:
Direct Mail: 95%
Magazines: 5%
Founded: 1964
Marketers of term life & group health insurance.

BUSINESS PLANNERS & CONSULTANTS INC
370 Lexington Ave (Suite 909)
New York, NY 10017-6503
Telephone: (212) 972-1970, FAX: (212) 972-1126
Pres: Kevin S. Foley
Conducts Business: U.S.
Employees: 20
Primary Market Served: Business & Consumer
Advertising/Marketing Budget Related to Direct Marketing: 0-25%
Direct Marketing ad budget:
Direct Mail: 10%
Newspapers: 20%

Telephone: 70%

Gross sales or billing: $1,200,000

Insurance administration (TPA); basically short term disability (Statutory NY). Broker, property casualty, life & health.

CMI DIRECT

130 Cook Ave (Suite 101)
Pasadena, CA 91107-7320
Telephone: (951) 300-1700, FAX: (866) 723-5433, Web Site: www.cmidirect.net
Pres & CEO: Charles F. Murray
CFO: Jim Aeling
Mktg Dir: Dana Kelley
Conducts Business: U.S.
Employees: 33
Primary Market Served: Consumer
Advertising/Marketing Budget Related to Direct Marketing: 76-100%
Founded: 1979

Direct marketing services company. Specializes in telemarketer insurance products through financial institutions, & other organizations.

CNA

333 S Wabash Ave
Chicago, IL 60604-4107
Telephone: (312) 822-5000, Toll Free: (800) 262-2000, E-Mail: cna_help@cna.com, Web Site: www.cna.com
Chmn Bd & CEO: Thomas F. Motamed
Exec VP & CFO: D. Craig Mense
Sr VP & CIO: Ray Oral
Chief Risk Officer: Mark Verheyen
Underwriting Dir: Katherine Fenwick
Conducts Business: U.S.
Employees: 16,000
Primary Market Served: Business & Consumer
Catalog available online
Gross sales or billing: $10,000,000,000
Insurance carrier.

CANADA BROKERLINK INSURANCE

Subs. of ING Canada
17520 111th Ave
Edmonton, AB, Canada T55 OA2
Telephone: (780) 474-8911, FAX: (780) 479-0573, Web Site: www.brokerlink.ca
Reg Mktg: Chris Miller
Conducts Business: Canada
Primary Market Served: Consumer
Direct Marketing ad budget: $25,000
Direct Mail: 30%
Magazines: 5%
Newspapers: 20%
TV/Radio: 45%

Founded: 1960

Sell general insurance by mail to homeowners, business owners & auto owners on a mass merchandising basis.

CAPITAL INSURANCE GROUP (CIG)

2300 Garden Rd
Monterey, CA 93940-5326
Telephone: (831) 233-5500, Web Site: www.ciginsurance.com
Corp Mktg Mgr: Sandie Borthwick

CAREFIRST BLUE CROSS BLUE SHIELD

840 First St NE
Washington, DC 20002-8046
Telephone: (202) 479-8000, FAX: (301) 470-8049, Web Site: www.carefirst.com
Pres & CEO: Chet Burrell
VP: Daniel Winn MD
Vice Chmn: Edward J. Basan
COO: Michael L. Daly
Dir Pub Rels: Michael Sullivan
Conducts Business: Worldwide
Employees: 5,400
Primary Market Served: Business & Consumer
Catalog available online
Indirect online sales

Health insurance marketer.

CARHILL ENTERPRISES INC

1232 Washington Ave (Suite 300)
Saint Louis, MO 63103-1983
Telephone: (314) 621-7646, Web Site: www.cahillinsight.com
Owner: Andrew Hillin

CATERPILLAR INSURANCE SERVICES CORP

Subs. of Caterpillar Inc
2120 West End Ave
Nashville, TN 37203
Telephone: (615) 386-5800, Web Site: www.cat.com
Primary Market Served: Business & Consumer
Founded: 1981

Insurance company providing insurance to business & consumers using Caterpillar machinery.

CELTIC LIFE INSURANCE CO

233 S Wacker Dr (Suite 700)
Chicago, IL 60606-6300
Telephone: (312) 332-5401, FAX: (312) 441-0341, E-Mail: info@celtic-net.com, Web Site: www.celtic-net.com

Chmn, Pres & CEO: Frederick J. Manning
Sr VP & CFO: Lewis R. Marszalek
Sr VP, Admin: Blake A. Westerfield
COO: James P. Daly
VP, HR: Barbara Basham
Primary Market Served: Business & Consumer
Catalog available online

Group health insurance.

CENTRAL STATES HEALTH & LIFE CO OF OMAHA

1212 N 96th St
Omaha, NE 68114
Telephone: (402) 397-1111, Toll Free: (800) 826-6587, FAX: (402) 391-3772, Web Site: www.cso.com
Chmn: Richard T. Kizer
Pres: T. Edward Kizer
Sr VP, Opers: Jeffrey J. Wanning
Sr VP & CFO: Leonard A. Pacer
VP & CIO: David W. Dibben
Employees: 650
Primary Market Served: Consumer
Catalog available online
Advertising/Marketing Budget Related to Direct Marketing: 26-50%
Founded: 1932
Gross sales or billing: $78,900,000

Sell credit card insurance.

CENTRAL STATES INDEMNITY

Subs. of Berkshire Hathaway Inc
1212 N 96th St
Omaha, NE 68114-2274
Telephone: (402) 997-8000, (402) 397-1111, Toll Free: (800) 445-6500, Web Site: www.csi-omaha.com
Pres: John Kizer
Exec VP: Kevin Moran
Sr VP Mktg: Mike Hoody
Asst VP: Mark Spack
Conducts Business: U.S.
Employees: 450
Primary Market Served: Business & Consumer
Advertising/Marketing Budget Related to Direct Marketing: 76-100%
Direct Marketing ad budget:
Direct Mail: 50%
Telephone: 50%
Founded: 1977
Gross sales or billing: $54,000,000

Provider of payment protection insurance: Life, disability, involuntary unemployment & family leave insurance.

CHAIRMAN'S MARKETING GROUP LLC

8 Lafayette Rd W
Princeton, NJ 08540-2428
Telephone: (732) 745-4700

Primary Market Served: Consumer

CHARTIS
70 Pine St (fl 22)
New York, NY 10270-0001
Telephone: (212) 770-8013, Web Site:
www.chartisinsurance.com/pcg
CEO: Peter D. Hancock
Primary Market Served: Consumer

CIGNA INTERNATIONAL
1601 Chestnut St, 2 Liberty Pl (fl 53)
Philadelphia, PA 19192-0003
Telephone: (215) 761-1741, FAX:
(215) 761-5515, Web Site: www.
cigna.com
Chmn & CEO CIGNA Corp: H. Edward Hanway
Exec VP & CFO: Michael W. Bell
Exec VP HR & Svcs CIGNA Corp:
John M. Murabito
Sr VP Bus Devel: Michael Ross
Exec VP & Gen Counsel CIGNA Corp:
Carol Ann Petren
Employees: 27,000
Primary Market Served: Consumer
Founded: 1792
Gross sales or billing: $1,200,000,000
Discount brokerage services.

CIVIL SERVICE EMPLOYEES INSURANCE GROUP
2121 N California Blvd (Suite 555)
Walnut Creek, CA 94596-3501
Telephone: (415) 274-7803, (925) 817-6300, Toll Free: (800) 282-6848,
Web Site: www.cseinsurance.com
Sr VP Field Opers & Mktg Devel: Kelli
Schulhofer
Exec VP Prods & Svcs: Dave Brinker
CFO & Sr VP: Stefan Dobrus
Pres & CEO: Pierre Bize
Conducts Business: U.S.
Employees: 300
Primary Market Served: Business &
Consumer
Catalog available online
Indirect online sales
Founded: 1949
Gross sales or billing: $74,000,000

Market personal lines, small commercial & life insurance products through independent agents & financial institutions to both public & non-public employees.

COLONIAL LIFE INSURANCE CO TEXAS
2600 West Freeway
Fort Worth, TX 76113

Telephone: (817) 390-2350, Toll Free:
(888) 227-5119, FAX: (817) 390-2209, E-Mail: insurance@
colonialinsurance.com, Web Site:
www.colonialinsurance.com
Pres: William B. Hampton
Conducts Business: U.S.
Primary Market Served: Consumer
Catalog available online
Founded: 1978

Insurance underwriters for individual life insurance policies.

COLUMBIAN MUTUAL LIFE INSURANCE CO
Vestal Pkwy E
Binghamton, NY 13902-4600
Telephone: (607) 724-2472, Toll Free:
(800) 423-9765
Pres & CEO: Thomas E. Rattmann
Conducts Business: U.S.
Employees: 292
Primary Market Served: Business &
Consumer
Catalog available online
Advertising/Marketing Budget Related
to Direct Marketing: 0-25%
Direct Marketing ad budget: $20,000
Founded: 1903

Mutual life insurance company licensed in 50 states, the District of Columbia, the Commonwealth of Puerto Rico & the Virgin Islands. Products sold directly include life insurance, guaranteed issue senior life, annuity & IRA products.

COMBINED INSURANCE CO OF AMERICA
1000 Milwaukee Ave Fl 1
Glenview, IL 60025-2424
Telephone: (847) 953-8116, Toll Free:
(800) 490-1322, FAX: (847) 953-8070, Web Site: www.
combinedinsurance.com
VP Mktg: Rebecca Mills
Chmn & CEO: Doug Wendt
Primary Market Served: Consumer

COMMERCIAL TRAVELERS MUTUAL INSURANCE CO
70 Genesee St
Utica, NY 13502-3503
Telephone: (315) 797-5200, Toll Free:
(800) 422-6200, FAX: (315) 797-3198, E-Mail: comtravl@
commercialtravelers.com, Web Site:
www.commercialtravelers.com
Chmn Bd: Richard Griffith
CEO & Pres: Paul H. Trevvett
Conducts Business: U.S.
Employees: 97
Primary Market Served: Business &
Consumer

Catalog available online
Advertising/Marketing Budget Related
to Direct Marketing: 0-25%
Direct Marketing ad budget:
Direct Mail: 100%
Founded: 1883
Gross sales or billing: $34,800,000

Student accident insurance pre-school through college, life & disability income insurance for small employers.

CONSECO INC
11825 N Pennsylvania Ave
Carmel, IN 46032-4555
Telephone: (317) 817-6100, FAX:
(317) 817-2847, Web Site: www.
conseco.com
Pres: Dan R. Bardin
VP Bus Devel: Mark A Cecil
Exec VP: Brad Corbin
Sr VP Strategic Plng: Barbara S. Stewart
Conducts Business: U.S.
Employees: 4,000
Primary Market Served: Consumer
Advertising/Marketing Budget Related
to Direct Marketing: 76-100%
Founded: 1979
Gross sales or billing: $4,467,400,000

Life insurance for the 50+ market.
Medicare supplement & term insurance.

CONTINENTAL WESTERN GROUP
aka CWG. Operating Unit of W.R.
Berkley Corp
11201 Douglas Ave
Des Moines, IA 50322
Telephone: (515) 473-3000, Toll Free:
(800) 533-0303, FAX: (515) 473-3015, Web Site: www.cwgins.com
Pres: Michael G Connor
CEO: Bradley S. Kuster
VP Prod Mngmt: Aaron M. Larson
AVP Agency Sls: Mike Elam
Conducts Business: U.S.
Primary Market Served: Consumer
Founded: 1925

Sell insurance to owners of antique & collectible automobiles.

COUNTRY FINANCIAL
PO Box 2020
Bloomington, IL 61702-2020
Telephone: (309) 821-3000
Mgr, Agency Promos: Jennifer Manning
Primary Market Served: Business &
Consumer

COVERDELL & CO INC
Subsidiary of Vertrue Inc.
8770 W Bryn Mawr Ave (Suite 1000)

Chicago, IL 60631-3515
Telephone: (404) 881-2227, Toll Free:
(800) 992-2196, FAX: (404) 881-
2222, Web Site: www.coverdell.com
Pres: Michael Owens
VP, Client & Mktg Svc: Susan Pavloff
Conducts Business: U.S.
Primary Market Served: Business &
Consumer
Catalog available online
Founded: 1963
Gross sales or billing: $4,700,000

Sell insurance through magazine coupon advertising & direct mail solicitation, primarily within the rural &
financial institution markets.

CUNA MUTUAL GROUP
5910 Mineral Point Rd
Madison, WI 53705-4498
Telephone: (608) 238-5851, Toll Free:
(800) 356-2644, FAX: (608) 231-
8839, Web Site: www.cunamutual.
com
Chmn: Loretta M. Burd
Pres, CEO & Dir: Jeff Post
Exec VP & CFO: Jeffrey D. Holley
Bus Mngmt & Analysis Leader: Chris
Kennedy
Conducts Business: Worldwide
Employees: 5,500
Primary Market Served: Business &
Consumer
Catalog available online
Indirect online sales
Founded: 1926
Gross sales or billing: $2,800,000,000

Insurance company serving credit
unions & their members. Handle life,
health & casualty policies.

CUNNINGHAM GROUP
7234 W North Ave (Suite 101)
Elmwood Park, IL 60707-4200
Telephone: (708) 848-2300, Toll Free:
(800) 962-1224, FAX: (708) 848-
2174, E-Mail: cunngroup@cg-ins.
com, Web Site: www.cg-ins.com
Pres: James H. Cunningham
Employees: 25
Primary Market Served: Business &
Consumer
Advertising/Marketing Budget Related
to Direct Marketing: 76-100%
Founded: 1947
Gross sales or billing: $2,900,000

User of direct marketing for insurance.

DESJARDINS FINANCIAL
  SECURITIES
Div. of La Societe Financiere Des
Caisses Desjardins Inc
200 Ave des Commandeurs
Levis, QC, Canada G6V 6R2

Telephone: (418) 838-7870, FAX:
(418) 833-5985, Web Site: www.
desjardinsfinancialsecurity.com
VP, Pub Affairs & Commun: Daniel
Roussel
Sr VP, HR & Advisory Svcs: Lise Bor-
deleau
CEO: Monique Leroux
Pres & COO: Richard Fortier
Conducts Business: Canada
Employees: 1,215
Primary Market Served: Business &
Consumer
Gross sales or billing: $745,000,000

Sell life & disability insurance, annuities & pension funds to individuals,
groups & credit unions.

DIRECT AUTO INSURANCE
1281 Murfreesboro Pike Ste 150
Nashville, TN 37217-2437
Telephone: (615) 399-4859, Web Site:
www.directgeneral.com
VP Mktg: Tara Harrington
Primary Market Served: Consumer

DIRECTORY OF AMERICAN
  BUSINESS & INSURANCE
  ATTORNEYS
130 Church St (#303)
New York, NY 10007-2906
Telephone: (732) 458-7788, Toll Free:
(800) 445-7995, FAX: (732) 458-
7710, E-Mail: staff@abialaw.com,
Web Site: www.abialaw.com
Pres: George Wilson
Asst: Donald Simpson
Conducts Business: U.S.
Primary Market Served: Business &
Consumer

Association of insurance & business attorneys.

DIVERSIFIED HEALTHCARE
  SERVICES
800 E Campbell Rd (Suite 399)
Richardson, TX 75081
Telephone: (972) 238-1492, FAX:
(972) 907-8283, Web Site: www.
dhscorp.com
Owner & Pres: Jerry O'Connor
Conducts Business: U.S.
Primary Market Served: Business &
Consumer

Medical billing & collection agency.

THE DOCTOR'S CO
185 Greenwood Rd
Napa, CA 94558
Telephone: (707) 226-0176, E-Mail:
info@thedoctors.com, Web Site:
www.thedoctors.com
Pres: R. Anderson
Primary Market Served: Business

Founded: 1976
Medical malpractice insurance for doctors.

ELECTRIC INSURANCE CO
75 Sam Fonzo Dr
Beverly, MA 01915-1000
Telephone: (978) 921-2080, Toll Free:
(800) 227-2757, FAX: (978) 524-
5583, E-Mail: sales@
electricinsurance.com, Web Site:
www.electricinsurance.com
Mktg Coord: Jennifer Fielding
Mktg Mgr: Mike Sullivan
Conducts Business: U.S.
Primary Market Served: Business &
Consumer
Founded: 1966

Auto & home insurance.

EMPIRE BLUE CROSS &
  BLUE SHIELD
1 Liberty Plz (Suite 1300)
New York, NY 10006-1419
Telephone: (212) 476-1000, Toll Free:
(877) 476-7111, FAX: (212) 476-
1281, Web Site: www.empireblue.
com
CMO: Jack Smith
Pres & Gen Mgr: Brian Griffin
Primary Market Served: Business &
Consumer

Health insurance provider.

EMPLOYERS INSURANCE
10375 Professional Cir
Reno, NV 89521-4802
Telephone: (775) 327-2677, Web Site:
www.employers.com
VP Corp Mktg: Ty Vukelich

EQUITABLE LIFE &
  CASUALTY INSURANCE
  CO
Three Triad Ctr
Salt Lake City, UT 84180-1200
Telephone: (801) 579-3400, FAX:
(801) 579-3789, Web Site: www.
equilife.com
Pres & CEO: E. Rod Ross
Chief Mktg Officer: Larry Thomas
Actuary: Rick Klar
Treas: Kristine S. Christensen
Mktg Svcs Dir: Louis Trani
Legal Counsel: Ken Surfass
Conducts Business: U.S.
Employees: 140
Primary Market Served: Consumer
Founded: 1935
Gross sales or billing: $125,719,941
Life & health insurance for the elderly.

FCIA MANAGEMENT CO INC

Great American Insurance Co
125 Park Ave (fl 14)
New York, NY 10017-5529
Telephone: (212) 885-1500, FAX:
(212) 885-1535, E-Mail: service@
fcia.com, Web Site: www.fcia.com
Pres: Lindley Franklin
Conducts Business: U.S.
Employees: 120
Primary Market Served: Business
Catalog available online
Direct Marketing ad budget:
Direct Mail: $12,000
Founded: 1991

Manage & administer credit & political
risk insurance policies.

FARM BUREAU INSURANCE

7373 W Saginaw Hwy, Box 30400
Lansing, MI 48917
Telephone: (517) 323-7000, Toll Free:
(800) 292-2680, FAX: (517) 327-
0208, Web Site: www.
farmbureauinsurance-mi.com
Pres: Wayne Wood
Dir: Greg Waldie
Exec VP: Jim Robinson
VP, Mktg: Kevin P. Kelly
Conducts Business: U.S.
Employees: 700
Primary Market Served: Business &
Consumer
Catalog available online
Direct Marketing ad budget: $500,000
Newspapers: 90%
TV/Radio: 10%

Marketer of multiple line insurance
products.

FARMERS INSURANCE

4680 Wilshire Blvd
Los Angeles, CA 90010
Telephone: (410) 338-1633, (410) 366-
1000, Toll Free: (800) 327-6377,
FAX: (410) 554-1926, Web Site:
www.farmers.com
VP Mktg: John Ingersoll
Employees: 18,000
Primary Market Served: Consumer
Founded: 1928

Personal insurance including auto &
homeowners.

FIDELITY SECURITY LIFE INSURANCE CO

3130 Broadway
Kansas City, MO 64111-2406
Telephone: (816) 756-1060, Toll Free:
(800) 648-8624, FAX: (816) 968-
0580, E-Mail: info@fslins.com, Web
Site: www.fslins.com
Pres & Treas: Richard F. Jones
Sr VP, Mktg: David Smith

Sr VP: Michael E. Hall
VP: Mark L. Burley
Asst VP: Dana L. Hamilton
Conducts Business: U.S.
Employees: 300
Primary Market Served: Business &
Consumer
Catalog available online
Advertising/Marketing Budget Related
to Direct Marketing: 30%
Founded: 1969

Third party endorsement & broad market insurance.

FOREMOST INSURANCE GROUP

Div. of Farmers Insurance Co
PO Box 2450
Grand Rapids, MI 49501-2450
Telephone: (616) 956-8241, Toll Free:
(800) 527-3905, FAX: (800) 325-
1507, Web Site: www.foremost.com
Pres: Steve Boshoven
Sr VP Mktg: Nancy Treul
Asst VP Claims: Dennis Squibb
VP Fin: Jeff Pepper
VP, Commun: John Kalinka
Dir, Mktg: Mike Cok
Dir, Direct Mktg: Randy Slotten
Mgr, List Mngmt/Direct Mail: David
Simmonds
Conducts Business: U.S., Canada
Employees: 2,300
Primary Market Served: Consumer
Direct Marketing ad budget:
$4,000,000
Gross sales or billing: $1,500,000,000

Insurer of auto, homeowners, mobile
homes & recreational vehicles. Complete turnkey marketing programs.

FORESTERS

789 Don Mills Rd
Toronto, ON, Canada M3C 1T9
Telephone: (416) 467-2544, Web Site:
www.foresters.com
Primary Market Served: Business

FORETHOUGHT FINANCIAL SERVICES INC

Subs. of Hillenbrand Industries
1 Forethought Ctr
Batesville, IN 47006-1279
Telephone: (812) 934-7139, Toll Free:
(800) 331-8853, FAX: (812) 934-
8564, Web Site: www.forethought.
com
Pres & CEO: John Graf
Conducts Business: U.S.
Employees: 160
Primary Market Served: Business &
Consumer

Founded: 1985
Sell pre-need funeral insurance through
independent funeral homes.

GEICO DIRECT

Subs. of GEICO Corp
1 GEICO Plaza
Washington, DC 20076-0005
Telephone: (301) 986-2842, Toll Free:
(800) 841-3000, FAX: (301) 986-
2068, Web Site: www.geico.com
Pres & CEO: Olza M. Nicely
VP, Mktg: Ted Ward
Conducts Business: U.S.
Employees: 18,400
Primary Market Served: Consumer
Advertising/Marketing Budget Related
to Direct Marketing: 76-100%
Gross sales or billing: $4,324,200,000

Market auto insurance.

GALLAGHER AFFINITY

Div. of Arthur J Gallagher & Co
8430 Enterprise Cir
Lakewood Ranch, FL 34202
Telephone: (941) 757-1445, Toll Free:
(888) 437-6611, Web Site: www.
gallagher-affinity.com
Pres: Kevin Garvin
CEO: Douglas D. Furbush III
Primary Market Served: Business &
Consumer
Founded: 2001

Insurance programs, benefits and association management services provider.

GERBER LIFE INSURANCE CO

Subs. of Gerber Products Co
1311 Mamaroneck Ave
White Plains, NY 10605-5221
Telephone: (914) 272-4000, Toll Free:
(800) 704-2180, FAX: (914) 272-
4099, Web Site: www.gerberlife.com
CEO: Wesley Protheroe
Sr VP, Mktg: Peter Mendelson
Mktg Mgr: Andrea Borgelt
Dir, Creative Svcs: Sharon Langel
Conducts Business: U.S., Puerto Rico,
and Canada
Employees: 200
Primary Market Served: Consumer
Advertising/Marketing Budget Related
to Direct Marketing: 76-100%
Direct Marketing ad budget:
Direct Mail: 50%
Magazines: 15%
Newspapers: 10%
Online: 10%
TV/Radio: 15%
Founded: 1967

Gross sales or billing: $148,000,000

Supplementary life & health insurance policies sold using various direct response techniques to budget-minded people of all ages.

GOLDEN RULE INSURANCE CO

7440 Woodland Dr, Golden Rule Bldg
Indianapolis, IN 46278-1719
Telephone: (317) 297-4123, FAX: (317) 297-0908, Web Site: www. goldenrule.com
Pres. Fin Svcs: Richard Merril
Media Svcs Mgr: Jo Ann Robinson
Conducts Business: U.S.
Primary Market Served: Business & Consumer

Health & life insurance company.

GREAT-WEST LIFE

8515 E Orchard Rd
Greenwood Village, CO 80111
Toll Free: (800) 537-2033, Web Site: www.greatwest.com
Pres & CEO: Mitchell T.G. Graye
Mktg: Michelle Buckalew
Conducts Business: U.S.
Employees: 6,600
Primary Market Served: Business

Pension insurance.

GUARANTEE TRUST LIFE INSURANCE CO

1275 Milwaukee Ave (Suite 100)
Glenview, IL 60025-2489
Telephone: (847) 298-0670, FAX: (847) 298-1215, E-Mail: pr@gtlic. com, Web Site: www.gtlic.com
Pres & CEO: Richard S. Holson III
Sr VP Mktg: B. Montgomery Edson
VP, Direct Mktg: Mike Haas
VP Govt Rels: Jeff Burman
Conducts Business: U.S.
Employees: 274
Primary Market Served: Consumer
Founded: 1936
Gross sales or billing: $279,000,000

Marketer of life insurance.

THE GUARDIAN LIFE INSURANCE CO

7 Hanover Sq (fl 14)
New York, NY 10004-4013
Telephone: (212) 598-8000, Web Site: www.guardianlife.com
Interim Exec VP: Brad Thomas
Primary Market Served: Business & Consumer

GUIDEONE INSURANCE

1111 Ashworth Rd
West Des Moines, IA 50265-3537

Toll Free: (877) 448-4331, Web Site: www.guideone.com
Sr Mktg Specialist: Jason Darrah
Chmn Bd, Pres & CEO: Jim Wallace
Primary Market Served: Business

THE HARTFORD FINANCIAL SERVICES INC

Div. of Hartford Life Insurance Co
200 Executive Blvd
Southington, CT 06489-1058
Telephone: (860) 547-5000, (860) 843-8070, FAX: (860) 547-2680, Web Site: www.thehartford.com
Chmn & CEO: Ramani Ayer
Pres, COO & Dir: Thomas M. Marra
Exec VP & Gen Counsel: Alan J. Kreczko
Exec VP & CFO: David M. Johnson
AVP Mktg: Daniel Lavoie
Exec VP Grp Benefits Division: Ronald R. Gendreau
Employees: 31,000
Primary Market Served: Consumer
Catalog available online
Advertising/Marketing Budget Related to Direct Marketing: 76-100%
Founded: 1994
Gross sales or billing: $26,000,000,000

Life insurance.

HEALTH ALLIANCE PLAN

2850 W Grand Blvd
Detroit, MI 48202-2692
Telephone: (248) 443-1075, FAX: (248) 443-8851, E-Mail: alandin1@ hapcorp.org, Web Site: www. hapcorp.org
Dir Adv, Commun & Direct Mktg: Anita Landino

HEALTHPLAN SERVICES

3501 E Frontage Rd
Tampa, FL 33607
Telephone: (813) 289-1000, Toll Free: (800) 545-6441, Web Site: www. healthplan.com
Sr VP Sls: Jay McLauchlin
Pres & CEO: Jeff Bak
Conducts Business: U.S.
Employees: 600
Primary Market Served: Business & Consumer
Founded: 1970

Manage & administer small group and individual benefit health plan.

HIGHMARK BLUE CROSS BLUE SHIELD

120 Fifth Ave (Suite 1044)
Pittsburgh, PA 15222-3099
Telephone: (412) 544-7000, FAX: (412) 544-5350, Web Site: www. highmark.com

Chmn: J. Robert Baum
Pres & CEO: William Winkenwerder Jr
EVP: S. Tyrone Alexander
EVP, CFO, & Treas: Nanette P. De Turk
Primary Market Served: Business & Consumer
Founded: 1996

Individual & group health insurance.

HOMESTEADERS LIFE CO

5700 Westown Pkwy
West Des Moines, IA 50266-8214
Telephone: (515) 440-7777, Toll Free: (800) 477-3633, E-Mail: service@ homesteaderslife.com, Web Site: www.homesteaderslife.com
Mktg Mgr: Karen King
VP Mktg: Dean Lambert
Direct Mail: Pam Davis
Conducts Business: U.S.
Primary Market Served: Business
Advertising/Marketing Budget Related to Direct Marketing: 0-25%
Direct Marketing ad budget: $1,000,000
Direct Mail: 100%
Founded: 1906

Pre-need insurance marketer.

HORACE MANN EDUCATORS CORP

1 Horace Mann Plaza
Springfield, IL 62715-0002
Telephone: (217) 789-2500, FAX: (217) 788-5161, Web Site: www. horacemann.com
Chmn: Joseph J. Malone
CEO & Pres Elect: Marita Zuraitis
Pres & CEO: Peter H. Heckman
Exec VP: Douglas W. Reynolds
Sr VP Mktg: Robert B. Joyner
VP & CIO: Mark Hansen
Conducts Business: U.S.
Employees: 2,400
Primary Market Served: Consumer
Catalog available online
Founded: 1945
Gross sales or billing: $873,800,000

Multi-line insurance company that targets teachers & other school employees in the U.S. Homeowners auto, individual & group life insurance & retirement annuities.

ING

dba Relia Star Insurance Co
20 Washington Ave S
Minneapolis, MN 55401-1908
Telephone: (612) 342-7061, Toll Free: (800) 333-6965, FAX: (612) 372-5339, Web Site: www.ing.com
Chmn: Henk Breukink

Chmn: Peter Elverding
Employees: 118,000
Primary Market Served: Business &
Consumer
Gross sales or billing: $163,000,000

Sell insurance plans through brokers including all financial services.

ING USA ANNUITY & LIFE INS CO
Div. of ING
909 Locust St
Des Moines, IA 50309-2899
Telephone: (515) 698-7100, FAX:
(515) 698-2001, Web Site: www.ing-
usa.com
Corp Commun: Cynthia M. Schaus
Employees: 900
Primary Market Served: Business &
Consumer

Insurance equities, annuities & life.

INFINITY INSURANCE CO
3700 Colonnade Pkwy (Suite 600)
Birmingham, AL 35243-3219
Toll Free: (800) 527-5412, Web Site:
www.infinityauto.com
AVP Natl Mktg: Greg Fasking
Primary Market Served: Business

INSURANCE.COM
29000 Aurora Rd
Solon, OH 44139-1843
Telephone: (440) 715-0075, Web Site:
www.insurance.com
Customer Commun Mgr: Karen Im-
brogno
Primary Market Served: Business

INTELLIQUOTE INSURANCE SERVICES
5170 Golden Foothill Pkwy
El Dorado Hills, CA 95762-9658
Toll Free: (800) 543-3467, Web Site:
www.intelliquote.com
Pres & CEO: Gary Lardy
Primary Market Served: Business

HERBERT L JAMISON & CO LLC
100 Executive Dr (Suite 200)
West Orange, NJ 07052-3362
Telephone: (973) 731-0806, Toll Free:
(800) 526-4766, (800) JAMISON,
FAX: (973) 731-3035, Web Site:
www.jamisongroup.com
SVP Sls Mktg: Christopher J. Serreino
Sr VP Sls Mktg: Anthony F. Bavaro
VP: Noel Santiago
Exec VP: Robert Frattarda
Conducts Business: Worldwide
Employees: 100
Primary Market Served: Business &
Consumer

Catalog available online
Indirect online sales
Advertising/Marketing Budget Related
to Direct Marketing: 51-75%
Founded: 1938

Insurance brokerage.

JOHN HANCOCK FINANCIAL SERVICES INC
Subs. of Manulife Financial
601 Congress St, Box 111
Boston, MA 02117
Telephone: (617) 572-6000, Toll Free:
(800) 732-5543, FAX: (617) 572-
6451, Web Site: www.johnhancock.
com
Pres & CEO: Dominic D'Alessandro
PR Coord: Melissa Salmon
Pres, CEO & Dir: John D. Des Prez III
Sr VP Bus Devel & Gen Counsel: Jean-
Paul Bisnaire
Chmn Bd: Arthur R. Sawchuck
Dir: John M. Cassaday
Conducts Business: U.S., Canada, Eu-
rope
Employees: 21,287
Primary Market Served: Business &
Consumer
Founded: 1862

Life insurance company with several
subsidiaries.

KELSEY NATIONAL CORP
3030 S Bundy Dr
Los Angeles, CA 90066
Telephone: (310) 390-1000, Toll Free:
(800) 366-5656, FAX: (310) 390-
3158, E-Mail: info@kelsey.com,
Web Site: www.kelsey.com
Chmn & CEO: Van Kelsey
Pres: Mark Kelsey
VP, Sls: Warren Blumberg
Sec/Treas & COO: Van Kelsey III
Controller: Brian K. Buhler
Conducts Business: U.S.
Primary Market Served: Business &
Consumer
Catalog available online
Advertising/Marketing Budget Related
to Direct Marketing: 76-100%
Founded: 1964

Insurance TPA (Third Party Administrator) & marketer specializing in small
business & association group employee
benefits nationwide.

KEMPER CORP
1 E Wacker Dr
Chicago, IL 60601-1883
Telephone: (312) 661-4600, Toll Free:
(800) 733-7366, FAX: (312) 494-
6995, Web Site: www.kemper.com
Chmn: Richard C. Vie

Pres, CEO & Chmn: Donald G. South-
well
Exec VP, CFO & Dir: Eric J. Draught
Sr VP: Scott Renwick
VP, Chief Acctg Officer: Richard
Roeske
Conducts Business: U.S.
Employees: 7,000
Primary Market Served: Business &
Consumer
Catalog available online
Advertising/Marketing Budget Related
to Direct Marketing: 0-25%
Gross sales or billing: $8,000,000,000

Mid-west multiple line insurer.

LANCER INSURANCE CO
Div. of Lancer Financial Group
PO Box 9004
Long Beach, NY 11561-9004
Telephone: (516) 431-4441, Toll Free:
(800) 782-8902, FAX: (516) 889-
5111, E-Mail: roneill@lancer-ins.
com, Web Site: www.lancer-ins.com
Pres & CEO: David P. Delaney Jr.
VP, Safety & Engrng: Bob Crescenzo
Exec VP: Timothy D. Delaney
Exec VP: Thomas Theiler
Sr VP, Customer Svc: Randy O'Neill
Conducts Business: U.S.
Employees: 475
Primary Market Served: Business
Catalog available online
Indirect online sales
Advertising/Marketing Budget Related
to Direct Marketing: 51-75%
Direct Marketing ad budget: $100,000
Direct Mail: 60%
Magazines: 25%
Telephone: 15%
Founded: 1945
Gross sales or billing: $275,000,000

Provides commercial automobile &
physical damage insurance coverage to
motor coaches, municipal & school
buses, vanpools, limousines, long-haul
truck owner/operations, oil heat distributors in Northeast U.S. Complete drug
testing services. Also provides commercial automobile & physical damage
insurance coverage to the car rental industry & personal auto and umbrella
coverage to active & retired teachers &
school administrators in NJ.

L'ENTRAIDE ASSURANCE
520 Charest Blvd E (fl1), Quebec-
Centre Station
Quebec, QC, Canada G2J 0A2
Telephone: (418) 658-0663, FAX:
(418) 658-5065, E-Mail: service@
lentraide.com, Web Site: www.
lentraide.com
Chmn, Pres & CEO: Gaetan Gagne
Primary Market Served: Business

LIBERTY LIFE INSURANCE CO

Subs. of Liberty Corp.
2000 Wade Hampton Blvd
Greenville, SC 29615-1064
Telephone: (864) 609-8111, Toll Free:
(800) 344-5834 (Mktg), FAX: (864)
609-4411, Web Site: www.
libertycorp.com
Pres: Robert Evans
Sr VP: Judith Tshibangu
Primary Market Served: Consumer

Life insurance.

LIBERTY MUTUAL GROUP, INC

Subs. of Liberty Mutual Holding Company, Inc
175 Berkeley St
Boston, MA 02116-5066
Telephone: (617) 357-9500, Toll Free:
(800) 837-5274, Web Site: www.
libertymutual.com
Chmn Bd, Pres & CEO: Edmund F.
Kelly
Exec VP & CIO: A. Alexander Fontanes
Exec VP, Personal Markets: J. Paul
Condrin III
Exec VP, Comml Markets: David H.
Long
VP Direct Mktg: Debra Shear
Conducts Business: South America,
East Asia, Spain, Portugal, Poland,
Turkey
Employees: 40,000
Primary Market Served: Consumer
Catalog available online
Indirect online sales
Gross sales or billing: $390,000,000

Direct writing insurance company.

LINCOLN FINANCIAL GROUP

aka Lincoln Financial Corp
150 N Radnor Chester Rd
Radnor, PA 19087
Telephone: (215) 448-1400, Toll Free:
(877) 275-5462, FAX: (215) 448-
3962, Web Site: www.lfg.com
CEO & Pres: Dennis R. Glass
CFO: Randal J. Freitag
Dir: William J. Avery
Conducts Business: Worldwide
Employees: 10,744
Primary Market Served: Business &
Consumer
Direct online sales
Advertising/Marketing Budget Related
to Direct Marketing: 0-25%
Founded: 1905

Gross sales or billing: $1,316,000,000
Market life insurance products & investment services. Mutual funds & financial planning.

LONG & FOSTER INSURANCE

14501 George Carter Way
Chantilly, VA 20151-1770
Telephone: (703) 653-8500
Pres: James Maiden
Primary Market Served: Business

MANULIFE FINANCIAL INC

200 Bloor St E
Toronto, ON, Canada M4W 1E5
Telephone: (416) 229-4515, Toll Free:
(800) 387-0990, FAX: (416) 229-
3028, Web Site: www.manulife.com
Pres & CEO: Donald A. Guloien
Exec VP, Human Resources & Commun: Stephanie E. Kingsmill
Conducts Business: Canada, U.S.
Primary Market Served: Business &
Consumer
Founded: 1887
Gross sales or billing: $1,000,000,000

Market life & health insurance & annuity to credit card holders & members of associations through direct mail & agency sales force.

MARSH AFFINITY GROUP SERVICES

500 W Monroe St (Suite 2400)
Chicago, IL 60661
Toll Free: (800) 621-3008, Web Site:
www.seaburychicago.com
Sr VP, Mktg: Joan O'Sullivan
Primary Market Served: Business &
Consumer
Founded: 1949

Life, health & professional liability insurance, through association sponsorship, for healthcare professionals, accountants & retired persons.

MARSH US CONSUMER

12421 Meredith Dr
Urbandale, IA 50398-9001
Telephone: (515) 365-6102
Mng Dir: Mark M. Poole
CEO: Liz Flynn
Primary Market Served: Business

MASSMUTUAL FINANCIAL GROUP

1295 State St
Springfield, MA 01111-0001
Telephone: (413) 788-8411, FAX:
(413) 744-8889, E-Mail: name@
www.massmutual.com, Web Site:
www.massmutual.com

Pres & CEO: Stuart Reese
Dir of Media & PR: James Lacey
Dir Distr Mktg: David Vermette
Conducts Business: U.S., Chile, Argentina, Bermuda, Luxembourg, Hong
Kong, Japan, Taiwan & Macal
Employees: 28,000
Primary Market Served: Business &
Consumer
Advertising/Marketing Budget Related
to Direct Marketing: 0-25%
Founded: 1851

Diversified insurance & financial services organization.

MEDCO INSURANCE CO

1515 S 75th St
Omaha, NE 68124-1618
Toll Free: (800) 228-6080, E-Mail:
clientservices@gomedico.com, Web
Site: www.gomedico.com
Primary Market Served: Business

MEEMIC INSURANCE CO

1685 N Opdyke Rd
Auburn Hills, MI 48326-2656
Toll Free: (888) 463-3642, Web Site:
www.meemic.com

MERASTAR INSURANCE CO

Subsidiary of Unitrin
5600 Brainerd Rd (Suite 1A)
Chattanooga, TN 37411-5336
Toll Free: (800) 637-2782, FAX: (800)
369-1430, E-Mail: merastar.assist.
team@unitrindirect.com, Web Site:
www.merastar.com
CEO: Tim Brunn
VP Mktg: Don Smith
Dir Mktg: Allyson Bowman
Sr Mktg Mgr: Paul A. Boyles
Mktg Mgr: William J. Capone
VP Sys: Ken Lytle
Conducts Business: U.S.
Employees: 250
Primary Market Served: Business &
Consumer
Catalog available online
Indirect online sales
Advertising/Marketing Budget Related
to Direct Marketing: 76-100%
Direct Marketing ad budget:
$1,500,000
Direct Mail: $1,500,000
Founded: 1974
Gross sales or billing: $30,000,000

Marketer of personal lines of insurance products through employer-sponsored payroll deduction.

METLIFE INTERNATIONAL

2701 Queens Plaza N (#4E-148)
Long Island City, NY 11101-4020
Telephone: (212) 578-3128

VP Direct Mktg: Hallie Harenski

METROPOLITAN PROPERTY & CASUALTY INS

700 Quaker Ln
Warwick, RI 02886-6681
Telephone: (401) 827-2104
Dir: Kevin Raymond
Primary Market Served: Business

THE MIDLAND CO

7000 Midland Blvd
Amelia, OH 45102-2608
Telephone: (513) 943-7200
VP Mktg: Joe David
Primary Market Served: Business &
Consumer

MILLER'S FIRST INSURANCE COMPANIES

111 E Fourth St, PO Box 220
Alton, IL 62002
Telephone: (618) 463-3636, Toll Free:
(800) 558-0500, FAX: (618) 463-
3614, Web Site: www.millersfirst.
com
Pres & CEO: George Milnor
Conducts Business: U.S.
Primary Market Served: Consumer
Catalog available online
Founded: 1888

Homeowner and auto insurance.

MINNESOTA LIFE

Subs of Securian Financial Group, Inc
400 Robert St N
Saint Paul, MN 55101
Telephone: (651) 665-3500, Toll Free:
(888) 237-1838, FAX: (651) 665-
4488, Web Site: www.minnesotalife.
com; www.securian.com
Pres, Chmn & CEO: Robert L. Senkler
Pres & Dir: Randy F. Wallake
Dir Mktg: Paula Bilitz
Conducts Business: U.S., Puerto Rico
Employees: 5,000
Primary Market Served: Business &
Consumer
Gross sales or billing: $2,093,664,000

Provider of insurance, annuities & mutual funds.

MUTUAL OF OMAHA

Mutual of Omaha Plaza (fl 7)
Omaha, NE 68175-0001
Telephone: (402) 342-7600, Toll Free:
(800) 775-6000, FAX: (402) 351-
2775, Web Site: www.
mutualofomaha.com
Chmn & CEO: Daniel P. Neary
Exec VP & CFO: David A. Diamond
Exec VP, Info Svcs: James L. Hanson
Sr VP: Tom Graham
Sr VP DTC Mktg: Stephen Abels

Conducts Business: Worldwide
Employees: 4,867
Primary Market Served: Business &
Consumer
Catalog available online
Founded: 1909
Gross sales or billing: $4,200,000,000

Insurance & financial services.

NATIONAL GENERAL INSURANCE

Subs. of Ally Financial Inc
PO Box 3199
Winston-Salem, NC 27102-3199
Toll Free: (888) 293-5108, Web Site:
www.nationalgeneral.com
Chmn, Pres & CEO: Michael Karfun-
kel
Pres: Byron Storms
CFO: Michael Weiner
Exec VP & Chief Mktg Officer: Barry
Karfunkel
Conducts Business: U.S.
Primary Market Served: Consumer
Catalog available online
Indirect online sales

Sell auto & home insurance.

NGL INSURANCE GROUP

Subs. of National Guardian Life
Two E Gilman St (Stop 1)
Madison, WI 53703-1494
Telephone: (608) 257-5611, Toll Free:
(800) 548-2962, FAX: (608) 257-
9340, Web Site: www.nglic.com
Pres & CEO: Mark L. Solverud
Chmn: John Larson
Treas, Dir Corp Svcs: Robert A. Mucci
VP & Dir Mktg: Steven M. Phelps
VP, Gen Counsel & Asst Sec: Matthew
J. Dew III
Employees: 177
Primary Market Served: Business &
Consumer
Catalog available online
Indirect online sales
Founded: 1984
Gross sales or billing: $253,000,000

Life insurance.

NATIONWIDE MUTUAL INSURANCE CO

1 Nationwide Blvd
Columbus, OH 43215-2220
Telephone: (614) 249-7111, Toll Free:
(800) 882-2822, FAX: (614) 854-
3676, Web Site: www.nationwide.
com
Chmn: Arden L. Shisler
Vice Chmn: James F. Patterson
CEO: Stephen S Rasmussen
Exec VP & CIO: Gail G. Snyder
CFO: Lawrence A. Hilsheimer

Conducts Business: U.S., Puerto Rico,
Virgin Islands, Germany
Employees: 36,000
Primary Market Served: Business &
Consumer
Catalog available online
Gross sales or billing: $22,000,000,000

Market automobile, fire, life, health &
casualty insurance for the individual,
family & business. Involved in providing associated financial services such
as mutual funds.

NEW ENGLAND LIFE INSURANCE CO

Subsidiary of MetLife
501 Boylston St
Boston, MA 02110
Telephone: (617) 578-2000, FAX:
(617) 536-2393, Web Site: www.
nefn.metlife.com
Sr VP, Mktg: George Maloof
Dir Computer Opers: Thomas Yang
Pres: C. Robert Henricson
Conducts Business: U.S.
Employees: 4,000
Primary Market Served: Business &
Consumer
Catalog available online
Founded: 1835
Gross sales or billing: $162,000,000

Insurance & financial services organization.

NEW YORK LIFE INSURANCE CO/AARP

5505 W Cypress St (Suite 300)
Tampa, FL 33607-1707
Telephone: (813) 288-5500, FAX:
(813) 288-5256, Web Site: www.
nylaarp.com
Sr VP: Thomas Kelly
VP, Mktg: Ralph Cohen
Corp VP, Mktg: Victoria Buhrow
First VP Mktg: Victoria Vilaret
Conducts Business: Worldwide
Employees: 10,000
Primary Market Served: Consumer
Direct online sales
Advertising/Marketing Budget Related
to Direct Marketing: 76-100%
Direct Marketing ad budget:
$25,000,000

Financial service company. Provide individual & group life & long term care
insurance.

NORTH AMERICA LIFE INSURANCE CO

1010 Ranch Rd 620 S (Suite 215)
Lakeway, TX 78734-5639
Telephone: (512) 347-1835, Web Site:
www.nagrp.com
Primary Market Served: Consumer

NORTH AMERICAN CO FOR LIFE & HEALTH INSURANCE

525 W Van Buren St Ste 1200
Chicago, IL 60607-3820
Telephone: (312) 648-7600, Toll Free: (800) 800-3656, FAX: (312) 648-7796, Web Site: www.nacolah.com
CEO: Ihor Hron
Adv Dir: Dan Miller
Mktg: Evelyn Pletch
Conducts Business: U.S.
Primary Market Served: Business & Consumer
Advertising/Marketing Budget Related to Direct Marketing: 0-25%
Founded: 1905

Life & health insurance & annuities.

OXFORD HEALTH PLANS, INC

48 Monroe Turnpike
Trumbull, CT 06611
Toll Free: (800) 889-7658, FAX: (203) 459-6464, E-Mail: info@speedmat.com, Web Site: www.oxhp.com
Primary Market Served: Business & Consumer

Healthcare insurance.

PPI BENEFIT SOLUTIONS

10 Research Pkwy
Wallingford, CT 06492-1963
Toll Free: (888) 674-0046, FAX: (203) 468-9886, E-Mail: clientservices@ppibenefits.com, Web Site: www.ppibenefits.com
Pres: Luis Nunes
Conducts Business: U.S.
Employees: 52
Primary Market Served: Business

Sell pension plans & group insurance to associations & individual employers.

PARCEL INSURANCE PLAN INC

PO Box 66708, Saint Louis, MO 63166-6708
Subs. of Brown & Brown Insurance
9666 Olive Blvd (Suite 200)
Saint Louis, MO 63132-3012
Telephone: (314) 692-0300, Toll Free: (800) 325-7390, FAX: (314) 692-7598, E-Mail: office@pipinsure.com, Web Site: www.pipinsure.com
Pres: Charles Smith Jr.
VP: Ric Victores
Mktg Dir: Scott Gehner
Conducts Business: U.S.
Employees: 15
Primary Market Served: Business
Indirect online sales
Advertising/Marketing Budget Related to Direct Marketing: 0-25%

Direct Marketing ad budget:
Direct Mail: 25%
Magazines: 5%
Telephone: 70%
Founded: 1966

Sell UPS, parcel post & air cargo insurance at low cost. Offer reduced record-keeping. Sell direct to high volume small parcel shippers. Mailing address: PO Box 66708, Saint Louis, MO 63166-6708.

PARTNERS HEALTH

901 Market St (Suite 500)
Philadelphia, PA 19107
Telephone: (215) 849-9600, Toll Free: (800) 553-0784, E-Mail: sroberts@healthpart.com, Web Site: www.healthpart.com
Pres & CEO: William George
Sr VP Bus Developer: Judy B. Harrington
Sr VP Chief Medical Officer: Vicki Sessoms
Sr VP Opers & COO: Elaine Markezin
Conducts Business: U.S.
Employees: 550
Primary Market Served: Business & Consumer
Founded: 1985

HMO.

PEARL INSURANCE GROUP LLC

1200 E Glen Ave
Peoria Heights, IL 61616-5325
Telephone: (309) 688-9000, Web Site: www.pearlinsurance.com
Exec VP, Chief Sls & Mktg Officer: Michael Murphy
Primary Market Served: Business

PEMCO INSURANCE COS

325 Eastlake Ave E
Seattle, WA 98109-5466
Telephone: (206) 628-4000, Toll Free: (800) 467-3626, FAX: (206) 628-5886, Web Site: www.pemco.com
CEO, Pres & Chmn: Stanley W. McNaughton
Sr VP & COO: Steve Miller
VP Chief Mktg Officer: Rod Brooks
Commun Mgr: Jon Osterberg
Conducts Business: U.S.
Employees: 1,150
Primary Market Served: Consumer
Founded: 1949
Gross sales or billing: $232,000,000

Group of insurance companies offering auto, home, boat, excess personal liability & life insurance to the general public & the educational industry in Washington.

PENN MUTUAL

600 Dresher Rd
Horsham, PA 19044-2204
Telephone: (215) 956-8083, FAX: (215) 956-8368, Web Site: www.pennmutual.com
Chmn & CEO: Robert E. Chappell
Pres & COO: Daniel J. Toran
Mktg Support Grp Mgr: Wendy A. Madonna
Mktg Support Grp Mgr: Judy Nigro
Dir Prog Mktg: Tracy Marrocco
Conducts Business: U.S.
Employees: 600
Primary Market Served: Business & Consumer
Advertising/Marketing Budget Related to Direct Marketing: 0-25%
Founded: 1847
Gross sales or billing: $250,000,000

Life insurance & financial services.

PEOPLES BENEFIT LIFE INSURANCE CO

Div. of Aegon USA
300 Eagleview Blvd
Exton, PA 19341-1155
Telephone: (610) 648-5000, FAX: (610) 648-5348
Mktg Dir: Lou Whalen
Conducts Business: U.S.
Employees: 2,000
Primary Market Served: Consumer
Direct Marketing ad budget: $85,000,000

Market life & health insurance & related financial services through multimedia direct response to the general public, credit card files, credit unions, veterans & other affinity groups, customer lists & association members.

THE PHILADELPHIA CONTRIBUTORSHIP INSURANCE CO

212 S Fourth St
Philadelphia, PA 19106-3787
Telephone: (215) 627-1752, Toll Free: (800) 346-9229, E-Mail: info@contributorship.com, Web Site: www.contributorship.com
VP, Mktg: Joan Saracino
Primary Market Served: Consumer
Catalog available online
Founded: 1752

Homeowners insurance.

PHYSICIANS MUTUAL INSURANCE CO

2600 Dodge St
Omaha, NE 68131

Telephone: (402) 633-1604, Toll Free: (888) 932-7642, FAX: (402) 633-1604, Web Site: www.physiciansmutual.com
Chmn: William R. Hamsa
Pres & CEO: Robert A. Reed
Exec VP & COO: Edward W. Graycar
Mgr: Mike Story
Conducts Business: U.S.
Employees: 1,000
Primary Market Served: Consumer
Catalog available online
Advertising/Marketing Budget Related to Direct Marketing: 76-100%
Founded: 1902

Individual health & accident supplementary insurance. Individual life insurance.

PLYMOUTH ROCK ASSURANCE

PO Box 906
Lincroft, NJ 07738-0906
Telephone: (732) 978-6255, Web Site: www.highpointins.com
Admin Asst.: Donna Diehl
Pres & CEO: Gerry Wilson
Primary Market Served: Business & Consumer

PREMERA BLUE CROSS

3900 E Sprague Ave (Bldg 1)
Spokane, WA 99202-4847
Telephone: (425) 670-4000, Toll Free: (800) 422-0032, FAX: (425) 670-5853, Web Site: www.premera.com
Chief Mktg Officer & Exec VP Sls: C. Marion Butler
DM: Chris Wickizer
Exec VP & CFO: Kent Marquardt
Sr Mgr Producer Rels & Mktg: Kelly Jones
Conducts Business: U.S.
Primary Market Served: Business & Consumer

Marketer of health insurance products.

THE PRINCIPAL FINANCIAL GROUP

711 High St
Des Moines, IA 50392-0330
Telephone: (515) 247-5111, Toll Free: (800) 986-3343, FAX: (515) 246-5475, Web Site: www.principal.com
Chmn, Pres & CEO: Larry D. Zimpleman
Exec VP & CFO: Michael H. Gersie
VP, Mktg: Mike Beer
Conducts Business: Worldwide
Employees: 15,200
Primary Market Served: Business & Consumer
Catalog available online

Gross sales or billing: $9,800,000,000
Insurance.

PROFILE COVERAGE CORP

PO Box 9081
Melville, NY 11747-9081
Telephone: (631) 981-7600, FAX: (631) 981-7681, E-Mail: info@profileinsure.com, Web Site: www.profileinsure.com
Pres: Louis Pellegrino
Conducts Business: U.S.
Employees: 28
Primary Market Served: Business
Advertising/Marketing Budget Related to Direct Marketing: 0-25%
Gross sales or billing: $3,600,000

Full service insurance agency selling personal, commercial & health insurance.

THE PROGRESSIVE CORP

6300 Wilson Mills Rd
Mayfield Village, OH 44143-2182
Telephone: (440) 461-5000, Toll Free: (800) PROGRESSIVE, (800) 776-4737, FAX: (800) 456-6590, Web Site: www.progressive.com
Chmn: Peter B. Lewis
Pres & CEO: Glen M. Renwick
CFO: Brian C. Domeck
CIO: Raymond M. Voelker
VP: Jeffrey W. Basch
Employees: 27,778
Primary Market Served: Business & Consumer
Catalog available online
Direct online sales
Advertising/Marketing Budget Related to Direct Marketing: 26-50%
Founded: 1965
Gross sales or billing: $14,786,400,000

Leader in nonstandard, high-risk personal auto insurance. Standard-risk and preferred auto insurance, personal use coverage (motorcycles, recreational vehicles & snowmobiles), collateral insurance for auto lenders, directors' & officers' insurance & employee misconduct insurance.

PROTECTIVE LIFE CORP

PO Box 770
Deerfield, IL 60015-0770
Telephone: (847) 948-8988, Toll Free: (800) 323-5771, FAX: (847) 948-1156, Web Site: www.protective.com
Chmn, Pres & CEO: John D. Johns
Vice Chmn & CFO: Richard J. Bielen
Exec VP & COO: Carolyn M. Johnson
Sr VP: Brent Griggs
Sr VP: Thomas D. Keyes
Conducts Business: U.S.
Employees: 180
Primary Market Served: Business

Catalog available online
Direct Marketing ad budget:
Magazines: $500,000
Gross sales or billing: $150,000,000

Sell credit insurance via direct marketing.

PROTECTIVE LIFE INSURANCE CO

Div. of Protective Life Corp
2801 Hwy 280 S
Birmingham, AL 35223-2488
Telephone: (205) 268-1000, Toll Free: (800) 866-3555, FAX: (205) 868-3086, Web Site: www.protective.com
Pres: John E. Johns
Sr VP, Fin Institutions Insurance Div: Steven A. Schultz
Conducts Business: U.S., Guam
Employees: 1,000
Primary Market Served: Business & Consumer
Direct Marketing ad budget: $250,000
Founded: 1907

Sell life, accidental death, accident, health (disability) & investment products through direct marketing methods.

REASSURE AMERICA LIFE INSURANCE CO

Affiliate of Swiss Re
1275 Sandusky Rd
Jacksonville, IL 62650
Toll Free: (800) 637-4475, FAX: (217) 291-2398, Web Site: www.swissre.com
Pres: W. Weldon Wilson
Conducts Business: U.S.
Employees: 128
Primary Market Served: Consumer
Founded: 1950
Gross sales or billing: $52,200,000

Sell life, accident & health insurance to consumers by direct response techniques.

REGIT INC

1200 Roosevelt Rd (Suite 115)
Glen Ellyn, IL 60137
Telephone: (630) 495-1500, Toll Free: (800) 537-9786, FAX: (630) 495-1611, E-Mail: regit@regitinc.com, Web Site: www.regitinc.com
Pres: Donna Freestate
Mktg Dir: Marilyn Smaron
Conducts Business: U.S.
Primary Market Served: Consumer

Market health insurance to real estate professionals.

REMARK USA

Subs. of Reinsurers Marketing BV Amstelveen Holland
3033 Campus Dr (Suite W205)

Minnetonka, MN 55441-2702
Telephone: (952) 938-4699, FAX:
(952) 988-8500, E-Mail: jessica.
sbragia@remarkgroup.com, Web
Site: www.remarkamericas.com
CEO: Michael Levison
Pres: Brad Smith
Chief Mktg Officer: Jessica Sbragia
Conducts Business: U.S., Canada, U.
K., Holland, Australia
Primary Market Served: Consumer
Advertising/Marketing Budget Related
to Direct Marketing: 76-100%
Direct Marketing ad budget:
Direct Mail: 100%
Gross sales or billing: $2,700,000

Design & implement direct marketing
programs which provide life & accident
insurance offers to customers of financial institutions, insurance companies
& banks.

RESERVE NATIONAL INSURANCE CO

PO Box 138801
Oklahoma City, OK 73113-8801
Telephone: (405) 848-7931, Web Site:
www.reservenational.com
Sr VP Opers: Orin Crossley

RESPONSE INSURANCE

PO Box 4079
Scranton, PA 18505-6079
Telephone: (203) 634-7255, Toll Free:
(800) 518-2984, FAX: (203) 634-
7319, E-Mail: webcs@response.com,
Web Site: www.response.com
Exec VP & COO: John Ammendola
VP, Fin: George Kowalsky
VP, Customer Svc & Sls: Kathleen A.
Gleeson
Primary Market Served: Consumer
Founded: 1995

Direct writer of auto insurance.

SCA PROMOTIONS INC

3030 Lyndon B Johnson Fwy (Suite
300)
Dallas, TX 75234
Telephone: (214) 860-3700, Toll Free:
(888) 860-3700, FAX: (214) 860-
3723, E-Mail: scainfo@scapromo.
com, Web Site: www.scapromo.com
Pres & Founder: Robert Hamman
Mktg Coord: Nancy Rodriguez
Conducts Business: U.S., Canada
Employees: 40
Primary Market Served: Business
Catalog available online
Advertising/Marketing Budget Related
to Direct Marketing: 0-25%

Founded: 1986
Offers fixed fee solutions for jumbo
prize funding, conditional prize fulfillment & over redemption protection, to
eliminate risk in promotional programs
such as contests, internet games and
telecards.

SAFECO INSURANCE CO

4333 Brooklyn NE
Seattle, WA 98185-0001
Telephone: (206) 545-5000, Toll Free:
(800) 332-3226, FAX: (206) 545-
5767/5651, Web Site: www.safeco.
com
Pres & CEO: Paula Rosput Reynolds
Exec VP & Chief Legal Officer: Arthur
Chong
Exec VP, Insurance Opers: Mike
Hughes
AVP Mktg: DeAnna Kerrick
Exec VP & CFO: Ross Kari
CIO: William Jenks
Conducts Business: U.S.
Employees: 7,000
Primary Market Served: Business &
Consumer
Catalog available online
Indirect online sales
Advertising/Marketing Budget Related
to Direct Marketing: 26-50%
Founded: 1923
Gross sales or billing: $6,200,000,000

Insurance & financial products sold to
consumers.

SAFEWARE, THE INSURANCE AGENCY INC

6500 Busch Blvd (Suite 233)
Columbus, OH 43229
Telephone: (614) 781-1492, Toll Free:
(800) 800-1492, FAX: (614) 781-
0559, E-Mail: service@safeware.
com, Web Site: www.safeware.com
Pres & CFO: James Johnson
Dir: Arthur Heggen
Conducts Business: Worldwide
Employees: 24
Primary Market Served: Business &
Consumer
Catalog available online
Indirect online sales
Advertising/Marketing Budget Related
to Direct Marketing: 76-100%
Direct Marketing ad budget: $250,000
Magazines: 10%
Telephone: 90%
Founded: 1982
Gross sales or billing: $3,000,000

Insurance for computer owners for
business & personal uses. Covers computers against theft, fire, power surges,
natural disasters & while in transit.

SAVINGS BANK LIFE INSURANCE CO OF MA (SBLI)

1 Linscott Rd
Woburn, MA 01801-2001
Telephone: (781) 938-3500, Web Site:
www.sbli.com
VP, Dir: Rose Cahill
Primary Market Served: Consumer

SELMAN & CO

6110 Parkland Blvd
Cleveland, OH 44124-4187
Telephone: (440) 646-9336, Toll Free:
(800) 735-6262, FAX: (440) 646-
9339, E-Mail: ldenning@
selmaninsurance.com, Web Site:
www.sel-co.com
Chmn: John L. Selman
Pres: David L. Selman
Mktg Dir: Laura Denning
Conducts Business: U.S.
Employees: 100
Primary Market Served: Consumer
Catalog available online
Direct online sales
Advertising/Marketing Budget Related
to Direct Marketing: 51-75%
Founded: 1905

Insurance agency/third-party administration specializing in direct marketing
of life & health, property & casualty insurance to professional associations &
financial institutions.

SENTRY LIFE INSURANCE CO

Subs. of Sentry Insurance Co
1800 Northpoint Dr
Stevens Point, WI 54481
Telephone: (715) 346-6000, FAX:
(715) 346-7028, E-Mail: infoctr@
coredcs.com, Web Site: www.sentry.
com
Pres & CEO: Dale Schuh
VP & COO: Bob Recko
Conducts Business: U.S.
Primary Market Served: Business &
Consumer

Sell life, health, auto, home, commercial, group & individual insurance, also
retirement planning.

SHELBY INSURANCE COMPANIES

2 Perimeter Park S (Suite 423E)
Birmingham, AL 35243-3282
Toll Free: (800) 443-1573, FAX: (877)
837-8203, Web Site: www.vesta.com
Sr VP, CFO & Treas: W. Perry Cronin
VP Mktg: Howard Barber

Primary Market Served: Business & Consumer

Property casualty insurance company; markets through independent agents. Providing homeowners, automobile, dwelling fire, umbrella (personal catastrophe). Non-standard automobile and other insurance needs.

SPECTRUM ECOMMERCE
26023 Acero (Suite 100)
Mission Viejo, CA 92691-7942
Telephone: (949) 600-7900, Web Site: elifemarketers.com
Pres: Sy Alter
Primary Market Served: Consumer

STANDARD LIFE
1245 Sherbrooke St W
Montreal, QC, Canada H3G 1G3
Telephone: (514) 499-8855, Toll Free: (877) 499-9555, FAX: (514) 499-4908, Web Site: www.standardlife.ca
Pres & CEO: Charles Guay
Sr VP Retail Markets: Dennis Berthiaume
Sr VP Grp Savings & Retirement: Anthony Cardone
CFO: Christian Martineau
Sr VP Legal & Compliance: Penny Westman
Conducts Business: U.S., Canada
Primary Market Served: Business & Consumer
Catalog available online
Gross sales or billing: $30,000,000

Direct marketer to promote healthcare insurance coverage through mailings.

STARMOUNT LIFE INSURANCE CO
8485 Goodwood Blvd
Baton Rouge, LA 70806-7878
Telephone: (225) 926-2888, Toll Free: (888) 729-5433, (888) 729-7827, E-Mail: info@starmountlife.com, Web Site: www.starmountlife.com
Chmn: Hans J. Sternberg
Pres: Erich Sternberg
Exec VP: Donna Sternberg
Mktg Coord: Julie Andre
Exec VP: Deborah Sternberg
Conducts Business: U.S.
Employees: 160
Primary Market Served: Consumer
Catalog available online
Direct online sales
Advertising/Marketing Budget Related to Direct Marketing: 76-100%
Direct Marketing ad budget:
Direct Mail: 95%
Newspapers: 5%
Founded: 1983

Gross sales or billing: $40,000,000
Life, accident & health insurance.

STATE FARM INSURANCE COS
1 State Farm Plaza
Bloomington, IL 61710-0001
Telephone: (309) 766-2311, FAX: (309) 766-3621, Web Site: www.statefarm.com
Chmn & CEO: Edward B. Rust Jr.
Vice Chmn, CFO & Treas: Michael L. Tipsord
Vice Chmn & CMO: Michael C. Davidson
Vice Chmn & CAO: James E. Rutrough
Sr Exec VP: Jack W. North
Dir, Database Mktg: Don Lynn
Conducts Business: U.S., Canada
Employees: 57,000
Primary Market Served: Business & Consumer
Catalog available online
Indirect online sales
Advertising/Marketing Budget Related to Direct Marketing: 51-75%
Direct Marketing ad budget:
Direct Mail: $7,000,000
Founded: 1922

STATE MUTUAL INSURANCE CO
PO Box 153
Rome, GA 30162-0153
Telephone: (706) 291-1054, FAX: (706) 291-9459
VP: J. Gary Barton
Employees: 11
Primary Market Served: Business & Consumer
Gross sales or billing: $19,600,000
Sells all forms of insurance.

SUNLIFE OF CANADA
1 Sunlife Executive Park
Wellesley Hills, MA 02481
Telephone: (781) 237-6030, Toll Free: (800) SUNLIFE, FAX: (781) 446-1779, Web Site: www.sunlife-usa.com
CEO: Donald A. Stewart
Corp Dir: Krystyna T. Hoeg
Corp Dir: David Kerr
Conducts Business: Worldwide
Primary Market Served: Business & Consumer
Catalog available online
Gross sales or billing: $6,100,000,000
Group individuals & annuities.

JOHN SUTHERLAND & ASSOCIATES
6275 Lusk Blvd

San Diego, CA 92121-2731
Telephone: (858) 535-1139, Toll Free: (800) 545-9591, FAX: (858) 535-9124
CEO: Smokey Sutherland
Dir: Joanne Garcia
Conducts Business: U.S.
Employees: 10
Primary Market Served: Consumer
Gross sales or billing: $900,000

Water bed insurance.

SYMETRA FINANCIAL
777 108th Ave (Suite 1200)
Bellevue, WA 98004-5135
Telephone: (425) 256-8000, Toll Free: (800) 426-7355, FAX: (425) 256-5737, Web Site: www.symetra.com
Chmn: Lowndes A. Smith
Pres & CEO: Thomas M. Marra
Asst VP & Dir, Commun: Colin Johnson
Dir: Peter S. Burgess
Exec VP & COO: Roger F. Harbin
Sr VP Gen Agency & Advisor Distr: Allyn D. Close
Conducts Business: U.S.
Employees: 1,200
Primary Market Served: Business & Consumer
Founded: 1923
Gross sales or billing: $1,500,000,000

Life insurance company selling through independent agents & financial planners. Regional offices: Atlanta, GA; Chicago, IL; Fountain Valley, CA; Redmond, WA.

TIAA-CREF
730 Third Ave
New York, NY 10017
Telephone: (212) 490-9000, FAX: (212) 916-6505, Web Site: www.tiaa-cref.org
Head Mktg: Jamie Depeau
Conducts Business: U.S., Canada
Employees: 3,800
Primary Market Served: Business & Consumer

Sell pensions & insurance to education market.

TEXAS FARM BUREAU INSURANCE COS
7420 Fish Pond Rd
Waco, TX 76710-1010
Telephone: (254) 751-2688, Web Site: www.txfb-ins.com
VP Mktg: Kimberly Kemper
Primary Market Served: Consumer

TRANSAMERICA LIFE & PROTECTION
520 Park Ave

Baltimore, MD 21201-4500
Telephone: (410) 209-5617, Web Site:
www.aegondms.com

TRANSAMERICA LIFE INSURANCE CO

Subs. of Aegon
4333 Edgewood Rd NE
Cedar Rapids, IA 52499
Telephone: (319) 398-8511, Toll Free:
(800) 558-9011, FAX: (319) 369-
2825, Web Site: www.transamerica.
com
Chmn & Pres: Larry M. Norman
Exec VP, COO & Dir: Brenda K. Clan-
cey
Sr VP & CFO: Darryl D. Button
Conducts Business: U.S.
Employees: 300
Primary Market Served: Consumer
Indirect online sales
Direct Marketing ad budget:
Direct Mail: $25,000
Gross sales or billing: $139,000,000

Sell life insurance.

TRANSAMERICA OCCIDENTAL LIFE CO

Subs. of Aegon USA
1150 S Olive St (T-24)
Los Angeles, CA 90015
Telephone: (213) 742-3111, FAX:
(213) 741-6623, Web Site: www.
transamerica.com
Pres & Chmn: Ron Wagley
Sr VP & CIO: Eric Goodman
VP & COO: Paul Reaburn
VP, Counsel & Sec: Craig D. Vermie
Conducts Business: U.S., Canada, Eu-
rope, Hong Kong, Puerto Rico,
Guam, Virgin Islands
Employees: 3,700
Primary Market Served: Business &
Consumer
Direct Marketing ad budget:
Direct Mail: $1,000,000
Founded: 1911
Gross sales or billing: $2,100,000,000

Promote the sale of life insurance & related financial services to the general
public.

TRANSAMERICA RETIREMENT SERVICES

1150 S Olive St (#T-9-10)
Los Angeles, CA 90015-2211
Telephone: (213) 742-3363, Web Site:
www.ta-retirement.com
VP Mktg: Dave Shute

Provides companies with retirement
plan benefits for their employees. Services include turn-key retirement plans,

profit sharing, defined benefit & new
comparability plans for clients & third
party administrators

THE TRAVELERS INSURANCE COS

1 Tower Sq (#9PB-B)
Hartford, CT 06183-0001
Telephone: (860) 277-8252, (651) 317-
2685, FAX: (860) 954-7691, Web
Site: www.travelers.com
VP Corp Commun Adv: Joan Palm
Mktg Mgr: Patrick Todd
Primary Market Served: Business &
Consumer
Founded: 1864

Insurance & financial services.

TRIGON BLUE CROSS/BLUE SHIELD

602 S Jefferson St, PO Box 13047
Roanoke, VA 24011
Telephone: (540) 853-5000, Toll Free:
(800) 553-3164, FAX: (540) 853-
3053, Web Site: www.trigon.com
Pres: Tom Snead
Mktg Dir: James Hicks
Direct Response Mgr: Lora Lee Hart
Primary Market Served: Business &
Consumer
Advertising/Marketing Budget Related
to Direct Marketing: 51-75%

Health insurance.

21ST CENTURY INSURANCE

Owned by AIG
6301 Owensmouth Ave
Woodland Hills, CA 91367
Telephone: (818) 704-3700, FAX:
(818) 226-1198, E-Mail:
executiveoffice@21st.com, Web
Site: www.21st.com
Chmn: Robert M. Sandler
Pres & CEO: Bruce W. Marlow
Mktg Mgr: Bernarda Durate
Employees: 2,500
Primary Market Served: Consumer
Founded: 1958
Gross sales or billing: $1,375,300,000

Insurance company.

2-10 HOME BUYERS WARRANTY

10375 E Harvard Ave, 1 Denver High-
lands (Suite 100)
Denver, CO 80231-3966
Telephone: (720) 747-6000, Web Site:
www.2-10.com
Gen Mgr Direct Sls: Frederick Diehl

USAA

United Services Automobile Association

9800 Fredericksburg Rd, USAA Build-
ing
San Antonio, TX 78240-4100
Telephone: (512) 498-6524, FAX:
(512) 498-8000
Chmn: Gen Herres
Pres: Edwin L. Rosane
Sr VP Mktg: Kenneth A. McClure
VP Sales: Art Settles
Exec Dir, Mktg Svcs: Barbara Shields
Conducts Business: Worldwide
Primary Market Served: Business &
Consumer
Direct Marketing ad budget:
$2,700,000
Telephone: 100%

Offer a complete line of life & health
insurance & annuities.

USI AFFINITY

Subs. of USI Holdings Corp
1 International Plz (Suite 400)
Philadelphia, PA 19113-1535
Telephone: (610) 833-2876, Toll Free:
(800) 625-2876, FAX: (610) 265-
2876, E-Mail: info@usiaffinity.com,
Web Site: www.brcorp.com
Chmn, Pres & CEO: Alan Zink
VP, Mktg: Anne Keenan
VP: James A. Young
VP: Jose Rivera
Sr VP: Joseph B. Kaiser
Conducts Business: U.S.
Employees: 115
Primary Market Served: Consumer
Direct Marketing ad budget:
Direct Mail: $800,000
Magazines: $30,000
Founded: 1944

Insurance administrators. Branch Offices: Chicago, IL, Boston, MA & Washington, DC.

USI AFFINITY COLLEGIATE INSURANCE RESOURCES

3070 Riverside Dr
Columbus, OH 43221-2547
Telephone: (614) 486-5388, Web Site:
www.collegiateinsuranceresources.
com
COO: Jeff Roedel

UNIFORMED SERVICES BENEFIT ASSOCIATION

10895 Grandview Dr (Suite 350)
Overland Park, KS 66210
Toll Free: (800) 368-7021, Web Site:
www.usba.com
Pres & CEO: Col Robin A. Snyder
USAF (Ret)
Conducts Business: U.S.
Employees: 68
Primary Market Served: Consumer
Catalog available online
Indirect online sales

Advertising/Marketing Budget Related to Direct Marketing: 76-100%
Direct Marketing ad budget: $1,100,000
Direct Mail: 30%
Magazines: 40%
Newspapers: 30%
Founded: 1959
Gross sales or billing: $25,000,000

Sell life insurance, health insurance & financial services to military veterans & federal employees.

THE UNION LABOR LIFE INSURANCE CO

Div. of Ullico Inc
8403 Colesville Rd
Silver Spring, MD 20910-6331
Telephone: (202) 962-2945, FAX: (202) 962-8429, E-Mail: info@ullico.com, Web Site: www.unioncare.com
Chmn, Pres & CEO: Mark E. Singleton
Mktg Mgr, Direct Mktg: Tammi Leathers
Dir Mktg Indus Life Insurance & Illustration Actuary: Blaine Barham
Conducts Business: U.S., Canada
Employees: 1,520
Primary Market Served: Consumer
Advertising/Marketing Budget Related to Direct Marketing: 76-100%
Direct Marketing ad budget: $2,400,000
Direct Mail: 100%
Founded: 1925
Gross sales or billing: $539,000,000

Insurance programs for third party clients.

UNITED INVESTORS LIFE INSURANCE CO

Div. of Torchmark Corp
2001 3rd Ave S Bsmt, Box 10207
Birmingham, AL 35233-2196
Telephone: (205) 325-4300, Toll Free: (800) 288-2722, FAX: (205) 325-4157, Web Site: www.uilic.com
Pres & CEO: Anthony McWhorter
Sr VP, Chief Actuary: Thomas Aycock
VP, Mktg: Ross Stagner
VP, Controller: James L. Mayton Jr.
Conducts Business: U.S.
Employees: 100
Primary Market Served: Business & Consumer
Gross sales or billing: $339,000,000

Sell life insurance to consumers.

UNUM CORP

2211 Congress St (Suite B118)
Portland, ME 04122
Telephone: (207) 770-2211, Toll Free: (800) 421-0344, FAX: (207) 770-4510, Web Site: www.unum.com
Pres & CEO: Thomas R. Watjen
Exec VP, CFO & Chief Actuary: Robert C. Greving
Exec VP & Gen Counsel: Charles Glick
Pres & CEO Unum US: Kevin P. McCarthy
Conducts Business: U.S., Canada, U.K., France
Employees: 4,000
Primary Market Served: Business & Consumer
Gross sales or billing: $1,500,000,000

Insurance marketer.

WELLMARK BLUE CROSS & BLUE SHIELD OF IOWA

PO Box 9232, 1331 Grand Ave
Des Moines, IA 50306-9232
Telephone: (515) 376-4500, Toll Free: (800) 524-9242, FAX: (515) 323-7722, Web Site: www.wellmark.com
Chmn & CEO: John Forsyth
Primary Market Served: Business & Consumer

Health insurance & financial service.

WESTERN-SOUTHERN LIFE

400 Broadway
Cincinnati, OH 45202-3312
Telephone: (513) 629-1800, Web Site: www.westernsouthernlife.com
Mktg Officer: Jim DeLuca
Primary Market Served: Consumer

XL ENVIRONMENTAL

Div. of Capital Ltd
505 Eagleview Blvd
Exton, PA 19341-1119
Telephone: (610) 968-9500, Toll Free: (800) 327-1414, FAX: (610) 458-9109, E-Mail: webinfo.xli@xlgroup.com, Web Site: www.xlenvironmental.com
VP Mktg & Commun NA: Sarah German
Conducts Business: U.S.
Employees: 468
Primary Market Served: Business
Advertising/Marketing Budget Related to Direct Marketing: 0-25%
Founded: 1985
Gross sales or billing: $32,200,000

Insurance for hazardous waste companies.

ZURICH

1400 American Ln
Schaumburg, IL 60196-5452
Telephone: (847) 605-3712, Toll Free: (800) 382-2150, FAX: (847) 605-6403, Web Site: www.zurichna.com
CEO: Martin Senn
Pres Programs & Direct Markets: Tina Mallie
VP, Direct Mktg: Kathleen Trautmann
Exec VP: David Banks
Employees: 1,200
Primary Market Served: Business & Consumer
Catalog available online
Founded: 1996
Gross sales or billing: $19,800,000,000

Sell life insurance & annuities.

Merchandise & Services (16)

A&B EQUIPMENT CO
2101 Riverside Dr
Fort Worth, TX 76103-2120
Telephone: (817) 332-8361, Toll Free:
(800) 426-0683, FAX: (817) 332-
8430
Gen Mgr: Holly Hughes
Conducts Business: U.S.
Employees: 25
Primary Market Served: Business
Advertising/Marketing Budget Related
to Direct Marketing: 26-50%
Direct Marketing ad budget: $50,000
Direct Mail: 100%

Sell construction equipment to construction companies.

A&P
2 Paragon Dr
Montvale, NJ 07645
Telephone: (201) 573-9700, Toll Free:
(866) 44 FRESH, FAX: (201) 505-
3054, E-Mail: apcustomerrel@aptea.
com, Web Site: www.aptea.com
Pres & CEO: Paul Hertz
Chmn Bd: Greg Mays
Dir Mktg & Adv: Beth Curran
Employees: 38,000
Primary Market Served: Consumer
Gross sales or billing: $6,800,000,000

Retail supermarket chain.

A LA CARTE
Div. of David Scott Industries
5610 W Bloomingdale Rd
Chicago, IL 60639
Telephone: (773) 745-5900, Toll Free:
(800) 723-2370, FAX: (773) 237-
3075, E-Mail: service@alacarteline.
com, Web Site: www.alacarteline.
com
Pres: Mike Shulkin
Conducts Business: U.S.
Employees: 25
Primary Market Served: Business &
Consumer
Catalog available online
Indirect online sales
Gross sales or billing: $1,000,000

Direct mail marketer of incentives, executive gifts & gourmet foods. Decorator of all types of cans & tins.
Manufacturer of private label microwave popcorn & candies.

AAA UMBRELLA CO INC
230 Pegasus Ave
Northvale, NJ 07647-1904

Telephone: (201) 784-3242, Toll Free:
(800) 426-7446, FAX: (201) 226-
0041, E-Mail: sales@aaaumbrella.
com, Web Site: www.aaaumbrella.
com
Pres: Jeff Nanus
Conducts Business: U.S., Canada
Employees: 18
Primary Market Served: Business

Umbrellas as premium items.

ACCO BRANDS CORP
Four Corporate Dr
Lake Zurich, IL 60047-8997
Telephone: (800) 222-6462, FAX:
(800) 247-1317, Web Site: www.
accobrands.com
Pres & CEO: Boris Elisman
Conducts Business: US, Canada, Europe
Employees: 500
Primary Market Served: Business &
Consumer

Manufacturer of office, school & computer supplies & furniture sold through commercial & mass market retailers.

ADM PRODUCTIONS INC
40 Seaview Blvd
Port Washington, NY 11050-4618
Telephone: (516) 484-6900, Toll Free:
(800) ADM-DIAL, FAX: (516) 621-
2531, Web Site: www.admpro.com
Pres & CEO: Anthony DeMartino
VP & CFO: Angelo DeMartino
Producer: John Dunn
Employees: 50
Primary Market Served: Business
Advertising/Marketing Budget Related
to Direct Marketing: 26-50%
Direct Marketing ad budget:
Direct Mail: 20%
Magazines: 20%
Newspapers: 20%
TV/Radio: 20%
Telephone: 20%
Founded: 1981
Gross sales or billing: $16,000,000

Specialize in creating & producing dynamic corporate image, sales/marketing & training films & videos. Majority of clients are corporate.

ADP INC
aka Automatic Data Processing, Inc
1 ADP Blvd
Roseland, NJ 07068-1728
Telephone: (973) 974-5000, Toll Free:
(800) 225-5237, FAX: (973) 974-
3334, Web Site: www.adp.com
Pres & CEO: Carlos Rodriguez

Exec VP Worldwide Sales & Mktg:
Edward B. Flynn III
Conducts Business: U.S.
Employees: 46,000
Primary Market Served: Business
Founded: 1949
Gross sales or billing: $7,800,000,000

Leading provider of payroll & employer related services in U.S.

ADT LLC
dba ADT Security Services
1501 Yamato Rd
Boca Raton, FL 33431
Telephone: (561) 988-3600, FAX:
(561) 988-3673, Web Site: www.adt.
com
Pres & CEO: Naren K. Gurshaney
Sr VP & Chief Mktg Officer: Jerri De-
Vard
Primary Market Served: Business &
Consumer
Catalog available online
Gross sales or billing: $11,000,000,000
Manufacture of anti-theft devices.

AFA SERVICE CORP
3495 Piedmont Rd NE 11
Atlanta, GA 30305
Telephone: (404) 237-2964, (404) 262-
2729, Web Site: www.arbys.com
Pres & Chief Mktg Officer: Debbie
Pike
Primary Market Served: Business

Create & produce all creative materials for Arby's Roast Beef Restaurants.

AIN PLASTICS INC
Div. of Thyssen Kruup Materials NA,
Inc
60 Fullerton Ave
Yonkers, NY 10704
Telephone: (914) 668-6800, Toll Free:
(800) 431-2451, FAX: (914) 668-
8820, Web Site: www.ainplastics.
com
Sls Mgr: John Colleluori
Conducts Business: U.S., Canada
Employees: 250
Primary Market Served: Business &
Consumer
Catalog available online
Direct online sales
Advertising/Marketing Budget Related
to Direct Marketing: 51-75%
Founded: 1970
Gross sales or billing: $10,000,000

Plastic, sheet, rod, tube, film & accessories.

AON INNOVATIVE SOLUTIONS

200 East Randolph St
Chicago, IL 60601
Telephone: (312) 381-1000, Web Site:
www.aon.com
Pres & CEO: Gregory C. Case
Global Chief Mktg & Commun Officer: Philip B. Clement
Primary Market Served: Business

Provider of customer services & technology support solutions for Fortune 500 companies.

APW-WRIGHT LINE

Div. of Applied Power Inc
160 Gold Star Blvd
Worcester, MA 01606
Telephone: (508) 852-4300, Toll Free:
(800) 225-7348, FAX: (508) 852-3060, Web Site: www.wrightline.com
Mktg Commun Dir: Sandy Flanagan
Conducts Business: Worldwide
Employees: 850
Primary Market Served: Business
Advertising/Marketing Budget Related to Direct Marketing: 0-25%

Manufacturer of specialty filing systems & office furnishings. Manufacturer of LAN management, engineering environment, multi-media environment & technical furniture solutions.

ARI

2523 S McDonough Rd
Orchard Hill, GA 30266
Telephone: (770) 227-8222, Toll Free:
(800) 241-5064, FAX: (770) 227-9190, Web Site: www.halt.com
Pres: J. Gordon Dixon
Conducts Business: U.S.
Employees: 35
Primary Market Served: Business
Catalog available online

Aerosol manufacturer.

ASE TECHNOLOGIES INC

226 Lowell St
Wilmington, MA 01887-3074
Telephone: (978) 658-0009, FAX:
(978) 658-9990, E-Mail: info@ase-tech.com, Web Site: www.ase-tech.com
Pres: Jay Baumgarten
Primary Market Served: Business

Sell software & services for high speed laser printers, data conversion, open printing.

AT&T INC

208 S Akard St
Dallas, TX 75202
Telephone: (210) 821-4105, Web Site:
www.att.com
Chmn & CEO: Randall L. Stephenson
Sr Exec VP & Global Mktg Officer:
Cathy M. Coughlin
Conducts Business: Worldwide
Primary Market Served: Business &
Consumer

Promote international long distance telecommunications services & equipment.

A+E TELEVISION NETWORKS LLC

235 E 45th St
New York, NY 10017
Telephone: (212) 210-1400, FAX:
(212) 210-1326, E-Mail:
aefeedback@aenetworks.com, Web
Site: www.aenetworks.com
Chmn: Abbe Raven
Pres & CEO: Nancy Dubuc
Conducts Business: U.S., Canada
Primary Market Served: Consumer
Catalog available online
Direct online sales

ABBOTT PRODUCTS

86 Finnell Dr
Weymouth, MA 02188-1126
Telephone: (781) 331-2030, Toll Free:
(800) 392-7700, FAX: (781) 331-2030, E-Mail: abbottproducts@comcast.net, Web Site:
abbottbingoproducts.com
Conducts Business: U.S., Canada
Primary Market Served: Business &
Consumer
Direct Marketing ad budget: $200,000
Direct Mail: 100%
Gross sales or billing: $50,000,000

Sell bingo equipment & supplies to distributors & organizations for fundraising. Branches throughout the U.S. & Canada.

ACCOONA CORP

101 Hudson St (Suite 3606)
Jersey City, NJ 07302-3915
Telephone: (201) 557-9388, Web Site:
www.accoona.com
VP: Shelley Rochester
Primary Market Served: Consumer

ACCOUNTEMPS

Div. of Robert Half International Inc
2884 Sand Hill Rd (Suite 200)
Menlo Park, CA 94025-7059
Telephone: (650) 234-6000, Toll Free:
(800) 803-8367, FAX: (650) 234-6998, Web Site: www.accountemps.com
Chmn. & CEO: Harold M. Messmer Jr.
Exec Dir: Andrew Denka
Conducts Business: U.S., Canada, U.
K., Israel, Europe
Primary Market Served: Business
Advertising/Marketing Budget Related to Direct Marketing: 0-25%

Provides professional accountants & financial executives to industry on a temporary basis. Use direct mail to sell temporary employment services to corporate controllers & financial executives.

ACCUSPLIT INC

3090 Independence Dr Ste 150
Livermore, CA 94551-9423
Telephone: (925) 226-0888, Toll Free:
(800) 935-1996, FAX: (925) 463-0147, E-Mail: sales@accusplit.com,
Web Site: www.accusplit.com
Pres: W. Ron Sutton
VP, Natl Team Sls Div: Steve Simmons
Conducts Business: Worldwide
Employees: 14
Primary Market Served: Business &
Consumer
Catalog available online
Direct online sales
Advertising/Marketing Budget Related to Direct Marketing: 76-100%
Direct Marketing ad budget: $160,000
Direct Mail: $50,000
Magazines: $60,000
Newspapers: $10,000
TV/Radio: $5,000
Telephone: $20,000
Founded: 1972

Manufacture stopwatches, sports watches, cycle computers & pedometers for sports, industry, auto racing, horse racing & sailing. Also, import & distribute fitness products.

ACE HARDWARE CORP

2200 Kensington Ct
Oak Brook, IL 60523-2100
Telephone: (630) 990-6600, FAX:
(630) 990-6838, Web Site: www.
acehardware.com
Chmn Bd: David Ziegler
Pres & CEO: John Venhuizen
Exec VP Mdsg Adv Mktg & Paint:
John J. Surane
Primary Market Served: Business &
Consumer
Catalog available online
Direct online sales

Distribute power tools & hardware.

ACHIEVE GLOBAL

Subs. of Times Mirror
8875 Hidden River Pkwy (Suite 400)
Tampa, FL 33637

Telephone: (813) 631-5500, Toll Free: (800) 566-0630, FAX: (813) 631-5796, Web Site: www.achieveglobal.com
CEO: Sharon Daniels
Conducts Business: Worldwide
Employees: 1,850
Primary Market Served: Business
Founded: 1972

Marketer of training programs to business organizations designed to strengthen sales, customer service & management.

ACTIVISION VALUE

7800 Equitable Dr (Suite 200)
Eden Prairie, MN 55344
Telephone: (952) 918-9400, FAX: (952) 918-9560
Gen Mgr: Dave Oxford
Conducts Business: U.S.
Primary Market Served: Business & Consumer

Computer software & services for both business & personal use.

ACTIVSTYLE

1701 Broadway St NE
Minneapolis, MN 55413-2638
Telephone: (612) 520-9333, Toll Free: (800) 651-6223, FAX: (612) 520-9300, Web Site: www.activstyle.com
Pres: Keith Trowbridge
Conducts Business: U.S., Canada
Primary Market Served: Business & Consumer
Catalog available online
Indirect online sales

Manufacturer of healthcare products for incontinence & medical supplies.

AD INFINITUM BOOKS

7 N MacQuesten Pkwy
Mount Vernon, NY 10550-1811
Telephone: (914) 664-5930, Toll Free: (800) 697-0402, FAX: (914) 664-2642, E-Mail: aibservice@adinfinitumbooks.com, Web Site: www.adinfinitumbooks.com
Pres: William Brandon

ADVENTURE CREATIONS INC

2077 Harbor Blvd (#B)
Costa Mesa, CA 92625-2630
Telephone: (949) 515-3600, FAX: (949) 515-3933, E-Mail: sales@adv-creations.com, Web Site: www.adv-creations.com
Pres: Dale Frankhouse
Conducts Business: Worldwide
Employees: 6
Primary Market Served: Business
Catalog available online

Indirect online sales
Advertising/Marketing Budget Related to Direct Marketing: 0-25%
Founded: 1981

Large inflatables used for advertising; helium & cold air inflatables in stock & custom made.

AEROVOX INC

167 John Vertente Blvd
New Bedford, MA 02745-1221
Telephone: (508) 994-9661, Toll Free: (888) AEROVOX, FAX: (508) 995-3000, E-Mail: sales1@aerovox.com, Web Site: www.aerovox.com
Pres & COO: Bob Elliott
Sr VP: F. Randal Hunt
Mktg Mgr: Al Sembos
Mktg Mgr: Dan Filkins
Mktg Mgr: Enrique Sanches Jr
Conducts Business: Worldwide
Employees: 1,500
Primary Market Served: Business & Consumer
Catalog available online
Indirect online sales
Advertising/Marketing Budget Related to Direct Marketing: 0-25%
Founded: 1922
Gross sales or billing: $111,600,000

AC & power DC capacitors, DC film capacitors, aluminum electrolytic capacitors, power factor correction capacitors & EMI filters.

AFFINION GROUP

6 High Ridge Park
Stamford, CT 06905-1327
Telephone: (203) 956-1000, Toll Free: (800) 251-2148, Web Site: www.affiniongroup.com
CEO: Todd H. Siegel

AFFINITY EXPRESS

2200 Point Blvd (Suite 130)
Elgin, IL 60123
Telephone: (847) 930-3200, FAX: (847) 930-3299, E-Mail: kellyg@affinityexpress.com, Web Site: www.affinityexpress.com
VP Mktg: Kelly Glass
Conducts Business: U.S., Canada
Employees: 300
Primary Market Served: Business & Consumer
Catalog available online
Direct online sales
Advertising/Marketing Budget Related to Direct Marketing: 76-100%
Direct Marketing ad budget:
Direct Mail: 15%
Online: 70%
Telephone: 15%

Founded: 2000

Builds online identity programs for corporations, colleges, retail organizations and service organizations. Full service product fulfillment company.

AFFINITY4

999 Waterside Dr (Suite 1910)
Norfolk, VA 23510-3319
Telephone: (757) 465-4602, Web Site: www.affinity4.com
Pres & CEO: Stephen Halliday
Primary Market Served: Business & Consumer

AGCO SPRA-COUP

Div. of Willknight Inc
4205 River Green Pkwy
Duluth, GA 30096
Telephone: (320) 231-9400, FAX: (320) 231-9413, Web Site: www.agcocorp.com
Pres: Dale Jones
HR Mgr: Paulette Hagen
Conducts Business: U.S., Canada
Primary Market Served: Business & Consumer
Direct Marketing ad budget:
Magazines: 99%
Newspapers: 1%

Manufacturer of liquid & granular fertilizing application equipment.

AHRENSDORF & ASSOCIATES

PO Box 7494
Saint Davids, PA 19087-7494
Telephone: (610) 971-0500, FAX: (610) 971-9530, E-Mail: leeahrensdorf@att.net
Pres: Lee Ahrensdorf
Primary Market Served: Business

Executive search consultant.

AIR AMBULANCE NETWORK INC

3607 Alt 19 Ste A
Palm Harbor, FL 34683-1412
Telephone: (727) 934-3999, Toll Free: (800) 327-1966, FAX: (727) 937-0276, Web Site: www.airambulancenetwork.com
Chmn & Pres: Richard Hunter
Dir: Barbara Hunter
Sr Flight Coord: Sherry Gincel
Conducts Business: Worldwide
Employees: 8
Primary Market Served: Business & Consumer
Direct Marketing ad budget:
Direct Mail: $250,000
Telephone: $500,000
Founded: 1991

Gross sales or billing: $650,000

Toll-free, 24-hour air ambulance service.

AIR FRANCE
125 W 55th St
New York, NY 10019
Telephone: (212) 830-4000, FAX: (212) 830-4244, Web Site: www. airfrance.us
Conducts Business: U.S., Canada
Primary Market Served: Business & Consumer

Full-service marketer to generate sales of Air France Airlines.

AIR-LEC INDUSTRIES INC
3300 Commercial Ave
Madison, WI 53714-1458
Telephone: (608) 244-4754, FAX: (608) 246-7676, E-Mail: info@air-lec.com, Web Site: www.air-lec.com
Pres: John T. Lunenschloss
Sls & Svc: Harold Clute
Conducts Business: Worldwide
Employees: 8
Primary Market Served: Business
Founded: 1921

Heavy duty automatic industrial door operating equipment & aquatic weed cutters sold direct to users.

AIR-SCENT INTERNATIONAL
290 Alpha Dr, RIDC Industrial Park
Pittsburgh, PA 15238-2906
Toll Free: (800) 247-0770, FAX: (412) 252-2000, E-Mail: laura@aromaresource.com, Web Site: www. airscent.com
Pres: A. Zlotnik
Gen Mgr: A. Howard
Conducts Business: U.S., Canada
Employees: 50
Primary Market Served: Business
Catalog available online
Indirect online sales
Advertising/Marketing Budget Related to Direct Marketing: 0-25%
Direct Marketing ad budget:
Direct Mail: 10%
Magazines: 80%
Telephone: 10%
Founded: 1946

Manufacturer of air freshener products & systems. Scented specialty items.

AIRLINES REPORTING CORP
3000 Wilson Blvd Ste 300
Arlington, VA 22201-3862
Telephone: (703) 816-8135, FAX: (703) 816-8104, E-Mail: corpcom@arccorp.com, Web Site: www. arccorp.com

VP & CFO: Alfred Altschul
Campaign Mktg Database Analyst: Arthur Redman
VP & Gen Counsel: Kathleen O. Agiropolous
VP Tech Svcs: Randy Black
VP HR: Mike Gilliland
Primary Market Served: Business
Catalog available online
Indirect online sales

Accredit & maintain a list of travel agencies based in U.S.A.

AIROMAT CORP
2916 Engle Rd
Fort Wayne, IN 46809-1198
Telephone: (260) 747-7408, Toll Free: (800) 348-4905, FAX: (260) 747-7409, E-Mail: airomat@airomat.com, Web Site: www.mymatting.com
Pres, CEO & Mktg Dir: Joanne Feasel
Opers Mgr: Pam Peters

THE AKADINE PRESS INC
120 Bloomingdale Rd (Suite 100)
White Plains, NY 10605-1522
Telephone: (914) 747-0777, FAX: (914) 747-0778, Web Site: www. commonreader.com
Pres: James Mustich Jr
Mktg Dir: Lisa Camilly
Conducts Business: Worldwide
Primary Market Served: Business & Consumer
Catalog available online
Direct online sales

Sell books.

ALAMO RENT A CAR
Owned by Enterprise Holdings
600 Corporate Park Dr
Saint Louis, MO 63105
Telephone: (314) 512-2880, Web Site: www.alamo.com
Pres & CEO: Pamela Nicholson
Chief Strategy Officer & Exec VP Global Sls & Mktg: Greg Stubblefield
Chief Mktg & Commun Officer: Patrick T. Farrell
Conducts Business: U.S.
Employees: 6,000
Primary Market Served: Business & Consumer
Catalog available online
Gross sales or billing: $539,000,000

Rental car company.

ALARMINGYOU.COM
One Town Center Rd
Boca Raton, FL 33486-1002
Telephone: (714) 981-2900, Web Site: www.alarmingyou.com

Mng Partner: Dave Saenz

ALL STAR CARTS & VEHICLES
1565-D Fifth Industrial Ct
Bay Shore, NY 11706-3434
Telephone: (631) 666-5252, Toll Free: (800) 831-3166, FAX: (631) 666-1319, Web Site: www.allstarcarts.com
Pres: Stephen Kronrad
VP: Robert Kronrad
Sls: Robert Smith
Conducts Business: Worldwide
Employees: 51
Primary Market Served: Business
Catalog available online
Indirect online sales
Advertising/Marketing Budget Related to Direct Marketing: 0-25%
Direct Marketing ad budget:
Direct Mail: 5%
Magazines: 20%
Online: 75%
Founded: 1978
Gross sales or billing: $4,400,000

Ice cream, hot dog & hot food pushcarts, trailers, trucks & kiosks for food & merchandising. Sell to individuals & companies.

ALL-STATE LEGAL
All-State International Inc
1 Commerce Dr
Cranford, NJ 07016-3508
Telephone: (908) 272-0800, Toll Free: (800) 222-0510, FAX: (800) 634-5184, E-Mail: sjacobs@aslegal.com, Web Site: www.aslegal.com
CEO: Robert Busch
Conducts Business: US
Employees: 230
Primary Market Served: Business
Catalog available online
Indirect online sales
Advertising/Marketing Budget Related to Direct Marketing: 26-50%
Direct Marketing ad budget: $7,500,000
Founded: 1954
Gross sales or billing: $47,000,000

Serve the legal profession & corporations with engraving, printing, office products, legal specialty products & corporate outfits. Branch offices in Fort Wayne, IN & Los Angeles.

ALLERGAN INC
2525 DuPont Dr
Irvine, CA 92612-1531
Telephone: (714) 246-4500, Toll Free: (800) 347-4500, FAX: (714) 246-6987, Web Site: www.allergan.com
Chmn & CEO: David E.I. Pyott

Exec VP Fin & Bus Devel, CFO: Jeffrey L. Edwards
Conducts Business: Worldwide
Employees: 6,770
Primary Market Served: Business & Consumer
Catalog available online
Founded: 1948
Gross sales or billing: $3,000,000,000
Provider of specialty therapeutic products.

ALLOYD BRANDS
SBU of Tegrant Corp
1401 Pleasant St
Dekalb, IL 60115-2663
Telephone: (815) 756-8451, Toll Free: (800) 756-7639, FAX: (815) 756-5187/9192, Web Site: www.alloyd.com
Pres: William M. Kelly
Sls & Mktg Mgr: Rob Van Gilse
Conducts Business: Worldwide
Employees: 560
Primary Market Served: Business
Founded: 1961
Gross sales or billing: $41,900,000
A custom thermoformer & manufacturer of packaging machinery.

ALMOST HEAVEN GROUP
RP-NFOA
HC 67 Box 539 BB
Renick, WV 24966
Telephone: (304) 645-2310, FAX: (304) 497-2698, E-Mail: art@almostheaven.net, Web Site: www.almostheaven.net
Mktg Dir: Art Glick
Conducts Business: Worldwide
Employees: 232
Primary Market Served: Business & Consumer
Catalog available online
Indirect online sales
Direct Marketing ad budget: $372,000
Direct Mail: 50%
Magazines: 50%
Founded: 1976
Gross sales or billing: $28,700,000
Leisure & computer related companies.

ALPHA SUPPLY INC
1225 Hollis
Bremerton, WA 98310-3611
Telephone: (360) 373-3302, Toll Free: (800) 257-4211, FAX: (360) 377-9235
Pres: Tom Orme
Mgr: Al Clever
Conducts Business: Worldwide
Employees: 10
Primary Market Served: Business & Consumer
Catalog available online

Advertising/Marketing Budget Related to Direct Marketing: 76-100%
Direct Marketing ad budget:
Direct Mail: 60%
Magazines: 35%
Telephone: 5%
Founded: 1968
Gross sales or billing: $4,000,000
Sell jewelers' supplies, equipment & lapidary supplies.

ALSTOM SIGNALING INC
1025 John St
West Henrietta, NY 14586-9781
Telephone: (585) 279-2228, Web Site: www.alstomsignalingsolutions.com
Mktg Commun/Graphics Specialist: James Heinlein
Primary Market Served: Business & Consumer

ALTIRIS
Subs. of Symantec.
588 W 400 St
Lindon, UT 84042
Telephone: (801) 226-8500, Toll Free: (888) 252-5551, FAX: (801) 226-8506, Web Site: www.symantec.com
Employees: 180
Primary Market Served: Business & Consumer
Catalog available online
Direct online sales
Advertising/Marketing Budget Related to Direct Marketing: 26-50%
Founded: 1983
Developer of leading disaster recovery & remote access software.

AMANET
dba American Manufacturing Network
7001 Eton Ave # B
Canoga Park, CA 91303-2112
Telephone: (818) 786-1113, FAX: (818) 786-5736, E-Mail: info@amanet-usa.com, Web Site: www.amanet.com
Pres: Sandip Desai
Gen Mgr: Leonor Towell
Sls Mgr: Lorene Tremblay
Conducts Business: U.S.
Employees: 20
Primary Market Served: Business
Indirect online sales
Advertising/Marketing Budget Related to Direct Marketing: 0-25%
Gross sales or billing: $2,800,000
Custom component manufacturer of all types of machining including CNC mills, lathes, metal stamping & sheet metal parts for industrial & aerospace applications.

AMATEUR ELECTRONIC SUPPLY LLC
5710 W Good Hope Rd
Milwaukee, WI 53223
Telephone: (414) 558-0333, Toll Free: (800) 558-0411, FAX: (414) 358-3337, Web Site: www.aesham.com
Dir: Mike Hansen
Mgr: Bruce Lapointe
Mgr: Ben Taeusch
Branch Mgr: Dale Porray
Conducts Business: U.S.
Primary Market Served: Business & Consumer
Catalog available online
Direct online sales
Provide electronics for amateur radio buffs.

AMAZON.COM
440 Terry Ave N
Seattle, WA 98109
Telephone: (206) 266-1000, Web Site: www.amazon.com
Pres, CEO & Chmn: Jeffrey Bezos
Sr VP & CFO: Thomas J. Szkutak
Sr VP, Bus Devel: Jeffrey M. Blackburn
Sr VP, Consumer Bus: Jeffrey A. Wilke
Online retail company.

AMCAT TELEPROFIT INC
300 Johnny Bench Dr (# 120)
Oklahoma City, OK 73104-2476
Telephone: (405) 216-8080, Toll Free: (800) 364-5518, FAX: (405) 216-8063, E-Mail: smart@amcat.com, Web Site: www.amcat.com
Pres: Richard Costello
Chmn: Mark Costello
Primary Market Served: Business & Consumer
Founded: 1990
Affordable, predictive dialing systems for small & medium size business.

AMERICAN AUTOMOBILE ASSOCIATION
aka AAA
1000 AAA Dr
Heathrow, FL 32746
Telephone: (407) 444-8000, Web Site: www.aaa.com
Pres & CEO: Robert L. Darbelnet
Sr Exec VP & COO: Marshall L. Doney
VP & CFO: John Schaffer

AMERICAN BRONZING CO
Div. of Bronze Shoe Co
1313 Alum Creek Dr
Columbus, OH 43209-2706

Telephone: (614) 252-7388, Toll Free: (800) 423-5678, FAX: (614) 252-4602, E-Mail: bronzeinfo@bronshoe.com, Web Site: www.abcbronze.com
Pres: Robert Kaynes Jr.
VP, Mktg & Sls: Diane Taylor
Sls Dir: John Falor
Conducts Business: U.S.
Employees: 90
Primary Market Served: Consumer
Catalog available online
Direct online sales
Advertising/Marketing Budget Related to Direct Marketing: 51-75%
Direct Marketing ad budget:
Direct Mail: 95%
Magazines: 5%
Founded: 1934
Gross sales or billing: $1,500,000
Bronzed baby shoes for consumers.

AMERICAN CIVIL DEFENSE ASSOCIATION
12162 S Business Park Dr (Suite 208)
Draper, UT 84020
Telephone: (801) 501-0077, Toll Free: (800) 425-5397, FAX: (888) 425-5339, E-Mail: info@tacda.org, Web Site: www.tacda.org
Exec Dir: Sharon Packer
Conducts Business: U.S.
Employees: 3
Primary Market Served: Business & Consumer
Catalog available online
Indirect online sales
Founded: 1962
Sell medical emergency triage tags to civil defense directors, hospitals, rescue, fire departments & large industry.

AMERICAN CRANE & EQUIPMENT CORP
531 Old Swede Rd
Douglassville, PA 19518-1205
Telephone: (610) 385-4876, Toll Free: (877) 877-6778, FAX: (610) 385-3191, E-Mail: info@americancrane.com, Web Site: www.americancrane.com
Pres: Oddvar Norheim
VP & CFO: Dave Hope
Conducts Business: Worldwide
Employees: 105
Primary Market Served: Business & Consumer
Catalog available online
Advertising/Marketing Budget Related to Direct Marketing: 0-25%
Direct Marketing ad budget: $100,000
Founded: 1972
Gross sales or billing: $15,000,000
Manufacturer of electric overhead cranes & hoists.

AMERICAN DERMATOLOGICAL CORP
dba Dermatique
PO Box 565014
Miami, FL 33256-5014
Telephone: (305) 573-0763, Toll Free: (888) 573-0763, FAX: (305) 573-1704, E-Mail: info@dermatique.com, Web Site: www.dermatique.com
Pres: William J. O'Malley
VP: Thomas O'Malley
Conducts Business: Worldwide
Employees: 10
Primary Market Served: Consumer
Catalog available online
Direct online sales
Advertising/Marketing Budget Related to Direct Marketing: 0-25%
Sell skin care products to women.

AMERICAN GREETINGS CORP
1 American Rd
Cleveland, OH 44144
Telephone: (216) 252-7300, FAX: (216) 252-6778, Web Site: www.americangreetings.com
Chmn: Morry Weiss
Co CEO: Zev Weiss
Co CEO: Jeffrey Weiss
Primary Market Served: Business & Consumer
Advertising/Marketing Budget Related to Direct Marketing: 76-100%
Import greeting cards & gift items.

AMERICAN HEALTH & SAFETY INC
Div. of LabSource
325 Industrial Cir
Stoughton, WI 53589
Telephone: (630) 413-5662, Toll Free: (800) 522-7554, FAX: (800) 326-3245, Web Site: www.ahsafety.com
Pres & CEO: David Gust
Conducts Business: U.S.
Employees: 34
Primary Market Served: Business
Catalog available online
Founded: 1980
Nationwide distributor of personal safety equipment & supplies.

AMERICAN HEALTHWAYS
701 Cool Springs Blvd
Franklin, TN 37067-2697
Telephone: (615) 665-7716, FAX: (615) 665-7697, Web Site: www.americanhealthways.com
Info Tech: Regina Seider
Primary Market Served: Business & Consumer

Advertising/Marketing Budget Related to Direct Marketing: 26-50%
For-profit health care company with 70 diabetes, cardiac & respiratory disease management treatment centers across the country.

AMERICAN LOCKER SECURITY SYSTEMS INC
Subs. of American Locker Group Inc
PO Box 169
Coppell, TX 75019-0169
Telephone: (817) 329-1600, Toll Free: (800) 828-9118, E-Mail: info@americanlocker.com, Web Site: www.americanlocker.com
Pres, COO & Treas: Roy J. Glosser
CFO: Paul M. Zadins
VP, Mktg: Jonathan M. Ruttenberg
VP, Mfg: Jim Panho
VP & Gen Mgr: David L. Henderson
Conducts Business: Worldwide
Employees: 88
Primary Market Served: Business & Consumer
Catalog available online
Indirect online sales
Advertising/Marketing Budget Related to Direct Marketing: 0-25%
Direct Marketing ad budget: $80,000
Direct Mail: 15%
Magazines: 85%
Founded: 1931
Gross sales or billing: $24,000,000
Manufacture coin & key operated lockers which are marketed through direct salesmen & distributors nationwide to municipalities, private sectors & industrial corporations.

AMERICAN MOVIE CLASSICS HOLDING CORP
Div. of Rainbow Programming
220 Jericho Quadrangle
Jericho, NY 11753
Telephone: (516) 803-3000, FAX: (516) 803-3003, Web Site: www.amctv.com
Pres: Ed Carroll
VP: Theana Apostolou
VP: Joshua Berger
VP, Production: Mary Conlon
VP, Res: Sean Fassett
Conducts Business: U.S.
Primary Market Served: Business & Consumer
Cable television programmer offering a channel of classic American films to cable television companies.

AMERICAN OSTOMY SUPPLY
13400 Lakefront Dr
Earth City, MO 63045-1516

Telephone: (314) 291-2900, Toll Free: (800) 858-5858, FAX: (800) 545-0065
Opers Mgr: Lisa Juenger
Conducts Business: U.S., Asia, Europe
Employees: 28
Primary Market Served: Business & Consumer
Advertising/Marketing Budget Related to Direct Marketing: 76-100%

Mail order marketer of medical supplies.

AMERICAN 3B SCIENTIFIC

2189 Flintstone Dr (Suite O)
Tucker, GA 30084-5023
Telephone: (770) 492-9111, Web Site: www.a3bs.com
Mktg Mgr: Mark Dresser
Conducts Business: U.S., Canada, Brazil
Primary Market Served: Business
Catalog available online
Direct online sales
Advertising/Marketing Budget Related to Direct Marketing: 0-25%
Direct Marketing ad budget:
Direct Mail: 75%
Online: 25%

AMERICAN TOURISTER

Subs. of Samsonite International S.A.
575 West St (Suite 110)
Mansfield, MA 02048-1160
Toll Free: (800) 765-2247, Web Site: www.americantourister.com
Chmn & CEO: Tim Parker
Conducts Business: U.S.
Primary Market Served: Business & Consumer
Catalog available online
Direct online sales
Founded: 1933

Luggage & travel accessories.

AMERICA'S FINEST PET DOORS

Patio Pacific Inc
202 Tank Farm Rd (Suite F1)
San Luis Obispo, CA 93401-7520
Telephone: (805) 781-7700 X201, Toll Free: (800) 826-2871, FAX: (805) 781-9734, E-Mail: alan@petdoors.com, Web Site: www.petdoors.com
Pres: Alan Lethers
Opers Mgr: Cheri Segovia
Conducts Business: U.S., Canada
Employees: 10
Primary Market Served: Business & Consumer
Catalog available online
Indirect online sales
Advertising/Marketing Budget Related to Direct Marketing: 0-25%
Direct Marketing ad budget:

Magazines: 40%
Online: 60%
Founded: 1973
Gross sales or billing: $3,500,000

Pet doors.

AMERICRAFT - THE GIFT BROKERS INC

210 Lockes Village Rd
Wendell, MA 01379
Telephone: (978) 544-7330, Toll Free: (800) 866-2723, FAX: (978) 544-2771, E-Mail: info@americraft.us, Web Site: www.americraft.us
Pres: Robert M. Cabral Jr
Project Mgr: Patricia J. Mitchell
Employees: 2
Primary Market Served: Business
Advertising/Marketing Budget Related to Direct Marketing: 0-25%
Founded: 1978
Gross sales or billing: $5,000,000

Product sourcing & development for mail order merchants. Provide innovative niche specific merchandise & reliable, personalized drop shipped items.

AMIGO MOBILITY INTERNATIONAL INC

6693 Dixie Hwy
Bridgeport, MI 48722-9725
Telephone: (989) 777-0910, Toll Free: (800) 692-6446, FAX: (989) 777-8184, E-Mail: info@myamigo.com, Web Site: www.myamigo.com
Founder & Pres: Alan Thieme
Mktg Commun Mgr: Janet Princing
Opers Mgr: Mike Labrake
Mktg Mgr: Frances E. Hetzuer
Dir Fin & Admin: Mike Galer
Dir New Bus: Janet Hausbeck
VP: Beth Thieme
Conducts Business: Worldwide
Employees: 50
Primary Market Served: Business & Consumer
Founded: 1968

Power operated vehicles.

AMREL

3445 Fletcher Ave
El Monte, CA 91731
Telephone: (626) 443-6818, Toll Free: (800) 654-9838, FAX: (626) 443-8600, E-Mail: amrel@amrel.com, Web Site: www.amrel.com
CEO: Edward Chen
Mktg Coord: Alice Chang
Conducts Business: Worldwide
Employees: 100
Primary Market Served: Business & Consumer
Catalog available online
Indirect online sales

Advertising/Marketing Budget Related to Direct Marketing: 76-100%
Founded: 1989
Gross sales or billing: $25,000,000

Rugged mobile computer, programmable power supplies, and electronic loads manufacturer.

AMSTERDAM PRINTING

Div. of Holland USA, Inc
166 Wallins Corners Rd
Amsterdam, NY 12010-1899
Telephone: (518) 842-6000, Toll Free: (800) 203-9917, FAX: (518) 843-5204, E-Mail: customerservice@amsterdamprinting.com, Web Site: www.amsterdamprinting.com
Chmn & CEO: Glenn Taylor
Pres: Kevin Kirbey
Conducts Business: U.S., Canada, Europe
Employees: 585
Primary Market Served: Business
Catalog available online
Direct online sales
Advertising/Marketing Budget Related to Direct Marketing: 76-100%
Founded: 1898
Gross sales or billing: $10,000,000

Direct mail marketer of business forms, imprinted promotional items, & human resources products.

AMTELCO

4800 Curtin Dr
McFarland, WI 53558
Telephone: (608) 838-4194, Toll Free: (800) 356-9148, FAX: (608) 838-8998, E-Mail: info@amtelco.com, Web Site: www.amtelco.com
CEO: Joseph W. Everly
Conducts Business: Worldwide
Employees: 110
Primary Market Served: Business
Catalog available online
Founded: 1977

Manufacture & develop telemessaging equipment.

ANDREA ELECTRONICS CORP

RP-NFOA
65 Orville Dr (Suite 1)
Bohemia, NY 11716-2517
Telephone: (631) 719-1800, Toll Free: (800) 442-7787, FAX: (631) 719-1950, Web Site: www.andreaelectronics.com
Chmn & CEO: Frank A.D. Andrea Jr
Co-Pres & COO: John Andrea
Co-Pres: Douglas Andrea
VP, Pub Rels: Molly Jankey
Employees: 80
Primary Market Served: Business

Founded: 1934
Gross sales or billing: $6,000,000

Airborne intercom & telecommunication products sold to the government & to industry.

ANGELICA IMAGE APPAREL

Div. of Angelica Corp
7700 Forsyth Blvd (Suite 1010)
Saint Louis, MO 63105-1821
Telephone: (314) 854-3800, Toll Free: (800) 235-8410, Web Site: www.angelica.com
Chmn, CEO & Pres: Stephen M. O'Hara
VP & CEO: James W. Shaffer
Conducts Business: U.S.
Employees: 5,000
Primary Market Served: Business & Consumer

Manufacturer of uniforms & career apparel for healthcare, hospitality, retail & industrial applications.

THE ANIMAL MEDICAL CENTER

510 E 62nd St
New York, NY 10065-8314
Telephone: (212) 838-8100, FAX: (212) 832-9630, Web Site: www.amcny.org
Pub Rels Dir & Devel: Karen Aiken
CEO: Cynthia Phipps
Conducts Business: U.S.
Primary Market Served: Consumer

Non-profit veterinary hospital, research institute & educational center.

ANNE KLEIN

1411 Broadway Rm 2002
New York, NY 10018-3762
Web Site: www.anneklein.com
CEO: Gregg I. Marks
Conducts Business: U.S., Canada
Primary Market Served: Business & Consumer

Retailer of women's clothing.

ANRITSU CO

Div. of Anritsu Corp
490 Jarvis Dr
Morgan Hill, CA 95037
Telephone: (408) 778-2000, Toll Free: (800) 267-4878, FAX: (408) 776-1744, Web Site: www.us.anritsu.com
VP, Telecommuns: Don Mulder
VP, Engrng Dir & Gen Mgr: Frank Tiernan
VP & Gen Mgr Americas Sls Region: Wade Hulon
Conducts Business: Worldwide
Employees: 4,000
Primary Market Served: Business

Advertising/Marketing Budget Related to Direct Marketing: 0-25%
Direct Marketing ad budget:
Direct Mail: $30,000
Magazines: $90,000
Founded: 1895
Gross sales or billing: $80,000,000

Microwave & telecommunications test & measurement equipment to commercial, government, domestic & international markets.

APPLE INC

1 Infinite Loop
Cupertino, CA 95014-2083
Telephone: (408) 996-1010, FAX: (408) 996-0275, Web Site: www.apple.com
CEO: Tim Cook
Sr VP Worldwide Mktg: Philip W. Schiller
Conducts Business: Worldwide
Employees: 14,000
Primary Market Served: Business & Consumer

Manufacturer of personal computers for business, home & education.

ARBUS CAPITAL LTD

RP-NFOA
1320 Tower Rd
Schaumburg, IL 60173
Telephone: (847) 290-9600, FAX: (847) 290-9601
Owner: Stephen Jauzapaitis
Conducts Business: U.S.
Employees: 5
Primary Market Served: Business

Business brokerage firm.

ARCELORMITTAL

1 S Dearborn St
Chicago, IL 60603-2302
Telephone: (312) 899-3440, FAX: (312) 899-3504, Web Site: www.mittalsteel.com
CEO: Louis Schorsch
Primary Market Served: Business & Consumer
Catalog available online
Gross sales or billing: $12,900,000,000

Manufacturers of steel & steel products.

ARCELORMITTAL

RP-NFOA
139 Modena Rd
Coatesville, PA 19320-4036
Telephone: (610) 383-2000, FAX: (610) 383-5036, Web Site: www.arcelormittal.com
Gen Mgr: Edward Frey
Dir Prod Control: Bob Insetta
Primary Market Served: Business

Advertising/Marketing Budget Related to Direct Marketing: 76-100%
Direct Marketing ad budget:
Direct Mail: $100,000
Magazines: $200,000

Producer of carbon, alloy & clad plate & sheet steels.

ARCH TELECOM INC

RP-NFOA
210 Barton Springs (Suite 275)
Austin, TX 78704
Telephone: (512) 492-0735, Toll Free: (800) 890-7575, FAX: (512) 495-7101, Web Site: www.archtelecom.com
Pres: Charles Russo
Dir: John Llorens
Mktg Dir: Steve Cortez
Mgr: Randy Rice
Conducts Business: U.S.
Primary Market Served: Business & Consumer
Catalog available online
Indirect online sales

Provides 800 line services.

ARGENT TRADING LLC

521 5th Ave Rm 2200
New York, NY 10175-2900
Telephone: (212) 697-8800, FAX: (212) 697-8606, Web Site: www.Argenttrading.com
Chmn Bd: Jose Canino
CEO & Pres: Rafael Corral
COO & Pres: John Ende
Exec VP & Gen Counsel: Gregg Young
Exec VP Acq: Bill Levitz
Sls Coord: Kiki Mosterion
Primary Market Served: Business
Catalog available online
Advertising/Marketing Budget Related to Direct Marketing: 0-25%
Founded: 1958

Marketing services.

ARISTOKRAFT INC

Div. of Fortune Brands
1 Masterbrand Cabinets Dr
Jasper, IN 47547-0420
Telephone: (812) 482-2527, FAX: (812) 482-9872, Web Site: www.aristokraft.com
Pres: Greg Stoner
Sr VP & CFO: Steve Svetik
Exec VP, Sls: Gary G. Lautzenhiser
Exec VP, Mktg: Neil P. Lynch
Exec VP, HR: Rick Mullis
Conducts Business: U.S.
Employees: 2,300
Primary Market Served: Business & Consumer
Catalog available online

Advertising/Marketing Budget Related to Direct Marketing: 0-25%
Founded: 1954
Gross sales or billing: $250,000,000
Manufacturer of kitchen & bath cabinets & vanities.

ARNAUD'S
813 Bienville St
New Orleans, LA 70112-3121
Telephone: (504) 523-0611, Toll Free: (866) 230-8895, FAX: (504) 581-7908, Web Site: www.arnauds.com
Owner: Jane Casbarian
Owner: Archie Casbarian
Sls & Mktg Dir: Lisa Sins
Assoc Sls Dir: Debbie Ryall
Conducts Business: U.S.
Employees: 50
Primary Market Served: Consumer
Catalog available online
Indirect online sales

Restaurant featuring French Creole cuisine.

ARQUEST INC
14 Scotto Farm Ln
Millstone Twp, NJ 08535-9426
Telephone: (609) 395-9500, Toll Free: (888) 270-8378, (888) ARQUEST, FAX: (609) 395-9778, Web Site: www.arquest.com
Pres & COO: Matthew J. Rinaldi
VP, Sls & Mktg: M. Reid Macfarlan
Mktg & Bus Devel: Scott Traister
Conducts Business: U.S., Canada, Mexico, Russia
Employees: 500
Primary Market Served: Business
Advertising/Marketing Budget Related to Direct Marketing: 0-25%
Founded: 2004
Gross sales or billing: $63,100,000
Private label disposable diapers, training & swim pants for infants.

ARROW CO
Div. of Cabot Corp
5457 W 79th St
Indianapolis, IN 46268-1675
Telephone: (317) 692-6666, FAX: (317) 692-6769, Web Site: www.aearo.com
Mktg Dir: Susan Chaille
Conducts Business: Worldwide
Primary Market Served: Business & Consumer

Manufacturer of hearing protection & noise abatement products.

ARROWHEAD MOUNTAIN SPRING WATER
Div. of Perrier Group of America
PO Box 628

Wilkes Barre, PA 18703-0628
Toll Free: (800) 873-7775, Web Site: www.arrowheadwater.com
Pres & CEO: Donald W. Wood
VP: Russel Rogers
Corp Sec Dir Bd: Ross Drysdale
Dir Bd: Patty McGinley
Dir Bd: Michael Nicolichuk
Conducts Business: U.S.
Employees: 1,500
Primary Market Served: Business & Consumer
Catalog available online
Direct online sales
Founded: 1894

Sell coffee & coffee equipment, bottled drinking water & water filtration equipment to both residential & commercial customers.

ASHLAND INC
50 E Rivercenter Blvd (Suite 1600)
Covington, KY 41011-1678
Telephone: (859) 815-3333, Web Site: www.ashland.com
Chmn & CEO: James J. O'Brien
Sr VP & CFO: Lamar M. Chambers
Sr VP & Gen Counsel: David L. Hausrath
VP & Pres Ashland Distr: Robert M. Craycraft
VP HR & Communs: Susan B. Esler
Conducts Business: Worldwide
Primary Market Served: Business
Advertising/Marketing Budget Related to Direct Marketing: 0-25%

Manufactures chemical specialty products for a variety of markets.

ASIAEXP
1835 NE Miami Gardens Dr
Miami, FL 33179-5035
Telephone: (305) 675-5969, Web Site: www.asiaexp.com
Sr VP: Richard Goldberg

ASSET MARKETING SERVICES INC
14101 Southcross Dr W
Burnsville, MN 55337-6902
Telephone: (952) 707-7000, Web Site: www.amsi-corp.com
VP Mktg: Richard Bauer
Primary Market Served: Consumer
Catalog available online
Direct online sales

ASSOCIATED PHOTO
PO Box 188218
Erlanger, KY 41018-8218
Telephone: (859) 344-1460, Toll Free: (800) 727-2580, FAX: (859) 282-0032
Pres: Fred Mosher

VP: Carla Steinbrunner
Conducts Business: U.S.
Employees: 4
Primary Market Served: Business & Consumer
Direct Marketing ad budget:
Direct Mail: 90%
Magazines: 5%
Telephone: 5%
Founded: 1912
Gross sales or billing: $685,000

Replacement photo lamps & specialty photo cards.

ASSOCIATED TEXTILE RENTAL SERVICES
548 Saint Paul St
Rochester, NY 14605-1735
Telephone: (585) 454-5988, Toll Free: (800) 639-4624, Web Site: www.associatedtextile.com
Pres: David Abelove
Sr VP: Anthony Barbato
Conducts Business: U.S.
Employees: 175
Primary Market Served: Business
Catalog available online
Gross sales or billing: $13,000,000

Linens & uniform sales & rentals.
Mailing address: PO Box 6510, Utica, NY 13504.

ASTROLOGER'S FUND INC
370 Lexington Ave Rm 416, New York, NY 10017-6503
Subs. of New York Astrology Center
7913 Bay Pkwy (#A7)
Brooklyn, NY 11214
Telephone: (212) 949-7275, FAX: (212) 608-6964, E-Mail: books@afund.com, Web Site: www.afund.com
Dir: Henry Weingarten
Conducts Business: Worldwide
Employees: 4
Primary Market Served: Consumer
Catalog available online
Direct online sales
Founded: 1968

Mail order sales of books & audio & video tapes. Specialize in astrology, multi-dimensional healing & new age consciousness.

AUDIO & VIDEO LABS INC
Div. of Audio & Video Labs Inc
7905 N Route 130
Pennsauken, NJ 08110-1402
Telephone: (856) 663-9030, Toll Free: (800) 468-9353, FAX: (856) 661-3450, E-Mail: info@discmakers.com, Web Site: www.discmakers.com
Chmn: Morris Ballen
Dir, Mktg & E-Commerce: Lee Sowers

Conducts Business: Worldwide
Primary Market Served: Business &
  Consumer
Catalog available online
Indirect online sales
Advertising/Marketing Budget Related
  to Direct Marketing: 26-50%
Direct Marketing ad budget:
  $1,000,000
Direct Mail: 60%
Magazines: 20%
Telephone: 20%
Founded: 1946

Manufacturer of CD-Rom, CD-audio &
cassettes. Complete printing & packaging.

AUDIOVOX

180 Marcus Blvd
Hauppauge, NY 11788-3794
Telephone: (631) 436-6550, FAX:
  (631) 273-5939, Web Site: www.
  voxxintl.com
Pres, CEO, Dir: Patrick M. Lavelle
VP & Chief Mktg Officer: Ann M.
  Boutcher
Conducts Business: U.S., Canada,
  Mexico, Europe, Far East, S America
Employees: 940
Primary Market Served: Business &
  Consumer
Direct Marketing ad budget:
Direct Mail: 20%
Magazines: 50%
Newspapers: 20%
Telephone: 10%
Founded: 1960
Gross sales or billing: $456,700,000

Mobile & consumer electronics & accessories

AUTODESK INC

111 McInnis Pkwy
San Rafael, CA 94903
Telephone: (415) 507-5000, FAX:
  (415) 507-5100, Web Site: www.
  autodesk.com
Pres & CEO: Carl Bass
Chief Mktg Officer & Sr VP: Chris
  Bradshaw
Sr VP Indus Strategy & Mktg: Andrew
  Anagnost
Conducts Business: Worldwide
Primary Market Served: Business
Catalog available online
Direct online sales

Software manufacturer.

AUTOMATION CONTROL
PRODUCTS

1725 Windward Concourse (Suite 300)
Alpharetta, GA 30005

Telephone: (678) 990-0945, FAX:
  (678) 990-0951, E-Mail: info@
  thinmanager.com, Web Site: www.
  thinmanager.com
Pres & CEO: Matt Crandell
Chief Tech Officer: Tim Caine
VP Mktg: Tom Jordan
Conducts Business: U.S.
Employees: 50
Primary Market Served: Business &
  Consumer

Management software developer.

AUTOMATION MAILING &
SHIPPING SOLUTIONS INC

Subs. of Automated Fastening Inc
1138 W Ninth St
Cleveland, OH 44113-1060
Telephone: (216) 241-4487, Toll Free:
  (800) 883-7935, FAX: (216) 241-
  5918, E-Mail: service@
  mailshipsolutions.com, Web Site:
  www.mailshipsolutions.com
CEO & Pres: James W. Johnson
Conducts Business: U.S.
Employees: 15
Primary Market Served: Business
Catalog available online
Direct online sales
Advertising/Marketing Budget Related
  to Direct Marketing: 26-50%
Direct Marketing ad budget:
Direct Mail: 50%
Online: 50%
Founded: 1941
Gross sales or billing: $2,000,000

Mailroom equipment & accessories,
shipping supplies, postage meters, folders, inserters & bar code printers (postal discounts).

AUTOMOTIVE
HEADPHONES

44648 Mound Rd (# 161)
Sterling Heights, MI 48314-1322
Telephone: (586) 292-6166
Asst: Kim Jankowski
Primary Market Served: Business &
  Consumer

AVNET INC

2211 S 47th St
Phoenix, AZ 85034
Telephone: (480) 643-2000, FAX:
  (480) 643-7240, Web Site: www.
  avnet.com
Chmn & CEO: Rick Hamada
Pres Electronics Mktg Global: Gerry
  Frey
Employees: 11,800
Primary Market Served: Business
Catalog available online
Direct online sales
Founded: 1921

Gross sales or billing: $15,681,000,000
Distributors of semi-conductors, electromechanical components & production tools.

B&G LIEBERMAN CO INC

2420 Distribution St
Charlotte, NC 28203
Telephone: (704) 376-0717, Toll Free:
  (800) 438-0346, FAX: (800) 248-
  2696, E-Mail: bgl@bglieberman.
  com, Web Site: www.bglieberman.
  com
Pres: Gerald Lieberman
VP: Larry Lieberman
Conducts Business: U.S., Canada
Employees: 40
Founded: 1949

Sell tailoring supplies & equipment to
department stores, clothiers, dry
cleaners & tailors. Uniform rentals.

B BUNCH CO INC

9619 N 21st Dr
Phoenix, AZ 85021-1895
Telephone: (602) 997-6452, FAX:
  (602) 997-7266, E-Mail: sales@
  bbunch.com, Web Site: www.
  bbunch.com
COO: Ed Bunch
Primary Market Served: Business &
  Consumer
Founded: 1968

Pre & post paper equipment processing.

BFS CREDIT SERVICES CO

Div. of Bridgestone/Firestone Inc
6275 Eastland Rd
Brook Park, OH 44142-1301
Telephone: (216) 362-5094, FAX:
  (216) 362-5236, E-Mail:
  lupinettijim@bfsusa.com
Pres: L.A. Ehmke
Sls Promo Mgr: Jim Lupinetti
Conducts Business: U.S.
Primary Market Served: Consumer

Conduct the direct marketing sales of
merchandise, credit offerings, clubs &
services to account holder base & new
account prospects.

BGE HOME PRODUCTS &
SERVICES INC

1409 Tangiere Dr (Suite A)
Baltimore, MD 21220-2878
Toll Free: (888) 243-4663, Web Site:
  www.bgehome.com
VP Mktg: Catherine M. Davenport
Primary Market Served: Business &
  Consumer

BMI HOME DECORATING

Div. of BMI Group Inc
6917 Catalpa Ct
Spring Grove, IL 60081
Telephone: (815) 675-3703, FAX:
(815) 675-3703, E-Mail: bmigroup@
aol.com
Owner: Betty Meyn
Owner: George Meyn
Conducts Business: U.S., Canada
Employees: 3
Primary Market Served: Business &
Consumer
Advertising/Marketing Budget Related
to Direct Marketing: 26-50%
Direct Marketing ad budget: $10,000
Magazines: 100%
Founded: 1978
Gross sales or billing: $150,000

Sell fabrics & wallpaper at discount
prices.

BOC GASES

Div. of BOC Group
575 Mountain Ave
Murray Hill, NJ 07974
Telephone: (908) 464-8100, Toll Free:
(800) 262-4273, FAX: (410) 749-
4073, E-Mail: info@linde.com, Web
Site: www.boc-gases.com
Mktg: Grace Mauro
Conducts Business: U.S.
Primary Market Served: Business &
Consumer

Principal products sold through Welding Supply Distributors: oxygen, acety-
lene, nitrogen, argon, helium,
hydrogen, carbon dioxide, MAPP,
medical gases, special gases, food
gases, cylinders & liquid cylinders.

BP

4101 Winfield Rd (Suite 100)
Warrenville, IL 60555-3522
Telephone: (630) 821-3000, Toll Free:
(800) 638-5672, Web Site: www.bp.
com
Employees: 11,000
Primary Market Served: Business &
Consumer

Marketing, refining & transportation.

BYK-GARDNER USA

9104 Guilford Rd
Columbia, MD 21046-2677
Telephone: (310) 483-6500, Web Site:
www.byk.com
VP & Gen Mgr: Michael Gogoel
Primary Market Served: Business &
Consumer

BADGE-A-MINIT

345 N Lewis Ave
Oglesby, IL 61348-9776

Telephone: (815) 883-8822, Toll Free:
(800) 223-4103, FAX: (815) 883-
9696, Web Site: www.badgeaminit.
com
Chmn Bd & Treas: Malcolm Roebuck
Conducts Business: U.S.
Employees: 105
Primary Market Served: Business &
Consumer
Catalog available online
Direct online sales
Advertising/Marketing Budget Related
to Direct Marketing: 76-100%
Direct Marketing ad budget:
Magazines: 100%

Manufacturer of badge making equipment.

BAKER & TAYLOR INC

2550 W Tyvola Rd (#300)
Charlotte, NC 28217-4579
Telephone: (704) 998-3100, Toll Free:
(800) 775-1800, FAX: (704) 998-
3316, E-Mail: btinfo@btol.com, Web
Site: www.btol.com
VP, Mktg: Conny Koury
Mktg Dir: Joanne Young
Chmn, Pres & CEO: Richard Wills
Exec VP & COO: Marshall A. Wright
Exec VP & CFO: James C. Melton
Conducts Business: Worldwide
Employees: 3,750
Primary Market Served: Business
Catalog available online
Direct online sales
Advertising/Marketing Budget Related
to Direct Marketing: 26-50%
Founded: 1828
Gross sales or billing: $2,200,000,000

Distributor of books, video & music to
retailers & libraries worldwide.

BAKER CORP

3020 Old Ranch Pkwy (Suite 220)
Seal Beach, CA 90740-8805
Telephone: (562) 430-6262
Mktg Mgr: Lore McKenna

BALDUCCI ENTERPRISES INC

12920 Cloverleaf Center Dr (Suite B)
Germantown, MD 20874
Telephone: (240) 403-2440, FAX:
(240) 403-2520
CEO: Barbara Parasco
Primary Market Served: Business &
Consumer

Sell gourmet food.

BALDWIN FILTERS

A CLARCOR Co
4400 E Hwy 30
Kearney, NE 68848-6010

Telephone: (308) 234-1951, Toll Free:
(800) 822-5394, FAX: (800) 828-
4453, E-Mail: info@baldwinfilter.
com, Web Site: www.baldwinfilter.
com
Pres: Sam Ferrise
VP, Branded Sls: Jay Hussey
HR: Mike Sandgeroth
Sls: Julie Sheckler
Conducts Business: U.S., Europe, Aus-
tralia, Mexico
Employees: 850
Primary Market Served: Business &
Consumer
Catalog available online
Indirect online sales
Founded: 1936
Gross sales or billing: $100,000,000

Manufacturer of filters.

BALE CO

222 Public St
Providence, RI 02940
Toll Free: (800) 822-5350, FAX: (401)
831-5500, Web Site: www.bale.com
Mktg Mgr: Jane Byrne
Conducts Business: U.S.
Primary Market Served: Business &
Consumer
Catalog available online
Direct online sales
Advertising/Marketing Budget Related
to Direct Marketing: 76-100%

Manufacturer of jewelry & award products - customized pins, trophy & plaque
services. Also, honor awards for
schools, hospitals, industry & government.

BALFOUR

Div. of Commemorative Brands Inc
PO Box 149107
Austin, TX 78714-9107
Telephone: (512) 444-0571, FAX:
(512) 440-1138, Web Site: www.
artcarved.com
Pres: Dave Fiore
VP, Mktg: Dennis Reed
Conducts Business: Worldwide
Employees: 1,000
Primary Market Served: Business &
Consumer
Advertising/Marketing Budget Related
to Direct Marketing: 0-25%
Founded: 1914

Markets sports accessories & jewelry
to retailers & manufactures class rings.

BANKERS WARRANTY GROUP

Subs. Bankers Financial Corp
11101 Roosevelt Blvd N
Saint Petersburg, FL 33716-2340

Toll Free: (800) 431-5843, E-Mail: info@bankerswarrantygroup.com, Web Site: www. bankerswarrantygroup.com
Gen Mgr: Dawn Morris
VP Sls: Michael Kelly
Conducts Business: U.S, Canada, Caribbean
Employees: 300
Primary Market Served: Business
Advertising/Marketing Budget Related to Direct Marketing: 0-25%
Direct Marketing ad budget:
Direct Mail: 40%
Telephone: 60%
Founded: 1981

Extended warranties, telemarketing, parts distribution, product fulfillment.

BARNESANDNOBLE.COM

76 Ninth Ave (fl 9)
New York, NY 10011
Telephone: (212) 414-6000, Toll Free: (800) THE-BOOK, FAX: (212) 414-6140, E-Mail: service@ barnesandnoble.com, Web Site: www.barnesandnoble.com
Chmn: Leonard S. Riggio
CEO: Michael P. Huseby
CEO Retail Grp: Mitchell S. Klipper
Chief Mdsg Officer: Jaime Carey
Conducts Business: Worldwide
Primary Market Served: Business & Consumer
Catalog available online
Direct online sales
Advertising/Marketing Budget Related to Direct Marketing: 76-100%
Gross sales or billing: $419,800,000

Mail order division of Barnes & Noble.

BARTON-COTTON

3030 Waterview Ave (Suite 100)
Baltimore, MD 21230-3520
Telephone: (410) 247-4800, Toll Free: (800) 348-1102, FAX: (410) 536-0491, E-Mail: info@bartoncotton.com, Web Site: www.bartoncotton.com
CEO: Rob Dragonette
VP: Dawn Brelsford
Dir, Client Svcs: Rosemarie Carlyle
Primary Market Served: Business
Founded: 1928

Manufacture greeting cards.

BAUDVILLE INC

5380 52nd St SE
Grand Rapids, MI 49512-9702
Telephone: (616) 698-0889, Toll Free: (800) 728-0888, FAX: (616) 698-0554, E-Mail: service@baudville.com, Web Site: www.baudville.com
Pres: Debra Sikanas
CEO: Bill Darooge

Employees: 64
Primary Market Served: Business & Consumer
Founded: 1983
Gross sales or billing: $4,100,000

Computer software; specialty paper & accessories for award certificates & badges.

BAUSCH & LOMB INC

1 Bausch & Lomb Pl
Rochester, NY 14604-2701
Telephone: (585) 338-6000, Toll Free: (800) 344-8815, FAX: (585) 338-6007, Web Site: www.bausch.com
Chmn & CEO: Gerald M. Ostrov
Sr VP, Opers: Gerhard Bauer
VP, Pres, US Vision Care: Robert J. Moore
Dir Sls, Retinal Prods, US: Edward Kennedy
Corp VP Commun & Investor Rels: Barbara M. Kelley
Sr Mgr Publicity & Prof Mtgs: Tor Constantino
Employees: 13,000
Primary Market Served: Business & Consumer
Catalog available online
Founded: 2007
Gross sales or billing: $2,292,400,000

Healthcare & optic company.

BAY MANUFACTURING

Div. of Hemco Inc
PO Box 1250
Milan, OH 44846-1250
Telephone: (419) 499-4602, FAX: (419) 499-4603, Web Site: www.baymfg.com
Pres: M.J. McGuire
Adv Mgr: Cheryl Graziani
Sec & Treas: Deb McGuire
Conducts Business: Worldwide
Employees: 8
Primary Market Served: Business & Consumer
Catalog available online
Direct Marketing ad budget:
Magazines: 100%
Founded: 1939
Gross sales or billing: $300,000

Sell specialty boating accessories, outboard long shaft kits, swim platforms, outboard motor brackets & replacement skegs.

BAYER CORP CONSUMER CARE DIVISION

100 Bayer Blvd, P.O. Box 915
Whippany, NJ 07981-0915
Telephone: (862) 404-3000, Web Site: www.consumercare.bayer.com

Pres Consumer Care Div: Erica L. Mann
Conducts Business: Worldwide
Primary Market Served: Business & Consumer

Diversified pharmaceutical company with worldwide operations. Manufacturer & marketer of prescription & over-the-counter medicines.

BAYLOR HEALTH CARE SYSTEM

3500 Gaston Ave
Dallas, TX 75246-2017
Telephone: (214) 820-4901, Toll Free: (800) 4Baylor, FAX: (214) 820-7499, Web Site: www.baylorhealth.com
CEO: Joel T. Allison
Pres & COO: Gary D. Brock
Employees: 13,000
Primary Market Served: Business & Consumer
Catalog available online
Advertising/Marketing Budget Related to Direct Marketing: 26-50%
Founded: 1903

Provide healthcare services.

BEACON SHOE CO INC

11 Worthington Access Dr Stop 1
Maryland Heights, MO 63043-3804
Telephone: (636) 488-5444, FAX: (636) 488-3103
Pres: Robert Tucker
Conducts Business: U.S.
Primary Market Served: Consumer

Warehouse of women's footwear.

BEAR COMPUTER SYSTEMS INC

PO Box 559001
Dallas, TX 75355
Telephone: (818) 509-0459, Toll Free: (800) 252-1691, FAX: (818) 769-3055, E-Mail: info@bearcom.com, Web Site: www.bearcom.com
Chmn: John Watson
Pres & CEO: Jerry Denham
Chief Mktg Officer: Kent Huffman
Conducts Business: U.S., Canada, Europe, Asia
Employees: 10
Primary Market Served: Business
Catalog available online
Direct online sales
Advertising/Marketing Budget Related to Direct Marketing: 0-25%
Founded: 1982
Gross sales or billing: $1,000,000

Software & integrated print solutions.

BECKMAN COULTER INC

250 S Kraemer Blvd

Brea, CA 92821-6232
Telephone: (714) 993-5321, Toll Free:
(800) 526-3821, FAX: (800) 232-
3828, Web Site: www.
beckmancoulter.com
Pres & CEO: Scott Garrett
Pres: Tom Joyce
Conducts Business: Worldwide
Employees: 6,900
Primary Market Served: Business
Gross sales or billing: $857,000,000

Develops, manufactures & markets automated systems & supplies for life science research & clinical diagnostic
laboratories which advance biological
discovery & diagnosis of disease. Products include instruments, accessories,
software & consumables for sample
preparation, separation, detection,
measurement & data handling.

BECKMANN CONVERTING INC

14 Park Dr, PO Box 390
Amsterdam, NY 12010-5340
Telephone: (518) 842-0073, FAX:
(518) 842-0282, E-Mail: ppiusz@
beckmannconverting.com, Web Site:
www.beckmannconverting.com
CEO: Klaus Beckmann
VP Sls & Mktg: Scott Ayers
Gen Mgr: Peter Piusz
Conducts Business: Worldwide
Employees: 35
Primary Market Served: Business
Advertising/Marketing Budget Related
to Direct Marketing: 76-100%
Founded: 2006
Gross sales or billing: $5,100,000

Contract ultrasonic & hot melt gravure
laminating processes to manufacture
precision laminates of non-woven films
& fabrics.

BEEMAK PLASTICS INC

Subs of Jordan Industries Inc
16711 Knott Ave
La Mirada, CA 90638-6013
Telephone: (310) 886-5880, Toll Free:
(800) 421-4393, FAX: (310) 764-
0330, E-Mail: info@beemak.com,
Web Site: www.beemak.com
Pres: Chris Braun
VP Mktg: Dwight Lewis
VP Sls: Julia Alty
Conducts Business: U.S., Canada
Employees: 100
Primary Market Served: Business
Catalog available online
Direct online sales
Founded: 1951
Gross sales or billing: $8,200,000

Manufacturer of plastic holders & racks
to display brochures, pamphlets, books,
magazines, forms or "take one" pur-

poses. Custom injection molding,
acrylic fabrication & in-house imprint-
ing & fulfillment services. We also produce all of our holders in almost any
PMS color.

BEHLEN MANUFACTURING CO

4025 E 23rd St
Columbus, NE 68601-3448
Telephone: (402) 564-3111, FAX:
(402) 563-7405, E-Mail: behlen@
megavision.com, Web Site: www.
behlenmfg.com
Chmn & CEO: Tony F. Raimondo
VP, Sls: John Bowes
Gen Mgr: John Underwood
Conducts Business: U.S.
Employees: 800
Primary Market Served: Business
Founded: 1936
Gross sales or billing: $68,000,000

Pre-engineered metal buildings, grain
bins & agriculturally related products,
animal confinement & livestock equipment.

BELK STORES SERVICES INC

Div. of Belk Inc.
2801 W Tyvola Rd
Charlotte, NC 28217-4500
Telephone: (704) 357-1000, FAX:
(704) 357-1782, Web Site: www.
belk.com
Chmn: John M. Belk
Pres, Mktg: H. McKay Belk
Primary Market Served: Consumer
Catalog available online
Direct online sales
Advertising/Marketing Budget Related
to Direct Marketing: 0-25%
Retail.

BERMAN GROUP

18 Tarleton Rd
Newton Center, MA 02459-1733
Telephone: (617) 426-0870, FAX:
(617) 719-1505, E-Mail: rob@
bermanusa.com, Web Site: www.
bermanusa.com
Pres: Robert S. Berman
Conducts Business: Worldwide
Employees: 10
Primary Market Served: Business
Advertising/Marketing Budget Related
to Direct Marketing: 76-100%
Founded: 1905
Gross sales or billing: $5,000,000

Manufacturer of genuine leather wallets, diaries & notebooks for stationery,
luggage & promotional product gift
trades.

BIC CORP

1 BIC Way (Suite 1)
Shelton, CT 06484-6299
Telephone: (203) 783-2000, FAX:
(203) 783-2081, Web Site: www.
bicworld.com
CEO: Mario Guevara
Conducts Business: Worldwide
Employees: 1,500
Primary Market Served: Business &
Consumer
Gross sales or billing: $300,000,000

Manufacturer of disposable lighters,
shavers, writing instruments & White
Out.

BIJOUX TERNER

6950 NW 77th Ct
Miami, FL 33126-2714
Telephone: (305) 500-7500, Toll Free:
(800) 262-3614, FAX: (305) 262-
9286, E-Mail: customerservice@
bijouxterner.com, Web Site: www.
bijouxterner.com
Pres & CEO: Moni Terner
VP: Rosa Terner
Conducts Business: Worldwide
Employees: 250
Primary Market Served: Business &
Consumer

Sell high fashion custom jewelry.

THE BIL-RAY ALUMINUM SIDING CORP OF QUEENS INC

The Bil-Ray Group
102 Jericho Tpke
New Hyde Park, NY 11040-4507
Telephone: (516) 616-4200, Toll Free:
(800) 474-4415, FAX: (516) 616-
4030, Web Site: www.homeclub.com
Chmn: Ferdinando L. Assinin
CEO: Charles G. Le Poin
Mktg Dir: Robert Silverman
Mktg Mgr: Tom Langon
Employees: 32
Primary Market Served: Consumer
Founded: 1949

General home improvement contractors.

BIOSCIENCES-AMERSHAM

Subs. of GE Healthcare
800 Centennial Ave, PO Box 1327
Piscataway, NJ 08855-1327
Telephone: (732) 457-8000, FAX:
(732) 457-0557, Web Site: www.
amersham.com
CEO & Sr VP: Joe Hogan
Exec VP & CIO: Russel P. Mayer
Exec VP & CFO: Kathryn McCarthy
CTO: Michael J. Barber
Gen Mgr, Opers: Raphael Strosin
Primary Market Served: Business

Catalog available online

Sell labeling detection & analysis of biological molecules for the life science research community.

STANLEY BLACK & DECKER INC

1000 Stanley Dr
New Britain, CT 06053
Telephone: (860) 225-5111, Web Site: www.stanleyblackanddecker.com
Chmn & CEO: John F. Lundgren
Pres & COO: James M. Loree
Conducts Business: U.S.
Employees: 25,500
Primary Market Served: Business & Consumer
Founded: 1910

Manufacturer of power tool accessories & replacement service parts for all Black & Decker household products.

BLACK ENTERTAINMENT TELEVISION INC

Div. of Viacomm
1235 W St NE
Washington, DC 20018-1211
Telephone: (202) 608-2000, Web Site: www.bet.com
Chmn & CEO: Debra Lee
Exec VP Mktg: Vicky Free
Conducts Business: U.S.
Employees: 450
Primary Market Served: Business & Consumer

Producer of music videos, black college sports, news & family entertainment.

BLANCHARD & CO INC

909 Poydras St (Suite 1900)
New Orleans, LA 70112
Telephone: (504) 837-3010, Toll Free: (800) 880-4653, FAX: (504) 837-4884, Web Site: www.blanchardonline.com
CEO: Donald W. Doyle Jr.
COO: Michael McGoey
CFO: Debra L. Cash
Sr VP Sls: L. Craig Baudot
Conducts Business: Worldwide
Employees: 85
Primary Market Served: Consumer
Catalog available online
Direct online sales
Advertising/Marketing Budget Related to Direct Marketing: 51-75%
Direct Marketing ad budget:
Direct Mail: 25%
Magazines: 25%
Newspapers: 40%
TV/Radio: 10%
Founded: 1975

Market rare U.S. coins & precious metals to investors & collectors.

DICK BLICK HOLDINGS INC

Subs. of Dick Blick Co
PO Box 1267
Galesburg, IL 61402-1267
Telephone: (309) 343-6181, FAX: (309) 343-5785, E-Mail: admin@dickblick.com, Web Site: www.dickblick.com
Pres, CEO: Bob Buchsbaum
Conducts Business: Worldwide
Employees: 550
Primary Market Served: Business & Consumer
Catalog available online
Direct online sales
Founded: 1911

Sells art & educational materials to schools, hospitals & individual consumers & "handy helpers" for the home, yard & garden. Branch in Emmaus, PA.

BLOOMINGDALE'S DIRECT

aka Bloomingdale's by Mail Ltd
1000 Third Ave (fl 11)
New York, NY 10022
Telephone: (212) 705-2000, Toll Free: (800) 777-0000, FAX: (212) 705-2805, Web Site: www.bloomingdales.com
Chmn & CEO: Tony Spring
Exec VP Mktg: Frank Berman
Employees: 381
Primary Market Served: Consumer
Founded: 2001
Gross sales or billing: $64,700,000

Catalog & mail order houses for apparel, accessories, gifts, cosmetics, housewares & more.

BLUE CORAL SLICK 50

6718 Gentle Bend Dr, Houston, TX 77069-1716
Div. of Shell Oil Products US (SOPUS)
910 Louisiana St, One Shell Plaza
Houston, TX 77002-4916
Telephone: (713) 241-6161, Toll Free: (800) 416-1600, FAX: (713) 241-4044, E-Mail: SCD-ConsumerSolutions@Shell.com, Web Site: www.bluecoral.com
VP Shell Lubricants: Doug Boyle
PR: Deborah Breazeale
Corp Affairs: Nino Polomo
Sponsorship & Events: Victoria Moreno
Primary Market Served: Business & Consumer
Founded: 1927

Manufacturer of oil additive designed to reduce engine wear and other car care products. Slick 50 engine & fuel treatments & Blue Coral car wash.

BLUESTEM BRANDS

6509 Flying Cloud Dr
Eden Prairie, MN 55344-3307
Telephone: (952) 656-3700, Web Site: www.fingerhut.com
VP, New Customer Acq Mktg: Jennifer Kemp
Primary Market Served: Business & Consumer

BLUEWATER YACHTS

811 E Maple
Mora, MN 55051-1224
Telephone: (320) 679-3811, FAX: (320) 679-3820, E-Mail: bluewater@ncis.com, Web Site: www.bluewateryacht.com
Pres & Owner: Steve Klapmeier
Owner: Jolie Klapmeier
Mktg Dir: Kari Boster
Conducts Business: U.S., Canada, Europe, Asia, S. America
Employees: 60
Primary Market Served: Consumer
Indirect online sales
Founded: 1954

Custom luxury yachts.

BOBCAT CO

Div. of Doosan Infracore
250 E Beaton Dr
West Fargo, ND 58078
Telephone: (701) 241-8700, FAX: (701) 241-8704, Web Site: www.bobcat.com
Pres: Rich Goldsbury
Conducts Business: Worldwide
Employees: 1,800
Primary Market Served: Business & Consumer
Catalog available online
Indirect online sales
Advertising/Marketing Budget Related to Direct Marketing: 0-25%
Founded: 1947

Manufacturer of BOBCAT loaders & excavators.

BODY BY JAKE GLOBAL LLC

11611 San Vicente Blvd Ste 610
Los Angeles, CA 90049-6506
Telephone: (310) 571-7101, FAX: (310) 571-7107, E-Mail: info@bodybyjake.com, Web Site: www.bodybyjake.com
Pres: Phil Scotti
CFO: Kevin Gallagher
Employees: 10
Primary Market Served: Business
Catalog available online
Direct online sales
Gross sales or billing: $1,100,000

Production, marketing & licensing.

BOEING CO
100 N Riverside
Chicago, IL 60606
Telephone: (312) 544-2000, FAX:
(312) 544-2082, Web Site: www.
boeing.com
Chmn, Pres & CEO: W. James McNerney Jr.
Vice Chmn, Pres & COO: Dennis A.
Muilenburg
Exec VP & CFO: Greg Smith
Chief Tech Officer: John J. Tracy
Primary Market Served: Business
Catalog available online

Aerospace industry.

BOISE CASCADE HOLDINGS LLC
1111 W Jefferson St (Suite 300)
Boise, ID 83702-5389
Telephone: (208) 384-6451, FAX:
(208) 384-7189, E-Mail:
mediarelations@bc.com, Web Site:
www.bc.com
Chmn & CEO: William Thomas Stephens
Sr VP & CFO: Thomas E. Carlile
VP, HR & Commun: John Sahlberg
Conducts Business: U.S., U.K., Australia, Canada, Mexico, New Zealand
Employees: 10,191
Primary Market Served: Business
Catalog available online
Direct online sales
Founded: 1957
Gross sales or billing: $5,780,000,000

Delivers office, building and paper solutions.

BOLIND INC
PO Box 18714
Boulder, CO 80308-1714
Telephone: (303) 443-3142, FAX:
(303) 443-9889, Web Site: www.
bolind.com
Pres: Katherine Lukoskie
VP: Bruce F. Lindeke
Conducts Business: U.S.
Employees: 25
Primary Market Served: Business &
Consumer
Catalog available online
Direct online sales
Advertising/Marketing Budget Related
to Direct Marketing: 76-100%
Founded: 1956

Stationery & return address label manufacturer selling to distributors & the consumer. Also produce a gift catalog.

BONTEX
1207 Hunakai St
Honolulu, HI 96816-4614
Telephone: (540) 261-2181, FAX:
(540) 261-3784, E-Mail: bontex@
bontex.com, Web Site: www.bontex.
com
Pres: J.C. Kostelni
VP: Charles Kostelini
Sls Dir: Larry Morris
Conducts Business: Worldwide
Employees: 250
Primary Market Served: Business
Catalog available online
Indirect online sales
Direct Marketing ad budget: $100,000
Direct Mail: 10%
Magazines: 10%
Newspapers: 10%
TV/Radio: 70%
Gross sales or billing: $45,000,000

Producers of Bontex wet web elastomeric impregnated fiberboard/nonwovens.

BOUNDLESS CORP
1916 State Route 96
Phelps, NY 14532-9705
Telephone: (631) 962-1500, Toll Free:
(800) 231-5445, FAX: (631) 962-
1505, E-Mail: sales@boundless.com,
Web Site: www.boundless.com
Chmn & CEO: Xitian Wang
CFO: Xiangi Cheng
VP & Dir: Yuangie Jin
VP: Delong Song
Direct Mail Mgr: Jim Catalano
Conducts Business: U.S.
Employees: 300
Primary Market Served: Business &
Consumer
Catalog available online
Advertising/Marketing Budget Related
to Direct Marketing: 51-75%
Founded: 1969
Gross sales or billing: $6,000,000

Manufacturer of display terminals from text to multi-console all the way to X, which now includes network computers.

BOWERS & MERENA AUCTIONS
18061 Fitch
Irvine, CA 92614-6018
Telephone: (949) 253-0916, Toll Free:
(800) 458-4646, FAX: (949) 253-
4091, E-Mail: auction@
bowersandmerena.com, Web Site:
www.bowersandmerena.com
Pres: Stephen Deeds
Dir: Jeff Ambio
Dir: Debbie McDonald
Adv Dir: Chris Karstedt
Primary Market Served: Business &
Consumer
Founded: 1953

Auction house.

BOYD GAMING CORP
3883 Howard Hughes Pkwy (fl 9)
Las Vegas, NV 89169
Telephone: (702) 792-7200, FAX:
(702) 792-7313, Web Site: www.
boydgaming.com
Pres & CEO: Keith E. Smith
Chmn: William S. Boyd
Exec. VP & Chief Bus Devel Officer:
Robert L. Boughner
Exec VP & COO: Paul J. Chakmak
Employees: 18,300
Primary Market Served: Business &
Consumer
Gross sales or billing: $2,278,000,000

Resort & casino operator in Nevada, New Jersey, Illinois, Indiana, Iowa, Kansas, Louisiana, and Mississippi.

THE BRADFORD GROUP
9333 N Milwaukee Ave
Niles, IL 60714-1303
Telephone: (847) 966-2770, FAX:
(847) 581-8630, Web Site: www.
collectiblestoday.com
Pres & CEO: Rich Tinberg
Sr VP & Gen Mgr: Shay Gallagher
VP, Opers: Robert Del Cielo
VP, Legal: Joel Platt
Mktg Svcs Dir: Karen Cox
Mgr: Allison Fox
Conducts Business: Worldwide
Primary Market Served: Business &
Consumer
Catalog available online
Direct online sales
Founded: 1973

Exchange trading, buying & selling of collector's plates. Offers of recommended plates are made periodically.

BRADFORD HEALTH SERVICES
2101 Magnolia Ave S (Suite 518)
Birmingham, AL 35205-2853
Telephone: (205) 251-7753, Toll Free:
(800) 217-2849, Web Site: www.
bradfordhealth.com
Pres & CEO: Jerry Crowder
Conducts Business: U.S.
Employees: 350
Primary Market Served: Business &
Consumer
Catalog available online
Advertising/Marketing Budget Related
to Direct Marketing: 76-100%
Direct Marketing ad budget:
Direct Mail: $50,000
Magazines: $20,000
Newspapers: $20,000
TV/Radio: $400,000
Telephone: $25,000

Gross sales or billing: $20,000,000

Dedicated to making recovery from alcohol & other chemical dependencies available to the general public.

BRADY CORP

W H Brady Co
6555 W Good Hope Rd
Milwaukee, WI 53223
Telephone: (414) 358-6600, Toll Free: (800) 541-1686, FAX: (800) 292-2289, Web Site: www.bradycorp. com
Pres & CEO: Frank M. Jaehnert
Pres, Brady Americas: Matt O. Williamson
Pres, Direct Mktg Americas: Tom Felmer
Sr VP & CEO: David Mathieson
Sr VP, HR: Michael O. Oliver
Conducts Business: Worldwide
Employees: 8,000
Primary Market Served: Business
Catalog available online
Indirect online sales
Founded: 1914
Gross sales or billing: $1,300,000,000

Manufacturer of industrial identification products for electronic, electrical, telecommunications & automotive markets.

BRADY MARKETING CO INC

1331 N California Blvd (Suite 320)
Walnut Creek, CA 94596-4563
Telephone: (925) 676-1300, Toll Free: (800) 326-6080, FAX: (925) 676-3082, E-Mail: info@bradymarketing. com, Web Site: www. bradymarketing.com
Pres: Frank Brady
VP, Fin: Lorraine Brady
Conducts Business: U.S.
Employees: 25
Primary Market Served: Business & Consumer

Supply consumers with replacement coffee carafes, shaver parts, food processor parts & accessories.

BRAHMIN LEATHER WORKS

77 Alden Rd
Fairhaven, MA 02719
Telephone: (508) 994-4000, Toll Free: (800) 229-2428, FAX: (508) 994-4153, Web Site: www.brahminusa. com
Pres: William R. Martin
VP: Joan Martin
Acct Sls Exec: David Patton
Primary Market Served: Business & Consumer
Catalog available online

Direct online sales

Manufacture men's & women's high end hand bags & leather accessories.

BRIDGESTONE AMERICAS INC

535 Marriott Dr, PO Box 140990
Nashville, TN 37214-0990
Telephone: (615) 937-1000, Toll Free: (800) 543-7522, FAX: (615) 937-3721, Web Site: www. bridgestonetire.com
CEO & Pres: Gary Garfield
COO: Eduardo Minardi
Chief Administrative Officer: Christine Karbowiak
Primary Market Served: Business & Consumer

Manufacture & distribute tires as well as other rubber products.

BRISTOL-MYERS SQUIBB CO

345 Park Ave
New York, NY 10154
Telephone: (212) 546-4000, FAX: (212) 546-9544, Web Site: www. bms.com
CEO: Lamberto Andreotti
Exec VP & CFO: Charles Bancroft
Exec VP & Chief Comml Officer: Giovanni Caforio MD
Exec VP & Chief Scientific Officer: Francis Cuss
Conducts Business: Worldwide
Employees: 43,000
Primary Market Served: Business
Catalog available online
Gross sales or billing: $18,000,000,000

A diversified company whose principle businesses are pharmaceuticals, consumer products, nutritional & medical devices.

BROADVISION INC

1700 Seaport Blvd (Suite 210)
Redwood City, CA 94063-5579
Telephone: (650) 295-0716, Toll Free: (866) 246-4887, FAX: (650) 364-3425, E-Mail: sales@broadvision. com, Web Site: www.broadvision. com
Pres & CEO: Dr. Pehong Chen
CFO: Dr. Shin-Yuan Tzou
VP Strategy, Product Mngmt & Mktg: Peter Chu
Primary Market Served: Business & Consumer
Catalog available online
Indirect online sales
Founded: 1993

Offer a comprehensive application system optimized for enabling global Fortune 1000 companies to establish direct consumer connection & obtain higher

profit margin through dynamically marketing & selling goods & services online on a personalized one-to-one basis.

BROCADE COMMUNICATIONS SYSTEMS INC

Subs. of EMC Corp
130 Holger Way
San Jose, CA 95134
Telephone: (408) 333-8000, FAX: (408) 333-8101, E-Mail: info@ brocade.com, Web Site: www. brocade.com
Chmn: Dave House
CEO: Lloyd Carney
Chief Tech Officer & VP Corp Devel & Emerging Bus: Ken Cheng
Chief Mktg Officer: Christine Heckert
Primary Market Served: Business
Catalog available online
Advertising/Marketing Budget Related to Direct Marketing: 0-25%

Design, manufacture & market network communication systems. Supplier of information switching products.

BROOKFIELD OFFICE PROPERTIES

250 Vesey St (fl 15), Brookfield Place
New York, NY 10281
Telephone: (212) 417-7000, FAX: (212) 417-7214, Web Site: brookfieldofficeproperties.com
CEO: Dennis Friedrich
Pres & Global COO: Tom Farley
Global Chief Investment Officer: G. Mark Brown
CFO: Bryan Davis
Employees: 2,014
Primary Market Served: Business
Gross sales or billing: $1,028,000,000

Commercial & real estate.

BROOKS SPORTS INC

19820 North Creek Pkwy #200, Bothell, WA 98011-8227
PO Box 31509
Seattle, WA 98103-1509
Telephone: (425) 402-1632, Toll Free: (800) 227-6657, FAX: (425) 489-1975, Web Site: www. brooksrunning.com
Pres, CEO & Dir: James M. Weber
VP Mktg: Dave Larson
Conducts Business: Worldwide
Employees: 150
Primary Market Served: Business
Catalog available online
Direct online sales
Advertising/Marketing Budget Related to Direct Marketing: 0-25%
Founded: 1914

Gross sales or billing: $21,000,000

Manufacturer & marketer of technical athletic footwear, apparel & accessories.

BROWN-FORMAN CORP

850 Dixie Hwy
Louisville, KY 40210
Telephone: (502) 585-1100, FAX: (502) 774-7876, E-Mail: brownforman@b-f.com, Web Site: www. brown-forman.com
Chmn & CEO: Paul C. Varga
VP, Dir Corp Commun: Philip Lynch
Conducts Business: Worldwide
Employees: 3,750
Primary Market Served: Consumer
Indirect online sales
Founded: 1870
Gross sales or billing: $2,218,000

Producer of quality consumer products.

BROWN SHOE CO

Div. of Brown Group
8300 Maryland Ave, PO Box 29
Saint Louis, MO 63105-3645
Telephone: (314) 854-4000, FAX: (314) 854-4274, Web Site: www. brownshoe.com
Chmn Bd & CEO: Ronald Fromm
Pres & COO: Diane M. Sullivan
Pres, NY Div: Richard M. Ausick
Sr VP & CFO: Mark E. Hood
Sr VP: Douglas Koch
Primary Market Served: Business
Catalog available online
Indirect online sales

Marketer of women's, men's & children's brand name footwear.

TONY BROWN PRODUCTIONS

2214 Frederick Douglass Blvd (Suite 124)
New York, NY 10026
Telephone: (718) 264-2226, FAX: (718) 264-1914, E-Mail: mail@tbol. net, Web Site: www.tonybrown.com
Pres: Tony Brown
Mktg Dir: Jim Cannaday
Primary Market Served: Consumer

Sell video cassettes to public.

BUENA VISTA WINERY

18000 Old Winery Rd
Sonoma, CA 95476
Telephone: (707) 252-7117, Toll Free: (800) 678-8504, FAX: (707) 252-0392, Web Site: www. buenavistawinery.com
Pres, Boisset Family Estates: Jean-Charles Boisset
Conducts Business: Worldwide
Employees: 75

Primary Market Served: Business & Consumer
Catalog available online

BUICK

Div. of General Motors Corp
300 Renaissance Center
Detroit, MI 48265-3000
Telephone: (313) 556-5000, Toll Free: (800) 521-7300, FAX: (313) 556-5108, Web Site: www.buick.com
US VP Buick-GMC: Duncan Aldred
VP Buick-GMC Mktg: Tony DiSalle
Buick-GMC US Adv & Promotions Dir: Sandra Moore
Buick-GMC US Product Mktg Dir: Roger McCormack
Employees: 280,000
Primary Market Served: Business & Consumer
Catalog available online
Indirect online sales

Automotive manufacturer.

BULL HN INFORMATION SYSTEMS

285 Billerica Rd (Suite 200)
Chelmsford, MA 01824-4174
Telephone: (978) 294-6000, FAX: (978) 294-7999, Web Site: www. bull.com/us
Dir Commun: Steve Puleo
Conducts Business: Worldwide
Employees: 7,178
Primary Market Served: Business

BUNN-O-MATIC CORP

1400 Stevenson Dr
Springfield, IL 62703-4291
Telephone: (217) 529-6601, FAX: (217) 529-6622, E-Mail: bunn@ bunn.com, Web Site: www.bunn.com
CFO: Gene Wilkin
VP: Bill Taylor
Mktg Mgr: Lisa McCloud
Conducts Business: Worldwide
Primary Market Served: Business & Consumer
Catalog available online
Advertising/Marketing Budget Related to Direct Marketing: 0-25%
Direct Marketing ad budget:
Direct Mail: 100%
Founded: 1958

Manufactures coffee brewers, coffee grinders, iced tea brewers, hot water machines, coffee filters, coffee warmers, coffee decanters, water conditioning systems, espresso coffee brewers & espresso coffee grinders.

BUNZL DISTRIBUTION USA, INC

aka BUNZL

1 Cityplace Dr Ste 200
Saint Louis, MO 63141-7067
Telephone: (314) 997-5959, Toll Free: (888) 997-5959, FAX: (314) 997-1405, Web Site: www. bunzldistribution.com
Pres: Patrick Larmon
Sr VP Strategic Devel: Terry Frank
Dir Comp Svcs & ECommerce: John Pestka
VP Strategic Vendor Devel: Dave Fisher
Conducts Business: U.S.
Employees: 3,625
Primary Market Served: Business
Gross sales or billing: $946,100,000

Supplies a range of products including outsourced food packaging, disposable supplies, and cleaning and safety products to food processors, supermarkets, retailers, convenience stores and other users. Bunzl Distribution is the largest division of Bunzl plc, an international distribution and outsourcing group headquartered in London.

BURLINGTON COAT FACTORY

1830 Route 130 N
Burlington, NJ 08016
Telephone: (609) 387-7800, FAX: (609) 387-7071, Web Site: www. burlingtoncoatfactory.com
Pres & CEO: Thomas A. Kingsbury
Exec VP & CFO: Todd Weyhrich
Exec VP & Chief Mdsg Officer: Paul Metcalf
Exec VP & Chief Mktg Officer: Bart Sichel
Primary Market Served: Consumer

Retail warehouse.

BURLINGTON INDUSTRIES INC

804 Green Valley Rd (Ste 300)
Greensboro, NC 27408-7039
Telephone: (336) 379-2000, FAX: (336) 379-2498, Web Site: www. burlington.com
Pres & COO: George Henderson
CEO: William A. Klopman
Primary Market Served: Business & Consumer

Textile manufacturing company.

BURLINGTON NORTHERN & SANTA FE LLC

aka BNSF Railway Co
2650 Lou Menk Dr
Fort Worth, TX 76131-2830
Telephone: (817) 878-2000, Toll Free: (800) 795-2673, FAX: (817) 333-7593, Web Site: www.bnsf.com
Pres & CEO: Carl R. Ice

Exec VP Law & Corp Affairs: Roger Nober
Exec VP & Chief Mktg Officer: Stevan B. Bobb
Exec VP Opers: Gregory C. Fox
Exec VP & CFO: Julie A. Piggott
Conducts Business: U.S.
Employees: 43,000
Primary Market Served: Business
Catalog available online

BURNS INC

350 Mariano S Bishop Blvd
Fall River, MA 02721-2365
Telephone: (508) 675-0381, Toll Free: (800) 341-2200, FAX: (508) 677-1300, Web Site: www.burnstools.com
Chmn Bd: John M. Burns Sr.
VP, Treas & Co-Owner: Jeffery M. Burns
Conducts Business: U.S.
Employees: 30
Primary Market Served: Business & Consumer
Catalog available online
Direct online sales
Advertising/Marketing Budget Related to Direct Marketing: 26-50%
Founded: 1934

Marketer of industrial power tools.

BUSHNELL OUTDOOR PRODUCTS

9200 Cody
Overland Park, KS 66214-1734
Telephone: (913) 752-3400, Toll Free: (800) 423-3537, FAX: (913) 752-3550, Web Site: www.bushnell.com
Pres: Joe Messner
CFO: Dave Broadbent
Media Rels: Jen Messelt
Conducts Business: Worldwide
Primary Market Served: Business
Catalog available online
Indirect online sales

Optical products: binoculars, telescopes, spotting scopes, rifle scopes, sunglass, laser range finders, speed guns, digital navigation, night vision, helmets and goggles.

BUSINESS AUTOMATION SYSTEMS INC

6949 Charlotte Pike Ste 106
Nashville, TN 37209-4200
Telephone: (615) 329-4585, FAX: (615) 320-0206, Web Site: www.bas-solutions.com
Pres: Raymond E. Ingram
Office Mgr: Ardith Ingram
Proj Mgr: Pamela Blackall
Conducts Business: U.S.
Employees: 13

Primary Market Served: Business & Consumer
Founded: 1985

Computer support services.

BUSINESS GRAPHICS INC

188 W Industrial Dr (Suite 428)
Elmhurst, IL 60126-1612
Telephone: (815) 338-8222, Toll Free: (800) 435-4874, FAX: (815) 338-2652, E-Mail: busgraph@mc.net, Web Site: www.businessgraphics.com
Pres: Luke Johnsos
Sec & Treas: Judith Johnsos
Conducts Business: U.S.
Employees: 4
Primary Market Served: Business
Catalog available online
Direct online sales
Advertising/Marketing Budget Related to Direct Marketing: 51-75%
Direct Marketing ad budget:
Direct Mail: $50,000
Founded: 1981
Gross sales or billing: $1,000,000

Sells printed products to the business community, restaurants, hotels & hospitals.

BUSINESSONLINE

701 B St (Suite 1000)
San Diego, CA 92101-8109
Telephone: (619) 699-0767, Web Site: www.businessol.com
CEO: Thad Kahlow

BUTLER SCHEIN ANIMAL HEALTH

400 Metro Pl N Ste 100
Dublin, OH 43017-3340
Telephone: (614) 761-9095, Toll Free: (888) 691-2724, FAX: (888) 329-3861, Web Site: www.butlerschein.com
Chmn, Pres & CEO: Kevin Vasquez
VP Mktg & Sls Svcs: Davey L. Stone
Reg Mgr: Mike Stone
Pres Comml Div: Kim Allen
VP Bus Devel: Ben Coe
Natl Dir Equine Sls Devel: Jeannie Jeffery
Reg Mgr: Bob Anderson
Reg Mgr: Dawn Burdette
Reg Mgr: Mike Powers
Conducts Business: U.S., Worldwide
Primary Market Served: Business
Catalog available online

Veterinarian supplies & drugs.

BUTLER SPECIALTY CO

8200 S Chicago Ave
Chicago, IL 60617-1804

Telephone: (773) 221-1200, Toll Free: (800) 799-2857, FAX: (773) 221-5892, Web Site: www.butlerspecialty.net
Chmn: Burton Bergman
Vice Chmn: Burt Fainman
Pres: David Bergman
Conducts Business: Worldwide
Employees: 25
Primary Market Served: Business
Catalog available online
Advertising/Marketing Budget Related to Direct Marketing: 0-25%
Founded: 1930

Manufacturer of accent furniture, lamps, wall curios, globes, consoles & benches.

H E BUTT GROCERY CO

aka H-E-B Grocery Stores
646 S Main Ave
San Antonio, TX 78204-1210
Telephone: (210) 938-8357, Toll Free: (800) 432-3113, FAX: (210) 938-7511, Web Site: www.heb.com
Chmn & CEO: Charles Butt
COO: Bob Loeffler
Conducts Business: U.S.
Employees: 76,000
Primary Market Served: Consumer
Founded: 1905

Full-service grocery store chain throughout Texas.

C & J CLARK AMERICA INC

aka Clarks
156 Oak St
Newton Upper Falls, MA 02464
Telephone: (617) 964-1222, Toll Free: (800) 925-4315, FAX: (617) 243-4213, Web Site: www.clarks.com
Pres: Robert Infantino
Primary Market Served: Business & Consumer

Retailer & wholesaler of footwear & accessories.

CA INC

1 Ca Plz Ste 100
Islandia, NY 11749-5303
Toll Free: (800) 225-5224, FAX: (631) 342-3300, E-Mail: info@ca.com, Web Site: www.ca.com
Pres & CEO: John A. Swainson
EVP, Gen Mgr Worldwide Sls: George Fischer
EVP, Chief Mktg Officer: Donald R. Friedman
Conducts Business: Worldwide
Employees: 14,500
Primary Market Served: Business
Founded: 1976

Gross sales or billing: $3,943,000,000

Develops, licenses & supports more than 500 integrated products that include enterprise computing & information management, application development, manufacturing & financial applications.

CBT DIRECT
905 E Martin Luther King Jr Dr Ste 500
Tarpon Springs, FL 34689-4830
Telephone: (727) 724-8994, Toll Free: (877) 872-4646, FAX: (727) 797-9143, Web Site: www.cbtdirect.com
Pres: Frank Coleman
VP, Mktg: Jamie Sene
VP, Opers: Kim Cardinale
Sr Training Advisor: Robert Roy
Conducts Business: Worldwide
Employees: 250
Primary Market Served: Business & Consumer
Advertising/Marketing Budget Related to Direct Marketing: 0-25%
Founded: 1991
Gross sales or billing: $51,000,000

Online and computer-based training for the IT industry.

CCA GLOBAL PARTNERS
670 N Commercial St
Manchester, NH 03101-1160
Telephone: (603) 626-0333, Web Site: www.ccaglobal.com
VP Mktg: Terri Daniels
Primary Market Served: Business & Consumer

CCC OF AMERICA
8080 Tristar Dr #106, Irving, TX 75063-2811
102 Decker Ct (Suite 204)
Irving, TX 75062
Telephone: (214) 206-3130, Toll Free: (800) 935-2222, FAX: (214) 206-3134, Web Site: www.cccofamerica.com
Editor: Gabe Huck
Catalog available online
Direct online sales
Founded: 1983

Manufacturer of children's animated videos.

CCI SOLUTIONS
1342 88th Ave SE, PO Box 481
Olympia, WA 98507-0481
Telephone: (360) 943-5378, Toll Free: (800) 426-8664, FAX: (360) 754-1566, (800) 339-TAPE, E-Mail: info@ccisolutions.com, Web Site: www.ccisolutions.com
Pres: Bob Schmidt

CEO: Denny Bradley
Sls & Adv Mgr: Jerry Lamb
Conducts Business: U.S., Canada
Employees: 47
Primary Market Served: Business & Consumer
Advertising/Marketing Budget Related to Direct Marketing: 76-100%
Direct Marketing ad budget: $100,000
Direct Mail: 80%
Magazines: 20%
Founded: 1976
Gross sales or billing: $8,000,000

Audio cassette tape supply, sound reinforcement equipment, audio/visual equipment.

CD UNIVERSE
101 N Plains Ind Rd
Wallingford, CT 06492-2165
Telephone: (203) 294-1648, Toll Free: (800) 231-7937, FAX: (203) 294-0391, Web Site: www.cduniverse.com
CEO: Chris Beilman
Primary Market Served: Consumer
Direct online sales

Internet retailer of music, movies and video games.

CDMO INC
PO Box 765
Deer Park, NY 11729-0765
Telephone: (631) 242-8820, FAX: (631) 242-5761, E-Mail: cdsales@cdmo.com, Web Site: www.cdmo.com
Conducts Business: U.S.
Primary Market Served: Consumer
Catalog available online
Direct online sales

Distribute DVD, CD, VHS & other recording formats.

CDW CORP
Headquarters & Business Technology Center
200 N Milwaukee Ave
Vernon Hills, IL 60061
Telephone: (847) 465-6000, (847) 371-6090, Web Site: www.cdw.com
Chmn & CEO: Thomas E. Richards
Sr VP & Chief Mktg Officer: Neal J. Campbell
Sr VP, Gen Counsel & Corp Sec: Christine A. Leahy
Sr VP Opers & Chief Info Officer: Jonathan J. Stevens
Sr VP & CFO: Ann E. Ziegler
Primary Market Served: Business & Consumer

Founded: 1984

Provider of technology solutions for business, government, education and healthcare.

CMEINFO.COM
500 Corporate Pkwy (Suite 300)
Birmingham, AL 35242
Telephone: (205) 991-9188, Toll Free: (800) 284-8433, FAX: (800) 284-5964, Web Site: www.cmeinfo.com
Mktg Dir: Rich Frankel
Primary Market Served: Business & Consumer

Video & audio continuing medical education program for doctors.

CRM LEARNING
2720 Loker Ave W (Suite Q)
Carlsbad, CA 92010-6606
Telephone: (760) 431-9800, Toll Free: (800) 421-0833, FAX: (760) 931-5792, E-Mail: sales@crmlearning.com, Web Site: www.crmlearning.com
Partner & CEO: Peter Jordan
Mktg Dir: Lindy Caulder
Sls: Pan Clavert
Employees: 38
Primary Market Served: Business
Catalog available online
Direct online sales
Gross sales or billing: $6,000,000

Training videos for businesses, government, healthcare & education.

CSI
1059 Powers Rd
Conklin, NY 13748-1400
Telephone: (607) 775-7905, Web Site: www.cleanersupply.com
Pres: Jeff Schapiro
Primary Market Served: Business & Consumer

CTB/MCGRAW-HILL LLC
20 Ryan Ranch Rd
Monterey, CA 93940
Telephone: (800) 538-9547, FAX: (800) 282-0266, E-Mail: customer_service_ind@ctb.com, Web Site: www.ctb.com
Pres: Ellen Haley
COO: Sandor Nagy
VP Sls: David Seitter
Conducts Business: U.S.
Primary Market Served: Business
Catalog available online
Direct online sales

Central testing bureau for McGraw-Hill for grades K-12.

CTC CORP
Subs. of Starson Services Corp

254 Benmont Ave
Bennington, VT 05201
Telephone: (802) 442-6371, FAX: (802) 442-8526
Owner: Bruce Laumeister
Treas & Sec: Wayne Massari
Sls Mgr: Philip Jordan
Conducts Business: U.S., Canada
Employees: 100
Primary Market Served: Business & Consumer

Wholesale & retail photo-finishing lab.

CVT PRODUCTION INC

50906 Rothbury Dr
Granger, IN 46530-6291
Telephone: (574) 247-0647, Web Site: www.destinationfitness.com
Pres: Mark Lange
Primary Market Served: Business & Consumer
Catalog available online
Indirect online sales

Produce & distribute scenic workout video tapes for home exercise equipment.

CYRO INDUSTRIES

379 Interpace Pkwy Ste 1
Parsippany, NJ 07054-1131
Telephone: (973) 541-8000, Toll Free: (800) 631-5384, FAX: (973) 442-6117, (973) 442-6135, Web Site: www.cyro.com
Pres: John Medina
VP: W.M. Lowman
Gen Mgr Sheet Products: D.L. Quinlan
Conducts Business: U.S., Latin America
Employees: 750
Primary Market Served: Business
Founded: 1976

Manufacturer of acrylic sheet & molding compounds, plus polycarbonate sheet, all sold to a variety of markets.

CABLE SHOPPING NETWORK

15945 N 76th St
Scottsdale, AZ 85260-1781
Telephone: (480) 624-4446, Web Site: www.shopcsntv.com
Dir Mktg: Steven Harris
Primary Market Served: Business & Consumer

CABLEVISION SYSTEMS CORP

111 Stewart Ave
Bethpage, NY 11714
Telephone: (516) 803-2300, FAX: (516) 803-3134, Web Site: www.cablevision.com
Chmn: Charles F. Dolan
CEO: James L. Dolan
Vice Chmn & CFO: Gregg G. Seibert
Pres: Brian G. Sweeney
COO: Kristin A. Dolan
Primary Market Served: Consumer
Catalog available online
Direct online sales
Founded: 1973

Cable television, digital cable, movies-on-demand & VoIP telephony. Controls Madison Square Garden, NY Knicks, NY Rangers & Radio City Music Hall.

CADIE PRODUCTS CORP

151 E 11th St
Paterson, NJ 07524-1228
Telephone: (973) 278-8300, FAX: (973) 278-0303, E-Mail: emeyers@cadie.com, Web Site: www.cadieproducts.com
Pres: Edwin W. Meyers
VP: Bob Appelbaum
VP: Dan Kellenberger
VP: Kenneth Meyers
Conducts Business: Worldwide
Employees: 70
Primary Market Served: Consumer
Catalog available online
Advertising/Marketing Budget Related to Direct Marketing: 26-50%
Founded: 1939
Gross sales or billing: $10,000,000

Supplier of mail order specialties to catalog houses & space advertisers. Manufacture & distribute extensive cleaning products to supermarkets & mass merchandisers.

CAESARS ENTERTAINMENT CORP

1 Caesars Palace Dr
Las Vegas, NV 89109
Telephone: (702) 407-6000, Toll Free: (800) 634-6001, FAX: (702) 407-6037, Web Site: www.caesars.com
Chmn, CEO & Pres: Gary Loveman
Exec VP & CFO: Donald Colvin
Global Pres Destination Markets: Tom Jenkin
Exec VP & Chief Mktg Officer: Tariq M. Shaukat
Conducts Business: U.S.
Employees: 67,000
Primary Market Served: Business & Consumer
Catalog available online
Indirect online sales
Gross sales or billing: $8,570,000,000

Casino & entertainment company.

CAFE LANGO

Div. of Jeffrey Norton Publishers Inc
PO Box 400
Sharon Springs, NY 13459-0400
Telephone: (203) 453-1456, Toll Free: (800) 243-1234, FAX: (203) 453-5110, E-Mail: mail@cafelango.com, Web Site: www.audioforum.com
Pres: Jeffrey Norton
Acctg Mgr: Laura McGrady
Conducts Business: Worldwide
Employees: 10
Primary Market Served: Consumer
Catalog available online
Indirect online sales
Advertising/Marketing Budget Related to Direct Marketing: 76-100%
Direct Marketing ad budget: $400,000
Founded: 1972
Gross sales or billing: $2,000,000

Sell quality self-instructional language courses on CDs, audio & video cassettes as well as music, literature & personal development programs.

CALICO CORNERS

Div. of Everfast
203 Gale Ln
Kennett Square, PA 19348-1764
Telephone: (610) 444-9700, Toll Free: (800) 213-6366, FAX: (610) 444-1221, Web Site: www.calicocorners.com
CEO: Bert Kerstetter
Primary Market Served: Consumer
Founded: 1948

Retail stores across U.S. specializing in fabrics for the home, custom labor services & custom upholstery furniture.

CALIFORNIA INSTITUTE OF TECHNOLOGY

Industrial Relations Ctr 1-90
Pasadena, CA 91125-9000
Telephone: (626) 395-3746, FAX: (626) 795-7174, E-Mail: execedu@caltech.edu, Web Site: www.irc.caltech.edu
Dir, Opers & Mktg: Anne Campbell
Dir: Gaylord Nichols
Conducts Business: Worldwide
Primary Market Served: Business
Catalog available online
Direct online sales
Advertising/Marketing Budget Related to Direct Marketing: 76-100%
Direct Marketing ad budget:
Direct Mail: 94%
Magazines: 2%
Online: 4%
Founded: 1891

Develop & provide executive educational programs that focus on effective leadership in world class organizations. Programs also provide a leadership perspective that addresses critical, strategic & competitive issues.

CALIFORNIA MUSTANG PARTS & ACCESSORIES

19400 San Jose Ave
City of Industry, CA 91748
Telephone: (909) 598-3383, Toll Free: (800) 775-0101, FAX: (909) 598-5611, E-Mail: csmustang@cal-mustang.com, Web Site: www.cal-mustang.com
Pres: Gary Lovett
Conducts Business: U.S.
Employees: 2
Primary Market Served: Business & Consumer
Catalog available online
Direct online sales
Advertising/Marketing Budget Related to Direct Marketing: 26-50%
Direct Marketing ad budget:
Direct Mail: 20%
Magazines: 60%
TV/Radio: 20%
Founded: 1976
Gross sales or billing: $200,000

Parts & accessories for Ford Mustang automobiles.

CAMPBELL SOUP CO

1 Campbell Pl
Camden, NJ 08103-1701
Telephone: (856) 342-4800, Toll Free: (800) 257-8443, FAX: (856) 342-3878, Web Site: www.campbellsoupcompany.com
Pres & CEO: Denise M. Morrison
Sr VP & Chief Mktg Officer: Michael P. Senackerib
Employees: 24,000
Primary Market Served: Business & Consumer
Catalog available online
Direct online sales
Founded: 1869
Gross sales or billing: $7,343,000,000

Food manufacturers.

CANINE COMPANIONS FOR INDEPENDENCE

PO Box 446
Santa Rosa, CA 95402-0446
Telephone: (707) 577-1700, Toll Free: (800) 572-2275, FAX: (707) 577-1711, E-Mail: info@cci.org, Web Site: www.caninecompanions.org
Pres, Bd of Dirs: Jean Schulz
Devel Dir: Jennifer Conroy
CEO: Corey Hudson
Conducts Business: U.S.
Employees: 140
Primary Market Served: Consumer
Advertising/Marketing Budget Related to Direct Marketing: 0-25%
Founded: 1975

Gross sales or billing: $12,665,333
Non-profit organization providing dogs for the disabled.

CAPEZIO BALLET MAKERS INC

1 Campus Rd
Totowa, NJ 07512
Telephone: (973) 595-9000, Toll Free: (800) 533-1887, FAX: (800) 595-9120, E-Mail: info@capezio.com, Web Site: www.capezio.com
Pres & Vice Chmn: Michael Terlizzi
Employees: 400
Primary Market Served: Business & Consumer
Catalog available online
Direct online sales
Gross sales or billing: $23,000,000

Retail store chain & manufacturers of dancewear products.

CAPITOL CONCIERGE INC

1400 "I" St NW (Suite 750)
Washington, DC 20005
Telephone: (202) 223-4765, FAX: (202) 833-2287, E-Mail: onlineconcierge@capitolconcierge.com, Web Site: www.capitolconcierge.com
CEO: Lynda Ellis
Employees: 100
Primary Market Served: Business & Consumer
Founded: 1987

Corporate concierge services for commercial & residential buildings.

CARAUSTAR

5000 Austell-Powder Springs Rd (# 300)
Austell, GA 30106-3227
Telephone: (770) 948-3101, E-Mail: info@caraustar.com, Web Site: www.caraustar.com
Chmn: James E. Rogers
Pres, CEO & Dir: Michael J. Keough
Sr VP, CFO & Dir: Ronald J. Domanico
VP, Gen Counsel & Sec: Wilma E. Beaty
VP: Gregory B. Cottrell
Conducts Business: U.S.
Employees: 30
Primary Market Served: Business
Catalog available online
Gross sales or billing: $989,000,000

Manufacturer of paper, tubes, cores & cans.

CARD TECHNOLOGY INC

Div. of NBS
10925 Bren Rd E
Hopkins, MN 55343-9613

Telephone: (201) 845-7373, FAX: (201) 845-3337, E-Mail: info@nbstech.com, Web Site: www.nbstech.com
Pres: Fred Muller
VP, DM: Teresa Luke
Conducts Business: U.S.
Employees: 250
Primary Market Served: Business & Consumer
Gross sales or billing: $16,400,000

Manufacture & distribute embossing related equipment to the health care, banking & retail markets.

ER CARPENTER

Div. of Carpenter Co
302 Highland Dr
Taylor, TX 76574
Telephone: (512) 365-5833, Toll Free: (800) 234-9105, FAX: (512) 352-6025, Web Site: www.carpenter.com
Pres & CEO: Stan Yukevich
Dir: Judie Carpenter
Dir: Dan Schecter
Dir: Ken Thompsen
Conducts Business: U.S.
Employees: 100
Primary Market Served: Business
Catalog available online
Indirect online sales
Advertising/Marketing Budget Related to Direct Marketing: 0-25%
Founded: 1903

Manufacturers of polyester quilt batting, pillow forms & craft fiber, mattress pads & bed pillows.

CARROT-TOP INDUSTRIES INC

328 Elizabeth Brady Rd
Hillsborough, NC 27278-9540
Telephone: (919) 732-6200, Toll Free: (800) 628-3524, FAX: (919) 732-5526, E-Mail: service@carrot-top.com, Web Site: www.carrot-top.com
Pres: Dwight A. Morris
Dir, Mktg: Eric Pennington
Conducts Business: U.S., Canada, Mexico
Employees: 20
Primary Market Served: Business & Consumer
Catalog available online
Direct online sales
Advertising/Marketing Budget Related to Direct Marketing: 76-100%
Direct Marketing ad budget:
Direct Mail: 75%
Telephone: 25%
Founded: 1980
Gross sales or billing: $4,800,000

Sell flags, flag poles, banners, trophies & plaques. Also, sell supplies for meetings & conventions.

CARSON'S

Subs. of The Bon-Ton Stores Inc
331 W Wisconsin Ave
Milwaukee, WI 53203-2201
Telephone: (414) 347-1152, FAX: (414) 278-5748, Web Site: www. carsons.com
Pres & CEO: Brendan L. Hoffman
Exec VP & Chief Mktg Officer: Luis Fernandez
Conducts Business: U.S.
Employees: 18,000
Primary Market Served: Consumer
Advertising/Marketing Budget Related to Direct Marketing: 0-25%
Founded: 1854

CATERPILLAR INC

501 SW Jefferson Ave
Peoria, IL 61630
Telephone: (309) 675-0545, Web Site: www.cat.com
Chmn & CEO: Doug Oberhelman
Grp Pres & CFO: Bradley M. Halverson
Exec VP Law and Pub Policy: James B. Buda
Sr VP: David P. Bozeman
VP Sls & Mktg: Paolo Fellin
Primary Market Served: Business
Gross sales or billing: $55,656,000,000

Manufacturer of construction and mining equipment, diesel and natural gas engines, industrial gas turbines and diesel-electric locomotives.

CEDAR FRESH PRODUCTS

Div. of Arbor American Corp
4207 University Dr
Coral Gables, FL 33146-1140
Telephone: (305) 870-9390, Web Site: www.cedarfresh.com
Pres: Jay Butera
Pres & CEO: Jonathan Mayer
Conducts Business: U.S.
Employees: 45
Primary Market Served: Business
Catalog available online
Direct online sales

Manufacturer & distributor of housewares business-to-business.

CELESTIAL SEASONINGS

Subs. of The Hain Celestial Group Inc
4600 Sleepytime Dr
Boulder, CO 80301-3292
Telephone: (303) 530-5300, Toll Free: (800) 351-8175, FAX: (303) 581-1249, Web Site: www. celestialseasonings.com
Chmn, Pres & CEO: Irwin David Simon
CEO, Hain Celestial US: John Carroll
Chief Mktg Officer, Grocery & Snacks: Maureen M. Putman

Conducts Business: U.S., Canada, Europe, Australia
Employees: 220
Primary Market Served: Consumer
Catalog available online
Direct online sales
Founded: 1969
Gross sales or billing: $70,000,000

Manufacturer of green, herbal, wellness and other specialty teas.

CENTER FOR CREATIVE LEADERSHIP

1 Leadership Pl
Greensboro, NC 27410-9427
Telephone: (336) 545-2810, FAX: (336) 282-3284, E-Mail: info@ccl. org, Web Site: www.ccl.org
CEO & Pres: John Ryan
Sr VP Res & Innovation: David G. Altman
VP HR: Paul Draeger
Exec VP Global Leadership Devel: Lily M. Kelly-Radford Ph.D.
VP: Portia Mount
Conducts Business: Worldwide
Employees: 350
Primary Market Served: Business
Catalog available online
Direct online sales
Advertising/Marketing Budget Related to Direct Marketing: 0-25%
Direct Marketing ad budget: $550,000
Direct Mail: $500,000
Magazines: $50,000
Founded: 1970
Gross sales or billing: $24,000,000

Non-profit organization. Research based management training institution. Produce management training seminars, assessment instruments & publications of general interest to managers, leaders & human resource professionals.

CENTER FOR PROFESSIONAL DEVELOPMENT

Subs. of Florida State University
555 W Pensacola St (#2027), Turnbull Conference Ctr
Tallahassee, FL 32306-1640
Telephone: (850) 487-1691, (850) 644-8004, FAX: (850) 644-2589, Web Site: www.Learningforlife.fsu.com
Facilities Dir: Suzanne Harrell
Assoc Dir: Susann Rudasill
Mktg Dir: Jean Martin
Dir: Bill Lindner
Conducts Business: U.S.
Employees: 50
Primary Market Served: Business & Consumer
Direct Marketing ad budget: $150,000
Direct Mail: 70%

Magazines: 5%
Newspapers: 20%
TV/Radio: 5%
Founded: 1980
Gross sales or billing: $2,750,000

Design & implementation of continuing education programs to audiences primarily in southeastern United States. Operate urban & rural meeting & conference centers for regional & national programs. Also offer online programs.

CENTERCORE GROUP INC

aka Kobico LLC & Domore
201 Industrial Park
Marked Tree, AR 72365
Toll Free: (800) 686-0821, FAX: (870) 358-3330, Web Site: www. centercoregroup.com
Pres: Ralph Berger
Conducts Business: U.S., Canada, Mexico
Employees: 20
Primary Market Served: Business
Founded: 1957
Gross sales or billing: $8,000,000

Contract furniture seating, open-plan systems, wall panels, wood casegoods & seating & custom products.

CENTERPOINT ENERGY

800 LaSalle Ave
Minneapolis, MN 55402-2006
Telephone: (612) 372-4664, FAX: (612) 321-4873, E-Mail: mgc-businessinformation@ centerpointenergy.com, Web Site: www.minnegasco.centerpointenergy. com
Pres & CEO: David M. McClanahan
Prod Mgr: Kelly O'Keefe
Exec VP & Gen Counsel: Scott Rozzell
Grp Pres Regulated Opers: Thomas R. Standish
Exec VP & CFO: Gary L. Whitlock
Primary Market Served: Consumer
Founded: 1959

Gas industry, sales & marketing, business & management, household appliance merchandising, public utilities, energy.

CENTRAL SHIPPEE INC

46 Star Lake Rd
Bloomingdale, NJ 07403-1244
Telephone: (973) 838-1100, Toll Free: (800) 631-8968, FAX: (973) 838-8273, Web Site: www. centralshippee.com
Chmn Bd: Donald A. Hubner
VP, Opers: Eric Hubner
Conducts Business: U.S.
Employees: 29
Primary Market Served: Business & Consumer

Founded: 1945

Sell flameproof felt for display & exhibits. Also, tablecloths, banners, Velcro compatible fabrics & banners.

CERTAINTEED CORP

Div. of St. Gobain
750 E Swedesford Rd
Valley Forge, PA 19482
Telephone: (610) 341-7000/7739, Toll Free: (800) 233-8990, FAX: (610) 341-7777, Web Site: www. certainteed.com
VP, Mktg: Marcia Hannah
Pres & CEO: Peter Dachowski
Sr VP: Gianpaolo Caccini
VP: David Sharpe
VP & CFO: Robert Statile
Primary Market Served: Business & Consumer
Catalog available online
Founded: 1904

Insulation, siding, roofing & windows.

CESSNA AIRCRAFT CO

Subs. of Textron Inc
One Cessna Blvd
Wichita, KS 67215-1400
Telephone: (316) 517-6000, Toll Free: (800) 4-CESSNA, FAX: (316) 517-6640, Web Site: www.cessna.com
CEO: Scott Ernest
Sr VP Sls & Mktg: Kriya Shortt
Conducts Business: Worldwide
Employees: 7,500
Primary Market Served: Business & Consumer
Advertising/Marketing Budget Related to Direct Marketing: 26-50%
Founded: 1927

Aircraft manufacturer of general aviation products for business & utility use.

CHABIN CONCEPTS

2515 Ceanothus Ave (Suite 100)
Chico, CA 95973-7720
Telephone: (530) 345-0364, FAX: (530) 345-6417, E-Mail: chabininc@aol.com
Pres: Audrey Taylor
Employees: 5
Primary Market Served: Business
Founded: 1989

Industrial development & recruitment.

CHAMPION

A Gardner Denver Co
1800 Gardner Expressway
Quincy, IL 62305-9364
Telephone: (217) 222-5400, FAX: (217) 228-8260, Web Site: www. championpneumatic.com
Chmn: Ross J. Centanni

Pres, CEO & Dir: Barry L. Pennypacker
VP, Fin & CFO: Helen W. Cornell
VP, Corp Controller: David J. Antoniuk
VP & Gen Mgr: Winfried Kaiser
Conducts Business: Worldwide
Employees: 150
Primary Market Served: Business
Catalog available online
Advertising/Marketing Budget Related to Direct Marketing: 0-25%
Founded: 1919

Air compressor manufacturer.

CHANEL INC

9 W 57th St (fl 44)
New York, NY 10019
Telephone: (212) 688-5055, Toll Free: (800) 550-0005, FAX: (212) 752-1851, Web Site: www.chanel.com
Global CEO: Maureen Chiquet
Pres, US & COO: John Galantic
VP Mktg Svcs: Steve Caputo
Primary Market Served: Business & Consumer

High fashion house specializing in luxury merchandise.

CHAR-BROIL

1442 Belfast Ave
Columbus, GA 31904-4432
Telephone: (706) 571-7000, Web Site: www.charbroil.com
VP Mktg: Rob Schwing

CHARTER COMMUNICATIONS

400 Atlantic St
Stamford, CT 06901
Telephone: (203) 905-7801, Web Site: www.charter.com
Pres & CEO: Thomas M. Rutledge
COO: John Bickham
Exec VP & CFO: Christopher L. Winfrey
Exec VP & Chief Mktg Officer: Jonathan Hargis
Employees: 15,500
Primary Market Served: Consumer
Catalog available online
Indirect online sales
Advertising/Marketing Budget Related to Direct Marketing: 76-100%
Founded: 1975
Gross sales or billing: $5,500,000,000

Advanced digital technology for home & office via cable network systems.

CHASE INDUSTRIES, INC

dba Chase Doors
10021 Commerce Park Dr
Cincinnati, OH 45246-1333

Telephone: (513) 860-5565, Toll Free: (800) 543-4455, FAX: (800) 245-7045, Web Site: www.chasedoors.com
Pres: Bob Muir
VP, Sls: Mike Hegner
VP, Mktg: Rory Falato
Conducts Business: U.S.
Employees: 200
Primary Market Served: Business
Advertising/Marketing Budget Related to Direct Marketing: 0-25%
Founded: 1932
Gross sales or billing: $14,700,000

Manufacturer of double-acting impact traffic doors. Chase's product line includes strip doors and sliding fire and pharmaceutical doors.

CHATTANOOGA SHOOTING SUPPLIES INC

2600 Walker Rd
Chattanooga, TN 37421-1285
Telephone: (423) 894-3007, Toll Free: (800) 251-4808, FAX: (423) 855-5513, Web Site: www. chattanoogashooting.com
CFO: David Dodson
Sls Mgr: Jim Post
Pur Mgr: Chris Means
Primary Market Served: Business

Wholesaler of guns & reloading supplies.

CHOICE COURIER SYSTEMS INC

1 Whitehall St (fl 12)
New York, NY 10004-2138
Telephone: (212) 370-1999, FAX: (212) 370-0440, Web Site: www. choicecourier.com
Chmn: Ed Katz
Pres CEO: Michael Katz
Conducts Business: U.S.
Employees: 1,200
Primary Market Served: Consumer
Direct Marketing ad budget: $1,000,000
Direct Mail: 50%
Magazines: 15%
Newspapers: 25%
TV/Radio: 10%
Founded: 1964

Messenger & courier service. Conduct surveys of traffic needs.

CHOICE HOTELS INTERNATIONAL

1 Choice Hotels Cir (#400)
Rockville, MD 20850-5140
Telephone: (301) 592-5000, Web Site: www.choicehotels.com
Pres & CEO: Stephen Joyce
Exec VP & COO: Patrick Pacious

CFO: David White
Sr VP Performance Analytics: William Carlson
Sr VP Brand Strategy & Mktg: Alexandra Jaritz
Employees: 1,860
Primary Market Served: Business & Consumer
Gross sales or billing: $544,700,000

International lodging company.

CHOICE POINT
1000 Alderman Dr
Alpharetta, GA 30005
Telephone: (770) 752-6000, Toll Free: (800) 342-5339, FAX: (770) 752-6005, Web Site: www.choicepoint.com
Chmn & CEO: Derek V. Smith
Pres, COO & Dir: Douglas C. Curling
CFO: David E. Trine
CTO: Stanley M. Garrison
VP, Precision Mktg: Bernadette L. Randall
Primary Market Served: Business & Consumer
Catalog available online

Public records information network.

CHRISTIAN BRANDS
5226 S 31st Pl
Phoenix, AZ 85040-3742
Telephone: (602) 243-5200, Toll Free: (800) 521-2914, FAX: (602) 232-1855, Web Site: www.christian-brands.com
Pres: Paul DiGiovanni
VP: Tom DiGiovanni
Dir Mktg: Mary Ellen Wanamaker
Conducts Business: U.S.
Employees: 90
Primary Market Served: Business & Consumer
Catalog available online
Direct online sales
Advertising/Marketing Budget Related to Direct Marketing: 0-25%
Direct Marketing ad budget:
Direct Mail: 65%
Online: 35%
Founded: 1948

Church supplies & religious articles.

CINCINNATI BELL INC
221 E 4th St
Cincinnati, OH 45202-4137
Toll Free: (888) CIN-BELL, Web Site: www.cincinnatibell.com
Pres & CEO: Theodore H. Torbeck
CFO: Leigh Fox
Conducts Business: U.S.
Employees: 2,500

Primary Market Served: Consumer
Regional, integrated communications company.

CINTAS
6800 Cintas Blvd, PO Box 625737
Cincinnati, OH 45262-5737
Telephone: (513) 459-1200, Web Site: www.cintas.com
CEO: Scott D. Farmer
Pres & COO: J. Philip Holloman
Sr VP Fin & CFO: William C. Gale
Conducts Business: U.S.
Employees: 2,700
Primary Market Served: Business

Manufacturer, distributor & renter of industrial uniforms.

CIRCLE K STORES INC
Subs. of Alimentation Couche-Tard (Canada)
935 E Tallmadge Ave
Akron, OH 44310-3566
Telephone: (330) 630-6300, Web Site: www.cirlcek.com
Pres & CEO: Brian Hannasch
Conducts Business: Worldwide
Employees: 14,000
Primary Market Served: Consumer
Direct Marketing ad budget:
Direct Mail: 100%

Convenience store operator.

CLAMPITT PAPER CO
9207 Ambassador Row
Dallas, TX 75247-4506
Telephone: (214) 638-3300, FAX: (214) 634-7837, E-Mail: dcrew@clampitt.com, Web Site: www.clampitt.com
Chmn: Donald Clampitt
Office Mgr: Candie Garcia
Mktg: Whitney Robinson
Sls: Tommy Liska
Conducts Business: U.S.
Employees: 74
Primary Market Served: Business & Consumer
Catalog available online
Indirect online sales
Founded: 1941

Wholesale distributor of fine papers.

THE CLARK GRAVE VAULT CO
375 E Fifth Ave
Columbus, OH 43201-2819
Telephone: (614) 294-3761, FAX: (614) 299-2324, Web Site: www.clarkvault.com
Pres: David A. Beck
VP, Mfg: Mark A. Beck
VP, Mktg: Douglas Beck
Conducts Business: U.S., Canada

Employees: 100
Primary Market Served: Business
Catalog available online
Indirect online sales
Founded: 1898

Manufacturer of metal burial vaults. Also, metal working & stamping.

CLEARSALEING INC
8415 Pulsar Pl Ste 477
Columbus, OH 43240-4093
Telephone: (614) 448-2688, Toll Free: (800) 592-0463, Web Site: www.clearsaleing.com
CEO: Michael Lanese
Mktg Mgr: Adam Hritzak

CLEGG INDUSTRIES INC
19032 S Vermont Ave
Gardena, CA 90248-4412
Telephone: (310) 225-3800, FAX: (800) 250-9851, E-Mail: sales@clegg.xo.com, Web Site: www.cleggonline.com
Pres: Kevin Clegg
VP Mktg: Frank Bennett
Primary Market Served: Business & Consumer
Catalog available online
Founded: 1987
Gross sales or billing: $20,000,000

Manufacturer of light, sound & voice promotional products.

CLEMENTE NOVELTIES INC
301 Lafayette St
Utica, NY 13502-4311
Telephone: (315) 732-4145, FAX: (315) 732-2251, E-Mail: clemente@6org.com
Pres: Anthony Clemente
VP: Andrew J. Scarafile
Conducts Business: U.S.
Employees: 15
Primary Market Served: Business & Consumer
Founded: 1950
Gross sales or billing: $6,000,000

Direct marketing to profit organizations & school fundraising.

THE CLOROX CO
1221 Broadway
Oakland, CA 94612-1888
Telephone: (510) 271-7000, FAX: (510) 832-1463, Web Site: www.thecloroxcompany.com
Chmn & CEO: Donald R. Knauss
Exec VP & COO: George Roeth
Exec VP & COO: Benno Dorer
Sr VP & Chief Mktg Officer: Thomas P. Britanik
Conducts Business: Worldwide
Employees: 8,400

Primary Market Served: Consumer
Advertising/Marketing Budget Related
to Direct Marketing: 0-25%
Direct Marketing ad budget:
Direct Mail: $500,000
TV/Radio: $500,000
Founded: 1913
Gross sales or billing: $5,600,000,000
Manufacturer of consumer products.

CLUETT PEABODY
48 W 38th St
New York, NY 10018-6248
Telephone: (212) 984-8900, FAX:
(212) 984-8910, Web Site: www.
arrowshirt.com
Pres: James Williams
Conducts Business: Worldwide
Employees: 4,000
Primary Market Served: Business &
Consumer
Advertising/Marketing Budget Related
to Direct Marketing: 0-25%
Gross sales or billing: $650,000,000

COASTAL TOOL & SUPPLY
510 New Park Ave
West Hartford, CT 06110
Telephone: (860) 233-8213, Toll Free:
(877) 551-8665, FAX: (860) 233-
6295, E-Mail: sales@coastaltool.
com, Web Site: www.coastaltool.
com
Pres: Robert S. Ludgin
Webmaster: Todd Mogren
Conducts Business: Worldwide
Employees: 10
Primary Market Served: Business &
Consumer
Catalog available online
Direct online sales
Advertising/Marketing Budget Related
to Direct Marketing: 0-25%
Founded: 1980
Gross sales or billing: $5,000,000
Power tools, hand tools & related accessories.

COBALT
Unit of ADP Dealer Services
605 5th Ave S (Suite 800)
Seattle, WA 98104-3888
Telephone: (206) 269-6363, Toll Free:
(800) 909-8244, Web Site: www.
cobalt.com
Pres & CEO: John W. Holt

THE COCA-COLA CO
PO Box 1734
Atlanta, GA 30301-1734
Telephone: (404) 676-2121, Toll Free:
(800) 438-2653, FAX: (404) 676-
6792, Web Site: www.cocacola.com
Chmn & CEO: Muhtar Kent

CFO: Gary P. Fayard
Chief Mktg & Comml Officer: Joseph
V. Tripodi
Employees: 71,000
Primary Market Served: Business &
Consumer
Founded: 1886
Gross sales or billing: $5,080,000,000
Manufacture, distribute & market syrups & concentrates for soft drinks. Also process citrus products & manufacture orange juice & other juices & beverages.

COLE-PARMER INSTRUMENT CO
625 E Bunker Ct
Vernon Hills, IL 60061-1844
Telephone: (847) 549-7600, Toll Free:
(800) 323-4340, FAX: (847) 247-
2929, E-Mail: info@coleparmer.com,
Web Site: www.coleparmer.com
VP & CRM: Mark Graves
Dir Catalog Production & Planning:
Bob Guttosch
Pres: Andy Greenawalt
Dir, Global Mktg: Mary Blase
Conducts Business: Worldwide
Employees: 280
Primary Market Served: Business
Catalog available online
Indirect online sales
Advertising/Marketing Budget Related
to Direct Marketing: 76-100%
Direct Marketing ad budget:
Direct Mail: 90%
Magazines: 8%
Telephone: 2%
Founded: 1955
Distributor of laboratory & research equipment.

COLGATE-PALMOLIVE CO
300 Park Ave
New York, NY 10022-7499
Telephone: (212) 310-2000, Toll Free:
(800) 468-6502, FAX: (212) 310-
2475, Web Site: www.colgate.com
Pres & CEO: Ian M. Cook
Chief Mktg Officer: Nigel B. Burton
VP Global Adv: Jeff Salguero
VP Global Design & Packaging: William H. Lunderman
Conducts Business: U.S.
Employees: 37,000
Primary Market Served: Consumer
Founded: 1806
Gross sales or billing: $17,000,000,000
Manufactures & sells household products.

COLLECTIBLES TODAY NETWORK, LTD
dba Collectibles Today. Part of the
Bradford Group.
9200 N Maryland Ave
Niles, IL 60105
Toll Free: (800) 323-5577 #6, Web
Site: www.collectiblestoday.com
Pres: Richard W. Tinberg
Conducts Business: U.S., Canada
Employees: 6
Primary Market Served: Consumer
Advertising/Marketing Budget Related
to Direct Marketing: 76-100%
Sell direct mail collectibles to consumers.

COLLEGIATE CAP & GOWN
Div. of Herff Jones Inc
1000 N Market St
Champaign, IL 61820-3009
Telephone: (217) 351-9500, FAX:
(217) 351-9214, Web Site: www.
herff-jones.com
Natl Sls Mgr: Ken Langlois
Plant Mgr: Peter Slamkowski
Adv & Promo Dir: John Moore
Gen Mgr Cap & Gown Div: Tom Tanton
Conducts Business: U.S.
Employees: 500
Primary Market Served: Business
Founded: 1926
Manufacture, rent & sell graduation caps & gowns. Manufacture & sell choir apparel to churches & schools. Also, pulpit robes, academic outfits & judicial robes.

COMCAST SPECTACOR LP
3601 S Broad St Ste 1, Wells Fargo
Center
Philadelphia, PA 19148-5250
Telephone: (215) 336-3600, Toll Free:
(800) 298-4200, FAX: (215) 389-
9518, E-Mail: info@comcast-
spectacor.com, Web Site: www.
comcast-spectacor.com
Chmn: Edward M. Snider
Pres & COO: David A. Scott
Pres Global Spectrum: John Page
Exec VP Bus Devel: Mike Sheehey
Sr VP Strategic Growth Initiatives:
Dan Gallagher
CFO: Gary Rostick
Conducts Business: U.S.
Primary Market Served: Business &
Consumer
Advertising/Marketing Budget Related
to Direct Marketing: 0-25%
Founded: 1967
Sports & entertainment company.

COMMEMORATIVE BRANDS INC

7211 Circle S Rd, PO Box 149079
Austin, TX 78714-9770
Telephone: (512) 444-0571, FAX: (512) 444-0065
Adv: Theresa Aradi
Conducts Business: U.S.
Primary Market Served: Business
Advertising/Marketing Budget Related to Direct Marketing: 76-100%
Founded: 1996

Sell jewelry.

COMMSCOPE INC

1100 CommScope Pl SE
Hickory, NC 28603
Telephone: (828) 324-2200, Toll Free: (800) 982-1708, Web Site: www.commscope.com
Pres & CEO: Marvin S. Edwards Jr.
Sr VP Global Mktg: Fiona Nolan
Conducts Business: Worldwide
Employees: 11,251
Primary Market Served: Business
Advertising/Marketing Budget Related to Direct Marketing: 0-25%
Founded: 1937
Gross sales or billing: $2,195,100,000

A global designer, manufacturer, and supplier of communications equipment, services, and systems

THE COMPANY STORE INC

Div. of Hanover Direct Inc
455 Park Plaza Dr
La Crosse, WI 54601-4445
Telephone: (608) 785-1400, FAX: (608) 791-5790, Web Site: www.thecompanystore.com
Pres, Home Fashions: Jeffrey C. Potts
VP, Telemktg: Patrick Kelly
Mktg Mgr: Mark Freedman
Conducts Business: U.S.
Employees: 800
Primary Market Served: Consumer
Advertising/Marketing Budget Related to Direct Marketing: 76-100%
Founded: 1911

Direct marketer & manufacturer of comforters, pillows & other natural fiber & down-filled items.

COMPHEALTH

6440 Millrock Dr (Suite 175)
Salt Lake City, UT 84121-5892
Telephone: (801) 930-3000, Toll Free: (800) 453-3030, FAX: (801) 930-4517, E-Mail: info@comphealth.com, Web Site: www.comphealth.com
Pres: Michael Reinholtz
Conducts Business: U.S.
Employees: 150

Primary Market Served: Business
Founded: 1985

Permanent and temporary physician staffing.

CONCEPT COMMUNICATIONS CO

154 S Pinnacle Dr
Romeoville, IL 60446-4614
Telephone: (630) 829-8450, Toll Free: (800) 323-3524, FAX: (630) 629-8415, E-Mail: info@cstore1.com, Web Site: www.cstore1.com
Pres: Rudolf Orisek
VP, Opers: Tim Orisek
VP, Mktg: Martin Orisek
Primary Market Served: Business
Catalog available online
Direct online sales
Founded: 1987

Marketing agent - sell merchandise to gas stations & convenience stores.

CONDOLINK

Subs. of LDM Enterprises
3012 N 93rd St
Omaha, NE 68134-4716
Telephone: (402) 592-3525, Toll Free: (800) 877-9600, FAX: (402) 592-4122, E-Mail: info@condolink.com, Web Site: www.condolink.com
Pres: Linda Miller
Mktg Dir: Tim Whiteman
Conducts Business: Worldwide
Employees: 10
Primary Market Served: Business & Consumer
Founded: 1978

Clearinghouse for resales & rentals of resort condominium time sharing.

THE CONFERENCE BOARD INC

845 Third Ave
New York, NY 10022-6679
Telephone: (212) 759-0900, FAX: (212) 980-7014, Web Site: www.conference-board.org
Pres & CEO: Jonathan Spector
Sr VP, Opers: Salvatore J. Vitale
Exec VP & COO: Joan S. Dargery
Dir Consumer Res Ctr: Lynn Franco
Conducts Business: Worldwide
Employees: 200
Primary Market Served: Business
Catalog available online
Founded: 1916
Gross sales or billing: $55,900,000

Business research institute with offices in San Ramon, CA; Washington, DC; Chicago, IL; Ottawa, ON, Canada; Brussels, Belgium; New York and Hong Kong.

CONFORM PACIFIC

PO Box 1658
Lomita, CA 90717-5658
Toll Free: (800) CONFORM, FAX: (310) 496-2880, E-Mail: info@smartblock.com, Web Site: www.smartblock.com
Conducts Business: U.S.
Primary Market Served: Business
Founded: 1988

Manufacture construction materials.

CONMIO INC

570 Fashion Ave (Rm 1104)
New York, NY 10018-1629
Telephone: (917) 583-2651, Web Site: www.conmio.com
Sr VP: Floyd Weintraub

CONSUMER BENEFIT SERVICES INC

1620 Bond St
Naperville, IL 60563-0131
Telephone: (630) 420-6200, Toll Free: (800) 657-8309, FAX: (630) 420-2294, E-Mail: dcarlson@consumerbenefit.com, Web Site: www.consumerbenefit.com
Pres: David Carlson

CONSUMER CREDIT ADVOCATES INC

4746 S 900th E (Suite 240)
Salt Lake City, UT 84117
Telephone: (801) 265-9333, FAX: (801) 265-9595
Primary Market Served: Business & Consumer
Founded: 1989

Debt consolidators.

CONSUMER'S ENERGY

Div. of CMS Energy
212 W Michigan Ave
Jackson, MI 49201-2277
Telephone: (517) 788-0550, Toll Free: (800) 805-0490, FAX: (517) 788-1859, E-Mail: businesscenter@consumerenergy.com, Web Site: www.consumersenergy.com
Pres, CEO & Dir: David W. Joos
Exec VP & CFO: Thomas J. Webb
Sr VP & Gen Counsel: James E. Brunner
Sr VP & HR: John M. Butler
Sr VP: William E. Garrity
Primary Market Served: Business & Consumer

Electric & gas utility company.

CONVERSIONVOODOO.COM

10601 Tierrasanta Blvd (# G-371)
San Diego, CA 92124-2616

Telephone: (858) 625-4203, Web Site: www.conversionvoodoo.com

CONVERTIBLE SERVICE

5126 N Walnut Grove Ave
San Gabriel, CA 91776-2026
Telephone: (626) 285-2255, Toll Free: (800) 333-1140, FAX: (626) 285-9004, Web Site: www.convertibleparts.com
Owner: Paul Terry
Mgr: Ron Hayes
Conducts Business: Worldwide
Employees: 8
Primary Market Served: Business & Consumer
Catalog available online
Direct online sales
Advertising/Marketing Budget Related to Direct Marketing: 0-25%
Direct Marketing ad budget: $45,000
Direct Mail: 30%
Magazines: 50%
Online: 20%
Founded: 1982
Gross sales or billing: $400,000

Manufactures & sells convertible top mechanism parts.

COOPER COMMUNITIES INC

903 N 47th St
Rogers, AR 72756
Telephone: (479) 246-6500, Toll Free: (800) 648-6401, FAX: (479) 855-6256, E-Mail: coopernet@ccias.com, Web Site: www.cooper-communities.com
Chmn, Pres & CEO: John Cooper Jr.
Sr VP & CFO: Kent Burger
Pres, Cooper Land Dev: Randy Brucker
Pres, Cooper Homes Inc: Daniel W. Cooper
Conducts Business: U.S.
Employees: 600
Primary Market Served: Business & Consumer
Catalog available online
Advertising/Marketing Budget Related to Direct Marketing: 51-75%
Direct Marketing ad budget:
Direct Mail: $6,000,000
Telephone: $500,000
Founded: 1954
Gross sales or billing: $169,000,000

Develop entire communities & sell to middle-income consumers in about four states.

COOPER TIRE & RUBBER CO INC

dba Coopertires
701 Lima Ave
Findlay, OH 45840-2315
Telephone: (419) 423-1321, Toll Free: (800) 537-9523, FAX: (419) 424-4212, E-Mail: cooperinfo@coopertire.com, Web Site: www.coopertire.com
Chmn, Pres & CEO: Roy V. Armes
Sr VP & Chief Human Resources Officer: Brenda Harmon
VP & CFO: Brad Hughes
Conducts Business: U.S., Europe, Middle East, China, Mexico
Employees: 13,355
Primary Market Served: Business
Direct Marketing ad budget: $42,555
Founded: 1914
Gross sales or billing: $2,900,000,000

Manufacture and sale of replacement tires, including passenger, light truck, motorcycle and racing.

COPTECH INC

219 Water St
Saugus, MA 01906-1948
Telephone: (781) 935-2679, Toll Free: (800) 934-1560, FAX: (781) 935-7673, Web Site: www.coptechinc.com
Pres: Tom Cherry
Primary Market Served: Business

COSCO INDUSTRIES INC

7220 W Wilson Ave
Chicago, IL 60706-4706
Telephone: (708) 867-5800, Toll Free: (800) 323-0253, FAX: (800) 323-0275
Pres & Gen Mgr: John Anthony
VP & Sec: Paul C. Becker
Sls Mgr: Liz Schmidt
Conducts Business: Worldwide
Primary Market Served: Business

Manufacturer of marking devices & machines.

COSMO INTERNATIONAL

601 Fairway Dr
Deerfield Beach, FL 33441-1867
Telephone: (954) 798-4500, FAX: (954) 798-4514
Pres: J.F. Belmont
Mktg Mgr: Felipe Martinez
Primary Market Served: Business & Consumer

Manufacture fragrances.

COTTA TRANSMISSION CO

1301 Prince Hall Dr
Beloit, WI 53511
Telephone: (608) 368-5600, FAX: (608) 368-5605, E-Mail: sales@cotta.com, Web Site: www.cotta.com
Pres: Matt Modek
VP: John Duncan Thompson
Mktg Dir: Larry Mowell

Conducts Business: U.S.
Primary Market Served: Business
Catalog available online
Advertising/Marketing Budget Related to Direct Marketing: 0-25%
Direct Marketing ad budget:
Direct Mail: 2%
Magazines: 98%
Founded: 1909

Sells industrial gearboxes to OEMs in a variety of industries.

THE COUNTRY BED SHOP

328 Richardson Rd
Ashby, MA 01431
Telephone: (978) 386-7550, FAX: (978) 386-7263, E-Mail: alan@countrybed.com, Web Site: www.countrybed.com
Pres: Alan Pease
Conducts Business: U.S.
Primary Market Served: Consumer
Catalog available online
Indirect online sales
Founded: 1975

Manufacture early American wood furniture.

COVERDELL CANADA CORPORATION

1801 McGill College Ave (Suite 725)
Montreal, QC, Canada H3A 2N4
Telephone: (514) 847-7800
Primary Market Served: Business

COX COMMUNICATIONS INC

Div. of Cox Enterprises
1400 Lake Hearn Dr
Atlanta, GA 30319-1464
Telephone: (404) 843-5000, Toll Free: (888) 566-7751, FAX: (404) 269-2243, Web Site: www.cox.com
Pres: Patrick J. Esser
Exec VP, Chief Opers Officer: Jill Campbell
Exec VP Product Mgmt & Devel: Len Barlik
Sr VP & Chief Mktg & Sls Officer: Mark Greatrex
Sr VP Product Mktg: David Pugliese
Sr VP Brand Mktg, Adv & Social Media: Joseph J. Rooney
Conducts Business: U.S.
Employees: 825
Primary Market Served: Business & Consumer
Catalog available online
Indirect online sales
Advertising/Marketing Budget Related to Direct Marketing: 26-50%
Gross sales or billing: $133,000,000

COYNE AMERICAN INSTITUTE

330 N Green St
Chicago, IL 60607-1300
Telephone: (773) 935-2520, Toll Free: (800) 999-5220, FAX: (773) 935-2920, Web Site: www.coyneamerican.edu
Pres: Russell Freeman
VP: Lee Mueller
Indus Rep: Bill Austin
Conducts Business: U.S.
Employees: 200
Primary Market Served: Consumer
Catalog available online
Founded: 1899

Industrial training organization in the areas of electronics technician, electrical maintenance, air conditioning, refrigeration, heating & computer systems skills.

THE CRACKER BOX INC

PO Box 114
Blooming Glen, PA 18911-0114
Telephone: (215) 443-7777, FAX: (215) 443-7777, E-Mail: walter@ crackerboxkits.com, Web Site: www.crackerboxkits.com
Pres: Paul T. Caine
Conducts Business: Worldwide
Primary Market Served: Consumer
Catalog available online
Direct online sales
Founded: 1971

Catalog of 223 original beaded ornament kits.

CRAFT-DISTON INDUSTRIES

Subs. of Architectural Art Mfg. Inc
PO Box 12492
Wichita, KS 67277-2492
Telephone: (316) 838-4291, Toll Free: (800) 835-0028, FAX: (316) 838-8502, Web Site: www.craftdiston.com
Pres & Owner: John J. Murphy
VP & Gen Mgr: Carl Fry
Conducts Business: U.S., Mexico, Caribbean, Peru, Argentina, Chile
Employees: 30
Primary Market Served: Business & Consumer
Catalog available online
Indirect online sales
Advertising/Marketing Budget Related to Direct Marketing: 26-50%
Founded: 1985
Gross sales or billing: $4,000,000

Shower & tub enclosures, mirrored closet doors to glass houses & plumbing wholesalers.

CRANE PUMPS & SYSTEMS INC

aka CP&S
420 Third St
Piqua, OH 45356-3918
Telephone: (937) 773-2442, FAX: (937) 773-2238, E-Mail: cranepumps@cranepumps.com, Web Site: www.cranepumps.com
Pres: Vincent Buffa
VP Sls & Mktg: Brian O'Toole
Dir Mktg: Chuck Drake
Conducts Business: Worldwide
Employees: 811
Primary Market Served: Business
Catalog available online
Indirect online sales
Gross sales or billing: $89,800,000

Pumps, end suction, regen turbine, self-priming, vertical multistage, sump pumps & condensate return systems for OEM & industrial markets.

CREATIVE HEALTH PRODUCTS

5148 Saddle Ridge Rd
Plymouth, MI 48170
Telephone: (734) 996-5900, Toll Free: (800) 742-4478, FAX: (734) 996-4650, Web Site: www.chponline.com
Pres: Marlene Donoghue
VP, Sec: W.C. Donoghue
Sls Mgr: Robin Mack
Mgr: Debbie Schooley
Conducts Business: Worldwide
Employees: 10
Primary Market Served: Business & Consumer
Catalog available online
Direct online sales
Advertising/Marketing Budget Related to Direct Marketing: 76-100%
Direct Marketing ad budget:
Direct Mail: 37%
Magazines: 1%
Online: 62%
Founded: 1976
Gross sales or billing: $1,500,000

Fitness testing products.

CREATIVE TEACHING ASSOCIATES

23505 Auberry Rd
Clovis, CA 93619-9648
Telephone: (559) 291-6626, Toll Free: (800) 767-4282, FAX: (559) 291-2953, Web Site: www.mastercta.com
Pres & CEO: Richard Wiebe
Sls & Mktg Mgr: Laurie Long
Conducts Business: Worldwide
Employees: 35
Primary Market Served: Business
Catalog available online
Advertising/Marketing Budget Related to Direct Marketing: 0-25%

Direct Marketing ad budget:
Direct Mail: $15,000
Magazines: $5,000
Telephone: $1,500
Founded: 1971
Gross sales or billing: $3,000,000

Manufacturer & marketer of teaching materials such as games, teaching/learning activities & books for math, science, language & reading for grades K-12.

CREATIVITY INTERNATIONAL

4930 Cascade Rd SE
Ada, MI 49546
Telephone: (616) 956-0053, FAX: (616) 956-6957
Pres: Sheri Lewis
Pres: Charles J. Lewis
Employees: 3
Primary Market Served: Consumer
Founded: 1978
Gross sales or billing: $120,000

Sell educational material to professional photographers via direct mail.

CREST HEALTHCARE SUPPLY

195 S Third St
Dassel, MN 55325-4511
Toll Free: (800) 328-8908, (800) 369-9207, Web Site: www.cresthealthcare.com
Pres: Larry Lautt
Mktg & Sls Dir: Paul Kritzeck
IT: Adam Simons
IT: Chad Ardoff
Conducts Business: U.S., Canada, Puerto Rico
Employees: 80
Primary Market Served: Business
Catalog available online
Indirect online sales
Advertising/Marketing Budget Related to Direct Marketing: 76-100%
Founded: 1967
Gross sales or billing: $10,000,000

Direct marketer of hospital signal systems, nurse call equipment, pillow speakers, bed maintenance & accessories, general maintenance, fire protection security & surveillance, blood pressure equipment, healthcare TV, lighting fixtures & exam lamps, cubicle curtains, track & hardware, special orders, repair services, casters, wheelchair parts & signage.

CRESTLINE SPECIALTIES, INC

Div. of Geiger Brothers
70 Mt Hope Ave
Lewiston, ME 04241

Telephone: (207) 777-7075, Toll Free: (866) 488-4975, FAX: (207) 784-5038, E-Mail: info@crestline.com, Web Site: www.crestline.com
VP & Gen Mgr: Judy Paradis
Conducts Business: U.S.
Employees: 62
Primary Market Served: Business
Gross sales or billing: $8,200,000

Advertising specialties & custom imprinted products for industry, education & associations.

CRONIN & CO
50 Nye Rd
Glastonbury, CT 06033-2196
Telephone: (860) 659-0514, Web Site: www.cronin-co.com
Partner & COO: Kimberly Manning
Primary Market Served: Business & Consumer

A T CROSS CO
1 Albion Rd
Lincoln, RI 02865-3700
Telephone: (401) 333-1200, Toll Free: (800) 282-7677, FAX: (401) 334-2861, Web Site: www.cross.com
Pres & CEO: David Whalen
VP, Fin, CFO: Kevin F. Mahoney
VP Legal & HR: Tina C. Benik
VP Strategic Devel: Robin Boss Dorman
Pres Cross Accessory Division: Charles S. Mellen
Conducts Business: U.S., Canada, Europe, Asia, Bermuda, Puerto Rico
Employees: 900
Primary Market Served: Business
Catalog available online
Direct online sales
Founded: 1846
Gross sales or billing: $139,000,000

Manufacturer & marketer of fine writing instruments & gifts.

CROSS COUNTRY AUTOMOTIVE SERVICES
1 Cabot Rd
Medford, MA 02155-5117
Telephone: (781) 393-9300, Web Site: www.cchs.com
Dir, Mktg & Communs: Katherine Bassick
Primary Market Served: Business

CROSS COUNTRY TRAVCORPS
6551 Park of Commerce Blvd
Boca Raton, FL 33487-8247
Toll Free: (800) 530-6125, FAX: (561) 998-8533, Web Site: www.crosscountrytravcorps.com
Pres & CEO: Joseph A. Boshart

VP, Corp Devel & Strategy: Victor Kalafa
Conducts Business: U.S.
Employees: 1,200
Primary Market Served: Consumer
Advertising/Marketing Budget Related to Direct Marketing: 0-25%
Founded: 1978
Gross sales or billing: $655,400,000
Healthcare staffing.

CUISINART
Div. of Conair Corp
1 Cummings Point Rd
Stamford, CT 06902-7901
Telephone: (203) 975-4600, FAX: (203) 975-4660, E-Mail: marketing@cuisinart.com, Web Site: www.cuisinart.com
CEO: Leandro Rizzuto Jr.
Dir Mktg Commun: Mary Rodgers
Conducts Business: Worldwide
Primary Market Served: Business & Consumer
Founded: 1971

Food processors & stainless steel cookware, blenders, toasters, coffee makers & cooking accessories.

CULINARY PARTS UNLIMITED
840 Folsom St
San Francisco, CA 94107
Toll Free: (800) 543-7549, FAX: (415) 495-5141, Web Site: www.culinaryparts.com
Mgr: Mike Hanika
Conducts Business: U.S., Canada
Employees: 12
Primary Market Served: Business & Consumer
Advertising/Marketing Budget Related to Direct Marketing: 76-100%
Direct Marketing ad budget: $100,000
Direct Mail: 70%
Magazines: 25%
Newspapers: 5%
Gross sales or billing: $2,000,000

Replacement parts & accessories for high-end kitchenware, both European & domestic products.

CUSTOM DIRECT
8245 N Union Blvd
Colorado Springs, CO 80920-4456
Telephone: (410) 679-3300
VP, Opers: Dale Dabbs
Primary Market Served: Consumer

CYTEC INDUSTRIES INC
1405 Buffalo St
Olean, NY 14760-1139

Telephone: (716) 372-9650, FAX: (716) 372-1594, Web Site: www.conap.com
Pur Mgr: Bill Work
Admin: Marsha Topec
Conducts Business: Worldwide
Employees: 100
Primary Market Served: Business
Catalog available online
Founded: 1958

Supplies epoxy & polyurethane resin systems for potting & encapsulation, conformal coatings, adhesives, sealants, tooling resin systems & elastomers for the defense, aerospace, electronic, biomedical, computer, automotive & related markets.

DCA
889 S Matlack St
West Chester, PA 19382
Telephone: (610) 344-7488, Toll Free: (800) 638-6684, FAX: (610) 431-6500, E-Mail: ortho@dentalcorp.com, Web Site: www.dentalcorp.com
Pres: Don Taylor
Conducts Business: U.S., Canada, Europe, S. America, Asia, Africa
Employees: 5
Primary Market Served: Business & Consumer
Catalog available online
Direct online sales
Advertising/Marketing Budget Related to Direct Marketing: 0-25%
Direct Marketing ad budget: $100,000
Founded: 1982
Gross sales or billing: $2,500,000

Sell orthodontic supplies.

DIA - NIELSEN USA INC
Subs. of DIA - Nielsen GmbH Duren Germany
41 Twosome Dr (Unit 5)
Moorestown, NJ 08057
Telephone: (856) 642-9700, Toll Free: (800) 893-6361, FAX: (856) 642-9709, Web Site: www.dianielsen.com
Mng Dir: Richard Tillinghast
Conducts Business: N. America, S. America
Employees: 10
Primary Market Served: Business
Catalog available online
Advertising/Marketing Budget Related to Direct Marketing: 0-25%
Founded: 1978

Manufacturer of consumable products for industrial, medical and gaming markets.

DMB REALTY NETWORK
20789 N Pima Rd (Suite 250)
Scottsdale, AZ 85255-7206

Telephone: (480) 515-0148, Web Site: www.dmbrealty.com
Mktg Communs: Gina Canzonetta

DMC CORP
Subs. of DMC Inc Paris France
10 Basin Dr (Suite 130)
Kearny, NJ 07032
Telephone: (973) 589-0606, Toll Free: (800) 275-4117, FAX: (973) 589-8931, Web Site: www.dmc-usa.com
VP Mktg: Steve Mancuso
Conducts Business: Worldwide
Employees: 100
Primary Market Served: Business & Consumer
Catalog available online
Direct online sales
Advertising/Marketing Budget Related to Direct Marketing: 0-25%
Direct Marketing ad budget: $100
Founded: 1934
Gross sales or billing: $21,500,000

Craft manufacturer sells to specialty & mass market outlets. Wool broadwoven fabric and wholesale nondurable goods knitting mill.

DPC COMPUTERS
42 Melnick Dr
Monsey, NY 10952
Telephone: (845) 426-3790, Toll Free: (866) 513-CORP, FAX: (845) 426-6275, E-Mail: learnmore@salestax.com, Web Site: www.salestax.com
Pres & CEO: David Polatseck
Sls Dir & CFO: Abe Brach
VP Prof Svcs: Anthony Ward
Conducts Business: U.S., Canada
Employees: 15
Primary Market Served: Business
Catalog available online
Direct online sales
Advertising/Marketing Budget Related to Direct Marketing: 51-75%
Direct Marketing ad budget: $200,000
Direct Mail: 25%
Magazines: 25%
Telephone: 50%
Founded: 1991
Gross sales or billing: $2,000,000

Sales tax compliance software. Provides current sales & use tax rates by zip code & covers the entire U.S., its territories & Canada. Provides stand alone systems & integration files. Provides CD-Rom of sales tax forms.

DA-LITE SCREEN CO INC
3100 N Detroit St
Warsaw, IN 46582-2288
Telephone: (574) 267-8101, Toll Free: (800) 622-3737, FAX: (574) 267-7804, E-Mail: info@da-lite.com, Web Site: www.da-lite.com

Pres, CEO: Richard Lundin
Sr VP, Sls & Mktg: Judy Loughran
Mktg Coord: Dawn J. Stiles
Dir Mktg: Wendy Long
Conducts Business: Worldwide
Employees: 600
Primary Market Served: Business
Catalog available online
Indirect online sales
Advertising/Marketing Budget Related to Direct Marketing: 26-50%
Direct Marketing ad budget: $1,300,000
Founded: 1909

Projection screens, computer furniture, lecterns & audio visual equipment.

DAIRY FARMERS OF AMERICA INC
10220 N Ambassador Dr Suite 1000
Kansas City, MO 64153-2327
Telephone: (816) 801-6455, Toll Free: (888) 332-6455, FAX: (816) 801-6456, E-Mail: webmail@dfamilk.com, Web Site: www.dfamilk.com
Pres & CEO: Richard P. Smith
Exec VP: Mark Korsmeyer
Sr VP, Fin: David Meyer
Sr VP & Chief Fluid Mktg Officer: John Wilson
Employees: 4,000
Primary Market Served: Business & Consumer
Founded: 1998
Gross sales or billing: $7,800,000,000

Produce & distribute dairy products.

DAMILIC CORP
601 Dover Rd Ste 7
Rockville, MD 20850-1275
Telephone: (301) 251-2960, Toll Free: (800) 276-7749, FAX: (301) 251-8591, E-Mail: info@realsig.com, Web Site: www.realsig.com
Pres: Robert Olding
Conducts Business: U.S., Canada, Europe, Central & S. America
Employees: 7
Primary Market Served: Business
Catalog available online
Founded: 1998

Manufacturer of automatic signature machines which write signatures (with notes or postscripts) or calligraphy. Operates as an attachment to an IBM/PC or compatible with automatic paper feeding.

DANKER LABORATORIES INC
6805 33rd St E, Box 1899
Sarasota, FL 34243

Toll Free: (800) 237-9641, FAX: (800) 665-5086, E-Mail: sales@dankerlabs.com, Web Site: www.dankerlabs.com
Owner: Frederick Danker
Office Mgr & Exec Asst: Gwen Norris
Gen Mgr: Kevin Hing
Conducts Business: U.S., Canada
Employees: 15
Primary Market Served: Business
Catalog available online
Direct online sales
Advertising/Marketing Budget Related to Direct Marketing: 0-25%
Founded: 1958

Manufactures contact lenses, solutions & cases. Sell to ophthalmologists, optometrists, opticians, hospitals, pharmacies & drug wholesalers.

DANSK
Subs. of Lenox Corp
PO Box 2006
Bristol, PA 19007-0806
Telephone: (914) 697-6400, Toll Free: (800) 326-7528, FAX: (914) 697-6464, Web Site: www.dansk.com
CEO: Peter Cameron
Primary Market Served: Business & Consumer
Founded: 1954

Manufacturer of tabletop goods.

DASSAULT FALCON JET CORP
dba Dassault Aviation
200 Riser Rd
Little Ferry, NJ 07643-1226
Telephone: (201) 440-6700, FAX: (201) 541-4515, Web Site: www.dassaultfalcon.com
Chmn: Charles Edelstone
Pres, CEO & Dir: John Rosanvallon
Sr VP, Fin & Admin: J. Morgan Young
Conducts Business: U.S.
Primary Market Served: Business & Consumer
Founded: 1963

Business aircraft services.

DATACAL ENTERPRISES
1345 N Mondel Dr
Gilbert, AZ 85233
Telephone: (480) 813-3100, Toll Free: (800) 223-0123, FAX: (480) 545-8090, E-Mail: info@datacal.com, Web Site: www.datacal.com
Pres: Jim Lunt
Primary Market Served: Business & Consumer
Catalog available online
Direct online sales

Founded: 1999

Computer, accessories, video & CD computer training.

DATALEVER CORP
1515 Walnut St (Suite 200)
Boulder, CO 80302-5429
Telephone: (303) 541-1515, Web Site: www.datalever.com
VP: Ed Sugg
Primary Market Served: Business

DATAPOINT USA INC
8122 Datapoint Dr (Suite 300)
San Antonio, TX 78229-3264
Telephone: (210) 614-9977, FAX: (210) 614-2297, E-Mail: info@ datapointusa.com, Web Site: www. datapointusa.com
Pres: John Perkins
Conducts Business: Worldwide
Employees: 1,500
Primary Market Served: Business
Founded: 1968
Gross sales or billing: $208,000,000

Local area networks & network servers, enterprise-wide system integration, networked video conferencing & PCs.

DAVID DAUBER & ASSOCIATES
50 Lexington Ave (Suite 173)
New York, NY 10010
Telephone: (212) 564-1728, FAX: (212) 208-4524, E-Mail: advancedbc@aol.com
Pres: David Dauber
Conducts Business: U.S.
Primary Market Served: Business
Catalog available online
Advertising/Marketing Budget Related to Direct Marketing: 26-50%
Founded: 1991

Assists companies in establishing mail order & internet Visa/MasterCard merchant accounts & database management and provide secure gateways, web hosting and web creation.

THE DAVIS CENTER
19 State Route 10 (Suite 25)
Succasunna, NJ 07876-1750
Telephone: (862) 251-4637, FAX: (862) 251-4642, E-Mail: info@ thedaviscenter.com, Web Site: www. thedaviscenter.com
Pres & Founder: Dorinne S. Davis
Office Mgr: Nancy Puckett-Dunn
Conducts Business: U.S. Worldwide, (Europe, Asia, other)
Employees: 4
Primary Market Served: Business & Consumer
Catalog available online

Advertising/Marketing Budget Related to Direct Marketing: 0-25%
Direct Marketing ad budget:
Direct Mail: $3,000
Magazines: $1,000
Newspapers: $1,000
Founded: 1998

Services for general education, therapy, hearing & speech.

DAYDOTS
1801 Riverbend W Dr
Fort Worth, TX 76118
Telephone: (817) 590-4500, Toll Free: (800) 321-3687, FAX: (800) 438-7002, E-Mail: customercare@ daydots.com, Web Site: www. daydots.com
Pres: Mike Milliorn
Exec VP & CFO: Peter Currie
VP, Sls: Rob Heidemann
Mktg Mgr: Karen Combs
Primary Market Served: Business
Catalog available online
Direct online sales
Founded: 1985

Manufacture pressure sensitive labels for food retailers. Distribution of food safety products for restaurants.

DAYS INNS WORLDWIDE INC
Div. Wyndham Worldwide Corp
1 Sylvan Way Ste 2
Parsippany, NJ 07054-3879
Telephone: (973) 753-6000, Toll Free: (800) 441-1618, Web Site: www. daysinn.com
Pres: Clyde Guinn
Sr VP Mktg & Commun: Alyson Johnson
Conducts Business: Worldwide
Primary Market Served: Business & Consumer
Catalog available online
Advertising/Marketing Budget Related to Direct Marketing: 0-25%
Founded: 1970

International mid-market hotel chain.

DEERE & CO
dba John Deere
One John Deere Pl
Moline, IL 61625
Telephone: (309) 765-8000, FAX: (309) 748-0114, Web Site: www. deere.com
Chmn & CEO: Samuel R. Allen
Sr VP & CFO: Rajesh Kalathur
VP Corp Commun & Global Brand Mgmt: Francis B. Emerson
VP Corp Strategy & Bus Devel: David C. Larson
Conducts Business: Worldwide

Primary Market Served: Business & Consumer
Catalog available online
Indirect online sales
Advertising/Marketing Budget Related to Direct Marketing: 0-25%
Founded: 1921

Manufacturer of portable outdoor power equipment.

DEL WEBB
100 Bloomfield Hills Pkwy Ste 150
Bloomfield Hills, MI 48304-2957
Telephone: (248) 644-7300, Toll Free: (888) 717-9777, FAX: (248) 433-4598, Web Site: www.delwebb.com
Chmn: William J. Pulite
Pres & CEO: Richard J. Dugas Jr.
Exec VP & CFO: Roger A. Cregg
Exec VP, HR: Leo J. Taylor
Sr VP & Gen Counsel: John R. Stroller
Primary Market Served: Business & Consumer
Catalog available online

Home builders–55 yrs. & over, active adult retirement community.

DELL COMPUTER CORP
RP-NFOA
One Dell Way
Round Rock, TX 78682
Telephone: (512) 338-4400, FAX: (512) 283-6161, Web Site: www.dell. com
Chmn & CEO: Michael S. Dell
Sr VP & Chief Mktg Officer: Karen H. Quintos
Primary Market Served: Business & Consumer
Advertising/Marketing Budget Related to Direct Marketing: 76-100%

Design, manufacture, & direct market personal computers.

DELMMAR COMMUNICATIONS
920 N Ashland Dr
Cameron, MO 64429
Telephone: (816) 632-1583, Toll Free: (800) 872-2627, FAX: (816) 632-5107, E-Mail: sales@eradiostore. com, Web Site: www.delmmar.com
Mktg Dir: Connie Lintner
Primary Market Served: Business
Catalog available online
Direct online sales
Founded: 1987

Distributor for Motorola radius division radios & Jobcom by Ritroin 2 way radios

DELSTAR TECHNOLOGIES INC
Subs. of SWM

601 Industrial Dr
Middletown, DE 19709
Telephone: (302) 378-8888, Toll Free:
(800) 521-6713, FAX: (302) 378-4482, Web Site: www.delstarinc.com
CEO: Mark Abrahams
VP, Sls & Mktg: D. Timothy Cullen
Conducts Business: U.S., Canada, Europe
Employees: 132
Primary Market Served: Business & Consumer
Catalog available online
Direct online sales
Direct Marketing ad budget:
Direct Mail: $20,000
Magazines: $100,000
Newspapers: $10,000
Founded: 1946
Gross sales or billing: $74,600,000

Manufactures extruded plastic netting used in various applications including filtration, parts protection, grocery store case liners, automotive, aquaculture & fencing.

DELTA UPSILON INTERNATIONAL FRATERNITY

8705 Founders Rd, Box 68942
Indianapolis, IN 46268
Telephone: (317) 875-8900, FAX:
(317) 876-1629, E-Mail: ihq@deltau.org, Web Site: www.deltau.org
Exec Dir: Justin Kirk
Assoc Exec Dir: Karl Grindel
Conducts Business: U.S., Canada
Employees: 11
Primary Market Served: Consumer
Catalog available online
Direct online sales
Advertising/Marketing Budget Related to Direct Marketing: 0-25%
Direct Marketing ad budget:
Direct Mail: $10,000
Magazines: $100,000
Founded: 1834

Headquarters for Delta Upsilon International Fraternity chapters in the U.S. & Canada. Offers fraternity related items.

DELUXE LABORATORIES INC

Div. of Rank of London
5433 Fernwood Ave
Hollywood, CA 90027
Telephone: (323) 462-6171, FAX:
(323) 960-7016, E-Mail: steven.vananda@bydeluxe.com, Web Site: www.bydeluxe.com
Pres, CEO: Peter Pacitti
Exec VP & CFO: Tom Vale
VP, Mktg: Dierdre Kurnett
VP & Gen Mgr: Michael Jackman
Conducts Business: U.S., Canada

Employees: 1,200
Primary Market Served: Business
Catalog available online
Indirect online sales
Advertising/Marketing Budget Related to Direct Marketing: 0-25%

Full-service video tape duplication, packaging & fulfillment services.

DENVER TAX SOFTWARE INC

PO Box 632285
Littleton, CO 80163-2285
Telephone: (303) 796-7780, Toll Free:
(800) 326-6686, FAX: (888) 326-6686, Web Site: www.denvertax.com
Owner & Pres: Dave Kaufmann
Primary Market Served: Business
Catalog available online
Direct online sales

Tax software to CPAs.

DERMAC LABS INC

dba Touch of Mink
PO Box 5268
Salem, OR 97304-0268
Telephone: (503) 399-8181, Toll Free:
(800) 547-9164, FAX: (503) 581-7439, Web Site: www.touchofmink.com
Pres & CEO: John Simpson
Conducts Business: U.S., Taiwan
Employees: 22
Primary Market Served: Business & Consumer
Advertising/Marketing Budget Related to Direct Marketing: 76-100%
Founded: 1970
Gross sales or billing: $1,800,000

Manufacturer of skin & hair care products. Supply hotel amenities. Private packaging for private labels.

DESERET BOOK

PO Box 30178
Salt Lake City, UT 84130-0178
Telephone: (801) 534-1515, Toll Free:
(800) 453-4532, FAX: (801) 517-3392, Web Site: www.deseretbook.com
Mgr: Rex T. Carlisle Jr.
Dir: Mark Standing
Conducts Business: Worldwide
Employees: 3
Primary Market Served: Consumer
Founded: 1871

Retail, mail & phone order sales of books & other related book store merchandise with emphasis on religion.

DETAILS INTERACTIVE LLC

30 Manchester Dr
Westfield, NJ 07090-2265

Telephone: (917) 331-0685, E-Mail:
mark@detailsinteractive.com, Web Site: www.detailsinteractive.com

THE DETROIT INSTITUTE OF ARTS

5200 Woodward Ave
Detroit, MI 48202
Telephone: (313) 833-7900, FAX:
(313) 833-1390, Web Site: www.dia.org
Dir, Pres & CEO: Graham W. Beal
Exec VP & COO: Annmarie Erickson
Conducts Business: U.S.
Primary Market Served: Business & Consumer
Catalog available online
Direct online sales
Gross sales or billing: $55,400,000

Museum wholesale & retail merchandise.

DEVELOPMENT DIMENSIONS INTERNATIONAL

1225 Washington Pike
Bridgeville, PA 15017-2838
Telephone: (412) 257-0600, Toll Free:
(800) 933-4463, FAX: (412) 220-2942, E-Mail: info@ddiworld.com, Web Site: www.ddiworld.com
Owner & Pres: William C. Byham
Pres: Bob Rogers
Cons DDI Direct: Jane Miller Rollman
Primary Market Served: Business

Human resources training & consulting.

DEVRY EDUCATION GROUP

3005 Highland Pkwy
Downers Grove, IL 60515-5799
Telephone: (630) 515-7700, Toll Free:
(800) 73-DEVRY, E-Mail: inquiries@devrygroup.com, Web Site: www.devryeducationgroup.com
Pres & CEO: Daniel Hamburger
Sr Dir Global Commun: Ernie Gibble
Conducts Business: U.S., Canada
Employees: 4,800
Primary Market Served: Consumer
Gross sales or billing: $933,000,000

Global provider of educational services.

DEXTA CORP

962 Kaiser Rd
Napa, CA 94558
Telephone: (707) 255-2454, Toll Free:
(800) 733-3982, FAX: (707) 255-8520, Web Site: www.dexta.com
Pres: Paul Rusin

Primary Market Served: Business
Sell medical & dental equipment factory direct.

DIAGRAPH CORP
One Missouri Research Park Dr
Saint Charles, MO 63304-5685
Telephone: (636) 300-2000, Toll Free: (800) 722-1125, FAX: (636) 300-2004, E-Mail: info@diagraph.com, Web Site: www.diagraph.com
Mktg Dir: Bill Myers
Prod Mgr: Jackie Goodell
Conducts Business: U.S.
Primary Market Served: Business
Catalog available online
Founded: 1896

Industrial marking products including labels, ink jet printers & label printer applicators.

DIDIT
330 Old Country Rd (Suite 206)
Mineola, NY 11501-4143
Telephone: (212) 631-0157, Web Site: www.did-it.com
Exec Chmn: Kevin Lee
Primary Market Served: Consumer

DIEBOLD INC
5995 Mayfair Rd, PO Box 3077
North Canton, OH 44720-8077
Telephone: (330) 490-4000, Toll Free: (800) DIEBOLD, Web Site: www.diebold.com
Pres & CEO: Andy W. Mattes
Exec VP & COO: George S. Meyers Jr.
Exec VP Electronic Security: Tony Byerly
Sr VP Strategic Projects: Stefan E. Merz
Conducts Business: Worldwide
Employees: 15,500
Primary Market Served: Business
Catalog available online
Direct online sales
Advertising/Marketing Budget Related to Direct Marketing: 26-50%
Founded: 1859
Gross sales or billing: $2,900,000,000
Sells ATM machines & supplies.

DIGDEV DIRECT
260 SW Natura Ave (fl 2)
Deerfield Beach, FL 33441
Telephone: (954) 949-9500, Web Site: www.foundationmediagroup.com
Primary Market Served: Business & Consumer

DINEEQUITY INC
450 N Brand Blvd (fl 7)
Glendale, CA 91203-4415
Toll Free: (866) 995-DINE, Web Site: dineequity.com
Chmn & CEO: Julia A. Stewart
CFO: Tom W. Emrey
Pres Applebee's International Inc: Steven R. Layt
Sr VP Commun & Pub Affairs: Scott Remy
Conducts Business: U.S., Canada, Japan
Primary Market Served: Consumer
Catalog available online
Advertising/Marketing Budget Related to Direct Marketing: 0-25%
Founded: 1958
Gross sales or billing: $349,000,000

Operator & franchiser of IHOP & Applebees restaurants.

DINN BROTHERS INC
The Trophy People
221 Interstate Dr
West Springfield, MA 01089
Telephone: (413) 750-3466, Toll Free: (800) 628-9657, FAX: (800) 876-7497, E-Mail: sales@dinntrophy.com, Web Site: www.dinntrophy.com
Pres: Bill Dinn
Sls Mgr: Michael Dinn
Conducts Business: U.S.
Primary Market Served: Business & Consumer
Catalog available online
Founded: 1956
Gross sales or billing: $8,400,000

Sell trophies & awards direct to schools, clubs & organizations.

DIRECT ENERGY
2225 Sheppard Ave E (Suite 100)
Toronto, ON, Canada M2J 5C2
Telephone: (416) 758-8700, Toll Free: (800) 348-2999
Exec VP: Anna Filipopoulas
Primary Market Served: Business & Consumer

DIRECT SUPPLY INC
6767 N Industrial Rd
Milwaukee, WI 53223
Telephone: (414) 358-2805, Toll Free: (800) 634-7328, FAX: (414) 358-2397, E-Mail: deardirect@directs.com, Web Site: www.directsupply.net
Pres & CEO: Robert J. Hillis
Conducts Business: U.S.
Employees: 600
Primary Market Served: Consumer
Catalog available online
Direct online sales
Founded: 1985
Gross sales or billing: $89,900,000
Provide long-term healthcare equipment to nursing home facilities.

DIRECTV LLC
2230 E Imperial Hwy
El Segundo, CA 90245
Telephone: (310) 535-5000, FAX: (310) 535-5225, Web Site: www.directv.com
Chmn, Pres & CEO: Michael White
Exec VP & CFO: Patrick T. Doyle
Exec VP & Chief Tech Officer: Romulo C. Pontual
Primary Market Served: Business
Founded: 1990

Sell direct broadcast satellite service to American consumers.

DIRXION
1859 Bowles Ave (Suite 100)
Saint Louis, MO 63026-1936
Telephone: (636) 717-2300, Web Site: www.dirxion.com
Mktg Mgr: Jennifer Graham

DISCOVERY COMMUNICATIONS INC
One Discovery Pl
Silver Spring, MD 20910
Telephone: (240) 662-2000, FAX: (240) 662-1868, Web Site: corporate.discovery.com
Founder & Chmn: John Hendricks
Pres & CEO: David Zaslav
Pres Adv Sls: Joe Abruzzese
Chief Commun Officer, Sr Exec VP Corp Mktg & Affairs: David C. Leavy
Chief Human Resources & Global Diversity Officer: Adria Alpert-Romm
Primary Market Served: Business & Consumer
Founded: 1982

Worldwide cable network: Discovery Channel, The Learning Channel, Animal Planet, Science Channel, OWN: Oprah Winfrey Network, The Hub, Military Channel, Destination America & Velocity. Discovery showcase networks & multimedia on-line.

DISCOVERY TOYS
3037 Independence Dr (Suite G)
Livermore, CA 94551-7676
Telephone: (925) 606-2600, Toll Free: (800) 426-4777, FAX: (925) 370-0289, Web Site: www.discoverytoysinc.net
Conducts Business: U.S., Canada, Japan
Employees: 171
Primary Market Served: Consumer

Founded: 1978

Sell developmental books, toys & games via home demonstration.

DOALL CO

1480 S Wolf Rd
Wheeling, IL 60090-6514
Telephone: (847) 824-1122, Toll Free: (800) 92-DOALL, FAX: (847) 699-7524, E-Mail: info@doall.com, Web Site: www.doall.com
Chmn & Pres: Michael Wilkie
COO: Clifford Gordon
Mktg Dir: Bruno Gruaz
Primary Market Served: Business
Catalog available online
Direct online sales

Provide industrial supplies & metal capital equipment for industries.

DOCTOR'S BEST INC

197 Avenida La Pata (#A)
San Clemente, CA 92673-6307
Telephone: (949) 498-3628, Toll Free: (800) 333-6977, FAX: (800) 754-2036, (949) 498-3952, E-Mail: info@drbvitamins.com, Web Site: www.drbvitamins.com
Pres: Ken Halvorsrude
VP Corp Opers: Peter Dunphy
COO: Evan Falchuk
Conducts Business: U.S.
Employees: 11
Primary Market Served: Business & Consumer
Catalog available online
Indirect online sales
Advertising/Marketing Budget Related to Direct Marketing: 0-25%
Direct Marketing ad budget: $225,000
Founded: 1990
Gross sales or billing: $3,000,000

Sell nutritional (food) supplements, primarily wholesale to mail order catalogers.

DOMINION RETAIL INC

120 Tredegar St
Richmond, VA 23219-4306
Telephone: (804) 819-2268, Web Site: www.dom.com
Mng Dir: R. Michael Rose
Primary Market Served: Business & Consumer

EDWARD DON & CO

9801 Adam Don Pkwy
Woodridge, IL 60517-8136
Telephone: (708) 442-9400, Toll Free: (800) 777-4366, FAX: (708) 442-0436, Web Site: www.don.com
Chmn: Robert E. Don
Pres & CEO: Steven R. Don
COO & CFO: Jim Jones

VP: Jim Lyman
VP, HR: Mark Scheider
Conducts Business: U.S., Caribbean, U. K., Korea
Employees: 1,500
Primary Market Served: Business
Catalog available online
Direct online sales
Advertising/Marketing Budget Related to Direct Marketing: 0-25%
Founded: 1921

Distributor of food service equipment & supplies.

DOUGLAS PRESS INC

2810 Madison St
Bellwood, IL 60104-2256
Telephone: (708) 547-8400, Toll Free: (800) 323-0705, FAX: (708) 547-0296, Web Site: www.douglaspress.com
Pres: Frank Fienberg
VP, Mktg: Debra Fienberg
Conducts Business: U.S., Canada, Australia, U.K., Belgium
Employees: 250
Primary Market Served: Business
Catalog available online
Direct online sales
Gross sales or billing: $24,000,000

Manufacturer of games of chance used by non-profit organizations, state lotteries & sales promotion agencies.

THE DOW CHEMICAL CO

2030 Dow Center
Midland, MI 48674
Telephone: (989) 636-1000, Toll Free: (800) 258-2436, FAX: (989) 832-1556, Web Site: www.dow.com
Chmn, CEO & Pres: Andrew Liveris
Exec VP, Chief Sustainability Officer & CIO: David E. Kepler II
Exec VP & CFO: Bill Weideman
Conducts Business: Worldwide
Employees: 53,000
Primary Market Served: Business
Catalog available online
Gross sales or billing: $57,000,000,000

International chemical company.

DOW CORNING CORP

PO Box 994
Midland, MI 48686-0994
Telephone: (989) 496-4400, Toll Free: (800) 248-2481, FAX: (989) 496-4572, Web Site: www.dowcorning.com
Chmn, Pres & CEO: Robert D. Hansen
Exec VP & CFO: J. Donald Sheets
Sr VP & CTO: Gregg A. Zank
VP & Chief HR Officer: Mike Conway
VP & CIO: Kristy Folkwein
Conducts Business: Worldwide
Employees: 9,000

Primary Market Served: Business
Catalog available online
Indirect online sales
Founded: 1943

Develop, manufacture & market silicones, related specialty chemical materials, hyperpure polycrystalline silicon, silicon-source chemicals & certain specialty healthcare products.

DRAGICH AUTO LITERATURE

PO Box 1024
Princeton, MN 55371-4024
Telephone: (763) 389-8600, FAX: (763) 389-8222, E-Mail: mail@dragich.com, Web Site: www.dragich.com
Pres: John Dragich
Primary Market Served: Business & Consumer
Founded: 1974

Sell books on automobiles.

DRAWING BOARD INC

101 E 9th St
Waynesboro, PA 17268-2200
Telephone: (301) 739-4487, Toll Free: (800) 527-9530, FAX: (800) 253-1838, E-Mail: customerservice@drawingboard.com, Web Site: www.drawingboard.com
Pres: Mark Ladouceur
Conducts Business: U.S.
Primary Market Served: Business & Consumer

Sell imprinted stationery, labels, business forms, Christmas cards & continuous forms supplies to individuals & small business firms by direct mail & space advertising.

DREIS & KRUMP MANUFACTURING CO

481 Governors Hwy (Suite 2)
Peotone, IL 60468
Telephone: (708) 258-1200, FAX: (708) 258-9682, E-Mail: chicago@dreis-krump.com, Web Site: www.dreis-krump.com
Pres: R. Wolfer
VP, Fin: A. Anderson
Conducts Business: Worldwide
Employees: 50
Primary Market Served: Business
Advertising/Marketing Budget Related to Direct Marketing: 0-25%
Direct Marketing ad budget:
Magazines: 100%
Founded: 1899
Gross sales or billing: $8,000,000

Manufacturer of metal forming equipment sold worldwide.

DREXEL UNIVERSITY GOODWIN COLLEGE OF PROFESSIONAL STUDIES
3001 Market St (Suite 100), One Drexel Plaza
Philadelphia, PA 19104
Telephone: (215) 895-2159, E-Mail: goodwin@drexel.edu, Web Site: goodwin.drexel.edu
Dean: William F. Lynch Ph.D.
Sr Dir Strategic Mktg, Commun and Enrollment Mgmt: Denise McLeod
Dir Fin & Plng: Charlotte Ford
Conducts Business: U.S.
Employees: 73
Primary Market Served: Business

Markets continuing professional education non-credit seminars, conferences & workshops for professionals. Key audiences: government employees, engineers, entrepreneurs & managers. Programs offered nationally.

THE DU-RITE GROUP INC
103 S Van Brunt St
Englewood, NJ 07631-3437
Telephone: (201) 387-7000, FAX: (201) 385-8513, E-Mail: information@duriteconstruction.com, Web Site: www.duriteconstruction.com
VP: Dennis Zysman
VP: Gary Zysman
Conducts Business: U.S.
Primary Market Served: Business

Construction company.

DUGGAN & BROWN INC
1617 Old York Rd
Abington, PA 19001
Telephone: (215) 657-3400, FAX: (215) 657-6119, E-Mail: john@dugganandbrown.com, Web Site: www.dugganandbrown.com
Partner: John Duggan
Conducts Business: U.S.
Employees: 10
Primary Market Served: Business
Advertising/Marketing Budget Related to Direct Marketing: 76-100%
Founded: 1973
Gross sales or billing: $50,000,000

Mail order marketing firm.

DUNCAN AVIATION
3701 Aviation Rd, Lincoln Airport
Lincoln, NE 68524
Telephone: (402) 475-2611, Toll Free: (800) 228-4277, FAX: (402) 475-5541, Web Site: www.duncanaviation.com
Chmn: J. Robert Duncan
Pres: Aaron C. Hilkemann
Exec VP & COO: Mark Matthes

CFO: Jeff Lake
Gulfstream Tech Rep: John Kauppila
Conducts Business: Worldwide
Employees: 525
Primary Market Served: Business
Catalog available online
Indirect online sales
Advertising/Marketing Budget Related to Direct Marketing: 26-50%
Gross sales or billing: $123,000,000

Sell & service corporate aircraft.

DUNCRAFT INC
102 Fisherville Rd
Concord, NH 03303-9020
Telephone: (603) 224-0200, Toll Free: (800) 593-5656, FAX: (603) 226-3735, E-Mail: info@duncraft.com, Web Site: www.duncraft.com
CEO: Michael M. Dunn
Pres: Sharon Dunn
Conducts Business: U.S.
Employees: 55
Primary Market Served: Business & Consumer
Catalog available online
Direct online sales
Advertising/Marketing Budget Related to Direct Marketing: 76-100%
Direct Marketing ad budget: $1,000,000
Direct Mail: 90%
Online: 10%
Founded: 1952
Gross sales or billing: $6,900,000

Retail-wholesale mail order company selling wild bird supplies to the nation.

E I DUPONT DE NEMOURS & CO
aka DuPont
1007 Market St
Wilmington, DE 19898
Telephone: (302) 774-1000, Toll Free: (800) 441-7515, FAX: (302) 774-7321, Web Site: www.dupont.com
Chmn Bd & CEO: Ellen Kullman
Exec VP & CFO: Nicholas C. Fanandakis
Sr VP Corp Strategy: David Bills
VP Corp Commun: AnnaMaria DeSalva
Primary Market Served: Business & Consumer
Founded: 1802

Operates in six principal business segments: chemical, fibers, polymers, petroleum & diversified business.

DURACELL
Div. of Proctor & Gamble
14 Research Dr
Bethel, CT 06801

Toll Free: (800) 551-2355, Web Site: www.duracell.com
Pres: Stassi Anastassov
Primary Market Served: Business & Consumer
Founded: 1916

Manufacturer of Duracell Alkaline & specialty batteries for consumer & OEM markets; manufacturer of professional products for B to B market.

THE DURHAM MANUFACTURING CO
201 Main St
Durham, CT 06422-2108
Telephone: (860) 349-3427, Toll Free: (800) 243-3774, FAX: (860) 349-8572, (800) 782-5499, E-Mail: info@durhammfg.com, Web Site: www.durhammfg.com
Chmn: Herbert Patterson
Pres: Richard Patterson
VP, Prod Devel: John Mansfield
VP, Sls & Mktg: Joe Soja
Conducts Business: U.S., Canada, U.K., Mexico
Employees: 240
Primary Market Served: Business
Catalog available online
Indirect online sales
Advertising/Marketing Budget Related to Direct Marketing: 0-25%
Direct Marketing ad budget: $60,000
Founded: 1922
Gross sales or billing: $44,000,000

Manufacturer of quality steel office products: literature racks, data processing files, security & first aid boxes, industrial storage bins, cabinets & racks.

THE DWYER GROUP
1020 N University Parks Dr
Waco, TX 76707-3863
Telephone: (254) 759-5850, Web Site: www.dwyergroup.com
VP Mktg: Bob Walker

DWYER INSTRUMENTS INC
102 Indiana Hwy 212
Michigan City, IN 46360-1956
Telephone: (219) 879-8868, Web Site: www.dwyer-inst.com
Mktg Mgr: Robert Thompson
Primary Market Served: Business

DX ENGINEERING
PO Box 1491
Akron, OH 44309-1491
Toll Free: (800) 777-0703, FAX: (330) 572-3279, E-Mail: info@comteksystems.com, Web Site: www.comteksystems.com
Pres: Thomas J. Hayes
Pur Agent: M.C. Hayes

Conducts Business: U.S.
Employees: 7
Primary Market Served: Business
Catalog available online
Direct online sales
Advertising/Marketing Budget Related
to Direct Marketing: 0-25%
Direct Marketing ad budget:
Direct Mail: 51%
Telephone: 49%
Founded: 1975
Gross sales or billing: $600,000

Manufacture point-of-sale systems.

DYNAMICS RESEARCH CORP

60 Frontage Rd
Andover, MA 01810
Telephone: (978) 475-9090, Toll Free:
(800) 522-4321, FAX: (978) 475-
8205, Web Site: www.drc.com
VP, Mktg: Edward Johnson
CFO: David Keleher
Employees: 1,600
Primary Market Served: Business &
Consumer
Founded: 1955
Gross sales or billing: $259,000,000

Computer software manufacturer &
content delivery services.

EMC CORP

176 South St
Hopkinton, MA 01748
Toll Free: (888) 438-3622, Web Site:
www.emc.com
Sr VP, Corp Mktg: David A. Donatelli
Adv & Brand Strategy: Kim Chrystie
Exec VP: Jeremy Burton
Conducts Business: Worldwide
Employees: 500
Primary Market Served: Business
Advertising/Marketing Budget Related
to Direct Marketing: 0-25%
Founded: 1979
Gross sales or billing: $11,155,090,000

Supplier of innovative, high-performance information storage products &
related services for mainframe, open
systems & AS400 computers.

EMED CO INC

PO Box 369
Buffalo, NY 14240-0369
Telephone: (716) 626-1616, Toll Free:
(800) 442-3633, FAX: (716) 626-
1630, E-Mail: customerservice@
emedco.com, Web Site: www.
emedco.com
Mktg Dir: Ron Doiel
Mktg Dir: Scott Wardour
Mdsg Mgr: David Ewen
Cust Svc Mgr: Bill Arnold
Mgr: Nick Colca

Conducts Business: U.S.
Primary Market Served: Business
Catalog available online
Direct online sales
Advertising/Marketing Budget Related
to Direct Marketing: 76-100%
Direct Marketing ad budget:
Direct Mail: 95%
Telephone: 5%

Manufacturer of identification products: signs, labels, tags, markers.

EMS TECHNOLOGIES

660 Engineering Dr
Norcross, GA 30092
Telephone: (770) 263-9200, FAX:
(770) 447-4405, Web Site: www.
ems-t.com
Pres: Paul Domorski
Exec VP, CFO & Treas: Don T. Scartz
VP, Gen Counsel: Timothy C. Reis
VP, Bus Opers: Joanne Walker
VP: Gary Shell
Primary Market Served: Business &
Consumer
Catalog available online

Industrial manufacturer.

ETTSI PREMIUMS & INCENTIVES

301 Indigo Dr
Daytona Beach, FL 32114-1134
Telephone: (386) 271-0204, Web Site:
www.ettsi.com
Owner, CEO: Frank Bertalli

EXL

10 Exchange Pl
Jersey City, NJ 07302-3918
Telephone: (201) 748-4729
Methodology: Krishna Mehta

EARTHRISE

Subs. of Earthrise Trading Co
2151 Michelson Dr (Suite 258)
Irvine, CA 92648
Telephone: (949) 623-0980, FAX:
(949) 623-0990, E-Mail: info@
earthrise.com, Web Site: www.
earthrise.com
Mktg Dir: Rob Kelly
Primary Market Served: Consumer
Founded: 1982

Health food manufacturer.

EASTERN MICHIGAN UNIVERSITY

1000 College Pl
Ypsilanti, MI 48197
Telephone: (734) 487-1849, FAX:
(734) 484-1151, Web Site: www.
emich.edu
Pres: Susan W. Martin PhD

CFO: John Lumm
VP Commun: Walter Kraft
VP Advancement: Tom Stevick
Exec VP & Provost: Kim Schatzel
Conducts Business: U.S.
Employees: 2,400
Primary Market Served: Business &
Consumer
Catalog available online
Founded: 1849
Gross sales or billing: $85,000,000

Market all aspects of the university to a
national market.

EASTERN MOUNTAIN SPORTS

1 Vose Farm Rd
Peterborough, NH 03458-2122
Telephone: (603) 924-9571, Toll Free:
(888) 463-6367, FAX: (603) 924-
4320, Web Site: www.ems.com
CEO: William Manzee
VP E-commerce & Strategic Bus: Scott
Barrett
Dir Mktg: Kate Lynch
Conducts Business: U.S.
Employees: 500
Primary Market Served: Consumer
Direct Marketing ad budget:
Direct Mail: 100%
Founded: 1967

Retailer of outdoor clothing & equipment.

EASTMAN CHEMICAL CO

200 S Wilcox Dr
Kingsport, TN 37660-5147
Telephone: (423) 229-2000, Toll Free:
(800) 325-4330, E-Mail: eastman1@
eastman.com, Web Site: www.
eastman.com
CEO: Mark J. Costa
COO: Ronald C. Lindsay
Exec VP & CFO: Curt E. Espeland
Exec VP: Brad A. Lich
Primary Market Served: Business

Specialty chemical company.

DAVID EASTON INC

5 Union Sq W (fl 3)
New York, NY 10003-3315
Telephone: (212) 334-3820, FAX:
(212) 334-3821, Web Site: www.
davideastoninc.com
Owner & Pres: David Easton
Primary Market Served: Business &
Consumer

Interior design.

EASYLINK SERVICES INTERNATIONAL CORP

33 Knightsbridge Rd
Piscataway, NJ 08854

Toll Free: (800) 828-7115, FAX: (732) 652-3810, E-Mail: sales@easylink. com, Web Site: www.easylink.com
CEO: Tom Stallings
VP, Sls & Mktg: Jim Walsh
Primary Market Served: Business

Designs, develops & markets variety of business to business facsimile transmission services including fax to fax, desktop to fax, enhanced fax & broadcast services designed to reduce the cost of sending as international fax.

EATON CORP
8609 Six Forks Rd
Raleigh, NC 27615-2966
Telephone: (216) 523-4400, Toll Free: (800) 356-5794, FAX: (216) 523-4787, Web Site: www.eaton.com
Chmn, Pres & CEO: Alexander M. Cutler
Exec VP & CFO: Richard H. Fearon
Sr VP: Craig Arnold
VP & CIO: William W. Blausey Jr.
VP: Richard P. Jacobs
Mktg Mgr: Kristin Somers
Conducts Business: U.S., Canada
Employees: 60,000
Primary Market Served: Business
Catalog available online
Founded: 1893
Gross sales or billing: $12,300,000,000

Manufacture & sell electrical & electronic controls to industrial & construction customers.

EBAY INC
2065 Hamilton Ave
San Jose, CA 95125
Telephone: (408) 376-7400, Toll Free: (800) 322-7400, Web Site: www.ebayinc.com
Pres & CEO: Dave Wenig
Sr VP & CFO: Scott Schenkel
Sr VP & Chief Commun Officer: Dan Tarman
Sr VP & Chief Tech Officer: Steve Fisher
Founded: 1995

Online marketplace.

ECOLAB PROFESSIONAL PRODUCTS
Div. of Ecolab Inc
370 N Wabasha St, Ecolab Ctr
Saint Paul, MN 55102-2233
Telephone: (651) 293-4248, FAX: (651) 225-3025, E-Mail: ecolabs@ecolabs.com, Web Site: www.ecolab.com
Dir Mktg: Mark Miller
Conducts Business: U.S., Canada
Employees: 350
Primary Market Served: Business

Advertising/Marketing Budget Related to Direct Marketing: 26-50%
Direct Marketing ad budget:
Direct Mail: 25%
Magazines: 75%
Founded: 1923
Gross sales or billing: $3,800,000,000

Infection control & cleaning products for healthcare & institutional/commercial buildings.

ECONOMY HANDICRAFTS
932 46th St
Brooklyn, NY 11219
Telephone: (718) 431-9300, Toll Free: (800) 216-1601, FAX: (718) 431-9309, Web Site: www.vanguardcrafts.com
Pres: Eric Schwedock
Conducts Business: U.S.
Employees: 21
Primary Market Served: Business & Consumer
Catalog available online
Indirect online sales
Advertising/Marketing Budget Related to Direct Marketing: 0-25%
Direct Marketing ad budget:
Direct Mail: 75%
Magazines: 25%
Founded: 1959
Gross sales or billing: $1,700,000

Generalized & specialized arts & crafts supplies. Sell to institutions such as schools, hospitals & correctional facilities, as well as to individuals.

EDO INTERACTIVE
3841 Green Hills Village Dr (Suite 425)
Nashville, TN 37215-2632
Telephone: (615) 297-6080, Web Site: www.edointeractive.com
Dir Mktg: Constance Baker

EDROY PRODUCTS CO INC
245 N Midland Ave, PO Box 998
Nyack, NY 10960-0998
Telephone: (845) 358-6600, Toll Free: (800) 233-8803, FAX: (845) 358-4098, E-Mail: sales@edroyproducts.com, Web Site: www.edroyproducts.com
Pres: Steve Stoltze
Conducts Business: U.S., Canada
Employees: 5
Primary Market Served: Business
Catalog available online
Advertising/Marketing Budget Related to Direct Marketing: 0-25%
Direct Marketing ad budget:
Magazines: 100%
Founded: 1937

Magnifiers & low vision aids.

EDUCATION DIRECT
Div. of A Thompson Co
925 Oak St
Scranton, PA 18515
Telephone: (570) 342-7701, FAX: (570) 961-4851, Web Site: www.educationdirect.com
Pres: David Beach
Conducts Business: Worldwide
Employees: 50
Primary Market Served: Consumer
Catalog available online
Advertising/Marketing Budget Related to Direct Marketing: 76-100%

Marketer of educational training products to industry, consumers & government.

EDUCATIONAL COIN CO
PO Box 892
Highland, NY 12528-0892
Telephone: (845) 691-6100, Web Site: www.educationalcoin.com
Dir Mktg: Robin Danziger

EDUCATIONAL INSIGHTS, INC
Subs of Learning Resources
152 W Walnut St Ste 201
Gardena, CA 90248-3147
Telephone: (310) 884-2000, Toll Free: (888) 591-9334, FAX: (310) 886-8850, E-Mail: service@edin.com, Web Site: www.educationalinsights.com
Pres & COO: Jim Whitney
CEO: C. Reid Calcott
VP Prod Devel: Pat Sarka
VP Mktg: Mark J. Mallardi
Conducts Business: U.S., Canada, U.K.
Employees: 100
Primary Market Served: Business
Catalog available online
Indirect online sales
Advertising/Marketing Budget Related to Direct Marketing: 26-50%
Direct Marketing ad budget:
Direct Mail: 90%
Magazines: 5%
Telephone: 5%
Founded: 1962
Gross sales or billing: $7,500,000

Manufacturer of educational toys, games & computer software for both school & home use.

EDUCATIONAL TESTING SERVICE
660 Rosedale Rd
Princeton, NJ 08541
Telephone: (609) 921-9000, FAX: (609) 734-5410, Web Site: www.ets.org
Pres & CEO: Walt MacDonald

VP Mktg & Pub Affairs: Scott Nelson
Conducts Business: Worldwide
Employees: 2,433
Primary Market Served: Business &
  Consumer
Catalog available online
Direct online sales
Founded: 1947
Gross sales or billing: $860,000,000

SAT'S, PSAT'S, High school tests,
GRE, GMAT, TOEFL, NAP.

EDUTREK
155 N 400 W (Suite 150)
Salt Lake City, UT 84103-1132
Toll Free: (801) 716-3924, Web Site:
  edutrek.com

College selection & financial aid advice services

EFFECTIVE PROMOTIONS
INC
PO Box 210
Fort Johnson, NY 12070-0210
Telephone: (518) 274-0291, Toll Free:
  (888) 467-3514, FAX: (518) 274-
  0290, Web Site: www.efpromotions.
  com
Pres: Patricia M. O'Brien
Employees: 10
Primary Market Served: Business &
  Consumer
Catalog available online
Direct online sales

Direct mail marketing of poly bags.

EIRE DIRECT
720 N Franklin (Suite 310)
Chicago, IL 60610-3512
Telephone: (312) 640-4000, FAX:
  (312) 640-0324, E-Mail: info@
  eiredirect.com, Web Site: www.
  eiredirect.com
Partner: Ellen Best
Partner: Jim Kearney
Primary Market Served: Business &
  Consumer
Catalog available online
Advertising/Marketing Budget Related
  to Direct Marketing: 26-50%
Founded: 1996

U.S. office for the national telephone
company of Ireland.

ELI JOURNALS
Div. of Mosaic Media Inc
2222 Sedwick Rd (Ste 101)
Durham, NC 27713-2658
Telephone: (585) 203-5248, Toll Free:
  (800) 223-8720, FAX: (585) 292-
  4392, Web Site: www.elijournals.
  com
CEO: Greg Lindberg
Conducts Business: U.S., Canada, U.K.

Primary Market Served: Business
Catalog available online
Direct online sales
Advertising/Marketing Budget Related
  to Direct Marketing: 76-100%
Direct Marketing ad budget:
Direct Mail: 50%
Online: 50%

Publish self-study computer training
materials and newsletters.

EMERGENCY ESSENTIALS
INC
362 Commerce Loop #B, Orem, UT
  84058-5157
653 N 1500th W
Orem, UT 84057-2831
Telephone: (801) 222-9596, FAX:
  (801) 222-9598, E-Mail:
  webmaster@beprepared.com, Web
  Site: www.beprepared.com
CEO & Pres: David Sheets
VP: Don Pectol
VP: Matt Nettesheim
Conducts Business: U.S.
Primary Market Served: Business &
  Consumer
Catalog available online
Direct online sales
Founded: 1987

Specialize in home storage, first aid &
camping equipment.

EMPEROR CLOCK LLC
PO Box 960
Amherst, VA 24521
Toll Free: (800) 642-0011, FAX: (434)
  946-1420, E-Mail: emperor@
  emperorclock.com, Web Site: www.
  emperorclock.com
VP: Eleanor Carpenter
Customer Svc Mgr: Julie George
Conducts Business: Worldwide
Employees: 25
Primary Market Served: Business &
  Consumer
Catalog available online
Indirect online sales
Advertising/Marketing Budget Related
  to Direct Marketing: 76-100%
Direct Marketing ad budget:
Direct Mail: 70%
Magazines: 20%
Newspapers: 1%
Online: 9%
Founded: 1969

Manufacturer of do-it-yourself grandfather clock kits & fully assembled
grandfather clocks, wall and mantel
clocks.

EMPIRE SCIENTIFIC
151 E Industry Ct
Deer Park, NY 11729-5713

Telephone: (631) 595-9206, Toll Free:
  (800) 645-7220, FAX: (631) 595-
  9384, (800) 343-5733, E-Mail:
  sales@empirescientific.com, Web
  Site: www.empirescientific.com
Pres: Jeffrey English
VP: Spencer Slipko
Conducts Business: U.S., Australia, Ja-
  pan, England, Canada, Sweden, Italy
Employees: 30
Primary Market Served: Business
Catalog available online
Indirect online sales
Direct Marketing ad budget:
Direct Mail: $150,000
Magazines: $50,000
Telephone: $50,000
Gross sales or billing: $4,000,000

Manufacturer of video camcorder batteries, cellular phone & cordless phone
batteries.

ENCORE MARKETING
INTERNATIONAL
4501 Forbes Blvd
Lanham, MD 20706-4236
Telephone: (301) 459-8020, Toll Free:
  (800) 846-9398, FAX: (301) 731-
  0525, E-Mail: customerservice@
  encoremarketing.com, Web Site:
  www.encoremarketing.com
CEO: Stanley Plotnick
Pres: Stephen Klein
EVP Mktg: Dave Gallimore
VP Mktg: Bonnie Kasander
Conducts Business: U.S., Canada, Eu-
  rope
Employees: 200
Primary Market Served: Consumer
Catalog available online
Direct online sales
Advertising/Marketing Budget Related
  to Direct Marketing: 76-100%
Direct Marketing ad budget: $45,000
Online: 25%
Telephone: 75%
Founded: 1978
Gross sales or billing: $75,000,000

Offer a variety of branded and un-
branded discount clubs & loyalty programs.

ENERGIZER HOLDINGS INC
533 Maryville University Dr
Saint Louis, MO 63141
Telephone: (314) 985-2000, Toll Free:
  (800) 383-7323, FAX: (636) 733-
  4001, Web Site: www.energizer.com
CEO: Ward M. Klein
Pres & CEO Energizer Personal Care:
  David Hatfield
Exec VP & CFO: Daniel J. Sescleifer
Conducts Business: Worldwide

Primary Market Served: Business & Consumer

Manufacturer of batteries & personal care products.

ENERPAC

Div. of Applied Power Inc
PO Box 9010
Menomonee Falls, WI 53052-9010
Telephone: (262) 781-6600, Toll Free:
  (800) 433-2766, FAX: (262) 781-
  1028, Web Site: www.enerpac.com
Chmn & Pres: Bob Arzbacher
Global Mktg Mgr: Larry Rothering
Mktg Commun Lead Mgr: Kandy
  Raether
Conducts Business: Worldwide
Employees: 500
Primary Market Served: Business &
  Consumer
Advertising/Marketing Budget Related
  to Direct Marketing: 0-25%
Founded: 1910

Specialize in sale & design of hydraulic tools & equipment.

ENNIS INC

2441 Presidential Pkwy
Midlothian, TX 76065-3723
Telephone: (972) 775-9801, Toll Free:
  (800) 962-0944, FAX: (800) 645-
  8339, Web Site: www.ennis.com
Chmn, Pres & CEO: Keith S. Walters
Exec VP & Treas: Michael D. Magill
VP, Opers: Terry Pennington
VP, Fin, CFO & Sec: Richard L. Travis
  Jr.
VP, Admin & Dir: Ronald M. Graham
Primary Market Served: Business
Catalog available online
Direct online sales
Gross sales or billing: $584,000,000

Manufacturer of business forms & promotional & commercial products. Toll free fax: (800) 972-3100.

ENTERGY

639 Loyola Ave (Suite 300)
New Orleans, LA 70113-7106
Telephone: (504) 576-4000, Toll Free:
  (800) ENTERGY, FAX: (504) 576-
  4428, Web Site: www.entergy.com
Chmn & CEO: J. Wayne Leonard
Pres & COO: Richard Smith
Exec VP & CFO: Leo Denault
Exec VP, Opers: Mark T. Savoff
Exec VP: Curt L. Hebert Jr.
Conducts Business: U.S.
Primary Market Served: Business &
  Consumer
Gross sales or billing: $11,000,000,000
Public utility.

ENTERPREX INTERNATIONAL CORP

12101 Clark St Ste G
Arcadia, CA 91006-6031
Telephone: (626) 256-1444, FAX:
  (626) 256-1404, E-Mail: premium@
  enterprex.com, Web Site: www.
  enterprex.com
Pres: Walter Yuan
VP: Dennis Chen
Conducts Business: U.S.
Employees: 7
Primary Market Served: Business &
  Consumer
Catalog available online
Advertising/Marketing Budget Related
  to Direct Marketing: 0-25%
Founded: 1973
Gross sales or billing: $4,000,000

Marketer of consumer premium merchandise.

ENTERPRISE IRELAND

345 Park Ave (17th fl)
New York, NY 10154-0037
Telephone: (212) 371-3600, FAX:
  (212) 371-6398, Web Site: www.
  enterprise-ireland.com
CEO: Frank Ryan
Dir Americas: Marina Donohoe
East Coast Mgr: Tom Cusak
Exec Dir: Gerry Murphy
Conducts Business: Australia, Central,
  N., S. America, Europe, Far East
  Realm
Employees: 16
Primary Market Served: Business &
  Consumer
Advertising/Marketing Budget Related
  to Direct Marketing: 0-25%
Founded: 1991
Gross sales or billing: $7,000,000,000

Agency of Irish government established to promote & develop exports from Ireland. Irish government trade & technology division.

ENTERTAINMENT MUSIC MARKETING CORP

dba EMMC
795 Foxhurst Rd
Baldwin, NY 11510-3530
Telephone: (631) 243-0600, FAX:
  (631) 243-0605, E-Mail:
  emmcmusic@aol.com, Web Site:
  www.emmcmusic.com
VP & Owner: Jeffrey Saltzman
Opers Mgr: Michael Wentz
Conducts Business: Worldwide
Employees: 9
Primary Market Served: Business
Catalog available online
Direct online sales
Advertising/Marketing Budget Related
  to Direct Marketing: 26-50%

Direct Marketing ad budget:
Direct Mail: $20,000
Magazines: $6,000
Telephone: $6,000
Founded: 1976
Gross sales or billing: $1,400,000

Importer & supplier of musical instruments, including string instruments, amplifiers & PA systems. Also, electronic pianos, sing-a-long machines & tapes.

ESCO CORP

2141 NW 25th Ave
Portland, OR 97210-2578
Telephone: (503) 228-2141, FAX:
  (503) 778-6682, Web Site: www.
  escocorp.com
VP & Gen Mgr Mining Div: Jim
  Songer
Gen Mgr Sls & Mktg, NA & SA: Tim
  Elbel
Gen Mgr Construction Div: Pat Fonner
Process Devel Svcs: John Hemmingson
Conducts Business: Worldwide
Employees: 2,000
Primary Market Served: Business
Advertising/Marketing Budget Related
  to Direct Marketing: 0-25%
Direct Marketing ad budget: $500,000

Manufacture & sell earth moving equipment to the mining & construction markets. Dredging & forestry products.

ESCORT INC

5440 Westchester Rd
West Chester, OH 45069-2950
Telephone: (513) 870-8500, Toll Free:
  (800) 964-3138, FAX: (513) 870-
  8509, E-Mail: sales@escortradar.
  com, Web Site: www.escortradar.
  com
CEO: Greg Blair
Pres & COO: John Larson
VP Sls & Mktg: Gary Oppito
Adv & DM Mgr: Kim Schmidt
Conducts Business: U.S.
Employees: 250
Primary Market Served: Consumer
Advertising/Marketing Budget Related
  to Direct Marketing: 76-100%
Gross sales or billing: $20,200,000

Manufacturer & marketer of the passport line of radar & laser detectors.

ESPRIT LINE CO LTD USA

11 Heronvue Rd
Greenwich, CT 06831-2906
Telephone: (203) 629-5124
Pres & CEO: Noboru Otani

ESSELTE AMERICAS

An Esselte Co

225 Broadhollow Rd
Melville, NY 11747-2340
Telephone: (631) 675-5700, Toll Free:
(800) 645-6051, FAX: (631) 622-
1970, Web Site: www.curtis.com
Pres & CEO: Magnus Nicolin
Conducts Business: U.S., Canada, Eu-
rope, Mexico
Primary Market Served: Business &
Consumer

Manufacturer of computer accessories,
furniture, printer sound enclosures &
microfilm storage products.

ESTEE LAUDER INC
767 Fifth Ave
New York, NY 10153
Telephone: (212) 572-4200, FAX:
(212) 893-7782, Web Site: www.
esteelauder.com
Exec Chmn: William Lauder
Pres & CEO: Fabrizio Freda
Grp Pres: John Demsey
Exec VP Res & Devel, Product Innova-
tion & Brand Product Devel: Carl
Haney
Exec VP & CFO: Tracey T. Travis
Style & Image Dir: Aerin Lauder
Primary Market Served: Consumer
Catalog available online
Direct online sales
Founded: 1946

Development, marketing & selling of
skin care & fragrance products.

ETHYL CORP
330 S Fourth St, PO Box 2189
Richmond, VA 23218
Telephone: (804) 788-5000, FAX:
(804) 788-5688, Web Site: www.
ethyl.com
Chmn & CEO: Bruce C. Gotwald
Pres & COO: Thomas E. Gotwald
VP, HR & External Affairs: Henry C.
Page Jr
Conducts Business: Worldwide
Employees: 1,800
Primary Market Served: Business
Advertising/Marketing Budget Related
to Direct Marketing: 0-25%
Founded: 1887
Gross sales or billing: $1,030,000,000

Develops, manufactures & blends per-
formance-enhancing fuel & lubricant
additives marketed worldwide to refin-
ers & others who sell petroleum products for use in transportation &
industrial equipment. Ethyl additives
increase the value of gasoline, diesel &
heating fuels, as well as lubricants for
engines, automatic transmission, gears
& hydraulic & industrial equipment.

**EVEREX COMPUTER
SYSTEMS INC**
48319 Fremont Blvd
Fremont, CA 94538-6580
Toll Free: (800) 383-7391, (866) 850-
8835, FAX: (510) 683-2186, E-Mail:
customerservice@everex.com, Web
Site: www.everex.com
Pres: Yale Ma
Gen Mgr & VP, Sls: John Lin
Conducts Business: Worldwide
Primary Market Served: Business
Catalog available online
Direct online sales
Founded: 1983
Gross sales or billing: $500,000,000

Manufacture computer peripherals &
personal computer systems.

**EXECUTIVE ENTERPRISES
INC**
12 Skyline Dr
Hawthorne, NY 10532-2133
Telephone: (860) 701-5900, Toll Free:
(800) 831-8333, FAX: (860) 701-
5909, (800) 250-3861, E-Mail: info@
eeiconferences.com, Web Site: www.
eeiconferences.com
CEO: Glenn Shapiro
COO & CFO: David Berks
Sr Mktg Mgr: Sally Sheffield
Conducts Business: U.S., Canada
Employees: 35
Primary Market Served: Business
Catalog available online
Indirect online sales
Advertising/Marketing Budget Related
to Direct Marketing: $2MM%
Direct Marketing ad budget:
Direct Mail: 99.8%
Telephone: 0.2%
Founded: 1971
Gross sales or billing: $15,000,000

Conduct seminars & conferences for
corporate executives, attorneys, engineers, accountants, bankers, insurance
companies, human resource executives
& government employees.

**EXECUTIVE PROTECTION
PRODUCTS INC**
351 Second St
Napa, CA 94559
Telephone: (707) 253-7142, FAX:
(707) 253-7149, E-Mail: services@
epsecuritysolutions.com, Web Site:
epsecuritysolutions.com
Pres: Gene Kelly
Primary Market Served: Business

Security consultation & systems to
schools, government agencies & corporations.

**EXPERIENCE IN SOFTWARE
INC**
2029 Durant Ave Ste 201
Berkeley, CA 94704-1564
Telephone: (510) 644-0694, Toll Free:
(800) 678-7008, FAX: (510) 644-
3823, Web Site: www.
projectkickstart.com
Pres: Roy A. Nierenberg
Mktg Mgr: Carolyn Burd
Conducts Business: Worldwide
Employees: 4
Primary Market Served: Business &
Consumer
Catalog available online
Indirect online sales
Advertising/Marketing Budget Related
to Direct Marketing: 76-100%
Direct Marketing ad budget:
Direct Mail: 85%
Magazines: 15%
Founded: 1983

Software publisher.

**EXPRESSIONS CUSTOM
FURNITURE**
Div. of Century Furniture Industries
401 11th St NW, PO Box 608
Hickory, NC 28603-0608
Telephone: (828) 328-1851, FAX:
(828) 328-2176, Web Site: www.
expressionsfurniture.com
Conducts Business: U.S.
Employees: 40
Primary Market Served: Business &
Consumer

Custom furniture, case goods & accessories; manufacturer & retailer.

F P INTERNATIONAL
34175 Ardenwood Blvd
Fremont, CA 94555-3653
Telephone: (650) 261-5300, Toll Free:
(800) 866-9946, FAX: (650) 361-
1713, Web Site: www.fpintl.com
VP Mktg: Larry Lenhart
Mktg Mgr: Jim Jensen
VP, Sls: Harry Reynolds
Sr VP Sls & Mktg: Joe Nezwek
Conducts Business: U.S.
Employees: 500
Primary Market Served: Business
Catalog available online
Indirect online sales
Advertising/Marketing Budget Related
to Direct Marketing: 0-25%
Founded: 1967
Gross sales or billing: $100,000,000

Manufacture protective packing materials.

FAFCO INC
435 Otterson Dr
Chico, CA 95928-8207

Telephone: (530) 332-2100, Toll Free: (800) 994-7652, FAX: (530) 332-2109, Web Site: www.fafco.com
Chmn, Pres & CEO: Freeman A. Ford
Sls & Mktg Coord: Suzanne Caraveo
Employees: 62
Primary Market Served: Business & Consumer
Catalog available online
Indirect online sales
Founded: 1969
Gross sales or billing: $7,900,000

Manufacture solar pool heating energy panels & thermal energy & ice cool storage systems.

FLM GRAPHICS CORP
123 Lehigh Dr
Fairfield, NJ 07004-3095
Telephone: (973) 575-9450, E-Mail: info@flmgraphics.com, Web Site: www.flmgraphics.com
CIO: Mark Hahn
Pres: Vince Fiorello
Founder & CEO: Frank L. Misischia
VP: Peter Burke
Conducts Business: U.S., Canada, Puerto Rico, Caribbean
Employees: 75
Primary Market Served: Business & Consumer
Catalog available online
Direct Marketing ad budget: $250,000
Direct Mail: 50%
Magazines: 50%
Gross sales or billing: $19,000,000

Process to professional photographers, industrial photo departments, schools, school photographers & advanced amateurs. Includes signs, posters, murals & banners, point of purchase & exhibitors.

FMC CORP
1735 Market St
Philadelphia, PA 19103
Telephone: (215) 299-6000, FAX: (215) 299-5998, Web Site: www.fmc.com
Chmn, Pres & CEO: William G. Walter
Sr VP & CFO: William K. Foster
CIO: Michael F. Giesler
VP, Gen Mgr: Theodore H. Butz
VP, Treas: Thomas C. Deas Jr.
Conducts Business: Worldwide
Employees: 21,000
Primary Market Served: Business
Catalog available online
Founded: 1884
Gross sales or billing: $3,800,000,000

Performance & industrial chemicals, machinery & equipment for industry & agriculture.

FTD COMPANIES INC
3113 Woodcreek Dr
Downers Grove, IL 60515
Telephone: (630) 719-7800, Web Site: www.ftdcompanies.com
Pres & CEO: Robert S. Apatoff
Exec VP & CFO: Becky A. Sheehan
Sr VP Consumer Div: Lawrence B. Plawsky
Conducts Business: U.S., Canada
Primary Market Served: Business & Consumer
Catalog available online
Direct online sales
Advertising/Marketing Budget Related to Direct Marketing: 26-50%
Floral & gifting company.

FAIRFIELD INDUSTRIES INC
1111 Gillingham Ln
Sugar Land, TX 77478-2865
Telephone: (281) 275-7500, Toll Free: (800) 231-9809, FAX: (281) 275-7550, E-Mail: jblattman@fairfield.com, Web Site: www.fairfield.com
Pres & CEO: Walt Pharris
Sls Mgr: Dennis Clark
Sls Rep: Jim Blattman
Sls Rep: Mary Rafipour
Sls Rep: Nick Shilcock
Conducts Business: U.S.
Primary Market Served: Business
Catalog available online
Gross sales or billing: $250,000

Packaging experts in meeting industrial sub-contracting needs: shrink wrapping, labeling, skin packaging, assembly & poly bagging.

FALCON PRODUCTS INC
Subs. of CF Group
810 W Highway 25 70
Newport, TN 37821-8044
Telephone: (314) 991-9200, Toll Free: (800) 873-3252, FAX: (314) 991-9227, E-Mail: info@falconproducts.com, Web Site: www.falconproducts.com
Chmn & CEO: Frank Jacobs
CFO & VP, Fin: Mike Dreller
Sr VP, Quality: Richard Hnatek
VP, Sls: Stephen Cohen
VP, Sys Tech & Devel: Mike Kula
Conducts Business: Worldwide
Employees: 2,000
Primary Market Served: Business
Catalog available online
Advertising/Marketing Budget Related to Direct Marketing: 0-25%
Direct Marketing ad budget: $200,000
Magazines: 100%
Founded: 1959

Gross sales or billing: $113,000,000
Commercial furniture for healthcare, foodservice, office & lodging industries.

FALCON SAFETY PRODUCTS
25 Imclone Dr, Box 1229
Branchburg, NJ 08876
Telephone: (908) 707-4900, FAX: (908) 707-8855, Web Site: www.falconsafety.com
Pres: Phil Lapin
CFO: Greg Mas
VP, Mfg: Ron Maurer
VP, Mktg & Sls: Andy Steinman
Conducts Business: Worldwide
Employees: 60
Primary Market Served: Business & Consumer
Catalog available online
Advertising/Marketing Budget Related to Direct Marketing: 51-75%
Direct Marketing ad budget:
Direct Mail: 20%
Magazines: 80%
Founded: 1953
Gross sales or billing: $15,000,000

Computer/office accessories, marine accessories; boat horns & mooring compensators.

FAMOUS SMOKE SHOP INC
1100 Conroy Pl, Easton, PA 18040-6657
90 Mort Dr
Easton, PA 18040-9202
Telephone: (610) 559-7000, Toll Free: (800) 672-5544, FAX: (610) 559-7170, E-Mail: info@famous-smoke.com, Web Site: www.famous-smoke.com
Pres: Arthur Zaretsky
Conducts Business: U.S.
Employees: 60
Primary Market Served: Business & Consumer
Catalog available online
Direct online sales
Advertising/Marketing Budget Related to Direct Marketing: 76-100%
Direct Marketing ad budget:
Direct Mail: 70%
Online: 30%
Founded: 1939
Gross sales or billing: $2,800,000

Sell brand & off-brand named cigars at discounts. Mailing list available.

FARROW GROUP
2001 Huron Church Rd
Windsor, ON, Canada N9C 2L6
Telephone: (519) 966-3003, E-Mail: info@farrow.com, Web Site: www.farrow.com
Chmn & CEO: Rick Farrow

Pres: Randy Motley
Vice Chmn: John Farrow
Conducts Business: U.S.
Employees: 350
Primary Market Served: Business & Consumer
Indirect online sales
Advertising/Marketing Budget Related to Direct Marketing: 0-25%
Founded: 1910
Gross sales or billing: $158,000,000

Our mission is to be the leading provider of superior customs brokerage, logistics and systems solutions which contribute to the success and profitability of North American companies engaged in international trade.

FASSON ROLL DIV

Div. of Avery Dennison Corp
5750 Heisley Rd
Mentor, OH 44060-1830
Telephone: (440) 354-7900, FAX: (440) 358-4712, (440) 358-6025, Web Site: www.fasson.com
Grp VP Fasson Roll Worldwide: Christian Simcic
Conducts Business: U.S., Canada, Europe
Employees: 160
Primary Market Served: Business

Manufactures & sells roll stock pressure sensitive materials to companies that make labels. Branches: Rancho Cucamonga, CA; Peachtree City & Atlanta, GA; Chicago, IL; Fort Wayne, IN; Kansas City, MO; Greensboro, NC; Cranbury, NJ; Quakertown, PA; Dallas, TX; Kent, WA; Neenah, WI.

FAULTLESS STARCH/BON AMI CO

1025 W Eighth St
Kansas City, MO 64101-1200
Telephone: (816) 842-1230, FAX: (816) 842-3417, E-Mail: info@faultless.com, Web Site: www.faultless.com
Chmn & Co-CEO: Gordon T. Beaham III
Pres & Co-CEO: David G. Beaham
VP, Treas & Co-CEO: Robert B. Beaham
VP: Ben Stark
Primary Market Served: Consumer
Catalog available online

Manufacture household cleaners, garden tools & products.

FEDEX CORP

3965 Airways Blvd
Memphis, TN 38116-5017
Telephone: (901) 369-3600, FAX: (901) 395-5082, Web Site: www.fedex.com
Chmn, Pres & CEO: Frederick W. Smith
Exec VP, Mktg Devel & Corp Commun: T Michael Glenn
Conducts Business: Worldwide
Employees: 300,000
Primary Market Served: Business & Consumer
Founded: 1971

Specialize in transportation of high priority business goods & documents.

GEORGE FENCIK ASSOCIATES

Div. of GFA Marketing Group
1006 Arnold Ave
Point Pleasant, NJ 08742
Telephone: (732) 295-8092, Toll Free: (800) 443-6743, FAX: (732) 295-1729, E-Mail: gfencik@aol.com
Pres: George Fencik
Conducts Business: U.S., Canada, Japan, Switzerland
Employees: 5
Primary Market Served: Business & Consumer
Advertising/Marketing Budget Related to Direct Marketing: 26-50%
Founded: 1979

Sell health and beauty aids - housewares & consumer products.

FINE ARCHITECTURAL METALSMITHS

Div. of New England Tool Co Ltd
PO Box 30
Chester, NY 10918
Telephone: (845) 651-7550, FAX: (845) 651-7857, Web Site: www.iceforge.com
CEO: Ed Mack
Art Dir: Rhoda Weber Mack
Conducts Business: U.S.
Primary Market Served: Business & Consumer
Advertising/Marketing Budget Related to Direct Marketing: 51-75%
Direct Marketing ad budget:
Direct Mail: 30%
Magazines: 65%
Telephone: 5%
Founded: 1981

Ornamental iron gates with electronic openers. Ornamental iron & aluminum fencing. Ornamental iron, aluminum, stainless & brass railings. Ornamental iron furniture & sheet metal fabrications. Custom lighting. Sold to industrial parks, businesses, homeowners, architects & interior designers.

FINLEY PRODUCTS INC

1333 Beaconfield Ln
Lancaster, PA 17601-5344
Telephone: (717) 735-8200, Toll Free: (888) 626-5301, FAX: (717) 735-8210, E-Mail: fininfo@finleyproducts.com, Web Site: www.2X4basics.com
Pres: Howard Livingston
VP Sls Mktg: Fin Livingston Jr.
Conducts Business: Worldwide
Employees: 10
Primary Market Served: Consumer
Catalog available online
Indirect online sales
Advertising/Marketing Budget Related to Direct Marketing: 76-100%
Founded: 2001

Outdoor furniture & storage equipment, shed kits, deck bench brackets, a multifunction roofing tool, a portable desk for construction & architecture design

FIRE MOUNTAIN GEMS

1 Fire Mountain Way
Grants Pass, OR 97526-2373
Telephone: (541) 956-7890, Toll Free: (800) 355-2137, (800) 423-2319, FAX: (541) 470-GEMS, E-Mail: questions@firemtn.com, Web Site: www.firemtn.com
Pres: Stuart Freedman
Mgr, Direct Response: Rex T. Carlisle
VP Mktg: Christlin Freedman
Admin & Mktg: Lisa Emonds
Conducts Business: U.S., Canada
Employees: 180
Primary Market Served: Business & Consumer
Catalog available online
Direct online sales
Advertising/Marketing Budget Related to Direct Marketing: 51-75%
Direct Marketing ad budget:
Direct Mail: 90%
Magazines: 10%
Founded: 1973

Wholesale jewelry components, beads & findings.

FIRST MEDIA COMMUNICATIONS INC

9149 Jones Ct
Brentwood, TN 37027-8537
Telephone: (615) 661-0826, FAX: (615) 661-4084, Web Site: www.first-media.com
Pres: James L. Berk II
Employees: 2
Primary Market Served: Business & Consumer
Catalog available online
Direct online sales

Gross sales or billing: $100,000

Music publishing, musical instruments and supplies.

FISHER-PRICE
Div. of Mattel Inc
636 Girard Ave
East Aurora, NY 14052-1824
Telephone: (716) 687-3000, FAX:
(716) 687-3636, Web Site: www.
fisherprice.com
CEO: Bryan Stockton
CFO: Kevin M. Farr
Exec VP Global Enterprise: David All-
mark
Exec VP Global Brand Teams: Geoff
Walker
Conducts Business: U.S.
Employees: 850
Primary Market Served: Business &
Consumer
Catalog available online
Direct online sales
Gross sales or billing: $76,500,000

Manufacture toys for catalog & retail sales.

FISHER SCIENTIFIC
A Fisher Scientific Co
300 Industry Dr
Pittsburgh, PA 15275-1001
Toll Free: (800) 766-7000, FAX: (800)
772-7702, Web Site: www.fishersci.
com
Safety Dir: Carl Shaw
Mktg Mgr: Tim Zeh
Mktg Mgr: Scott Daly
Conducts Business: U.S.
Employees: 450
Primary Market Served: Business
Founded: 1902

Sell safety products & controlled environments.

FITNESS QUEST
1400 Raff Rd SW
Canton, OH 44750-2320
Telephone: (330) 478-0755, Toll Free:
(800) 321-9236, FAX: (330) 479-
9213, E-Mail: customersupport@
fitnessquest.com, Web Site: www.
fitnessquest.com
Pres: Robert R. Schnabel Jr
VP, Bus Devel: Craig Waters
VP, Mktg: Mike Clark
Conducts Business: U.S.
Employees: 147
Primary Market Served: Consumer
Catalog available online
Direct online sales
Advertising/Marketing Budget Related
to Direct Marketing: 0-25%

Gross sales or billing: $35,300,000

Consumer direct company specializing in health-oriented products sold through direct marketing.

FITNESS USA SUPER CENTERS
7091 Orchard Lake Rd (Suite 300)
West Bloomfield, MI 48322
Telephone: (248) 737-7200, Toll Free:
(800) GET-FIT-1, FAX: (248) 932-
3300, Web Site: www.fitnessusa.com
Pres & CEO: Larry Gurney
Mgr: Michael Winger
Primary Market Served: Consumer
Catalog available online
Indirect online sales
Founded: 1958

Full service health spa for men & wom-
en.

FLEXCON
1 FLEXcon Industrial Pk
Spencer, MA 01562-2643
Telephone: (508) 885-8200, Web Site:
www.flexcon.com
Dir, Corp Communs: Joyce Laffin
Primary Market Served: Business &
Consumer

THE FLINCHBAUGH CO INC
245 Beshore School Rd
Manchester, PA 17345
Telephone: (717) 266-2202, FAX:
(717) 266-7055, E-Mail:
flinchbaugh@blazenet.net, Web Site:
www.flinchbaugh.com
Owner & Pres: Gregory Jenkins
Owner & Exec VP: Kurt Weber
Conducts Business: U.S., Canada, Aus-
tralia, U.S. Virgin Islands
Employees: 50
Primary Market Served: Business &
Consumer
Catalog available online
Indirect online sales
Advertising/Marketing Budget Related
to Direct Marketing: 0-25%
Direct Marketing ad budget:
Direct Mail: 20%
Magazines: 80%
Founded: 1936
Gross sales or billing: $3,000,000

Incline wheelchair lifts, stair climbs, dumbwaiters & custom machine work to dealers or direct.

FLORIDA A&M UNIVERSITY
Div. of Journalism
510 Orr Dr (Suite 4003)
Tallahassee, FL 32307
Telephone: (850) 599-3379, E-Mail:
sjgc@famu.edu, Web Site: sjgc.
famu.edu

Dean: Dr. Ann Wead
Dir: Dorothy Bland
Conducts Business: U.S.
Primary Market Served: Consumer

Educational institution that prepares students for opportunities in broadcast journalism, magazine production, newspaper production through courses in mass communications & public relations.

FLORIDA POWER & LIGHT CO
Subs. of NextEra Energy Inc
700 Universe Blvd
Juno Beach, FL 33408
Telephone: (305) 552-3552, Toll Free:
(800) 468-8243, FAX: (305) 552-
2487, Web Site: www.fpl.com
Chmn, Pres & CEO: James L. Robo
Vice Chmn, CFO & Exec VP Fin: Mor-
ay P. Dewhurst
VP Strategy & Corp Devel: Mark E.
Hickson
Pres: Eric Silagy
Conducts Business: U.S.
Primary Market Served: Business &
Consumer
Founded: 1925

Electricity utility in Florida. PO Box 14000, Juno Beach, FL 33408.

FLUID METERING INC
dba Fmi
5 Aerial Way (Suite 500)
Syosset, NY 11791-5593
Telephone: (516) 922-6050, Toll Free:
(800) 223-3388, FAX: (516) 624-
8261, E-Mail: pumps@fmipump.
com, Web Site: www.fmipump.com
Pres: Henry Pinkerton III
Adv Mktg: Herb Warner
Adv: George Bienenstock
Conducts Business: Worldwide
Employees: 60
Primary Market Served: Business &
Consumer
Catalog available online
Indirect online sales
Advertising/Marketing Budget Related
to Direct Marketing: 0-25%
Direct Marketing ad budget:
Direct Mail: 20%
Magazines: 80%
Founded: 1959
Gross sales or billing: $1,940,000

Manufactures valveless rotating & re-
ciprocating piston metering pumps. Industrial business to business supplier.

FLUKE BIOMEDICAL
Div. of Fluke Corp
6920 Seaway Blvd
Everett, WA 98203-5829

Telephone: (425) 347-6100, Toll Free: (800) 850-4608, FAX: (425) 446-5116, Web Site: www. flukebiomedical.com
CEO: R. Kerry Clark
Exec VP, Global Communs: Shelley Bird
Exec VP Strategy & Corp Devel: Vivek Jain
Dir Mktg: Karen Higley
Conducts Business: Worldwide
Employees: 150
Primary Market Served: Business & Consumer
Catalog available online
Indirect online sales
Advertising/Marketing Budget Related to Direct Marketing: 76-100%
Founded: 1966
Gross sales or billing: $14,600,000

Manufactures biomedical test & simulation products. Biomedical test, diagnostic imaging, radiation oncology, radiation safety, nuclear medicine, nuclear power systems, & asset management capabilities.

FM HOWELL & CO
79 Pennsylvania Ave
Elmira, NY 14902-1455
Telephone: (607) 734-6291, FAX: (607) 735-0464, E-Mail: best@howellpkg.com, Web Site: www. howellpkg.com
Chmn & CEO: George Howell
Dir: Stephen D. Duff
Employees: 275
Primary Market Served: Business
Gross sales or billing: $21,000,000

Manufacture paperboard packing & thermoform plastic packaging.

FOLLETT SCHOOL SOLUTIONS INC
Div. of Follett Corp
1340 Ridgeview Dr
McHenry, IL 60050
Telephone: (815) 759-1700, Toll Free: (888) 511-5114, FAX: (800) 852-5458, E-Mail: customerservice@follett.com, Web Site: www.flr.follett.com
Pres & CEO: Mary Lee Schneider
Conducts Business: Worldwide
Employees: 600
Primary Market Served: Business
Catalog available online
Advertising/Marketing Budget Related to Direct Marketing: 51-75%
Founded: 1948

Wholesaler to schools of audiovisual materials & online services for grades K-12.

FOOTE-JONES/ILLINOIS GEAR
Div. of Regal Beloit
2914 Industrial Ave
Aberdeen, SD 57402-1089
Telephone: (605) 225-0360, FAX: (605) 225-0567, Web Site: www. footejones.com
VP & Gen Mgr: Louis Ertel
Natl Sls Mgr: Daniel Ward
Conducts Business: U.S., S. America
Employees: 300
Primary Market Served: Business
Advertising/Marketing Budget Related to Direct Marketing: 0-25%
Direct Marketing ad budget:
Direct Mail: 10%
Magazines: 85%
Telephone: 5%
Founded: 1962
Gross sales or billing: $50,000,000

Custom gears & shafts, standard & special gear boxes.

FORD MOTOR CO
One American Rd
Dearborn, MI 48126-2798
Telephone: (313) 845-8540, Toll Free: (800) 555-5259, FAX: (313) 845-6073, Web Site: www.ford.com
Chmn: William Clay Ford
Pres & CEO: Alan Mulally
COO: Mark Fields
Exec VP Global Mktg Sls & Svc: James D. Farley
Exec VP & Pres Americas: Joseph R. Hinrichs
Exec VP & CFO: Robert L. Shanks
Conducts Business: Worldwide
Employees: 245,000
Primary Market Served: Business & Consumer
Catalog available online
Indirect online sales
Founded: 1903
Gross sales or billing: $173,000,000,000

Automotive manufacturer.

FOREMOST INDUSTRIAL EXCHANGE
Subs. of Mared Industries
15222 Keswick St
Van Nuys, CA 91405-1068
Telephone: (818) 988-6900, FAX: (818) 787-0293
Chmn: Edward Guttenberg
Pres: Larry Phillips
Sec: Paul Cirino
Conducts Business: U.S.
Employees: 150
Primary Market Served: Business
Gross sales or billing: $25,600,000

Business-to-business supplier of cutting tools & abrasives.

FOUR CORNERS DIRECT INC
8520 S Tamiami Trl Unit 2
Sarasota, FL 34238-3001
Telephone: (941) 364-8585
Pres: Martin Lothman
Primary Market Served: Business & Consumer

4IMPRINT INC
101 Commerce St
Oshkosh, WI 54901
Telephone: (920) 236-7272, Toll Free: (877) 446-7746, (888) 298-8190, FAX: (800) 355-5043, E-Mail: administrator@4imprint.com, Web Site: www.4imprint.com
Pres: Kevin Lyons-Tarr
VP Admin: Mary Curtin
VP Sls & Mktg: Greg Ebel
Conducts Business: U.S., U.K.; Germany; France; Hong Kong
Employees: 350
Primary Market Served: Business
Catalog available online
Direct online sales
Advertising/Marketing Budget Related to Direct Marketing: 76-100%
Direct Marketing ad budget: $4,000,000
Direct Mail: $4,000,000
Founded: 1985

Imprinted promotional products.

LARRY FOX & CO LTD
PO Box 729
Valley Stream, NY 11582-0729
Telephone: (516) 791-7929, Toll Free: (800) 397-7923, FAX: (516) 791-1022, E-Mail: larry@larryfox.com, Web Site: www.larryfox.com
Pres: Ellen Ingber
VP: Larry Fox
Conducts Business: U.S., Australia, Canada, Japan, Germany
Employees: 7
Primary Market Served: Business & Consumer
Catalog available online
Direct online sales
Advertising/Marketing Budget Related to Direct Marketing: 26-50%
Direct Marketing ad budget:
Direct Mail: 80%
Magazines: 15%
Newspapers: 5%
Founded: 1961

Promotional & advertising specialties. Stock Firematic items for direct sales to firefighters, emergency medical personnel & fire departments.

FRAGRANCE INTERNATIONAL INC
398 E Rayen Ave
Youngstown, OH 44505
Telephone: (330) 747-3341, Toll Free:
(888) 547-8355, FAX: (330) 747-
3343, E-Mail: comments@kisstell.
com, Web Site: www.kisstell.com
Pres: Brad Levy
VP: Judy Levy
Conducts Business: U.S.
Employees: 50
Primary Market Served: Business &
Consumer
Catalog available online
Direct online sales
Advertising/Marketing Budget Related
to Direct Marketing: 0-25%
Direct Marketing ad budget:
Direct Mail: 25%
Online: 25%
Telephone: 50%
Founded: 1978

Perfumes, colognes, health & beauty
aids.

THE FRANKLIN MINT
Subs. of Sequential Brands Group Inc
486 Thomas Jones Way Ste 240
Exton, PA 19341-2561
Telephone: (610) 497-4800, Toll Free:
(800) THE-MINT, FAX: (610) 497-
4956, E-Mail: support@franklinmint.
com, Web Site: www.franklinmint.
com
CEO: Yehuda Shmidman
CFO: Gary Klein
Grp Pres Brand Mgmt: Rick Platt
Chief Mktg Officer: Jameel Spencer
Conducts Business: Worldwide
Employees: 40
Primary Market Served: Business &
Consumer
Catalog available online
Direct online sales
Advertising/Marketing Budget Related
to Direct Marketing: 76-100%
Founded: 1964

Creator & marketer of fine collectibles,
home decor & luxury products. Product
lines offer originally designed items in
a diverse range of artistic genres: sculpture, Franklin Heirloom Dolls, fashion
jewelry, Franklin Mint Precision Models, home accessories, historic & artistic arms reproductions, games &
collector plates.

FREEMAN DECORATING CO
909 Newark Tpke
Kearny, NJ 07032-4307
Telephone: (201) 998-6006

FRITO-LAY
Div. of PepsiCo Americas Foods
7701 Legacy Dr
Plano, TX 75024-4099
Telephone: (972) 334-7000, Toll Free:
(800) 352-4477, FAX: (972) 334-
2019, Web Site: www.fritolay.com
CEO, PepsiCo Americas Foods: Brian
Cornell
Pres Frito-Lay, NA: Tom Greco
Conducts Business: U.S.
Primary Market Served: Business &
Consumer
Catalog available online
Manufacturer of snack foods for retail
sales.

FUJIFILM HOLDINGS AMERICA CORP
Subs. of Fujifilm Corp, Tokyo, Japan
200 Summit Lake Dr
Valhalla, NY 10595-1356
Telephone: (914) 789-8100, Toll Free:
(800) 755-3854, FAX: (914) 789-
8295, Web Site: www.fujifilmusa.
com
Pres & CEO: Go Miyazaki
Pres: Shigeru Sano
VP, Gen Counsel & Sec: Judy Melillo
Conducts Business: U.S.
Primary Market Served: Business &
Consumer
Catalog available online
Manufacture & sell cameras & film.

FUJITSU TRANSACTION SOLUTIONS INC
Subs. of Fujitsu LTD
2791 Telecom Pkwy
Richardson, TX 75082-3523
Telephone: (972) 963-2300, Toll Free:
(800) 340-4425, Web Site: www.
fujitsu.com
Pres & CEO: Masao Teramoto
COO: Ed Soladay
Sr VP: Keith McNamara
Sr VP: Bill Witte
Reg VP, Sls: Don Cramb
Conducts Business: U.S., Canada
Employees: 1,400
Primary Market Served: Business
Catalog available online
Indirect online sales
Gross sales or billing: $120,000,000

Develop, manufacture & market retail
point-of-sale (POS) systems, automated
teller machines (ATMs) & handheld
computer systems.

THE FULLER THEOLOGICAL SEMINARY
135 N Oakland Ave
Pasadena, CA 91182
Telephone: (626) 584-5200, Toll Free:
(800) 235-2222, FAX: (626) 584-
5449, Web Site: www.fuller.edu

Pres: Mark Labberton
Exec Dir Integrated Mktg & Commun:
Joyce V. Hiendarto
Conducts Business: U.S.
Primary Market Served: Business &
Consumer
Catalog available online
Direct online sales
Founded: 1947
Gross sales or billing: $78,400,000

G&S FRUIT PACKERS LLC
16600 County Rd 25 S
Weirsdale, FL 32195
Telephone: (352) 821-2251, Toll Free:
(800) 949-9074, FAX: (352) 821-
0278, E-Mail: info@gsfruitpackers.
com, Web Site: www.gsfruitpackers.
com
Owner: Pete Spyke
Conducts Business: Worldwide
Primary Market Served: Business &
Consumer
Catalog available online
Founded: 1879

Fulfillment company specializing in
Florida & tropical fruit.

G H BASS & CO
Div. of Phillips Van Huesen
200 Madison Ave
New York, NY 10016-3903
Telephone: (212) 381-3900, FAX:
(212) 381-3950, E-Mail: help@
ghbass.com, Web Site: www.ghbass.
com
Pres: Kristin Kohler Burrows
Conducts Business: U.S.
Employees: 5,000
Primary Market Served: Business &
Consumer
Catalog available online
Direct online sales
Founded: 1876
Gross sales or billing: $600,000,000
Shoes wholesaler.

GE LIGHTING NORTH AMERICA
Div. of General Electric
1975 Noble Rd
Cleveland, OH 44112-6300
Telephone: (216) 266-2121, FAX:
(216) 266-2930, Web Site: www.
gelighting.com/na
Pres & CEO Lighting: Maryrose Syl-
vester
Primary Market Served: Business &
Consumer

Light bulbs & other commercial electrical equipment.

GN NETCOM
77 Northeastern Blvd

Nashua, NH 03062-3128
Telephone: (603) 598-1100, Toll Free: (800) 345-8639, FAX: (603) 598-1122, Web Site: www.jabra.com
Conducts Business: U.S., Canada
Employees: 350
Primary Market Served: Business
Catalog available online
Advertising/Marketing Budget Related to Direct Marketing: 0-25%
Founded: 1987
Gross sales or billing: $100,000

Manufactures professional, lightweight wireless and corded telephone headsets.

GACO WESTERN INC

200 W Mercer St (Suite 202)
Seattle, WA 98119-3958
Telephone: (206) 575-0450, Toll Free: (800) 456-4226, FAX: (206) 575-0587, E-Mail: info@gaco.com, Web Site: www.gaco.com
Pres: Peter Davis
Mktg Dir: Kyle Sherk
Admin Asst to Pres: Yolanda Sewell
Conducts Business: Worldwide
Employees: 51
Primary Market Served: Business & Consumer
Catalog available online
Direct online sales
Founded: 1955

Manufactures & distributes waterproofing systems, architectural coatings & sprayed-in-place polyurethane foam insulation.

GALEN WILLIAMS LANDSCAPING & GARDEN DESIGN

Seven Oyster Shores Rd
East Hampton, NY 11937-1103
Telephone: (631) 324-6220, FAX: (631) 329-3684
Pres: Galen Williams
Primary Market Served: Business & Consumer

Landscape architects.

GALL'S INC

Subs. Aramark Uniform & Career Apparel
2680 Palumbo Dr
Lexington, KY 40509-1234
Telephone: (859) 266-7227, Toll Free: (800) 477-7766, FAX: (859) 268-5954, E-Mail: help-desk@galls.com, Web Site: www.galls.com
Pres: Thomas Vozzo
CFO: David Solomon
CIO: Robert McCormack
Conducts Business: U.S.
Employees: 450

Primary Market Served: Business & Consumer
Catalog available online
Direct online sales
Founded: 1967

Public safety equipment supplier.

GAMBRO INC

14143 Denver W Pkwy
Lakewood, CO 80401
Telephone: (303) 232-6800, Toll Free: (800) 525-2623, FAX: (303) 222-6810, Web Site: www.gambro.com
Pres & CEO: David B. Perez
COO: Teresa W. Ayers
VP: Frank Corbin
VP, Opers: Gary Heath
Dir, Mktg: Anne Bonelli
Conducts Business: U.S.
Employees: 7
Primary Market Served: Business
Catalog available online
Advertising/Marketing Budget Related to Direct Marketing: 0-25%
Founded: 1984
Gross sales or billing: $6,000,000

Incentive suppliers & distributors.

GAMMA PHOTO LABS LLC

222 N Des Plains
Chicago, IL 60661-1120
Telephone: (312) 337-0022, FAX: (312) 337-3753, Web Site: www.photobition.com
Pres: Doug Goddard
VP, Opers: Ray Pryor
Office Mgr: Patricia Andrews
Conducts Business: U.S.
Employees: 135
Primary Market Served: Business & Consumer
Catalog available online
Advertising/Marketing Budget Related to Direct Marketing: 0-25%
Direct Marketing ad budget: $40,000

Full-service custom photo lab.

GANNETT CO INC

7950 Jones Branch Dr
Mc Lean, VA 22107-0150
Telephone: (703) 854-6000, FAX: (703) 854-2046, Web Site: www.gannett.com
Pres & CEO: Gracia C. Martore
Sr VP & Chief Mktg Officer: Maryam Banikarim
Employees: 50,000
Primary Market Served: Business & Consumer
Gross sales or billing: $8,000,000,000

Communication media & newspapers.

GARON PRODUCTS INC

PO Box 1924

Wall, NJ 07719-1924
Telephone: (732) 449-1776, Toll Free: (800) 631-5380, FAX: (732) 449-6937, Web Site: www.garonproducts.com
Pres: Arthur M. Crowley
Mktg Dir: Tara Crowley
Conducts Business: U.S.
Primary Market Served: Business
Catalog available online
Direct online sales
Direct Marketing ad budget:
Direct Mail: 85%
Telephone: 15%

Manufacturer of industrial & construction maintenance products. Sell to business & industrial markets largely through direct mail catalogs.

GAYLORD BROTHERS

PO Box 4901
Syracuse, NY 13221-4901
Telephone: (315) 634-8440, Web Site: www.gaylord.com
VP Sls & Mktg: Coleen Gagliardo
Conducts Business: U.S.
Primary Market Served: Business

Furniture, office & library supplies. Mailing address: PO Box 4901, Syracuse, NY 13221.

GELCO INFORMATION NETWORK

10700 Prairie Lakes Dr
Eden Prairie, MN 55344
Telephone: (952) 947-1500, Toll Free: (800) 444-6588, FAX: (952) 947-1525, Web Site: www.gelco.com
Pres: Neil Vill
VP, Prods & Mktg: Ralph Bernstein
Conducts Business: U.S., Canada
Employees: 300
Primary Market Served: Business
Advertising/Marketing Budget Related to Direct Marketing: 0-25%
Founded: 1894

A worldwide provider of complete, outsourced trade fund & travel expense management solutions to U.S. & multinational Fortune 1000 companies & government agencies.

GEMALTO INC

dba Gem Plus Card Services
101 Park Dr
Montgomeryville, PA 18936-9613
Telephone: (215) 390-2000, E-Mail: us.sales@gemalto.com, Web Site: www.gemalto.com
VP-Pres, VP Sys: Eric Soulliard
Conducts Business: U.S., Canada, S. America
Employees: 400
Primary Market Served: Business

Advertising/Marketing Budget Related
to Direct Marketing: 0-25%
Direct Marketing ad budget:
Magazines: 100%
Founded: 1953
Gross sales or billing: $29,800,000

Manufacturer of semiconductors & related devices, magnetic stripe & smart cards. Sell to financial, retail, travel, entertainment & oil industries. Firm also produces magnetic tape for use on financial transaction cards.

GENERAL ELECTRIC CO
3135 Easton Tpke
Fairfield, CT 06828-0001
Telephone: (203) 373-2211, FAX:
(203) 373-3131, Web Site: www.ge.
com
Chmn & CEO: Jeffrey R. Immelt
Sr VP & CFO: Jeffrey S. Bornstein
Sr VP & Chief Mktg Officer: Beth
Comstock
Primary Market Served: Business &
Consumer

Diversified manufacturer of technology
& services.

GENERAL PENCIL CO INC
67 Fleet St
Jersey City, NJ 07306
Telephone: (201) 653-5351, FAX:
(201) 653-2298, E-Mail: info@
generalpencil.com, Web Site: www.
generalpencil.com
Pres & CEO: James Weissenborn
Primary Market Served: Business &
Consumer
Catalog available online
Direct online sales
Founded: 1864

Manufactures wood-cased pencils for
the art, craft, office, drafting & bowling
industries.

GENERAL PHYSICS CORP
6095 Marshalee Dr (Suite 300)
Elkridge, MD 21075
Telephone: (410) 379-3600, Toll Free:
(800) 727-6677, FAX: (410) 540-
5302, E-Mail: info@gpworldwide.
com, Web Site: www.gpworldwide.
com
Head Engrng: Ben Parks
CEO: Jerome I. Feldman
Head Training: Jim Barnes
Primary Market Served: Business

Training & engineering services.

GENERAL VITAMIN CORP
10700 World Trade Blvd (Ste 102)
Raleigh, NC 27617-4220
Telephone: (919) 929-5785, Toll Free:
(800) 323-8432, FAX: (919) 929-
2458, E-Mail: support@
generalvitamin.com, Web Site: www.
generalvitamin.com
VP: A.C. Bushnel
Conducts Business: U.S.
Primary Market Served: Business &
Consumer

Sell vitamins through direct response
marketing.

GENETICA DNA
LABORATORIES INC
8740 Montgomery Rd (Suite 11)
Cincinnati, OH 45236-2100
Telephone: (513) 985-9777, Toll Free:
(800) 433-6848, FAX: (513) 985-
9983, Web Site: www.genetica.com
Pres & Founder: Elizabeth Panke M.
D.; Ph.D.
Conducts Business: North & South
America, Africa
Employees: 15
Primary Market Served: Business &
Consumer
Catalog available online
Direct online sales
Founded: 1996

Commercial provider of DNA testing services. Services include DNA paternity tests, DNA family relationship tests, and DNA identity tests to the general public as well as to healthcare, legal professionals and embassies throughout the United States and worldwide.

GEORGIA POWER
Subs. of Southern Co
241 Ralph McGill Blvd NE
Atlanta, GA 30308-3374
Telephone: (404) 506-3440
Pres & CEO: Paul Bowers
Exec VP, CFO, Treas & Comptroller:
Ron Hinson
Exec VP External Affairs: Craig Barrs
Primary Market Served: Business &
Consumer

Utility company.

GERBER PRODUCTS CO
Subs. of Nestle Group
12 Vreeland Rd (fl 2)
Florham Park, NJ 07932
Telephone: (973) 593-7500, Toll Free:
(800) 284-9488, Web Site: www.
gerber.com
Head Nestle Nutrition North America:
Kurt T. Schmidt
Integrated Mktg Mgr: Bernadette Tor-
torella
Conducts Business: Worldwide
Employees: 3,500

Primary Market Served: Consumer
Advertising/Marketing Budget Related
to Direct Marketing: 26-50%
Founded: 1928
Gross sales or billing: $1,300,000,000

Baby food, baby care & baby wear.

GERO VITA
1835 Newport Blvd (Suite A109, #439)
Costa Mesa, CA 92627-5007
Toll Free: (888) 382-9175, Web Site:
www.gvi.com
Pres: Tuong Nyugen
VP: Jim Chiang
Employees: 100
Primary Market Served: Consumer
Catalog available online
Direct online sales
Gross sales or billing: $26,000,000

Vitamins.

GET SEEN MEDIA GROUP
5115 Wilshire Blvd (Apt 235)
Los Angeles, CA 90036-4371
Telephone: (323) 424-4669, Web Site:
www.getseenmedia.com
CEO: Frank Mustafa

GETRONICS
RP-NFOA
100 Ames Pond Dr (Suite 200)
Tewksbury, MA 01876-1240
Telephone: (978) 625-5000, Web Site:
www.getronics.com
Vice Chmn & Exec VP: Kevin Roche
Primary Market Served: Business &
Consumer

Manufacture & sell software & services.

GHIRARDELLI CHOCOLATE
CO
1111 139th Ave
San Leandro, CA 94578
Telephone: (510) 483-6970, Toll Free:
(800) 877-9338, FAX: (510) 297-
2649, Web Site: www.ghirardelli.
com
Pres & CEO: Martin E. Thompson
CFO: Martin Hug
VP Mktg: Vicki Isip
VP Sls: Rob Budowski
Conducts Business: U.S.
Primary Market Served: Business
Catalog available online
Direct online sales
Founded: 1852
Gross sales or billing: $35,800,000

Manufacturer & marketer of premium
chocolate products.

GLAMOUR SHOTS LICENSING

Subs. of Candid Color Systems
1300 Metropolitan Ave
Oklahoma City, OK 73108
Telephone: (405) 947-8747, Toll Free: (888) GLAMOUR-SHOTS, FAX: (405) 951-7343, Web Site: www.glamourshots.com
Pres: Jack Counts
Primary Market Served: Consumer
Catalog available online

Fashion photography.

GLAS-COL

711 Hulman St, PO Box 2128
Terre Haute, IN 47808
Telephone: (812) 235-6167, FAX: (812) 234-6975, Web Site: www.i-2-r.com
Conducts Business: U.S.
Primary Market Served: Business

Manufacturer of laboratory devices.

GLAXOSMITHKLINE USA

5 Crescent Dr
Philadelphia, PA 19112
Toll Free: (888) 825-5249, Web Site: us.gsk.com
CEO: Sir Andrew Witty
Pres North America Pharmaceuticals: Deirdre Connelly
Conducts Business: Worldwide
Employees: 100,000
Primary Market Served: Consumer
Catalog available online
Indirect online sales
Founded: 1715

Pharmaceutical manufacturer selling to wholesalers. Sell over-the-counter products to retail industries.

GLOBAL SPECIALTIES

Div. of Interplex Electronics Inc
994 N Colony Rd (Unit 305)
Wallingford, CT 06492-5902
Telephone: (203) 272-3285, FAX: (203) 272-4330, Web Site: www.globalspecialties.com
Exec VP: John Pease
VP & Gen Mgr: Eric Blauvelt
Conducts Business: Worldwide
Employees: 56
Primary Market Served: Business

Manufacture electronic testing & prototyping equipment.

GLOBE TICKET & LABEL CO

350 Randy Rd (Suite 1)
Carol Stream, IL 60188-1831

Telephone: (404) 762-9711, Toll Free: (800) 523-5968, FAX: (404) 762-7019, Web Site: www.globeticket.com
Pres, CFO & Exec VP: Bob Puleo
Bus Devel Dir: Philip Raines
Conducts Business: U.S., U.K.
Employees: 320
Primary Market Served: Business
Indirect online sales
Direct Marketing ad budget: $100,000
Direct Mail: 20%
Magazines: 75%
Newspapers: 5%
Founded: 1868
Gross sales or billing: $30,000,000

Manufacturer of printed products (tickets, tags, labels, transfers, parking checks, data processing cards) & commercial publications.

GO AHEAD VACATIONS

Subs. of EF Education
One Education St
Cambridge, MA 02141
Telephone: (617) 619-1000, Toll Free: (800) 242-4686, FAX: (617) 619-1001, E-Mail: goahead@et.com, Web Site: www.goaheadvacations.com
Pres: Louise Jillian
Exec VP: Chris O'Brien
Conducts Business: U.S.
Primary Market Served: Consumer

Business vacation & travel agency.

GOLD MEDAL PRODUCTS CO

10700 Medallion Dr
Cincinnati, OH 45241-4807
Telephone: (513) 769-7676, Toll Free: (800) 543-0862, FAX: (800) 542-1496, E-Mail: info@gmpopcorn.com, Web Site: www.gmpopcorn.com
Pres: Dan Kroeger
Natl Sls Mgr: Chris Petroff
Dir Mktg: Stephanie Goodin
Conducts Business: Worldwide
Primary Market Served: Business & Consumer
Catalog available online
Advertising/Marketing Budget Related to Direct Marketing: 0-25%
Founded: 1931

Concession equipment and supplies for fund-raising purposes. Branches: Orlando, FL; Chicago, IL; Indianapolis, IN; New Orleans, LA; Greensboro, NC; Pittsburgh, PA; Nashville, TN.

GOLDEN FLEECE DESIGNS INC

441 S Victory Blvd

Burbank, CA 91502-2353
Telephone: (818) 848-7724, FAX: (818) 566-7100, Web Site: www.mandonia.com
Chmn & CEO: Symeon D. Argyropoulos
VP: Maria Argyropoulos
VP: Antoinette Argyropoulos
Conducts Business: U.S., Canada, Caribbean, U.K., Japan, Greece
Employees: 20
Primary Market Served: Business & Consumer
Catalog available online
Direct online sales
Advertising/Marketing Budget Related to Direct Marketing: 0-25%
Direct Marketing ad budget: $50,000
Direct Mail: $20,000
Magazines: $15,000
Online: $15,000
Founded: 1970

Marine & industrial canvas, canvas products & covers, flags, duffle & tote bags, promotional goods. Nautical gifts manufacturers, exporters & wholesale supplier to the U.S. government.

GOLDEN GATE TRANSPORTATION DISTRICT

1011 Anderson Dr
San Rafael, CA 94901
Telephone: (415) 921-5858, FAX: (415) 923-2014, Web Site: www.goldengate.org
Pres: John J. Moylan
First VP: Albert J. Boro
Second VP: Tom Ammiano
Dir: Harold C. Brown Jr.
Dir: Gerald D. Cochran
Conducts Business: U.S.
Primary Market Served: Business
Catalog available online

Purchasing division for the transportation industry.

GOODYEAR TIRE & RUBBER CO

200 Innovation Way
Akron, OH 44316-0001
Telephone: (330) 796-2121, Toll Free: (800) 321-2136, FAX: (330) 796-2222, Web Site: www.goodyear.com
Chmn, Pres & CEO: Richard J Kramer
Exec VP & CFO: Laura Thompson
Sr VP Global Commun: Paul Fitzhenry
VP Bus Devel: Scott Honnold
Conducts Business: U.S.
Employees: 69,000
Primary Market Served: Business & Consumer
Founded: 1894

Gross sales or billing: $19,500,000,000

Manufacturer & marketer of passenger, truck & farm tires for replacement markets.

W R GRACE & CO

7500 Grace Dr
Columbia, MD 21044
Telephone: (410) 531-4000, FAX: (410) 531-4367, Web Site: www. grace.com
Pres & COO: Fred Festa
Conducts Business: Worldwide
Employees: 6,500
Primary Market Served: Business
Founded: 1899
Gross sales or billing: $2,800,000,000

Specialty chemicals & specialized healthcare company.

GRAINGER INDUSTRIAL SUPPLY

Div. of WW Grainger Inc
1657 Shermer Rd
North Brook, IL 60062
Telephone: (847) 498-5900, FAX: (847) 498-3402, Web Site: www. grainger.com
Chmn, Pres & CEO: James T. Ryan
Sr VP & Grp Pres Americas: Court Carruthers
Sr VP & CFO: Ronald L. Jadin
Sr VP & Grp Pres Global Supply Chain & Intl: D.G. Macpherson
Conducts Business: U.S., Canada
Employees: 350
Primary Market Served: Business
Catalog available online
Direct online sales
Advertising/Marketing Budget Related to Direct Marketing: 0-25%
Direct Marketing ad budget:
Direct Mail: 85%
Magazines: 5%
Telephone: 10%
Founded: 1927

Specialty distribution of replacement parts for MRO, food & bottled water equipment.

GRAPHIK DIMENSIONS LTD

2103 Brentwood St
High Point, NC 27263
Telephone: (336) 887-3500, Toll Free: (800) 221-0262, FAX: (336) 887-3773, E-Mail: customercare@ pictureframes.com, Web Site: www. pictureframes.com
Pres: Joan Feinsod
VP: Dave Shelton
Conducts Business: Worldwide
Employees: 120
Primary Market Served: Business & Consumer

Catalog available online
Direct online sales
Advertising/Marketing Budget Related to Direct Marketing: 76-100%
Founded: 1966

Manufacture picture frames.

GREAT WESTERN SUPPLY

2828 Forest Ln (Suite 2000)
Dallas, TX 75234
Telephone: (972) 481-6100, Toll Free: (800) 527-2782, FAX: (972) 481-6215, Web Site: www.proforma.com/ greatwesternsupply
CEO: Joseph Salatino
Conducts Business: U.S.
Employees: 200
Primary Market Served: Business
Catalog available online
Advertising/Marketing Budget Related to Direct Marketing: 0-25%
Founded: 1972
Gross sales or billing: $25,000,000

Business to business telemarketing wholesaler of office supplies and computer supplies. Advertising specialty items for business promotions.

GROVE ENTERPRISES INC

618 Dog Branch Rd
Brasstown, NC 28902-8750
Telephone: (828) 837-9200, Toll Free: (800) 438-8155, FAX: (828) 837-2216, E-Mail: judy@grove-ent.com, Web Site: www.grove-ent.com
Pres: Robert Grove
CEO: Judy A. Grove
Conducts Business: Worldwide
Employees: 14
Primary Market Served: Business & Consumer
Catalog available online
Direct online sales
Advertising/Marketing Budget Related to Direct Marketing: 76-100%
Direct Marketing ad budget:
Direct Mail: 90%
Magazines: 10%
Founded: 1979
Gross sales or billing: $3,500,000

Shortwave, scanner radios & accessories, computer sales & service & web page design. Publisher of monthly magazine, Monitoring Times.

GROVER CO

PO Box 41844
Mesa, AZ 85274-1844
Telephone: (480) 827-8011, FAX: (480) 827-8014
Pres: Rande Grover
VP: John Grover
Conducts Business: Worldwide
Employees: 10
Primary Market Served: Consumer

Advertising/Marketing Budget Related to Direct Marketing: 0-25%
Direct Marketing ad budget:
Direct Mail: 50%
Newspapers: 40%
TV/Radio: 5%
Telephone: 5%

Sell the Marathon Mill & Kenwood Bread Mixer plus the whole grains for use in the mixer through mail order. Also sell Mountain House freeze-dried foods.

GROWING FAMILY PORTRAITS

2003 Western Ave (Suite 460)
Seattle, WA 98121-2185
Telephone: (206) 587-0333, Web Site: www.silversand.com

GUIDING EYES FOR THE BLIND

611 Granite Springs Rd
Yorktown Heights, NY 10598
Telephone: (914) 245-4042, Toll Free: (800) 942-0149, FAX: (914) 245-1609, Web Site: www.guidingeyes. org
Pres & CEO: Bill Badger
Dir: Carolyn Kihm
Comptroller: Jerry Attard
Conducts Business: U.S.
Primary Market Served: Business & Consumer
Gross sales or billing: $20,434,061

Guide dog training school.

GULFSTREAM AEROSPACE CORP

Subs. of General Dynamics Co
500 Gulfstream Rd, PO Box 2206
Savannah, GA 31408-2206
Telephone: (912) 965-3000, E-Mail: info@gulfstream.com, Web Site: www.gulfstream.com
Pres: Larry Flynn
CFO: Dan Clare
Sr VP Worldwide Sls & Mktg: Scott Neal
Conducts Business: Worldwide
Employees: 13,500
Primary Market Served: Business
Founded: 1978

Manufacture Gulfstream Business Jet Aircraft; special requirement jet aircraft for government & military purposes.

HCI DIRECT

3369 Progress Dr
Bensalem, PA 19020
Telephone: (215) 244-9600, Toll Free: (888) 765-0062, FAX: (215) 244-0328, Web Site: www.silkies.com
Pres & CEO: John F. Biagini

VP & CFO: William J. Kelly
Mktg Dir: Darrell Edwards
Conducts Business: Worldwide
Primary Market Served: Business &
    Consumer
Catalog available online
Direct online sales
Advertising/Marketing Budget Related
    to Direct Marketing: 76-100%
Direct Marketing ad budget:
Direct Mail: 90%
Online: 1%
Telephone: 9%
Gross sales or billing: $53,100,000

Direct marketing company for women's
goods and services. Primary service is
hosiery.

HP INDIGO & INKJET PRESS
    SOLUTIONS
Div. of Hewlett-Packard
1115 SE 164th Ave (suite 210)
Vancouver, WA 98683
Telephone: (360) 975-5000, Web Site:
    www.hp.com
Sr VP Inkjet & Printing Solutions: Ste-
    phen Nigro

Manufacturer and seller of large format, commercial & industrial printers.

HAGEMEYER - NORTH
    AMERICA
1460 Tobias Gadson Blvd
Charleston, SC 29407-4793
Telephone: (843) 745-2400, FAX:
    (843) 745-6942, E-Mail: info@
    hagemeyerna.com, Web Site: www.
    hagemeyerna.com
Exec VP: Lisa A. Mitchell
Mgr Mktg Design Services: Anna
    McGuiness
Conducts Business: U.S.
Employees: 17,600
Primary Market Served: Business
Founded: 1900
Gross sales or billing: $1,500,000,000
Industrial supplies.

HAIN CELESTIAL GROUP
    INC
4600 Sleepytime Dr
Boulder, CO 80301
Toll Free: (800) 434-4246, Web Site:
    www.hain-celestial.com
Chmn, Pres & CEO: Irwin David Si-
    mon
Exec VP & CFO: Stephen J. Smith
Exec VP & CEO Hain Celestial US:
    John Carroll
Chief Mktg Officer Grocery & Snacks:
    Maureen M. Putman
Employees: 2,131
Primary Market Served: Business
Catalog available online

Gross sales or billing: $900,000,000
Manufacturer of 200 products-cookies,
snack bars, cereals, soups & chilies.
Primarily sold through distributors &
retailed through health stores & health
food section of supermarkets.

HALE INDIAN RIVER
    GROVES INC
PO Box 691237
Vero Beach, FL 32969-1237
Toll Free: (800) 356-7264, FAX: (877)
    329-4253, E-Mail: marketing@
    halegroves.com, Web Site: www.
    hales.com
Pres: Stephen Hale III
VP: Daniel Keith Bryan
Conducts Business: U.S.
Employees: 400
Primary Market Served: Business &
    Consumer
Catalog available online
Direct online sales
Advertising/Marketing Budget Related
    to Direct Marketing: 76-100%
Direct Marketing ad budget:
Direct Mail: 75%
Magazines: 10%
Newspapers: 10%
TV/Radio: 5%
Founded: 1948

Sell Indian River citrus for family,
business gifts & personal use. Also
truckload shipments for fund-raisers.

HALL-ERICKSON INC
98 E Naperville Rd (Suite 200)
Westmont, IL 60559-2199
Telephone: (630) 434-7779, FAX:
    (630) 434-1216
Pres: Peter H. Erickson
Primary Market Served: Business
Advertising/Marketing Budget Related
    to Direct Marketing: 0-25%

Exposition management company.

HALLMARK CARDS INC
2501 McGee Trafficway
Kansas City, MO 64108
Telephone: (816) 274-5111, Toll Free:
    (800) 425-5627, FAX: (816) 274-
    7276, Web Site: www.hallmark.com
Pres & CEO: Donald J. Hall Jr.
Pres North America: David E. Hall
Conducts Business: U.S.
Employees: 31,800
Primary Market Served: Business &
    Consumer
Gross sales or billing: $3,900,000,000
Social expression company.

HALLS KANSAS CITY
211 Nichols Rd
Kansas City, MO 64112

Telephone: (816) 274-3222, Toll Free:
    (800) 624-4034, FAX: (816) 274-
    3220, E-Mail: contact@halls.com,
    Web Site: www.halls.com
Pres & CEO: Kelly Cole
Conducts Business: U.S.
Primary Market Served: Consumer
Catalog available online
Indirect online sales

Specialty women's retail clothing store.

HALSOM HOME CARE INC
Subs of Tuscan Inc
7905 Clyo Rd
Centerville, OH 45459
Telephone: (937) 438-6600, Toll Free:
    (800) 345-5438, FAX: (937) 438-
    6620, E-Mail: main@halsom.com,
    Web Site: www.halsom.com
Pres: Mike Zelinskas
Conducts Business: U.S.
Employees: 11
Primary Market Served: Business &
    Consumer
Founded: 1936

Distributor of medical supplies to
physicians & home care products to individuals.

HAMILTON BEACH BRANDS
    INC
Subs. of NACCO Industries
4421 Waterfront Dr
Glen Allen, VA 23060-3375
Telephone: (804) 273-9777, FAX:
    (804) 527-7142, Web Site: www.
    hamiltonbeach.com
Pres & CEO: Gregory H. Trepp
Sr VP North America Sls & Mktg: R.
    Scott Tidey
VP & CFO: James H. Taylor
Primary Market Served: Business &
    Consumer

Manufacturer of small appliances.

THE HAMILTON GROUP
    LTD INC
Subs. of The Bradford Exchange
7018 A C Skinner Pkwy (#300)
Jacksonville, FL 32256
Telephone: (904) 279-1300, FAX:
    (904) 279-1414, Web Site: www.
    collectibletoday.com
VP, Mktg: Debbie Montalao
Gen Mgr: Bernard Fazer
Employees: 330
Primary Market Served: Consumer
Advertising/Marketing Budget Related
    to Direct Marketing: 76-100%
Gross sales or billing: $135,000,000
Direct marketing firm.

HAMILTON WATCH
Swatch Group US

1200 Harbor Blvd
Weehawken, NJ 07086-6728
Telephone: (201) 271-1400, Toll Free:
(800) 243-8463, Web Site: www.
hamiltonwatches.com
Mgr: Dennis Phillips
Conducts Business: U.S., Canada, Europe, Asia, & S. America
Employees: 19
Primary Market Served: Business
Advertising/Marketing Budget Related
to Direct Marketing: 0-25%
Founded: 1892

Manufacture & distribute complete collection of watches for retail & fine jewelry store trade & customized watches for awards as incentives.

HAMMACHER SCHLEMMER & CO INC

9307 N Milwaukee Ave
Niles, IL 60714
Telephone: (847) 581-8600, Toll Free:
(800) 233-4800, FAX: (847) 581-
8616, Web Site: www.hammacher.
com
CEO: Richard W. Tinberg
Gen Mgr: Fred Barnes
Conducts Business: Worldwide
Primary Market Served: Business &
Consumer
Catalog available online
Direct online sales
Founded: 1848

Publish 12 catalogs annually, with circulation exceeding 30,000,000 copies. In addition Hammacher has a retail store located in New York.

HAMPTON MARKETING CORP

19 Industrial Blvd
Medford, NY 11763
Telephone: (516) 924-1335, Toll Free:
(800) 229-1019, FAX: (516) 924-
1669, Web Site: www.
hamptonstamp.com
CEO: R.F. Gallagher
Pres: Ronald T. Gallagher
Opers Mgr: Steven Gallagher
Conducts Business: U.S., Canada
Employees: 41
Primary Market Served: Business &
Consumer
Catalog available online
Direct online sales
Advertising/Marketing Budget Related
to Direct Marketing: 51-75%
Direct Marketing ad budget:
Direct Mail: 45%
Magazines: 20%
Newspapers: 30%
Telephone: 5%

Founded: 1978

Supplier of premium & mail order products both imported & domestic. Includes: manufacture of fine rubber stamps & accessories, self-inking, creative rubber stamps for the craft industry, short run custom or personalized labels, various personalized products, ink, ink pads & bar code printing. Contract rubber stamp programs.

HANLEY WOOD LLC

Owned by affiliates of JP Morgan Partners LLC
1 Thomas Cir NW (Suite 600)
Washington, DC 20005-5803
Telephone: (202) 452-0800, FAX:
(202) 785-1974, Web Site: www.
hanleywood.com
CEO: Frank Anton
VP Mktg: Ann Seltz
Exec Dir E-Media: Andreas Schmidt
Employees: 630
Primary Market Served: Business &
Consumer
Founded: 1976
Gross sales or billing: $180,000,000

Magazine publisher & trade show producer. Four divisions: Media; Exhibitions; Marketing; Intelligence.

HANNA INSTRUMENTS INC

584 Park East Dr
Woonsocket, RI 02895
Telephone: (401) 765-7500, Toll Free:
(800) 426-6287, FAX: (401) 765-
7575, E-Mail: custsvc@hannainst.
com, Web Site: www.hannainst.com
Pres: Martino Nardo
VP: Pamela Nardo
Conducts Business: Worldwide
Primary Market Served: Business
Catalog available online
Direct online sales
Founded: 1986
Gross sales or billing: $12,000,000

Manufacturer & distributor of water quality instruments.

THE HANOVER SHOE CO

Subs. of C J Clark Ltd
156 Oak St
Newton, MA 02464
Telephone: (617) 964-1222, FAX:
(617) 243-4210, Web Site: www.
clarks.com
Pres & CEO: Bob Infantino
Conducts Business: U.S.
Employees: 1,500
Primary Market Served: Consumer
Advertising/Marketing Budget Related
to Direct Marketing: 0-25%

Founded: 1899

Sell men's shoes through catalogs & other direct response methods.

CHRIS HANSEN

Subs. of Crompton & Knowles Corp
16300 W Lincoln Ave
New Berlin, WI 53151-2837
Telephone: (414) 607-5700, FAX:
(414) 607-5704, Web Site: www.chr-hansen.com
Pres, N American Div: Leif Naergaard
Mktg Commun Mgr: Cindy Stoebich
Conducts Business: Worldwide
Employees: 400
Primary Market Served: Business
Gross sales or billing: $100,000

Manufacturer of food ingredients, flavor, color, food additives, sweeteners, spices & seasonings.

HANSEN CORP

Div. of Minebea Corp
901 S First St
Princeton, IN 47670-2369
Telephone: (812) 385-3415, FAX:
(812) 385-3013, E-Mail: sales@
hansen-motor.com, Web Site: www.
hansen-motor.com
Pres & Gen Mgr: William K. Poyner
Controller: W. Michael Hollars
Dir, IT: Bonnie Reeves
Design Engrng Mgr: Lincoln Dreher
Conducts Business: U.S., Canada, Europe, Asia
Employees: 400
Primary Market Served: Business
Catalog available online
Indirect online sales
Advertising/Marketing Budget Related
to Direct Marketing: 0-25%
Direct Marketing ad budget:
Direct Mail: 5%
Magazines: 15%
Online: 80%
Founded: 1908

Design, manufacture & sale of custom timing motors, chart drives, DC Servo motors, clock movements, steppers, BLDC actuator & brake motors.

HARBOUR BAY INC

32 Thunderbird Dr
Oakland, NJ 07436-2211
Telephone: (845) 368-2857, FAX:
(845) 368-2349
Pres: Richard Fleming
Conducts Business: U.S., Canada
Employees: 3
Primary Market Served: Business &
Consumer
Indirect online sales
Advertising/Marketing Budget Related
to Direct Marketing: 0-25%
Direct Marketing ad budget: $100,000

Direct Mail: 85%
Magazines: 10%
Newspapers: 5%
Founded: 1994
Gross sales or billing: $500,000
Seller of tobacco accessories for cigars, pipes and cigarettes.

HARLAND FINANCIAL SOLUTIONS INC

605 Crescent Executive Ct (Suite 600)
Lake Mary, FL 32746
Telephone: (407) 804-6600, Toll Free: (800) 815-5592, FAX: (407) 829-6702, Web Site: www.harlandfinancialsolutions.com
Pres: John O'Malley
Sr VP & CTO: Dan Larlee
Sr VP, Strategic Initiatives: Helen Beckel
Exec VP: Stan Muir
VP Bus Devel & Strategic Mktg: Scott Hansen
Employees: 120
Primary Market Served: Business & Consumer
Catalog available online

Market software & technical support.

JOHN HARLAND CO

2939 Miller Rd
Decatur, GA 30035-4038
Telephone: (770) 981-5580, Toll Free: (800) 723-3690, FAX: (770) 593-5367, E-Mail: jhhwebmaster@harland.net, Web Site: www.harland.net
Pres & CEO: Tim Tuff
Sr VP & Gen Counsel: Phil Theodore
Sr VP: John C. Walters
Pub Rels: Dan Coleman
Conducts Business: U.S., Canada
Employees: 7,000
Primary Market Served: Business
Catalog available online
Direct online sales
Founded: 1923
Gross sales or billing: $560,000,000

Produces business forms, checks & stamps.

HARRIS CORP

1025 W NASA Blvd
Melbourne, FL 32919-0001
Telephone: (321) 727-9100, Toll Free: (800) 442-7747, E-Mail: webmaster@harris.com, Web Site: harris.com
Pres & CEO: William M. Brown
Sr VP & CFO: Miguel Lopez

Primary Market Served: Business
Global communications company with core capabilities in wireless, office & digital television systems & microelectronics information processing defense communications.

THE HARTZ MOUNTAIN CORP

dba Hartz
400 Plaza Dr
Secaucus, NJ 07094-3605
Telephone: (201) 271-4800, Toll Free: (800) 275-1414, FAX: (201) 271-0068, Web Site: www.hartz.com
Pres & CEO: Bob Shipley
VP, Mktg: Julianne Krauss
Conducts Business: U.S.
Employees: 1,600
Primary Market Served: Business & Consumer
Founded: 1926
Gross sales or billing: $189,300,000

Manufacture & sell pet products.

HASCO FIRST PHOTO

Div. of Hasco International Inc
3613 Mueller Rd
Saint Charles, MO 63301
Telephone: (636) 946-5115, FAX: (636) 946-7148, Web Site: www.growingfamily.com
Chmn & CEO: Raymond W. Harmon
Pres: Dave Van Vliet
Mktg Dir: Jim Grabowski
Conducts Business: U.S., Canada, Japan, Australia, New Zealand, France
Primary Market Served: Consumer

Infant & newborn photography.

HEALTH CARE CONCEPTS INC

3011 N IH-35
Austin, TX 78722
Telephone: (512) 479-8508, Toll Free: (800) 628-4201, FAX: (512) 479-8741
Pres: Charles R. Denham
Conducts Business: U.S.
Employees: 10
Primary Market Served: Business

Medical research company.

HEALTH CARE LOGISTICS

450 Town St
Circleville, OH 43113-2244
Toll Free: (800) 848-1633, Web Site: www.healthcarelogistics.com
Mktg Mgr: Diane Taylor
Primary Market Served: Business

HEALTH O METER

9500 W 55th St (Suite C)

Countryside, IL 60525-7110
Telephone: (708) 377-0600, Toll Free: (800) 815-6615, FAX: (708) 377-0601, E-Mail: HomProCS@homscales.com, Web Site: www.homscales.com
Mktg Svcs Mgr: Barbara Vook
Mktg Mgr Medical Sls: Art Swanson
Conducts Business: U.S.
Primary Market Served: Business & Consumer

Manufacture scales.

THE HEALTHY BACK STORE

10300 Southard Dr
Beltsville, MD 20705-2107
Telephone: (703) 339-1700, Toll Free: (800) 4 MY BACK, FAX: (703) 339-0671, E-Mail: service@healthyback.com, Web Site: www.healthyback.com
Pres: Tony Mazlish
VP: Cliff Levin
Conducts Business: U.S.
Employees: 45
Primary Market Served: Business & Consumer
Catalog available online
Direct online sales
Advertising/Marketing Budget Related to Direct Marketing: 0-25%
Direct Marketing ad budget: $250,000
Direct Mail: 25%
Newspapers: 50%
TV/Radio: 25%
Founded: 1993
Gross sales or billing: $10,000,000

Back care products such as ergonomic office seating, car seat supports & back-friendly beds.

HECHT RUBBER CORP

6161 Phillips Hwy
Jacksonville, FL 32216-5920
Telephone: (904) 731-3401, Toll Free: (800) 872-3401, FAX: (904) 730-0066, Web Site: www.hechtrubber.com
Pres: Larry M. Hecht
CFO: Stuart Hecht
Conducts Business: Worldwide
Employees: 33
Primary Market Served: Business & Consumer
Catalog available online
Advertising/Marketing Budget Related to Direct Marketing: 26-50%
Direct Marketing ad budget:
Direct Mail: 70%
Magazines: 10%
Newspapers: 1%
Telephone: 19%

Founded: 1944

Manufacturer & distributor of rubber products for business, industry, government & safety. Sell products through direct mail.

W C HELLER & CO

201 W Wabash St
Montpelier, OH 43543-1840
Telephone: (419) 485-3176, FAX: (419) 485-8694
Pres: R.L. Heller
VP: Andrew M. Heller
Conducts Business: U.S.
Employees: 4
Primary Market Served: Business & Consumer
Catalog available online
Advertising/Marketing Budget Related to Direct Marketing: 26-50%
Direct Marketing ad budget:
Direct Mail: 60%
Magazines: 10%
Newspapers: 10%
Telephone: 20%
Founded: 1891
Gross sales or billing: $500,000

Manufacturers of wood library furniture such as book shelving, counters, tables & study carrels. Sold to schools, public & private libraries, offices & hospitals. Custom cabinets for anyone.

HELLO DIRECT

Subs. of GN Netcom
77 Northeastern Blvd
Nashua, NH 03062-3128
Telephone: (408) 972-1990, Toll Free: (800) 435-5634, FAX: (408) 972-8155, Web Site: www.hello-direct.com
VP, Mktg: Ron Becht
Gen Mgr: Terry Flynn
Cntrl: Brian Ronan
Sls Dir: James Smith
Conducts Business: U.S.
Employees: 300
Primary Market Served: Business & Consumer
Direct online sales
Founded: 1987
Gross sales or billing: $26,000,000

Sell telephone systems & accessories, including headsets, handsets, fax machines & accessories, voice mail, auto attendant, teleconferencing units & small key telephone systems. Home & business offices are included.

HELLY-HANSEN

3326 160th Ave SE, #200, Bellevue, WA 98008-6418
4101 C St NE (Suite 200)
Auburn, WA 98002

Toll Free: (800) 435-5901, FAX: (425) 649-3740, Web Site: www.hellyhansen.com
CEO: Peter Sjolander
VP & Gen Mgr USA: Filip Francke
Primary Market Served: Business
Catalog available online
Direct online sales
Founded: 1877
Gross sales or billing: $25,000,000

Manufacturer and seller of high quality, protective technical gear for work and sport.

HELMAN GROUP LTD

1621 Beacon Pl
Oxnard, CA 93033
Telephone: (805) 487-7772, FAX: (805) 487-9975, E-Mail: barryh@helmangroup.com, Web Site: www.helmangroup.com
Pres: Andy Helman
Mgr, Sls: Lisa Latimer
CEO: Barry Helman
Conducts Business: U.S., Canada, Japan, Europe, Taiwan, Korea, Hong Kong
Employees: 50
Primary Market Served: Business
Indirect online sales
Advertising/Marketing Budget Related to Direct Marketing: 0-25%
Founded: 1969
Gross sales or billing: $30,000,000

Manufacturer of mail order products. Distribution & sales to retail accounts in the U.S. & Canada.

HELZBERG DIAMONDS

Subs. of Berkshire Hathaway
1825 Swift St
North Kansas City, MO 64116-3606
Telephone: (816) 842-7780, Toll Free: (800) HELZBERG, FAX: (816) 480-0294, Web Site: www.helzberg.com
Chmn & CEO: Beryl Raff
Sr VP & Chief Mktg Officer: Becky Higgins
Sr VP Mktg, E-Commerce & Distr: Pat Duncan
Conducts Business: U.S.
Employees: 3,000
Primary Market Served: Consumer
Catalog available online
Direct online sales
Advertising/Marketing Budget Related to Direct Marketing: 26-50%
Founded: 1915
Gross sales or billing: $479,700,000

Retail jewelry store.

HERMAN MILLER INC

855 E Main Ave
Zeeland, MI 49464

Telephone: (616) 654-3000, FAX: (616) 654-5234, E-Mail: investor@hermanmiller.com, Web Site: www.hermanmiller.com
Chmn: Michael A. Volkema
Pres, CEO & Dir: Brian C. Walker
CFO: Greg Bylsma
Treas & Chief Acctg Officer: Jeff Stutz
Conducts Business: Worldwide
Employees: 3,500
Primary Market Served: Business
Catalog available online
Indirect online sales
Gross sales or billing: $1,900,000,000

Manufacturer of office furniture systems, desks & seating products.

HERR FOODS INC

20 Herr Dr
Nottingham, PA 19362
Telephone: (610) 932-9330, Toll Free: (800) 344-3777, FAX: (610) 932-2137, E-Mail: info@herrs.com, Web Site: www.herrs.com
Chmn & CEO: J.M. Herr
Pres: Edwin Herr
Sr VP HR: Richard White
Sr VP Sls & Mktg: Daryl Thomas
Employees: 1,400
Primary Market Served: Consumer
Catalog available online
Direct online sales
Founded: 1946
Gross sales or billing: $165,000,000

Snack foods.

HERRINGTON

Three Symmes Dr
Londonderry, NH 03053
Telephone: (603) 437-1600, Toll Free: (800) 903-2878, FAX: (603) 437-1340, (603) 437-3492, E-Mail: customerservice@herringtoncatalog.com, Web Site: www.herringtoncatalog.com
Pres & Owner: Lee R. Herrington
Controller: Norm Beauchesne
Conducts Business: U.S.
Employees: 64
Primary Market Served: Consumer
Catalog available online
Direct online sales
Founded: 1980

Sell upscale products: audio, video, photography, motoring, golf, boating & skiing accessories to consumers via online and mail order catalog.

HEWLETT-PACKARD CO

3000 Hanover St
Palo Alto, CA 94304-1185
Telephone: (650) 857-1501, Toll Free: (800) 752-0900, FAX: (650) 857-5518, Web Site: www.hp.com
Pres & CEO: Meg Whitman

Exec VP & CFO: Catherine A. Lesjak
Chief Strategy Officer: Mohamad Ali
Exec VP & Chief Tech Officer: Martin Fink
Exec VP & Chief Mktg & Commun Officer: Henry Gomez
Employees: 156,000
Primary Market Served: Business & Consumer
Catalog available online
Direct online sales
Gross sales or billing: $91,600,000,000

Manufacturer of electronic equipment for measurement analysis & computation.

HILTON HHONORS
Div. of Hilton Worldwide
7930 Jones Branch Dr
McLean, VA 22102
Telephone: (703) 883-1000, Web Site: hhonors.hilton.com
Exec VP Comml Svcs: Jeff Diskin
Sr Dir Global Fitness: Jodi Sullivan
VP Restaurant Concepts: Beth Scott
Primary Market Served: Business

Membership-based guest loyalty program.

HIPCRICKET INC
4400 Carillon Pt # 4
Kirkland, WA 98033-7353
Telephone: (425) 452-1111, Web Site: www.hipcricket.com
CMO: Jeff Hasen

THE HISTORICAL RESEARCH CENTER INTERNATIONAL INC
2107 Corporate Dr
Boynton Beach, FL 33426-6645
Telephone: (561) 732-5263, Toll Free: (800) 985-9956, FAX: (561) 940-7991, E-Mail: custsvc@names.com, Web Site: www.historicalresearchcenter.net
Founder: Michael Walshe
Employees: 40
Primary Market Served: Consumer
Catalog available online
Direct online sales
Advertising/Marketing Budget Related to Direct Marketing: 76-100%
Direct Marketing ad budget:
Direct Mail: 10%
Newspapers: 10%
TV/Radio: 70%
Telephone: 10%
Founded: 1988

Retail heraldic products.

HOBSONS
50 E Business Way (Suite 300)
Cincinnati, OH 45241-2398
Telephone: (513) 985-4186, Web Site: www.hobsons.com
Dir Student Mktg: Daniela Locreille
Educational professionals offering higher education CRM & other tools for student recruitment, enrollment management & student retention

HOLLISTER INC
2000 Hollister Dr
Libertyville, IL 60048
Telephone: (847) 680-1000, Toll Free: (888) 740-8999, FAX: (847) 680-2123, Web Site: www.hollister.com
Pres: V. George Maliekel
VP, Global Mktg Officer: Brian Luedtke
Conducts Business: U.S.
Primary Market Served: Business
Catalog available online
Indirect online sales

Developer, manufacturer & marketer of healthcare products.

HOLY CROSS HOSPITAL
4725 N Federal Hwy
Fort Lauderdale, FL 33308-4670
Telephone: (954) 771-8000, FAX: (954) 229-8597, Web Site: www.holy-cross.com
Pres & CEO: Patrick A. Taylor MD
Sr VP & COO: Luisa Gutman
Sr VP & Administrator, HealthPlex: Mark R. Dissette
Chief Medical Officer: Kenneth Homer MD
Conducts Business: U.S.
Employees: 1,400
Primary Market Served: Business & Consumer

Not-for-profit, privately owned, religiously affiliated facility under the direction of the Sisters of Mercy.

THE HOME DEPOT INC
2455 Paces Ferry Rd
Atlanta, GA 30339-1834
Telephone: (770) 433-8211, Toll Free: (800) 466-3337, FAX: (770) 384-2356, Web Site: www.homedepot.com
Chmn & CEO: Francis C. Blake
Exec VP, Corp Svcs & CFO: Carol B. Tome
Exec VP, HR: Timothy M. Crow
Sr VP & Chief Mktg Officer: Trish Mueller
Conducts Business: U.S., Canada
Employees: 364,000
Primary Market Served: Business & Consumer
Catalog available online
Direct online sales
Founded: 1978

Gross sales or billing: $78,000,000,000
Home improvement specialty retailer.

HOME INTERIORS & GIFTS INC
1649 Frankford Rd W
Carrollton, TX 75007-4605
Telephone: (972) 695-1000, FAX: (972) 695-1112
Pres & CEO: Mike Lohner
Primary Market Served: Consumer

HONEYWELL
RP-NFOA
101 Columbia Rd
Morristown, NJ 07962
Telephone: (973) 455-2000, FAX: (973) 455-4807, Web Site: www.honeywell.com
Chmn & CEO: David M. Cote
Sr VP & CFO: Tom Szlosek
Corp VP, Chief Strategy & Mktg Officer: Rhonda Germany
Conducts Business: Worldwide
Employees: 132,000
Primary Market Served: Business
Advertising/Marketing Budget Related to Direct Marketing: 0-25%
Gross sales or billing: $6,200,000,000

Global controls company providing products, systems & services that increase comfort, environmental protection, energy conservation, productivity & safety in homes & buildings, industry, aviation & space.

THE HOPE CO INC
12777 Pennridge Dr
Bridgeton, MO 63044
Telephone: (314) 739-7254, Toll Free: (800) 325-4026, FAX: (314) 739-7786, E-Mail: info@hopecompany.com
Pres & CEO: John H. Finnegan, Sr
Mktg Dir: John H. Finnegan, Jr
Conducts Business: U.S.
Primary Market Served: Business
Catalog available online

Manufacture chemical home care products.

HORMEL FOODS CORP
One Hormel Pl
Austin, MN 55912-3680
Telephone: (507) 437-5611, Toll Free: (800) 523-4635, FAX: (507) 437-5158, Web Site: www.hormelfoods.com
Chmn, Pres & CEO: Jeffrey M. Ettinger
Exec VP & CFO: Jody H. Feragen
VP Mktg Foodservice: Jeffrey R. Baker
VP Mktg Grocery Products: Luis G. Marconi

VP Mktg Meat Products: Steven J. Venenga
Primary Market Served: Business
Catalog available online
Indirect online sales

Meat packing & food processing.

HUBERT CO
9555 Dry Fork Rd
Harrison, OH 45030-1994
Telephone: (513) 367-8767, Toll Free: (800) 543-7374, FAX: (513) 367-8823, Web Site: www.hubert.com
Pres: C. Bart Kohler
VP, Mktg: Andy Hallock
Dir Mktg: Mark Woodrow
Conducts Business: Worldwide
Employees: 309
Primary Market Served: Business
Catalog available online
Direct online sales
Founded: 1946

Food service store furnishings, equipment & supplies. Food service industry, merchandising displays, equipment & supplies.

HY CITE CORP
dba Royal Prestige & Ocean Blue
333 Holtzman Rd
Madison, WI 53713-2109
Telephone: (608) 273-3373, Toll Free: (877) 494-2289, FAX: (608) 273-0936, Web Site: www.hycite.com
Pres & CEO: Erik S. Johnson
Mktg Supvr: Cybell Abrei
Employees: 175
Primary Market Served: Consumer
Founded: 1959
Gross sales or billing: $5,900,000

Cookware, cutlery, water filters, air purifiers & China flatware.

HY-KO PRODUCTS CO
60 Meadow Ln
Northfield, OH 44067-1415
Telephone: (330) 467-7446, Web Site: www.hy-ko.com
Project Supvr: Sarah Shebesta
Primary Market Served: Business & Consumer

HYATT HOTELS CORP
71 S Wacker Dr
Chicago, IL 60606-4716
Telephone: (312) 750-1234, FAX: (312) 780-5289, Web Site: www.hyatt.com
Exec Chmn Bd: Thomas J. Pritzker
Pres & CEO: Mark Hoplamazian
Exec VP & CFO: Gebhard F. Rainer
Global Head Mktg & Brand Strategy: John Wallis

Conducts Business: U.S., Canada, Caribbean
Primary Market Served: Business & Consumer
Direct Marketing ad budget: $20,000,000
Direct Mail: 50%
Magazines: 20%
Newspapers: 20%
TV/Radio: 10%

Hotel management & development corporation.

HYATT LEGAL PLANS INC
A MetLife Co
1111 Superior Ave E (Suite 800)
Cleveland, OH 44114-2529
Telephone: (216) 241-0022, FAX: (216) 694-4305, Web Site: www.legalplans.com
CEO: William H. Brooks
VP Opers & Gen Counsel: Andrew Kohn
CFO: Michael Penzer
Mktg Dir: Marcia Bowers
Employees: 82
Primary Market Served: Business & Consumer
Catalog available online
Indirect online sales
Advertising/Marketing Budget Related to Direct Marketing: 0-25%
Founded: 1977
Gross sales or billing: $8,200,000

Group Legal services provider through 4,600 participating law firms in the U.S.

HYGIENIC FABRICS & FILTERS INC
1301 Erie Ave, PO Box 1005
Sheboygan, WI 53082-1005
Telephone: (920) 457-7383, Toll Free: (800) 876-2009, FAX: (920) 457-2558, Web Site: www.hyfab.com
Pres, Sls: John F. Wilson Jr
VP: Thomas Laiken
Employees: 6
Primary Market Served: Business & Consumer
Catalog available online
Direct online sales
Advertising/Marketing Budget Related to Direct Marketing: 0-25%
Founded: 1936

Manufacturer of filter cloths sold to the food processing industry & household soft goods sold via catalog.

IBM CORP
1 New Orchard Rd
Armonk, NY 10504-1725

Telephone: (914) 765-1900, FAX: (914) 765-6633, Web Site: www.ibm.com
Pres & CEO: Virginia M. Rometty
Sr VP & CFO, Fin & Enterprise Transformation: Martin Schroeter
Sr VP Mktg & Commun: Jon C. Iwata
Sr VP Corp Strategy: Kenneth M. Keverian
Sr VP Sls & Distr: Bruno V. Di Leo
Conducts Business: U.S.
Employees: 400,000
Primary Market Served: Business

Global technology & innovation company.

IDMS INC
560 Broadhollow Rd (Suite 109)
Melville, NY 11747-3702
Telephone: (631) 249-7744, Toll Free: (800) 582-5831, FAX: (631) 249-4425, E-Mail: sales@idmsinc.com, Web Site: www.idmsinc.com
Pres: Jeff Goldstein
Mktg: Leslie Goldstein
Conducts Business: U.S.
Employees: 6
Primary Market Served: Business & Consumer
Catalog available online
Direct online sales
Advertising/Marketing Budget Related to Direct Marketing: 26-50%
Direct Marketing ad budget: $50,000
Online: $50,000
Founded: 1984
Gross sales or billing: $1,500,000

Custom software development & developer of integrated computer network solutions. Targeting primarily wholesalers, distributors, manufacturers & accountants. Specializing in EDI, telecommunications & bar coding.

INX INTERNATIONAL INK CO
150 N Martingale Rd (Suite 700)
Schaumburg, IL 60173
Toll Free: (800) 631-7956, FAX: (847) 969-9758, E-Mail: info@inxink.com, Web Site: www.inxinternational.com
Pres: Rick Clendenning
VP, Fin: Bryce Kristo
Conducts Business: U.S., Canada
Employees: 1,300
Primary Market Served: Business
Advertising/Marketing Budget Related to Direct Marketing: 0-25%
Founded: 1991
Gross sales or billing: $360,000,000
Manufacturer of printing ink & coding.

ITT EDUCATIONAL SERVICES INC

13000 N Meridian St
Carmel, IN 46082
Telephone: (317) 706-9200, Web Site: www.ittesi.com
Chmn Bd & CEO: Kevin M. Modany
Exec VP & CFO: Daniel M. Fitzpatrick
Exec VP, Chief Mktg Officer: Glen E. Tanner
Sr VP Mktg: Jill M. Minnick
Sr VP Opers: Barry S. Smith
Conducts Business: U.S.
Primary Market Served: Consumer
Catalog available online
Direct online sales
Advertising/Marketing Budget Related to Direct Marketing: 76-100%
Direct Marketing ad budget: $50,000,000
Founded: 1968

Owner & operator of more than 135 technical colleges providing accredited, technology-orientated undergraduate & graduate degree programs.

ITW BEE LEITZKE

Div of Illinois Tool Works
2000 Industrial Rd
Iron Ridge, WI 53035-9535
Telephone: (920) 625-2342, FAX: (920) 625-2643, Web Site: www.itwbeeleitzke.com
COO: Barth Leatherman
Pres: Jerry DeWitz
Mktg Mgr: Mark Simmons
Conducts Business: U.S., Canada
Primary Market Served: Business
Founded: 1929

Fasteners & industrial components, industrial distribution. Manufacture fasteners.

ITW VORTEC

Div. of Illinois Tool Works
10125 Carver Rd
Cincinnati, OH 45242
Telephone: (513) 891-7474, Toll Free: (800) 441-7475, FAX: (513) 891-4092, E-Mail: techsupport@vortec.com, Web Site: www.vortec.com
Gen Mgr: Michael Parker
Mktg Supvr: Dave Kremp
Matls Coord: Sandy Baggett
Conducts Business: Worldwide
Primary Market Served: Business
Catalog available online
Founded: 1961

Manufacture new technology items such as specialized compressed air appliances that cool, reduce air consumption & lower plant noise level. Sell to all types of industrial customers through direct marketing promotions.

THE IAMS CO

8700 Mason Montgomery Rd`
Mason, OH 45040
Toll Free: (800) 675-3849, Web Site: www.iams.com
Sr VP Global Snacks & Pet Care: Daniel S. Rajczak
Conducts Business: U.S., Canada
Employees: 1,000
Primary Market Served: Consumer
Founded: 1946
Gross sales or billing: $118,300,000

Supplier of premium pet food.

ICLIMBER INC

315 W Verdugo Ave (Suite 101)
Burbank, CA 91502-2484
Telephone: (818) 567-3030, Web Site: www.iclimber.com
VP Sls & Mktg: Allen Horwitz
Primary Market Served: Consumer

I/D/E/A INC

One Idea Way
Caldwell, ID 83605-6900
Telephone: (208) 459-6357, Toll Free: (800) 635-9261, FAX: (208) 459-6484, Web Site: www.relyonidea.com
CEO: Paul Kaye
Controller & VP: Anita Kiser
Conducts Business: U.S., Canada
Employees: 70
Primary Market Served: Business

Business-to-business printed product marketer.

IDEAL INDUSTRIES INC

Becker Pl
Sycamore, IL 60178
Telephone: (815) 895-5181, Toll Free: (800) 435-0705, FAX: (815) 895-4800, E-Mail: ideal_industries@idealindustries.com, Web Site: www.idealindustries.com
VP Mktg: Glenn Hollister
Primary Market Served: Business

Manufacture of electrical products through distributions.

IDEARC MEDIA CORP

2200 W Airfield Dr
Dallas, TX 75261
Telephone: (972) 453-7797
Mgr Mktg Res: David Bernstein
Primary Market Served: Consumer

ILOOP MOBILE INC

25 Metro Dr (Suite 210)
San Jose, CA 95110-1338
Telephone: (408) 907-3360, Web Site: www.iloopmobile.com
Exec VP Mobile Strategy: Michael Becker

IMPERIAL SUPPLIES

789 Armed Forces Dr
Green Bay, WI 54304-4527
Telephone: (920) 494-5403, Toll Free: (800) 558-2808, FAX: (800) 553-8769, Web Site: www.imperialsupplies.com
Pres: Rob Gilson
VP, Mktg: Mitchell Mittlestadt
Dir Mktg: Pauline Schuster
Mktg Mgr: Nicole Alboushi
Conducts Business: U.S.
Employees: 120
Primary Market Served: Business & Consumer
Catalog available online
Indirect online sales
Advertising/Marketing Budget Related to Direct Marketing: 0-25%
Founded: 1958

Wholesaler & nationwide distributor of maintenance supplies.

INDIUM CORP OF AMERICA

34 Robinson Rd
Clinton, NY 13323-1419
Telephone: (315) 853-4900, Toll Free: (800) 446-3486, FAX: (800) 221-5759, E-Mail: askus@indium.com, Web Site: www.indium.com
Chmn & CEO: William N. Macartney III
Pres: Gregory P. Evans
Mgr: Kevin Moore
Conducts Business: Worldwide
Employees: 240
Primary Market Served: Business
Catalog available online
Advertising/Marketing Budget Related to Direct Marketing: 0-25%
Direct Marketing ad budget:
Direct Mail: 5%
Magazines: 90%
Telephone: 5%
Founded: 1934
Gross sales or billing: $30,000,000

Manufacturer of indium metal & specialty solders & alloys.

INFOMART

1950 Stemmons Fwy (Suite1000)
Dallas, TX 75207
Telephone: (214) 800-8000, FAX: (214) 800-8100, Web Site: www.infomartusa.com
Pres: Tom Jones
Property Mgr: Jay Stone
Conducts Business: Worldwide
Primary Market Served: Business & Consumer
Advertising/Marketing Budget Related to Direct Marketing: 76-100%

Real estate & trade show educational facility.

INGRAM BOOK GROUP

Div. of Ingram Industries Inc
One Ingram Blvd
La Vergne, TN 37086
Telephone: (615) 793-5000, Toll Free:
(800) 937-8000, FAX: (800) 876-
0186, Web Site: www.ipage.
ingrambook.com
Pres, IBC: Jim Chandler
CEO, Ingram Book Grp: Mike Lovett
VP, Mktg, IBG: Kelley Maier
VP, Sls & Mktg: Tom Jones
Conducts Business: Worldwide
Employees: 3,500
Primary Market Served: Business
Catalog available online
Advertising/Marketing Budget Related
to Direct Marketing: 0-25%
Founded: 1969

A leading wholesaler of trade books,
spoken audio, and magazines. Operating units include Ingram Book Company, Ingram Periodicals Inc., Ingram
International, Ingram Library Services
Inc, Spring Arbor Distributors Inc.,
Tennessee Book Company, Ingram
Fulfillment Services, and Ingram Customer Systems.

INSIGHT DIRECT INC

Div. of Insight Enterprises Inc
6820 S Harl Ave
Tempe, AZ 85283-4318
Telephone: (480) 333-3001, Toll Free:
(800) 467-4448, FAX: (480) 902-
1180, Web Site: www.insight.com
Pres: Tim A. Crown
CEO: Eric Crown
VP, Opers: Denny Chittick
VP, Sls: Rick Ridart
VP, Mktg: Dan Sager
Corp Communs: Valerie Paxton
Conducts Business: U.S., Canada, US
Virgin Islands
Employees: 550
Primary Market Served: Business &
Consumer
Advertising/Marketing Budget Related
to Direct Marketing: 76-100%
Direct Marketing ad budget:
Direct Mail: $1,000,000
Magazines: $6,000,000
Founded: 1986
Gross sales or billing: $245,000,000

Distribution company selling computer
& electronic components, peripherals
& software.

INSTITUTE FOR INTERNATIONAL RESEARCH INC

708 Third Ave (4th fl)
New York, NY 10017-4103
Telephone: (212) 661-3500, Toll Free:
(800) 345-8016, FAX: (212) 599-
2192, E-Mail: register@iirusa.com,
Web Site: www.iir-ny.com
Gen Mgr & Fin Dir: Debra Chipman
VP, Mktg: Roxanne John
Mktg Dir: Yemil Martinez
Conducts Business: Worldwide
Employees: 75
Primary Market Served: Business
Direct Marketing ad budget:
Direct Mail: 98%
Magazines: 2%

Business information company that organizes conferences & training programs for mid to senior level
executives.

INSTITUTE FOR NATURAL RESOURCES

2352 Stanwell Dr
Concord, CA 94520
Telephone: (925) 687-0860, FAX:
(925) 609-2820, E-Mail: dcheung@
biocorp.com
CEO, Pres & Owner: Barry Meltzer
VP: Deborah Cheung
Primary Market Served: Consumer
Catalog available online
Direct online sales

Conducts scientific seminars for professionals.

THE INSTRUMENT WORKSHOP

PO Box 1060
Ashland, OR 97520-0050
Telephone: (541) 552-0989, Toll Free:
(800) 442-6038, FAX: (541) 488-
5846, E-Mail: shop77@fortepiano.
com, Web Site: www.fortepiano.com
Partner: Lutz Bungart
Partner: Martha Bungart
Conducts Business: Worldwide
Primary Market Served: Business &
Consumer
Catalog available online
Indirect online sales
Advertising/Marketing Budget Related
to Direct Marketing: 51-75%
Direct Marketing ad budget:
Direct Mail: 75%
Magazines: 20%
Telephone: 5%
Founded: 1969
Gross sales or billing: $100,000

Parts & plans for early keyboard instruments: harpsichords, clavichords, virginals, forte pianos, hammer dulcimers,
harps, sitars & zithers.

INTEGRETEL INC

5883 Rue Ferrari
San Jose, CA 95138-1857
Telephone: (408) 362-4000, FAX:
(408) 362-2795, Web Site: www.
integretel.com
CEO: Joe Lynam
Pres: Ken Dawson
Primary Market Served: Business
Direct Marketing ad budget:
Direct Mail: 15%
Magazines: 80%
Newspapers: 5%
Founded: 1988

Telephone billing company & service
agency.

INTEGRITY MUSIC INC

800 Hillcrest Rd (Suite 6)
Mobile, AL 36695-3906
Telephone: (251) 633-9000, FAX:
(251) 633-5202, Web Site: www.
integritymusic.com
Pres: Mike Coleman
Dir: Jean C. Coleman
Conducts Business: Worldwide
Employees: 218
Primary Market Served: Consumer
Catalog available online
Direct online sales
Founded: 1987

Producer and publisher of Christian
music products.

INTEL CORP

2200 Mission College Blvd
Santa Clara, CA 95052
Telephone: (408) 765-8080, Toll Free:
(800) 548-4725, FAX: (408) 765-
6187, Web Site: www.intel.com
Chmn Bd: Andy D. Bryant
CEO: Brian M. Krzanich
Pres: Renee J. James
Exec VP & CFO: Stacy J. Smith
Exec VP, Gen Mgr Sls & Mktg: Thomas M. Kilroy
Exec VP, Gen Mgr Tech & Mfg Grp:
William M. Holt
VP & Chief Mktg Officer: Deborah S.
Conrad
Conducts Business: Worldwide
Employees: 94,100
Primary Market Served: Business &
Consumer
Founded: 1968
Gross sales or billing: $35,382,000,000

Semiconductor chip designer and manufacturer.

INTERFACEFLOR LLC

1503 Orchard Hill Rd
La Grange, GA 30240-5709
Telephone: (706) 882-1891, Toll Free:
(800) 336-0225, FAX: (706) 882-
0500, Web Site: www.interfaceflor.
com
Pres & CEO: David Hobbs
VP Mktg: Tracy Cook

Conducts Business: Worldwide
Employees: 1,500
Primary Market Served: Business
Advertising/Marketing Budget Related
  to Direct Marketing: 0-25%
Founded: 1923
Gross sales or billing: $190,000,000

Manufactures carpet tile & six foot
goods. Markets tiles under the Interface
& Interface Retail names in 90 different countries.

INTERGRAPH CORP

170 Graphics Dr
Madison, AL 35758
Telephone: (256) 730-2000, Toll Free:
  (800) 345-4856, FAX: (256) 730-
  2048, Web Site: www.intergraph.
  com
Pres & CEO: R. Halsey Wise
Sr VP & Treas: Larry J. Laster
Exec VP & COO: R. Reid French Jr
VP & CAO: Steven Cost
VP: David Vance Lucas
Primary Market Served: Business &
  Consumer
Founded: 1969

Design, manufacture, market & support
turnkey computer-aided engineering,
design & graphics.

INTERNATIONAL CRYSTAL MANUFACTURING CO

10 N Lee St
Oklahoma City, OK 73102
Telephone: (405) 236-3741, Toll Free:
  (800) 252-6780, FAX: (405) 235-
  1904, E-Mail: info@icmfg.com, Web
  Site: www.icmfg.com
Pres: Dana Guy
VP & Gen Sls Mgr: Steve Webb
Mktg Mgr: Mark Handley
Pur & Inventory Mgr: Barbara Thomp-
  son
Conducts Business: U.S.
Employees: 30
Primary Market Served: Business &
  Consumer
Catalog available online
Direct online sales
Advertising/Marketing Budget Related
  to Direct Marketing: 76-100%
Direct Marketing ad budget:
Online: 25%
Telephone: 75%
Founded: 1967

Manufacture crystals & related items.

INTERNATIONAL PAPER

6400 Poplar Ave
Memphis, TN 38197-0100

Telephone: (901) 419-9000, Toll Free:
  (800) 207-4003, E-Mail:
  internationalpaper.comm@ipaper.
  com, Web Site: www.
  internationalpaper.com
Chmn Bd & CEO: John V. Faraci
Sr VP & CFO: Carol L. Roberts
Sr VP Corp Devel: C. Cato Ealy
Employees: 60,000
Primary Market Served: Business &
  Consumer
Gross sales or billing: $22,000,000,000

A global paper and packaging company
with manufacturing operations in North
America, Europe, Latin America, Asia
and North Africa, complemented by an
extensive North American merchant
distribution system.

INTERNATIONAL SPECIALIZED BOOK SERVICES INC

dba Isbs
920 NE 58th Ave (Suite 300)
Portland, OR 97213
Telephone: (503) 287-3093, Toll Free:
  (800) 944-6190, FAX: (503) 280-
  8832, E-Mail: isbs_sales@isbs.com,
  Web Site: www.isbscatalog.com
Gen Mgr: Rod Walker
Mktg Mgr: Tamna Greenfield
Sec: Carl D. Dyess
Conducts Business: Worldwide
Employees: 15
Primary Market Served: Business &
  Consumer
Catalog available online
Indirect online sales
Advertising/Marketing Budget Related
  to Direct Marketing: 26-50%
Founded: 1976
Gross sales or billing: $2,000,000

Represent over 60 book publishers exclusively. 80% of business is by direct
mail marketing to libraries, companies,
retail outlets & special interest individuals. Self-maintained database/com-
puter mailing lists. Also represent
English speaking foreign publishers.

INTRA BUSINESS SYSTEMS INC

PO Box 6681
South Bend, IN 46660-6681
Telephone: (574) 257-7940, FAX:
  (574) 257-7944, E-Mail: info@
  intrabusinesssystems.com, Web Site:
  www.intrabusinesssystems.com
Owner: John Kampars
Conducts Business: U.S.
Primary Market Served: Business &
  Consumer
Advertising/Marketing Budget Related
  to Direct Marketing: 76-100%
Direct Marketing ad budget: $72,000

Direct Mail: 5%
Magazines: 95%
Founded: 2000
Gross sales or billing: $500,000

Remanufacturer of laser printer & cop-
ier toner cartridges & office supplies.

INTROMARK INC

217 Ninth St
Pittsburgh, PA 15222-3506
Telephone: (412) 288-1300, Toll Free:
  (800) 851-6030 X1368, FAX: (412)
  338-0497, E-Mail: licensing@
  intromark.com
Mng Dir: Richard Resnick
Licensing Mgr: John Adkins
Mktg Coord: Brian Frattaroli
Conducts Business: Worldwide
Employees: 9
Primary Market Served: Business &
  Consumer
Gross sales or billing: $700,000

Invention licensing and marketing service organization specializing in new
products.

INVACARE CONTINUING CARE GROUP

Div. of Invacare Corp
1848 Craig Rd
Saint Louis, MO 63146-4712
Telephone: (519) 659-1395, Toll Free:
  (800) 347-5440, FAX: (636) 519-
  0044, Web Site: www.invacare-ccg.
  com
Mgr: Victoria Cote
Conducts Business: U.S., Canada, S.
  America, Middle East, Far East, Eu-
  rope
Primary Market Served: Business
Catalog available online
Advertising/Marketing Budget Related
  to Direct Marketing: 0-25%

Manufacture electric & manual hospital
beds & related patient room furniture
sold direct to the end user through local
representation.

INVACARE SUPPLY GROUP

9 Industrial Rd
Milford, MA 01757-3588
Telephone: (508) 429-1000, Toll Free:
  (800) 225-4792, FAX: (508) 429-
  1581, E-Mail: service.isg@invacare.
  com, Web Site: www.
  invacaresupplygroup.com
VP, Fin: Paul Patsuno
VP Cust Svc: Steve Biles
VP MIS: Paul Jandron
Conducts Business: U.S.
Employees: 100
Primary Market Served: Business
Advertising/Marketing Budget Related
  to Direct Marketing: 76-100%

Direct Marketing ad budget:
Direct Mail: $500,000
Founded: 1975
Gross sales or billing: $60,000,000

Wholesaler of durable medical equipment. Distribution centers in Holliston, MA; Rancho Cucamonga, CA; Grand Prairie, TX; Atlanta, GA; South Bend, IN & Edison, NJ.

INWAVE INTERNET
PO Box 8243, Janesville, WI 53547-8243
1131 W Enterprise Dr
Janesville, WI 53546
Toll Free: (888) 469-2831, FAX: (608) 752-8981, Web Site: www.inwave. com
Pres: Mark Mitchell
Primary Market Served: Business & Consumer
Catalog available online
Advertising/Marketing Budget Related to Direct Marketing: 76-100%
Direct Marketing ad budget:
Direct Mail: 85%
Magazines: 15%
Founded: 1992

Small electronics equipment.

IOMEGA CORP
4059 S 1900 W
Roy, UT 84067
Telephone: (801) 332-1000, Toll Free: (888) 446-6342, FAX: (801) 332-3158, Web Site: www.iomega.com
Pres & CEO: Thomas Kampfer
CFO: Preston Romm
VP, Sls: Peter Wharton
Conducts Business: Worldwide
Primary Market Served: Business
Catalog available online
Direct online sales
Founded: 1980
Gross sales or billing: $400,000,000

Develop, manufacture & sell high-performance removable mass storage products for desktop computers. Patented Bernoulli Technology provides unlimited data storage capability by combining the removability of floppy drives with the high capacity & performance of rigid drives. Bernoulli drives are distributed through dealers/distributors domestically & internationally.

ISUZU MOTORS AMERICA LLC
Subs. of Isuzu Motors Ltd
1400 S Douglass Rd (Suite 100)
Anaheim, CA 92806
Telephone: (562) 229-5000, Toll Free: (800) 255-6727, FAX: (562) 229-5463, Web Site: www.isuzu.com
Dir Mktg, Comml Trucks: Brian Tabel
Dir Sls & Mktg, PowerTrain Div: John Dutcher
Conducts Business: US
Primary Market Served: Consumer
Catalog available online
Indirect online sales
Founded: 1975

Distributor of commercial vehicles & diesel engines.

ITOCHU CHEMICALS AMERICA INC
660 White Plains Rd #3Fl, Tarrytown, NY 10591-5104-POST
360 Hamilton Ave (Suite 610)
White Plains, NY 10601-1842
Telephone: (914) 333-7800, Toll Free: (800) 423-6870, FAX: (914) 333-7848, Web Site: www.itochu-sc.com
Controller: Alex Tabaco
Pres: Bob Yamashita
Mktg Mgr: Shin Ishii
Conducts Business: Worldwide
Employees: 30
Primary Market Served: Business & Consumer

Pharmaceutical company that sells information storage products, including magnetic media, video related products & thermal facsimile paper to OEMs, distributors & major accounts.

JLG INDUSTRIES INC
One JLG Dr
McConnellsburg, PA 17233
Telephone: (717) 485-5161, Toll Free: (877) JLG-SELL, FAX: (717) 485-6417, E-Mail: comments@jlg.com, Web Site: www.jlg.com
CEO: William J. Lasky
Sr VP, Sls & Mktg Devel: Craig Paylor
VP: Dale Robertson
VP, Cust Support Svcs: John Louderback
VP, Mktg: Dan Sandonato
Mktg Commun Specialist: Mark Eckert
Conducts Business: Worldwide
Employees: 3,770
Primary Market Served: Business & Consumer
Catalog available online
Indirect online sales
Advertising/Marketing Budget Related to Direct Marketing: 0-25%
Direct Marketing ad budget:
Magazines: 100%
Founded: 1969
Gross sales or billing: $1,056,168

World's leading producer of mobile aerial work platforms and a leading manufacturer of telescopic material handlers and hydraulic excavators marketed under the JLG and Gradall Trademarks.

JT INTERNATIONAL
500 Frank W Burr Blvd (Suite 24)
Teaneck, NJ 07666-6802
Telephone: (201) 871-1210, Web Site: www.jti.com
Dir Portfolio Brand & Trade Strategy: Dirk Skogerson
Primary Market Served: Consumer

JAFF MARKETING GROUP INC
20603 Rhodes Rd
Spring, TX 77388-3714
Telephone: (281) 353-0004, FAX: (281) 288-0970
Pres: Frank J. Vross
Conducts Business: U.S.
Primary Market Served: Consumer
Advertising/Marketing Budget Related to Direct Marketing: 76-100%
Direct Marketing ad budget:
Direct Mail: 100%
Founded: 1972

Varied consumer products for the ultimate consumer, by mail order.

JARDEN CORP
2381 NW Executive Center Dr
Boca Raton, FL 33431
Telephone: (561) 912-4395, Web Site: www.jarden.com
Exec Chmn: Martin E. Franklin
Vice Chmn, Pres & CFO: Ian G. Ashken
CEO: James E. Lillie
Primary Market Served: Business & Consumer

Consumer products company.

JAZ HOLDINGS LLC
dba Regent Book Co
PO Box 37, Bldg 5
Liberty Corner, NJ 07938-0037
Telephone: (973) 574-7600, Toll Free: (800) 999-9554, FAX: (973) 944-5073, E-Mail: webmaster@ regentbook.com, Web Site: www. regentbook.com
Pres: Janice Zucker
VP: Joshua Zucker
Mgr: Charlene Iacobacci
Conducts Business: U.S.
Primary Market Served: Business
Catalog available online
Indirect online sales
Gross sales or billing: $6,500,000

Sell all types of books to libraries & schools.

JENNY PRODUCTS INC

850 N Pleasant Ave
Somerset, PA 15501-1069
Telephone: (814) 445-3400, FAX:
(814) 445-2280, Web Site: www.
jennyproducts.com
Pres: Peter Leiss
CFO, VP, Sec & Treas: Daniel Leiss
Svc Mgr: Donald Ryan
Prodn Mgr: Dennis Young
Office Mgr: Heather Brougher
Conducts Business: U.S., Canada, Middle East, Europe
Employees: 11
Primary Market Served: Business &
Consumer
Advertising/Marketing Budget Related
to Direct Marketing: 0-25%

Manufacture & sell high pressure hot
water, cold water & steam cleaners to
reps, distributors & jobbers.

JERDEN RECORDS/ SPEECHWORKS

Subs. of SoundWorks USA Inc
17725 NE 65th St (Suite A-160)
Redmond, WA 98052
Telephone: (425) 882-3344, Toll Free:
(888) 401-4487, FAX: (425) 882-
3494, E-Mail: jerden@aol.com, Web
Site: www.soundworks.net
Pres: G.B. Dennon
VP & COO: Robert L. Wikstrom
Conducts Business: U.S.
Employees: 7
Primary Market Served: Business &
Consumer
Catalog available online
Direct online sales
Advertising/Marketing Budget Related
to Direct Marketing: 51-75%
Founded: 1991

Audio publisher that packages, manufactures & markets music, spoken word
& video products via radio, TV & the
Internet to consumers.

JOBSCOPE CORP

Subs. of Gower Corp
355 Woodruff Rd (Suite 406)
Greenville, SC 29607-3481
Telephone: (864) 458-3143, Toll Free:
(800) 443-5794, FAX: (864) 234-
4852, E-Mail: marketing@jobscope.
com, Web Site: www.jobscope.com
Pres: Hunter Park
VP, Sls: Bob Parrott
Mktg Dir: Dan Bryant
Sls Mgr: Jeff Maddox
Conducts Business: U.S., Canada, Europe
Employees: 65
Primary Market Served: Business
Catalog available online

Advertising/Marketing Budget Related
to Direct Marketing: 51-75%
Founded: 1980

Marketer of MFG software to Make-to-
Order & Engineer-to-Order manufacturers. Also aviation component repair
manufacturers.

JOFCO INC

402 E 13th St, PO Box 71
Jasper, IN 47547-0071
Telephone: (812) 482-5154, Toll Free:
(800) 23-JOFCO, FAX: (812) 634-
2392, E-Mail: furniture@jofco.com,
Web Site: www.jofco.com
Pres & CEO: Bill Rubino
Pur Dir: Steve Fleck
Mktg Svcs: Gene Luebbehusen
Conducts Business: U.S., Canada, Pacific Rim Area
Employees: 300
Primary Market Served: Business
Catalog available online
Indirect online sales
Advertising/Marketing Budget Related
to Direct Marketing: 0-25%
Direct Marketing ad budget: $50,000
Founded: 1922

Manufacturers of wood office furniture
& upholstered seating.

JOHNSON & JOHNSON

One Johnson & Johnson Plaza
New Brunswick, NJ 08903
Telephone: (732) 524-0400, FAX:
(732) 214-0332, Web Site: www.jnj.
com
Chmn Bd & CEO: Alex Gorsky
Grp Worldwide Chmn: Sandra E. Peterson
Chief Scientific Officer & Worldwide
Chmn Pharmaceuticals: Paulus Stoffels MD
VP Fin & CFO: Dominic J. Caruso
VP & Gen Counsel: Michael H. Ullmann
VP Global HR: Peter M. Fasolo PhD
Conducts Business: Worldwide
Employees: 128,300
Primary Market Served: Business &
Consumer
Founded: 1886

Manufacturer of healthcare products &
provider of related services for the consumer, pharmaceutical & professional
markets.

JONES INTERNATIONAL LTD

9697 E Mineral Ave
Centennial, CO 80112

Telephone: (303) 792-3111, Toll Free:
(800) 525-7002, FAX: (303) 784-
8508, E-Mail: publicrelations@jones.
com, Web Site: www.jones.com
Pres & CEO: Glen Jones
Grp VP & CFO: Timothy J. Burke
VP Mktg: Kim Ketchel
Conducts Business: U.S., U.K.
Employees: 2,000
Primary Market Served: Business &
Consumer

Sixty systems across country provide
services to subscribers. Online University (take courses online).

JOSLIN PHOTO PUZZLE CO

PO Box 914
Southampton, PA 18966-0914
Telephone: (215) 357-8346, FAX:
(215) 357-0307, E-Mail: 2832@
comcast.net, Web Site: www.
jigsawpuzzle.com
Owner: Marcia S. Joslin
Prodn Engr: Jeffrey L. Joslin
Conducts Business: Worldwide
Primary Market Served: Business &
Consumer
Catalog available online
Indirect online sales
Founded: 1972

Manufacturer of jigsaw puzzles for
sales promotions, advertising campaigns & premium promotions. Also,
personalized photo jigsaw puzzles &
precut blank jigsaw puzzles for heat
transfers.

JOSTENS, INC

3601 Minnesota Dr (Suite 400)
Minneapolis, MN 55435-6008
Telephone: (952) 830-3300, FAX:
(952) 830-3293, Web Site: www.
jostens.com
Pres & CEO: Michael Bailey
CIO: Alden Sutherland
Sr VP & Gen Mgr Printing & Emerging
Mkts: Timothy M. Larson
Mktg Mgr: Chris Johnson
Dir Commun: Richard Stoebe
Employees: 6,700
Primary Market Served: Business &
Consumer
Founded: 1897
Gross sales or billing: $850,000,000

Class rings, graduation announcements,
caps & gowns, yearbooks, diplomas,
customized awards & plaques & photography packages.

JUNIOR'S CHEESECAKE

386 Flatbush Ave Ext at Dekalb Ave
Brooklyn, NY 11238

Telephone: (718) 852-5257, Toll Free: (800) 458-6467, FAX: (718) 260-9849, E-Mail: info@ juniorscheesecake.com, Web Site: www.juniorscheesecake.com
Pres: Walter Rosen
VP: Marvin Rosen
Mktg Mgr: Alan Rosen
Primary Market Served: Consumer
Founded: 1950

Cheesecake restaurant, bakery, cafe & bar.

JUSTTHINK INC
85 Cranford Way
Sherwood Park, AB, Canada T8H0H9
Telephone: (780) 416-0244
Pres: Jesse Willms
Primary Market Served: Business & Consumer

K-TEL INTERNATIONAL
555 Pioneer Creek Dr, Maple Plain, MN 55359-9008
7500 Wayzata Blvd (Suite 28)
Golden Valley, MN 55426-1682
Telephone: (204) 889-5430, Toll Free: (800) 665-5021, FAX: (612) 559-6803, Web Site: www.ktel.com
Pres: Bill McMahon
VP & Gen Mgr: Mary Kuehn
Founder: Philip Kives
Primary Market Served: Consumer
Founded: 1968

Distributor of music.

KEH.COM
4900 Highlands Pkwy SE
Smyrna, GA 30082-5132
Telephone: (770) 333-4200, Toll Free: (800) 342-5534, FAX: (770) 333-4242, E-Mail: sales@keh.com, Web Site: www.keh.com
Pres: W. King Grant Jr.
Gen Mgr: Pat Mulherin
Sls Mgr: Ed Warrick
Conducts Business: Worldwide
Employees: 30
Primary Market Served: Business & Consumer
Catalog available online
Direct online sales
Advertising/Marketing Budget Related to Direct Marketing: 76-100%
Founded: 1979

Buy, sell & trade new & used photographic equipment to professionals, amateurs & collectors. Catalog available.

KHL ENGINEERED PACKAGING SOLUTIONS
Div. of AMCOR Sunrise
6600 Valley View St

Buena Park, CA 90620
Telephone: (714) 690-6361
Mktg Coord: Selena Jimenez
Primary Market Served: Business & Consumer

KTM SPORTMOTORCYCLE USA INC
1119 Milan Ave
Amherst, OH 44001-1319
Telephone: (440) 985-3553, FAX: (440) 985-3060, Web Site: www.ktmusa.com
Controller: John Eric Burleson
CFO: Patrick Prugger
Dir: Stefan Pierer
Pur: Harald Plockinger
Conducts Business: U.S.
Primary Market Served: Business

Importer of Austrian-built racing motorcycles.

KADANT JOHNSON INC
805 Wood St
Three Rivers, MI 49093
Telephone: (269) 278-1715, FAX: (269) 279-5980, Web Site: www.kadantjohnson.com
Pres: Rudi Leerentueld
Pres, Kadant Canada: Mike Soucy
PR Mgr: Steve Manos
Mgr: Ivan Kroupa
Primary Market Served: Business
Catalog available online

Manufacture steam specialty items for the pulp & paper industry.

KANO LABORATORIES
1000 E Thompson Ln
Nashville, TN 37211
Telephone: (615) 833-4101, Toll Free: (800) 311-3374, FAX: (615) 833-5790, Web Site: www.kanolabs.com
Chmn: P.R. Zimmerman
Pres: Peter Zimmerman
Conducts Business: U.S., Canada, Europe, Japan, Middle East
Employees: 15
Primary Market Served: Business & Consumer
Catalog available online
Direct online sales
Founded: 1939

Marketer of industrial strength specialty chemicals, penetrating oil & lubricants.

KANSAS CITY CHIEFS
One Arrowhead Dr
Kansas City, MO 64129
Telephone: (816) 920-9300, Toll Free: (888) 99-CHIEFS, FAX: (816) 923-4719, Web Site: www.kcchiefs.com
Chmn & CEO: Clark Hunt

Sr VP Bus Opers: Bill Chapin
CFO: Dan Crumb
VP Bus Devel: Tyler Epp
VP Commun: Ted Crews
VP Admin: Kirsten Krug
VP Stadium Opers: David Young
Conducts Business: U.S.
Primary Market Served: Business & Consumer
Direct Marketing ad budget: $150,000
Direct Mail: 25%
Newspapers: 25%
TV/Radio: 50%

Season & group professional football ticket sales.

KAPLAN INC
Subs. of Graham Holdings Co
6301 Kaplan University Ave
Fort Lauderdale, FL 33309
Telephone: (954) 515-3993, Web Site: www.kaplan.com
Chmn: Andrew S. Rosen
CEO: Thomas C. Leppert
CFO: Matthew Seelye
Exec VP Strategy & Innovation: Darrell Splithoff
Chief Learning Officer: Bror Saxberg
CIO: Edward Hanapole
Gen Counsel & Chief Compliance Officer: Janice L. Block
Sr VP Mktg: Melissa Mack
Employees: 24,000
Primary Market Served: Business & Consumer
Founded: 1938
Gross sales or billing: $1,700,000,000

Company that prepares students for college & graduate school entrance exams.

KAYLOR'S SCHOOL SUPPLY
4152 Hwy 75 N
Albertville, AL 35951
Telephone: (256) 878-1200, Toll Free: (800) 239-9999, FAX: (800) 239-9998, E-Mail: sales@kaylorsinc.com, Web Site: www.kaylorsinc.com
Pres: Jesse Kaylor
VP: Dan Kaylor
Primary Market Served: Business & Consumer

School supplies.

KEENELAND ASSOCIATION INC
4201 Versailles Rd, PO Box 1690
Lexington, KY 40588-1690
Telephone: (859) 254-3412, Toll Free: (800) 456-3412, FAX: (859) 255-2484, Web Site: www.keeneland.com
Pres & CEO: Nick Nicholson
VP: Harvie Wilkinson

Commun Dir: R. James Williams
Sls Dir: W.B. Rogers Beasley
Treas: Jessica A. Green
Conducts Business: U.S., E. Asia, S. America, Australia, Canada, Europe, Middle East
Employees: 125
Primary Market Served: Consumer
Catalog available online
Indirect online sales
Founded: 1936
Gross sales or billing: $700,000,000

Thoroughbred race track & auction company.

KELCO SUPPLY CO

2000 176th St NW (Suite 203)
Big Lake, MN 55309-8020
Telephone: (763) 493-1260, Toll Free: (800) 328-7720, FAX: (763) 493-1261, E-Mail: info@kelcosupply.com, Web Site: www.kelcosupply.com
Mktg Mgr: Lori Adamson
Owner, Pres, CEO & CFO: Alicia Carr
Conducts Business: U.S.
Employees: 25
Primary Market Served: Business & Consumer
Advertising/Marketing Budget Related to Direct Marketing: 76-100%
Direct Marketing ad budget:
Direct Mail: 100%
Gross sales or billing: $4,000,000

Sell funeral, church, school, nursing home, hospital & emergency supplies.

JJ KELLER & ASSOCIATES INC

3003 W Breezewood Ln
Neenah, WI 54957-0368
Telephone: (920) 722-2848, Toll Free: (800) 327-6868, FAX: (800) 727-7516, E-Mail: thines@jjkeller.com, Web Site: www.jjkeller.com/jjk
Chmn: Robert Keller
Pres: James Keller
VP, Publications & Prods: Terrence Quirk
Corp Creative Mgr: Thomas A. Hines
Conducts Business: U.S., Canada
Employees: 1,200
Primary Market Served: Business
Catalog available online
Direct online sales
Founded: 1953

Publishes training materials, videos, software, training seminars & workshops & services dealing with government regulations & management systems for the transportation, chemical process & healthcare industries, including permits & licenses.

KENDALL PRODUCTS/DRI-DEK

PO Box 8656
Naples, FL 34101-8656
Telephone: (239) 643-2244, Toll Free: (800) 348-2398, FAX: (800) 828-4248, E-Mail: info@dri-dek.com, Web Site: www.dri-dek.com
Pres & CEO: Lee Dees
Dir Mktg & Sls: Linda Bell
Mgr: Scott Lilly
Conducts Business: Worldwide
Primary Market Served: Business & Consumer
Catalog available online
Direct online sales

Distributor of industrial services & safety products.

KENNAMETAL INC

1600 Technology Way
Latrobe, PA 15650-0231
Toll Free: (800) 222-9327, FAX: (800) 521-3319, E-Mail: mcs-na.service@kennmetal.com, Web Site: www.kennametal.com
Pres & CEO: Carlos M. Cardoso
VP: James R. Breisinger
VP: Raj Datt
VP: David W. Greenfield
VP: Dr William Y. Hsu
Employees: 14,000
Primary Market Served: Business
Catalog available online
Direct online sales
Founded: 1938

Manufacture tools & systems for metal cutting, mining & construction.

KENSINGTON COMPUTER PRODUCTS GROUP

Div. of ACCO Brands
333 Twin Dolphin Dr (6th fl)
Redwood Shores, CA 94065
Telephone: (650) 572-2700, FAX: (650) 267-2800, Web Site: www.kensington.com
Exec VP & Pres Computer Prods Grp: Christopher Franey
Conducts Business: U.S.
Employees: 45
Primary Market Served: Business & Consumer
Catalog available online
Direct online sales

Manufacturer of computer power protection, input & security devices & accessories and provider of computer peripheral & software product accessories.

KERR-HAYS CO

PO Box 711
Ligonier, PA 15658-0711

Telephone: (724) 238-6694, FAX: (724) 238-7440
Pres: Laura Widing
Conducts Business: U.S.
Primary Market Served: Business & Consumer

Manufacturer of custom gifts & premiums.

KEY WEST ALOE HOLDINGS LLC

Div. of Key West Fragrance & Cosmetic Factory Inc
PO Box 19547
Fort Lauderdale, FL 33318-0547
Telephone: (305) 883-3166, FAX: (305) 883-3185, Web Site: www.keywestaloe.com
CEO & Pres: Nalin Patel
Conducts Business: U.S., Canada, Central America, Caribbean, Hawaii, Switzerland, Italy, Korea, Iceland, Saudi Arabia, Singapore
Employees: 50
Primary Market Served: Business & Consumer
Catalog available online
Advertising/Marketing Budget Related to Direct Marketing: 26-50%
Founded: 1971

Manufacture & sell aloe based cosmetics: skin care, bath, hair care, suntan products & fragrances for both male & female via mail order, wholesale, private label & retail.

KIMBERLY-CLARK CORP

2100 Winchester Rd
Neenah, WI 54956
Telephone: (920) 721-2000, Toll Free: (888) 525-8388, FAX: (920) 721-7722, Web Site: www.kimberly-clark.com
Chmn Bd & CEO: Thomas J. Falk
Exec VP: Robert E. Abernathy
Pres Global Health Care: Joanne B. Bauer
Sr VP & CFO: Mark A. Buthman
Sr VP & Chief HR Officer: Lizanne C. Gottung
Sr VP & Gen Counsel: Thomas J. Mielke
Pres Global Brands & Innovation: Anthony J. Palmer
Conducts Business: Worldwide
Employees: 64,000
Primary Market Served: Consumer
Gross sales or billing: $16,700,000,000

Feminine care, infant care, adult care & household products.

KNOLL GROUP

Subs. of Westinghouse Electric Corp
76 Ninth Ave (11th fl)

New York, NY 10011
Telephone: (212) 343-4000, FAX:
  (212) 343-4180
VP, Mktg: Andrew Coco
Conducts Business: U.S., Canada
Employees: 100
Primary Market Served: Business &
  Consumer
Advertising/Marketing Budget Related
  to Direct Marketing: 0-25%
Direct Marketing ad budget: $300,000
Gross sales or billing: $400,000,000

Manufacture & market office furniture,
seating, desk accessories, textiles, executive & residential furniture & case
goods.

KOEZE CO
P.O. Box 9470
Grand Rapids, MI 49509
Toll Free: (800) 555-9688, E-Mail:
  service@koezedirect.com, Web Site:
  www.koeze.com
Pres: Jeff Koeze
Mktg Mgr: Tom Lakos
Conducts Business: U.S.
Primary Market Served: Consumer

Manufacture & sell consumer nut products.

KOZAK AUTO DRYWASH INC
Eight S Lyon St
Batavia, NY 14020-1802
Telephone: (716) 343-8111, Toll Free:
  (800) 237-9927, FAX: (585) 343-
  3732, E-Mail: info@kozak.com,
  Web Site: www.dryautowash.com
Pres, CFO & Mktg Dir: Edward R.
  Harding
VP: Carol Harding
Conducts Business: Worldwide
Employees: 7
Primary Market Served: Business &
  Consumer
Catalog available online
Indirect online sales
Advertising/Marketing Budget Related
  to Direct Marketing: 76-100%
Direct Marketing ad budget: $75,000
Direct Mail: 80%
Magazines: 10%
Newspapers: 10%
Founded: 1926
Gross sales or billing: $700,000

Manufacturer of a Drywash cloth that
cleans & polishes cars without water.
Sell to dealers, funeral directors & individual consumers. Consumer list totals
about 265M names. Also sells complete
line of car care accessories. Mailmaster
(printing & mailing) division located at
same address is capable of complete

lettershop operations including printing, folding, Cheshire labeling & mail
stuffing.

KREG TOOL CO
201 Campus Dr
Huxley, IA 50124-9760
Telephone: (515) 597-6400, Web Site:
  www.kregtool.com
VP Sls & Mktg: Brad Lilienthal

KROSS INC
dba Kross Kits
25682 Springbrook Ave Ste 140
Santa Clarita, CA 91350-2433
Telephone: (661) 284-3557, Toll Free:
  (800) 456-3699, FAX: (661) 257-
  1914, Web Site: www.krosskits.com
Pres: Robert M. James
Conducts Business: U.S., Canada
Employees: 12
Primary Market Served: Business &
  Consumer

Supply auto emergency, first aid &
earthquake kits & other items for credit
card merchandising, premium & advertising specialty programs.

L&L MANAGEMENT
751 N Fair Oaks Ave
Pasadena, CA 91103-3069
Telephone: (626) 568-0338, FAX:
  (626) 568-9165
Owner: Joe Brown
Conducts Business: U.S., Canada
Employees: 1
Primary Market Served: Business &
  Consumer
Advertising/Marketing Budget Related
  to Direct Marketing: 0-25%
Direct Marketing ad budget:
Direct Mail: 65%
Magazines: 25%
Telephone: 10%
Founded: 1984

Audio/video cassette duplication company providing high volume cassette
copies for direct marketing or promotional purposes. Also provides on-site
recording of conferences.

L BRANDS INC
3 Limited Pkwy
Columbus, OH 43230
Telephone: (614) 415-7000, FAX:
  (614) 415-7440, Web Site: www.lb.
  com
Chmn & CEO: Leslie H. Wexner
Exec VP & CFO: Stuart Burgdoerfer
COO: Charles C. McGuigan
Primary Market Served: Consumer

Clothing and accessory retailer.

LGP GEM LTD
10 W 46th St (Suite 4A)
New York, NY 10036-4515
Telephone: (212) 840-2510, FAX:
  (212) 302-6182, E-Mail: sales@
  lgpltd.com, Web Site: www.lgpltd.
  com
Pres & CEO: Isaac Pollak
Exec VP: Arlene Rubin
Conducts Business: Worldwide
Employees: 16
Primary Market Served: Business
Founded: 1980

Fashion jewelry and watches design
and manufacture for direct mail industry.

LS RECORDS
1225 Apache Ln
Madison, TN 37115
Telephone: (615) 868-7171, FAX:
  (615) 860-7665, E-Mail: ls654@
  home.com, Web Site: www.
  cristylane.com
Pres: Lee Stoller
CFO, VP & Mktg Mgr: Kevin Stoller
Conducts Business: Worldwide
Employees: 7
Primary Market Served: Business &
  Consumer
Direct Marketing ad budget:
  $1,000,000
Magazines: 34%
Newspapers: 33%
TV/Radio: 33%
Gross sales or billing: $1,500,000

Television marketing & music publishing.

LACROSSE FOOTWEAR INC
Subs. of ABC-MART Inc
17634 NE Airport Way
Portland, OR 97230-4999
Telephone: (503) 262-0110, Toll Free:
  (800) 323-2668, FAX: (503) 262-
  0115, E-Mail: customerservice@
  lacrossefootwear.com, Web Site:
  www.lacrossefootwear.com
Pres: Koya Oba
Conducts Business: U.S.
Employees: 303
Primary Market Served: Business &
  Consumer
Catalog available online
Advertising/Marketing Budget Related
  to Direct Marketing: 0-25%
Founded: 1897
Gross sales or billing: $107,798,000

Rainwear, specialty clothing & footwear to direct marketers.

LAITRAM MACHINERY
Subs. of The Laitram Corp
220 Laitram Ln

Harahan, LA 70123
Telephone: (504) 733-6000, FAX:
(504) 733-6111
Pres & Gen Mgr: Flemming Frederick-son
CFO: Laurie Oerthing
Mktg Mgr: Cindy Foremaster
Conducts Business: U.S., U.K., Europe
Primary Market Served: Business

Manufacturer of food processing equipment.

LAKE SHORE INDUSTRIES
1817 Poplar St
Erie, PA 16508-0427
Toll Free: (800) 458-0463, FAX: (814)
453-4293, E-Mail: info@lsisigns.
com, Web Site: www.lsisigns.com
Pres & CEO: Leo Bruno
Adv & Mktg: Shirley Bruno
Acct: Marie Bartlett
Conducts Business: U.S., Canada
Employees: 16
Primary Market Served: Business &
Consumer
Catalog available online
Founded: 1908
Gross sales or billing: $1,700,000

Cast aluminum signs & markers, fabricated signs, acrylic signs, vinyl graphics, ADA signs, commercial castings.

LAMINEX INC
Div. of D&K Group Inc
4209 Pleasant Rd
Fort Mill, SC 29708-9328
Telephone: (704) 679-4170, Toll Free:
(800) 438-8850, FAX: (704) 679-8453, Web Site: www.laminex.com
Pres: Tim Long
Conducts Business: Worldwide
Employees: 135
Primary Market Served: Business
Founded: 1945

Manufacture hardware & software for photo I.D. & security cards. Sell by direct mail to schools, colleges, government & industry.

LAND O' LAKES INC
4001 Lexington Ave
Arden Hills, MN 55122
Telephone: (651) 481-2222, Toll Free:
(800) 328-9680, FAX: (651) 481-2000, Web Site: www.landolakesinc.
com
Pres & CEO: Chris Policinski
Sr VP & CFO: Daniel E. Knutson
Sr VP & Chief Mktg Officer: Barry
Wolfish
Conducts Business: U.S.
Employees: 8,500
Primary Market Served: Consumer

Gross sales or billing: $7,200,000,000
Food processing & marketing; farm supplies.

LANDMARK GRAPHICS CORP
Subs. of Halliburton
2107 Citywest Blvd
Houston, TX 77042-3051
Telephone: (713) 839-2000, FAX:
(713) 839-2015, Web Site: www.
landmarksoftware.com
VP Landmark Software & Svcs: Nagaraj Srinivasan
Dir Global Sls, Bus Devel & Opers:
Ken Powell
Dir Strategy: Michael Jones
Employees: 1,900
Primary Market Served: Business &
Consumer
Catalog available online

Manufacture seismic interpretation software.

LANDSCAPE FORMS INC
431 Lawndale Ave
Kalamazoo, MI 49048
Telephone: (616) 381-0490, Toll Free:
(800) 430-6209, FAX: (616) 381-3455, E-Mail: specify@
landscapeforms.com, Web Site:
www.landscapeforms.com
Pres: Bill Main
CFO: Conrad Sutter
Mktg Svc Mgr: Janis L. Etzcorn
Conducts Business: U.S.
Primary Market Served: Business
Catalog available online

Manufacture exterior furniture for commercial spaces.

LARAN COMMUNICATIONS INC
26W482 Blair St
Winfield, IL 60190-1109
Telephone: (630) 690-2141, FAX:
(630) 690-2143, Web Site: www.
web-ads.com
Owner: Lawrence E. Spiegel
Conducts Business: U.S.
Primary Market Served: Business &
Consumer
Catalog available online
Founded: 1991

Provider of on-line advertising for direct marketers.

LATHEM TIME CORP
200 Selig Dr SW
Atlanta, GA 30336
Telephone: (404) 691-0400, Toll Free:
(800) 241-4990, FAX: (404) 696-6048, Web Site: www.lathem.com
Pres: William Lathem

CFO: Ann Hooper
Mktg Mgr: Lance Whipple
Conducts Business: Worldwide
Employees: 185
Primary Market Served: Business
Advertising/Marketing Budget Related
to Direct Marketing: 51-75%
Direct Marketing ad budget:
Direct Mail: 30%
Magazines: 70%
Founded: 1919

Manufacturer of time clocks & automated time & attendance systems.

LAUGHLIN ASSOCIATES INC
2533 N Carson St
Carson City, NV 89706
Telephone: (775) 883-8484, Toll Free:
(888) 273-8152, FAX: (775) 883-4874
Pres & CEO: Lewis E. Laughlin
COO & Exec VP: Robert Seligman
VP Mktg & Sls: Meghan Cole
Conducts Business: U.S.
Employees: 32
Primary Market Served: Business &
Consumer
Catalog available online
Direct online sales
Advertising/Marketing Budget Related
to Direct Marketing: 0-25%
Founded: 1972
Gross sales or billing: $4,000,000

Resident agents.

LAWN DOCTOR INC
142 State Route 34
Holmdel, NJ 07733-2092
Telephone: (732) 946-0029, Toll Free:
(800) 631-5660, FAX: (732) 946-9089, Web Site: www.lawndoctor.
com
Pres & CEO: Scott Frith
Conducts Business: U.S.
Employees: 72
Primary Market Served: Consumer
Advertising/Marketing Budget Related
to Direct Marketing: 51-75%
Founded: 1967
Gross sales or billing: $75,000,000

Franchised lawn care service. Has 500 franchises in 40 states.

LEA & PERRINS INC
15-01 Pollitt Dr
Fair Lawn, NJ 07410
Telephone: (201) 791-1600, FAX:
(201) 791-8945, Web Site: www.
leaperrins.com
CEO: Ralph Abrams
CFO: Brian Duffy
Mktg Dir: Michael Schwartzman
Employees: 100

Primary Market Served: Consumer

Manufacturer of condiments (steak & barbeque sauces).

LEADERSHIP SOFTWARE CORP

PO Box 725
Nyack, NY 10960
Telephone: (845) 358-0406, Toll Free: (800) 872-0068, FAX: (845) 358-0359, E-Mail: info@leadersoft.com, Web Site: www.leadersoft.com
Pres: Roger W. Seiler
VP: Sally Marmion
Conducts Business: Worldwide
Employees: 2
Primary Market Served: Business & Consumer
Catalog available online
Direct online sales
Advertising/Marketing Budget Related to Direct Marketing: 76-100%
Founded: 1992

Software publisher of memory training products & Human Resources software for performance assessment & planning & CBT.

LEARNCOM HR CONSULTING & TRAINING

Div. of Learning Communications Inc
5520 Trabuco Rd
Irvine, CA 92620-5705
Telephone: (515) 440-0890, Toll Free: (800) 698-8263, FAX: (515) 221-3149, E-Mail: nhartline@learncom.com, Web Site: www.learncomhr.com
VP, Sls: Jacqueline Hendrick
Conducts Business: Worldwide
Employees: 45
Primary Market Served: Business
Catalog available online
Direct online sales
Advertising/Marketing Budget Related to Direct Marketing: 51-75%
Direct Marketing ad budget:
Direct Mail: 50%
Magazines: 10%
Telephone: 40%
Founded: 1950

Produce & distribute video based training products in the areas of environmental & safety compliance, EEO & affirmative action compliance, labor relations issues & general management.

LEARNING CARE GROUP

21333 Haggerty Rd (Suite 300)
Novi, MI 48375-5537
Telephone: (248) 697-9115, Web Site: www.learningcaregroup.com
Chief Mktg Officer: Stacy DeWalt

LEARNING COMMUNICATIONS LLC

5520 Trabuco Rd
Irvine, CA 92620-5705
Toll Free: (800) 622-3610, FAX: (949) 727-4323, E-Mail: sales@learncom.com, Web Site: www.learncom.com
Pres: Lloyd Singer
Conducts Business: Worldwide
Employees: 14
Primary Market Served: Business
Advertising/Marketing Budget Related to Direct Marketing: 0-25%
Founded: 1985

Training videos, human resources management, safety & sexual harassment.

LEVI STRAUSS & CO

1155 Battery St
San Francisco, CA 94111
Telephone: (415) 501-6000, FAX: (415) 501-7112, Web Site: www.levistrauss.com
Chmn Bd: Stephen C. Neal
Pres & CEO: Chip Bergh
Exec VP & CFO: Harmit Singh
Employees: 10,600
Primary Market Served: Business & Consumer
Catalog available online
Direct online sales
Gross sales or billing: $4,100,000,000

Manufacturer of men's & women's apparel.

LEXISNEXIS

A member of the Reed Elsevier Plc Group
125 Park Ave (Suite 2200)
New York, NY 10017
Telephone: (212) 309-8100, FAX: (800) 437-8674, Web Site: www.lexisnexis.com
CEO: Mike Walsh
Exec VP & CFO: Ed Cassar
Exec VP Opers: Alex Watson
Exec VP Strategy & Bus Devel: Andrew Matuch
Exec VP & Chief Tech Officer: Jeff Reihl
Conducts Business: Worldwide
Employees: 12,000
Primary Market Served: Business
Founded: 1966

LexisNexis is a provider of data & information for the legal, corporate, government & academic markets via the web & other media.

LIBERTY ORCHARDS CO INC

117 Mission Ave, PO Box C
Cashmere, WA 98815

Telephone: (509) 782-2191, Toll Free: (800) 888-5696, FAX: (509) 782-1487, E-Mail: service@libertyorchards.com, Web Site: www.libertyorchards.com
Pres & CEO: Greg Taylor
CFO: Brad Thomas
VP, Sls & Mktg: J. Mike Rainey
Wholesale Admin Asst: Kathy Paine
Materials & Pur Mgr: Jim Johnson
Conducts Business: U.S.
Employees: 80
Primary Market Served: Business & Consumer
Catalog available online
Direct online sales
Founded: 1920
Gross sales or billing: $14,400,000

Manufacturer of candy.

LIEBERT CORP

Subs. of Emerison Electric Co
1050 Dearborn Dr, PO Box 29186
Columbus, OH 43085
Telephone: (614) 841-6700, Toll Free: (800) LIEBERT, FAX: (614) 841-6022, Web Site: www.liebert.com
Pres: Robert Bauer
Pres, Liebert North America: Scott Dysert
VP & Gen Mgr: Steve Madara
VP & Gen Mgr: Randy MacCleary
VP, Mktg: Kevin Stoll
Conducts Business: Worldwide
Employees: 5,100
Primary Market Served: Business
Catalog available online
Advertising/Marketing Budget Related to Direct Marketing: 26-50%
Gross sales or billing: $358,000,000

Manufacturer of computer support equipment.

LIFEBOAT DISTRIBUTION

Div. of Programmers Paradise Inc
1157 Shrewsbury Ave
Shrewsbury, NJ 07702
Telephone: (732) 389-8950, FAX: (732) 389-9227, Web Site: www.programmersparadise.com
Pres: Bill Willet
VP, Mktg: Jeff Largiader
Primary Market Served: Business

Distribute computer software to dealers.

LIFELOCK

60 E Rio Salado Pkwy Ste 400
Tempe, AZ 85281-9129
Telephone: (480) 457-2007, Web Site: www.lifelock.com
VP Mktg: Andrew Wyant
Primary Market Served: Business & Consumer

LIFETIPS
240 Commercial St (Suite 3B)
Boston, MA 02109-1386
Telephone: (617) 886-9001, Web Site:
www.lifetips.com
Pres: Byron White
Primary Market Served: Consumer

LIGHT SOURCES INC
6220 Indian River Rd (Suite I)
Virginia Beach, VA 23464-3514
Telephone: (757) 424-8636, Toll Free:
(800) 882-8834, FAX: (757) 424-
6186, E-Mail: lightsources@
earthlink.net, Web Site: www.
lightsourcesinc.com
Pres: Marty Pfiefer
Conducts Business: U.S., Canada
Employees: 3
Primary Market Served: Business &
Consumer
Catalog available online
Advertising/Marketing Budget Related
to Direct Marketing: 0-25%
Direct Marketing ad budget:
Direct Mail: 80%
Magazines: 20%
Founded: 1977
Gross sales or billing: $350,000

Direct sales of special lamps for studio,
audiovisual, photographic, micro-
graphic, reprographic, communication
& medical equipment. Sell to schools,
churches, hospitals, libraries, museums,
theatres, television, publishers, banks,
photographers & industries using visual
aids & reproduction equipment.

LIONSGATE TELEVISION CORP
Div. of Lionsgate Entertainment Inc
2700 Colorado Ave (Suite 200)
Santa Monica, CA 90404-5502
Telephone: (310) 449-9200, FAX:
(310) 255-3870, Web Site: www.
lionsgate.com
CEO: Jon Feltheimer
Vice Chmn: Michael Burns
Co-COO & Pres Motion Picture Group:
Steve Beeks
Co-COO: Brian Goldsmith
Gen Counsel & Chief Strategic Officer:
Wayne Levin
CFO: James W. Barge
Conducts Business: Worldwide
Employees: 40
Primary Market Served: Business
Catalog available online

Televison production company.

A LISS & CO INC
51-55 59th Pl
Woodside, NY 11377-7408
Telephone: (718) 728-0600, Toll Free:
(800) 221-0938, FAX: (718) 728-
1227, E-Mail: alissco@aol.com
CEO: Jerold Liss
Pres: Jeffrey Liss
Conducts Business: Worldwide
Employees: 27
Primary Market Served: Business
Direct Marketing ad budget: $650,000
Founded: 1936
Gross sales or billing: $5,300,000

Distribute & sell materials handling, industrial & safety equipment & office
furniture. Expertise in storage & manual methods of in-plant movement.

LLADRO USA INC
Subs. of Lladro S.A.
One Lladro Dr
Moonachie, NJ 07074-1019
Telephone: (201) 807-1177, Toll Free:
(800) 634-9088, FAX: (201) 807-
1293, E-Mail: customer-services@
us.lladro.com, Web Site: www.
lladro.com
Pres: Rosa Lladro
CEO, Lladro USA: Brent McDaneld
Global Sls Dir: Fernando Gallego
Employees: 100
Primary Market Served: Business &
Consumer
Founded: 1953
Gross sales or billing: $16,600,000

Distribute porcelain figurines.

LO-AD COMMUNICATIONS
150 E Colorado Blvd (Suite 210)
Pasadena, CA 91105
Telephone: (626) 304-7750, FAX:
(626) 304-2716, Web Site: www.lo-
ad.com
CFO: Dennis Hammilton
Mng Dir: Kris Flynn
Acct Exec: Christine David
Primary Market Served: Business

International service bureau. Communication company.

LO INK SPECIALTIES
PO Box 530B
Kennebunkport, ME 04046-1821
Telephone: (207) 967-9110, Toll Free:
(800) 777-6471, FAX: (800) 895-
6465, E-Mail: rwatson@loink.com,
Web Site: www.loink.com
Pres: Robert C. Watson III
Conducts Business: U.S., Canada
Employees: 1
Primary Market Served: Business
Catalog available online
Direct online sales
Advertising/Marketing Budget Related
to Direct Marketing: 76-100%
Direct Marketing ad budget:
Direct Mail: 90%

Magazines: 10%
Founded: 1985
Gross sales or billing: $500,000

Sell to architects, surveyors, engineers
& contractors.

LOCKHEED MARTIN CORP
6801 Rockledge Dr
Bethesda, MD 20817
Telephone: (301) 897-6000, Web Site:
www.lockheedmartin.com
Chmn, Pres & CEO: Marillyn A. Hew-
son
Exec VP & CFO: Bruce L. Tanner
Primary Market Served: Business

Design & produce strategic missiles,
spacecraft, aircraft, electronic systems;
communications & intelligence systems; ocean & information systems;
technical information & management
services.

LOCTITE CORP
Div. of Henkel Corp-Industrial
1001 Trout Brook Crossing
Rocky Hill, CT 06067
Telephone: (860) 571-5100, Toll Free:
(800) 562-8483, (800) LOCTITE,
FAX: (860) 571-5465, Web Site:
www.loctite.com
Corp Commun Adv: Mike Bruno
Conducts Business: U.S., Canada,
Mexico
Employees: 400
Primary Market Served: Business &
Consumer
Catalog available online
Direct online sales
Founded: 1997

Manufacturer of adhesives, sealants, lubricants & coatings.

LOGICAL COMPUTER SELECTIONS
18 Winding Way
Short Hills, NJ 07078-2530
Telephone: (212) 949-2290, Toll Free:
(800) 949-2701, FAX: (212) 697-
5786, E-Mail: info@logicomputer.
com, Web Site: www.logicomputer.
com
Pres: Satish Bhalerao
Conducts Business: U.S., Asia
Employees: 19
Primary Market Served: Business &
Consumer
Catalog available online
Direct online sales
Advertising/Marketing Budget Related
to Direct Marketing: 0-25%
Direct Marketing ad budget:
Direct Mail: 100%
Founded: 1989

Gross sales or billing: $5,000,000

Sell & service micro computers & install local area networks. Distributors of micro computer tapes & backup systems. Also, provide services for systems integration & software development.

LORILLARD TOBACCO CO
PO Box 10529
Greensboro, NC 27404-0529
Telephone: (336) 335-7000, Toll Free: (877) 703-0386, FAX: (336) 373-6917, E-Mail: externalaffairs@lortobco.com, Web Site: www.lorillard.com
Chmn, Pres & CEO: Murray S. Kessler
Exec VP Fin, Planning & CFO: David H. Taylor
Exec VP Legal & External Affairs, Gen Counsel & Sec: Ronald S. Milstein
Exec VP Production Opers: Charles E. Hennighausen
Exec VP Mktg & Sls: Randy B. Spell
VP, Controller & Chief Acctg Officer: Anthony B. Petitt
Primary Market Served: Business & Consumer
Founded: 1760
Gross sales or billing: $3,500,000,000
Manufacture & sell cigarettes.

LOS ANGELES KINGS
1111 S Figueroa
Los Angeles, CA 90015
Telephone: (213) 742-7100, Toll Free: (888) KINGS-LA, FAX: (213) 742-7296, Web Site: kings.nhl.com
Owner: Philip F. Anschutz
Owner: Edward P. Roski Jr.
Pres & Gen Mgr: Dean Lombardi
Pres Bus Opers: Luc Robitaille
VP Fin: Joe Leibfried
VP Mktg: Jonathan Lowe
Conducts Business: U.S., Canada
Primary Market Served: Business & Consumer
Catalog available online
Direct online sales
Advertising/Marketing Budget Related to Direct Marketing: 26-50%
Founded: 1967

Professional hockey team.

LOVING PROMISES & MORE
1429 Commerce Ave
Longview, WA 98632
Telephone: (360) 425-8466, Toll Free: (800) 999-6909
Pres: Linda Vickers
Conducts Business: U.S.
Employees: 6

Primary Market Served: Consumer
Sell lingerie & lovers products through home parties & retail.

LUCE CORP
Div. of American Metaseal of CT
336 Putnam Ave, Box 4124
Hamden, CT 06517
Telephone: (203) 787-0281, FAX: (203) 230-2753
Pres & Mktg Mgr: Timothy F. Pagnam
VP: Mary Pagnam
Sec & VP: Julia Pagnam
Conducts Business: U.S.
Employees: 8
Primary Market Served: Business & Consumer
Direct Marketing ad budget: $5,000
Gross sales or billing: $500,000

Blue magic krispy kans, mail order companies, wholesale distributors & retail stores.

LUGGAGE BASE
670 S Frontage Rd
Nipomo, CA 93444-9148
Telephone: (805) 929-8191, Toll Free: (888) 832-1201, FAX: (805) 929-8192, E-Mail: service@luggagebase.com, Web Site: www.luggagebase.com
Owner: Joe Williams
Owner: Susan Williams
Employees: 4
Primary Market Served: Business & Consumer
Catalog available online
Direct online sales
Advertising/Marketing Budget Related to Direct Marketing: 0-25%
Founded: 1971

Name brand luggage, travel gear, bookbags, backpacks & briefcases at discount prices.

LUNDBERG FAMILY FARMS
Div. of Wehah-Lundberg, Inc.
PO Box 369, 5370 Church St
Richvale, CA 95974-0369
Telephone: (530) 882-4551, FAX: (530) 882-4500, E-Mail: info@lundberg.com, Web Site: www.lundberg.com
Chmn: Wendell Lundberg
VP, Sls & Mktg: Tim O'Donnell
Conducts Business: Worldwide
Employees: 140
Primary Market Served: Business & Consumer
Direct Marketing ad budget:
Direct Mail: $10,000
Magazines: $70,000
Telephone: $24,000
Founded: 1937

Gross sales or billing: $8,900,000
Grow & market whole grain, brown rice & rice products.

LUSTER CARE PRODUCTS
8854 Frost Ave
Saint Louis, MO 63134-1044
Telephone: (636) 272-1885, Toll Free: (800) 291-5223, FAX: (636) 272-1869, Web Site: www.lusterlace.com
Pres: Robert Flores
Member: Loretta Dwyre
Conducts Business: U.S.
Employees: 6
Primary Market Served: Business
Catalog available online
Direct online sales
Advertising/Marketing Budget Related to Direct Marketing: 51-75%
Founded: 1995
Gross sales or billing: $700,000

Sell to wholesale distributors & jobbers. Products are part of a metal polishing system (patented). Luster Lace was developed specifically for polishing round & tubular objects such as brass hand & foot rails, metal furniture, auto parts & brass beds. Luster Pad is perfect for flat & uneven surfaces, brass sinks, engine parts, motorcycle & auto rims, etc. Luster Seal, newest product, is a metal sealant excellent for sealing metals against damage from oxidation.

MBI INC
47 Richards Ave
Norwalk, CT 06857-0001
Telephone: (203) 853-2000, E-Mail: webmail@mbi-inc.com, Web Site: www.mbi-inc.com
Personnel Mgr: Thomas Reese
CEO: Peter Magiathlin
CFO: Michael Wilbur
Employees: 600
Primary Market Served: Consumer
Founded: 1969
Gross sales or billing: $500,000,000

Market collectibles through The Danbury Mint, The Postal Commemorative Society, The Easton Press, and The Danbury Mint, UK.

MCI COMMUNICATIONS SERVICES INC
Subs. of Verizon Communications; dba Verizon Enterprise Solutions Services
One Verizon Way
Basking Ridge, NJ 07920-1097
Toll Free: (877) 297-7816, Web Site: www.mci.com
Sr VP & Global Pres: Christopher Formant

Global Pres Enterprise Sls: Mike Lanman
Chief Mktg Officer: John Harrobin
Chief Info Officer: Ajay Waghray
Conducts Business: Worldwide
Primary Market Served: Consumer

Design, construction and operation of networks, information systems and mobile technologies for businesses and governments.

MDE MARKETING
55 Lehman St
Mahwah, NJ 07430-3050
Telephone: (201) 891-7010, Web Site: www.wdemarketing.com
Mktg Dir: Ken Ebling

MGI MANAGEMENT INSTITUTE
12 Skyline Dr
Hawthorne, NY 10532
Telephone: (914) 428-6500, Toll Free: (800) 932-0191, FAX: (914) 428-0773, E-Mail: mgiusa@aol.com, Web Site: www.mgi.org
VP: Gerard Cunningham
Engr: Mark Luciono
Conducts Business: Worldwide
Employees: 12
Primary Market Served: Business
Catalog available online
Indirect online sales
Advertising/Marketing Budget Related to Direct Marketing: 76-100%
Founded: 1968

Develop & administer database learning programs, both print-based and online, for many professional associates.

MGM GRAND DETROIT
1777 3rd St
Detroit, MI 48226-2561
Toll Free: (877) 888-2121, Web Site: www.mgmgrand.com/det
Database Mktg Mgr: Synthia Adams

MPBS INDUSTRIES
2820 E Washington Blvd
Los Angeles, CA 90023-4217
Telephone: (323) 268-8514, Toll Free: (800) 421-6265, FAX: (323) 268-6305, Web Site: www.mpbs.com
Pres: Michael Dernburg
Gen Mgr: Philip Lopes
Mktg: Jim Kallenberg
Conducts Business: Worldwide
Employees: 30
Primary Market Served: Business
Advertising/Marketing Budget Related to Direct Marketing: 0-25%

Gross sales or billing: $7,000,000
Distributor of equipment & supplies for industrial meat & food processing & packaging.

MPS MULTIMEDIA INC
1222 S Amphlett Blvd
San Mateo, CA 94402-1906
Telephone: (650) 872-7100, FAX: (650) 872-7133, E-Mail: sales@gospg.com, Web Site: www.selectmedia.com
Pres & CEO: Steve Chen
VP & Mktg Dir: Edgar Chen
Primary Market Served: Business & Consumer
Catalog available online
Indirect online sales
Resale & distribution of CD-ROM titles.

MTS SYSTEMS CORP
14000 Technology Dr
Eden Prairie, MN 55344-2247
Telephone: (952) 937-4000, Toll Free: (800) 328-2255, FAX: (952) 937-4515, E-Mail: info@mts.com, Web Site: www.mts.com
Chmn: Sidney W. Emery Jr.
Pres, CEO & Dir: Laura B. Hamilton
VP & CFO: Susan E. Knight
Treas & Dir: Paul Runice
Primary Market Served: Business
Gross sales or billing: $421,000,000

Industrial services: make testing equipment for testing materials, structures & vehicles.

MACY'S MARKETING
aka Advertex Communications
151 W 34th St (fl 17)
New York, NY 10001-2101
Telephone: (212) 695-4400, FAX: (212) 494-1517, Web Site: www.macys.com
Chmn, Pres & CEO: Terry J. Lundgren
Exec VP & CFO: Karen M. Hoquet
Chief Mktg Officer: Martine Reardon
CIO: Larry A. Lewark
Conducts Business: U.S.
Employees: 188,000
Primary Market Served: Consumer
Catalog available online
Direct online sales
Founded: 1820
Gross sales or billing: $26,970,000,000

Retail department store.

MAGNAFLUX
Div. of Illinois Works Inc
3624 W Lake Ave
Glenview, IL 60026-1215

Telephone: (847) 657-5300, FAX: (847) 657-5388, Web Site: www.magnaflux.com
Gen Mgr: Steve Groeninger
Sls & Mktg Mgr: Kevin Walker
Conducts Business: Worldwide
Employees: 100
Primary Market Served: Business
Catalog available online
Advertising/Marketing Budget Related to Direct Marketing: 51-75%
Founded: 1927
Gross sales or billing: $50,000,000

Non-destructive testing equipment & materials.

MAGNATAG VISIBLE SYSTEMS
Div. of WA Krapf Inc
2031 O'Neill Rd
Macedon, NY 14502-8953
Telephone: (315) 986-3033, FAX: (315) 986-4000, Web Site: www.magnatag.com
Pres: Wallace Krapf
Info Sys Mgr: Doug Weeks
Conducts Business: U.S.
Primary Market Served: Business & Consumer

Mail order house specializing in magnetic scheduling systems.

MAGNET LLC
Seven Chamber Dr, PO Box 605
Washington, MO 63090
Telephone: (636) 239-5661, Toll Free: (800) 458-9457, FAX: (636) 239-4490, E-Mail: contactus@themagnetgroup.com, Web Site: www.magnetllc.com
Pres & CEO: Bill Korowitz
COO: Tom Gorgonne
CFO: Paul Leone
Exec VP: David Kagel
VP, Sls: Darryl Haddox
Primary Market Served: Business
Catalog available online
Indirect online sales

Promotional magnet supplier.

THE MAGNI CO INC
Div. of The Magni Group Inc
7106 Wellington Point Rd
McKinney, TX 75070-5705
Telephone: (972) 540-2050, Toll Free: (800) 645-9199, FAX: (972) 540-1057, E-Mail: sales@magnico.com, Web Site: www.magnico.com; www.magnilife.com
Pres: Evan Reynolds
VP: Darlene Reynolds
Conducts Business: U.S., U.K., Australia, Canada
Employees: 7

Primary Market Served: Business & Consumer
Catalog available online
Direct online sales
Advertising/Marketing Budget Related to Direct Marketing: 26-50%
Founded: 1982
Gross sales or billing: $3,950,000

Health products in North America & Australia.

THE MAINE PHOTOGRAPHIC WORKSHOPS

2 Central St
Rockport, ME 04856-5936
Telephone: (207) 236-8581, Toll Free: (877) 577-7700, FAX: (207) 236-2558, E-Mail: info@theworkshops.com, Web Site: www.theworkshops.com
Dir: David H. Lyman
Conducts Business: U.S., France, Italy
Employees: 20
Primary Market Served: Business
Advertising/Marketing Budget Related to Direct Marketing: 0-25%

Create & offer workshops & training programs for working professionals in film, video & photography.

MAJESTIC PRODUCTS CO

Subs. of Vermont Castings Group
149 Cleveland Dr
Paris, KY L5T 2N6-40361
Telephone: (859) 987-0740, Web Site: majesticproducts.com
Chmn & CEO: Ricardo Leon
Sr VP Sls & Customer Svc: Jess Baldwin
Conducts Business: U.S., Canada, Europe
Employees: 350
Primary Market Served: Business & Consumer
Catalog available online
Direct Marketing ad budget:
Direct Mail: 25%
Magazines: 50%
Newspapers: 10%
TV/Radio: 5%
Telephone: 10%

Manufacture wood & gas stoves.

MALCO PRODUCTS INC

361 Fairview Ave
Barberton, OH 44203
Telephone: (330) 753-0361, Toll Free: (800) 253-2526, FAX: (330) 753-2025, Web Site: www.malcopro.com
Pres: Stuart Glauberman
VP: Jay Glauberman
Mgr: Dave Pennell
Mgr: Todd West

Conducts Business: Worldwide
Employees: 200
Primary Market Served: Business & Consumer
Catalog available online
Direct online sales

Chemical specialty manufacturer supplying automotive chemicals & specialty chemicals to direct marketing & fundraising companies under the Malco or private label.

MALM CHEMICAL CORP

Dept WEB-5, PO Box 300
Pound Ridge, NY 10576-0300
Telephone: (914) 764-5775, FAX: (914) 764-5386, E-Mail: custserv1@malms.com, Web Site: www.malms.com
Pres: Jay Kolinsky
Conducts Business: U.S., Canada
Primary Market Served: Business & Consumer
Catalog available online
Direct online sales
Advertising/Marketing Budget Related to Direct Marketing: 76-100%
Founded: 1979

Automotive wax, polishes & high speed applicators.

EF MALONEY INC

257 Mamaroneck Ave (Suite 208)
Mamaroneck, NY 10543-2686
Telephone: (718) 549-7000, FAX: (718) 549-6320, E-Mail: efmaloney@aol.com, Web Site: www.efmaloney.com
Pres: E. F. Maloney
VP: Thomas J. Carney
Conducts Business: U.S.
Employees: 16
Primary Market Served: Business & Consumer
Catalog available online
Advertising/Marketing Budget Related to Direct Marketing: 26-50%
Founded: 1953
Gross sales or billing: $1,000,000

Distributor of equipment & furniture to schools, institutions & offices.

THE MALONEY GROUP

Five E 22nd St
New York, NY 10010-5315
Telephone: (212) 777-6655, FAX: (212) 777-6600
Pres: Antoinette Maloney
Primary Market Served: Business
Founded: 1991

Marketing firm, new business consultant.

MANE SOLUTIONS

314 Fifth Ave
New York, NY 10001-3606
Telephone: (212) 736-0306, FAX: (212) 239-2039
Pres: Kenneth McBride
Conducts Business: U.S., Europe
Employees: 6
Primary Market Served: Consumer

Hair replacement.

MANNING MATERIALS

Div. of Canamould Max
680 Ben Franklin Hwy E, PO Box 250
Birdsboro, PA 19508-0250
Telephone: (610) 385-6797, Toll Free: (800) 445-1719, FAX: (610) 385-7524, E-Mail: mmsupport@manningmaterials.com, Web Site: www.manningmaterials.com
Pres: Drew Seibert
Gen Mgr Sls, VP Mktg: Matthew Thomas
Project Mgr: Greg Gates
Employees: 30
Primary Market Served: Business & Consumer
Catalog available online
Founded: 1980

Maintenance products for cleaning & sealing of stucco.

MARATHON NORCO AEROSPACE INC

Subs. of Transdigm Group
8301 Imperial Rd
Waco, TX 76712-6588
Telephone: (254) 776-0650, FAX: (254) 776-6558, Web Site: www.mptc.com
Pres & CEO: Nicolas Howley
Pres (Marathon): Al Rodriguez
VP & CFO: Gregory Rufus
Conducts Business: U.S.
Employees: 250
Primary Market Served: Business
Catalog available online
Direct Marketing ad budget: $500,000
Direct Mail: 50%
Magazines: 50%
Gross sales or billing: $26,000,000

Manufacturer of ni-cad batteries for airframe OEMs, government & commercial OEMs.

MARCOR REMEDIATION INC

3900 Vero Rd
Halethorpe, MD 21227-1510
Telephone: (410) 785-0001, Toll Free: (800) 547-0128, FAX: (410) 771-0348, E-Mail: info@marcor.com, Web Site: www.marcor.com
VP, Sls & Mktg: Steve Silicato

Dir Corp Commun: Dr. Joan Warfield
 Blazucki
Conducts Business: U.S.
Employees: 586
Primary Market Served: Business
Catalog available online
Indirect online sales
Founded: 1980

Full-service environmental contracting firm, with regional operations throughout the US. Services include emergency response, model remediation, IAQ, industrial cleaning & vacuuming, environmental site assessments, UST testing, clean-up & removal, soil & groundwater remediation, waste water treatment, as well as asbestos, disaster recovery, lead & other hazard abatement.

MARK JAMES & ASSOCIATES INC

PO Box 429
Oswego, IL 60543-0429
Telephone: (630) 548-8100, FAX:
 (630) 548-6107, E-Mail: info@
 markjamesassociates.com, Web Site:
 www.markjamesassociates.com/
 contact.html
Pres: Ted Fujii
Office Mgr: Sharon Geltner
Conducts Business: U.S., Australia,
 Canada, Europe
Employees: 2
Primary Market Served: Business
Founded: 1961
Gross sales or billing: $200,000

Manufacturer's representative of merchandise ranging from collectibles & household goods to cameras & watches. Develops & supplies merchandise offers to direct mail industry & premium incentive markets.

MARKETING AND PRODUCT STRATEGY

Globalink Inc
Nine Centennial Dr
Peabody, MA 01960
Telephone: (978) 977-2000, Toll Free:
 (800) 825-5897, FAX: (781) 238-
 0986, Web Site: www.lhsl.com
Sr VP, Mktg & Corp Communs: Ellen
 Spooren
Sr VP: Robert Weideman
Sr VP, Worldwide Sls: Gerald Calabrese
Primary Market Served: Business &
 Consumer

Translation software & in-house translation service.

MARKETING RESULTS INC

604 Libertyville Pl

Sicklerville, NJ 08081
Telephone: (856) 740-3334, FAX:
 (856) 740-3335, Web Site: www.
 marketingresults.net
CEO: Patrice Gianni
Pres: Gary A. Border
Dir: Kevin McElroy
Dir, Mktg: Alisa Mirabal
Sr Acct Exec: Craig Border
Sr Acct Exec: Rebecca Perger
Conducts Business: U.S., Canada
Employees: 10
Primary Market Served: Business &
 Consumer
Catalog available online
Advertising/Marketing Budget Related
 to Direct Marketing: 51-75%
Direct Marketing ad budget:
Direct Mail: $1,500,000
Magazines: $25,000
Newspapers: $100,000
TV/Radio: $500,000
Telephone: $200,000
Gross sales or billing: $3,500,000

Marketer in the casino gaming, lodging, food, beverage & cellular communications industries.

MARKWINS INTERNATIONAL CORP

22067 Ferrero Pkwy
City of Industry, CA 91789
Telephone: (909) 595-8898, FAX:
 (909) 595-8820, Web Site: www.
 markwins.com
Pres & CEO: Eric Chen
CFO: Julie Hsu
Exec VP, Gen Mgr: Mac Ritchie
Sr VP, Sls: Matt Allen
Sr VP, Mktg: Shawn Haynes
Conducts Business: U.S., Canada, Norway, Sweden, Denmark
Employees: 60
Primary Market Served: Business
Catalog available online
Advertising/Marketing Budget Related
 to Direct Marketing: 0-25%

Cosmetics manufacturers supplying specialty health & beauty aids to direct marketers in 20 countries.

MARMELSTEIN INC

760 S Fourth St
Philadelphia, PA 19147
Telephone: (215) 925-9862, FAX:
 (215) 925-3889
Pres & Owner: Judy Buchsbaum
Conducts Business: U.S.
Employees: 20
Primary Market Served: Business &
 Consumer
Advertising/Marketing Budget Related
 to Direct Marketing: 26-50%

Textile distributor to both consumer & business.

THE MARMON GROUP LLC

181 W Madison St Ste 2500
Chicago, IL 60602-4505
Telephone: (312) 372-9500, FAX:
 (312) 845-5305, Web Site: www.
 marmon.com
Pres & CEO: Frank S. Ptak
Div Pres: Kelly E. Dier
Sr VP & Gen Counsel: Robert W.
 Webb
VP, HR: Larry Rist
Conducts Business: Worldwide
Employees: 27,000
Primary Market Served: Business &
 Consumer
Advertising/Marketing Budget Related
 to Direct Marketing: 0-25%
Gross sales or billing: $7,000,000,000

International association of more than 60 auto manufacturing & service companies.

MARY KAY COSMETICS INC

16251 Dallas Pkwy
Addison, TX 75001-6801
Telephone: (972) 687-6300, Toll Free:
 (800) MARY KAY, FAX: (972) 687-
 1611, Web Site: www.marykay.com
Exec Chmn: Richard R. Rogers
Pres & CEO: David B. Holl
CIO: Kregg Jodie
Chief Mktg Officer: Sheryl Adkins-
 Green
CFO: Deborah Gibbins
Conducts Business: Worldwide
Employees: 4,500
Primary Market Served: Consumer
Catalog available online
Direct online sales
Founded: 1985
Gross sales or billing: $2,250,000,000

Manufacturer & marketer of personal care products through 200,000 independent beauty consultants.

MARY OF PUDDIN HILL INC

938 Cambridge Dr
Duncanville, TX 75137-4602
Telephone: (903) 455-2651, Toll Free:
 (800) 545-8889, FAX: (903) 455-
 4522, E-Mail: customerservice@
 puddinhill.com, Web Site: www.
 puddinhill.com
Pres: Ron Massey
Conducts Business: U.S.
Employees: 118
Primary Market Served: Consumer
Catalog available online
Direct online sales
Advertising/Marketing Budget Related
 to Direct Marketing: 51-75%
Direct Marketing ad budget:
Direct Mail: 100%
Founded: 1839

Gross sales or billing: $3,600,000

Sell fruit cakes, candies & other food gifts by direct mail.

MASCO CORP
21001 Van Born Rd
Taylor, MI 48180
Telephone: (313) 274-7400, FAX: (313) 792-6135, E-Mail: webmaster@mascohq.com, Web Site: www.masco.com
Chmn: Richard A. Manoogian
Pres, CEO & Dir: Timothy Wadhams
Exec VP & COO: Donald J. DeMarie Jr.
VP, Corp Devel & CFO: John G. Sznewajs
VP & CIO: Timothy J. Monteith
Primary Market Served: Business & Consumer
Catalog available online
Indirect online sales

Building & home improvement products.

WB MASON CO
59 Centre St
Brockton, MA 02303
Toll Free: (800) 773-4488, Web Site: www.wbmason.com
Pres & CEO: Leo J. Meehan Jr.
Dir Mktg: Lindsay Picard
Primary Market Served: Consumer

Office products merchandiser.

MASTERPIECE STUDIOS INC
PO Box 8700
Mankato, MN 56002-8700
Telephone: (507) 388-8788, Toll Free: (800) 447-0219, FAX: (507) 344-4606, E-Mail: masterpiecestudios@masterpiecestudios.com, Web Site: www.masterpiecestudios.com
Exec VP, Sls & Mktg: Doug Faust
Pres: John Kind
Conducts Business: U.S., Canada
Employees: 215
Primary Market Served: Business & Consumer
Gross sales or billing: $27,600,000

Manufacture & distribute stationery & copy paper for use in small presses & office copiers.

MASTERVISION INC
969 Park Ave
New York, NY 10028
Telephone: (212) 879-0448, Toll Free: (800) 876-0091, FAX: (212) 744-3560, E-Mail: stadin1@aol.com, Web Site: www.mastervision.com
Pres: Richard N. Stadin
Conducts Business: Worldwide
Employees: 10

Primary Market Served: Business & Consumer
Direct Marketing ad budget:
Direct Mail: 25%
Magazines: 25%
Newspapers: 25%
Online: 25%
Founded: 1980

Produce & market cultural & educational TV, video cassettes, disks, how-to's & books in the arts, humanities & sciences.

MATTEL INC
333 Continental Blvd
El Segundo, CA 90245-5012
Telephone: (310) 252-2000, FAX: (310) 252-2180, Web Site: www.mattel.com
Chmn & CEO: Bryan Stockton
CFO: Kevin Farr
Exec VP Global Brands Team: Tim Kilpin
Employees: 25,000
Primary Market Served: Consumer
Founded: 1945
Gross sales or billing: $5,650,200,000

Manufacturer of family products.

MAUI JIM INC
8300 N Allen Rd
Peoria, IL 61615
Telephone: (309) 691-3700, FAX: (309) 683-2202, Web Site: www.mauijim.com
Pres: Walter Hester
VP, Mktg: Chris Abbruzzese
Primary Market Served: Business & Consumer
Catalog available online
Direct online sales

Vision care products & services, sunglasses.

MAZDA MOTOR OF AMERICA INC
Div. of Mazda Corp
7755 Irvine Center Dr
Irvine, CA 92623
Telephone: (949) 727-1990, Toll Free: (800) 222-6500, FAX: (949) 727-6101, Web Site: www.mazdausa.com
Pres & CEO: James J. O'Sullivan
Sr VP, US Opers Group: Robert Davis
CFO & Sr VP Fin, Admin & IT: Jim Lievois
VP Mktg: Russell Wager
VP US Sls Opers: Ron Stettner
Employees: 860
Primary Market Served: Business
Catalog available online
Indirect online sales

Gross sales or billing: $300,000,000

Parts & accessories & automotive distributor.

MCDONALD OBSOLETE PARTS CO
6458 W Eureka Rd
Rockport, IN 47635
Telephone: (812) 359-4965, FAX: (812) 359-5555, E-Mail: parts@mcdonaldparts.com, Web Site: www.mcdonaldparts.com
Pres & Owner: Marjorie McDonald
Parts Specialist: Robert McDonald
Parts Buyer: Will McDonald
Conducts Business: U.S.
Primary Market Served: Business & Consumer
Catalog available online
Indirect online sales
Advertising/Marketing Budget Related to Direct Marketing: 26-50%
Direct Marketing ad budget: $2,500
Founded: 1974
Gross sales or billing: $150,000

Obsolete Ford, Lincoln & Mercury parts to the public & dealers.

MCFEELY'S SQUARE DRIVE SCREWS
PO Box 44976
Madison, WI 53744-4976
Telephone: (434) 846-2729, Toll Free: (800) 443-7937, FAX: (804) 847-7136, E-Mail: tech@mcfeelys.com, Web Site: www.mcfeelys.com
Pres: James C. Ray
Tech Dir: Daren Lawrence
Opers Mgr: Ron Pegran
Conducts Business: U.S.
Employees: 35
Primary Market Served: Business & Consumer
Catalog available online
Indirect online sales
Advertising/Marketing Budget Related to Direct Marketing: 0-25%
Direct Marketing ad budget: $1,000,000
Direct Mail: $900,000
Magazines: $100,000
Founded: 1978

Supply square drive screws for the woodworking market.

MCGRUFF SPECIALTY PRODUCTS OFFICE
Div. of National Crime Prevention Council
1 Prospect St
Amsterdam, NY 12010

Telephone: (518) 842-4388, Toll Free: (888) 776-7763, FAX: (800) 995-5121, E-Mail: mcgruff@spocentral.com, Web Site: www.mcgruffspo.com
Pres & CEO: Alfonso E. Lendhart
Exec Dir: Tibby Milne
Dir: Carolyn Cullen
Conducts Business: U.S.
Primary Market Served: Business
Catalog available online
Direct online sales
Advertising/Marketing Budget Related to Direct Marketing: 76-100%

Crime prevention educational products.

MCKENZIE TAXIDERMY SUPPLY
PO Box 480
Granite Quarry, NC 28072-0480
Telephone: (704) 279-7985, Toll Free: (800) 279-7985, Web Site: www.mckenziesp.com
CEO: Kevin McKenzie
Dir, IT: Barry McKenzie
Mgr: Eric Cantrall
Primary Market Served: Business & Consumer
Catalog available online
Direct online sales

Taxidermy supplies.

MCNICHOLS CO
PO Box 30300
Tampa, FL 33630-3300
Telephone: (813) 282-3828, FAX: (813) 288-9342, E-Mail: sales@mcnichols.com, Web Site: www.mcnichols.com
Mktg Dir: William J. Tuxhorn
Adv Dir: Sharon Robertson
Conducts Business: U.S., Mexico, Canada, Puerto Rico, Costa Rica, Chile, Colombia, Venezuela, Panama
Employees: 315
Primary Market Served: Business
Catalog available online
Indirect online sales
Advertising/Marketing Budget Related to Direct Marketing: 76-100%
Direct Marketing ad budget:
Direct Mail: 80%
Magazines: 8%
Online: 10%
Telephone: 2%
Founded: 1952
Gross sales or billing: $95,000,000

Distributor of specialty metals.

MEDTRONIC INC
710 Medtronic Pkwy NE
Minneapolis, MN 55432

Telephone: (763) 514-4000, Toll Free: (800) 328-2518, FAX: (763) 514-4879, Web Site: www.medtronic.com
Chmn & CEO: Omar Ishrak
Sr VP Strategy & Bus Devel: Geoffrey Martha
Sr VP & CFO: Gary Ellis
Sr VP & Chief Scientific, Clinical and Regulatory Officer: Richard E. Kuntz
Conducts Business: Worldwide
Employees: 37,000
Primary Market Served: Consumer
Advertising/Marketing Budget Related to Direct Marketing: 51-75%
Founded: 1949
Gross sales or billing: $12,300,000,000

Implantable pacing systems, heart valves, cardiopulmonary pumps, cardiac ablation systems, leads, angioplasty catheters, drug pumps, spinal stimulators & blood management products sold to doctors & hospitals. 40 U.S. locations & 120 international offices & facilities.

MEGGER
427 Bronze Way
Dallas, TX 75237-1019
Telephone: (214) 330-3539, Web Site: www.megger.com
Dir Mktg: Elsa Cantu
Primary Market Served: Business & Consumer

MEGUIAR'S INC
17991 Mitchell S, PO Box 92623
Irvine, CA 92614-6015
Telephone: (949) 752-8000, Toll Free: (800) 347-5700, FAX: (949) 752-6659, Web Site: www.meguiars.com
Pres & CEO: Barry Meguiar
Employees: 225
Primary Market Served: Business & Consumer
Founded: 1901
Gross sales or billing: $26,500,000

Surface cleaners, polishes & waxes for cars, boats, planes, wood, fiberglass, plastics & marble.

MENARDI MIKROPUL LLC
1 Maxwell Dr
Trenton, SC 29847
Telephone: (803) 663-6551, Toll Free: (800) 321-3218, FAX: (803) 663-4029, E-Mail: info@menardifilters.com, Web Site: www.menardifilters.com
Mgr: Lisa Hayes
Conducts Business: U.S., Canada
Employees: 150
Primary Market Served: Business
Catalog available online

Advertising/Marketing Budget Related to Direct Marketing: 0-25%
Direct Marketing ad budget: $200,000
Direct Mail: 20%
Magazines: 20%
Telephone: 60%
Founded: 2000
Gross sales or billing: $9,100,000

Manufacture & service filtration products for air pollution control & product recovery in chemical, mineral, food & other industries.

MENTOR CORP
201 Mentor Dr
Santa Barbara, CA 93111-3340
Telephone: (805) 879-6000, Toll Free: (800) 525-0245, FAX: (805) 964-2712, Web Site: www.mentorcorp.com
Chmn: Joseph E. Whitters
Pres, CEO & Dir: Joshua H. Levine
VP, HR: Cathryn Ullery
VP & CFO: Michael O'Neil
VP & COO: Edward S. Northrop
Employees: 950
Primary Market Served: Business
Catalog available online
Founded: 1969
Gross sales or billing: $300,000,000

Manufacturer of medical devices for plastic & reconstructive surgery, clinical & consumer health care.

MERCK & CO INC
1 Merck Dr
Whitehouse Station, NJ 08889
Telephone: (908) 423-1000, Web Site: www.merck.com
Chmn & CEO: Kenneth C. Frazier
Exec VP & Pres Mfg Division: Willie A. Deese
Exec VP & CIO: Clark Golestani
Exec VP & CFO: Peter N. Kellogg
Exec VP & Chief Medical Officer: Michael Rosenblatt MD
Conducts Business: U.S., Canada, Europe
Employees: 60,000
Primary Market Served: Business & Consumer
Gross sales or billing: $22,600,000,000

Pharmaceuticals & health products for humans.

MERISEL
127 W 30th St (5th fl)
New York, NY 10001
Telephone: (212) 594-4800, FAX: (212) 594-4488, E-Mail: corp@merisel.com, Web Site: www.merisel.com
VP, Mktg: Leslie Sinfield
Conducts Business: U.S.

Primary Market Served: Business

Distributor of computer products, and software sales.

MERSCO MEDICAL
1411 E Wells Ave
Pierre, SD 57501
Telephone: (605) 224-6687, Toll Free: (800) 234-1881, FAX: (605) 322-1801
Reg Admin: Steve Statz
Conducts Business: U.S.
Employees: 80
Primary Market Served: Consumer
Advertising/Marketing Budget Related to Direct Marketing: 51-75%

Home healthcare.

METSO MINERALS/WS TYLER
Div. of North American Vibrating Equipment
20965 Crossroads Cir
Waukesha, WI 53186
Telephone: (803) 699-4200, (262) 717-2500, FAX: (262) 717-2501, E-Mail: minerals.info.csr@metso.com, Web Site: www.metsominerals.com
Conducts Business: U.S., Canada, Central & South America
Employees: 550
Primary Market Served: Business & Consumer
Advertising/Marketing Budget Related to Direct Marketing: 0-25%

Manufacture & sell mining equipment.

FRED MEYER JEWELERS INC
Div. of Fred Meyer Inc
3800 SE 22nd Ave
Portland, OR 97202
Telephone: (503) 232-8844, Toll Free: (800) 457-5977, FAX: (503) 797-7616, Web Site: www.fredmeyerjewelers.com
Pres & CEO: Ed Dayoob
VP, Strategic Plng & Bus Devel: Mark Funasaki
Employees: 3,000
Primary Market Served: Consumer
Catalog available online
Direct online sales
Founded: 1973
Gross sales or billing: $259,000,000
Fine jewelry.

MICKWEE GROUP INC
5600 Mowry School Rd Ste 230
Newark, CA 94560-5800
Telephone: (510) 651-6522, FAX: (510) 770-9682, E-Mail: info@generatemarketing.com, Web Site: www.generatemarketing.com
Pres: Ron Mickwee
Client Grp Dir: Ann Mickwee
Conducts Business: U.S.
Employees: 35
Primary Market Served: Business
Advertising/Marketing Budget Related to Direct Marketing: 26-50%
Direct Marketing ad budget:
Direct Mail: 10%
Telephone: 90%

Provide third-party direct marketing services to the computer industry. Services include telemarketing (outbound & inbound) & direct mail.

MICRO PLASTICS INC
PO Box 149
Flippin, AR 72634
Telephone: (870) 453-2261, Toll Free: (800) 466-1467, FAX: (870) 453-8676, E-Mail: mpsales@microplastics.com, Web Site: www.microplastics.com
Pres: Tom Hill
Nat'l Sls Mgr: Bruce Sanders
Mktg & Adv: Tammy Killian
Creative Mktg Devel: Tony Wilson
Conducts Business: U.S., Canada, U.K., Mexico, South America, Central America, Far East
Employees: 350
Primary Market Served: Business & Consumer
Catalog available online
Direct online sales
Advertising/Marketing Budget Related to Direct Marketing: 26-50%
Founded: 1961

Manufacture & sell nylon & plastic hardware & fasteners to distributors & O.E.M. manufacturers.

MICROFLUIDICS CORP
Subs. of MFIC Corp
90 Glacier Dr (#1000)
Westwood, MA 02090-1818
Telephone: (617) 969-5452, Toll Free: (800) 370-5452, FAX: (617) 965-1213, E-Mail: info@mfics.com, Web Site: www.microfluidicscorp.com
CEO: Michael C. Ferrara
Pres & COO: Robert Bruno
VP Sls & Mktg: Thomas Hoarty
Conducts Business: U.S., Canada, Europe, Asia
Employees: 53
Primary Market Served: Business
Advertising/Marketing Budget Related to Direct Marketing: 26-50%
Founded: 1984
Gross sales or billing: $15,600,000

MICRON CORP
89 Access Rd (Suite 5), Norwood Airport Business Park
Norwood, MA 02062-5234
Telephone: (781) 769-5771, Toll Free: (800) 456-0734, FAX: (781) 762-3531, E-Mail: info@microncorp.com, Web Site: www.microncorp.com
Pres: William Theos
VP, Sls: John Theos
VP Mfg: Charles W. Theos
Conducts Business: U.S.
Employees: 30
Primary Market Served: Business
Catalog available online
Direct online sales
Advertising/Marketing Budget Related to Direct Marketing: 0-25%
Founded: 1982
Gross sales or billing: $3,200,000

Assemble printed circuit boards, surface mount and through hole.

MID WEST FLOOR CO INC
2714 Breckenridge Industrial Ct
Saint Louis, MO 63144
Telephone: (314) 647-6060, FAX: (314) 647-9189, E-Mail: sales@mid-westfloor.com, Web Site: www.mid-westfloor.com
Pres: Virgil Hendricks
Sls: Kasie Wright
Conducts Business: U.S.
Employees: 100
Primary Market Served: Consumer
Catalog available online
Advertising/Marketing Budget Related to Direct Marketing: 0-25%
Direct Marketing ad budget: $50,000
Direct Mail: 100%
Founded: 1939
Gross sales or billing: $10,000,000

THE MIDDLEBY CORP
1400 Toastmaster Dr
Elgin, IL 60120-9272
Telephone: (847) 741-3300, FAX: (847) 741-0015, E-Mail: sales@middleby.com, Web Site: www.middleby.com
Pres & CEO: Selim A. Bassoul
VP & CFO: Timothy J. Fitzgerald
Investor Rels & PR: Darcy Bretz
Conducts Business: Worldwide
Employees: 1,282
Primary Market Served: Business
Gross sales or billing: $403,431,000

Manufacturer of commercial cooking equipment.

MIDLAND MARKETING GROUP
PO Box 8576
Saint Joseph, MO 64508-8576

Telephone: (816) 261-9007, FAX: (816) 233-0859, E-Mail: info@ midlandmarketinggroup.com, Web Site: www.midlandmarketinggroup. com
Pres: Gary Gerchen
Primary Market Served: Consumer
Greeting card distributor.

THE MILLARD GROUP
7301 N Cicero Ave
Lincolnwood, IL 60712-1613
Telephone: (847) 674-4100, Toll Free: (800) 339-6876, FAX: (847) 677-0790, E-Mail: sales@millardgroup. com, Web Site: www.millardgroup. com
Pres: Larry Kugler
Conducts Business: U.S.
Employees: 2,300
Primary Market Served: Business
Catalog available online
Gross sales or billing: $50,000,000

Contract custodial services to major commercial, medical & educational facilities.

MILWAUKEE ELECTRIC TOOL CORP
Div of Techtronic Industries Co Ltd, Hong Kong
13135 W Lisbon Rd
Brookfield, WI 53005-2550
Telephone: (262) 781-3600, Toll Free: (800) 729-3878, FAX: (800) 638-9582, Web Site: www. milwaukeetool.com
Pres: Steven P. Richman
Pres Sls: Darrell Hendrix
Conducts Business: U.S., Canada
Employees: 2,075
Primary Market Served: Business & Consumer
Catalog available online
Founded: 1924

Manufacture power tools & heavy-duty electric tools for contractors & industry.

MINITAB INC
1829 Pine Hall Rd
State College, PA 16801-3008
Telephone: (814) 238-3280, Toll Free: (800) 448-3555, FAX: (814) 238-4383, E-Mail: sales@minitab.com, Web Site: www.minitab.com
CEO: Barbara Ryan
Conducts Business: U.S., Canada, Europe, Asia, Australia, U.K., South America
Employees: 300
Primary Market Served: Business & Consumer
Catalog available online

Direct online sales
Founded: 1972

Provider of quality improvement software: Minitab Statistical Software, Quality Companion by Minitab & Quality Trainer by Minitab. Also provide a complete solution for Six Sigma & other projects. Companies that rely on Minitab software & services include Toshiba, DuPont & Boeing.

MIRACLE EAR
Subs. of Amplifon SpA
5000 Cheshire Pkwy N
Minneapolis, MN 55446
Toll Free: (800) 464-8002, FAX: (763) 268-4365, Web Site: www.miracle-ear.com
Pres & CEO, Amplifon USA: Heinz Ruch
Chief Fin Officer: Jerry Knuston
VP Miracle-Ear: Vera Peterson
Conducts Business: U.S., Canada, Puerto Rico, Australia, Spain, Mexico
Employees: 600
Primary Market Served: Consumer
Catalog available online
Advertising/Marketing Budget Related to Direct Marketing: 26-50%
Direct Marketing ad budget:
Direct Mail: $4,000,000
TV/Radio: $6,000,000
Telephone: $2,000,000
Founded: 1948
Gross sales or billing: $96,000,000

Manufacture hearing aids.

MISSCO CORP
PO Box 321400, PO Box 5349
Flowood, MS 39232-1400
Telephone: (601) 948-8600, Toll Free: (800) 647-5333, FAX: (601) 987-3038
Supvr: Jim Scholtens
Proj Coord: Monique Chatman
VP, Sls: Mel Edmonds
Sls: Tracy Echols
Conducts Business: U.S.
Primary Market Served: Business & Consumer
Catalog available online

Sells office & school supplies, furniture & equipment.

MR G'S ENTERPRISES
5613 Elliott Reeder Rd
Fort Worth, TX 76117-6013
Telephone: (817) 831-3501, FAX: (817) 831-0638, E-Mail: mrgs@ mrgusa.com, Web Site: www. mrgusa.com
Owner: Glenn Garrison
Conducts Business: Worldwide
Employees: 12

Primary Market Served: Business & Consumer
Catalog available online
Indirect online sales
Advertising/Marketing Budget Related to Direct Marketing: 76-100%
Direct Marketing ad budget:
Magazines: 100%
Founded: 1974
Gross sales or billing: $500,000

Autofasteners, rechrome plastic service & screw kits for 922 models.

MR WASH CAR WASH
3817 Dupont Ave
Kensington, MD 20895
Telephone: (301) 933-4858, Web Site: www.mrwash.com
Adv & Mktg Dir: Jody Weinstein
Primary Market Served: Consumer
Catalog available online

Car wash services.

MOBILE FUSION
165 S Union Blvd Ste 405
Lakewood, CO 80228-2210
Telephone: (720) 963-8000, Toll Free: (800) 431-8556, Web Site: www. mobile-fusion.com
Mng Partner: Joel Morrow

MODERNAGE CUSTOM DIGITAL IMAGING LABS
555 8th Ave (Rm 2003)
New York, NY 10018-4651
Telephone: (212) 997-1800, Toll Free: (800) 997-2510, FAX: (212) 869-4796, E-Mail: info@modernage.com, Web Site: www.modernage.com
Pres & Co-Owner: Kenneth Troiano
VP & Co-Owner: Richard Troiano
Conducts Business: U.S.
Employees: 120
Primary Market Served: Business & Consumer
Catalog available online
Direct online sales
Advertising/Marketing Budget Related to Direct Marketing: 0-25%
Direct Marketing ad budget:
Direct Mail: 10%
Magazines: 40%
Newspapers: 50%
Founded: 1944

A full service custom photographic lab specializing in single roll development (E-6, C-41 & B&W); duratrans, duraflex or C-prints to any size; photo-composites, dupes, B&W silver gelatin prints, murals & overlaminating; full color & B&W airbrushing, retouching & restoration services. Complete digital imaging, hi-res drum scans to hi-res color negative, transparency or B&W

outputs. Computer generated slides, design & layout. Direct digital C-prints & inkjet printing.

MOEN INC

Subs. of Fortune Brands Home & Security
25300 Al Moen Dr
North Olmsted, OH 44070-5619
Telephone: (440) 962-2000, Web Site: www.moen.com
Pres: David Lingafelter
VP & CFO: Patrick Hallinan
VP Global Brand Mktg: Tim McDonough
VP Global Strategic Devel: Mike Pickett

Design and manufacture of kitchen & bathroom faucets.

MOLSON COORS BREWING CO

1225 17th St (Ste 3200)
Denver, CO 80202-5536
Telephone: (303) 927-2337, Toll Free: (800) 665-7661, Web Site: www.molsoncoors.com
Chmn Bd: Peter H. Coors
Vice Chmn Bd: Andrew T. Molson
Pres & CEO: Peter Swinburn
Pres & CEO Intl: Kandy Anand
Pres & CEO Canada: Stewart Glendinning
Global CFO: Gavin Hattersley
Pres & CEO Europe: Mark Hunter
Global Chief People & Legal Officer: Samuel Walker
Global Chief Supply Chain Officer: Celso White
Primary Market Served: Business & Consumer
Catalog available online
Founded: 1913

Beer brewing & distribution company.

THURSTON MOORE COUNTRY LTD

304 W Due West Ave
Madison, TN 37115-4511
Telephone: (615) 868-7448, FAX: (615) 868-3738
Pres: Thurston Moore
Treas: Tracy Guerriero
Conducts Business: Worldwide
Employees: 3
Primary Market Served: Business & Consumer
Advertising/Marketing Budget Related to Direct Marketing: 0-25%
Direct Marketing ad budget:
Direct Mail: 100%
Founded: 1975

Gross sales or billing: $200,000
Specialize in personality dollar bills, custom brochures, full color post cards, business cards & bookmarks.

JACQUES MORET INC

RP-NFOA
1411 Broadway (fl 8)
New York, NY 10018
Telephone: (212) 354-2400, FAX: (212) 354-5544, E-Mail: info@moret.com, Web Site: www.moret.com
Asst to VP Mktg: Joanne Paolucci
Conducts Business: U.S., China
Employees: 55
Primary Market Served: Business
Advertising/Marketing Budget Related to Direct Marketing: 0-25%
Founded: 1975

Sell active wear clothing & apparel to all levels of distribution.

MORITT, HOCK, HAMROFF & HOROWITZ

400 Garden City Plaza
Garden City, NY 11530-3327
Telephone: (516) 873-2000, FAX: (516) 873-2010, E-Mail: lhauser@morritthock.com, Web Site: www.morritthock.com
Pres: Neil J. Moritt
Dir Bus Devel: Laura Hauser
Partner: Alan Hock
Employees: 35
Primary Market Served: Business
Founded: 1980

Attorneys.

THOMAS MOSER CABINETMAKERS

149 Main St
Freeport, ME 04032
Telephone: (207) 865-4519, Toll Free: (800) 708-9041, FAX: (207) 865-6539, E-Mail: freeportshowroom@thosmoser.com, Web Site: www.thosmoser.com
Mktg Dir: Gretchen Kruysman
HR: Cindy Violet
Conducts Business: U.S.
Employees: 100
Primary Market Served: Business & Consumer
Advertising/Marketing Budget Related to Direct Marketing: 26-50%
Founded: 1973
Gross sales or billing: $7,000,000

Handcrafted solid wood furniture to direct users, architects & designers for residential, corporate & institutional use.

MOSTAD & CHRISTENSEN

PO Box 1709
Oak Harbor, WA 98277-1709
Telephone: (360) 679-4164, Toll Free: (800) 654-1654, FAX: (360) 679-4167, E-Mail: marketing@mostad.com, Web Site: www.mostad.com
Editor: Shirlee Christensen
Pres: Arvid Mostad
Office Mgr: Michael Coppage
Conducts Business: U.S., Canada
Employees: 9
Primary Market Served: Business

Provide marketing services such as newsletters & brochures to CPAs.

MOTIENT COMMUNICATIONS

11700 Plaza America Dr Ste 900
Reston, VA 20190-4774
Telephone: (847) 478-4330, Toll Free: (800) 752-2672, FAX: (703) 758-6111
VP System Engrng & Solutions: Deborah Peterson
Employees: 487
Primary Market Served: Business & Consumer
Founded: 1988

Owns & operates an integrated terrestrial/satellite network & provides a variety of mobile communications solutions for the transportation, field service, wireless email & telemetry markets.

MOTOR COACH INDUSTRIES INTERNATIONAL INC

aka MCI
1700 E Golf Rd
Schaumburg, IL 60173
Telephone: (847) 285-2000, Toll Free: (800) 624-2622, Web Site: www.mcicoach.com
Pres & CEO: Tom Sorrells III
Sr VP Sls & Mktg: Pete Cotter
Conducts Business: U.S., Canada, Taiwan, Australia
Employees: 2,000
Primary Market Served: Business
Founded: 1975
Gross sales or billing: $6,924,000,000

Distribution of OEM coach & bus parts to the transit & inter-city fleet companies.

MUSEUM MASTERS INC

185 E 85th St (Suite 27B)
New York, NY 10028
Telephone: (212) 360-7100, (917) 273-8710, FAX: (212) 360-7102, E-Mail: MMIMarilyn@aol.com, Web Site: www.museummasters.com

Pres: Marilyn Goldberg
Conducts Business: U.S., Canada, Europe, Japan, Korea
Employees: 5
Primary Market Served: Business
Direct Marketing ad budget: $100,000
Direct Mail: 50%
Magazines: 50%
Founded: 1980
Gross sales or billing: $1,000,000

Design & produce boutique items using images of the masters, i.e., Picasso, Van Gogh, Gaughin, Degas, Toulouse-Lautrec, Matisse, Warhol & Haring. Also, licensing of these images & merchandising for exhibitions & special events.

MUSIC CHOICE

650 Dresher Rd
Horsham, PA 19044-2204
Telephone: (215) 784-5840, Web Site: www.musicchoice.com
Pres: David Devessa
Sr VP, Sls: Christina Tancredi
Conducts Business: U.S.
Employees: 120
Primary Market Served: Business & Consumer
Founded: 1991

Provide commercial free CD music service to businesses & consumers.

MUSKEGON POWER TOOL CORP

2357 Whitehall Rd
North Muskegon, MI 49445
Telephone: (231) 766-2194, Toll Free: (800) 635-5465, FAX: (231) 766-3846
Pres: William A. Seyferth
Conducts Business: Worldwide
Employees: 5
Primary Market Served: Business & Consumer
Catalog available online
Advertising/Marketing Budget Related to Direct Marketing: 26-50%

Sell professional portable power tools to contractors via direct mail.

MXENERGY INC

595 Summer St (Suite 300)
Stamford, CT 06901-1407
Telephone: (203) 356-1318, Web Site: www.mxenergy.com
Mktg Mgr: Caroline Antunez

MYRON CORP

205 Maywood Ave
Maywood, NJ 07607-1000
Telephone: (201) 843-6464, Toll Free: (877) 803-3358, FAX: (201) 843-8390, Web Site: www.myron.com

Pres: Marie Adler-Kravecas
CEO: Jim Adler
Conducts Business: U.S., Canada
Employees: 1,000
Primary Market Served: Business
Catalog available online
Direct online sales
Founded: 1955
Gross sales or billing: $100,000

Sell imprinted pocket & desk appointment diaries, laser engraved pens & market business to business gifts.

MYSTIC STAMP CO INC

9700 Mill St
Camden, NY 13316
Toll Free: (866) 660-7147, FAX: (800) 385-4919, E-Mail: info@mysticstamp.com, Web Site: www.mysticstamp.com
Pres: Donald J. Sundman
Mktg Mgr: Linda Stevens
Conducts Business: U.S., Canada
Employees: 100
Primary Market Served: Consumer
Catalog available online
Direct online sales
Advertising/Marketing Budget Related to Direct Marketing: 26-50%
Founded: 1923
Gross sales or billing: $19,900,000

Sell retail & wholesale postage stamps to collectors by mail.

NCR CORP

3097 Satellite Blvd
Duluth, GA 30096
Telephone: (937) 445-1936, Toll Free: (800) CALL-NCR, FAX: (937) 445-1682, Web Site: www.ncr.com
Chmn & CEO: Bill Nuti
Exec VP Industry & Field Opers and Corp Devel: John G. Bruno
Exec VP Svcs: Peter Dorsman
Sr VP, CFO & Chief Acctg Officer: Bob Fishman
Primary Market Served: Business
Catalog available online
Founded: 1884

Computer systems; business information processing systems.

NPI

14901 Trinity Blvd
Fort Worth, TX 76155
Telephone: (214) 634-2288, FAX: (682) 503-8214, E-Mail: sales@npisorters.com, Web Site: www.npisorters.com
Mktg Mgr: Michelle Ramirez
Primary Market Served: Business

NATIONAL AUTO WARRANTY

100 Mall Pkwy
Wentzville, MO 63385-4816
Toll Free: (800) 649-1620
Chief Mktg Officer: Shawn Morris
Primary Market Served: Consumer

NATIONAL BULK EQUIPMENT INC

12838 Stainless Dr
Holland, MI 49424
Telephone: (616) 399-2220, FAX: (616) 399-7365, E-Mail: sales@nbe-inc.com, Web Site: www.nbe-inc.com
Pres: Todd Reed
CEO: Joe Reed
Exec VP, Opers: Dave Denhof
VP: Ellen Kaines
Conducts Business: U.S.
Employees: 65
Primary Market Served: Business
Catalog available online
Indirect online sales
Advertising/Marketing Budget Related to Direct Marketing: 0-25%
Direct Marketing ad budget: $100,000
Founded: 1977
Gross sales or billing: $6,000,000

Manufacturer of mixing, storing & conveying equipment for use with dry bulk materials. Also handle pastes & liquids.

NATIONAL EMBLEM SALES

Div. of The American Legion National Headquarters
PO Box 36460
Indianapolis, IN 46206-0460
Telephone: (317) 630-1247, Toll Free: (888) 453-4466, FAX: (317) 630-1381, E-Mail: emblem@legion.org, Web Site: www.emblem.legion.org
Div Dir: Jeffrey Brown
Mktg Mgr: Kevin Carruthers
Conducts Business: U.S.
Employees: 35
Primary Market Served: Business & Consumer
Catalog available online
Direct online sales
Advertising/Marketing Budget Related to Direct Marketing: 76-100%
Founded: 1919

Sell regalia to American Legion members & posts.

NATIONAL 4-H SUPPLY SERVICE

Div. of National 4-H Council
7100 Connecticut Ave
Chevy Chase, MD 20815

Telephone: (301) 961-2959, FAX: (301) 961-2937, E-Mail: 4hsupply@fourhcouncil.edu, Web Site: www.fourhcouncil.edu
Sr VP: Edwin M. Gershon
Dir Natl 4-H Supply Svc: Kelly Carpenter
Conducts Business: U.S.
Employees: 15
Primary Market Served: Business & Consumer
Catalog available online
Direct online sales
Advertising/Marketing Budget Related to Direct Marketing: 26-50%
Direct Marketing ad budget: $300,000
Direct Mail: 60%
Online: 40%
Founded: 1924
Gross sales or billing: $4,500,000

Goods & services to the 4-H.

NATIONAL GALLERY OF ART GIFT SHOP

4th & Constitution Ave NW
Washington, DC 20565
Telephone: (202) 842-6466, Toll Free: (800) 697-9350, FAX: (202) 842-4043, Web Site: www.nga.gov
Chmn: John Wilmerding
Pres: Victoria P. Sant
Gallery Dir: Earl A. Powell III
Conducts Business: U.S.
Employees: 70
Primary Market Served: Consumer
Catalog available online
Indirect online sales

Sell fine art reproductions & posters to the general public.

NATIONAL RAILROAD PASSENGER CORP

dba Amtrak
60 Massachusetts Ave NE
Washington, DC 20002
Telephone: (202) 906-3000, Toll Free: (800) USA-RAIL, FAX: (202) 906-3306, Web Site: www.amtrak.com
Pres & CEO: Joseph H. Boardman
Chief Mktg & Sls Officer: Matt Hardison
CFO: Gerald Sokol Jr.
CIO: Jason Molfetas
VP Opers: DJ Stadtler
Employees: 19,000
Primary Market Served: Business & Consumer
Catalog available online
Direct online sales
Founded: 1971
Gross sales or billing: $2,042,000,000

Rail passenger service.

NATIONAL SEMINARS GROUP

Div. of Rockhurst University Continuing Education Center
6901 W 63rd St (Suite 300)
Shawnee Mission, KS 66202-4005
Telephone: (913) 432-7755, Toll Free: (800) 258-7246, FAX: (913) 432-0824, E-Mail: cstserv@natsem.com, Web Site: www.natsem.com
Exec Dir & Founder: Mark Truitt
VP Mktg: Janette Novack
Mgr: Gary Weinberg
Facilities Mgr: Helena Conley
Conducts Business: U.S.
Employees: 200
Primary Market Served: Business
Catalog available online
Direct online sales
Advertising/Marketing Budget Related to Direct Marketing: 76-100%
Founded: 1978

One of the nation's leading business training seminar companies.

NATIONWIDE BEAUTY & BARBER SUPPLY

2600 Erie Blvd E
Syracuse, NY 13224-1287
Telephone: (315) 446-9026, FAX: (315) 446-8943, E-Mail: sales@nationwidebeauty.com, Web Site: www.nationwidebeauty.com
Pres: Norman Kassel
VP & Sec: Richard Kassel
Conducts Business: U.S., Puerto Rico
Employees: 25
Primary Market Served: Business & Consumer
Catalog available online
Indirect online sales
Direct Marketing ad budget:
Direct Mail: $120,000
Newspapers: $2,000
Telephone: $30,000
Gross sales or billing: $3,000,000

Mail order wholesale beauty & barber supplies to trade & retail consumers.

NATIONWIDE DISPLAYS INC

100 Christopher St
Ronkonkoma, NY 11779
Telephone: (631) 467-2034, FAX: (631) 467-2079, E-Mail: info@nationwidedisplays.com, Web Site: www.nationwidedisplays.com
Pres: Bill Griffith
VP Sls: Steve Griffith
Conducts Business: U.S., Canada
Employees: 15
Primary Market Served: Business
Catalog available online
Indirect online sales
Direct Marketing ad budget: $75,000
Direct Mail: 100%

Founded: 1990

Portable & custom exhibits for industry installation & dismantling. Serving North America & Europe.

NAVISTAR

2701 Navistar Dr
Lisle, IL 60532-3637
Telephone: (331) 332-5000, Web Site: www.navistar.com
Pres & CEO: Troy Clarke
Exec VP & CFO: Walter G. Borst
Exec VP & COO: Jack Allen
Sr VP Strategy & Planning and Pres Global & Specialty Bus: Eric Tech
Conducts Business: U.S.
Employees: 13,000
Primary Market Served: Business & Consumer
Catalog available online
Indirect online sales
Direct Marketing ad budget: $500,000
Direct Mail: 90%
Telephone: 10%
Gross sales or billing: $4,000,000,000

International medium & heavy duty trucks, school buses, parts, service, engines & financing to businesses.

NAVITAR INC

200 Commerce Dr
Rochester, NY 14623-3506
Telephone: (585) 359-4000, Toll Free: (800) 828-6778, FAX: (585) 359-4999, E-Mail: info@navitar.com, Web Site: www.navitar.com
Co-Pres: Julian Goldstein
Co-Pres: Jeremy Goldstein
COO: Thomas McCune
CFO: Mark Smith
Conducts Business: Worldwide
Employees: 50
Primary Market Served: Business
Catalog available online
Direct Marketing ad budget:
Direct Mail: 25%
Magazines: 25%
Telephone: 50%

Manufacturer of optical lenses & audio visual equipment.

NESTLE HEALTHCARE NUTRITION

Div. of Nestle USA
12 Vreeland Rd (fl 2), PO Box 697
Florham Park, NJ 07932
Toll Free: (800) 422-2752, Web Site: www.nestle-nutrition.com
Chief Mktg & Medical Sls Officer: Rick Klauser
VP Mktg: Barbara McCartney
VP Retail Sls: Steve Goodyear
Primary Market Served: Business

Manufacture nutrition supplements.

NETWORK TELEPHONE SERVICES INC
dba Pacific Marketing
21135 Erwin St
Woodland Hills, CA 91367-3713
Telephone: (818) 992-4300, Toll Free: (800) 727-6874, FAX: (818) 992-8415, Web Site: www.nts.net
CEO: Joseph Preston
Pres: Gary Passon
VP Mktg: David Wood
Employees: 500
Primary Market Served: Business & Consumer
Gross sales or billing: $56,200,000
Service bureau for 800, 900 & 976 telephone lines.

NEUTRON INDUSTRIES
Subs. of State Industrial Products Inc
7107 N Black Canyon Hwy
Phoenix, AZ 85021-7619
Telephone: (602) 864-0090, Toll Free: (888) 712-7127, FAX: (602) 357-3996, (877) 646-7337, E-Mail: questions@neutronindustries.com, Web Site: www.neutronindustries.com
Pres & COO, St Indus Prods: Robert San Julian
Mktg Mgr: T. J. McDowell
Conducts Business: U.S., Canada, U.K.
Employees: 225
Primary Market Served: Business
Catalog available online
Indirect online sales
Advertising/Marketing Budget Related to Direct Marketing: 76-100%
Direct Marketing ad budget:
Direct Mail: 60%
Telephone: 40%
Founded: 1978

Sell maintenance, cleaning & repair products to industrial institutions & commercial accounts.

NEVCO SCOREBOARD CO
301 E Harris Ave
Greenville, IL 62246-2193
Telephone: (618) 664-0360, Toll Free: (800) 851-4040, FAX: (618) 664-0398, E-Mail: sales@nevcoscoreboards.com, Web Site: www.nevcoscoreboards.com
Pres: MG Nevinger
Mktg Staff, Dir: Tom Harnetiaux
Admin Coord: Angie Rankers
Conducts Business: Worldwide
Employees: 92
Primary Market Served: Consumer
Catalog available online
Indirect online sales
Founded: 1934

Gross sales or billing: $5,600,000
Manufacture scoreboards for sporting events.

THE NEW PIPER AIRCRAFT INC
2926 Piper Dr
Vero Beach, FL 32960-1955
Telephone: (772) 567-4361, FAX: (772) 978-6573, E-Mail: marketing@piper.com, Web Site: www.newpiper.com
Pres & CEO: James K. Bass
VP Sls: Bob Kromer
Conducts Business: Worldwide
Employees: 100
Primary Market Served: Business & Consumer
Catalog available online
Advertising/Marketing Budget Related to Direct Marketing: 51-75%
Founded: 1937

Manufactures the world's only complete line of piston aircraft for personal, business & utility use.

NEW YORK POWER AUTHORITY
123 Main St (Mailroom 10-B)
White Plains, NY 10601-3170
Telephone: (914) 681-6200, E-Mail: info@nypa.gov, Web Site: www.nypa.gov
Chmn: John R. Koelmel
Vice Chmn: Joanne M. Mahoney
Pres & CEO: Gil C. Quiniones
COO: Ed Welz
Exec VP & CFO: Donald A. Russak
Sr VP Strategic Planning: Robert F. Lurie
Primary Market Served: Business & Consumer
Catalog available online

Promotes energy efficiency to customers of New York Power.

NEW YORK-PRESBYTERIAN/ COLUMBIA UNIVERSITY MEDICAL CENTER
630 W 168th St
New York, NY 10032
Telephone: (212) 305-2500, FAX: (212) 305-8023, Web Site: www.nyp.org
CEO: Steven J. Corwin MD
Pres: Robert F. Kelly
Exec VP, CFO, & Treas: Phyllis R. F. Lantos
Sr VP & Chief Info Officer: Aurelia G. Boyer
VP Mktg & Chief Mktg Officer: David A. Feinberg
Conducts Business: U.S.
Employees: 25

Primary Market Served: Business & Consumer
Founded: 1928
Gross sales or billing: $18,180,612
Provide medical care & related health services.

NEWELL RUBBERMAID, INC
3 Glenlake Pkwy
Atlanta, GA 30328
Telephone: (770) 418-7000, Web Site: www.newellrubbermaid.com
Primary Market Served: Business & Consumer

NICKLAUS COMPANIES LLC
11780 US Hwy 1 (Suite 500)
North Palm Beach, FL 33408-3042
Telephone: (561) 227-0300, FAX: (561) 227-0548, Web Site: www.nicklaus.com
Chmn: Jack Nicklaus
Sr VP Mktg, Licensing & Commun: Andrew O'Brien
Conducts Business: Worldwide
Employees: 500
Primary Market Served: Business & Consumer
Catalog available online
Direct online sales
Advertising/Marketing Budget Related to Direct Marketing: 0-25%
Founded: 1970

Golf courses design, development of golf & real estate communities and the marketing & licensing of golf products and services.

NILODOR INC
10966 Industrial Pkwy NW
Bolivar, OH 44612-8991
Telephone: (330) 874-1017, Toll Free: (800) 443-4321, FAX: (330) 874-3366, E-Mail: info@nilodor.com, Web Site: www.nilodor.com
Pres: Les W. Mitson
VP, Sls: Kurt Peterson
VP Mktg: Todd Sauser
Conducts Business: U.S.
Employees: 33
Primary Market Served: Business & Consumer
Advertising/Marketing Budget Related to Direct Marketing: 0-25%
Founded: 1954
Gross sales or billing: $3,100,000
Manufacturer of deodorizing products & cleaners.

NIMLOK
7420 N Lehigh Ave
Niles, IL 60714

Telephone: (847) 647-1012, Toll Free: (800) 233-8870, FAX: (847) 647-2044, E-Mail: info@nimlok.com, Web Site: www.nimlok.com
Pres: Simon Perutz
Dir: Dave Fugiel
Conducts Business: U.S.
Employees: 68
Primary Market Served: Business
Catalog available online
Advertising/Marketing Budget Related to Direct Marketing: 26-50%
Gross sales or billing: $20,000,000
Display & exhibit systems: portable panel systems, pop-ups, tabletop displays & custom modular exhibit systems: exhibit shipping cases; aluminum truss system.

NISSAN NORTH AMERICA INC

One Nissan Way
Franklin, TN 37067
Telephone: (615) 725-1000, Web Site: www.nissanusa.com
CEO: Carlos Ghosn
Chmn Mgmt Com for North America: Jose Munoz
Exec VP & Chief Planning Officer: Andy Palmer
Corp VP North America & Sr. Pres R&D: Kunio Nakaguro
VP Mktg Commun & Media: Jon Brancheau
VP Sls: Derrick Hatami
VP Fin: Carlos Servin
Conducts Business: U.S.
Primary Market Served: Consumer
Catalog available online
Sales, marketing & distribution of Nissan & Infiniti automobiles in the US.

NORMAN CONTROL CO

Div. of Coffman Manufacturing Corp
305 Cary Point Dr
Cary, IL 60013-2974
Telephone: (847) 639-5721, FAX: (847) 639-5755, E-Mail: susan@coffmanmfg.com, Web Site: www.coffmanmfg.com
Pres: Richard Coffman
Co-Owner: Susan Coffman
Conducts Business: U.S.
Employees: 23
Primary Market Served: Business & Consumer
Direct Marketing ad budget:
Direct Mail: 50%
Magazines: 50%
Founded: 1948

Gross sales or billing: $1,000,000
Institutional laundry equipment - dumpers, carts, hamper dumpers, hydraulic dumpers, barrel dumpers, lighted inspection tables & towel counting units.

NORMAN ROCKWELL MUSEUM

9 Glendale Rd, Rte 183
Stockbridge, MA 01262
Telephone: (413) 298-4100, Toll Free: (800) 742-9450, FAX: (413) 298-4144, E-Mail: emazzer@nrm.org, Web Site: www.nrm.org
Dir: Laurie Norton Moffatt
Dir: Terry Smith
Commun Coord: Ellen S. Mazzer
Store Mgr: Mike Duffy
Conducts Business: Worldwide
Employees: 63
Primary Market Served: Business & Consumer
Direct online sales
Advertising/Marketing Budget Related to Direct Marketing: 0-25%
Founded: 1967
Gross sales or billing: $4,197,553
Sells exclusive Norman Rockwell books, prints, signed lithographs & gift items through gift shop & website.

NORTHERN CROSS

Div. of Barancorp
214 N 2100 Rd
Lecompton, KS 66050
Telephone: (785) 887-6010, Toll Free: (800) 625-7233, FAX: (785) 887-6263
Pres & CEO: Dennis A. Baranski
Conducts Business: U.S., Canada, Japan, Western Europe
Primary Market Served: Business & Consumer
Catalog available online
Founded: 1984
Manufacturers of safety & survival products for distribution to industry, wholesalers, retailers & individuals. Distributes its proprietary products & other safety & survival products produced by other manufacturers in the field.

NORTHERN SAFETY CO INC

PO Box 4250
Utica, NY 13504-4250
Telephone: (315) 793-4900, Web Site: www.northernsafety.com
Pres: Neil Sexton
Primary Market Served: Business

NORTHERN TOOL & EQUIPMENT INC

2800 Southcross Dr W
Burnsville, MN 55306-6936
Telephone: (952) 894-9510, Toll Free: (800) 221-0516, FAX: (952) 894-1020, Web Site: www.northerntool.com
Chmn & CEO: Donald L. Kotula
Pres: Chuck Albrecht
CFO: Tom Erickson
VP & Mktg Dir: Jay Berlin
Mktg Dir: Kevin Huggett
Conducts Business: Worldwide
Employees: 2,000
Catalog available online
Direct online sales
Advertising/Marketing Budget Related to Direct Marketing: 51-75%
Direct Marketing ad budget:
Direct Mail: 75%
Magazines: 10%
Newspapers: 5%
TV/Radio: 10%
Founded: 1981
Gross sales or billing: $349,000,000
Mail order marketer of industrial & consumer tools.

NORWOOD PROMOTIONAL PRODUCTS

14421 Myerlake Cir
Clearwater, FL 33760-2840
Telephone: (317) 275-2500, Toll Free: (800) 959-9138, FAX: (317) 275-2570, Web Site: www.norwood.com
Sr VP, Chief Mktg Officer: Jim Simone
Pres: Paul Lage MAS
VP Mktg & Mdsg: Andy Roth
Employees: 3,500
Primary Market Served: Business
Founded: 1989
Gross sales or billing: $330,000,000
Supply promotional products sold through distributors.

NUANCE SPEECH SOLUTIONS

One Wayside Rd
Burlington, MA 01803
Telephone: (781) 565-5000, FAX: (781) 565-5001, E-Mail: sales@speechworks.com, Web Site: www.nuance.com
Pres Speech Solutions Div: Stuart Patterson
Exec VP, Worldwide Mktg: Steve Chambers
CEO: Paul Ricci
Sr VP Mktg & Global Strategy: Robert J. Weidman

Primary Market Served: Business

Develop advanced speech recognition software for the call-center & telephone market.

NUCOR CORP
1915 Rexford Rd Ste 400
Charlotte, NC 28211-3888
Telephone: (704) 366-7000, FAX: (704) 362-4208, E-Mail: info@nucor.com, Web Site: nucor.com
Pres: Daniel D'Micco
Primary Market Served: Business
Founded: 1966

Manufacture steel & steel products.

NUNATURALS
2220 W Second Ave (Suite 1)
Eugene, OR 97402-7112
Telephone: (541) 344-9785, Toll Free: (800) 753-4372, FAX: (541) 343-0915, E-Mail: info@nunaturals.com, Web Site: www.nunaturals.com
Pres: Warren Sablosky
Gen Mgr: Travis Debacker
Conducts Business: U.S.
Employees: 8
Primary Market Served: Business & Consumer
Catalog available online
Indirect online sales
Founded: 1989

Vitamins, nutrients & herbs.

NAT NUSSBAUM & ASSOCIATES INC
1440 Coral Ridge Dr
Coral Springs, FL 33071-5433
Telephone: (954) 345-9131, FAX: (954) 345-0786, E-Mail: nlnmktg@aol.com
Pres: Nathan Nussbaum
Conducts Business: U.S., Canada, U.K., Australia
Employees: 1
Primary Market Served: Business
Advertising/Marketing Budget Related to Direct Marketing: 26-50%
Direct Marketing ad budget:
Direct Mail: 70%
Magazines: 5%
Newspapers: 5%
Telephone: 20%
Founded: 1992
Gross sales or billing: $400,000

Sell jewelry, electronics & other items to the mail order industry.

NUTRITIONAL RESEARCH ASSOCIATES INC
407 E Broad St
South Whitley, IN 46787-1001

Telephone: (260) 723-4931, Toll Free: (800) 456-4931, FAX: (260) 723-6297, E-Mail: info@nrfeeds.com, Web Site: www.nrfeeds.com
Pres: Barbara Pook
Mgr: Kerry Flater
Conducts Business: U.S., Canada, Australia, Singapore, Mexico, Caribbean, Latin America
Employees: 11
Primary Market Served: Business & Consumer
Advertising/Marketing Budget Related to Direct Marketing: 26-50%
Direct Marketing ad budget: $25,000
Magazines: 100%
Founded: 1934
Gross sales or billing: $2,000,000

Small animal nutritional products. Small animal & bird cages & equipment. Caged bird seed mixes & nutritional supplies. Small animal complete feeds. Horse, goat, & other livestock supplements.

OSRAM SYLVANIA
Subs. of OSRAM GmbH
100 Endicott St
Danvers, MA 01923-3782
Telephone: (978) 777-1900, Toll Free: (800) LIGHTBULB, FAX: (978) 750-2152, Web Site: www.sylvania.com
Pres & CEO: Jes Munk Hansen
Primary Market Served: Business

Lighting manufacturer.

OAKWOOD HOMES CORP
7800 McCloud Rd
Greensboro, NC 27409-9634
Telephone: (336) 664-2400, Toll Free: (800) 822-0633, FAX: (336) 315-3249, Web Site: www.oakwoodhomes.com
Pres: Dale Holmgren
Conducts Business: U.S.
Employees: 1,200
Primary Market Served: Consumer
Catalog available online
Direct Marketing ad budget: $1,000,000
Gross sales or billing: $150,000,000

Homes to the public.

THE OCCASIONS GROUP
1750 Tower Blvd
North Mankato, MN 56003-1706
Telephone: (507) 625-6464
VP, Sls & Mktg: Jean Andersen

OFF THE WALL MAGNETICS LLC
60 SE Main St
Portland, OR 97214-3320

Toll Free: (800) 337-2637, Web Site: www.4thefridge.com
Pres: Page Mesher

OFFICE DEPOT
6600 N Military Trl
Boca Raton, FL 33496-2434
Telephone: (561) 438-4800, Toll Free: (800) 463-3768, FAX: (561) 438-4001, Web Site: www.officedepot.com
Chmn & CEO: Roland C. Smith
Exec VP & CFO: Stephen E. Hare
Exec VP E-Commerce: Mike Kirschner
Exec VP Mktg: Tim Rea
Employees: 52,000
Primary Market Served: Business & Consumer
Founded: 1986
Gross sales or billing: $15,000,000,000

Office products distributor.

OLAN MILLS INC
6060 Shallowford Rd
Chattanooga, TN 37421-1611
Telephone: (423) 622-5141, Toll Free: (800) 251-6320, FAX: (423) 629-8128, Web Site: www.olanmills.com
Chmn & CEO: Robert L. McDowell
CIO: Steve Kraus
Dir Mktg: Lynette Darr
Conducts Business: U.S., Canada, U.K.
Employees: 4,000
Primary Market Served: Consumer
Advertising/Marketing Budget Related to Direct Marketing: 76-100%
Founded: 1932
Gross sales or billing: $156,700,000

Portrait sales company.

OLEDA & CO INC
7700 Camp Bowie W
Fort Worth, TX 76116-6450
Telephone: (817) 731-1147, Toll Free: (800) 731-4247, FAX: (817) 731-1149, E-Mail: oleda@oleda.com, Web Site: www.oleda.com
Pres: Oleda Baker
VP, Bus Devel: James Haun
Conducts Business: Worldwide
Primary Market Served: Consumer
Catalog available online
Direct online sales
Advertising/Marketing Budget Related to Direct Marketing: 51-75%
Founded: 1969

Anti-aging, beauty, fitness & health national mail order company. Products sold through various mail order media, including TV. Sold in bulk to countries outside U.S.

OLIVER OF ADRIAN INC
PO Box 189

Adrian, MI 49221-0189
Telephone: (517) 263-2132, Toll Free:
　(877) 668-0885, FAX: (517) 265-
　8698, E-Mail: info@
　oliverinstrument.com, Web Site:
　www.oliverofadrian.com
Sec: Mary Smith
VP: Neal Garrison
Conducts Business: Worldwide
Employees: 6
Primary Market Served: Business &
　Consumer
Catalog available online
Advertising/Marketing Budget Related
　to Direct Marketing: 0-25%
Direct Marketing ad budget: $4,000
Online: $360
Telephone: $140
Founded: 1913
Gross sales or billing: $900,000

Manufacture a complete line of metalworking machine tools such as automatic & manual drill grinders,
automatic & manual cutter & tool
grinders & point thinning machines.
Customers include major cutting tool
manufacturers, automotive firms, construction equipment companies & farm
equipment manufacturers.

OLYMPIA SALES INC

215 Moody Rd
Enfield, CT 06083-3207
Telephone: (860) 749-0751, Toll Free:
　(800) 338-9992, FAX: (860) 814-
　4451, E-Mail: info@olympiasales.
　net, Web Site: www.olympiasales.us
Chmn: Arthur O'Hara
Pres & Dir: Thomas A. O'Hara
Mktg Dir: Diane Spiro
Conducts Business: U.S.
Employees: 40
Primary Market Served: Business &
　Consumer
Catalog available online
Indirect online sales
Founded: 1966
Gross sales or billing: $7,200,000

Manufacturer & distributor of greeting
cards, stationary, and office supplies.

OMAHA VACCINE CO

Div. of CSR
11143 Mockingbird Dr
Omaha, NE 68137-2332
Telephone: (402) 731-9600, Toll Free:
　(800) 367-4444, FAX: (800) 242-
　9447, E-Mail: customerservice@
　OmahaVaccine.com, Web Site:
　www.omahavaccine.com
Chmn & CEO: Scott Remington
VP: Jim Hoing
Conducts Business: Worldwide
Employees: 90

Primary Market Served: Business &
　Consumer
Catalog available online
Direct online sales
Market animal health & animal related
products.

OMNI FARM

1369 Calloway Gap Rd
West Jefferson, NC 28694
Telephone: (336) 982-3475, Toll Free:
　(800) TREE-FARM, FAX: (336)
　982-4163, E-Mail: omnifarm@
　omnifarm.com, Web Site: www.
　omnifarm.com
Pres: Hal F. Gimlin
Exec Dir: Pat Herbert
Conducts Business: U.S.
Employees: 11
Primary Market Served: Business &
　Consumer
Catalog available online
Direct online sales
Advertising/Marketing Budget Related
　to Direct Marketing: 76-100%
Direct Marketing ad budget: $30,000
Direct Mail: 50%
Online: 50%
Founded: 1972
Gross sales or billing: $1,000,000

Sell real Christmas trees, wreaths, gar-
lands, greenery & Christmas tree stands
through catalogs & direct to consumer.

ON-HAND ADHESIVES INC

940 Telser Rd
Lake Zurich, IL 60047-6714
Telephone: (847) 437-7773, Toll Free:
　(800) 323-5158, FAX: (847) 437-
　8006, E-Mail: help@on-hand.com,
　Web Site: www.on-hand.com
Chmn Bd & CEO: George L. Cooper
Pres: Michael Cooper
Sec & Treas: Margaret Cooper
Conducts Business: U.S.
Employees: 20
Primary Market Served: Business
Catalog available online
Direct online sales
Direct Marketing ad budget:
Direct Mail: $75,000
Telephone: $25,000
Gross sales or billing: $3,000,000

Industrial distributor of adhesives with
branch offices in Milwaukee, Saint
Louis & Los Angeles.

1-800-FLOWERS.COM

1 Old Country Rd (Suite 500)
Carle Place, NY 11514-1847
Telephone: (516) 237-6000, Web Site:
　www.1800flowers.com
Dir, Third Party Mktg: Jill Eastman Vi-
dal

Primary Market Served: Business &
　Consumer

1-800-MATTRESS.COM

1000 S Oyster Bay Rd
Hicksville, NY 11801-3527
Toll Free: (800) 327-7720, Web Site:
　www.1800mattress.com
Pres & CEO: Napoleon Barragan
Conducts Business: U.S.
Employees: 280
Primary Market Served: Business &
　Consumer
Catalog available online
Direct online sales
Advertising/Marketing Budget Related
　to Direct Marketing: 0-25%
Direct Marketing ad budget:
　$5,500,000
Direct Mail: $150,000
Magazines: $260,000
Newspapers: $340,000
TV/Radio: $4,000,000
Founded: 1976
Gross sales or billing: $170,000,000

Sell mattresses, box springs & bedding
accessories via the Internet.

100% REAL ESTATE INC

1810 Lee Rd
Orlando, FL 32810-5702
Toll Free: (800) 454-3422, E-Mail:
　rcs@100percentflorida.com, Web
　Site: www.100percentflorida.com
Pres: Robert C. Sinclair
VP: Colby Sinclair
Conducts Business: U.S., Japan, Cen-
　tral America, Korea
Employees: 33
Primary Market Served: Business &
　Consumer
Advertising/Marketing Budget Related
　to Direct Marketing: 51-75%
Direct Marketing ad budget: $28,000
Direct Mail: 15%
Magazines: 35%
Newspapers: 50%
Gross sales or billing: $60,000,000

Real estate broker specializing in businesses, warehouses, office buildings &
land in Florida.

ONEIDA LTD

Div. of Oneida Ltd
163-181 Kenwood Ave
Oneida, NY 13421-2829
Telephone: (315) 361-3000, Toll Free:
　(888) 263-7195, FAX: (315) 361-
　3700, Web Site: www.oneida.com
Pres & CEO: James E. Joseph
EVP & CFO: Andrew G. Church
CIO & SVP, IT: Rob Hack
EVP: W. Tim Runyan
CMO & SVP Strat Plng: David Sank
Conducts Business: Worldwide

Employees: 905
Primary Market Served: Business &
Consumer
Catalog available online
Direct online sales
Advertising/Marketing Budget Related
to Direct Marketing: 0-25%
Founded: 1880
Gross sales or billing: $350,800,000

Manufacturer and supplier of flatware,
hollow ware & giftware, crystal and
glass products.

OPEN TEXT INC
275 Frank Tompa Dr
Waterloo, ON, Canada N2L 0A1
Telephone: (519) 888-9933, Toll Free:
(800) 499-6544, FAX: (519) 888-
0677, E-Mail: support@opentext.
com, Web Site: www.opentext.com
Chmn: P. Thomas Jenkins
Pres, CEO & Dir: John Shackleton
CFO: Paul J. McFeeters
Exec VP, Bus Devel: M. William For-
quer
Exec VP, Worldwide Sls: John A.
Kirkham
Conducts Business: U.S.
Employees: 2,700
Primary Market Served: Business &
Consumer
Advertising/Marketing Budget Related
to Direct Marketing: 51-75%
Founded: 1971
Gross sales or billing: $595,000,000

Software developer. Publishes a calen-
daring/group scheduling software program called OnTime for the IBM PC's
& compatibles. Markets to Fortune
1000 & government agencies that have
a need for an organizational tool to better manage their time & schedule group
meetings. Publish OnTime for Windows Network version & On Time Enterprise for Novell Netware, Banyan
Vines & Windows NT.

OPRYLAND
Div. of Gaylord Entertainment Co
2800 Opryland Dr
Nashville, TN 37214-1200
Telephone: (615) 889-1000, FAX:
(615) 871-7741, E-Mail: info@
gaylordhotels.com, Web Site: www.
oprylandhotels.com
Pres: Jerry Sevigny
Conducts Business: U.S.
Employees: 4,000
Primary Market Served: Business &
Consumer

Meeting, convention & entertainment
destination.

ORACLE CORP
RP-NFOA

500 Oracle Pkwy
Redwood Shores, CA 94065-1675
Telephone: (650) 506-7000, Toll Free:
(800) 633-0738, FAX: (650) 506-
7200, Web Site: www.oracle.com
Chmn Bd: Jeffrey O. Henley
CEO: Larry Ellison
Pres & CFO: Safra A. Catz
Pres: Mark Hurd
Chief Mktg Officer: Judith Sim
Group VP Product Mktg: Robert
Shrimp
Conducts Business: Worldwide
Primary Market Served: Business &
Consumer
Founded: 1977

Supplier of database management software & services.

ORCHARD SUPPLY HARDWARE
Subs. of Sears Holdings Corp
6450 Via Del Oro St
San Jose, CA 95119
Telephone: (408) 281-3500, FAX:
(408) 225-0388, Web Site: www.osh.
com
CEO: Jerry Post
CFO: Michael Baumann
VP, Mktg: Rick Saunders
Employees: 7,000
Primary Market Served: Consumer
Founded: 1931

Hardware.

OSMONICS INC
5951 Clearwater Dr
Minnetonka, MN 55343-8990
Telephone: (952) 264-3937, Toll Free:
(800) 605-6698, FAX: (952) 536-
3301, Web Site: www.osmonics.com
CEO: D. Dean Spatz
Exec VP, Bus Devel, Strategy, Sls &
Mktg: Ed Fierko
Sr VP, Sls & Mktg: Roger Miller
VP, Fin & Admin: L. Lee Runzheimer
Corp Commun Mgr: Kay A. Kettwig
Mktg Coord: Karen Schurmann
Conducts Business: Worldwide
Employees: 1,350
Primary Market Served: Business
Catalog available online
Advertising/Marketing Budget Related
to Direct Marketing: 0-25%
Founded: 1969
Gross sales or billing: $160,000,000

Manufacturer of high technology
equipment, controls & components that
purify water, separate and handle fluids, remove dissolved solids, concen-
trate wastes and enable clean water to
be recycled or discharged to environment.

OTTO ENVIRONMENTAL SYSTEMS OF NORTH AMERICA
12700 General Dr, PO Box 410251
Charlotte, NC 28273
Telephone: (704) 588-9191, Toll Free:
(800) 227-5885, FAX: (704) 588-
5250, E-Mail: info@otto-usa.com,
Web Site: www.otto-usa.com
CEO: Steve Stradtman
Dir Opers: Brenda Beaver

Manufacture bins & two-wheeled trash
carts for material recycling & solid
wastes.

OUR DESIGNS INC
1212 W Fourth Plain Blvd
Vancouver, WA 98660-2023
Telephone: (859) 282-5500, Toll Free:
(800) 382-5252, FAX: (859) 282-
5508, E-Mail: sales@ourdesigns.
com, Web Site: www.ourdesigns.
com
CEO: Mike Daugherty
Pres: Carol Daugherty
Employees: 22
Primary Market Served: Business &
Consumer
Catalog available online
Direct online sales
Advertising/Marketing Budget Related
to Direct Marketing: 51-75%
Founded: 1981
Gross sales or billing: $2,600,000

Direct mail for firefighters, police officers, EMTs & paramedics.

P & H MINING EQUIPMENT
Subs. of Joy Global Inc
4400 W National Ave
Milwaukee, WI 53214-3639
Telephone: (414) 671-4400, FAX:
(414) 671-7618, Web Site: www.
phmining.com
Chmn: John Hanson
Pres & CEO: Michael W. Sutherlin
CFO & Treas: James H. Woodward Jr.
Exec VP & COO: Mark E. Readinger
Exec VP: Edward L. Doheny II
Conducts Business: Worldwide
Employees: 13,700
Primary Market Served: Business
Catalog available online
Founded: 1884
Gross sales or billing: $2,000,000,000

Manufacture & distribution of equipment for pulp and paper-making machinery, surface & underground mining.

PC/NAMETAG INC
124 Horizon Dr
Verona, WI 53593

Telephone: (608) 845-1850, Toll Free:
(800) 233-9767, E-Mail: sales@
pcnametag.com, Web Site: www.
pcnametag.com
Pres: Nick Topitzes
Sls Asst: Darren Walker
Employees: 45
Primary Market Served: Business
Catalog available online
Direct online sales
Advertising/Marketing Budget Related
to Direct Marketing: 76-100%
Founded: 1980

Sell meeting & conference supplies.

PI INC
213 Dennis St
Athens, TN 37303-2995
Telephone: (423) 745-6213, FAX:
(423) 745-7039, Web Site: www.pi-
inc.com
Pres: Jeff Beene
Conducts Business: Worldwide
Employees: 500
Primary Market Served: Business
Catalog available online
Indirect online sales

Supplier of injection molded plastic
components.

PVC PLASTICS CO
4406 E Morgan Ave
Evansville, IN 47715-2254
Telephone: (812) 476-3592, Toll Free:
(800) 782-7527, FAX: (812) 474-
4531
Pres: William D. Smith
Conducts Business: U.S.
Employees: 35
Primary Market Served: Business &
Consumer
Founded: 1965

Plumbing wholesaler & distributor of
plastic pipes, valves, fittings, pumps &
drainage products.

PACCAR INC
777 106th Ave NE
Bellevue, WA 98004-5027
Telephone: (425) 468-7400, FAX:
(425) 468-8216, Web Site: www.
paccar.com
Chmn & CEO: Mark C. Piggott
Dir: Alison J. Carnwath
Dir: John M. Fluke
Pres: Thomas Plimpton
VP & CIO: Janice Skredsvig
Employees: 21,000
Primary Market Served: Business
Catalog available online
Indirect online sales
Gross sales or billing: $16,000,000,000

Manufacturer of heavy duty trucks &
industrial winches.

PACE INC
255 Air Tool Dr
Southern Pines, NC 28387-3433
Telephone: (910) 695-7223, FAX:
(910) 695-1594, E-Mail: support@
paceworldwide.com, Web Site:
www.paceworldwide.com/index.asp
CEO & Pres: Paul Dunham
Mktg: Sandra Dunham
Primary Market Served: Business

Assembly, rework & repair of highly
advanced electronics including printed
circuit assemblies. Manufactures fume
extraction systems.

PACE UNIVERSITY
1 Pace Plaza
New York, NY 10038
Telephone: (212) 346-1781, Toll Free:
(866) 722-3338, FAX: (212) 346-
1821, Web Site: www.pace.edu
Pres: Stephen Friedman
Exec VP & CFO: Robert C. Almon
VP Enrollment & Placement: Robina
Schepp
VP & Chief Mktg Officer for Univer-
sity Rels: Frederica N. Wald
Conducts Business: U.S.
Primary Market Served: Business &
Consumer
Founded: 1862

Sell Pace University education to both
adolescents & adults.

PACIFIC CYCLE INC
dba Mongoose, Schwinn & GT
Subs of Dorel Industries (CN)
4902 Hammersly Rd
Madison, WI 53711
Telephone: (608) 268-2468, Toll Free:
(800) 724-9466, FAX: (847) 236-
3692, (847) 573-0602, E-Mail: info@
pacificcycle.com, Web Site: www.
pacificcycle.com
Pres & CEO: Jeff Frehner
Exec VP Mktg: Bruno Maier
Conducts Business: Worldwide
Employees: 360
Primary Market Served: Business
Gross sales or billing: $80,700,000

Manufacturer & distributor of Mongoose Pro, Mongoose, MGX, Road-
master & Flexible Flyer brand name
recreation equipment.

PACIFIC PROPELLER INC
Subs. of Precision Aerospace Corp
5802 S 228th St
Kent, WA 98032-1810
Telephone: (253) 872-7767, Toll Free:
(800) 722-7767, FAX: (253) 872-
7221, E-Mail: jheikke@pacprop.
com, Web Site: www.
pacificpropeller.com

VP & Gen Mgr: Jeff Heikke
Prod Sls Mgr: Al Hayward
Sls & Mktg Dir: Don Lownds
Conducts Business: U.S., Canada
Primary Market Served: Business &
Consumer
Direct Marketing ad budget: $72,000
Direct Mail: 26%
Magazines: 74%
Founded: 1946

Manufacture, distribution, servicing &
maintenance of aircraft propellers.

PAL HEALTH TECHNOLOGIES
1805 Riverway Dr
Pekin, IL 61554-9309
Telephone: (309) 347-8785, Toll Free:
(800) 223-2957, FAX: (309) 477-
4456, Web Site: www.palhealth.com
VP: Lois Barnum
Conducts Business: U.S.
Employees: 180
Primary Market Served: Business
Catalog available online
Gross sales or billing: $15,000,000

Manufacture & market national & international prescription orthotics & in-
soles.

PARAGON LABORATORIES
20433 Earl St
Torrance, CA 90503-2414
Telephone: (310) 370-1563, Toll Free:
(800) 231-3670, FAX: (310) 370-
7354, E-Mail: sales@
paragonlabsusa.com, Web Site:
www.paragonlabsusa.com
CEO: Jay Kaufman
COO: Richard Kaufman
Conducts Business: Worldwide
Employees: 50
Primary Market Served: Business &
Consumer
Gross sales or billing: $22,000,000

Manufacturer, distributor & packager
of nutritional supplements, life cycle
products & weight reduction products.

PARKER STEEL CO
4239 Monroe St, Box 2883
Toledo, OH 43606-1943
Telephone: (419) 473-2481, Toll Free:
(800) 333-4140, FAX: (419) 471-
2655, Web Site: www.metricmetal.
com
Pres & CEO: Paul Goldner
Pres: Jerry Hidalgo
VP: Mark Goldner
Mktg: Sharon Goldner
Sls Mgr: Jeff Meyer
Conducts Business: U.S., Canada,
Mexico
Employees: 23

Primary Market Served: Business
Catalog available online
Indirect online sales
Founded: 1955
Gross sales or billing: $6,300,000

Steel warehouse specializing in metric sizes.

PARKER SYSTEMS INC
2880 Yadkin Rd
Chesapeake, VA 23323-0360
Telephone: (757) 485-2955, Toll Free: (866) 472-7537, FAX: (757) 487-5872, E-Mail: info@parkersystemsinc.com, Web Site: www.parkersystemsinc.com
Pres: Ellen Parker
Opers Dir: John Parker
Sls Mgr: Pam McSwain
Conducts Business: Worldwide
Employees: 28
Primary Market Served: Business
Catalog available online
Advertising/Marketing Budget Related to Direct Marketing: 0-25%
Direct Marketing ad budget:
Direct Mail: 30%
Magazines: 10%
Online: 50%
Telephone: 10%
Founded: 1970

Manufacture oil spill cleaning equipment & erosion control products.

PASLODE
Div. of Illinois Tool Works
888 Forest Edge Dr
Vernon Hills, IL 60061-8117
Telephone: (847) 634-1900, Toll Free: (800) 222-6990, FAX: (847) 634-6602, E-Mail: tech@paslode.com, Web Site: www.paslode.com
Mgr: Martin Jahn
Sls Mgr: Mark Boutelle
Bus Unit Mgr: Chuck Heinlen
Conducts Business: U.S., Canada, West Europe, Japan, Australia
Employees: 900
Primary Market Served: Business
Catalog available online
Indirect online sales
Founded: 1935
Gross sales or billing: $150,000,000

Manufacturer & marketer of cordless & pneumatic fastening systems for construction, remodeling & industrial applications.

PASTERNACK ENTERPRISES INC
PO Box 16759
Irvine, CA 92623-6759
Telephone: (949) 261-1920, Web Site: www.pasternack.com

Pres: Chuck Becker
Primary Market Served: Business

PEERLESS RATTAN
687 Miller Rd
Plainwell, MI 49080-9538
Telephone: (269) 685-1858, Toll Free: (877) 611-2263, E-Mail: sales@peerlessrattan.com, Web Site: www.peerlessrattan.com
Owner: Helen Cribbs
Conducts Business: U.S.
Primary Market Served: Business & Consumer
Catalog available online
Indirect online sales
Advertising/Marketing Budget Related to Direct Marketing: 0-25%
Gross sales or billing: $200,000

Mail order house specializing in raw materials of rattan, chair cane webbing, seagrass, basketry reeds, ash splint & fiber rush.

PENNSTREET BAKERY
Div. of Savory Foods
900 Hynes SW
Grand Rapids, MI 49507
Telephone: (616) 241-2583, Toll Free: (800) 84-CAKES, FAX: (616) 241-6332, Web Site: www.pennstreet.com
Pres: Dan Abraham
Conducts Business: U.S.
Employees: 30
Primary Market Served: Business & Consumer
Catalog available online
Direct online sales
Advertising/Marketing Budget Related to Direct Marketing: 0-25%
Founded: 1972

Mail order bakery goods.

PENSKE LOGISTICS
Div. of Penske Corp
Rte 10 Green Hills
Reading, PA 19603
Toll Free: (800) 529-6531, FAX: (610) 775-2449, E-Mail: info.penskelogistics@penske.com, Web Site: www.penskelogistics.com
Pres: Marc Althen
Exec VP Opers: Terry Miller
Sr VP Fin: Paul Ott
Sr VP Sls: Joe Carlier
Sr VP Global Products: Andy Moses
Conducts Business: U.S.
Employees: 10,000
Primary Market Served: Business
Catalog available online
Indirect online sales
Founded: 1969

Gross sales or billing: $2,100,000,000
Provider of integrated logistics services and supply chain management.

PENTON LEARNING SYSTEMS INC
535 Fifth Ave (fl 8)
New York, NY 10017-8011
Telephone: (212) 885-2700, FAX: (212) 885-2703, E-Mail: info@iqpc.com, Web Site: www.iqpc.com
Cust Svc Dir: Patti Kahwaty
Conducts Business: U.S.
Employees: 60
Primary Market Served: Business

Marketer of business educational materials.

PERFECTION TIP CO/ CAMPING PRODUCTS CO
Subs. of Parrish Enterprises
1340 W Cowles St
Long Beach, CA 90803
Telephone: (562) 491-0076, Toll Free: (800) 525-4835, FAX: (562) 435-7599
Pres: J. Parrish
Gen Mgr: David Hill
Conducts Business: Worldwide
Employees: 12
Primary Market Served: Business
Gross sales or billing: $800,000

Manufacture guides/tips for fishing rods. Manufacture & import camping products (i.e., backpack stoves, lanterns, slingshots/ammo, butane fuel) for outdoor sports.

PERFORMANCE MEDIA SOLUTIONS INC & TRUEWORX INC
4001 S Decatur Blvd (#37-425)
Las Vegas, NV 89103-5860
Telephone: (866) 827-7077
Pres: Clive Stanley
Primary Market Served: Business & Consumer

PERNOD RICARD USA
Div. of Joseph E Seagram & Sons
100 Manhattanville Rd
Purchase, NY 10577-2134
Telephone: (914) 848-4800, Web Site: www.pernod-ricard-usa.com
Sr VP of Mktg: Kevin Fennessey
DM Dir: Mary Ellen Griffin
Sr VP Spirits Mktg: Matt Aeppli
Conducts Business: Worldwide
Primary Market Served: Business & Consumer

Producer of premium liquors & wines.

PERRYGRAF

25W550 Geneva Rd (Suite 1934)
Carol Stream, IL 60188-2225
Telephone: (630) 665-3333, Toll Free:
(800) 323-4433, FAX: (630) 665-
3491, E-Mail: info2@
americanperrygraf.com, Web Site:
www.perrygraf.com
Dir Sls & Mktg: Don Hoff
Mktg Dir: Cathie Smith
Sls Mgr: Karen Vidoni
Conducts Business: Worldwide
Employees: 35
Primary Market Served: Business
Catalog available online
Advertising/Marketing Budget Related
to Direct Marketing: 76-100%
Direct Marketing ad budget: $300,000
Direct Mail: 85%
Magazines: 5%
Telephone: 10%
Founded: 1934
Gross sales or billing: $5,000,000

Design & manufacture slide-charts,
wheel-charts & pop-up calendars.

RJ PERSSON ENTERPRISES INC

1208 Kent Ave (Suite 101)
Montrose, CO 81402-5228
Telephone: (303) 249-6000, FAX:
(303) 249-0800
Pres: Richard Persson
Conducts Business: U.S., Canada
Primary Market Served: Consumer
Founded: 1982

List owner with databases for opportunity seekers.

PETEDGE

100 Cummings Ctr (307B)
Beverly, MA 01915-6107
Telephone: (978) 998-8100, Toll Free:
(800) 738-3343, FAX: (978) 887-
8499, E-Mail: support@petedge.com,
Web Site: www.petedge.com
Pres: Andrew Katz
VP, Fin & Opers: Dale Robinson
Primary Market Served: Business &
Consumer
Catalog available online
Direct online sales

Mail order pet supplies.

PFAELZER BROTHERS

Div. of Hickory Farms Inc
1505 Holland Rd
Maumee, OH 43537
Telephone: (419) 893-7611, Toll Free:
(800) 345-9290, FAX: (419) 893-
0164, Web Site: www.
phaelzerbrothers.com
CEO, Pres & Chmn: John J. Langdon
Sr VP, Bus Devel: Ike Herb

VP, HR: Amy Heaton
VP, Sls & Mktg: Erik Long
VP & CFO: Mark Wagner
Conducts Business: U.S., Japan
Employees: 30
Primary Market Served: Business &
Consumer
Catalog available online
Direct online sales
Advertising/Marketing Budget Related
to Direct Marketing: 76-100%

Sell gourmet beef steak gift packs &
beef snack products via direct mail.
Sell beef snacks to distribution companies.

PFIZER INC

235 E 42nd St
New York, NY 10017
Telephone: (212) 733-2323, Web Site:
www.pfizer.com
Chmn Bd & CEO: Ian C. Read
Exec VP Bus Opers & CFO: Frank
D'Amelio
Exec VP Strategy, Portfolio & Comml
Opers: Laurie Olson
Exec VP & Chief Medical Officer: Freda
C. Lewis-Hall
Conducts Business: Worldwide
Employees: 87,000
Primary Market Served: Business &
Consumer
Catalog available online
Founded: 1849
Gross sales or billing: $48,371,000,000

Make & market agricultural, chemical,
pharmaceutical & food products.

PHARMAVITE CORP LLC (HQ)

Subs. of Otsuka
8510 Balboa
Northridge, CA 91325-3583
Telephone: (818) 221-6200, Toll Free:
(800) 423-2405, FAX: (818) 221-
6618, Web Site: www.pharmavite.
com
VP Bus Devel: Tom Zimmerman
Pres & CEO: Connie Barry
Exec VP & CFO: Steve Chopp
Conducts Business: U.S., Canada, Japan
Employees: 850
Primary Market Served: Consumer
Gross sales or billing: $108,900,000

Manufacture vitamins & skin care
products. Fulfill internationally continuity for customer.

PHILIP MORRIS USA INC

Subs. of Altria Group Inc
6601 W Broad St
Richmond, VA 23230-1701

Telephone: (804) 274-2000, FAX:
(804) 484-8231, Web Site: www.
philipmorrisusa.com
Pres & CEO: Cliff B. Fleet
Sr VP Smokable Mfg: Gregory H. Ray
VP & Gen Mgr, Marlboro: K.C.
Crosthwaithe
Primary Market Served: Business
Catalog available online
Indirect online sales
Advertising/Marketing Budget Related
to Direct Marketing: 0-25%

Manufacture & sell tobacco & food
products.

PHILLIPS KILN SERVICE LTD

2607 Dakota Ave Ste 2
South Sioux City, NE 68776-3256
Telephone: (402) 494-6837, Toll Free:
(800) 831-0876, FAX: (402) 494-
6858, E-Mail: info@kilm.com, Web
Site: www.kiln.com
Chmn: Eric Bertness
Pres: Daryl Austin
VP, Intl Sls: Walter M. Gebhart
Conducts Business: U.S., Canada
Employees: 60
Primary Market Served: Business
Catalog available online

Provide replacement parts, installation
& repair of industrial rotary equipment.

PHOENIX LEARNING GROUP INC

141A Millwell Dr
Maryland Heights, MO 63043-2509
Telephone: (314) 569-0211, Toll Free:
(800) 221-1274, FAX: (314) 569-
2834, E-Mail: dealersales@
phoenixlearninggroup.com, Web
Site: www.phoenixlearninggroup.
com
VP Market Devel: Kathy Longsworth
VP, Opers & Mngmt: Erin Bryant
Customer Svc Mgr: Rhonda Sterling
Sls Rep: Antoinette Montegrande
Sls Rep: Shane Egan
Conducts Business: Worldwide
Employees: 25
Primary Market Served: Business &
Consumer
Catalog available online
Direct online sales
Direct Marketing ad budget:
Direct Mail: 10%
Magazines: 20%
Online: 40%
Telephone: 30%
Founded: 1973

Market video cassette & multimedia
programs in fields of health, business
& industry. Also, film & video programs in education, social services &
television.

PHOENIX POKE BOATS INC

106 Bethford Rd
McKee, KY 40447
Telephone: (606) 965-2803, E-Mail:
  pokeboat@pokeboat.com, Web Site:
  www.pokeboat.com
Pres: Tom G. Wilson
Conducts Business: Worldwide
Primary Market Served: Consumer
Catalog available online
Indirect online sales
Advertising/Marketing Budget Related
  to Direct Marketing: 0-25%
Direct Marketing ad budget:
Direct Mail: 10%
Magazines: 60%
Telephone: 30%
Founded: 1973

Manufacture & direct market small
boats & duck boats.

PHOTOWORKS

1 American Rd
Cleveland, OH 44144-2301
Telephone: (206) 281-1390, Toll Free:
  (800) PHOTOWORKS, FAX: (206)
  284-5357, E-Mail: info@
  photoworks.com, Web Site: www.
  photoworks.com
Chmn: Joseph W. Waechter
Pres & CEO: Andy L. Wood
CFO: David M. Douglass
VP Bus Devel: David Kaill
VP Engrng: Dan Zimmerman
Conducts Business: U.S., Canada
Employees: 400
Primary Market Served: Consumer
Catalog available online
Direct online sales
Advertising/Marketing Budget Related
  to Direct Marketing: 0-25%
Direct Marketing ad budget:
Direct Mail: $4,000,000
Founded: 1976
Gross sales or billing: $11,000,000

Specialize in 35mm motion picture
photographic film & processing for
consumers.

PHYSICAL THERAPY
INSTITUTE INC

12630 Monte Vista Rd (Suite 204)
Poway, CA 92064
Telephone: (858) 485-7103
Owner: Mary Hall
Primary Market Served: Consumer
Physical therapy.

PHYSICIANS PLANNING
ASSOCIATION SERVICES

350 Fairway Dr (Suite 200), Hillsboro
  Executive Center N
Deerfield Beach, FL 33441-1834
Telephone: (954) 571-1877, Toll Free:
  (800) 221-2168, FAX: (954) 571-
  8582, E-Mail: insurance@
  assnservices.com, Web Site: www.
  physiciansplanning.com
Chmn: Patricia Arden
Sr VP: Stuart Liebowitz
Insurance Mgr: Michael Haggerty
Membership Svc Mgr: Joseph Santoli
Conducts Business: U.S.
Employees: 25
Primary Market Served: Business &
  Consumer
Catalog available online
Indirect online sales
Advertising/Marketing Budget Related
  to Direct Marketing: 76-100%
Direct Marketing ad budget:
Direct Mail: $600,000
Founded: 1963
Gross sales or billing: $11,000,000

Provide economic & financial benefits
to physicians, dentists & professionals
through American Professional Practice
Association, National Association of
Residents & Interns & National Association of the Professions.

THE PILLSBURY CO

Subs. of General Mills
PO Box 9452, General Mills Inc
Minneapolis, MN 55440-9452
Telephone: (763) 764-7600, Toll Free:
  (800) 248-7310, FAX: (763) 764-
  8330, Web Site: www.pillsbury.com
Chmn Bd & CEO: Kendall J. Powell
Exec VP, Gen Counsel, Chief Compli-
  ance & Risk Mgmt Officer & Sec:
  Roderick A. Palmore
Exec VP & Global Human Resources:
  Michael L. Davis
Exec VP & COO, US: Ian R. Friendly
Exec VP Global Strategy Growth &
  Mktg Innovation: Y. Marc Belton
Exec VP Supply Chain: John Church
Exec VP Innovation Technology &
  Quality: Peter C. Erickson
Sr VP Sls & Channel Devel: Shawn P.
  O'Grady
Exec VP & COO, Intl: Christopher D.
  O'Leary
Sr VP & Chief Mktg Officer: Mark W.
  Addicks
Conducts Business: Worldwide
Primary Market Served: Consumer
Catalog available online
Indirect online sales

International food, drink, restaurant &
retail company.

THE PIN MAN

PO Box 52817
Tulsa, OK 74152-0187
Telephone: (918) 587-2405, FAX:
  (918) 745-2162, Web Site: www.
  positivepin.com
Pres: Bern L. Gentry
VP: Michelle Gentry
Sec & Treas: Eric Cahn
Conducts Business: Canada, Germany,
  England, France
Employees: 8
Primary Market Served: Business &
  Consumer
Advertising/Marketing Budget Related
  to Direct Marketing: 51-75%
Direct Marketing ad budget: $75,000
Magazines: 100%
Founded: 1973
Gross sales or billing: $1,000,000

Custom & stock lapel pins, totes, pens,
pencils, mugs, smocks, plaques, awards
& teacher gifts.

PINE CASTLE ANIMAL
HOSPITAL

5250 S Orange Ave
Orlando, FL 32809
Telephone: (407) 855-5010
Owner: Craig Lautenschlager DVM
Primary Market Served: Consumer
Animal hospital.

PINKERTON SECURITY &
INVESTIGATION SERVICES

Subs Securitas Security Services USA,
  Inc
2 Campus Dr
Parsippany, NJ 07054-4499
Telephone: (973) 397-2276, Toll Free:
  (800) 724-1616, FAX: (973) 397-
  2491, Web Site: www.ci-pinkerton.
  com
Pres: Ron Long
VP Sls & Mktg: Bruce Scherer
Conducts Business: Worldwide
Primary Market Served: Business
Advertising/Marketing Budget Related
  to Direct Marketing: 26-50%
Founded: 1850

Security & investigative agency.

PIZZA HUT INC

Subs. of Yum! Brands Inc
7100 Corporate Dr
Plano, TX 75024
Telephone: (972) 338-7700, Toll Free:
  (866) 298-6986, FAX: (972) 338-
  6869, Web Site: www.pizzahut.com
CEO: Scott Bergen
Pres: David Gibbs
Chief Mktg Officer: Carrie Walsh
Primary Market Served: Business &
  Consumer
Restaurant franchiser.

POLAROID CORP
4350 Baker Rd
Minnetonka, MN 55343-8684
Telephone: (781) 386-2000, Toll Free:
(800) 765-2764, FAX: (781) 386-
3263, E-Mail: marketing@polaroid.
com, Web Site: www.polaroid.com
CEO: Scott W. Hardy
Primary Market Served: Business &
Consumer

Design, manufacture & market worldwide a variety of products primarily in
instant imaging recording.

POLY ONE CORP
33587 Walker Rd
Avon Lake, OH 44012
Telephone: (440) 930-1000, Toll Free:
(866) POLY-ONE, FAX: (440) 930-
1428, Web Site: www.polyone.com
Pres, CEO & Chmn Bd: Steve Newlin
Sr VP & CFO: W. David Wilson
Sr VP, CIO & HR: Kenneth M. Smith
Sr VP & Gen Mgr: Bernard Baert
Sr VP: Michael E. Kahler
Conducts Business: Worldwide
Primary Market Served: Business
Catalog available online
Indirect online sales
Advertising/Marketing Budget Related
to Direct Marketing: 0-25%
Gross sales or billing: $1,000,000,000

Business-to-business marketer of plastic raw materials.

POLYNESIAN CULTURAL
CENTER
2255 Kuhio Ave (Suite 1010)
Honolulu, HI 96815-2648
Telephone: (808) 293-3333, Toll Free:
(800) 367-7060, FAX: (888) 722-
7339, E-Mail: internetrez@
polynesia.com, Web Site: www.
polynesia.com
Chmn: Ted Jacobson
Pres: Lester W.B. Moore
Sr VP, Mktg & Sls: Alfred Grace
VP, Fin: Greg Gollaher
Retail Sls & Mktg Mgr: Eric Workman
Conducts Business: U.S.
Employees: 1,000
Primary Market Served: Business &
Consumer
Catalog available online
Indirect online sales
Advertising/Marketing Budget Related
to Direct Marketing: 0-25%
Founded: 1963
Gross sales or billing: $1,000,000

Merchandiser of South Pacific crafts &
goods. Producer & distributor of Polynesian videos, audios, books & IMAX
films.

POSITION TECHNOLOGIES
INC
2000 S Batavia Ave (Suite 351)
Geneva, IL 60134-3300
Telephone: (630) 262-5300, FAX:
(630) 232-2998, Web Site: www.
positiontech.com
Pres: Ken Johnson
Primary Market Served: Business

POSTY CARDS INC
1600 Olive St
Kansas City, MO 64127-2539
Telephone: (816) 231-2323, Toll Free:
(800) 554-5018, FAX: (888) 577-
3800, E-Mail: customerservice@
postycards.com, Web Site: www.
postycards.com
Pres: Lance H. Jessee
Mktg Dir: Janet Coats
Conducts Business: Worldwide
Employees: 38
Primary Market Served: Business &
Consumer
Catalog available online
Indirect online sales
Advertising/Marketing Budget Related
to Direct Marketing: 0-25%
Founded: 1948
Gross sales or billing: $4,000,000

Manufacture & market greeting cards
& calendars.

POWER & TELEPHONE
SUPPLY
44 Hull St # 2
Randolph, VT 05060-1102
Toll Free: (800) 451-4381, FAX: (802)
234-5006, E-Mail: cablesales@
ptsupply.com, Web Site: www.
ptsupply.com/enterprise
Dir Sls: Cyrus Parker
Mktg Coord: Valerie Wild
Conducts Business: U.S.
Primary Market Served: Business
Catalog available online
Advertising/Marketing Budget Related
to Direct Marketing: 51-75%
Founded: 1946

Distributor of communication cables,
wire, supplies & equipment, test equipment, fiber optic & security cameras.

POWER MUSIC
P.O. Box 3030
Salt Lake City, UT 84110
Telephone: (801) 292-2418, Toll Free:
(800) 777-BEAT, FAX: (801) 292-
2462, Web Site: www.powermusic.
com
Owner: Richard Petty
Mktg Dir: Jodie Erickson
Primary Market Served: Business &
Consumer

Direct online sales
Advertising/Marketing Budget Related
to Direct Marketing: 76-100%

Exercise music tapes for health clubs &
aerobics instructors & a new line of
music tapes for home workouts.

PRACTICING LAW
INSTITUTE
1177 Avenue of the Americas
New York, NY 10036-2714
Telephone: (212) 824-5700, Toll Free:
(800) 260 4PLI, FAX: (800) 321-
0093, E-Mail: info@pli.edu, Web
Site: www.pli.edu
Exec Dir: Victor J. Rubino
Direct Mktg Mgr: Nadine Hovan
Assoc Dir Mktg: Arlene Bein
Conducts Business: Worldwide
Employees: 160
Primary Market Served: Business
Direct online sales
Founded: 1933

Help lawyers maintain their compe-
tence by keeping up with changes in
the law resulting from new statutes, decisions, regulations & developments in
the social & economic climate. Offer
programs, specialized law books,
audio, videotapes & online services.

PRATT CORP
3035 N Shadeland Ave (Suite 100)
Indianapolis, IN 46226-6231
Telephone: (317) 924-3201, Toll Free:
(800) 428-7728, FAX: (317) 927-
0653, Web Site: www.prattcorp.com
Pres: Daniel D. Pratt Jr
VP: Thomas Pratt
Conducts Business: U.S
Employees: 100
Primary Market Served: Business

Manufacturer of promotional banners,
flags, bunting, pennants, sign kits &
balloons.

PREMIER FARNELL CORP
4180 Highlander Pkwy
Richfield, OH 44286-9352
Telephone: (216) 525-4300, Toll Free:
(800) 458-3222, FAX: (216) 525-
4509, E-Mail: information@
premierfarnell.com, Web Site: www.
premierfarnell.com
Pres Premier Holding Inc: Peter D.
Costello
VP Premier Farnell Corp: Joseph Dap-
rile
Head Corp Commun: Jenny Peters
Conducts Business: Worldwide
Employees: 4,100
Primary Market Served: Business
Founded: 1966

Gross sales or billing: $905,100,000

Manufacture fire-fighting equipment; distribute electronic components, industrial maintenance & repair products.

PREMIER PACKAGING CORP

PO Box 352
Victor, NY 14564-0352
Toll Free: (877) 924-8460, FAX: (585) 924-8753, E-Mail: info@ premiercustompkg.com, Web Site: www.premiercustompkg.com
VP: Paul Dougherty
Acct Exec: Peter Ashe
Acct Exec: Glenn Marino
Sls & Mktg Mgr: David Denn
Sls Support Mgr: Bryan William
Conducts Business: U.S., Canada
Employees: 40
Primary Market Served: Business
Advertising/Marketing Budget Related to Direct Marketing: 0-25%
Direct Marketing ad budget: $40,000
Founded: 1989

Manufacture custom packaging for all forms of media to be mailed/delivered to end user.

PRIME

Div. of Prime Resources
1100 Boston Ave
Bridgeport, CT 06610
Telephone: (203) 331-9100, Toll Free: (800) 873-7746, FAX: (203) 330-0123, Web Site: www.primeline.com
Pres: Rick Brenner
Conducts Business: Worldwide
Employees: 18
Primary Market Served: Business
Catalog available online
Direct online sales
Direct Marketing ad budget: $150,000
Direct Mail: 50%
Magazines: 35%
Newspapers: 10%
Telephone: 5%

Manufacturer of battery operated pencil sharpeners, telephone indexes, desk sets, organizers & office accessories.

PRINCESS HOUSE INC

470 Miles Standish Blvd
Taunton, MA 02780
Telephone: (508) 823-0711, (508) 832-6800, Toll Free: (800) 622-0039, FAX: (508) 823-5182, Web Site: www.princesshouse.com
Chmn Bd: James Northrop
Pres: Timothy J. Brown
Sr Mgr Programs: Stefani Shea
Unit Organizer: Lavena Pleva
Conducts Business: U.S., Canada, Mexico, U.K., Australia

Employees: 600
Primary Market Served: Consumer
Catalog available online
Gross sales or billing: $150,000,000

Direct sales (party plan) of crystal & porcelain tabletop products as well as other home decorative & gift items.

THE PRINCETON REVIEW

24 Prime Pkwy (Suite 201)
Natick, MA 01760
Toll Free: (800) 273-8439, E-Mail: prep@review.com, Web Site: www.princetonreview.com
CEO: Kate Eberle Walker
Primary Market Served: Consumer

Test preparation and college admission services company.

THE PROCTER & GAMBLE CO

1 Procter & Gamble Plaza
Cincinnati, OH 45201
Telephone: (513) 983-1100, Web Site: www.pg.com
Chmn Bd, Pres & CEO: Alan G. Lafley
Vice Chmn Global Opers: Werner Geissler
CFO: Jon R. Moeller
Global Consumer & Market Knowledge Officer: Joan M. Lewis
Global Brand Building Officer: Marc S. Pritchard
Global Customer Bus Devel Officer: Carolyn M. Tastad
Conducts Business: Worldwide
Employees: 77,300
Primary Market Served: Business & Consumer
Founded: 1837

Manufacture & market laundry, cleaning & personal care products, pharmaceuticals, food & beverages.

PROFESSIONAL BINDING PRODUCTS INC

2192-A Anchor Ct
Thousand Oaks, CA 91320
Toll Free: (800) 443-7557, (800) 545-9413, E-Mail: sales@probinding.com, Web Site: www.probinding.com
Pres: Michael Drew
Primary Market Served: Business & Consumer

Marketer & distributor of laminating & binding machines.

PROFILE MAILING SERVICE INC

575 Underhill Blvd (Suite 132)
Syosset, NY 11791-3416
Telephone: (516) 802-3974

Pres: Marc Goldstein
Conducts Business: U.S.
Employees: 9
Primary Market Served: Business
Advertising/Marketing Budget Related to Direct Marketing: 0-25%
Direct Marketing ad budget:
Direct Mail: 50%
Magazines: 20%
Newspapers: 20%
Telephone: 10%
Founded: 1992
Gross sales or billing: $1,300,000

Standard mailing services, data processing, laser personalization & fulfillment services.

PROGRESS SOFTWARE CORP

14 Oak Park
Bedford, MA 01730
Telephone: (781) 280-4000, Toll Free: (800) 477-6473, FAX: (781) 280-4095, Web Site: www.progress.com
Pres & CEO: Joseph W. Allsop
Conducts Business: Worldwide
Primary Market Served: Business
Catalog available online
Gross sales or billing: $405,376

Application development & database software.

PROJECTION VIDEO SERVICES

5803 Rolling Rd (Suite 207)
Springfield, VA 22152-1056
Telephone: (703) 912-1334, Toll Free: (800) 377-7650, FAX: (703) 912-1350, Web Site: www.projection.com
Pres: Dave Campbell
Corp Dir Mktg & Commun: Nancy DeBrosse
Conducts Business: U.S.
Employees: 150
Primary Market Served: Business & Consumer
Gross sales or billing: $7,000,000

Audio-visual & computer rental service firm with branches in Boston, New York, New Orleans, Philadelphia, Washington D.C., San Francisco & Anaheim.

PROTECTION ONE INC

1035 N Third St (Suite 101)
Lawrence, KS 66044
Telephone: (785) 856-5500, Toll Free: (800) GET-HELP, Web Site: www.protectionone.com
Pres, CEO & Dir: Richard Ginsburg
Exec VP & COO: Peter J. Pefanis
Dir Mktg: Robert McClarin
Exec VP & CFO: Darius G. Nevin

Sr VP: Joseph Sanchez
Mgr: Nancy Roll
Primary Market Served: Consumer
Gross sales or billing: $270,000,000

Security alarm service.

PRUDENT PUBLISHING CO

65 Challenger Rd
Ridgefield Park, NJ 07660-2111
Telephone: (201) 641-7900, FAX:
  (800) 772-1144
Chmn Bd Dirs: Alan Solow
Mktg Dir: Tony Patella
Conducts Business: U.S., Canada
Employees: 80
Primary Market Served: Business &
  Consumer
Gross sales or billing: $7,900,000

Sell custom imprinted Christmas cards.

FRED PRYOR SEMINARS

Div. of Park University Enterprises
5700 Broadmoor St (Suite 300)
Mission, KS 66202-2415
Telephone: (913) 967-8518, Toll Free:
  (800) 780-8476, FAX: (913) 967-
  8849, E-Mail: customerservice@
  pryor.com, Web Site: www.pryor.
  com
CEO: Lauren Wright
Pres: John Brown
Mktg Supvr: Janet Turner
Conducts Business: U.S., U.K., Aus-
  tralia, New Zealand, Germany
Employees: 90
Primary Market Served: Business
Catalog available online
Direct online sales

Provide business & educational semi-
nars/audio & video cassettes.

PUTT PUTT FUN CENTERS

300 S Liberty St (Suite 100)
Winston-Salem, NC 27101-5279
Telephone: (336) 714-3950, Toll Free:
  (866) PUTT-PUTT, FAX: (336) 714-
  3955, Web Site: www.puttputt.com
CEO: David Callahan
Conducts Business: U.S., Canada, Leb-
  anon, Japan, Indonesia
Primary Market Served: Business &
  Consumer
Catalog available online
Advertising/Marketing Budget Related
  to Direct Marketing: 0-25%

Sell equipment & supplies to family
amusement centers including clothing,
equipment, resale merchandise, promotional & operational supplies & construction materials. Offer supply &
design services for miniature golf, driving ranges, batting cages, go-carts,
bumper boats & indoor soft play.

QC SUPPLY LLC

PO Box 581
Schuyler, NE 68661-0581
Telephone: (402) 352-3167, Web Site:
  www.qcsupply.com
Pres: Lonnie Kitt
Primary Market Served: Business &
  Consumer

QUADRANT ENGINEERING PLASTIC PRODUCTS

PO Box 14235
Reading, PA 19612-4235
Telephone: (610) 320-6600, Toll Free:
  (800) 366-0300, FAX: (610) 320-
  6868, Web Site: www.quadrantepp.
  com
Pres & CEO: Glen Steady
VP, Mktg: Earl Wester
Mktg Commun Mgr: Kress Swartz
CEO: Michael Kotch
Conducts Business: U.S., Canada,
  Mexico, Europe, Far East
Primary Market Served: Business
Catalog available online
Indirect online sales
Advertising/Marketing Budget Related
  to Direct Marketing: 51-75%

Industrial plastics.

THE QUAKER OATS CO

Div. of PepsiCo Americas Foods
PO Box 049003
Chicago, IL 60604-9003
Telephone: (312) 821-1000, Toll Free:
  (800) 367-6287, FAX: (312) 222-
  8323, Web Site: www.quakeroats.
  com
CEO, PepsiCo Americas Foods: Brian
  Cornell
Pres Quaker Foods & Snacks, NA: Jose
  Luis Prado
Primary Market Served: Business &
  Consumer
Catalog available online
Indirect online sales

Foods & beverages.

QUILL CORP

Subs. of Staples Inc
100 Schelter Rd
Lincolnshire, IL 60069
Telephone: (847) 876-3535, Toll Free:
  (800) 789-1331, Web Site: www.
  quill.com
Pres: Sergio Pereira
VP Mktg: Kayrle Sieber
VP Mdsg: Kevin Wood
Conducts Business: U.S., Canada
Employees: 1,000
Primary Market Served: Business

Sell office products to business & professional people.

R&S INDUSTRIES CORP

1065 Appalachian Trl
Chesterfield, MO 63017-1948
Telephone: (314) 781-5400, FAX:
  (314) 781-5169, E-Mail:
  sendeverything@
  miraclepolishingcloth.com, Web
  Site: www.miraclepolishingcloth.
  com
Pres & Co-Owner: Ronald B. Schwartz
VP & Co-Owner: Steven Rubin
Conducts Business: Worldwide
Employees: 10
Primary Market Served: Consumer
Catalog available online
Indirect online sales
Advertising/Marketing Budget Related
  to Direct Marketing: 76-100%
Direct Marketing ad budget: $500,000
Direct Mail: 80%
Magazines: 20%
Founded: 1965
Gross sales or billing: $2,000,000

Manufacture "Miracle Polishing
Cloth," a chemically treated cotton
cloth which cleans, polishes & protects
ANY surface.

RACER'S EQUIPMENT WAREHOUSE

111 Commerce Dr
Warwick, RI 02886-2429
Telephone: (401) 348-6010, Toll Free:
  (800) 556-2864, FAX: (401) 348-
  6023, E-Mail: scott@racers-eq.com,
  Web Site: www.racers-eq.com
Pres: Ralph Accinno
HR: Nancy Accinno
VP Fin: Peter Accinno
Conducts Business: Worldwide
Employees: 25
Primary Market Served: Business
Advertising/Marketing Budget Related
  to Direct Marketing: 0-25%
Direct Marketing ad budget:
Direct Mail: 60%
TV/Radio: 20%
Telephone: 20%
Founded: 1965
Gross sales or billing: $3,700,000

High performance auto parts & accessories.

RAINBOW ART GLASS

1761 Rte 34 S
Wall, NJ 07727-3935
Telephone: (732) 681-6003, Toll Free:
  (800) 526-2356, FAX: (732) 681-
  4984, E-Mail: info@rainbowartglass.
  com, Web Site: www.
  rainbowartglass.com
Pres: Charles M. Longo
VP: Anthony Longo
Conducts Business: U.S., Canada, Europe

Employees: 29
Primary Market Served: Business &
    Consumer
Founded: 1965
Gross sales or billing: $4,500,000

Manufacture stained glass lamp kits,
supplies & other stained glass items.
Sell both wholesale & retail.

RALEY'S BEL AIR MARKETS

Div. of Raley's
500 W Capitol Ave
West Sacramento, CA 95605-2696
Telephone: (916) 373-3333, FAX:
    (916) 373-6351, Web Site: www.
    raleys.com
Pres & CEO: Bill Coyne
Conducts Business: U.S.
Employees: 15,000
Primary Market Served: Consumer
Founded: 1935
Gross sales or billing: $3,400,000,000

Supermarket chain in Northern California.

RAND MATERIAL HANDLING EQUIPMENT CO INC

Div. of Lab Safety Supply Inc
PO Box 5195
Janesville, WI 53547-5195
Telephone: (401) 751-7657, Toll Free:
    (800) 366-2300, FAX: (800) 755-
    7263, E-Mail: cs@randmh.com, Web
    Site: www.randmh.com
Pres: James Fitzgerald Sr
Primary Market Served: Business
Founded: 1972

Material handling & packaging products sold to a wide range of businesses,
wholesalers, manufacturers & government agencies.

RAPIDS WHOLESALE EQUIPMENT

6201 S Gateway Dr
Marion, IA 52302-9430
Telephone: (319) 447-1670, Toll Free:
    (800) 472-7431, FAX: (319) 447-
    1680, (800) 858-0327, E-Mail:
    judys@rapidswholesale.com, Web
    Site: www.rapidswholesale.com
VP: Diane Dodds
Pres: Joe Schmitt
VP Mktg: Joe Dodds
VP: Geri Schmitt
Conducts Business: U.S.
Employees: 48
Primary Market Served: Business
Founded: 1936
Gross sales or billing: $14,800,000

Supplier & manufacturer of refrigeration, beer & restaurant equipment, food
service equipment & furniture.

RAYCOM SPORTS

Div. of Raycom Media
1900 W Morehead St
Charlotte, NC 28208-5228
Telephone: (704) 378-4456/4400,
    FAX: (704) 378-4465, E-Mail:
    whicks@raycomsports.com, Web
    Site: raycomsports.com
Pres: Ken Haines
Dir ACC Properties: Lisa Shaw
Sls Dir: Jim Brannon
Dir Event Acctg: Stephanie Miller
Employees: 50
Primary Market Served: Business &
    Consumer
Direct online sales
Founded: 1979

Documentary, sports & entertainment
programs produced for TV & sold to
sports fans & video distributors on a
national level.

READING FOR EDUCATION

180 Freedom Ave
Murfreesboro, TN 37129-0071
Telephone: (615) 896-3800
Pres: Elijah Collard

RECOGNITION PRODUCTS INTERNATIONAL

8706 Commerce Dr (Suite 6)
Easton, MD 21601-6903
Telephone: (410) 820-0022, Toll Free:
    (800) 292-7354, FAX: (410) 820-
    5044, E-Mail: info@
    recognitionproducts.com, Web Site:
    www.shoprecognitionproducts.com
CEO: Donald A. Schwartz
Pres: Charles W. Bresloff
Controller: Vickie Sharp
Sls Mgr: Mike Ridge
VP: Kay Stein
Conducts Business: U.S.
Employees: 9
Primary Market Served: Business &
    Consumer
Catalog available online
Direct online sales
Advertising/Marketing Budget Related
    to Direct Marketing: 0-25%
Direct Marketing ad budget:
Direct Mail: 20%
Online: 80%
Founded: 2000
Gross sales or billing: $2,100,000

Manufactures wholesale awards recognition and promotional products including medals, emblematic jewelry &
plaques.

RECOGNITION SYSTEMS (DOT WORKS)

30 Harbor Park Dr
Port Washington, NY 11050
Telephone: (516) 625-5000, FAX:
    (516) 625-1507, E-Mail: wade@
    dotworks.com, Web Site: www.
    dotworks.com
Mktg Dir: John Bender
VP: Linda McLuster
Mktg Mgr: Liz Barrington
Conducts Business: U.S., Canada
Employees: 15
Primary Market Served: Business

Distributor of graphic arts, films &
chemicals.

RECORDING FOR THE BLIND & DYSLEXIC INC

20 Roszel Rd
Princeton, NJ 08540-9983
Telephone: (609) 452-0606, Toll Free:
    (800) 221-4792, FAX: (609) 520-
    7996, E-Mail: info@rfbd.org, Web
    Site: www.rfbd.org
Mail Mktg Dir: JoAnne Rygiel
Pres: John Kelly
Publ Editor: Paula Whitcomb
Conducts Business: U.S., Canada,
    Mexico, Europe
Employees: 200
Primary Market Served: Business &
    Consumer
Catalog available online
Direct online sales
Advertising/Marketing Budget Related
    to Direct Marketing: 0-25%
Founded: 1948

Educational & professional audio tapes
& computer discs for visually impaired
& learning disabled nationwide.

JP REDINGTON & CO

PO Box 429
Huntington, NY 11743
Telephone: (631) 754-0111, FAX:
    (631) 757-0878
Pres: Marie Ricciardi
Conducts Business: U.S., Europe, Asia
Employees: 5
Primary Market Served: Consumer
Advertising/Marketing Budget Related
    to Direct Marketing: 0-25%
Founded: 1897
Gross sales or billing: $1,000,000

Manufactures public building furniture.
Church pews

REED EXHIBITIONS

Div. of Reed Elsevier plc
383 Main Ave
Norwalk, CT 06851-1500
Telephone: (203) 840-4800, Toll Free:
    (888) 745-7644, FAX: (203) 840-
    5805, E-Mail: inquiry@reedexpo.
    com, Web Site: www.reedexpo.com
Chmn & CEO: Mike Rusbridge
Reg Pres The Americas: Chet Burchett

COO: Chris Rees
Primary Market Served: Business & Consumer

Trade show management. Acts as relationship broker - identifying, targeting, attracting and matching the needs of buyers and suppliers.

REGAL WARE INC

1675 Reigle Dr
Kewaskum, WI 53040-8923
Telephone: (262) 626-2121, E-Mail: pseitz@regalware.com, Web Site: www.regalware.com
Pres & CEO: Jeffrey A. Reigle
COO: Douglas J. Reigle
Dir Commun: Pat Seitz
Conducts Business: U.S., Canada, Mexico, Europe, Japan, Central America, South America, Philippines, New Zealand
Employees: 500
Primary Market Served: Business
Catalog available online
Direct online sales
Advertising/Marketing Budget Related to Direct Marketing: 0-25%
Founded: 1945

Manufacturer of stainless steel and cast aluminum cookware for direct marketing and retail companies.

REID SUPPLY CO

2265 Black Creek Rd
Muskegon, MI 49444-2673
Telephone: (231) 777-3951, Toll Free: (800) 253-0421, FAX: (231) 767-3882, E-Mail: mail@reidsupply.com, Web Site: www.reidsupply.com
Mktg Dir: Greg Palmer
Conducts Business: Worldwide
Primary Market Served: Business
Catalog available online
Direct online sales
Advertising/Marketing Budget Related to Direct Marketing: 51-75%
Founded: 1948

Global industrial supplies distributor.

RELIABLE TECHNOLOGIES INC

55 S Commercial St
Manchester, NH 03101
Telephone: (603) 644-2528, Toll Free: (800) 346-7890, FAX: (603) 627-5553, Web Site: www.tei-imaging.com
Mktg & Sls Mgr: Sarah Scheffer
Sls Mngr: Nancy Warner
Customer Svc Mgr: Scott Spaulding
Svc Mgr: Matt Morin
Svc Supvr: Julian Reynolds
Conducts Business: Worldwide
Employees: 75

Primary Market Served: Business & Consumer
Catalog available online
Advertising/Marketing Budget Related to Direct Marketing: 76-100%
Gross sales or billing: $5,000,000
Direct marketing of computer supplies, accessories, & add-ons.

RELIANT ENERGY

Div. of NRG Energy
1201 Fannin St
Houston, TX 77002
Telephone: (713) 497-7794, Toll Free: (866) 222-7100, Web Site: www.reliant.com
Pres: Elizabeth Killinger
Sr VP & Chief Mktg Officer: Sicily Dickenson

Retail energy service provider.

RENT-A-CENTER INC

5501 Headquarters Dr
Plano, TX 75024
Telephone: (972) 801-1100, Toll Free: (800) 275-2996, FAX: (972) 943-0113, Web Site: www.rentacenter.com
CEO: Robert D. Davis
Pres & COO: Mitchell Fadel
Sr VP Mktg & Chief Customer Officer: Rita E. Bargerhuff
Primary Market Served: Business & Consumer
Catalog available online
Direct online sales
Founded: 1986
Gross sales or billing: $2,400,000,000

A rent-to-own industry.

REPLOGLE GLOBES INC

2801 S 25th Ave
Broadview, IL 60155-4500
Telephone: (708) 343-0900, FAX: (708) 343-0923, E-Mail: info@replogleglobes.com, Web Site: www.replogleglobes.com
Co-Pres & Treas: Ed Dieschbourg
Pres: Dan Dillon
National Acct Mgr: Rodney Wachowiak
New Bus Devel: Dell Torgerson
Sls Mgr: Bob Mitchell
Export Sls Mgr: Patricia Boling
Special Accts Mgr: Jane Quinn
Conducts Business: Worldwide
Employees: 150
Primary Market Served: Business
Catalog available online
Indirect online sales
Advertising/Marketing Budget Related to Direct Marketing: 0-25%
Direct Marketing ad budget:
Direct Mail: 30%
Magazines: 65%

Telephone: 5%
Founded: 1930
Manufacturer of geographical globes.

REXCRAFT WEDDING INVITATIONS

Div. of Artco
One Stationery Pl
Rexburg, ID 83441
Telephone: (208) 359-1000, Toll Free: (800) 635-3898, FAX: (800) 826-2712, E-Mail: cs@rexcraft.com, Web Site: www.rexcraft.com
Pres: Garth Miller
Direct Mail Mktg Coord: Blair Taylor
Conducts Business: U.S., Canada, Australia
Primary Market Served: Consumer
Catalog available online
Indirect online sales
Advertising/Marketing Budget Related to Direct Marketing: 76-100%
Direct Marketing ad budget:
Magazines: 100%
Founded: 1910

Sell a varied line of wedding invitations, napkins imprinted in foil & miscellaneous reception & gift items.

RHODE ISLAND NOVELTY

5 Industrial Rd
Cumberland, RI 02864-4714
Telephone: (401) 335-3300, Toll Free: (800) 528-5599, FAX: (800) 448-1775, E-Mail: info@rinovelty.com, Web Site: www.rinovelty.com
Webmaster/Sys Admin: Scott Bloodworth
Primary Market Served: Business
Catalog available online
Direct online sales
Founded: 1986

RICCI LEE HUBBART ASSOCIATES INC

PO Box 1694
Cupertino, CA 95015-1694
Telephone: (408) 725-1242, FAX: (408) 716-2704, E-Mail: susan@riccilee.com, Web Site: www.riccilee.com
Pres: Susan Hubbart
Primary Market Served: Business
Founded: 1992

Search consultant agency.

RICH BRANDS

1819 E Morten Ave (Suite 110)
Phoenix, AZ 85020-4661
Telephone: (602) 889-4800, Toll Free: (877) 856-1753, FAX: (602) 889-4830, E-Mail: sales@esscentualbrands.com, Web Site: esscentualbrands.com

Pres: Mark Grodsky
Direct Mktg Mgr: Susan Baler
Conducts Business: U.S., Europe
Employees: 500
Primary Market Served: Consumer
Catalog available online
Direct online sales
Gross sales or billing: $15,600,000

Manufacturer and distributor of personal care products and room fragrances.

RICH PRODUCTS CORP

One Robert Rich Way
Buffalo, NY 14213-1701
Telephone: (716) 878-8000, Toll Free: (800) 828-2021, FAX: (716) 878-8765, Web Site: www.richs.com
Chmn: Robert E. Rich Jr
Vice Chmn: Melinda R. Rich
Pres, CEO & Dir: William G. Gisel Jr.
Exec VP, CFO: James Deuschle
Sr VP, CIO: Paul Klein
Conducts Business: U.S., Canada
Employees: 6,500
Primary Market Served: Business & Consumer
Catalog available online
Direct online sales
Advertising/Marketing Budget Related to Direct Marketing: 0-25%
Founded: 1983
Gross sales or billing: $2,400,000

Sell tickets & merchandise.

RICHARDSON ELECTRONICS LTD

40 W 267 Keslinger Rd
Lafox, IL 60147
Telephone: (630) 208-2200, FAX: (630) 208-2550, E-Mail: edg@rell.com, Web Site: www.rell.com
CEO & Pres: E.J. Richardson
CFO: Kathleen Dvorak
VP, Worldwide Sls: Robert Prince
VP, Mktg Opers: Brad Knechtal
Mktg Mgr: Julie Gentry
Conducts Business: Worldwide
Primary Market Served: Business & Consumer
Catalog available online
Indirect online sales
Advertising/Marketing Budget Related to Direct Marketing: 0-25%
Direct Marketing ad budget: $1,200,000
Direct Mail: 10%
Magazines: 40%
Online: 50%
Founded: 1947
Gross sales or billing: $625,000,000

Global provider of "engineered solutions," serving the RF and wireless communications, industrial power conversion, and display systems markets. Delivers engineered solutions for its

customers' needs through product manufacturing, systems integration, prototype design and manufacture, testing and logistics.

RIO BRANDS

Div. of All-Luminum Products Inc
10981 Decatur Rd
Philadelphia, PA 19154-3297
Telephone: (215) 632-2800, FAX: (215) 824-1172
Chmn: Bob Cohen
Pres: Warren Cohen
Exec VP, Sls & Mktg: Mark J. Cohen
Conducts Business: U.S.
Employees: 1,650
Primary Market Served: Business
Founded: 1947
Gross sales or billing: $18,900,000

Manufacturer of folding tables, folding cots & beach chairs. Importer of office chairs. Sell to all warehouse clubs, mass merchants, drug stores & department stores.

RIO GRANDE

Div. of The Bell Group
7500 Bluewater Rd NW
Albuquerque, NM 87121-1962
Telephone: (505) 839-3000, Toll Free: (800) 545-6566, FAX: (800) 965-2329, E-Mail: info@riogrande.com, Web Site: www.riogrande.com
CEO: Andrea Hill
Pres: Hugh Bell
Conducts Business: Worldwide
Employees: 400
Primary Market Served: Business
Catalog available online
Direct online sales
Advertising/Marketing Budget Related to Direct Marketing: 76-100%
Direct Marketing ad budget:
Direct Mail: 100%
Founded: 1944
Gross sales or billing: $31,000,000

Wholesale distributor of supplies to the jewelry industry.

RJ REYNOLDS TOBACCO CO

Subs. of Reynolds American Inc
PO Box 2959
Winston Salem, NC 27102
Telephone: (336) 741-5111, Toll Free: (800) 341-5211, Web Site: www.rjrt.com
Pres & Chief Comml Officer: Andrew D. Gilchrist
Exec VP Consumer Mktg: J. Brice O'Brien
Exec VP Trade Mktg: Robert D. Stowe
CFO: Mark A. Peters
Primary Market Served: Consumer

Tobacco company.

C H ROBINSON WORLDWIDE INC

14701 Charlson Rd
Eden Prairie, MN 55347-5076
Telephone: (952) 937-8500, FAX: (952) 937-6740, E-Mail: info@chrobinson.com, Web Site: www.chrobinson.com
Chmn, CEO & Pres: John P. Wiehoff
Sr VP: Jim Butts
VP: Molly M. DuBois
VP: Linda Feuss
VP, HR: Laura Gillund
Conducts Business: Worldwide
Employees: 3,700
Primary Market Served: Business
Advertising/Marketing Budget Related to Direct Marketing: 0-25%
Gross sales or billing: $6,600,000,000

Third party provider of all modes of transportation.

ROBINSON HOME PRODUCTS

170 Lawrence Bell Dr (Suite 110)
Buffalo, NY 14221-8484
Telephone: (716) 685-6300, FAX: (716) 685-4916
VP, Mktg: Joan Skerker
VP, Admin: Larry Skerker
VP: Robert Skerker
Conducts Business: U.S., Canada, Europe, Far East
Employees: 61
Primary Market Served: Business & Consumer
Gross sales or billing: $80,000,000

Kitchen housewares, including cutlery, kitchen tools, promotional sets, gift sets & gadgets.

ROCKWELL AUTOMATION

1201 S 2nd St
Milwaukee, WI 53204-2410
Telephone: (414) 382-2000, FAX: (414) 382-4444, Web Site: www.rockwellautomation.com
Pres, CEO & Chmn: Keith Nosbusch
Sr VP & CFO: Theodore D. Crandall
Sr VP: John D. Cohn
Sr VP: Steven A. Eisenbrown
Sr VP: Douglas M. Hagerman
Conducts Business: Worldwide
Employees: 4,000
Primary Market Served: Business
Catalog available online
Founded: 1952

Complete line of predictive maintenance tools including portable vibration meters, data collectors, analyzers, balancing machines, on-line surveillance systems, protection monitors & predictive maintenance software. Full range of technical consultation services & a comprehensive set of training courses to complement the wide family of products. These services assist its customers in establishing & successfully implementing an effective predictive maintenance program.

ROHM & HAAS CO
100 S Independence Mall W
Philadelphia, PA 19106-2320
Telephone: (215) 592-3000, Toll Free: (877) 288-5881, FAX: (215) 592-3377, Web Site: www.rohmhaas.com
Chmn & CEO: Raj L. Gupta
Pres & COO: J. Michael Fitzpatrick
VP: Gray Wirth
VP: Phillip J. Lewis MD
VP: Richard J. Lovely
Primary Market Served: Business
Catalog available online
Direct online sales

Manufacturers of specialty chemicals.

ROLAND PRODUCTS INC
3400 W Olympic Blvd
Los Angeles, CA 90019
Telephone: (323) 731-1111, Toll Free: (800) 321-2226, FAX: (323) 731-9585, E-Mail: salesinfo@rolandinc.com, Web Site: www.rolandinc.com
Pres: Frances Ro
Conducts Business: U.S., Canada
Primary Market Served: Consumer
Catalog available online
Direct online sales
Advertising/Marketing Budget Related to Direct Marketing: 26-50%
Direct Marketing ad budget:
Magazines: 25%
Newspapers: 25%
TV/Radio: 50%
Founded: 1989

High end European houseware & kitchenware sold to North American consumers.

ROLL INTERNATIONAL CORP
11444 W Olympic Blvd (fl 10)
Los Angeles, CA 90064-1557
Telephone: (310) 966-5700, FAX: (310) 914-4747, Web Site: www.roll.com
Chmn: Stewart Resnick
Co-Chmn: Lynda R. Resnick
Sr VP & Chief Tax Officer: Jordan P. Weiss
Employees: 2,600
Primary Market Served: Consumer
Founded: 1957
Gross sales or billing: $1,400,000,000
Collectibles.

RONCO CORP
21344 Superior St, Chatsworth, CA 91311-4312
1779 Wells Branch Pkwy (#110B-337)
Austin, TX 78728
Toll Free: (800) 486-1806, E-Mail: customerservice@ronco.com, Web Site: www.ronco.com
Pres: Terry Tigner
VP Mktg: Christian Darby
Employees: 200
Primary Market Served: Business & Consumer
Gross sales or billing: $41,300,000,000
Direct response television advertising.

ROSE DISPLAYS LTD
35 Congress St
Salem, MA 01970-5529
Telephone: (978) 219-8100, Web Site: www.rosedisplays.com
Dir, Mktg: Melissa Santos
Primary Market Served: Business

ROSS METALS
27 W 47 St
New York, NY 10036-2806
Telephone: (212) 869-1407, Toll Free: (800) 654-ROSS
Pres: Jack Angel Ross
Exec Supvr: Karin Zakarian
Sls Mgr: Sally Singh
Telemarketing Dir: Armida Moultrie
Conducts Business: Worldwide
Employees: 30
Primary Market Served: Business
Catalog available online
Direct online sales
Founded: 1974

Wholesale jewelry company.

ROTO-ROOTER SERVICES CO
Div. of Roto-Rooter Group
255 E Fifth St, 2500 First Financial Center
Cincinnati, OH 45202-4726
Telephone: (513) 762-6690, FAX: (513) 762-6590, Web Site: www.rotorooter.com
Pres & COO: Richard Arguilla
Sr VP Bus Devel: Robert Goldschmidt
Dir Pub Rels: Paul Abrams
Primary Market Served: Business & Consumer
Advertising/Marketing Budget Related to Direct Marketing: 0-25%
Provider of plumbing repair & drain cleaning services.

ROW RESOURCES INC
260 Main St (Ste 110)
Northport, NY 11768-1738
Telephone: (631) 261-0525

Pres: Kenneth Rowland
Primary Market Served: Business

ROWE POTTERY WORKS INC
404 England St
Cambridge, WI 53523
Telephone: (608) 423-3363, Toll Free: (800) 356-5003, FAX: (608) 423-4273, E-Mail: sales@rowepottery.com, Web Site: www.rowepottery.com
Pres: James Rowe
Dir, Mktg: Greg Sanders
Primary Market Served: Business & Consumer
Catalog available online
Direct online sales
Advertising/Marketing Budget Related to Direct Marketing: 0-25%

Retail manufacturer of pottery & wrought iron.

ROYAL CANADIAN MINT
320 Sussex Dr
Ottawa, ON, Canada K2J 2G6
Telephone: (613) 993-1912
Primary Market Served: Business

ROYAL CANIN
500 Fountain Lakes Blvd (Suite 100)
Saint Charles, MO 63301-4354
Telephone: (636) 926-0003, Web Site: www.royalcanin.us
Dir Mktg: Ann Hudson
Primary Market Served: Consumer

RUSH INDUSTRIES, INC
263 Horton Hwy
Mineola, NY 11501-2255
Telephone: (516) 741-0346, FAX: (516) 741-0348, Web Site: www.rushindustries.com
Pres: Esra Sheena
Conducts Business: U.S.
Employees: 11
Primary Market Served: Consumer
Catalog available online
Direct online sales
Direct Marketing ad budget:
Direct Mail: 50%
Magazines: 50%
Founded: 1977

General merchandise.

RUSKIN, MOSCOU, FALTISCHEK, PC
190 EAB Plaza (15th fl East Tower)
Uniondale, NY 11556
Telephone: (516) 663-6600, FAX: (516) 663-6601, E-Mail: info@rmfpc.com, Web Site: www.rmfpc.com
Mng Partner: Michael Faltischek

Mktg & Pub Affairs Dir: Barbara L. Cerrone
Conducts Business: U.S.
Employees: 120
Primary Market Served: Business
Advertising/Marketing Budget Related to Direct Marketing: 0-25%

Law firm.

RUTLAND PRODUCTS

38 Merchants Row
Rutland, VT 05701-2853
Toll Free: (800) 544-1307, FAX: (802) 775-5262, E-Mail: sales@rutland. com, Web Site: www.rutland.com
Pres: Thomas P. Martin
Conducts Business: U.S., Canada
Primary Market Served: Business & Consumer
Advertising/Marketing Budget Related to Direct Marketing: 26-50%
Founded: 1883

Manufacturer of products related to chimney sweeping & hearth products.

SCI MANAGEMENT

1929 Allen Pkwy
Houston, TX 77019-2506
Telephone: (713) 525-7783, Web Site: www.sci-corp.com
Mng Dir Mktg: Russell Richmond

SLM CORP

aka Sallie Mae
300 Continental Dr
Newark, DE 19713
Web Site: www.salliemae.com
CEO: Raymond J. Quinlan
Exec VP Banking: Joseph DePaulo
Exec VP & Gen Counsel: Laurent C. Lutz
Exec VP & CFO: Steven J. McGarry
Conducts Business: U.S.
Primary Market Served: Business & Consumer
Catalog available online
Gross sales or billing: $9,100,000,000

Financial services company specializing in education.

SA-SO

525 N Great Southwest Pkwy
Arlington, TX 76011
Telephone: (972) 641-4911, Toll Free: (800) 752-4294, FAX: (972) 660-3684, E-Mail: info@sa-so.com, Web Site: www.sa-so.com
Co-Owner: Joe Nussbaum
Co-Owner: Becky Nussbaum
Conducts Business: U.S.
Primary Market Served: Business & Consumer
Catalog available online
Direct online sales

Advertising/Marketing Budget Related to Direct Marketing: 51-75%
Founded: 1948

Supplier of industrial & municipal safety equipment products. Sell to industries & government by direct mail.

SAFEGUARD BUSINESS SYSTEMS INC

8585 N Stemmons Fwy (Suite 600N)
Dallas, TX 75247-3824
Telephone: (214) 905-3935, Toll Free: (800) 523-2422, FAX: (800) 439-8423, Web Site: www.gosafeguard. com
Pres: Tim Broadhead
VP: Elizabeth Jones
VP: David Miller
VP: Lauren Pickwoad
VP: Mark Roggenkamp
Conducts Business: U.S., Canada
Employees: 850
Primary Market Served: Business & Consumer
Direct Marketing ad budget: $1,300,000
Founded: 1956
Gross sales or billing: $86,900,000

Served the small business community for more than 47 years with business management solutions such as continuous & laser computer checks & forms, accounting software, one-write accounting, gift certificate & records management solutions.

SAFTI FIRST

Div. of O'Keeffe's Architectural Building Products Inc
100 N Hill Dr (Suite 12)
Brisbane, CA 94005-1010
Telephone: (415) 824-4900, Toll Free: (888) 653-3333, FAX: (415) 824-5900, (888) 653-4444, E-Mail: info@ safti.com, Web Site: www.safti.com
Chmn & Pres: William O'Keeffe Jr.
Pres & CEO: William O'Keefe
Sr VP & CFO: William H. Hernandez
VP Sls & Mktg: Kathryn O'Keeffe
VP Sls: Mike Vicarra
Conducts Business: U.S., China, Saudi Arabia, Mexico, France
Employees: 70
Primary Market Served: Business
Catalog available online
Indirect online sales
Advertising/Marketing Budget Related to Direct Marketing: 26-50%
Founded: 1961
Gross sales or billing: $17,000,000

San Francisco based manufacturer of fire rated glazing & framing systems, standard custom skylight systems & ar-

chitectural building products for residential, commercial & industrial buildings.

SAGE SOFTWARE INC

6561 Irvine Center Dr
Irvine, CA 92618-2118
Telephone: (949) 753-1222, Toll Free: (800) 854-3415, FAX: (949) 753-0374, Web Site: www.sagesoftware. com
Acting CFO: Andrew Griffith
Exec VP & CIO: John D. Bartz
Exec VP, Mktg: Dennis Frahman
Sr VP, HR: Beccie C. Dawson
Sr VP, Fin: Marshall Ford
Conducts Business: U.S., Canada
Employees: 230
Primary Market Served: Business & Consumer
Catalog available online
Advertising/Marketing Budget Related to Direct Marketing: 0-25%
Direct Marketing ad budget: $1,000,000
Direct Mail: 50%
Telephone: 50%
Founded: 1985
Gross sales or billing: $300,000,000

Sell accounting & business-related software to small & medium-sized businesses.

SAKS FIFTH AVENUE

Subs. of Hudson's Bay Co
12 E 49th St (fl 2)
New York, NY 10017-1088
Telephone: (212) 940-5195, FAX: (212) 940-5339, Web Site: www. saksfifthavenue.com
Pres: Marigay McKee
Chief Mktg Officer: Mark Briggs
Conducts Business: U.S.
Primary Market Served: Business & Consumer
Advertising/Marketing Budget Related to Direct Marketing: 26-50%
Founded: 1924

Department store specializing in luxury items.

SALES & MARKETING MANAGEMENT MAGAZINE

Div. of Bill Communications
770 Broadway
New York, NY 10003
Toll Free: (800) 821-6897, FAX: (905) 470-8561, E-Mail: joyce.cooney@ nielsen.com, Web Site: www. salesandmarketing.com
Grp Publr: Dan Corcoran
Online Editor: Stacy Straczynski
Editor In Chief: Michael McCue
Editor in Chief: Jennifer Juergens
Exec Editor: Lorrie Freifeld

Conducts Business: Worldwide
Primary Market Served: Business &
  Consumer
Catalog available online
Direct online sales
Advertising/Marketing Budget Related
  to Direct Marketing: 26-50%
Direct Marketing ad budget:
  $100,000,000
Direct Mail: 90%
Magazines: 5%
Telephone: 5%

Market books, data & directories to the
sales & marketing community.

SALES SERVICE/AMERICA INC

85 S Bragg St (Suite 600)
Alexandria, VA 22312-2793
Telephone: (703) 813-2400
VP Sls & Msdg: Greg Magnani
Primary Market Served: Consumer

Fine art print & posters, bags, banners,
buttons, printed certificates, flags, jewelry, pencils, pens, embroidered promotional gifts, thermometers, tote boxes,
signs, porcelain cups & mugs

SAMSONITE INTERNATIONAL SA

575 West St (Suite 110)
Mansfield, MA 02048-1160
Telephone: (508) 851-1400, Toll Free:
  (800) 547-BAGS, FAX: (303) 373-
  8715, Web Site: www.samsonite.com
Chmn & CEO: Timothy Charles Parker
CFO: Kyle Francis Gendreau
Pres, The Americas: Tom Korbas
Conducts Business: U.S.
Primary Market Served: Business &
  Consumer
Catalog available online
Direct online sales
Advertising/Marketing Budget Related
  to Direct Marketing: 0-25%
Founded: 1910

Manufacture & sell luggage.

SAN FRANCISCO BAY AREA RAPID TRANSIT DISTRICT (BART)

800 Madison St
Oakland, CA 94607-2622
Telephone: (510) 464-6000, FAX:
  (510) 464-7103, Web Site: www.
  bart.gov
Gen Mgr: Thomas E. Margro
VP: Gail Murray
Dir: Joel Keller
Dir: Bob Franklin
Dir: Carole Ward Allen
Conducts Business: U.S.
Employees: 3,400
Primary Market Served: Consumer

Catalog available online
Direct online sales
Founded: 1946

Public transportation agency serving
four counties in the Bay Area with over
76 miles of track.

SANDY CORP

Div. of General Physics
300 E Big Beaver Rd (Suite 500)
Troy, MI 48083
Toll Free: (800) 733-4739, FAX: (248)
  729-4701, E-Mail: info@sandycorp.
  com, Web Site: www.sandycorp.com
Pres: Frederic Strickland
Sr VP: Dave Gugalal
Employees: 151
Primary Market Served: Business
Advertising/Marketing Budget Related
  to Direct Marketing: 0-25%
Founded: 1911
Gross sales or billing: $42,000,000

Full service performance improvement
company. Helps clients close the gap
between current performance & their
full potential. Services include consulting, research, training & communication tools & media.

SANI SERV

PO Box 1089
Mooresville, IN 46158-5089
Telephone: (317) 831-7030, FAX:
  (317) 381-7036, Web Site: www.
  saniserv.com
Pres: Rob McAfee
VP, Sls & Mktg: Stephen Dowling
Conducts Business: Worldwide
Employees: 100
Primary Market Served: Business
Catalog available online
Indirect online sales
Advertising/Marketing Budget Related
  to Direct Marketing: 26-50%
Founded: 1929
Gross sales or billing: $20,000,000

Manufactures Soft Serv ice cream &
milkshakes. Also batch freezers & cap-
puccino machines.

SANTA FE NATURAL TOBACCO CO

PO Box 25140
Santa Fe, NM 87504-5140
Telephone: (505) 982-4257, Web Site:
  www.nascigs.com
Consumer Relationship Mktg Mgr: Jo-
  hanna Stein
Primary Market Served: Business

SATORI SOFTWARE INC

1301 5th Ave (Suite 2200)
Seattle, WA 98101-2676

Telephone: (206) 357-2900, Toll Free:
  (800) 553-6477, FAX: (206) 357-
  2901, E-Mail: sales@satorisoftware.
  com, Web Site: www.satorisoftware.
  com
VP Sls: Joe Skop
Pres: Hugh Rogovy
Conducts Business: U.S., UK
Employees: 20
Primary Market Served: Business &
  Consumer
Catalog available online
Direct online sales
Advertising/Marketing Budget Related
  to Direct Marketing: 26-50%
Founded: 1982
Gross sales or billing: $1,800,000

Mailroom address correction & postal
presorting software is sold to print
shops, large companies, or list management services.

SAUNDERS MANUFACTURING CO INC

65 Nickerson Hill Rd
Readfield, ME 04355
Telephone: (207) 685-3385, Toll Free:
  (800) 341-4674, FAX: (207) 685-
  9918, E-Mail: jsherwood@saunders-
  usa.com, Web Site: www.saunders-
  usa.com
CEO & Owner: John Rosmarin
CFO & COO: Dann Harriman
VP Sls: Michael Stanga
Mktg Mgr: Tracy Kastning
Web Mktg Mgr: Jennifer Sherwood
Conducts Business: USA, Canada,
  Mexico, EU, Australia
Employees: 70
Primary Market Served: Business
Catalog available online
Indirect online sales
Advertising/Marketing Budget Related
  to Direct Marketing: 0-25%
Direct Marketing ad budget:
Online: 100%
Founded: 1947

Manufacturer of metal & plastic office
products, especially aluminum holders
for business forms, clipboards & sheet-
holders. Also manufacture specialty
printed clipboards for sports plays as
well as general office supplies. Distributor of UHU glue adhesives & Ticket
Board police products.

SCAN OPTICS INC

169 Progress Dr, Manchester, CT
  06040-2242
169 Progress Dr
Manchester, CT 06040-2294
Telephone: (860) 645-7878, Toll Free:
  (800) 745-6001, FAX: (860) 645-
  7995, E-Mail: info@scanoptics.com,
  Web Site: www.scanoptics.com

Chmn: James C. Mavel
CEO: Gideon Agar
Pres: Raymond Griffin
Sr VP & COO: Richard Lieberfarb
Exec VP: Raymond Parker
Employees: 183
Primary Market Served: Business
Founded: 1968
Gross sales or billing: $28,741,000

Computer services & software sold to companies involved in large volume datacapturing for data processing.

HENRY SCHEIN INC
135 Duryea Rd
Melville, NY 11747-3834
Telephone: (631) 843-5500, Toll Free: (800) 472-4346, FAX: (631) 843-5658, E-Mail: custserv@ henryschein.com, Web Site: www. henryschein.com
Chmn & CEO: Stanley Bergman
Pres & COO: James P. Breslawski
Exec VP, CAO & Dir: Gerald A. Benjamin
Exec VP Bus Devel: Mark E. Mlotek
Sr Advisor: Leonard A. David
Conducts Business: U.S., Canada, Europe
Employees: 1,500
Primary Market Served: Business & Consumer
Catalog available online
Direct online sales
Founded: 1932
Gross sales or billing: $5,100,000,000

Sell pharmaceutical, medical, dental & veterinary supplies to health care professionals & institutional customers.

SCHNUCK MARKETS INC
11420 Lackland Rd
Saint Louis, MO 63146-6928
Telephone: (314) 994-9900, FAX: (314) 994-4465, Web Site: www. schnucks.com
Chmn & CEO: Scott C. Schnuck
Pres: Todd Schnuck
Sr VP, Sls & Mktg: Randy Wedel
Sr Analyst: Mark Dagestad
Adv Dir: Joyce Reese
Conducts Business: U.S.
Employees: 15,000
Primary Market Served: Business & Consumer
Catalog available online
Direct online sales
Advertising/Marketing Budget Related to Direct Marketing: 0-25%
Direct Marketing ad budget:
Direct Mail: 85%
Magazines: 10%

Newspapers: 5%

Grocery items to consumers; also offer services in most of our stores - pharmacy, video rental, carry-out foods, photo finishing, bakery, check cashing services, Western Union, etc.

SCHOOL SPECIALTY INC
dba Brodhead Garrett, Frey Scientific, EPS & Childcraft
W6316 Design Dr
Greenville, WI 54942-8404
Telephone: (920) 734-5712, Toll Free: (888) 388-3224, FAX: (920) 734-5112, E-Mail: info@schoolspecialty. com, Web Site: www. schoolspecialty.com
Chmn Bd: Terry L. Lay
CEO: David J. Vander Zanden
Exec VP & CFO: David Vander Ploeg
Exec VP Dir Mktg: David Johnson
Commun & Investor Rels: Mark Fleming
Conducts Business: U.S.
Employees: 2,800
Primary Market Served: Business
Founded: 1959
Gross sales or billing: $1,043,200,000

Supplier of industrial, vocational & technical equipment to secondary & post secondary schools.

SCOPE 1
6490 S Sprinkle Rd
Kalamazoo, MI 49004-9706
Telephone: (269) 323-1333, Toll Free: (877) 7SCOPE1, Web Site: www. scope1.com
Pres: William English
Primary Market Served: Consumer

SCORECARDS USA
200 Circuit Dr
North Kingstown, RI 02852-0298
Telephone: (401) 294-4049, Toll Free: (800) 553-4154, FAX: (401) 294-4076, E-Mail: sales@scorecardsusa. com, Web Site: www.scorecardsusa. com
Treas: Dennis Glass
Pres: Ed Bouclin
Mgr: Heidi Lee Strickland
Conducts Business: U.S.
Primary Market Served: Business
Advertising/Marketing Budget Related to Direct Marketing: 26-50%
Direct Marketing ad budget:
Direct Mail: 75%
Magazines: 15%
Telephone: 10%

Golf scorecards.

SCOTT SIGN SYSTEMS INC
Div. of Identity Group

7525 Pennsylvania Ave (Unit 102)
Sarasota, FL 34243-5065
Telephone: (941) 355-5171, Toll Free: (800) 237-9447, FAX: (941) 351-1787, E-Mail: mail@scottsigns.com, Web Site: www.scottsigns.com
Pres: Steve Evans
Art Dir: Jennifer Adkins
Conducts Business: Worldwide
Employees: 100
Primary Market Served: Business & Consumer
Catalog available online
Indirect online sales
Founded: 1957
Gross sales or billing: $8,000,000

Manufacturer of dimensional letters, logos & graphics. Also, custom fabrication of signing products.

SCOTTS-SIERRA HORTICULTURAL
14111 Scottslawn Rd
Marysville, OH 43041
Toll Free: (888) 270-3714, Web Site: www.scottscompany.com
Chm & CEO: Jim Hagedorn
Conducts Business: U.S., Canada, Europe, Australia
Employees: 300
Primary Market Served: Business & Consumer
Advertising/Marketing Budget Related to Direct Marketing: 0-25%
Direct Marketing ad budget:
Direct Mail: 10%
Magazines: 10%
TV/Radio: 80%
Gross sales or billing: $100,000,000

Manufacture & sell controlled release fertilizers, soils & plant protection products to the nursery, greenhouse, turf & landscape & retail industries.

SCULPTURE HOUSE INC
405 Skillman Rd, PO Box 69
Skillman, NJ 08558
Telephone: (609) 466-2986, FAX: (888) 529-1980, E-Mail: customercare@sculpturehouse.com, Web Site: www.sculpturehouse.com
Pres: Bruner Barrie
Conducts Business: United States & Puerto Rico
Employees: 25
Primary Market Served: Business & Consumer
Catalog available online
Direct online sales
Founded: 1883

Sell sculpting supplies, tools & materials.

SEA BEAR

605 30th St
Anacortes, WA 98221
Telephone: (360) 293-4661, Toll Free:
(800) 645-3474, FAX: (888) 487-
6427, Web Site: www.seabear.com
Pres & CEO: Mike Mondello
VP, Fin: Dan Jondal
VP Direct to Consumer: Patti Fisher
Conducts Business: U.S., Canada, Ja-
pan, Hong Kong, Taiwan
Primary Market Served: Business &
Consumer
Catalog available online
Direct online sales
Founded: 1957

Gift pack smoked salmon, oysters &
mussels. No refrigeration required.

SEARS HOME IMPROVEMENT PRODUCTS & SERVICES

Subs. of Sears Holdings Corp
3333 Beverly Rd
Hoffman Estates, IL 60179
Toll Free: (800) 424-2047, Web Site:
www.searshomeservices.com
Chmn & CEO, Sears Holdings: Edward
S. Lampert
Sr VP & Pres, Home Services: Arun
Arora
Primary Market Served: Consumer
Catalog available online

Home renovations and product installa-
tions.

SEARS, ROEBUCK & CO

Subs. of Sears Holdings Corp
3333 Beverly Rd
Hoffman Estates, IL 60179
Telephone: (847) 286-2500, FAX:
(847) 286-7829, Web Site: www.
sears.com
Chmn & CEO, Sears Holdings: Edward
S. Lampert
Exec VP, Chief Mdsg Officer & Pres:
Ronald D. Boire
Conducts Business: U.S., Canada,
Mexico
Employees: 320,000
Primary Market Served: Consumer
Founded: 1886
Gross sales or billing: $21,000,000,000

Integrated retailer of general merchandise.

SECO-LARM USA INC

16842 Millikan Ave
Irvine, CA 92606
Telephone: (949) 261-2999, Toll Free:
(800) 662-0800, FAX: (949) 261-
7326, E-Mail: info@seco-larm.com,
Web Site: www.seco-larm.com
VP: Michael Block

Mktg Dir: Joe Kovar
Mgr: Lawrence Hwang
Conducts Business: Worldwide
Employees: 20
Primary Market Served: Business &
Consumer
Catalog available online
Advertising/Marketing Budget Related
to Direct Marketing: 0-25%
Founded: 1971
Gross sales or billing: $4,400,000

Dealer direct & export of vehicle, residential & commercial security systems
& access.

SEIKO CORP OF AMERICA

Subs. of Seiko Holdings Corp, Tokyo
1111 MacArthur Blvd
Mahwah, NJ 07430
Telephone: (201) 529-3316, E-Mail:
custserv@seikousa.com, Web Site:
www.seikousa.com
Pres & CEO: Yoshikatsu Kawada
Exec VP Sls & Mktg: Les Perry
Primary Market Served: Business &
Consumer

Sell watches & clocks.

SELECT COMFORT CORP

9800 59th Ave N
Minneapolis, MN 55442
Telephone: (763) 551-7000, Toll Free:
(888) 411-2188, FAX: (763) 551-
7826, Web Site: www.selectcomfort.
com
CEO: William McLaughlin
Sr VP, CIO: Ernest Park
Sr VP, CFO: James C. Raube
Media Dir: Lynn Ferrin
Conducts Business: U.S.
Primary Market Served: Consumer
Catalog available online
Direct online sales
Advertising/Marketing Budget Related
to Direct Marketing: 100%
Founded: 1987
Gross sales or billing: $806,000,000

Manufacture & sell adjustable firmness
sleep systems-air beds.

SELLSTROM MANUFACTURING CO

2050 Hammond Dr
Schaumburg, IL 60173-3810
Telephone: (847) 358-2000, Toll Free:
(800) 323-7402, FAX: (847) 358-
8564, E-Mail: sellstrom@sellstrom.
com, Web Site: www.sellstrom.com
Pres & CEO: David Peters
VP, Sls & Mktg: Rusty Franklin
Mktg Coord: Melissa Heard
Conducts Business: Worldwide
Employees: 101
Primary Market Served: Business

Advertising/Marketing Budget Related
to Direct Marketing: 0-25%
Founded: 1923
Gross sales or billing: $7,100,000

Diversified manufacturer of industrial
safety products.

SENCORE INC

3200 Sencore Dr
Sioux Falls, SD 57107
Telephone: (605) 339-0100, Toll Free:
(800) SEN-CORE, FAX: (605) 339-
0317, E-Mail: sales@sencore.com,
Web Site: www.sencore.com
Chmn & Pres: Al Bowden
Exec VP: Doug Bowden
Sls & Mktg Mgr: Jeffrey Murray
Conducts Business: U.S., Canada, Pu-
erto Rico, Mexico, France
Employees: 250
Primary Market Served: Business
Catalog available online
Advertising/Marketing Budget Related
to Direct Marketing: 76-100%
Founded: 1958
Gross sales or billing: $32,000,000

Manufacturer of electronic test equipment.

SENSIENT TECHNOLOGIES

2526 Baldwin St
Saint Louis, MO 63106
Telephone: (314) 889-7600, Toll Free:
(800) 325-8110, FAX: (314) 658-
7318, Web Site: www.sensient-tech.
com
Chmn, Pres & CEO: Kenneth P. Man-
ning
Sr VP & CFO: Steve Cordier
Gen Mgr: Terry Anderson
Conducts Business: Worldwide
Employees: 300
Primary Market Served: Business
Direct Marketing ad budget: $100,000
Founded: 1904
Gross sales or billing: $90,000,000

Manufacturers of certified (FD&C/
D&C) natural colorants supplied to
food, drug, beverage, cosmetic, baking,
pet food industries & pharmaceutical.

SENSORY EFFECTS POWDER SYSTEM

231 Rock Industrial Park Dr
Bridgeton, MO 63044
Telephone: (314) 291-5444, Toll Free:
(800) 422-5444, FAX: (314) 291-
3289, E-Mail: info@sensoryeffects.
com
Sls & Mktg Dir: Tiffany Tyler
Conducts Business: U.S., Central
America
Primary Market Served: Consumer

Advertising/Marketing Budget Related to Direct Marketing: 0-25%
Direct Marketing ad budget:
Direct Mail: 90%
Telephone: 10%
Founded: 1972

Vitamite non-dairy beverage powders for people who are lactose-intolerant.

JA SEXAUER
Subsidiary of Wilmar Industries
570 Taxter Rd (Ste 230)
Elmsford, NY 10523-2365
Telephone: (914) 472-7501, Toll Free: (800) 431-1872, FAX: (914) 472-5834, Web Site: www.jasmro.com
Pres, CEO Wilmar: Armond Waxman
Sr VP Wilmar: William Sanford
Mktg Dir: Rick Coalter
Conducts Business: U.S., Canada
Primary Market Served: Business
Catalog available online
Direct online sales
Advertising/Marketing Budget Related to Direct Marketing: 0-25%
Founded: 1921

Distributor of plumbing, heating, air conditioning & electrical maintenance products to institutional, commercial & government markets.

SHELL OIL CO
Subs. of Dutch Royal Shell
PO Box 2463
Houston, TX 77252
Telephone: (713) 241-6161, Web Site: www.shell.us
Dir Upstream Americas & Pres: Marvin Odum
Mktg Alliance Implementation Mgr: Sergio Roldan
Primary Market Served: Consumer

Oil and gas producer.

SHERMAN SPECIALTY TOY CO INC
300 Jericho Quadrangle (Suite 240)
Jericho, NY 11753-2719
Telephone: (516) 861-6420, (516) 546-7400, Toll Free: (800) 645-6513, FAX: (516) 861-1033, (800) 853-8697, E-Mail: orders@shermanspecialty.com, Web Site: www.shermanspecialty.com
Pres: Stuart Krosser
Mktg Mgr: Guy Abbate
Mktg: Shawn Hood
Conducts Business: Worldwide
Employees: 99
Primary Market Served: Business
Catalog available online
Direct online sales
Advertising/Marketing Budget Related to Direct Marketing: 0-25%

Gross sales or billing: $19,000,000
Market inexpensive toys used as premiums and a full line of party novelties.

SHILLCRAFT INC
2530 Riva Rd (Suite 308)
Annapolis, MD 21401-7414
Telephone: (410) 682-3060, Toll Free: (800) 638-1542, FAX: (410) 682-3130, Web Site: www.shillcraft.com
Mktg Mgr: Joyce Wehberg
Conducts Business: U.S., Canada
Employees: 24
Primary Market Served: Business & Consumer
Advertising/Marketing Budget Related to Direct Marketing: 76-100%

Sell latch hook kits for making rugs, wall hangings, pillow covers plus related needlecraft items to retail stores, chains & direct to the consumer-primarily female.

SHIPPING SOLUTIONS
PO Box 1067, Ferndale, WA 98248-1067-POST
PO Box 22267
Eagan, MN 55122-0267
Telephone: (651) 905-1727, Toll Free: (888) 890-7447, FAX: (651) 905-1827, E-Mail: info@shipsolutions.com, Web Site: www.shipsolutions.com
Pres: David M. Noah
Chief Tech Officer: Robert Hale
Employees: 5
Primary Market Served: Business
Catalog available online

Sell software to international trading companies.

SHOP.COM
Subs. of Market America Inc
3301 NE 1st Ave
Miami, FL 33137
Toll Free: (866) 420-1709, E-Mail: customerservice@shop.com, Web Site: www.shop.com
CEO: JR Ridinger
COO: Vince Hunt
Conducts Business: U.S.
Employees: 150
Primary Market Served: Business & Consumer
Founded: 1997
Gross sales or billing: $34,500,000

Online shopping portal. Builds custom malls & stores.

SHOPSMITH INC
6530 Poe Ave
Dayton, OH 45414

Telephone: (937) 898-6070, Toll Free: (800) 543-7586, FAX: (937) 890-5197, Web Site: www.shopsmith.com
Chmn & CEO: John R. Folkerth
Pres: Robert Folkerth
CFO: Mark May
Dir Mktg Mgr: Karen Seabach
Conducts Business: U.S., Canada, England
Employees: 93
Primary Market Served: Business & Consumer
Founded: 1972
Gross sales or billing: $11,000,000

Manufacture & sell woodworking power tools direct to the general public through direct mail & direct sales.

SHOWTIME NETWORKS INC
Subs. of Viacom Inc
1633 Broadway
New York, NY 10019
Telephone: (212) 708-1600, FAX: (212) 708-1450, Web Site: www.sho.com
Chmn & CEO: Matthew Blank
Pres: David Nevins
Conducts Business: U.S.
Employees: 575
Primary Market Served: Consumer
Founded: 1976

Premium-cable television network.

SILICON GRAPHICS INC
RP-NFOA
46600 Landing Pkwy
Fremont, CA 94538-6420
Telephone: (510) 933-8300, Web Site: www.sgi.com
CEO: Robert Ewald
Primary Market Served: Business & Consumer

Manufacture 3-D computer graphic systems; some software development.

SIMON PROPERTY GROUP
115 W Washington St
Indianapolis, IN 46204
Telephone: (317) 636-1600, FAX: (317) 263-7925, Web Site: www.shopsimon.com
VP, Corp Mktg: Shari Simon
Conducts Business: U.S., Europe
Employees: 4,000
Primary Market Served: Business

Develop & operate enclosed shopping malls, strip centers & mixed use centers.

SIMPLEX GRINNELL
50 Technology Dr
Westminster, MA 01441-0001

Telephone: (978) 731-2500, Toll Free: (800) SIMPLEX, FAX: (978) 731-7856, Web Site: www. simplexgrinnel.com
Pres: Dean S. Seavers
VP & CFO: Mike Ford
VP, Mktg: Dave Baer
Dir, Mktg Commun: Chris Woodcock
Conducts Business: Worldwide
Employees: 3,000
Primary Market Served: Business
Catalog available online
Advertising/Marketing Budget Related to Direct Marketing: 26-50%
Founded: 2001
Gross sales or billing: $1,800,000,000

Manufacture recorders & fire alarm systems for industrial companies.

SIMPSON ELECTRIC CO
dba Lac Du Flambeau Band of Lake Superior Chippewa Indians
520 Simpson Ave, PO Box 99
Lac Du Flambeau, WI 54538-0099
Telephone: (715) 588-3311, FAX: (715) 588-3327, E-Mail: cservice@ simpsonelectric.com, Web Site: www.simpsonelectric.com
CEO: William Conn
Conducts Business: U.S., Europe, Asia, South America
Employees: 100
Primary Market Served: Business
Catalog available online
Founded: 1934
Gross sales or billing: $10,000,000

Manufacturer of analog & digital instrumentation; electrical & electronic test equipment & accessories, panel meters & controllers.

SIRIUSXM RADIO INC
1221 Avenue of the Americas
New York, NY 10020
Telephone: (212) 584-5100, Web Site: www.siriusxm.com
CEO: James E. Meyer
Pres & Chief Content Officer: Scott Greenstein
Exec VP & Chief Administrative Officer: Dara Altman
Exec VP & Gen Counsel: Patrick L. Donnelly
Exec VP & CFO: David J. Frear
Primary Market Served: Business & Consumer

Satellite radio provider.

SKULLDUGGERY
5433 E La Palma Ave
Anaheim, CA 92807-2022
Telephone: (714) 777-6425, Toll Free: (800) 3 FOSSIL, FAX: (714) 832-1215, Web Site: www.skullduggery.com

Chmn & Pres: Peter Koehl
VP, Mktg: Emmy Koehl
Conducts Business: Worldwide
Employees: 9
Primary Market Served: Business & Consumer

Manufacture & sell museum quality fossil replicas to artists, executives, physicians, dentists, scholars, geologists, anthropologists & those with interest in the earth's past, present & future.

SKYMALL INC
1520 E Pima St
Phoenix, AZ 85034-4600
Telephone: (602) 254-9777, Toll Free: (800) SKY-MALL, FAX: (602) 254-6075, Web Site: www.skymall.com
CEO: Kevin Weiss
Primary Market Served: Consumer
Catalog available online
Direct online sales
Founded: 1990
Gross sales or billing: $100,000,000

Consumer mail order products. In-flight direct response shopping service.

SKYPOINT COMMUNICATIONS INC
7340 Mark St
Loretto, MN 55357
Telephone: (763) 548-2600, FAX: (763) 548-2610, E-Mail: info@ skypoint.com, Web Site: www.skypoint.com
Pres: Greg Kemmitz
Sls & Mktg Mgr: Bruce Morrows
Primary Market Served: Business
Catalog available online
Founded: 1994

Internet services provider.

SLEEPY'S INC
dba Sleepy's
1000 S Oyster Bay Rd
Hicksville, NY 11801-3527
Telephone: (516) 844-8800, Toll Free: (800) sleepys, FAX: (516) 844-8847, Web Site: www.sleepys.com
Pres: David Acker
CFO: Joseph Graci
Conducts Business: U.S.
Employees: 2,000
Primary Market Served: Consumer
Founded: 1957
Gross sales or billing: $394,000,000
Bedding retailer.

SLIFTER
307 7th Ave (Rm 2104)
New York, NY 10001-6089
Telephone: (212) 488-2222, Web Site: www.slifter.com

Dir Corp Communs: Michelle Barna

AO SMITH CORP
11270 W Park Pl (Suite 1200)
Milwaukee, WI 53224-3643
Telephone: (414) 359-4000, FAX: (414) 359-4064, Web Site: www.aosmith.com
Chmn & CEO: Paul W. Jones
Exec VP & CFO: Terry M. Murphy
Sr VP IT: Randall S. Bednar
Exec VP: Christopher L. Mapes
Exec VP Corp Tech: Ronald E. Massa
Primary Market Served: Business
Catalog available online
Gross sales or billing: $2,100,000,000

Water heaters, electric motors & protective coatings.

SMITHFIELD FOODS
Subs. of WH Group Limited
200 Commerce St
Smithfield, VA 23430
Toll Free: (800) 276-6158, Web Site: www.smithfieldfoods.com
Pres & CEO: C. Larry Pope
Pres & COO Pork Grp: George H. Richter
Exec VP & Chief Synergy Officer: Robert W. Manly IV
CFO: Kenneth M. Sullivan
Exec VP & Chief Commodity Hedging Officer: Dhamu Thamodaran
Exec VP & Chief Sustainability Officer: Dennis H. Treacy
Conducts Business: U.S.
Primary Market Served: Business & Consumer
Advertising/Marketing Budget Related to Direct Marketing: 26-50%
Global food company.

TOM SNYDER PRODUCTIONS
Div. of Scholastic
100 Talcott Ave Ste 6
Watertown, MA 02472-5715
Telephone: (617) 926-6000, Toll Free: (800) 342-0236, FAX: (800) 304-1254, E-Mail: ask@tomsnyder.com, Web Site: www.tomsnyder.com
Gen Mgr: Richard Abrams
Channel Mgr, Mktg: Kim Goodman
VP Mktg: John Caroll
VP & Chief Academic Officer: David Dockerman
Dir Fin & Admin: Arlene Hawkins
Dir Prod Mngmt: Liza Debus
Dir Natl Sls: Brian McKean
Employees: 80
Primary Market Served: Business & Consumer
Catalog available online
Direct online sales

Founded: 1980

Sell educational software & technology.

SOCIAL STUDIES SCHOOL SERVICE

10200 Jefferson Blvd
Culver City, CA 90232-0802
Telephone: (310) 839-2436, Toll Free: (800) 421-4246, FAX: (310) 839-2249, (800) 944-5432, E-Mail: access@socialstudies.com, Web Site: www.socialstudies.com
Co-Pres: Irwin Levin
Co-Pres: Sanford Weiner
CEO: David Weiner
Chief Educ Officer: Aaron Willis
Conducts Business: U.S., Canada
Employees: 65
Primary Market Served: Business & Consumer
Catalog available online
Direct online sales
Founded: 1965

Distributor of a wide variety of supplementary curriculum materials for educators.

SOLARCOM

One Sun Ct
Norcross, GA 30092
Telephone: (770) 449-6116, Toll Free: (888) SUN-DATA, FAX: (770) 448-7726, Web Site: www.solarcom.net
Chmn & CEO: Eric Prockow
Vice Chmn: John Crilly
Pres Solarcom LLC: Ted Glahn
Pres Atlantic Global Sys: Bill Woerner
VP Mktg: Randy Hicks
Gen Mgr: Jim Johnson
Mktg Coord: Barbara Ingram
Conducts Business: U.S., Europe, S. America, Australia, Japan, China
Employees: 356
Primary Market Served: Business
Catalog available online
Direct online sales
Advertising/Marketing Budget Related to Direct Marketing: 0-25%
Direct Marketing ad budget:
Direct Mail: 10%
Magazines: 50%
TV/Radio: 40%
Founded: 1976
Gross sales or billing: $250,000,000

An independent business & technology solutions provider that delivers system integration, data management, groupware solutions, Lan/Wan solutions, product delivery & lease/financing services.

SOLITRON DEVICES INC

3301 Electronics Way

West Palm Beach, FL 33407-4636
Telephone: (561) 848-4311, FAX: (561) 863-5946, E-Mail: sales@solitrondevices.com, Web Site: www.solitrondevices.com
Chmn, Pres, CFO & CEO: Shevach Saraf
Dir Opers: Jesse Quinn
Dir: Dr. Jacob A. Davis
Dir: Joseph Schlig
Conducts Business: U.S.
Employees: 80
Primary Market Served: Business
Catalog available online
Advertising/Marketing Budget Related to Direct Marketing: 0-25%
Direct Marketing ad budget: $60,000
Founded: 1959
Gross sales or billing: $8,000,000

Manufactures & markets semiconductor & related products primarily to the defense & aerospace industries.

SONY ELECTRONICS INC

Subs. of Sony Corp of America
16530 Via Esprillo
San Diego, CA 92127
Telephone: (858) 942-2400, Web Site: www.sony.com
Pres & COO: Mike Fasulo
VP Corp Commun: John Dolak
Conducts Business: U.S.
Primary Market Served: Business

Marketer of consumer electronics.

SONY PICTURES HOME ENTERTAINMENT

Subs. of Sony Corp
10202 W Washington Blvd (Rm 7814), SPP Bldg
Culver City, CA 90232-3119
Telephone: (310) 244-4000, FAX: (310) 244-1544, Web Site: www.cthe.com
Pres: Man Jit Singh
Conducts Business: U.S., Canada
Employees: 120
Primary Market Served: Consumer
Advertising/Marketing Budget Related to Direct Marketing: 0-25%

Video distribution company.

SOUTHEAST TOYOTA DISTRIBUTORS LLC

100 Jim Moran Blvd
Deerfield Beach, FL 33442
Telephone: (954) 429-2000, Web Site: www.jmfamily.com
Pres: Kenneth Czubay
Mktg Mgr: Grant Wilson
Primary Market Served: Business & Consumer
Catalog available online

Toyota parts & services.

SOUTHERN FLAVORING CO INC

1330 Norfolk Ave
Bedford, VA 24523-2223
Telephone: (540) 586-8565, Toll Free: (800) 765-8565, FAX: (540) 586-8568, E-Mail: tom@southernflavoring.com, Web Site: www.southernflavoring.com
Pres: Earle Thomas Messier
VP, Mktg: John P. Messier
Conducts Business: U.S.
Employees: 20
Primary Market Served: Business & Consumer
Catalog available online
Indirect online sales
Founded: 1929

Liquid food flavorings & colors.

HUCK SPAULDING ENTERPRISES

Rte 85, New Scotland Rd
Voorheesville, NY 12186
Telephone: (518) 768-2070, Toll Free: (888) 982-8866, FAX: (518) 768-2240, E-Mail: orders@spaulding-rogers.com, Web Site: www.spaulding-rogers.com
CEO: Huck Spaulding
Pres & Sec: William Lawyer
Vice-CEO: Josephine Spaulding
VP: Jeff Lawyer
VP & Treas: Bobbi DeFranco
Pur Agent: Bob Weineski
Conducts Business: Worldwide
Employees: 56
Primary Market Served: Business & Consumer
Catalog available online
Indirect online sales
Founded: 1956

Huck Spaulding Ent Inc. distributor of products by Spaulding & Rogers Mfg Inc & Spaulding Color Corp for tattoo equipment & supplies used by tattoo artists, plastic surgeons, research institutes, veterinarians, ophthalmologists & many other professionals. Also manufacture body jewelry, piercing kits & piercing supplies.

SPEAKERS GUILD INC

78 Old Kings Hwy, PO Box 1540
Sandwich, MA 02563-1540
Telephone: (508) 888-6702, Toll Free: (800) 343-4530, FAX: (508) 888-6771, E-Mail: info@speakersguild.com, Web Site: www.speakersguild.com
Pres: Phil Frankio
Owner: Edward Larkin
Conducts Business: U.S., Canada
Employees: 6
Primary Market Served: Business

Catalog available online
Indirect online sales
Advertising/Marketing Budget Related
to Direct Marketing: 26-50%
Direct Marketing ad budget: $150,000
Direct Mail: 95%
Telephone: 5%
Founded: 1978
Gross sales or billing: $6,500,000

Provide public speakers & seminar leaders for meetings & conventions.

SPEAR ENGINEERING CO

3107 N Stone Ave
Colorado Springs, CO 80907
Telephone: (719) 471-9850
Pres: Spencer Katalin
VP: Joann Wall
Conducts Business: U.S.
Employees: 8
Primary Market Served: Business & Consumer
Direct Marketing ad budget:
Direct Mail: 90%
Magazines: 10%

Manufacture & sell a line of name-plates & signs. Solicit orders through magazine ads & direct mail. Mailing address: PO Box 7025, Colorado Springs, CO 80933.

SPECIALIZED PRODUCTS CO

1100 S Kimball Ave
Southlake, TX 76092
Telephone: (817) 329-6647, Toll Free: (800) 866-5353, FAX: (800) 234-8286, E-Mail: spc@specialized.net, Web Site: www.specialized.net
Pres: Pete Smith
Exec Asst: Lisa Oldham
Conducts Business: Worldwide
Employees: 49
Primary Market Served: Business
Catalog available online
Direct online sales
Advertising/Marketing Budget Related
to Direct Marketing: 76-100%
Founded: 1965
Gross sales or billing: $20,000,000

Sells tool kits, tools & test equipment for installation and maintenance of telecom, computers, fiber optics, LAN & electronic systems. Sells extensive line of instrument shipping cases, complete range of products for field service & depot repair. 400+ page full color catalog.

SPECIALTY STORE SERVICES INC

454 Jarvis Ave
Des Plaines, IL 60018
Telephone: (847) 470-7000, Toll Free: (888) 441-4440, FAX: (847) 470-5355, Web Site: www. specialtystoreservices.com
Pres: Malcom Finke
VP, Opers: Evan Finke
VP Adv: Eric Weinstein
Employees: 85
Primary Market Served: Business
Catalog available online
Direct online sales
Advertising/Marketing Budget Related
to Direct Marketing: 76-100%
Founded: 1987
Gross sales or billing: $11,800,000

Manufacturers of displays, fixtures and retail store supplies.

SPECTRA MERCHANDISING INTERNATIONAL INC

4230 N Normandy
Chicago, IL 60634
Telephone: (773) 202-8408, FAX: (773) 202-8409
Pres: Patricia Schoenberg
VP: Alex Greenwood
Conducts Business: U.S., Mexico, Europe, Australia, Canada
Employees: 60
Primary Market Served: Business
Advertising/Marketing Budget Related
to Direct Marketing: 0-25%
Founded: 1981

Consumer electronics; audio, video, calculators & telephones.

SPECTRUM CHEMICALS & LABORATORY PRODUCTS

14422 S San Pedro St
Gardena, CA 90248-2027
Telephone: (310) 516-8000, Web Site: www.spectrumchemical.com
Dir, EBus: Larry Hilton
Primary Market Served: Business

SPEED-MAT

374 South St
Biddeford, ME 04005
Telephone: (207) 294-4358, Toll Free: (800) 882-7017, FAX: (207) 882-9279, E-Mail: info@speed-mat.com, Web Site: www.speed-mat.com
Pres: Harry F. Esterly
VP, Treas & Mktg Mgr: Diana E. Esterly
Conducts Business: Worldwide
Employees: 7
Primary Market Served: Business & Consumer
Indirect online sales
Advertising/Marketing Budget Related
to Direct Marketing: 76-100%
Direct Marketing ad budget: $30,000
Direct Mail: 10%
Magazines: 80%

Telephone: 10%
Founded: 1973

SPINNEYBECK ENTERPRISES

425 Crosspoint Pkwy (Ste 100)
Getzville, NY 14068-1609
Telephone: (716) 446-2380, Toll Free: (800) 482-7777, FAX: (716) 446-2396, E-Mail: sales@spinneybeck. com, Web Site: www.spinneybeck. com
Pres: Roger Wall
VP, Opers Mngmt: Jack Wolf
VP, Fin: Susanne Francis
Employees: 60
Primary Market Served: Business & Consumer
Catalog available online
Indirect online sales
Founded: 1962
Gross sales or billing: $11,800,000

Wholesale Italian upholstery leather supplier.

SPRING-GREEN LAWN CARE CORP

11909 Spaulding School Dr
Plainfield, IL 60544
Telephone: (815) 436-8777, FAX: (815) 436-9056, Web Site: www. spring-green.com
Pres: Thomas W. Hofer
Primary Market Served: Business

Sell lawn care franchises.

SPRINGS GLOBAL INC

Div. of Spring Industries
110 5th Ave (fl 5)
New York, NY 10011-5647
Telephone: (888) 926-7888, Web Site: www.springs.com
Pres: Tom O'Connor
Conducts Business: Worldwide
Employees: 18,000
Primary Market Served: Business

Sell home textiles & furnishings to department & chain stores.

SQUADRON MAIL ORDER

1115 Crowley Dr
Carrollton, TX 75011-1312
Telephone: (972) 242-8663, Toll Free: (877) 414-0434, FAX: (972) 242-3775, E-Mail: mailorder@squadron. com, Web Site: www.squadron.com
Pres: Jerry Campbell
Mktg Dir: Charles Harransky
Conducts Business: Worldwide
Employees: 40
Primary Market Served: Consumer
Catalog available online
Indirect online sales
Direct Marketing ad budget: $300,000

Direct Mail: 80%
Magazines: 20%
Gross sales or billing: $3,000,000
Sell plastic models & military books with an emphasis on aviation.

STANDARD COMMUNICATIONS CORP
Subs. of Marantz of Japan Inc
6260 Sequence Dr
San Diego, CA 92121-4358
Telephone: (858) 546-5300, Toll Free: (800) 745-2445, FAX: (858) 546-5301, E-Mail: satcommsales@stdcom.com, Web Site: www.standardcomm.com
Pres & CEO: Ron Blanchard
Conducts Business: U.S.
Employees: 140
Primary Market Served: Business
Advertising/Marketing Budget Related to Direct Marketing: 0-25%
Direct Marketing ad budget:
Direct Mail: 100%
Founded: 1969
Gross sales or billing: $60,000,000
Commercial satellite receivers.

STANLEY SUPPLY & SERVICES
335 Willow St
North Andover, MA 01845-5921
Telephone: (978) 682-9844, Toll Free: (800) 225-5370, FAX: (800) 743-8141, Web Site: www.stanleysupplyservices.com
Pres: Holly Tsourides
VP Global Sls: Bruce Westcott
Conducts Business: Worldwide
Employees: 133
Primary Market Served: Business
Catalog available online
Direct online sales
Advertising/Marketing Budget Related to Direct Marketing: 76-100%
Founded: 1963
Gross sales or billing: $33,000,000
Direct mail distributor of hardware, industrial equipment, mail-order house & electronic parts.

STARCHTECH
720 Florida Ave S (#A)
Golden Valley, MN 55426-1704
Telephone: (763) 545-5400, Toll Free: (800) 597-7225, FAX: (763) 545-9450, Web Site: www.starchtech.com
CEO: Ed Boehmer
Gen Mgr, Sls: Dean Bartels
Inside Sls: Charlie Pyle
Dir, Opers: Matt Niles
Plant Mgr: Gary Barbo
Primary Market Served: Business

Catalog available online
Indirect online sales
Founded: 1997
Biodegradable packing materials.

STARCREST PRODUCTS OF CALIFORNIA INC
3660 Brennan Ave
Perris, CA 92599
Telephone: (909) 943-2011, FAX: (909) 943-2971, E-Mail: tmc@tstonramp.com
Pres: T.M. Calandra
VP: Michael Donnelly
Mdse Mgr: Frank Hartless
Dir Acct & HR: Betty Abramson
Conducts Business: U.S.
Employees: 1,700
Primary Market Served: Consumer
Advertising/Marketing Budget Related to Direct Marketing: 76-100%
Direct Marketing ad budget: $42,000,000
Direct Mail: 100%
Founded: 1976
Gross sales or billing: $300,000,000
Mail order sales of consumer products.

STARKEY LABORATORIES
6700 Washington Ave S
Eden Prairie, MN 55344-3405
Telephone: (952) 941-6401, Web Site: www.starkey.com
Sr Dir, Mktg & Communs: Chris McCormick
Primary Market Served: Business & Consumer

STARZ ENTERTAINMENT LLC
8900 Liberty Cir
Englewood, CO 80112-7057
Telephone: (855) 807-2929, Web Site: www.starz.com
CEO: Chris Albrecht
Pres: Glenn Curtis
Exec VP Mktg: Nancy McGee
Sr VP Consumer Mktg: Kelly Bumann
Primary Market Served: Consumer
Premium movie service provider.

STATWARE
90 Main St (Suite 213A)
Centerbrook, CT 06409
Telephone: (860) 767-9000, FAX: (860) 767-3145, E-Mail: info@statware.net, Web Site: www.powerlist.com
Pres: Richard Lepoutre
Provide software to list brokers & list managers.

STEELCASE INC
901 44th St SE
Grand Rapids, MI 49508
Telephone: (616) 247-2710, FAX: (616) 475-2270, Web Site: www.steelcase.com
Chmn: Robert C. Pew III
Pres, CEO & Dir: James P. Hackett
Exec VP & CFO: David C. Sylvester
Exec VP & CIO: John S. Dean
Sr VP: Mark A. Baker
Employees: 13,000
Primary Market Served: Business & Consumer
Catalog available online
Founded: 1912
Manufacture office furniture.

STERLING FLUID SYSTEMS
2005 Dr Martin Luther King St, PO Box 7026
Indianapolis, IN 46202-1165
Telephone: (317) 925-9661, Toll Free: (800) 879-0182, FAX: (317) 924-7388, Web Site: www.peerlesspump.com
Pres: Dean Douglas
VP, Sls & Mktg: John Kahren
CFO: David Baker
Conducts Business: Worldwide
Employees: 200
Primary Market Served: Business
Direct Marketing ad budget:
Direct Mail: 25%
Magazines: 75%
Founded: 1923
Manufacturer of chemical processing pumps sold by authorized representatives nationally & internationally.

STERLING JEWELERS INC
Subs. of Signet Group
375 Ghent Rd
Akron, OH 44333-4601
Telephone: (330) 668-5000, FAX: (330) 668-5052, E-Mail: webmaster@jewels.com, Web Site: www.sterlingjewelers.com
Pres & CEO: Mark Light
Chmn: Terry Burman
Exec VP & CFO: Robert Trabucco
Sr VP, Mktg: George Murray
Employees: 10,000
Primary Market Served: Consumer
Advertising/Marketing Budget Related to Direct Marketing: 26-50%
Founded: 1906
Gross sales or billing: $1,300,000,000
Retail jewelry.

STERLING NAME TAPE INC
Nine Willow St, PO Box 939
Winsted, CT 06098

Telephone: (860) 379-5142, Toll Free: (800) 654-5210, FAX: (860) 379-0394, E-Mail: postman@sterlingtape.com, Web Site: www.sterlingtape.com
Pres: James Barrett
Conducts Business: U.S., Canada, Europe, Mexico
Employees: 4
Primary Market Served: Business & Consumer
Catalog available online
Direct online sales
Direct Marketing ad budget: $35,000
Direct Mail: 50%
Magazines: 50%
Founded: 1901

Manufacturer of personalized garment labels.

STEWART ENTERPRISES INC

1333 S Clearview Pkwy
Jefferson, LA 70121-1014
Telephone: (504) 729-1400, Toll Free: (800) 535-6017, FAX: (504) 729-1984, Web Site: www.stewartenterprises.com
Pres & CEO: Thomas J. Crawford
Chmn Bd: Frank B. Stewart Jr.
Direct Mktg Mgr: Kellie Ferrara
Integrated Mktg Commun Dir: Connie P. Ernst
Conducts Business: United States & Puerto Rico
Employees: 5,400
Primary Market Served: Consumer
Catalog available online
Advertising/Marketing Budget Related to Direct Marketing: 5-10%
Founded: 1910
Gross sales or billing: $487,000,000

Funeral home, cemetery owner & operator.

STEWART-MACDONALD

21 N Shafer, PO Box 900
Athens, OH 45701
Telephone: (740) 592-3021, Toll Free: (800) 848-2273, FAX: (740) 593-7922, E-Mail: hostetler@stewmac.com, Web Site: www.stewmac.com
Founder: C.E. Stewart
Co-Founder: Bill MacDonald
VP: Jay Hostetler
Builder: Dan Erlewine
Builder: Don MacRostie
Conducts Business: Worldwide
Employees: 15
Primary Market Served: Business & Consumer
Catalog available online
Direct online sales
Direct Marketing ad budget:
Direct Mail: 80%

Magazines: 20%
Manufacturer & distributor of fretted musical instruments, kits, parts & supplies.

KIRK STIEFF CO

Div. of Lenox
1414 Radcliffe St
Bristol, PA 19007
Telephone: (267) 525-7800, Toll Free: (800) 635-3669, Web Site: www.lenox.com
Conducts Business: U.S.
Employees: 400
Primary Market Served: Business & Consumer
Advertising/Marketing Budget Related to Direct Marketing: 0-25%

Manufacturer & designer of sterling silver, pewter & silverplate flatware, holloware & decorative accessories.

STIMPSON CO INC

1515 SW 13th Ct
Pompano Beach, FL 33069-4789
Telephone: (954) 946-3500, Toll Free: (877) 765-0748, FAX: (954) 941-1921, E-Mail: customerservice@stimpson.com, Web Site: www.stimpson.com
VP Sls & Mktg: Bill Rauff
Conducts Business: U.S., Canada, U.K.
Employees: 450
Primary Market Served: Business
Catalog available online
Indirect online sales
Advertising/Marketing Budget Related to Direct Marketing: 26-50%
Direct Marketing ad budget:
Magazines: 100%
Founded: 1852
Gross sales or billing: $41,500,000

Sell industrial fasteners & attaching machinery.

STONWURKS

13218 Kerry Ln
Eden Prairie, MN 55346-3140
Telephone: (785) 526-7847, Toll Free: (888) 884-7881, FAX: (785) 526-7841, E-Mail: stonwurks@stonwurks.com, Web Site: www.stonwurks.com
VP: Kirk Meyer
Sls Mgr: Lloyd Frigon
Office Mgr: Joan Caskey
Conducts Business: U.S.
Employees: 5
Primary Market Served: Business & Consumer
Advertising/Marketing Budget Related to Direct Marketing: 76-100%

Founded: 1992
Fabricator of panelized light-weight stone.

STORE SMART EXPRESS/ VISUAL HORIZONS

180 Metro Park
Rochester, NY 14623-2610
Telephone: (585) 424-5300, Toll Free: (800) 424-1011, FAX: (585) 424-1064, E-Mail: cs@storesmart.com, Web Site: www.storesmart.com
VP & Founder: Reenie Fiengold
Mktg Mgr: Stan Fiengold
Catalog available online
Indirect online sales
Founded: 1997

Free full color catalog full of things to protect, store & organize. Clear vinyl peel & stick pockets are sized to fit business cards, 3 1/2 disks & CD-ROMs. With over 300 more sizes & the ability to have the pockets customized, the uses are endless. All products & services guaranteed. Phone/fax orders welcomed. Accepting Master Charge, VISA & American Express.

STRATEGY CORPS LLC

201 Summit View Dr (Suite 250), Summit Bldg
Brentwood, TN 37027-4645
Telephone: (615) 221-8381, Toll Free: (888) 577-6933, FAX: (615) 221-8479, E-Mail: info@strategycorps.com, Web Site: www.strategycorps.com
Chmn: William King
DM Mgr: Christie Skelley
Sls: David Crook
Employees: 16
Primary Market Served: Business
Advertising/Marketing Budget Related to Direct Marketing: 26-50%
Direct Marketing ad budget:
Direct Mail: 50%
Magazines: 50%
Founded: 2000
Gross sales or billing: $1,200,000

Sell accounts receivable software to banking institutions & other businesses to facilitate banks' efforts in selling small business loans & insurance products.

STRATUS TECHNOLOGIES

111 Powder Mill Rd
Maynard, MA 01754-3409
Telephone: (978) 461-7000, Toll Free: (800) 787-2887, FAX: (978) 461-3670, Web Site: www.stratus.com
Pres & CEO: David J. Laurello
Mktg Dir: Sue Lawrence-Longo
Primary Market Served: Business

Founded: 1980
Industrial manufacturers of computers.

STRAW HAT COOPERATIVE CORP

18 Crow Canyon Ct (Suite 150)
San Ramon, CA 94583-1669
Telephone: (925) 837-3400, FAX: (925) 820-1080, E-Mail: info@strawhatpizza.com, Web Site: www.strawhatpizza.com
Pres & CEO: Joshua Richman
Dir Mktg: Kevin Johnson
Reg Dir: Lee Dubrow
Conducts Business: U.S.
Employees: 1,000
Primary Market Served: Consumer
Founded: 1987
Gross sales or billing: $20,000,000

Franchised company of individually owned & operated pizza restaurants.

STREAM INTERNATIONAL

20 William St (Suite 310)
Wellesley, MA 02481-4145
Telephone: (781) 304-1800, Toll Free: (888) 264-5834, FAX: (781) 575-6999, Web Site: www.stream.com
CEO: Steven D.R. Moore
VP, Mktg: Deb Keeman

Customer relationship management & customer care services.

STURBRIDGE YANKEE WORKSHOP INC

90 Blueberry Rd
Portland, ME 04102-1924
Telephone: (207) 774-9045, Toll Free: (800) 343-1144, FAX: (207) 774-2561, Web Site: www.sturbridgeyankee.com
Pres: Thomas Binnie
Sr Fin Analyst: John Alexander
Gen Mgr: Gary Boisvert
Conducts Business: U.S.
Employees: 75
Primary Market Served: Consumer
Catalog available online
Direct online sales
Advertising/Marketing Budget Related to Direct Marketing: 76-100%
Founded: 1953

Fine home furnishings & accessories.

STURGES SPORTSWEAR

7752 NC 48
Battleboro, NC 27809
Telephone: (252) 446-0096, Toll Free: (866) 532-6748, FAX: (252) 977-3932, E-Mail: estu73123@aol.com, Web Site: www.sturgessportswear.com
Co-Pres: Johnny Sturges
Co-Pres: Eddie Sturges

Conducts Business: U.S., Japan, Mexico, Canada
Employees: 150
Primary Market Served: Business & Consumer
Catalog available online
Indirect online sales
Advertising/Marketing Budget Related to Direct Marketing: 76-100%
Founded: 1978

Wholesale supplier of T-shirts, denim, sweatwear & ladies leisure wear to the imprintable sportswear industry.

SUEZ ENERGY NORTH AMERICA

1990 Post Oak Blvd (Suite 1900)
Houston, TX 77056-3831
Telephone: (713) 636-0000, FAX: (713) 636-1364, Web Site: www.tractebelpowerinc.com
Pres & CEO: Zin Smati
Sr VP & Gen Counsel: Bart Clark
Sr VP, HR: Mike Thompson
Exec VP, Bus Devel: Paul Gevicchi
Exec VP & CFO: Geert Peeters
Conducts Business: Worldwide
Employees: 47,000
Primary Market Served: Business
Founded: 1895
Gross sales or billing: $11,000,000,000

Independent power & industrial energy.

SUNBEAM PRODUCTS INC

dba Jarden Consumer Solutions
2381 NW Executive Center Dr
Boca Raton, FL 33431
Telephone: (561) 912-4100, FAX: (561) 912-4567, Web Site: www.sunbeam.com
CEO: James E. Lillie
VP Mktg: Matt Ragland
Primary Market Served: Business & Consumer
Catalog available online
Direct online sales

Manufacture & sell small kitchen appliances, scales & therapeutic products.

SUNDANCER JEWELRY CO INC

5921 Office Blvd NE (Suite A)
Albuquerque, NM 87109
Telephone: (505) 345-7475, FAX: (505) 345-7561, E-Mail: sales@sundancer.net, Web Site: www.sundancer.net
Pres: Steven Stacy
Primary Market Served: Business
Catalog available online
Founded: 1973

Manufacture jewelry.

SUNOCO INC

Subs. of Energy Transfer Partners LP
Mellon Bank Ctr, 1735 Market St (Suite LL)
Philadelphia, PA 19103-7583
Telephone: (215) 977-3000, FAX: (215) 977-3409, Web Site: www.sunocoinc.com
Chmn & CEO: Kelcy L. Warren
Pres & COO: Marshall McCrea
CFO: Martin Salinas
Sr VP, Gen Counsel & Sec: Thomas P. Mason
Chief Compliance Officer: Greg Brazaitis
Primary Market Served: Business & Consumer
Advertising/Marketing Budget Related to Direct Marketing: 76-100%
Direct Marketing ad budget:
Direct Mail: 5%
Magazines: 5%
Newspapers: 10%
TV/Radio: 80%
Founded: 1886

Markets gasoline under the Sunoco brand through retail outlets & convenience stores in 23 states.

SUNRISE MEDICAL INC

6899 Winchester Cir (Suite 200)
Boulder, CO 80301-3696
Telephone: (303) 218-4500, Toll Free: (800) 333-4000, FAX: (303) 218-4949, Web Site: www.sunrisemedical.com
Pres & CEO: Thomas Rossnagel
VP Mktg: Bob Kaenel
Conducts Business: U.S., Canada
Employees: 2,298
Primary Market Served: Business
Catalog available online
Advertising/Marketing Budget Related to Direct Marketing: 0-25%
Direct Marketing ad budget:
Direct Mail: 35%
Magazines: 35%
Telephone: 30%
Founded: 1898
Gross sales or billing: $175,500,000

Electric, manual & crank-free manual beds, dining, resident & commons area furnishings, nationwide direct sales force & leasing programs. Sell to healthcare, hospital & retirement industry.

SUNSTAR

Div. of Strategic Planning
4635 W Foster Ave
Chicago, IL 60630-1709
Telephone: (773) 777-4000, FAX: (773) 777-1417, E-Mail: dominico@sunstar.com, Web Site: www.sunstar.com

CEO: Hiroo Kaneda
Pres: Shigeto Yasuoka
VP: Lawrence Farrell
Gen Mgr: Noboru Masuda
Primary Market Served: Business & Consumer
Catalog available online
Indirect online sales
Gross sales or billing: $44,300,000

Represents pharmaceutical company based in Japan. Oral care, health and beauty.

SUPELCO INC
Div. of Sigma-Aldrich Co
595 N Harrison Rd
Bellefonte, PA 16823-6217
Telephone: (814) 359-3441, Toll Free: (800) 359-3041, FAX: (814) 359-3044, E-Mail: supelco@sial.com, Web Site: www.sigma-aldrich.com
Pres: Russell Gant
VP, Mktg: Shailesh Maingi
Conducts Business: Worldwide
Primary Market Served: Business
Advertising/Marketing Budget Related to Direct Marketing: 51-75%
Founded: 1966

Separations technology & supportive products for analysts in the petroleum/chemicals, life sciences, environmental & food & beverage markets; such as high resolution GC, capillary & HPLC products as well as a full line of accessories & chemical standards.

SWEEPSTAKES CLEARINGHOUSE
Subs. of Allied Marketing Group Inc
2000 E Lamar Blvd
Dallas, TX 76006
Telephone: (214) 915-7100, Toll Free: (800) 481-2631, FAX: (214) 915-7458, E-Mail: customersupport@sweepstakesclearinghouse.com, Web Site: www.schstore.com
Pres: Steven Hammond
COO: Julia Gostic
Conducts Business: U.S., Canada
Employees: 200
Primary Market Served: Consumer
Advertising/Marketing Budget Related to Direct Marketing: 76-100%
Direct Marketing ad budget:
Direct Mail: 100%
Founded: 1984

Discount consumer mail order marketer.

SYLVAN LEARNING INC
1001 Fleet St (fl 9)
Baltimore, MD 21202
Telephone: (410) 843-8000, Toll Free: (800) 31-SUCCESS, FAX: (410) 843-8057, E-Mail: pr@sylvanlearning.com, Web Site: www.sylvanlearning.com
CEO: Jeffrey Cohen
Chief Growth Officer: Barbara Timm-Brock
Chief Mktg Officer: Julia Fitzgerald
Chief Academic Officer: Lynn A. Fontana PhD
CFO: John McAuliffe
Chief Tech Officer: Eric Wenck
Chief People Officer: Sasha Shultz
Conducts Business: U.S., Canada, Germany, Guam, Spain
Primary Market Served: Consumer
Catalog available online
Direct Marketing ad budget: $15,000,000
Direct Mail: 10%
Magazines: 5%
Newspapers: 25%
TV/Radio: 55%
Telephone: 5%
Founded: 1979

Tutoring provider.

SYMANTEC
350 Ellis St
Mountain View, CA 94043-2202
Telephone: (408) 517-8000, FAX: (408) 517-8186, Web Site: www.symantec.com
Pres & CEO: Michael Brown
Exec VP, COO: Stephen Gillett
Exec VP & CFO: Thomas Seifert
Exec VP, Gen Counsel & Sec: Scott Taylor
Employees: 17,100
Primary Market Served: Business & Consumer
Catalog available online
Direct online sales
Founded: 1982
Gross sales or billing: $5,199,400,000

Manufacture & market network security software for consumers and businesses and computer software systems.

SYNGENTA
410 Swing Rd
Greensboro, NC 27409-2012
Telephone: (336) 632-6000, FAX: (336) 632-7065
Conducts Business: U.S.
Employees: 1,500
Primary Market Served: Business & Consumer

Agricultural chemical manufacturer.

SYNTELLECT
Div. of Enghouse Systems, Ltd.
2095 W Pinnacle Peak Rd Ste 110
Phoenix, AZ 85027-1262
Telephone: (602) 789-2800, Toll Free: (800) 788-9733, FAX: (602) 789-2899, Web Site: www.syntellect.com
Chmn & CEO: Anthony Carollo
Pres: Steve Dodenhoff
VP & CFO: Timothy V. Vatuone
Dir Sls & Mktg: Andy Klune
Conducts Business: U.S., Canada
Employees: 45
Primary Market Served: Business

Design, manufacture & sell telecommunication equipment.

SYSTEM PAVERS
3750 S Susan St (Suite 200)
Newport Beach, CA 92704-6964
Telephone: (949) 263-8300, Web Site: www.systempavers.com
VP Mktg: Katherine Fotch
Primary Market Served: Business & Consumer

SYSTEMAX INC
dba Infotel Distributors and Tiger Direct
11 Harbor Park Dr
Port Washington, NY 11050
Telephone: (516) 608-7000, FAX: (516) 6208-7001, Web Site: www.systemax.com
Chmn Bd & CEO: Richard Leeds
VP Mktg: Scott Strunk
Conducts Business: U.S., Canada
Employees: 3,287
Primary Market Served: Business & Consumer
Gross sales or billing: $2,345,200,000

Direct marketer of computers and related products to businesses in North America and Europe. Through nearly 20 catalogs and a dozen Web sites, Systemax offers more than 100,000 brand-name and private-label items. Systemax also assembles its own computers, which are sold under the Systemax and Ultra brands.

TD AMERITRADE HOLDING CORP
200 S 108th Ave
Omaha, NE 68154
Toll Free: (800) 237-8692, Web Site: www.amtd.com
Pres & CEO: Fred Tomczyk
Exec VP & COO: Marv Adams
Pres Retail Distr: Tom Bradley
Exec VP & CFO: William J. Gerber
Exec VP & Chief Risk Officer: David Kimm

TDS TELECOM
525 Junction Rd
Madison, WI 53717-2152

Telephone: (608) 664-4119, Web Site:
www.tdstelecom.com
Dir, Consumer Mktg: Shane West

TNT PACKAGING INC
2390 NW 149th St
Miami, FL 33054
Telephone: (305) 633-2556, (305) 769-
0616, Toll Free: (800) 327-6085,
FAX: (305) 769-0619, E-Mail:
tntpackaging@bellsouth.net, Web
Site: www.tntpackaging.com
Gen Mgr: Jeffrey Tokayer
Mgr Sls: Barry Tokayer
Conducts Business: Worldwide
Employees: 14
Primary Market Served: Business
Catalog available online
Indirect online sales
Direct Marketing ad budget: $446,000
Founded: 1981
Gross sales or billing: $2,700,000

Direct mail marketers & manufacturers
of corrugated solid fiber boxes & "lu-
cite" products, bins, shipping cartons,
office supplies & files.

TXU ENERGY
6555 Sierra Dr
Irving, TX 77002-6336
Telephone: (972) 868-8345, Web Site:
www.txu.com
Dir Mktg: Eddie Otto

TARGET CORP
1000 Nicollet Mall
Minneapolis, MN 55403
Telephone: (612) 304-6073, Web Site:
www.target.com
Exec VP, Gen Counsel & Sec: Timothy
Baer
Exec VP & CIO: Robert DeRodes
Exec VP Property Devel: John Griffith
Exec VP & CFO: John Mulligan
Exec VP & Chief Mktg Officer: Jeffrey
J. Jones II
Exec VP HR: Jodeen Kozlak
Exec VP Stores: Tina Schiel
Exec VP Mdsg & Supply Chain: Ka-
thryn Tesija
Pres Community Rels: Laysha L. Ward
Founded: 1946

Upscale discount retailer.

TAYLOR CORP
1725 Roe Crest Dr
North Mankato, MN 56003-1806
Telephone: (507) 625-2828, FAX:
(507) 625-3388
Pres: Bradley J. Schreier
VP Sls & Mktg: Gary Zellmer
VP Social Div: Jean Andersen
Christmas Mgr: Patricia Savig
DM Div Mgr: Paul Schleich

Conducts Business: U.S., Canada
Employees: 100
Primary Market Served: Business &
Consumer

Holding company - imprinted items,
stationary pens, business cards & greeting cards.

TAYLOR-STILES DIVISION
Littleford Day Inc
7451 Empire Dr
Florence, KY 41042
Telephone: (859) 525-7600, Toll Free:
(800) 365-8555, FAX: (859) 525-
1446, E-Mail: sales@littleford.com,
Web Site: www.littleford.com
Pres & CEO: Donald Steedman
Mktg Mgr: William R. Barker
Conducts Business: Worldwide
Employees: 150
Primary Market Served: Business
Catalog available online
Advertising/Marketing Budget Related
to Direct Marketing: 51-75%
Founded: 1882

Manufacture & market size reduction,
waste reclamation & recycling equipment to various processing industries.

TECHNI-TOOL INC
1547 N Trooper Rd
Worcester, PA 19490
Telephone: (610) 941-2400, Toll Free:
(800) 832-4866, FAX: (800) 854-
8665, E-Mail: sales@techni-tool.
com, Web Site: www.techni-tool.
com
Pres: Paul Weiss
VP, Mktg: David Weitner
Exec VP: Steven Weiss
Exec VP: Stuart Weiss
VP, Sls: Michael Ryan
Conducts Business: Worldwide
Employees: 235
Primary Market Served: Business
Catalog available online
Direct online sales
Advertising/Marketing Budget Related
to Direct Marketing: 76-100%
Direct Marketing ad budget:
$1,000,000
Founded: 1959
Gross sales or billing: $50,000,000

Supplier of tools, tool kits, soldering,
test equipment & instrumentation for
electronic production, assembly & repair.

TEKTRONIX INC
14200 SW Karl Braun Dr
Beaverton, OR 97077
Telephone: (503) 627-7111, Toll Free:
(800) 833-9200, FAX: (503) 627-
3247, Web Site: www.tektronix.com
Chmn, Pres & CEO: Rick Wills

VP, Sls: Richard McBee
Mktg Mgr: Steve Dawson
Sr VP & CFO: Colin L. Slade
Sr VP Corp Devel, Gen Counsel &
Sec: James F. Dalton
VP & Gen Mgr: Bob Agnes
Employees: 4,400
Primary Market Served: Business
Catalog available online
Gross sales or billing: $1,100,000,000

Manufacture electronic measurement,
communications & display equipment.

TELCORDIA
TECHNOLOGIES
One Telcordia Dr
Piscataway, NJ 08854-4151
Telephone: (732) 699-2000, FAX:
(973) 829-2458, Web Site: www.
telcordia.com
CEO: Richard Smith
Sr VP Mktg: Graham Palmer
Tech Licensing Dir: Andrew Dudek
Exec VP Global Sls Mktg: Patrick Jog-
gerst
Primary Market Served: Business

Telecommunications research & software.

TELECT INC
23321 E Knox Ave
Liberty Lake, WA 99019-9461
Telephone: (509) 926-6000, FAX:
(509) 926-8915, E-Mail: getinfo@
telect.com, Web Site: www.telect.
com
Pres & CEO: Wayne E. Williams
Exec VP & CFO: Stan Hilbert
Founder & Chmn Bd: Bill Williams Jr.
Dir Corp Controller: Mike Drew
Dir Global Quality: Kelly Jones
Primary Market Served: Business
Catalog available online
Direct online sales

Manufacture telecommunications hardware.

TELEFLORA
11444 W Olympic Blvd (fl 4)
Los Angeles, CA 90064-1546
Telephone: (310) 966-3586, Web Site:
www.teleflora.com
Dir, Partner Mktg: Pamela Ng
Primary Market Served: Business &
Consumer

TELEFONIX INC
2340 Ernie Kruger Cir
Waukegan, IL 60087-3224
Telephone: (847) 244-4500, Web Site:
www.telefonixinc.com
VP, Sls Mktg: Allison Burke
Primary Market Served: Business

TENNESSEE VALLEY AUTHORITY

400 W Summit Hill Dr
Knoxville, TN 37902-1499
Telephone: (865) 632-2101, Web Site:
  www.tva.gov
Pres & CEO: Bill Johnson
Exec VP & COO: Chip Pardee
Exec VP & CFO: John Thomas
Exec VP & Gen Counsel: Ralph Rodgers
Exec VP & Chief External Rels Officer: Rob Manning
Sr VP HR & Commun: Kathy Black
Primary Market Served: Business
Catalog available online
Founded: 1933
Gross sales or billing: $9,100,000,000

Electrical utility.

TENSAR INTERNATIONAL CORPORATION

2500 Northwinds Pkwy (Suite 500)
Alpharetta, GA 30009-2247
Telephone: (404) 250-1290, Web Site:
  www.tensarcorp.com
VP Mktg: Tim Oliver
Primary Market Served: Business

TERMINIX INTERNATIONAL, THE TRUGREEN COMPANIES

860 Ridge Lake Blvd
Memphis, TN 38120-9434
Telephone: (901) 766-1105, Web Site:
  www.trugreenchemlawn.com
Sr VP: Norman Goldenberg
Primary Market Served: Business &
  Consumer

TESSCO INC

RP-NFOA
11126 McCormick Rd
Hunt Valley, MD 21031
Telephone: (410) 229-1000, Toll Free:
  (800) 508-5444, FAX: (410) 527-
  0005, E-Mail: webhelp@tessco.com,
  Web Site: www.tessco.com
CEO: Robert B. Barnhill Jr.
Conducts Business: U.S., Canada
Employees: 100
Primary Market Served: Business &
  Consumer
Founded: 1952

Distributor of wireless communications
products.

TETLEY USA INC

Subs. of Tata Global Beverages
155 Chestnut Ridge Rd
Montvale, NJ 07645-1156
Telephone: (201) 571-0300, Web Site:
  www.tetleyusa.com
Reg Pres: Steve Rice

Sr VP Sls & Mktg: David Allen
Conducts Business: U.S.
Primary Market Served: Business &
  Consumer

Tea manufacturer.

TEXAS INDUSTRIES INC

1341 W Mockingbird Ln
Dallas, TX 75247
Telephone: (972) 647-6700, FAX:
  (972) 647-3878, Web Site: www.txi.
  com
Chmn: Robert D. Rogers
Pres: Melvin G. Brekhus
Exec VP & CFO: Richard M. Fowler
VP, Steel: Tommy A. Valenta
Primary Market Served: Business
Catalog available online
Gross sales or billing: $996,000,000

Manufacture & sell cement, concrete,
steel & masonry products.

TEXWIPE CO

1210 S Park Dr
Kernersville, NC 27284-3104
Telephone: (201) 684-1800, Toll Free:
  (800) TEXWIPE, FAX: (201) 684-
  1801, E-Mail: info@texwipe.com,
  Web Site: www.texwipe.com
Pres & CEO: William Paley
Prod Mktg Mgr: Mark King
Facilities Mgr: Larry Ruvolo
Corp Acct Mgr: Tim Daly
Conducts Business: Worldwide
Employees: 200
Primary Market Served: Business
Catalog available online
Indirect online sales
Advertising/Marketing Budget Related
  to Direct Marketing: 26-50%
Founded: 1964

Manufacturer of contamination & control products for hospitals, laboratories
& clear rooms.

THEIDEACLUB.COM & DUMAS MARTIN CONSULTING

101 W Mission Blvd (Suite 110-147)
Pomona, CA 91766-1245
Telephone: (909) 620-4772, FAX:
  (909) 629-4739, Web Site: www.
  theideaclub.com
Pres & CEO: Dumas Martin Jr.
Co-Founder & VP: Eleanora O. Murph
Conducts Business: U.S.
Employees: 5
Primary Market Served: Business &
  Consumer
Catalog available online
Direct online sales
Advertising/Marketing Budget Related
  to Direct Marketing: 0-25%
Direct Marketing ad budget:

Direct Mail: $2,000
Magazines: $3,000
Newspapers: $5,000
Online: $5,000
TV/Radio: $2,000
Telephone: $5,000
Founded: 1993

Idea development consulting service.

THERMAL PRODUCT SOLUTIONS

Div. of Lunaire Ltd
PO Box 150
White Deer, PA 17887-0150
Telephone: (570) 538-7200, Toll Free:
  (800) 586-2473
Pres: Michael Grausam
VP: Stuart Lunick
VP: Arthur Campbell
VP Engrng: Troy Boring
Application Engrng Mgr: Glenn Cun-
  ningham
Mktg Coord: Erin Hall
Conducts Business: Worldwide
Employees: 250
Primary Market Served: Business
Catalog available online
Indirect online sales
Advertising/Marketing Budget Related
  to Direct Marketing: 0-25%
Direct Marketing ad budget: $90,000
Direct Mail: 20%
Magazines: 80%
Founded: 1932
Gross sales or billing: $20,000,000

Test chambers for the simulation of environmental conditions - temperature,
humidity, altitude, pressure & combined environments. Burn-in, temperature cycling, thermal shock, stress
screening, precision lab ovens, vacuum
& clean room ovens. Sell to all industries & the government.

THERMO PRO

1600 Distribution Dr (Suite D)
Duluth, GA 30097
Telephone: (678) 475-1647, Toll Free:
  (800) 523-5542, FAX: (678) 475-
  1747, Web Site: www.thermopro.
  com
Pres: David Gould
VP: Michael L. Gould
Mktg Mgr: Nancy Prossick
Conducts Business: U.S., Canada,
  Great Britain, France
Employees: 30
Primary Market Served: Business &
  Consumer
Catalog available online
Advertising/Marketing Budget Related
  to Direct Marketing: 0-25%

Founded: 1970

Manufacturer & distributor of storage containers, magazine displays & literature organizers.

THETFORD CORP

7101 Jackson Rd
Ann Arbor, MI 48103
Telephone: (734) 769-6000, Toll Free: (800) 543-1219, FAX: (734) 769-2023, Web Site: www.thetford.com
Pres & CEO: John Arlen
VP, Opers: Don Ternes
Mktg Mgr: Armin Luzi
Conducts Business: Worldwide
Employees: 275
Primary Market Served: Business & Consumer
Catalog available online
Direct Marketing ad budget: $400,000
Founded: 1963
Gross sales or billing: $75,000,000

Manufacturer of sanitation products & systems for recreational vehicle & marine industries.

THOMAS COMPUTER CORP

809 Irma Ave
Orlando, FL 32803-3806
Telephone: (407) 855-2020, Toll Free: (800) 621-3906, FAX: (407) 426-2805, E-Mail: hildap@ thomascompute.com, Web Site: www.thomascomputer.com
Pres: Charles Green
VP: Douglas Polkosky
VP: Hilda Polkosky
Treas & Sec: Stanley Green
Conducts Business: Worldwide
Employees: 16
Primary Market Served: Business & Consumer
Indirect online sales
Advertising/Marketing Budget Related to Direct Marketing: 76-100%
Founded: 1965

Marketer of computers, supplies & accessories.

THOMAS KLISE/CRIMSON MULTIMEDIA

PO Box 720
Mystic, CT 06355-0720
Toll Free: (800) 937-0092, FAX: (860) 536-5141, E-Mail: info@crimsoninc.com, Web Site: www.crimsoninc.com
Pres: Molly Klise
Conducts Business: U.S.
Employees: 13
Primary Market Served: Business
Catalog available online
Indirect online sales

Advertising/Marketing Budget Related to Direct Marketing: 76-100%
Direct Marketing ad budget:
Direct Mail: 90%
Magazines: 5%
Newspapers: 5%
Founded: 1994
Gross sales or billing: $2,500,000

Educational & entertainment software for school & library use.

THORLO INC

2210 Newton Dr, PO Box 5399
Statesville, NC 28687
Telephone: (704) 872-6522, Toll Free: (888) 846-7567, FAX: (704) 838-7005, Web Site: www.thorlo.com
VP, Mktg: Robert Ravich
Employees: 350
Primary Market Served: Consumer
Founded: 1953

Sock manufacturer.

THOUGHT TECHNOLOGY LTD

2180 Belgrave Ave
Montreal, QC, Canada H4A 2L8
Telephone: (514) 489-8251, Toll Free: (800) 361-3651, FAX: (514) 489-8255, E-Mail: lawrence@ thoughttechnology.com, Web Site: www.thoughttechnology.com
Pres: Hal K. Myers
VP & Co-Founder: Lawrence Klein
Sales & Mktg Mgr: Shawn Tian
Conducts Business: Worldwide
Employees: 45
Primary Market Served: Business
Catalog available online
Advertising/Marketing Budget Related to Direct Marketing: 0-25%
Direct Marketing ad budget:
Direct Mail: 50%
Magazines: 25%
Telephone: 25%
Founded: 1974

Manufacturer of Bio-feedback equipment.

THOUSAND TRAILS LP

2 N Riverside Plz (Suite 800)
Chicago, IL 60606-2682
Telephone: (214) 618-7200, Toll Free: (800) 205-0606, FAX: (214) 618-7324, Web Site: www.1000trails.com
Pres & CEO: John Malone
CFO: Bryan D. Reed
VP, Sls & Mktg: R. Gerald Gelinas
VP, Gen Counsel: Walter B. Jaccard
VP HR: David McCrum
Conducts Business: U.S.
Employees: 2,400
Primary Market Served: Consumer
Catalog available online

Indirect online sales
Advertising/Marketing Budget Related to Direct Marketing: 51-75%
Gross sales or billing: $72,000,000

Sell memberships to a private resort network. Campsites in the US & British Columbia & recreational facilities.

THREE GEORGES AND THE NUTHOUSE

558 S Broad St
Mobile, AL 36603-1124
Telephone: (334) 433-1689, FAX: (334) 433-3364, E-Mail: sales@ threegeorges.com, Web Site: www.threegeorges.com
Pres & CEO: Scott Gonzales
VP: Siobhan Gonzales
Conducts Business: U.S.
Employees: 15
Primary Market Served: Business & Consumer
Catalog available online
Direct online sales

Marketer of shelled pecans & fruit cakes sold wholesale & retail.

3M POST-IT CUSTOM PRINTED PRODUCTS

3M Center Bldg
Saint Paul, MN 55144-1001
Toll Free: (800) 328-2407, Web Site: www.3m.com
Mktg & Comm Mgr: Mindy Shea
Nat Sls Mgr: Tim Mogck
Primary Market Served: Business

TIMBER CREST FARMS

4791 Dry Creek Rd
Healdsburg, CA 95448
Telephone: (707) 433-8251, FAX: (707) 433-8255, E-Mail: tcf@sonic.net, Web Site: www.sonic.net/tcf
Owner: Ronald E. Waltenspiel
Mktg Dir: Ruth Waltenspiel
Conducts Business: Worldwide
Employees: 17
Primary Market Served: Business & Consumer
Catalog available online
Direct online sales
Advertising/Marketing Budget Related to Direct Marketing: 0-25%
Direct Marketing ad budget:
Direct Mail: 10%
Magazines: 80%
Newspapers: 10%
Founded: 1957
Gross sales or billing: $4,000,000

Grow, process & package dried fruits, nuts, dried tomatoes & gift packs.

TIMBERLAND LLC

Subs. of VF Corp

200 Domain Dr
Stratham, NH 03885
Telephone: (603) 772-9500, Toll Free:
(888) 802-9947, Web Site: www.
timberland.com
Pres: Patrik Frisk
Conducts Business: U.S.
Employees: 600
Primary Market Served: Consumer
Direct online sales
Advertising/Marketing Budget Related
to Direct Marketing: 0-25%
Direct Marketing ad budget:
Direct Mail: 100%
Founded: 1955
Gross sales or billing: $2,000,000,000
Manufacturer and retailer of outdoor
footwear and apparel.

TIME PRODUCTS INTERNATIONAL

501 Pierce St
Del Rio, TX 78840-5456
Telephone: (847) 459-8885, FAX:
(847) 459-8111, E-Mail: cttpi@aol.
com, Web Site: www.tpi2000.com
Pres: Herbert Kwok
Sr VP, Mktg: Edward Gusfield
VP: Paul Berko
Employees: 20
Primary Market Served: Business &
Consumer
Advertising/Marketing Budget Related
to Direct Marketing: 0-25%
Direct Marketing ad budget:
Direct Mail: 100%
Founded: 1977
Gross sales or billing: $8,000,000

Small electronic consumer-type items -
clocks, calculators & radios to direct
mail & mail order. Also, promotional
products.

TIME/SYSTEM

150 Front St (Fl 1 Bldg C)
Chicopee, MA 01013
Toll Free: (800) 637-9942, FAX: (800)
269-3075, E-Mail: customerservice@
timesystem.us, Web Site: www.
timesystem.us
Pres: Sheryl Hofmann
Conducts Business: U.S., Canada
Employees: 50
Primary Market Served: Business &
Consumer
Advertising/Marketing Budget Related
to Direct Marketing: 0-25%
Direct Marketing ad budget: $250,000
Founded: 1981

Manufacturer & distributor of productivity tools & training (i.e. paper-based
management systems, software, workshops).

TIME WARNER INC

1 Time Warner Ctr
New York, NY 10019-8016
Telephone: (212) 484-8000, Web Site:
www.timewarner.com
Chmn & CEO: Jeffrey L. Bewkes
Exec VP & CFO: Howard M. Averill
Exec VP & Gen Counsel: Paul T. Cap-
puccio
Exec VP, Corp Mktg & Commun: Gary
L. Ginsberg
Exec VP Global Pub Policy: Carol A.
Melton
Exec VP, Intl & Corp Strategy: Olaf
Olafsson
Primary Market Served: Business &
Consumer

Media & entertainment company with
businesses in television networks, film
& TV entertainment and publishing.

TIMM MEDICAL TECHNOLOGIES, INC

150 Saunders Rd (Suite 120)
Lake Forest, IL 60045-2524
Telephone: (952) 947-9410, Toll Free:
(800) 438-8592, FAX: (952) 947-
9411, Web Site: www.timmmedical.
com
Founder & Chmn: Gerry Timm
Pres & CEO: Gerry Mattys
CFO: Bill Cook
Mgr: Camille Christianson
Employees: 120
Primary Market Served: Business &
Consumer
Catalog available online
Direct online sales
Founded: 1997

Markets impotence & incontinence diagnostic & management products to
doctors, pharmacists & consumers.

TOLAND HOME AND GARDEN INC

273 N Otto St
Port Townsend, WA 98368-9780
Telephone: (504) 893-9503, Toll Free:
(800) 989-6287, E-Mail: info@
tolandhomeandgarden.com, Web
Site: www.tolandhomeandgarden.
com
Owner: Bruce Solly
Consultant: David T. Sands
Consultant: Jill Sands
Conducts Business: U.S.
Employees: 125
Primary Market Served: Business
Catalog available online
Advertising/Marketing Budget Related
to Direct Marketing: 51-75%

Manufacturer of personalized door &
car mats, accent rugs & pillows; including decorated flags, comfort mats &
computer mouse pads.

TOMAHAWK LIVE TRAP CO

PO Box 323
Tomahawk, WI 54487-0323
Telephone: (715) 453-3550, Toll Free:
(800) 272-8727, FAX: (715) 453-
4326, E-Mail: trapem@livetrap.com,
Web Site: www.livetrap.com
Pres: Greg Smith
Sls & Fin Exec: Mary S. Smith
Conducts Business: U.S., Canada, Ar-
gentina, Brazil, England, Germany,
Mexico
Employees: 45
Primary Market Served: Business &
Consumer
Catalog available online
Direct online sales
Founded: 1925

Traps & cages that capture animals
alive & unharmed. Animal traps, cages
& squeeze cages, animal control poles
& protection gloves.

THE TORO CO

8111 Lyndale Ave S
Bloomington, MN 55420
Telephone: (952) 888-8801, Toll Free:
(800) 348-2424, FAX: (952) 887-
8258, E-Mail: companyinfo@
thetorocompany.com, Web Site:
www.thetorocompany.com
Chmn & CEO: Mike Hoffman
VP, Treas & CFO: Renee J. Peterson
VP HR & Bus Devel: Peter M. Ram-
stad
Conducts Business: Worldwide
Primary Market Served: Consumer
Catalog available online
Indirect online sales

Provider of innovative turf, landscape,
rental & construction equipment and irrigation & outdoor lighting solutions.

TOTER INC

841 Meacham Rd
Statesville, NC 28677
Telephone: (704) 872-8171, Toll Free:
(800) 424-0422, FAX: (704) 878-
0734, E-Mail: info@toter.com, Web
Site: www.toter.com
Pres, CEO: Larry Boppe
VP, Sls & Mktg: John Scott
CFO: Jeff Gilliam
Conducts Business: U.S., Japan
Employees: 400
Primary Market Served: Business &
Consumer
Direct Marketing ad budget:
Magazines: 100%
Gross sales or billing: $65,000,000

Manufacture molded polyethylene roll-
out cart systems for commercial & residential recycling & refuse collection.

Special office carts are available for confidential documents, office paper & aluminum can recycling.

TOYOTA MOTOR SALES USA INC

19001 S Western Ave
Torrance, CA 90501
Telephone: (310) 468-4000, Toll Free: (800) 331-4331, FAX: (310) 468-7841, Web Site: www.toyota.com
Exec Chmn: Yoshima Inaba
Pres & CEO: Kazuo Ohara
VP North America Bus Strategy: Nihar Patel
VP Mktg: Flaurel English
VP Retail Market Devel: Ernest Bastien
VP Corp Commun: Steven Curtis
Sr VP: Robert C. Daly
Grp VP & CFO: Tracey C. Doi
VP Vehicle Mktg & Commun: Alec Hagey
VP Mktg: Jack Hollis
Employees: 8,900
Primary Market Served: Business & Consumer
Catalog available online
Indirect online sales
Gross sales or billing: $2,147,500,000

Corporate headquarters office for sales division within America.

TRANCOS INC

6800 Koll Center Pkwy (Ste 170)
Pleasanton, CA 94566-7044
Telephone: (650) 364-3110, Web Site: www.trancos.com
CEO: Brian Nelson

TRANSCAT

35 Vantage Point Dr
Rochester, NY 14624-1175
Telephone: (585) 352-9460, Toll Free: (800) 800-5001, FAX: (585) 352-1486, Web Site: www.transcat.com
Chairman: Carl E. Sassano
Pres, CEO & COO: Charles P. Hadeed
VP Fin CFO: John J. Zimmer
VP HR: John A. DeVoldre
VP Mktg: Jay F. Woychick
Conducts Business: Worldwide
Employees: 238
Primary Market Served: Business
Catalog available online
Direct online sales
Advertising/Marketing Budget Related to Direct Marketing: 51-75%
Direct Marketing ad budget: $1,000,000
Founded: 1964
Gross sales or billing: $66,500,000

Distributor of calibration & test instruments. Also offers calibration services.

TRANSEMANTICS INC

1337 Connecticut Ave NW (4th fl)
Washington, DC 20036
Telephone: (202) 362-2505, FAX: (202) 686-5603, E-Mail: ili@transemantics.com, Web Site: www.transemantics.com
Dir: Marie-Laurence Wax
Mgr: Allen B. Cooperman
Conducts Business: U.S., Europe
Employees: 26
Primary Market Served: Business
Advertising/Marketing Budget Related to Direct Marketing: 76-100%
Founded: 1970
Gross sales or billing: $1,500,000

All aspects of foreign language communication, including, but not limited to: translating, interpreting, cultural analysis of promotional material aimed at foreign markets, typesetting, audio-visual narration, subtitling, tape transcription, language & culture research.

TRI-CHEM INC

681 Main St Ste 24, Bldg 24
Belleville, NJ 07109-3471
Telephone: (973) 751-9200, FAX: (973) 450-1260, (973) 450-1057, E-Mail: paints@trichem.com, Web Site: www.trichem.com
CEO: Andy McKnight
VP, Sls: Linda Musgrove
Opers Mgr: Kathleen Bodrato
Conducts Business: Worldwide
Employees: 250
Primary Market Served: Consumer
Advertising/Marketing Budget Related to Direct Marketing: 76-100%
Direct Marketing ad budget:
Direct Mail: 90%
Magazines: 4%
Newspapers: 5%
Telephone: 1%
Founded: 1950
Gross sales or billing: $420,000

Direct selling company. Sell fashion painting supply items to 10,000 independent dealers (in-home demonstrators).

TRI TECH LABORATORIES INC

1000 Robins Rd
Lynchburg, VA 24504-3516
Telephone: (434) 845-7073, FAX: (434) 847-4360, Web Site: www.tritechlabs.com
Pres: Ron Rogers
Conducts Business: U.S.
Primary Market Served: Business
Direct Marketing ad budget:
Direct Mail: 65%
Magazines: 15%
Newspapers: 5%

TV/Radio: 15%
Sell cosmetics, toiletries, food, household products, jewelry & giftware to independent sales agents.

TRICOR BRAUN

2145 Internationale Pkwy Ste 800
Woodridge, IL 60517-4830
Telephone: (708) 385-9333, FAX: (708) 385-3015, Web Site: www.tricorbraun.com
Chmn: Ken Kranzberg
Pres & CEO: Keith Strope
Exec VP, Design: Craig Sawicki
Conducts Business: U.S., Canada, Mexico, Central America, South America, Europe, Asia
Employees: 300
Primary Market Served: Business
Catalog available online
Advertising/Marketing Budget Related to Direct Marketing: 0-25%

Packaging, design & supply, focus on containers for cosmetic-personal care & household chemicals & fragrance.

TRILITHIC

9710 Park Davis Dr
Indianapolis, IN 46235-2390
Telephone: (317) 423-6604, Web Site: www.trilithic.com
Dir, Mktg & Communs: Karalee Slayton
Primary Market Served: Business

TRISTAR PRODUCTS

492 US Hwy 46 E
Fairfield, NJ 07004
Telephone: (973) 575-5400, FAX: (973) 683-6708, E-Mail: infotp@tristarproductsinc.com, Web Site: www.tristarproductsinc.com
Pres & CEO: Keith Mirchandani
VP & CFO: Steve Souers
Producer: Chris Bonanno
Dir Production: John Glouatts
Dir HR: Elizabeth Sandman
Primary Market Served: Business
Catalog available online
Direct online sales

International direct response marketing company. Markets products through TV, retail & catalog advertising.

TRITON COLLEGE

2000 Fifth Ave
River Grove, IL 60171
Telephone: (708) 456-0300, FAX: (708) 583-3121, Web Site: www.triton.edu
Pres: Patricia Granados
Dir Mktg Svcs: Sam Tolia
Conducts Business: U.S.

Primary Market Served: Business & Consumer
Catalog available online
Founded: 1964

Two year community college & business employee training facility.

TRUE VALUE CO
8600 W Bryn Mawr Ave
Chicago, IL 60631-3579
Telephone: (773) 695-5000, Web Site: www.truevaluecompany.com
Pres & CEO: John Hartman
Sr VP Mktg & Chief Customer Officer: Blake Fohl
Sr VP & Chief Mdsg Officer: Ken Goodgame
Sr VP & CFO: Dave Shadduck
Sr VP & COO: Abhinav Shukla
Primary Market Served: Consumer

Retailer-owned hardware cooperative.

TRUGREEN/CHEMLAWN
RP-NFOA
461 Enterprise Dr
Lewis Center, OH 43035-9424
Telephone: (614) 846-1800, Toll Free: (800) TRUE-GREEN, FAX: (614) 431-0155, Web Site: www.trugreen.com
Chmn: George W. Tamke
CEO: J. Patrick Speinhour
Sr VP & CFO: Steve J. Martin
Branch Mgr: Al Karow
Conducts Business: U.S., Canada
Employees: 700
Primary Market Served: Business & Consumer
Advertising/Marketing Budget Related to Direct Marketing: 76-100%

Offer quality lawn, tree & shrub care to residential & commercial customers.

TRUITT BROTHERS INC
1105 Front St NE
Salem, OR 97301-1034
Telephone: (503) 362-3674, Toll Free: (800) 547-8712, FAX: (503) 588-2868, E-Mail: truittbrothers@truittbros.com, Web Site: www.truittbros.com
Pres: Peter Truitt
VP: David Truitt
Gen Mgr Spec Prods: Jeff Geyer
Mktg Mgr: Roger Plant
Food Svc Sls Dir: Rod Friesen
Conducts Business: U.S., Pacific Rim, Mexico
Employees: 350
Primary Market Served: Business

Produce shelf stable canned, tray & pouched products for institutional, wholesale & retail markets.

TUPPERWARE BRANDS CORP
14901 S Orange Blossom Trail
Orlando, FL 32837
Telephone: (407) 826-5050, Toll Free: (800) 366-3800, FAX: (407) 826-8874, Web Site: www.tupperwarebrands.com
Chmn & CEO: Rick Goings
Pres & COO: Simon Hemus
Grp Pres Europe, Africa & Middle East: R. Glenn Drake
Sr VP Global Mktg & Strategy: Gavin Little
Sr VP Global Product Mktg: William J. Wright
VP Global Pub Rels & Women's Initiative: Elinor Steele
Conducts Business: Worldwide
Primary Market Served: Consumer
Catalog available online
Direct online sales

Developer, manufacturer and distributor of storage, preparation and organization housewares.

20TH CENTURY FOX TELEVISION
10201 W Pico Blvd
Los Angeles, CA 90064-2606
Telephone: (310) 369-4636, FAX: (310) 969-0468, Web Site: www.foxstudios.com
Co-Chmn & Pres: Gary Newman
Co-Chmn & Pres: Dana Walden
Exec VP & CFO: Robert Barron
Conducts Business: International (except U.S., Canada)
Employees: 400
Primary Market Served: Business & Consumer
Catalog available online
Advertising/Marketing Budget Related to Direct Marketing: 51-75%
Founded: 1983

Production & distribution of television programming.

TYCO ELECTRONICS CORP
Subs. of TE Connectivity Ltd
1050 Westlakes Dr
Berwyn, PA 19312
Telephone: (610) 893-9800, Web Site: www.te.com
Chmn & CEO: Tom Lynch
Exec VP & CFO: Robert Hau
Exec VP & Chief Tech Officer: Rob Shaddock
Sr VP Strategy & Bus Devel: Brad Gambill
Sr VP & Chief Mktg Officer: Amy Shah
Conducts Business: U.S.
Primary Market Served: Business
Catalog available online

Indirect online sales
Advertising/Marketing Budget Related to Direct Marketing: 0-25%
Founded: 1957

Broad based materials science company. Develop & supply high performance products (many based on radiation chemistry) for the electronics, aerospace, processed electrical power, construction, telecommunications & consumer industries.

TYCO VALVES & CONTROLS
Div. of Tyco International Ltd
10707 Clay Rd (#200)
Houston, TX 77041-5497
Telephone: (713) 986-4665, Toll Free: (800) 343-0990, FAX: (713) 937-5466, Web Site: www.tycovalves.com
Chmn & CEO: Edward D. Breen
VP, Mktg: Mark Fucich
VP, Sls & Dist: Gene Crouch
Mgr, Mktg Svcs: Darrel Desrochers
Conducts Business: Worldwide
Employees: 594
Primary Market Served: Business
Catalog available online

Manufacturer of Butterfly Valves: ANSI Class 150/300 2"-36," AWWA 3"-96," Resilient Seat 1"-48," PTFE Lined 2"-12." Check Valves 2"-48." Electric, pneumatic and hydraulic actuators & accessories for quarter turn valves.

U-HAUL INTERNATIONAL
2727 N Central Ave
Phoenix, AZ 85004
Telephone: (602) 263-6011, Toll Free: (800) GO-UHAUL, FAX: (602) 263-6598, Web Site: www.uhaul.com
Chmn & CEO: Joe Shoen
Pres: John C. Taylor
VP U-Haul Bus Consultants: James P. Shoen
Conducts Business: U.S., Canada
Primary Market Served: Business & Consumer
Catalog available online
Indirect online sales
Advertising/Marketing Budget Related to Direct Marketing: 0-25%
Founded: 1945

Truck & trailer rentals.

UGL EQUIS CORP
161 N Clark St (Suite 2400)
Chicago, IL 60601-3221
Telephone: (312) 424-8000, FAX: (312) 424-8080, Web Site: www.equiscorp.com
Pres & CEO: David Montross

Exec VP & CFO: Larry O'Drobinak
Mktg Coord: Lawrence Perea
HR: Linda Gamino
Commun: Megan Brody
Conducts Business: U.S.
Primary Market Served: Business &
Consumer
Catalog available online
Founded: 1984

Real estate tenant representation.

USX
600 Grant St
Pittsburgh, PA 15219
Telephone: (412) 433-1121, E-Mail:
webmaster@usx.com, Web Site:
www.usx.com
Chmn & CEO USX Corp: Thomas J.
Usher
Vice Chmn & CFO: Robert M. Hernan-
dez
Public Affairs Mgr: John Armstrong
Primary Market Served: Business &
Consumer

Manufacture iron & steel products &
oil company.

ULTIMATE OFFICE
PO Box 688
Farmingdale, NJ 07727-0688
Telephone: (732) 780-6911, Toll Free:
(800) 631-2233, FAX: (732) 780-
9833, Web Site: www.ultoffice.com
Pres: Donald McGee
Database Mgr: Michele Scott
Conducts Business: U.S.
Employees: 25
Primary Market Served: Business
Advertising/Marketing Budget Related
to Direct Marketing: 76-100%
Direct Marketing ad budget:
Direct Mail: 90%
Online: 10%

Manufacture & supply magnetic visual
scheduling boards. Sell through direct
mail to known inquirers & buyers of direct mail items.

ULTIMATE PRODUCTS INC
RP-NFOA
1151 Bay Blvd (Suite D)
Chula Vista, CA 91911-2669
Telephone: (813) 881-1575, Toll Free:
(800) 477-4287, FAX: (813) 881-
1831, E-Mail: office@ultimatehat.
com, Web Site: www.ultimatehat.
com
Pres: Monica McGrath
Conducts Business: Worldwide
Employees: 8
Primary Market Served: Business &
Consumer
Catalog available online
Direct online sales

Founded: 1987
Manufacturer of nautical belts & jewelry.

ULTRA DIRECT MARKETING INC
PO Box 1575
Jackson, NJ 08527
Telephone: (732) 364-8337, Toll Free:
(800) 365-8587, FAX: (732) 364-
9598, E-Mail: contact@ultradirect.
com, Web Site: www.ultradirect.com
Pres: Randi Hersh
Conducts Business: U.S.
Employees: 5
Primary Market Served: Business
Catalog available online
Direct online sales

Sell computer supplies & accessories.

UNADILLA LAMINATED PRODUCTS
Div. of Unadilla Silo Co Inc
32 Clifton St
Unadilla, NY 13849
Telephone: (607) 369-9341, FAX:
(607) 369-3608, E-Mail: info@
unalam.com, Web Site: www.
unalam.com
Pres: Craig H. Van Cott
VP, Sls: Phillip Holowacz
Conducts Business: U.S., Canada
Employees: 75
Primary Market Served: Business &
Consumer
Advertising/Marketing Budget Related
to Direct Marketing: 0-25%
Direct Marketing ad budget:
Direct Mail: 50%
Magazines: 50%
Founded: 1906

Manufacturer of glue laminated wood
arches, beams & trusses.

UNICOM ELECTRIC INC
565 Brea Canyon Rd Ste A
Walnut, CA 91789-3004
Telephone: (626) 964-7873, Toll Free:
(800) 346-6668, FAX: (626) 964-
7880, E-Mail: info@unicomlink.
com, Web Site: www.unicomlink.
com
Pres: Jeffrey Lo
Sls Mgr: Sam Hen
Conducts Business: U.S., Canada
Employees: 32
Primary Market Served: Business &
Consumer
Catalog available online
Advertising/Marketing Budget Related
to Direct Marketing: 0-25%
Founded: 1986

Gross sales or billing: $3,100,000
Network hardware to the enterprise &
Soho market.

UNICOM GOVERNMENT INC
RP-NFOA
Div. UNICOM Global
2553 Dulles View Dr (Suite 100)
Herndon, VA 20171-5228
Telephone: (703) 502-2000, FAX:
(703) 463-5011, Web Site:
unicomgov.com
CEO: Corry S. Hong
Conducts Business: U.S.
Primary Market Served: Business
Catalog available online
Advertising/Marketing Budget Related
to Direct Marketing: 26-50%

Provider of computer hardware & software products to federal government.

UNILEVER BEST FOODS
Subs. of Unilever United States
800 Sylvan Ave
Englewood Cliffs, NJ 07632
Telephone: (201) 567-8000, FAX:
(201) 871-8257, E-Mail:
comments@unilever.com, Web Site:
www.unilever.com
Pres Unilever Foods: Antoine De Saint-
Affrique
Pres Unilever North America: Kees
Kruythoff
Conducts Business: Worldwide
Primary Market Served: Consumer
Catalog available online

Maker & seller of condiments.

UNION SWITCH & SIGNAL INC
Subs. of Ansaldo Signal NV
1000 Technology Dr
Pittsburgh, PA 15219-3120
Telephone: (412) 688-2400, Toll Free:
(800) 351-1520, FAX: (412) 688-
2399, Web Site: www.switch.com
Prod Mngmt Dir: Robert Galbraith
VP Sls & Mktg: John P. Dolan
Conducts Business: Worldwide
Employees: 950
Primary Market Served: Business
Advertising/Marketing Budget Related
to Direct Marketing: 0-25%
Direct Marketing ad budget: $200,000
Direct Mail: $100,000
Magazines: $100,000
Founded: 1881
Gross sales or billing: $270,900,000

Supplier of traditional & modern signal
& control products & systems for Class
1, Regional & Short Line Railroads,
transit & commuter applications; offer

individual products, turnkey systems, maintenance & repair, engineering & service.

UNISYS
801 Lakeview Dr (Ste 100)
Blue Bell, PA 19422
Telephone: (215) 986-4011, Toll Free: (800) 874-8647, FAX: (215) 986-2312, Web Site: www.unisys.com
Chmn & CEO: J. Edward Coleman
Sr VP & Chief Mktg Officer: Quincy Allen
Sr VP & CFO: Janet B. Haugen
Sr VP & Chief Info Officer: Suresh Mathews
Sr VP & Pres Global Sls: Jeff Renzi
Conducts Business: Worldwide
Employees: 23,000
Primary Market Served: Business
Catalog available online
Advertising/Marketing Budget Related to Direct Marketing: 0-25%
Founded: 1886

Information technology company.

UNITED AIR SPECIALISTS INC
Subs. of Clareor Inc
4440 Creek Rd
Cincinnati, OH 45242
Telephone: (513) 891-0400, Toll Free: (800) 992-4422, FAX: (513) 891-4882, E-Mail: uas@uasinc.com, Web Site: www.uasinc.com
Pres: Rich Larson
VP, Mktg: Pam Curry
Conducts Business: Worldwide
Employees: 230
Primary Market Served: Business & Consumer
Catalog available online
Indirect online sales
Advertising/Marketing Budget Related to Direct Marketing: 51-75%
Direct Marketing ad budget: $230,000
Direct Mail: $130,000
Magazines: $45,000
Newspapers: $30,000
Online: $25,000
Founded: 1966

Manufacturer & distributor of electronic air cleaners for commercial & industrial use.

UNITED SECURITY PRODUCTS INC
PO Box 785
Poway, CA 92074-0785
Telephone: (858) 413-0149, Toll Free: (800) 227-1592, FAX: (858) 413-0124, E-Mail: usp@unitedsecurity.com, Web Site: www.unitedsecurity.com
Pres: Ted Greene

Conducts Business: Worldwide
Employees: 32
Primary Market Served: Business & Consumer
Catalog available online
Founded: 1972
Gross sales or billing: $3,900,000

Manufacturer of burglar & fire alarm equipment.

UNITED STAFFING SYSTEMS
130 William St (fl 5)
New York, NY 10038
Toll Free: (800) 972-9525, FAX: (646) 224-8393, Web Site: www.unitedstaffing.com
Pres: Barry Saide
Primary Market Served: Business & Consumer
Catalog available online

Full-service personnel agency.

US BRANDING GROUP LLC
PO Box 540957
Lake Worth, FL 33467
Telephone: (561) 966-8090
Primary Market Served: Business & Consumer

US GAS & ELECTRIC
333 Mamaroneck Ave (#490)
White Plains, NY 10605
Telephone: (888) 947-7880, FAX: (888) 400-1230, E-Mail: salesinfo@usgande.com, Web Site: www.usgande.com
Pres & CEO: Douglas Marcille Esq.
Exec VP Energy Supply & Bus Devel: Brian Rose
COO: Joseph Casey
Exec VP & CFO: David Weinberg
Founded: 2002

Commercial & residential energy provider.

US PLAYING CARD CO
Subs. of Jarden Corp
300 Gap Way
Erlanger, KY 41018-3160
Toll Free: (800) 543-2273, FAX: (859) 815-7566, E-Mail: sales@usplayingcard.com, Web Site: www.usplayingcard.com
Pres: Marc Hill
Sr VP Mktg: Roy Gifford
Conducts Business: U.S., Canada, Europe
Primary Market Served: Business
Advertising/Marketing Budget Related to Direct Marketing: 0-25%
Founded: 1867

Manufacturer of playing cards & calendars.

UNIVERSAL CORP
1501 N Hamilton St
Richmond, VA 23230
Telephone: (804) 359-9311, FAX: (804) 254-3582, Web Site: www.universalcorp.com
Chmn & CEO: Henry H. Harrell
Pres: Allen King
Primary Market Served: Business
Founded: 1918

Importers & exporters of tobacco leaf.

UNIVERSAL ENGINEERING CORP
800 First Ave NW
Cedar Rapids, IA 52405-3999
Telephone: (319) 365-0441, Toll Free: (800) 366-2051, FAX: (319) 369-5440, E-Mail: info@universalcrusher.com, Web Site: www.universalcrusher.com
CEO: Daniel Ferguson
CFO: Tom J. Werning
Sls & Mktg Mgr: Gerry Mangrich
Conducts Business: Worldwide
Employees: 60
Primary Market Served: Business
Catalog available online
Direct Marketing ad budget:
Magazines: 100%
Founded: 1906
Gross sales or billing: $10,000,000

Manufacture rock crushers, shredders & apron feeders.

UNIVERSAL SECURITY INSTRUMENTS INC
11407 Cronhill Dr (Suite A)
Owings Mills, MD 21117-6218
Telephone: (410) 363-3000, FAX: (410) 363-2218, E-Mail: sales@universalsecurity.com, Web Site: www.universalsecurity.com
CEO, Sec & Treas: James B. Huff
Pres: Harvey B. Grossblatt
Office Mgr: Susie Bowles
Conducts Business: U.S.
Employees: 15
Primary Market Served: Business & Consumer
Catalog available online
Direct online sales
Founded: 1969
Gross sales or billing: $35,800,000

Designs and sells smoke alarms, carbon monoxide alarms and outdoor floodlights in retail stores. Smoke alarms for the hearing impaired are sold to distributors by USI Electric subsidiary.

UNIVERSAL TRAINING
736 N Western Ave (Suite 323)
Lake Forest, IL 60045

Telephone: (847) 235-2170, E-Mail: information@universaltraining.com, Web Site: www.universaltraining.com
Pres & Co-Owner: Carl Ruggiero
Dir Mktg & PR: Maureen Smith-McKee
Sr Cons & Co-Owner: Mary Carolan
Sr Cons & Co-Owner: John Doyle
Conducts Business: U.S., Canada & Mexico
Employees: 25
Primary Market Served: Business
Direct online sales
Advertising/Marketing Budget Related to Direct Marketing: 0-25%
Founded: 1968
Gross sales or billing: $2,000,000

Custom training.

UNIWAY MANAGEMENT CORP

dba Ucac Financial Services
5182A Old Dixie Hwy
Forest Park, GA 30297
Telephone: (404) 363-6200, Toll Free: (888) 386-4929, FAX: (404) 363-8848, E-Mail: uniway@bellsouth.net, Web Site: www.uniway.com
Pres: Robert C. Hardy
Chmn Bd: Robert W. Carter
Conducts Business: U.S.
Employees: 11
Primary Market Served: Consumer
Advertising/Marketing Budget Related to Direct Marketing: 51-75%
Founded: 1979
Gross sales or billing: $1,500,000

Consumer services & franchise continuing/club programs & consumer products - wholesalers/distributors.

UPSTART

Div. of Highsmith Co
PO Box 8010
Madison, WI 53708-8010
Telephone: (920) 563-9571, FAX: (800) 448-5828, Web Site: www.highsmith.com
Gen Mgr Dist: Bill Flood
Conducts Business: U.S.
Employees: 15
Primary Market Served: Business & Consumer
Direct Marketing ad budget:
Direct Mail: 95%
Magazines: 5%

Sell posters, bookmarks, T-shirts, buttons, sweatshirts, books, plastic book bags, certificates, mobiles, bulletin board decorators & balloons to libraries & schools.

URBAN MAPPING INC

690 Fifth St (Suite 200)
San Francisco, CA 94107-1517
Telephone: (415) 946-8170, Web Site: www.urbanmapping.com
CEO: Ian White

UTILITIES SUPPLY CORP

Subs. of F W Webb
50 Everberg Rd
Woburn, MA 01801-1019
Telephone: (781) 395-9023, Toll Free: (800) 343-7555, FAX: (800) 232-8726, (781) 395-2329, E-Mail: jge@fwwebb.com, Web Site: www.uscosupply.com
Opers Mgr: John Everett
Conducts Business: Worldwide
Employees: 35
Primary Market Served: Business & Consumer
Catalog available online
Direct online sales
Advertising/Marketing Budget Related to Direct Marketing: 76-100%
Direct Marketing ad budget: $100,000
Direct Mail: 50%
Magazines: 40%
Telephone: 10%

Distributor of thermoplastic piping products & accessories, environmental, plumbing & heating products.

VALDAWN WATCH CO

2910 Thomson Ave (6th fl)
Long Island City, NY 11101-2939
Telephone: (201) 807-1110, FAX: (201) 807-0228
Pres: Mark Schell
Mktg Dir: Amy Burdick
Conducts Business: U.S.
Employees: 15
Primary Market Served: Business
Advertising/Marketing Budget Related to Direct Marketing: 26-50%
Gross sales or billing: $3,500,000

Design & manufactures custom watches.

VALENTI CLASSICS

9848 S 57th St
Franklin, WI 53132-8680
Telephone: (262) 835-2070, FAX: (262) 835-2575, Web Site: www.valenticlassics.com
CEO: Steve Valenti

VALENTINE RESEARCH INC

10280 Alliance Rd
Cincinnati, OH 45242-4710
Telephone: (513) 984-8900, Toll Free: (800) 331-3030, FAX: (513) 984-8976, E-Mail: sales@valentine1.com, Web Site: www.valentine1.com
Pres: Michael D. Valentine
Dir Mktg: Pete Kaufman
Conducts Business: U.S., Canada
Primary Market Served: Consumer
Catalog available online
Direct online sales

Vertically integrated electronic products & radar locators manufacturer & direct marketer.

VANCE INDUSTRIES INC

5617 W Howard St
Niles, IL 60714-4011
Telephone: (847) 375-8900, FAX: (847) 375-6818, E-Mail: vance@vanceind.com, Web Site: www.vanceind.com
Chmn & CEO: William Rapp
Pres: Jim Schleiter
Mktg Svcs Mgr: Lisa Walker
Retail Div: John Kensey
Conducts Business: U.S., Canada, Europe
Employees: 70
Primary Market Served: Business & Consumer
Advertising/Marketing Budget Related to Direct Marketing: 0-25%
Direct Marketing ad budget:
Direct Mail: 35%
Magazines: 55%
Telephone: 10%

Manufacturer of cutting boards, drawer organizers, kitchen sinks & bar sinks.

THE VANE BROTHERS CO

2100 Frankfurst Ave
Baltimore, MD 21226-1026
Telephone: (410) 631-5096, FAX: (410) 631-7781, E-Mail: webmaster@vanebros.com, Web Site: www.vanebros.com
Pres: Duff Hughes
Mktg Dir: Don Glenn
Primary Market Served: Business

Marine transportation of petroleum products & sale of bunker fuel to ships.

VEER

119 14th St NW (Suite 400)
Calgary, AB, Canada T2N IZ6
Telephone: (403) 234-7901, Web Site: www.veer.com
Mktg Mgr: Marla Clarke
Primary Market Served: Business

VENTYX

400 Perimeter Center Ter NE Ste 500
Atlanta, GA 30346-1231
Telephone: (770) 952-8444, Toll Free: (800) 868-0497, FAX: (770) 955-2977, E-Mail: support@ventyx.com, Web Site: www.ventyx.com
Pres: Gregory Dukat

VP, Mktg: Steve Roth
Event Mktg Mgr: Martha Thompson
Mktg Coord: Ronnie Norton
Conducts Business: Worldwide
Employees: 1,000
Primary Market Served: Business
Founded: 1976

Software development company, EAM.

VERIAD
Subs. of Moore Wallace
650 Columbia St
Brea, CA 92821-2912
Telephone: (714) 990-2700, Toll Free:
(800) 962-0658, FAX: (800) 962-
0658, E-Mail: info@veriad.com,
Web Site: www.veriad.com
Pres: Cal Laird
Owner: David G. Smith
CEO Moore Wallace: Mark A. Angel-
som
VP Customer Tech: Denise Milano
Lead Svc Mgr: Laura Richards
Info Tech Mgr: Micke Clemens
Conducts Business: U.S., Canada
Employees: 165
Primary Market Served: Business
Catalog available online
Direct online sales
Founded: 1958

Manufacturer of pressure sensitive labels supplied direct to hospitals, business & industry.

VERTEX INC
1041 Old Cassatt Rd
Berwyn, PA 19312
Telephone: (610) 640-4200, Toll Free:
(800) 355-3500, FAX: (610) 640-
5892, Web Site: www.vertexinc.com
Pres & CEO: Jeff Westphal
VP, Mktg: Gerry Hurley
VP Commun & Pub Affairs: Alex
Smith
Conducts Business: U.S., Canada
Employees: 160
Primary Market Served: Business
Catalog available online
Indirect online sales
Founded: 1978

Developer & marketer of computer
software for tax-related applications.
Products are used for the calculation of
taxes by companies doing business in
several states. Sales tax software covers
all taxing jurisdictions in the U.S. &
Canada. Payroll software interfaces
with payroll systems to calculate federal, state & local withholding taxes. Telecommunication tax software provides
utility tax rate information for all taxing jurisdictions in the U.S.

VIACOM INC
dba Viacom

1515 Broadway
New York, NY 10036-8901
Telephone: (212) 258-6000, FAX:
(212) 258-6464, Web Site: www.
viacom.com
Exec Chmn: Sumner E. Redstone
Pres, CEO & Dir: Philippe Dauman
Exec VP, Corp Commun: Carl D. Folta
COO: Thomas E. Dooley
CFO & Exec VP Strategy & Corp De-
vel: Wade Davis
Exec VP HR & Admin: Scott M. Mills
Primary Market Served: Business &
Consumer

Entertainment & publishing.

VIAHEALTH
1425 Portland Ave
Rochester, NY 14621-3001
Telephone: (585) 922-4000, (585) 922-
3677, FAX: (585) 922-3929, Web
Site: www.viahealth.org
Pres: Mark Clement
Dir: Joseph Vasile
Sr VP: Dr. Richard Gangemi
VP, Fin Svcs: John Midolo
Dept Chief: John Schriver
Mktg: Mike Tedesco
Conducts Business: U.S.
Employees: 6,000
Primary Market Served: Business &
Consumer
Catalog available online
Advertising/Marketing Budget Related
to Direct Marketing: 0-25%
Direct Marketing ad budget:
Direct Mail: 50%
Newspapers: 25%
TV/Radio: 25%
Gross sales or billing: $202,000,000

Inpatient & ambulatory healthcare to
community.

VIATECH PUBLISHING
SOLUTIONS INC
1440 5th Ave
Bay Shore, NY 11706-4147
Telephone: (631) 968-8500, Toll Free:
(800) 645-8558, FAX: (631) 968-
0830, Web Site: www.viatechpub.
com
COO: Ron Simmons
VP, Natl Sls: Thomas Bergenholtz
Conducts Business: U.S., Canada,
Mexico
Employees: 500
Primary Market Served: Business
Catalog available online
Indirect online sales
Advertising/Marketing Budget Related
to Direct Marketing: 0-25%
Founded: 1906

Manufacture loose leaf binders & accessories. On demand printing & fulfillment services.

VICTORY CORPS
2730 Nevada Ave N
New Hope, MN 55427
Telephone: (763) 561-5600, Toll Free:
(800) 328-6120, FAX: (763) 561-
8523, E-Mail: cs@victorycorps.com,
Web Site: www.victorycorps.com
Pres: Dennis Flaherty
Sls Mgr: Brian Knoop
Mktg Coord: Stacy Handeland
Mktg Mgr: Polly Fossum
Conducts Business: U.S., Canada
Employees: 70
Primary Market Served: Business &
Consumer
Catalog available online
Direct online sales
Direct Marketing ad budget: $225,000
Direct Mail: 30%
Magazines: 20%
Online: 30%
Telephone: 20%
Founded: 1904
Gross sales or billing: $10,000,000

Retail catalog sales of flags, flag poles,
custom banners, parade floats & float
kits, sign and banner displays, trade
show displays and accessories.

VIERK NATIONAL SUPPLY
2300 Commonwealth Ave
North Chicago, IL 60064
Telephone: (847) 869-4318, Toll Free:
(800) 428-7548, FAX: (847) 689-
4412, Web Site: www.vierk.com
CFO: Amber Swift
Conducts Business: U.S.
Employees: 11
Primary Market Served: Business
Catalog available online
Indirect online sales
Advertising/Marketing Budget Related
to Direct Marketing: 76-100%
Direct Marketing ad budget:
Direct Mail: $240,000
Telephone: $18,000
Founded: 1949
Gross sales or billing: $2,600,000

Wholesale distributor of plumbing/
heating & industrial supplies.

VIEW VIDEO INC/ARCADIA
ENTERTAINMENT CORP
PO Box 77
Saugerties, NY 12477
Telephone: (845) 246-9955, FAX:
(845) 246-9966, E-Mail: sales@
view.com, Web Site: www.view.com
Pres & Founder: Bob Karcy
Conducts Business: Worldwide
Employees: 15
Primary Market Served: Business &
Consumer
Catalog available online
Direct online sales

Advertising/Marketing Budget Related to Direct Marketing: 26-50%
Founded: 1984

Pre-recorded home video cassettes. Broadcast quality programming in the following core areas: art, classical music, opera, dance, jazz & pop music, parenting/children's interactive, sports, modern lifestyles.

VIKING PUMP INC

Div. of IDEX Corp
406 State St, Box 8
Cedar Falls, IA 50613-0008
Telephone: (319) 266-1741, FAX: (319) 273-8157, E-Mail: info@vikingpump.com, Web Site: www.vikingpump.com
Mktg Mgr: James Mayer
VP, Mktg & Sls: Kevin Rhodes
VP, Domestic Mktg: W. Vogel
Mktg Dir: James Murphy
Conducts Business: Worldwide
Employees: 770
Primary Market Served: Business
Catalog available online
Direct online sales
Advertising/Marketing Budget Related to Direct Marketing: 0-25%
Direct Marketing ad budget:
Direct Mail: 10%
Magazines: 90%
Founded: 1911

Manufacturer of positive displacement rotary pumps. Marketed through a worldwide distribution organization to petroleum, chemical & petrochemical industries. Food, pulp and paper manufacturers & most other process industries.

VILLAGE WEAVERS

418 Villita St Ste 800
San Antonio, TX 78205-2910
Telephone: (210) 222-0776, E-Mail: shop@villageweavers.com, Web Site: www.villageweavers.com
Pres: Chris Van Wyk

VIRCO MANUFACTURING CORP

Hwy 65 S
Conway, AR 72033
Telephone: (501) 329-2901, Toll Free: (800) 448-4726, FAX: (800) 258-7367, E-Mail: info@virco.com, Web Site: www.virco.com
VP, Mktg: Randal Smith
VP: Glen Parish
Facilities Mgr: Don Curran
Corp Copywriter: Bob Roskos
Primary Market Served: Business & Consumer
Catalog available online

Direct online sales
School & office furniture manufacturer.

VIRGINIA PORT AUTHORITY

Commonwealth of Virginia
600 World Trade Ctr
Norfolk, VA 23510-1781
Telephone: (757) 683-8000, Toll Free: (800) 446-8098, FAX: (757) 683-2897, Web Site: www.portofvirginia.com
Dir Port Promo: Linda Ford
Conducts Business: U.S., Worldwide
Employees: 150

Provides port services (transportation) to importers, exporters, S/S lines, railroads & motor carriers.

VISIBLE COMPUTER SUPPLY CORP

Subs. of Wallace Computer Services Inc
1750 Wallace Ave
Saint Charles, IL 60174
Telephone: (630) 377-2586, Toll Free: (800) 323-0628, FAX: (800) 233-2016, Web Site: www.wallace.com
Gen Mgr: Paul Kasanders
Conducts Business: U.S.
Primary Market Served: Business
Direct Marketing ad budget:
Direct Mail: 90%
Telephone: 10%

Supplier of tax forms.

VISUAL HORIZONS

180 Metro Park
Rochester, NY 14623-2610
Telephone: (585) 424-5300, Toll Free: (800) 424-1011, FAX: (800) 424-5411, E-Mail: cs@visualhorizons.com, Web Site: www.visualhorizons.com
Pres: Stanley Z. Feingold
VP, Co-Founder: Reenie Feingold
Conducts Business: U.S., Australia, England, Germany, India
Employees: 10
Primary Market Served: Business
Catalog available online
Indirect online sales
Advertising/Marketing Budget Related to Direct Marketing: 76-100%
Founded: 1971
Gross sales or billing: $2,000,000

Free 56-page full-color catalog includes "Presentation Survival Skills," offering advice for the beginner to the power presenter. Offer up-to-date selection of stock slides & overheads, LCD panels, projectors, laminating & binding equipment, laser pointers &

thousands of hard-to-find products at competitive prices. Some services include 35mm slide duplication, creation of custom slides & overheads, PC/MAC scans & imaging of slides & overheads from PC/MAC files such as PowerPoint, Corel Draw, Freelance etc.

VITA-MIX CORP

8615 Usher Rd
Cleveland, OH 44138-2199
Telephone: (440) 235-4840, Toll Free: (800) VITA-MIX, FAX: (440) 235-3726, E-Mail: service@vitamix.com, Web Site: www.vitamix.com
Pres: John Barnard
Chmn Bd Dirs: W. G. Barnard
Mktg Asst: Kristi Poltrone
Comml Mktg Mgr: DeAnne Hrabak
Conducts Business: Worldwide
Employees: 125
Primary Market Served: Consumer
Catalog available online
Direct online sales
Founded: 1921

Manufacturer of multi-purpose small kitchen appliances.

VITASOY USA INC

1 New England Way
Ayer, MA 01432-1514
Telephone: (978) 772-6880, Toll Free: (800) VITA-SOY, FAX: (978) 772-6881, E-Mail: info@vitasoy-usa.com, Web Site: www.vitasoy-usa.com
Pres & CEO: Walter Riglian
Conducts Business: U.S.
Employees: 90
Primary Market Served: Business & Consumer
Catalog available online
Founded: 1940
Gross sales or billing: $50,000,000

Process & manufacture soy-based food products for retail consumption under Vitasoy, Azumaya & Nasoya labels.

VIVENDI SA

800 Third Ave
New York, NY 10022
Telephone: (212) 572-7000, FAX: (212) 572-1080, Web Site: www.vivendi.com
Chmn Mgmt Bd: Jean-Francois Dubos
Sr Exec VP Commun & Pub Affairs: Simon Gillham
CFO: Herve Philippe
Conducts Business: Worldwide
Primary Market Served: Business & Consumer
Catalog available online
Direct online sales

Founded: 1853

Consumer-focused, performance driven, values-based global media and communications company. Headquartered in Paris.

VIVITAR CORP
1600 N Desert Dr (Suite 101)
Tempe, AZ 85281-1798
Toll Free: (800) 592-9541, FAX: (909) 348-6390, Web Site: www.vivitar.com
Pres: Clifford Montgomery
Conducts Business: Worldwide
Employees: 150
Primary Market Served: Business & Consumer
Catalog available online
Advertising/Marketing Budget Related to Direct Marketing: 51-75%
Founded: 1938

Distributor of wide range of photographic items.

VOLKSWAGEN GROUP OF AMERICA INC
Subs. of Volkswagen AG
2200 Ferdinand Porsche Dr
Herndon, VA 20171
Telephone: (248) 754-5000, Web Site: www.volkswagengroupamerica.com
Pres & CEO: Michael Horn
COO: Mark McNabb
VP Sls: Mark Barnes
VP Customer Experience: Robert Martell
VP Mktg: Vinay Shahani
VP Mktg & Strategy: Joerg Sommer
VP After Sls: Don Stephenson
VP Brand Commun: Scott Vazin
Conducts Business: U.S., Canada
Employees: 5,900
Primary Market Served: Consumer
Catalog available online
Indirect online sales
Advertising/Marketing Budget Related to Direct Marketing: 0-25%

Manufacturer and distributor of automobiles.

VOLVO CARS OF NORTH AMERICA LLC
Subs. of AB Volvo
1 Volvo Dr, PO Box 914
Northvale, NJ 07647-0914
Telephone: (201) 768-7300, Toll Free: (800) 458-1552, E-Mail: customercare@volvocars.com, Web Site: www.volvocars.com
Pres & CEO: Tony Nicolosi
VP & CFO: Tim Fissinger
VP Mktg & Product Devel: Tassos Panos

Exec VP Grp Truck Sls & Mktg Americas: Dennis Slagle
Conducts Business: U.S., Canada
Employees: 4,500
Primary Market Served: Business & Consumer
Advertising/Marketing Budget Related to Direct Marketing: 0-25%
Gross sales or billing: $207,200,000

Import & market cars from Sweden.

ED VOYLES HYUNDAI INC
2135 Cobb Pkwy SE
Smyrna, GA 30080-7632
Telephone: (770) 952-8881, Toll Free: (877) 579-0642, FAX: (770) 612-9396, Web Site: www.edvoyleshyundai.com
Pres: Charles Edwin Voyles
Dir Internet Sls: Mike Cotter
Conducts Business: U.S.
Employees: 129
Primary Market Served: Business & Consumer
Catalog available online
Indirect online sales
Advertising/Marketing Budget Related to Direct Marketing: 0-25%
Direct Marketing ad budget:
Direct Mail: 20%
Magazines: 15%
Newspapers: 50%
Telephone: 15%

Auto & truck repairs; transportation services; small business accounting & services.

VULCAN INFORMATION PACKAGING
Div. of Ebsco Industries
PO Box 29
Vincent, AL 35178
Telephone: (205) 672-2241, Toll Free: (800) 633-4526, FAX: (205) 672-1276, Web Site: www.vulcan-online.com
CEO: J.T. Stephens
VP: Franklin Barn
Pur Mgr: Glen Jones
Conducts Business: U.S.
Employees: 300
Primary Market Served: Business & Consumer
Catalog available online
Direct online sales
Advertising/Marketing Budget Related to Direct Marketing: 26-50%
Founded: 1950

Manufacture loose leaf binders, magazine storage collectors, index tabs plus custom binders.

VULCAN MATERIALS CO
1200 Urban Ctr Dr

Birmingham, AL 35242
Telephone: (205) 298-3000, FAX: (205) 298-2960, Web Site: www.vulcanmaterials.com
Chmn, Pres & CEO: Donald M. James
Sr VP: Guy M. Badgett III
Sr VP: Danny R. Shepherd
Sr VP: Ronald G. Mc Abee
Sr VP: Daniel F. Sansone
Primary Market Served: Business
Advertising/Marketing Budget Related to Direct Marketing: 0-25%
Founded: 1909

Construction materials & chemicals.

WTS MEDIA
2841 Hickory Valley Rd, PO Box 8277
Chattanooga, TN 37421
Telephone: (423) 894-9427, Toll Free: (800) 251-7228, FAX: (423) 894-7281, E-Mail: customerservice@wtsmedia.com, Web Site: www.wts-tape.com
Pres & CEO: Tom Salley Sr.
Conducts Business: U.S.
Employees: 40
Primary Market Served: Business & Consumer
Catalog available online
Direct online sales
Advertising/Marketing Budget Related to Direct Marketing: 76-100%
Founded: 1977

Audio, video, CD and DVD duplication service. Blank audio and video media sales. Professional presentation products, including projectors, microphones, screens and lecterns.

WAG/AERO GROUP
1216 North Rd
Lyons, WI 53148
Telephone: (262) 763-9586, Toll Free: (800) 558-6868, FAX: (262) 763-7595, E-Mail: wagaero-sales@wagaero.com, Web Site: www.wagaero.com
Pres: Mary Myers
Mktg Dir: Mary Pat Henningfield
Buyer: Mary Meinen
Sls Dir: Sandy Hana
Conducts Business: Worldwide
Employees: 32
Primary Market Served: Business & Consumer
Catalog available online
Direct online sales
Advertising/Marketing Budget Related to Direct Marketing: 76-100%
Direct Marketing ad budget:
Direct Mail: 80%
Magazines: 5%
Online: 15%

Founded: 1961

Aircraft replacement parts, remanufacture exhaust systems, engine mounts & seatbelts.

WALMART STORES INC
702 SW 8th St
Bentonville, AR 72716
Telephone: (479) 273-4000, Toll Free: (800) 925-6278, FAX: (479) 277-1830, Web Site: www.walmart.com
Chmn: S. Robson Walton
Pres & CEO: Doug McMillon
Exec VP & CFO: Charles M. Holley Jr.
Exec VP & Gen Counsel: Karen Roberts
Exec VP & Chief Mdsg & Mktg Officer: Duncan Mac Naughton
Exec VP & Chief Mktg Officer: Stephen F. Quinn
Employees: 2,200,000
Primary Market Served: Consumer
Catalog available online
Indirect online sales
Gross sales or billing: $476,000,000,000

Discount retailer.

WARNACO SWIMWEAR INC
Div. of Speedo
1201 W 5th St (Suite T1200)
Los Angeles, CA 90017-1493
Telephone: (323) 726-1262, FAX: (323) 724-6931, Web Site: www.speedo.com
Pres, Speedo North America: Sherry Waterson
Pres, Designer Swimwear: Paul Schneider
COO: Larry Burak
CFO: Michelle Pascoe
VP, Mktg Speedo: Craig Brommers
Conducts Business: U.S.
Employees: 400
Primary Market Served: Business & Consumer
Catalog available online
Direct online sales
Gross sales or billing: $18,100,000

Sportswear & swimwear manufacturer & retailer.

WASHINGTON GAS ENERGY SERVICES
13865 Sunrise Valley Dr (Suite 200)
Herndon, VA 20171-6189
Telephone: (703) 793-7500, Web Site: www.wges.com
Mgr Residential Mktg: Maria Frazzini

WASHINGTON NATIONAL OPERA
2700 F St NW, Kennedy Center for the Arts
Washington, DC 20566
Telephone: (202) 467-4600, Toll Free: (800) 444-1324, Web Site: www.kennedy-center.org/wno
Music Dir: Philippe Auguin
Exec Dir: Michael L. Mael
Artistic Dir: Francesca Zambello
Conducts Business: U.S., Canada, Germany, U.K., France, Italy, Japan
Primary Market Served: Business & Consumer
Catalog available online
Direct online sales
Advertising/Marketing Budget Related to Direct Marketing: 51-75%
Founded: 1956

Ticket sales to performances of the opera, to subscribers, single ticket buyers, corporate accounts & civic organizations.

ANDREW D WASHTON BOOKS ON THE FINE ARTS
168 Irving Ave
Port Chester, NY 10573
Telephone: (914) 933-0479, E-Mail: andrew@washtonbooks.com, Web Site: www.washtonbooks.com
Pres: Andrew Washton
VP: Ruth Washton
Conducts Business: U.S., Canada, Europe, Far East
Employees: 1
Primary Market Served: Business & Consumer
Catalog available online
Direct online sales
Advertising/Marketing Budget Related to Direct Marketing: 0-25%
Direct Marketing ad budget: $5,000
Direct Mail: 90%
Magazines: 5%
Newspapers: 5%
Founded: 1982
Gross sales or billing: $100,000

Antiquarian book dealer in the fine arts. Sell to dealers of art, museums, scholars, libraries, collectors of art. Carry mostly out-of-print books.

WATERS CORP
34 Maple St
Milford, MA 01757-3696
Telephone: (508) 482-2000, Toll Free: (800) 252-4752, FAX: (508) 872-1990, Web Site: www.waters.com
Pres & CEO: Douglas A. Berthiaume
Employees: 2,500
Primary Market Served: Business
Catalog available online
Founded: 1958
Gross sales or billing: $350,000,000
Laboratory instruments.

WAYTEK
2440 Galpin Ct
Chanhassen, MN 55317-0690
Telephone: (952) 465-0431, Web Site: www.waytekwire.com
Mktg: Sonia Johnson
Primary Market Served: Business

WEBB DESIGNS INC
PO Box 1405
El Cajon, CA 92022-1405
Telephone: (619) 596-6400, Toll Free: (800) 262-9322, FAX: (619) 596-4511, E-Mail: awebb@webbshade.com, Web Site: www.webbshade.com
Pres: Allison Webb Untiedt
VP, R&D: Tony Webb
Dir: Chris Latko
Conducts Business: U.S., Canada, Mexico
Employees: 18
Primary Market Served: Business
Catalog available online
Direct Marketing ad budget: $12,000
Founded: 1946
Gross sales or billing: $1,400,000

Weaving mill & manufacturer of woven wood window shades.

THE WEDDING PAGES
195 Broadway
New York, NY 10007
Telephone: (212) 219-8555, Toll Free: (800) 843-4983, FAX: (212) 219-1929, Web Site: www.theknot.com
Chmn & CEO: David Liu
Pres & CMO: Janet Scardino
COO & Dir: Sandra Stiles
CFO, Treas & Sec: Richard Szefc
CTO: Armando Cardenas-Nolazsco
Conducts Business: U.S.
Employees: 80
Primary Market Served: Business & Consumer
Catalog available online
Direct online sales
Advertising/Marketing Budget Related to Direct Marketing: 26-50%
Direct Marketing ad budget: $300,000
Direct Mail: $200,000
Telephone: $100,000
Founded: 1982
Gross sales or billing: $72,000,000

Database marketing to brides & grooms. A complete bridal marketing system for wedding professionals.

WEIGHT WATCHERS INTERNATIONAL
675 Avenue of the Americas (fl 6)
New York, NY 10010-5117
Telephone: (516) 390-1400, FAX: (516) 390-1302, Web Site: www.weight-watchers.com

Pres & CEO: James R. Chambers
Pres North America: Lesya Lysyj
Chief Strategy Officer: Michael Echenberg
Chief Product Officer: Catherine Ulrich
Primary Market Served: Consumer
Founded: 1963

Commercial weight loss company.

WEINGEROFF ENTERPRISES INC

One Weingeroff Blvd
Cranston, RI 02910-4019
Telephone: (401) 467-2200, FAX: (401) 785-1320, Web Site: www. weingeroff.com
Chmn: Frederick L. Weingeroff
Pres: Gregg Weingeroff
Mktg Dir: Lisa Weingeroff
Mgr: Mona Hirson
Controller: Anthony P. Santucci
Conducts Business: Worldwide
Employees: 300
Primary Market Served: Business
Advertising/Marketing Budget Related to Direct Marketing: 0-25%
Direct Marketing ad budget: $500,000
Direct Mail: 30%
Magazines: 10%
Newspapers: 10%
TV/Radio: 50%
Founded: 1957
Gross sales or billing: $3,000,000

Supplier of premium incentives & continuity programs to the direct mail trade & TV markets.

WESCO

225 W Station Square Dr (Suite 700)
Pittsburgh, PA 15219
Telephone: (412) 454-2200, Toll Free: (800) 343-1201, E-Mail: info@ wesco.com, Web Site: www. wescodist.com
Chmn & CEO: Roy W. Haley
Sr VP & COO: John J. Engel
Sr VP, CFO & CAO: Stephen A. Van Oss
VP: William E. Cenk
VP: William M. Goodwin
Corp Controller: Timothy A. Hibbard
Conducts Business: U.S.
Employees: 80
Primary Market Served: Business & Consumer
Advertising/Marketing Budget Related to Direct Marketing: 0-25%
Direct Marketing ad budget:
Direct Mail: 25%
Magazines: 25%
Telephone: 50%
Founded: 1885

Electrical & electronics distributor & contractor.

WEST BEND

Brand of Focus Electrics LLC
2845 Wingate St
West Bend, WI 53095
Telephone: (262) 334-5107, Toll Free: (866) 290-1851, FAX: (262) 334-6800, Web Site: www.focuselectrics. com
Pres: Mike Carpenter
VP Prod Devel: Brian Beesley
Dir Prod Devel: Howard Kaney
Conducts Business: Worldwide
Employees: 40
Primary Market Served: Business & Consumer
Catalog available online
Direct online sales
Advertising/Marketing Budget Related to Direct Marketing: 0-25%
Founded: 1911
Gross sales or billing: $11,000,000

Manufacturer of quality electrical appliances, electronics & stainless steel cookware.

WEST FARM FOODS (BRANCH)

520 Albany St
Caldwell, ID 83605
Telephone: (208) 459-3687, FAX: (208) 459-9135, Web Site: www. westfarm.com
Pres: John Miller
Conducts Business: U.S.
Employees: 90
Primary Market Served: Business

Dairy products.

WESTCON

520 White Plains Rd (Ste 100)
Tarrytown, NY 10591-5167
Telephone: (914) 829-7000, FAX: (914) 829-7137, Web Site: www. westcon.com
Pres & CEO: Tom Dolan
Exec VP & CFO: John P. O'Malley
Exec VP: Anthony Daley
Sr VP Opers: Brian Westfield
CMO: Duncan Potter
Conducts Business: U.S.
Employees: 25
Primary Market Served: Business
Catalog available online
Direct online sales
Advertising/Marketing Budget Related to Direct Marketing: 76-100%

Electronic trade show management company.

WESTERN PSYCHOLOGICAL SERVICES

625 Alaska Ave
Torrance, CA 90503-5124
Telephone: (310) 478-2061, Toll Free: (800) 648-8857, FAX: (310)) 478-7838, E-Mail: marketing@ wpspublish.com, Web Site: www. wpspublish.com
Pres: Jeffrey Manson
Mktg Dir: Brian Thomas
Primary Market Served: Business & Consumer
Catalog available online
Direct online sales
Founded: 1948

Publisher of psychological and educational assessments.

WESTLAKE PLASTICS CO

PO Box 127
Lenni, PA 19052-0127
Telephone: (610) 459-1000, Toll Free: (800) 999-1700, FAX: (610) 459-1084, Web Site: www. westlakeplastics.com
Sls & Mktg Dir Indus Prods: Tony Caballero
Mktg Dir: Amy Gaylord
Sls Mgr: James Abbott
Pur Mgr: Elizabeth McKenna
Employees: 68
Primary Market Served: Business
Advertising/Marketing Budget Related to Direct Marketing: 76-100%
Founded: 1958
Gross sales or billing: $7,000,000

Custom bag manufacturer. All types & sizes. Plain or printed for packaging & protection.

WHIRLPOOL CORP

2000 N M-63
Benton Harbor, MI 49022-2692
Telephone: (269) 923-5000, E-Mail: info@whirlpool.com, Web Site: www.whirlpoolcorp.com
Chmn & CEO: Jeff Fettig
Exec VP & CFO: Larry Venturelli
Pres US Opers: Joseph T. Liotine
Exec VP Global Product Org: David Szczupak
Conducts Business: Worldwide
Primary Market Served: Business & Consumer
Gross sales or billing: $19,000,000,000

Manufacturer and marketer of major home appliances.

WHITAKER NATIONAL

533 Fourth Ave (12th fl)
Huntington, WV 25701-1318
Telephone: (304) 525-0852, Toll Free: (800) 377-8721, FAX: (304) 525-0874, Web Site: www.neshold.com
Vice Chmn, Pres, & CEO: Vincent Morra
COO: G. Scott Dillon
CFP: William G. Keely

Conducts Business: U.S.
Employees: 17
Primary Market Served: Business
Gross sales or billing: $5,500,000

Emergency room management.

WHITE CAP WHOLESALE CONTRACTORS SUPPLIES

Div. of White Cap Industries Inc
PO Box 1770
Costa Mesa, CA 92628-1770
Toll Free: (800) 944-8322, FAX: (866) 791-8396, E-Mail: customerservice@ whitecap.com, Web Site: www. whitecapdirect.com
Pres: Greg Grosch
VP & Sls Mgr: Rik Gagnon
Sec: Diane Galbreath
Mktg Dir: Terry Anderson
Conducts Business: U.S.
Employees: 400
Primary Market Served: Business & Consumer
Advertising/Marketing Budget Related to Direct Marketing: 76-100%
Founded: 1976
Gross sales or billing: $80,000,000

Sell construction tools & accessories to the construction trade.

WHITING & DAVIS

171 Commonwealth Ave
Attleboro Falls, MA 02763-1152
Telephone: (508) 699-4412, Toll Free: (800) 876-MESH, FAX: (508) 695-7606, E-Mail: info@ whitinganddavis.com, Web Site: www.whitinganddavis.com
Pres: David Youngerman
Conducts Business: Worldwide
Employees: 50
Primary Market Served: Business & Consumer
Catalog available online
Advertising/Marketing Budget Related to Direct Marketing: 0-25%
Direct Marketing ad budget: $50,000
Direct Mail: 55%
Magazines: 25%
Newspapers: 20%
Founded: 1991
Gross sales or billing: $8,000,000

Safety glove manufacturer. Safety products used in meat, pork & poultry slaughter facilities.

WHITMAN PUBLISHING LLC

3101 Clairmont Rd
Atlanta, GA 30329
Toll Free: (800) 546-2995, FAX: (256) 246-1116, E-Mail: info@ whitmanbooks.com, Web Site: www. whitmanbooks.com
Gen Mgr: Dawn Burbank

Conducts Business: U.S., Canada
Employees: 15
Primary Market Served: Business & Consumer
Advertising/Marketing Budget Related to Direct Marketing: 51-75%
Direct Marketing ad budget:
Direct Mail: 70%
Magazines: 20%
Newspapers: 10%
Founded: 1916

Sell stamps & stamp supplies to collectors (60% by mail direct to the consumer). Balance of business is jobber or dealer direct.

WIDEBAND BY KARS

PO Box 1785
New Rochelle, NY 10802-1785
Telephone: (212) 691-9000, FAX: (212) 691-9835, E-Mail: info@ widebandjewelry.com, Web Site: www.widebandjewelry.com
Pres: Richard M. Korwin
Conducts Business: U.S.
Employees: 10
Primary Market Served: Business
Catalog available online
Founded: 1951

Jewelry manufacturer.

LT MOSES WILLARD INC

3972 Bach Buxton Rd
Amelia, OH 45102-1014
Telephone: (513) 248-5500, Toll Free: (800) 621-8956, FAX: (513) 831-0548, E-Mail: info@ltmoses.com, Web Site: www.ltmoses.com
Owner: Christopher L. Nordloh
Conducts Business: U.S., Canada, Europe
Employees: 19
Primary Market Served: Business
Advertising/Marketing Budget Related to Direct Marketing: 0-25%
Direct Marketing ad budget:
Online: 100%
Founded: 1971
Gross sales or billing: $1,500,000

Manufacturer of handmade museum reproductions, lighting, folk art & accessories.

WILTON ARMETALE

Plumb & Square Sts
Mount Joy, PA 17552
Telephone: (717) 653-4444, Toll Free: (800) 553-2048, FAX: (717) 653-6573, E-Mail: cservice@armetale. com, Web Site: www.armetale.com
Chmn Bd: Fred Wilton
Chief Mktg Officer: Dan Helmer
Pres: David Meckley
Conducts Business: U.S., Canada, Japan, Germany

Employees: 180
Primary Market Served: Business & Consumer
Catalog available online
Direct online sales
Founded: 1892

Manufacturer of aluminum tableware, gifts & decorative accessories.

WILTON INDUSTRIES INC

2240 W 75th St
Woodridge, IL 60517
Telephone: (630) 963-1818, Toll Free: (800) 794-5866, FAX: (630) 963-7196, E-Mail: info@wilton.com, Web Site: www.wilton.com
Pres & CEO: Vincent Naccarato
VP & Gen Mgr: Marvin Oakes
Conducts Business: Worldwide
Employees: 500
Primary Market Served: Business & Consumer
Catalog available online
Direct online sales

Distributor of cake decorating, candy making & bakeware products, picture frames & fashion kitchenware products & gadgets.

WINDSOR VINEYARDS

205 Concourse Blvd
Santa Rosa, CA 95403-8258
Toll Free: (800) 289-9463, (800) 741-6070, E-Mail: webmaster@ windsorvineyards.com, Web Site: www.windsorvineyards.com
Principal: Patrick Roney
Principal: Leslie Rudd
Admin Asst: Gina Bertoli
Conducts Business: U.S.
Employees: 160
Primary Market Served: Business & Consumer
Catalog available online
Direct online sales
Founded: 1959
Gross sales or billing: $14,200,000

Sell premium California wines with personalized labels.

HARRY WINSTON INC

718 Fifth Ave
New York, NY 10019
Telephone: (212) 245-2000, FAX: (212) 489-0016, E-Mail: hw@ harrywinston.com, Web Site: www. harry-winston.com
Pres: Thomas O'Neill
VP, Wholesale: Steven Shonebarger
Primary Market Served: Business & Consumer

Retail jeweler.

WOMANSHIP
137 Conduit St
Annapolis, MD 21401
Telephone: (410) 267-6661, FAX:
(410) 263-2036, E-Mail: sail@
womanship.com, Web Site: www.
womanship.com
Pres & Founder: Suzanne Pogell
Conducts Business: U.S., Canada, British Virgin Islands, Europe (Greece,
Turkey, France), New Zealand
Employees: 100
Primary Market Served: Consumer
Direct online sales
Advertising/Marketing Budget Related
to Direct Marketing: 0-25%
Direct Marketing ad budget:
Direct Mail: 70%
Magazines: 15%
Newspapers: 10%
Telephone: 5%
Founded: 1984

Sailing school for women by women &
publisher of videos, articles & books
on collaborative learning & the issues
of women's & men's learning styles.

WORKING ASSETS
RP-NFOA
dba CREDO
101 Market St (Suite 700)
San Francisco, CA 94105
Toll Free: (800) 668-9253, FAX: (415)
371-1046, Web Site: www.
workingassets.com
CEO: Laura Scher
Pres: Michael Kieschnick
Employees: 107
Primary Market Served: Consumer
Founded: 1985
Gross sales or billing: $14,200,000

Long distance phone company & credit
card.

WORLD KITCHEN INC
1 Steuben St
Corning, NY 14830-2900
Telephone: (607) 377-8000, Toll Free:
(800) 999-3436, FAX: (607) 377-
8946, Web Site: www.worldkitchen.
com
Pres & CEO: Joseph T. Mallof
Sr VP: James A. Sharman
VP, Sls & Mktg: Dennis Brown
Conducts Business: Worldwide
Employees: 20,000
Primary Market Served: Consumer
Catalog available online
Direct online sales

Manufacturer of housewares.

WORLD WRESTLING
   ENTERTAINMENT INC
dba WWE
1241 E Main St
Stamford, CT 06902
Telephone: (203) 352-8600, FAX:
(203) 359-5180, Web Site: www.
wwe.com
Chmn & CEO: Vincent K. McMahon
Exec VP TV Production: Kevin Dunn
Exec VP Talent, Live Events & Creative: Paul Levesque
Pres WWE Studios: Michael Luisi
Chief Brand Officer: Stephanie McMahon
Chief Revenue & Mktg Officer: Michelle D. Wilson
Conducts Business: U.S., Italy, France,
Germany, Australia, Saudi Arabia,
Japan, England, New Zealand
Employees: 560
Primary Market Served: Consumer
Catalog available online
Direct online sales
Gross sales or billing: $415,300,000

Integrated media and entertainment
company.

WORLEYPARSONS
Subs. of Parsons Corp
2675 Morgantown Rd
Reading, PA 19607
Telephone: (610) 855-2000, FAX:
(610) 885-2001, Web Site: www.
worleyparsons.com
Chmn & CEO: John Grill
Dir, Corp Commun: Don Lassus
Sr VP: Robert Martin
Exec VP: W. Jeffrey Osborne
Conducts Business: Worldwide
Employees: 700
Primary Market Served: Business
Founded: 1995

Global business unit of Parsons Corporation consolidating petroleum, chemical & power project services into one
global entity. Full service design centers in Pasadena, CA; Reading, PA;
Houston, TX & London, UK. Worldwide network of project offices. Provides full-service engineering services.

XEROX CORP
45 Glover Ave, PO Box 4505
Norwalk, CT 06856-4505
Toll Free: (800) 275-9376, Web Site:
www.xerox.com
Chmn & CEO: Ursula M. Burns
Corp Exec VP: Lynn Blodgett
Corp Exec VP Corp Strategy & Asia
Opers: James A. Firestone
Corp Exec VP & CFO: Kathryn Mikells
Corp Exec VP & Pres Tech: Armando
Zagalo de Lima
Corp Exec VP & Pres Svcs: Robert
Zapfel
Conducts Business: U.S.
Employees: 140,000
Primary Market Served: Business &
Consumer
Catalog available online
Founded: 1906

Business process & document management company.

XILINX INC
2100 Logic Dr
San Jose, CA 95124-3400
Telephone: (408) 559-7778, FAX:
(408) 559-7114, Web Site: www.
xilinx.com
Pres CEO & Chmn: William Roelandts
Conducts Business: U.S., Canada, Europe, Asia
Employees: 3,295
Primary Market Served: Business
Founded: 1984
Gross sales or billing: $1,842,739,000

FPGA semiconductors & related software.

YEAR ONE INC
Year One Inc
Braselton, GA 30517
Telephone: (706) 658-2140, FAX:
(706) 654-5355, E-Mail: info@
yearone.com, Web Site: www.
yearone.com
Pres: Kevin King
VP, Opers: Mike King
Conducts Business: U.S., Canada, Europe
Employees: 175
Primary Market Served: Business &
Consumer
Catalog available online
Indirect online sales
Advertising/Marketing Budget Related
to Direct Marketing: 76-100%
Direct Marketing ad budget:
$1,500,000
Direct Mail: 66%
Magazines: 33%
TV/Radio: 1%
Founded: 1981

Mail order antique & classic automobile parts.

YENKIN-MAJESTIC
1920 Leonard Ave
Columbus, OH 43219
Telephone: (614) 253-8511, FAX:
(614) 253-6327
VP, Pur: John Gerhold
Conducts Business: U.S., Canada, Europe, Middle East
Employees: 600
Primary Market Served: Business &
Consumer
Direct Marketing ad budget: $400,000
Magazines: 10%
Newspapers: 40%

TV/Radio: 50%
Founded: 1920
Gross sales or billing: $60,000,000

Manufacturers & marketers of a complete line of coatings, selling to industry, paint stores, discount store & home improvement store chains.

YOUR CHOICE OR MINE

128 N Kingston St
San Mateo, CA 94401-2063
Telephone: (650) 340-7959, FAX: (650) 340-0449
Pres: Stacy Weiss Elliott
VP: Thomas Elliott
Conducts Business: U.S., Canada
Employees: 2
Primary Market Served: Business
Indirect online sales
Direct Marketing ad budget: $20,000
Direct Mail: 50%
Magazines: 25%
Newspapers: 25%
Founded: 1985
Gross sales or billing: $1,500,000

Custom manufacture executive gifts, premiums, employee awards for advertising agencies, retailers, manufacturers, trade associations & corporate awards.

ZIG ZIGLAR CORP

5050 W Park Blvd (Suite 700)
Plano, TX 75093
Telephone: (972) 233-9191, Toll Free: (800) 527-0306, FAX: (469) 321-7556, E-Mail: info@ziglar.com, Web Site: www.zigziglar.com
Founder: Zig Ziglar
Pres: Tom Ziglar
COO: Richard Oates
Fin Mgr: Gail R. Arnett
Consultant: Bryan Flanagan
Consultant: Amy Jones
Conducts Business: Worldwide
Employees: 35
Primary Market Served: Business & Consumer
Catalog available online
Direct online sales
Direct Marketing ad budget:
Direct Mail: $100,000
Newspapers: $25,000
TV/Radio: $10,000
Telephone: $200,000
Gross sales or billing: $4,600,000

Promote motivational materials for training & development: books, cassettes, video tapes & seminars. Speakers bureau, customized training.

ZIM-AMERICAN ISRAELI SHIPPING CO INC

Subs. of Zim Israel Navigation Co Ltd

1110 South Ave
Staten Island, NY 10314
Telephone: (718) 313-1950, Web Site: www.zim.com
Mktg & Sls: Andrew Monestero
Conducts Business: Worldwide
Employees: 180
Founded: 1948

Ocean shipping.

ZIMMERMAN IRRIGATION INC

Div. of Trickl-EEZ
3550 Chambersburg Rd
Biglerville, PA 17307
Telephone: (717) 337-2727, Toll Free: (800) 452-5699, FAX: (717) 337-1785, E-Mail: info@trikl-eez.com, Web Site: www.trickl-eez.com
Pres: John Nye
VP: Sandra Nye
Mgr: Ron Mihalek
Inside Sls: Ken Ketterman
Conducts Business: U.S.
Employees: 5
Primary Market Served: Business & Consumer
Catalog available online
Indirect online sales
Advertising/Marketing Budget Related to Direct Marketing: 0-25%
Direct Marketing ad budget:
Direct Mail: 70%
Magazines: 10%
Newspapers: 20%
Founded: 1973
Gross sales or billing: $1,500,000

Sell irrigation supplies, primarily agricultural & supplies for vegetable growing needs.

ZIMMERMAN-MCDONALD MACHINERY INC

2272 Weldon Pkwy
Saint Louis, MO 63146-3206
Telephone: (314) 291-9360, FAX: (314) 291-2981, E-Mail: zimsales@zimmermanmcdonald.com, Web Site: www.zimmermanmcdonald.com
CEO: Stan Zimmerman
Pres: Brad Zimmerman
Employees: 15
Primary Market Served: Business & Consumer
Catalog available online
Advertising/Marketing Budget Related to Direct Marketing: 51-75%
Direct Marketing ad budget:
Direct Mail: 90%
Telephone: 10%
Founded: 1982

Sell machinery for metalworking & fabrication.

ZOTOS INTERNATIONAL

Div. of Shiseido Cosmetics America Ltd
100 Tokeneke Rd
Darien, CT 06820-4894
Telephone: (203) 655-8911, Toll Free: (800) 242-9283, (800) 242-WAVE, FAX: (203) 656-7890, E-Mail: HumanResources@zotosintl.com, Web Site: www.zotos.com
Pres, CEO & COO: Ron Krassin
VP, Sls & Sls Dir: Bruce Selan
VP, Mktg: Wolf Heim
VP, Mktg Core Brands: Richard Stella
Conducts Business: Worldwide
Employees: 450
Primary Market Served: Business & Consumer
Catalog available online
Indirect online sales
Gross sales or billing: $900,000,000

Manufacturer of hair care & color products & personal care items for salons. Products sold through professional beauty supply stores, salons & online retailers.

Publishers (17)

ABC CLIO
130 Cremona
Santa Barbara, CA 93117
Telephone: (805) 968-1911, FAX:
(805) 685-9685, E-Mail: elott@abc-
clio.com, Web Site: www.abc-clio.
com
Pres: Becky Snyder
Conducts Business: U.S.
Employees: 12
Primary Market Served: Business
Advertising/Marketing Budget Related
to Direct Marketing: 26-50%
Direct Marketing ad budget:
Direct Mail: 75%
Magazines: 25%
Gross sales or billing: $1,200,000

Educational reference, software & educational videos for the K-12 & higher
education market.

ACP MEDICINE
Pub by Web Md
69 John St S (Suite 310)
Hamilton, ON, Canada L8N 2B9
Telephone: (905) 522-8526, Toll Free:
(855) 647-6511, FAX: (905) 522-
9273, E-Mail: acpmedicine@
deckerpublishing.com, Web Site:
acpmedicine.com
Editor in Chief: Elizabeth Nabel MD
Conducts Business: Worldwide
Employees: 27
Primary Market Served: Business &
Consumer
Catalog available online
Direct online sales
Direct Marketing ad budget:
Direct Mail: 92%
Magazines: 5%
Telephone: 3%
Founded: 1978

Publish medical information services
for physicians.

ASM PRESS
Div. of American Society for Micro-
biology
1752 N St NW
Washington, DC 20036-2904
Telephone: (202) 737-3600, Toll Free:
(800) 546-2416, FAX: (202) 942-
9342, E-Mail: books@asmusa.org,
Web Site: www.asmpress.org
Mktg Mgr: Courtenay Brown
Mktg Program Coord: Alaina Scalercio
Mktg Asst: Bridget McGee
Conducts Business: U.S., Canada
Employees: 9
Primary Market Served: Business &
Consumer
Catalog available online
Indirect online sales

Advertising/Marketing Budget Related
to Direct Marketing: 51-75%
Direct Marketing ad budget: $300,000
Direct Mail: 80%
Magazines: 20%
Gross sales or billing: $3,000,000

Scientific publications for the microbi-
ologist.

AARDVARK ENTERPRISES
Proprietorship of J. Alvin Speers
204 Millbank Dr SW
Calgary, AB, Canada T2Y 2H9
Telephone: (360) 779-5374
Proprietor: J. Alvin Speers
Conducts Business: U.S., Canada
Employees: 1
Primary Market Served: Business &
Consumer
Advertising/Marketing Budget Related
to Direct Marketing: 26-50%
Direct Marketing ad budget: $5,000
Direct Mail: 70%
Magazines: 10%
Newspapers: 10%
Telephone: 10%
Founded: 1962

Publisher of books. Catalogue of 114 titles.

HARRY N ABRAMS INC
Subs. of Le Martiniere Group
115 W 18th St (fl 5)
New York, NY 10011-4113
Telephone: (212) 206-7715, FAX:
(212) 645-8437, Web Site: www.
hnabooks.com
Pres & CEO: Michael Jacobs
VP Mktg: Maggie Kneip
Conducts Business: Worldwide
Employees: 94
Primary Market Served: Business &
Consumer
Founded: 1949
Gross sales or billing: $11,400,000

Publisher of art, photographic & illustrated gift books syndicated to other
mail order companies.

**ACCELERATED LEARNING
FOUNDATION**
118 N Court St
Fairfield, IA 52556-2811
Telephone: (641) 954-5443, Toll Free:
(800) 289-2377, FAX: (641) 954-
5851, E-Mail: info@
gamesforthinkers.org, Web Site:
www.gamesforthinkers.org
Pres: Layman G. Allen
Conducts Business: Worldwide
Primary Market Served: Business &
Consumer

Catalog available online
Direct online sales
Founded: 1962

Publisher of educational games that
teach logic, math, science, language,
word structures & strategy.

ACTIVE PARENTING
1220 Kennestone Cir Ste 130
Marietta, GA 30066-6022
Telephone: (770) 429-0565, Toll Free:
(800) 825-0060, (800) 235-7755,
FAX: (770) 429-0334, E-Mail:
cservice@activeparenting.com, Web
Site: www.activeparenting.com
Founder & Pres: Michael H. Popkin
Ph.D.
Mktg Mgr: Virginia Murray
Employees: 17
Primary Market Served: Business &
Consumer
Catalog available online
Direct online sales
Founded: 1983

Video-based programs & books for parents.

**ADVANSTAR
COMMUNICATIONS INC**
24950 Country Club Blvd (Ste 200)
North Olmstead, OH 44070-5351
Telephone: (440) 243-8100, Toll Free:
(800) 225-4569, FAX: (440) 891-
2651, E-Mail: info@advanstar.com,
Web Site: www.advanstarlists.com
CEO: Joe Loggia
Exec VP Healthcare, Dental & Market
Devel: Georgiann Decenzo
Exec VP, Chief Administrative Officer
& CFO: Thomas Ehardt
Exec VP, Customer Devel & Pres, Li-
censing: Chris Demoulin
VP, Pub Opers: Francis Heid
Conducts Business: U.S., Canada, U.
K., Germany, France, Brazil, Hong
Kong
Employees: 1,500
Primary Market Served: Business
Catalog available online
Indirect online sales
Advertising/Marketing Budget Related
to Direct Marketing: 26-50%
Founded: 1987

Business information company serving
specialized markets with top business
and professional publications, exhibitions and conferences, numerous web-
based communities, direct marketing &
database and reference products and
services. Target market sectors in automotive aftermarket, fashion, healthcare,
pharmaceutical, science, licensing, dental & veterinary.

AGATE PUBLISHING

1501 Madison St
Evanston, IL 60202-2033
Telephone: (847) 475-4457, Toll Free:
(800) 326-4430, FAX: (312) 751-
7334, Web Site: www.surreybooks.
com
Publr, Publicity Dir & Spec Mkts Mgr:
Susan Schwartz
Conducts Business: U.S.
Employees: 4
Primary Market Served: Business &
Consumer
Advertising/Marketing Budget Related
to Direct Marketing: 0-25%
Founded: 1982

Publishers of health, travel & career
books & cookbooks distributed to catalogs, retail stores, schools & used as
premiums & incentives. Direct mail
sales to in-house list.

AGORA INC

14 W Mount Vernon Pl
Baltimore, MD 21201-5125
Telephone: (410) 783-8499, FAX:
(410) 783-8414, E-Mail: csteam@
agorapublishinggroup.com, Web
Site: www.agora-inc.com
Chmn & Pres: William Bonner
CEO: Miles Norin
CFO: Bob Comppon
Publr: Kathleen Peddicord
VP: Beth Dent
Conducts Business: U.S., England,
France, Germany, So Africa, Austral-
ia, Panama City
Employees: 500
Primary Market Served: Business &
Consumer
Catalog available online
Indirect online sales
Advertising/Marketing Budget Related
to Direct Marketing: 76-100%
Direct Marketing ad budget:
Direct Mail: 40%
Online: 60%
Founded: 1979

Publishers & marketers of health, travel
& financial newsletters & books, children's books & academic titles.

AHC MEDIA

3525 Piedmont Rd NE (Suite 400)
Atlanta, GA 30305-1562
Telephone: (404) 262-7436, FAX:
(404) 262-7837
Mktg Dir: Steve Ackerman
Conducts Business: Worldwide
Employees: 95
Primary Market Served: Business &
Consumer
Direct Marketing ad budget:
Direct Mail: $3,800,000

Gross sales or billing: $11,000,000
Publish & sell newsletters & books, primarily health-related, to hospitals,
medical & legal audiences. Continuing
medical, nursing & dental education.

ALFRED PUBLISHING CO INC

16320 Roscoe Blvd (Suite 100)
Van Nuys, CA 91406-1216
Telephone: (818) 891-5999, Toll Free:
(800) 292-6122, FAX: (818) 893-
5560, E-Mail: sales@alfred.com,
Web Site: www.alfred.com
CEO: Ron Manus
Pres: Morty Manus
Chief Mktg Officer: Andrew Surmani
Pub Rels & Social Media Mgr: Marina
Terteryan
Conducts Business: Worldwide
Employees: 275
Primary Market Served: Business &
Consumer
Catalog available online
Direct online sales
Advertising/Marketing Budget Related
to Direct Marketing: 0-25%
Direct Marketing ad budget:
Direct Mail: 40%
Magazines: 40%
Telephone: 20%
Founded: 1922
Gross sales or billing: $31,000,000

Publisher of sheet music for instrument,
vocal & classroom use, music-related
software, DVD, MIDI, and CD titles.

ALL STAR DIRECTORIES

2200 Alaskan Way (Suite 200)
Seattle, WA 98121
Toll Free: (888) 404-8043, FAX: (707)
667-1524, Web Site: www.
allstardirectories.com
Pres & CEO: Doug Brown
VP, Mktg: Dave Sampson
Primary Market Served: Business &
Consumer

ALLYN & BACON

Div. of Pearson Higher Education
1 Lake St
Upper Saddle River, NJ 07458-1813
Telephone: (617) 848-7216, FAX:
(781) 455-1220
Assoc Publr: Stephen Dragin
Conducts Business: Worldwide
Employees: 120
Primary Market Served: Business &
Consumer
Advertising/Marketing Budget Related
to Direct Marketing: 76-100%

Gross sales or billing: $3,000,000
Publisher of professional & reference
books sold to educators, psychologists,
audiologists & speech pathologists.

AMACOM BOOKS

Div. of American Management Associ-
ation
1601 Broadway
New York, NY 10019-7434
Telephone: (212) 903-8376, FAX:
(212) 903-8083, E-Mail:
customerservice@amanet.org, Web
Site: www.amacombooks.org
Publr: Hank Kennedy
DM Dir: Harriet Weitzner
Spec Sls Mgr: Renita Hanfling
Conducts Business: U.S.
Employees: 40
Primary Market Served: Business &
Consumer
Catalog available online
Direct online sales
Advertising/Marketing Budget Related
to Direct Marketing: 26-50%

Business book publisher selling a variety of titles to the professional business
community.

AMERICA DIRECT BOOK SERVICE CUSTOM PUBLISHING

Div. of Gigo.com, Inc
1805 Spring Valley Rd
Ossining, NY 10562-1637
Telephone: (914) 271-3640, FAX:
(914) 271-3641, E-Mail: info@
americadirectbook.com, Web Site:
www.americadirectbook.com
CEO: Arthur G. Heydendael

Publishing-on-Demand & custom publishing.

AMERICAN BIOGRAPHICAL INSTITUTE INC

5126 Bur Oak Cir
Raleigh, NC 27612-3101
Telephone: (919) 781-8710, FAX:
(919) 781-8712
Pres: Janet Evans
Chmn: Arlene Calhoun
Conducts Business: Worldwide
Employees: 22
Primary Market Served: Business &
Consumer
Advertising/Marketing Budget Related
to Direct Marketing: 76-100%
Direct Marketing ad budget: $150,000
Direct Mail: 100%
Founded: 1967
Gross sales or billing: $1,500,000

Publisher of biographical reference
books sold primarily to individuals &
libraries.

AMERICAN COLLEGE OF PHYSICIANS

190 N Independence Mall W
Philadelphia, PA 19106-1572
Telephone: (215) 351-2600, Toll Free:
   (800) 523-1546, FAX: (215) 351-
   2686, Web Site: www.acponline.org
CEO: Steven E Weinberger MD
COO: Wayne H Bylsma PhD
Sr VP: Patrick Alguire MD
Sr VP: Michael S Barr MD
Sr VP: Robert B Doherty
CFO: Ralph L Hibbs Jr
Dir, Mktg & Bus Logistics: Nancy
   Matthews
Conducts Business: Worldwide
Employees: 450
Primary Market Served: Business
Catalog available online
Direct online sales
Advertising/Marketing Budget Related
   to Direct Marketing: 26-50%
Founded: 1915
Gross sales or billing: $66,000,000

Publisher of medical journals distributed to members & sold to individuals.

AMERICAN CRAFT COUNCIL

1224 Marshall St NE (Suite 200)
Minneapolis, MN 55413-1089
Telephone: (212) 274-0630, FAX:
   (212) 274-0650, E-Mail: council@
   craftcouncil.org, Web Site: www.
   craftcouncil.org
Editor in Chief: Andrew Wagner
Publr: John Gourlay
Conducts Business: U.S.
Employees: 28
Primary Market Served: Consumer
Founded: 1943

Non-profit membership organization to
stimulate interest in museum & gallery
quality crafts. Publisher of bi-monthly
American Craft magazine.

AMERICAN EXPRESS PUBLISHING CORP

Subs. of American Express
1120 Avenue Of The Americas Fl 9
New York, NY 10036-6700
Telephone: (212) 382-5600, Toll Free:
   (888) 461-6180, FAX: (212) 827-
   6496, E-Mail: aepc@custmersvc.
   com, Web Site: www.amexpub.com
Pres & CEO: Ed Kelly
COO & Gen Mgr: Anthony Morgano
Sr VP & CMO: Mark Stanich
VP: Stacy Staaterman
Editor: Lisa Gabor
Conducts Business: U.S.
Employees: 300
Primary Market Served: Consumer
Catalog available online

Direct online sales
Publisher of magazines about travel &
leisure, food & wines. Also, newsletters, one college magazine & a magazine for college student cardmembers.

AMERICAN HISTORIC INNS INC

PO Box 669
Dana Point, CA 92629-0669
Telephone: (949) 497-2232, Toll Free:
   (800) 397-4667, FAX: (949) 497-
   9228, E-Mail: comments@iloveinns.
   com, Web Site: www.iloveinns.com
Pres, CEO & Publisher: Deborah Ed-
   wards Sakach
Prod Devel Mgr & Editor: Stephen Sa-
   kach
Editor: Joshua Prizer
Editor: Tim Sakach
Employees: 12
Primary Market Served: Consumer
Catalog available online
Direct online sales
Founded: 1981
Gross sales or billing: $1,000,000

Bed & Breakfast books & promotions.

AMERICAN INSTITUTE OF PHYSICS

2 Huntington Quadrangle (Suite 1NO1)
Melville, NY 11747-4502
Telephone: (516) 576-2200, Toll Free:
   (800) 892-8259, FAX: (516) 576-
   2374, E-Mail: aipinfo@aip.org, Web
   Site: www.aip.org
Exec Dir & CEO: H. Frederick Dylla
VP, Publ: John Haynes
Conducts Business: Worldwide
Employees: 240
Primary Market Served: Business &
   Consumer
Catalog available online
Direct online sales
Advertising/Marketing Budget Related
   to Direct Marketing: 0-25%
Direct Marketing ad budget:
Direct Mail: 20%
Magazines: 40%
Online: 40%
Founded: 1931

Publisher of journals, magazines & databases sold to the scientific community & libraries.

AMERICAN KENNEL CLUB

260 Madison Ave
New York, NY 10016-2401
Telephone: (212) 696-8200, FAX:
   (212) 696-8217, (212) 696-8299,
   Web Site: www.akc.org
Pres & CEO: Dennis B. Sprung
COO: Daryl Hendricks
CFO: Peter W. Farnsworth

Dir, Commun: Lisa Peterson
Conducts Business: U.S.
Employees: 450
Primary Market Served: Consumer
Catalog available online
Direct online sales
Advertising/Marketing Budget Related
   to Direct Marketing: 26-50%
Direct Marketing ad budget:
Direct Mail: 90%
Telephone: 10%
Founded: 1884
Gross sales or billing: $72,700,000

AKC Kennel Gazette is the official
publication of the American Kennel
Club. Editorial content for breeders &
exhibitors of pure-bred dogs. AKC is a
registry body of pure-bred dogs & governing body of dog events.

AMERICAN MATHEMATICAL SOCIETY

201 Charles St, PO Box 6248
Providence, RI 02904-2294
Telephone: (401) 455-4000, Toll Free:
   (800) 321-4267, FAX: (401) 331-
   3842, E-Mail: ams@ams.org, Web
   Site: www.ams.org
Exec Dir: Donald McClure
Assoc Exec Dir: Robert M. Harington
Publr: Sergei Gelfand
Mgr, Sales Admin: Lori Sprague
Conducts Business: Worldwide
Employees: 160
Primary Market Served: Business &
   Consumer
Catalog available online
Direct online sales
Advertising/Marketing Budget Related
   to Direct Marketing: 0-25%
Founded: 1888
Gross sales or billing: $24,760,000

A non-profit organization that publishes books, journals & videotapes in
its effort to promote research mathematics. Sells publications & rents several mailing lists, all maintained daily.

AMERICAN TECHNICAL PUBLISHERS INC

10100 Orland Pkwy
Orland Park, IL 60467-5756
Telephone: (708) 957-1100, Toll Free:
   (800) 323-3471, FAX: (708) 957-
   1101, E-Mail: service@
   americantech.net, Web Site: www.
   atplearning.com
Pres: Robert Deisinger
VP, Edit: Jonathan Gosse
VP, Mktg: J. David Holloway
Conducts Business: U.S.
Employees: 32
Primary Market Served: Business &
   Consumer
Catalog available online

Direct online sales
Advertising/Marketing Budget Related
to Direct Marketing: 76-100%
Founded: 1898

Technical training materials for education & industry.

THE AMERICAN VINTAGE LIBRARY

Div. of Vintage Newspapers
PO Box 48621
Los Angeles, CA 90048-0621
Telephone: (310) 552-3176, Toll Free:
(800) 235-1919, Web Site: www.
vintagelibrary.com
VP: Jack Wayne
Conducts Business: U.S.
Primary Market Served: Business &
Consumer
Advertising/Marketing Budget Related
to Direct Marketing: 76-100%
Founded: 1976

Original newspapers every day since
1880. 35 major dailies to choose from.
Newspaper comes custom leather-
bound & personalized, for a marriage
day, birthday, retirement or any special
day.

AMOS PRESS, INC

aka Amos Publishing
911 Vandemark Rd
Sidney, OH 45365
Telephone: (937) 498-2111, FAX:
(937) 498-0876, Web Site: www.
amospress.com
Pres: Bill Fay
Mktg Dir: Margie Bruns
Employees: 125
Primary Market Served: Business &
Consumer
Catalog available online
Indirect online sales
Direct Marketing ad budget:
Direct Mail: 40%
Magazines: 10%
Online: 40%
Telephone: 10%
Founded: 1876
Gross sales or billing: $49,000,000

Amos Publishing is a niche publishing
company producing 15 different magazines for a variety of markets including
stamp and coin collectors, automotive
enthusiasts and crafters.

ARCHAEOLOGY MAGAZINE

Archaeological Institute of America
36-36 33rd St
Long Island City, NY 11106
Telephone: (718) 472-3050, FAX:
(718) 472-3051, E-Mail:
production@archaeology.org, Web
Site: www.archaeology.org

Pres: Brian Rose
Editor-in-Chief: Claudia Valentino
Conducts Business: Worldwide
Employees: 20
Primary Market Served: Consumer
Direct online sales
Advertising/Marketing Budget Related
to Direct Marketing: 51-75%
Founded: 1948

Magazine & journal publisher.

ARIZONA HIGHWAYS MAGAZINE

Div. of Arizona Dept of Transportation
2039 W Lewis Ave
Phoenix, AZ 85009-2819
Telephone: (602) 712-2200, FAX:
(602) 254-4505, E-Mail: editor@
arizonahighways.com, Web Site:
www.arizonahighways.com
Publr: Win Holden
Ed: Robert Stieve
Art Dir: Barbara Glynn Denney
Mktg: Debbie Klein
Conducts Business: U.S.
Employees: 58
Primary Market Served: Business &
Consumer
Catalog available online
Direct online sales
Advertising/Marketing Budget Related
to Direct Marketing: 76-100%
Direct Marketing ad budget:
$1,500,000
Direct Mail: 89%
Magazines: 4%
Newspapers: 1%
TV/Radio: 5%
Telephone: 1%
Founded: 1925
Gross sales or billing: $7,587,000

Publisher of Arizona Highways magazine, a travel publication exploring the
state featuring full-color photography
& Arizona travel-related books, videotapes, maps & gifts.

THE ARIZONA REPUBLIC

200 E Van Buren St
Phoenix, AZ 85004-2238
Telephone: (602) 444-8000, Web Site:
www.azcentral.com
VP, Digital Audience Devel: Mark Hi-
land
Exec Editor: Nicole Carroll
Primary Market Served: Consumer

ARMY TIMES PUBLISHING CO

6883 Commercial Dr
Springfield, VA 22151-4202
Telephone: (703) 750-9000, Toll Free:
(800) 336-4590, FAX: (703) 750-
8129, E-Mail: cust-svc@atpco.com,
Web Site: www.armytimes.com

Pres & CEO: Elaine Howard
Dir, Product Mktg: John Lee
Conducts Business: U.S., Foreign,
APO-FPO
Employees: 337
Primary Market Served: Business &
Consumer
Catalog available online
Direct online sales
Gross sales or billing: $19,200,000

Sell both new & renewal orders by
mail & telephone to Army Times,
Navy Times, Air Force Times, Federal
Times, Defense News & Space News.

ART NEWS MAGAZINE

Div. of Artnews LLC
48 W 38th St (fl 9)
New York, NY 10018-0042
Telephone: (212) 398-1690, FAX:
(212) 819-0394, E-Mail: info@
artnews.com, Web Site: www.
artnews.com
Publr: Milton Esterow
Exec Editor: Robin Cembalest
Conducts Business: Worldwide
Employees: 40
Primary Market Served: Consumer
Direct online sales
Founded: 1902

Magazine publisher specializing in the
fine arts.

THE ART OF SELF PROMOTION

1012 Park Ave, PO Box 23
Hoboken, NJ 07030-4334
Telephone: (201) 653-0783, FAX:
(201) 222-2494, E-Mail: ilise@
marketing-mentor.com, Web Site:
www.artofselfpromotion.com
Dir: Ilise Benun
Conducts Business: U.S.
Employees: 1
Primary Market Served: Business
Catalog available online
Direct online sales
Advertising/Marketing Budget Related
to Direct Marketing: 76-100%
Direct Marketing ad budget: $10,000
Direct Mail: 90%
Telephone: 10%
Founded: 1990
Gross sales or billing: $100,000

Publisher of The Art of Self Promotion,
a newsletter for self-employed professionals, marketing services & talents.
Inquiries regarding private consulta-
tions are welcome.

ARTECH HOUSE

Subs. of Horizon House Publications
Inc
685 Canton St

Norwood, MA 02062-2610
Telephone: (781) 769-9750, FAX:
(781) 769-6334, E-Mail: artech@
artechhouse.com, Web Site: www.
artechhouse.com
Dir Sls, Mktg & Bus Devel: John W.
Stone
Conducts Business: Worldwide
Employees: 27
Primary Market Served: Business
Catalog available online
Indirect online sales
Advertising/Marketing Budget Related
to Direct Marketing: 76-100%
Direct Marketing ad budget: $250,000
Direct Mail: 75%
Magazines: 15%
Online: 10%
Founded: 1969

Publisher of professional books for engineers & managers in nanotechnology, biomedical engineering, telecommunications, optoelectronics, microwave, radar, antennas, & other high-tech areas. Sell to corporate, university & individual technical community.

ASPEN PUBLISHERS INC

Subs. of Wolters Kluwer Group
76 Ninth Ave (fl 7)
New York, NY 10011-5201
Telephone: (212) 771-0600, Toll Free:
(800) 638-8437, Web Site: www.
aspenpublishers.com
Chief Mktg Officer: Alan Scott
VP, Bus Devel: Aaron Yaverski
Mktg Dir: Ann Marie Cocchia
Conducts Business: Worldwide
Employees: 165
Primary Market Served: Business &
Consumer
Founded: 1958

Publisher of professional books, journals, newsletters & manuals primarily in health care, allied health, public administration, corporate administration, law & nursing markets.

ASSOCIATED CONSTRUCTION PUBLICATIONS

1200 Madison Ave (Suite LL20)
Indianapolis, IN 46225
Telephone: (317) 423-7080, FAX:
(317) 423-7094, Web Site: www.
acppubs.com
Primary Market Served: Business
Advertising/Marketing Budget Related
to Direct Marketing: 0-25%
Founded: 1901

Provide construction & business news for contractors, public officials & construction industry materials & equipment suppliers in Iowa, Kansas, Nebraska & Western & Northeastern Missouri.

ATLANTA JOURNAL & CONSTITUTION

Div. of Cox Enterprises
223 Perimeter Center Pkwy
Atlanta, GA 30303
Telephone: (404) 526-5151, Web Site:
www.ajc.com
Publr: Amy Glennon
VP, Mktg: Amy Chown

Publisher of newspaper, also providing direct mail services.

THE ATLANTIC MONTHLY

RP-NFOA
600 New Hampshire Ave NW Fl 4
Washington, DC 20037-2403
Telephone: (202) 266-6000, Toll Free:
(800) 234-2411, FAX: (202) 266-
6001, Web Site: www.theatlantic.
com
Chmn: David Bradley
Publr-at-Large: John Fox Sullivan
Pres, The Atlantic: M. Scott Havens
VP, Mktg & Strategic Partnerships: Zazie Lucke
Conducts Business: Worldwide
Employees: 80
Primary Market Served: Consumer
Catalog available online
Direct online sales
Founded: 1857

Publisher of The Atlantic Monthly magazine.

ATLANTIC PUBLICATION GROUP LLC

1796 Balfoure Dr
Charleston, SC 29407-3103
Telephone: (843) 747-0025, FAX:
(843) 744-0816, E-Mail: info@
atlanticpublicationgrp.com, Web
Site: www.atlanticpublicationgrp.
com
Pres: Richard Barry
VP, Opers: Warren Darby
Publ Svcs Dir: Ashley Arnsdorff
Sr Art Dir: Bob Durand
Conducts Business: U.S., U.K., Japan
Employees: 20
Primary Market Served: Business &
Consumer
Advertising/Marketing Budget Related
to Direct Marketing: 76-100%
Direct Marketing ad budget:
Direct Mail: 90%
Magazines: 10%
Gross sales or billing: $2,500,000

Specializing in developing customized organizational magazines surrounding the specific needs of various organizations. Publishing programs offered range from consultation to full scale magazine production.

AUGSBURG FORTRESS PUBLISHERS

Publishing House of the Evangelical
Lutheran Church in America
100 S Fifth St (Suite 600)
Minneapolis, MN 55402-1242
Telephone: (612) 330-3300, Toll Free:
(800) 426-0115, FAX: (612) 330-
3455, E-Mail: info@
augsburgfortress.org, Web Site:
www.augsburgfortress.org
Pres: Rev. Beth A. Lewis
Publr: Tim Paulson
Sr VP Sls & Mktg: Tim Blevins
VP Fin: John Rahja
VP HR: Sandra Middendorf
Conducts Business: U.S., Canada
Employees: 225
Primary Market Served: Consumer
Catalog available online
Direct online sales
Advertising/Marketing Budget Related
to Direct Marketing: 51-75%
Gross sales or billing: $36,000,000

Provide education resource materials; theological, children's & other books; music; worship resources for the congregations of the Evangelical Lutheran Church in America. Also, offers most of these materials to others, including bookstores. Publisher of the following periodicals: Christ In Our Home, Word In Season, Davey & Goliath's Devotions. Mailing address: PO Box 1209, Minneapolis, MN 55440-1209.

AUGUST HOME PUBLISHING CO

2200 Grand Ave
Des Moines, IA 50312-5306
Telephone: (515) 875-7000, FAX:
(515) 333-5441, Web Site: www.
augusthome.com
CEO & Owner: Donald Peschke
Employees: 150
Primary Market Served: Business &
Consumer
Catalog available online
Indirect online sales
Founded: 1979
Gross sales or billing: $16,800,000

Woodworking & other related magazines.

AVIATION BOOK CO

7201 Perimeter Rd S (Suite C)
Seattle, WA 98108-3804
Telephone: (206) 767-5232, FAX:
(206) 763-3428, E-Mail: sales@
aviationbook.com, Web Site: www.
aviationbook.com

Pres: Nancy Griffith
Conducts Business: U.S., Canada
Employees: 8
Primary Market Served: Business &
  Consumer
Catalog available online
Direct online sales
Advertising/Marketing Budget Related
  to Direct Marketing: 51-75%
Founded: 1982

Publishes & sells aviation books & pilot supplies.

BAI

Div. of Bank Administration Institute
115 S La Salle St (Suite 3300)
Chicago, IL 60603-3801
Telephone: (312) 683-2464, FAX:
  (312) 683-2373, E-Mail: info@bai.
  org, Web Site: www.bai.org
Pres, CEO: Deborah Bianucci
Mng Dir, Corp Mktg: Jack Thurston
Conducts Business: U.S.
Employees: 20
Primary Market Served: Business
Advertising/Marketing Budget Related
  to Direct Marketing: 51-75%
Direct Marketing ad budget:
Direct Mail: 80%
Telephone: 20%
Founded: 1922

Training & educational products for entry & mid-level staff at financial institutions.

BCR ENTERPRISES INC

3025 Highland Pkwy (Suite 200)
Downers Grove, IL 60515-5668
Telephone: (630) 986-1432, Toll Free:
  (800) 227-1234, FAX: (630) 323-
  5324, Web Site: www.bcr.com
Pres: Jerry A. Goldstone
Gen Mgr: Fred Knight
Sls Mgr: Michael Leahy
Mktg: Angela Boling
Ed: Eric Krapf
Conducts Business: U.S., Canada
Employees: 26
Primary Market Served: Business
Catalog available online
Advertising/Marketing Budget Related
  to Direct Marketing: 76-100%
Direct Marketing ad budget:
  $2,100,000
Founded: 1971
Gross sales or billing: $14,000,000

Marketer of publications & training
programs on communications network
technologies.

BJU PRESS

1700 Wade Hampton Blvd
Greenville, SC 29614
Telephone: (864) 242-5100, Toll Free:
  (800) 845-5731, FAX: (864) 271-
  8151, (800) 525-8398, E-Mail:
  bjupinfo@bjupress.com, Web Site:
  www.bjupress.com
Production Dir: Jim Davis
CEO: Steve Smith
Mktg & Sls Dir: John Cross
Conducts Business: U.S., Canada, Aus-
  tralia
Employees: 350
Primary Market Served: Business &
  Consumer
Catalog available online
Direct online sales
Founded: 1973

Publisher of textbooks for Christian
schools & juvenile fiction.

BLS INC

501 N Lincoln St
Wilmington, DE 19805-3047
Telephone: (302) 631-1616, Toll Free:
  (800) 545-7766, FAX: (302) 631-
  1619, E-Mail: bls@tutorsystems.
  com, Web Site: www.tutorsystems.
  com
Pres: Bradford Siegfried
Conducts Business: U.S.
Primary Market Served: Business &
  Consumer
Catalog available online

Educational software publisher.

BABCOX PUBLICATIONS LLC

3550 Embassy Pkwy
Akron, OH 44333-8318
Telephone: (330) 670-1234, FAX:
  (330) 670-0874, E-Mail: bbabcox@
  babcox.com, Web Site: www.
  babcox.com
Pres & CEO: Bill Babcox
eMedia & Audience Devel: Brad
  Mitchell
Conducts Business: U.S., Canada
Employees: 65
Primary Market Served: Business
Catalog available online
Direct online sales
Advertising/Marketing Budget Related
  to Direct Marketing: 0-25%
Founded: 1921
Gross sales or billing: $5,000,000

Monthly updated lists of automotive
aftermarket firms. Special databases
available.

BALL PUBLISHING

Div. of Burpee Horticulture Co.
622 Town Rd, PO Box 1660
West Chicago, IL 60186
Telephone: (630) 231-3675, FAX:
  (630) 231-5254, E-Mail: info@
  ballpublishing.com, Web Site: www.
  ballpublishing.com
Publr & Sales Mgr: Paul Black
Conducts Business: Worldwide
Employees: 21
Primary Market Served: Consumer
Catalog available online
Founded: 1937

Books & monthly magazines for professional horticulturists. We sell direct
to growers, educators & academic libraries.

BALTIMORE MAGAZINE

Div. of Rosebud Entertainment LLC
1000 Lancaster St (Suite 400)
Baltimore, MD 21202-4632
Telephone: (410) 752-4200, Toll Free:
  (800) 935-0838, FAX: (410) 625-
  0280, E-Mail: blori@
  baltimoremagazine.net, Web Site:
  www.baltimoremagazine.net
COO: Richard Basoco
Dir Mktg & Sls: Sally Ann Davis
Circulation Dir: Lori Birney
Conducts Business: U.S.
Employees: 30
Primary Market Served: Consumer
Catalog available online
Direct online sales
Advertising/Marketing Budget Related
  to Direct Marketing: 0-25%
Direct Marketing ad budget: $75,000
Direct Mail: 100%
Founded: 1907

Magazine presents lifestyle features &
articles for the Baltimore metropolitan
area.

BANKER & TRADESMAN

Div. of The Warren Group
280 Summer St
Boston, MA 02210-1131
Telephone: (617) 428-5100, FAX:
  (617) 428-5119, Web Site: www.
  bankerandtradesman.com
CEO & Publr: Timothy M. Warren Jr.
Pres & COO: David Lovins
Circulation & Mktg Coord: Natasha
  Carter
Conducts Business: U.S.
Employees: 75
Primary Market Served: Business
Direct online sales
Advertising/Marketing Budget Related
  to Direct Marketing: 76-100%
Direct Marketing ad budget:
Direct Mail: 40%
Magazines: 20%
Online: 30%
TV/Radio: 10%

Founded: 1872

Publisher of weekly banking, financial & real estate newspapers in Massachusetts.

BANTAM DELL PUBLISHING GROUP INC

RP-NFOA
Div. of Random House, Inc
1745 Broadway
New York, NY 10019
Telephone: (212) 782-9000, FAX: (212) 940-7381, Web Site: www. bantam-dell.atrandom.com
Conducts Business: U.S.
Primary Market Served: Consumer
Catalog available online
Direct online sales

Publisher of mass market paperbacks, trade & hardcover books. Direct marketing business is through hardcover & paperback continuity programs.

BARBOUR PUBLISHING INC

1810 Barbour Dr
Uhrichsville, OH 44683-1084
Telephone: (740) 922-6045, FAX: (740) 922-5948, (800) 220-5948, E-Mail: info@barbourbooks.com, Web Site: www.barbourbooks.com
Pres: Tim Martins
Mktg Dir: Mary Burns
Primary Market Served: Business & Consumer
Founded: 1981

Christian book publisher.

BARTERNEWS

24446 Caswell Ct
Laguna Niguel, CA 92677
Telephone: (949) 831-0607, FAX: (949) 831-9378, E-Mail: bmeyer@barternews.com, Web Site: www. barternews.com
Publr: Robert B. Meyer
Opers Mgr: Marcia Meyer
Conducts Business: U.S., Australia, New Zealand
Employees: 8
Primary Market Served: Business
Indirect online sales
Advertising/Marketing Budget Related to Direct Marketing: 26-50%
Direct Marketing ad budget: $90,000
Direct Mail: 50%
Magazines: 25%
Newspapers: 25%
Founded: 1980
Gross sales or billing: $250,000

National magazine reporting on how barter is done for small business, corporate America & International countertrade.

BASELINE FT

3415 S Sepulveda Blvd (Suite 200)
Los Angeles, CA 90034-6032
Telephone: (212) 254-8235, (310) 393-9999, Toll Free: (800) 242-7546, FAX: (212) 529-3330, E-Mail: info@baseline.hollywood.com, Web Site: www.baseline.hollywood.com
Pres: Rafi Gordon
Conducts Business: Worldwide
Employees: 15
Primary Market Served: Business & Consumer
Founded: 1986

Sell reference products relating to motion picture industry to libraries & movie buffs. Online database service to entertainment industry.

BAUER PUBLISHING CO

270 Sylvan Ave
Englewood Cliffs, NJ 07632-2523
Telephone: (201) 569-6699, FAX: (201) 569-5303, Web Site: www.bauerpublishing.com
Pres & CEO: Hubert Boehle
Sr VP Production: Richard Buchert
Sr VP Subscriptions & Licensing: Dennis Cohen
Conducts Business: U.S.
Employees: 200
Primary Market Served: Consumer
Catalog available online
Indirect online sales

Periodical publisher.

BAXTER BROS INC

1030 E Putnam Ave
Greenwich, CT 06830
Telephone: (203) 637-4559, Toll Free: (866) 280-1924, FAX: (203) 637-4550, E-Mail: info@baxterinvestment.com, Web Site: www.baxterinvestment.com
Pres: William J. Baxter Jr.
Fulfillment Mgr: S. Asher
Conducts Business: U.S., Canada
Employees: 10
Primary Market Served: Business & Consumer
Advertising/Marketing Budget Related to Direct Marketing: 0-25%
Founded: 1959

Publish a financial-economic advisory bulletin for paid subscribers once a month.

MEL BAY PUBLICATIONS INC

Four Industrial Dr
Pacific, MO 63069-0066
Toll Free: (800) 8-MELBAY, FAX: (636) 257-5062, E-Mail: email@melbay.com, Web Site: www.melbay.com
Pres: William Bay
VP: Bryndon Bay
Editor: John Zardin
Editor: Louis Hornbuster
Editor: David Barrett
Conducts Business: Worldwide
Employees: 57
Primary Market Served: Business & Consumer
Catalog available online
Indirect online sales
Advertising/Marketing Budget Related to Direct Marketing: 26-50%
Founded: 1947

Instructional music books for a wide variety of instruments & styles of play. Also, many of the books have complimenting music cassettes, CDs & videos.

BEDFORD/ST MARTIN'S

Subs. of Bedford, Freeman & Worth Publishing Group LLC
75 Arlington St
Boston, MA 02116
Telephone: (617) 426-7440, FAX: (617) 426-8582, Web Site: www.bedfordstmartins.com
Pres & Publr: Charles Christensen
Adv & Promo Mgr: Hope Tompkins
Employees: 60
Primary Market Served: Consumer
Catalog available online
Advertising/Marketing Budget Related to Direct Marketing: 51-75%
Founded: 1981

Publishers of college English, history, communications & political science books.

BELCARO GROUP INC

dba shopathome.com
7100 E Belleview Ave (Suite 208)
Greenwood Village, CO 80111-1634
Telephone: (303) 843-0302, Web Site: www.shopathome.com
Pres: Marc Braunstein
VP: Claudia Braunstein
Primary Market Served: Business & Consumer

Online coupon and direct response company.

BELVOIR MEDIA GROUP LLC

800 Connecticut Ave
Norwalk, CT 06854

Telephone: (203) 857-3100, FAX: (203) 857-3103, E-Mail: customer_service@belvoir.com, Web Site: www.belvoir.com
Chmn Bd & CEO: Robert Englander
Exec VP: Timothy H. Cole
COO: Phil Penny
Production Dir: Chris Burt
Conducts Business: U.S., Canada
Employees: 50
Primary Market Served: Business & Consumer
Catalog available online
Direct online sales
Direct Marketing ad budget:
Direct Mail: 100%
Founded: 1972

Publisher of reader-focused magazines, newsletters, books, web sites and electronic media.

BERKSHIRE DIRECT INC
616 Main St
Williamstown, MA 01267
Telephone: (413) 458-1721, FAX: (413) 458-1727, E-Mail: info@berkshiredirect.com, Web Site: www.berkshiredirect.com
Owner: Allen Jezouit
Project Mgr: Elinor Goodwin
Project Mgr: Kimberly Ciola
Conducts Business: Worldwide
Employees: 5
Primary Market Served: Business & Consumer
Catalog available online
Indirect online sales
Advertising/Marketing Budget Related to Direct Marketing: 26-50%
Direct Marketing ad budget: $2,000,000
Direct Mail: 100%
Founded: 2001
Gross sales or billing: $2,000,000

Publish Gardeners' Marketplace, Back-to-Basics Marketplace, Backyard Living Marketplace, and Cooperative Advertising Media.

CHANNING L BETE CO INC
One Community Pl
South Deerfield, MA 01373
Toll Free: (800) 477-4776, FAX: (800) 499-6464, E-Mail: custscvs@channing.bete.com, Web Site: www.channing-bete.com
Pres & CEO: Michael Bete
Exec VP & COO: Robert Underhill
Sr VP Adv & Publg Dir: Carol W. Wentworth-Bete
Sr VP & Dir Mktg & Sls: Daniel C. Carmody
Conducts Business: U.S., Canada, U.K., Australia, Japan
Employees: 345

Primary Market Served: Business
Catalog available online
Founded: 1954

Publish a wide range of consumer information booklets. Booklets are sold via direct mail, telemarketing & direct sale to government, business, industry, health organizations, educational institutions & religious organizations.

BETTERWAY BOOKS
Div. of FW Publications
10151 Carver Rd (Suite 200)
Blue Ash, OH 45242-4760
Telephone: (513) 531-2222, Toll Free: (800) 289-0963, FAX: (513) 531-4744, Web Site: www.fwpublications.com/books.asp
Pres: Sara Domville
Mktg Dir: Karen Cooper
Conducts Business: Worldwide
Catalog available online

With nearly 3,000 titles in print and nearly a century of publishing history, F+W is one of the largest enthusiast book publishers in the world. Imprints include books on crafts, woodworking, painting, fine art, writing and more.

BLACK ENTERPRISE MAGAZINE
Div. of Earl G. Graves Ltd
260 Madison Ave (fl 11)
New York, NY 10016
Telephone: (212) 242-8000, FAX: (212) 886-9618, Web Site: www.blackenterprise.com
Chmn Bd: Earl G. Graves Sr.
Pres & CEO: Earl Butch Graves
Exec VP, Corp Sls: Michael Graves
Conducts Business: U.S.
Employees: 96
Primary Market Served: Consumer
Direct Marketing ad budget:
Direct Mail: 20%
Magazines: 30%
Newspapers: 30%
TV/Radio: 20%
Founded: 1970
Gross sales or billing: $35,000,000

Publish monthly magazine Black Enterprise & Black consumer inserts.

BLETHEN MAINE NEWSPAPERS INC
390 Congress St, PO Box 1460
Portland, ME 04104-5009
Telephone: (207) 791-6650, FAX: (207) 791-6925, Web Site: www.mainetoday.com
Pres: Joe Michaud
CEO & Publr: Chuck Cochrane
CFO Central Maine Newspapers: Gary Zemrak

Exec Producer: Brian Becker
Dir HR Central Maine Newspapers: Karne O'Connor
Primary Market Served: Business & Consumer
Newspaper publisher.

THE BLUE BOOK BUILDING & CONSTRUCTION NETWORK
800 E Main St
Jefferson Valley, NY 10535
Toll Free: (800) 431-2584, FAX: (914) 243-0287, E-Mail: info@thebluebook.com, Web Site: www.thebluebook.com
Mktg Opers Supvr: Kelly Meyering

BOARDROOM INC
281 Tresser Blvd (fl 8)
Stamford, CT 06901-3284
Telephone: (203) 973-5900, FAX: (203) 967-3086, Web Site: www.bottomlinepublications.com
Founder & Chmn: Marty Edelston
Pres: Marjory Abrams
COO & Publr: Sarah Hiner
Exec VP Mktg: Brian Kurtz
Conducts Business: U.S., Canada, Australia
Employees: 89
Primary Market Served: Consumer
Catalog available online
Direct online sales
Advertising/Marketing Budget Related to Direct Marketing: 76-100%
Direct Marketing ad budget:
Direct Mail: 55%
Magazines: 5%
Newspapers: 5%
Online: 10%
TV/Radio: 20%
Telephone: 5%
Founded: 1971

Publish newsletters & books in the categories of health, finance, consumer issues, psychology, retirement planning & taxes for the executive at home.

BOOK PASSAGE CAFE
51 Tamal Vista Blvd
Corte Madera, CA 94925-1145
Telephone: (415) 927-0960, Toll Free: (800) 999-7909, FAX: (415) 924-3838, Web Site: www.BookPassage.com
Pres & Chmn Bd: Elaine Petrocelli
Retail Mgr: Janel Feierbend
Conducts Business: Worldwide
Employees: 50
Primary Market Served: Consumer
Catalog available online

Direct online sales

Retail & mail order sales of travel books, guides, maps & language aids. Also, complete retail line of books.

BOOK PUBLISHING INFORMATION KIT

Div. of Para Publishing
530 Ellwood Ridge
Santa Barbara, CA 93117-1047
Telephone: (805) 968-7277, Toll Free: (800) PARAPUB, FAX: (805) 968-1379, E-Mail: danpoynter@ parapublishing.com, Web Site: www. parapublishing.com
Publr: Dan Poynter
Office Mgr: Becky Carbone
Conducts Business: Worldwide
Employees: 6
Primary Market Served: Business & Consumer
Catalog available online
Direct online sales
Advertising/Marketing Budget Related to Direct Marketing: 76-100%
Founded: 1969
Publish books & mailing lists.

BOOKS ON TAPE

Div. of Random House
400 Hahn Rd
Westminster, MD 21157-4627
Toll Free: (800) 733-3000, Web Site: www.booksontape.com
Conducts Business: U.S.
Employees: 100
Primary Market Served: Business & Consumer
Catalog available online
Direct online sales
Advertising/Marketing Budget Related to Direct Marketing: 0-25%
Direct Marketing ad budget:
Online: 100%
Founded: 1975
Manufacture & sell recordings of full-length audiobooks, from classics to current bestsellers.

BOOTH MICHIGAN

PO Box 2168
Grand Rapids, MI 49503
Telephone: (616) 222-5824, FAX: (616) 222-5318, Web Site: www. boothnewspapers.com
Dir, Projects: Renee Hampton
Mktg & Sls Dir: Larry Dodge
Mktg Mgr: Monique Van Epps
Sls Mgr: Kim Brown
Acct Mgr: Steve Davis
Primary Market Served: Business & Consumer
Corporate office of eight newspapers throughout Michigan.

THE BOSTON GLOBE

Subs. of The New York Times Co.
135 Morrissey Blvd
Boston, MA 02125
Telephone: (617) 929-2000, Toll Free: (888) MY-GLOBE, FAX: (617) 929-2606, Web Site: www.bostonglobe. com
Publr: Christopher M. Mayer
Editor: Brian McGrory
Conducts Business: U.S.
Primary Market Served: Business & Consumer
Catalog available online
Indirect online sales
Publishes Daily & Sunday newspapers.

R R BOWKER

630 Central Ave
New Providence, NJ 07974
Toll Free: (888) BOWKER-2 (269-5372), FAX: (908) 771-8699, Web Site: www.bowker.com
Gen Mgr: Sharon Lubrano
Database publisher of information references & directories available in print, CD-ROM, internet, online & tape for libraries & the publishing trade. Major titles include Books in Print, Ulrich's International Periodicals Directory, American Library Directory, American Book Trade Directory, Broadcasting & Cable Yearbook & Literary Market Place.

BOWTIE INC

3 Burroughs Ave
Irvine, CA 92618-2804
Telephone: (949) 855-8822, FAX: (949) 855-1850, E-Mail: mevans@ bowtieinc.com, Web Site: www. animalnetwork.com
List Mgr: Michael Evans
Conducts Business: U.S., Canada
Primary Market Served: Business & Consumer
Magazine publisher & list manager of 25 magazines.

BOYS' LIFE & SCOUTING MAGAZINES

Subs. of Boy Scouts of America
1325 W Walnut Hill Ln, PO Box 152079
Irving, TX 75015-2079
Telephone: (972) 580-2000, Toll Free: (866) 584-6589, FAX: (972) 580-2079, Web Site: www.boyslife.org
Natl Commissioner: Donald D. Belcher
Pres: John C. Cushman III
Mng Ed: J.D. Owen
Sr Ed: Michael Goldman
Conducts Business: U.S.
Primary Market Served: Consumer

Founded: 1911
Gross sales or billing: $12,000,000
Publish two magazines by Boy Scouts of America totaling 2.2 million in paid circulation. Each magazine has special direct response rates for mail order advertisers.

BRANT PUBLICATIONS INC

110 Greene St (PH2)
New York, NY 10012-3824
Telephone: (212) 941-2800, FAX: (212) 941-2885, Web Site: www. interviewmagazine.com
Publr: Sandra J. Brant
VP & Assoc Publr: David Hamilton
Circ Dir: Donald Liebling
Adv Dir: Cynthia Zabel
Adv Dir: Jennifer Norton
Conducts Business: Worldwide
Primary Market Served: Business & Consumer
Publisher of Art in America, The Magazine Antiques & Interview.

BRENTWOOD BENSON MUSIC PUBLISHING

101 Winners Cir N
Brentwood, TN 37027-5352
Telephone: (615) 261-3400, Toll Free: (800) 846-7664, FAX: (615) 261-3381, E-Mail: choral@ brentwoodbensonmusic.com, Web Site: www.brentwoodbenson.com
Dir Mktg: Rob Collins
VP Print Prod: Jonathan Crumpton
Conducts Business: U.S.
Primary Market Served: Business & Consumer
Catalog available online
Direct online sales
Advertising/Marketing Budget Related to Direct Marketing: 76-100%
Direct Marketing ad budget:
Direct Mail: 80%
Magazines: 10%
Online: 10%
Founded: 1902
Christian music & publishing company selling direct to the public & through retail stores.

BROADWAY BOOKS

Subs. Random House
1745 Broadway
New York, NY 10019
Telephone: (212) 782-9644, FAX: (212) 782-8338, E-Mail: bwaypub@ randomhouse.com, Web Site: www. randomhouse.com/broadway
Publr: Molly Stern
Conducts Business: Worldwide
Employees: 70
Primary Market Served: Consumer

Catalog available online
Direct online sales
Founded: 1996

Publisher of adult non & selective fiction. Audio division with "Books on Tape."

BROADWAY PLAY PUBLISHING INC

224 E 62nd St
New York, NY 10065-8201
Telephone: (212) 772-8334, FAX: (212) 772-8358, E-Mail: sara@broadwayplaypubl.com, Web Site: www.broadwayplaypubl.com
Pres: C.W.D. Gould
Conducts Business: U.S.
Employees: 3
Primary Market Served: Business & Consumer
Advertising/Marketing Budget Related to Direct Marketing: 76-100%
Direct Marketing ad budget:
Direct Mail: $20,000
Founded: 1982
Gross sales or billing: $500,000

Publisher of plays.

BULLETIN OF THE ATOMIC SCIENTISTS

1155 E 60th St
Chicago, IL 60637-2745
Telephone: (773) 702-6301, FAX: (773) 980-6932, E-Mail: admin@thebulletin.org, Web Site: www.thebulletin.org
Exec Dir: Kennette Benedict
Editor: Mindy Kay Bricker
Fin Dir: Lisa McCabe
Conducts Business: Worldwide
Employees: 8
Primary Market Served: Business & Consumer
Advertising/Marketing Budget Related to Direct Marketing: 0-25%
Founded: 1945

Journal dedicated to informing policy leaders & the public about risks to humanity from nuclear weapons, nuclear energy, climate change & biotechnology. By publishing expert analysis, convening scientists & policymakers & tracking trends with the Doomsday Clock, provide knowledge & solutions for a safer world.

THE BUREAU OF NATIONAL AFFAIRS, INC

Subs. of Bloomberg
1801 S Bell St
Arlington, VA 22202-4506
Telephone: (703) 341-3000, Toll Free: (800) 372-1033, FAX: (703) 341-1688, Web Site: www.bna.com

Chmn: Paul Wojcik
Pres & Publr: Darren P. McKewen
VP & Chief Mktg Officer: Lisa A. Fitzpatrick
VP & Grp Publr, Book Division: Margret S. Hullinger
Conducts Business: U.S., Canada, Europe, Japan
Employees: 1,200
Primary Market Served: Business
Catalog available online
Direct online sales
Direct Marketing ad budget:
   $3,000,000
Direct Mail: 80%
Magazines: 20%
Founded: 1929

A publisher of print & electronic news & information services, reporting on developments in business, economics, law, taxation, labor relations, environmental protection, & other public policy issues. Products include specialized information services, books, research reports, web information services, software & printing services.

BUSINESS PUBLISHERS INC

2222 Sedwick Rd
Durham, NC 27713-2655
Toll Free: (800) 223-8720, FAX: (800) 508-2592, E-Mail: custserv@bpinews.com, Web Site: www.bpinews.com
CEO: Greg Lindberg
Conducts Business: Worldwide
Employees: 60
Primary Market Served: Business
Catalog available online
Direct online sales
Advertising/Marketing Budget Related to Direct Marketing: 51-75%
Direct Marketing ad budget:
Direct Mail: 80%
Telephone: 20%
Founded: 1963

Washington newsletter specialists covering energy, environment, education, health, grants, transportation, law, construction & natural & human resources. Over 40 titles for high-level government & private sector executives.

CCH INC

Div. of Walters Klumer
2700 Lake Cook Rd
Riverwoods, IL 60015-3888
Telephone: (847) 267-7000, Toll Free: (888) 224-7377, Web Site: www.cchgroup.com
Pres & CEO: Karen Abramson
Conducts Business: Worldwide
Employees: 7,613
Primary Market Served: Business
Catalog available online

Gross sales or billing: $537,000,000
Principal products include publication of loose leaf current news reports & books, primarily on tax & business law subjects; corporate services to lawyers.

CRB

Div. of Barchart Inc
209 W Jackson Blvd (Suite 200)
Chicago, IL 60606-6940
Telephone: (312) 554-8456, Toll Free: (800) 621-5271, FAX: (312) 939-4135, E-Mail: info@crbtrader.com, Web Site: www.crbtrader.com
Pres: Eero Pikat
Editor-in-Chief: Chris Lown
Conducts Business: U.S., Canada, Europe, Far East
Employees: 10
Primary Market Served: Business & Consumer
Catalog available online
Direct online sales
Advertising/Marketing Budget Related to Direct Marketing: 26-50%
Direct Marketing ad budget:
Direct Mail: 40%
Magazines: 60%
Founded: 1934

Financial publishing company. Publish products used by traders, money managers & brokers active in the futures & options markets. Maintains an historical database on many futures, options & cash markets as well as stock indices. Available in printed chart format, floppy diskette, CD-ROM or via the internet.

CSPI/NUTRITION ACTION HEALTH LETTER

1220 L St NW Ste 300
Washington, DC 20005-4053
Telephone: (202) 332-9110, FAX: (202) 265-4954, E-Mail: cspi@cspinet.org, Web Site: www.cspinet.org
Pres: Kathleen O'Reilly
Sec: Michael F. Jacobson Ph.D.
Treas: Mark A. Ingram
Bd Member: Tom Gegax
Bd Member: William Corr
Conducts Business: U.S., Canada
Employees: 60
Primary Market Served: Consumer
Catalog available online
Direct online sales
Advertising/Marketing Budget Related to Direct Marketing: 76-100%
Direct Marketing ad budget:
   $5,000,000
Direct Mail: 100%
Founded: 1971
Gross sales or billing: $16,000,000

CALIBRE PRESS INC

200 Green St (Suite 200)
San Francisco, CA 94111-1356
Telephone: (214) 545-3060, Toll Free:
(800) 323-0037, FAX: (866) 225-
4273, Web Site: www.calibrepress.
com
Consultant: Charles Remsberg
Consultant: Dave Smith
Sls Mgr: Steve Hirst
Conducts Business: Worldwide
Employees: 14
Primary Market Served: Consumer
Catalog available online
Advertising/Marketing Budget Related
to Direct Marketing: 51-75%
Founded: 1979
Gross sales or billing: $2,700,000

Law enforcement training media &
seminars.

CAMPAIGNS & ELECTIONS MAGAZINE

1901 N Moore St (Suite 1105)
Arlington, VA 22209-1718
Telephone: (703) 778-4028, Toll Free:
(800) 771-8252, FAX: (703) 778-
4024, Web Site: www.
campaignsandelections.com
Publr: Shane Greer
VP, Sls & Bus: Emily Leonard
Schoenthaler
Editor: Shane D'April
Conducts Business: U.S., Canada, S.
America, Europe
Employees: 15
Primary Market Served: Business
Catalog available online
Indirect online sales
Advertising/Marketing Budget Related
to Direct Marketing: 51-75%
Direct Marketing ad budget:
Direct Mail: 55%
Magazines: 35%
Newspapers: 10%
Gross sales or billing: $3,000,000

Magazine for people in politics. Our
10,000 readers are elected officials,
campaign managers & other political
leaders.

CAMPMOR INC

400 Corporate Dr
Mahwah, NJ 07430-3606
Telephone: (201) 335-9064, Toll Free:
(800) 525-4784, FAX: (201) 236-
3601, Web Site: www.campmor.com
Chmn: Morton Jarashow
Pres: Daniel Jarashow
Conducts Business: Worldwide
Employees: 100
Primary Market Served: Consumer
Advertising/Marketing Budget Related
to Direct Marketing: 26-50%

Direct Marketing ad budget:
$1,500,000
Direct Mail: 90%
Magazines: 5%
Newspapers: 5%
Gross sales or billing: $19,000,000

Catalog publisher and retailer.

CANADIAN BUSINESS

Div. of CB Media Ltd
1 Mount Pleasant Rd (fl 11)
Toronto, ON, Canada M4Y 2Y5
Telephone: (416) 596-5100, FAX:
(416) 764-1200, Web Site: www.
canadianbusiness.com
Dir & Mktg: Soomi Kwak
Conducts Business: Canada
Primary Market Served: Business &
Consumer

Publisher of Canada's national business
magazine. Mailing list consists of professionals & business executives.

CAPTAN ASSOCIATES INC

744 Durham Rd
Brick, NJ 08724-1064
Telephone: (732) 840-1244, FAX:
(732) 840-1211
Pres: Clara Bluestein
Conducts Business: U.S., Canada, Eu-
rope, S. America
Primary Market Served: Business
Advertising/Marketing Budget Related
to Direct Marketing: 0-25%
Direct Marketing ad budget:
Direct Mail: 30%
Magazines: 60%
Telephone: 10%
Founded: 1976

Publish & sell books & periodicals providing technology consulting to management, research & development
personnel of industrial firms.

CARROLL PUBLISHING

4701 Sangamore Rd (Suite S155)
Bethesda, MD 20816-2532
Telephone: (301) 263-9800, Toll Free:
(800) 336-4240, FAX: (301) 263-
9801, E-Mail: info@carrollpub.com,
Web Site: www.carrollpub.com
Pres: Thomas E. Carroll
Conducts Business: U.S.
Employees: 25
Primary Market Served: Business
Catalog available online
Direct online sales
Founded: 1973

Government directory & organization
chart publisher; all levels in print & online. Also, defense organizational
charts in print & online.

CATHOLIC DIGEST

Published by Bayard Magazine Group,
division of Bayard, Inc.
Sponsored by Augustinians of the As-
sumption.
1 Montauk Ave (Suite 2)
New London, CT 06320-4967
Toll Free: (800) 321-0411, E-Mail:
catholicdigest@bayardinc.com, Web
Site: www.catholicdigest.com
Editor in Chief: Danielle Bean
Production Dir: Paul Bourque
Art Dir: Jeff McCall
Circulation Dir: Valerie Westrate
Adv Acct Exec: Sue Lachapelle
Conducts Business: U.S.
Employees: 40
Primary Market Served: Consumer
Direct online sales
Advertising/Marketing Budget Related
to Direct Marketing: 76-100%
Founded: 1936

Publisher of a digest-size magazine 11
times a year.

THE CATHOLIC UNIVERSITY OF AMERICA PRESS

620 Michigan Ave NE, Leahy Hall
(Rm 240)
Washington, DC 20064
Telephone: (202) 319-5052, FAX:
(202) 319-4985, E-Mail: cua-press@
cua.edu, Web Site: cuapress.cua.edu
Dir: Trevor C. Lipscombe
Mng Editor: Theresa Walker
Mktg Mgr: Brian Roach
Conducts Business: Worldwide
Primary Market Served: Business &
Consumer
Catalog available online
Direct online sales
Advertising/Marketing Budget Related
to Direct Marketing: 0-25%
Founded: 1939

Publisher of scholarly books.

MARSHALL CAVENDISH CORP

Subs. of Cavendish Times Publishing
Group
99 White Plains Rd
Tarrytown, NY 10591-5502
Telephone: (914) 332-8888, Toll Free:
(800) 821-9881, FAX: (914) 332-
1888, Web Site: www.
marshallcavendish.com
Pres: Albert Lee
VP, Mktg: Richard Farley
Sr Editor: Liu Ling
Sr Editor of Mathematics: Varsha Pri-
malani
Conducts Business: U.S., Canada, U.
K., Australia
Employees: 35

Primary Market Served: Business
Catalog available online
Direct online sales
Advertising/Marketing Budget Related
   to Direct Marketing: 0-25%
Founded: 1970

Publisher of school & library books.
Specialize in encyclopedias.

CENGAGE LEARNING
Ult. Parent Apax Partners Inc.
10650 Toebben Dr
Independence, KY 41051-5100
Toll Free: (800) 354-9706, FAX: (800)
   487-8488, Web Site: www.delmar.
   com
Sr VP & CIO: Carl Urbania
CFO: Emanuel Guzman
Exec VP Sls & Mktg: Rich Foley
Employees: 275
Primary Market Served: Business &
   Consumer
Catalog available online
Direct online sales
Advertising/Marketing Budget Related
   to Direct Marketing: 0-25%
Founded: 1945

Education & training information provider.

CHAIN STORE GUIDE
Div. of Lebhar-Friedman Inc
3922 Coconut Palm Dr Ste 300
Tampa, FL 33619-1389
Toll Free: (800) 927-9292, FAX: (813)
   627-6882, E-Mail: info@csgis.com,
   Web Site: www.csgis.com
Res Dir: Mike Jarvis
Natl Acct Mgr: Kathy Marshall
Dir Sls & Mktg: Carmen Vasquez-Per-
ez
Publr: Art Sciarrotta
Conducts Business: U.S., Canada, Eu-
   rope, Asia
Employees: 75
Primary Market Served: Business
Catalog available online
Direct online sales
Advertising/Marketing Budget Related
   to Direct Marketing: 76-100%
Direct Marketing ad budget: $450,000
Direct Mail: $300,000
Magazines: $50,000
Telephone: $100,000
Founded: 1932
Gross sales or billing: $7,000,000

Maintain company data from all major
retail & food service segments to provide prospect lists to manufacturers &
suppliers to these industries.

CHEMICAL WEEK
140 E 45th St (Rm 4000)
New York, NY 10017-9304

Telephone: (212) 621-4900, FAX:
   (212) 621-4800, E-Mail:
   clientservices@chemweek.com, Web
   Site: www.chemweek.com
Group VP - Publr: Lyn Tattum
Global Sls Dir: John Mennella
Conducts Business: U.S.
Primary Market Served: Business &
   Consumer
Publish trade magazine.

CHICAGO MAGAZINE
Owned by K-3 Communications
435 N Michigan Ave (Suite 1100)
Chicago, IL 60611-4031
Telephone: (312) 222-8999, FAX:
   (312) 222-0287, Web Site: www.
   chicagomag.com
Publr: Tom Conradi
Editor-in-Chief: Elizabeth Fenner
Acting Design Dir: Nicole Dudka
Exec Editor: Terrance Noland
Mng Editor Digital: Luke Seemann
Conducts Business: U.S., Canada
Employees: 55
Primary Market Served: Business &
   Consumer
Catalog available online
Direct online sales
Founded: 1970

Sell Chicago magazine to both advertisers & consumers who are interested
in the Chicago Area.

CHIEF EXECUTIVE
   MAGAZINE
Div. of Chief Executive Group
1 Sound Shore Dr (Suite 100)
Greenwich, CT 06830-7251
Telephone: (203) 930-2700, FAX:
   (203) 930-2701, Web Site: www.
   chiefexecutive.net
Pres & Chmn: Wayne Cooper
CEO & Publr: Marshall Cooper
Editor in Chief: J.P. Donlon
Conducts Business: Worldwide
Employees: 50
Primary Market Served: Business
Catalog available online
Founded: 1977

Business publication written primarily
by & for chief executive officers in
American industry.

CHIEF MARKETER AND
   MULTICHANNEL
   MERCHANT
249 W 17th St
New York, NY 10011-5390
Telephone: (212) 204-4228
Primary Market Served: Consumer

CHINA BOOKS &
   PERIODICALS INC
360 Swift Ave (#48)
South San Francisco, CA 94080
Telephone: (650) 872-7076, Toll Free:
   (800) 818-2017, FAX: (650) 872-
   7808, E-Mail: info@chinabooks.
   com, Web Site: www.chinabooks.
   com
Pres: Greg Jones
CEO: Erik Noyes
Editor: Chris Rosyn
Conducts Business: Worldwide
Employees: 15
Primary Market Served: Business &
   Consumer
Catalog available online
Direct online sales
Advertising/Marketing Budget Related
   to Direct Marketing: 51-75%
Direct Marketing ad budget: $100,000
Direct Mail: $90,000
Magazines: $5,000
Telephone: $5,000
Founded: 1960
Gross sales or billing: $1,000,000

Books, periodicals & software from
China & Far East. Sold to schools, libraries, businesses & consumers.

CHRISTIAN BOOK
   DISTRIBUTORS INC
140 Summit St
Peabody, MA 01960-5156
Telephone: (978) 532-5300, FAX:
   (978) 977-5010, E-Mail: javedisian@
   chrbook.com, Web Site: www.
   chrbook.com
Pres: Ray Hendrickson
VP, Catalog Sls: Ken Davis
Mgr: Gary Lussier
Conducts Business: Worldwide
Employees: 300
Primary Market Served: Business &
   Consumer
Catalog available online
Direct online sales
Advertising/Marketing Budget Related
   to Direct Marketing: 76-100%
Founded: 1978
Gross sales or billing: $76,000,000

Distributor of Christian books by mail
order.

THE CHRISTIAN SCIENCE
   PUBLISHING SOCIETY
210 Massachusetts Ave
Boston, MA 02115-3195
Telephone: (617) 450-2000, E-Mail:
   info@christianscience.com, Web
   Site: jsh.christianscience.com
Mng Publr, Fin & Opers: Patrick Haf-
ford
Publ Mgr: John Selover
Ed: David T. Cook

Conducts Business: Worldwide
Primary Market Served: Consumer
Indirect online sales
Advertising/Marketing Budget Related
   to Direct Marketing: 76-100%
Direct Marketing ad budget:
Direct Mail: $3,000,000
Founded: 1898

Publisher of The Christian Science
Monitor & other products.

CHRISTIANITY TODAY INC

465 Gundersen Dr
Carol Stream, IL 60188-2415
Telephone: (630) 260-6200, FAX:
   (630) 260-0114, Web Site: www.
   christianitytoday.com
Ed-in-Chief & CEO: Harold B. Smith
Sr VP: Vicki Howard
VP, Mktg: Carol Thompson
VP: Terumi Echols
Exec Admin: Paulette De Paul
Conducts Business: Worldwide
Employees: 100
Primary Market Served: Business &
   Consumer
Catalog available online
Direct online sales
Direct Marketing ad budget:
Direct Mail: 90%
Magazines: 10%

Publisher of nine evangelical Christian
magazines, continuity books & cassettes.

CLASSIC MOTORBOOKS INC

Subs. of Motorbooks International Pub-
   lishers & Wholesalers Inc
400 1st Ave N (Suite 300)
Minneapolis, MN 55401
Telephone: (715) 294-3345, Toll Free:
   (800) 826-6600, FAX: (715) 294-
   4448, Web Site: www.motorbooks.
   com
VP, Global Publ: Tim Parker
Conducts Business: Worldwide
Employees: 70
Primary Market Served: Consumer
Advertising/Marketing Budget Related
   to Direct Marketing: 51-75%
Direct Marketing ad budget: $420,000
Gross sales or billing: $16,000,000

Publish books about motorcars. Distribute own books & books published by
others to bookstores & automotive aviation aftermarket. Retail titles to customers who respond to catalog
featuring 6,000 titles.

CLEMENT
COMMUNICATIONS

Subs. of Brady Corporation
PO Box 398
Buffalo, NY 14240

Toll Free: (800) 253-6368, E-Mail:
   customerservice@clement.com, Web
   Site: www.clement.com
Pres: George Clement
Gen Mgr: Chris Fontes
VP Mktg: Pam Scott
VP Sales: Bill Kearns
Conducts Business: U.S., Canada,
   Great Britain
Employees: 38
Primary Market Served: Business
Advertising/Marketing Budget Related
   to Direct Marketing: 0-25%
Founded: 1919
Gross sales or billing: $10,000,000

Full service employee communications
company focused on providing awareness, education & reinforcement tools
to help organizations communicate
more effectively to all levels within an
organization.

COBBLESTONE PUBLISHING

30 Grove St (Suite C)
Peterborough, NH 03458-1453
Telephone: (603) 924-7209, Toll Free:
   (800) 821-0115, FAX: (603) 924-
   7380, E-Mail: customerservice@
   caruspub.com, Web Site: www.
   cobblestonepub.com
Mktg Mgr: Manuela Meier
Conducts Business: Worldwide
Employees: 14
Primary Market Served: Consumer
Advertising/Marketing Budget Related
   to Direct Marketing: 51-75%
Founded: 1979

Publisher of special interest children's
magazines & related ancillary products.

COIN WORLD

Div. of Amos Press Inc
911 Vandemark Rd
Sidney, OH 45365-8974
Telephone: (937) 498-0800, Toll Free:
   (800) 253-4555, FAX: (937) 498-
   0812, E-Mail: cwcustomerservice@
   coinworld.com, Web Site: www.
   coinworld.com
Ed: Beth Deisher
Circ Mgr: Terri Wise
Conducts Business: U.S.
Employees: 27
Primary Market Served: Consumer
Catalog available online
Direct online sales
Advertising/Marketing Budget Related
   to Direct Marketing: 51-75%
Direct Marketing ad budget:
Direct Mail: 90%
Magazines: 5%
Telephone: 5%

Founded: 1960
Weekly publication containing national
& international news & picture coverage plus features on U.S. & world
coins, tokens, medals & paper money
for beginner, intermediate & advanced
collectors.

COLD SPRING HARBOR LAB
PRESS

dba CSHL Press
500 Sunnyside Blvd
Woodbury, NY 11797-2924
Telephone: (516) 422-4100, Toll Free:
   (800) 843-4388, FAX: (516) 422-
   4097, E-Mail: cshpress@cshl.edu,
   Web Site: www.cshlpress.com
Exec Dir: John Inglis
Book Sls Mgr: Elizabeth Powers
Fin Dir: Stephen Nussbaum
Opers Mgr: Nancy Hodson
Book Devel Mgr, Mktg & Sls Dir: Jan
   Argentine
Dir Serials Mktg & Sls: Wayne Manos
Cust Svc: Geraldine Jaitlin
Conducts Business: U.S., Canada,
   Worldwide
Employees: 45
Primary Market Served: Business &
   Consumer
Catalog available online
Direct online sales
Advertising/Marketing Budget Related
   to Direct Marketing: 0-25%
Direct Marketing ad budget: $380,000
Direct Mail: 90%
Magazines: 10%
Founded: 1933
Gross sales or billing: $7,300,000

Publishes & sells books, journals, DVD
& CD to scientists.

COLLECTOR BOOKS &
AMERICAN QUILTERS
SOCIETY

Div. of Schroeder Publishing Co Inc
5801 Kentucky Dam Rd, PO Box 3009
Paducah, KY 42003-9323
Telephone: (270) 898-6211, Toll Free:
   (800) 626-5420, FAX: (270) 898-
   8890, E-Mail: info@collectorbooks.
   com, Web Site: www.collectorbooks.
   com
CEO: Bill Shroeder Sr.
Pres: Bill Schroeder Jr.
Sec & Treas: Meredith Schroeder
Credit Mgr: Rick Loyd
Office Mgr: Paula Bunting
Conducts Business: U.S., Canada
Employees: 65
Primary Market Served: Business &
   Consumer
Catalog available online
Indirect online sales

Advertising/Marketing Budget Related
to Direct Marketing: 51-75%
Direct Marketing ad budget:
Direct Mail: $250,000
Magazines: $150,000
Founded: 1973

Publisher of the American Quilter
Magazine. Also, sell books on quilting,
antiques & collectibles through mail order.

COLLEGESOURCE INC

dba "Career Guidance Foundation"
8090 Engineer Rd
San Diego, CA 92111
Telephone: (858) 560-8051, Toll Free:
(800) 854-2670, FAX: (858) 278-
8960, Web Site: www.collegesource.
com
Owner: Harry Cooper
CEO: Kerry Cooper
VP: Annette Crone
Conducts Business: Worldwide
Primary Market Served: Business
Founded: 1971

Non-profit publishing firm servicing
the education community, libraries and
government agencies.

COLUMBIA JOURNALISM
REVIEW

Subs. of Columbia University Graduate
School of Journalism
729 Seventh Ave (fl 3)
New York, NY 10019
Telephone: (212) 854-2718, Toll Free:
(888) 625-7782, FAX: (212) 854-
8367, Web Site: www.cjr.org
Publr: Dennis F. Giza
Conducts Business: U.S.
Primary Market Served: Business &
Consumer
Founded: 1961

Bimonthly magazine devoted to monitoring the performance of the news media.

THE COLUMBIAN

PO Box 180
Vancouver, WA 98666-0180
Telephone: (360) 694-3391, FAX:
(360) 735-4503, Web Site: www.
columbian.com
Pres & Publr: Scott Campbell
Editor: Lou Brancaccio
Circ & Production Dir: Marc Dailey
Adv Dir: Teresa Keplinger
Employees: 220
Primary Market Served: Business &
Consumer
Advertising/Marketing Budget Related
to Direct Marketing: 0-25%
Direct Marketing ad budget:
Direct Mail: 20%

Newspapers: 80%
Founded: 1890
Daily newspaper publisher.

THE COLUMBUS DISPATCH

34 S 3rd St
Columbus, OH 43215
Telephone: (614) 461-5000, FAX:
(614) 461-7551, E-Mail: csmith@
the.dispatch.com, Web Site: www.
dispatch.com
Chmn, Publr: John F. Wolfe
Pres & CEO: Michael J. Fiorile

COMMONWEALTH
BUSINESS MEDIA INC

2 Penn Plz E Ste 2, 400 Windsor Corp
Park
Newark, NJ 07105-2251
Telephone: (609) 371-7700, Toll Free:
(800) 221-5488, FAX: (609) 371-
7879, Web Site: www.cbizmedia.
com
Creative Svcs Dir: Robert Bertrand
Conducts Business: Worldwide
Employees: 800
Primary Market Served: Business
Direct online sales
Founded: 2000

Products include magazines and direc-
tories for the international trade and
transportation market, including The
Journal of Commerce, Traffic World,
Air Cargo World, PIERS, The Pocket
List of Railroad Officials, The Official
Railway Guide, Pacific Shipper, The
Florida Shipper, Shipping Digest, Gulf
Shipper, Canadian Sailings, Official
Export Guide, U.S. Custom House
Guide, Transportation Telephone Tick-
ler, Musical America International Di-
rectory of the Performing Arts and
others.

COMMUNICATION
CREATIVITY

209 Church St
Buena Vista, CO 81211
Telephone: (720) 344-4388, Toll Free:
(800) 331-8355, FAX: (866) 685-
0307, E-Mail: steve@steveheimberg.
com, Web Site: www.
communicationcreativity.com
Pres: Marilyn Ross
VP, Production: Tom Ross
Mktg Dir: Ann Markham
Mgr: Steve Heimberg
Conducts Business: U.S.
Employees: 5
Primary Market Served: Consumer
Catalog available online

Indirect online sales
Publisher of innovative nonfiction
books. Specialize in business, advertis-
ing/PR, lifestyle, career strategies &
publishing "how-to" reference.

CONCORDIA PUBLISHING
HOUSE

3558 S Jefferson
Saint Louis, MO 63118-3910
Telephone: (314) 268-1000, Toll Free:
(800) 325-3040, FAX: (314) 268-
1329, E-Mail: order@cph.org, Web
Site: www.cph.org
Pres & CEO: Bruce G. Kintz
VP, Corp Counsel: Jonathan D. Schultz
Exec Dir, Fin: Peggy Anderson
Exec Dir, IT: Steve Harris
Exec Dir, Mktg & Sls: Larry Padgett
Conducts Business: Worldwide
Employees: 350
Primary Market Served: Business &
Consumer
Catalog available online
Direct online sales
Advertising/Marketing Budget Related
to Direct Marketing: 26-50%
Direct Marketing ad budget:
Direct Mail: $1,000,000
Magazines: $100,000
Telephone: $50,000
Founded: 1869
Gross sales or billing: $35,000,000

Publisher of religious materials.

CONDE NAST

4 Times Sq
New York, NY 10036-6561
Telephone: (212) 286-2860, FAX:
(212) 880-8289, Web Site: www.
condenast.com
Chmn: S.I. Newhouse Jr.
Pres: Robert Sauerberg
Consumer Mktg Production Dir: Naomi
Farber
Conducts Business: U.S.
Primary Market Served: Consumer

Magazine publisher utilizing direct
mail in subscription acquisition & renewal efforts for Vogue, Architectural
Digest, Glamour, Mademoiselle, Self,
GQ, Vanity Fair, Gourmet, Bon Appetit, Brides, Details & Allure. Also, handle The New Yorker, Conde Nast
Traveller, House & Garden, Conde
Nast Sports for Women.

CONNELL
COMMUNICATIONS INC

Affiliated with International Data
Group
45 Main St Ste 102
Peterborough, NH 03458-2433

Telephone: (603) 924-7271, Toll Free: (800) 677-8847, FAX: (603) 924-7013
Conducts Business: Worldwide
Employees: 55
Primary Market Served: Consumer
Consumer magazine publisher.

CONSUMERS DIGEST INC
520 Lake Cook Rd (Suite 500)
Deerfield, IL 60015-5633
Telephone: (847) 607-3000, FAX: (847) 763-0200, E-Mail: postmaster@consumersdigest.com, Web Site: www.consumersdigest.com
Publr: Randy Weber
Conducts Business: U.S.
Primary Market Served: Consumer
Direct Marketing ad budget:
Direct Mail: 100%
Founded: 1960

Publisher of Consumers Digest & Your Money magazines.

CONSUMERS UNION
101 Truman Ave
Yonkers, NY 10703-1057
Telephone: (914) 378-2000, FAX: (914) 378-2906, Web Site: www.consumersunion.org
VP, External Affairs & Info Svcs: Chris Meyer
Commun Dir: David Butler
Conducts Business: U.S.
Primary Market Served: Consumer
Advertising/Marketing Budget Related to Direct Marketing: 76-100%

Publisher of Consumer Reports Magazine, Consumer Reports Travel Newsletter & Consumer Reports Health Newsletter.

DAVID C COOK
Subs. of Cook Communications Ministries
4050 Lee Vance View
Colorado Springs, CO 80918-7102
Telephone: (719) 536-0100, Toll Free: (800) 323-7543, FAX: (719) 536-3232, Web Site: www.davidccook.com
Pres & CEO: Chris Doombos
Exec VP: Alyson Bruu
Exec VP: Bob Beever
CFO & Controller: David Hatchell
Editor: C. Elvan Olmstead
Conducts Business: Worldwide
Employees: 400
Primary Market Served: Business & Consumer
Catalog available online
Direct online sales

Founded: 1875
Publish Christian books.

COOKBOOK PUBLISHERS INC
9825 Widmer Rd
Lenexa, KS 66285-5920
Telephone: (913) 492-5900, Toll Free: (800) 227-7282, FAX: (913) 492-5947, E-Mail: info@cookbookpublishers.com, Web Site: www.cookbookpublishers.com
Chmn: Dennis Evans
Pres & CEO: Kevin Derry
Conducts Business: U.S., Canada
Employees: 150
Primary Market Served: Consumer
Catalog available online
Indirect online sales
Advertising/Marketing Budget Related to Direct Marketing: 76-100%
Founded: 1947
Gross sales or billing: $5,000,000

Publish personalized & specialty cookbooks for individuals & organizations. Also, specialty cookbooks for retail.

CORNHUSKER PRESS
Div. of Dutton-Lainson Co
451 W Second St
Hastings, NE 68902-0729
Telephone: (402) 462-4141, FAX: (402) 460-4612, E-Mail: dlsales@dutton-lainson.com, Web Site: www.dutton-lainson.com
Pres: Charles R. Hermes
VP & CFO: David N. Brandt
VP, Sls & Mktg: Mark Bliss
VP: Jeremy L. Daniels
Conducts Business: U.S.
Employees: 60
Primary Market Served: Business & Consumer
Catalog available online
Direct online sales
Direct Marketing ad budget: $100,000
Direct Mail: 50%
Magazines: 20%
Newspapers: 5%
TV/Radio: 10%
Telephone: 15%
Founded: 1935
Gross sales or billing: $34,000,000

Sell limited edition prints, books & greeting cards on both the wholesale & retail level.

COUNCIL ON FOREIGN RELATIONS INC
dba Foreign Affairs (Magazine)
58 E 68th St, The Harold Pratt House
New York, NY 10021-5953

Telephone: (212) 434-9400, FAX: (212) 861-2759, E-Mail: editor@foreignaffairs.com, Web Site: www.foreignaffairs.org
Editor & Peter G. Peterson Chmn: Gideon Rose
Publr: Lynda Hammes
Adv Dir: Edward Welsh
Mktg Dir: Emilie Harkin
Primary Market Served: Consumer
Direct online sales
Advertising/Marketing Budget Related to Direct Marketing: 0-25%
Direct Marketing ad budget:
Direct Mail: 90%
Magazines: 1%
Telephone: 9%
Founded: 1922

Non-profit organization publishing magazine six times a year. Dedicated to improving the understanding of U.S. foreign policy & international affairs through the free & civil exchange of ideas.

COUNTRY SAMPLER GROUP
Div. of Emmis Publishing
707 Kautz Rd
Saint Charles, IL 60174
Telephone: (630) 377-8000, FAX: (630) 377-8194, Web Site: www.sampler.com
Pres & CEO: Margaret Borst
VP, Circ: Denise Boba
VP, Prodn: William Lowry
Conducts Business: Worldwide
Employees: 40
Primary Market Served: Business & Consumer
Indirect online sales
Advertising/Marketing Budget Related to Direct Marketing: 51-75%
Direct Marketing ad budget:
Direct Mail: 93%
Magazines: 5%
Telephone: 2%
Founded: 1984
Gross sales or billing: $12,000,000

Publisher of national consumer home decorating & craft magazines: Country Sampler Decorating Ideas, Country Sampler, Decorate with Paint, Country Marketplace & a trade magazine, Country Business. Also do custom publishing.

CRAIN COMMUNICATIONS INC
1155 Gratiot Ave
Detroit, MI 48207-2997
Telephone: (313) 446-6000, FAX: (313) 446-1616, Web Site: www.crain.com
Chmn: Keith Crain
Pres: Rance Crain

Exec VP: Bill Morrow
Dir Corp Commun: Jim Parks
Conducts Business: Worldwide
Employees: 1,000
Primary Market Served: Business &
 Consumer
Direct online sales
Founded: 1916

Publisher of over 30 business, consumer & trade magazines including Advertising Age, Automotive News, Crain's Chicago, Detroit, New York & Cleveland Business. Extensive use of direct mail in selling advertising, subscriptions & registration to professional conferences.

CREATIVE PUBLISHING INTERNATIONAL

400 First Ave N (Suite 400)
Minneapolis, MN 55401
Telephone: (612) 344-8100, FAX:
 (612) 344-8691, E-Mail: sales@
 creativepub.com, Web Site: www.
 creativepub.com
Pres & CEO: Ken Fund
Conducts Business: Worldwide
Employees: 85
Primary Market Served: Business &
 Consumer
Catalog available online
Indirect online sales
Advertising/Marketing Budget Related
 to Direct Marketing: 26-50%
Founded: 1969

Sell continuity series via mail & telephone. Also sell single titles direct to retail & educational markets. Provide comprehensive custom publishing & creative services for books, magazines, catalogs, brochures, ads & direct mail packages.

CREATIVE TEACHING PRESS

6262 Katella Ave
Cypress, CA 90630-5204
Telephone: (714) 895-5047, Toll Free:
 (800) 287-8879
Pres: Jim Connelly
Primary Market Served: Business &
 Consumer

THE CRICKET MAGAZINE GROUP

Div. of Carus Publishing
70 E Lake St (Ste 300)
Chicago, IL 60601-5945
Telephone: (603) 924-7209, Toll Free:
 (800) 821-0115, FAX: (815) 224-
 6615, E-Mail: customerservice@
 caruspub.com, Web Site: www.
 cricketmag.com
Chmn & CEO: Andre Carus

Publr & Ed-in-Chief: Marianne Carus
CFO: Jason Patenaude
Conducts Business: Worldwide
Employees: 50
Primary Market Served: Business &
 Consumer
Catalog available online
Direct online sales
Advertising/Marketing Budget Related
 to Direct Marketing: 76-100%
Founded: 1973
Gross sales or billing: $6,000,000

Children's magazine publisher. Sell subscriptions via direct mail, space ads, package inserts, agents, bookstores & schools.

CROSS COUNTRY STITCHING

PO Box 180
Quakertown, PA 18951-0180
Telephone: (215) 529-6430, Toll Free:
 (800) 231-8108, FAX: (215) 529-
 6434, Web Site: www.
 crosscountrystitching.com
Pres: Allen Coleman
Co-Owner: Linda Coleman
Conducts Business: Worldwide
Primary Market Served: Business &
 Consumer
Catalog available online
Direct online sales
Advertising/Marketing Budget Related
 to Direct Marketing: 51-75%
Direct Marketing ad budget:
Direct Mail: 90%
Magazines: 10%
Founded: 1982

Publisher of Needlecraft Designs & Projects & Counted Cross Stitch Magazine.

CURRICULUM ASSOCIATES INC

153 Rangeway Rd
North Billerica, MA 01862-2013
Telephone: (978) 667-8000, FAX:
 (978) 667-5706, E-Mail: cainfo@
 curriculumassociates.com, Web Site:
 www.curriculumassociates.com
Pres: Frank E. Ferguson
VP, Sls & Mktg: Katherine Harvey
Mktg Mgr: Jackie Dawson
Conducts Business: U.S.
Employees: 70
Primary Market Served: Business
Advertising/Marketing Budget Related
 to Direct Marketing: 0-25%
Founded: 1969

Publisher selling educational materials direct to schools.

CYGNUS BUSINESS MEDIA

1233 Janesville Ave

Fort Atkinson, WI 53538-2738
Telephone: (203) 227-4037, Toll Free:
 (800) 547-7377, FAX: (203) 227-
 4245, Web Site: www.cygnus.com
CEO: John French
CFO: Paul Bonaiuto
VP, HR & Commun: Ed Wood
Conducts Business: Worldwide
Employees: 450
Primary Market Served: Business
Catalog available online
Direct online sales
Founded: 1937
Gross sales or billing: $247,000,000

Publish business-to-business trade magazines. Also create & develop company sponsored publications, trade shows & online business information sites & magazines.

DRG

269 S Jefferson
Berne, IN 46711
Telephone: (260) 589-4000, FAX:
 (260) 589-8093, Web Site: www.
 drgnetwork.com
CEO: David McKee
Primary Market Served: Business &
 Consumer

DAILY COMMERCIAL NEWS & CONSTRUCTION RECORD

Div of Reed Construction Data
500 Hood Rd (4th fl)
Markham, ON, Canada L3R 9Z3
Telephone: (905) 752-5408, Toll Free:
 (800) 465-6475, FAX: (905) 752-
 5450, (888) 396-9413, E-Mail:
 dcnonl@reedbusiness.com, Web
 Site: www.dcnonl.com
Ed: Patrick McConnell
Circ Mgr: Sonia Kalra-ali
VP & Mng Dir: Mark Casaletto
Customer Care Coord: Christine Taka-
 shima
Mktg Mgr: Michelle Smith
Conducts Business: Canada
Primary Market Served: Business &
 Consumer

Daily newspaper for the building & construction marketplace in Ontario, Canada.

DAILY RECORD & DISPATCH CO

99 W Broad St
Dunn, NC 28334-6031
Telephone: (910) 891-1234, FAX:
 (910) 891-5253, Web Site: www.
 mydailyrecord.com
Editor & Publr: Bart Adams
Mng Editor: Lisa Farmer
Adv Dir: Maria House

Conducts Business: U.S.
Employees: 50
Primary Market Served: Business &
  Consumer
Catalog available online
Direct online sales
Advertising/Marketing Budget Related
  to Direct Marketing: 0-25%
Direct Marketing ad budget:
Newspapers: 80%
Telephone: 20%
Founded: 1950

Newspapers.

DANTE UNIVERSITY PRESS
PO Box 812158
Wellesley, MA 02482-0014
Telephone: (781) 790-1059, FAX:
  (781) 790-1056, E-Mail: dante@
  danteuniversity.org, Web Site: www.
  danteuniversity.org
Pres: Adolph Caso
VP: Josephine Tanner
Conducts Business: Worldwide
Primary Market Served: Business &
  Consumer
Catalog available online
Advertising/Marketing Budget Related
  to Direct Marketing: 0-25%
Direct Marketing ad budget:
Magazines: 100%
Founded: 1976

Renaissance thought & letters, Italian
language & linguistics, Italian-Ameri-
can history & culture, bilingual education; reprints, translations, programmed
learning.

THE DARTNELL CORP
Div. of Eli Research
2272 Airport Rd S
Naples, FL 34112
Telephone: (585) 240-7301, Toll Free:
  (800) 447-4030, FAX: (585) 292-
  4392, E-Mail: customerservice@
  dartnellcorp.com, Web Site: www.
  dartnellcorp.com
Publr: Kenneth Kahn
Dir Editorial: Claude Werder
Editor: Paula P. Willits Ed. D.
Editor: Cynthia Gomez
Editor: Robert L. Dilenschnieder
Editor: David Dee
Employees: 350
Primary Market Served: Business
Catalog available online
Direct online sales
Advertising/Marketing Budget Related
  to Direct Marketing: 76-100%
Founded: 1917

Dedicated to supplying diverse business audiences with informational, instructional & motivational training
materials, including books & manuals,
newsletters, videos, planners, audiocas-
sette programs & a speakers bureau.
Materials provide valuable training information for salespeople, supervisors,
managers, secretaries, human resource
professionals & customer service representatives.

DICK DAVIS DIGEST
176 North St
Salem, MA 01970-1648
Telephone: (978) 745-5532, FAX:
  (978) 745-1283, E-Mail: marketing@
  dickdavis.com, Web Site: www.
  dickdavis.com
Pres: Don Hanrahan
Gen Mgr: Roberta Norman
Conducts Business: U.S., Canada
Primary Market Served: Business &
  Consumer
Advertising/Marketing Budget Related
  to Direct Marketing: 51-75%
Direct Marketing ad budget:
Direct Mail: 85%
Newspapers: 15%
Founded: 1982

Bi-weekly financial newsletter that is
marketed to serious investors & financial professionals.

DAVIS PUBLICATIONS INC
50 Portland St
Worcester, MA 01608-2013
Telephone: (508) 754-7201, Toll Free:
  (800) 533-2847, FAX: (508) 753-
  3834, Web Site: www.davisart.com
Chmn: Mark Davis
Pres: Wyatt Wade
Conducts Business: U.S., Canada
Employees: 35
Primary Market Served: Business &
  Consumer
Catalog available online
Indirect online sales
Advertising/Marketing Budget Related
  to Direct Marketing: 76-100%
Founded: 1901
Gross sales or billing: $8,000,000

Publish art educational work.

DEFENSE NEWS MEDIA
GROUP
Subs Army Times Publishing Co
6883 Commercial Dr
Springfield, VA 22151-4202
Telephone: (703) 848-0490, FAX:
  (703) 848-0480, E-Mail: mgrant@
  atpco.com, Web Site: www.
  defensenews.com
Dir Mktg: Maurice Grant

DENTAL ECONOMICS
Div. of PennWell Corp
1421 S Sheridan Rd
Tulsa, OK 74112
Toll Free: (800) 331-4633, E-Mail:
  christopherp@pennwell.com, Web
  Site: www.dentaleconomics.com
Publr: Christopher Page
Editor: Chris Salerno DDS
Mng Editor: Zachary Kulsrud
Conducts Business: U.S.
Primary Market Served: Business &
  Consumer

Business journal for the dental profession.

DENTAL PRODUCTS
REPORT
Div. of MEDEC Dental Communica-
  tions
641 Lexington Ave Fl 8
New York, NY 10022-4503
Telephone: (847) 441-3700, FAX:
  (847) 441-3702, Web Site: www.
  dentalproducts.net
Publr Emeritus: Dolph Sharp
Conducts Business: Worldwide
Employees: 33
Primary Market Served: Business
Founded: 1967

Publisher of dental publications with
lists of dentists & dental labs available
for rental.

DIRECT RESPONSE
CONSULTING
6849 Old Dominion Dr (Suite 320)
McLean, VA 22101
Telephone: (703) 749-3100, FAX:
  (703) 749-0962, E-Mail: info@drcs.
  com, Web Site: www.drcs.com
Partner: Jerry Watson
Partner: Byron Hughery
Conducts Business: U.S.
Employees: 2
Primary Market Served: Business
Direct Marketing ad budget:
Direct Mail: $200,000
Gross sales or billing: $1,000,000

Publish personal biographical books for
libraries & the general public. Directories for organizations. Fund-raising.

DISCOVER PUBLICATIONS
6797 N High St (Suite 213)
Worthington, OH 43085-2533
Telephone: (877) 872-3080, FAX:
  (614) 431-3324, E-Mail: info@
  discoverpubs.com, Web Site: www.
  discoverpubs.com
Pres: Leo Zupan

DOANE
77 Westport Plaza (Suite 250)
Saint Louis, MO 63146-3121
Telephone: (314) 569-2700, Toll Free:
  (866) 647-0918, FAX: (314) 569-
  1083, Web Site: www.doane.com

CEO: Lynn O. Henderson
VP & Mgr: Dick Stiltz
Mng Dir: Ken P. Morrison
Circ Dir: Shanon Weaver
Primary Market Served: Business & Consumer
Catalog available online
Direct online sales
Founded: 1920

Information & publishing.

DOVER PUBLICATIONS INC

Subs. of Courier Corp
31 E Second St
Mineola, NY 11501
Telephone: (516) 294-7000, FAX: (516) 742-6953, Web Site: www. doverpublications.com
Pres: Frank Fontana
VP Mktg: Ken Katzman
Conducts Business: Worldwide
Primary Market Served: Business & Consumer
Catalog available online
Direct online sales
Founded: 1943

Publish original & out-of-print books in such fields as art, music, physical & natural sciences, crafts, needlework, linguistics, orientalia, anthropology, children's coloring books & cooking books. Books sold to individuals & institutions via direct mail, space ads, web & retail stores.

DOW JONES & CO

Subs News Corp
PO Box 300
Princeton, NJ 08543-0300
Telephone: (609) 520-4000, FAX: (212) 416-4348, Web Site: www. dowjones.com/corp/index.html
Pres: Todd Larson
Chief Commun Officer: Bethany Sherman
VP, Corp Affairs: Howard Hoffman
Conducts Business: Worldwide
Employees: 7,400
Primary Market Served: Business & Consumer
Catalog available online
Indirect online sales
Founded: 1882
Gross sales or billing: $1,700,000,000

Publisher of the Wall Street Journal, Barron's, The Asian Wall Street Journal, The Asian Wall Street Weekly, Wall Street Journal/Europe, Dow Jones New Wires, Ottaway Newspapers, Inc. Also, Broadcast News Services, Dow Jones Interactive Publishing, WSJ Interactive Edition & Smart Money Magazine.

DOW THEORY FORECASTS

7412 Calumet Ave
Hammond, IN 46324
Telephone: (219) 931-6480, Toll Free: (800) 233-5922, FAX: (219) 931-6487, E-Mail: custserv@ horizonpublishing.com, Web Site: www.dowtheory.com
Pres: Charles Follett
VP & Editor: Richard Moroney
Mng Editor: Bob Sweet
Editor: Charles Carlson
Analyst: David Wright
Primary Market Served: Business & Consumer
Catalog available online
Direct online sales
Founded: 1946

Investment newsletter covering investment grade & income-oriented stocks.

EDC PUBLISHING

Div. of Educational Development Corp
PO Box 470663
Tulsa, OK 74147-0663
Telephone: (918) 622-4522, Toll Free: (800) 475-4522, FAX: (800) 747-4509, Web Site: www.edcpub.com
Chmn, Pres & CEO: Randall White
Conducts Business: U.S.
Employees: 100
Primary Market Served: Business & Consumer
Advertising/Marketing Budget Related to Direct Marketing: 0-25%
Founded: 1963
Gross sales or billing: $30,000,000

Children's educational books (USBORNE). Activity kits (kid kits).

EAGLE PUBLISHING

One Massachusetts Ave NW
Washington, DC 20001
Telephone: (202) 216-0600, FAX: (202) 216-0612, Web Site: www. eaglepub.com
Chmn: Thomas L. Phillips
Pres: Jeffrey J. Carneal
VP Opers & CFO: Jon Heimerman
Conducts Business: U.S.
Employees: 220
Primary Market Served: Business & Consumer
Advertising/Marketing Budget Related to Direct Marketing: 0-25%
Direct Marketing ad budget:
Direct Mail: 100%
Founded: 1993
Gross sales or billing: $8,300,000

National weekly newspaper featuring political topics. Sold through direct mail subscriptions.

ECKANKAR

Eckankar Religion of the Light & Sound of God
PO Box 27300
Minneapolis, MN 55427
Telephone: (612) 544-3001, Toll Free: (800) 327-5113, FAX: (612) 474-1127, Web Site: www.eckankar.org
Natl Sls & Mktg Mgr: John Kulick
Conducts Business: U.S., Canada, Australia, New Zealand, Europe
Employees: 1
Primary Market Served: Business & Consumer
Founded: 1969

Distributor of books on Eckankar religion to booksellers, wholesalers & consumers.

THE ECONOMIST NEWSPAPER NA INC

Div. of The Economist Newspaper Group Inc
750 3rd Ave (fl 5)
New York, NY 10017
Telephone: (212) 554-0600, FAX: (212) 586-1191, Web Site: www. economist.com
Chief Revenue Officer: David Kaye
Head Sls: Joe Parsons
Head Client Solutions: Suzanne Hopkins
Conducts Business: Worldwide
Primary Market Served: Business & Consumer
Catalog available online
Direct online sales
Founded: 1843

International weekly magazine devoted to report & commentary from a global perspective on business, politics, finance, science & technology.

EDITORIAL PROJECTS IN EDUCATION INC

6935 Arlington Rd (Suite 100)
Bethesda, MD 20814-5233
Telephone: (301) 280-3100, Toll Free: (800) 346-1834, FAX: (301) 280-3250, Web Site: www.edweek.org
Pres & Publr: Virginia B. Edwards
Gen Mgr: Michele Givens
Adv Dir: Michael McKenna
Primary Market Served: Business & Consumer
Founded: 1981

Publishes Education Week-weekly national newspaper for school administrators. Teacher's magazine-monthly for K-12 teachers.

EDUCATORS PROGRESS SERVICE INC

aka FreeTeachingAids.com

214 Center St
Randolph, WI 53956-1408
Telephone: (920) 326-3126, Toll Free:
(888) 951-4469, Web Site: www.
freeteachingaids.com
Pres & Publr: Kathy Nehmer
Conducts Business: Worldwide
Employees: 5
Primary Market Served: Business &
Consumer
Advertising/Marketing Budget Related
to Direct Marketing: 26-50%
Founded: 1934

Publisher of guides to free materials.
Sell to schools, libraries, nursing
homes, health & youth centers, prisons
& industry.

EDWARD ELGAR
PUBLISHING INC

Nine Dewey Ct, The William Pratt
House
Northampton, MA 01060-3815
Telephone: (413) 584-5551, FAX:
(413) 584-9933, E-Mail: sales@e-
elgar.com, Web Site: www.e-elgar.
com
VP: Richard Henning
Promo Mgr: Katy Wight
Publ Asst: Tara Gorvine
Conducts Business: Worldwide
Employees: 5
Primary Market Served: Business &
Consumer
Catalog available online
Indirect online sales
Advertising/Marketing Budget Related
to Direct Marketing: 51-75%
Direct Marketing ad budget: $300,000
Direct Mail: 100%
Founded: 1986
Gross sales or billing: $3,000,000

Academic monographs & reference
books on Economics, Politics & Business to libraries, academics & professionals.

ELKS MAGAZINE

Div. of BPO Elks of the USA
2750 N Lakeview Ave
Chicago, IL 60614-1889
Telephone: (773) 755-4700, FAX:
(773) 775-4792, E-Mail: elksmag@
elks.org, Web Site: www.elks.org
Editor & Publr: Cheryl T. Stachura
Adv Coord: Briseida Hernandez
Dir Circulation: Phil Claiborne
Conducts Business: U.S.
Employees: 40
Primary Market Served: Business &
Consumer
Advertising/Marketing Budget Related
to Direct Marketing: 0-25%

Founded: 1922
Monthly magazine (July/Aug & Dec/
Jan issues combined) with heavy direct-to-consumer advertising. Reaches
1.1 million households.

ELSEVIER

360 Park Ave S
New York, NY 10010-1710
Telephone: (212) 633-3805, FAX:
(212) 633-3880, Web Site: www.
elsevier.com
CEO: Ron Mobed
Primary Market Served: Business

EMPLOYMENT PUBLISHING
INC

175 Strafford Ave
Wayne, PA 19087-3317
Telephone: (610) 975-4539, FAX:
(610) 687-7860, E-Mail: jfannin@
employment911.com
Pres: Jake Fannin

EN ESPANOL PUBLISHING
GROUP LLC

250 S Beverly Dr (#301)
Beverly Hills, CA 90212-3831
Telephone: (310) 248-2680
Pres: Michaelle Fastlicht
Primary Market Served: Business &
Consumer

ENCYCLOPAEDIA
BRITANNICA INC

RP-NFOA
331 N LaSalle St
Chicago, IL 60654-2682
Telephone: (312) 347-7159, Toll Free:
(800) 323-1229, FAX: (312) 294-
2104, Web Site: www.britannica.com
Pres: Jorge Cauz
Sr VP, Chief Mktg Officer: Greg Bar-
low
Sr VP & Editor: Dale Hoiberg
Conducts Business: U.S., Canada
Primary Market Served: Business &
Consumer
Direct Marketing ad budget:
Direct Mail: 60%
Magazines: 5%
TV/Radio: 35%

Obtain leads for Encyclopaedia Britannica through all direct response media. Product is sold to a demographic
cross-section, primarily families with
children. Marketer of children & adult
products via mail order. Also performs
telemarketing services for outside clients.

ENTREPRENEUR MEDIA INC

2445 McCabe Way (Suite 400)
Irvine, CA 92614

Telephone: (949) 261-2325, Toll Free:
(800) 274-6229, FAX: (949) 261-
0234, Web Site: www.entrepreneur.
com
CEO: Peter Shea
VP & Editor-in-Chief: Amy Cosper
Conducts Business: U.S., Canada
Employees: 100
Primary Market Served: Consumer
Catalog available online

Publisher of Entrepreneur magazines:
Entrepreneur de Mexico, Entrepreneur
Japan, Entrepreneur Philippines & En-
trepreneur International.

ENVIRONMENTAL LAW
INSTITUTE

2000 "L" St NW (Suite 200)
Washington, DC 20036-4919
Telephone: (202) 939-3800, FAX:
(202) 939-3868, E-Mail: law@eli.
org, Web Site: www.eli.org
Pres: Leslie Carothers
VP Devel: Martin Dickinson
VP Fin & Admin: Elliot D
VP Res & Policy: Elissa Parker
VP, Publications & Assoc: Scott
Schang
Conducts Business: U.S.
Employees: 60
Primary Market Served: Business
Catalog available online
Gross sales or billing: $5,300,000

Publish & market books, journals,
newsletters & loose-leaf services on environmental & natural resources law &
policy. Publish Environmental Law Reporter (ELR).

ESQUIRE MAGAZINE

Div. of Hearst Corp
300 W 57th St (21st fl)
New York, NY 10019
Telephone: (212) 649-4020, FAX:
(212) 649-4303, E-Mail: esquire@
hearst.com, Web Site: www.esquire.
com
Editor in Chief: David Granger
Editor: Nick Sullivan
Editorial Dir: Helene F. Rubinstein
Design Dir: David Curcurito
Mng Editor: John Kenney
Dir Photography: Michael Norseng
Conducts Business: U.S., Canada
Primary Market Served: Business &
Consumer

Publisher of Esquire Magazine. Use
various direct marketing techniques in
circulation subscription efforts.

ESSENCE
COMMUNICATIONS INC

135 W 50th St (4th fl)
New York, NY 10020-1201

Telephone: (212) 522-1212, FAX: (212) 921-5173, Web Site: www.essence.com
Publr & CEO: Edward Lewis
Pres: Michele Ebanks
Conducts Business: U.S.
Employees: 150
Primary Market Served: Consumer
Catalog available online
Direct online sales
Advertising/Marketing Budget Related to Direct Marketing: 76-100%
Direct Marketing ad budget:
Direct Mail: $10,400,000
TV/Radio: $400,000
Telephone: $45,000
Founded: 1968
Gross sales or billing: $97,000,000

Publish Essence Magazine, Latina Magazine & The Essence By Mail Catalog.

F&W MEDIA INC
10151 Carver Rd (Suite 200)
Blue Ash, OH 45242-4760
Telephone: (513) 531-2690, FAX: (513) 531-0293, Web Site: www.fwmedia.com
Chmn & CEO: David Nussbaum
COO & CFO: Jim Ogle
Pres: Sara Domville
Pres: David Blansfield
VP, Commun: Stacie Berger
Conducts Business: U.S., Canada, English-speaking countries
Employees: 300
Primary Market Served: Business & Consumer
Direct online sales
Advertising/Marketing Budget Related to Direct Marketing: 51-75%
Direct Marketing ad budget:
Direct Mail: 90%
Magazines: 10%
Founded: 1913

Publish magazines, books & courses for freelance artists, crafters, designers, woodworkers & writers. Mail several million pieces per year to solicit subscriptions, sell books & home study courses in writing, art, woodworking & design.

FDANEWS
300 N Washington St (Suite 200)
Falls Church, VA 22046-3431
Telephone: (703) 538-7600, Toll Free: (888) 838-5578, FAX: (703) 538-7676, E-Mail: customerservice@fdanews.com, Web Site: www.fdanews.com
Pres: Cindy Carter
Publ: Matt Salt
Mktg Dir: Allison King
Sr Mktg Mgr: Alka Desai

Conducts Business: U.S., Canada, Worldwide
Employees: 30
Primary Market Served: Business & Consumer
Catalog available online
Direct online sales
Advertising/Marketing Budget Related to Direct Marketing: 26-50%
Founded: 1976
Gross sales or billing: $6,100,000

Premier provider of regulation, legislative and business news and information to the pharmaceutical, medical device and biotech industries.

FW MEDIA
4700 E Galbraith Rd
Cincinnati, OH 45236-2726
Telephone: (513) 531-2690, Web Site: www.fwpublications.com
VP Consumer Mktg: Sara DeCarlo
Primary Market Served: Business & Consumer

FACTS ON FILE INC
Subs. of Infobase Holdings Inc
132 W 31st St (17th fl)
New York, NY 10001
Telephone: (212) 967-8800, Toll Free: (800) 322-8755, FAX: (212) 678-3633, Web Site: www.infobasepublishing.com
Pres & CEO: Mark McDonnell
CFO: James Housely
Edit Dir & Electronic Publ Dir: Laurie Likoff
Conducts Business: U.S., U.K.
Employees: 125
Primary Market Served: Business & Consumer
Catalog available online
Direct online sales
Advertising/Marketing Budget Related to Direct Marketing: 0-25%

Book, electronic reference & trade publisher.

FAIRCHILD BOOKS
Div. of Bloomsbury Publishing Plc
1385 Broadway
New York, NY 10018
Telephone: (212) 419-5292, Web Site: www.fairchildbooks.com
Publr: Priscilla McGeehon
Head Sls, Americas: Derek Stordahl
Conducts Business: U.S., Canada
Employees: 20
Primary Market Served: Business & Consumer
Catalog available online
Advertising/Marketing Budget Related to Direct Marketing: 76-100%
Direct Marketing ad budget: $500,000
Direct Mail: 90%

Newspapers: 5%
Telephone: 5%
Gross sales or billing: $2,000,000

Textile, apparel, design and merchandising, retail, interior design to 2 and 4 year colleges and universities, high schools and professionals.

FAIRCHILD FASHION MEDIA
Div. of Conde Nast
750 Third Ave
New York, NY 10017-2703
Telephone: (212) 286-2860, Web Site: www.condenast.com/fairchild
Pres & CEO: Gina Sanders
Editorial Dir: Peter W. Kaplan
Chief Mktg Officer: Melissa Brecher
Conducts Business: Worldwide
Employees: 726
Primary Market Served: Business & Consumer
Founded: 1889
Gross sales or billing: $350,000,000

Publisher of trade & consumer magazines serving the retail & industrial industries.

THE FAMILY HANDYMAN
Subs. of Reader's Digest Inc
2915 Commers Dr (Suite 700)
Eagan, MN 55121-2398
Telephone: (651) 454-9200, FAX: (651) 994-2250
Publr: Mike Rielly
Ed-in-Chief: Gary Havens
Circ Mgr: Craig Reynolds
Conducts Business: U.S., Canada
Employees: 52
Primary Market Served: Consumer
Advertising/Marketing Budget Related to Direct Marketing: 51-75%
Direct Marketing ad budget: $6,000,000
Direct Mail: 100%
Gross sales or billing: $27,000,000

Magazine for do-it-yourself homeowners.

FARM JOURNAL INC
Div. of Tribune Co
30 S 15th St Ste 900, Center Sq W
Philadelphia, PA 19102-4803
Telephone: (215) 557-8937, FAX: (215) 568-4238
Pres: Roger Randall
VP, Publ Svc: Earl Ainsworth
Conducts Business: U.S.
Employees: 230
Primary Market Served: Business & Consumer
Advertising/Marketing Budget Related to Direct Marketing: 0-25%
Direct Marketing ad budget:

Magazines: $100,000
Founded: 1877
Gross sales or billing: $35,000,000
Magazine publisher.

FARM PROGRESS CO

Subs. of Rural Press Ltd Inc
255 38th Ave (Suite P)
Saint Charles, IL 60174-5410
Telephone: (630) 690-5600, FAX:
    (630) 462-2202, E-Mail: dwilson@
    farmprogress.com, Web Site: www.
    farmprogress.com
VP Mktg Opers: Sara Hess
Conducts Business: Worldwide
Employees: 200
Primary Market Served: Business &
    Consumer
Indirect online sales
Advertising/Marketing Budget Related
    to Direct Marketing: 0-25%
Founded: 1841
Gross sales or billing: $45,000,000

Publisher of specialized agricultural
publications serving producers & agri-
businesses database management.

FARRAR STRAUS & GIROUX INC

18 W 18th St Fl 7
New York, NY 10011-4675
Telephone: (212) 741-6900, Web Site:
    us.macmillan.com/fsg.aspx
Pres & Publr: Jonathan Galassi
Conducts Business: Worldwide
Employees: 95
Primary Market Served: Business
Catalog available online
Indirect online sales
Advertising/Marketing Budget Related
    to Direct Marketing: 0-25%
Founded: 1946

Publisher of books for adults & children.

FERGUSON PUBLISHING CO

Div. of Infobase Publishing
132 W 31st St (17 fl)
New York, NY 10001-3406
Telephone: (800) 322-8755, FAX:
    (800) 678-3633, Web Site: www.
    infobasepublishing.com
Conducts Business: U.S.
Employees: 70
Primary Market Served: Business
Advertising/Marketing Budget Related
    to Direct Marketing: 51-75%
Founded: 1939
Gross sales or billing: $8,200,000

Publisher of career education books
and reference materials. Offer the publications to direct mail companies for
their mailings.

FINANCIAL PUBLISHING CO

Div. of Carleton
1251 N Eddy St (Suite 202)
South Bend, IN 46617-1478
Toll Free: (800) 247-3214, FAX: (574)
    243-6060, Web Site: www.financial-
    publishing.com
VP, Engrng, Res & Devel & Tech: De-
    borah Grounds
Conducts Business: U.S., Canada
Employees: 25
Primary Market Served: Business
Catalog available online
Indirect online sales
Direct Marketing ad budget:
Direct Mail: 88%
Magazines: 12%

Publisher of financial books, rate
charts, schedules, micro computer software, electronic calculators & internet
products.

THE FINANCIAL TIMES GROUP

Div. of Pearson Plc
1330 Avenue of the Americas
New York, NY 10019-5436
Telephone: (212) 641-6500, Web Site:
    www.ft.com
CEO: John Ridding
Editor: Lionel Barber
Global Comml Dir & Dep CEO: Ben
    Hughes
Dep Dir Global Commun & Head
    Commun, Americas: Darcy Kelly
Primary Market Served: Business &
    Consumer

CARL FISCHER MUSIC

65 Bleecker St Fl 8
New York, NY 10012-2420
Telephone: (212) 777-0900, Toll Free:
    (800) 762-2328, FAX: (212) 477-
    6996, E-Mail: cf-info@carlfischer.
    com, Web Site: www.carlfischer.com
CEO: Lauren Keiser
VP Sls & Mktg: Chris Scialfa
Mktg Mgr: Alfred Fredel
Mktg Asst: Tiffany Sumner
Conducts Business: Worldwide
Employees: 40
Primary Market Served: Business &
    Consumer
Catalog available online
Advertising/Marketing Budget Related
    to Direct Marketing: 0-25%
Direct Marketing ad budget: $300,000
Direct Mail: 80%
Magazines: 20%
Founded: 1872

Sheet music & music products to dealers & consumers.

FLORIDA TODAY

AKA Cape Publications, Inc. Owned
    by Gannett Co Inc
1 Gannett Plz
Melbourne, FL 32940
Telephone: (321) 242-3500, Toll Free:
    (877) 424-0156, FAX: (321) 242-
    3729, Web Site: www.floridatoday.
    com
Exec Ed: Terry Eberle
Bus Devel Dir: Greg Watson
Sls & Mktg: Patricia Shoff
Mktg & Community Affairs: Gina Kai-
    ser
Employees: 600
Primary Market Served: Business &
    Consumer
Founded: 1966
Gross sales or billing: $34,700,000

Newspaper publishing company.

FOOD CHEMICAL NEWS

Div. of CRC Press Inc
901 N Glebe Rd (Suite 200)
Arlington, VA 22203-1853
Telephone: (202) 887-6320, Toll Free:
    (888) 732-7070, FAX: (202) 887-
    6335, E-Mail: cs@foodregulation.
    com, Web Site: www.
    foodchemicalnews.com
Ed of Food Chemical News: Jay
    Fletcher
Mktg Dir: Amy Mitrani
Conducts Business: U.S.
Employees: 20
Primary Market Served: Business
Indirect online sales
Advertising/Marketing Budget Related
    to Direct Marketing: 76-100%
Direct Marketing ad budget:
Direct Mail: 90%
Telephone: 10%
Founded: 1959

Newsletters & reports on food regulations & environmental regulations.

FORBES INC

90 Fifth Ave
New York, NY 10011
Telephone: (212) 620-1887, Toll Free:
    (800) 295-0893, Web Site: www.
    forbes.com
Sr VP, Consumer Mktg & Bus Devel:
    Nina LaFrance
Conducts Business: U.S., Canada
Employees: 700
Primary Market Served: Consumer
Advertising/Marketing Budget Related
    to Direct Marketing: 76-100%
Founded: 1917

Magazine for business executives & investors.

FORUM PUBLISHING CO
383 E Main St
Centerport, NY 11721-1538
Telephone: (631) 754-5000, Toll Free: (800) 635-7654, FAX: (631) 754-0630, E-Mail: forumpublishing@aol.com, Web Site: www.forum123.com
Pres: Martin B. Stevens
Conducts Business: U.S.
Employees: 9
Primary Market Served: Business
Catalog available online
Direct online sales
Advertising/Marketing Budget Related to Direct Marketing: 0-25%
Direct Marketing ad budget:
Direct Mail: 25%
Magazines: 25%
Telephone: 50%
Founded: 1981
Gross sales or billing: $1,400,000

Publishers of trade magazines, connecting retail stores with wholesale merchandise.

FRANKLIN ESTIMATING SYSTEMS
2391 S 1560 W Ste B
Woods Cross, UT 84087-2378
Telephone: (801) 303-6083, Toll Free: (800) 346-7363, FAX: (801) 303-4540, E-Mail: management@franklinestimating.com, Web Site: www.fesys.com
Owner: Gregory Harrison
Conducts Business: U.S., Canada
Employees: 21
Primary Market Served: Business
Catalog available online
Indirect online sales
Advertising/Marketing Budget Related to Direct Marketing: 51-75%
Direct Marketing ad budget: $120,000
Direct Mail: $50,000
Magazines: $50,000
Telephone: $20,000
Founded: 1917

Publisher of Estimating Guides to the Graphic Arts. Catalogs include: Franklin Offset Catalog, Franklin Small Press Catalog, Franklin Estimator for Windows & Power Macintosh (Computer Estimating Software for Printers). Also Data Manager, a turnkey system for collecting time, storing, sorting & reporting the time & production information.

FULCRUM PUBLISHING
4690 Table Mountain Dr (Suite 100)
Golden, CO 80403
Telephone: (303) 277-1623, Toll Free: (800) 992-2908, FAX: (303) 279-7111, Web Site: www.fulcrum-books.com

Publr: Sam Scinta
Mktg Mgr: Melanie Roth
Publishing Asst: Katie O'Neill
Conducts Business: U.S.
Employees: 25
Primary Market Served: Business & Consumer
Catalog available online
Direct online sales
Advertising/Marketing Budget Related to Direct Marketing: 0-25%
Founded: 1984

Books for gardeners, teachers, librarians & professors.

GALE
RP-NFOA
Subs. of Cengage Learning
27500 Drake Rd
Farmington Hills, MI 48331-3535
Telephone: (248) 699-4253, Web Site: www.gale.cengage.com
Conducts Business: Worldwide
Primary Market Served: Business
Catalog available online
Founded: 1954

Information publisher providing data in print & electronic formats.

GARLINGHOUSE CO
174 Oakwood Dr, Glastonbury, CT 06033-2432
Sub of: Virtual Mktg Concepts
2121 Boundary St (Suite 208), Burnside Bldg
Beaufort, SC 29902-6812
Telephone: (703) 547-4115, Toll Free: (800) 235-5700, FAX: (703) 222-9705, Web Site: www.familyhomeplans.com
Publr & CEO: James D. McNair lll
Conducts Business: U.S., Canada
Employees: 50
Primary Market Served: Business & Consumer
Catalog available online
Direct online sales
Direct Marketing ad budget: $250,000
Direct Mail: 15%
Magazines: 50%
Newspapers: 5%
Telephone: 30%
Founded: 1907
Gross sales or billing: $5,000,000

Publishers of Home Plan books and magazines; blueprint sales to public through books & magazines.

GAZETTE COMMUNICATIONS INC
dba Decisionmark; Gazette Direct Mktg Svcs; The Gazette & KCRG-TV 9
500 Third Ave SE, Box 511

Cedar Rapids, IA 52406
Telephone: (319) 398-8211, Toll Free: (800) 397-8211, FAX: (319) 368-8834, Web Site: www.gazettecommunications.com
Exec VP & CFO: Ken Slaughter
Pres & COO: Charles M. Peters
CEO: Joe F. Hladky
Mgr Mktg & Promos: Stacie Bedford
Conducts Business: U.S.
Employees: 700
Primary Market Served: Business & Consumer
Founded: 1883
Gross sales or billing: $34,700,000

Companies include a daily newspapers, an ABC affiliate broadcast station, a shoppers network, commercial printing, and online services. Over 300,000 Eastern Iowans read, tune in, or log onto their products daily.

GEBBIE PRESS INC
PO Box 1000
New Paltz, NY 12561-0017
Telephone: (845) 255-7560, FAX: (888) 345-2790, E-Mail: gebbiepress@pipeline.com, Web Site: www.gebbieinc.com
Ed, Publr & Pres: Mark Gebbie
Assoc Ed: Barbara A. Edelman
Conducts Business: U.S.
Employees: 2
Primary Market Served: Business
Catalog available online
Indirect online sales
Founded: 1954
Gross sales or billing: $100,000

Publish All-in-One media directory including all daily, weekly, Black & Hispanic newspapers; all radio, TV, Black & Hispanic stations; consumer magazines, trade press, business periodicals & farm press. Also available as text files on CD or as an online subscription service.

GEMINI PUBLISHING CO
PO Box 57931
Webster, TX 77598-7931
Telephone: (281) 316-4276, E-Mail: getgirls@getgirls.com, Web Site: www.getgirls.com
Pres & Owner: Don Diebel
VP: Michele Diebel
Conducts Business: U.S., Canada, Europe, Asia
Employees: 3
Primary Market Served: Business & Consumer
Catalog available online
Direct online sales
Advertising/Marketing Budget Related to Direct Marketing: 0-25%
Direct Marketing ad budget: $10,000

Direct Mail: 10%
Newspapers: 5%
Online: 80%
Telephone: 5%
Founded: 1978
Gross sales or billing: $90,000

Books, cassettes, videos, CDs & DVDs to help men meet, attract & succeed with women. Free 4-page catalog available upon request. Market products to single men & our books to mail order businesses.

GENIUM PUBLISHING

79 The Mall, PO Box 46
Amsterdam, NY 12010
Telephone: (518) 842-4111, FAX:
(518) 842-1843, E-Mail: sales@
genium.com, Web Site: www.
genium.com
Mktg Dir: Paul Hans
Conducts Business: U.S., Canada, Europe
Employees: 7
Primary Market Served: Business & Consumer
Catalog available online
Direct online sales
Advertising/Marketing Budget Related to Direct Marketing: 76-100%
Direct Marketing ad budget:
Direct Mail: 100%
Founded: 1984
Gross sales or billing: $1,000,000

Technical books & manuals, health & safety booklets, manuals, videotapes & software & vocational training videotapes.

PETER GLENN PUBLICATIONS

777 E Atlantic Ave (Suite C2337)
Delray Beach, FL 33483
Telephone: (561) 404-4290, Toll Free:
(888) 332-6700, FAX: (561) 892-5786, E-Mail: gregjames@pgdirect.
com, Web Site: www.pgdirect.com
CEO & Publr: Gregory James
Dir: L Chip Brill
Dir: Umberto Guido III
Conducts Business: Worldwide
Employees: 9
Primary Market Served: Business & Consumer
Catalog available online
Direct online sales
Advertising/Marketing Budget Related to Direct Marketing: 51-75%
Founded: 1956

Publishing house for the entertainment industry.

GLOBAL DEMAND PUBLISHING INC

101 B Middle St (Suite 101 B)
Jacksonville, NC 28546-6798
Telephone: (910) 937-0562, FAX:
(910) 455-1937, E-Mail:
globaldemandpublishing@yahoo.
com
Mktg: Louann Driver
Founded: 2005

GLOBE SPECIALTY PRODUCTS INC

9 Latti Farm Rd
Millbury, MA 01527-2132
Telephone: (508) 871-1900
Pres: David Dickerson
Primary Market Served: Business & Consumer

GOLF DIGEST CO

Subs. of Conde Nast
20 Westport Rd Ste 320, PO Box 850
Wilton, CT 06897-4550
Telephone: (203) 761-5100, FAX:
(203) 371-2572, Web Site: www.
golfdigest.com
Pres & Publr: Peter King Hunsinger
Chmn & Editor: Jery Tarde
Conducts Business: U.S., Canada
Employees: 325
Primary Market Served: Business & Consumer
Catalog available online
Direct online sales
Advertising/Marketing Budget Related to Direct Marketing: 76-100%
Gross sales or billing: $7,700,000

Publish Golf Digest, Golf World, & Golf Shop Operations. Special event publications include programs for the Masters & U.S. Opens. Other products include books, videos, golf schools, custom research & a variety of events conducted by NYT Event Sports Marketing.

GOODHEART-WILLCOX PUBLISHER

18604 W Creek Dr
Tinley Park, IL 60477-6243
Telephone: (708) 687-5000, Toll Free:
(800) 323-0440, FAX: (708) 687-0315, E-Mail: custserv@g-w.com,
Web Site: www.g-w.com
Pres: John F. Flanagan
VP, Sls & Mktg: Todd Scheffers
Conducts Business: Worldwide
Employees: 65
Primary Market Served: Business & Consumer
Catalog available online
Indirect online sales
Founded: 1921

Gross sales or billing: $26,500,000

Publisher of industrial/technical, family & consumer sciences & career textbooks for education, industry & individuals.

GOODMAN MEDIA GROUP INC

250 W 57th St (Suite 710)
New York, NY 10107
Telephone: (212) 262-2247, FAX:
(212) 262-2278, E-Mail: jgoodman@
gmgpub.com, Web Site: www.
goodmanmediagroup.dev.
hotresponse.com
Publr: Jason Goodman
Sls Dir: Deena E. Brown
Primary Market Served: Consumer
Founded: 1995

Small consumer publishing firm publishing various topics, including collectibles, Victorian & women's magazines.

GOVERNING MAGAZINE

1100 Connecticut Ave NW (Suite 1300)
Washington, DC 20036-4109
Telephone: (202) 862-8802, Web Site:
www.governing.com
Circulation Dir: Paula Lawrence
Primary Market Served: Business & Consumer

GRADE FINDERS INC

1500 Spring Garden St (fl 12)
Philadelphia, PA 19130
Toll Free: (800) 777-8074, E-Mail:
info@gradefinders.com, Web Site:
www.gradefinders.com
CEO: William A. Subers
Pres: Mark Subers
Conducts Business: Worldwide
Employees: 7
Primary Market Served: Business
Catalog available online
Direct online sales
Founded: 1967

Publish a directory of paper manufacturers, distributors & converters. List the brand names produced by each.

THE GREAT AMARILLO DIRECTORY

Div. of Yellow Book
2400 Lakeview Dr (Suite 113)
Amarillo, TX 79109-1532
Telephone: (806) 353-5155, FAX:
(806) 359-2974, Web Site: www.
worldpages.com
Pres & CEO: Joe Walsh
VP: John Beaver
Primary Market Served: Business

Catalog available online
Publish telephone directories.

GREENWOOD PUBLISHING GROUP INC

Div. of Houghton Mifflin Harcourt
PO Box 6926, PO Box 5007
Portsmouth, NH 03802-6926
Telephone: (203) 226-3571, FAX: (203) 222-1502, E-Mail: sales@greenwood.com, Web Site: www.greenwood.com
Pres: Wayne Smith
Mktg Consultant: Roland Ochsenbein
Conducts Business: Worldwide
Employees: 264
Primary Market Served: Business & Consumer
Founded: 1967
Gross sales or billing: $29,700,000

Publish scholarly, professional & reference books, newsletters & journals for the academic & professional markets. Approximately 700 original titles per year. Backlist contains over 12,000 titles in social sciences & humanities. Imprints: Auburn House, Praeger Publishers, Greenwood Press, Bergin & Garvey, Quorum Books.

GROWING CHILD, INC

Subs. of Dunn & Hargitt
PO Box 2505
West Lafayette, IN 47996-2505
Telephone: (765) 464-0920, Toll Free: (800) 927-7289, FAX: (765) 423-4495, E-Mail: service@growingchild.com, Web Site: www.growingchild.com
Pres: Dennis Dunn
Conducts Business: U.S., Canada
Employees: 45
Primary Market Served: Business & Consumer
Catalog available online
Direct online sales
Founded: 1971

Publisher of child-development materials & commodities investment charts.

GRUBER & ALLISON INC

7487 Falls Rd W
Boynton Beach, FL 33437
Telephone: (561) 752-9960, FAX: (561) 752-0085
Pres: J.H. Gruber
Conducts Business: U.S., Canada, Europe
Employees: 6
Primary Market Served: Business & Consumer
Advertising/Marketing Budget Related to Direct Marketing: 0-25%

Founded: 1991
Newsletters.

GUILFORD PUBLICATIONS INC

72 Spring St (4th fl)
New York, NY 10012-4050
Telephone: (212) 431-9800, Toll Free: (800) 365-7006, FAX: (212) 966-6708, E-Mail: info@guilford.com, Web Site: www.guilford.com
Pres: Robert Matloff
Mktg Dir: Marian Robinson
Sls Mgr: Anne Patota
Conducts Business: Worldwide
Employees: 55
Primary Market Served: Business & Consumer
Catalog available online
Direct online sales
Advertising/Marketing Budget Related to Direct Marketing: 51-75%
Founded: 1973

Publish professional & trade books, DVDs, newsletters & journals in psychology & psychiatry, family therapy, learning disabilities, addictions, gender issues, education, & geography.

GULF PUBLISHING CO

2 Greenway Plz (Ste 1020)
Houston, TX 77046-0208
Telephone: (713) 529-4301, FAX: (713) 520-4433, E-Mail: publications@gulfpub.com, Web Site: www.gulfpub.com
Pres & CEO: John T. Royall
Publr: Ron Higgins
Publr: Bret Ronk
Conducts Business: Worldwide
Employees: 160
Primary Market Served: Business
Catalog available online
Indirect online sales
Founded: 1916

Publish specialized books & software for engineering & scientific professionals.

HDA INC

944 Anglum Rd
Saint Louis, MO 63042
Telephone: (314) 770-2222, Toll Free: (800) 533-4350, FAX: (314) 770-1454, E-Mail: plans@hdainc.com, Web Site: www.designamerica.com
Pres: Robert Ketterer
Sls Mgr: Michael Kirchwehm
Conducts Business: U.S., Canada
Employees: 27
Primary Market Served: Business & Consumer
Advertising/Marketing Budget Related to Direct Marketing: 0-25%

Direct Marketing ad budget: $60,000
Direct Mail: 12%
Magazines: 80%
TV/Radio: 8%
Founded: 1910
Gross sales or billing: $2,000,000

Blueprints, project plans, how-to books; Sunset, Ortho, BH&G & Sterling magazines.

HAMMOCK PUBLISHING INC

814 Church St (Suite 201)
Nashville, TN 37203
Telephone: (615) 690-3400, FAX: (615) 690-3401, E-Mail: info@hammock.com, Web Site: www.hammock.com
Pres: John Lavey
Dir Sls: Steve Sullivan
Admin Dir: Julia Boklage
Conducts Business: U.S.
Primary Market Served: Business & Consumer
Catalog available online
Founded: 1991

Publishing-base relationship marketing. Publish custom magazine, newsletter & internet based services.

HAR COURT INC

9400 Southpark Center Loop
Orlando, FL 32819-8647
Telephone: (407) 345-2000, FAX: (407) 345-1052
Mktg: Katie Lile
Primary Market Served: Business
Publishing.

HARCOURT EDUCATIONAL MEASUREMENT

Div. of Psychological Corp
19500 Bulverde Rd
San Antonio, TX 78259-3701
Telephone: (210) 299-1061, Toll Free: (800) 211-8378, FAX: (800) 232-1223, Web Site: www.harcourtassessment.com
Pres: Eugene T. Paslov
Mktg Dir: Wayne Gressett
Exhibits Mgr: Liz Huggins
DM Mgr: Terrie Dittman
Conducts Business: U.S., Canada, Australia, U.K.
Employees: 35
Primary Market Served: Business & Consumer
Advertising/Marketing Budget Related to Direct Marketing: 51-75%
Direct Marketing ad budget:
Direct Mail: 90%
Magazines: 5%
Telephone: 5%

Founded: 1968

Retail publication & distribution of educational books, kits, video & microcomputer software to professionals working in public & private schools, colleges, universities, hospitals & clinics. Wholesale distribution to college & university bookstores.

HARLEQUIN ENTERPRISES LTD

Subs. of Torstar Corp.
225 Duncan Mill Rd
Don Mills, ON, Canada M3B 3K9
Telephone: (416) 445-5860, FAX:
(416) 445-8655, E-Mail:
customer_ecare@harlequin.ca, Web
Site: www.eharlequin.com
Pres & COO: Dana Hayes
Exec VP, New Bus Devel & Strategy:
Pamela Layock
Exec VP, Retail Mktg & Sls: Craig
Swinwood
VP, Direct Mail & Readers Svc: Christina Clifford
Conducts Business: Worldwide
Employees: 1,000
Primary Market Served: Business &
Consumer
Catalog available online
Direct online sales
Direct Marketing ad budget:
$30,000,000
Direct Mail: 100%
Gross sales or billing: $583,000,000

Publish & market paperback books in 13 languages in over 90 countries.

HARPERCOLLINS

Subs of News Corp
10 E 53rd St
New York, NY 10022-5299
Telephone: (212) 207-7000, Toll Free:
(800) 242-7737, FAX: (212) 207-
7145, Web Site: www.harpercollins.
com
Pres & CEO: Brian Murray
Chief Mktg Officer: Barnaby Dawe
VP Indep Retailing: Carl Lennertz
Conducts Business: U.S.
Employees: 1,425
Primary Market Served: Business &
Consumer
Gross sales or billing: $165,200,000

The company's publishing groups include HarperCollins General Books (imprints such as Perennial, Quill), HarperCollins Children's Book Group, HarperCollins UK, HarperCollins Canada, HarperCollins India, and HarperCollins Australia/New Zealand. Its Zondervan unit publishes bibles and Christian books. The company's e-book imprint is PerfectBound.

HARPER'S MAGAZINE

Harper's Magazine Foundation
666 Broadway (11th fl)
New York, NY 10012
Telephone: (212) 420-5720, FAX:
(212) 228-5889, Web Site: www.
harpers.org
Pres & Publr: John R. MacArthur
VP & Gen Mgr: Lynn Carlson
VP Pub Rels: Giulia Melucci
Conducts Business: Worldwide
Primary Market Served: Consumer
Catalog available online
Direct online sales
Founded: 1850

Published since 1850, Harper's Magazine is the oldest monthly magazine in America. Marketed to an intelligent, literate audience of thought-leaders through direct mail & other direct response advertising.

HARVARD BUSINESS REVIEW

Subs. of Harvard Business School Publishing
60 Harvard Way
Boston, MA 02163
Telephone: (617) 783-7410, FAX:
(617) 783-7493, Web Site: hbr.org
Editor in Chief: Adi Ignatius
Editor: Amy Bernstein
Grp Publr: Joshua Macht
Sr Dir Consumer Mktg: Elaine Spencer
Sls & Mktg Coord: Nicole Palermo
Conducts Business: Worldwide
Employees: 40
Primary Market Served: Business &
Consumer
Advertising/Marketing Budget Related
to Direct Marketing: 51-75%

In-depth articles report timely business problems affecting marketing, general management, executive training & organization mergers. Subscribers are upper level management executives.

HARVARD BUSINESS SCHOOL PUBLISHING

60 Harvard Way
Boston, MA 02163-1001
Telephone: (617) 783-7400, Web Site:
www.harvardbusiness.org
VP Global Sales & Mktg: Ian Fanton
Sr Dir Global Mktg: Peter Walsh
Sr Dir Consumer Mktg: Elaine Spencer
Primary Market Served: Business

HATTON-BROWN PUBLISHERS INC

225 Hanrick St
Montgomery, AL 36104-3317
Telephone: (334) 834-1170, FAX:
(334) 834-4525, E-Mail: webman@
hattonbrown.com, Web Site: www.
hattonbrown.com
Co-Publr: David E. Knight
COO: Dianne C. Sullivan
Conducts Business: Worldwide
Employees: 23
Primary Market Served: Business &
Consumer

Publisher of trade magazine serving the forestry & wood products markets. Brochure design & database management.

HAYMARKET GROUP LTD

12 W 37th St
New York, NY 10018-7480
Telephone: (212) 239-0855, FAX:
(212) 967-4184, Web Site: www.
chocalatiermagazine.com
Pres: Michael Schneider
Adv Dir: Elizabeth Hall
Prodn Dir: Christina Van der Walt
Cir Dir: Charles Squires
Conducts Business: U.S., Canada
Employees: 12
Primary Market Served: Consumer
Catalog available online
Direct online sales
Advertising/Marketing Budget Related
to Direct Marketing: 26-50%
Gross sales or billing: $1,100,000

Publisher of Chocolatier & Pastry Art & Design magazines.

HEALTH AFFAIRS

Div. of Project Hope
7500 Old Georgetown Rd (Suite 600)
Bethesda, MD 20814-6800
Telephone: (301) 656-7401, FAX:
(301) 654-2845, Web Site: www.
healthaffairs.org
Publr: John Iglehart
Circ & Mktg Dir: Georgie Goldston
Exec Dir: Don Metz
Primary Market Served: Business
Catalog available online
Direct online sales
Advertising/Marketing Budget Related
to Direct Marketing: 0-25%
Founded: 1981

Bi-monthly health policy journal.

HEALTH SCIENCES CONSORTIUM

300 Silver Cedar Ct
Chapel Hill, NC 27514-1696
Telephone: (919) 942-8731, FAX:
(919) 942-3689, E-Mail: tony.
penta@edtsi.com, Web Site: www.
healthsciencesconsortium.org
Exec Dir: Frank B. Penta Edd
Mktg Dir: Jack Adcox

Publications Dir: Tony Penta
Conducts Business: U.S., Canada
Employees: 10
Primary Market Served: Business
Catalog available online
Indirect online sales
Advertising/Marketing Budget Related
to Direct Marketing: 76-100%
Direct Marketing ad budget:
Direct Mail: 95%
Magazines: 5%
Founded: 1971
Gross sales or billing: $1,000,000

Publishers of instructional video &
computer-based programs in the health
sciences.

HEARLIHY & CO

1002 E Adams, PO Box 1747
Pittsburg, KS 66762
Toll Free: (800) 622-1000, (866) 622-
1003, FAX: (800) 443-2260, Web
Site: www.hearlihy.com
Pres & CEO: Harvey Dean
Treas & Sec: Sandra Hearlihy
Supvr: Beth Garrison
Conducts Business: U.S.
Primary Market Served: Business &
Consumer
Catalog available online
Direct online sales
Advertising/Marketing Budget Related
to Direct Marketing: 51-75%
Direct Marketing ad budget:
Direct Mail: 80%
Telephone: 20%
Founded: 1969

Publisher of Educational Curriculum
for Technology Education & Life
Skills.

THE HEARST CORP

300 W 57th St
New York, NY 10019-3741
Telephone: (212) 649-2000, FAX:
(212) 649-2108, Web Site: www.
hearst.com/magazines/
Chmn Bd: William R. Hearst III
CEO: Frank A. Bennack Jr
Pres & COO: Steven R. Swartz
Sr VP & Chief Legal & Devel Officer:
James M. Asher
Sr VP, Fin & Admin: Ronald J. Doer-
fler
Conducts Business: U.S.
Employees: 17,000
Primary Market Served: Business &
Consumer
Catalog available online
Direct online sales
Founded: 1887
Gross sales or billing: $4,520,000,000
Magazine publisher.

HEARST MAGAZINES

Subs. of The Hearst Corporation
300 W 57th St (fl 19)
New York, NY 10019-3741
Telephone: (212) 649-2824, FAX:
(212) 765-3528, Web Site: www.
hearst.com/magazines
Pres: David Carey
Pres, Mktg Publishing Dir: Michael A.
Clinton
Editorial Dir: Ellen Levine
Employees: 20,000
Primary Market Served: Business &
Consumer
Catalog available online
Direct online sales

Newspapers, magazines, radio & television.

HEARTLAND BOATING MAGAZINE

319 N Fourth St (Suite 650)
Saint Louis, MO 63102
Telephone: (314) 241-4310, Toll Free:
(800) 366-9630, FAX: (314) 241-
4207, E-Mail: info@
heartlandboating.com, Web Site:
www.heartlandboating.com
Publr & Ed: Nelson Spencer
Sls Mgr: Kathryn Burns
Conducts Business: U.S.
Employees: 6
Primary Market Served: Consumer
Advertising/Marketing Budget Related
to Direct Marketing: 76-100%
Direct Marketing ad budget: $35,000
Direct Mail: 90%
Magazines: 5%
TV/Radio: 5%
Founded: 1989
Gross sales or billing: $500,000

Boating magazine for those interested
& active in boating in mid-America.

HEARTSTRINGS PRESS

Div. of Gramma's Graphics Inc
49 Starview Pl, Dept DMMP-GL
Lancaster, VA 22503
Telephone: (804) 462-0884, Toll Free:
(800) 462-0884, FAX: (716) 462-
0884, E-Mail: sue@grandloving.
com, Web Site: www.grandloving.
com
Co-author: Julie Carlson
Sec & Treas: F.B. Johnson
Pres: Sue Johnson
Conducts Business: Worldwide
Primary Market Served: Business &
Consumer
Catalog available online
Indirect online sales
Advertising/Marketing Budget Related
to Direct Marketing: 26-50%

Founded: 1980

Grandloving: Making Memories with
Your Grandchildren (newly released
5th edition), Heartstrings Press features
anecdotes & ideas from over 350
grandparents, parents & grandchildren
worldwide. Includes over 250 innovative, inexpensive activities for grandparents to do with or mail to their
grandchildren. Three hundred & eight
pages include illustrated projects, index
& guide to the best children's books &
products. and updated to include new
technology & social networking methods.

HELDREF PUBLICATIONS

Div. of Helen Dwight Reid Educational
Foundation
1319 18th St NW
Washington, DC 20036-1802
Telephone: (202) 296-6267, (215) 625-
8900, FAX: (202) 296-5149, Web
Site: www.heldref.org
Exec Dir Gen Counsel: Douglas Kirk-
patrick
Mktg Dir: Katie Pfund
Circ Dir: Fred Huber
Art Dir: Sergey Ivanov
Conducts Business: Worldwide
Employees: 80
Primary Market Served: Business &
Consumer
Catalog available online
Indirect online sales
Advertising/Marketing Budget Related
to Direct Marketing: 51-75%
Direct Marketing ad budget:
Direct Mail: $250,000

Publisher of scholarly journals & magazines.

HEMMINGS MOTOR NEWS

PO Box 256
Bennington, VT 05201
Toll Free: (800) 227-4373, FAX: (802)
447-9631, Web Site: www.hmn.com
Publr & Ed-in-Chief: Jim Maneto
Primary Market Served: Business &
Consumer

Publish a monthly magazine for collectors of antique automobiles, listing
cars, parts, supplies & services.

THE HERALD & REVIEW

Div. of Lee Enterprises
601 E William St
Decatur, IL 62525-1190
Telephone: (217) 429-5151, FAX:
(217) 421-6913, E-Mail: hrdirect@
herald-review.com, Web Site: www.
herald-review.com
Editor: Tim Cain
Editor: David Dawson
Editor: Jeana Matherly

Editor: Todd Nelson
Editor: Scott Perry
Employees: 300
Primary Market Served: Business & Consumer
Catalog available online
Direct online sales
Founded: 1873

Publisher of specialty magazines, guides & brochures; also direct mail, list rental, lettershop & postal center.

HIGHLIGHTS FOR CHILDREN

1800 Watermark Dr
Columbus, OH 43215-1035
Telephone: (614) 487-2601, Toll Free: (800) 848-8922, FAX: (614) 487-2700, Web Site: www.highlights.com
CEO: Kent S. Johnson
Exec Asst: Amy Maynard
VP Mktg: Shelly Stotzer
Conducts Business: U.S., Canada, Taiwan, Sweden, China, Singapore, Indonesia, Thailand, Korea
Employees: 600
Primary Market Served: Consumer
Catalog available online
Direct online sales
Advertising/Marketing Budget Related to Direct Marketing: 26-50%
Founded: 1946
Gross sales or billing: $120,000,000

Monthly magazine for children 2-12. Also sell books & other educational materials to parents, teachers & schools.

HIGHSCOPE EDUCATIONAL RESEARCH FOUNDATION

600 N River St
Ypsilanti, MI 48198-2898
Toll Free: (800) 587-5639, FAX: (734) 485-0704, E-Mail: info@highscope.org, Web Site: www.highscope.org
Pres: Larry Schweinhart
Curriculum Devel: Ann Epstein
Early Childhood Educ: Beth Marshall
Res: Tomoko Wakabayashi
Educational Svcs: Gavin Haque
Fin & Opers: Theresa Schenk
Sls & Mktg: Carrie Hernandez
Publications: Nancy Brickman
Conducts Business: U.S., U.K., Canada, Netherlands, Mexico, Singapore
Employees: 65
Primary Market Served: Business & Consumer
Catalog available online
Indirect online sales
Advertising/Marketing Budget Related to Direct Marketing: 0-25%

Founded: 1970

Educational books, videos & recordings for educators & educational researchers working primarily with early childhood education.

HOKE COMMUNICATIONS INC

54 Adams St
Garden City, NY 11530
Telephone: (516) 746-6700, FAX: (516) 294-8141
Pres: Stuart W. Boysen III
Publr: Henry Reed Hoke III
Conducts Business: Worldwide
Employees: 2
Primary Market Served: Business & Consumer
Advertising/Marketing Budget Related to Direct Marketing: 76-100%
Direct Marketing ad budget:
Direct Mail: 50%
Telephone: 50%
Founded: 1938

Publishing company.

HOLLYWOOD FILM ARCHIVE

8391 Beverly Blvd (PMB 321)
Los Angeles, CA 90048
Telephone: (323) 655-4968, Web Site: www.hfarchive.com
Pres: D. Richard Baer
Admin Dir: Howard Schiller
Conducts Business: Worldwide
Employees: 3
Primary Market Served: Business & Consumer
Catalog available online
Advertising/Marketing Budget Related to Direct Marketing: 26-50%
Direct Marketing ad budget:
Direct Mail: 60%
Magazines: 10%
Newspapers: 20%
Online: 5%
Telephone: 5%
Founded: 1972
Gross sales or billing: $200,000

Publisher of movie & TV reference material; also distributes similar works to entertainment industry, libraries & the public.

HOME PLANNERS

Wholly Owned by Hanley-Wood Inc
3275 W Ina Rd (Suite 110)
Tucson, AZ 85741-2152
Telephone: (520) 297-8200, FAX: (520) 297-6219, E-Mail: sales@homeplanners.com, Web Site: www.homeplanners.com
Pres: Nick Foley
Mktg Dir: Julie Turetzky

Conducts Business: U.S., Canada
Employees: 80
Primary Market Served: Business & Consumer
Catalog available online
Indirect online sales
Advertising/Marketing Budget Related to Direct Marketing: 76-100%
Direct Marketing ad budget:
Direct Mail: 10%
Magazines: 90%
Founded: 1946

Publisher of home plan books & construction blueprints. Sell directly to consumers, home builders & bookstores.

HORTICULTURE MAGAZINE

Div. of F+W Media Inc
10151 Carver Rd (Suite 200)
Cincinnati, OH 45242
Telephone: (513) 531-2690, FAX: (513) 891-7153, Web Site: www.hortmag.com
Publr: Patty Dunning
Editor: Meghan Shinn
Conducts Business: U.S., Canada, Mexico, Europe
Employees: 30
Primary Market Served: Business & Consumer
Advertising/Marketing Budget Related to Direct Marketing: 76-100%
Direct Marketing ad budget:
Direct Mail: $600,000
Telephone: $50,000
Founded: 1904
Gross sales or billing: $8,000,000

Published eight times each year - gardening magazine for avid amateur gardeners.

HUMAN RESOURCE DEVELOPMENT PRESS

22 Amherst Rd
Amherst, MA 01002-9709
Telephone: (413) 253-3488, Toll Free: (800) 822-2801, FAX: (413) 253-3490, E-Mail: info@hrdpress.com, Web Site: www.hrdpress.com
CEO: Gregory Carkhuff
Publr: Robert Carkhuff
Employees: 21
Primary Market Served: Business
Founded: 1972
Gross sales or billing: $3,568,850

Publishing company that caters to the training & human research development market. Provide a line of customized resources to the training professional & novice that are cost & time effective.

IDG ENTERPRISE

Subs. of International Data Group
492 Old Connecticut Path, PO Box 9208
Framingham, MA 01701-9208
Telephone: (508) 872-0080, Web Site: www.idgenterprise.com
Pres & CEO: Michael Friedenberg
Pres, IDG Strategic Mktg Svcs & IDG Global Solutions Grp: Matt Yorke
Sr VP/Grp Publr & Chief Mktg Officer: Bob Melk
Conducts Business: Worldwide
Employees: 144
Primary Market Served: Business
Advertising/Marketing Budget Related to Direct Marketing: 0-25%
Founded: 1987
Gross sales or billing: $20,900,000

Publishing firm dedicated to the information processing industry, written with a management perspective.

IHS MARKIT

321 Inverness Dr S
Englewood, CO 80112-5895
Telephone: (303) 858-6187, Toll Free: (800) 447-2273, Web Site: www.ihs.com
Chmn & CEO: Jerre L. Stead
Pres & COO: Lance Uggla
Conducts Business: Worldwide
Employees: 8,800
Primary Market Served: Business & Consumer
Catalog available online
Founded: 1928

Publisher of critical information, analytics and solutions for the major industries & markets that drive economies worldwide.

INC MAGAZINE

Seven World Trade Center
New York, NY 10007-2195
Telephone: (212) 389-5377, FAX: (617) 248-8090, E-Mail: mail@inc.com, Web Site: www.inc.com
Pres: Bob LaPointe
Editor-in-Chief: Eric Schurenberg
Conducts Business: Worldwide
Primary Market Served: Business
Advertising/Marketing Budget Related to Direct Marketing: 26-50%

Publisher of monthly business magazine for growing companies. Also market management books & conferences & seminars, information services, planning guides, special reprints & newsletters. Conferences and seminars.

IDEALS PUBLICATIONS INC

2636 Elm Hill Pike (Suite 120), PO Box 305301

Nashville, TN 37214-3162
Telephone: (615) 333-0478, FAX: (615) 781-1447, Web Site: www.idealspublications.com
Pres: Simon Waterlow
Publr: Pat Pingry
Conducts Business: U.S., Canada
Employees: 30
Primary Market Served: Consumer
Direct online sales
Advertising/Marketing Budget Related to Direct Marketing: 76-100%

Publisher of Ideals Magazine, a six-issue per year publication dealing with traditional ideals & values. Also publish general interest books, specialty cookbooks & popular children's books.

IMPACT PUBLISHING INC

Potentials Unlimited
3409 47th Ave E
Bradenton, FL 34203-3974
Telephone: (941) 739-2611, Toll Free: (800) 4-A-NEW-ME, FAX: (941) 756-0315, Web Site: www.potentialsunlimited.com
Pres: Stephanie Banfill
Conducts Business: Worldwide
Employees: 10
Primary Market Served: Business & Consumer
Catalog available online
Direct online sales
Advertising/Marketing Budget Related to Direct Marketing: 0-25%
Founded: 1975

Publisher of self-help, motivational & educational audio & video tapes. Ten different series with over 180 titles, including English, Spanish & French language versions; new MP3 titles available.

INDIAN COUNTRY TODAY MEDIA NETWORK

Div. of Oneida Nation Enterprises, LLC
590 Madison Ave
New York, NY 10022
Telephone: (212) 600-2086, Web Site: www.indiancountrytodaymedianetwork.com
Publr & CEO: Ray Halbritter
Primary Market Served: Consumer

INDIANAPOLIS NEWSPAPERS INC

307 N Pennsylvania St
Indianapolis, IN 46204
Telephone: (317) 444-4444, FAX: (317) 633-9414, Web Site: www.indystar.com
Pres & Publr: Karen Crotchfelt
Dir Mktg & Sls Distr: Bryan Sturgeon

VP & Editor: Jeff Taylor
Employees: 1,300
Primary Market Served: Business & Consumer
Gross sales or billing: $76,000,000

Publishes The Indianapolis Star & The Indianapolis News for the state of Indiana. Also provides on-line service specializing in auto racing information, Indiana basketball & local news.

INFORMATION FOR PUBLIC AFFAIRS, INC

dba State Net
2101 K St
Sacramento, CA 95816-4920
Telephone: (916) 444-0840, Toll Free: (800) 726-4566, FAX: (916) 446-5369, E-Mail: info@statenet.com, Web Site: www.statenet.com
Employees: 200
Primary Market Served: Business
Founded: 1970
Gross sales or billing: $15,600,000

Provide on-line services for access to state & federal legislative & regulatory information.

INSTITUTE OF MANAGEMENT & ADMINISTRATION (IOMA)

Subs. of Bureau of National Affairs
3 Bethesda Metro Center (Suite 250)
Bethesda, MD 20814-5377
Telephone: (703) 341-3500, Toll Free: (800) 372-1033, FAX: (800) 253-0332, Web Site: www.ioma.com
Conducts Business: United States
Primary Market Served: Business
Catalog available online
Direct online sales

Newsletters for professionals specializing in law office management, insurance, accounting, corporate finance, corporate compensation & benefits, manufacturing, finance, or design/construction.

INSTITUTIONAL INVESTOR INC

225 Park Ave S
New York, NY 10003
Telephone: (212) 224-3300, FAX: (212) 224-3592, Web Site: www.institutionalinvestor.com
Chmn: Diane Alfano
CEO: Jane Wilkinson
Mng Dir & Grp Publr: Allison Adams
Editor: Michael Peltz
Dir Bus Devel: Tracy Redmond Fenton
Exec Dir Sls: Kristin Zammit
Conducts Business: Worldwide
Primary Market Served: Business
Direct online sales

Advertising/Marketing Budget Related
to Direct Marketing: 76-100%
Financial publishers.

INSTITUTIONAL REAL ESTATE INC

2274 Camino Ramon
San Ramon, CA 94583
Telephone: (925) 244-0500, FAX:
(925) 244-0520, Web Site: www.irei.
com
VP Mktg: Sandy Terranova
Primary Market Served: Business

INSURANCE PUBLICATIONS INC

Broker World
9404 Reeds Rd, PO Box 11310
Overland Park, KS 66207-1010
Telephone: (913) 383-9191, Toll Free:
(800) 762-3387, FAX: (913) 383-
1247, E-Mail: brokerwrld@primary.
net, Web Site: www.
brokerworldmag.com
Publr: Stephen P. Howard
Ed: Sharon A. Chace
Production Mgr: Betsy Masters
Circ Dir: Patty L. Godfrey
Sales Mgr: Rita S. Reeves
Comptroller: Holly Lang
Mktg Coord: Hope E. Howard
Conducts Business: U.S.
Employees: 10
Primary Market Served: Business
Catalog available online
Direct online sales
Founded: 1981

Publisher of trade magazine.

INTEREX

34 Hunt Rd
Amesbury, MA 01913
Telephone: (978) 388-8755, Toll Free:
(800) INTEREX, FAX: (978) 388-
8747, Web Site: www.
interexhibits.com
CEO: Ronald W. Evans
Pres: Tamara C. Olbres
Exec Dir: Darryl Armstrong
Adv Mgr: Kathy Schwartz
Conducts Business: Worldwide
Employees: 38
Primary Market Served: Business
Catalog available online
Indirect online sales
Advertising/Marketing Budget Related
to Direct Marketing: 26-50%
Users group for Hewlett-Packard.

INTERNATIONAL DIRECT MEDIA CO & INFORMATION PUBLISHING CO

2801 39th Ave (Suite 100)
San Francisco, CA 94116-2744
Telephone: (415) 661-4730, E-Mail:
infopubsf@aol.com, Web Site: www.
bookwormproductions.com
Pres: Don D. Flaten
VP & Gen Mgr: A.R. Wrenn
Conducts Business: U.S., Canada
Employees: 6
Primary Market Served: Business &
Consumer
Advertising/Marketing Budget Related
to Direct Marketing: 51-75%
Direct Marketing ad budget:
Direct Mail: 80%
Magazines: 20%
Founded: 1984

General giftware merchandise, educational books, videos & tapes.

INTERNATIONAL MARINE

The McGraw-Hill Cos
90 Mechanic St
Camden, ME 04843-1844
Telephone: (207) 236-4837, FAX:
(207) 236-6314, Web Site: www.
internationalmarine.com
Ed Dir: Jon Eaton
Acq Ed: Thomas McCarthy
Mng Ed: Deborah Oliver
Conducts Business: Worldwide
Employees: 10
Primary Market Served: Consumer
Catalog available online
Founded: 1969

Publisher & retailer of nautical books.
Send quarterly catalog to customer list.

INTERNATIONAL MASTERS PUBLISHERS INC

948 Plaza Dr
Montoursville, PA 17754-2400
Toll Free: (800) 570-5718, E-Mail:
customerservice@imp-usa.com, Web
Site: www.imponline.com
Gen Counsel & Corp Sec: Rhonda Gornitsky
Employees: 300
Primary Market Served: Consumer
Founded: 1979
Gross sales or billing: $300,000,000
Full service DM continuity publisher.

JIST PUBLISHING

Div. of New Mountain Learning LLC
875 Montreal Way
Saint Paul, MN 55102
Toll Free: (800) 328-4564, FAX: (800)
328-1452, E-Mail: educate@emcp.
com, Web Site: jist.emcp.com

VP & Publr: Linda Hein
Conducts Business: Worldwide
Employees: 45
Primary Market Served: Business &
Consumer
Catalog available online
Direct online sales
Direct Marketing ad budget:
Direct Mail: 75%
Magazines: 15%
Telephone: 10%
Founded: 1981

Career development, job search & educational training books, videos & software.

JAZZTIMES MAGAZINE INC

85 Quincy Ave (Suite 2)
Quincy, MA 02169-6764
Telephone: (617) 706-9110, FAX:
(617) 536-0102, E-Mail: info@
jazztimes.com, Web Site: www.
jazztimes.com
Publr: Lee Mergner
Conducts Business: Worldwide
Employees: 10
Primary Market Served: Business &
Consumer
Indirect online sales
Direct Marketing ad budget:
Direct Mail: 40%
TV/Radio: 60%
Founded: 1970

Magazine which covers the spectrum
from historical styles to the sounds of
today with reviews of new releases &
reissues, profiles of artists & jazz news
here & abroad.

THE JEWISH PUBLICATION SOCIETY

2100 Arch St
Philadelphia, PA 19103
Telephone: (215) 832-0600, Toll Free:
(800) 234-3151, FAX: (215) 568-
2017, Web Site: www.jewishpub.org
Dir: Barry L. Schwartz
Mng Editor: Carol Hupping
Dir Devel & Cmty Rels: Sarah Kroloff
Segal
Acctg Mgr: Trisha Lubrant
Conducts Business: Worldwide
Employees: 18
Primary Market Served: Business
Catalog available online
Founded: 1888

Non-profit publishing company. Publish books to promote Jewish culture &
experience.

JONES PUBLISHING INC

N7450 Aanstad Rd, PO Box 5000
Iola, WI 54945-5000

Telephone: (715) 445-5000, Toll Free: (800) 331-0038, FAX: (715) 445-4053, E-Mail: jonespub@ jonespublishing.com, Web Site: www.jonespublishing.com
Founder: Joe Jones
Pres: Ryan Jones
Conducts Business: Worldwide
Employees: 34
Primary Market Served: Business & Consumer
Catalog available online
Direct online sales
Founded: 1987

JOSSEY-BASS INC PUBLISHERS

Subs. of John Wiley & Sons, Inc
One Montgomery St (Suite 1200)
San Francisco, CA 94104-4505
Telephone: (415) 433-1740, FAX: (415) 433-0499, Web Site: www. josseybass.com
Mgr: Steve Robinson
Conducts Business: U.S., Canada
Employees: 154
Primary Market Served: Business & Consumer
Advertising/Marketing Budget Related to Direct Marketing: 26-50%

Professional books (hardcover & paperback) & journals in the fields of management, social & behavioral sciences, education (K-12 & higher education), non-profit sector, health administration & public administration.

THE JOURNAL NEWS

Subs. of The Gannett Co Inc
1133 Westchester Ave (Suite N110)
White Plains, NY 10604
Telephone: (914) 694-9300, FAX: (914) 696-8152, Web Site: www. nyjournalnews.com
Publr: Janet Hasson
Editor: Cyndee Royle
Conducts Business: U.S.
Primary Market Served: Business & Consumer

Total market coverage of Westchester, Putnam & Rockland Counties, NY through newspaper inserts.

JOURNAL OF COMMERCE GROUP

Div. of the Economist Group Ltd
2 Penn Plz E (Suite 4)
Newark, NJ 07105-2251
Telephone: (973) 848-7000, FAX: (973) 848-7004, Web Site: www.joc. com
Pres: Bill Ralph
Sr VP, Mktg: Steve Brennen
Conducts Business: Worldwide
Employees: 400

Primary Market Served: Business
Advertising/Marketing Budget Related to Direct Marketing: 76-100%
Founded: 1827

Publisher of several publications & web sites covering logistics, trade & transportation.

JOURNAL STAR

Subs. of Copley Press Inc
One News Plaza
Peoria, IL 61643
Telephone: (309) 686-3026, FAX: (309) 686-3265, Web Site: www. pjstar.com
Publr: John McConnell
Promo Pub Affairs Mgr: Joy M. Anderson
Conducts Business: US
Primary Market Served: Consumer

Daily newspaper & Copley newspaper.

KCI COMMUNICATIONS INC

Subs. of National Information Corp
7600A Leesburg Pike, West Building (Suite 300)
Falls Church, VA 22043
Telephone: (703) 394-4931, FAX: (703) 905-8100, Web Site: www.kci-com.com
Pres: Walter Pearce
Conducts Business: U.S., Canada, Europe
Employees: 35
Primary Market Served: Consumer
Catalog available online
Direct online sales
Direct Marketing ad budget:
Direct Mail: 100%

Publisher of financial newsletters & books.

KET

Kentucky Educational Television
600 Cooper Dr
Lexington, KY 40502-1669
Telephone: (859) 258-7000, Toll Free: (800) 432-0951, FAX: (606) 258-7396, E-Mail: rgriffin@ket.org, Web Site: www.ket.org
Exec Dir & CEO: Shae Hopkins
Sr Dir, Mktg & Online Content: Tim Bischoff
Sr Dir, Production Opers: Nike Brower
Sr Dir, Education: Nancy Carpenter
Sr Dir, Programming: Craig Cornwall
Sr Dir Tech: Fred Engel
Sr Dir, Fin & Admin: Linda Hume
Sr Dir, External Affairs: Julie Schmidt
Conducts Business: U.S.
Primary Market Served: Business & Consumer
Catalog available online

KALMBACH PUBLISHING CO

21027 Crossroads Cir, PO Box 1612
Waukesha, WI 53187-1612
Telephone: (262) 796-8776, Toll Free: (800) 558-1544, FAX: (262) 796-1143, Web Site: www.kalmbach.com
Pres: Charles R. Croft
Conducts Business: Worldwide
Employees: 300
Primary Market Served: Consumer
Advertising/Marketing Budget Related to Direct Marketing: 51-75%

Publisher of hobby & leisure magazines such as Model Railroader, Astronomy, Dollhouse Miniature & 4 other magazine titles in addition to a full line of related hobby books, calendars, posters & videos. Sold to consumers, bookstores, hobby shops, newsstands & wholesalers.

KAPLAN PUBLISHING

205 W Randolph St (Suite 200)
Chicago, IL 60606-1814
Telephone: (312) 606-8905, Toll Free: (800) 245-2665, FAX: (312) 606-8985, Web Site: www. kaplanpublishing.com
Chmn & CEO: Andrew S. Rosen
Pres: Thomas C. Leppert
CFO: Matthew Seelye
Exec VP, Strategy & Innovation: Darrell Splithoff
Conducts Business: Worldwide
Employees: 20
Primary Market Served: Business
Catalog available online
Direct online sales
Advertising/Marketing Budget Related to Direct Marketing: 26-50%
Direct Marketing ad budget: $500,000
Direct Mail: 10%
Magazines: 60%
Newspapers: 20%
TV/Radio: 5%
Telephone: 5%

Trade publishing & distribution company.

KAPPA PUBLISHING GROUP

Subs. of Games Magazine
6198 Butler Pike (Suite 200)
Blue Bell, PA 19422-2606
Telephone: (215) 643-6385, FAX: (215) 628-3571, Web Site: www. kappapublishing.com
Pres: Despina McNulty
Asst VP: Janis Weiner
Editor in Chief: R. Wayne Schmitt-berger
Circulation Dir: Dave Tyler
Adv Mgr: Connie Kolkka
Conducts Business: Canada

Primary Market Served: Business & Consumer
Catalog available online
Direct online sales

Sell puzzle & game magazines.

KENSINGTON PUBLISHING CORP

119 W 40th St (fl 21)
New York, NY 10018-2522
Telephone: (212) 407-1500, Toll Free: (800) 221-2647, FAX: (212) 407-1590, Web Site: www.kensingtonbooks.com
Pres: Steven Zacharius
Dir Publicity: Karen Auerbach
Conducts Business: Worldwide
Employees: 87
Primary Market Served: Consumer
Catalog available online
Founded: 1974
Gross sales or billing: $57,000,000

Sell books to consumers. Topics include: romance, mystery, true crime, biography, fiction, health, self-help, suspense & horror.

KEY COMMUNICATIONS INC

385 Garrisonville Rd (Suite 116), PO Box 569
Garrisonville, VA 22554
Telephone: (540) 720-5584, FAX: (540) 720-5687, E-Mail: usglass@aol.com, Web Site: www.key-com.com
Publr: Debra A. Levy
Conducts Business: Worldwide
Employees: 17
Primary Market Served: Business
Indirect online sales
Advertising/Marketing Budget Related to Direct Marketing: 0-25%
Direct Marketing ad budget:
Direct Mail: 99%
Telephone: 1%
Founded: 1966

Magazines, editorial & ad space.

KEYBOARD WORKSHOP

Subs. of Duane Shinn Publications
PO Box 700
Medford, OR 97501-0047
Telephone: (541) 664-7052, FAX: (541) 664-7052, E-Mail: duane@playpiano.com, Web Site: www.playpiano.com
Owner: Duane Shinn
Conducts Business: U.S., Canada
Employees: 4
Primary Market Served: Consumer
Catalog available online
Direct online sales

Advertising/Marketing Budget Related to Direct Marketing: 51-75%
Direct Marketing ad budget:
Direct Mail: $75,000
Magazines: $10,000
Online: $100,000
Founded: 1965
Gross sales or billing: $400,000

Music courses, books, cassettes to mail order retailers such as catalog houses. Drop-ship for most accounts. Also create non-music products to be manufactured & marketed by other marketers.

KIMBO EDUCATIONAL

Div. of United Sound Arts Inc
Ten N Third Ave
Long Branch, NJ 07740-7045
Telephone: (732) 229-4949, Toll Free: (800) 631-2187, FAX: (732) 870-3340, E-Mail: service@kimboed, Web Site: www.kimboed.com
CEO: Gertrude Kimble
Pres: James Kimble
Sr VP: Jeffrey Kimble
Conducts Business: U.S., Canada, Australia, Japan, Singapore, New Zealand, Great Britain
Employees: 1
Primary Market Served: Business & Consumer
Catalog available online
Direct online sales
Direct Marketing ad budget:
Direct Mail: 75%
Telephone: 25%
Founded: 1962
Gross sales or billing: $2,000,000

Produce compact discs, DVD's for the educational marketplace & parent/teacher stores. Main area of concentration is on early childhood, yet products for middle grade & adult fitness programs are also released.

KING FEATURES

300 W 57th St (fl 15)
New York, NY 10019-3741
Telephone: (212) 455-4000, FAX: (212) 682-8332
Pres: T.R. Shepard III
Conducts Business: Worldwide
Primary Market Served: Business & Consumer

Syndicate comic strips for newspapers & license merchandising.

THE KIPLINGER WASHINGTON EDITORS INC

1100 13th St NW (Suite 750)
Washington, DC 20005-4364

Telephone: (202) 887-6400, Toll Free: (800) 544-0155, FAX: (202) 496-1817, Web Site: www.kiplinger.com
Pres: Knight A. Kiplinger
Sr VP & CFO: Corbin M. Wilkes
Vice Chmn & VP: Todd L. Kipplinger
Dir Mktg: Larry Fishbein
Conducts Business: U.S.
Employees: 220
Primary Market Served: Business & Consumer
Catalog available online
Direct online sales
Advertising/Marketing Budget Related to Direct Marketing: 51-75%
Founded: 1923
Gross sales or billing: $24,300,000

Publisher of Kiplinger Personal Finance Magazine & The Kiplinger Newsletters.

B KLEIN PUBLICATIONS

PO Box 970392
Boca Raton, FL 33497-0392
Telephone: (561) 496-3316, FAX: (561) 496-5546, E-Mail: bkleinpub@aol.com
Pres: Bernard Klein
VP: Betty Klein
Conducts Business: Worldwide
Employees: 6
Primary Market Served: Business & Consumer
Advertising/Marketing Budget Related to Direct Marketing: 51-75%
Direct Marketing ad budget: $150,000
Direct Mail: 70%
Magazines: 10%
Newspapers: 10%
Telephone: 10%
Founded: 1946
Gross sales or billing: $1,000,000

Reference books, directories, mailing lists & consulting services.

KOLBE CORP

2355 E Camelback Rd (Suite 610)
Phoenix, AZ 85016-9040
Telephone: (602) 840-9770, Toll Free: (800) 642-2822, FAX: (602) 952-2706, E-Mail: info@kolbe.com, Web Site: www.kolbe.com
CEO: David Kolbe
Pres Kolbe Intl: William K. Rapp
Chmn Bd: Kathryn Kolbe
VP Mktg & Communs: Jerry Cobb
Conducts Business: Worldwide
Employees: 20
Primary Market Served: Business & Consumer
Direct online sales

Founded: 1975

Online, print, and audio/video materials for self awareness, both personal & in business; team building, change management & placement in organizational development.

WILLIAM S KONECKY ASSOCIATES INC

72 Ayers Point Rd
Old Saybrook, CT 06475
Telephone: (860) 388-0878, FAX: (860) 388-0273
Pres: William Konecky
VP: Sean Konecky
Primary Market Served: Business

Book publishers for Art & Military History.

KRAUSE PUBLICATIONS INC

Subs of F+W Media Inc
700 E State St
Iola, WI 54990
Telephone: (715) 445-2214, FAX: (715) 445-4087, Web Site: www. krausebooks.com
Editor: Tom Bartsch
Conducts Business: Worldwide
Employees: 400
Primary Market Served: Business & Consumer
Catalog available online
Direct online sales
Founded: 1952

Publish books & periodicals in the following areas: collector cars, sports cards & sports memorabilia, records, coins, crafts, firearms, comic books & toy collecting, turkey hunting, deer hunting, trapping & rural building. Books & subscriptions are sold through direct marketing techniques to hobbyists & investors.

LAKESIDE PUBLISHING CO LLC

990 Grove St
Evanston, IL 60201-6510
Telephone: (847) 491-6440, FAX: (847) 491-0459, E-Mail: cs@ centurysports.net, Web Site: www. centurysports.net
Pres: Norman Jacobs
Circ Mgr: Richard Kent
Conducts Business: U.S.
Employees: 15
Primary Market Served: Consumer
Catalog available online
Direct online sales
Advertising/Marketing Budget Related to Direct Marketing: 0-25%
Founded: 1969
Gross sales or billing: $20,000,000

Baseball digest & cruise travel

LANDAUER CORP

3100 NW 101st St (Suite A)
Urbandale, IA 50322-3867
Telephone: (515) 287-2144, Toll Free: (800) 557-2144, FAX: (515) 276-5102, E-Mail: info@landauercorp. com, Web Site: www.landauercorp. com
Pres: Jeramy Landauer
Conducts Business: U.S.
Employees: 10
Primary Market Served: Business & Consumer
Catalog available online
Indirect online sales
Advertising/Marketing Budget Related to Direct Marketing: 0-25%
Founded: 1991

Christmas cards, gifts & books.

LANDMARK COMMUNICATIONS INC

11300 Atlantis Pl (Suite F)
Alpharetta, GA 30022
Telephone: (770) 813-1000, Web Site: www.landmarkcommunications.net
Pres: Mark Roundtree
VP: Gabriel Sterling
Dir Res & Database Mgmt: Mike Seigle
Conducts Business: U.S.
Primary Market Served: Business & Consumer

Full service political consulting and communications firm.

LAS VEGAS REVIEW JOURNAL

Div. of Don Rey Media Group
1111 W Bonanza Rd, PO Box 70
Las Vegas, NV 89125
Telephone: (702) 383-0211, FAX: (702) 383-4646, Web Site: www.lvrj. com
Publ Dir: Steve Coffeen
Publr: Sherman R. Frederick
Editor: Thomas Mitchel
Gen Mgr: Alan B. Fleming
Dir Adv: Bob Brown
Conducts Business: U.S.
Employees: 817
Primary Market Served: Business & Consumer
Catalog available online
Indirect online sales
Advertising/Marketing Budget Related to Direct Marketing: 0-25%
Direct Marketing ad budget:
Direct Mail: 25%
Newspapers: 25%
Telephone: 50%

Newspaper.

LAWYERS & JUDGES PUBLISHING CO INC

PO Box 30040
Tucson, AZ 85751-0040
Telephone: (520) 323-1500, FAX: (520) 323-0055, E-Mail: sales@ lawyersandjudges.com, Web Site: www.lawyersandjudges.com
Pres: Steve Weintraub
Primary Market Served: Business & Consumer
Founded: 1963

Publisher of print & digital resources in the various forensic fields.

LAWYER'S WEEKLY PUBLICATIONS

10 Milk St (Suite 1000)
Boston, MA 02108-4620
Telephone: (617) 451-7300, FAX: (617) 451-0132, Web Site: www. lawyersweekly.com
CEO: Jeff Baskies
Assoc Publr: Paul J. Martinek
Conducts Business: U.S.
Employees: 120
Primary Market Served: Business
Direct Marketing ad budget:
Direct Mail: 50%
Newspapers: 50%
Founded: 1972

Publish a statewide weekly legal newspaper in the states of Massachusetts, Rhode Island, Michigan, Missouri, North Carolina, Ohio & Virginia. Also publish newsletters, books & other services for attorneys in Massachusetts & New England, plus a biweekly newspaper, Lawyers Weekly USA. Sell New England attorney's kits & marketing services for those wishing to promote directly to attorneys.

LAZAR MEDIA GROUP INC

334 E Bay St (PMB 156)
Charleston, SC 29401
Toll Free: (877) 579-0222, FAX: (843) 577-5542, E-Mail: email@ lazarshopping.com, Web Site: www. lazarmedia.com
CEO: Elysa Lazar
Conducts Business: U.S.
Primary Market Served: Business & Consumer
Catalog available online
Direct online sales
Founded: 1986

Full service publisher of consumer books.

LEADERSHIP DIRECTORIES INC

1407 Broadway (#318)
New York, NY 10018-3853

Telephone: (212) 627-4140, FAX:
(212) 645-0931, E-Mail: info@
leadershipdirectories.com, Web Site:
www.leadershipdirectories.com
Chmn Bd: William W. Cressley
CEO: Gretchen G. Teichgraeber
VP, Sls & Mktg: Adam Bernacki
VP, Admin & Treas: Jim Gee
Chief Info Officer: Brian F. Hanley
VP, Products & Content: Sue Healy
VP, Washington, DC: Imogene Akins
Hutchinson
Conducts Business: U.S.
Employees: 60
Primary Market Served: Business
Catalog available online
Advertising/Marketing Budget Related
to Direct Marketing: 76-100%

Publisher of directories on corporations, federal & state government. Rent
mailing lists of corporate, state & federal managers & buyers.

LEISURE ARTS INC

104 Champs Blvd (#100)
Maumelle, AR 72113-6738
Telephone: (501) 868-8800, Web Site:
www.leisurearts.com
Editorial Dir: Susan Wiles
Primary Market Served: Business &
Consumer

HAL LEONARD CORP

7777 W Bluemound Rd, Box 13819
Milwaukee, WI 53213
Telephone: (414) 774-3630, FAX:
(414) 774-3259, Web Site: www.
halleonard.com
Chmn & CEO: Keith Mardak
Pres: Larry Morton
Sr Sls & Mktg Mgr: Brad Smith
Adv Mgr: Jim Meinhardt
Conducts Business: Worldwide
Employees: 370
Primary Market Served: Business &
Consumer
Founded: 1947

Music publisher selling to distributors.

LERNER PUBLISHING
GROUP

1251 Washington Ave N
Minneapolis, MN 55401
Telephone: (612) 332-3344, Toll Free:
(800) 328-4929, FAX: (800) 332-
1132, E-Mail: info@lernerbooks.
com, Web Site: www.lernerbooks.
com
Chmn Bd: Harry Lerner
CEO: Adam Lerner
Exec VP & CFO: Margaret Wunderlich
Exec VP Sls: David Wexler
Conducts Business: U.S.
Employees: 100

Primary Market Served: Business &
Consumer
Catalog available online
Indirect online sales
Founded: 1959
Gross sales or billing: $8,100,000

Publisher of books for young people,
grades K-12 & distributed to schools,
libraries & bookstores.

LEXISNEXIS MATTHEW
BENDER

1275 Broadway
Albany, NY 12204-2628
Telephone: (518) 487-3000, Toll Free:
(800) 424-4200, E-Mail: lexisnexis@
matthewbender, Web Site: www.
bender.lexisnexis.com
CEO: Mike Walsh
CEO: Mark Kelsey
CEO, Mktg & Bus Solutions: Phil Liv-
ingston
Sr VP & Chief Mktg Officer: Lisa Ago-
na
Conducts Business: Worldwide
Employees: 1,400
Primary Market Served: Business
Advertising/Marketing Budget Related
to Direct Marketing: 26-50%

Publishing company specializing in legal, tax & business publications & software for lawyers, accountants &
business people.

PETER LI EDUCATION
GROUP

2621 Dryden Rd (Suite 300)
Dayton, OH 45439
Telephone: (937) 293-1415, Toll Free:
(800) 523-4625, FAX: (937) 293-
1310, Web Site: www.peterli.com
Chmn: Peter Li
Pres, Publr: Bret Thomas
VP, Opers: Cathy Helmers
VP, Mktg: Terry Perkins
Corp Circulation Dir: Rosemary
Walker
Mktg Mgr: Amy Baird
Conducts Business: Worldwide
Employees: 100
Primary Market Served: Consumer
Catalog available online
Direct online sales
Founded: 1971

Serves the educational & religious education markets nationwide as a publisher of magazines and teaching resources
for school administrators, teachers &
students.

LIFE-STUDY FELLOWSHIP
FOUNDATION INC

90 Heights Rd
Darien, CT 06820

Telephone: (203) 655-1436, FAX:
(203) 655-1392, Web Site: www.
lifestudyfellowship.com
Pres: Theodore E. Lundberg
Exec VP: Michael Donnelly
VP, Mktg: Michael Keane
VP, Fin: John Keane Jr.
Conducts Business: Worldwide
Employees: 85
Primary Market Served: Consumer
Advertising/Marketing Budget Related
to Direct Marketing: 51-75%
Direct Marketing ad budget:
Direct Mail: 80%
Newspapers: 20%
Founded: 1939

Publisher of inspirational books &
pamphlets.

LIGUORI PUBLICATIONS

One Liguori Dr
Liguori, MO 63057-9999
Telephone: (636) 464-2500, Toll Free:
(800) 325-9521, FAX: (800) 325-
9526, E-Mail: liguori@liguori.org,
Web Site: www.liguori.org
Pres: Rev Donald Willard
Publr: Virgil Tipton
Mktg Mgr: Angela Baumann
Bi-lingual Mktg Specialist: Rhina Por-
tillo
Conducts Business: Worldwide
Primary Market Served: Business &
Consumer
Catalog available online
Direct online sales
Advertising/Marketing Budget Related
to Direct Marketing: 76-100%
Founded: 1947

Publisher of the Liguorian magazine,
parish bulletins, trade books on spirituality, prayer & Christian living & religious education materials, Spanish &
English.

LINGUISYSTEMS

3100 Fourth Ave
East Moline, IL 61244-9700
Telephone: (309) 755-2300, Toll Free:
(800) 776-4332, FAX: (800) 577-
4555, E-Mail: service@
linguisystems.com, Web Site: www.
linguisystems.com
Co-Owner: Linda Bowers
Co-Owner: Rosemary Huisingh
Ed: Mark Barrett
Ed: Paul Johnson
Ed: Carolyn Lo Giudice
Conducts Business: U.S., Europe, Can-
ada
Employees: 45
Primary Market Served: Business &
Consumer
Catalog available online
Direct online sales

Advertising/Marketing Budget Related to Direct Marketing: 76-100%
Direct Marketing ad budget:
Direct Mail: 100%
Founded: 1984

Publisher of language & critical thinking materials for speech language pathologists, special educators & regular education teachers.

LINKS MAGAZINE
10 Executive Park Rd (Suite 202)
Hilton Head Island, SC 29928
Telephone: (843) 842-6200, FAX: (843) 842-6233, Web Site: www.linksmagazine.com
Pres & Publr: Jack Purcell
Editorial Dir: Nancy Purcell
Dir Consumer Mktg: Lori Masaoay
Conducts Business: U.S., Canada
Employees: 25
Primary Market Served: Consumer
Direct online sales
Advertising/Marketing Budget Related to Direct Marketing: 0-25%
Direct Marketing ad budget:
Direct Mail: 50%
Magazines: 25%
Online: 20%
Telephone: 5%
Founded: 1988

Golf magazine.

LIPPINCOTT, WILLIAMS & WILKINS
Subs. of Wolters Kluwer Health
351 W Camden St
Baltimore, MD 21201-2436
Telephone: (410) 528-4000, Toll Free: (800) 638-0672, FAX: (410) 528-8597, E-Mail: customerservice@lww.com, Web Site: www.lww.com
Pres, Domestic Mktg: Rick Perry
Pres, Periodicals: Carole Pippen
Conducts Business: Worldwide
Employees: 350
Primary Market Served: Business & Consumer
Catalog available online
Direct online sales
Advertising/Marketing Budget Related to Direct Marketing: 26-50%
Founded: 1890
Gross sales or billing: $49,300,000

Publisher of medical, nursing (software), allied health, scientific books, journals, periodicals & newspapers.

LIVE DESIGN
249 W 17th St
New York, NY 10011
Telephone: (212) 204-4268, FAX: (212) 204-4291, Web Site: livedesignonline.com

Assoc Publr & Editorial Dir: David Johnson
Editorial Coord: Lisa Murphy
Conducts Business: U.S., Canada, Europe, Asia
Primary Market Served: Business

A creative and technical journal for live entertainment professionals in lighting, staging, and projection. Provides designers, programmers, and technicians with tips and trends, news and reviews of the latest gear, reports from the field, and industry viewpoint and commentary.

LLEWELLYN PUBLICATIONS
Div. of Llewellyn Worldwide Ltd
2143 Wooddale Dr
Woodbury, MN 55125-2989
Telephone: (651) 291-1970, Toll Free: (877) 639-9753, FAX: (651) 291-1908, Web Site: www.llewellyn.com
Owner: Carl L. Weschcke
Publr: Bill Krause
VP: Gabe Weschcke
Sls Dir: Rhonda Ogren
Conducts Business: U.S., Canada, U.K., Australia, New Zealand, Mexico
Employees: 75
Primary Market Served: Business & Consumer
Advertising/Marketing Budget Related to Direct Marketing: 51-75%
Direct Marketing ad budget: $500,000
Founded: 1901

Oldest "new age" book & periodical publisher in North America. Books on astrology, wicca, yoga, meditation, magic, tarot & alternative health. English & Spanish language titles. Also publish New Worlds magazine & Flux - YA fiction & Midnight Inc - adult mystery fiction.

LOMBARDI PUBLISHING CORP
PO Box 428
Vaughan, ON, Canada L0J 1C0
Toll Free: (866) 744-3579, FAX: (905) 856-9416, E-Mail: customerservice@lombardipublishing.com, Web Site: www.lombardipublishing.com
Pres: Adrian Newman
Primary Market Served: Business & Consumer

M2MEDIA 360
1030 W Higgins Rd (Suite 230)
Park Ridge, IL 60068
Telephone: (760) 318-7000, E-Mail: cnaughton@m2media360.com, Web Site: www.m2media360.com
Pres: Marion Minor
Sr VP & Grp Publr: Charles Forman

Ed-in-Chief: Richard Brandes
Mktg Specialist: Cheryl Naughton
Conducts Business: U.S.
Employees: 10
Primary Market Served: Business & Consumer
Advertising/Marketing Budget Related to Direct Marketing: 0-25%
Gross sales or billing: $4,800,000

Trade publications for green industry.

MTS PUBLISHING
800 W 5th Ave (Suite 204A)
Naperville, IL 60563-4925
Telephone: (630) 955-9750, Toll Free: (800) 332-4655, FAX: (630) 955-9787, E-Mail: info@midwesttruckshopper.com, Web Site: www.midwesttruckshopper.com
Pres: Stephen Shumate
Shareholder: Robert Quigley
Conducts Business: U.S., Canada, Mexico
Employees: 7
Primary Market Served: Business & Consumer
Catalog available online
Direct online sales
Advertising/Marketing Budget Related to Direct Marketing: 76-100%
Gross sales or billing: $2,000,000

Publisher of crossword puzzles sold on subscription basis.

MAGAZINE PUBLISHERS OF AMERICA
The Association of Magazine Media
757 3rd Ave (fl 11)
New York, NY 10017-2194
Telephone: (212) 872-3700, FAX: (212) 888-4217, E-Mail: mpa@magazine.org, Web Site: www.magazine.org
Pres & CEO: Mary Berner
Exec VP, Communs & Events: Meredith Wagner
Chief Mktg Officer: Christopher Kevorkian
Dir Consumer Mktg, Members Svcs, IMAG: Suzette Kraemer
Exec VP, Govt Affairs: James C. Cregan
Sr VP, Legislative & Regulatory Policy: Rita Cohen
Sr VP, Digital Strategy & Initiatives: Ethan Grey
VP, Creative Svcs: Patty Bogie
Conducts Business: Worldwide
Employees: 50
Primary Market Served: Consumer
Catalog available online
Founded: 1919

Gross sales or billing: $2,425,000,000

Magazine industry association. Supports the marketing & Washington activities of over 800 U.S. magazines, representing 60% of total ABC circulation. Branch Office in Washington, DC.

MAGNA PUBLICATIONS INC
2718 Dryden Dr
Madison, WI 53704-3086
Telephone: (608) 246-3590, FAX: (608) 246-3597, Web Site: www. magnapubs.com
Pres: Bill Haight
VP: David Burns
Mng Editor: Catherine Stover
Mktg Svcs Specialist: Theresa Girardi
Conducts Business: U.S., Canada
Employees: 35
Primary Market Served: Business
Catalog available online
Direct online sales
Advertising/Marketing Budget Related to Direct Marketing: 76-100%
Direct Marketing ad budget: $3,000,000
Direct Mail: 85%
Magazines: 5%
Newspapers: 5%
Telephone: 5%
Founded: 1971
Gross sales or billing: $6,000,000

Subscription newsletters to colleges, universities.

MAJORIUM
aka The American Management Development Group, Inc
2025 Main St
Stevens Point, WI 54481-3019
Telephone: (715) 342-1018, Toll Free: (800) 654-4935, FAX: (715) 342-1118, E-Mail: sales@majorium.com, Web Site: www.letstalkselling.com
CEO: Timothy Bednarz Ph.D.
Partner: Shirley Bednarz Ph.D.
Conducts Business: U.S.
Employees: 8
Primary Market Served: Business

Management programs for professional service businesses (Doctors, Lawyers, etc.) & small middle business management manuals. Training for sales, sales management & speaking consulting.

MANCOMM INC
317 W 4th St
Davenport, IA 52801
Telephone: (563) 323-6245, Toll Free: (877) 626-2666, FAX: (563) 323-0804, E-Mail: 411@mancomm.com, Web Site: mancomm.com
Pres: Benjamin Mangan
Primary Market Served: Consumer

Founded: 1988

Safety & compliance publisher of regulatory products, training tools & resources.

MARKETSHARE PUBLICATIONS INC
Subs. of Marketshare Group Inc.
7171 W 95th St (Suite 310)
Overland Park, KS 66212-2249
Telephone: (877) 880-8068, FAX: (913) 217-2895, Web Site: www. marketsharegroup.com
Pres & CEO: Howard L. Payne
Conducts Business: U.S.
Employees: 20
Primary Market Served: Business & Consumer
Founded: 1985

Direct response card pack publisher.

MARQUIS WHO'S WHO VENTURES LLC
100 Connell Dr, Ste 2300
Berkeley Heights, NJ 07922
Telephone: (908) 279-0100, Toll Free: (844) 394-6946, E-Mail: info@ marquisww.com, Web Site: www. marquiswhoswho.com
CEO: Fred Marks
Conducts Business: Worldwide
Primary Market Served: Business & Consumer
Catalog available online
Indirect online sales
Founded: 1898

Publisher of comprehensive biographical information available in print & online. Major Marquis Who's Who publications include Who's Who in America and Who's Who in the World.

MARSHALL & SWIFT
777 S Figueroa St (fl 12)
Los Angeles, CA 90017-5878
Telephone: (213) 683-9000, FAX: (213) 683-9010, Web Site: www. marshallswift.com
Mktg Dir: Leslie Lake
Mktg Res Analyst: Linda Jovanelly
Conducts Business: U.S., Canada
Primary Market Served: Business
Catalog available online
Founded: 1932

Publisher of building cost information.

MARTINDALE-HUBBELL
Div. of Reed Elsevier Inc
121 Chanlon Rd
New Providence, NJ 07974
Telephone: (908) 771-7777, Toll Free: (800) 526-4902, FAX: (908) 771-8704, Web Site: www.martindale. com

CEO: Mike Walsh
CEO: Mark Kelsey
CEO, Mktg & Bus Solutions: Phil Livingston
Sr VP, Chief Mktg Officer: Lisa Agona
VP, Database Prodn: Dean Hollister
Sr Mktg Dir: Marilyn Canning
Conducts Business: Worldwide
Primary Market Served: Consumer
Founded: 1868

Publisher of The Martindale-Hubbell Law Directory in hardcopy, on CD-ROM, online through Lexis/Nexis & on the Internet; containing listings of over 900,000 lawyers & law firms worldwide. Other publications include Law Digest, a summary of laws from each of the 50 states and 75 countries; Martindale-Hubbell Law Directory's International Edition, designed for the international legal community and Martindale-Hubbell Bar Register of Preeminent Lawyers, listing law practices designated as outstanding by members of the legal community.

MARYLAND PENNYSAVER
1342 Charwood Rd
Hanover, MD 21076
Toll Free: (888) 899-8992, Web Site: www.mdpennysaver.com
VP, Sls: Chris Shertzer
Conducts Business: U.S.
Employees: 330
Primary Market Served: Business & Consumer
Catalog available online
Indirect online sales
Advertising/Marketing Budget Related to Direct Marketing: 76-100%
Direct Marketing ad budget:
Direct Mail: 100%
Founded: 1979

Saturation mailed shopper appearing weekly in over 1,284,300 households in MD & VA. Display advertising, inserts & circulars plus web press printing.

MAYO CLINIC
200 First St SW
Rochester, MN 55905
Telephone: (507) 284-2511, Web Site: www.mayoclinic.org
CEO & Pres: John H. Noseworthy
CFO: Jeffrey W. Bolton
Chief Mktg & Pub Affairs Officer: John La Forgia
Chair, Mktg Div: Misty Hathaway
Chair, External Rels Div: Chris Gade
Brand Mngmt: Amy Davis
Conducts Business: U.S., Germany, Chile, Japan, Netherlands, Saudi Arabia
Employees: 52,194

Primary Market Served: Business & Consumer
Direct online sales
Advertising/Marketing Budget Related to Direct Marketing: 0-25%
Gross sales or billing: $5,234,000,000

Produce & market reliable health information products to general consumers, including newsletters, books, CD-ROM & on-line services.

MCCLATCHY CO
2100 "Q" St
Sacramento, CA 95816-6899
Telephone: (916) 321-1855, FAX: (916) 321-1869, Web Site: www.mcclatchy.com
Pres & CEO: Patrick J. Talamantes
VP, News & Washington Editor: Anders Gyllenhaal
VP, Corp Devel, Gen Counsel & Sec: Karole Morgan-Prager
Dir Commun: Peter Tira
Employees: 16,791
Primary Market Served: Business & Consumer
Founded: 1857
Gross sales or billing: $1,675,200,000

Newspaper company.

MCDOUGAL LITTELL
Div. of Houghton Mifflin Co
1560 Sherman Ave, PO Box 1667
Evanston, IL 60201
Telephone: (847) 869-2300, FAX: (847) 869-0841, Web Site: www.mcdougallittell.com
Pres: Rita Schaefer
Ed-in-Chief: Susan Schaffrath
Conducts Business: U.S.
Employees: 300
Primary Market Served: Business
Direct online sales
Advertising/Marketing Budget Related to Direct Marketing: 0-25%
Direct Marketing ad budget: $650,000
Direct Mail: $200,000
Telephone: $450,000
Founded: 1969
Gross sales or billing: $204,000,000

Educational text books for marketing to High, Junior High & Middle Schools.

MCFARLAND & CO INC PUBLISHERS
960 NC Hwy 88 W, PO Box 611
Jefferson, NC 28640-0611
Telephone: (336) 246-4460, Toll Free: (800) 253-2187, FAX: (336) 246-5018, E-Mail: info@mcfarlandpub.com, Web Site: www.mcfarlandpub.com
Pres: Robert Franklin
Exec Editor: Steve Wilson

Exec VP: Rhonda Herman
Dir Fin & Admin: Margie Turnmire
Sls Mgr: Karl-Heinz Roseman
Conducts Business: Worldwide
Employees: 45
Primary Market Served: Consumer
Catalog available online
Direct online sales
Advertising/Marketing Budget Related to Direct Marketing: 0-25%
Direct Marketing ad budget:
Direct Mail: 60%
Magazines: 15%
Newspapers: 5%
Online: 20%
Founded: 1979

Scholarly & reference books.

THE MCGRAW-HILL FINANCIAL
1221 Ave of the Americas
New York, NY 10020-1095
Telephone: (212) 904-2000, Web Site: www.mhfi.com
Pres, CEO & Chmn: Harold W. McGraw III
Exec VP, CFO: Jack F. Callahan
Exec VP, Human Resources: John Berisford
Exec VP & CIO: Bruce D. Marcus
Exec VP, Corp Affairs: D. Edward Smyth
Exec VP Global Strategy: Charles L. Teschner Jr.
Exec VP & Gen Counsel: Kenneth M. Vittor
VP, Govt Affairs: Cynthia Braddon
Conducts Business: U.S.
Employees: 20,214
Primary Market Served: Business & Consumer
Gross sales or billing: $6,255,100,000

Content and analytics company serving the capital and commodity markets.

MCKNIGHT'S LONG-TERM CARE NEWS
An imprint of Haymarket Media Group, UK
One Northfield Plaza (Suite 521)
Northfield, IL 60093
Telephone: (847) 784-8706, Toll Free: (800) 558-1703, FAX: (847) 784-9346, E-Mail: mltcn-webmaster@mltcn.com, Web Site: www.mcknightsonline.com
VP, Assoc Publr & Editorial Dir: John O'Connor
Natl Sls Mgr: Karmen Maurer
Circ Mgr: Sherry Oommen
Conducts Business: Worldwide
Primary Market Served: Business

McKnight's long term care news publications.

MCMURRY INC
1010 E Missouri Ave
Phoenix, AZ 85014-2602
Telephone: (602) 395-5850, Web Site: www.mcmurry.com
Sr Dir Database Mktg: Joseph Abeyta

MEDCOM INC
6060 Phyllis Dr
Cypress, CA 90630
Toll Free: (800) 877-1443, FAX: (714) 891-3140, E-Mail: lhammonds@medcominc.com, Web Site: www.medcominc.com
CEO: Bill Williams
VP, Sls & Mktg: Michael Zoradi
Mktg Mgr: Lisa Hammonds
Conducts Business: Worldwide
Employees: 70
Primary Market Served: Business
Catalog available online
Direct online sales
Direct Marketing ad budget: $25
Direct Mail: 80%
Telephone: 20%

Produce & market training educational materials in the health care field.

MEDIA TWO
1014 W 36th St
Baltimore, MD 21211-2415
Telephone: (410) 828-0120, FAX: (410) 825-1002, Web Site: www.mediatwo.com
Pres: Jonathan Witty
Mktg Coord: Bethany Vellucci

MEDICAL ECONOMICS MAGAZINE
Div. of Thomson
24950 Country Club Blvd (Suite 200)
North Olmsted, OH 44070-5351
Telephone: (440) 243-8100, FAX: (440) 891-2735, Web Site: medicaleconomics.modernmedicine.com/about
Editor-in-Chief: Tara Sultz
Mng Editor: Lois A. Bowers
Sr Editor: Jeffrey Bendix
Sr Editor: Morgan Lewis Jr.
Conducts Business: U.S.
Primary Market Served: Business
Catalog available online
Indirect online sales

Lists of nurse, pharmacy, medical, lab, physician, medical equipment & supplies manufacturers, nursing home personnel & hospital personnel. $3MM+ healthcare professionals. Also offer direct response postcard decks for pharmacists, registered nurses & physicians.

MEISTER MEDIA WORLDWIDE

37733 Euclid Ave
Willoughby, OH 44094-5992
Telephone: (440) 942-2000, Toll Free:
(800) 572-7740, FAX: (440) 975-
3447, E-Mail: info@meistermedia.
com, Web Site: www.meistermedia.
com
Chmn & CEO: Gary T. Fitzgerald
Vice Chmn: William Miller
Pres: Michael DeLuca
VP, Bus Devel: K. Elliot Nowels
Dir Mktg: Brian Dunay
Conducts Business: Worldwide
Employees: 116
Primary Market Served: Business &
Consumer
Catalog available online
Direct online sales
Advertising/Marketing Budget Related
to Direct Marketing: 0-25%
Direct Marketing ad budget: $700,000
Direct Mail: 80%
Magazines: 10%
Online: 10%
Gross sales or billing: $11,700,000

Publish monthly & annual farm publications sold online & via direct mail.
Books, CD, DVD & video. Crop pro-
tection/pest control, fertilizer/nutrition,
fruits & vegetables, ornamental horticulture, plant breeding, precision &
sustainable agriculture.

MENTORING MINDS

4882 Hightech Dr
Tyler, TX 75703-2613
Telephone: (903) 509-4002
Primary Market Served: Consumer

MEREDITH CORP

1716 Locust St
Des Moines, IA 50309-3023
Telephone: (515) 284-3000, FAX:
(515) 284-2700, Web Site: www.
meredith.com
Pres & CEO: Stephen M. Lacy
VP & CFO: Joseph H. Ceryanec
Chief Devel Officer & Gen Counsel:
John S. Zieser
Pres, Meredith Nat Media Grp: Tom
Harty
Pres, Media Local Media Grp: Paul
Karpowicz
Exec VP, Chief Mktg Officer: Nancy
Weber
Corp Controller: Steven M. Cappaert
Employees: 3,300
Primary Market Served: Business &
Consumer
Founded: 1902
Gross sales or billing: $1,600,000,000

Publisher of magazines & tradebooks
on TV broadcasting & marketing.

THE MIAMI HERALD MEDIA CO

1 Herald Plaza
Miami, FL 33132-1609
Telephone: (305) 350-2111
Mgr, Direct Mktg Sls: Sylvia Schenck-
er
Primary Market Served: Business

MIDWEST PUBLISHING INC

10844 N 23rd Ave
Phoenix, AZ 85029-4924
Telephone: (602) 943-1244, FAX:
(602) 331-0702
Employees: 275
Primary Market Served: Business &
Consumer
Gross sales or billing: $30,500,000

MISSOURI LIFE INC

501 High St (# A)
Boonville, MO 65233-1211
Telephone: (660) 882-9898, Toll Free:
(800) 492-2593, FAX: (660) 882-
9899, E-Mail: info@missourilife.
com, Web Site: www.missourilife.
com
Publr: Greg Wood
Exec Office Mgr: Amy Stapleton
VP: Danita Allen Wood
Conducts Business: U.S.
Employees: 8
Primary Market Served: Business &
Consumer
Catalog available online
Direct online sales
Advertising/Marketing Budget Related
to Direct Marketing: 26-50%
Founded: 1973

Statewide magazine & printing & publishing company.

MITCHELL INTERNATIONAL

Thomson Publishing Corp
6220 Greenwich Dr
San Diego, CA 92122-5913
Telephone: (858) 368-7000, FAX:
(858) 238-9111, Web Site: www.
mitchell.com
Pres & CEO: James Lindner
Exec VP, Sls, Svc, Prod Mngmt &
Mktg: Todd Mavis
Sr VP, Natl Sls: Bob Schachte
Mktg Dir: Chris Andrews
Conducts Business: U.S., Canada
Employees: 500
Primary Market Served: Business
Founded: 1946
Gross sales or billing: $80,000,000

Furnish technical automotive repair information to the body shop, general repair shops & insurance industries via
online services & publications.

MONKEYSHINES PUBLISHERS

North Carolina Learning Institute for
Fitness & Education
1608 Ilchester Ct
Greensboro, NC 27401
Telephone: (336) 292-6999, FAX:
(336) 292-6999, E-Mail: mkshines@
nr.infi.net, Web Site: www.
monkeyshinespublishers.com
Pres: Phyllis B. Goldman
Catalog available online
Indirect online sales
Founded: 1987

Educational resource material for K-12.

MORGAN KAUFMANN PUBLISHERS INC

Div. of Elsevier
30 Corporate Dr (Suite 400)
Burlington, MA 01803
Telephone: (781) 313-4700, E-Mail:
order@mkp.com, Web Site: www.
mkp.com
VP: Amy Pedersen
Mng Dir: Suzanne BeDell
Fin Dir: Jill Espinola
Employees: 24
Primary Market Served: Business &
Consumer
Catalog available online
Direct online sales
Advertising/Marketing Budget Related
to Direct Marketing: 76-100%
Founded: 1984

Computer books, database management, science behind graphics books.
Catalogs in bookstores.

MORRIS VISITORS PUBLICATIONS LLC

Div. of Morris Communications
699 Broad St (Suite 500)
Augusta, GA 30901
Telephone: (305) 892-6644, FAX:
(305) 892-1005, E-Mail:
mvpcustomerservice@morris.com,
Web Site: www.
morrisvisitorpublications.com
Conducts Business: U.S., Caribbean
Employees: 120
Primary Market Served: Business &
Consumer
Direct online sales
Advertising/Marketing Budget Related
to Direct Marketing: 51-75%
Direct Marketing ad budget:
Direct Mail: 60%
Magazines: 25%
Online: 5%
TV/Radio: 5%
Telephone: 5%

Publishers specializing in magazines
and travel guides.

MOTHER EARTH NEWS MAGAZINE

Subs. of Ogden Publications Inc
1503 SW 42nd St
Topeka, KS 66609-1265
Telephone: (785) 274-4300, Toll Free:
(800) 678-5779, FAX: (785) 274-
4305, E-Mail: bwelch@ogdenpubs.
com, Web Site: www.cappers.com
Gen Mgr Pubns & Publr: Bryan Welch
Ed-in-Chief: Richard Backus
Ed-in-Chief: Kathryn C. Compton
Ed-in-Chief: Robyn Griggs Lawrence
Ed-in-Chief: David Schimke
Conducts Business: U.S., Canada
Employees: 67
Primary Market Served: Consumer
Catalog available online
Direct online sales
Advertising/Marketing Budget Related
to Direct Marketing: 76-100%
Direct Marketing ad budget:
Direct Mail: 95%
Newspapers: 5%
Founded: 1879

Publisher of two tabloids & one bi-
monthly magazine aimed at 50+ C&D
counties nationally, biweekly. Use direct mail & space advertising to secure
salesmen & subscriptions for biweekly
magazines.

MOTHER JONES MAGAZINE

222 Sutter St (Suite 600)
San Francisco, CA 94108-4457
Telephone: (415) 321-1700, Web Site:
www.motherjones.com
CEO: Madeleine Buckingham
Publr: Steven Katz
VP, Strategy & Bus Devel: Kevin Wal-
ter
Dir: Jane Butcher
Conducts Business: U.S., Canada
Employees: 40
Primary Market Served: Consumer
Catalog available online
Direct online sales
Founded: 1976
Gross sales or billing: $9,500,000

Non-profit educational organization
dedicated to the dissemination of information & ideas necessary for a just society & a healthy democracy. Publisher
of Mother Jones Magazine.

MOTT MEDIA LLC

1130 Fenway Cir
Fenton, MI 48430
Telephone: (810) 714-4280, FAX:
(810) 714-2077, E-Mail: info@
mottmedia.com, Web Site: www.
mottmedia.com
Pres: William Hoetger
VP: Joyce Bohn
Conducts Business: U.S., Canada

Employees: 14
Primary Market Served: Business &
Consumer
Catalog available online
Indirect online sales
Advertising/Marketing Budget Related
to Direct Marketing: 26-50%
Direct Marketing ad budget: $50,000
Direct Mail: 20%
Magazines: 70%
Telephone: 10%
Gross sales or billing: $1,200,000

Publisher of trade & textbook materials
designed for the Christian school &/or
bookstore market. Owner of the Home-
schooling Book Club.

MOUNTAIN PRESS PUBLISHING CO

PO Box 2399
Missoula, MT 59806-2399
Telephone: (406) 728-1900, Toll Free:
(800) 234-5308, FAX: (406) 728-
1635, E-Mail: info@mountain-press.
com, Web Site: mountain-press.com
Owner & Publr: John A. Rimel
Bus Mgr: Rob Williams
History Editor: Gwen McKenna
Conducts Business: U.S., Canada
Employees: 12
Primary Market Served: Business &
Consumer
Catalog available online
Indirect online sales
Advertising/Marketing Budget Related
to Direct Marketing: 26-50%
Direct Marketing ad budget:
Direct Mail: 80%
Magazines: 6%
Newspapers: 4%
Online: 10%
Founded: 1948
Gross sales or billing: $1,200,000

Publish books on geology, western
Americana & natural science. Titles
sold through book trade & direct mail.

MIKE MURACH & ASSOCIATES INC

4340 N Knoll Ave
Fresno, CA 93722-7825
Telephone: (559) 440-9071, Toll Free:
(800) 221-5528, FAX: (559) 440-
0963, E-Mail: murachbooks@
murach.com, Web Site: www.
murach.com
Pres: Mike Murach
Mktg Dir: Judy Taylor
Dir Mktg: Cyndi Vasquez
Employees: 12
Primary Market Served: Business &
Consumer
Catalog available online
Direct online sales

Advertising/Marketing Budget Related
to Direct Marketing: 76-100%
Direct Marketing ad budget:
Direct Mail: 90%
Magazines: 10%
Founded: 1972

Publishers of PC & mainframe computer books.

MUSIC SALES CORP

180 Madison Ave (fl 24)
New York, NY 10016
Telephone: (212) 254-2100, FAX:
(212) 254-2013, E-Mail: info@
musicsales.com, Web Site: www.
musicsales.com
Pres: Barrie Edwards
VP, G Schirmer: Kristin Lancino
CFO: John Castaldo
VP: Tomas Wise
VP, Admin & Opers: Denise Maurin
Conducts Business: U.S.
Employees: 100
Primary Market Served: Business &
Consumer
Catalog available online
Direct online sales
Advertising/Marketing Budget Related
to Direct Marketing: 0-25%
Direct Marketing ad budget:
Direct Mail: 40%
Magazines: 60%
Founded: 1935
Gross sales or billing: $7,600,000

Music books for musicians & fans.

NADA APPRAISAL GUIDES

3186 Airway Ave (Unit K)
Costa Mesa, CA 92626
Telephone: (714) 556-8511, Toll Free:
(800) 966-6232, FAX: (714) 957-
0302, E-Mail: info@nadaguides.com,
Web Site: www.nadaguides.com
Pres & CEO: Donald D. Christy Jr.
VP & Gen Mgr: Lenny Sims
Conducts Business: U.S., Canada,
Mexico, Puerto Rico
Employees: 32
Primary Market Served: Business &
Consumer
Catalog available online
Indirect online sales
Advertising/Marketing Budget Related
to Direct Marketing: 26-50%
Founded: 1933

Publisher of used value guides for cars,
boats, RV's, motorcycles, mobile
homes, airplanes, helicopters, vans,
limousines, mobile homes, & commercial trucks.

NCP SOLUTIONS

11100 Wildlife Center Dr
Reston, VA 20190-5362

Telephone: (703) 438-6000, Toll Free: (800) 822-9919, FAX: (703) 438-3570, Web Site: www.nwf.org
Pres: Mark VanPatten
VP, Promo Activities: Diane Snyder
Conducts Business: U.S., Worldwide
Employees: 375
Primary Market Served: Business & Consumer
Catalog available online
Advertising/Marketing Budget Related to Direct Marketing: 0-25%
Founded: 1936

Wildlife conservation, educational materials, magazine publishing & merchandise catalog.

NAR PRODUCTIONS
Div. of NAR Associates
PO Box 233
Barryville, NY 12719-0233
Telephone: (845) 557-8713, FAX: (845) 557-6770, E-Mail: info@aodceus.com, Web Site: www.aodceus.com
Conducts Business: U.S.
Employees: 5
Primary Market Served: Business & Consumer
Catalog available online
Indirect online sales
Advertising/Marketing Budget Related to Direct Marketing: 76-100%
Founded: 1977

Publishing & communications firm.

NATIONAL ARCHIVES & RECORDS ADMINISTRATION
700 Pennsylvania Ave NW
Washington, DC 20408-0001
Telephone: (202) 357-5000, Toll Free: (866) 325-7208, Web Site: www.archives.gov
Archivist of the US: David S. Ferriero
Dep Archivist of the US: Debra Steidel Wall
COO: William J. Bosanko
Chief Strategy & Commun Officer: Donna Garland
Chief Innovation Officer: Pamela Wright
Chief Info Officer: Michael Walsh
CFO: Micah Cheatham
Inspector Gen: Paul Brachfeld
Conducts Business: U.S.
Employees: 40
Primary Market Served: Business & Consumer
Catalog available online
Advertising/Marketing Budget Related to Direct Marketing: 51-75%
Direct Marketing ad budget: $350,000
Direct Mail: 75%
Magazines: 20%

Newspapers: 5%
Gross sales or billing: $2,000,000

Publishers of historically significant federal records. Microforms, finding aids, guides & periodicals are sold to individuals, schools, libraries, research centers & genealogists. Museum shop & catalogs.

NATIONAL AUDUBON SOCIETY
225 Varick St
New York, NY 10014
Telephone: (212) 979-3000, FAX: (212) 979-3188, Web Site: www.audubon.org
Pres & CEO: David Yarnold
CFO: Mary Beth Henson
Chief Devel Officer: Kimberly Keller
COO: Susan Lunden
Chief Conservation Officer: Peg R. Olsen
Chief Info Officer: Andy Roos
Conducts Business: U.S.
Employees: 600
Primary Market Served: Consumer
Advertising/Marketing Budget Related to Direct Marketing: 51-75%
Direct Marketing ad budget: $4,000,000
Gross sales or billing: $11,000,000

Publisher of leading environmental magazine.

NATIONAL CATHOLIC REPORTER PUBLISHING CO INC
115 E Armour Blvd
Kansas City, MO 64111-1203
Telephone: (816) 531-0538, Toll Free: (800) 444-8910, FAX: (816) 968-2268, Web Site: www.ncronline.org
Publr: Thomas Fox
Editor: Dennis Coday
Editor at Large: Tom Roberts
Adv/Prod Dir: Vicki Breashears
Mktg Dir: Sara Wiercinski
Conducts Business: Worldwide
Employees: 30
Primary Market Served: Business & Consumer
Direct online sales
Advertising/Marketing Budget Related to Direct Marketing: 76-100%
Direct Marketing ad budget: $1,000,000
Direct Mail: 99%
Magazines: 1%
Newspapers: 1%
Founded: 1964
Gross sales or billing: $5,500,000

An independent newsweekly sold primarily through direct mail. Sell a homily service for churches by mail.

NATIONAL CRIME PREVENTION COUNCIL
One Prospect St
Amsterdam, NY 12010
Telephone: (518) 842-4388, Toll Free: (888) 776-7763, FAX: (800) 995-5121, E-Mail: mcgruff@spocentral.com, Web Site: www.mcgruffspo.com
Acting Mktg Dir: Anna Podolec
Employees: 20
Primary Market Served: Business & Consumer
Catalog available online
Direct online sales

National publication on safety.

NATIONAL ENQUIRER
Subs. of American Media Inc
4 New York Plaza
New York, NY 10004
Telephone: (212) 545-4800, Web Site: www.nationalenquirer.com
Chmn & CEO: David Pecker
Exec VP, Chief Mktg Officer: Kevin Hyson
Exec VP, Consumer Mktg: Dave Leckey
Editor in Chief: Tony Frost
Adv Dir: Lorelis Marte
Conducts Business: U.S., Canada, Puerto Rico
Employees: 1,500
Primary Market Served: Consumer

Publisher of National Enquirer, Star, Globe, Country Weekly, Country Music, All to World, Mira, National Examiner, Sun, Weekly World News, Mini Mages. Our publications are proven direct response vehicles.

NATIONAL GEOGRAPHIC SOCIETY
1145 17th St NW
Washington, DC 20036-4688
Telephone: (202) 862-8638, Toll Free: (800) 373-1717, Web Site: www.nationalgeographic.com
Chmn & CEO: John Fahey
Chmn Emeritus: Gilbert Grosvenor
Exec VP: Terrence B. Adamson
Pres, National Geographic Television: Brooke Runnette
Exec VP, Pres National Geographic Publishing and Digital Media: Declan Moore
Chief Mktg Officer: Amy Maniatis
Editor in Chief, National Geographic Magazine: Chris Johns
Conducts Business: Worldwide
Employees: 1,400
Catalog available online
Indirect online sales
Advertising/Marketing Budget Related to Direct Marketing: 51-75%

Founded: 1888
Magazine publisher, educational products.

NATIONAL JOURNAL GROUP

600 New Hampshire Ave NW
Washington, DC 20037
Telephone: (202) 739-8400, Toll Free: (800) 613-6701, FAX: (202) 833-8069, Web Site: www.nationaljournal.com
Pres: Bruce Gottlieb
Editor: Charles Green
Exec Editor: Adam B. Kushner
Dep Editor in Chief: Patricia Wilson
Primary Market Served: Business & Consumer

NATIONAL REVIEW

215 Lexington Ave
New York, NY 10016
Telephone: (212) 679-7330, FAX: (212) 849-2852, Web Site: www.nationalreview.com
Editor: Richard Lowry
Exec Publr: Scott Budd
Adv Dir: Jim Fowler
Conducts Business: U.S.
Employees: 50
Primary Market Served: Consumer
Catalog available online
Advertising/Marketing Budget Related to Direct Marketing: 76-100%
Direct Marketing ad budget:
Direct Mail: 100%
Founded: 1955
Gross sales or billing: $8,000,000
Magazine publisher.

NATIONAL TECHNICAL INFORMATION SERVICE

Div. of US Dept of Commerce
5301 Shawnee Rd
Alexandria, VA 22312-2379
Telephone: (703) 605-6000, FAX: (703) 605-6900, Web Site: www.ntis.gov
Dir: Ron Lawson
Conducts Business: Worldwide
Employees: 350
Primary Market Served: Business & Consumer
Advertising/Marketing Budget Related to Direct Marketing: 0-25%
Direct Marketing ad budget:
Direct Mail: $20,000
Magazines: $20,000
Newspapers: $20,000
Founded: 1945

A central clearing house & government wide resource for scientific technical engineering & other business-related information, with three million titles.

Provides a wide range of products & services including online, world wide web, audiovisual materials, CD ROM & more.

THE NATIONAL UNDERWRITER CO

5081 Olympic Blvd
Erlanger, KY 41018-3164
Toll Free: (800) 543-0874, FAX: (856) 692-2246, E-Mail: customerservice@nuco.com, Web Site: www.nuco.com
Pres: Garry Baumgartner
VP, Mktg: Peggy Walker
Pur Mgr: Steve Johnston
Conducts Business: U.S.
Employees: 160
Primary Market Served: Business
Catalog available online
Direct online sales
Advertising/Marketing Budget Related to Direct Marketing: 26-50%
Founded: 1897

Weekly newspapers, monthly magazines & 100 book and software publications for the insurance industry & other financial service fields.

NATURAL HISTORY MAGAZINE

American Museum of Natural History
105 W NC Highway 54 (Suite 265), PMB 204
Durham, NC 27713-6650
Telephone: (646) 356-6500, FAX: (646) 356-6511, E-Mail: nhmag@naturalhistorymag.com, Web Site: www.naturalhistorymag.com
Ed-in-Chief: Peter G. Brown
Publr: Charles Harris
Prodn Dir: Meredith Miller
Conducts Business: Worldwide
Employees: 35
Primary Market Served: Consumer
Catalog available online
Direct online sales
Advertising/Marketing Budget Related to Direct Marketing: 26-50%
Founded: 1900
Gross sales or billing: $12,500,000

Monthly magazine (ten issues annually) published by the American Museum of Natural History.

NATURE PUBLISHING GROUP

75 Varick St (fl 9)
New York, NY 10013-1917
Telephone: (212) 726-9200, FAX: (212) 696-9006, Web Site: www.nature.com
Mng Dir: Steven Inchcoombe
Editor in Chief: Phillip Campbell

Exec VP, Chief Tech Officer: Howard Ratner
Bus Intelligence Unit Dir: Peter Collins
Mktg Dir: David Hoole
Comml Dir: Dean Sanderson
Conducts Business: Worldwide
Primary Market Served: Business
Catalog available online
Direct online sales
Advertising/Marketing Budget Related to Direct Marketing: 0-25%

Publisher of scientific journals.

NAVAL INSTITUTE PRESS

Div. of US Naval Institute
291 Wood Rd
Annapolis, MD 21402-5034
Telephone: (410) 268-6110, Toll Free: (800) 233-8764, FAX: (410) 571-1703, E-Mail: webmaster@usni.org, Web Site: www.usni.org/navalinstitutepress
Prod Asst: Carol Parkinson
Publr: William Miller
Dir: Rick Russell
Conducts Business: Worldwide
Employees: 60
Primary Market Served: Business & Consumer
Catalog available online
Direct online sales
Direct Marketing ad budget: $350,000
Founded: 1873

The book-publishing imprint of the U. S. Naval Institute, a private professional society for members of the military services and civilians who share an interest in naval & maritime affairs. Membership includes a subscription to the monthly magazine Proceedings, substantial discounts on more than 800 books, art prints, & photographs available from the press. Direct mail is used extensively to generate new members & to promote book sales among members & non-members.

NEO-TECH PUBLISHING CO

2435 W Horizon Ridge Pkwy (Suite 100)
Henderson, NV 89052-5787
Telephone: (702) 891-0303, FAX: (702) 795-8393
Gen Mgr: Steve Rapella
Primary Market Served: Consumer
Self help books.

NEVADA MAGAZINE

401 N Carson St Ste 100, Carson City, NV 89701-4221
401 N Carson St
Carson City, NV 89701-4221

Telephone: (775) 687-5416, FAX:
(775) 687-6159, E-Mail: editor@
nevadamagazine.com, Web Site:
www.nevadamagazine.com
Publr: Joyce Hollister
Editor: Matt Brown
Assoc Editor: Charlie Johnston
Events Editor: Ann Henderson
Dir Sls: Carrie Roussel
Conducts Business: U.S., Canada
Employees: 10
Primary Market Served: Consumer
Catalog available online
Direct online sales
Advertising/Marketing Budget Related
to Direct Marketing: 76-100%
Founded: 1936

Travel & leisure magazine of The Real
West.

NEW DIRECTIONS PUBLISHING CORP

80 Eighth Ave (fl 19)
New York, NY 10011-7146
Telephone: (212) 255-0230, FAX:
(212) 255-0231, E-Mail: editorial@
ndbooks.com, Web Site: www.
ndbooks.com
Pres: Barbara Epler
Exec VP: Laurie Callahan
VP, Sr Editor, Dir Foreign Rights: Declan Spring
Publicity & Mktg Dir: Tom Roberge
Conducts Business: Worldwide
Employees: 10
Primary Market Served: Consumer
Catalog available online
Founded: 1936

NEW ENGLAND JOURNAL OF MEDICINE

Div. of Massachusetts Medical Society
860 Winter St
Waltham, MA 02451-1430
Telephone: (781) 893-3800, FAX:
(781) 893-7729, Web Site: www.
nejm.org
VP Publr: Chris Lynch
Ed: Marsha Angell
Exec Publ Svcs Dir: William H. Paige
Exec Worldwide Sls & Mktg Dir: Art
Wilschek
Conducts Business: Worldwide
Employees: 270
Primary Market Served: Business

Weekly medical journal directed to
physicians, residents, medical students,
researchers, libraries, hospitals & other
professionals in the medical field.

NEW JERSEY MONTHLY

55 Park Pl
Morristown, NJ 07960-3924
Telephone: (973) 539-8230, FAX:
(973) 538-2953, E-Mail: research@
njmonthly.com, Web Site: www.
njmonthly.com
Editor: Ken Schlager
Mng Editor: Deborah Carter
Strategic Mktg Mgr: Diana Stroup
Conducts Business: U.S.
Employees: 40
Primary Market Served: Consumer
Advertising/Marketing Budget Related
to Direct Marketing: 26-50%
Founded: 1976

Statewide monthly consumer magazine
with articles relating to New Jersey.

NEW TRACK MEDIA LLC

201 E Fifth St (Suite 1110), PNC Center
Cincinnati, OH 45202
Telephone: (513) 421-6500, FAX:
(513) 421-1244, E-Mail: lriggs@
newtrackmedia.com, Web Site:
www.newtrackmedia.com
Pres & CEO: Stephen J. Kent
CFO: Mark F. Arnett
Publr: Lisa O'Bryan
VP, Circulation: Nicole McGuire
Primary Market Served: Business &
Consumer

NEW WIN PUBLISHING INC

Div. of Academic Learning Co
9682 Telstar Ave (Suite 110)
El Monte, CA 91731-3009
Telephone: (626) 448-3448, FAX:
(626) 602-3817, E-Mail: info@
AcademicLearningCompany.com,
Web Site: www.newwinpublishing.
com
Publr: Frank Gil
Conducts Business: U.S.
Employees: 3
Primary Market Served: Business &
Consumer
Advertising/Marketing Budget Related
to Direct Marketing: 0-25%
Founded: 1989

Publisher of non-fiction, trade titles,
cookbooks, craft & how-to books. Also
publish outdoor sports books under
Winchester Press imprint.

THE NEW YORK TIMES CO

620 8th Ave
New York, NY 10018-1618
Telephone: (212) 556-1234, Web Site:
www.nytimes.com
Chmn & Publr: Arthur O. Sulzberger
Jr.
Pres & CEO: Mark Thompson
Vice Chmn: Michael Golden
Exec VP & CFO: James M. Follo
Exec VP, Gen Counsel: Kenneth Richieri
Exec Editor: Jill Abramson
Exec VP, Print Products & Svcs Grp:
Roland Caputo
Exec VP, Digital Products & Svcs Grp:
Denise Warren
VP, Corp Commun: Eileen Murphy
VP, Res & Devel Opers: Michael Zimbalist
Exec Dir Digital Subscription Mktg:
James Dunn
Conducts Business: U.S., Canada
Primary Market Served: Business &
Consumer
Gross sales or billing: $3,300,000,000

Agency promotes subscriptions of The
New York Times newspapers.

THE NEW YORKER MAGAZINE

4 Times Sq
New York, NY 10036
Telephone: (212) 286-2860, FAX:
(212) 286-4168, Web Site: www.
newyorker.com
Editor-in-Chief: Dave Remnick
VP & Publr: Lisa Hughes
Assoc Publr: Beth Lusko
Adv Dir: Risa Aronson
Book Publ Dir: Andrea Abbott
Sales Devel Dir: Kris Weinisch
Conducts Business: U.S.
Employees: 350
Primary Market Served: Business &
Consumer
Founded: 1925

Weekly publication.

THE NEWS TRIBUNE

Subs. of McClatchy Co.
1950 S State St
Tacoma, WA 98405-2817
Telephone: (253) 597-8742, E-Mail:
customerservice@thenewstribune.
com, Web Site: www.
thenewstribune.com
Exec. Editor, Sr VP: Karen Peterson
Mng Editor: Dale Phelps
Primary Market Served: Consumer
Founded: 1880

Business newspaper publisher.

NEWSDAY

Subs. of Cablevision.
235 Pinelawn Rd
Melville, NY 11747-4250
Toll Free: (800) 639-7329, Web Site:
www.newsday.com
Publr: Fred Groser
Editor: Deborah Henley
Dir Circulation: Patrick Tornabene
Primary Market Served: Consumer
Catalog available online
Gross sales or billing: $50,000,000
Newspaper publisher.

NEXTSCREEN LLC
8121 Bee Caves Rd, #100, Austin, TX
 78746-4938
8868 Research Blvd Ste 108
Austin, TX 78758-6446
Telephone: (512) 892-8682, Web Site:
 www.avguide.com
Ed-in-Chief: Harry Pearson
Publr & VP: Mark Fisher
Editor: Roy Gregory
Editor: Chris Martens
Conducts Business: Worldwide
Employees: 18
Primary Market Served: Consumer
Catalog available online
Indirect online sales
Advertising/Marketing Budget Related
 to Direct Marketing: 0-25%
Founded: 1998
Gross sales or billing: $2,000,000

Publishes bi-monthly journal, The Absolute Sound, about high end audio
equipment & music.

THE NIELSEN CO
85 Broad St
New York, NY 10004
Toll Free: (800) 864-1224, Web Site:
 www.nielsen.com
Chmn & CEO: David Calhoun
Vice Chair: Susan Whiting
Vice Chair: Rick Kash
Conducts Business: U.S.
Employees: 42,000
Primary Market Served: Business
Catalog available online
Indirect online sales
Advertising/Marketing Budget Related
 to Direct Marketing: 51-75%
Founded: 1964
Gross sales or billing: $9,000,000

Global information and measurement
company.

NIELSEN TRADE DIMENSIONS
40 Danbury Rd
Wilton, CT 06897-4406
Telephone: (203) 222-5750, Toll Free:
 (800) 291-0410, FAX: (203) 222-
 5701, E-Mail: tradedimensions.
 info@nielsen.com, Web Site: www.
 tradedimensions.com
Dir Mktg: Carley Staron
Dir Res Opers: Thomas Donato
Acct Rep: Tracey Jason
Conducts Business: U.S., Canada
Employees: 14
Primary Market Served: Business &
 Consumer
Catalog available online
Direct online sales
Advertising/Marketing Budget Related
 to Direct Marketing: 26-50%

Gross sales or billing: $3,000,000
Customized retail databases for consumer packaged goods manufacturers.
Directories on the supermarket, convenience store, mass merchandiser/
chain drug industries, plus a directory
of retail tenants.

NIGHTINGALE-CONANT CORP
6245 W Howard St
Niles, IL 60714-3403
Telephone: (847) 647-0300, Toll Free:
 (800) 557-1660, FAX: (847) 647-
 7145, Web Site: www.nightingale.
 com
Pres: Vic Conant
Sr VP, Publ & Bus Devel: Gary Chapel
VP, Mktg: Sara Pond
Dir, New Prod Devel: Dan Strutzel
Dir, HR: Michael Burgess
Conducts Business: U.S., Canada, U.
 K., Australia
Employees: 250
Primary Market Served: Business &
 Consumer
Catalog available online
Direct online sales
Advertising/Marketing Budget Related
 to Direct Marketing: 51-75%
Direct Marketing ad budget:
 $20,000,000
Direct Mail: 80%
Magazines: 6%
Telephone: 14%
Gross sales or billing: $50,000,000

Publisher of audio & video cassette
programs sold to individuals & companies via direct marketing & distributors. Syndicated radio program to
stations & sponsors via direct marketing.

NIGHTINGALE RESOURCES
6 Chestnut St
Cold Spring, NY 10516-2517
Telephone: (718) 338-3976, (212) 753-
 5383, Toll Free: (800) 953-9929
Owner & Pres: Lila Teich Gold
Conducts Business: Worldwide
Primary Market Served: Business &
 Consumer
Indirect online sales
Founded: 1981

Publishes children's, history & cookery
books. Judaica. Reprint 1st Jewish (Kosher) cookbook published in English.

NIHON KEIZAI SHIMBUN AMERICA INC
1325 Ave of the Americas (Ste 2500)
New York, NY 10019

Telephone: (212) 261-6230, FAX:
 (212) 261-6239, Web Site: www.
 nikkeius.com
Ed: Kenji Fukasawa
Conducts Business: U.S., Canada, S.
 America
Employees: 60
Primary Market Served: Business &
 Consumer
Advertising/Marketing Budget Related
 to Direct Marketing: 26-50%
Direct Marketing ad budget:
Direct Mail: 50%
Magazines: 20%
Newspapers: 20%
TV/Radio: 5%
Telephone: 5%

Sells subscriptions to the Nikkei
Weekly, a Japanese business & economic newspaper written in English.

THE NONPROFIT TIMES
Publication of the Davis Information
 Group
201 Littleton Rd (Suite 120)
Morris Plains, NJ 07950-2939
Telephone: (973) 401-0202, FAX:
 (973) 401-0404, Web Site: www.
 nptimes.com
Publr: Willy Morgan
CEO: John McIlquham
Conducts Business: U.S.
Employees: 10
Primary Market Served: Business
Advertising/Marketing Budget Related
 to Direct Marketing: 0-25%
Direct Marketing ad budget: $100,000
Direct Mail: 70%
Telephone: 30%
Gross sales or billing: $1,000,000

National monthly publication for non-
profit organizations.

NORDSKOG PUBLISHING CO
Subs. of Nordskog Industries
4562 Westinghouse St (Suite E)
Ventura, CA 93003-5797
Telephone: (805) 642-2070, FAX:
 (805) 642-1862, Web Site: www.
 nordskogpublishing.com
Publr: Jerry Nordskog
Mng Editor: Desta Garret
Mktg & Promos Mgr: Eugene Cling-
 man
Editor: Kimberly Winters Woods
Conducts Business: U.S., Canada
Employees: 12
Primary Market Served: Consumer
Catalog available online
Direct online sales
Advertising/Marketing Budget Related
 to Direct Marketing: 26-50%
Direct Marketing ad budget: $100,000
Direct Mail: 50%
Magazines: 40%

TV/Radio: 10%
Founded: 1968
Gross sales or billing: $2,000,000
Monthly periodical. Special consumer interest.

NUCLEAR PLANT JOURNAL
1400 Opus Pl (Suite 904)
Downers Grove, IL 60515
Telephone: (630) 858-6161, FAX: (630) 852-8787, Web Site: www. nuclearplantjournal.com
Sr Publr & Editor: Newal Agnihotri
Publr & Sls Mgr: Anu Agnihotri
Conducts Business: Worldwide
Employees: 4
Primary Market Served: Business
Catalog available online
Direct online sales
Advertising/Marketing Budget Related to Direct Marketing: 0-25%
Founded: 1983

Mailing list of subscribers available for rental. Subscribers are primarily engineers, scientists & managers in the nuclear power industry. List is BPA audited & updated every other month.

NYREV INC
dba New York Review of Books
435 Hudson St (Ste 300)
New York, NY 10014-3949
Telephone: (212) 757-8070, FAX: (212) 333-5374, E-Mail: mail@ nybooks.com, Web Site: www. nybooks.com
CEO: Rea Hederman
Ed: Barbara Epstein
Ed: Robert Silvers
Conducts Business: Worldwide
Employees: 35
Primary Market Served: Consumer
Catalog available online
Direct online sales
Advertising/Marketing Budget Related to Direct Marketing: 0-25%
Direct Marketing ad budget:
Direct Mail: 60%
Magazines: 30%
Newspapers: 10%
Founded: 1963
Gross sales or billing: $3,200,000

Magazine - 20 times/year.

OAG WORLDWIDE
3025 Highland Pkwy (Suite 200)
Downers Grove, IL 60515
Telephone: (630) 515-5300, FAX: (630) 515-5301, E-Mail: custsvc@ oag.com, Web Site: www.oag.com
Mgr, Customer Direct Mktg: Bonita Glader
Conducts Business: Worldwide
Employees: 800

Primary Market Served: Business & Consumer
Catalog available online
Direct online sales
Advertising/Marketing Budget Related to Direct Marketing: 0-25%

Distributor & publisher of printed & electronic travel information & other travel related publications.

OAKSTONE PUBLISHING LLC
Div. of Haights Cross Communications LLC
2700 Corporate Dr (Suite 100)
Birmingham, AL 35242
Telephone: (205) 991-5188, Toll Free: (800) 952-0690, FAX: (205) 995-4656, E-Mail: info@ oakstonepublishing.com, Web Site: www.oakstonepublishing.com
Pres & CEO: Diane L. Munson
Sr VP, Opers & HR: Connie Fleming
VP, Sls: Steven R. Cummings
VP, Nat & Strategic Sls: Mary Ellen Garling
Employees: 100
Primary Market Served: Business & Consumer
Advertising/Marketing Budget Related to Direct Marketing: 51-75%
Founded: 1975

Publishes audiotapes and compact discs & computer software for medical & dental continuing education & wellness, safety & financial newsletters and calendars sold to organizations for distribution to their employees.

OIL & GAS JOURNAL
Subs. of PennWell Publishing Co
1421 S Sheridan Rd
Tulsa, OK 74112-6600
Telephone: (918) 835-3161, Toll Free: (800) 331-4463, FAX: (918) 832-9497, Web Site: www.pennwell.com; www.ogj.com
Presentation Ed: Robert G. Lair
Conducts Business: Worldwide
Primary Market Served: Business & Consumer
Catalog available online
Direct online sales
Advertising/Marketing Budget Related to Direct Marketing: 0-25%

Weekly trade magazine covering all aspects of the petroleum industry. Maintain & rent mailing list of subscribers & prospects.

OMNIGRAPHICS INC
PO Box 8002
Aston, PA 19014-8002

Telephone: (610) 461-3548, Toll Free: (800) 234-1340, FAX: (800) 875-1340, E-Mail: info@omnigraphics. com, Web Site: www.omnigraphics. com
Chmn: Frederick G. Ruffner Jr.
Pres & Publr: Peter E. Ruffner
Sr VP: Matthew Barbour
Conducts Business: Worldwide
Employees: 35
Primary Market Served: Business & Consumer
Catalog available online
Direct online sales
Advertising/Marketing Budget Related to Direct Marketing: 76-100%
Direct Marketing ad budget:
Direct Mail: 83%
Magazines: 15%
Telephone: 2%
Founded: 1985

Reference publisher serving the library, school, business & institutional markets.

THE ORANGE COUNTY REGISTER
Owned by Freedom Communications, Inc.
625 N Grand Ave
Santa Ana, CA 92701
Toll Free: (877) 469-7344, E-Mail: customerservice@ocregister.com, Web Site: www.ocregister.com
Pres: Eric Spitz
Publr: Aaron Kushner
VP, Mktg: Lelani Kroeker
VP, Nat Sls & Direct Mktg: Steve Bentz
Primary Market Served: Business & Consumer
Founded: 1905

Newspaper.

ORBIS BOOKS
Subs. of Maryknoll Fathers & Brothers
PO Box 302, Price Bldg
Maryknoll, NY 10545-0302
Telephone: (914) 941-7636 X2576, Toll Free: (800) 258-5838, FAX: (914) 941-7005, E-Mail: orbisbooks@maryknoll.org, Web Site: www.orbisbooks.com
Mktg Mgr: Bernadette Price
Conducts Business: Worldwide
Employees: 20
Primary Market Served: Business & Consumer
Catalog available online
Indirect online sales
Advertising/Marketing Budget Related to Direct Marketing: 26-50%
Direct Marketing ad budget:
Direct Mail: 70%
Magazines: 30%

Founded: 1970
Gross sales or billing: $2,400,000

Not for profit publisher of books on religion/politics, ecology, interreligious dialogue, comparative religion, world religions, spirituality, peace studies, ethnic studies, women's issues & missiology.

OUR SUNDAY VISITOR PUBLISHING

Div. of Our Sunday Visitor Inc
200 Noll Plaza
Huntington, IN 46750
Telephone: (260) 356-8400, Toll Free: (800) 348-2440, FAX: (260) 356-8472, E-Mail: athomas@osv.com, Web Site: www.osv.com
Publr: Greg Erlandson
Mktg Dir Books: Jill Kurtz
Circulation Mgr: Amy Thomas
Conducts Business: Worldwide
Employees: 53
Primary Market Served: Business & Consumer
Catalog available online
Direct online sales
Advertising/Marketing Budget Related to Direct Marketing: 0-25%
Founded: 1912

Publish & market a wide variety of books & periodicals to Catholic readers. Also market general religious & educational titles.

OXFORD UNIVERSITY PRESS INC

198 Madison Ave
New York, NY 10016
Telephone: (212) 726-6000, FAX: (212) 726-6455, Web Site: global.oup.com
Pres, US & Publr: Niko Pfund
Conducts Business: Worldwide
Employees: 255
Primary Market Served: Business & Consumer
Catalog available online

Sell books to retailers, distributors & through direct mail to academics, professionals & businessmen. Branch offices located worldwide.

PC WORLD

Div. of IDG Communications Inc
501 2nd St
San Francisco, CA 94107-1496
Telephone: (415) 243-0500, FAX: (415) 442-1891, Web Site: www.pcworld.com
Pres & CEO: Jeff Edman
Editorial Dir: Steve Fox
Conducts Business: Worldwide
Employees: 80

Primary Market Served: Business & Consumer

International data group company. Publisher of computer related magazines & newspapers.

PESI LLC

aka Professional Education Systems Institute
200 Spring St (Ste A)
Eau Claire, WI 54703-3663
Toll Free: (800) 844-8260, FAX: (800) 554-9775, E-Mail: info@pesi.com, Web Site: www.pesi.com
Exec Dir: Rick Olson
VP Mktg: Jane Kemper
Conducts Business: U.S., Canada
Employees: 40
Primary Market Served: Business & Consumer
Founded: 1979
Gross sales or billing: $4,500,000

Provide continuing education programs for legal, nursing, construction, financial, general business & real estate professions. Also, publish & market medical & law-oriented audio tapes.

PMIC

4727 Wilshire Blvd (Suite 300)
Los Angeles, CA 90010-3873
Telephone: (323) 954-0224, Toll Free: (800) 633-4215, FAX: (323) 954-0253, Web Site: pmiconline.stores.yahoo.net
Pres: James Davis
Primary Market Served: Business & Consumer
Catalog available online
Direct online sales
Founded: 1989

Publish medical books.

PACE COMMUNICATIONS INC

1301 Carolina St
Greensboro, NC 27401-1032
Telephone: (336) 378-6065, FAX: (336) 275-2864, Web Site: www.pacecommunications.com
CEO: Bonnie McElveen-Hunter
Chief Mktg & Sls Officer: Craig Waller
Pres, Ecommerce: Cindy Marshall
VP Custom Publishing & Mktg Svcs: Jaci Ponzoni
Mktg Res Mgr: Emily Wright
Dir HR: Gol Casper
Conducts Business: Worldwide
Primary Market Served: Business & Consumer

Publish In Flight magazine & trade publication.

PALADIN PRESS

Subs. of Paladin Enterprises Inc
7077 Winchester Cir, Gunbarrel Tech Center
Boulder, CO 80301-3505
Telephone: (303) 443-7250, Toll Free: (800) 392-2400, FAX: (303) 442-8741, E-Mail: service@paladin-press.com, Web Site: www.paladin-press.com
Pres & Publr: Peder C. Lund
Ed Dir: Jon Ford
Sls Dir: Wendy Mannatt
Conducts Business: Worldwide
Employees: 25
Primary Market Served: Business & Consumer
Catalog available online
Direct online sales
Direct Marketing ad budget: $100,000
Direct Mail: 20%
Magazines: 80%
Founded: 1970

Mail order publisher specializing in books & videos on survival, self-defense, martial arts, weaponry & military & police science. Market is primarily men, 21 to 50 years.

PANOPTIC ENTERPRISES

PO Box 11220
Burke, VA 22009-1220
Telephone: (703) 451-5953, Toll Free: (800) 594-4766, FAX: (703) 451-5953, E-Mail: panoptic@fedgovcontracts.com, Web Site: www.fedgovcontracts.com
Pres: Vivina McVay
VP: Barry McVay
Conducts Business: U.S.
Employees: 2
Primary Market Served: Business & Consumer
Catalog available online
Indirect online sales
Advertising/Marketing Budget Related to Direct Marketing: 51-75%
Direct Marketing ad budget: $15,000
Direct Mail: 94%
Magazines: 2%
Newspapers: 2%
Online: 2%
Founded: 1982
Gross sales or billing: $45,000

Books, pamphlets, seminars on how to win federal contracts. Sold nationwide to businesses of all sizes plus individuals interested in starting a business or working in this field.

PARA PUBLISHING

PO Box 8206
Santa Barbara, CA 93118-8206

Telephone: (805) 968-7277, Toll Free: (800) PARAPUB, FAX: (805) 986-1379, E-Mail: danpoynter@ parapublishing.com, Web Site: www. parapublishing.com
Publr: Dan Poynter
Office Mgr: Becky Carbone
Conducts Business: Worldwide
Employees: 6
Primary Market Served: Business & Consumer
Catalog available online
Direct online sales
Advertising/Marketing Budget Related to Direct Marketing: 26-50%
Founded: 1969

Books & information for writers & publishers.

PARLAY INTERNATIONAL
712 Bancroft Rd (#505)
Walnut Creek, CA 94598
Telephone: (510) 601-1000, FAX: (510) 601-1008, E-Mail: info@ parlay.com, Web Site: www.parlay. com
Pres & CEO: Robert Lester
Employees: 2
Primary Market Served: Business
Catalog available online
Direct online sales
Founded: 1987

PASTIME PUBLICATIONS INC
Div. of Pastime Company
99 Kalamath St
Denver, CO 80223-1549
Telephone: (303) 534-7867, Toll Free: (888) 650-8665, FAX: (630) 214-7600, E-Mail: post@ pastimecompany.com, Web Site: www.pastimecompany.com
Pres: Carl A. Nelson
Opers: Mike Draper
Conducts Business: Worldwide
Employees: 20
Primary Market Served: Business & Consumer
Catalog available online
Indirect online sales
Direct Marketing ad budget:
Direct Mail: 50%
Telephone: 50%
Founded: 1990
Gross sales or billing: $250,000

PATH TO PURCHASE INSTITUTE
8550 W Bryn Mawr Ave (Suite 200)
Chicago, IL 60631-3731
Telephone: (847) 675-7400, Web Site: www.p2pi.org
Mktg Analyst: Meggie Smolen

Primary Market Served: Business & Consumer

PATIENT NEWS
3909 Witmer Rd (#1080)
Niagara Falls, NY 14305-1239
Telephone: (705) 457-4030, Toll Free: (800) 667-0268, FAX: (705) 457-4067, E-Mail: jbishop@patientnews. com, Web Site: www.patientnews. com
VP, Sls & Mktg: Joanne Bishop
Employees: 50
Primary Market Served: Business & Consumer
Founded: 1993

PEARSON EDUCATION
Div. of Pearson plc
One Lake St
Upper Saddle River, NJ 07458-1813
Telephone: (201) 236-7000, FAX: (201) 236-3290, Web Site: www. pearsoned.com
CEO: John Fallon
CFO: Robin Freestone
CEO, North American Education: Will Ethridge
Sr VP Communs: Wendy Spiegel
Conducts Business: Worldwide
Employees: 19,186
Primary Market Served: Business
Catalog available online
Direct online sales
Advertising/Marketing Budget Related to Direct Marketing: 0-25%
Founded: 1998
Gross sales or billing: $5,073,700,000

Publisher of textbooks, workbooks & other materials for K-12 elementary schools, higher education & professional markets. Also operates assessment & skill development divisions.

PEARSON VUE
Subs. of Pearson Education Inc
5601 Green Valley Dr
Bloomington, MN 55437-1099
Telephone: (952) 681-3000, Web Site: home.pearsonvue.com
President: Robert Whelan
Sr VP & CFO: Doug Kennedy
Sr VP, Products & Svcs: Ron Lancaster
Sr VP Bus Devel: Don Wagner
Conducts Business: Worldwide
Primary Market Served: Business & Consumer
Founded: 1994

Online testing services company

PENGUIN GROUP USA INC
Div. of Pearson Education
375 Hudson St
New York, NY 10014

Telephone: (212) 366-2000, Web Site: www.us.penguingroup.com
Chmn & CEO: John Makinson
CEO: David Shanks
CFO: Jim Crofton
Sr VP, Distr: Jim Clark
Pres: Susan Petersen Kennedy
Exec VP, Bus Opers: Doug Whiteman
Sr VP, Legal Affairs: Alex Gigante
Conducts Business: U.S., Canada
Employees: 200
Primary Market Served: Business & Consumer
Catalog available online
Direct online sales
Advertising/Marketing Budget Related to Direct Marketing: 76-100%
Direct Marketing ad budget: $15,000,000
Direct Mail: 95%
Magazines: 4%
Telephone: 1%

Book publisher specializing in books for business professionals, teachers & consumers. Book sales are made by direct mail.

PENNSYLVANIA STATE UNIVERSITY PRESS
820 N University Dr (Suite C)
University Park, PA 16802-1012
Telephone: (814) 865-1327, Toll Free: (800) 326-9180, FAX: (814) 863-1408, Web Site: www.psupress.org
Editor in Chief: Patrick H. Alexander
Mng Editor: Cherene Howard
Exec Editor Art & Humanities: Eleanor Goodman
Mktg & Sls Mgr: Tony Sanfilippo
Production Coord: Patty Mitchell
Editorial Asst: Cali Buckley
Conducts Business: U.S., U.K., Canada
Employees: 26
Primary Market Served: Business & Consumer
Catalog available online
Direct online sales
Advertising/Marketing Budget Related to Direct Marketing: 26-50%
Direct Marketing ad budget: $205,980
Direct Mail: 45%
Magazines: 49%
Newspapers: 5%
TV/Radio: 1%
Founded: 1956
Gross sales or billing: $2,000,000

Scholarly books in the subject areas of history, art history, philosophy, political science, Pennsylvania history & regional interest.

PENNWELL PUBLISHING
1421 S Sheridan Rd
Tulsa, OK 74112

Telephone: (918) 835-3161, Toll Free: (800) 331-4463, E-Mail: headquarters@pennwell.com, Web Site: www.pennwell.com
Pres & CEO: Brian Biochlini
Exec VP & CFO: Mark C. Wilmonth
VP: Jim Enos
VP, Digital Media: Tom Citorino
Circulation Mgr: Linda Thomas
Conducts Business: U.S., Canada, Europe, Asia
Employees: 10
Primary Market Served: Business
Catalog available online
Advertising/Marketing Budget Related to Direct Marketing: 51-75%
Direct Marketing ad budget: $500,000
Direct Mail: 75%
Magazines: 15%
TV/Radio: 5%
Telephone: 5%
Founded: 1910
Gross sales or billing: $5,000,000

Conferences, trade shows & exhibitions.

PENSIONS & INVESTMENTS

Div. of Crain Communication Inc
711 3rd Ave
New York, NY 10017-4014
Telephone: (212) 210-0100, FAX: (212) 210-0117, Web Site: www.pionline.com
Grp Publr: William T. Bisson
VP & Publr: Christopher Battaglia
Promo Dir: Michelle DeMarco
Adv Sls Dir: Richard Scanlon
Conducts Business: U.S., Canada, Europe
Employees: 50
Primary Market Served: Business
Advertising/Marketing Budget Related to Direct Marketing: 26-50%
Founded: 1973

Newspaper edited for financial executives in corporations, governments, banks, insurance companies & money management firms. Readers make investment, financing, real estate, employee benefits, leasing, brokerage & cash management decisions for their firms.

PERSONAL ACHIEVEMENT INSTITUTE

PO Box 6543, One Speaking Success Rd
Kingman, AZ 86402-6543
Telephone: (928) 753-7546, Toll Free: (800) 321-1225, FAX: (928) 753-7554, E-Mail: burt@burtdubin.com, Web Site: www.speakingbizsuccess.com
Pres: Burt Dubin
Conducts Business: Worldwide

Employees: 3
Primary Market Served: Business & Consumer
Catalog available online
Direct online sales
Advertising/Marketing Budget Related to Direct Marketing: 76-100%
Direct Marketing ad budget:
Online: 100%
Founded: 1978

Write & publish the Speaking Success System - a system for the mastery of the business skills & platform expertise a speaker needs.

PERSONNEL POLICY SERVICE INC

PO Box 7697
Louisville, KY 40257-0697
Telephone: (502) 899-5102, Toll Free: (800) 437-3735, FAX: (800) 755-7011, E-Mail: info@ppspublishers.com, Web Site: www.ppspublishers.com
Pres: John C. Norman Jr.
Conducts Business: U.S.
Primary Market Served: Business
Catalog available online
Direct online sales

Publisher of loose leaf services & newsletters. Mailing address: PO Box 7967, Louisville, KY 40257-0697.

PETERSON'S

Div. of Thomson Corp
2000 Lenox Dr
Lawrenceville, NJ 08648-2314
Telephone: (609) 896-1800, FAX: (609) 896-1811, E-Mail: custsvc@petersons.com, Web Site: www.petersons.com
Pres: Mary E. Gatsch
VP, Mktg: Michael H. Fleischner
Conducts Business: Worldwide
Employees: 200
Primary Market Served: Business & Consumer
Catalog available online
Direct online sales
Founded: 1966

Education publishing in the areas of college search and selection, test preparation, and financial aid online and in print.

PLAYBOY ENTERPRISES INC

9346 Civic Center Dr (#200)
Beverly Hills, CA 90210-3604
Telephone: (310) 860-1215, Web Site: www.playboyenterprises.com
CEO: Scott N. Flanders
Chief Mktg Officer: Kristin Patrick
Exec VP Bus Affairs & Gen Counsel: Rachel Sagan

Exec VP & Chief Revenue Officer: Matthew A. Nordby
Sr VP, HR: Kendice Briggs
Chief Content Officer, Editorial Dir: Jimmy Jellinek
Exec VP, CFO: Christopher Pachler
Pres, Playboy Media: David Israel
VP, Pub Rels: Theresa Hennessey
Conducts Business: Worldwide
Employees: 643
Primary Market Served: Consumer
Gross sales or billing: $193,700,000

An international publishing & entertainment company that publishes Playboy magazine & related media, including newsstand specials & calendars; licenses 16 foreign editions of Playboy magazine; operates a direct marketing business including the Playboy & Critics' Choice Video catalogs; creates & distributes programming for domestic pay television, worldwide home video & international television; markets the Playboy trademarks on apparel, accessories & products for consumers around the world.

PNEUMA BOOKS

25 Hunter Ct
Elkton, MD 21921-1762
Telephone: (410) 441-8200, FAX: (410) 441-8201, E-Mail: gettingstarted@pneumabooks.com, Web Site: www.pneumabooks.com
Employees: 8
Primary Market Served: Business & Consumer
Advertising/Marketing Budget Related to Direct Marketing: 76-100%
Direct Marketing ad budget: $110,000
Direct Mail: $40,000
Magazines: $60,000
Telephone: $10,000
Founded: 1971
Gross sales or billing: $1,200,000

Publisher & wholesaler of financial, how-to & spare time or new career books & manuals. Interested parties should remit three dollars for complete information package, including catalogs, procedures, distributor forms, etc.

THE POHLY CO

437 D St (Apt 2F)
Boston, MA 02210-1983
Telephone: (617) 451-1700, Toll Free: (800) 383-0888, FAX: (617) 338-7767, E-Mail: info@pohlyco.com, Web Site: www.pohlyco.com
Pres: Diana Pohly
Conducts Business: U.S.

Primary Market Served: Business & Consumer

Specializes in custom publishing, consulting, online content and creative services.

POKER PLAYER
Sub. of Gambling Times Inc
13701 Riverside Dr Ste 300
Sherman Oaks, CA 91423-2447
Telephone: (310) 674-3365, FAX: (310) 674-3205, E-Mail: ard@ gamblingtimes.com, Web Site: www. gamblingtimes.com
Pres: Stanley R. Sludikoff
Mng Editor: A.R. Dyck
Editor: Lou Krieger
Conducts Business: Worldwide
Primary Market Served: Business & Consumer
Catalog available online
Indirect online sales
Founded: 1971
Gross sales or billing: $900,000
Magazines.

POWERS TELEVISION MARKETING
9731 Variel Ave
Chatsworth, CA 91311-4315
Telephone: (818) 700-1522, FAX: (818) 700-1527, E-Mail: mpowers@ mpowers.com, Web Site: www. mpowers.com
Pres: Melvin Powers
Conducts Business: Worldwide
Employees: 21
Primary Market Served: Business & Consumer
Catalog available online
Direct online sales
Direct Marketing ad budget:
Direct Mail: 40%
Magazines: 25%
Newspapers: 10%
TV/Radio: 25%
Gross sales or billing: $4,000,000

Publisher of mail order books & seminars. Also act as television consultant.

PRAKKEN PUBLICATIONS INC
2851 Boardwalk St
Ann Arbor, MI 48104
Telephone: (734) 975-2800, Toll Free: (800) 530-9673, FAX: (734) 975-2787, Web Site: www.techdirections. com; www.eddigest.com
Pres & Bus Mgr: Turalee Barlow
Mng Editor Tech Directions Magazine: Suzanne Peckham
Mng Editor Education Digest Journal: Pamela Moore
Circulation Mgr: Vanessa Revelli

Book & Adv Sls Mgr: Matt Knope
Conducts Business: Worldwide
Employees: 6
Primary Market Served: Business & Consumer
Catalog available online
Direct online sales
Advertising/Marketing Budget Related to Direct Marketing: 51-75%
Direct Marketing ad budget: $50,000
Direct Mail: 20%
Magazines: 30%
Online: 50%
Founded: 1934
Gross sales or billing: $500,000

Publishers of The Education Digest, Tech Directions Magazine, Machinists' Ready Reference & other technology & career-technical education books, video, and CD-ROM.

PRESS-ENTERPRISE CO
Div. of A H Belo Corp
3450 14th St
Riverside, CA 92501
Telephone: (951) 684-1200, FAX: (951) 368-9022, Web Site: www.pe. com
Publr & CEO: Ronald Redfern
Employees: 800
Primary Market Served: Business & Consumer
Advertising/Marketing Budget Related to Direct Marketing: 0-25%
Founded: 1878

Newspaper-Western Riverside County & South Central San Bernardino County, 162,551 daily & 170,748 circulation on Sundays.

THEODORE PRESSER CO
588 N Gulph Rd Ste B
King Of Prussia, PA 19406-2831
Telephone: (610) 592-1222, FAX: (610) 592-1229, E-Mail: webmaster@presser.com, Web Site: www.presser.com
Pres & CEO: Sonya Kim Heil
Mktg Mgr: Dwight Munroe
Conducts Business: U.S., Canada, Mexico
Employees: 50
Primary Market Served: Business
Catalog available online
Direct online sales
Direct Marketing ad budget:
Direct Mail: 67%
Magazines: 33%
Founded: 1783

Music publishers, selling sheet music & music books to music dealers.

PRESTWICK HOUSE INC
PO Box 658
Clayton, DE 19938-0658

Telephone: (302) 659-2070, Web Site: www.prestwickhouse.com
Gen Mgr: Keith Bergstrom
Primary Market Served: Business & Consumer

PRIME MEDIA EQUINE GROUP
656 Quince Orchard Rd
Gaithersburg, MD 20878
Telephone: (301) 977-3900, FAX: (301) 990-9015, Web Site: www. equisearch.com
Pres & CEO: Dean Nelson
Exec VP & Publr: Susan Harding
Sr VP: Steve Parr
Sr VP & CFO: Kevin Neary
Conducts Business: U.S., Canada, Europe
Primary Market Served: Business & Consumer
Catalog available online
Indirect online sales

Publisher of Equus, Practical Horseman, Dressage Today, Horse & Rider & The Arabian Horse.

PRINCETON BOOK CO PUBLISHERS
dba Princeton Book Company-Dance Horizons
614 Rte 130
Hightstown, NJ 08520-2651
Telephone: (609) 426-0602, Toll Free: (800) 220-7149, FAX: (609) 426-1344, E-Mail: pbc@dancehorizons. com, Web Site: www.dancehorizons. com
Pres: Charles H. Woodford
Internet Coord: John McMenamin
Customer Svc: Marcia Sylvester
Conducts Business: Worldwide
Employees: 7
Primary Market Served: Business & Consumer
Catalog available online
Direct online sales
Advertising/Marketing Budget Related to Direct Marketing: 76-100%
Direct Marketing ad budget:
Direct Mail: 25%
Online: 75%
Founded: 1975
Gross sales or billing: $1,000,000

Dance books, videos, DVDs, and non-fiction books.

PRITCHETT & HULL ASSOCIATES INC
3440 Oakcliff Rd NE (Suite 110)
Atlanta, GA 30340-3079

Telephone: (770) 451-0602, Toll Free: (800) 241-4925, FAX: (770) 454-7130, E-Mail: phsales@p-h.com, Web Site: www.p-h.com
Pres: Cecily Shull
Conducts Business: U.S., Canada
Employees: 11
Primary Market Served: Business & Consumer
Catalog available online
Advertising/Marketing Budget Related to Direct Marketing: 51-75%
Founded: 1973

Publisher of patient education materials for hospitals & medical offices.

PRIVACY JOURNAL

PO Box 28577
Providence, RI 02908-0577
Telephone: (401) 274-7861, FAX: (401) 274-4747, E-Mail: orders@privacyjournal.net, Web Site: www.privacyjournal.net
Publr: Robert Ellis Smith
Asst to Publr: Lee Shoreham
Conducts Business: USA
Employees: 3
Primary Market Served: Business & Consumer
Catalog available online
Direct online sales
Founded: 1974
Gross sales or billing: $500,000

Monthly newsletter on credit reports, mailing lists, telemarketing, wiretaps, Internet & other privacy issues. Subscription: $125/year.

PRO CD INC

Div. of Info USA Inc
5711 S 86th Cir
Omaha, NE 68127
Toll Free: (800) 992-3766, FAX: (402) 750-0020
VP: Bruce Lowry
Mktg Acct Exec: Melissa Powers
Primary Market Served: Business & Consumer
Catalog available online
Direct online sales
Advertising/Marketing Budget Related to Direct Marketing: 76-100%
Direct Marketing ad budget:
Direct Mail: 95%
Telephone: 5%

Provider of every published telephone listing on CD-ROM for consumers, retailers & corporate networks.

PROFESSIONAL PHOTOGRAPHER MAGAZINE

Subs. of Professional Photographers of America

229 Peachtree St NE (Suite 2200), International Tower
Atlanta, GA 30303-1608
Telephone: (404) 522-8600, Toll Free: (800) 786-6277, FAX: (404) 614-6405, E-Mail: csc@ppa.com, Web Site: www.ppa.com
CEO: David Trust
Commun Mgr: Amy Walkes
Adv Mgr: Danielle Chavannes
Sr Mgr Pubns: Kris Delaney
Conducts Business: U.S., Canada
Employees: 50
Primary Market Served: Business & Consumer
Direct online sales
Advertising/Marketing Budget Related to Direct Marketing: 26-50%
Direct Marketing ad budget:
Direct Mail: 90%
Magazines: 10%

Monthly magazine for photographers.

PROFESSIONAL TRAINING ASSOCIATES INC

46 S Linden St (Suite C)
Duquesne, PA 15110-1091
Telephone: (412) 460-0266, FAX: (412) 460-0269, E-Mail: info@ptainc.com, Web Site: www.ptainc.com
Chmn & Pres: Greg Ashman
Dir VP Trng: John Curcio
VP: William Tomlinson
Conducts Business: U.S., Canada
Employees: 4
Primary Market Served: Business
Catalog available online
Indirect online sales
Advertising/Marketing Budget Related to Direct Marketing: 76-100%

Environmental & safety training & customized course development for industrial, commercial, manufacturing, construction, consulting, government and education sectors. Courses include Asbestos, Lead-Based Paint, HAZWOPER, Confined Space Entry and Construction Safety Outreach.

PROGRESSIVE BUSINESS PUBLICATIONS

Div. of American Future Systems Inc
370 Technology Dr
Malvern, PA 19355-1315
Telephone: (610) 695-8600, Toll Free: (800) 220-5000, FAX: (610) 647-8089, E-Mail: customer_service@pbp.com, Web Site: www.pbp.com
Pres: Ed Satell
Conducts Business: Worldwide
Primary Market Served: Business
Advertising/Marketing Budget Related to Direct Marketing: 76-100%
Direct Marketing ad budget:

Direct Mail: 25%
Telephone: 75%

Publisher of subscription newsletters & posters for business.

PROMO MAGAZINE

Div. of Penton Business Media Inc
249 W 17th St (3rd fl)
New York, NY 10011
Telephone: (203) 358-9900, Toll Free: (800) 927-5007, FAX: (203) 358-5816, E-Mail: larry.jaffee@penton.com, Web Site: www.promomagazine.com
Editor in Chief: Larry Jaffee
Group Publr: Leslie Bacon
Exec Editor: Patricia Odell
Primary Market Served: Business
Founded: 1987

Promotional marketing magazine.

THE PSYCHOLOGICAL CORP

Subs. of Harcourt Inc
Harcourt Educational Measurement
19500 Bulverde Rd
San Antonio, TX 78259
Toll Free: (800) 211-8378, FAX: (800) 232-1223, Web Site: www.psychcorp.com
Pres & CEO: Michael Hansen
Pres, The Psychological Corp: Aurelio Prifitera
SVP: Jean Shiunko
VP: Scott Barnes
VP: Jim Hill
Catalog available online
Indirect online sales

Publishing company.

PUBLICATIONS INTERNATIONAL LTD

7373 N Cicero Ave
Lincolnwood, IL 60712-1613
Telephone: (847) 676-3470, Toll Free: (800) 595-8484, FAX: (847) 676-3671, Web Site: www.pubint.com
Founder & CEO: Louis Weber
VP, Special Markets: Jerry Kurtzweil
Exec VP, Children's Books & Digital: Jennifer Goldstein
Co-editions & Special Sls Mgr: Grant Sargent
Conducts Business: U.S.
Employees: 210
Primary Market Served: Consumer
Catalog available online
Indirect online sales
Advertising/Marketing Budget Related to Direct Marketing: 26-50%
Founded: 1967

Gross sales or billing: $45,600,000

Consumer based publisher specializing in the areas of cookbooks, children's, health, automobile, sports, crafts, lifestyle & consumer information.

QUAYSIDE PUBLISHING GROUP

400 1st Ave N (Suite 400)
Minneapolis, MN 55401-1721
Telephone: (612) 344-8100, FAX: (612) 344-8691, Web Site: www. quaysidepub.com
Pres & CEO: Ken Fund
Conducts Business: Worldwide
Employees: 70
Primary Market Served: Consumer

QUEUE INC

80 Hathaway Dr
Stratford, CT 06615-7304
Telephone: (203) 335-0906, Toll Free: (800) 232-2224, FAX: (800) 775-2729, E-Mail: jdk@queueinc.com, Web Site: www.qworkbooks.com
CEO: Jonathan Kantrowitz
Controller: Peter Uhrynowski
Conducts Business: U.S., Canada, Far & Near East, Europe, Australia
Employees: 30
Primary Market Served: Business & Consumer
Catalog available online
Direct online sales
Advertising/Marketing Budget Related to Direct Marketing: 76-100%
Founded: 1980
Gross sales or billing: $4,000,000

Publish educational software & CD-ROM.

RANDOM HOUSE DIRECT MARKETING

Div. of Random House
1745 Broadway
New York, NY 10019-4305
Telephone: (212) 572-4985, Toll Free: (800) 678-5681, FAX: (212) 572-6018, Web Site: www. randomhousedirect.com
Dir Mktg: Tom Downing
VP & Gen Mgr: Lisa Faith Phillips
Sr Mktg Mgr: Lyn Hastings
Conducts Business: U.S.
Primary Market Served: Consumer
Catalog available online
Direct online sales
Advertising/Marketing Budget Related to Direct Marketing: 76-100%
Direct Marketing ad budget: $5,000,000

Direct Mail: 100%

Responsible for direct mailings of select Random House titles & development of Conde Nast direct mail book products.

RANDOM LENGTHS PUBLICATIONS INC

450 Country Club Rd (#240)
Eugene, OR 97401-6078
Telephone: (541) 686-9925, Toll Free: (888) 686-9925, FAX: (541) 686-9629, (800) 874-7979, E-Mail: rlmail@rlpi.com, Web Site: www. randomlengths.com
Publr: Jon Anderson
Mktg Dir: Nancy West
Conducts Business: Worldwide
Primary Market Served: Business
Catalog available online
Direct online sales
Advertising/Marketing Budget Related to Direct Marketing: 76-100%
Direct Marketing ad budget:
Direct Mail: 100%
Founded: 1958

Newsletters, directory to wood products & related industries.

THE READER'S DIGEST ASSOCIATION INC

750 3rd Ave
New York, NY 10017-2703
Toll Free: (800) 310-6261, Web Site: www.rda.com
Pres & CEO: Robert E. Guth
Sr VP Global HR: Susan Cummiskey
Sr VP & Global Chief Info Officer: Joe Held
Sr VP, Gen Counsel & Sec: Andrea Newborn
Exec VP, Bus Opers: Albert L. Perruzza
VP Global Commun: Susan Fraysse Russ
Exec VP & CFO: Paul Tomkins
Conducts Business: Worldwide
Employees: 1,800
Primary Market Served: Consumer
Gross sales or billing: $2,000,000,000

Global publisher & direct mail marketer of magazines, books & home entertainment products.

REDBOOK MAGAZINE

Div. of Hearst Corp
300 W 57th St
New York, NY 10019
Telephone: (212) 649-2000, Toll Free: (800) 888-0008, FAX: (212) 581-7605, Web Site: www.redbookmag. com
Editor in Chief: Jill Herzig
Exec Editor: Meredith Rollins

Creative Dir: Holland Utley
Mng Editor: Kim Cheney
Special Proj Dir: Lori Berger
Conducts Business: Worldwide
Primary Market Served: Consumer

Mail order section "Shopping with Redbook" (incorporates travel, school, camps, crafts & gardens) carries direct response advertising. "Catalogue Review" is published once a year in August for catalog advertising.

REDLEAF PRESS

Div. of Think Small
10 Yorkton Ct
Saint Paul, MN 55117-1065
Telephone: (651) 641-6621, Toll Free: (800) 423-8309, FAX: (800) 641-0115, E-Mail: jvoltz@redleafpress. org, Web Site: www.redleafpress.org
Publr: Linda Hein
Editor-in-Chief: David Heath
Mktg Mgr: Joanne Voltz
Sls Mgr: Inga Weberg
Opers Mgr: Paul Bloomer
Conducts Business: U.S.
Employees: 25
Primary Market Served: Business
Catalog available online
Direct online sales
Direct Marketing ad budget:
Direct Mail: 60%
Online: 35%
Telephone: 5%
Founded: 1976

Resources for early childhood education specifically books. Sell to early childhood professionals, organizations, schools, libraries, corporations, military & individuals.

REED ELSEVIER

Lexis Nexis
125 Park Ave (fl 23)
New York, NY 10017-8503
Telephone: (212) 309-8100, FAX: (212) 309-8187, Web Site: www. reedelsevier.com
CEO: Erik Engstrom
CFO: Duncan Palmer
Conducts Business: Worldwide
Employees: 2,000
Primary Market Served: Business & Consumer

Book publishing & packaging firm.

REGNERY PUBLISHING

Div. of Eagle Publishing
1 Massachusetts Ave NW
Washington, DC 20001-1401
Telephone: (202) 216-0600, FAX: (202) 216-0612, Web Site: www. regnery.com
Pres & Publr: Marji Ross
Mktg & Publicity: Patricia Jackson

Conducts Business: U.S.
Employees: 100
Primary Market Served: Consumer
Catalog available online
Direct online sales
Advertising/Marketing Budget Related to Direct Marketing: 76-100%
Direct Marketing ad budget:
Direct Mail: 100%
Founded: 1947
Gross sales or billing: $9,100,000

Book publishers.

REIMAN PUBLICATIONS

5400 S 60th St
Greendale, WI 53129
Telephone: (414) 423-0100, Toll Free: (800) 344-6913, FAX: (414) 423-3840, Web Site: www.reimanpub.com
Chmn: Roy Reiman
Pres: Russel Denson
Sr VP, Catalog & Tour Mktg: Phil Minix
Sr Circulation Bus Analyst: Kevin Nangle
VP: Heidi Reuter Lloyd
Conducts Business: U.S., Canada
Employees: 525
Primary Market Served: Consumer
Catalog available online
Direct online sales
Advertising/Marketing Budget Related to Direct Marketing: 76-100%
Direct Marketing ad budget:
Direct Mail: 100%
Founded: 1965
Gross sales or billing: $56,100,000

Publisher of Country, Country EXTRA, Country Woman, Country Discoveries, Crafting Traditions, Birds & Blooms, Farm & Ranch Living, Reminisce, Reminisce EXTRA, Taste of Home & Quick Cooking & Country Store (catalog).

REMEDY MAGAZINE

Div of MediZine Healthy Living
500 Fifth Ave (Suite 1900)
New York, NY 10110
Telephone: (212) 695-2223, FAX: (212) 695-2936, E-Mail: info@rmedizine.com, Web Site: www.medizine.com
Chief Revenue Officer: Suzanne Polizzi
Pres & CEO: Traver Hutchins
Assoc Mktg Mgr: Jenna Chessari
Employees: 100
Primary Market Served: Consumer
Catalog available online
Advertising/Marketing Budget Related to Direct Marketing: 0-25%
Founded: 1992
Gross sales or billing: $10,000,000

REMILON LLC

100 View St Ste 202
Mountain View, CA 94041-1374
Telephone: (650) 425-7511, Web Site: www.remilon.com
Co-CEO: Adrian Ridner

RENO GAZETTE JOURNAL

Div. of Gannett Corp
955 Kuenzli St
Reno, NV 89520
Telephone: (775) 788-6200, FAX: (775) 788-6563
Publr: Sue Clark Johnson
Community Mktg Mgr: Robert Boisson
Asst to Publr: Kim Foster
Primary Market Served: Business & Consumer

Advertising (newspaper). Sell advertising space & newspaper distributor.

RESOURCE PUBLICATIONS INC

5369 Camden Ave (Suite 260)
San Jose, CA 95124-5809
Telephone: (408) 286-8505, Toll Free: (888) 273-7782, FAX: (408) 287-8748, E-Mail: info@rpinet.com, Web Site: www.rpinet.com
Pres & Publr: William Burns
Mktg Mgr: Josh Burns
Ministry Consultant: Caroline Thomas
Conducts Business: U.S.
Employees: 8
Primary Market Served: Business & Consumer
Catalog available online
Indirect online sales
Advertising/Marketing Budget Related to Direct Marketing: 51-75%
Direct Marketing ad budget:
Direct Mail: 5%
Magazines: 10%
Online: 55%
Telephone: 30%
Founded: 1973
Gross sales or billing: $800,000

Books, periodicals, software, music services, videos & custom book packaging.

RIZZOLI INTERNATIONAL PUBLICATIONS INC

dba Universe Publishing Div
300 Park Ave S (3rd fl)
New York, NY 10010
Telephone: (212) 387-3400, FAX: (212) 387-3535
Pres: Marco Ausenda
Publr & VP: Charles Miers
Conducts Business: U.S.
Employees: 50
Primary Market Served: Business
Founded: 1975

Gross sales or billing: $7,700,000

Publisher of art, architecture, photography, gardening, fashion, design, lifestyle, music & culinary books.

THE ROBLIN GROUP INC

405 Tarrytown Rd (Ste 1545)
White Plains, NY 10607
Telephone: (914) 686-7221, FAX: (914) 372-1028, E-Mail: freethingsusa@yahoo.com, Web Site: www.freethingsusa.com
Pres: Robert Kalian
VP: Linda Kalian
Mktg Mgr: Dennis Kalian
Conducts Business: U.S.
Employees: 7
Primary Market Served: Business & Consumer
Catalog available online
Direct online sales
Advertising/Marketing Budget Related to Direct Marketing: 76-100%
Direct Marketing ad budget:
Direct Mail: 80%
Magazines: 20%
Founded: 1980

Direct marketing of books & reports to business & consumers. Publishes nonfiction paperback books to general public via direct marketing & through dealers.

RODALE INC

RP-NFOA
400 S 10th St
Emmaus, PA 18098
Telephone: (610) 967-5171, FAX: (610) 967-8963, Web Site: www.rodaleinc.com
Chmn & CEO: Maria Rodale
Exec VP, Gen Counsel & Chief Admin Officer: Paul A. McGinley
Exec VP & CFO: Thomas A. Pogash
Sr VP & Gen Mgr, Digital & New Brand Devel: Anthony Astarita
Sr VP Intl: Robert Novick
Sr VP HR: Tracey Pierce
Sr VP Audience Devel & E-Tail Mktg: Joyce Shirer
VP & Publr: Mary Ann Naples
Conducts Business: U.S., Canada, Europe
Employees: 1,000
Primary Market Served: Business & Consumer
Direct Marketing ad budget: $80,000,000
Gross sales or billing: $200,000,000

Publisher of Prevention, Organic Gardening, Bicycling, New Woman, Runner's World, Backpacker, Mountain Bike, Men's Health Magazine, American Woodworker, Men's Confidential

Newsletter & other newsletters. Also consumer books on health, nutrition, exercise, gardening & bicycling.

ROGERS PUBLISHING LTD
333 Blour St E (6th fl)
Toronto, ON, Canada M4W 1G9
Telephone: (416) 935-7777, FAX: (416) 935-3597, Web Site: www. rogerspublishing.ca
Pres & CEO: Brian Segal
Sr VP Circulation & Devel: Michael J. Fox
VP, Consumer Mktg: Tracey McKinley
VP Bus Plng: Immee Chee Wah
Conducts Business: Canada
Primary Market Served: Business & Consumer
Founded: 1887
Gross sales or billing: $1,200,000,000

Publisher of Canadian consumer magazines. Also, offer subscriber lists for rental.

SNL FINANCIAL
One SNL Plaza, PO Box 2124
Charlottesville, VA 22902
Telephone: (434) 977-1600, FAX: (434) 977-4466, E-Mail: support@ sni.com, Web Site: www.snl.com
Pres: Mike Chinn
Conducts Business: U.S.
Primary Market Served: Business
Catalog available online
Indirect online sales

Researcher & publisher specializing in financial services.

SRDS
Part of Kantar Media
1700 E Higgins Rd Ste 500
Des Plaines, IL 60018-5610
Toll Free: (800) 851-7737, FAX: (847) 375-5001, Web Site: www.srds.com
VP, Publr: Joseph Hayes
VP Client Sales & Svc: Trish Delauner
Dir: Lindsay H Morrison
Dir Mktg Res: Joe Hardin
Conducts Business: Worldwide
Employees: 200
Primary Market Served: Business
Catalog available online
Indirect online sales
Direct Marketing ad budget:
Direct Mail: 25%
Founded: 1919

Publisher of SRDS Direct Marketing List Source and SRDS Direct Net List, research services with information on available mailing lists for rent or purchase. Pinpoints the sources & describes more than 68,000 mailing lists.

ST MEDIA GROUP INTERNATIONAL
dba "Signs of the Times"; "Visual Mdsg & Str Design"; "Big Picture" & "Signs & Screen Printing"
11262 Cornell Park Dr
Cincinnati, OH 45242-1812
Telephone: (513) 421-2050, Toll Free: (800) 925-1110, FAX: (513) 421-5144, E-Mail: customer@ stmediagroup.com, Web Site: www. signweb.com
Pres & CEO: Tedd Swormstedt
CFO: Brian Foos
Publr Signs of Times: Wade Swormstedt
Grp Publr: Steve Duccilli
Conducts Business: Worldwide
Employees: 45
Primary Market Served: Business
Catalog available online
Direct online sales
Advertising/Marketing Budget Related to Direct Marketing: 0-25%
Founded: 1906
Gross sales or billing: $10,100,000

A global provider of trade information across multiple media divisions: "ST Publications", "ST Events", "ST Online", "ST Books".

THE SAILING CO
Subs. of Miller Sports Group Publishing
PO Box 420235
Palm Coast, FL 32142-0235
Toll Free: (866) 436-2460, FAX: (401) 848-5048, Web Site: www. sailingworld.com
Publr: Sally Helm
Mktg Dir: George Brengle
Conducts Business: Worldwide
Employees: 60
Primary Market Served: Business & Consumer

Magazine written for those who enjoy cruising under sail.

ST LOUIS POST-DISPATCH
900 N Tucker Blvd
Saint Louis, MO 63101
Telephone: (314) 340-8000, Toll Free: (800) 365-0820, FAX: (314) 340-3140, Web Site: www.stltoday.com
Publr: Terry Egger
Editor in Chief: Gilbert Bailon
Newsroom Administrator: Marcia Koenig
Dep Mng Editor: Adam Goodman
Dep Mng Editor: Bob Rose
Conducts Business: U.S.
Employees: 1,500
Primary Market Served: Business & Consumer

Gross sales or billing: $26,100,000
Daily & Sunday newspaper.

SALEM MEDIA GROUP
4880 Santa Rosa Rd
Camarillo, CA 93012
Telephone: (804) 987-0400, E-Mail: info@salem.cc, Web Site: salemmedia.com
CEO: Edward Atsinger III
Dir Adv: Dave Santrella
Pres: David Evans
Exec VP & CFO: Evan Masyr
Primary Market Served: Business & Consumer
Founded: 1986

Broadcaster, publisher and Internet content provider for Christian audiences.

SALES LEADS
601 Heritage Dr (Suite 111)
Jupiter, FL 33458-2777
Toll Free: (866) 725-3753, FAX: (866) 702-5558, E-Mail: info@ salesleadsinc.com, Web Site: www. salesleadsinc.com
Pres: John B. Beecher
Co-Founder: La Verne Beecher
VP & Ed: Michael Beecher
Conducts Business: U.S., Canada
Employees: 3
Primary Market Served: Business
Catalog available online
Direct online sales
Advertising/Marketing Budget Related to Direct Marketing: 76-100%
Direct Marketing ad budget: $30,000
Direct Mail: 90%
Telephone: 10%
Founded: 1959

Newsletter geared towards industrial salespeople who wish to obtain qualified leads on industrial expansions throughout the U.S. & Canada.

SAN ANTONIO EXPRESS-NEWS
Div. of Hearst Communications Inc
Ave E & Third St
San Antonio, TX 78205
Telephone: (210) 250-2000, E-Mail: feedabck@express-news.net, Web Site: www.expressnews.com
Exec VP Adv: Ray McCutcheon
VP Mktg: Catherine Ferguson
Founded: 1865

South Texas newspaper publisher.

SAN FRANCISCO CHRONICLE
Subs. of Hearst Corp
901 Mission St
San Francisco, CA 94103

Telephone: (415) 777-1111, FAX:
(415) 536-5178, Web Site: www.
sfgate.com
Chmn & Publr: Frank J. Vega
Exec VP & Editor: Ward H. Bushee
Conducts Business: U.S.
Primary Market Served: Business &
Consumer
Advertising/Marketing Budget Related
to Direct Marketing: 0-25%

Publish two daily newspapers (one
morning, one evening) & one combined
Sunday paper.

SAN JOSE MERCURY NEWS
750 Ridder Park Dr
San Jose, CA 95190
Telephone: (408) 920-5000, FAX:
(408) 288-8060, Web Site: www.
mercurynews.com
Pres & Publr: Steve Rossi
VP & Editor: David Butler
VP Adv & Mktg: Pete Casillas
Circulation Dir: Dan Smith
Employees: 1,530
Primary Market Served: Business &
Consumer
Direct online sales
Advertising/Marketing Budget Related
to Direct Marketing: 0-25%
Founded: 1851

Daily newspaper.

SCHOLASTIC INC
557 Broadway
New York, NY 10012-3919
Telephone: (212) 343-6100, Toll Free:
(800) SCHOLASTIC, FAX: (212)
343-6484, Web Site: www.
scholastic.com
Chmn, Pres & CEO: Richard Robinson
Pres, Trade Publ: Ellie Berger
Exec VP & Pres Scholastic Media: De-
borah A Forte
Exec VP, CFO & CAO: Maureen
O'Connell
Sr VP, Corp Commun & Media Rels:
Kyle Good
Exec VP, Gen Counsel & Sec: Andrew
S Hedden
Exec VP & Pres Scholastic Education:
Margery W Mayer
Exec VP & Pres Book Clubs & E-Com-
merce: Judith A Newman
Exec VP & Pres Consumer & Prof
Publ: Hugh Roome
Pres, Scholastic Classroom & Com-
munity Grp: Greg Worrell
Conducts Business: U.S., Canada, U.
K., Australia, New Zealand
Employees: 1,075
Primary Market Served: Business &
Consumer

Gross sales or billing: $206,000,000
Market educational periodicals, paperback & hard cover books, software &
textbooks primarily to the educational
market. Also market through wholesale, retail, public library & to selected
at-home consumer markets. Publish
Home Office Computing magazine.

**SCHOOL ANNUAL
PUBLISHING CO**
2568 Park Center Blvd
State College, PA 16801-3005
Toll Free: (800) 436-6030, E-Mail:
yearbook@schoolannual.com, Web
Site: www.schoolannual.com
COO & VP: Nancy Stone
Customer Svc Supvr: Brenda Pollock
Sls Rep: Bernard Kalt
Sls Rep: Tonya Daher
Conducts Business: Worldwide
Primary Market Served: Business &
Consumer
Catalog available online
Indirect online sales
Advertising/Marketing Budget Related
to Direct Marketing: 76-100%
Founded: 1953

Publisher of yearbooks, church directories, calendars, and agenda planners.

SCHOOLWISE PRESS
1167 Bosworth St
San Francisco, CA 94131-2801
Telephone: (415) 337-7971, Toll Free:
(800) 247-8443 x 202, FAX: (415)
337-1146, E-Mail: info@
schoolwisepress.com, Web Site:
www.schoolwisepress.com
Pres & Editor: Steve Rees
Tech Dir: Greg Smith
Prod Mgr: Robert Ross
Mktg Dir: Alison Nakashima
Sr Project Mgr: Lee Smith Seiden
Conducts Business: U.S.
Primary Market Served: Business &
Consumer

Publishers of books & information
services about schools.

SCOTT PUBLICATIONS, INC
2145 W Sherman Blvd
Muskegon, MI 49441-3434
Telephone: (231) 755-2200, Toll Free:
(866) 733-9382, FAX: (231) 755-
1003, Web Site: www.
scottpublications.com
Pres: Robert H. Keessen

**SCRIPPS NETWORKS
INTERACTIVE INC**
9721 Sherrill Blvd
Knoxville, TN 37932-3330

Toll Free: (865) 560-2700, Web Site:
scrippsnetworksinteractive.com
Chmn, Pres & CEO: Kenneth W. Lowe
Pres, Scripps Networks: John Lansing
Pres, Ad Sls & Mktg & Branded Enter-
tainment: Steven Gigliotti
Exec VP, Content Distr & Mktg: Henry
Ahn
Exec VP, Strategy & Planning: Jim
Clayton
Exec VP, Opers & Chief Tech Officer:
Mark Hale
Exec VP, Fin: Lori Hickok

Developer of high-profile lifestyle-ori-
ented content for many media platforms including television, digital,
mobile & publishing.

SEATTLE MAGAZINE
Subs. of Tiger Oak Publications
1518 1st Ave S (Suite 500)
Seattle, WA 98134-1456
Telephone: (206) 284-1750, Toll Free:
(800) 637-0334, FAX: (206) 284-
2550, E-Mail: customerservice@
seattlemag.com, Web Site: www.
seattlemag.com
Publr: R. Craig Bednar
Editorial Dir: Rachel Hart
Promos, Sls Devel Dir: Jamie Peha
Promos Coord: Elizabeth Tveit
Conducts Business: U.S.
Employees: 75
Primary Market Served: Business &
Consumer
Founded: 1966
Gross sales or billing: $7,000,000

Travel & lifestyle publication, published twelve times a year, for the
greater northwest region. Provides
service-oriented articles on travel, lodging, the outdoors, the environment,
people, business & topical issues im-
portant to the region; on food & restaurants & home related subjects.

**SECOND RENAISSANCE
BOOKS**
2121 Alton Pkwy (Suite 250)
Irvine, CA 92606-4926
Telephone: (860) 354-5448, Toll Free:
(800) 729-6149, FAX: (860) 355-
7161, Web Site: www.
aynrandbookstore.com
Pres & CEO: Yaron Brook
Conducts Business: Worldwide
Employees: 6
Primary Market Served: Business &
Consumer
Catalog available online
Direct online sales
Advertising/Marketing Budget Related
to Direct Marketing: 76-100%
Direct Marketing ad budget: $100,000
Direct Mail: 100%

Founded: 1985
Gross sales or billing: $600,000

Books & taped lectures to individuals interested in ideas & principles of individualism, reason & freedom.

SELECT PRESS
40 Phillip Terr
Novato, CA 94945
Telephone: (415) 209-9838, E-Mail: selectpr@aol.com
Editor: Roderick Crandall
Conducts Business: Worldwide
Employees: 4
Primary Market Served: Business & Consumer
Direct Marketing ad budget:
Direct Mail: $50,000
Telephone: $10,000
Founded: 1986

Publish various publications for business. Divisions market to lawyers, academics & managers.

SERENITY
PO Box 168
Maria Stein, OH 45860-0168
Telephone: (419) 925-1215, Toll Free: (800) 869-1684, FAX: (419) 925-1216, E-Mail: serenity@bright.net, Web Site: www.serenitymusic.com
Pres & Owner: Jim Moeller
Conducts Business: U.S.
Employees: 9
Primary Market Served: Business & Consumer
Catalog available online
Direct online sales
Advertising/Marketing Budget Related to Direct Marketing: 26-50%
Direct Marketing ad budget: $100,000
Direct Mail: 50%
Magazines: 50%
Gross sales or billing: $500,000

Production & distribution of new age & classical music & books.

SEYBOLD PUBLICATIONS
Div. of The Joss Group, LLC
PO Box 682
Gilbertsville, PA 19525
Telephone: (610) 327-3958, Toll Free: (888) 544-7104, FAX: (888) 463-4814, E-Mail: molly@thejossgroup, Web Site: www.seyboldreports.com
Mktg Dir: Dorothy Engel
Conducts Business: Worldwide
Primary Market Served: Business
Catalog available online
Indirect online sales
Founded: 1971

Computer publications.

SHUTTERBUG
Div. of Primedia Enthusiast Group
1415 Chaffee Dr Ste 10
Titusville, FL 32780-7936
Telephone: (321) 269-3212, FAX: (321) 255-3146, Web Site: www.shutterbug.net
Publr: Ron Leach
Conducts Business: U.S.
Primary Market Served: Consumer
Catalog available online
Direct online sales
Advertising/Marketing Budget Related to Direct Marketing: 0-25%

Monthly photographic equipment magazine for advanced, amateur & professional photographers, featuring reviews, news & test reports.

SIMMONS-BOARDMAN PUBLISHING CORP
55 Broad St (fl 26)
New York, NY 10004
Telephone: (212) 620-7200, Toll Free: (800) 257-5091, Web Site: www.simmonsboardman.com
Chmn & Pres: Arthur J. McGinnis Jr.
Co-Owner & Dir: Ms Pat McGinnis
Dir: Ms Kim McGinnis
Grp Publr: Jonathan Chalon
Controller: Allen Morrell
Conducts Business: Worldwide
Employees: 70
Primary Market Served: Business
Advertising/Marketing Budget Related to Direct Marketing: 26-50%
Direct Marketing ad budget:
Direct Mail: 47%
Telephone: 53%
Founded: 1910

Trade/business publications in the following markets: commercial banking; railroads and rail transit; shipping maritime; intermodal transportation; rail track & maintenance. Railway Educational Bureau & Book Division in Omaha, NE. Conferences relating to the maritime & rail industries.

SIMON & SCHUSTER INC
Div. of CBS Corp.
1230 Ave of the Americas
New York, NY 10020
Telephone: (212) 698-7000, Toll Free: (800) 223-2348, Web Site: www.simonandschuster.com
Pres & CEO: Carolyn Reidy
Exec VP & Publr: Jonathan Karp
Exec VP, Sls & Mktg: Michael Selleck
Sr VP, Mktg: Liz Perl
Conducts Business: U.S.
Primary Market Served: Consumer

Operate book clubs & continuity programs. Sell direct to the consumer through various direct response media.

SINGLE SCENE NEWS
1928 E Laguna Dr
Tempe, AZ 85282-5913
Telephone: (480) 945-6746, FAX: (480) 945-6746, E-Mail: publisher@azsinglescene.com, Web Site: www.azsinglescene.com
Publr: Janet Jacobsen
Publr: Jeff Jacobsen
Publr: Harlan Jacobsen
Conducts Business: U.S.
Employees: 2
Primary Market Served: Business & Consumer
Indirect online sales
Advertising/Marketing Budget Related to Direct Marketing: 0-25%
Direct Marketing ad budget:
Direct Mail: 40%
Newspapers: 60%
Founded: 1972

Monthly service newspaper of news, advice & events for single adults.

SMART PRACTICE
Div. of Smart Health
3400 E McDowell Rd
Phoenix, AZ 85008-7899
Toll Free: (800) 522-0800, FAX: (800) 522-8329, E-Mail: info@smartpractice.com, Web Site: www.smartpractice.com
Pres & CEO: Dr. Curt Hamann
Co-Founder: Naomi Rhode
VP: Beth Hamann
VP Mktg & Sls: Scott Maloney
Conducts Business: Worldwide
Employees: 340
Primary Market Served: Business
Catalog available online
Direct online sales
Direct Marketing ad budget:
Direct Mail: $1,500,000
Gross sales or billing: $100,000,000

Dental & medical supplies plus practice promotional products to medical professionals, veterinarians & real estate professionals.

SMITHSONIAN ENTERPRISES
Smithsonian Institution
420 Lexington Ave
New York, NY 10170-0002
Telephone: (212) 916-1300, Toll Free: (800) 766-2149, FAX: (212) 490-0058, Web Site: www.smithsonianmag.com
Pres: Christopher A. Liedel
VP, Adv Sls & Mktg: Stephen P. Giannetti
Mktg Dir: Judy Glassman
Consumer Mktg Dir: Lisa Dunham
Editor in Chief: Michael Caruso
Conducts Business: U.S.

Employees: 100
Primary Market Served: Consumer
Catalog available online
Direct online sales
Advertising/Marketing Budget Related
to Direct Marketing: 51-75%
Direct Marketing ad budget:
Direct Mail: 100%
Founded: 1981

Publishes monthly magazine. Articles cover science, history, fine & folk art, & the environment. Membership in Smithsonian National Associates includes magazine subscription. Use direct mail to promote to literate audience.

SOURCEBOOKS INC

1935 Brookdale Rd (Suite 139)
Naperville, IL 60563-7994
Telephone: (630) 961-3900, Toll Free:
(800) 432-7444, FAX: (630) 961-
2168, Web Site: www.sourcebooks.
com
Publisher & CEO: Dominique Raccah

Independent publisher of authors in various subjects and styles in both the physical and digital formats.

SOUTH-WESTERN PUBLISHING

Subs. of The Thomson Corp
5191 Natorp Blvd
Madison, OH 45040
Telephone: (513) 299-1000, FAX:
(513) 527-6992
Pres: Bob Lynch
Conducts Business: Worldwide
Employees: 700
Primary Market Served: Business
Advertising/Marketing Budget Related
to Direct Marketing: 51-75%
Direct Marketing ad budget:
Direct Mail: $1,000,000

Publisher of business administration & educational materials for collegiate & secondary schools.

SOUTHERN PROGRESS CORP

Subs. of Time Inc
2100 Lake Shore Dr
Birmingham, AL 35209-6721
Telephone: (205) 877-6000, FAX:
(205) 877-6283, Web Site: www.
southernprogress.com
Pres & CEO: Tom K. Angelillo
Exec VP: Bruce Akin
Conducts Business: U.S.
Employees: 750
Primary Market Served: Business &
Consumer
Founded: 1886

Gross sales or billing: $84,500,000
Publisher of Southern Living, Progressive Farmer, Southern Accents, Cooking Light, Southern Living Vacations, Oxmoor House Books, Weight Watchers & Coastal Living.

SPOKEN ARTS

195 S White Rock Rd
Holmes, NY 12531-5406
Telephone: (845) 878-9600, Toll Free:
(800) 326-4090, FAX: (845) 878-
9009, E-Mail: sales@
spokenartsmedia.com, Web Site:
www.spokenartsmedia.com
Pres: Daniel Welsh
COO: Susan Welsh
Conducts Business: US
Employees: 3
Primary Market Served: Business &
Consumer
Catalog available online
Indirect online sales
Direct Marketing ad budget: $150,000
Direct Mail: 100%
Gross sales or billing: $300,000

Motion picture/video production. Language arts, children's tales, cassettes, videos, multimedia cassettes, audio books & read-a-longs. Sell to educational institutions, libraries, distributors & dealers.

THE SPOKESMAN-REVIEW

Div. of Cowles Publishing Co
PO Box 2160
Spokane, WA 99210-2160
Telephone: (509) 459-5060, FAX:
(509) 459-5083, E-Mail: shaunh@
spokesman.com, Web Site: www.
spokane.net
Dir, Mktg & Sls: Shaun Higgins
Primary Market Served: Business &
Consumer

Business newspaper publisher.

SPORTING CLAYS LTD

317 S Washington Ave (Suite 201)
Titusville, FL 32976-3539
Telephone: (321) 268-5010, FAX:
(321) 267-7216, E-Mail: sales@
sportingclays.net, Web Site: www.
sportingclays.net
Publr: Dan Wade
Sales: Eileen Meister
Conducts Business: Worldwide
Primary Market Served: Consumer

Monthly magazines, sporting clays.

THE SPORTING NEWS

Subs. of American City Business Journals
120 W Morehead St Ste 310
Charlotte, NC 28202-1826

Telephone: (704) 973-1546, Toll Free:
(800) 443-1886, FAX: (704) 973-
1552, Web Site: www.sportingnews.
com
Pres & Publr: Jeff Price
Conducts Business: Worldwide
Employees: 120
Primary Market Served: Consumer
Catalog available online
Direct online sales
Advertising/Marketing Budget Related
to Direct Marketing: 76-100%
Direct Marketing ad budget:
Direct Mail: $3,500,000
Magazines: $250,000
Newspapers: $100,000
TV/Radio: $1,700,000
Telephone: $250,000
Founded: 1886
Gross sales or billing: $60,000,000

SPRINGER SCIENCE & BUSINESS MEDIA LLC

233 Spring St
New York, NY 10013
Telephone: (212) 460-1500, FAX:
(212) 460-1575, Web Site: www.
springer.com
CEO: Derk Haank
COO: Martin Mos
CFO: Ulrich Vest
Exec VP Corp Communs: Eric Merkel-
Sobotta
Exec VP Mktg: Juliane Ritt
Conducts Business: Worldwide
Employees: 400
Primary Market Served: Business &
Consumer
Catalog available online
Direct online sales
Founded: 1842
Gross sales or billing: $44,700,000

Scientific, medical & technical publisher of books & journals.

STANDARD & POOR'S CORP

Div. of McGraw-Hill Companies, Inc.
55 Water St
New York, NY 10041-0004
Telephone: (212) 438-2000, FAX:
(212) 438-7375, Web Site: www.
standardandpoors.com
Pres: Douglas L. Peterson
Sr VP Fin: Edward J. Haran
Sr VP Mktg & Commun: Catherine J.
Mathis
Sr VP & Chief Info Officer: Joseph D.
Sniado
VP HR: Sheila M. O'Neill
Conducts Business: U.S., Europe, Asia
Employees: 7,500
Primary Market Served: Business
Catalog available online
Founded: 1906

Gross sales or billing: $2,400,000,000

Marketer of financial & business information to investors, financial institutions, libraries & corporations.

STANDARD PUBLISHING

Subs. of Standex International
8805 Governor's Hill Dr (Suite 400)
Cincinnati, OH 45249
Telephone: (513) 931-4050, Toll Free: (800) 543-1301, FAX: (877) 867-5751, Web Site: www.standardpub. com
Pres & CEO: Matthew Thibeau
VP Sls & Mktg: Steven Couture
Conducts Business: U.S., Canada, U. K., Australia, New Zealand
Primary Market Served: Business & Consumer
Catalog available online
Direct online sales
Advertising/Marketing Budget Related to Direct Marketing: 0-25%
Founded: 1866

Publish dated curriculum, summer vacation school products, Bible centered books, games & church supplies. Sell to churches direct through company owned stores (15) & religious bookstores (5000). Also a commercial printer.

STAR TRIBUNE MEDIA CO

425 Portland Ave S
Minneapolis, MN 55488
Telephone: (612) 673-4000, FAX: (612) 673-4359, Web Site: www. startribunecompany.com
Publr & CEO: Michael J. Klingensmith
Editor & Sr VP: Nancy Barnes
Sr VP, Circulation: Steven H. Alexander
Sr VP & Gen Counsel: Randy Lebedoff
Sr VP Digital: Jim Bernard
Sr VP Opers: Kevin Desmond
Chief Revenue Officer: Jeff Griffing
Primary Market Served: Consumer
Founded: 1867

Daily newspaper & consumer periodical publications.

STAYWELL/KRAMES

Subs. of Vivendi Universal
1100 Grundy Ln (#2)
San Bruno, CA 94066
Telephone: (650) 742-0400, FAX: (650) 244-4568, Web Site: www. staywell.com
Pres & CEO: Patrick Clifford
Pres & CEO Staywell Insurance: Don Davis
Sr VP, Sls: Jean Neiner
Conducts Business: U.S., Canada, Australia, Europe
Employees: 150

Primary Market Served: Business
Catalog available online
Indirect online sales
Advertising/Marketing Budget Related to Direct Marketing: 76-100%
Founded: 1974

Publish full-color booklets, brochures & posters on numerous health & safety topics for physicians, hospitals & corporations.

STECK-VAUGHN

Div. of Harcourt Education
10801 N Mopac Expy (Bldg 3)
Austin, TX 78759-5415
Telephone: (512) 343-8227, Toll Free: (800) 531-5015, (877) 866-2586, FAX: (512) 795-3617, (877) 265-2730, E-Mail: info@steck-vaughn. com, Web Site: www.steck-vaughn. com
Pres & CEO: Richard J. Casabonne
Pres, Educational Trade Unit: James P. Levy
Exec VP, Opers: Floyd D. Rogers
VP & CFO: Todd Wehner
Gen Mgr: Carol Wolf
Conducts Business: Worldwide
Employees: 300
Primary Market Served: Consumer
Catalog available online
Direct online sales
Advertising/Marketing Budget Related to Direct Marketing: 51-75%
Founded: 1936

Supplemental publisher of educational workbooks, books, software & manipulatives for school, library, international & direct marketing markets.

STEPHENS PUBLISHING CO

311 W Perkins Ave
Sandusky, OH 44870-4805
Telephone: (419) 626-5592, Toll Free: (800) 236-5592, FAX: (419) 626-9333, Web Site: www. stephenspublishing.com
Pres: Craig S. Stephens
Conducts Business: U.S., Canada, England
Employees: 102
Primary Market Served: Business
Catalog available online
Direct online sales

Publisher of 15 professional journals.

STERLING PUBLISHING CO INC

Subs. of Barnes & Noble.
387 Park Ave S (fl 5)
New York, NY 10016-8898

Telephone: (212) 532-7160, Toll Free: (800) 367-9692, FAX: (212) 213-2495, Web Site: www. sterlingpublishing.com
Exec VP: Theresa Thompson
Conducts Business: U.S., Canada, U. K., Australia, New Zealand
Employees: 250
Primary Market Served: Business
Advertising/Marketing Budget Related to Direct Marketing: 0-25%
Direct Marketing ad budget: $500,000
Direct Mail: 60%
Magazines: 20%
Newspapers: 10%
Telephone: 10%
Founded: 1949
Gross sales or billing: $28,100,000

Self help and how to books.

MARTHA STEWART LIVING OMNIMEDIA

601 W 26th St (Fl 9)
New York, NY 10001-1101
Telephone: (212) 827-8000, Web Site: www.marthastewart.com
Sr VP Consumer Mktg Dir: Richard Fontaine
Primary Market Served: Business & Consumer

STRANG COMMUNICATIONS CO

600 Rinehart Rd
Lake Mary, FL 32746-4898
Telephone: (407) 333-0600, FAX: (407) 333-7100, E-Mail: magcustsvc@strang.com, Web Site: www.strang.com
Pres & Ed: Stephen Strang
Circ Dir: Larry Bregel
Retailing Editor: Andy Butcher
Editor: J. Lee Grudy
Sr Editor: Rafael Serrano
Conducts Business: U.S.
Employees: 100
Primary Market Served: Business & Consumer
Catalog available online
Direct online sales
Direct Marketing ad budget:
Direct Mail: $500,000

Christian magazine service that publishes Charisma, Ministries Today, SpiritLed Woman, Christian Retailing, New Man & Vida Cristiana.

STRESS MARKET

PO Box 127
Port Angeles, WA 98362-0017
Telephone: (360) 457-9223, Toll Free: (800) 578-7377, FAX: (360) 457-9466, E-Mail: info@stressmarket. com, Web Site: www.stressmarket. com

Pres: Tim Lownstein
Conducts Business: U.S.
Employees: 3
Primary Market Served: Business &
    Consumer
Catalog available online
Direct online sales
Advertising/Marketing Budget Related
    to Direct Marketing: 76-100%
Direct Marketing ad budget:
Direct Mail: 30%
Magazines: 30%
Online: 40%
Founded: 1978
Gross sales or billing: $100,000

Educational books & cassettes, stress
meters, biofeedback & holographic music. Health Master, fitness, nutrition,
psychology, biodots, stress cards & re-
laxation.

SUCCESSFUL FARMING

Div. of Meredith Publishing Co
1716 Locust St
Des Moines, IA 50309-3023
Telephone: (515) 284-2143, Toll Free:
    (800) 678-2711, FAX: (515) 284-
    3127
Pres & Publr: Chris Little
Magazine Grp VP: Jerry Ward
Publr: Jim Cornick
DM Mgr: Cathy Porepp
Conducts Business: U.S.
Primary Market Served: Consumer

Publish a mail order marketplace section in each of 12 issues per year. The
magazine itself provides decision making business help to large, professional
farm families.

SUNBURST DIGITAL INC

3150 W Higgins Rd (Suite 140)
Hoffman Estates, IL 60169
Toll Free: (800) 321-7511, E-Mail:
    sales@sunburst.com, Web Site:
    www.sunburst.com
Pres & CEO: Dan Figurski
Conducts Business: Worldwide
Employees: 180
Primary Market Served: Consumer
Catalog available online
Indirect online sales
Advertising/Marketing Budget Related
    to Direct Marketing: 76-100%
Direct Marketing ad budget:
Direct Mail: 95%
Magazines: 1%
Telephone: 4%
Founded: 1973

Produce & distribute video, computer
software & print instructional materials
for use in elementary & secondary
schools, colleges, hospitals, public
agencies & homes. Products are mar-

keted by direct mail & telemarketing to
school teachers, librarians & administrators.

SUNRISE GREETINGS

2501 McGee St
Kansas City, MO 64108-2615
Telephone: (812) 336-4045, Toll Free:
    (800) 457-4045, FAX: (812) 336-
    8712, E-Mail: info@interart.com,
    Web Site: www.interartdistribution.
    com
CEO: Susan Hare
Art Dir: Sara Davis
Dir, Seasonal Cards: Kandy Schwandt
Conducts Business: U.S., U.K., Canada
Employees: 475
Primary Market Served: Business
Catalog available online
Advertising/Marketing Budget Related
    to Direct Marketing: 0-25%
Founded: 1974
Gross sales or billing: $22,000,000

Greeting card publisher, stationery &
paper gifts.

SUNSET MAGAZINE

Subs. of Time Inc Magazine Co
80 Willow Rd
Menlo Park, CA 94025
Telephone: (650) 321-3600, FAX:
    (650) 328-6215
Circ Dir: Christina Olsen
Circ Mktg Mgr: Jalayne Forrester
Circ Mktg Mgr: Karen Gallion
Circ Mktg Mgr: Pamela Miller
Conducts Business: U.S.
Employees: 300
Primary Market Served: Consumer
Direct Marketing ad budget:
Direct Mail: $4,000,000
TV/Radio: $600,000
Telephone: $200,000
Founded: 1898
Gross sales or billing: $100,000,000

Publish Sunset Books & Sunset Mag-
azineRO serving 13 Western States.

SURE-FIRE BUSINESS
SUCCESS CATALOG

50 Follen St (#507)
Cambridge, MA 02138
Telephone: (617) 547-6372, FAX:
    (617) 547-0061, E-Mail: drjlant@
    worldprofit.com, Web Site: www.
    worldprofit.com
Pres: Jeffrey Lant
Conducts Business: Worldwide
Employees: 2
Primary Market Served: Business &
    Consumer
Catalog available online
Direct online sales
Advertising/Marketing Budget Related
    to Direct Marketing: 76-100%

Direct Marketing ad budget:
Online: 100%
Founded: 1979

Books, card decks, and software to help
businesses grow. See web site for details.

SURPLUS RECORD

Subs. of Free Markets
20 N Wacker Dr (Suite 2400)
Chicago, IL 60606-3181
Telephone: (312) 372-9077, Toll Free:
    (800) 622-5449, FAX: (312) 372-
    6537, E-Mail: surplus@
    surplusrecord.com, Web Site: www.
    surplusrecord.com
Publr: T.C. Scanlan
CEO: Glen Meakem
Sr VP: Doug Wnorowski
Conducts Business: Worldwide
Employees: 20
Primary Market Served: Business
Catalog available online
Advertising/Marketing Budget Related
    to Direct Marketing: 76-100%
Founded: 1924

Surplus machine tools. Publisher of
Catalog/Index of Available Capital
Equipment.

SUSSEX PUBLISHERS INC

115 E 23rd St (9th fl)
New York, NY 10010
Telephone: (212) 260-7210, FAX:
    (212) 260-7445, Web Site: www.
    blues-buster.com
Editor in Chief: Kaja Perina
Exec Editor: Lysi Ma
Creative Dir: Ed Levine
Sr Editor: Jay Dixit
Assoc Editor: Carlin Flora
Primary Market Served: Business &
    Consumer
Catalog available online
Direct online sales

Publish magazines.

THOMSON REUTERS

195 Broadway Fl 4
New York, NY 10007-3124
Telephone: (212) 367-6300, Toll Free:
    (800) 950-1216, FAX: (212) 367-
    6301, Web Site: www.riahome.com
Mktg Dir: John Hartnett
Mktg Mgr: David O'Toole
Conducts Business: U.S.
Primary Market Served: Business
Catalog available online
Direct online sales
Advertising/Marketing Budget Related
    to Direct Marketing: 0-25%
Direct Marketing ad budget:
Direct Mail: 40%

Telephone: 60%

Publish insightful analysis & practical guidance of laws & regulations for CPA's, corporate tax & finance, human resource professionals & attorneys. Sell through mail order & national sales force.

TL ENTERPRISES INC

Affinity Group Inc
2575 Vista Del Mar Dr
Ventura, CA 93001-3920
Telephone: (805) 667-4100, FAX: (805) 667-4419
Pres: Joe McAdams
Employees: 300
Primary Market Served: Business & Consumer
Advertising/Marketing Budget Related to Direct Marketing: 76-100%

Publisher & marketer of magazines, clubs & ancillary products.

TT PUBLISHING

Div. of American Trucking Associations
950 N Gleb Rd
Arlington, VA 22203
Telephone: (703) 838-1770, FAX: (703) 838-0285, Web Site: www.ttnews.com
Publr: Bob Rast
Publr: Howard Abramson
VP & Assoc Publr Mktg & Circulation: Paul Rosenthal
Conducts Business: U.S., Canada, Mexico
Employees: 38
Primary Market Served: Business
Catalog available online
Direct online sales
Advertising/Marketing Budget Related to Direct Marketing: 0-25%
Direct Marketing ad budget:
Direct Mail: $100,000
Magazines: $5,000
Newspapers: $5,000
Telephone: $10,000
Founded: 1933
Gross sales or billing: $8,200,000

Publish weekly newspaper "Transport Topics", & monthly magazines "Light & Medium Truck" & "Utility Fleet Management."

THE TAUNTON PRESS

63 S Main St, PO Box 5506
Newtown, CT 06470-2344
Telephone: (203) 426-8171, Toll Free: (800) 477-8727, FAX: (203) 426-3434, Web Site: www.taunton.com
Pres: Suzanne Roman
EVP: Tim Rahr
COO: Tom Luxeder
Production Mgr: Phil Van Kirk

Sr VP, CMO: Janine Scolpino
Conducts Business: U.S., Canada
Employees: 270
Primary Market Served: Business & Consumer
Gross sales or billing: $26,000,000

Publisher of magazines, books & videos.

TAX MANAGEMENT INC

Subs. of The Bureau of National Affairs Inc
3 Bethesda Metro Ctr (Suite 250), BNA Customer Contact Center
Bethesda, MD 20814-5377
Telephone: (202) 452-4200, FAX: (202) 496-6013
Pres: Dave McFarlend
Adv & Commun Mgr: Barbara Patrick
Promo Mgr: Gretchen Zekiel
Conducts Business: Worldwide
Primary Market Served: Business

Publisher of professionally oriented tax & related business services for lawyers, accountants, executives & financial planners.

THE TEACHING CO

4151 Lafayette Center Dr
Chantilly, VA 20151-1232
Telephone: (703) 502-7300, Toll Free: (800) 832-2412, FAX: (703) 378-3819, Web Site: www.teach12.com
Pres: Thomas Rollins
Dir, Mktg Production: Jason Smigel
Primary Market Served: Business & Consumer
Founded: 1990

Make educational audio & video cassettes featuring teachers & professors from leading universities & high schools. Sold through mail order & retail.

TECHNOLOGY REVIEW

Subs. of Massachusetts Institute of Technology
1 Main St (Suite 7), MIT Bldg W59
Cambridge, MA 02142-1599
Telephone: (617) 475-8000, FAX: (617) 258-5850, Web Site: www.technologyreview.com
Publr & CEO: R. Bruce Journey
VP Circulation & Consumer Mktg: Heather Holmes
Ed: John Benditt
VP & GM: Martha Connors
Mktg Dir: Marcy Dill
Conducts Business: Worldwide
Employees: 20
Primary Market Served: Business & Consumer
Catalog available online
Advertising/Marketing Budget Related to Direct Marketing: 26-50%

Direct Marketing ad budget:
Direct Mail: $2,000,000
Founded: 1899

MIT's national magazine on technological innovation across the full spectrum of technologies & industries. Coverage concentrated on areas of high technology where progress is most rapid, such as biotechnology, information technology & materials science. Coverage also provided of innovation in mature industries, such as transportation, construction & energy technology.

TELECOMMUNICATIONS REPORTS INTERNATIONAL INC

Part of Aspen Publishers
1015 15th St NW (fl 10)
Washington, DC 20005-2605
Telephone: (202) 312-6060, Toll Free: (800) 234-1660, FAX: (202) 312-6111, E-Mail: bhammond@tr.com, Web Site: www.tr.com
Pres: Robert Becker
Mng Ed: Brian Hammond
Conducts Business: U.S.
Primary Market Served: Business
Catalog available online
Direct online sales

Publisher of newsletters, directories & manuals to the telecommunications industry.

TELEMEDIA COMMUNICATIONS US

25 Sheppard Ave W (Suite 100)
North York, ON, Canada M2N 6S7
Telephone: (416) 733-7600, Toll Free: (800) 461-3773 U.S., (888) 290-1466 Can., FAX: (416) 733-3563, E-Mail: info@transcontinental.ca, Web Site: www.transcontinental.com
Chmn: Remi Marcoux
Pres & CEO: Luc Desjardins
COO: Francois Oliver
VP & CFO: Benoit Huard
Conducts Business: U.S.
Employees: 14,476
Primary Market Served: Consumer
Founded: 1976
Gross sales or billing: $2,100,000,000

Publisher of consumer magazines.

TELEPHONY

Div. of Intertec Publishing Corp
One IBM Plaza (23rd fl)
Chicago, IL 60611
Telephone: (312) 595-1080, Toll Free: (800) 458-0479, FAX: (312) 595-0295, Web Site: www.internettelephony.com
Pres: Cameron Bishop
Div VP: Larry Lannon

Mktg Dir: Bill McDonough
Tele Publr: Mark Hickey
Conducts Business: Worldwide
Employees: 100
Primary Market Served: Business
Founded: 1901

Publisher of the weekly journal of tele-communications - Telephony, monthly journal of telecommunications - Global Telephony. Also publisher of telecom-munications books. Sponsor telecom-munications seminars.

TEN SPEED PRESS
Subs. of Philip Wood, Inc.
6001 Shellmound St 4th Fl, PO Box 7123
Emeryville, CA 94608-1988
Telephone: (510) 559-1600, Toll Free: (800) 841-BOOK, FAX: (510) 559-1629, E-Mail: order@tenspeed.com, Web Site: www.tenspeed.com
Pres & CEO: Phillip R. Wood
Publicity Mgr: Lisa Regul
Customer Svc: Shelley Davidson
Conducts Business: U.S., U.K., Cana-da, Australia, New Zealand, South Africa, Singapore, India
Employees: 75
Primary Market Served: Business & Consumer
Catalog available online
Direct online sales
Advertising/Marketing Budget Related to Direct Marketing: 0-25%
Gross sales or billing: $24,000,000

Book, poster & audiotape publisher. Sell to wholesalers, distributors, book-stores, libraries & specialty accounts.

TERRITORIAL NEWSPAPERS
Div. of Wick Communications
3280 E Hemisphere Loop (Suite 180), PO Box 27087
Tucson, AZ 85726-7087
Telephone: (520) 294-1200, FAX: (520) 294-4040, Web Site: www.azbiz.com
Publr: Thomas P. Lee
List Coord: James Werner
Employees: 50

TEXAS MONTHLY
Subs. of Emmis Communications
816 Congress Ave Ste 1700
Austin, TX 78701-2643
Telephone: (512) 320-6900, Toll Free: (800) 759-2000, FAX: (512) 476-9007, E-Mail: info@texasmonthly.com, Web Site: www.texasmonthly.com
Publr: Michael R. Levy
Sr VP Sls & Mktg: April Brumley Hin-kle
Sr VP & Gen Mgr: Lorelei Calvert

Office Mgr: Angela Clawson
Dir: Charlie Llewelin
Dir: Cynthia Winer
Conducts Business: U.S.
Employees: 125
Primary Market Served: Consumer
Catalog available online
Indirect online sales
Founded: 1973

Publish a monthly general interest con-sumer magazine for Texans.

THIEME MEDICAL PUBLISHERS INC
dba Thieme New York
333 7th Ave Rm 500
New York, NY 10001-5122
Telephone: (212) 760-0888, Toll Free: (800) 782-3488, FAX: (212) 947-1112, E-Mail: info@thieme.com, Web Site: www.thieme.com
Pres: Brian Scanlon
Dir Online Div: Sigrid Lesch
Online Mktg: Cornelia Schulze
Mktg: Verena Dieme
Employees: 50
Primary Market Served: Business
Catalog available online
Direct online sales
Advertising/Marketing Budget Related to Direct Marketing: 51-75%
Direct Marketing ad budget:
Direct Mail: 70%
Online: 30%
Founded: 1995
Gross sales or billing: $13,800,000

Publisher of medical books & journals.

THOMAS NELSON
HarperCollins Christian Publishing
PO Box 141000
Nashville, TN 37214
Telephone: (615) 889-9000, Toll Free: (800) 251-4000, FAX: (615) 889-5940, Web Site: www.thomasnelson.com
Pres & CEO: Mark Schoenwald
Conducts Business: U.S.
Primary Market Served: Business & Consumer
Advertising/Marketing Budget Related to Direct Marketing: 26-50%
Direct Marketing ad budget:
Direct Mail: 40%
Magazines: 10%
TV/Radio: 10%
Telephone: 40%
Founded: 1798
Gross sales or billing: $250,000

Bibles & Christian books, audio & vid-eo tapes to churches & consumers.

THOMPSON PUBLISHING GROUP INC
1020 19th St NW (Suite 350)
Washington, DC 20036-6107
Telephone: (202) 872-4000, Toll Free: (800) 677-3789, FAX: (800) 999-5661, E-Mail: service@thompson.com, Web Site: www.thompson.com
Grp Sls: Steve Ackerman
Conducts Business: U.S., Canada
Employees: 300
Primary Market Served: Business
Catalog available online
Direct online sales
Advertising/Marketing Budget Related to Direct Marketing: 51-75%
Direct Marketing ad budget:
Direct Mail: 65%
Online: 10%
Telephone: 25%
Founded: 1972

Publish loose-leaf reference services & newsletters. Thompson Publishing Services division in Tampa, Florida provides database systems, 800 cus-tomer service number, distribution, cashiering & other related fulfillment services to publishers, associations & government agencies. A brochure list-ing these services is available by call-ing (800) 677-3789.

THOMSON WEST
Subs. of Thomson Corp
610 Opperman Dr
Eagan, MN 55164
Telephone: (651) 687-7000, Toll Free: (800) 328-9378, FAX: (651) 687-7849, E-Mail: jeff.patrios@thomsonreuters.com, Web Site: www.thomson.com
Pres & CEO: Peter Warwick
Sr VP, HR: Tom Moran
Exec VP, Chief Strategy Officer: Charles B. Cater
Sr Dir Mktg: Jeff Patrios
Conducts Business: Worldwide
Employees: 7,000
Primary Market Served: Business
Catalog available online
Direct online sales
Advertising/Marketing Budget Related to Direct Marketing: 51-75%
Direct Marketing ad budget: $25,000,000
Founded: 1876
Gross sales or billing: $935,000,000

A legal publisher, headquartered in Ea-gan, MN, supplying legal professionals with print & electronic source materials including WESTLAW, a computer-as-sisted legal research service; West's Le-gal Directory(TM); West CD-ROM

Telephone: (703) 854-3400, Toll Free: (800) 872-0001, E-Mail: accuracy@usatoday.com, Web Site: www.usatoday.com
Pres & Publr: Larry Kramer
Sr VP, Adv: Lee Jones
Dir, Inside Sls & New Bus: Ellen Dobrin
Dir, Commun: Heidi Zimmerman
Conducts Business: U.S.
Primary Market Served: Business

Direct response classified advertising space marketed to mail order & catalog advertisers.

UNITY SCHOOL OF CHRISTIANITY

1901 NW Blue Pkwy
Unity Village, MO 64065-0001
Telephone: (816) 254-3550, FAX: (816) 251-3554, E-Mail: unity@unityonline.org, Web Site: www.unityonline.org
Sr Dir Mktg: Kim West
VP Mktg: Tim Ipema
Dir: Charles Rickert Filmore
Dir: Rev. Gregory Guice
Conducts Business: Worldwide
Employees: 600
Primary Market Served: Consumer
Catalog available online
Direct online sales

Publisher of four different religious magazines sold to consumers by subscription.

UNIVERSITY OF CHICAGO PRESS

1427 E 60th St
Chicago, IL 60637
Telephone: (773) 702-7700, FAX: (773) 702-9756, Web Site: www.press.uchicago.edu
Dir: Garrett P. Kiely
Conducts Business: U.S., Canada, U.K., Europe, Japan, Australia
Employees: 200
Primary Market Served: Business & Consumer
Catalog available online
Direct online sales
Advertising/Marketing Budget Related to Direct Marketing: 26-50%
Direct Marketing ad budget: $400,000
Direct Mail: 100%

Publishers of scholarly books, journals & references.

UNIVERSITY OF OKLAHOMA PRESS

4100 28th Ave NW
Norman, OK 73069-8218

Toll Free: (800) 627-7377, FAX: (405) 364-5798, Web Site: www.oupress.com
Dir: John Drayton
Editor-in-Chief & Assoc Dir: Charles E. Rankin
Conducts Business: Worldwide
Primary Market Served: Business & Consumer
Catalog available online
Direct online sales
Direct Marketing ad budget:
Direct Mail: 100%
Founded: 1929

Publish books.

UNIVERSITY PRESS OF AMERICA INC

Div. of D. Rowman & Littlefield Publishing Group
4501 Forbes Blvd (Suite 200)
Lanham, MD 20706
Telephone: (301) 459-3366, Toll Free: (800) 462-6420, FAX: (301) 429-5748, E-Mail: custserv@rowman.com, Web Site: www.univpress.com
Bus Dir, Mktg: Dean Roxanis
Conducts Business: Worldwide
Employees: 10
Primary Market Served: Business & Consumer
Catalog available online
Direct online sales
Advertising/Marketing Budget Related to Direct Marketing: 0-25%
Direct Marketing ad budget:
Direct Mail: 50%
Online: 50%
Founded: 1975
Gross sales or billing: $3,000,000

Publisher of scholarly monographs, college texts, professional books & reprints. Owns National Book Network, distributor of independent trade book publishers.

URBAN RESPONSE LLC

Subs. of James Direct, Inc.
500 S Prospect Ave
Hartville, OH 44632-9403
Telephone: (330) 877-0800, Toll Free: (866) 550-3501, FAX: (330) 877-0802
Pres: James DiCola
Primary Market Served: Consumer

VALUE LINE PUBLISHING INC

Div. of Value Line Inc
220 E 42nd St
New York, NY 10017
Telephone: (212) 907-1500, FAX: (212) 818-9747, Web Site: www.valueline.com
Mktg Dir: Lawrence Freeman

Conducts Business: Worldwide
Employees: 340
Primary Market Served: Business & Consumer
Direct online sales
Advertising/Marketing Budget Related to Direct Marketing: 76-100%
Founded: 1931

Investment publications, electronic products, mutual funds, asset management & investment research.

VAN DAM INC

121 W 27th St (Ste 1102)
New York, NY 10001-6261
Telephone: (212) 929-0416, Toll Free: (800) UNFOLDS, FAX: (212) 929-0426, E-Mail: info@vandam.com, Web Site: www.vandam.com
Pres: Stephan C. VanDam
Conducts Business: Worldwide
Primary Market Served: Business & Consumer

Produce pop-up maps & guides.

VERMONT MEDIA PUBLISHING CO

Deerfield Valley News
PO Box 310
West Dover, VT 05356-0310
Telephone: (802) 464-3388, FAX: (802) 464-7255, E-Mail: publisher@vermontmedia.com, Web Site: www.dvalnews.com
Publr: Randy Capitani
Gen Mgr: Victoria Capitani
Founded: 1966

Southern Vermont newspaper publishing company.

THE VESTAL PRESS LTD

Div. of The Rowman & Littlefield Publishing Group
4501 Forbes Blvd (Suite 200)
Lanham, MD 20706
Telephone: (301) 459-3366, Toll Free: (800) 462-6420, FAX: (301) 429-5746, E-Mail: sburnett@rowman.com, Web Site: www.nbnbooks.com
Sr VP NBN Mktg: Marianne Bohr
Dir Sls Admin: Lita Orner
VP Mktg: Linda May
Conducts Business: Worldwide
Employees: 150
Primary Market Served: Consumer
Catalog available online
Indirect online sales
Advertising/Marketing Budget Related to Direct Marketing: 0-25%
Direct Marketing ad budget: $10,000
Direct Mail: 70%
Magazines: 25%
Newspapers: 5%

Founded: 1961

Publish & sell books on technical antiquarian hobbies, early entertainment history (including film), woodcarving.

VISUAL REFERENCE PUBLICATIONS

Subs. of Milton B Conhaim Inc
302 Fifth Ave
New York, NY 10001
Telephone: (212) 279-7000, Toll Free: (800) 251-4545, FAX: (212) 279-7014
VP, Mktg: John Burr
VP & Publr: Lawrence Fuersich
Conducts Business: Worldwide
Employees: 30
Primary Market Served: Business

Publications & books for retailers, advertising agencies, designers & architects.

WALCH PUBLISHING

40 Walch Dr
Portland, ME 04103-1286
Telephone: (207) 772-2846, Toll Free: (800) 558-2846, FAX: (207) 772-3105, E-Mail: customerservice@ walch.com, Web Site: www.walch.com
CEO: John Thoreson
Pres: Al Noyes
Controller Dir Fin: Jim Walker
Publr: Betty Merti
Conducts Business: U.S., Canada, U.K., Singapore
Employees: 35
Primary Market Served: Business & Consumer
Catalog available online
Indirect online sales
Advertising/Marketing Budget Related to Direct Marketing: 76-100%
Direct Marketing ad budget:
Direct Mail: 96%
Magazines: 4%
Founded: 1927
Gross sales or billing: $6,000,000

Educational materials for teachers & students in middle school & high school; sell directly to teachers as well as through distributors & retail stores.

WALKER PUBLISHING CO INC

Div. of Bloomsbury Publishing
175 Fifth Ave (Frnt 4)
New York, NY 10010-7728
Telephone: (212) 727-8300, Toll Free: (800) 289-2553, FAX: (212) 727-0984
Pres: George Gibson
CFO & Controller: Theodore Rosenfeld

Conducts Business: Worldwide
Employees: 30
Primary Market Served: Business & Consumer

Publisher of books; adult & juvenile fiction & non-fiction.

WARNER PRESS

1201 E Fifth St
Anderson, IN 46012
Telephone: (765) 644-7721, Toll Free: (800) 741-7721, FAX: (765) 640-8005, E-Mail: wporders@ warnerpress.org, Web Site: www. warnerpress.com
Sls Mgr: Regina Jackson
Primary Market Served: Business & Consumer
Founded: 1881

Religious publications.

WARREN COMMUNICATIONS NEWS

2115 Ward Ct NW
Washington, DC 20037-1209
Telephone: (202) 872-9200, Toll Free: (800) 771-9202, FAX: (202) 318-8350, E-Mail: info@warren-news. com, Web Site: www.warren-news. com
Pres & Editor: Dan Warren
Exec Publr & Chmn: Paul Warren
Publr: Albert Warren
Assoc Mng Editor: Edie Herman
Sr Editor: Mark Seavy
Sr Editor: Jeff Berman
Conducts Business: U.S.
Employees: 50
Primary Market Served: Business
Catalog available online
Direct online sales
Advertising/Marketing Budget Related to Direct Marketing: 26-50%
Founded: 1945

Publish reference books & newsletters about the telecommunications industry.

WARREN, GORHAM & LAMONT INC

Div. of Thomson Reuters
195 Broadway
New York, NY 10007-3100
Telephone: (617) 423-2020, Web Site: ria.thomsonreuters.com
Telemktg Dir: Dan Antman
Conducts Business: U.S., Canada
Primary Market Served: Business
Advertising/Marketing Budget Related to Direct Marketing: 76-100%

Publishing firm specializing in tax & legal accounting, IS & HR publications for professionals.

THE WASHINGTON MONTHLY CO

1200 18th St NW (Suite 330)
Washington, DC 20036-2556
Telephone: (202) 955-9010, FAX: (202) 955-9011, E-Mail: editors@ washingtonmonthly.com, Web Site: www.washingtonmonthly.com
Publr: Diane Straus Tucker
Ed-in-Chief: Paul Glastris
VP, Opers & Mktg: Carl Iseli
VP, Circulation & Bus: Claire Iseli
Conducts Business: U.S.
Employees: 8
Primary Market Served: Business & Consumer
Founded: 1969

National magazine covering politics, government & public affairs.

THE WASHINGTON POST

Div. of The Washington Post Co
1150 15th St NW
Washington, DC 20071
Telephone: (202) 334-6000, Toll Free: (800) 627-1150, E-Mail: letters@ washpost.com, Web Site: www. washingtonpost.com
Chmn & CEO: Donald E. Graham
VP at Large: Leonard Downie Jr.
Deputy Mng Editor: Milton Coleman
Conducts Business: U.S., Europe
Employees: 3,600
Primary Market Served: Consumer
Direct online sales
Advertising/Marketing Budget Related to Direct Marketing: 0-25%
Founded: 1977

Newspaper publisher.

WASHINGTON POST DIGITAL

1150 15th St NW
Washington, DC 20071
Telephone: (202) 334-9900
Mng Editor, Digital: Emilio Garcia-Ruiz
Primary Market Served: Business & Consumer

THE WASHINGTONIAN

1828 "L" St NW (Suite 200)
Washington, DC 20036
Telephone: (202) 296-3600, E-Mail: editorial@washingtonian.com, Web Site: www.washingtonian.com
Circ Dir & Controller: Michael Johnson
Adv Dir: Edward Mansfield
Conducts Business: U.S.
Employees: 50
Primary Market Served: Consumer
Catalog available online

Advertising/Marketing Budget Related
to Direct Marketing: 0-25%
Founded: 1965

Monthly magazine for an educated &
affluent consumer audience.

WATERING INC/HEMMINGS MOTOR NEWS
222 W Main St
Bennington, VT 05201-2103
Telephone: (802) 442-3101, Toll Free:
(800) 227-4373, FAX: (802) 447-
1561, E-Mail: hmnmail@hemmings.
com, Web Site: www.hemmings.com
Chmn Bd: Ray Shaw
Conducts Business: Worldwide
Employees: 100
Primary Market Served: Consumer
Catalog available online
Direct online sales
Advertising/Marketing Budget Related
to Direct Marketing: 51-75%
Founded: 1954
Gross sales or billing: $32,000,000

Publisher of periodicals & books for
the antique, classic & special interest
auto hobby market.

WEISS RESEARCH INC
Subs. of Weiss Group LLC
4400 Northcorp Pkwy
Palm Beach Gardens, FL 33410
Telephone: (561) 627-3300, Toll Free:
(800) 291-8545, FAX: (561) 625-
6685, Web Site: www.weissinc.com
CEO & Pres: Martin D. Weiss Ph. D.
Conducts Business: U.S.
Employees: 200
Primary Market Served: Business &
Consumer
Catalog available online
Direct online sales
Founded: 1971

Publisher of financial newsletters with
economic & stock market analysis.

WENNER MEDIA LLC
1290 Ave of the Americas (fl 2)
New York, NY 10104-0298
Telephone: (212) 484-1616, FAX:
(212) 484-1713
Chmn Bd & Pres: Jann S. Wenner
COO: John Gruber
Conducts Business: U.S., Canada
Employees: 300
Primary Market Served: Business &
Consumer
Founded: 1967
Gross sales or billing: $33,400,000

Publisher of Rolling Stone Magazine,
US, The Entertainment Magazine &
Men's Journal.

WESTGROUP
Div. of The Thomson Corp
610 Opperman Dr
Eagan, MN 55123-1340
Toll Free: (800) 344-5008, Web Site:
www.westgroup.com
Pres & CEO Westgroup: Brian Hall
VP Strategic Devel: Lee Bongiolatti
Conducts Business: U.S., Canada, Eu-
rope, Japan
Primary Market Served: Business
Advertising/Marketing Budget Related
to Direct Marketing: 26-50%
Direct Marketing ad budget:
Direct Mail: 85%
Magazines: 5%
Telephone: 10%

Sells quality law books in areas of the
law having national & international appeal. Sales are primarily to practicing
attorneys.

WESTWOOD PUBLISHING CO
Div. of The Gil Boyne Group Inc
700 S Central Ave
Glendale, CA 91204
Telephone: (818) 242-1159, FAX:
(818) 247-9379
Pres: Mark T. Gilboyne
Gen Mgr: Jon Younquist
Conducts Business: U.S., Canada, Ma-
laysia, New Zealand, South Africa,
Australia, U.K.
Employees: 6
Primary Market Served: Business &
Consumer
Direct Marketing ad budget: $130,000
Direct Mail: 70%
Magazines: 30%
Gross sales or billing: $835,000

Mail order publisher of hypnotism,
mind power & holistic studies books.
Cassettes, courses & videotapes. Operate state licensed vocational school to
train hypnotherapists.

WHITE MANE PUBLISHING CO INC
73 W Burd St
Shippensburg, PA 17257-1259
Telephone: (717) 532-2237, Toll Free:
(888) 948-6263, FAX: (717) 532-
6110, E-Mail: marketing@
whitemane.com, Web Site: www.
whitemane.com
Opers Dir: Denise Logan
Conducts Business: U.S.
Employees: 10
Primary Market Served: Business &
Consumer
Catalog available online
Indirect online sales
Advertising/Marketing Budget Related
to Direct Marketing: 0-25%

Direct Marketing ad budget:
Direct Mail: 50%
Magazines: 20%
Newspapers: 15%
TV/Radio: 5%
Telephone: 10%
Founded: 1987

MICHAEL WIESE PRODUCTIONS
3940 Laurel Canyon Blvd (#1111)
Studio City, CA 91604
Telephone: (818) 379-8799, Toll Free:
(800) 833-5738, FAX: (818) 986-
3408, Web Site: www.mwp.com
Pres: Michael Wiese
VP: Ken Lee
Conducts Business: Worldwide
Employees: 3
Primary Market Served: Business &
Consumer
Catalog available online
Direct online sales
Advertising/Marketing Budget Related
to Direct Marketing: 0-25%
Direct Marketing ad budget:
Direct Mail: 80%
Magazines: 20%

Health & educational infomercials,
books, videos & audios & books for
film & video professionals. Also, network television documentaries.

WILDLIFE EDUCATION LTD
1260 Audubon Rd
Park Hills, KY 41011-1904
Telephone: (858) 513-7600, FAX:
(858) 513-7660, E-Mail: animals@
zoobooks.com, Web Site: www.
zoobooks.com
Publr: Ed Shadek
Sls Mgr: Kurt Von Hertsenberg
Online Mktg Mgr: Debi S. Ives
Circ Mgr: Jay Hillis
Conducts Business: Worldwide
Primary Market Served: Consumer
Direct online sales
Founded: 1980

Publish wildlife magazines and books
for children.

JOHN WILEY & SONS CANADA LTD
Subs. of John Wiley & Sons Inc
5353 Dundaf St W
Etobicoke, ON, Canada M9B 6H8
Telephone: (416) 236-4433, FAX:
(416) 236-4448, Web Site: www.
wiley.com
Pres: Diane Wood
Prodn Mgr: Karen Bryan
Conducts Business: Canada
Employees: 90

Primary Market Served: Business

Professional, reference & trade books sold to educational & research institutions, industry professionals & libraries.

JOHN WILEY & SONS INC

111 River St
Hoboken, NJ 07030-5774
Telephone: (201) 748-6000, FAX: (201) 748-6088, E-Mail: info@wiley. com, Web Site: www.wiley.com
Chmn Bd: Peter Booth Riley
Pres & CEO: William J. Pesce
Sr VP, Corp Commun: Deborah E. Wiley
Dir: Bradford Wiley II
VP, Retail Sls: Jack Day
Conducts Business: U.S., Canada, Europe, Australia, India, S.E. Asia
Employees: 4,900
Primary Market Served: Business & Consumer
Catalog available online
Direct online sales
Advertising/Marketing Budget Related to Direct Marketing: 51-75%
Direct Marketing ad budget:
Direct Mail: 95%
Magazines: 5%
Founded: 1807
Gross sales or billing: $1,100,000,000

Publisher of scientific, technical, business law, professional medical books & other related materials.

WILLIS MUSIC CO

7380 Industrial Rd, PO Box 548
Florence, KY 41042-0548
Telephone: (859) 283-2050, Toll Free: (800) 354-9799, FAX: (859) 283-1784, E-Mail: ordpt@willis-music. com, Web Site: www.willismusic. com
Owner: Edward R. Cranley
Pres: Kevin Cranley
Conducts Business: Worldwide
Employees: 150
Primary Market Served: Business & Consumer
Catalog available online
Direct Marketing ad budget:
Direct Mail: 50%
Magazines: 15%
Newspapers: 25%
TV/Radio: 10%
Founded: 1899

Music publishers. Also, musical instruments & accessories, music & stationery racks, musical gifts & collectors' items.

THE HW WILSON CO

950 University Ave
Bronx, NY 10452

Telephone: (718) 588-8400, Toll Free: (800) 367-6770, FAX: (800) 590-1617, E-Mail: custserv@hwwilson. com, Web Site: www.hwwilson.com
Pres & CEO: Harold Regan
VP, Sls & Mktg: Deborah V. Loeding
Conducts Business: Worldwide
Employees: 500
Primary Market Served: Business
Catalog available online
Direct online sales
Founded: 1898

Publisher of indexes, abstracts, reference books, videotapes, online database vendor & CD-ROM products.

WINN DEVON

aka CAP & Winn Devon; Div of Encore Art Group
6311 Westminster Hwy (Unit 110)
Richmond, BC, Canada V7C 4V4
Telephone: (206) 763-9544, Toll Free: (800) 875-4150, FAX: (206) 762-1389, Web Site: www.winndevon. com
Pres: Lisa Krieger
Creative Dir: Niki Krieger
Conducts Business: Worldwide
Employees: 60
Primary Market Served: Business
Founded: 1977
Gross sales or billing: $4,400,000

Publisher & distributor of original artworks, fine art posters and limited edition prints.

WINSLOW PUBLISHING

550 Eglinton Ave W
Toronto, ON, Canada M5N 3A8
Telephone: (416) 789-4733, E-Mail: winslow@interlog.com, Web Site: www.winslowpublishing.com
Owner & Pres: Michelle West
VP: Lawrence Merkur
Conducts Business: U.S., Canada
Employees: 2
Primary Market Served: Business & Consumer
Catalog available online
Indirect online sales
Advertising/Marketing Budget Related to Direct Marketing: 0-25%
Direct Marketing ad budget:
Direct Mail: 100%
Founded: 1981

Publish & sell books. Also, sell craft supplies & novelties.

WOLFE PUBLISHING CO INC

2180 Gulfstream (Suite A)
Prescott, AZ 86301-6182

Telephone: (928) 445-7810, Toll Free: (800) 899-7810, FAX: (928) 778-5124, E-Mail: wolfepub@riflemag. com, Web Site: www.riflemagazine. com
Pres & Publr: Mark Harris
Conducts Business: Worldwide
Employees: 11
Primary Market Served: Business & Consumer
Catalog available online
Founded: 1965

We publish magazines, books & art prints. Product is sold to dealers & retail consumers.

WOMAN'S MISSIONARY UNION

100 Missionary Ridge, PO Box 830010
Birmingham, AL 35283-0010
Telephone: (205) 991-8100, FAX: (205) 991-4990, E-Mail: email@ wmu.org, Web Site: www.wmu.org
Mktg Svcs Dir: Dolores Jackson
Conducts Business: U.S.
Employees: 160
Primary Market Served: Consumer
Catalog available online
Direct online sales
Advertising/Marketing Budget Related to Direct Marketing: 0-25%
Founded: 1888

Publisher of Christian Missions materials, including New Hope books.

WOMAN'S DAY SPECIAL INTEREST PUBLICATIONS

Subs. of Hachette Filipacchi Magazines Publications Inc
1633 Broadway (42nd fl)
New York, NY 10019
Telephone: (212) 767-6000, FAX: (212) 767-5612, Web Site: www. womensday.com
Assoc Publr: Lynne Dominick
Conducts Business: U.S.
Primary Market Served: Consumer

Publisher of 39 special interest consumer magazines sold exclusively at supermarkets & retail outlets.

WOODALL PUBLISHING CO LP

Affinity Group
2575 Vista Del Mar Dr
Ventura, CA 93001
Telephone: (805) 667-4100, Toll Free: (800) 323-9076, FAX: (805) 667-4468, Web Site: www.woodalls.com
Chmn Bd, Affinity: Stephen Adams
CEO, Pres, Dir, Affinity: Michael A. Shneider
CFO & Sr VP: Thomas F. Wolfe

Pres & CEO Woodall: Linda L.
  ProFaiser
Pres & CEO Camping World: Marcus
  Lemonis
Conducts Business: U.S., Canada
Employees: 55
Primary Market Served: Consumer
Direct Marketing ad budget:
Direct Mail: 50%
Magazines: 10%
Newspapers: 40%
Founded: 1935

Monthly publications & annual directory for the Campground Industry.

WORDRIGHT ENTERPRISES INC
431 Dogwood Terr
Buffalo Grove, IL 60089-1820
Telephone: (847) 215-5190, Web Site:
  www.globalsources.com
Trade Shows Mgr: Alexis Schmookler
Conducts Business: Worldwide
Primary Market Served: Business

Business to business e-commerce.

THE WORLD BANK
1818 "H" St NW
Washington, DC 20433
Telephone: (202) 473-1000, FAX:
  (202) 477-6391, Web Site: www.
  worldbank.org
Pres: Jim Yong Kim
Media Mgr: Amy L. Stilwell
Mgr Corp Commun: Carl Hanton
Press Officer: Cynthia Case
Sr Commun Officer: Maya Brahmam
Conducts Business: Worldwide
Employees: 10,000
Primary Market Served: Business &
  Consumer
Catalog available online
Indirect online sales
Advertising/Marketing Budget Related
  to Direct Marketing: 0-25%
Founded: 1945

Publications department disseminates
economic & development research produced by World Bank.

WORLD BOOK INC
233 N Michigan Ave (Suite 2000)
Chicago, IL 60601-5805
Telephone: (312) 729-5800, Toll Free:
  (800) 255-1750, FAX: (312) 729-
  5600, Web Site: www.worldbook.
  com
Pres: Don Keller
Conducts Business: U.S., Canada
Employees: 178
Primary Market Served: Consumer
Catalog available online
Indirect online sales

Advertising/Marketing Budget Related
  to Direct Marketing: 51-75%
Direct Marketing ad budget:
  $6,000,000
Direct Mail: $1,000,000
Magazines: $2,000,000
Newspapers: $1,000,000
TV/Radio: $1,000,000
Telephone: $1,000,000
Founded: 1917
Gross sales or billing: $31,000,000

Market encyclopedias (print & CD-ROM) & other reference resources to consumers, schools & libraries.

WORLD PUBLICATIONS INC
460 N Orlando Ave (Suite 200)
Winter Park, FL 32789
Telephone: (407) 628-4802, FAX:
  (407) 628-7061, Web Site: www.
  worldpub.net
Chmn: Jonas Bonnier
CEO: Terry Snow
COO: Dan Altman
VP Consumer Mktg: Bruce Miller
VP Production Opers: Lisa Earlywine
Conducts Business: U.S., Canada
Employees: 65
Primary Market Served: Business &
  Consumer
Catalog available online
Direct online sales
Advertising/Marketing Budget Related
  to Direct Marketing: 76-100%
Gross sales or billing: $350,000,000

Consumer sports-related publications
& trade publications for the sports &
boating industries, food & garden.

WORLDVU LLC
1906 E Pratt St
Baltimore, MD 21231-1925
Telephone: (410) 522-4223, FAX:
  (410) 522-4233, E-Mail: info@
  worldvu.com, Web Site: www.
  worldvu.com
Pres & Publr: Merry Law
Assoc Publr: Wayne Winkler
Conducts Business: Worldwide
Employees: 3
Primary Market Served: Business
Catalog available online
Indirect online sales
Advertising/Marketing Budget Related
  to Direct Marketing: 76-100%
Direct Marketing ad budget:
Direct Mail: 96%
Magazines: 2%
Telephone: 2%

Publisher of practical information for
businesses worldwide, including the
Guide to Worldwide Postal-Code Address Formats.

WRITER'S DIGEST BOOKS
Div. of F&W Publications
10151 Carver Rd (Suite 200)
Blue Ash, OH 45242-4760
Telephone: (513) 531-2690, Toll Free:
  (800) 666-0963, Web Site: www.
  fwpublications.com
Pres Book Publ & Book Clubs: William Budge Wallis
Conducts Business: Worldwide
Employees: 300
Primary Market Served: Business &
  Consumer
Direct online sales
Advertising/Marketing Budget Related
  to Direct Marketing: 0-25%
Founded: 1921

Publish instructional books for writers,
artists, songwriters, woodworkers &
photographers.

WYANDOTTE WEST COMMUNICATIONS INC
PO Box 12003
Kansas City, KS 66112-0003
Telephone: (913) 788-5565, FAX:
  (913) 788-9812, E-Mail: news@
  wyandottewest.com, Web Site: www.
  wyandottewest.com
Pres: Murrel W. Bland
Gen Mgr & Ed: Joe Keefhaver
Sls & Mktg Mgr: Jamie Ralston
Sls: Mickey Johns
Production Ed: Sarah Abend
Conducts Business: U.S.
Employees: 7
Primary Market Served: Business &
  Consumer
Catalog available online
Direct online sales
Advertising/Marketing Budget Related
  to Direct Marketing: 0-25%
Direct Marketing ad budget: $15,000
Direct Mail: 10%
Newspapers: 10%
Telephone: 80%
Founded: 1968
Gross sales or billing: $465,000

Community weekly newspaper. Sell
subscriptions to consumers & ads to
consumers and businesses.

WYCLIFFE BIBLE TRANSLATORS
7500 W Camp Wisdom Rd
Dallas, TX 75236-5629
Telephone: (972) 708-7522, Web Site:
  www.wycliffe.org
Sustained Giving Mgr: Pixie Christensen
Primary Market Served: Consumer

YANKEE PUBLISHING INC
1121 Main St

Dublin, NH 03444
Telephone: (603) 563-8111, FAX:
(603) 563-8732, Web Site: www.
yankeemagazine.com
Chmn: C. Robertson Trowbridge
Conducts Business: U.S.
Employees: 100
Primary Market Served: Consumer

Publisher of Yankee Magazine, Old
Farmers Almanac, Travel Guide to
New England.

YELLOW BOOK USA

Div. of hibu Inc.
398 RXR Plaza
Uniondale, NY 11556-0398
Telephone: (516) 730-1900, Toll Free:
(800) 666-8230, FAX: (845) 278-
3299, Web Site: www.yellowbook.
com
Chief Comml Officer & CEO, hibu
US: Bob Gregerson
Conducts Business: U.S.
Employees: 35
Primary Market Served: Business
Founded: 1972

Publish local telephone directories &
other specialized publications.

YOGA JOURNAL / ACTIVE
INTEREST MEDIA

475 Sansome St (Suite 850)
San Francisco, CA 94111-3135
Telephone: (415) 591-0555, Web Site:
www.yogajournal.com
Grp Circulation Dir: Barbara Besser

ZIFF DAVIS MEDIA INC

28 E 28th St (11th fl)
New York, NY 10016
Telephone: (212) 503-5100, FAX:
(212) 503-5023, Web Site: www.
ziffdavis.com
CEO: Vivek Shah
COO: Steve Horowitz
Editor in Chief: Dan Costa
CFO: Andy Johns
Sr VP, Sls & Mktg: Eric Koepele
Primary Market Served: Business &
Consumer

Magazine publisher.

ZONDERVAN CORP

Div. of Harper Collins Publishers
5300 Patterson Ave SE
Grand Rapids, MI 49530
Telephone: (616) 698-6900, Toll Free:
(800) 727-3060, FAX: (616) 698-
3235, Web Site: www.zondervan.
com
Pres & CEO: Bruce Ryskamp
EVP & CFO: Gary Wicker
EVP: Scott Bolinder
Conducts Business: Worldwide

Employees: 340
Primary Market Served: Business
Catalog available online
Direct online sales
Founded: 1932
Gross sales or billing: $38,600,000

Company specializing in the publication & sale of books, Bibles, curriculum & software.

Subscription Agencies (18)

This section lists agencies that distribute, sell or market magazines and newspapers to various segments of the public and industry.

AMERICAN PREFERRED READER'S SERVICE INC

1975 E Sunrise Blvd Ste 800
Fort Lauderdale, FL 33304-1455
Telephone: (954) 767-6022, Toll Free: (888) 482-2443, FAX: (954) 767-6065, E-Mail: jfarrell@amerpref.com, Web Site: www.amerpref.com
Pres: James H. Farrell Sr.
VP Mktg: Caryn Farrell
Agency Acct Exec: Leslie S. Smith
Conducts Business: U.S.
Employees: 100
Primary Market Served: Business & Consumer
Founded: 1985
Gross sales or billing: $2,000,000

Distribute family oriented magazines, wholesale & retail.

BELLTOWER TECHNOLOGIES LLC

2089 N Collins Blvd (Suite 200)
Richardson, TX 75080
Telephone: (214) 220-8000, Web Site: www.belltowertech.com
CEO: Michael Martin
Sr VP Devel: Shaun Dawson
VP & Vice Chmn Devel: Tim Klein
Primary Market Served: Business
Indirect online sales
Founded: 2002

Food recall and withdrawal communication solutions provider.

COMMUNICATION RESOURCES INC

23 Market
Beaufort, SC 29906-9184
Telephone: (330) 266-1489, Toll Free: (800) 992-2144, FAX: (330) 493-3158, E-Mail: service@comresources.com, Web Site: www.comresources.com
Pres: Randall S. Coy
COO: Kelly Brown
Conducts Business: U.S., Canada
Employees: 25
Primary Market Served: Business & Consumer
Advertising/Marketing Budget Related to Direct Marketing: 76-100%

Periodical publications & newsletter related materials.

CUSTOMIZED NEWSPAPER ADVERTISING

aka CNA

319 E Fifth St
Des Moines, IA 50309
Telephone: (515) 244-2145, Toll Free: (800) 227-7636, FAX: (515) 244-4855, Web Site: www.cnaads.com
Exec Dir: Bill Monroe
Sales & Mktg Dir: Susan Patterson Plank
Asst Dir: Chris Mudge
Employees: 15
Primary Market Served: Business

CNA facilitates multi-newspaper and on-line planning and placement locally or nationwide.

DAYTON DAILY NEWS

Div. of Cox Enterprises
1611 S Main St, Cox Ohio Publishing, Media Ctr
Dayton, OH 45409-2547
Telephone: (937) 222-5700, Toll Free: (888) 397-6397, FAX: (937) 225-2153, E-Mail: daytondaily@coxohio.com, Web Site: www.daytondailynews.com
Publr: Kevin Riley
Conducts Business: U.S.
Employees: 1,000
Primary Market Served: Business & Consumer
Advertising/Marketing Budget Related to Direct Marketing: 0-25%
Gross sales or billing: $58,300,000

Sells newspapers.

DETROIT NEWSPAPERS

615 W Lafayette Blvd
Detroit, MI 48226
Telephone: (313) 222-2300, FAX: (313) 496-5400, E-Mail: newsroom@detnews.com, Web Site: www.freep.com
Editor & Publr: Jonathan Wolman
Managing Editor: Donald W Nauss
Deputy Managing Editor: Gary Miles
Primary Market Served: Business & Consumer

Agent for Detroit News & Detroit Free Press.

EBSCO RECEPTION ROOM SUBSCRIPTION SERVICES

Div. of EBSCO Investment Services Inc
PO Box 830460
Birmingham, AL 35283-0460

Telephone: (205) 991-1409, Toll Free: (800) 527-5901, FAX: (205) 995-1621, Web Site: www.ebsco.com/errss
Pres: J.T. Stephens
VP & Gen Mgr: Jack H. Breard
Office Mgr: Susie Sims
Conducts Business: U.S., Canada
Employees: 55
Primary Market Served: Business
Direct online sales
Advertising/Marketing Budget Related to Direct Marketing: 76-100%
Direct Marketing ad budget:
Direct Mail: 100%
Founded: 1980

Provide professional offices, barber & beauty shops & business offices with one-order, one-invoice purchasing of magazines & journal subscriptions at savings up to 50%.

IN-SYNC PUBLICATIONS

800 Knob Hill Ave
Redondo Beach, CA 90277
Telephone: (310) 543-9045, FAX: (310) 543-9035, E-Mail: insyncpubs@aol.com, Web Site: www.insyncpubs.com
Owner: Robert Christy
VP: Julie Christy
Conducts Business: Worldwide
Employees: 3
Primary Market Served: Business & Consumer
Catalog available online
Indirect online sales
Advertising/Marketing Budget Related to Direct Marketing: 76-100%
Direct Marketing ad budget:
Direct Mail: 100%
Founded: 1987
Gross sales or billing: $180,000

Sales & service of motion picture & video equipment to the professional market. Our newspaper tries to put buyer & seller together.

MERRILL CORP

Subs. of Merrill Corp
4110 Clearwater Rd
Saint Cloud, MN 56301
Telephone: (320) 656-5000, FAX: (320) 656-5163
CEO & Chmn: John W Castro
COO, DataSite & Intl: Rick R Atterbury
Primary Market Served: Business

Company print program.

O'CURRANCE INC
11747 S Lonepeak Pkwy (Suite 100)
Draper, UT 84020-6876
Telephone: (801) 736-0500, Toll Free:
(888) 628-7726, FAX: (801) 736-
0510, E-Mail: sales@ocurrance.com,
Web Site: www.ocurance.com
CEO: Pankaj Dhanuka
Dir Sales: Adam Miller
Primary Market Served: Business &
Consumer
Founded: 1994

Call center.

PERIODICAL PUBLISHER'S SERVICE BUREAU INC
653 W Fallbrook Ave
Fresno, CA 93711
Telephone: (419) 626-0623, Toll Free:
(888) 206-0350, FAX: (419) 626-
4576, Web Site: www.ppsb.com
Pres & CEO: Richard Hasselbaum
Conducts Business: Worldwide
Primary Market Served: Business &
Consumer
Catalog available online
Founded: 1910

Subscription sales & reader service
processing.

THE PLAIN DEALER
1801 Superior Ave E
Cleveland, OH 44114-2107
Telephone: (216) 999-5000, Toll Free:
(800) 362-0727, FAX: (216) 999-
6356, Web Site: www.plaindealer.
com
Pres & Publr: Terrence C.Z. Egger
Editor: Debra Adams Simmons
Sr VP Sales & Mktg: Andrea Hogben
Managing Editor: Thomas Fladung
Dir Mktg & Community Affairs: Shir-
ley D Stineman
Conducts Business: U.S.
Employees: 1,520
Primary Market Served: Consumer
Catalog available online
Direct online sales
Advertising/Marketing Budget Related
to Direct Marketing: 0-25%
Direct Marketing ad budget:
Direct Mail: 10%
Magazines: 5%
Newspapers: 50%
Online: 15%
TV/Radio: 10%
Telephone: 10%
Founded: 1842
Gross sales or billing: $220,000,000

Ohio's largest newspaper. Selling ads,
classifieds, subscriptions, article reprints online.

PUBLISHERS CLEARING HOUSE
382 Channel Dr
Port Washington, NY 11050-2297
Telephone: (516) 883-5432, FAX:
(516) 767-4567, E-Mail: cirving@
pch.com, Web Site: www.pch.com
Chmn: Robin B. Smith
Pres & CEO: Andrew Goldberg
Conducts Business: U.S., Canada, U.K.
Employees: 500
Primary Market Served: Consumer
Catalog available online
Direct online sales
Advertising/Marketing Budget Related
to Direct Marketing: 76-100%
Direct Marketing ad budget:
Direct Mail: 90%
Telephone: 10%
Founded: 1953
Gross sales or billing: $625,000,000

Publishers Clearing House is a leading
multi-channel direct marketer of value-
based consumer products and magazines and a respected leader in the direct marketing industry.

RAPID CITY JOURNAL
507 Main St
Rapid City, SD 57701-2733
Telephone: (605) 394-8300, FAX:
(605) 394-8462, E-Mail:
classifieds@rapidcityjournal.com,
Web Site: www.rapidcityjournal.com
Publr: Barbara Soderlin
Online Sls Mgr: Debbie Renner
Interim Editor: Justin Breen
Interactive Products Mgr: Christopher
Donahue
HR Mgr: Laurel Grove
Employees: 220
Primary Market Served: Business &
Consumer
Catalog available online
Gross sales or billing: $19,100,000

Sells to western South Dakota area.
Printing, want ads, newspapers.

SUBSCRIPTIONAGENCY. COM INC
365 E Central Ave
Winter Haven, FL 33880
Telephone: (863) 229-2557, Toll Free:
(866) 590-6247, FAX: (866) 890-
6247, E-Mail: info@
subscriptionagency.com, Web Site:
www.subscriptionagency.com
Pres: Melanie Truesdell
Conducts Business: U.S.
Primary Market Served: Business &
Consumer
Catalog available online
Direct online sales
Founded: 2003

Gross sales or billing: $2,600,000
Magazine subscription clearinghouse &
fulfillment agency.

SYNAPSE GROUP INC
Subs. of Time Inc.
225 High Ridge Rd, East Building
Stamford, CT 06905-3038
Telephone: (203) 595-8255, FAX:
(203) 329-8237, E-Mail:
webmaster@synapsemail.com, Web
Site: www.synapsegroupinc.com
CEO: Jeff Blatt
Sr VP Mktg: Michel Wright
EVP Sales & Partnership Mktg: Sebas-
tien Bilodeau
Conducts Business: U.S.
Employees: 300
Primary Market Served: Consumer
Advertising/Marketing Budget Related
to Direct Marketing: 76-100%
Direct Marketing ad budget:
Direct Mail: 100%
Founded: 1991

Marketing.

TIME OUT NEW YORK
475 10th Ave (12th fl)
New York, NY 10018
Telephone: (646) 432-3000, FAX:
(212) 677-9665, E-Mail: tnew@
kable.com, Web Site: www.timeout.
com/newyork/
Mktg Dir: Michael Rucker
Editor: Michael Martin
Primary Market Served: Consumer

Weekly arts and entertainment guide to
New York City.

TIMES PUBLISHING CO
205 W 12th St
Erie, PA 16534-0011
Telephone: (814) 870-1600, FAX:
(814) 870-1808, E-Mail: terry.
cascioli@timesnews.com
Pres & Publr: Rosanne Cheeseman
VP Sls & Mktg: Terry Cascioli
Conducts Business: Newspaper
Employees: 250
Direct online sales
Founded: 1888

Newspaper for Erie County, PA.

TIMES UNION
Div. of Hearst
Box 15000, News Plaza
Albany, NY 12212
Telephone: (518) 454-5694, FAX:
(518) 454-5628, Web Site: www.
timesunion.com
Online Ed: Patti Hart
Online Exec Producer: Paul Block
VP & Editor: Rex Smith

Primary Market Served: Business &
Consumer
Local Newspaper.

UNIVERSITY SUBSCRIPTION SERVICE

1213 Butterfield Rd
Downers Grove, IL 60515
Telephone: (630) 960-3233, Toll Free:
(888) 877-1213, FAX: (630) 960-
3246, Web Site: www.ussmag.com
Pres: Pethi Velu
VP: Param Velu
Conducts Business: U.S.
Employees: 30
Primary Market Served: Consumer
Catalog available online
Indirect online sales
Advertising/Marketing Budget Related
to Direct Marketing: 0-25%
Direct Marketing ad budget:
$2,000,000
Founded: 1974
Gross sales or billing: $8,000,000

Sell subscriptions to consumer magazines to teachers, college students &
educators by direct mail, space advertising, publication inserts & through
college bookstores.

WORLD PRESS REVIEW

Div. of All Media Inc
700 Broadway
New York, NY 10003
Telephone: (212) 982-8880, Web Site:
www.worldpressreview.com
Publr & Founder: Teri Schure
Ed-in-Chief: Alice Chasan
Prod & Design Mgr: Laura R. Custus
Adv Coord: Louisa D. Kearney
Conducts Business: Worldwide
Employees: 19
Primary Market Served: Consumer
Indirect online sales
Founded: 1997
Gross sales or billing: $400,000

Monthly magazine & website of the
foreign press with translated feature articles, commentary & cartoons from
leading publications throughout the
world. 95% subscription sold.

AESU INC
3922 Hickory Ave
Baltimore, MD 21211-1834
Telephone: (410) 366-5494, Toll Free: (800) 638-7640, FAX: (410) 366-6999, E-Mail: res@aesu.com, Web Site: www.aesu.com
Principal (Pres): Beth Satren
Mgr: Karoline Bowman
Pres: Fritz Satran
Dir: Lisabeth Satran
Conducts Business: Worldwide
Employees: 25
Primary Market Served: Business & Consumer
Catalog available online
Indirect online sales
Advertising/Marketing Budget Related to Direct Marketing: 26-50%
Founded: 1977
Gross sales or billing: $10,000,000

International tour operators. Incentive travel & specialty tours.

AIFS
1 High Ridge Park
Stamford, CT 06905-1322
Telephone: (203) 399-5000, Toll Free: (866) 906-2437, FAX: (203) 599-5590, E-Mail: info@aifs.com, Web Site: www.aifs.com
Pres & CEO: William Gertz
VP Mktg: Kim Fleming
Founded: 1964

Cultural exchange organization with global offices in 6 countries.

ABSOLUTE RESERVATION CENTER INC
150 E Wildmere Ave (#108)
Longwood, FL 32750-5464
Telephone: (407) 660-9995, Web Site: www.arcfun.com
Primary Market Served: Business & Consumer

ACADEMIC TRAVEL ABROAD INC
1920 N St NW (Suite 200)
Washington, DC 20036-1652
Telephone: (202) 785-9000, Toll Free: (800) 556-7896, FAX: (202) 342-0317, Web Site: www.academictravel.com
Chmn: David T. Parry
Pres: Kate Simpson
Exec VP: Chase Poffenberger
VP Fin & Admin: Sarah Saleh
Conducts Business: U.S., Canada
Employees: 45
Primary Market Served: Business & Consumer

Founded: 1947
Gross sales or billing: $13,750,000
Tour operators for tours around the world.

AIRTRAN AIRWAYS
Subs. of Southwest Airlines
1800 Phoenix Blvd (Suite 104)
Atlanta, GA 30349-5569
Telephone: (678) 254-7999, Toll Free: (800) 247-8726, Web Site: www.airtran.com

ALEXANDER + ROBERTS
53 Summer St
Keene, NH 03431-3318
Telephone: (603) 357-5033, Toll Free: (800) 221-2216, FAX: (603) 357-4548, E-Mail: info@generaltours.com, Web Site: www.generaltours.com
Pres: Robert Drumm
Dir Opers: Beth Karlicek
Conducts Business: U.S.
Employees: 25
Primary Market Served: Business & Consumer
Direct Marketing ad budget: $50,000
Direct Mail: 25%
Newspapers: 75%
Founded: 1947
Gross sales or billing: $15,000,000

Tour packages including airfare to Russia, Eastern Europe, Israel, Egypt, Morocco, Middle East, Japan, China, Orient, India & Turkey.

AMBASSADOR PROGRAMS
1956 Ambassador Way
Spokane, WA 99224-4012
Telephone: (509) 568-7800, Toll Free: (800) 669-7882, FAX: (877) 284-4517, Web Site: www.peopletopeople.com
Primary Market Served: Business & Consumer
Founded: 1995

Develops and delivers educational travel programs for students in the United States and internationally.

AMERICAN AIRLINES INC
Subs. of American Airlines Group Inc.
4333 Amon Carter Blvd
Fort Worth, TX 76155-2605
Telephone: (817) 963-1234, FAX: (817) 967-2841, Web Site: www.aa.com
CEO: William Douglas Parker
CFO: Derek J. Kerr
VP: Derek DeCross
Conducts Business: Worldwide

Employees: 90,000
Primary Market Served: Business & Consumer
Founded: 1934
Provides scheduled airline services.

AMERISTAR CASINOS INC
3773 Howard Hughes Pkwy (Suite 490)
Las Vegas, NV 89169-0949
Telephone: (702) 567-7000, FAX: (702) 369-8860, Web Site: www.ameristarcasinos.com
CEO & Dir: Gordon R. Kanofsky
Pres: Lawrence A. Hodges
CFO: Thomas M. Steinbauer
Primary Market Served: Consumer
Founded: 1954

Develops, owns, and operates casinos and related facilities in the United States.

ELIZABETH ARDEN SPAS LLC
300 Main St (fl 8)
Stamford, CT 06901-3033
Telephone: (203) 905-1700, FAX: (203) 905-1716, Web Site: www.reddoorspas.com
CEO & Pres: W Todd Walter
CFO: Robert Broadhead
Chief Mktg Officer & Sr VP: Lisa Hagen
Conducts Business: U.S.
Employees: 4,200
Primary Market Served: Consumer
Direct online sales
Advertising/Marketing Budget Related to Direct Marketing: 0-25%
Direct Marketing ad budget: $500,000
Direct Mail: 100%
Founded: 1910
Gross sales or billing: $200,000,000

Spa and salon services and beauty and hair retail products to consumers.

AUSTRALIAN TOURIST COMMISSION
6100 Center Drive
Los Angeles, CA 90045
Telephone: (310) 695-3200, Web Site: www.australia.com
Primary Market Served: Consumer
Catalog available online
Direct online sales
Advertising/Marketing Budget Related to Direct Marketing: 0-25%
Gross sales or billing: $200,000

Promotes travel to Australia to U.S. & Canadian citizens.

AVIS WORLD HEADQUARTERS
6 Sylvan Way
Parsippany, NJ 07054-3826
Telephone: (973) 496-3500, Web Site:
www.avis.com
CEO & COO: Larry De Shon
CFO: David B. Wyshner
Conducts Business: Worldwide
Employees: 11,000
Primary Market Served: Business &
Consumer

Provide rental car services to business
& leisure travelers.

BAHAMAS MINISTRY OF TOURISM
1200 S Pine Island Rd (Suite 750)
Fort Lauderdale, FL 33324-4413
Telephone: (954) 236-9292, Toll Free:
(800) 422-4262, Web Site: www.
bahamas.com
Sr Dir Commun: Nalini Bethel
Primary Market Served: Business &
Consumer

BEAU RIVAGE RESORT & CASINO
dba Beau Rivage
875 Beach Blvd
Biloxi, MS 39530-4299
Telephone: (228) 386-7111, FAX:
(228) 386-7730, Web Site: www.
beaurivage.com
Primary Market Served: Business &
Consumer
Founded: 2006

Operates as a resort and casino

BEST WESTERN INTERNATIONAL
6201 N 24th Pkwy
Phoenix, AZ 85016-2023
Telephone: (602) 957-4200, FAX:
(623) 780-6199, Web Site: www.
bestwestern.com
CEO & Pres: David Kong
Founder: M. K. Guertin
Founded: 1946

Owns and operates a chain of hotels.

BLUE STRAWBERRY RESORTS LLC
444 Brickell Ave., Ste. 51-859
Miami, FL 33131
Telephone: (756) 513-1456, Toll Free:
(800) 873-1440, Web Site: www.
bluestrawberry-resorts.com
CEO: Erika Garcia

Represents over 400 beachfront & golf
course view hotel rooms

BROADMOOR HOTEL INC
1 Lake Ave
Colorado Springs, CO 80906-4269
Telephone: (719) 623-5112, Toll Free:
(866) 837-9520, FAX: (719) 577-
5738, Web Site: www.broadmoor.
com
Pres & CEO: Jack Damioli
Dir Communs: Allison Scott
Dir Natl Sls Mid-Atlantic Region:
Laurie Meacham
Dir Natl Sls Mid-West Region: Tammy
Page Boettner
Conducts Business: U.S.
Employees: 1,500
Primary Market Served: Business &
Consumer
Catalog available online
Direct online sales
Founded: 1891
Gross sales or billing: $52,000,000

Full-service hotel & resort.

BROTHERHOOD AMERICA'S OLDEST WINERY LTD
100 Brotherhood Plaza Dr
Washingtonville, NY 10992-2262
Telephone: (845) 496-3661, FAX:
(845) 496-8720, E-Mail: contact@
brotherhoodwinery.net, Web Site:
www.brotherhoodwinery.net
VP & Winemaker: Cesar Baeza
Winemaker: Bob Barrow
Conducts Business: U.S.
Employees: 40
Primary Market Served: Consumer
Catalog available online
Direct online sales
Advertising/Marketing Budget Related
to Direct Marketing: 0-25%
Founded: 1839

Conduct tours & wine tastings. Produce
a diversified line of quality wine for local, regional & national distribution.

CALLAWAY GARDENS
Subs. of Ida Cason Callaway Founda-
tion
17800 US Hwy 27
Pine Mountain, GA 31822-2000
Telephone: (706) 663-2281, Toll Free:
(800) CALLAWAY, FAX: (706)
663-6812, E-Mail: info@
callawaygardens.com, Web Site:
www.callawaygardens.com/where-
to-stay
CEO & Pres: William Doyle III
Conducts Business: U.S.
Employees: 1,100
Primary Market Served: Business &
Consumer
Catalog available online
Direct online sales
Advertising/Marketing Budget Related
to Direct Marketing: 0-25%
Founded: 1958
Full-service destination resort. Com-
plete stores & products division head-
quartered at Callaway Gardens for
retail & catalog sales of food items.

CARNIVAL CRUISE LINES
3655 NW 87th Ave
Miami, FL 33178-2418
Telephone: (212) 599-2600, Web Site:
www.carnival.com
CEO & Chmn: Micky Arison
Primary Market Served: Business &
Consumer

CHATEAU LE COMBE
Subs. of Commonwealth Hospitality
10111 Bellamy Hill
Edmonton, AB, Canada T5J 1N7
Telephone: (780) 428-6611, Toll Free:
(800) 661-8801, FAX: (780) 425-
6564, E-Mail: info@chateaulecombe.
com, Web Site: www.
chateaulecombe.com
Gen Mgr: Ike Janacek
Conducts Business: U.S., Canada
Employees: 250
Primary Market Served: Business &
Consumer
Direct Marketing ad budget:
Magazines: 60%
Newspapers: 5%
Online: 35%

307 room luxury hotel in downtown
Edmonton. Meeting & convention facilities to accommodate up to 800 persons. Full food & beverage facilities.

COAST HOTELS LIMITED
dba Coast Hotels & Resorts
600 Stewart St (Suite 1920)
Seattle, WA 98101-1238
Telephone: (206) 826-2700, FAX:
(206) 826-2701, Web Site: www.
coasthotels.com
Pres & CEO: Dave Cottler
EVP & COO: Doug Rigoni
Corp Dir Mktg: Joe Figone
Conducts Business: Worldwide
Primary Market Served: Business &
Consumer
Catalog available online
Direct online sales
Advertising/Marketing Budget Related
to Direct Marketing: 51-75%
Direct Marketing ad budget:
Direct Mail: 40%
Magazines: 10%
Newspapers: 50%
Founded: 1972

Operator of resorts & conference centers.

COLLETTE VACATIONS
162 Middle St
Pawtucket, RI 02860-1013
Telephone: (401) 728-3805, FAX:
(401) 727-9014, E-Mail: czesk@
collettetours.com, Web Site: www.
collettevacations.com
CEO & Pres: Daniel J. Sullivan
CFO: John Galvin
Founded: 1918

Tour operator, offers escorted tours in
the United States.

THE CONTEST CENTER
59 DeGarmo Hills Rd
Wappingers Falls, NY 12590-2101
Telephone: (845) 297-4833, E-Mail:
contestcen@aol.com, Web Site:
www.contestcen.com
Owner, Pres: Frank Rubin
Conducts Business: U.S., Canada, Eng-
land, Australia
Employees: 1
Primary Market Served: Consumer
Catalog available online
Indirect online sales
Advertising/Marketing Budget Related
to Direct Marketing: 76-100%
Direct Marketing ad budget: $10,000
Direct Mail: $10,000
Founded: 1980
Gross sales or billing: $150,000

Online contests.

DELTA VACATIONS
Sub. of MLT Vacations
700 Central Ave.
Atlanta, GA 30354
Telephone: (404) 559-2270, Toll Free:
(800) 800-1504, Web Site: www.
deltavacations.com
Primary Market Served: Consumer
Catalog available online
Direct online sales
Advertising/Marketing Budget Related
to Direct Marketing: 51-75%
Founded: 1981

Air-inclusive vacation packages to over
120 destinations worldwide.

DESTINATIONS IRELAND & BEYOND
91 Broadway (Suite 1)
Kingston, NY 12401-6017
Toll Free: (800) 832-1848, FAX: (845)
810-7678, E-Mail: info@digbtravel.
com, Web Site: www.allgolftravel.
com/tours
Pres: Declan O'Brien
Conducts Business: Worldwide
Primary Market Served: Business &
Consumer
Catalog available online

Advertising/Marketing Budget Related
to Direct Marketing: 0-25%
Founded: 1990

Luxury custom-designed tours.

DAN DIPERT TRAVEL SERVICE INC
7301 W Pioneer Pkwy
Arlington, TX 76013-2804
Telephone: (817) 543-3700, Toll Free:
(800) 433-5335, FAX: (817) 543-
3728, Web Site: www.dandipert.com
Pres & CEO: Dan W. Dipert
COO: Autumn Dipert Brown
Sls & Mktg Dir: Linda Dipert
Conducts Business: U.S., Canada
Employees: 25
Primary Market Served: Business &
Consumer
Catalog available online
Advertising/Marketing Budget Related
to Direct Marketing: 51-75%
Direct Marketing ad budget: $200,000
Direct Mail: 70%
Newspapers: 30%
Founded: 1970

Travel agency specializing in retail &
wholesale escorted tours, retail travel
& motorcoach charter.

DISNEY VACATION CLUB
Subs. of Walt Disney Co.
200 Celebration Pl
Kissimmee, FL 34747
Telephone: (407) 566-3000, Toll Free:
(800) 500-3990, FAX: (407) 566-
3393
SVP & Gen Mgr: Ken Potrock
Primary Market Served: Consumer
Catalog available online
Direct online sales
Founded: 1991

Vacation ownership business.

WALT DISNEY PARKS & RESORTS
1375 N Buena Vista Dr
Lake Buena Vista, FL 32830-8402
Telephone: (407) 824-2222, FAX:
(407) 566-5700, Web Site: www.
disneyworld.com
Pres: George A. Kalogridis

Theme parks and resorts.

DOUBLETREE SUITES BY HILTON
400 Soldiers Field Rd
Boston, MA 02134-1893
Telephone: (617) 783-0090, Toll Free:
(800) 222-TREE, FAX: (617) 783-
0897, E-Mail: doubletree1@hilton.
com
Conducts Business: U.S.

Employees: 5,200
Primary Market Served: Business &
Consumer
Catalog available online
Direct online sales
Direct Marketing ad budget:
$1,000,000
Direct Mail: 30%
Magazines: 35%
Newspapers: 35%
Gross sales or billing: $464,000,000

Provide travelers with first class suites,
services & amenities, innovative restaurants & lounges. Flexible meeting &
banquet rooms. Relaxing health & fitness facilities.

E-MILES.COM
5800 Tennyson Pkwy., Ste. 600
Plano, TX 75024
Telephone: (214) 743-5555, Web Site:
www.e-miles.com
VP: Brad Harraman

ELMWOOD SPA
18 Elm St
Toronto, ON, Canada M5G 1G7
Telephone: (416) 964-4515, Toll Free:
(877) 284-6348, E-Mail: spa@
elmwoodspa.com, Web Site: www.
elmwoodspa.com
Sr Mgr Sls & Mktg: Gwen Hayes

Day Spa.

EMPIRE CITY CASINO AT YONKERS RACEWAY
810 Yonkers Ave
Yonkers, NY 10704-2030
Telephone: (914) 968-4200, Web Site:
www.empirecitygaming.com
Adv Mgr: Clare Galterio

Harness racing & video casino gaming
machines.

ENTERPRISE RENT-A-CAR
600 Corporate Park Dr
Saint Louis, MO 63105-4204
Telephone: (314) 512-5000, FAX:
(314) 512-4706, Web Site: www.
enterprise.com
Chmn & CEO: Andrew C. Taylor
Pres & COO: Pamela M. Nicholson
Founded: 1957

American car rental company.

EVENTFUL INC
12626 High Bluff Dr., Ste. 100
San Diego, CA 92130
Telephone: (858) 882-0360, FAX:
(858) 964-4640, Web Site: www.
eventful.com
CEO: Jordan Glazier

VP Mktg & Artist Rels: Holly Anderson
Primary Market Served: Business & Consumer
Founded: 2004

Digital media company serving entertainment consumers and event marketers.

EXPEDIA INC
333 108th Ave NE (Suite 300)
Bellevue, WA 98004-5736
Telephone: (425) 679-7200, Web Site: www.expedia.com
CEO: Dara Khosrowshahi
CFO & EVP: Mark D. Okerstrom
Primary Market Served: Business & Consumer
Founded: 1996

Operates as an online travel company in the United States & internationally.

FOUR SEASONS HOTELS & RESORTS
1165 Leslie St (Suite 600)
Toronto, ON, Canada M3C 2K8
Telephone: (416) 449-1750, Toll Free: (800) 819-5053, FAX: (416) 441-4437, Web Site: www.fourseasons.com
CEO & Pres: Allen Smith
CFO: John M. Davison
Conducts Business: U.S., Canada
Primary Market Served: Business & Consumer
Catalog available online
Direct online sales
Founded: 1960

Hotel chain.

GRAND CIRCLE TRAVEL
347 Congress St
Boston, MA 02210-1230
Telephone: (617) 350-7500, Toll Free: (800) 959-0405, FAX: (617) 346-6030, Web Site: www.gct.com
Chmn Bd: Allan Lewis
Vice Chmn: Harriet Lewis
VP, Pub Rels: Priscilla O'Reilly
CEO: Vince Cook
EVP: Mark C. Frevert
Conducts Business: U.S.
Employees: 3,000
Primary Market Served: Consumer
Catalog available online
Direct online sales
Advertising/Marketing Budget Related to Direct Marketing: 76-100%
Direct Marketing ad budget:
Direct Mail: 75%
Telephone: 25%
Founded: 1958

Gross sales or billing: $577,000,000
International travel for retired Americans.

GRAND PACIFIC RESORTS
5900 Pasteur Ct (#200)
Carlsbad, CA 92009-7336
Telephone: (760) 827-4100, Toll Free: (800) 374-7779, Web Site: www.grandpacificresorts.com
VP Resort Opers: Doreen Bechard
Gen Mgr: Greg Veal
VP Sls & Bus Devel: Sherri Weeks
Founded: 1991

A vacation ownership company, manages resort properties in California.

HAPPY TRAILS RESORT
17200 W Bell Rd
Surprise, AZ 85374-9740
Telephone: (623) 584-0066, Toll Free: (800) 872-4579, FAX: (623) 546-6293, E-Mail: happytrails@uccinc.net, Web Site: www.htresort.com
Assn Mgr: Beth McWilliams
Conducts Business: U.S.
Employees: 40
Primary Market Served: Business & Consumer
Founded: 1984

Adult recreational vehicle & mobile home resort. Lots are owned by occupants.

HERSHEY PARK
Div. of HERCO
100 W Hershey Park Dr
Hershey, PA 17033-2727
Telephone: (717) 534-3149, Toll Free: (800) HERSHEY, E-Mail: info@hersheypa.com, Web Site: www.hersheypark.com
Chmn: James E. Nevels
Pres & CEO: John P. (J.P.) Bilbrey
Conducts Business: U.S.
Primary Market Served: Business & Consumer
Founded: 1907

90-acre theme park.

HERTZ CORP
Subs. of Ford Motor Co
225 Brae Blvd
Park Ridge, NJ 07656
Telephone: (201) 307-2000, FAX: (201) 307-2644, Web Site: www.hertz.com
Conducts Business: Worldwide
Primary Market Served: Business & Consumer

Rent-A-Car service for businesses & leisure travelers.

HILTON GRAND VACATIONS CO
dba Hilton Resorts Corporation
6355 Metrowest Blvd (Suite 180)
Orlando, FL 32835-6203
Telephone: (407) 722-3100, FAX: (407) 521-3112, Web Site: www.hiltongrandvacations.com
Pres: Mark D. Wang
CFO: Johann Murray
SVP Mktg: Dennis DeLorenzo
Founded: 1992

Develops, markets, and operates vacation ownership resorts.

HILTON HOTELS CORP
7930 Jones Branch Dr (Suite 100)
Mc Lean, VA 22102-3389
Telephone: (703) 883-1000, Toll Free: (800) HILTONS, FAX: (310) 205-3670, Web Site: www.hilton.com
CEO: Christopher Nassetta
CFO: Kevin J. Jacobs
Pres Devel: Ian R. Carter
Conducts Business: Worldwide
Primary Market Served: Business & Consumer
Catalog available online
Indirect online sales
Advertising/Marketing Budget Related to Direct Marketing: 0-25%
Founded: 1919
Gross sales or billing: $8,000,000,000

Engaged in the ownership, leasing, management, development, and franchising of hotels, resorts, and timeshare properties worldwide.

HOBART & WILLIAM SMITH COLLEGES
300 Pulteney St
Geneva, NY 14456-3304
Telephone: (315) 781-3540, Toll Free: (800) 852-2256, FAX: (315) 781-3400, Web Site: www.hws.edu
Pres & Trustee: Mark D. Gearen
Conducts Business: U.S.
Employees: 4
Primary Market Served: Consumer
Catalog available online
Founded: 1822
Gross sales or billing: $69,100,000

Educational & research institution.

HOLIDAY TRAVEL OF AMERICA
6405 El Camino Real
Carlsbad, CA 92009-2802
Telephone: (760) 431-8600, Toll Free: (888) 732-2479, FAX: (760) 431-3131, E-Mail: sales@htoa.com, Web Site: www.htoa.com
Founder & CEO: Richard J. Romanello
Primary Market Served: Business

Catalog available online
Founded: 1988
Wholesaler & provider of travel certificates.

HOLIDAY VACATIONS

2727 Henry Ave, PO Box 87
Eau Claire, WI 54701-6828
Telephone: (715) 834-5555, Toll Free:
(800) 826-2266, FAX: (715) 834-8554, E-Mail: info@
holidayvacations.net, Web Site:
www.holidayvacations.net
Dir Worldwide Opers: Greg Barnes
Employees: 100
Primary Market Served: Consumer

Tour company & travel agency.

HOMEAWAY.COM INC

1011 W Fifth St (Suite 300)
Austin, TX 78703-5363
Telephone: (512) 684-1100, Toll Free:
(877) 228-3145, Web Site: www.
homeaway.com
CFO: Rebecca Lynn Atchison
Primary Market Served: Business &
Consumer
Founded: 2004

Online vacation rental property marketplace that enables property owners and managers to market properties for rental to vacation travelers.

INDIANAPOLIS MOTOR
SPEEDWAY

4790 W 16th St
Indianapolis, IN 46222-2550
Telephone: (317) 492-8500, FAX:
(317) 492-6571, Web Site: www.
indianapolismotorspeedway.com
Primary Market Served: Business &
Consumer
Founded: 1909

Owns & operates a racing facility for motorsports.

INTERCONTINENTAL
HOTELS GROUP

Three Ravinia Dr (Suite 100)
Atlanta, GA 30346-2149
Toll Free: (800) 621-0555, FAX: (801)
975-1846, Web Site: www.
ichotelsgroup.com
Chmn: Patrick Cescau
CEO: Richard Solomons
CFO: Paul Edgecliffe-Johnson
Primary Market Served: Consumer
Gross sales or billing: $2,020,300,000

Hotels & resorts.

KUWAIT AIRWAYS CORP

400 Kelby St (Suite 41)
Fort Lee, NJ 07024-2938

Telephone: (201) 582-9222, Toll Free:
(800) 4-KUWAIT, FAX: (212) 947-8113, E-Mail: nyc@kuwait-airways.
com, Web Site: www.kuwait-airways.com
Chmn & Mng Dir: Rasha A. Al-Roumi
Primary Market Served: Consumer
International airlines.

LEXINGTON LUGGAGE
LIMITED

793 Lexington Ave (Frnt 1)
New York, NY 10065-8161
Telephone: (212) 223-0698, Toll Free:
(800) 822-0404, FAX: (212) 753-3298, E-Mail: sales@
lexingtonluggage.com, Web Site:
www.lexingtonluggage.com
Conducts Business: U.S.
Employees: 15
Primary Market Served: Business &
Consumer
Advertising/Marketing Budget Related
to Direct Marketing: 26-50%
Founded: 1949

Sell luggage, attache cases, brief cases, garment bags & fine pens at wholesale prices.

LIVE NATION

9348 Civic Center Dr Lobby
Beverly Hills, CA 90210-3642
Telephone: (310) 867-7000, Web Site:
www.livenation.com
CEO: Mike Rapino
Primary Market Served: Business &
Consumer

Concert promoter.

LOEWS HOTELS, INC

Div. of Loews Corp
667 Madison Ave (fl 7)
New York, NY 10065-8087
Telephone: (212) 521-2000, Toll Free:
(866) 563-9792, FAX: (212) 521-2379, Web Site: www.loewshotels.
com
SVP Asset Mngmt: Constantine S. Dimas
SVP Acquisitions & Devel: Michael
Palmeri
Conducts Business: Worldwide
Employees: 5,000
Primary Market Served: Business &
Consumer
Advertising/Marketing Budget Related
to Direct Marketing: 0-25%
Founded: 1946

Hotel chain.

THE LOS ANGELES
CONVENTION & VISITORS
BUREAU

333 S Hope St (fl 18)
Los Angeles, CA 90071-1406
Telephone: (213) 624-7300, Toll Free:
(800) 366-6116, FAX: (213) 627-9746, Web Site: discoverlosangeles.
com
CEO: Mark S. Liberman
Conducts Business: U.S., China, Japan,
England
Employees: 75
Primary Market Served: Business
Catalog available online
Advertising/Marketing Budget Related
to Direct Marketing: 26-50%
Direct Marketing ad budget:
Direct Mail: 20%
Magazines: 20%
Newspapers: 20%
Online: 20%
TV/Radio: 20%
Founded: 1977

Resource for visitor information.

LUFTHANSA GERMAN
AIRLINES

1640 Hempstead Tpke
East Meadow, NY 11554-1040
Telephone: (516) 296-9200, FAX:
(516) 296-9386, Web Site: www.
lufthansa-usa.com
CEO & Chmn: Carsten Spohr
Conducts Business: Worldwide.
Primary Market Served: Business &
Consumer
Advertising/Marketing Budget Related
to Direct Marketing: 0-25%
Founded: 1955

Global airline.

MIRAGE RESORTS, INC.

Subs. MGM Resorts International.
3400 Las Vegas Blvd S
Las Vegas, NV 89109-8923
Telephone: (702) 693-7111, FAX:
(702) 791-7446, Web Site: www.
mirageresorts.com
Chm. & CEO: James J. Murren
Primary Market Served: Business &
Consumer

Operates casino-based entertainment resorts

MARRIOTT
INTERNATIONAL INC

10400 Fernwood Rd
Bethesda, MD 20817-1102
Telephone: (301) 380-3000, (301) 380-1791, E-Mail: internet.customer.
care@marriott.com, Web Site: www.
marriott.com
CEO: Arne M. Sorenson Jr.

Conducts Business: Worldwide
Primary Market Served: Business & Consumer
Founded: 1971

Diversified hospitality company involved in lodging & services.

MARRIOTT OWNERSHIP RESORTS SALES & MARKETING

dba Marriott Vacation Club International
6649 Westwood Blvd (Suite 500)
Orlando, FL 32821-6066
Telephone: (407) 206-6000, Toll Free: (800) 850-6674, FAX: (407) 206-6097, Web Site: www.marriottvacationclub.com
Pres: Stephen P. Weisz
Chief HR Officer: Michael E. Yonker
Primary Market Served: Consumer
Founded: 1983

Marketer of time-share resorts.

MONTBLEU RESORT CASINO AND SPA

Subs. of Tropicana Casinos and Resorts
55 Hwy 50
Stateline, NV 89449
Telephone: (775) 586-2126, Toll Free: (888) 829-7630, FAX: (775) 588-3515, Web Site: www.montbleuresort.com
Gen Mgr: Timothy Tretton
Employees: 1,500
Primary Market Served: Consumer
Catalog available online
Indirect online sales
Advertising/Marketing Budget Related to Direct Marketing: 26-50%
Founded: 1979

Hotel casino resort.

NEW ZEALAND TOURISM BOARD

501 Santa Monica Blvd (Suite 300)
Santa Monica, CA 90401-2443
Telephone: (310) 395-7480, (310) 395-5453, FAX: (310) 395-5453, E-Mail: nzinfo@nztb.govt.nz, Web Site: www.purenz.com
Conducts Business: Globally
Employees: 10
Primary Market Served: Consumer
Advertising/Marketing Budget Related to Direct Marketing: 0-25%
Founded: 1901

New Zealand tourism information.

1000 ISLANDS INTERNATIONAL TOURISM COUNCIL

43373 Collins Landing Rd

Alexandria Bay, NY 13607-2210
Telephone: (315) 482-2520, Toll Free: (800) 847-5263, (800) 456-2267, FAX: (315) 482-5906, E-Mail: info@visit1000islands.com, Web Site: www.visit1000islands.com/visitorinfo/
Exec Dir: Gary de Young
PR Mgr: Tillie Youngs
Conducts Business: U.S., Canada
Employees: 8
Primary Market Served: Consumer
Catalog available online
Advertising/Marketing Budget Related to Direct Marketing: 26-50%
Direct Marketing ad budget: $235,000
Direct Mail: 15%
Magazines: 5%
Newspapers: 10%
TV/Radio: 70%
Gross sales or billing: $581,000

Tourist promotion agency for the Thousand Islands International region, covering southeastern Ontario & Jefferson County, NY.

ORLANDO/ ORANGE COUNTY CONVENTION & VISITOR'S BUREAU

6700 Forum Dr (Suite 100)
Orlando, FL 32821-8086
Telephone: (407) 354-5568, Web Site: visitorlando.com
Exec Dir: Kathie Canning
Primary Market Served: Business & Consumer

BUCK OWENS' CRYSTAL PALACE

2800 Buck Owens Blvd
Bakersfield, CA 93308-6314
Telephone: (661) 328-7560, FAX: (805) 328-7565, E-Mail: mhufford@buckowens.com, Web Site: www.buckowens.com
Gen Mgr: Mathy Hufford
Primary Market Served: Consumer

Live country music venue, general store & restaurant.

PAN PACIFIC HOTEL & RESORTS AMERICA

2125 Terry Ave
Seattle, WA 98121-2709
Telephone: (206) 264-8111, Toll Free: (877) 324-4856, FAX: (206) 654-5049, Web Site: www.panpacific.com
Conducts Business: U.S.
Employees: 479
Primary Market Served: Business & Consumer
Advertising/Marketing Budget Related to Direct Marketing: 26-50%

Founded: 1986
Gross sales or billing: $16,100,000
330 room hotel.

PETER PAN BUS LINES INC

1776 Main St
Springfield, MA 01103-1027
Telephone: (413) 781-3320, Toll Free: (800) 343-9999, FAX: (413) 747-7626, E-Mail: info@peterpanbus.com, Web Site: www.peterpanbus.com
CEO & Pres: Peter A. Picknelly
COO: Brian Stefano
SVP Maintenance: Thomas Picknally
Dir HR: Anne Miller
Controller: Maurice Brodeur
Dir Mktg: Danielle Veronesi
Conducts Business: U.S., Canada
Employees: 750
Primary Market Served: Business & Consumer
Advertising/Marketing Budget Related to Direct Marketing: 0-25%
Direct Marketing ad budget: $700,000
Direct Mail: 10%
Magazines: 10%
Newspapers: 50%
TV/Radio: 30%
Founded: 1933
Gross sales or billing: $53,900,000

Motorcoach transportation available for charter & tour throughout U.S. & Canada.

POTAWATOMI BINGO CASINO

1721 W Canal St
Milwaukee, WI 53233-2655
Telephone: (414) 645-6888, Toll Free: (800) PAYS-BIG, FAX: (414) 847-7727, Web Site: www.paysbig.com
CFO: Rodney Ferguson
Gen Mgr: Mike Goodrich
Mktg Dir: Kristina Potrykus
Primary Market Served: Business & Consumer
Founded: 1991

Owns & operates a casino.

PRINCESS CRUISES (HQ)

24844 Avenue Rockefeller
Santa Clarita, CA 91355-3467
Telephone: (661) 753-0000, Toll Free: (800) (774)-6237, FAX: (661) 284-4747, Web Site: www.princesscruises.com
Pres: Jan Swartz
Conducts Business: U.S., Canada
Employees: 22,900
Primary Market Served: Business & Consumer
Founded: 1965

Market cruise vacations.

RCI LLC

9998 N Michigan Rd
Carmel, IN 46032-9640
Telephone: (317) 805-9000, FAX:
(317) 805-9335, Web Site: www.rci.
com
CEO & Pres Europe & Middle East:
Peter Giamalva
CEO Global Vacation Network: John
Paul Nichols
CIO & EVP: Philippe Guionnet
Conducts Business: Worldwide
Employees: 1,200
Primary Market Served: Consumer
Founded: 1974

Leisure travel company that provides
exchange service for timeshare owners.

RESORTS CASINO HOTEL

1133 Boardwalk
Atlantic City, NJ 08401-7329
Telephone: (609) 334-6000, Toll Free:
(800) 336-6378, FAX: (609) 340-
6349, Web Site: www.resortsac.com
Sr VP, Opers: Steve Callendary
EVP Fin & Asst Gen Mgr: Francis X.
McCarthy
Reg VP Mktg: Mary Beth Wilkes
Conducts Business: U.S.
Employees: 3,000
Primary Market Served: Consumer
Catalog available online
Direct online sales
Founded: 1978

Hotel & casino.

ROYAL CARIBBEAN
INTERNATIONAL LTD

1050 Caribbean Way
Miami, FL 33132-2028
Telephone: (305) 539-6000, FAX:
(305) 374-7354, Web Site: www.
royalcaribbean.com
SVP Intl: Michael W. Bayley
Primary Market Served: Consumer
Founded: 1969

Owns and operates cruise ships in the
United States and internationally.

SABRE HOLDINGS INC

3150 Sabre Dr
Southlake, TX 76092-2103
Telephone: (682) 605-1000, FAX:
(682) 605-7239, Web Site: www.
sabre.com
CEO & Pres: Thomas Klein
CFO & EVP: Richard A. Simonson
Primary Market Served: Business
Founded: 1960

Provides technology solutions to travel
& tourism industry in the United States
and internationally.

SEASHORE VACATIONS

11 Executive Park Rd
Hilton Head Island, SC 29928-4781
Telephone: (843) 785-2191, Toll Free:
(800) 845-0077, FAX: (843) 785-
6450, E-Mail: seashorehhi@hargray.
com, Web Site: www.seashorehhi.
com
Rental Mgr: Buddy Konecny
Conducts Business: U.S.
Employees: 4
Primary Market Served: Business &
Consumer
Advertising/Marketing Budget Related
to Direct Marketing: 51-75%
Direct Marketing ad budget: $30,000
Direct Mail: 100%

Rental agents for condos, villas &
homes.

SOUTH SEAS ISLAND
RESORT

5400 Plantation Rd
Captiva Island, FL 33924
Toll Free: (866) 565-5089, FAX: (941)
482-2470, Web Site: www.southseas.
com
Primary Market Served: Business &
Consumer
Catalog available online
Indirect online sales

Own & operate nine beachfront properties.

STARWOOD HOTELS &
RESORTS WORLDWIDE
INC

1 Star Pt
Stamford, CT 06902-8911
Telephone: (203) 964-6000, FAX:
(914) 640-8310, Web Site: www.
starwoodhotels.com
Chief Admin Officer & Gen Counsel:
Kenneth S. Siegel
Founded: 1969

Operates as a hotel & leisure company
worldwide.

STEPPIN' OUT & SEE
AMERICA

1140 N Town Center Dr (#360)
Las Vegas, NV 89144-0501
Telephone: (702) 798-6522, FAX: 702
798-6562, E-Mail: sales@see-
america.net, Web Site:
steppinoutseeamerica.com
CEO: Bob Colton

Sell all catalogs for national coupon
books.

THE STRATOSPHERE LAS
VEGAS

Subs. of AREP

2000 Las Vegas Blvd S
Las Vegas, NV 89104-2507
Telephone: (702) 380-7777, Toll Free:
(800) 998-6937, FAX: (702) 383-
4755, Web Site: www.
stratospherehotel.com
Gen Mgr: Paul Hobson
Primary Market Served: Business &
Consumer
Founded: 1999

Hotel & casino.

SUPER 8 HOTELS
WORLDWIDE

Subs. of Wyndham Worldwide Corpo-
ration
1 Sylvan Way
Parsippany, NJ 07054-3887
Toll Free: (800) 800-8000, FAX: (720)
535-2199, Web Site: www.super8.
com
Pres: John Valetta
Conducts Business: U.S., Canada, Chi-
na
Primary Market Served: Business &
Consumer
Catalog available online
Direct online sales
Advertising/Marketing Budget Related
to Direct Marketing: 0-25%
Direct Marketing ad budget:
Direct Mail: 15%
Magazines: 2%
Online: 40%
TV/Radio: 40%
Telephone: 3%
Founded: 1974
Gross sales or billing: $1,300,000,000

Promote Super 8 Motels to users of
economy lodging throughout the
United States & Canada.

TAUCK WORLD DISCOVERY

10 Norden Pl
Norwalk, CT 06855-1454
Telephone: (203) 899-6760, Web Site:
www.tauck.com
Dir Direct & Interactive Mktg: Cheryl
DeMichael

TRAVEL PLANNERS INC

381 Park Ave S
New York, NY 10016-8806
Telephone: (212) 532-1660, Toll Free:
(800) 221-3531, FAX: (212) 532-
1556, Web Site: www.tphousing.com
Co-Founder: Ray Vastola
Co-Founder: Ira Malin
Exec Dir: Lisa Baez
New Bus Devel Dir: Penny Kent
Dir Corp Rels: Beth McEntee-Rome
Conducts Business: U.S., Canada, W.
Europe, Orient
Primary Market Served: Business
Catalog available online

Founded: 1980

Marketer of discounted travel programs for conventions, meetings & individual business travel.

TRAVELCLICK
300 N Martingale Rd
Schaumburg, IL 60173-2407
Telephone: (847) 585-5016
Events Mgr: Sharon Fulton
Primary Market Served: Business & Consumer

TREASURE CHEST
304 Park Ave S
New York, NY 10010-4301
Telephone: (212) 590-2332, Web Site: treasurechestonline.com
Primary Market Served: Consumer

USA HOSTS LTD
365 Canal St (Suite 1400)
New Orleans, LA 70130-1123
Telephone: (504) 524-8687, FAX: (504) 524-8842, Web Site: www.usahosts.com
CEO: Terrence J. Epton
Conducts Business: Worldwide
Employees: 6
Primary Market Served: Business
Advertising/Marketing Budget Related to Direct Marketing: 0-25%

Provides destination services for special events, corporate meetings, conventions, and incentive group travels in North America.

VAIL RESORTS INC
390 Interlocken Crescent (#1000)
Broomfield, CO 80021-8056
Telephone: (303) 404-1800, FAX: (303) 404-6415, Web Site: www.vailresorts.com
Chmn Bd & CEO: Robert A. Katz
EVP & Chief Mktg Officer: Kirsten A. Lynch
Primary Market Served: Consumer

Operates ski resorts in Vail and Keystone, Colorado.

VIRTUOSO LTD
1001 SW Klickitat Way (Suite 105)
Seattle, WA 98134-1161
Telephone: (206) 625-0969, Web Site: www.virtuoso.com

WATER'S EDGE RESORT & SPA
Owned & operated by DGG Properties Co., Inc.
1525 Boston Post Rd
Westbrook, CT 06498-2044

Telephone: (860) 399-5901, Toll Free: (800) 222-5901, FAX: (860) 399-8644, Web Site: www.watersedgeresort.com
Pres & Treas: Michael Datillo
Gen Mgr: Tina Datillo
Conducts Business: U.S.
Employees: 300
Primary Market Served: Business & Consumer
Catalog available online
Indirect online sales
Advertising/Marketing Budget Related to Direct Marketing: 0-25%
Founded: 1986

Full service shoreline resort & vacation club with restaurant.

WEST END DIVING CENTERS INC
12464 Natural Bridge Rd
Bridgeton, MO 63044-2321
Telephone: (314) 209-7200, Toll Free: (888) 843-3483, E-Mail: info@2dive.com, Web Site: www.westenddiving.com
Pres: Doug Goergens
Founded: 1960

Professional diving center & retail store.

WESTERN RIVER EXPEDITIONS
7258 Racquet Club Dr
Salt Lake City, UT 84121-4599
Telephone: (801) 942-6669, Toll Free: (866) 904-1160, FAX: (801) 942-8514, Web Site: www.westernriver.com
CEO: Brian Merrill
Mktg Dir: Kam Wixom
Employees: 12
Primary Market Served: Business & Consumer
Catalog available online
Indirect online sales
Advertising/Marketing Budget Related to Direct Marketing: 76-100%
Direct Marketing ad budget:
Direct Mail: 50%
Magazines: 25%
Newspapers: 25%
Founded: 1961
Gross sales or billing: $5,000,000

Whitewater rafting trips in Grand Canyon, Colorado River in Utah through Westwater & Cataract Canyons, Green River & Salmon River in Idaho.

WINDSTAR CRUISES
Subs. of Ambassadors International Cruise Group Company
2101 4th Ave (Suite 210)
Seattle, WA 98121-2392

Telephone: (206) 292-9606, Toll Free: (800) 258-SAIL, FAX: (206) 340-0975, E-Mail: info@windstarcruises.com, Web Site: www.windstarcruises.com
EVP Fleet Opers: Captain Nico Corbijn
VP Marine Hotel Opers: Nick Burger
Conducts Business: U.S., Canada
Employees: 12
Primary Market Served: Business & Consumer
Catalog available online
Direct online sales
Advertising/Marketing Budget Related to Direct Marketing: 26-50%
Direct Marketing ad budget: $100,000
Direct Mail: 50%
Magazines: 50%
Founded: 1984
Gross sales or billing: $144,000,000

Cruises: mostly Americans & Canadians; ages 20-75, mid to upper income.

WYNDHAM HOTEL GROUP
1 Sylvan Way (fl 3)
Parsippany, NJ 07054-3887
Telephone: (973) 753-8925, Web Site: www.cendant.com
Sr Dir Loyalty & Mktg: Florence Ho
Primary Market Served: Consumer

YOUR MAN TOURS
100 N Sepulveda Blvd (Suite 1700)
El Segundo, CA 90245-5655
Telephone: (310) 649-3820, FAX: (310) 649-2118, E-Mail: ymt@earthlink.net, Web Site: www.ymtvacations.com
Pres: William Price
Conducts Business: U.S., Canada
Employees: 120
Primary Market Served: Consumer
Catalog available online
Indirect online sales
Advertising/Marketing Budget Related to Direct Marketing: 76-100%
Direct Marketing ad budget: $3,500,000
Direct Mail: 20%
Magazines: 12%
Newspapers: 25%
TV/Radio: 38%
Telephone: 5%
Founded: 1967
Gross sales or billing: $30,000,000

Travel tour operator selling direct to the general public.

Direct Marketers — Geographic Index

ALABAMA

Alfa Insurance (15), PO Box 11000, Montgomery, 36191-0001

Award Co of America (6), 3200 Rice Mine Rd, Tuscaloosa, 35406-1510

Bradford Health Services (16), 2101 Magnolia Ave S (Suite 518), Birmingham, 35205-2853

BuyFilters.com LLC (5), PO Box 581, Silverhill, 36576

CMEinfo.com (16), 500 Corporate Pkwy (Suite 300), Birmingham, 35242

Compass Bank (14), 15 20th St S, Birmingham, 35233-2011

EBSCO Reception Room Subscription Services (18), PO Box 830460, Birmingham, 35283-0460

Fathers of St Edmund Southern Missions Inc (1), 1428 Broad St, Selma, 36701-4300

GameTime Inc (11), 150 Playcore Dr, Fort Payne, 35967

Gothic Arch Greenhouses Inc (8), 309 Glenwood St, Mobile, 36606-1741

Hatton-Brown Publishers Inc (17), 225 Hanrick St, Montgomery, 36104-3317

Infinity Insurance Co (15), 3700 Colonnade Pkwy (Suite 600), Birmingham, 35243-3219

Integrity Music Inc (16), 800 Hillcrest Rd (Suite 6), Mobile, 36695-3906

Intergraph Corp (16), 170 Graphics Dr, Madison, 35758

Robert James Co Inc (10), 930 Marketta Spur Rd, Moody, 35004

Jeffers & Co (5), 310 W Saunders Rd, Dothan, 36301

Kappler Protective Apparel & Fabrics (2), 55 Grimes Dr, PO Box 490, Guntersville, 35976

Kaylor's School Supply (16), 4152 Hwy 75 N, Albertville, 35951

Long's Electronics Inc (3), 2630 S Fifth Ave, Irondale, 35210-1209

MAX Federal Credit Union (14), 2785 Zelda Rd, Montgomery, 36106-2698

Oakstone Publishing LLC (17), 2700 Corporate Dr (Suite 100), Birmingham, 35242

Priester Pecan Co Inc (4), 208 E Old Fort Rd, Fort Deposit, 36032-4012

Protective Life Insurance Co (15), 2801 Hwy 280 S, Birmingham, 35223-2488

Redstone Federal Credit Union (1), 220 Wynn Dr NW, Huntsville, 35893-0001

Regions (14), 1900 5th Ave N Ste 300, Birmingham, 35203-2669

Regitar USA Inc (9), 2575 Container Dr, Montgomery, 36109

Shelby Insurance Companies (15), 2 Perimeter Park S (Suite 423E), Birmingham, 35243-3282

Southern Poverty Law Center (1), 400 Washington Ave, Montgomery, 36104-4344

Southern Progress Corp (17), 2100 Lake Shore Dr, Birmingham, 35209-6721

Three Georges and the Nuthouse (16), 558 S Broad St, Mobile, 36603-1124

Tidbits Media (17), 1430 I-85 Pkwy (Suite 301), Montgomery, 36106-3635

United Investors Life Insurance Co (15), 2001 3rd Ave S Bsmt, Box 10207, Birmingham, 35233-2196

University of Alabama (13), 624 Paul W Bryant Dr, Tuscaloosa, 35487

Vulcan Information Packaging (16), PO Box 29, Vincent, 35178

Vulcan Materials Co (16), 1200 Urban Ctr Dr, Birmingham, 35242

Woman's Missionary Union (17), 100 Missionary Ridge, PO Box 830010, Birmingham, 35283-0010

ALASKA

Oomingmak Musk Ox Producers Co-operative (6), 604 "H" St, Anchorage, 99501

Rural Alaska Community Action Program Inc (1), 731 E 8th Ave, Anchorage, 99501-3772

St Lawrence Island Original Ivory Co-operative (6), PO Box 189, Gambell, 99742

ARIZONA

Alliance Defense Fund (1), 15100 N 90th St, Scottsdale, 85260-2901

American Federation of Astrologers (1), 6535 S Rural Rd, Tempe, 85283-3746

Animal Health Express, Inc (5), 3301 N Freeway Rd, Tucson, 85705-5015

Antique Electronic Supply (3), 6221 S Maple Ave, Tempe, 85283

Arizona Highways Magazine (17), 2039 W Lewis Ave, Phoenix, 85009-2819

The Arizona Republic (17), 200 E Van Buren St, Phoenix, 85004-2238

Avnet Inc (16), 2211 S 47th St, Phoenix, 85034

B Bunch Co Inc (16), 9619 N 21st Dr, Phoenix, 85021-1895

Benevilla (1), 16752 Greenwood St, 16752 N. Greasewood St., Surprise, 85378

Best Western International (19), 6201 N 24th Pkwy, Phoenix, 85016-2023

Cable Shopping Network (16), 15945 N 76th St, Scottsdale, 85260-1781

Christian Brands (16), 5226 S 31st Pl, Phoenix, 85040-3742

Community Food Bank (1), 3003 S Country Club Rd (Ste 221), Tucson, 85713-4084

Con-Cor International (11), 8101 E Research Ct Ste 101, Tucson, 85710-6758

Crosstown Traders Inc (2), 3740 E 34th St, Tucson, 85710

DMB Realty Network (16), 20789 N Pima Rd (Suite 250), Scottsdale, 85255-7206

DataCal Enterprises (16), 1345 N Mondel Dr, Gilbert, 85233

Desert Rat Truck Centers (12), 3705 S Palo Verde St, Tucson, 85713-5401

Drumbeat Indian Arts Inc (6), 4143 N 16th St (Suite 1), Phoenix, 85016-5351

Fairytale Brownies (4), 4610 E Cotton Center Blvd (Suite 100), Phoenix, 85040-8898

Food for the Hungry Inc (1), 1224 E Washington St, Phoenix, 85034-1102

Grand Canyon Association (1), PO Box 399, Grand Canyon, 86023

Grand Canyon University (13), 3300 W Camelback Rd, Phoenix, 85017-1097

Grover Co (16), PO Box 41844, Mesa, 85274-1844

Happy Trails Resort (19), 17200 W Bell Rd, Surprise, 85374-9740

Home Planners (17), 3275 W Ina Rd (Suite 110), Tucson, 85741-2152

Insight Direct Inc (16), 6820 S Harl Ave, Tempe, 85283-4318

Kolbe Corp (17), 2355 E Camelback Rd (Suite 610), Phoenix, 85016-9040

Lawyers & Judges Publishing Co Inc (17), PO Box 30040, Tucson, 85751-0040

LifeLock (16), 60 E Rio Salado Pkwy Ste 400, Tempe, 85281-9129

Make-A-Wish Foundation of America (1), 4742 N 24th St (Suite 400), Phoenix, 85016-4862

McMurry Inc (17), 1010 E Missouri Ave, Phoenix, 85014-2602

Mechanical Breakdown Administrators Inc (14), 9419 E San Salvador (Suite 105), Scottsdale, 85258-5510

Midwest Publishing Inc (17), 10844 N 23rd Ave, Phoenix, 85029-4924

Mountain West Supply Co (3), 5116 E Charter Oak, Scottsdale, 85254

Naturmed (7), 661 E Howards Rd, Camp Verde, 86322

Neutron Industries (16), 7107 N Black Canyon Hwy, Phoenix, 85021-7619

Nu-Parr Swimwear (2), 929 E Indian School Rd, Phoenix, 85014-4745

Personal Achievement Institute (17), PO Box 6543, One Speaking Success Rd, Kingman, 86402-6543

PetSmart Inc (5), 19601 N 27th Ave, Phoenix, 85027-4010

Rich Brands (16), 1819 E Morten Ave (Suite 110), Phoenix, 85020-4661

Sedona Labs (7), 260 Justin Dr, Cottonwood, 86326

Sierra Scientific Inc (9), 1005 N 50th St (Suite 150), Phoenix, 85008-0117

Single Scene News (17), 1928 E Laguna Dr, Tempe, 85282-5913

SkyMall Inc (16), 1520 E Pima St, Phoenix, 85034-4600

Smart Practice (17), 3400 E McDowell Rd, Phoenix, 85008-7899

Syntellect (16), 2095 W Pinnacle Peak Rd Ste 110, Phoenix, 85027-1262

Territorial Newspapers (17), 3280 E Hemisphere Loop (Suite 180), PO Box 27087, Tucson, 85726-7087

U-Haul International (16), 2727 N Central Ave, Phoenix, 85004

University of Phoenix (13), 1625 W Fountainhead Pkwy, Tempe, 85282-2371

Vemma Nutrition Co (7), 1621 W Rio Salado Pkwy, Tempe, 85012

Vitamin Research Products (7), 260 Justin Dr, Cottonwood, 86326

Vivitar Corp (16), 1600 N Desert Dr (Suite 101), Tempe, 85281-1798

Wolfe Publishing Co Inc (17), 2180 Gulfstream (Suite A), Prescott, 86301-6182

ARKANSAS

CenterCore Group Inc (16), 201 Industrial Park, Marked Tree, 72365

Cooper Communities Inc (16), 903 N 47th St, Rogers, 72756

Creative Irish Gifts (6), 3801 Woodland Heights Rd Ste 100, Little Rock, 72212-2410

Holland Wildflower Farm (8), 290 O'Neil Ln, Elkins, 72727

Lafferty Equipment Manufacturing Inc (9), 5614 Oak Grove Rd, North Little Rock, 72118

Leisure Arts Inc (17), 104 Champs Blvd (#100), Maumelle, 72113-6738

Micro Plastics Inc (16), PO Box 149, Flippin, 72634

Reliance Electric (9), 5711 RS Boreham Jr St, Fort Smith, 72901-8301

AG Russell Knives Inc (11), 2900 S 26th St, Rogers, 72758-8571

Virco Manufacturing Corp (16), Hwy 65 S, Conway, 72033

WalMart Stores Inc (16), 702 SW 8th St, Bentonville, 72716

CALIFORNIA

ABC Clio (17), 130 Cremona, Santa Barbara, 93117

AGIA Insurance Services (15), 1155 Eugenia Pl, Carpinteria, 93013-2061

Abbeon Cal Inc (9), 123 Gray Ave, Santa Barbara, 93101-1809

Accountants' Supply House (10), PO Box 1186, Lancaster, 93584-1186

Accountemps (16), 2884 Sand Hill Rd (Suite 200), Menlo Park, 94025-7059

ACCUSPLIT Inc (16), 3090 Independence Dr Ste 150, Livermore, 94551-9423

Adventure Creations Inc (16), 2077 Harbor Blvd (#B), Costa Mesa, 92625-2630

Air Power USA (12), 8366 Isis Ave, Los Angeles, 90045

Aircraft Spruce & Specialty Co (12), 225 Airport Cir, Corona, 92880-2527

Alfred Publishing Co Inc (17), 16320 Roscoe Blvd (Suite 100), Van Nuys, 91406-1216

Allergan Inc (16), 2525 DuPont Dr, Irvine, 92612-1531

Alliance of Area Business Publications (1), 1970 E Grand Ave (Suite 300), Redondo Beach, 90245-5038

Amanet (16), 7001 Eton Ave # B, Canoga Park, 91303-2112

American Association of Critical-Care Nurses (1), 101 Columbia, Aliso Viejo, 92656-4109

American Council on Exercise (1), 4851 Paramount Dr, San Diego, 92123

The American Film Institute (1), 2021 N Western Ave, Los Angeles, 90027-1657

American Historic Inns Inc (17), PO Box 669, Dana Point, 92629-0669

American Horse Products (11), 31896 Plaza Dr (Suite C4), San Juan Capistrano, 92675

American Society on Aging (1), 575 Market St (Suite 2100), San Francisco, 94105-2869

The American Vintage Library (17), PO Box 48621, Los Angeles, 90048-0621

America's Finest Pet Doors (16), 202 Tank Farm Rd (Suite F1), San Luis Obispo, 93401-7520

Amrel (16), 3445 Fletcher Ave, El Monte, 91731

Amvac Chemical Corp (8), 4100 E Washington Blvd, Los Angeles, 90023-4406

Ancient Circles (6), 190 North St, Willits, 95490-3420

Anritsu Co (16), 490 Jarvis Dr, Morgan Hill, 95037

Anthem Blue Cross (15), 1 Wellpoint Way, Westlake Village, 91362-3893

Apple Inc (16), 1 Infinite Loop, Cupertino, 95014-2083

Aramark Uniform Services (2), 115 N First St, Burbank, 91502-1856

Art.com (8), 2100 Powell St 13th Fl, Emeryville, 94608-1893

Astronomical Society of the Pacific (1), 390 Ashton Ave, San Francisco, 94112-1722

Audio-Digest Foundation (1), 450 N Brand Blvd (Suite 900), Glendale, 91203-2397

Audio Editions Books-on-Cassette & CD (3), PO Box 6930, Auburn, 95604-6930

Australian Tourist Commission (19), 6100 Center Drive, Los Angeles, 90045

Autobytel Inc (12), 18872 MacArthur Blvd (Suite 200), Irvine, 92612-1448

Autodesk Inc (16), 111 McInnis Pkwy, San Rafael, 94903

Avery Dennison Corp (10), 50 Pointe Dr, Brea, 92821-3699

The Ayn Rand Institute (1), 2121 Alton Pkwy (Suite 250), Irvine, 92606-4926

Back Designs Inc (7), PO Box 2810, Novato, 94948-2810

Bailey's Inc (9), 1210 Commerce Ave (Suite 8), Woodland, 95776

Baker Corp (16), 3020 Old Ranch Pkwy (Suite 220), Seal Beach, 90740-8805

Balboa Life & Casualty (15), 3349 Michelson (Suite 200), Irvine, 92623-9702

Bamboo Sourcery (8), 666 Wagnon Rd, Sebastopol, 95472-9546

Banana Republic (2), 2 Folsom St, San Francisco, 94105

Bank of the West (14), 300 S Grand Ave, Los Angeles, 90071-3109

Barely Nothings Lingerie (2), 530 W Tefft St, Nipomo, 93444

BarterNews (17), 24446 Caswell Ct, Laguna Niguel, 92677

Baseline FT (17), 3415 S Sepulveda Blvd (Suite 200), Los Angeles, 90034-6032

Bathroom Machineries (8), 495 Main St, Murphys, 95247

Beauty Naturally (7), PO Box 4005, Burlingame, 94011-4005

Beckman Coulter Inc (16), 250 S Kraemer Blvd, Brea, 92821-6232

Beemak Plastics Inc (16), 16711 Knott Ave, La Mirada, 90638-6013

Beeman Precision Airguns (11), 10652 Bloomfield Ave, Santa Fe Springs, 90670-3912

Bennett Marine Video (3), 2321 Abbot Kinney Blvd (Suite 101), Venice, 90291-4876

Better Tools For Industry (9), 9525 Pathway St, Santee, 92071

Bick International (6), PO Box 854, Van Nuys, 91408-0854

Biomerica Inc (7), 17571 Von Karman Ave, Irvine, 92614-6207

Blue Shield Life (15), 50 Beale St, San Francisco, 94105-1813

Blue Shield of California (15), 50 Beale St, San Francisco, 94105-1808

Body by Jake Global LLC (16), 11611 San Vicente Blvd Ste 610, Los Angeles, 90049-6506

Book Passage Cafe (17), 51 Tamal Vista Blvd, Corte Madera, 94925-1145

Book Publishing Information Kit (17), 530 Ellwood Ridge, Santa Barbara, 93117-1047

Bountiful Gardens (8), 1712 S Main St (Suite D), Willits, 95490-4400

Bowers & Merena Auctions (16), 18061 Fitch, Irvine, 92614-6018

BowTie Inc (17), 3 Burroughs Ave, Irvine, 92618-2804

Brady Marketing Co Inc (16), 1331 N California Blvd (Suite 320), Walnut Creek, 94596-4563

BroadVision Inc (16), 1700 Seaport Blvd (Suite 210), Redwood City, 94063-5579

Brocade Communications Systems Inc (16), 130 Holger Way, San Jose, 95134

Buena Vista Home Entertainment (3), 500 S Buena Vista St, Burbank, 91521

Buena Vista Winery (16), 18000 Old Winery Rd, Sonoma, 95476

BusinessOnline (16), 701 B St (Suite 1000), San Diego, 92101-8109

C&T Bridge Supplies (11), 3532 Katella Ave (Suite 103), Los Alamitos, 90720-3138

CAIG Laboratories Inc (9), 12200 Thatcher Ct, Poway, 92064

CDMI Inc (1), 711 Pacific Coast Hwy (Unit 118), Huntington Beach, 92648-5051

CMI Direct (15), 130 Cook Ave (Suite 101), Pasadena, 91107-7320

CRM Learning (16), 2720 Loker Ave W (Suite Q), Carlsbad, 92010-6606

CTB/McGraw-Hill LLC (16), 20 Ryan Ranch Rd, Monterey, 93940

Cable Car Clothiers/Robert Kirk Ltd (2), 110 Sutter St (Suite 108), San Francisco, 94104

Cable Connection (3), 1035 Mission Ct, Fremont, 94539

Calbiochem-Novabiochem Corp (9), 10394 Pacific Ctr Ct, San Diego, 92121-4340

Calibre Press Inc (17), 200 Green St (Suite 200), San Francisco, 94111-1356

California Chamber of Commerce (1), 1215 K St (Suite 1400), Sacramento, 95814

California Institute of Technology (16), Industrial Relations Ctr 1-90, Pasadena, 91125-9000

California Mustang Parts & Accessories (16), 19400 San Jose Ave, City of Industry, 91748

California Society of CPA's (1), 1800 Gateway Dr (Suite 200), San Mateo, 94404-4072

Cane & Basket Supply Co (8), 1283 S Cochran Ave, Los Angeles, 90019-2846

Canine Companions for Independence (16), PO Box 446, Santa Rosa, 95402-0446

The Caning Shop (11), 926 Gilman St, Berkeley, 94710

Capital Insurance Group (CIG) (15), 2300 Garden Rd, Monterey, 93940-5326

Carabella Collection (2), 17662 Armstrong Ave, Irvine, 92614

Cardflex Financial Services (14), 2900 Bristol Ave (bldg F), Costa Mesa, 92626-5981

Chabin Concepts (16), 2515 Ceanothus Ave (Suite 100), Chico, 95973-7720

Charisma Brands LLC (6), 23482 Peralta Dr Ste A, Laguna Hills, 92653-1733

Children of the Night (1), 14530 Sylvan St, Van Nuys, 91411

China Books & Periodicals Inc (17), 360 Swift Ave (#48), South San Francisco, 94080

City of Cerritos (1), 18125 Bloomfield Ave, Cerritos, 90703

City of Hope National Medical Center (1), 1500 E Duarte Rd, Duarte, 91010

Civil Service Employees Insurance Group (15), 2121 N California Blvd (Suite 555), Walnut Creek, 94596-3501

Clegg Industries Inc (16), 19032 S Vermont Ave, Gardena, 90248-4412

Clients & Profits Worldwide (14), 4755 Oceanside Blvd (#200), Oceanside, 92056-3056

The Clorox Co (16), 1221 Broadway, Oakland, 94612-1888

CollegeSource Inc (17), 8090 Engineer Rd, San Diego, 92111

Conform Pacific (16), PO Box 1658, Lomita, 90717-5658

CM Connolly (1), 7220 Greenhaven Dr (Suite 7), Sacramento, 95831-3592

Continuing Education of the Bar (CEB) (1), 2100 Franklin St Ste 500, Oakland, 94612-3098

ConversionVoodoo.com (16), 10601 Tierrasanta Blvd (# G-371), San Diego, 92124-2616

Convertible Service (16), 5126 N Walnut Grove Ave, San Gabriel, 91776-2026

Coppa Woodworking, Inc (8), 1231 Paraiso Ave, San Pedro, 90731

Corona-Lotus Inc (4), 50 Francisco St, San Francisco, 94133-2107

Countrywide Financial Corp (14), 45 Park Granada, Calabasas, 91302

Creative Teaching Associates (16), 23505 Auberry Rd, Clovis, 93619-9648

Creative Teaching Press (17), 6262 Katella Ave, Cypress, 90630-5204

Culinary Parts Unlimited (16), 840 Folsom St, San Francisco, 94107

Custom Toll Free (5), 10940 Wilshire Blvd (fl 17), Los Angeles, 90024

Cuvaison Inc (4), 1221 Duhig Rd, Napa, 94559

DFS Group Limited (5), 525 Market St, First Market Tower, San Francisco, 94105-2708

D'Lights (8), 2107 Chico Ave, South El Monte, 91733-1606

Dairy Council of California (1), 2151 Michelson Dr (Suite 235), Irvine, 92612-1339

Dalrada Financial Corp (14), 11956 Bernardo Plaza Dr (Suite 516), San Diego, 92128-2538

Data Direct Networks (3), 9351 Deering Ave, Chatsworth, 91311

Davis Instruments Corp (8), 3465 Diablo Ave, Hayward, 94545-2746

Delta Tech Industries (12), 1901 S Vineyard Ave # 7, Ontario, 91761-7747

DeLuxe Laboratories Inc (16), 5433 Fernwood Ave, Hollywood, 90027

Dexta Corp (16), 962 Kaiser Rd, Napa, 94558

Dharma Trading Co (2), 1805 S McDowell Blvd Ext (Suite D), Petaluma, 94954-6945

DineEquity Inc (16), 450 N Brand Blvd (fl 7), Glendale, 91203-4415

Dinyari Inc (9), 500 Phelan Ave, San Jose, 95112-2506

DIRECTV LLC (16), 2230 E Imperial Hwy, El Segundo, 90245

Discovery Toys (16), 3037 Independence Dr (Suite G), Livermore, 94551-7676

Diversified Photo Supply Corp (10), 333 W Alondra Blvd (Suite C), Gardena, 90248-2428

Doctor's Best Inc (16), 197 Avenida La Pata (#A), San Clemente, 92673-6307

The Doctor's Co (15), 185 Greenwood Rd, Napa, 94558

Donor Services Group (1), 6715 W Sunset Blvd, Los Angeles, 90028-7107

Dr Jays (2), 7720 Kenamar Ct (Suite C), San Diego, 92121-2425

Draper's & Damon's (2), 9 Pasteur (Suite 200), Irvine, 92618-3804

Dream Products Inc (5), 412 Dream Ln, Van Nuys, 91496-0001

Dynamic Development Co (12), 25512 Pampero Cir, Mission Viejo, 92691-5436

Dynamic Engineering (3), 150 Dubois St (Suite C), Santa Cruz, 95060-2114

EOS International Inc (5), 1902 Wright Pl (fl 2), Carlsbad, 92008

ETR Associates (7), 100 Enterprise Way (Suite G300), Scotts Valley, 95066

Earthrise (16), 2151 Michelson Dr (Suite 258), Irvine, 92648

eBay Inc (16), 2065 Hamilton Ave, San Jose, 95125

Educational Insights, Inc (16), 152 W Walnut St Ste 201, Gardena, 90248-3147

Electronic Arts Inc (3), 209 Redwood Shores Pkwy, Redwood City, 94065-1175

Elite Debit (14), 11450 Sheldon St, Sun Valley, 91352-1121

En ESPANOL Publishing Group LLC (17), 250 S Beverly Dr (#301), Beverly Hills, 90212-3831

Enterprex International Corp (16), 12101 Clark St Ste G, Arcadia, 91006-6031

Entrepreneur Media Inc (17), 2445 McCabe Way (Suite 400), Irvine, 92614

Epson America (10), 3840 Kilroy Airport Way, Long Beach, 90806-2469

ESignal (14), 3955 Point Eden Way, Hayward, 94545-3720

Eventful Inc (19), 12626 High Bluff Dr., Ste. 100, San Diego, 92130

Everex Computer Systems Inc (16), 48319 Fremont Blvd, Fremont, 94538-6580

Excelligence Learning Corp (5), 2 Lower Ragsdale Dr (Suite 125), Monterey, 93940-7810

Executive Protection Products Inc (16), 351 Second St, Napa, 94559

Experience In Software Inc (16), 2029 Durant Ave Ste 201, Berkeley, 94704-1564

F P International (16), 34175 Ardenwood Blvd, Fremont, 94555-3653

FAFCO Inc (16), 435 Otterson Dr, Chico, 95928-8207

Farmers Insurance (15), 4680 Wilshire Blvd, Los Angeles, 90010

Fireman's Fund Insurance Co (14), 777 San Marin Dr, Novato, 94998-0002

First Advantage Membership Services (14), 12395 First American Way, Poway, 92064-6897

Fisher Investments (14), 13100 Skyline Blvd, Woodside, 94062-4542

Forecaster Publishing Co Inc (14), 19623 Ventura Blvd, Tarzana, 91356

Foremost Industrial Exchange (16), 15222 Keswick St, Van Nuys, 91405-1068

Rich Fox & Associates Inc (1), 175 Chaparral Rd, Carmel Valley, 93924-9634

Frederick's of Hollywood Group Inc (2), 6255 Sunset Blvd (fl 6), Los Angeles, 90028-7403

Freestyle Photographic Supplies (5), 5124 Sunset Blvd, Los Angeles, 90027-9897

Fresno Oxygen (9), 2825 S Elm Ave (#101), Fresno, 93706-5460

The Fuller Theological Seminary (16), 135 N Oakland Ave, Pasadena, 91182

GBH Communications (3), 1309 S Myrtle Ave, Monrovia, 91016-4150

Gallery of Cats (6), 26136 Galvez Ct, Valencia, 91355-3349

Gateway Inc (3), 7565 Irvine Center Dr, Irvine, 92618

Geary's of Beverly Hills (6), 351 N Beverly Dr, Beverly Hills, 90210-4794

Gero Vita (16), 1835 Newport Blvd (Suite A109, #439), Costa Mesa, 92627-5007

Get Seen Media Group (16), 5115 Wilshire Blvd (Apt 235), Los Angeles, 90036-4371

Ghirardelli Chocolate Co (16), 1111 139th Ave, San Leandro, 94578

Golden Fleece Designs Inc (16), 441 S Victory Blvd, Burbank, 91502-2353

Golden Gate Transportation District (16), 1011 Anderson Dr, San Rafael, 94901

Goodwill Industries of San Francisco (1), 1580 Mission St, San Francisco, 94103-2513

Grand Pacific Resorts (19), 5900 Pasteur Ct (#200), Carlsbad, 92009-7336

Gump's By Mail Inc (6), 135 Post St, San Francisco, 94108

Gun Video Catalog/LMP (11), 4585 Murphy Canyon Rd, San Diego, 92123-4318

The Gymboree Corp (2), 500 Howard St, San Francisco, 94105-3000

Hadley Fruit Orchards Inc (4), 47993 Seminole Dr, Cabazon, 92230

Harbor Freight Tools (9), 3491 Mission Oaks Blvd, Camarillo, 93012-5034

Harris Direct (1), 21250 Califa St (Suite 114), Woodland Hills, 91367-5023

Harwil Corp (9), 541 Kinetic Dr, Oxnard, 93030

Hear Music (3), 100 N Crescent Dr, Beverly Hills, 90210

Helman Group Ltd (16), 1621 Beacon Pl, Oxnard, 93033

Herbalife International of America Inc (7), PO Box 80210, Los Angeles, 90080

Hewlett-Packard Co (16), 3000 Hanover St, Palo Alto, 94304-1185

Hireko Golf (11), 16185 Stephens St, City of Industry, 91745

Holiday Travel of America (19), 6405 El Camino Real, Carlsbad, 92009-2802

Hollywood Film Archive (17), 8391 Beverly Blvd (PMB 321), Los Angeles, 90048

Home Safeguard Industries (9), 29706 Baden Pl, Malibu, 90265

Hot Topic Inc (2), 18305 E San Jose Ave, City of Industry, 91748

Houlihan Lokey Howard & Zukin (14), 10250 Constellation Blvd (fl 5), Los Angeles, 90067

Howard Rice Nemerovski Canady Falk & Rabkin (14), 3 Embarcadero Ctr (fl 7), San Francisco, 94111-4078

Hydra Group LLC (9), 10940 Wilshire Blvd (Fl 11), Los Angeles, 90024

IClimber Inc (16), 315 W Verdugo Ave (Suite 101), Burbank, 91502-2484

iLoop Mobile Inc (16), 25 Metro Dr (Suite 210), San Jose, 95110-1338

In-Sync Publications (18), 800 Knob Hill Ave, Redondo Beach, 90277

Information for Public Affairs, Inc (17), 2101 K St, Sacramento, 95816-4920

Institute For Natural Resources (16), 2352 Stanwell Dr, Concord, 94520

Institute of Reading Development (1), Five Commercial Blvd, Novato, 94949

Institutional Real Estate Inc (17), 2274 Camino Ramon, San Ramon, 94583

Integretel Inc (16), 5883 Rue Ferrari, San Jose, 95138-1857

Intel Corp (16), 2200 Mission College Blvd, Santa Clara, 95052

IntelliQuote Insurance Services (15), 5170 Golden Foothill Pkwy, El Dorado Hills, 95762-9658

International Direct Media Co & Information Publishing Co (17), 2801 39th Ave (Suite 100), San Francisco, 94116-2744

International Wine Accessories Inc (4), 1445 N McDowell Blvd, Petaluma, 94954

Intuit (10), 2632 Marine Way, Mountain View, 94043

Involve Social (1), 44288 Fremont Blvd, Fremont, 94538-6000

Isuzu Motors America LLC (16), 1400 S Douglass Rd (Suite 100), Anaheim, 92806

JDR Microdevices (3), 4101 Dublin Blvd (Suite F120), Dublin, 94568

Jaffe Brothers Natural Foods (4), 28560 Lilac Rd, Valley Center, 92082

Jafra Cosmetics International Inc (7), 2451 Townsgate Rd, Westlake Village, 91361

Jameco Electronics (3), 1355 Shoreway Rd, Belmont, 94002

Jazzercise Inc (2), 2460 Impala Dr, Carlsbad, 92008

Jossey-Bass Inc Publishers (17), One Montgomery St (Suite 1200), San Francisco, 94104-4505

KCET (1), 2900 W Alameda Ave #600, Burbank, 91505-4268

KHL Engineered Packaging Solutions (16), 6600 Valley View St, Buena Park, 90620

KPBS FM/TV (1), 5200 Campanile Dr San Diego State Univ, San Diego, 92182-1901

Kelsey National Corp (15), 3030 S Bundy Dr, Los Angeles, 90066

Kensington Computer Products Group (16), 333 Twin Dolphin Dr (6th fl), Redwood Shores, 94065

Kross Inc (16), 25682 Springbrook Ave Ste 140, Santa Clarita, 91350-2433

L&L Management (16), 751 N Fair Oaks Ave, Pasadena, 91103-3069

The LadyBug Co (8), 12857 Oroville Quincy Hwy, Berry Creek, 95916

Lamkin Corp (11), 6530 Gateway Park Dr, San Diego, 92154-7510

Lark in the Morning (5), PO Box 1176, Mendocino, 95460

Larkwood Group LLC (1), 4096 Piedmont Ave (Suite 214), Oakland, 94611-5221

LearnCom HR Consulting & Training (16), 5520 Trabuco Rd, Irvine, 92620-5705

Learning Communications LLC (16), 5520 Trabuco Rd, Irvine, 92620-5705

Levi Strauss & Co (16), 1155 Battery St, San Francisco, 94111

Lexus Division of Toyota (12), 19001 S Western Ave (Suite L100), Torrance, 90501-1106

LibertyTree Press (5), 100 Swan Way, Oakland, 94621-1428

LifeScript (7), 4000 MacArthur Blvd, Newport Beach, 92660

Lionsgate Television Corp (16), 2700 Colorado Ave (Suite 200), Santa Monica, 90404-5502

Live Nation (19), 9348 Civic Center Dr Lobby, Beverly Hills, 90210-3642

LO-AD Communications (16), 150 E Colorado Blvd (Suite 210), Pasadena, 91105

Location Sound Corp (3), 10639 Riverside Dr, North Hollywood, 91602-2355

Longevity Pure Medicine (7), 10415 Ravenwood Ct, Los Angeles, 90077-2517

The Los Angeles Convention & Visitors Bureau (19), 333 S Hope St (fl 18), Los Angeles, 90071-1406

Los Angeles Kings (16), 1111 S Figueroa, Los Angeles, 90015

The Los Angeles Lakers Inc (11), 555 N Nash St, El Segundo, 90245

Lotions & Lace (2), 3960 Garner Rd, Riverside, 92501

Luggage Base (16), 670 S Frontage Rd, Nipomo, 93444-9148

Lundberg Family Farms (16), PO Box 369, 5370 Church St, Richvale, 95974-0369

MPBS Industries (16), 2820 E Washington Blvd, Los Angeles, 90023-4217

MPS Multimedia Inc (16), 1222 S Amphlett Blvd, San Mateo, 94402-1906

MRV Communications (3), 20415 Nordhoff St, Chatsworth, 91311

Making It Big (2), 525 Portal St, Cotati, 94931-3023

Markwins International Corp (16), 22067 Ferrero Pkwy, City of Industry, 91789

Marshall & Swift (17), 777 S Figueroa St (fl 12), Los Angeles, 90017-5878

Matt & Kumpany Kuzins (1), 1512 14th St, Sacramento, 95814

Mattel Inc (16), 333 Continental Blvd, El Segundo, 90245-5012

Mazda Motor of America Inc (16), 7755 Irvine Center Dr, Irvine, 92623

McClatchy Co (17), 2100 "Q" St, Sacramento, 95816-6899

McKesson Corp (7), 1 Post St, San Francisco, 94104-5203

Medcom Inc (17), 6060 Phyllis Dr, Cypress, 90630

Medic Alert Foundation (1), 5226 Pirrone Court, Salida, 95368

Meguiar's Inc (16), 17991 Mitchell S, PO Box 92623, Irvine, 92614-6015

Mentor Corp (16), 201 Mentor Dr, Santa Barbara, 93111-3340

Merchant E-Solutions (14), 3600 Bridge Pkwy (Suite 102), Redwood City, 94065

Mickwee Group Inc (16), 5600 Mowry School Rd Ste 230, Newark, 94560-5800

Microbiz Corp (3), 655 Oak Grove Ave (#493), Menlo Park, 94026-0493

Mitchell International (17), 6220 Greenwich Dr, San Diego, 92122-5913

Mitsubishi Digital Electronics America Inc (3), 10833 Valley View St (Suite 300), Cypress, 90630

Mitsubishi Motors North America Inc (1), 6400 Katella Ave, Cypress, 90630

Moby Wrap Inc (2), PO Box 1066, Chico, 95927-1066

Modern Postcard (10), 1675 Faraday Ave, Carlsbad, 92008-7314

Monex Deposit Co (14), 4910 Birch St Ste 103, Newport Beach, 92660-2188

Moon Shine Trading Co (4), 1250-A Harter Ave, Woodland, 95776-6134

Mother Jones Magazine (17), 222 Sutter St (Suite 600), San Francisco, 94108-4457

Motion Picture & Television Fund (1), 23388 Mulholland Dr, Woodland Hills, 91364-2733

Multi-Level Marketing International Association (MLMIA) (1), 119 Stanford Ct, Irvine, 92612-1671

Mike Murach & Associates Inc (17), 4340 N Knoll Ave, Fresno, 93722-7825

Murad Inc (7), 2121 Rosecrans Ave (Floor 5), El Segundo, 90245-4744

Musician's Friend (5), PO Box 5111, Westlake Village, 91359-5111

Mustek Inc (3), 3002 Dow Ave (Suite 210), Tustin, 92780-7234

Mylan Enterprises (7), 18563 Ventura Blvd (#272), Tarzana, 91356

NADA Appraisal Guides (17), 3186 Airway Ave (Unit K), Costa Mesa, 92626

Narrow Way (6), 712 Moraga Rd, Lafayette, 94549-4916

National Pen Corp (6), 12121 Scripps Summit Dr (Suite 200), San Diego, 92131-4609

National University (1), 11355 N Torrey Pines Rd, La Jolla, 92037-1013

Nestle USA (4), 800 N Brand Blvd, Glendale, 91203-1216

NetSpend (14), 1825 S Grant St (Suite 800), San Mateo, 94402-2663

Network Telephone Services Inc (16), 21135 Erwin St, Woodland Hills, 91367-3713

New & Unique Videos (3), 7323 Rondel Ct, San Diego, 92119

New Wave Media Inc (5), 5858 Horton St (Ste 300), Emeryville, 94608

New Win Publishing Inc (17), 9682 Telstar Ave (Suite 110), El Monte, 91731-3009

New Zealand Tourism Board (19), 501 Santa Monica Blvd (Suite 300), Santa Monica, 90401-2443

No Load FundX (14), 235 Montgomery St (Suite 1049), San Francisco, 94104-2994

Nordskog Publishing Co (17), 4562 Westinghouse St (Suite E), Ventura, 93003-5797

Nowell's Inc (8), 615 Irwin St, San Rafael, 94901-3940

Oakley Inc (2), 1 Icon, Foothill Ranch, 92610-3000

Oracle Corp (16), 500 Oracle Pkwy, Redwood Shores, 94065-1675

The Orange County Register (17), 625 N Grand Ave, Santa Ana, 92701

Orchard Supply Hardware (16), 6450 Via Del Oro St, San Jose, 95119

Orion Telescopes & Binoculars (11), 89 Hangar Way, Watsonville, 95076

Buck Owens' Crystal Palace (19), 2800 Buck Owens Blvd, Bakersfield, 93308-6314

PC World (17), 501 2nd St, San Francisco, 94107-1496

PMIC (17), 4727 Wilshire Blvd (Suite 300), Los Angeles, 90010-3873

Pacific Sportswear Co Inc (5), 6160 Fairmount Ave (Suite F), San Diego, 92120-3427

PAPYRUS (5), 500 Chadbourne Rd, Fairfield, 94534-9656

Para Publishing (17), PO Box 8206, Santa Barbara, 93118-8206

Paradise Galleries (6), 23482 Peralta Dr, Laguna Hills, 92653

Paragon Laboratories (16), 20433 Earl St, Torrance, 90503-2414

Parlay International (17), 712 Bancroft Rd (#505), Walnut Creek, 94598

Parmer Books (6), 7644 Forrestal Rd, San Diego, 92120-2203

Pasternack Enterprises Inc (16), PO Box 16759, Irvine, 92623-6759

Patagonia (2), 259 W Santa Clara St, Ventura, 93001-2545

PayPal Inc (14), 2211 N First St, San Jose, 95131

Peet's Coffee & Tea Inc (4), 1776 4th St, Berkeley, 94710-1711

Perfection Tip Co/Camping Products Co (16), 1340 W Cowles St, Long Beach, 90803

Periodical Publisher's Service Bureau Inc (18), 653 W Fallbrook Ave, Fresno, 93711

Petco Animal Supplies (5), 9125 Rehco Rd, San Diego, 92121-2270

Pharmavite Corp LLC (HQ) (16), 8510 Balboa, Northridge, 91325-3583

PhotoStamps.com (5), 1990 E Grand Ave, El Segundo, 90245-5013

Physical Therapy Institute Inc (16), 12630 Monte Vista Rd (Suite 204), Poway, 92064

Planned Parenthood Mar Monte (1), 1691 The Alameda, San Jose, 95126-2203

Bud Plant Illustrated Books (6), 3809 Laguna Ave, Palo Alto, 94306-2629

Plastic View ATC (9), 4585 Runway (Suite B), Simi Valley, 93063

Playboy Enterprises Inc (17), 9346 Civic Center Dr (#200), Beverly Hills, 90210-3604

Poker Player (17), 13701 Riverside Dr Ste 300, Sherman Oaks, 91423-2447

Porta-Bote International (11), 1074 Independence Ave, Mountain View, 94043-1602

Powers Television Marketing (17), 9731 Variel Ave, Chatsworth, 91311-4315

Press-Enterprise Co (17), 3450 14th St, Riverside, 92501

Princess Cruises (HQ) (19), 24844 Avenue Rockefeller, Santa Clarita, 91355-3467

Professional Binding Products Inc (16), 2192-A Anchor Ct, Thousand Oaks, 91320

Progressive Energy Corp (5), 650 Corte Raquel, San Marcos, 92069-7320

Quartermaster Uniform & Equipment Co (2), PO Box 4147, Cerritos, 90703-4147

Quick Draw Clip Systems Inc (9), 4869 McGrath St (Suite 130), Ventura, 93003-7767

Raley's Bel Air Markets (16), 500 W Capitol Ave, West Sacramento, 95605-2696

Real Goods Trading Corp (5), 13771 S Hwy 101, Hopland, 95449

Recycled Software Inc (3), 3764 Serenity Trl, Palm Springs, 92262-9774

RedEnvelope Inc (6), 4840 Eastgate Mall, San Diego, 92121-1977

Redwood City Seed Co (8), PO Box 361, Redwood City, 94064-0361

Remilon LLC (17), 100 View St Ste 202, Mountain View, 94041-1374

Rose Resnick Lighthouse for the Blind & Visually Impaired (1), 214 Van Ness Ave, San Francisco, 94102

Resource Publications Inc (17), 5369 Camden Ave (Suite 260), San Jose, 95124-5809

Ricci Lee Hubbart Associates Inc (16), PO Box 1694, Cupertino, 95015-1694

Road Runner Sports Inc (11), 5553 Copley Dr, San Diego, 92111-7904

Roland Products Inc (16), 3400 W Olympic Blvd, Los Angeles, 90019

Roll International Corp (16), 11444 W Olympic Blvd (fl 10), Los Angeles, 90064-1557

Rosicrucian Order AMORC (1), 1342 Naglee Ave, San Jose, 95191

Rosland Capital LLC (14), 429 Santa Monica Blvd (Suite 450), Santa Monica, 90401-3401

SF Global Sourcing Inc (3), 3626 Geary Blvd, San Francisco, 94118

Safti First (16), 100 N Hill Dr (Suite 12), Brisbane, 94005-1010

Sage Software Inc (16), 6561 Irvine Center Dr, Irvine, 92618-2118

Salem Media Group (17), 4880 Santa Rosa Rd, Camarillo, 93012

San Francisco Bay Area Rapid Transit District (BART) (16), 800 Madison St, Oakland, 94607-2622

San Francisco Chronicle (17), 901 Mission St, San Francisco, 94103

San Francisco Herb & Natural Food Co (4), 240 Stockton St (#400), San Francisco, 94108

San Francisco Victoriana Inc (9), 2070 Newcomb Ave, San Francisco, 94124

San Jose Mercury News (17), 750 Ridder Park Dr, San Jose, 95190

Santa Barbara Greenhouses (8), 721 Richmond Ave, Oxnard, 93030-7229

Schoolwise Press (17), 1167 Bosworth St, San Francisco, 94131-2801

Charles Schwab & Co Inc (14), 211 Main St, San Francisco, 94105-1905

SECO-LARM USA Inc (16), 16842 Millikan Ave, Irvine, 92606

Second Renaissance Books (17), 2121 Alton Pkwy (Suite 250), Irvine, 92606-4926

See's Candies Inc (4), 20600 S Alameda St, Carson, 90810-1105

Select Press (17), 40 Phillip Terr, Novato, 94945

Shield Healthcare (7), 27911 Franklin Pkwy, Valencia, 91355-4110

Silicon Graphics Inc (16), 46600 Landing Pkwy, Fremont, 94538-6420

Skullduggery (16), 5433 E La Palma Ave, Anaheim, 92807-2022

Smith & Noble (8), 1181 California Ave, Corona, 92881

SOAR Inflatables (11), 20 Healdsburg Ave, Healdsburg, 95448

Social Studies School Service (16), 10200 Jefferson Blvd, Culver City, 90232-0802

Soitenly Stooges (6), 1415 Gardena Ave, Glendale, 91204-2709

Sony Electronics Inc (16), 16530 Via Esprillo, San Diego, 92127

Sony Pictures Home Entertainment (16), 10202 W Washington Blvd (Rm 7814), SPP Bldg, Culver City, 90232-3119

Southern California Gas Co (1), 1919 S State College Blvd, Anaheim, 92806-6114

Specialty Equipment Market Association (1), 1575 S Valley Vista Dr, Diamond Bar, 91765-3914

Spectrum Chemicals & Laboratory Products (16), 14422 S San Pedro St, Gardena, 90248-2027

Spectrum eCommerce (15), 26023 Acero (Suite 100), Mission Viejo, 92691-7942

Standard Communications Corp (16), 6260 Sequence Dr, San Diego, 92121-4358

Starcrest Products of California Inc (16), 3660 Brennan Ave, Perris, 92599

StayWell/Krames (17), 1100 Grundy Ln (#2), San Bruno, 94066

Straw Hat Cooperative Corp (16), 18 Crow Canyon Ct (Suite 150), San Ramon, 94583-1669

Student Union at SJSU (1), 1 Washington Sq (Suite 1400), San Jose, 95192-0038

Sunset Magazine (17), 80 Willow Rd, Menlo Park, 94025

John Sutherland & Associates (15), 6275 Lusk Blvd, San Diego, 92121-2731

Symantec (16), 350 Ellis St, Mountain View, 94043-2202

System Pavers (16), 3750 S Susan St (Suite 200), Newport Beach, 92704-6964

TechBA - Fumec (1), 1737 1st St (Suite 110), San Jose, 95112-4522

TL Enterprises Inc (17), 2575 Vista Del Mar Dr, Ventura, 93001-3920

Tailwinds Inc (6), 775 E Blithedale (#166), Mill Valley, 94941-1554

Teleflora (16), 11444 W Olympic Blvd (fl 4), Los Angeles, 90064-1546

Ten Speed Press (17), 6001 Shellmound St 4th Fl, PO Box 7123, Emeryville, 94608-1988

TheIdeaClub.com & Dumas Martin Consulting (16), 101 W Mission Blvd (Suite 110-147), Pomona, 91766-1245

TigerDirect Inc (3), 1940 E Mariposa Ave, El Segundo, 90245

Timber Crest Farms (16), 4791 Dry Creek Rd, Healdsburg, 95448

Timberline Geodesics (8), 2015 Blake St, Berkeley, 94704

Time Motion Tools (9), 12778 Brook-printer Pl, Poway, 92064

Toyota Motor Sales USA Inc (16), 19001 S Western Ave, Torrance, 90501

Toys To Grow On (11), 2695 E Dominguez St, Carson, 90895

Trancos Inc (16), 6800 Koll Center Pkwy (Ste 170), Pleasanton, 94566-7044

Transamerica Occidental Life Co (15), 1150 S Olive St (T-24), Los Angeles, 90015

TransAmerica Retirement Services (15), 1150 S Olive St (#T-9-10), Los Angeles, 90015-2211

20th Century Fox Television (16), 10201 W Pico Blvd, Los Angeles, 90064-2606

21st Century Insurance (15), 6301 Owensmouth Ave, Woodland Hills, 91367

U-Bild (8), 821B S Tremont St Ste B, Oceanside, 92054-4158

USC Viterbi School of Engineering (1), 3650 McClintock Ave, Olin Hall (Suite 5), Los Angeles, 90089-1451

Ultimate Products Inc (16), 1151 Bay Blvd (Suite D), Chula Vista, 91911-2669

Unicom Electric Inc (16), 565 Brea Canyon Rd Ste A, Walnut, 91789-3004

United Farm Workers of America, AFL-CIO (1), 29700 Woodford-Tehachapi Rd, Keene, 93531

United Security Products Inc (16), PO Box 785, Poway, 92074-0785

US Tax Shield (14), 17328 Ventura Blvd, Encino, 91316-3904

United Systems c/o Biomed (7), 2354 Stanwell Dr, Concord, 94520-4822

Universal Studios Inc (3), 100 Universal City (Plz #3), Universal City, 91608-1138

University of California Irvine Extension (1), Pereira Dr W (Bldg 234), Irvine, 92697-5700

Urban Mapping Inc (16), 690 Fifth St (Suite 200), San Francisco, 94107-1517

Varian Medical Systems (9), 3100 Hansen Way, Palo Alto, 94304

Veriad (16), 650 Columbia St, Brea, 92821-2912

Visa USA (14), 900 Metro Center Blvd, Foster City, 94404-2173

Warnaco Swimwear Inc (16), 1201 W 5th St (Suite T1200), Los Angeles, 90017-1493

Warner Bros (3), 4000 Warner Blvd, Burbank, 91522-0001

Warrior Custom Golf Inc (11), 15 Mason (Suite A), Irvine, 92618-2707

Mal Warwick Associates (1), 2550 9th St (Suite 103), Berkeley, 94710-2551

Webb Designs Inc (16), PO Box 1405, El Cajon, 92022-1405

Wells Fargo (14), 420 Montgomery St, San Francisco, 94163

West Marine Inc (11), 500 Westridge Dr, Watsonville, 95076-4171

Western Psychological Services (16), 625 Alaska Ave, Torrance, 90503-5124

Westwood Publishing Co (17), 700 S Central Ave, Glendale, 91204

White Cap Wholesale Contractors Supplies (16), PO Box 1770, Costa Mesa, 92628-1770

Michael Wiese Productions (17), 3940 Laurel Canyon Blvd (#1111), Studio City, 91604

Simon Wiesenthal Center (1), 1399 S Roxbury Dr Ste 100, Los Angeles, 90035-4709

Williams-Sonoma Inc (8), 3250 Van Ness Ave, San Francisco, 94109-1012

Windsor Vineyards (16), 205 Concourse Blvd, Santa Rosa, 95403-8258

Winetasting.com (4), 578 Gateway Dr, Napa, 94558-7517

Woodall Publishing Co LP (17), 2575 Vista Del Mar Dr, Ventura, 93001

Sylvia Woods Harp Center (11), PO Box 816, Montrose, 91021

Woodwind & Brasswind Inc (5), PO Box 7479, Westlake Village, 91359

Working Assets (16), 101 Market St (Suite 700), San Francisco, 94105

Xilinx Inc (16), 2100 Logic Dr, San Jose, 95124-3400

Yoga Journal / Active Interest Media (17), 475 Sansome St (Suite 850), San Francisco, 94111-3135

Your Choice Or Mine (16), 128 N Kingston St, San Mateo, 94401-2063

Your Man Tours (19), 100 N Sepulveda Blvd (Suite 1700), El Segundo, 90245-5655

Zoological Society of San Diego (1), 2920 Zoo Dr, PO Box 120551, San Diego, 92112

COLORADO

Accellos Inc (12), 90 S Cascade Ave (Suite 1200), Colorado Springs, 80903-1678

American Indian College Fund (1), 8333 Greenwood Blvd, Denver, 80221

American Numismatic Association (1), 818 N Cascade Ave, Colorado Springs, 80903-3279

Arrow Electronics Inc (3), 76459 S Lima St, Englewood, 80112

Belcaro Group Inc (17), 7100 E Belleview Ave (Suite 208), Greenwood Village, 80111-1634

Birthday Keepsakes (6), 1323 S Garfield Ave, Loveland, 80537-6334

Bolind Inc (16), PO Box 18714, Boulder, 80308-1714

Broadmoor Hotel Inc (19), 1 Lake Ave, Colorado Springs, 80906-4269

DV Burrell Seed Growers Co (8), 405 N Main St, Rocky Ford, 81067

Celestial Seasonings (16), 4600 Sleepytime Dr, Boulder, 80301-3292

Coast to Coast Inc (1), PO Box 6574, Englewood, 80155-6574

Communication Creativity (17), 209 Church St, Buena Vista, 81211

Compassion International (1), 12290 Voyager Pkwy, Colorado Springs, 80921-3694

David C Cook (17), 4050 Lee Vance View, Colorado Springs, 80918-7102

Creative Learning Systems Inc (9), 1140 Boston Ave (Unit A), Longmont, 80501-5890

Current USA Inc (6), 1025 E Woodmen Rd, Colorado Springs, 80920-3181

Custom Direct (16), 8245 N Union Blvd, Colorado Springs, 80920-4456

DataLever Corp (16), 1515 Walnut St (Suite 200), Boulder, 80302-5429

Denver Metro Convention & Visitors Bureau (1), 1555 California St (Suite 300), Denver, 80202

Denver Tax Software Inc (16), PO Box 632285, Littleton, 80163-2285

Eagle Claw Fishing Tackle (11), 4245 E 46th Ave, Denver, 80216-3219

Estes Industries (11), 1295 "H" St, Penrose, 81240

Federal Citizen Information Center (5), Consumer Information Catalog, Pueblo, 81009

Fulcrum Publishing (17), 4690 Table Mountain Dr (Suite 100), Golden, 80403

Gaiam Inc (9), PO Box 3095, Boulder, 80307-3095

Gambro Inc (16), 14143 Denver W Pkwy, Lakewood, 80401

Gates Corp (9), 1551 Wewatta St, Denver, 80202

Golden Bison LLC (4), 1395 S Platte River Dr, Denver, 80223-3467

Golf Card International (1), 64 Inverness Dr E, Englewood, 80112

Gorsuch Ltd (2), 263 E Gore Creek Dr, Vail, 81657

Great-West Life (15), 8515 E Orchard Rd, Greenwood Village, 80111

Hain Celestial Group Inc (16), 4600 Sleepytime Dr, Boulder, 80301

IHS Markit (17), 321 Inverness Dr S, Englewood, 80112-5895

Jason Natural Personal Care Products (7), 4600 Sleepytime Dr, Boulder, 80301-3284

Jones International Ltd (16), 9697 E Mineral Ave, Centennial, 80112

Leanin' Tree Inc (6), 6055 Longbow Dr, Box 9800, Boulder, 80301

Lillian Vernon Corp (6), 800 E Woodman Rd, Colorado Springs, 80920

MGMA-ACMPE (1), 104 Inverness Terr Dr E, Englewood, 80112-5306

Miller Stockman (2), 8500 Zuni St, Denver, 80260-5007

Mobile Fusion (16), 165 S Union Blvd Ste 405, Lakewood, 80228-2210

Molson Coors Brewing Co (16), 1225 17th St (Ste 3200), Denver, 80202-5536

National Institute for Trial Advocacy (1), 1685 38th St, Boulder, 80301-2735

National Jewish Health (1), 1400 Jackson St, Denver, 80206-2761

National Multiple Sclerosis Society (1), 900 S Broadway (Suite) 210, Denver, 80209-4269

Native American Rights Fund (1), 1506 Broadway, Boulder, 80302-6217

Paladin Press (17), 7077 Winchester Cir, Gunbarrel Tech Center, Boulder, 80301-3505

Pastime Publications Inc (17), 99 Kalamath St, Denver, 80223-1549

RJ Persson Enterprises Inc (16), 1208 Kent Ave (Suite 101), Montrose, 81402-5228

Renton's Inc (10), 10107 Quarry Hill Pl, Parker, 80134-3748

The Right Start Inc (5), 3000 E Third Ave (#15), Denver, 80206

Rocky Mountain Chocolate Factory (4), 265 Turner Dr, Durango, 81303-7941

Society of American Magicians Inc (1), 4927 S Oak Ct, Littleton, 80127

Spear Engineering Co (16), 3107 N Stone Ave, Colorado Springs, 80907

Starz Entertainment LLC (16), 8900 Liberty Cir, Englewood, 80112-7057

Stickers 'N' Stuff Inc (6), 245 W Sycamore Ln, Louisville, 80027-2235

Sunrise Medical Inc (16), 6899 Winchester Cir (Suite 200), Boulder, 80301-3696

TAB Boards International Inc (14), 11031 Sheridan Blvd, Westminster, 80020-3201

Tecra Tools Inc (9), 2925 S Umatilla St, Englewood, 80110-1217

Trumble Greetings (6), 6055 Longbow Dr, Boulder, 80301-3203

2-10 Home Buyers Warranty (15), 10375 E Harvard Ave, 1 Denver Highlands (Suite 100), Denver, 80231-3966

Vail Resorts Inc (19), 390 Interlocken Crescent (#1000), Broomfield, 80021-8056

Weston Distance Learning Inc (13), 2001 Lowe St, Fort Collins, 80525-3474

Wilsons Leather (2), 7401 Boone Ave N, Brooklyn Park, 55428

CONNECTICUT

AIFS (19), 1 High Ridge Park, Stamford, 06905-1322

AETNA - Marketing Product & Communication (14), 151 Farmington Ave, Hartford, 06156

Affinion Group (16), 6 High Ridge Park, Stamford, 06905-1327

American Radio Relay League (1), 225 Main St, Newington, 06111-1494

AmeriCares (1), 88 Hamilton Ave, Stamford, 06902-3100

Anheuser-Busch Inc Promotional Products Group (6), 20 Constitution Blvd S, Shelton, 06484

Anthem Blue Cross Blue Shield (15), 370 Bassett Rd, North Haven, 06473

Elizabeth Arden Spas LLC (19), 300 Main St (fl 8), Stamford, 06901-3033

Association of Bridal Consultants (1), 56 Danbury Rd (Suite 11), New Milford, 06776-2521

Baxter Bros Inc (17), 1030 E Putnam Ave, Greenwich, 06830

Belvoir Media Group LLC (17), 800 Connecticut Ave, Norwalk, 06854

BIC Corp (16), 1 BIC Way (Suite 1), Shelton, 06484-6299

RC Bigelow Inc (4), 201 Black Rock Tpke, Fairfield, 06825-5512

Stanley Black & Decker Inc (16), 1000 Stanley Dr, New Britain, 06053

Boardroom Inc (17), 281 Tresser Blvd (fl 8), Stamford, 06901-3284

CD Universe (16), 101 N Plains Ind Rd, Wallingford, 06492-2165

Catholic Digest (17), 1 Montauk Ave (Suite 2), New London, 06320-4967

Century Photo (10), PO Box 308, Newtown, 06470-0308

Chadwick's of Boston Inc (2), 500 Bic Dr (Bldg 4), Milford, 06461

Champion America Inc (10), 28 Flax Mill Rd, Branford, 06405-2803

Charter Communications (16), 400 Atlantic St, Stamford, 06901

Chief Executive Magazine (17), 1 Sound Shore Dr (Suite 100), Greenwich, 06830-7251

Clairol Inc (7), One Blachley Rd, Stamford, 06922-0003

Coastal Tool & Supply (16), 510 New Park Ave, West Hartford, 06110

Cooper Surgical Inc (7), 75 Corporate Dr, Trumbull, 06611

Crabtree & Evelyn Ltd (4), 777 Post Rd E, Westport, 06880

Cronin & Co (16), 50 Nye Rd, Glastonbury, 06033-2196

Cuisinart (16), 1 Cummings Point Rd, Stamford, 06902-7901

Droll Yankees Inc (8), 55 Lathrop Rd Ext, Plainfield, 06374-1965

Duracell (16), 14 Research Dr, Bethel, 06801

The Durham Manufacturing Co (16), 201 Main St, Durham, 06422-2108

ESPN (5), ESPN Plaza, Bristol, 06010

Engineering Services & Products Co (9), 1395 John Fitch Blvd, South Windsor, 06074-1029

Esprit Line Co Ltd USA (16), 11 Heronvue Rd, Greenwich, 06831-2906

Florian Tools (8), 157 Water St, Southington, 06489-3018

Fox Valley Systems Inc (9), 5A Production Dr, Brookfield, 06804

Gems Sensors & Controls (9), One Cowles Rd, Plainville, 06062-1198

General Electric Co (16), 3135 Easton Tpke, Fairfield, 06828-0001

Global Specialties (16), 994 N Colony Rd (Unit 305), Wallingford, 06492-5902

Golf Digest Co (17), 20 Westport Rd Ste 320, PO Box 850, Wilton, 06897-4550

Good Directions Co Inc (8), 20 Commerce Dr, Danbury, 06810-4131

Guideposts (1), 39 Old Ridgebury Rd Ste 2AB, Danbury, 06810-5122

The Hartford Financial Services Inc (15), 200 Executive Blvd, Southington, 06489-1058

Hobby Surplus Sales (11), 287 Main St, New Britain, 06050-2202

Janice's LLC (8), 30 Arbor St (#3), Hartford, 06106-1215

Jaypro Sports (11), 976 Hartford Tpke, Waterford, 06385-4044

William S Konecky Associates Inc (17), 72 Ayers Point Rd, Old Saybrook, 06475

LIMRA International (1), 300 Day Hill Rd, Windsor, 06095-1783

Lego Direct Marketing (11), 555 Taylor Rd, Enfield, 06082-2372

Life-Study Fellowship Foundation Inc (17), 90 Heights Rd, Darien, 06820

Loctite Corp (16), 1001 Trout Brook Crossing, Rocky Hill, 06067

Luce Corp (16), 336 Putnam Ave, Box 4124, Hamden, 06517

MBI Inc (16), 47 Richards Ave, Norwalk, 06857-0001

Matthews 1812 House Inc (4), 250 Kent Rd S, Cornwall Bridge, 06754

Moore Medical LLC (7), 1690 New Britain Ave Ste A, Farmington, 06032-3361

MxEnergy Inc (16), 595 Summer St (Suite 300), Stamford, 06901-1407

Mystic Seaport Museum Stores (6), 75 Greenmanville Ave, Mystic, 06355-0990

NETC (5), 215 Knob Hill, Hamden, 06518

Nielsen Trade Dimensions (17), 40 Danbury Rd, Wilton, 06897-4406

Nodine's Smokehouse (4), 65 Fowler Ave, Torrington, 06790-6529

Olympia Sales Inc (16), 215 Moody Rd, Enfield, 06083-3207

Oxford Health Plans, Inc (15), 48 Monroe Turnpike, Trumbull, 06611

PPI Benefit Solutions (15), 10 Research Pkwy, Wallingford, 06492-1963

PTI Pyramid Technologies LLC (10), 45 Gracey Ave, Meriden, 06451-2284

Pachmayr Ltd (11), 475 Smith St, Middletown, 06457-1529

People's United Bank (14), 850 Main St, Bridgeport, 06604-4917

Pitney Bowes (10), 1 Elmcroft Rd, Stamford, 06926-0700

Richard M Pordes LLC (1), 99 Dolphin Cove Quay, Stamford, 06902-7716

Prime (16), 1100 Boston Ave, Bridgeport, 06610

Queue Inc (17), 80 Hathaway Dr, Stratford, 06615-7304

Reed Exhibitions (16), 383 Main Ave, Norwalk, 06851-1500

Rinfret Ltd (8), 354 Greenwich Ave, Greenwich, 06830-6522

S&S Worldwide (11), 75 Mill St, Colchester, 06415-0513

SSHC Inc/Radiant Heating Commercial Applications (9), Four Custom Dr, Old Saybrook, 06475-4008

Save the Children Federation Inc (1), 501 Kingss Hwy E (Suite 400), Fairfield, 06825

Scan Optics Inc (16), 169 Progress Dr, Manchester, 06040-2294

Silo-Hunt Hill Farm (8), 44 Upland Rd, New Milford, 06776-2199

Soundprints (6), 353 Main Ave, Norwalk, 06851-1552

Sovereign Bank New England (14), 140 Hebron Ave, Glastonbury, 06033-4239

Starwood Hotels & Resorts Worldwide Inc (19), 1 Star Pt, Stamford, 06902-8911

Statware (16), 90 Main St (Suite 213A), Centerbrook, 06409

Sterling Name Tape Inc (16), Nine Willow St, PO Box 939, Winsted, 06098

Stew Leonard's (4), 100 Westport Ave, Norwalk, 06851

Synapse Group Inc (18), 225 High Ridge Rd, East Building, Stamford, 06905-3038

Tauck World Discovery (19), 10 Norden Pl, Norwalk, 06855-1454

The Taunton Press (17), 63 S Main St, PO Box 5506, Newtown, 06470-2344

Thomas Klise/Crimson Multimedia (16), PO Box 720, Mystic, 06355-0720

Torqmaster International (9), 200 Harvard Ave, Stamford, 06902-6230

The Travelers Insurance Cos (15), 1 Tower Sq (#9PB-B), Hartford, 06183-0001

Tricor Direct Inc (9), 20 Thompson Rd, Branford, 06405-2842

Tuttle (2), 23 Village Ln, Wallingford, 06492

Tyson Associates Inc (17), 246 Federal Rd (Suite D23), Brookfield, 06804

US Games Systems Inc (11), 179 Ludlow St, Stamford, 06902

Water's Edge Resort & Spa (19), 1525 Boston Post Rd, Westbrook, 06498-2044

Webster Bank (14), 145 Bank St Fl 1, Waterbury, 06702-2211

White Flower Farm (8), PO Box 50, Litchfield, 06759

World Wrestling Entertainment Inc (16), 1241 E Main St, Stamford, 06902

Xerox Corp (16), 45 Glover Ave, PO Box 4505, Norwalk, 06856-4505

Zotos International (16), 100 Tokeneke Rd, Darien, 06820-4894

DELAWARE

AAA Mid-Atlantic Insurance Groups (15), 1 River Pl, Wilmington, 19801-5125

Advanced Machinery (9), 2 McCullough Dr, New Castle, 19720

AstraZeneca (7), 1800 Concord Pike A3C-122, Wilmington, 19850

BLS Inc (17), 501 N Lincoln St, Wilmington, 19805-3047

The Bank of New York/Delaware (14), 100 White Clay Center Dr (102), Newark, 19711-5478

Chick Harness & Supply Inc (11), 18011 S Dupont Hwy, Harrington, 19952-2135

DelStar Technologies Inc (16), 601 Industrial Dr, Middletown, 19709

E I DuPont De Nemours & Co (16), 1007 Market St, Wilmington, 19898

WL Gore & Associates Inc (2), 555 Paper Mill Rd, Newark, 19711

Kennel Vet (11), 28424 Seaford Rd, Laurel, 19956

MXT Card Services, LLC (14), 2 Penns Way (Suite 201), New Castle, 19720-2407

Prestwick House Inc (17), PO Box 658, Clayton, 19938-0658

SLM Corp (16), 300 Continental Dr, Newark, 19713

Signature Styles LLC (2), 2711 Centerville Rd (Suite 400), Wilmington, 19808

Winterthur Museum & Country Estate (6), 5105 Kennett Pike, Wilmington, 19735

DISTRICT OF COLUMBIA

AAAS/Science (1), 1200 New York Ave NW, Washington, 20005-3928

AARP (1), 601 E St NW, Washington, 20049-0003

ADRFCO (1), 1612 K St NW (Suite 1102), Washington, 20006-2849

AFL-CIO (1), 815 16th St NW, Washington, 20006

AMVETS National Service Foundation (1), 4647 Forbes Blvd, Lanham, 20706

ASM Press (17), 1752 N St NW, Washington, 20036-2904

Academic Travel Abroad Inc (19), 1920 N St NW (Suite 200), Washington, 20036-1652

ActionAid (1), 1420 K St NW (Suite 900), Washington, 20005-2507

African Wildlife Foundation (1), 1400 16th St NW (Suite 120), Washington, 20036-2249

American Association for Justice (1), 777 6th St NW (Suite 200), The Leonard M Ring Law Center, Washington, 20001-3707

American Association of University Women (1), 1111 16th St NW, Washington, 20036-4809

American Bankers Association (1), 1120 Connecticut Ave NW, Washington, 20036-3959

American Chemical Society (1), 1155 16th St NW, Washington, 20036-4839

American College of Cardiology (1), 2400 N St NW, Washington, 20037-1153

American Forests (1), 1220 L St NW (Suite 750), Washington, 20005-4079

American Humane Association (1), 1400 16th St NW Ste 360, Washington, 20036-2215

American Institute for Cancer Research (1), 1759 R St NW, Washington, 20009-2570

American Psychological Association (1), 750 First St NE, Washington, 20002-4242

American Red Cross (1), 2025 East St NW (Suite 100), National HQ, Washington, 20006-5009

American Society of Interior Designers (1), 718 7th St NW (Floor 4), Washington, 20001

Americans for Peace Now (1), 2100 M St NW (Suite 619), Washington, 20037-1269

Arent Fox LLP (9), 1050 Connecticut Ave NW, Washington, 20036

Association of American Publishers (1), 455 Massachusetts Ave NW (Suite 700), Washington, 20001-2777

The Atlantic Monthly (17), 600 New Hampshire Ave NW Fl 4, Washington, 20037-2403

Black Entertainment Television Inc (16), 1235 W St NE, Washington, 20018-1211

B'nai B'rith International (1), 1120 20th St NW (Suite 300 N), Washington, 20036

Born Free USA (1), PO Box 32160, Washington, 20007

CSPI/Nutrition Action Health Letter (17), 1220 L St NW Ste 300, Washington, 20005-4053

Capitol Concierge Inc (16), 1400 "I" St NW (Suite 750), Washington, 20005

Care2 (1), 1100 15th S NW (Suite 600), Washington, 20005-1759

Carefirst Blue Cross Blue Shield (15), 840 First St NE, Washington, 20002-8046

The Catholic University of America Press (17), 620 Michigan Ave NE, Leahy Hall (Rm 240), Washington, 20064

Center for Science in the Public Interest (1), 1220 L St NW Ste 300, Washington, 20005-4053

Children's Hospital Foundation (1), 801 Roeder Rd, Silver Spring, 20910

Citizens Against Government Waste (1), 1301 Pennsylvania Ave NW Ste 1075, Washington, 20004-1707

Civil War Preservation Trust (1), 1156 15th St NW (Suite 900), Washington, 20005-4761

Council for Advancement and Support of Education (1), 1307 New York Ave NW (Suite 1000), Washington, 20005-4701

Defenders of Wildlife (1), 1130 17th St NW, Washington, 20036-4604

Democratic Congressional Campaign Committee (1), 430 S Capitol St SE, Washington, 20003

Eagle Publishing (17), One Massachusetts Ave NW, Washington, 20001

Edison Electric Institute (1), 701 Pennsylvania Ave NW, Washington, 20004-2696

Environmental Defense Fund (1), 1875 Connecticut Ave NW (# 600), Washington, 20009-5739

Environmental Law Institute (17), 2000 "L" St NW (Suite 200), Washington, 20036-4919

Food & Water Watch (1), 1616 P St NW, Washington, 20036-1408

Fund for Public Interest Research (1), 218 D St SE Fl 2, Washington, 20003-1900

GEICO Direct (15), 1 GEICO Plaza, Washington, 20076-0005

Georgetown University Law Center (13), 600 New Jersey Ave NW, Washington, 20001

Georgetown University McDonough School of Business (1), 37th & O Streets, NW, Washington, 20057

Governing Magazine (17), 1100 Connecticut Ave NW (Suite 1300), Washington, 20036-4109

Graduate School USA (1), 600 Maryland Ave SW, Washington, 20024

Hanley Wood LLC (16), 1 Thomas Cir NW (Suite 600), Washington, 20005-5803

Heldref Publications (17), 1319 18th St NW, Washington, 20036-1802

The Humane Society of the US (1), 2100 L St NW, Washington, 20037

ICMA Retirement Corp (14), 777 N Capitol St NE (Suite 600), Washington, 20002

The Interfaith Alliance (1), 1250 24th NW (Suite 300), Washington, 20037

International City/County Management Association (1), 777 N Capitol St NE (Suite 500), Washington, 20002-4201

International Fellowship of Christians and Jews (1), PO Box 96105, Washington, 20090-6105

The Kiplinger Washington Editors Inc (17), 1100 13th St NW (Suite 750), Washington, 20005-4364

Lautman Maska Neill & Co (1), 1730 Rhode Island Ave NW (Suite 301), Washington, 20036-3120

Market Development Group Inc (1), 1832 Connecticut Ave N, 1832 Connecticut Avenue, NW, Washington, 20009

NARAL Pro-Choice America (1), 1156 15th St NW (Suite 700), Washington, 20005-1704

National Archives & Records Administration (17), 700 Pennsylvania Ave NW, Washington, 20408-0001

National Association of Home Builders (1), 1201 15th St NW, Washington, 20005-2800

National Committee to Preserve Social Security & Medicare (1), 10 "G" St NE (Suite 600), Washington, 20002-4215

National Gallery of Art Gift Shop (16), 4th & Constitution Ave NW, Washington, 20565

National Geographic Society (17), 1145 17th St NW, Washington, 20036-4688

National Journal Group (17), 600 New Hampshire Ave NW, Washington, 20037

National Law Enforcement Officers Memorial Fund (1), 901 E St NW Ste 100, Washington, 20004-2025

National League for Nursing (1), 2600 Virginia Ave NW (#8), Washington, 20037-1905

National Osteoporosis Foundation (1), 1150 17th St NW (Suite 850), Washington, 20037-1216

National Railroad Passenger Corp (16), 60 Massachusetts Ave NE, Washington, 20002

The National Restaurant Association Educational Foundation (1), 2055 L St NW, Washington, 20036

National Retail Federation Inc (1), 1101 New York Ave, Washington, 20005

National Society of Collegiate Scholars (1), 2000 M St NW Ste 600, Washington, 20036-3328

National Trust for Historic Preservation (1), 2600 Virginia Ave NW (Suite 1000), Washington, 20037-1922

Network for Good (1), 1140 Connecticut Ave NW (Suite 700), Washington, 20036-4011

OMP (1), 1133 19th St NW (Suite 300), Washington, 20036-3610

Ocean Conservancy (1), 1300 19th St NW, Washington, 20036

Overseas Private Investment Corp (OPIC) (14), 1100 New York Ave NW, Washington, 20527

Paralyzed Veterans of America (1), 801 18th St NW, Washington, 20006-3517

People for the American Way (1), 1101 15th St NW (Suite 600), Washington, 20005-5023

Pharmaceutical Care Management Association (1), 325 7th St NW, Washington, 20004

Population Connection (1), 2120 L St NW (Suite 500), Washington, 20037-1534

Portland Cement Association (1), 1150 Connecticut Ave NW, Washington, 20036

Regnery Publishing (17), 1 Massachusetts Ave NW, Washington, 20001-1401

SOS Children's Villages - USA (1), 1001 Connecticut Ave NW Ste 1250, Washington, 20036-5520

Society for Neuroscience (1), 1121 14th St NW (Suite 1010), Washington, 20005-5642

Special Olympics International (1), 1133 19th St NW Ste 1200, Washington, 20036-3604

Sustainable Forestry Initiative Inc (1), 2121 K St NW (Suite 750), Washington, 20037

Telecommunications Reports International Inc (17), 1015 15th St NW (fl 10), Washington, 20005-2605

Thompson Publishing Group Inc (17), 1020 19th St NW (Suite 350), Washington, 20036-6107

Transemantics Inc (16), 1337 Connecticut Ave NW (4th fl), Washington, 20036

Travelex America Inc (14), 1152 15th St NW (fl 7), Washington, 20005

USO Inc (1), PO Box 96860, Washington, 20077-7677

Union Privilege, AFL-CIO (1), 1100 1st St NW (Suite 850), Washington, 20002

United Nations Foundation (1), 1750 Pennsylvania Ave NW (#300), Washington, 20006-4502

US Chamber of Commerce (1), 1615 "H" St NW, Washington, 20062-2000

US Department of Commerce (1), 1401 Constitution Ave NW, Washington, 20230

US News & World Report (17), 1050 Thomas Jefferson St NW, Washington, 20007

US Travel Association (1), 1100 New York Ave NW (Suite 450), Washington, 20005-6130

The Urban Land Institute (1), 1025 Thomas Jefferson St NW (Suite 500W), Washington, 20007-5201

Warren Communications News (17), 2115 Ward Ct NW, Washington, 20037-1209

The Washington Monthly Co (17), 1200 18th St NW (Suite 330), Washington, 20036-2556

Washington National Opera (16), 2700 F St NW, Kennedy Center for the Arts, Washington, 20566

The Washington Post (17), 1150 15th St NW, Washington, 20071

Washington Post Digital (17), 1150 15th St NW, Washington, 20071

The Washingtonian (17), 1828 "L" St NW (Suite 200), Washington, 20036

The World Bank (17), 1818 "H" St NW, Washington, 20433

World Wildlife Fund (1), 1250 24th St NW PO Box 97180, Washington, 20090-7180

YWCA of the USA (1), 2025 M St NW (Suite 550), Washington, 20036-3320

FLORIDA

AAA Auto Club South (1), 1515 N Westshore Blvd, Tampa, 33607-4599

ADT LLC (16), 1501 Yamato Rd, Boca Raton, 33431

Absolute Reservation Center Inc (19), 150 E Wildmere Ave (#108), Longwood, 32750-5464

Achieve Global (16), 8875 Hidden River Pkwy (Suite 400), Tampa, 33637

Action Direct Inc (11), 14285 SW 142nd St, Miami, 33186

Air Ambulance Network Inc (16), 3607 Alt 19 Ste A, Palm Harbor, 34683-1412

AlarmingYou.com (16), One Town Center Rd, Boca Raton, 33486-1002

American Automobile Association (16), 1000 AAA Dr, Heathrow, 32746

American College of Physician Executives (1), 400 N Ashley Dr (Suite 400), Tampa, 33602-4322

American Dermatological Corp (16), PO Box 565014, Miami, 33256-5014

American Nicaraguan Foundation (1), 1000 NW 57th Ct Ste 770, Miami, 33126-3288

American Preferred Reader's Service Inc (18), 1975 E Sunrise Blvd Ste 800, Fort Lauderdale, 33304-1455

Arnet Pharmaceutical (7), 2525 Davie Rd, Davie, 33317

AsiaEXP (16), 1835 NE Miami Gardens Dr, Miami, 33179-5035

Assurant Group (15), 1 Chase Manhattan Plaza, New York, 10005-1401

AvMed Health Plan Inc (1), 9400 S Dadeland Blvd (Suite 120), Miami, 33156-2823

Bahamas Ministry of Tourism (19), 1200 S Pine Island Rd (Suite 750), Fort Lauderdale, 33324-4413

Bankers Warranty Group (16), 11101 Roosevelt Blvd N, Saint Petersburg, 33716-2340

Battery Pros Inc (9), 161 1st St, Horseshoe Beach, 32648-0054

Bell Performance Inc (9), 1340 Bennett Dr, Longwood, 32750-7623

Bethesda Hospital Foundation (1), 2815 S Seacrest Blvd, Boynton Beach, 33435-7934

Bijoux Terner (16), 6950 NW 77th Ct, Miami, 33126-2714

Blue Cross Blue Shield of Florida (15), 4800 Deerwood Corporate Campus Pkwy, Jacksonville, 32246

Blue Strawberry Resorts LLC (19), 444 Brickell Ave., Ste. 51-859, Miami, 33131

Boca Java (4), 200 S Biscayne Blvd Ste 1818, Miami, 33131-2329

Brooke Distributors Inc (3), 16250 NW 52nd Ave, Miami, 33014

Buggies Unlimited (12), 3510 Port Jacksonville Pkwy, Jacksonville, 32226

CBT Direct (16), 905 E Martin Luther King Jr Dr Ste 500, Tarpon Springs, 34689-4830

Carnival Cruise Lines (19), 3655 NW 87th Ave, Miami, 33178-2418

Cedar Fresh Products (16), 4207 University Dr, Coral Gables, 33146-1140

Center for Professional Development (16), 555 W Pensacola St (#2027), Turnbull Conference Ctr, Tallahassee, 32306-1640

Chain Store Guide (17), 3922 Coconut Palm Dr Ste 300, Tampa, 33619-1389

Champs Corp (11), 311 Manatee Ave W, Bradenton, 34205

Champs Software Inc (3), 1255 N Vantage Point Dr, Crystal River, 34429

Checks by Phone/Checks by Web (14), 9770 S Military Trail (Suite 380), Boynton Beach, 33436

Chico's FAS Inc (2), 11215 Metro Pkwy, Fort Myers, 33966-1206

Corona Cigar Co (5), 7792 W Sand Lake Rd, Orlando, 32819

Cosmo International (16), 601 Fairway Dr, Deerfield Beach, 33441-1867

Cross Country Travcorps (16), 6551 Park of Commerce Blvd, Boca Raton, 33487-8247

Crystek Corp (9), 12730 Commonwealth Dr, Fort Myers, 33913

Cushman Fruit Co Inc (4), 1884 Indian Rd W, West Palm Beach, 33406

DS Services of North America LP (4), 200 Eagles Blvd, Lakeland, 33810

Danker Laboratories Inc (16), 6805 33rd St E, Box 1899, Sarasota, 34243

The Dartnell Corp (17), 2272 Airport Rd S, Naples, 34112

Databazaar.com (10), 12070 Miramar Pkwy, Miramar, 33025

Davidoff of Geneva Inc (6), 3001 Gateway Centre Pkwy N, Pinellas Park, 33782-6124

Decal Shop (10), 1849 Foster Dr, Jacksonville, 32216

DigDev Direct (16), 260 SW Natura Ave (fl 2), Deerfield Beach, 33441

Disney Vacation Club (19), 200 Celebration Pl, Kissimmee, 34747

Walt Disney Parks & Resorts (19), 1375 N Buena Vista Dr, Lake Buena Vista, 32830-8402

ETTSI Premiums & Incentives (16), 301 Indigo Dr, Daytona Beach, 32114-1134

Eagle Asset Management Inc (14), 880 Carillon Pkwy, Saint Petersburg, 33716

Ecklers (12), 5200 S Washington Ave, Titusville, 32780-7316

Edwin Watts Golf (11), 20 Hill Ave, Fort Walton Beach, 32548

Encircle (14), 1691 NW 107th Ave, Miami, 33172

FIU Online (1), 11200 SW 8th St (Marc 210), Miami, 33199

Florida A&M University (16), 510 Orr Dr (Suite 4003), Tallahassee, 32307

Florida Credit Union (14), PO Box 5549, Gainesville, 32627

Florida Gift Fruit Shippers Association (1), 5500 W Concord Ave, Orlando, 32808-7700

Florida Institute of CPA's (1), 325 W College Ave, Tallahassee, 32301

Florida Power & Light Co (16), 700 Universe Blvd, Juno Beach, 33408

Florida Today (17), 1 Gannett Plz, Melbourne, 32940

Food for the Poor Inc (1), 6401 Lyons Rd, Coconut Creek, 33073-3602

Four Corners Direct Inc (16), 8520 S Tamiami Trl Unit 2, Sarasota, 34238-3001

G&S Fruit Packers LLC (16), 16600 County Rd 25 S, Weirsdale, 32195

G-Neil Direct Mail (10), 720 International Pkwy, PO Box 450939, Sunrise, 33345-0939

Gallagher Affinity (15), 8430 Enterprise Cir, Lakewood Ranch, 34202

Galloway Farms (8), 7790 SW 87th Ave, Miami, 33173-3506

Peter Glenn Publications (17), 777 E Atlantic Ave (Suite C2337), Delray Beach, 33483

W W Grainger Inc (5), 4514 19th St Ct E, Bradenton, 34203-3709

Graves Lapidary Co (9), 1800 N Andrews Ave, Pompano Beach, 33069-1421

Gruber & Allison Inc (17), 7487 Falls Rd W, Boynton Beach, 33437

Gulf Coast Data Supply Inc (3), 5455 Rowe Trl, Milton, 32571-9556

HR Direct (10), PO Box 452049, Sunrise, 33345-2049

HSN Inc (5), 1 HSN Dr, Saint Petersburg, 33729

Hale Indian River Groves Inc (16), PO Box 691237, Vero Beach, 32969-1237

The Hamilton Collection (6), 7018 A C Skinner Pkwy (Suite 300), Jacksonville, 32256-6975

The Hamilton Group Ltd Inc (16), 7018 A C Skinner Pkwy (#300), Jacksonville, 32256

Har Court Inc (17), 9400 Southpark Center Loop, Orlando, 32819-8647

Harland Financial Solutions Inc (16), 605 Crescent Executive Ct (Suite 600), Lake Mary, 32746

Harris Corp (16), 1025 W NASA Blvd, Melbourne, 32919-0001

HealthPlan Services (15), 3501 E Frontage Rd, Tampa, 33607

Hecht Rubber Corp (16), 6161 Phillips Hwy, Jacksonville, 32216-5920

Hilton Grand Vacations Co (19), 6355 Metrowest Blvd (Suite 180), Orlando, 32835-6203

The Historical Research Center International Inc (16), 2107 Corporate Dr, Boynton Beach, 33426-6645

Hoffman Mint (6), 1400 NW 65th Pl, Fort Lauderdale, 33309-1902

Holy Cross Hospital (16), 4725 N Federal Hwy, Fort Lauderdale, 33308-4670

Hot Sauce Harry's (4), 1077 Innovation Ave Unit 109, North Port, 34289-9345

Hyatt Fruit Co (4), PO Box 639, Vero Beach, 32961-0639

IMPACT Publishing Inc (17), 3409 47th Ave E, Bradenton, 34203-3974

InfoSource Inc (3), 1300 City View Ctr, Oviedo, 32755-5530

Jarden Corp (16), 2381 NW Executive Center Dr, Boca Raton, 33431

Marlin P Jones & Associates Inc (3), 8380 Resource Rd, West Palm Beach, 33404

Kaplan Inc (16), 6301 Kaplan University Ave, Fort Lauderdale, 33309

Karaoke USA (5), 1185 Gooden Xing, Largo, 33778

Kellyco Metal Detector Distributors (11), 1085 Belle Ave, Winter Springs, 32708

Kendall Products/Dri-Dek (16), PO Box 8656, Naples, 34101-8656

Key West Aloe Holdings LLC (16), PO Box 19547, Fort Lauderdale, 33318-0547

B Klein Publications (17), PO Box 970392, Boca Raton, 33497-0392

Lazydays RV Center (12), 6131 Lazydays Blvd, Seffner, 33584-2968

LeadFlash (14), 6700 Broken Sound Pkwy NW, Boca Raton, 33487-5701

Levenger (5), 420 S Congress Ave Ste 101, Delray Beach, 33445-4696

Life Extension Foundation (7), 3600 W Commercial Blvd Ste 100, Fort Lauderdale, 33309-3324

Ligonier Ministries (5), 421 Ligonier Ct, Sanford, 32771-8608

LOTSolutions (14), 10151 Deerwood Park Blvd (Suite 200-330), Jacksonville, 32256-0564

MDR (7), 14101 NW Fourth St, Sunrise, 33325-6209

The Mark Group (2), 1155 Broken Sound Pkwy NW, Boca Raton, 33487

Marriott Ownership Resorts Sales & Marketing (19), 6649 Westwood Blvd (Suite 500), Orlando, 32821-6066

Maus & Hoffman Inc (2), 225 SE 6th Ave, Fort Lauderdale, 33301

McNichols Co (16), PO Box 30300, Tampa, 33630-3300

Melitta USA (4), 13925 58th St N, Clearwater, 33760-3721

The Miami Herald Media Co (17), 1 Herald Plaza, Miami, 33132-1609

National Council on Compensation Insurance Inc (1), 901 Peninsula Corp Cir, Boca Raton, 33487

National Golf Foundation (1), 501 N Hwy A1A, Jupiter, 33477-4577

National Parkinson Foundation (1), 200 SE 1st St (Suite 800), Miami, 33131-1909

The New Piper Aircraft Inc (16), 2926 Piper Dr, Vero Beach, 32960-1955

New York Life Insurance Co/AARP (15), 5505 W Cypress St (Suite 300), Tampa, 33607-1707

Nicklaus Companies LLC (16), 11780 US Hwy 1 (Suite 500), North Palm Beach, 33408-3042

Norwood Promotional Products (16), 14421 Myerlake Cir, Clearwater, 33760-2840

Nova Southeastern University Fischler College of Education (1), 1750 NE 167th St, North Miami Beach, 33162-3017

Nat Nussbaum & Associates Inc (16), 1440 Coral Ridge Dr, Coral Springs, 33071-5433

Office Depot (16), 6600 N Military Trl, Boca Raton, 33496-2434

OfficeMax Inc (10), 6600 N Military Trail, Boca Raton, 33496

100% Real Estate Inc (16), 1810 Lee Rd, Orlando, 32810-5702

Orlando/ Orange County Convention & Visitor's Bureau (19), 6700 Forum Dr (Suite 100), Orlando, 32821-8086

Pango Pango Swimwear Corp (2), 1909 E Atlantic Blvd, Pompano Beach, 33060-6562

Physicians Planning Association Services (16), 350 Fairway Dr (Suite 200), Hillsboro Executive Center N, Deerfield Beach, 33441-1834

Pine Castle Animal Hospital (16), 5250 S Orange Ave, Orlando, 32809

The Professional Golfers' Association of America (1), 100 Avenue of the Champions, Palm Beach Gardens, 33410-9601

Racer Walsh Co (12), 1849 Foster Dr, Jacksonville, 32216-3104

Remington College (13), 500 International Pkwy (Suite 200), Heathrow, 32746-5627

Royal Caribbean International Ltd (19), 1050 Caribbean Way, Miami, 33132-2028

The Sailing Co (17), PO Box 420235, Palm Coast, 32142-0235

St Petersburg/Clearwater Area CVB (1), 13805 58th St N (Suite 2-200), Clearwater, 33760-3716

Sales Leads (17), 601 Heritage Dr (Suite 111), Jupiter, 33458-2777

Saunders Military Insignia (6), PO Box 1831, Naples, 34106-1831

Scott Sign Systems Inc (16), 7525 Pennsylvania Ave (Unit 102), Sarasota, 34243-5065

Seta Corp of Boca Inc (5), 6400 E Rogers Cir, Boca Raton, 33499-0002

Shop.com (16), 3301 NE 1st Ave, Miami, 33137

Shutterbug (17), 1415 Chaffee Dr Ste 10, Titusville, 32780-7936

Solitron Devices Inc (16), 3301 Electronics Way, West Palm Beach, 33407-4636

South Seas Island Resort (19), 5400 Plantation Rd, Captiva Island, 33924

Southeast Toyota Distributors LLC (16), 100 Jim Moran Blvd, Deerfield Beach, 33442

The Sperry & Hutchinson Co Inc (6), 1625 S Congress Ave, Delray Beach, 33445

Sporting Clays Ltd (17), 317 S Washington Ave (Suite 201), Titusville, 32976-3539

Stimpson Co Inc (16), 1515 SW 13th Ct, Pompano Beach, 33069-4789

Strang Communications Co (17), 600 Rinehart Rd, Lake Mary, 32746-4898

SubscriptionAgency.com Inc (18), 365 E Central Ave, Winter Haven, 33880

Sullivan-Victory Groves (4), 990 US-1, Rockledge, 32955

Sun Harvest Citrus (6), 14601 Six Mile Cypress Pkwy, Fort Myers, 33912-4307

Sunbeam Products Inc (16), 2381 NW Executive Center Dr, Boca Raton, 33431

Sunburst Farms Inc (8), 2200 NW 70th Ave, Miami, 33122-1816

Sunshine Discount Crafts (11), 12335 62nd St N, Largo, 33773

TNT Packaging Inc (16), 2390 NW 149th St, Miami, 33054

Thomas Computer Corp (16), 809 Irma Ave, Orlando, 32803-3806

Thompson Cigar Co (6), 5401 Hangar Ct, Tampa, 33634

Trend Magazines Inc (17), 490 First Ave S (8th fl), Saint Petersburg, 33701

Trophyland USA Inc (5), 7001 W 20th Ave, Hialeah, 33014

Tupperware Brands Corp (16), 14901 S Orange Blossom Trail, Orlando, 32837

Unicol Inc (17), 11590 SW Ninth Ct, Pembroke Pines, 33025-4324

US Branding Group LLC (16), PO Box 540957, Lake Worth, 33467

Venus Fashion, Inc (2), 11711 Marco Beach Dr, Jacksonville, 32224

Wasserman Uniform Co (2), 700 NW 57th Pl, Fort Lauderdale, 33309

Richard Weiner Consultant (14), 1814 NE Miami Gardens Dr (Suite 904), North Miami Beach, 33179-5043

Weiss Research Inc (17), 4400 Northcorp Pkwy, Palm Beach Gardens, 33410

Wood Carvers Supply Inc (9), 3031 Placida Rd (Ste 7), Englewood, 34224-8547

World Publications Inc (17), 460 N Orlando Ave (Suite 200), Winter Park, 32789

Wrisco Industries Inc (8), 355 Hiatt Dr (Suite B), Palm Beach Gardens, 33418-7106

GEORGIA

AFA Service Corp (16), 3495 Piedmont Rd NE 11, Atlanta, 30305

AFLAC (15), 1932 Wynnton Rd, Columbus, 31999

AGCO Inc (9), 2782 Simpson Cir, Norcross, 30071

AMC Inc (2), 240 Peachtree St NW (Suite 2200), Atlanta, 30303-1327

ARI (16), 2523 S McDonough Rd, Orchard Hill, 30266

Active Parenting (17), 1220 Kennestone Cir Ste 130, Marietta, 30066-6022

AdvanceMe Inc (14), 2015 Vaughn Rd NW (Suite 500), Kennesaw, 30144-7831

Agco Spra-Coup (16), 4205 River Green Pkwy, Duluth, 30096

AHC Media (17), 3525 Piedmont Rd NE (Suite 400), Atlanta, 30305-1562

AirTran Airways (19), 1800 Phoenix Blvd (Suite 104), Atlanta, 30349-5569

John Alden Life Insurance Co/North Star Marketing (15), 11465 Johns Creek Pkwy (Suite 160), Duluth, 30097-1573

American Cancer Society (1), 1599 Clifton Rd NE, Atlanta, 30329-4251

American Family Life Assurance Co of Columbus (AFLAC) (15), 1932 Wynnton Rd, Columbus, 31999-0001

American Megatrends Inc (3), 5555 Oakbrook Pkwy (Suite 200), Norcross, 30093-2286

American 3B Scientific (16), 2189 Flintstone Dr (Suite O), Tucker, 30084-5023

Ames Taping Tool System Inc (9), 1380 Beverage Dr Ste W, Stone Mountain, 30083-2133

Arthritis Foundation (1), 1355 W Peachtree St NW (fl 6), Atlanta, 30309-2922

Ashworth College (13), 6625 The Corner Pkwy, Norcross, 30092

Assurant Solutions Preneed Division (15), 260 Interstate North Cir SE, Atlanta, 30339-2110

Astral Brands LLC (7), 3715 Northside Pkwy (Suite 200), Atlanta, 30327

Atlanta Cutlery Corp (11), 2147 Gees Mill Rd NE, Conyers, 30013-1333

Atlanta Journal & Constitution (17), 223 Perimeter Center Pkwy, Atlanta, 30303

Automation Control Products (16), 1725 Windward Concourse (Suite 300), Alpharetta, 30005

Automod (12), 3353 W Hospital Ave, Atlanta, 30341-3419

Ballard Designs (8), 1670 Defoor Ave, Atlanta, 30318-7528

Benchmark Brands Inc (5), 1375 Peachtree St NE (Suite 600), Norcross, 30309-3170

Bland Farms (4), 1126 Raymond Bland Rd, Glennville, 30427

Boys & Girls Clubs of America National Headquarters (1), 1275 Peachtree St NE, Atlanta, 30309-3506

Beverly Bremer Silver Shop (6), 3164 Peachtree Rd NE, Atlanta, 30305-1853

Byron Plantation (4), 500 Atlantic Ave, Vidalia, 30474-3705

Callaway Gardens (19), 17800 US Hwy 27, Pine Mountain, 31822-2000

Caraustar (16), 5000 Austell-Powder Springs Rd (# 300), Austell, 30106-3227

CARE USA (1), 151 Ellis St NE, Atlanta, 30303-2420

Carvel Corp (4), 5620 Glenridge Dr NE, Atlanta, 30342

Char-Broil (16), 1442 Belfast Ave, Columbus, 31904-4432

Char-Broil Grill Lover's Catalog (8), 1442 Belfast Ave, Columbus, 31904

Choice Point (16), 1000 Alderman Dr, Alpharetta, 30005

City of LaGrange (1), 200 Ridley Ave, PO Box 430, LaGrange, 30240

The Coca-Cola Co (16), PO Box 1734, Atlanta, 30301-1734

Collector's Armoury Ltd (6), PO Box 2948, McDonough, 30253-1743

Concurrent Computer Corp (3), 4375 River Green Pkwy, Duluth, 30096-2572

Cox Communications Inc (16), 1400 Lake Hearn Dr, Atlanta, 30319-1464

Dr Ho's (7), 150 Stewart Pkwy, Greensboro, L6E 1A4-30642

Delta Vacations (19), 700 Central Ave., Atlanta, 30354

Direct Gardening Association (1), PO Box 429, La Grange, 30241

EMS Technologies (16), 660 Engineering Dr, Norcross, 30092

First Data Merchant Services (14), 5565 Glenridge (Suite 2000), Connector NE, Atlanta, 30342

Fiserv (14), 4411 E Jones Bridge Rd, Norcross, 30092-1615

GE Money (14), 4125 Windward Plaza Dr, Alpharetta, 30005-8738

Georgia Institute of Technology (1), North Ave, Atlanta, 30332

Georgia Power (16), 241 Ralph McGill Blvd NE, Atlanta, 30308-3374

Golden Key International Honour Society (1), 1040 Crown Pointe Pkwy (Suite 900), Atlanta, 30338-4724

Graham Field Health Products Inc (7), 2935 Northeast Pkwy, Atlanta, 30360-2808

Gulfstream Aerospace Corp (16), 500 Gulfstream Rd, PO Box 2206, Savannah, 31408-2206

Habitat For Humanity International (1), 121 Habitat St, Americus, 31709-3499

John Harland Co (16), 2939 Miller Rd, Decatur, 30035-4038

Herschend Family Entertainment (5), 5445 Triangle Pkwy (Ste 200), Norcross, 30092

Hobby Builders Supply (11), 2388 Pleasantdale Rd, Atlanta, 30340

Home Decorators Collection Inc (8), 3074 Chastain Meadows Pkwy, Marietta, 30066-3356

The Home Depot Inc (16), 2455 Paces Ferry Rd, Atlanta, 30339-1834

IPS - Sendero Corp (14), 230 Scientific Dr (Suite 800), Norcross, 30092-2909

In Touch Ministries (1), PO Box 7900, Atlanta, 30357

InterContinental Hotels Group (19), Three Ravinia Dr (Suite 100), Atlanta, 30346-2149

InterfaceFlor LLC (16), 1503 Orchard Hill Rd, La Grange, 30240-5709

International Manufacturing Co (8), 216 Main St, Whitesburg, 30185-3203

KEH.com (16), 4900 Highlands Pkwy SE, Smyrna, 30082-5132

Kalmed Dental Products Inc (7), 3048 Alberta Dr, Marietta, 30062-1513

L6 Holdings Corp (14), 6555 Sugarloaf Pkwy (Suite 307), Duluth, 30097-4934

Landmark Communications Inc (17), 11300 Atlantis Pl (Suite F), Alpharetta, 30022

Lathem Time Corp (16), 200 Selig Dr SW, Atlanta, 30336

Magnolia Hall (8), 49 Bryant St, Jasper, 30143

MAP International (1), 2200 Glynco Pkwy, Brunswick, 31521

Montag & Caldwell Inc (14), 3455 Peachtree Rd NE (Suite 1200), Atlanta, 30326-3248

Morris Visitors Publications LLC (17), 699 Broad St (Suite 500), Augusta, 30901

Moultrie Manufacturing Co (8), 1403 Hwy 133 S, Moultrie, 31788

NCR Corp (16), 3097 Satellite Blvd, Duluth, 30096

Newell Rubbermaid, Inc (16), 3 Glenlake Pkwy, Atlanta, 30328

North Point Resources (1), 4400 North Point Pkwy (Suite 152), Alpharetta, 30022-2429

Omega Research & Development (12), 981 N Burnt Hickory Rd, Douglasville, 30134

Pritchett & Hull Associates Inc (17), 3440 Oakcliff Rd NE (Suite 110), Atlanta, 30340-3079

Professional Photographer Magazine (17), 229 Peachtree St NE (Suite 2200), International Tower, Atlanta, 30303-1608

Ranger Joe's International Military Supply (2), 325 Farr Rd, Columbus, 31907

Raven's Nest Herbals, LLC (7), PO Box 370, Duluth, 30096

River Street Sweets (4), 13 E River St, Savannah, 31401

Schermer Pecans (4), 819 S Veterans Blvd, Glennville, 30427-8000

Solarcom (16), One Sun Ct, Norcross, 30092

Sportime International (11), 3155 Northwoods Pkwy, Norcross, 30071

State Mutual Insurance Co (15), PO Box 153, Rome, 30162-0153

Summit Industries Inc (5), 839 Pickens Industrial Dr, Marietta, 30062

Sunnyland Farms Inc (4), PO Box 8200, Albany, 31706-8200

Suntrust Banks Inc (14), 303 Peachtree Center Ave NE (Suite 320), Atlanta, 30303-1280

Technical Association of the Pulp & Paper Industry (1), 15 Technology Pkwy S (Suite 115), Norcross, 30092-2923

Tensar International Corporation (16), 2500 Northwinds Pkwy (Suite 500), Alpharetta, 30009-2247

Thermo Pro (16), 1600 Distribution Dr (Suite D), Duluth, 30097

United Community Bank (14), 63 Hwy 51 S, Blairsville, 30512

Uniway Management Corp (16), 5182A Old Dixie Hwy, Forest Park, 30297

Ventyx (16), 400 Perimeter Center Ter NE Ste 500, Atlanta, 30346-1231

Ed Voyles Hyundai Inc (16), 2135 Cobb Pkwy SE, Smyrna, 30080-7632

Walk Thru The Bible Ministries Inc (1), 555 Triangle Pkwy (Suite 250), Norcross, 30092

Welcomemat Services Inc (9), 3348 Peachtree Rd (Suite 1095), Atlanta, 30326-1400

Whitman Publishing LLC (16), 3101 Clairmont Rd, Atlanta, 30329

Year One Inc (16), Year One Inc, Braselton, 30517

HAWAII

Bank of Hawaii (14), PO Box 2900, Honolulu, 96846-0001

Bontex (16), 1207 Hunakai St, Honolulu, 96816-4614

Central Pacific Bank (14), 220 S King St, Honolulu, 96813-4530

First Hawaiian Bank (14), 999 Bishop St Ste 3200, Honolulu, 96813-4424

Hawaiian Host Inc (4), 500 Alakawa St (Suite 111), Honolulu, 96817-4576

Islands Tropicals (6), PO Box 1989, Keaau, 96749-1989

Polynesian Cultural Center (16), 2255 Kuhio Ave (Suite 1010), Honolulu, 96815-2648

IDAHO

Angler's Catalog Co (11), 3551 W Deerfield Dr, Eagle, 83616

Boise Cascade Holdings LLC (16), 1111 W Jefferson St (Suite 300), Boise, 83702-5389

Bosom Buddy Breast Forms (7), 2417 Bank Dr (Suite 201), Boise, 83705-0731

Brookhollow Cards (10), 1 Stationary Pl, Rexburg, 83440-3567

Cascade Outfitters (11), 604 E 45th St, Boise, 83714-4848

Cattle Kate (2), 6701 W State St, Boise, 83714-7412

Cougar Mountain Software (14), 7180 Potomac Dr, Boise, 83704

Gibson Auer LLC (7), PO Box 228, Victor, 83455-0228

I/D/E/A Inc (16), One Idea Way, Caldwell, 83605-6900

Rexcraft Wedding Invitations (16), One Stationery Pl, Rexburg, 83441

Seastrom Manufacturing Co Inc (3), 456 Seastrom St, Twin Falls, 83301

Sunshine Minting Inc (14), 7600 N Mineral Dr (Suite 700), Coeur D'Alene, 83815-9170

West Farm Foods (Branch) (16), 520 Albany St, Caldwell, 83605

ILLINOIS

A La Carte (16), 5610 W Bloomingdale Rd, Chicago, 60639

AAA-Chicago Motor Club (1), 975 Meridian Lake Dr, Aurora, 60504-4904

ACCO Brands Corp (16), Four Corporate Dr, Lake Zurich, 60047-8997

AMA Insurance Agency Inc (15), 515 N State St, Chicago, 60654

AON Center (15), 200 E Randolph St, Chicago, 60601-6436

Aon Innovative Solutions (16), 200 East Randolph St, Chicago, 60601

Abbott (7), 100 Abbott Park Rd, Abbott Park, 60064-3502

Ace Hardware Corp (16), 2200 Kensington Ct, Oak Brook, 60523-2100

Affinity Express (16), 2200 Point Blvd (Suite 130), Elgin, 60123

Agate Publishing (17), 1501 Madison St, Evanston, 60202-2033

Alexian Brothers Bonaventure House (1), 825 W Wellington Ave, Chicago, 60657

Alloyd Brands (16), 1401 Pleasant St, Dekalb, 60115-2663

Allstate Motor Club Inc (13), PO Box 3094, Arlington Heights, 60006-3094

Alzheimer's Association (1), 225 N Michigan Ave, Fl 17, Chicago, 60601-7757

American Association of Individual Investors (1), 625 N Michigan Ave, Chicago, 60611-3110

American Bar Association (1), 321 N Clark St, Chicago, 60654-5000

American Health Information Management Association (1), 233 N Michigan Ave (21st fl), Chicago, 60601-5519

American Library Association-Publishing Services (1), 50 E Huron St, Chicago, 60611

American Lung Association (1), 55 W Wacker Dr (Suite 1150), Chicago, 60601

American Medical Association (1), 515 N State St, Chicago, 60610

American Science & Surplus (9), 7410 N Lehigh Ave, Niles, 60714-4024

American Technical Publishers Inc (17), 10100 Orland Pkwy, Orland Park, 60467-5756

Anatomical Chart Co (7), 2700 Lake Cook Rd, Riverwoods, 60015

Appraisal Institute (1), 200 W Madison St Ste 1500, Chicago, 60606-3515

Arbus Capital Ltd (16), 1320 Tower Rd, Schaumburg, 60173

ArcelorMittal (16), 1 S Dearborn St, Chicago, 60603-2302

Armbrust Paper Tubes Inc (10), 6255 S Harlem Ave, Chicago, 60638-3990

BAI (17), 115 S La Salle St (Suite 3300), Chicago, 60603-3801

BCR Enterprises Inc (17), 3025 Highland Pkwy (Suite 200), Downers Grove, 60515-5668

BMI Home Decorating (16), 6917 Catalpa Ct, Spring Grove, 60081

BP (16), 4101 Winfield Rd (Suite 100), Warrenville, 60555-3522

Badge-A-Minit (16), 345 N Lewis Ave, Oglesby, 61348-9776

Ball Publishing (17), 622 Town Rd, PO Box 1660, West Chicago, 60186

Bank One (14), One Bank One Plaza, Chicago, 60670

Bankers Life & Casualty Co (15), 600 W Chicago Ave, Chicago, 60654-2800

Baxter Healthcare, Renal Division (7), One Baxter Pkwy, Deerfield, 60015-4625

Beltone Corp (3), 2601 Patriot Blvd, Glenview, 60026-8023

Benet Academy (1), 2200 Maple Ave, Lisle, 60532-2393

William Blair & Co LLC (14), 222 W Adams St, Chicago, 60606-5312

Dick Blick Holdings Inc (16), PO Box 1267, Galesburg, 61402-1267

Blue Cross Blue Shield of Illinois (15), 300 E Randolph St, Chicago, 60601

Boeing Co (16), 100 N Riverside, Chicago, 60606

The Bradford Group (16), 9333 N Milwaukee Ave, Niles, 60714-1303

Braintree Payment Solutions LLC (14), 833 W Jackson Blvd (Suite 500), Chicago, 60607-5400

Brand New Products LLC (4), 2503 N Clark St (#280), Chicago, 60614

Broadcast Electronics Inc (3), 4100 N 24th St, Quincy, 62305

Brokers/Consultants Inc (15), 1332 Dartmouth Rd, Flossmoor, 60422-1905

Brookfield Zoo (1), 3300 Golf Rd, Brookfield, 60513-1060

Bulletin of the Atomic Scientists (17), 1155 E 60th St, Chicago, 60637-2745

Bunker Hill Auctions (6), 21 Foxhurst Ln, Millbrook, 60536

Bunn-O-Matic Corp (16), 1400 Stevenson Dr, Springfield, 62703-4291

Business Graphics Inc (16), 188 W Industrial Dr (Suite 428), Elmhurst, 60126-1612

Butler Specialty Co (16), 8200 S Chicago Ave, Chicago, 60617-1804

C&S Sales Inc (9), 150 Carpenter Ave, Wheeling, 60090

CCH Inc (17), 2700 Lake Cook Rd, Riverwoods, 60015-3888

CCIM Institute (1), 430 N Michigan Ave (Suite 800), Chicago, 60611-4011

CDW Corp (16), 200 N Milwaukee Ave, Vernon Hills, 60061

CNA (15), 333 S Wabash Ave, Chicago, 60604-4107

CRB (17), 209 W Jackson Blvd (Suite 200), Chicago, 60606-6940

Calendar Marketing Association (1), 214 N Hale St, Wheaton, 60187-5115

Career Education Corp (1), 231 N Martingale Rd Ste 100, Schaumburg, 60173-2007

CashNetUSA II LLC (14), 200 W Jackson Blvd (Suite 1400), Chicago, 60606-6941

Caterpillar Inc (16), 501 SW Jefferson Ave, Peoria, 61630

Catholic Church Extension Society (1), 150 S Wacker Dr (Suite 2000), Chicago, 60606-4103

Celtic Life Insurance Co (15), 233 S Wacker Dr (Suite 700), Chicago, 60606-6300

Champion (16), 1800 Gardner Expressway, Quincy, 62305-9364

Chicago Convention & Tourism Bureau (1), 2301 S Lakeshore Dr, Chicago, 60616-1490

Chicago Magazine (17), 435 N Michigan Ave (Suite 1100), Chicago, 60611-4031

Christianity Today Inc (17), 465 Gundersen Dr, Carol Stream, 60188-2415

Clubs of America (6), 484 W Wagner Rd, Lakemoor, 60051

Coin Laundry Association (1), 1S660 Midwest Rd (Suite 205), Oakbrook Terrace, 60181-4738

Cole-Parmer Instrument Co (16), 625 E Bunker Ct, Vernon Hills, 60061-1844

Cole's Appliance & Furniture Co (8), 4026 Lincoln Ave, Chicago, 60618-3097

Collectibles Today Network, Ltd (16), 9200 N Maryland Ave, Niles, 60105

Collegiate Cap & Gown (16), 1000 N Market St, Champaign, 61820-3009

Combined Insurance Co of America (15), 1000 Milwaukee Ave Fl 1, Glenview, 60025-2424

Concept Communications Co (16), 154 S Pinnacle Dr, Romeoville, 60446-4614

Consumer Benefit Services Inc (16), 1620 Bond St, Naperville, 60563-0131

Consumers Digest Inc (17), 520 Lake Cook Rd (Suite 500), Deerfield, 60015-5633

Cortz Inc (5), 320 Industrial Dr, West Chicago, 60185-1817

Cosco Industries Inc (16), 7220 W Wilson Ave, Chicago, 60706-4706

Cosmetique, Inc (13), 859 West End Ct, Vernon Hills, 60061

Country Financial (15), PO Box 2020, Bloomington, 61702-2020

Country Sampler Group (17), 707 Kautz Rd, Saint Charles, 60174

Coverdell & Co Inc (15), 8770 W Bryn Mawr Ave (Suite 1000), Chicago, 60631-3515

Coyne American Institute (16), 330 N Green St, Chicago, 60607-1300

Crate & Barrel (8), 1250 Techny Rd, Northbrook, 60062-5419

Creative Catalogs Corp (6), 1005 101st St, Lemont, 60439-9642

The Cricket Magazine Group (17), 70 E Lake St (Ste 300), Chicago, 60601-5945

Cunningham Group (15), 7234 W North Ave (Suite 101), Elmwood Park, 60707-4200

Custom Accessories (11), 5900 Ami Dr, Richmond, 60071-8968

Da-Lite Screen Co Inc (16), 3100 N Detroit St, Warsaw, 46582-2288

Dairy Management Inc (1), 10255 W Higgins Rd (Suite 900), Rosemont, 60018

Deere & Co (16), One John Deere Pl, Moline, 61625

Design Toscano, Inc (6), 1400 Morse Ave, Elk Grove Village, 60007-5722

DeVry Education Group (16), 3005 Highland Pkwy, Downers Grove, 60515-5799

Discover Financial Services (14), 2500 Lake Cook Rd, Riverwoods, 60015-1838

Divine Word Missionaries (1), 1835 Waukegan Rd, Techny, 60082-6099

DoAll Co (16), 1480 S Wolf Rd, Wheeling, 60090-6514

Edward Don & Co (16), 9801 Adam Don Pkwy, Woodridge, 60517-8136

Douglas Press Inc (16), 2810 Madison St, Bellwood, 60104-2256

Douglas Shaw & Associates (1), 1717 Park St Ste 300, Naperville, 60563-4864

Dreis & Krump Manufacturing Co (16), 481 Governors Hwy (Suite 2), Peotone, 60468

Dutch Gardens USA Inc (8), PO Box 2999, Bloomington, 61702-2999

Easter Seals (1), 233 S Wacker Dr (Suite 2400), Chicago, 60606-6410

Eire Direct (16), 720 N Franklin (Suite 310), Chicago, 60610-3512

Elks Magazine (17), 2750 N Lakeview Ave, Chicago, 60614-1889

Ellis Systems Corp (9), 28457 N Ballard Dr Ste F, Lake Forest, 60045-4545

Encyclopaedia Britannica Inc (17), 331 N LaSalle St, Chicago, 60654-2682

Event 360 Inc (1), 55 E Jackson Blvd (Suite 1010), Chicago, 60604

FTD Companies Inc (16), 3113 Woodcreek Dr, Downers Grove, 60515

Farm Progress Co (17), 255 38th Ave (Suite P), Saint Charles, 60174-5410

Farrington Transportation (12), 553 S Joliet Rd (Suite B), Bolingbrook, 60440-3631

FEEDING AMERICA (1), 35 E Wacker Dr (Suite 2000), Chicago, 60601-2200

The Field Museum (1), 1400 S Lake Shore Dr, Chicago, 60605-2827

First to the Finish Inc (7), 1325 N Broad St, Carlinville, 62626-9770

Caimin Flannery & Associates (14), 4275 Stableford Ln, Naperville, 60564-9768

Flight Form Cases Inc (9), 6543 S Laramie Ave, Bedford Park, 60638

Follett School Solutions Inc (16), 1340 Ridgeview Dr, McHenry, 60050

Frog Tool Co Ltd (11), 2169 IL Rte 26, Dixon, 61021-9217

GE Partnership Marketing Group (14), 200 N Martingale Rd, Schaumburg, 60173

Gamma Photo Labs LLC (16), 222 N Des Plains, Chicago, 60661-1120

General Binding Corp (10), One GBC Plaza, Northbrook, 60062

General Growth Properties (5), 110 N Wacker Dr, Chicago, 60606-1511

Glenview State Bank (14), 800 Waukegan Rd, Glenview, 60025-4300

Globe Ticket & Label Co (16), 350 Randy Rd (Suite 1), Carol Stream, 60188-1831

Golden Trophy (4), 3548 N Kostner Ave, Chicago, 60641

Goodheart-Willcox Publisher (17), 18604 W Creek Dr, Tinley Park, 60477-6243

Grainger Industrial Supply (16), 1657 Shermer Rd, North Brook, 60062

WW Grainger Inc (9), 100 Grainger Pkwy, Lake Forest, 60045

The Great Books Foundation (1), 35 E Wacker Dr (Suite 400), Chicago, 60601-2298

Guarantee Trust Life Insurance Co (15), 1275 Milwaukee Ave (Suite 100), Glenview, 60025-2489

HIMSS (1), 33 W Monroe St Ste 1700, Chicago, 60603-5616

Hall-Erickson Inc (16), 98 E Naperville Rd (Suite 200), Westmont, 60559-2199

Hamakor Judaica Inc (5), 4150 Dempster Dt, Skokie, 60076

The Hamilton Collection (6), 7018 A C Skinner Pkwy (Suite 300), Jacksonville, 32256-6975

Hammacher Schlemmer & Co Inc (16), 9307 N Milwaukee Ave, Niles, 60714

Handi-Ramp Inc (7), 510 North Ave, Libertyville, 60048-2025

Harper College (1), 1200 W Algonquin Rd, Palatine, 60067-7373

Harris Bancorp Inc (14), 111 W Monroe St (fl 21W), Chicago, 60603-4096

Health O Meter (16), 9500 W 55th St (Suite C), Countryside, 60525-7110

Heller Financial (14), 500 W Monroe St (fl 44), Chicago, 60661-3671

The Herald & Review (17), 601 E William St, Decatur, 62525-1190

Hollister Inc (16), 2000 Hollister Dr, Libertyville, 60048

Home 123 Mortgage (14), 2033 Milwaukee Ave (Suite 237), Riverwoods, 60015

Hoover's Mfg Co (2), 4133 Progress Blvd, PO Box 547, Peru, 61354-1125

Horace Mann Educators Corp (15), 1 Horace Mann Plaza, Springfield, 62715-0002

House of Wesley Inc (8), 1704 Morrissey Dr, Bloomington, 61704-7107

Hyatt Hotels Corp (16), 71 S Wacker Dr, Chicago, 60606-4716

INX International Ink Co (16), 150 N Martingale Rd (Suite 700), Schaumburg, 60173

Ideal Industries Inc (16), Becker Pl, Sycamore, 60178

Indus-Tool (12), 300 N Oakley Blvd, Chicago, 60612

The Innovation Machine (1), 30 S Wacker Dr (Suite 2200), Chicago Mercantile Exchange, Chicago, 60606-7452

Institute of Real Estate Management (1), 430 N Michigan Ave, Chicago, 60611-4090

Inter7 Internet Technologies Inc (3), 219 S Prospect St, Galena, 61036-2119

Iroquois Products (10), 2220 W 56th St, Chicago, 60636-3900

JC Whitney (12), 225 N Michigan Ave (Suite 9), Chicago, 60601-7757

Joint Commission (1), 1 Renaissance Blvd, Oakbrook Terrace, 60181-4805

Journal Star (17), One News Plaza, Peoria, 61643

K-Log (8), 1224 27th St, Zion, 60099-2673

Kaplan Publishing (17), 205 W Randolph St (Suite 200), Chicago, 60606-1814

Kemper Corp (15), 1 E Wacker Dr, Chicago, 60601-1883

Lakeside Publishing Co LLC (17), 990 Grove St, Evanston, 60201-6510

LaPreferida Inc (4), 3400 W 35th St, Chicago, 60632

Laran Communications Inc (16), 26W482 Blair St, Winfield, 60190-1109

Learning Seed (3), 641 W Lake St (#301), Chicago, 60661

Lesman Instrument Co (9), 135 Bernice Dr, Bensenville, 60106-3366

Life Fitness (11), 5100 N River Rd, Schiller Park, 60176

Lincoln Park Zoo (1), 2001 N Clark St, Chicago, 60614

LinguiSystems (17), 3100 Fourth Ave, East Moline, 61244-9700

Loyola University Chicago (1), 820 N Michigan Ave, Chicago, 60611-2147

M2Media 360 (17), 1030 W Higgins Rd (Suite 230), Park Ridge, 60068

MTS Publishing (17), 800 W 5th Ave (Suite 204A), Naperville, 60563-4925

Magnaflux (16), 3624 W Lake Ave, Glenview, 60026-1215

Mark James & Associates Inc (16), PO Box 429, Oswego, 60543-0429

The Marmon Group LLC (16), 181 W Madison St Ste 2500, Chicago, 60602-4505

Marsh Affinity Group Services (15), 500 W Monroe St (Suite 2400), Chicago, 60661

Maui Jim Inc (16), 8300 N Allen Rd, Peoria, 61615

McDougal Littell (17), 1560 Sherman Ave, PO Box 1667, Evanston, 60201

McKnight's Long-Term Care News (17), One Northfield Plaza (Suite 521), Northfield, 60093

McMaster-Carr Supply Co (HQ) (9), 600 County Line Rd, Elmhurst, 60126-2081

Medill IMC/Northwestern University (1), 1870 Campus Dr, Evanston, 60208-0885

Melaniphy & Associates, Inc (8), 6348 N Milwaukee Ave (Suite 198), Chicago, 60646

Mercy Home for Boys & Girls (1), 1140 W Jackson Blvd, Chicago, 60607-2906

Methode Electronics Inc (9), 7401 W Wilson Ave, Chicago, 60706

Meyer Partners (1), 1701 E Woodfield Rd (Suite 425), Schaumburg, 60173-5313

Mid America Designs Inc (12), 17082 N US Hwy 45, Effingham, 62401-6764

Mid America Motorworks (12), 17082 N US Hwy 45, Effingham, 62401-7107

The Middleby Corp (16), 1400 Toastmaster Dr, Elgin, 60120-9272

The Millard Group (16), 7301 N Cicero Ave, Lincolnwood, 60712-1613

The Miller Group (5), 1610 Design Way, Dupo, 62239-1820

MillerCoors LLC (4), 250 S Wacker Dr Ste 800, Chicago, 60606-5888

Miller's First Insurance Companies (15), 111 E Fourth St, PO Box 220, Alton, 62002

Morkes Chocolates (4), 1890 N Rand Rd, Palatine, 60074

Morningstar Inc (14), 22 W Washington St, Chicago, 60602

The Morton Arboretum (1), 4100 Illinois (Route 53), Lisle, 60532-1293

Motor Coach Industries International Inc (16), 1700 E Golf Rd, Schaumburg, 60173

Muscular Dystrophy Association (1), 222 S Riverside Plaza (Suite 1500), Chicago, 60606

National Association of Publishers Representatives (1), 2800 W Higgins Rd (Suite 440), Hoffman Estates, 60169

National Association of Realtors (1), 430 N Michigan Ave, Chicago, 60611-4087

National Luggage Dealers Association (1), 1817 Elmdale Ave, Glenview, 60625-1355

Navistar (16), 2701 Navistar Dr, Lisle, 60532-3637

Nevco Scoreboard Co (16), 301 E Harris Ave, Greenville, 62246-2193

Nightingale-Conant Corp (17), 6245 W Howard St, Niles, 60714-3403

Nimlok (16), 7420 N Lehigh Ave, Niles, 60714

Norman Control Co (16), 305 Cary Point Dr, Cary, 60013-2974

North American Co for Life & Health Insurance (15), 525 W Van Buren St Ste 1200, Chicago, 60607-3820

The Northern Trust Co (14), 50 S LaSalle St, Chicago, 60603-1003

Nuclear Plant Journal (17), 1400 Opus Pl (Suite 904), Downers Grove, 60515

Nuveen Investments (14), 333 W Wacker Dr, Chicago, 60606

OAG Worldwide (17), 3025 Highland Pkwy (Suite 200), Downers Grove, 60515

OMSI Inc (1), 9480 N Demazenod Dr, Belleville, 62223-1159

Olesuk Financial Services (14), 5206 W Elm St (#100), McHenry, 60050-4000

On-Hand Adhesives Inc (16), 940 Telser Rd, Lake Zurich, 60047-6714

Professional Education Institute (13), 7020 High Grove Blvd, Chicago, 60527-7637

Paasche Airbrush Co (10), 4311 N Normandy Ave, Chicago, 60634-1395

PAL Health Technologies (16), 1805 Riverway Dr, Pekin, 61554-9309

Paris Presents Inc (7), 3800 Swanson Ct, Gurnee, 60031-1226

Paslode (16), 888 Forest Edge Dr, Vernon Hills, 60061-8117

Path to Purchase Institute (17), 8550 W Bryn Mawr Ave (Suite 200), Chicago, 60631-3731

Pearl Insurance Group LLC (15), 1200 E Glen Ave, Peoria Heights, 61616-5325

Perrygraf (16), 25W550 Geneva Rd (Suite 1934), Carol Stream, 60188-2225

Personal Creations (6), 1005 101st St Ste A, Lemont, 60439-9628

Polyair Packaging (9), 808 E 113th St, Chicago, 60628

Polyline LLC (3), 845 N Church St, Elmhurst, 60126

The Popcorn Factory (4), 13970 W Laurel Dr, Lake Forest, 60045-4533

Position Technologies Inc (16), 2000 S Batavia Ave (Suite 351), Geneva, 60134-3300

Prevent Blindness America (1), 211 W Wacker Dr (Suite 1700), Chicago, 60606-1375

Print Services Distribution Association (1), 330 N Wabash Ave (Suite 2000), Chicago, 60611

Protective Life Corp (15), PO Box 770, Deerfield, 60015-0770

Publications International Ltd (17), 7373 N Cicero Ave, Lincolnwood, 60712-1613

The Quaker Oats Co (16), PO Box 049003, Chicago, 60604-9003

Quill Corp (16), 100 Schelter Rd, Lincolnshire, 60069

Quill Lincolnshire Inc (10), 100 Schelter Rd, Lincolnshire, 60069

Reassure America Life Insurance Co (15), 1275 Sandusky Rd, Jacksonville, 62650

Reb Storage Systems International (9), 4556 W Grand Ave, Chicago, 60639-4734

REGIT Inc (15), 1200 Roosevelt Rd (Suite 115), Glen Ellyn, 60137

Renaissance Greeting Cards Inc (5), 3113 Woodcreek Dr, Downers Grove, 60515

Replogle Globes Inc (16), 2801 S 25th Ave, Broadview, 60155-4500

Richardson Electronics Ltd (16), 40 W 267 Keslinger Rd, Lafox, 60147

Robert Marketing Inc (5), 17 The Court of Island Point, Northbrook, 60062-3210

Rock-Tred Corp (9), 405 N Oakwood Ave, Waukegan, 60085

SRDS (17), 1700 E Higgins Rd Ste 500, Des Plaines, 60018-5610

Sears Home Improvement Products & Services (16), 3333 Beverly Rd, Hoffman Estates, 60179

Sears, Roebuck & Co (16), 3333 Beverly Rd, Hoffman Estates, 60179

Sedgwick Moran Detert & Arnold LLP (9), 1 N Wacker Dr (Suite 4200), Chicago, 60606-2862

Seedburo Equipment Co (8), 2293 S Mount Prospect Rd, Des Plaines, 60018-1810

Sellstrom Manufacturing Co (16), 2050 Hammond Dr, Schaumburg, 60173-3810

LH Selman Ltd (6), 410 S Michigan Ave Ste 207, Chicago, 60605-1448

Shape LLC (3), 2105 Corporate Dr, Addison, 60101

Simply Batteries Inc (7), 105 N 1st St, De Kalb, 60115

Solar Cine Products Inc (5), 4247 S Kedzie Ave, Chicago, 60632

Sourcebooks Inc (17), 1935 Brookdale Rd (Suite 139), Naperville, 60563-7994

Specialty Store Services Inc (16), 454 Jarvis Ave, Des Plaines, 60018

Spectra Merchandising International Inc (16), 4230 N Normandy, Chicago, 60634

Spilsbury Puzzle Co (11), 70 W Madison St (Suite 2300), Chicago, 60602-4250

Spring-Green Lawn Care Corp (16), 11909 Spaulding School Dr, Plainfield, 60544

Star Silkscreen Design Inc (2), 2281 Hubbard Ave, Decatur, 62526-2149

State Farm Insurance Cos (15), 1 State Farm Plaza, Bloomington, 61710-0001

Sunburst Digital Inc (17), 3150 W Higgins Rd (Suite 140), Hoffman Estates, 60169

Sunstar (16), 4635 W Foster Ave, Chicago, 60630-1709

Surplus Record (17), 20 N Wacker Dr (Suite 2400), Chicago, 60606-3181

Svoboda Collins LLC (5), 1 North Franklin (Suite 1500), Chicago, 60606

Taylor Capital Group, Inc (14), 9550 W Higgins Rd, Rosemont, 60018-4906

Telefonix Inc (16), 2340 Ernie Kruger Cir, Waukegan, 60087-3224

Telephony (17), One IBM Plaza (23rd fl), Chicago, 60611

Tempco Electric Heater Corp (9), 607 N Central Ave, Wood Dale, 60191-1452

Thoma Cressey Bravo (14), 300 N La Salle Dr (Suite 4300), Chicago, 60654-3422

Thousand Trails LP (16), 2 N Riverside Plz (Suite 800), Chicago, 60606-2682

Timm Medical Technologies, Inc (16), 150 Saunders Rd (Suite 120), Lake Forest, 60045-2524

Tower Hobbies/Hobbico (11), 2904 Research Rd, Champaign, 61822

Trans Union Corp (14), 555 W Adams St, Chicago, 60661-3614

Travelclick (19), 300 N Martingale Rd, Schaumburg, 60173-2407

Tribune Co (17), 435 N Michigan Ave, Chicago, 60611-4041

Tricor Braun (16), 2145 Internationale Pkwy Ste 800, Woodridge, 60517-4830

Triton College (16), 2000 Fifth Ave, River Grove, 60171

True Value Co (16), 8600 W Bryn Mawr Ave, Chicago, 60631-3579

Tyndale House Publishers (17), 351 Executive Dr, Carol Stream, 60188

UGL Equis Corp (16), 161 N Clark St (Suite 2400), Chicago, 60601-3221

ULTA Salon Cosmetics Fragrance (7), 1000 Remington Blvd, Bolingbrook, 60440

US Foodservice (4), 9399 W Higgins Rd Ste 500, Rosemont, 60018-4992

Universal Hovercraft (11), 1204 Third St S, Cordova, 61242

Universal Training (16), 736 N Western Ave (Suite 323), Lake Forest, 60045

University of Chicago GSB (1), 450 N Cityfront Plaza Dr (Suite 514), Chicago, 60611-4316

University of Chicago Press (17), 1427 E 60th St, Chicago, 60637

University of Illinois College of LAS, Office of Advancement (1), 702 S Wright St MC-446, 2090 Lincoln Hall, Urbana, 61801

University of Illinois Foundation (1), 1305 W Green St (MC-386), Urbana, 61801-2962

University Subscription Service (18), 1213 Butterfield Rd, Downers Grove, 60515

Vance Industries Inc (16), 5617 W Howard St, Niles, 60714-4011

Vierk National Supply (16), 2300 Commonwealth Ave, North Chicago, 60064

Visible Computer Supply Corp (16), 1750 Wallace Ave, Saint Charles, 60174

Walgreens Co (7), 200 Wilmont Rd, Deerfield, 60015

Washington Mutual Home Loan, Inc (14), 75 N Fairway Dr, Vernon Hills, 60061-1846

Wilton Industries Inc (16), 2240 W 75th St, Woodridge, 60517

Winston Marketing Group (8), PO Box 7985, Elk Grove Village, 60009-7985

Wordright Enterprises Inc (17), 431 Dogwood Terr, Buffalo Grove, 60089-1820

World Book Inc (17), 233 N Michigan Ave (Suite 2000), Chicago, 60601-5805

World Future Society (1), 333 N La-Salle St, Chicago, 60654

Zoro Tools Inc (9), 1000 Asbury Dr (Suite 1), Buffalo Grove, 60089-4551

Zurich (15), 1400 American Ln, Schaumburg, 60196-5452

INDIANA

Abbey Press (6), One Hill Dr, Saint Meinrad, 47577-1004

Airomat Corp (16), 2916 Engle Rd, Fort Wayne, 46809-1198

Amazon Drygoods (2), 3788 Wilson St, Osgood, 47037

The American Legion National Headquarters (1), 5745 Lee Rd, John H. Geiger Operations Ctr, Indianapolis, 46216

American Stationery Co Inc (10), 100 N Park Ave, Box 207, Peru, 46970

Anthem Corporate Communications (15), 120 Monument Cir, Indianapolis, 46204

Anthem Inc (7), 120 Monument Cir, Indianapolis, 46204

Aristokraft Inc (16), 1 Masterbrand Cabinets Dr, Jasper, 47547-0420

Arrow Co (16), 5457 W 79th St, Indianapolis, 46268-1675

Associated Construction Publications (17), 1200 Madison Ave (Suite LL20), Indianapolis, 46225

Bart's Watersports (11), 7581 E 800th N, North Webster, 46555-9604

Berger's Table Pad Co (8), 1501 W Market St, Indianapolis, 46222

Bits & Pieces Inc (11), PO Box 4150, Lawrenceburg, 47025

Vera Bradley (2), 12420 Stonebridge Rd, Roanoke, 46783

Breck's Bulbs (8), PO Box 65, Guilford, 47022

CVT Production Inc (16), 50906 Rothbury Dr, Granger, 46530-6291

Children's Better Health Institute (1), 1100 Waterway Blvd, Indianapolis, 46202

Conseco Inc (15), 11825 N Pennsylvania Ave, Carmel, 46032-4555

DRG (17), 269 S Jefferson, Berne, 46711

Da-Lite Screen Co Inc (16), 3100 N Detroit St, Warsaw, 46582-2288

Delta Upsilon International Fraternity (16), 8705 Founders Rd, Box 68942, Indianapolis, 46268

DirectBuy Inc (1), 8450 Broadway, Merrillville, 46410

Dow Theory Forecasts (17), 7412 Calumet Ave, Hammond, 46324

Dwyer Instruments Inc (16), 102 Indiana Hwy 212, Michigan City, 46360-1956

e-Pipeconnection (9), 4406 E Morgan Ave, Evansville, 47715-2254

Elkhart Cases (2), 3605 Cooper Dr, Elkhart, 46514

Fielder's Choice Direct (8), 306 N Main St, Monticello, 47960-2133

Financial Publishing Co (17), 1251 N Eddy St (Suite 202), South Bend, 46617-1478

Forethought Financial Services Inc (15), 1 Forethought Ctr, Batesville, 47006-1279

Gardens Alive! Inc (8), PO Box 4028, Lawrenceburg, 47025

Glas-Col (16), 711 Hulman St, PO Box 2128, Terre Haute, 47808

Gohn Brothers (5), 105 S Main St, Middlebury, 46540

Golden Rule Insurance Co (15), 7440 Woodland Dr, Golden Rule Bldg, Indianapolis, 46278-1719

Growing Child, Inc (17), PO Box 2505, West Lafayette, 47996-2505

Hansen Corp (16), 901 S First St, Princeton, 47670-2369

ITT Educational Services Inc (16), 13000 N Meridian St, Carmel, 46082

Indianapolis Motor Speedway (19), 4790 W 16th St, Indianapolis, 46222-2550

Indianapolis Newspapers Inc (17), 307 N Pennsylvania St, Indianapolis, 46204

Intra Business Systems Inc (16), PO Box 6681, South Bend, 46660-6681

Ivy Tech Community College of Indiana (13), 50 W Fall Creek Pkwy N Dr, Indianapolis, 46208-5752

James Medical Rents & Sales Inc (7), 7821 Coldwater Rd Ste A, Fort Wayne, 46825-8412

Jofco Inc (16), 402 E 13th St, PO Box 71, Jasper, 47547-0071

Kitchen Kompact Inc (8), 911 E 11th St, Jeffersonville, 47130-4142

Liberty Fund Inc (1), 8335 Allison Pointe Trail (Suite 300), Indianapolis, 46250-1684

Lure Craft (11), 513 W Central Ave, Lagrange, 46761

McDonald Obsolete Parts Co (16), 6458 W Eureka Rd, Rockport, 47635

Mead Johnson Co (7), 2400 W Lloyd Expwy, Evansville, 47721-0001

Merrimade Stationery Co LLC (10), 275 Billerca Rd, Chelmsford, 01824-4113

National Emblem Sales (16), PO Box 36460, Indianapolis, 46206-0460

Nutritional Research Associates Inc (16), 407 E Broad St, South Whitley, 46787-1001

Our Sunday Visitor Publishing (17), 200 Noll Plaza, Huntington, 46750

PVC Plastics Co (16), 4406 E Morgan Ave, Evansville, 47715-2254

Pratt Corp (16), 3035 N Shadeland Ave (Suite 100), Indianapolis, 46226-6231

Professional Creations (5), 1220 Church St, New Castle, 47362

RCI LLC (19), 9998 N Michigan Rd, Carmel, 46032-9640

Relaxo-Bak Inc (7), 4956 W 300 N, Anderson, 46011

Roche Diagnostics Corp (7), 9115 Hague Rd, Indianapolis, 46256-1045

The RYTEX Co (10), 100 N Park Ave, Peru, 46970-1701

Sailrite Enterprises, Inc (11), 2390 E 100 S, Columbia City, 46725-8751

Sani Serv (16), PO Box 1089, Mooresville, 46158-5089

Scott's Dog Supply Inc (11), 2619 Cressmoor Cir, Indianapolis, 46234-7020

Simon Property Group (16), 115 W Washington St, Indianapolis, 46204

Sony DADC (3), 1800 N Fruitridge Ave, Terre Haute, 47804

Sterling Fluid Systems (16), 2005 Dr Martin Luther King St, PO Box 7026, Indianapolis, 46202-1165

Stile-Tile Like Metal Roofing (9), 7800 State Rd (#60), Sellersburg, 47172

Sur La Table (8), PO Box 840, Brownsburg, 46112

Teachers Credit Union (1), 110 S Main St, South Bend, 46601-1833

Threefold (9), 5151 N Shadeland Ave, Indianapolis, 46226-2603

Touch of Class Catalog (8), 709 W 12th St, Huntingburg, 47542-8915

Trilithic (16), 9710 Park Davis Dr, Indianapolis, 46235-2390

Warner Press (17), 1201 E Fifth St, Anderson, 46012

IOWA

ARAG (15), 400 Locust St (Suite 480), Des Moines, 50309

Accelerated Learning Foundation (17), 118 N Court St, Fairfield, 52556-2811

Aegon USA Investment Management, Inc (14), 4333 Edgewood Rd NE, Cedar Rapids, 52499-3830

Agri Drain Corp (9), 1462 340th St, Adair, 50002

August Home Publishing Co (17), 2200 Grand Ave, Des Moines, 50312-5306

Aviva USA Corp (14), 611 Fifth Ave, Des Moines, 50309

Continental Western Group (15), 11201 Douglas Ave, Des Moines, 50322

Customized Newspaper Advertising (18), 319 E Fifth St, Des Moines, 50309

Foundation for Chiropractic Education & Research (1), 380 Wright Rd, Norwalk, 50211-1661

Frontier Natural Products Co-op (7), 3021 78th St, PO Box 299, Norway, 52318

Gazette Communications Inc (17), 500 Third Ave SE, Box 511, Cedar Rapids, 52406

GuideOne Insurance (15), 1111 Ashworth Rd, West Des Moines, 50265-3537

Hagie Manufacturing Co (9), 721 Central Ave W, PO Box 273, Clarion, 50525

Homesteaders Life Co (15), 5700 Westown Pkwy, West Des Moines, 50266-8214

ING USA Annuity & Life Ins Co (15), 909 Locust St, Des Moines, 50309-2899

Iowa Medical Society (1), 515 E Locust St (#400), Des Moines, 50309

Iowa Student Loan Liquidity Corp (1), 6805 Vista Dr, Ashford I Bldg, West Des Moines, 50266-9362

J&P Cycles (12), 13225 Circle Dr, Anamosa, 52205-7321

John Deere Financial (14), 6400 NW 86th St, PO Box 6600, Johnston, 50131-6600

Kreg Tool Co (16), 201 Campus Dr, Huxley, 50124-9760

Landauer Corp (17), 3100 NW 101st St (Suite A), Urbandale, 50322-3867

Life Investors Insurance Co of America (14), 4333 Edgewood Rd NE, Cedar Rapids, 52499-0001

Mi-T-M Corp (9), 8650 Enterprise Dr, Peosta, 52068-9433

Mancomm Inc (17), 317 W 4th St, Davenport, 52801

Marsh US Consumer (15), 12421 Meredith Dr, Urbandale, 50398-9001

Maxon Furniture Inc (10), 505 Ford Ave, Muscatine, 52761-5662

Meredith Corp (17), 1716 Locust St, Des Moines, 50309-3023

Midwest Technology Products & Services (9), 2600 Bridgeport Dr, Sioux City, 51111

PPC (9), PO Box 246, Johnston, 50131

Pioneer Hi-Bred International Inc (4), 7100 NW 62nd Ave, PO Box 1000, Johnston, 50131-1000

The Principal Financial Group (15), 711 High St, Des Moines, 50392-0330

Profit Potentials Inc (1), 1 Foreign Candy Dr, Hull, 51239-7719

Rapids Wholesale Equipment (16), 6201 S Gateway Dr, Marion, 52302-9430

Successful Farming (17), 1716 Locust St, Des Moines, 50309-3023

Transamerica Life Insurance Co (15), 4333 Edgewood Rd NE, Cedar Rapids, 52499

Universal Engineering Corp (16), 800 First Ave NW, Cedar Rapids, 52405-3999

Veridian Credit Union (1), PO Box 6000 1827 Ansborough Ave, Waterloo, 50704

Viking Pump Inc (16), 406 State St, Box 8, Cedar Falls, 50613-0008

Wellmark Blue Cross & Blue Shield of Iowa (15), PO Box 9232, 1331 Grand Ave, Des Moines, 50306-9232

KANSAS

Bushnell Corporation (11), 9200 Cody St, Overland Park, 66214-1734

Bushnell Outdoor Products (16), 9200 Cody, Overland Park, 66214-1734

Cessna Aircraft Co (16), One Cessna Blvd, Wichita, 67215-1400

Cookbook Publishers Inc (17), 9825 Widmer Rd, Lenexa, 66285-5920

Craft-Diston Industries (16), PO Box 12492, Wichita, 67277-2492

Dean & Deluca Brands Inc (4), 2526 E 36th Cir N, Wichita, 67219-2300

Ebersole Lapidary Supply Inc (11), 5830 W Hendryx St, Wichita, 67209-1234

The Fuller Brush Co (5), One Fuller Way, Great Bend, 67530

GTM Sportswear (2), PO Box 8, Manhattan, 66505-0008

Goddard Manufacturing Co (8), 109 S Mill St, Logan, 67646-5112

Hearlihy & Co (17), 1002 E Adams, PO Box 1747, Pittsburg, 66762

Industrial Uniform Co Inc (2), 902 E Indianapolis St, Wichita, 67211-2407

Insurance Publications Inc (17), 9404 Reeds Rd, PO Box 11310, Overland Park, 66207-1010

Kansas State University Division of Continuing Education (1), 13 College Ct Bldg, Manhattan, 66506-6005

Marketshare Publications Inc (17), 7171 W 95th St (Suite 310), Overland Park, 66212-2249

Mother Earth News Magazine (17), 1503 SW 42nd St, Topeka, 66609-1265

National Seminars Group (16), 6901 W 63rd St (Suite 300), Shawnee Mission, 66202-4005

Northern Cross (16), 214 N 2100 Rd, Lecompton, 66050

Payless ShoeSource Inc (2), 3231 SE 6th Ave, Topeka, 66607-2260

Peruvian Connection Ltd (2), 24535 McLouth Rd, Tonganoxie, 66086-3132

Player Piano Co Inc (11), 704 E Douglas Ave, Wichita, 67202-2745

Protection One Inc (16), 1035 N Third St (Suite 101), Lawrence, 66044

Fred Pryor Seminars (16), 5700 Broadmoor St (Suite 300), Mission, 66202-2415

SW Caging Corp (14), 5342 NW 25th St, Topeka, 66618-3738

The Saint Francis Community Services (1), 509 E Elm St, Salina, 67401

Sprint Corp (3), 6391 Sprint Pkwy, Overland Park, 66251-4300

Stanley Home Products (8), 1 Fuller Way, Great Bend, 67530-2466

Sunshine Unlimited Inc (9), 303 W Normal Dr, Lindsborg, 67456-1519

Uniformed Services Benefit Association (15), 10895 Grandview Dr (Suite 350), Overland Park, 66210

Vet Vax (11), 1203 E Hwy 24-40, Tonganoxie, 66086-9507

Wyandotte West Communications Inc (17), PO Box 12003, Kansas City, 66112-0003

KENTUCKY

Abbey of Gethsemani (1), 3642 Monks Rd, Trappist, 40051

American Printing House for the Blind (7), 1839 Frankfort Ave, Louisville, 40206-0085

Ashland Inc (16), 50 E Rivercenter Blvd (Suite 1600), Covington, 41011-1678

Associated Photo (16), PO Box 188218, Erlanger, 41018-8218

Baron/Barclay Bridge Supplies (11), 3600 Chamberlain Ln (Suite 206), Louisville, 40241

Brown-Forman Corp (16), 850 Dixie Hwy, Louisville, 40210

Camping World Inc (11), Box 90018, Bowling Green, 42102-9018

Cengage Learning (17), 10650 Toebben Dr, Independence, 41051-5100

Christian Appalachian Project (1), 485 Ponderosa Dr, Paintsville, 41240

Collector Books & American Quilters Society (17), 5801 Kentucky Dam Rd, PO Box 3009, Paducah, 42003-9323

Donna Salyers' Fabulous-Bridal Inc (2), 25 W Robbins St, Covington, 41011-3005

Fauntleroy Supply Co/Wing Supply (11), 820 N Main St, Greenville, 42345

Gall's Inc (16), 2680 Palumbo Dr, Lexington, 40509-1234

House of Onyx, Inc (6), 120 N Main St, The Aaron Bldg, Greenville, 42345-1504

Humana Inc (7), 500 W Main St, Louisville, 40202

Jefferson National (14), 10350 Ormsby Park Pl (Suite 600), Louisville, 40223-6175

KCEOC Community Action Partnership Inc (1), PO Box 490, Barbourville, 40906-0490

KET (17), 600 Cooper Dr, Lexington, 40502-1669

Keeneland Association Inc (16), 4201 Versailles Rd, PO Box 1690, Lexington, 40588-1690

Kentucky Bankers Association (1), 600 W Main St (Suite 400), Louisville, 40202-2998

Majestic Products Co (16), 149 Cleveland Dr, Paris, L5T 2N6-40361

The National Underwriter Co (17), 5081 Olympic Blvd, Erlanger, 41018-3164

Papa John's International (4), 2002 Papa John's Blvd, Louisville, 40299-2333

Party Kits & Equestrian Gifts (6), 10920 Plantside Dr Ste C, Louisville, 40299-6113

Personnel Policy Service Inc (17), PO Box 7697, Louisville, 40257-0697

J Peterman Co (5), 400 Old Vine St Ste 200, Lexington, 40507-1910

Phoenix Poke Boats Inc (16), 106 Bethford Rd, McKee, 40447

Sweet Tooth Candies (4), 1020 Saratoga St, Newport, 41071-2129

Taylor-Stiles Division (16), 7451 Empire Dr, Florence, 41042

US Cavalry (6), 2855 Centennial Ave, Radcliff, 40160-9000

US Playing Card Co (16), 300 Gap Way, Erlanger, 41018-3160

Veneer Factory Outlet (8), 6521 Jacob Dr, Westport, 40077

WILD Flavors Inc (4), 1261 Pacific Ave, Erlanger, 41018-1260

Wildlife Education Ltd (17), 1260 Audubon Rd, Park Hills, 41011-1904

Willis Music Co (17), 7380 Industrial Rd, PO Box 548, Florence, 41042-0548

Xcelerated Investments Inc (14), 2940 Hebron Park Dr (Suite 307), Hebron, 41048-9573

LOUISIANA

AllBrands.com Sewing Machine Superstore (11), 20415 Highland Rd, Baton Rouge, 70817-7348

Amaryllis Inc (8), 4350 Pine Ridge Rd., Baton Rouge, 70809

Arnaud's (16), 813 Bienville St, New Orleans, 70112-3121

Baton Rouge Conventions & Visitors Bureau (1), 359 3rd St Ste A, Baton Rouge, 70801-1310

Blanchard & Co Inc (16), 909 Poydras St (Suite 1900), New Orleans, 70112

Blue Cross Blue Shield of Louisiana (15), 5525 Reitz Ave, Baton Rouge, 70809-3802

Community Coffee Co (4), 3332 Partridge Ln (Bldg A), Baton Rouge, 70809-2413

Durio Nursery (8), 5853 Hwy 182, Opelousas, 70570

Entergy (16), 639 Loyola Ave (Suite 300), New Orleans, 70113-7106

Great Chefs Television Publishing (6), 747 Magazine St, New Orleans, 70130

Laitram Machinery (16), 220 Laitram Ln, Harahan, 70123

Louisiana State Museum (1), 701 Chartres St, New Orleans, 70116-3205

Orient Expressed Imports Inc (2), 3446 Magazine St, New Orleans, 70115

Starmount Life Insurance Co (15), 8485 Goodwood Blvd, Baton Rouge, 70806-7878

Stewart Enterprises Inc (16), 1333 S Clearview Pkwy, Jefferson, 70121-1014

Stuller Inc (2), 302 Rue Louis XIV, Lafayette, 70508

Jimmy Swaggart Ministries (1), 8919 World Ministry Ave Ste B, Baton Rouge, 70810-9007

USA Hosts Ltd (19), 365 Canal St (Suite 1400), New Orleans, 70130-1123

MAINE

Akers Ski Inc (11), 51 Akers Way, Andover, 04216

Antique & Collectible Tools Inc (11), 27 Fickett Rd, Pownal, 04069

LL Bean Inc (2), 15 Casco St, Freeport, 04033-0001

Blethen Maine Newspapers Inc (17), 390 Congress St, PO Box 1460, Portland, 04104-5009

Clarin by Hussey Seating (5), 38 Dyer St Ext, North Berwick, 03906-6763

Crestline Specialties, Inc (16), 70 Mt Hope Ave, Lewiston, 04241

Cuddledown Inc (8), 14 Yarmouth Junction, Yarmouth, 04096

DeLorme Mapping (3), 2 DeLorme Dr, Yarmouth, 04096

Ducktrap River Fish Farm (4), 57 Little River Dr, Belfast, 04915

Fieldstone Gardens Inc (8), 55 Quaker Ln, Vassalboro, 04989-3816

Gimbels of Maine Inc (6), 14 Commercial St, Boothbay Harbor, 04538-1821

Hebron Academy (1), 309 Paris Rd, Hebron, 04238-0309

International Marine (17), 90 Mechanic St, Camden, 04843-1844

The Jackson Laboratory JAX Research Systems (1), 600 Main St, Bar Harbor, 04609-1523

Lo Ink Specialties (16), PO Box 530B, Kennebunkport, 04046-1821

The Maine Photographic Workshops (16), 2 Central St, Rockport, 04856-5936

Maine Potato Board (1), 744 Main St (Rm 1), Presque Isle, 04769

Thomas Moser Cabinetmakers (16), 149 Main St, Freeport, 04032

Nowetah's American Indian Store & Museum (6), 2 Colegrove Rd, New Portland, 04961-3821

PowerPay (14), 320 Cumberland Ave, Portland, 04101

Renaissance Greeting Cards Inc (5), 3113 Woodcreek Dr, Downers Grove, 60515

Saunders Manufacturing Co Inc (16), 65 Nickerson Hill Rd, Readfield, 04355

Speed-Mat (16), 374 South St, Biddeford, 04005

Sturbridge Yankee Workshop Inc (16), 90 Blueberry Rd, Portland, 04102-1924

TD Bank NA (14), 70 Gray Rd, Falmouth, 04105-2019

Thorndike Press (17), 10 Water St Ste 310, Waterville, 04901-6566

Unum Corp (15), 2211 Congress St (Suite B118), Portland, 04122

Walch Publishing (17), 40 Walch Dr, Portland, 04103-1286

MARYLAND

ADRA International (1), 12501 Old Columbia Pike, Silver Spring, 20904-6601

AESU Inc (19), 3922 Hickory Ave, Baltimore, 21211-1834

AIIM International (1), 1100 Wayne Ave (Suite 1100), Silver Spring, 20910-5616

AMVETS National Service Foundation (1), 4647 Forbes Blvd, Lanham, 20706

Accounting with Debits and Credits with Coates & Hutchinson PC (14), PO Box 561, Odenton, 21113

Accuracy in Media Inc (1), 4350 E West Hwy (Suite 555), Bethesda, 20814

Aegon Direct Marketing Services Inc (15), 100 Light St Fl B1, Baltimore, 21202-1098

AGORA Inc (17), 14 W Mount Vernon Pl, Baltimore, 21201-5125

Air Force Sergeants Association (1), 5211 Auth Rd, Suitland, 20746-4339

Aircraft Owners & Pilots Association (1), 421 Aviation Way, Frederick, 21701-4756

American Breast Cancer Foundation (1), 10400 Little Patuxent Pkwy (Suite 480), Columbia, 21044

American Capital (15), 2 Bethesda Metro Ctr 14th Fl, Bethesda, 20814-5390

American Kidney Fund (1), 6110 Executive Blvd (Suite 1010), Rockville, 20852

American Nurses' Association (1), 8515 Georgia Ave (Suite 400), Silver Spring, 20006-3492

American Running Association (1), 4405 East-West Hwy (Suite 405), Bethesda, 20814-4522

American Speech-Language-Hearing Association (1), 2200 Research Blvd, Rockville, 20850-3289

Association for Financial Professionals (14), 4520 East West Hwy (Suite 750), Bethesda, 20814-3574

BGE Home Products & Services Inc (16), 1409 Tangiere Dr (Suite A), Baltimore, 21220-2878

BYK-Gardner USA (16), 9104 Guilford Rd, Columbia, 21046-2677

Balducci Enterprises Inc (16), 12920 Cloverleaf Center Dr (Suite B), Germantown, 20874

Baltimore Magazine (17), 1000 Lancaster St (Suite 400), Baltimore, 21202-4632

Joseph A Bank Clothiers Inc (2), 500 Hanover Pike, Hampstead, 21074-2002

Barton-Cotton (16), 3030 Waterview Ave (Suite 100), Baltimore, 21230-3520

Bill Me Later Inc (14), 9690 Deereco Rd (fl 7), Timonium, 21093-6936

Blaine Window Hardware Inc (9), 17319 Blaine Dr, Hagerstown, 21740

Blissliving Home (8), 5515 Security Ln (Suite 1100), Rockville, 20852-5009

Books on Tape (17), 400 Hahn Rd, Westminster, 21157-4627

BrightFocus Foundation (1), 22512 Gateway Ctr Dr, Clarksburg, 20871-2005

CDR Fundraising Group (1), 16900 Science Dr (Suite 210), Bowie, 20715-4412

Carroll Publishing (17), 4701 Sangamore Rd (Suite S155), Bethesda, 20816-2532

Catholic Relief Services (1), 228 Lexington St, Baltimore, 21201-3443

Chesapeake Bay Foundation (1), 6 Herndon Ave, Annapolis, 21403-4503

Children's Hospital Foundation (1), 801 Roeder Rd, Silver Spring, 20910

Choice Hotels International (16), 1 Choice Hotels Cir (#400), Rockville, 20850-5140

CitiFinancial Credit Co (14), 300 Saint Paul Pl, Baltimore, 21202-2120

ClearOne Advantage (14), 1501 S Clinton St (320), Baltimore, 21224

The Country House Inc (6), 805 E Main St, Salisbury, 21804-5024

Cystic Fibrosis Foundation (1), 6931 Arlington Rd (fl 2), Bethesda, 20814-5231

DB Alex Brown Inc (14), 100 International Dr (fl 22), Baltimore, 21202-3298

Daedalus Books Inc (5), PO Box 6000, Columbia, 21046-6000

Damilic Corp (16), 601 Dover Rd Ste 7, Rockville, 20850-1275

Discovery Communications Inc (16), One Discovery Pl, Silver Spring, 20910

Editorial Projects in Education Inc (17), 6935 Arlington Rd (Suite 100), Bethesda, 20814-5233

Encore Marketing International (16), 4501 Forbes Blvd, Lanham, 20706-4236

Epilepsy Foundation (1), 8301 Professional Pl E (Suite 200), Landover, 20785-2353

Foundation Fighting Blindness (1), 7168 Columbia Gateway Dr Ste 100, Columbia, 21046-3256

Alan Furman & Co (2), 12250 Rockville Pike (Suite 270), Rockville, 20852

General Physics Corp (16), 6095 Marshalee Dr (Suite 300), Elkridge, 21075

W R Grace & Co (16), 7500 Grace Dr, Columbia, 21044

Health Affairs (17), 7500 Old Georgetown Rd (Suite 600), Bethesda, 20814-6800

The Healthy Back Store (16), 10300 Southard Dr, Beltsville, 20705-2107

Hopkins Medical Products (7), 5 Greenwood Pl, Baltimore, 21208-2763

Institute of Management & Administration (IOMA) (17), 3 Bethesda Metro Center (Suite 250), Bethesda, 20814-5377

Jos A Bank Clothiers Inc (2), 500 Hanover Pike, Hampstead, 21074-2002

The Jewish Federation of Greater Washington (1), 6101 Montrose Rd (Suite 100), North Bethesda, 20852-4816

Kaiser Foundation Health Plan of the Mid-Atlantic States Inc (1), 2101 E Jefferson St, Rockville, 20852-4908

Lilypons Water Gardens (8), 6800 Lilypons Rd, Adamstown, 21710-8606

Lippincott, Williams & Wilkins (17), 351 W Camden St, Baltimore, 21201-2436

Lockheed Martin Corp (16), 6801 Rockledge Dr, Bethesda, 20817

MARCOR Remediation Inc (16), 3900 Vero Rd, Halethorpe, 21227-1510

Marriott International Inc (19), 10400 Fernwood Rd, Bethesda, 20817-1102

Maryland Pennysaver (17), 1342 Charwood Rd, Hanover, 21076

The Maryland Saddlery Inc (11), 14924 Falls Rd, Butler, 21023

McCormick & Co Inc (4), 18 Loveton Cir, Sparks, 21152-9202

Media Two (17), 1014 W 36th St, Baltimore, 21211-2415

Medifast Inc (4), 11445 Cronhill Dr Ste 200, Owings Mills, 21117-2270

Mr Wash Car Wash (16), 3817 Dupont Ave, Kensington, 20895

NAACP (1), 4805 Mount Hope Dr, Baltimore, 21215-3206

NASA Federal Credit Union (1), 500 Prince Georges Blvd, Upper Marlboro, 20774-8732

NASW Assurance Services Inc (1), 50 Citizens Way (Suite 304), Frederick, 21701

NEA's Member Benefits Corp (1), 900 Clopper Rd, Gaithersburg, 20878-1360

NTL Institute (1), 8380 Colesville Rd (Suite 560), Silver Spring, 20910-6262

National Foundation for Cancer Research (1), 4600 E West Hwy (Suite 525), Bethesda, 20814-6900

National 4-H Supply Service (16), 7100 Connecticut Ave, Chevy Chase, 20815

National Gallery of Art Gift Shop (16), 4th & Constitution Ave NW, Washington, 20565

Naval Institute Press (17), 291 Wood Rd, Annapolis, 21402-5034

Pallottine Center for Apostolic Causes Inc/St Jude Shrine (1), 308 N Paca St, Baltimore, 21201

Penny Wise Office Products (10), 6911 Laurel Bowie Rd (Suite 209), Bowie, 20715-1712

Planet Cotton (2), 8001 Cessna Ave, Gaithersburg, 20879-4116

Pneuma Books (17), 25 Hunter Ct, Elkton, 21921-1762

Prime Media Equine Group (17), 656 Quince Orchard Rd, Gaithersburg, 20878

Print Products International (9), 9030 Junction Dr, Annapolis Junction, 20701

Recognition Products International (16), 8706 Commerce Dr (Suite 6), Easton, 21601-6903

Rollyson Financial Group (14), 150 Oak Dr, Pasadena, 21122-4421

Shillcraft Inc (16), 2530 Riva Rd (Suite 308), Annapolis, 21401-7414

Albert S Smyth Co Inc (6), 2020 York Rd, Timonium, 21093

Sylvan Learning Inc (16), 1001 Fleet St (fl 9), Baltimore, 21202

T Rowe Price Associates Inc (14), 100 E Pratt St (fl 4), Baltimore, 21202-1081

Tax Management Inc (17), 3 Bethesda Metro Ctr (Suite 250), BNA Customer Contact Center, Bethesda, 20814-5377

Tax Reduction Institute (14), 13200 Executive Park Ter, Germantown, 20874-5313

Tessco Inc (16), 11126 McCormick Rd, Hunt Valley, 21031

Texada Capital Corp (14), 62 Greenwood Shoals, Grasonville, 21638-9659

Transamerica Life & Protection (15), 520 Park Ave, Baltimore, 21201-4500

The Union Labor Life Insurance Co (15), 8403 Colesville Rd, Silver Spring, 20910-6331

United Communications Group (17), 9737 Washingtonian Blvd (Suite 100), Two Washingtonian Center, Gaithersburg, 20878-7364

US Pharmacopeia (1), 12601 Twinbrook Pkwy, Rockville, 20852-1790

Universal Security Instruments Inc (16), 11407 Cronhill Dr (Suite A), Owings Mills, 21117-6218

University Press of America Inc (17), 4501 Forbes Blvd (Suite 200), Lanham, 20706

The Vane Brothers Co (16), 2100 Frankfurst Ave, Baltimore, 21226-1026

The Vestal Press Ltd (17), 4501 Forbes Blvd (Suite 200), Lanham, 20706

Vietnam Veterans of America (1), 8719 Colesville Rd (Suite 100), Silver Spring, 20910-3710

Womanship (16), 137 Conduit St, Annapolis, 21401

WorldVu LLC (17), 1906 E Pratt St, Baltimore, 21231-1925

MASSACHUSETTS

A-T Surgical Manufacturing Co (2), 115 Clemente St, Holyoke, 01040-5644

APW-Wright Line (16), 160 Gold Star Blvd, Worcester, 01606

ASE Technologies Inc (16), 226 Lowell St, Wilmington, 01887-3074

Abbott Products (16), 86 Finnell Dr, Weymouth, 02188-1126

Academic Management Services (14), 463 Swansea Mall Dr, Swansea, 02777-4119

Aerovox Inc (16), 167 John Vertente Blvd, New Bedford, 02745-1221

Alfa Aesar-A Johnson Matthey Co (9), 26 Partridge Rd, Ward Hill, 01835-8099

Alfa CTP Systems (10), 554 Clark Rd # 2, Tewksbury, 01876-1631

AliMed Inc (7), 297 High St, Dedham, 02026-2898

Amergent (1), 9 Centennial Dr Unit 201, Peabody, 01960-7940

American Institute for Economic Research (1), 250 Division St, Great Barrington, 01230-1198

American Student Assistance (1), 100 Cambridge St (Suite 1600), Boston, 02114-2567

American Tourister (16), 575 West St (Suite 110), Mansfield, 02048-1160

Americraft - The Gift Brokers Inc (16), 210 Lockes Village Rd, Wendell, 01379

Appalachian Mountain Club (1), 5 Joy St, Boston, 02108-1490

Artech House (17), 685 Canton St, Norwood, 02062-2610

Association of Marian Helpers (1), Eden Hill, Stockbridge, 01263

Atlantic Spice Co (4), 2 Shore Rd, North Truro, 02652

BJ's Wholesale Club Inc (13), 25 Research Dr, Westborough, 01582

Bank Boston (14), 100 Federal St, Boston, 02110

Banker & Tradesman (17), 280 Summer St, Boston, 02210-1131

The Bauman Group (14), 50 Main St, Ashland, 01721-3113

Bedford/St Martin's (17), 75 Arlington St, Boston, 02116

Bentley University (13), 175 Forest St, Waltham, 02452-4705

Berkshire Direct Inc (17), 616 Main St, Williamstown, 01267

Berkshire Record Outlet Inc (3), Rte 102 Pleasant St, Lee, 01238-9804

Berman Group (16), 18 Tarleton Rd, Newton Center, 02459-1733

Berway Visual Products Inc (3), 668 Main St (Suite 10), Wilmington, 01887

Channing L Bete Co Inc (17), One Community Pl, South Deerfield, 01373

The Black Dog Tavern Co Inc (2), PO Box 2219, 20 Beach St Extension, Vineyard Haven, 02568

Blue Raven Technology (3), 110 Fordham Rd, Wilmington, 01887-2165

Bose Corp (3), 100 The Mountain Rd, Framingham, 01701-9168

The Boston Co Asset Management LLC (14), 1 Boston Pl, Boston, 02108-4407

The Boston Globe (17), 135 Morrissey Blvd, Boston, 02125

Brahmin Leather Works (16), 77 Alden Rd, Fairhaven, 02719

Bruce Medical Supply (7), 411 Waverly Oaks Rd (Suite 154), Waltham, 02452

Brylane (2), PO Box 8320, Taunton, 02780

Bull HN Information Systems (16), 285 Billerica Rd (Suite 200), Chelmsford, 01824-4174

Burns Inc (16), 350 Mariano S Bishop Blvd, Fall River, 02721-2365

C & J Clark America Inc (16), 156 Oak St, Newton Upper Falls, 02464

Cape Cod Cupola Co Inc (8), 78 State Rd, North Dartmouth, 02747-2994

Casual Male Retail Group (2), 555 Turnpike St, Canton, 02021-2724

Chelsea Clock Co Inc (6), 284 Everett Ave, Chelsea, 02150-1598

Christian Book Distributors Inc (17), 140 Summit St, Peabody, 01960-5156

The Christian Science Publishing Society (17), 210 Massachusetts Ave, Boston, 02115-3195

Citizens Bank (14), 28 State St, Boston, 02109

Clark's Corvair Parts, Inc (12), 400 Mohawk Trl, Shelburne Falls, 01370-8503

Cohasset Colonials (8), 14 S Pleasant St, Ashburnham, 01430-1649

Josiah R Coppersmythe (8), 10 Mill Pond Rd, Harwich, 02645-1205

Coptech Inc (16), 219 Water St, Saugus, 01906-1948

The Country Bed Shop (16), 328 Richardson Rd, Ashby, 01431

Country Curtains Inc (8), P.O. Box 955, Stockbridge, 01262

Country Dance and Song Society (1), 116 Pleasant St (Suite 345), Easthampton, 01027-2759

Cross Country Automotive Services (16), 1 Cabot Rd, Medford, 02155-5117

The Cross Country Group LLC (13), 1 Cabot Rd, Medford, 02155-5117

Curriculum Associates Inc (17), 153 Rangeway Rd, North Billerica, 01862-2013

DMB Financial (14), 500 Cummings Center (Suite 5450), Beverly, 01915-6519

Dana-Farber Cancer Institute (1), 450 Brookline Ave, Boston, 02215-5450

Dante University Press (17), PO Box 812158, Wellesley, 02482-0014

Datum Timing, Test & Measurement (9), 34 Tozer Rd, Beverly, 01915

Dave's Soda & Pet City (5), 151 Springfield St, Agawam, 01001-1553

DaVinci Direct (1), 36 Cordage Park Cir (Suite 339), Plymouth, 02360-7320

Dick Davis Digest (17), 176 North St, Salem, 01970-1648

Davis Publications Inc (17), 50 Portland St, Worcester, 01608-2013

Deloitte & Touche (14), 200 Berkeley St (#820), Boston, 02116

Diamond Machining Technology (9), 85 Hayes Memorial Dr, Marlborough, 01752-1831

Dinn Brothers Inc (16), 221 Interstate Dr, West Springfield, 01089

Doubletree Suites by Hilton (19), 400 Soldiers Field Rd, Boston, 02134-1893

Dover Saddlery (11), 525 Great Rd, Littleton, 01460-6221

Dynamics Research Corp (16), 60 Frontage Rd, Andover, 01810

EMC Corp (16), 176 South St, Hopkinton, 01748

Eastern Bank (14), 265 Franklin St, Boston, 02110

89 Degrees (9), 25 Burlington Mall Rd (Suite 610), Burlington, 01803-4100

Elderhostel Inc (1), 650 Suffolk St (#300), Lowell, 01854-3694

Electric Insurance Co (15), 75 Sam Fonzo Dr, Beverly, 01915-1000

Edward Elgar Publishing Inc (17), Nine Dewey Ct, The William Pratt House, Northampton, 01060-3815

Faire Harbour Limited (5), 44 Captain Pierce Rd, Scituate, 02066-2644

Fallon Community Health Plan (1), 10 Chestnut St, Worcester, 01608-2898

Fidelity Investments (14), 82 Devonshire St, Boston, 02109-3605

FLEXcon (16), 1 FLEXcon Industrial Pk, Spencer, 01562-2643

GCC Printers (10), 209 Burlington Rd, Bedford, 01730

GRP Funding LLC (14), 1350 Main St (fl 4), Springfield, 01103-1664

Getronics (16), 100 Ames Pond Dr (Suite 200), Tewksbury, 01876-1240

Globe Specialty Products Inc (17), 9 Latti Farm Rd, Millbury, 01527-2132

Go Ahead Vacations (16), One Education St, Cambridge, 02141

Grand Circle Travel (19), 347 Congress St, Boston, 02210-1230

The Hanover Shoe Co (16), 156 Oak St, Newton, 02464

Harvard Business Review (17), 60 Harvard Way, Boston, 02163

Harvard Business School - Executive Education (1), Soldiers Field, Teele Hall, Boston, 02163-1000

Harvard Business School Publishing (17), 60 Harvard Way, Boston, 02163-1001

Harvard Pilgrim Health Care (7), 93 Worcester St, Wellesley, 02481-3609

Hitchcock Shoes Inc (2), 225 Beal St, Hingham, 02043-1543

Human Resource Development Press (17), 22 Amherst Rd, Amherst, 01002-9709

IDG Enterprise (17), 492 Old Connecticut Path, PO Box 9208, Framingham, 01701-9208

Interex (17), 34 Hunt Rd, Amesbury, 01913

International Fund for Animal Welfare (1), 290 Summer St, Yarmouth Port, 02675-1734

Invacare Supply Group (16), 9 Industrial Rd, Milford, 01757-3588

Investors Marketing Services (14), 168 Centre St, Danvers, 01923-1321

JazzTimes Magazine Inc (17), 85 Quincy Ave (Suite 2), Quincy, 02169-6764

Jeffrey Lant Associates Inc (5), 50 Follen St (Suite 507), Cambridge, 02138

J Jill Group, Inc (2), 4 Batterymarch Park, Quincy, 02169

John Hancock Financial Services Inc (15), 601 Congress St, Box 111, Boston, 02117

Johnny Appleseed's Inc (2), 35 Village Rd (Suite 500), Middleton, 01949-1236

KAR Graphics (8), PO Box 2430, Mashpee, 02649

Will Kirkpatrick Shorebird Decoys Inc (6), 124 Forest Ave, Hudson, 01749-2840

Lahey Clinic (1), 41 Mall Rd, Burlington, 01805-0002

The Law Offices of James Sokolove (14), 93 Worcester St # 101, Wellesley Hills, 02481-3609

Lawyer's Weekly Publications (17), 10 Milk St (Suite 1000), Boston, 02108-4620

Legal Sea Foods Inc (4), 1 Seafood Way, Boston, 02210-2702

Lemee's Inc (8), 138 Robinson St, Hanson, 02341

Liberty Mutual Group, Inc (15), 175 Berkeley St, Boston, 02116-5066

Lifetips (16), 240 Commercial St (Suite 3B), Boston, 02109-1386

Litle & Co (14), 900 Chelmsford St, Lowell, 01851-8100

MFS Investment Management (14), 500 Boylston St, Boston, 02116-3740

Magellan's Catalog (5), PO Box 3390, Chelmsford, 01824-0990

Mardiron Optics (11), Four Spartan Cir, Stoneham, 02180

Marian Helpers Center (1), 2 Prospect Hill Rd, Stockbridge, 01262

Marketing and Product Strategy (16), Nine Centennial Dr, Peabody, 01960

WB Mason Co (16), 59 Centre St, Brockton, 02303

Massachusetts Horticultural Society (1), 900 Washington St, Wellesley, 02482

MassMutual Financial Group (15), 1295 State St, Springfield, 01111-0001

Mercury International Trading (2), 20 Alice Agnew Dr, North Attleboro, 02763-1036

Merrimade Stationery Co LLC (10), 275 Billerca Rd, Chelmsford, 01824-4113

Microfluidics Corp (16), 90 Glacier Dr (#1000), Westwood, 02090-1818

Micron Corp (16), 89 Access Rd (Suite 5), Norwood Airport Business Park, Norwood, 02062-5234

Millipore Corp (9), 75 Wiggins Ave, Bedford, 01730-2337

Morgan Kaufmann Publishers Inc (17), 30 Corporate Dr (Suite 400), Burlington, 01803

Murder by Mail (1), PO Box 789, West Tisbury, 02575

NEBS (10), 500 Main St, Groton, 01471-0001

NNE Marketing (1), 105 Paul Revere Rd, Concord, 01742-4817

National Fire Protection Association (1), 1 Batterymarch Park Bsmt, Quincy, 02169-7484

New England Cheesemaking Supply Co (4), 54B Whately Rd Ste B, South Deerfield, 01373-9608

New England Journal of Medicine (17), 860 Winter St, Waltham, 02451-1430

New England Life Insurance Co (15), 501 Boylston St, Boston, 02110

Newport Creative Communications (1), 33 Railroad Ave, Duxbury, 02332-3884

Norman Rockwell Museum (16), 9 Glendale Rd, Rte 183, Stockbridge, 01262

Nourse Farms (8), 41 River Rd, South Deerfield, 01373

Nuance Speech Solutions (16), One Wayside Rd, Burlington, 01803

OSRAM Sylvania (16), 100 Endicott St, Danvers, 01923-3782

Oxfam America (1), 226 Causeway St (5th fl), Boston, 02114-2206

PNC Global Investment Servicing (14), 66 Broadway Ste 3, Lynnfield, 01940-2369

Partners Village Store (11), 865 Main Rd, Westport, 02790-4315

PartyLite Gifts Inc (8), 600 Cordwainer Dr, Norwell, 02061

PetEdge (16), 100 Cummings Ctr (307B), Beverly, 01915-6107

Peter Pan Bus Lines Inc (19), 1776 Main St, Springfield, 01103-1027

Philips Lifeline (7), 111 Lawrence St, Framingham, 01702-8156

The Pohly Co (17), 437 D St (Apt 2F), Boston, 02210-1983

Potpourri Group Inc (6), 101 Billerica Ave - Bldg 2, North Billerica, 01862

Princess House Inc (16), 470 Miles Standish Blvd, Taunton, 02780

The Princeton Review (16), 24 Prime Pkwy (Suite 201), Natick, 01760

PRO Chemical & Dye Inc (10), 126 Shove St, Fall River, 02724-2039

Progress Software Corp (16), 14 Oak Park, Bedford, 01730

Putnam Investments (14), 1 Post Office Sq, Boston, 02109-2106

RBS Citizens Financial Group Inc (14), 770 Legacy Pl (MLP 250), Dedham, 02026-6837

Reebok International Ltd (2), 1895 JW Foster Blvd, Canton, 02021

The Reggio Register Co Inc (8), 31 Jytek Rd, Leominster, 01453-5934

The Renovator's Supply Inc (9), Renovator's Old Mill, Millers Falls, 01349

Rent Mother Nature (4), PO Box 380193, Cambridge, 02238

LW Robbins Associates (1), 201 Summer St, Holliston, 01746-2258

Roman Research Inc/Simply Whispers Earring (2), 800 Franklin St, Hanson, 02341

Rose Displays Ltd (16), 35 Congress St, Salem, 01970-5529

SC Direct (2), 400 Manley St Ste 1, West Bridgewater, 02379-1085

Samsonite International SA (16), 575 West St (Suite 110), Mansfield, 02048-1160

Savings Bank Life Insurance Co of MA (SBLI) (15), 1 Linscott Rd, Woburn, 01801-2001

Shaker Workshops (8), 14 S Pleasant St, Ashburnham, 01430-1649

Simmons College (1), 300 The Fenway, Boston, 02115-5898

Simplex Grinnell (16), 50 Technology Dr, Westminster, 01441-0001

Small Business Service Bureau Inc (1), 554 Main St, PO Box 15014, Worcester, 01615-2014

Tom Snyder Productions (16), 100 Talcott Ave Ste 6, Watertown, 02472-5715

Speakers Guild Inc (16), 78 Old Kings Hwy, PO Box 1540, Sandwich, 02563-1540

Stanley Supply & Services (16), 335 Willow St, North Andover, 01845-5921

Staples Inc (10), 500 Staples Dr, Framingham, 01702-4474

State Street Global Advisors (14), 1 Lincoln St (fl 33), Boston, 02111-2901

Stratus Technologies (16), 111 Powder Mill Rd, Maynard, 01754-3409

Stream International (16), 20 William St (Suite 310), Wellesley, 02481-4145

Sunlife of Canada (15), 1 Sunlife Executive Park, Wellesley Hills, 02481

Sure-Fire Business Success Catalog (17), 50 Follen St (#507), Cambridge, 02138

THD Inc (1), 80 Hayden Ave (Suite 300), Lexington, 02421-7962

Talbots (2), 1 Talbots Dr, Hingham, 02043-1583

Technology Review (17), 1 Main St (Suite 7), MIT Bldg W59, Cambridge, 02142-1599

Thermo Fisher Scientific Inc (9), 81 Wyman St, Waltham, 02451-1223

Thomson Research (14), 22 Thompson Pl, Boston, 02210

Time/System (16), 150 Front St (Fl 1 Bldg C), Chicopee, 01013

The Tog Shop Inc (2), 30 Tozer Rd, Beverly, 01915

Tully & Holland Inc (14), 20 William St Ste 135, Wellesley, 02481-4133

UMass Dartmouth (1), 285 Old Westport Rd, North Dartmouth, 02747-2356

UndercoverWear Inc (2), 30 Commerce Way (Unit 2), Tewksbury, 01876

UniFirst Corp (2), 68 Jonspin Rd, Wilmington, 01887

Utilities Supply Corp (16), 50 Everberg Rd, Woburn, 01801-1019

The Vantage Group Inc (14), 90 Canal St, Boston, 02114

Village Software Inc (3), 76 Summer St (Suite 600), Boston, 02110-1267

Vitasoy USA Inc (16), 1 New England Way, Ayer, 01432-1514

WGBH Educational Foundation (1), 1 Guest St, Brighton, 02135-2016

Waters Corp (16), 34 Maple St, Milford, 01757-3696

WearGuard Corp (2), 141 Longwater Dr, Norwell, 02061-1683

WESCO (16), 225 W Station Square Dr (Suite 700), Pittsburgh, 15219

Whiting & Davis (16), 171 Commonwealth Ave, Attleboro Falls, 02763-1152

Williamsburg Blacksmiths Inc (8), 26 Williams St, Williamsburg, 01096

MICHIGAN

Admore Inc (10), 24707 Wood Ct, Macomb, 48042-5378

Amerisure Insurance Cos (15), 26777 Halsted Rd, Farmington Hills, 48331-3586

Amigo Mobility International Inc (16), 6693 Dixie Hwy, Bridgeport, 48722-9725

Automotive Headphones (16), 44648 Mound Rd (# 161), Sterling Heights, 48314-1322

Baudville Inc (16), 5380 52nd St SE, Grand Rapids, 49512-9702

Booth Michigan (17), PO Box 2168, Grand Rapids, 49503

Bronner's Christmas Wonderland (6), 25 Christmas Ln, Frankenmuth, 48734-1807

Buick (16), 300 Renaissance Center, Detroit, 48265-3000

Citizens Republic Bank (14), 328 S Saginaw St, Flint, 48502-1923

Cold Stream Farm (8), 8585 N Stephens Rd, Free Soil, 49411

Con-Way Freight (12), 2211 Old Earhart Rd Ste 100, Ann Arbor, 48105-2963

Consumer's Energy (16), 212 W Michigan Ave, Jackson, 49201-2277

Crain Communications Inc (17), 1155 Gratiot Ave, Detroit, 48207-2997

Creative Health Products (16), 5148 Saddle Ridge Rd, Plymouth, 48170

Creativity International (16), 4930 Cascade Rd SE, Ada, 49546

DaimlerChrysler Corp (12), 1000 Chrysler Dr (CIMS 485-06-73), Auburn Hills, 48326-2766

Del Webb (16), 100 Bloomfield Hills Pkwy Ste 150, Bloomfield Hills, 48304-2957

The Detroit Institute of Arts (16), 5200 Woodward Ave, Detroit, 48202

Detroit Newspapers (18), 615 W Lafayette Blvd, Detroit, 48226

Do-It Corp (9), 1201 Blue Star Hwy, PO Box 592, South Haven, 49090-0592

The Dow Chemical Co (16), 2030 Dow Center, Midland, 48674

Dow Corning Corp (16), PO Box 994, Midland, 48686-0994

Eastern Michigan University (16), 1000 College Pl, Ypsilanti, 48197

Elderly Instruments (5), 1100 N Washington, Lansing, 48906

Family Christian Stores (5), 5300 Patterson Ave SE, Grand Rapids, 49530

Farm Bureau Insurance (15), 7373 W Saginaw Hwy, Box 30400, Lansing, 48917

Fitness USA Super Centers (16), 7091 Orchard Lake Rd (Suite 300), West Bloomfield, 48322

Ford Motor Co (16), One American Rd, Dearborn, 48126-2798

Foremost Insurance Group (15), PO Box 2450, Grand Rapids, 49501-2450

Gale (17), 27500 Drake Rd, Farmington Hills, 48331-3535

Golf Haus (11), 700 N Pennsylvania Ave, Lansing, 48906-5319

Grower's Supply Co (8), 2326 Bishop Circle E, Dexter, 48130-1566

Health Alliance Plan (15), 2850 W Grand Blvd, Detroit, 48202-2692

Herman Miller Inc (16), 855 E Main Ave, Zeeland, 49464

HighScope Educational Research Foundation (17), 600 N River St, Ypsilanti, 48198-2898

Indoor Gardening Supplies (8), PO Box 527, Dexter, 48130

J&L Industrial Supply (9), 20921 Lahser Rd, Southfield, 48034-4432

Kadant Johnson Inc (16), 805 Wood St, Three Rivers, 49093

Kingsley North Inc (11), 910 Brown St, PO Box 216, Norway, 49870

Koeze Co (16), P.O. Box 9470, Grand Rapids, 49509

Landscape Forms Inc (16), 431 Lawndale Ave, Kalamazoo, 49048

Learning Care Group (16), 21333 Haggerty Rd (Suite 300), Novi, 48375-5537

Leslie Shoe Co Inc (2), 480 N Second St, Rogers City, 49779-1367

Local Search Association (1), 820 Kirts Blvd (Suite 100), Troy, 48084-4836

MGM Grand Detroit (16), 1777 3rd St, Detroit, 48226-2561

MSU Federal Credit Union (1), 3777 West Rd, East Lansing, 48823-8029

Masco Corp (16), 21001 Van Born Rd, Taylor, 48180

Mary Maxim Inc (11), 2001 Holland Ave, Port Huron, 48061-5019

Meemic Insurance Co (15), 1685 N Opdyke Rd, Auburn Hills, 48326-2656

Michigan Apple Committee (1), 13750 S Sedona Pkwy (Suite 3), Lansing, 48906-8101

Mott Media LLC (17), 1130 Fenway Cir, Fenton, 48430

Muskegon Power Tool Corp (16), 2357 Whitehall Rd, North Muskegon, 49445

National Bulk Equipment Inc (16), 12838 Stainless Dr, Holland, 49424

The Newman Group Computer Services Corp (3), 2577 Newport Rd, Ann Arbor, 48103-2274

Okun Brothers Shoes Inc (2), 179 Portage Rd, Kalamazoo, 49007-4801

Oliver of Adrian Inc (16), PO Box 189, Adrian, 49221-0189

Parts Place Inc (12), 5510 E 10 Mile Rd, Warren, 48091-3899

Peerless Rattan (16), 687 Miller Rd, Plainwell, 49080-9538

Pennstreet Bakery (16), 900 Hynes SW, Grand Rapids, 49507

Phone Bank Systems Inc (1), 4990 Northwind Dr (Suite 235), East Lansing, 48823-5091

Prakken Publications Inc (17), 2851 Boardwalk St, Ann Arbor, 48104

Reid Supply Co (16), 2265 Black Creek Rd, Muskegon, 49444-2673

Resumate Inc (3), 2500 Packard St (Suite 200), Ann Arbor, 48104

Sandy Corp (16), 300 E Big Beaver Rd (Suite 500), Troy, 48083

Schoolcraft College (1), 18600 Haggerty Rd, Livonia, 48152-2696

Scope 1 (16), 6490 S Sprinkle Rd, Kalamazoo, 49004-9706

Scott Publications, Inc (17), 2145 W Sherman Blvd, Muskegon, 49441-3434

B Shackman & Co Inc (6), 9964 W Miller Dr, Galesburg, 49053

Society of Manufacturing Engineers (1), One SME Dr, PO Box 930, Dearborn, 48121

Steelcase Inc (16), 901 44th St SE, Grand Rapids, 49508

Teachers' Discovery (5), 2741 Paldan Dr, Auburn Hills, 48326-1827

Terumo Cardiovascular Systems Corp (5), 6200 Jackson Rd, Ann Arbor, 48103-9586

Thetford Corp (16), 7101 Jackson Rd, Ann Arbor, 48103

Troy Biologicals Inc (7), 1238 Rankin Dr, Troy, 48083

University Bank (14), 2015 Washtenaw Ave, Ann Arbor, 48104

Whirlpool Corp (16), 2000 N M-63, Benton Harbor, 49022-2692

Wholesale Tool Co (9), 12155 Stephens Dr, Warren, 48089

Wysong Corp (7), 7550 Eastman Ave, Midland, 48642-7779

Zondervan Corp (17), 5300 Patterson Ave SE, Grand Rapids, 49530

MINNESOTA

Activision Value (16), 7800 Equitable Dr (Suite 200), Eden Prairie, 55344

ActivStyle (16), 1701 Broadway St NE, Minneapolis, 55413-2638

Agilis Co (14), 2380 Crossroads Blvd, Albert Lea, 56007-4001

Allianz Life Insurance Co of North America (15), 5701 Golden Hills Dr, PO Box 1344, Minneapolis, 55416-1297

American Academy of Neurology (1), 201 Chicago Ave, Minneapolis, 55415-1126

American Craft Council (17), 1224 Marshall St NE (Suite 200), Minneapolis, 55413-1089

The American Phytopathological Society (1), 3340 Pilot Knob Rd, Saint Paul, 55121-2055

Ameriprise Financial Services Inc (14), 70100 Ameriprise Financial Center, Minneapolis, 55474-0023

Apothecary Products Inc (7), 11750 12th Ave S, Burnsville, 55337-1297

Art Instruction Schools (13), 3400 Technology Dr, Minneapolis, 55418-6000

Asset Marketing Services Inc (16), 14101 Southcross Dr W, Burnsville, 55337-6902

Augsburg Fortress Publishers (17), 100 S Fifth St (Suite 600), Minneapolis, 55402-1242

Aveda Corp (7), 4000 Pheasant Ridge Dr, Blaine, 55449

Bellacor (8), 251 1st Ave, N (Suite 900), Minneapolis, 55401

Best Buy (3), 7601 Penn Ave S, Richfield, 55423-3683

Bluestem Brands (16), 6509 Flying Cloud Dr, Eden Prairie, 55344-3307

Bluewater Yachts (16), 811 E Maple, Mora, 55051-1224

Card Technology Inc (16), 10925 Bren Rd E, Hopkins, 55343-9613

Centerpoint Energy (16), 800 LaSalle Ave, Minneapolis, 55402-2006

Charmaster (8), 2307 Hwy 2 W, Grand Rapids, 55744-2152

Classic Motorbooks Inc (17), 400 1st Ave N (Suite 300), Minneapolis, 55401

Classic Thermographers (10), 1680 Roe Crest Dr, North Mankato, 56003-2658

Courage Cards & Gifts (1), 3915 Golden Valley Rd Courage Ctr, Golden Valley, 55422-4249

Creative Banner Assemblies (9), 2730 Nevada Ave, Minneapolis, 55427-2807

Creative Publishing International (17), 400 First Ave N (Suite 400), Minneapolis, 55401

Crest Healthcare Supply (16), 195 S Third St, Dassel, 55325-4511

Digi International (3), 11001 Bren Rd E, Minnetonka, 55343-4410

Digi-Key Corp (3), 701 Brooks Ave S, Thief River Falls, 56701

Dragich Auto Literature (16), PO Box 1024, Princeton, 55371-4024

Eckankar (17), PO Box 27300, Minneapolis, 55427

Ecolab Professional Products (16), 370 N Wabasha St, Ecolab Ctr, Saint Paul, 55102-2233

Eichten's Hidden Acres (4), 16809 310th St, PO Box 216, Center City, 55012

The Family Handyman (17), 2915 Commers Dr (Suite 700), Eagan, 55121-2398

Farm Home Offices (10), 6739 12th Ave S, Richfield, 55423

Gelco Information Network (16), 10700 Prairie Lakes Dr, Eden Prairie, 55344

General Mills Inc (8), One General Mills Blvd, Minneapolis, 55426

Gillette Children's Specialty Healthcare (1), 200 University Ave E, Saint Paul, 55101-2507

Greater Public (1), 401 N 3rd St (Suite 370), Minneapolis, 55401-1350

Hazelden (7), PO Box 11, Center City, 55012-0011

Heartland America (3), 8085 Century Blvd, Chaska, 55318

James J Hill Reference Library (1), 80 4th St W, Saint Paul, 55102-1605

Historic Aviation (12), 640 Taft St NE, Minneapolis, 55413-2815

Hormel Foods Corp (16), One Hormel Pl, Austin, 55912-3680

ING (15), 20 Washington Ave S, Minneapolis, 55401-1908

JIST Publishing (17), 875 Montreal Way, Saint Paul, 55102

Jostens, Inc (16), 3601 Minnesota Dr (Suite 400), Minneapolis, 55435-6008

K-tel International (16), 7500 Wayzata Blvd (Suite 28), Golden Valley, 55426-1682

Kelco Supply Co (16), 2000 176th St NW (Suite 203), Big Lake, 55309-8020

Land O' Lakes Inc (16), 4001 Lexington Ave, Arden Hills, 55122

Lazard Middle Market LLC (14), 80 S 8th St, Minneapolis, 55402

Lerner Publishing Group (17), 1251 Washington Ave N, Minneapolis, 55401

Llewellyn Publications (17), 2143 Wooddale Dr, Woodbury, 55125-2989

MTS Systems Corp (16), 14000 Technology Dr, Eden Prairie, 55344-2247

Marshall Fields Dept Stores (5), 7235 France Ave S, Minneapolis, 55435-4337

Masterpiece Studios Inc (16), PO Box 8700, Mankato, 56002-8700

Mayo Clinic (17), 200 First St SW, Rochester, 55905

Medtronic (7), 710 Medtronic Pkwy, Minneapolis, 55432-5604

Medtronic Inc (16), 710 Medtronic Pkwy NE, Minneapolis, 55432

Merrill Corp (18), 4110 Clearwater Rd, Saint Cloud, 56301

Minnesota Life (15), 400 Robert St N, Saint Paul, 55101

Minnesota Multi Housing Association (1), 1600 W 82nd St (Suite 110), Bloomington, 55431-1411

Minnesota Public Radio (1), 480 Cedar St, Saint Paul, 55101-2230

Miracle Ear (16), 5000 Cheshire Pkwy N, Minneapolis, 55446

Northern Tool & Equipment Inc (16), 2800 Southcross Dr W, Burnsville, 55306-6936

The Occasions Group (16), 1750 Tower Blvd, North Mankato, 56003-1706

Osmonics Inc (16), 5951 Clearwater Dr, Minnetonka, 55343-8990

Patterson Dental (10), 1031 Mendota Heights Rd, Saint Paul, 55120-1419

Pearson VUE (17), 5601 Green Valley Dr, Bloomington, 55437-1099

The Pillsbury Co (16), PO Box 9452, General Mills Inc, Minneapolis, 55440-9452

Piper Jaffray (14), 800 Nicollet Mall (Suite 1000), Minneapolis, 55402-7036

Polaroid Corp (16), 4350 Baker Rd, Minnetonka, 55343-8684

Quayside Publishing Group (17), 400 1st Ave N (Suite 400), Minneapolis, 55401-1721

RBC Dain Rauscher Inc (14), 60 S Sixth St, Minneapolis, 55402-4422

Redleaf Press (17), 10 Yorkton Ct, Saint Paul, 55117-1065

ReMark USA (15), 3033 Campus Dr (Suite W205), Minnetonka, 55441-2702

C H Robinson Worldwide Inc (16), 14701 Charlson Rd, Eden Prairie, 55347-5076

Rockler Woodworking & Hardware (8), 4365 Willow Dr, Medina, 55340

The Schwan Food Co (5), 115 W College Dr, Marshall, 56258-1747

Select Comfort Corp (16), 9800 59th Ave N, Minneapolis, 55442

Shipping Solutions (16), PO Box 22267, Eagan, 55122-0267

Skypoint Communications Inc (16), 7340 Mark St, Loretto, 55357

The Sportsman's Guide Inc (11), 411 Farwell Ave, South Saint Paul, 55075-2428

Star Tribune Media Co (17), 425 Portland Ave S, Minneapolis, 55488

Starchtech (16), 720 Florida Ave S (#A), Golden Valley, 55426-1704

Starkey Laboratories (16), 6700 Washington Ave S, Eden Prairie, 55344-3405

Stonwurks (16), 13218 Kerry Ln, Eden Prairie, 55346-3140

Stratford Hall (10), 1680 Roe Crest Dr, North Mankato, 56003-2658

Target Corp (16), 1000 Nicollet Mall, Minneapolis, 55403

Taylor Corp (16), 1725 Roe Crest Dr, North Mankato, 56003-1806

Taymark Inc (1), 4875 White Bear Pkwy, White Bear Lake, 55110

Thomson West (17), 610 Opperman Dr, Eagan, 55164

3M Post-It Custom Printed Products (16), 3M Center Bldg, Saint Paul, 55144-1001

The Toro Co (16), 8111 Lyndale Ave S, Bloomington, 55420

Turncraft Clocks Inc (6), 4310 Shoreline Dr, Spring Park, 55384-9722

US Bancorp (14), 800 Nicollet Mall, Minneapolis, 55402-7014

US Bank (14), 200 S 6th St, Minneapolis, 55402-1403

University of Minnesota (1), 100 Church St SE (3 Morrill Hal)l, Minneapolis, 55455

University of Minnesota Alumni Association (1), 200 Oak St SE (Suite 200), Minneapolis, 55455-2040

Victory Corps (16), 2730 Nevada Ave N, New Hope, 55427

Waytek (16), 2440 Galpin Ct, Chanhassen, 55317-0690

We-No-Nah Canoe Inc (11), 1252 Bundy Blvd, Box 247, Winona, 55987-4872

Westgroup (17), 610 Opperman Dr, Eagan, 55123-1340

Wilsons Leather (2), 7401 Boone Ave N, Brooklyn Park, 55428

Win Craft Inc (5), 1124 W Fifth St, PO Box 888, Winona, 55987

Wolters Kluwer Financial Services (14), 100 S 5th St (Suite 700), Minneapolis, 55402-1219

Xcel Energy (5), 414 Nicollet Mall (GO 6), Minneapolis, 55401-1927

MISSISSIPPI

ACBL (1), 6575 Windchase Dr, Horn Lake, 38637-1523

Beau Rivage Resort & Casino (19), 875 Beach Blvd, Biloxi, 39530-4299

FNC INC (14), 1214 Office Park Dr, Oxford, 38655-3597

Forestry Suppliers Inc (9), 205 W Rankin St, PO Box 8397, Jackson, 39284-6126

Historical Replications Inc (8), 3908 N State St, Jackson, 39206-5752

Kelly's Kids (2), 391 Liberty Rd, Natchez, 39120

MISSCO Corp (16), PO Box 321400, PO Box 5349, Flowood, 39232-1400

Quality Products Inc (10), 2415 Hwy 45 N, PO Box 564, Columbus, 39703

Uncle Ben's Inc (4), 1098 N Broadway St, Greenville, 38701-2004

University of Southern Mississippi (1), 118 College Dr (Box 5016), Hattiesburg, 39406-0001

MISSOURI

Alamo Rent A Car (16), 600 Corporate Park Dr, Saint Louis, 63105

American Century Investments (14), 4500 Main St, Box 418210, Kansas City, 64111

American Ostomy Supply (16), 13400 Lakefront Dr, Earth City, 63045-1516

American Recreation Products Inc (11), 1224 Fern Ridge Pkwy, Saint Louis, 63141-4404

Angelica Image Apparel (16), 7700 Forsyth Blvd (Suite 1010), Saint Louis, 63105-1821

Anheuser-Busch Inc Promotional Products Group (6), 20 Constitution Blvd S, Shelton, 06484

Anthem Blue Cross Blue Shield (15), 1831 Chestnut St (#1), Saint Louis, 63103-2275

Association of the Miraculous Medal (1), 1811 W Saint Joseph St, Perryville, 63775-1598

Bass Pro Shops (11), 1935 S Campbell Ave, Springfield, 65807

Mel Bay Publications Inc (17), Four Industrial Dr, Pacific, 63069-0066

Beacon Shoe Co Inc (16), 11 Worthington Access Dr Stop 1, Maryland Heights, 63043-3804

Big Brothers Big Sisters of Greater Kansas City (1), 1709 Walnut St, Kansas City, 64108

Bissinger French Confections (4), 1600 N Broadway, Saint Louis, 63102

Brown Shoe Co (16), 8300 Maryland Ave, PO Box 29, Saint Louis, 63105-3645

Bunzl Distribution USA, Inc (16), 1 Cityplace Dr Ste 200, Saint Louis, 63141-7067

Burger's Ozark Country Cured Hams Inc (4), 32819 Hwy 87, California, 65018

CTA Inc (5), 1625 Larkin Williams Rd, Fenton, 63026-1205

Carhill Enterprises Inc (15), 1232 Washington Ave (Suite 300), Saint Louis, 63103-1983

CheckMark Communications (4), 1111 Chouteau Ave, Saint Louis, 63102-1025

Children International (1), 2000 E Red Bridge Rd, Kansas City, 64131-3694

Clarkson Eyecare (5), 217 Clarkson Rd, Ellisville, 63011-2219

Commerce Bancshares Inc (14), 8000 Forsyth Blvd (CBIR-1), Saint Louis, 63105-1707

Con-Way Truckload (12), 4701 E 32nd St, Joplin, 64804

Concordia Publishing House (17), 3558 S Jefferson, Saint Louis, 63118-3910

Copilevitz & Canter, LLC (14), 310 W 20th St (Suite 300), Kansas City, 64108-2025

DWS Investments Service Co (14), 210 W 10th St, Kansas City, 64105-1614

Dairy Farmers of America Inc (16), 10220 N Ambassador Dr Suite 1000), Kansas City, 64153-2327

Deck the Walls Inc (5), 221 First Executive Ave, Saint Peters, 63376-1697

Delmmar Communications (16), 920 N Ashland Dr, Cameron, 64429

Diagraph Corp (16), One Missouri Research Park Dr, Saint Charles, 63304-5685

Dirxion (16), 1859 Bowles Ave (Suite 100), Saint Louis, 63026-1936

Doane (17), 77 Westport Plaza (Suite 250), Saint Louis, 63146-3121

Eggs by Byrd (10), HC 3 Box 3653, Wappapello, 63966-9727

Energizer Holdings Inc (16), 533 Maryville University Dr, Saint Louis, 63141

Enterprise Rent-A-Car (19), 600 Corporate Park Dr, Saint Louis, 63105-4204

Faultless Starch/Bon Ami Co (16), 1025 W Eighth St, Kansas City, 64101-1200

Fidelity Security Life Insurance Co (15), 3130 Broadway, Kansas City, 64111-2406

Fiorella's Jack Stack Barbecue (4), 13441 Holmes Rd, Kansas City, 64145

First Banks Inc (14), 135 N Meramec Ave, Clayton, 63105

Garden Botanika Inc (7), 8500 Valcour Ave, Saint Louis, 63123

H&R Block Inc (14), 1 H&R Block Way, Kansas City, 64105-1905

HDA Inc (17), 944 Anglum Rd, Saint Louis, 63042

Hallmark Cards Inc (16), 2501 McGee Trafficway, Kansas City, 64108

Halls Kansas City (16), 211 Nichols Rd, Kansas City, 64112

Hasco First Photo (16), 3613 Mueller Rd, Saint Charles, 63301

Heartland Boating Magazine (17), 319 N Fourth St (Suite 650), Saint Louis, 63102

Helzberg Diamonds (16), 1825 Swift St, North Kansas City, 64116-3606

The Hope Co Inc (16), 12777 Pennridge Dr, Bridgeton, 63044

InteliSpend Prepaid Solutions (5), 1400 S Highway Dr, Fenton, 63099

Invacare Continuing Care Group (16), 1848 Craig Rd, Saint Louis, 63146-4712

Edward Jones (14), 12555 Manchester Rd, Des Peres, 63131-3710

Kansas City Chiefs (16), One Arrowhead Dr, Kansas City, 64129

EC Kraus Home Wine & Beer Making Supplies (4), 733 S Northern Blvd, PO Box 7850, Independence, 64054

Liguori Publications (17), One Liguori Dr, Liguori, 63057-9999

Luster Care Products (16), 8854 Frost Ave, Saint Louis, 63134-1044

Lutheran Church Extension Fund - Missouri Synod (1), 10733 Sunset Office Dr (Suite 300), Sunset Corporate Center, Saint Louis, 63127-1020

Luzier Personalized Cosmetics (7), 5601 E 135th St, Grandview, 64030

Magna-Tel Inc (5), 775 S Kingshighway St, Cape Girardeau, 63703

Magna Visual Inc (9), 9400 Watson Rd, Saint Louis, 63126

Magnet LLC (16), Seven Chamber Dr, PO Box 605, Washington, 63090

Maverick Ventures Product Line (5), 15698 Ferncreek Dr, Chesterfield, 63017-0702

Joyce Meyer Ministries (1), 700 Grace Pkwy, Fenton, 63026-5390

Mid West Floor Co Inc (16), 2714 Breckenridge Industrial Ct, Saint Louis, 63144

Midcontinent Financial Center Inc (14), 3401 W Broadway Bus Park Ct (Suite 205), Columbia, 65203-0393

Midland Marketing Group (16), PO Box 8576, Saint Joseph, 64508-8576

Missouri Landscape & Nursery Association (1), 16072 Pike 9292, Bowling Green, 63334

Missouri Life Inc (17), 501 High St (# A), Boonville, 65233-1211

National Auto Warranty (16), 100 Mall Pkwy, Wentzville, 63385-4816

National Catholic Reporter Publishing Co Inc (17), 115 E Armour Blvd, Kansas City, 64111-1203

National Research Center for College & University Admissions (1), 3651 NE Ralph Powell Rd, Lees Summit, 64064-2357

National Seminars Group (16), 6901 W 63rd St (Suite 300), Shawnee Mission, 66202-4005

PFI Western Stores Inc (2), 2816 S Ingram Mill Rd, Springfield, 65804

Parcel Insurance Plan Inc (15), 9666 Olive Blvd (Suite 200), Saint Louis, 63132-3012

Phoenix Learning Group Inc (16), 141A Millwell Dr, Maryland Heights, 63043-2509

Posty Cards Inc (16), 1600 Olive St, Kansas City, 64127-2539

R&S Industries Corp (16), 1065 Appalachian Trl, Chesterfield, 63017-1948

Royal Canin (16), 500 Fountain Lakes Blvd (Suite 100), Saint Charles, 63301-4354

St Louis Post-Dispatch (17), 900 N Tucker Blvd, Saint Louis, 63101

St Louis Slot Machine Co (6), 9617 Dielman Rock Island Industrial Dr, Saint Louis, 63132-2149

Schnuck Markets Inc (16), 11420 Lackland Rd, Saint Louis, 63146-6928

Sensient Technologies (16), 2526 Baldwin St, Saint Louis, 63106

Sensory Effects Powder System (16), 231 Rock Industrial Park Dr, Bridgeton, 63044

Soft Surroundings (2), 1100 N Lindbergh Blvd, Saint Louis, 63132-2914

Stark Brothers Nurseries & Orchards (8), PO Box 1800, Louisiana, 63353

Sunrise Greetings (17), 2501 McGee St, Kansas City, 64108-2615

Townsend Communications LLC (17), 20 E Gregory Blvd, Kansas City, 64114

Uniforms & Scrubs.com (7), 910 Kehrs Mill Rd (Suite 106), Ballwin, 63011-2404

Unity School of Christianity (17), 1901 NW Blue Pkwy, Unity Village, 64065-0001

Upbeat Inc (9), 211 N Lindbergh Blvd (fl 2), Saint Louis, 63141-7838

Vehicle Assurance (5), 3902 S Old Hwy 94, Saint Charles, 63304

Veterans of Foreign Wars of the US (1), 406 W 34th St, Kansas City, 64111-2736

Washington University (1), 1 Brookings Dr, Saint Louis, 63130-4899

Watts Radiant (9), 4500 E Progress Pl, Springfield, 65803

West End Diving Centers Inc (19), 12464 Natural Bridge Rd, Bridgeton, 63044-2321

Westhoff Machine Co (9), 9462 Watson Industrial Park, Saint Louis, 63126

Gilbert H Wild & Son Inc (8), 2944 State Hwy 37, Reeds, 64859

Zimmerman-McDonald Machinery Inc (16), 2272 Weldon Pkwy, Saint Louis, 63146-3206

MONTANA

Mountain Press Publishing Co (17), PO Box 2399, Missoula, 59806-2399

Photographer's Formulary Inc (9), 7079 Hwy 83 N, Condon, 59826

Ranch House Meat Co (4), 1313 Grand Ave (Suite 1), Billings, 59102

St Labre Indian School (1), PO Box 77, Ashland, 59003-0077

Sims Stoves (11), 7452 Burlington Ave, Billings, 59106

NEBRASKA

AccuTrade Inc (14), 1005 Ameritrade Pl, Bellevue, 68005

Alpha Dog Marketing Inc (1), 9060 Andermatt Dr Ste 101, Lincoln, 68526-9644

Arbor Capital 1 (14), 1414 Harney St (Suite 400), Omaha, 68102-2255

Arbor Day Foundation (1), 100 Arbor Ave, Nebraska City, 68410

Back to the Bible (5), 6400 Cornhusker Hwy, Lincoln, 68507-3123

Baldwin Filters (16), 4400 E Hwy 30, Kearney, 68848-6010

Behlen Manufacturing Co (16), 4025 E 23rd St, Columbus, 68601-3448

Burden Sales Co (9), 1015 W O St, Lincoln, 68528-1322

Cabela's Inc (11), 1 Cabela Dr, Sidney, 69160-1001

Central States Health & Life Co of Omaha (15), 1212 N 96th St, Omaha, 68114

Central States Indemnity (15), 1212 N 96th St, Omaha, 68114-2274

Commercial Federal Bank (14), 13220 California St (Suite 100), Omaha, 68154-5228

Condolink (16), 3012 N 93rd St, Omaha, 68134-4716

Cornhusker Press (17), 451 W Second St, Hastings, 68902-0729

Duncan Aviation (16), 3701 Aviation Rd, Lincoln Airport, Lincoln, 68524

Father Flanagan's Boy's Home (1), 14100 Crawford St, Boys Town, 68010-7520

GWR Wealth Management (14), 900 S 74th Plaza (Suite 400), Omaha, 68114

Garden Perennials (8), 85261 Hwy 15, Wayne, 68787-7097

KV Vet Supply Co, Inc (5), 3190 N Rd (#245), David City, 68632-5142

Medco Insurance Co (15), 1515 S 75th St, Omaha, 68124-1618

Medibadge Inc (5), PO Box 12307, Omaha, 68112-0307

Missionary Society of St Columban (1), PO Box 10, Saint Columbans, 68056-0010

Mutual of Omaha (15), Mutual of Omaha Plaza (fl 7), Omaha, 68175-0001

Omaha Creative Group Inc (4), 11030 O St, Omaha, 68137-2346

Omaha Fixture International (8), 10320 "J" St, Omaha, 68127-1092

Omaha Steaks Inc (4), 11030 "O" St, Omaha, 68137-2346

Omaha Vaccine Co (16), 11143 Mockingbird Dr, Omaha, 68137-2332

Oriental Trading Co Inc (5), 5455 S 90th St, Omaha, 68127-3501

Phillips Kiln Service LTD (16), 2607 Dakota Ave Ste 2, South Sioux City, 68776-3256

Physicians Mutual Insurance Co (15), 2600 Dodge St, Omaha, 68131

Pro CD Inc (17), 5711 S 86th Cir, Omaha, 68127

QC Supply LLC (16), PO Box 581, Schuyler, 68661-0581

Speedway (12), PO Box 81906, Lincoln, 68501-1906

Surplus Center (9), 1015 W "O" St, Lincoln, 68528-1322

TD Ameritrade Holding Corp (16), 200 S 108th Ave, Omaha, 68154

TransFirst ePayment Services (14), 13220 Birch Dr (Suite 110), Omaha, 68164-5434

Wellness Councils of America (1), 17002 Marcy St (Suite 140), Omaha, 68118-2933

Wimmer's Meat Products Inc (4), 126 W Grant St, PO Box 286, West Point, 68788-0286

NEVADA

Ameristar Casinos Inc (19), 3773 Howard Hughes Pkwy (Suite 490), Las Vegas, 89169-0949

BluBlocker Corp (2), 3350 Palm Ctr Dr, Las Vegas, 89103-5668

Boyd Gaming Corp (16), 3883 Howard Hughes Pkwy (fl 9), Las Vegas, 89169

Caesars Entertainment Corp (16), 1 Caesars Palace Dr, Las Vegas, 89109

California Pacific Research & New Generation (7), 300 Brinkby Ave (Suite 200), Reno, 89509-4359

EMPLOYERS Insurance (15), 10375 Professional Cir, Reno, 89521-4802

Enco Manufacturing Co (9), 400 Nevada Pacific Hwy, Fernley, 89408

Ethel M Chocolates Inc (4), 1 Sunset Way, Henderson, 89014

IDC, Ltd (1), 2500 Paseo Verde Pkwy, Henderson, 89074-7117

Las Vegas Review Journal (17), 1111 W Bonanza Rd, PO Box 70, Las Vegas, 89125

Laughlin Associates Inc (16), 2533 N Carson St, Carson City, 89706

Longevity Network Ltd (7), 2764 N Green Valley Pkwy (Suite 401), Henderson, 89014-2121

Mirage Resorts, Inc. (19), 3400 Las Vegas Blvd S, Las Vegas, 89109-8923

MontBleu Resort Casino and Spa (19), 55 Hwy 50, Stateline, 89449

Morcon Industrial Specialty Inc (9), 658 Hardy Way (Suite 2), Mesquite, 89027-3914

Neo-Tech Publishing Co (17), 2435 W Horizon Ridge Pkwy (Suite 100), Henderson, 89052-5787

Nevada Commission on Tourism (1), 401 N Carson St, Carson City, 89701-4221

Nevada Magazine (17), 401 N Carson St, Carson City, 89701-4221

Patagonia Mail Order Inc (2), 8550 White Fir St, Reno, 89523-2050

Performance Media Solutions Inc & TrueWorx Inc (16), 4001 S Decatur Blvd (#37-425), Las Vegas, 89103-5860

Reno Gazette Journal (17), 955 Kuenzli St, Reno, 89520

Spalding Laboratories Inc (7), PO Box 10000, Reno, 89510-9928

Sportif Mail Order Inc (2), 1415 Greg St (Suite 101), Sparks, 89431

Steppin' Out & See America (19), 1140 N Town Center Dr (#360), Las Vegas, 89144-0501

The Stratosphere Las Vegas (19), 2000 Las Vegas Blvd S, Las Vegas, 89104-2507

TVC Enterprises and the TV Collector Magazine (6), 6704 Fruit Flower Ave, Las Vegas, 89130

Zappos.com (2), 400 Stewart Ave (Suite A), Las Vegas, 89101-2914

NEW HAMPSHIRE

Alexander + Roberts (19), 53 Summer St, Keene, 03431-3318

Brookstone Co (3), 1 Innovation Way, Merrimack, 03054-4873

CCA Global Partners (16), 670 N Commercial St, Manchester, 03101-1160

Cobblestone Publishing (17), 30 Grove St (Suite C), Peterborough, 03458-1453

Connell Communications Inc (17), 45 Main St Ste 102, Peterborough, 03458-2433

Custom Miniatures (6), 19 Winnhaven Dr, Hudson, 03051-4748

Dartmouth-Hitchcock (1), Hinman Box 7070, One Medical Center Dr, Lebanon, 03756-1000

Duncraft Inc (16), 102 Fisherville Rd, Concord, 03303-9020

Eastern Mountain Sports (16), 1 Vose Farm Rd, Peterborough, 03458-2122

Emerson Ecologics (7), 1230 Elm St (Suite 301), Manchester, 03101-1336

GN Netcom (16), 77 Northeastern Blvd, Nashua, 03062-3128

Garnet Hill Inc (2), 231 Main St, Franconia, 03580

Greenwood Publishing Group Inc (17), PO Box 6926, PO Box 5007, Portsmouth, 03802-6926

Hampshire Pewter Co (6), Route 108 Box 350 (#201), Somersworth, 03878-1564

Harman's Cheese & Country Store Inc (4), 1400 Rte 117, Sugar Hill, 03586

Hello Direct (16), 77 Northeastern Blvd, Nashua, 03062-3128

Herrington (16), Three Symmes Dr, Londonderry, 03053

Information Unlimited Inc (11), 19 Brook Rd, Mont Vernon, 03057

Kenmore Stamp Co (6), 119 West St, PO Box 331, Milford, 03055-4855

Littleton Coin Co Inc (6), 1309 Mt Eustis Rd, Littleton, 03561

MFE Instruments (9), 32 Hampshire Rd, Salem, 03079

Northeast Hinge Distributors Inc (9), 261 Proctor Hill Rd, Hollis, 03049

Paymentech (14), Four Northeastern Blvd, Salem, 03079-5916

Reliable Technologies Inc (16), 55 S Commercial St, Manchester, 03101

Rubber Stamps of America (6), 1110 Main St, Dublin, 03444

Solar Components Corp (9), 121 Valley St, Manchester, 03103-0237

Timberland LLC (16), 200 Domain Dr, Stratham, 03885

Village Coin Shop (6), 51C Plaistow Rd, Plaistow, 03865

Whitehorse Gear (11), 107 E Conway Rd, Center Conway, 03813-4012

Yankee Publishing Inc (17), 1121 Main St, Dublin, 03444

NEW JERSEY

A&P (16), 2 Paragon Dr, Montvale, 07645

AAA Umbrella Co Inc (16), 230 Pegasus Ave, Northvale, 07647-1904

ADP Inc (16), 1 ADP Blvd, Roseland, 07068-1728

Accoona Corp (16), 101 Hudson St (Suite 3606), Jersey City, 07302-3915

Ad-Lib Advertising Inc (10), 109 White Oak Ln (Suite 72A), Old Bridge, 08857

Aerosoles (2), PO Box 1916, Edison, 08818-1916

Affinity Federal Credit Union (1), 73 Mountainview Blvd, Basking Ridge, 07920

All-State Legal (16), 1 Commerce Dr, Cranford, 07016-3508

Allyn & Bacon (17), 1 Lake St, Upper Saddle River, 07458-1813

American General Co (15), 3600 State Rte 66, Neptune, 07753

Analytical Measurements (9), 22 Mountain View Dr, Chester, 07930-3104

Anda Inc (7), 400 Interpace Pkwy (Corporate Ctr 3), Parsippany, 07054

Anything Goes (6), 321 Main St, Allenhurst, 07711-1037

Arquest Inc (16), 14 Scotto Farm Ln, Millstone Twp, 08535-9426

The Art of Self Promotion (17), 1012 Park Ave, PO Box 23, Hoboken, 07030-4334

Audio & Video Labs Inc (16), 7905 N Route 130, Pennsauken, 08110-1402

Avis World Headquarters (19), 6 Sylvan Way, Parsippany, 07054-3826

BOC Gases (16), 575 Mountain Ave, Murray Hill, 07974

Basic Adhesives Inc (9), 60 Webro Rd, Clifton, 07012

Bauer Publishing Co (17), 270 Sylvan Ave, Englewood Cliffs, 07632-2523

Bayer Corp Consumer Care Division (16), 100 Bayer Blvd, P.O. Box 915, Whippany, 07981-0915

Bed Bath & Beyond (8), 650 Liberty Ave, Union, 07083-8107

J&H Berge/The Lab Mart (7), 4111 S Clinton Ave, South Plainfield, 07080

Berkeley College (13), 44 Rifle Camp Rd, West Paterson, 07424

Biosciences-Amersham (16), 800 Centennial Ave, PO Box 1327, Piscataway, 08855-1327

R R Bowker (17), 630 Central Ave, New Providence, 07974

Brim Electronics Inc (3), 120 Home Pl, Lodi, 07644

Burlington Coat Factory (16), 1830 Route 130 N, Burlington, 08016

Butler Distributing Co (3), 730 Fairfield Ave, Kenilworth, 07033-2012

CIT (14), 1 CIT Dr, Livingston, 07039-5703

CYRO Industries (16), 379 Interpace Pkwy Ste 1, Parsippany, 07054-1131

Cadie Products Corp (16), 151 E 11th St, Paterson, 07524-1228

Campbell Soup Co (16), 1 Campbell Pl, Camden, 08103-1701

Campmor Inc (17), 400 Corporate Dr, Mahwah, 07430-3606

Capezio Ballet Makers Inc (16), 1 Campus Rd, Totowa, 07512

Captan Associates Inc (17), 744 Durham Rd, Brick, 08724-1064

Caswell-Massey Co Ltd (7), 29 Northfield Ave, Edison, 08837

Center for Professional Advancement (13), 190 Route 18 (Suite 203), East Brunswick, 08816-1407

Central Shippee Inc (16), 46 Star Lake Rd, Bloomingdale, 07403-1244

Chairman's Marketing Group LLC (15), 8 Lafayette Rd W, Princeton, 08540-2428

Commonwealth Business Media Inc (17), 2 Penn Plz E Ste 2, 400 Windsor Corp Park, Newark, 07105-2251

Coronis Building Systems Inc (9), 92 Columbus Jobstown Rd, PO Box 200, Columbus, 08022

DIA - Nielsen USA Inc (16), 41 Twosome Dr (Unit 5), Moorestown, 08057

DMC Corp (16), 10 Basin Dr (Suite 130), Kearny, 07032

Dassault Falcon Jet Corp (16), 200 Riser Rd, Little Ferry, 07643-1226

The Davis Center (16), 19 State Route 10 (Suite 25), Succasunna, 07876-1750

Days Inns Worldwide Inc (16), 1 Sylvan Way Ste 2, Parsippany, 07054-3879

Delicious Orchards (4), 320 Rte 34, Colts Neck, 07722-2430

Details Interactive LLC (16), 30 Manchester Dr, Westfield, 07090-2265

Diamond Essence (2), 1115 Innman Ave (Suite 333), Edison, 08820

Diapers.com (5), PO Box 483, Jersey City, 07303

Discovery (9), 12 Christopher Way Ste 202, Eatontown, 07724-3331

DNE Nutraceuticals Inc (7), 700 Central Ave, Farmingdale, 07727

Dow Jones & Co (17), PO Box 300, Princeton, 08543-0300

Dr Leonard's Healthcare Corp (7), 100 Nixon Ln, Edison, 08837-3804

The Du-Rite Group Inc (16), 103 S Van Brunt St, Englewood, 07631-3437

EWA & Miniature Cars USA Inc (11), 369 Springfield Ave, PO Box 188, Berkeley Heights, 07922-0188

EXL (16), 10 Exchange Pl, Jersey City, 07302-3918

EasyLink Services International Corp (16), 33 Knightsbridge Rd, Piscataway, 08854

Edmund Optics Inc (9), 101 E Gloucester Pike, Barrington, 08007-1331

Educational Testing Service (16), 660 Rosedale Rd, Princeton, 08541

Etchworld (11), 176-180 Fifth Ave, Hawthorne, 07506

FLM Graphics Corp (16), 123 Lehigh Dr, Fairfield, 07004-3095

Falcon Safety Products (16), 25 Imclone Dr, Box 1229, Branchburg, 08876

George Fencik Associates (16), 1006 Arnold Ave, Point Pleasant, 08742

Financial Executives International (1), 1250 Headquarters Plaza (fl 7), Morristown, 07960

Flaghouse Inc (5), 601 Flaghouse Dr, Hasbrouck Heights, 07604

Foote, Francisco & Co (1), 19 Beverly Rd, West Caldwell, 07006-6501

Fran's Basket House, Inc (8), 295 Rte 10 E, Succasunna, 07876-1380

Freeman Decorating Co (16), 909 Newark Tpke, Kearny, 07032-4307

Garon Products Inc (16), PO Box 1924, Wall, 07719-1924

General Pencil Co Inc (16), 67 Fleet St, Jersey City, 07306

Gerber Products Co (16), 12 Vreeland Rd (fl 2), Florham Park, 07932

The Graph Co (14), PO Box 961, Vineland, 08362-0961

Haband Co Inc (2), 110 Bauer Dr, Oakland, 07436-3105

Hamilton Watch (16), 1200 Harbor Blvd, Weehawken, 07086-6728

Handy Store Fixtures Inc (8), 337 Sherman Ave, Newark, 07114-1592

Hanover Direct Inc (5), 1200 Harbor Blvd, Weehawken, 07086

Harbour Bay Inc (16), 32 Thunderbird Dr, Oakland, 07436-2211

The Hartz Mountain Corp (16), 400 Plaza Dr, Secaucus, 07094-3605

Herbach & Rademan Co (9), 353 Crider Ave, Moorestown, 08057

Hertz Corp (19), 225 Brae Blvd, Park Ridge, 07656

Hillside Wire Cloth Co (9), 109 Roosevelt Ave, Belleville, 07109

Honeywell (16), 101 Columbia Rd, Morristown, 07962

The IEI Corp (6), 29 Emmons Dr Ste A30, Princeton, 08540-5994

Institute of Management Accountants Inc (1), Ten Paragon Dr (Suite 1), Montvale, 07645-1718

JT International (16), 500 Frank W Burr Blvd (Suite 24), Teaneck, 07666-6802

Herbert L Jamison & Co LLC (15), 100 Executive Dr (Suite 200), West Orange, 07052-3362

Jaz Holdings LLC (16), PO Box 37, Bldg 5, Liberty Corner, 07938-0037

Johnson & Johnson (16), One Johnson & Johnson Plaza, New Brunswick, 08903

Journal of Commerce Group (17), 2 Penn Plz E (Suite 4), Newark, 07105-2251

Kimbo Educational (17), Ten N Third Ave, Long Branch, 07740-7045

King Pharmaceuticals, Inc (7), 132 Windsor Rd, Tenafly, 07670

Kuwait Airways Corp (19), 400 Kelby St (Suite 41), Fort Lee, 07024-2938

Lawn Doctor Inc (16), 142 State Route 34, Holmdel, 07733-2092

Lea & Perrins Inc (16), 15-01 Pollitt Dr, Fair Lawn, 07410

Lifeboat Distribution (16), 1157 Shrewsbury Ave, Shrewsbury, 07702

Lin Terry (6), 185 6th Ave Ste 4, Paterson, 07524-1247

Lincoln Educational Services Corp (13), 200 Executive Dr (Suite 340), West Orange, 07052-3303

Lladro USA Inc (16), One Lladro Dr, Moonachie, 07074-1019

Logical Computer Selections (16), 18 Winding Way, Short Hills, 07078-2530

MCI Communications Services Inc (16), One Verizon Way, Basking Ridge, 07920-1097

MDE Marketing (16), 55 Lehman St, Mahwah, 07430-3050

Marketing Results Inc (16), 604 Libertyville Pl, Sicklerville, 08081

Marquis Who's Who Ventures LLC (17), 100 Connell Dr, Ste 2300, Berkeley Heights, 07922

Martindale-Hubbell (17), 121 Chanlon Rd, New Providence, 07974

Medco Health Solutions Inc (7), 100 Parsons Pond Dr, Franklin Lakes, 07417-2604

Merck & Co Inc (16), 1 Merck Dr, Whitehouse Station, 08889

Metro Speedgear (11), 70 Okner Pkwy (Suite A), Livingston, 07039

Metropolitan Window Fashions at Fabricland (8), 855 Rte 22, North Plainfield, 07060-3619

Meylan Corp (9), 543 Valley Rd (Suite 1), Montclair, 07043-1844

Multiple Sclerosis Association of America (1), 375 Kings Hwy N, Cherry Hill, 08034

Myron Corp (16), 205 Maywood Ave, Maywood, 07607-1000

National Association for Printing Leadership (1), 75 W Century Rd (Suite 100), Paramus, 07652-1461

Nestle HealthCare Nutrition (16), 12 Vreeland Rd (fl 2), PO Box 697, Florham Park, 07932

New Jersey Institute for Continuing Legal Education (1), 1 Constitution Sq, New Brunswick, 08901-1587

New Jersey Monthly (17), 55 Park Pl, Morristown, 07960-3924

The NonProfit Times (17), 201 Littleton Rd (Suite 120), Morris Plains, 07950-2939

Novartis Pharmaceuticals Corp (7), 1 Health Plaza (Bldg 701 Rm 060), East Hanover, 07936-1016

Numark Brands (7), 164 Northfield Ave, Edison, 08837

Pearson Education (17), One Lake St, Upper Saddle River, 07458-1813

Peterson's (17), 2000 Lenox Dr, Lawrenceville, 08648-2314

Phillips-Van Heusen Corp (2), 200 Madison Ave, New York, 10016

Pilani's Live in Style (2), 284 Steelmanville Rd, Egg Harbor Township, 08234-7806

Pinkerton Security & Investigation Services (16), 2 Campus Dr, Parsippany, 07054-4499

Plymouth Rock Assurance (15), PO Box 906, Lincroft, 07738-0906

Princeton Book Co Publishers (17), 614 Rte 130, Hightstown, 08520-2651

Prudent Publishing Co (16), 65 Challenger Rd, Ridgefield Park, 07660-2111

Prudential Financial (14), 751 Broad St, Newark, 07102-2195

Qualco, Inc (8), 225 Passaic St, Passaic, 07055-6414

Rainbow Art Glass (16), 1761 Rte 34 S, Wall, 07727-3935

Recording for the Blind & Dyslexic Inc (16), 20 Roszel Rd, Princeton, 08540-9983

Resorts Casino Hotel (19), 1133 Boardwalk, Atlantic City, 08401-7329

Jacques C Schiff Jr Inc (5), 195 Main St, Ridgefield Park, 07660

Schwartz & Co (6), 12 Cook Ln, Verona, 07044-2002

Sculpture House Inc (16), 405 Skillman Rd, PO Box 69, Skillman, 08558

Seiko Corp of America (16), 1111 MacArthur Blvd, Mahwah, 07430

Seton Hall University (1), 400 South Orange Ave, South Orange, 07079-2646

Shiseido Cosmetics America (7), 366 Princeton-Hightstown Rd, East Windsor, 08520

Skinder-Strauss Associates (14), 890 Mountain Ave (Suite 300), New Providence, 07974

Software Assistance International Ltd (3), 85 Moraine Rd, Morris Plains, 07950

Songbird Hearing Inc (7), 210 N Center Dr, North Brunswick, 08902

Robert A Stanger & Co Inc (14), 1129 Broad St, Shrewsbury, 07702

The Suburban Chamber of Commerce (14), 71 Summit Ave Ste 1, Summit, 07901-3690

Super 8 Hotels Worldwide (19), 1 Sylvan Way, Parsippany, 07054-3887

The Supplies Guys (3), 268 Greenwood Ave, Midland Park, 07432-1445

Symrise (7), 300 North St, Teterboro, 07608-1204

Telcordia Technologies (16), One Telcordia Dr, Piscataway, 08854-4151

Tetley USA Inc (16), 155 Chestnut Ridge Rd, Montvale, 07645-1156

Thomas Scientific (9), 1654 High Hill Rd, Swedesboro, 08085

Tidewater Workshop (8), 1 No New York Rd (Suite 15), Galloway, 08205

Toys "R" Us (11), 1 Geoffrey Way, Wayne, 07470-2066

Transaction Publishers (17), 10 Corporate Pl S (Suite 102), Piscataway, 08854-6148

Tri-Chem Inc (16), 681 Main St Ste 24, Bldg 24, Belleville, 07109-3471

Tristar Products (16), 492 US Hwy 46 E, Fairfield, 07004

UBS Wealth Management US (14), 1200 Harbor Blvd, Weehawken, 07086-6728

Ultimate Office (16), PO Box 688, Farmingdale, 07727-0688

Ultra Direct Marketing Inc (16), PO Box 1575, Jackson, 08527

Unilever Best Foods (16), 800 Sylvan Ave, Englewood Cliffs, 07632

United Retail Inc (2), 365 W Passaic St (Suite 230), Rochelle Park, 07662-3017

Utretch Art Supplies (10), 6 Corporate Dr Ste 1, Cranbury, 08512-3616

Vcom International Multi-Media Corp (3), 55 Ruta Ct, PO Box 3171, South Hackensack, 07606

Vitamin Specialties Co (7), 500 Halls Mill Rd, Freehold, 07728

Volvo Cars of North America LLC (16), 1 Volvo Dr, PO Box 914, Northvale, 07647-0914

Weichert Co (14), 1625 State Route 10, Morris Plains, 07950-2905

John Wiley & Sons Inc (17), 111 River St, Hoboken, 07030-5774

Workforce Advantage USA (13), 66 Elmora Ave, Elizabeth, 07202-1630

Wyndham Hotel Group (19), 1 Sylvan Way (fl 3), Parsippany, 07054-3887

NEW MEXICO

American Society of Radiologic Technologists (1), 15000 Central Ave SE, Albuquerque, 87123-3909

The Bell Group Rio Grande (5), 7500 Bluewater Rd NW, Albuquerque, 87121-1962

ClingZ Inc (9), 541 Laser Dr NE, Rio Rancho, 87124-4518

Gallup Inter-Tribal Indian Ceremonial (1), 206 W Coal Ave, Gallup, 87301-6306

Hooleon Corp (3), 304 W Denby Ave, PO Box 589, Melrose, 88124

Indian Arts & Crafts Association (1), 4010 Carlisle NE (Suite C), Albuquerque, 87107

Indian House Records & Tapes (3), 27 Valencia Rd, Taos, 87571

Rio Grande (16), 7500 Bluewater Rd NW, Albuquerque, 87121-1962

Santa Fe Natural Tobacco Co (16), PO Box 25140, Santa Fe, 87504-5140

Santa Fe School of Cooking (4), 125 N Guadalupe St, Santa Fe, 87501

Sundancer Jewelry Co Inc (16), 5921 Office Blvd NE (Suite A), Albuquerque, 87109

NEW YORK

ABC Carpet & Home (8), 888 Broadway at E 19th St, New York, 10003-1280

ACN USA (1), 725 Leonard St, Brooklyn, 11222-2350

ADM Productions Inc (16), 40 Seaview Blvd, Port Washington, 11050-4618

AIG Accident & Health (15), 70 Pine St (50th fl), New York, 10270

AIG Marketing (15), 70 Pine St (40th fl), New York, 10270-0002

AIN Plastics Inc (16), 60 Fullerton Ave, Yonkers, 10704

Aon Consulting New York (15), 199 Water St (fl 12), New York, 10038-3551

APSCO (11), 7994 CR Ten, Davenport Center, 13751

ASPCA (1), 424 E 92nd St, New York, 10028-6804

AXA Equitable (15), 1290 Ave of the Americas (fl 7), New York, 10104-0101

A+E Television Networks LLC (16), 235 E 45th St, New York, 10017

Harry N Abrams Inc (17), 115 W 18th St (fl 5), New York, 10011-4113

Active Web Group (9), 30 Oser Ave (Suite 500), Hauppauge, 11788

Ad Infinitum Books (16), 7 N MacQuesten Pkwy, Mount Vernon, 10550-1811

Adirondack Direct (10), 3040 48th Ave, Long Island City, 11101

The Advertising Council Inc (1), 815 2nd Ave (fl 9), New York, 10017-4511

Air France (16), 125 W 55th St, New York, 10019

The Akadine Press Inc (16), 120 Bloomingdale Rd (Suite 100), White Plains, 10605-1522

All Star Carts & Vehicles (16), 1565-D Fifth Industrial Ct, Bay Shore, 11706-3434

Alliance Bernstein (14), 1345 Ave of the Americas, New York, 10105-0302

CM Almy & Son Inc (5), 28 Kaysal Ct, Armonk, 10504

ALSTOM Signaling Inc (16), 1025 John St, West Henrietta, 14586-9781

Amacom Books (17), 1601 Broadway, New York, 10019-7434

America Direct Book Service Custom Publishing (17), 1805 Spring Valley Rd, Ossining, 10562-1637

American Arbitration Association (1), 120 Broadway (fl 15), New York, 10271-0016

American Bible Society (1), 1865 Broadway, New York, 10023-7505

American Civil Liberties Union Foundation (1), 125 Broad St (fl 18), New York, 10004-2454

American Express Co (14), 200 Vesey St (fl 47, New York, 10285-0002

American Express Publishing Corp (17), 1120 Avenue Of The Americas Fl 9, New York, 10036-6700

American Foundation for the Blind Inc (1), 2 Penn Plaza (Suite 1102), New York, 10121-1100

American Institute of Chemical Engineers (1), 120 Wall St (fl 23), New York, 10005-4020

American Institute of CPAs (1), 1211 Avenue of the Americas (Suite 1900), New York, 10036-8775

American Institute of Physics (17), 2 Huntington Quadrangle (Suite 1NO1), Melville, 11747-4502

American International Group (15), 70 Pine St (fl 50), New York, 10270

American Kennel Club (17), 260 Madison Ave, New York, 10016-2401

American Management Association (1), 1601 Broadway, New York, 10019-7434

American Movie Classics Holding Corp (16), 220 Jericho Quadrangle, Jericho, 11753

American National Standards Institute (1), 25 W 43rd St (fl 4), New York, 10036

American Securities Capital Partners (15), 666 3rd Ave (fl 29), New York, 10017-4030

Amnesty International USA (1), Five Penn Plaza (fl 16), New York, 10001-1823

Amref Health Africa in the USA (1), 4 W 43rd St (Floor 2), New York, 10036-7408

Amsterdam Printing (16), 166 Wallins Corners Rd, Amsterdam, 12010-1899

Amsterdam Printing (5), 166 Wallins Corners Rd, Amsterdam, 12010

Andrea Electronics Corp (16), 65 Orville Dr (Suite 1), Bohemia, 11716-2517

The Angler's Den (11), 11 W Main St (Suite 4), Pawling, 12564-1341

The Animal Medical Center (16), 510 E 62nd St, New York, 10065-8314

Ann Inc (2), 7 Times Square Tower (Fl 14), New York, 10036

Anne Klein (16), 1411 Broadway Rm 2002, New York, 10018-3762

Anti-Defamation League (1), 605 3rd Ave (fl 9), New York, 10158-0102

Antiquarian Booksellers Association of America Inc (1), 20 W 44th St, New York, 10036

Arbor Commercial Mortgage (14), 333 Earle Ovington Blvd, Uniondale, 11553-3610

Archaeology Magazine (17), 36-36 33rd St, Long Island City, 11106

Argent Trading LLC (16), 521 5th Ave Rm 2200, New York, 10175-2900

Armento Inc (5), 1011 Military Rd, PO Box 39, Buffalo, 14217-0039

Art News Magazine (17), 48 W 38th St (fl 9), New York, 10018-0042

Aspen Publishers Inc (17), 76 Ninth Ave (fl 7), New York, 10011-5201

Associated Textile Rental Services (16), 548 Saint Paul St, Rochester, 14605-1735

Association for Computing Machinery (1), 2 Penn Plaza (Suite 701), New York, 10121-0701

Assurant Group (15), 1 Chase Manhattan Plaza, New York, 10005-1401

Astoria Federal Savings (14), 1 Astoria Federal Plaza, Lake Success, 11042-1076

Astrologer's Fund Inc (16), 7913 Bay Pkwy (#A7), Brooklyn, 11214

At Last Naturals (7), PO Box 338, North Salem, 10560-0338

Audio Classics Ltd (3), 3501 Vestal Rd, Vestal, 13850-2244

Audiovox (16), 180 Marcus Blvd, Hauppauge, 11788-3794

Avon Products Inc (7), 777 Third Ave, New York, 10017

Axis Capital (14), 430 Park Ave (fl 2), New York, 10022-3539

BBC Worldwide Americas Inc (3), 1120 Ave of the Americas (Fl 5), New York, 10036-6700

BMG Columbia House (13), 1 Penn Plaza, New York, 10119-0002

BNY Mellon (14), 1 Wall St, New York, 10286

Bachrach Clothing Inc (2), 323 W 39th St (Fl 11), New York, 10018

Maurice Badler Fine Jewelry Ltd (2), 485 Park Ave, New York, 10022-1228

Bantam Dell Publishing Group Inc (17), 1745 Broadway, New York, 10019

BarnesandNoble.com (16), 76 Ninth Ave (fl 9), New York, 10011

Bausch & Lomb Inc (16), 1 Bausch & Lomb Pl, Rochester, 14604-2701

Beckmann Converting Inc (16), 14 Park Dr, PO Box 390, Amsterdam, 12010-5340

Beluga Bar by Caviarteria (4), 75 Murray St, New York, 10007

Benetton USA (2), 601 Fifth Ave, New York, 10017-1024

Bergdorf Goodman (2), 625 Madison Ave (fl 14), New York, 10022

Better Health Fitness (11), 5302 New Utrecht Ave, Brooklyn, 11219-4139

The Bil-Ray Aluminum Siding Corp of Queens Inc (16), 102 Jericho Tpke, New Hyde Park, 11040-4507

Black Enterprise Magazine (17), 260 Madison Ave (fl 11), New York, 10016

Bliss World LLC (5), 200 Vesey St (fl 25), New York, 10281

Bloomingdale's Direct (16), 1000 Third Ave (fl 11), New York, 10022

The Blue Book Building & Construction Network (17), 800 E Main St, Jefferson Valley, 10535

Bobley-Harmann Corp (5), 200 Tradezone Ave, Ronkonkoma, 11779

The Body Shop Inc (7), 575 5th Ave, New York, 10017

Bookspan (13), 2 Park Ave (fl 10), New York, 10016-5604

Boundless Corp (16), 1916 State Route 96, Phelps, 14532-9705

The Bowery Mission (1), 432 Park Ave S (fl 3), New York, 10016

Brant Publications Inc (17), 110 Greene St (PH2), New York, 10012-3824

Bristol-Myers Squibb Co (16), 345 Park Ave, New York, 10154

Broadway Books (17), 1745 Broadway, New York, 10019

Broadway Play Publishing Inc (17), 224 E 62nd St, New York, 10065-8201

Bronson Nutritionals LLC (7), 70 Commerce St, Hauppauge, 11788-3962

Bronx Council on the Arts (1), 1738 Hone Ave, Bronx, 10461-1486

Brookfield Office Properties (16), 250 Vesey St (fl 15), Brookfield Place, New York, 10281

Brooks Brothers (2), 346 Madison Ave (fl 10), New York, 10017-3788

Brotherhood America's Oldest Winery Ltd (19), 100 Brotherhood Plaza Dr, Washingtonville, 10992-2262

Arthur Brown & Bro Inc (10), 2 W 45th St Frnt 1, New York, 10036-4214

Tony Brown Productions (16), 2214 Frederick Douglass Blvd (Suite 124), New York, 10026

Burberry (2), 444 Madison Ave, New York, 10022-6903

Business Planners & Consultants Inc (15), 370 Lexington Ave (Suite 909), New York, 10017-6503

CA Inc (16), 1 Ca Plz Ste 100, Islandia, 11749-5303

CDMO Inc (16), PO Box 765, Deer Park, 11729-0765

CNY Awards & Apparel Inc (5), 106 New Hartford Shopping Center, New Hartford, 13413

CSI (16), 1059 Powers Rd, Conklin, 13748-1400

Cablevision Systems Corp (16), 111 Stewart Ave, Bethpage, 11714

Cablexpress Technologies (10), 5404 S Bay Rd, Syracuse, 13212-3801

Cafe Lango (16), PO Box 400, Sharon Springs, 13459-0400

Cambridge Educational (12), 132 W 31st St Fl 17, New York, 10001-3406

Canyon Marketing (7), 920 S Oyster Bay Rd, Hicksville, 11801

Carestream Health Inc (7), 150 Verona St, Rochester, 14608

Catholic Charities - Brooklyn & Queens (1), 191 Joralemon St, Brooklyn, 11201-4306

Marshall Cavendish Corp (17), 99 White Plains Rd, Tarrytown, 10591-5502

Chanel Inc (16), 9 W 57th St (fl 44), New York, 10019

Channel 13 WNET Catalog Division (5), 825 8th Ave, New York, 10019

Chartis (15), 70 Pine St (fl 22), New York, 10270-0001

Chem-Tainer Industries Inc (9), 361 Neptune Ave, North Babylon, 11704

Chemical Week (17), 140 E 45th St (Rm 4000), New York, 10017-9304

Chief Marketer and Multichannel Merchant (17), 249 W 17th St, New York, 10011-5390

Children's Aid Society (1), 711 3rd Ave (Suite 700), New York, 10017

Choice Courier Systems Inc (16), 1 Whitehall St (fl 12), New York, 10004-2138

Christian Herald Association (1), 432 Park Ave S (fl 3), New York, 10016

Church Pension Fund (1), 19 E 34th St, New York, 10016

Citi Cards / Citicorp Credit Services (14), 1 Court Sq, Long Island City, 11120-0001

Citibank (14), 399 Park Ave, New York, 10022-4699

Citigroup Inc (14), 399 Park Ave, New York, 10043-0001

Clement Communications (17), PO Box 398, Buffalo, 14240

Clemente Novelties Inc (16), 301 Lafayette St, Utica, 13502-4311

Cluett Peabody (16), 48 W 38th St, New York, 10018-6248

Coach (2), 516 W 34th St, New York, 10001-1394

Cold Spring Harbor Lab Press (17), 500 Sunnyside Blvd, Woodbury, 11797-2924

Colgate-Palmolive Co (16), 300 Park Ave, New York, 10022-7499

Collector's Teapot (6), 10 Broeck Ave, Kingston, 12401

The College Board (1), 250 Vesey St, New York, 10281

Colonial Redi-Record Corp (10), 1225 36th St, Brooklyn, 11218-2023

Columbia Journalism Review (17), 729 Seventh Ave (fl 3), New York, 10019

Columbia University, Annual Fund Programs (5), 622 W 113th St (MC4520), New York, 10025-7982

Columbian Mutual Life Insurance Co (15), Vestal Pkwy E, Binghamton, 13902-4600

Commercial Travelers Mutual Insurance Co (15), 70 Genesee St, Utica, 13502-3503

Concern Worldwide (1), 355 Lexington Ave Fl 19, New York, 10017-6603

Conde Nast (17), 4 Times Sq, New York, 10036-6561

The Conference Board Inc (16), 845 Third Ave, New York, 10022-6679

Conmio Inc (16), 570 Fashion Ave (Rm 1104), New York, 10018-1629

Consumers Union (17), 101 Truman Ave, Yonkers, 10703-1057

The Contest Center (19), 59 DeGarmo Hills Rd, Wappingers Falls, 12590-2101

Cooper Vision (7), 370 Woodcliff Dr (Suite 200), Fairport, 14450

Cornell Lab of Ornithology (1), 159 Sapsucker Woods Rd, Ithaca, 14850-1923

Cosgrove Associates (14), 747 Third Ave (fl 16l), New York, 10017-2803

Council on Foreign Relations Inc (17), 58 E 68th St, The Harold Pratt House, New York, 10021-5953

Covenant House International Headquarters (1), 460 W 41st St, New York, 10036

Crohn's & Colitis Foundation of America (1), 733 3rd Ave (Suite 510), New York, 10017-3210

Cuba Cheese Shoppe (4), 53 Genesee St, Cuba, 14727-1199

Cytec Industries Inc (16), 1405 Buffalo St, Olean, 14760-1139

DPC Computers (16), 42 Melnick Dr, Monsey, 10952

David Dauber & Associates (16), 50 Lexington Ave (Suite 173), New York, 10010

Day Runner Direct (10), 101 Oneil Rd, Sidney, 13838-1055

DealerTrack (14), 1111 Marcus Ave (fl 3), New Hyde Park, 11042-2039

Dental Products Report (17), 641 Lexington Ave Fl 8, New York, 10022-4503

Destinations Ireland & Beyond (19), 91 Broadway (Suite 1), Kingston, 12401-6017

Deutsche Bank Alex Brown Inc (14), 60 Wall St, New York, 10005

Diamonds By Rennie Ellen (6), 15 W 47th St (Rm 503), New York, 10036

Didit (16), 330 Old Country Rd (Suite 206), Mineola, 11501-4143

The Dime Savings Bank of New York FSB (14), 589 5th Ave, New York, 10017

Dimmock Hill Golf Course Pro Shop (11), 638 Dimmock Hill Rd, Binghamton, 13905-9801

DineWise (4), 500 Bi-County Blvd (Suite 400), Farmingdale, 11735-3996

Christian Dior Perfumes (7), 151 W 34th St, New York, 10001

Direct Brands Inc (13), W 34th St (fl 5), 1 Penn Plaza, New York, 10119-0002

The Direct Marketing Association (1), 1333 Broadway (Suite 301), New York, 10018

The Direct Marketing Club of New York Inc (1), 54 Adams St, Garden City, 11530-3918

Directory of American Business & Insurance Attorneys (15), 130 Church St (#303), New York, 10007-2906

Disc Makers (3), 150 W 25th St (#402), New York, 10001

Diversified Investment Advisors (14), 440 Mamaroneck Ave, Harrison, 10528-2421

Doctors Without Borders (1), 333 7th Ave (fl 2), New York, 10001-5004

DoubleVerify (9), 575 8th Ave (fl 7), New York, 10018-3186

Dover Publications Inc (17), 31 E Second St, Mineola, 11501

Down Home Comforts (8), 126 County Rte 3, Putnam Station, 12861

The Dreyfus Corp (14), 200 Park Ave, New York, 10166

Drug Policy Alliance (1), 131 W 33 St (fl 15), New York, 10001-2938

E-Z-EM Inc (7), 1111 Marcus Ave (Suite M-60), Lake Success, 11042

EMED Co Inc (16), PO Box 369, Buffalo, 14240-0369

ESL Federal Credit Union (14), 225 Chestnut St, Rochester, 14604

David Easton Inc (16), 5 Union Sq W (fl 3), New York, 10003-3315

The Economist Newspaper NA Inc (17), 750 3rd Ave (fl 5), New York, 10017

Economy Handicrafts (16), 932 46th St, Brooklyn, 11219

Edroy Products Co Inc (16), 245 N Midland Ave, PO Box 998, Nyack, 10960-0998

Educational Coin Co (16), PO Box 892, Highland, 12528-0892

Effective Promotions Inc (16), PO Box 210, Fort Johnson, 12070-0210

Elsevier (17), 360 Park Ave S, New York, 10010-1710

Emigrant Savings Bank (14), 5 E 42nd St, New York, 10017-6904

Empire Blue Cross & Blue Shield (15), 1 Liberty Plz (Suite 1300), New York, 10006-1419

Empire City Casino at Yonkers Raceway (19), 810 Yonkers Ave, Yonkers, 10704-2030

Empire Coffee & Tea Co (4), 568 9th Ave Frnt 1, New York, 10036-3726

Empire Scientific (16), 151 E Industry Ct, Deer Park, 11729-5713

Enterprise Ireland (16), 345 Park Ave (17th fl), New York, 10154-0037

Entertainment Music Marketing Corp (16), 795 Foxhurst Rd, Baldwin, 11510-3530

Episcopal Relief & Development (1), 815 2nd Ave (fl 7), New York, 10017-4503

Esquire Magazine (17), 300 W 57th St (21st fl), New York, 10019

Esselte Americas (16), 225 Broadhollow Rd, Melville, 11747-2340

Essence Communications Inc (17), 135 W 50th St (4th fl), New York, 10020-1201

Essential Products Co Inc (7), 90 Water St, New York, 10005-3511

Estee Lauder Inc (16), 767 Fifth Ave, New York, 10153

Executive Enterprises Inc (16), 12 Skyline Dr, Hawthorne, 10532-2133

Eyeglass Service Industries (2), 481 Sunrise Hwy, Lynbrook, 11563

The FX Matt Brewing Co (4), 830 Varick St, Utica, 13502-4001

FCIA Management Co Inc (15), 125 Park Ave (fl 14), New York, 10017-5529

Facts On File Inc (17), 132 W 31st St (17th fl), New York, 10001

Fairchild Books (17), 1385 Broadway, New York, 10018

Fairchild Fashion Media (17), 750 Third Ave, New York, 10017-2703

Farrar Straus & Giroux Inc (17), 18 W 18th St Fl 7, New York, 10011-4675

Fashion Institute of Technology Library (1), 7th Ave at 27th St, New York, 10001-5992

Ferguson Publishing Co (17), 132 W 31st St (17 fl), New York, 10001-3406

Ferrara Bakery & Cafe Inc (4), 195 Grand St, New York, 10013

Fifth Avenue Committee (1), 621 DeGraw St, Brooklyn, 11217

Films Media Group (3), 132 W 31st St (Fl 17), New York, 10001-3406

Michael C Fina (6), 500 Park Ave (Frnt A), New York, 10022-1606

The Financial Times Group (17), 1330 Avenue of the Americas, New York, 10019-5436

Fine Architectural Metalsmiths (16), PO Box 30, Chester, 10918

Carl Fischer Music (17), 65 Bleecker St Fl 8, New York, 10012-2420

Fisher-Price (16), 636 Girard Ave, East Aurora, 14052-1824

Fluid Metering Inc (16), 5 Aerial Way (Suite 500), Syosset, 11791-5593

FM Howell & Co (16), 79 Pennsylvania Ave, Elmira, 14902-1455

Forbes Inc (17), 90 Fifth Ave, New York, 10011

Ford Foundation Office of Communications (5), 320 E 43rd St, New York, 10017-4816

Forum Publishing Co (17), 383 E Main St, Centerport, 11721-1538

Four Seasons Solar Products LLC (8), 5005 Veterans Memorial Hwy, Holbrook, 11741

Fowler's Chocolates Inc (4), 100 River Rock Dr (Suite 102), Buffalo, 14207-2163

Larry Fox & Co Ltd (16), PO Box 729, Valley Stream, 11582-0729

Franciscan Friars of the Atonement - Graymoor (1), Rte Nine, Garrison, 10524

Franciscan Mission Associates (1), 274-280 W Lincoln Ave, Mount Vernon, 10550-2509

Freeport Music Inc (11), 65 Clove Ave, Farmingville, 11738-1630

French Trade Office Embassy of France (1), 1700 Broadway Ste 3201, New York, 10019-5925

FreshDirect (5), 23-30 Borden Ave, Long Island City, 11101-4515

A I Friedman Inc (10), 44 W 18th St, New York, 10011

Fujifilm Holdings America Corp (16), 200 Summit Lake Dr, Valhalla, 10595-1356

G H Bass & Co (16), 200 Madison Ave, New York, 10016-3903

GMG Productions Inc (3), 346 Baltustrol Cr, Roslyn, 11021

Galen Williams Landscaping & Garden Design (16), Seven Oyster Shores Rd, East Hampton, 11937-1103

The Gallery Shop (6), 1285 Elmwood Ave, Albright-Knox Art Gallery, Buffalo, 14222-1096

Gay Men's Health Crisis (1), 446 W 33rd St, New York, 10001-2601

Gaylord Brothers (16), PO Box 4901, Syracuse, 13221-4901

Gebbie Press Inc (17), PO Box 1000, New Paltz, 12561-0017

Genium Publishing (17), 79 The Mall, PO Box 46, Amsterdam, 12010

Gerber Life Insurance Co (15), 1311 Mamaroneck Ave, White Plains, 10605-5221

Girl Scouts of the USA (1), 420 Fifth Ave, New York, 10018-2729

Glens Falls Hospital Foundation (1), 126 South St, Glens Falls, 12801-4321

Glenview Capital Management (14), 767 Fifth Ave (fl 44), New York, 10153-0023

Global Computer Corp (3), 100 Oakland Ave, Port Jefferson, 11777

Global Equipment Co Inc (9), 11 Harbor Park Dr, Port Washington, 11050

Go Promos (5), PO Box 698, Amsterdam, 12010-0698

Godiva Chocolatier (4), 333 W 34th St Fl 6, New York, 10001-2566

Gold Medal Hair Products Inc (7), 330 Conklin St, Farmingdale, 11735-2609

Goodman Media Group Inc (17), 250 W 57th St (Suite 710), New York, 10107

Government of India Tourist Office (1), 1270 Ave of the Americas (Suite 1808), New York, 10020-1700

Grandma Brown's Beans Inc (4), 5837 Scenic Ave, Mexico, 13114

Gridley & Co LLC (14), 10 E 53rd St (fl 24), New York, 10022-5070

Gruppo Levey & Co (14), 122 E 42nd St (fl 46), New York, 10168-0002

The Guardian Life Insurance Co (15), 7 Hanover Sq (fl 14), New York, 10004-4013

Guiding Eyes for the Blind (16), 611 Granite Springs Rd, Yorktown Heights, 10598

Guilford Publications Inc (17), 72 Spring St (4th fl), New York, 10012-4050

HSBC Bank USA, NA (14), 452 5th Ave, New York, 10018

Hampshire Agency (14), 33 Great Neck Rd (#7), Great Neck, 11021-3335

Hampton Marketing Corp (16), 19 Industrial Blvd, Medford, 11763

HarperCollins (17), 10 E 53rd St, New York, 10022-5299

Harper's Magazine (17), 666 Broadway (11th fl), New York, 10012

HAVE Inc (3), 350 Power Ave, Hudson, 12534-2448

Haymarket Group Ltd (17), 12 W 37th St, New York, 10018-7480

HealthRight International (1), 240 Greene St, New York, 10012

The Hearst Corp (17), 300 W 57th St, New York, 10019-3741

Hearst Magazines (17), 300 W 57th St (fl 19), New York, 10019-3741

Hermes of Paris (2), 55 E 59th St (#3), New York, 10022

Tommy Hilfiger (2), 601 W 26th St (#500), New York, 10001-1142

Hobart & William Smith Colleges (19), 300 Pulteney St, Geneva, 14456-3304

Hoke Communications Inc (17), 54 Adams St, Garden City, 11530

Homespun Tapes Music Instruction (3), PO Box 340, Woodstock, 12498-0340

House of Oldies (6), 35 Carmine St Frnt 1, New York, 10014-4429

IBM Corp (16), 1 New Orchard Rd, Armonk, 10504-1725

IDMS Inc (16), 560 Broadhollow Rd (Suite 109), Melville, 11747-3702

INC Magazine (17), Seven World Trade Center, New York, 10007-2195

Illy Caffe North America (4), 800 Westchester Ave (Suite S440), Rye Brook, 10573-1329

Independent Living Aids (7), 137 Rano Rd, Buffalo, 14207

Indian Country Today Media Network (17), 590 Madison Ave, New York, 10022

Indium Corp of America (16), 34 Robinson Rd, Clinton, 13323-1419

Institute for International Research Inc (16), 708 Third Ave (4th fl), New York, 10017-4103

Institute for Student Achievement (1), 1 Old Country Rd Ste 250, Carle Place, 11514-1818

Institute of Business Forecasting (1), 350 Northern Blvd, Great Neck, 11021-4809

Institutional Advancement Programs Inc (1), 65 Main St (#208), Tuckahoe, 10707

Institutional Investor Inc (17), 225 Park Ave S, New York, 10003

Instructor's Choice Dancewear (2), 5020 Sunrise Hwy, Massapequa Park, 11762-2913

International Advertising Association (1), 747 3rd Ave (fl 2), New York, 10017-2878

International Irrigation Systems (8), 291 Riverview Blvd, St. Catherines, L2T 3N3

International Planned Parenthood Federation Western Hemisphere Region Inc (1), 125 Maiden Ln (9th Fl), New York, 10038-5063

Itochu Chemicals America Inc (16), 360 Hamilton Ave (Suite 610), White Plains, 10601-1842

JDRF (1), 26 Broadway (fl 15), New York, 10004-1838

JP Morgan Chase & Co (14), 270 Park Ave (10th fl), New York, 10017-2070

The Jordan Edmiston Group Inc (14), 150 E 52nd St (18th fl), New York, 10022-6260

The Journal News (17), 1133 Westchester Ave (Suite N110), White Plains, 10604

Junior's Cheesecake (16), 386 Flatbush Ave Ext at Dekalb Ave, Brooklyn, 11238

Kaplan Test Prep (1), 395 Hudson St, New York, 10014

Kensington Publishing Corp (17), 119 W 40th St (fl 21), New York, 10018-2522

Key Bank National Association (14), 19 Corporate Woods Blvd, Albany, 12211-2345

King Features (17), 300 W 57th St (fl 15), New York, 10019-3741

Calvin Klein Cosmetics Co (7), 205 W 39th St, New York, 10018

Knoll Group (16), 76 Ninth Ave (11th fl), New York, 10011

Kozak Auto Drywash Inc (16), Eight S Lyon St, Batavia, 14020-1802

LGP GEM LTD (16), 10 W 46th St (Suite 4A), New York, 10036-4515

LIM College (1), 12 E 53rd St, New York, 10022-5268

Lancer Insurance Co (15), PO Box 9004, Long Beach, 11561-9004

Latest Products Corp (7), 36 Orchard Dr, Woodbury, 11797-2830

Leadership Directories Inc (17), 1407 Broadway (#318), New York, 10018-3853

Leadership Software Corp (16), PO Box 725, Nyack, 10960

League of American Orchestras (1), 33 W 60th St (5th fl), New York, 10023-7905

Leucadia National Corp (14), 315 Park Ave S (fl 20), New York, 10010-3649

The Leukemia & Lymphoma Society (1), 3 International Dr (Suite 200), Rye Brook, 10573

Lexington Luggage Limited (19), 793 Lexington Ave (Frnt 1), New York, 10065-8161

LexisNexis (16), 125 Park Ave (Suite 2200), New York, 10017

LexisNexis Matthew Bender (17), 1275 Broadway, Albany, 12204-2628

The Library of America (13), 14 E 60th St, New York, 10022-1006

Life Technologies (9), 3175 Staley Rd, Grand Island, 14072-2028

Lifetime Brands Inc (8), 1000 Stewart Ave, Garden City, 11530

A Liss & Co Inc (16), 51-55 59th Pl, Woodside, 11377-7408

Listening Library Inc, Random House Audio (3), 1745 Broadway, New York, 10019

Live Design (17), 249 W 17th St, New York, 10011

Loehmann's (2), 2500 Halsey St, Bronx, 10461-3637

Loews Hotels, Inc (19), 667 Madison Ave (fl 7), New York, 10065-8087

Lufthansa German Airlines (19), 1640 Hempstead Tpke, East Meadow, 11554-1040

M&M Health Care Apparel Co (2), 1541 60th St, Brooklyn, 11219-5023

MGI Management Institute (16), 12 Skyline Dr, Hawthorne, 10532

MJA International (7), 31 Stonywell Ct, Dix Hills, 11746-5424

MSC Industrial Supply Co (9), 75 Maxess Rd, Melville, 11747-3151

Macy's Marketing (16), 151 W 34th St (fl 17), New York, 10001-2101

Madisonavegifts.com (6), 325 Barben Ave, Watertown, 13601-4503

Magazine Publishers of America (17), 757 3rd Ave (fl 11), New York, 10017-2194

Magnaplan Corp (10), 1320 State Rte 9 (#3314), Champlain, 12919-5412

Magnatag Visible Systems (16), 2031 O'Neill Rd, Macedon, 14502-8953

Maison Glass Delicacies (4), 3180 US 9, Cold Spring, 10516

MALM Chemical Corp (16), Dept WEB-5, PO Box 300, Pound Ridge, 10576-0300

EF Maloney Inc (16), 257 Mamaroneck Ave (Suite 208), Mamaroneck, 10543-2686

The Maloney Group (16), Five E 22nd St, New York, 10010-5315

Mane Solutions (16), 314 Fifth Ave, New York, 10001-3606

Manhattan College (1), Manhattan College Pkwy, Bronx, 10471-3915

March of Dimes Foundation (1), 1275 Mamaroneck Ave, White Plains, 10605

Markertek Video Supply (3), 1 Tower Dr, PO Box 397, Saugerties, 12477-4386

Maryknoll Fathers & Brothers (1), 55 Ryder Rd, 55 Ryder Rd, Ossining, Ossining, 10562

MasterCard Worldwide (14), 2000 Purchase St, Purchase, 10577-2509

Mastervision Inc (16), 969 Park Ave, New York, 10028

The McGraw-Hill Financial (17), 1221 Ave of the Americas, New York, 10020-1095

McGruff Specialty Products Office (16), 1 Prospect St, Amsterdam, 12010

Medco Supply Co Inc (7), 500 Fillmore Ave, Tonawanda, 14150

Medical Letter Inc (1), 145 Huguenot St (Suite 312), New Rochelle, 10801-7537

Memorial Sloan Kettering Cancer Center (1), 1275 York Ave, New York, 10065

Merisel (16), 127 W 30th St (5th fl), New York, 10001

Merrill Lynch International Inc (14), 250 Vesey St (fl 12), Four World Financial Center, New York, 10281-1023

MetLife International (15), 2701 Queens Plaza N (#4E-148), Long Island City, 11101-4020

Metropolis Magazine (2), 205 Lexington Ave (fl 17), New York, 10016

Metropolitan Museum of Art (8), 1000 Fifth Ave, New York, 10028

The Metropolitan Opera (1), 30 Lincoln Center, New York, 10023

Mini City Ltd (12), 799 Holt Rd Ste 170, Webster, 14580-9188

Frank Mittermeier Inc (11), 3577 E Tremont Ave, Bronx, 10455-2008

Modernage Custom Digital Imaging Labs (16), 555 8th Ave (Rm 2003), New York, 10018-4651

Mohawk Lifts (9), 65 Vrooman Ave, PO Box 110, Amsterdam, 12010

Jacques Moret Inc (16), 1411 Broadway (fl 8), New York, 10018

Morgan Stanley (14), 1585 Broadway, New York, 10036

Moritt, Hock, Hamroff & Horowitz (16), 400 Garden City Plaza, Garden City, 11530-3327

Museum Masters Inc (16), 185 E 85th St (Suite 27B), New York, 10028

The Museum of Modern Art (5), 11 W 53rd St, New York, 10019-5497

Music Barn Inc (6), PO Box 1083, Niagara Falls, 14304-0383

Music Sales Corp (17), 180 Madison Ave (fl 24), New York, 10016

Mutual of America Life Insurance Co (14), 320 Park Ave, New York, 10022-6839

Mystic Stamp Co Inc (16), 9700 Mill St, Camden, 13316

NBTY Inc (7), 2100 Smithtown Ave, Ronkonkoma, 11779-7347

NYSARC, Inc (1), 393 Delaware Ave, Delmar, 12054

NAR Productions (17), PO Box 233, Barryville, 12719-0233

National Association for Female Executives (1), 2 Park Ave (fl 10), New York, 10016-5604

National Audubon Society (17), 225 Varick St, New York, 10014

National Basketball Association (1), 645 Fifth Ave, New York, 10022

National Crime Prevention Council (17), One Prospect St, Amsterdam, 12010

National Enquirer (17), 4 New York Plaza, New York, 10004

National Medical Fellowships (1), 347 5th Ave (Suite 510), New York, 10016-5007

National Review (17), 215 Lexington Ave, New York, 10016

Nationwide Beauty & Barber Supply (16), 2600 Erie Blvd E, Syracuse, 13224-1287

Nationwide Displays Inc (16), 100 Christopher St, Ronkonkoma, 11779

Nature Publishing Group (17), 75 Varick St (fl 9), New York, 10013-1917

Navitar Inc (16), 200 Commerce Dr, Rochester, 14623-3506

Neighborhood Cleaners Association International (1), 252 W 29th St, New York, 10001

Neuberger & Berman Management (14), 605 3rd Ave (fl 21), New York, 10158-3698

New Directions Publishing Corp (17), 80 Eighth Ave (fl 19), New York, 10011-7146

New York & Co (2), 33 W 34th St, New York, 10001

New York Blood Center Inc (1), 310 E 67th St, New York, 10021

New York Easter Seal Society (1), 40th W 37th St (Suite 503), Development Office, New York, 10018-7345

New York Findings (6), 72 Bowery, New York, 10013

New York Foundation For The Arts (1), 20 Jay St (fl 7), Brooklyn, 11201-8352

New York Landmarks Conservancy (1), One Whitehall St, New York, 10004

New York Philharmonic (1), 10 Lincoln Ctr Plaza, Avery Fisher Hall, New York, 10023-6970

New York Power Authority (16), 123 Main St (Mailroom 10-B), White Plains, 10601-3170

New York-Presbyterian/Columbia University Medical Center (16), 630 W 168th St, New York, 10032

New York Road Runners (13), Nine E 89th St, New York, 10128

The New York Times Co (17), 620 8th Ave, New York, 10018-1618

New York University (1), 11 W 42nd St (Rm 431), New York, 10036-8083

New York University Medical Center (1), 550 First Ave, New York, 10016

The New Yorker Magazine (17), 4 Times Sq, New York, 10036

Newsday (17), 235 Pinelawn Rd, Melville, 11747-4250

The Nielsen Co (17), 85 Broad St, New York, 10004

Nightingale Resources (17), 6 Chestnut St, Cold Spring, 10516-2517

Nihon Keizai Shimbun America Inc (17), 1325 Ave of the Americas (Ste 2500), New York, 10019

North Shore Animal League America Inc (1), 25 Davis Ave, Port Washington, 11050

Northern Safety Co Inc (16), PO Box 4250, Utica, 13504-4250

Nyrev Inc (17), 435 Hudson St (Ste 300), New York, 10014-3949

Old World Mouldings Inc (9), 821 Lincoln Ave, Bohemia, 11716

Oliver Wyman (14), 1166 Avenue of the Americas, New York, 10036-2726

1-800-Flowers.com (16), 1 Old Country Rd (Suite 500), Carle Place, 11514-1847

1-800-Mattress.com (16), 1000 S Oyster Bay Rd, Hicksville, 11801-3527

1000 Islands International Tourism Council (19), 43373 Collins Landing Rd, Alexandria Bay, 13607-2210

One World Projects (6), 43 Ellicott Ave, Batavia, 14020-2010

Oneida Ltd (16), 163-181 Kenwood Ave, Oneida, 13421-2829

Oppenheimer Funds (14), 225 Liberty St (fl 11), 2 World Financial Ctr, New York, 10281-1005

Orbis Books (17), PO Box 302, Price Bldg, Maryknoll, 10545-0302

Our Lady of Victory Homes of Charity (1), 780 Ridge Rd, Lackawanna, 14218-1682

Oxford University Press Inc (17), 198 Madison Ave, New York, 10016

Pace University (16), 1 Pace Plaza, New York, 10038

Parkinson's Disease Foundation (1), 1359 Broadway (Suite 1509), New York, 10018

Patient News (17), 3909 Witmer Rd (#1080), Niagara Falls, 14305-1239

Penguin Group USA Inc (17), 375 Hudson St, New York, 10014

Pensions & Investments (17), 711 3rd Ave, New York, 10017-4014

Penton Learning Systems Inc (16), 535 Fifth Ave (fl 8), New York, 10017-8011

Pernod Ricard USA (16), 100 Manhattanville Rd, Purchase, 10577-2134

Petsky Prunier LLC (14), 60 Broad St (Ste 3810), New York, 10004-2329

Pfizer Inc (16), 235 E 42nd St, New York, 10017

Phillips-Van Heusen Corp (2), 200 Madison Ave, New York, 10016

Planned Parenthood Federation of America (1), 434 W 33rd St, New York, 10001-2600

Polo Ralph Lauren (2), 625 Madison Ave, New York, 10022

Pontifical Mission Societies in the US (1), 70 W 36th St (fl 8), New York, 10018-1256

Practicing Law Institute (16), 1177 Avenue of the Americas, New York, 10036-2714

Premier Packaging Corp (16), PO Box 352, Victor, 14564-0352

ST Preston & Son Inc (8), 102 Main St Wharf, Greenport, 11944-1422

PricewaterhouseCoopers LLP (14), 300 Madison Ave (fl 24), New York, 10017

Profile Coverage Corp (15), PO Box 9081, Melville, 11747-9081

Profile Mailing Service Inc (16), 575 Underhill Blvd (Suite 132), Syosset, 11791-3416

Promo Magazine (17), 249 W 17th St (3rd fl), New York, 10011

Promotion Marketing Association (PMA) Inc (1), 650 1st Ave (Suite 2-SW), New York, 10016-3207

Publishers Clearing House (18), 382 Channel Dr, Port Washington, 11050-2297

Puritan's Pride (7), 2100 Smithtown Ave, Ronkonkoma, 11779-7347

Putnam Rolling Ladder Co Inc (5), 32 Howard St, New York, 10013-3112

Random House Children's Books (13), 1745 Broadway (fl 10), New York, 10019

Random House Direct Marketing (17), 1745 Broadway, New York, 10019-4305

The Reader's Digest Association Inc (17), 750 3rd Ave, New York, 10017-2703

Recognition Systems (Dot Works) (16), 30 Harbor Park Dr, Port Washington, 11050

Redbook Magazine (17), 300 W 57th St, New York, 10019

Redcats USA (2), 463 Fashion Ave (#1603), New York, 10018-7421

JP Redington & Co (16), PO Box 429, Huntington, 11743

Reed Elsevier (17), 125 Park Ave (fl 23), New York, 10017-8503

Reliable Racing Supply (11), 643 Upper Glen St (Suite B), Queensbury, 12804-2014

Remedy Magazine (17), 500 Fifth Ave (Suite 1900), New York, 10110

Research To Prevent Blindness Inc (1), 360 Lexington Ave (fl 22), New York, 10017

Retawmatic Corp (9), 14911 41st Ave, Flushing, 11355-1025

Rich Products Corp (16), One Robert Rich Way, Buffalo, 14213-1701

Pete Rickard Inc (11), 115 Roy Walsh Rd, Cobleskill, 12043-4422

Rizzoli International Publications Inc (17), 300 Park Ave S (3rd fl), New York, 10010

Robinson Home Products (16), 170 Lawrence Bell Dr (Suite 110), Buffalo, 14221-8484

The Roblin Group Inc (17), 405 Tarrytown Rd (Ste 1545), White Plains, 10607

Rochester Institute of Technology (1), 55 Lomb Memorial Dr, Rochester, 14623-5602

RocketWear (2), 101 W 57th St (#15 D), New York, 10019

Ross Metals (16), 27 W 47 St, New York, 10036-2806

Row Resources Inc (16), 260 Main St (Ste 110), Northport, 11768-1738

Rush Industries, Inc (16), 263 Horton Hwy, Mineola, 11501-2255

Ruskin, Moscou, Faltischek, PC (16), 190 EAB Plaza (15th fl East Tower), Uniondale, 11556

SIFMA (1), 120 Broadway (fl 35), New York, 10271-0080

St Joseph's College (1), 245 Clinton Ave, Brooklyn, 11205-3602

Saks Fifth Avenue (16), 12 E 49th St (fl 2), New York, 10017-1088

Sales & Marketing Management Magazine (16), 770 Broadway, New York, 10003

Salesian Missions (1), 2 Le Fevres Ln, New Rochelle, 10801-5710

Sam Ash Music Direct (5), PO Box 9047, Hicksville, 11802

Sanky Communications Inc (1), 599 11th Ave (fl 6), New York, 10036-2110

The Sausage Maker Inc (4), 1500 Clinton St (Bldg 7), Buffalo, 14206-3099

Henry Schein Inc (16), 135 Duryea Rd, Melville, 11747-3834

Scholastic Inc (17), 557 Broadway, New York, 10012-3919

Sesame Workshop (1), 1 Lincoln Plaza, New York, 10023-7163

JA Sexauer (16), 570 Taxter Rd (Ste 230), Elmsford, 10523-2365

Sherman Specialty Toy Co Inc (16), 300 Jericho Quadrangle (Suite 240), Jericho, 11753-2719

Showtime Networks Inc (16), 1633 Broadway, New York, 10019

Simmons-Boardman Publishing Corp (17), 55 Broad St (fl 26), New York, 10004

Simon & Schuster Inc (17), 1230 Ave of the Americas, New York, 10020

Simplicity Pattern Co Inc/Style Patterns Ltd/New Look English Pattern Co Ltd (8), 261 Madison Ave (fl 4), New York, 10016-3906

SiriusXM Radio Inc (16), 1221 Avenue of the Americas, New York, 10020

Sleepy's Inc (16), 1000 S Oyster Bay Rd, Hicksville, 11801-3527

Slifter (16), 307 7th Ave (Rm 2104), New York, 10001-6089

The Smile Train (1), 41 Madison Ave (fl 28), New York, 10010-2325

Smithsonian Enterprises (17), 420 Lexington Ave, New York, 10170-0002

Peter J Solomon Co (14), 1345 Avenue of the Americas, New York, 10105

Sotheby's (6), 1334 York Ave at 72nd St, New York, 10021-4806

Spa-Finder Inc (7), 333 SE 2nd Ave (Suite 3750), New York, 33131

Spadet (7), 178 Columbus Ave (#230119), New York, 10023

Huck Spaulding Enterprises (16), Rte 85, New Scotland Rd, Voorheesville, 12186

Spectronics Corp (9), 956 Brush Hollow Rd, Westbury, 11590-1731

Spiegel Brands Inc (2), 110 William St (11th Fl), New York, 10038-3945

Spinneybeck Enterprises (16), 425 Crosspoint Pkwy (Ste 100), Getzville, 14068-1609

Spoken Arts (17), 195 S White Rock Rd, Holmes, 12531-5406

Springer Science & Business Media LLC (17), 233 Spring St, New York, 10013

Springs Global Inc (16), 110 5th Ave (fl 5), New York, 10011-5647

Standard & Poor's Corp (17), 55 Water St, New York, 10041-0004

Stellar Technology Inc (9), 237 Commerce Dr, Amherst, 14228-2302

Sterling Publishing Co Inc (17), 387 Park Ave S (fl 5), New York, 10016-8898

Martha Stewart Living Omnimedia (17), 601 W 26th St (Fl 9), New York, 10001-1101

Stock Drive Products (5), 2101 Jericho Tpke, New Hyde Park, 11040

Stokes Seeds Inc (8), 2495 Walden Ave (# 800), Buffalo, 14225-4767

Store Smart Express/Visual Horizons (16), 180 Metro Park, Rochester, 14623-2610

Paul Stuart (2), Madison Ave & 45th St, New York, 10017

Sunbilt Solar Products (8), 109-10 180th St, Jamaica, 11433-2622

Sunrise Business Products (10), 69 E Jericho Tpke, Mineola, 11501

Sunshine Glassworks Ltd (11), 111 Industrial Pkwy, Buffalo, 14227-2712

Sussex Publishers Inc (17), 115 E 23rd St (9th fl), New York, 10010

Syracuse University (1), 900 S Crouse Ave, Syracuse, 13244-0001

Systemax Inc (16), 11 Harbor Park Dr, Port Washington, 11050

Thomson Reuters (17), 195 Broadway Fl 4, New York, 10007-3124

TIAA-CREF (15), 730 Third Ave, New York, 10017

Talas (10), 330 Morgan Ave, Brooklyn, 11211

Team Cheer (2), 131 Main St (Ste 2), Geneseo, 14454-1242

Theatre Development Fund Inc (1), 520 8th Ave (Suite 801), New York, 10018-6507

Thieme Medical Publishers Inc (17), 333 7th Ave Rm 500, New York, 10001-5122

Things Deco (6), 130 E 18th St (Suite 8F), New York, 10003-2416

Thirteen/WNET (1), 825 Eighth Ave, New York, 10019

Thomson Reuters LPC (14), 3 Times Sq, New York, 10036

Tiffany & Co (6), 600 Madison Ave (fl 4), New York, 10022-1689

Time Inc (17), 1271 6th Ave, New York, 10020-1300

Time Out New York (18), 475 10th Ave (12th fl), New York, 10018

Time Warner Inc (16), 1 Time Warner Ctr, New York, 10019-8016

Times Union (18), Box 15000, News Plaza, Albany, 12212

Todaro Brothers Mail Order Co (4), 555 Second Ave (Front A), New York, 10016-6346

Torah Umesorah Publications (5), 620 Foster Ave, Brooklyn, 11230

Transcat (16), 35 Vantage Point Dr, Rochester, 14624-1175

Transit Treasure Inc (12), 311 E 38th St (Suite 19B), New York, 10016-0748

TransitCenter Inc (1), 1 Whitehall St (fl 17), New York, 10004

Travel Planners Inc (19), 381 Park Ave S, New York, 10016-8806

Treasure Chest (19), 304 Park Ave S, New York, 10010-4301

Triumph Learning (17), 136 Madison Ave (fl 7), New York, 10016-6711

The Trumpet Club (17), 578 Broadway (Rm 807), New York, 10012

truTV (17), 1 Time Warner Ctr, New York, 10019-6038

UCEA (1), PO Box 1168, New York, 10040-0815

UNICEF (1), 3 United Nations Plaza, New York, 10017

Unadilla Laminated Products (16), 32 Clifton St, Unadilla, 13849

United Business Media (17), 600 Community Dr (Ste 1), Manhasset, 11030-3818

United Jewish Appeal Federation of New York (1), 130 E 59th St, New York, 10022-1302

United Jewish Communities (1), 25 Broadway (fl 17), New York, 10004-1015

United Nations Federal Credit Union (1), 2401 44th Rd (fl 7) Ct Sq Pl, Long Island City, 11101-4605

United Spinal Association (1), 120-34 Queens Blvd (#320), Kew Gardens, 11415

United Staffing Systems (16), 130 William St (fl 5), New York, 10038

United States Bronze Sign Co Inc (1), 811 Second Ave, New Hyde Park, 11040

US Digital Transactions Corporation (14), 228 Park Ave S, New York, 10003-1502

US Fund for UNICEF (6), 125 Maiden Ln, New York, 10038-4912

US Gas & Electric (16), 333 Mamaroneck Ave (#490), White Plains, 10605

United States Tennis Association (1), 70 W Red Oak Ln, White Plains, 10604-3610

Unitron Ltd (9), 73 Mall Dr, Commack, 11725-5703

University at Buffalo Center for Entrepreneurial Leadership (5), 77 Goodell St (Ste 201), Buffalo, 14203

Urbani Truffles USA Corp (4), 10 West End Ave, New York, 10023

Valdawn Watch Co (16), 2910 Thomson Ave (6th fl), Long Island City, 11101-2939

Value Line Publishing Inc (17), 220 E 42nd St, New York, 10017

Van Dam Inc (17), 121 W 27th St (Ste 1102), New York, 10001-6261

Vanderbilt Advertising (14), 220 E 42nd St (fl 6), New York, 10017-5806

Vector Marketing Corp (5), 1116 E State St, Olean, 14760-3814

Verizon Communications Inc (3), 140 West St LBBY 1, New York, 10013

Veronis Suhler Stevenson LLC (14), 55 E 52nd St (fl 33), New York, 10055-0007

Viacom Inc (16), 1515 Broadway, New York, 10036-8901

Viahealth (16), 1425 Portland Ave, Rochester, 14621-3001

Viatech Publishing Solutions Inc (16), 1440 5th Ave, Bay Shore, 11706-4147

Victor Machinery Exchange (9), 56 Bogart St, Brooklyn, 11206-3817

Video Artists International (3), 109 Wheeler Ave, Pleasantville, 10570

VIEW Video Inc/Arcadia Entertainment Corp (16), PO Box 77, Saugerties, 12477

Visual Horizons (16), 180 Metro Park, Rochester, 14623-2610

Visual Reference Publications (17), 302 Fifth Ave, New York, 10001

Vitamin Power Inc (7), 75 Commerce Dr, Hauppauge, 11788

Vivendi SA (16), 800 Third Ave, New York, 10022

Walker Publishing Co Inc (17), 175 Fifth Ave (Frnt 4), New York, 10010-7728

Warren, Gorham & Lamont Inc (17), 195 Broadway, New York, 10007-3100

Andrew D Washton Books On the Fine Arts (16), 168 Irving Ave, Port Chester, 10573

Wathne Ltd (2), 156 W 56 St, New York, 10019

The Wedding Pages (16), 195 Broadway, New York, 10007

Weight Watchers International (16), 675 Avenue of the Americas (fl 6), New York, 10010-5117

Welch Allyn, Inc (9), 4341 State Street Rd, Skaneateles Falls, 13153-5300

Wenner Media LLC (17), 1290 Ave of the Americas (fl 2), New York, 10104-0298

Westcon (16), 520 White Plains Rd (Ste 100), Tarrytown, 10591-5167

Wideband by Kars (16), PO Box 1785, New Rochelle, 10802-1785

The HW Wilson Co (17), 950 University Ave, Bronx, 10452

Wine Enthusiast Cos (4), 333 N Bedford Rd, Mount Kisco, 10549-1158

Winmill & Co (14), 11 Hanover Sq, New York, 10005-2818

Harry Winston Inc (16), 718 Fifth Ave, New York, 10019

Woman's Day Special Interest Publications (17), 1633 Broadway (42nd fl), New York, 10019

Women's Sports Foundation (1), 1899 Hempstead Turnpike, Eisenhower Park, East Meadow, 11554-1099

World Kitchen Inc (16), 1 Steuben St, Corning, 14830-2900

World Press Review (18), 700 Broadway, New York, 10003

Yellow Book USA (17), 398 RXR Plaza, Uniondale, 11556-0398

Your Move Chess & Games (11), 832 N Broadway, North Massapequa, 11758

David Yurman Enterprises LLC (5), 24 Vestry St, New York, 10013-1903

Ziff Davis Media Inc (17), 28 E 28th St (11th fl), New York, 10016

Zim-American Israeli Shipping Co Inc (16), 1110 South Ave, Staten Island, 10314

NORTH CAROLINA

Air Chek Inc (9), PO Box 2000, Naples, 28760-5000

Ambient Shapes Inc (7), 856 21st Street Dr SE, Hickory, 28602-8376

American Baseball Coaches Association (1), 4101 Piedmont Pkwy (Suite C), Greensboro, 27410

American Biographical Institute Inc (17), 5126 Bur Oak Cir, Raleigh, 27612-3101

Asheville Compassionate Communication Center (13), 150 E Chestnut St (#1), Asheville, 28801-2337

B&G Lieberman Co Inc (16), 2420 Distribution St, Charlotte, 28203

Babyshoe.com (6), 306 Hebron St, Hendersonville, 28739-5210

Baker & Taylor Inc (16), 2550 W Tyvola Rd (#300), Charlotte, 28217-4579

Bank of America (14), 100 N Tryon St, Charlotte, 28255

Bob Barker Co Inc (5), 134 N Main St, Fuquay Varina, 27526-0429

Battleground Antiques Inc (6), 3910 US Hwy 70 E, New Bern, 28560

Belk Stores Services Inc (16), 2801 W Tyvola Rd, Charlotte, 28217-4500

Bencone Uniform Connection (2), 1855 Runnymede Rd, Winston Salem, 27104-3109

Blue Cross Blue Shield of North Carolina (15), PO Box 2291, Durham, 27702-2291

Boy Scouts of America/National Supply Group (1), 2109 Westinghouse Blvd, Charlotte, 28273-6310

Branch Banking & Trust Co (14), 200 W 2nd St, Winston-Salem, 27101

Brooks Equipment Co (9), 10926 David Taylor Dr (Ste 300), Charlotte, 28262

Burlington Industries Inc (16), 804 Green Valley Rd (Ste 300), Greensboro, 27408-7039

Business Publishers Inc (17), 2222 Sedwick Rd, Durham, 27713-2655

CMS Inc (14), 2650 Pilgrim Ct, Winston Salem, 27106-5238

Camellia Forest Nursery (8), 620 Hwy 54 W, Chapel Hill, 27516-7955

Carolina Biological Supply Co (9), 2700 York Rd, Burlington, 27215-3387

Carrot-Top Industries Inc (16), 328 Elizabeth Brady Rd, Hillsborough, 27278-9540

Center for Creative Leadership (16), 1 Leadership Pl, Greensboro, 27410-9427

Chadsworth's 1-800-Columns (8), 277 N Front St, Wilmington, 28401-3907

Charlotte Chamber of Commerce (1), 330 S Tryon St (Ste 200), Charlotte, 28202-1923

CommScope Inc (16), 1100 CommScope Pl SE, Hickory, 28603

Computer Dynamics Inc (3), 3030 Whitehall Park Dr, Charlotte, 28273

The Ben Craig Center (1), 8701 Mallard Creek Rd # 106, Charlotte, 28262-6007

Daily Record & Dispatch Co (17), 99 W Broad St, Dunn, 28334-6031

The Dartnell Corp (17), 2272 Airport Rd S, Naples, 34112

Direct SAT TV LLC (3), 1930 N Poplar St (Ste 21), Southern Pines, 28387-7092

Dorothy's Ruffled Originals Inc (8), 6721 Market St, Wilmington, 28405-3703

Eaton Corp (16), 8609 Six Forks Rd, Raleigh, 27615-2966

Eli Journals (16), 2222 Sedwick Rd (Ste 101), Durham, 27713-2658

Expressions Custom Furniture (16), 401 11th St NW, PO Box 608, Hickory, 28603-0608

Foundation of FirstHealth (1), 150 Applecross Rd, Pinehurst, 28374-8520

Gardens Of The Blue Ridge Inc (8), PO Box 10, Pineola, 28662

Gateway Bank and Trust (14), 2235 Gateway Access Point (Ste 200), Raleigh, 27607-3076

General Vitamin Corp (16), 10700 World Trade Blvd (Ste 102), Raleigh, 27617-4220

Global Demand Publishing Inc (17), 101 B Middle St (Suite 101 B), Jacksonville, 28546-6798

Gould & Goodrich (2), 709 E McNeil St, Lillington, 27546

Billy Graham Evangelistic Association (1), 1 Billy Graham Pkwy, Charlotte, 28201-0001

Graphik Dimensions Ltd (16), 2103 Brentwood St, High Point, 27263

Grove Enterprises Inc (16), 618 Dog Branch Rd, Brasstown, 28902-8750

Hallelujah Acres (5), 916 Cox Rd (Ste 210), Gastonia, 28054-3434

Hanesbrands Inc (2), 1000 E Hanes Mill Rd, Winston Salem, 27105-1384

Happy Jack Inc (11), 2122 US 258, Snow Hill, 28580

Health Sciences Consortium (17), 300 Silver Cedar Ct, Chapel Hill, 27514-1696

House of Eyes (2), 2222 A Patterson St (Ste A), Greensboro, 27407-2539

IHFRA (1), 209 S Main, High Point, 27260

ISA-The International Society of Automation (1), 67 T W Alexander Dr, Research Triangle Park, 27709

Inmar (14), 635 Vine St, Winston-Salem, 27101-4185

The Inspiration Networks (1), PO Box 7750, Charlotte, 28241

JR Cigar (5), 2589 Eric Ln, Burlington, 27215

Jerry's Artarama (10), 3060 Wake Forest Rd, Raleigh, 27609

Kayne & Son Custom Hardware Inc (8), 100 Daniel Ridge Rd, Candler, 28715-9434

Kayser-Roth Corp Inc (2), 102 Corporate Center Blvd, Greensboro, 27408

King's Chandelier Co (6), 729 S Van Buren Rd (Hwy 14 S), Eden, 27288-5321

Klingspor's Woodworking Shop (9), 856 21st St Dr SE, Hickory, 28602

Lending Tree/Home Loan Center (14), 11115 Rushmore Dr, Charlotte, 28277-3442

Lenovo (3), 1009 Think Pl, Morrisville, 27560-9002

Local Government Federal Credit Union (14), 323 W Jones St (Ste 600), Raleigh, 27603-1369

Lorillard Tobacco Co (16), PO Box 10529, Greensboro, 27404-0529

Lowe's Companies Inc (8), 1000 Lowes Blvd, Mooresville, 28117-8520

Markson Scientific LLC (9), 336 E Montgomery St, Henderson, 27536-4618

McFarland & Co Inc Publishers (17), 960 NC Hwy 88 W, PO Box 611, Jefferson, 28640-0611

McKenzie Taxidermy Supply (16), PO Box 480, Granite Quarry, 28072-0480

Monkeyshines Publishers (17), 1608 Ilchester Ct, Greensboro, 27401

National General Insurance (15), PO Box 3199, Winston-Salem, 27102-3199

National Wholesale Co Inc (2), 400 National Blvd, Lexington, 27292-2631

Natural History Magazine (17), 105 W NC Highway 54 (Suite 265), PMB 204, Durham, 27713-6650

Nucor Corp (16), 1915 Rexford Rd Ste 400, Charlotte, 28211-3888

Oakwood Homes Corp (16), 7800 McCloud Rd, Greensboro, 27409-9634

Omni Farm (16), 1369 Calloway Gap Rd, West Jefferson, 28694

One Hanes Place Catalog (2), 450 W Hanes Mill Rd, Winston Salem, 27105

Otto Environmental Systems of North America (16), 12700 General Dr, PO Box 410251, Charlotte, 28273

Overton's Inc (11), 111 Red Banks Rd, Greenville, 27858-5702

PHE Inc (5), PO Box 8200, Hillsborough, 27278-8200

Pace Communications Inc (17), 1301 Carolina St, Greensboro, 27401-1032

Pace Inc (16), 255 Air Tool Dr, Southern Pines, 28387-3433

Preferred Communications (3), 410 Central Ave, Butner, 27509-1916

The Professional Putters Association (1), 300 S Liberty St (Suite 100), Winston Salem, 27101-5279

Putt Putt Fun Centers (16), 300 S Liberty St (Suite 100), Winston-Salem, 27101-5279

Raycom Sports (16), 1900 W Morehead St, Charlotte, 28208-5228

Replacements Ltd (8), 1089 Knox Rd, Greensboro, 27420-6029

RJ Reynolds Tobacco Co (16), PO Box 2959, Winston Salem, 27102

Sandy Mush Herb Nursery (8), 316 Surrett Cove Rd, Leicester, 28748

Sara Lee Direct Home Shopping (2), 1000 E Hanes Mill Rd, Winston-Salem, 27105-1384

SipcamAdvan (5), 2525 Meridian Pkwy (Suite 350), Durham, 27713-2261

The Sporting News (17), 120 W Morehead St Ste 310, Charlotte, 28202-1826

Standard Tools & Equipment Co (9), 4810 Clover Rd, Greensboro, 27405-9607

Sterling Business Services (14), 202 Dunhagan Pl, Cary, 27511-5049

Sturges Sportswear (16), 7752 NC 48, Battleboro, 27809

Syngenta (16), 410 Swing Rd, Greensboro, 27409-2012

Tafford Uniforms (2), PO Box 481912, Charlotte, 28269

Texwipe Co (16), 1210 S Park Dr, Kernersville, 27284-3104

ThorLo Inc (16), 2210 Newton Dr, PO Box 5399, Statesville, 28687

Toter Inc (16), 841 Meacham Rd, Statesville, 28677

Turner Greenhouses (8), US Hwy 117 S, PO Box 1260, Goldsboro, 27533

UMI Publications Inc (17), 6100 Orr Rd, Charlotte, 28213-6326

Uwharrie Capital Corp (14), PO Box 338, Albemarle, 28002-0338

VF Imagewear (2), 105 Corporate Center Blvd, Greensboro, 27408

Village Interiors Carpet One (8), 3203 Hwy 70 SE, Newton, 28658

Wake Forest University Baptist Medical Center (1), Medical Center Blvd, Winston Salem, 27157-0001

NORTH DAKOTA

Acme Tools (8), 1705 13th Ave N, Grand Forks, 58203-2304

Alerus Financial National Assoc (14), 401 Demers Ave Ste 100, Grand Forks, 58201-4574

Bobcat Co (16), 250 E Beaton Dr, West Fargo, 58078

Northern Greenhouse Sales (8), PO Box 42, Neche, 58265-0042

Swanson Health Products (4), 4075 40th Ave SW, Fargo, 58104-3912

Telpro Inc (9), 7251 S 42nd St, Grand Forks, 58201

OHIO

ASM International (1), 9639 Kinsman Rd, Materials Park, 44073-0002

AcuSport Corp (11), 1 Hunter Pl, Bellefontaine, 43311-3001

Adams Manufacturing Co (9), 9790 Midwest Ave, Cleveland, 44125-2497

Advanstar Communications Inc (17), 24950 Country Club Blvd (Ste 200), North Olmstead, 44070-5351

American Bronzing Co (16), 1313 Alum Creek Dr, Columbus, 43209-2706

American Greetings Corp (16), 1 American Rd, Cleveland, 44144

American Insurance Administrators Inc (15), 3070 Riverside Dr, Columbus, 43221

American Modern Insurance Group (15), 7000 Midland Blvd, Amelia, 45102-2607

American Trim (9), 1005 W Grand Ave, Lima, 45801

AmeriMark Direct LLC (2), 6864 Engle Rd, Middleburg Heights, 44130

Amos Press, Inc (17), 911 Vandemark Rd, Sidney, 45365

Associated Materials (8), 3773 State Rd, Cuyahoga Falls, 44223-2603

Automation Mailing & Shipping Solutions Inc (16), 1138 W Ninth St, Cleveland, 44113-1060

BBS & Associates (1), 130 Springside Dr (Suite 200), Akron, 44333-4553

BFS Credit Services Co (16), 6275 Eastland Rd, Brook Park, 44142-1301

Babcox Publications LLC (17), 3550 Embassy Pkwy, Akron, 44333-8318

Barbour Publishing Inc (17), 1810 Barbour Dr, Uhrichsville, 44683-1084

RG Barry Corp (2), 13405 Yarmouth Rd NW, Pickerington, 43147-8493

Eddie Bauer Groveport Service Center (2), 6600 Alum Creek Dr, Groveport, 43125

Bay Manufacturing (16), PO Box 1250, Milan, 44846-1250

Betterway Books (17), 10151 Carver Rd (Suite 200), Blue Ash, 45242-4760

Bigelow Electronics (3), 186 E Jefferson St, Bluffton, 45817-0125

Bluestone Perennials Inc (8), 7211 Middle Ridge Rd, Madison, 44057-3050

Butler Schein Animal Health (16), 400 Metro Pl N Ste 100, Dublin, 43017-3340

C2G (3), 3555 Kettering Blvd, Moraine, 45439

COSE (1), 240 Huron Rd E (Suite 200), Cleveland, 44115-1722

Campbell Tools Co (9), 125 N Tecumseh Rd, Springfield, 45504-3404

Charter One Bank (14), 1215 Superior Ave, Cleveland, 44114-3299

Chase Industries, Inc (16), 10021 Commerce Park Dr, Cincinnati, 45246-1333

Cincinnati Bell Inc (16), 221 E 4th St, Cincinnati, 45202-4137

Cinmar LP (8), 5566 West Chester Rd, West Chester, 45069-2914

Cintas (16), 6800 Cintas Blvd, PO Box 625737, Cincinnati, 45262-5737

Circle K Stores Inc (16), 935 E Tallmadge Ave, Akron, 44310-3566

The Clark Grave Vault Co (16), 375 E Fifth Ave, Columbus, 43201-2819

ClearSaleing Inc (16), 8415 Pulsar Pl Ste 477, Columbus, 43240-4093

Cleveland Clinic Foundation (1), 9500 Euclid Ave (AC311), Cleveland, 44195-0001

Cleveland Institute of Electronics (13), 1776 E 17th St, Cleveland, 44114-3636

The Cleveland Orchestra (1), 11001 Euclid Ave, Cleveland, 44106-1796

Coin World (17), 911 Vandemark Rd, Sidney, 45365-8974

Coldwater Creek (2), 5389 E Provident Dr, Cincinnati, 45246

The Columbus Dispatch (17), 34 S 3rd St, Columbus, 43215

Companion Plants (8), 7247 N Coolville Ridge Rd, Athens, 45701

Consolidated Electronics Inc (3), 705 Watervliet Ave, Dayton, 45420

Consolidated Plastics Co Inc (9), 4700 Prosper Rd, Stow, 44224-1068

Continental Supply Inc (9), 7505 James Dr, Cleveland, 44133

Cooper Tire & Rubber Co Inc (16), 701 Lima Ave, Findlay, 45840-2315

Cornerstone Brands Inc (5), 5568 W Chester Rd, West Chester, 45069

Crane Pumps & Systems Inc (16), 420 Third St, Piqua, 45356-3918

Dalco Electronics (3), 425 S Pioneer Blvd, Springboro, 45066-1180

Dayton Daily News (18), 1611 S Main St, Cox Ohio Publishing, Media Ctr, Dayton, 45409-2547

Decko Products Inc (4), 2105 Superior St, Sandusky, 44870

Diebold Inc (16), 5995 Mayfair Rd, PO Box 3077, North Canton, 44720-8077

Disabled American Veterans (1), PO Box 14301, Cincinnati, 45250-0301

Discover Publications (17), 6797 N High St (Suite 213), Worthington, 43085-2533

DX Engineering (16), PO Box 1491, Akron, 44309-1491

ElectroWarmth Products LLC (8), 513 Market St, Danville, 43014

Ellerbusch Instrument Co (9), 4505 Vine St, Cincinnati, 45217-1617

Escort Inc (16), 5440 Westchester Rd, West Chester, 45069-2950

Express LLC (2), 1 Express Dr, Columbus, 43230

F&W Media Inc (17), 10151 Carver Rd (Suite 200), Blue Ash, 45242-4760

FW Media (17), 4700 E Galbraith Rd, Cincinnati, 45236-2726

Fasson Roll Div (16), 5750 Heisley Rd, Mentor, 44060-1830

Fifth Third Bank (14), 38 Fountain Square Plz, Cincinnati, 45202-3102

First Merit Bank (HQ) (14), III Cascade Plaza (7 fl), Akron, 44308-1124

FirstGroup America (12), 600 Vine St (Suite 1400), Cincinnati, 45202-2426

Fitness Quest (16), 1400 Raff Rd SW, Canton, 44750-2320

Four Wheel Drive Hardware LLC (12), 44488 State Rte 14, Columbiana, 44408-9540

Fox Lite, Inc (9), 8300 Dayton Springfield Rd, Fairborn, 45324

Fragrance International Inc (16), 398 E Rayen Ave, Youngstown, 44505

GE Lighting North America (16), 1975 Noble Rd, Cleveland, 44112-6300

Genetica DNA Laboratories Inc (16), 8740 Montgomery Rd (Suite 11), Cincinnati, 45236-2100

Gerstner Woodworks (6), 20 Gerstner Way, Dayton, 45402-8408

Ghent Manufacturing Inc (10), 2999 Henkle Dr, Lebanon, 45036-9260

Gilson Co Inc (9), 7975 N Central Dr, Lewis Center, 43035

Gold Medal Products Co (16), 10700 Medallion Dr, Cincinnati, 45241-4807

Goodyear Tire & Rubber Co (16), 200 Innovation Way, Akron, 44316-0001

Grimes Horticulture Inc (8), 11335 Concord Hambden Rd, Concord, 44077-0640

Halsom Home Care Inc (16), 7905 Clyo Rd, Centerville, 45459

Havel's Inc (7), 3726 Lonsdale St, Cincinnati, 45227-3651

Health Care Logistics (16), 450 Town St, Circleville, 43113-2244

W C Heller & Co (16), 201 W Wabash St, Montpelier, 43543-1840

Hickory Farms (4), 1505 Holland Rd, PO Box 219, Maumee, 43537-0219

Highlights For Children (17), 1800 Watermark Dr, Columbus, 43215-1035

Hobsons (16), 50 E Business Way (Suite 300), Cincinnati, 45241-2398

The HoneyBaked Ham Co (4), 6145 Merger Dr, Holland, 43528-8430

Horticulture Magazine (17), 10151 Carver Rd (Suite 200), Cincinnati, 45242

Hubert Co (16), 9555 Dry Fork Rd, Harrison, 45030-1994

Huntington Bancshares (14), 41 S High St Fl 1, Columbus, 43215-6167

HY-KO Products Co (16), 60 Meadow Ln, Northfield, 44067-1415

Hyatt Legal Plans Inc (16), 1111 Superior Ave E (Suite 800), Cleveland, 44114-2529

ITW Vortec (16), 10125 Carver Rd, Cincinnati, 45242

The Iams Co (16), 8700 Mason Montgomery Rd`, Mason, 45040

Improvements (8), 8879 West Chester Rd, West Chester, 45069-2914

Insurance.com (15), 29000 Aurora Rd, Solon, 44139-1843

K-D Lamp Co (12), 101 Parker Dr, Andover, 44003-9456

KTM Sportmotorcycle USA Inc (16), 1119 Milan Ave, Amherst, 44001-1319

Kao Brands (9), 2535 Spring Grove Ave, Cincinnati, 45214

Kett Tool Co (9), 5055 Madison Rd, Cincinnati, 45227

Key Bank (14), 127 Public Sq, Cleveland, 44114

Knott's Berry Farm Foods (4), 1 Strawberry Ln, Orrville, 44667-0280

The Kroger Co (4), 1014 Vine St (Suite 1000), Cincinnati, 45202-1100

L Brands Inc (16), 3 Limited Pkwy, Columbus, 43230

Laser Label Technologies Inc (10), 4560 Darrow Rd, Stow, 44224-1888

Lehman's (8), 4779 Kidron Rd, Dalton, 44618

AM Leonard Inc (8), 241 Fox Dr, Piqua, 45356

Peter Li Education Group (17), 2621 Dryden Rd (Suite 300), Dayton, 45439

Liebert Corp (16), 1050 Dearborn Dr, PO Box 29186, Columbus, 43085

Lion Apparel (2), 7200 Poe Ave (# 400), Dayton, 45414-2547

Luxottica Retail (2), 4000 Luxottica Pl, Mason, 45040-8114

MCCS (14), 9111 Duke Blvd, Mason, 45040-8999

Macy's Inc (5), 7 W Seventh St, Cincinnati, 45202

Malco Products Inc (16), 361 Fairview Ave, Barberton, 44203

Mary's Plant Farm & Landscaping (8), 2410 Lanes Mill Rd, Hamilton, 45013-9181

T Marzetti Co Inc (4), 1105 Schrock Rd (Suite 300), Columbus, 43229-1146

Robert J Matthews Co (7), 2780 Richville Dr SE, Massillon, 44646-8396

Medical Economics Magazine (17), 24950 Country Club Blvd (Suite 200), North Olmsted, 44070-5351

Meister Media Worldwide (17), 37733 Euclid Ave, Willoughby, 44094-5992

Micro Center (3), 4119 Leap Rd, Hilliard, 43026

The Midland Co (15), 7000 Midland Blvd, Amelia, 45102-2608

Midwest Center for Stress & Anxiety Inc (7), 106 N Church St (Suite 200), PO Box 205, Oak Harbor, 43449

Moen Inc (16), 25300 Al Moen Dr, North Olmsted, 44070-5619

Moto Franchise Corp (3), 444 Lake Center Dr, Dayton, 45459

National City Bank (14), 1900 E Ninth St, Cleveland, 44114

Nationwide Mutual Insurance Co (15), 1 Nationwide Blvd, Columbus, 43215-2220

Natural Essentials Inc (5), 1800 Miller Pkwy, Streetsboro, 44241-5067

New Track Media LLC (17), 201 E Fifth St (Suite 1110), PNC Center, Cincinnati, 45202

Nilodor Inc (16), 10966 Industrial Pkwy NW, Bolivar, 44612-8991

O'Brien Manufacturing (9), 117 Industry Rd, Marietta, 45750-9355

Parker Hannifin Corp (9), 6035 Parkland Blvd, Cleveland, 44124-4186

Parker Steel Co (16), 4239 Monroe St, Box 2883, Toledo, 43606-1943

Parts Express (3), 725 Pleasant Valley Dr, Springboro, 45066-1158

Pfaelzer Brothers (16), 1505 Holland Rd, Maumee, 43537

PharmArt (6), 450 Town St, Circleville, 43113

Photoworks (16), 1 American Rd, Cleveland, 44144-2301

The Plain Dealer (18), 1801 Superior Ave E, Cleveland, 44114-2107

Plas-Tanks Industries Inc (9), 39 Standen Dr, Hamilton, 45015

Poly One Corp (16), 33587 Walker Rd, Avon Lake, 44012

Premier Farnell Corp (16), 4180 Highlander Pkwy, Richfield, 44286-9352

The Procter & Gamble Co (16), 1 Procter & Gamble Plaza, Cincinnati, 45201

The Progressive Corp (15), 6300 Wilson Mills Rd, Mayfield Village, 44143-2182

Rod's Western Palace (2), 3099 Silver Dr D, Columbus, 43224-3945

Roto-Rooter Services Co (16), 255 E Fifth St, 2500 First Financial Center, Cincinnati, 45202-4726

ST Media Group International (17), 11262 Cornell Park Dr, Cincinnati, 45242-1812

Safeware, The Insurance Agency Inc (15), 6500 Busch Blvd (Suite 233), Columbus, 43229

Schneider Saddlery (11), 8255 E Washington St, Chagrin Falls, 44023

The Scotts Co LLC (8), 14111 Scottslawn Rd, Marysville, 43041

Scotts-Sierra Horticultural (16), 14111 Scottslawn Rd, Marysville, 43041

Selman & Co (15), 6110 Parkland Blvd, Cleveland, 44124-4187

Serenity (17), PO Box 168, Maria Stein, 45860-0168

Shopsmith Inc (16), 6530 Poe Ave, Dayton, 45414

Shortage Control Inc & SC Video (5), 22643 Ascoa Ct, Strongsville, 44149-4700

The JM Smucker Co (4), 1 Strawberry Ln, Orrville, 44667-0280

South-Western Publishing (17), 5191 Natorp Blvd, Madison, 45040

Sporty's Preferred Living (5), 2001 Sportys Dr, Clermont County Airport, Batavia, 45103-9719

Standard Publishing (17), 8805 Governor's Hill Dr (Suite 400), Cincinnati, 45249

Stephens Publishing Co (17), 311 W Perkins Ave, Sandusky, 44870-4805

Sterling Jewelers Inc (16), 375 Ghent Rd, Akron, 44333-4601

Stewart-MacDonald (16), 21 N Shafer, PO Box 900, Athens, 45701

Summit Racing Equipment (12), 1200 Southeast Ave, Tallmadge, 44278-3161

Support Plus (7), 5581 Hudson Industrial Pkwy, PO Box 2599, Hudson, 44236-5019

Things Remembered (6), 5500 Avion Park Dr, Highland Heights, 44143-1992

TruGreen/ChemLawn (16), 461 Enterprise Dr, Lewis Center, 43035-9424

USI Affinity Collegiate Insurance Resources (15), 3070 Riverside Dr, Columbus, 43221-2547

United Air Specialists Inc (16), 4440 Creek Rd, Cincinnati, 45242

United Church Homes (1), 170 E Center St, Marion, 43301-1806

University of Akron (1), 302 E Butchel Ln, Akron, 44325-0001

Urban Response LLC (17), 500 S Prospect Ave, Hartville, 44632-9403

Vagabond Creations Inc (10), 2560 Lance Dr, Dayton, 45409-1581

Valentine Research Inc (16), 10280 Alliance Rd, Cincinnati, 45242-4710

K Van Bourgondien & Sons Inc (8)

Vita-Mix Corp (16), 8615 Usher Rd, Cleveland, 44138-2199

West Shore Distributors (8), 31060 Clemens Rd, Westlake, 44145-1005

Western-Southern Life (15), 400 Broadway, Cincinnati, 45202-3312

What on Earth (5), 5581 Hudson Industrial Pkwy, Hudson, 44236-5019

Lt Moses Willard Inc (16), 3972 Bach Buxton Rd, Amelia, 45102-1014

Writer's Digest Books (17), 10151 Carver Rd (Suite 200), Blue Ash, 45242-4760

Yenkin-Majestic (16), 1920 Leonard Ave, Columbus, 43219

OKLAHOMA

Amcat TeleProfit Inc (16), 300 Johnny Bench Dr (# 120), Oklahoma City, 73104-2476

American Counseling Association (1), 305 N Beech Cir, Broken Arrow, 74012-2293

American Fidelity Assurance Co (15), 2000 N Classen Blvd, PO Box 25523, Oklahoma City, 73125

Blue Cross Blue Shield of Oklahoma (15), 1400 S Boston Ave, Tulsa, 74119-3612

Dental Economics (17), 1421 S Sheridan Rd, Tulsa, 74112

EDC Publishing (17), PO Box 470663, Tulsa, 74147-0663

Feed the Children (1), 333 N Meridian, Oklahoma City, 73107

Glamour Shots Licensing (16), 1300 Metropolitan Ave, Oklahoma City, 73108

International Crystal Manufacturing Co (16), 10 N Lee St, Oklahoma City, 73102

Jantz Supply Koval Knives (9), 309 W Main, PO Box 584, Davis, 73030

Kraftbilt (10), 6504 E 44th St, Tulsa, 74145-4614

Loves Travel Stops & Country Stores (5), 10601 N Pennsylvania, Oklahoma City, 73120-4198

Lowrance Electronics (11), 12000 E Skelly Dr, Tulsa, 74128

Oil & Gas Journal (17), 1421 S Sheridan Rd, Tulsa, 74112-6600

Oklahoma Dept of Commerce (1), 900 N Stiles Ave, Oklahoma City, 73104-3234

Optronics Inc (11), 401 S 41st St E, Muskogee, 74403

Oral Roberts University (1), Graduate Ctr (7th fl), 7777 S Lewis Ave, Tulsa, 74171

PennWell Publishing (17), 1421 S Sheridan Rd, Tulsa, 74112

The Pin Man (16), PO Box 52817, Tulsa, 74152-0187

Reserve National Insurance Co (15), PO Box 138801, Oklahoma City, 73113-8801

Sportsmith LLC (11), 5925 S 118th Ave, Tulsa, 74146-6827

StatSoft Inc (9), 2300 E 14th St, Tulsa, 74104

Don Stewart Association (1), PO Box 21004, Tulsa, 74121-1004

University of Oklahoma Press (17), 4100 28th Ave NW, Norman, 73069-8218

OREGON

Almore International Inc (7), 10950 SW 5th St #270, Beaverton, 97005

Hanna Andersson Corp (2), 608 NE 19th Ave, Portland, 97232

Bridge City Tool Works Inc (9), 2545 SW Spring Garden St (Suite 120), Portland, 97219-3942

Brownell Holly Farms (6), 17251 S Clackamas River Dr, Oregon City, 97045-9493

Catch The Wind Kite Shop (11), 266 SE Hwy 101, Lincoln City, 97367-2749

Church Extension Plan (14), 4070 27th Ct SE (Suite 210), Salem, 97302-1359

Columbia Sportswear (2), 14375 NW Science Park Dr, Portland, 97229

Compass Electronics (9), 397 SW Stringtown Rd, Forest Grove, 97116

Dermac Labs Inc (16), PO Box 5268, Salem, 97304-0268

Esco Corp (16), 2141 NW 25th Ave, Portland, 97210-2578

Fire Mountain Gems (16), 1 Fire Mountain Way, Grants Pass, 97526-2373

Gossler Farms Nursery (8), 1200 Weaver Rd, Springfield, 97478-9663

Harry & David Holdings Inc (4), 2500 S Pacific Hwy, Medford, 97501-8724

IPD Co Inc (12), 11744 NE Ainsworth Cir, Portland, 97220

Informal Education Products (11), 2517 SE Mailwell Dr, Milwaukie, 97222-7329

The Instrument Workshop (16), PO Box 1060, Ashland, 97520-0050

International Society for Technology in Education (1), 180 W 8th Ave (Suite 300), Eugene, 97401-2916

International Specialized Book Services Inc (16), 920 NE 58th Ave (Suite 300), Portland, 97213

Keyboard Workshop (17), PO Box 700, Medford, 97501-0047

LaCrosse Footwear Inc (16), 17634 NE Airport Way, Portland, 97230-4999

Leslie Jordan (2), 1930 NW 24th Ave, Portland, 97210

Lithia Motors Inc (12), 360 E Jackson St, Medford, 97501-5892

Fred Meyer Jewelers Inc (16), 3800 SE 22nd Ave, Portland, 97202

Nike Inc (2), 1 SW Bowerman Dr, Beaverton, 97005-0979

Nomadics Tipi Makers (11), 17671 Snow Creek Rd, Bend, 97701-9149

NuNaturals (16), 2220 W Second Ave (Suite 1), Eugene, 97402-7112

Off the Wall Magnetics LLC (16), 60 SE Main St, Portland, 97214-3320

Oregon Freeze Dry Inc (4), 525 25th Ave SW, Albany, 97321-3900

Pacific Botanicals LLC (7), 4840 Fish Hatchery Rd, Grants Pass, 97527-9547

Pacific Spirit Corp (6), 1334 Pacific Ave, Forest Grove, 97116-2315

Portland Rescue Mission (1), PO Box 3713, Portland, 97208-3713

Random Lengths Publications Inc (17), 450 Country Club Rd (#240), Eugene, 97401-6078

Ronell Clock Co (5), PO Box 5510, Grants Pass, 97527

Stock Yards Packing Co Inc (4), 2500 S Pacific Hwy, Medford, 97501

Tektronix Inc (16), 14200 SW Karl Braun Dr, Beaverton, 97077

Norm Thompson Outfitters Inc (2), 3188 NW Aloclek Dr, Hillsboro, 97124

Tillamook County Creamery Association (4), 4185 Hwy 101 N, Tillamook, 97141-7770

Truitt Brothers Inc (16), 1105 Front St NE, Salem, 97301-1034

Universal Tea Co Inc (4), 16655 SW 72nd Ave (Ste 200), Tigard, 97224

Woodcrafters Lumber Sales Inc (9), 212 NE Sixth Ave, Portland, 97232-2976

PENNSYLVANIA

A-Mark Inc (15), 715 Twining Rd (Suite 118), Dresher, 19025-1832

ACP Medicine (17), 69 John St S (Suite 310), Hamilton, L8N 2B9

ASTM International (1), 100 Barr Harbor Dr, West Conshohocken, 19428-2959

Acurian (7), 2 Walnut Grove (Suite 375), Horsham, 19044-2286

Advanced Medical Nutrition Inc (7), 600 Boyce Rd, Pittsburgh, 15205-9742

Advanta Corp (14), 625 West Ridge Pike, Conshohocken, 19428

Ahrensdorf & Associates (16), PO Box 7494, Saint Davids, 19087-7494

Air-Scent International (16), 290 Alpha Dr, RIDC Industrial Park, Pittsburgh, 15238-2906

American College of Physicians (17), 190 N Independence Mall W, Philadelphia, 19106-1572

American Crane & Equipment Corp (16), 531 Old Swede Rd, Douglassville, 19518-1205

American Eagle Outfitters (2), 77 Hot Metal St, Pittsburgh, 15203-2382

American Mint LLC (6), 5051 Louise Dr, Mechanicsburg, 17055-4927

American Period Lighting Inc (8), 3004 Columbia Ave, Lancaster, 17603-4001

AmerisourceBergen (7), 1300 Morris Ave, Chesterbrook, 19087-5559

Ames-Tru-Temper (8), 465 Railroad Ave, Camp Hill, 17011-5611

Aon's Affinity Insurance Services Inc (15), 159 E County Line Rd, Hatboro, 19040-1218

Arbill Safety Products (9), 10450 Drummond Rd, Philadelphia, 19154

ArcelorMittal (16), 139 Modena Rd, Coatesville, 19320-4036

Arrowhead Mountain Spring Water (16), PO Box 628, Wilkes Barre, 18703-0628

Wendell August Forge Inc (6), 390 Lincoln Ave, Grove City, 16127

Black Box Corp (3), 1000 Park Dr, Lawrence, 15055-1018

Blair Corp (2), 220 Hickory St, Warren, 16366-0001

W Atlee Burpee Co (8), 300 Park Ave, Warminster, 18974-4860

CJ Hummul Co (11), PO Box 522, 422 Third St, Nescopeck, 18635-0522

Calico Corners (16), 203 Gale Ln, Kennett Square, 19348-1764

Harriet Carter Gifts Inc (6), PO Box 427, Montgomeryville, 18936-0427

Center for eBusiness & Advanced IT (1), 5340 Fryling Rd (Suite 201), Erie, 16510-4672

CertainTeed Corp (16), 750 E Swedesford Rd, Valley Forge, 19482

Charming Shoppes Inc. (2), 3750 State Rd, Bensalem, 19020-5903

Cherry Brothers LLC/Cherrydale (1), 707 N Valley Forge Rd, Lansdale, 19446

Children's Hospital of Pittsburgh (1), 4401 Penn Ave, Pittsburgh, 15224

CIGNA International (15), 1601 Chestnut St, 2 Liberty Pl (fl 53), Philadelphia, 19192-0003

Comcast Spectacor LP (16), 3601 S Broad St Ste 1, Wells Fargo Center, Philadelphia, 19148-5250

Wm F Comly & Son Inc (9), 1825 E Boston St, Philadelphia, 19125-1201

The Cracker Box Inc (16), PO Box 114, Blooming Glen, 18911-0114

Cross Country Stitching (17), PO Box 180, Quakertown, 18951-0180

DCA (16), 889 S Matlack St, West Chester, 19382

Dansk (16), PO Box 2006, Bristol, 19007-0806

Day-Timer (13), 1 Willow Ln, East Texas, 18046

Delaware Investments (14), 2005 Market St, Philadelphia, 19103-7042

Dentsply International (7), 221 West Philadelphia St, York, 17401

Destination Maternity Corp (2), 456 N Fifth St, Philadelphia, 19123-4007

Development Dimensions International (16), 1225 Washington Pike, Bridgeville, 15017-2838

Diakon Lutheran Social Ministries (1), 798 Hausman Rd (Suite 300), Allentown, 18104-9108

Dorothy Biddle Service (8), 348 Greeley Lake Rd, Greeley, 18425-9749

Drawing Board Inc (16), 101 E 9th St, Waynesboro, 17268-2200

Drexel University Goodwin College of Professional Studies (16), 3001 Market St (Suite 100), One Drexel Plaza, Philadelphia, 19104

Drug Information Association (1), 800 Enterprise Rd (Suite 200), Horsham, 19044-3595

Duggan & Brown Inc (16), 1617 Old York Rd, Abington, 19001

Easthill Group Inc (12), 263 Shoemaker Rd, Pottstown, 19464-6433

Education Direct (16), 925 Oak St, Scranton, 18515

Education Management Corp (1), 210 6th Ave (fl 33), Pittsburgh, 15222-2603

Elite Sportswear LP (2), 2136 N 13th St (Suite A), Reading, 19604-1213

Employment Publishing Inc (17), 175 Strafford Ave, Wayne, 19087-3317

Entrepreneur Partners (14), 2000 Market St Ste 720, Philadelphia, 19103-3214

Everfast Inc (8), 203 Gale Ln, Kennett Square, 19348-1735

FMC Corp (16), 1735 Market St, Philadelphia, 19103

Family Album (6), 4887 Newport Rd, Kinzers, 17535-9793

Famous Smoke Shop Inc (16), 90 Mort Dr, Easton, 18040-9202

Farm Journal Inc (17), 30 S 15th St Ste 900, Center Sq W, Philadelphia, 19102-4803

Federated Investors Co (14), 1001 Liberty Ave, Federated Investors Tower, Pittsburgh, 15222-3779

Finley Products Inc (16), 1333 Beaconfield Ln, Lancaster, 17601-5344

Fisher Scientific (16), 300 Industry Dr, Pittsburgh, 15275-1001

Fitness Systems Manufacturing Corp (7), 1745 Portland Ave, Wyomissing, 19609

Flickinger's Nursery (8), Rte 85, Beyer, 16211

The Flinchbaugh Co Inc (16), 245 Beshore School Rd, Manchester, 17345

Fox Chase Cancer Center (1), 333 Cottman Ave, Philadelphia, 19111-2497

The Franklin Mint (16), 486 Thomas Jones Way Ste 240, Exton, 19341-2561

Paul Fredrick Menstyle (2), 223 W Poplar St, Fleetwood, 19522

French Creek Sheep & Wool Co Inc (2), 600 Pine Swamp Rd, Elverson, 19520

Gary's Perennials, LLC (8), 1122 E Welsh Rd, Maple Glen, 19002-2224

Gemalto Inc (16), 101 Park Dr, Montgomeryville, 18936-9613

General Nutrition Corp (7), 300 6th Ave Fl 2, Pittsburgh, 15222-2511

Gilman's Lapidary Supply (11), 726 Durham St, Hellertown, 18055-1926

GlaxoSmithKline USA (16), 5 Crescent Dr, Philadelphia, 19112

Grade Finders Inc (17), 1500 Spring Garden St (fl 12), Philadelphia, 19130

HCI Direct (16), 3369 Progress Dr, Bensalem, 19020

Harriet Carter Gifts, Inc (6), 425 Stump Rd, Montgomeryville, 18936-9631

Heldref Publications (17), 1319 18th St NW, Washington, 20036-1802

Herr Foods Inc (16), 20 Herr Dr, Nottingham, 19362

The Hershey Co (4), 100 Crystal A Dr, Hershey, 17033-9524

Hershey Park (19), 100 W Hershey Park Dr, Hershey, 17033-2727

Highmark Blue Cross Blue Shield (15), 120 Fifth Ave (Suite 1044), Pittsburgh, 15222-3099

The History Book Club Inc (13), 1225 S Market St, Mechanicsburg, 17055

Home-Sew Inc (11), 1825 W Market St, PO Box 4099, Bethlehem, 18018-0099

Homecraft Veneer & Woodworker Supply (8), 1102 Manor Ave, Latrobe, 15650-4506

Hook & Hackle Co Inc (11), 607 Ann St Rear, Homestead, 15120

William B Hugg Enterprise Inc Swim Wear & Accessories (11), 44 W Butler Ave, Ambler, 19002-4517

ICIS Inc (2), 1908 Ringing Rock Rd, Upper Black Eddy, 18912

Industrial Instruments & Supplies Inc (9), 125 James Way, Southampton, 18966

Intelligent Direct (9), 10 1st St, Wellsboro, 16901-8167

International Masters Publishers Inc (17), 948 Plaza Dr, Montoursville, 17754-2400

Intromark Inc (16), 217 Ninth St, Pittsburgh, 15222-3506

JLG Industries Inc (16), One JLG Dr, McConnellsburg, 17233

Jenny Products Inc (16), 850 N Pleasant Ave, Somerset, 15501-1069

The Jewish Publication Society (17), 2100 Arch St, Philadelphia, 19103

Joslin Photo Puzzle Co (16), PO Box 914, Southampton, 18966-0914

Kappa Publishing Group (17), 6198 Butler Pike (Suite 200), Blue Bell, 19422-2606

Kennametal Inc (16), 1600 Technology Way, Latrobe, 15650-0231

Kerr-Hays Co (16), PO Box 711, Ligonier, 15658-0711

The Kraft Heinz Co (4), One PPG Pl, Pittsburgh, 15222

Lake Shore Industries (16), 1817 Poplar St, Erie, 16508-0427

Lefty's Corner (6), 601 Nichols St, PO Box 615, Clarks Summit, 18411-1487

Lenox Group Inc (6), 1414 Radcliffe St, Bristol, 19007-5413

Lincoln Financial Group (15), 150 N Radnor Chester Rd, Radnor, 19087

MMS Education (5), 105 Terry Dr (Suite 120), Newtown, 18940-1872

Mylan NV (7), 1000 Mylan Blvd, Canonsburg, 15317

Manning Materials (16), 680 Ben Franklin Hwy E, PO Box 250, Birdsboro, 19508-0250

Marmelstein Inc (16), 760 S Fourth St, Philadelphia, 19147

McPherson Associates Inc (1), 1235 Westlakes Dr (Suite 130), Berwyn, 19312-2412

Minitab Inc (16), 1829 Pine Hall Rd, State College, 16801-3008

Music Choice (16), 650 Dresher Rd, Horsham, 19044-2204

New Pig Corp (9), 1 Pork Ave, Tipton, 16684

NutriSystem Inc (7), 600 Office Center Dr, Fort Washington, 19034-3232

Omnigraphics Inc (17), PO Box 8002, Aston, 19014-8002

One Point (10), 101 Poplar St Unit 2, Scranton, 18509-2745

Orbit Manufacturing Co (9), 1507 W Park Ave, Perkasie, 18944

PNC Bank Corp (14), 249 5th Ave Ste 1200, One PNC Plaza, Pittsburgh, 15222-2707

Partners Health (15), 901 Market St (Suite 500), Philadelphia, 19107

Penn Herb Co Ltd (7), 10601 Decatur Rd (Suite 2), Philadelphia, 19154-3293

Penn Mutual (15), 600 Dresher Rd, Horsham, 19044-2204

Penn State Hazleton (1), 76 University Dr, Hazleton, 18202-8025

Pennsylvania Firebacks (8), 50 Levick St, Philadelphia, 19111

Pennsylvania State University Press (17), 820 N University Dr (Suite C), University Park, 16802-1012

Penske Logistics (16), Rte 10 Green Hills, Reading, 19603

Peoples Benefit Life Insurance Co (15), 300 Eagleview Blvd, Exton, 19341-1155

Pfaltzgraff Co (8), 140 E Market St, York, 17401-1219

The Philadelphia Contributorship Insurance Co (15), 212 S Fourth St, Philadelphia, 19106-3787

Philadelphia Museum of Art (1), PO Box 7646, Philadelphia, 19101-7646

Pittsburgh Parks Conservancy (1), 2000 Technology Dr (Suite 300), Pittsburgh, 15219-3137

Pocket Nurse Enterprises Inc (7), 610 Frankfort Rd, Monaca, 15061-2218

Presque Isle Wine Cellars Inc (4), 9440 W Main Rd, North East, 16428

Theodore Presser Co (17), 588 N Gulph Rd Ste B, King Of Prussia, 19406-2831

Professional Training Associates Inc (17), 46 S Linden St (Suite C), Duquesne, 15110-1091

Progressive Business Publications (17), 370 Technology Dr, Malvern, 19355-1315

Quadrant Engineering Plastic Products (16), PO Box 14235, Reading, 19612-4235

RMA-The Risk Management Association (1), 1801 Market St (Suite 300), Philadelphia, 19103-1628

Raybuck Autobody Parts (12), 2829 Saint John Rd, Punxsutawney, 15767-8501

Response Insurance (15), PO Box 4079, Scranton, 18505-6079

Rio Brands (16), 10981 Decatur Rd, Philadelphia, 19154-3297

Rodale Inc (17), 400 S 10th St, Emmaus, 18098

Rohm & Haas Co (16), 100 S Independence Mall W, Philadelphia, 19106-2320

SAE International (6), 400 Commonwealth Dr, Warrendale, 15086-7511

SEI (14), One Freedom Valley Dr, Oaks, 19456-9989

Safe Publications Inc (11), PO Box 74, Doylestown, 18901-0074

Sage Financial Group (14), 300 Barr Harbor Dr (Suite 200), Five Tower Bridge, West Conshohocken, 19428

School Annual Publishing Co (17), 2568 Park Center Blvd, State College, 16801-3005

Schultz & Williams Inc (1), 325 Chestnut St (Suite 700), Philadelphia, 19106-2616

Sculptz (2), 1150 Northbrook Dr (Suite 200), Feasterville Trevose, 19053-8409

Seybold Publications (17), PO Box 682, Gilbertsville, 19525

Sickafus Sheepskins (2), 8373 Rte 183, Strausstown, 19559

Society of Financial Service Professionals (1), 19 Campus Blvd (Suite 225), Newtown Square, 19073-3239

Stagestep Inc (5), 4701 Bath St (# 46), Philadelphia, 19137

Star Sprinkler Inc (9), 1400 Pennbrook Pkwy, Lansdale, 19446-3840

The StayWell Co (7), 780 Township Line Rd, Yardley, 19067-4200

Kirk Stieff Co (16), 1414 Radcliffe St, Bristol, 19007

Sunoco Inc (16), Mellon Bank Ctr, 1735 Market St (Suite LL), Philadelphia, 19103-7583

Supelco Inc (16), 595 N Harrison Rd, Bellefonte, 16823-6217

Sure Fit Inc (8), 8000 Quarry Rd (Suite C), Alburtis, 18011-9599

TABcom (5), 1 Maplewood Dr, Hazleton, 18202-9790

Techni-Tool Inc (16), 1547 N Trooper Rd, Worcester, 19490

Teva Pharmaceuticals USA (7), 1090 Horsham Rd, North Wales, 19454-1090

Thermal Product Solutions (16), PO Box 150, White Deer, 17887-0150

Times Publishing Co (18), 205 W 12th St, Erie, 16534-0011

ToonUp Coach (13), 11 West Ave (Suite 220), Wayne, 19087-3224

Tova Corp (7), 1200 Wilson Dr, Studio Park, West Chester, 19380

Tyco Electronics Corp (16), 1050 Westlakes Dr, Berwyn, 19312

UPMC Health Plan (1), 600 Grant St, Pittsburgh, 15219

USI Affinity (15), 1 International Plz (Suite 400), Philadelphia, 19113-1535

USX (16), 600 Grant St, Pittsburgh, 15219

Union Switch & Signal Inc (16), 1000 Technology Dr, Pittsburgh, 15219-3120

Unisys (16), 801 Lakeview Dr (Ste 100), Blue Bell, 19422

Universal Vintage Tire Co (11), 2994 Elizabethtown Rd, Hershey, 17033

University of Pennsylvania (1), 3451 Walnut St, 601 Franklin Bldg, Philadelphia, 19104-6285

University of Pennsylvania - Veterinary Medicine (Development) (1), 3800 Spruce St (Suite 172E), Philadelphia, 19104-4192

Vanguard (14), 100 Vanguard Blvd, Malvern, 19355

Vaxserve (7), 54 Glenmaura Ntl Blvd (Suite 301), Moosic, 18507-2101

Vertex Inc (16), 1041 Old Cassatt Rd, Berwyn, 19312

WESCO (16), 225 W Station Square Dr (Suite 700), Pittsburgh, 15219

Western Pennsylvania Conservancy (1), 800 Waterfront Dr Fl 2, Pittsburgh, 15222-4718

Westlake Plastics Co (16), PO Box 127, Lenni, 19052-0127

Whirley Drink Works (5), 618 Fourth Ave, Warren, 16365

White Mane Publishing Co Inc (17), 73 W Burd St, Shippensburg, 17257-1259

The Wig Co (2), 1391 McLaughlin Run Rd, Pittsburgh, 15241

Wilton Armetale (16), Plumb & Square Sts, Mount Joy, 17552

WinterSilks LLC (2), 100 Murray Dr, Warren, 16368-0001

Wire Works (9), 200 Keystone Rd (Suite 1), Chester, 19013

Woolrich Inc (2), 2 Mill St, Woolrich, 17779

WorleyParsons (16), 2675 Morgantown Rd, Reading, 19607

XL Environmental (15), 505 Eagleview Blvd, Exton, 19341-1119

Yves Rocher North America Inc (7), 102 Pickering Way (Suite 300), Exton, J4G2V7-19341-1330

Zimmerman Irrigation Inc (16), 3550 Chambersburg Rd, Biglerville, 17307

PUERTO RICO

Caribe Direct Inc (6), 107 Calle Tres Hermanos, San Juan, 00907-2306

RHODE ISLAND

AAA Southern New England (1), 110 Royal Little Dr, Providence, 02904-1860

APC by Schneider Electric (3), 132 Fairgrounds Rd, West Kingston, 02889

Advanced Financial Services (14), 25 Enterprise Dr, Middletown, 02842-7233

American Catalog Mailers Association (1), PO Box 41211, Providence, 02940-1211

American Mathematical Society (17), 201 Charles St, PO Box 6248, Providence, 02904-2294

Amica Insurance (15), 100 Amica Way, Lincoln, 02865-1158

Bale Co (16), 222 Public St, Providence, 02940

Bizzaro Rubber Stamps (6), PO Box 292, Greenville, 02828-0292

Brigade Quartermasters Ltd (11), 177 Georgia Ave, Providence, 02905-4422

CVS Caremark (7), 1 CVS Dr, Woonsocket, 02895-6146

Collette Vacations (19), 162 Middle St, Pawtucket, 02860-1013

A T Cross Co (16), 1 Albion Rd, Lincoln, 02865-3700

Domestic Bank (14), 15 Park Row W, Providence, 02903-1104

Emblem & Badge Inc (6), 16 Sunnyside Ave, Johnston, 02919-5318

Embrace Home Loans (14), 25 Enterprise Ctr, Middletown, 02842-7233

Hanna Instruments Inc (16), 584 Park East Dr, Woonsocket, 02895

Hasbro Inc (11), 1027 Newport Ave, Pawtucket, 02861-2500

Home Loan Investment Bank (14), One Home Loan Plaza (Suite 3), Warwick, 02886

Klitzner Industries (6), 530 Wellington Ave (Suite 4), Cranston, 02910-2950

Metropolitan Property & Casualty Ins (15), 700 Quaker Ln, Warwick, 02886-6681

Plan International USA (1), 155 Plan Way, Warwick, 02886-1099

Posh Papers (6), 73 Terrace Ave, Riverside, 02915-4726

Privacy Journal (17), PO Box 28577, Providence, 02908-0577

Racer's Equipment Warehouse (16), 111 Commerce Dr, Warwick, 02886-2429

Rhode Island Novelty (16), 5 Industrial Rd, Cumberland, 02864-4714

Ross-Simons (6), 9 Ross Simons Dr, Cranston, 02920-4475

Scorecards USA (16), 200 Circuit Dr, North Kingstown, 02852-0298

Union Federal Savings Bank (14), 1565 Mineral Spring Ave, North Providence, 02904

Weingeroff Enterprises Inc (16), One Weingeroff Blvd, Cranston, 02910-4019

SOUTH CAROLINA

Atlantic Publication Group LLC (17), 1796 Balfoure Dr, Charleston, 29407-3103

BJU Press (17), 1700 Wade Hampton Blvd, Greenville, 29614

Blue Cross Blue Shield of South Carolina (15), I-20 E at Alpine Rd, Columbia, 29219

Carter & Holmes Inc (8), 629 Mendenhall Rd, Newberry, 29108-6351

Communication Resources Inc (18), 23 Market, Beaufort, 29906-9184

Craig/Vartorella International Marketing & Advertising Inc (1), 277 Peckwood Rd, Camden, 29020

Garlinghouse Co (17), 2121 Boundary St (Suite 208), Burnside Bldg, Beaufort, 29902-6812

Hagemeyer - North America (16), 1460 Tobias Gadson Blvd, Charleston, 29407-4793

Hyman's (2), 5809 N Rhett Ave, Hanahan, 29410-2510

Jobscope Corp (16), 355 Woodruff Rd (Suite 406), Greenville, 29607-3481

Jones School Supply Co Inc (6), PO Box 2909, Irmo, 29063-4009

Laminex Inc (16), 4209 Pleasant Rd, Fort Mill, 29708-9328

Lazar Media Group Inc (17), 334 E Bay St (PMB 156), Charleston, 29401

Liberty Life Insurance Co (15), 2000 Wade Hampton Blvd, Greenville, 29615-1064

Links Magazine (17), 10 Executive Park Rd (Suite 202), Hilton Head Island, 29928

The MR Group Inc (9), 2042 Dogwood Rd, Charleston, 29414

Manchester Farms Inc (4), 8126 Garners Ferry Rd, Columbia, 29209-9402

Medals of America (6), 114 Southchase Blvd, Fountain Inn, 29644-9019

Menardi Mikropul LLC (16), 1 Maxwell Dr, Trenton, 29847

Mergent Inc (14), 580 Kingslet Park Dr, Fort Mill, 29715-6403

George W Park Seed Co Inc (8), 3507 Cokesbury Rd, Hodges, 29653

Seashore Vacations (19), 11 Executive Park Rd, Hilton Head Island, 29928-4781

Shakespeare Co (11), 6111 Shakespeare Rd, Columbia, 29223

Springs Global Inc (16), 110 5th Ave (fl 5), New York, 10011-5647

Voyageur Inc (11), 111 Kayaker Way, Easley, 29642-2433

SOUTH DAKOTA

Dakota Digital (12), 4510 W 61st St N, Sioux Falls, 57107-0639

Foote-Jones/Illinois Gear (16), 2914 Industrial Ave, Aberdeen, 57402-1089

Great Western Bank (14), 100 N Phillips Ave, Sioux Falls, 57104-6715

Mersco Medical (16), 1411 E Wells Ave, Pierre, 57501

Native American Heritage Association (1), 12085 Quaal Rd, Black Hawk, 57718

Rapid City Journal (18), 507 Main St, Rapid City, 57701-2733

St Joseph's Indian School (1), 1301 N Main St, Chamberlain, 57325-1656

Sencore Inc (16), 3200 Sencore Dr, Sioux Falls, 57107

TENNESSEE

ALSAC - St Jude (1), 262 Danny Thomas Pl, Memphis, 38105-1905

American General Life & Accident Insurance (15), American General Ctr, Nashville, 37250

American Healthways (16), 701 Cool Springs Blvd, Franklin, 37067-2697

AmMed Direct (7), 1971 Tennessee Ave N, Parsons, 38363-5049

Ansar Inc (1), 6651 Bethesda Arno Rd, Thompsons Station, 37179-9216

BMI (1), 10 Music Sq E, Nashville, 37203-4321

Brentwood Benson Music Publishing (17), 101 Winners Cir N, Brentwood, 37027-5352

Bridgestone Americas Inc (16), 535 Marriott Dr, PO Box 140990, Nashville, 37214-0990

Business Automation Systems Inc (16), 6949 Charlotte Pike Ste 106, Nashville, 37209-4200

Catalog Music Corp (3), 4301 Hillsboro Rd (Suite 320), PO Box 159297, Nashville, 37215

Caterpillar Insurance Services Corp (15), 2120 West End Ave, Nashville, 37203

Chattanooga Shooting Supplies Inc (16), 2600 Walker Rd, Chattanooga, 37421-1285

Comdata Corp (14), 5301 Maryland Way, Brentwood, 37027

Direct Auto Insurance (15), 1281 Murfreesboro Pike Ste 150, Nashville, 37217-2437

Ducks Unlimited (1), 1 Waterfowl Way, Memphis, 38120-2351

Eastman Chemical Co (16), 200 S Wilcox Dr, Kingsport, 37660-5147

Edo Interactive (16), 3841 Green Hills Village Dr (Suite 425), Nashville, 37215-2632

Falcon Products Inc (16), 810 W Highway 25 70, Newport, 37821-8044

FedEx Corp (16), 3965 Airways Blvd, Memphis, 38116-5017

First Media Communications Inc (16), 9149 Jones Ct, Brentwood, 37027-8537

First Tennessee Bank (14), 165 Madison Ave, Memphis, 38103-2725

Fleet One LLC (14), 613 Bakertown Rd, Antioch, 37013-2657

Formal Approach (2), 281 W Old Andrew Johnson Hwy, Jefferson City, 37760-1805

Fostoria Industries Inc (9), 114 Roscoe Fitz Rd, Johnson City, 37615

Genesco Inc (2), 1415 Murfreesboro Rd (Suite 190), Nashville, 37217-2895

Graceland (6), 3734 Elvis Presley Blvd, Memphis, 38116-4106

Hammock Publishing Inc (17), 814 Church St (Suite 201), Nashville, 37203

Ideals Publications Inc (17), 2636 Elm Hill Pike (Suite 120), PO Box 305301, Nashville, 37214-3162

Ingram Book Group (16), One Ingram Blvd, La Vergne, 37086

International Paper (16), 6400 Poplar Ave, Memphis, 38197-0100

Journeys (2), 1415 Murfreesboro Pike Ste 181, Genesco Park, Nashville, 37217-2829

Kano Laboratories (16), 1000 E Thompson Ln, Nashville, 37211

LS Records (16), 1225 Apache Ln, Madison, 37115

Lee's Nursery (8), 233 Lee's Dr, McMinnville, 37110-6939

LifeWay Christian Resources (1), 1 Lifeway Plaza, Nashville, 37234-1002

Lifeway Christian Stores (5), 1 LifeWay Plaza, Nashville, 37234

Lucky Heart Cosmetics Inc (7), 390 Mulberry St, Memphis, 38103-4212

Memphis Net & Twine Co Inc (11), 2481 Matthews Ave, Memphis, 38108

Merastar Insurance Co (15), 5600 Brainerd Rd (Suite 1A), Chattanooga, 37411-5336

Thurston Moore Country Ltd (16), 304 W Due West Ave, Madison, 37115-4511

National Federation of Independent Business (1), 53 Century Blvd (Suite 250), Nashville, 37214-4618

Nissan North America Inc (16), One Nissan Way, Franklin, 37067

No Load Fund Investor (14), PO Box 3029, Brentwood, 37024-3029

Nylon Net Co (11), 1340 Farmville Rd, Memphis, 38122

Olan Mills Inc (16), 6060 Shallowford Rd, Chattanooga, 37421-1611

Opryland (16), 2800 Opryland Dr, Nashville, 37214-1200

PI Inc (16), 213 Dennis St, Athens, 37303-2995

Reading for Education (1), 180 Freedom Ave, Murfreesboro, 37129-6926

Reading for Education (16), 180 Freedom Ave, Murfreesboro, 37129-0071

Scripps Networks Interactive Inc (17), 9721 Sherrill Blvd, Knoxville, 37932-3330

ServiceMaster Co (8), 860 Ridge Lake Blvd, Memphis, 38120-9434

Smart Dog Products (11), 1009 S College St, Winchester, 37398

Strategy Corps LLC (16), 201 Summit View Dr (Suite 250), Summit Bldg, Brentwood, 37027-4645

Tennessee Valley Authority (16), 400 W Summit Hill Dr, Knoxville, 37902-1499

Terminix International, The Trugreen Companies (16), 860 Ridge Lake Blvd, Memphis, 38120-9434

Thomas Nelson (17), PO Box 141000, Nashville, 37214

Time Logistics Inc (12), 1406 Nashville Hwy, Columbia, 38401

Tinsley Tool Supply Inc (9), 8038 Canter Ln, Powell, 37849-3143

Tractor Supply Co (5), 5401 Virginia Way, Brentwood, 37027

The United Methodist Publishing House (17), 201 8th Ave S, Nashville, 37203-3919

VF Imagewear (2), 105 Corporate Center Blvd, Greensboro, 27408

WTS Media (16), 2841 Hickory Valley Rd, PO Box 8277, Chattanooga, 37421

The Wexner Companies Inc (2), 418 S Grove Park Rd, Memphis, 38117-3518

TEXAS

A&B Equipment Co (16), 2101 Riverside Dr, Fort Worth, 76103-2120

AAFES (5), 3911 S Walton Walker Blvd, Dallas, 75236-1598

AT&T Inc (16), 208 S Akard St, Dallas, 75202

Accountants Education Group (10), 8111 Lyndon B Johnson Fwy Ste 1345, Dallas, 75251-1354

American Airlines (12), 4333 Amon Carter Blvd, Fort Worth, 76155-2605

American Airlines Inc (19), 4333 Amon Carter Blvd, Fort Worth, 76155-2605

American College of Emergency Physicians (1), 1125 Executive Cir, Irving, 75038-2522

American General Life Insurance Co (15), 2929 Allen Pkwy, Houston, 77019-2155

American Health & Life Insurance Co (15), 3001 Meacham Blvd (Suite 200), Fort Worth, 76137

American Heart Association (1), 7272 Greenville Ave, Dallas, 75231-5129

American Locker Security Systems Inc (16), PO Box 169, Coppell, 75019-0169

Amplify Federal Credit Union (1), 607 Congress Ave, Austin, 78758

MD Anderson Cancer Center - Children's Art Project (1), 6900 Fannin St (Suite FHB 1 1000), Houston, 77030-3800

Anglicans United & Latimer Press (1), 904 Forest Hill Ct, Cedar Hill, 75104-5712

Annie's Attic LLC (11), 1 Annie Ln, Big Sandy, 75755-9400

Antique Rose Emporium (8), 9300 Lueckemeyer Rd, Brenham, 77833-6453

Arch Telecom Inc (16), 210 Barton Springs (Suite 275), Austin, 78704

Astro Air, LP (9), 1653 N Bolton, Jacksonville, 75766

Balfour (16), PO Box 149107, Austin, 78714-9107

Baylor Health Care System (16), 3500 Gaston Ave, Dallas, 75246-2017

Bear Computer Systems Inc (16), PO Box 559001, Dallas, 75355

Bearingpoint Inc (14), 100 Crescent Court (Suite 700), Dallas, 75201-2112

Beauticontrol Cosmetics Inc (7), 2121 Midway Rd, Carrollton, 75006-5039

BellTower Technologies LLC (18), 2089 N Collins Blvd (Suite 200), Richardson, 75080

BenefitMall (15), 485 Lyndon B Johnson Fwy (Suite 1100), Dallas, 75244-6025

Blue Coral Slick 50 (16), 910 Louisiana St, One Shell Plaza, Houston, 77002-4916

Carol Bond Health Foods (7), 334 Main St, Liberty, 77575-4806

Boys' Life & Scouting Magazines (17), 1325 W Walnut Hill Ln, PO Box 152079, Irving, 75015-2079

Brown's Omaha Plant Farms (8), 110 McLean Ave, Omaha, 75571

Burlington Northern & Santa Fe LLC (16), 2650 Lou Menk Dr, Fort Worth, 76131-2830

H E Butt Grocery Co (16), 646 S Main Ave, San Antonio, 78204-1210

CCC of America (16), 102 Decker Ct (Suite 204), Irving, 75062

CPM Delta 1, Inc (11), 10830 Sanden Dr, Dallas, 75238

Careington International (7), 7400 Gaylord Pkwy (fl 3), Frisco, 75034-9463

ER Carpenter (16), 302 Highland Dr, Taylor, 76574

Brad Cecil & Associates (1), 2115 Arlington Downs Rd, Arlington, 76011-8210

Charity Dynamics (1), 3721 Executive Center Dr (Suite 100), Austin, 78731-1615

Charlotte Ford Trunks (11), PO Box 495, Dumas, 79029

CheckVantage (14), 26 Long Creek Rd, Austin, 78737-9303

Clampitt Paper Co (16), 9207 Ambassador Row, Dallas, 75247-4506

Collider Media (9), 619 Congress Ave Ste B, Austin, 78701-3024

Collin Street Bakery (4), 401 W Seventh Ave, Corsicana, 75110-6362

Collis Curve Catalog Sales (7), 6110 California Rd, Brownsville, 78521

Colonial Life Insurance Co Texas (15), 2600 West Freeway, Fort Worth, 76113

Comerica Inc (14), 1717 Main St, Dallas, 75201-4612

Commemorative Brands Inc (16), 7211 Circle S Rd, PO Box 149079, Austin, 78714-9770

Computer Station Corp (3), 6611 Bissonnet St (Suite 107), Houston, 77074

The Container Store (8), 500 Freeport Pkwy Ste 100, Coppell, 75019-3998

Corpus Christi Museum of Science & History (1), 1900 N Chaparral St, Corpus Christi, 78401-1114

Crazy Crow Trading Post (11), 1801 Airport Rd, PO Box 847, Pottsboro, 75076-3094

D/FW Grocers Association (1), 3044 Old Denton Rd (Suite 111), Carrollton, 75007-5074

Datapoint USA Inc (16), 8122 Datapoint Dr (Suite 300), San Antonio, 78229-3264

Daydots (16), 1801 Riverbend W Dr, Fort Worth, 76118

Dell Computer Corp (16), One Dell Way, Round Rock, 78682

Digital Speech Systems (3), 1241 N Glenville Dr, Richardson, 75081-2412

Dan Dipert Travel Service Inc (19), 7301 W Pioneer Pkwy, Arlington, 76013-2804

Diversified Healthcare Services (15), 800 E Campbell Rd (Suite 399), Richardson, 75081

Dunham & Co (1), 6111 W Plano Pkwy (Suite 2700), Plano, 75093

The Dwyer Group (16), 1020 N University Parks Dr, Waco, 76707-3863

E-Miles.com (19), 5800 Tennyson Pkwy., Ste. 600, Plano, 75024

Educational First Steps (1), 2815 Gaston Ave, Dallas, 75226

Eilenberger's Bakery Inc (4), 512 N John St, Palestine, 75801-2725

Ennis Inc (16), 2441 Presidential Pkwy, Midlothian, 76065-3723

Fairfield Industries Inc (16), 1111 Gillingham Ln, Sugar Land, 77478-2865

Finck Cigar Co (5), 6100 West Ave, PO Box 831007, San Antonio, 78283-1007

Fossil (2), 901 S Central Expy, Richardson, 75080

Frito-Lay (16), 7701 Legacy Dr, Plano, 75024-4099

Frost Bank (14), 100 W Houston St (Ste 100), San Antonio, 78205-1400

Fujitsu Transaction Solutions Inc (16), 2791 Telecom Pkwy, Richardson, 75082-3523

Galveston Bay Foundation (1), 17330 Hwy 3 (TX-3), Webster, 77598-4133

Gemini Publishing Co (17), PO Box 57931, Webster, 77598-7931

Golfsmith International Inc (11), 11000 Middle Fiskville Rd, Austin, 78753-3152

The Great Amarillo Directory (17), 2400 Lakeview Dr (Suite 113), Amarillo, 79109-1532

Great Western Supply (16), 2828 Forest Ln (Suite 2000), Dallas, 75234

Greater Fort Worth Builders Association (1), 100 E 15th St Ste 600, Fort Worth, 76102-6569

Gulf Publishing Co (17), 2 Greenway Plz (Ste 1020), Houston, 77046-0208

Harcourt Educational Measurement (17), 19500 Bulverde Rd, San Antonio, 78259-3701

Harvard Square Records (3), PO Box 19517, Austin, 78760-9517

Health Care Concepts Inc (16), 3011 N IH-35, Austin, 78722

Conrad N Hilton College of Hotel & Restaurant Management University of Houston (1), 229 CN Hilton Hotel College, Houston, 77204-3028

Home Interiors & Gifts Inc (16), 1649 Frankford Rd W, Carrollton, 75007-4605

HomeAway.com Inc (19), 1011 W Fifth St (Suite 300), Austin, 78703-5363

Idearc Media Corp (16), 2200 W Airfield Dr, Dallas, 75261

Infomart (16), 1950 Stemmons Fwy (Suite1000), Dallas, 75207

International Academy - Compounding Pharmacists (1), 4638 Riverstone Blvd Ste 100, Missouri City, 77459-6157

International Currency LLC (11), 8725 Eastex Fwy, Beaumont, 77708-1307

Investors Alliance Inc (1), 300 Bowie St (Suite 100A), Austin, 78703

JC Penney Inc (5), 6501 Legacy Dr, Plano, 75024-3612

Jaff Marketing Group Inc (16), 20603 Rhodes Rd, Spring, 77388-3714

KMA Direct Communications (1), 10334 Brockwood Rd, Dallas, 75238

King Ranch Saddle Shop (8), 120 S 6th St, Kingsville, 78363

Susan G Komen for the Cure (1), 5005 LBJ Fwy (Suite 250), Dallas, 75244-6125

Landmark Graphics Corp (16), 2107 Citywest Blvd, Houston, 77042-3051

Life Line Screening (7), 901 S Mopac Expressway, Austin, 78746

Lift Outreach (1), 7370 Dogwood Pk, Richland Hills, 76118-6403

Lockhart Industries Inc (9), 9610 Skillman St, Dallas, 75243-8202

The Magni Co Inc (16), 7106 Wellington Point Rd, McKinney, 75070-5705

Marathon Norco Aerospace Inc (16), 8301 Imperial Rd, Waco, 76712-6588

Mary Kay Cosmetics Inc (16), 16251 Dallas Pkwy, Addison, 75001-6801

Mary of Puddin Hill Inc (16), 938 Cambridge Dr, Duncanville, 75137-4602

Mastergrip Inc (11), 3410 Century Cir, Irving, 75062-4904

Megger (16), 427 Bronze Way, Dallas, 75237-1019

The Menninger Foundation (1), 2801 Gessner Dr, Menninger Clinic, Houston, 77280

Mentoring Minds (17), 4882 Hightech Dr, Tyler, 75703-2613

Michael's (11), 8000 Bent Branch, Irving, 75063-6023

Miracle of Aloe (7), 4401 Diplomacy Ave, Dallas, 75261-2688

Mr G's Enterprises (16), 5613 Elliott Reeder Rd, Fort Worth, 76117-6013

MoneyGram International (14), 2828 N Harwood (fl 15), Dallas, 75201

MultiView (1), 7701 Las Colinas Ridge (Suite 800), Irving, 75063-7555

NPI (16), 14901 Trinity Blvd, Fort Worth, 76155

NRS (11), 1410 S Fm 51, Decatur, 76234-2416

National Motor Club of America Inc (1), 130 E John Carpenter Fwy, Irving, 75062-2708

National Pecan Co (4), 5757 Main St (Suite 205), Frisco, 75034

Naveen Jindal School of Management (1), 800 W Campbell Rd (SM 42), Richardson, 75080-3021

Neiman-Marcus Group (8), 4121 Pinnacle Point Drive # 100, Dallas, 75211-1570

NestFamily.com (3), PO Box 293446, Lewisville, 75029

NextScreen LLC (17), 8868 Research Blvd Ste 108, Austin, 78758-6446

Nissan Motor Acceptance Corp (14), 8900 Freeport Pkwy, Irving, 75063

No Fault Sports Products (11), 2101 Briarglen Dr, Houston, 77027-3711

North America Life Insurance Co (15), 1010 Ranch Rd 620 S (Suite 215), Lakeway, 78734-5639

Oblate Missions (1), 323 Oblate Dr, PO Box 659432, San Antonio, 78265-9432

Oleda & Co Inc (16), 7700 Camp Bowie W, Fort Worth, 76116-6450

Orange Leap (1), 13800 Montfort Dr (Suite 220), Dallas, 75240-4347

Pecan Producers International (4), 2131 E State Hwy 31, Corsicana, 75151-1301

Pier 1 Imports Inc (8), 100 Pier 1 Pl, Fort Worth, 76102-2600

Pittman & Davis Inc (4), 801 N Expressway 77, Harlingen, 78552

Pizza Hut Inc (16), 7100 Corporate Dr, Plano, 75024

Powr-Flite, a Tacony Co (9), 3101 Wichita Ct, Fort Worth, 76140-1755

The Psychological Corp (17), 19500 Bulverde Rd, San Antonio, 78259

Reliant Energy (16), 1201 Fannin St, Houston, 77002

Rent-A-Center Inc (16), 5501 Headquarters Dr, Plano, 75024

Rhythm Band Inc (11), 1316 E Lancaster Ave, Fort Worth, 76102-6634

RobbinsKersten Direct (1), 855 E Collins Blvd, Richardson, 75081-2251

Ronco Corp (16), 1779 Wells Branch Pkwy (#110B-337), Austin, 78728

Rose Electronics (3), 10707 Stancliff Rd, Houston, 77099

SCA Promotions Inc (15), 3030 Lyndon B Johnson Fwy (Suite 300), Dallas, 75234

SCI Management (16), 1929 Allen Pkwy, Houston, 77019-2506

SWBC (14), 9311 San Pedro Ave (Suite 600), San Antonio, 78216-4459

Sa-So (16), 525 N Great Southwest Pkwy, Arlington, 76011

Sabre Holdings Inc (19), 3150 Sabre Dr, Southlake, 76092-2103

Safeguard Business Systems Inc (16), 8585 N Stemmons Fwy (Suite 600N), Dallas, 75247-3824

Sally Beauty Supply LLC (7), 3001 Colorado Blvd, Denton, 76210

San Antonio Express-News (17), Ave E & Third St, San Antonio, 78205

Shell Oil Co (16), PO Box 2463, Houston, 77252

Society of Petroleum Engineers (1), 222 Palisades Creek Dr, Richardson, 75080-2040

Specialized Association Services (1), 130 E John Carpenter Fwy, Irving, 75062-2708

Specialized Products Co (16), 1100 S Kimball Ave, Southlake, 76092

Sport Supply Group (11), 1901 Diplomat Dr, Dallas, 75234

Squadron Mail Order (16), 1115 Crowley Dr, Carrollton, 75011-1312

START International (9), 4270 Airborn Dr, Addison, 75001-5182

Steck-Vaughn (17), 10801 N Mopac Expy (Bldg 3), Austin, 78759-5415

Suez Energy North America (16), 1990 Post Oak Blvd (Suite 1900), Houston, 77056-3831

Sweepstakes Clearinghouse (16), 2000 E Lamar Blvd, Dallas, 76006

TWL Knowledge Group (3), 4101 International Pkwy, Carrollton, 75007

TXU Energy (16), 6555 Sierra Dr, Irving, 77002-6336

Tandy Leather Co (11), 1900 SE Loop 820, Fort Worth, 76140-1003

Texas Children's Hospital (1), 6621 Fannin St, Houston, 77030

Texas Farm Bureau Insurance Cos (15), 7420 Fish Pond Rd, Waco, 76710-1010

Texas Industries Inc (16), 1341 W Mockingbird Ln, Dallas, 75247

Texas Monthly (17), 816 Congress Ave Ste 1700, Austin, 78701-2643

Texas Parks & Wildlife Dept (1), 4200 Smith School Rd, Austin, 78744

Texas Refinery Corp (9), 840 N Main St, Fort Worth, 76106-9419

Time Products International (16), 501 Pierce St, Del Rio, 78840-5456

Tools for Wellness (7), 2900 N Quinlan Rd (Suite B240-217), Austin, 78732

TransFirst Holdings Inc (14), 5400 Lyndon B Johnson Fwy (Suite 900), Dallas, 75240-1054

Tucker Electronics Co (3), 1717 Reserve St, Garland, 75042

Tyco Valves & Controls (16), 10707 Clay Rd (#200), Houston, 77041-5497

USAA (15), 9800 Fredericksburg Rd, USAA Building, San Antonio, 78240-4100

USAA Alliance Services Marketing (14), 9800 Fredericksburg Rd, San Antonio, 78288-0141

Universal Fidelity Corp (14), 16325 Westheimer Rd, Houston, 77082-1233

University of North Texas (1), 1155 Union Cir #311277, Denton, 76203-5017

University of Texas School of Law (1), 727 E Dean Keeton St, Continuing Legal Education, Austin, 78705-3224

Village Weavers (16), 418 Villita St Ste 800, San Antonio, 78205-2910

Vintage Wood Works (8), 9195 Hwy 34 S, Quinlan, 75474

Visionworks of America Inc (7), 175 E Houston St (Floor 6), San Antonio, 78205-2210

WRS Group Ltd (7), 5045 Franklin Ave, Waco, 76710-6919

Whole Foods Market Inc (4), 550 Bowie St (Ste 99), Austin, 78703-4644

Wildseed Farms (8), 100 Legacy Dr, PO Box 3000, Fredericksburg, 78624

Williamson-Dickie Manufacturing Co (2), 509 W Vickery Blvd, Fort Worth, 76104

Wycliffe Bible Translators (17), 7500 W Camp Wisdom Rd, Dallas, 75236-5629

Zale Corp (6), 901 W Walnut Hill Ln, Irving, 75038-1001

Zig Ziglar Corp (16), 5050 W Park Blvd (Suite 700), Plano, 75093

UTAH

Altiris (16), 588 W 400 St, Lindon, 84042

American Civil Defense Association (16), 12162 S Business Park Dr (Suite 208), Draper, 84020

Basic Research (7), 5742 Harold Gatty Dr, Salt Lake City, 84116-3762

Best Friends Animal Society (1), 5001 Angel Canyon Rd, Kanab, 84741-5000

CHG (7), 6440 S Millrock Dr (Suite 175), Salt Lake City, 84121

CollegeAmerica (1), 4021 S 700 E (Suite 300), Salt Lake City, 84107-2184

Comphealth (16), 6440 Millrock Dr (Suite 175), Salt Lake City, 84121-5892

Consumer Credit Advocates Inc (16), 4746 S 900th E (Suite 240), Salt Lake City, 84117

Deseret Book (16), PO Box 30178, Salt Lake City, 84130-0178

EduTrek (16), 155 N 400 W (Suite 150), Salt Lake City, 84103-1132

Emergency Essentials Inc (16), 653 N 1500th W, Orem, 84057-2831

Equitable Life & Casualty Insurance Co (15), Three Triad Ctr, Salt Lake City, 84180-1200

Franklin Estimating Systems (17), 2391 S 1560 W Ste B, Woods Cross, 84087-2378

InterContinental Hotels Group (19), Three Ravinia Dr (Suite 100), Atlanta, 30346-2149

Iomega Corp (16), 4059 S 1900 W, Roy, 84067

Love To Learn Inc (5), 741 N State Rd 198, Salem, 84653

Merrick Bank (14), 10705 S Jordan Gtwy (Suite 200), South Jordan, 84095-3977

O'Currance Inc (18), 11747 S Lonepeak Pkwy (Suite 100), Draper, 84020-6876

1-800-Contacts (7), 261 Data Dr, Draper, 84020

Power Music (16), P.O. Box 3030, Salt Lake City, 84110

Propay USA Inc (14), 3400 N Ashton Blvd (Suite 200), Lehi, 84043-5310

Sundance Catalog Co (6), 3865 W 2400 S, Salt Lake City, 84120-7212

Tamrac Inc (2), 154 E 21st St, Ogden, 84401

Ultradent Products Inc (7), 505 W 10200 S, South Jordan, 84095-3935

Western River Expeditions (19), 7258 Racquet Club Dr, Salt Lake City, 84121-4599

VERMONT

American Meadows Inc & Vermont Wild Flowers Farm (8), 2438 Shelburne Rd., Ste. 1, Shelburne, 05482

Authentic Designs (8), 154 Mill Rd, West Rupert, 05776-9716

Brown & Jenkins Trading Co (4), 3929 Vermont Rt 15, Jeffersonville, 05464

CTC Corp (16), 254 Benmont Ave, Bennington, 05201

Communication Industries Corp (10), 117 J L H Memorial Dr, Grafton, 05146-0116

Dakin Farm (4), 5797 Rte 7, Ferrisburgh, 05456-9798

Gardener's Supply Co (8), 128 Intervale Rd, Burlington, 05401-2804

Green Mountain Coffee Roasters, Inc (4), 33 Coffee Ln, Waterbury, 05676

Harrington's of Vermont Inc (4), 210 E Main St, Richmond, 05477-7721

Hearthside Quilts & Supplies (11), 90 Mechanicsville Rd, PO Box 610, Hinesburg, 05461

Hemmings Motor News (17), PO Box 256, Bennington, 05201

International Coins & Currency Inc (6), 62 Ridge St, Montpelier, 05602

Le Jardin Du Gourmet (8), 1354 Memorial Dr, Saint Johnsbury Center, 05863

Maple Grove Farms of Vermont Inc (4), 1052 Portland St, Saint Johnsbury, 05819-2815

McGaw Graphics (6), 6378 Route 7A, Manchester Center, 05250

National Pension Service Inc (14), 40 Main St (Suite 300), Burlington, 05401-8433

The Orvis Co Inc (11), 4180 Main St, Manchester, 05254

Perennial Pleasures Nursery (8), 63 Brickhouse Rd, East Hardwick, 05836

Power & Telephone Supply (16), 44 Hull St # 2, Randolph, 05060-1102

Rutland Products (16), 38 Merchants Row, Rutland, 05701-2853

Spates The Florist (8), PO Box 407, Newport, 05855-5729

Sugarbush Farm Inc (4), 591 Sugarbush Farm Rd, Woodstock, 05091

Tuttle Printing & Engraving (10), 414 Quality Ln, Rutland, 05702

The Vermont Country Store (5), 5650 Main St, Manchester Center, 05255-9711

Vermont Media Publishing Co (17), PO Box 310, West Dover, 05356-0310

Vermont Ski Areas Association (1), 26 State St, PO Box 368, Montpelier, 05601

Vermont Teddy Bear Co (6), 6655 Shelburne Rd, Shelburne, 05482

Watering Inc/Hemmings Motor News (17), 222 W Main St, Bennington, 05201-2103

VIRGINIA

ARE Press (1), 215 67th St, Virginia Beach, 23451-2061

Affinity4 (16), 999 Waterside Dr (Suite 1910), Norfolk, 23510-3319

Airlines Reporting Corp (16), 3000 Wilson Blvd Ste 300, Arlington, 22201-3862

American Diabetes Association (1), 1701 N Beauregard St, Alexandria, 22311-1733

American Society of Civil Engineers (1), 1801 Alexander Bell Dr, Reston, 20191-4382

American Trucking Association (1), 950 N Glebe Rd (Suite 210), Arlington, 22203-4181

Army Times Publishing Co (17), 6883 Commercial Dr, Springfield, 22151-4202

Association for Facilities Engineering (1), 8200 Greensboro Dr (Suite 400), McLean, 22102

Association for Talent Development (1), 1640 King St, Alexandria, 22314

Association of Fundraising Professionals (1), 4300 Wilson Blvd (Suite 300), Arlington, 22203-4179

The Bureau of National Affairs, Inc (17), 1801 S Bell St, Arlington, 22202-4506

CMS LLC (1), 1900 Campus Commons Dr (Suite 450), Reston, 20191-1559

Campaigns & Elections Magazine (17), 1901 N Moore St (Suite 1105), Arlington, 22209-1718

CARFAX Inc (12), 5860 Trinity Pkwy (Suite 600), Centreville, 20120-1998

Cartouche Ltd (6), 100 S Early St, Alexandria, 22304

Chartifacts (6), 3221 Marlboro Ct, Richmond, 23225-0654

ChildFund International (1), 2821 Emerywood Pkwy, Richmond, 23294

ChildFund International (1), 2821 Emerywood Pkwy, Richmond, 23294-3726

Christian Broadcasting Network Inc (1), 977 Centerville Tpke, Virginia Beach, 23463-1001

Christian Relief Services Charities Inc (1), 8301 Richmond Hwy, Alexandria, 22309

Coastal Training Technologies Corp (7), 500 Studio Dr, Virginia Beach, 23452-1175

The Colonial Williamsburg Foundation (1), PO Box 1776, Williamsburg, 23187-1776

Conservation International (1), 2011 Crystal Dr (Suite 500), Arlington, 22202

Council of Better Business Bureaus - BBBOnline (1), 3033 Wilson Blvd Ste 600, Arlington, 22201-3863

Craver Mathews Smith & Co (1), 1900 Campus Commons Dr (Suite 450), Reston, 20191-1559

Crutchfield Corp (3), 1 Crutchfield Pk, Charlottesville, 22911-9097

DSP Inc USA (10), 216 3rd St NE (Suite C), Charlottesville, 22902

Darden School Foundation Executive Foundation (1), 100 Darden Blvd, Charlottesville, 22903

Defense News Media Group (17), 6883 Commercial Dr, Springfield, 22151-4202

Direct Response Consulting (17), 6849 Old Dominion Dr (Suite 320), McLean, 22101

Direct Sports Supply (11), 1720 Curve Rd, Pearisburg, 24134

Dominion Retail Inc (16), 120 Tredegar St, Richmond, 23219-4306

Eberle & Associates Inc (1), 1420 Spring Hill Rd (Suite 490), McLean, 22102-3006

Edible Landscaping (8), 361 Spirit Ridge Ln, Afton, 22920

S Wallace Edwards & Sons Inc (4), PO Box 25, Surry, 23883-0025

Emperor Clock LLC (16), PO Box 960, Amherst, 24521

Envelope Manufacturers Association (1), 500 Montgomery St (Suite 550), Alexandria, 22314-1581

Ethyl Corp (16), 330 S Fourth St, PO Box 2189, Richmond, 23218

Evergreen Enterprises Inc (8), 5915 Midlothian Tpke, Richmond, 23225-5917

FDAnews (17), 300 N Washington St (Suite 200), Falls Church, 22046-3431

Food Chemical News (17), 901 N Glebe Rd (Suite 200), Arlington, 22203-1853

Freddie Mac (14), 8200 Jones Branch Dr, McLean, 22102-3110

Fundamentals Co Inc (1), 411 Euclid Ave, Bristol, 24201

Gannett Co Inc (16), 7950 Jones Branch Dr, Mc Lean, 22107-0150

Genworth Financial Inc (14), 6620 W Broad St, Richmond, 23230

The Jane Goodall Institute (1), 1595 Spring Hill Rd (Suite 550), Vienna, 22182-4100

HSP Direct (1), 20130 Lakeview Center Plaza, Ashburn, 20147

Hamilton Beach Brands Inc (16), 4421 Waterfront Dr, Glen Allen, 23060-3375

Harris Connect LLC (1), 1400 Crossways Blvd, Chesapeake, 23320

Heartstrings Press (17), 49 Starview Pl, Dept DMMP-GL, Lancaster, 22503

Heaven & Earth (5), 1255 Fordham Dr (Suite 120), Virginia Beach, 23464

Hilton HHonors (16), 7930 Jones Branch Dr, McLean, 22102

Hilton Hotels Corp (19), 7930 Jones Branch Dr (Suite 100), Mc Lean, 22102-3389

Independent Insurance Agents & Brokers of America (1), 127 S Peyton St, Alexandria, 22314

International Auto Parts (12), 4351 Seminole Trail, Charlottesville, 22911

International Sign Association (1), 1001 N Fairfax St (Suite 301), Alexandria, 22314-1587

Intersections (14), 3901 Stonecroft Blvd, Chantilly, 20151-1032

KCI Communications Inc (17), 7600A Leesburg Pike, West Building (Suite 300), Falls Church, 22043

Key Communications Inc (17), 385 Garrisonville Rd (Suite 116), PO Box 569, Garrisonville, 22554

Liberty Tax Service (14), 1716 Corporate Landing Pkwy, Virginia Beach, 53454-5681

Light Sources Inc (16), 6220 Indian River Rd (Suite I), Virginia Beach, 23464-3514

Long & Foster Insurance (15), 14501 George Carter Way, Chantilly, 20151-1770

George Mason University School of Management (1), 4400 University Dr (MS 1B1), Fairfax, 22030-4422

Mead Westvaco Consumer & Office Products (10), 501 S 5th St, Richmond, 23219-0501

Military Officers Association of America (1), 201 N Washington St, Alexandria, 22314-2539

Military Order of the Purple Heart Svc (1), PO Box 49, Annandale, 22003-0049

MINDset Direct (1), 1700 N Jefferson St, Arlington, 22205-2817

Motient Communications (16), 11700 Plaza America Dr Ste 900, Reston, 20190-4774

The Motley Fool (14), 123 N Pitt St, Alexandria, 22314-3128

Music Treasures Co (6), PO Box 9138, Richmond, 23227-0138

NCP Solutions (17), 11100 Wildlife Center Dr, Reston, 20190-5362

National Active & Retired Federal Employees Association (1), 606 N Washington St, Alexandria, 22314-1914

National Association of Federal Credit Unions (14), 3138 10th St N, Arlington, 22201-2160

National Association of Professional Insurance Agents (1), 400 N Washington St, Alexandria, 22314-2353

National Automated Clearing House Association (1), 13450 Sunrise Valley Dr (Suite 100), Herndon, 20171

National Community Pharmacists Association (1), 100 Daingerfield Rd, Alexandria, 22314

National Contract Management Association (1), 21740 Beaumeade Cir (Suite 125), Ashburn, 20147-6237

National Court Reporters Association (1), 12030 Sunrise Valley Dr (Suite 400), Reston, 20191

National Defense Industrial Association (1), 2111 Wilson Blvd (Suite 400), Arlington, 22201-3061

National Relief Charities (1), 13318 Airport Dr, Elkwood, 22718-1760

National Rifle Association of America (1), 11250 Waples Mill Rd, Fairfax, 22030-7400

National Right to Work Legal Defense Foundation (1), 8001 Braddock Rd, Springfield, 22160-2115

National Rural Electric Cooperative Association (1), 4301 Wilson Blvd, Arlington, 22203-1860

National School Boards Association Inc (1), 1680 Duke St (fl 2), Alexandria, 22314-3493

National Technical Information Service (17), 5301 Shawnee Rd, Alexandria, 22312-2379

National Wildlife Federation (1), 11100 Wildlife Center Dr, Reston, 20190-5362

The Nature Conservancy (1), 4245 N Fairfax Dr (Suite 100), Arlington, 22203-1606

Navy Federal Credit Union (14), 820 Follin Ln SE, Vienna, 22180-4907

Newspaper Association of America (1), 4401 Wilson Blvd (Suite 900), Arlington, 22203-4195

Operation Smile Inc (1), 3641 Faculty Blvd, Virginia Beach, 23453-8000

PBS Distribution (3), 2100 Crystal Dr, Arlington, 22202

Panoptic Enterprises (17), PO Box 11220, Burke, 22009-1220

Parker Systems Inc (16), 2880 Yadkin Rd, Chesapeake, 23323-0360

Philip Morris USA Inc (16), 6601 W Broad St, Richmond, 23230-1701

The Plow & Hearth Inc (8), 7021 Wolftown-Hood Rd, Madison, 22727-2200

Project HOPE (1), 255 Carter Hall Ln, Millwood, 22646-0255

Projection Video Services (16), 5803 Rolling Rd (Suite 207), Springfield, 22152-1056

Rappahannock Electric Cooperative (1), 247 Industrial Ct, Fredericksburg, 22408-2443

SCA Direct (1), 11200 Waples Mill Rd (Suite 150), Fairfax, 22030-7418

SNL Financial (17), One SNL Plaza, PO Box 2124, Charlottesville, 22902

Sales Service/America Inc (16), 85 S Bragg St (Suite 600), Alexandria, 22312-2793

The Salvation Army National Headquarters (1), 615 Slaters Ln, Alexandria, 22314-1112

Shades of Light (8), 4924 W Broad St, Richmond, 23230-3122

Smithfield Foods (16), 200 Commerce St, Smithfield, 23430

Society for Human Resource Management (1), 1800 Duke St (Suite 100), Alexandria, 22314-3499

Software AG USA (3), 11700 Plaza America Dr (Suite 700), Reston, 20190

Southern Flavoring Co Inc (16), 1330 Norfolk Ave, Bedford, 24523-2223

Specialized Information Publishers Association (1), 8229 Boone Blvd (Suite 260), Vienna, 22182

Strongwell (9), 400 Commonwealth Ave, Bristol, 24201-3800

TT Publishing (17), 950 N Gleb Rd, Arlington, 22203

The Teaching Co (17), 4151 Lafayette Center Dr, Chantilly, 20151-1232

Tri Tech Laboratories Inc (16), 1000 Robins Rd, Lynchburg, 24504-3516

Tridium Inc (9), 3951 Westerre Pkwy, Richmond, 23233-1317

Trigon Blue Cross/Blue Shield (15), 602 S Jefferson St, PO Box 13047, Roanoke, 24011

Trout Unlimited (1), 1777 N Kent St (Suite 100), Arlington, 22209-3800

UNICOM Government Inc (16), 2553 Dulles View Dr (Suite 100), Herndon, 20171-5228

USA TODAY (17), 7950 Jones Branch Dr, Mc Lean, 22102-3302

United Way Worldwide (1), 701 N Fairfax St, Alexandria, 22314-2058

Universal Corp (16), 1501 N Hamilton St, Richmond, 23230

VW Credit (14), 2200 Ferdinand Porsche Dr, Herndon, 20171-5884

K Van Bourgondien & Sons Inc (8)

Van Groesbeck & Co (1), 2124 Hanover Ave, Richmond, 23220

The Virginia Diner Inc (4), 322 W Main St, Wakefield, 23888-2940

Virginia Home For Boys & Girls (1), 8716 W Broad St, Richmond, 23294

Virginia Port Authority (16), 600 World Trade Ctr, Norfolk, 23510-1781

Volkswagen Group of America Inc (16), 2200 Ferdinand Porsche Dr, Herndon, 20171

Volunteers of America (1), 1660 Duke St, Alexandria, 22314

Wakefield Peanut Co (4), 11253 General Mahone Hwy (Rte 460), Wakefield, 23888

Washington Gas Energy Services (16), 13865 Sunrise Valley Dr (Suite 200), Herndon, 20171-6189

Washington Marketing Group (1), 5155 N 37th St, Arlington, 22207

Young America's Foundation (1), 11480 Commerce Park Dr (fl 6), Reston, 20191-1556

WASHINGTON

All Star Directories (17), 2200 Alaskan Way (Suite 200), Seattle, 98121

Alpha Supply Inc (16), 1225 Hollis, Bremerton, 98310-3611

Amazon.com (16), 440 Terry Ave N, Seattle, 98109

Ambassador Programs (19), 1956 Ambassador Way, Spokane, 99224-4012

Ampersand Press (11), 750 Lake St, Port Townsend, 98368-2216

Aviation Book Co (17), 7201 Perimeter Rd S (Suite C), Seattle, 98108-3804

Birthday Express Inc (5), 11220-120th Ave NE, Kirkland, 98033

Brooks Sports Inc (16), PO Box 31509, Seattle, 98103-1509

Brown & Co (8), 8527 Semiahmoo Dr, Blaine, 98230

CCI Solutions (16), 1342 88th Ave SE, PO Box 481, Olympia, 98507-0481

Coast Hotels Limited (19), 600 Stewart St (Suite 1920), Seattle, 98101-1238

Coastal Hotel Group (1), 15375 SE 30th Pl (Suite 290), Bellevue, 98007-6500

Cobalt (16), 605 5th Ave S (Suite 800), Seattle, 98104-3888

The Columbian (17), PO Box 180, Vancouver, 98666-0180

Crystal Records Inc (3), 28818 NE Hancock Rd, Camas, 98607

Ebbets Field Flannels Inc (2), 562 First Ave S (Suite 200), Seattle, 98104

Expedia Inc (19), 333 108th Ave NE (Suite 300), Bellevue, 98004-5736

Fancy Fronds (8), 40830 172nd St SE, Gold Bar, 98251-9453

Financial Services International Corp (14), 701 Fifth Ave (#4200), Seattle, 98104

Fluke Biomedical (16), 6920 Seaway Blvd, Everett, 98203-5829

Gaco Western Inc (16), 200 W Mercer St (Suite 202), Seattle, 98119-3958

GaelSong (6), PO Box 15356, Seattle, 98115-0356

Gift Services Inc (6), 1800 W Fourth Plain Blvd (Suite 120B), Vancouver, 98660-1367

Grizzly Industrial Inc (9), 1821 Valencia St, Bellingham, 98229-4746

Growing Family Portraits (16), 2003 Western Ave (Suite 460), Seattle, 98121-2185

HP Indigo & Inkjet Press Solutions (16), 1115 SE 164th Ave (suite 210), Vancouver, 98683

Helly-Hansen (16), 4101 C St NE (Suite 200), Auburn, 98002

HipCricket Inc (16), 4400 Carillon Pt # 4, Kirkland, 98033-7353

Michael Jaffe Stamps Inc/Brookman Stamp Co (6), 6300 NE St James Rd, Vancouver, 98663

Brian Jenner Inc (6), 2810 W Kennewick Ave #E, Pasco, 99302-2466

Jerden Records/SpeechWorks (16), 17725 NE 65th St (Suite A-160), Redmond, 98052

Laplink Software Inc (3), 610 108th Ave NE (Suite 610), Bellevue, 98004-5125

Liberty Orchards Co Inc (16), 117 Mission Ave, PO Box C, Cashmere, 98815

Loving Promises & More (16), 1429 Commerce Ave, Longview, 98632

Masterworks (1), 19462 Powder Hill Pl NE Ste 100, Poulsbo, 98370-7472

Mostad & Christensen (16), PO Box 1709, Oak Harbor, 98277-1709

Nautilus Inc (11), 17750 SE 6th Way, Vancouver, 98683-5535

Nelson Crab Inc (4), 3088 Kindred Ave, Tokeland, 98590

The News Tribune (17), 1950 S State St, Tacoma, 98405-2817

Nordstrom Inc (2), 1617 6th Ave, Seattle, 98101

Northwest Laboratories (9), 241 S Holden St, Seattle, 98108

Orion (1), 33926 9th Ave S, Federal Way, 98003-6708

Our Designs Inc (16), 1212 W Fourth Plain Blvd, Vancouver, 98660-2023

Outdoor Research (11), 2203 First Ave S (Suite 700), Seattle, 98134-1424

PACCAR Inc (16), 777 106th Ave NE, Bellevue, 98004-5027

Pacific Propeller Inc (16), 5802 S 228th St, Kent, 98032-1810

Pan Pacific Hotel & Resorts America (19), 2125 Terry Ave, Seattle, 98121-2709

PEMCO Insurance Cos (15), 325 Eastlake Ave E, Seattle, 98109-5466

Premera Blue Cross (15), 3900 E Sprague Ave (Bldg 1), Spokane, 99202-4847

REI-Recreational Equipment Inc (11), 6750 S 228th St, Kent, 98032

Recreational Equipment Inc (11), 6750 S 228th St, Kent, 98032-4803

Russell Investments (14), 1301 Second Ave (18th Fl), Seattle, 98101

Safeco Insurance Co (15), 4333 Brooklyn NE, Seattle, 98185-0001

Satori Software Inc (16), 1301 5th Ave (Suite 2200), Seattle, 98101-2676

Sea Bear (16), 605 30th St, Anacortes, 98221

Seattle Magazine (17), 1518 1st Ave S (Suite 500), Seattle, 98134-1456

Daniel Smith Inc (10), 4150 1st Ave S, Seattle, 98134

Spokane Teachers Credit Union (14), 1620 N Signal Dr, Liberty Lake, 99019-9517

The Spokesman-Review (17), PO Box 2160, Spokane, 99210-2160

Starbucks Corp (4), 2401 Utah Ave S, PO Box 34067, Seattle, 98134

Stress Market (17), PO Box 127, Port Angeles, 98362-0017

Symetra Financial (15), 777 108th Ave (Suite 1200), Bellevue, 98004-5135

Telect Inc (16), 23321 E Knox Ave, Liberty Lake, 99019-9461

Think Ink (10), 9709 Riverbend Dr, Bothell, 98011-4030

3D Mail Results (5), 6205 S 231st St, Kent, 98032-3208

Toland Home and Garden Inc (16), 273 N Otto St, Port Townsend, 98368-9780

University of Washington Educational Outreach (1), 2012 Skagit Ln (Miller Hall Box 353600), Seattle, 98195-3600

Virtuoso Ltd (19), 1001 SW Klickitat Way (Suite 105), Seattle, 98134-1161

Windstar Cruises (19), 2101 4th Ave (Suite 210), Seattle, 98121-2392

World Vision Inc (1), PO Box 9716, Dept W, Federal Way, 98063-9716

Zones Inc (3), 1102 15th St SW (Suite 102), Auburn, 98001-6509

WEST VIRGINIA

Almost Heaven Group (16), HC 67 Box 539 BB, Renick, 24966

Bike Nashbar (11), PO Box 1455, Crab Orchard, 25827-1455

Darco International Inc (9), 810 Memorial Blvd, Huntington, 25701-7002

The Legal Studies Forum (1), 101 Law School Dr, Morgantown, 26505

Mountain Craft Shop Co (11), 7901 Proctor Creek Rd, RR1 Box 122, Proctor, 26055

National Humane Education Society (1), 3731 Berryville Pike, Charles Town, 25415

Sunshine Farm & Gardens (8), HC 67 Box 539B, Renick, 24966

Whitaker National (16), 533 Fourth Ave (12th fl), Huntington, 25701-1318

Woodcraft Supply Corp LLC (9), 1177 Rosemar Rd, Parkersburg, 26105-8272

WISCONSIN

AW Direct Inc (12), 1125 Deming Way, Madison, 53717-1953

Air-Lec Industries Inc (16), 3300 Commercial Ave, Madison, 53714-1458

Amateur Electronic Supply LLC (16), 5710 W Good Hope Rd, Milwaukee, 53223

American Appraisal Associates (14), 411 E Wisconsin Ave (Suite 1900), Milwaukee, 53202-4466

American Family Insurance Group (15), 6000 American Pkwy, Madison, 53783-0001

American Girl Brands LLC (6), 8400 Fairway Pl, Middleton, 53562-2548

American Health & Safety Inc (16), 325 Industrial Cir, Stoughton, 53589

American Society for Quality (1), 600 N Plankinton Ave, Milwaukee, 53203

Amtelco (16), 4800 Curtin Dr, McFarland, 53558

Artful Home (8)

As We Change (7), 250 City Center, Oshkosh, 54901

Associated Bag Co (10), 400 W Boden St, Milwaukee, 53207-7120

Assurant Health (15), 501 W Michigan St, Milwaukee, 53203-2706

Brady Corp (16), 6555 W Good Hope Rd, Milwaukee, 53223

BrownCor International (5), 500 W Oklahoma Ave, Milwaukee, 53207

BUYSEASONS Inc (5), 5915 S Moorland Rd, New Berlin, 53151

C&H Distributors LLC (9), 770 S 70th St, PO Box 14770, Milwaukee, 53214-0770

Camelot Enterprises (9), 8234 199th Ave, Bristol, 53104-9701

Carson's (16), 331 W Wisconsin Ave, Milwaukee, 53203-2201

Centaur Forge LLC (9), 117 N Spring St, Burlington, 53105-1532

Cherry Tree Toys Inc (11), 12446 W State Rd 81, Beloit, 53511-8049

The Company Store Inc (16), 455 Park Plaza Dr, La Crosse, 54601-4445

The Computer Supply People (3), N93 W14636 Whitaker Way, Menomonee Falls, 53051

Conney Safety Products LLC (7), 3202 Latham Dr, Madison, 53744-4190

Cornerstone Business Services Inc (14), 200 S Washington St (Suite 205), Green Bay, 54301

Cotta Transmission Co (16), 1301 Prince Hall Dr, Beloit, 53511

Credit Union Executives Society (1), 5510 Research Park Dr, Fitchburg, 53711-5377

CUNA Mutual Group (15), 5910 Mineral Point Rd, Madison, 53705-4498

CUNA - Trade Association (1), 5710 Mineral Point Rd, Madison, 53705-4454

Cygnus Business Media (17), 1233 Janesville Ave, Fort Atkinson, 53538-2738

Demco Inc (10), 4810 Forest Run Rd, Madison, 53704-7338

Direct Supply Inc (16), 6767 N Industrial Rd, Milwaukee, 53223

Drs Foster & Smith Inc (2), 2253 Airpark Rd, PO Box 100, Rhinelander, 54501-0100

Dozier Equipment International (9), 770 S 70th St, PO Box 88031, Milwaukee, 53288

Duluth Trading Co Inc (8), 170 Countryside Dr, PO Box 200, Belleville, 53508-0200

Eastbay Running Store Inc (2), 111 S First Ave, Wausau, 54401

Educators Progress Service Inc (17), 214 Center St, Randolph, 53956-1408

Elemental Scientific LLC (9), 1607 N Richmond St, Appleton, 54911-3553

Enerpac (16), PO Box 9010, Menomonee Falls, 53052-9010

Fair Indigo (2), 579 Donofrio Dr (Suite 104), Madison, 53719-2838

FatWallet (14), 100 E Grand Ave, Beloit, 53511-6255

Figi's Inc (4), 3200 S Central Ave, Marshfield, 54404-2000

4Imprint Inc (16), 101 Commerce St, Oshkosh, 54901

Guaranty Bank (14), 4000 W Brown Deer Rd, Brown Deer, 53209

Chris Hansen (16), 16300 W Lincoln Ave, New Berlin, 53151-2837

Harley-Davidson Inc (12), 3700 W Juneau Ave, Milwaukee, 53208-2865

Herrschners Inc (11), 2800 Hoover Rd, Stevens Point, 54492-0001

Holiday Vacations (19), 2727 Henry Ave, PO Box 87, Eau Claire, 54701-6828

Hy Cite Corp (16), 333 Holtzman Rd, Madison, 53713-2109

Hygienic Fabrics & Filters Inc (16), 1301 Erie Ave, PO Box 1005, Sheboygan, 53082-1005

ITW Bee Leitzke (16), 2000 Industrial Rd, Iron Ridge, 53035-9535

Imperial Supplies (16), 789 Armed Forces Dr, Green Bay, 54304-4527

International Foundation of Employee Benefit Plans (1), 18700 W Bluemound Rd, Brookfield, 53045-2936

INWAVE Internet (16), 1131 W Enterprise Dr, Janesville, 53546

Jockey International Global Inc (2), 2300 60th St, Kenosha, 53140-3822

Jones Publishing Inc (17), N7450 Aanstad Rd, PO Box 5000, Iola, 54945-5000

JW Jung Seed Co (8), 335 S High St, Randolph, 53957-0001

Kalmbach Publishing Co (17), 21027 Crossroads Cir, PO Box 1612, Waukesha, 53187-1612

JJ Keller & Associates Inc (16), 3003 W Breezewood Ln, Neenah, 54957-0368

Kester's Wild Game Food Nurseries Inc (8), 4582 Hwy 116 E, Omro, 54963

Kimberly-Clark Corp (16), 2100 Winchester Rd, Neenah, 54956

Klockit (6), PO Box 636, N3211 Country Rd H, Lake Geneva, 53147-0636

Krause Publications Inc (17), 700 E State St, Iola, 54990

Lab Safety Supply Inc (5), 401 S Wright Rd, Box 1368, Janesville, 53547-1368

Lakewood Products LLC (11), 3188 Bowling Green Ln, Suamico, 54173

Leather Unlimited Corp (2), 7155 Co Rd B, PO Box L, Belgium, 53004

Hal Leonard Corp (17), 7777 W Bluemound Rd, Box 13819, Milwaukee, 53213

Lorman Education Services (1), 2510 Alpine Rd, Eau Claire, 54703-9560

Magna Publications Inc (17), 2718 Dryden Dr, Madison, 53704-3086

Majorium (17), 2025 Main St, Stevens Point, 54481-3019

Mason Companies Inc (2), 1251 First Ave, Chippewa Falls, 54729-1408

McClure & Zimmerman (8), 335 S High St, Randolph, 53956-1425

McFeely's Square Drive Screws (16), PO Box 44976, Madison, 53744-4976

Metso Minerals/WS Tyler (16), 20965 Crossroads Cir, Waukesha, 53186

Milwaukee Electric Tool Corp (16), 13135 W Lisbon Rd, Brookfield, 53005-2550

NBI Inc (1), PO Box 3067, Eau Claire, 54702-3067

NGL Insurance Group (15), Two E Gilman St (Stop 1), Madison, 53703-1494

Nancy's Notions LLC (11), 333 Beichl Ave, Beaver Dam, 53916-0683

Nasco (5), 901 Janesville Ave, Fort Atkinson, 53538-2497

National Business Furniture Inc (10), 735 N Water St Ste 440, Milwaukee, 53202-4103

Nelson-Jameson Inc (9), 2400 E Fifth St, PO Box 647, Marshfield, 54449-0647

Norscot Group (5), 1000 W Donges Bay Rd, Mequon, 53092

Northwestern Mutual (14), 720 E Wisconsin Ave, Milwaukee, 53202-4703

OfficeFurniture.com (8), 80 S 70th St, West Allis, 53214

P & H Mining Equipment (16), 4400 W National Ave, Milwaukee, 53214-3639

PC/Nametag Inc (16), 124 Horizon Dr, Verona, 53593

PESI LLC (17), 200 Spring St (Ste A), Eau Claire, 54703-3663

Pacific Cycle Inc (16), 4902 Hammersly Rd, Madison, 53711

Pegasus Auto Racing Supplies Inc (12), 2475 S 179th St, New Berlin, 53146-2150

Pleasant Company (11), 8400 Fairway Pl, Middleton, 53562

Potawatomi Bingo Casino (19), 1721 W Canal St, Milwaukee, 53233-2655

Prairie Nursery (8), W5875 Dyke Ave, Westfield, 53964-8579

Priests of the Sacred Heart (1), 6889 S Lovers Ln Rd, Hales Corners, 53130-0900

RBC Funds (14), PO Box 702, Milwaukee, 53201-0701

Rainbow Group LLC (11), 8233 Forsythia St Ste 120, Middleton, 53562-1496

Rand Material Handling Equipment Co Inc (16), PO Box 5195, Janesville, 53547-5195

Referee Enterprises (1), 2017 Lathrop Ave, Racine, 53405

Regal Ware Inc (16), 1675 Reigle Dr, Kewaskum, 53040-8923

Reiman Publications (17), 5400 S 60th St, Greendale, 53129

Renaissance Learning (5), 2911 Peach St, Wisconsin Rapids, 54494

Rockwell Automation (16), 1201 S 2nd St, Milwaukee, 53204-2410

Rowe Pottery Works Inc (16), 404 England St, Cambridge, 53523

Ruud Lighting Inc (9), 9201 Washington Ave, Racine, 53406-3772

Sax Arts & Crafts (10), PO Box 1579, Appleton, 54912-1579

School Specialty Inc (16), W6316 Design Dr, Greenville, 54942-8404

Sentry Life Insurance Co (15), 1800 Northpoint Dr, Stevens Point, 54481

Silver Star Brands (6), 250 City Center, Oshkosh, 54901

Simpson Electric Co (16), 520 Simpson Ave, PO Box 99, Lac Du Flambeau, 54538-0099

AO Smith Corp (16), 11270 W Park Pl (Suite 1200), Milwaukee, 53224-3643

Snap-on Inc (9), 2801 80th St, Kenosha, 53141-1410

Society of the Divine Savior (1), 1303 Milwaukee Dr, New Holstein, 53062

Sony Creative Software (3), 8215 Greenway Blvd (Suite 400), Middleton, 53562-3685

Sportime International (11), 3155 Northwoods Pkwy, Norcross, 30071

Storage Battery Systems Inc (12), N 56 W 16665 Ridgewood Dr, Menomonee Falls, 53051

The Swiss Colony Inc (4), 112 7th Ave, Monroe, 53566-1364

TDS Telecom (16), 525 Junction Rd, Madison, 53717-2152

Tackle Craft (11), W5043 480th Ave, Ellsworth, 54011-5209

Thrivent Financial for Lutherans (14), 4321 N Ballard Rd, Appleton, 54919-0001

Tomahawk Live Trap Co (16), PO Box 323, Tomahawk, 54487-0323

Total Training Solutions LLC (5), PO Box 310, Waunakee, 53597-0310

Uline (5), 12575 Uline Dr, Pleasant Prairie, 53158-3686

Uncharted Country Publishing (17), 408 S Baldwin St, Madison, 53703-4805

University of Wisconsin-Madison School of Business (1), 975 University Ave, Madison, 53706

Upstart (16), PO Box 8010, Madison, 53708-8010

Valenti Classics (16), 9848 S 57th St, Franklin, 53132-8680

Wag/Aero Group (16), 1216 North Rd, Lyons, 53148

Wm K Walthers Inc (11), 5601 W Florist Ave, Milwaukee, 53218

West Bend (16), 2845 Wingate St, West Bend, 53095

Wind in the Rigging (11), 123 E Main St, PO Box 249, Port Washington, 53074-0249

Wisconsin Historical Foundation (1), 816 State St, Madison, 53706

WYOMING

Queen Bee Gardens (4), 262 E Main St, Lovell, 82431-2102

Sierra Trading Post (2), 5025 Campstool Rd, Cheyenne, 82007-1816

Unicover Corp (6), 1 Unicover Ctr, Cheyenne, 82008-0001

Woodworker's Supply Inc (11), 1108 N Glenn Rd, Casper, 82601

CANADA

Alberta

Aardvark Enterprises (17), 204 Millbank Dr SW, Calgary, T2Y 2H9

Canada Brokerlink Insurance (15), 17520 111th Ave, Edmonton, T55 OA2

Chateau Le Combe (19), 10111 Bellamy Hill, Edmonton, T5J 1N7

ENMAX Corp (9), 141 - 50 Ave SE, Calgary, T2G 4S7

Fitter International Inc (1), 3050 - 2600 Portland St SE, Calgary, T2G 4M6

JustThink Inc (16), 85 Cranford Way, Sherwood Park, T8H0H9

Veer (16), 119 14th St NW (Suite 400), Calgary, T2N IZ6

British Columbia

British Columbia Automobile Association (15), 4567 Canada Way, Burnaby, V5G 4T1

House of Orange (2), PO Box 444, Brentwood Bay, V8M 1R3

PacNet Services Ltd (14), 595 Howe St (fl 4), Vancouver, V6C 2T5

Winn Devon (17), 6311 Westminster Hwy (Unit 110), Richmond, V7C 4V4

Manitoba

Arctic Trading Co Inc (6), Kelsey & Bernier Sts, Box 910, Churchill, R0B 0E0

Winnipeg Art Gallery (1), 300 Memorial Blvd, Winnipeg, R3C 1V1

Nova Scotia

Bear Woods Supply Co Inc (11), PO Box 275, Cornwallis, B0S 1H0

Ontario

ACP Medicine (17), 69 John St S (Suite 310), Hamilton, L8N 2B9

Alzheimer Society of Canada (1), 20 Eglinton Ave W (Suite 1600), Toronto, M4R 1K8

Bell & Howell Ltd (9), 5650 Yonge St (Suite 1802), North York, M2M 4G3

Berry Hill Ltd (8), 75 Burwell Rd, Saint Thomas, N5P 3R5

The Bombay Co (8), 98 Orfus Rd., Toronto, M6A 1L9

CAA Auto Club & Travel Agency Inc (1), 60 Commerce Valley Dr E, Thornhill, L3T 7P9

Canadian Blood Services (1), 1800 Alta Vista Dr, Ottawa, K1G 4J5

Canadian Business (17), 1 Mount Pleasant Rd (fl 11), Toronto, M4Y 2Y5

Canadian Institute of Chartered Accountants (1), 277 Wellington St W, Toronto, M5V 3H2

Daily Commercial News & Construction Record (17), 500 Hood Rd (4th fl), Markham, L3R 9Z3

Direct Energy (16), 2225 Sheppard Ave E (Suite 100), Toronto, M2J 5C2

Efstonscience Inc (3), 1 High Meadow Pl (Unit 5), Toronto, M9L 0A3

Elmwood Spa (19), 18 Elm St, Toronto, M5G 1G7

Farrow Group (16), 2001 Huron Church Rd, Windsor, N9C 2L6

Foresters (15), 789 Don Mills Rd, Toronto, M3C 1T9

Four Seasons Hotels & Resorts (19), 1165 Leslie St (Suite 600), Toronto, M3C 2K8

GE Canada (9), 2300 Meadowvale Blvd, Mississauga, L5N 5P9

Gifts Corp (6), 130 Bell Farm Rd (Unit 2), Barrie, L4M 6J4

Harlequin Enterprises Ltd (17), 225 Duncan Mill Rd, Don Mills, M3B 3K9

Ideal Industries (Canada) Corp (9), 33 Fuller Rd, Ajax, L1S 2E1

International Irrigation Systems (8), 291 Riverview Blvd, St. Catherines, L2T 3N3

John Hancock Retirement Plan Services (14), 200 Bloor St W - ET6, Toronto, M4W1E5

The Kidney Foundation of Canada/ Greater Ontario Branch (1), 1599 Hurontario St (Suite 201), Hamilton, L5G 4S1

Lombardi Publishing Corp (17), PO Box 428, Vaughan, L0J 1C0

Manulife Financial Inc (15), 200 Bloor St E, Toronto, M4W 1E5

Northern Response International (8), 50 Staples Ave - Richmond Hill, Toronto, L4B O47

Open Text Inc (16), 275 Frank Tompa Dr, Waterloo, N2L 0A1

PC Ontario Fund (1), 401-19 Duncan St, Toronto, M5H 3H1

Peak Impact Inc (14), Meriline RPO Box 78029, Ottawa, K2E 1B1

Psion Teklogix Inc (3), 2100 Meadowvale Blvd, Mississauga, L5N 719

Rogers Publishing Ltd (17), 333 Blour St E (6th fl), Toronto, M4W 1G9

Royal Bank of Canada (14), 200 Bay St, Royal Bank Plaza, Toronto, M5J 2J5

Royal Canadian Mint (16), 320 Sussex Dr, Ottawa, K2J 2G6

SDI Marketing (14), 65 International Blvd (Suite 200), Toronto, M9W 6L9

Sears Canada Inc (5), 290 Yonge St (Suite 700), Toronto, M5B 2C3

SickKids Foundation (1), 525 University Ave (fl 14), Toronto, M5G 2L3

Steptoe & Wife Antiques Ltd (8), 225 Nugget Ave, Unit 2, Scarborough, M1S 3L2

Telemedia Communications US (17), 25 Sheppard Ave W (Suite 100), North York, M2N 6S7

Stephen Thomas (1), 184 Front St E (Suite 501), Toronto, M5A 4N3

TigerDirect.ca (3), 55 E Beaver Creek Rd (Unit G), Richmond Hill, L4B 1E5

Toronto Hydro-Electric System (1), 14 Carlton St, Toronto, M5B 1K5

UNICEF Canada (1), 2200 Yonge St (#1100), Toronto, M4S 2C6

United Way Toronto & York Region (1), 26 Wellington St E (fl 12), Toronto, M5E 1S2

John Wiley & Sons Canada Ltd (17), 5353 Dundaf St W, Etobicoke, M9B 6H8

Winslow Publishing (17), 550 Eglinton Ave W, Toronto, M5N 3A8

World Vision Canada (1), 1 World Dr, Mississauga, L5T 2Y4

Prince Edward Island

Vesey's Seeds Ltd (8), PO Box 9000, Charlottetown, C1A 8K6

Quebec

Cancer Research Society (1), 625 President Kennedy Ave (Suite 402), Montreal, H3A 3S5

Coverdell Canada Corporation (16), 1801 McGill College Ave (Suite 725), Montreal, H3A 2N4

Desjardins Financial Securities (15), 200 Ave des Commandeurs, Levis, G6V 6R2

L'Entraide Assurance (15), 520 Charest Blvd E (fl1), Quebec-Centre Station, Quebec, G2J 0A2

Marimac Inc (8), 6395 Cote deLiesse, Montreal, H4T 1E5

Promotional Product Professionals of Canada (1), 455 Fenelon Blvd (Suite 202), Dorval, H9S 5T8

Standard Life (15), 1245 Sherbrooke St W, Montreal, H3G 1G3

Thought Technology Ltd (16), 2180 Belgrave Ave, Montreal, H4A 2L8

A

A&B Equipment Co, Fort Worth, TX (16)
A La Carte, Chicago, IL (16)
A-T Surgical Manufacturing Co, Holyoke, MA (2)
AAA Auto Club South, Tampa, FL (1)
AAA-Chicago Motor Club, Aurora, IL (1)
AAA Umbrella Co Inc, Northvale, NJ (16)
ABC Carpet & Home, New York, NY (8)
ABC Clio, Santa Barbara, CA (17)
ACBL, Horn Lake, MS (1)
ACCO Brands Corp, Lake Zurich, IL (16)
ACP Medicine, Hamilton, ON, Canada (17)
ADM Productions Inc, Port Washington, NY (16)
ADP Inc, Roseland, NJ (16)
ADRFCO, Washington, DC (1)
ADT LLC, Boca Raton, FL (16)
AESU Inc, Baltimore, MD (19)
AFA Service Corp, Atlanta, GA (16)
AFL-CIO, Washington, DC (1)
AGCO Inc, Norcross, GA (9)
AIG Accident & Health, New York, NY (15)
AIIM International, Silver Spring, MD (1)
AIN Plastics Inc, Yonkers, NY (16)
AMA Insurance Agency Inc, Chicago, IL (15)
AMC Inc, Atlanta, GA (2)
AON Center, Chicago, IL (15)
Aon Consulting New York, New York, NY (15)
Aon Innovative Solutions, Chicago, IL (16)
APC by Schneider Electric, West Kingston, RI (3)
APSCO, Davenport Center, NY (11)
APW-Wright Line, Worcester, MA (16)
ARAG, Des Moines, IA (15)
ARE Press, Virginia Beach, VA (1)
ARI, Orchard Hill, GA (16)
ASE Technologies Inc, Wilmington, MA (16)
ASM Press, Washington, DC (17)
ASTM International, West Conshohocken, PA (1)
AT&T Inc, Dallas, TX (16)
Aardvark Enterprises, Calgary, AB, Canada (17)
Abbeon Cal Inc, Santa Barbara, CA (9)
Abbey of Gethsemani, Trappist, KY (1)
Abbey Press, Saint Meinrad, IN (6)
Abbott, Abbott Park, IL (7)
Abbott Products, Weymouth, MA (16)
Harry N Abrams Inc, New York, NY (17)
Absolute Reservation Center Inc, Longwood, FL (19)
Academic Management Services, Swansea, MA (14)
Academic Travel Abroad Inc, Washington, DC (19)
Accelerated Learning Foundation, Fairfield, IA (17)
Accountants Education Group, Dallas, TX (10)
Accountants' Supply House, Lancaster, CA (10)
Accountemps, Menlo Park, CA (16)
Accounting with Debits and Credits with Coates & Hutchinson PC, Odenton, MD (14)
Accuracy in Media Inc, Bethesda, MD (1)
ACCUSPLIT Inc, Livermore, CA (16)
AccuTrade Inc, Bellevue, NE (14)
Ace Hardware Corp, Oak Brook, IL (16)
Achieve Global, Tampa, FL (16)
Action Direct Inc, Miami, FL (11)
Active Parenting, Marietta, GA (17)
Active Web Group, Hauppauge, NY (9)
Activision Value, Eden Prairie, MN (16)
ActivStyle, Minneapolis, MN (16)
AcuSport Corp, Bellefontaine, OH (11)
Ad-Lib Advertising Inc, Old Bridge, NJ (10)
Adams Manufacturing Co, Cleveland, OH (9)
Adirondack Direct, Long Island City, NY (10)
Admore Inc, Macomb, MI (10)

Advanced Machinery, New Castle, DE (9)
Advanced Medical Nutrition Inc, Pittsburgh, PA (7)
Advanstar Communications Inc, North Olmstead, OH (17)
Adventure Creations Inc, Costa Mesa, CA (16)
The Advertising Council Inc, New York, NY (1)
Aerovox Inc, New Bedford, MA (16)
AETNA - Marketing Product & Communication, Hartford, CT (14)
Affinity Express, Elgin, IL (16)
Affinity4, Norfolk, VA (16)
Agate Publishing, Evanston, IL (17)
Agco Spra-Coup, Duluth, GA (16)
Agilis Co, Albert Lea, MN (14)
AGORA Inc, Baltimore, MD (17)
Agri Drain Corp, Adair, IA (9)
AHC Media, Atlanta, GA (17)
Ahrensdorf & Associates, Saint Davids, PA (16)
Air Ambulance Network Inc, Palm Harbor, FL (16)
Air Chek Inc, Naples, NC (9)
Air France, New York, NY (16)
Air-Lec Industries Inc, Madison, WI (16)
Air Power USA, Los Angeles, CA (12)
Air-Scent International, Pittsburgh, PA (16)
Aircraft Spruce & Specialty Co, Corona, CA (12)
Airlines Reporting Corp, Arlington, VA (16)
The Akadine Press Inc, White Plains, NY (16)
Alamo Rent A Car, Saint Louis, MO (16)
John Alden Life Insurance Co/North Star Marketing, Duluth, GA (15)
Alexander + Roberts, Keene, NH (19)
Alfa Aesar-A Johnson Matthey Co, Ward Hill, MA (9)
Alfa CTP Systems, Tewksbury, MA (10)
Alfred Publishing Co Inc, Van Nuys, CA (17)
AliMed Inc, Dedham, MA (7)
All Star Carts & Vehicles, Bay Shore, NY (16)
All Star Directories, Seattle, WA (17)
All-State Legal, Cranford, NJ (16)
AllBrands.com Sewing Machine Superstore, Baton Rouge, LA (11)
Allergan Inc, Irvine, CA (16)
Alliance Bernstein, New York, NY (14)
Alliance of Area Business Publications, Redondo Beach, CA (1)
Allianz Life Insurance Co of North America, Minneapolis, MN (15)
Alloyd Brands, Dekalb, IL (16)
Allyn & Bacon, Upper Saddle River, NJ (17)
Almore International Inc, Beaverton, OR (7)
Almost Heaven Group, Renick, WV (16)
CM Almy & Son Inc, Armonk, NY (5)
Alpha Supply Inc, Bremerton, WA (16)
ALSTOM Signaling Inc, West Henrietta, NY (16)
Altiris, Lindon, UT (16)
Alzheimer Society of Canada, Toronto, ON, Canada (1)
Amacom Books, New York, NY (17)
Amanet, Canoga Park, CA (16)
Amaryllis Inc, Baton Rouge, LA (8)
Amateur Electronic Supply LLC, Milwaukee, WI (16)
Amazon Drygoods, Osgood, IN (2)
Ambassador Programs, Spokane, WA (19)
Ambient Shapes Inc, Hickory, NC (7)
Amcat TeleProfit Inc, Oklahoma City, OK (16)
American Airlines Inc, Fort Worth, TX (19)
American Appraisal Associates, Milwaukee, WI (14)
American Arbitration Association, New York, NY (1)
American Association for Justice, Washington, DC (1)

American Bankers Association, Washington, DC (1)
American Bar Association, Chicago, IL (1)
American Biographical Institute Inc, Raleigh, NC (17)
American Capital, Bethesda, MD (15)
American Century Investments, Kansas City, MO (14)
American Civil Defense Association, Draper, UT (16)
American College of Physicians, Philadelphia, PA (17)
American Counseling Association, Broken Arrow, OK (1)
American Crane & Equipment Corp, Douglassville, PA (16)
American Express Co, New York, NY (14)
American Family Insurance Group, Madison, WI (15)
American Family Life Assurance Co of Columbus (AFLAC), Columbus, GA (15)
American Federation of Astrologers, Tempe, AZ (1)
American Fidelity Assurance Co, Oklahoma City, OK (15)
American Forests, Washington, DC (1)
American Foundation for the Blind Inc, New York, NY (1)
American General Co, Neptune, NJ (15)
American General Life Insurance Co, Houston, TX (15)
American Greetings Corp, Cleveland, OH (16)
American Health & Life Insurance Co, Fort Worth, TX (15)
American Health & Safety Inc, Stoughton, WI (16)
American Health Information Management Association, Chicago, IL (1)
American Healthways, Franklin, TN (16)
American Institute of Chemical Engineers, New York, NY (1)
American Institute of CPAs, New York, NY (1)
American Institute of Physics, Melville, NY (17)
American Insurance Administrators Inc, Columbus, OH (15)
American International Group, New York, NY (15)
American Library Association-Publishing Services, Chicago, IL (1)
American Locker Security Systems Inc, Coppell, TX (16)
American Management Association, New York, NY (1)
American Mathematical Society, Providence, RI (17)
American Meadows Inc & Vermont Wild Flowers Farm, Shelburne, VT (8)
American Medical Association, Chicago, IL (1)
American Megatrends Inc, Norcross, GA (3)
American Modern Insurance Group, Amelia, OH (15)
American Movie Classics Holding Corp, Jericho, NY (16)
American Ostomy Supply, Earth City, MO (16)
American Period Lighting Inc, Lancaster, PA (8)
American Preferred Reader's Service Inc, Fort Lauderdale, FL (18)
American Printing House for the Blind, Louisville, KY (7)
American Psychological Association, Washington, DC (1)
American Recreation Products Inc, Saint Louis, MO (11)
American Red Cross, Washington, DC (1)
American Running Association, Bethesda, MD (1)
American Science & Surplus, Niles, IL (9)
American Society for Quality, Milwaukee, WI (1)
American Society of Interior Designers, Washington, DC (1)

American Society on Aging, San Francisco, CA (1)

American Speech-Language-Hearing Association, Rockville, MD (1)

American Student Assistance, Boston, MA (1)

American Technical Publishers Inc, Orland Park, IL (17)

American 3B Scientific, Tucker, GA (16)

American Tourister, Mansfield, MA (16)

American Trim, Lima, OH (9)

American Trucking Association, Arlington, VA (1)

The American Vintage Library, Los Angeles, CA (17)

Americans for Peace Now, Washington, DC (1)

America's Finest Pet Doors, San Luis Obispo, CA (16)

Americraft - The Gift Brokers Inc, Wendell, MA (16)

Amerisure Insurance Cos, Farmington Hills, MI (15)

Ames Taping Tool System Inc, Stone Mountain, GA (9)

Amica Insurance, Lincoln, RI (15)

Amigo Mobility International Inc, Bridgeport, MI (16)

AmMed Direct, Parsons, TN (7)

Amos Press, Inc, Sidney, OH (17)

Ampersand Press, Port Townsend, WA (11)

Amrel, El Monte, CA (16)

Amsterdam Printing, Amsterdam, NY (16)

Amsterdam Printing, Amsterdam, NY (5)

Amtelco, McFarland, WI (16)

Amvac Chemical Corp, Los Angeles, CA (8)

Analytical Measurements, Chester, NJ (9)

Anatomical Chart Co, Riverwoods, IL (7)

Ancient Circles, Willits, CA (6)

Anda Inc, Parsippany, NJ (7)

Hanna Andersson Corp, Portland, OR (2)

Andrea Electronics Corp, Bohemia, NY (16)

Angelica Image Apparel, Saint Louis, MO (16)

Angler's Catalog Co, Eagle, ID (11)

Anglicans United & Latimer Press, Cedar Hill, TX (1)

Anheuser-Busch Inc Promotional Products Group, Shelton, CT (6)

Ann Inc, New York, NY (2)

Anne Klein, New York, NY (16)

Annie's Attic LLC, Big Sandy, TX (11)

Anritsu Co, Morgan Hill, CA (16)

Anthem Blue Cross, Westlake Village, CA (15)

Anthem Blue Cross Blue Shield, Saint Louis, MO (15)

Anthem Corporate Communications, Indianapolis, IN (15)

Antiquarian Booksellers Association of America Inc, New York, NY (1)

Antique & Collectible Tools Inc, Pownal, ME (11)

Antique Electronic Supply, Tempe, AZ (3)

Aon's Affinity Insurance Services Inc, Hatboro, PA (15)

Apothecary Products Inc, Burnsville, MN (7)

Apple Inc, Cupertino, CA (16)

Appraisal Institute, Chicago, IL (1)

Arbill Safety Products, Philadelphia, PA (9)

Arbus Capital Ltd, Schaumburg, IL (16)

ArcelorMittal, Chicago, IL (16)

ArcelorMittal, Coatesville, PA (16)

Arch Telecom Inc, Austin, TX (16)

Arctic Trading Co Inc, Churchill, MB, Canada (6)

Arent Fox LLP, Washington, DC (9)

Argent Trading LLC, New York, NY (16)

Aristokraft Inc, Jasper, IN (16)

Arizona Highways Magazine, Phoenix, AZ (17)

Armbrust Paper Tubes Inc, Chicago, IL (10)

Armento Inc, Buffalo, NY (5)

Army Times Publishing Co, Springfield, VA (17)

Arnet Pharmaceutical, Davie, FL (7)

Arquest Inc, Millstone Twp, NJ (16)

Arrow Co, Indianapolis, IN (16)

Arrow Electronics Inc, Englewood, CO (3)

Arrowhead Mountain Spring Water, Wilkes Barre, PA (16)

The Art of Self Promotion, Hoboken, NJ (17)

Artech House, Norwood, MA (17)

Arthritis Foundation, Atlanta, GA (1)

Asheville Compassionate Communication Center, Asheville, NC (13)

Ashland Inc, Covington, KY (16)

Ashworth College, Norcross, GA (13)

Aspen Publishers Inc, New York, NY (17)

Associated Construction Publications, Indianapolis, IN (17)

Associated Photo, Erlanger, KY (16)

Associated Textile Rental Services, Rochester, NY (16)

Association for Computing Machinery, New York, NY (1)

Association for Facilities Engineering, McLean, VA (1)

Association for Financial Professionals, Bethesda, MD (14)

Association for Talent Development, Alexandria, VA (1)

Association of American Publishers, Washington, DC (1)

Association of Bridal Consultants, New Milford, CT (1)

Association of Marian Helpers, Stockbridge, MA (1)

Assurant Group, New York, NY (15)

Assurant Health, Milwaukee, WI (15)

Assurant Solutions Preneed Division, Atlanta, GA (15)

Astral Brands LLC, Atlanta, GA (7)

Astro Air, LP, Jacksonville, TX (9)

Astronomical Society of the Pacific, San Francisco, CA (1)

At Last Naturals, North Salem, NY (7)

Atlanta Cutlery Corp, Conyers, GA (11)

Atlantic Publication Group LLC, Charleston, SC (17)

Atlantic Spice Co, North Truro, MA (4)

Audio & Video Labs Inc, Pennsauken, NJ (16)

Audio Classics Ltd, Vestal, NY (3)

Audio-Digest Foundation, Glendale, CA (1)

Audiovox, Hauppauge, NY (16)

August Home Publishing Co, Des Moines, IA (17)

Wendell August Forge Inc, Grove City, PA (6)

Authentic Designs, West Rupert, VT (8)

Autodesk Inc, San Rafael, CA (16)

Automation Control Products, Alpharetta, GA (16)

Automation Mailing & Shipping Solutions Inc, Cleveland, OH (16)

Automod, Atlanta, GA (12)

Automotive Headphones, Sterling Heights, MI (16)

Avery Dennison Corp, Brea, CA (10)

Aviation Book Co, Seattle, WA (17)

Avis World Headquarters, Parsippany, NJ (19)

Avnet Inc, Phoenix, AZ (16)

Award Co of America, Tuscaloosa, AL (6)

The Ayn Rand Institute, Irvine, CA (1)

B

B Bunch Co Inc, Phoenix, AZ (16)

BAI, Chicago, IL (17)

BCR Enterprises Inc, Downers Grove, IL (17)

BGE Home Products & Services Inc, Baltimore, MD (16)

BJ's Wholesale Club Inc, Westborough, MA (13)

BJU Press, Greenville, SC (17)

BLS Inc, Wilmington, DE (17)

BMI, Nashville, TN (1)

BMI Home Decorating, Spring Grove, IL (16)

BNY Mellon, New York, NY (14)

BOC Gases, Murray Hill, NJ (16)

BP, Warrenville, IL (16)

BYK-Gardner USA, Columbia, MD (16)

Babcox Publications LLC, Akron, OH (17)

Babyshoe.com, Hendersonville, NC (6)

Back Designs Inc, Novato, CA (7)

Back to the Bible, Lincoln, NE (5)

Badge-A-Minit, Oglesby, IL (16)

Bahamas Ministry of Tourism, Fort Lauderdale, FL (19)

Baker & Taylor Inc, Charlotte, NC (16)

Balboa Life & Casualty, Irvine, CA (15)

Balducci Enterprises Inc, Germantown, MD (16)

Baldwin Filters, Kearney, NE (16)

Bale Co, Providence, RI (16)

Balfour, Austin, TX (16)

Ballard Designs, Atlanta, GA (8)

Bamboo Sourcery, Sebastopol, CA (8)

Bank Boston, Boston, MA (14)

Bank of America, Charlotte, NC (14)

Bank of Hawaii, Honolulu, HI (14)

The Bank of New York/Delaware, Newark, DE (14)

Bank One, Chicago, IL (14)

Banker & Tradesman, Boston, MA (17)

Bankers Warranty Group, Saint Petersburg, FL (16)

Barbour Publishing Inc, Uhrichsville, OH (17)

Bob Barker Co Inc, Fuquay Varina, NC (5)

BarnesandNoble.com, New York, NY (16)

Baron/Barclay Bridge Supplies, Louisville, KY (11)

RG Barry Corp, Pickerington, OH (2)

BarterNews, Laguna Niguel, CA (17)

Barton-Cotton, Baltimore, MD (16)

Bart's Watersports, North Webster, IN (11)

Baseline FT, Los Angeles, CA (17)

Basic Adhesives Inc, Clifton, NJ (9)

Bass Pro Shops, Springfield, MO (11)

Bathroom Machineries, Murphys, CA (8)

Baton Rouge Conventions & Visitors Bureau, Baton Rouge, LA (1)

Battery Pros Inc, Horseshoe Beach, FL (9)

Battleground Antiques Inc, New Bern, NC (6)

Baudville Inc, Grand Rapids, MI (16)

The Bauman Group, Ashland, MA (14)

Bausch & Lomb Inc, Rochester, NY (16)

Baxter Bros Inc, Greenwich, CT (17)

Bay Manufacturing, Milan, OH (16)

Mel Bay Publications Inc, Pacific, MO (17)

Bayer Corp Consumer Care Division, Whippany, NJ (16)

Baylor Health Care System, Dallas, TX (16)

LL Bean Inc, Freeport, ME (2)

Bear Computer Systems Inc, Dallas, TX (16)

Bear Woods Supply Co Inc, Cornwallis, NS, Canada (11)

Bearingpoint Inc, Dallas, TX (14)

Beau Rivage Resort & Casino, Biloxi, MS (19)

Beauty Naturally, Burlingame, CA (7)

Beckman Coulter Inc, Brea, CA (16)

Beckmann Converting Inc, Amsterdam, NY (16)

Beemak Plastics Inc, La Mirada, CA (16)

Beeman Precision Airguns, Santa Fe Springs, CA (11)

Behlen Manufacturing Co, Columbus, NE (16)

Belcaro Group Inc, Greenwood Village, CO (17)
Bell & Howell Ltd, North York, ON, Canada (9)
The Bell Group Rio Grande, Albuquerque, NM (5)
Bell Performance Inc, Longwood, FL (9)
Bellacor, Minneapolis, MN (8)
BellTower Technologies LLC, Richardson, TX (18)
Beltone Corp, Glenview, IL (3)
Beluga Bar by Caviarteria, New York, NY (4)
Belvoir Media Group LLC, Norwalk, CT (17)
Bencone Uniform Connection, Winston Salem, NC (2)
BenefitMall, Dallas, TX (15)
Benetton USA, New York, NY (2)
Bentley University, Waltham, MA (13)
J&H Berge/The Lab Mart, South Plainfield, NJ (7)
Berger's Table Pad Co, Indianapolis, IN (8)
Berkeley College, West Paterson, NJ (13)
Berkshire Direct Inc, Williamstown, MA (17)
Berkshire Record Outlet Inc, Lee, MA (3)
Berman Group, Newton Center, MA (16)
Berry Hill Ltd, Saint Thomas, ON, Canada (8)
Berway Visual Products Inc, Wilmington, MA (3)
Channing L Bete Co Inc, South Deerfield, MA (17)
Better Health Fitness, Brooklyn, NY (11)
Better Tools For Industry, Santee, CA (9)
BIC Corp, Shelton, CT (16)
Bick International, Van Nuys, CA (6)
Bigelow Electronics, Bluffton, OH (3)
Bijoux Terner, Miami, FL (16)
Biomerica Inc, Irvine, CA (7)
Biosciences-Amersham, Piscataway, NJ (16)
Bissinger French Confections, Saint Louis, MO (4)
Bizzaro Rubber Stamps, Greenville, RI (6)
Stanley Black & Decker Inc, New Britain, CT (16)
Black Box Corp, Lawrence, PA (3)
Black Entertainment Television Inc, Washington, DC (16)
Blaine Window Hardware Inc, Hagerstown, MD (9)
William Blair & Co LLC, Chicago, IL (14)
Bland Farms, Glennville, GA (4)
Blethen Maine Newspapers Inc, Portland, ME (17)
Dick Blick Holdings Inc, Galesburg, IL (16)
Blue Coral Slick 50, Houston, TX (16)
Blue Cross Blue Shield of Florida, Jacksonville, FL (15)
Blue Cross Blue Shield of Illinois, Chicago, IL (15)
Blue Cross Blue Shield of Louisiana, Baton Rouge, LA (15)
Blue Cross Blue Shield of Oklahoma, Tulsa, OK (15)
Blue Cross Blue Shield of South Carolina, Columbia, SC (15)
Blue Raven Technology, Wilmington, MA (3)
Blue Shield Life, San Francisco, CA (15)
Blue Shield of California, San Francisco, CA (15)
Bluestem Brands, Eden Prairie, MN (16)
Bluestone Perennials Inc, Madison, OH (8)
B'nai B'rith International, Washington, DC (1)
Bobcat Co, West Fargo, ND (16)
Bobley-Harmann Corp, Ronkonkoma, NY (5)
Body by Jake Global LLC, Los Angeles, CA (16)
Boeing Co, Chicago, IL (16)
Boise Cascade Holdings LLC, Boise, ID (16)
Bolind Inc, Boulder, CO (16)
Bontex, Honolulu, HI (16)
Book Publishing Information Kit, Santa Barbara, CA (17)
Books on Tape, Westminster, MD (17)
Booth Michigan, Grand Rapids, MI (17)
Bosom Buddy Breast Forms, Boise, ID (7)
The Boston Co Asset Management LLC, Boston, MA (14)

The Boston Globe, Boston, MA (17)
Boundless Corp, Phelps, NY (16)
Bountiful Gardens, Willits, CA (8)
Bowers & Merena Auctions, Irvine, CA (16)
BowTie Inc, Irvine, CA (17)
Boyd Gaming Corp, Las Vegas, NV (16)
The Bradford Group, Niles, IL (16)
Bradford Health Services, Birmingham, AL (16)
Vera Bradley, Roanoke, IN (2)
Brady Corp, Milwaukee, WI (16)
Brady Marketing Co Inc, Walnut Creek, CA (16)
Brahmin Leather Works, Fairhaven, MA (16)
Branch Banking & Trust Co, Winston-Salem, NC (14)
Brand New Products LLC, Chicago, IL (4)
Brant Publications Inc, New York, NY (17)
Brentwood Benson Music Publishing, Brentwood, TN (17)
Bridgestone Americas Inc, Nashville, TN (16)
Brigade Quartermasters Ltd, Providence, RI (11)
Brim Electronics Inc, Lodi, NJ (3)
Bristol-Myers Squibb Co, New York, NY (16)
British Columbia Automobile Association, Burnaby, BC, Canada (15)
Broadcast Electronics Inc, Quincy, IL (3)
Broadmoor Hotel Inc, Colorado Springs, CO (19)
BroadVision Inc, Redwood City, CA (16)
Broadway Play Publishing Inc, New York, NY (17)
Brocade Communications Systems Inc, San Jose, CA (16)
Brokers/Consultants Inc, Flossmoor, IL (15)
Bronson Nutritionals LLC, Hauppauge, NY (7)
Bronx Council on the Arts, Bronx, NY (1)
Brooke Distributors Inc, Miami, FL (3)
Brookfield Office Properties, New York, NY (16)
Brookhollow Cards, Rexburg, ID (10)
Brooks Equipment Co, Charlotte, NC (9)
Brooks Sports Inc, Seattle, WA (16)
Brown & Co, Blaine, WA (8)
Arthur Brown & Bro Inc, New York, NY (10)
Brown Shoe Co, Saint Louis, MO (16)
BrownCor International, Milwaukee, WI (5)
Brownell Holly Farms, Oregon City, OR (6)
Brown's Omaha Plant Farms, Omaha, TX (8)
Bruce Medical Supply, Waltham, MA (7)
Buena Vista Home Entertainment, Burbank, CA (3)
Buena Vista Winery, Sonoma, CA (16)
Buick, Detroit, MI (16)
Bull HN Information Systems, Chelmsford, MA (16)
Bulletin of the Atomic Scientists, Chicago, IL (17)
Bunker Hill Auctions, Millbrook, IL (6)
Bunn-O-Matic Corp, Springfield, IL (16)
Bunzl Distribution USA, Inc, Saint Louis, MO (16)
Burberry, New York, NY (2)
Burden Sales Co, Lincoln, NE (9)
The Bureau of National Affairs, Inc, Arlington, VA (16)
Burger's Ozark Country Cured Hams Inc, California, MO (4)
Burlington Industries Inc, Greensboro, NC (16)
Burlington Northern & Santa Fe LLC, Fort Worth, TX (16)
Burns Inc, Fall River, MA (16)
DV Burrell Seed Growers Co, Rocky Ford, CO (8)
Bushnell Corporation, Overland Park, KS (11)
Bushnell Outdoor Products, Overland Park, KS (16)
Business Automation Systems Inc, Nashville, TN (16)
Business Graphics Inc, Elmhurst, IL (16)
Business Planners & Consultants Inc, New York, NY (15)
Business Publishers Inc, Durham, NC (17)

Butler Distributing Co, Kenilworth, NJ (3)
Butler Schein Animal Health, Dublin, OH (16)
Butler Specialty Co, Chicago, IL (16)
BUYSEASONS Inc, New Berlin, WI (5)
Byron Plantation, Vidalia, GA (4)

C

C&H Distributors LLC, Milwaukee, WI (9)
C & J Clark America Inc, Newton Upper Falls, MA (16)
C&S Sales Inc, Wheeling, IL (9)
C&T Bridge Supplies, Los Alamitos, CA (11)
C2G, Moraine, OH (3)
CA Inc, Islandia, NY (16)
CAA Auto Club & Travel Agency Inc, Thornhill, ON, Canada (1)
CAIG Laboratories Inc, Poway, CA (9)
CBT Direct, Tarpon Springs, FL (16)
CCA Global Partners, Manchester, NH (16)
CCH Inc, Riverwoods, IL (17)
CCI Solutions, Olympia, WA (16)
CCIM Institute, Chicago, IL (1)
CDW Corp, Vernon Hills, IL (16)
CHG, Salt Lake City, UT (7)
CIT, Livingston, NJ (14)
CMEinfo.com, Birmingham, AL (16)
CNA, Chicago, IL (15)
CNY Awards & Apparel Inc, New Hartford, NY (5)
CPM Delta 1, Inc, Dallas, TX (11)
CRB, Chicago, IL (17)
CRM Learning, Carlsbad, CA (16)
CSI, Conklin, NY (16)
CTB/McGraw-Hill LLC, Monterey, CA (16)
CTC Corp, Bennington, VT (16)
CVT Production Inc, Granger, IN (16)
CYRO Industries, Parsippany, NJ (16)
Cabela's Inc, Sidney, NE (11)
Cable Connection, Fremont, CA (3)
Cable Shopping Network, Scottsdale, AZ (16)
Cablexpress Technologies, Syracuse, NY (10)
Caesars Entertainment Corp, Las Vegas, NV (16)
Calbiochem-Novabiochem Corp, San Diego, CA (9)
Calendar Marketing Association, Wheaton, IL (1)
California Chamber of Commerce, Sacramento, CA (1)
California Institute of Technology, Pasadena, CA (16)
California Mustang Parts & Accessories, City of Industry, CA (16)
California Society of CPA's, San Mateo, CA (1)
Callaway Gardens, Pine Mountain, GA (19)
Cambridge Educational, New York, NY (12)
Camelot Enterprises, Bristol, WI (9)
Campaigns & Elections Magazine, Arlington, VA (17)
Campbell Soup Co, Camden, NJ (16)
Campbell Tools Co, Springfield, OH (9)
Canadian Business, Toronto, ON, Canada (17)
Canadian Institute of Chartered Accountants, Toronto, ON, Canada (1)
Cancer Research Society, Montreal, QC, Canada (1)
Cane & Basket Supply Co, Los Angeles, CA (8)
The Caning Shop, Berkeley, CA (11)
Cape Cod Cupola Co Inc, North Dartmouth, MA (8)
Capezio Ballet Makers Inc, Totowa, NJ (16)
Capitol Concierge Inc, Washington, DC (16)
Captan Associates Inc, Brick, NJ (17)
Caraustar, Austell, GA (16)
Card Technology Inc, Hopkins, MN (16)
Care2, Washington, DC (1)

CARE USA, Atlanta, GA (1)

Carefirst Blue Cross Blue Shield, Washington, DC (15)

Carestream Health Inc, Rochester, NY (7)

CARFAX Inc, Centreville, VA (12)

Caribe Direct Inc, San Juan, PR (6)

Carnival Cruise Lines, Miami, FL (19)

Carolina Biological Supply Co, Burlington, NC (9)

ER Carpenter, Taylor, TX (16)

Carroll Publishing, Bethesda, MD (17)

Carrot-Top Industries Inc, Hillsborough, NC (16)

Carter & Holmes Inc, Newberry, SC (8)

Cartouche Ltd, Alexandria, VA (6)

Carvel Corp, Atlanta, GA (4)

Casual Male Retail Group, Canton, MA (2)

Caterpillar Inc, Peoria, IL (16)

Caterpillar Insurance Services Corp, Nashville, TN (15)

The Catholic University of America Press, Washington, DC (17)

Cattle Kate, Boise, ID (2)

Marshall Cavendish Corp, Tarrytown, NY (17)

Cedar Fresh Products, Coral Gables, FL (16)

Celtic Life Insurance Co, Chicago, IL (15)

Cengage Learning, Independence, KY (17)

Centaur Forge LLC, Burlington, WI (9)

Center for Creative Leadership, Greensboro, NC (16)

Center for Professional Advancement, East Brunswick, NJ (13)

Center for Professional Development, Tallahassee, FL (16)

CenterCore Group Inc, Marked Tree, AR (16)

Central Pacific Bank, Honolulu, HI (14)

Central Shippee Inc, Bloomingdale, NJ (16)

Central States Indemnity, Omaha, NE (15)

Century Photo, Newtown, CT (10)

CertainTeed Corp, Valley Forge, PA (16)

Cessna Aircraft Co, Wichita, KS (16)

Chabin Concepts, Chico, CA (16)

Chadsworth's 1-800-Columns, Wilmington, NC (8)

Chain Store Guide, Tampa, FL (17)

Champion, Quincy, IL (16)

Champion America Inc, Branford, CT (10)

Champs Software Inc, Crystal River, FL (3)

Chanel Inc, New York, NY (16)

Channel 13 WNET Catalog Division, New York, NY (5)

Charisma Brands LLC, Laguna Hills, CA (6)

Charlotte Ford Trunks, Dumas, TX (11)

Charmaster, Grand Rapids, MN (8)

Charter One Bank, Cleveland, OH (14)

Chartifacts, Richmond, VA (6)

Chase Industries, Inc, Cincinnati, OH (16)

Chateau Le Combe, Edmonton, AB, Canada (19)

Chattanooga Shooting Supplies Inc, Chattanooga, TN (16)

Checks by Phone/Checks by Web, Boynton Beach, FL (14)

CheckVantage, Austin, TX (14)

Chelsea Clock Co Inc, Chelsea, MA (6)

Chem-Tainer Industries Inc, North Babylon, NY (9)

Chemical Week, New York, NY (17)

Cherry Tree Toys Inc, Beloit, WI (11)

Chicago Magazine, Chicago, IL (17)

Chick Harness & Supply Inc, Harrington, DE (11)

Chico's FAS Inc, Fort Myers, FL (2)

Chief Executive Magazine, Greenwich, CT (17)

Children of the Night, Van Nuys, CA (1)

Children's Hospital Foundation, Silver Spring, MD (1)

China Books & Periodicals Inc, South San Francisco, CA (17)

Choice Hotels International, Rockville, MD (16)

Choice Point, Alpharetta, GA (16)

Christian Book Distributors Inc, Peabody, MA (17)

Christian Brands, Phoenix, AZ (16)

Christian Broadcasting Network Inc, Virginia Beach, VA (1)

Christianity Today Inc, Carol Stream, IL (17)

Church Pension Fund, New York, NY (1)

Cintas, Cincinnati, OH (16)

Citi Cards / Citicorp Credit Services, Long Island City, NY (14)

Citibank, New York, NY (14)

Citizens Against Government Waste, Washington, DC (1)

Citizens Bank, Boston, MA (14)

City of LaGrange, LaGrange, GA (1)

Civil Service Employees Insurance Group, Walnut Creek, CA (15)

Clampitt Paper Co, Dallas, TX (16)

Clarin by Hussey Seating, North Berwick, ME (5)

The Clark Grave Vault Co, Columbus, OH (16)

Classic Thermographers, North Mankato, MN (10)

Clegg Industries Inc, Gardena, CA (16)

Clement Communications, Buffalo, NY (17)

Clemente Novelties Inc, Utica, NY (16)

Cleveland Institute of Electronics, Cleveland, OH (13)

Clients & Profits Worldwide, Oceanside, CA (14)

Clubs of America, Lakemoor, IL (6)

Cluett Peabody, New York, NY (16)

Coast Hotels Limited, Seattle, WA (19)

Coastal Hotel Group, Bellevue, WA (1)

Coastal Tool & Supply, West Hartford, CT (16)

The Coca-Cola Co, Atlanta, GA (16)

Coin Laundry Association, Oakbrook Terrace, IL (1)

Cold Spring Harbor Lab Press, Woodbury, NY (17)

Cold Stream Farm, Free Soil, MI (8)

Coldwater Creek, Cincinnati, OH (2)

Cole-Parmer Instrument Co, Vernon Hills, IL (16)

Collector Books & American Quilters Society, Paducah, KY (17)

Collector's Armoury Ltd, McDonough, GA (6)

Collector's Teapot, Kingston, NY (6)

CollegeSource Inc, San Diego, CA (17)

Collegiate Cap & Gown, Champaign, IL (16)

Collin Street Bakery, Corsicana, TX (4)

Collis Curve Catalog Sales, Brownsville, TX (7)

Colonial Redi-Record Corp, Brooklyn, NY (10)

Columbia Journalism Review, New York, NY (17)

The Columbian, Vancouver, WA (17)

Columbian Mutual Life Insurance Co, Binghamton, NY (15)

Comcast Spectacor LP, Philadelphia, PA (16)

Comdata Corp, Brentwood, TN (14)

Comerica Inc, Dallas, TX (14)

Commemorative Brands Inc, Austin, TX (16)

Commerce Bancshares Inc, Saint Louis, MO (14)

Commercial Federal Bank, Omaha, NE (14)

Commercial Travelers Mutual Insurance Co, Utica, NY (15)

Commonwealth Business Media Inc, Newark, NJ (17)

CommScope Inc, Hickory, NC (16)

Communication Industries Corp, Grafton, VT (10)

Communication Resources Inc, Beaufort, SC (18)

Community Coffee Co, Baton Rouge, LA (4)

Companion Plants, Athens, OH (8)

Compass Bank, Birmingham, AL (14)

Compass Electronics, Forest Grove, OR (9)

Comphealth, Salt Lake City, UT (16)

Computer Station Corp, Houston, TX (3)

The Computer Supply People, Menomonee Falls, WI (3)

Con-Way Truckload, Joplin, MO (12)

Concept Communications Co, Romeoville, IL (16)

Concordia Publishing House, Saint Louis, MO (17)

Concurrent Computer Corp, Duluth, GA (3)

Condolink, Omaha, NE (16)

The Conference Board Inc, New York, NY (16)

Conform Pacific, Lomita, CA (16)

Conney Safety Products LLC, Madison, WI (7)

Consolidated Electronics Inc, Dayton, OH (3)

Consolidated Plastics Co Inc, Stow, OH (9)

Consumer Credit Advocates Inc, Salt Lake City, UT (16)

Consumer's Energy, Jackson, MI (16)

Continental Supply Inc, Cleveland, OH (9)

Continuing Education of the Bar (CEB), Oakland, CA (1)

Convertible Service, San Gabriel, CA (16)

David C Cook, Colorado Springs, CO (17)

Cooper Communities Inc, Rogers, AR (16)

Cooper Surgical Inc, Trumbull, CT (7)

Cooper Tire & Rubber Co Inc, Findlay, OH (16)

Cooper Vision, Fairport, NY (7)

Coppa Woodworking, Inc, San Pedro, CA (8)

Josiah R Coppersmythe, Harwich, MA (8)

Coptech Inc, Saugus, MA (16)

Cornell Lab of Ornithology, Ithaca, NY (1)

Cornerstone Business Services Inc, Green Bay, WI (14)

Cornhusker Press, Hastings, NE (17)

Corona-Lotus Inc, San Francisco, CA (4)

Coronis Building Systems Inc, Columbus, NJ (9)

Corpus Christi Museum of Science & History, Corpus Christi, TX (1)

Cortz Inc, West Chicago, IL (5)

Cosco Industries Inc, Chicago, IL (16)

Cosgrove Associates, New York, NY (14)

Cosmo International, Deerfield Beach, FL (16)

Cotta Transmission Co, Beloit, WI (16)

Cougar Mountain Software, Boise, ID (14)

Council for Advancement and Support of Education, Washington, DC (1)

Council of Better Business Bureaus - BBBOnline, Arlington, VA (1)

Country Dance and Song Society, Easthampton, MA (1)

Country Financial, Bloomington, IL (15)

Country Sampler Group, Saint Charles, IL (17)

Countrywide Financial Corp, Calabasas, CA (14)

Courage Cards & Gifts, Golden Valley, MN (1)

Coverdell & Co Inc, Chicago, IL (15)

Coverdell Canada Corporation, Montreal, QC, Canada (16)

Cox Communications Inc, Atlanta, GA (16)

Craft-Diston Industries, Wichita, KS (16)

The Ben Craig Center, Charlotte, NC (1)

Craig/Vartorella International Marketing & Advertising Inc, Camden, SC (1)

Crain Communications Inc, Detroit, MI (17)

Crane Pumps & Systems Inc, Piqua, OH (16)

Craver Mathews Smith & Co, Reston, VA (1)

Crazy Crow Trading Post, Pottsboro, TX (11)

Creative Health Products, Plymouth, MI (16)

Creative Learning Systems Inc, Longmont, CO (9)

Creative Publishing International, Minneapolis, MN (17)

Creative Teaching Associates, Clovis, CA (16)

Creative Teaching Press, Cypress, CA (17)

Crest Healthcare Supply, Dassel, MN (16)

Crestline Specialties, Inc, Lewiston, ME (16)

The Cricket Magazine Group, Chicago, IL (17)

Cronin & Co, Glastonbury, CT (16)

A T Cross Co, Lincoln, RI (16)

Cross Country Automotive Services, Medford, MA (16)

The Cross Country Group LLC, Medford, MA (13)

Cross Country Stitching, Quakertown, PA (17)

Crystal Records Inc, Camas, WA (3)

Crystek Corp, Fort Myers, FL (9)

Cuba Cheese Shoppe, Cuba, NY (4)

Cuisinart, Stamford, CT (16)

Culinary Parts Unlimited, San Francisco, CA (16)

CUNA Mutual Group, Madison, WI (15)

Cunningham Group, Elmwood Park, IL (15)

Curriculum Associates Inc, North Billerica, MA (17)

Cushman Fruit Co Inc, West Palm Beach, FL (4)

Custom Accessories, Richmond, IL (11)

Custom Miniatures, Hudson, NH (6)

Customized Newspaper Advertising, Des Moines, IA (18)

Cuvaison Inc, Napa, CA (4)

Cygnus Business Media, Fort Atkinson, WI (17)

Cytec Industries Inc, Olean, NY (16)

D

DB Alex Brown Inc, Baltimore, MD (14)

DCA, West Chester, PA (16)

D/FW Grocers Association, Carrollton, TX (1)

DIA - Nielsen USA Inc, Moorestown, NJ (16)

D'Lights, South El Monte, CA (8)

DMC Corp, Kearny, NJ (16)

DPC Computers, Monsey, NY (16)

DRG, Berne, IN (17)

DS Services of North America LP, Lakeland, FL (4)

DWS Investments Service Co, Kansas City, MO (14)

Da-Lite Screen Co Inc, Warsaw, IN (16)

Daedalus Books Inc, Columbia, MD (5)

Daily Commercial News & Construction Record, Markham, ON, Canada (17)

Daily Record & Dispatch Co, Dunn, NC (17)

DaimlerChrysler Corp, Auburn Hills, MI (12)

Dairy Council of California, Irvine, CA (1)

Dairy Farmers of America Inc, Kansas City, MO (16)

Dairy Management Inc, Rosemont, IL (1)

Dakin Farm, Ferrisburgh, VT (4)

Dakota Digital, Sioux Falls, SD (12)

Dalco Electronics, Springboro, OH (3)

Dalrada Financial Corp, San Diego, CA (14)

Damilic Corp, Rockville, MD (16)

Danker Laboratories Inc, Sarasota, FL (16)

Dansk, Bristol, PA (16)

Dante University Press, Wellesley, MA (17)

The Dartnell Corp, Naples, FL (17)

Dassault Falcon Jet Corp, Little Ferry, NJ (16)

Data Direct Networks, Chatsworth, CA (3)

Databazaar.com, Miramar, FL (10)

DataCal Enterprises, Gilbert, AZ (16)

DataLever Corp, Boulder, CO (16)

Datapoint USA Inc, San Antonio, TX (16)

Datum Timing, Test & Measurement, Beverly, MA (9)

David Dauber & Associates, New York, NY (16)

Davidoff of Geneva Inc, Pinellas Park, FL (6)

The Davis Center, Succasunna, NJ (16)

Dick Davis Digest, Salem, MA (17)

Davis Instruments Corp, Hayward, CA (8)

Davis Publications Inc, Worcester, MA (17)

Day Runner Direct, Sidney, NY (10)

Day-Timer, East Texas, PA (13)

Daydots, Fort Worth, TX (16)

Days Inns Worldwide Inc, Parsippany, NJ (16)

Dayton Daily News, Dayton, OH (18)

DealerTrack, New Hyde Park, NY (14)

Decal Shop, Jacksonville, FL (10)

Decko Products Inc, Sandusky, OH (4)

Deere & Co, Moline, IL (16)

Del Webb, Bloomfield Hills, MI (16)

Delaware Investments, Philadelphia, PA (14)

Dell Computer Corp, Round Rock, TX (16)

Delmmar Communications, Cameron, MO (16)

Deloitte & Touche, Boston, MA (14)

DelStar Technologies Inc, Middletown, DE (16)

Delta Tech Industries, Ontario, CA (12)

DeLuxe Laboratories Inc, Hollywood, CA (16)

Demco Inc, Madison, WI (10)

Democratic Congressional Campaign Committee, Washington, DC (1)

Dental Economics, Tulsa, OK (17)

Dental Products Report, New York, NY (17)

Denver Metro Convention & Visitors Bureau, Denver, CO (1)

Denver Tax Software Inc, Littleton, CO (16)

Dermac Labs Inc, Salem, OR (4)

Desjardins Financial Securities, Levis, QC, Canada (15)

Destinations Ireland & Beyond, Kingston, NY (19)

The Detroit Institute of Arts, Detroit, MI (16)

Detroit Newspapers, Detroit, MI (18)

Deutsche Bank Alex Brown Inc, New York, NY (14)

Development Dimensions International, Bridgeville, PA (16)

Dexta Corp, Napa, CA (16)

Dharma Trading Co, Petaluma, CA (2)

Diagraph Corp, Saint Charles, MO (16)

Diamonds By Rennie Ellen, New York, NY (6)

Diebold Inc, North Canton, OH (16)

DigDev Direct, Deerfield Beach, FL (16)

Digi International, Minnetonka, MN (3)

Digi-Key Corp, Thief River Falls, MN (3)

Digital Speech Systems, Richardson, TX (3)

The Dime Savings Bank of New York FSB, New York, NY (14)

Dimmock Hill Golf Course Pro Shop, Binghamton, NY (11)

DineWise, Farmingdale, NY (4)

Dinn Brothers Inc, West Springfield, MA (16)

Dan Dipert Travel Service Inc, Arlington, TX (19)

Direct Energy, Toronto, ON, Canada (16)

Direct Gardening Association, La Grange, GA (1)

The Direct Marketing Association, New York, NY (1)

The Direct Marketing Club of New York Inc, Garden City, NY (1)

Direct Response Consulting, McLean, VA (17)

Direct SAT TV LLC, Southern Pines, NC (3)

Directory of American Business & Insurance Attorneys, New York, NY (15)

DIRECTV LLC, El Segundo, CA (16)

Discover Financial Services, Riverwoods, IL (14)

Discovery Communications Inc, Silver Spring, MD (16)

Diversified Healthcare Services, Richardson, TX (15)

Diversified Investment Advisors, Harrison, NY (14)

Diversified Photo Supply Corp, Gardena, CA (10)

Divine Word Missionaries, Techny, IL (1)

DNE Nutraceuticals Inc, Farmingdale, NJ (7)

Do-It Corp, South Haven, MI (9)

DoAll Co, Wheeling, IL (16)

Doane, Saint Louis, MO (17)

Doctor's Best Inc, San Clemente, CA (16)

The Doctor's Co, Napa, CA (15)

Domestic Bank, Providence, RI (14)

Dominion Retail Inc, Richmond, VA (16)

Edward Don & Co, Woodridge, IL (16)

Dorothy Biddle Service, Greeley, PA (8)

Dorothy's Ruffled Originals Inc, Wilmington, NC (8)

Doubletree Suites by Hilton, Boston, MA (19)

Douglas Press Inc, Bellwood, IL (16)

Dover Publications Inc, Mineola, NY (17)

The Dow Chemical Co, Midland, MI (16)

Dow Corning Corp, Midland, MI (16)

Dow Jones & Co, Princeton, NJ (17)

Dow Theory Forecasts, Hammond, IN (17)

Dozier Equipment International, Milwaukee, WI (9)

Dragich Auto Literature, Princeton, MN (16)

Drawing Board Inc, Waynesboro, PA (16)

Dreis & Krump Manufacturing Co, Peotone, IL (16)

Drexel University Goodwin College of Professional Studies, Philadelphia, PA (16)

The Dreyfus Corp, New York, NY (14)

Droll Yankees Inc, Plainfield, CT (8)

Drug Policy Alliance, New York, NY (1)

Drumbeat Indian Arts Inc, Phoenix, AZ (6)

The Du-Rite Group Inc, Englewood, NJ (16)

Ducks Unlimited, Memphis, TN (1)

Ducktrap River Fish Farm, Belfast, ME (4)

Duggan & Brown Inc, Abington, PA (16)

Duncan Aviation, Lincoln, NE (16)

Duncraft Inc, Concord, NH (16)

E I DuPont De Nemours & Co, Wilmington, DE (16)

Duracell, Bethel, CT (16)

The Durham Manufacturing Co, Durham, CT (16)

Dwyer Instruments Inc, Michigan City, IN (16)

DX Engineering, Akron, OH (16)

Dynamic Development Co, Mission Viejo, CA (12)

Dynamic Engineering, Santa Cruz, CA (3)

Dynamics Research Corp, Andover, MA (16)

E

e-Pipeconnection, Evansville, IN (9)

E-Z-EM Inc, Lake Success, NY (7)

EBSCO Reception Room Subscription Services, Birmingham, AL (18)

EDC Publishing, Tulsa, OK (17)

EMC Corp, Hopkinton, MA (16)

EMED Co Inc, Buffalo, NY (16)

EMS Technologies, Norcross, GA (16)

EOS International Inc, Carlsbad, CA (5)

ESL Federal Credit Union, Rochester, NY (14)

EWA & Miniature Cars USA Inc, Berkeley Heights, NJ (11)

Eagle Claw Fishing Tackle, Denver, CO (11)

Eagle Publishing, Washington, DC (17)

Eastbay Running Store Inc, Wausau, WI (2)

Eastern Bank, Boston, MA (14)

Eastern Michigan University, Ypsilanti, MI (16)

Easthill Group Inc, Pottstown, PA (12)

Eastman Chemical Co, Kingsport, TN (16)

David Easton Inc, New York, NY (16)

EasyLink Services International Corp, Piscataway, NJ (16)

Eaton Corp, Raleigh, NC (16)

Ebbets Field Flannels Inc, Seattle, WA (2)

Ebersole Lapidary Supply Inc, Wichita, KS (11)

Eckankar, Minneapolis, MN (17)

Ecklers, Titusville, FL (12)

Ecolab Professional Products, Saint Paul, MN (16)

The Economist Newspaper NA Inc, New York, NY (17)

Economy Handicrafts, Brooklyn, NY (16)

Edible Landscaping, Afton, VA (8)

G

G&S Fruit Packers LLC, Weirsdale, FL (16)

G H Bass & Co, New York, NY (16)

G-Neil Direct Mail, Sunrise, FL (10)

GBH Communications, Monrovia, CA (3)

GCC Printers, Bedford, MA (10)

GE Canada, Mississauga, ON, Canada (9)

GE Lighting North America, Cleveland, OH (16)

GE Money, Alpharetta, GA (14)

GE Partnership Marketing Group, Schaumburg, IL (14)

GMG Productions Inc, Roslyn, NY (3)

GN Netcom, Nashua, NH (16)

GRP Funding LLC, Springfield, MA (14)

GWR Wealth Management, Omaha, NE (14)

Gaco Western Inc, Seattle, WA (16)

Gaiam Inc, Boulder, CO (9)

Gale, Farmington Hills, MI (17)

Galen Williams Landscaping & Garden Design, East Hampton, NY (16)

Gallagher Affinity, Lakewood Ranch, FL (15)

The Gallery Shop, Buffalo, NY (6)

Gall's Inc, Lexington, KY (16)

Gallup Inter-Tribal Indian Ceremonial, Gallup, NM (1)

Gambro Inc, Lakewood, CO (16)

GameTime Inc, Fort Payne, AL (11)

Gamma Photo Labs LLC, Chicago, IL (16)

Gannett Co Inc, Mc Lean, VA (16)

Gardens Of The Blue Ridge Inc, Pineola, NC (8)

Garlinghouse Co, Beaufort, SC (17)

Garon Products Inc, Wall, NJ (16)

Gary's Perennials, LLC, Maple Glen, PA (8)

Gates Corp, Denver, CO (9)

Gateway Inc, Irvine, CA (3)

Gaylord Brothers, Syracuse, NY (16)

Gazette Communications Inc, Cedar Rapids, IA (17)

Gebbie Press Inc, New Paltz, NY (17)

Gelco Information Network, Eden Prairie, MN (16)

Gemalto Inc, Montgomeryville, PA (16)

Gemini Publishing Co, Webster, NY (17)

Gems Sensors & Controls, Plainville, CT (9)

General Binding Corp, Northbrook, IL (10)

General Electric Co, Fairfield, CT (16)

General Pencil Co Inc, Jersey City, NJ (16)

General Physics Corp, Elkridge, MD (16)

General Vitamin Corp, Raleigh, NC (16)

Genesco Inc, Nashville, TN (2)

Genetica DNA Laboratories Inc, Cincinnati, OH (16)

Genium Publishing, Amsterdam, NY (17)

Genworth Financial Inc, Richmond, VA (14)

Georgetown University Law Center, Washington, DC (13)

Georgetown University McDonough School of Business, Washington, DC (1)

Georgia Power, Atlanta, GA (16)

Gerstner Woodworks, Dayton, OH (6)

Getronics, Tewksbury, MA (16)

Ghent Manufacturing Inc, Lebanon, OH (10)

Ghirardelli Chocolate Co, San Leandro, CA (16)

Gibson Auer LLC, Victor, ID (7)

Gift Services Inc, Vancouver, WA (6)

Gillette Children's Specialty Healthcare, Saint Paul, MN (1)

Gilman's Lapidary Supply, Hellertown, PA (11)

Gilson Co Inc, Lewis Center, OH (9)

Glas-Col, Terre Haute, IN (16)

Peter Glenn Publications, Delray Beach, FL (17)

Glenview State Bank, Glenview, IL (14)

Global Computer Corp, Port Jefferson, NY (3)

Global Equipment Co Inc, Port Washington, NY (9)

Global Specialties, Wallingford, CT (16)

Globe Specialty Products Inc, Millbury, MA (17)

Globe Ticket & Label Co, Carol Stream, IL (16)

Go Promos, Amsterdam, NY (5)

Goddard Manufacturing Co, Logan, KS (8)

Gohn Brothers, Middlebury, IN (5)

Gold Medal Hair Products Inc, Farmingdale, NY (7)

Gold Medal Products Co, Cincinnati, OH (16)

Golden Fleece Designs Inc, Burbank, CA (16)

Golden Gate Transportation District, San Rafael, CA (16)

Golden Rule Insurance Co, Indianapolis, IN (15)

Golden Trophy, Chicago, IL (4)

Golf Digest Co, Wilton, CT (17)

Good Directions Co Inc, Danbury, CT (8)

Goodheart-Willcox Publisher, Tinley Park, IL (17)

Goodyear Tire & Rubber Co, Akron, OH (16)

WL Gore & Associates Inc, Newark, DE (2)

Gossler Farms Nursery, Springfield, OR (8)

Gothic Arch Greenhouses Inc, Mobile, AL (8)

Gould & Goodrich, Lillington, NC (2)

Governing Magazine, Washington, DC (17)

Government of India Tourist Office, New York, NY (1)

W R Grace & Co, Columbia, MD (16)

Grade Finders Inc, Philadelphia, PA (17)

Graham Field Health Products Inc, Atlanta, GA (7)

Grainger Industrial Supply, North Brook, IL (16)

WW Grainger Inc, Lake Forest, IL (9)

Grand Canyon University, Phoenix, AZ (13)

Grandma Brown's Beans Inc, Mexico, NY (4)

Graphik Dimensions Ltd, High Point, NC (16)

Graves Lapidary Co, Pompano Beach, FL (9)

The Great Amarillo Directory, Amarillo, TX (17)

Great Chefs Television Publishing, New Orleans, LA (6)

Great-West Life, Greenwood Village, CO (15)

Great Western Supply, Dallas, TX (16)

Greater Fort Worth Builders Association, Fort Worth, TX (1)

Green Mountain Coffee Roasters, Inc, Waterbury, VT (4)

Greenwood Publishing Group Inc, Portsmouth, NH (17)

Grimes Horticulture Inc, Concord, OH (8)

Grove Enterprises Inc, Brasstown, NC (16)

Grower's Supply Co, Dexter, MI (8)

Growing Child, Inc, West Lafayette, IN (17)

Gruber & Allison Inc, Boynton Beach, FL (17)

Gruppo Levey & Co, New York, NY (14)

Guaranty Bank, Brown Deer, WI (14)

The Guardian Life Insurance Co, New York, NY (15)

GuideOne Insurance, West Des Moines, IA (15)

Guiding Eyes for the Blind, Yorktown Heights, NY (16)

Guilford Publications Inc, New York, NY (17)

Gulf Coast Data Supply Inc, Milton, FL (3)

Gulf Publishing Co, Houston, TX (17)

Gulfstream Aerospace Corp, Savannah, GA (16)

Gun Video Catalog/LMP, San Diego, CA (11)

H

H&R Block Inc, Kansas City, MO (14)

HCI Direct, Bensalem, PA (16)

HDA Inc, Saint Louis, MO (17)

HR Direct, Sunrise, FL (10)

HSBC Bank USA, NA, New York, NY (14)

HSP Direct, Ashburn, VA (1)

Habitat For Humanity International, Americus, GA (1)

Hadley Fruit Orchards Inc, Cabazon, CA (4)

Hagemeyer - North America, Charleston, SC (16)

Hagie Manufacturing Co, Clarion, IA (9)

Hain Celestial Group Inc, Boulder, CO (16)

Hale Indian River Groves Inc, Vero Beach, FL (16)

Hall-Erickson Inc, Westmont, IL (16)

Hallmark Cards Inc, Kansas City, MO (16)

Halsom Home Care Inc, Centerville, OH (16)

Hamilton Beach Brands Inc, Glen Allen, VA (16)

Hamilton Watch, Weehawken, NJ (16)

Hammacher Schlemmer & Co Inc, Niles, IL (16)

Hammock Publishing Inc, Nashville, TN (17)

Hampshire Agency, Great Neck, NY (14)

Hampshire Pewter Co, Somersworth, NH (6)

Hampton Marketing Corp, Medford, NY (16)

Handi-Ramp Inc, Libertyville, IL (7)

Hanley Wood LLC, Washington, DC (16)

Hanna Instruments Inc, Woonsocket, RI (16)

Chris Hansen, New Berlin, WI (16)

Hansen Corp, Princeton, IN (16)

Happy Trails Resort, Surprise, AZ (19)

Har Court Inc, Orlando, FL (17)

Harbor Freight Tools, Camarillo, CA (9)

Harbour Bay Inc, Oakland, NJ (16)

Harcourt Educational Measurement, San Antonio, TX (17)

Harland Financial Solutions Inc, Lake Mary, FL (16)

John Harland Co, Decatur, GA (16)

Harlequin Enterprises Ltd, Don Mills, ON, Canada (17)

Harley-Davidson Inc, Milwaukee, WI (12)

Harman's Cheese & Country Store Inc, Sugar Hill, NH (4)

HarperCollins, New York, NY (17)

Harris Bancorp Inc, Chicago, IL (14)

Harris Corp, Melbourne, FL (16)

Harry & David Holdings Inc, Medford, OR (4)

The Hartz Mountain Corp, Secaucus, NJ (16)

Harvard Business Review, Boston, MA (17)

Harvard Business School Publishing, Boston, MA (17)

Harvard Pilgrim Health Care, Wellesley, MA (7)

Hatton-Brown Publishers Inc, Montgomery, AL (17)

HAVE Inc, Hudson, NY (3)

Hazelden, Center City, MN (7)

Health Affairs, Bethesda, MD (17)

Health Care Concepts Inc, Austin, TX (16)

Health Care Logistics, Circleville, OH (16)

Health O Meter, Countryside, IL (16)

HealthPlan Services, Tampa, FL (15)

Health Sciences Consortium, Chapel Hill, NC (17)

The Healthy Back Store, Beltsville, MD (16)

Hearlihy & Co, Pittsburg, KS (17)

The Hearst Corp, New York, NY (17)

Hearst Magazines, New York, NY (17)

Hearthside Quilts & Supplies, Hinesburg, VT (11)

Heartland America, Chaska, MN (3)

Heartstrings Press, Lancaster, VA (17)

Hecht Rubber Corp, Jacksonville, FL (16)

Heldref Publications, Washington, DC (17)

Heller Financial, Chicago, IL (14)

W C Heller & Co, Montpelier, OH (16)

Hello Direct, Nashua, NH (16)

Helly-Hansen, Auburn, WA (16)

Helman Group Ltd, Oxnard, CA (16)

Hemmings Motor News, Bennington, VT (17)

The Herald & Review, Decatur, IL (17)

Herbach & Rademan Co, Moorestown, NJ (9)

Herbalife International of America Inc, Los Angeles, CA (7)
Herman Miller Inc, Zeeland, MI (16)
Hermes of Paris, New York, NY (2)
Herschend Family Entertainment, Norcross, GA (5)
The Hershey Co, Hershey, PA (4)
Hershey Park, Hershey, PA (19)
Hertz Corp, Park Ridge, NJ (19)
Hewlett-Packard Co, Palo Alto, CA (16)
Hickory Farms, Maumee, OH (4)
Highmark Blue Cross Blue Shield, Pittsburgh, PA (15)
HighScope Educational Research Foundation, Ypsilanti, MI (17)
Hillside Wire Cloth Co, Belleville, NJ (9)
Hilton HHonors, McLean, VA (16)
Hilton Hotels Corp, Mc Lean, VA (19)
Hireko Golf, City of Industry, CA (11)
Hoffman Mint, Fort Lauderdale, FL (6)
Hoke Communications Inc, Garden City, NY (17)
Holiday Travel of America, Carlsbad, CA (19)
Holland Wildflower Farm, Elkins, AR (8)
Hollister Inc, Libertyville, IL (16)
Hollywood Film Archive, Los Angeles, CA (17)
Holy Cross Hospital, Fort Lauderdale, FL (16)
The Home Depot Inc, Atlanta, GA (16)
Home Planners, Tucson, AZ (17)
Home Safeguard Industries, Malibu, CA (9)
HomeAway.com Inc, Austin, TX (19)
Homecraft Veneer & Woodworker Supply, Latrobe, PA (4)
Homespun Tapes Music Instruction, Woodstock, NY (3)
Homesteaders Life Co, West Des Moines, IA (15)
The HoneyBaked Ham Co, Holland, OH (4)
Honeywell, Morristown, NJ (16)
Hook & Hackle Co Inc, Homestead, PA (11)
Hooleon Corp, Melrose, NM (3)
Hoover's Mfg Co, Peru, IL (2)
The Hope Co Inc, Bridgeton, MO (16)
Hopkins Medical Products, Baltimore, MD (7)
Hormel Foods Corp, Austin, MN (16)
Horticulture Magazine, Cincinnati, OH (17)
Houlihan Lokey Howard & Zukin, Los Angeles, CA (14)
House of Eyes, Greensboro, NC (2)
House of Oldies, New York, NY (6)
House of Onyx, Inc, Greenville, KY (6)
House of Orange, Brentwood Bay, BC, Canada (2)
Howard Rice Nemerovski Canady Falk & Rabkin, San Francisco, CA (14)
Hubert Co, Harrison, OH (16)
William B Hugg Enterprise Inc Swim Wear & Accessories, Ambler, PA (11)
Human Resource Development Press, Amherst, MA (17)
Humana Inc, Louisville, KY (7)
Huntington Bancshares, Columbus, OH (14)
HY-KO Products Co, Northfield, OH (16)
Hyatt Fruit Co, Vero Beach, FL (4)
Hyatt Hotels Corp, Chicago, IL (16)
Hyatt Legal Plans Inc, Cleveland, OH (16)
Hygienic Fabrics & Filters Inc, Sheboygan, WI (16)
Hyman's, Hanahan, SC (2)

I

IBM Corp, Armonk, NY (16)
ICIS Inc, Upper Black Eddy, PA (2)
IDG Enterprise, Framingham, MA (17)
IDMS Inc, Melville, NY (16)

IHS Markit, Englewood, CO (17)
INC Magazine, New York, NY (17)
ING, Minneapolis, MN (15)
ING USA Annuity & Life Ins Co, Des Moines, IA (15)
INX International Ink Co, Schaumburg, IL (16)
IPD Co Inc, Portland, OR (12)
IPS - Sendero Corp, Norcross, GA (14)
ISA-The International Society of Automation, Research Triangle Park, NC (1)
ITW Bee Leitzke, Iron Ridge, WI (16)
ITW Vortec, Cincinnati, OH (16)
I/D/E/A Inc, Caldwell, ID (16)
Ideal Industries (Canada) Corp, Ajax, ON, Canada (9)
Ideal Industries Inc, Sycamore, IL (16)
Illy Caffe North America, Rye Brook, NY (4)
IMPACT Publishing Inc, Bradenton, FL (17)
Imperial Supplies, Green Bay, WI (16)
Improvements, West Chester, OH (8)
In-Sync Publications, Redondo Beach, CA (18)
Independent Insurance Agents & Brokers of America, Alexandria, VA (1)
Independent Living Aids, Buffalo, NY (7)
Indian Arts & Crafts Association, Albuquerque, NM (1)
Indian House Records & Tapes, Taos, NM (3)
Indianapolis Motor Speedway, Indianapolis, IN (19)
Indianapolis Newspapers Inc, Indianapolis, IN (17)
Indium Corp of America, Clinton, NY (16)
Indus-Tool, Chicago, IL (12)
Industrial Instruments & Supplies Inc, Southampton, PA (9)
Industrial Uniform Co Inc, Wichita, KS (2)
Infinity Insurance Co, Birmingham, AL (15)
Infomart, Dallas, TX (16)
Information for Public Affairs, Inc, Sacramento, CA (17)
Information Unlimited Inc, Mont Vernon, NH (11)
InfoSource Inc, Oviedo, FL (3)
Ingram Book Group, La Vergne, TN (16)
Insight Direct Inc, Tempe, AZ (16)
Institute for International Research Inc, New York, NY (17)
Institute of Management Accountants Inc, Montvale, NJ (1)
Institute of Management & Administration (IOMA), Bethesda, MD (17)
Institute of Reading Development, Novato, CA (1)
Institute of Real Estate Management, Chicago, IL (1)
Institutional Advancement Programs Inc, Tuckahoe, NY (1)
Institutional Investor Inc, New York, NY (17)
Institutional Real Estate Inc, San Ramon, CA (17)
Instructor's Choice Dancewear, Massapequa Park, NY (2)
The Instrument Workshop, Ashland, OR (16)
Insurance.com, Solon, OH (15)
Insurance Publications Inc, Overland Park, KS (17)
Integretel Inc, San Jose, CA (16)
Intel Corp, Santa Clara, CA (16)
IntelliQuote Insurance Services, El Dorado Hills, CA (15)
Inter7 Internet Technologies Inc, Galena, IL (3)
Interex, Amesbury, MA (17)
InterfaceFlor LLC, La Grange, GA (16)
Intergraph Corp, Madison, AL (16)
International Academy - Compounding Pharmacists, Missouri City, TX (1)
International Advertising Association, New York, NY (1)

International City/County Management Association, Washington, DC (1)
International Crystal Manufacturing Co, Oklahoma City, OK (16)
International Direct Media Co & Information Publishing Co, San Francisco, CA (17)
International Foundation of Employee Benefit Plans, Brookfield, WI (1)
International Irrigation Systems, St. Catherines, ON, Canada (8)
International Manufacturing Co, Whitesburg, GA (8)
International Paper, Memphis, TN (16)
International Sign Association, Alexandria, VA (1)
International Specialized Book Services Inc, Portland, OR (16)
International Wine Accessories Inc, Petaluma, CA (4)
Intersections, Chantilly, VA (14)
Intra Business Systems Inc, South Bend, IN (16)
Intromark Inc, Pittsburgh, PA (16)
Intuit, Mountain View, CA (10)
Invacare Continuing Care Group, Saint Louis, MO (16)
Invacare Supply Group, Milford, MA (16)
Investors Alliance Inc, Austin, TX (1)
Investors Marketing Services, Danvers, MA (14)
INWAVE Internet, Janesville, WI (16)
Iomega Corp, Roy, UT (16)
Iowa Medical Society, Des Moines, IA (1)
Iroquois Products, Chicago, IL (10)
Islands Tropicals, Keaau, HI (6)
Itochu Chemicals America Inc, White Plains, NY (16)

J

J&L Industrial Supply, Southfield, MI (9)
JC Whitney, Chicago, IL (12)
JDR Microdevices, Dublin, CA (3)
JDRF, New York, NY (1)
JIST Publishing, Saint Paul, MN (17)
JLG Industries Inc, McConnellsburg, PA (16)
JR Cigar, Burlington, NC (5)
Jaffe Brothers Natural Foods, Valley Center, CA (4)
Jameco Electronics, Belmont, CA (3)
James Medical Rents & Sales Inc, Fort Wayne, IN (7)
Robert James Co Inc, Moody, AL (10)
Herbert L Jamison & Co LLC, West Orange, NJ (15)
Jantz Supply Koval Knives, Davis, OK (9)
Jarden Corp, Boca Raton, FL (16)
Jason Natural Personal Care Products, Boulder, CO (7)
Jaypro Sports, Waterford, CT (11)
Jaz Holdings LLC, Liberty Corner, NJ (16)
JazzTimes Magazine Inc, Quincy, MA (17)
Jeffers & Co, Dothan, AL (5)
Jefferson National, Louisville, KY (14)
Jeffrey Lant Associates Inc, Cambridge, MA (5)
Jenny Products Inc, Somerset, PA (16)
Jerden Records/SpeechWorks, Redmond, WA (16)
Jerry's Artarama, Raleigh, NC (10)
The Jewish Publication Society, Philadelphia, PA (17)
Jobscope Corp, Greenville, SC (16)
Jockey International Global Inc, Kenosha, WI (2)
Jofco Inc, Jasper, IN (16)
John Deere Financial, Johnston, IA (14)
John Hancock Financial Services Inc, Boston, MA (15)
John Hancock Retirement Plan Services, Toronto, ON, Canada (14)
Johnson & Johnson, New Brunswick, NJ (16)

Edward Jones, Des Peres, MO (14)
Jones International Ltd, Centennial, CO (16)
Marlin P Jones & Associates Inc, West Palm Beach, FL (3)
Jones Publishing Inc, Iola, WI (17)
Jones School Supply Co Inc, Irmo, SC (6)
Joslin Photo Puzzle Co, Southampton, PA (16)
Jossey-Bass Inc Publishers, San Francisco, CA (17)
Jostens, Inc, Minneapolis, MN (16)
The Journal News, White Plains, NY (17)
Journal of Commerce Group, Newark, NJ (17)
JustThink Inc, Sherwood Park, AB, Canada (16)

K

K-D Lamp Co, Andover, OH (12)
KAR Graphics, Mashpee, MA (8)
KCET, Burbank, CA (1)
KEH.com, Smyrna, GA (16)
KET, Lexington, KY (17)
KHL Engineered Packaging Solutions, Buena Park, CA (16)
KMA Direct Communications, Dallas, TX (1)
KTM Sportmotorcycle USA Inc, Amherst, OH (16)
KV Vet Supply Co, Inc, David City, NE (5)
Kadant Johnson Inc, Three Rivers, MI (16)
Kalmed Dental Products Inc, Marietta, GA (7)
Kano Laboratories, Nashville, TN (16)
Kansas City Chiefs, Kansas City, MO (16)
Kansas State University Division of Continuing Education, Manhattan, KS (1)
Kao Brands, Cincinnati, OH (9)
Kaplan Inc, Fort Lauderdale, FL (16)
Kaplan Publishing, Chicago, IL (17)
Kappa Publishing Group, Blue Bell, PA (17)
Kappler Protective Apparel & Fabrics, Guntersville, AL (2)
Karaoke USA, Largo, FL (5)
Kaylor's School Supply, Albertville, AL (16)
Kayne & Son Custom Hardware Inc, Candler, NC (8)
Kelco Supply Co, Big Lake, MN (16)
JJ Keller & Associates Inc, Neenah, WI (16)
Kellyco Metal Detector Distributors, Winter Springs, FL (11)
Kelsey National Corp, Los Angeles, CA (15)
Kemper Corp, Chicago, IL (15)
Kendall Products/Dri-Dek, Naples, FL (16)
Kennametal Inc, Latrobe, PA (16)
Kennel Vet, Laurel, DE (11)
Kensington Computer Products Group, Redwood Shores, CA (16)
Kentucky Bankers Association, Louisville, KY (1)
Kerr-Hays Co, Ligonier, PA (16)
Kester's Wild Game Food Nurseries Inc, Omro, WI (8)
Kett Tool Co, Cincinnati, OH (9)
Key Bank, Cleveland, OH (14)
Key Bank National Association, Albany, NY (14)
Key Communications Inc, Garrisonville, VA (17)
Key West Aloe Holdings LLC, Fort Lauderdale, FL (16)
The Kidney Foundation of Canada/Greater Ontario Branch, Hamilton, ON, Canada (1)
Kimbo Educational, Long Branch, NJ (17)
King Features, New York, NY (17)
King Ranch Saddle Shop, Kingsville, TX (8)
King's Chandelier Co, Eden, NC (6)
Kingsley North Inc, Norway, MI (11)
The Kiplinger Washington Editors Inc, Washington, DC (17)

Will Kirkpatrick Shorebird Decoys Inc, Hudson, MA (6)
Kitchen Kompact Inc, Jeffersonville, IN (8)
B Klein Publications, Boca Raton, FL (17)
Klingspor's Woodworking Shop, Hickory, NC (9)
Klockit, Lake Geneva, WI (6)
Knoll Group, New York, NY (16)
Knott's Berry Farm Foods, Orrville, OH (4)
Kolbe Corp, Phoenix, AZ (17)
Susan G Komen for the Cure, Dallas, TX (1)
William S Konecky Associates Inc, Old Saybrook, CT (17)
Kozak Auto Drywash Inc, Batavia, NY (16)
The Kraft Heinz Co, Pittsburgh, PA (4)
Kraftbilt, Tulsa, OK (10)
Krause Publications Inc, Iola, WI (17)
The Kroger Co, Cincinnati, OH (4)
Kross Inc, Santa Clarita, CA (16)

L

L&L Management, Pasadena, CA (16)
L6 Holdings Corp, Duluth, GA (14)
LGP GEM LTD, New York, NY (16)
LS Records, Madison, TN (16)
Lab Safety Supply Inc, Janesville, WI (5)
LaCrosse Footwear Inc, Portland, OR (16)
The LadyBug Co, Berry Creek, CA (8)
Lafferty Equipment Manufacturing Inc, North Little Rock, AR (9)
Laitram Machinery, Harahan, LA (16)
Lake Shore Industries, Erie, PA (16)
Lakewood Products LLC, Suamico, WI (11)
Laminex Inc, Fort Mill, SC (16)
Lancer Insurance Co, Long Beach, NY (15)
Landauer Corp, Urbandale, IA (2)
Landmark Communications Inc, Alpharetta, GA (17)
Landmark Graphics Corp, Houston, TX (16)
Landscape Forms Inc, Kalamazoo, MI (16)
Laplink Software Inc, Bellevue, WA (3)
LaPreferida Inc, Chicago, IL (4)
Laran Communications Inc, Winfield, IL (16)
Lark in the Morning, Mendocino, CA (5)
Las Vegas Review Journal, Las Vegas, NV (17)
Laser Label Technologies Inc, Stow, OH (10)
Latest Products Corp, Woodbury, NY (7)
Lathem Time Corp, Atlanta, GA (16)
Laughlin Associates Inc, Carson City, NV (16)
Lautman Maska Neill & Co, Washington, DC (1)
Lawyers & Judges Publishing Co Inc, Tucson, AZ (17)
Lawyer's Weekly Publications, Boston, MA (17)
Lazer Media Group Inc, Charleston, SC (17)
Lazard Middle Market LLC, Minneapolis, MN (14)
Leadership Directories Inc, New York, NY (17)
Leadership Software Corp, Nyack, NY (16)
LeadFlash, Boca Raton, FL (14)
League of American Orchestras, New York, NY (1)
Leanin' Tree Inc, Boulder, CO (6)
LearnCom HR Consulting & Training, Irvine, CA (16)
Learning Communications LLC, Irvine, CA (16)
Leather Unlimited Corp, Belgium, WI (2)
Lefty's Corner, Clarks Summit, PA (6)
Legal Sea Foods Inc, Boston, MA (4)
The Legal Studies Forum, Morgantown, WV (1)
Lehman's, Dalton, OH (8)
Leisure Arts Inc, Maumelle, AR (17)
Lenox Group Inc, Bristol, PA (6)
L'Entraide Assurance, Quebec, QC, Canada (15)
AM Leonard Inc, Piqua, OH (8)

Hal Leonard Corp, Milwaukee, WI (17)
Lerner Publishing Group, Minneapolis, MN (17)
Leslie Jordan, Portland, OR (2)
Lesman Instrument Co, Bensenville, IL (9)
Leucadia National Corp, New York, NY (14)
Levenger, Delray Beach, FL (5)
Levi Strauss & Co, San Francisco, CA (16)
Lexington Luggage Limited, New York, NY (19)
LexisNexis, New York, NY (17)
LexisNexis Matthew Bender, Albany, NY (17)
Lexus Division of Toyota, Torrance, CA (12)
Liberty Orchards Co Inc, Cashmere, WA (16)
LibertyTree Press, Oakland, CA (5)
The Library of America, New York, NY (13)
Liebert Corp, Columbus, OH (16)
Life Extension Foundation, Fort Lauderdale, FL (7)
Life Fitness, Schiller Park, IL (11)
Life Technologies, Grand Island, NY (9)
Lifeboat Distribution, Shrewsbury, NJ (16)
LifeLock, Tempe, AZ (16)
Lifetime Brands Inc, Garden City, NY (8)
Light Sources Inc, Virginia Beach, VA (16)
Ligonier Ministries, Sanford, FL (5)
Liguori Publications, Liguori, MO (17)
Lilypons Water Gardens, Adamstown, MD (8)
Lin Terry, Paterson, NJ (6)
Lincoln Educational Services Corp, West Orange, NJ (13)
Lincoln Financial Group, Radnor, PA (15)
LinguiSystems, East Moline, IL (17)
Lion Apparel, Dayton, OH (2)
Lionsgate Television Corp, Santa Monica, CA (16)
Lippincott, Williams & Wilkins, Baltimore, MD (17)
A Liss & Co Inc, Woodside, NY (16)
Lithia Motors Inc, Medford, OR (12)
Live Design, New York, NY (17)
Live Nation, Beverly Hills, CA (19)
Lladro USA Inc, Moonachie, NJ (16)
Llewellyn Publications, Woodbury, MN (17)
LO-AD Communications, Pasadena, CA (16)
Lo Ink Specialties, Kennebunkport, ME (16)
Local Search Association, Troy, MI (1)
Location Sound Corp, North Hollywood, CA (3)
Lockheed Martin Corp, Bethesda, MD (16)
Loctite Corp, Rocky Hill, CT (16)
Loews Hotels, Inc, New York, NY (19)
Logical Computer Selections, Short Hills, NJ (16)
Lombardi Publishing Corp, Vaughan, ON, Canada (17)
Long & Foster Insurance, Chantilly, VA (15)
Longevity Pure Medicine, Los Angeles, CA (7)
Long's Electronics Inc, Irondale, AL (3)
Lorillard Tobacco Co, Greensboro, NC (16)
The Los Angeles Convention & Visitors Bureau, Los Angeles, CA (19)
Los Angeles Kings, Los Angeles, CA (16)
The Los Angeles Lakers Inc, El Segundo, CA (11)
Lotions & Lace, Riverside, CA (2)
LOTSolutions, Jacksonville, FL (14)
Lowe's Companies Inc, Mooresville, NC (8)
Luce Corp, Hamden, CT (16)
Lufthansa German Airlines, East Meadow, NY (19)
Luggage Base, Nipomo, CA (16)
Lundberg Family Farms, Richvale, CA (16)
Lure Craft, Lagrange, IN (11)
Luster Care Products, Saint Louis, MO (16)
Lutheran Church Extension Fund - Missouri Synod, Saint Louis, MO (1)

M

M&M Health Care Apparel Co, Brooklyn, NY (2)
M2Media 360, Park Ridge, IL (17)
MFE Instruments, Salem, NH (9)
MGI Management Institute, Hawthorne, NY (16)
MGMA-ACMPE, Englewood, CO (1)
Mi-T-M Corp, Peosta, IA (9)
Mirage Resorts, Inc., Las Vegas, NV (19)
MJA International, Dix Hills, NY (7)
MPBS Industries, Los Angeles, CA (16)
MPS Multimedia Inc, San Mateo, CA (16)
The MR Group Inc, Charleston, SC (9)
MRV Communications, Chatsworth, CA (3)
MSC Industrial Supply Co, Melville, NY (9)
MTS Publishing, Naperville, IL (17)
MTS Systems Corp, Eden Prairie, MN (16)
Mylan NV, Canonsburg, PA (7)
Macy's Inc, Cincinnati, OH (5)
Magellan's Catalog, Chelmsford, MA (5)
Magna Publications Inc, Madison, WI (17)
Magna-Tel Inc. Cape Girardeau, MO (5)
Magna Visual Inc, Saint Louis, MO (9)
Magnaflux, Glenview, IL (16)
Magnaplan Corp, Champlain, NY (10)
Magnatag Visible Systems, Macedon, NY (16)
Magnet LLC, Washington, MO (16)
The Magni Co Inc, McKinney, TX (16)
The Maine Photographic Workshops, Rockport, ME (16)
Maine Potato Board, Presque Isle, ME (1)
Maison Glass Delicacies, Cold Spring, NY (4)
Majestic Products Co, Paris, KY (16)
Majorium, Stevens Point, WI (17)
Malco Products Inc, Barberton, OH (16)
MALM Chemical Corp, Pound Ridge, NY (16)
EF Maloney Inc, Mamaroneck, NY (16)
The Maloney Group, New York, NY (16)
Manchester Farms Inc, Columbia, SC (4)
Manning Materials, Birdsboro, PA (16)
Manulife Financial Inc, Toronto, ON, Canada (15)
MAP International, Brunswick, GA (1)
Maple Grove Farms of Vermont Inc, Saint Johnsbury, VT (4)
Marathon Norco Aerospace Inc, Waco, TX (16)
March of Dimes Foundation, White Plains, NY (1)
MARCOR Remediation Inc, Halethorpe, MD (16)
Mardiron Optics, Stoneham, MA (11)
Marimac Inc, Montreal, QC, Canada (8)
Mark James & Associates Inc, Oswego, IL (16)
Marketing and Product Strategy, Peabody, MA (16)
Marketing Results Inc, Sicklerville, NJ (16)
Marketshare Publications Inc, Overland Park, KS (17)
Markson Scientific LLC, Henderson, NC (9)
Markwins International Corp, City of Industry, CA (16)
Marmelstein Inc, Philadelphia, PA (16)
The Marmon Group LLC, Chicago, IL (16)
Marquis Who's Who Ventures LLC, Berkeley Heights, NJ (17)
Marriott International Inc, Bethesda, MD (19)
Marsh Affinity Group Services, Chicago, IL (15)
Marsh US Consumer, Urbandale, IA (15)
Marshall & Swift, Los Angeles, CA (17)
Maryland Pennysaver, Hanover, MD (17)
The Maryland Saddlery Inc, Butler, MD (11)
Mary's Plant Farm & Landscaping, Hamilton, OH (8)
T Marzetti Co Inc, Columbus, OH (4)
Masco Corp, Taylor, MI (16)
Mason Companies Inc, Chippewa Falls, WI (2)

Massachusetts Horticultural Society, Wellesley, MA (1)
MassMutual Financial Group, Springfield, MA (15)
MasterCard Worldwide, Purchase, NY (14)
Masterpiece Studios Inc, Mankato, MN (16)
Mastervision Inc, New York, NY (16)
Robert J Matthews Co, Massillon, OH (7)
Maui Jim Inc, Peoria, IL (16)
Maverick Ventures Product Line, Chesterfield, MO (5)
Maxon Furniture Inc. Muscatine. IA (10)
Mayo Clinic, Rochester, MN (17)
Mazda Motor of America Inc, Irvine, CA (16)
McClatchy Co, Sacramento, CA (17)
McClure & Zimmerman, Randolph, WI (8)
McCormick & Co Inc, Sparks, MD (4)
McDonald Obsolete Parts Co, Rockport, IN (16)
McDougal Littell, Evanston, IL (17)
McFeely's Square Drive Screws, Madison, WI (16)
McGaw Graphics, Manchester Center, VT (6)
The McGraw-Hill Financial, New York, NY (17)
McGruff Specialty Products Office, Amsterdam, NY (16)
McKenzie Taxidermy Supply, Granite Quarry, NC (16)
McKesson Corp, San Francisco, CA (7)
McKnight's Long-Term Care News, Northfield, IL (17)
McMaster-Carr Supply Co (HQ), Elmhurst, IL (9)
McNichols Co, Tampa, FL (16)
Mead Johnson Co, Evansville, IN (7)
Mead Westvaco Consumer & Office Products, Richmond, VA (10)
Mechanical Breakdown Administrators Inc, Scottsdale, AZ (14)
Medco Health Solutions Inc, Franklin Lakes, NJ (7)
Medco Insurance Co, Omaha, NE (15)
Medco Supply Co Inc, Tonawanda, NY (7)
Medcom Inc, Cypress, CA (17)
Medibadge Inc, Omaha, NE (5)
Medical Economics Magazine, North Olmsted, OH (17)
Medical Letter Inc, New Rochelle, NY (1)
Medtronic, Minneapolis, MN (7)
Megger, Dallas, TX (16)
Meguiar's Inc, Irvine, CA (16)
Meister Media Worldwide, Willoughby, OH (17)
Melaniphy & Associates, Inc, Chicago, IL (8)
Memphis Net & Twine Co Inc, Memphis, TN (11)
Menardi Mikropul LLC, Trenton, SC (16)
The Menninger Foundation, Houston, TX (1)
Mentor Corp, Santa Barbara, CA (16)
Merastar Insurance Co, Chattanooga, TN (15)
Merck & Co Inc, Whitehouse Station, NJ (16)
Mercury International Trading, North Attleboro, MA (2)
Meredith Corp, Des Moines, IA (17)
Mergent Inc, Fort Mill, SC (14)
Merisel, New York, NY (16)
Merrick Bank, South Jordan, UT (14)
Merrill Corp, Saint Cloud, MN (18)
Merrill Lynch International Inc, New York, NY (14)
Methode Electronics Inc, Chicago, IL (9)
Metro Speedgear, Livingston, NJ (11)
Metropolitan Museum of Art, New York, NY (8)
Metropolitan Property & Casualty Ins, Warwick, RI (15)
Metso Minerals/WS Tyler, Waukesha, WI (16)
Meylan Corp, Montclair, NJ (9)
The Miami Herald Media Co, Miami, FL (17)
Michigan Apple Committee, Lansing, MI (1)
Mickwee Group Inc, Newark, CA (16)

Micro Center, Hilliard, OH (3)
Micro Plastics Inc, Flippin, AR (16)
Microbiz Corp, Menlo Park, CA (3)
Microfluidics Corp, Westwood, MA (16)
Micron Corp, Norwood, MA (16)
Mid America Designs Inc, Effingham, IL (12)
Mid America Motorworks, Effingham, IL (12)
Midcontinent Financial Center Inc, Columbia, MO (14)
The Middleby Corp, Elgin, IL (16)
The Midland Co, Amelia, OH (15)
Midwest Center for Stress & Anxiety Inc, Oak Harbor, OH (7)
Midwest Publishing Inc, Phoenix, AZ (17)
Midwest Technology Products & Services, Sioux City, IA (9)
Military Officers Association of America, Alexandria, VA (1)
Military Order of the Purple Heart Svc, Annandale, VA (1)
The Millard Group, Lincolnwood, IL (16)
The Miller Group, Dupo, IL (5)
Millipore Corp, Bedford, MA (9)
Milwaukee Electric Tool Corp, Brookfield, WI (16)
Mini City Ltd, Webster, NY (12)
Minitab Inc, State College, PA (16)
Minnesota Life, Saint Paul, MN (15)
Minnesota Multi Housing Association, Bloomington, MN (1)
Minnesota Public Radio, Saint Paul, MN (1)
Miracle of Aloe, Dallas, TX (7)
MISSCO Corp, Flowood, MS (16)
Missouri Landscape & Nursery Association, Bowling Green, MO (1)
Missouri Life Inc, Boonville, MO (17)
Mr G's Enterprises, Fort Worth, TX (16)
Mitchell International, San Diego, CA (17)
Frank Mittermeier Inc, Bronx, NY (11)
Modern Postcard, Carlsbad, CA (10)
Modernage Custom Digital Imaging Labs, New York, NY (16)
Mohawk Lifts, Amsterdam, NY (9)
Molson Coors Brewing Co, Denver, CO (16)
Montag & Caldwell Inc, Atlanta, GA (14)
Moon Shine Trading Co, Woodland, CA (4)
Moore Medical LLC, Farmington, CT (7)
Thurston Moore Country Ltd, Madison, TN (16)
Morcon Industrial Specialty Inc, Mesquite, NV (9)
Jacques Moret Inc, New York, NY (16)
Morgan Kaufmann Publishers Inc, Burlington, MA (17)
Morgan Stanley, New York, NY (14)
Moritt, Hock, Hamroff & Horowitz, Garden City, NY (16)
Morkes Chocolates, Palatine, IL (4)
Morris Visitors Publications LLC, Augusta, GA (17)
Thomas Moser Cabinetmakers, Freeport, ME (16)
Mostad & Christensen, Oak Harbor, WA (16)
Motient Communications, Reston, VA (16)
Motion Picture & Television Fund, Woodland Hills, CA (1)
The Motley Fool, Alexandria, VA (14)
Motor Coach Industries International Inc, Schaumburg, IL (16)
Mott Media LLC, Fenton, MI (17)
Mountain Craft Shop Co, Proctor, WV (11)
Mountain Press Publishing Co, Missoula, MT (17)
Mountain West Supply Co, Scottsdale, AZ (3)
Multi-Level Marketing International Association (MLMIA), Irvine, CA (1)
Mike Murach & Associates Inc, Fresno, CA (17)
Murder by Mail, West Tisbury, MA (1)

Muscular Dystrophy Association, Chicago, IL (1)
Museum Masters Inc, New York, NY (16)
The Museum of Modern Art, New York, NY (5)
Music Choice, Horsham, PA (16)
Music Sales Corp, New York, NY (17)
Music Treasures Co, Richmond, VA (6)
Muskegon Power Tool Corp, North Muskegon, MI (16)
Mustek Inc, Tustin, CA (3)
Mutual of America Life Insurance Co, New York, NY (14)
Mutual of Omaha, Omaha, NE (15)
Myron Corp, Maywood, NJ (16)
Mystic Seaport Museum Stores, Mystic, CT (6)

N

NADA Appraisal Guides, Costa Mesa, CA (17)
NBTY Inc, Ronkonkoma, NY (7)
NCP Solutions, Reston, VA (17)
NCR Corp, Duluth, GA (16)
NEBS, Groton, MA (10)
NGL Insurance Group, Madison, WI (15)
NPI, Fort Worth, TX (16)
NTL Institute, Silver Spring, MD (1)
Nancy's Notions LLC, Beaver Dam, WI (11)
NAR Productions, Barryville, NY (17)
Nasco, Fort Atkinson, WI (5)
National Active & Retired Federal Employees Association, Alexandria, VA (1)
National Archives & Records Administration, Washington, DC (17)
National Association for Female Executives, New York, NY (1)
National Association for Printing Leadership, Paramus, NJ (1)
National Association of Publishers Representatives, Hoffman Estates, IL (1)
National Association of Realtors, Chicago, IL (1)
National Automated Clearing House Association, Herndon, VA (1)
National Bulk Equipment Inc, Holland, MI (16)
National Business Furniture Inc, Milwaukee, WI (10)
National Catholic Reporter Publishing Co Inc, Kansas City, MO (17)
National City Bank, Cleveland, OH (14)
National Community Pharmacists Association, Alexandria, VA (1)
National Contract Management Association, Ashburn, VA (1)
National Council on Compensation Insurance Inc, Boca Raton, FL (1)
National Court Reporters Association, Reston, VA (1)
National Crime Prevention Council, Amsterdam, NY (17)
National Emblem Sales, Indianapolis, IN (16)
National Fire Protection Association, Quincy, MA (1)
National Foundation for Cancer Research, Bethesda, MD (1)
National 4-H Supply Service, Chevy Chase, MD (16)
National Golf Foundation, Jupiter, FL (1)
National Journal Group, Washington, DC (17)
National Law Enforcement Officers Memorial Fund, Washington, DC (1)
National League for Nursing, Washington, DC (1)
National Luggage Dealers Association, Glenview, IL (1)
National Medical Fellowships, New York, NY (1)
National Motor Club of America Inc, Irving, TX (1)
National Pecan Co, Frisco, TX (4)
National Pen Corp, San Diego, CA (6)

National Pension Service Inc, Burlington, VT (14)
National Railroad Passenger Corp, Washington, DC (16)
The National Restaurant Association Educational Foundation, Washington, DC (1)
National Retail Federation Inc, Washington, DC (1)
National Right to Work Legal Defense Foundation, Springfield, VA (1)
National Rural Electric Cooperative Association, Arlington, VA (1)
National School Boards Association Inc, Alexandria, VA (1)
National Seminars Group, Shawnee Mission, KS (16)
National Society of Collegiate Scholars, Washington, DC (1)
National Technical Information Service, Alexandria, VA (17)
The National Underwriter Co, Erlanger, KY (17)
Nationwide Beauty & Barber Supply, Syracuse, NY (16)
Nationwide Displays Inc, Ronkonkoma, NY (16)
Nationwide Mutual Insurance Co, Columbus, OH (15)
Natural Essentials Inc, Streetsboro, OH (5)
The Nature Conservancy, Arlington, VA (1)
Nature Publishing Group, New York, NY (17)
Nautilus Inc, Vancouver, WA (11)
Naval Institute Press, Annapolis, MD (17)
Navistar, Lisle, IL (16)
Navitar Inc, Rochester, NY (16)
Navy Federal Credit Union, Vienna, VA (14)
Neighborhood Cleaners Association International, New York, NY (1)
Nelson Crab Inc, Tokeland, WA (4)
Nelson-Jameson Inc, Marshfield, WI (9)
Nestle HealthCare Nutrition, Florham Park, NJ (16)
Nestle USA, Glendale, CA (4)
Network Telephone Services Inc, Woodland Hills, CA (16)
Neuberger & Berman Management, New York, NY (14)
Neutron Industries, Phoenix, AZ (16)
New & Unique Videos, San Diego, CA (3)
New England Cheesemaking Supply Co, South Deerfield, MA (4)
New England Journal of Medicine, Waltham, MA (17)
New England Life Insurance Co, Boston, MA (15)
New Jersey Institute for Continuing Legal Education, New Brunswick, NJ (1)
New Pig Corp, Tipton, PA (9)
The New Piper Aircraft Inc, Vero Beach, FL (16)
New Track Media LLC, Cincinnati, OH (17)
New Win Publishing Inc, El Monte, CA (17)
New York Blood Center Inc, New York, NY (1)
New York Easter Seal Society, New York, NY (1)
New York Findings, New York, NY (6)
New York Foundation For The Arts, Brooklyn, NY (1)
New York Landmarks Conservancy, New York, NY (1)
New York Power Authority, White Plains, NY (16)
New York-Presbyterian/Columbia University Medical Center, New York, NY (16)
The New York Times Co, New York, NY (17)
New York University Medical Center, New York, NY (1)
The New Yorker Magazine, New York, NY (17)
Newell Rubbermaid, Inc, Atlanta, GA (16)
The Newman Group Computer Services Corp, Ann Arbor, MI (3)
Newspaper Association of America, Arlington, VA (1)

Nicklaus Companies LLC, North Palm Beach, FL (16)
The Nielsen Co, New York, NY (17)
Nielsen Trade Dimensions, Wilton, CT (17)
Nightingale-Conant Corp, Niles, IL (17)
Nightingale Resources, Cold Spring, NY (17)
Nihon Keizai Shimbun America Inc, New York, NY (17)
Nilodor Inc, Bolivar, OH (16)
Nimlok, Niles, IL (16)
Nissan Motor Acceptance Corp, Irving, TX (14)
No Fault Sports Products, Houston, TX (11)
No Load FundX, San Francisco, CA (14)
Nodine's Smokehouse, Torrington, CT (4)
Nomadics Tipi Makers, Bend, OR (11)
The NonProfit Times, Morris Plains, NJ (17)
Norman Control Co, Cary, IL (16)
Norman Rockwell Museum, Stockbridge, MA (16)
Norscot Group, Mequon, WI (5)
North American Co for Life & Health Insurance, Chicago, IL (15)
Northeast Hinge Distributors Inc, Hollis, NH (9)
Northern Cross, Lecompton, KS (16)
Northern Greenhouse Sales, Neche, ND (8)
Northern Safety Co Inc, Utica, NY (16)
The Northern Trust Co, Chicago, IL (14)
Northwest Laboratories, Seattle, WA (9)
Northwestern Mutual, Milwaukee, WI (14)
Norwood Promotional Products, Clearwater, FL (16)
Nourse Farms, South Deerfield, MA (8)
Novartis Pharmaceuticals Corp, East Hanover, NJ (7)
Nowell's Inc, San Rafael, CA (8)
Nu-Parr Swimwear, Phoenix, AZ (2)
Nuance Speech Solutions, Burlington, MA (16)
Nuclear Plant Journal, Downers Grove, IL (17)
Nucor Corp, Charlotte, NC (16)
NuNaturals, Eugene, OR (16)
Nat Nussbaum & Associates Inc, Coral Springs, FL (16)
Nutritional Research Associates Inc, South Whitley, IN (16)
Nuveen Investments, Chicago, IL (14)
Nylon Net Co, Memphis, TN (11)

O

OAG Worldwide, Downers Grove, IL (17)
OSRAM Sylvania, Danvers, MA (16)
Oakley Inc, Foothill Ranch, CA (2)
Oakstone Publishing LLC, Birmingham, AL (17)
O'Brien Manufacturing, Marietta, OH (9)
Ocean Conservancy, Washington, DC (1)
O'Currance Inc, Draper, UT (18)
Office Depot, Boca Raton, FL (16)
OfficeFurniture.com, West Allis, WI (8)
OfficeMax Inc, Boca Raton, FL (10)
Oil & Gas Journal, Tulsa, OK (17)
Oklahoma Dept of Commerce, Oklahoma City, OK (1)
Old World Mouldings Inc, Bohemia, NY (9)
Olesuk Financial Services, McHenry, IL (14)
Oliver of Adrian Inc, Adrian, MI (16)
Olympia Sales Inc, Enfield, CT (16)
Omaha Fixture International, Omaha, NE (8)
Omaha Steaks Inc, Omaha, NE (4)
Omaha Vaccine Co, Omaha, NE (16)
Omni Farm, West Jefferson, NC (16)
Omnigraphics Inc, Aston, PA (17)
On-Hand Adhesives Inc, Lake Zurich, IL (16)
1-800-Contacts, Draper, UT (7)
1-800-Flowers.com, Carle Place, NY (16)

Promotion Marketing Association (PMA) Inc, New York, NY (1)

Promotional Product Professionals of Canada, Dorval, QC, Canada (1)

Protective Life Corp, Deerfield, IL (15)

Protective Life Insurance Co, Birmingham, AL (15)

Prudent Publishing Co, Ridgefield Park, NJ (16)

Prudential Financial, Newark, NJ (14)

Fred Pryor Seminars, Mission, KS (16)

Psion Teklogix Inc, Mississauga, ON, Canada (3)

Putnam Investments, Boston, MA (14)

Putnam Rolling Ladder Co Inc, New York, NY (5)

Putt Putt Fun Centers, Winston-Salem, NC (16)

Q

QC Supply LLC, Schuyler, NE (16)

Quadrant Engineering Plastic Products, Reading, PA (16)

The Quaker Oats Co, Chicago, IL (16)

Qualco, Inc, Passaic, NJ (8)

Quality Products Inc, Columbus, MS (10)

Quartermaster Uniform & Equipment Co, Cerritos, CA (2)

Queen Bee Gardens, Lovell, WY (4)

Queue Inc, Stratford, CT (17)

Quick Draw Clip Systems Inc, Ventura, CA (9)

Quill Corp, Lincolnshire, IL (16)

Quill Lincolnshire Inc, Lincolnshire, IL (10)

R

RBC Dain Rauscher Inc, Minneapolis, MN (14)

RBS Citizens Financial Group Inc, Dedham, MA (14)

RMA-The Risk Management Association, Philadelphia, PA (1)

Racer Walsh Co, Jacksonville, FL (12)

Racer's Equipment Warehouse, Warwick, RI (16)

Rainbow Art Glass, Wall, NJ (16)

Rainbow Group LLC, Middleton, WI (11)

Ranch House Meat Co, Billings, MT (4)

Rand Material Handling Equipment Co Inc, Janesville, WI (16)

Random Lengths Publications Inc, Eugene, OR (17)

Ranger Joe's International Military Supply, Columbus, GA (2)

Rapid City Journal, Rapid City, SD (18)

Rapids Wholesale Equipment, Marion, IA (16)

Raybuck Autobody Parts, Punxsutawney, PA (12)

Raycom Sports, Charlotte, NC (16)

Reading for Education, Murfreesboro, TN (1)

Reb Storage Systems International, Chicago, IL (9)

Recognition Products International, Easton, MD (16)

Recognition Systems (Dot Works), Port Washington, NY (16)

Recording for the Blind & Dyslexic Inc, Princeton, NJ (16)

Recycled Software Inc, Palm Springs, CA (3)

RedEnvelope Inc, San Diego, CA (6)

Redleaf Press, Saint Paul, MN (17)

Redwood City Seed Co, Redwood City, CA (8)

Reed Elsevier, New York, NY (17)

Reed Exhibitions, Norwalk, CT (16)

Referee Enterprises, Racine, WI (1)

Regal Ware Inc, Kewaskum, WI (16)

The Reggio Register Co Inc, Leominster, MA (8)

Regitar USA Inc, Montgomery, AL (9)

Reid Supply Co, Muskegon, MI (16)

Relaxo-Bak Inc, Anderson, IN (7)

Reliable Racing Supply, Queensbury, NY (11)

Reliable Technologies Inc, Manchester, NH (16)

Reliance Electric, Fort Smith, AR (9)

Renaissance Greeting Cards Inc, Downers Grove, IL (5)

Renaissance Learning, Wisconsin Rapids, WI (5)

Reno Gazette Journal, Reno, NV (17)

The Renovator's Supply Inc, Millers Falls, MA (9)

Rent-A-Center Inc, Plano, TX (16)

Rent Mother Nature, Cambridge, MA (4)

Renton's Inc, Parker, CO (10)

Replacements Ltd, Greensboro, NC (8)

Replogle Globes Inc, Broadview, IL (16)

Research To Prevent Blindness Inc, New York, NY (1)

Rose Resnick Lighthouse for the Blind & Visually Impaired, San Francisco, CA (1)

Resource Publications Inc, San Jose, CA (17)

Resumate Inc, Ann Arbor, MI (3)

Retawmatic Corp, Flushing, NY (9)

Rhode Island Novelty, Cumberland, RI (16)

Rhythm Band Inc, Fort Worth, TX (11)

Ricci Lee Hubbart Associates Inc, Cupertino, CA (16)

Rich Products Corp, Buffalo, NY (16)

Richardson Electronics Ltd, Lafox, IL (16)

Pete Rickard Inc, Cobleskill, NY (11)

Rio Brands, Philadelphia, PA (16)

Rio Grande, Albuquerque, NM (16)

River Street Sweets, Savannah, GA (4)

Rizzoli International Publications Inc, New York, NY (17)

Robert Marketing Inc, Northbrook, IL (5)

C H Robinson Worldwide Inc, Eden Prairie, MN (16)

Robinson Home Products, Buffalo, NY (16)

The Roblin Group Inc, White Plains, NY (17)

Rock-Tred Corp, Waukegan, IL (9)

RocketWear, New York, NY (2)

Rockler Woodworking & Hardware, Medina, MN (8)

Rockwell Automation, Milwaukee, WI (16)

Rocky Mountain Chocolate Factory, Durango, CO (4)

Rodale Inc, Emmaus, PA (17)

Rod's Western Palace, Columbus, OH (2)

Rogers Publishing Ltd, Toronto, ON, Canada (17)

Rohm & Haas Co, Philadelphia, PA (16)

Rollyson Financial Group, Pasadena, MD (14)

Roman Research Inc/Simply Whispers Earring, Hanson, MA (2)

Ronco Corp, Austin, TX (16)

Ronell Clock Co, Grants Pass, OR (5)

Rose Displays Ltd, Salem, MA (16)

Rose Electronics, Houston, TX (3)

Rosicrucian Order AMORC, San Jose, CA (1)

Rosland Capital LLC, Santa Monica, CA (14)

Ross Metals, New York, NY (16)

Ross-Simons, Cranston, RI (6)

Roto-Rooter Services Co, Cincinnati, OH (16)

Row Resources Inc, Northport, NY (16)

Rowe Pottery Works Inc, Cambridge, WI (16)

Royal Bank of Canada, Toronto, ON, Canada (14)

Royal Canadian Mint, Ottawa, ON, Canada (16)

Rubber Stamps of America, Dublin, NH (6)

Rural Alaska Community Action Program Inc, Anchorage, AK (1)

Ruskin, Moscou, Faltischek, PC, Uniondale, NY (16)

Rutland Products, Rutland, VT (16)

Ruud Lighting Inc, Racine, WI (9)

S

S&S Worldwide, Colchester, CT (11)

SC Direct, West Bridgewater, MA (2)

SCA Promotions Inc, Dallas, TX (15)

SDI Marketing, Toronto, ON, Canada (14)

SEI, Oaks, PA (14)

SF Global Sourcing Inc, San Francisco, CA (3)

SIFMA, New York, NY (1)

SLM Corp, Newark, DE (16)

SNL Financial, Charlottesville, VA (17)

SRDS, Des Plaines, IL (17)

SSHC Inc/Radiant Heating Commercial Applications, Old Saybrook, CT (9)

ST Media Group International, Cincinnati, OH (17)

SWBC, San Antonio, TX (14)

Sa-So, Arlington, TX (16)

Sabre Holdings Inc, Southlake, TX (19)

Safe Publications Inc, Doylestown, PA (11)

Safeco Insurance Co, Seattle, WA (15)

Safeguard Business Systems Inc, Dallas, TX (16)

Safeware, The Insurance Agency Inc, Columbus, OH (15)

Safti First, Brisbane, CA (16)

Sage Financial Group, West Conshohocken, PA (14)

Sage Software Inc, Irvine, CA (16)

The Sailing Co, Palm Coast, FL (17)

The Saint Francis Community Services, Salina, KS (1)

St Lawrence Island Original Ivory Cooperative, Gambell, AK (6)

St Louis Post-Dispatch, Saint Louis, MO (17)

St Louis Slot Machine Co, Saint Louis, MO (6)

St Petersburg/Clearwater Area CVB, Clearwater, FL (1)

Saks Fifth Avenue, New York, NY (16)

Salem Media Group, Camarillo, CA (17)

Sales & Marketing Management Magazine, New York, NY (16)

Sales Leads, Jupiter, FL (17)

Salesian Missions, New Rochelle, NY (1)

Sally Beauty Supply LLC, Denton, TX (7)

Sam Ash Music Direct, Hicksville, NY (5)

Samsonite International SA, Mansfield, MA (16)

San Francisco Chronicle, San Francisco, CA (17)

San Francisco Herb & Natural Food Co, San Francisco, CA (4)

San Francisco Victoriana Inc, San Francisco, CA (9)

San Jose Mercury News, San Jose, CA (17)

Sandy Corp, Troy, MI (16)

Sani Serv, Mooresville, IN (16)

Santa Barbara Greenhouses, Oxnard, CA (8)

Santa Fe Natural Tobacco Co, Santa Fe, NM (16)

Satori Software Inc, Seattle, WA (16)

Saunders Manufacturing Co Inc, Readfield, ME (16)

Saunders Military Insignia, Naples, FL (6)

The Sausage Maker Inc, Buffalo, NY (4)

Save the Children Federation Inc, Fairfield, CT (1)

Sax Arts & Crafts, Appleton, WI (10)

Scan Optics Inc, Manchester, CT (16)

Henry Schein Inc, Melville, NY (16)

Schermer Pecans, Glennville, GA (4)

Jacques C Schiff Jr Inc, Ridgefield Park, NJ (5)

Schneider Saddlery, Chagrin Falls, OH (11)

Schnuck Markets Inc, Saint Louis, MO (16)

Scholastic Inc, New York, NY (17)

School Annual Publishing Co, State College, PA (17)

School Specialty Inc, Greenville, WI (16)

Schoolwise Press, San Francisco, CA (17)

Schultz & Williams Inc, Philadelphia, PA (1)

Scorecards USA, North Kingstown, RI (16)

Scott Sign Systems Inc, Sarasota, FL (16)
The Scotts Co LLC, Marysville, OH (8)
Scott's Dog Supply Inc, Indianapolis, IN (11)
Scotts-Sierra Horticultural, Marysville, OH (16)
Sculpture House Inc, Skillman, NJ (16)
Sea Bear, Anacortes, WA (16)
Seashore Vacations, Hilton Head Island, SC (19)
Seattle Magazine, Seattle, WA (17)
SECO-LARM USA Inc, Irvine, CA (16)
Second Renaissance Books, Irvine, CA (17)
Seedburo Equipment Co, Des Plaines, IL (8)
Seiko Corp of America, Mahwah, NJ (16)
Select Press, Novato, CA (17)
Sellstrom Manufacturing Co, Schaumburg, IL (16)
LH Selman Ltd, Chicago, IL (6)
Sencore Inc, Sioux Falls, SD (16)
Sensient Technologies, Saint Louis, MO (16)
Sentry Life Insurance Co, Stevens Point, WI (15)
Serenity, Maria Stein, OH (17)
JA Sexauer, Elmsford, NY (16)
Seybold Publications, Gilbertsville, PA (17)
B Shackman & Co Inc, Galesburg, MI (6)
Shades of Light, Richmond, VA (8)
Shakespeare Co, Columbia, SC (11)
Shape LLC, Addison, IL (3)
Shelby Insurance Companies, Birmingham, AL (15)
Sherman Specialty Toy Co Inc, Jericho, NY (16)
Shield Healthcare, Valencia, CA (7)
Shillcraft Inc, Annapolis, MD (16)
Shipping Solutions, Eagan, MN (16)
Shop.com, Miami, FL (16)
Shopsmith Inc, Dayton, OH (16)
Shortage Control Inc & SC Video, Strongsville, OH (5)
Sierra Scientific Inc, Phoenix, AZ (9)
Silicon Graphics Inc, Fremont, CA (16)
Silver Star Brands, Oshkosh, WI (6)
Simmons-Boardman Publishing Corp, New York, NY (17)
Simon Property Group, Indianapolis, IN (16)
Simplex Grinnell, Westminster, MA (16)
Simplicity Pattern Co Inc/Style Patterns Ltd/New Look English Pattern Co Ltd, New York, NY (8)
Simpson Electric Co, Lac Du Flambeau, WI (16)
Sims Stoves, Billings, MT (11)
Single Scene News, Tempe, AZ (17)
SiriusXM Radio Inc, New York, NY (16)
Skinder-Strauss Associates, New Providence, NJ (14)
Skullduggery, Anaheim, CA (16)
Skypoint Communications Inc, Loretto, MN (16)
Small Business Service Bureau Inc, Worcester, MA (1)
Smart Dog Products, Winchester, TN (11)
Smart Practice, Phoenix, AZ (17)
AO Smith Corp, Milwaukee, WI (16)
Smithfield Foods, Smithfield, VA (16)
The JM Smucker Co, Orrville, OH (4)
Snap-on Inc, Kenosha, WI (9)
Tom Snyder Productions, Watertown, MA (16)
SOAR Inflatables, Healdsburg, CA (11)
Social Studies School Service, Culver City, CA (16)
Society for Human Resource Management, Alexandria, VA (1)
Society of Financial Service Professionals, Newtown Square, PA (1)
Society of Manufacturing Engineers, Dearborn, MI (1)
Software AG USA, Reston, VA (3)
Software Assistance International Ltd, Morris Plains, NJ (3)
Solar Cine Products Inc, Chicago, IL (5)

Solar Components Corp, Manchester, NH (9)
Solarcom, Norcross, GA (16)
Solitron Devices Inc, West Palm Beach, FL (16)
Sony Electronics Inc, San Diego, CA (16)
Sotheby's, New York, NY (6)
Soundprints, Norwalk, CT (6)
South Seas Island Resort, Captiva Island, FL (19)
South-Western Publishing, Madison, OH (17)
Southeast Toyota Distributors LLC, Deerfield Beach, FL (16)
Southern California Gas Co, Anaheim, CA (1)
Southern Flavoring Co Inc, Bedford, VA (16)
Southern Progress Corp, Birmingham, AL (17)
Sovereign Bank New England, Glastonbury, CT (14)
Spa-Finder Inc, New York, NY (7)
Spadet, New York, NY (7)
Spalding Laboratories Inc, Reno, NV (7)
Spates The Florist, Newport, VT (8)
Huck Spaulding Enterprises, Voorheesville, NY (16)
Speakers Guild Inc, Sandwich, MA (16)
Spear Engineering Co, Colorado Springs, CO (16)
Specialized Association Services, Irving, TX (1)
Specialized Information Publishers Association, Vienna, VA (1)
Specialized Products Co, Southlake, TX (16)
Specialty Store Services Inc, Des Plaines, IL (16)
Spectra Merchandising International Inc, Chicago, IL (16)
Spectronics Corp, Westbury, NY (9)
Spectrum Chemicals & Laboratory Products, Gardena, CA (16)
Speed-Mat, Biddeford, ME (16)
The Sperry & Hutchinson Co Inc, Delray Beach, FL (6)
Spinneybeck Enterprises, Getzville, NY (16)
Spokane Teachers Credit Union, Liberty Lake, WA (14)
Spoken Arts, Holmes, NY (17)
The Spokesman-Review, Spokane, WA (17)
Sport Supply Group, Dallas, TX (11)
Sportif Mail Order Inc, Sparks, NV (2)
Sportime International, Norcross, GA (11)
Spring-Green Lawn Care Corp, Plainfield, IL (16)
Springer Science & Business Media LLC, New York, NY (17)
Springs Global Inc, New York, NY (16)
Sprint Corp, Overland Park, KS (3)
Stagestep Inc, Philadelphia, PA (5)
Standard & Poor's Corp, New York, NY (17)
Standard Communications Corp, San Diego, CA (16)
Standard Life, Montreal, QC, Canada (15)
Standard Publishing, Cincinnati, OH (17)
Robert A Stanger & Co Inc, Shrewsbury, NJ (14)
Stanley Supply & Services, North Andover, MA (16)
Staples Inc, Framingham, MA (10)
Star Sprinkler Inc, Lansdale, PA (9)
Starbucks Corp, Seattle, WA (4)
Starchtech, Golden Valley, MN (16)
Stark Brothers Nurseries & Orchards, Louisiana, MO (8)
Starkey Laboratories, Eden Prairie, MN (16)
START International, Addison, TX (9)
State Farm Insurance Cos, Bloomington, IL (15)
State Mutual Insurance Co, Rome, GA (15)
StatSoft Inc, Tulsa, OK (9)
StayWell/Krames, San Bruno, CA (17)
Steelcase Inc, Grand Rapids, MI (16)
Stellar Technology Inc, Amherst, NY (9)
Stephens Publishing Co, Sandusky, OH (17)
Steptoe & Wife Antiques Ltd, Scarborough, ON, Canada (8)
Sterling Fluid Systems, Indianapolis, IN (16)

Sterling Name Tape Inc, Winsted, CT (16)
Sterling Publishing Co Inc, New York, NY (17)
Stew Leonard's, Norwalk, CT (4)
Stewart-MacDonald, Athens, OH (16)
Martha Stewart Living Omnimedia, New York, NY (17)
Kirk Stieff Co, Bristol, PA (16)
Stile-Tile Like Metal Roofing, Sellersburg, IN (9)
Stimpson Co Inc, Pompano Beach, FL (16)
Stock Drive Products, New Hyde Park, NY (5)
Stock Yards Packing Co Inc, Medford, OR (4)
Stonwurks, Eden Prairie, MN (16)
Strang Communications Co, Lake Mary, FL (17)
Strategy Corps LLC, Brentwood, TN (16)
Stratford Hall, North Mankato, MN (10)
The Stratosphere Las Vegas, Las Vegas, NV (19)
Stratus Technologies, Maynard, MA (16)
Stress Market, Port Angeles, WA (17)
Strongwell, Bristol, VA (9)
Sturges Sportswear, Battleboro, NC (16)
SubscriptionAgency.com Inc, Winter Haven, FL (18)
Suez Energy North America, Houston, TX (16)
Sugarbush Farm Inc, Woodstock, VT (4)
Sullivan-Victory Groves, Rockledge, FL (4)
Summit Industries Inc, Marietta, GA (5)
Summit Racing Equipment, Tallmadge, OH (12)
Sun Harvest Citrus, Fort Myers, FL (6)
Sunbeam Products Inc, Boca Raton, FL (16)
Sunbilt Solar Products, Jamaica, NY (8)
Sunburst Farms Inc, Miami, FL (8)
Sundancer Jewelry Co Inc, Albuquerque, NM (16)
Sunlife of Canada, Wellesley Hills, MA (15)
Sunnyland Farms Inc, Albany, GA (4)
Sunoco Inc, Philadelphia, PA (16)
Sunrise Business Products, Mineola, NY (10)
Sunrise Greetings, Kansas City, MO (17)
Sunrise Medical Inc, Boulder, CO (16)
Sunshine Discount Crafts, Largo, FL (11)
Sunshine Farm & Gardens, Renick, WV (8)
Sunshine Glassworks Ltd, Buffalo, NY (11)
Sunshine Minting Inc, Coeur D'Alene, ID (14)
Sunshine Unlimited Inc, Lindsborg, KS (9)
Sunstar, Chicago, IL (16)
Suntrust Banks Inc, Atlanta, GA (14)
Supelco Inc, Bellefonte, PA (16)
Super 8 Hotels Worldwide, Parsippany, NJ (19)
Sur La Table, Brownsburg, IN (8)
Sure-Fire Business Success Catalog, Cambridge, MA (17)
Surplus Center, Lincoln, NE (9)
Surplus Record, Chicago, IL (17)
Sussex Publishers Inc, New York, NY (17)
Svoboda Collins LLC, Chicago, IL (5)
The Swiss Colony Inc, Monroe, WI (4)
Symantec, Mountain View, CA (16)
Symetra Financial, Bellevue, WA (15)
Symrise, Teterboro, NJ (7)
Syngenta, Greensboro, NC (16)
Syntellect, Phoenix, AZ (16)
System Pavers, Newport Beach, CA (16)
Systemax Inc, Port Washington, NY (16)

T

T Rowe Price Associates Inc, Baltimore, MD (14)
TAB Boards International Inc, Westminster, CO (14)
Thomson Reuters, New York, NY (17)
TIAA-CREF, New York, NY (15)
TL Enterprises Inc, Ventura, CA (17)
TNT Packaging Inc, Miami, FL (16)

TT Publishing, Arlington, VA (17)
TVC Enterprises and the TV Collector Magazine, Las Vegas, NV (6)
TWL Knowledge Group, Carrollton, TX (3)
TABcom, Hazleton, PA (5)
Tackle Craft, Ellsworth, WI (11)
Tailwinds Inc, Mill Valley, CA (6)
Talas, Brooklyn, NY (10)
Tamrac Inc, Ogden, UT (2)
Tandy Leather Co, Fort Worth, TX (11)
The Taunton Press, Newtown, CT (17)
Tax Management Inc, Bethesda, MD (17)
Tax Reduction Institute, Germantown, MD (14)
Taylor Capital Group, Inc, Rosemont, IL (14)
Taylor Corp, North Mankato, MN (16)
Taylor-Stiles Division, Florence, KY (16)
Taymark Inc, White Bear Lake, MN (1)
Teachers' Discovery, Auburn Hills, MI (5)
The Teaching Co, Chantilly, VA (17)
Team Cheer, Geneseo, NY (2)
Techni-Tool Inc, Worcester, PA (16)
Technical Association of the Pulp & Paper Industry, Norcross, GA (1)
Technology Review, Cambridge, MA (17)
Tektronix Inc, Beaverton, OR (16)
Telcordia Technologies, Piscataway, NJ (16)
Telecommunications Reports International Inc, Washington, DC (17)
Telect Inc, Liberty Lake, WA (16)
Teleflora, Los Angeles, CA (16)
Telefonix Inc, Waukegan, IL (16)
Telephony, Chicago, IL (17)
Telpro Inc, Grand Forks, ND (9)
Tempco Electric Heater Corp, Wood Dale, IL (9)
Ten Speed Press, Emeryville, CA (17)
Tennessee Valley Authority, Knoxville, TN (16)
Tensar International Corporation, Alpharetta, GA (16)
Terminix International, The Trugreen Companies, Memphis, TN (16)
Tessco Inc, Hunt Valley, MD (16)
Tetley USA Inc, Montvale, NJ (16)
Teva Pharmaceuticals USA, North Wales, PA (7)
Texas Industries Inc, Dallas, TX (16)
Texas Parks & Wildlife Dept, Austin, TX (1)
Texas Refinery Corp, Fort Worth, TX (9)
Texwipe Co, Kernersville, NC (16)
Theatre Development Fund Inc, New York, NY (1)
TheIdeaClub.com & Dumas Martin Consulting, Pomona, CA (16)
Thermal Product Solutions, White Deer, PA (16)
Thermo Fisher Scientific Inc, Waltham, MA (9)
Thermo Pro, Duluth, GA (16)
Thetford Corp, Ann Arbor, MI (16)
Thieme Medical Publishers Inc, New York, NY (17)
Things Deco, New York, NY (6)
Things Remembered, Highland Heights, OH (6)
Think Ink, Bothell, WA (10)
Thirteen/WNET, New York, NY (1)
Thoma Cressey Bravo, Chicago, IL (14)
Thomas Computer Corp, Orlando, FL (16)
Thomas Klise/Crimson Multimedia, Mystic, CT (16)
Thomas Nelson, Nashville, TN (17)
Thomas Scientific, Swedesboro, NJ (9)
Stephen Thomas, Toronto, ON, Canada (1)
Thompson Publishing Group Inc, Washington, DC (17)
Thomson Research, Boston, MA (14)
Thomson Reuters LPC, New York, NY (14)
Thomson West, Eagan, MN (17)
Thorndike Press, Waterville, ME (17)

Thought Technology Ltd, Montreal, QC, Canada (16)
3D Mail Results, Kent, WA (5)
Three Georges and the Nuthouse, Mobile, AL (16)
3M Post-It Custom Printed Products, Saint Paul, MN (16)
Tidbits Media, Montgomery, AL (17)
TigerDirect.ca, Richmond Hill, ON, Canada (3)
TigerDirect Inc, El Segundo, CA (3)
Tillamook County Creamery Association, Tillamook, OR (4)
Timber Crest Farms, Healdsburg, CA (16)
Timberline Geodesics, Berkeley, CA (8)
Time Inc, New York, NY (17)
Time Motion Tools, Poway, CA (9)
Time Products International, Del Rio, TX (16)
Time/System, Chicopee, MA (16)
Time Warner Inc, New York, NY (16)
Times Union, Albany, NY (18)
Timm Medical Technologies, Inc, Lake Forest, IL (16)
Tinsley Tool Supply Inc, Powell, TN (9)
Todaro Brothers Mail Order Co, New York, NY (4)
Toland Home and Garden Inc, Port Townsend, WA (16)
Tomahawk Live Trap Co, Tomahawk, WI (16)
Torah Umesorah Publications, Brooklyn, NY (5)
Toronto Hydro-Electric System, Toronto, ON, Canada (1)
Torqmaster International, Stamford, CT (9)
Total Training Solutions LLC, Waunakee, WI (5)
Toter Inc, Statesville, NC (16)
Townsend Communications LLC, Kansas City, MO (17)
Toyota Motor Sales USA Inc, Torrance, CA (16)
Trans Union Corp, Chicago, IL (14)
Transaction Publishers, Piscataway, NJ (17)
Transamerica Occidental Life Co, Los Angeles, CA (15)
Transcat, Rochester, NY (16)
Transemantics Inc, Washington, DC (16)
TransFirst Holdings Inc, Dallas, TX (14)
Transit Treasure Inc, New York, NY (12)
Travel Planners Inc, New York, NY (19)
Travelclick, Schaumburg, IL (19)
The Travelers Insurance Cos, Hartford, CT (15)
Trend Magazines Inc, Saint Petersburg, FL (17)
Tri Tech Laboratories Inc, Lynchburg, VA (16)
Tribune Co, Chicago, IL (17)
Tricor Braun, Woodridge, IL (16)
Tricor Direct Inc, Branford, CT (9)
Trigon Blue Cross/Blue Shield, Roanoke, VA (15)
Trilithic, Indianapolis, IN (16)
Tristar Products, Fairfield, NJ (16)
Triton College, River Grove, IL (16)
Trophyland USA Inc, Hialeah, FL (5)
Trout Unlimited, Arlington, VA (1)
Troy Biologicals Inc, Troy, MI (7)
TruGreen/ChemLawn, Lewis Center, OH (16)
Truitt Brothers Inc, Salem, OR (16)
Trumble Greetings, Boulder, CO (6)
The Trumpet Club, New York, NY (17)
truTV, New York, NY (17)
Tucker Electronics Co, Garland, TX (3)
Tully & Holland Inc, Wellesley, MA (14)
Turncraft Clocks Inc, Spring Park, MN (6)
Tuttle, Wallingford, CT (2)
Tuttle Printing & Engraving, Rutland, VT (10)
20th Century Fox Television, Los Angeles, CA (16)
Tyco Electronics Corp, Berwyn, PA (16)
Tyco Valves & Controls, Houston, TX (16)
Tyndale House Publishers, Carol Stream, IL (17)

U

U-Bild, Oceanside, CA (8)
U-Haul International, Phoenix, AZ (16)
UBS Wealth Management US, Weehawken, NJ (14)
UGL Equis Corp, Chicago, IL (16)
UNICEF, New York, NY (1)
UNICEF Canada, Toronto, ON, Canada (1)
USAA, San Antonio, TX (15)
USX, Pittsburgh, PA (16)
Uline, Pleasant Prairie, WI (5)
Ultimate Office, Farmingdale, NJ (16)
Ultimate Products Inc, Chula Vista, CA (16)
Ultra Direct Marketing Inc, Jackson, NJ (16)
UMass Dartmouth, North Dartmouth, MA (1)
Unadilla Laminated Products, Unadilla, NY (16)
Uncharted Country Publishing, Madison, WI (17)
Uncle Ben's Inc, Greenville, MS (4)
Unicol Inc, Pembroke Pines, FL (17)
Unicom Electric Inc, Walnut, CA (16)
UNICOM Government Inc, Herndon, VA (16)
Unicover Corp, Cheyenne, WY (6)
Uniforms & Scrubs.com, Ballwin, MO (7)
Union Federal Savings Bank, North Providence, RI (14)
Union Switch & Signal Inc, Pittsburgh, PA (16)
Unisys, Blue Bell, PA (16)
United Air Specialists Inc, Cincinnati, OH (16)
United Business Media, Manhasset, NY (17)
United Church Homes, Marion, OH (1)
United Communications Group, Gaithersburg, MD (17)
United Community Bank, Blairsville, GA (14)
United Investors Life Insurance Co, Birmingham, AL (15)
United Security Products Inc, Poway, CA (16)
United Spinal Association, Kew Gardens, NY (1)
United Staffing Systems, New York, NY (16)
US Bancorp, Minneapolis, MN (14)
US Bank, Minneapolis, MN (14)
US Branding Group LLC, Lake Worth, FL (16)
United States Bronze Sign Co Inc, New Hyde Park, NY (1)
US Chamber of Commerce, Washington, DC (1)
US Department of Commerce, Washington, DC (1)
US Foodservice, Rosemont, IL (4)
US Fund for UNICEF, New York, NY (6)
US Games Systems Inc, Stamford, CT (11)
US News & World Report, Washington, DC (17)
USA Hosts Ltd, New Orleans, LA (19)
USA TODAY, Mc Lean, VA (17)
US Pharmacopeia, Rockville, MD (1)
US Playing Card Co, Erlanger, KY (16)
US Travel Association, Washington, DC (1)
United Systems c/o Biomed, Concord, CA (7)
United Way Toronto & York Region, Toronto, ON, Canada (1)
Unitron Ltd, Commack, NY (9)
Universal Corp, Richmond, VA (16)
Universal Engineering Corp, Cedar Rapids, IA (16)
Universal Fidelity Corp, Houston, TX (14)
Universal Hovercraft, Cordova, IL (11)
Universal Security Instruments Inc, Owings Mills, MD (16)
Universal Studios Inc, Universal City, CA (3)
Universal Training, Lake Forest, IL (16)
Universal Vintage Tire Co, Hershey, PA (11)
University Bank, Ann Arbor, MI (14)
University of Akron, Akron, OH (1)
University of Alabama, Tuscaloosa, AL (13)
University of Chicago Press, Chicago, IL (17)

University of Illinois Foundation, Urbana, IL (1)
University of Oklahoma Press, Norman, OK (17)
University Press of America Inc, Lanham, MD (17)
Unum Corp, Portland, ME (15)
Upbeat Inc, Saint Louis, MO (9)
Upstart, Madison, WI (16)
The Urban Land Institute, Washington, DC (1)
Urbani Truffles USA Corp, New York, NY (4)
Utilities Supply Corp, Woburn, MA (16)
Utretch Art Supplies, Cranbury, NJ (10)

V

VF Imagewear, Greensboro, NC (2)
Vagabond Creations Inc, Dayton, OH (10)
Valdawn Watch Co, Long Island City, NY (16)
Value Line Publishing Inc, New York, NY (17)
K Van Bourgondien & Sons Inc, (8)
Van Dam Inc, New York, NY (17)
Vance Industries Inc, Niles, IL (16)
Vanderbilt Advertising, New York, NY (14)
The Vane Brothers Co, Baltimore, MD (16)
Vanguard, Malvern, PA (14)
Varian Medical Systems, Palo Alto, CA (9)
Vaxserve, Moosic, PA (7)
Vcom International Multi-Media Corp, South Hackensack, NJ (3)
Veer, Calgary, AB, Canada (16)
Vemma Nutrition Co, Tempe, AZ (7)
Veneer Factory Outlet, Westport, KY (8)
Ventyx, Atlanta, GA (16)
Venus Fashion, Inc, Jacksonville, FL (2)
Veriad, Brea, CA (16)
Veridian Credit Union, Waterloo, IA (1)
Verizon Communications Inc, New York, NY (3)
Vermont Teddy Bear Co, Shelburne, VT (6)
Veronis Suhler Stevenson LLC, New York, NY (14)
Vertex Inc, Berwyn, PA (16)
Vet Vax, Tonganoxie, KS (11)
Veterans of Foreign Wars of the US, Kansas City, MO (1)
Viacom Inc, New York, NY (16)
Viahealth, Rochester, NY (16)
Viatech Publishing Solutions Inc, Bay Shore, NY (16)
Victor Machinery Exchange, Brooklyn, NY (9)
Victory Corps, New Hope, MN (16)
Video Artists International, Pleasantville, NY (3)
Vierk National Supply, North Chicago, IL (16)
VIEW Video Inc/Arcadia Entertainment Corp, Saugerties, NY (16)
Viking Pump Inc, Cedar Falls, IA (16)
Village Coin Shop, Plaistow, NH (6)
Village Interiors Carpet One, Newton, NC (8)
Village Software Inc, Boston, MA (3)
Vintage Wood Works, Quinlan, TX (8)
Virco Manufacturing Corp, Conway, AR (16)
The Virginia Diner Inc, Wakefield, VA (4)
Virginia Home For Boys & Girls, Richmond, VA (1)
Visa USA, Foster City, CA (14)
Visible Computer Supply Corp, Saint Charles, IL (16)
Visual Horizons, Rochester, NY (16)
Visual Reference Publications, New York, NY (17)
Vitamin Power Inc, Hauppauge, NY (7)
Vitamin Research Products, Cottonwood, AZ (7)
Vitasoy USA Inc, Ayer, MA (16)
Vivendi SA, New York, NY (16)
Vivitar Corp, Tempe, AZ (16)
Volvo Cars of North America LLC, Northvale, NJ (16)

Voyageur Inc, Easley, SC (11)
Ed Voyles Hyundai Inc, Smyrna, GA (16)
Vulcan Information Packaging, Vincent, AL (16)
Vulcan Materials Co, Birmingham, AL (16)

W

WRS Group Ltd, Waco, TX (7)
WTS Media, Chattanooga, TN (16)
Wag/Aero Group, Lyons, WI (16)
Walch Publishing, Portland, ME (17)
Walker Publishing Co Inc, New York, NY (17)
Wm K Walthers Inc, Milwaukee, WI (11)
Warnaco Swimwear Inc, Los Angeles, CA (16)
Warner Press, Anderson, IN (17)
Warren Communications News, Washington, DC (17)
Warren, Gorham & Lamont Inc, New York, NY (17)
Washington Marketing Group, Arlington, VA (1)
The Washington Monthly Co, Washington, DC (17)
Washington Mutual Home Loan, Inc, Vernon Hills, IL (14)
Washington National Opera, Washington, DC (16)
Washington Post Digital, Washington, DC (17)
Andrew D Washton Books On the Fine Arts, Port Chester, NY (16)
Wasserman Uniform Co, Fort Lauderdale, FL (2)
Waters Corp, Milford, MA (16)
Water's Edge Resort & Spa, Westbrook, CT (19)
Wathne Ltd, New York, NY (2)
Watts Radiant, Springfield, MO (9)
Waytek, Chanhassen, MN (16)
We-No-Nah Canoe Inc, Winona, MN (11)
WearGuard Corp, Norwell, MA (2)
Webb Designs Inc, El Cajon, CA (16)
Webster Bank, Waterbury, CT (14)
The Wedding Pages, New York, NY (16)
Weichert Co, Morris Plains, NJ (14)
Weingeroff Enterprises Inc, Cranston, RI (16)
Weiss Research Inc, Palm Beach Gardens, FL (17)
Welcomemat Services Inc, Atlanta, GA (9)
Wellmark Blue Cross & Blue Shield of Iowa, Des Moines, IA (15)
Wellness Councils of America, Omaha, NE (1)
Wells Fargo, San Francisco, CA (14)
Wenner Media LLC, New York, NY (17)
WESCO, Pittsburgh, PA (16)
West Bend, West Bend, WI (16)
West Farm Foods (Branch), Caldwell, ID (16)
West Marine Inc, Watsonville, CA (16)
West Shore Distributors, Westlake, OH (8)
Westcon, Tarrytown, NY (16)
Western Pennsylvania Conservancy, Pittsburgh, PA (1)
Western Psychological Services, Torrance, CA (16)
Western River Expeditions, Salt Lake City, UT (19)
Westgroup, Eagan, MN (17)
Westhoff Machine Co, Saint Louis, MO (9)
Westlake Plastics Co, Lenni, PA (16)
Weston Distance Learning Inc, Fort Collins, CO (13)
Westwood Publishing Co, Glendale, CA (17)
Whirley Drink Works, Warren, PA (5)
Whirlpool Corp, Benton Harbor, MI (16)
Whitaker National, Huntington, WV (16)
White Cap Wholesale Contractors Supplies, Costa Mesa, CA (16)
White Flower Farm, Litchfield, CT (8)
White Mane Publishing Co Inc, Shippensburg, PA (17)
Whitehorse Gear, Center Conway, NH (11)
Whiting & Davis, Attleboro Falls, MA (16)

Whitman Publishing LLC, Atlanta, GA (16)
Wholesale Tool Co, Warren, MI (9)
Wideband by Kars, New Rochelle, NY (16)
Michael Wiese Productions, Studio City, CA (17)
WILD Flavors Inc, Erlanger, KY (4)
Wildseed Farms, Fredericksburg, TX (8)
John Wiley & Sons Canada Ltd, Etobicoke, ON, Canada (17)
John Wiley & Sons Inc, Hoboken, NJ (17)
Lt Moses Willard Inc, Amelia, OH (16)
Williamsburg Blacksmiths Inc, Williamsburg, MA (8)
Williamson-Dickie Manufacturing Co, Fort Worth, TX (2)
Willis Music Co, Florence, KY (17)
The HW Wilson Co, Bronx, NY (17)
Wilton Armetale, Mount Joy, PA (16)
Wilton Industries Inc, Woodridge, IL (16)
Wimmer's Meat Products Inc, West Point, NE (4)
Windsor Vineyards, Santa Rosa, CA (16)
Windstar Cruises, Seattle, WA (19)
Wine Enthusiast Cos, Mount Kisco, NY (4)
Winmill & Co, New York, NY (14)
Winn Devon, Richmond, BC, Canada (17)
Winslow Publishing, Toronto, ON, Canada (17)
Harry Winston Inc, New York, NY (16)
Wire Works, Chester, PA (9)
Wolfe Publishing Co Inc, Prescott, AZ (17)
Wood Carvers Supply Inc, Englewood, FL (9)
Woodcraft Supply Corp LLC, Parkersburg, WV (9)
Woodcrafters Lumber Sales Inc, Portland, OR (9)
Woodwind & Brasswind Inc, Westlake Village, CA (5)
Woodworker's Supply Inc, Casper, WY (11)
Wordright Enterprises Inc, Buffalo Grove, IL (17)
Workforce Advantage USA, Elizabeth, NJ (13)
The World Bank, Washington, DC (17)
World Future Society, Chicago, IL (1)
World Publications Inc, Winter Park, FL (17)
WorldVu LLC, Baltimore, MD (17)
WorleyParsons, Reading, PA (16)
Wrisco Industries Inc, Palm Beach Gardens, FL (8)
Writer's Digest Books, Blue Ash, OH (17)
Wyandotte West Communications Inc, Kansas City, KS (17)
Wysong Corp, Midland, MI (7)

X

XL Environmental, Exton, PA (15)
Xerox Corp, Norwalk, CT (16)
Xilinx Inc, San Jose, CA (16)

Y

Year One Inc, Braselton, GA (16)
Yellow Book USA, Uniondale, NY (17)
Yenkin-Majestic, Columbus, OH (16)
Your Choice Or Mine, San Mateo, CA (16)
Your Move Chess & Games, North Massapequa, NY (11)
Yves Rocher North America Inc, Exton, PA (7)

Z

Zale Corp, Irving, TX (6)
Ziff Davis Media Inc, New York, NY (17)
Zig Ziglar Corp, Plano, TX (16)
Zimmerman Irrigation Inc, Biglerville, PA (16)

A

A&P, Montvale, NJ (16)
A La Carte, Chicago, IL (16)
AAA Auto Club South, Tampa, FL (1)
AAA-Chicago Motor Club, Aurora, IL (1)
AAA Mid-Atlantic Insurance Groups, Wilmington, DE (15)
AAA Southern New England, Providence, RI (1)
AAFES, Dallas, TX (5)
ABC Carpet & Home, New York, NY (8)
ACBL, Horn Lake, MS (1)
ACCO Brands Corp, Lake Zurich, IL (16)
ACP Medicine, Hamilton, ON, Canada (17)
ADRFCO, Washington, DC (1)
ADT LLC, Boca Raton, FL (16)
AESU Inc, Baltimore, MD (19)
AFL-CIO, Washington, DC (1)
AGCO Inc, Norcross, GA (9)
AGIA Insurance Services, Carpinteria, CA (15)
AIG Accident & Health, New York, NY (15)
AIG Marketing, New York, NY (15)
AIN Plastics Inc, Yonkers, NY (16)
ALSAC - St Jude, Memphis, TN (1)
AMA Insurance Agency Inc, Chicago, IL (15)
AMVETS National Service Foundation, Lanham, MD (1)
AON Center, Chicago, IL (15)
Aon Consulting New York, New York, NY (15)
APC by Schneider Electric, West Kingston, RI (3)
APSCO, Davenport Center, NY (11)
ARAG, Des Moines, IA (15)
ARE Press, Virginia Beach, VA (1)
ASM International, Materials Park, OH (1)
ASM Press, Washington, DC (17)
AT&T Inc, Dallas, TX (16)
AW Direct Inc, Madison, WI (12)
A+E Television Networks LLC, New York, NY (16)
Aardvark Enterprises, Calgary, AB, Canada (17)
Abbey of Gethsemani, Trappist, KY (1)
Abbey Press, Saint Meinrad, IN (6)
Abbott, Abbott Park, IL (7)
Abbott Products, Weymouth, MA (16)
Harry N Abrams Inc, New York, NY (17)
Absolute Reservation Center Inc, Longwood, FL (19)
Academic Management Services, Swansea, MA (14)
Academic Travel Abroad Inc, Washington, DC (19)
Accelerated Learning Foundation, Fairfield, IA (17)
Accoona Corp, Jersey City, NJ (16)
Accountants Education Group, Dallas, TX (10)
Accountants' Supply House, Lancaster, CA (10)
Accuracy in Media Inc, Bethesda, MD (1)
ACCUSPLIT Inc, Livermore, CA (16)
AccuTrade Inc, Bellevue, NE (14)
Ace Hardware Corp, Oak Brook, IL (16)
Acme Tools, Grand Forks, ND (8)
Action Direct Inc, Miami, FL (11)
Active Parenting, Marietta, GA (17)
Activision Value, Eden Prairie, MN (16)
ActivStyle, Minneapolis, MN (16)
Acurian, Horsham, PA (7)
Advanced Financial Services, Middletown, RI (14)
Advanced Machinery, New Castle, DE (9)
Advanced Medical Nutrition Inc, Pittsburgh, PA (7)
The Advertising Council Inc, New York, NY (1)
Aegon Direct Marketing Services Inc, Baltimore, MD (15)
Aegon USA Investment Management, Inc, Cedar Rapids, IA (14)
Aerovox Inc, New Bedford, MA (16)

AETNA - Marketing Product & Communication, Hartford, CT (14)
Affinity Express, Elgin, IL (16)
Affinity Federal Credit Union, Basking Ridge, NJ (1)
Affinity4, Norfolk, VA (16)
Agate Publishing, Evanston, IL (17)
Agco Spra-Coup, Duluth, GA (16)
Agilis Co, Albert Lea, MN (14)
AGORA Inc, Baltimore, MD (17)
AHC Media, Atlanta, GA (17)
Air Ambulance Network Inc, Palm Harbor, FL (16)
Air Chek Inc, Naples, NC (9)
Air Force Sergeants Association, Suitland, MD (1)
Air France, New York, NY (16)
Air Power USA, Los Angeles, CA (12)
Aircraft Owners & Pilots Association, Frederick, MD (1)
Aircraft Spruce & Specialty Co, Corona, CA (12)
The Akadine Press Inc, White Plains, NY (16)
Akers Ski Inc, Andover, ME (11)
Alamo Rent A Car, Saint Louis, MO (16)
John Alden Life Insurance Co/North Star Marketing, Duluth, GA (15)
Alerus Financial National Assoc, Grand Forks, ND (14)
Alexander + Roberts, Keene, NH (19)
Alexian Brothers Bonaventure House, Chicago, IL (1)
Alfa CTP Systems, Tewksbury, MA (10)
Alfa Insurance, Montgomery, AL (15)
Alfred Publishing Co Inc, Van Nuys, CA (17)
AliMed Inc, Dedham, MA (7)
All Star Directories, Seattle, WA (17)
AllBrands.com Sewing Machine Superstore, Baton Rouge, LA (11)
Allergan Inc, Irvine, CA (16)
Alliance Bernstein, New York, NY (14)
Alliance Defense Fund, Scottsdale, AZ (1)
Allianz Life Insurance Co of North America, Minneapolis, MN (15)
Allstate Motor Club Inc, Arlington Heights, IL (13)
Allyn & Bacon, Upper Saddle River, NJ (17)
Almore International Inc, Beaverton, OR (7)
Almost Heaven Group, Renick, WV (16)
CM Almy & Son Inc, Armonk, NY (5)
Alpha Supply Inc, Bremerton, WA (16)
ALSTOM Signaling Inc, West Henrietta, NY (16)
Altiris, Lindon, UT (16)
Alzheimer Society of Canada, Toronto, ON, Canada (1)
Alzheimer's Association, Chicago, IL (1)
Amacom Books, New York, NY (17)
Amaryllis Inc, Baton Rouge, LA (8)
Amateur Electronic Supply LLC, Milwaukee, WI (16)
Amazon Drygoods, Osgood, IN (2)
Ambassador Programs, Spokane, WA (19)
Ambient Shapes Inc, Hickory, NC (7)
Amcat TeleProfit Inc, Oklahoma City, OK (16)
American Airlines, Fort Worth, TX (12)
American Airlines Inc, Fort Worth, TX (19)
American Arbitration Association, New York, NY (1)
American Association of Critical-Care Nurses, Aliso Viejo, CA (1)
American Association of Individual Investors, Chicago, IL (1)
American Bar Association, Chicago, IL (1)
American Bible Society, New York, NY (1)
American Biographical Institute Inc, Raleigh, NC (17)

American Breast Cancer Foundation, Columbia, MD (1)
American Bronzing Co, Columbus, OH (16)
American Capital, Bethesda, MD (15)
American Catalog Mailers Association, Providence, RI (1)
American Century Investments, Kansas City, MO (14)
American Civil Defense Association, Draper, UT (16)
American Civil Liberties Union Foundation, New York, NY (1)
American College of Cardiology, Washington, DC (1)
American College of Emergency Physicians, Irving, TX (1)
American College of Physician Executives, Tampa, FL (1)
American Council on Exercise, San Diego, CA (1)
American Counseling Association, Broken Arrow, OK (1)
American Craft Council, Minneapolis, MN (17)
American Crane & Equipment Corp, Douglassville, PA (16)
American Dermatological Corp, Miami, FL (16)
American Diabetes Association, Alexandria, VA (1)
American Express Co, New York, NY (14)
American Express Publishing Corp, New York, NY (17)
American Family Insurance Group, Madison, WI (15)
American Family Life Assurance Co of Columbus (AFLAC), Columbus, GA (15)
American Federation of Astrologers, Tempe, AZ (1)
American Fidelity Assurance Co, Oklahoma City, OK (15)
The American Film Institute, Los Angeles, CA (1)
American Forests, Washington, DC (1)
American Foundation for the Blind Inc, New York, NY (1)
American General Life & Accident Insurance, Nashville, TN (15)
American General Life Insurance Co, Houston, TX (15)
American Girl Brands LLC, Middleton, WI (6)
American Greetings Corp, Cleveland, OH (16)
American Health & Life Insurance Co, Fort Worth, TX (15)
American Health Information Management Association, Chicago, IL (1)
American Healthways, Franklin, TN (16)
American Heart Association, Dallas, TX (1)
American Historic Inns Inc, Dana Point, CA (17)
American Horse Products, San Juan Capistrano, CA (11)
American Indian College Fund, Denver, CO (1)
American Institute of Chemical Engineers, New York, NY (1)
American Institute of CPAs, New York, NY (1)
American Institute of Physics, Melville, NY (17)
American Insurance Administrators Inc, Columbus, OH (15)
American International Group, New York, NY (15)
American Kennel Club, New York, NY (17)
The American Legion National Headquarters, Indianapolis, IN (1)
American Library Association-Publishing Services, Chicago, IL (1)
American Locker Security Systems Inc, Coppell, TX (16)
American Lung Association, Chicago, IL (1)
American Mathematical Society, Providence, RI (17)

American Meadows Inc & Vermont Wild Flowers Farm, Shelburne, VT (8)

American Megatrends Inc, Norcross, GA (3)

American Mint LLC, Mechanicsburg, PA (6)

American Movie Classics Holding Corp, Jericho, NY (16)

American Nicaraguan Foundation, Miami, FL (1)

American Nurses' Association, Silver Spring, MD (1)

American Ostomy Supply, Earth City, MO (16)

American Period Lighting Inc, Lancaster, PA (8)

American Preferred Reader's Service Inc, Fort Lauderdale, FL (18)

American Printing House for the Blind, Louisville, KY (7)

American Psychological Association, Washington, DC (1)

American Radio Relay League, Newington, CT (1)

American Red Cross, Washington, DC (1)

American Running Association, Bethesda, MD (1)

American Science & Surplus, Niles, IL (9)

American Securities Capital Partners, New York, NY (15)

American Society for Quality, Milwaukee, WI (1)

American Society of Interior Designers, Washington, DC (1)

American Society of Radiologic Technologists, Albuquerque, NM (1)

American Society on Aging, San Francisco, CA (1)

American Speech-Language-Hearing Association, Rockville, MD (1)

American Stationery Co Inc, Peru, IN (10)

American Student Assistance, Boston, MA (1)

American Technical Publishers Inc, Orland Park, IL (17)

American Tourister, Mansfield, MA (16)

The American Vintage Library, Los Angeles, CA (17)

Americans for Peace Now, Washington, DC (1)

America's Finest Pet Doors, San Luis Obispo, CA (16)

AmerisourceBergen, Chesterbrook, PA (7)

Ameristar Casinos Inc, Las Vegas, NV (19)

Ames-Tru-Temper, Camp Hill, PA (8)

Amica Insurance, Lincoln, RI (15)

Amigo Mobility International Inc, Bridgeport, MI (16)

AmMed Direct, Parsons, TN (7)

Amos Press, Inc, Sidney, OH (17)

Amplify Federal Credit Union, Austin, TX (1)

Amrel, El Monte, CA (16)

Anatomical Chart Co, Riverwoods, IL (7)

Ancient Circles, Willits, CA (6)

Anda Inc, Parsippany, NJ (7)

MD Anderson Cancer Center - Children's Art Project, Houston, TX (1)

Hanna Andersson Corp, Portland, OR (2)

Angelica Image Apparel, Saint Louis, MO (16)

Angler's Catalog Co, Eagle, ID (11)

The Angler's Den, Pawling, NY (11)

Anglicans United & Latimer Press, Cedar Hill, TX (1)

Anheuser-Busch Inc Promotional Products Group, Shelton, CT (6)

Animal Health Express, Inc, Tucson, AZ (5)

The Animal Medical Center, New York, NY (16)

Ann Inc, New York, NY (2)

Anne Klein, New York, NY (16)

Annie's Attic LLC, Big Sandy, TX (11)

Anthem Blue Cross, Westlake Village, CA (15)

Anthem Blue Cross Blue Shield, North Haven, CT (15)

Anthem Blue Cross Blue Shield, Saint Louis, MO (15)

Anthem Corporate Communications, Indianapolis, IN (15)

Antiquarian Booksellers Association of America Inc, New York, NY (1)

Antique & Collectible Tools Inc, Pownal, ME (11)

Antique Electronic Supply, Tempe, AZ (3)

Antique Rose Emporium, Brenham, TX (8)

Anything Goes, Allenhurst, NJ (6)

Aon's Affinity Insurance Services Inc, Hatboro, PA (15)

Apothecary Products Inc, Burnsville, MN (7)

Apple Inc, Cupertino, CA (16)

Appraisal Institute, Chicago, IL (1)

Arbor Capital 1, Omaha, NE (14)

Arbor Day Foundation, Nebraska City, NE (1)

ArcelorMittal, Chicago, IL (16)

Arch Telecom Inc, Austin, TX (16)

Archaeology Magazine, Long Island City, NY (17)

Arctic Trading Co Inc, Churchill, MB, Canada (6)

Elizabeth Arden Spas LLC, Stamford, CT (19)

Arent Fox LLP, Washington, DC (9)

Aristokraft Inc, Jasper, IN (16)

Arizona Highways Magazine, Phoenix, AZ (17)

The Arizona Republic, Phoenix, AZ (17)

Armbrust Paper Tubes Inc, Chicago, IL (10)

Armento Inc, Buffalo, NY (5)

Army Times Publishing Co, Springfield, VA (17)

Arnaud's, New Orleans, LA (16)

Arrow Co, Indianapolis, IN (16)

Arrow Electronics Inc, Englewood, CO (3)

Arrowhead Mountain Spring Water, Wilkes Barre, PA (16)

Art.com, Emeryville, CA (8)

Art Instruction Schools, Minneapolis, MN (13)

Art News Magazine, New York, NY (17)

Arthritis Foundation, Atlanta, GA (1)

As We Change, Oshkosh, WI (7)

Ashworth College, Norcross, GA (13)

Aspen Publishers Inc, New York, NY (17)

Asset Marketing Services Inc, Burnsville, MN (16)

Associated Photo, Erlanger, KY (16)

Association for Computing Machinery, New York, NY (1)

Association for Facilities Engineering, McLean, VA (1)

Association for Talent Development, Alexandria, VA (1)

Association of American Publishers, Washington, DC (1)

Association of Bridal Consultants, New Milford, CT (1)

Association of Marian Helpers, Stockbridge, MA (1)

Association of the Miraculous Medal, Perryville, MO (1)

Assurant Group, New York, NY (15)

Assurant Health, Milwaukee, WI (15)

Astral Brands LLC, Atlanta, GA (7)

AstraZeneca, Wilmington, DE (7)

Astro Air, LP, Jacksonville, TX (9)

Astrologer's Fund Inc, Brooklyn, NY (16)

Astronomical Society of the Pacific, San Francisco, CA (1)

At Last Naturals, North Salem, NY (7)

Atlanta Cutlery Corp, Conyers, GA (11)

The Atlantic Monthly, Washington, DC (17)

Atlantic Publication Group LLC, Charleston, SC (17)

Atlantic Spice Co, North Truro, MA (4)

Audio & Video Labs Inc, Pennsauken, NJ (16)

Audio Classics Ltd, Vestal, NY (3)

Audio-Digest Foundation, Glendale, CA (1)

Audio Editions Books-on-Cassette & CD, Auburn, CA (3)

Audiovox, Hauppauge, NY (16)

Augsburg Fortress Publishers, Minneapolis, MN (17)

August Home Publishing Co, Des Moines, IA (17)

Wendell August Forge Inc, Grove City, PA (6)

Australian Tourist Commission, Los Angeles, CA (19)

Authentic Designs, West Rupert, VT (8)

Autobytel Inc, Irvine, CA (12)

Automation Control Products, Alpharetta, GA (16)

Automod, Atlanta, GA (12)

Automotive Headphones, Sterling Heights, MI (16)

Avery Dennison Corp, Brea, CA (10)

Aviation Book Co, Seattle, WA (17)

Avis World Headquarters, Parsippany, NJ (19)

Aviva USA Corp, Des Moines, IA (14)

Avon Products Inc, New York, NY (7)

Award Co of America, Tuscaloosa, AL (6)

Axis Capital, New York, NY (14)

B

B Bunch Co Inc, Phoenix, AZ (16)

BBC Worldwide Americas Inc, New York, NY (3)

BBS & Associates, Akron, OH (1)

BFS Credit Services Co, Brook Park, OH (16)

BGE Home Products & Services Inc, Baltimore, MD (16)

BJ's Wholesale Club Inc, Westborough, MA (13)

BJU Press, Greenville, SC (17)

BLS Inc, Wilmington, DE (17)

BMG Columbia House, New York, NY (13)

BMI Home Decorating, Spring Grove, IL (16)

BNY Mellon, New York, NY (14)

BOC Gases, Murray Hill, NJ (16)

BP, Warrenville, IL (16)

BYK-Gardner USA, Columbia, MD (16)

Babyshoe.com, Hendersonville, NC (6)

Bachrach Clothing Inc, New York, NY (2)

Back Designs Inc, Novato, CA (7)

Back to the Bible, Lincoln, NE (5)

Badge-A-Minit, Oglesby, IL (16)

Maurice Badler Fine Jewelry Ltd, New York, NY (2)

Bahamas Ministry of Tourism, Fort Lauderdale, FL (19)

Balboa Life & Casualty, Irvine, CA (15)

Balducci Enterprises Inc, Germantown, MD (16)

Baldwin Filters, Kearney, NE (16)

Bale Co, Providence, RI (16)

Balfour, Austin, TX (16)

Ball Publishing, West Chicago, IL (17)

Ballard Designs, Atlanta, GA (8)

Baltimore Magazine, Baltimore, MD (17)

Bamboo Sourcery, Sebastopol, CA (8)

Banana Republic, San Francisco, CA (2)

Bank Boston, Boston, MA (14)

Joseph A Bank Clothiers Inc, Hampstead, MD (2)

Bank of America, Charlotte, NC (14)

Bank of Hawaii, Honolulu, HI (14)

The Bank of New York/Delaware, Newark, DE (14)

Bank One, Chicago, IL (14)

Bankers Life & Casualty Co, Chicago, IL (15)

Bantam Dell Publishing Group Inc, New York, NY (17)

Barbour Publishing Inc, Uhrichsville, OH (17)

Barely Nothings Lingerie, Nipomo, CA (2)

Bob Barker Co Inc, Fuquay Varina, NC (5)

BarnesandNoble.com, New York, NY (16)

Baron/Barclay Bridge Supplies, Louisville, KY (11)

RG Barry Corp, Pickerington, OH (2)

Bart's Watersports, North Webster, IN (11)

Baseline FT, Los Angeles, CA (17)

Bass Pro Shops, Springfield, MO (11)
Bathroom Machineries, Murphys, CA (8)
Baton Rouge Conventions & Visitors Bureau, Baton Rouge, LA (1)
Battleground Antiques Inc, New Bern, NC (6)
Baudville Inc, Grand Rapids, MI (16)
Eddie Bauer Groveport Service Center, Groveport, OH (2)
Bauer Publishing Co, Englewood Cliffs, NJ (17)
The Bauman Group, Ashland, MA (14)
Bausch & Lomb Inc, Rochester, NY (16)
Baxter Bros Inc, Greenwich, CT (17)
Bay Manufacturing, Milan, OH (16)
Mel Bay Publications Inc, Pacific, MO (17)
Bayer Corp Consumer Care Division, Whippany, NJ (16)
Baylor Health Care System, Dallas, TX (16)
Beacon Shoe Co Inc, Maryland Heights, MO (16)
LL Bean Inc, Freeport, ME (2)
Bear Woods Supply Co Inc, Cornwallis, NS, Canada (11)
Beau Rivage Resort & Casino, Biloxi, MS (19)
Beauticontrol Cosmetics Inc, Carrollton, TX (7)
Beauty Naturally, Burlingame, CA (7)
Bed Bath & Beyond, Union, NJ (8)
Bedford/St Martin's, Boston, MA (17)
Beeman Precision Airguns, Santa Fe Springs, CA (11)
Belcaro Group Inc, Greenwood Village, CO (17)
Belk Stores Services Inc, Charlotte, NC (16)
Bell & Howell Ltd, North York, ON, Canada (9)
Bell Performance Inc, Longwood, FL (9)
Bellacor, Minneapolis, MN (8)
Beltone Corp, Glenview, IL (3)
Beluga Bar by Caviarteria, New York, NY (4)
Belvoir Media Group LLC, Norwalk, CT (17)
Bencone Uniform Connection, Winston Salem, NC (2)
BenefitMall, Dallas, TX (15)
Benevilla, Surprise, AZ (1)
Bentley University, Waltham, MA (13)
Bergdorf Goodman, New York, NY (2)
Berger's Table Pad Co, Indianapolis, IN (8)
Berkeley College, West Paterson, NJ (13)
Berkshire Direct Inc, Williamstown, MA (17)
Berkshire Record Outlet Inc, Lee, MA (3)
Berry Hill Ltd, Saint Thomas, ON, Canada (8)
Berway Visual Products Inc, Wilmington, MA (3)
Best Buy, Richfield, MN (3)
Better Health Fitness, Brooklyn, NY (11)
Better Tools For Industry, Santee, CA (9)
BIC Corp, Shelton, CT (16)
Bick International, Van Nuys, CA (6)
Bigelow Electronics, Bluffton, OH (3)
RC Bigelow Inc, Fairfield, CT (4)
Bijoux Terner, Miami, FL (16)
Bike Nashbar, Crab Orchard, WV (11)
The Bil-Ray Aluminum Siding Corp of Queens Inc, New Hyde Park, NY (16)
Biomerica Inc, Irvine, CA (7)
Birthday Express Inc, Kirkland, WA (5)
Bissinger French Confections, Saint Louis, MO (4)
Bits & Pieces Inc, Lawrenceburg, IN (11)
Bizzaro Rubber Stamps, Greenville, RI (6)
Stanley Black & Decker Inc, New Britain, CT (16)
The Black Dog Tavern Co Inc, Vineyard Haven, MA (2)
Black Enterprise Magazine, New York, NY (17)
Black Entertainment Television Inc, Washington, DC (16)
Blaine Window Hardware Inc, Hagerstown, MD (9)
Blair Corp, Warren, PA (2)

William Blair & Co LLC, Chicago, IL (14)
Blanchard & Co Inc, New Orleans, LA (16)
Bland Farms, Glennville, GA (4)
Blethen Maine Newspapers Inc, Portland, ME (17)
Dick Blick Holdings Inc, Galesburg, IL (16)
Bliss World LLC, New York, NY (5)
Bloomingdale's Direct, New York, NY (16)
Blue Coral Slick 50, Houston, TX (16)
Blue Cross Blue Shield of Florida, Jacksonville, FL (15)
Blue Cross Blue Shield of Illinois, Chicago, IL (15)
Blue Cross Blue Shield of Louisiana, Baton Rouge, LA (15)
Blue Cross Blue Shield of Oklahoma, Tulsa, OK (15)
Blue Cross Blue Shield of South Carolina, Columbia, SC (15)
Blue Raven Technology, Wilmington, MA (3)
Blue Shield Life, San Francisco, CA (15)
Blue Shield of California, San Francisco, CA (15)
Bluestem Brands, Eden Prairie, MN (16)
Bluestone Perennials Inc, Madison, OH (8)
Bluewater Yachts, Mora, MN (16)
Boardroom Inc, Stamford, CT (17)
Bobcat Co, West Fargo, ND (16)
Bobley-Harmann Corp, Ronkonkoma, NY (5)
The Body Shop Inc, New York, NY (7)
Bolind Inc, Boulder, CO (16)
The Bombay Co, Toronto, ON, Canada (8)
Carol Bond Health Foods, Liberty, TX (7)
Book Passage Cafe, Corte Madera, CA (17)
Book Publishing Information Kit, Santa Barbara, CA (17)
Books on Tape, Westminster, MD (17)
Bookspan, New York, NY (13)
Booth Michigan, Grand Rapids, MI (17)
Born Free USA, Washington, DC (1)
Bose Corp, Framingham, MA (3)
Bosom Buddy Breast Forms, Boise, ID (7)
The Boston Co Asset Management LLC, Boston, MA (14)
The Boston Globe, Boston, MA (17)
Boundless Corp, Phelps, NY (16)
Bountiful Gardens, Willits, CA (8)
Bowers & Merena Auctions, Irvine, CA (16)
The Bowery Mission, New York, NY (1)
BowTie Inc, Irvine, CA (17)
Boy Scouts of America/National Supply Group, Charlotte, NC (1)
Boyd Gaming Corp, Las Vegas, NV (16)
Boys & Girls Clubs of America National Headquarters, Atlanta, GA (1)
Boys' Life & Scouting Magazines, Irving, TX (17)
The Bradford Group, Niles, IL (16)
Bradford Health Services, Birmingham, AL (16)
Vera Bradley, Roanoke, IN (2)
Brady Marketing Co Inc, Walnut Creek, CA (16)
Brahmin Leather Works, Fairhaven, MA (16)
Branch Banking & Trust Co, Winston-Salem, NC (14)
Brand New Products LLC, Chicago, IL (4)
Brant Publications Inc, New York, NY (17)
Breck's Bulbs, Guilford, IN (8)
Beverly Bremer Silver Shop, Atlanta, GA (6)
Brentwood Benson Music Publishing, Brentwood, TN (17)
Bridge City Tool Works Inc, Portland, OR (9)
Bridgestone Americas Inc, Nashville, TN (16)
Brigade Quartermasters Ltd, Providence, RI (11)
British Columbia Automobile Association, Burnaby, BC, Canada (15)
Broadmoor Hotel Inc, Colorado Springs, CO (19)
BroadVision Inc, Redwood City, CA (16)

Broadway Books, New York, NY (17)
Broadway Play Publishing Inc, New York, NY (17)
Brokers/Consultants Inc, Flossmoor, IL (15)
Bronner's Christmas Wonderland, Frankenmuth, MI (6)
Bronson Nutritionals LLC, Hauppauge, NY (7)
Bronx Council on the Arts, Bronx, NY (1)
Brookfield Zoo, Brookfield, IL (1)
Brookhollow Cards, Rexburg, ID (10)
Brooks Brothers, New York, NY (2)
Brooks Equipment Co, Charlotte, NC (9)
Brookstone Co, Merrimack, NH (3)
Brotherhood America's Oldest Winery Ltd, Washingtonville, NY (19)
Brown & Co, Blaine, WA (8)
Brown & Jenkins Trading Co, Jeffersonville, VT (4)
Arthur Brown & Bro Inc, New York, NY (10)
Brown-Forman Corp, Louisville, KY (16)
Tony Brown Productions, New York, NY (16)
BrownCor International, Milwaukee, WI (5)
Brownell Holly Farms, Oregon City, OR (6)
Brown's Omaha Plant Farms, Omaha, TX (8)
Bruce Medical Supply, Waltham, MA (7)
Brylane, Taunton, MA (2)
Buena Vista Home Entertainment, Burbank, CA (3)
Buena Vista Winery, Sonoma, CA (16)
Buggies Unlimited, Jacksonville, FL (12)
Buick, Detroit, MI (16)
Bulletin of the Atomic Scientists, Chicago, IL (17)
Bunker Hill Auctions, Millbrook, IL (6)
Bunn-O-Matic Corp, Springfield, IL (16)
Burberry, New York, NY (2)
Burden Sales Co, Lincoln, NE (9)
Burger's Ozark Country Cured Hams Inc, California, MO (4)
Burlington Coat Factory, Burlington, NJ (16)
Burlington Industries Inc, Greensboro, NC (16)
Burns Inc, Fall River, MA (16)
W Atlee Burpee Co, Warminster, PA (8)
DV Burrell Seed Growers Co, Rocky Ford, CO (8)
Bushnell Corporation, Overland Park, KS (11)
Business Automation Systems Inc, Nashville, TN (16)
Business Planners & Consultants Inc, New York, NY (15)
Butler Distributing Co, Kenilworth, NJ (3)
H E Butt Grocery Co, San Antonio, TX (16)
BUYSEASONS Inc, New Berlin, WI (5)
Byron Plantation, Vidalia, GA (4)

C

C&H Distributors LLC, Milwaukee, WI (9)
C & J Clark America Inc, Newton Upper Falls, MA (16)
C&S Sales Inc, Wheeling, IL (9)
C&T Bridge Supplies, Los Alamitos, CA (11)
CAA Auto Club & Travel Agency Inc, Thornhill, ON, Canada (1)
CAIG Laboratories Inc, Poway, CA (9)
CBT Direct, Tarpon Springs, FL (16)
CCA Global Partners, Manchester, NH (16)
CCI Solutions, Olympia, WA (16)
CD Universe, Wallingford, CT (16)
CDMI Inc, Huntington Beach, CA (1)
CDMO Inc, Deer Park, NY (16)
CDW Corp, Vernon Hills, IL (16)
CHG, Salt Lake City, UT (7)
CJ Hummul Co, Nescopeck, PA (11)
CMEinfo.com, Birmingham, AL (16)
CMI Direct, Pasadena, CA (15)

CMS Inc, Winston Salem, NC (14)

CNA, Chicago, IL (15)

CNY Awards & Apparel Inc, New Hartford, NY (5)

CPM Delta 1, Inc, Dallas, TX (11)

CRB, Chicago, IL (17)

CSI, Conklin, NY (16)

CSPI/Nutrition Action Health Letter, Washington, DC (17)

CTA Inc, Fenton, MO (5)

CTC Corp, Bennington, VT (16)

CVS Caremark, Woonsocket, RI (7)

CVT Production Inc, Granger, IN (16)

Cabela's Inc, Sidney, NE (11)

Cable Car Clothiers/Robert Kirk Ltd, San Francisco, CA (2)

Cable Connection, Fremont, CA (3)

Cable Shopping Network, Scottsdale, AZ (16)

Cablevision Systems Corp, Bethpage, NY (16)

Cablexpress Technologies, Syracuse, NY (10)

Cadie Products Corp, Paterson, NJ (16)

Caesars Entertainment Corp, Las Vegas, NV (16)

Cafe Lango, Sharon Springs, NY (16)

Calbiochem-Novabiochem Corp, San Diego, CA (9)

Calendar Marketing Association, Wheaton, IL (1)

Calibre Press Inc, San Francisco, CA (17)

Calico Corners, Kennett Square, PA (16)

California Mustang Parts & Accessories, City of Industry, CA (16)

California Pacific Research & New Generation, Reno, NV (3)

California Society of CPA's, San Mateo, CA (1)

Callaway Gardens, Pine Mountain, GA (19)

Cambridge Educational, New York, NY (12)

Camellia Forest Nursery, Chapel Hill, NC (8)

Camelot Enterprises, Bristol, WI (9)

Campbell Soup Co, Camden, NJ (16)

Campbell Tools Co, Springfield, OH (9)

Camping World Inc, Bowling Green, KY (11)

Campmor Inc, Mahwah, NJ (17)

Canada Brokerlink Insurance, Edmonton, AB, Canada (15)

Canadian Blood Services, Ottawa, ON, Canada (1)

Canadian Business, Toronto, ON, Canada (17)

Cancer Research Society, Montreal, QC, Canada (1)

Cane & Basket Supply Co, Los Angeles, CA (8)

Canine Companions for Independence, Santa Rosa, CA (16)

The Caning Shop, Berkeley, CA (11)

Canyon Marketing, Hicksville, NY (7)

Cape Cod Cupola Co Inc, North Dartmouth, MA (8)

Capezio Ballet Makers Inc, Totowa, NJ (16)

Capitol Concierge Inc, Washington, DC (16)

Carabella Collection, Irvine, CA (2)

Card Technology Inc, Hopkins, MN (16)

Care2, Washington, DC (1)

CARE USA, Atlanta, GA (1)

Career Education Corp, Schaumburg, IL (1)

Carefirst Blue Cross Blue Shield, Washington, DC (15)

Careington International, Frisco, TX (7)

Carestream Health Inc, Rochester, NY (7)

CARFAX Inc, Centreville, VA (12)

Caribe Direct Inc, San Juan, PR (6)

Carnival Cruise Lines, Miami, FL (19)

Carrot-Top Industries Inc, Hillsborough, NC (16)

Carson's, Milwaukee, WI (16)

Carter & Holmes Inc, Newberry, SC (8)

Harriet Carter Gifts Inc, Montgomeryville, PA (6)

Cartouche Ltd, Alexandria, VA (6)

Carvel Corp, Atlanta, GA (4)

Cascade Outfitters, Boise, ID (11)

Casual Male Retail Group, Canton, MA (2)

Caswell-Massey Co Ltd, Edison, NJ (7)

Catalog Music Corp, Nashville, TN (3)

Catch The Wind Kite Shop, Lincoln City, OR (11)

Caterpillar Insurance Services Corp, Nashville, TN (15)

Catholic Charities - Brooklyn & Queens, Brooklyn, NY (1)

Catholic Digest, New London, CT (17)

Catholic Relief Services, Baltimore, MD (1)

The Catholic University of America Press, Washington, DC (17)

Cattle Kate, Boise, ID (2)

Celestial Seasonings, Boulder, CO (16)

Celtic Life Insurance Co, Chicago, IL (15)

Cengage Learning, Independence, KY (17)

Center for Professional Development, Tallahassee, FL (16)

Center for Science in the Public Interest, Washington, DC (1)

Centerpoint Energy, Minneapolis, MN (16)

Central Pacific Bank, Honolulu, HI (14)

Central Shippee Inc, Bloomingdale, NJ (16)

Central States Health & Life Co of Omaha, Omaha, NE (15)

Central States Indemnity, Omaha, NE (15)

Century Photo, Newtown, CT (10)

CertainTeed Corp, Valley Forge, PA (16)

Cessna Aircraft Co, Wichita, KS (16)

Chadsworth's 1-800-Columns, Wilmington, NC (8)

Chadwick's of Boston Inc, Milford, CT (2)

Chairman's Marketing Group LLC, Princeton, NJ (15)

Champs Corp, Bradenton, FL (11)

Chanel Inc, New York, NY (16)

Channel 13 WNET Catalog Division, New York, NY (5)

Char-Broil Grill Lover's Catalog, Columbus, GA (8)

Charisma Brands LLC, Laguna Hills, CA (6)

Charlotte Chamber of Commerce, Charlotte, NC (1)

Charlotte Ford Trunks, Dumas, TX (11)

Charmaster, Grand Rapids, MN (8)

Charming Shoppes Inc., Bensalem, PA (2)

Charter Communications, Stamford, CT (16)

Charter One Bank, Cleveland, OH (14)

Chartifacts, Richmond, VA (6)

Chartis, New York, NY (15)

Chateau Le Combe, Edmonton, AB, Canada (19)

Chem-Tainer Industries Inc, North Babylon, NY (9)

Chemical Week, New York, NY (17)

Cherry Tree Toys Inc, Beloit, WI (11)

Chicago Convention & Tourism Bureau, Chicago, IL (1)

Chicago Magazine, Chicago, IL (17)

Chick Harness & Supply Inc, Harrington, DE (11)

Chico's FAS Inc, Fort Myers, FL (2)

Chief Marketer and Multichannel Merchant, New York, NY (17)

ChildFund International, Richmond, VA (1)

ChildFund International, Richmond, VA (1)

Children of the Night, Van Nuys, CA (1)

Children's Aid Society, New York, NY (1)

Children's Better Health Institute, Indianapolis, IN (1)

Children's Hospital Foundation, Silver Spring, MD (1)

Children's Hospital of Pittsburgh, Pittsburgh, PA (1)

China Books & Periodicals Inc, South San Francisco, CA (17)

Choice Courier Systems Inc, New York, NY (16)

Choice Hotels International, Rockville, MD (16)

Choice Point, Alpharetta, GA (16)

Christian Appalachian Project, Paintsville, KY (1)

Christian Book Distributors Inc, Peabody, MA (17)

Christian Brands, Phoenix, AZ (16)

Christian Broadcasting Network Inc, Virginia Beach, VA (1)

Christian Herald Association, New York, NY (1)

Christian Relief Services Charities Inc, Alexandria, VA (1)

The Christian Science Publishing Society, Boston, MA (17)

Christianity Today Inc, Carol Stream, IL (17)

Church Extension Plan, Salem, OR (14)

CIGNA International, Philadelphia, PA (15)

Cincinnati Bell Inc, Cincinnati, OH (16)

Cinmar LP, West Chester, OH (8)

Circle K Stores Inc, Akron, OH (16)

Citibank, New York, NY (14)

CitiFinancial Credit Co, Baltimore, MD (14)

Citigroup Inc, New York, NY (14)

Citizens Against Government Waste, Washington, DC (1)

Citizens Bank, Boston, MA (14)

City of Cerritos, Cerritos, CA (1)

City of Hope National Medical Center, Duarte, CA (1)

City of LaGrange, LaGrange, GA (1)

Civil Service Employees Insurance Group, Walnut Creek, CA (15)

Clairol Inc, Stamford, CT (7)

Clampitt Paper Co, Dallas, TX (16)

Clarin by Hussey Seating, North Berwick, ME (5)

Clark's Corvair Parts, Inc, Shelburne Falls, MA (12)

Clarkson Eyecare, Ellisville, MO (5)

Classic Motorbooks Inc, Minneapolis, MN (17)

Classic Thermographers, North Mankato, MN (10)

Clegg Industries Inc, Gardena, CA (16)

Clemente Novelties Inc, Utica, NY (16)

Cleveland Institute of Electronics, Cleveland, OH (13)

The Cleveland Orchestra, Cleveland, OH (1)

ClingZ Inc, Rio Rancho, NM (9)

The Clorox Co, Oakland, CA (16)

Clubs of America, Lakemoor, IL (6)

Cluett Peabody, New York, NY (16)

Coach, New York, NY (2)

Coast Hotels Limited, Seattle, WA (19)

Coast to Coast Inc, Englewood, CO (1)

Coastal Tool & Supply, West Hartford, CT (16)

Cobblestone Publishing, Peterborough, NH (17)

The Coca-Cola Co, Atlanta, GA (16)

Cohasset Colonials, Ashburnham, MA (8)

Coin World, Sidney, OH (17)

Cold Spring Harbor Lab Press, Woodbury, NY (17)

Cold Stream Farm, Free Soil, MI (8)

Coldwater Creek, Cincinnati, OH (2)

Cole's Appliance & Furniture Co, Chicago, IL (8)

Colgate-Palmolive Co, New York, NY (16)

Collectibles Today Network, Ltd, Niles, IL (16)

Collector Books & American Quilters Society, Paducah, KY (17)

Collector's Armoury Ltd, McDonough, GA (6)

Collector's Teapot, Kingston, NY (6)

The College Board, New York, NY (1)

CollegeAmerica, Salt Lake City, UT (1)

Collider Media, Austin, TX (9)

Collin Street Bakery, Corsicana, TX (4)

Collis Curve Catalog Sales, Brownsville, TX (7)

Colonial Life Insurance Co Texas, Fort Worth, TX (15)

The Colonial Williamsburg Foundation, Williamsburg, VA (1)

Columbia Journalism Review, New York, NY (17)

Columbia University, Annual Fund Programs, New York, NY (5)
The Columbian, Vancouver, WA (17)
Columbian Mutual Life Insurance Co, Binghamton, NY (15)
Combined Insurance Co of America, Glenview, IL (15)
Comcast Spectacor LP, Philadelphia, PA (16)
Comdata Corp, Brentwood, TN (14)
Comerica Inc, Dallas, TX (14)
Wm F Comly & Son Inc, Philadelphia, PA (9)
Commercial Federal Bank, Omaha, NE (14)
Commercial Travelers Mutual Insurance Co, Utica, NY (15)
Communication Creativity, Buena Vista, CO (17)
Communication Resources Inc, Beaufort, SC (18)
Community Coffee Co, Baton Rouge, LA (4)
Companion Plants, Athens, OH (8)
The Company Store Inc, La Crosse, WI (16)
Compass Bank, Birmingham, AL (14)
Compass Electronics, Forest Grove, OR (9)
Computer Station Corp, Houston, TX (3)
The Computer Supply People, Menomonee Falls, WI (3)
Con-Cor International, Tucson, AZ (11)
Concordia Publishing House, Saint Louis, MO (17)
Conde Nast, New York, NY (17)
Condolink, Omaha, NE (16)
Connell Communications Inc, Peterborough, NH (17)
Conney Safety Products LLC, Madison, WI (7)
Conseco Inc, Carmel, IN (15)
Conservation International, Arlington, VA (1)
Consolidated Electronics Inc, Dayton, OH (3)
Consolidated Plastics Co Inc, Stow, OH (9)
Consumer Credit Advocates Inc, Salt Lake City, UT (16)
Consumers Digest Inc, Deerfield, IL (17)
Consumer's Energy, Jackson, MI (16)
Consumers Union, Yonkers, NY (17)
The Contest Center, Wappingers Falls, NY (19)
Continental Supply Inc, Cleveland, OH (9)
Continental Western Group, Des Moines, IA (15)
Convertible Service, San Gabriel, CA (16)
David C Cook, Colorado Springs, CO (17)
Cookbook Publishers Inc, Lenexa, KS (17)
Cooper Communities Inc, Rogers, AR (16)
Coppa Woodworking, Inc, San Pedro, CA (8)
Josiah R Coppersmythe, Harwich, MA (8)
Cornell Lab of Ornithology, Ithaca, NY (1)
Cornerstone Brands Inc, West Chester, OH (5)
Cornerstone Business Services Inc, Green Bay, WI (14)
Cornhusker Press, Hastings, NE (17)
Corona Cigar Co, Orlando, FL (5)
Corona-Lotus Inc, San Francisco, CA (4)
Coronis Building Systems Inc, Columbus, NJ (9)
Corpus Christi Museum of Science & History, Corpus Christi, TX (1)
Cortz Inc, West Chicago, IL (5)
Cosgrove Associates, New York, NY (14)
Cosmetique, Inc, Vernon Hills, IL (13)
Cosmo International, Deerfield Beach, FL (16)
Council for Advancement and Support of Education, Washington, DC (1)
Council of Better Business Bureaus - BBBOnline, Arlington, VA (1)
Council on Foreign Relations Inc, New York, NY (17)
The Country Bed Shop, Ashby, MA (16)
Country Curtains Inc, Stockbridge, MA (8)
Country Dance and Song Society, Easthampton, MA (1)

Country Financial, Bloomington, IL (15)
The Country House Inc, Salisbury, MD (6)
Country Sampler Group, Saint Charles, IL (17)
Countrywide Financial Corp, Calabasas, CA (14)
Courage Cards & Gifts, Golden Valley, MN (1)
Covenant House International Headquarters, New York, NY (1)
Coverdell & Co Inc, Chicago, IL (15)
Cox Communications Inc, Atlanta, GA (16)
Coyne American Institute, Chicago, IL (16)
Crabtree & Evelyn Ltd, Westport, CT (4)
The Cracker Box Inc, Blooming Glen, PA (16)
Craft-Diston Industries, Wichita, KS (16)
Craig/Vartorella International Marketing & Advertising Inc, Camden, SC (1)
Crain Communications Inc, Detroit, MI (17)
Crazy Crow Trading Post, Pottsboro, TX (11)
Creative Banner Assemblies, Minneapolis, MN (9)
Creative Catalogs Corp, Lemont, IL (16)
Creative Health Products, Plymouth, MI (16)
Creative Irish Gifts, Little Rock, AR (6)
Creative Publishing International, Minneapolis, MN (17)
Creative Teaching Press, Cypress, CA (17)
Creativity International, Ada, MI (16)
Credit Union Executives Society, Fitchburg, WI (1)
The Cricket Magazine Group, Chicago, IL (17)
Crohn's & Colitis Foundation of America, New York, NY (1)
Cronin & Co, Glastonbury, CT (16)
Cross Country Stitching, Quakertown, PA (17)
Cross Country Travcorps, Boca Raton, FL (16)
Crosstown Traders Inc, Tucson, AZ (2)
Crutchfield Corp, Charlottesville, VA (3)
Crystal Records Inc, Camas, WA (17)
Cuba Cheese Shoppe, Cuba, NY (4)
Cuddledown Inc, Yarmouth, ME (8)
Cuisinart, Stamford, CT (16)
Culinary Parts Unlimited, San Francisco, CA (16)
CUNA Mutual Group, Madison, WI (15)
CUNA - Trade Association, Madison, WI (1)
Cunningham Group, Elmwood Park, IL (15)
Current USA Inc, Colorado Springs, CO (6)
Cushman Fruit Co Inc, West Palm Beach, FL (4)
Custom Direct, Colorado Springs, CO (16)
Custom Miniatures, Hudson, NH (6)
Cuvaison Inc, Napa, CA (4)
Cystic Fibrosis Foundation, Bethesda, MD (1)

D

DB Alex Brown Inc, Baltimore, MD (14)
DCA, West Chester, PA (16)
DMC Corp, Kearny, NJ (16)
Dr Ho's, Greensboro, GA (7)
DRG, Berne, IN (17)
DS Services of North America LP, Lakeland, FL (4)
DWS Investments Service Co, Kansas City, MO (14)
Daedalus Books Inc, Columbia, MD (5)
Daily Commercial News & Construction Record, Markham, ON, Canada (17)
Daily Record & Dispatch Co, Dunn, NC (17)
DaimlerChrysler Corp, Auburn Hills, MI (12)
Dairy Council of California, Irvine, CA (1)
Dairy Farmers of America Inc, Kansas City, MO (16)
Dairy Management Inc, Rosemont, IL (1)
Dakin Farm, Ferrisburgh, VT (4)
Dakota Digital, Sioux Falls, SD (12)
Dalco Electronics, Springboro, OH (3)
Dalrada Financial Corp, San Diego, CA (14)

Dana-Farber Cancer Institute, Boston, MA (1)
Dansk, Bristol, PA (16)
Dante University Press, Wellesley, MA (17)
Darden School Foundation Executive Foundation, Charlottesville, VA (1)
Dartmouth-Hitchcock, Lebanon, NH (1)
Dassault Falcon Jet Corp, Little Ferry, NJ (16)
Databazaar.com, Miramar, FL (10)
DataCal Enterprises, Gilbert, AZ (16)
Davidoff of Geneva Inc, Pinellas Park, FL (6)
DaVinci Direct, Plymouth, MA (1)
The Davis Center, Succasunna, NJ (16)
Dick Davis Digest, Salem, MA (17)
Davis Instruments Corp, Hayward, CA (8)
Davis Publications Inc, Worcester, MA (17)
Day Runner Direct, Sidney, NY (10)
Day-Timer, East Texas, PA (13)
Days Inns Worldwide Inc, Parsippany, NJ (16)
Dayton Daily News, Dayton, OH (18)
Dean & Deluca Brands Inc, Wichita, KS (4)
Decal Shop, Jacksonville, FL (10)
Deck the Walls Inc, Saint Peters, MO (5)
Decko Products Inc, Sandusky, OH (4)
Deere & Co, Moline, IL (16)
Del Webb, Bloomfield Hills, MI (16)
Delicious Orchards, Colts Neck, NJ (4)
Dell Computer Corp, Round Rock, TX (16)
DeLorme Mapping, Yarmouth, ME (3)
DelStar Technologies Inc, Middletown, DE (16)
Delta Tech Industries, Ontario, CA (12)
Delta Upsilon International Fraternity, Indianapolis, IN (16)
Delta Vacations, Atlanta, GA (19)
Democratic Congressional Campaign Committee, Washington, DC (1)
Dental Economics, Tulsa, OK (17)
Dentsply International, York, PA (7)
Denver Metro Convention & Visitors Bureau, Denver, CO (1)
Dermac Labs Inc, Salem, OR (16)
Deseret Book, Salt Lake City, UT (16)
Desert Rat Truck Centers, Tucson, AZ (12)
Design Toscano, Inc, Elk Grove Village, IL (6)
Desjardins Financial Securities, Levis, QC, Canada (15)
Destinations Ireland & Beyond, Kingston, NY (19)
The Detroit Institute of Arts, Detroit, MI (16)
Detroit Newspapers, Detroit, MI (18)
DeVry Education Group, Downers Grove, IL (16)
Dharma Trading Co, Petaluma, CA (2)
Diakon Lutheran Social Ministries, Allentown, PA (1)
Diamond Essence, Edison, NJ (2)
Diamond Machining Technology, Marlborough, MA (9)
Diamonds By Rennie Ellen, New York, NY (6)
Didit, Mineola, NY (16)
DigDev Direct, Deerfield Beach, FL (16)
Digi International, Minnetonka, MN (3)
Digi-Key Corp, Thief River Falls, MN (3)
The Dime Savings Bank of New York FSB, New York, NY (14)
Dimmock Hill Golf Course Pro Shop, Binghamton, NY (11)
DineEquity Inc, Glendale, CA (16)
DineWise, Farmingdale, NY (4)
Dinn Brothers Inc, West Springfield, MA (16)
Christian Dior Perfumes, New York, NY (7)
Dan Dipret Travel Service Inc, Arlington, TX (19)
Direct Auto Insurance, Nashville, TN (15)
Direct Energy, Toronto, ON, Canada (16)
Direct Gardening Association, La Grange, GA (1)

Direct SAT TV LLC, Southern Pines, NC (3)
Direct Sports Supply, Pearisburg, VA (11)
Direct Supply Inc, Milwaukee, WI (16)
DirectBuy Inc, Merrillville, IN (1)
Directory of American Business & Insurance Attorneys, New York, NY (15)
Disabled American Veterans, Cincinnati, OH (1)
Discovery, Eatontown, NJ (9)
Discovery Communications Inc, Silver Spring, MD (16)
Discovery Toys, Livermore, CA (16)
Disney Vacation Club, Kissimmee, FL (19)
Diversified Healthcare Services, Richardson, TX (15)
Diversified Photo Supply Corp, Gardena, CA (10)
Divine Word Missionaries, Techny, IL (1)
DNE Nutraceuticals Inc, Farmingdale, NJ (7)
Do-It Corp, South Haven, MI (9)
Doane, Saint Louis, MO (17)
Doctor's Best Inc, San Clemente, CA (16)
Drs Foster & Smith Inc, Rhinelander, WI (2)
Doctors Without Borders, New York, NY (1)
Domestic Bank, Providence, RI (14)
Dominion Retail Inc, Richmond, VA (16)
Donna Salyers' Fabulous-Bridal Inc, Covington, KY (2)
Dorothy Biddle Service, Greeley, PA (8)
Dorothy's Ruffled Originals Inc, Wilmington, NC (8)
Doubletree Suites by Hilton, Boston, MA (19)
DoubleVerify, New York, NY (16)
Dover Publications Inc, Mineola, NY (17)
Dow Jones & Co, Princeton, NJ (17)
Dow Theory Forecasts, Hammond, IN (17)
Down Home Comforts, Putnam Station, NY (8)
Dozier Equipment International, Milwaukee, WI (9)
Dr Jays, San Diego, CA (2)
Dr Leonard's Healthcare Corp, Edison, NJ (7)
Dragich Auto Literature, Princeton, MN (16)
Draper's & Damon's, Irvine, CA (2)
Drawing Board Inc, Waynesboro, PA (16)
Dream Products Inc, Van Nuys, CA (5)
The Dreyfus Corp, New York, NY (14)
Droll Yankees Inc, Plainfield, CT (8)
Drug Information Association, Horsham, PA (1)
Drug Policy Alliance, New York, NY (1)
Drumbeat Indian Arts Inc, Phoenix, AZ (6)
Ducks Unlimited, Memphis, TN (1)
Ducktrap River Fish Farm, Belfast, ME (4)
Duluth Trading Co Inc, Belleville, WI (8)
Duncraft Inc, Concord, NH (16)
E I DuPont De Nemours & Co, Wilmington, DE (16)
Duracell, Bethel, CT (16)
Durio Nursery, Opelousas, LA (8)
Dutch Gardens USA Inc, Bloomington, IL (8)
Dynamic Development Co, Mission Viejo, CA (12)
Dynamic Engineering, Santa Cruz, CA (3)
Dynamics Research Corp, Andover, MA (16)

E

e-Pipeconnection, Evansville, IN (9)
EDC Publishing, Tulsa, OK (17)
EMS Technologies, Norcross, GA (16)
EOS International Inc, Carlsbad, CA (5)
ESL Federal Credit Union, Rochester, NY (14)
ESPN, Bristol, CT (5)
ETR Associates, Scotts Valley, CA (7)
EWA & Miniature Cars USA Inc, Berkeley Heights, NJ (11)
Eagle Asset Management Inc, Saint Petersburg, FL (14)

Eagle Claw Fishing Tackle, Denver, CO (11)
Eagle Publishing, Washington, DC (17)
Earthrise, Irvine, CA (16)
Eastbay Running Store Inc, Wausau, WI (2)
Easter Seals, Chicago, IL (1)
Eastern Michigan University, Ypsilanti, MI (16)
Eastern Mountain Sports, Peterborough, NH (16)
Easthill Group Inc, Pottstown, PA (12)
David Easton Inc, New York, NY (16)
Ebbets Field Flannels Inc, Seattle, WA (2)
Eberle & Associates Inc, McLean, VA (1)
Ebersole Lapidary Supply Inc, Wichita, KS (11)
Eckankar, Minneapolis, MN (17)
Ecklers, Titusville, FL (12)
The Economist Newspaper NA Inc, New York, NY (17)
Economy Handicrafts, Brooklyn, NY (16)
Edible Landscaping, Afton, VA (8)
Editorial Projects in Education Inc, Bethesda, MD (17)
Edmund Optics Inc, Barrington, NJ (9)
Education Direct, Scranton, PA (16)
Educational Testing Service, Princeton, NJ (16)
Educators Progress Service Inc, Randolph, WI (17)
S Wallace Edwards & Sons Inc, Surry, VA (4)
Edwin Watts Golf, Fort Walton Beach, FL (11)
Effective Promotions Inc, Fort Johnson, NY (16)
Efstonscience Inc, Toronto, ON, Canada (3)
Eggs by Byrd, Wappapello, MO (10)
Eichten's Hidden Acres, Center City, MN (4)
89 Degrees, Burlington, MA (9)
Eilenberger's Bakery Inc, Palestine, TX (4)
Eire Direct, Chicago, IL (16)
Elderhostel Inc, Lowell, MA (1)
Elderly Instruments, Lansing, MI (5)
Electric Insurance Co, Beverly, MA (15)
Electronic Arts Inc, Redwood City, CA (3)
ElectroWarmth Products LLC, Danville, OH (8)
Elemental Scientific LLC, Appleton, WI (9)
Edward Elgar Publishing Inc, Northampton, MA (17)
Elite Sportswear LP, Reading, PA (2)
Elkhart Cases, Elkhart, IN (2)
Elks Magazine, Chicago, IL (17)
Emblem & Badge Inc, Johnston, RI (6)
Embrace Home Loans, Middletown, RI (14)
Emergency Essentials Inc, Orem, UT (16)
Emerson Ecologics, Manchester, NH (7)
Emigrant Savings Bank, New York, NY (14)
Emperor Clock LLC, Amherst, VA (16)
Empire Blue Cross & Blue Shield, New York, NY (15)
Empire Coffee & Tea Co, New York, NY (4)
En ESPANOL Publishing Group LLC, Beverly Hills, CA (17)
Enco Manufacturing Co, Fernley, NV (9)
Encore Marketing International, Lanham, MD (16)
Encyclopaedia Britannica Inc, Chicago, IL (17)
Energizer Holdings Inc, Saint Louis, MO (16)
Enerpac, Menomonee Falls, WI (16)
Engineering Services & Products Co, South Windsor, CT (9)
ENMAX Corp, Calgary, AB, Canada (9)
Entergy, New Orleans, LA (16)
Enterprex International Corp, Arcadia, CA (16)
Enterprise Ireland, New York, NY (16)
Entrepreneur Media Inc, Irvine, CA (17)
Entrepreneur Partners, Philadelphia, PA (14)
Envelope Manufacturers Association, Alexandria, VA (1)
Epilepsy Foundation, Landover, MD (1)
Episcopal Relief & Development, New York, NY (1)

Epson America, Long Beach, CA (10)
Equitable Life & Casualty Insurance Co, Salt Lake City, UT (15)
Escort Inc, West Chester, OH (16)
Esquire Magazine, New York, NY (17)
Esselte Americas, Melville, NY (16)
Essence Communications Inc, New York, NY (17)
Essential Products Co Inc, New York, NY (7)
Estee Lauder Inc, New York, NY (16)
Estes Industries, Penrose, CO (11)
Etchworld, Hawthorne, NJ (11)
Ethel M Chocolates Inc, Henderson, NV (4)
Eventful Inc, San Diego, CA (19)
Excelligence Learning Corp, Monterey, CA (5)
Expedia Inc, Bellevue, WA (19)
Experience In Software Inc, Berkeley, CA (16)
Expressions Custom Furniture, Hickory, NC (16)
Eyeglass Service Industries, Lynbrook, NY (2)

F

F&W Media Inc, Blue Ash, OH (17)
FAFCO Inc, Chico, CA (16)
FDAnews, Falls Church, VA (17)
FIU Online, Miami, FL (1)
FLM Graphics Corp, Fairfield, NJ (16)
FNC INC, Oxford, MS (14)
FTD Companies Inc, Downers Grove, IL (16)
FW Media, Cincinnati, OH (17)
Facts On File Inc, New York, NY (17)
Fairchild Books, New York, NY (17)
Fairchild Fashion Media, New York, NY (17)
Faire Harbour Limited, Scituate, MA (5)
Fairytale Brownies, Phoenix, AZ (4)
Falcon Safety Products, Branchburg, NJ (16)
Fallon Community Health Plan, Worcester, MA (1)
Family Album, Kinzers, PA (6)
Family Christian Stores, Grand Rapids, MI (5)
The Family Handyman, Eagan, MN (17)
Famous Smoke Shop Inc, Easton, PA (16)
Fancy Fronds, Gold Bar, WA (8)
Farm Bureau Insurance, Lansing, MI (15)
Farm Home Offices, Richfield, MN (10)
Farm Journal Inc, Philadelphia, PA (17)
Farm Progress Co, Saint Charles, IL (17)
Farmers Insurance, Los Angeles, CA (15)
Farrow Group, Windsor, ON, Canada (16)
Father Flanagan's Boy's Home, Boys Town, NE (1)
Fathers of St Edmund Southern Missions Inc, Selma, AL (1)
FatWallet, Beloit, WI (14)
Faultless Starch/Bon Ami Co, Kansas City, MO (16)
Fauntleroy Supply Co/Wing Supply, Greenville, KY (11)
Federal Citizen Information Center, Pueblo, CO (5)
Federated Investors Co, Pittsburgh, PA (14)
FedEx Corp, Memphis, TN (16)
Feed the Children, Oklahoma City, OK (1)
George Fencik Associates, Point Pleasant, NJ (16)
Ferrara Bakery & Cafe Inc, New York, NY (4)
Fidelity Investments, Boston, MA (14)
Fidelity Security Life Insurance Co, Kansas City, MO (15)
The Field Museum, Chicago, IL (1)
Fieldstone Gardens Inc, Vassalboro, ME (8)
Fifth Avenue Committee, Brooklyn, NY (1)
Fifth Third Bank, Cincinnati, OH (14)
Figi's Inc, Marshfield, WI (4)
Financial Services International Corp, Seattle, WA (14)
The Financial Times Group, New York, NY (17)

Finck Cigar Co, San Antonio, TX (5)
Fine Architectural Metalsmiths, Chester, NY (16)
Finley Products Inc, Lancaster, PA (16)
Fiorella's Jack Stack Barbecue, Kansas City, MO (4)
Fire Mountain Gems, Grants Pass, OR (16)
Fireman's Fund Insurance Co, Novato, CA (14)
First Advantage Membership Services, Poway, CA (14)
First Banks Inc, Clayton, MO (14)
First Data Merchant Services, Atlanta, GA (14)
First Hawaiian Bank, Honolulu, HI (14)
First Media Communications Inc, Brentwood, TN (16)
First Merit Bank (HQ), Akron, OH (14)
First to the Finish Inc, Carlinville, IL (7)
Carl Fischer Music, New York, NY (17)
Fisher Investments, Woodside, CA (14)
Fisher-Price, East Aurora, NY (16)
Fitness Quest, Canton, OH (16)
Fitness Systems Manufacturing Corp, Wyomissing, PA (7)
Fitness USA Super Centers, West Bloomfield, MI (16)
Fitter International Inc, Calgary, AB, Canada (1)
Caimin Flannery & Associates, Naperville, IL (14)
FLEXcon, Spencer, MA (16)
Flickinger's Nursery, Beyer, PA (8)
Flight Form Cases Inc, Bedford Park, IL (9)
The Flinchbaugh Co Inc, Manchester, PA (16)
Florian Tools, Southington, CT (8)
Florida A&M University, Tallahassee, FL (16)
Florida Credit Union, Gainesville, FL (14)
Florida Gift Fruit Shippers Association, Orlando, FL (1)
Florida Power & Light Co, Juno Beach, FL (16)
Florida Today, Melbourne, FL (17)
Fluid Metering Inc, Syosset, NY (16)
Fluke Biomedical, Everett, WA (16)
Food for the Hungry Inc, Phoenix, AZ (1)
Food for the Poor Inc, Coconut Creek, FL (1)
Forbes Inc, New York, NY (17)
Ford Foundation Office of Communications, New York, NY (5)
Ford Motor Co, Dearborn, MI (16)
Forecaster Publishing Co Inc, Tarzana, CA (14)
Foremost Insurance Group, Grand Rapids, MI (15)
Forethought Financial Services Inc, Batesville, IN (15)
Formal Approach, Jefferson City, TN (2)
Fossil, Richardson, TX (2)
Fostoria Industries Inc, Johnson City, TN (9)
Foundation for Chiropractic Education & Research, Norwalk, IA (1)
Foundation of FirstHealth, Pinehurst, NC (1)
Four Corners Direct Inc, Sarasota, FL (16)
Four Seasons Hotels & Resorts, Toronto, ON, Canada (19)
Four Seasons Solar Products LLC, Holbrook, NY (8)
Four Wheel Drive Hardware LLC, Columbiana, OH (12)
Fox Chase Cancer Center, Philadelphia, PA (1)
Larry Fox & Co Ltd, Valley Stream, NY (16)
Fox Lite, Inc, Fairborn, OH (9)
Fragrance International Inc, Youngstown, OH (16)
Franciscan Friars of the Atonement - Graymoor, Garrison, NY (1)
Franciscan Mission Associates, Mount Vernon, NY (1)
The Franklin Mint, Exton, PA (16)
Fran's Basket House, Inc, Succasunna, NJ (8)
Frederick's of Hollywood Group Inc, Los Angeles, CA (2)

Paul Fredrick Menstyle, Fleetwood, PA (2)
Freeport Music Inc, Farmingville, NY (11)
Freestyle Photographic Supplies, Los Angeles, CA (5)
French Creek Sheep & Wool Co Inc, Elverson, PA (2)
FreshDirect, Long Island City, NY (5)
Fresno Oxygen, Fresno, CA (9)
A I Friedman Inc, New York, NY (10)
Frito-Lay, Plano, TX (16)
Frog Tool Co Ltd, Dixon, IL (11)
Frontier Natural Products Co-op, Norway, IA (7)
Fujifilm Holdings America Corp, Valhalla, NY (16)
Fulcrum Publishing, Golden, CO (17)
The Fuller Theological Seminary, Pasadena, CA (16)
Fund for Public Interest Research, Washington, DC (1)
Fundamentals Co Inc, Bristol, VA (1)
Alan Furman & Co, Rockville, MD (2)

G

G&S Fruit Packers LLC, Weirsdale, FL (16)
G H Bass & Co, New York, NY (16)
GCC Printers, Bedford, MA (10)
GE Canada, Mississauga, ON, Canada (9)
GE Lighting North America, Cleveland, OH (16)
GE Partnership Marketing Group, Schaumburg, IL (14)
GEICO Direct, Washington, DC (15)
GMG Productions Inc, Roslyn, NY (3)
GRP Funding LLC, Springfield, MA (14)
Gaco Western Inc, Seattle, WA (16)
Gaiam Inc, Boulder, CO (9)
Galen Williams Landscaping & Garden Design, East Hampton, NY (16)
Gallagher Affinity, Lakewood Ranch, FL (15)
Gallery of Cats, Valencia, CA (6)
The Gallery Shop, Buffalo, NY (6)
Galloway Farms, Miami, FL (8)
Gall's Inc, Lexington, KY (16)
Gallup Inter-Tribal Indian Ceremonial, Gallup, NM (1)
GameTime Inc, Fort Payne, AL (11)
Gamma Photo Labs LLC, Chicago, IL (16)
Gannett Co Inc, Mc Lean, VA (16)
Garden Botanika Inc, Saint Louis, MO (7)
Garden Perennials, Wayne, NE (8)
Gardener's Supply Co, Burlington, VT (8)
Gardens Alive! Inc, Lawrenceburg, IN (8)
Gardens Of The Blue Ridge Inc, Pineola, NC (8)
Garlinghouse Co, Beaufort, SC (17)
Garnet Hill Inc, Franconia, NH (2)
Gates Corp, Denver, CO (9)
Gateway Bank and Trust, Raleigh, NC (14)
Gateway Inc, Irvine, CA (3)
Gay Men's Health Crisis, New York, NY (1)
Gazette Communications Inc, Cedar Rapids, IA (17)
Geary's of Beverly Hills, Beverly Hills, CA (6)
Gemini Publishing Co, Webster, TX (17)
General Binding Corp, Northbrook, IL (10)
General Electric Co, Fairfield, CT (16)
General Mills Inc, Minneapolis, MN (8)
General Nutrition Corp, Pittsburgh, PA (7)
General Pencil Co Inc, Jersey City, NJ (16)
General Vitamin Corp, Raleigh, NC (16)
Genesco Inc, Nashville, TN (2)
Genetica DNA Laboratories Inc, Cincinnati, OH (16)
Genium Publishing, Amsterdam, NY (17)
Genworth Financial Inc, Richmond, VA (14)

Georgetown University Law Center, Washington, DC (13)
Georgetown University McDonough School of Business, Washington, DC (1)
Georgia Power, Atlanta, GA (16)
Gerber Life Insurance Co, White Plains, NY (15)
Gerber Products Co, Florham Park, NJ (16)
Gero Vita, Costa Mesa, CA (16)
Gerstner Woodworks, Dayton, OH (6)
Getronics, Tewksbury, MA (16)
Ghent Manufacturing Inc, Lebanon, OH (10)
Gibson Auer LLC, Victor, ID (7)
Gift Services Inc, Vancouver, WA (6)
Gifts Corp, Barrie, ON, Canada (6)
Gillette Children's Specialty Healthcare, Saint Paul, MN (1)
Gilman's Lapidary Supply, Hellertown, PA (11)
Gilson Co Inc, Lewis Center, OH (9)
Gimbels of Maine Inc, Boothbay Harbor, ME (6)
Girl Scouts of the USA, New York, NY (1)
Glamour Shots Licensing, Oklahoma City, OK (16)
GlaxoSmithKline USA, Philadelphia, PA (16)
Peter Glenn Publications, Delray Beach, FL (17)
Glens Falls Hospital Foundation, Glens Falls, NY (1)
Glenview Capital Management, New York, NY (14)
Glenview State Bank, Glenview, IL (14)
Global Equipment Co Inc, Port Washington, NY (9)
Globe Specialty Products Inc, Millbury, MA (17)
Go Ahead Vacations, Cambridge, MA (16)
Go Promos, Amsterdam, NY (5)
Goddard Manufacturing Co, Logan, KS (8)
Godiva Chocolatier, New York, NY (4)
Gohn Brothers, Middlebury, IN (5)
Gold Medal Hair Products Inc, Farmingdale, NY (7)
Gold Medal Products Co, Cincinnati, OH (16)
Golden Bison LLC, Denver, CO (4)
Golden Fleece Designs Inc, Burbank, CA (16)
Golden Rule Insurance Co, Indianapolis, IN (15)
Golden Trophy, Chicago, IL (4)
Golf Card International, Englewood, CO (1)
Golf Digest Co, Wilton, CT (17)
Golf Haus, Lansing, MI (11)
Golfsmith International Inc, Austin, TX (11)
Good Directions Co Inc, Danbury, CT (8)
Goodheart-Willcox Publisher, Tinley Park, IL (17)
Goodman Media Group Inc, New York, NY (17)
Goodwill Industries of San Francisco, San Francisco, CA (1)
Goodyear Tire & Rubber Co, Akron, OH (16)
WL Gore & Associates Inc, Newark, DE (2)
Gorsuch Ltd, Vail, CO (2)
Gossler Farms Nursery, Springfield, OR (8)
Gothic Arch Greenhouses Inc, Mobile, AL (8)
Governing Magazine, Washington, DC (17)
Government of India Tourist Office, New York, NY (1)
Graceland, Memphis, TN (6)
Graduate School USA, Washington, DC (1)
Billy Graham Evangelistic Association, Charlotte, NC (1)
Graham Field Health Products Inc, Atlanta, GA (7)
Grand Canyon University, Phoenix, AZ (13)
Grand Circle Travel, Boston, MA (19)
Grandma Brown's Beans Inc, Mexico, NY (4)
The Graph Co, Vineland, NJ (14)
Graphik Dimensions Ltd, High Point, NC (16)
Graves Lapidary Co, Pompano Beach, FL (9)
Great Chefs Television Publishing, New Orleans, LA (6)
Great Western Bank, Sioux Falls, SD (14)

Greater Fort Worth Builders Association, Fort Worth, TX (1)

Green Mountain Coffee Roasters, Inc, Waterbury, VT (4)

Greenwood Publishing Group Inc, Portsmouth, NH (17)

Gridley & Co LLC, New York, NY (14)

Grizzly Industrial Inc, Bellingham, WA (9)

Grove Enterprises Inc, Brasstown, NC (16)

Grover Co, Mesa, AZ (16)

Growing Child, Inc, West Lafayette, IN (17)

Gruber & Allison Inc, Boynton Beach, FL (17)

Guarantee Trust Life Insurance Co, Glenview, IL (15)

Guaranty Bank, Brown Deer, WI (14)

The Guardian Life Insurance Co, New York, NY (15)

Guideposts, Danbury, CT (1)

Guiding Eyes for the Blind, Yorktown Heights, NY (16)

Guilford Publications Inc, New York, NY (17)

Gulf Coast Data Supply Inc, Milton, FL (3)

Gump's By Mail Inc, San Francisco, CA (6)

Gun Video Catalog/LMP, San Diego, CA (11)

H

H&R Block Inc, Kansas City, MO (14)

HCI Direct, Bensalem, PA (16)

HDA Inc, Saint Louis, MO (17)

HR Direct, Sunrise, FL (10)

HSBC Bank USA, NA, New York, NY (14)

HSN Inc, Saint Petersburg, FL (5)

Haband Co Inc, Oakland, NJ (2)

Habitat For Humanity International, Americus, GA (1)

Hadley Fruit Orchards Inc, Cabazon, CA (4)

Hagie Manufacturing Co, Clarion, IA (9)

Hale Indian River Groves Inc, Vero Beach, FL (16)

Hallelujah Acres, Gastonia, NC (5)

Hallmark Cards Inc, Kansas City, MO (16)

Halls Kansas City, Kansas City, MO (16)

Halsom Home Care Inc, Centerville, OH (16)

Hamakor Judaica Inc, Skokie, IL (5)

Hamilton Beach Brands Inc, Glen Allen, VA (16)

The Hamilton Collection, Jacksonville, FL (6)

The Hamilton Group Ltd Inc, Jacksonville, FL (16)

Hammacher Schlemmer & Co Inc, Niles, IL (16)

Hammock Publishing Inc, Nashville, TN (17)

Hampshire Agency, Great Neck, NY (14)

Hampshire Pewter Co, Somersworth, NH (6)

Hampton Marketing Corp, Medford, NY (16)

Handi-Ramp Inc, Libertyville, IL (7)

Hanesbrands Inc, Winston Salem, NC (2)

Hanley Wood LLC, Washington, DC (16)

Hanover Direct Inc, Weehawken, NJ (5)

The Hanover Shoe Co, Newton, MA (16)

Happy Trails Resort, Surprise, AZ (19)

Harbor Freight Tools, Camarillo, CA (9)

Harbour Bay Inc, Oakland, NJ (16)

Harcourt Educational Measurement, San Antonio, TX (17)

Harland Financial Solutions Inc, Lake Mary, FL (16)

Harlequin Enterprises Ltd, Don Mills, ON, Canada (17)

Harman's Cheese & Country Store Inc, Sugar Hill, NH (4)

HarperCollins, New York, NY (17)

Harper's Magazine, New York, NY (17)

Harrington's of Vermont Inc, Richmond, VT (4)

Harris Bancorp Inc, Chicago, IL (14)

Harry & David Holdings Inc, Medford, OR (4)

The Hartford Financial Services Inc, Southington, CT (15)

The Hartz Mountain Corp, Secaucus, NJ (16)

Harvard Business Review, Boston, MA (17)

Harvard Business School - Executive Education, Boston, MA (1)

Harvard Pilgrim Health Care, Wellesley, MA (7)

Harvard Square Records, Austin, TX (3)

Hasbro Inc, Pawtucket, RI (11)

Hasco First Photo, Saint Charles, MO (16)

Hatton-Brown Publishers Inc, Montgomery, AL (17)

Havel's Inc, Cincinnati, OH (7)

Haymarket Group Ltd, New York, NY (17)

Hazelden, Center City, MN (7)

Health O Meter, Countryside, IL (16)

HealthPlan Services, Tampa, FL (15)

HealthRight International, New York, NY (1)

The Healthy Back Store, Beltsville, MD (16)

Hear Music, Beverly Hills, CA (3)

Hearlihy & Co, Pittsburg, KS (17)

The Hearst Corp, New York, NY (17)

Hearst Magazines, New York, NY (17)

Hearthside Quilts & Supplies, Hinesburg, VT (11)

Heartland America, Chaska, MN (3)

Heartland Boating Magazine, Saint Louis, MO (17)

Heartstrings Press, Lancaster, VA (17)

Heaven & Earth, Virginia Beach, VA (5)

Hecht Rubber Corp, Jacksonville, FL (16)

Heldref Publications, Washington, DC (17)

W C Heller & Co, Montpelier, OH (16)

Hello Direct, Nashua, NH (16)

Helzberg Diamonds, North Kansas City, MO (16)

Hemmings Motor News, Bennington, VT (17)

The Herald & Review, Decatur, IL (17)

Herbach & Rademan Co, Moorestown, NJ (9)

Herr Foods Inc, Nottingham, PA (16)

Herrington, Londonderry, NH (16)

Herrschners Inc, Stevens Point, WI (11)

Herschend Family Entertainment, Norcross, GA (5)

The Hershey Co, Hershey, PA (4)

Hershey Park, Hershey, PA (19)

Hertz Corp, Park Ridge, NJ (19)

Hewlett-Packard Co, Palo Alto, CA (16)

Hickory Farms, Maumee, OH (4)

Highlights For Children, Columbus, OH (17)

Highmark Blue Cross Blue Shield, Pittsburgh, PA (15)

HighScope Educational Research Foundation, Ypsilanti, MI (17)

James J Hill Reference Library, Saint Paul, MN (1)

Conrad N Hilton College of Hotel & Restaurant Management University of Houston, Houston, TX (1)

Hilton Hotels Corp, Mc Lean, VA (19)

Hireko Golf, City of Industry, CA (11)

Historic Aviation, Minneapolis, MN (12)

Historical Replications Inc, Jackson, MS (8)

The Historical Research Center International Inc, Boynton Beach, FL (16)

The History Book Club Inc, Mechanicsburg, PA (13)

Hitchcock Shoes Inc, Hingham, MA (2)

Hobart & William Smith Colleges, Geneva, NY (19)

Hobby Builders Supply, Atlanta, GA (11)

Hobby Surplus Sales, New Britain, CT (11)

Hoffman Mint, Fort Lauderdale, FL (6)

Hoke Communications Inc, Garden City, NY (17)

Holiday Vacations, Eau Claire, WI (19)

Holland Wildflower Farm, Elkins, AR (8)

Hollywood Film Archive, Los Angeles, CA (17)

Holy Cross Hospital, Fort Lauderdale, FL (16)

Home Decorators Collection Inc, Marietta, GA (8)

The Home Depot Inc, Atlanta, GA (16)

Home Interiors & Gifts Inc, Carrollton, TX (16)

Home Loan Investment Bank, Warwick, RI (14)

Home Planners, Tucson, AZ (17)

Home-Sew Inc, Bethlehem, PA (11)

HomeAway.com Inc, Austin, TX (19)

Homecraft Veneer & Woodworker Supply, Latrobe, PA (8)

Homespun Tapes Music Instruction, Woodstock, NY (3)

The HoneyBaked Ham Co, Holland, OH (4)

Hook & Hackle Co Inc, Homestead, PA (11)

Hooleon Corp, Melrose, NM (3)

Hoover's Mfg Co, Peru, IL (2)

Hopkins Medical Products, Baltimore, MD (7)

Horace Mann Educators Corp, Springfield, IL (15)

Horticulture Magazine, Cincinnati, OH (17)

Hot Topic Inc, City of Industry, CA (2)

House of Eyes, Greensboro, NC (2)

House of Oldies, New York, NY (6)

House of Onyx, Inc, Greenville, KY (6)

House of Orange, Brentwood Bay, BC, Canada (2)

House of Wesley Inc, Bloomington, IL (8)

Howard Rice Nemerovski Canady Falk & Rabkin, San Francisco, CA (14)

William B Hugg Enterprise Inc Swim Wear & Accessories, Ambler, PA (11)

Humana Inc, Louisville, KY (7)

The Humane Society of the US, Washington, DC (1)

Hy Cite Corp, Madison, WI (16)

HY-KO Products Co, Northfield, OH (16)

Hyatt Fruit Co, Vero Beach, FL (4)

Hyatt Hotels Corp, Chicago, IL (16)

Hyatt Legal Plans Inc, Cleveland, OH (16)

Hygienic Fabrics & Filters Inc, Sheboygan, WI (16)

Hyman's, Hanahan, SC (2)

I

ICIS Inc, Upper Black Eddy, PA (2)

IDC, Ltd, Henderson, NV (1)

IDMS Inc, Melville, NY (16)

The IEI Corp, Princeton, NJ (6)

IHS Markit, Englewood, CO (17)

ING, Minneapolis, MN (15)

ING USA Annuity & Life Ins Co, Des Moines, IA (15)

IPD Co Inc, Portland, OR (12)

ISA-The International Society of Automation, Research Triangle Park, NC (1)

ITT Educational Services Inc, Carmel, IN (16)

The Iams Co, Mason, OH (16)

IClimber Inc, Burbank, CA (16)

Ideals Publications Inc, Nashville, TN (17)

Idearc Media Corp, Dallas, TX (16)

Illy Caffe North America, Rye Brook, NY (4)

IMPACT Publishing Inc, Bradenton, FL (17)

Imperial Supplies, Green Bay, WI (16)

Improvements, West Chester, OH (8)

In-Sync Publications, Redondo Beach, CA (18)

In Touch Ministries, Atlanta, GA (1)

Independent Living Aids, Buffalo, NY (7)

Indian Country Today Media Network, New York, NY (17)

Indian House Records & Tapes, Taos, NM (3)

Indianapolis Motor Speedway, Indianapolis, IN (19)

Indianapolis Newspapers Inc, Indianapolis, IN (17)

Indoor Gardening Supplies, Dexter, MI (8)

Indus-Tool, Chicago, IL (12)

Industrial Uniform Co Inc, Wichita, KS (2)

Infomart, Dallas, TX (16)
Informal Education Products, Milwaukie, OR (11)
Information Unlimited Inc, Mont Vernon, NH (11)
Insight Direct Inc, Tempe, AZ (16)
Institute For Natural Resources, Concord, CA (16)
Institute of Management Accountants Inc, Montvale, NJ (1)
Institute of Reading Development, Novato, CA (1)
Institutional Advancement Programs Inc, Tuckahoe, NY (1)
Instructor's Choice Dancewear, Massapequa Park, NY (2)
The Instrument Workshop, Ashland, OR (16)
Integrity Music Inc, Mobile, AL (16)
Intel Corp, Santa Clara, CA (16)
InteliSpend Prepaid Solutions, Fenton, MO (5)
InterContinental Hotels Group, Atlanta, GA (19)
The Interfaith Alliance, Washington, DC (1)
Intergraph Corp, Madison, AL (16)
International Advertising Association, New York, NY (1)
International Auto Parts, Charlottesville, VA (12)
International Coins & Currency Inc, Montpelier, VT (6)
International Crystal Manufacturing Co, Oklahoma City, OK (16)
International Direct Media Co & Information Publishing Co, San Francisco, CA (17)
International Foundation of Employee Benefit Plans, Brookfield, WI (1)
International Fund for Animal Welfare, Yarmouth Port, MA (1)
International Irrigation Systems, St. Catherines, ON, Canada (8)
International Manufacturing Co, Whitesburg, GA (8)
International Marine, Camden, ME (17)
International Masters Publishers Inc, Montoursville, PA (17)
International Paper, Memphis, TN (16)
International Planned Parenthood Federation Western Hemisphere Region Inc, New York, NY (1)
International Society for Technology in Education, Eugene, OR (1)
International Specialized Book Services Inc, Portland, OR (16)
International Wine Accessories Inc, Petaluma, CA (4)
Intersections, Chantilly, VA (14)
Intra Business Systems Inc, South Bend, IN (16)
Intromark Inc, Pittsburgh, PA (16)
Intuit, Mountain View, CA (10)
Investors Alliance Inc, Austin, TX (1)
INWAVE Internet, Janesville, WI (16)
Iowa Medical Society, Des Moines, IA (1)
Iowa Student Loan Liquidity Corp, West Des Moines, IA (1)
Islands Tropicals, Keaau, HI (6)
Isuzu Motors America LLC, Anaheim, CA (16)
Itochu Chemicals America Inc, White Plains, NY (16)
Ivy Tech Community College of Indiana, Indianapolis, IN (13)

J

J&L Industrial Supply, Southfield, MI (9)
JC Penney Inc, Plano, TX (5)
JC Whitney, Chicago, IL (12)
JDR Microdevices, Dublin, CA (3)
JDRF, New York, NY (1)
JIST Publishing, Saint Paul, MN (17)
JLG Industries Inc, McConnellsburg, PA (16)
JP Morgan Chase & Co, New York, NY (14)

JR Cigar, Burlington, NC (5)
JT International, Teaneck, NJ (16)
Jaff Marketing Group Inc, Spring, TX (16)
Jaffe Brothers Natural Foods, Valley Center, CA (4)
Michael Jaffe Stamps Inc/Brookman Stamp Co, Vancouver, WA (6)
Jafra Cosmetics International Inc, Westlake Village, CA (7)
Jameco Electronics, Belmont, CA (3)
Herbert L Jamison & Co LLC, West Orange, NJ (15)
Janice's LLC, Hartford, CT (8)
Jantz Supply Koval Knives, Davis, OK (9)
Jarden Corp, Boca Raton, FL (16)
Jason Natural Personal Care Products, Boulder, CO (7)
Jaypro Sports, Waterford, CT (11)
Jazzercise Inc, Carlsbad, CA (2)
JazzTimes Magazine Inc, Quincy, MA (17)
Jeffers & Co, Dothan, AL (5)
Jefferson National, Louisville, KY (14)
Jeffrey Lant Associates Inc, Cambridge, MA (5)
Brian Jenner Inc, Pasco, WA (6)
Jenny Products Inc, Somerset, PA (16)
Jerden Records/SpeechWorks, Redmond, WA (16)
Jerry's Artarama, Raleigh, NC (10)
The Jewish Federation of Greater Washington, North Bethesda, MD (1)
J Jill Group, Inc, Quincy, MA (2)
Jockey International Global Inc, Kenosha, WI (2)
John Deere Financial, Johnston, IA (14)
John Hancock Financial Services Inc, Boston, MA (15)
Johnny Appleseed's Inc, Middleton, MA (2)
Johnson & Johnson, New Brunswick, NJ (16)
Joint Commission, Oakbrook Terrace, IL (1)
Jones International Ltd, Centennial, CO (16)
Marlin P Jones & Associates Inc, West Palm Beach, FL (3)
Jones Publishing Inc, Iola, WI (17)
The Jordan Edmiston Group Inc, New York, NY (14)
Joslin Photo Puzzle Co, Southampton, PA (16)
Jossey-Bass Inc Publishers, San Francisco, CA (17)
Jostens, Inc, Minneapolis, MN (16)
The Journal News, White Plains, NY (17)
Journal Star, Peoria, IL (17)
Journeys, Nashville, TN (2)
JW Jung Seed Co, Randolph, WI (8)
Junior's Cheesecake, Brooklyn, NY (16)
JustThink Inc, Sherwood Park, AB, Canada (16)

K

K-tel International, Golden Valley, MN (16)
KAR Graphics, Mashpee, MA (8)
KCET, Burbank, CA (1)
KCI Communications Inc, Falls Church, VA (17)
KEH.com, Smyrna, GA (16)
KET, Lexington, KY (17)
KHL Engineered Packaging Solutions, Buena Park, CA (16)
KMA Direct Communications, Dallas, TX (1)
KPBS FM/TV, San Diego, CA (1)
KV Vet Supply Co, Inc, David City, NE (5)
Kalmbach Publishing Co, Waukesha, WI (17)
Kano Laboratories, Nashville, TN (16)
Kansas City Chiefs, Kansas City, MO (16)
Kansas State University Division of Continuing Education, Manhattan, KS (1)
Kaplan Inc, Fort Lauderdale, FL (16)
Kaplan Test Prep, New York, NY (1)
Kappa Publishing Group, Blue Bell, PA (17)

Kappler Protective Apparel & Fabrics, Guntersville, AL (2)
Kaylor's School Supply, Albertville, AL (16)
Kayne & Son Custom Hardware Inc, Candler, NC (8)
Kayser-Roth Corp Inc, Greensboro, NC (2)
Keeneland Association Inc, Lexington, KY (16)
Kelco Supply Co, Big Lake, MN (16)
Kellyco Metal Detector Distributors, Winter Springs, FL (11)
Kelly's Kids, Natchez, MS (2)
Kelsey National Corp, Los Angeles, CA (15)
Kemper Corp, Chicago, IL (15)
Kendall Products/Dri-Dek, Naples, FL (16)
Kenmore Stamp Co, Milford, NH (6)
Kennel Vet, Laurel, DE (11)
Kensington Computer Products Group, Redwood Shores, CA (16)
Kensington Publishing Corp, New York, NY (17)
Kerr-Hays Co, Ligonier, PA (16)
Kester's Wild Game Food Nurseries Inc, Omro, WI (8)
Kett Tool Co, Cincinnati, OH (9)
Key Bank, Cleveland, OH (14)
Key Bank National Association, Albany, NY (14)
Key West Aloe Holdings LLC, Fort Lauderdale, FL (16)
Keyboard Workshop, Medford, OR (17)
The Kidney Foundation of Canada/Greater Ontario Branch, Hamilton, ON, Canada (1)
Kimberly-Clark Corp, Neenah, WI (16)
Kimbo Educational, Long Branch, NJ (17)
King Features, New York, NY (17)
King Pharmaceuticals, Inc, Tenafly, NJ (7)
King Ranch Saddle Shop, Kingsville, TX (8)
King's Chandelier Co, Eden, NC (6)
Kingsley North Inc, Norway, MI (11)
The Kiplinger Washington Editors Inc, Washington, DC (17)
Will Kirkpatrick Shorebird Decoys Inc, Hudson, MA (6)
B Klein Publications, Boca Raton, FL (17)
Calvin Klein Cosmetics Co, New York, NY (7)
Klingspor's Woodworking Shop, Hickory, NC (9)
Klitzner Industries, Cranston, RI (6)
Klockit, Lake Geneva, WI (6)
Knoll Group, New York, NY (16)
Knott's Berry Farm Foods, Orrville, OH (4)
Koeze Co, Grand Rapids, MI (16)
Kolbe Corp, Phoenix, AZ (17)
Susan G Komen for the Cure, Dallas, TX (1)
Kozak Auto Drywash Inc, Batavia, NY (16)
The Kraft Heinz Co, Pittsburgh, PA (4)
Kraftbilt, Tulsa, OK (10)
EC Kraus Home Wine & Beer Making Supplies, Independence, MO (4)
Krause Publications Inc, Iola, WI (17)
The Kroger Co, Cincinnati, OH (4)
Kross Inc, Santa Clarita, CA (16)
Kuwait Airways Corp, Fort Lee, NJ (19)

L

L&L Management, Pasadena, CA (16)
L Brands Inc, Columbus, OH (16)
L6 Holdings Corp, Duluth, GA (14)
LIMRA International, Windsor, CT (1)
LS Records, Madison, TN (16)
LaCrosse Footwear Inc, Portland, OR (16)
The LadyBug Co, Berry Creek, CA (8)
Lahey Clinic, Burlington, MA (1)

Lake Shore Industries, Erie, PA (16)
Lakeside Publishing Co LLC, Evanston, IL (17)
Land O' Lakes Inc, Arden Hills, MN (16)
Landauer Corp, Urbandale, IA (17)
Landmark Communications Inc, Alpharetta, GA (17)
Landmark Graphics Corp, Houston, TX (16)
Laplink Software Inc, Bellevue, WA (3)
LaPreferida Inc, Chicago, IL (4)
Laran Communications Inc, Winfield, IL (16)
Lark in the Morning, Mendocino, CA (5)
Las Vegas Review Journal, Las Vegas, NV (17)
Laughlin Associates Inc, Carson City, NV (16)
Lawn Doctor Inc, Holmdel, NJ (16)
Lawyers & Judges Publishing Co Inc, Tucson, AZ (17)
Lazar Media Group Inc, Charleston, SC (17)
Lazydays RV Center, Seffner, FL (12)
Le Jardin Du Gourmet, Saint Johnsbury Center, VT (8)
Lea & Perrins Inc, Fair Lawn, NJ (16)
Leadership Software Corp, Nyack, NY (16)
LeadFlash, Boca Raton, FL (14)
Leanin' Tree Inc, Boulder, CO (6)
Learning Seed, Chicago, IL (3)
Leather Unlimited Corp, Belgium, WI (2)
Lefty's Corner, Clarks Summit, PA (6)
Legal Sea Foods Inc, Boston, MA (4)
Lego Direct Marketing, Enfield, CT (11)
Lehman's, Dalton, OH (8)
Leisure Arts Inc, Maumelle, AR (17)
Lemee's Inc, Hanson, MA (8)
Lending Tree/Home Loan Center, Charlotte, NC (14)
AM Leonard Inc, Piqua, OH (8)
Hal Leonard Corp, Milwaukee, WI (17)
Lerner Publishing Group, Minneapolis, MN (17)
Leslie Shoe Co Inc, Rogers City, MI (2)
Leucadia National Corp, New York, NY (14)
The Leukemia & Lymphoma Society, Rye Brook, NY (1)
Levenger, Delray Beach, FL (5)
Levi Strauss & Co, San Francisco, CA (16)
Lexington Luggage Limited, New York, NY (19)
Lexus Division of Toyota, Torrance, CA (12)
Peter Li Education Group, Dayton, OH (17)
Liberty Fund Inc, Indianapolis, IN (1)
Liberty Life Insurance Co, Greenville, SC (15)
Liberty Mutual Group, Inc, Boston, MA (15)
Liberty Orchards Co Inc, Cashmere, WA (16)
Liberty Tax Service, Virginia Beach, VA (14)
LibertyTree Press, Oakland, CA (5)
The Library of America, New York, NY (13)
Life Extension Foundation, Fort Lauderdale, FL (7)
Life Fitness, Schiller Park, IL (11)
Life Investors Insurance Co of America, Cedar Rapids, IA (14)
Life Line Screening, Austin, TX (7)
Life-Study Fellowship Foundation Inc, Darien, CT (17)
LifeLock, Tempe, AZ (16)
Lifetips, Boston, MA (16)
Lifeway Christian Stores, Nashville, TN (5)
Light Sources Inc, Virginia Beach, VA (16)
Ligonier Ministries, Sanford, FL (5)
Liguori Publications, Liguori, MO (17)
Lillian Vernon Corp, Colorado Springs, CO (6)
Lilypons Water Gardens, Adamstown, MD (8)
Lin Terry, Paterson, NJ (6)
Lincoln Educational Services Corp, West Orange, NJ (13)
Lincoln Financial Group, Radnor, PA (15)
Lincoln Park Zoo, Chicago, IL (1)

LinguiSystems, East Moline, IL (17)
Links Magazine, Hilton Head Island, SC (17)
Lion Apparel, Dayton, OH (2)
Lippincott, Williams & Wilkins, Baltimore, MD (17)
Listening Library Inc, Random House Audio, New York, NY (3)
Lithia Motors Inc, Medford, OR (12)
Litle & Co, Lowell, MA (14)
Littleton Coin Co Inc, Littleton, NH (6)
Live Nation, Beverly Hills, CA (19)
Lladro USA Inc, Moonachie, NJ (16)
Llewellyn Publications, Woodbury, MN (17)
Local Government Federal Credit Union, Raleigh, NC (14)
Local Search Association, Troy, MI (1)
Loctite Corp, Rocky Hill, CT (16)
Loehmann's, Bronx, NY (2)
Loews Hotels, Inc, New York, NY (19)
Logical Computer Selections, Short Hills, NJ (16)
Lombardi Publishing Corp, Vaughan, ON, Canada (17)
Longevity Network Ltd, Henderson, NV (7)
Longevity Pure Medicine, Los Angeles, CA (7)
Lorillard Tobacco Co, Greensboro, NC (16)
Los Angeles Kings, Los Angeles, CA (16)
The Los Angeles Lakers Inc, El Segundo, CA (11)
Lotions & Lace, Riverside, CA (2)
LOTSolutions, Jacksonville, FL (14)
Louisiana State Museum, New Orleans, LA (1)
Love To Learn Inc, Salem, UT (5)
Loves Travel Stops & Country Stores, Oklahoma City, OK (5)
Loving Promises & More, Longview, WA (16)
Lowe's Companies Inc, Mooresville, NC (8)
Lowrance Electronics, Tulsa, OK (11)
Luce Corp, Hamden, CT (16)
Lucky Heart Cosmetics Inc, Memphis, TN (7)
Lufthansa German Airlines, East Meadow, NY (19)
Luggage Base, Nipomo, CA (16)
Lundberg Family Farms, Richvale, CA (16)
Lure Craft, Lagrange, IN (11)
Lutheran Church Extension Fund - Missouri Synod, Saint Louis, MO (1)
Luzier Personalized Cosmetics, Grandview, MO (7)

M

M&M Health Care Apparel Co, Brooklyn, NY (2)
M2Media 360, Park Ridge, IL (17)
MBI Inc, Norwalk, CT (16)
MCCS, Mason, OH (14)
MCI Communications Services Inc, Basking Ridge, NJ (16)
MDR, Sunrise, FL (7)
MFS Investment Management, Boston, MA (14)
Mi-T-M Corp, Peosta, IA (9)
Mirage Resorts, Inc., Las Vegas, NV (19)
MMS Education, Newtown, PA (5)
MPS Multimedia Inc, San Mateo, CA (16)
MRV Communications, Chatsworth, CA (3)
MTS Publishing, Naperville, IL (17)
MXT Card Services, LLC, New Castle, DE (14)
Macy's Inc, Cincinnati, OH (5)
Macy's Marketing, New York, NY (16)
Madisonavegifts.com, Watertown, NY (6)
Magazine Publishers of America, New York, NY (17)
Magellan's Catalog, Chelmsford, MA (5)
Magnaplan Corp, Champlain, NY (10)
Magnatag Visible Systems, Macedon, NY (16)
The Magni Co Inc, McKinney, TX (16)

Magnolia Hall, Jasper, GA (8)
Maine Potato Board, Presque Isle, ME (1)
Maison Glass Delicacies, Cold Spring, NY (4)
Majestic Products Co, Paris, KY (16)
Make-A-Wish Foundation of America, Phoenix, AZ (1)
Making It Big, Cotati, CA (2)
Malco Products Inc, Barberton, OH (16)
MALM Chemical Corp, Pound Ridge, NY (16)
EF Maloney Inc, Mamaroneck, NY (16)
Manchester Farms Inc, Columbia, SC (4)
Mancomm Inc, Davenport, IA (17)
Mane Solutions, New York, NY (16)
Manhattan College, Bronx, NY (1)
Manning Materials, Birdsboro, PA (16)
Manulife Financial Inc, Toronto, ON, Canada (15)
MAP International, Brunswick, GA (1)
Maple Grove Farms of Vermont Inc, Saint Johnsbury, VT (4)
March of Dimes Foundation, White Plains, NY (1)
Mardiron Optics, Stoneham, MA (11)
Marian Helpers Center, Stockbridge, MA (1)
Marimac Inc, Montreal, QC, Canada (8)
The Mark Group, Boca Raton, FL (2)
Markertek Video Supply, Saugerties, NY (3)
Marketing and Product Strategy, Peabody, MA (16)
Marketing Results Inc, Sicklerville, NJ (16)
Marketshare Publications Inc, Overland Park, KS (17)
Marmelstein Inc, Philadelphia, PA (16)
The Marmon Group LLC, Chicago, IL (16)
Marquis Who's Who Ventures LLC, Berkeley Heights, NJ (17)
Marriott International Inc, Bethesda, MD (19)
Marriott Ownership Resorts Sales & Marketing, Orlando, FL (19)
Marsh Affinity Group Services, Chicago, IL (15)
Marshall Fields Dept Stores, Minneapolis, MN (5)
Martindale-Hubbell, New Providence, NJ (17)
Mary Kay Cosmetics Inc, Addison, TX (16)
Mary of Puddin Hill Inc, Duncanville, TX (16)
Maryknoll Fathers & Brothers, Ossining, NY (1)
Maryland Pennysaver, Hanover, MD (17)
The Maryland Saddlery Inc, Butler, MD (11)
Mary's Plant Farm & Landscaping, Hamilton, OH (8)
T Marzetti Co Inc, Columbus, OH (4)
Masco Corp, Taylor, MI (16)
Mason Companies Inc, Chippewa Falls, WI (16)
George Mason University School of Management, Fairfax, VA (1)
WB Mason Co, Brockton, MA (16)
Massachusetts Horticultural Society, Wellesley, MA (1)
MassMutual Financial Group, Springfield, MA (15)
MasterCard Worldwide, Purchase, NY (14)
Mastergrip Inc, Irving, TX (11)
Masterpiece Studios Inc, Mankato, MN (16)
Mastervision Inc, New York, NY (16)
Matt & Kumpany Kuzins, Sacramento, CA (1)
Mattel Inc, El Segundo, CA (16)
Matthews 1812 House Inc, Cornwall Bridge, CT (4)
Robert J Matthews Co, Massillon, OH (7)
Maui Jim Inc, Peoria, IL (16)
MAX Federal Credit Union, Montgomery, AL (14)
Mary Maxim Inc, Port Huron, MI (11)
Maxon Furniture Inc, Muscatine, IA (10)
Mayo Clinic, Rochester, MN (17)
McClatchy Co, Sacramento, CA (17)
McClure & Zimmerman, Randolph, WI (8)
McCormick & Co Inc, Sparks, MD (4)
McDonald Obsolete Parts Co, Rockport, IN (16)

McFarland & Co Inc Publishers, Jefferson, NC (17)

McFeely's Square Drive Screws, Madison, WI (16)

The McGraw-Hill Financial, New York, NY (17)

McKenzie Taxidermy Supply, Granite Quarry, NC (16)

McKesson Corp, San Francisco, CA (7)

Mead Johnson Co, Evansville, IN (7)

Mead Westvaco Consumer & Office Products, Richmond, VA (10)

Mechanical Breakdown Administrators Inc, Scottsdale, AZ (14)

Medals of America, Fountain Inn, SC (6)

Medibadge Inc, Omaha, NE (5)

Medic Alert Foundation, Salida, CA (1)

Medifast Inc, Owings Mills, MD (4)

Medill IMC/Northwestern University, Evanston, IL (1)

Medtronic, Minneapolis, MN (7)

Medtronic Inc, Minneapolis, MN (16)

Megger, Dallas, TX (16)

Meguiar's Inc, Irvine, CA (16)

Meister Media Worldwide, Willoughby, OH (17)

Melaniphy & Associates, Inc, Chicago, IL (8)

Memorial Sloan Kettering Cancer Center, New York, NY (1)

Memphis Net & Twine Co Inc, Memphis, TN (11)

The Menninger Foundation, Houston, TX (1)

Mentoring Minds, Tyler, TX (17)

Merastar Insurance Co, Chattanooga, TN (15)

Merck & Co Inc, Whitehouse Station, NJ (16)

Meredith Corp, Des Moines, IA (17)

Merrick Bank, South Jordan, UT (14)

Merrill Lynch International Inc, New York, NY (14)

Merrimade Stationery Co LLC, Chelmsford, MA (10)

Mersco Medical, Pierre, SD (16)

Methode Electronics Inc, Chicago, IL (9)

Metro Speedgear, Livingston, NJ (11)

Metropolis Magazine, New York, NY (2)

Metropolitan Museum of Art, New York, NY (8)

The Metropolitan Opera, New York, NY (1)

Metso Minerals/WS Tyler, Waukesha, WI (16)

Fred Meyer Jewelers Inc, Portland, OR (16)

Meylan Corp, Montclair, NJ (9)

Michael's, Irving, TX (11)

Michigan Apple Committee, Lansing, MI (1)

Micro Center, Hilliard, OH (3)

Micro Plastics Inc, Flippin, AR (16)

Mid America Designs Inc, Effingham, IL (12)

Mid America Motorworks, Effingham, IL (12)

Mid West Floor Co Inc, Saint Louis, MO (16)

Midcontinent Financial Center Inc, Columbia, MO (14)

The Midland Co, Amelia, OH (15)

Midland Marketing Group, Saint Joseph, MO (16)

Midwest Center for Stress & Anxiety Inc, Oak Harbor, OH (7)

Midwest Publishing Inc, Phoenix, AZ (17)

Midwest Technology Products & Services, Sioux City, IA (9)

Military Officers Association of America, Alexandria, VA (1)

Military Order of the Purple Heart Svc, Annandale, VA (1)

Miller Stockman, Denver, CO (2)

MillerCoors LLC, Chicago, IL (4)

Miller's First Insurance Companies, Alton, IL (15)

Milwaukee Electric Tool Corp, Brookfield, WI (16)

Mini City Ltd, Webster, NY (12)

Minitab Inc, State College, PA (16)

Minnesota Life, Saint Paul, MN (15)

Minnesota Public Radio, Saint Paul, MN (1)

Miracle Ear, Minneapolis, MN (16)

Miracle of Aloe, Dallas, TX (7)

MISSCO Corp, Flowood, MS (16)

Missouri Life Inc, Boonville, MO (17)

Mr G's Enterprises, Fort Worth, TX (16)

Mr Wash Car Wash, Kensington, MD (16)

Mitsubishi Digital Electronics America Inc, Cypress, CA (3)

Mitsubishi Motors North America Inc, Cypress, CA (1)

Frank Mittermeier Inc, Bronx, NY (11)

Modernage Custom Digital Imaging Labs, New York, NY (16)

Molson Coors Brewing Co, Denver, CO (16)

Monex Deposit Co, Newport Beach, CA (14)

MoneyGram International, Dallas, TX (14)

Montag & Caldwell Inc, Atlanta, GA (14)

MontBleu Resort Casino and Spa, Stateline, NV (19)

Moon Shine Trading Co, Woodland, CA (4)

Thurston Moore Country Ltd, Madison, TN (16)

Morcon Industrial Specialty Inc, Mesquite, NV (9)

Morgan Kaufmann Publishers Inc, Burlington, MA (17)

Morgan Stanley, New York, NY (14)

Morkes Chocolates, Palatine, IL (4)

Morningstar Inc, Chicago, IL (14)

Morris Visitors Publications LLC, Augusta, GA (17)

Thomas Moser Cabinetmakers, Freeport, ME (16)

Mother Earth News Magazine, Topeka, KS (17)

Mother Jones Magazine, San Francisco, CA (17)

Motient Communications, Reston, VA (16)

Motion Picture & Television Fund, Woodland Hills, CA (1)

The Motley Fool, Alexandria, VA (14)

Moto Franchise Corp, Dayton, OH (3)

Mott Media LLC, Fenton, MI (17)

Moultrie Manufacturing Co, Moultrie, GA (8)

Mountain Craft Shop Co, Proctor, WV (11)

Mountain Press Publishing Co, Missoula, MT (17)

Mountain West Supply Co, Scottsdale, AZ (3)

Multi-Level Marketing International Association (MLMIA), Irvine, CA (1)

Mike Murach & Associates Inc, Fresno, CA (17)

Murad Inc, El Segundo, CA (7)

Murder by Mail, West Tisbury, MA (1)

Muscular Dystrophy Association, Chicago, IL (1)

The Museum of Modern Art, New York, NY (5)

Music Barn Inc, Niagara Falls, NY (6)

Music Choice, Horsham, PA (16)

Music Sales Corp, New York, NY (17)

Music Treasures Co, Richmond, VA (6)

Muskegon Power Tool Corp, North Muskegon, MI (16)

Mustek Inc, Tustin, CA (3)

Mutual of Omaha, Omaha, NE (15)

Mylan Enterprises, Tarzana, CA (7)

Mystic Seaport Museum Stores, Mystic, CT (6)

Mystic Stamp Co Inc, Camden, NY (16)

N

NAACP, Baltimore, MD (1)

NADA Appraisal Guides, Costa Mesa, CA (17)

NASW Assurance Services Inc, Frederick, MD (1)

National General Insurance, Winston-Salem, NC (15)

NBI Inc, Eau Claire, WI (1)

NBTY Inc, Ronkonkoma, NY (7)

NCP Solutions, Reston, VA (17)

NEA's Member Benefits Corp, Gaithersburg, MD (1)

NGL Insurance Group, Madison, WI (15)

NTL Institute, Silver Spring, MD (1)

NYSARC, Inc, Delmar, NY (1)

Nancy's Notions LLC, Beaver Dam, WI (11)

NAR Productions, Barryville, NY (17)

Narrow Way, Lafayette, CA (6)

Nasco, Fort Atkinson, WI (5)

National Active & Retired Federal Employees Association, Alexandria, VA (1)

National Archives & Records Administration, Washington, DC (17)

National Association for Female Executives, New York, NY (1)

National Association of Professional Insurance Agents, Alexandria, VA (1)

National Association of Realtors, Chicago, IL (1)

National Audubon Society, New York, NY (17)

National Auto Warranty, Wentzville, MO (16)

National Automated Clearing House Association, Herndon, VA (1)

National Basketball Association, New York, NY (1)

National Business Furniture Inc, Milwaukee, WI (10)

National Catholic Reporter Publishing Co Inc, Kansas City, MO (17)

National City Bank, Cleveland, OH (14)

National Committee to Preserve Social Security & Medicare, Washington, DC (1)

National Community Pharmacists Association, Alexandria, VA (1)

National Contract Management Association, Ashburn, VA (1)

National Court Reporters Association, Reston, VA (1)

National Crime Prevention Council, Amsterdam, NY (17)

National Defense Industrial Association, Arlington, VA (1)

National Emblem Sales, Indianapolis, IN (16)

National Enquirer, New York, NY (17)

National Foundation for Cancer Research, Bethesda, MD (1)

National 4-H Supply Service, Chevy Chase, MD (16)

National Gallery of Art Gift Shop, Washington, DC (16)

National Humane Education Society, Charles Town, WV (1)

National Jewish Health, Denver, CO (1)

National Journal Group, Washington, DC (17)

National Law Enforcement Officers Memorial Fund, Washington, DC (1)

National League for Nursing, Washington, DC (1)

National Luggage Dealers Association, Glenview, IL (1)

National Medical Fellowships, New York, NY (1)

National Motor Club of America Inc, Irving, TX (1)

National Osteoporosis Foundation, Washington, DC (1)

National Pecan Co, Frisco, TX (4)

National Pension Service Inc, Burlington, VT (14)

National Railroad Passenger Corp, Washington, DC (16)

The National Restaurant Association Educational Foundation, Washington, DC (1)

National Retail Federation Inc, Washington, DC (1)

National Review, New York, NY (17)

National Rifle Association of America, Fairfax, VA (1)

National Right to Work Legal Defense Foundation, Springfield, VA (1)

National Society of Collegiate Scholars, Washington, DC (1)

National Technical Information Service, Alexandria, VA (17)

National University, La Jolla, CA (1)

National Wholesale Co Inc, Lexington, NC (2)

National Wildlife Federation, Reston, VA (1)

Nationwide Beauty & Barber Supply, Syracuse, NY (16)

Nationwide Mutual Insurance Co, Columbus, OH (15)

Natural Essentials Inc, Streetsboro, OH (5)

Natural History Magazine, Durham, NC (17)

The Nature Conservancy, Arlington, VA (1)

Nautilus Inc, Vancouver, WA (11)

Naval Institute Press, Annapolis, MD (17)

Naveen Jindal School of Management, Richardson, TX (1)

Navistar, Lisle, IL (16)

Neiman-Marcus Group, Dallas, TX (8)

Nelson Crab Inc, Tokeland, WA (4)

Neo-Tech Publishing Co, Henderson, NV (17)

NestFamily.com, Lewisville, TX (3)

NetSpend, San Mateo, CA (14)

Network Telephone Services Inc, Woodland Hills, CA (16)

Neuberger & Berman Management, New York, NY (14)

Nevada Commission on Tourism, Carson City, NV (1)

Nevada Magazine, Carson City, NV (17)

Nevco Scoreboard Co, Greenville, IL (16)

New & Unique Videos, San Diego, CA (3)

New Directions Publishing Corp, New York, NY (17)

New England Cheesemaking Supply Co, South Deerfield, MA (4)

New England Life Insurance Co, Boston, MA (15)

New Jersey Institute for Continuing Legal Education, New Brunswick, NJ (1)

New Jersey Monthly, Morristown, NJ (17)

New Pig Corp, Tipton, PA (9)

The New Piper Aircraft Inc, Vero Beach, FL (16)

New Track Media LLC, Cincinnati, OH (17)

New Wave Media Inc, Emeryville, CA (5)

New Win Publishing Inc, El Monte, CA (17)

New York Blood Center Inc, New York, NY (1)

New York Easter Seal Society, New York, NY (1)

New York Landmarks Conservancy, New York, NY (1)

New York Life Insurance Co/AARP, Tampa, FL (15)

New York Philharmonic, New York, NY (1)

New York Power Authority, White Plains, NY (16)

New York-Presbyterian/Columbia University Medical Center, New York, NY (16)

New York Road Runners, New York, NY (13)

The New York Times Co, New York, NY (17)

New York University Medical Center, New York, NY (1)

The New Yorker Magazine, New York, NY (17)

New Zealand Tourism Board, Santa Monica, CA (19)

Newell Rubbermaid, Inc, Atlanta, GA (16)

The Newman Group Computer Services Corp, Ann Arbor, MI (3)

The News Tribune, Tacoma, WA (17)

Newsday, Melville, NY (17)

Newspaper Association of America, Arlington, VA (1)

NextScreen LLC, Austin, TX (17)

Nicklaus Companies LLC, North Palm Beach, FL (16)

Nielsen Trade Dimensions, Wilton, CT (17)

Nightingale-Conant Corp, Niles, IL (17)

Nightingale Resources, Cold Spring, NY (17)

Nihon Keizai Shimbun America Inc, New York, NY (17)

Nike Inc, Beaverton, OR (2)

Nilodor Inc, Bolivar, OH (16)

Nissan North America Inc, Franklin, TN (16)

No Load Fund Investor, Brentwood, TN (14)

No Load FundX, San Francisco, CA (14)

Nodine's Smokehouse, Torrington, CT (4)

Nomadics Tipi Makers, Bend, OR (11)

Nordskog Publishing Co, Ventura, CA (17)

Nordstrom Inc, Seattle, WA (2)

Norman Control Co, Cary, IL (16)

Norman Rockwell Museum, Stockbridge, MA (16)

Norscot Group, Mequon, WI (5)

North America Life Insurance Co, Lakeway, TX (15)

North American Co for Life & Health Insurance, Chicago, IL (15)

North Shore Animal League America Inc, Port Washington, NY (1)

Northeast Hinge Distributors Inc, Hollis, NH (9)

Northern Cross, Lecompton, KS (16)

Northern Greenhouse Sales, Neche, ND (8)

Northern Response International, Toronto, ON, Canada (8)

Northwestern Mutual, Milwaukee, WI (14)

Nourse Farms, South Deerfield, MA (8)

Nova Southeastern University Fischler College of Education, North Miami Beach, FL (1)

Novartis Pharmaceuticals Corp, East Hanover, NJ (7)

Nowell's Inc, San Rafael, CA (8)

Nowetah's American Indian Store & Museum, New Portland, ME (6)

Nu-Parr Swimwear, Phoenix, AZ (2)

Numark Brands, Edison, NJ (7)

NuNaturals, Eugene, OR (16)

NutriSystem Inc, Fort Washington, PA (7)

Nutritional Research Associates Inc, South Whitley, IN (16)

Nuveen Investments, Chicago, IL (14)

Nylon Net Co, Memphis, TN (11)

Nyrev Inc, New York, NY (17)

O

OAG Worldwide, Downers Grove, IL (17)

Oakley Inc, Foothill Ranch, CA (2)

Oakstone Publishing LLC, Birmingham, AL (17)

Oakwood Homes Corp, Greensboro, NC (16)

O'Brien Manufacturing, Marietta, OH (9)

Ocean Conservancy, Washington, DC (1)

O'Currance Inc, Draper, UT (18)

Office Depot, Boca Raton, FL (16)

OfficeMax Inc, Boca Raton, FL (10)

Oil & Gas Journal, Tulsa, OK (17)

Okun Brothers Shoes Inc, Kalamazoo, MI (2)

Olan Mills Inc, Chattanooga, TN (16)

Old World Mouldings Inc, Bohemia, NY (9)

Oleda & Co Inc, Fort Worth, TX (16)

Olesuk Financial Services, McHenry, IL (14)

Oliver of Adrian Inc, Adrian, MI (16)

Olympia Sales Inc, Enfield, CT (16)

Omaha Creative Group Inc, Omaha, NE (4)

Omaha Steaks Inc, Omaha, NE (4)

Omaha Vaccine Co, Omaha, NE (16)

Omni Farm, West Jefferson, NC (16)

Omnigraphics Inc, Aston, PA (17)

1-800-Contacts, Draper, UT (7)

1-800-Flowers.com, Carle Place, NY (16)

1-800-Mattress.com, Hicksville, NY (16)

One Hanes Place Catalog, Winston Salem, NC (2)

100% Real Estate Inc, Orlando, FL (16)

1000 Islands International Tourism Council, Alexandria Bay, NY (19)

Oneida Ltd, Oneida, NY (16)

Oomingmak Musk Ox Producers Cooperative, Anchorage, AK (6)

Open Text Inc, Waterloo, ON, Canada (16)

Opryland, Nashville, TN (16)

Optronics Inc, Muskogee, OK (11)

Oracle Corp, Redwood Shores, CA (16)

Oral Roberts University, Tulsa, OK (1)

The Orange County Register, Santa Ana, CA (17)

Orbis Books, Maryknoll, NY (17)

Orchard Supply Hardware, San Jose, CA (16)

Orient Expressed Imports Inc, New Orleans, LA (2)

Oriental Trading Co Inc, Omaha, NE (5)

Orion Telescopes & Binoculars, Watsonville, CA (11)

Orlando/ Orange County Convention & Visitor's Bureau, Orlando, FL (19)

The Orvis Co Inc, Manchester, VT (11)

Our Designs Inc, Vancouver, WA (16)

Our Lady of Victory Homes of Charity, Lackawanna, NY (1)

Our Sunday Visitor Publishing, Huntington, IN (17)

Overton's Inc, Greenville, NC (11)

Buck Owens' Crystal Palace, Bakersfield, CA (19)

Oxford Health Plans, Inc, Trumbull, CT (15)

Oxford University Press Inc, New York, NY (17)

P

PBS Distribution, Arlington, VA (3)

PC Ontario Fund, Toronto, ON, Canada (1)

PC World, San Francisco, CA (17)

PESI LLC, Eau Claire, WI (17)

PFI Western Stores Inc, Springfield, MO (2)

PHE Inc, Hillsborough, NC (5)

PMIC, Los Angeles, CA (17)

PNC Bank Corp, Pittsburgh, PA (14)

PNC Global Investment Servicing, Lynnfield, MA (14)

PPC, Johnston, IA (9)

Professional Education Institute, Chicago, IL (13)

PVC Plastics Co, Evansville, IN (16)

Paasche Airbrush Co, Chicago, IL (10)

Pace Communications Inc, Greensboro, NC (17)

Pace University, New York, NY (16)

Pachmayr Ltd, Middletown, CT (11)

Pacific Botanicals LLC, Grants Pass, OR (7)

Pacific Propeller Inc, Kent, WA (16)

Pacific Spirit Corp, Forest Grove, OR (6)

Paladin Press, Boulder, CO (17)

Pallottine Center for Apostolic Causes Inc/St Jude Shrine, Baltimore, MD (1)

Pan Pacific Hotel & Resorts America, Seattle, WA (19)

Pango Pango Swimwear Corp, Pompano Beach, FL (2)

Panoptic Enterprises, Burke, VA (17)

Papa John's International, Louisville, KY (4)

PAPYRUS, Fairfield, CA (5)

Para Publishing, Santa Barbara, CA (17)

Paradise Galleries, Laguna Hills, CA (6)

Paragon Laboratories, Torrance, CA (16)

Paralyzed Veterans of America, Washington, DC (1)

George W Park Seed Co Inc, Hodges, SC (8)

Parker Hannifin Corp, Cleveland, OH (9)

Parmer Books, San Diego, CA (6)

Partners Health, Philadelphia, PA (15)

Partners Village Store, Westport, MA (11)

Parts Express, Springboro, OH (3)

Parts Place Inc, Warren, MI (12)

Party Kits & Equestrian Gifts, Louisville, KY (6)

Pastime Publications Inc, Denver, CO (17)

Patagonia, Ventura, CA (2)

Patagonia Mail Order Inc, Reno, NV (2)

Path to Purchase Institute, Chicago, IL (17)
Patient News, Niagara Falls, NY (17)
PayPal Inc, San Jose, CA (14)
Peak Impact Inc, Ottawa, ON, Canada (14)
Pearson VUE, Bloomington, MN (17)
Pecan Producers International, Corsicana, TX (4)
Peerless Rattan, Plainwell, MI (16)
Peet's Coffee & Tea Inc, Berkeley, CA (4)
Pegasus Auto Racing Supplies Inc, New Berlin, WI (12)
PEMCO Insurance Cos, Seattle, WA (15)
Penguin Group USA Inc, New York, NY (17)
Penn Herb Co Ltd, Philadelphia, PA (7)
Penn Mutual, Horsham, PA (15)
Penn State Hazleton, Hazleton, PA (1)
Pennstreet Bakery, Grand Rapids, MI (16)
Pennsylvania Firebacks, Philadelphia, PA (8)
Pennsylvania State University Press, University Park, PA (17)
Peoples Benefit Life Insurance Co, Exton, PA (15)
People's United Bank, Bridgeport, CT (14)
Perennial Pleasures Nursery, East Hardwick, VT (8)
Performance Media Solutions Inc & TrueWorx Inc, Las Vegas, NV (16)
Periodical Publisher's Service Bureau Inc, Fresno, CA (18)
Pernod Ricard USA, Purchase, NY (16)
Personal Achievement Institute, Kingman, AZ (17)
Personal Creations, Lemont, IL (6)
RJ Persson Enterprises Inc, Montrose, CO (16)
Petco Animal Supplies, San Diego, CA (5)
PetEdge, Beverly, MA (16)
Peter Pan Bus Lines Inc, Springfield, MA (19)
J Peterman Co, Lexington, KY (5)
Peterson's, Lawrenceville, NJ (17)
PetSmart Inc, Phoenix, AZ (5)
Pfaelzer Brothers, Maumee, OH (16)
Pfaltzgraff Co, York, PA (8)
Pfizer Inc, New York, NY (16)
PharmArt, Circleville, OH (6)
Pharmavite Corp LLC (HQ), Northridge, CA (16)
The Philadelphia Contributorship Insurance Co, Philadelphia, PA (15)
Philips Lifeline, Framingham, MA (7)
Phillips-Van Heusen Corp, New York, NY (2)
Phoenix Learning Group Inc, Maryland Heights, MO (16)
Phoenix Poke Boats Inc, McKee, KY (16)
Photographer's Formulary Inc, Condon, MT (9)
Photoworks, Cleveland, OH (16)
Physical Therapy Institute Inc, Poway, CA (16)
Physicians Mutual Insurance Co, Omaha, NE (15)
Physicians Planning Association Services, Deerfield Beach, FL (16)
Pilani's Live in Style, Egg Harbor Township, NJ (2)
The Pillsbury Co, Minneapolis, MN (16)
The Pin Man, Tulsa, OK (16)
Pine Castle Animal Hospital, Orlando, FL (16)
Pioneer Hi-Bred International Inc, Johnston, IA (4)
Pittman & Davis Inc, Harlingen, TX (4)
Pizza Hut Inc, Plano, TX (16)
The Plain Dealer, Cleveland, OH (18)
Plan International USA, Warwick, RI (1)
Planet Cotton, Gaithersburg, MD (2)
Planned Parenthood Federation of America, New York, NY (1)
Planned Parenthood Mar Monte, San Jose, CA (1)
Bud Plant Illustrated Books, Palo Alto, CA (6)
Plastic View ATC, Simi Valley, CA (9)
Playboy Enterprises Inc, Beverly Hills, CA (17)
Player Piano Co Inc, Wichita, KS (11)

Pleasant Company, Middleton, WI (11)
The Plow & Hearth Inc, Madison, VA (8)
Plymouth Rock Assurance, Lincroft, NJ (15)
Pneuma Books, Elkton, MD (17)
Pocket Nurse Enterprises Inc, Monaca, PA (7)
The Pohly Co, Boston, MA (17)
Poker Player, Sherman Oaks, CA (17)
Polaroid Corp, Minnetonka, MN (16)
Polo Ralph Lauren, New York, NY (2)
Polyair Packaging, Chicago, IL (9)
Polynesian Cultural Center, Honolulu, HI (16)
The Popcorn Factory, Lake Forest, IL (4)
Population Connection, Washington, DC (1)
Porta-Bote International, Mountain View, CA (11)
Portland Cement Association, Washington, DC (1)
Posh Papers, Riverside, RI (6)
Posty Cards Inc, Kansas City, MO (16)
Potawatomi Bingo Casino, Milwaukee, WI (19)
Potpourri Group Inc, North Billerica, MA (6)
Power Music, Salt Lake City, UT (16)
Powers Television Marketing, Chatsworth, CA (17)
Prairie Nursery, Westfield, WI (8)
Prakken Publications Inc, Ann Arbor, MI (17)
Preferred Communications, Butner, NC (3)
Premera Blue Cross, Spokane, WA (15)
Presque Isle Wine Cellars Inc, North East, PA (4)
Press-Enterprise Co, Riverside, CA (17)
ST Preston & Son Inc, Greenport, NY (8)
Prestwick House Inc, Clayton, DE (17)
Priester Pecan Co Inc, Fort Deposit, AL (4)
Priests of the Sacred Heart, Hales Corners, WI (1)
Prime Media Equine Group, Gaithersburg, MD (17)
Princess Cruises (HQ), Santa Clarita, CA (19)
Princess House Inc, Taunton, MA (16)
Princeton Book Co Publishers, Hightstown, NJ (17)
The Princeton Review, Natick, MA (16)
The Principal Financial Group, Des Moines, IA (15)
Print Products International, Annapolis Junction, MD (9)
Pritchett & Hull Associates Inc, Atlanta, GA (17)
Privacy Journal, Providence, RI (17)
Pro CD Inc, Omaha, NE (17)
PRO Chemical & Dye Inc, Fall River, MA (10)
The Procter & Gamble Co, Cincinnati, OH (16)
Professional Binding Products Inc, Thousand Oaks, CA (16)
The Professional Golfers' Association of America, Palm Beach Gardens, FL (1)
Professional Photographer Magazine, Atlanta, GA (17)
The Professional Putters Association, Winston Salem, NC (1)
Profit Potentials Inc, Hull, IA (1)
The Progressive Corp, Mayfield Village, OH (15)
Progressive Energy Corp, San Marcos, CA (5)
Project HOPE, Millwood, VA (1)
Projection Video Services, Springfield, VA (16)
Promotion Marketing Association (PMA) Inc, New York, NY (1)
Protection One Inc, Lawrence, KS (16)
Protective Life Insurance Co, Birmingham, AL (15)
Prudent Publishing Co, Ridgefield Park, NJ (16)
Publications International Ltd, Lincolnwood, IL (17)
Publishers Clearing House, Port Washington, NY (18)
Puritan's Pride, Ronkonkoma, NY (7)
Putnam Investments, Boston, MA (14)
Putnam Rolling Ladder Co Inc, New York, NY (5)
Putt Putt Fun Centers, Winston-Salem, NC (16)

Q

QC Supply LLC, Schuyler, NE (16)
The Quaker Oats Co, Chicago, IL (16)
Quartermaster Uniform & Equipment Co, Cerritos, CA (2)
Quayside Publishing Group, Minneapolis, MN (17)
Queen Bee Gardens, Lovell, WY (4)
Queue Inc, Stratford, CT (17)
Quick Draw Clip Systems Inc, Ventura, CA (9)

R

R&S Industries Corp, Chesterfield, MO (16)
RBC Dain Rauscher Inc, Minneapolis, MN (14)
RBC Funds, Milwaukee, WI (14)
RBS Citizens Financial Group Inc, Dedham, MA (14)
REI-Recreational Equipment Inc, Kent, WA (11)
Racer Walsh Co, Jacksonville, FL (12)
Rainbow Art Glass, Wall, NJ (16)
Rainbow Group LLC, Middleton, WI (11)
Raley's Bel Air Markets, West Sacramento, CA (16)
Ranch House Meat Co, Billings, MT (4)
Random House Children's Books, New York, NY (13)
Random House Direct Marketing, New York, NY (17)
Ranger Joe's International Military Supply, Columbus, GA (2)
Rapid City Journal, Rapid City, SD (18)
Raven's Nest Herbals, LLC, Duluth, GA (7)
Raybuck Autobody Parts, Punxsutawney, PA (12)
Raycom Sports, Charlotte, NC (16)
RCI LLC, Carmel, IN (19)
The Reader's Digest Association Inc, New York, NY (17)
Reading for Education, Murfreesboro, TN (1)
Real Goods Trading Corp, Hopland, CA (5)
Reassure America Life Insurance Co, Jacksonville, IL (15)
Reb Storage Systems International, Chicago, IL (9)
Recognition Products International, Easton, MD (16)
Recording for the Blind & Dyslexic Inc, Princeton, NJ (16)
Recreational Equipment Inc, Kent, WA (11)
Recycled Software Inc, Palm Springs, CA (3)
Redbook Magazine, New York, NY (17)
Redcats USA, New York, NY (2)
RedEnvelope Inc, San Diego, CA (6)
JP Redington & Co, Huntington, NY (16)
Redwood City Seed Co, Redwood City, CA (8)
Reebok International Ltd, Canton, MA (2)
Reed Elsevier, New York, NY (17)
Reed Exhibitions, Norwalk, CT (16)
Referee Enterprises, Racine, WI (1)
The Reggio Register Co Inc, Leominster, MA (8)
Regions, Birmingham, AL (14)
REGIT Inc, Glen Ellyn, IL (15)
Regnery Publishing, Washington, DC (17)
Reiman Publications, Greendale, WI (17)
Relaxo-Bak Inc, Anderson, IN (7)
Reliable Racing Supply, Queensbury, NY (11)
Reliable Technologies Inc, Manchester, NH (16)
ReMark USA, Minnetonka, MN (15)
Remedy Magazine, New York, NY (17)
Renaissance Learning, Wisconsin Rapids, WI (5)
Reno Gazette Journal, Reno, NV (17)
The Renovator's Supply Inc, Millers Falls, MA (9)
Rent-A-Center Inc, Plano, TX (16)
Rent Mother Nature, Cambridge, MA (4)

Replacements Ltd, Greensboro, NC (8)

Research To Prevent Blindness Inc, New York, NY (1)

Rose Resnick Lighthouse for the Blind & Visually Impaired, San Francisco, CA (1)

Resorts Casino Hotel, Atlantic City, NJ (19)

Resource Publications Inc, San Jose, CA (17)

Response Insurance, Scranton, PA (15)

Retawmatic Corp, Flushing, NY (9)

Rexcraft Wedding Invitations, Rexburg, ID (16)

Rhythm Band Inc, Fort Worth, TX (11)

Rich Brands, Phoenix, AZ (16)

Rich Products Corp, Buffalo, NY (16)

Richardson Electronics Ltd, Lafox, IL (16)

Pete Rickard Inc, Cobleskill, NY (11)

The Right Start Inc, Denver, CO (5)

Rinfret Ltd, Greenwich, CT (8)

River Street Sweets, Savannah, GA (4)

RJ Reynolds Tobacco Co, Winston Salem, NC (16)

Road Runner Sports Inc, San Diego, CA (11)

LW Robbins Associates, Holliston, MA (1)

Robinson Home Products, Buffalo, NY (16)

The Roblin Group Inc, White Plains, NY (17)

Roche Diagnostics Corp, Indianapolis, IN (7)

RocketWear, New York, NY (2)

Rockler Woodworking & Hardware, Medina, MN (8)

Rocky Mountain Chocolate Factory, Durango, CO (4)

Rodale Inc, Emmaus, PA (17)

Rod's Western Palace, Columbus, OH (2)

Rogers Publishing Ltd, Toronto, ON, Canada (17)

Roland Products Inc, Los Angeles, CA (16)

Roll International Corp, Los Angeles, CA (16)

Rollyson Financial Group, Pasadena, MD (14)

Roman Research Inc/Simply Whispers Earring, Hanson, MA (2)

Ronco Corp, Austin, TX (16)

Ronell Clock Co, Grants Pass, OR (5)

Rose Electronics, Houston, TX (3)

Rosicrucian Order AMORC, San Jose, CA (1)

Rosland Capital LLC, Santa Monica, CA (14)

Ross-Simons, Cranston, RI (6)

Roto-Rooter Services Co, Cincinnati, OH (16)

Rowe Pottery Works Inc, Cambridge, WI (16)

Royal Bank of Canada, Toronto, ON, Canada (14)

Royal Canin, Saint Charles, MO (16)

Royal Caribbean International Ltd, Miami, FL (19)

Rubber Stamps of America, Dublin, NH (6)

Rural Alaska Community Action Program Inc, Anchorage, AK (1)

Rush Industries, Inc, Mineola, NY (16)

AG Russell Knives Inc, Rogers, AR (11)

Rutland Products, Rutland, VT (16)

The RYTEX Co, Peru, IN (10)

S

S&S Worldwide, Colchester, CT (11)

SC Direct, West Bridgewater, MA (2)

SEI, Oaks, PA (14)

SLM Corp, Newark, DE (16)

SSHC Inc/Radiant Heating Commercial Applications, Old Saybrook, CT (9)

SW Caging Corp, Topeka, KS (14)

SWBC, San Antonio, TX (14)

Sa-So, Arlington, TX (16)

Safe Publications Inc, Doylestown, PA (11)

Safeco Insurance Co, Seattle, WA (15)

Safeguard Business Systems Inc, Dallas, TX (16)

Safeware, The Insurance Agency Inc, Columbus, OH (15)

Sage Financial Group, West Conshohocken, PA (14)

Sage Software Inc, Irvine, CA (16)

The Sailing Co, Palm Coast, FL (17)

Sailrite Enterprises, Inc, Columbia City, IN (11)

The Saint Francis Community Services, Salina, KS (1)

St Joseph's College, Brooklyn, NY (1)

St Lawrence Island Original Ivory Cooperative, Gambell, AK (6)

St Louis Post-Dispatch, Saint Louis, MO (17)

St Louis Slot Machine Co, Saint Louis, MO (6)

St Petersburg/Clearwater Area CVB, Clearwater, FL (1)

Saks Fifth Avenue, New York, NY (16)

Salem Media Group, Camarillo, CA (17)

Sales & Marketing Management Magazine, New York, NY (16)

Sales Service/America Inc, Alexandria, VA (16)

Salesian Missions, New Rochelle, NY (1)

Sally Beauty Supply LLC, Denton, TX (7)

Sam Ash Music Direct, Hicksville, NY (5)

Samsonite International SA, Mansfield, MA (16)

San Francisco Bay Area Rapid Transit District (BART), Oakland, CA (16)

San Francisco Chronicle, San Francisco, CA (17)

San Francisco Herb & Natural Food Co, San Francisco, CA (4)

San Francisco Victoriana Inc, San Francisco, CA (9)

San Jose Mercury News, San Jose, CA (17)

Sandy Mush Herb Nursery, Leicester, NC (8)

Santa Barbara Greenhouses, Oxnard, CA (8)

Santa Fe School of Cooking, Santa Fe, NM (4)

Sara Lee Direct Home Shopping, Winston-Salem, NC (2)

Satori Software Inc, Seattle, WA (16)

Saunders Military Insignia, Naples, FL (6)

The Sausage Maker Inc, Buffalo, NY (4)

Save the Children Federation Inc, Fairfield, CT (1)

Savings Bank Life Insurance Co of MA (SBLI), Woburn, MA (15)

Henry Schein Inc, Melville, NY (16)

Schermer Pecans, Glennville, GA (4)

Jacques C Schiff Jr Inc, Ridgefield Park, NJ (5)

Schneider Saddlery, Chagrin Falls, OH (11)

Schnuck Markets Inc, Saint Louis, MO (16)

Scholastic Inc, New York, NY (17)

School Annual Publishing Co, State College, PA (17)

Schoolwise Press, San Francisco, CA (17)

Charles Schwab & Co Inc, San Francisco, CA (14)

Schwartz & Co, Verona, NJ (6)

Scope 1, Kalamazoo, MI (16)

Scott Sign Systems Inc, Sarasota, FL (16)

The Scotts Co LLC, Marysville, OH (8)

Scott's Dog Supply Inc, Indianapolis, IN (11)

Scotts-Sierra Horticultural, Marysville, OH (16)

Sculpture House Inc, Skillman, NJ (16)

Sculptz, Feasterville Trevose, PA (2)

Sea Bear, Anacortes, WA (16)

Sears Canada Inc, Toronto, ON, Canada (5)

Sears Home Improvement Products & Services, Hoffman Estates, IL (16)

Sears, Roebuck & Co, Hoffman Estates, IL (16)

Seashore Vacations, Hilton Head Island, SC (19)

Seattle Magazine, Seattle, WA (17)

SECO-LARM USA Inc, Irvine, CA (16)

Second Renaissance Books, Irvine, CA (17)

Seedburo Equipment Co, Des Plaines, IL (8)

See's Candies Inc, Carson, CA (4)

Seiko Corp of America, Mahwah, NJ (16)

Select Comfort Corp, Minneapolis, MN (16)

Select Press, Novato, CA (17)

Selman & Co, Cleveland, OH (15)

LH Selman Ltd, Chicago, IL (6)

Sensory Effects Powder System, Bridgeton, MO (16)

Sentry Life Insurance Co, Stevens Point, WI (15)

Serenity, Maria Stein, OH (17)

ServiceMaster Co, Memphis, TN (8)

Sesame Workshop, New York, NY (1)

Seta Corp of Boca Inc, Boca Raton, FL (5)

Seton Hall University, South Orange, NJ (1)

B Shackman & Co Inc, Galesburg, MI (6)

Shades of Light, Richmond, VA (8)

Shaker Workshops, Ashburnham, MA (8)

Shakespeare Co, Columbia, SC (11)

Shape LLC, Addison, IL (3)

Shelby Insurance Companies, Birmingham, AL (15)

Shell Oil Co, Houston, TX (16)

Shield Healthcare, Valencia, CA (7)

Shillcraft Inc, Annapolis, MD (16)

Shiseido Cosmetics America, East Windsor, NJ (7)

Shop.com, Miami, FL (16)

Shopsmith Inc, Dayton, OH (16)

Showtime Networks Inc, New York, NY (16)

Shutterbug, Titusville, FL (17)

Sickafus Sheepskins, Strausstown, PA (2)

Sierra Trading Post, Cheyenne, WY (2)

Signature Styles LLC, Wilmington, DE (2)

Silicon Graphics Inc, Fremont, CA (16)

Silo-Hunt Hill Farm, New Milford, CT (8)

Silver Star Brands, Oshkosh, WI (6)

Simon & Schuster Inc, New York, NY (17)

Simplicity Pattern Co Inc/Style Patterns Ltd/New Look English Pattern Co Ltd, New York, NY (8)

Simply Batteries Inc, De Kalb, IL (7)

Sims Stoves, Billings, MT (11)

Single Scene News, Tempe, AZ (17)

SipcamAdvan, Durham, NC (5)

SiriusXM Radio Inc, New York, NY (16)

Skinder-Strauss Associates, New Providence, NJ (14)

Skullduggery, Anaheim, CA (16)

SkyMall Inc, Phoenix, AZ (16)

Sleepy's Inc, Hicksville, NY (16)

Smart Dog Products, Winchester, TN (11)

The Smile Train, New York, NY (1)

Smith & Noble, Corona, CA (8)

Daniel Smith Inc, Seattle, WA (10)

Smithfield Foods, Smithfield, VA (16)

Smithsonian Enterprises, New York, NY (17)

The JM Smucker Co, Orrville, OH (4)

Albert S Smyth Co Inc, Timonium, MD (6)

Snap-on Inc, Kenosha, WI (9)

Tom Snyder Productions, Watertown, MA (16)

SOAR Inflatables, Healdsburg, CA (11)

Social Studies School Service, Culver City, CA (16)

Society for Human Resource Management, Alexandria, VA (1)

Society of American Magicians Inc, Littleton, CO (1)

Society of Petroleum Engineers, Richardson, TX (1)

Society of the Divine Savior, New Holstein, WI (1)

Soft Surroundings, Saint Louis, MO (2)

Software Assistance International Ltd, Morris Plains, NJ (3)

Soitenly Stooges, Glendale, CA (6)

Solar Cine Products Inc, Chicago, IL (5)

Solar Components Corp, Manchester, NH (9)

Songbird Hearing Inc, North Brunswick, NJ (7)

Sony Pictures Home Entertainment, Culver City, CA (16)

Sotheby's, New York, NY (6)

Soundprints, Norwalk, CT (6)

South Seas Island Resort, Captiva Island, FL (19)

Southeast Toyota Distributors LLC, Deerfield Beach, FL (16)

Southern California Gas Co, Anaheim, CA (1)
Southern Flavoring Co Inc, Bedford, VA (16)
Southern Poverty Law Center, Montgomery, AL (1)
Southern Progress Corp, Birmingham, AL (17)
Sovereign Bank New England, Glastonbury, CT (14)
Spa-Finder Inc, New York, NY (7)
Spadet, New York, NY (7)
Spalding Laboratories Inc, Reno, NV (7)
Spates The Florist, Newport, VT (8)
Huck Spaulding Enterprises, Voorheesville, NY (16)
Spear Engineering Co, Colorado Springs, CO (16)
Specialized Information Publishers Association, Vienna, VA (1)
Specialty Equipment Market Association, Diamond Bar, CA (1)
Spectrum eCommerce, Mission Viejo, CA (15)
Speed-Mat, Biddeford, ME (16)
Spiegel Brands Inc, New York, NY (2)
Spilsbury Puzzle Co, Chicago, IL (11)
Spinneybeck Enterprises, Getzville, NY (16)
Spokane Teachers Credit Union, Liberty Lake, WA (14)
Spoken Arts, Holmes, NY (17)
The Spokesman-Review, Spokane, WA (17)
Sportif Mail Order Inc, Sparks, NV (2)
Sporting Clays Ltd, Titusville, FL (17)
The Sporting News, Charlotte, NC (17)
The Sportsman's Guide Inc, South Saint Paul, MN (11)
Sportsmith LLC, Tulsa, OK (11)
Sporty's Preferred Living, Batavia, OH (5)
Springer Science & Business Media LLC, New York, NY (17)
Squadron Mail Order, Carrollton, TX (16)
Stagestep Inc, Philadelphia, PA (5)
Standard Life, Montreal, QC, Canada (15)
Standard Publishing, Cincinnati, OH (17)
Stanley Home Products, Great Bend, KS (8)
Staples Inc, Framingham, MA (10)
Star Silkscreen Design Inc, Decatur, IL (2)
Star Sprinkler Inc, Lansdale, PA (9)
Star Tribune Media Co, Minneapolis, MN (17)
Starbucks Corp, Seattle, WA (4)
Starcrest Products of California Inc, Perris, CA (16)
Stark Brothers Nurseries & Orchards, Louisiana, MO (8)
Starkey Laboratories, Eden Prairie, MN (16)
Starmount Life Insurance Co, Baton Rouge, LA (15)
Starz Entertainment LLC, Englewood, CO (16)
State Farm Insurance Cos, Bloomington, IL (15)
State Mutual Insurance Co, Rome, GA (15)
State Street Global Advisors, Boston, MA (14)
StatSoft Inc, Tulsa, OK (9)
Steck-Vaughn, Austin, TX (17)
Steelcase Inc, Grand Rapids, MI (16)
Steptoe & Wife Antiques Ltd, Scarborough, ON, Canada (8)
Sterling Jewelers Inc, Akron, OH (16)
Sterling Name Tape Inc, Winsted, CT (16)
Stew Leonard's, Norwalk, CT (4)
Don Stewart Association, Tulsa, OK (1)
Stewart Enterprises Inc, Jefferson, LA (16)
Stewart-MacDonald, Athens, OH (16)
Martha Stewart Living Omnimedia, New York, NY (17)
Stickers 'N' Stuff Inc, Louisville, CO (6)
Kirk Stieff Co, Bristol, PA (16)
Stile-Tile Like Metal Roofing, Sellersburg, IN (9)
Stock Yards Packing Co Inc, Medford, OR (4)
Stokes Seeds Inc, Buffalo, NY (8)
Stonwurks, Eden Prairie, MN (16)

Strang Communications Co, Lake Mary, FL (17)
Stratford Hall, North Mankato, MN (10)
The Stratosphere Las Vegas, Las Vegas, NV (19)
Straw Hat Cooperative Corp, San Ramon, CA (16)
Stress Market, Port Angeles, WA (17)
Strongwell, Bristol, VA (9)
Paul Stuart, New York, NY (2)
Stuller Inc, Lafayette, LA (2)
Sturbridge Yankee Workshop Inc, Portland, ME (16)
Sturges Sportswear, Battleboro, NC (16)
SubscriptionAgency.com Inc, Winter Haven, FL (18)
The Suburban Chamber of Commerce, Summit, NJ (14)
Successful Farming, Des Moines, IA (17)
Sugarbush Farm Inc, Woodstock, VT (4)
Sullivan-Victory Groves, Rockledge, FL (4)
Summit Industries Inc, Marietta, GA (5)
Summit Racing Equipment, Tallmadge, OH (12)
Sun Harvest Citrus, Fort Myers, FL (6)
Sunbeam Products Inc, Boca Raton, FL (16)
Sunbilt Solar Products, Jamaica, NY (8)
Sunburst Digital Inc, Hoffman Estates, IL (17)
Sunburst Farms Inc, Miami, FL (8)
Sundance Catalog Co, Salt Lake City, UT (6)
Sunlife of Canada, Wellesley Hills, MA (15)
Sunnyland Farms Inc, Albany, GA (4)
Sunoco Inc, Philadelphia, PA (16)
Sunset Magazine, Menlo Park, CA (17)
Sunshine Discount Crafts, Largo, FL (11)
Sunshine Farm & Gardens, Renick, WV (8)
Sunshine Glassworks Ltd, Buffalo, NY (11)
Sunshine Minting Inc, Coeur D'Alene, ID (14)
Sunshine Unlimited Inc, Lindsborg, KS (9)
Sunstar, Chicago, IL (16)
Suntrust Banks Inc, Atlanta, GA (14)
Super 8 Hotels Worldwide, Parsippany, NJ (19)
The Supplies Guys, Midland Park, NJ (3)
Support Plus, Hudson, OH (7)
Sur La Table, Brownsburg, IN (8)
Sure-Fire Business Success Catalog, Cambridge, MA (17)
Surplus Center, Lincoln, NE (9)
Sussex Publishers Inc, New York, NY (17)
John Sutherland & Associates, San Diego, CA (15)
Svoboda Collins LLC, Chicago, IL (5)
Jimmy Swaggart Ministries, Baton Rouge, LA (1)
Sweepstakes Clearinghouse, Dallas, TX (16)
Sweet Tooth Candies, Newport, KY (4)
The Swiss Colony Inc, Monroe, WI (4)
Sylvan Learning Inc, Baltimore, MD (16)
Symantec, Mountain View, CA (16)
Symetra Financial, Bellevue, WA (15)
Synapse Group Inc, Stamford, CT (18)
Syngenta, Greensboro, NC (16)
System Pavers, Newport Beach, CA (16)
Systemax Inc, Port Washington, NY (16)

T

T Rowe Price Associates Inc, Baltimore, MD (14)
TD Bank NA, Falmouth, ME (14)
TIAA-CREF, New York, NY (15)
TL Enterprises Inc, Ventura, CA (17)
TVC Enterprises and the TV Collector Magazine, Las Vegas, NV (6)
TABcom, Hazleton, PA (5)
Tackle Craft, Ellsworth, WI (11)
Tafford Uniforms, Charlotte, NC (2)
Tailwinds Inc, Mill Valley, CA (6)
Talas, Brooklyn, NY (10)

Talbots, Hingham, MA (2)
Tamrac Inc, Ogden, UT (2)
Tandy Leather Co, Fort Worth, TX (11)
The Taunton Press, Newtown, CT (17)
Tax Reduction Institute, Germantown, MD (14)
Taylor Capital Group, Inc, Rosemont, IL (14)
Taylor Corp, North Mankato, MN (16)
Taymark Inc, White Bear Lake, MN (1)
The Teaching Co, Chantilly, VA (17)
Team Cheer, Geneseo, NY (2)
Technology Review, Cambridge, MA (17)
Teleflora, Los Angeles, CA (16)
Telemedia Communications US, North York, ON, Canada (17)
Ten Speed Press, Emeryville, CA (17)
Terminix International, The Trugreen Companies, Memphis, TN (16)
Tessco Inc, Hunt Valley, MD (16)
Tetley USA Inc, Montvale, NJ (16)
Texas Children's Hospital, Houston, TX (1)
Texas Farm Bureau Insurance Cos, Waco, TX (15)
Texas Monthly, Austin, TX (17)
Texas Parks & Wildlife Dept, Austin, TX (1)
Theatre Development Fund Inc, New York, NY (1)
TheIdeaClub.com & Dumas Martin Consulting, Pomona, CA (16)
Thermo Fisher Scientific Inc, Waltham, MA (9)
Thermo Pro, Duluth, GA (16)
Thetford Corp, Ann Arbor, MI (16)
Things Deco, New York, NY (6)
Things Remembered, Highland Heights, OH (6)
Think Ink, Bothell, WA (10)
Thirteen/WNET, New York, NY (1)
Thomas Computer Corp, Orlando, FL (16)
Thomas Nelson, Nashville, TN (17)
Stephen Thomas, Toronto, ON, Canada (1)
Thompson Cigar Co, Tampa, FL (6)
Norm Thompson Outfitters Inc, Hillsboro, OR (2)
ThorLo Inc, Statesville, NC (16)
Thorndike Press, Waterville, ME (17)
Thousand Trails LP, Chicago, IL (16)
Three Georges and the Nuthouse, Mobile, AL (16)
Threefold, Indianapolis, IN (9)
Thrivent Financial for Lutherans, Appleton, WI (14)
Tidbits Media, Montgomery, AL (17)
Tidewater Workshop, Galloway, NJ (8)
Tiffany & Co, New York, NY (6)
TigerDirect.ca, Richmond Hill, ON, Canada (3)
Tillamook County Creamery Association, Tillamook, OR (4)
Timber Crest Farms, Healdsburg, CA (16)
Timberland LLC, Stratham, NH (16)
Timberline Geodesics, Berkeley, CA (8)
Time Inc, New York, NY (17)
Time Out New York, New York, NY (18)
Time Products International, Del Rio, TX (16)
Time/System, Chicopee, MA (16)
Time Warner Inc, New York, NY (16)
Times Union, Albany, NY (18)
Timm Medical Technologies, Inc, Lake Forest, IL (16)
Todaro Brothers Mail Order Co, New York, NY (4)
The Tog Shop Inc, Beverly, MA (2)
Tomahawk Live Trap Co, Tomahawk, WI (16)
Tools for Wellness, Austin, TX (7)
Torah Umesorah Publications, Brooklyn, NY (5)
The Toro Co, Bloomington, MN (16)
Toter Inc, Statesville, NC (16)
Touch of Class Catalog, Huntingburg, IN (8)
Tova Corp, West Chester, PA (7)
Tower Hobbies/Hobbico, Champaign, IL (11)

Townsend Communications LLC, Kansas City, MO (17)

Toyota Motor Sales USA Inc, Torrance, CA (16)

Toys "R" Us, Wayne, NJ (11)

Toys To Grow On, Carson, CA (11)

Tractor Supply Co, Brentwood, TN (5)

Transaction Publishers, Piscataway, NJ (17)

Transamerica Life Insurance Co, Cedar Rapids, IA (15)

Transamerica Occidental Life Co, Los Angeles, CA (15)

TransFirst ePayment Services, Omaha, NE (14)

Transit Treasure Inc, New York, NY (12)

TransitCenter Inc, New York, NY (1)

Travelclick, Schaumburg, IL (19)

The Travelers Insurance Cos, Hartford, CT (15)

Travelex America Inc, Washington, DC (14)

Treasure Chest, New York, NY (19)

Trend Magazines Inc, Saint Petersburg, FL (17)

Tri-Chem Inc, Belleville, NJ (16)

Tribune Co, Chicago, IL (17)

Trigon Blue Cross/Blue Shield, Roanoke, VA (15)

Triton College, River Grove, IL (1)

Triumph Learning, New York, NY (17)

Trophyland USA Inc, Hialeah, FL (5)

True Value Co, Chicago, IL (16)

TruGreen/ChemLawn, Lewis Center, OH (16)

Trumble Greetings, Boulder, CO (6)

The Trumpet Club, New York, NY (17)

truTV, New York, NY (17)

Tucker Electronics Co, Garland, TX (3)

Tupperware Brands Corp, Orlando, FL (16)

Turncraft Clocks Inc, Spring Park, MN (6)

Turner Greenhouses, Goldsboro, NC (8)

Tuttle, Wallingford, CT (2)

20th Century Fox Television, Los Angeles, CA (16)

21st Century Insurance, Woodland Hills, CA (15)

Tyndale House Publishers, Carol Stream, IL (17)

U

U-Bild, Oceanside, CA (8)

U-Haul International, Phoenix, AZ (16)

UBS Wealth Management US, Weehawken, NJ (14)

UCEA, New York, NY (1)

UGL Equis Corp, Chicago, IL (16)

UMI Publications Inc, Charlotte, NC (17)

UNICEF, New York, NY (1)

UNICEF Canada, Toronto, ON, Canada (1)

USAA, San Antonio, TX (15)

USAA Alliance Services Marketing, San Antonio, TX (14)

USI Affinity, Philadelphia, PA (15)

USO Inc, Washington, DC (1)

USX, Pittsburgh, PA (16)

Ultimate Products Inc, Chula Vista, CA (16)

Ultradent Products Inc, South Jordan, UT (7)

UMass Dartmouth, North Dartmouth, MA (1)

Unadilla Laminated Products, Unadilla, NY (16)

Uncharted Country Publishing, Madison, WI (17)

UndercoverWear Inc, Tewksbury, MA (2)

Unicom Electric Inc, Walnut, CA (16)

Unicover Corp, Cheyenne, WY (6)

UniFirst Corp, Wilmington, MA (2)

Uniformed Services Benefit Association, Overland Park, KS (15)

Unilever Best Foods, Englewood Cliffs, NJ (16)

Union Federal Savings Bank, North Providence, RI (14)

The Union Labor Life Insurance Co, Silver Spring, MD (15)

Union Privilege, AFL-CIO, Washington, DC (1)

United Air Specialists Inc, Cincinnati, OH (16)

United Business Media, Manhasset, NY (17)

United Church Homes, Marion, OH (1)

United Community Bank, Blairsville, GA (14)

United Farm Workers of America, AFL-CIO, Keene, CA (1)

United Investors Life Insurance Co, Birmingham, AL (15)

United Jewish Appeal Federation of New York, New York, NY (1)

United Jewish Communities, New York, NY (1)

The United Methodist Publishing House, Nashville, TN (17)

United Nations Federal Credit Union, Long Island City, NY (1)

United Retail Inc, Rochelle Park, NJ (2)

United Security Products Inc, Poway, CA (16)

United Spinal Association, Kew Gardens, NY (1)

United Staffing Systems, New York, NY (16)

US Bancorp, Minneapolis, MN (14)

US Bank, Minneapolis, MN (14)

US Branding Group LLC, Lake Worth, FL (16)

United States Bronze Sign Co Inc, New Hyde Park, NY (1)

US Cavalry, Radcliff, KY (6)

US Department of Commerce, Washington, DC (1)

US Digital Transactions Corporation, New York, NY (14)

US Fund for UNICEF, New York, NY (6)

US Games Systems Inc, Stamford, CT (11)

US News & World Report, Washington, DC (17)

US Tax Shield, Encino, CA (14)

US Travel Association, Washington, DC (1)

United Systems c/o Biomed, Concord, CA (7)

United Way Toronto & York Region, Toronto, ON, Canada (1)

Unitron Ltd, Commack, NY (9)

Unity School of Christianity, Unity Village, MO (17)

Universal Hovercraft, Cordova, IL (11)

Universal Security Instruments Inc, Owings Mills, MD (16)

Universal Studios Inc, Universal City, CA (3)

Universal Tea Co Inc, Tigard, OR (4)

Universal Vintage Tire Co, Hershey, PA (11)

University at Buffalo Center for Entrepreneurial Leadership, Buffalo, NY (5)

University of Akron, Akron, OH (1)

University of Alabama, Tuscaloosa, AL (13)

University of California Irvine Extension, Irvine, CA (1)

University of Chicago GSB, Chicago, IL (1)

University of Chicago Press, Chicago, IL (17)

University of Illinois Foundation, Urbana, IL (1)

University of Minnesota, Minneapolis, MN (1)

University of Minnesota Alumni Association, Minneapolis, MN (1)

University of Oklahoma Press, Norman, OK (17)

University of Pennsylvania, Philadelphia, PA (1)

University of Southern Mississippi, Hattiesburg, MS (1)

University of Texas School of Law, Austin, TX (1)

University of Wisconsin-Madison School of Business, Madison, WI (1)

University Press of America Inc, Lanham, MD (17)

University Subscription Service, Downers Grove, IL (18)

Uniway Management Corp, Forest Park, GA (16)

Unum Corp, Portland, ME (15)

Upbeat Inc, Saint Louis, MO (9)

Upstart, Madison, WI (16)

Urban Response LLC, Hartville, OH (17)

Urbani Truffles USA Corp, New York, NY (4)

Utilities Supply Corp, Woburn, MA (16)

Utretch Art Supplies, Cranbury, NJ (10)

Uwharrie Capital Corp, Albemarle, NC (14)

V

VW Credit, Herndon, VA (14)

Vail Resorts Inc, Broomfield, CO (19)

Valentine Research Inc, Cincinnati, OH (16)

Value Line Publishing Inc, New York, NY (17)

K Van Bourgondien & Sons Inc, (8)

Van Dam Inc, New York, NY (17)

Vance Industries Inc, Niles, IL (16)

Vanderbilt Advertising, New York, NY (14)

Vanguard, Malvern, PA (14)

The Vantage Group Inc, Boston, MA (14)

Vcom International Multi-Media Corp, South Hackensack, NJ (3)

Vector Marketing Corp, Olean, NY (5)

Vehicle Assurance, Saint Charles, MO (5)

Vemma Nutrition Co, Tempe, AZ (7)

Veneer Factory Outlet, Westport, KY (8)

Venus Fashion, Inc, Jacksonville, FL (2)

Veridian Credit Union, Waterloo, IA (1)

Verizon Communications, New York, NY (3)

Vermont Ski Areas Association, Montpelier, VT (1)

Vermont Teddy Bear Co, Shelburne, VT (6)

Vesey's Seeds Ltd, Charlottetown, PE, Canada (8)

The Vestal Press Ltd, Lanham, MD (17)

Vet Vax, Tonganoxie, KS (11)

Veterans of Foreign Wars of the US, Kansas City, MO (1)

Viacom Inc, New York, NY (16)

Viahealth, Rochester, NY (16)

Victor Machinery Exchange, Brooklyn, NY (9)

Victory Corps, New Hope, MN (16)

Video Artists International, Pleasantville, NY (3)

Vietnam Veterans of America, Silver Spring, MD (1)

VIEW Video Inc/Arcadia Entertainment Corp, Saugerties, NY (16)

Village Coin Shop, Plaistow, NH (6)

Village Interiors Carpet One, Newton, NC (8)

Village Software Inc, Boston, MA (3)

Vintage Wood Works, Quinlan, TX (8)

Virco Manufacturing Corp, Conway, AR (16)

The Virginia Diner Inc, Wakefield, VA (4)

Virginia Home For Boys & Girls, Richmond, VA (1)

Visa USA, Foster City, CA (14)

Visionworks of America Inc, San Antonio, TX (7)

Vita-Mix Corp, Cleveland, OH (16)

Vitamin Power Inc, Hauppauge, NY (7)

Vitamin Research Products, Cottonwood, AZ (7)

Vitamin Specialties Co, Freehold, NJ (7)

Vitasoy USA Inc, Ayer, MA (16)

Vivendi SA, New York, NY (16)

Vivitar Corp, Tempe, AZ (16)

Volkswagen Group of America Inc, Herndon, VA (16)

Volunteers of America, Alexandria, VA (1)

Volvo Cars of North America LLC, Northvale, NJ (16)

Voyageur Inc, Easley, SC (11)

Ed Voyles Hyundai Inc, Smyrna, GA (16)

Vulcan Information Packaging, Vincent, AL (16)

W

WGBH Educational Foundation, Brighton, MA (1)

WRS Group Ltd, Waco, TX (7)

WTS Media, Chattanooga, TN (16)

Wag/Aero Group, Lyons, WI (16)

Wake Forest University Baptist Medical Center, Winston Salem, NC (1)

Wakefield Peanut Co, Wakefield, VA (4)

Walch Publishing, Portland, ME (17)

Walgreens Co, Deerfield, IL (7)

Walk Thru The Bible Ministries Inc, Norcross, GA (1)

Walker Publishing Co Inc, New York, NY (17)

WalMart Stores Inc, Bentonville, AR (16)

Wm K Walthers Inc, Milwaukee, WI (11)

Warnaco Swimwear Inc, Los Angeles, CA (16)

Warner Bros, Burbank, CA (3)

Warner Press, Anderson, IN (17)

Washington Marketing Group, Arlington, VA (1)

The Washington Monthly Co, Washington, DC (17)

Washington National Opera, Washington, DC (16)

The Washington Post, Washington, DC (17)

Washington Post Digital, Washington, DC (17)

Washington University, Saint Louis, MO (1)

The Washingtonian, Washington, DC (17)

Andrew D Washton Books On the Fine Arts, Port Chester, NY (16)

Wasserman Uniform Co, Fort Lauderdale, FL (2)

Watering Inc/Hemmings Motor News, Bennington, VT (17)

Water's Edge Resort & Spa, Westbrook, CT (19)

Wathne Ltd, New York, NY (2)

Watts Radiant, Springfield, MO (9)

We-No-Nah Canoe Inc, Winona, MN (11)

WearGuard Corp, Norwell, MA (2)

Webster Bank, Waterbury, CT (14)

The Wedding Pages, New York, NY (16)

Weichert Co, Morris Plains, NJ (14)

Weight Watchers International, New York, NY (16)

Richard Weiner Consultant, North Miami Beach, FL (14)

Weiss Research Inc, Palm Beach Gardens, FL (17)

Welch Allyn, Inc, Skaneateles Falls, NY (9)

Welcomemat Services Inc, Atlanta, GA (9)

Wellmark Blue Cross & Blue Shield of Iowa, Des Moines, IA (15)

Wells Fargo, San Francisco, CA (14)

Wenner Media LLC, New York, NY (17)

WESCO, Pittsburgh, PA (16)

West Bend, West Bend, WI (16)

West Marine Inc, Watsonville, CA (11)

Western Pennsylvania Conservancy, Pittsburgh, PA (1)

Western Psychological Services, Torrance, CA (16)

Western River Expeditions, Salt Lake City, UT (19)

Western-Southern Life, Cincinnati, OH (15)

Westhoff Machine Co, Saint Louis, MO (9)

Weston Distance Learning Inc, Fort Collins, CO (13)

Westwood Publishing Co, Glendale, CA (17)

The Wexner Companies Inc, Memphis, TN (2)

What on Earth, Hudson, OH (5)

Whirlpool Corp, Benton Harbor, MI (16)

White Cap Wholesale Contractors Supplies, Costa Mesa, CA (16)

White Flower Farm, Litchfield, CT (8)

White Mane Publishing Co Inc, Shippensburg, PA (17)

Whitehorse Gear, Center Conway, NH (11)

Whiting & Davis, Attleboro Falls, MA (16)

Whitman Publishing LLC, Atlanta, GA (16)

Wholesale Tool Co, Warren, MI (9)

Michael Wiese Productions, Studio City, CA (17)

The Wig Co, Pittsburgh, PA (2)

WILD Flavors Inc, Erlanger, KY (4)

Gilbert H Wild & Son Inc, Reeds, MO (8)

Wildlife Education Ltd, Park Hills, KY (17)

Wildseed Farms, Fredericksburg, TX (8)

John Wiley & Sons Inc, Hoboken, NJ (17)

Williams-Sonoma Inc, San Francisco, CA (8)

Williamsburg Blacksmiths Inc, Williamsburg, MA (8)

Willis Music Co, Florence, KY (17)

Wilsons Leather, Brooklyn Park, MN (2)

Wilton Armetale, Mount Joy, PA (16)

Wilton Industries Inc, Woodridge, IL (16)

Wimmer's Meat Products Inc, West Point, NE (4)

Win Craft Inc, Winona, MN (5)

Wind in the Rigging, Port Washington, WI (11)

Windsor Vineyards, Santa Rosa, CA (16)

Windstar Cruises, Seattle, WA (19)

Wine Enthusiast Cos, Mount Kisco, NY (4)

Winetasting.com, Napa, CA (4)

Winmill & Co, New York, NY (14)

Winnipeg Art Gallery, Winnipeg, MB, Canada (1)

Winslow Publishing, Toronto, ON, Canada (17)

Harry Winston Inc, New York, NY (16)

Winston Marketing Group, Elk Grove Village, IL (8)

WinterSilks LLC, Warren, PA (2)

Wire Works, Chester, PA (9)

Wolfe Publishing Co Inc, Prescott, AZ (17)

Woman's Missionary Union, Birmingham, AL (17)

Womanship, Annapolis, MD (16)

Woman's Day Special Interest Publications, New York, NY (17)

Wood Carvers Supply Inc, Englewood, FL (9)

Woodall Publishing Co LP, Ventura, CA (17)

Woodcraft Supply Corp LLC, Parkersburg, WV (9)

Woodcrafters Lumber Sales Inc, Portland, OR (9)

Sylvia Woods Harp Center, Montrose, CA (11)

Woodwind & Brasswind Inc, Westlake Village, CA (5)

Woodworker's Supply Inc, Casper, WY (11)

Woolrich Inc, Woolrich, PA (2)

Workforce Advantage USA, Elizabeth, NJ (13)

Working Assets, San Francisco, CA (16)

The World Bank, Washington, DC (17)

World Book Inc, Chicago, IL (17)

World Future Society, Chicago, IL (1)

World Kitchen Inc, Corning, NY (16)

World Press Review, New York, NY (18)

World Publications Inc, Winter Park, FL (17)

World Vision Inc, Federal Way, WA (1)

World Wrestling Entertainment Inc, Stamford, CT (16)

Wrisco Industries Inc, Palm Beach Gardens, FL (8)

Writer's Digest Books, Blue Ash, OH (17)

Wyandotte West Communications Inc, Kansas City, KS (17)

Wycliffe Bible Translators, Dallas, TX (17)

Wyndham Hotel Group, Parsippany, NJ (19)

Wysong Corp, Midland, MI (7)

X

Xcel Energy, Minneapolis, MN (5)

Xerox Corp, Norwalk, CT (16)

Y

YWCA of the USA, Washington, DC (1)

Yankee Publishing Inc, Dublin, NH (17)

Year One Inc, Braselton, GA (16)

Yenkin-Majestic, Columbus, OH (16)

Young America's Foundation, Reston, VA (1)

Your Man Tours, El Segundo, CA (19)

Your Move Chess & Games, North Massapequa, NY (11)

David Yurman Enterprises LLC, New York, NY (5)

Yves Rocher North America Inc, Exton, PA (7)

Z

Zale Corp, Irving, TX (6)

Ziff Davis Media Inc, New York, NY (17)

Zig Ziglar Corp, Plano, TX (16)

Zimmerman Irrigation Inc, Biglerville, PA (16)

Zimmerman-McDonald Machinery Inc, Saint Louis, MO (16)

Zoological Society of San Diego, San Diego, CA (1)

Zotos International, Darien, CT (16)

Zurich, Schaumburg, IL (15)

Consultants, Recruiters, Collection & Finance (20) — Geographic Index

ALABAMA

FotoBed.com, 4630 Old Looney Mill Rd, Birmingham, 35243-2607

ARIZONA

Billin Medina-Warren, 8655 E Via de Ventura (#G200), Scottsdale, 85258-3300

CDMC/Carefree Direct Marketing Corp, PO Box 3737, 8001 E Serene St, Carefree, 85377-3737

Robert DeLay, 4121 E Via del Cuculin, Tucson, 85718-3320

Direct Marketing Insights Inc, 15970 W Edgemont Ave, Goodyear, 85395-8112

Kennedy Inner Circle, 15433 N Tatum Blvd (Suite 104), Phoenix, 85032-4231

Smith-Browning Direct Inc, 45 Camielle Ct, Sedona, 86336-5977

Andrew Yoelin & Co, 5524 E Waltann Ln, Scottsdale, 85254-1701

CALIFORNIA

ADM Marketing, 908 N Hollywood Way, Burbank, 91505-2815

Access Business Communications Inc, 5611 Ocean Terrace Dr, Huntington Beach, 92648-7511

Allen, Matkins, Leck, Gamble & Mallory, 515 S Figueroa St (fl 9), Los Angeles, 90071-3398

Anderson/Skow, 690 Texas St, San Francisco, 94107-2941

Diana Baty, 109 Sullivan Dr, Moraga, 94556-1211

Blatteis Communications, 2335 W Hedding St, San Jose, 95128-1327

Bloom, Hergott, Diemer, Rosenthal and Laviolette LLP, 150 S Rodeo Dr (fl 3), Beverly Hills, 90212-2410

Bristol Associates Inc, 5777 W Century Blvd (Suite 865), Los Angeles, 90045-5696

Brown, Van Remmen, Kanuit, Inc, 840 Apollo St (Suite 300), El Segundo, 90245-4763

Browning, Jacobson & Klein LLP, 9595 Wilshire Blvd (Suite 601), Beverly Hills, 90212-2506

Coleman Frost LLP, 429 Santa Monica Blvd (Suite 700), Santa Monica, 90401-3435

The Copy Works, 12668 Camino Emparrado, San Diego, 92128-1404

Decker Communications Inc, 575 Market St (Suite 1925), San Francisco, 94105

Patricia Dowd Inc, 5300 San Jacinto Ave, Atascadero, 93422-2940

Employers Group, 400 Continental Blvd Ste 300, El Segundo, 90245-5080

Equity Management Inc, 4365 Executive Dr Ste 1000, San Diego, 92121-2192

Gartner Inc, 1650 Technology Dr Ste 500, San Jose, 95110-3838

HDI Group, 1 Embarcadero Ctr (Suite 500), San Francisco, 94111-3610

Robert Half International Inc, 2884 Sand Hill Rd (Suite 200), Menlo Park, 94025

Harvest Communications, 2400 Washington Ave (Suite 411), Redding, 96001-2827

IJHANA, 409 W Olympic Blvd (Apt 7062), Los Angeles, 90015-1635

JK Associates LLC, 445 Sherman Ave (Suite W), Palo Alto, 94306-1828

Jasek Enterprises, 1000 Deep Wood Dr, Westlake Village, 91362-4215

Joffrey Long Consultants, 17045 Chatsworth St, Granada Hills, 91344-5845

LN Marketing Associates, 25 Seki Ct, Emerald Hills, 94062-3401

Ladd Associates Inc, 2527 Fillmore St, San Francisco, 94115

MVI Marketing Ltd, 1053 Trevor Way, San Luis Obispo, 93401-4549

Martineau & Associates, 1770 Oakdell Dr, Menlo Park, 94025

McKee Consulting LLC, 1404 W Country Club Ln, Escondido, 92026-1660

Paul Nelson Direct Marketing, 2411 Sixth St, Santa Monica, 90405

New American Dimensions, 6955 La Tijera Blvd (Suite B), Los Angeles, 90045-1932

Odenza Marketing Group, 4445 Eastgate Mall (Suite 200), San Diego, V5G 4L7-92121-1971

James Robert Parish Consulting, 4338 Gentry Ave (Suite 1), Studio City, 91604-1764

Mary Anne Parshall Consulting Inc, 616 Corte Regalo, Camarillo, 93010-9107

Pillsbury Winthrop Shaw Pittman LLP, 725 S Figueroa St (Suite 2800), Los Angeles, 90017-5406

Proven Prospects Inc, 275 Arboleda Rd, Santa Barbara, 93110-1703

Public Issues Management, 902 Rose Ave, Piedmont, 94611-4343

Publication Fulfillment Svcs, 10564 Progress Way (Suite D), Cypress, 90630-4712

Neil Ransick Marketing, 212 Teresita Blvd, San Francisco, 94127-1729

Research Boston Corp, 1160 Brown Ave, Lafayette, 94549-3102

Response ADvantage, 8635 Falmouth (#301), Playa Del Rey, 90293-8281

Responsys, 1100 Grundy Ln (#3), San Bruno, 94066-3065

Rhino Marketing Inc, 515 S Flower St (fl 36), Los Angeles, V3B 5H6-90071-2221

Russ, August & Kabat, 12424 Wilshire Blvd (Suite 1200), Los Angeles, 90025

Schus & Co, 1458 Royal Blvd, Glendale, 91201

Sharf Woodward & Associates Inc, 5900 Sepulveda Blvd (Suite 104), Sherman Oaks, 91411

Southwest Consultants, 17045 Chatsworth St, Granada Hills, 91344-5845

Transamerican Mailing, 355 State Pl, Escondido, 92029-1359

Unisfair, 1450 Fashion Island Blvd (Suite 500), San Mateo, 94404-2077

WPG Americas Inc, 5285 Hellyer Ave (Suite 150), San Jose, 95138

Whitewing Labs, 17939 Chatsworth St (#408), Granada Hills, 91344

Zoe Marketing, 5132 Meadows del Mar, San Diego, 92130-4854

COLORADO

About Books Inc, 1001 Taurus Dr, Colorado Springs, 80906-1133

The Contrino Group, 2770 Arapahoe Rd Ste 132, Lafayette, 80026-8016

Jungle Consulting, 13795 Tewkesbury Ct, Colorado Springs, 80908

Legrand Hart, 1625 Broadway (Suite 200), Denver, 80202

Qwest, 1801 California St, Denver, 80202-5555

CONNECTICUT

The Aldrich Group, 43 Sherman Hill Rd D-104, Woodbury, 06798

Alexander & Co LLC, 178 Water St, Stonington, 06378

Blum & Co LLC, 81 Clinton St, Fairfield, 06824-6908

Bowman Circulation Marketing, 56 Ritch Ave W (fl 2), Greenwich, 06830-6918

Reggie Brady Marketing Solutions LLC, 198 Scribner Ave, Norwalk, 06854-1324

Ciarlo Consulting LLC, 39 Gary Ave, Waterbury, 06704-2034

Circulation Specialists Inc, 2 Corporate Dr (#945), Shelton, 06484-4694

Communication Managers, LLC, 604 Federal Rd, Brookfield, 06804-2070

John Condon & Associates, 38 Angus Ln, Greenwich, 06831-4402

Connecticut Marketing Associates, 12 Godfrey Pl (Suite 3), Wilton, 06897

Corry Direct Marketing LLC, 109 Limekiln Rd, Ridgefield, 06877-3418

Direct Advantage Partners, 69 Bluff Ave (Suite 100), Rowayton, 06853-1802

Direct Dynamics LLC, 85 Emanuel Church Rd, Killingworth, 06419

The Edbraham Group, PO Box 753, Westbrook, 06498-0753

JS Eliezer Associates Inc, 300 Atlantic St (fl 7), Stamford, 06901-3522

Growth Platforms Institute, 68 St Johns (Suite 200), Wilton, 06897

Imagination Works, 24 Primrose Dr, Trumbull, 06611-5043

Victoria James Executive Search Inc, 11 Stonefence Ln, South Kent, 06785-1307

Lev & Berlin, 200 Connecticut Ave (Suite 10), Norwalk, 06854-1907

Madison Executive Search, 54 Danbury Rd (Suite 368), Ridgefield, 06877

Mangieri/Hull Solutions LLC, One Riverside Rd, Sandy Hook, 06482

The Marketing Alliance, 127 Field Point Dr, Fairfield, 06824-6374

Marvel Associates, 199 Sound Beach Ave, Box 504, Old Greenwich, 06870-1711

Mission: A Consulting Group, 36 Cross Hwy, Westport, 06880-2141

Platinum Press, 37 Route 80, Killingworth, 06419-1429

Polestar Group, 20 N Canton Rd, West Simsbury, 06092

The Rusin Group, LLC, 30 Hollow Tree Pl, Wilton, 06897

Smith Hanley Associates, 107 John St Ste 201, Southport, 06890-1466

Frederick Wershaw Management Co, 111 Black Rock Rd, Stamford, 06903-1430

Windsor House, Two Industrial Rd, Windsor Locks, 06096

DELAWARE

Epic Research LLC, 300 Centennial Cir, Greenville, 19807-2130

The Jackson Consulting Group Ltd, PO Box 246, Middletown, 19709

Mail Management Enterprises, 5616 Galestown Reliance Rd, Seaford, 19973-6044

Modern Mail, PO Box 674, Bear, 19701-0674

Morris James Hitchens & Williams, 500 Delaware Ave (Suite 1500), PO Box 2306, Wilmington, 19801-1494

DISTRICT OF COLUMBIA

Baker & Hostetler LLP, 1050 Connecticut Ave NW (Suite 1100), Washington, 20036-5304

Center For Information Policy Leadership, 2200 Pennsylvania Ave NW, Hunton & Williams, LLP, Washington, 20037-1701

National Economic Research Associates Inc, 1255 23rd St NW (Suite 600), Washington, 20037

VMF Inc, 3313 Ross Pl NW, Washington, 20008

Venable LLP Conference Center, 575 7th St NW, Washington, 20004-1607

FLORIDA

AVD Marketing, 4113 Trenton Ave, Hollywood, 33026-4923

Ability Commerce, 1300 NW 17th Ave (Suite 200), Delray Beach, 33445-2560

Allpro Direct Marketing, 11626 Prosperous Dr, Odessa, 33556

JoAnna Brandi & Co Inc, 7491 N Federal Hwy C-5 (#304), Boca Raton, 33487

The Catalog Consultancy, 3285 West Brookfield Way, Vero Beach, 32966-3164

Thomas Dawson, 40 Casa Bella Cir, Palm Coast, 32137-1223

Direct Mail Systems, 12450 Automobile Blvd, Clearwater, 33762

Executive Connections LLC, 8466 Lockwood Ridge Rd (#330), Sarasota, 34243-2951

Jonathan Friedman, 3720 N 37th Ter, Hollywood, 33021

IZEA, 1000 Legion Pl (Suite 1600), Orlando, 32801-1060

Ideas in SEO, 758 NE 90 St (Unit 514), Miami, 33138

JZ Marketing, 4532 Varsity Cir, Lehigh Acres, 33971

Kforce Inc, 1001 E Palm Ave, Tampa, 33605-3551

Leads-Plus Inc, PO Box 400, Killarney, 34740-0400

Life Works Inc, 2817 Evans St, Hollywood, 33020-1119

MRI Norwalk, 2334 S Cypress Bend Dr (Suite 11), Pompano Beach, 33069-4488

Mr Fantastic LLC, 55739 Holiday Cr, Astor, 32102-7991

Muldoon & Baer Inc, 130 Banyan Isle Rd, Palm Beach Gardens, 33416-4601

Open Systems Services, 330 SW 27 Ave (Suite 402), Miami, 33135

Postal En Espanol Inc, 8325 W Hillsborough Ave, Tampa, 33615-3805

Ridenour & Associates, 4125 Moss Oak Pl, Sarasota, 34231-2935

The Schmidt Group International Inc, 298 Peppertree Dr S, Vero Beach, 32963

Seklemian Newell Inc (CRMC), 1521 Alton Rd (Suite 138), Miami Beach, 33139-3301

Snyder Glenn J & Assocs, 49 Quail Ln, Jacksonville Beach, 32250

UCI/Dream Giveaways, 19321-C US Hwy 19 N (Suite 605), Clearwater, 33764

West Companies Inc, 7155 Savoy Ct, Seminole, 33776-4329

GEORGIA

AS Kleeman & Associates, 1416 Spyglass Hill Dr, Duluth, 30097-5948

Equifax Credit Information Services Inc, 1550 Peachtree NW, Atlanta, 30309

Morris & Fellows, 6105 Blue Stone Rd NE (Suite A), Atlanta, 30328-3885

Plexus Marketing Group Inc, PO Box 76380, Bldg G, Atlanta, 30358-1380

Kurt Salmon Associates Inc, 1355 Peachtree St NE (Suite 900), Atlanta, 30309-3266

HAWAII

Pohaku Inc, 44-103 Puuohalai Pl, Kaneohe, 96744-2545

ILLINOIS

A Plus Marketing Ltd, 1300 Barclay Blvd, Buffalo Grove, 60089-4500

Actuarial Enterprises Ltd, 920 N Franklin St (Suite 401), Chicago, 60610-3186

Applications Development Corp, 3101 Wolf Ct, Dekalb, 60115-8257

BennettBaker Ltd, 33 W Monroe St (Suite 2110), Chicago, 60603-5414

Brothers & Thompson PC, 180 N Stetson Ave Ste 4425, Chicago, 60601-6733

Burtch Works LLC, 1560 Sherman Ave (fl 10), Evanston, 60201-5017

Peter N Carey & Associates Inc, 184 Briarwood Loop, Oak Brook, 60523-8713

Catalog Marketing Group, 2770 Sheridan Rd, Evanston, 60201-1728

CORS, 1 Pierce Pl (Suite 295), Itasca, 60143-1253

DM Info, 308 Royce Woods Ct, Naperville, 60565

Duggan & Brown Inc, 118 Appletree St, Barrington, 60010

Equity Residential Properties, Two N Riverside Plaza (Suite 400), Chicago, 60606-2624

FunME Events, PO Box 463, Dekalb, 60115-0463

GasPedal, 333 W North Ave (Suite 500), Chicago, 60610-1293

Glazer-Kennedy Insider Circle, 8430 W Bryn Mawr Ave (Suite 575), Chicago, 60631-3497

HealthInfo Direct, 1528 Sandburg Dr, Schaumburg, 60173-2183

High Note Media Inc, 5315 N Clark (#218), Chicago, 60640-2290

IMV, 1400 E Touhy Ave (Suite 250), Des Plaines, 60018-3339

Jacobsohn Consulting Associates, PO Box 236, Highland Park, 60035-0236

Kannon Consulting Inc, 2314 N Lincoln Park W (Apt 14S), Chicago, 60614-3462

KesTry, 209 E Lake Shore Dr (#6E), Chicago, 60611-1307

Kobs Strategic Consulting, 222 N Columbus Dr (#2202), Chicago, 60601-7819

Herbert Krug & Associates Inc, 500 Davis St (Suite 812), Evanston, 60201-4655

Learning Resources Institute, 2235 Durand Dr, Downers Grove, 60515

Steve Lytle, 425 W Randolph St, Chicago, 60606-1530

MCDM Strategic Direct Marketing, 12864 Bradford Ln, Plainfield, 60585-2244

Marketing Highway, 1416 Gordon Ter, Deerfield, 60015-4739

Marnell Database Marketing, 119 W Chestnut St (Suite 3E), Chicago, 60610-3288

Northern Illinois Consulting Inc, PO Box 7157, Libertyville, 60048-7157

O'Keefe Henry Direct Inc, 707 Lake Cook Rd (Suite 285), Deerfield, 60015-4933

PCG, Inc, 1S935 Tanglewood Dr (#121), Batavia, 60510-9511

James R Perdiew & Co, 1405 Afton Cir, Inverness, 60010-5702

S Pernick & Associates, 1616 Sheridan Rd (Unit 2H), Wilmette, 60091-1884

Productive Strategies Inc, 2 Northfield Plaza (Suite 365), Northfield, 60093-1272

Quigley Consulting Group, 1775 W Broadland Ln, Lake Forest, 60045-4817

Shapes Marketing Inc, 2086 Saint Johns Ave (Apt 207), Highland Park, 60035-2461

Silliker Inc, 111 E Wacker Dr (Suite 2300), Chicago, 60601-4214

SourceLink, 500 Park Blvd (Suite 1245), Itasca, 60143-2610

SpencerStuart, 353 N Clark (Suite 2400), Chicago, 60654-3479

Tesar Reynes Inc, 333 N Michigan Ave (Suite 2226), Chicago, 60601-4035

Training Consultants Inc, 1415 Sheridan Rd, Highland Park, 60035

WTB Associates Inc, 4020 Bunker Ln, Wilmette, 60091

ZS Associates, 1800 Sherman Ave, Evanston, 60201

INDIANA

ACCENT Marketing Services LLC, 400 Missouri Ave (Suite 100), Jeffersonville, 47130-3086

ChaCha Mobile Answers, 14550 Clay Terrace Blvd (Suite 130), Carmel, 46032-3653

Rescott LLC Marketing & Technology, 5856 Poole Pl (Suite 263), Noblesville, 46062-7608

Brent Slinkard Consultant, 1048 W 17th St, Bloomington, 47404-3338

IOWA

Brokers International Ltd, 1200 E Main St, Panora, 50216-1100

Gazette Direct Marketing Co, 500 Third Ave SE, Cedar Rapids, 52401-1945

The Stelter Co, 10435 New York Ave, Des Moines, 50322-3774

TitanTV Media, 818 Dows Rd SE, Cedar Rapids, 52403-7000

KANSAS

Rich Becker & Associates/Pump-Em-Up Publishing, In Public Relations, 9225 Woodstone Ln, Lenexa, 66219-1959

J Schmid & Associates Inc, 5800 Foxridge Dr (Suite 200), Mission, 66202-2333

StrategicOne, 6700 Antioch Rd (Suite 110), Overland Park, 66204-1200

WDS Marketing & Public Relations, 8232 Hadley St, Overland Park, 66204-3542

KENTUCKY

PackStream LLC, 2400 Dundee Rd, Louisville, 40205-2047

MARYLAND

American Marketing & Communication Corp, 14201 Pennsylvania Ave, Hagerstown, 21742-1665

Amtower & Co Federal Direct, PO Box 314, Highland, 20777-0314

Arlen Communications Inc, 7315 Wisconsin Ave (Suite 705E), Bethesda, 20814

Creative Synergy Inc, 13660 Spinning Wheel Dr, Germantown, 20874-2819

Daly Communications, 5630 Wisconsin Ave (#903), Chevy Chase, 20815-4456

Iris Marketing, 1303 Harling Ct, Bel Air, 21015-5029

PMG, 7160 Columbia Gateway Dr (Suite 300), Columbia, 21046-2134

ProjectSense, 602 Whispering Wind Ct, Gaithersburg, 20877-3418

Roland Advisors, 4 Norwood Rd, Annapolis, 21401-1227

Webb Mason, 10830 Gilroy Rd, Hunt Valley, 21031-4312

MASSACHUSETTS

Accenture, 800 Boylston St (#2300), Boston, 02199

Atlantic-ACM, One Beacon St (fl 34), Boston, 02108

Bernheimer Associates, 10 Laurel Ave, Wellesley, 02481-7534

ClickSquared, 280 Summer St (Suite 600), Boston, 02210-1131

CopyDirect, 39 Forge Dr, Plymouth, 02360-2508

Cramer, 425 University Ave, Norwood, 02062-2636

Mary Culnan, 175 Forest St, Smith Technology Ctr 322, Waltham, 02452

MJ Curran & Associates Inc, 304 Newbury St (Apt 509), Boston, 02115

DBMCatalyst, 152 Railroad St, Holliston, 01746-2165

The Devereux Group, 47 Locust St, Little Harbour, Marblehead, 01945-2935

Directives/Targeted Marketing and Communications, 1022 Avalon Way, Plymouth, 02360-7777

Executive Search International, 1525 Centre St, Newton, 02461-1200

The Forum Corp, 265 Franklin St (Suite 400), Boston, 02110-3182

Gilchrist & Partners, 542 Mass Ave, Boston, 02118-1439

iKnowtion LLC, 25 Burlington Mall Rd (Suite 409), Burlington, 01803-4156

Kochevar Research Associates, PO Box 290010, Charlestown, 02129-0201

Kowal & Associates Inc, 620 Massachusetts Ave, Cambridge, 02139-3376

Arthur D Little Inc, 1 Federal St (fl 28), Boston, 02110-2011

LoyaltyOne, 3 Bessom St (Suite 211), Marblehead, 01945-2372

Market Recognition, 112 Prescott Rd, Boxborough, 01719-1121

Monster Worldwide, 133 Boston Post Rd (#15), Weston, 02493-2525

Percipio Media, LLC, 201 Broadway (Suite 7), Cambridge, 02139-1955

Productivity Development Group Inc, PO Box 488, Westford, 01886

The Results Group, 65 E India Row (Suite 37F), Harbor Towers, Boston, 02110-3323

Bruce Rhodes, 83 Victoria Rd, Sudbury, 01776-3139

Alan Rosenspan & Associates, 34 Summit Ave, Sharon, 02067-2149

Statistical Innovations Inc, 375 Concord Ave, Belmont, 02478-3084

Systems Analytics Inc, 946 Great Plain Ave (#125), Needham, 02492-3030

Teres Consulting Inc, Nine Magnolia St, Framingham, 01701-4913

The Yankee Group, One Liberty Sq (fl 7), Boston, 02109-4868

MICHIGAN

Advertising Network Solutions, 109 N Washington St, Oxford, 48371-4670

BJT Management Group, 8303 Baileau Oaks Dr NE, Ada, 49301-9764

Customer Retention Solutions, 7837 S Sprinkle Rd, Portage, 49002-9432

Directions Marketing, 505 Green Rd, Ann Arbor, 48105

Marketing Solutions, 28252 Woodworth Way, Lathrup Village, 48076-2518

Signature Inc, 4701 Midway Dr, Ann Arbor, 48103

Urban Science Applications Inc, 200 Renaissance Ctr (Suite 1800), Detroit, 48243-1306

MINNESOTA

Clario Analytics, 7684 Golden Triangle Dr, Eden Prairie, 55344-3732

DWS Associates, 1032 Saint Johns Bay, Saint Paul, 55129-8537

Ecoenvelopes, 17800 George Moran Dr, Eden Prairie, 55347

Engagenextgen LLC, 5463 Bartlett Blvd, Mound, 55364-1605

Group 3 Marketing, 1907 Wayzata Blvd (Suite 200), Wayzata, 55391-2070

IC System Inc, PO Box 64378, Saint Paul, 55164

Independent Consultant, 2307 Boxwood Ave E, Saint Paul, 55119-5670

Ovative/Group LLC, 701 Washington Ave N (#400), Minneapolis, 55401-0096

Product to Market LLC, 4536 County Rd 4 SW, Cokato, 55321-4220

RDO Marketing LLC, 4820 W 77th St (Suite 120), Minneapolis, 55435-4809

Reichert & Associates Inc, PO Box 268, Grand Marais, 55604

Schulte Associates, 2807 Polk St NE, Minneapolis, 55418-2954

Solutran, 3600 Holly Ln (Suite 60), Plymouth, 55447

Stockham Consulting, 7300 Butterscotch Rd, Eden Prairie, 55346-3233

Whitney Worldwide Inc, 553 Hayward Ave N (Suite 250), Saint Paul, 55128-9006

MISSOURI

Avantus, 2463 Schuetz Rd, Maryland Heights, 63043-3314

Colarelli Meyer & Associates Inc, 7751 Carondelet Ave (Suite 302), Saint Louis, 63105-3316

Collinger & Associates, 590 Sarah Ln (Apt 401), Saint Louis, 63141-6968

Hemisphere Marketing, 6437 Washington St, Kansas City, 64113-1731

LandaJob, 222 W Gregory Blvd (Suite 304), Kansas City, 64114-1127

Masten Publishing Systems, PO Box 6074, Chesterfield, 63006-6074

Outsourcing Solutions Inc, PO Box 407, Wentzville, 63385-0407

NEBRASKA

First of Omaha Merchant Processing, 1620 Dodge St, Omaha, 68197

Integrated Marketing Solutions (IMS), 30108 Kimberly Dr, Ashland, 68003-3806

West Corp, 11808 Miracle Hills Dr, Omaha, 68154

NEVADA

Pamela Cotrupe, 129 S Royal Ascot Dr, Las Vegas, 89144-4309

NEW HAMPSHIRE

ASH Recruitment Solutions, PO Box 888, Exeter, 03833-0888

Concept Communications, 400 Amherst St, Nashua, 03063-1241

DM Assistance Inc, 155 Fleet St, Portsmouth, 03801-4050

Rapid Insight Inc, 53 Technology Ln (Suite 112), Conway, 03818-5804

NEW JERSEY

Allen Consulting, 89 Middletown Rd, Holmdel, 07733-2203

Alliance Direct Marketing Solutions LLC, 665 Newark Ave (Suite 408), Jersey City, 07306

American Catalog Partnerships LLC, 392 Morris Ave, Summit, 07901-4734

BBC Direct Mktg Svcs, 361 Oak Shade Rd, Shamong, 08088

Baier Stein Direct, 211 Dryden Rd, Bernardsville, 07924-1108

Capell & Associates, 601 Central Ave, Barnegat Light, 08006

Caugherty Hahn Communications, 233 Rock Rd (Suite 248), Glen Rock, 07452-1708

The Chubb Corp, 15 Mountainview Rd, Warren, 07059

Didactic Systems, PO Box 457, Cranford, 07016-0457

E Media Advantage, Six Hamilton Ln, Livingston, 07039-2006

Gillespie Magazine Marketing & Publishing, 3450 Princeton Pike, Lawrenceville, 08648

International Corp, 225 Division Ave, Hasbrouck Heights, 07604-1719

JRB Marketing Group, 93 Einstein Way, East Windsor, 08512-2549

Judith Kennerk, 11 Scott Ave, Princeton Junction, 08550-1005

Leaps & Bounds LLC, 100 Old Palisades Rd (Suite 2409), Fort Lee, 07024-7021

Libey-Concordia, 811 Church Rd (Suite 105), Cherry Hill, 08002

Marketing Systems Analysis, 108 N Washington Ave, Ventnor, 08406-1961

Marketsmith Inc, 14 Walsh Dr (Floor 200), Parsippany, 07054-1063

Medavante, 100 American Metro Blvd (Suite 106), Hamilton, 08619-2319

Milrod Executive Search, 22 Riverside Dr, Princeton, 08540-4017

OSG Billing, 100 W Forest Ave (Suite G), Englewood, 07631-4033

Practical Computer Solutions, 154 Brentwood Dr, South Orange, 07079-1141

Privacy & Information Practices Advisory, 10 Gristmill Ln, Saddle River, 07458-1317

Response Design Corp, 5541 Simpson Ave, Ocean City, 08226-1258

Smith O'Keefe & Associates, 1566 Somers Point Rd, Egg Harbor Township, 08234-8514

Thinkalytics, 440 Millburn Ave, Millburn, 07041-1210

Tucker Capital Corp, 234 Nassau St (Suite 3), Princeton, 08542-4614

USY Consulting Inc, 50 Highwood Dr, Dumont, 07628-2608

Vertical Media Group, 2200 N Central Rd, Fort Lee, 07024-7557

Williams, Caliri, Miller & Otley, 1428 Rte 23, Wayne, 07474-5826

NEW MEXICO

Deborah Hoffman Copywriting, 306 Sagebrush Dr, Corrales, 87048-8552

NEW YORK

Ad Hoc Marketing Resources Inc, 15 W 72nd St, New York, 10023

Adecco Employment Services, 175 Broadhollow Rd, Melville, 11747-4902

Agency.com, 488 Madison Ave (fl 22), New York, 10022

American Society of Mechanical Engineers, Three Park Ave, New York, 10016-5990

Analytic Recruiting Inc, 144 E 44th St Ste 301, New York, 10017-4055

Arich Corp, 150 Central Park S (Suite 3210), New York, 10019-1566

Auriemma Consulting Group, 120 Broadway (Ste 3401), New York, 10271-3400

Black & Co, 232 Madison Ave (Suite 1400), New York, 10016

The Boston Consulting Group, 430 Park Ave Fl 14, New York, 10022-3528

Boyden Global Executive Search, 3 Manhattanville Rd (Suite 104), Building 3, Purchase, 10577-2116

Capgemini Americas Outsourcing, 623 Fifth Ave (fl 33), New York, 10022

Career Blazers, 5 W 37th St (fl 5), New York, 10018-5384

Andrea B Cautela, 111 Worth St, New York, 10013-4008

Cohen & Co, 281 Hicks St, Brooklyn, 11201-4508

Communispond Inc, 5 Lauras Ln, East Hampton, 11937-5916

Crandall Associates Inc, 6 Litchfield Rd # 316, Port Washington, 11050-3815

John Cummings & Partners LLC, Six Blair Rd, Armonk, 10504-2522

DB Consulting, 550 Mamaroneck Ave, Harrison, 10528

DCJ Consulting, 6749 Exeter St, Forest Hills, 11375-4150

Chet Dalzell, 145 E 29th St (Apt 6D), New York, 10016-8146

Daniel Gonzalez & Associates, 939 8th Ave (#300), New York, 10019-4205

Davis & Gilbert, 1740 Broadway, New York, 10019-4379

Bert Davis Executive Search, 425 Madison Ave (fl 14), New York, 10017-1110

Denmark Francisco, 684 9th Ave (fl 4), New York, 10036-3612

Direct Marketers On Call Inc (DMOC), 45 Christopher St (Apt 4A), New York, 10014-3585

Direct Ventures Inc, 720 Milton Rd (Apt W4D), Rye, 10580-3252

EBM Direct Marketing Services LLC, 39 Seaview Ln, Port Washington, 11050-1737

Eastern Collection Corp, 16 Barclay Dr, Sag Harbor, 11963-4316

Edelman Direct Marketing Inc, 75 Fairview Ave, Great Neck, 11023-1350

eMarketing Strategy Group, 155 E 34th St (Suite 20-C), New York, 10016-4718

Ernan Roman Direct Marketing Corp, 3 Melrose Ln, Little Neck, 11363-1220

Ernst & Young LLP, 5 Times Sq, New York, 10036-6527

Cynthia Fields & Co (CFC), 230 W 22nd St, New York, 10011-2701

FlarePath LLC, PO Box 111, Canaan, 12029-0111

Focus on the ROI, 97 Gem Ln, Massapequa Park, 11762-3222

Furguiele & Co Inc, 276 Read Ave, Crestwood, 10707

Global Marketing Group Ltd, 119 W 57th St (Suite 1405), New York, 10019-2401

Barbara Gold, 10 W 15th (Apt 1924), New York, 10011-6850

Goodman & Co, PO Box 835, New York, 10024-0540

GreenPath Sustainability Consultants, 13 Windgate Dr, New City, 10956-4434

Grey Birch Group LLC, 64 Sycamore Ln, Irvington, 10533-1931

Gordon W Grossman Inc, 254 Salem Rd, Pound Ridge, 10576-1320

Gundersen Partners LLC, 30 Irving Pl (fl 2), New York, 10003

Hal Levy & Associates, 186 Mohonk Rd, High Falls, 12440-5229

Elizabeth Hartman, 5 Azalea Dr, Syosset, 11791-2802

Hauser List Services, NMIS, 2545 Hempstead Tpke (Suite 401), East Meadow, 11554-2144

Howard-Sloan-Koller Group, 300 E 42nd St Fl 15, New York, 10017-5925

EA Hughes & Co, 200 Park Ave S (Suite 1608), New York, 10003-1521

IPG, 532 W 22nd St (Apt 3C), New York, 10011-1117

Imagine 360 Marketing, 1123 Broadway (Suite 902), New York, 10010-2007

Infomorphosis/Marketing Solutions, 152 W 20th St (Suite D), New York, 10011-3635

JLMC, 15 Park Row (17E), New York, 10038-2301

Jack Schecterson visualmarketing Consultants, 5316 251st Pl, Little Neck, 11362-1711

Kenzer Group, LLC, One Penn Plaza (Suite 6300), New York, 10119

Liz Kislik Associates LLC, 100 Merrick Rd (Suite 505E), Rockville Centre, 11570-4834

Richard Law, 166 E 3rd St, Deer Park, 11729-5307

Nancy Liss, 233 E 32nd St, New York, 10016-6336

Lister Butler Inc, 445 Park Ave (Suite 1401), New York, 10022-8626

Loeb & Loeb Inc, 345 Park Ave, New York, 10154-0004

MLB Associates, 1936 Saranac Ave (Suite 2-300), Lake Placid, 12946-1114

Mapping Analytics, 120 Allens Creek Rd, Rochester, 14618-3306

Marketrac Inc, 300 Roosevelt Way, Westbury, 11590-6700

Shannon McDonald, 205 W 88 St (#9D), New York, 10024

McKinsey & Co, 55 E 52nd St (fl 21), New York, 10055-0183

Media Recruiting Group Inc, 1 Bridge St (Suite P2), Irvington, 10533-1575

Adrian Miller Direct Marketing, 43 Park Ave, Port Washington, 11050-4010

Fred Milman Associates, 23 Selina Ct, Glen Cove, 11542-3048

MIMAARTS LLC, 535 Fifth Ave (fl 31), New York, 10017-3667

NAK Marketing & Communications, 575 Madison Ave (Suite 700), New York, 10022-8512

Oak Knoll Limited Liability Co, 7 Hastings Ct, South Salem, 10590-2517

Glen Orenstein, 2959 Judith Dr, Merrick, 11566-5448

Paul, Hastings, Janofsky & Walker LLP, 75 E 55th St, Park Avenue Tower, New York, 10022-3205

Publishing Fulfillment Consulting LLC, 85 Settlers Hill Rd, Brewster, 10509-5210

Lynda Raihofer & Associates LLC, 48 Young Ave, Pelham, 10803-1724

Rainwater Associates Inc, 135 E 71st St, New York, 10021-4258

Redwood Partners Ltd, 60 E 42nd St (Rm 1820), New York, 10165-6210

Reed Smith Hall Dickler Advertising & Law Marketing Group, 599 Lexington Ave (Floor 29), New York, 10022

Retrieval Masters Creditors Bureau Inc, 4 Westchester Plz (Suite 110), Elmsford, 10523-1615

Ross Culbert & Lavery, 900 Broadway (#401), New York, 10003

Anne Ruth, 6 Alden Pl Apt 1D, Bronxville, 10708-4846

SIGMA Marketing Group LLC, 1850 S Winton Rd, Rochester, 14618-3923

SKO-Brenner-American, 841 Merrick Rd CS 9320, Baldwin, 11510-9320

Sandler Techworks, 525 E 82nd St (Suite 2G), New York, 10028-7148

Satisfaction Software Inc, 8711 150th St, Jamaica, 11435-3107

Schupak Group Inc, 595 Madison Ave (Room 1900), New York, 10022-1958

Severini Communications LLC, 2025 W Broadway 16K, New York, 10023

Shasho Jones Direct Inc, 145 W 67th St (#4D), New York, 10023-5930

David Shepard Associates Inc, 332 Altessa Blvd, Melville, 11747-5222

Kate Shifman Consulting, 179 Saint Johns Pl (Apt 2), Brooklyn, 11217-3417

Ray Slyper Associates, 420 E 72nd St (Suite 2L), New York, 10021

Smart Source Direct, 1185 Ave of the Americas (fl 27), News America Marketing, New York, 10036-2603

Debbie Sorace, 70 Edwards Pl, Valley Stream, 11580-3143

Stagg Direct Marketing Inc, 11 Gorham Rd, Scarsdale, 10583-1117

Stephen-Bradford Search, 555th Ave (Rm 300), New York, 10017-9288

Stephens Inc, 65 E 55th St (Floor 22), New York, 10022-3369

Elizabeth Streitz & Associates, 255 W 108th St (Suite 9A), New York, 10025

TSI, 350 Northern Blvd (Suite 308), Albany, 12204-1028

TeleManagement Search, 6 Litchfield Rd (Suite 316), Port Washington, 11050-3815

Tolliver Inc, 303 5th Ave (Rm 206), New York, 10016-6690

Towers Watson, 875 Third Ave, New York, 10022

Karen Tripi Associates, 305 Madison Ave (Suite 2319), New York, 10165-6209

The Troyanos Group Ltd, 106 N Broadway (fl 3), Irvington, 10533-1262

Gilbert Tweed Associates, 415 Madison Ave (fl 20), New York, 10017

WLA Inc, 535 5th Ave (Floor 31), New York, 10017-3667

Wakefield Talabisco International, 11 E 44th St (Rm 1206), New York, 10017-3608

Steve Wexler Creative Group, PO Box 219, Farmingville, 11738-0219

Winston & Winston PC, 295 Madison Ave, New York, 10017

Winterberry Group, 60 Broad St (Suite 3810), New York, 10004-2329

Brian Wolfe, 418 E 59th St (Apt 26A), New York, 10022-2378

RL Zapin Associates Inc, 708 Third Ave (fl 6), New York, 10017

Neil Zelenetz & Associates, 219 Kings Point Rd, East Hampton, 11937-3047

Zimmerman Business Consulting Inc, 44 E 92nd St (Suite 5B), New York, 10128-1319

NORTH CAROLINA

AKS Marketing & Media, 200 Chimeneas Pl, Chapel Hill, 27517-8389

Altman Dedicated Direct, 853 Academy St, Rural Hall, 27045-9329

Beechtree Assoc Inc, 216 Whisperwood Dr (Suite 100), Cary, 27511

Clarity Group LLC, 600 Market St (Suite 302), Chapel Hill, 27516-4057

ClementDIRECT, 72109 Moseley, Chapel Hill, 27517-8574

T A Cook Consultants Inc, 9212 Falls of Neuse Rd (Suite 201), Raleigh, 27615-2483

Direct Marketing Resources, 517 Highland Forest Dr, Charlotte, 28270-0848

Direct Marketing Resources Group Inc, 4501 Newborn Ave (Suite 130-253), Raleigh, 27610-1550

Group f/64, 1050 Arbor Rd, Winston-Salem, 27104

PrintCom Consulting Group, 1020 Farm Creek Rd, Waxhaw, 28173-7793

RSM McGladrey Inc, 4725 Piedmont Row Dr (Suite 300), Charlotte, 28210-4280

RW Consulting, 452 Sondley Woods Pl, Asheville, 28805

OHIO

The Ad Farm, 4041 W Central Ave, Ottawa Hills, 43606-2526

American Tax Associates Inc, 31 E Whittier St, Columbus, 43206-2026

Richard L Bencin & Associates, 2616 Hidden Canyon Dr, Brecksville, 44141-3530

Dovetail Art & Design Inc, 113 Wade Dr, Dover, 44622-9460

Eadon Ventures, 11224 Reeder Ave NE, Alliance, 44601-8332

Interactive Search Group, 35104 Euclid Ave (Suite 303), Cleveland, 44094

Kramer & Associates, 8044 Montgomery Rd (Suite 200), Bank One Towers, Cincinnati, 45236-2926

L3 Virtual Solutions LLC, 450 Township Rd (#208), Marengo, 43334

Laven & Loeb Inc, 2163 Halcyon Rd, Beachwood, 44122-1301

Mac Murray Petersen & Shuster LLP, 6530 W Campus Oval (Suite 210), New Albany, 43054-7069

Mastery Marketing Group, 2525 Tiller Ln, Columbus, 43231-2267

Richard Saunders International, 3849 Edwards Rd, Cincinnati, 45244

Sedlak, 22901 Millcreek Blvd (Suite 600), Metropolitan Plaza, Highland Hills, 44122-5724

Skystone Ryan, 635 W Seventh St (Suite 107), Cincinnati, 45203

TeleDevelopment Services Inc, PO Box 502, Richfield, 44286-0502

Transglobal Consultants Inc, 3210 Glastonbury Cir NW, Canton, 44708-1174

Wind River Group, 900 State Mill Rd, Akron, 44319-2138

OREGON

Effective Marketing Associates, Inc, 3525 Riverknoll Way, West Linn, 97068-3641

Interface Engineering, 708 SW Third Ave (Suite 400), Portland, 97204

Michel Consulting, 61903 Brokentop Dr, Bend, 97702-1085

SLR Associates, 3300 NW 185th Ave (PMB 268), Portland, 97229-3406

PENNSYLVANIA

The Beam Group, 414 Mill Creek Rd, Gladwyne, 19035-1519

Brandywine Consulting Group Inc, 1398 Morstein Rd (Suite 4), West Chester, 19380-5848

Col Voce Consulting, 551 Newcomen Rd, Exton, 19341-1938

Corpora Consulting, 42 W Market St, Bethlehem, 18018-5703

Direct Marketing Consultant, 399 Sherman Ave, Sharon, 16146-3953

The Diversified Services Group Inc, 303 W Lancaster Ave (Suite 2E), Wayne, 19087-3938

Denny Hatch Associates Inc, 310 Gaskill St, Philadelphia, 19147-1503

David Heneberry Associates, 111 Reynolds Ln, West Grove, 19390-1371

Infomercial Monitoring Service Inc, 10 N Church St (Suite 200), West Chester, 19380-3000

The Keystone Equities Group, 1003 Egypt Rd, Oaks, 19456-1155

Kistler-Tiffany Companies LLC, 1205 Westlakes Dr (Suite 290), Berwyn, 19312-2405

LTD Supply Chain, 3 Black Horse Cir, Downingtown, 19335-1552

Ken Malek Associates Inc, PO Box 383, Yardley, 19067-8383

Management Science Associates Inc, 6565 Penn Ave, Pittsburgh, 15206-4490

McBee Associates Inc, 997 Old Eagle School Rd (Suite 205), Wayne, 19087-1706

Media Management Services Inc, 105 Terry Dr (Suite 120), Newton, 18940-1872

Medina Associates, 12 Hilltop Rd, Rose Valley, 19086-6243

National Mail/Marketing Corp, 390 Reed Rd (fl 13), Broomall, 19008-4008

NigroNewMedia, 4004 Hermitage Hills Blvd (Apt 20), Hermitage, 16148-3420

Raab Associates, 730 Yale Ave, Swarthmore, 19081-1805

Spectrum Retail Associates, 10 E Athens Ave (Suite 200), Ardmore, 19003

Grant Thornton LLP, Two Commerce Square (Suite 3100), Philadelphia, 19103

Wesley R Weber & Associates, 405 Brookmeade Dr, West Chester, 19380

RHODE ISLAND

Mac McIntosh Inc, 601 Pendar Rd, North Kingstown, 02852-6620

Spaide, Kuipers & Co, 42 Second St, Newport, 02840

SOUTH CAROLINA

Blexrud Direct, 215 Indian Wells Dr, Spartanburg, 29306-6625

SOUTH DAKOTA

Bull Dog Media Group Inc, PO Box 463, Madison, 57042-0463

TENNESSEE

The Buffkin Group LLC, 10 Cadillac Dr (Suite 190), Brentwood, 37027

LucidView, 80 Rolling Links Blvd, Oak Ridge, 37830-9023

Marketing Consulting Services, 2669 Suffolk St, Kingsport, 37660-5803

TEXAS

ABCO Inc, 1621 Wall St, Dallas, 75215-1864

Audience Research & Development, 2440 Lofton Ter, Fort Worth, 76109-1123

Creating Selling Opportunities, 2902 W Lane Dr (Suite E), Houston, 77027

Creditcards.com, 9430 Research Blvd (Suite IV400), Austin, 78759-5769

Dodson & Associates, 16302 Shadybank Dr, Dallas, 75248-2957

Echotouch Corp, 5907 Carry Back Ln, Austin, 78746-1448

GC Services, 6330 Gulfton, Houston, 77081

Gibson Direct Inc, 204 Plantation Dr, Coppell, 75019-3232

Glengarry Marketing, 2303 RR 620 S Unit 135-150, Austin, 78734

Ed Golden & Associates, 7303 Shoal Creek Blvd, Austin, 78757-2028

Hatchholdings LLC, 5832 Broadwell Dr, Plano, 75093-4717

The Herman Group, 7112 Viridian Ln, Austin, 78739-2092

International Direct Marketing Consultants Inc, 3419 Westminster Ave, Dallas, 75205-1387

International Resource Management Co, 3008 Spring Valley Dr, Bedford, 76021-4245

Lion's Share Marketing Group, Inc, 5410 Schumacher Ln, Houston, 77056-6810

Moran Direct Inc, 710 N Post Oak Rd (Suite 520), Houston, 77024-3858

ProSource, 1502 Augusta Dr (Suite 100), Houston, 77057-2454

Pursuant Group, 5151 Beltline Rd (Suite 900), Dallas, 75254-6757

Savitz, 13747 Montfort Dr (Suite 117), Dallas, 75240-4499

Sheshunoff Management Services, 901 S Mo Pac Expy (Suite 140), Austin, 78746-5759

Shisler and Associates, 14917 Oaks North Dr (Suite 113), Dallas, 75254-7631

The Sound Direct Marketing Group, PO Box 162527, Austin, 78716-2527

TALX Corp, 14755 Preston Rd (Suite 525), Dallas, 75254-7898

VERMONT

Continuity Shippers Association, 2351 N Bridgewater Rd, Saddlebow Farm, Woodstock, 05091-9670

de Rham & Co Inc, 590 Danby Mountain Rd, Dorset, 05251

Coleman W Hoyt Consultant, 2351 N Bridgewater Rd, Saddlebow Farm, Woodstock, 05091-9670

Printmark, 432 Johnson Rd, East Montpelier, 05651-4250

Raphel Marketing, 211 North Ave, Saint Johnsbury, 05819-1626

Timberline Interactive, 5 Park St (Suite 2), Middlebury, 05753-1169

Windward Group, 241 Spinnaker Ln, Shelburne, 05482-7779

VIRGINIA

F Curtis Barry & Co, 2104 Willowick Ln, Henrico, 23238-3616

Blagman Creative/Direct Response, 13269 Triple Crown Loop, Gainesville, 20155-6668

Chapman Cubine Adams & Hussey, 1600 Wilson Blvd (Suite 300), Arlington, 22209-2505

Click2Mail, 3103 10th St N (Suite 201), Arlington, 22201-2191

Communications Unlimited Inc, 10129 Deepwood Cir, Richmond, 23238-4241

Dan Smolen Direct Search LLC, 44 Lightfoot Dr, Stafford, 22554-8509

DeHart & Darr Associates, 1360 Beverly Rd (Suite 201), McLean, 22101-3647

Erlandson Associates, 222 W Market St, Leesburg, 20176-2709

Foxhall Corporation, 6849 Old Dominion Dr (Suite 320), McLean, 22101-3791

Graduate Management Admission Council, 11921 Freedom Dr (Suite 300), Reston, 20190

NEW Customer Service Companies Inc, 22894 Pacific Blvd, Sterling, 20166-6722

Production Solutions, 1953 Gallows Rd (Suite 600), Vienna, 22182-3988

RedEngine Digital, 1485 Chain Bridge Rd (Suite 305), Mc Lean, 22101-4501

The Services Group (TSG), 2101 Wilson Blvd (Suite 700), Arlington, 22201-3060

Stateside Associates, 2300 Clarendon Blvd (Suite 407), Arlington, 22201-3300

Technical Assistance Research Programs (TARP), 2425 Wilson Blvd (Suite 400), Arlington, 22201

Turtle Bay Management Co Inc, 209 86th St (Suite E), Virginia Beach, 23451

Wagner Hines & Avary Inc, 218 N Lee St, Alexandria, 22314

West Cary Group, 5 W Cary St, Richmond, 23220-5609

WASHINGTON

brandUNITY Inc, PO Box 4512, Rollingbay, 98061-0512

Emailogics Inc/Emailbrain, 8100 NE Parkway Dr (Suite 300), Vancouver, 98662-7954

Sentinel Peak LLC, 15600 Redmond Way, Redmond, 98052

Strofina Inc, 10200 NE Garibaldi Loop, Bainbridge Island, 98110-3976

The Write Answers Copywriting & Consulting, 816 Peace Portal Dr (#82), Blaine, 98230-4010

WEST VIRGINIA

Marketing/Media Dynamics Inc, 197 Shannondale Rd, Harpers Ferry, 25425-4564

WISCONSIN

ABR Employment Services, 1402 Pankratz St (Suite 101), Madison, 53704-4046

Einhorn Associates Inc, 2675 N Mayfair Rd (Suite 410), Milwaukee, 53226

Hunter Business Group LLC, 4650 N Port Washington Rd Stop 8, Milwaukee, 53212-1078

The Kaiser Group Inc, 237 South St, Waukesha, 53186

Dorothy Kerr & Associates, 1509 E Standish Pl, Milwaukee, 52317-1960

Market Square Communications Inc, 1100 Centerpoint Dr (Suite 203), Stevens Point, 54481-2849

Miglautsch Marketing Inc, 555 S Industrial Dr (Suite 5), Hartland, 53029

NuEdge Systems, 4900 W Brown Deer Rd, Brown Deer, 53223

CANADA

Ontario

Cameron & Co, 83 Duggan Ave, Toronto, M4V 1Y1

Figurs*, 39a Fourth St, Toronto, M8V 2Y2

News Marketing Canada, 100 King St W (Suite 7000), One First Canadian Place, Toronto, M5X 1A4

Quebec

CakeMail Inc, 4020 St-Ambroise (Suite 145), Montreal, H4C 2C7

Ken Elo, 3863 Laval, Montreal, H2W 2H9

Komunik, 1500 St Patrick, Montreal, H3K 0A3

Publications Groupe RR International Inc, 2322 Sherbrooke E, Montreal, H2K 1E5

Consultants, Recruiters, Collection & Finance (20)

A PLUS MARKETING LTD
1300 Barclay Blvd
Buffalo Grove, IL 60089-4500
Telephone: (847) 537-1166, FAX:
  (847) 537-5611, Web Site: www.
  aplusmarketing.com
Pres: Greg Alberts
Founded: 1983

ABCO INC
1621 Wall St
Dallas, TX 75215-1864
Telephone: (214) 565-1191, Web Site:
  www.abcoinc.com
Pres: Leon Kaplan
COO: Elia Peres
CFO: Scott Jeffrey
Founded: 1956

**ABR EMPLOYMENT
  SERVICES**
Div. of Forward Service Corp
1402 Pankratz St (Suite 101)
Madison, WI 53704-4046
Telephone: (608) 244-3526, FAX:
  (608) 244-8279, E-Mail: info@
  abrjobs.com, Web Site: www.
  abrjobs.com
Mgr: Deborah Schaefer

ADM MARKETING
908 N Hollywood Way
Burbank, CA 91505-2815
Toll Free: (888) 800-1001
Founder: Stephen Farr-Jones

AKS MARKETING & MEDIA
200 Chimeneas Pl
Chapel Hill, NC 27517-8389
Telephone: (919) 240-5496
CEO: Markus Wilhelm
Primary Market Served: Business &
  Consumer

**ASH RECRUITMENT
  SOLUTIONS**
PO Box 888
Exeter, NH 03833-0888
Telephone: (603) 778-8888, E-Mail: t.
  hall@ashrecruit.com, Web Site:
  www.ashrecruit.com
Principal: Anthony Hall
Primary Market Served: Business
Advertising/Marketing Budget Related
  to Direct Marketing: 76-100%
Founded: 2001

AVD MARKETING
4113 Trenton Ave
Hollywood, FL 33026-4923

Telephone: (954) 410-9000, Web Site:
  www.avdmarketing.com
Principal: Andre Doren
Primary Market Served: Business &
  Consumer

ABILITY COMMERCE
A Marketing Concepts Company
1300 NW 17th Ave (Suite 200)
Delray Beach, FL 33445-2560
Telephone: (561) 330-3151, Web Site:
  www.abilitycommerce.com
Pres: Terence Jukes
Founder & CEO: Diane Buzzeo
VP: Debbie Longo
VP Fin: David Faidley
Dir Tech: Patrick Reineke
Dir Sales & Mktg: Shawn Ellen

ABOUT BOOKS INC
1001 Taurus Dr
Colorado Springs, CO 80906-1133
Telephone: (719) 632-8226, FAX:
  (719) 471-2182, E-Mail: infoabi2@
  about-books.com, Web Site: www.
  about-books.com
Pres: Tom Ross

**ACCENT MARKETING
  SERVICES LLC**
400 Missouri Ave (Suite 100)
Jeffersonville, IN 47130-3086
Telephone: (812) 206-6200, Web Site:
  www.accentonline.com
Pres & CEO: Kevin Foley

ACCENTURE
800 Boylston St (#2300)
Boston, MA 02199
Telephone: (617) 488-4000, FAX:
  (617) 488-4001, Web Site: www.
  accenture.com
Assoc Partner: Robert Mann Jr.

**ACCESS BUSINESS
  COMMUNICATIONS INC**
5611 Ocean Terrace Dr
Huntington Beach, CA 92648-7511
Toll Free: (800) 675-2415, Web Site:
  www.abcimarketing.com
Pres: Jack Bogle

**ACTUARIAL ENTERPRISES
  LTD**
920 N Franklin St (Suite 401)
Chicago, IL 60610-3186
Telephone: (312) 397-0099, E-Mail:
  jay@actentltd.com
Pres: Jay M. Jaffe

THE AD FARM
4041 W Central Ave
Ottawa Hills, OH 43606-2526
Telephone: (419) 720-5676, Web Site:
  www.theadfarm.com
Pres: Jonathan Downing
Founded: 2008

**AD HOC MARKETING
  RESOURCES INC**
15 W 72nd St
New York, NY 10023
Telephone: (212) 595-1800, FAX:
  (212) 656-1860, E-Mail:
  adhocmrktg@aol.com, Web Site:
  www.members.aol.com/adhocmrktg
Pres: Karen Hochman

**ADECCO EMPLOYMENT
  SERVICES**
175 Broadhollow Rd
Melville, NY 11747-4902
Telephone: (631) 844-7800, Web Site:
  www.adecco.com
Mktg: Ed Blust

**ADVERTISING NETWORK
  SOLUTIONS**
109 N Washington St
Oxford, MI 48371-4670
Telephone: (248) 475-7845, Web Site:
  www.adnetworksolutions.com
Pres: Jeff Fasseel
Primary Market Served: Business &
  Consumer

AGENCY.COM
Sub of The Designory Inc.
488 Madison Ave (fl 22)
New York, NY 10022
Telephone: (212) 358-2600, FAX:
  (212) 358-2604, Web Site: www.
  agency.com
Worldwide CEO: David Eastman
Founded: 1995

THE ALDRICH GROUP
43 Sherman Hill Rd D-104
Woodbury, CT 06798
Telephone: (860) 274-7693, (203) 263-
  5505, FAX: (203) 263-5572, E-Mail:
  jeff.aldrich@aldrichsearch.com, Web
  Site: www.aldrichsearch.com
Principal: Jeff Aldrich
Dir Bus Devel Opers: J Andrew Hib-
  bert
Dir IT & Fulfillment Opers: P Daniel
  Riley

ALEXANDER & CO LLC
178 Water St

Stonington, CT 06378
Telephone: (860) 535-9160, FAX:
(860) 535-9161, E-Mail: jraandco@
aol.com
Pres: James R. Alexander

ALLEN CONSULTING
89 Middletown Rd
Holmdel, NJ 07733-2203
Telephone: (732) 946-2711, FAX:
(732) 946-8032, E-Mail: sylvia@
allenconsulting.com, Web Site:
www.allenconsulting.com
Pres: Sylvia Allen

**ALLEN, MATKINS, LECK,
GAMBLE & MALLORY**
515 S Figueroa St (fl 9)
Los Angeles, CA 90071-3398
Telephone: (213) 622-5555, FAX:
(213) 620-8816, E-Mail:
communications@allenmatkins.com,
Web Site: www.allenmatkins.com
Mng Partner: Brian Leck
Oper Partner: George T McDonnell

**ALLIANCE DIRECT
MARKETING SOLUTIONS
LLC**
665 Newark Ave (Suite 408)
Jersey City, NJ 07306
Telephone: (201) 863-1360, Toll Free:
(888) 455-2367, FAX: (201) 863-
3910, E-Mail: vteran@
alliancedirectleads.com, Web Site:
www.alliancedirectleads.com
Pres: Vivian Teran
Conducts Business: US
Employees: 10
Primary Market Served: Business &
Consumer
Direct online sales
Advertising/Marketing Budget Related
to Direct Marketing: 0-25%
Founded: 2002
Gross sales or billing: $200,000

List broker of business, consumer,
email, data processing and printing.

**ALLPRO DIRECT
MARKETING**
11626 Prosperous Dr
Odessa, FL 33556
Telephone: (888) 679-0255, (727) 375-
1502, Toll Free: (866) 472-3982,
FAX: (727) 499-7999, Web Site:
www.allprodirectmarketing.com
Primary Market Served: Business &
Consumer
Founded: 1982

Full service direct mail & printing service.

**ALTMAN DEDICATED
DIRECT**
853 Academy St
Rural Hall, NC 27045-9329
Telephone: (336) 969-9538, FAX:
(336) 969-0187, E-Mail: saltman@
AltmanDedicatedDirect.com, Web
Site: www.altmandedicateddirect.
com
Pres: Shari Altman
Founded: 1999

**AMERICAN CATALOG
PARTNERSHIPS LLC**
392 Morris Ave
Summit, NJ 07901-4734
Telephone: (908) 598-1947
Chmn: Theodore Pamperin

**AMERICAN MARKETING &
COMMUNICATION CORP**
14201 Pennsylvania Ave
Hagerstown, MD 21742-1665
Telephone: (240) 625-9225, FAX:
(240) 625-9235, E-Mail: info@
amcc1.com, Web Site: www.
americanmarketingcc.com
Pres & CEO: Lisa C. Boyle

**AMERICAN SOCIETY OF
MECHANICAL ENGINEERS**
Three Park Ave
New York, NY 10016-5990
Telephone: (973) 882-1167, Toll Free:
(800) 843-2763, FAX: (973) 882-
1717, E-Mail: infocentral@asme.org,
Web Site: www.asme.org
Chair: J. R. Sims

**AMERICAN TAX
ASSOCIATES INC**
31 E Whittier St
Columbus, OH 43206-2026
Telephone: (614) 443-5343, FAX:
(614) 443-0279
Pres: Dale H. Durley

**AMTOWER & CO FEDERAL
DIRECT**
PO Box 314
Highland, MD 20777-0314
Telephone: (240) 882-9546, E-Mail:
markamtower@gmail.com, Web
Site: www.federaldirect.net
Partner: Mark Amtower
Founded: 1985

ANALYTIC RECRUITING INC
144 E 44th St Ste 301
New York, NY 10017-4055

Telephone: (212) 545-8511, FAX:
(212) 545-8520, E-Mail: rita@
analyticrecruiting.com, Web Site:
www.analyticrecruiting.com
Pres: Rita Raz
Founded: 1980

Experienced in Database Marketing,
Marketing Analytics, Digital Analytics
& Strategy, Customer Insights & Marketing Management. Works with clients in matching skills, career goals &
positions.

ANDERSON/SKOW
690 Texas St
San Francisco, CA 94107-2941
Toll Free: (888) 983-0880, Web Site:
www.andersonskow.com
Pres: Kathi Skow
Primary Market Served: Business &
Consumer

**APPLICATIONS
DEVELOPMENT CORP**
3101 Wolf Ct
Dekalb, IL 60115-8257
Toll Free: (815) 754-7432, Web Site:
www.appdevcorp.com
CEO: John Jencks
Founded: 1995

ARICH CORP
150 Central Park S (Suite 3210)
New York, NY 10019-1566
Telephone: (212) 247-1800, FAX:
(212) 247-2231, Web Site: www.
arichinc.com
Pres & CEO: Richard F. Gray

**ARLEN COMMUNICATIONS
INC**
7315 Wisconsin Ave (Suite 705E)
Bethesda, MD 20814
Telephone: (301) 656-7940, E-Mail:
info@arlencom.com, Web Site:
www.arlencom.com
Pres: Gary Arlen

Research & consulting firm.

**AS KLEEMAN &
ASSOCIATES**
1416 Spyglass Hill Dr
Duluth, GA 30097-5948
Telephone: (770) 752-0500, FAX:
(770) 752-0066
Pres: Alan Kleeman

ATLANTIC-ACM
One Beacon St (fl 34)
Boston, MA 02108

Telephone: (617) 720-3700, FAX:
(617) 720-1077, E-Mail: atlantic@
atlantic-acm.com, Web Site: www.
atlantic-acm.com
CEO: Judy Reed Smith
Pres: Fedor Smith

AUDIENCE RESEARCH & DEVELOPMENT
2440 Lofton Ter
Fort Worth, TX 76109-1123
Telephone: (817) 924-6922, FAX:
(817) 924-7539, E-Mail: jgumbert@
ar-d.com, Web Site: www.ar-d.com
Principal & Sr VP: Jim Willi
Pres & CEO: Jerry Gumbert
Chief Mktg Svcs Officer: Robin Hoff-
man

AURIEMMA CONSULTING GROUP
120 Broadway (Ste 3401)
New York, NY 10271-3400
Telephone: (516) 333-4800, FAX:
(516) 333-4815, E-Mail: info@acg.
net, Web Site: www.acg.net
Pres: Michael Auriemma
Exec VP: Marc Sacher

AVANTUS
2463 Schuetz Rd
Maryland Heights, MO 63043-3314
Telephone: (314) 994-3449, Web Site:
www.avantus.com
Pres: Louis R. Capobianco
Primary Market Served: Business &
Consumer

BBC DIRECT MKTG SVCS
dba BBC Worldwide
361 Oak Shade Rd
Shamong, NJ 08088
Telephone: (609) 268-9919, Toll Free:
(877) 786-4389, FAX: (609) 268-
9939, E-Mail: csr@bbcglobal.com,
Web Site: www.bbcglobal.com
Pres: Clarence Reichenbach Jr.
VP: C. Stephen Reichenbach
Opers Mgr: Rachel McCormick
Conducts Business: U.S., Canada
Primary Market Served: Business

3PL Transportation Logistics, Warehousing & Distribution.

BJT MANAGEMENT GROUP
8303 Baileau Oaks Dr NE
Ada, MI 49301-9764
Telephone: (616) 682-0369, Web Site:
www.bjtmgt.com
Pres & CEO: Robert Ostertag
Primary Market Served: Consumer

Provides management services to companies

BAIER STEIN DIRECT
211 Dryden Rd
Bernardsville, NJ 07924-1108
Telephone: (908) 781-7849, Web Site:
www.directcopy.com
Pres: Donna Baier Stein
Founded: 2011

BAKER & HOSTETLER LLP
1050 Connecticut Ave NW (Suite
1100)
Washington, DC 20036-5304
Telephone: (202) 861-1500, FAX:
(202) 861-1783, E-Mail:
wschweitzer@bakerlaw.com, Web
Site: www.bakerlaw.com
Partner: William H. Schweitzer
Mng Partner: Jeffrey H Paravano
Exec Partner: R Steven Kestner

F CURTIS BARRY & CO
2104 Willowick Ln
Henrico, VA 23238-3616
Telephone: (804) 740-8743, FAX:
(804) 740-6179, E-Mail: cbarry@
fcbco.com, Web Site: www.fcbco.
com
Pres: Curt Barry

DIANA BATY
109 Sullivan Dr
Moraga, CA 94556-1211
Telephone: (202) 689-5332
Primary Market Served: Consumer

THE BEAM GROUP
414 Mill Creek Rd
Gladwyne, PA 19035-1519
Telephone: (215) 988-2100, FAX:
(215) 988-1558, Web Site: www.
beamgroup.com
Pres: Russell Glicksman
Founded: 1989

RICH BECKER & ASSOCIATES/PUMP-EM-UP PUBLISHING, IN PUBLIC RELATIONS
9225 Woodstone Ln
Lenexa, KS 66219-1959
Telephone: (913) 894-9530, FAX:
(913) 894-9530, E-Mail: rbecker@
kc.rr.com
Pres: Rich Becker

BEECHTREE ASSOC INC
216 Whisperwood Dr (Suite 100)
Cary, NC 27511
Telephone: (919) 852-1800, FAX:
(919) 852-4400, E-Mail: jfoliano@
aol.com
Pres: Jay Foliano

RICHARD L BENCIN & ASSOCIATES
2616 Hidden Canyon Dr
Brecksville, OH 44141-3530
Telephone: (440) 526-6726, FAX:
(440) 546-1623, E-Mail: rlbencin@
netzero.net, Web Site: www.rlbencin.
com
Pres: Richard L. Bencin
Conducts Business: Worldwide
Employees: 4
Primary Market Served: Business
Founded: 1981
Gross sales or billing: $1,000,000

Recruiting services for both the direct
marketing & center industries.

BENNETTBAKER LTD
33 W Monroe St (Suite 2110)
Chicago, IL 60603-5414
Telephone: (312) 252-8883, FAX:
(312) 252-8209, E-Mail: nbennett@
bennettwheelless.com, Web Site:
www.bennettbaker.com
CEO/Founder: Neysa Bennett
Recruiter: Heather Baker
Conducts Business: U.S.
Employees: 2
Primary Market Served: Business
Advertising/Marketing Budget Related
to Direct Marketing: 76-100%
Direct Marketing ad budget:
Direct Mail: 70%
Telephone: 30%
Founded: 1987

Executive search firm for the direct
marketing and internet marketing industries.

BERNHEIMER ASSOCIATES
10 Laurel Ave
Wellesley, MA 02481-7534
Telephone: (781) 237-8910, FAX:
(781) 239-2932, E-Mail: wsbii@
hotmail.com, Web Site: bernheimer.
com
Pres: Walter Bernheimer II

BILLIN MEDINA-WARREN
8655 E Via de Ventura (#G200)
Scottsdale, AZ 85258-3300
Telephone: (972) 951-7291
Principal: Billin Medina-Warren
Founded: 2010

BLACK & CO
232 Madison Ave (Suite 1400)
New York, NY 10016
Telephone: (212) 867-5533, FAX:
(212) 447-0785, E-Mail:
wblack6340@aol.com
Pres: William Black

BLAGMAN CREATIVE/ DIRECT RESPONSE
13269 Triple Crown Loop
Gainesville, VA 20155-6668
Telephone: (703) 743-2493, E-Mail:
jackbee21@comcast.net
Pres: Jack Blagman

BLATTEIS COMMUNICATIONS
2335 W Hedding St
San Jose, CA 95128-1327
Telephone: (901) 356-0090, Web Site:
www.blatteis.com
Owner: Beatrice Blatteis
Primary Market Served: Business &
Consumer

BLEXRUD DIRECT
215 Indian Wells Dr
Spartanburg, SC 29306-6625
Telephone: (864) 583-7399, FAX:
(864) 583-7399, E-Mail: blexrud@
bellsouth.net
Pres: Tom Blexrud
Partner: Paul Starck
Conducts Business: U.S.
Employees: 1
Primary Market Served: Business &
Consumer
Advertising/Marketing Budget Related
to Direct Marketing: 0-25%
Founded: 1987

Direct marketing consulting services.

BLOOM, HERGOTT, DIEMER, ROSENTHAL AND LAVIOLETTE LLP
150 S Rodeo Dr (fl 3)
Beverly Hills, CA 90212-2410
Telephone: (310) 859-6800, FAX:
(310) 860-6820, E-Mail: sfb@bhdrl.
com
Partner: Stephen F. Breimer
Founded: 1971

BLUM & CO LLC
81 Clinton St
Fairfield, CT 06824-6908
Telephone: (203) 255-4813, FAX:
(203) 255-3936, E-Mail: e-blum@att.
net, Web Site: www.blumdirect.com
Pres: Sandra J. Blum

THE BOSTON CONSULTING GROUP
430 Park Ave Fl 14
New York, NY 10022-3528
Telephone: (212) 446-2800
Lead Researcher: Ginny Woodis
CIO: Robbert Kuppens
Founded: 1984

BOWMAN CIRCULATION MARKETING
56 Ritch Ave W (fl 2)
Greenwich, CT 06830-6918
Telephone: (917) 913-6172, E-Mail:
nicole@nicolebowman.com, Web
Site: www.nicolebowman.com
Pres: Nicole Bowman
Conducts Business: U.S.
Primary Market Served: Business &
Consumer
Indirect online sales
Founded: 2004

Consulting consumer marketing to publishers of magazines & newsletters.

BOYDEN GLOBAL EXECUTIVE SEARCH
3 Manhattanville Rd (Suite 104), Building 3
Purchase, NY 10577-2116
Telephone: (914) 747-0093, E-Mail:
inquiry@boyden.com, Web Site:
www.boyden.com
Mng Dir: Tim C. McNamara
CEO: Trina Gordon

REGGIE BRADY MARKETING SOLUTIONS LLC
198 Scribner Ave
Norwalk, CT 06854-1324
Telephone: (203) 838-8138, Web Site:
www.reggiebrady.com
Pres: Regina Brady

JOANNA BRANDI & CO INC
7491 N Federal Hwy C-5 (#304)
Boca Raton, FL 33487
Telephone: (561) 279-0027, E-Mail:
joanna@returnonhappiness.com,
Web Site: www.returnonhappiness.
com
Pres: JoAnna Brandi

Training, consulting & research in customer & employee loyalty & happi-
ness. Twenty one years of helping
companies create customer-caring cultures.

BRANDUNITY INC
PO Box 4512
Rollingbay, WA 98061-0512
Telephone: (206) 842-4948, FAX:
(206) 842-4958, E-Mail: admin@
brandunity.com, Web Site: www.
brandunity.com
Pres: Ann Jensen Warman
CTO: David J Warman
Conducts Business: Worldwide
Employees: 4
Primary Market Served: Business &
Consumer
Indirect online sales

Advertising/Marketing Budget Related
to Direct Marketing: 0-25%
Direct Marketing ad budget:
Direct Mail: 25%
Magazines: 25%
Online: 50%
Founded: 2003
Gross sales or billing: $1,000,000

Integrated brand marketing, strategies
& creative services.

BRANDYWINE CONSULTING GROUP INC
1398 Morstein Rd (Suite 4)
West Chester, PA 19380-5848
Telephone: (610) 696-5872, FAX:
(610) 429-1954, Web Site: www.
brandywineconsulting.com
Mng Partner: Benjamin J. Ventresca Jr.

BRISTOL ASSOCIATES INC
5777 W Century Blvd (Suite 865)
Los Angeles, CA 90045-5696
Telephone: (310) 670-0525, FAX:
(310) 670-4075, E-Mail: lfarber@
bristolassoc.com, Web Site: www.
bristolassoc.com
Acct Exec: Laurie Stern
Pres: Ben Farber
VP: Steven Kessler
Founded: 1967

BROKERS INTERNATIONAL LTD
1200 E Main St
Panora, IA 50216-1100
Telephone: (641) 755-2775, FAX:
(641) 755-4201
Commun Specialist: Sara Tokheim
Founded: 1955

BROTHERS & THOMPSON PC
180 N Stetson Ave Ste 4425
Chicago, IL 60601-6733
Telephone: (312) 372-2909, FAX:
(312) 704-6693, E-Mail:
hthompson@brothersthompson.net,
Web Site: www.brothersthompson.
net
Partner: Alan W. Brothers
Partner: Hubert O Thompson
Founded: 1997

BROWN, VAN REMMEN, KANUIT, INC
840 Apollo St (Suite 300)
El Segundo, CA 90245-4763
Telephone: (310) 640-0777, FAX:
(310) 640-0606, E-Mail: info@
bvksearch.com, Web Site: www.
bvksearch.com
Pres & CEO: Roger Van Remmen
Founded: 1981

BROWNING, JACOBSON & KLEIN LLP

9595 Wilshire Blvd (Suite 601)
Beverly Hills, CA 90212-2506
Telephone: (310) 247-8777, FAX:
(310) 247-1827
Co-Owner: Kenneth L. Browning
Founded: 1995

THE BUFFKIN GROUP LLC

10 Cadillac Dr (Suite 190)
Brentwood, TN 37027
Telephone: (615) 988-2582, E-Mail:
info@thebuffkingroup.com, Web
Site: www.thebuffkingroup.com
Mng Partner: Craig Buffkin
Primary Market Served: Business

Executive recruitment firm specializing
in the digital direct marketing, healthcare, technology, digital media, financial services ad non-profit sectors.

BULL DOG MEDIA GROUP INC

PO Box 463
Madison, SD 57042-0463
Telephone: (605) 256-9103, Web Site:
www.commissionsoup.com
Pres/Co-Founder: Darin Namken
CEO & Co-Founder: Todd Knodel
Dir & Co-Founder: Chad Ekroth
Opers Mgr: Camelyn Sims

BURTCH WORKS LLC

1560 Sherman Ave (fl 10)
Evanston, IL 60201-5017
Telephone: (847) 440-8550, FAX:
(847) 440-8556, Web Site: www.
burtchworks.com
Exec Recruiter: Sandy Marmitt

CDMC/CAREFREE DIRECT MARKETING CORP

PO Box 3737, 8001 E Serene St
Carefree, AZ 85377-3737
Telephone: (480) 488-4227, FAX:
(480) 488-2841
Pres: Stephen R. Warsaw

CAKEMAIL INC

4020 St-Ambroise (Suite 145)
Montreal, QC, Canada H4C 2C7
Telephone: (514) 316-1550, Web Site:
www.cakemail.com
Primary Market Served: Business
Founded: 2007

CAMERON & CO

83 Duggan Ave
Toronto, ON, Canada M4V 1Y1
Telephone: (416) 268-2326
Owner: Wade Cameron

Primary Market Served: Business &
Consumer

CAPELL & ASSOCIATES

601 Central Ave
Barnegat Light, NJ 08006
Telephone: (201) 572-8774, FAX:
(609) 494-7369, E-Mail: contact@
capellandassociates.com, Web Site:
www.capell&associates.com
Pres: E Daniel Capell

CAPGEMINI AMERICAS OUTSOURCING

623 Fifth Ave (fl 33)
New York, NY 10022
Telephone: (212) 314-8000, FAX:
(212) 314-8001
CEO: Dave Bonner

CAREER BLAZERS

5 W 37th St (fl 5)
New York, NY 10018-5384
Telephone: (212) 719-3232, FAX:
(212) 221-0452
Pres: Allen Bowers

PETER N CAREY & ASSOCIATES INC

184 Briarwood Loop
Oak Brook, IL 60523-8713
Telephone: (630) 573-4260, Toll Free:
(877) PNCAREY, FAX: (630) 573-
0529, E-Mail: pncarey1@sbcglobal.
net
Pres: Peter N. Carey
Conducts Business: U.S.
Employees: 2
Primary Market Served: Business &
Consumer
Advertising/Marketing Budget Related
to Direct Marketing: 0-25%
Direct Marketing ad budget:
Direct Mail: 100%
Founded: 1996

Executive recruiting for direct marketing and graphic arts industries.

THE CATALOG CONSULTANCY

3285 West Brookfield Way
Vero Beach, FL 32966-3164
Telephone: (772) 226-7740, FAX:
(772) 226-7740, E-Mail:
catalog321@aol.com, Web Site:
www.catalogconsultant.com

CATALOG MARKETING GROUP

2770 Sheridan Rd
Evanston, IL 60201-1728
Telephone: (847) 864-8089
Pres: E. Herbert Krug

Primary Market Served: Business

CAUGHERTY HAHN COMMUNICATIONS

233 Rock Rd (Suite 248)
Glen Rock, NJ 07452-1708
Telephone: (201) 251-7778, FAX:
(201) 251-7779, Web Site: www.
chcomm.com
Pres & CEO: Lisa C. Hahn

ANDREA B CAUTELA

111 Worth St
New York, NY 10013-4008
Telephone: (212) 577-5920
Primary Market Served: Consumer

CENTER FOR INFORMATION POLICY LEADERSHIP

at Hunton & Williams, LLP
2200 Pennsylvania Ave NW, Hunton &
Williams, LLP
Washington, DC 20037-1701
Telephone: (202) 778-2264, FAX:
(202) 778-2201, Web Site: www.
policyleaders.com
Pres: Martin E Abrams
VP & Sr Policy Counselor: Markus B
Heyder

CHACHA MOBILE ANSWERS

14550 Clay Terrace Blvd (Suite 130)
Carmel, IN 46032-3653
Telephone: (317) 660-6680, Web Site:
partners.chacha.com
Chief Sls & Mktg Officer: Jay Highley

CHAPMAN CUBINE ADAMS & HUSSEY

1600 Wilson Blvd (Suite 300)
Arlington, VA 22209-2505
Telephone: (703) 248-0025, Web Site:
www.ahadirect.com
Chmn & Founder: James Hussey
Pres: Kim Cubine
Exec VP: Lon-Given Chapman
Principal & Founder: Greg Adams
Principal & Sr VP: Pete Carter
Principal & Sr VP: Jenny Allen
Principal & VP Fin: John Wanda
Sr VP Production: Shannon Murphy
Primary Market Served: Business &
Consumer

THE CHUBB CORP

15 Mountainview Rd
Warren, NJ 07059
Telephone: (908) 903-2000, FAX:
(908) 903-2027, Web Site: www.
chubb.com
Sr VP Customer & Mktg Intel: Jeff
Hoffman

CIARLO CONSULTING LLC
39 Gary Ave
Waterbury, CT 06704-2034
Telephone: (203) 232-6655

CIRCULATION SPECIALISTS INC
2 Corporate Dr (#945)
Shelton, CT 06484-4694
Telephone: (888) 315-2472, FAX:
(888) 315-2507
Pres: Greg Wolfe
CEO: John LeBrun
Exec VP: Beverly Chaloux

CLARIO ANALYTICS
7684 Golden Triangle Dr
Eden Prairie, MN 55344-3732
Telephone: (952) 653-0980, Toll Free:
(866) 849-3341, FAX: (952) 653-
5900, E-Mail: sales@clarioanalytics.
com, Web Site: www.clarioanalytics.
com
CEO: Bill Flach
Pres: Randy Erdahl
Mng Principal: Scott Spencer
CTO: Matt Redlon
CFO: John Miller
Employees: 22
Primary Market Served: Business
Advertising/Marketing Budget Related
to Direct Marketing: 0-25%
Direct Marketing ad budget: $20,000
Direct Mail: 50%
Online: 50%
Founded: 2002
Gross sales or billing: $1,500,000
Specializes in analyzing vast quantities
of consumer data to help companies
that have large information databases
market more efficiently.

CLARITY GROUP LLC
600 Market St (Suite 302)
Chapel Hill, NC 27516-4057
Telephone: (919) 932-6036, Web Site:
www.claritygroupinc.com
Founder & CEO: Craig Wood
Sr VP: Ret Boney

CLEMENTDIRECT
72109 Moseley
Chapel Hill, NC 27517-8574
Telephone: (919) 338-2853, FAX:
(206) 338-2511, Web Site: www.
clementdirect.com
Pres: Coy Clement
Founded: 2000

CLICK2MAIL
3103 10th St N (Suite 201)
Arlington, VA 22201-2191
Telephone: (703) 521-9029, Toll Free:
(866) 665-2787, FAX: (703) 358-
8811, E-Mail: info@click2mail.com,
Web Site: www.click2mail.com
Pres & CEO: Lee Garvey
Bus Devel Mgr: Karla Humphrey
Conducts Business: U.S.
Primary Market Served: Business &
Consumer
Catalog available online
Direct online sales
Advertising/Marketing Budget Related
to Direct Marketing: 51-75%
Direct Marketing ad budget: $25,000
Direct Mail: 50%
Online: 50%
Founded: 2003

CLICKSQUARED
280 Summer St (Suite 600)
Boston, MA 02210-1131
Telephone: (781) 622-1611, Toll Free:
(866) 402-5425, FAX: (857) 246-
7645, E-Mail: info@clicksquared.
com, Web Site: www.clicksquared.
com
CEO: Sam Zales
Sr VP Svcs & Opers: Mark Mosholder
Mng Dir - Europe: Greg Garnys
Dir European Strategy & Analysis
Team: Adam Crisp
Chief Tech Officer: Michael McGonagle
Provider of email & cross-channel database marketing solutions, including
self-service email to automated, real-
time customer engagement.

COHEN & CO
281 Hicks St
Brooklyn, NY 11201-4508
Telephone: (718) 875-5065, FAX:
(718) 875-5065, E-Mail:
herbertjcohen@aol.com
Pres: Herbert J. Cohen

COL VOCE CONSULTING
551 Newcomen Rd
Exton, PA 19341-1938
Telephone: (215) 266-2992, Web Site:
www.colvoce.com
Pres: Diane Rodwell
Primary Market Served: Business &
Consumer

COLARELLI MEYER & ASSOCIATES INC
7751 Carondelet Ave (Suite 302)
Saint Louis, MO 63105-3316
Telephone: (314) 721-1860, Toll Free:
(800) 459-4548, FAX: (314) 721-
1992, E-Mail: cmaconsult@
cmaconsult.com, Web Site: www.
cmaconsult.com
Partner: Dan Bean

Sr VP: Jami Wolfe
Partner: Joseph Hoffman
Sr VP: Jay Staley
Sr VP: Terence Bostic
Sr VP: Jennifer Nguyen

COLEMAN FROST LLP
429 Santa Monica Blvd (Suite 700)
Santa Monica, CA 90401-3435
Telephone: (310) 576-7312, Web Site:
www.colemanfrost.com
Partner: JB Frost
Partner: Derrick F Coleman
Founded: 2003

COLLINGER & ASSOCIATES
590 Sarah Ln (Apt 401)
Saint Louis, MO 63141-6968
Telephone: (314) 432-2058, FAX:
(314) 991-9797, E-Mail: bcmktr@
aol.com
Pres: William Collinger

COMMUNICATION MANAGERS, LLC
604 Federal Rd
Brookfield, CT 06804-2070
Telephone: (203) 775-4213, FAX:
(203) 775-6413, E-Mail: etalian@
communicationmanagers.com, Web
Site: www.communicationmanagers.
com
Principal: Elizabeth Talian

COMMUNICATIONS UNLIMITED INC
10129 Deepwood Cir
Richmond, VA 23238-4241
Telephone: (804) 754-7242, E-Mail:
communicationsunlimited@verizon.
net
VP: Robert Carter

COMMUNISPOND INC
5 Lauras Ln
East Hampton, NY 11937-5916
Telephone: (631) 907-8010, Toll Free:
(800) 529-5925, FAX: (631) 907-
8011, Web Site: www.
communispond.com
Pres: Kevin Daley
CEO: William Rosenthal
VP & Gen Mgr: Dale L Klamfoth
VP Mktg: Kathleen Richardson
Founded: 1969

CONCEPT COMMUNICATIONS
400 Amherst St
Nashua, NH 03063-1241
Telephone: (603) 577-9810, Web Site:
www.conceptcommusa.com
Dir: John Fayad

JOHN CONDON & ASSOCIATES

38 Angus Ln
Greenwich, CT 06831-4402
Telephone: (203) 869-7006, FAX:
(203) 622-1488
Pres & Owner: John Condon Jr.

CONNECTICUT MARKETING ASSOCIATES

12 Godfrey Pl (Suite 3)
Wilton, CT 06897
Telephone: (203) 761-9556, FAX:
(203) 761-9763
VP: Steve R. Lake
Founded: 1988

CONTINUITY SHIPPERS ASSOCIATION

2351 N Bridgewater Rd, Saddlebow
Farm
Woodstock, VT 05091-9670
Telephone: (802) 672-3634
Exec Dir: Coleman Hoyt
Founded: 1996

THE CONTRINO GROUP

2770 Arapahoe Rd Ste 132
Lafayette, CO 80026-8016
Telephone: (303) 664-1290, Web Site:
www.thecontrinogroup.com
Pres: Kathleen Contrino

T A COOK CONSULTANTS INC

9212 Falls of Neuse Rd (Suite 201)
Raleigh, NC 27615-2483
Telephone: (919) 510-8142, FAX:
(919) 510-8143, E-Mail: info-us@
tacook.com, Web Site: www.tacook.
com
Primary Market Served: Consumer

THE COPY WORKS

12668 Camino Emparrado
San Diego, CA 92128-1404
Telephone: (858) 676-6757, Web Site:
www.thecopyworks.com
Owner: Susan Fantle

COPYDIRECT

39 Forge Dr
Plymouth, MA 02360-2508
Telephone: (508) 732-9900, Web Site:
www.belindabrewster.com
Primary Market Served: Business &
Consumer

CORPORA CONSULTING

42 W Market St
Bethlehem, PA 18018-5703
Telephone: (215) 313-9229
Pres: Placido Corpora

CORRY DIRECT MARKETING LLC

109 Limekiln Rd
Ridgefield, CT 06877-3418
Telephone: (203) 438-1478, FAX:
(203) 431-0217, E-Mail: tom@
corrydirect.com, Web Site: www.
corrydirect.com
Pres: Thomas P. Corry

CORS

1 Pierce Pl (Suite 295)
Itasca, IL 60143-1253
Telephone: (630) 250-8677, Toll Free:
(800) 323-1352, FAX: (630) 250-
7362, E-Mail: resume@cors.com,
Web Site: www.cors.com
Mktg Commun Supvr: Therese De-
Francesco

PAMELA COTRUPE

129 S Royal Ascot Dr
Las Vegas, NV 89144-4309
Telephone: (818) 624-0087

CRAMER

425 University Ave
Norwood, MA 02062-2636
Telephone: (781) 278-2387, Web Site:
www.crameronline.com
Dir Mktg: Rebecca Hodgkins
Sr VP Fin: Greg Martin
Chmn Bd: Tom Martin
Sr VP Event Svcs: Chris Martin
CEO: Thom Faria
VP Mktg Solutions: Brent Turner
Pres, Creative Svcs: Richard Sturchio
Exec VP Opers: Tim Martin

CRANDALL ASSOCIATES INC

6 Litchfield Rd # 316
Port Washington, NY 11050-3815
Telephone: (516) 767-6800, E-Mail:
joyce@crandallassociates.com, Web
Site: www.crandallassociates.com
Pres: Wendy Weber
Founded: 1973

CREATING SELLING OPPORTUNITIES

2902 W Lane Dr (Suite E)
Houston, TX 77027
Telephone: (713) 622-6936, FAX:
(713) 622-2924, E-Mail: annci@
sbcglobal.net
Owner: Ann C. Iverson

CREATIVE SYNERGY INC

13660 Spinning Wheel Dr
Germantown, MD 20874-2819
Telephone: (301) 515-9397, Web Site:
kimschwalm.com
Pres: Kim Krause Schwalm

CREDITCARDS.COM

9430 Research Blvd (Suite IV400)
Austin, TX 78759-5769
Telephone: (512) 996-8663, Web Site:
www.creditcards.com
VP Strategic Mktg: Jody Farmer
CEO: Christopher J Speltz
VP Opers: Jeff Witmire
VP Devel: Cesar A Gonzalez

MARY CULNAN

175 Forest St, Smith Technology Ctr
322
Waltham, MA 02452
Telephone: (781) 891-2773, E-Mail:
mculnan@bentley.edu

Professor Emeritus, Information &
Process Management, Bentley College.

JOHN CUMMINGS & PARTNERS LLC

Six Blair Rd
Armonk, NY 10504-2522
Telephone: (914) 273-4691, FAX:
(914) 206-3007, E-Mail: john@
dbmscan.com, Web Site: www.
dbmscan.com
Pres: John J. Cummings
Partner: Robert Cummings

MJ CURRAN & ASSOCIATES INC

304 Newbury St #509, Boston, MA
02115-2839-POST
304 Newbury St (Apt 509)
Boston, MA 02115
Telephone: (617) 247-7700, FAX:
(617) 267-6429
Pres: Martin J. Curran

CUSTOMER RETENTION SOLUTIONS

7837 S Sprinkle Rd
Portage, MI 49002-9432
Telephone: (269) 324-7385
Pres: David Disser

DB CONSULTING

550 Mamaroneck Ave
Harrison, NY 10528
Telephone: (914) 698-2008, E-Mail:
darcybev@yahoo.com
CEO: Darcy Bevelacqua
CEO & Partner: Kandal Antik
Partner: Mark Wilcox

DBMCATALYST

152 Railroad St
Holliston, MA 01746-2165
Telephone: (339) 227-7591
Principal: Ann McCartan

DCJ CONSULTING
6749 Exeter St
Forest Hills, NY 11375-4150
Telephone: (718) 575-8357
Primary Market Served: Consumer

DM ASSISTANCE INC
155 Fleet St
Portsmouth, NH 03801-4050
Telephone: (603) 964-6156
Pres: Wes DeVries
Sec: Sharon Brown

DM INFO
308 Royce Woods Ct
Naperville, IL 60565
Telephone: (630) 357-0732, FAX:
   (630) 527-8136, E-Mail: dminfo@
   dmcsweeney.com
Owner: David McSweeney
Conducts Business: U.S.
Primary Market Served: Business &
   Consumer
Advertising/Marketing Budget Related
   to Direct Marketing: 76-100%
Founded: 2003

Database and program analysis, list
brokerage utilities, non-profit and direct marketers services.

DWS ASSOCIATES
1032 Saint Johns Bay
Saint Paul, MN 55129-8537
Telephone: (602) 321-6512, Web Site:
   www.dwstevenson.com
CEO: Dudley Stevenson
Founded: 1982

DALY COMMUNICATIONS
5630 Wisconsin Ave (#903)
Chevy Chase, MD 20815-4456
Telephone: (301) 951-9110, E-Mail:
   speaker@johnjaydaly.com, Web
   Site: www.johnjaydaly.com
Pres: John Jay Daly

CHET DALZELL
145 E 29th St (Apt 6D)
New York, NY 10016-8146
Telephone: (212) 725-2294
Primary Market Served: Consumer

DAN SMOLEN DIRECT
   SEARCH LLC
44 Lightfoot Dr
Stafford, VA 22554-8509
Telephone: (703) 835-9900, FAX:
   (703) 835-9966, E-Mail: dsmolen@
   dansmolen.com, Web Site: www.
   dansmolen.com
Pres: Daniel T. Smolen
Conducts Business: U.S.
Employees: 2

Primary Market Served: Business &
   Consumer
Advertising/Marketing Budget Related
   to Direct Marketing: 76-100%
Direct Marketing ad budget:
Direct Mail: 15%
Newspapers: 85%
Founded: 2005

Executive search services for direct
marketing, interactive marketing &
consumer insights.

DANIEL GONZALEZ &
   ASSOCIATES
939 8th Ave (#300)
New York, NY 10019-4205
Telephone: (212) 682-0333
Pres: Daniel Gonzalez
Founded: 1989

DAVIS & GILBERT
1740 Broadway
New York, NY 10019-4379
Telephone: (212) 468-4800, FAX:
   (212) 468-4888, Web Site: www.
   dglaw.com
Partner: Ronald R. Urbach

BERT DAVIS EXECUTIVE
   SEARCH
Bert Davis Publishing Placement Con-
   sultants
425 Madison Ave (fl 14)
New York, NY 10017-1110
Telephone: (212) 838-4000, FAX:
   (212) 935-3291, E-Mail: info@
   bertdavis.com, Web Site: www.
   bertdavis.com
Pres: Bert Davis
Sr VP: Kathy Berlowe
Mktg & Research Dir: Kristi Johnston
Exec VP: Sally Dougan
Primary Market Served: Business &
   Consumer
Founded: 1977

THOMAS DAWSON
40 Casa Bella Cir
Palm Coast, FL 32137-1223
Telephone: (303) 250-9000

DE RHAM & CO INC
590 Danby Mountain Rd
Dorset, VT 05251
Telephone: (802) 867-0155, Toll Free:
   (888) 867-0155, FAX: (802) 867-
   0361, Web Site: www.derham.com
Pres: Abbott de Rham
Conducts Business: U.S.
Primary Market Served: Business &
   Consumer

Founded: 1993
Automated speech solutions for direct
marketers. End-to-end services for customer service and marketing call center, direct marketing consulting.

DECKER
   COMMUNICATIONS INC
575 Market St (Suite 1925)
San Francisco, CA 94105
Telephone: (415) 543-8100, Toll Free:
   (877) 485-0700, FAX: (415) 543-
   8103, E-Mail: info@
   deckercommunications.com, Web
   Site: www.deckercommunications.
   com
Chmn & Founder: Bert Decker
CEO: Ben Decker
Pres: Kelly Decker
VP Sales: Terry Lee
COO: John Tarman

DEHART & DARR
   ASSOCIATES
1360 Beverly Rd (Suite 201)
McLean, VA 22101-3647
Telephone: (703) 448-1000, FAX:
   (703) 790-3460
VP: Daniel Smith
Consultant: Anne Darr

ROBERT DELAY
4121 E Via del Cuculin
Tucson, AZ 85718-3320
Telephone: (520) 615-8235

DENMARK FRANCISCO
684 9th Ave (fl 4)
New York, NY 10036-3612
Telephone: (212) 444-8157, Web Site:
   www.dsfnyc.com
Primary Market Served: Consumer

THE DEVEREUX GROUP
47 Locust St, Little Harbour
Marblehead, MA 01945-2935
Telephone: (781) 631-9213, FAX:
   (781) 639-3044, E-Mail: roeser@
   devereuxgroup.com, Web Site: www.
   devereuxgroup.com
Pres: Prugh Roeser

DIDACTIC SYSTEMS
PO Box 457
Cranford, NJ 07016-0457
Telephone: (908) 276-5413, FAX:
   (908) 276-7174, E-Mail: didacticra@
   aol.com
Pres: Erwin Rausch

DIRECT ADVANTAGE
   PARTNERS
69 Bluff Ave (Suite 100)

Rowayton, CT 06853-1802
Telephone: (203) 286-7100
Mng Partner: Steve Mason

DIRECT DYNAMICS LLC
85 Emanuel Church Rd
Killingworth, CT 06419
Telephone: (860) 614-4816, E-Mail:
info@direct-dynamics.com, Web
Site: direct-dynamics.com
Mng Partner: Francis Barkyoumb

DIRECT MAIL SYSTEMS
12450 Automobile Blvd
Clearwater, FL 33762
Telephone: (727) 573-1985, Toll Free:
(800) 683-6245, FAX: (727) 573-
1747, E-Mail: info@direct-mail-
systems.com, Web Site: www.direct-
mail-systems.com
Pres: Roger Pennington

DIRECT MARKETERS ON
CALL INC (DMOC)
45 Christopher St (Apt 4A)
New York, NY 10014-3585
Telephone: (212) 691-1942, FAX:
(212) 924-1331, E-Mail: info@
dmoc-inc.com, Web Site: www.
dmoc-inc.com
Pres: Heather Frayne
Opers Mgr: Nicole Allen
Comptroller: Amy Gotbetter
Employees: 6
Primary Market Served: Business &
Consumer
Indirect online sales
Advertising/Marketing Budget Related
to Direct Marketing: 76-100%
Direct Marketing ad budget:
Direct Mail: 50%
Magazines: 50%
Founded: 1989

Freelance and consulting service for
the direct marketing industry, servicing
ad agencies, and corporations in the
New York Metro Region.

DIRECT MARKETING
CONSULTANT
399 Sherman Ave
Sharon, PA 16146-3953
Telephone: (724) 699-0230
Direct Mktg Consultant: Lynne Nigro

DIRECT MARKETING
INSIGHTS INC
15970 W Edgemont Ave
Goodyear, AZ 85395-8112
Telephone: (843) 817-7488, E-Mail:
jimp@dminsights.com, Web Site:
www.dminsights.com

Pres: James L. Padgitt
Expert direct response consulting help
for entrepreneurial owners of catalog &
ecommerce businesses.

DIRECT MARKETING
RESOURCES
517 Highland Forest Dr
Charlotte, NC 28270-0848
Telephone: (704) 845-5890, Toll Free:
(888) 644-4DMR, E-Mail: dan@
dmresources.com, Web Site: www.
dmresources.com
Pres: Daniel J. Sullivan
Conducts Business: U.S.
Employees: 4
Primary Market Served: Business &
Consumer
Advertising/Marketing Budget Related
to Direct Marketing: 26-50%
Direct Marketing ad budget:
Direct Mail: 20%
Telephone: 80%
Founded: 1988
Gross sales or billing: $1,000,000
Executive search firm specializing in
the direct marketing industry, both cor-
porate and agency and all functional
areas.

DIRECT MARKETING
RESOURCES GROUP INC
4501 Newborn Ave (Suite 130-253)
Raleigh, NC 27610-1550
Telephone: (919) 231-2728, Toll Free:
(800) 517-5253, Web Site: www.
improvedmarketingresults.com
CEO & Video Producer: George Wehmann

DIRECT VENTURES INC
720 Milton Rd (Apt W4D)
Rye, NY 10580-3252
Telephone: (914) 833-9842, FAX:
(914) 834-3883, E-Mail: bsideroff@
directventuresmcinc.wm
Pres: Barry Sideroff

DIRECTIONS MARKETING
505 Green Rd
Ann Arbor, MI 48105
Telephone: (734) 930-2820, FAX:
(734) 930-9189, E-Mail: directions@
directions.com.eg, Web Site: www.
directions.com.eg
Pres: Bruce S. Moyer

DIRECTIVES/TARGETED
MARKETING AND
COMMUNICATIONS
1022 Avalon Way
Plymouth, MA 02360-7777

Telephone: (215) 546-7817, Web Site:
www.directivesmarketing.com
Pres: Carolyn Gould
Founded: 1988
Specializes in multi-channel, integrated
marketing and communications. Over
the years, its clients have included consumer and business-to-business marketers, ranging from small retailers to
Fortune 200 companies. Experienced in
all types of industry segments - from
fashion to finance, technology to travel,
health to hard goods - and a wide variety of communications channels - bricks
and mortar, catalog, internet, solo direct mail, telemarketing, publishing,
advertising, and television.

THE DIVERSIFIED SERVICES
GROUP INC
303 W Lancaster Ave (Suite 2E)
Wayne, PA 19087-3938
Telephone: (610) 989-1710, FAX:
(610) 989-1730, E-Mail: rfgrieb@
dsg-network.com, Web Site: www.
dsg-network.com
Principal & Founder: Robert F. Grieb
Principal: Borden Ayers
Founded: 1989

DODSON & ASSOCIATES
16302 Shadybank Dr
Dallas, TX 75248-2957
Telephone: (972) 931-9200
Principal: Gordon O. Dodson

DOVETAIL ART & DESIGN
INC
113 Wade Dr
Dover, OH 44622-9460
Telephone: (330) 343-3764, Web Site:
www.dovetailart.com
Primary Market Served: Consumer

PATRICIA DOWD INC
5300 San Jacinto Ave
Atascadero, CA 93422-2940
Telephone: (805) 985-8243, E-Mail:
pdowd@pdisearch.com, Web Site:
www.pdisearch.com
Pres: Patricia Dowd

The first recruiter to specialize in database marketing placing all levels of database marketing professionals since
1988.

DUGGAN & BROWN INC
118 Appletree St
Barrington, IL 60010
Telephone: (847) 381-8484, FAX:
(847) 381-8499, E-Mail: evan@
dugganandbrown.com, Web Site:
www.dugganandbrown.com
Partner: Evan Brown

Founded: 1977
Mail order marketing firm.

E MEDIA ADVANTAGE

Six Hamilton Ln
Livingston, NJ 07039-2006
Telephone: (917) 994-3685, FAX:
(973) 455-1312, E-Mail: tnevitt@
emediaadvantage.com, Web Site:
emediaadvantage.com
Pres: Toni Nevitt

EBM DIRECT MARKETING SERVICES LLC

39 Seaview Ln
Port Washington, NY 11050-1737
Telephone: (516) 874-7839, Web Site:
www.ebmdirectmarketing.com
Member: Eric Mohr
Founded: 1996

EADON VENTURES

11224 Reeder Ave NE
Alliance, OH 44601-8332
Telephone: (330) 418-4298, Web Site:
www.eadonventures.com
Pres: David Conway

EASTERN COLLECTION CORP

16 Barclay Dr
Sag Harbor, NY 11963-4316
Telephone: (631) 563-2112, Toll Free:
(800) 243-1204, FAX: (631) 563-
2471, E-Mail: ecc1626@aol.com
Pres: Arleen Rossi

ECHOTOUCH CORP

5907 Carry Back Ln
Austin, TX 78746-1448
Telephone: (512) 327-5638, Web Site:
www.echotouch.com
CEO: Brian McClure

ECOENVELOPES

17800 George Moran Dr
Eden Prairie, MN 55347
Telephone: (612) 605-4885, Toll Free:
(888) 428-4364, FAX: (651) 392-
8924, E-Mail: info@ecoenvelopes.
com, Web Site: www.ecoenvelopes.
com
Founder & CEO: Ann DeLaVergne

THE EDBRAHAM GROUP

PO Box 753
Westbrook, CT 06498-0753
Telephone: (860) 664-4120, Web Site:
www.theedbrahamgroup.com
Principal: Shirley Edbrooke
Primary Market Served: Business

EDELMAN DIRECT MARKETING INC

75 Fairview Ave
Great Neck, NY 11023-1350
Telephone: (516) 829-9398
Pres: Robert Edelman
Pres Consumer Mktg & Global Crea-
tive Dir: Mitch Markson
Founded: 1984

EFFECTIVE MARKETING ASSOCIATES, INC

aka EMA
3525 Riverknoll Way
West Linn, OR 97068-3641
Telephone: (503) 657-5859, FAX:
(503) 657-5886, Web Site: www.e-
m-a.com
Pres: Stephen B. Garner
Founded: 1983

EINHORN ASSOCIATES INC

2675 N Mayfair Rd (Suite 410)
Milwaukee, WI 53226
Telephone: (414) 453-4488, FAX:
(414) 453-4831, Web Site: www.
einhornassociates.com
Pres: Stephen Einhorn
VP: Jaclyn Christiansen
Sr Analyst: Greg Wagner
Sr Analyst: Alvin Vitangcol
CFO: Nancy Einhorn

JS ELIEZER ASSOCIATES INC

300 Atlantic St (fl 7)
Stamford, CT 06901-3522
Telephone: (203) 658-1300
Pres: Andrew Gruber
Founded: 1964

EMAILOGICS INC/ EMAILBRAIN

8100 NE Parkway Dr (Suite 300)
Vancouver, WA 98662-7954
Telephone: (866) 873-3019, Web Site:
www.emailbrain.com
Bus Devel: Stephanie Lazardi

EMARKETING STRATEGY GROUP

155 E 34th St (Suite 20-C)
New York, NY 10016-4718
Telephone: (212) 679-6486, Web Site:
www.ruthstevens.com
Pres: Ruth Stevens

EMPLOYERS GROUP

400 Continental Blvd Ste 300
El Segundo, CA 90245-5080
Toll Free: (800) 748-8484, Web Site:
www.employesgroup.com
Mktg Mgr: Nicole Vierzba

Primary Market Served: Consumer
Human Resources consulting firm offering custom consulting services,
training, seminars, publications &
products

ENGAGENEXTGEN LLC

5463 Bartlett Blvd
Mound, MN 55364-1605
Telephone: (952) 905-4474
Primary Market Served: Consumer

EPIC RESEARCH LLC

300 Centennial Cir
Greenville, DE 19807-2130
Telephone: (302) 467-5445, Web Site:
www.epicresearch.net
Chief Mktg Officer: Ben Brake

EQUIFAX CREDIT INFORMATION SERVICES INC

1550 Peachtree NW
Atlanta, GA 30309
Telephone: (404) 885-8000, Toll Free:
(800) 685-5000, FAX: (404) 885-
8988, Web Site: www.equifax.com
Chmn & CEO: Richard F. Smith
VP & Chief Mktg Officer: Paul J.
Springman

EQUITY MANAGEMENT INC

4365 Executive Dr Ste 1000
San Diego, CA 92121-2192
Telephone: (858) 558-2500, FAX:
(858) 558-2547, Web Site: www.
equitymanagementinc.com
Chmn & CEO: Glen Konkle

EQUITY RESIDENTIAL PROPERTIES

Two N Riverside Plaza (Suite 400)
Chicago, IL 60606-2624
Telephone: (312) 474-1300, FAX:
(312) 474-8703, E-Mail:
mgraycraddock@eqr.com, Web Site:
www.eqr.com
Corp Mktg Dir: Mary Gray Craddock

ERLANDSON ASSOCIATES

222 W Market St
Leesburg, VA 20176-2709
Telephone: (703) 669-0889, E-Mail:
bgerlandso@aol.com
Pres: Barbara Erlandson

ERNAN ROMAN DIRECT MARKETING CORP

3 Melrose Ln
Little Neck, NY 11363-1220

Telephone: (718) 225-4151, FAX:
(718) 225-4889, E-Mail: ernan@
erdm.com, Web Site: www.erdm.
com
Pres: Ernan Roman
Sr Partner: Scott Hornstein
Conducts Business: U.S.
Primary Market Served: Business &
Consumer
Advertising/Marketing Budget Related
to Direct Marketing: 76-100%
Founded: 1983

Integrated direct marketing and consen-
sual opt-in marketing consulting services.

ERNST & YOUNG LLP
5 Times Sq
New York, NY 10036-6527
Telephone: (212) 773-6146, FAX:
(312) 879-4000, Web Site: www.ey.
com
Dir Direct Mktg Distr: Ingrid McGuire

EXECUTIVE CONNECTIONS
LLC
8466 Lockwood Ridge Rd (#330)
Sarasota, FL 34243-2951
Telephone: (941) 323-8300, Web Site:
www.executiveconnectionsllc.com
CEO: Jeff Gundersen
Chief Coaching Officer: Lorraine
White
Mktg Dir: Jackie Bivins
Search Consultant: Paula Fontana
Conducts Business: U.S.
Employees: 8
Primary Market Served: Business &
Consumer
Catalog available online
Direct online sales
Advertising/Marketing Budget Related
to Direct Marketing: 51-75%
Direct Marketing ad budget: $100,000
Founded: 2003
Gross sales or billing: $5,000,000

Specializes in executive search consulting and executive coaching.

EXECUTIVE SEARCH
INTERNATIONAL
1525 Centre St
Newton, MA 02461-1200
Telephone: (617) 527-8787, E-Mail:
info@execsearchintl.com, Web Site:
www.execsearchintl.com
Mng Partner: Les Gore

CYNTHIA FIELDS & CO
(CFC)
230 W 22nd St
New York, NY 10011-2701
Telephone: (212) 242-6063
Owner: Cynthia Fields

FIGURS*
39a Fourth St
Toronto, ON, Canada M8V 2Y2
Telephone: (416) 826-9083
Primary Market Served: Business

FIRST OF OMAHA
MERCHANT PROCESSING
Subs. of First National Bank of Omaha
1620 Dodge St
Omaha, NE 68197
Telephone: (402) 341-0500, Toll Free:
(800) 228-2443
Chmn: Bruce Lawitzen

FLAREPATH LLC
PO Box 111
Canaan, NY 12029-0111
Telephone: (212) 927-1296
Co-Pres: Mark Oberski

FOCUS ON THE ROI
97 Gem Ln
Massapequa Park, NY 11762-3222
Telephone: (917) 620-1838
Primary Market Served: Consumer

THE FORUM CORP
265 Franklin St (Suite 400)
Boston, MA 02110-3182
Telephone: (617) 523-7300, Toll Free:
(800) 367-8611, FAX: (617) 371-
3300, E-Mail: forum@forum.com,
Web Site: www.forum.com
Pres & CEO: Ed Boswell

FOTOBED.COM
4630 Old Looney Mill Rd
Birmingham, AL 35243-2607
Toll Free: (888) 368-6233, E-Mail:
service@fotobed.com, Web Site:
www.fotobed.com
Pres: John Castleberry

FOXHALL CORPORATION
6849 Old Dominion Dr (Suite 320)
McLean, VA 22101-3791
Telephone: (703) 749-3126
Pres: Bryon Hughey
Primary Market Served: Business &
Consumer

JONATHAN FRIEDMAN
3720 N 37th Ter
Hollywood, FL 33021
Telephone: (954) 416-3419
Primary Market Served: Business &
Consumer

FUNME EVENTS
Div. of Creative Marketing Enterprises
Inc
PO Box 463

Dekalb, IL 60115-0463
Toll Free: (800) 386-6321, FAX: (815)
787-3100, E-Mail: funMEevents@
aol.com, Web Site: www.
funMEevents.com
Pres: Michael T. Embrey

FURGIUELE & CO INC
276 Read Ave
Crestwood, NY 10707
Telephone: (914) 793-0045, FAX:
(914) 779-6447, E-Mail: fci@fcidms.
com, Web Site: www.fcidms.com
Pres: Joseph Furgiuele

GC SERVICES
6330 Gulfton
Houston, TX 77081
Telephone: (713) 777-4441, FAX:
(713) 776-6535, E-Mail: marketing.
communications@gcserv.com, Web
Site: www.gcserv.com
Pres: Frank Taylor

GARTNER INC
1650 Technology Dr Ste 500
San Jose, CA 95110-3838
Telephone: (408) 468-8000, Toll Free:
(800) 419-3282, FAX: (408) 954-
1780, E-Mail: tom.mccall@gartner.
com, Web Site: www.gartner.com
Sr Dir, Pub Rels: Tom McCall

GASPEDAL
333 W North Ave (Suite 500)
Chicago, IL 60610-1293
Telephone: (312) 932-9000, Web Site:
www.gaspedal.net
CEO: Andy Sernovitz
Primary Market Served: Business &
Consumer

GAZETTE DIRECT
MARKETING CO
Subs. of Gazette Co
500 Third Ave SE
Cedar Rapids, IA 52401-1945
Telephone: (319) 399-5997, FAX:
(319) 399-5998, Web Site: www.
gazette.com
CEO & Pub: Joe Haldy

GIBSON DIRECT INC
204 Plantation Dr
Coppell, TX 75019-3232
Telephone: (972) 462-7580, FAX:
(972) 304-9202
Pres: Steve E. Gibson

GILCHRIST & PARTNERS
542 Mass Ave
Boston, MA 02118-1439
Telephone: (617) 314-4096, Toll Free:
(866) 617-5070

**GILLESPIE MAGAZINE
MARKETING &
PUBLISHING**
Div. of Gillespie
3450 Princeton Pike
Lawrenceville, NJ 08648
Telephone: (609) 895-0200, FAX:
(609) 895-0222, Web Site: www.
gillespie.com
Exec VP Mng Dir: Jamie Pack

**GLAZER-KENNEDY INSIDER
CIRCLE**
8430 W Bryn Mawr Ave (Suite 575)
Chicago, IL 60631-3497
Telephone: (410) 825-8600, Web Site:
www.dankennedy.com
Pres: William Glazer

GLENGARRY MARKETING
2303 RR 620 S Unit 135-150
Austin, TX 78734
Toll Free: (800) 883-1924
CEO: Robert Stutz
Founded: 2004

**GLOBAL MARKETING
GROUP LTD**
119 W 57th St (Suite 1405)
New York, NY 10019-2401
Telephone: (212) 247-6060, FAX:
(212) 586-5446, E-Mail: kimglobal@
aol.com, Web Site: www.
gmgsolution.com
Pres: Kenneth Miller

BARBARA GOLD
10 W 15th (Apt 1924)
New York, NY 10011-6850
Telephone: (917) 750-4038
Primary Market Served: Consumer

ED GOLDEN & ASSOCIATES
7303 Shoal Creek Blvd
Austin, TX 78757-2028
Telephone: (512) 458-8222, FAX:
(512) 454-3536
Pres: Ed Golden

GOODMAN & CO
PO Box 835
New York, NY 10024-0540
Telephone: (212) 579-0020, Web Site:
www.goodmancompany.com
Chmn & CEO: Susan Goodman
Primary Market Served: Business &
Consumer

**GRADUATE MANAGEMENT
ADMISSION COUNCIL**
11921 Freedom Dr (Suite 300)
Reston, VA 20190

Telephone: (703) 668-9813, Web Site:
www.mba.com
Primary Market Served: Business

**GREENPATH
SUSTAINABILITY
CONSULTANTS**
13 Windgate Dr
New City, NY 10956-4434
Telephone: (914) 980-8346
Pres: David Refkin

GREY BIRCH GROUP LLC
64 Sycamore Ln
Irvington, NY 10533-1931
Telephone: (914) 479-5088, Web Site:
www.greybirch.com
Principal: Anne Schaeffer

GORDON W GROSSMAN INC
254 Salem Rd
Pound Ridge, NY 10576-1320
Telephone: (914) 238-9387, FAX:
(914) 238-1635
Pres: Gordon W. Grossman

GROUP F/64
1050 Arbor Rd
Winston-Salem, NC 27104
Telephone: (336) 748-8272, FAX:
(336) 748-8780
Pres: Cynthia Skaar

GROUP 3 MARKETING
800 Wayzata Blvd E, #201, Wayzata,
MN 55391-1764
1907 Wayzata Blvd (Suite 200)
Wayzata, MN 55391-2070
Telephone: (952) 475-3269, Toll Free:
(888) 571-6554, FAX: (952) 449-
0403, E-Mail: info@
group3marketing.com, Web Site:
www.group3marketing.com
Pres: Bart Foreman

**GROWTH PLATFORMS
INSTITUTE**
68 St Johns (Suite 200)
Wilton, CT 06897
Telephone: (203) 529-0500, E-Mail:
info@growthplatforms.org, Web
Site: www.growthplatforms.org
Pres, Consulting: Neil Kleinfeld

**GUNDERSEN PARTNERS
LLC**
30 Irving Pl (fl 2)
New York, NY 10003
Telephone: (212) 677-7660, FAX:
(212) 358-0275, Web Site: www.
gundersenpartners.com
Principal: Steven Gundersen
Mgr Opers: Ed Steffen

Founded: 1984

HDI GROUP
1 Embarcadero Ctr (Suite 500)
San Francisco, CA 94111-3610
Telephone: (415) 794-3320, Web Site:
www.hobbsdirect.com
Pres: Michele Hobbs
Primary Market Served: Business &
Consumer

HAL LEVY & ASSOCIATES
186 Mohonk Rd
High Falls, NY 12440-5229
Telephone: (845) 687-4400
Pres: Hal Levy

**ROBERT HALF
INTERNATIONAL INC**
2884 Sand Hill Rd (Suite 200)
Menlo Park, CA 94025
Telephone: (650) 234-6000, FAX:
(650) 234-6930, E-Mail:
webmaster@rhi.com, Web Site:
www.rhii.com
CEO: Harold M. Messmer Jr

ELIZABETH HARTMAN
5 Azalea Dr
Syosset, NY 11791-2802
Telephone: (516) 650-8862
VP: Elizabeth Hartman

**HARVEST
COMMUNICATIONS**
2400 Washington Ave (Suite 411)
Redding, CA 96001-2827
Toll Free: (800) 303-6405, FAX: (800)
926-8038, Web Site: www.harvest-
communications.com
Admin: Jeanelle Couch

**DENNY HATCH ASSOCIATES
INC**
310 Gaskill St
Philadelphia, PA 19147-1503
Telephone: (215) 627-9103, FAX:
(215) 627-6610, E-Mail:
dennyhatch@yahoo.com, Web Site:
www.dennyhatch.com
Pres: Denny Hatch

HATCHHOLDINGS LLC
5832 Broadwell Dr
Plano, TX 75093-4717
Telephone: (214) 505-4697
Principal: William Randall

**HAUSER LIST SERVICES,
NMIS**
2545 Hempstead Tpke (Suite 401)
East Meadow, NY 11554-2144

Telephone: (516) 935-8603, FAX: (516) 935-8626, E-Mail: david@ hausernet.com, Web Site: www. hausertrack.com
Chmn: Barry Hauser
EVP: David Hauser

HEALTHINFO DIRECT
1528 Sandburg Dr
Schaumburg, IL 60173-2183
Telephone: (630) 936-9465
Principal: Matthew Stone

HEMISPHERE MARKETING
6437 Washington St
Kansas City, MO 64113-1731
Telephone: (816) 444-5439, Web Site: www.hemispheremarketing.com
Owner: Gina Valentino

DAVID HENEBERRY ASSOCIATES
111 Reynolds Ln
West Grove, PA 19390-1371
Telephone: (203) 778-0692, FAX: (203) 778-0699
Pres: David Heneberry

THE HERMAN GROUP
7112 Viridian Ln
Austin, TX 78739-2092
Telephone: (336) 210-3547, E-Mail: info@hermangroup.com, Web Site: www.hermangroup.com
CEO: Joyce L. Gioia

HIGH NOTE MEDIA INC
5315 N Clark (#218)
Chicago, IL 60640-2290
Telephone: (773) 980-6873, Web Site: www.highnotemedia.com

DEBORAH HOFFMAN COPYWRITING
306 Sagebrush Dr
Corrales, NM 87048-8552
Telephone: (505) 440-8725
Primary Market Served: Consumer

HOWARD-SLOAN-KOLLER GROUP
300 E 42nd St Fl 15
New York, NY 10017-5925
Telephone: (212) 661-5250, FAX: (212) 557-9178, E-Mail: ekoller@ hsksearch.com, Web Site: www. hsksearch.com
Pres: Edward R. Koller Jr.
Dir, Res: Steven Unger

COLEMAN W HOYT CONSULTANT
2351 N Bridgewater Rd, Saddlebow Farm
Woodstock, VT 05091-9670
Telephone: (802) 672-3634, FAX: (802) 672-5116, E-Mail: cwhoyt@ vermontel.net
Principal: Coleman W. Hoyt

EA HUGHES & CO
200 Park Ave S (Suite 1608)
New York, NY 10003-1521
Telephone: (212) 689-4600, FAX: (212) 689-4975, E-Mail: hr@ eahughes.com, Web Site: www. eahughes.com
Pres: Elaine A. Hughes

HUNTER BUSINESS GROUP LLC
4650 N Port Washington Rd Stop 8
Milwaukee, WI 53212-1078
Telephone: (414) 203-8060, Toll Free: (800) 423-4010, FAX: (414) 203-8225, E-Mail: hunter@ hunterbusiness.com, Web Site: www. hunterbusiness.com
Pres: Victor Hunter
COO: Nedra Sadorf

IC SYSTEM INC
PO Box 64378
Saint Paul, MN 55164
Toll Free: (800) 443-4123, Web Site: www.icsystem.com
Pres & CEO: John Erickson
Dir Mktg: Eric Johannes
Conducts Business: U.S.
Primary Market Served: Business & Consumer
Founded: 1938

Nationally licensed & bonded account collection services company.

IJHANA
409 W Olympic Blvd (Apt 7062)
Los Angeles, CA 90015-1635
Telephone: (213) 268-4283, Toll Free: (888) 421-9222, E-Mail: info@ ijhana.com, Web Site: www.ijhana. com
Managing Partner & CTO: Kevin Calloway
Mng Partner: Thomas Dillmann
Global technology consulting firm

IMV
1400 E Touhy Ave (Suite 250)
Des Plaines, IL 60018-3339
Telephone: (847) 297-1404, FAX: (847) 297-5010, E-Mail: sales@ imvinfo.com, Web Site: www. imvlimited.com

VP: Gail Prochaska

IPG
532 W 22nd St (Apt 3C)
New York, NY 10011-1117
Telephone: (646) 229-2255
Primary Market Served: Consumer

IZEA
1000 Legion Pl (Suite 1600)
Orlando, FL 32801-1060
Telephone: (321) 332-6830, Web Site: www.izea.com
Internet Mktg Specialist: Ashley Edwards

IDEAS IN SEO
758 NE 90 St (Unit 514)
Miami, FL 33138
Telephone: (786) 280-6051
Primary Market Served: Business & Consumer

IKNOWTION LLC
25 Burlington Mall Rd (Suite 409)
Burlington, MA 01803-4156
Telephone: (781) 494-9989, Web Site: www.iknowtion.com
Mng Partner: William Duffy

IMAGINATION WORKS
24 Primrose Dr
Trumbull, CT 06611-5043
Telephone: (203) 377-1747, FAX: (203) 377-7401, E-Mail: jim@ imaginationworks.net, Web Site: www.imaginationworks.net
Principal: Jim Lang

IMAGINE 360 MARKETING
1123 Broadway (Suite 902)
New York, NY 10010-2007
Telephone: (212) 313-9616, Web Site: www.i360m.com
Pres & CEO: Yael Penn

INDEPENDENT CONSULTANT
2307 Boxwood Ave E
Saint Paul, MN 55119-5670
Telephone: (612) 239-6572
Consultant: Mary Scundi

INFOMERCIAL MONITORING SERVICE INC
10 N Church St (Suite 200)
West Chester, PA 19380-3000
Telephone: (610) 328-6902, FAX: (610) 328-6791, E-Mail: catanese@ imstv.com, Web Site: www.imstv. com
Pres & CEO: Samuel R. Catanese

INFOMORPHOSIS/ MARKETING SOLUTIONS
152 W 20th St (Suite D)
New York, NY 10011-3635
Telephone: (212) 366-6216, FAX:
(212) 255-4784, E-Mail: dfain@nyc.
rr.com
Principal: Deborah Fain

INTEGRATED MARKETING SOLUTIONS (IMS)
30108 Kimberly Dr
Ashland, NE 68003-3806
Telephone: (402) 486-3151, FAX:
(402) 486-3161
Pres: Chris Peterson

INTERACTIVE SEARCH GROUP
35104 Euclid Ave (Suite 303)
Cleveland, OH 44094
Telephone: (216) 255-3388, Web Site:
www.isgstaffingnow.com
Pres: Jason Peterson

INTERFACE ENGINEERING
708 SW Third Ave (Suite 400)
Portland, OR 97204
Telephone: (503) 382-2266, FAX:
(503) 382-2262, E-Mail: solutions@
interfaceengineering.com, Web Site:
www.ieice.com
Pres & Treas: Omid Nabipoor
Sr VP: David Pickett
Principal: Joel Cruz
Assoc Principal: Andrew Briones
Assoc Principal: David Chesley
Founded: 1969

Consulting engineering firm designing
mechanical, electrical lighting, telecommunications fire safety and life
safety systems.

INTERNATIONAL CORP
225 Division Ave
Hasbrouck Heights, NJ 07604-1719
Telephone: (201) 203-3083, Web Site:
www.datadirectsolutions.com
Primary Market Served: Consumer

INTERNATIONAL DIRECT MARKETING CONSULTANTS INC
3419 Westminster Ave
Dallas, TX 75205-1387
Telephone: (214) 443-9494, FAX:
(214) 443-9512, E-Mail:
billmcnutt@charter.net, Web Site:
www.dmtrademissions.com
Pres: William McNutt III

INTERNATIONAL RESOURCE MANAGEMENT CO
3008 Spring Valley Dr
Bedford, TX 76021-4245
Telephone: (817) 861-9191, FAX:
(817) 277-0868, E-Mail: james@
irmco.net, Web Site: www.irmco.net
Dir: James E. Johnson

IRIS MARKETING
1303 Harling Ct
Bel Air, MD 21015-5029
Telephone: (443) 742-1232
Pres: Vayia Skinner

JK ASSOCIATES LLC
445 Sherman Ave (Suite W)
Palo Alto, CA 94306-1828
Telephone: (650) 838-9816, FAX:
(650) 838-9867, Web Site: www.jk-
associates.com
Pres: Judith W. Kincaid

JLMC
15 Park Row (17E)
New York, NY 10038-2301
Telephone: (917) 476-3072
Primary Market Served: Consumer

JRB MARKETING GROUP
93 Einstein Way
East Windsor, NJ 08512-2549
Telephone: (301) 758-2334, FAX:
(302) 348-2490, E-Mail: jrblitman@
gmail.com
Principal & CEO: Joan Blitman

JZ MARKETING
4532 Varsity Cir
Lehigh Acres, FL 33971
Telephone: (239) 693-7567, Web Site:
www.jzmktg.com
Primary Market Served: Business &
Consumer

JACK SCHECTERSON VISUALMARKETING CONSULTANTS
5316 251st Pl
Little Neck, NY 11362-1711
Telephone: (718) 225-3536
Pres: Jack Schecterson

THE JACKSON CONSULTING GROUP LTD
PO Box 246
Middletown, DE 19709
Telephone: (302) 378-0218, Toll Free:
(866) 450-7005, FAX: (302) 378-
0219, E-Mail: djack98489@aol.com,
Web Site: www.jcg-ltd.com
Chmn: Donald R. Jackson

JACOBSOHN CONSULTING ASSOCIATES
Div. of American Slicing Machine Co
PO Box 236
Highland Park, IL 60035-0236
Telephone: (312) 543-3330, E-Mail:
jacobsohnr@aol.com
Pres: Richard H. Jacobsohn
Conducts Business: U.S., Canada, Eu-
rope, Japan
Employees: 10
Primary Market Served: Business &
Consumer
Advertising/Marketing Budget Related
to Direct Marketing: 51-75%
Direct Marketing ad budget:
Direct Mail: 50%
Online: 50%
Founded: 1904
Gross sales or billing: $5,000,000

Consulting for direct sales of consumer
products through direct mail, magazines & credit cards, syndicated to oil
& credit card companies, catalogs, internet.

VICTORIA JAMES EXECUTIVE SEARCH INC
11 Stonefence Ln
South Kent, CT 06785-1307
Telephone: (203) 750-8838 X101,
FAX: (203) 547-6284, E-Mail:
vjames@victoriajames.com, Web
Site: www.victoriajames.com
Pres: Victoria James

JASEK ENTERPRISES
1000 Deep Wood Dr
Westlake Village, CA 91362-4215
Telephone: (805) 379-2871, FAX:
(805) 379-9839
Pres: Alexander M. Kushner

JOFFREY LONG CONSULTANTS
17045 Chatsworth St
Granada Hills, CA 91344-5845
Telephone: (818) 635-1777, Web Site:
www.southwestbancorp.com
Pres: Joffrey Long

JUNGLE CONSULTING
13795 Tewkesbury Ct
Colorado Springs, CO 80908
Telephone: (702) 596-4366
Owner & CEO: Gary Moore
Primary Market Served: Business

Dental practice consultants

THE KAISER GROUP INC
237 South St
Waukesha, WI 53186

Telephone: (262) 544-4971, FAX: (262) 544-6271, Web Site: www.kaisergrp.com
Pres: Peter Kaiser

KANNON CONSULTING INC
2314 N Lincoln Park W (Apt 14S)
Chicago, IL 60614-3462
Telephone: (312) 346-2244, FAX: (312) 346-3665, Web Site: www.kannon.com
Pres: Barbara Cohen

KEN ELO
3863 Laval
Montreal, QC, Canada H2W 2H9
Telephone: (514) 926-6945
Mktg Consultant: Kenza Elouazzani
Primary Market Served: Business & Consumer

KENNEDY INNER CIRCLE
15433 N Tatum Blvd (Suite 104)
Phoenix, AZ 85032-4231
Telephone: (602) 269-3111, FAX: (602) 269-3113
Pres: Dan S. Kennedy

JUDITH KENNERK
11 Scott Ave
Princeton Junction, NJ 08550-1005
Telephone: (609) 240-2876
Primary Market Served: Consumer

KENZER GROUP, LLC
One Penn Plaza (Suite 6300)
New York, NY 10119
Telephone: (212) 308-4300, FAX: (917) 534-6280, E-Mail: info@kenzergroup.com, Web Site: kenzergroup.com
Chmn: Robert Kenzer

DOROTHY KERR & ASSOCIATES
1509 E Standish Pl
Milwaukee, WI 52317-1960
Telephone: (414) 228-0335, FAX: (414) 228-0337
Pres: Dorothy Kerr
Strategic planning, copywriting, marketing evaluation, mentoring.

KESTRY
209 E Lake Shore Dr (#6E)
Chicago, IL 60611-1307
Telephone: (312) 664-6060, FAX: (312) 664-6059, E-Mail: kkestnbaum@earthlink.net
Pres: Kate Kestnbaum
Conducts Business: U.S.
Primary Market Served: Business & Consumer

Advertising/Marketing Budget Related to Direct Marketing: 76-100%
Founded: 1967
Marketing consulting services.

THE KEYSTONE EQUITIES GROUP
1003 Egypt Rd
Oaks, PA 19456-1155
Telephone: (610) 415-6300, Toll Free: (800) 715-9905, FAX: (610) 415-6328, Web Site: www.keystoneequities.com
Pres: William B. Fretz Jr.
Chmn: Richard A. Hansen
Mng Dir: Kevin M. Leigh
Mng Dir: Mark A. Zimmer
Exec Dir: Jack Freeman
Exec Dir: L. Keith Fretz
Exec Dir: John J. Harrison
Sr VP: Noel J. Atkinson
Employees: 15
Primary Market Served: Business
Indirect online sales
Advertising/Marketing Budget Related to Direct Marketing: 26-50%
Direct Marketing ad budget: $25,000
Direct Mail: 25%
Newspapers: 75%
Founded: 2003
Gross sales or billing: $5,000,000
Investment banking services (capital & M&A advisory) for direct marketing companies.

KFORCE INC
1001 E Palm Ave
Tampa, FL 33605-3551
Telephone: (813) 552-2394, Web Site: www.kforce.com

LIZ KISLIK ASSOCIATES LLC
100 Merrick Rd (Suite 505E)
Rockville Centre, NY 11570-4834
Telephone: (516) 568-2932, FAX: (516) 568-2936, Web Site: www.lizkislik.com
Pres: Liz Kislik
Exec Asst: Lauren Norris
Specialize in assessment, training, coaching and mentoring for all aspects of management, organizational design and customer care.

KISTLER-TIFFANY COMPANIES LLC
1205 Westlakes Dr (Suite 290)
Berwyn, PA 19312-2405
Telephone: (610) 722-3300, Toll Free: (866) 250-5413, Web Site: www.ktadv.com
Partner: David Kovach

KOBS STRATEGIC CONSULTING
222 N Columbus Dr (#2202)
Chicago, IL 60601-7819
Telephone: (312) 938-4430, FAX: (847) 934-1194, E-Mail: kobs4ksc@aol.com
Pres: Jim Kobs
Advertising/Marketing Budget Related to Direct Marketing: 76-100%
Founded: 1989

KOCHEVAR RESEARCH ASSOCIATES
PO Box 290010
Charlestown, MA 02129-0201
Telephone: (617) 242-4332, FAX: (617) 242-8009, E-Mail: kra@bigfoot.com, Web Site: www.kochevarresearch.com
Pres: John J. Kochevar

KOMUNIK
1500 St Patrick
Montreal, QC, Canada H3K 0A3
Telephone: (514) 904-0710, Web Site: www.komunik.com
VP Sls: Patrick Gagne
Primary Market Served: Business

KOWAL & ASSOCIATES INC
620 Massachusetts Ave
Cambridge, MA 02139-3376
Telephone: (617) 577-0700, FAX: (617) 577-0500, E-Mail: pkowal@kowalassociates.com, Web Site: www.kowalassociates.com
Pres: G. Paul Kowal
Employees: 5
Founded: 1988
Assists companies improve the connection with their customers & prospects by helping them create a customer-centric corporate culture.

KRAMER & ASSOCIATES
8044 Montgomery Rd (Suite 200), Bank One Towers
Cincinnati, OH 45236-2926
Telephone: (513) 792-5700, Toll Free: (800) 281-1400, FAX: (513) 792-5709, E-Mail: eservice@kramerandassociates.com, Web Site: www.kramerandassociates.com
Mngmt Dir: Lyn Kramer

HERBERT KRUG & ASSOCIATES INC
500 Davis St (Suite 812)
Evanston, IL 60201-4655
Telephone: (847) 864-0550, FAX: (847) 864-0575
Pres: E Herbert Krug

L3 VIRTUAL SOLUTIONS LLC
450 Township Rd (#208)
Marengo, OH 43334
Telephone: (740) 625-6535, Web Site:
www.l3vs.com
Mktg Commun Consultant: Lark Lamontagne

LN MARKETING ASSOCIATES
25 Seki Ct
Emerald Hills, CA 94062-3401
Telephone: (650) 368-7181
Pres: Lisa Nash
Primary Market Served: Business &
Consumer

LTD SUPPLY CHAIN
3 Black Horse Cir
Downingtown, PA 19335-1552
Telephone: (610) 458-3636, FAX:
(610) 458-8039, E-Mail: tomc@
ltdsupplychain.com, Web Site: www.
ltdsupplychain.com
Pres: Thomas W. Craig

LADD ASSOCIATES INC
2527 Fillmore St
San Francisco, CA 94115
Telephone: (415) 921-1001, FAX:
(415) 921-2311, E-Mail: info@
laddassociates.com, Web Site:
laddassociates.com
Pres: Jack W. Ladd

LANDAJOB
222 W Gregory Blvd (Suite 304)
Kansas City, MO 64114-1127
Telephone: (816) 523-1881, Toll Free:
(800) 931-8806, FAX: (816) 523-
1876, E-Mail: adstaff@landajobnow.
com, Web Site: www.landajobnow.
com
Pres: Landa Williams

LAVEN & LOEB INC
2163 Halcyon Rd
Beachwood, OH 44122-1301
Telephone: (216) 291-3483, (623) 217-
2101, E-Mail: alaven@lavenandloeb.
com; vtaylor@lavenandloeb.com,
Web Site: www.lavenandloeb.com
Pres: Ava Laven
VP: Richard Loeb
Admin Mgr: Victor Taylor
Conducts Business: U.S.
Employees: 4
Primary Market Served: Business
Catalog available online
Advertising/Marketing Budget Related
to Direct Marketing: 0-25%
Founded: 2004

RICHARD LAW
166 E 3rd St
Deer Park, NY 11729-5307
Telephone: (917) 267-8293
Primary Market Served: Consumer

LEADS-PLUS INC
PO Box 400
Killarney, FL 34740-0400
Toll Free: (800) 548-4571, E-Mail:
eurekaman43@hotmail.com, Web
Site: www.salesprospectingexpert.
com
Pres: Gordie Allen

LEAPS & BOUNDS LLC
100 Old Palisades Rd (Suite 2409)
Fort Lee, NJ 07024-7021
Telephone: (201) 947-5459
Mng Dir: Jerry Reisberg

LEARNING RESOURCES INSTITUTE
Lilly Associates Inc
2235 Durand Dr
Downers Grove, IL 60515
Telephone: (630) 963-0398
Mng Dir: Sam Lilly

LEGRAND HART
1625 Broadway (Suite 200)
Denver, CO 80202
Telephone: (303) 298-8470, FAX:
(303) 298-8570, Web Site: www.
legrandhart.com
CEO: DeeDee Legrand-Hart

LEV & BERLIN
200 Connecticut Ave (Suite 10)
Norwalk, CT 06854-1907
Telephone: (203) 838-8500, Toll Free:
(800) 377-4508, FAX: (203) 854-
1652, E-Mail: info@levberlin.com,
Web Site: www.levberlin.com
Counsel: Bruce Lev

LIBEY-CONCORDIA
811 Church Rd (Suite 105)
Cherry Hill, NJ 08002
Toll Free: (877) 903-9448, FAX: (856)
885-5068, E-Mail: libey@libey.com,
Web Site: www.libey.com
Pres: Donald R. Libey

LIFE WORKS INC
2817 Evans St
Hollywood, FL 33020-1119
Telephone: (954) 929-8428, Toll Free:
(888) 780-9400, FAX: (954) 925-
3365, Web Site: www.healthwagon.
com
Pres: Doug Brown
Sells Health & Wellness Products

LION'S SHARE MARKETING GROUP, INC
5410 Schumacher Ln
Houston, TX 77056-6810
Telephone: (713) 686-4252, Web Site:
www.lionsshare.com
Owner: Sharon Lyon
Primary Market Served: Consumer

NANCY LISS
233 E 32nd St
New York, NY 10016-6336
Telephone: (646) 418-5000
Primary Market Served: Consumer

LISTER BUTLER INC
445 Park Ave (Suite 1401)
New York, NY 10022-8626
Telephone: (212) 951-6100, FAX:
(212) 481-0230, Web Site: www.
listerbutler.com
Pres & CEO: Anita K. Hersh

ARTHUR D LITTLE INC
1 Federal St (fl 28)
Boston, MA 02110-2011
Telephone: (617) 532-9550, FAX:
(617) 261-6630, Web Site: www.
adlittle-us.com
CEO: Michael Tram

LOEB & LOEB INC
345 Park Ave
New York, NY 10154-0004
Telephone: (212) 407-4000, Web Site:
www.loeb.com
Partner: James Taylor

LOYALTYONE
3 Bessom St (Suite 211)
Marblehead, MA 01945-2372
Telephone: (781) 990-8844, Web Site:
www.speechrep.com
Primary Market Served: Business &
Consumer

LUCIDVIEW
80 Rolling Links Blvd
Oak Ridge, TN 37830-9023
Toll Free: (888) 582-4384, Web Site:
www.lucidview.com
Pres: Gordon Bell

STEVE LYTLE
425 W Randolph St
Chicago, IL 60606-1530
Telephone: (312) 894-7000

MCDM STRATEGIC DIRECT MARKETING
12864 Bradford Ln
Plainfield, IL 60585-2244

Telephone: (815) 436-5194, FAX: (815) 439-5941

Pres: Mike Capetanakis

Produces leads via all online & office media. Expertise in customer retention & copywriting.

MLB ASSOCIATES

1936 Saranac Ave (Suite 2-300)
Lake Placid, NY 12946-1114
Telephone: (518) 523-2371, FAX: (518) 523-9011, E-Mail: mlbassoc@aol.com, Web Site: www.mlbassociates.com
Exec Search-Database Mktg: Mary Lou Brown

MRI NORWALK

Div. of MRI Management Recruiters International
2334 S Cypress Bend Dr (Suite 11)
Pompano Beach, FL 33069-4488
Telephone: (203) 926-1200, FAX: (203) 926-1211, E-Mail: jbgurn@mricoastalgroup.com, Web Site: www.mricoastalgroup.com
Pres: Jim Gurn

MVI MARKETING LTD

1053 Trevor Way
San Luis Obispo, CA 93401-4549
Telephone: (805) 239-2994, (805) 459-4455, FAX: (805) 239-2947, E-Mail: info@mvimarketing.com, Web Site: www.mvimarketing.com
Pres: Elizabeth Chatelain
CEO: Marty Hurwitz

MAC MCINTOSH INC

601 Pendar Rd
North Kingstown, RI 02852-6620
Telephone: (401) 294-7730, Toll Free: (800) 944-5553, FAX: (401) 679-0176, E-Mail: info@sales-lead-experts.com, Web Site: www.sales-lead-experts.com
Pres: M.H. McIntosh

MAC MURRAY PETERSEN & SHUSTER LLP

6530 W Campus Oval (Suite 210)
New Albany, OH 43054-7069
Telephone: (614) 939-9955, FAX: (614) 939-9955, E-Mail: dbryson@mpslawyers.com, Web Site: www.mpslawyers.com
Attorney & Partner: Helen Mac Murray
Office Mgr: Destiny Bryson

MADISON EXECUTIVE SEARCH

54 Danbury Rd (Suite 368)
Ridgefield, CT 06877

Telephone: (203) 431-6565, FAX: (203) 431-6060, E-Mail: mimi@directexec.com, Web Site: www.directexec.com
Partner: M. Ward Perrott
Partner: Mimi D'Amelio

MAIL MANAGEMENT ENTERPRISES

5616 Galestown Reliance Rd
Seaford, DE 19973-6044
Telephone: (410) 883-3224, FAX: (410) 883-3392, E-Mail: mailmgt@aol.com, Web Site: www.mailmanagemententerprises.com
Pres: Jacquelyn McPeak

KEN MALEK ASSOCIATES INC

RP-NFOA
PO Box 383
Yardley, PA 19067-8383
Telephone: (215) 579-2070, FAX: (215) 860-3498, Web Site: www.kenmalek.com
Pres: Kenneth Malek

MANAGEMENT SCIENCE ASSOCIATES INC

6565 Penn Ave
Pittsburgh, PA 15206-4490
Telephone: (412) 362-2000, Toll Free: (800) MSA-INFO, FAX: (412) 363-5598, E-Mail: info@msa.com, Web Site: www.msa.com
Pres: Dr Alfred A. Kuehn
Mgr, Mktg Communs: Sharon Motta

MANGIERI/HULL SOLUTIONS LLC

One Riverside Rd
Sandy Hook, CT 06482
Telephone: (203) 270-4800, FAX: (203) 270-4815, E-Mail: chris@mhrecruiters.com, Web Site: www.mhrecruiters.com
Pres & Owner: Christopher J. Mangieri

MAPPING ANALYTICS

120 Allens Creek Rd
Rochester, NY 14618-3306
Telephone: (585) 271-6490, Toll Free: (877) 893-6490, FAX: (585) 271-1132, E-Mail: sales@mappinganalytics.com, Web Site: www.mappinganalytics.com
Pres: Ralph Rothfelder
Office Mgr: Kate Ralston
Sr Sls Consultant: George Bauman
Conducts Business: U.S.
Employees: 10
Primary Market Served: Business
Advertising/Marketing Budget Related to Direct Marketing: 0-25%

Founded: 1989
Gross sales or billing: $2,000,000

Decision support for sales & marketing professionals who are interested in customer profiling, site selection, sale & service territory management & design.

MARKET RECOGNITION

112 Prescott Rd
Boxborough, MA 01719-1121
Telephone: (978) 314-0127, Web Site: www.marketrecognition.com
VP: Jane Shurtleff

MARKET SQUARE COMMUNICATIONS INC

1100 Centerpoint Dr (Suite 203)
Stevens Point, WI 54481-2849
Telephone: (715) 344-4609, FAX: (715) 344-6885
Pres: Ann Garber

THE MARKETING ALLIANCE

127 Field Point Dr
Fairfield, CT 06824-6374
Telephone: (203) 254-0474
Principal: James McAlister

MARKETING CONSULTING SERVICES

2669 Suffolk St
Kingsport, TN 37660-5803
Telephone: (423) 288-5866, FAX: (423) 288-5576
Pres: John Buckles

MARKETING HIGHWAY

1416 Gordon Ter
Deerfield, IL 60015-4739
Telephone: (312) 502-3732, E-Mail: info@marketinghighway.com, Web Site: www.marketinghighway.com
Mng Partner: Sid Liebenson

MARKETING/MEDIA DYNAMICS INC

197 Shannondale Rd
Harpers Ferry, WV 25425-4564
Telephone: (304) 725-1119
Pres: Mary Sue Jedele

MARKETING SOLUTIONS

28252 Woodworth Way
Lathrup Village, MI 48076-2518
Telephone: (248) 443-5252, FAX: (248) 443-5252
Pres: Allen Weaks

MARKETING SYSTEMS ANALYSIS

Div. of SCI, LLC

108 N Washington Ave
Ventnor, NJ 08406-1961
Telephone: (609) 487-9340, FAX:
(866) 214-3208, E-Mail: ernie@
schell.com, Web Site: www.schell.
com
Pres: Ernest H. Schell
Conducts Business: U.S., U.K.
Employees: 2
Primary Market Served: Business &
Consumer
Advertising/Marketing Budget Related
to Direct Marketing: 76-100%
Direct Marketing ad budget:
Direct Mail: 10%
Online: 90%
Founded: 1987

Publishes online guide for direct commerce systems & services

MARKETRAC INC
300 Roosevelt Way
Westbury, NY 11590-6700
Telephone: (516) 365-4330, FAX:
(516) 365-5789
Pres: Louise Donnelly

MARKETSMITH INC
14 Walsh Dr (Floor 200)
Parsippany, NJ 07054-1063
Telephone: (973) 889-0006, Web Site:
www.marketsmithinc.com
VP Mktg: Davey Rosenbaum

MARNELL DATABASE MARKETING
119 W Chestnut St (Suite 3E)
Chicago, IL 60610-3288
Telephone: (312) 944-3511
Pres: Thomas J. Marnell

MARTINEAU & ASSOCIATES
1770 Oakdell Dr
Menlo Park, CA 94025
Telephone: (650) 326-5030, FAX:
(650) 329-0883
Partner: Catherine Martineau

MARVEL ASSOCIATES
199 Sound Beach Ave, Box 504
Old Greenwich, CT 06870-1711
Telephone: (203) 637-4777
Pres: Hunter M. Marvel

MASTEN PUBLISHING SYSTEMS
PO Box 6074
Chesterfield, MO 63006-6074
Telephone: (636) 527-1810, Toll Free:
(800) 616-9476, E-Mail: steve@
mastensystems.com, Web Site: www.
mastensystems.com
CEO: Steve Masten

MASTERY MARKETING GROUP
2525 Tiller Ln
Columbus, OH 43231-2267
Telephone: (203) 544-8997, (703) 938-
0101, Toll Free: (800) MKT-0121,
FAX: (203) 544-8397, (703) 938-
0144, E-Mail: info@masterymg.com,
Web Site: www.masterymktgrp.com
Pres: Paul Hall

MCBEE ASSOCIATES INC
997 Old Eagle School Rd (Suite 205)
Wayne, PA 19087-1706
Telephone: (610) 964-9680, Web Site:
www.mcbeeassociates.com
Dir, Mktg: Tanya McTaggart

SHANNON MCDONALD
205 W 88 St (#9D)
New York, NY 10024
Telephone: (917) 838-2057
Primary Market Served: Consumer

MCKEE CONSULTING LLC
1404 W Country Club Ln
Escondido, CA 92026-1660
Telephone: (760) 738-8200, Web Site:
www.trainyourcallcenter.com
Partner: Sally Cordova

MCKINSEY & CO
55 E 52nd St (fl 21)
New York, NY 10055-0183
Telephone: (212) 446-7000, FAX:
(212) 446-8575, Web Site: www.
mckinsey.com
Knowledge Opers Coord: Kelly
Brennan
Employees: 14,190
Gross sales or billing: $4,370,000,000

MEDAVANTE
100 American Metro Blvd (Suite 106)
Hamilton, NJ 08619-2319
Telephone: (609) 528-9413, Web Site:
www.metavante.com
Primary Market Served: Consumer

MEDIA MANAGEMENT SERVICES INC
105 Terry Dr (Suite 120)
Newton, PA 18940-1872
Telephone: (215) 579-8590, Toll Free:
(800) 523-5948, FAX: (215) 579-
8589, Web Site: www.
mmseducation.com
VP: Connie Schofer

MEDIA RECRUITING GROUP INC
1 Bridge St (Suite P2)
Irvington, NY 10533-1575

Telephone: (914) 591-5511, FAX:
(914) 591-8911, E-Mail: resume@
mediarecruiting.com, Web Site:
www.mediarecruiting.com
Exec VP: Steve Goldberg

MRG are leaders in executive search
for digital media sales and marketing
placements including: sales, marketing/
SEO/SEM, social media marketing. We
also place within other mediums (like
print). Launched in 2009, MRG also
has a Digital Sales & Marketing Course
Division designed to empower media
professionals in today's rapidly changing times.

MEDINA ASSOCIATES
12 Hilltop Rd
Rose Valley, PA 19086-6243
Telephone: (610) 565-8836, FAX:
(610) 565-8184, E-Mail:
kurtmedina@aol.com, Web Site:
www.medinaassociates.com
Pres: Kurt Medina
Conducts Business: U.S.
Employees: 2
Primary Market Served: Consumer
Advertising/Marketing Budget Related
to Direct Marketing: 76-100%
Direct Marketing ad budget:
$20,000,000
Direct Mail: 20%
Magazines: 10%
TV/Radio: 60%
Telephone: 10%
Founded: 1991

Direct response marketing consulting
specializing in the 50 plus mature market.

MICHEL CONSULTING
61903 Brokentop Dr
Bend, OR 97702-1085
Telephone: (541) 633-7838
Pres: Bill Michel

MIGLAUTSCH MARKETING INC
555 S Industrial Dr (Suite 5)
Hartland, WI 53029
Telephone: (262) 369-3900, FAX:
(262) 369-3915, E-Mail: info@
migmar.com, Web Site: www.
migmar.com
Owner: John Miglautsch

ADRIAN MILLER DIRECT MARKETING
43 Park Ave
Port Washington, NY 11050-4010
Telephone: (516) 767-9288, E-Mail:
amiller@adrianmiller.com, Web Site:
www.adrianmiller.com
Pres: Adrian Miller

FRED MILMAN ASSOCIATES
23 Selina Ct
Glen Cove, NY 11542-3048
Telephone: (516) 625-8075, FAX:
   (516) 625-5927, E-Mail: fmilman@
   compuserve.com
Pres: Fred Milman

**MILROD EXECUTIVE
   SEARCH**
22 Riverside Dr
Princeton, NJ 08540-4017
Telephone: (609) 683-8787, FAX:
   (609) 683-8221
Pres: Jane Milrod

MIMAARTS LLC
535 Fifth Ave (fl 31)
New York, NY 10017-3667
Telephone: (212) 584-1810
Primary Market Served: Consumer

**MISSION: A CONSULTING
   GROUP**
Div. of Mission Inc
36 Cross Hwy
Westport, CT 06880-2141
Telephone: (203) 227-9475, FAX:
   (203) 227-6512, E-Mail: info@
   mission-consulting.com, Web Site:
   www.mission-consulting.com
Mng Partner: Dorothy E. Curran

MR FANTASTIC LLC
c/o Billue, 1345 Ellis Pl, Bowling
   Green, KY 42104-0602
55739 Holiday Cr
Astor, FL 32102-7991
Telephone: (407) 719-2020, E-Mail:
   sbillue@usa2net.net, Web Site:
   www.stanbillue.com
Pres & Owner: Stan Billue
Conducts Business: Worldwide
Employees: 5
Primary Market Served: Business
Catalog available online
Indirect online sales
Direct Marketing ad budget: $120,000
Direct Mail: 10%
Magazines: 10%
Newspapers: 10%
Online: 20%
Telephone: 50%
Founded: 1983
Gross sales or billing: $1,000,000

Audio & video tapes and live seminars
for telemarketing sales training, motivation, and consulting.

MODERN MAIL
PO Box 674
Bear, DE 19701-0674
Telephone: (302) 391-1200, Web Site:
   www.triggermarketing.com

Pres: Doug Ainsworth

MONSTER WORLDWIDE
133 Boston Post Rd (#15)
Weston, MA 02493-2525
Toll Free: (888) MONSTER, Web Site:
   www.monster.com
VP CRM: Matthew Resteghini

MORAN DIRECT INC
710 N Post Oak Rd (Suite 520)
Houston, TX 77024-3858
Telephone: (713) 880-3725, FAX:
   (713) 263-7647, E-Mail: rmoran@
   morandirect.com, Web Site: www.
   morandirect.com
Pres: Ron Moran

MORRIS & FELLOWS
6105 Blue Stone Rd NE (Suite A)
Atlanta, GA 30328-3885
Telephone: (404) 250-0225
Pres Fin: Cheri Morris
Office Mgr: Ginger Pepper

**MORRIS JAMES HITCHENS
   & WILLIAMS**
500 Delaware Ave (Suite 1500), PO
   Box 2306
Wilmington, DE 19801-1494
Telephone: (302) 888-6800, FAX:
   (302) 571-1750, Web Site: www.
   morrisjames.com
Partner: Edward M. McNally

MULDOON & BAER INC
130 Banyan Isle Rd
Palm Beach Gardens, FL 33416-4601
Telephone: (561) 630-0999, FAX:
   (561) 630-9466, Web Site: www.
   muldoonandbaer.com
Pres: Katie Muldoon
VP: J. Baer

**NAK MARKETING &
   COMMUNICATIONS**
575 Madison Ave (Suite 700)
New York, NY 10022-8512
Telephone: (212) 505-9290, Web Site:
   www.nakcomm.com
Pres: Thaddeus Kubis

**NATIONAL ECONOMIC
   RESEARCH ASSOCIATES
   INC**
1255 23rd St NW (Suite 600)
Washington, DC 20037
Telephone: (202) 466-3510, FAX:
   (202) 466-3605, E-Mail: andrew.
   carron@nera.com, Web Site: www.
   nera.com
Pres: Dr Andrew Carron

**NATIONAL MAIL/
   MARKETING CORP**
390 Reed Rd (fl 13)
Broomall, PA 19008-4008
Telephone: (610) 544-8200, FAX:
   (610) 544-1819, Web Site: www.
   natlmail.com
Pres: Vince Jennings

**PAUL NELSON DIRECT
   MARKETING**
2411 Sixth St
Santa Monica, CA 90405
Telephone: (310) 392-9533
Creative Dir: Paul Nelson

**NEW AMERICAN
   DIMENSIONS**
6955 La Tijera Blvd (Suite B)
Los Angeles, CA 90045-1932
Telephone: (310) 670-6800
Pres: David Morse

**NEW CUSTOMER SERVICE
   COMPANIES INC**
22894 Pacific Blvd
Sterling, VA 20166-6722
Telephone: (703) 707-1582, Web Site:
   www.newcorp.com
Primary Market Served: Consumer

NEWS MARKETING CANADA
100 King St W (Suite 7000), One First
   Canadian Place
Toronto, ON, Canada M5X 1A4
Telephone: (416) 775-3000, FAX:
   (416) 775-3055, E-Mail:
   spetkovich@newsmarketing.ca, Web
   Site: www.newsmarketing.ca
Sr VP: Adam North

NIGRONEWMEDIA
4004 Hermitage Hills Blvd (Apt 20)
Hermitage, PA 16148-3420
Telephone: (724) 699-0230
Primary Market Served: Consumer

**NORTHERN ILLINOIS
   CONSULTING INC**
PO Box 7157
Libertyville, IL 60048-7157
Telephone: (847) 828-1999, Web Site:
   www.cmsbusiness.com
Pres: John Coxon
Primary Market Served: Business &
   Consumer

NUEDGE SYSTEMS
Div. of Metavante Corp
4900 W Brown Deer Rd
Brown Deer, WI 53223
Toll Free: (800) 236-3282, Web Site:
   www.nuedgesystems.com

Pres & CEO: Frank R. Martire

OSG BILLING
100 W Forest Ave (Suite G)
Englewood, NJ 07631-4033
Telephone: (201) 871-1100, Web Site:
www.osgbilling.com
Sr Mktg Coord: Alexandria Pasckvale

**OAK KNOLL LIMITED
LIABILITY CO**
7 Hastings Ct
South Salem, NY 10590-2517
Telephone: (914) 533-0208
Principal: Charles Prescott
Primary Market Served: Business &
Consumer

**ODENZA MARKETING
GROUP**
4445 Eastgate Mall (Suite 200)
San Diego, CA V5G 4L7-92121-1971
Telephone: (866) 883-2968, Web Site:
www.odenza.com
Mktg Mgr: Pav Sangha
Conducts Business: U.S. & Canada
Employees: 30
Direct online sales
Advertising/Marketing Budget Related
to Direct Marketing: 0-25%
Direct Marketing ad budget:
Direct Mail: 25%
Magazines: 65%
Online: 10%
Founded: 2001
Marketing firm.

**O'KEEFE HENRY DIRECT
INC**
707 Lake Cook Rd (Suite 285)
Deerfield, IL 60015-4933
Telephone: (847) 681-9200, FAX:
(847) 681-9299, Web Site: www.
okeefehenrydirect.com
Pres: Peter Henry

OPEN SYSTEMS SERVICES
330 SW 27 Ave (Suite 402)
Miami, FL 33135
Telephone: (305) 541-1970
Pres: Alexander Lopez

GLEN ORENSTEIN
2959 Judith Dr
Merrick, NY 11566-5448
Telephone: (516) 359-8785
Primary Market Served: Consumer

**OUTSOURCING SOLUTIONS
INC**
PO Box 407
Wentzville, MO 63385-0407

Telephone: (847) 419-1790, FAX:
(847) 419-1818
EVP & Chief Mktg Officer: Steven K.
Richards

OVATIVE/GROUP LLC
701 Washington Ave N (#400)
Minneapolis, MN 55401-0096
Telephone: (612) 886-1010, Web Site:
www.ovative.com

PCG, INC
1S935 Tanglewood Dr (#121)
Batavia, IL 60510-9511
Telephone: (630) 482-9300, FAX:
(630) 454-3750, E-Mail: sasmith@
pcgnow.com, Web Site: www.
pcgnow.com
Partner: Meg Goodman

PMG
7160 Columbia Gateway Dr (Suite
300)
Columbia, MD 21046-2134
Telephone: (410) 290-0667, Web Site:
www.pmgdirect.net
Pres: Rick Powell

PACKSTREAM LLC
2400 Dundee Rd
Louisville, KY 40205-2047
Telephone: (502) 552-9624, Web Site:
www.packstream.com
CEO: Erik Nelson

**JAMES ROBERT PARISH
CONSULTING**
4338 Gentry Ave (Suite 1)
Studio City, CA 91604-1764
Telephone: (818) 753-9455, FAX:
(818) 505-6509, E-Mail: jrparish@
sbcglobal.net, Web Site: www.
jamesrobertparish.com
Pres & Owner: James Robert Parish

**MARY ANNE PARSHALL
CONSULTING INC**
616 Corte Regalo
Camarillo, CA 93010-9107
Telephone: (805) 445-7522, FAX:
(805) 445-8876
CEO: Mary Ann Parshall
Primary Market Served: Business &
Consumer
Catalog available online
Indirect online sales

**PAUL, HASTINGS,
JANOFSKY & WALKER
LLP**
75 E 55th St, Park Avenue Tower
New York, NY 10022-3205

Telephone: (212) 318-6037, FAX:
(212) 319-4090, E-Mail:
robertsherman@paulhastings.com,
Web Site: www.paulhastings.com
DMA Gen Counsel: Robert Sherman
Esq.

PERCIPIO MEDIA, LLC
201 Broadway (Suite 7)
Cambridge, MA 02139-1955
Telephone: (617) 995-7855

JAMES R PERDIEW & CO
1405 Afton Cir
Inverness, IL 60010-5702
Telephone: (847) 842-8525, FAX:
(847) 842-8518, E-Mail: jrpco@
perdiew.com, Web Site: www.
perdiew.com
Pres: James R. Perdiew

S PERNICK & ASSOCIATES
1616 Sheridan Rd (Unit 2H)
Wilmette, IL 60091-1884
Telephone: (847) 256-0115
Conducts Business: U.S., Canada
Primary Market Served: Business &
Consumer
Founded: 1989

Telemanagement of outsourced programs.

**PILLSBURY WINTHROP
SHAW PITTMAN LLP**
725 S Figueroa St (Suite 2800)
Los Angeles, CA 90017-5406
Telephone: (213) 488-7100, Web Site:
www.pillsburywinthrop.com
Partner: Deborah Thoren-Peden

PLATINUM PRESS
37 Route 80
Killingworth, CT 06419-1429
Telephone: (860) 663-3882, FAX:
(718) 825-5065, E-Mail:
herbertjcohen@aol.com
Pres: Herbert Cohen

**PLEXUS MARKETING
GROUP INC**
PO Box 76380, Bldg G
Atlanta, GA 30358-1380
Telephone: (770) 390-9692, Toll Free:
(800) 9-PLEXUS, FAX: (770) 390-
9693, Web Site: www.
plexusmarketing.com
Pres: Michael McClellan

POHAKU INC
44-103 Puuohalai Pl
Kaneohe, HI 96744-2545
Telephone: (319) 653-2569, Web Site:
www.gopohaku.com

Pres & CEO: Wendy Gady
Primary Market Served: Business &
Consumer

POLESTAR GROUP
20 N Canton Rd
West Simsbury, CT 06092
Telephone: (860) 658-4992
Pres: Peter Brinkerhoff

POSTAL EN ESPANOL INC
8325 W Hillsborough Ave
Tampa, FL 33615-3805
Telephone: (813) 885-8888, Web Site:
www.postalenespanol.com
Gen Mgr & Mktg Consultant: Jeff Devin

**PRACTICAL COMPUTER
SOLUTIONS**
154 Brentwood Dr
South Orange, NJ 07079-1141
Telephone: (973) 761-6099, FAX:
(215) 243-8283, E-Mail: dbsteig@
alum.mit.edu, Web Site: www.
donsteig.com
Pres: Donald B. Steig

**PRINTCOM CONSULTING
GROUP**
1020 Farm Creek Rd
Waxhaw, NC 28173-7793
Telephone: (704) 843-5350, FAX:
(704) 843-5352, E-Mail: printcom@
aol.com
Pres: William Lamparter

PRINTMARK
432 Johnson Rd
East Montpelier, VT 05651-4250
Telephone: (802) 229-9743, FAX:
(802) 229-9746, E-Mail: alex@
printmark.net, Web Site: www.
printmark.net
Pres: Alex Brown

**PRIVACY & INFORMATION
PRACTICES ADVISORY**
10 Gristmill Ln
Saddle River, NJ 07458-1317
Telephone: (201) 887-2157

PRODUCT TO MARKET LLC
4536 County Rd 4 SW
Cokato, MN 55321-4220
Telephone: (320) 286-9997
Owner: Mark Koivisto
Primary Market Served: Business

PRODUCTION SOLUTIONS
1953 Gallows Rd (Suite 600)
Vienna, VA 22182-3988
Telephone: (703) 734-5700

Pres & CEO: George Lizama

**PRODUCTIVE STRATEGIES
INC**
2 Northfield Plaza (Suite 365)
Northfield, IL 60093-1272
Telephone: (847) 446-0008, FAX:
(847) 446-0211, E-Mail: pkrone@
productivestrategies.com, Web Site:
www.productivestrategies.com
Pres: Philip Krone

**PRODUCTIVITY
DEVELOPMENT GROUP
INC**
PO Box 488
Westford, MA 01886
Telephone: (978) 692-1818, FAX:
(978) 692-5080, E-Mail: info@
martinstankard.com
Pres: Martin F. Stankard

PROJECTSENSE
602 Whispering Wind Ct
Gaithersburg, MD 20877-3418
Telephone: (240) 476-1677, Web Site:
www.projectsense.net

PROSOURCE
1502 Augusta Dr (Suite 100)
Houston, TX 77057-2454
Telephone: (713) 667-3690, FAX:
(713) 660-9629, Web Site: www.
prosourcedev.com
VP Mktg: April Merrill
Primary Market Served: Business &
Consumer

PROVEN PROSPECTS INC
275 Arboleda Rd
Santa Barbara, CA 93110-1703
Telephone: (805) 448-6253, Web Site:
www.provemprospects.com
CEO: Ben Kennedy

**PUBLIC ISSUES
MANAGEMENT**
902 Rose Ave
Piedmont, CA 94611-4343
Telephone: (510) 654-9114, FAX:
(510) 654-0196
Principal: Karen Joffe

**PUBLICATION
FULFILLMENT SVCS**
aka Edwards-Pullin Consulting
10564 Progress Way (Suite D)
Cypress, CA 90630-4712
Telephone: (714) 226-9785, FAX:
(714) 226-9733, E-Mail: janpullin@
pfsmag.com, Web Site: www.
pfsmag.com
Pres: Jan Edwards-Pullin

**PUBLICATIONS GROUPE RR
INTERNATIONAL INC**
2322 Sherbrooke E
Montreal, QC, Canada H2K 1E5
Telephone: (514) 521-8148
VP Opers: Diane Tanguay
Primary Market Served: Business &
Consumer

**PUBLISHING FULFILLMENT
CONSULTING LLC**
85 Settlers Hill Rd
Brewster, NY 10509-5210
Telephone: (845) 278-2800, Web Site:
www.fulfillmentconsulting.com
Pres: William Dugan

PURSUANT GROUP
5151 Beltline Rd (Suite 900)
Dallas, TX 75254-6757
Telephone: (214) 866-7700, E-Mail:
info@pursuant.com, Web Site: www.
pursuant.com
CEO: Trent Ricker
VP, Mktg: Cassandra Bennett
Primary Market Served: Consumer

**QUIGLEY CONSULTING
GROUP**
1775 W Broadland Ln
Lake Forest, IL 60045-4817
Telephone: (847) 604-6773
Pres: Robert Quigley

QWEST
1801 California St
Denver, CO 80202-5555
Telephone: (303) 992-1400, Toll Free:
(800) 603-6000, FAX: (303) 896-
8515, Web Site: www.qwest.com
Chmn & CEO: Eduard R. Mueller

RDO MARKETING LLC
4820 W 77th St (Suite 120)
Minneapolis, MN 55435-4809
Telephone: (952) 746-7585

RSM MCGLADREY INC
4725 Piedmont Row Dr (Suite 300)
Charlotte, NC 28210-4280
Telephone: (980) 233-4700, Web Site:
www.rsmmcgladrey.com
Sr Dir Mktg Svcs & Brand: Eric Webb
Primary Market Served: Business &
Consumer

RW CONSULTING
452 Sondley Woods Pl
Asheville, NC 28805
Telephone: (828) 299-3645, Web Site:
www.rwconsulting.net
Pres: Bob Weinberg
Conducts Business: U.S.

Employees: 2
Primary Market Served: Business &
    Consumer
Advertising/Marketing Budget Related
    to Direct Marketing: 51-75%
Founded: 1996

Provide strategic and database analytic
services to direct and database marketers. Expertise includes business evalua-
tions, program and product
improvement and database conceptual
design.

RAAB ASSOCIATES
730 Yale Ave
Swarthmore, PA 19081-1805
Telephone: (914) 241-2117, FAX:
    (914) 241-0080, E-Mail: info@
    raabassociates.com, Web Site: www.
    raabassociates.com
Partner: David M. Raab

**LYNDA RAIHOFER &
    ASSOCIATES LLC**
48 Young Ave
Pelham, NY 10803-1724
Telephone: (914) 738-8282
Owner: Lynda Raihofer

**RAINWATER ASSOCIATES
    INC**
135 E 71st St
New York, NY 10021-4258
Telephone: (212) 861-2856, FAX:
    (212) 861-1729, E-Mail: rainwine@
    aol.com
Pres: Michael Michaelson

NEIL RANSICK MARKETING
212 Teresita Blvd
San Francisco, CA 94127-1729
Telephone: (415) 664-6728
Principal Owner: Neil Ransick

RAPHEL MARKETING
RP-NFOA
211 North Ave
Saint Johnsbury, VT 05819-1626
Telephone: (802) 751-8802, FAX:
    (802) 751-8804, E-Mail: neil@
    raphel.com, Web Site: www.raphel.
    com
Pres: Neil Raphel

RAPID INSIGHT INC
53 Technology Ln (Suite 112)
Conway, NH 03818-5804
Telephone: (603) 447-0240, Web Site:
    www.rapidinsightinc.com

REDENGINE DIGITAL
1485 Chain Bridge Rd (Suite 305)
Mc Lean, VA 22101-4501

Telephone: (703) 556-6951, Web Site:
    www.redenginedigital.com
Pres: Liz Murphy

REDWOOD PARTNERS LTD
60 E 42nd St (Rm 1820)
New York, NY 10165-6210
Telephone: (212) 843-8585, FAX:
    (212) 843-9093, E-Mail: info@
    redwoodpartners.com, Web Site:
    www.redwoodpartners.com
Mng Dir: Michael D. Flannery

**REED SMITH HALL
    DICKLER ADVERTISING &
    LAW MARKETING GROUP**
599 Lexington Ave (Floor 29)
New York, NY 10022
Telephone: (212) 549-0377, FAX:
    (212) 521-5450, Web Site: www.
    reedsmith.com
Exec Partner: Douglas Wood
Asst Mktg VP: Andrea Mouzakis

**REICHERT & ASSOCIATES
    INC**
PO Box 268
Grand Marais, MN 55604
Telephone: (218) 387-1095, E-Mail:
    reichertln@aol.com
Pres: Leo N. Reichert

**RESCOTT LLC MARKETING
    & TECHNOLOGY**
5856 Poole Pl (Suite 263)
Noblesville, IN 46062-7608
Telephone: (317) 816-0700, Web Site:
    www.rescott.com
Pres: Toby Reeves

RESEARCH BOSTON CORP
1160 Brown Ave
Lafayette, CA 94549-3102
Telephone: (978) 225-8030, FAX:
    (267) 295-8704, Web Site: www.
    researchboston.com
Pres: Paul Teplitz

RESPONSE ADVANTAGE
8635 Falmouth (#301)
Playa Del Rey, CA 90293-8281
Telephone: (310) 577-0389, Web Site:
    www.responseadvantage.com
Pres: Stephanie Beckman

RESPONSE DESIGN CORP
5541 Simpson Ave
Ocean City, NJ 08226-1258
Telephone: (609) 601-5866, Toll Free:
    (800) 366-4732, FAX: (609) 788-
    3619, E-Mail: rdc@responsedesign.
    com, Web Site: www.
    responsedesign.com

Pres: Kathryn E. Jackson

RESPONSYS
1100 Grundy Ln (#3)
San Bruno, CA 94066-3065
Telephone: (650) 745-1700, Web Site:
    www.responsys.com
Chief Mktg Officer: Scott Olrich

THE RESULTS GROUP
aka Verdant Results Group
65 E India Row (Suite 37F), Harbor
    Towers
Boston, MA 02110-3323
Telephone: (617) 227-0229, Web Site:
    www.verdant-results-group.com
Pres: Vincent Vassallo

**RETRIEVAL MASTERS
    CREDITORS BUREAU INC**
4 Westchester Plz (Suite 110)
Elmsford, NY 10523-1615
Telephone: (914) 592-0055, Toll Free:
    (800) 666-8097, FAX: (914) 345-
    5023, E-Mail: info@retrievalmasters.
    com, Web Site: www.
    retrievalmasters.com
Pres: Michael Ghort

RHINO MARKETING INC
515 S Flower St (fl 36)
Los Angeles, CA V3B 5H6-90071-
    2221
Telephone: (604) 472-3240, Toll Free:
    (877) 605-7022, FAX: (604) 637-
    5619, Web Site: www.rhino.ca
Chief Rhino: Doug Morneau
Primary Market Served: Business &
    Consumer

BRUCE RHODES
83 Victoria Rd
Sudbury, MA 01776-3139
Telephone: (978) 443-8389
Pres: Bruce Rhodes

RIDENOUR & ASSOCIATES
333 W North Ave #354, Chicago, IL
    60610-1293
4125 Moss Oak Pl
Sarasota, FL 34231-2935
Telephone: (312) 787-8228, FAX:
    (312) 787-8528, E-Mail:
    ssridenour@aol.com, Web Site:
    www.ridenourassociates.com
Pres: Suzanne S. Ridenour

ROLAND ADVISORS
4 Norwood Rd
Annapolis, MD 21401-1227
Telephone: (410) 268-3648
Principal: Donald Roland
Primary Market Served: Business &
    Consumer

ALAN ROSENSPAN & ASSOCIATES

34 Summit Ave
Sharon, MA 02067-2149
Telephone: (781) 784-2228, Web Site:
www.alanrosenspan.com
Pres: Alan Rosenspan

ROSS CULBERT & LAVERY

900 Broadway (#401)
New York, NY 10003
Telephone: (212) 206-0044, Web Site:
www.rclnyc.com
Pres: Peter Ross

THE RUSIN GROUP, LLC

30 Hollow Tree Pl
Wilton, CT 06897
Telephone: (203) 529-3257

RUSS, AUGUST & KABAT

12424 Wilshire Blvd (Suite 1200)
Los Angeles, CA 90025
Telephone: (310) 826-7474, FAX:
(310) 826-6991, E-Mail: info@
raklaw.com, Web Site: www.raklaw.
com
Pres, Mng Partner: Larry C. Russ

ANNE RUTH

6 Alden Pl Apt 1D
Bronxville, NY 10708-4846
Telephone: (914) 337-7931
Marketing: Anne Ruth

SIGMA MARKETING GROUP LLC

1850 S Winton Rd
Rochester, NY 14618-3923
Telephone: (585) 473-7300, Toll Free:
(888) 277-9837, FAX: (585) 473-
0332, E-Mail: mbush@
sigmamarketing.com, Web Site:
www.sigmamarketing.com; www.
jthgearanalytics.com (Blog)
CEO: Kenyon Blunt
CFO: Jaime Sanchez
Exec VP Client Svcs: Jim Dellavilla
SVP Strategy & Mktg: Martha Bush
Chief Technology Officer: Mike Fuqua
Employees: 85
Founded: 1985
Gross sales or billing: $15,300,000

Analytics+Strategy+Technology=Making it Work. SIGMA Marketing turns data into customer intelligence & innovative marketing solutions: online & offline. Our direct & digital solutions focus on multichannel marketing strategies, data & technology integration, web analytics & sales enablement. We build long term customer relationships and drive Marketing ROI.

SKO-BRENNER-AMERICAN

841 Merrick Rd CS 9320
Baldwin, NY 11510-9320
Telephone: (516) 771-4400, Toll Free:
(800) 645-3390, FAX: (516) 771-
7810, E-Mail: collect@skobrenner.
com, Web Site: www.skobrenner.
com
Chmn & CEO: Stuart Brenner

SLR ASSOCIATES

3300 NW 185th Ave (PMB 268)
Portland, OR 97229-3406
Telephone: (503) 645-0675
Pres: Stacy Rollins

KURT SALMON ASSOCIATES INC

Subs. of Management Consulting
Group PLC
1355 Peachtree St NE (Suite 900)
Atlanta, GA 30309-3266
Telephone: (404) 892-0321, FAX:
(404) 898-9590, E-Mail:
infoksaweb@kurtsalmon.com, Web
Site: www.kurtsalmon.com
Chmn: Mark Wietecha
CEO: Jerry T. Black
CFO: William Beckemeyer
CIO: Bruce Seeber
VP & Pres Health Care Div: James Berarducci
Editorial Mgr: Katherine Lombardo
Conducts Business: Worldwide
Employees: 60
Catalog available online
Indirect online sales
Founded: 1935

Global management consultant that specializes in health care providers. Strategy, facility planning & information technology for multi-hospital systems, community hospitals, academic medical centers, children's hospitals, & physician group practices in the US. Also serves retail & consumer products industries.

SANDLER TECHWORKS

525 E 82nd St (Suite 2G)
New York, NY 10028-7148
Telephone: (917) 697-9678, Web Site:
www.sandlertechworks.com
Primary Market Served: Consumer

SATISFACTION SOFTWARE INC

8711 150th St
Jamaica, NY 11435-3107
Telephone: (732) 382-8736, FAX:
(732) 382-8736, E-Mail: db@biink.
com
Pres: David Beardsley

RICHARD SAUNDERS INTERNATIONAL

3849 Edwards Rd
Cincinnati, OH 45244
Telephone: (513) 271-9911, FAX:
(513) 271-9966, E-Mail: doug@
eurekaranch.com, Web Site: www.
eurekaranch.com
Pres: Douglas B. Hall

SAVITZ

13747 Montfort Dr (Suite 117)
Dallas, TX 75240-4499
Telephone: (310) 642-4799, FAX:
(310) 642-7795, E-Mail: lmoran@
savitzfieldandfocus.com, Web Site:
www.savitzfieldandfocus.com
Mgr: Lynn Moran

J SCHMID & ASSOCIATES INC

5800 Foxridge Dr (Suite 200)
Mission, KS 66202-2333
Telephone: (913) 236-8988, FAX:
(913) 236-8987, E-Mail: info@
jschmid.com, Web Site: www.
jschmid.com
Pres & Chief Creative Officer: Lois
Boyle

THE SCHMIDT GROUP INTERNATIONAL INC

298 Peppertree Dr S
Vero Beach, FL 32963
Telephone: (772) 492-0073, FAX:
(772) 492-0293, E-Mail:
catalogprofit@att.net, Web Site:
www.the-schmidt-group.com
Pres: Alfred M. Schmidt Jr.

SCHULTE ASSOCIATES

2807 Polk St NE
Minneapolis, MN 55418-2954
Telephone: (612) 788-1673, FAX:
(612) 788-1147, E-Mail: schulte@
nmoa.org, Web Site: www.nmoa.org/
schulte
Pres: John D. Schulte

SCHUPAK GROUP INC

595 Madison Ave (Room 1900)
New York, NY 10022-1958
Telephone: (212) 582-4210
CEO: Donald Schupak

SCHUS & CO

1458 Royal Blvd
Glendale, CA 91201
Telephone: (818) 550-8100, E-Mail:
sschus@aol.com
Pres: Stephanie Schus

SEDLAK
22901 Millcreek Blvd (Suite 600), Metropolitan Plaza
Highland Hills, OH 44122-5724
Telephone: (216) 206-4700, FAX: (216) 206-4840, E-Mail: info@jasedlak.com, Web Site: www.jasedlak.com
Pres: Jeffrey B. Graves
Mktg Commun: N. Evans

SEKLEMIAN NEWELL INC (CRMC)
1521 Alton Rd (Suite 138)
Miami Beach, FL 33139-3301
Telephone: (310) 622-5405, FAX: (520) 842-7344, Web Site: www.thecrmc.com
Pres: Devon Wylie

Customer Relationship Management Conference (CRMC).

SENTINEL PEAK LLC
15600 Redmond Way
Redmond, WA 98052
Telephone: (360) 293-7271, Web Site: www.sentinel-peak.com
Principal: Bart Pestarino

THE SERVICES GROUP (TSG)
2101 Wilson Blvd (Suite 700)
Arlington, VA 22201-3060
Telephone: (703) 528-7444, FAX: (703) 522-2329, E-Mail: tsq@tsginc.com, Web Site: www.tsginc.com
CEO: Hugh Doyle

SEVERINI COMMUNICATIONS LLC
2025 W Broadway 16K
New York, NY 10023
Telephone: (917) 734-3991, E-Mail: mark@severinicommunications.com, Web Site: www.severinicommunications.com
Pres: Mark Severini
Mng Dir: Jose Gonzalez
Primary Market Served: Consumer

SHAPES MARKETING INC
2086 Saint Johns Ave (Apt 207)
Highland Park, IL 60035-2461
Telephone: (847) 291-1110, FAX: (847) 291-1308, Web Site: www.shapesmarket.com
Chmn: John L. Shapin
Pres: Margaret Shapin

SHARF WOODWARD & ASSOCIATES INC
5900 Sepulveda Blvd (Suite 104)
Sherman Oaks, CA 91411
Telephone: (818) 988-2200, Toll Free: (877) 482-6687, Web Site: www.swjobs.com
Owner: Bernie Sharf

SHASHO JONES DIRECT INC
145 W 67th St (#4D)
New York, NY 10023-5930
Telephone: (212) 929-2300, E-Mail: glenda@sjdirect.com, Web Site: www.sjdirect.com
Pres: Glenda Shasho Jones
Pres: Rey Cruz
Founded: 1991

Catalog consulting, branding & creative development.

DAVID SHEPARD ASSOCIATES INC
332 Altessa Blvd
Melville, NY 11747-5222
Telephone: (516) 271-5567, FAX: (516) 271-5589, E-Mail: davidshepard@dsadirect.com, Web Site: www.dsadirect.com
Pres: David B. Shepard

SHESHUNOFF MANAGEMENT SERVICES
901 S Mo Pac Expy (Suite 140)
Austin, TX 78746-5759
Telephone: (512) 472-4000, Toll Free: (800) 477-1772, FAX: (512) 479-8189, E-Mail: info@smslp.com, Web Site: www.ashesh.com
Partner: Alex Sheshunoff

KATE SHIFMAN CONSULTING
179 Saint Johns Pl (Apt 2)
Brooklyn, NY 11217-3417
Telephone: (917) 710-0219
Primary Market Served: Consumer

SHISLER AND ASSOCIATES
14917 Oaks North Dr (Suite 113)
Dallas, TX 75254-7631
Telephone: (972) 387-8656
Partner: Jack Shisler

SIGNATURE INC
4701 Midway Dr
Ann Arbor, MI 48103
Telephone: (734) 426-2000, FAX: (734) 426-2109, E-Mail: johnagno@signatureseries.com, Web Site: www.mentoringandcoaching.com
Pres: John Agno

SILLIKER INC
111 E Wacker Dr (Suite 2300)
Chicago, IL 60601-4214
Telephone: (708) 957-7878, FAX: (708) 957-3798, E-Mail: cjx@netcom.com, Web Site: www.silliker.com
Dir, Mktg Commun: Jessica Sawyer-Lueck

SKYSTONE RYAN
635 W Seventh St (Suite 107)
Cincinnati, OH 45203
Telephone: (513) 241-6778, FAX: (513) 241-0551, E-Mail: cincinnati@skystoneryan.com, Web Site: www.skystoneryan.com
Pres: J. Patrick Ryan

BRENT SLINKARD CONSULTANT
1048 W 17th St
Bloomington, IN 47404-3338
Telephone: (812) 336-1111
Pres: Brent Slinkard

RAY SLYPER ASSOCIATES
420 E 72nd St (Suite 2L)
New York, NY 10021
Telephone: (212) 439-0710
Pres: Ray Slyper

SMART SOURCE DIRECT
Div. of News America Marketing
1185 Ave of the Americas (fl 27), News America Marketing
New York, NY 10036-2603
Telephone: (617) 375-0404, FAX: (617) 425-0115, Web Site: www.newsamerica.com

SMITH-BROWNING DIRECT INC
45 Camielle Ct
Sedona, AZ 86336-5977
Telephone: (928) 203-9420
VP: Timothy C. Smith
Co Owner: Elizabeth Smith

SMITH HANLEY ASSOCIATES
107 John St Ste 201
Southport, CT 06890-1466
Telephone: (203) 319-4300, Toll Free: (888) 221-2900, FAX: (203) 319-4320, Web Site: www.smithhanley.com
Pres: Tom Hanley
Mng Dir: Jacqueline Paige
Recruiter: Eda Zullo
Recruiter: Peg Hoerres
Recruiter: Kim McStocker
Recruiter: Nikki Quist
Employees: 100

Founded: 1980

Highly specialized recruiting firm with long term dedicated professionals focusing on the needs of our clients.

SMITH O'KEEFE & ASSOCIATES

1566 Somers Point Rd
Egg Harbor Township, NJ 08234-8514
Telephone: (609) 653-0400, Toll Free: (800) 222-0461, FAX: (609) 653-6483, E-Mail: info@smithokeefe. com, Web Site: www.smithokeefe. com
CEO: Kenneth P. Smith

SNYDER GLENN J & ASSOCS

49 Quail Ln
Jacksonville Beach, FL 32250
Telephone: (904) 246-6223, FAX: (904) 246-6229
Owner: Glenn J. Snyder

SOLUTRAN

3600 Holly Ln (Suite 60)
Plymouth, MN 55447
Telephone: (763) 559-2225, Toll Free: (888) 765-8872, FAX: (763) 559-8872, E-Mail: solutions@solutran. com, Web Site: www.solutran.com
Pres & CEO: Barry J. Nordstrand

DEBBIE SORACE

70 Edwards Pl
Valley Stream, NY 11580-3143
Telephone: (516) 659-5614
Primary Market Served: Consumer

THE SOUND DIRECT MARKETING GROUP

PO Box 162527
Austin, TX 78716-2527
Telephone: (512) 306-0879
Pres: Robert Rogin

SOURCELINK

500 Park Blvd (Suite 1245)
Itasca, IL 60143-2610
Toll Free: (866) 947-6872, Web Site: www.sourcelink.com
Pres & CEO: Don McKenzie

SOUTHWEST CONSULTANTS

17045 Chatsworth St
Granada Hills, CA 91344-5845
Telephone: (818) 635-1777, Web Site: www.southwestbancorp.com
Pres: Joffrey Long

SPAIDE, KUIPERS & CO

42 Second St
Newport, RI 02840

Telephone: (610) 668-8296, FAX: (610) 579-3844, E-Mail: spaide@ spaidekuipers.com, Web Site: www. spaidekuipers.com
Principal: William J. Spaide

SPECTRUM RETAIL ASSOCIATES

10 E Athens Ave (Suite 200)
Ardmore, PA 19003
Telephone: (610) 645-9520, Toll Free: (800) 570-6565, FAX: (610) 645-9524
Chmn: Scott C. Borowsky
Dir: Eileen Vogel

Specializes in direct sales, catalog and graphic arts.

SPENCERSTUART

353 N Clark (Suite 2400)
Chicago, IL 60654-3479
Telephone: (312) 822-0088, FAX: (312) 822-0116, Web Site: www. spencerstuart.com
Chmn: Kevin M Connelly
CEO: David S Daniel
Mng Dir N America: Michael J Anderson
CFO & Chief Admin Officer: Richard M Kurkow
Conducts Business: U.S., Canada, Worldwide
Employees: 1,400
Primary Market Served: Business
Gross sales or billing: $435,000,000

Senior level executive search for CEOs/general managers and key functional leaders. Clients include leading direct and interactive marketing companies and suppliers/agencies to the industry.

STAGG DIRECT MARKETING INC

11 Gorham Rd
Scarsdale, NY 10583-1117
Telephone: (914) 725-3990, FAX: (914) 472-7298
Pres: Phyllis C. Stagg

STATESIDE ASSOCIATES

2300 Clarendon Blvd (Suite 407)
Arlington, VA 22201-3300
Telephone: (703) 525-7466 X228
Pres & CEO: Constance Campanella
Primary Market Served: Business

STATISTICAL INNOVATIONS INC

375 Concord Ave
Belmont, MA 02478-3084

Telephone: (617) 489-4490, FAX: (617) 489-4499, E-Mail: statisticalinnovations@gmail.com, Web Site: www. statisticalinnovations.com
Pres: Jay Magidson

THE STELTER CO

10435 New York Ave
Des Moines, IA 50322-3774
Toll Free: (800) 331-6881
Creative Dir: Beverly Hutney

STEPHEN-BRADFORD SEARCH

555th Ave (Rm 300)
New York, NY 10017-9288
Telephone: (212) 221-6333, X346, Toll Free: (800) 720-0922, FAX: (212) 391-7826, E-Mail: info@ stephenbradford.com, Web Site: www.stephenbradford.com
Pres: Erika Weinstein

STEPHENS INC

65 E 55th St (Floor 22)
New York, NY 10022-3369
Telephone: (212) 891-1777, Web Site: www.stephens.com
Mng Dir: Ken Wasik

STOCKHAM CONSULTING

7300 Butterscotch Rd
Eden Prairie, MN 55346-3233
Telephone: (952) 250-2206
Mktg Consultant: Maria Stockham

STRATEGICONE

6700 Antioch Rd (Suite 110)
Overland Park, KS 66204-1200
Telephone: (913) 342-9100 x102, Web Site: www.strategic-one.com
Pres: Mike Rogers
Primary Market Served: Business & Consumer

ELIZABETH STREITZ & ASSOCIATES

255 W 108th St (Suite 9A)
New York, NY 10025
Telephone: (212) 749-3152
Pres: Elizabeth Streitz

STROFINA INC

10200 NE Garibaldi Loop
Bainbridge Island, WA 98110-3976
Telephone: (206) 855-9681
Pres: Jordan Levine
Founded: 2010

Database application development company.

SYSTEMS ANALYTICS INC
946 Great Plain Ave (#125)
Needham, MA 02492-3030
Telephone: (781) 444-4837, E-Mail:
　info@systemsanalytics.com, Web
　Site: www.systemsanalytics.com
Pres: John Zhang

TALX CORP
RP-NFOA
Div. of Equifax
14755 Preston Rd (Suite 525)
Dallas, TX 75254-7898
Telephone: (972) 755-2100, FAX:
　(972) 755-2080, E-Mail:
　consulting@managementinsights.
　com, Web Site: www.
　managementinsights.com
Dir TCI Services: Gayle Malone
Client Svcs Relations: Kelly Connel

TSI
350 Northern Blvd (Suite 308)
Albany, NY 12204-1028
Telephone: (518) 463-5555, FAX:
　(518) 463-4504, E-Mail: tsi@capital.
　net, Web Site: www.tsidrivers.com
Pres: Peter Mirabille

**TECHNICAL ASSISTANCE
RESEARCH PROGRAMS
(TARP)**
2425 Wilson Blvd (Suite 400)
Arlington, VA 22201
Telephone: (703) 524-1456, FAX:
　(703) 524-6374, Web Site: www.
　tarp.com
Pres: John Goodman

**TELEDEVELOPMENT
SERVICES INC**
PO Box 502
Richfield, OH 44286-0502
Telephone: (330) 659-4441, FAX:
　(330) 659-4442, E-Mail: jkaplan@
　teledevelopment.com, Web Site:
　www.teledevelopment.com
Founder & Pres: Jon E. Kaplan

**TELEMANAGEMENT
SEARCH**
6 Litchfield Rd (Suite 316)
Port Washington, NY 11050-3815
Telephone: (516) 767-6990, FAX:
　(516) 767-6980, E-Mail: connie@
　tmrecruiters.com, Web Site: www.
　tmrecruiters.com
Pres: Connie Caroli

TERES CONSULTING INC
Nine Magnolia St
Framingham, MA 01701-4913
Telephone: (508) 872-4922, FAX:
　(253) 595-6748, E-Mail: info@
　teresconsulting.com, Web Site:
　www.teresconsulting.com
Principal: Wayne Teres

TESAR REYNES INC
333 N Michigan Ave (Suite 2226)
Chicago, IL 60601-4035
Telephone: (312) 726-1900, E-Mail:
　tony@tesar-reynes.com, Web Site:
　www.tesar-reynes.com
Partner: Anthony Reynes

THINKALYTICS
440 Millburn Ave
Millburn, NJ 07041-1210
Telephone: (973) 671-1590, Web Site:
　www.thinkalytics.com
Primary Market Served: Consumer

GRANT THORNTON LLP
Two Commerce Square (Suite 3100)
Philadelphia, PA 19103
Telephone: (215) 561-4200, FAX:
　(215) 561-1066, Web Site: www.
　grantthornton.com
Mng Partner: Richard Gebert

TIMBERLINE INTERACTIVE
5 Park St (Suite 2)
Middlebury, VT 05753-1169
Telephone: (802) 388-8377, Web Site:
　www.timberlineinteractive.com
Pres & CEO: Bud Reed

TITANTV MEDIA
Owned by Turnstone & Capital CBC
　New Media
818 Dows Rd SE
Cedar Rapids, IA 52403-7000
Telephone: (319) 365-5597, Toll Free:
　(800) 365-7629, FAX: (319) 365-
　5694, E-Mail: mktg@titantv.com,
　Web Site: www.titantv.com
Pres & COO: Mark Effron

TOLLIVER INC
303 5th Ave (Rm 206)
New York, NY 10016-6690
Telephone: (212) 758-7344, FAX:
　(212) 750-8617, E-Mail: tolliver12@
　aol.com
Pres: Susan Taliaferro

TOWERS WATSON
Subs. of The Wyatt Co
875 Third Ave
New York, NY 10022
Telephone: (212) 725-7550, FAX:
　(212) 644-7432, Web Site: www.
　towerswatson.com
Mktg Dir: Bob Crane

**TRAINING CONSULTANTS
INC**
1415 Sheridan Rd
Highland Park, IL 60035
Telephone: (847) 432-9428, FAX:
　(847) 432-9318, E-Mail: wetrain2@
　home.com
Pres: Andrea Crane

TRANSAMERICAN MAILING
355 State Pl
Escondido, CA 92029-1359
Telephone: (760) 745-5343, Web Site:
　www.transdirect.com
VP: Heather Benjamin

**TRANSGLOBAL
CONSULTANTS INC**
Div. of International Services Group
3210 Glastonbury Cir NW
Canton, OH 44708-1174
Telephone: (330) 477-6450, E-Mail:
　transglobal@earthlink.net
Dir: Lawrence J Chaido

KAREN TRIPI ASSOCIATES
305 Madison Ave (Suite 2319)
New York, NY 10165-6209
Telephone: (212) 972-5258, FAX:
　(212) 599-3809, E-Mail: karen@
　karentripi.com, Web Site: www.
　karentripi.com
Pres: Karen Tripi

**THE TROYANOS GROUP
LTD**
106 N Broadway (fl 3)
Irvington, NY 10533-1262
Telephone: (914) 479-1801, FAX:
　(914) 993-9554, E-Mail: dennis@
　troyanosgroup.com, Web Site: www.
　troyanosgroup.com
Pres: Dennis Troyanos
Employees: 4
Primary Market Served: Business
Founded: 1991

Executive search in the direct marketing industry.

TUCKER CAPITAL CORP
234 Nassau St (Suite 3)
Princeton, NJ 08542-4614
Telephone: (609) 924-5710, FAX:
　(609) 924-5027, E-Mail: info@
　tuckercapital.com, Web Site: www.
　tuckercapital.com
Mng Dir: Craig L. Battle

**TURTLE BAY
MANAGEMENT CO INC**
209 86th St (Suite E)
Virginia Beach, VA 23451

Telephone: (757) 422-2760, FAX:
(757) 422-1434, E-Mail: jimlant@
turtlebaymanagement.com, Web
Site: www.turtlebaymanagement.
com
Principal: Jim Lant

**GILBERT TWEED
ASSOCIATES**
415 Madison Ave (fl 20)
New York, NY 10017
Telephone: (212) 758-3000, FAX:
(212) 832-1040, E-Mail: hrdptgt@
gmail.com, Web Site: www.
gilberttweed.com
Owner & CEO: Janet Tweed

UCI/DREAM GIVEAWAYS
19321-C US Hwy 19 N (Suite 605)
Clearwater, FL 33764
Telephone: (727) 536-2777, Web Site:
www.dreamgiveaways.com
Primary Market Served: Business &
Consumer

USY CONSULTING INC
50 Highwood Dr
Dumont, NJ 07628-2608
Telephone: (201) 585-7402, FAX:
(201) 585-2754, E-Mail:
usyconsulting@hotmail.com
Pres: Reizo Yoshida

UNISFAIR
1450 Fashion Island Blvd (Suite 500)
San Mateo, CA 94404-2077
Telephone: (866) 354-4030, Web Site:
www.unisfair.com
Mktg Mgr: Nhien Le
Primary Market Served: Business

**URBAN SCIENCE
APPLICATIONS INC**
200 Renaissance Ctr (Suite 1800)
Detroit, MI 48243-1306
Telephone: (313) 259-9900, Web Site:
www.urbanscience.com
Global Practice Dir: Mark Yuhn

VMF INC
3313 Ross Pl NW
Washington, DC 20008
Telephone: (202) 966-3361, FAX:
(202) 362-8409, E-Mail: veflei@aol.
com
Pres: Virginia Fleischman

**VENABLE LLP
CONFERENCE CENTER**
575 7th St NW
Washington, DC 20004-1607

Telephone: (202) 344-4860, (202) 344-
4000, Toll Free: (888) VENABLE,
FAX: (202) 344-8300, E-Mail:
info@venable.com, Web Site: www.
venable.com
Partner: Ian Volner

VERTICAL MEDIA GROUP
2200 N Central Rd
Fort Lee, NJ 07024-7557
Telephone: (201) 245-7935
Pres: Jeff Holland

**WDS MARKETING & PUBLIC
RELATIONS**
8232 Hadley St
Overland Park, KS 66204-3542
Telephone: (913) 362-4541, FAX:
(913) 362-7342, E-Mail: bwilson@
wdspr.com, Web Site: www.wdspr.
com
Owner: Becky S. Wilson

WLA INC
535 5th Ave (Floor 31)
New York, NY 10017-3667
Telephone: (212) 584-1810
CEO: Worth Linen
Primary Market Served: Business &
Consumer

WPG AMERICAS INC
Subs. of WPG Holdings.
5285 Hellyer Ave (Suite 150)
San Jose, CA 95138
Telephone: (408) 392-8100, FAX:
(408) 436-9551, E-Mail:
notherncalifornia.sales@
wpgamericas.com, Web Site: www.
wpgamericas.com
Pres: Rich Davis
VP, Supplier Mktg: Dave Bowers

Global distributor of semiconductors,
passive, electro-mechanical and display
products.

WTB ASSOCIATES INC
4020 Bunker Ln
Wilmette, IL 60091
Telephone: (847) 251-4188
Chmn: William T. Bringham Sr.
Pres: William T. Bringham Jr.

**WAGNER HINES & AVARY
INC**
218 N Lee St
Alexandria, VA 22314
Telephone: (703) 684-7740, FAX:
(703) 548-3721
Chmn: Robert Avary

**WAKEFIELD TALABISCO
INTERNATIONAL**
11 E 44th St (Rm 1206)
New York, NY 10017-3608
Telephone: (212) 661-8600, FAX:
(212) 661-8832, Web Site: www.
wtali.com
Pres: Barbara Talabisco

WEBB MASON
10830 Gilroy Rd
Hunt Valley, MD 21031-4312
Telephone: (410) 785-1111, Web Site:
www.webbmason.com
HR Dir: Marty Levine
Primary Market Served: Business

**FREDERICK WERSHAW
MANAGEMENT CO**
111 Black Rock Rd
Stamford, CT 06903-1430
Telephone: (203) 329-3000, FAX:
(203) 329-3044
Pres: Frederick I. Wershaw

**WESLEY R WEBER &
ASSOCIATES**
405 Brookmeade Dr
West Chester, PA 19380
Telephone: (610) 909-8040, E-Mail:
wesweber@aol.com
Pres: Wesley R. Weber

WEST CARY GROUP
5 W Cary St
Richmond, VA 23220-5609
Toll Free: (804) 343-2029
Primary Market Served: Consumer

WEST COMPANIES INC
7155 Savoy Ct
Seminole, FL 33776-4329
Telephone: (212) 319-7069
Pres: Larry J. West
Founded: 1984

Mergers & acquisitions for direct marketing & e commerce cos.

WEST CORP
11808 Miracle Hills Dr
Omaha, NE 68154
Toll Free: (800) 841-9000, FAX: (402)
963-1602, E-Mail: sales@west.com,
Web Site: www.west.com
VP, Mktg: Mark Meudt

**STEVE WEXLER CREATIVE
GROUP**
PO Box 219
Farmingville, NY 11738-0219
Telephone: (631) 736-6565, Web Site:
www.wexdirect.com
CEO: Steve Wexler

WHITEWING LABS
17939 Chatsworth St (#408)
Granada Hills, CA 91344
Toll Free: (800) 950-3030, FAX: (818)
240-2785, E-Mail: service@
whitewing.com, Web Site: www.
whitewing.com
Pres: Cynthia A. Kolke

WHITNEY WORLDWIDE INC
553 Hayward Ave N (Suite 250)
Saint Paul, MN 55128-9006
Telephone: (651) 748-5000, Toll Free:
(800) 597-0227, FAX: (651) 748-
4000, Web Site: www.whitneyworld.
com
Pres & CEO: Les Layton

**WILLIAMS, CALIRI, MILLER
& OTLEY**
1428 Rte 23
Wayne, NJ 07474-5826
Telephone: (973) 694-0800, FAX:
(973) 694-0302, Web Site: www.
wcmolaw.com
Administrator: Barbara Jerchower

WIND RIVER GROUP
900 State Mill Rd
Akron, OH 44319-2138
Telephone: (330) 644-7774, FAX:
(330) 645-2045
Pres: Ed Jacobs

WINDSOR HOUSE
Div. of Windsor Marketing
Two Industrial Rd
Windsor Locks, CT 06096
Telephone: (860) 627-5927, FAX:
(860) 627-0252, E-Mail: ahalley@
windsormarketing.com, Web Site:
windsormarketing.com
Pres & Treas: Kevin Armata

WINDWARD GROUP
241 Spinnaker Ln
Shelburne, VT 05482-7779
Telephone: (802) 985-3631, Web Site:
www.windwardgroup.us
Mng Partner: Rebecca Jewett

WINSTON & WINSTON PC
295 Madison Ave
New York, NY 10017
Telephone: (212) 922-9483, FAX:
(212) 532-2722, Web Site: www.
winstonandwinston.com
Sr Partner: Arthur Winston

WINTERBERRY GROUP
Subs. of Petsky Prunier LLC
60 Broad St (Suite 3810)
New York, NY 10004-2329

Telephone: (212) 842-6000, FAX:
(212) 842-6010, E-Mail: info@
winterberrygroup.com, Web Site:
www.winterberrygroup.com
Sr Mng Dir: Bruce Biegel

BRIAN WOLFE
418 E 59th St (Apt 26A)
New York, NY 10022-2378
Telephone: (516) 840-3748
Primary Market Served: Consumer

**THE WRITE ANSWERS
COPYWRITING &
CONSULTING**
816 Peace Portal Dr (#82)
Blaine, WA 98230-4010
Toll Free: (888) 331-0322, Web Site:
www.thewriteanswers.com
Resultant: Peter Britton

THE YANKEE GROUP
RP-NFOA
One Liberty Sq (fl 7)
Boston, MA 02109-4868
Telephone: (617) 598-7200, E-Mail:
info@yankeegroup.com, Web Site:
www.yankeegroup.com
Chief Strategy Officer: Berge Ayvazian

ANDREW YOELIN & CO
5524 E Waltann Ln
Scottsdale, AZ 85254-1701
Telephone: (602) 482-6214, E-Mail:
corpdating@aol.com
Pres: Andrew Yoelin

ZS ASSOCIATES
1800 Sherman Ave
Evanston, IL 60201
Telephone: (847) 492-3600, FAX:
(847) 864-6280, E-Mail: inquiry@
zsassociates.com, Web Site: www.
zsassociates.com
Founder & Co Chmn Bd: Andris Zoltners

RL ZAPIN ASSOCIATES INC
708 Third Ave (fl 6)
New York, NY 10017
Telephone: (212) 297-6248, E-Mail:
roni@rlzapinassociates.com, Web
Site: www.rlzapinassociates.com
Pres: Roni L. Zapin
Primary Market Served: Business &
Consumer

**NEIL ZELENETZ &
ASSOCIATES**
219 Kings Point Rd
East Hampton, NY 11937-3047
Telephone: (516) 746-2981, E-Mail:
nzelenetz@aol.com

Pres: Neil Zelenetz

**ZIMMERMAN BUSINESS
CONSULTING INC**
44 E 92nd St (Suite 5B)
New York, NY 10128-1319
Telephone: (212) 860-3107, FAX:
(212) 860-7730, E-Mail: ljzzbci@
aol.com, Web Site: www.zbcinc.com
Pres: Leonard J. Zimmerman

ZOE MARKETING
5132 Meadows del Mar
San Diego, CA 92130-4854
Telephone: (858) 408-1700
Pres: Russell Levine

Full Service Direct Mail Companies (21) — Geographic Index

ALABAMA

Mail Enterprises LLC, 3810 5th Ct N, Birmingham, 35222-1308

NCP Solutions, 5200 E Lake Blvd, Birmingham, 35217

ARIZONA

Cactus Mailing Company, 16121 N 78th St, Scottsdale, 85260

The Market Builder Inc, 5135 E Ingram St (Suite 2), Mesa, 85205-3465

ARKANSAS

Sumotext, Inc, 10825 Financial Centre Pkwy Ste 123, Little Rock, 72211-3557

CALIFORNIA

Active Voice, 354 Pine St, Ste 700, San Francisco, 94104

Chewning Direct Marketing, 4 Candlebush, Irvine, 92603-3727

Direct Mail Center, 1099 Mariposa St, San Francisco, 94107

Dufford Marketing, 2233 Brigden Rd, Pasadena, 91104-3304

Professional Print & Mail Inc, 2818 E Hamilton Ave, Fresno, 93721-3209

Towne AllPoints, 3441 W MacArthur Blvd, Santa Ana, 92704

COLORADO

Advanced Direct Marketing Inc, 712 E Eisenhower Blvd, Loveland, 80537-3920

DMXENGAGE, 8955 E Nichols Ave (Suite 200), Centennial, 80112-3498

Eagle:xm, 5105 E 41st Ave, Denver, 80216-4420

Mountain Media Enterprises, 102 Rome Ct, Fort Collins, 80524

CONNECTICUT

Harty Integrated Solutions, 25 James St, Box 324, New Haven, 06513-0324

The Marketing Advantage Inc, 1200 High Ridge Rd., Stamford, 06905

Marketing Solutions Unlimited LLC, 109 Talcott Rd, West Hartford, 06110-1228

Media Horizons Inc, 40 Richards Ave, Norwalk, 06854-2320

Phoenix Marketing Group LLC, 24 Woods Way, Redding, 06896

WordCom Inc, 56 Main St, PO Box 308, Ellington, 06029-3360

FLORIDA

Cox Target Media Inc, 805 Executive Center Dr W (Suite 100), St. Petersburg, 33702

DME Holdings, 2441 Bellevue Ave, Daytona Beach, 32114

Hill Mailing & Printing of Florida Inc, PO Box 3331, Brandon, 33509-3331

Innovative Marketing Direct Inc, 3200 Henderson Blvd (Suite 100), Tampa, 33609-3054

MediaWorks Advertising & Marketing Inc, 725 W Granada Blvd (Suite 12), Ormond Beach, 32174

Nordis Technologies Inc, 4401 NW 124th Ave, Coral Springs, 33065-7636

Progressive Communications, 1001 Sand Pond Rd, Lake Mary, 32746-3354

Tribune Direct Orlando, 633 N Orange Ave, Orlando, 32801

GEORGIA

AtlantaPrintAndMail.com Inc, 1820 Briarwood Industrial Ct NE (Suite 7), Atlanta, 30329-2198

Image Makers Marketing Inc, 1843 Blackwater Dr, Marietta, 30066-6713

Loyaltyworks Inc, 2299 Perimeter Park Dr (Suite 150), Atlanta, 30341-1333

Stezzi Direct Inc, 3404 Oakcliff Rd (Suite C-3), Atlanta, 30340

ILLINOIS

Active Graphics Inc, 5500 W 31st St, Cicero, 60804-3957

FMP Direct Inc, 1019 W Park Ave, Libertyville, 60048

First Class Inc, 5410 W Roosevelt Rd (Unit 222), Chicago, 60644-1570

Inte Q, 1815 S Meyers Rd, Oakbrook Terrace, 60181

Integrated Merchandising Systems LLC, 8338 Austin Ave, Morton Grove, 60053-3209

Liberty Creative Solutions, 18625 W Creek Dr, Tinley Park, 60477-6247

NPN360 Inc, 1400 S Wolf Rd (Suite 102), Wheeling, 60090-6524

Premier Print and Services Group Inc, 10 S Riverside Plz (Suite 1810), Chicago, 60606

Printing Arts, 2001 W 21st St, Broadview, 60155

Programmers Investment Corp, 125 E Algonquin Rd, Arlington Heights, 60005

Tribune Direct LLC, 505 Northwest Ave (Suite A), Northlake, 60164-1662

INDIANA

Bacompt Systems Inc, 12742 Hamilton Crossing Blvd, Carmel, 46032-5422

L & D Mail Masters, 110 Security Pkwy, New Albany, 47150

KANSAS

MarketAide Services Inc, PO Box 190, Hutchinson, 67504-0190

KENTUCKY

Icon Marketing Communications, 2320 Grandview Dr, Fort Mitchell, 41017

MAINE

GG Direct, 351 Riverside Industrial Pkwy, Portland, 04103-1415

MARYLAND

DataLab USA, 202561 Goldenrod Ln, Germantown, 20876-4063

EU Services, 649 N Horners Ln, Rockville, 20850-1233

Precision Solutions, 11221 Dolfield Blvd (Suite 103), Owings Mills, 21117

Suman Inc, 10805 Whiterim Dr, Potomac, 20854-1786

MASSACHUSETTS

B&W Press Inc, 401 E Main St, Georgetown, 01833-2513

DS Graphics Inc, 120 Stedman St, Lowell, 01851

Direct Results, 2005 Riverdale St, West Springfield, 01089-1067

The Field Companies Fulfillment Center Inc, 385 Pleasant St, PO Box 78, Watertown, 02471-0078

Mail Computer Service, 321 Manley St, West Bridgewater, 02379

Tiziani Whitmyre Inc, Sharon Commerce Center, 2 Commercial St, Sharon, 02067

Universal Wilde, 26 Dartmouth St, Westwood, 02090

MICHIGAN

ICS Marketing Services, 4225 Legacy Pkwy, Lansing, 48911-4246

MINNESOTA

Driasi, 7930 Century Blvd, Chanhassen, 55317-8001

IWCO Direct, 7951 Powers Blvd, Chanhassen, 55317-9502

ProPhase Marketing Inc, 6321 Bury Dr (Suite 19), Eden Prairie, 55346-1739

Taylor Communications, 1725 Roe Crest Dr, North Mankato, 56003

MISSOURI

AdSell Companies, 5001 Southwest Ave, Saint Louis, 63110-3427

American Direct Marketing Resources Inc, 400 Chesterfield Ctr (Suite 500), Chesterfield, 63017-7703

Creative Marketing Programs of Kansas City, 412 Oak St, Kansas City, 64106-1133

Emfluence, 106 W 11th St (Suite 2220), Kansas City, 64105-1823

Gabriel Group, 3190 Rider Trail S, Earth City, 63045

Sales Development Associates Inc, 7850 Manchester Rd, Saint Louis, 63143-2710

NEBRASKA

Aradius Group, 4700 "F" St, Omaha, 68117

NEW JERSEY

CCG Marketing Solutions, 14 Henderson Dr, West Caldwell, 07006-6608

CCI Direct Mail, 521 Gotham Pkwy, Carlstadt, 07072

Hummel Integrated Marketing Solutions, 850 Springfield Rd, Union, 07083-8614

ICS Corp, 100 Friars Blvd, West Deptford, 08086

MRC Marketing, 12 Lincoln Blvd (Suite 103), Emerson, 07630

PromarkDirect Inc, PO Box 258, Ramsey, 07446-0258

Redi-Direct Marketing Inc, 5 Audrey Pl, Fairfield, 07004

Telebrands Corp, One Telebrands Plz, Fairfield, 07004

Trimensions Inc, 1 Eagle St, Englewood, 07631

NEW YORK

Adrea Rubin Marketing Inc, 19 W 44th St (Suite 1415), New York, 10036-6101

Advertising Distributors of America Inc, 200 Trade Zone Dr, Ronkonkoma, 11779

Cathedral Corp, 632 Ellsworth Rd, Griffiss Technology Park, Rome, 13441

Compu-Mail Direct Marketing, 3235 Grand Island Blvd, Grand Island, 14072

Design Distributors, Inc, 300 Marcus Blvd, Deer Park, 11729-4500

The Horah Group, 351 Manville Rd (Suite 105), Pleasantville, 10570-2166

Katalyst Partners Inc, 307 7th Ave (Suite 2401), New York, 10001

Lazarus Direct Inc, 50 Charles Lindbergh Blvd (Suite 504), Uniondale, 11553-3650

LOG-ON, 520 8th Ave (Floor 14), New York, 10018

Manhattan Media Services Inc, 271 Madison Ave (Suite 905), New York, 10016

North American Communications Inc, 7 Edgemont Rd, Katonah, 10536

Quality Letter Service Inc, 22 W 32nd St (Floor 10), New York, 10001-3807

Relationship1, 1 Blue Hill Plz (Suite 1523), Pearl River, 10965-3175

Star Direct Mail, 118 Louisiana Ave., Brooklyn, 11207

UniWorld Group, 1 Metro Tech Center N (Fl 11), Brooklyn, 11201

NORTH CAROLINA

Advanced Direct, 4221 Tudor Ln, Greensboro, 27410-8105

Everest Direct Mail & Marketing, 9 SW Pack Sq (Suite 202), Asheville, 28801

RCS Response Technologies Inc, 6420 Rea Rd (Suite 210), Charlotte, 28217

OHIO

Haines Direct, 8050 Freedom Ave NW, North Canton, 44720

OREGON

McIntyre Direct Group LLC, 700 N Hayden Island Dr (Suite 390), Portland, 97217-8185

PENNSYLVANIA

Alcom, 140 Christopher Ln, Harleysville, 19438

Direct Mail Service Inc, 939 W North Ave, Pittsburgh, 15233-1605

Forecast Direct Marketing Group, 37 Terminal Way, Pittsburgh, 15219

MSP Inc, 155 Commerce Dr, Freedom, 15042-9202

PlusNetMarketing Inc, 600 Eagleview Blvd (Suite 300), Exton, 19341

Signature Communications Inc, 417 N 8th St (Suite 401), Philadelphia, 19123

RHODE ISLAND

Catalog Design Studios, 8 Barnes St, Providence, 02906-1517

SOUTH CAROLINA

Nelson Printing Corp - Direct Marketers of Charleston, 100 Columbus St, Charleston, 29403

TENNESSEE

Baber Direct Marketing, 4222 Pilot Dr, Memphis, 38118

DNI Corp, 711 Spence Ln, Nashville, 37217

MailNow Inc, 305 Donelson Pike (Suite B), PO Box 140290, Nashville, 37214

TEXAS

The EZ-Forms Co, 317 Sidney Baker S (#317), Kerrville, 78028

GS Marketing, 1345 Enclave Pkwy, Houston, 77077-2026

iDfour, 1001 S Dairy Ashford St (Suite 450), Houston, 77077-2386

PremierIMS Inc, 11101 Ella Blvd, Houston, 77067

Thomas Printworks, 707 West Rd, Houston, 77038-2505

Topp Direct Marketing, 701 Palm Valley Dr W, Harlingen, 78552-9039

VIRGINIA

Communications Corp of America, 13195 Freedom Way, Boston, 22713-4114

Huntsinger & Jeffer, 809 Brook Hill Cir, Richmond, 23227-2503

L & E Meridian, 8000 Corporate Ct, Springfield, 22153

Lawrence Direct Marketing Inc, 22 John Marshall St (Suite B), Warrenton, 20186

O'Connell Meier LLC, 5221 Franconia Rd (Suite 10252), Alexandria, 22310

O'Neill Marketing Co, 10805 Main St (Suite 400), Fairfax, 22030

Taradel LLC, 4805 Lake Brook Dr (Suite 140), Glen Allen, 23060-9278

WASHINGTON

Kaye-Smith, 4101 Oakesdale Ave SW, Renton, 98057-4817

WISCONSIN

AB Data Ltd, 4057 N Wilson Dr, Milwaukee, 53211-1848

AM Solutions, 100 Interstate Blvd, Edgerton, 53534-9399

The Marek Group, W228 N821 Westmound Dr, Waukesha, 53186

Prospect Direct Inc, 2266 N Prospect Ave (Suite 336), Milwaukee, 53202-6306

CANADA

British Columbia

PDQ Post Group, 19134 95A Ave (Unit 7), Surrey, V4N 4P2

Ontario

Data Communications Management Corp, 9195 Torbram Rd, Brampton, L6S 6H2

Data Direct Group Inc, 1-2001 Drew Rd, Mississauga, L5S 1S4

Direct Response Media Group, 2285 Wyecroft Rd, Oakville, L6L 5L7

The Interprovincial Group, 1315 Morningside Ave, Scarborough, M1B 3C5

Prism Data Services Ltd, 200-1599 Hurontario St, Mississauga, L5G 4S1

Saatchi & Saatchi Canada, 175 Bloor St E, South Tower (Suite 1300), Toronto, M4W 3R9

Spring Global Delivery Solutions, 3170 Orlando Dr (Unit 3), Mississauga, L4V 1R5

Westminster International Inc, 4-50 Valleywood Dr, Markham, L3R 6E9

Quebec

Harling Marketing Inc, 18103 Rte Transcanadienne, Kirkland, H9J 3Z4

Full Service Direct Mail Companies (21)

AB DATA LTD
4057 N Wilson Dr
Milwaukee, WI 53211-1848
Telephone: (414) 963-7800, FAX:
(414) 963-7899, E-Mail:
dmservices@abdata.com, Web Site:
dms.abdata.com
Co-Mng Dir: Charles Pruitt
Co-Mng Dir: Thomas R Glenn
Founded: 1980
Direct marketing services company
providing printing, direct mail, database management & digital marketing
solutions.

ACTIVE GRAPHICS INC
5500 W 31st St
Cicero, IL 60804-3957
Telephone: (708) 656-8900, FAX:
(708) 656-2176, E-Mail: support@
active-us.com, Web Site: www.
active-us.com
Pres: Jeremy Hayes
Brand marketing company specializing
in digital print, fulfillment services,
large format printing & marketing software solutions.

ACTIVE VOICE
354 Pine St, Ste 700
San Francisco, CA 94104
Telephone: (415) 487-2000, FAX:
(415) 487-2260, E-Mail: info@
activevoice.net, Web Site: www.
activevoice.net
Exec Dir: Ellen Schneider
Nonprofit network of strategists that assist the public policy sector in developing story-centric media campaigns to
advance social change.

**ADREA RUBIN MARKETING
INC**
19 W 44th St (Suite 1415)
New York, NY 10036-6101
Telephone: (212) 983-0020, FAX:
(212) 983-1057, E-Mail: info@
adrearubin.com, Web Site: www.
adrearubin.com
CEO: Adrea Rubin
Pres: Lisa Pollack
Employees: 20
Integrated direct marketing agency.

ADSELL COMPANIES
5001 Southwest Ave
Saint Louis, MO 63110-3427
Telephone: (314) 773-0500, FAX:
(314) 773-0555, E-Mail: marks@
adsell.com, Web Site: www.adsell.
com

Pres: Mark W Shocker
Founded: 1934
Full-service printing, direct mail, ful-
fillment & custom finishing company.

ADVANCED DIRECT
4221 Tudor Ln, Greensboro, NC
27410-8105
4221 Tudor Ln
Greensboro, NC 27410-8105
Telephone: (336) 299-0800, Toll Free:
(800) 786-2812, FAX: (336) 299-
2619, E-Mail: info@advdirectinc.
com, Web Site: www.advdirectinc.
com
Pres: Jeff Burkett

**ADVANCED DIRECT
MARKETING INC**
712 E Eisenhower Blvd
Loveland, CO 80537-3920
Telephone: (970) 669-9800, FAX:
(970) 669-1920, E-Mail: sales@
admimail.com, Web Site: www.
admimail.com
Pres: Dennis DenBoer
Founded: 1988
Digital printing services, offset printing, direct to press printing, short run
color printing, mailing lists and direct
mail services company.

**ADVERTISING
DISTRIBUTORS OF
AMERICA INC**
200 Trade Zone Dr
Ronkonkoma, NY 11779
Telephone: (631) 231-5700, FAX:
(631) 434-1063
Pres & CEO: Dominick Iannaccone
Lettershop, direct mail, printing & ful-
fillment services company.

ALCOM
140 Christopher Ln
Harleysville, PA 19438
Telephone: (215) 513-1600, E-Mail:
stucker@alcomprinting.com, Web
Site: www.alcomprinting.com
Pres & CEO: Donald Eichman
Mng Dir: Douglas Yeager
Dir Mktg: Sharon Tucker
Conducts Business: U.S.
Primary Market Served: Business &
Consumer
Founded: 1960
Integrated print, direct mail marketing
& business development solutions com-
pany.

AM SOLUTIONS
100 Interstate Blvd
Edgerton, WI 53534-9399
Telephone: (800) 410-6245, E-Mail:
fschulze@amsolutionswi.com, Web
Site: www.amsolutionswi.com
Pres: Fred Schulze
VP Opers: Eric Stein
Midwest marketing services provider
specializing in direct mail marketing.

**AMERICAN DIRECT
MARKETING RESOURCES
INC**
400 Chesterfield Ctr (Suite 500)
Chesterfield, MO 63017-7703
Telephone: (636) 532-7703, FAX:
(636) 532-2427, E-Mail: admr@
admr.com, Web Site: www.
americandirectmarketing.com
Pres: Ed Smith
Advertising/Marketing Budget Related
to Direct Marketing: Full-service advertising company specializing in direct mail.%
Founded: 1983

ARADIUS GROUP
4700 "F" St
Omaha, NE 68117
Telephone: (402) 734-4400, Toll Free:
(800) 369-0033, FAX: (402) 734-
7492, E-Mail: info@aradiusgroup.
com, Web Site: www.aradiusgroup.
com
CEO: Steve Hayes
Pres: Chuck Kinzer Jr
Chief Mktg Officer: Bob Redmond
Primary Market Served: Business
Full-service digital marketing & print-
ing services company.

**ATLANTAPRINTANDMAIL.
COM INC**
1820 Briarwood Industrial Ct NE
(Suite 7)
Atlanta, GA 30329-2198
Telephone: (404) 321-6222, E-Mail:
info@mymailingservice.com, Web
Site: www.mymailingservice.com
Pres: Marc Sherman
Primary Market Served: Business &
Consumer
Founded: 1990
Full-service direct mail marketing com-
pany..

B&W PRESS INC
401 E Main St
Georgetown, MA 01833-2513

Telephone: (978) 352-6100, Toll Free: (877) 246-3467, FAX: (978) 352-5955, E-Mail: csr@bwpress.com, Web Site: www.bwpress.com
Pres & Treas: Paul Beegan
Plant Mgr: Dan Kimball
Conducts Business: U.S., Canada
Employees: 47
Primary Market Served: Business & Consumer
Direct Marketing ad budget: $300,000
Direct Mail: 40%
Magazines: 50%
Telephone: 10%
Founded: 1966
Gross sales or billing: $12,550,000

Specialty printing company that designs & prints direct mail marketing products.

BABER DIRECT MARKETING

4222 Pilot Dr
Memphis, TN 38118
Telephone: (901) 332-6300, Toll Free: (800) 847-7040, FAX: (901) 332-6441, E-Mail: info@baberweb.com, Web Site: www.baberweb.com
Pres: Michael Baber
Customer Svc Mgr: Denise Ellison
Creative Dir: Jayme McKeever
Opers: Vivian Hines
Primary Market Served: Business

Full service online and print/direct mail marketing services company.

BACOMPT SYSTEMS INC

12742 Hamilton Crossing Blvd
Carmel, IN 46032-5422
Telephone: (317) 574-7474, Toll Free: (800) 533-7109, FAX: (317) 574-7475, E-Mail: customer.service@ bacompt.com, Web Site: www.bacompt.com
VP: Dwayne Hurt
Chief Strategy Officer: Larry Bauer
Mktg Dir: Lisa Thomas
Primary Market Served: Business

Marketing company specializing in shelf-edge communications for retail businesses.

CCG MARKETING SOLUTIONS

14 Henderson Dr
West Caldwell, NJ 07006-6608
Telephone: (973) 808-0009, Toll Free: (866) 902-2807, FAX: (973) 808-9740, E-Mail: info@corpcomm.com, Web Site: home.corpcomm.com
Pres & CEO: Simon Hooks
Pres: James Pinkin
Dir Mktg & Bus Devel: Robert Ross
Conducts Business: U.S.

Primary Market Served: Business & Consumer
Founded: 1966

Full-service integrated marketing solutions provider.

CACTUS MAILING COMPANY

16121 N 78th St
Scottsdale, AZ 85260
Telephone: (480) 443-1442, Toll Free: (888) 632-5282, FAX: (866) 828-7794, E-Mail: info@cactusmailing.com, Web Site: www.cactusmailing.com
Pres: Michael Ryan
Conducts Business: U.S.
Primary Market Served: Business
Founded: 2001

Direct mail marketing company specializing in postcard marketing.

CATALOG DESIGN STUDIOS

8 Barnes St
Providence, RI 02906-1517
Telephone: (866) 849-4264, E-Mail: sfletcher@catalogdesignstudios.com, Web Site: www.catalogdesignstudios.com
Creative Dir: Sarah Fletcher
Conducts Business: U.S.
Primary Market Served: Business & Consumer

Direct mail and creative services company specializing in catalog design, production & consultation.

CATHEDRAL CORP

632 Ellsworth Rd, Griffiss Technology Park
Rome, NY 13441
Telephone: (315) 338-0021, Toll Free: (800) 698-0299, FAX: (315) 338-5874, E-Mail: sales@ cathedralstewardship.com, Web Site: www.cathedralcorporation.com
Pres & COO: Marianne W. Gaige
VP Mktg: Larry J. Beasley

CCI DIRECT MAIL

521 Gotham Pkwy
Carlstadt, NJ 07072
Telephone: (201) 507-5200, E-Mail: sales@ccidirectmail.com, Web Site: ccidirectmail.com
Pres: Joseph Pisano
Conducts Business: U.S.
Primary Market Served: Consumer
Founded: 1992

Full-service direct mail marketing company.

CHEWNING DIRECT MARKETING

4 Candlebush
Irvine, CA 92603-3727
Telephone: (949) 854-5401, FAX: (949) 743-8395, E-Mail: hchewning@cdmdirect.com, Web Site: www.cdmdirect.com
Pres: Hugh Chewning
Primary Market Served: Business & Consumer

Direct mail copywriting, consulting & strategy company.

COMMUNICATIONS CORP OF AMERICA

13195 Freedom Way
Boston, VA 22713-4114
Telephone: (540) 547-1700, FAX: (540) 302-8015, E-Mail: contact@ cca.net, Web Site: www.cca.net
Pres: Steven R. Fisher
VP Sales & Mktg: Douglas Knoche
Conducts Business: U.S.
Primary Market Served: Business
Founded: 1971

Full-service direct mail production facility specializing in continuous form printing, data processing, personalization, finishing & mail processing.

COMPU-MAIL DIRECT MARKETING

3235 Grand Island Blvd
Grand Island, NY 14072
Telephone: (716) 775-8001, Toll Free: (800) 255-0607, FAX: (716) 775-5681, E-Mail: marketing@compu-mail.com, Web Site: compu-mail.com
Pres: Michael Vitch
VP Opers: Andy Severson
Mktg Dir: Paul Vander Horst
Conducts Business: U.S.
Primary Market Served: Business

Direct mail marketing and print services company.

COX TARGET MEDIA INC

Subs. Cox Media Group.
805 Executive Center Dr W (Suite 100)
St. Petersburg, FL 33702
Telephone: (727) 399-3000, Toll Free: (800) 678-2743, FAX: (727) 399-3061, E-Mail: info@coxtarget.com, Web Site: www.coxtarget.com
Pres & CEO: Michael Vivio
Chief Info Officer: Chris Cate
VP Mktg: Lisa Sullivan
Primary Market Served: Consumer

Founded: 1968

Integrated direct marketing services company connecting companies and customers through its Valpak, Savings. com & Favado businesses.

CREATIVE MARKETING PROGRAMS OF KANSAS CITY

412 Oak St
Kansas City, MO 64106-1133
Telephone: (816) 472-6843, Toll Free: (800) 373-6843, FAX: (816) 472-8184, E-Mail: getresults@cmpkc. com, Web Site: www.cmpkc.com
Pres: Dwight W Orr
Primary Market Served: Business & Consumer
Founded: 1985

Full-service marketing firm specializing in digital marketing, database & CRM solutions for healthcare, retail and other consumer & B2B segments.

DNI CORP

711 Spence Ln
Nashville, TN 37217
Telephone: (615) 313-7000, Web Site: www.dnicorp.com
CEO: Jono Huddleston
Founded: 1984

Direct marketing fulfillment, mail presort services & statement processing company.

DS GRAPHICS INC

120 Stedman St
Lowell, MA 01851
Telephone: (978) 970-1359, E-Mail: sales@dsgraphics.com, Web Site: www.dsgraphics.com
VP Mailing Svcs: Justin Pallis
Pres: Jeffrey Pallis
Founded: 1993

Full-service marketing company specializing in digital strategy, print & mail services, logistics and branding solutions.

DATA COMMUNICATIONS MANAGEMENT CORP

9195 Torbram Rd
Brampton, ON, Canada L6S 6H2
Telephone: (905) 791-3151, Toll Free: (800) 268-0128, FAX: (905) 791-3277, E-Mail: info@datacm.com, Web Site: www.datacm.com
Pres: Michael Sifton
Pres: Gregory J Cochrane
CFO: James Lorimer
CTO: Karl Spangler
Conducts Business: Canada, U.S.

Primary Market Served: Business & Consumer
Founded: 1959

Multi-channel marketing communications company.

DATA DIRECT GROUP INC

1-2001 Drew Rd
Mississauga, ON, Canada L5S 1S4
Telephone: (905) 564-0150, FAX: (905) 564-7246, E-Mail: info@ datadirect.ca, Web Site: datadirect.ca
Owner & Pres: Ebraham Sesook
Founded: 1994

Full-service, fully integrated direct marketing company.

DATALAB USA

202561 Goldenrod Ln
Germantown, MD 20876-4063
Telephone: (301) 972-1430, Toll Free: (800) 972-1430, E-Mail: information@datalabusa.com, Web Site: datalabusa.com
Exec VP Bus Devel: Hans Aigner
COO: Olga Aigner
CIO: Ryder Warehall
CFO: Larissa Warehall
Primary Market Served: Business & Consumer

Marketing services company specializing in data sourcing, data processing, analytics and data warehousing.

DESIGN DISTRIBUTORS, INC

300 Marcus Blvd
Deer Park, NY 11729-4500
Telephone: (631) 242-2000, FAX: (631) 242-7367, E-Mail: info@ designdistributors.com, Web Site: www.designdistributors.com
Pres: Adam Avrick
Conducts Business: U.S. & Canada
Primary Market Served: Business
Advertising/Marketing Budget Related to Direct Marketing: Full-service direct marketing solutions company.%

DIRECT MAIL CENTER

1099 Mariposa St
San Francisco, CA 94107
Telephone: (415) 252-1600, FAX: (415) 252-9100, E-Mail: dmc@ directmailctr.com, Web Site: www. directmailctr.com
Gen Mgr: Pierre Smit
Acct Mgr: Ray Leung
Conducts Business: U.S.
Primary Market Served: Business
Founded: 1983

Full-service mailing & printing company.

DIRECT MAIL SERVICE INC

939 W North Ave
Pittsburgh, PA 15233-1605
Telephone: (412) 471-6300, FAX: (412) 321-6061, E-Mail: info@ dirmailserv.com, Web Site: www. dirmailserv.com
Pres: David Marconi
Conducts Business: U.S.
Primary Market Served: Business

Full-service direct mail services provider.

DIRECT RESPONSE MEDIA GROUP

2285 Wyecroft Rd
Oakville, ON, Canada L6L 5L7
Telephone: (905) 465-1233, Toll Free: (866) 993-0600, FAX: (905) 465-1228, E-Mail: info@drmg.ca, Web Site: www.drmg.com
Pres: Jason Bradbury
VP Fin: David Vander Ploeg
Founded: 1996

Direct mail marketing company specializing in the design, printing & delivery of direct mail advertising.

DIRECT RESULTS

2005 Riverdale St
West Springfield, MA 01089-1067
Telephone: (413) 732-8310, FAX: (413) 732-8361
Pres: John Epstein
Conducts Business: U.S.

Local, direct mail services company.

DME HOLDINGS

2441 Bellevue Ave
Daytona Beach, FL 32114
Telephone: (877) 720-0082, E-Mail: info@dmedelivers.com, Web Site: dmedelivers.com
Pres & Gen Mgr: Mike Panaggio
VP: Kathy Wise
Office Mgr: Mike Dunn
CMO: Rob Carll
Conducts Business: U.S.
Employees: 100
Primary Market Served: Business & Consumer
Founded: 1982

Full-service direct marketing agency.

DMXENGAGE

8955 E Nichols Ave (Suite 200)
Centennial, CO 80112-3498
Telephone: (303) 339-9300, FAX: (303) 388-6363, E-Mail: workwithus@dmxengage.com, Web Site: dmxengage.com
Pres: Mark Mayfield
Conducts Business: U.S.
Primary Market Served: Business

Founded: 1991

Integrated behavioral marketing company offering marketing, data, print & fulfillment services.

DRIASI
7930 Century Blvd
Chanhassen, MN 55317-8001
Telephone: (952) 556-5600, Toll Free: (800) 688-0760, FAX: (952) 556-8200, E-Mail: tpa@driasi.com, Web Site: www.driasi.com
Pres & CEO: Jennifer Toal
Exec VP: Scott Allison
CFO & Exec VP: Dave Kaldor
Conducts Business: U.S., Canada
Employees: 130
Primary Market Served: Business & Consumer
Founded: 1982

Business administration, customer service & marketing support services company.

DUFFORD MARKETING
2233 Brigden Rd
Pasadena, CA 91104-3304
Telephone: (626) 665-2268, E-Mail: donnduff@aol.com
Pres: Donn Dufford
Conducts Business: U.S.

Specialized marketing consultancy.

EU SERVICES
649 N Horners Ln
Rockville, MD 20850-1233
Telephone: (301) 424-3300, Toll Free: (800) 230-3362, FAX: (301) 424-3696, E-Mail: marketing@euservices.com, Web Site: www.euservices.com
Pres: Russ Stewart
Mktg Mgr: Art Simpson
Employees: 360
Founded: 1968

Full-service direct mail marketing services company.

THE EZ-FORMS CO
317 Sidney Baker S (#317)
Kerrville, TX 78028
Telephone: (281) 667-4414, FAX: (281) 667-4415, E-Mail: ezformscontactus@gmail.com, Web Site: www.ez-forms.com
Gen Mgr: Ed Marion
Conducts Business: U.S.
Primary Market Served: Business
Founded: 1986

E-Form automation products & services company.

EAGLE:XM
5105 E 41st Ave
Denver, CO 80216-4420
Telephone: (303) 320-5411, Toll Free: (800) 426-5376, FAX: (303) 393-6584, E-Mail: extendedmedia@eaglexm.com, Web Site: www.eaglexm.com
Pres: Mark Steputis
Sr VP: Joel Susel
VP, Database Mktg: David Born
VP Finance: Denis Rice
VP Sales: Scott Nordstrom
Conducts Business: U.S.
Primary Market Served: Business

Cross-channel customer engagement solutions company that utilizes data intelligence & marketing automation.

EMFLUENCE
106 W 11th St (Suite 2220)
Kansas City, MO 64105-1823
Telephone: (816) 472-4455, Toll Free: (877) 81-EMAIL, FAX: (816) 472-8855, E-Mail: expert@emfluence.com, Web Site: www.emfluence.com
Mktg Mgr: David Cacioppo
COO: Chris Cacioppo
Controller: Marlana Allaman
Dir Devel: Jacob Schwartz
Conducts Business: U.S.
Primary Market Served: Business
Founded: 2003

Full-service digital marketing agency.

EVEREST DIRECT MAIL & MARKETING
Subs. of Lake Holdings LLC
9 SW Pack Sq (Suite 202)
Asheville, NC 28801
Telephone: (866) 811-1553, E-Mail: info@everestdmm.com, Web Site: www.everestdmm.com
Pres: Maddison Lake
Pres: Casey Hildreth
Conducts Business: U.S.
Primary Market Served: Business
Founded: 2014

Direct mail & marketing developers of promotional & transactional print and mail for small & large businesses.

FMP DIRECT INC
1019 W Park Ave
Libertyville, IL 60048
Telephone: (847) 816-1919, Toll Free: (800) 995-3343, FAX: (847) 816-1969, E-Mail: info@fmpdirect.com, Web Site: www.fmpdirect.com
CEO: Michael Wilmet
Pres: Rachel Wilmet
Conducts Business: U.S.
Employees: 9
Primary Market Served: Business

Catalog available online
Indirect online sales
Advertising/Marketing Budget Related to Direct Marketing: 0-25%
Direct Marketing ad budget:
Direct Mail: $50,000
Magazines: $30,000
Telephone: $20,000
Founded: 1987
Gross sales or billing: $4,000,000

Exclusively offer the National Credit Register (145 million credit qualified individuals), the New Movers Register (1.8 million monthly new movers), the New Credit Additions File (1.5 million monthly) & the Access America Databank (166 million American shoppers). All lists are complete with demographics, mail order buyer, donor information & financial lifestyle data. Also provide creative, production & fulfillment services.

THE FIELD COMPANIES FULFILLMENT CENTER INC
385 Pleasant St, PO Box 78
Watertown, MA 02471-0078
Telephone: (617) 926-5550, Toll Free: (800) 346-6552, FAX: (617) 924-9011, E-Mail: info@fieldcompanies.com, Web Site: www.fieldcompanies.com
Pres & Treas: Joseph McDonald
Founded: 1975

E-commerce, fulfillment, mailing services, data processing & electronic printing solutions company.

FIRST CLASS INC
5410 W Roosevelt Rd (Unit 222)
Chicago, IL 60644-1570
Telephone: (773) 378-1009, FAX: (773) 378-1018, Web Site: www.firstclassinc.com
Owner & Pres: Lonna Schulz
Conducts Business: U.S.
Primary Market Served: Business
Founded: 1992

Full-service direct mail services company.

FORECAST DIRECT MARKETING GROUP
37 Terminal Way
Pittsburgh, PA 15219
Telephone: (412) 481-4977, FAX: (412) 481-0872, Web Site: forecastdirect.com
Pres: William Ferari
Conducts Business: U.S.
Primary Market Served: Business

Founded: 1988
Direct mail marketing services company.

GG DIRECT
351 Riverside Industrial Pkwy
Portland, ME 04103-1415
Telephone: (207) 772-0414, FAX:
(207) 871-1444, E-Mail: data@
ggdirect.com, Web Site: www.
ggdirect.com
Pres: Ted Woodward
Partner: Al Brewer
Primary Market Served: Business

Full-service direct marketing company
offering direct mail services, mailing
lists & database management.

GS MARKETING
1345 Enclave Pkwy
Houston, TX 77077-2026
Telephone: (713) 580-3900, FAX:
(713) 580-5935, E-Mail: contactus@
gsmarketing.com, Web Site: www.
gsmarketing.com
VP: Shelley Washburn
VP & Gen Mgr: Claudia Esquivel

Full-service direct marketing & digital
agency.

GABRIEL GROUP
3190 Rider Trail S
Earth City, MO 63045
Telephone: (314) 743-5700, FAX:
(314) 743-5800, E-Mail: sales@
gabrielgr.com, Web Site: gabrielgr.
com
Pres: Arthur Kerckhoff
CEO: David Hawkins
Conducts Business: U.S.
Primary Market Served: Business
Founded: 1983

Direct mail services company offering
fundraising, marketing support services, printing services and creative development.

HAINES DIRECT
Div. of Haines & Co Inc
8050 Freedom Ave NW
North Canton, OH 44720
Telephone: (866) 879-6379, E-Mail:
sales@haines-direct.com, Web Site:
www.haines-direct.com
VP: Ashley Williams
VP: Jim Countryman
Founded: 1970

In-house direct mail services company.

HARLING MARKETING INC
dba Harling Direct
18103 Rte Transcanadienne
Kirkland, QC, Canada H9J 3Z4
Telephone: (514) 695-1430, FAX:
(514) 695-0530, E-Mail: info@
harlingdirect.com, Web Site: www.
harlingdirect.com
Pres: Randy Yates
Conducts Business: Canada
Primary Market Served: Business
Founded: 1959

Marketing support services company
specializing in Direct mail, third party
fulfillment logistics, inventory management, warehousing, database management, consumer loyalty programs, sales
rep distribution, kit assembly, contest
management & Internet services.

HARTY INTEGRATED SOLUTIONS
25 James St, Box 324
New Haven, CT 06513-0324
Telephone: (203) 562-5112, Toll Free:
(800) 654-0562, FAX: (203) 782-
9168, E-Mail: gplatt@hartynet.com,
Web Site: www.hartynet.com
Pres: George R. Platt
Primary Market Served: Business
Founded: 1900

Marketing & custom web content solutions company.

HILL MAILING & PRINTING OF FLORIDA INC
PO Box 3331
Brandon, FL 33509-3331
Telephone: (813) 258-5220, Toll Free:
(888) 662-6951, FAX: (813) 944-
2882, E-Mail: mail@hillmailing.
com, Web Site: hillmailing.com
Pres: Robert Lee
Primary Market Served: Business

Full-service direct mail & printing
company.

THE HORAH GROUP
351 Manville Rd (Suite 105)
Pleasantville, NY 10570-2166
Telephone: (914) 495-3200, E-Mail:
dgoldsmith@horah.com, Web Site:
www.horah.com
Pres: Richard Goldsmith
Conducts Business: U.S.
Primary Market Served: Business

Collection of direct marketing companies offering a full range of strategic,
creative and direct marketing services.

HUMMEL INTEGRATED MARKETING SOLUTIONS
850 Springfield Rd
Union, NJ 07083-8614
Telephone: (908) 688-5300, FAX:
(908) 688-6020, E-Mail: info@
hummelsolutions.com, Web Site:
www.hummelsolutions.com
Pres: John Hummel
Conducts Business: U.S.
Primary Market Served: Business
Founded: 1884

Direct mail & commercial printing
company.

HUNTSINGER & JEFFER
809 Brook Hill Cir
Richmond, VA 23227-2503
Telephone: (804) 266-2499, FAX:
(804) 266-8563, E-Mail: info@
huntsinger-jeffer.com, Web Site:
www.huntsinger-jeffer.com
Pres: Victoria Lester
Sr Writer: Kelly Woodward
List Servs Dir: Shannon Holleman
Sr Copywriter: Willis Turner
Conducts Business: U.S.
Primary Market Served: Business
Founded: 1964

Direct marketing company specializing
in nonprofits and membership organizations.

ICS CORP
100 Friars Blvd
West Deptford, NJ 08086
Telephone: (215) 427-3355, E-Mail:
mefstathios@ics-corporation.com,
Web Site: www.ics-corporation.com
Pres: Matthew Bastian
Conducts Business: U.S.
Primary Market Served: Business
Founded: 1965

Direct mail & marketing services company.

ICS MARKETING SERVICES
Div. of Progressive Impressions Inter-
national
4225 Legacy Pkwy
Lansing, MI 48911-4246
Telephone: (517) 394-1890, Toll Free:
(888) 394-1890, FAX: (517) 394-
7408, E-Mail: sales@icshq.com,
Web Site: icshq.com
Sr VP & Chmn: Marty Jerick
Pres: Ken Orr
Sr VP Sls & Mktg: Kevin Harlow
Conducts Business: U.S.
Employees: 50
Primary Market Served: Business &
Consumer
Advertising/Marketing Budget Related
to Direct Marketing: 26-50%
Direct Marketing ad budget:
Direct Mail: 50%
Online: 50%

Founded: 1990

Advanced marketing and technological solutions for business growth.

IWCO DIRECT

7951 Powers Blvd
Chanhassen, MN 55317-9502
Telephone: (952) 474-0961, FAX: (952) 474-6467, Web Site: www. iwco.com
CEO: Jim Anderson
COO: Joe Morrison
Exec VP: Steve Myrvold
Pres: Mike Ertel
Exec VP & Chief Mktg Officer: Dave Johannes
Conducts Business: U.S.
Employees: 600
Primary Market Served: Business
Founded: 1916

Offers a full array of direct mail production services including sheet-fed and continuous form printing, variable data printing solutions, personalization, lettershop, response management, fulfillment, presorting, commingling & international mailing.

ICON MARKETING COMMUNICATIONS

2320 Grandview Dr
Fort Mitchell, KY 41017
Telephone: (859) 647-7271, FAX: (859) 647-0615, E-Mail: shawn@ iconmc.com, Web Site: iconmc.com
VP: Shawn Murdock
Conducts Business: U.S.
Primary Market Served: Business
Founded: 1997

Brand marketing & strategy company.

IDFOUR

1001 S Dairy Ashford St (Suite 450)
Houston, TX 77077-2386
Telephone: (281) 497-7606, FAX: (281) 497-7616, E-Mail: scotthaney@interdirectusa.com, Web Site: www.idfour.com
Chmn: Scott Haney
Chief Mktg Exec: Rick Mulinix
Conducts Business: U.S.
Primary Market Served: Business

Data, analytics, marketing & marketplace services company.

IMAGE MAKERS MARKETING INC

1843 Blackwater Dr
Marietta, GA 30066-6713
Telephone: (770) 926-9552, FAX: (770) 926-9558, E-Mail: elaine. gossett@immmail.com, Web Site: www.imagemakersmarketing.com
Pres: Elaine Gossett

Exec VP & Creative Dir: Steve Gossett
Conducts Business: U.S.
Primary Market Served: Business & Consumer
Founded: 1980

Full-service advertising & marketing agency.

INNOVATIVE MARKETING DIRECT INC

3200 Henderson Blvd (Suite 100)
Tampa, FL 33609-3054
Telephone: (813) 873-7909, FAX: (813) 873-7918, E-Mail: mail@ innovativedirectmail.com, Web Site: www.innovativedirectmail.com
Pres: Jonathan Kass
Conducts Business: U.S.
Primary Market Served: Business & Consumer
Founded: 2007

Direct mail marketing company specializing in the automotive industry.

INTE Q

1815 S Meyers Rd
Oakbrook Terrace, IL 60181
Telephone: (630) 874-2424, Web Site: www.inteqinsights.com
Pres & CEO: Jeffrey Harris
VP: Steven Kietz
Chmn: Mike Byrne
Conducts Business: U.S.
Primary Market Served: Consumer
Founded: 1998

Customer loyalty program and customer relationship management (CRM) services provider.

INTEGRATED MERCHANDISING SYSTEMS LLC

8338 Austin Ave
Morton Grove, IL 60053-3209
Toll Free: (877) 467-1200, E-Mail: doug.carlson@imsfastpak.com, Web Site: www.imsfastpak.com
CEO: Rick Remick
CFO: Carolyn Close
VP: Doug Carlson
VP Mktg: Todd Cromheecke
Conducts Business: U.S., Canada
Primary Market Served: Business & Consumer
Founded: 1985

Merchandise warehousing & fulfillment company.

THE INTERPROVINCIAL GROUP

dba Interprovincial Printing Ltd & Interpro Mailings Ltd
1315 Morningside Ave

Scarborough, ON, Canada M1B 3C5
Telephone: (416) 283-5555, FAX: (416) 283-6643, E-Mail: info@ interprovincialgroup.com, Web Site: www.interprovincialgroup.com
Mgr: Lee Barker
Conducts Business: Canada
Primary Market Served: Business & Consumer

Full-service printing & mail services company.

KATALYST PARTNERS INC

307 7th Ave (Suite 2401)
New York, NY 10001
Telephone: (203) 257-4277, E-Mail: bpetisi@katalystresponse.com, Web Site: www.katalystresponse.com
Pres: Bob Petisi
Sr VP & Gen Mgr: Nate Snelson
Conducts Business: U.S.
Primary Market Served: Business & Consumer

Full-service direct marketing agency.

KAYE-SMITH

4101 Oakesdale Ave SW
Renton, WA 98057-4817
Telephone: (425) 228-8600, Toll Free: (800) 822-9987, FAX: (425) 291-3167, E-Mail: info@kayesmith.com, Web Site: www.kayesmith.com
Sls Mgr: Alex Smith
Pres: Randy Gifford
Sales Mgr: Joan St Marie
Primary Market Served: Business & Consumer
Founded: 1958

Full-service direct mail marketing & business communications company.

L & E MERIDIAN

8000 Corporate Ct
Springfield, VA 22153
Telephone: (703) 913-0300, Toll Free: (800) 555-1556, FAX: (703) 913-7052, E-Mail: estimating@l-e.com, Web Site: www.l-e.com
VP Acct Svcs: Sylvia Pearson
Primary Market Served: Business & Consumer
Founded: 1986

High volume data management, direct mail processing and digital printing company.

L & D MAIL MASTERS

110 Security Pkwy
New Albany, IN 47150
Telephone: (812) 981-7161, FAX: (812) 981-7169, E-Mail: info@ ldmailmasters.com, Web Site: www. ldmailmasters.com
Pres: Diane Fischer

Conducts Business: U.S.
Primary Market Served: Business
Founded: 1986

Full-service direct marketing agency.

LAWRENCE DIRECT MARKETING INC
22 John Marshall St (Suite B)
Warrenton, VA 20186
Telephone: (540) 349-9278, FAX:
(540) 347-7885, E-Mail: james@
lawrencedirect.com, Web Site: www.
lawrencedirect.com
Pres: E. Michael Lawrence
VP Client Svcs: James Lawrence
Conducts Business: U.S.
Primary Market Served: Consumer
Founded: 1987

Full-service direct response agency.

LAZARUS DIRECT INC
50 Charles Lindbergh Blvd (Suite 504)
Uniondale, NY 11553-3650
Telephone: (516) 880-7000, E-Mail:
inquiries@lazarusdirect.com, Web
Site: www.lazarusmarketing.com
Pres: Candy Kaye
Co-Owner & Pres: Donna Garda
Conducts Business: U.S.
Primary Market Served: Consumer
Advertising/Marketing Budget Related
to Direct Marketing: Direct market-
ing service provider specializing in
direct mail production, data process-
ing, personalization & lettershop
functions.%
Founded: 1975

LIBERTY CREATIVE SOLUTIONS
18625 W Creek Dr
Tinley Park, IL 60477-6247
Telephone: (708) 633-7450, FAX:
(708) 633-7449, E-Mail: info@
libertycreativesolutions.com, Web
Site: www.libertycreativesolutions.
com
Mktg Coord: Angela Hipelius
Pres Sls: Jeff Hofer
Primary Market Served: Consumer
Founded: 1964

Full-service marketing, design, printing
& mailing company.

LOG-ON
520 8th Ave (Floor 14)
New York, NY 10018
Telephone: (212) 279-4567, E-Mail:
sales@log-on.org, Web Site: www.
log-on.org
Pres & CEO: Dan Arnowitz
Pres: Dan Cantelmo
Conducts Business: U.S.

Primary Market Served: Business &
Consumer
Founded: 1987

Full-service direct mail, printing, fulfillment & design company.

LOYALTYWORKS INC
Div. of Incentive Solutions Group of
Companies
2299 Perimeter Park Dr (Suite 150)
Atlanta, GA 30341-1333
Telephone: (678) 539-5000, Toll Free:
(800) 844-5000, FAX: (678) 539-
5173, Web Site: www.loyaltyworks.
com
Exec VP, Client Svcs: Steve Damerow
Sr VP Mktg: Mark Herbert
Conducts Business: U.S., Canada
Employees: 80
Primary Market Served: Business &
Consumer
Advertising/Marketing Budget Related
to Direct Marketing: 76-100%

Designs, builds & manages loyalty &
incentive marketing programs, from
recognition & performance improvement programs to complete consumer
relationship marketing solutions.

MRC MARKETING
An MRC Media Group Company
12 Lincoln Blvd (Suite 103)
Emerson, NJ 07630
Telephone: (201) 406-9471, FAX:
(201) 986-0361, Web Site: www.
mrcmarketing.net
VP New Bus Devel: Susan Rector
Pres: Dave Rector
Primary Market Served: Consumer

Full-service, in-house, consumer &
business to business marketing company.

MSP INC
155 Commerce Dr
Freedom, PA 15042-9202
Telephone: (724) 774-3244, Toll Free:
(800) 876-3211, FAX: (724) 774-
6996, E-Mail: info@msp-pgh.com,
Web Site: www.msp-pgh.com
Pres: Richard E. Bushee III
Mktg: Doug Wright
VP Sales & Mktg: Luke Teboul
Primary Market Served: Business &
Consumer
Founded: 1953

Full-service direct mail marketing company.

MAIL COMPUTER SERVICE
321 Manley St
West Bridgewater, MA 02379

Telephone: (508) 584-6490, Toll Free:
(800) 640-8530, FAX: (508) 584-
2890
Pres: Ron Menconi
Primary Market Served: Consumer
Founded: 1988

Data processing, database management,
fulfillment & direct mail services company.

MAIL ENTERPRISES LLC
3810 5th Ct N
Birmingham, AL 35222-1308
Telephone: (205) 595-4945, Toll Free:
(800) 595-4945, FAX: (205) 595-
4943, E-Mail: sswedenburg@
mailent.com, Web Site: www.
mailent.com
CEO: Scott Swedenburg
Partner: Ricky Miskelley
Partner: Doug Lackey
Conducts Business: U.S.
Primary Market Served: Business &
Consumer
Advertising/Marketing Budget Related
to Direct Marketing: 76-100%
Direct Marketing ad budget:
Direct Mail: 95%
Telephone: 5%
Founded: 1964

Direct mail services company.

MAILNOW INC
dba xDateMarketing.com
305 Donelson Pike (Suite B), PO Box
140290
Nashville, TN 37214
Telephone: (615) 844-4244, FAX:
(615) 208-9757, E-Mail: randall@
xdatemarketing.com, Web Site:
www.xdatemarketing.com
Pres: Randall Putala
Primary Market Served: Business
Founded: 2012

Direct mail marketing program specializing in the insurance industry.

MANHATTAN MEDIA SERVICES INC
271 Madison Ave (Suite 905)
New York, NY 10016
Telephone: (212) 808-4077, FAX:
(212) 808-4080, E-Mail: mmorello@
manhmedia.com, Web Site: www.
manhmedia.com
Pres & CEO: Marianna Morello
COO: Celia Mollica
Sr Acct Exec: Marcello Morello
Controller: Jackie Redger
Conducts Business: U.S.
Employees: 10
Primary Market Served: Consumer
Advertising/Marketing Budget Related
to Direct Marketing: 76-100%

Direct Marketing ad budget:
Magazines: 70%
Newspapers: 30%
Founded: 1995
Gross sales or billing: $30,000,000

Full service direct response/branding advertising agency specializing in place print media at substantially discounted rates.

THE MAREK GROUP

W228 N821 Westmound Dr
Waukesha, WI 53186
Telephone: (262) 549-8900, FAX: (262) 49-8910, E-Mail: info@ marekgroup.com, Web Site: www. marekgroup.com
Pres: Fuzzy Marek
Pres: Tami Marek-Loper
CFO: Chris Dolney
Chief Strategy Officer: Jay Thomas
Founded: 1972

Full-service field marketing & sales support services company.

THE MARKET BUILDER INC

5135 E Ingram St (Suite 2)
Mesa, AZ 85205-3465
Telephone: (480) 641-6200, FAX: (480) 641-6239, E-Mail: info@ themarketbuilder.com, Web Site: www.themarketbuilder.com
Pres: Keith Lawson
Sec Treas: Peggy Lawson
VP & Gen Mgr: Brian Lawson
VP Opers: Paul Lawson
Conducts Business: U.S.
Primary Market Served: Consumer
Founded: 1992

Traditional & electronic direct marketing services company.

MARKETAIDE SERVICES INC

PO Box 190
Hutchinson, KS 67504-0190
Telephone: (785) 825-7161, Toll Free: (800) 204-2433, FAX: (785) 825-4697, E-Mail: creative@marketaide. com, Web Site: www.marketaide. com
Media Dir: Kendi Carlgren
Direct Mail Mgr: Derryl Hill
Conducts Business: U.S.
Primary Market Served: Consumer

Procurement, processing & direct mail services company.

THE MARKETING ADVANTAGE INC

1200 High Ridge Rd.
Stamford, CT 06905
Telephone: (203) 968-8400, FAX: (501) 968-8301, E-Mail: info@ marketingadvantage.com, Web Site: www.marketingadvantage.com
Owner: John Keon PhD
Conducts Business: U.S.
Primary Market Served: Consumer
Direct online sales
Founded: 1985

Marketing & sales analytics company specializing in pharmaceutical, biotech, healthcare & medical device companies.

MARKETING SOLUTIONS UNLIMITED LLC

109 Talcott Rd
West Hartford, CT 06110-1228
Telephone: (860) 523-0670, FAX: (860) 523-0675, E-Mail: info@ msuprint.com, Web Site: msuprint. com
Pres: Heidi Buckley
Conducts Business: U.S.
Primary Market Served: Consumer
Founded: 1991

Print & direct mail services company.

MCINTYRE DIRECT GROUP LLC

700 N Hayden Island Dr (Suite 390)
Portland, OR 97217-8185
Telephone: (503) 516-4592, FAX: (503) 286-7622, E-Mail: marcia@ mcintyredirectgroup.com, Web Site: mcintyredirectgroup.com
Pres: Marcia Mantz
Founder: Susan McIntyre
VP Mktg: Carrie Chapin
Conducts Business: U.S.
Primary Market Served: Business & Consumer
Founded: 1991

Full service agency & consulting firm for catalogers.

MEDIA HORIZONS INC

40 Richards Ave
Norwalk, CT 06854-2320
Telephone: (203) 857-0770, FAX: (203) 857-0296, E-Mail: info@ mediahorizons.com, Web Site: www. mediahorizons.com
Pres & CEO: James Kabakow
Sr VP, New Bus: Tom Reynolds
Sr VP, Mktg: Liz Russell
Conducts Business: U.S.
Employees: 53
Primary Market Served: Consumer
Founded: 1988

Full service direct marketing & media company. Services include strategic planning, media buying (alternative media, print & broadcast), direct mail, website development, e-mail and alternative media program management.

MEDIAWORKS ADVERTISING & MARKETING INC

725 W Granada Blvd (Suite 12)
Ormond Beach, FL 32174
Telephone: (386) 676-4608, E-Mail: scott@mediaworksusa.com, Web Site: www.mediaworksusa.com
Pres: Scott Reid
Sr Partner Client Svcs: Marcia Malys
Conducts Business: U.S.
Primary Market Served: Consumer
Founded: 1996

Cable advertising & marketing company specializing in direct mail printing, radio/audio & TV/video production and campaign management & tracking.

MOUNTAIN MEDIA ENTERPRISES

102 Rome Ct
Fort Collins, CO 80524
Telephone: (970) 493-2499, FAX: (970) 493-3598, E-Mail: info@ mountain-media.com, Web Site: fortcollinsdigitalprinting.com
Pres: Mark Hoyle
Co-Owner: Sonny Schaus
Primary Market Served: Consumer

Full-service digital printing and direct mail services company.

NCP SOLUTIONS

Subs. of Harland Clarke Corp.
5200 E Lake Blvd
Birmingham, AL 35217
Telephone: (250) 849-5200, Web Site: www.ncprint.com
CEO: Mark Harris
VP, Direct Mktg: Joseph Tetstone
Conducts Business: U.S.
Primary Market Served: Business
Founded: 1974

Print & digital media communication company specializing in transactional & marketing communications, electronic services & mail services.

NPN360 INC

1400 S Wolf Rd (Suite 102)
Wheeling, IL 60090-6524
Telephone: (847) 215-7300, FAX: (847) 215-7314, E-Mail: sales@ npn360.com, Web Site: www. npn360.com
Pres: Artie Collins
Exec VP: Jeff Greenbury
Employees: 30
Primary Market Served: Business

Founded: 1985

Full-service direct mail production company specializing in print (forms, letters, brochures, envelopes), personalization, bindery and lettershop.

NELSON PRINTING CORP - DIRECT MARKETERS OF CHARLESTON

100 Columbus St
Charleston, SC 29403
Telephone: (843) 723-7233, FAX: (843) 723-8098, E-Mail: info@nelsonprint.com, Web Site: nelsonprint.com
Pres: Eric Nelson
Primary Market Served: Business & Consumer
Founded: 2014

Full-service print and direct mail marketing company.

NORDIS TECHNOLOGIES INC

4401 NW 124th Ave
Coral Springs, FL 33065-7636
Telephone: (954) 323-5500, Toll Free: (800) 208-1169, FAX: (954) 323-0100, E-Mail: help@nordistechnologies.com, Web Site: www.nordistechnologies.com
Pres & CEO: Ronnie Selinger
Sr VP & Gen Mgr: Richard O'Rourke
Mktg Mgr: Deborah Risch
Conducts Business: U.S.
Employees: 100
Primary Market Served: Business
Advertising/Marketing Budget Related to Direct Marketing: 76-100%
Direct Marketing ad budget:
Direct Mail: 90%
Magazines: 10%
Founded: 1989

Print & digital communications solutions company.

NORTH AMERICAN COMMUNICATIONS INC

7 Edgemont Rd
Katonah, NY 10536
Telephone: (914) 273-8620, E-Mail: info@nacmail.com, Web Site: www.nacmail.com
CEO: Rob Herman
CEO: Nick Robinson
Conducts Business: U.S.
Employees: 2,000
Primary Market Served: Business & Consumer
Founded: 1979

Privately owned, integrated direct mail manufacturer.

O'CONNELL MEIER LLC

5221 Franconia Rd (Suite 10252)
Alexandria, VA 22310
Telephone: (703) 635-2893, Toll Free: (866) 391-1415, FAX: (703) 739-0478, E-Mail: info@omdirect.com, Web Site: www.omdirect.com
Pres: Rich Meier
CEO & Creative Dir: Lynn O'Connell
Primary Market Served: Business & Consumer
Founded: 1989

Marketing communications firm specializing in campaigns that integrate traditional, interactive and emerging marketing techniques.

O'NEILL MARKETING CO

10805 Main St (Suite 400)
Fairfax, VA 22030
Telephone: (703) 934-0272, FAX: (703) 934-0273, E-Mail: info@oneillmarketing.com, Web Site: www.oneillmarketing.com
Pres: Rita O'Neill
Primary Market Served: Business & Consumer

Full-service direct marketing and data management company.

PDQ POST GROUP

19134 95A Ave (Unit 7)
Surrey, BC, Canada V4N 4P2
Telephone: (604) 888-0676, Toll Free: (888) 998-9878, FAX: (604) 888-4467, E-Mail: sales@pdqpostgroup.com, Web Site: www.pdqpostgroup.com
Pres: Lorraine Duclos
Gen Mgr: Pam Erikson
Conducts Business: U.S., Canada
Primary Market Served: Consumer
Founded: 1991

Lettershop & direct mail management company.

PHOENIX MARKETING GROUP LLC

24 Woods Way
Redding, CT 06896
Telephone: (203) 544-7033, E-Mail: bseide@phoenix-marketing.com, Web Site: www.phoenix-marketing.com
Pres: Bruce Seide
Conducts Business: U.S.
Primary Market Served: Business
Founded: 1991

Direct marketing industry consulting company.

PLUSNETMARKETING INC

600 Eagleview Blvd (Suite 300)
Exton, PA 19341
Telephone: (610) 458-0707, E-Mail: info@pnmarketing.com, Web Site: www.plusnetmarketing.com
CEO: Edward Devlin
COO: Susan Widen
Chief Tech Officer: Jon Hayward
Sr VP Sales: Dave Nazaruk
VP Mktg: Kim Brockway
Primary Market Served: Consumer
Founded: 1999

Promotions and targeted marketing services company.

PRECISION SOLUTIONS

11221 Dolfield Blvd (Suite 103)
Owings Mills, MD 21117
Telephone: (443) 870-3079, FAX: (443) 548-2954, E-Mail: info@precisionsolutions.net, Web Site: www.precisionsolutions.net
Pres: Mike Scudder
Conducts Business: U.S.
Primary Market Served: Business & Consumer
Founded: 2007

Full-service printing and direct mail services company.

PREMIER PRINT AND SERVICES GROUP INC

10 S Riverside Plz (Suite 1810)
Chicago, IL 60606
Telephone: (312) 648-2266, Toll Free: (800) 648-3677, FAX: (312) 648-1361, Web Site: www.premierprint.com
Pres: Ronald La Bine
CFO & COO: Chuck Blazevich
Conducts Business: U.S.
Primary Market Served: Consumer
Founded: 1984

Full service marketing communications & print services company.

PREMIERIMS INC

11101 Ella Blvd
Houston, TX 77067
Telephone: (832) 608-6400, FAX: (832) 608-6420, E-Mail: contact@mailplex.com, Web Site: www.premiercompany.com
CEO: Norm Pegram
Pres: Geno Baiamonte
Conducts Business: U.S.
Primary Market Served: Business & Consumer
Founded: 2008

Full-service direct mail marketing company.

PRINTING ARTS

2001 W 21st St
Broadview, IL 60155

Telephone: (708) 938-1600, FAX:
(708) 938-1717, E-Mail:
webcontact@printarts.com, Web
Site: printarts.com
Pres: John Ropski
Conducts Business: U.S.
Primary Market Served: Business
Founded: 1994

Full-service packaging & commercial
printing company.

PRISM DATA SERVICES LTD

200-1599 Hurontario St
Mississauga, ON, Canada L5G 4S1
Telephone: (905) 278-5556, FAX:
(905) 278-6603, E-Mail: sales@
prism-data.com, Web Site: www.
prism-data.com
Pres: William Cram
VP: Dave Quinn
Conducts Business: Canada
Primary Market Served: Business

Mail and address management services
company.

PROPHASE MARKETING INC

6321 Bury Dr (Suite 19)
Eden Prairie, MN 55346-1739
Telephone: (952) 974-1100, Toll Free:
(800) 969-6400, FAX: (952) 974-
7874, E-Mail: sales@ppmi.com,
Web Site: prophasemarketing.com
Pres & CEO: Mike Pietrini
COO: Craig Whaley
Dir Tech: John Nadler
Dir New Bus Devel: Kelly Whalen
Primary Market Served: Business &
Consumer
Founded: 1986

Full-service marketing & software solutions company.

PROFESSIONAL PRINT &
MAIL INC

2818 E Hamilton Ave
Fresno, CA 93721-3209
Telephone: (559) 237-7468, Toll Free:
(800) 654-7468, FAX: (559) 237-
4929, E-Mail: info@printfresno.com,
Web Site: www.printfresno.com
Pres & CEO: Doug Carlile
Dir Sales: Ed Caz
Primary Market Served: Consumer
Founded: 1985

Full-service commercial printer & direct mail marketing company.

PROGRAMMERS
INVESTMENT CORP

125 E Algonquin Rd
Arlington Heights, IL 60005

Telephone: (224) 265-6000, FAX:
(224) 265-6142, E-Mail: pic@pic-
online.com, Web Site: www.pic-
online.com
CEO: Gary W. Scherer
Pres: Rick Ziemek
CIO: Jim Heck

Order management company specializing in direct mail and e-commerce.

PROGRESSIVE
COMMUNICATIONS

1001 Sand Pond Rd
Lake Mary, FL 32746-3354
Telephone: (407) 333-9500, Toll Free:
(800) 571-9407, FAX: (407) 333-
7979, E-Mail: info@
progressivecommunications.com,
Web Site:
progressivecommunications.com
Pres: Mark Mills
Founded: 1975

Full-service marketing company specializing in commercial printing, design, mail and fulfillment.

PROMARKDIRECT INC

PO Box 258
Ramsey, NJ 07446-0258
Telephone: (201) 489-0532, Toll Free:
(800) 776-6275, FAX: (201) 489-
2680, E-Mail: solutions@
promarkdirect.com, Web Site: www.
promarkdirect.com
Pres: Donna Johns
Founded: 1977

Full service marketing & advertising
agency specializing in multichannel
strategic marketing solutions.

PROSPECT DIRECT INC

2266 N Prospect Ave, Ste 336, Milwaukee, WI 53202-6306
2266 N Prospect Ave (Suite 336)
Milwaukee, WI 53202-6306
Telephone: (414) 271-3313, FAX:
(414) 271-4244, E-Mail: info@
prospect-direct.com, Web Site: www.
prospect-direct.com
Pres: Jill Cohen

Direct mail fundraising company specializing in Jewish non-profit organizations.

QUALITY LETTER SERVICE
INC

the lettersmiths(R) "the datasmarts"(R)
22 W 32nd St (Floor 10)
New York, NY 10001-3807
Telephone: (212) 268-3400, FAX:
(212) 268-3401, E-Mail: info@
qletter.com, Web Site: www.qletter.
com
Pres: Gary Weinberg

VP Opers: Robert Weinberg
Full-service print, mail and fulfillment
services company.

RCS RESPONSE
TECHNOLOGIES INC

6420 Rea Rd (Suite 210)
Charlotte, NC 28217
Telephone: (704) 522-1919, FAX:
(704) 522-9092, E-Mail: results@
rcsdirect.com, Web Site: www.
rcsdirect.com
Pres & COO: Joseph A Rowell
IT Mgr: Brandon Sproul
Founded: 1987

Direct marketing firm specializing in
direct mail, telemarketing, fax & email
campaigns.

REDI-DIRECT MARKETING
INC

5 Audrey Pl
Fairfield, NJ 07004
Telephone: (973) 808-4500, E-Mail:
sales@redidirect.com, Web Site:
www.redidirect.com
CEO: Tom Buckley
Primary Market Served: Business
Founded: 1990

Full-service, multi-channel direct marketing company.

RELATIONSHIP1

1 Blue Hill Plz (Suite 1523)
Pearl River, NY 10965-3175
Telephone: (845) 732-8300, E-Mail:
inforequest@relationship1.com, Web
Site: www.relationship1.com
CEO & Pres: David L. Ganz
COO: Howard W. Mertz
Conducts Business: U.S., Canada, Eu-
rope
Primary Market Served: Business &
Consumer
Founded: 1993

Build and maintain customized marketing databases from which we offer
analysis, modeling, and reporting; direct mail and catalog lettershop; list
brokerage; strategic consulting.

SAATCHI & SAATCHI
CANADA

Subs. of Saatchi & Saatchi
175 Bloor St E, South Tower (Suite
1300)
Toronto, ON, Canada M4W 3R9
Telephone: (416) 359-9595, FAX:
(416) 866-4111, Web Site: saatchi.ca
Exec VP & Mng Dir: Stuart Payne
Pres: John McCarter
Pres: Brian Sheppard

Primary Market Served: Consumer

Full-service, integrated communications company.

SALES DEVELOPMENT ASSOCIATES INC

7850 Manchester Rd
Saint Louis, MO 63143-2710
Telephone: (314) 862-8828, FAX:
  (314) 862-8829, E-Mail: patb@
  sdastl.com, Web Site: www.sdastl.
  com
Pres: Patricia Biggerstaff
Founded: 1989

Strategic marketing and sales company.

SIGNATURE COMMUNICATIONS INC

417 N 8th St (Suite 401)
Philadelphia, PA 19123
Telephone: (215) 922-3022, FAX:
  (215) 922-3033, Web Site: www.
  signatureteam.com
Principal: Tony DeMarco
Conducts Business: U.S.
Primary Market Served: Business &
  Consumer
Founded: 1981

Full-service marketing communications company.

SPRING GLOBAL DELIVERY SOLUTIONS

3170 Orlando Dr (Unit 3)
Mississauga, ON, Canada L4V 1R5
Telephone: (905) 678-2770, E-Mail:
  spring.cs.ca@springglobalmail.com,
  Web Site: www.spring-gds.com
VP Americas: Lou LaForet
Conducts Business: Worldwide
Primary Market Served: Business &
  Consumer
Founded: 2001

Provides international mail, parcel & return services to businesses.

STAR DIRECT MAIL

118 Louisiana Ave.
Brooklyn, NY 11207
Telephone: (718) 257-3500, Toll Free:
  (877) 978-2762, FAX: (718) 649-
  5470, Web Site: www.stardirectmail.
  com
Dir: Chaim Gansburg
Founded: 1988

Print & mailing service provider to the direct mail & marketing industry.

STEZZI DIRECT INC

3404 Oakcliff Rd (Suite C-3)
Atlanta, GA 30340
Telephone: (770) 448-9900, Toll Free:
  (800) 954-5100, FAX: (770) 448-
  9480, E-Mail: info@stezzi.com, Web
  Site: www.stezzi.com
Pres: Joseph Stezzi
Fulfillment Dir: James Haublein
Founded: 1986

Full-service commercial printing and direct mail marketing company.

SUMAN INC

10805 Whiterim Dr
Potomac, MD 20854-1786
Telephone: (301) 461-7625, E-Mail:
  anil.chaturvedi@sumaninc.com, Web
  Site: www.sumaninc.com
CEO & Pres: Dr Anil Chaturvedi
Employees: 2
Primary Market Served: Business
Direct online sales
Founded: 1999

Sell state-of-the-art marketing analytic solutions to marketing companies. Products include EZ Predict & EZ Map for direct marketing.

SUMOTEXT, INC

10825 Financial Centre Pkwy Ste 123
Little Rock, AR 72211-3557
Toll Free: (800) 480-1248, Web Site:
  www.sumotext.com

TARADEL LLC

4805 Lake Brook Dr (Suite 140)
Glen Allen, VA 23060-9278
Telephone: (804) 364-8444, Toll Free:
  (800) 481-1656, FAX: (888) 241-
  3023, E-Mail: info@taradel.com,
  Web Site: www.taradel.com
Pres: James Fitzgerald
CFO: Tom McNally
VP Bus Devel: Wendy Urquhart
Dir Mktg: Chris Barr
Primary Market Served: Business &
  Consumer
Founded: 2003

Full-service direct mail, print advertising and digital marketing services company.

TAYLOR COMMUNICATIONS

Sub. of Taylor Corp.
1725 Roe Crest Dr
North Mankato, MN 56003
Toll Free: (800) 755-6405, Web Site:
  www.taylorcommunications.com
Pres: Mark O'Leary
Sr VP: Jeff Crump
Sr VP: Ben Cutting
Sr VP Sales: Joe Zappa
CEO: Charlie Hipp
Conducts Business: Worldwide
Primary Market Served: Business

Founded: 1912

Full-service print & digital communications company specializing in the healthcare, financial services, retail and industrial markets.

TELEBRANDS CORP

One Telebrands Plz
Fairfield, NJ 07004
Telephone: (973) 247-8777, Web Site:
  www.telebrands.com
Pres: A.J. Khubani
EVP Opers: Bala Iyer
VP Mktg: Shail Prasad
VP Fin: Bob Barnett
VP Sales: Angelo Bianco
Conducts Business: Worldwide
Primary Market Served: Business &
  Consumer
Founded: 1983

Direct television marketing company and creator of the "As Seen On TV" logo & trade category.

THOMAS PRINTWORKS

707 West Rd
Houston, TX 77038-2505
Telephone: (832) 201-2000, Toll Free:
  (800) 656-8883, FAX: (832) 201-
  2001, E-Mail: info@seebridgemedia.
  com, Web Site: www.
  thomasprintworks.com
Pres & Founder: Don Lawler
Mgr: Tony Robinson
Conducts Business: U.S.
Primary Market Served: Business &
  Consumer

Full-service print, mail & reprographic services company.

TIZIANI WHITMYRE INC

Sharon Commerce Center, 2 Commercial St
Sharon, MA 02067
Telephone: (781) 793-9380, FAX:
  (781) 793-9395, E-Mail: info@tizinc.
  com, Web Site: www.tizinc.com
CEO: Robert Tiziani
Pres: Rick Whitmyre
Prin: Jason Dodd
Primary Market Served: Consumer

Marketing agency specializing in revenue generation & frand development for B2B & life science companies.

TOPP DIRECT MARKETING

701 Palm Valley Dr W
Harlingen, TX 78552-9039
Telephone: (956) 421-5750, FAX:
  (956) 421-5721, E-Mail: info@
  toppmarketing.com, Web Site: www.
  toppmarketing.com
CEO: John W. Topp

Founded: 1983

Full-service direct mail marketing company.

TOWNE ALLPOINTS

3441 W MacArthur Blvd
Santa Ana, CA 92704
Telephone: (714) 540-3095, Toll Free:
(800) 243-8099, FAX: (714) 540-
4192, E-Mail: info@towne.com,
Web Site: www.towne.com
Chmn & Owner: Deborah Griffith
Founded: 1953

Direct marketing & fulfillment services company.

TRIBUNE DIRECT LLC

Div. of Tribune Publishing
505 Northwest Ave (Suite A)
Northlake, IL 60164-1662
Telephone: (708) 836-2700, Toll Free:
(800) 545-9657, FAX: (708) 836-
0605, Web Site: tribunedirect.com
Dir Mktg Svcs: Tim Street
Primary Market Served: Business &
Consumer

Full-service direct response marketing company.

TRIBUNE DIRECT ORLANDO

633 N Orange Ave
Orlando, FL 32801
Telephone: (407) 420-5100, E-Mail:
kkeenan@tribunedirect.com, Web
Site: www.
orlandosentinelmediagroup.com/
DirectMail
Direct Mail Mgr: Kevin Keenan

Full-service provider of strategic, targeted , direct mail marketing solutions.

TRIMENSIONS INC

1 Eagle St
Englewood, NJ 07631
Telephone: (201) 816-8820, FAX:
(201) 816-8870, E-Mail: jghossn@
trimensionsinc.com, Web Site: www.
trimensionsinc.com
CEO: John Ghossn

Full-service design & production company specializing in educational & promotional materials and products.

UNIVERSAL WILDE

26 Dartmouth St
Westwood, MA 02090
Telephone: (781) 251-2700, FAX:
(781) 251-2613, E-Mail: marketing@
universalwilde.com, Web Site: www.
universalwilde.com
Pres: Stephen J Flood
Corp Mktg & New Bus Devel Dir: William Gentes

New Busn Devt: Tome Andrade
New Busn Devt: Nancy Harhut
New Busn Devt: Jim Bailey
Conducts Business: U.S.
Primary Market Served: Business
Founded: 1868

Provider of full-service marketing solutions including agency services, offset & digital print, direct mail services emails, membership cards and automated fulfillment & distribution programs.

UNIWORLD GROUP

1 Metro Tech Center N (Fl 11)
Brooklyn, NY 11201
Telephone: (212) 219-1600, FAX:
(212) 219-6395, E-Mail: newbiz@
uwqny.com, Web Site: www.uwg.is
Dir: Monique Nelson
Dir: Chris Jimenez
Founded: 1969

Advertising & marketing agency specializing in multicultural communications and creative development.

WESTMINSTER INTERNATIONAL INC

4-50 Valleywood Dr
Markham, ON, Canada L3R 6E9
Telephone: (416) 494-6245, Toll Free:
(866) 635-8050, FAX: (905) 771-
9349, E-Mail: info@westminster.ca,
Web Site: www.westminster.ca
Pres: Nancy Holmes
Conducts Business: Canada
Primary Market Served: Business
Advertising/Marketing Budget Related
to Direct Marketing: Data management, lettershop, direct mail, print & fulfillment services company.%
Founded: 1986

WORDCOM INC

56 Main St, PO Box 308
Ellington, CT 06029-3360
Telephone: (860) 875-7373, Toll Free:
(800) 822-0622, FAX: (860) 872-
2713, E-Mail: sales@wordcom-inc.
com, Web Site: www.wordcom-inc.
com
Chmn Bd & CEO: George Wachtel
Pres: Christopher Wachtel
Sr VP: Tim Berger
VP Mktg: Steve Morris
Conducts Business: U.S.
Primary Market Served: Business
Founded: 1981

Full-service marketing company & producer of direct mail campaigns.

Computer Services, Data Processing, List & Subscription Fulfillment Companies (22) — Geographic Index

ARIZONA

Infolure, 1705 W Parkside Ln, Phoenix, 85027-1333

JDA Software Group Inc, 14400 N 87th St, Scottsdale, 85260-3649

Professional Marketing Associates, 405 W Fairmont Dr, Tempe, 85282-2007

ARKANSAS

Acxiom Corp, 601 E 3rd St, Little Rock, 72201-1709

CognitiveDATA Inc, 500 President Clinton Ave (Suite 301), Little Rock, 72201-1760

CALIFORNIA

AccountMate Software Corp, 1445 Technology Ln (Suite A5), Petaluma, 94954-7613

AcquireWEB Inc, 1065 E Hillsdale Blvd (Suite 310), Foster City, 94404-1689

Adobe Systems Inc, 345 Park Ave, San Jose, 95110-2704

Aptimus, 199 Fremont St (Suite 1800), San Francisco, 94105

Business Objects Americas, Inc, 3030 Orchard Pkwy, San Jose, 95134-2028

CAM Commerce Solutions, 17075 Newhope St (Suite A), Fountain Valley, 92708-4299

Christian Resource Management, 2322 N Batavia (Suite 108), Orange, 92865-2000

Cisco Systems Inc, 170 W Tasman Dr, San Jose, 95134-1700

COMPITSS Inc, 1000 Business Center Dr (Suite 107), Newbury Park, 91320-1237

Contact Center Compliance, 350 E St (Suite 100), Santa Rosa, 95404-4438

CoreLogic Inc, 40 Pacifica (Suite 900), Irvine, 92618

CrownPeak Technology Inc, 5880 W Jefferson Blvd (Suite G), Los Angeles, 90016-3160

The Customer Connection Inc, 960 S Andreasen Dr (Suite B), Escondido, 92029-1964

DMRA, 201 San Antonio Cir (Suite 280), Mountain View, 94040-1256

Demandbase Inc, 680 Folsom (Suite 400), San Francisco, 94107

ESRI, 380 New York St, Redlands, 92373-8118

FileMaker Inc, 5201 Patrick Henry, Santa Clara, 95054-1164

Fujitsu America Inc, 1250 E Arques Ave MS 122, Sunnyvale, 94085-3470

Hitachi Data Systems, 2845 Lafayette St, Santa Clara, 95050-2639

Information Sources Inc, 2175 Cactus Ct Apt 1, Walnut Creek, 94595-2531

Input Systems Inc, 16308 Orange Ave, Paramount, 90723

Integrated Marketing Technology Inc, 2269 Chestnut St (#992), San Francisco, 94123-2600

Island Pacific Inc, 17310 Red Hill Ave Ste 320, Irvine, 92614-5600

KXEN Inc, 300 California St (Suite 220), San Francisco, 94104-1410

King Computer Services Inc, 3115 Foothill Blvd (#M250), La Crescenta, 91214-2691

Magento, 10441 Jefferson Blvd (Suite 200), Culver City, 90232-3512

Mailer's Software, 22382 Avenida Empresa, Rancho Santa Margarita, 92688-2112

Melissa Data Corp, 22382 Avenida Empresa, Rancho Santa Margarita, 92688-2112

MindFireInc, 30 Corporate Park (Suite 400), Irvine, 92606-5133

Old Vine Marketing, 147 Old Vine Way, Napa, 94558-7028

Phoenix Technologies Ltd, 910 E Hamilton Ave (Suite 110), Campbell, 95008-0612

QMSI, 5800 Ager Beswick Rd, Montague, 96064-9423

Response Management Technologies Inc, 2550 9th St (Suite 103), Berkeley, 94710-2516

Salford Systems, 9685 Via Excelencia (Suite 208), San Diego, 92126-7500

Savicom, 44 Montgomery St (Suite 1600), San Francisco, 94104-4703

Sybase Inc, 1 Sybase Dr, Dublin, 94568-7976

TheLaw.net Corp, 6640 Lusk Blvd (Suite A205), San Diego, 92121-2777

TRUSTe, 835 Market St (Suite 800), San Francisco, 94103-1905

Vision Solutions, 15300 Barranca Pkwy, Irvine, 92618

Western Digital Corp, 3355 Michelson Dr (Suite 100), Irvine, 92612-5694

Yousendit Inc, 1919 S Bascom Ave (fl 3), Campbell, 95008-2220

COLORADO

Complete Mailing Solutions, Inc, 3001 S Tejon St, Englewood, 80110-1316

Core Technologies, 1245 Pearl St (Suite 202), Boulder, 80302-5253

Corporate Express US Inc, One Environmental Way, Broomfield, 80021

Covalent Marketing, 2021 S Ogden St, Denver, 80210-4134

Demographic Research Co, 1552 Pennsylvania St, Denver, 80203

Direct Data Capture Ltd, 4611 Plettner Ln (Suite 130), Evergreen, 80439-7396

Dovetail, 1221 W Mineral Ave (Suite 102), Littleton, 80120-4544

Global IntelliSystems, 1153 Bergen Pkwy (Suite 455), Evergreen, 80439-9501

Jeppesen, 55 Inverness Dr E, Englewood, 80112-5412

KBM Group, 2051 Dogwood St (Suite 220), Louisville, 80027

Oracle Data Cloud, 10075 Westmoor Dr (Suite 105), Broomfield, 80021-2570

RealData Services Inc, 322 Van Dorn Dr, Glenwood Springs, 81601-9524

Rigden Inc, PO Box 17187, Boulder, 80308-0187

TeleTech, 9197 S Peoria St, Englewood, 80112-5833

Wiland Direct, 6309 Monarch Park Pl (Suite 201), Longmont, 80503-7198

CONNECTICUT

Connex International Inc, 50 Federal Rd, Danbury, 06810-6129

Data Square LLC, 733 Summer St (Suite 601), Stamford, 06901-1035

Fairfield Marketing Group Inc, 830 Sport Hill Rd, Easton, 06612-1241

Interactive Marketing Solutions, 777 Summer St (Suite 502), Stamford, 06901-1042

MDF Systems, 780 James P Casey Rd, Bristol, 06010-8537

Pitney Bowes Software Systems, One Elmcroft Rd, Stamford, 06926-0700

Shepard's Inc, 32 Henry St, Bethel, 06801

Software Marketing Associates Inc, 1086 Elm St (Suite 200), Rocky Hill, 06067-2341

Suntel Inc, 2321 Whitney Ave (Suite 401A, Hamden, 06518-3541

Wired Assets Data Corp, 284 Riversville Rd, Greenwich, 06831-3253

FLORIDA

Alvion LLC, 2503 Del Prado Blvd (Suite 502), Cape Coral, 33904

August Marketing, 4704 W Neptune St (Suite 200), Tampa, 33629-5502

Citrix Systems, Inc, 851 W Cypress Creek Rd, Fort Lauderdale, 33309-2040

Computer Solutions Inc, 13701 SW 88th St (Suite 306), Bldg H33, Miami, 33186-1309

Data Partners Inc, 12857 Banyan Creek Dr, Fort Myers, 33908-3083

Geoscape, 2100 W Flagler St (fl 2), Miami, 33135-1619

The Information Engine, 9105 Hammock Edge Pl, Bradenton, 34212-3254

Latin Force Group LLC, 2100 W Flagler St (#2), Miami, 33135-1619

Logicnology Inc, 720 International Pkwy, Sunrise, 33325-6219

MarketLeverage, 701 International Pkwy (Suite 200), Lake Mary, 32746-5624

Parker Software, 4767 New Broad St, Orlando, 32814

Precision Play Media / MarketLeverage, 701 International Pkwy (Suite 200), Lake Mary, 32746-5624

PrimeNet, 2100 Palmetto St (Suite A), Clearwater, 33765-2101

Rapid Progress Marketing & Modeling LLC, 1760 Delaware Ave NE, Saint Petersburg, 33703-5439

Support Services Corp, 69 Daniels Pkwy (Suite 29-252), Fort Myers, 33901

Time Customer Service Inc, One N Dale Mabry Hwy, Tampa, 33609-2700

V12 Data, 2319 Oak Myrtle Ln (#104), Wesley Chapel, 33544

GEORGIA

Airs Inc, 4080 Hwy 92, Douglasville, 30135-4404

Colinear Systems, 2650 Holcomb Bridge Rd (Suite 610), Alpharetta, 30022-5343

Computer Business Services Inc, 205 W Forsyth St, PO Box A, Americus, 31709-3533

First Wave Technologies Inc, 7000 Central Pkwy NE (Suite 330), Atlanta, 30328-4589

Gates Marketing, 3909 Oakcliff Industrial Ct, Atlanta, 30340-3408

Infor, 13560 Morris Rd (Suite 4100), Alpharetta, 30004

Nexxlinx (HQ), 3565 Piedmont Rd NE (Bldg 2, Suite 100), Atlanta, 30305-8204

North American Mailing Technologies Inc, 141 B Buford Dr, Lawrenceville, 30045-4926

O2 Consulting Inc, 7760 Landowne Dr, Atlanta, 30350-1064

Peachtree Data Inc, 2905 Premiere Pkwy (Suite 200), Duluth, 30097-5275

Performance Direct Inc, 3525 Piedmont Rd, Atlanta, 30305-1530

PossibleNOW Inc, 4400 River Green Pkwy, Duluth, 30096-8316

Premiere Global Services Inc, 3280 Peachtree Rd NE (Suite 1000), Atlanta, 30305-2451

Stibo Systems, 3550 George Busbee Pkwy NW (Suite 350), Kennesaw, 30144-2122

Touch-Base Computing, PO Box 213, Silver Creek, 30173

HAWAII

DataCraft Inc, 28 Kainehe St (Suite A-1), Kailua, 96734-6130

ILLINOIS

ACG/Computech Direct, 2155 Stonington Ave (Suite 215), Hoffman Estates, 60195-2058

The Allant Group, 2056 Westings Ave (Suite 500), Naperville, 60563-2485

Alterian, 35 Wacker Dr (Suite 200), Chicago, 60601-2104

Anthem Marketing, 549 W Randolph St (Suite 702), Chicago, 60661-1478

Audience Identification Inc, PO Box 3305, Lisle, 60532-8305

Cogensia, 100 W Hillcrest Blvd (Suite 406), Schaumburg, 60195-3108

DKP & Associates, Inc, 8340 N Lincoln Ave (Suite 100), Skokie, 60077-2462

Daystar Data Group Inc, 155 W Central Rd, Schaumburg, 60195-1945

Direct Logic Solutions, 4507 N Sterling Ave (Suite 402), Peoria, 61615-3860

Information Command Inc, 411 W Ontario St (Apt 225), Chicago, 60654-6954

Integrated Business Services Inc, 736 N Western Ave (Suite 125), Lake Forest, 60045-1820

Kable Fulfillment Services, 16 S Wesley Ave, Mount Morris, 61054-1473

MarketerNet LLC, 233 S Wacker Dr (Suite 1800), Sears Tower, Chicago, 60606-6462

Omeda, 555 Huehl Rd, Northbrook, 60062-2336

Partners Marketing Inc, 1750 E Main St (Suite 10), Saint Charles, 60174-2363

Peak Computer Systems, 6400 W Main St (Suite 1A), Belleville, 62223

Phoenix Data Processing LLC, One Oak Hill Center (Suite 301), Westmont, 60559-5540

SPSS Inc, 200 W Madison St (Suite 2300), Chicago, 60606-3416

Scientific Computing Associates Corp, 212 Lathrop Ave, River Forest, 60305-2121

Spectrum Data, 131 N 3rd St, Oregon, 61061-1410

Strategic Data Intelligence LLC, 555 Skokie Blvd (Suite 255), Northbrook, 60062-2812

SubscriberMail LLC, 3333 Warrenville Rd (Suite 530), Lisle, 60532-4551

Valid USA Inc, 1011 Warrenville Rd (Suite 450), Lisle, 60532

INDIANA

Fifth Gear LLC, 9100 Purdue Rd (Suite 400), Indianapolis, 46268-1180

Service Net Warranty LLC, 650 Missouri Ave, Jeffersonville, 47130-3081

IOWA

BWB Marketing Services, PO Box 802, Ankeny, 50021-0802

B2E Direct Marketing Inc, 209 S Main St, Grimes, 50111-2192

CDS Global, 1901 Bell Ave, Des Moines, 50315-1099

KANSAS

Datasystem Solutions Inc, 6310 Lamar Ave (Suite 200), Overland Park, 66202-4284

Lexinet Corp, 701 N Union St, Council Grove, 66846-9358

Ruf Strategic Solutions, 1533 E Spruce St, Olathe, 66061-3698

KENTUCKY

DirecTech Holding Company Inc, 33 W Second St (Suite 504), Maysville, 41056

MARYLAND

Barcoding Inc, 2220 Boston St (Floor 2), Baltimore, 21231-3058

Data Services Inc, 31516 Winterplace Pkwy, Salisbury, 21804-1882

Decision Software Inc, 6911 Old Landover Rd, Hyattsville, 20785-1503

Group 1 Software Inc, 4200 Parliament Pl (Suite 600), Lanham, 20706-1844

Lewis Direct, 325 E Oliver St, Baltimore, 21202-2948

Lotame Solutions, 8850 Stanford Blvd (Suite 2000), Columbia, 21045-4726

MMI Direct LLC, 7160 Columbia Gateway Dr (Suite 300), Columbia, 21046-2134

Merkle Inc, 7001 Columbia Gateway Dr, Columbia, 21046-2289

Saturn Corp, 4701 Lydell Rd, Hyattsville, 20781-1117

Sisk Fulfillment Service Inc, 1900 Industrial Park Dr, Box 463, Federalsburg, 21632-2667

Stockton Inc, 8341 Beechcraft Ave, Gaithersburg, 20879-1509

MASSACHUSETTS

Access International, 1035 Cambridge St (Suite 22), Cambridge, 02141-1154

Bitstream Inc, 500 Nickerson Rd, Marlborough, 01752-4695

CommercialWare Inc, 24 Prime Park Way, Cochituate Pl, Natick, 01760

Computerworld DataBase Div, 1 Speen St, Framingham, 01701-4644

Customer Portfolios LLC, 88 Black Falcon Ave, Boston, 02210-2425

D&B Sales and Marketing Solutions, 460 Totten Pond Rd, Waltham, 02451-1908

Datamatics Technologies, 56 Middlesex Tpke (Suite 250), Burlington, 01803-4973

Direxxis Inc, 250 1st Ave (Suite 102), Needham, 02494-2847

Elcom International Inc, Ten Oceana Way, Norwood, 02062-2601

Equifax Database Marketing, 500 Edgewater Dr (Suite 525), Wakefield, 01880-6222

FreshAddress Inc, 36 Crafts St, Newton, 02458-1249

GMC Software Technology Inc, 529 Main St (Suite 205), Charlestown, 02129-1121

Global Ware Solutions, 200 Ward Hill Ave, Haverhill, 01835-6972

Inforonics Global Services LLC, 25 Porter Rd (Suite 4), Littleton, 01460-1434

Intellidyn Corp, 72 Sharp St (Suite A9), Hingham, 02043-4362

Ipswitch Inc, 83 Hartwell Ave, Lexington, 02421-3116

L-Com Inc, 45 Beechwood Dr, North Andover, 01845-1023

Neolane, 275 Washington St (Floor 3), Newton, 02458-1611

NetProspex Inc, 318 Bear Hill Rd, Waltham, 02451-1095

PTC, 140 Kendrick St (Suite C120), Needham, 02494-2743

Pluris Inc, 550 Cochituate Rd (Suite 7), Framingham, 01701-4600

Portrait International Inc, 125 Summer St (Floor 16), Boston, 02110-1636

3Com Corp, 350 Campus Dr, Marlborough, 01752-3082

Window Book Inc, 300 Franklin St, Cambridge, 02139-3781

Zircon Co Inc, 67 Aurora Ln, Salem, 01970-6803

Zoom Information Inc, 307 Waverley Oaks Rd, Waltham, 02452

MICHIGAN

ANCOR, 1911 Woodslee Dr, Troy, 48083-2236

CRK Computer Services, 335 Applewood Ln, Bloomfield Hills, 48302-1103

Dundee Internet Services Inc, PO Box 102, Dundee, 48131-0102

MarketNet Services LLC, 14998 Cleveland St (Suite E), Spring Lake, 49456-8993

Renkim Corp, 13333 Allen Rd, Southgate, 48195-2216

Sage Direct Inc, 3400 Raleigh Ave SE, Grand Rapids, 49512-2042

TechniServe Inc, 2065 Livernois Rd, Troy, 48083-1737

Thomson Tax & Accounting, 7322 Newman Blvd, Dexter, 48130

MINNESOTA

Artful Dragon Press Inc, 14108 Lake St Ext, Minnetonka, 55345-3019

Corporate Graphics Direct Marketing Solutions, 1170 Grey Fox Rd, Arden Hills, 55112-6908

eBureau LLC, 25 6th Ave N, Saint Cloud, 56303-4729

FG Companies, 901 Twelve Oaks Center Dr (Suite 934), Wayzata, 55391-4721

Fair Isaac Corp, 2665C Long Lake Rd, Saint Paul, 55113-2538

Lorton Data Inc, 2 Pine Tree Dr (Suite 302), Arden Hills, 55112-3715

OPIN Systems Inc, 7900 International Dr (Suite 410), Minneapolis, 55425-8900

MISSOURI

Data Dash Inc, 3928 Delor St, Saint Louis, 63116-3316

Direct Marketing Audit Systems, 3159 Fee Fee Rd (Suite 221), Bridgeton, 63044-3299

Inquiry Intelligence Systems, 18 N Central Dr, O'Fallon, 63366

Marco Data Service, 12537 Peter Moore Ln, De Soto, 63020-4760

Savvis Inc, 1 Savvis Pkwy, Town and Country, 63017-5827

Wooden Computer Services, 13358 Windbrooke Ln, Saint Louis, 63146-2224

NEBRASKA

Data University, 6550 S 34th St, Lincoln, 68516-5454

PRIORITY Data Systems Inc, 5035 S 110th St, Omaha, 68137-2376

UAA Clearinghouse, 6912 N 97th Cir, Omaha, 68122-1010

NEW HAMPSHIRE

NextMark Inc, 33 S Main St (fl 3), Hanover, 03755-2048

PC Connection, Route 101A, 730 Milford Rd, Merrimack, 03054-4631

TomTom North American, 11 Lafayette St, Lebanon, 03766-1445

NEW JERSEY

Accurate Marketing Systems, 122 Voorhis Ave, River Edge, 07661-1522

Applied Info Group, 100 Market St, Kenilworth, 07033-1722

Business Development Solutions Inc, 311 Hadleigh Dr, Cherry Hill, 08003-1979

(C) Systems LLC, 510 Thornall St (Suite 310), Edison, 08837-2207

Commerce Register Inc, 190 Godwin Ave, Midland Park, 07432-1841

Commercial Data Processing Inc, 264 Passaic Ave, Fairfield, 07004-2531

COREMedia Systems Inc, 695 US Hwy 46 (Suite 403), Fairfield, 07004-1561

Cornwell Data Services Inc, 352 Evelyn St, Paramus, 07652-2908

Createch Marketing, 180 Summit Ave (Suite 203), Montvale, 07645-1722

D&B, 3 Sylvan Way (Suite 1), Parsippany, 07054-3821

The Data Base Inc, 1710 Hwy 35, Oakhurst, 07755

DataBridge Marketing Systems Corp, 16A Forshee Cir, Montvale, 07645-1772

DirectSmile LLC, 300 Broadacres Dr (fl 4), Bloomfield, 07003-3153

Easy Analytic Software Inc, 101 Haag Ave, Bellmawr, 08031-2506

The Fidelis Group Inc, 223 Gates Rd (Unit A), Little Ferry, 07643-1900

Freestyle Solutions, 9 Campus Dr (Suite 1), Parsippany, 07054-4412

Global Turnkey Systems Inc, 2001 US Highway 46 (Suite 203), Parsippany, 07054-1315

GrayHair Software, 124 Gaither Dr (Suite 160), Mount Laurel, 08054-1719

Heritage Direct, 1710 Hwy 35, Oakhurst, 07755-2910

IPacesetters, 135 Chestnut Ridge Rd, Montvale, 07645-1152

Millions By Marketing Inc, 88 E Main St (Suite 338), Mendham, 07945-1832

Publishers Computer Corp, 209 Main St, New Milford, 07646-1733

Raritan Inc, 400 Cottontail Ln, Somerset, 08873-1238

The Total Mailing System, 551 Mid-Atlantic Pkwy, West Deptford, 08066

Veratad Technologies LLC, 500 Frank W Burr Blvd (Suite 14), Teaneck, 07666-6802

NEW YORK

Alliant, 301 Fields Ln , North Center, Brewster, 10509-2621

Anchor Computer Inc, 1900 New Hwy, Farmingdale, 11735-1537

BCC Software Inc, 75 Josons Dr, Rochester, 14623-3494

Blue Hill Marketing Solutions Inc, 1 Blue Hill Plaza (Suite 1674), Pearl River, 10965-6159

Bureau Van Dijk, 40 Wall St (fl 27), New York, 10005-1364

CRC Data Systems, 47-10 32nd Pl, Long Island City, 11101

Cambey & West Inc, 120 N Rte 9W, Congers, 10920-1729

Center for International Earth Science Information Network, 61 Rte 9 W, Palisades, 10964-1707

Collective - The Audience Engine, 99 Park Ave (fl 5), New York, 10016-1601

Cross Country Computer Corp, 570 S Research Pl, Central Islip, 11722-4415

CyberData, 20 Max Ave, Hicksville, 11801-1419

D&D Associates Inc, PO Box 9150, Garden City, 11530-9150

DMRS Group Inc, 304 Park Ave S (fl 11), New York, 10010-4305

Datran Media, 345 Hudson St (Suite 500), New York, 10014-7402

Direct Access Marketing Services Inc, 6851 Jericho Tpke (Suite 245), Syosset, 11791-3063

Drake Direct, 225 E 46th St (Penthouse D), New York, 10017-2928

Enertex Marketing, 99 Madison Ave (Floor 10), New York, 10016-7419

Fulcrum, 70 W 40th St (fl 10), New York, 10018-2621

The Hyiad Group, 400 Garden City Plz (Suite 403), Garden City, 11530-3336

Insight Out of Chaos, 80 Broad St (Suite 2503), New York, 10004-3325

Walter Karl Inc, 2 Blue Hill Plaza (fl 3), Pearl River, 10965-3115

MBS, 570 S Research Pl, Central Islip, 11722-4415

MESA Media & Entertainment Services Alliancce, 39 N Bayles Ave, Port Washington, 11050-2930

Mercury Commerce Inc, 1100 Shames Dr (Suite 200), Westbury, 11590

The Merging Technologies Group LLC, 175K Commerce Dr, Hauppauge, 11788-3920

PNT Marketing Services, Inc, 2420 Jackson Ave, Long Island City, 11101-4323

Pegg Nadler Associates Inc, 400 E 77th St (Suite 16b), New York, 10075-2337

Professional Advertising Systems Inc, 200 Business Park Dr (Suite 304), Armonk, 10504-1751

Profit Center Software Inc, 50 Charles Lindbergh Blvd, Uniondale, 11553-3626

QED Marketing Inc, 570 Research Pl, Central Islip, 11722-4415

Return Path Inc, 3 Park Ave S (Floor 41), New York, 10016-5902

SmartFocus Inc, 545 5th Ave (Rm 1000), New York, 10011-4650

SofTrek Corp, 30 Bryant Woods N, Amherst, 14228-3601

Type-A-Scan Inc, 39 W 19th St (fl 7), New York, 10011-4251

LG Wilson & Associates, 14 N Chatsworth Ave (Suite 5J), Larchmont, 10538-2103

XMPIE Inc, 485 Lexington Ave (fl 10), New York, 10017-2652

NORTH CAROLINA

Conclusive Analytics, Inc, 13620 Reese Blvd (Suite 300), Huntersville, 28078-6453

Quaero Corp, 1930 Camden Rd (Suite 2060), Charlotte, 28203-5900

SAS Institute, 100 SAS Campus Dr, Cary, 27513-2414

Technekes LLC, 1927 S Tryon St (Suite 310), Charlotte, 28203-4688

Web Decisions, 303 Pisgah Church Rd (Suite 2A), Greensboro, 27455-2756

Wheaton Group, 201 Bolinas Ct, Chapel Hill, 27517-8344

Yankelovich Inc, 400 Meadowmont Village Cir (Suite 431), Chapel Hill, 27517-7505

OHIO

Alltel Publishing Corp, 100 Executive Pkwy, Hudson, 44236-1630

CTRAC Information Solutions, 16855 Foltz Pkwy, Strongsville, 44149-5517

International Data Management - a Dmh Marketing Partners Co, 490 White Pond Dr, Akron, 44320-1122

NFocus Consulting Inc, 1594 Hubbard Dr, Lancaster, 43130-8124

Reynolds & Reynolds Co, One Reynolds Way, Kettering, 45430-1586

SBDP Corp, 4208 Airport Rd, Cincinnati, 45226-1646

Teradata Corp, 10000 Innovation Dr, Miamisburg, 45342-4927

OKLAHOMA

A La Mode Inc, 3705 W Memorial Rd (Suite 402), Oklahoma City, 73134-1507

Data Management & Marketing Services LLC, 508 N Aster Ave, Broken Arrow, 74012-9446

Marketing Information Network, 120 N Bryant Ave (Suite A1), Edmond, 73034-6300

Myriad Systems Inc, 2627 E-I-44 Service Rd, Oklahoma City, 73111-8302

OREGON

AccuDirect Response, 205 SE Spokane St (Suite 325), Portland, 97202

PacificEast, 4900 SW Griffith Dr (Suite 251), Beaverton, 97005-2977

PENNSYLVANIA

Advanced Software Applications Corp, 500 Millers Run Rd (Suite 201), Morgan, 15064-9733

Echo Data Group, 121 N Shirk Rd, New Holland, 17557-9714

Elliott Marketing Group Inc, 2281 Sidgefield Ln, Pittsburgh, 15241-2713

The IDT Group, 1650 Market St (Floor 36), Philadelphia, 19103-7334

Innovative Systems Inc, 790 Holiday Dr, Pittsburgh, 15220-8127

LSSiData, 1 Sentry Pkwy (Suite 6000), Blue Bell, 19422-2310

Mac Direct, 185 Discovery Drive, Colmar, 18915

Mail Movers & Mailing Services, 325 S 69th St, Upper Darby, 19082-4213

Neat Co, 1601 Market St (Suite 3500), Philadelphia, 19103-2301

Sungard Computer Services, 680 E Swedesford Rd, Wayne, 19087

Telephone Look-Up Service Co, 301 Oxford Valley Rd (Suite 304B), Yardley, 19067-7709

Volt Delta, 1 Sentry Pkwy E (Suite 6000), Blue Bell, 19422-2310

PUERTO RICO

Database Marketing Services, PO Box 2995, Guaynabo, 00970-2995

SOUTH CAROLINA

Blackbaud Inc, 2000 Daniel Island Dr, Charleston, 29492-7541

TENNESSEE

Data Intelligence Group, 9045 Carothers Pkwy (Suite 200), Franklin, 37067-1799

TEXAS

ACTIVE Network LLC, 717 N Harwood St (Suite 2500), Dallas, 75201

Alliance Data, 7500 Dallas Pkwy Ste 700, Plano, 75024-4006

Artemis International Solutions Corp, 401 Congress Ave (Suite 2650), Austin, 78701-3708

BT Americas, 7301 North State Hwy 161 (Suite 400), Irving, 75039-2802

Bowman & Partners, 1914 Spring Dr (Suite 101), Roanoke, 76262-7416

Convio Inc, 11501 Domain Dr (Suite 200), Austin, 78758-3406

Data Dallas Corp, 1111 W Mockingbird Ln (Suite 300), Dallas, 75247-5017

Harte-Hanks, 9601 Mc Allister Freeway (Suite 610), San Antonio, 78216

Hoover's Inc, 5800 Airport Blvd, Austin, 78752-4204

MLS Data Management Solutions, 6115 Camp Bowie Blvd (Suite 200), Fort Worth, 76116-5500

ReachForce, 2711 W Anderson Ln (Suite 200), Austin, 78757

Trinity Technical Group, Inc, 2118 Royal Dominion Court, Arlington, 76006-4836

Xerox Services, 2828 N Haskell Ave, Dallas, 75204-2909

VERMONT

AIDC (American International Distribution Corp), 89 Winter Sport Ln, Williston, 05495-0080

Datamann Inc, 1994 Hartford Ave, Wilder, 05088

Global-Z International Inc, 395 Shields Dr, Bennington, 05201-9810

VIRGINIA

CACI International Inc, 1100 N Glebe Rd, Arlington, 22201-4714

DM Data Solutions LLC, 7508 Manigold Ct, Alexandria, 22315-3838

Data Management Inc, 8300 Greensboro Dr (Suite 800), Mc Lean, 22102-3661

Eloqua Inc, 1921 Gallows Rd (Suite 250), Vienna, 22182-3994

Marketing 1by1 Inc, 11350 Random Hills Rd, Fairfax, 22030-6044

Relevate Group Inc, 6883 Commercial Dr, Springfield, 22159-0310

Strategic Software Systems LLC, 1508 Willow Lawn Dr (Suite 111), Richmond, 23230-3421

WASHINGTON

Concur, 601 108th Ave NE (Suite 1000), Bellevue, 98004-4750

Intelius Inc, 500 108th Ave (fl 22), Bellevue, 98004-5500

Microsoft Corp, 1 Microsoft Way, Redmond, 98052-8300

Tableau Software, 837 N 34th St (Suite 200), Seattle, 98103-8965

WISCONSIN

Advanced Concepts Inc, 8875 N 55th St (Suite 200), Milwaukee, 53223-2311

Arrow Companies, LLC, 1501 Wisconsin St (#2), Delavan, 53115-1471

Communication Logistics, Inc, 2040 Jay Mar Rd (Suite 2), Plover, 54467-3257

TEC Mailing Solutions, LLC, 712 Lois Dr, Sun Prairie, 53590-1100

WennSoft, 1970 S Calhoun Rd, New Berlin, 53151-2214

CANADA

Nova Scotia

Epic Marketing Solutions, 6054 Quinpool Rd, Halifax, B3L 1A1

The Oyster Group, 33 Thorne Ave (Unit 2), Dartmouth, B3B 2E7

Ontario

Andsor Research Inc, 40 Richview Rd (Suite 1501), Etobicoke, M9A 5C1

Complete Mailing Service, 8 Dohme Ave, Toronto, M4B 1Y8

Cornerstone Group of Companies, 20 Eglinton Ave W (Floor 4), Toronto, M4R 1K8

LoyaltyOne, 438 University Ave (Suite 600), Toronto, M5G 2L1

Northern Response (International) Ltd, 50 Staples Ave, Richmond Hill, Toronto, L4B 0A7

Promotional Products Fulfillment & Distribution Ltd, 80 William Smith Dr, Whitby, L1N 9W1

Wilson, Hugh & Associate Consultants Ltd, Four Long Bridge Rd, Thornhill, L4J 1L5

Quebec

Coveo Solutions Inc, 3175 des Quatre Bourgeois (Suite 200), Quebec, G1W 2K7

Computer Services, Data Processing, List & Subscription Fulfillment Companies (22)

A LA MODE INC
3705 W Memorial Rd (Suite 402)
Oklahoma City, OK 73134-1507
Telephone: (405) 359-6587, Toll Free:
(800) ALAMODE, FAX: (405) 359-
8612, Web Site: www.alamode.com
Chief Exec Officer: Jay Shafer
Primary Market Served: Consumer
Founded: 1985

Develops desktop, mobile & web tools for the real estate & mortgage industries.

ACG/COMPUTECH DIRECT
2155 Stonington Ave (Suite 215)
Hoffman Estates, IL 60195-2058
Telephone: (847) 843-3200, FAX:
(847) 843-8060, E-Mail: info@acg-
computech-direct.com, Web Site:
www.acg-computech-direct.com
Pres: Rick Botthof

Offers a comprehensive package of database, data hygiene & processing, and list rental fulfillment services.

AIDC (AMERICAN INTERNATIONAL DISTRIBUTION CORP)
89 Winter Sport Ln
Williston, VT 05495-0080
Toll Free: (800) 678-2432, FAX: (802)
864-7749, E-Mail: jmacon@aidcvt.
com, Web Site: www.aidcvt.com
Pres & CEO: Marilyn R. McConnell
Chief Opers: Michael Pelland
Founded: 1986

Fulfillment and distribution business serving a prestigious group of clients with offices worldwide.

ACCESS INTERNATIONAL
1035 Cambridge St (Suite 22)
Cambridge, MA 02141-1154
Telephone: (617) 218-5000, Toll Free:
(877) 433-9097, FAX: (617) 494-
8404, E-Mail: info@accessint.com,
Web Site: www.accessint.com
Pres: Bill Wood
Employees: 70
Founded: 1978

Fundraising through implementation of Enterprise. An extremely flexible & robust software designed to facilitate all aspects of fundraising including individual-based marketing and list management, database segmentation, contact management, document management, high volume donation/pledge processing, membership benefits, special events, capital and endowment campaigns, annual funds, integrated planned giving, statistical analysis and reporting and receipting.

ACCOUNTMATE SOFTWARE CORP
1445 Technology Ln (Suite A5)
Petaluma, CA 94954-7613
Telephone: (707) 774-7500, FAX:
(707) 774-7590, E-Mail:
information@accountmate.com, Web
Site: www.accountmate.com
CEO & Pres: David Dierke
Chief Tech Officer: Tommy Tan
COO: David Render
Dir Tech Svcs: Charles Ocat
Founded: 1984

Provides accounting and business management software for businesses.

ACCUDIRECT RESPONSE
205 SE Spokane St (Suite 325)
Portland, OR 97202
Telephone: (503) 223-2076, Web Site:
accdirectnw.com
Primary Market Served: Consumer

Helping clients connect with their target customers for all direct marketing needs.

ACCURATE MARKETING SYSTEMS
122 Voorhis Ave
River Edge, NJ 07661-1522
Telephone: (201) 265-5198
VP: Barry Holmes

ACQUIREWEB INC
1065 E Hillsdale Blvd (Suite 310)
Foster City, CA 94404-1689
Telephone: (650) 212-2233, FAX:
(650) 212-2234, E-Mail: sales@
aquireweb.com, Web Site: www.
acquireWEB.com
Pres & CEO: Albert Gadbut
Gen Mgr: Jay Dean
Primary Market Served: Business
Founded: 2001

Helping marketers gain an integrated understanding of customer identity across all contact channels enables an integrated customer relationship and marketing program.

ACTIVE NETWORK LLC
717 N Harwood St (Suite 2500)
Dallas, TX 75201
Telephone: (858) 964-6064, Toll Free:
(877) 228-4808, Web Site: www.
activenetwork.com
Sr VP: Darko Dejanovic
Pres: Mark Hall Trivette
Sr Acct Mgr: Sejal Pietrzak
Conducts Business: Worldwide
Primary Market Served: Business
Founded: 1999

Data management services & software provider for activities & events industry.

ACXIOM CORP
601 E 3rd St
Little Rock, AR 72201-1709
Telephone: (501) 342-1000, FAX:
(501) 342-3913, Web Site: www.
acxiom.com
Pres & CEO: Scott E. Howe
Exec VP & CFO: Warren C. Jenson
Exec VP & Chief Prod Officer: Philip
("Phil") L. Mui
Conducts Business: U.S., Europe, Asia-
Pacific & South America.

Marketing services & information technology company.

ADOBE SYSTEMS INC
345 Park Ave
San Jose, CA 95110-2704
Telephone: (408) 536-6000, Toll Free:
(800) 833-6687, FAX: (408) 537-
6000, Web Site: www.adobe.com
Pres & CEO: Shantanu Narayen
EVP & CFO: Mark Garrett
Sr VP & Chief Mktg Officer: Ann
Lewnes
Sr VP & Gen Mgr Digital Media: David Wadhwani
Sr VP People & Places: Donna Morris
Conducts Business: Worldwide
Employees: 6,677
Primary Market Served: Consumer
Founded: 1982
Gross sales or billing: $2,575,000,000

Sell software through OEM's, retail & via direct mail business-to-business.

ADVANCED CONCEPTS INC
8875 N 55th St (Suite 200)
Milwaukee, WI 53223-2311
Telephone: (414) 362-9640, FAX:
(414) 362-9646, E-Mail: info@
advanced-concepts.com, Web Site:
www.advanced-concepts.com
Pres: Jeff Wohlfahrt
VP Opers: Mary A. Kunze

Custom computer programming services.

ADVANCED SOFTWARE APPLICATIONS CORP
500 Millers Run Rd (Suite 201)
Morgan, PA 15064-9733
Telephone: (412) 220-9300, FAX:
(412) 220-3878, E-Mail: asa@
asacorp.com, Web Site: www.
asacorp.com
Exec Officer, Pres & Dir: Bill Goss-man
CMO: Ken Ramoutar

Provides analytical and decisioning solutions to businesses in various industries worldwide.

AIRS INC
4080 Hwy 92
Douglasville, GA 30135-4404
Telephone: (770) 949-0133, FAX:
(770) 949-2773, E-Mail: estacks@
aol.com
Pres: Ed Stacks

THE ALLANT GROUP
2056 Westings Ave (Suite 500)
Naperville, IL 60563-2485
Toll Free: (800) 367-7311, FAX: (630)
355-3090, E-Mail: dirwin@
allantgroup.com, Web Site: www.
allantgroup.com
EVP Sales & Mktg: Dave Irwin
CEO, Pres & Dir: Terrence E. McCarthy
CFO: Tamara L. Affrunti
Founded: 1984

Provides cross channel marketing and advertising services.

ALLIANCE DATA
7500 Dallas Pkwy Ste 700
Plano, TX 75024-4006
Telephone: (972) 348-5100, E-Mail:
info@thealliedgrp.com, Web Site:
www.alliancedata.com
Pres Retail Svcs: Ed Heffernan
Primary Market Served: Consumer

Provider of data-driven loyalty and marketing campaigns.

ALLIANT
301 Fields Ln , North Center
Brewster, NY 10509-2621
Telephone: (845) 276-2600, FAX:
(845) 276-2605, Web Site: www.
alliantdata.com
Co-Founder, CEO & Pres: JoAnne
Monfradi Dunn
Co-Founder & VP Mktg & Compliance: Rick Witsell
Co-Founder & CFO: Gregory Dunn
VP Database Devel & Tech: Bill Adam
VP Sales Bus Devel: Donna Hamilton

Primary Market Served: Business
Develops predictive segmentation solutions for direct-to-consumer marketers.

ALLTEL PUBLISHING CORP
Subs. of Alltel Corp
100 Executive Pkwy
Hudson, OH 44236-1630
Telephone: (330) 650-7100, FAX:
(330) 650-7883, Web Site: www.
alltel.com
Pres: Jerry Weaver

ALTERIAN
35 Wacker Dr (Suite 200)
Chicago, IL 60601-2104
Telephone: (312) 704-1700, FAX:
(312) 704-1701, Web Site: www.
alterian.com
CEO & Dir: Heath Davies
Deputy Chmn & Interim Head Mngmt
Team: Lain Barrie Johnson
Primary Market Served: Business &
Consumer
Founded: 2000

Engages in the design & development of software tools for marketing & customer insight for sale under license through third party business partner organizations.

ALVION LLC
2503 Del Prado Blvd (Suite 502)
Cape Coral, FL 33904
Telephone: (239) 574-8600, Toll Free:
(877) 528-7800, FAX: (239) 574-8551, Web Site: www.alvion.com
CEO: Robert Sher

ANCHOR COMPUTER INC
1900 New Hwy
Farmingdale, NY 11735-1537
Telephone: (631) 293-6100, FAX:
(631) 293-0891, Web Site: www.
anchorcomputer.com
Founder & CEO: Len Schenker
Pres. Anchor Retail Solutions: Mark
Schenker
Dir Bus Devel: Brenda Matheson
VP: Debra Schenker
VP Ecommerce Svcs: Nancy Atwood
Conducts Business: U.S. & Canada
Primary Market Served: Business &
Consumer
Founded: 1974

Provides data processing services & software solutions for direct & digital marketing professionals in the U.S. and Canada.

ANCOR
aka Anchor Information Management
1911 Woodslee Dr
Troy, MI 48083-2236

Telephone: (248) 740-8866, Toll Free:
(800) 229-3860, FAX: (248) 740-9025, Web Site: www.anchorinfo.
com
Chmn Bd & CFO: Stephen Chapman
Exec Officer: James DeLong
Founded: 1993

Ancor Information Management, LLC operates as an outsourcing provider of customized print & electronic document services for communication & membership programs.

ANDSOR RESEARCH INC
40 Richview Rd (Suite 1501)
Etobicoke, ON, Canada M9A 5C1
Telephone: (416) 245-8073, FAX:
(416) 240-8473
Pres: Andrei Sorin

Computer Systems Design & related services.

ANTHEM MARKETING
549 W Randolph St (Suite 702)
Chicago, IL 60661-1478
Telephone: (312) 441-0382
Mng Partner & CEO: John Keenan
Partner & COO: Christopher N. Carroll
Primary Market Served: Business &
Consumer

Providing solutions that help businesses gain strategic advantages. Your competitive edge in a complex and ever-changing marketplace.

APPLIED INFO GROUP
100 Market St
Kenilworth, NJ 07033-1722
Telephone: (908) 241-7007, FAX:
(9080 241-7088, Web Site: www.
appliedinfogroup.com
Pres: Mitchell Rubin
Mgr HR: Frank A. Nasta

Provides email & database marketing services.

APTIMUS
199 Fremont St (Suite 1800)
San Francisco, CA 94105
Telephone: (415) 896-2123, FAX:
(415) 896-2561
Founder & Chmn Bd: Timothy C.
Choate
Sr VP Sls: Michael Mayor
VP Tech: Lance J. Nelson
Sr VP Mktg & Media Svcs: Michael
Sullivan
Corp Sec & Gen Counsel: David H.
Davis

Founded: 1997

Provides digital media solutions. Advertising & optimization platform provides results-driven campaign solutions to advertisers in various digital media channels.

ARROW COMPANIES, LLC

1501 Wisconsin St (#2)
Delavan, WI 53115-1471
Telephone: (262) 724-8822, FAX: (262) 724-8824, Web Site: www. arrowcompanies.com
Pres: Jerry Voors

Provides warehousing, distribution and internet fulfillment.

ARTEMIS INTERNATIONAL SOLUTIONS CORP

401 Congress Ave (Suite 2650)
Austin, TX 78701-3708
Telephone: (512) 201-8222, FAX: (512) 874-8900, Web Site: www. aisc.com
CEO: Scott Brighton
Pres.: Randall Jacobs
CFO: Andrew Simon Price
VP: Christopher Smith
Sr VP, Sec & Gen Counsel: Charles F. Savoni
Founded: 1998

Provides enterprise project & resource management solutions.

ARTFUL DRAGON PRESS INC

14108 Lake St Ext
Minnetonka, MN 55345-3019
Telephone: (612) 221-8908, Web Site: www.artfuldragon.com
Pres: John Arleth
Primary Market Served: Business & Consumer

Company offers printing in books, calendars, catalogs, magazines, booklets, brochures, CD's Labels.

AUDIENCE IDENTIFICATION INC

PO Box 3305
Lisle, IL 60532-8305
Telephone: (630) 435-0460, FAX: (630) 435-0470, E-Mail: rmarsh@ audienceid.com
Pres: Ronald K. Marsh
Gen Mgr.: Russell Sams

AUGUST MARKETING

4704 W Neptune St (Suite 200)
Tampa, FL 33629-5502

Telephone: (561) 747-1325, Toll Free: (866) 242-4414, E-Mail: sbarret@ augustmktg.com, Web Site: www. augustmktg.com
VP Mktg: Lorna Berry
Primary Market Served: Business & Consumer

Direct marketing agency.

BCC SOFTWARE INC

Subs. of Bowe Bell & Howell
75 Josons Dr
Rochester, NY 14623-3494
Telephone: (585) 272-9130, Toll Free: (800) 453-3130, FAX: (585) 272-9141, Web Site: www.bccsoftware. com
Pres: K. Jon Runstrom
VP Finance: Ken Kathan
Exec VP: Christopher G. Lien
Exec VP Res & Devel: Erik Runstrom
Sr VP: Jim Mann
Conducts Business: U.S.
Employees: 65
Primary Market Served: Business
Advertising/Marketing Budget Related to Direct Marketing: 0-25%
Direct Marketing ad budget: $800,000
Founded: 1978

Develops mailing software solutions for professional mailers.

BT AMERICAS

Subs. of BT Group
7301 North State Hwy 161 (Suite 400)
Irving, TX 75039-2802
Telephone: (972) 830-8169, FAX: (703) 755-6740, Web Site: www. btglobalservices.com
Pub Rels Mgr: Diane Noe
CFO: Andrew McCauley
Pub Rels Mgr: Eileen Connolly
Advisory Chmn: Timothy Patrick Flynn
Founded: 1982

Provides information & communications technology services.

BWB MARKETING SERVICES

PO Box 802
Ankeny, IA 50021-0802
Telephone: (515) 986-1992, Web Site: www.bwbmarketing.com
Pres: Keith Snow
Primary Market Served: Business & Consumer

B2E DIRECT MARKETING INC

209 S Main St
Grimes, IA 50111-2192
Telephone: (515) 986-1992, Web Site: www.bwbmarketing.com

Pres: Keith Snow

BARCODING INC

2220 Boston St (Floor 2)
Baltimore, MD 21231-3058
Telephone: (410) 385-8532, Toll Free: (888) 860-SCAN, (888) 860-7226, FAX: (410) 385-8559, E-Mail: info@barcoding.com, Web Site: www.barcoding.com
CEO: Jay Steinmetz
Pres: Shane Snyder
Dir, Mktg: David Shapiro
Dir Prof Svcs.: Joe Santini
Employees: 50
Founded: 1998
Gross sales or billing: $20,000,000

Designs, develops, implements and supports barcode and wireless technology for warehouse management, package tracking, lead and order automation. Our complete solutions include hardware, software and professional services. Contact us for a free solutions guide and consultation.

BITSTREAM INC

500 Nickerson Rd
Marlborough, MA 01752-4695
Telephone: (617) 497-6222, FAX: (617) 868-0784, Web Site: www. bitstream.com
Exec Chmn: Amos Kaminski
CFO, Principal Acctg Officer & VP: James P. Dore
Chief Tech Officer & VP: John S. Collins
VP Engrng: Constantine Kisons
VP Res & Devel: Sampo Kaasila
Founded: 1981

A software development company, provides mobile browsing, fonts and font rendering & automated marketing communication and print production solutions.

BLACKBAUD INC

2000 Daniel Island Dr
Charleston, SC 29492-7541
Telephone: (843) 216-6200, Toll Free: (800) 443-9441, FAX: (843) 216-6100, Web Site: www.blackbaud. com
Pres & CEO: Michael "Mike" Gianoni
Pres Gen Markets Bus: Kevin W. Mooney
Primary Market Served: Business & Consumer

Provides software and related services designed specifically for non-profit organizations.

BLUE HILL MARKETING SOLUTIONS INC

dba LiftEngine
1 Blue Hill Plaza (Suite 1674)
Pearl River, NY 10965-6159
Telephone: (845) 627-6600, FAX:
(845) 735-3985, E-Mail: sales@
liftengine.com, Web Site: www.
liftengine.com
Pres & Co-Founder: Keith Huntoon
Exec VP & Co-Founder: Scott Marko-
witz
Primary Market Served: Business &
Consumer

Direct marketing solutions company
specializing in connecting clients to
their best customers through online personalization, database and segmentation strategies.

BOWMAN & PARTNERS

1914 Spring Dr (Suite 101)
Roanoke, TX 76262-7416
Toll Free: (888) 817-1948, E-Mail:
info@bowman-partners.com, Web
Site: www.bowman-partners.com
Principal: Paul Bowman
Primary Market Served: Business &
Consumer

Helping companies acquire, retain and
grow a more profitable customer base.

BUREAU VAN DIJK

40 Wall St (fl 27)
New York, NY 10005-1364
Telephone: (212) 797-3550, FAX:
(212) 797-3555, E-Mail: newyork@
bvdinfo.com, Web Site: www.
bvdinfo.com
Mktg Dir Americas: Leela Hauser
Mgr: Anarew Cowley
Primary Market Served: Business &
Consumer

Information on companies that helps
you generate more business opportunities from prospects and customers.

BUSINESS DEVELOPMENT SOLUTIONS INC

311 Hadleigh Dr
Cherry Hill, NJ 08003-1979
Telephone: (856) 787-1500, E-Mail:
info@hdsdatabase.com, Web Site:
www.bdsdatabase.com
Pres: Robert Bloom
Dir Software Devel: Steve LoCastro
Primary Market Served: Business &
Consumer

Focused on helping business-to-business & business-to-consumer marketers
of all sizes identify, analyze, & serve
their customers & prospects more effectively.

BUSINESS OBJECTS AMERICAS, INC

3030 Orchard Pkwy
San Jose, CA 95134-2028
Telephone: (408) 953-6000, FAX:
(408) 953-6001, Web Site: www.
businessobjects.com

Provides enterprise business intelligence software enabling organizations
to track, understand, & manage enterprise performance.

(C) SYSTEMS LLC

510 Thornall St (Suite 310)
Edison, NJ 08837-2207
Telephone: (732) 548-6100, FAX:
(732) 548-3883, Web Site: www.
csystemsllc.net
Founder & CEO: Lee Hornstein
Dir Opers: Heather Austen

Providing the highest quality Database,
Web and IT support services & committed to bringing customers innovative solutions to their challenges.

CACI INTERNATIONAL INC

1100 N Glebe Rd
Arlington, VA 22201-4714
Telephone: (703) 841-7800, FAX:
(703) 841-7882, Web Site: www.
caci.com
Pres & CEO CACI: Gregory R. Brad-
ford
Exec VP, PR & Bus Communs: Jody
A. Brown

Engages in the development & implementation of systems integration solutions for federal, state & local and
commercial customers.

CAM COMMERCE SOLUTIONS

17075 Newhope St (Suite A)
Fountain Valley, CA 92708-4299
Telephone: (714) 241-9241, FAX:
(714) 241-9893, Web Site: www.
camcommerce.com
VP Sls & Mktg: Chester Ritchie
Founded: 1983

Develops, markets, installs, and services integrated point-of-sale, ERP, electronic payment processing, inventory
control, eCommerce shopping cart, &
management reporting solutions for
small to medium size retailers.

CDS GLOBAL

Subs. of The Hearst Corp
1901 Bell Ave
Des Moines, IA 50315-1099
Telephone: (515) 246-6837, FAX:
(515) 246-6687, E-Mail: dluther@
cdsfulfillment.com, Web Site: www.
cdsglobal.com
CEO & Pres: Debra A. Janssen
CFO: Paul Polus
Founded: 1972

Provides outsourced business solutions
to various industries.

CRC DATA SYSTEMS

Affiliate of Opinion Access Corp
47-10 32nd Pl
Long Island City, NY 11101
Telephone: (718) 729-2622, E-Mail:
jrafael@opinionaccess.com, Web
Site: www.opinionaccess.com
VP Bus Devel: Lance Hoffman
Founded: 1994

Provides data collection, tabulating,
coding, data entry & printing services
to companies performing market research activities.

CRK COMPUTER SERVICES

335 Applewood Ln
Bloomfield Hills, MI 48302-1103
Telephone: (248) 569-3050, FAX:
(248) 569-5259, E-Mail:
information@crkusa.com, Web Site:
www.crkusa.com
Pres: Dan Neagoe
Founded: 1974

Provider of Direct Marketing Computer
Services, specializing in complete database design with CRM functionality
and list rental maintenance with on-line
counts, business and consumer merge/
purge and magazine fulfillment. In
house FASTforward, zip modeling and
decease suppression, match back analysis, data enhancement, data append,
postal presorts, ink-jet tape creation
and email marketing.

CTRAC INFORMATION SOLUTIONS

16855 Foltz Pkwy
Strongsville, OH 44149-5517
Telephone: (440) 572-1000, FAX:
(440) 572-3330, E-Mail: ctrac@
ctrac.com, Web Site: www.ctrac.com
VP Systems & Opers: Robert J. Ku-
bicki
CEO & Pres: Mike Adams
Exec VP: Gary Seits
Dir Bus Devel: Susan Williamson
VP Sls & Data /entry: L. A. Miklosko

Provides database/document development, management, storage, & recovery solutions.

CAMBEY & WEST INC

120 N Rte 9W

Congers, NY 10920-1729
Telephone: (845) 267-3006, FAX: (845) 267-3503, E-Mail: info@ cambeywest.com, Web Site: www. cambeywest.com
Dir Bus Devel: Jane Giles

Full service - from front end mail processing & cashiering to lettershop, e-commerce and automated data feeds. Dynamic Internet-based system with continual enhancements

CENTER FOR INTERNATIONAL EARTH SCIENCE INFORMATION NETWORK

61 Rte 9 W
Palisades, NY 10964-1707
Telephone: (845) 365-8988, FAX: (845) 365-8922, E-Mail: ciesin. info@ciesin.columbia.edu, Web Site: www.ciesin.org
Dir: Robert S. Chen

Provide information that would help scientists, decision-makers, and the public better understand the changing relationship between human beings and the environment.

CHRISTIAN RESOURCE MANAGEMENT

2322 N Batavia (Suite 108)
Orange, CA 92865-2000
Telephone: (714) 974-0754, FAX: (714) 974-7845, E-Mail: CRMOrange@aol.com, Web Site: www.crmorange.com
Pres: Craig Bryson

Serves Christian organizations with the expertise to handle the full range of services needed to effectively minister in a professional & personal way.

CISCO SYSTEMS INC

170 W Tasman Dr
San Jose, CA 95134-1700
Telephone: (408) 526-4000, Toll Free: (800) 553-NETS, FAX: (408) 526-4100, Web Site: www.cisco.com
Chmn & CEO: John T. Chambers
Pres & COO: Gary B. Moore

Provides products for transporting data, voice, & video within buildings, across campuses & globally.

CITRIX SYSTEMS, INC

851 W Cypress Creek Rd
Fort Lauderdale, FL 33309-2040
Telephone: (954) 267-3000, FAX: (954) 267-3101, Web Site: www. citrix.com
Pres & CEO: Mark B. Templeton

Exec VP, CFO & COO: David J. Henshall
Sr VP Customer Experience: Catherine Courage
Primary Market Served: Business & Consumer

Designs, develops & markets technology solutions that allow applications to be delivered, supported & shared on-demand.

COGENSIA

A CAC Group Co
100 W Hillcrest Blvd (Suite 406)
Schaumburg, IL 60195-3108
Telephone: (847) 805-9800, FAX: (847) 805-9313, E-Mail: info@cac-group.com, Web Site: www. cogensia.com
Pres & CEO: Bradley Rukstales

Provides breakthrough data-driven marketing strategies & solutions, empowering clients with resources to build sustainable customer relationships & maximize marketing ROI.

COGNITIVEDATA INC

Sub. of Merkle
500 President Clinton Ave (Suite 301)
Little Rock, AR 72201-1760
Telephone: (501) 975-7580, Toll Free: (866) 243-7883, FAX: (501) 975-7681, E-Mail: info@cognitivedata. com, Web Site: www.cognitivedata. com
Founder & CEO: Rod Ford
Primary Market Served: Business & Consumer
Founded: 2001

Provides customer & marketing data solutions.

COLINEAR SYSTEMS

2650 Holcomb Bridge Rd (Suite 610)
Alpharetta, GA 30022-5343
Telephone: (770) 643-0000, Toll Free: (800) COLINEAR, FAX: (770) 643-0265, E-Mail: sales@colinear.com, Web Site: www.colinear.com
Pres: Lloyd Merriam
Founded: 1984

Engages in the design & development of a personal computer-based application for mail-order management.

COLLECTIVE - THE AUDIENCE ENGINE

99 Park Ave (fl 5)
New York, NY 10016-1601
Telephone: (646) 722-8550, FAX: (646) 442-6529, Web Site: www. collective.com
Founder & CEO: Joe Apprendi

Pres & Chief Revenue Officer: Jill R. Botway
CFO: Aman Verjee
Sr VP Natl Sls: Todd Benedict
Chief Architect: Chris Putnam
Primary Market Served: Consumer
Founded: 2005

Marketing agency, providing multi-screen advertising solutions that help brands connect with their audience.

COMMERCE REGISTER INC

190 Godwin Ave
Midland Park, NJ 07432-1841
Telephone: (201) 445-3000, FAX: (201) 445-5806, E-Mail: cri@ comreginc.com, Web Site: www. comreginc.com
Pres: Charles Greer
IT Exec: Robert Vermilye

Commerce Register Incorporated (CRI) is a data processing service bureau specializing in providing both standard and custom solutions to the direct mail.

COMMERCIAL DATA PROCESSING INC

264 Passaic Ave
Fairfield, NJ 07004-2531
Telephone: (973) 882-1660, Toll Free: (800) 242-3731, FAX: (973) 882-0387, Web Site: www.dataprocess. com
Founder, Chmn Bd & CEO: Tom Fahmie

Provides information management solutions that enable customers to outsource various tasks in the U.S. Also provides paper document storage and archiving & post office box management services.

COMMERCIALWARE INC

Div. of Datadvantage
24 Prime Park Way, Cochituate Pl
Natick, MA 01760
Telephone: (508) 655-7500, FAX: (508) 647-9495, Web Site: www. commercialware.com
VP Sls: Chris Sarne
VP Client Svcs: Denise Gibbons
VP Mktg: Laura Naylor
Founded: 1975

Provides software solutions for cross-channel retailers.

COMMUNICATION LOGISTICS, INC

2040 Jay Mar Rd (Suite 2)
Plover, WI 54467-3257
Telephone: (715) 341-6180, FAX: (715) 341-7971, Web Site: www. comloginc.com
Pres Creative/Mktg Svcs: Sarah Straub

Primary Market Served: Business

Progressive marketing company providing expert service to direct marketers across the nation.

COMPITSS INC
1000 Business Center Dr (Suite 107)
Newbury Park, CA 91320-1237
Telephone: (805) 823-2286, E-Mail:
info@compitss.com, Web Site:
www.compitss.com
Pres: Al Lakshmanan

Provides technology services.

COMPLETE MAILING SERVICE
8 Dohme Ave
Toronto, ON, Canada M4B 1Y8
Telephone: (416) 755-7761, Toll Free:
(888) 683-2501, FAX: (416) 755-8231, E-Mail: sales@
completemailing.com, Web Site:
www.completemailing.com

Direct mail & marketing solutions company.

COMPLETE MAILING SOLUTIONS, INC
3001 S Tejon St
Englewood, CO 80110-1316
Telephone: (303) 761-0681, Toll Free:
(888) 843-9937, FAX: (303) 761-7837, Web Site: www.comp-mail.com
Founded: 1979

Premium mailing & printing equipment, along with digital document processing & logistics software solutions by trusted brands.

COMPUTER BUSINESS SERVICES INC
205 W Forsyth St, PO Box A
Americus, GA 31709-3533
Telephone: (229) 924-4408, Toll Free:
(866) 924-4408, FAX: (229) 924-3644, E-Mail: nelson@combusser.
com, Web Site: www.combusser.com
VP & CEO: Bill Bennett
CIO: Chris Dill
Project Mgr: Crystal Mays
Conducts Business: U.S.
Employees: 30
Primary Market Served: Business
Advertising/Marketing Budget Related to Direct Marketing: 0-25%
Direct Marketing ad budget: $100,000
Telephone: 100%
Founded: 1974
Gross sales or billing: $5,000,000

Providing data processing services to governmental & business communities.

COMPUTER SOLUTIONS INC
13701 SW 88th St (Suite 306), Bldg H33
Miami, FL 33186-1309
Telephone: (305) 558-7000, FAX:
(305) 557-0003, E-Mail: info@
csiflorida.com, Web Site: www.
csiflorida.com
VP: Ernie Smith

Full service software development organization providing solutions for Multi-channel, Fulfillment, Catalog & Mail Order companies.

COMPUTERWORLD DATABASE DIV
Div. of Computer World Inc
1 Speen St
Framingham, MA 01701-4644
Telephone: (508) 879-0700, Toll Free:
(800) 343-6474, FAX: (508) 875-4394, Web Site: www.
computerworld.com
Pres: Matthew Sweeney

CONCLUSIVE ANALYTICS, INC
13620 Reese Blvd (Suite 300)
Huntersville, NC 28078-6453
Telephone: (704) 887-5600, FAX:
(704) 887-5601, E-Mail: info@
conclusivemarketing.com, Web Site:
www.conclusiveanalytics.com
Pres & CEO: Mark Rees
Co-Founder Chief Tech Officer: William Brennan
CFO: Lisa McAllister
Exec VP Bus Devel Mgrs Acquisitions: Jay Buford
Exec VP & Gen Mgr Charlotte: Rod Rapp
Founded: 1997

Provides Software-as-a-Service based sales & marketing analytics solution.

CONCUR
601 108th Ave NE (Suite 1000)
Bellevue, WA 98004-4750
Telephone: (425) 702-590-5000, Toll Free: (800) 401-8412, FAX: (425) 590-5999, Web Site: www.concur.com
Pres: Elena Donio
Founded: 1993

Provider of integrated travel & expense management solutions.

CONNEX INTERNATIONAL INC
50 Federal Rd
Danbury, CT 06810-6129
Telephone: (203) 731-5400, Toll Free:
(800) 426-6639, FAX: (203) 730-9060, E-Mail: marketing@
connexintl.com, Web Site: www.
connexintl.com
Pres: Debora Volansky
Controller: Dom Mercurio
Dir Opers: Jill Tino
VP & Dir Bus Devel: April Pereyra
Dir Info Tech: James Adanuncio
Founded: 1981

Provides audio, Web, & event solutions.

CONTACT CENTER COMPLIANCE
350 E St (Suite 100)
Santa Rosa, CA 95404-4438
Telephone: (707) 303-4437, Toll Free:
(800) 308-0258, Web Site: www.dnc.com
CEO: Michael Kovatch
Primary Market Served: Business & Consumer

CONVIO INC
11501 Domain Dr (Suite 200)
Austin, TX 78758-3406
Telephone: (512) 652-2600, Toll Free:
(888) 528-9501, FAX: (512) 652-2699, Web Site: www.convio.com
Co-Founder, Chief Strategy Officer & Dir: Vinay K. Bhagat
Chief Tech Officer: David G. Hart
VP Corp Communs: Susan Tull
VP Consulting: Brian Hauf
VP Customer Support Svcs: Dave Hendrix
Founded: 1999

Provides on-demand constituent engagement solutions that enable nonprofit organizations to raise funds, advocate for change & cultivate relationships with donors, activists, volunteers, alumni & other constituents in North America.

CORE TECHNOLOGIES
1245 Pearl St (Suite 202)
Boulder, CO 80302-5253
Telephone: (614) 231-3031, Toll Free:
(866) 624-5927, FAX: (303) 395-1474, E-Mail: support@core-tech.
com, Web Site: www.mailware.com
CEO: Bruce Kowkabany
Primary Market Served: Consumer

CORELOGIC INC
Subs of MacDonald, Dettwiler & Assocs LTD
40 Pacifica (Suite 900)
Irvine, CA 92618

Telephone: (949) 214-1000, Toll Free: (800) 426-1466, Web Site: www.corelogic.com
Pres & CEO: Frank Martell
Sr Exec VP: Barry Sando
CFO: Jim Balas
Conducts Business: Worldwide
Primary Market Served: Consumer
Founded: 1978

Global property information, analytics and data-enabled services provider.

COREMEDIA SYSTEMS INC
695 US Hwy 46 (Suite 403)
Fairfield, NJ 07004-1561
Telephone: (973) 276-0882, FAX: (973) 276-0891, Web Site: www.coremedia-systems.com
Co-Founder & CEO: Glenn DeKraker
Primary Market Served: Business & Consumer
Founded: 1992

Develops & delivers media software solutions to direct response agencies, media agencies & marketers in North America.

CORNERSTONE GROUP OF COMPANIES
20 Eglinton Ave W (Floor 4)
Toronto, ON, Canada M4R 1K8
Telephone: (416) 932-9555, FAX: (416) 932-9566, E-Mail: info@cstonecanada.com, Web Site: www.cstonecanada.com
CEO & Pres: Ossie Hinds
VP Fin: Dan Vickruck
COO: Bob Coles
Sr VP: Don Lange
Sr VP Fundraising Svcs Group: Justin Webb
Conducts Business: U.S., Canada
Employees: 275
Primary Market Served: Business & Consumer
Founded: 1987
Gross sales or billing: $25,000,000

Canadian supplier of information-based products & services: List brokerage, list management, list processing, data products, fundraising services, publishing services & marketing database services.

CORNWELL DATA SERVICES INC
352 Evelyn St
Paramus, NJ 07652-2908
Telephone: (201) 261-1050, FAX: (201) 261-7569, E-Mail: info@cornwelldata.com, Web Site: www.cornwelldata.com
Pres: Peter Cornwell
Mktg: Judy Piretra

Conducts Business: U.S.
Employees: 30
Catalog available online
Direct Marketing ad budget: $10,000
Founded: 1967
Gross sales or billing: $2,000,000

Data processing solutions and list services.

CORPORATE EXPRESS US INC
Subs. of Staples Inc
One Environmental Way
Broomfield, CO 80021
Telephone: (303) 664-2000, Toll Free: (888) 238-6329, FAX: (303) 664-3474, Web Site: www.cexp.com
VP Mktg: Medio Waldt
Founded: 1985

Markets & distributes office & computer products.

CORPORATE GRAPHICS DIRECT MARKETING SOLUTIONS
1170 Grey Fox Rd
Arden Hills, MN 55112-6908
Telephone: (651) 494-1740, Toll Free: (800) 728-2615, FAX: (651) 494-1750, E-Mail: contact@cgdms.com, Web Site: www.cgids.com
Mktg Dir: Mark Wilkes
Primary Market Served: Business & Consumer

Direct marketing & customer communications.

COVALENT MARKETING
2021 S Ogden St
Denver, CO 80210-4134
Telephone: (303) 588-7754, Web Site: www.covalentmarketing.com
Principal: Stanton Willins
Primary Market Served: Business

COVEO SOLUTIONS INC
3175 des Quatre Bourgeois (Suite 200)
Quebec, QC, Canada G1W 2K7
Telephone: (418) 263-1111, FAX: (418) 263-1221, Web Site: www.coveo.com
COO: Guy Gauvin

Provides enterprise search applications using its search & relevance technology platform.

CREATECH MARKETING
180 Summit Ave (Suite 203)
Montvale, NJ 07645-1722
Telephone: (201) 326-3000, Toll Free: (866) 808-1050, Web Site: www.createchmarketing.com

VP Opers & Product Mngmt: Elaine Cohen
Primary Market Served: Consumer

Direct mail & emarketing service provider.

CROSS COUNTRY COMPUTER CORP
570 S Research Pl
Central Islip, NY 11722-4415
Telephone: (631) 334-1810, E-Mail: inquiry@crosscountrycomputer.com, Web Site: www.crosscountrycomputer.com
Principal, Pres & CEO: Thomas Berger
Primary Market Served: Business & Consumer

Specializes in bringing strategic solutions within the reach of all companies seeking to evolve their methods and turn the ROI equation back in their favor.

CROWNPEAK TECHNOLOGY INC
5880 W Jefferson Blvd (Suite G)
Los Angeles, CA 90016-3160
Telephone: (310) 841-5920, FAX: (310) 841-5913, Web Site: www.crownpeak.com
CEO & Dir: Jim Howard
COO: Jim Yares
Founded: 2001

Develops Software-as-a-Service Web experience management & optimization solutions to organizations in the U.S. & internationally.

THE CUSTOMER CONNECTION INC
960 S Andreasen Dr (Suite B)
Escondido, CA 92029-1964
Telephone: (760) 489-8339, Toll Free: (800) 477-7166, FAX: (760) 489-1075, E-Mail: contact@custcon.com, Web Site: www.thecustomerconnection.com
Pres: Judd Goldfedder
Founded: 1979

Creating & maintaining relationship marketing programs.

CUSTOMER PORTFOLIOS LLC
88 Black Falcon Ave
Boston, MA 02210-2425
Telephone: (617) 224-9501, E-Mail: getstarted@customerportfolios.com, Web Site: www.customerportfolios.com
CEO: Perry Cooper
Founder & COO: Augio MacCurrach

Chief Mktg Officer & Lead Strategist: Nick Godfrey
Founded: 2001

Full-service digital marketing platform that is custom-built for your business.

CYBERDATA
20 Max Ave
Hicksville, NY 11801-1419
Telephone: (516) 942-8000, FAX: (516) 942-0800, E-Mail: info@cyberdata.com, Web Site: www.cyberdata.com
CEO & Pres: Ralph Potente
Co-Chief Exec Officer: Harry Stalnaker
Founded: 1989

Provides information management & delivery services.

D&B
3 Sylvan Way (Suite 1)
Parsippany, NJ 07054-3821
Telephone: (973) 605-6000, FAX: (973) 605-6920, Web Site: www.dnb.com
Sr Dir Mktg: Tariq Sharif
Credit reporting services industry.

D&B SALES AND MARKETING SOLUTIONS
460 Totten Pond Rd
Waltham, MA 02451-1908
Telephone: (781) 672-9200, Toll Free: (800) 590-0065, FAX: (781) 672-9290, Web Site: www.b2bsalesandmarketing.com
Pres & CEO: Steven W. Alesio

D&D ASSOCIATES INC
PO Box 9150
Garden City, NY 11530-9150
Telephone: (516) 326-8800, Toll Free: (800) 554-0347
Pres: Marvin Nagourney

DKP & ASSOCIATES, INC
8340 N Lincoln Ave (Suite 100)
Skokie, IL 60077-2462
Telephone: (847) 933-9808, FAX: (847) 933-9821, E-Mail: dpearlman@dkpassociates.com, Web Site: www.dkpassociates.com
Pres: Deborah E. Pearlman
VP: Jeff Erickson

DM DATA SOLUTIONS LLC
7508 Manigold Ct
Alexandria, VA 22315-3838
Telephone: (703) 415-6222, Web Site: www.dmdatasolutions.com
Pres: Mike Thornsbury
Primary Market Served: Business

DMRA
201 San Antonio Cir (Suite 280)
Mountain View, CA 94040-1256
Telephone: (650) 559-9988, FAX: (650) 559-0149, E-Mail: mikeg@dmrainc.com, Web Site: www.dmrainc.com
CEO: Michael E. Green
Primary Market Served: Business

providing database, analytical & processing services, and market research to corporations utilizing direct marketing & other forms of direct communications.

DMRS GROUP INC
304 Park Ave S (fl 11)
New York, NY 10010-4305
Telephone: (212) 590-2340, FAX: (212) 590-2341, E-Mail: bgrossman@dmrsgroup.com, Web Site: www.dmrsgroup.com
Pres: Bernice Grossman

Assists companies to better manage marketing information.

THE DATA BASE INC
1710 Hwy 35
Oakhurst, NJ 07755
Telephone: (732) 531-4600, FAX: (732) 531-4798, E-Mail: don.nissim@heritagedirectdm.com, Web Site: www.heritagedirectdm.com
Pres: Donald Nissim
Founded: 1989

DATA DALLAS CORP
1111 W Mockingbird Ln (Suite 300)
Dallas, TX 75247-5017
Telephone: (214) 638-2007, Web Site: www.datadallas.com
Pres: Gerald Garcia

U.S. based technology & business services firm with nearly three decades of experience in IBM mainframe & business process outsourcing.

DATA DASH INC
3928 Delor St
Saint Louis, MO 63116-3316
Telephone: (314) 832-5788, Toll Free: (800) 211-5988, FAX: (314) 832-5775, E-Mail: info@datadash.com, Web Site: www.datadash.com
Pres: Sue Morton

Providing high quality data & document services.

DATA INTELLIGENCE GROUP
9045 Carothers Pkwy (Suite 200)
Franklin, TN 37067-1799

Telephone: (615) 861-3301, Web Site: www.wedigdata.com
COO & Co-Founder: Robert (Robby) Cucullu
CEO & Co-Founder: Karen M. Richards

DATA MANAGEMENT & MARKETING SERVICES LLC
508 N Aster Ave
Broken Arrow, OK 74012-9446
Telephone: (918) 994-7272, Web Site: www.dm-ms.net

DATA MANAGEMENT INC
8300 Greensboro Dr (Suite 800)
Mc Lean, VA 22102-3661
Telephone: (703) 893-5627, Toll Free: (800) 334-8331, FAX: (703) 356-1698, E-Mail: info@data-management.com, Web Site: www.data-management.com
CEO & Pres: Jim Strasbourger
Conducts Business: U.S.
Employees: 45
Primary Market Served: Business & Consumer
Advertising/Marketing Budget Related to Direct Marketing: 0-25%
Founded: 1961

Provide total solutions for analysis and modeling, CRM, data enrichment & hosted Database Management.

DATA PARTNERS INC
12857 Banyan Creek Dr
Fort Myers, FL 33908-3083
Telephone: (239) 267-8762, Toll Free: (866) 423-1818, FAX: (239) 267-9043, E-Mail: info@data-partners.com, Web Site: www.datapartners.com
Co-Founder & Pres: Brigid Berry
Co-Founder & Dir Sls & Mktg Dir,: Jody Pelfrey
Conducts Business: U.S.
Employees: 21
Primary Market Served: Business
Indirect online sales
Founded: 2002
Gross sales or billing: $3,800,000

Customized data and data solutions in direct marketing and collections industries.

DATA SERVICES INC
31516 Winterplace Pkwy
Salisbury, MD 21804-1882
Telephone: (410) 546-2206, Toll Free: (800) 432-4066, FAX: (410) 546-2274, Web Site: www.dataservicesinc.com

Dir Fin & Admin: Bernadette M. Dowling
Pres & CEO: Jerry Messer
VP & Dir Mktg: Bridget Amabili
Founded: 1967

Provides U.S., Canadian & international Database Management, Data Quality, Data Enhancement and Email Services to Direct & Data-Driven Marketers across the globe.

DATA SQUARE LLC
733 Summer St (Suite 601)
Stamford, CT 06901-1035
Telephone: (203) 964-9733, FAX: (203) 964-0783, E-Mail: info@ datasquare.com, Web Site: www. datasquare.com
Head Client Rels: Devyani Sadh
Chief Fin & Chief Enterprise Svcs Officer: Rajinder Gauri
Head Strategic Planning: Mark Greene
Sr VP & Solutions Exec: Michael Dolan
Primary Market Served: Business
Founded: 1999

Provides business intelligence solutions for B2B and B2C sectors.

DATA UNIVERSITY
6550 S 34th St
Lincoln, NE 68516-5454
Telephone: (402) 742-2179, Toll Free: (866) 328-2848, E-Mail: info@ datauniversity.com, Web Site: www. datauniversity.org
Pres & CEO: Mark Graham

Provides marketers with information, training & consultation regarding leveraging internal & external marketing data to accomplish customer acquisition, cultivation & retention goals.

DATABASE MARKETING SERVICES
PO Box 2995
Guaynabo, PR 00970-2995
Telephone: (787) 792-7005
Pres: Kenneth Sewell
Primary Market Served: Business & Consumer

DATABRIDGE MARKETING SYSTEMS CORP
16A Forshee Cir
Montvale, NJ 07645-1772
Telephone: (201) 690-6319, Web Site: www.databridgemarketing .com
Pres: Jim Frustieri
Primary Market Served: Business & Consumer

Provides database marketing & building services to corporatemarketing organizations.

DATACRAFT INC
dba Akamai Data Solutions
28 Kainehe St (Suite A-1)
Kailua, HI 96734-6130
Telephone: (808) 263-5583, FAX: (808) 262-4101, E-Mail: akamaidatasolutions@dcraftinc.com, Web Site: www.akamaidatasolutions.com
Pres: Steven Hinaga
Primary Market Served: Business & Consumer
Founded: 1997

Creative problem solving & personal approach providing you with customized & accurate processing.

DATAMANN INC
1994 Hartford Ave
Wilder, VT 05088
Telephone: (802) 295-6600, Toll Free: (800) 451-4263, FAX: (802) 296-3623, Web Site: www.datamann.com
Pres: John Mann
CFO: Kathy Reagan

Specializing in the implementation & development of innovative software solutions which can transform the operational performance of mail order, fulfillment or multi-channel retail businesses.

DATAMATICS TECHNOLOGIES
56 Middlesex Tpke (Suite 250)
Burlington, MA 01803-4973
Telephone: (781) 425-5240, FAX: (781) 425-5232, Web Site: www. datamaticstech.com
Vice Chmn & CEO: Rahul L. Kanodia

DATASYSTEM SOLUTIONS INC
6310 Lamar Ave (Suite 200)
Overland Park, KS 66202-4284
Telephone: (913) 362-6969, FAX: (913) 362-6383, E-Mail: sales@ mutipub.com, Web Site: www. datasystem.com
Founder & CEO: Gay Manning
Pres & COO: Lorna Fenimore
CTO: Nancy Spear
Dir Client Devel: Robert Tonchuk
Dir Software Devel: Tony Prettyman
Founded: 1985

Provider of subscription management software.

DATRAN MEDIA
345 Hudson St (Suite 500)
New York, NY 10014-7402
Telephone: (212) 706-9781, FAX: (212) 706-9758, Web Site: www. datranmedia.com

Chief Mktg Officer: Dennis Syracuse
Primary Market Served: Business

Provides marketing & advertising services.

DAYSTAR DATA GROUP INC
155 W Central Rd
Schaumburg, IL 60195-1945
Telephone: (847) 202-0100, FAX: (847) 202-0107, E-Mail: sales@ daystardg.com, Web Site: www. daystardg.com
Pres: Jim Calhoun
Conducts Business: U.S.
Employees: 24
Primary Market Served: Consumer
Advertising/Marketing Budget Related to Direct Marketing: 0-25%
Founded: 1990

Daystar creates and delivers client-focused database marketing solutions. From marketing databases to metrics and analysis, from campaign management and execution to data processing and list services, Daystar combines technology-based solutions with practical direct marketing expertise to help you leverage data to make better marketing decisions faster.

DECISION SOFTWARE INC
6911 Old Landover Rd
Hyattsville, MD 20785-1503
Telephone: (301) 459-9000, FAX: (301) 459-3072, E-Mail: info@ dsoftware.biz, Web Site: www. dsimarketingservices.com
Pres & Founder: Jeff Fowler
Dir Client Svcs: Eli Black
Conducts Business: U.S.
Employees: 14
Primary Market Served: Business
Indirect online sales
Advertising/Marketing Budget Related to Direct Marketing: 0-25%
Founded: 1989

DSI provides database design & hosting services as well as campaign management software. Clients include BB & BC catalogers, insurance, manufacturing, fundraisers, retailers, energy & utility and publishers.

DEMANDBASE INC
680 Folsom (Suite 400)
San Francisco, CA 94107
Telephone: (415) 683-2660, E-Mail: info@demandbase.com, Web Site: www.demandbase.com
Sr Mgr Demand Gen: Chris Golec
Chief Mktg Officer: Peter Isaacson
CFO: Tony Russo
Chief Revenue Officer: Don Wight
Chief Product Officer: Alan Fletcher
Primary Market Served: Business

Founded: 2006

Account-Based Marketing platform & services provider.

DEMOGRAPHIC RESEARCH CO

1552 Pennsylvania St
Denver, CO 80203
Telephone: (310) 766-5590, FAX: (303) 831-9181, Web Site: www. drcmodel.com
Pres & CEO: Richard P. Li
Founded: 1975

Modeling service & software development firm in the direct marketing industry.

DIRECT ACCESS MARKETING SERVICES INC

6851 Jericho Tpke (Suite 245)
Syosset, NY 11791-3063
Telephone: (516) 364-2777, FAX: (516) 364-0644, E-Mail: info@ daxcess.com, Web Site: www. daxcess.com
Pres: Thomas Saracco
VP, Sls & Mktg: Neil Mason

Marketing database & list processing servicescompany.

DIRECT DATA CAPTURE LTD

4611 Plettner Ln (Suite 130)
Evergreen, CO 80439-7396
Telephone: (631) 547-5500, FAX: (631) 547-6800, E-Mail: jan@ datacapture.com, Web Site: www. datacapture.com
Pres: Jan A. Trevalyan

DIRECT LOGIC SOLUTIONS

4507 N Sterling Ave (Suite 402)
Peoria, IL 61615-3860
Telephone: (309) 688-5500, FAX: (309) 688-5502, E-Mail: nedbarrett@ direct-logic.com, Web Site: www. direct-logic.com
Pres: Edward V. Barrett
CEO: Chris Cusack
VP, Client Analytics: Jeff Muckler
Conducts Business: U.S., Canada, Europe
Primary Market Served: Business & Consumer
Indirect online sales
Founded: 1999

Direct response consulting services.

DIRECT MARKETING AUDIT SYSTEMS

3159 Fee Fee Rd (Suite 221)
Bridgeton, MO 63044-3299

Telephone: (314) 739-7480, FAX: (314) 739-7284, Web Site: www. dmasinc.com
Pres: Dennis Hupp

DIRECTECH HOLDING COMPANY INC

33 W Second St (Suite 504)
Maysville, KY 41056
Toll Free: (866) 550-5030, E-Mail: ceo@directech.com, Web Site: www. directech.com
CEO: Thomas Beaudreau
Pres: Bernard J. Schafer
Founded: 2004

Provides electronic home products.

DIRECTSMILE LLC

300 Broadacres Dr (fl 4)
Bloomfield, NJ 07003-3153
Telephone: (973) 338-9368, Web Site: www.directsmile.com
VP: Mike Beard

Services industry.

DIREXXIS INC

250 1st Ave (Suite 102)
Needham, MA 02494-2847
Telephone: (781) 444-7900, FAX: (781) 444-7909, Web Site: www. direxxismarketing.com
CEO & Pres: Steve Scruton
COO: Chris Piper
Chief Tech Officer: Rick Kollmeyer
Chief Mktg Officer: William Fayenweather
Primary Market Served: Business
Founded: 2004

Provides distributed marketing software solutions globally.

DOVETAIL

1221 W Mineral Ave (Suite 102)
Littleton, CO 80120-4544
Telephone: (303) 904-4771, FAX: (303) 904-4776, E-Mail: welcome@ dovetailnet.com, Web Site: www. dovetailnet.com
VP Bus Devel: Jeff Barela
Pres: Paul Vannett
Conducts Business: U.S., Canada
Employees: 12
Primary Market Served: Business
Advertising/Marketing Budget Related to Direct Marketing: 0-25%
Founded: 1995

Builds and manages marketing databases for business-to-consumer companies.

DRAKE DIRECT

225 E 46th St (Penthouse D)
New York, NY 10017-2928

Telephone: (212) 759-1225, (914) 299-4956, FAX: (212) 759-9756, E-Mail: Rhonda@DrakeDirect.com, Web Site: www.drakedirect.com
Pres: Rhonda Knehans Drake
VP: Perry Drake

Management & usage of customer data in the corporate sector.

DUNDEE INTERNET SERVICES INC

PO Box 102
Dundee, MI 48131-0102
Telephone: (734) 529-5331, FAX: (734) 529-5085, E-Mail: pat@ dundee.net, Web Site: mailing-list-services.com/dundee.net
CEO: Patricia K. Roundtree
CTO: Richard Roundtree

Full featured Email List Management & Marketing Service provider.

EASY ANALYTIC SOFTWARE INC

101 Haag Ave
Bellmawr, NJ 08031-2506
Telephone: (856) 931-5780, FAX: (856) 931-4115, Web Site: www. easidemographics.com
Pres: Robert M. Katz
Chief Tech Officer: Edward A. Sussman
Founded: 1995

Offers demographic estimates, forecasts services.

EBUREAU LLC

25 6th Ave N
Saint Cloud, MN 56303-4729
Telephone: (320) 534-5000, FAX: (320) 534-5020, Web Site: www. ebureau.com
CEO, Pres, Chief Strategy Officer, COO & Dir: Gordon Meyer
CFO: Nancy Deaton
Exec VP Bus Devel: Mark Doman
Exec VP Bus Devel: David Dowhan
Sr VP & Gen Mgr Audience Targeting Solutions: Jeremy Longinotti
Founded: 2004

Offers a suite of predictive analytics & real-time information solutions to consumer-facing businesses.

ECHO DATA GROUP

121 N Shirk Rd
New Holland, PA 17557-9714
Toll Free: (800) 511-3870, E-Mail: sroberts@echodata.com, Web Site: www.echodata.com
CEO: Stephen H. Roberts
VP Sls & Mktg: Jonathan Roberts

Founded: 1983
Full service fulfillment company,

ELCOM INTERNATIONAL INC
Ten Oceana Way
Norwood, MA 02062-2601
Telephone: (781) 501-4000, FAX: (781) 762-1540, Web Site: www. elcominternational.com
Chmn & Exec VP: William Lock
Fin Dir: David Elliott
CEO: Gregory D. King

Develops & licenses automated procurement software applications that enable companies to conduct interactive electronic commerce.

ELLIOTT MARKETING GROUP INC
2281 Sidgefield Ln
Pittsburgh, PA 15241-2713
Telephone: (412) 831-1183
Pres: John Elliott
Founded: 1999

ELOQUA INC
1921 Gallows Rd (Suite 250)
Vienna, VA 22182-3994
Telephone: (703) 584-2750, Web Site: www.eloqua.com
Pres: Dorian E. Daley
Co-Founder & Chief Tech Officer: Steven K. Woods
Primary Market Served: Consumer
Founded: 1999

Provides on-demand revenue performance management software solutions for businesses.

ENERTEX MARKETING
99 Madison Ave (Floor 10)
New York, NY 10016-7419
Telephone: (212) 532-3115, FAX: (212) 532-1878, E-Mail: info@ enertexmarketing.com, Web Site: www.enertexmarketing.com
Pres: Chuck Greene
Exec VP: Alphonse Ingenito
VP: Tom Holm

Provides direct marketing campaign planning and execution, data processing, list brokerage & list management services.

EPIC MARKETING SOLUTIONS
6054 Quinpool Rd
Halifax, NS, Canada B3L 1A1
Telephone: (902) 455-5100, Toll Free: (888) 323-6263, FAX: (902) 455-5103, E-Mail: info@epicmarketing. ca, Web Site: www.epicmarketing.ca

Pres: Ash Chugh
Primary Market Served: Business

Data marketing & consulting.

EQUIFAX DATABASE MARKETING
Subs. of Equifax
500 Edgewater Dr (Suite 525)
Wakefield, MA 01880-6222
Telephone: (781) 876-2000, Toll Free: (800) 660-5125, FAX: (781) 246-3720, E-Mail: monica.baker@ equifax.com, Web Site: www. equifax.com/databaseservices
Senior VP Multi-Channel Retail & Catalog: Kevin McShane
VP Sls & Mktg: Ned McMullen
Founded: 2002

Offers marketing database hosting services & industry-specific data models, business processes, & management reports.

ESRI
380 New York St
Redlands, CA 92373-8118
Telephone: (909) 793-2853, Web Site: www.esri.com
Bus Solutions Mgr: Simon Thompson

Offer the expertise you need to solve real-world problems & grow your business.

FG COMPANIES
901 Twelve Oaks Center Dr (Suite 934)
Wayzata, MN 55391-4721
Telephone: (952) 476-8900, E-Mail: mmelius@fgcompanies.com, Web Site: www.fgcompanies.com
Mng Dir: Mark Van Ert
Primary Market Served: Business

Advisory firm focused on the consumer finance & commercial finance industries.

FAIR ISAAC CORP
2665C Long Lake Rd
Saint Paul, MN 55113-2538
Telephone: (651) 636-4509, E-Mail: info@fairisaac.com, Web Site: www. fairisaac.com
CEO: Mark N. Greene

Provides analytics & decision making services including credit scoring.

FAIRFIELD MARKETING GROUP INC
Div. of FMG Inc
830 Sport Hill Rd
Easton, CT 06612-1241

Telephone: (203) 261-5585 X202, (203) 261-5568, FAX: (203) 261-0884, E-Mail: info@ fairfieldmarketing.com, Web Site: www.fairfieldmarketing.com
Pres: Edward Washchilla Jr.

Data base mailing lists & computer processing lettershop services.

THE FIDELIS GROUP INC
223 Gates Rd (Unit A)
Little Ferry, NJ 07643-1900
Telephone: (410) 721-3450, Web Site: www.thefidelisgroup.net
Pres/ CEO: Livleen Singh
Primary Market Served: Business & Consumer

Develop software & provides IT solutions.

FIFTH GEAR LLC
9100 Purdue Rd (Suite 400)
Indianapolis, IN 46268-1180
Telephone: (317) 631-0907, FAX: (317) 631-6585, Web Site: www. infifthgear.com
CFO: Donald J.B. Van Der Wiel
VP Tech: Robert Mcilvaine
VP Planning Assessment: Jeff Dahltorp
VP Client Success: Rick Hall
VP Sls & Mktg: Blake Vaughn
Primary Market Served: Business & Consumer
Founded: 1982

Infuses order fulfillment, customer care, product personalization, & ecommerce technology into a direct-to-consumer experience for the catalog and direct-to-consumer retail industry worldwide.

FILEMAKER INC
5201 Patrick Henry
Santa Clara, CA 95054-1164
Telephone: (408) 987-7000, FAX: (408) 987-3823, Web Site: www. filemaker.com
CEO & Pres: Dominique Philippe Goupil
Co-Founder: Randy Komisar
CFO & VP: David Williams
Chief Tech Officer & VP: Steven Marcek
Chief Admin Officer & Sr VP: Bill Epling
Founded: 1986

Develops & delivers software to create custom business solutions for individuals & organizations.

FIRST WAVE TECHNOLOGIES INC
7000 Central Pkwy NE (Suite 330)
Atlanta, GA 30328-4589

Telephone: (678) 672-3100, Web Site: www.firstwave.com
CEO: Richard Brock
Computer software service business.

FREESTYLE SOLUTIONS
c/o DBA Dyda Comp Development Corp, 11 Commerce Way #D, Totowa, NJ 07512-1154
9 Campus Dr (Suite 1)
Parsippany, NJ 07054-4412
Telephone: (973) 237-9415, Toll Free: (800) 858-3666, FAX: (973) 237-9043, E-Mail: sales@dydacomp.com, Web Site: www.dydacomp.com
CEO: Fred Lizza
CFO: Paul Kincaid
VP Mktg: Laura Hills
VP Sales: Mark Brandwein

FRESHADDRESS INC
36 Crafts St
Newton, MA 02458-1249
Telephone: (617) 965-4500, Toll Free: (800) 321-3009, FAX: (617) 965-4551, Web Site: www.freshaddress.com
Co-Founder & CEO: Bill Kaplan
Co-Founder & Pres: Austin Bliss
Chief Systems Engr: Austin Jordan
VP Client Svcs: Nicole Campbell
Dir Strategic Sls: Mark Rafferty
Conducts Business: U.S.
Employees: 25
Primary Market Served: Business
Advertising/Marketing Budget Related to Direct Marketing: 0-25%
Founded: 1999

Provides services to help companies build and update their e-mail address databases and manage, monitor, and improve their e-mail deliverability.

FUJITSU AMERICA INC
Subs. of Fujitsu Limited
1250 E Arques Ave MS 122
Sunnyvale, CA 94085-3470
Telephone: (408) 746-6000, Toll Free: (800) 831-3183, FAX: (408) 992-2674, E-Mail: solutions@us.fujitsu.com, Web Site: www.fujitsu.com
Sr VP Sls & Mktg & Strategy: Matthew Goldman

Offers an extensive portfolio of business technology services, cloud services, computing platforms & industry solutions.

FULCRUM
70 W 40th St (fl 10)
New York, NY 10018-2621
Telephone: (212) 651-7000, Toll Free: (888) 245-9450

CEO: Richard Vermillion
Relationship marketing & innovation, offering sophisticated analytical solutions, groundbreaking technologies, & winning campaign strategies that help companies improve marketing performance & customer relationships.

GMC SOFTWARE TECHNOLOGY INC
529 Main St (Suite 205)
Charlestown, MA 02129-1121
Toll Free: (800) 250-1850, FAX: (617) 241-5665, Web Site: www.gmc.net
Pres & Gen Mgr GMC North America: Steve Francis
Primary Market Served: Business

Designs & develops customer communications management (CCM) software.

GATES MARKETING
3909 Oakcliff Industrial Ct
Atlanta, GA 30340-3408
Telephone: (770) 455-9662, FAX: (770) 455-8785
Pres: Robert Gates
Founded: 2009

GEOSCAPE
2100 W Flagler St (fl 2)
Miami, FL 33135-1619
Telephone: (305) 860-1460, FAX: (305) 860-6161, Web Site: www.geoscape.com
CEO: David Perez
Mng Dir & Sr Partner: Cesar M. Melgoza
Founded: 2003

Operates as a strategy & market intelligence company.

GLOBAL INTELLISYSTEMS
1153 Bergen Pkwy (Suite 455)
Evergreen, CO 80439-9501
Telephone: (970) 315-3637, Toll Free: (800) 707-7074, FAX: (970) 432-7190, Web Site: www.globalintellisystems.com
CEO/Founder: John Brogan
Primary Market Served: Business & Consumer

Company offers email marketing, delivery monitoring, mobile messaging, surveying, confirmed opt-in, advanced list analysis & data services.

GLOBAL TURNKEY SYSTEMS INC
2001 US Highway 46 (Suite 203)
Parsippany, NJ 07054-1315

Telephone: (973) 331-1010, FAX: (973) 331-0042, E-Mail: sales@gtsystems.com, Web Site: www.gtsystems.com
Pres & CEO: Al Alteslane
VP Prod Mktg: Karen Tiesling
Founded: 1969

Develops enterprise resource planning solutions.

GLOBAL WARE SOLUTIONS
200 Ward Hill Ave
Haverhill, MA 01835-6972
Toll Free: (800) 469-7500, FAX: (978) 469-7373, E-Mail: sales@gwsmail.com, Web Site: www.globalwaresolutions.com
Pres: Michael T. Liess
CFO & Member Exec Team: John P. Viliesis
Founded: 1978

Provides ecommerce & supply chain management solutions.

GLOBAL-Z INTERNATIONAL INC
395 Shields Dr
Bennington, VT 05201-9810
Telephone: (802) 445-1011, FAX: (802) 445-1016, E-Mail: info@globalz.com, Web Site: www.globalz.com
Pres: Sasha Garder
Exec VP: Dimitri Garder
VP Opers: Ed Barbeau
Chief Mktg Officer: Ted Haas
Founded: 1989

GRAYHAIR SOFTWARE
124 Gaither Dr (Suite 160)
Mount Laurel, NJ 08054-1719
Telephone: (856) 727-9372, FAX: (856) 727-1315, Web Site: www.grayhairsoftware.com
Founder, CEO & Pres: Cameron Bellamy
Dir Bus Devel: Josh McCaully
Market Research Dir: Robert Tiedeken
VP Prod Mngmt & Mktg: Raymond T. Chin
VP Client Svcs: Therese Powers
Primary Market Served: Consumer
Founded: 2000

Provides mail tracking & address quality products & services for the direct mail industry.

GROUP 1 SOFTWARE INC
Subs. of Pitney Bowes
4200 Parliament Pl (Suite 600)
Lanham, MD 20706-1844

Telephone: (301) 731-2300, Toll Free: (888) 413-6763, FAX: (301) 731-0360, E-Mail: info@g1.com, Web Site: www.g1.com
Pres: Michael Hickey
Mktg: Nick Smith

Provides software for database marketing, electronic document systems & mailing efficiency.

HARTE-HANKS
9601 Mc Allister Freeway (Suite 610)
San Antonio, TX 78216
Telephone: (210) 829-9000, FAX: (210) 829-9403, Web Site: www.hartehanks.com
Pres & CEO: Robert Allan Philpott
Exec VP & CFO: Douglas "Doug" C. Shepard

Provides a full range of specialized, co-ordinated, & integrated direct marketing services to companies in a wide variety of industries.

HERITAGE DIRECT
1710 Hwy 35
Oakhurst, NJ 07755-2910
Telephone: (732) 531-2212, FAX: (732) 531-4798, Web Site: www.actionmarkets.com
Pres: Donald Nissim
Founded: 1982

Specializes in Direct Marketing, Sales Promotions, Event Marketing.

HITACHI DATA SYSTEMS
2845 Lafayette St
Santa Clara, CA 95050-2639
Telephone: (408) 970-1000, FAX: (408) 727-8036, Web Site: www.hds.com
CEO: Jack Domme
Founded: 1989

Provides information infrastructure, data storage solutions & services for organizations.

HOOVER'S INC
Subs. of Dun & Bradstreet
5800 Airport Blvd
Austin, TX 78752-4204
Telephone: (512) 374-4500, FAX: (512) 374-4051, Web Site: www.hoovers.com
Pres & CEO, Dun & Bradstreet: Robert Carrigan

Offers proprietary business information through our online platform & integrated workflow solutions.

THE HYIAD GROUP
400 Garden City Plz (Suite 403)
Garden City, NY 11530-3336

Telephone: (516) 433-3800, FAX: (516) 822-6670, Web Site: www.thehyaidgroup.com
Pres: Richard Levinson
VP & Comptroller: Barbara Cheny
VP, Client Svcs: Janine Levinson
VP, HR: Tom Monks
VP, Sls: Tom Clarken
Conducts Business: U.S.
Employees: 300
Primary Market Served: Business
Founded: 1969

THE IDT GROUP
1650 Market St (Floor 36)
Philadelphia, PA 19103-7334
Telephone: (215) 487-4420, FAX: (215) 487-3110, Web Site: www.idthospitality.com
Pres: Harry W. Rivkin
Founded: 1988

Serves the Guest Management needs of the hospitality industry with high-value, customized database-driven solutions that support hotel & resort database & Internet marketing, sales, CRM, revenue management & operations.

INFOLURE
Subs. of Datalure
1705 W Parkside Ln
Phoenix, AZ 85027-1333
Telephone: (602) 308-6700, FAX: (602) 308-6801, E-Mail: glenn.gottfried@infolure.com, Web Site: www.infolure.com
COO & Founder: Gene Hanson
VP Sls & Bus Devel of Infolure: Perry Kahn
Dir Prod & Bus Devel of Datalure: Keith Goodnight
Dir Sls & Bus Develop Datalure: Will Turner
Employees: 25
Primary Market Served: Business
Advertising/Marketing Budget Related to Direct Marketing: 76-100%
Direct Marketing ad budget: $100,000
Direct Mail: 10%
Magazines: 90%
Founded: 1992
Gross sales or billing: $10,000,000

Offers support services for direct marketing & accounts receivable markets.

INFOR
13560 Morris Rd (Suite 4100)
Alpharetta, GA 30004
Telephone: (678) 319-8000, Web Site: www.infor.com
CEO: Charles Phillips
Primary Market Served: Business & Consumer

Founded: 2002
Innovative, exciting key player in the enterprise software space.

INFORMATION COMMAND INC
411 W Ontario St (Apt 225)
Chicago, IL 60654-6954
Telephone: (312) 245-1111, Toll Free: (800) 376-6654, FAX: (312) 245-1128, E-Mail: gon@phonebiz2000.com, Web Site: www.info2u.com

Specializes in Business Organizations & Telecommunications.

THE INFORMATION ENGINE
9105 Hammock Edge Pl
Bradenton, FL 34212-3254
Telephone: (904) 645-6000, Web Site: www.informationeng.com
Primary Market Served: Business & Consumer

INFORMATION SOURCES INC
dba TecTrends
2175 Cactus Ct Apt 1
Walnut Creek, CA 94595-2531
Telephone: (510) 525-6220, FAX: (510) 525-1568, Web Site: www.tectrends.com
Pres: Ruth Koolish

Computer & network security company.

INFORONICS GLOBAL SERVICES LLC
25 Porter Rd (Suite 4)
Littleton, MA 01460-1434
Telephone: (315) 261-7525, FAX: (978) 698-7500, E-Mail: info@inforonics.com, Web Site: www.inforonics.com
Dir Tech Svcs: Joe Venskus
VP: Candace Verhulst
Founded: 1962

IT service management company, provides IT service management & outsourced technical support services.

INNOVATIVE SYSTEMS INC
790 Holiday Dr
Pittsburgh, PA 15220-8127
Telephone: (412) 937-9300, Toll Free: (800) 622-6390, FAX: (412) 937-9309, E-Mail: info@innovativesystems.com, Web Site: www.innovativesystems.com
Founder, Chmn Bd, CEO & Pres: Robert J. Colonna
Exec VP Opers: Jeff Canter

Founded: 1968

Delivers enterprise customer information solutions & database consulting services to banking, insurance, financial services, retail, & hospitality industries worldwide.

INPUT SYSTEMS INC

16308 Orange Ave
Paramount, CA 90723
Telephone: (562) 634-1170, Toll Free: (800) 327-9337, FAX: (562) 634-0993, E-Mail: info@sweepssoftware.com, Web Site: www.sweepssoftware.com
Pres: Harley D. Hancock
Founded: 1974

INQUIRY INTELLIGENCE SYSTEMS

18 N Central Dr
O'Fallon, MO 63366
Telephone: (636) 240-1800, Toll Free: (800) 467-2329, FAX: (636) 281-1517, E-Mail: sales@iqsalespro.com, Web Site: www.inquiry-tracking.com
Owner: Mike Moss
Sls Exec: Daniel Moss
Fin Exex: Janice Crawford
Founded: 1986

INSIGHT OUT OF CHAOS

80 Broad St (Suite 2503)
New York, NY 10004-3325
Telephone: (212) 935-0044, FAX: (212) 742-0469, E-Mail: info@iooc.com, Web Site: www.iooc.com
Pres: Spencer Hapoienu

Offers database design & maintenance, interpreting data, processing raw transaction data, direct mail design, printing, & data entry services.

INTEGRATED BUSINESS SERVICES INC

736 N Western Ave (Suite 125)
Lake Forest, IL 60045-1820
Telephone: (847) 735-1690, Toll Free: (800) 451-5478, Web Site: www.medbase200.com
Pres: Samuel Tartamella
Founded: 1982

Provides marketing lists & deployment services to American & Canadian firms and brokers.

INTEGRATED MARKETING TECHNOLOGY INC

2269 Chestnut St (#992)
San Francisco, CA 94123-2600

Telephone: (415) 699-2280, FAX: (917) 591-5333, E-Mail: information@imtnetwork.com, Web Site: www.imtnetwork.com
Pres & CEO: James Tucker
Conducts Business: Worldwide
Employees: 15
Primary Market Served: Business
Indirect online sales
Advertising/Marketing Budget Related to Direct Marketing: 0-25%
Direct Marketing ad budget:
Direct Mail: 20%
Online: 80%
Founded: 1993
Gross sales or billing: $10,000,000

An outsourced marketing database provider. Specializes in building, housing and maintaining marketing data and performing critical marketing analysis.

INTELIUS INC

500 108th Ave (fl 22)
Bellevue, WA 98004-5500
Telephone: (425) 974-6100, Web Site: www.intelius.com
CEO: Naveen Jain
Founded: 2003

Telephone communications services.

INTELLIDYN CORP

72 Sharp St (Suite A9)
Hingham, MA 02043-4362
Telephone: (781) 741-5503, Toll Free: (866) 773-5756, FAX: (781) 741-5545, E-Mail: kmf@intellidyn.com, Web Site: www.intellidyn.com
Founder, CEO & Pres: Peter E. Harvey
Sr VP Client Svcs: Jack Wallace
Employees: 24
Primary Market Served: Business
Catalog available online
Direct online sales
Advertising/Marketing Budget Related to Direct Marketing: 0-25%
Founded: 1998

Data Integration/warehousing, analytic, strategic planning, database marketing & targeted list sales sold to Fortune 100 companies such as Chase, AOL, and Household Finance.

INTERACTIVE MARKETING SOLUTIONS

777 Summer St (Suite 502)
Stamford, CT 06901-1042
Telephone: (203) 653-2762, FAX: (203) 653-2767, E-Mail: solutions@ims-dm.com
CEO: Frank Rigano

Primary Market Served: Business & Consumer

Developing innovative list and database management software and services designed to help businesses succeed in their marketing efforts by mitigating the challenges imposed by privacy & consumer opt-out legislation.

INTERNATIONAL DATA MANAGEMENT - A DMH MARKETING PARTNERS CO

490 White Pond Dr
Akron, OH 44320-1122
Telephone: (330) 869-8500, FAX: (330) 869-4027, Web Site: www.idmi.com
Exec VP: Christopher Moore
Primary Market Served: Business & Consumer

Full service database management customized to meet each organization's specific fundraising needs,

IPACESETTERS

135 Chestnut Ridge Rd
Montvale, NJ 07645-1152
Telephone: (201) 391-1500, FAX: (201) 391-8357, Web Site: www.ipacesetters.com
Chief Exec Officer: Tim Searcy
Founder & Pres: Carla Kidd
Exec Chmn: Gerard A. DeBiasi
Controller: Richard Sauter
Primary Market Served: Consumer
Founded: 1988

Provides customer acquisition, customer retention, loyalty & win-back, lead generation, appointment setting & bilingual marketing services.

IPSWITCH INC

83 Hartwell Ave
Lexington, MA 02421-3116
Telephone: (781) 676-5700, FAX: (781) 676-5710, Web Site: www.whatsupgold.com
CEO & Founder: Roger Greene
CIO: Azmi Jafarey
VP Mktg & Prod Mngmt: Ronnie Ray
Founded: 1991

Develops information technology software to produce solutions & services to businesses in the areas of network administrators, network managers,& information technology users.

ISLAND PACIFIC INC

Div. of Synaro & Subs. of 3Q Holdings Limited
17310 Red Hill Ave Ste 320

Irvine, CA 92614-5600
Telephone: (949) 476-2212, Toll Free: (800) 569-1122, FAX: (949) 476-0177, Web Site: www.islandpacific. com
CEO: David Rosen
Chief Tech Officer: Jay Fisher
Founded: 2004

Offers merchandise management software solutions for retailers. It also offers point of sale software & systems.

JDA SOFTWARE GROUP INC

Subs. of RedPrairie Corp.
14400 N 87th St
Scottsdale, AZ 85260-3649
Telephone: (480) 308-3000, Toll Free: (800) 479-7382, FAX: (480) 308-3001, E-Mail: info@jda.com, Web Site: www.jda.com
Exec VP, Chief Mktg Officer: Kevin Iaquinto
Primary Market Served: Business
Founded: 1985

Provides enterprise software solutions worldwide.

JEPPESEN

55 Inverness Dr E
Englewood, CO 80112-5412
Telephone: (303) 799-9090, Toll Free: (800) 353-2107, Web Site: www. jeppesen.com
CEO: Mark Van Tine
Pres: Thomas Wede
VP Quality & Bus Oper Svcs: Marilyn Aragon
Primary Market Served: Consumer

Provides data acquisition & analysis, all levels of customer support, product development, sales and marketing, executive offices and more.

KBM GROUP

A Wunderman company
2051 Dogwood St (Suite 220)
Louisville, CO 80027
Toll Free: (800) 579-1950, E-Mail: sales@kbmg.com, Web Site: www. kbmg.com
CEO: Dave DeMarsh
Pres & COO: Bret Harper
VP Mktg Commun: Adam Woods
Sr VP, New Busn Devt: Joe Bank
CFO: Jason Dodge
Conducts Business: Worldwide
Primary Market Served: Business & Consumer
Founded: 1997

Data analytics and technology integration marketing services company.

KXEN INC

300 California St (Suite 220)

San Francisco, CA 94104-1410
Telephone: (415) 904-4160, FAX: (415) 904-9041, Web Site: www. kxen.com
CEO: John Ball
CTO & Founder: Erik Marcado
Sr VP Corp Opers: Xavier Haffreingue
Sr VP Bus Devel: Bruno Delahaye
VP Prod Mngmt: Marco Casalaina

Provides predictive analytics solutions.

KABLE FULFILLMENT SERVICES

Subs. of Kable Media Services, Inc.
16 S Wesley Ave
Mount Morris, IL 61054-1473
Telephone: (815) 734-4151, FAX: (815) 734-5228
Pres & CEO: Michael P. Duloc

Provides magazine subscription services, as well as product & merchandise fulfillment for publishers & direct marketers.

WALTER KARL INC

Div. of Donnelley Marketing Company
2 Blue Hill Plaza (fl 3)
Pearl River, NY 10965-3115
Telephone: (845) 620-0700, FAX: (845) 620-1885, E-Mail: info@ walterkarl.infousa.com, Web Site: www.walterkarl.com
Pres Strategic Info Mngmt: John Barth
Sr VP Client Opers: Kathy Elter
VP Bus Devel: Laurence Liebson
Gen Mgr Prod & Mktg: Lori Colantuono
Employees: 100
Founded: 1957

Walter Karl, the industry's leading direct and interactive marketing firm, is the "marketing partner" of over 500 management and brokerage clients in all B2B and consumer areas. Our marketing power is derived from our talented and experienced professionals who provide large company services with individual attention and commitment.

KING COMPUTER SERVICES INC

3115 Foothill Blvd (#M250)
La Crescenta, CA 91214-2691
Telephone: (818) 951-5240, E-Mail: kingsoftware@aol.com, Web Site: www.kingcomputerservices.com
Pres: Morrison J. Budlong
Founded: 1984

Computer software systems analysis & design, custom computer programming prepackaged software services.

L-COM INC

45 Beechwood Dr
North Andover, MA 01845-1023
Telephone: (978) 682-6936, FAX: (978) 689-9484, Web Site: www.L-com.com
CEO Pres & Dir: Jon A. Jensen
COO: Zig Woronko
Founded: 1982

LSSIDATA

Subs. of VoltDelta
1 Sentry Pkwy (Suite 6000)
Blue Bell, PA 19422-2310
Telephone: (610) 276-4300, Toll Free: (800) 210-9021, FAX: (610) 567-5698, E-Mail: info@lssi.net, Web Site: www.lssidata.com
CEO & Pres: J. A McMaster
Sr VP & CIO: Ronnie Strickland
Dir Prod Mngmt: Mike McGuire
VP & Gen Mgr: Richard Kurtz
Conducts Business: Worldwide
Primary Market Served: Business & Consumer
Founded: 1995

Directory assistance.

LATIN FORCE GROUP LLC

2100 W Flagler St (#2)
Miami, FL 33135-1619
Telephone: (305) 860-1460, FAX: (305) 860-6161, Web Site: www. latinforce.com
Pres: Cesar M. Melgoza
Founded: 2002

LEWIS DIRECT

325 E Oliver St
Baltimore, MD 21202-2948
Telephone: (410) 539-5100, FAX: (410) 539-4700
Exec VP: James G. Dickman
Founded: 1930

Dedicated to the integration of market research, proven strategies, effective creative solutions, cost-conscious production & data analysis into accountable and actionable results.

LEXINET CORP

701 N Union St
Council Grove, KS 66846-9358
Telephone: (620) 767-7000, FAX: (620) 767-7100, E-Mail: tlc@ lexinetcorporation.com
CEO: Tom Davis
Primary Market Served: Business & Consumer

Develop & implement flexible, creative & personalized direct marketing programs for any organization.

LOGICNOLOGY INC
720 International Pkwy
Sunrise, FL 33325-6219
Telephone: (954) 851-1200, FAX:
(954) 846-8552
Pres: Terry Jukes

LORTON DATA INC
2 Pine Tree Dr (Suite 302)
Arden Hills, MN 55112-3715
Telephone: (651) 203-8200, FAX:
(651) 203-8299, Web Site: www.
lortondata.com
CEO: Tony Evans
VP Solutions: Pamela Corbeille-Lepel
Conducts Business: U.S.
Employees: 20
Primary Market Served: Business
Direct online sales
Direct Marketing ad budget:
Direct Mail: 100%
Founded: 1989
Gross sales or billing: $2,500,000

Database services to the direct marketing industry to help businesses improve
their ROI of their direct marketing dollars.

LOTAME SOLUTIONS
8850 Stanford Blvd (Suite 2000)
Columbia, MD 21045-4726
Telephone: (410) 379-2195, FAX:
(410) 379-2198, Web Site: www.
lotame.com
Founder, CEO & Dir: Andrew Mon-
fried
CFO: Michael Sullivan
Founded: 2006

Operates an independent data management platform (DMP) for publishers,
marketers, & agencies to collect, unify,
protect, & activate audience data.

LOYALTYONE
438 University Ave (Suite 600)
Toronto, ON, Canada M5G 2L1
Telephone: (416) 228-6500, Web Site:
www.loyalty.com; www.airmiles.ca
CEO, Pres & Member Exec Commit-
tee: Bryan A. Pearson
CFO & Sr VP: Todd March
Founded: 1991

A global provider of loyalty strategy,
loyalty programs, customer analytics
and relationship marketing with 1400
associates across North America.

MBS
570 S Research Pl
Central Islip, NY 11722-4415
Telephone: (631) 851-5000, Web Site:
www.mbsinsight.com
CEO: John Healy
Pres: Lissa Napolillo

Sr VP: Kelly Kennedy
Primary Market Served: Business &
Consumer

MDF SYSTEMS
780 James P Casey Rd
Bristol, CT 06010-8537
Telephone: (860) 584-4750, Toll Free:
(800) 426-3752, FAX: (860) 584-
4759, Web Site: www.mdfsystems.
com
Pres: Richard Kovitch
Founded: 2006

Advertising, Promotional & trade show
services.

MESA MEDIA & ENTERTAINMENT SERVICES ALLIANCCE
39 N Bayles Ave
Port Washington, NY 11050-2930
Telephone: (516) 767-6720, Web Site:
www.mesalliance.org/
Exec Dir: Guy Finley
Exec Dir: Martin Porter
Primary Market Served: Business &
Consumer

Provides information resources to entertainment technology professionals

MLS DATA MANAGEMENT SOLUTIONS
6115 Camp Bowie Blvd (Suite 200)
Fort Worth, TX 76116-5500
Telephone: (817) 989-3800, FAX:
(817) 989-3899, Web Site: www.
mlsc.com
Pres: John Kirkland
Mktg Mgr: Manda Bilby
Founded: 1982

A member company as mailing list systems. At MLS, we help you collect, integrate, organize, store and interpret the
data your business generates. We specialize in acquisition marketing, data
quality, data warehousing and business
intelligence solutions.

MMI DIRECT LLC
7160 Columbia Gateway Dr (Suite
300)
Columbia, MD 21046-2134
Telephone: (410) 561-1500, FAX:
(410) 561-0833, Web Site: www.
mmidirect.com
Sr VP Sls & Mktg: John Bell
Founded: 1972

Provides data processing & database
marketing solutions. Offers Web-based
reporting, database design & maintenance, analytic & data, list rental fulfillment, & database services.

MAC DIRECT
185 Discovery Drive
Colmar, PA 18915
Telephone: (215) 822-5775, Toll Free:
(800) 278-1154, FAX: (215) 822-
7977, E-Mail: info@macdirect.com,
Web Site: www.macdirect.com
Gallery Dir: Lauren Carline

Provides Binding, Color Prints, Consul-
tations.

MAGENTO
10441 Jefferson Blvd (Suite 200)
Culver City, CA 90232-3512
Telephone: (310) 954-8012, Web Site:
www.magento.com
Co-Founder & COO: Roy Rubin
Founded: 2001

Provides eCommerce software &
eCommerce platforms solutions worldwide.

MAIL MOVERS & MAILING SERVICES
325 S 69th St
Upper Darby, PA 19082-4213
Telephone: (610) 888-6969, (610) 734-
1220, FAX: (610) 734-1200, E-Mail:
mailmovers@rcn.com, Web Site:
www.mailmoversandmore.com

Design print & mail - a direct mail marketing specialist. Full color menus -
brochures - flyers - business cards -
postcards for any size business.

MAILER'S SOFTWARE
Div. of Melissa Data Co
22382 Avenida Empresa
Rancho Santa Margarita, CA 92688-
2112
Telephone: (949) 858-3000, Toll Free:
(800) 635-4772, FAX: (949) 589-
5211, E-Mail: info@melissadata.
com, Web Site: www.
mailerssoftware.com
Pres & Founder: Raymond F. Melissa
COO: Gary Van Roekel
Chief Tech Officer: Phil Maitino
VP Info Systems: John Melissa
VP Mktg: Greg Brown

Provider of data quality & address verification software.

MARCO DATA SERVICE
12537 Peter Moore Ln
De Soto, MO 63020-4760
Telephone: (636) 337-3109, FAX:
(636) 586-1938
Owner: Barbara Marco
Founded: 1986

Computer business solutions.

MARKETERNET LLC

233 S Wacker Dr (Suite 1800), Sears Tower
Chicago, IL 60606-6462
Telephone: (312) 775-9320, Toll Free: (888) 443-3684, FAX: (312) 775-9328, E-Mail: info@marketernet. com, Web Site: www.marketernet. com

Provides consumer marketing services for the automotive, banking, real estate & credit union industries.

MARKETING 1BY1 INC

Subs. of Conexance MD SAS.
11350 Random Hills Rd
Fairfax, VA 22030-6044
Telephone: (703) 934-6020, FAX: (703) 591-3049, Web Site: marketing1by1.com
CEO: Keith Wardell
COO: John McCardell
VP Software Devel: Freddy Feliz

Develops marketing automation software solutions.

MARKETING INFORMATION NETWORK

120 N Bryant Ave (Suite A1)
Edmond, OK 73034-6300
Telephone: (405) 516-1215, FAX: (405) 516-1230, Web Site: www.minokc.com
Pres: Scott R. Chilcutt
Founded: 1989

Provides data card content & list research solutions.

MARKETLEVERAGE

Subs. of PrecisionPlay Media, Inc.
701 International Pkwy (Suite 200)
Lake Mary, FL 32746-5624
Telephone: (407) 268-7700, FAX: (407) 268-7654, Web Site: www. precisionplaymedia.com
CEO: Michael Jenkins
Founded: 2004

Internet affiliate marketing network & offers online marketing services.

MARKETNET SERVICES LLC

14998 Cleveland St (Suite E)
Spring Lake, MI 49456-8993
Telephone: (616) 847-7992, FAX: (616) 847-7994, Web Site: www. marketnetservices.com
Pres: J. T. McDonald
Sr VP Sls & Mktg: Steve Sprunger
Founded: 1996

Develops lead management software for clients to capture, respond to, distribute & track leads from all sources.

MELISSA DATA CORP

22382 Avenida Empresa
Rancho Santa Margarita, CA 92688-2112
Telephone: (949) 858-3000, Toll Free: (800) 800-6245, FAX: (949) 589-5211, E-Mail: sales@melissadata. com, Web Site: www.melissadata. com
Founder, CEO & Pres: Raymond Melissa
COO: Gary Van Rockel
Conducts Business: U.S., Canada
Employees: 75
Primary Market Served: Business
Catalog available online
Direct online sales
Founded: 1985

Provides mailing software, databases, programming tools, business and consumer lists, data enhancement and hygiene services.

MERCURY COMMERCE INC

1100 Shames Dr (Suite 200)
Westbury, NY 11590
Telephone: (212) 307-7001, FAX: (646) 219-3982, E-Mail: info@ mercury-commerce.com, Web Site: www.mercury-commerce.com
Pres: Jeff Eisenberg
Conducts Business: U.S.
Primary Market Served: Business
Catalog available online
Indirect online sales
Advertising/Marketing Budget Related to Direct Marketing: 0-25%
Direct Marketing ad budget:
Direct Mail: 97%
Newspapers: 3%
Founded: 1999

Provides custom & web-based integration solutions for bulk-ship & drop-ship supply partners.

THE MERGING TECHNOLOGIES GROUP LLC

175K Commerce Dr
Hauppauge, NY 11788-3920
Telephone: (631) 435-2955, FAX: (631) 952-0664, E-Mail: info@mt-group.com, Web Site: www.mt-group.com
Primary Market Served: Business
Founded: 1997

IT solutions provider.

MERKLE INC

7001 Columbia Gateway Dr
Columbia, MD 21046-2289
Telephone: (443) 542-4000, Toll Free: (877) 9MERKLE, FAX: (443) 542-4758, Web Site: www.merkleinc.com
Chmn & CEO: David S. Williams
CFO & Exec VP: Jean Holder
Exec VP Quantitative Mktg & Pres Merkle APAC: Zhengda Shen
Pres Response Svcs: Bill Sayre
Employees: 785
Founded: 1971
Gross sales or billing: $27,000,000

Operates as a customer relationship marketing agency.

MICROSOFT CORP

RP-NFOA
1 Microsoft Way
Redmond, WA 98052-8300
Telephone: (425) 882-8080, FAX: (425) 936-8000, Web Site: www. microsoft.com/msft
CEO: Satya Nadella

Microsoft Corporation develops, manufactures, licenses, sells & supports software products.

MILLIONS BY MARKETING INC

88 E Main St (Suite 338)
Mendham, NJ 07945-1832
Telephone: (973) 222-0011, Web Site: www.millionsbymarketing.com
CEO: Greg Morris

Provides marketing solutions for your organization & are dedicated to outsourcing a full suite of marketing services.

MINDFIREINC

30 Corporate Park (Suite 400)
Irvine, CA 92606-5133
Telephone: (949) 474-4418, Web Site: www.mindfireinc.com
VP: Joseph Manos
Primary Market Served: Consumer

Marketing automation for agencies and marketing servicesproviders.

MYRIAD SYSTEMS INC

2627 E-I-44 Service Rd
Oklahoma City, OK 73111-8302
Telephone: (405) 478-9000, Toll Free: (866) 505-1730, FAX: (405) 478-8315, E-Mail: sales@myriadsystems. com, Web Site: www.myriadsystems. com
Pres: Charles Riney
Founded: 2005

US based software outsourcing company that focuses on highly qualitative, timely delivered & cost-effective software development & testing services.

NEAT CO

1601 Market St (Suite 3500)
Philadelphia, PA 19103-2301

Telephone: (215) 382-3300, Toll Free: (866) 632-8732, FAX: (215) 386-2536, Web Site: neatco.com
Chmn & CEO: Jeff Dickerson
CFO: Dan Doyle
Sr VP Product Mngmt: Harris Somanoff
Primary Market Served: Consumer
Founded: 2002

Provides scanners, cloud services & other solutions to accountants, real estate agents, small business owners, legal companies, insurance & other industries.

NEOLANE
275 Washington St (Floor 3)
Newton, MA 02458-1611
Telephone: (617) 467-6760, FAX: (617) 467-6701, Web Site: www.neolane.com
CEO, Pres & Dir: Stephane Dehoche
Co-Pres & Dir: Gilles Queru
CFO: Michael Lerendu
Founded: 2006

Provides enterprise marketing software.

NETPROSPEX INC
318 Bear Hill Rd
Waltham, MA 02451-1095
Toll Free: (888) 826-4877, E-Mail: sales@netprospex.com, Web Site: www.netprospex.com
Chmn & Co-Founder: Gary Halliwell
CEO: Michael C Bird
CFO: Thomas "Tom" C Rauker
Chief Mktg Officer: Derek Slayton
VP Mktg: Maribeth Ross
Primary Market Served: Business & Consumer
Founded: 2006

Provides contact data to sales & marketing professionals.

NEXTMARK INC
Partnered with Adslot limited
33 S Main St (fl 3)
Hanover, NH 03755-2048
Telephone: (603) 643-1307, FAX: (603) 643-1662, Web Site: www.nextmark.com
Founder, Chmn Bd, CEO & Pres: Joseph Pych
Dir Opers: John Swindell
Founded: 1999

Provides technology solutions for media planning, operations & sales.

NEXXLINX (HQ)
3565 Piedmont Rd NE (Bldg 2, Suite 100)
Atlanta, GA 30305-8204

Telephone: (770) 250-0349, Toll Free: (877) 747-0658, Web Site: www.nexxlinx.com
Chmn & CEO: Craig Mento
VP Sls: William I. Coffeen III
Chief Mktg Officer: Doug Morgan
A business communication solution provider.

NFOCUS CONSULTING INC
1594 Hubbard Dr
Lancaster, OH 43130-8124
Telephone: (740) 654-5809, Toll Free: (800) 675-5809, FAX: 740 654-0934, Web Site: www.nfocusconsulting.com
Pres: Douglas Cronin
Founded: 1989

Data and technology company hosting some of the largest compiled databases in the country, creating scalable solutions for your direct marketing needs & budget.

NORTH AMERICAN MAILING TECHNOLOGIES INC
141 B Buford Dr
Lawrenceville, GA 30045-4926
Telephone: (770) 962-5833
Owner/Operator: Cassandra Lee
Primary Market Served: Business & Consumer

NORTHERN RESPONSE (INTERNATIONAL) LTD
50 Staples Ave, Richmond Hill
Toronto, ON, Canada L4B 0A7
Telephone: (905) 737-6698, Toll Free: (866) 584-1694, FAX: (905) 737-0099, E-Mail: general@nresponse.com, Web Site: www.shopnorthern.com
Owner: Richard Stacey
Founded: 1984

O2 CONSULTING INC
7760 Landowne Dr
Atlanta, GA 30350-1064
Telephone: (404) 384-3990
Pres: Timothy Olzer
Founded: 2010

OLD VINE MARKETING
147 Old Vine Way
Napa, CA 94558-7028
Telephone: (707) 694-9647, E-Mail: info@oldvinemarketing.com, Web Site: www.oldvinemarketing.com
Owner: Steven Bowden

Founded: 2006

Addresses the demand for more sophisticated & effective direct marketing strategies for the wine industry.

OMEDA
555 Huehl Rd
Northbrook, IL 60062-2336
Telephone: (847) 564-8900, FAX: (847) 564-1203, Web Site: www.omeda.com
Pres: Aaron Oberman
Founded: 1980

Provides online outsourced integrated database management & email marketing services.

OPIN SYSTEMS INC
7900 International Dr (Suite 410)
Minneapolis, MN 55425-8900
Telephone: (952) 567-2444, Toll Free: (800) 888-1804, FAX: (651) 994-7828, E-Mail: judywy@opin.com, Web Site: www.opin.com
CEO: Ray Pinson
Assoc Dir Mktg: Judy Wise
Founded: 1986

ORACLE DATA CLOUD
10075 Westmoor Dr (Suite 105)
Broomfield, CO 80021-2570
Toll Free: (800) 633-0738, E-Mail: thedatahotline@oracle.com, Web Site: cloud.oracle.com
Gen Mgr: Omar Tawakol
CEO & Pres: Eric Roza
Primary Market Served: Business

Provider of consumer data used to inform and measure marketing.

THE OYSTER GROUP
33 Thorne Ave (Unit 2)
Dartmouth, NS, Canada B3B 2E7
Toll Free: (877) 405-4858, E-Mail: fdrinnan@theoystergroup.ca, Web Site: www.theoystergroup.ca
Founder & CEO: Faith Drinnan

PC CONNECTION
Route 101A, 730 Milford Rd
Merrimack, NH 03054-4631
Telephone: (603) 683-2167, Toll Free: (800) 800-0014, FAX: (603) 683-5773, E-Mail: pr@pcconnection.com, Web Site: www.pcconnection.com, macconnection.com
Pres & CEO: Timothy McGrath
Sr VP Corp Mktg & Creative Svcs: David Beffa-Negrini
Sr VP Treas & CFO: Jack Ferguson
Sr VP HR: Bradley Mousseau
Corp Communs: Lynn McKensie
Conducts Business: U.S., Canada, Europe

Employees: 1,000
Primary Market Served: Business &
Consumer
Catalog available online
Direct online sales
Founded: 1982

Provider of a full range of information
technology solutions to business, government & education markets.

PNT MARKETING SERVICES, INC

2420 Jackson Ave
Long Island City, NY 11101-4323
Telephone: (718) 433-4063, Toll Free:
(888) 768-2210, FAX: (914) 428-
0504, E-Mail: tony@
pntmarketingservices.com, Web Site:
www.pntmarketingservices.com
Co-CEO: Tony Coretto
Partner: Phil Jarymiszyn
Dir Client Svcs: Adam Isler
CTI: Michael Zeoli
Mktg & Engagement Mgr: Erin Frank-
lin
Conducts Business: U.S.
Employees: 20
Primary Market Served: Business
Indirect online sales
Advertising/Marketing Budget Related
to Direct Marketing: 0-25%
Direct Marketing ad budget: $20,000
Direct Mail: 25%
Online: 75%
Founded: 1988
Gross sales or billing: $3,900,000

PNT provides marketing support services (database marketing, data mining
& analytics, list management, technology support & strategy consulting) to
the financial services & other industries.

PTC

140 Kendrick St (Suite C120)
Needham, MA 02494-2743
Telephone: (781) 370-5000, Toll Free:
(877) 275-4782, Web Site: www.ptc.
com
Pres & CEO: James E. Heppelman
Exec VP & Chief Mktg Officer: Char-
lie Ungashick
Founded: 1982

Direct marketer of a wide range of information technology products & services, including computer systems,
software & peripheral equipment, networking communications, system con-
figuration, and repair.

PACIFICEAST

4900 SW Griffith Dr (Suite 251)
Beaverton, OR 97005-2977

Toll Free: (800) 665-8400, Web Site:
www.pacificeast.com
CEO: Garth Froese
Primary Market Served: Business &
Consumer

Empowers businesses with consumer,
customer and business information.

PARKER SOFTWARE

4767 New Broad St
Orlando, FL 32814
Toll Free: (800) 680-7712, Web Site:
www.parker-software.com
CEO: Stephen Parker
Fin Dir: Julia Parker
Tech Dir: Daniel Tallentire
Primary Market Served: Business &
Consumer
Founded: 2003

Develops innovative software aimed at
online companies.

PARTNERS MARKETING INC

1750 E Main St (Suite 10)
Saint Charles, IL 60174-2363
Telephone: (630) 524-9901, FAX:
(630) 524-9909, E-Mail: georgeb@
partnersmarketing.com, Web Site:
www.partnersmarketing.com
VP, Opers: Jerry Jones
EVP & Gen Mgr: George Bardenheier
Jr.
Conducts Business: U.S., Canada
Primary Market Served: Consumer
Founded: 1992

Marketing consulting with expertise for
marketing projects and services to ex-
pecting, new and experienced parents.

PEACHTREE DATA INC

2905 Premiere Pkwy (Suite 200)
Duluth, GA 30097-5275
Telephone: (678) 987-4600, Web Site:
www.peachtreedata.com
Pres: Richard West
Primary Market Served: Business &
Consumer
Founded: 1994

Line of business includes providing
computer processing & data preparation services.

PEAK COMPUTER SYSTEMS

Div of Peak Communications Inc
6400 W Main St (Suite 1A)
Belleville, IL 62223
Telephone: (618) 398-5612, E-Mail:
info@peaknet.net, Web Site: www.
peaknet.net
Pres: Grant Wuller

PEGG NADLER ASSOCIATES INC

400 E 77th St (Suite 16b)
New York, NY 10075-2337
Telephone: (212) 861-0846, E-Mail:
pegg@peggnadler.com
Pres: Pegg Nadler
Primary Market Served: Business

Marketing and Advertising

PERFORMANCE DIRECT INC

3525 Piedmont Rd
Atlanta, GA 30305-1530
Telephone: (678) 608-2820, Toll Free:
(800) 869-2300, FAX: (404) 869-
2547, E-Mail: info@performancede.
com
Pres & CEO: Carter S.D. Taylor

Marketing & consulting services.

PHOENIX DATA PROCESSING LLC

One Oak Hill Center (Suite 301)
Westmont, IL 60559-5540
Telephone: (630) 654-4400, FAX:
(630) 654-4470, E-Mail: sales@
phoenixdataprocessing.com, Web
Site: www.phoenixdataprocessing.
com
CEO Telematch: Peg Kuman
Brand Develop Dir: Scott Johnson
Founded: 1982

Provides data processing, analytics, &
database services to the direct marketing industry.

PHOENIX TECHNOLOGIES LTD

910 E Hamilton Ave (Suite 110)
Campbell, CA 95008-0612
Telephone: (408) 570-1000, Toll Free:
(800) 677-7305, FAX: (408) 570-
1001, Web Site: www.phoenix.com
CEO & Pres: Richard J. Geruson
Founded: 1979

Designs, develops & supports core system software/personal computers basic
input-output system products for computing devices.

PITNEY BOWES SOFTWARE SYSTEMS

One Elmcroft Rd
Stamford, CT 06926-0700
Telephone: (203) 356-5000, Toll Free:
(800) 624-5377, FAX: (203) 351-
7336, Web Site: www.pitneybowes.
com
Pres & CEO: Marc Blautenbach

Sells & finances, rents & services integrated mail & document management
systems.

PLURIS INC
550 Cochituate Rd (Suite 7)
Framingham, MA 01701-4600
Telephone: (508) 663-1100, FAX:
(508) 663-1060, E-Mail: info@
plurismarketing.com, Web Site:
www.plurismarketing.com
Co-Founder, CEO & Dir: Michael Caccavale
Primary Market Served: Consumer
Founded: 2001

Offers direct marketing, analytics &
strategy, marketing enablement, offer
management, digital messaging & media
measurement services.

PORTRAIT INTERNATIONAL INC
Subs. of Pitney Bowes Inc
125 Summer St (Floor 16)
Boston, MA 02110-1636
Telephone: (617) 457-5200, Web Site:
www.portraitsoftware.com
Exec VP: Mark Smith

POSSIBLENOW INC
4400 River Green Pkwy
Duluth, GA 30096-8316
Telephone: (770) 255-1020, FAX:
(770) 255-1025, Web Site: www.
dncsolution.com
Founder, CEO & Pres: Scott Frey
COO: Rick Stauffer
Founded: 2000

Provides customer engagement & enterprise
preference management solutions.

PRECISION PLAY MEDIA / MARKETLEVERAGE
701 International Pkwy (Suite 200)
Lake Mary, FL 32746-5624
Telephone: (407) 805-8800, Web Site:
www.precisionplaymedia.com
CEO: Michael Jenkins

PREMIERE GLOBAL SERVICES INC
3280 Peachtree Rd NE (Suite 1000)
Atlanta, GA 30305-2451
Telephone: (404) 262-8400, Toll Free:
(800) 546-1541, FAX: (404) 262-
8540, Web Site: www.pgi.com
Chmn & CEO & Founder: Boland
Jones
Pres: Theodore P. Schrafft
Chief Tech Officer: David M. Guthrie
Primary Market Served: Business &
Consumer
Catalog available online

Indirect online sales
Provide audio teleconferencing services,
blast faxing & fax-on-demand, automated
recording replay programs, as
well as training & educational consultants.

PRIMENET
Subs. of Journal Communications
2100 Palmetto St (Suite A)
Clearwater, FL 33765-2101
Telephone: (651) 405-4000, FAX:
(651) 405-4100, Web Site: www.
pnms.com
Pres & Owner: Mark Keefe
Founded: 1962

Certified full-service direct marketing
company that provides integrated online
& print direct marketing services
for Fortune 500 companies & regional
& local businesses.

PRIORITY DATA SYSTEMS INC
5035 S 110th St
Omaha, NE 68137-2376
Telephone: (402) 592-2550, Toll Free:
(877) 273-7774, FAX: (402) 592-
5052, E-Mail: sales@pdomaha.com,
Web Site: www.priority-data.com
Dir Bus Devel: John Dunn
Founded: 1979

Provides proprietary rating solutions &
information management services in
the U.S.

PROFESSIONAL ADVERTISING SYSTEMS INC
200 Business Park Dr (Suite 304)
Armonk, NY 10504-1751
Telephone: (914) 765-0500, FAX:
(914) 765-0503, E-Mail: info@
paslists.com, Web Site: www.
paslists.com
Pres: Eric Raskin
Founded: 2000

Provides Guiding Eyes for the Blind
with expert computer services.

PROFESSIONAL MARKETING ASSOCIATES
405 W Fairmont Dr
Tempe, AZ 85282-2007
Telephone: (480) 829-0131, FAX:
(480) 829-9202, Web Site: www.
pmafulfillment.com
Pres: Chris Roth
Founded: 2003

PROFIT CENTER SOFTWARE INC
50 Charles Lindbergh Blvd

Uniondale, NY 11553-3626
Telephone: (516) 414-6300, Toll Free:
(888) 446-6240, FAX: (516) 414-
6304, E-Mail: jmarrah@profitcenter.
com, Web Site: www.profitcenter.
com
Pres & CEO: John Marrah
Exec VP Prod Devel: Matthew Ehrlich
Sr VP Customer Svc: Gloria Tyson
Exec VP Application Devel: Solomon
Niyazov
VP Sls: Peter Steinle
Conducts Business: U.S. & Canada
Advertising/Marketing Budget Related
to Direct Marketing: 76-100%
Founded: 2002

Engages in the design, development,
sales, implementation & support of
Web-based business automation solutions
for multichannel direct marketing
companies.

PROMOTIONAL PRODUCTS FULFILLMENT & DISTRIBUTION LTD
80 William Smith Dr
Whitby, ON, Canada L1N 9W1
Telephone: (905) 668-5060, Toll Free:
(800) 263-4678, FAX: (905) 668-
1195, E-Mail: sales@ppfd.com, Web
Site: www.ppfd.com
CEO: Gilbert Kee
Founded: 1986

Positioned to execute traditional marketing
programs while still embracing
the electronic revolution.

PUBLISHERS COMPUTER CORP
209 Main St
New Milford, NJ 07646-1733
Telephone: (201) 261-3700, FAX:
(201) 261-9110, E-Mail: mail@
publisherscomputer.com, Web Site:
www.publisherscomputer.com
Pres: Andrew Johnston

QED MARKETING INC
570 Research Pl
Central Islip, NY 11722-4415
Telephone: (631) 851-4254
Pres: Peter Muzzy
Primary Market Served: Business &
Consumer

Data Processing Services.

QMSI
5800 Ager Beswick Rd
Montague, CA 96064-9423
Telephone: (530) 459-0910, Web Site:
www.quintmail.com

QUAERO CORP
1930 Camden Rd (Suite 2060)
Charlotte, NC 28203-5900
Telephone: (704) 414-0200, FAX:
(704) 414-2195, Web Site: www.
quaero.com
Founder, CEO & Pres: Naras Eecham-
badi
Exec VP & Mng Dir Mktg Performace
Mngmt: Lane Michel
Founded: 1999

Interactive media & entertainment
company, providing various marketing
& customer engagement agency services.

RAPID PROGRESS MARKETING & MODELING LLC
1760 Delaware Ave NE
Saint Petersburg, FL 33703-5439
Telephone: (727) 528-8578, Web Site:
www.rpmsquared.com
Pres: Scott Terry

Specialize in providing our clients with
consulting, planning & strategy development, cutting-edge modeling, internet & direct marketing services,
databases & state-of-the-art professional training courses.

RARITAN INC
400 Cottontail Ln
Somerset, NJ 08873-1238
Telephone: (732) 764-8886, FAX:
(732) 764-8887, Web Site: www.
raritan.com
Chmn & CEO: Ching-I Hsu
VP Fin: Joe Delong
Founded: 1985

Develops & delivers power management, infrastructure management, & se-
rial solutions for data centers of various
sizes in the U.S. & internationally.

REACHFORCE
2711 W Anderson Ln (Suite 200)
Austin, TX 78757
Telephone: (844) 254-5405, E-Mail:
info@reachforce.com, Web Site:
www.reachforce.com
CEO: Bob Riazzi
Conducts Business: U.S.
Primary Market Served: Business
Founded: 2005

Provider of B2B marketing data quality
management services.

REALDATA SERVICES INC
322 Van Dorn Dr
Glenwood Springs, CO 81601-9524
Telephone: (970) 945-2456, FAX:
(970) 945-5356, E-Mail: rick@
realdataservices.com, Web Site:
www.realdataservices.com
VP: Rick Hilleary

RELEVATE GROUP INC
6883 Commercial Dr
Springfield, VA 22159-0310
Telephone: (703) 658-8300, Toll Free:
(800) 523-7346, FAX: (703) 658-
8301, E-Mail: sales@relevategroup.
com, Web Site: www.relevategroup.
com
Dir Opers: Carolyn Tate
CEO & CFO: Steven Rao
Chief Tech Officer: Noreen Thomas
VP Database Info Tech: Jarom Hagen
Founded: 1979

Relevate builds, manages & analyzes
data in order to provide behavioral targeting & data driven solutions. Solutions include Telematch phone append,
database marketing & campaign management, data enhancement, proprietary new mover & auto owner data,
merge/purge, modeling & analytics &
email append & solutions.

RENKIM CORP
13333 Allen Rd
Southgate, MI 48195-2216
Telephone: (734) 374-8300, FAX:
(734) 374-9165, E-Mail: info@
renkim.com, Web Site: www.renkim.
com
CEO: Kevin Gaffer
Founded: 1982

Provides print & mail solutions for collection letters, automotive leasing &
loan billing, health care billing & cred-
it/financial billing.

RESPONSE MANAGEMENT TECHNOLOGIES INC
aka RMT
2550 9th St (Suite 103)
Berkeley, CA 94710-2516
Telephone: (510) 843-8180, FAX:
(510) 843-8020, E-Mail: info@
respmgt.com, Web Site: www.
respmgt.com
Pres: Julie Weidenbach

RETURN PATH INC
3 Park Ave S (Floor 41)
New York, NY 10016-5902
Telephone: (212) 905-5500, FAX:
(212) 905-5501, Web Site: www.
returnpath.biz
Co-Founder, Chmn & CEO: Matthew
Blumberg
Co-Founder & Pres: George Bilbrey
CFO: Lisa A. Mogensen

Founded: 1999

Provides Email intelligence solutions
that provide brands with data-driven insights, commercial applications and expertise to maximize inbox placement
and impact & protect their users &
brands.

REYNOLDS & REYNOLDS CO
One Reynolds Way
Kettering, OH 45430-1586
Telephone: (937) 485-2000, Toll Free:
(800) 883-3031, FAX: (866) 268-
5407, Web Site: www.reyrey.com
Founder, Chmn & CEO: Robert Brock-
man
Pres: Ron Lamb
Founded: 1866

Delivers the software, business forms
and supplies & professional services
that support all areas of automotive retailing for car dealers & automakers.

RIGDEN INC
PO Box 17187
Boulder, CO 80308-0187
Telephone: (303) 442-8190, FAX:
(303) 442-8686, E-Mail: rigden@
rigden.com, Web Site: www.rigden.
com
Pres: James Jobson

RUF STRATEGIC SOLUTIONS
1533 E Spruce St
Olathe, KS 66061-3698
Telephone: (913) 782-8544, Toll Free:
(800) 829-8544, FAX: (913) 782-
0150, Web Site: www.ruf.com
Founder: Jacob F. Ruf
Founded: 1976

Database marketing company, designs
& delivers marketing & business intelligence solutions to organizations.

SAS INSTITUTE
100 SAS Campus Dr
Cary, NC 27513-2414
Telephone: (919) 677-8000, FAX:
(919) 677-4444, Web Site: www.sas.
com
Chmn Bd, CEO & Pres: Dr. James H.
Goodnight
Primary Market Served: Business &
Consumer

Provides business analytics software &
services to the business intelligence
market.

SBDP CORP
4208 Airport Rd
Cincinnati, OH 45226-1646

Telephone: (513) 871-7019, FAX: (513) 871-0134, E-Mail: info@sbdp.com, Web Site: www.sbdp.com
Pres: William R. Fryer
Founded: 1971

Provides accurate timely & simple solutions to the direct mail marketplace.

SPSS INC
200 W Madison St (Suite 2300)
Chicago, IL 60606-3416
Telephone: (312) 651-3000, Toll Free: (800) 543-2185, FAX: (312) 651-3668, E-Mail: sales@spss.com, Web Site: www.spss.com
Pres: Sabine Schlig

Develops & markets integrated statistical software.

SAGE DIRECT INC
3400 Raleigh Ave SE
Grand Rapids, MI 49512-2042
Telephone: (616) 940-8311, Toll Free: (800) 729-8310, FAX: (616) 940-3383, E-Mail: sageinc@sagedirect.com, Web Site: www.sagedirect.com
Pres: Gary Sage
VP: Pamela Sage

Provides a wide array of mailing, marketing, document processing & database services to companies & organizations throughout North America, including hundreds of banks & credit unions.

SALFORD SYSTEMS
9685 Via Excelencia (Suite 208)
San Diego, CA 92126-7500
Telephone: (619) 543-8880, FAX: (619) 543-8888, Web Site: www.salford-systems.com
Founder & Pres: Dr. Dan Steinberg
Primary Market Served: Business & Consumer
Founded: 1983

Specializes in providing new generation data mining & choice modeling software & consultation services.

SATURN CORP
4701 Lydell Rd
Hyattsville, MD 20781-1117
Telephone: (301) 772-7000, Toll Free: (800) USA-0090, FAX: (301) 386-4538, E-Mail: sales@saturncorp.com, Web Site: www.saturncorp.com
CEO & Pres: Fielding Yost
Dir New Bus Devel: Opal Scott
Founded: 1981

Develops & offers online constituent relationship management or database management solutions for organiza-

tions with various chapters, regional offices, international offices, & affiliate databases.

SAVICOM
44 Montgomery St (Suite 1600)
San Francisco, CA 94104-4703
Telephone: (415) 983-0990, FAX: (415) 445-9999, E-Mail: sales@savicom.net, Web Site: www.savicom.net
CEO: Ted Bernard
VP Worldwide Sls: Patrick B. Scoggin
Employees: 28
Primary Market Served: Business
Founded: 1996
Gross sales or billing: $6,500,000

Hosts web based list management and e-mail delivery services to marketers, agencies, and publishers.

SAVVIS INC
1 Savvis Pkwy
Town and Country, MO 63017-5827
Telephone: (314) 628-7000, Toll Free: (800) 728-8471, FAX: (703) 667-6298
Supvr Mktg: Vincent DiMemmo

SCIENTIFIC COMPUTING ASSOCIATES CORP
212 Lathrop Ave
River Forest, IL 60305-2121
Telephone: (708) 771-4567, FAX: (708) 771-4569, E-Mail: sca@scausa.com, Web Site: www.scausa.com
Branch Mgr: Ching-Tl Liu

Statistical software developer & consulting services provider.

SERVICE NET WARRANTY LLC
650 Missouri Ave
Jeffersonville, IN 47130-3081
Telephone: (812) 258-4700, Toll Free: (812) 258-4722, FAX: (812) 258-4693, Web Site: www.servicenet.com
CEO: Kevin Callahan
CFO: Wayne Schwertley
Exec VP Sls: Greg Gadbois
Primary Market Served: Consumer
Founded: 1996

Delivers warranty and service solutions to manufacturers and retailers worldwide.

SHEPARD'S INC
32 Henry St
Bethel, CT 06801

Telephone: (203) 830-8300, Toll Free: (800) 243-0993, FAX: (203) 794-1296, E-Mail: mleahy@shepardsinc.com, Web Site: www.shepardsinc.com
Pres: Michael Goodman
VP: Michael Leahy
Founded: 1900

Full service logistics company that offers a wide array of scalable solutions, from transportation to order fulfillment.

SISK FULFILLMENT SERVICE INC
1900 Industrial Park Dr, Box 463
Federalsburg, MD 21632-2667
Telephone: (410) 754-8141, FAX: (410) 754-8223, Web Site: www.siskfulfillment.com
Pres: John Phillips

Provides order fulfillment solutions.

SMARTFOCUS INC
545 5th Ave (Rm 1000)
New York, NY 10011-4650
Telephone: (425) 460-1000, (646) 356-1169, Web Site: www.smartfocus.com
CEO: Rob Mullen
Chief Mktg Officer: Jess Stephens

Experience in personalization marketing intelligence & business strategy.

SOFTREK CORP
30 Bryant Woods N
Amherst, NY 14228-3601
Telephone: (716) 691-2800, Toll Free: (800) 442-9211, FAX: (716) 691-2828, Web Site: www.softrek.com
Dir Bus Devel: Steven Birnbaum
VP: Bob Girardi
Dir Client Solutions: Sherry Blum
Founded: 1987

Provides donor management software, and online fundraising and decision support tools for nonprofit organizations.

SOFTWARE MARKETING ASSOCIATES INC
1086 Elm St (Suite 200)
Rocky Hill, CT 06067-2341
Telephone: (860) 721-8929, FAX: (860) 257-9679, E-Mail: sma@sma-promail.com, Web Site: www.sma-promail.com
Exec VP: Denise S. Lunden
Founded: 1981

Custom computer programming services industry.

SPECTRUM DATA
131 N 3rd St

Oregon, IL 61061-1410
Telephone: (815) 732-6567, FAX:
(815) 732-7035
Owner: David Murray
Owner: Ed Messenger
Primary Market Served: Business &
Consumer
Founded: 1989

Direct marketing company.

STIBO SYSTEMS
3550 George Busbee Pkwy NW (Suite
350)
Kennesaw, GA 30144-2122
Telephone: (770) 425-3282, FAX:
(770) 425-3012, Web Site: www.
stibocatalog.com
Pres: Andreas Lorenzen
Sr VP Bus Devel: Charlie Lawhorn
Founded: 1976

Develops master data management
(MDM) solutions to gather, manage,
publish, and share product information
and digital assets.

STOCKTON INC
8341 Beechcraft Ave
Gaithersburg, MD 20879-1509
Telephone: (301) 527-1550, FAX:
(301) 527-1503, E-Mail: info@
stocktoninc.com, Web Site: www.
stocktoninc.com
Pres: Stephen Strack

STRATEGIC DATA
INTELLIGENCE LLC
555 Skokie Blvd (Suite 255)
Northbrook, IL 60062-2812
Telephone: (847) 897-5707, FAX:
(847) 897-5715, E-Mail: info@
sdintelligence.com, Web Site: www.
sdintelligence.com
CEO & Principal: Michael Brostoff
Bus Mgr: Irene Diehl
Conducts Business: U.S.
Primary Market Served: Business
Founded: 2007

Data hygiene for direct and email companies. Develop, maintain and host
marketing databases, call center solutions.

STRATEGIC SOFTWARE
SYSTEMS LLC
1508 Willow Lawn Dr (Suite 111)
Richmond, VA 23230-3421
Telephone: (804) 288-8827x110, Web
Site: www.sss1.com
Mng Partner: William Hungerford
Primary Market Served: Business &
Consumer
Founded: 1994

Data warehousing for banks & marketers.

SUBSCRIBERMAIL LLC
3333 Warrenville Rd (Suite 530)
Lisle, IL 60532-4551
Telephone: (630) 303-5000, FAX:
(630) 303-5100, Web Site: www.
subscribermail.com
Founder, CEO & Pres: Jordan Ayan
Founded: 2001

Email marketing services provider.

SUNGARD COMPUTER
SERVICES
Div. of Sungard Data Systems
680 E Swedesford Rd
Wayne, PA 19087
Telephone: (484) 582-5673, E-Mail:
GetInfo@SunGard.com, Web Site:
www.sungard.com
Pres & CEO: Russell Fradin

Provides software & processing solutions for financial services, education
& the public sector.

SUNTEL INC
2321 Whitney Ave (Suite 401A
Hamden, CT 06518-3541
Telephone: (203) 287-9114, FAX:
(203) 248-3883, E-Mail: info@
suntelinc.com, Web Site: www.
suntelinc.com
Mgr: Sachin Parikh

SUPPORT SERVICES CORP
69 Daniels Pkwy (Suite 29-252)
Fort Myers, FL 33901
Telephone: (239) 332-5300, FAX:
(239) 332-4555, E-Mail: s.ward@ss-
corp.com, Web Site: www.ss-corp.
com
Pres: Stephen Ward

Provides everything any marketer
could need for Direct Marketing List
Management, List Acquisition, Mapping, Data Processing, & Database
Marketing Services.

SYBASE INC
1 Sybase Dr
Dublin, CA 94568-7976
Telephone: (925) 236-5000, FAX:
(925) 236-4321, Web Site: www.
sybase.com/product/datawarehousing
Sr VP & Gen Mgr North America Re-
gion: Jay Foreman
Exec Officer: James S. Wambach
Primary Market Served: Consumer
Founded: 1984

Provides enterprise data base management, business intelligence & analytics,
and mobile messaging solutions for individual & corporate customers in the
United States & internationally.

TEC MAILING SOLUTIONS,
LLC
712 Lois Dr
Sun Prairie, WI 53590-1100
Telephone: (608) 825-8525, Toll Free:
(866) 379-9437, FAX: (608) 825-
8526, E-Mail: info@tecmailing.com
Pres: Brian Euclide
Mgr Info Tec: Mark Henry

Service provider to the mailing and distribution industries.

TABLEAU SOFTWARE
837 N 34th St (Suite 200)
Seattle, WA 98103-8965
Telephone: (206) 633-3400, FAX:
(206) 633-3004, Web Site: www.
tableausoftware.com
Chmn, CEO & Co-Founder: Christian
Chabot
CFO: Thomas "Tom" Walker
Chief Mktg Officer: Elissa Fink
Primary Market Served: Consumer

Offers analytics software.

TECHNEKES LLC
1927 S Tryon St (Suite 310)
Charlotte, NC 28203-4688
Telephone: (704) 342-2900, FAX:
(704) 342-2975, Web Site: www.
technekes.com
Pres & COO: Steve Amedio
Founded: 2000

Line of business includes performing
commercial business, marketing, opinion & other economic research.

TECHNISERVE INC
2065 Livernois Rd
Troy, MI 48083-1737
Telephone: (248) 989-0100, FAX:
(248) 989-0111, E-Mail: info@
techni-serve.com, Web Site: www.
techni-serve.com
CEO & CFO: Nancy Gardner
Pres & CTO: Kim Schooley
Primary Market Served: Business &
Consumer

Provides software and services that
support customers' core business functions.

TELEPHONE LOOK-UP
SERVICE CO
301 Oxford Valley Rd (Suite 304B)
Yardley, PA 19067-7709
Telephone: (215) 321-0706, Toll Free:
(800) 366-0706, FAX: (215) 321-
3229, E-Mail: computer@
telephonelookup.com, Web Site:
www.telephonelookup.com
Pres: Michael W. Schoedler

Founded: 1975
Telephone solicitation services.

TELETECH
9197 S Peoria St
Englewood, CO 80112-5833
Telephone: (303) 397-8100, Toll Free: (800) TELETECH, FAX: (303) 397-8199, E-Mail: solutions@TeleTech.com, Web Site: www.teletech.com
CEO: Kenneth Tuchman

Customer management, business-process & database-marketing solutions.

TERADATA CORP
10000 Innovation Dr
Miamisburg, OH 45342-4927
Telephone: (937) 242-4800, Web Site: www.teradata.com
Solutions Mktg VP: Sam Gragg
Primary Market Served: Business & Consumer

Sells analytic data platforms, applications & related services.

THELAW.NET CORP
6640 Lusk Blvd (Suite A205)
San Diego, CA 92121-2777
Telephone: (858) 554-0583, Web Site: www.thelaw.net
Pres: Mark Whitney

THOMSON TAX & ACCOUNTING
7322 Newman Blvd
Dexter, MI 48130
Toll Free: (800) 968-8900, FAX: (734) 426-3750, E-Mail: jack.larue@thomson.com, Web Site: www.cs.thomson.com
Sr VP: Jack LaRue
Founded: 1979

Professional tax & accounting software & solutions for accountants & tax professionals.

3COM CORP
350 Campus Dr
Marlborough, MA 01752-3082
Telephone: (508) 323-5000, FAX: (508) 323-1111
Exec VP, CEO H3C & COO H3C: Shusheng Zheng
VP Corp Branding & Communs: Catherine Derr
Founded: 1979

Develops enterprise networking solutions worldwide.

TIME CUSTOMER SERVICE INC
A Time Warner Co
One N Dale Mabry Hwy
Tampa, FL 33609-2700
Telephone: (813) 878-6100, Toll Free: (800) 723-NCOA, FAX: (813) 878-6452, Web Site: www.timecustomerservice.com
Pres: Tim Adams

Provides fulfillment services such as stock acquisition & management, publisher statement creation & promotion analysis.

TOMTOM NORTH AMERICAN
Subs. of Sony Corp of America
11 Lafayette St
Lebanon, NH 03766-1445
Telephone: (603) 643-0330, Toll Free: (800) 331-7881, FAX: (603) 653-0249, Web Site: www.tomtom.com
Chief Admin Officer: George Bremser
Founded: 1983

Provides digital map data & traffic information for business & consumer applications.

THE TOTAL MAILING SYSTEM
551 Mid-Atlantic Pkwy
West Deptford, NJ 08066
Telephone: (856) 628-8800, FAX: (856) 628-8810, Web Site: www.ttms.com
Pres.: Robert Powell
Founded: 1983

TOUCH-BASE COMPUTING
PO Box 213
Silver Creek, GA 30173
Telephone: (706) 378-0964, E-Mail: sales@touchbase.com, Web Site: www.touchbase.com
Pres: Philip Boylan
VP Special Mktg: Keith Camille

TRINITY TECHNICAL GROUP, INC
2118 Royal Dominion Court
Arlington, TX 76006-4836
Telephone: (817) 879-7907, E-Mail: info@trinitytechnicalgroup.com, Web Site: www.trinitytechnicalgroup.com
COO: Ben F. Bruce
Primary Market Served: Business & Consumer

TRUSTE
835 Market St (Suite 800)
San Francisco, CA 94103-1905
Telephone: (415) 520-3490, FAX: (415) 520-3420, Web Site: www.truste.org
VP Mktg: Dave Deasy

Founded: 1997
Online privacy solutions provider

TYPE-A-SCAN INC
39 W 19th St (fl 7)
New York, NY 10011-4251
Telephone: (212) 367-8406, FAX: (212) 691-8134, E-Mail: info@typeascan.com, Web Site: www.typeascan.com
Founded: 1966

Dynamic & technically advanced organization providing a host of direct marketing services.

UAA CLEARINGHOUSE
6912 N 97th Cir
Omaha, NE 68122-1010
Telephone: (402) 991-2810, Web Site: www.uaaclearinghouse.com
Pres: Mark Shada
Contact: Bill Meyer

Provides the direct mail industry with a practical solution for reducing the cost & waste associated with undeliverable as addressed mail.

V12 DATA
2319 Oak Myrtle Ln (#104)
Wesley Chapel, FL 33544
Telephone: (813) 960-7800, FAX: (813) 960-7811, E-Mail: info@v12data.com, Web Site: www.v12data.com
Pres & Bd Member: Anders Ekman
Exec VP: Scott Busby
VP Tech Svcs: Brent Cosgrove
Primary Market Served: Business & Consumer
Founded: 1978

Offers a variety of software solutions designed to address the data quality and business intelligence issues of the marketplace.

VALID USA INC
Subs. of Valid SA
1011 Warrenville Rd (Suite 450)
Lisle, IL 60532
Telephone: (630) 852-8200, Toll Free: (855) 825-4387, E-Mail: info@validusa.com, Web Site: www.validusa.com
VP Mktg Opers: Marty Kurpiel
Gen Mgr: Chuck Wittenmeyer
Conducts Business: Worldwide
Primary Market Served: Business
Founded: 2012

Provides solutions for data, payments, identity, mobile & targeted brand messaging.

VERATAD TECHNOLOGIES LLC
500 Frank W Burr Blvd (Suite 14)
Teaneck, NJ 07666-6802
Telephone: (201) 510-6000, FAX: (201) 510-6036, Web Site: www. veratad.com
Mng Dir: John E. Ahrens
Conducts Business: U.S.
Employees: 8
Primary Market Served: Business
Direct online sales
Advertising/Marketing Budget Related to Direct Marketing: 0-25%
Direct Marketing ad budget:
Direct Mail: 60%
Magazines: 5%
Telephone: 35%
Founded: 2002

Specializing in age and identity authentication, online tools, resourcing billions of public and government records with results in seconds. Volume pricing available.

VISION SOLUTIONS
15300 Barranca Pkwy
Irvine, CA 92618
Telephone: (949) 253-6500, Toll Free: (800) 683-4667, FAX: (949) 253-6501, E-Mail: info@visionsolutions. com, Web Site: www. visionsolutions.com
Pres & CEO: Nicolaas Vlok
Founded: 1990

Provides cloud protection and recovery high availability, disaster recovery, migration, virtual machine protection, & cross-platform data sharing solutions for Windows, Linux, AIX, IBM Power Systems & cloud computing for small and midsize businesses.

VOLT DELTA
Subs. of Volt Information Svcs
1 Sentry Pkwy E (Suite 6000)
Blue Bell, PA 19422-2310
Telephone: (610) 825-7720, FAX: (610) 567-5698, Web Site: www. voltdelta.com
CEO: Robert Pines

WEB DECISIONS
303 Pisgah Church Rd (Suite 2A)
Greensboro, NC 27455-2756
Telephone: (336) 545-7817 x100
CEO: Kim Addington
Chief Mktg Officer: Scott Ashby
Primary Market Served: Business

Database driven marketing solutions.

WENNSOFT
1970 S Calhoun Rd
New Berlin, WI 53151-2214

Telephone: (262) 821-4100, FAX: (262) 821-3838, Web Site: www. wennsoft.com
CEO: John G. Jazwiec
Founded: 1995

Provides solutions to automate & optimize business processes in organizations.

WESTERN DIGITAL CORP
3355 Michelson Dr (Suite 100)
Irvine, CA 92612-5694
Telephone: (949) 672-7000, FAX: (949) 672-7837, Web Site: www. westerndigital.com
Pres & CEO: Stephen "Steve" D. Milligen

Global provider of solutions for the collection, storage, management, protection & use of digital content, including audio and video.

WHEATON GROUP
201 Bolinas Ct
Chapel Hill, NC 27517-8344
Telephone: (919) 969-8859, FAX: (425) 675-6014, E-Mail: jim. wheaton@wheatongroup.com, Web Site: www.wheatongroup.com
Principal: Cynthia Wheaton
Principal: Jim Wheaton
Principal: Boris Gendelev
Principal: Leo Sterk
Conducts Business: U.S.
Employees: 6
Primary Market Served: Business & Consumer
Founded: 2000

Builds and maintains marketing databases. Specializes in data mining and direct and database marketing consulting.

WILAND DIRECT
6309 Monarch Park Pl (Suite 201)
Longmont, CO 80503-7198
Telephone: (303) 485-8686, Web Site: www.wilanddirect.com
CEO & Pres: Phillip Wiland
CFO: Michael Gaffney
Founded: 2004

Operates as a marketing intelligence company serving companies & organizations in the U.S.

WILSON, HUGH & ASSOCIATE CONSULTANTS LTD
Four Long Bridge Rd
Thornhill, ON, Canada L4J 1L5
Telephone: (905) 764-5312
Pres: Hugh Wilson

LG WILSON & ASSOCIATES
14 N Chatsworth Ave (Suite 5J)
Larchmont, NY 10538-2103
Telephone: (914) 649-5928, E-Mail: lisa@lgwilson.com, Web Site: www. lgwilson.com
Pres: Lisa Wilson

Provides strategic fundraising solutions that combine relationship marketing, creative development & information technology.

WINDOW BOOK INC
300 Franklin St
Cambridge, MA 02139-3781
Telephone: (617) 395-4500, Toll Free: (800) 524-0380, FAX: (617) 395-5900, E-Mail: sales@windowboo. com, Web Site: www.windowbook. com
CEO & Founder: Jeffrey Peoples
Founded: 1988

Providing computer programming services.

WIRED ASSETS DATA CORP
284 Riversville Rd
Greenwich, CT 06831-3253
Telephone: (203) 340-2316, Web Site: www.wiredassets.com
Pres & CFO: Dean Eaker

WOODEN COMPUTER SERVICES
13358 Windbrooke Ln
Saint Louis, MO 63146-2224
Telephone: (314) 576-1124
Pres: Roger Wooden
Founded: 1994

XMPIE INC
485 Lexington Ave (fl 10)
New York, NY 10017-2652
Telephone: (212) 479-5166, FAX: (212) 888-2061, Web Site: www. xmpie.com
Co-Founder Chmn, Pres & CEO: Dr Jacob Aizikowitz
Founded: 2000

Provides data publishing software that unites customer databases & creative content to help print service providers, creatives/designers, marketing service firms & small-to-medium sized businesses.

XEROX SERVICES
2828 N Haskell Ave
Dallas, TX 75204-2909
Telephone: (214) 841-6111, Toll Free: (800) 275-9376, Web Site: www.acs-inc.com

Chmn Bd & CEO: Ursula M. Burns M.
  Burns
Pres Xerox Services: Lynn Blodgett
Chief Mktg Officer: Christa Carone

Provides BPO & IT outsourcing to
commercial, non-profit organizations
& government agencies.

YANKELOVICH INC
400 Meadowmont Village Cir (Suite
  431)
Chapel Hill, NC 27517-7505
Telephone: (919) 932-8600, FAX:
  (919) 932-8629, Web Site: www.
  yankelovich.com
CFO: Jim Cain
Founded: 1958

Provides generational marketing consulting services, with specialty in market research & analysis, segmentation
& consulting solutions.

YOUSENDIT INC
1919 S Bascom Ave (fl 3)
Campbell, CA 95008-2220
Telephone: (408) 879-9118, Web Site:
  www.yousendit.com

ZIRCON CO INC
67 Aurora Ln
Salem, MA 01970-6803
Telephone: (978) 741-7000, FAX:
  (978) 532-0012
Pres: Curtis B. Flory III
Founded: 1973

Providing turnkey vendors, computer
systems.

ZOOM INFORMATION INC
dba ZoomInfo
307 Waverley Oaks Rd
Waltham, MA 02452
Telephone: (781) 693-7500, FAX:
  (781) 693-7510, Web Site: www.
  zoominfo.com
Founder, CEO & Chief Scientist & Dir:
  Yonatan Stern
CFO: Steven D. Hill
VP, Engrng: Eugenia Gillan
Chief Tech Officer: Leo Laferriere
VP Bus Devel: Don Wynns

Provides business-to-business (B2B)
data and business information solutions
for customers in sales, marketing, recruiting, or other businesses.

List Brokers & Compilers (23) — Geographic Index

ARIZONA

Best Mailing Lists Inc, 7507 E Tanque Verde Rd, Best Mailing Lists Inc, Tucson, 85715-3667

Healthy Offers Inc, 10799 N 90th St (Suite 200), Scottsdale, 85260

CALIFORNIA

Avrick Direct Inc, PO Box 1449, Goleta, 93116-1449

Byrum & Fleming, 321 San Anselmo Ave, San Anselmo, 94960-2647

Carney Direct Marketing, 15510 Rockfield Blvd (Suite A), Irvine, 92618-2792

Computerized Research & Development Inc, 1708 Maple Grove Ln, Lincoln, 95648

Direct List Technology Inc, 1582 N Batavia St (Suite 3), Orange, 92867-3544

DS Direct Response, 5314 Palos Verdes Blvd, Torrance, 90505

Homeowners Marketing Services Inc, 12444 Victory Blvd (Floor 2), North Hollywood, 91606-3156

Infocore Inc, 5973 Avenida Encinas (Suite 218), Carlsbad, 92008

InfoMat Inc, 21171 S Western (Suite 260), Torrance, 90501

List Alliance Inc, 3000 Danville Blvd (Suite 519), Alamo, 94507

List Pro of America, 3089-C Clairemont Dr (Suite 267), San Diego, 92117-6802

List Team, 22287 Mulholland Hwy (Suite 408), Calabasas, 91302

ListGIANT, 2475 Townsgate Rd (Floor 1), Westlake Village, 91361

ListSource, 40 Pacifica (Suite 900), Irvine, 92618

Martin Worldwide Inc, 638 Lindero Canyon Rd (Suite 200), Oak Park, 91377

Names in the News, 1890 Grand Ave (Suite 1365), Oakland, 94612

NetHawk Interactive, 1255 Park Ave (Suite D), Emeryville, 94608-3679

Peppermill Marketing Inc, 8335 W Sunset Blvd (Suite 246), Los Angeles, 90069-1529

SK&A, 2601 Main St (Suite 650), Irvine, 92614-4228

George Sterne Agency Inc, 747 S Mission Rd (Suite 2200), Fallbrook, 92088

COLORADO

Data-Dynamix Inc, PO Box 140118, Denver, 80214-0118

Datahouse Inc, 2153 Sable Chase Dr, Colorado Springs, 80920

I-Behavior Inc, 2051 Dogwood St (Suite 220), Louisville, 80027-3042

MailGraphics Inc, 1668 Valtec Ln (Suite F), Boulder, 80301-4635

CONNECTICUT

Andrew Associates Inc, 6 Pearson Way, Enfield, 06082

Evergreen Marketing, 2 Corporate Dr (Suite 945), Shelton, 06484

Gelderman Group Inc, 19 Junction Rd, Brookfield, 06804

Key Marketing Advantage LLC, 7 Edmund Rd (Suite 100), Newtown, 06470-1632

Macromark Inc, 39 Old Ridgebury Rd (Suite 23), Danbury, 06810

Market Data Retrieval, 6 Armstrong Rd (Suite 301), Shelton, 06484

Pont Media Direct, 10 E Meadow Ln, Norwalk, 06851-2902

RMI Direct Marketing Inc, 44 Old Ridgebury Rd (Plz 1), Danbury, 06810-5107

Sound Beach Marketing Partners LLC, Two Rocky Point Rd, Old Greenwich, 06870

Statlistics, 51-53 Kenosia Ave, Danbury, 06810

DISTRICT OF COLUMBIA

Commonwealth Lists, 1615 L St NW (Suite 1000), Washington, 22036

List America, 1832 Connecticut Ave NW, Washington, 20016

Packer List Inc, 612 E Capitol St NE, Washington, 20003

FLORIDA

AccuData Integrated Marketing, 5220 Summerlin Commons Blvd (Suite 200), Fort Myers, 33907-2150

Alesco Data Group LLC, 5276 Summerlin Commons Way (Suite 703), Fort Myers, 33907-2159

Alliance Strategies Group Inc, 7700 Congress Ave (Suite 3115), Boca Raton, 33487

American Database Marketing Inc, 12627 San Jose Blvd (#603), Jacksonville, 32223-8642

BB Direct Inc, 2503 Del Prado Blvd (Suite 504), Cape Coral, 33904

Computermail South Inc, 200 Second Ave S (Suite 160), Saint Petersburg, 33701-4313

The Data Group, 425 S Avalon Park Blvd, Orlando, 32828-6703

Dresden Direct Inc, 109 Saint Edward Pl, Palm Beach Gardens, 33418-4606

Dunhill International List Co Inc, 6400 Congress Ave (Suite 1750), Boca Raton, 33487-2898

Gulf Coast List Service, 16350 Bruce B Downs Blvd (#47645), Tampa, 33646

Kroll Direct Marketing Inc, 3914 Netherlee Way, Wellington, 33449

Leadcreations.com LLC, 12717 W Sunrise Blvd (Suite 312), Fort Lauderdale, 33323

List Source Direct, 55 SE 2nd Ave, Delray Beach, 33444

ListAbility Inc, 20845 Loggia Ct, Venice, 34293

LISTS Inc, 2950 Halcyon Ln (Suite 401), Jacksonville, 32223

Mastermailer Inc, 3700 N 29th Ave (Suite 203), Hollywood, 33020-1019

MetaResponse Group Inc, 700 W Hillsboro Blvd (Suite 4-107), Deerfield Beach, 33441-1619

Nexxa Group Inc, 12734 Kenwood Ln (Suite 87), Fort Myers, 33907-5638

Political Resources Inc, PO Box 1403, Lake Worth, 33460-1403

SalesLeads.tv Inc, 2701 NW 2nd Ave (Suite 213), Boca Raton, 33431

Worldata, 3000 N Military Trl, Boca Raton, 33431-6321

GEORGIA

Alpha List Marketing Inc, 4880 Lower Roswell Ave (Suite 165), Box 512, Marietta, 30068-5611

A Caldwell List Co Inc, 3295 River Exchange Dr (Suite 380), Norcross, 30092-4238

Capitol Hill Lists LLC, 1668 Rambling Rill Cir, Statham, 30666

Dirmark Group Inc, 75 Long Cir, Roswell, 30075

Equifax Online Marketing, 1550 Peachtree St NE, Atlanta, 30309-2402

Goldleaf Data Inc, 5400 Laurel Springs Pkwy (Suite 104), Suwanee, 30024-6060

Homeowner Data Services Inc, 1424 N Brown Rd (Suite 400), Lawrenceville, 30043-8107

MSNI Inc, 70 Mansell Ct (Suite 100), Roswell, 30076-4857

TouchPoint Data Solutions Inc, 13010 Morris Rd (Bldg 1, Suite 600), Alpharetta, 30004

ILLINOIS

American Hotel Register Co, 100 S Milwaukee Ave Ste 100, Vernon Hills, 60061-4321

American Student Marketing LLC, 430 Park Ave, Highland Park, 60035-2638

Cross Marketing USA, 1310 N Ritchie Ct (Suite 16-C), Chicago, 60610-8401

Direct Response Services, 111 Northlane Dr, Glen Carbon, 62034

Farm Market iD, 170 Quail Ridge Dr, Westmont, 60559

GlaserDirect Inc, 800 Roosevelt Rd (Bldg B, Suite 200), Glen Ellyn, 50137-5839

Infutor Data Solutions, One Lincoln Center, 18W140 Butterfield Rd (Suite 1020), Oakbrook Terrace, 60181

MNI, 1633 Central St, Evanston, 60201-1505

MSI List Marketing, 738 E Dundee Rd (Suite 321), Palatine, 60074-2858

Marketing Economics Inc, 1636 N Wells (#3112), Chicago, 60614-6023

Midwest Lists & Media Ltd, 9333 N Milwaukee Ave, Niles, 60714

Tri-Media Marketing Services Inc, 3330 Old Glenview Rd (Suite 2), Wilmette, 60091-2963

INDIANA

Harris Marketing Inc, 6100 N Keystone Ave (Suite 427), Indianapolis, 46220-2428

IOWA

HR Direct Inc, 508 N 2nd St, Fairfield, 52556-2464

KANSAS

Midwest Direct Marketing Inc, 501 N Webster, Spring Hill, 66083

KENTUCKY

American Clearinghouse Inc, 2201 Plantside Dr, Louisville, 40299-1940

MARYLAND

All American List Corp, 8903 Presidential Pkwy (Suite 201), Upper Marlboro, 20772

Mary Elizabeth Granger & Associates Inc, 110 West Rd (Suite 235), Baltimore, 21204-2343

Namebank, 1001 Cathedral St, Baltimore, 21201

National Fundraising Lists, 16900 Science Dr (Suite 210), Bowie, 20715-4412

The Right Lists Ltd, 305 Beckwith St, Gaithersburg, 20878-5603

MASSACHUSETTS

Act One Lists, 237 Washington St (Floor 2), Marblehead, 01945-3334

Advantage List Marketing Inc, 780 Marshall St, Holliston, 01746-1438

Commercial Mailing Lists, 26 Carver Rd, Framingham, 01701-4493

Direct Channel Inc, 234 W Center St Ste 2, West Bridgewater, 02379-1633

Healy List Marketing, 153 Andover St (Suite 108A), Danvers, 01923-1450

Intelitec, 154 Taylor St, Granby, 01033-9526

MGM Mailing Lists, Ten Leslin Ln, South Sandwich, 02563

MICHIGAN

Advertising That Works, 6375 Westmoor Rd, Bloomfield Hills, 48301-1360

MISSOURI

Crosslists Cross & Co, PO Box 230, Lone Jack, 64070

MCH Strategic Data, 601 E Marshall St, Sweet Springs, 65351-9613

Sorkins Inc, PO Box 411067, Saint Louis, 63141

NEBRASKA

ACTON International Ltd, 5760 Cornhusker Hwy (Suite 2), Lincoln, 68507-3121

B2BAdvantage, 1020 E 1st St, Papillion, 68046

CAS Inc, 10303 Crown Point Ave, Omaha, 68134-1061

Cole Information Services, 17041 Lakeside Hills Plz (Suite 2), Omaha, 68130-4677

Compass Ventures, 808 P St (Suite 300), Lincoln, 68508-1383

Hugo Dunhill Mailing Lists Inc, 11211 John Galt Blvd, Omaha, 68137

First Direct Inc, 1508 J F Kennedy Dr (Suite 103), Bellevue, 68005-6611

InfoUSA, 1020 E 1st St, Papillion, 68046

Infogroup Media Solutions, 1020 E 1st St, Papillion, 68046

US Data Corp, 17310 Wright St (Suite 100), Omaha, 68130

NEVADA

Collins List Exchange Inc, 2312 N Green Valley Pkwy (Suite 2922), Henderson, 89014-3118

Exhibitrac Direct Marketing, 1930 Village Center Cir (Suite 3-637), Las Vegas, 89134

NEW HAMPSHIRE

F1rstMark Inc, 25 Vintinner Rd, Campton, 03223

Market Street Lists Inc, 7 Pleasant St, PO Box 850, Exeter, 03833-0850

NEW JERSEY

ALC Inc, 750 College Rd E (Suite 201), Princeton, 08540

Borelli Direct Marketing Inc, PO Box 5085, Kendall Park, 08824-5085

Conrad Direct Inc, 300 Knickerbocker Rd, Cresskill, 07626-1350

Dataline Inc, 5 Vaughn Dr (Suite 307), Princeton, 08540-6313

Ethnic Technologies LLC, 600 Huyler St (Suite 5), South Hackensack, 07606-1734

Focus USA Inc, 95 N State Route 17, Paramus, 07652

Global DM Solutions Inc, 416 Main St, Boonton, 07005-1714

Jamax Direct LLC, 375 Sylvan Ave (Suite 2), Englewood Cliffs, 07632-2714

List Service Direct Inc, 2 Christie Heights St, Leonia, 07605-2233

NCRI List Management, 455 Sylvan Ave, Englewood Cliffs, 07632-2703

Redi-Data Inc, 5 Audrey Pl, Fairfield, 07004-3401

Specialists Marketing Services Inc, 777 Terrace Ave (Suite 401), Hasbrouck Heights, 07604

Splashnet Inc, 20 Gloria Ln, Fairfield, 07004

Trinity Direct LLC, 10 Park Pl (Bldg 5), Butler, 07405

Vision Marketing Inc, 455 Sylvan Ave, Englewood Cliffs, 07632-2703

NEW YORK

ASL Marketing Inc, 2 Dubon Ct, Farmingdale, 11735-1008

Adpress Inc, 135 E 54th St (Penthouse F), New York, 10022-4539

AmeriList Inc, 40 Ramland Rd S (Suite 203B), Orangeburg, 10962

Belardi/Ostroy, 39 Broadway (Floor 32), New York, 10006

Complete Mailing Lists LLC, 190 E Post Rd, White Plains, 10601

Contact Marketing LLC, 228 Park Ave S, New York, 10003-1502

CoverClicks Media Inc, 817 Broadway (Floor 5), New York, 10003-4709

Directory of Major Malls Inc, PO Box 837, Nyack, 10960-0837

Donnelley Marketing, 2 Blue Hill Plz (Suite 1662), Pearl River, 10965-3115

DunnData Co, 2022 Rte 22 S, Patterson Business Park E, Brewster, 10509-5946

Eclipse Direct Marketing, 173 Mineola Blvd (Suite 402), Mineola, 11501-2555

Leon Henry Inc, 200 N Central Ave (Suite 220), Hartsdale, 10530-9915

Horizon Lists, 13 N Rockland (Suite 4), Congers, 10463

Hotline List Corp, 1071 Ave of the Americas, New York, 10018

Infinite Media Concepts Inc, 190 E Post Rd, White Plains, 10601-4912

JF Direct Marketing Inc, 34 Beach Rd, Ossining, 10562

LS Direct Marketing, 4 Suffern Pl, Suffern, 10901

Lake Group Media Inc, 1 Byram Brook Pl, Armonk, 10504

LeadGen Media Group LLC, 1324 Forest Ave (Suite 401), Staten Island, 10302-2044

List Advisor Inc, 500 Bi County Blvd (Suite 125), Farmingdale, 11735-3996

List Strategies Inc, 244 Madison Ave (Suite 1950), New York, 10016-2817

Mazzone Marketing Group LLC, PO Box 40536, Brooklyn, 11204-0536

MeritDirect, 2 International Dr, Rye Brook, 10573

Net 60 LLC, 228 Park Ave S (Suite 83872), New York, 10003-1502

PMX Agency, 5 Hanover Sq, New York, 10004-2614

Research & Response International Inc, 250 W 57th St (Suite 1326), New York, 10107-1309

Rickard Squared, 190 Motor Pkwy (Suite 103), Hauppauge, 11788-5159

SIE (Select Information Exchange), 175 W 79th St, New York, 10024

3 Gen Co, 544 Empire Blvd, Brooklyn, 11225

USADATA Inc, 477 Madison Ave (Suite 1220), New York, 10022-5839

Fred Woolf List Co Inc, PO Box 346, Somers, 10589-0346

NORTH CAROLINA

The Book of Lists, 120 W Morehead St (Suite 100), Charlotte, 28202-1854

FJ Associates LLC, PO Box 12771, Wilmington, 28405-0138

Multimedia Lists Inc, Asheville

Roseberry Direct List Management & Brokerage, 265 Timberline Trl, Elon, 27244-8088

OHIO

Matt Brown & Associates Inc, 707 Miamisburg-Centerville Rd (Suite 227), Dayton, 45459

Hippo Direct, PO Box 391313, Solon, 44139

List Marketing Group Inc, 19885 Detroit Rd (Suite 207), Cleveland, 44116-1815

PENNSYLVANIA

IDR Marketing Partners LLC, 1125 Lancaster Ave Ste 2, Berwyn, 19312-2601

Listmasters Direct Mail Services, 10300 Drummond Rd, Philadelphia, 19154

MarketForce Corp, 101 W Eagle Rd (Suite 284), Havertown, 19083-2244

Neighborhood Greetings, 6951 Allentown Blvd (Suite D), Harrisburg, 17112

Paramount Lists Inc, 3126 Peach St, Erie, 16508-2734

WS Ponton Inc, 3030 William Pitt Way, Pittsburgh, 15238

SWAT Marketing Team, 433 S Broad St, PO Box 464, Grove City, 16127

SOUTH CAROLINA

Rein Associates LLC, 209 Waltrip St (Unit 5), Conway, 29526-8384

TENNESSEE

Altair Customer Intelligence, 341 Cool Springs Blvd, Franklin, 37067

Beach List Direct Inc, 4605 Villa Green Dr, Nashville, 37215-4331

Triax Data Inc, 8911 Linksvue Dr, Knoxville, 37922-5254

TEXAS

AccuList Inc, 258 Ceremonial Ridge, San Antonio, 78260-6444

Fred E Allen Inc, 2726 W Ferguson, Mount Pleasant, 75455-6516

AllMedia Inc, 1400 Preston Rd (Suite 400), Plano, 75093

American Direct Marketing Services Inc, 14800 Landmark Blvd (Suite 190), Dallas, 75254-6900

Business Extension Bureau, 4802 Travis St, Houston, 77002-9740

Hometown Mailing Lists & Direct Mail, 6119 Greenville Ave (Suite 169), Dallas, 75206

Manning Media International, 2128 Surrey Ln, McKinney, 75070

Market Approach Consulting Services LP, 111 E Center St, Lorena, 76655-9651

Names in the Mail Inc, 10710 Shiloh Rd, Dallas, 75228-2640

TKLi, 3700 Standridge Dr (Suite 210), The Colony, 75056-4149

UTAH

American Name Services Inc, 774 South 400 East, Orem, 84097

VERMONT

New England List Services Inc, 171 Mountain View Dr, Danville, 05828-9641

VIRGINIA

All-n-One List Marketing Inc, PO Box 862, Fishersville, 22939-0862

American Mailing Lists Corp, 9625 Surveyor Ct (Suite 400), Manassas, 20110

Atlantic List Company Inc, 2300 9th St S (Suite 301), Arlington, 22204-2345

Carol Enters List Co Inc, 9663-C Main St, Fairfax, 22032

GreatLists.com, PO Box 623, Herndon, 20172

IDM Inc, 11951 Freedom Dr (Suite 400), Reston, 20190-5686

Infocus Marketing Inc, 4245 Sigler Rd, Warrenton, 20187-3940

Omega List Co, 1420 Spring Hill Rd (Suite 490), McLean, 22102-3028

Pinnacle List Co, 2800 Shirlington Rd (Suite 970), Arlington, 22206-3613

Response Unlimited, 284 Shalom Rd, Waynesboro, 22980-7349

Robertson Mailing List Co, 113 E Market St (Suite 300), Leesburg, 20176

TMA Direct Inc, 2000 Edmund Halley Dr (Suite 250), Reston, 20191

Washington Lists Inc, 6849 Old Dominion Dr (Suite 320), McLean, 22101

WASHINGTON

Compact Information Systems, 7120 185th Ave NE (Suite 150), Redmond, 98052-0576

Mailing Lists Plus Inc, 13104 SE Newport Way, PMB 203, Bellevue, 98006

Marketry Inc, 4122 Factoria Blvd SE (Suite 400), Bellevue, 98006-4275

WISCONSIN

McCarthy Media Group Inc, 1088 Stonewood Crossing, Sun Prairie, 53590-4405

CANADA

British Columbia

JR Direct Response International Inc, 201-4841 Delta St, Delta, V4K 2T9

JS Direct Address Ltd, 1429 Dominion St (#203), North Vancouver, V7J 1B4

Ontario

Fixed Address Marketing Inc, 136 Pinnacle Tr, Aurora, L4G 7G7

InfoCanada, 1290 Central Pkwy W (Suite 500), Mississauga, L5C 4R9

List Brokers & Compilers (23)

ALC INC
750 College Rd E (Suite 201)
Princeton, NJ 08540
Telephone: (609) 580-2800, Toll Free:
(800) 252-5478, FAX: (609) 580-
2888, E-Mail: info@alc.com, Web
Site: www.alc.com
CEO: Donn Rappaport
Mktg Mgr: Susan Rappaport
Conducts Business: U.S.
Primary Market Served: Business
Founded: 1978

Direct & digital data marketing services provider.

ASL MARKETING INC
2 Dubon Ct
Farmingdale, NY 11735-1008
Telephone: (516) 248-6100, FAX:
(516) 248-6364, E-Mail: info@
aslmarketing.com, Web Site: www.
aslmarketing.com
Fin Dir: Andrew Belth
Pres: Steven Stolls
Pres & CEO: Janice Kaye
Primary Market Served: Business &
Consumer
Founded: 2012

Direct marketing company specializing in student marketing data.

ACCUDATA INTEGRATED MARKETING
Div. of Compact Information Systems
5220 Summerlin Commons Blvd (Suite 200)
Fort Myers, FL 33907-2150
Telephone: (239) 425-4400, Toll Free:
(800) 732-3440, FAX: (239) 425-
4401, E-Mail: info@accudata.com,
Web Site: www.accudata.com
Pres: Bree Verrengia
Media Rels: Denise Abbattista
Pres: Nate Petel
Sr Dir Product Mktg: Dustin Williams
Dir Mktg: Karen Blanchard

Fully integrated marketing solutions company.

ACCULIST INC
dba AccuList USA
258 Ceremonial Ridge
San Antonio, TX 78260-6444
Telephone: (210) 807-9940, Toll Free:
(877) 505-8747, FAX: (210) 494-
5478, E-Mail: sales@acculistusa.
com, Web Site: www.acculistusa.
com
Pres & Founder: David Kanter
Info Servs Mgr: Jon Buckley
Conducts Business: Canada, U.S.
Primary Market Served: Business

Founded: 1988
List and insert media broker.

ACT ONE LISTS
237 Washington St (Floor 2)
Marblehead, MA 01945-3334
Telephone: (781) 639-1919, Toll Free:
(800) 228-5478, FAX: (781) 639-
2733, E-Mail: info@act1lists.com,
Web Site: www.actonelists.com
Pres & CEO: Steven Cushinsky
Primary Market Served: Business
Founded: 1993

Full-service mailing, telephone, fax, and email list broker, manager & compiler.

ACTON INTERNATIONAL LTD
5760 Cornhusker Hwy (Suite 2)
Lincoln, NE 68507-3121
Telephone: (402) 905-9566, E-Mail:
info@acton.com, Web Site: www.
acton.com
CEO: Frank Lambert
CEO: Kraig Prange
Conducts Business: Worldwide
Primary Market Served: Business
Founded: 1975

Full-service direct marketing agency specializing in managed data solutions.

ADPRESS INC
135 E 54th St (Penthouse F)
New York, NY 10022-4539
Telephone: (212) 679-1710, FAX:
(212) 532-9508, E-Mail:
adpressinc@aol.com, Web Site:
www.adpressinc.com
Pres: Bill Meyer

ADVANTAGE LIST MARKETING INC
780 Marshall St
Holliston, MA 01746-1438
Telephone: (508) 429-4400, FAX:
(508) 429-7117, E-Mail: markm@
advantagelist.com, Web Site: www.
advantagelist.com
Pres: Mark J. Murphy
Primary Market Served: Business &
Consumer
Founded: 1989

Direct mail and email list provider.

ADVERTISING THAT WORKS
6375 Westmoor Rd
Bloomfield Hills, MI 48301-1360

Telephone: (248) 757-2878, FAX:
(248) 626-2264, Web Site: www.
advthatworks.com
Pres & Owner: Steven Bartley
Conducts Business: U.S.
Primary Market Served: Business &
Consumer
Founded: 1986

Direct mail sales lead compiler specializing in home sales, mortgages and name recordings.

ALESCO DATA GROUP LLC
5276 Summerlin Commons Way (Suite 703)
Fort Myers, FL 33907-2159
Telephone: (239) 275-5006, Toll Free:
(800) 701-6531, FAX: (239) 275-
7737, E-Mail: lists@alescodata.com,
Web Site: www.alescodata.com
CEO: Michael Sklorenko
CEO: Paul Theriot
Primary Market Served: Business
Founded: 2001

Integrated direct marketing services company providing mailing lists, marketing data and related services for direct mail, email, telemarketing & voice messaging campaigns.

ALL AMERICAN LIST CORP
Div. of DirectMail.com
8903 Presidential Pkwy (Suite 201)
Upper Marlboro, MD 20772
Telephone: (301) 420-5760, Toll Free:
(888) 690-2252, FAX: (301) 420-
5765, E-Mail: info@allamericanlist.
com, Web Site: www.allamericanlist.
com
Pres: Robert Salta
Principal: Kirk Swain
Primary Market Served: Business &
Consumer

Email, business & consumer lists brokerage company.

ALL-N-ONE LIST MARKETING INC
PO Box 862
Fishersville, VA 22939-0862
Telephone: (703) 717-5621, FAX:
(703) 286-5418, E-Mail: info@
allinonelistmarketing.com, Web Site:
www.allinonelistmarketing.com
Pres: Greg Sholes
Primary Market Served: Business

Full-service list brokerage & management company specializing in Christian, Evangelical, Conservative and other religious lists.

FRED E ALLEN INC
2726 W Ferguson
Mount Pleasant, TX 75455-6516
Telephone: (903) 572-1701, FAX:
(903) 572-1703
Pres: Fred Allen
Primary Market Served: Business

Mail list broker & manager.

ALLIANCE STRATEGIES GROUP INC
7700 Congress Ave (Suite 3115)
Boca Raton, FL 33487
Telephone: (561) 499-3201, E-Mail:
info@asgroupinc.com, Web Site:
www.asgroupinc.com
Mng Member: Bryan G Rudnick
Partner: David J Thompson
Primary Market Served: Business &
Consumer

Provides marketing support services,
including list rentals, for conservative
causes.

ALLMEDIA INC
1400 Preston Rd (Suite 400)
Plano, TX 75093
Telephone: (469) 467-9100, FAX:
(214) 291-5431, E-Mail: brokerage@
allmediainc.com, Web Site: www.
allmediainc.com
Pres: Laura McClendon
VP: Rick Becker
Conducts Business: Worldwide
Primary Market Served: Business &
Consumer
Founded: 1981

Provides targeted media for measurable
results. Account teams provide expert
advice to marketers regarding the purchase and use of email, postal & telemarketing prospect lists & related data
management services. Help clients implement lead generation programs, insert media & online media to meet
marketing goals.

ALPHA LIST MARKETING INC
4880 Lower Roswell Ave (Suite 165),
Box 512
Marietta, GA 30068-5611
Telephone: (404) 995-7049, FAX:
(404) 601-0826
Pres: Judy Kelly
Conducts Business: U.S.
Primary Market Served: Business
Founded: 1991

List brokerage firm.

ALTAIR CUSTOMER INTELLIGENCE
341 Cool Springs Blvd

Franklin, TN 37067
Telephone: (615) 468-6800, Toll Free:
(800) 241-6631, FAX: (615) 468-
6878, E-Mail: asales@altairci.com,
Web Site: www.altairci.com
VP Sls & Mktg: David Hadaway
Pres: Steve Collins
Co-Founder & CFO: Mike Mullican
Employees: 30
Primary Market Served: Business
Direct online sales
Founded: 2001

Marketing services company specializing in data management, analytics and
reporting.

AMERICAN CLEARINGHOUSE INC
2201 Plantside Dr
Louisville, KY 40299-1940
Telephone: (502) 499-4185, Toll Free:
(800) 944-6361
Owner: Renee Jones
Conducts Business: U.S.
Primary Market Served: Business
Founded: 1988

Data mapping, database marketing and
mailing list company.

AMERICAN DATABASE MARKETING INC
12627 San Jose Blvd (#603)
Jacksonville, FL 32223-8642
Telephone: (888) 565-7724, FAX:
(888) 270-4338, E-Mail: admdun@
cs.com, Web Site: www.admlists.
com
Sls Dir: Brant Turner
Primary Market Served: Business &
Consumer
Founded: 1979

List provider for direct mail, telemarketing & email marketing campaigns.

AMERICAN DIRECT MARKETING SERVICES INC
Subs. of Casson Media Group Inc.
14800 Landmark Blvd (Suite 190)
Dallas, TX 75254-6900
Telephone: (214) 634-2361, Toll Free:
(800) 527-5080, FAX: (214) 905-
3829, Web Site: www.dmlist.com
Office Mgr: Mike Casson
Pres: Scott Casson
Primary Market Served: Business &
Consumer
Founded: 1975

Financial services marketing company
specializing in investor leads, investor
lists and affluent consumer lists for direct mail, email, telemarketing & investor relations campaigns.

AMERICAN HOTEL REGISTER CO
100 S Milwaukee Ave Ste 100
Vernon Hills, IL 60061-4321
Telephone: (708) 743-4163, FAX:
(708) 564-5797, Web Site: www.
americanhotel.com
Pres: James Leahy
Mktg Analyst: Lisa Falk

AMERICAN MAILING LISTS CORP
9625 Surveyor Ct (Suite 400)
Manassas, VA 20110
Telephone: (571) 292-5806, FAX:
(571) 292-5807, E-Mail: dorothy@
amlc.info, Web Site: amlc.info.
575elmp01.blackmesh.com
Pres: Richard Viguerie
Primary Market Served: Business &
Consumer
Founded: 1965

Provider of donor lists for Republican,
Conservative and charitable fundraising
campaigns.

AMERICAN NAME SERVICES INC
774 South 400 East
Orem, UT 84097
Telephone: (801) 235-8061, Toll Free:
(800) 434-1851, FAX: (801) 764-
0613, E-Mail: sales@
americannameservices.com, Web
Site: www.americannameservices.
com
Pres: Jill Grammer-Williams
VP Prodn: Jen Langston
VP Sales: Patti Thompson
VP Bus Devel: Jerry Williams
Conducts Business: Worldwide
Primary Market Served: Business
Founded: 1995

Full-service agency specializing in list
brokerage, list management & data
processing.

AMERICAN STUDENT MARKETING LLC
430 Park Ave
Highland Park, IL 60035-2638
Telephone: (847) 432-4329, FAX:
(847) 432-4811, E-Mail: admin@
asmdm.com, Web Site: www.
asmdm.com
VP: Larry Gerber
Primary Market Served: Business
Founded: 1998

Provider of permission-based student
marketing data & campaign management.

AMERILIST INC
40 Ramland Rd S (Suite 203B)
Orangeburg, NY 10962
Telephone: (845) 362-6737, Toll Free:
(800) 457-2899, FAX: (845) 362-
6433, E-Mail: info@amerilist.com,
Web Site: www.amerilist.com
Pres: Ravi Buckredan
Conducts Business: Canada, U.S.
Founded: 2002

Provider of targeted mailing, telemarketing, email lists, data processing, data enhancement, printing & advertising services.

ANDREW ASSOCIATES INC
6 Pearson Way
Enfield, CT 06082
Telephone: (860) 253-0000, FAX:
(860) 253-0007, E-Mail: mmccarthy@andrewdm.com, Web Site:
www.andrewdm.com
Pres & Treas: Judith Knapp
Pres: Graeme Bazarian
Dir Mktg & Bus Devel: Mary McCarthy
Conducts Business: U.S.
Primary Market Served: Business & Consumer

Marketing, advertising & data management company.

ATLANTIC LIST COMPANY INC
2300 9th St S (Suite 301)
Arlington, VA 22204-2345
Telephone: (703) 528-7482, FAX:
(703) 528-7492, E-Mail:
ingridloukota@atlanticlist.com, Web
Site: www.atlanticlist.com
Pres & CEO: Ingrid Loukota
COO: Maia Worden
Conducts Business: U.S.
Primary Market Served: Business

List brokerage & management firm.

AVRICK DIRECT INC
PO Box 1449
Goleta, CA 93116-1449
Telephone: (805) 683-6551, FAX:
(805) 683-6553, E-Mail: doreen@
avrick.com, Web Site: avrickdirect.
com
COO: Doreen Ellen Burk
Conducts Business: Worldwide
Primary Market Served: Business & Consumer
Direct online sales
Founded: 1996

Direct marketing company specializing in data compilation.

BB DIRECT INC
2503 Del Prado Blvd (Suite 504)
Cape Coral, FL 33904
Telephone: (866) 501-6273, FAX:
(239) 573-8764, E-Mail: info@
bbdirect.com, Web Site: www.
bbdirect.com
Owner & List Sls Mgr: Brian Berg
Primary Market Served: Business
Founded: 2003

Provider of mailing lists, database hygiene & integrated direct marketing data.

BEACH LIST DIRECT INC
4605 Villa Green Dr
Nashville, TN 37215-4331
Telephone: (615) 356-1100, E-Mail:
cbeach@beachlistdirect.com, Web
Site: www.beachlistdirect.com
Mng Dir: Clay Beach
Prodn Mgr: Joy Miller
Acctg Mgr: Angie Smith
Conducts Business: U.S.
Primary Market Served: Business & Consumer
Founded: 1994

Direct marketing and data processing services for the mailing list and marketing database industries.

BELARDI/OSTROY
39 Broadway (Floor 32)
New York, NY 10006
Telephone: (212) 924-1300, FAX:
(212) 381-1745, E-Mail: katel@
belardiostroy.com, Web Site:
belardiostroy.com
Chmn & CEO: Andy Ostroy
Pres: Donna Belardi
Conducts Business: U.S.
Primary Market Served: Consumer
Founded: 1997

Multi-channel direct marketing agency specializing in data management, customer acquisition & retention and creative services.

BEST MAILING LISTS INC
7507 E Tanque Verde Rd, Best Mailing
Lists Inc
Tucson, AZ 85715-3667
Telephone: (520) 885-0400, Toll Free:
(800) 692-2378, FAX: (520) 885-
3100, E-Mail: best@bestmailing.
com, Web Site: www.bestmailing.
com
Pres: Karen J Kirsch
VP: Herbert Kirsch
Conducts Business: Worldwide
Employees: 15
Primary Market Served: Business
Founded: 1984

Direct marketing mailing lists & sales leads provider.

THE BOOK OF LISTS
Div. of American City Business Journals
120 W Morehead St (Suite 100)
Charlotte, NC 28202-1854
Telephone: (800) 433-4565, Web Site:
www.bizjournals.com/bizbooks
Gen Mgr: Whitney Shaw
Primary Market Served: Business & Consumer

The Business Journals' annual compilation of the leading buyers, businesses and employers in more than 60 of the U.S.'s most dynamic markets.

BORELLI DIRECT MARKETING INC
PO Box 5085
Kendall Park, NJ 08824-5085
Telephone: (732) 940-1500, E-Mail:
joe@borellidirect.com, Web Site:
www.borellidirect.com
Owner: Joe Borelli
Conducts Business: U.S.
Primary Market Served: Business & Consumer
Founded: 2006

List brokerage for direct mail, email & telemarketing campaigns.

MATT BROWN & ASSOCIATES INC
707 Miamisburg-Centerville Rd (Suite 227)
Dayton, OH 45459
Telephone: (937) 434-3949, Toll Free:
(800) 233-3949, FAX: (937) 434-
6272, E-Mail: mba@mbalists.com,
Web Site: www.mbalists.com
Pres: Bernice Willis
Primary Market Served: Business & Consumer
Founded: 1987

Direct marketing services company specializing in direct mail, email, mobile & telemarketing.

B2BADVANTAGE
Div. of Infogroup Inc
1020 E 1st St
Papillion, NE 68046
Telephone: (402) 836-5683, E-Mail:
info@b2b-advantage.com, Web Site:
www.b2b-advantage.com
Pres & CEO: Joe Tropeano
Conducts Business: U.S.
Primary Market Served: Consumer
Founded: 2012

Database marketing company specializing in helping marketers through the use of transactional modeled data.

BUSINESS EXTENSION BUREAU

4802 Travis St
Houston, TX 77002-9740
Telephone: (713) 528-5568, Toll Free: (800) 969-5568, FAX: (713) 528-1648, E-Mail: ronr@bebtexas.com, Web Site: bebtexas.com
Pres & CEO: Ron Royall
VP Sales: Ro Royall
Conducts Business: U.S.
Primary Market Served: Business
Founded: 1960

Full-service mail marketing services company.

BYRUM & FLEMING

321 San Anselmo Ave
San Anselmo, CA 94960-2647
Telephone: (415) 457-1700, Toll Free: (800) 850-1711, E-Mail: hilary@byrumfleming.com, Web Site: www.byrumfleming.com
Partner: Robert Fleming
Customer Svc: Hilary Doyle
Conducts Business: U.S.
Primary Market Served: Business & Consumer
Founded: 1995

List management & brokerage firm.

CAS INC

10303 Crown Point Ave
Omaha, NE 68134-1061
Telephone: (402) 964-9998, Toll Free: (866) 461-4693, FAX: (402) 963-2103, E-Mail: sales@cas-online.com, Web Site: www.cas-online.com
Pres: Jared M. Wright
Exec VP: Joe Evans
CEO: JoAnn Mitchell
Pres: Scott Swanson
Primary Market Served: Business
Founded: 1981

Database marketing products and services company.

A CALDWELL LIST CO INC

3295 River Exchange Dr (Suite 380)
Norcross, GA 30092-4238
Telephone: (770) 662-0255, Toll Free: (800) 241-7425, FAX: (770) 662-0351, E-Mail: guidance@caldwell-list.com, Web Site: www.caldwell-list.com
Pres: Cheslie Lachnicht
Conducts Business: U.S.
Primary Market Served: Business

Mail list broker.

CAPITOL HILL LISTS LLC

1668 Rambling Rill Cir
Statham, GA 30666

Telephone: (770) 725-9596, E-Mail: grant@capitolhilllists.com, Web Site: capitolhilllists.com
Pres: Paul Kilgore
Primary Market Served: Business

List brokerage, management and data services company.

CARNEY DIRECT MARKETING

15510 Rockfield Blvd (Suite A)
Irvine, CA 92618-2792
Telephone: (949) 581-5100, Toll Free: (800) 240-3349, E-Mail: pete@carneydirect.com, Web Site: www.carneydirect.com
Pres: Pete Carney
Conducts Business: U.S.
Primary Market Served: Business
Founded: 1991

List management and brokerage company.

COLE INFORMATION SERVICES

17041 Lakeside Hills Plz (Suite 2)
Omaha, NE 68130-4677
Toll Free: (800) 403-5894, E-Mail: info@coleinformation.com, Web Site: www.coleinformation.com
CEO: Jim Eggleston
CFO: Vickie Neville
Chmn: Greg Elsberry
Conducts Business: U.S., Canada
Primary Market Served: Business
Catalog available online
Indirect online sales
Founded: 1947

Sales prospect listing company.

COLLINS LIST EXCHANGE INC

2312 N Green Valley Pkwy (Suite 2922)
Henderson, NV 89014-3118
Telephone: (702) 369-6015, FAX: (702) 920-8115, E-Mail: listinfo@collinslist.com, Web Site: www.collinslist.com
Owner & Pres: Melody Collins
Conducts Business: U.S.
Primary Market Served: Business

Full-service list management & brokerage company specializing in consumer response files.

COMMERCIAL MAILING LISTS

Subs. of The Forman Group Ltd
26 Carver Rd
Framingham, MA 01701-4493

Telephone: (508) 879-2647, Toll Free: (800) 875-8345, FAX: (508) 879-2911
Pres: Bruce Forman
Conducts Business: U.S.
Primary Market Served: Business

List brokerage for marketing, direct mail, email and telemarketing.

COMMONWEALTH LISTS

Steve Cram & Associates
1615 L St NW (Suite 1000)
Washington, DC 22036
Telephone: (202) 831-6202, FAX: (202) 831-6203, E-Mail: info@commonwealthlists.com, Web Site: www.commonwealthlists.com
Pres: Sara Holt
Founded: 1983

List brokerage and management company specializing in the non-profit sector.

COMPACT INFORMATION SYSTEMS

7120 185th Ave NE (Suite 150)
Redmond, WA 98052-0576
Telephone: (425) 869-1379, Toll Free: (800) 632-1379, FAX: (425) 558-2638, E-Mail: pat@compactlists.com, Web Site: www.compactlists.com
Founder, CEO & Pres: Pat Wiley
Mgr: Lori Wiley
Primary Market Served: Business & Consumer
Founded: 1988

Online mailing lists & data hygiene services company.

COMPASS VENTURES

808 P St (Suite 300)
Lincoln, NE 68508-1383
Telephone: (402) 438-3222, FAX: (402) 438-3439, E-Mail: info@compassventures.com, Web Site: www.compassventures.com
Partner: Michelle Brown
Partner: Todd Love
Partner: John Hartmann
Conducts Business: U.S., Canada
Primary Market Served: Business & Consumer
Founded: 2005

Source information compiler and data services company for business and consumer products.

COMPLETE MAILING LISTS LLC

190 E Post Rd
White Plains, NY 10601

Telephone: (914) 771-6640, Toll Free: (866) 314-5478, FAX: (914) 771-6645, E-Mail: info@completemailinglists.com, Web Site: completemailinglists.com
Mng Partner: Eric Woolf
Pres: Bill Woods
Conducts Business: U.S.
Primary Market Served: Business
Founded: 2006

Targeted mailing list compiler and brokerage.

COMPUTERIZED RESEARCH & DEVELOPMENT INC
1708 Maple Grove Ln
Lincoln, CA 95648
Telephone: (916) 434-5690, E-Mail: info@computerizedresearch.com, Web Site: www.cradinc.com
Pres: Judy Groom
Conducts Business: U.S.
Primary Market Served: Business
Founded: 1979

Mail list compiler specializing in state board licensees.

COMPUTERMAIL SOUTH INC
200 Second Ave S (Suite 160)
Saint Petersburg, FL 33701-4313
Telephone: (727) 579-1000, FAX: (727) 823-5474, E-Mail: sales@computermailsouth.com, Web Site: www.computermailsouth.com
Pres: John L. Cissna
Primary Market Served: Business & Consumer
Founded: 1976

Mailing list broker.

CONRAD DIRECT INC
300 Knickerbocker Rd
Cresskill, NJ 07626-1350
Telephone: (201) 567-3200, FAX: (201) 567-1530, E-Mail: listinfo@conraddirect.com, Web Site: www.conraddirect.com
Pres & CEO: Jerry Gould
Exec VP: Barbara Schonwald
VP, Opers: Tom Colwell
VP: Steve Maier
VP: Sharon Traina
Conducts Business: U.S.
Primary Market Served: Business
Founded: 1982

Direct marketing firm specializing in list management, list brokerage, online marketing, merge-purge, creative services, print & production management & alternative media.

CONTACT MARKETING LLC
228 Park Ave S

New York, NY 10003-1502
Telephone: (201) 530-0200, E-Mail: info@contactmarketing.net, Web Site: www.contactmarketing.net
Pres: Ari Ginsberg
Conducts Business: U.S.
Primary Market Served: Business

Direct marketing company specializing in direct mail & email marketable databases.

COVERCLICKS MEDIA INC
817 Broadway (Floor 5)
New York, NY 10003-4709
Telephone: (646) 434-1413, E-Mail: info@coverclicksmail.com, Web Site: www.coverclicks.com
CEO: Joshua Blumenfeld
Primary Market Served: Business & Consumer
Founded: 2001

Performance-based online marketing company.

CROSS MARKETING USA
1310 N Ritchie Ct (Suite 16-C)
Chicago, IL 60610-8401
Telephone: (312) 440-3700, Toll Free: (866) 440-3700, FAX: (312) 943-5813, E-Mail: ronbernstein@crossmarketing.us, Web Site: www.crossmarketing.us
VP: Ronald A. Bernstein
Primary Market Served: Consumer

CROSSLISTS CROSS & CO
PO Box 230
Lone Jack, MO 64070
Telephone: (816) 697-3306, FAX: (816) 697-3317, E-Mail: info@crosscompany.com, Web Site: www.crosscompany.com
CEO: Joy Pettid
Dir List Brokerage & Data Acquisition: JoAnn Alberts
Conducts Business: U.S.
Primary Market Served: Business & Consumer
Founded: 1980

Direct marketing data company specializing in the Catholic market.

DATA-DYNAMIX INC
PO Box 140118
Denver, CO 80214-0118
Telephone: (720) 855-9282, Toll Free: (888) 314-0078, FAX: (720) 855-9099, E-Mail: sales@data-dynamix.com, Web Site: www.data-dynamix.com
Pres: Brent Fankhauser
Dir Opers: Kevin Layton
Admin Asst: Brian Tellinghuisen
Dir Sls: Susan Duchin

Conducts Business: U.S., Canada, U.K.
Primary Market Served: Business & Consumer
Indirect online sales
Founded: 2000

List brokerage & direct mail company specializing in emerging technologies.

THE DATA GROUP
425 S Avalon Park Blvd
Orlando, FL 32828-6703
Toll Free: (800) 262-5609, E-Mail: questions@thedatagroup.com, Web Site: thedatagroup.com
Primary Market Served: Business

Data management, business optimization & marketing services company.

DATAHOUSE INC
2153 Sable Chase Dr
Colorado Springs, CO 80920
Toll Free: (866) 640-3282, E-Mail: data@datahouseinc.com, Web Site: www.datahouseinc.com
Pres: Richard Mestas
Conducts Business: U.S.
Primary Market Served: Business & Consumer
Catalog available online
Indirect online sales
Founded: 2003

Direct marketing list provider and data processing services firm.

DATALINE INC
5 Vaughn Dr (Suite 307)
Princeton, NJ 08540-6313
Telephone: (609) 452-6014, FAX: (609) 951-0025, E-Mail: psobel@datalinedata.com, Web Site: datalinedata.com
Pres & CEO: Paul Sobel
Exec VP & CMO: Linda Sadler
Sr VP: Lorrie Latzen
Primary Market Served: Business & Consumer
Founded: 2000

Provider of consumer marketing information, digital audiences and custom modeling & analytic services.

DIRECT CHANNEL INC
234 W Center St Ste 2
West Bridgewater, MA 02379-1633
Telephone: (508) 588-4448, FAX: (508) 588-4644, E-Mail: sales@directchannel.com, Web Site: www.directchannel.com
Pres: Paul O'Neill
Primary Market Served: Consumer

Direct advertising agency specializing in lists.

DIRECT LIST TECHNOLOGY INC

1582 N Batavia St (Suite 3)
Orange, CA 92867-3544
Telephone: (714) 772-3282, Toll Free: (888) 341-1117, FAX: (714) 772-6947, E-Mail: info@directlist.com, Web Site: www.directlist.com
Pres: Eran Salu
Primary Market Served: Consumer
Founded: 1987

Full-service data marketing company offering targeted data, direct mail, email and lead generation marketing services.

DIRECT RESPONSE SERVICES

aka R Co Inc
111 Northlane Dr
Glen Carbon, IL 62034
Telephone: (618) 288-8811, Toll Free: (800) 795-5478, FAX: (618) 288-3005, E-Mail: drs@drslist.com, Web Site: www.drslist.com
Pres: Kenneth Petersen
Conducts Business: U.S.
Primary Market Served: Consumer

Full-service database marketing services company.

DIRECTORY OF MAJOR MALLS INC

PO Box 837
Nyack, NY 10960-0837
Telephone: (845) 348-7000, Toll Free: (800) 898-6255, Web Site: shoppingcenters.com
Pres: Tama J. Shor
Primary Market Served: Business & Consumer

Detailed information & primary contacts for the major shopping centers & malls in the U.S. & Canada.

DIRMARK GROUP INC

75 Long Cir
Roswell, GA 30075
Telephone: (678) 245-1831, Toll Free: (888) 221-4968, E-Mail: dirmarkonline@dirmark.com, Web Site: dirmark.com
Pres: Michael Newton
Conducts Business: U.S., Canada
Primary Market Served: Business & Consumer
Founded: 1984

Business, consumer & email lists and database analytics services company.

DONNELLEY MARKETING

Div. of info USA
2 Blue Hill Plz (Suite 1662)

Pearl River, NY 10965-3115
Telephone: (201) 476-2300, FAX: (201) 476-2151, Web Site: www.infousa.com
Pres, Donnelley Group: Ed Mallin
HR Dir: Barbara Klumack

DRESDEN DIRECT INC

109 Saint Edward Pl
Palm Beach Gardens, FL 33418-4606
Telephone: (561) 622-3400
Pres: Phillip Dresden
Conducts Business: U.S.
Primary Market Served: Business & Consumer
Founded: 1989

DS DIRECT RESPONSE

5314 Palos Verdes Blvd
Torrance, CA 90505
Telephone: (310) 251-1830, E-Mail: info@dsdirectresponse.com, Web Site: dsdirectresponse.com
Pres & Owner: Debra Stanley
CEO: Christopher Barnes
Conducts Business: U.S.
Primary Market Served: Consumer

Integrated marketing company and list provider.

HUGO DUNHILL MAILING LISTS INC

11211 John Galt Blvd
Omaha, NE 68137
Telephone: (800) 223-6454, FAX: (402) 255-9099, E-Mail: sales@hdml.com, Web Site: www.hdml.com
Mktg Mgr: Annette Mercado
Conducts Business: U.S.
Employees: 50
Primary Market Served: Business
Direct online sales
Founded: 1939

Mailing lists, email lists, medical leads & sales leads.

DUNHILL INTERNATIONAL LIST CO INC

6400 Congress Ave (Suite 1750)
Boca Raton, FL 33487-2898
Telephone: (561) 998-7800, Toll Free: (800) 386-4455, FAX: (561) 998-7880, E-Mail: dunhill@dunhills.com, Web Site: www.dunhills.com
Pres: Robert Dunhill
VP: Candy Dunhill
VP Opers: Cindy Dunhill
Conducts Business: U.S.
Employees: 25
Primary Market Served: Business & Consumer

Founded: 1938

Specializing in business and consumer categories such as executives by job function, professionals, vacationers, investors, business owners and more. Maintains 30,000 list categories. Inquire about e-mail appending and list management.

DUNNDATA CO

2022 Rte 22 S, Patterson Business Park E
Brewster, NY 10509-5946
Telephone: (845) 278-1200, Web Site: www.dunndataco.com
Pres & CEO: Stephen Dunn
COO: Rosy Faver
Dir Sales & Mktg: Jennifer Schmidt
Primary Market Served: Business & Consumer
Founded: 2007

Direct marketing list and data brokerage company.

ECLIPSE DIRECT MARKETING

173 Mineola Blvd (Suite 402)
Mineola, NY 11501-2555
Telephone: (212) 931-8344, FAX: (516) 493-9122, E-Mail: jkaiser@eclipsedm.com, Web Site: www.eclipsedm.com
Mng Partner: Kris Thelen
Pres: Jane Kaiser
Mng Partner: John Hammersley
Mng Partner: John Kiggins
CFO: Michael Cuffee
Conducts Business: U.S.
Primary Market Served: Consumer

List broker and list management services provider.

CAROL ENTERS LIST CO INC

9663-C Main St
Fairfax, VA 22032
Telephone: (703) 425-0052, FAX: (703) 425-0056, E-Mail: listmanagement@carolenters.com, Web Site: www.carolenters.com
Pres: Barbara Sims
Primary Market Served: Consumer
Founded: 1993

List management & brokerage firm specializing in the non-profit sector.

EQUIFAX ONLINE MARKETING

Div. of Equifax Inc
1550 Peachtree St NE
Atlanta, GA 30309-2402

Telephone: (404) 885-8000, Web Site:
www.equifax.com/business/online-
marketing
Conducts Business: Worldwide
Primary Market Served: Business &
Consumer

Data-driven digital marketing services
provider.

ETHNIC TECHNOLOGIES LLC

600 Huyler St (Suite 5)
South Hackensack, NJ 07606-1734
Telephone: (201) 440-8923, Toll Free:
(866) 333-8324, FAX: (201) 440-
2168, E-Mail: karens@
ethnictechnologies.com, Web Site:
www.ethnictechnologies.com
CEO: Zachary Wilhoit
Sls Dir: Karen Sinisi
Conducts Business: U.S.
Primary Market Served: Consumer
Founded: 1997

Provider of multicultural marketing
data, ethnic identification software and
ethnic data appending services.

EVERGREEN MARKETING

Div. of Circulation Specialists Inc.
2 Corporate Dr (Suite 945)
Shelton, CT 06484
Telephone: (203) 822-7782, E-Mail:
jchiavelli@evergreenmarketing.com,
Web Site: www.evergreenmarketing.
com
VP, Brokerage & Mngmt: Jim Chiavel-
li
Conducts Business: U.S., U.K.
Primary Market Served: Consumer
Founded: 1986

Marketing services, list brokerage and
list management company.

EXHIBITRAC DIRECT MARKETING

1930 Village Center Cir (Suite 3-637)
Las Vegas, NV 89134
Telephone: (702) 824-9651, Toll Free:
(866) 988-6601, FAX: (702) 824-
9376, E-Mail: sales@exhibitrac.com,
Web Site: www.exhibitrac.com
Pres: Kyle Landrum
Natl Sales Mgr: Dave Scherschel
Primary Market Served: Business
Founded: 1996

Marketing company specializing in
trade show exhibitor lists.

FJ ASSOCIATES LLC

PO Box 12771
Wilmington, NC 28405-0138
Telephone: (910) 452-2643, FAX:
(630) 982-1056
Pres: Fran Milberg

VP: Jeffrey Milberg
Conducts Business: U.S.
Employees: 2
Primary Market Served: Business &
Consumer
Founded: 1999

Direct marketing consultancy specializing in the contact center industry.

FARM MARKET ID

170 Quail Ridge Dr
Westmont, IL 60559
Telephone: (844) 487-6322, E-Mail:
sales@farmmarketid.com, Web Site:
www.farmmarketid.com
Pres: Steve Rao
VP Mktg: Peg Kuman
Conducts Business: U.S.
Primary Market Served: Business &
Consumer
Founded: 1973

Data marketing solutions company specializing in the agricultural industry.

FIRST DIRECT INC

1508 J F Kennedy Dr (Suite 103)
Bellevue, NE 68005-6611
Telephone: (402) 403-0000, Toll Free:
(866) 363-9575, FAX: (402) 403-
0001, E-Mail: sales@
firstdirectmarketing.com, Web Site:
www.firstdirectmarketing.com
Partner: Joel Buhr
Conducts Business: U.S.
Primary Market Served: Business
Direct online sales
Founded: 2005

Mailing lists, data processing, printing,
mail services, campaign management,
direct marketing consulting services.

F1RSTMARK INC

25 Vintinner Rd
Campton, NH 03223
Telephone: (603) 726-4800, Toll Free:
(800) 729-2600, FAX: (603) 726-
4840, E-Mail: sales@firstmark.com,
Web Site: www.firstmark.com
Pres: Michael H. Pomerantz
Conducts Business: U.S.
Primary Market Served: Consumer
Founded: 1987

List & data management services provider.

FIXED ADDRESS MARKETING INC

136 Pinnacle Tr
Aurora, ON, Canada L4G 7G7
Telephone: (905) 750-0029, E-Mail:
dockeray@fixedaddressmarketing.
com, Web Site: www.
fixedaddressmarketing.com
Pres: Tara Dockeray

Conducts Business: Canada
Primary Market Served: Consumer
Founded: 1995

Direct marketing, list brokerage and
list management services company.

FOCUS USA INC

95 N State Route 17
Paramus, NJ 07652
Telephone: (201) 489-2525, FAX:
(201) 489-4499, E-Mail: info@focus-
usa-l.com, Web Site: www.focus-
usa-l.com
Dir Adv: Chicca D'Agostino
Pres: Amy Carraher
Conducts Business: U.S.

List broker and data management services company.

GELDERMAN GROUP INC

19 Junction Rd
Brookfield, CT 06804
Telephone: (203) 740-9000, FAX:
(203) 702-7096, E-Mail:
geldermangroup@earthlink.net
Pres: Harriet Schopjer
Primary Market Served: Consumer

List brokerage for consumer marketers.

GLASERDIRECT INC

800 Roosevelt Rd (Bldg B, Suite 200)
Glen Ellyn, IL 50137-5839
Telephone: (630) 469-2075, Toll Free:
(888) 380-1356, FAX: (630) 790-
5244, E-Mail: info@glaserdirect.
com, Web Site: www.glaserdirect.
com
CEO: Joseph Glaser
Sr VP: Barb Toschak
Sr VP: Bert Des Rosiers
Conducts Business: U.S.
Employees: 12
Primary Market Served: Business &
Consumer
Founded: 1974

Full-service list brokerage & list management company.

GLOBAL DM SOLUTIONS INC

416 Main St
Boonton, NJ 07005-1714
Telephone: (973) 402-2205, Toll Free:
(866) 402-2205, FAX: (973) 402-
2305, E-Mail: contact@
globaldmsolutions.com, Web Site:
www.globaldmsolutions.com
Pres: Sheila Donovan

Global contact data management services company.

GOLDLEAF DATA INC

5400 Laurel Springs Pkwy (Suite 104)

Suwanee, GA 30024-6060
Toll Free: (888) 936-3282, E-Mail:
info@goldleafdata.com, Web Site:
goldleafdata.com
Pres: Jason Butler
Primary Market Served: Consumer
Founded: 2003

Supplier of mailing lists and consumer
data.

MARY ELIZABETH GRANGER & ASSOCIATES INC

110 West Rd (Suite 235)
Baltimore, MD 21204-2343
Telephone: (410) 842-1170, FAX:
(410) 842-1185, E-Mail: info@
maryegranger.com, Web Site: www.
maryegranger.com
Pres & Owner: Bonnie Granger
VP: Kris Matthews
Sr Acct Mgr: Linda Martin
CFO: Carol Vorwerck
Conducts Business: U.S.
Employees: 10
Primary Market Served: Consumer
Catalog available online
Indirect online sales
Founded: 1983

Mailing list brokerage and management
services.

GREATLISTS.COM

PO Box 623
Herndon, VA 20172
Telephone: (703) 821-8130, FAX:
(703) 821-8243, E-Mail: info@
greatlists.com, Web Site: greatlists.
com
Pres: Phil Dismukes
Primary Market Served: Business &
Consumer
Founded: 1979

Supplier of domestic USA and international B2B and professional marketing
lists.

GULF COAST LIST SERVICE

16350 Bruce B Downs Blvd (#47645)
Tampa, FL 33646
Telephone: (813) 962-3594, FAX:
(813) 907-8463, E-Mail: tg@
gulfcoastlist.com
Owner: Tina Genovese
Conducts Business: U.S.
Primary Market Served: Consumer
Founded: 1986

National mail, email and telemarketing
lists provider.

HR DIRECT INC

Sub. of AstroView, Inc
508 N 2nd St
Fairfield, IA 52556-2464

Telephone: (641) 472-7188, FAX:
(641) 472-5729, E-Mail: info@
hrdirect.net, Web Site: www.hrdirect.
net
Pres: David Hawthorne

Mailing list brokerage & management
company.

HARRIS MARKETING INC

6100 N Keystone Ave (Suite 427)
Indianapolis, IN 46220-2428
Telephone: (317) 251-9729, FAX:
(317) 251-9733, E-Mail:
hmdataindy@msn.com, Web Site:
www.listsandmail.com
Pres: Janet Harris
Primary Market Served: Consumer

List brokerage specializing in the Indianapolis market.

HEALTHY OFFERS INC

dba Medicx Media Solutions
10799 N 90th St (Suite 200)
Scottsdale, AZ 85260
Telephone: (480) 614-0060, FAX:
(480) 614-0160, E-Mail: info@
medicxmedia.com, Web Site: www.
medicxmedia.com
Pres & CEO: Michael Weintraub
Sr VP Opers: Frank Hicks
Primary Market Served: Business &
Consumer
Founded: 2006

Data-driven programmatic media &
marketing solutions company specializing in pharmaceutical, OTC, health,
wellness, consumer packaged good &
personal care brands.

HEALY LIST MARKETING

153 Andover St (Suite 108A)
Danvers, MA 01923-1450
Toll Free: (800) 281-8956, FAX: (978)
336-0463, E-Mail: info@
healylistmarketing.com, Web Site:
www.healylistmarketing.com
Principal: Jim Healy
Primary Market Served: Consumer

Transactional consumer database company.

LEON HENRY INC

200 N Central Ave (Suite 220)
Hartsdale, NY 10530-9915
Telephone: (914) 285-3456, FAX:
(914) 285-3450, E-Mail: lh@
leonhenryinc.com, Web Site: www.
leonhenryinc.com
Exec VP: Gail Henry
Conducts Business: U.S., Canada, U.K.
Primary Market Served: Business &
Consumer
Indirect online sales

Founded: 1956
Insert media and mailing list brokerage
firm.

HIPPO DIRECT

PO Box 391313
Solon, OH 44139
Telephone: (440) 519-0730, FAX:
(440) 519-0727, E-Mail:
rapidresponse@hippodirect.com,
Web Site: www.hippodirect.com
Pres: Greg Branstetter
Founded: 192

Mailing list & email list brokerage and
database marketing company.

HOMEOWNER DATA SERVICES INC

1424 N Brown Rd (Suite 400)
Lawrenceville, GA 30043-8107
Telephone: (770) 925-9000, FAX:
(770) 925-8977, E-Mail: hdsi@
newhomedata.net, Web Site: www.
newhomedata.net
Pres: George F. O'Neil
Primary Market Served: Consumer

HOMEOWNERS MARKETING SERVICES INC

12444 Victory Blvd (Floor 2)
North Hollywood, CA 91606-3156
Toll Free: (888) 743-3037, E-Mail:
inquiry@
homeownersmarketingservices.com,
Web Site: www.
homeownersmarketingservices.com
Pres: Barry Weiner
HR: Laura Friedman
Conducts Business: U.S.
Founded: 1967

Provider of mailing or telemarketing
lists of new homeowners.

HOMETOWN MAILING LISTS & DIRECT MAIL

6119 Greenville Ave (Suite 169)
Dallas, TX 75206
Toll Free: (800) 798-4811, E-Mail:
tinkham@hometownlists.com, Web
Site: www.hometownlists.com
Pres & Broker: Wes Tinkham
Conducts Business: U.S.
Primary Market Served: Business &
Consumer
Founded: 1995

Business & consumer direct mailing
lists provider.

HORIZON LISTS

13 N Rockland (Suite 4)
Congers, NY 10463

Telephone: (845) 300-4932, E-Mail: sales@horizonlists.com, Web Site: www.horizonlists.com
Primary Market Served: Consumer

Full-service marketing firm specializing in list brokerage, list management and email marketing services.

HOTLINE LIST CORP

1071 Ave of the Americas
New York, NY 10018
Telephone: (212) 840-8135, FAX: (212) 840-8139
Pres: Bonnie Dursi

Direct marketing list brokerage.

I-BEHAVIOR INC

A KBM Group company
2051 Dogwood St (Suite 220)
Louisville, CO 80027-3042
Telephone: (303) 228-5000, E-Mail: ib-sales@i-behavior.com, Web Site: www.i-behavior.com
Pres & CEO: Dave DeMarsh
Other: Adam Woods
Gen Mgr: Joe Bank
Mng Dir: Jason Dodge
Conducts Business: Worldwide
Primary Market Served: Business & Consumer

Provider of consumer and business transaction data for multi-channel merchants.

IDM INC

Integrated Direct Marketing
11951 Freedom Dr (Suite 400)
Reston, VA 20190-5686
Telephone: (703) 547-4961, E-Mail: info@integrated-dm.com, Web Site: www.idm.us.com
Pres: Chad Slater
Exec VP Client Svcs: Rocky Beal
Conducts Business: U.S., Canada
Employees: 15
Primary Market Served: Business & Consumer
Founded: 2003

Data intelligence and marketing advisory firm that provides custom data solutions for the needs of multi-channel direct marketers.

IDR MARKETING PARTNERS LLC

dba Brandshare
1125 Lancaster Ave Ste 2
Berwyn, PA 19312-2601
Telephone: (610) 993-0500, FAX: (610) 993-9938, E-Mail: idr@idronline.com, Web Site: www.idronline.com
Pres: Douglas Guyer
Primary Market Served: Consumer

Founded: 1984

Marketing agency that connects retailers and consumers with appropriate brands.

INFINITE MEDIA CONCEPTS INC

dba Mailinglists.com
190 E Post Rd
White Plains, NY 10601-4912
Telephone: (914) 948-8300, FAX: (914) 949-1605, Web Site: mailinglists.com
Pres: Steven Sheck
VP Sales: Becky Santaniello
Primary Market Served: Consumer
Founded: 1993

Mailing list brokerage and management data & analysis products & services company.

INFOUSA

Div. of Infogroup Inc
1020 E 1st St
Papillion, NE 68046
Toll Free: (800) 835-5856, Web Site: www.infousa.com
Pres: Amit Khanna
Conducts Business: U.S.
Primary Market Served: Business & Consumer
Founded: 1972

Provider of business & consumer mailing lists, sales leads & end-to-end marketing services.

INFOCANADA

An InfoGroup company
1290 Central Pkwy W (Suite 500)
Mississauga, ON, Canada L5C 4R9
Toll Free: (800) 565-7224, FAX: (905) 803-7195, E-Mail: info@infocanada.ca, Web Site: infogroup.infocanada.ca
Pres: Dan Cadieux
Pres: Anna Tchirova
Primary Market Served: Business & Consumer

Provider of data-driven and multi-channel marketing solutions.

INFOCORE INC

5973 Avenida Encinas (Suite 218)
Carlsbad, CA 92008
Telephone: (760) 607-2500, FAX: (760) 607-2505, E-Mail: info@infocore.com, Web Site: www.infocore.com
Pres & CEO: Kitty Kolding
Pres: Amy McNabb
Sr VP: Denise Covington
Conducts Business: Worldwide
Primary Market Served: Business & Consumer

Direct online sales
Founded: 1992

Strategic marketing data sourcing company.

INFOCUS MARKETING INC

4245 Sigler Rd
Warrenton, VA 20187-3940
Toll Free: (800) 708-5478, FAX: (866) 708-5478, E-Mail: sales@infocusmarketing.com, Web Site: www.infocusmarketing.com
Dir Mktg: Tom Heim
Dir Devel: Maggie Powers
Primary Market Served: Business & Consumer
Founded: 1990

List management direct mail marketing services company to national trade associations.

INFOGROUP MEDIA SOLUTIONS

Div. of Infogroup Inc
1020 E 1st St
Papillion, NE 68046
Telephone: (800) 223-2194, E-Mail: infogroupmediasolutions@infogroup.com, Web Site: www.infogroupmediasolutions.com
Pres: Gretchen Littlefield
Exec VP: Karen Mayhew
Sr VP & Gen Mgr: Stephanie Ceruolo
VP Mktg: Akshay Gandotra
Primary Market Served: Business & Consumer

Data, technology, marketing resources & list strategies company.

INFOMAT INC

21171 S Western (Suite 260)
Torrance, CA 90501
Telephone: (310) 212-5944, FAX: (310) 212-3026, E-Mail: listmgr@infomatbiz.com, Web Site: www.infomatbiz.com
Pres: Craig A Huey
Primary Market Served: Business
Founded: 1972

Postal & email list brokerage and management company.

INFUTOR DATA SOLUTIONS

One Lincoln Center, 18W140 Butterfield Rd (Suite 1020)
Oakbrook Terrace, IL 60181
Telephone: (312) 348-7900, E-Mail: sales@infutor.com, Web Site: www.infutor.com
CEO: Gary Walter
COO: Jeff Beard
CFO: Drew Plisco
CTO: John Barnes
Primary Market Served: Consumer

Founded: 2003
Full-service data solutions provider.

INTELITEC
154 Taylor St
Granby, MA 01033-9526
Telephone: (413) 467-9476, E-Mail:
info@intelitec.com, Web Site:
intelitec.com
Pres: Joseph Furnia
Conducts Business: U.S., Germany,
Europe
Primary Market Served: Business &
Consumer
Founded: 1991

Specialty multi-channel marketing solutions using web crawling and traditional data channels to create customer
targeting.

JF DIRECT MARKETING INC
34 Beach Rd
Ossining, NY 10562
Telephone: (914) 762-1975, FAX:
(914) 762-9247, E-Mail: jfdirect@
bestweb.net, Web Site: www.
jfdirectmarketing.com
Pres: John Ferrini
Conducts Business: U.S.
Primary Market Served: Business &
Consumer
Founded: 1992

A full service direct marketing company consisting of list brokerage, list
management, e-mail marketing, list
compilation, data appending, M/P, lettershop & fulfillment.

JR DIRECT RESPONSE
INTERNATIONAL INC
201-4841 Delta St
Delta, BC, Canada V4K 2T9
Telephone: (604) 940-0277, Toll Free:
(877) 940-0277, FAX: (604) 946-
1419, E-Mail: contactus@jrdirect.
com, Web Site: www.jrdirect.com
Gen Mgr: John Flame
Primary Market Served: Business &
Consumer
Founded: 1989

Marketing & data services company
specializing in list brokerage & management, data processing, copywriting
and consulting services.

JS DIRECT ADDRESS LTD
1429 Dominion St (#203)
North Vancouver, BC, Canada V7J
1B4
Telephone: (604) 987-1282, FAX:
(604) 987-1283, E-Mail: jim.slight@
jsdirect.com, Web Site: www.
jsdirect.com
Pres: Jim Slight

Conducts Business: Canada
Founded: 1992
Direct marketing agency specializing
in list brokerage and list management.

JAMAX DIRECT LLC
375 Sylvan Ave (Suite 2)
Englewood Cliffs, NJ 07632-2714
Telephone: (201) 569-4540
Pres & Owner: David Malamed
Conducts Business: U.S.
Primary Market Served: Consumer
Founded: 2007

Full-service direct response marketing
agency.

KEY MARKETING
ADVANTAGE LLC
7 Edmund Rd (Suite 100)
Newtown, CT 06470-1632
Telephone: (203) 491-2200, FAX:
(203) 491-2201, E-Mail: info@
keymarketingadvantage.com, Web
Site: keymarketingcorp.com
Pres: Linda Bridson
Conducts Business: U.S.
Primary Market Served: Business &
Consumer
Founded: 2003

Provider of list brokerage & management, marketing & analytic services
and the development of proprietary
B2B & B2C database resources.

KROLL DIRECT
MARKETING INC
3914 Netherlee Way
Wellington, FL 33449
Telephone: (609) 275-2900, E-Mail:
lee@krolldirect.com, Web Site:
www.krolldirect.com
Pres: Leland Kroll
Dir Sales: Gwen Coryell
Conducts Business: U.S.
Primary Market Served: Consumer
Catalog available online
Founded: 1989

Provider of list brokerage, list management, list compilation, alternative media and mobile marketing service.

LS DIRECT MARKETING
4 Suffern Pl
Suffern, NY 10901
Telephone: (845) 357-1238, E-Mail:
info@lsdirect.com, Web Site: www.
lsdirect.com
Pres & CEO: Jeff Horowitz
Co-Founder & VP: Chris Knoebel
Dir Sales: Kathy Goldrich
Primary Market Served: Consumer

Founded: 1997
Direct mail marketing company and list
provider.

LAKE GROUP MEDIA INC
1 Byram Brook Pl
Armonk, NY 10504
Telephone: (914) 925-2400, FAX:
(914) 925-2499, E-Mail: ryan.lake@
lakegroupmedia.com, Web Site:
www.lakegroupmedia.com
CEO: Ryan Lake
Sr VP: Karen Lake
Sr VP: Joe Robinson
Primary Market Served: Business &
Consumer
Founded: 1961

Direct marketing agency and list brokerage specializing in the direct mail,
email & online channels.

LEADCREATIONS.COM LLC
12717 W Sunrise Blvd (Suite 312)
Fort Lauderdale, FL 33323
Telephone: (305) 851-0999, FAX:
(707) 281-0421, E-Mail: info@
leadcreations.com, Web Site: www.
leadcreations.com
Fin Mgr: Umut Vadar
Conducts Business: Worldwide
Primary Market Served: Business &
Consumer
Founded: 2006

Digital marketing and lead generation
company.

LEADGEN MEDIA GROUP
LLC
1324 Forest Ave (Suite 401)
Staten Island, NY 10302-2044
Telephone: (888) 206-3738, FAX:
(888) 206-3796, E-Mail: info@
leadgenmediagroup.com, Web Site:
www.leadgenmediagroup.com
CEO: Scott Mauer
Dir Opers: Austin Mauer
Conducts Business: U.S.
Primary Market Served: Consumer
Founded: 2010

Search engine marketing services company.

LIST ADVISOR INC
500 Bi County Blvd (Suite 125)
Farmingdale, NY 11735-3996
Telephone: (631) 777-2900, FAX:
(631) 777-3050
Pres: Thomas R. Frenz
Conducts Business: U.S.
Primary Market Served: Consumer
Founded: 1986

Database marketing, direct mail & list
consultancy.

LIST ALLIANCE INC
3000 Danville Blvd (Suite 519)
Alamo, CA 94507
Telephone: (925) 820-3151, E-Mail:
    info@listalliance.com, Web Site:
    www.listalliance.com
Pres: Randy Robertson
Primary Market Served: Business &
    Consumer
Founded: 2004

Customer acquisition company specializing in list brokerage services, direct strategy planning and customized promotional database solutions.

LIST AMERICA
Div. of Market Development Group Inc
1832 Connecticut Ave NW
Washington, DC 20016
Telephone: (202) 298-9206, FAX:
    (202) 244-7294, Web Site: mdginc.
    org
Grp VP: Gerry Gretschel
Conducts Business: Worldwide
Founded: 1979

List brokerage & list management services company specializing in the global nonprofit community.

LIST MARKETING GROUP INC
19885 Detroit Rd (Suite 207)
Cleveland, OH 44116-1815
Telephone: (216) 990-2000, E-Mail:
    fran@listmarketinggroup.com, Web
    Site: www.listmarketinggroup.com
CEO: Frances Anderson
Conducts Business: U.S.
Primary Market Served: Business &
    Consumer
Founded: 1998

Direct marketing company specializing in list services.

LIST PRO OF AMERICA
3089-C Clairemont Dr (Suite 267)
San Diego, CA 92117-6802
Telephone: (858) 483-1410, E-Mail:
    listpro@swmall.com, Web Site:
    swmall.com/listpro
Founder: Diane O'Brien
Conducts Business: U.S.
Primary Market Served: Consumer
Founded: 1988

Marketing services company specializing in targeted mailing lists.

LIST SERVICE DIRECT INC
2 Christie Heights St
Leonia, NJ 07605-2233
Telephone: (201) 585-1447, Toll Free:
    (800) 371-5487, FAX: (201) 585-
    1732, E-Mail: info@listservicedirect.
    com, Web Site: www.
    listservicedirect.com
Pres & Owner: Micah Raskin
Conducts Business: U.S.
Primary Market Served: Business &
    Consumer

Sales lead distributor and provider of mailing lists, marketing data, sales leads and research data.

LIST SOURCE DIRECT
55 SE 2nd Ave
Delray Beach, FL 33444
Telephone: (561) 570-1287, E-Mail:
    info@listsourcedirect.com, Web Site:
    www.listsourcedirect
Pres: Sean Parke
Conducts Business: U.S.
Primary Market Served: Consumer
Founded: 2002

Marketing solutions company offering a full range of email, postal & telemarketing lists.

LIST STRATEGIES INC
244 Madison Ave (Suite 1950)
New York, NY 10016-2817
Telephone: (212) 767-1000, FAX:
    (212) 541-4408, E-Mail: info@
    liststrategies.com, Web Site: www.
    liststrategies.com
Pres: Joel Cooper
Exec VP & Partner: Sal Tisi
Conducts Business: U.S.
Primary Market Served: Business &
    Consumer
Founded: 1988

Full-service, personalized list brokerage.

LIST TEAM
22287 Mulholland Hwy (Suite 408)
Calabasas, CA 91302
Telephone: (818) 887-1166, Toll Free:
    (800) 553-2123, E-Mail: info@
    listteam.com, Web Site: www.
    listteam.com
Pres: Glenn Levine
Conducts Business: U.S.
Primary Market Served: Business &
    Consumer
Founded: 1984

Targeted list provider.

LISTABILITY INC
20845 Loggia Ct
Venice, FL 34293
Telephone: (866) 446-2055, E-Mail:
    info@listability.com, Web Site:
    www.listability.com
Partner: Carol Christopher Arnold

Partner: Shelli Dyer
Pres: Christopher Dyer
Conducts Business: U.S.
Primary Market Served: Business &
    Consumer

Company specializing in list brokerage services.

LISTGIANT
Subs. of Giant Partners
2475 Townsgate Rd (Floor 1)
Westlake Village, CA 91361
Toll Free: (800) 383-1381, E-Mail:
    contact@listgiant.com, Web Site:
    www.listgiant.com
Pres: Giovanni Barile
Conducts Business: U.S.
Primary Market Served: Business &
    Consumer
Founded: 2001

Direct marketing firm specializing in providing marketing lists for direct mail, telemarketing and email campaigns.

LISTMASTERS DIRECT MAIL SERVICES
10300 Drummond Rd
Philadelphia, PA 19154
Telephone: (215) 633-8200, E-Mail:
    sales@listmastersdirect.com, Web
    Site: www.listmastersdirect.com
Pres: David Geer
Conducts Business: U.S.
Primary Market Served: Business
Founded: 1985

Full-service direct mail marketing company.

LISTS INC
2950 Halcyon Ln (Suite 401)
Jacksonville, FL 32223
Telephone: (904) 733-6106, Toll Free:
    (800) 805-5478, FAX: (904) 730-
    7540, E-Mail: info@lists-inc.com,
    Web Site: www.lists-inc.com
Mgr: Pauline Aldridge
Conducts Business: U.S.
Primary Market Served: Business &
    Consumer
Founded: 1987

List compiler specializing in healthcare and medical direct marketing.

LISTSOURCE
Div. of CoreLogic
40 Pacifica (Suite 900)
Irvine, CA 92618
Telephone: (866) 774-3282, E-Mail:
    sales@corelogic.com, Web Site:
    www.listsource.com
Pres: Dave Hamilton
Conducts Business: U.S.
Primary Market Served: Consumer

Founded: 2007

Direct marketing company specializing in property, homeowner & demographic-based lead lists.

MCH STRATEGIC DATA
601 E Marshall St
Sweet Springs, MO 65351-9613
Telephone: (660) 335-6373, Toll Free: (800) 776-6373, FAX: (660) 335-4157, E-Mail: sales@mchdata.com, Web Site: mchdata.com
CEO: Peter Long
Pres: Amy Rambo
HR Dir: Larry Buchweitz
Conducts Business: U.S.
Primary Market Served: Business & Consumer
Founded: 1928

Email & data services company specializing in the education, healthcare, government & religious sectors.

MGM MAILING LISTS
Ten Leslin Ln
South Sandwich, MA 02563
Telephone: (508) 539-1300, Toll Free: (800) 660-5322, FAX: (508) 539-0700
Pres: Mark Linse
Conducts Business: U.S.
Primary Market Served: Business & Consumer
Founded: 1990

Mail list brokerage providing mailing lists of consumers & businesses for direct sales, lead generation, retail traffic & fundraising.

MNI
Manufacturers News Inc
1633 Central St
Evanston, IL 60201-1505
Telephone: (847) 864-7000, Toll Free: (888) 752-5200, FAX: (847) 332-1100, Web Site: mni.net
Pres & CEO: Thomas Dubin
VP: Scott Kartsounes
Conducts Business: U.S., Europe, China
Primary Market Served: Business
Catalog available online
Direct online sales
Founded: 1912

Publisher of detailed information profiling the manufacturing establishments and industrial distributors from original research.

MSI LIST MARKETING
738 E Dundee Rd (Suite 321)
Palatine, IL 60074-2858

Telephone: (847) 934-1111, FAX: (847) 890-6700, E-Mail: jeff@msilist.com, Web Site: www.msilist.com
Pres: Jeff Sutton
Conducts Business: U.S.
Primary Market Served: Business
Founded: 1984

Mailing list brokerage & management service specializing in direct mail to the investor marketplace.

MSNI INC
70 Mansell Ct (Suite 100)
Roswell, GA 30076-4857
Telephone: (770) 777-4121, Web Site: www.msniinc.com
Pres: Dan McDonald
Conducts Business: U.S.
Primary Market Served: Business & Consumer
Founded: 1999

Database & digital marketing firm offering proprietary solutions and mailing list services.

MACROMARK INC
39 Old Ridgebury Rd (Suite 23)
Danbury, CT 06810
Telephone: (845) 230-6300, FAX: (845) 278-0650, E-Mail: sales@macromark.com, Web Site: www.macromark.com
CEO & Pres: David Klein
Exec VP Sls: Adam Moran
Chmn: Rick Sarli
Sr VP Sls: Jennifer Luposello
Primary Market Served: Business & Consumer
Founded: 1985

Direct mail services company specializing in targeted lists.

MAILGRAPHICS INC
1668 Valtec Ln (Suite F)
Boulder, CO 80301-4635
Telephone: (303) 449-4053, E-Mail: questions@mailgraphics.com, Web Site: www.mailgraphics.com
Pres: Bruce Chiddister
Conducts Business: U.S.
Primary Market Served: Business & Consumer
Founded: 1997

Direct mail and database services company.

MAILING LISTS PLUS INC
13104 SE Newport Way, PMB 203
Bellevue, WA 98006
Telephone: (425) 451-3335, FAX: (425) 646-4485, E-Mail: info@mailinglistsplus.com, Web Site: www.mailinglistsplus.com

Pres: Carol Kollmann
Conducts Business: Worldwide
Primary Market Served: Business & Consumer
Founded: 1985

Full-service mail list broker and direct mail & email marketing services company.

MANNING MEDIA INTERNATIONAL
2128 Surrey Ln
McKinney, TX 75070
Telephone: (972) 562-6960, FAX: (972) 542-3336, E-Mail: info@manningmedia.com, Web Site: www.manningmedia.com
Pres: Mike Manning
Conducts Business: Worldwide
Primary Market Served: Business & Consumer

List supplier specializing in international direct marketing lists.

MARKET APPROACH CONSULTING SERVICES LP
111 E Center St
Lorena, TX 76655-9651
Telephone: (254) 857-1100, FAX: (254) 857-1000, E-Mail: wmclean@marketapproach.net, Web Site: www.marketapproach.net
Pres: Mark McLean
Sr VP Sales: Wade McLean
Dir Client Rels: Monica Rackley
Conducts Business: U.S.
Primary Market Served: Business
Founded: 2001

Provider of marketing lists and database services.

MARKET DATA RETRIEVAL
A Dun & Bradstreet Co
6 Armstrong Rd (Suite 301)
Shelton, CT 06484
Telephone: (203) 926-4800, Toll Free: (800) 333-8802, FAX: (203) 929-5253, E-Mail: mdrinfo@dnb.com, Web Site: schooldata.com
Pres: Mike Subrizi
Conducts Business: U.S.
Primary Market Served: Business & Consumer
Founded: 1969

Integrated marketing services agency specializing in education data.

MARKET STREET LISTS INC
7 Pleasant St, PO Box 850
Exeter, NH 03833-0850

Telephone: (603) 772-6666, Toll Free: (888) 675-5478, FAX: (603) 772-0184, E-Mail: info@market-street.com, Web Site: www.market-street.com
Pres: Christopher L. Velletri
Primary Market Served: Business & Consumer

Sales & marketing support products & services provider.

MARKETFORCE CORP
101 W Eagle Rd (Suite 284)
Havertown, PA 19083-2244
Telephone: (610) 356-5220, FAX: (610) 356-5110, E-Mail: davethomas@marketforcecorp.com, Web Site: www.marketforcecorp.com
CMO: Dave Thomas
Pres: Beth Dardes
Conducts Business: U.S., Canada
Primary Market Served: Business
Founded: 1984

Compiler of marketing related data on new businesses in the U.S. & Canada.

MARKETING ECONOMICS INC
1636 N Wells (#3112)
Chicago, IL 60614-6023
Telephone: (312) 642-2188, FAX: (312) 642-3091, E-Mail: codyh@meimedia.com, Web Site: www.meimedia.com
Pres: Cody Heiderer
Conducts Business: U.S.
Primary Market Served: Business & Consumer
Founded: 1987

Direct mail list brokerage.

MARKETRY INC
4122 Factoria Blvd SE (Suite 400)
Bellevue, WA 98006-4275
Telephone: (425) 451-1262, FAX: (425) 953-2957, E-Mail: greg@marketry.com, Web Site: www.marketry.com
Pres: Greg Swent
Conducts Business: U.S., Canada
Primary Market Served: Business
Founded: 1973

Full-service direct media brokerage firm.

MARTIN WORLDWIDE INC
638 Lindero Canyon Rd (Suite 200)
Oak Park, CA 91377
Toll Free: (888) 694-5478, Web Site: www.martinworldwide.net
Sr Mktg Consultant: Eddie Hren
Mktg Consultant: Jesse Sims

Primary Market Served: Business & Consumer

Direct marketing products provider specializing in lists.

MASTERMAILER INC
3700 N 29th Ave (Suite 203)
Hollywood, FL 33020-1019
Telephone: (954) 921-0000, Toll Free: (800) 771-5478, FAX: (954) 925-7900, Web Site: www.mastermailer.com
Pres: Theresa Bograkos
Conducts Business: U.S.
Primary Market Served: Business & Consumer
Founded: 1980

Full-service graphic design, printing, targeted mailing list and service company.

MAZZONE MARKETING GROUP LLC
PO Box 40536
Brooklyn, NY 11204-0536
Telephone: (718) 369-0001, Toll Free: (866) 928-5478, FAX: (718) 369-0099, E-Mail: info@mazzonemarketinggroup.com, Web Site: www.mazzonemarketinggroup.com
Pres: Michael R. Mazzone Jr
VP Sales: Kim Weitzell
Conducts Business: U.S.
Primary Market Served: Business & Consumer
Catalog available online
Direct online sales
Founded: 2007

Mailing list compiler, broker & manager. Specializing in niche markets, political donors, non-profit organizations, medical lists and many more.

MCCARTHY MEDIA GROUP INC
1088 Stonewood Crossing
Sun Prairie, WI 53590-4405
Telephone: (608) 329-6097, E-Mail: mmg.greenlinks@charter.net, Web Site: www.mccarthymediagroup.com
Pres: Michael McCarthy
Conducts Business: U.S.
Primary Market Served: Business & Consumer
Founded: 1997

Mailing list management & brokerage for business & consumer catalogs, niche publishers and business to consumer lead generation.

MERITDIRECT
2 International Dr
Rye Brook, NY 10573

Telephone: (914) 368-1000, FAX: (914) 368-1150, E-Mail: hq@meritdirect.com, Web Site: www.meritdirect.com
CEO: Rob Sanchez
Exec VP: Christopher Pickering
Exec VP: Mark Zilling
Conducts Business: Worldwide
Primary Market Served: Business & Consumer
Founded: 2000

Global, multi-channel integrated marketing products & services provider.

METARESPONSE GROUP INC
700 W Hillsboro Blvd (Suite 4-107)
Deerfield Beach, FL 33441-1619
Telephone: (954) 360-0644, FAX: (954) 360-7712, E-Mail: info@metaresponse.com, Web Site: www.metaresponse.com
Pres: Jerry Whiteway
Primary Market Served: Business & Consumer
Founded: 1999

Full-service list brokerage & list management company servicing the direct mail and e-mail needs of mailers within the financial newsletter, business-to-business and consumer markets.

MIDWEST DIRECT MARKETING INC
501 N Webster
Spring Hill, KS 66083
Telephone: (913) 686-2220, FAX: (913) 686-2320, E-Mail: info@midwestdm.com, Web Site: www.midwestdm.com
Pres: Scott Robbins
Conducts Business: U.S.
Primary Market Served: Business & Consumer
Founded: 1996

Mailing lists, alternative media, brokerage & management, database overlay & profile.

MIDWEST LISTS & MEDIA LTD
Subs. of The Bradford Group
9333 N Milwaukee Ave
Niles, IL 60714
Telephone: (847) 966-2770, FAX: (847) 966-8630, Web Site: www.thebradfordgroup.com
Mgr: Rich Tinberg
Conducts Business: Worldwide.
Primary Market Served: Business & Consumer

Direct mail services subsidiary of The Bradford Group of companies.

MULTIMEDIA LISTS INC
Asheville, NC
Toll Free: (800) 239-5478, E-Mail:
daniel@multimedialists.com, Web
Site: multimedialists.com
Pres: Daniel Klibanoff
Primary Market Served: Consumer
Founded: 2012

List brokerage and management company.

NCRI LIST MANAGEMENT
455 Sylvan Ave
Englewood Cliffs, NJ 07632-2703
Telephone: (201) 541-9500, FAX:
(201) 541-1944, E-Mail: info@
ncrilists.com, Web Site: www.
ncrilists.com
VP: Melissa Trotta
Conducts Business: U.S.
Primary Market Served: Business &
Consumer

Lists and marketing services company.

NAMEBANK
1001 Cathedral St
Baltimore, MD 21201
Telephone: (410) 864-0854, FAX:
(410) 864-0837, E-Mail: lists@
namebank.com, Web Site: www.
namebank.com
VP Svcs: Anne Kelly
Pres: Jenelle Ketcham
List Mgr: Sonia Vidal
Conducts Business: U.S.
Primary Market Served: Business &
Consumer

Provider of data management & direct
marketing strategies.

NAMES IN THE MAIL INC
10710 Shiloh Rd
Dallas, TX 75228-2640
Telephone: (972) 681-5701, Toll Free:
(800) 688-5701, FAX: (972) 681-
5786, E-Mail: nimnames@att.net
Pres: Judy Ashley

NAMES IN THE NEWS
1890 Grand Ave (Suite 1365)
Oakland, CA 94612
Telephone: (415) 989-3350, FAX:
(415) 433-7796, E-Mail:
susananstrand@nincal.com, Web
Site: www.nincal.com
CEO: Susan Anstrand
Partner & CFO: David Herrick
Pres: Suzie McGuire
Conducts Business: U.S.
Primary Market Served: Business
Founded: 1969

List brokerage and management company for nonprofit organizations.

NATIONAL FUNDRAISING LISTS
Div. of CDR Fundraising Group
16900 Science Dr (Suite 210)
Bowie, MD 20715-4412
Telephone: (410) 721-5700, FAX:
(410) 721-5795, E-Mail: info@
nflists.com, Web Site: www.nflists.
com
Sr VP: Diane Hardy
Acct Exec: Jennifer O'Baker
Primary Market Served: Business

List brokerage, list management & direct mail marketing list provider for
nonprofit organizations.

NEIGHBORHOOD GREETINGS
Member of the Allegra Network
6951 Allentown Blvd (Suite D)
Harrisburg, PA 17112
Telephone: (717) 839-6390, Toll Free:
(800) 332-9200, Web Site: ngp.
allegraharrisburg.com
Pres: Will Stone
Primary Market Served: Business &
Consumer
Founded: 1982

Direct mail marketing company & list
provider specializing in healthcare providers.

NET 60 LLC
228 Park Ave S (Suite 83872)
New York, NY 10003-1502
Telephone: (201) 833-9003, FAX:
(201) 301-8182, E-Mail: chaim@
net60.com, Web Site: net60.com
Pres: Chaim Lazar
Dir Opers: Sharon Nussbaum
VP Sales: Paula Markowitz
Primary Market Served: Business
Founded: 2003

Full-service list brokerage specializing
in list management.

NETHAWK INTERACTIVE
1255 Park Ave (Suite D)
Emeryville, CA 94608-3679
Telephone: (510) 595-2220, E-Mail:
info@nethawk.net, Web Site: www.
nethawk.net
Founder: Robert Mendez
VP: James McManis
VP Client Svcs: Carlotta Navarra
Conducts Business: U.S.
Primary Market Served: Business &
Consumer
Founded: 1998

Online B2B technology marketing and
advertising planning & management
company.

NEW ENGLAND LIST SERVICES INC
171 Mountain View Dr
Danville, VT 05828-9641
Telephone: (802) 684-1179, Toll Free:
(877) 252-2100, FAX: (802) 684-
2113, E-Mail: dave@nelists.com,
Web Site: www.nelists.com
Pres: David Hare
Conducts Business: U.S.
Primary Market Served: Consumer
Founded: 2001

Provider of targeted, consumer mailing
lists.

NEXXA GROUP INC
12734 Kenwood Ln (Suite 87)
Fort Myers, FL 33907-5638
Telephone: (239) 225-1516, Toll Free:
(800) 566-1217, E-Mail: info@
nexxagroup.com, Web Site: www.
nexxagroup.com
Pres: Holly Paulus
Conducts Business: U.S.
Primary Market Served: Business &
Consumer
Founded: 2005

Direct marketing data & database solutions provider.

OMEGA LIST CO
Subs. of Eberle Communications
Group
1420 Spring Hill Rd (Suite 490)
McLean, VA 22102-3028
Telephone: (703) 821-1890, FAX:
(703) 821-8794, E-Mail:
listmanager@omegalist.com, Web
Site: omegalist.com
List Mgr: Christine Tessier
Pres: Michael Hiban
Primary Market Served: Business &
Consumer
Founded: 1975

Direct mail list provider specializing in
charitable & political organizations.

PMX AGENCY
5 Hanover Sq
New York, NY 10004-2614
Telephone: (212) 387-0300, Toll Free:
(888) 960-0177, FAX: (212) 387-
7647, E-Mail: info@pmxagency.
com, Web Site: www.pmxagency.
com
Co-CEO: Chris Paradysz
Mktg Mgr: Mike Cousineau
Sr Mktg Mgr: Keisha Brescia
Exec VP: Sloan Seymour
CMO: Mary Beth Keelty
Conducts Business: U.S., Europe, Middle East
Employees: 800

Primary Market Served: Business &
Consumer
Founded: 1990

Global integrated marketing agency.

PACKER LIST INC
612 E Capitol St NE
Washington, DC 20003
Telephone: (202) 546-1889, FAX:
(202) 546-1897, E-Mail: dpacker@
packerlist.com, Web Site: www.
packerlist.com
Pres: Donna Packer
Conducts Business: U.S.
Founded: 1990

Full-service list broker & list manager.

PARAMOUNT LISTS INC
3126 Peach St
Erie, PA 16508-2734
Telephone: (814) 459-8787, Toll Free:
(800) 723-5478, FAX: (814) 459-
1398, E-Mail: info@paramountlists.
com, Web Site: www.
paramountdirectmarketing.com
Pres: Ralph Genovese
Primary Market Served: Business &
Consumer
Founded: 1972

Direct marketing mailing list & list
management provider.

PEPPERMILL MARKETING
INC
8335 W Sunset Blvd (Suite 246)
Los Angeles, CA 90069-1529
Toll Free: (866) 737-5478, E-Mail:
inquiry@peppermillmarketing.com,
Web Site: peppermillmarketing.com
Pres: Michael Franchino
Conducts Business: U.S.
Primary Market Served: Business &
Consumer
Direct online sales
Founded: 1993

Consumer & B2B direct mail and e-
mail marketing list brokerage & list
manager.

PINNACLE LIST CO
2800 Shirlington Rd (Suite 970)
Arlington, VA 22206-3613
Telephone: (703) 379-4394, FAX:
(703) 379-5312, E-Mail: holly@
pinnlistco.com, Web Site: www.
pinnlistco.com
Pres: Holly Ruble
List Mgmt Dir: Jennifer McLaughlin
Conducts Business: U.S.
Primary Market Served: Business &
Consumer

Full-service list brokerage & list management company specializing in the
political & nonprofit sectors.

POLITICAL RESOURCES INC
PO Box 1403
Lake Worth, FL 33460-1403
Toll Free: (800) 423-2677, FAX: (561)
533-0104, E-Mail: chess@
politicalresources.com, Web Site:
www.politicalresources.com
Pres: Carol Hess
Primary Market Served: Business &
Consumer
Founded: 1986

List brokerage and list management
company specializing in political, governmental and legal direct mail and
email lists.

PONT MEDIA DIRECT
10 E Meadow Ln
Norwalk, CT 06851-2902
Telephone: (203) 354-8074, FAX:
(203) 956-9227, E-Mail: stefanie@
listgoddess.com
Mng Partner: Stefanie Pont
Conducts Business: U.S., Canada, Eu-
rope & Asia
Primary Market Served: Business &
Consumer
Founded: 2004

List brokerage & marketing consulting
services.

WS PONTON INC
3030 William Pitt Way
Pittsburgh, PA 15238
Telephone: (412) 782-2360, Toll Free:
(800) 628-7806, FAX: (412) 782-
1109, E-Mail: info@wsponton.com,
Web Site: www.wsponton.com
VP, Sls: Joseph Marchese
Media Mgr: Marianne Rabinowitz
Conducts Business: U.S., Canada
Primary Market Served: Business &
Consumer

Provider of list broker services and
marketing data for direct mail campaigns, mailing lists, telemarketing
data & email lists.

RMI DIRECT MARKETING
INC
44 Old Ridgebury Rd (Plz 1)
Danbury, CT 06810-5107
Telephone: (203) 798-0448, FAX:
(203) 778-6130, E-Mail: info@
rmidirect.com, Web Site: www.
rmidirect.com
CEO: Tally Maffucci
Sr VP, Brokerage: Rich Leary
VP Bus Devel: Debbie McLain
Primary Market Served: Business &
Consumer

Founded: 1985
Direct marketing company offering list
brokerage & management, alternative
media and digital & creative services.

REDI-DATA INC
Subs. of Redi-Direct Inc
5 Audrey Pl
Fairfield, NJ 07004-3401
Telephone: (973) 227-4380, Toll Free:
(800) 635-5833, FAX: (973) 808-
5511, E-Mail: sales@redidata.com,
Web Site: www.redidata.com
Founder & CEO: Tom Buckley
Conducts Business: U.S.
Primary Market Served: Business &
Consumer
Founded: 2005

Provider of postal and email lists, data
services and direct marketing solutions.

REIN ASSOCIATES LLC
209 Waltrip St (Unit 5)
Conway, SC 29526-8384
Telephone: (843) 234-0422, Toll Free:
(888) 734-6462, FAX: (843) 234-
0428, E-Mail: info@reinassociates.
com, Web Site: reinassociates.com
Pres: Jack Rein
Conducts Business: U.S.
Primary Market Served: Consumer
Founded: 1977

Direct mail marketing support services
company.

RESEARCH & RESPONSE
INTERNATIONAL INC
250 W 57th St (Suite 1326)
New York, NY 10107-1309
Telephone: (212) 489-8610, FAX:
(212) 262-3474
Pres: George Collins
Primary Market Served: Consumer
Founded: 1985

Database marketing company specializing in consumer buying patterns in
the direct & online marketing arenas.

RESPONSE UNLIMITED
284 Shalom Rd
Waynesboro, VA 22980-7349
Telephone: (540) 943-6721, FAX:
(540) 943-0841, E-Mail: info@
responseunlimited.com, Web Site:
www.responseunlimited.com
Pres: Philip Zodhiates
Conducts Business: U.S.
Primary Market Served: Business &
Consumer

Mailing list management, list brokerage
and creative services company.

RICKARD SQUARED

190 Motor Pkwy (Suite 103)
Hauppauge, NY 11788-5159
Telephone: (631) 249-8710, FAX:
(631) 382-8248, E-Mail: mrickard@
rickard2.com, Web Site: rickard2.
com
Pres: Mark Rickard
Exec VP & COO: Jennifer Rickard
Primary Market Served: Consumer
Founded: 1986

Data-driven direct marketing products
& solutions company.

THE RIGHT LISTS LTD

305 Beckwith St
Gaithersburg, MD 20878-5603
Telephone: (301) 869-2020, E-Mail:
bfletch@rightlists.com, Web Site:
www.rightlists.com
Pres: Bill Fletcher
Conducts Business: U.S.
Primary Market Served: Business &
Consumer

Customized list brokerage services provider.

ROBERTSON MAILING LIST CO

113 E Market St (Suite 300)
Leesburg, VA 20176
Telephone: (703) 509-8441, FAX:
(888) 308-2572, E-Mail: vnorman@
rmlc.net, Web Site: www.rmlc.net
VP: Vickie L. Norman
Dir Mktg: Molly Rinaldi
Pres: Tammy Evans
Dir, Mktg & List Mngmt: Karen von
Kleeck
Primary Market Served: Business &
Consumer
Founded: 1987

List management & brokerage for political, charitable and conservative
mailers.

ROSEBERRY DIRECT LIST MANAGEMENT & BROKERAGE

265 Timberline Trl
Elon, NC 27244-8088
Telephone: (336) 532-1000, FAX:
(336) 532-1003, E-Mail: churteau@
roseberrydirect.com, Web Site:
roseberrydirect.com
Pres: Claudia Hurteau
Primary Market Served: Consumer
Founded: 2001

List rental services company.

SIE (SELECT INFORMATION EXCHANGE)

175 W 79th St
New York, NY 10024
Telephone: (212) 496-6435, FAX:
(212) 787-4269, Web Site: www.
siecom.com
List Mgr: Alex Wein
Pres: George Wein

SK&A

An IMS Health company
2601 Main St (Suite 650)
Irvine, CA 92614-4228
Toll Free: (800) 752-5478, FAX: (949)
476-9131, E-Mail: skasales@skainfo.
com, Web Site: www.skainfo.com
Pres: David Escalante
VP Fin: Jack Schember
Conducts Business: U.S.
Primary Market Served: Business &
Consumer
Founded: 1984

Leading provider of healthcare reference information in the United States.

SWAT MARKETING TEAM

433 S Broad St, PO Box 464
Grove City, PA 16127
Telephone: (412) 851-9700, FAX:
(412) 291-1155, E-Mail: cdbloch@
swatmarketingteam.com, Web Site:
swatmarketingteam.com
Pres: Christopher Bloch
Conducts Business: Worldwide
Primary Market Served: Business
Founded: 1999

Provides prospecting lists and databases to companies in the computer industry.

SALESLEADS.TV INC

2701 NW 2nd Ave (Suite 213)
Boca Raton, FL 33431
Telephone: (561) 239-0364, Toll Free:
(800) 590-5323, FAX: (561) 981-
8786, E-Mail: bear@salesleads.tv,
Web Site: www.salesleads.tv
Pres: John Fischer
Conducts Business: U.S.
Primary Market Served: Business &
Consumer
Founded: 1990

Full-service list broker and leads provider.

SORKINS INC

PO Box 411067
Saint Louis, MO 63141
Telephone: (314) 373-3975, E-Mail:
sales@sorkins.com, Web Site: www.
sorkins.com
Chmn & CEO: Murray L. Sorkin

Primary Market Served: Business &
Consumer

Publisher and list provider of business
& government information covering
the Missouri, Illinois & Kansas regions.

SOUND BEACH MARKETING PARTNERS LLC

Two Rocky Point Rd
Old Greenwich, CT 06870
Telephone: (203) 698-0708, FAX:
(203) 698-0712, E-Mail: thudock@
soundbeachmarketing.com, Web
Site: www.soundbeachmarketing.
com
Mng Owner: Terry Hudock
Conducts Business: U.S.
Primary Market Served: Business &
Consumer
Founded: 2001

List marketing services company.

SPECIALISTS MARKETING SERVICES INC

777 Terrace Ave (Suite 401)
Hasbrouck Heights, NJ 07604
Telephone: (201) 865-5800, FAX:
(201) 288-4295, E-Mail: info@sms-
inc.com, Web Site: www.sms-inc.
com
VP Sls & Mktg: Lon L. Mandel
Pres: Bruce Sherman
CFO: Nora Bush
Pres: Robin Neal
Exec VP: Susan Giampietro
Conducts Business: U.S.
Primary Market Served: Business &
Consumer
Founded: 1987

Data-driven, multi-channel marketing
company specializing in postal, digital
and insert media solutions.

SPLASHNET INC

Subs. of Redi-Direct Inc
20 Gloria Ln
Fairfield, NJ 07004
Telephone: (877) 244-9362, E-Mail:
contactus@splashnet.com, Web Site:
www.splashnet.com
Pres: Tom Buckley
Primary Market Served: Business

Provider of healthcare specialty email
lists and healthcare mailing lists.

STATLISTICS

An Alesco Co.
51-53 Kenosia Ave
Danbury, CT 06810
Telephone: (203) 778-8700, FAX:
(203) 778-4839, E-Mail: info@
statlistics.com, Web Site: www.
statlistics.com
CEO: John Papalia

Exec VP: Chris DeMartine
Mktg Dir: Tamara FitzGerald
Primary Market Served: Business

List management, list brokerage, E-commerce, merge/purge and data processing services provider.

GEORGE STERNE AGENCY INC

Subs. of PPAL
747 S Mission Rd (Suite 2200)
Fallbrook, CA 92088
Telephone: (760) 432-6913, Toll Free: (800) 772-8174, FAX: (760) 432-9570, E-Mail: info@ georgesterneagency.net, Web Site: georgesterneagency.net
Pres: Don Dominick
Pres: Claudia Dominick
Primary Market Served: Business & Consumer
Founded: 1974

List compiler specializing in the financial services industries.

TKLI

TKL Interactive Inc
3700 Standridge Dr (Suite 210)
The Colony, TX 75056-4149
Telephone: (972) 370-7878, Toll Free: (800) 789-3893, FAX: (972) 370-7879, E-Mail: info@tkli.com, Web Site: www.tkli.com
Pres: Ken Walker
Conducts Business: Worldwide
Primary Market Served: Business & Consumer
Catalog available online
Direct online sales
Founded: 1998

Full-service interactive agency, providing e-mail, direct mail, creative services, marketing strategy, execution and buys.

TMA DIRECT INC

2000 Edmund Halley Dr (Suite 250)
Reston, VA 20191
Telephone: (703) 547-4940, Toll Free: (877) TMA-5566, FAX: (703) 547-4979, E-Mail: info@tmadirect.com, Web Site: www.tmadirect.com
VP: Mike Murray
Conducts Business: U.S.
Primary Market Served: Business & Consumer
Founded: 1985

Full-service media agency specializing in list brokerage & management and data services.

3 GEN CO

544 Empire Blvd
Brooklyn, NY 11225

Telephone: (718) 484-4354
Pres: Moshe Kugel
Conducts Business: U.S.
Primary Market Served: Business & Consumer
Founded: 1989

Direct mail services company specializing in nonprofits.

TOUCHPOINT DATA SOLUTIONS INC

13010 Morris Rd (Bldg 1, Suite 600)
Alpharetta, GA 30004
Telephone: (770) 886-8611, FAX: (678) 686-1835, Web Site: touchpointdata.com
CEO: Max Korgman
Conducts Business: U.S.
Primary Market Served: Business & Consumer
Founded: 2003

Online consumer behavioral data compilation, prospect/customer email and social network marketing solutions provider.

TRI-MEDIA MARKETING SERVICES INC

3330 Old Glenview Rd (Suite 2)
Wilmette, IL 60091-2963
Toll Free: (800) 874-0338, E-Mail: neals@trimediaonline.com, Web Site: www.trimediaonline.com
Pres & Sls Mng: Neal Siegel
Conducts Business: U.S., Canada
Primary Market Served: Business
Catalog available online
Founded: 1989

Provides direct marketing and data & list services targeting Christian church leaders, homeschool families & consumers.

TRIAX DATA INC

8911 Linksvue Dr
Knoxville, TN 37922-5254
Telephone: (865) 971-4333, Toll Free: (888) 241-9559, FAX: (865) 971-4333, E-Mail: info@triaxdata.com, Web Site: www.triaxdata.com
Dir: Jonathan Brooks
Opers Mgr: Russell Brown
Primary Market Served: Consumer
Founded: 1996

Database marketing services provider for direct mail and telemarketing campaigns.

TRINITY DIRECT LLC

10 Park Pl (Bldg 5)
Butler, NJ 07405

Telephone: (973) 283-3600, FAX: (973) 283-3606, E-Mail: trinity. info@trinitydirect.net, Web Site: www.trinitydirect.net
Pres: John Kehoe
VP Sls & Mktg: Sean Kehoe
Conducts Business: U.S.
Primary Market Served: Business & Consumer
Founded: 1997

Direct mail marketing company specializing in list brokerage, list management and technology solutions.

US DATA CORP

17310 Wright St (Suite 100)
Omaha, NE 68130
Telephone: (402) 758-0290, Toll Free: (888) 578-3282, FAX: (402) 934-3885, E-Mail: info@ usdatacorporation.com, Web Site: www.usdatacorp.net
Mktg Dir: Erich Kaminsky
Conducts Business: U.S.
Primary Market Served: Business & Consumer
Founded: 1979

Marketing services company and provider of mailing lists, marketing data, sales leads & research data.

USADATA INC

477 Madison Ave (Suite 1220)
New York, NY 10022-5839
Toll Free: (800) 395-7707, E-Mail: info@usadata.com, Web Site: www. usadata.com
Data & Leads Group: Jon Rapkin
Primary Market Served: Business & Consumer
Founded: 2007

Direct marketing technology company that provides prospect lists, email marketing, display & social media advertising and data services through easy-to-use SaaS technology products.

VISION MARKETING INC

455 Sylvan Ave
Englewood Cliffs, NJ 07632-2703
Telephone: (201) 816-1560, FAX: (201) 816-1610, E-Mail: vminfo@ visionmarketing.com, Web Site: www.visionmarketing.com
Pres: Michael Young
Primary Market Served: Business & Consumer

Email & postal list brokerage specializing in the financial, insurance and telecommunications industries.

WASHINGTON LISTS INC

6849 Old Dominion Dr (Suite 320)
McLean, VA 22101

Telephone: (703) 749-3110, FAX:
   (703) 749-0960, E-Mail:
   emahoney@washingtonlists.com,
   Web Site: www.washingtonlists.com
Gen Mgr: Erin Mahoney
Conducts Business: U.S.
Primary Market Served: Business

List brokerage, management and rental
fulfillment services company.

FRED WOOLF LIST CO INC
PO Box 346
Somers, NY 10589-0346
Telephone: (914) 694-4466, Toll Free:
   (800) 431-1557, FAX: (914) 694-
   1710, E-Mail: info@woolflist.com,
   Web Site: www.woolflist.com
Pres: Fred Woolf
Sr VP: Sheila Woolf
Conducts Business: U.S.
Primary Market Served: Business &
   Consumer
Founded: 1972

List compiler and brokerage for the direct mail industry.

WORLDATA
3000 N Military Trl
Boca Raton, FL 33431-6321
Telephone: (561) 393-8200, Toll Free:
   (800) 331-8102, FAX: (561) 368-
   8345, E-Mail: hello@worldata.com,
   Web Site: www.worldata.com
Corp VP: Jay Schwedelson
Primary Market Served: Business &
   Consumer
Founded: 1975

Response marketing solutions company
specializing in new customer acquisition, lead generation and data hygiene.

ARIZONA

Mad Mimi, 14455 N Hayden Rd (Suite 219), Scottsdale, 85260

CALIFORNIA

Campaign Monitor, 631 Howard St (Suite 500), San Francisco, 94105

DAJ Direct Inc, 1501 Westcliff Dr (Suite 325), Newport Beach, 92660

Data.com, The Landmark, One Market (Suite 300), San Francisco, 94105

HomeData, PO Box 1449, Goleta, 93116-1149

MSI Direct Response Inc, 1501 Westcliff Dr (Suite 307), Newport Beach, 92660

VerticalResponse Inc, 550 Kearny St (Suite 710), San Francisco, 94108

COLORADO

Accutrend Data Corp, 7860 E Berry Place (Suite 200), Greenwood Village, 80111-2303

Agile Education Marketing LLC, 110 16th St (Suite 506), Denver, 80202

CONNECTICUT

Ginsburg Global LLC, 850 E Main St (Suite 501), Stamford, 06902

List Services Corporation, 6 Trowbridge Dr, PO Box 516, Bethel, 06801-0516

World Innovators Inc, 22 Bacon Rd, Roxbury, 06783-1817

DELAWARE

GetResponse Services Inc, 1011 Centre Rd (Suite 322), Wilmington, 19805

FLORIDA

Best ROI Lists, 7491 N Federal Hwy (Suite C5-324), Boca Raton, 33487

Lighthouse List Co, 27 SE 24th Ave (Suite 6), Pompano Beach, 33062-5346

Media Source Solutions, 31 Southeast 24th Ave (Suite 2), Pompano Beach, 33062

Newsmax List Management, PO Box 20989, West Palm Beach, 33416-0989

Outsource America Inc, 715 60th St Court E, Bradenton, 34208-6262

Titan List & Mailing Services Inc, 1020 NW 6th St (Suite D), Deerfield Beach, 33442

21st Century Marketing, 303 Alt Bay Club Cir (Suite 104), Altamonte Springs, 32701

GEORGIA

DataCentral Inc, 1235 Kennestone Cir NW (Suite F), Kennesaw, 30066

DirectInnovations Inc, 637 Pringle Dr, Suwanee, 30024

List Partners Inc, 3098 Piedmont Rd NE (Suite 200), Atlanta, 30305

MailChimp, 675 Ponce de Leon Ave NE (Suite 5000), Atlanta, 30308

ILLINOIS

ActiveCampaign Inc, 222 S Riverside Plz (Suite 810), Chicago, 60606

Mardevdm2, 2000 Clearwater Dr, Oak Brook, 60523

Medical Marketing Service Inc, 935 National Pkwy (Suite 93510), Schaumburg, 60173-5179

MARYLAND

Bethesda List Center Inc, 4300 Montgomery Ave (Suite 204-B), Bethesda, 20814-4463

Columbia Books & Information Services, 4340 East-West Hwy (Suite 300), Bethesda, 20814

InvestorPlace Lists, 9201 Corporate Blvd, Rockville, 20850-3202

Name Exchange, 880 N East St (Unit 201), Frederick, 21701-5045

MASSACHUSETTS

IDG List Services, 492 Old Connecticut Path, PO Box 9208, Framingham, 01701

NEBRASKA

William-Neil Associates, One Cabela Dr (Suite 2114), Sidney, 69160

NEW JERSEY

The Information Refinery Inc, 1 International Blvd (Suite 1200), Mahwah, 07495

LegaLists, 890 Mountain Ave (Suite 300), New Providence, 07974-1218

Profile America List Co Inc, 455 Sylvan Ave, Englewood Cliffs, 07632-2703

NEW YORK

Estee Marketing Group Inc, 800 Westchester Ave (Suite 614), Rye Brook, 10573

Hearst Business Media, 300 W 57th St, New York, 10019

IEEE Media, 3 Park Ave (fl 17), New York, 10016-5902

RAD Marketing, 167 Crary On-The-Park, Mount Vernon, 10550

The Rich List Co, PO Box 294, Wainscott, 11975-0294

Teikoku Databank America Inc, 780 3rd Ave (Floor 25), New York, 10017

ThomasNet RPM, 5 Penn Plz (Floor 17), New York, 10001

OKLAHOMA

Chilcutt Direct Marketing, 813 E 33rd St, Edmond, 73013-5407

PennWell Corp, 1421 S Sheridan Rd, Tulsa, 74112-6600

OREGON

Institute Lists, 1000 SW Broadway (Suite 1200), Portland, 97205

PENNSYLVANIA

AWeber Communications, 1100 Manor Dr, Chalfont, 18914

Great Lakes List Management, 3126 Peach St, Erie, 16508-2734

SOUTH CAROLINA

List Connection Inc, PO Box 1712, Simpsonville, 29681-1712

TENNESSEE

Emma, 9 Lea Ave, Nashville, 37210

List Managers & Owners (24)

ACCUTREND DATA CORP
7860 E Berry Place (Suite 200)
Greenwood Village, CO 80111-2303
Telephone: (303) 488-0011, FAX:
(303) 488-0133, E-Mail: info@
accutrend.com, Web Site: www.
accutrend.com
CEO: Vicki Reavis
Primary Market Served: Business &
Consumer
Founded: 1989

Directly acquires raw business records
from government jurisdictions and
standardizes, processes, links & up-
dates them daily.

ACTIVECAMPAIGN INC
222 S Riverside Plz (Suite 810)
Chicago, IL 60606
Toll Free: (800) 357-0402, E-Mail:
help@activecampaign.com, Web
Site: www.activecampaign.com
Pres: Jason VandeBoom
COO: Milos Srdjevic
CTO: Peter Evans
VP Mktg: Edward Angstadt
VP Fin: Tim Compton
Conducts Business: Worldwide
Primary Market Served: Business &
Consumer
Founded: 2003

Integrated marketing automation, email
marketing and automated sales CRM
platform.

**AGILE EDUCATION
MARKETING LLC**
110 16th St (Suite 506)
Denver, CO 80202
Toll Free: (866) 783-0241, E-Mail:
info@agile-ed.com, Web Site: www.
agile-ed.com
VP & Gen Mgr: Bob O'Dell
Mng Ptnr: Verlan Stephens
VP Corp Devel: Scott Brooks
Sr VP Bus Devel: Larry Sanek
VP Sales & Mktg: Jenny Schumacher
Conducts Business: U.S.
Primary Market Served: Business &
Consumer
Founded: 2009

Marketing solutions company specializing in education.

**AWEBER
COMMUNICATIONS**
1100 Manor Dr
Chalfont, PA 18914
Toll Free: (877) 293-2371, Web Site:
www.aweber.com
Pres & Owner: Tom Kulzer
COO: Sean Cohen

CTO: Brian Jones
CMO: Erik Harbison
Primary Market Served: Business &
Consumer
Founded: 1998

List management company specializing
in email marketing campaigns.

BEST ROI LISTS
Div. of Alliance Strategies Group
7491 N Federal Hwy (Suite C5-324)
Boca Raton, FL 33487
Telephone: (877) 301-5478, E-Mail:
info@bestroilists.com, Web Site:
www.bestroilists.com
Pres: Bryan Rudnick
Primary Market Served: Business &
Consumer

Marketing company specializing in
email list rentals.

**BETHESDA LIST CENTER
INC**
4300 Montgomery Ave (Suite 204-B)
Bethesda, MD 20814-4463
Telephone: (301) 986-1455, FAX:
(301) 907-4870, E-Mail: info@
bethesda-list.com, Web Site: www.
bethesda-list.com
Mktg Mgr: David James
Conducts Business: U.S., Canada,
Worldwide
Primary Market Served: Business
Indirect online sales
Founded: 1993

Full-service list manager and brokerage
specializing in publishers, associations,
seminar provider, catalogers and computer software & hardware companies.

CAMPAIGN MONITOR
631 Howard St (Suite 500)
San Francisco, CA 94105
Telephone: (888) 533-8098, E-Mail:
info@campaignmonitor.com, Web
Site: www.campaignmonitor.com
Pres: Alex Bard
COO: Craig Shull
CMO: Andrea Wildt
CTO: Herry Wiputra
Conducts Business: Worldwide
Employees: 250
Primary Market Served: Business &
Consumer
Founded: 2004

Provider of professional-grade email
marketing and automation software.

**CHILCUTT DIRECT
MARKETING**
813 E 33rd St

Edmond, OK 73013-5407
Telephone: (405) 726-8780, FAX:
(405) 726-8799, E-Mail: info@
cdmlist.com, Web Site: www.
cdmlist.com
Pres: Matt Chilcutt
VP: Jane McCoy
Conducts Business: U.S.
Primary Market Served: Business &
Consumer
Founded: 1980

Direct marketing company specializing
in list management & brokerage.

**COLUMBIA BOOKS &
INFORMATION SERVICES**
4340 East-West Hwy (Suite 300)
Bethesda, MD 20814
Telephone: (202) 464-1662, Toll Free:
(888) 265-0600, FAX: (202) 464-
1775, E-Mail: info@columbiabooks.
com, Web Site: www.
columbiabooks.com
Pres: Joel Poznansky
Primary Market Served: Business &
Consumer
Founded: 1965

Provider of compliance resources, print
directories, online databases and customized data delivery.

DAJ DIRECT INC
1501 Westcliff Dr (Suite 325)
Newport Beach, CA 92660
Telephone: (949) 722-0506, FAX:
(949) 722-8026, E-Mail: orders@
dajdirect.com, Web Site: www.
dajdirect.com
CEO & Pres: Daniel Jacobs
Exec VP: Robert Jacobs
Conducts Business: U.S.
Primary Market Served: Business &
Consumer
Catalog available online
Founded: 1993

List managers and brokerage specializing in business & financial opportunities, health & credit lists.

DATA.COM
Div. of Salesforce.com Inc
The Landmark, One Market (Suite 300)
San Francisco, CA 94105
Telephone: (415) 901-7000, Toll Free:
(800) 667-6389, Web Site: www.
data.com
Conducts Business: Worldwide
Primary Market Served: Business

Online directory of companies & business professionals, designed for multi-
channel (mail, email & phone) B2B
campaigns.

DATACENTRAL INC
1235 Kennestone Cir NW (Suite F)
Kennesaw, GA 30066
Telephone: (770) 218-8200, Toll Free:
(800) 411-5771, FAX: (770) 218-
8211, E-Mail: info@datacentralinc.
com, Web Site: www.datacentralinc.
com
Conducts Business: U.S.
Primary Market Served: Business &
Consumer
Founded: 2002

Full-service direct mail marketing company specializing in list, data, addressing, fulfillment & print services.

DIRECTINNOVATIONS INC
637 Pringle Dr
Suwanee, GA 30024
Telephone: (404) 402-2825, E-Mail:
htorgersen@directinnovations.biz,
Web Site: www.directinnovations.biz
Pres: Herb Torgersen
Primary Market Served: Business &
Consumer

Full-service direct marketing services and database/media management firm.

EMMA
9 Lea Ave
Nashville, TN 37210
Toll Free: (800) 595-4401, E-Mail:
hi@myemma.com, Web Site:
myemma.com
Owner: Clint Smith
Sr VP Mktg: Colby Cavanaugh
Conducts Business: Worldwide
Primary Market Served: Business &
Consumer
Founded: 2002

Email marketing software & services provider.

ESTEE MARKETING GROUP INC
800 Westchester Ave (Suite 614)
Rye Brook, NY 10573
Telephone: (914) 235-7080, FAX:
(914) 235-6518, E-Mail: info@
esteemarketing.com, Web Site:
www.esteemarketing.com
Pres: Chris Ragusa
Sr VP: Stan Madyda
Primary Market Served: Business &
Consumer
Founded: 1969

Direct marketing list services company specializing in list management, list brokerage, campaign/donor analyses, mail planning and insert media management & brokerage.

GETRESPONSE SERVICES INC
1011 Centre Rd (Suite 322)
Wilmington, DE 19805
Toll Free: (877) 362-4547, Web Site:
www.getresponse.com
Pres: Simon Grabowski
CMO: Daniel Brzezinski
CFO: Marta Zablocka-Peterson
CTO: Wojciech Zwiefka
Conducts Business: Worldwide
Primary Market Served: Business &
Consumer
Founded: 1997

Email marketing and online campaign management solutions company.

GINSBURG GLOBAL LLC
850 E Main St (Suite 501)
Stamford, CT 06902
Telephone: (203) 359-2420, FAX:
(203) 325-4443, E-Mail: gerry@
ginsburgglobal.com, Web Site: www.
ginsburgglobal.com
Pres: Gerry Ginsburg
Conducts Business: Worldwide
Primary Market Served: Business &
Consumer
Founded: 2007

International list manager & broker specializing in mailing lists, telemarketing lists, opt-in emails & SMS marketing.

GREAT LAKES LIST MANAGEMENT
3126 Peach St
Erie, PA 16508-2734
Telephone: (814) 456-2175, Toll Free:
(800) 964-5478, FAX: (814) 455-
1942, E-Mail: info@greatlakeslists.
com, Web Site: www.greatlakeslists.
com
Pres: Jay Stockhausen
Primary Market Served: Business &
Consumer

List management and direct marketing products & services company.

HEARST BUSINESS MEDIA
Div. of Hearst Communications Inc
300 W 57th St
New York, NY 10019
Telephone: (212) 649-2000, Web Site:
www.hearst.com/business-media
List Rentals Coord: Richard Malloch
Circ Dir: Gregory Dorn
Exec VP: Steven Hobbs
Exec VP: Thomas Cross
Conducts Business: Worldwide

Primary Market Served: Business &
Consumer

Global technology leader delivering information, insights, analytics and workflow solutions in the finance, healthcare and transportation markets.

HOMEDATA
Subs. of Avrick Direct Inc
PO Box 1449
Goleta, CA 93116-1149
Telephone: (805) 683-6551, FAX:
(805) 683-6553, E-Mail: doreen@
avrick.com, Web Site: avrickdirect.
com/homedata
Pres: Doreen Ellen Burk
Conducts Business: U.S.
Primary Market Served: Business &
Consumer
Direct online sales
Founded: 1982

The list compiler of new homeowner and new mover data to the direct marketing industry.

IDG LIST SERVICES
Div. of IDG
492 Old Connecticut Path, PO Box
9208
Framingham, MA 01701
Telephone: (508) 766-5633, E-Mail:
stozeski@idglist.com, Web Site:
www.idglist.com
Gen Mgr: Stephen Tozeski
Mktg Dir: Kim Pisano
Primary Market Served: Business &
Consumer

List management & brokerage services provider specializing in high tech B2B and prosumer direct marketing, lead generation & data intelligence.

IEEE MEDIA
3 Park Ave (fl 17)
New York, NY 10016-5902
Toll Free: (800) 261-2052, E-Mail:
ieeemedia@ieeeglobalspec.com,
Web Site: advertise.ieee.org
Direct Mail Mktg Mgr: Mark David
Primary Market Served: Business &
Consumer

Provides postal & email lists rentals of the IEEE Spectrum Masterfile.

THE INFORMATION REFINERY INC
1 International Blvd (Suite 1200)
Mahwah, NJ 07495
Telephone: (201) 529-2600, Toll Free:
(800) 529-9020, FAX: (201) 529-
4030, E-Mail: info@inforefinery.
com, Web Site: inforefinery.com
Pres: Gordon Clotworthy
EVP: Brian Clotworthy

Conducts Business: U.S.
Primary Market Served: Business &
   Consumer
Founded: 1986

Full-service list brokerage, list management & lead generation company.

INSTITUTE LISTS

Div. of Business Valuation Resources
1000 SW Broadway (Suite 1200)
Portland, OR 97205
Telephone: (917) 751-8439, E-Mail:
   info@institutelists.com, Web Site:
   institutelists.com
Pres, Institute Lists: Debra Goldfarb
Primary Market Served: Business

Business list and data management provider.

INVESTORPLACE LISTS

Div. of InvestorPlace Media LLC
9201 Corporate Blvd
Rockville, MD 20850-3202
Telephone: (601) 620-4135, FAX:
   (703) 940-7749, E-Mail: dferry@
   investormedia.com, Web Site: www.
   investorplacelists.com
VP: Dave Ferry
Primary Market Served: Business &
   Consumer

List management service for Investor-Place Media.

LEGALISTS

Div. of Lawyers Diary and Manual
   LLC
890 Mountain Ave (Suite 300)
New Providence, NJ 07974-1218
Telephone: (973) 642-1440 ext.109,
   FAX: (973) 642-3731, E-Mail:
   jwenzel@lawdiary.com, Web Site:
   www.lawdiary.com
List Mgr: Jill Wenzel
Conducts Business: U.S.
Primary Market Served: Business &
   Consumer

Provider of customized attorneys lists for qualified vendors.

LIGHTHOUSE LIST CO

27 SE 24th Ave (Suite 6)
Pompano Beach, FL 33062-5346
Telephone: (954) 489-3008, Toll Free:
   (800) 684-2180, FAX: (954) 489-
   0850, E-Mail: mtlistdude@aol.com,
   Web Site: www.lighthouselist.com
VP: Mark Traverso
Conducts Business: U.S., Canada
Primary Market Served: Business &
   Consumer
Founded: 1994

Full-service, integrated marketing agency specializing in lead generation and cost per lead marketing.

LIST CONNECTION INC

dba ListConnection.net
PO Box 1712
Simpsonville, SC 29681-1712
Telephone: (864) 962-0761, FAX:
   (864) 962-0769, E-Mail: leads@
   listconnection.net, Web Site: www.
   listconnection.net
VP List Mngmt & Sls: Ken Wood
Conducts Business: U.S., Canada
Primary Market Served: Business &
   Consumer

List management services provider.

LIST PARTNERS INC

3098 Piedmont Rd NE (Suite 200)
Atlanta, GA 30305
Telephone: (404) 350-0600, Toll Free:
   (800) 941-6562, E-Mail: contact@
   thelistinc.com, Web Site:
   listpartnersinc.com
Pres: Dave Currie
VP Client Svcs: David Thomson
VP Bus Devel: Billy Boydston
Sr List Mgr: Dan Mottern
VP Sls: Jennifer Groese
Conducts Business: U.S., Canada, U.K.
Primary Market Served: Business &
   Consumer
Founded: 1995

Sales intelligence company specializing in B2B sales & lead generation.

LIST SERVICES
CORPORATION

6 Trowbridge Dr, PO Box 516
Bethel, CT 06801-0516
Telephone: (203) 743-2600, E-Mail:
   info@listservices.com, Web Site:
   www.listservices.com
CEO: Joseph McCluskey
Primary Market Served: Business &
   Consumer
Founded: 1980

Data-driven relationship marketing company specializing in the operation of campaign platforms.

MSI DIRECT RESPONSE INC

1501 Westcliff Dr (Suite 307)
Newport Beach, CA 92660
Telephone: (949) 722-2524, FAX:
   (949) 650-0989, E-Mail: sales@
   mailingteam.com, Web Site:
   mailingteam.com
Acct Exec: Daniel Jacobs
Conducts Business: U.S.
Primary Market Served: Business &
   Consumer
Founded: 2003

List fulfillment data service specializing in affiliate mailing campaign support.

MAD MIMI

Subs. of GoDaddy.com LLC
14455 N Hayden Rd (Suite 219)
Scottsdale, AZ 85260
Telephone: (480) 505-8800, FAX:
   (480) 505-8844, E-Mail: support@
   madmimi.com, Web Site: madmimi.
   com
CEO: Blake Irving
Pres & COO: Scott Wagner
Conducts Business: Worldwide
Primary Market Served: Business &
   Consumer
Founded: 2008

Email marketing company.

MAILCHIMP

Subs. of The Rocket Science Group
675 Ponce de Leon Ave NE (Suite
   5000)
Atlanta, GA 30308
Telephone: (678) 999-0141, Web Site:
   mailchimp.com
Pres & Sls Mgr: Ben Chestnut
Chief Customer Officer: Dan Kurzius
COO: Farrah Kennedy
CFO: Rick Lynch
CMO: Tom Klein
Conducts Business: U.S.
Employees: 500
Primary Market Served: Business &
   Consumer
Founded: 2001

Marketing automation, email e-commerce & email marketing platform provider.

MARDEVDM2

2000 Clearwater Dr
Oak Brook, IL 60523
Toll Free: (800) 323-4958, FAX: (303)
   265-5457, E-Mail: info@
   mardevdm2.com, Web Site: www.
   mardevdm2.com
Dir Mktg: Jeff Adee
Mktg Program Specialist: Parin Mody
VP & Gen Mgr: Liz Baione
Conducts Business: U.S., Canada
Primary Market Served: Business &
   Consumer
Catalog available online
Indirect online sales
Founded: 1946

List manager and deliverer of industry-specific, targeted, highly responsive B2B direct marketing services, including database marketing, lead qualification, event marketing & market research.

MEDIA SOURCE SOLUTIONS

31 Southeast 24th Ave (Suite 2)
Pompano Beach, FL 33062

Telephone: (954) 788-0213, FAX: (954) 788-0215, Web Site: www. mediasourcesolutions.com
Pres List Bargains Div: Michele Volpe
Primary Market Served: Business & Consumer
Founded: 2003

Direct marketing company specializing in list management, email marketing, data services and display advertising.

MEDICAL MARKETING SERVICE INC

dba MMS Lists
935 National Pkwy (Suite 93510)
Schaumburg, IL 60173-5179
Telephone: (630) 350-1717, Toll Free: (800) 633-5478, E-Mail: sales@ mmslists.com, Web Site: www. mmslists.com
Pres: Richard M. Elliott
VP Mktg: Garth Elliott
CIO: Kirk Elliott
Conducts Business: U.S.
Primary Market Served: Business & Consumer
Founded: 1929

Data, email marketing services & list provider specializing in the healthcare industry.

NAME EXCHANGE

880 N East St (Unit 201)
Frederick, MD 21701-5045
Telephone: (301) 695-6140, FAX: (301) 695-5572, E-Mail: chris@ nameexchange.us, Web Site: nameexchange.us
Conducts Business: U.S.
Primary Market Served: Business & Consumer

Full-service list company specializing in direct mail fundraising.

NEWSMAX LIST MANAGEMENT

Div. of Newsmax Media Inc
PO Box 20989
West Palm Beach, FL 33416-0989
Telephone: (561) 674-0726, Toll Free: (800) 485-4350, FAX: (561) 494-0922, E-Mail: matthewd@newsmax. com, Web Site: www.newsmax.com/ advertise/list-management
Pres: Matthew D'Lando
Primary Market Served: Consumer

List management division of Newsmax Media Inc offering email list services, editorial content and marketing best practices.

OUTSOURCE AMERICA INC

715 60th St Court E
Bradenton, FL 34208-6262

Telephone: (941) 746-4555, Toll Free: (800) 729-5694, FAX: (441) 746-3595, E-Mail: sales@oaiworld.com, Web Site: www.oaiworld.com
VP: Catherine Morehead
Mktg Dir: Scott Stewart
Man Dir: Marilyn Forbes
Conducts Business: U.S.
Primary Market Served: Business & Consumer

Data entry, data management and fulfillment services company.

PENNWELL CORP

1421 S Sheridan Rd
Tulsa, OK 74112-6600
Telephone: (918) 831-9782, Toll Free: (800) 944-0937, E-Mail: kellib@ pennwell.com, Web Site: www. pennwell.com
Dental Group List Mgr: Kelli Berry
Primary Market Served: Business & Consumer
Founded: 1910

Provides subscriber & conference attendee lists for direct mail, email and telemarketing campaigns.

PROFILE AMERICA LIST CO INC

455 Sylvan Ave
Englewood Cliffs, NJ 07632-2703
Telephone: (201) 569-7272, FAX: (201) 569-5552, E-Mail: listmanager@profileamerica.com, Web Site: www.profileamerica.com
Sr VP: Kimberly Welch
Conducts Business: U.S.
Primary Market Served: Business & Consumer
Founded: 1990

List & data management company.

RAD MARKETING

167 Crary On-The-Park
Mount Vernon, NY 10550
Telephone: (914) 668-3563, FAX: (914) 668-4247, E-Mail: cabletowns@verizon.net
Pres: Robert Dadarria
Conducts Business: U.S.
Primary Market Served: Consumer
Founded: 1991

Seller of mailing lists from the Radio-Base & CableTowns databases.

THE RICH LIST CO

Div. of Leslie Mandel Enterprises Inc
PO Box 294
Wainscott, NY 11975-0294
Telephone: (212) 737-8917, FAX: (212) 861-5384, E-Mail: richlistco@ aol.com, Web Site: www.richlist.com
Pres & CEO: Leslie Mandel

Conducts Business: U.S.
Primary Market Served: Business & Consumer
Founded: 1968

Provider of direct marketing, mail and phone lists of wealthy investors & donors.

TEIKOKU DATABANK AMERICA INC

Subs. of Teikoku Databank Ltd
780 3rd Ave (Floor 25)
New York, NY 10017
Telephone: (212) 421-9805, FAX: (212) 421-9806, E-Mail: info@ teikoku.com, Web Site: www. teikoku.com
Pres & CEO: Shiro Shibuya
Conducts Business: Worldwide
Primary Market Served: Business
Founded: 1992

Provider of international business data, targeted lists and research services with a focus on North American and European markets.

THOMASNET RPM

Div. of Thomas Publishing Co
5 Penn Plz (Floor 17)
New York, NY 10001
Toll Free: (844) 851-8715, Web Site: rpm.thomasnet.com
Mktg: Shawn Fitzgerald
Dir: Brittany Asciolla
Conducts Business: U.S.
Primary Market Served: Business & Consumer

Full-service digital agency and lead generation provider specializing in manufacturers and industrial companies.

TITAN LIST & MAILING SERVICES INC

1020 NW 6th St (Suite D)
Deerfield Beach, FL 33442
Toll Free: (888) 345-7179, E-Mail: titanlms@bellsouth.net, Web Site: www.titanlists.com
Pres, Mngmt & Brokerage: Joan Piantadosi
Acct Mgr: Ron Zahn
Sales Mgr: Bob Caruso
Conducts Business: U.S.
Primary Market Served: Business & Consumer
Founded: 1998

Direct mail and mailing list services provider.

21ST CENTURY MARKETING

303 Alt Bay Club Cir (Suite 104)
Altamonte Springs, FL 32701

Telephone: (321) 663-4640, E-Mail: tony@21stcenturymarketingonline.com, Web Site: 21stcenturymarketingonline.com
Pres: Tony Giuliani
Primary Market Served: Business & Consumer

Multi-channel digital marketing and lead generation company specializing in email, SMS text and mobile marketing services.

VERTICALRESPONSE INC
Subs. of Deluxe Corporation
550 Kearny St (Suite 710)
San Francisco, CA 94108
Telephone: (866) 683-7842, E-Mail: askus@verticalresponse.com, Web Site: www.verticalresponse.com
Conducts Business: Worldwide
Primary Market Served: Business & Consumer
Founded: 2001

Provider of full suite of self-service marketing solutions including email, social media, event & direct mail marketing and online surveys.

WILLIAM-NEIL ASSOCIATES
One Cabela Dr (Suite 2114)
Sidney, NE 69160
Telephone: (800) 216-2214, FAX: (308) 254-6102, E-Mail: bobermier@william-neil.com, Web Site: www.william-neil.com
List Mgr: Beanie Obermier
Mgr: Pat Myers
Primary Market Served: Business & Consumer

List management provider for outdoor recreation merchandiser Cabela's Inc.

WORLD INNOVATORS INC
22 Bacon Rd
Roxbury, CT 06783-1817
Telephone: (860) 210-8088, FAX: (860) 210-7829, E-Mail: inquiry@worldinnovators.com, Web Site: www.worldinnovators.com
Pres: Anne M Peterson
Exec VP: Donna A Peterson
Dir Bus Devel: Greg Pesce
Conducts Business: U.S.
Primary Market Served: Consumer
Founded: 1980

B2B marketing campaign company specializing in global mailing and email lists.

Paper Suppliers (25) — Geographic Index

COLORADO

Bloomin Promotions, 3080 Valmont Rd, Boulder, 80301-2152

Idea Art Inc, 1005 E Woodmen Rd, Colorado Springs, 80920-3181

CONNECTICUT

AT Clayton & Co Inc, 300 Atlantic St (fl 7), Stamford, 06901-3513

Horizon Paper Co Inc, 1010 Washington Blvd, Stamford, 06901-2202

GEORGIA

Georgia-Pacific Corp LLC, PO Box 105605, Atlanta, 30348-5605

Unisource Worldwide, Inc, 6600 Governors Lake Pkwy, Norcross, 30071-1114

ILLINOIS

Amerikal Products, 2115 Northwestern Ave, Waukegan, 60087-4144

Midland Paper, 101 E Palatine Rd, Wheeling, 60090-9032

Myllykoski North America, 999 Oakmont Plaza Dr (Suite 200), Westmont, 60559-5517

Saint Mary's Paper Corp, 312 S Hale St, Wheaton, 60187

United Stationers, 1 Pkwy N Blvd, Deerfield, 60015-2559

Wade Paper Corp, 1141 Lake Cook Rd, Deerfield, 60015-5235

xpedx Stores Division, 3351 W Addison St, Chicago, 60618-4303

MASSACHUSETTS

Ecological Fibers Inc, 40 Pioneer Dr, Lunenburg, 01462-1699

Hampden Papers Inc, 100 Water St, Holyoke, 01040-6210

Sappi Fine Paper North America, 255 State St (fl 4), Boston, 02109-2618

MICHIGAN

Manistique Papers Inc, 453 S Mackinac Ave, Manistique, 49854

Millcraft of Michigan, 35255 Glendale St, Livonia, 48150-1254

MINNESOTA

American Solutions for Business, PO Box 218, Glenwood, 56334

NEW HAMPSHIRE

Monadnock Paper Mills Inc, 117 Antrim Rd, Bennington, 03442-4205

NEW JERSEY

Richard Bauer & Co Inc, 310 Cedar Ln (Fl 2-1), Teaneck, 07666-3441

Central Lewmar, 261 River Rd, Clifton, 07014-1551

Roosevelt Paper Co, One Roosevelt Dr, Mount Laurel, 08054-6312

NEW YORK

Bulkley Dunton Publishing Group, 250 W 34th St (Suite 2814), New York, 10119-2814

Central National-Gottesman Inc, 3 Manhattanville Rd, Purchase, 10577-2116

Finch Paper, One Glen St, Glens Falls, 12801-4439

Gould Paper Corp, 99 Park Ave (fl 10), New York, 10016-1500

ITOCHU International Inc, 335 Madison Ave, New York, 10017-4611

Mead Fine Paper Division, PO Box 400, Sidney, 13838-0400

Mohawk Fine Papers Inc, 465 Saratoga St, Cohoes, 12047-4626

Prestone Printing Co Inc, 4750 30th St, Long Island City, 11101-3404

OHIO

Elmers Products Inc, 460 Polaris Pkwy (Suite 500), Westerville, 43082-6091

Graphic Communications Holdings Inc, 5700 Darrow Rd (Suite 110), Hudson, 44236-5026

NewPage Corp, 8540 Gander Creek Dr, Miamisburg, 45342-5439

xpedx, 6285 Tri-Ridge Blvd, Loveland, 45140-8318

PENNSYLVANIA

Glatfelter, 96 S George St (Suite 500), York, 17401-1434

SOUTH CAROLINA

Bowater America Inc, 55 E Camperdown Way, Greenville, 29601-3511

Domtar Inc, 100 Kingsley Park Dr, Fort Mill, 29715-6476

TENNESSEE

Verso Paper, 6775 Lenox Center Ct (Suite 400), Memphis, 38115-4436

TEXAS

Olmsted-Kirk Paper Co, 2420 Butler, Dallas, 75235-7816

WASHINGTON

Longview Fibre Co, PO Box 639, 300 Fibre Way, Longview, 98632-7411

Weyerhaeuser Co, PO Box 9777, Federal Way, 98063-9777

WISCONSIN

American Fine Paper Co, 5793 Grande Market Dr, Appleton, 54913-8470

Appleton Coated LLC, 540 Prospect St, Combined Locks, 54113-1120

Label Colors Inc, W222N5710 Miller Way, Sussex, 53089-3988

Paperweight Development Corp, 825 E Wisconsin Ave, Appleton, 54911-3873

Paper Suppliers (25)

AMERICAN FINE PAPER CO
5793 Grande Market Dr
Appleton, WI 54913-8470
Telephone: (920) 733-6100, Toll Free:
(800) 458-5446, FAX: (920) 380-
8711, E-Mail: found@
americanfinepaper.com, Web Site:
www.americanfinepaper.com
Pres/Owner: David Grayson
Founded: 1981

Serves as the paper converter, printer
and merchant's source for truckload
quantities of bond, offset, kraft and
newsprint in rolls as well as skids of
sheets.

**AMERICAN SOLUTIONS FOR
BUSINESS**
PO Box 218
Glenwood, MN 56334
Telephone: (320) 634-5471, FAX:
(320) 634-5265, Web Site: www.
americanbus.com
COO: Craig McLain
VP & Sls Assoc: Rose Virnig
Dir Vendor Rels: Wayne Martin
Founded: 1981

Leading distributor of print, promotional products, office supplies, eCommerce and marketing solutions.

AMERIKAL PRODUCTS
2115 Northwestern Ave
Waukegan, IL 60087-4144
Telephone: (847) 244-3600, FAX:
(847) 244-2860, E-Mail: info@
amerikal.com, Web Site: www.
amerikal.com
Pres: R. Danielson
Founded: 1989

Pressroom solutions manufacturer dedicated solely to developing products that
offset petroleum usage, preserve natural resources, reduce energy costs, and
eliminate hazardous waste streams,
while improving work environments
for employees by eliminating unneces-
sary exposure to unsafe chemicals.

APPLETON COATED LLC
540 Prospect St
Combined Locks, WI 54113-1120
Telephone: (920) 788-3550, FAX:
(920) 687-3420, Web Site: www.
appletoncoated.com
Adv & Promotion Mgr: Ferko Goldinger
Founded: 1907

Manufactures and distributes coated
and specialty paper products.

RICHARD BAUER & CO INC
310 Cedar Ln (Fl 2-1)
Teaneck, NJ 07666-3441
Telephone: (201) 692-1005, Toll Free:
(800) 995-7881, FAX: (201) 692-
8626, E-Mail: info@richardbauer.
com, Web Site: www.richardbauer.
com
CEO: Robert Cipolaro
Pres: Burke Kimber
Founded: 1916

Printing and writing paper company.

BLOOMIN PROMOTIONS
3080 Valmont Rd
Boulder, CO 80301-2152
Telephone: (303) 443-3591, E-Mail:
flowers@bloomin.com, Web Site:
www.bloominpromotions.com
Pres: Don Martin

Worldwide authority on seed paper
products.

BOWATER AMERICA INC
Subs. of Bowater Inc
55 E Camperdown Way
Greenville, SC 29601-3511
Telephone: (864) 271-7733, Toll Free:
(800) 921-3244, FAX: (864) 282-
9320, E-Mail: hrsc@abitibibowater.
com, Web Site: www.bowater.com
Pres & CEO: David J. Paterson
Founded: 1977

Engages in the production of paper and
paper products.

**BULKLEY DUNTON
PUBLISHING GROUP**
Div. of International Paper
250 W 34th St (Suite 2814)
New York, NY 10119-2814
Telephone: (212) 863-1800, FAX:
(212) 863-1870, Web Site: www.
internationalpaper.com
Pres: George J. Doehner
EVP: Scott S. Bond
Founded: 1833

Offers coated, offset, specialty ground-
wood, opaque, and bulking book papers
for magazine, catalog, and book publishers in the U.S. Also provides a publishing service program.

CENTRAL LEWMAR
261 River Rd
Clifton, NJ 07014-1551
Telephone: (973) 622-6377, Toll Free:
(800) 772-7301, FAX: (973) 623-
4323, E-Mail: dan.watkoske@
expedx.com, Web Site: www.
centrallewmar.com

Pres & CEO: Leslie F. Stern
Founded: 2007

Printing and writing paper merchant
wholesalers.

**CENTRAL NATIONAL-
GOTTESMAN INC**
3 Manhattanville Rd
Purchase, NY 10577-2116
Telephone: (914) 696-9000, FAX:
(914) 696-1066, E-Mail: purchase@
cng-inc.com, Web Site: www.cng-
inc.com
CEO: Kenneth L. Wallach
Pres: Andrew Wallach
VP Opers: Edward J. Rapa
Founded: 1886

Through its subsidiaries, markets and
distributes pulp and paper in the US
and internationally.

AT CLAYTON & CO INC
300 Atlantic St (fl 7)
Stamford, CT 06901-3513
Telephone: (203) 658-1200, FAX:
(203) 658-1201, E-Mail:
webmaster@atclayton.com, Web
Site: www.atclayton.com
Chmn & CEO: Peter Harding

Develops and manages strategic programs for end users of paper.

DOMTAR INC
100 Kingsley Park Dr
Fort Mill, SC 29715-6476
Telephone: (270) 927-7204, Toll Free:
(803) 802-7500, FAX: (270) 927-
8714, Web Site: www.domtar.com
Mgr Communs: Stefan Nowicki
Founded: 2006

Engages in designing, manufacturing,
marketing, and distributing uncoated
freesheet paper.

ECOLOGICAL FIBERS INC
40 Pioneer Dr
Lunenburg, MA 01462-1699
Telephone: (978) 537-0003, FAX:
(978) 537-2238, E-Mail: jquill@
ecofibers.com
CEO: Stephen F. Quill
Pres: John A. Quill
Dir Sls & Mktg: Paul Zompa
Founded: 1972

Manufactures and sells cover materials
for book, decorative and specialty
packaging, photomount, and CD/multi-
media packaging industries worldwide.

ELMERS PRODUCTS INC
Subs. of Berwind Group

460 Polaris Pkwy (Suite 500)
Westerville, OH 43082-6091
Telephone: (614) 985-2600, Toll Free:
(800) 848-9400, FAX: (614) 985-
2605, E-Mail: comments@elmers.
com, Web Site: www.elmers.com
CEO & Pres: Roger Posacki
Dir Innovation & New Bus Devel: Joe
Wetli
Primary Market Served: Consumer
Founded: 1947

Manufactures consumer adhesives.

FINCH PAPER

dba Finch Paper Holdings, LLC
One Glen St
Glens Falls, NY 12801-4439
Telephone: (518) 793-2541, Toll Free:
(800) 833-9983, FAX: (518) 793-
7364, E-Mail: info@finchpaper.com,
Web Site: www.finchpaper.com
VP Sls & Mktg: Anthony T. McDowell
CEO & Pres: Debabrata Mukherjee Dr
CFO: Rob Baron
Founded: 1865

Paper mill, manufactures uncoated text
and cover, opaque, and digital papers.

GEORGIA-PACIFIC CORP LLC

PO Box 105605
Atlanta, GA 30348-5605
Telephone: (404) 652-4000, FAX:
(404) 230-7052, Web Site: www.gp.
com
CEO & Pres.: James B. Hannan
SVP & CFO: Tyler L. Woolson
Founded: 1927

Manufactures and markets tissue, pulp,
paper, packaging, building products,
and related chemicals worldwide.

GLATFELTER

96 S George St (Suite 500)
York, PA 17401-1434
Telephone: (717) 225-4711, Toll Free:
(866) 744-7380, FAX: (717) 225-
6834, E-Mail: info@glatfelter.com,
Web Site: www.glatfelter.com
Chmn & CEO: Dante C. Parrini
Founded: 1951

Global supplier of specialty paper and
engineered products.

GOULD PAPER CORP

99 Park Ave (fl 10)
New York, NY 10016-1500
Telephone: (212) 301-0001, Toll Free:
(800) 221-3043, FAX: (212) 481-
0392, Web Site: www.gouldpaper.
com
Chmn: Harry E. Gould
CFO & EVP: Carl Matthews
COO & EVP: David Berkowitz

Employees: 464
Founded: 1924
Gross sales or billing: $1,150,000,000

Distributes printing and business papers
& provides customer support services.

GRAPHIC COMMUNICATIONS HOLDINGS INC

5700 Darrow Rd (Suite 110)
Hudson, OH 44236-5026
Telephone: (330) 650-5522, FAX:
(330) 650-8998, E-Mail: info@
graphiccommunications.com, Web
Site: www.graphiccommunications.
com
CEO: Allan Dragone
Sr VP: John Patneau
Pres: Matthew Dawley
COO: Ken Flajs
Founded: 1979

Distributes printing and imaging papers, facility supplies and equipment,
and packaging materials and equipment.

HAMPDEN PAPERS INC

100 Water St
Holyoke, MA 01040-6210
Telephone: (413) 536-1000, FAX:
(413) 532-9161, Web Site: www.
hampdenpapers.com
VP Sls & Mktg: Bob Adams
Employees: 150
Founded: 1880
Gross sales or billing: $30,000,000

Manufactures fine converted coated papers and paperboards, and laminated
films and foils.

HORIZON PAPER CO INC

1010 Washington Blvd
Stamford, CT 06901-2202
Telephone: (203) 358-0855, Toll Free:
(866) 358-0855, FAX: (203) 358-
0828, Web Site: www.horizonpaper.
com
Chmn & CEO: Robert B. Obernier
Founded: 1978

Provides paper mill and paper products.

IDEA ART INC

1005 E Woodmen Rd
Colorado Springs, CO 80920-3181
Telephone: (719) 594-4100, Toll Free:
(800) 433-2278, FAX: (719) 534-
6313, E-Mail: customerservice@
ideaart.com, Web Site: www.ideaart.
com
Chmn: Chris Chamberlain

Paper Products For All Occasions.

ITOCHU INTERNATIONAL INC

335 Madison Ave
New York, NY 10017-4611
Telephone: (212) 818-8000, FAX:
(212) 818-8282, Web Site: www.
adpackusa.com
CEO & Pres: Yasuyuki Harada
CFO & Sr VP: Mamoru Seki
Founded: 1918

Engaged in trading operations.

LABEL COLORS INC

Sub. of Lauterbach Group, Mail Adver-
tising Supply Co Inc
W222N5710 Miller Way
Sussex, WI 53089-3988
Telephone: (262) 549-1730, Toll Free:
(800) 558-2126, FAX: (800) 784-
2591, Web Site: www.
lauterbachgroup.com
Pres: Shane Lauterbach
Dir Mktg: Derek Wilcox

Manufactures printing, marking, packaging, and converting products for direct response, food, beverage,
household, primary marking, and product security and authentication industries.

LONGVIEW FIBRE CO

PO Box 639, 300 Fibre Way
Longview, WA 98632-7411
Telephone: (360) 425-1550, FAX:
(360) 230-5135, E-Mail: info@
longviewfibre.com, Web Site: www.
longfibre.com
Pres: Randy Nebel
CFO: Heidi Pozzo
SVP Converted Prods: Ken D. Gettman
Founded: 1926

Manufactures and supplies kraft papers,
containerboards, and corrugated boxes
to customers in the US & internation-
ly.

MANISTIQUE PAPERS INC

Div. of Kruger Inc
453 S Mackinac Ave
Manistique, MI 49854
Telephone: (906) 341-2175, FAX:
(906) 341-5635
Pres: Leif Christensen

MEAD FINE PAPER DIVISION

Div. of The Mead Corp
PO Box 400
Sidney, NY 13838-0400
Toll Free: (800) 936-9811, Web Site:
www.mead.com

MIDLAND PAPER
101 E Palatine Rd
Wheeling, IL 60090-9032
Telephone: (847) 777-2700, Toll Free: (800) 323-8522, FAX: (847) 777-2552, E-Mail: whl@midlandpaper.com, Web Site: www.midlandpaper.com
CEO: E. Stanton Hooker
Pres & COO: Michael Graves
Founded: 1907

Engages in the distribution of printing and imaging paper, publication paper, packaging supplies and equipment, and facility supplies.

MILLCRAFT OF MICHIGAN
35255 Glendale St
Livonia, MI 48150-1254
Telephone: (734) 266-3710, Toll Free: (800) 482-0556, FAX: (734) 266-3705, Web Site: www.millcraft.com
COO & VP: John Orlando

independent merchant of paper, packaging and graphic arts products.

MOHAWK FINE PAPERS INC
465 Saratoga St
Cohoes, NY 12047-4626
Telephone: (518) 237-1740, Toll Free: (800) 843-6455, FAX: (518) 237-7394, E-Mail: info@mohawkpaper.com, Web Site: www.mohawkconnects.com
Chmn & CEO: Jr. Thomas D. O'Connor
Pres: Jack Haren
COO: Kevin P. Richard

Manufactures fine papers, envelopes, and specialty substrates for commercial and digital printing in North America, Europe, and Asia.

MONADNOCK PAPER MILLS INC
117 Antrim Rd
Bennington, NH 03442-4205
Telephone: (603) 588-3311, Toll Free: (800) 221-2159, FAX: (603) 588-3158, Web Site: www.monadnockpaper.com
Chmn & CEO: Richard G. Verney
VP Corp Communs: Geoff Verney
Dir Mktg: David Lunati
Founded: 1819

Designs, manufactures, and supplies paper products for customers in the United States and internationally.

MYLLYKOSKI NORTH AMERICA
999 Oakmont Plaza Dr (Suite 200)
Westmont, IL 60559-5517
Telephone: (203) 229-7400, Web Site: www.myllykoski.com
Dir Mktg: William Crane
Founded: 1977

Provides recycled and non-recycled ground wood paper products in North America and Europe.

NEWPAGE CORP
8540 Gander Creek Dr
Miamisburg, OH 45342-5439
Telephone: (937) 242-9345, Toll Free: (877) 855-7243, FAX: (937) 242-9327, Web Site: www.newpagecorp.com
Pres: Glenn R. Grill
CFO: Jay A. Epstein
SVP Opers: Laszlo M. Lukacs
Founded: 2012

Manufactures, markets, and distributes printing papers. Its products include coated,

OLMSTED-KIRK PAPER CO
2420 Butler
Dallas, TX 75235-7816
Telephone: (214) 637-2220, Toll Free: (800) 367-6526, FAX: (214) 637-2131, E-Mail: sales@okpaper.com, Web Site: www.okpaper.com
Chmn Bd & CEO: John Taylor
Pres: Robert Olmsted
Founded: 1905

Operates as a paper distributor in Texas.

PAPERWEIGHT DEVELOPMENT CORP
Subs. Appleton Papers Inc
825 E Wisconsin Ave
Appleton, WI 54911-3873
Telephone: (920) 734-9841, FAX: (920) 991-8796, Web Site: www.appletonideas.com
Chmn Bd: Mark R. Richards
CFO: Thomas J. Ferree
Pres: Tami L. Van Straten
Founded: 1907

Manufactures and sells coated paper products in the United States and internationally.

PRESTONE PRINTING CO INC
4750 30th St
Long Island City, NY 11101-3404
Telephone: (347) 468-7900, FAX: (347) 468-7885, E-Mail: info@prestoneprint.com, Web Site: www.prestoneprinting.com
Owner Pres: Rob Alder
Partner & VP Opers: Ira Wechsler

Partner & Plant Mgr: Tommy Politano
Full-service NYC printing facility.

ROOSEVELT PAPER CO
One Roosevelt Dr
Mount Laurel, NJ 08054-6312
Telephone: (856) 303-4100, (856) 303-4200, Toll Free: (800) 523-3470, FAX: (856) 642-1950, (856) 642-1949, Web Site: www.rooseveltpaper.com
Chmn Bd & CEO: Ted Kosloff
Pres: David Kosloff
Founder: Irving S. Kosloff
CFO: Tony Janulewicz
VP Sls: Dean Egan
Founded: 1932

Distributes and converts paper products.

SAINT MARY'S PAPER CORP
312 S Hale St
Wheaton, IL 60187
Telephone: (630) 668-6279, FAX: (630) 668-6292, Web Site: www.stmarys-paper.com
Pres: Walter Vail
Sr VP: Rick Howe III

SAPPI FINE PAPER NORTH AMERICA
Subs. of Sappi Fine Paper
255 State St (fl 4)
Boston, MA 02109-2618
Telephone: (617) 423-7300, FAX: (617) 423-5494, Web Site: www.sappi.com
CEO: Mark Gardner
CFO: Annette Luchene
Founded: 1854

Produces and supplies coated fine papers, pulp, and release papers in the United States and internationally.

UNISOURCE WORLDWIDE, INC
Subs. of Georgia Pacific
6600 Governors Lake Pkwy
Norcross, GA 30071-1114
Telephone: (770) 447-9000, Toll Free: (800) 864-7687, FAX: (770) 734-2000, Web Site: www.unisourcelink.com
Pres Supply Chain: Tom Shortt
CIO & SVP: Tim Kutz
Founded: 1968

Distributes and markets commercial printing and business imaging papers, facility supplies and equipment, and packaging materials and equipment in North America.

UNITED STATIONERS

1 Pkwy N Blvd
Deerfield, IL 60015-2559
Telephone: (847) 627-7000, FAX:
(847) 647-7001, Web Site: www.
unitedstationers.com
CEO & Dir: Randall W. Larrimore
Pres: Todd A. Shelton
CFO: Kathleen S. Dvorak
Founded: 1922

Supply Company distributes business
products, technology products, and janitorial and sanitation products for manufacturers and retailers in North
America.

VERSO PAPER

6775 Lenox Center Ct (Suite 400)
Memphis, TN 38115-4436
Telephone: (901) 369-4100, FAX:
(901) 369-4174, Web Site: www.
versopaper.com
CEO: David J. Paterson
CFO: Robert P. Mundy
VP: Peter H. Kesser

Engages in the manufacture and sale of
coated papers to catalog, magazine, insert, and commercial printing markets
in North America.

WADE PAPER CORP

1141 Lake Cook Rd
Deerfield, IL 60015-5235
Telephone: (847) 940-9777, Toll Free:
(800) 828-8318, FAX: (847) 940-
1077, E-Mail: info@wadepaper.com,
Web Site: www.wadepaper.com
Pres: Kevin P. Wade
Founded: 1986

Distributes printing paper to the catalogers, magazine publishers, and Web
printers.

WEYERHAEUSER CO

PO Box 9777
Federal Way, WA 98063-9777
Telephone: (253) 924-2345, Toll Free:
(800) 525-5440, FAX: (253) 924-
2685, Web Site: www.wy.com
Pres: Anne Giardini

XPEDX

Div. of Mead Paper Co
6285 Tri-Ridge Blvd
Loveland, OH 45140-8318
Telephone: (513) 965-2900, FAX:
(513) 965-2849, Web Site: www.
xpedx.com
Pres: Mary Laschinger
COO: James A. Connelly

Markets and distributes printing papers,
graphic supplies, printing press machines, and bindery and finishing
equipment.

XPEDX STORES DIVISION

3351 W Addison St
Chicago, IL 60618-4303
Telephone: (773) 442-6200, Toll Free:
(800) 600-0064, FAX: (630) 628-
6310, Web Site: www.epedxstores.
com
VP Mktg & Mdsg: Mike Cape

Envelope Manufacturers & Suppliers (26) — Geographic Index

CALIFORNIA

Golden State Envelopes, 31316 Via Colinas (Suite 106), Thousand Oaks, 91362-6717

CONNECTICUT

GBE Plus, 10 Midland St, Hartford, 06120-1118

FLORIDA

Double Envelope, 2500 NE 39th Ave, Gainesville, 32609-2098

ILLINOIS

Continental Envelope Corp, 1700 Averill Rd, Geneva, 60134-1668

Diamond Envelope Corp, 2270 White Oak Cir, Aurora, 60502-9675

Federal Envelope Co, 608 Country Club Dr, Bensenville, 60106-1303

Forest Envelope Co, 1958 University Ln, Lisle, 60532-2162

Gaw-O'Hara Envelope Co, 500 N Sacramento Blvd, Chicago, 60612-1024

Office Express Inc, 1320 Sherman Ave (Suite 104), Evanston, 60201-4381

Pactiv Corp, 1900 West Field Ct, Lake Forest, 60045-4828

Royal Envelope Corp, 4114 S Peoria St, Chicago, 60609-2521

Victor Envelope Co, 301 Arthur Ct, Bensenville, 60106-3381

INDIANA

Bowers Envelope Co, 5331 N Tacoma Ave, Indianapolis, 46220-3613

MARYLAND

Oles Envelope Corp, 532 E 25th St, Baltimore, 21218-5403

MASSACHUSETTS

Ames Specialty Packaging & Digital Print, 12 Tyler St, Somerville, 02143-3241

Mac Pac Inc, 90 Corporate Park Dr (Unit 1440), Pembroke, 02359-4935

Sheppard Envelope Co, 133 Southbridge St, Auburn, 01501-2503

Super Coups, 200 Cordwainer Dr (Suite 100), Norwell, 02061-1671

Worcester Envelope, 22 Millburn St, Auburn, 01501

MICHIGAN

Husky Envelope Products, 1225 E W Maple Rd, Walled Lake, 48390-3764

Wolf Envelope Co, 725 S Adams Rd, Birmingham, 48009-6902

MINNESOTA

MackayMitchell Envelope Co, 2100 Elm St SE, Minneapolis, 55414-2533

Quality Park Products, 1200 Washington Ave S (Suite 217), Minneapolis, 55415-1111

MISSISSIPPI

International Filing Corp LLC, 5370 Highway 42, Hattiesburg, 39401-1913

MISSOURI

American Mail-Well Envelope Co/St Louis Div, 101 Workman Ct, Eureka, 63025

Tension Corp, 819 E 19th St, Kansas City, 64108-1781

NEBRASKA

Burkley Envelope Co, 1600 N Chestnut, Wahoo, 68066-1000

NEW JERSEY

Sealed Air Corp, 200 Riverfront Blvd Ste 301, Elmwood Park, 07407-1038

United Envelope, 65 Railroad Ave, Ridgefield, 07657-2130

NEW YORK

Commercial Envelope Manufacturing Co Inc, 900 Grand Blvd, Deer Park, 11729-5745

Conformer Expansion Products Inc, 60 Cuttermill Rd (Suite 411), Great Neck, 11021-3104

Craig Envelope Corp, 1201 44th Ave, Long Island City, 11101-6917

Innovative Packaging of Westchester, Two Barrie Dr, Spring Valley, 10977-1617

Matt Industries Inc, One Dupli Park Dr, Syracuse, 13204-1436

Mercury Envelope Co Inc, 100 Merrick Rd (Suite 204E), Rockville Centre, 11570-4801

Poly-Flex Corp, 250 Executive Dr Ste S, Edgewood, 11717-8354

OHIO

American Church Inc, 525 Mcclurg Rd, Youngstown, 44512-6406

Ohio Envelope Manufacturing Co, 5161 W 164th St, Cleveland, 44142-1505

Specialty Envelope Inc, 4890 Spring Grove Ave, Cincinnati, 45232-1933

PENNSYLVANIA

North American Communications Inc (East), 141 NAC Dr, Duncansville, 16635-9428

Tri-State Envelope Corp, 20th & Market St, Ashland, 17921-1622

RHODE ISLAND

Admiral Packaging Inc, Ten Admiral St, Providence, 02908-3203

TEXAS

Love Envelopes Inc, 1130 Quaker St, Dallas, 75207-5604

VIRGINIA

ColorTree of Virginia Inc, 8000 Villa Park Dr, Richmond, 23228-6500

WASHINGTON

Cenveo Commercial Envelope Group, 1421 S Dean St, Seattle, 98144-2722

PAC Worldwide, 15435 NE 92nd St, Redmond, 98052-3516

WISCONSIN

Wisconsin Converting Inc, 1689 Morrow St, Green Bay, 54302-2605

CANADA

Ontario

Supremex Inc, 400 Humberline Dr, Etobicoke, M9W 5T3

Quebec

Montreal Envelope Inc, 7565 Boul Newman, Succ Lapierre LaSalle, Quebec, CP 3008-H8N 3H2

Supremex Inc, 7213 Cordner, La Salle, H8N 2J7

ADMIRAL PACKAGING INC
RP-NFOA
Ten Admiral St
Providence, RI 02908-3203
Telephone: (401) 274-7000, Toll Free: (800) 262-0027, FAX: (401) 331-1910, Web Site: www.admiralpkg.com
Pres: Harley Frank
Dir Press Svcs: Christopher Caito
Founded: 1898

Manufactures and supplies packaging products in the United States.

AMERICAN CHURCH INC
525 Mcclurg Rd
Youngstown, OH 44512-6406
Telephone: (330) 758-4545, Toll Free: (800) 250-7112, FAX: (800) 763-8772, E-Mail: sales@americanchurch.com, Web Site: www.americanchurch.com
Pres: Kyle Hamilton

Manufacturer of church offering envelopes.

AMERICAN MAIL-WELL ENVELOPE CO/ST LOUIS DIV
Div. of Cenveo
101 Workman Ct
Eureka, MO 63025
Telephone: (314) 966-2000, Toll Free: (800) 800-8845, FAX: (314) 966-4725, E-Mail: info@cenveo.com, Web Site: www.mail-well.com
Mgr: Frank Bow

AMES SPECIALTY PACKAGING & DIGITAL PRINT
12 Tyler St
Somerville, MA 02143-3241
Telephone: (617) 684-1000, Toll Free: (800) 521-2637, FAX: (617) 684-1264, E-Mail: info@amespage.com, Web Site: www.amespage.com
Sr Sls Exec: Scott Allen
Employees: 450
Founded: 1929
Gross sales or billing: $53,480,000

Offers envelope products, specialty packaging, on demand printing, and records and information management systems for healthcare, legal, financial, government, and insurance markets.

BOWERS ENVELOPE CO
5331 N Tacoma Ave
Indianapolis, IN 46220-3613
Telephone: (317) 253-4321, FAX: (317) 254-2231, Web Site: www.bowersenvelope.com
Pres: Tom Marshall
Founded: 1928

BURKLEY ENVELOPE CO
1600 N Chestnut
Wahoo, NE 68066-1000
Telephone: (402) 443-3010, FAX: (402) 443-4029, E-Mail: info@burkley.com, Web Site: www.burkley.com
Pres: Robert W. Burkley
Founded: 1891

A specialized supplier of high quality litho envelopes.

CENVEO COMMERCIAL ENVELOPE GROUP
1421 S Dean St
Seattle, WA 98144-2722
Telephone: (206) 682-7171, Toll Free: (800) 347-6989, FAX: (206) 329-2017, E-Mail: info@cenveo.com, Web Site: www.cenveo.com
VP Sls: Joe Ritchie

Global provider of print and related resources, offering solutions in the areas of envelopes, custom labels, specialty packaging, commercial print, publisher solutions and business documents.

COLORTREE OF VIRGINIA INC
8000 Villa Park Dr
Richmond, VA 23228-6500
Telephone: (804) 358-4245, FAX: (804) 358-0488, Web Site: www.colortree.com
CEO & Pres: Pat Patterson
CFO & Controller: Peter Dove
Dir Opers: Larry Thompson
Dir People & Devel: Deborah Taylor Clements
VP Sls: Mark Smith
Founded: 1988

Manufactures and distributes lithographic products to the direct mail industry.

COMMERCIAL ENVELOPE MANUFACTURING CO INC
Subs. of Cenveo Inc.
900 Grand Blvd
Deer Park, NY 11729-5745
Telephone: (631) 242-2500, FAX: (631) 242-6935, Web Site: www.commercial-envelope.com
Pres.: Alan J. Kristel

Founded: 1924
Envelope Manufacturing Co.

CONFORMER EXPANSION PRODUCTS INC
60 Cuttermill Rd (Suite 411)
Great Neck, NY 11021-3104
Telephone: (516) 504-6300, E-Mail: support@conformerinc.com, Web Site: www.conformerinc.com
Pres: Marvin Makofsky
Co-Founder & VP: Sari McConnell
VP & Gen Mgr: Bob Makofsky
Conducts Business: U.S., Canada
Primary Market Served: Business
Advertising/Marketing Budget Related to Direct Marketing: 0-25%
Founded: 1972

Created a full line of packaging designed specifically to save money on postage. Products offers performing presentation folders and portfolios for sales kits, meetings and events, and protective mailers and envelopes for the mail.

CONTINENTAL ENVELOPE CORP
1700 Averill Rd
Geneva, IL 60134-1668
Telephone: (630) 262-8080, Toll Free: (800) 621-8155, FAX: (630) 262-1450, E-Mail: sales@continentalenvelope.com, Web Site: www.continentalenvelope.com
Pres: Jacob Margulies

Full-service vendor with state-of-the-art facility that can deliver projects of almost any size and complexity.

CRAIG ENVELOPE CORP
1201 44th Ave
Long Island City, NY 11101-6917
Telephone: (718) 786-4277, Toll Free: (888) 272-4436, FAX: (718) 937-8178, E-Mail: info@craigenvelope.com, Web Site: www.craigenvelope.com
Pres: Lawrence Aaronson

One-stop shop for all of your envelope needs.

DIAMOND ENVELOPE CORP
2270 White Oak Cir, Aurora, IL 60504-9675
2270 White Oak Cir
Aurora, IL 60502-9675
Telephone: (630) 499-2800, FAX: (630) 499-2801
Pres & CEO: Alan Jania
VP & Gen Mgr: Michael Jania

VP Sls & Mktg: AJ Jania
Supply Chain Dir: Susan Jania
Office supplies and stationary company.

DOUBLE ENVELOPE
Div. of BSC Ventures
2500 NE 39th Ave
Gainesville, FL 32609-2098
Toll Free: (800) 543-5275, Web Site:
   www.double-envelope.com
Pres & CEO: Brian Sass

Specializes in the manufacturing of
commercial, custom printed and specialty envelopes - as well as photo bags
and print wallets.

FEDERAL ENVELOPE CO
608 Country Club Dr
Bensenville, IL 60106-1303
Telephone: (630) 595-2000, FAX:
   (630) 595-1212, E-Mail:
   postmaster@federalenvelope.com,
   Web Site: www.federalenvelope.com
Pres: Michael Shaw
Founded: 1965

Engages in the production and distribution of envelopes and printed materials.

FOREST ENVELOPE CO
RP-NFOA
1958 University Ln
Lisle, IL 60532-2162
Telephone: (630) 515-1200, FAX:
   (630) 515-1212, Web Site:
   forestenvelope.com
Pres: Jack Wagner
Gen Mgr: Judy Kern
Founded: 1976

Office supplies and stationary company.

GBE PLUS
Div. of Massachusetts Envelope Co
10 Midland St
Hartford, CT 06120-1118
Telephone: (860) 727-9100, Toll Free:
   (800) 842-0139, FAX: (860) 527-6041, Web Site: www.gbeplus.com
Contact: Bruce Newell

Printing publishers company.

GAW-O'HARA ENVELOPE CO
500 N Sacramento Blvd
Chicago, IL 60612-1024
Telephone: (773) 638-1200
Pres: Brian Dietrich
Fin Exec: Brian O'Hara
Chmn Bd: Rock P. Moran Jr

Stationery Product Manufacturing.

GOLDEN STATE ENVELOPES
31316 Via Colinas (Suite 106)
Thousand Oaks, CA 91362-6717
Telephone: (818) 865-7940, Toll Free:
   (800) 252-7600, FAX: (818) 865-0012, E-Mail: answers@golden-state-env.com, Web Site: www.golden-state-env.com
Pres: Mark W. Goggin

HUSKY ENVELOPE PRODUCTS
1225 E W Maple Rd
Walled Lake, MI 48390-3764
Telephone: (248) 624-7070, FAX:
   (248) 624-5990, E-Mail: bmuehl@huskyenvelope.com, Web Site: www.huskyenvelope.com
CEO & Treas: William E. Settle
Founded: 1975

Manufactures and supplies envelopes.

INNOVATIVE PACKAGING OF WESTCHESTER
Two Barrie Dr
Spring Valley, NY 10977-1617
Telephone: (845) 364-9500
Pres: Bruce Hollander

INTERNATIONAL FILING CORP LLC
Subs. of Cenveo Inc
5370 Highway 42
Hattiesburg, MS 39401-1913
Telephone: (601) 554-0521, FAX:
   (601) 554-0522, E-Mail: pcoerper@intfiling.com, Web Site: www.intfiling.com
Pres & CEO: Phil Coerper
CFO: John Kessler
Corp Dir & Support Svcs: Pat Stephens
Founded: 2002

Manufactures radiology film filing and
accessory products for healthcare market. Company offers radiology products, such as x-ray jackets, negative
preservers, x-ray mailers, and category
insert jackets; folders,

LOVE ENVELOPES INC
1130 Quaker St
Dallas, TX 75207-5604
Telephone: (214) 637-5900, Toll Free:
   (800) 569-5683, FAX: (214) 951-0469, E-Mail: sales.dallas@loveenvelopes.com, Web Site: www.loveenvelopes.com
Sls Mgr: Michael Love

Stationery product manufacturing.

MAC PAC INC
90 Corporate Park Dr (Unit 1440)
Pembroke, MA 02359-4935

Telephone: (781) 826-6900, FAX:
   (781) 826-6880, E-Mail: jsargeant@macpacinc.com, Web Site: www.macpacinc.com
Pres: Richard MacDowell
Mktg Dir: Julie Sargeant
Conducts Business: U.S., Canada
Catalog available online
Indirect online sales
Advertising/Marketing Budget Related
   to Direct Marketing: 0-25%
Founded: 1999

Decorative mailers envelopes ("Deco
Bags") and Decorative Bobble mailers
("Mac Pac Deco Bubble Bags").

MACKAYMITCHELL ENVELOPE CO
2100 Elm St SE
Minneapolis, MN 55414-2533
Telephone: (612) 331-9311, Toll Free:
   (800) 622-5299, FAX: (612) 331-3460, Web Site: www.mackayenvelope.com
Founder: Harvey B. Mackay
VP Natl Sls: Brian D. Bomberger
Founded: 1959

Manufactures and supplies plain and
printed envelopes for corporations and
small emerging companies.

MATT INDUSTRIES INC
PO Box 11500, Syracuse, NY 13218-1500-POST
dba Dupli Envelope & Graphics Corp
One Dupli Park Dr
Syracuse, NY 13204-1436
Telephone: (315) 472-1316, Toll Free:
   (800) 724-2477, FAX: (315) 422-3637, Web Site: www.duplionline.com
Pres: J. Kemper Matt Sr.
Founded: 1965

Manufactures and distributes envelopes
in the continental United States. Offers
on demand print products and services

MERCURY ENVELOPE CO INC
100 Merrick Rd (Suite 204E)
Rockville Centre, NY 11570-4801
Telephone: (516) 678-6744, FAX:
   (516) 678-6764, E-Mail:
   mercuryenvelope@aol.com
Pres: Scott Deutsch
VP: Maury Deutsch
Founded: 1974

Stationery Product Manufacturing .

MONTREAL ENVELOPE INC
aka Enveloppe Montreal Inc
7565 Boul Newman, Succ Lapierre La-Salle

Quebec, QC, Canada CP 3008-H8N 3H2
Telephone: (514) 331-7110, Toll Free: (800) 655-2709, FAX: (514) 748-7322, E-Mail: ybrochu@enveloppe-montreal.com, Web Site: www.enveloppe-montreal.com
Chmn Bd: Dany Paradis

Specialized in manufacturing all kinds of envelopes.

NORTH AMERICAN COMMUNICATIONS INC (EAST)
141 NAC Dr
Duncansville, PA 16635-9428
Telephone: (814) 696-3553, Toll Free: (800) 624-1533, FAX: (814) 696-1180, E-Mail: marketing@nacmail.com, Web Site: www.nacmail.com
Pres: Robert Herman
CEO: Nick Robinson
EVP: George Reed
Founded: 1934

International leader in direct mail marketing.

OFFICE EXPRESS INC
aka envelopesexpress.com
1320 Sherman Ave (Suite 104)
Evanston, IL 60201-4381
Toll Free: (888) 526-8438, FAX: (773) 341-7322, E-Mail: sales@envelopesexpress.com, Web Site: www.envelopesexpress.com
Pres: Bill Raspe
Founded: 1999

Office Express, Paper Products.

OHIO ENVELOPE MANUFACTURING CO
5161 W 164th St
Cleveland, OH 44142-1505
Telephone: (216) 267-2920, Toll Free: (800) 989-0336, FAX: (216) 267-1765, E-Mail: mgmt@ohioenvelope.com, Web Site: www.ohioenvelope.com
Pres: Rick Gould
Founded: 1936

Envelope Manufacturing Company specializes in converting customer printed sheets as well as producing all types and styles of envelopes.

OLES ENVELOPE CORP
532 E 25th St
Baltimore, MD 21218-5403
Telephone: (410) 243-1520, Toll Free: (800) 822-6537, FAX: (410) 366-7022, Web Site: www.olesenvelope.com
Chmn Bd: John R. Young

Founded: 1912

Produces custom printed envelopes through flexography, jet offset printing, and lithography conversion methods in the United States.

PAC WORLDWIDE
Subs. of PAC Worldwide
15435 NE 92nd St
Redmond, WA 98052-3516
Telephone: (425) 202-4000, Toll Free: (800) 535-0039, FAX: (425) 885-2934, Web Site: www.pac.com
CEO & Pres: Jim Boshaw
CFO: Jeff Snow
COO: Mark Samuelson
Founded: 1975

Manufacturer & distributor of custom-branded and stock protective packaging.

PACTIV CORP
1900 West Field Ct
Lake Forest, IL 60045-4828
Telephone: (847) 482-2000, Toll Free: (800) 828-2850, FAX: (847) 482-4738, Web Site: www.pactiv.com
CEO & Pres: Richard L. Wambold
CFO & SVP: Edward T. Walters
Dir: Thomas James Degnan
Founded: 1959

Manufactures & distributes food packaging and foodservice products.

POLY-FLEX CORP
250 Executive Dr Ste S
Edgewood, NY 11717-8354
Telephone: (631) 586-9500, FAX: (631) 586-6631, E-Mail: info@poly-flexcorp.com, Web Site: www.poly-flexcorp.com
Pres: Barry Neustein
Founded: 1977

Company provides printing of polyethylene films, and poly envelope for the direct mail industry.

QUALITY PARK PRODUCTS
Member Cenveo family of companies
1200 Washington Ave S (Suite 217)
Minneapolis, MN 55415-1111
Toll Free: (800) 828-7323, (800) 547-4252, FAX: (800) 398-9835, E-Mail: mktg@qualitypark.com, Web Site: www.qualitypark.com
Pres: Steve Kouroupas
VP Mktg & Strategic Bus Devel: Jim Bettinger
VP Sls , Office Prods: Mark Meinert

Envelopes & Mailing Supplies Manufacturer

ROYAL ENVELOPE CORP
4114 S Peoria St
Chicago, IL 60609-2521
Telephone: (773) 376-1212, Toll Free: (800) 279-0142, FAX: (773) 376-0011, E-Mail: info@royalenv.com, Web Site: www.royalenv.com
Pres: John Pusatera
Gen Mgr: Mike Pusatera
Gen Mgr: Matt Pusatera

Envelope manufacturing and lithographycompany.

SEALED AIR CORP
200 Riverfront Blvd Ste 301
Elmwood Park, NJ 07407-1038
Telephone: (201) 791-7600, FAX: (201) 703-4205, Web Site: www.sealedair.com
Pres & CEO: Jeroe Peribere
CFO: Carol Lowe
Founded: 1969

Provides packaging solutions including vacuum skin pack and laminated pouch for the food industry.

SHEPPARD ENVELOPE CO
133 Southbridge St
Auburn, MA 01501-2503
Telephone: (508) 791-5588, Toll Free: (800) 325-6622, FAX: (508) 754-3108, E-Mail: sales@sheppardenvelope.com, Web Site: www.sheppardenvelope.com
Pres: J Lincoln Spaulding

Office supplies and stationary company.

SPECIALTY ENVELOPE INC
4890 Spring Grove Ave
Cincinnati, OH 45232-1933
Telephone: (513) 542-4700, Toll Free: (800) 288-8884, FAX: (513) 542-5260, E-Mail: info@specialtyenevelope.com, Web Site: www.specialtyenevelope.com
Sls Mgr: Bill Herweh

Envelopes Manufacturer.

SUPER COUPS
Subs. of ADVO Inc
200 Cordwainer Dr (Suite 100)
Norwell, MA 02061-1671
Telephone: (508) 977-2000, Toll Free: (800) 626-2620, FAX: (508) 977-0644, Web Site: www.supercoups.com
Pres & Gen Mgr: David Murphy
Info Tech Mgr: Chris Valli
Fin Mgr: David Sullo

Direct mail advertising solutions to America's small businesses.

SUPREMEX INC
400 Humberline Dr
Etobicoke, ON, Canada M9W 5T3
Telephone: (416) 675-9370, Toll Free:
(800) 465-7603, FAX: (416) 675-
1952, (416) 848-8388, E-Mail: sales.
central@supremex.com, Web Site:
www.supremex.com
Chmn Bd: Robert Johnston
CEO & Gen Mgr: Stewart Emerson

Marketer of high quality stock and custom envelopes, labels and mailers.

SUPREMEX INC
7213 Cordner
La Salle, QC, Canada H8N 2J7
Telephone: (514) 595-0555, FAX:
(514) 595-1112, E-Mail: vente@
supremex.com, Web Site: www.
supremex.com
VP & Gen Mgr: Stewart Emerson
Founded: 1977

Manufactures and sells a range of stock
and custom envelopes, and related
products in Canada and the United
States.

TENSION CORP
819 E 19th St
Kansas City, MO 64108-1781
Telephone: (816) 471-3800, FAX:
(816) 283-1498, E-Mail: info@
tensioncorp.com, Web Site: www.
tension.com
Pres & CEO: William Berkley
COO: Bob Broadbear
Founded: 1886

Producers of envelopes, marketing directly to companies and organizations
across the country.

**TRI-STATE ENVELOPE
CORP**
20th & Market St
Ashland, PA 17921-1622
Telephone: (570) 875-0433, Toll Free:
(800) 233-3102, FAX: (570) 875-
0125, E-Mail: tsecny@attglobal.net,
Web Site: www.tristateenvelope.com
Pres: Joel Orgler
Conducts Business: U.S.
Employees: 500
Primary Market Served: Business &
Consumer
Advertising/Marketing Budget Related
to Direct Marketing: 76-100%
Founded: 1966

Envelope manufacturer producing
25,000,000 envelopes daily.

UNITED ENVELOPE
65 Railroad Ave
Ridgefield, NJ 07657-2130

Telephone: (201) 699-5800, Toll Free:
(800) 752-4012, FAX: (201) 313-
7177, Web Site: www.
unitedenvelope.com
VP: Steven Bunker

Envelope printing and manufacturing
company.

VICTOR ENVELOPE CO
301 Arthur Ct
Bensenville, IL 60106-3381
Telephone: (630) 616-2750, Web Site:
www.victorenvelope.com
Pres: Kent Dahlgren

Company specializes in custom envelope manufacturing.

**WISCONSIN CONVERTING
INC**
1689 Morrow St
Green Bay, WI 54302-2605
Telephone: (920) 437-6400, Toll Free:
(800) 544-1935, FAX: (920) 436-
4964, E-Mail: wci@
wisconsinconverting.com, Web Site:
www.wisconsinconverting.com
Pres: Rich Bierman
Employees: 50
Founded: 1987

Converters of ECO-SHIPPER(R) liner-
board utility mailers, DURA-BAG(R)
laminated, reinforced mailers; both
available in flat or gusseted, with or
without Peel & Seal Closure(TM).
Multi-color graphics. Sales to direct
marketers, catalog & fulfillment operations through national distribution.

WOLF ENVELOPE CO
725 S Adams Rd
Birmingham, MI 48009-6902
Telephone: (248) 687-2745, Toll Free:
(800) 258-5700, FAX: (248) 687-
2751, Web Site: www.wolfenvelope.
com
Pres: Hugh F. Mahler

WORCESTER ENVELOPE
22 Millburn St
Auburn, MA 01501
Telephone: (508) 832-5394, Toll Free:
(800) 343-1398, FAX: (508) 832-
3796, E-Mail: sales@
worcesterenvelope.com, Web Site:
www.worcester-envelope.com
Pres: Eldon Pond
Customer Svc Mgr & Sls: Mary Cutting
Gen Mgr: Scott Waterhouse

Specializes in the manufacturing of
printed media to the medium to large
volume mail industry, including envelope, form, and label.

ALABAMA

RayPress Corp, 380 Riverchase Pkwy E, Birmingham, 35244-1813

ARIZONA

White Electronic Designs, 3601 E University Dr, Phoenix, 85034-7217

ARKANSAS

Mays Mission for the Handicapped Inc, 604 Colonial Dr, Heber Springs, 72543-3425

CALIFORNIA

Apperson Inc, 13910 Cerritos Corporate Dr, Cerritos, 90703-2457

California Offset Printers, 620 W Elk Ave, Glendale, 91204

ColorEdge, 1919 Empire Ave, Burbank, 91504-3404

Creel Printing of California, 151 Kalmus Dr Ste H11, Costa Mesa, 92626-5971

Dome Printing, 340 Commerce Cir, Sacramento, 95815-4213

MailBlazer, 2020 S Eastwood Ave, Santa Ana, 92705-5208

Multi-Media Publishing & Packaging Inc, 14621 Titus St Ste A, Panorama City, 91402-4904

O'Neil Data Systems Inc, 12655 Beatrice St, Los Angeles, 90066-7300

PIP Postal Instant Press, 26722 Plaza, Mission Viejo, 92691

Precise Media Services Inc, 5678 E Concours Ave, Ontario, 91764

Shutterfly, 2800 Bridge Pkwy, Redwood City, 94065-1192

Sumi Printing, 1139 E Janis St, Carson, 90746-1306

TFC Inc, 690 Airpark Rd, Napa, 94558-7516

USDiscs, 2387 Buena Vista St, Duarte, 91010-3301

V3, 200 N Elevar St, Oxnard, 93030-7969

COLORADO

CPI Card Group, 10368 W Centennial Rd (Suite A), Littleton, 80127-4296

CONNECTICUT

Allied Printing Services Inc, 1 Allied Way, PO Box 850, Manchester, 06040-2728

Cenveo Inc, 1 Canterbury Green, Stamford, 06901-2032

Connecticut Color Inc, 127 Pomeroy Ave, Meriden, 06450-9210

National Graphics Inc, 248 Branford Rd, Route 139, North Branford, 06471-1303

Structural Graphics, 38 Plains Rd, Essex, 06426-1520

DELAWARE

Dupont Color Proofing, PO Box 80030, Wilmington, 19880-0030

Foxfire Printing & Packaging Inc, 750 Dawson Dr, Newark, 19713-3414

FLORIDA

BBF Integrated Solutions, 10950 Belcher Rd S, Largo, 33777-1438

Bellak Color Corp, 9730 NW 25th St, Miami, 33172-2201

Continental Plastic Card Co, 1801 Green Rd Ste B, Pompano Beach, 33064-1052

Dynacolor Graphics Inc, 950 SE 8th St, Hialeah, 33010

Globe Marketing Systems Inc, 11950 NW 39th St (Suite B), Coral Springs, 33065

Interprint Web & Sheetfed, 12350 US Hwy 19 N, Clearwater, 33764

Media Printing Corp, 4300 N Powerline Rd, Pompano Beach, 33073-3071

Modern Graphic Arts, 1527 102nd Ave N, Saint Petersburg, 33716-5049

Peninsular Printing of Daytona Beach Inc, 1814 Holsonback Dr, Daytona Beach, 32117-5112

Printing Corp of the Americas Inc (PCA), 620 SW 12th Ave, Fort Lauderdale, 33069

Rex Three Inc, 15431 SW 14th St, Sunrise, 33326

Rose Printing Co Inc, 2503 Jackson Bluff Rd, Tallahassee, 32304-4405

Solo Printing, 7860 NW 66th St, Miami, 33166-2708

Southeastern Printing, 950 SE 8th St, Hialeah, 33010

Think Shapes Mail, 5463 W Waters Ave (Suite 820), Tampa, 33634

GEORGIA

Atlanta Offset, 120 James Aldredge Blvd SW, Atlanta, 30336-2102

Beacon Printing & Graphics Inc, 1628A James P Rodgers Dr, Valdosta, 31601

Curtis 1000 Inc, 1725 Breckinridge Pkwy (Suite 500), Duluth, 30096-8994

IPD Printing & Distributing Inc, 5800 Peachtree Rd, Atlanta, 30341-2302

Naylor Inc, 350 Great Southwest Pkwy, Atlanta, 30336-2333

Sauers Group, Inc, 1585 Roadhaven Dr, Stone Mountain, 30083-1315

Williams Printing Co, 1240 Spring St NW, Atlanta, 30309-2808

Wise, 555 McFarland 400 Dr, Alpharetta, 30004-3375

HAWAII

Hagadone Printing Co, 274 Pu'uhale Rd, Honolulu, 96819-2234

IDAHO

Selkirk Press, 1714 Industrial Dr, PO Box 875, Sandpoint, 83864

ILLINOIS

A&H Lithoprint Inc, 2540 S 27th Ave, Broadview, 60155-3851

ABS Graphics, 901 S Rohlwing Rd (Suite M), Addison, 60101-4229

American Graphics Network Inc, 1701 E Lake Ave (Suite 270), Glenview, 60025-2088

American Slide-Chart Corp, 25W550 Geneva Rd, Carol Stream, 60188-2225

Aspen Packaging Corp, 5253 W Roosevelt Rd, Cicero, 60804-1222

Badger Press Inc, 32941 N Stone Manor Dr, Grayslake, 60030-3051

Benchmark Imaging & Display, 221 Lively Blvd, Elk Grove Village, 60007-1622

CDI Network Inc, 4311 Ariel Ct, Naperville, 60564-3188

Carqueville Graphics Inc, 1536 Bourbon Pkwy, Streamwood, 60107-1808

Classic Color, 2424 S 25th Ave, Broadview, 60155-3874

JJ Collins' Sons Inc, 7125 Janes Ave (Suite 200), Woodridge, 60517-2341

Continental Web Press Inc, 1430 Industrial Dr, Itasca, 60143-1848

Darwill, 11900 W Roosevelt Rd, Hillside, 60162-2069

Datamart Direct Inc, 279 Madsen Dr (Suite 101), Bloomingdale, 60108-2692

Dependable Business Forms, 843 South Myrtle Ave, Villa Park, 60181-3353

Des Plaines Printing Co, 1000 Executive Way, Des Plaines, 60018

Domino Amjet Inc, 1290 Lakeside Dr, Gurnee, 60031-2499

E&D Web Printing Inc, 1100A S Main St, Rochelle, 61068-3509

FCL Graphics Inc, 4600 N Olcott Ave, Harwood Heights, 60656

Stephen Fossler Co Inc, 1600 E Touhy Ave, Des Plaines, 60018-3607

The Garvey Group, 7400 N Lehigh Ave, Niles, 60714-4024

Impressions Unlimited Inc, PO Box 1349, Deerfield, 60015-6005

Innovative Plastic Printing Corp, 534 Congress Cir N, Roselle, 60172

Integrated Print & Graphics, 645 Stevenson Rd, South Elgin, 60177-1134

JD Graphic Co, 1101 Arthur Ave, Elk Grove Village, 60707

Jet LithoColor Inc, 1500 Centre Cir, Downers Grove, 60515

Kingery Printing Co, 3012 S Banker, Effingham, 62401-2900

Lake County Press Inc, PO Box 9209, Waukegan, 60079-9209

Lehigh Direct, 1900 S 25th Ave, Broadview, 60155-2800

MAR Graphics, 523 S Meyer Ave, Valmeyer, 62295-3120

Marking Specialists Group, 1000 Asbury Dr (Suite 2), Buffalo Grove, 60089-4551

Marvin Envelope & Paper Co, 2040 W North Ave, Chicago, 60647-5414

Metropolitan Graphic Arts, 930 Turret Ct, Mundelein, 60060-3821

O'Brien Document Solutions, 1273 Humbracht Cir, Bartlett, 60103-1606

PPS - Packaging Printing Specialists, 3915 Stern Ave, Saint Charles, 60174-5441

Perfect Plastic Printing Corp, 311 Kautz Rd (Suite 4), Saint Charles, 60174-5304

Plastic Graphic, 255 Industrial Dr, Wauconda, 60084-1078

Prime Graphics Inc, 501 N Central Ave, Wood Dale, 60191-1473

Print Management Partners, 701 Lee St (Suite 1050), Des Plaines, 60016-4572

Quantum Color, 6511 Oakton St, Morton Grove, 60053-2728

Rainbow Graphics Inc, 933 Tower Rd, Mundelein, 60060-3811

Schawk Inc, 1600 E Sherwin Ave, Des Plaines, 60018

Segerdahl Graphics Inc, 385 Gilman Ave, Wheeling, 60090-5807

SG360, 1351 S Wheeling Rd, Wheeling, 60090-5997

Specialty Print Communications Inc, 6019 W Howard St, Niles, 60714-4801

TempoGraphics Inc, 455 E North Ave, Carol Stream, 60188-2123

Triangle Printers Inc, 3737 Chase Ave, Skokie, 60076-4008

INDIANA

Newcomb Marketing Solutions, 605 E 9th St, Michigan City, 46360-3651

PIP Printing and Marketing Services, 6330 E 75th St (Suite 138), Indianapolis, 46250-2717

Shindigz, One Party Pl, South Whitley, 46787

IOWA

Fisher Group Inc, 1250 N Center Point Rd, Hiawatha, 52233-1226

The Printer Inc, 1220 Thomas Beck Rd, Des Moines, 50315-1068

KANSAS

Digital Vision Resources Group - DVRG, 8236 Nieman Rd, Lenexa, 66214-1507

Heart Thoughts Inc, 1480 N Stratford Ln, Wichita, 67206-1165

McCormick-Armstrong Co Inc, 1501 E Douglas, Wichita, 67211-1608

KENTUCKY

Allegra Marketing Services, 11750 Diode Court, Louisville, 40299-6424

CCL Label, 1187 Industrial Rd, Cold Spring, 41076

Fetter Printing Company Inc, 700 Locust Ln, Louisville, 40217-2997

Publishers Press Inc, 100 Frank E Simon Ave, Shepherdsville, 40165-6013

VG Reed & Sons, 1002 S 12th St, Louisville, 40210-1302

LOUISIANA

National Mail-It Inc, 9151 Youree Dr, Shreveport, 71115-3303

MAINE

The Dingley Press, 119 Lisbon St, Lisbon, 04250-6005

Formsource, 170 Summer St, Lewiston, 04240-7532

The Maine Connection, 246 Deering Ave, Univ of Maine School of Law, Portland, 04102-2837

MARYLAND

Editors Press Inc, 1701 Cabin Branch Dr, Hyattsville, 20785-3820

Image Checks, PO Box 2, Bel Air, 21014

McArdle Printing Co Inc, 800 Commerce Dr, Upper Marlboro, 20774-8792

Omni Print Inc, 9700 Philadelphia Ct, Lanham, 20706-4405

Tidewater Direct LLC, 300 Tidewater Dr, Centreville, 21617

MASSACHUSETTS

Arthur Blank & Co Inc, 225 Rivermoor St, Boston, 02132-4934

Boston Color Graphics, 755 Middlesex Tpke, Billerica, 01821-3927

CM Consulting Services, 7 Maple Ln, Marshfield, 02050-3466

48HourPrint.com, 33 Farnsworth St (Suite 2), Boston, 02210-1210

HubCast Inc, 500 Edgewater Dr (Suite 568), Wakefield, 01880-6222

Lasermax Roll Systems, 4 Suburban Park Dr, Billerica, 01821-3904

Linguistic Systems Inc, 201 Broadway, Cambridge, 02139

Pilgrim Printed Promotional Plastics, 1200 W Chestnut St, Brockton, 02301-5574

The Pond-Ekberg Co, 660 Broadway St, Chicopee, 01020-2400

Presskits, 8 Rose Ct Way, East Walpole, 02032-1185

UniGraphic Inc, 110 Commerce Way Ste 6, Woburn, 01801-1098

VistaPrint USA Inc, 95 Hayden Ave, Lexington, 02421-7942

MICHIGAN

Allegra Network, LLC, 47585 Galleon Dr, Plymouth, 48170-2466

Inland Press, 2001 W Lafayette Blvd, Detroit, 48216

John Henry Packaging, 5800 W Grand River Ave, Lansing, 48906-9111

Mitchell Graphics Inc, 2363 Mitchell Park Dr, Petoskey, 49770

Sheridan Books Inc, 613 E Industrial Dr, Chelsea, 48118-1536

Sir Speedy Grand Rapids, 4513 Broadmoor Ave SE (Suite A), Grand Rapids, 49512-5369

MINNESOTA

Ambassador Press, 1400 Washington Ave N, Minneapolis, 55411-3422

American Spirit Graphics Corp, 801 SE 9th St, Minneapolis, 55414-1306

Anderberg-Lund Printing, 6999 Oxford St, Saint Louis Park, 55426

Deluxe Corp, 3680 Victoria St N, Shoreview, 55126-2906

Japs-Olson Co, 7500 Excelsior Blvd, Saint Louis Park, 55426-4519

Nahan Printing Inc, 7000 Saukview Dr, Saint Cloud, 56303-0814

OlymPak, 6010 Earle Brown Dr (Suite 100), Minneapolis, 55430-4516

PGI Companies Inc, 11354 K-Tel Dr, Minnetonka, 55343-8868

Quill Healthcare, 8500 Wyoming Ave N, Minneapolis, 55445-1825

Schmidt, 1101 Frontage Rd NW, Byron, 55920

Western Graphics, 530 Wheeler St N, Saint Paul, 55104

MISSISSIPPI

Pearl River Graphics Printing, 404 Industrial Rd (Suite 1), Choctaw, 39350

MISSOURI

Cenveo Color Art Inc, 10300 Watson Rd, Saint Louis, 63127-1106

Creative Printing Services Inc, 34 N Brentwood Blvd, Saint Louis, 63105

Felco Printing & Mailing, 1910 Walnut St, Kansas City, 64108-1810

Greystone Graphics, 110 Geystone Ave, Kansas City, 66103

MWM Dexter Inc, 107 Washington Ave, Aurora, 65605-1461

US Tape & Label Corp, 2092 Westport Ctr Dr, Saint Louis, 63146-3564

Universal Printing, 1234 S Kingshighway Blvd, Saint Louis, 63110

Henry Wurst Inc, 1331 Saline St, North Kansas City, 64116-4410

NEBRASKA

Interstate Printing Co, 2002N 16th St, Omaha, 68110

Lancer Label, 301 S 74th St, Omaha, 68114

Redfield & Co Inc, 1901 Howard St, Omaha, 68102-2594

Surdell & Partners, 3738 S 149th St (Suite 109), Omaha, 68144-5564

NEVADA

Overnight Prints, 7582 Las Vegas Blvd (Suite 487), Las Vegas, 89123

Rapid Color Printing, 6445 Karms Park Ct, Las Vegas, 89118-1414

NEW HAMPSHIRE

Concord Litho, 92 Old Turnpike Rd, Concord, 03301-7305

Goss International, 121 Technology Dr, Durham, 03824-4716

Relyco, 121 Broadway, Dover, 03820-3299

Sterling Print & Mail System, 206 Concord St, Peterborough, 03458

NEW JERSEY

A&E Promotions LLC, 153 First Ave, Atlantic Highlands, 07716-0355

AC Pedreiro, 15 Diane Dr, Morganville, 07751-1370

Applied Printing Technologies, 77 Moonachie Ave, Moonachie, 07074-1801

The Ballantine Corp, 1700 Rte 23 N, Wayne, 07470-7536

CRW Graphics, 9100 Pennsauken Hwy, Pennsauken, 08110-1206

Clients First, 84 Elm St Ste 1, Westfield, 07090-2181

Driscoll Label Co Inc, 19 West St, East Hanover, 07936-2822

Federal Direct, 95 Main Ave Ste 2, Clifton, 07014-1749

Stephen Gould Paper Co Inc, 35 S Jefferson Rd, Whippany, 07981-1034

Hannecke Display Systems Inc, 91 Fulton St (#3), Boonton, 07005-1942

Hatteras Press Inc, 56 Park Rd, Tinton Falls, 07724-9715

Invitation Hotline, 68 Hawkins Rd, Manalapan, 07726

Jersey Printing Associates Inc, 153 First Ave, Atlantic Highlands, 07716-1265

Keystone Promotions Inc, 246 Washington Ave, Union, 07083

LP Thebault Co, 249 Pomeroy Rd, PO Box 169, Parsippany, 07054-3727

MediaTree, 77 E Haley Rd, Parsippany, 07054

Quadra Graphics Inc, PO Box 555, Cherry Hill, 08003-0555

Real Media Solutions, 77 Green Knolls Dr, Wayne, 07470-6123

The RONED Group, Six DeForest Ave, East Hanover, 07936

Sherwood Design & Development Center, One Kero Rd, Carlstadt, 07072

Unz & Co, 333 Cedar Ave (Suite 2), Middlesex, 08846-2400

NEW YORK

Andell Packaging Corp, 19 Nightingale Ct (Suite 2), Manhasset, 11030-4039

Benton Announcements Inc, 3006 Bailey Ave, Buffalo, 14215-2898

Center for Book Arts, 28 W 27th St (fl 3), New York, 10001-6906

Chase Media Group, 1520 Front St, Yorktown Heights, 10598-4638

Clean Lists Associates Inc, 122 E 42nd St (Suite 1700), New York, 10168-0002

DNP America Inc, 335 Madison Ave (3rd fl), New York, 10017-4616

Disc Graphics Inc, Ten Gilpin Ave, Hauppauge, 11788

Eastman Kodak Co, 343 State St, Rochester, 14650-0001

Essex Printing Co Inc, 14 Westminster Dr, Croton On Hudson, 10520-1008

The Flexi Group Inc, 2675 Henry Hudson Pkwy, Bronx, 10463

Hi-C Production, Nine Tottenham Pl, New Hyde Park, 11040-3516

Kodak Graphic Communications, 343 State St, Rochester, 14650-0002

Magjak Printing Corp, 114 Pearl St, Port Chester, 10573-4663

Media Link Communications, 321 E 22nd St (Suite 3K), New York, 10010

Official Offset Corp, 8600 New Horizons Blvd, Amityville, 11701-1183

PCI Paper Conversions Inc, 6761 Thompson Rd N, Syracuse, 13211-2119

PGS Printing & Graphics Services, 261 Birch Dr, Roslyn, 11576-3001

Printing Spectrum, 12 Research Way (Suite 1), East Setauket, 11733-3531

Sir Speedy Westbury, 75 State St, Westbury, 11590-5004

Spire Creative Group, 110 W 40th St (Rm 1702), New York, 10018-8508

SPIRE Printing & Packaging LLC, 501 5th Ave (Suite 811), New York, 10017-7849

Tucker Printers, 270 Middle Rd, Henrietta, 14467-9312

Web Graphics, PO Box 308, Glens Falls, 12801-0308

Wilen Group, 5 Wellwood Ave, Farmingdale, 11735-1213

William Charles Printing, 7 Fairchild Ct Ste 100, Plainview, 11803-1734

NORTH CAROLINA

The Hickory Printing Solutions LLC, 725 Reese Dr SW, Conover, 28613

Source 4 Inc, 16740 Birkdale Commons Pkwy (Suite 208), Huntersville, 28078-4462

OHIO

Ampac Holdings LLC, 12025 Tricon Rd, Cincinnati, 45246-1719

Angstrom Graphics, 4437 E 49th St, Cleveland, 44125

Caraustar Ashland Carton Plant, 600 Union St, Ashland, 44805

Champion Printing Inc, 2300 Montana Ave (Suite 319), Cincinnati, 45211-3829

Cyril-Scott Co, 3950 State Route 37 E, PO Box 310, Lancaster, 43130

The Gray Printing Co, 401 E North St, Fostoria, 44830-2828

Great Lakes Integrated, 4005 Clark Ave, Cleveland, 44109-1186

Hess Print Solutions, 3765 Sunnybrook Rd, Kent, 44240

Kreber Graphics Inc, 2580 Westbelt Dr, Columbus, 43228

Top USA Corp, 771 Dearborn Park Ln (Suite N), Worthington, 43085-5720

Univenture Inc, 13311 Industrial Pkwy, Marysville, 43040-9589

OKLAHOMA

Zed Marketing Group, 1210 Roosevelt St (Suite 220), Edmond, 73034-5176

OREGON

AKA Direct, 2415 North Ross Ave, Portland, 97227

PENNSYLVANIA

Action Mailers Inc, 90 Commerce Dr, Aston, 19014-3286

American Thermoplastic Co, 106 Gamma Dr, Pittsburgh, 15238-2985

Bartash Media Group, 5400 Grays Ave, Philadelphia, 19143-5897

Communifx Corp, 1253 Freedom Rd (Suite 500), Cranberry, 16066-4952

Consolidated Printing Inc, 5050 Parkside Ave, Philadelphia, 19131-4714

Fry Communications Inc, 800 W Church Rd, Mechanicsburg, 17055-3198

Graphic Arts Information Network (GAIN), 200 Deer Run Rd, Sewickley, 15143-2324

IBSDirect, 431 Yerkes Rd, King of Prussia, 19406-3556

Innovation Printing Inc, 11601 Caroline Rd, Philadelphia, 19154

Intelligencer Printing Co, 330 Eden Rd, Lancaster, 17601-4218

International Fulfillment Inc, 2800 Black Lake Pl (Suite C), Philadelphia, 19154-1024

McCourt Label Co, 20 Egbert Ln, Lewis Run, 16738-3802

National Mail Graphics Corp, 300 Old Mill Ln, Exton, 19341-2582

Neibauer Press, 20 Industrial Dr, Warminster, 18974-1433

Printing + Quick Copy, 8799 Frankford Ave, Philadelphia, 19136

Sir Speedy Newtown, 760 Newtown-Yardley Rd, Newtown, 18940-4500

Spring Hill Laser Services, PO Box 79, Sterling, 18463-0079

Valley Forge Tape & Label Co Inc, 119 Summit Dr, Exton, 19341

York Label, 405 Willow Springs Ln, York, 17405-6047

RHODE ISLAND

Colorlith Corp, 321 S Main St Ste 301, Providence, 02903-7109

The Foxon Co, 235 W Park St, Providence, 02908-4881

SOUTH DAKOTA

Western Web Printing, 4005 S Western Ave, Sioux Falls, 57105-6514

TENNESSEE

Arcade Marketing, Inc, 3800 Amnicola Hwy, Chattanooga, 37406-1003

Donihe Graphics Inc, 766 Brookside Dr, Kingsport, 37660-6614

King Printing Solutions, 531 Straight Creek Rd, New Tazewell, 37825

Morrison Printing Co, 1039 Walters Dr, Morristown, 37814-6133

National Mailroom Service Inc, 6924 Karns Crossing Ln, Knoxville, 37931-2571

TEXAS

ADS Media Group Inc, 15265 Capital Port (Suite 100), San Antonio, 78249-1350

American Color, 2010 Westridge Dr, Irving, 75038-2900

Clear Visions Inc, 121 Interpark Blvd (Suite 801), San Antonio, 78216

Dockery House Publishing Inc, 906 Main St (Suite B), Lindale, 75771

Graphic Arts Center, 2514 National Dr, Garland, 75041-2329

Graphics International Inc, 3883 Turtle Creek Blvd (Apt 1406), Dallas, 75219-4430

Lone Star Web Inc, 6730 Oakbrook Blvd, Dallas, 75235-4108

Nationwide Argosy Solutions LLC, 2500 W Loop S (Suite 500), Houston, 77027-4521

Paragon Printing & Mailing, 10423 McKalla Pl, Bldg A (Suite 100), Austin, 78758-4448

Performance Printing/ Optigraphics, 2929 N Stemmons Fwy, Dallas, 75247-6102

Shopguide.com, 3223 Commerce St, Amarillo, 79109-3275

Teraco Inc, 2080 Commerce Dr, Midland, 79703-7502

Texas Graphic Resource, 1234 Round Table Dr, Dallas, 75247-3504

Venture Encoding Service Inc, 4401 Cambridge, Fort Worth, 76155-2629

Williamson Printing, 6700 Denton Dr, Dallas, 75235-9827

Xpressdocs, 1000 Forest Park Blvd Ste 200, Fort Worth, 76110-1169

UTAH

AlphaGraphics World Headquarters, 268 S State St (Suite 300), Salt Lake City, 84111-5314

Westpro Inc, 2294 Mountain Vista Ln, Provo, 84606-6206

VERMONT

The Offset House Inc, 89 Sand Hill Rd, Essex Junction, 05452-3909

VIRGINIA

Aptara, Inc, 3110 Fairview Park Dr (Suite 900), Falls Church, 22042-4534

Catalogs America, 1 American Pl, Gordonsville, 22942

Datamatx Inc, 10430 Lakeridge Pkwy, Ashland, 23005-8124

Folder Factory Inc, 5421 Main St (Suite 300), Mount Jackson, 22843-9537

HBP, 2818 Fallfax Dr, Falls Church, 22042-2804

Industrial Arts & Graphics, 22714 Melrose Farm Ln, Middleburg, 20117

Membership Cards Only LLC, 8000 Towers Crescent Dr (Suite 1350), Vienna, 22182-6219

Progress Printing Co, 2677 Waterlick Rd, Lynchburg, 24502-4861

Stephenson Printing Inc, 5731 General Washington Dr, Alexandria, 22312

WASHINGTON

Labels West Inc, 17629 130th Ave NE, Woodinville, 98072

Sir Speedy Printing and Marketing Services, 7450 S Tacoma Way (Suite B1), Tacoma, 98409-3906

WISCONSIN

Arandell Corp, N82 W13118 Leon Rd, Menomonee Falls, 53051

Badger Press/Photographics Inc, 7325 30th Ave, Kenosha, 53142-4401

Graphic Communications Center, 3001 E Venture Dr, Box 357, Appleton, 54911-8309

Heavy Rotation, 3720 N Fratney St (Studios 3F), Milwaukee, 53212

Kwik-File, 619 N Commerce St, Sheboygan, 53081-3901

Mandel Co, 727 W Glendale Ave, Milwaukee, 53209-6509

Neenah Paper FR LLC, 1376 Kimberly Dr, Neenah, 54956-1641

NewsNotes LLC, 2348 Pinehurst Dr, Middleton, 53562

Outlook Group Corp, 1180 American Dr, Neenah, 54956-1306

Ripon Printers, 656 S Douglas St, Ripon, 54971-9044

Service Litho Print Inc, 50 W Fernau, Oshkosh, 54902-0875

Sir Speedy Green Bay, 333 Packerland Dr, Green Bay, 54303-4815

CANADA

Ontario

Crook & Grant Lithographers Ltd, 279 Yorkland Blvd, North York, M2J 1S5

Embassy Digital, 2880 Brighton Rd (Unit 1), Oakville, L6H 5S3

Grant's Mailing Services Inc, 2825 Argentia Rd (Unit 4), Mississauga, L5N 8G6

Litho-Web Inc, 730 Hardwick Rd, Bolton, L7E 5R4

PointOne Graphics Inc, 14 Vansco Rd, Toronto, M8Z 5J4

St Joseph Communications, 50 MacIntosh Blvd, Concord, L4K 4P3

TransContinental Yorkville - O'Keefe, Eight Tidemore Ave, Etobicoke, M9W 5H4

Quebec

Scientific Games Canada, 3000 Boul de l'Assomption, Montreal, H1N 3V5

Saskatchewan

PrintWest Communications Ltd, 1111 Eighth Ave, Regina, S4R 1E1

Printing & Related Services (27)

A&E PROMOTIONS LLC
153 First Ave
Atlantic Highlands, NJ 07716-0355
Telephone: (732) 275-1520, FAX:
(732) 275-1147, E-Mail: eveltri@
aepromo.com, Web Site: www.
promoplace.com
Pres: Eugene Veltri
Founded: 1987

Wholesale distribution of non-durable
goods.

A&H LITHOPRINT INC
2540 S 27th Ave
Broadview, IL 60155-3851
Telephone: (708) 345-1196, FAX:
(708) 345-1225, Web Site: www.
ahlithoprint.com
Pres: David Ashley

ABS GRAPHICS
901 S Rohlwing Rd (Suite M)
Addison, IL 60101-4229
Telephone: (630) 495-2400, FAX:
(630) 495-0728, E-Mail: info@
absinet.com, Web Site: www.absinet.
com
Pres: Ken VanderVeen
Mktg: Billy McCaleb
Founded: 1982

Provides integrated communications
marketing, and print media services in
the U.S.

AC PEDREIRO
15 Diane Dr
Morganville, NJ 07751-1370
Telephone: (732) 598-6766
Pres: Anna Pedreiro

ADS MEDIA GROUP INC
15265 Capital Port (Suite 100)
San Antonio, TX 78249-1350
Telephone: (210) 655-6613, FAX:
(210) 655-6269, Web Site: www.
adsmediagroup.com
VP Sls: Jim Stewart
Founder, Exec Chmn, CEO & Pres:
Clark R. Doyal
CIO: Stan Prescott
Primary Market Served: Consumer
Founded: 2001

Direct to the door delivery, provides
front door marketing services.

AKA DIRECT
2415 North Ross Ave
Portland, OR 97227
Telephone: (503) 467-2200, Toll Free:
(800) 647-8587, FAX: (503) 445-
0064, Web Site: www.akadirect.com

Pres & CEO: Wayne Modica
Primary Market Served: Consumer
Founded: 1968

Provide the most up-to-date, meaning-
ful, relevant data for effective planning,
budgeting, and analysis.

AMPAC HOLDINGS LLC
12025 Tricon Rd
Cincinnati, OH 45246-1719
Telephone: (513) 671-1777, Toll Free:
(800) 543-7030, FAX: (513) 671-
2920, Web Site: www.ampaconline.
com
CEO & Pres: John Baumann
Dir Tech Mktg Ampac Flexibles Performance Films: Tricia Reighard
Founded: 1966

Manufactures flexible packaging products.

ACTION MAILERS INC
Div. of The Action Group
90 Commerce Dr
Aston, PA 19014-3286
Telephone: (610) 859-0500, Toll Free:
(800) 258-5992, FAX: (610) 859-
0505, Web Site: www.actionmailer.
com
Pres: Daniel Dobbin
VP: Kathy Dobbin
Founded: 1972

**ALLEGRA MARKETING
SERVICES**
11750 Diode Court
Louisville, KY 40299-6424
Telephone: (502) 895-1530, FAX:
(502) 895-1624, Web Site: www.
allegra-east.com
Pres: Denise Spalding
Mktg Dir: Stephanie Samaro

ALLEGRA NETWORK, LLC
47585 Galleon Dr
Plymouth, MI 48170-2466
Telephone: (248) 596-8600, FAX:
(248) 596-8601, Web Site: www2.
allegranetwork.com
CEO: Mike Marcantonio
VP Fin & Admin: Laura Pierce-Marutz
Founded: 1976

Provides marketing, printing, &
graphic communication services to
small & mid-sized businesses in North
America.

**ALLIED PRINTING
SERVICES INC**
1 Allied Way, PO Box 850
Manchester, CT 06040-2728

Telephone: (860) 643-1101, Toll Free:
(800) 225-8777, (800) 224-8894,
FAX: (860) 646-7954, E-Mail:
allied@alliedprinting.com, Web Site:
www.alliedprinting.com
Pres: John G. Sommers
Mktg: Gunner Hicks
Founded: 1949

Operates as a printing & fulfillment
company.

**ALPHAGRAPHICS WORLD
HEADQUARTERS**
268 S State St (Suite 300)
Salt Lake City, UT 84111-5314
Telephone: (801) 595-7270, Toll Free:
(800) 955-6246, FAX: (801) 595-
7271, E-Mail: contactus@
alphagraphics.com, Web Site: www.
alphagraphics.com
Pres: Aaron T. Grohs
CFO, Treas & Sec: Randy Plant

Provides products & services for design, digital & offset printing, one-to-
one marketing, digital archiving &
mailing.

AMBASSADOR PRESS
1400 Washington Ave N
Minneapolis, MN 55411-3422
Telephone: (612) 521-0123, Toll Free:
(800) 544-9112, FAX: (612) 521-
4587, E-Mail: info@ambpress.com,
Web Site: www.ambpress.com
Owner: Barry Engle
Pres: Bernard Engle
Sls Exec: Josh Fieldman
Founded: 1960

Providing superior customer service in
the commercial printing industry.

AMERICAN COLOR
2010 Westridge Dr
Irving, TX 75038-2900
Telephone: (602) 333-1000, FAX:
(602) 333-1099, Web Site: www.
amcolor.com
Head Tech Svcs: Dave Norinski
Mgr: Jeff Geyer

**AMERICAN GRAPHICS
NETWORK INC**
1701 E Lake Ave (Suite 270)
Glenview, IL 60025-2088
Telephone: (847) 729-7220, FAX:
(847) 724-5080, E-Mail: info@
agninc.com, Web Site: www.agninc.
com
Pres: Wanda M. Sclaventis

Founded: 1977

Prints & distributes merchandise used for advertising.

AMERICAN SLIDE-CHART CORP

25W550 Geneva Rd
Carol Stream, IL 60188-2225
Telephone: (630) 665-3333, Toll Free: (800) 323-4433, FAX: (630) 665-3491, E-Mail: info2@ americanslidechart.com, Web Site: www.americanslidechart.com
Mgr: Don Hoff

Designing specialized dimensional tools that help leading companies sell smarter.

AMERICAN SPIRIT GRAPHICS CORP

801 SE 9th St
Minneapolis, MN 55414-1306
Telephone: (612) 623-3333, FAX: (612) 623-9314, E-Mail: asgc@asgc. com, Web Site: www.asgc.com
Chmn: A. Oscar Carlson
Pres & COO: Myron Angel
CEO: Darren Carlson
Exec VP: Lauren Drevlow
VP, Opers: Tim Franzen
Conducts Business: U.S.
Employees: 200
Founded: 1992

Quality 4 & 5 color heatset web offset commercial printer specializing in direct response formats, coupon books, publication inserts, brochures & small format catalogs. Featuring innovative in-line, press-finished formats for direct marketers. 2- 6-color sheetfed lithography. Inserting/mailing, personalization available through American Spirit Mailing.

AMERICAN THERMOPLASTIC CO

106 Gamma Dr
Pittsburgh, PA 15238-2985
Telephone: (412) 967-0900, Toll Free: (800) 245-6600, FAX: (412) 967-9990, E-Mail: atc@binders.com, Web Site: www.binders.com
Pres: S. Silberman
Mktg Exec: Joseph Sprumont
Founded: 1954

Manufactures custom-imprinted ring binders, index tabs, pocket folders, clipboards & related loose-leaf products.

ANDELL PACKAGING CORP

19 Nightingale Ct (Suite 2)
Manhasset, NY 11030-4039

Telephone: (718) 937-6500, FAX: (718) 482-9416
Pres: Sandor Schaeffer

provides display advertising service.

ANDERBERG-LUND PRINTING

6999 Oxford St
Saint Louis Park, MN 55426
Telephone: (952) 920-9720, Toll Free: (800) 231-9777, FAX: (952) 920-1103, E-Mail: sales@anderberglund. com, Web Site: www.anderberglund. com
Pres & CEO: Jack Anderberg

Innovative print solutions.

ANGSTROM GRAPHICS

4437 E 49th St
Cleveland, OH 44125
Telephone: (216) 271-5300, FAX: (216) 271-7650, E-Mail: wayne. angstrom@st-ives-usa.com, Web Site: www.angstromgraphics.com
Chmn, Pres & CEO: Wayne Angstrom
Pres & COO: Mark Berkey
Founded: 1918

Provides printing, omni channel & marketing solutions.

APPERSON INC

13910 Cerritos Corporate Dr
Cerritos, CA 90703-2457
Telephone: (562) 356-3333, Toll Free: (800) 877-2341, FAX: (562) 356-3310, E-Mail: sales@appersonprint. com, Web Site: www.appersonprint. com
CEO: R.P. Apperson
VP Intl Sls: Abel Garcia
Founded: 1955

Develops & delivers solutions for assessing performance & measuring success.

APPLIED PRINTING TECHNOLOGIES

77 Moonachie Ave
Moonachie, NJ 07074-1801
Telephone: (201) 896-6600, Toll Free: (888) 282-4141, FAX: (201) 896-6839, E-Mail: vpsales@ appliedprinting.com, Web Site: www.appliedprinting.com
Pres: Mike Voss
Founded: 1960

Offers digital prepress, printing, and finishing services.

APTARA, INC

3110 Fairview Park Dr (Suite 900)
Falls Church, VA 22042-4534

Telephone: (703) 352-0001, FAX: (703) 352-8862, E-Mail: info@ aptaracorp.com, Web Site: www. aptaracorp.com
Pres: William P. Penders
Founded: 1988

Provides digital content, learning & performance & business support services for various companies worldwide.

ARANDELL CORP

N82 W13118 Leon Rd
Menomonee Falls, WI 53051
Telephone: (262) 255-4400, Toll Free: (800) 558-8724, FAX: (262) 253-3162, E-Mail: jft@arandell.com, Web Site: www.arandell.com
Chmn Bd & CEO: James Treis
Pres, CFO & Dir: Bradley J. Hoffman
Founded: 1922

Operates as a Web offset printer in the U.S.

ARCADE MARKETING, INC

3800 Amnicola Hwy
Chattanooga, TN 37406-1003
Telephone: (423) 624-3301, FAX: (423) 622-4635, E-Mail: resumes@ arcadeinc.com
Pres & CEO: Serge Juredini
Sr VP Sls, Mktg & Devel: Diane Crecca

provides accounting, bookkeeping & related auditing services.

ASPEN PACKAGING CORP

5253 W Roosevelt Rd
Cicero, IL 60804-1222
Telephone: (708) 652-6444, Toll Free: (800) 367-5493, FAX: (708) 652-6444, E-Mail: sales@aspenpkg.com, Web Site: www.aspenpkg.com
Pres: Gary Stearns

Design, manufacture, provide replication, fulfillment & mailing services.

ATLANTA OFFSET

Subs. of Gannett Co Inc
120 James Aldredge Blvd SW
Atlanta, GA 30336-2102
Telephone: (404) 699-6200, FAX: (404) 699-1393, Web Site: www. gannett.com/about/map/offset.htm
Gen Mgr: Charlie Arthur

BBF INTEGRATED SOLUTIONS

Clondalkin Group Company
10950 Belcher Rd S
Largo, FL 33777-1438
Telephone: (727) 545-8703, Toll Free: (800) 666-8082, Web Site: www. bbfprinting.com

Chmn, Clondalkin Group Co: Mark
  Burgess
Founded: 1950

Provides innovative, specialized
printed & packaging solutions to a
broad range of customers & markets
through its three business platforms, including Direct Mail, Labels and Plastic
Cards.

BADGER PRESS INC
32941 N Stone Manor Dr
Grayslake, IL 60030-3051
Telephone: (847) 996-1190, E-Mail:
  info@badgerpressinc.com, Web Site:
  www.badgerpressinc.com
Pres: Sally O'Brien
Founded: 1983

Print & marketing service company.

BADGER PRESS/ PHOTOGRAPHICS INC
7325 30th Ave
Kenosha, WI 53142-4401
Telephone: (262) 658-1628, Toll Free:
  (800) 635-9773, FAX: (262) 658-
  0307
Pres: Todd Bundies

Full service offset & digital printing for
Southeastern Wisconsin & Northern Illinois.

THE BALLANTINE CORP
1700 Rte 23 N
Wayne, NJ 07470-7536
Telephone: (973) 305-1500, E-Mail:
  connect@ballantine.com, Web Site:
  www.ballantine.com
Dir Mktg & Digital: Ryan Cote
Founded: 1966

Helping companies implement successful direct marketing initiatives.

BARTASH MEDIA GROUP
5400 Grays Ave
Philadelphia, PA 19143-5897
Telephone: (215) 724-1700, Toll Free:
  (800) 599-9792, FAX: (215) 724-
  3313, Web Site: www.bartash.com
VP Fin & Admin: Keith Fisher
COO: Jack Riciutti
Acting Dir Sls: Rick Morrison
Primary Market Served: Consumer

BEACON PRINTING & GRAPHICS INC
1628A James P Rodgers Dr
Valdosta, GA 31601
Telephone: (912) 244-5634, Toll Free:
  (800) 227-7377, FAX: (912) 247-
  4405, E-Mail: sls@uspress.com, Web
  Site: www.uspress.com

Pres: Kent A. Buescher
Offers a full range of direct mail services including mailing lists, data services, inserting, inkjetting & more.

BELLAK COLOR CORP
9730 NW 25th St
Miami, FL 33172-2201
Telephone: (305) 854-8525, FAX:
  (305) 858-8783, Web Site: www.
  foilmania.com
Pres: Manuel Fernandez
Founded: 1960

Full service printer specializing in high
end offset & digital printing, along
with our exclusive BELLAK In-Line
Full Color Cold Foil Printing Process

BENCHMARK IMAGING & DISPLAY
Subs. of William McKinley Studios
221 Lively Blvd
Elk Grove Village, IL 60007-1622
Telephone: (847) 290-0002, FAX:
  (847) 290-8608, Web Site: www.
  benchmarkimaging.com
Pres: Bill McKinley
Founded: 1970

Provides portable display & large format printing services.

BENTON ANNOUNCEMENTS INC
3006 Bailey Ave
Buffalo, NY 14215-2898
Telephone: (716) 836-4100, FAX:
  (716) 836-4161
Chmn: Michael J. Guerra Sr.
Pres: Philip J. Guerra
VP: Michael J. Guerra Jr.
Conducts Business: U.S., Canada
Employees: 10
Primary Market Served: Business &
  Consumer
Advertising/Marketing Budget Related
  to Direct Marketing: 0-25%
Direct Marketing ad budget: $5,000
Telephone: 100%
Founded: 1935
Gross sales or billing: $600,000

Sell invitations with services that include embossing, leaf stamping, ther-
mography, printing, die cutting, gluing,
taping, numbering and scoring.

ARTHUR BLANK & CO INC
225 Rivermoor St
Boston, MA 02132-4934
Telephone: (617) 325-9600, Toll Free:
  (800) 776-7333, FAX: (617) 327-
  1235, E-Mail: abco@abco.com, Web
  Site: www.arthurblank.com
Chmn & CEO: Justin E. D'Angelo
CFO & Exec VP: Dab Fournier

Founded: 1934

Designs & manufactures private label
plastic cards in North America.

BOSTON COLOR GRAPHICS
755 Middlesex Tpke
Billerica, MA 01821-3927
Telephone: (978) 528-7999, Toll Free:
  (800) 767-0067, FAX: (978) 528-
  7609, E-Mail: sales@
  bostoncolorgraphics.com, Web Site:
  www.bostoncolorgraphics.com
Pres: Charles Noonan
Founded: 2003

BCG provides on-demand print, pre-
media and targeted, personalized communications.

CCL LABEL
1187 Industrial Rd
Cold Spring, KY 41076
Telephone: (859) 781-6161, Toll Free:
  (800) 422-6633, FAX: (859) 781-
  6339
VP: Eric Schaffer

CDI NETWORK INC
4311 Ariel Ct
Naperville, IL 60564-3188
Telephone: (708) 409-8585, FAX:
  (708) 409-8589, Web Site: www.
  cdinet.biz
Pres & CEO: Walter D. Schenk

CM CONSULTING SERVICES
15 Volunteer Rd, Hingham, MA
  02043-3684
7 Maple Ln
Marshfield, MA 02050-3466
Telephone: (781) 749-5000, FAX:
  (801) 749-5009, E-Mail:
  cmcalpine3@gmail.com
Acct Exec: Charles M. McAlpine

CPI CARD GROUP
10368 W Centennial Rd (Suite A)
Littleton, CO 80127-4296
Telephone: (303) 973-9311, FAX:
  (303) 973-8420, E-Mail: mbarber@
  cpicardgroup.com, Web Site: www.
  cpicardgroup.com
CEO, Pres & Dir: Steve Montross
CFO: Marvin S. Press
Conducts Business: U.S.
Primary Market Served: Business
Advertising/Marketing Budget Related
  to Direct Marketing: 0-25%
Founded: 1982
Gross sales or billing: $10,200,000

Manufactures plastic cards for retail,
grocery, financial, direct mail, and
many others. Visa/MasterCard certified.

CRW GRAPHICS
9100 Pennsauken Hwy
Pennsauken, NJ 08110-1206
Telephone: (856) 662-9111, Toll Free:
(800) 820-3000, FAX: (856) 665-
1789, E-Mail: service@crwgraphics.
com, Web Site: www.crwgraphics.
com
Chmn & CEO: Harriet Weiss
Pres: Mark Weiss
Founded: 1964

Operates as a commercial printing &
digital printing company in the U.S.

CALIFORNIA OFFSET
PRINTERS
620 W Elk Ave
Glendale, CA 91204
Telephone: (818) 291-1100, Toll Free:
(800) 280-6446, FAX: (818) 291-
1190, E-Mail: info@copprints.com,
Web Site: www.copprints.com
Pres CEO: William Rittwage
Founded: 1963

Provides web & digital printing services & direct mailing and fulfillment
services.

CARAUSTAR ASHLAND
CARTON PLANT
600 Union St
Ashland, OH 44805
Telephone: (419) 289-2666, FAX:
(419) 281-5415, Web Site: www.
caraustar.com
Chmn Bd: Daniel P. Casey

CARQUEVILLE GRAPHICS
INC
Subs. of Consolidated Graphics
1536 Bourbon Pkwy
Streamwood, IL 60107-1808
Telephone: (630) 837-4500, FAX:
(630) 837-4510, Web Site: www.
carqueville.com
Pres: Phillip J. Wicklander
Founded: 1864

Provides a wide range of commercial
printing services & solutions, including
label & specialty printing.

CATALOGS AMERICA
Div. of American Press LLC
1 American Pl
Gordonsville, VA 22942
Telephone: (540) 832-2253, Toll Free:
(800) 283-4666, FAX: (540) 832-
7253, E-Mail: dsayin@
catalogsamerica.com, Web Site:
www.catalogsamerica.com
Pres: Marshall J. Pettygrove

Provides lithographic printing services.

CENTER FOR BOOK ARTS
28 W 27th St (fl 3)
New York, NY 10001-6906
Telephone: (212) 481-0295, FAX:
(866) 708-8994, E-Mail: info@
centerforbookarts.org, Web Site:
www.centerforbookarts.org
Exec Dir: Alexander Campos
Mktg Mgr: Sara Bouchard
Founded: 1974

CENVEO COLOR ART INC
10300 Watson Rd
Saint Louis, MO 63127-1106
Telephone: (314) 966-2000, FAX:
(314) 966-4725, E-Mail:
mikedenny@cenveo.com, Web Site:
www.colorart.com
Contact: Mike Denny

Offers complete printing & binding
services for commercial, advertising,
magazine, periodical, catalog & directory printing.

CENVEO INC
1 Canterbury Green
Stamford, CT 06901-2032
Telephone: (410) 633-4200, Toll Free:
(800) 638-2850, FAX: (410) 633-
1202, Web Site: www.cenveo.com
Chmn & CEO: Robert G. Burton Sr.
COO: Mike Burton
CFO: Scott Goodwin
Pres: Rob G. Burton Jr.
Conducts Business: U.S. Asia, South
America & Central America

World leader in the management & distribution of print & related offerings.

CHAMPION PRINTING INC
Subs. of BSC Ventures, LLC.
2300 Montana Ave (Suite 319)
Cincinnati, OH 45211-3829
Telephone: (513) 541-1100, Toll Free:
(800) 543-1957, FAX: (513) 541-
9398, E-Mail: cpi@
championprintinginc.com, Web Site:
www.championprintinginc.com
Pres: Brian Sass
Pres: John Hassan

Commercial direct mail printer that
specializes in direct response products.

CHASE MEDIA GROUP
1520 Front St
Yorktown Heights, NY 10598-4638
Telephone: (914) 962-3871, FAX:
(914) 962-2040, Web Site: www.
chasemultimedia.com
Pres & Publr: Carla Chase
Classified Adv Mgr: Lisa Thomas
Chase Press Acct Exec: Glen Seaman
Mktg Mgr: Leslie Mancuso
Direct Mail Acct Exec: Amy Bambace

Conducts Business: U.S.
Primary Market Served: Consumer
Catalog available online
Direct online sales
Founded: 1958

Advertising shoppers, serving 355,949
homes weekly with 28 editions
throughout upper Westchester, Putnam,
Dutchess & Fairfield counties.

CLASSIC COLOR
2424 S 25th Ave
Broadview, IL 60155-3874
Telephone: (708) 484-0000, FAX:
(708) 344-2233, E-Mail: info@
classic-color.com, Web Site: www.
classic-color.com
Pres: Raymond E. Bell

Pre-media, digital artistry & innovative
printing.

CLEAN LISTS ASSOCIATES
INC
122 E 42nd St (Suite 1700)
New York, NY 10168-0002
Telephone: (212) 551-1013, FAX:
(212) 551-1107, E-Mail: cleanlists@
mindspring.com
Pres: Tamara Beck

CLEAR VISIONS INC
Subs. of R.R.
121 Interpark Blvd (Suite 801)
San Antonio, TX 78216
Telephone: (210) 496-6006, FAX:
(210) 496-9225, E-Mail:
bidrequest@clearvisionsinc.com,
Web Site: www.clearvisionsinc.com
Pres: Eric Koenigs
Founded: 1981

Operates as a full service print & mail
company.

CLIENTS FIRST
84 Elm St Ste 1
Westfield, NJ 07090-2181
Telephone: (908) 232-1200, Toll Free:
(800) 634-0040, FAX: (908) 233-
8833, E-Mail: info@clientsfirst.com,
Web Site: www.clientsfirst.com
Pres: Jeffrey Becker
Founded: 1981

Company's line of business includes
the wholesale distribution of stationery
& office supplies.

JJ COLLINS' SONS INC
7125 Janes Ave (Suite 200)
Woodridge, IL 60517-2341
Telephone: (630) 960-2525, Toll Free:
(800) 972-2296, FAX: (630) 960-
7487, E-Mail: sales@jjcollins.com,
Web Site: www.jjcollins.com

Pres: Jim Collins
Founded: 1878

Provides printing services.

COLOREDGE

1919 Empire Ave
Burbank, CA 91504-3404
Telephone: (818) 842-1121, Toll Free: (800) 300-3686, FAX: (818) 842-0280, E-Mail: john.davies@crushcreative.com, Web Site: www.coloredge.com
CEO & Pres: Guy Claudy
Sr. VP & Sls Mgr: John Davies

Provider of visual imaging solutions for luxury brands and retailers.

COLORLITH CORP

321 S Main St Ste 301
Providence, RI 02903-7109
Telephone: (508) 837-6100, Toll Free: (800) 556-7171, FAX: (508) 677-4466, E-Mail: lep@colorlith.net, Web Site: www.colorlith.net
Pres: Larry Pierce

COMMUNIFX CORP

1253 Freedom Rd (Suite 500)
Cranberry, PA 16066-4952
Telephone: (724) 935-8655, Web Site: www.communifax.com
CEO: Gene Ferruzza
VP Bus Devel & VP Promotional Mktg: Jill Zoria
Conducts Business: U.S.
Founded: 1988

Operates as a customer engagement agency in the U.S.

CONCORD LITHO

92 Old Turnpike Rd, Concord, NH 03301-7309
92 Old Turnpike Rd
Concord, NH 03301-7305
Telephone: (603) 225-3328, FAX: (603) 225-6120, E-Mail: print@concordlitho.com, Web Site: www.concordlitho.com
CEO: Peter Cook
Pres: Tom Cook
CFO: Marlin Kaufman
Founded: 1958

Full-service printing & direct marketing firm.

CONNECTICUT COLOR INC

127 Pomeroy Ave
Meriden, CT 06450-9210
Telephone: (203) 237-1400, FAX: (203) 440-3678, Web Site: www.connecticutcolor.com
Pres & Gen Mgr: Rick Herr
VP Dir Mktg: Nick Shostak

Founded: 2003

Provides commercial direct marketing print solutions.

CONSOLIDATED PRINTING INC

5050 Parkside Ave
Philadelphia, PA 19131-4714
Telephone: (215) 879-1400, Toll Free: (800) 347-0119, FAX: (215) 879-9130, Web Site: www.condrake.com
Pres: Michael George
Founded: 1965

CONTINENTAL PLASTIC CARD CO

1801 Green Rd Ste B
Pompano Beach, FL 33064-1052
Telephone: (954) 794-0040, Toll Free: (800) 543-0670, FAX: (954) 755-4493, E-Mail: info@continentalplasticcard.com, Web Site: www.continentalplasticcard.com
Owner: Tony Gardner

Provides quality printed plastic & magnetic products along with a full complement of support services.

CONTINENTAL WEB PRESS INC

1430 Industrial Dr
Itasca, IL 60143-1848
Telephone: (630) 773-1903, FAX: (630) 773-1909, E-Mail: inquires@continentalweb.com, Web Site: www.continentalweb.com
Pres: Diane Field
Chief Mktg Officer: Kenneth Field
Founded: 1974

Privately held printing company with facilities in Illinois & Kentucky.

CREATIVE PRINTING SERVICES INC

34 N Brentwood Blvd
Saint Louis, MO 63105
Telephone: (314) 863-4550, Toll Free: (800) 886-4551, FAX: (314) 863-6036, E-Mail: steve@cpsstl.com, Web Site: www.cpsstl.com
Contact: Steven M. Turner

CREEL PRINTING OF CALIFORNIA

151 Kalmus Dr Ste H11
Costa Mesa, CA 92626-5971
Telephone: (714) 540-7005, FAX: (714) 979-1496, Web Site: www.creelprint.com
CEO: Allan Creel
Pres: Alan Creel Jr.
Exec VP Sls & Mktg: Micah Armijo

Founded: 1999

Full service facility with capabilities ranging from pre-media, printing, binding, mailing, distribution & fulfillment.

CROOK & GRANT LITHOGRAPHERS LTD

279 Yorkland Blvd
North York, ON, Canada M2J 1S5
Telephone: (416) 499-1011, FAX: (416) 499-1821
Pres: Steve Crook

CURTIS 1000 INC

Subs. of American Business Products Inc
1725 Breckinridge Pkwy (Suite 500)
Duluth, GA 30096-8994
Telephone: (678) 380-9095, Toll Free: (877) 287-8715, FAX: (770) 717-1890, E-Mail: info@curtis1000.com, Web Site: www.curtis1000.com
Bus Segment Mgr: Chad Davis
Pres: Steve Geiger
Founded: 1882

Business communications company, provides direct marketing & communications process/print management solutions to organizations.

CYRIL-SCOTT CO

3950 State Route 37 E, PO Box 310
Lancaster, OH 43130
Telephone: (740) 654-2112, FAX: (740) 654-7712, E-Mail: mstephenson@cyrilscott.com, Web Site: www.cyrilscott.com
Pres: Chad Stephenson
Founded: 1959

DNP AMERICA INC

Div. of Dai Nippon Printing Co Ltd
335 Madison Ave (3rd fl)
New York, NY 10017-4616
Telephone: (212) 503-1060, FAX: (212) 679-0613
Fin: Sarah Clingman
Founded: 1974

Provides printing products & services, packaging supplies, security holograms & electronic devices in North & South America.

DARWILL

11900 W Roosevelt Rd
Hillside, IL 60162-2069
Telephone: (708) 236-4900, FAX: (708) 236-5820, Web Site: www.darwill.com
Co-CEO: Brandon Van Dyke
Co-CEO: Tony Van Dyke

VP Sls: Mark Pageau

Company performs direct marketing, personalized communications, POD storefronts & printing services.

DATAMART DIRECT INC
279 Madsen Dr (Suite 101)
Bloomingdale, IL 60108-2692
Telephone: (630) 307-7100, FAX:
(630) 307-8059, E-Mail: info@
datamartdirect.com, Web Site: www.
datamartdirect.com
CEO: Rosemary Bussert
Dir Digital Commons: Julie Leder
Founded: 1972

Marketing, variable digital printing, pod, mailing & fulfillment.

DATAMATX INC
10430 Lakeridge Pkwy
Ashland, VA 23005-8124
Telephone: (804) 365-1000, Toll Free:
(800) 943-5240, FAX: (804) 550-
2527, E-Mail: info@datamatx.com,
Web Site: www.datamatx.com
Pres: Harry Stevens
Founded: 1976

Full-service providers of high volume digital print & electronic transactional communications.

DELUXE CORP
3680 Victoria St N
Shoreview, MN 55126-2906
Telephone: (651) 483-7111, FAX:
(651) 481-4477, Web Site: www.
deluxe.com
CEO: Lee J. Schram
Sr VP & CFO: Terry D. Peterson
Founded: 1915

Check printer and personalized products & services provider.

DEPENDABLE BUSINESS FORMS
843 South Myrtle Ave
Villa Park, IL 60181-3353
Telephone: (630) 530-1734, FAX:
(630) 530-1789, E-Mail: j.zawaski@
comcast.net, Web Site: www.
dependablebusinessforms.com
Owner, Sls: John K. Zawaski
Founded: 1970

Stationery and Office Supplies industry.

DES PLAINES PRINTING CO
Div. of Des Plaines Publishing Co
1000 Executive Way
Des Plaines, IL 60018
Telephone: (847) 824-1111, Toll Free:
(800) 283-1776, FAX: (847) 824-
1112, E-Mail: custserv@dppc.com

CEO: Michael H. Ford

Provides typesetting, printing & mailing services.

DIGITAL VISION RESOURCES GROUP - DVRG
8236 Nieman Rd
Lenexa, KS 66214-1507
Telephone: (913) 402-5900, E-Mail:
info@dvrg.com, Web Site: www.
dvrg.com
Pres & CEO: Diane St Louis
Founded: 2006

Specializing in plastic card fulfillment.

THE DINGLEY PRESS
119 Lisbon St
Lisbon, ME 04250-6005
Telephone: (207) 353-4151, Toll Free:
(800) 317-4574, FAX: (207) 353-
9886, E-Mail: webrequest@dingley.
com, Web Site: www.dingley.com
Chmn Bd & CEO: Christopher A.
Pierce
Pres & COO: Robert Moore
Founded: 1928

Operates as a catalog printing company.

DISC GRAPHICS INC
10 Gilpin Ave, Hauppauge, NY 11788-
4724
Ten Gilpin Ave
Hauppauge, NY 11788
Telephone: (631) 234-1400, FAX:
(631) 234-1460, E-Mail: info@
discgraphics.com, Web Site: www.
discgraphics.com
Chmn Bd & CEO: Don Sinkin
Pres & Dir: Margaret Krumholz
Sr VP, Sls & Dir: Stephen Frey
Founded: 1969

Produces paper, plastic, foil-board & mini-flute packaging solutions.

DOCKERY HOUSE PUBLISHING INC
906 Main St (Suite B)
Lindale, TX 75771
Telephone: (903) 882-6900, FAX:
(903) 882-6902, E-Mail: questions@
dockerypublishing.com, Web Site:
www.dockerypublishing.com
Pres: Rod Dockery

DOME PRINTING
340 Commerce Cir
Sacramento, CA 95815-4213
Toll Free: (800) 343-3139
CEO: Tim Poole
CMO: Bob Poole
COO: Dave Baker

VP Fin: Eric Carle

One source for everything from creative services, digital printing, fulfillment & integrated business solutions, including custom client storefront solutions.

DOMINO AMJET INC
1290 Lakeside Dr
Gurnee, IL 60031-2499
Telephone: (847) 244-2501, FAX:
(847) 244-1421, Web Site: www.
dominoamjet.com
Pres & Gen Mgr: Gilles Buisson
Dir Mktg: Mark Meyer
Founded: 1978

Offers coding & printing solutions.

DONIHE GRAPHICS INC
Subs. of Graphics International Inc.
766 Brookside Dr
Kingsport, TN 37660-6614
Telephone: (423) 246-2800, Toll Free:
(800) 251-0337, FAX: (423) 246-
7297, Web Site: www.donihe.com
Plant Mgr: Shirley Ball
Founded: 1977

Provides commercial printing services.

DRISCOLL LABEL CO INC
19 West St
East Hanover, NJ 07936-2822
Telephone: (973) 585-7291, FAX:
(800) 342-1195, (973) 585-7295,
E-Mail: info@driscolllabel.com,
Web Site: www.driscolllabel.com
Pres: John Raguso

Custom printed pressure sensitive labels.

DUPONT COLOR PROOFING
Dupont Photopolymers & Electronic
Materials
PO Box 80030
Wilmington, DE 19880-0030
Toll Free: (800) 441-7515, FAX: (302)
892-8030, Web Site: www.dupont.
com/proofing
Chmn Bd & CEO: Ellen Kullman

Science & engineering to the global marketplace through innovative products, materials & services.

DYNACOLOR GRAPHICS INC
Div. of Franklin Dodd Communications
950 SE 8th St
Hialeah, FL 33010
Telephone: (305) 625-5388, Toll Free:
(800) 624-8840, FAX: (305) 888-
9903, E-Mail: dmail@dynacolor.
com, Web Site: www.dynacolor.com

Pres: Donald M. Duncanson

Line of business includes commercial printing & the lithographic process.

E&D WEB PRINTING INC

1100A S Main St
Rochelle, IL 61068-3509
Telephone: (708) 656-6600, Toll Free: (815) 562-5800, FAX: (708) 656-4154, E-Mail: info@eanddweb.com, Web Site: www.eanddweb.com
CEO: Christopher Love
Founded: 1964

Provides Web offset printing services.

EASTMAN KODAK CO

343 State St
Rochester, NY 14650-0001
Telephone: (585) 724-4000, Toll Free: (800) 698-3324, FAX: (585) 724-1089, Web Site: www.kodak.com
CEO: Jeffrey J. Clarke
CFO & Exec VP: John McMullen
CIO & Sr VP: Kim E. Van Gelder
Conducts Business: Worldwide
Primary Market Served: Business & Consumer
Catalog available online
Direct online sales
Advertising/Marketing Budget Related to Direct Marketing: 51-75%
Founded: 1880

Manufacturer & marketer of imaging products.

EDITORS PRESS INC

Subs. of Kelly Press Inc
1701 Cabin Branch Dr
Hyattsville, MD 20785-3820
Telephone: (301) 853-4900, Toll Free: (888) 853-4900, FAX: (301) 853-4961, Web Site: www.edpress.com
Pres: Michael Kelly

EMBASSY DIGITAL

Div. of Embassy Graphics Ltd
2880 Brighton Rd (Unit 1)
Oakville, ON, Canada L6H 5S3
Telephone: (905) 829-9969, Toll Free: (888) 477-8629, FAX: (905) 829-9429, E-Mail: info@embassydigital.com, Web Site: www.embassydigital.com
Opers Dir: Chris Whalen
Conducts Business: U.S., Canada
Primary Market Served: Business
Advertising/Marketing Budget Related to Direct Marketing: 51-75%
Direct Marketing ad budget: $40,000
Direct Mail: 60%
Telephone: 40%
Founded: 1990

Provides the latest in on demand print solutions.

ESSEX PRINTING CO INC

14 Westminster Dr
Croton On Hudson, NY 10520-1008
Telephone: (212) 688-4720, Toll Free: (800) 443-9113, FAX: (212) 308-2764, E-Mail: essexptg@aol.com, Web Site: www.essex-printing.com
Pres: Alvin B. Glaser

FCL GRAPHICS INC

4600 N Olcott Ave
Harwood Heights, IL 60656
Telephone: (708) 867-5500, Toll Free: (800) 274-3380, FAX: (708) 867-7768, Web Site: www.fclgraphics.com
Pres: Stephen Flood
VP Opers: Phil Bauman
Founded: 1973

Direct marketing printing company, provides digital printing services to small & large companies in the U.S.

FEDERAL DIRECT

95 Main Ave Ste 2
Clifton, NJ 07014-1749
Telephone: (973) 667-9800, Toll Free: (800) 927-5123, Web Site: www.feddirect.com
Sr VP: Angela Stubbs
Founded: 1926

Diversified provider of direct marketing services offering a broad range of capabilities in fulfillment, print & mailing services.

FELCO PRINTING & MAILING

1910 Walnut St
Kansas City, MO 64108-1810
Telephone: (816) 421-5164, Toll Free: (800) 467-0805, FAX: (816) 421-1607, E-Mail: jill@felco.net, Web Site: www.felco.net
Pres: Jill Dolling

Handles a wide variety of printing & direct mail projects.

FETTER PRINTING COMPANY INC

700 Locust Ln
Louisville, KY 40217-2997
Telephone: (502) 634-4771, Toll Free: (800) 234-4771, FAX: (502) 634-3587, E-Mail: info@fettergroup.com
CEO & Pres: Terry Gill
Sr VP: Ron Watkins
VP: Doug Amburgey
Founded: 1888

Operates as a label provider to the paint & coatings industry.

FISHER GROUP INC

1250 N Center Point Rd
Hiawatha, IA 52233-1226
Telephone: (319) 393-5405, FAX: (319) 393-2738, E-Mail: info@fishergroup.com, Web Site: www.fishergroup.com
Sr VP Sls & Mktg: Rick Sartorius
Founded: 1958

Full-service direct mail printer & lettershop, specializing in long-run inserted mailing packages & other communication tools such as magazines, self-mailers, & individual print components.

THE FLEXI GROUP INC

2675 Henry Hudson Pkwy
Bronx, NY 10463
Telephone: (718) 543-8699, Toll Free: (800) 665-8053, FAX: (718) 543-8609, E-Mail: info@flexigroup.com, Web Site: www.flexigroup.com
Gen Mgr Consumer SME: Michael Burke
Chief Mktg Officer: Marilyn Conyer

Provide a range of finance products and payment solutions to consumers & businesses through a network of retail and business partners.

FOLDER FACTORY INC

Div. of Gentile Brothers Screen Printing
5421 Main St (Suite 300)
Mount Jackson, VA 22843-9537
Telephone: (540) 984-8852, Toll Free: (800) 296-4321, FAX: (540) 477-9677, E-Mail: webmaster@folders.com, Web Site: www.folders.com
VP: Dave Gentile

FORMSOURCE

170 Summer St
Lewiston, ME 04240-7532
Telephone: (207) 782-3311, Toll Free: (877) 782-3311, FAX: (207) 783-0157, E-Mail: service@formsource1.com, Web Site: www.formsource1.com
Pres: Mark Hartnett

Offers professional design & marketing services

48HOURPRINT.COM

33 Farnsworth St (Suite 2)
Boston, MA 02210-1210
Toll Free: (800) 844-0599, Web Site: www.48hourprint.com
VP Mktg & Bus Devel: Peter Dammann

Operates as a printing services company.

STEPHEN FOSSLER CO INC
1600 E Touhy Ave
Des Plaines, IL 60018-3607
Telephone: (847) 635-7200, Toll Free: (800) 762-0030, FAX: (800) 424-9292, E-Mail: customerservice@fossler.com, Web Site: sfc.stephenfossler.com
Pres: John Trimberger

Produces embossed foil seals.

FOXFIRE PRINTING & PACKAGING INC
750 Dawson Dr
Newark, DE 19713-3414
Telephone: (302) 368-9466, Toll Free: (800) 497-0516, FAX: (302) 368-5164, E-Mail: info@foxfiresigns.com, Web Site: www.foxfiresigns.com
Founder & CEO: John Ferretti
Dir Bus Devel: Gunnar Spencer
Founded: 1997

Provides printing, data management & fulfillment services.

THE FOXON CO
235 W Park St
Providence, RI 02908-4881
Telephone: (401) 421-2386, Toll Free: (800) 556-6943, FAX: (401) 421-8996
Pres & Owner: William D. Ewing
Founded: 1992

Manufactures paper label from purchased materials; manufactures folding paperboard boxes; manufactures solid fiber boxes; tag printing service; manufactures paper packaging materials; plate making services.

FRY COMMUNICATIONS INC
800 W Church Rd
Mechanicsburg, PA 17055-3198
Telephone: (717) 766-0211, Toll Free: (800) 334-1429, FAX: (717) 691-0341, Web Site: www.frycomm.com
CEO: Michael T. Lukas
Dir Mfg: Mike Weber
Founded: 1934

Operates as an integrated communications company offering printing services, such as bindery, digital printing, on site co-mailing, distribution planning, and more.

THE GARVEY GROUP
aka Ed Garvey & Co
7400 N Lehigh Ave
Niles, IL 60714-4024
Telephone: (847) 647-1900, FAX: (847) 647-6550, E-Mail: info@thegarveygroup.com, Web Site: www.thegarveygroup.com

Owner, CEO & Pres: Ed J. Garvey Jr.
VP Sls: David Nolte

Provides print & distribution solutions to large-format, packaging, entertainment, retail, outdoor and environmental, transit, point-of-purchase/POS & signage markets in the U.S.

GLOBE MARKETING SYSTEMS INC
11950 NW 39th St (Suite B)
Coral Springs, FL 33065
Telephone: (954) 753-7173, Toll Free: (800) 382-9013, FAX: (954) 337-0650, Web Site: www.internetprintcenter.com
Pres: Dwight Jewett
Conducts Business: U.S.
Primary Market Served: Business

Full-service printing, mailing & statement processing company.

GOSS INTERNATIONAL
121 Technology Dr
Durham, NH 03824-4716
Telephone: (603) 749-6600, FAX: (603) 750-6860, Web Site: www.gossinternational.com
Pres & CEO: Richard Nichols

Supplies presses & finishing systems including automated & productive web offset presses for magazine, newspaper, packaging, catalog, direct mail & other printing applications.

STEPHEN GOULD PAPER CO INC
35 S Jefferson Rd
Whippany, NJ 07981-1034
Telephone: (973) 428-1500, FAX: (973) 428-5274, Web Site: www.stephengould.com
Pres: Michael Golden
Founded: 1939

Operates as a packaging & print solutions company providing product development services.

GRANT'S MAILING SERVICES INC
2825 Argentia Rd (Unit 4)
Mississauga, ON, Canada L5N 8G6
Telephone: (905) 826-1411, FAX: (905) 826-1450, E-Mail: mstephens@innovativeresponse.ca, Web Site: www.grants-mailing.ca
Pres: Norman Keyes

Full service direct mail, printing, fulfillment, shipping & computer services company.

GRAPHIC ARTS CENTER
2514 National Dr

Garland, TX 75041-2329
Telephone: (972) 543-1250, Toll Free: (800) 865-7086, FAX: (972) 271-8392
Principal: Calvin Jahn
Founded: 2003

Providing manufacturing, art copy, publishing & printing.

GRAPHIC ARTS INFORMATION NETWORK (GAIN)
200 Deer Run Rd
Sewickley, PA 15143-2324
Telephone: (412) 741-6860, Toll Free: (800) 910-4283, FAX: (412) 741-2311, E-Mail: printing@printing.org, Web Site: www.gain.net
Mktg Mgr: Rebecca Blunt

GRAPHIC COMMUNICATIONS CENTER
3001 E Venture Dr, Box 357
Appleton, WI 54911-8309
Telephone: (920) 733-4483, Toll Free: (800) 422-3696, FAX: (920) 733-1700
Pres: Harry Kachain

GRAPHICS INTERNATIONAL INC
3883 Turtle Creek Blvd (Apt 1406)
Dallas, TX 75219-4430
Telephone: (214) 352-7565, FAX: (214) 528-0114
Pres: L. Marcus Dean

THE GRAY PRINTING CO
401 E North St
Fostoria, OH 44830-2828
Telephone: (419) 435-6638
Pres: Robert A. Gray

GREAT LAKES INTEGRATED
4005 Clark Ave
Cleveland, OH 44109-1186
Telephone: (216) 651-1500, Toll Free: (800) 745-4846, FAX: (216) 651-8311, E-Mail: bbemer@glintergrated.com, Web Site: www.gll.com
Chmn Bd, Pres & CEO: James R. Schultz
Founded: 1931

Provides graphic communications tools & services.

GREYSTONE GRAPHICS
110 Geystone Ave
Kansas City, MO 66103

Telephone: (913) 342-1393, Toll Free: (800) 458-7407, FAX: (913) 621-4856, E-Mail: info@greystonegraphics.com, Web Site: www.greystonegraphics.com
CEO: Eugene Reynolds

HBP

2818 Fallfax Dr
Falls Church, VA 22042-2804
Telephone: (703) 289-9000, FAX: (703) 289-9143, E-Mail: info@hbp.com, Web Site: www.hbp.com
Sls & Mktg: Rick Jones
Founded: 1966

Provides commercial, digital & Web-to-print solutions.

HAGADONE PRINTING CO

274 Pu'uhale Rd
Honolulu, HI 96819-2234
Telephone: (808) 847-5310, Toll Free: (800) 491-4888, FAX: (808) 841-0094, E-Mail: sales@hagadoneprinting.com, Web Site: www.hagadoneprinting.com
Pres: Clint Schroeder
Founded: 1995

Offers commercial & publication printing services in Hawaii.

HANNECKE DISPLAY SYSTEMS INC

91 Fulton St (#3)
Boonton, NJ 07005-1942
Telephone: (973) 335-0434, FAX: (973) 335-1274, E-Mail: info.usa@hannecke.com, Web Site: www.hannecke.com
Sls Mgr: Hans Klein

HATTERAS PRESS INC

56 Park Rd
Tinton Falls, NJ 07724-9715
Telephone: (732) 223-9888, Toll Free: (800) 695-0719, FAX: (732) 223-1232, E-Mail: connect@hatteras.us, Web Site: www.hatterascpc.com
Pres: Charlie Duerr
Founded: 1983

Provides printing services. It offers pre-press, offset printing, digital printing, wide format printing, direct mail, cross media marketing, bindery & fulfillment services, as well as in house mailing, banners printing, digital, and wire-o binding services.

HEART THOUGHTS INC

1480 N Stratford Ln
Wichita, KS 67206-1165

Telephone: (316) 688-5781, Toll Free: (800) 524-2229, FAX: (316) 687-2846, Web Site: www.heart-thoughts.com
Pres: Grant Goodvin
Founded: 2004

Easy-to-use, pick-up-and-choose guide to assist you in your day-to-day experiences.

HEAVY ROTATION

3720 N Fratney St (Studios 3F)
Milwaukee, WI 53212
Telephone: (414) 384-5200, Toll Free: (800) 886-4759, FAX: (414) 434-9318, E-Mail: info@holoubekstudios.com, Web Site: heavytees.com
Pres: Brian Holoubek

Vintage t-shirts and irons-ons from the Verne Holoubek collection.

HESS PRINT SOLUTIONS

3765 Sunnybrook Rd
Kent, OH 44240
Toll Free: (800) 678-1222, E-Mail: info@hessprintsolutions.com, Web Site: www.thepressofohio.com
CFO: Jerry Haywood
VP Mktg & Sls: Michael A. Manley
Mktg Mgr: Sandy Showerman

Provides printing, binding & finishing services.

HI-C PRODUCTION

Nine Tottenham Pl
New Hyde Park, NY 11040-3516
Telephone: (516) 746-2142, FAX: (516) 294-1964, E-Mail: haponte435@aol.com
Pres: Hiram Aponte Jr

THE HICKORY PRINTING SOLUTIONS LLC

725 Reese Dr SW
Conover, NC 28613
Telephone: (828) 465-3431, Toll Free: (800) 442-5679, FAX: (828) 465-2517, E-Mail: gglisan@hickoryprinting.com, Web Site: www.hickoryprinting.com
Pres: George Glisan
Founded: 1917

Provides communication solutions to businesses & non-profit organizations in the U.S.

HUBCAST INC

500 Edgewater Dr (Suite 568)
Wakefield, MA 01880-6222
Telephone: (781) 221-7200, FAX: (781) 221-7223, Web Site: www.hubeast.com

CEO & Pres: Tim Corkery
Exec Chmn: Eric Schults
Dir Fin & Admin: Jason Pulsifer
VP Opers: Aron Blume
VP Prods & Tech: Adam Bellusci
Founded: 2005

Offers Web-based cloud print services for marketing and sales customers in large & small companies, enterprises, multi-national corporations, start-ups & Fortune 500 companies.

IPD PRINTING & DISTRIBUTING INC

Graphic Industries Inc
5800 Peachtree Rd
Atlanta, GA 30341-2302
Telephone: (770) 458-6351, FAX: (770) 454-6236, Web Site: www.rrdonnelley.com
Pres: George Gribble

Line of business includes commercial printing & the lithographic process.

IBSDIRECT

431 Yerkes Rd
King of Prussia, PA 19406-3556
Telephone: (610) 265-8210, FAX: (610) 265-7997, Web Site: www.ibsdm.com
CEO: George H. Schnyder
Pres: Theodore D. Sherwin
VP Mfg: Russ Kreider
Founded: 1932

Provides direct marketing services as well as services in the areas of printing & program management; strategic planning, marketing & research; account management; creative services; interactive media; fulfillment services/response management; & database analytics & reporting.

IMAGE CHECKS

PO Box 2
Bel Air, MD 21014
Toll Free: (800) 562-8768, FAX: (410) 676-8269, Web Site: www.imagechecks.com
Pres: Jim Browning

IMPRESSIONS UNLIMITED INC

PO Box 1349
Deerfield, IL 60015-6005
Telephone: (630) 705-6464, FAX: (630) 705-1598, E-Mail: info@impressionsunltd.com, Web Site: www.impressionsunltd.com
Pres: Ron Gion

INDUSTRIAL ARTS & GRAPHICS

22714 Melrose Farm Ln
Middleburg, VA 20117
Telephone: (540) 687-6770, Toll Free:
(866) 324-7746, FAX: (540) 687-
4678, E-Mail: gdrex@industrialarts.
us
Pres: George Drexel

Creative & visually effective graphic
communication products & services.

INLAND PRESS

Subs. of Detroit Legal News
2001 W Lafayette Blvd
Detroit, MI 48216
Telephone: (313) 961-6000, FAX:
(313) 961-7817, Web Site: www.
inlandpress.com
Pres: Bradley L. Thompson

One of metro Detroit's top printing
firms. Company prints brochures, annual reports, posters, catalogs & more.

INNOVATION PRINTING INC

11601 Caroline Rd
Philadelphia, PA 19154
Telephone: (215) 969-4600, FAX:
(215) 464-7664, Web Site: www.
innovationprinting.com
Pres: Jeff Jones
Controller: Bill Gray
VP: Dave Carpenter
VP: George Slater
Founded: 1973

Offers commercial printing services
with focuses on printing of the annual
reports. Its services include full-color
copying, digital, offset & mail merge
printing. Company primarily serves design, financial, software & pharmaceutical industries.

INNOVATIVE PLASTIC PRINTING CORP

534 Congress Cir N
Roselle, IL 60172
Telephone: (630) 539-4400, Toll Free:
(800) 238-7686, FAX: (630) 529-
2109, E-Mail: dan@innov8cards.
com, Web Site: www.innov8cards.
com
VP: Donald Faccomonto

INTEGRATED PRINT & GRAPHICS

645 Stevenson Rd
South Elgin, IL 60177-1134
Telephone: (847) 695-6777, FAX:
(847) 741-4090, E-Mail: info@
ipandginc.com, Web Site: www.
ipandginc.com
Sls Mgr: Douglas Marecek

Founded: 1990
Line of business includes commercial
printing & the lithographic process.

INTELLIGENCER PRINTING CO

330 Eden Rd
Lancaster, PA 17601-4218
Telephone: (717) 291-3100, Toll Free:
(800) 233-0107, FAX: (717) 569-
2643, Web Site: www.intellprinting.
com
Pres & CEO: Robert Mason
VP Sls: Dean Baker
Mktg & Bus Devel Mgr: Todd Foster
Founded: 1794

Provides printing services in the U.S.
specializing in offering heat set Web,
sheetfed, & digital printing services.

INTERNATIONAL FULFILLMENT INC

2800 Black Lake Pl (Suite C)
Philadelphia, PA 19154-1024
Telephone: (215) 638-8060, Toll Free:
(800) 962-8080, FAX: (215) 638-
8091, Web Site: www.ifionline.net
Pres: James Bowman
Founded: 1994

Subscription Fulfillment Services:
Magazine, Newspaper.

INTERPRINT WEB & SHEETFED

Subs. of Morten Enterprises
12350 US Hwy 19 N
Clearwater, FL 33764
Telephone: (727) 531-8957, Toll Free:
(800) 749-5152, FAX: (727) 536-
0647, E-Mail: customerservice@
printerusa.com, Web Site: www.
printerusa.com
Pres: James E. Morten

Offers printed products ranging from
catalogs, magazines & publications to
full color brochures & annual reports.
Services include file transfers, computer to plate digital.

INTERSTATE PRINTING CO

2002N 16th St
Omaha, NE 68110
Telephone: (402) 341-8028, Toll Free:
(800) 788-4177, FAX: (402) 341-
6168, E-Mail: printer@
interstateprinting.com, Web Site:
www.interstateprinting.com
Pres: Eugene W. Peter
Admin Asst: Karen Sasinski
Founded: 1917

Promotional product distributor.

INVITATION HOTLINE

68 Hawkins Rd
Manalapan, NJ 07726
Telephone: (732) 536-9115, Toll Free:
(800) 800-4355, FAX: (732) 972-
4875, E-Mail: info@
invitationhotline.com, Web Site:
www.invitationhotline.com

JD GRAPHIC CO

1101 Arthur Ave
Elk Grove Village, IL 60707
Telephone: (847) 364-4000, Toll Free:
(888) 364-6216, FAX: (847) 364-
4024, E-Mail: sakes@jdgraphic.com,
Web Site: www.jdgraphic.com
Owner & Pres: James DeBlasio Jr

JAPS-OLSON CO

7500 Excelsior Blvd
Saint Louis Park, MN 55426-4519
Telephone: (952) 932-9393, Toll Free:
(800) 548-2897, FAX: (612) 912-
1900, Web Site: www.japsolson.com
Chmn: Robert E. Murphy
CEO: Mike Beddor
Pres: Michael R. Murphy
CFO: Gary Petrangelo
Founded: 1907

Provides cross-media marketing solutions in the U.S.

JERSEY PRINTING ASSOCIATES INC

153 First Ave
Atlantic Highlands, NJ 07716-1265
Telephone: (732) 872-9654, FAX:
(732) 872-9309, E-Mail: sales@
jerseyprinting.com, Web Site: www.
jerseyprinting.com
Sls: Greg Heh
Founded: 1980

Tri-state area's premier commercial offset printing firm.

JET LITHOCOLOR INC

1500 Centre Cir
Downers Grove, IL 60515
Telephone: (630) 932-9000, Toll Free:
(800) 932-1538, (800) 932-1JET,
FAX: (630) 932-9101, E-Mail:
sales@jetlitho.com, Web Site: www.
jetlitho.com
CEO: George Bogdanovic
Dir Bus Devel: Randy Fox
Founded: 1947

Provides marketing & communication
solutions.

JOHN HENRY PACKAGING

5800 W Grand River Ave
Lansing, MI 48906-9111

Telephone: (707) 778-1250, Toll Free: (800) 327-5997, FAX: (707) 762-1253, Web Site: www.jhpackaging. com
Mktg Mgr: Dan Welty

KEYSTONE PROMOTIONS INC
246 Washington Ave
Union, NJ 07083
Telephone: (908) 688-6713, FAX: (908) 688-6645, E-Mail: mgunther_kpi@msn.com, Web Site: www.keystonepromotionsinc.com

KING PRINTING SOLUTIONS
531 Straight Creek Rd
New Tazewell, TN 37825
Telephone: (423) 626-7700, Toll Free: (800) 251-9236, FAX: (423) 526-5225, E-Mail: sales@kbfcorp.com, Web Site: www.kbfcorp.com
Pres: Jim King
Founded: 1972

providing companies with quality printed materials, including labels for packaged goods such as beverages, food products, pharmaceuticals, & household products.

KINGERY PRINTING CO
3012 S Banker
Effingham, IL 62401-2900
Telephone: (217) 347-5151, FAX: (217) 540-5400, Web Site: www.kingeryprinting.com
Pres: Mike Kingery
Founded: 1968

Provides commercial printing services.

KODAK GRAPHIC COMMUNICATIONS
343 State St
Rochester, NY 14650-0002
Telephone: (585) 724-0251, Toll Free: (800) 944-6171, FAX: (585) 724-0268, Web Site: www.kpgraphics. com
VP Market Segments & Packaging: Vic Stalam

Provides printing & proofing solutions.

KREBER GRAPHICS INC
2580 Westbelt Dr
Columbus, OH 43228
Telephone: (614) 529-5701, Toll Free: (800) 777-3501, FAX: (614) 777-4890, E-Mail: info@kreber.com, Web Site: www.kreber.com
Pres & CEO: Frank Kreber

Founded: 1947

Marketing agency with vast studio resources creating campaigns that invite & involve consumer participation.

KWIK-FILE
Subs. of Mayline Co Inc
619 N Commerce St
Sheboygan, WI 53081-3901
Telephone: (763) 572-1980, Toll Free: (800) 822-8037, FAX: (763) 572-0168, Web Site: www.mayline.com
VP Sls: Todd Nelson
Founded: 1995

Line of business includes the manufacturing of office furniture.

LP THEBAULT CO
Div. of EarthColor Inc.
249 Pomeroy Rd, PO Box 169
Parsippany, NJ 07054-3727
Telephone: (973) 884-1300, FAX: (973) 952-8282, E-Mail: info@earthcolor.com, Web Site: www.earthcolor.com
Chmn: Brian Thebault
CEO EarthColor: Robert Kashan

Line of business includes commercial or job printing such as bags, business forms, calendars, cards, & other printed material.

LABELS WEST INC
17629 130th Ave NE
Woodinville, WA 98072
Telephone: (425) 486-8484, Toll Free: (800) 540-3009, FAX: (425) 486-8488, Web Site: www.labelswest. com
Dir Sls & Mktg: Lance Wilson
Founded: 2003

Fast custom labels for all industries &environments.

LAKE COUNTY PRESS INC
PO Box 9209
Waukegan, IL 60079-9209
Telephone: (847) 336-4333, FAX: (847) 336-5846, Web Site: www.lakecountypress.com
CEO & Pres: Ralph Johnson
Sr VP & Dir Sls & Mktg: Peter Douglas
Primary Market Served: Business & Consumer
Founded: 1970

Engages in the production of printed products & multiple piece projects from one color reproduction through multi-color printing.

LANCER LABEL
Div. of Mail-Well

301 S 74th St
Omaha, NE 68114
Telephone: (402) 390-9119, Toll Free: (800) 228-7074, FAX: (800) 344-9456, E-Mail: customerservice@lancerlabel.com, Web Site: www.lancerlabel.com
Mfr Exec: Cory Blatz
Founded: 1973

Manufactures promotional materials. Products include labels, stickers, badges & decals.

LASERMAX ROLL SYSTEMS
4 Suburban Park Dr
Billerica, MA 01821-3904
Telephone: (978) 608-0500, FAX: (978) 608-0558, Web Site: www.lasermaxroll.com
Pres: Jeff Kewin
Founded: 1984

Manufactures & markets feeding, cutting, finishing, & folding equipment for the digital printing industry in the U.S. & internationally.

LEHIGH DIRECT
1900 S 25th Ave
Broadview, IL 60155-2800
Telephone: (708) 681-3612, FAX: (708) 681-4694, Web Site: www.lehighdirect.com
Customer Svc Mgr: Jennifer Evenson

Direct marketing company with unique & sophisticated highly personalized products for direct marketing applications.

LINGUISTIC SYSTEMS INC
201 Broadway
Cambridge, MA 02139
Toll Free: (877) 654-5006, FAX: (617) 528-7491, E-Mail: info@linguist.com, Web Site: www.linguist.com
Founder & Pres: Martin Roberts
VP Bus Devel: Mark Ettinger
Founded: 1967

Provides language service solutions in the U.S.

LITHO-WEB INC
730 Hardwick Rd
Bolton, ON, Canada L7E 5R4
Telephone: (905) 857-9111, Toll Free: (800) 490-6688, FAX: (905) 857-9112, E-Mail: sales@lithoweb.ca, Web Site: www.lithoweb.ca
Pres: Barry Moyer
Founded: 1970

Printing a huge assortment of commercial printed materials from the simple flyers to complex eight - color marketing collaterals, brochures, magazines and envelopes.

LONE STAR WEB INC
6730 Oakbrook Blvd
Dallas, TX 75235-4108
Telephone: (214) 638-4946, FAX:
(214) 630-4364, E-Mail: jerry@
lonestarweb.com, Web Site: www.
lonestarweb.com
CEO: Michael R. Hansen

Printing publishers company.

MAR GRAPHICS
523 S Meyer Ave
Valmeyer, IL 62295-3120
Toll Free: (800) 851-4460, Web Site:
www.margraphics.com
Pres & CEO: Rick Roever
Founded: 1961

Line of business includes Commercial
printing & the lithographic process.

MWM DEXTER INC
1310 E Kingsley St, #D, Springfield,
MO 65804-7216
107 Washington Ave
Aurora, MO 65605-1461
Telephone: (417) 841-1040, Toll Free:
(888) 833-1242, FAX: (417) 841-
1025, Web Site: www.mwmdexter.
com
Pres: Chris Dale
VP Sls & Mktg: Melissa Cole
Founded: 1922

Promotional printing services company
providing sheet fed printing, bindery &
finishing, fulfillment & mailing services.

MAGJAK PRINTING CORP
114 Pearl St
Port Chester, NY 10573-4663
Telephone: (914) 939-8800, Web Site:
www.magjak.com
CEO: Bruce Browning

MAILBLAZER
2020 S Eastwood Ave
Santa Ana, CA 92705-5208
Telephone: (714) 662-5396, Web Site:
www.mailblazer.com
Sls & Mktg Mgr: Ted Robison

THE MAINE CONNECTION
246 Deering Ave, Univ of Maine
School of Law
Portland, ME 04102-2837
Telephone: (207) 780-4355, FAX:
(207) 780-4239, E-Mail: mainelaw@
maine.edu
Pres: George E. Hopkins Jr.

MANDEL CO
727 W Glendale Ave
Milwaukee, WI 53209-6509

Telephone: (414) 271-6970, Toll Free:
(800) 888-6970, FAX: (414) 271-
1254, E-Mail: rick.mandel@
mandelcompany.com, Web Site:
www.mandelcompany.com
Pres: Rick Mandel

MARKING SPECIALISTS GROUP
1000 Asbury Dr (Suite 2)
Buffalo Grove, IL 60089-4551
Telephone: (847) 793-8100, Toll Free:
(800) 678-8073, FAX: (847) 793-
8109, E-Mail: info@marking-
specialists.com, Web Site: www.
marking-specialists.com
Pres: Cliff Modlin
Founded: 1977

Combine advanced technologies & the
highest quality materials to produce
domed decals, labels & other branding
products that appeal to the senses.

MARVIN ENVELOPE & PAPER CO
2040 W North Ave
Chicago, IL 60647-5414
Telephone: (773) 489-3300, Toll Free:
(800) 227-0011, FAX: (773) 489-
4783, E-Mail: marvinenvelope@aol.
com
Pres: Gordon M. Caplan
Founded: 2010

MAYS MISSION FOR THE HANDICAPPED INC
604 Colonial Dr
Heber Springs, AR 72543-3425
Telephone: (501) 362-7526, Toll Free:
(888) 503-7955, FAX: (501) 362-
7529, E-Mail: info@maysmission.
org, Web Site: www.maysmission.
org
Pres & Exec Dir: Sherry Niehaus
Prodn Mgr: Roland Stroud
DP Supvr: Brenda Johnson
Conducts Business: U.S.
Employees: 30
Primary Market Served: Business &
Consumer
Advertising/Marketing Budget Related
to Direct Marketing: 0-25%
Founded: 1972

Web printing, direct mail services, data
processing services.

MCARDLE PRINTING CO INC
Subs. of Bureau of National Affairs Inc
800 Commerce Dr
Upper Marlboro, MD 20774-8792
Telephone: (301) 390-8500, FAX:
(301) 390-8052, Web Site: www.
mcardleprinting.com

Pres: Lisa Arsenault
VP Opers: Jeff Emerson
Founded: 1946

Provides marketing services for businesses in the Washington-Baltimore region.

MCCORMICK-ARMSTRONG CO INC
1501 E Douglas
Wichita, KS 67211-1608
Telephone: (316) 264-1363, Toll Free:
(800) 733-1363, FAX: (316) 263-
4511, E-Mail: sales@
mccormickarmstrong.com, Web Site:
www.mccormickarmstrong.com
CEO & Pres: Jacob W. Shaffer
VP Sls & Mktg: Mark Trapanese
VP Sls & Mktg: Jere Ames-Johnson
Founded: 1912

Provides printing, finishing, distribution, & promotions & branding solutions.

MCCOURT LABEL CO
20 Egbert Ln
Lewis Run, PA 16738-3802
Toll Free: (800) 458-2390, FAX: (814)
362-4156, Web Site: www.
mccourtlabel.com
Pres: Dave Ferguson
Mktg Asst: Hilery Farrell
Primary Market Served: Consumer
Founded: 1896

Innovative labeling & packaging solutions.

MEDIA LINK COMMUNICATIONS
Div. of Robert Rose Enterprises
321 E 22nd St (Suite 3K)
New York, NY 10010
Telephone: (212) 674-8843, FAX:
(212) 260-8489, E-Mail: mlinkcom@
aol.com, Web Site: www.getprinted.
com
Pres: Robert Rose

MEDIA PRINTING CORP
4300 N Powerline Rd
Pompano Beach, FL 33073-3071
Telephone: (954) 984-7300, FAX:
(954) 984-7303
Pres: James Grubman

MEDIATREE
Div. of Telenations Inc
77 E Haley Rd
Parsippany, NJ 07054

Telephone: (973) 781-1070, Toll Free: (800) 475-8703, FAX: (973) 781-1071, E-Mail: sales@ mediatreegroup.com, Web Site: www.mediatreegroup.com
CEO: Bill Grassmyer
Sls Exec: Keith Simon
Conducts Business: U.S.
Employees: 15
Primary Market Served: Business
Catalog available online
Advertising/Marketing Budget Related to Direct Marketing: 0-25%
Founded: 1996
Gross sales or billing: $10,000,000

Promotional stored value content such as music downloads, ringtones & phone time. Plastic printing facility printing on premises.

MEMBERSHIP CARDS ONLY LLC
8000 Towers Crescent Dr (Suite 1350)
Vienna, VA 22182-6219
Toll Free: (800) 772-2737, E-Mail: rfaust@membershipcards.com, Web Site: www.membershipcards.com
Pres: Richard Faust

Manufactures all sorts of membership cards, loyalty cards, insurance cards, & direct mail packages.

METROPOLITAN GRAPHIC ARTS
930 Turret Ct
Mundelein, IL 60060-3821
Telephone: (847) 566-9502, Toll Free: (800) 755-5936, FAX: (847) 566-9584, E-Mail: gregs@mgaprinting.com, Web Site: www.mgaprinting.com
CEO: Joseph Szymanski
VP: Greg Szymanski
Founded: 1963

Commercial printing & the lithographic process.

MITCHELL GRAPHICS INC
2363 Mitchell Park Dr
Petoskey, MI 49770
Telephone: (231) 347-5650, Toll Free: (800) 583-9401, FAX: (231) 347-9255, E-Mail: mgi@ mitchellgraphics.com, Web Site: www.mitchellgraphics.com
Pres: Gary Fedus

Creative, print & direct mail expertise.

MODERN GRAPHIC ARTS
Subs. of Sandy Alexander Inc
1527 102nd Ave N
Saint Petersburg, FL 33716-5049

Telephone: (727) 579-1527, FAX: (727) 579-1528, Web Site: www.sandyinc.com
Opers Mgr: Sal Campanaro
Founded: 1989

Commercial Printing, Lithographic industry

MORRISON PRINTING CO
1039 Walters Dr
Morristown, TN 37814-6133
Telephone: (423) 586-4812, Toll Free: (800) 251-0975, FAX: (423) 586-0322, E-Mail: info@morrcom.com, Web Site: www.morrcom.com
Pres & CEO: Maudie Briggs

MULTI-MEDIA PUBLISHING & PACKAGING INC
14621 Titus St Ste A
Panorama City, CA 91402-4904
Telephone: (818) 341-7484, Toll Free: (800) 982-8138, FAX: (818) 341-2807, E-Mail: sales@mmppinc.com, Web Site: www.mmppinc.com
Pres: Luke Stefanki

One-stop source for professional custom packaging, duplication, packaging design, printing, product development, assembly & project management.

NAHAN PRINTING INC
7000 Saukview Dr
Saint Cloud, MN 56303-0814
Telephone: (320) 251-7611, E-Mail: info@nahan.com, Web Site: www.nahan.com
Pres: Mike Nahan
VP: Steve Burns
Founded: 1962

Commercial Print, Direct Mail & Digital Solutions service provider.

NATIONAL GRAPHICS INC
248 Branford Rd, Route 139
North Branford, CT 06471-1303
Telephone: (203) 481-2351, FAX: (203) 483-0256, E-Mail: inquiries@ natgraphics.com, Web Site: www.natgraphics.com
Mktg Exec: Tom Etzel
Founded: 1984

Printing & mailing of direct response components.

NATIONAL MAIL GRAPHICS CORP
300 Old Mill Ln
Exton, PA 19341-2582
Telephone: (610) 524-1600, FAX: (610) 524-7638, E-Mail: jsikorski@ nmgcorp.com, Web Site: www.nmgcorp.com

Pres & Owner: John Sikorski
Controller & CFO: Billie Bradley
VP & Gen Mgr: Bill Stewart
Founded: 1982

Offers digital, web, & envelope printing & prepressing services.

NATIONAL MAIL-IT INC
9151 Youree Dr
Shreveport, LA 71115-3303
Telephone: (318) 683-0093, Web Site: www.nationalmailit.com
CEO & Pres: Michael Riordan
Sr VP Strategic Mktg: Sherry Wax
Sr VP Sls & Mktg: Gary Garvey

Turn-Key Print Distribution Marketing Company that both targets & saturates your market area promoting your business by maximizing visual coverage & awareness.

NATIONAL MAILROOM SERVICE INC
6924 Karns Crossing Ln
Knoxville, TN 37931-2571
Telephone: (865) 862-4141, Toll Free: (866) 862-4141, FAX: (865) 862-4145, E-Mail: info@ nationalmailroom.com, Web Site: nationalmailroom.com
Pres: Ken Mayfield
Founded: 1954

Direct mail, fulfillment & printing services company.

NATIONWIDE ARGOSY SOLUTIONS LLC
2500 W Loop S (Suite 500)
Houston, TX 77027-4521
Telephone: (713) 961-4700, FAX: (713) 961-4701, Web Site: www.nationwidegraphics.com
Chmn Bd, CEO & Treas: Carl L. Norton
Founded: 1998

Provides commercial printing & related services.

NAYLOR INC
350 Great Southwest Pkwy
Atlanta, GA 30336-2333
Telephone: (404) 739-7280, FAX: (404) 739-7284, Web Site: www.naylorinc.com
CEO & Pres: Steve Naylor
Founded: 1965

Marketing communications company.

NEENAH PAPER FR LLC
Div. of Neenah Paper
1376 Kimberly Dr
Neenah, WI 54956-1641

Telephone: (920) 733-7341, Toll Free: (800) 558-8327, FAX: (920) 733-2975, E-Mail: info@foxriverpaper. com, Web Site: www.foxriverpaper. com
CEO, Pres & Dir: John P. O'Donnell
CFO, Sr VP & Treas: Bonnie C. Lind
Founded: 1883

Owns & operates real estate properties, mills & manufacturing assets that manufactures & supplies paper products.

NEIBAUER PRESS
20 Industrial Dr
Warminster, PA 18974-1433
Telephone: (215) 322-6200, Toll Free: (800) 322-6203, FAX: (215) 322-2495, E-Mail: info@neibauer.com, Web Site: www.neibauer.com
Pres: Nathan Neibauer
VP: Ruth Neibauer
Founded: 1955

Offer a full range of services from premium items to printing to personalization & mailing.

NEWCOMB MARKETING SOLUTIONS
605 E 9th St
Michigan City, IN 46360-3651
Telephone: (219) 874-3201, Toll Free: (800) 921-1221, FAX: (219) 874-8156, Web Site: www. newcombsolutions.com
Pres: Gloria Newcomb

Publishing, Allied & Printing Industries.

NEWSNOTES LLC
Div. of NAStar Inc.
2348 Pinehurst Dr
Middleton, WI 53562
Telephone: (608) 831-9600, Toll Free: (800) 676-9665, FAX: (608) 831-9665, E-Mail: sales@nastar-inc.com, Web Site: www.news-notes.com
Dir: John Short
Mktg Coord: Breonna Bleuel
Founded: 2004

Newspaper and commercial print advertising services company.

O'BRIEN DOCUMENT SOLUTIONS
1273 Humbracht Cir
Bartlett, IL 60103-1606
Telephone: (630) 830-0990, Toll Free: (800) 232-9595, FAX: (630) 830-0062, E-Mail: obrien_info@obinc. com, Web Site: www.obinc.com
CEO & Co-Founder: Kevin O'Brien

Founded: 1974

Acknowledged expert in innovative end-to-end solutions & services.

OFFICIAL OFFSET CORP
8600 New Horizons Blvd
Amityville, NY 11701-1183
Telephone: (631) 957-8500, Web Site: www.officialoffset.com
VP: Frank Paulino

Offer solutions beyond print.

THE OFFSET HOUSE INC
89 Sand Hill Rd
Essex Junction, VT 05452-3909
Telephone: (317) 849-5155, FAX: (317) 842-3324, Web Site: www. offsethouse.com
Pres: John McGrath
VP: Kevin McGrath
Founded: 1964

OLYMPAK
6010 Earle Brown Dr (Suite 100)
Minneapolis, MN 55430-4516
Telephone: (763) 504-5400, Toll Free: (800) 967-1705, FAX: (763) 504-5401, E-Mail: jgibas@olympak.com, Web Site: www.olympak.com
Sls: Colin White

Full service company with services ranging from market production & product fulfillment.

OMNI PRINT INC
9700 Philadelphia Ct
Lanham, MD 20706-4405
Telephone: (301) 731-7000, FAX: (301) 731-7001, E-Mail: info@ omniprint.net, Web Site: www. omniprint.net
Chmn & CEO: Kenneth A. Kaufman
Founded: 1971

Provides printing & mailing services specializing in the production of newsletters & direct mail pieces.

O'NEIL DATA SYSTEMS INC
12655 Beatrice St
Los Angeles, CA 90066-7300
Telephone: (310) 448-6400, FAX: (310) 577-7350, Web Site: www. oneildata.com
Pres & Gen Mgr: James Lucanish
Founder: William J. O'Neil
VP Sls Mktg: Mark Rosson
Conducts Business: U.S.
Founded: 1973

Provides publishing & marketing communication services & electronic & paper delivery solutions for enrollment kits, ID cards, direct mail campaigns, directories & catalogs.

OUTLOOK GROUP CORP
1180 American Dr
Neenah, WI 54956-1306
Telephone: (920) 727-7999, FAX: (920) 727-8529, E-Mail: info@ outlookgroup.com, Web Site: www. outlookgroup.com
CEO: John Cappy
Founded: 1977

Provides custom product packaging, direct marketing & printing.

OVERNIGHT PRINTS
A FarHeap Solutions Inc company
7582 Las Vegas Blvd (Suite 487)
Las Vegas, NV 89123
Toll Free: (888) 677-2000, E-Mail: service@overnightprints.com, Web Site: www.overnightprints.com
Conducts Business: U.S.
Primary Market Served: Business & Consumer
Founded: 2003

Online printing company specializing in mailing, direct mailing & list services.

PCI PAPER CONVERSIONS INC
6761 Thompson Rd N
Syracuse, NY 13211-2119
Telephone: (315) 437-1641, FAX: (315) 437-3634, E-Mail: sales@ padmaker.com, Web Site: www. padmaker.com
Contact: Peter McDermott

Custom manufacturer providing note pads, note cubes & stik-withit adhesive note pads to business for promotional & retail usage.

PGI COMPANIES INC
11354 K-Tel Dr
Minnetonka, MN 55343-8868
Telephone: (952) 933-5745, FAX: (952) 933-5864, E-Mail: ddallum@ pgicompanies.com, Web Site: www. pgicompanies.com
CFO: Chuck Belland
Founded: 1990

Provides handwork services including pick-n-pack of customer specific printed material.

PGS PRINTING & GRAPHICS SERVICES
Div of IDC Printing & Stationery
261 Birch Dr
Roslyn, NY 11576-3001
Telephone: (917) 880-5397, FAX: (866) 361-2957, E-Mail: sales@ pollack.com, Web Site: www. pollack.com

Founded: 1975

Specializes in affordable online printing, promotional items & print consulting.

PIP POSTAL INSTANT PRESS

Owned by Franchise Services Inc
26722 Plaza
Mission Viejo, CA 92691
Telephone: (949) 282-3800, FAX: (949) 282-3899, Web Site: www.pip.com
CEO: Don F. Lowe
VP Mktg: David Robidoux
Founded: 1996

Line of business includes owning or leasing franchises, patents, and copyrights which they in turn license others to use.

PPS - PACKAGING PRINTING SPECIALISTS

3915 Stern Ave
Saint Charles, IL 60174-5441
Telephone: (630) 513-8060, Toll Free: (877) 573-8060, FAX: (630) 513-8062, E-Mail: pps@ppsofil.com, Web Site: www.PPSofIL.com
VP: Ken Russo
Fin Exec: Denise Disieno
Conducts Business: U.S., Canada
Employees: 21
Primary Market Served: Business
Advertising/Marketing Budget Related to Direct Marketing: 51-75%
Direct Marketing ad budget: $100,000
Direct Mail: 75%
Telephone: 25%
Founded: 1983
Gross sales or billing: $7,000,000

Producers of membership cards, coupons, inserts, scratch off games, peel n reveal games, 3D specialty graphics

PRECISE MEDIA SERVICES INC

5678 E Concours Ave
Ontario, CA 91764
Telephone: (908) 481-3305, Toll Free: (800) 444-4217, FAX: (908) 481-3405, Web Site: www.precisemedia.com
Pres: Robert Miller
Founded: 1991

Line of business includes the manufacturing of phonograph records & prerecorded audio tapes and disks.

PARAGON PRINTING & MAILING

10423 McKalla Pl, Bldg A (Suite 100)
Austin, TX 78758-4448

Telephone: (512) 821-0222, FAX: (512) 821-0200, E-Mail: contact@paragonprinting.com, Web Site: www.paragonprinting.com
Pres: Don Murphy
Primary Market Served: Business & Consumer
Founded: 1981

Full-service printing, mailing & data processing company.

PEARL RIVER GRAPHICS PRINTING

An Enterprise of the Mississippi Band of Choctaw Indians
404 Industrial Rd (Suite 1)
Choctaw, MS 39350
Telephone: (601) 656-3636, FAX: (601) 650-3961, E-Mail: prgp@pearlriverprinting.com, Web Site: pearlriverprinting.com
Pres: Gerrard Cook
Conducts Business: U.S.
Primary Market Served: Business

Print & design company offering small & large format printing, full service copying & digital printing and graphic design.

PENINSULAR PRINTING OF DAYTONA BEACH INC

1814 Holsonback Dr
Daytona Beach, FL 32117-5112
Telephone: (386) 274-4837, FAX: (386) 274-5023, E-Mail: penprint@bellsouth.net, Web Site: www.peninsularprinting.com
Pres & Owner: William Maguire

PERFECT PLASTIC PRINTING CORP

311 Kautz Rd (Suite 4)
Saint Charles, IL 60174-5304
Telephone: (630) 584-1600, FAX: (630) 584-0648, E-Mail: ppp@perfectplastic.com, Web Site: www.perfectplastic.com
CEO: Matt Smoczynski
Founded: 1965

Manufactures plastic cards, provides creative services, personalization services & full service mail; fulfillment, printing & customer services.

PERFORMANCE PRINTING/ OPTIGRAPHICS

2929 N Stemmons Fwy, Dallas, TX 75247-6102
Div. of Pinnacle Brands Inc
2929 N Stemmons Fwy
Dallas, TX 75247-6102

Telephone: (214) 665-1038, Toll Free: (800) 727-27335, FAX: (214) 665-1090, Web Site: www.performancecompanies.com
Design & production of various promotional vehicles.

PILGRIM PRINTED PROMOTIONAL PLASTICS

Div. of Star Printing
1200 W Chestnut St
Brockton, MA 02301-5574
Telephone: (508) 436-6300, Toll Free: (800) 343-7810, FAX: (508) 580-3542, E-Mail: pilgrimsales@pilgrimplastics.com, Web Site: www.pilgrimplastics.com
Owner: Neal Abrams

Leading supplier of printed plastic to the promotional products & print distribution industries.

PIP PRINTING AND MARKETING SERVICES

6330 E 75th St (Suite 138)
Indianapolis, IN 46250-2717
Telephone: (317) 849-6244, Web Site: www.pip.com/pipindy
VP Mktg: David Robidoux
Primary Market Served: Consumer

Offers an array of marketing, printing & sign services.

PLASTIC GRAPHIC

255 Industrial Dr
Wauconda, IL 60084-1078
Telephone: (847) 487-2030, FAX: (847) 487-2050, E-Mail: bgrimespgc@sbcglobal.net, Web Site: www.plasticgraphic.com
VP, Sls: Brian Grimes
Founded: 1970

Specializes in printing on plastic.

POINTONE GRAPHICS INC

14 Vansco Rd
Toronto, ON, Canada M8Z 5J4
Telephone: (416) 255-8202, Toll Free: (866) 717-5722, FAX: (416) 255-6917, Web Site: www.point-one.com
Mktg Mgr: Tanya Low

Offers commercial printing services.

THE POND-EKBERG CO

660 Broadway St
Chicopee, MA 01020-2400
Telephone: (413) 594-7511, Toll Free: (800) 225-7511, FAX: (413) 594-2179, E-Mail: sales@pond-ekberg.com, Web Site: www.pond-ekberg.com
Pres: Jonathan Kratovil
Pres: Kevin Morris

Founded: 1999
Line of business includes commercial printing & the lithographic process.

PRESSKITS

Subs. of Ardmore Graphic Services Inc
8 Rose Ct Way
East Walpole, MA 02032-1185
Telephone: (781) 762-3003, Toll Free: (800) 472-3497, FAX: (781) 255-7791, Web Site: www.presskits.com
Pres: Tom Spiegel

PRIME GRAPHICS INC

501 N Central Ave
Wood Dale, IL 60191-1473
Telephone: (630) 227-1300, FAX: (630) 227-1823, E-Mail: moreinfo@primegraphicsinc.com, Web Site: www.primegraphicsinc.com
Mktg Exec: Cy Harris
Opers Exec: Sue Datavs

Printer & converter of innovative flexible packaging, shrink sleeves & decorative labels.

PRINT MANAGEMENT PARTNERS

701 Lee St (Suite 1050)
Des Plaines, IL 60016-4572
Telephone: (847) 699-2999, FAX: (847) 699-2935, Web Site: www.ourpartners.com
Pres: James O'Brien
CFO: Jim Grandos
Primary Market Served: Business

Providing creative business communications solutions using a portfolio of brands.

THE PRINTER INC

dba TPI
1220 Thomas Beck Rd
Des Moines, IA 50315-1068
Telephone: (515) 288-7241, FAX: (515) 288-9234, E-Mail: info@the-printer.com, Web Site: www.the-printer.com

Provide exciting new concepts, designs & templates. Design team create some fresh & innovative new looks for your direct marketing programs.

PRINTING + QUICK COPY

8799 Frankford Ave
Philadelphia, PA 19136
Telephone: (215) 331-5999, FAX: (215) 333-2577, E-Mail: copyman@aolcom
Owner: Bonnie Kaiser
Founded: 1984

PRINTING CORP OF THE AMERICAS INC (PCA)

620 SW 12th Ave
Fort Lauderdale, FL 33069
Telephone: (954) 781-8100, Toll Free: (866) 721-1722, FAX: (954) 781-8421, Web Site: www.pcaprinting.com
CEO: Murray Tuchman

Specialize in magazine & publication printing.

PRINTING SPECTRUM

12 Research Way (Suite 1)
East Setauket, NY 11733-3531
Telephone: (631) 689-1010, Web Site: www.printingspectrum.com
Owner: Jim Altebrando
Founded: 1987

Affordable Printing, small runs, big runs, design, fulfillment, CD's & more.

PRINTWEST COMMUNICATIONS LTD

Div. of PW Group
1111 Eighth Ave
Regina, SK, Canada S4R 1E1
Telephone: (306) 525-2304, Toll Free: (800) 236-6438, FAX: (306) 757-2439, E-Mail: general@printwest.com, Web Site: www.printwest.com
Contact: Keith Critchely
Founded: 1998

Provide everything for your printing or publishing project.

PROGRESS PRINTING CO

2677 Waterlick Rd
Lynchburg, VA 24502-4861
Telephone: (434) 239-9213, Toll Free: (800) 527-7804, FAX: (434) 237-1618, Web Site: www.progressprinting.net
Pres: Michael A. Thornton
Founded: 1962

Offers print project consulting, print management & control, consultative mailing & publication support services.

PUBLISHERS PRESS INC

100 Frank E Simon Ave
Shepherdsville, KY 40165-6013
Telephone: (502) 955-6526, FAX: (502) 955-5586, E-Mail: info@pubpress.com, Web Site: www.pubpress.com
Pres: Nicholas X. Simon
Exec VP: Michael J. Simon
VP Sls & Mktg: Dick Ryan
Founded: 1866

Provides commercial printing services to businesses & organizations.

QUADRA GRAPHICS INC

PO Box 555
Cherry Hill, NJ 08003-0555
Telephone: (856) 665-4060, FAX: (856) 665-7324, E-Mail: richard.nixon@qgi.com
Pres: Robert J. Camm
VP: Richard R. Nixon
Conducts Business: U.S.
Employees: 65
Primary Market Served: Business & Consumer
Gross sales or billing: $8,000,000

Electronic publishing & prepress printing & finishing services for direct marketing & publishing.

QUANTUM COLOR

6511 Oakton St
Morton Grove, IL 60053-2728
Telephone: (847) 967-3600, FAX: (847) 967-3610, Web Site: www.cpipress.com
Sr VP Worldwide Sls & Mktg: Bill Britts
Founded: 1992

Provides integrated printing & marketing automation services.

QUILL HEALTHCARE

8500 Wyoming Ave N
Minneapolis, MN 55445-1825
Telephone: (763) 493-7300, Toll Free: (800) 328-2179, FAX: (800) 328-0023, Web Site: www.medicalartspress.com
Founder: Mark Wexler
Founded: 1950

Sells professional printing & practice related essentials on mail order to healthcare professionals in the U.S.

RAINBOW GRAPHICS INC

933 Tower Rd
Mundelein, IL 60060-3811
Telephone: (847) 824-9600, E-Mail: jkoszuta@rainbowgraphics.com, Web Site: www.rainbowgraphics.com
Pres: Jeff Koszuta
Founded: 1982

Multi-color web offset lithographer with UV drying & variable cut-offs specializing in products for the direct mail market.

RAPID COLOR PRINTING

6445 Karms Park Ct
Las Vegas, NV 89118-1414
Telephone: (702) 792-6055, FAX: (702) 792-1437, Web Site: www.rapidcolor.com

Pres: David Huckabay

Multi-color web offset lithographer with UV drying & variable cut-offs specializing in products for the direct mail market.

RAYPRESS CORP

380 Riverchase Pkwy E
Birmingham, AL 35244-1813
Telephone: (205) 989-3731, FAX: (205) 989-7203, Web Site: www. raypress.com
VP Sls & Mktg: Robert Alden

Able to engineer custom labeling systems to meet your toughest application requirements.

REAL MEDIA SOLUTIONS

77 Green Knolls Dr
Wayne, NJ 07470-6123
Telephone: (973) 835-7060, Web Site: www.get-realmedia.com
Pres: Michael Aslett
Graphic Design: Robert M Bovasso

REDFIELD & CO INC

1901 Howard St
Omaha, NE 68102-2594
Telephone: (402) 341-0364, FAX: (402) 341-1454, Web Site: www. redfieldandcompany.com
Owner: Tom Beachler
Founded: 1883

Provides commercial printing services producing a wide variety of printed products that appeal to businesses both large and small.

VG REED & SONS

1002 S 12th St
Louisville, KY 40210-1302
Telephone: (502) 560-0100, Toll Free: (800) 635-9788, FAX: (502) 560-0197, E-Mail: info@vgreed.com, Web Site: www.vgreed.com
Pres: Howard Reed
Founded: 1938

Provides financial & commercial printing & fulfillment services.

RELYCO

121 Broadway
Dover, NH 03820-3299
Telephone: (603) 742-0999, Toll Free: (800) 777-7359, FAX: (603) 742-9993, E-Mail: info@relyco.com, Web Site: www.relyco.com
VP Mktg: Ronald Wimbley

Supplier of business printing & payment solutions to corporations, governments & institutions around the world.

REX THREE INC

15431 SW 14th St
Sunrise, FL 33326
Telephone: (954) 452-8301, Toll Free: (800) 782-6509, FAX: (954) 452-0569, E-Mail: info@rex3.com, Web Site: www.rexthree.com
Exec VP: Howard Shusterman
Founded: 1950

Specialties include print production, magazines, publishing, print on demand, interactive media, marketing, digital printing, asset management, inventory management, e-marketing, in house die cutting, etc.

RIPON PRINTERS

656 S Douglas St
Ripon, WI 54971-9044
Telephone: (920) 748-3136, Toll Free: (800) 321-3136, FAX: (920) 748-3741, E-Mail: info@riponprinters. com, Web Site: www.riponprinters. com
CEO & Pres: Andy Lyke
Mktg Dir: Carol Cluppert
Founded: 1962

Prints catalogs, direct mail publications, manuals & soft-cover educational products as well as offering marketing services.

THE RONED GROUP

Six DeForest Ave
East Hanover, NJ 07936
Telephone: (973) 386-1848, FAX: (973) 386-0969, E-Mail: info@ roned.com, Web Site: www.roned. com
Pres: Ronald N. Russo
Founded: 1968

Offset & process printing from typesetting to printing, finishing & fulfillment.

ROSE PRINTING CO INC

2503 Jackson Bluff Rd
Tallahassee, FL 32304-4405
Telephone: (850) 576-4151, Toll Free: (800) 227-3725, FAX: (850) 576-4153, E-Mail: roseprt@roseprinting. com, Web Site: www.roseprinting. com
Pres & Natl Sls Mgr: Charles Rosenberg
Direct online sales
Founded: 1932

Provides book manufacturing services for publishers in the U.S. specializing in printing case bound, soft cover, & saddle stitched books; magazines; catalogs; directories; trade journals; & mini-books, such as devotionals, minimanuals, value guides, pocket guides, and specialty products.

SAUERS GROUP, INC

1585 Roadhaven Dr
Stone Mountain, GA 30083-1315
Telephone: (770) 621-8888, Toll Free: (866) 458-5212, FAX: (770) 621-8866, E-Mail: info@sauersgroup. com, Web Site: www.sauersgroup. com
CEO & Pres: Richard S. Sauers
Founded: 1949

Engages in the businesses of communications, graphics, media, foundation & transport & logistics, offering design, printing, Website development, and DVD/CD replication services; & banners, posters, signs & promotional products.

SCHAWK INC

Div. of SGK Inc
1600 E Sherwin Ave
Des Plaines, IL 60018
Telephone: (847) 827-8424, Web Site: www.schawk.com
CEO: David A. Schawk
Founded: 1953

Brand development, activation and deployment company.

SCHMIDT

Div. of Taylor Corp
1101 Frontage Rd NW
Byron, MN 55920
Telephone: (507) 775-6400, FAX: (507) 775-6655, E-Mail: sls@ schmidt.com, Web Site: www. schmidt.com
Pres: Craig Monson

Provides innovative products, technologies & services that focus on the evolving needs personal & business of more than half of the Fortune 500 companies & millions of small businesses & consumers around the world.

SCIENTIFIC GAMES CANADA

Subs. of Scientific Games Corp
3000 Boul de l'Assomption
Montreal, QC, Canada H1N 3V5
Telephone: (514) 254-3000, FAX: (514) 254-1411, Web Site: www. scientificgames.com
Fin Dir: Sonia Verdy

SEGERDAHL GRAPHICS INC

385 Gilman Ave
Wheeling, IL 60090-5807
Telephone: (847) 850-8800, FAX: (847) 850-8801, Web Site: www. segerdahlgraphics.com
Chmn, CEO & Pres: Richard Joutras

Founded: 2002

Provides graphic solutions that include digital photography, direct to plate pre-media, sheet-fed printing with in-line UV & aqueous coating & imaging & mailing services.

SELKIRK PRESS
1714 Industrial Dr, PO Box 875
Sandpoint, ID 83864
Telephone: (208) 263-7523, FAX: (208) 263-2229, E-Mail: weprint@selkirkpress.com
Gen Mgr: Wesley Dustman
Founded: 1924

Full service printer offering in house graphic design, printing, copying, bindery & mailing services.

SERVICE LITHO PRINT INC
50 W Fernau
Oshkosh, WI 54902-0875
Telephone: (920) 231-3060, Toll Free: (800) 544-1493, FAX: (920) 231-1272, E-Mail: slp@service-litho.com
CEO: Steve Elbing
Founded: 1972

Specialty printing and packaging and related services including up to 48 pt substrates, lenticular, polypropylene tubs, removable pressure sensitive, UV printing, foil stamping, embossing, folding and gluing, and specialty point of sale.

SG360
1351 S Wheeling Rd
Wheeling, IL 60090-5997
Telephone: (847) 541-1080, FAX: (847) 541-5237, Web Site: www.sg360.com,
Chmn, Pres & CEO: Rick Joutras
CFO & Exec VP: Gary Gardner
Founded: 1956

Offers multi-channel marketing integration solutions.

SHERIDAN BOOKS INC
613 E Industrial Dr
Chelsea, MI 48118-1536
Telephone: (734) 475-9145, Toll Free: (800) 999-BOOK, FAX: (734) 475-7337, E-Mail: info@sheridanbooks.com, Web Site: www.sheridanbooks.com
Pres & COO: Pat Sticker
VP Sls & Mktg: Joe Thomsom
Founded: 1999

Operates as printing press.

SHERWOOD DESIGN & DEVELOPMENT CENTER
One Kero Rd

Carlstadt, NJ 07072
Telephone: (201) 372-3900, FAX: (201) 372-0917
Pres: Duncan Watson

SHINDIGZ
One Party Pl
South Whitley, IN 46787
Telephone: (219) 723-5171, Toll Free: (800) 314-8736, FAX: (219) 723-6976, E-Mail: csr@shindigz.com, Web Site: www.shindigz.com
Exec VP, Mktg: Wendy Moyle
Pres & CEO: Shep Moyle
Founded: 1926

Personalized party supplies & more.

SHOPGUIDE.COM
RP-NFOA
3223 Commerce St
Amarillo, TX 79109-3275
Telephone: (806) 351-0005, FAX: (806) 351-0059, E-Mail: info@shopguide.com, Web Site: www.shopguide.com
Pres: Donald J. Melancon
VP: Lloyd Kruckeberg

SHUTTERFLY
2800 Bridge Pkwy
Redwood City, CA 94065-1192
Telephone: (650) 610-5200, Web Site: www.shutterfly.com
Sr Mktg Mgr: Steven Marjon
Chief Mktg Officer: John Boris

SIR SPEEDY GRAND RAPIDS
4513 Broadmoor Ave SE (Suite A)
Grand Rapids, MI 49512-5369
Telephone: (616) 554-7777, Web Site: www.sirspeedy.com
Production Mgr: Eric O'Brien

SIR SPEEDY GREEN BAY
333 Packerland Dr
Green Bay, WI 54303-4815
Telephone: (920) 494-4236, FAX: (920) 494-4075, E-Mail: office@sirspeedygb.com, Web Site: www.sirspeedygb.com

SIR SPEEDY NEWTOWN
760 Newtown-Yardley Rd
Newtown, PA 18940-4500
Telephone: (215) 968-2080, Web Site: www.sirspeedynewtown.com
Primary Market Served: Consumer

SIR SPEEDY PRINTING AND MARKETING SERVICES
7450 S Tacoma Way (Suite B1)
Tacoma, WA 98409-3906

Telephone: (253) 473-0765), FAX: (253) 475-3012, Web Site: www.sirspeedy0905.com
Mktg Consultant: Lynnette Worrell

SIR SPEEDY WESTBURY
75 State St
Westbury, NY 11590-5004
Telephone: (516) 334-7400, Web Site: www.sirspeedyny.net
Primary Market Served: Consumer

SOLO PRINTING
7860 NW 66th St
Miami, FL 33166-2708
Telephone: (305) 594-8699, FAX: (305) 599-5245, Web Site: www.soloprinting.com
Mktg Dir: John Carr
VP Opers: Jorge Hernandez
Founded: 1985

Offers a full array of traditional print, binding, direct mail & fulfillment services along with many unique services such as spot gloss or dull UV, glitter & textured UV to highlight just a few.

SOURCE 4 INC
16740 Birkdale Commons Pkwy (Suite 208)
Huntersville, NC 28078-4462
Telephone: (704) 602-0110, Toll Free: (800) 541-5400, FAX: (704) 602-0119, E-Mail: source4newyork@source4.com, Web Site: www.source4.com
VP Tech Solutions: Gerald Via
Founded: 1978

Provides integrated business & marketing solutions for organizations.

SOUTHEASTERN PRINTING
950 SE 8th St
Hialeah, FL 33010
Telephone: (305) 855-8707, Toll Free: (800) 226-8221, FAX: (305) 888-9903, E-Mail: info@seprint.com, Web Site: www.seprint.com
Pres & Owner: Don Mader
Primary Market Served: Business
Founded: 1924

Full-service commercial/digital printing and mail services company.

SPECIALTY PRINT COMMUNICATIONS INC
6019 W Howard St
Niles, IL 60714-4801
Telephone: (847) 588-2580, FAX: (847) 588-2146, Web Site: www.specialtyprintcomm.com
CEO: Paul LeFebvre
Pres: Adam LeFebvre
VP Opers: John Gaspari

Founded: 1996

Provides loyalty, card issuance platform, marketing on demand, printing, inline, lettershop, binding & books printing services for direct marketers.

SPIRE CREATIVE GROUP

110 W 40th St (Rm 1702)
New York, NY 10018-8508
Telephone: (212) 391-0200, Web Site:
www.spirecreativegroup.com
Pres: Tom Sepanski

Creative firm dedicated to bringing powerful marketing tools to the most powerful brokers & leasing professionals in the commercial real estate sector.

SPIRE PRINTING & PACKAGING LLC

501 5th Ave (Suite 811)
New York, NY 10017-7849
Telephone: (212) 661-1157, E-Mail:
bweiser@spireprintingandpackaging.com, Web Site: www.
spireprintingandpackaging.com
Contact: Bruce Weiser
Primary Market Served: Consumer

Finding the perfect solutions to join concepts and designs with printing and packaging.

SPRING HILL LASER SERVICES

PO Box 79
Sterling, PA 18463-0079
Telephone: (570) 689-0970, FAX:
(570) 689-7915, E-Mail: kkshls@
icontech.com, Web Site: www.
springhilllaser.com
Founded: 1987

Direct mail production company specializing in database management, variable data printing, MICR printing (including rebate programs), barcoding & lettershop services.

ST JOSEPH COMMUNICATIONS

50 MacIntosh Blvd
Concord, ON, Canada L4K 4P3
Telephone: (905) 660-3111, FAX:
(905) 669-1972, Web Site: www.
stjoseph.com
Exec Chmn & CEO: Anthony Gagliano
CFO: Tim Zahavich
Founded: 1956

Communications company, provides marketing & communications solutions offering content, print media solutions.

STEPHENSON PRINTING INC

5731 General Washington Dr

Alexandria, VA 22312
Telephone: (703) 642-9000, Toll Free:
(800) 336-4637, FAX: (703) 354-
0384, E-Mail: gstephenson@
stephensonprinting.com, Web Site:
www.stephensonprinting.com
Pres & CEO: George W. Stephenson
Founded: 2001

Commercial printing on full web presses, sheet fed & digital presses.

STERLING PRINT & MAIL SYSTEM

Subs. of Sterling Business Corp
206 Concord St
Peterborough, NH 03458
Telephone: (603) 924-9401, Toll Free:
(800) 439-9401, FAX: (603) 924-
9247, E-Mail: sbc@sbc.mv.com,
Web Site: www.mv.com/ipusers/sbc
Pres: George A. Sterling
Founded: 1981

Ideas come to life with a full complement of graphic art services & special printing effects.

STRUCTURAL GRAPHICS

38 Plains Rd
Essex, CT 06426-1520
Telephone: (860) 767-2661, FAX:
(860) 767-2451, Web Site: www.
structuralgraphics.com
CEO: Michael Maguire
Founded: 1976

Designs & produces dimensional marketing materials.

SUMI PRINTING

1139 E Janis St
Carson, CA 90746-1306
Telephone: (310) 769-1600, Web Site:
www.getsumi.com
Co-Pres: Michael Sumi
Co-Pres: Roland Sumi
Founded: 1987

Provides full-service printing, packaging & binding services.

SURDELL & PARTNERS

3738 S 149th St (Suite 109)
Omaha, NE 68144-5564
Telephone: (402) 501-7400, Toll Free:
(800) 733-7765, FAX: (402) 733-
2083, E-Mail: info@surdellpartners.com, Web Site: www.surdellpartners.com
Principal & CEO: Daniel L. Surdell
Principal, COO & CFO: Pat Jung

Full-service advertising and marketing agency.

TFC INC

690 Airpark Rd

Napa, CA 94558-7516
Telephone: (707) 224-6161, Web Site:
www.tfcinc.com
Pres & Founder: Constance Hill
VP Mktg Execution Svcs: Dan Plunkett
Founded: 1988

Integrated marketing services provider.

TEMPOGRAPHICS INC

455 E North Ave
Carol Stream, IL 60188-2123
Telephone: (630) 462-8200, FAX:
(630) 462-0350, E-Mail: info@
tempographics.com
Pres: Peter Vouros
Founded: 1973

Market focus is direct mail & commercial printing.

TERACO INC

2080 Commerce Dr
Midland, TX 79703-7502
Toll Free: (888) 837-2261, Web Site:
www.teraco.com
Pres & CEO: Casey Campbell
VP & CFO: Craig McCune
VP Opers: Guy Meeker
Founded: 1962

Manufacturer of printed plastic promotions including plastic cards, business cards, luggage tags & environment friendly cards.

TEXAS GRAPHIC RESOURCE

1234 Round Table Dr
Dallas, TX 75247-3504
Telephone: (214) 630-2800, FAX:
(214) 630-0713
Contact: Jacques Cangelose

Main focus is in high-end digital and offset printing.

THINK SHAPES MAIL

5463 W Waters Ave (Suite 820)
Tampa, FL 33634
Telephone: (813) 885-2225, Toll Free:
(800) 889-4406, Web Site: www.
jigsawprinting.com
Founder: Jim O'Brien

Shaped mail, allows you to market your product or service in a way that is totally customized to you and your message.

TIDEWATER DIRECT LLC

300 Tidewater Dr
Centreville, MD 21617
Telephone: (410) 758-1500, FAX:
(410) 758-2478, Web Site: www.
tidewaterdirect.com
Pres: Ken Boone
VP Opers & Gen Mgr: Geoff Eisenberg

Founded: 1959
Provides commercial printing services.

TOP USA CORP

771 Dearborn Park Ln (Suite N)
Worthington, OH 43085-5720
Telephone: (614) 431-1601, Toll Free:
(800) 843-3381, FAX: (614) 431-
1239, E-Mail: info@topusa.com,
Web Site: www.topusa.com
Pres, Mktg: Pia Wendel

TRANSCONTINENTAL
YORKVILLE - O'KEEFE

Eight Tidemore Ave
Etobicoke, ON, Canada M9W 5H4
Telephone: (416) 741-1900, Toll Free:
(800) 361-9690, FAX: (416) 401-
2220, Web Site: www.
transcontinentalprinting.com
Founded: 1976

Innovative print solutions combined
with multiplatform strategies.

TRIANGLE PRINTERS INC

3737 Chase Ave
Skokie, IL 60076-4008
Telephone: (847) 675-3700, FAX:
(847) 674-1230, E-Mail: blevin@
triangleprinters.com, Web Site:
www.triangleprinters.com
Pres: David Saltzman
VP Bus Devel: Bonnie Dayan
VP Technology: Steve Farber
Employees: 45
Founded: 1955

Provides sheetfed and digital printing,
photography, design, bindery, mailing
and fulfillment for all marketing material. Also provides banners, signs, fleet
graphics, trade show graphics and
countertop displays. Manages entire
project in-house.

TUCKER PRINTERS

270 Middle Rd
Henrietta, NY 14467-9312
Telephone: (585) 359-3030, Web Site:
www.tuckerprinters.com
Pres: Michelle Yun
Plant Mgr: Anthony Antinetto

Full service, high quality offset printing
& packing company.

UNIGRAPHIC INC

110 Commerce Way Ste 6
Woburn, MA 01801-1098
Telephone: (781) 231-7200, FAX:
(781) 938-7727, E-Mail: info@uni-
graphic.com, Web Site: www.uni-
graphic.com
Pres: Bob Quinlan
CFO & COO: Michael Quinlan

Exec VP: Jack Quinlan
Founded: 1964

Provides digital and commercial printing & mailing services in New England
as well as retouching, prepress, bindery, digital proofing, & large format
printing services.

US TAPE & LABEL CORP

2092 Westport Ctr Dr
Saint Louis, MO 63146-3564
Telephone: (314) 824-4444, Toll Free:
(800) 569-1906, FAX: (314) 824-
4400, E-Mail: harrisonc@ustl.com,
Web Site: www.ustl.com
Pres: Jim Eiseman
VP & Gen Mgr: Jan Greis
Founded: 1950

Cost effective label & labeling solutions.

UNIVENTURE INC

13311 Industrial Pkwy
Marysville, OH 43040-9589
Telephone: (937) 645-4600, FAX:
(937) 645-4700, Web Site: www.
univenture.com
CEO: Ross O. Youngs
CFO: Larry George
Founded: 1988

Manufactures direct mail, packaging &
storage & presentation products.

UNIVERSAL PRINTING

1234 S Kingshighway Blvd
Saint Louis, MO 63110
Telephone: (314) 771-6900, FAX:
(314) 771-7987, E-Mail: info@
universalprintingco.com, Web Site:
www.universalprintingco.com

Provides printing services that offers
graphic arts.

UNZ & CO

Div. of Scott Printing Co
333 Cedar Ave (Suite 2)
Middlesex, NJ 08846-2400
Telephone: (732) 667-1020, Toll Free:
(800) 631-3098, FAX: (732) 868-
0260, E-Mail: unzco@unzco.com,
Web Site: www.unzco.com
Pres, Scott Printing Co: Daniel T. Scott
Founded: 1972

Resource for compliance products,
training & regulatory information - the
tools you need to help your business
run profitably & in full compliance
with industry regulations.

USDISCS

2387 Buena Vista St
Duarte, CA 91010-3301

Telephone: (626) 359-9955, Web Site:
www.usdiscs.com

V3

200 N Elevar St
Oxnard, CA 93030-7969
Telephone: (805) 981-2600, Toll Free:
(800) 882-1844, FAX: (805) 981-
1180, E-Mail: sales@printv3.com,
Web Site: www.printv3.com
Pres: Michael Szanger
Opers Mgr: Steve McCurry
Conducts Business: U.S.
Primary Market Served: Business
Founded: 1946

Print, packaging and direct mail services company.

VALLEY FORGE TAPE &
LABEL CO INC

119 Summit Dr
Exton, PA 19341
Telephone: (610) 524-8900, Toll Free:
(800) 345-1323, FAX: (610) 524-
8906, E-Mail: vfsales@vftl.com,
Web Site: www.vftl.com
Pres: Paul Myers
Gen Mgr: Dennis Hulton
Founded: 1962

Designs & manufactures printed labels.

VENTURE ENCODING
SERVICE INC

4401 Cambridge
Fort Worth, TX 76155-2629
Telephone: (817) 283-9500, FAX:
(817) 540-6966, E-Mail: sales@
venture-encoding.com, Web Site:
www.venture-encoding.com
CEO: Kenny Hargis
Founded: 1972

Offers paper & electronic communication solutions for the financial industry.

VISTAPRINT USA INC

95 Hayden Ave
Lexington, MA 02421-7942
Toll Free: (800) 961-2075, Web Site:
www.vistaprint.com
Pres & CEO: Robert Keane
CMO: Janet Holian
Pub Rels Mgr: Jason Keith
COO: Alex Schwotka
CPO: Anne Drapeau
Pub Rels Coord: Nick Gosselin
VP: Manya Chait
Conducts Business: Worldwide
Employees: 2,200
Primary Market Served: Business &
Consumer
Catalog available online
Direct online sales
Advertising/Marketing Budget Related
to Direct Marketing: 76-100%

Founded: 2000
Gross sales or billing: $515,800,000

The leading online supplier of high-quality, low-cost graphic design services & customized printed products to small business & consumers.

WEB GRAPHICS

PO Box 308
Glens Falls, NY 12801-0308
Telephone: (518) 792-6501, Toll Free: (800) 833-8863, FAX: (518) 792-9353, (800) 833-8861, E-Mail: proofs&pos@printatweb.com, Web Site: www.printatweb.com
Natl Sls Mgr: Bob Mongin
Dir Mfg: Michael Hart

Offers a complete line of custom printed products.

WESTERN GRAPHICS

530 Wheeler St N
Saint Paul, MN 55104
Telephone: (651) 603-6400, FAX: (651) 603-6401, E-Mail: info@westerngx.com, Web Site: www.westerngx.com
Pres: Timothy R Keran
Conducts Business: U.S.
Primary Market Served: Business
Advertising/Marketing Budget Related to Direct Marketing: Full-service print and business communications services provider.%
Founded: 1967

WESTERN WEB PRINTING

4005 S Western Ave
Sioux Falls, SD 57105-6514
Telephone: (605) 339-2383, Toll Free: (800) 843-6805, FAX: (605) 339-8323, E-Mail: info@westernwebprinting.com, Web Site: www.westernwebprinting.com
Acct Exec: Gary Peterson
Employees: 65
Founded: 1973
Gross sales or billing: $8,000,000

Fast turnaround design, print & mail all under one roof.

WESTPRO INC

2294 Mountain Vista Ln
Provo, UT 84606-6206
Telephone: (801) 373-2525, Toll Free: (800) 533-3885, FAX: (801) 373-8778, E-Mail: sales@westpro.net, Web Site: www.westpro.net

Specialize in embroidery & screen printing on custom apparel as well as promotional items, and gifts.

WHITE ELECTRONIC DESIGNS

3601 E University Dr
Phoenix, AZ 85034-7217
Telephone: (614) (602) 437-1520, FAX: (602) 437-9120, Web Site: www.whiteedc.com
CEO & Pres: Charles C. Leader
CFO & Sec: John W. Hohener
Founded: 1951

Designs, develops & manufactures defense & aerospace electronic components & systems for inclusion in high technology products.

WILEN GROUP

5 Wellwood Ave
Farmingdale, NY 11735-1213
Telephone: (631) 439-5000, FAX: (631) 439-4536, Web Site: www.wilengroup.com
CEO & Pres: Darrin Wilen
Sr VP Opers: Allison Rekus
Founded: 1981

Provides multi-platform services & solutions for clients marketing needs.

WILLIAM CHARLES PRINTING

7 Fairchild Ct Ste 100
Plainview, NY 11803-1734
Telephone: (516) 349-0900, FAX: (516) 349-0935, Web Site: www.williamcharlesprinting.com
Pres: Joseph Pelligrini
Mgr: Charles Pelligrini
Founded: 1935

Expert in fulfilling your visual communication needs at all phases of the process.

WILLIAMS PRINTING CO

Subs. of R.R. Donnelley & Sons Co
1240 Spring St NW
Atlanta, GA 30309-2808
Telephone: (404) 875-6611, Toll Free: (800) 950-7588, FAX: (404) 872-4025, Web Site: www.rrdonnelley.com
Pres: John R. Pope
Founded: 1922

Operates as a commercial printer in Atlanta.

WILLIAMSON PRINTING

6700 Denton Dr
Dallas, TX 75235-9827
Telephone: (214) 904-2100, Toll Free: (800) 843-5423, FAX: (214) 352-1842, E-Mail: jandagu@twpc.com, Web Site: www.wpcnet.com
CEO: Jerry Williamson

WISE

555 McFarland 400 Dr
Alpharetta, GA 30004-3375
Telephone: (770) 442-1060, Toll Free: (888) 815-9473, FAX: (770) 751-3599
COO & Gen Counsel: Charles E. Teets
Primary Market Served: Business & Consumer

Business forms manufacturer.

HENRY WURST INC

1331 Saline St
North Kansas City, MO 64116-4410
Telephone: (816) 842-3113, FAX: (816) 472-6221, E-Mail: info@henrywurst.com, Web Site: www.henrywurst.com
CEO: Michael S. Wurst
Mktg Mgr: Stephanie Fite
CFO: Kimberly Kimberly Macias-Lewis Macias-Lewis
COO: James E. Herbst
Founded: 1937

Marketing communications & printing company.

XPRESSDOCS

1000 Forest Park Blvd Ste 200
Fort Worth, TX 76110-1169
Telephone: (817) 870-4601, Toll Free: (866) 977-3627, FAX: (817) 870-1205, Web Site: www.xpressdocs.com
CEO & Dir: Eric D. Chandler
CFO: Scott B. Laver
COO: J. Scotty Parker
Founded: 2001

Provider of direct marketing solutions for organizations with large agent, dealer & franchise networks.

YORK LABEL

405 Willow Springs Ln
York, PA 17405-6047
Telephone: (717) 266-9675, FAX: (717) 266-9834, Web Site: www.yorklabel.com
VP Sls: John Attayek

ZED MARKETING GROUP

1210 Roosevelt St (Suite 220)
Edmond, OK 73034-5176
Telephone: (405) 348-8145, FAX: (405) 348-5541, E-Mail: zed@zedmktg.com, Web Site: www.zedmktg.com
Pres: Jim Zuckermandel

Lettershops, Mailing Services & Product Fulfillment Companies (28) — Geographic Index

ALABAMA

High Cotton, 2901 Alton Way, Birmingham, 35210

Wells Mailing, 4521 Troy Hwy, Montgomery, 36116-5121

ARIZONA

OnTrac, 2501 S Price Rd (Suite 201), Chandler, 85286-7897

SP Express, 7855 S River Pkwy (Suite 222), Tempe, 85284

ARKANSAS

LSC Marketing, 2207 Cantrell Rd, Little Rock, 72203

Mailmaster Corp, 5115 E Highland Dr, Jonesboro, 72401

CALIFORNIA

A&M Direct Mail Service Inc, 949 N Cataract Ave (Suite 1), San Dimas, 91773-1464

AD-Vantage Marketing, 455 Tesconi Cir, Santa Rosa, 95401-4619

Advanced Image Direct, 1415 S Acacia Ave, Fullerton, 92831-5317

Advantage Mailing Inc, PO Box 66013, Anaheim, 92816-6013

Adwest Mailers Inc, 19320 Londelius St, Northridge, 91324-3509

Arrow Mailing Services II Inc, 13040 Cerise Ave, Hawthorne, 90250-5523

Bullseye Marketing Inc, 9025 Owensmouth Ave, Canoga Park, 91304-1417

Business Services Network, 1275 Fairfax Ave Ste 103, San Francisco, 94124-1759

Complete Mailing Service Inc, 108 Dubois St, Santa Cruz, 95060-2109

Creative Mailing & Marketing, 879 W 190th St Ste 400, Gardena, 90248-4223

Fulfillment Express Inc, 7271 Paramount Blvd, Pico Rivera, 90660

Goodkind & Goodkind Direct Inc, 1433 11 St (Suite I), Arcata, 95521-5712

Imagine Fulfillment Services, 14245 Artesia Blvd, La Mirada, 90638

Iron Mountain Fulfillment Services, 565 Sinclair Frontage Rd, Milpitas, 95035

Jenco Productions Inc, 401 S J St, San Bernardino, 92410-2605

Mailing Source, 1760 Monrovia Ave (#C1), Costa Mesa, 92627

Matrix Manager, 1430 Blue Oaks Blvd (Suite 280), Roseville, 95747-5156

Service Mailers & Fulfillment Inc, 2468 E 26th St, Vernon, 90058-1214

Specialized Mailing Services Inc, 17451 Nichols Ln (Unit J), Huntington Beach, 92647

Taubenpost Inc, 20702 Linear Ln, Lake Forest, 92630

The UPS Store, Inc., 6060 Cornerstone Ct W, San Diego, 92121-3795

XPO, 3541 Lomita Blvd, Torrance, 90505-5016

COLORADO

First Data Corp, 6200 S Quebec St, Greenwood Village, 80111-4729

CONNECTICUT

BMI Fulfillment Services, 51-53 Kenosia Ave (Suite 2), Danbury, 06810-2304

Better Lists Inc, 64 Sunnyside Ave, Stamford, 06902-4792

Com-Pak, 225 Episcopal Rd, Berlin, 06037-7312

DST Output, 125 Ellington Rd, South Windsor, 06074-4112

Data-Mail Inc, 240 Hartford Ave, Newington, 06111-2054

Fosdick Fulfillment Corp, 26 Barnes Industrial Park Rd N, Wallingford, 06492

Meyer Fulfillment, 255 Long Beach Blvd, Stratford, 06615-7117

Mystic Logistics Inc, 2187 New London Tpke, South Glastonbury, 06073

3PL Worldwide Inc, 500 Bic Dr, Milford, 06461-1734

DELAWARE

Sheeran Direct Marketing, 71 Southgate Blvd, New Castle, 19720-2000

DISTRICT OF COLUMBIA

UNICOR- Services Business Group, 400 1st St NW, Washington, 20534-0004

US Postal Service-Library, 475 L'Enfant Plz SW, Washington, 20260-1540

FLORIDA

A-1 Direct Mail Marketing Inc, 11950 SW 128th St, Miami, 33186-5207

The Bureau Inc, 2809 SE Monroe St, Stuart, 34997-5904

Crane Duplicating Service Inc, 4915 Rattlesnake Hammock Rd, Naples, 34113-6959

DHL Express, 1200 S Pine Island Rd (Suite 600), Plantation, 33324

DHL Global Mail, 2700 S Commerce Pkwy (Suite 400), Weston, 33331-3631

Direct One Inc, 7224 Sandscove Ct (Suite 7), Winter Park, 32792-5921

Direct Response Marketing, 12450 Automobile Blvd, Clearwater, 33762

MBI Direct Mail, 710 W New Hampshire Ave, Deland, 32720-7231

Palm Coast Data LLC, 11 Commerce Blvd, Palm Coast, 32164-7961

Southern Fulfillment Services, 1650 90th Ave, Vero Beach, 32966

ThinkDirect Marketing Group, 8285 Bryan Dairy Rd (Suite 150), Largo, 33777-1306

GEORGIA

Innotrac Corp, 6465 E Johns Xing Ste 400, Duluth, 30097-1581

PBD Worldwide Fulfillment Services, 1650 Bluegrass Lakes Pkwy, Alpharetta, 30004-7714

United Parcel Service, 55 Glenlake Pkwy NE, Atlanta, 30328

HAWAII

Cardinal Mailing Services Ltd, 552 N Nimitz Hwy, Honolulu, 96817

IDAHO

ESP Printing & Mailing Inc, 317 E 37th St (Suite 5), Boise, 83714-6475

ILLINOIS

Advance Mailing Services Inc, 1130 Carolina Dr (Unit A), West Chicago, 60185-5163

Advantage Marketing Group, 1550 Howard St, Elk Grove Village, 60007

aNETorder/American Mailers, 820 Frontenac Rd, Naperville, 60563-1743

BFC, 1051 N Kirk Rd, Batavia, 60510-1438

Calmark Inc, 1400 W 44th St, Chicago, 60609-3332

Direct Mail Solutions LLC, 775 Kimberly Dr, Carol Stream, 60188-9407

Direct Mail Source, PO Box 8033, Wilmette, 60091-8033

The Envelope Connection Inc, 5660 N. Elston Ave., Chicago, 60646

Finishing Plus, Inc, 4546 W 47th St, Chicago, 60632

Form House Inc, 4640 S Kolmar Ave, Chicago, 60632

Hogard Business Services Inc, PO Box 748, Kankakee, 60901-0748

Johnson & Quin Inc, 7460 N Lehigh Ave, Niles, 60714-4099

KD Mailing & Fulfillment Service, 6850 N Central Park, Lincolnwood, 60712-2704

Mailways Enterprises Inc, 6105 Factory Rd (Suite 1), Crystal Lake, 60014-7965

Mid-Central Printing & Mailing Inc, 1225 Central Ave, Wilmette, 60091

Northwest Mailing Service Inc, 5501 W Grand Ave, Chicago, 60639-2909

Prodigy Mailing Services, 389 E South Frontage Rd, Bolingbrook, 60440-3029

Promotion Support Services Inc, 2832 5th St Ste 1, Rock Island, 61201-4027

Reliant Data Processing, 197 Alder Dr, North Aurora, 60542-1471

Source Link, 500 Park Blvd (Suite 1425), Itasca, 60143-2610

Strategic Marketing & Mailing, 3002 N Apollo Dr, PO Box 6013, Champaign, 61826-6013

ThreeSource Fulfillment, 655 Mulberry, Manteno, 60950-9219

Tripar International Inc, 20 Presidential Dr, Roselle, 60172

United Wire Service, 8512 N Allen Rd, Peoria, 61615-1527

Wit Postal Logistics LLC, 350 N La Salle Dr (Suite 1100), Chicago, 60654-5131

INDIANA

Faris Mailing Inc, 701 N Holt Rd Ste 3, Indianapolis, 46222-3455

The Order Fulfillment Group, 7313 Mayflower Park Dr, Zionsville, 46077-7903

Pentera Inc, 8650-G Commerce Park Pl, Indianapolis, 46268-3126

IOWA

AlanizMetroGroup, 1805 E Washington St, Mount Pleasant, 52641

The Pioneer Group, 316 W 5th St, Waterloo, 50701-5508

Promotion Fulfillment Ctr, 311 21st St, Camanche, 52730-9699

Rees Associates Inc, 1800 SW 2nd St, Des Moines, 50315-7147

KANSAS

Consolidated Mailing Corp, 5735 Kessler Ln, Shawnee Mission, 66203-2591

Midpoint National Inc, 1263 Southwest Blvd, Kansas City, 66103-1901

Southwest Publishing & Mailing Corp, 2600 NW Topeka Blvd, Topeka, 66617-1160

KENTUCKY

American Mailing Service Inc, 101 Armco Blvd, Ashland, 41101-7536

Blue Grass Mailing, Data & Fulfillment Services, 833 Nandino Blvd, Lexington, 40511-1202

dmh Marketing Partners - Louisville, 12101 Westport Rd, Louisville, 40245-1759

Premier Direct Marketing Inc, 7725 National Tpke (Unit 100), Louisville, 40214-4803

MARYLAND

BrightKey, 9050 Junction Dr Ste 2, Annapolis Junction, 20701-1134

DirectMail.com, 201 Skipjack Rd, Prince Frederick, 20678-3411

Distribution Postal Co Inc, 6202 Frankford Ave, Baltimore, 21206-4902

EU Services, 203 Log Canoe Cir, Stevensville, 21666-9270

Mail Advertising Services Inc, 15711 Pagano Ln, Darnestown, 20874-3115

A Rapid Mailing Inc, 8221 Preston Ct, Jessup, 20794-9368

ZIP Mailing Services Inc, 6304 Sheriff Rd (Suite Z), Landover, 20785-4361

MASSACHUSETTS

International Mailing Solutions LLC, 25 Corporate Dr (Suite 175), Burlington, 01803-4243

JLS Mailing Services Inc, 672 Crescent St, Brockton, 02302-3360

OnTime Companies, 201 Crescent Ave, Chelsea, 02150-3072

Arleen Smith Marketing Inc, 60 Mayflower Ln, Stoughton, 02072-3024

Staples Industrial, 500 Staples Dr, Framingham, 01702-4478

MICHIGAN

Alternate Marketing Networks Inc, 4675 32nd Ave Ste B, Hudsonville, 49426-8012

On-Demand Mail Services, 2083 Pontiac Rd Ste B, Auburn Hills, 48326-2485

Progressive Distribution Services Inc, 5505 36th St SE, Grand Rapids, 49512

Wolverine Solutions Group, 1601 Clay St, Detroit, 48211-1902

MINNESOTA

American Spirit Mailing, 401 13th Ave N, Howard Lake, 55349-0707

Archway Marketing Services, 19850 S Diamond Lake Rd, Rogers, 55374

Charnstrom, 5391 12th Ave E, Shakopee, 55379-1896

Ideagroup Mail Service, 4455 White Bear Pkwy, Saint Paul, 55110

Impact Mailing, 4600 Lyndale Ave N, Minneapolis, 55412-1408

Irresistible Ink Inc, 4444 Haines Rd, Duluth, 55811

Mail Handling Services, 7550 Corporate Way, Eden Prairie, 55344-2045

The John Roberts Co, 9687 E River Rd, Minneapolis, 55433

MISSISSIPPI

Sacred Heart League, 6050 Hwy 161 N, Walls, 38686-0001

MISSOURI

Impressions Direct, 2116 59th St, Saint Louis, 63110-2808

Innovative Industries Inc, 421 W Centennial Ave, Carthage, 64836-3528

NEVADA

The Bender Group, 345 Parr Cir, Reno, 89512

SilverState Marketing Solutions, 3585 E Patrick Ln (#200), Las Vegas, 89120-6211

Universal Distribution Services, 4910 Longley Ln (Suite 101), Reno, 89502

NEW HAMPSHIRE

Polaris Direct, 300 Technology Dr, Hooksett, 03106-2520

NEW JERSEY

A+ Letter Service, 200 Syracuse Ct, Lakewood, 08701

Advertising Mailers Inc, 60 Mayfield Ave (#4), Edison, 08837-3911

Alert Marketing, 160 Chubb Ave (#304), Lyndhurst, 07071

Barton & Cooney, 300 Richards Run, Burlington, 08016-2120

Direct Link Worldwide, 700 Dowd Ave, Elizabeth, 07201-2108

Direct Mail Depot Inc, 200 Circle Dr N, Piscataway, 08854-3705

Direct Market Designs Inc, 45 E 5th St, Paterson, 07524-1101

The First Occupational Center of New Jersey, 391 Lakeside Ave, Orange, 07050-2809

GMI Distribution, 305 Churchill Ave, Somerset, 08873

Gordon Management Inc, 60 Clyde Rd, Somerset, 08873-3486

The Hibbert Group, 400 Pennington Ave, Trenton, 08618-3105

Just Packaging Inc, 450 Oak Tree Ave, South Plainfield, 07080

Pitney Bowes International Mail Services, 158 Mount Olivet Ave, Newark, 07114-2114

Professional Mailing Services Inc, 12 Commerce St, Springfield, 07081-2996

Redi-Mail Direct Marketing Inc, 5 Audrey Pl, Fairfield, 07004-3401

Reliable Mail Service Inc, 121 Fieldcrest Ave Ste C, Edison, 08837-3658

Riverside Acquisition Group LLC, 365 New Albany Rd Ste A, Moorestown, 08057-1105

Shakespeare Mailing Service, 3107 Central Ave, Union City, 07087

Swan Packaging Fulfillment, 415 Hamburg Tpke (Suite G), Wayne, 07470-2164

NEW YORK

Access Direct Systems Inc, 91 Executive Blvd, Farmingdale, 11735-4710

Advanced Marketing Direct, 99 Thielman Dr, Buffalo, 14206-2365

Brigar Xpress Solutions, Inc, 5 Sand Creek Rd Ste 100, Albany, 12205-1400

The CPW Group, 60 Trade Zone Ct, Ronkonkoma, 11779-7395

Century Direct, 30-30 47th Ave (#3), Long Island City, 11101

Challenge Industries Inc, 950 Danby Rd (Suite 179), Ithaca, 14850-5793

Direct Mail of NY-PostHaste, 199 Albany Post Rd (Suite 158), Buchanan, 10511-1624

Direct Mail Trackers, 74 Southaven Ave (Suite D), Medford, 11763

Dispatch Letter Service, 545 W 45th St (fl 10), New York, 10036

Fulfillment Plus Inc, 889 Waverly Ave, Holtsville, 11742

G-Plex Direct Mail, 194 Morris Ave (Unit 7), Holtsville, 11742-1452

Graphnet Inc, 40 Fulton St Fl 28, New York, 10038-5074

Hand Assembly & Packaging Inc (HAPI), PO Box 617, Plainview, 11803-0019

Howell Marketing Services, 100 E Miller St, Elmira, 14904

Interstate EDP & Direct Mail Center Inc, 754 4th Ave, Brooklyn, 11232-1414

Key Computer Service of Chelsea, 227 E 56th St Rm 403, New York, 10022-3775

MVS Mailers Inc, 31 Crossways E Rd, Bohemia, 11716-1204

The Mailbox of Ithaca Inc, 1650 Hanshaw Rd, Ithaca, 14850-6348

Mailmen Inc, 15 Enter Ln, Hauppauge, 11749-4897

PDS International Mail Service, 85 Corporate Dr, Hauppauge, 11788

Prompt Direct, 66 Willow Ave (Suite 1), Staten Island, 10305-1848

TNT International Express, 68 S Service Rd (Suite 340, Melville, 11747-2358

US Monitor, 86 Maple Ave, New City, 10956-5019

Wolff/SMG, 1641 Commons Pkwy, Macedon, 14502-9190

NORTH CAROLINA

Excalibur Enterprises Inc, 4820 Bethania Station Rd, Winston Salem, 27105-1201

PBM Graphics, 415 Westcliff Rd, Greensboro, 27409

Trinity Road LLC, PO Box 7445, Charlotte, 28241-7445

OHIO

JC Direct Mail Inc, 4241 Williams Rd, Groveport, 43125

Macke Bindery Inc, 10355 Spartan Dr, Cincinnati, 45215

Marketing Communication Resource Inc, 4800 E 345th St, Willoughby, 44094-4607

PJ McNerney & Associates Inc, 440 Northland Blvd, Cincinnati, 45240

Vincent Graphics, LLC, PO Box 39, Box 386, Hilliard, 43026-0039

OREGON

Co-operations, 20049 SW 112th Ave, Tualatin, 97062

PENNSYLVANIA

ABDI, Inc Global Order Fulfillment, Ave A- Bldg 16, Buncher Commerce Park, Leetsdale, 15056-1304

FedEx Ground, 1000 FedEx Dr, Coraopolis, 15108-9373

Walter Garson Jr & Associates Inc, 1370 Adams Rd, Bensalem, 19020

Karol Media, 375 Stewart Rd, Wilkes-Barre, 18773-7600

Mailing Specialists Inc, 1130 Garden St, Greensburg, 15601

National Fulfillment Services, 100 Pine Ave, Holmes, 19043-1444

Pittsburgh Mailing, 4777 Streets Run Rd, Pittsburgh, 15236-1200

Radial Inc, 935 First Ave, King of Prussia, 19406

David J Thompson Mailing Corp, 21 Naus Way, Bloomsburg, 17815

RHODE ISLAND

The Allied Group, 25 Amflex Dr, Cranston, 02921

Mercury Print & Mail Co Inc, 1110 Central Ave, Pawtucket, 02861-2262

TENNESSEE

MT&L Card Products & Fulfillment Services, 2911 Kraft Dr, Nashville, 37204-3618

TEXAS

Alamo Mailing, 12716 O'Connor Rd, San Antonio, 78233

The Lead Connection Inc, 2300 W Morton St (Suite 131), Denison, 10543

QuantumDigital, 8702 Cross Park Dr., Austin, 78754-5235

The Service Center LTD, 6450 Clara St (Suite 100), Houston, 77041

Summit Direct Mail Inc, 1655 Terre Colony Ct, Dallas, 75212-6222

Zachry Associates Inc, 500 Chestnut (Suite 2000), Abilene, 79602

VIRGINIA

Centric Communications, 1048 W. 27th St., Norfolk, 23517

Direct Mail Solutions, 4500 Sarellen Rd, Richmond, 23231-4435

Oberthur Card Systems, 4250 Pleasant Valley Rd, Chantilly, 20151

WISCONSIN

Advanced Mail Inc, 2908 Melby St, Eau Claire, 54703-0564

Freedom Graphic Systems Inc, 1101 S Janesville St, Milton, 53563-1838

Integrated Mail Industries Ltd, 3450 W Hopkins St, Milwaukee, 53216-1700

JHL Mail Marketing Inc, 3100 Borham Ave, Stevens Point, 54481-5097

Quad/Graphics, N63 W23075 Hwy 74, Sussex, 53089-2827

CANADA

British Columbia

International Direct Response Services Ltd, 10159 Nordel Ct, Delta, V4G1J8

Ontario

The Added Touch, 156 Lakeshore Rd. E., Oakville, L6J 1H4

ArrowMail Canada, 1415 Janette Ave, Windsor, N8X 1Z1

Farrow Logistics, 6220 Westar Dr, Windsor, N9J 0B5

The Helicopter Group, 200 W Beaver Creek Rd (Unit 1), Richmond Hill, L4B 1B4

Interact Direct Marketing Inc, 787 Industrial Rd, London, N5V 4J4

Marco Sales & Incentives Ltd, 470 Hardy Rd, Brantford, N3V 6T1

Market Focus Direct, 550 Alden Rd (Suite 207), Markham, L3R 6A8

Post Linx Corp, 1170 Birchmount Rd, Scarborough, M1P 5E3

PostLink Corp, 1475 Startop Rd (Unit 8), Ottawa, K1B 3W5

Wood & Associates Direct Marketing Services Ltd, 9-1410 Bayly St., Pickering, L1W 3R3

Quebec

DXP Postexperts, 4575 Hickmore, Saint-Laurent, H4T 155

Lettershops, Mailing Services & Product Fulfillment Companies (28)

A&M DIRECT MAIL SERVICE INC
949 N Cataract Ave (Suite 1)
San Dimas, CA 91773-1464
Telephone: (909) 599-3905, (909) 579-0111, Toll Free: (800) 735-3905,
FAX: (909) 599-3516, E-Mail: mail@amdirectmail.com
Pres: Don Wooden
Employees: 20
Founded: 1969

A-1 DIRECT MAIL MARKETING INC
11950 SW 128th St
Miami, FL 33186-5207
Telephone: (305) 251-3187
Pres: William Bowne
Founded: 1987

A+ LETTER SERVICE
200 Syracuse Ct
Lakewood, NJ 08701
Telephone: (732) 905-2010, FAX: (732) 905-4662, E-Mail: aplus@aplusletter.com, Web Site: www.aplusletters.com
Pres: Raymond Finnegan
VP Sls & Mktg: Bob Barr
VP Opers: Dan Wilgus
Founded: 1986

ABDI, INC GLOBAL ORDER FULFILLMENT
Ave A- Bldg 16, Buncher Commerce Park
Leetsdale, PA 15056-1304
Telephone: (412) 741-1142, Toll Free: (800) 796-6471, FAX: (412) 741-4161, E-Mail: info@abdintl.com, Web Site: www.abdintl.com
Pres: Judy G. Cheteyan
CEO: Michael D. Cheteyan II
Founded: 1985

ACCESS DIRECT SYSTEMS INC
91 Executive Blvd
Farmingdale, NY 11735-4710
Telephone: (631) 420-0700, Web Site: www.accessdirect.com
Sales Exec: Lori Messina
Pres: John Dinozzi
Owner & Exec VP: John V. Dinozzi
Founded: 1971

AD-VANTAGE MARKETING
455 Tesconi Cir
Santa Rosa, CA 95401-4619
Telephone: (707) 578-8700, FAX: (707) 578-0258, E-Mail: info@ad-vantagemarketing.com, Web Site: ad-vantagemarketing.com
Dir: Glen Rankin
Sls: Aaron Rankin
Acct Mgr: Dave Rankin
Primary Market Served: Business
Founded: 1984

Full-service print and mailing services company.

THE ADDED TOUCH
156 Lakeshore Rd. E.
Oakville, ON, Canada L6J 1H4
Telephone: (905) 828-4041, Toll Free: (888) AD-TOUCH, FAX: (905) 338-1486, E-Mail: addedtouch@gmail.com, Web Site: www.addedtouch.com
Conducts Business: U.S., Canada
Employees: 20
Primary Market Served: Business & Consumer
Catalog available online
Indirect online sales
Advertising/Marketing Budget Related to Direct Marketing: 76-100%
Direct Marketing ad budget:
Direct Mail: 85%
Magazines: 10%
Newspapers: 5%
Founded: 1961
Gross sales or billing: $4,000,000

Sell unique, practical household items and call center/fulfillment services.

ADVANCE MAILING SERVICES INC
1130 Carolina Dr (Unit A)
West Chicago, IL 60185-5163
Telephone: (630) 293-0707, FAX: (630) 293-9268
Founded: 1988

ADVANCED IMAGE DIRECT
1415 S Acacia Ave
Fullerton, CA 92831-5317
Telephone: (714) 502-3900, Toll Free: (800) 540-3848, FAX: (714) 502-3901, Web Site: www.advancedimagedirect.com
VP Sales: Perry Wilson

ADVANCED MAIL INC
2908 Melby St
Eau Claire, WI 54703-0564
Telephone: (715) 839-8801, Toll Free: 888-624-5255, FAX: (715) 839-8906, Web Site: www.amailinc.com

Pres: Gary Dreher
Founded: 1986
Direct mail advertising.

ADVANCED MARKETING DIRECT
99 Thielman Dr
Buffalo, NY 14206-2365
Toll Free: (800) 696-7567, FAX: 716-821-5300, Web Site: www.amdirect.com
Owner: Robert Enderle
Founded: 1978

Direct Mail Advertising Services & Lithographic Commercial Printing.

ADVANTAGE MAILING INC
PO Box 66013
Anaheim, CA 92816-6013
Telephone: (714) 538-3881, Toll Free: (888) 909-6245, FAX: (714) 282-3903, Web Site: www.advantagemailinginc.com

Mailing, distribution & lettershop services.

ADVANTAGE MARKETING GROUP
RP-NFOA
1550 Howard St
Elk Grove Village, IL 60007
Telephone: (847) 952-2100, FAX: (847) 952-3348, Web Site: www.goamg.com

Direct mail advertising services.

ADVERTISING MAILERS INC
60 Mayfield Ave (#4)
Edison, NJ 08837-3911
Telephone: (732) 225-3404, Toll Free: (800) 427-8513, FAX: (732) 225-7429, E-Mail: admailers@aol.com

Lettershop services.

ADWEST MAILERS INC
19320 Londelius St
Northridge, CA 91324-3509
Telephone: (818) 982-3720, FAX: (818) 982-3786, E-Mail: sales@adwest.com, Web Site: www.adwest.com
Pres: Frank Grijalva
Founded: 1980

Direct mail advertising services.

ALAMO MAILING
12716 O'Connor Rd
San Antonio, TX 78233

Telephone: (210) 637-0404, FAX:
(210) 637-0081
Owner: Chad Elseth
Founded: 1952

ALANIZMETROGROUP
Div. of Qdmh
1805 E Washington St
Mount Pleasant, IA 52641
Telephone: (319) 385-7259, FAX:
(319) 385-2825, E-Mail: info@
alanizdirect.com, Web Site: www.
alanizdirect.com
Pres: Randy Seberg
Founded: 2000

Marketing products and services company.

ALERT MARKETING
160 Chubb Ave (#304)
Lyndhurst, NJ 07071
Web Site: www.alertmarketing.com
Pres: David Leyden
Founded: 2008

Management consulting services.

THE ALLIED GROUP
25 Amflex Dr
Cranston, RI 02921
Telephone: (401) 946-6100, Web Site:
www.thealliedgrp.com
Pres & CEO: Bob Clement
Founded: 1946

Marketing communications & Fulfillment Services

ALTERNATE MARKETING
NETWORKS INC
4675 32nd Ave Ste B
Hudsonville, MI 49426-8012
Telephone: (616) 662-6420, FAX:
(616) 662-6422, Web Site: www.
altmarknet.com
Chmn & CEO: Philip D. Miller
Founded: 1987

AMERICAN MAILING
SERVICE INC
Div. of The Gallaher Group
101 Armco Blvd
Ashland, KY 41101-7536
Telephone: (606) 329-2741, Toll Free:
(800) 678-8384, FAX: (606) 325-
8558, Web Site: www.
thegallahergroup.com
Pres: John Gallaher
Fin Exec: Stephanie Gallaher
Founded: 2001

Commercial printing.

AMERICAN SPIRIT MAILING
Div. of A.H.L. Services Inc
401 13th Ave N

Howard Lake, MN 55349-0707
Telephone: (320) 543-3737, FAX:
(320) 543-3228, E-Mail: asgc@asgc-
mail.com, Web Site: www.asgc.com
Founded: 2003

Direct mail advertising services.

ANETORDER/AMERICAN
MAILERS
820 Frontenac Rd
Naperville, IL 60563-1743
Telephone: (630) 579-8800, Web Site:
www.anetorder.com

ARCHWAY MARKETING
SERVICES
19850 S Diamond Lake Rd
Rogers, MN 55374
Telephone: (763) 428-3300, Toll Free:
(866) 779-9855 X1933, FAX: (763)
488-6803, E-Mail: info@archway.
com, Web Site: www.archway.com
Chmn: Edward J. Kolodzieski
Conducts Business: U.S., Canada
Employees: 2,400
Primary Market Served: Business
Advertising/Marketing Budget Related
to Direct Marketing: 0-25%
Founded: 1953
Gross sales or billing: $33,000,000

Provides marketing logistics, fulfillment & supply chain management services.

ARROW MAILING SERVICES
II INC
13040 Cerise Ave
Hawthorne, CA 90250-5523
Telephone: (310) 219-7740, FAX:
(310) 219-3335
Pres: Robert A. Tappan
Founded: 1965

Marketing consultants.

ARROWMAIL CANADA
1415 Janette Ave
Windsor, ON, Canada N8X 1Z1
Telephone: (313) 961-8334, FAX:
(313) 961-7849, E-Mail: info@
mailingcanada.com, Web Site: www.
mailingcanada.com

Manages the logistics of Canadian mail within Canada and internationally to the United States or any destination in the world.

BFC
1051 N Kirk Rd
Batavia, IL 60510-1438
Telephone: (630) 879-9240, Web Site:
www.bfcprint.com
Owner: Matt Novak
Pres: Joseph Novak Jr

HR Exec: Laura Pogwizd
Founded: 1975

Offset printing.

BMI FULFILLMENT
SERVICES
Subs. of Blumenfield Marketing Inc
51-53 Kenosia Ave (Suite 2)
Danbury, CT 06810-2304
Telephone: (203) 546-5580, FAX:
(203) 546-5575, E-Mail: barry@
bmigroup.com, Web Site: www.
bmigroup.com
CEO: Barry Blumenfield
Dir: Arthur Blumenfield
Founded: 1976

Order processing systems & services for direct marketers.

BARTON & COONEY
300 Richards Run
Burlington, NJ 08016-2120
Telephone: (609) 747-9300, FAX:
(609) 747-9700, E-Mail: pmdoyle@
bartoncooney.com, Web Site: www.
bartoncooney.com
Pres: Patrick Doyle
Controller: Linda Malin
Founded: 1920

Printing & Mailing

THE BENDER GROUP
345 Parr Cir
Reno, NV 89512
Telephone: (775) 788-8800, Toll Free:
(800) 621-9402, FAX: (775) 788-
8811, E-Mail: salesinfo@benderwhs.
com, Web Site: www.bendergroup.
com
CEO: Chris N Bender
Mgr Bus Devel: Jared Lindwall
Mgr, Bender Intl: William Dalton
Founded: 1945

BETTER LISTS INC
64 Sunnyside Ave
Stamford, CT 06902-4792
Telephone: (203) 324-4171, FAX:
(203) 358-0384, Web Site: www.
betterlists.com
Founded: 1964

Direct mail fulfillment & mailing resource.

BLUE GRASS MAILING,
DATA & FULFILLMENT
SERVICES
833 Nandino Blvd
Lexington, KY 40511-1202
Telephone: (859) 231-7272, Toll Free:
(800) 928-6245, FAX: (859) 259-
1214, E-Mail: info@bgmailing.com,
Web Site: www.bgmailing.com

Founded: 1974

BRIGAR XPRESS SOLUTIONS, INC
5 Sand Creek Rd Ste 100
Albany, NY 12205-1400
Telephone: (518) 438-7817, Toll Free:
(877) 437-7817, FAX: (518) 438-
0224, E-Mail: general@brigarxpress.
com, Web Site: www.brigarxpress.
com
Pres & CEO: Jack McGrath
HR Exec: Laura Polec
Sls Exec: Rich Trombley
Founded: 1990

Direct mail advertising services.

BRIGHTKEY
9050 Junction Dr Ste 2
Annapolis Junction, MD 20701-1134
Telephone: (301) 604-3305
Pres & CEO: Rita Hope Counts

BULLSEYE MARKETING INC
9025 Owensmouth Ave
Canoga Park, CA 91304-1417
Telephone: (818) 888-8700, Web Site:
www.bullseyeb2b.com
Pres: Scott Barker
Founded: 2005

Commercial Art/Graphic Designers.

THE BUREAU INC
2809 SE Monroe St
Stuart, FL 34997-5904
Telephone: (772) 283-8850, Web Site:
www.bureauinc.com
Pres: Resa Walton
Founded: 1975

Direct mail advertising services.

BUSINESS SERVICES NETWORK
1275 Fairfax Ave Ste 103
San Francisco, CA 94124-1759
Telephone: (415) 282-8161, FAX:
(415) 282-8176, E-Mail: sales@bsnc.
com, Web Site: www.bsnc.com
Pres: Harry Yue
HR Exec: Cindy Yue
Sls Exec: Steve Voris
Founded: 1984

THE CPW GROUP
60 Trade Zone Ct
Ronkonkoma, NY 11779-7395
Toll Free: (888) 641-7901
CEO: Lorraine Chaudhry-Ekinci
Pres: John P. Plate

CALMARK INC
1400 W 44th St
Chicago, IL 60609-3332

Telephone: (773) 247-7200, FAX:
(773) 247-3199, E-Mail: ljakobi@
calmark-inc.com, Web Site: www.
clamark-inc.com
Pres & CEO: James Fitzgerald
VP: Stephen Colella
Founded: 1960

Direct mail advertising services.

CARDINAL MAILING SERVICES LTD
552 N Nimitz Hwy
Honolulu, HI 96817
Telephone: (808) 538-3884, FAX:
(808) 521-1419, E-Mail: mail@
cardinalservicesltd.com, Web Site:
www.cardinalservicesltd.com
Pres: Malia Lageman

CENTRIC COMMUNICATIONS
1048 W. 27th St.
Norfolk, VA 23517
Telephone: (757) 622-2724, E-Mail:
info@centriccommunications.net,
Web Site: centriccommunications.net
CEO: J David Craig
Pres: Greg Jordan
Founded: 1959

CENTURY DIRECT
30-30 47th Ave (#3)
Long Island City, NY 11101
Telephone: (212) 349-0600, FAX:
(718) 349-9528, E-Mail: info@
centurydirect.net, Web Site: www.
centurydirect.net
Founded: 1932

Printing & mailing services to direct
mail marketing businesses.

CHALLENGE INDUSTRIES INC
950 Danby Rd (Suite 179)
Ithaca, NY 14850-5793
Telephone: (607) 272-8990, FAX:
(607) 277-7865, E-Mail: info@
aboutchallenge.org, Web Site: www.
aboutchallenge.org
Pres: Patrick McKee
HR Exec: Melissa Chiusano
Sls Exec: Russell Maracle
Founded: 1968

CHARNSTROM
5391 12th Ave E
Shakopee, MN 55379-1896
Telephone: (952) 403-0303, Toll Free:
(800) 328-2962, FAX: (800) 916-
3215, E-Mail: customerservice@
charnstrom.com, Web Site: www.
charnstrom.com
Pres: Greg Hedlund
VP: John Herntier

Founded: 1996

CO-OPERATIONS
20049 SW 112th Ave
Tualatin, OR 97062
Telephone: (503) 620-7977, Toll Free:
(866) 228-6362, FAX: (503) 620-
7917, E-Mail: info@fsipdx.com,
Web Site: www.fsipdx.com
CEO: Patricia Granum
Founded: 1993

COM-PAK
225 Episcopal Rd
Berlin, CT 06037-7312
Telephone: (856) 802-1900, Toll Free:
(856) 802-3097, E-Mail: info@com-
pak.com, Web Site: www.
marketpointdirect.com
Pres: Steve Walk
Founded: 2010

COMPLETE MAILING SERVICE INC
108 Dubois St
Santa Cruz, CA 95060-2109
Telephone: (831) 425-5556, FAX:
(831) 425-0306, E-Mail: info@
completemail.com, Web Site: www.
completemail.com
Founded: 1976

CONSOLIDATED MAILING CORP
5735 Kessler Ln
Shawnee Mission, KS 66203-2591
Telephone: (913) 262-4400, Toll Free:
(800) 706-6245, FAX: (913) 262-
7801, E-Mail: cmcmail@swbell.net,
Web Site: www.consolidatedmailing.
com
Sls Exec: Buz Prosser
Mgr: Karen Brennan
Founded: 1948

CRANE DUPLICATING SERVICE INC
4915 Rattlesnake Hammock Rd
Naples, FL 34113-6959
Telephone: (305) 280-6742, FAX:
(239) 732-8415, Web Site: www.
craneduplicating.com
Pres: Richard W. Price
Employees: 2
Founded: 2012

CREATIVE MAILING & MARKETING
Subs. of FYI Inc
879 W 190th St Ste 400
Gardena, CA 90248-4223
Telephone: (310) 637-7100, FAX:
(714) 998-9001, Web Site: www.
creativemandm.com

Pres & CEO: Phillip Hodgkins
Founded: 1998

DHL EXPRESS
1200 S Pine Island Rd (Suite 600)
Plantation, FL 33324
Telephone: (954) 888-7000, Toll Free:
(800) 225-5345, FAX: (954) 888-
7310, Web Site: www.dhl.com
VP: John Olin
HR Exec: Lorraine Rutenberg
Sls Exec: Debbie-Ann Scott
Fin Exec: Darryl Yearwood
Founded: 2004

DHL GLOBAL MAIL
Sub. of DPWN
2700 S Commerce Pkwy (Suite 400)
Weston, FL 33331-3631
Telephone: (954) 903-6300, Toll Free:
(866) 616-MAIL, FAX: (954) 903-
6310, E-Mail: contact@
dhlglobalmail.com, Web Site: www.
dhlglobalmail.com
VP: Beth Day
Founded: 1999

DMH MARKETING PARTNERS - LOUISVILLE
Div. of DNR Group.
12101 Westport Rd
Louisville, KY 40245-1759
Telephone: (502) 339-6442, E-Mail:
data@dmhmarketingpartners.com,
Web Site: www.
dmhmarketingpartners.com
Pres: David Redmon

Full service direct mail company.

DST OUTPUT
125 Ellington Rd
South Windsor, CT 06074-4112
Telephone: (860) 290-7337, Toll Free:
(800) 441-7587, Web Site: www.
dstoutput.com
VP Sls & Corp Commun: Cheryl Kananowicz

DXP POSTEXPERTS
4575 Hickmore
Saint-Laurent, QC, Canada H4T 155
Telephone: (514) 934-4545, E-Mail:
info@dxp-postexperts.com, Web
Site: www.postdestination.com
Gen Dir: Francois Paradis
Cust Lists Mgr: Claude Martineau
Conducts Business: Canada, U.S.
Primary Market Served: Business &
Consumer
Founded: 2014

Full-service direct mail marketing and
mail processing company.

DATA-MAIL INC
240 Hartford Ave
Newington, CT 06111-2054
Telephone: (860) 666-0399, FAX:
(860) 665-1226, E-Mail: aliceh@
data-mail.com, Web Site: www.data-
mail.com
Pres: Andrew J. Mandell
Dir Corp Devel: Mark Mandell
Founded: 1971

DIRECT LINK WORLDWIDE
700 Dowd Ave
Elizabeth, NJ 07201-2108
Telephone: (908) 289-0703, Toll Free:
(800) 223-7967, FAX: (908) 289-
0705, E-Mail: infousa@directlink.
com, Web Site: www.directlink.com
Pres: John Cucciniello
VP: Soren Mueller
Founded: 1986

Direct mail advertising services.

DIRECT MAIL DEPOT INC
200 Circle Dr N
Piscataway, NJ 08854-3705
Telephone: (732) 469-5900, FAX:
(732) 469-8414, E-Mail: sales@
directmaildepot.com, Web Site:
www.directmaildepot.com
COO: Carmen Ocello
Exec VP Sls & Mktg: Mitchell Gold-
klank
Conducts Business: U.S.
Employees: 250
Primary Market Served: Business
Advertising/Marketing Budget Related
to Direct Marketing: 0-25%
Direct Marketing ad budget: $50,000
Direct Mail: 100%
Founded: 1990

Specializing in laser personalization
and complete lettershop services. Serving the direct mail industry.

DIRECT MAIL OF NY-POSTHASTE
Div. of MCS Marketing Group Inc
199 Albany Post Rd (Suite 158)
Buchanan, NY 10511-1624
Telephone: (914) 736-2239
Sr Acct Rep: Christine Saluto

DIRECT MAIL SOLUTIONS
4500 Sarellen Rd
Richmond, VA 23231-4435
Telephone: (804) 254-8300, Toll Free:
(877) 367-0800, Web Site: www.
directmailsolutions.com
Dir Bus Devel: Stephanie Hoy
Pres & CEO: Chris Moore
CFO: Tom Rhodes
VP Opers: Scott Tozier
Founded: 1997

DIRECT MAIL SOLUTIONS LLC
775 Kimberly Dr
Carol Stream, IL 60188-9407
Telephone: (630) 653-6863, FAX:
(630) 653-7144, E-Mail: support@
dmspostal.com, Web Site: www.
dmspostal.com
Partner: Robert Hopkins
Partner: Bob Zunker
Partner: Jerry Gately
Employees: 10
Founded: 1998

Chicago area direct mail company.

DIRECT MAIL SOURCE
Div. of Women Entrepreneurs Inc
PO Box 8033
Wilmette, IL 60091-8033
Telephone: (847) 676-3744, E-Mail:
dms@directmailsource.net
Pres: Gail S. Izenstark

Specialized advertising/marketing
agency focused on direct mail advertising.

DIRECT MAIL TRACKERS
Div. of List Technology Systems
Group Inc
74 Southaven Ave (Suite D)
Medford, NY 11763
Telephone: (631) 758-0984, E-Mail:
info@dmtrackers.com, Web Site:
www.dmtrackers.com
Pres: Kevin Haining
Founded: 2002

DIRECT MARKET DESIGNS INC
45 E 5th St
Paterson, NJ 07524-1101
Telephone: (973) 925-9600, Web Site:
www.dmd-liberty.com
VP: Darwin Guarderas
Employees: 35
Founded: 2001

Catalog & mail order designs.

DIRECT ONE INC
7224 Sandscove Ct (Suite 7)
Winter Park, FL 32792-5921
Telephone: (407) 673-4500, FAX:
(407) 673-4501, E-Mail: wariagno@
directoneinc.com, Web Site: www.
directoneinc.com
CEO: Jeff Lauridsen
Exec VP: William G. Ariagno
Exec Mgr: Vicki Fosdyck
Conducts Business: U.S., Canada
Employees: 25
Primary Market Served: Business
Advertising/Marketing Budget Related
to Direct Marketing: 0-25%
Founded: 2004

Gross sales or billing: $4,000,000
Full service direct mail service.

DIRECT RESPONSE MARKETING
12450 Automobile Blvd
Clearwater, FL 33762
Telephone: (727) 573-1985, Toll Free: (800) 683-6245, FAX: (727) 573-1747, E-Mail: drmclwr@tampabay.rr.com, Web Site: www.dmsmails.com
Pres: Roger Pennington

DIRECTMAIL.COM
Div. of DM Group
201 Skipjack Rd
Prince Frederick, MD 20678-3411
Toll Free: (888) 690-2252, FAX: (301) 855-9810, Web Site: www.directmail.com
VP: Shawn Salta
VP: Robert Salta
VP: Kirk L. Swain
VP, Devel: Price Anderson
Conducts Business: U.S.
Employees: 20
Primary Market Served: Business
Direct online sales
Advertising/Marketing Budget Related to Direct Marketing: 0-25%
Direct Marketing ad budget:
Direct Mail: $200,000
Founded: 1972
Gross sales or billing: $3,000,000
Direct mail fund-raising counsel.

DISPATCH LETTER SERVICE
Subs. of Dispatch Graphics Inc
545 W 45th St (fl 10)
New York, NY 10036
Telephone: (212) 307-5943, FAX: (212) 307-6103, Web Site: www.dispatchletterservice.com
Pres & CEO: Paul A. Grech

DISTRIBUTION POSTAL CO INC
6202 Frankford Ave
Baltimore, MD 21206-4902
Telephone: (410) 488-1002, Toll Free: (800) 992-4525, FAX: (410) 488-2344, E-Mail: louishaber@distpost.com, Web Site: www.distpost.com
Pres: Louis Haber
Founded: 1979

EU SERVICES
203 Log Canoe Cir
Stevensville, MD 21666-9270
Telephone: (410) 643-7900, FAX: (410) 643-7933, E-Mail: clyde_sisk@siskmail.com, Web Site: www.siskmail.com

Pres: Clyde Sisk

ESP PRINTING & MAILING INC
317 E 37th St (Suite 5)
Boise, ID 83714-6475
Telephone: (208) 345-4644, Toll Free: (888) 845-7665, FAX: (208) 345-4765, E-Mail: info@espdirectmail.com
Pres: Ernest S. Puopolo
Direct mailing & custom printing services.

THE ENVELOPE CONNECTION INC
5660 N. Elston Ave.
Chicago, IL 60646
Telephone: (773) 774-4600, FAX: (773) 774-4601, E-Mail: sales@envelopeconnection.com, Web Site: envelopeconnection.com
VP Sls: Andrew Calvimontes

EXCALIBUR ENTERPRISES INC
4820 Bethania Station Rd
Winston Salem, NC 27105-1201
Telephone: (336) 744-5000, Toll Free: (800) 441-4193, FAX: (336) 767-8257, E-Mail: info@excaliburmail.com, Web Site: www.excaliburmail.com
Pres: Jackson D. Wilson Jr
COO: George Newstedt
VP: Mary Craig Tennille
Founded: 1972

FARIS MAILING INC
701 N Holt Rd Ste 3
Indianapolis, IN 46222-3455
Telephone: (317) 246-3315, FAX: (317) 246-3330, E-Mail: info@farismailing.net, Web Site: farismailing.com
Pres: Robert L. Faris Jr
Founded: 1968

FARROW LOGISTICS
Subs. of The Farrow Group
6220 Westar Dr
Windsor, ON, Canada N9J 0B5
Telephone: (844) 532-7769, E-Mail: info@farrowlogistics.com, Web Site: www.farrowlogistics.com
VP Canadian Opers: Scott Lane
Conducts Business: U.S., Canada
Employees: 500
Primary Market Served: Business
Indirect online sales
Advertising/Marketing Budget Related to Direct Marketing: 0-25%
Founded: 1911

Gross sales or billing: $30,000,000
Third party logistics, reduce cost, improve customer service, help build your Canadian market, time definite, returns logistics, pick a pack & more.

FEDEX GROUND
dba FedEx Ground Package System, Inc
1000 FedEx Dr
Coraopolis, PA 15108-9373
Telephone: (412) 269-1000, Toll Free: (800) 762-3725, FAX: (412) 747-4295, Web Site: www.fedex.com/us/ground/main
CEO & Pres: Henry J. Maier
EVP & COO: Michael P Mannion

FINISHING PLUS, INC
4546 W 47th St
Chicago, IL 60632
Telephone: (773) 523-5510, FAX: (773) 523-9155, E-Mail: info@finishingplus.com, Web Site: www.finishingplus.com
VP: Frank Puisis
Founded: 1928
Binding & finishing operations.

FIRST DATA CORP
6200 S Quebec St
Greenwood Village, CO 80111-4729
Telephone: (303) 488-8000, Toll Free: (800) 735-3362, Web Site: www.firstdata.com
VP Mktg: Lisa Fugate

THE FIRST OCCUPATIONAL CENTER OF NEW JERSEY
391 Lakeside Ave
Orange, NJ 07050-2809
Telephone: (973) 672-5800, FAX: (973) 672-0065, E-Mail: ocnj@ocnj.org, Web Site: www.ocnj.org
Pres & CEO: Rocco J. Meola
Admin Asst: Francine Faragi
Founded: 1954

FORM HOUSE INC
Div. of Diam International
4640 S Kolmar Ave
Chicago, IL 60632
Telephone: (773) 577-8500, E-Mail: ktalbot@theformhouse.com, Web Site: www.theformhouse.com
Sr VP: Keith Talbot
Gen Mgr Opers: Dennis Graf
Employees: 250
Founded: 2008
Gross sales or billing: $27,100,000

FOSDICK FULFILLMENT CORP

26 Barnes Industrial Park Rd N
Wallingford, CT 06492
Telephone: (203) 269-0211, Toll Free:
(800) 759-5588, FAX: (203) 679-
3290, E-Mail: sales@fosdickcorp.
com, Web Site: www.
fosdickfulfillment.com
CEO: William Pappas
CIO: John Konstantino
COO: Bob Formica
VP New Bus Dev: George C. Fanolis
Founded: 1999

FREEDOM GRAPHIC SYSTEMS INC

1101 S Janesville St
Milton, WI 53563-1838
Telephone: (608) 868-7007, Toll Free:
(800) 334-3540, FAX: (608) 868-
7006, E-Mail: information@fgs.com,
Web Site: www.
freedomgraphicsystems.com
CEO& Pres: Martin Liebert
Exec VP Sales & Mktg: Jon Singer
Dir Natl Accts: Joan Smuda
Founded: 1986

Operates as a direct mail marketing
company in the United States & Canada. Develops & manages direct mail
programs for its clients.

FULFILLMENT EXPRESS INC

7271 Paramount Blvd
Pico Rivera, CA 90660
Telephone: (562) 948-4400, Toll Free:
(800) 700-9295, FAX: (562) 948-
4459, E-Mail: information@fex.com,
Web Site: www.fex.com
Pres: Dieter Ammann
Founded: 1998

FULFILLMENT PLUS INC

889 Waverly Ave
Holtsville, NY 11742
Telephone: (631) 758-8300, FAX:
(631) 758-8360, E-Mail: jeff.
ehrlich@fulfillmentplusny.com, Web
Site: www.fulfillmentplusny.com
Pres: Jeffrey Ehrlich
Dir Mktg & Client Svcs: Jacqueline
Buonaiuto
Founded: 1983

G-PLEX DIRECT MAIL

194 Morris Ave (Unit 7)
Holtsville, NY 11742-1452
Telephone: (631) 447-9500, FAX: 631-
447-9518, Web Site: www.g-plex.net
Sls Mgr: Glen Faulhaber
VP: Marilyn Craig

Founded: 1975

A wide range of printing needs from
variable digital color printing to offset
lithography including full color sheet &
web printing, binding, stitching, die
cutting, embossing, foil stamping &
other specialized printing capabilities.

GMI DISTRIBUTION

Div. of Gordon Management Inc
305 Churchill Ave
Somerset, NJ 08873
Telephone: (732) 846-4800, FAX:
(732) 846-4709, E-Mail: keith@
gmidistribution.com, Web Site:
www.gmidistribution.com
Pres: Keith Gordon
Mgr: Joann Zemsky

WALTER GARSON JR & ASSOCIATES INC

1370 Adams Rd
Bensalem, PA 19020
Telephone: (215) 245-6610, FAX:
(215) 245-0281, E-Mail: walt@
garsonmail.com
Pres: Walter Garson Jr.
Employees: 25
Founded: 1977

Provides direct mail advertising services, offset printing advertising campaign services, promotional printing,
publication printing, stationery printing, bag printing, security instruments
printing, textile printing & technical
manual sheet printing.

GOODKIND & GOODKIND DIRECT INC

1433 11 St (Suite I)
Arcata, CA 95521-5712
Telephone: (712) 347-6114, Toll Free:
(800) 690-9342, FAX: (712) 347-
5754, E-Mail: mail@goodkind.com,
Web Site: www.goodkind.com
COO & CFO: Dan Goodkind
Pres: Kathi Goodkind
Founded: 1986

GORDON MANAGEMENT INC

aka GMI Distribution
60 Clyde Rd
Somerset, NJ 08873-3486
Telephone: (732) 846-4800, FAX:
(732) 846-4709, E-Mail: keith@
gmidistribution.com, Web Site:
www.gmidistribution.com
Pres: Keith Gordon
VP: Kenneth Gordon
Sales Exec: Linda Lynch
Founded: 1993

GRAPHNET INC

40 Fulton St Fl 28
New York, NY 10038-5074
Telephone: (212) 994-1100, Toll Free:
(800) 327-1800, FAX: (212) 994-
1188, E-Mail: custsvc@graphnet.
com, Web Site: www.graphnet.com
Pres & CEO: Yaakov Elkon
COO: Idan Elkon
VP Fin: Guy Conte
Founded: 1968

Provides integrated data messaging
technology & services.

HAND ASSEMBLY & PACKAGING INC (HAPI)

Div. of Your Mail Sack Inc
PO Box 617
Plainview, NY 11803-0019
Telephone: (718) 699-3400, FAX:
(718) 699-3409

Information service primarily engaged
in publishing directories, mailing lists
& collections or fact compilations.

THE HELICOPTER GROUP

200 W Beaver Creek Rd (Unit 1)
Richmond Hill, ON, Canada L4B 1B4
Telephone: (416) 222-3835, Web Site:
www.thehelicoptergroup.com
Pres: Kishan Gunasekaram
Founded: 1996

THE HIBBERT GROUP

400 Pennington Ave
Trenton, NJ 08618-3105
Telephone: (609) 394-7500, Toll Free:
(800) 545-4747, FAX: (609) 695-
6553, Web Site: www.hibbertco.com
Sr VP: Michelle Spedding
Co-Chmn & CEO: Timothy J Moonan
Co-Chmn: Thomas J Moonan
Sr VP Client Services: Rosemary M
Hober
Sr VP Info Tech: Kenneth J Swiatkow-
ski

HIGH COTTON

2901 Alton Way
Birmingham, AL 35210
Toll Free: (877) 838-2345, FAX: (205)
836-5587, E-Mail: sales@
highscottonusa.com, Web Site: www.
highcottonusa.com
Pres: Thomas S. McGahey
Conducts Business: U.S.
Employees: 100
Primary Market Served: Business &
Consumer
Advertising/Marketing Budget Related
to Direct Marketing: 76-100%

Founded: 1963

Full service direct marketing and fulfillment company - our suite of services include: database marketing, lists, data processing, printing, lettershop and fulfillment.

HOGARD BUSINESS SERVICES INC
PO Box 748
Kankakee, IL 60901-0748
Telephone: (815) 932-1835, FAX: (815) 932-4793, E-Mail: hogards@att.net, Web Site: www.hogardbusinessservices.com
Pres: Myrna Sullivan

Direct mail advertising services.

HOWELL MARKETING SERVICES
Div. of F.M. Howell & Co
100 E Miller St
Elmira, NY 14904
Telephone: (607) 734-6291, FAX: (607) 734-6759, E-Mail: jjs@howellmarketingservices.com, Web Site: www.howellmarketingservices.com
Pres: Katherine H. Roehlke

Prescription drug fulfillment & distribution services for the healthcare industry.

IDEAGROUP MAIL SERVICE
4455 White Bear Pkwy
Saint Paul, MN 55110
Telephone: (651) 490-2903, FAX: (651) 490-0728, E-Mail: ideagroup@visi.com
Owner: Steven Butler
Employees: 15
Founded: 1994
Gross sales or billing: $600,000

IMAGINE FULFILLMENT SERVICES
14245 Artesia Blvd
La Mirada, CA 90638
Telephone: (310) 217-4610, FAX: (310) 217-9632, E-Mail: andya@imaginefulfillment.com, Web Site: www.imaginefulfillment.com
Owner: Andy Arvidson
Co Owner: Jim Heffernan
Conducts Business: U.S.
Employees: 300
Primary Market Served: Business
Catalog available online
Advertising/Marketing Budget Related to Direct Marketing: 0-25%
Direct Marketing ad budget: $250,000
Direct Mail: 25%
Magazines: 25%
Newspapers: 25%

Telephone: 25%
Founded: 1998
Gross sales or billing: $20,000,000
Services include - pick, pack & ship. For direct mailers, e-commerce promotional items, sweepstakes, DRTV, POP.

IMPACT MAILING
4600 Lyndale Ave N
Minneapolis, MN 55412-1408
Telephone: (612) 521-6245, FAX: (612) 521-1349, E-Mail: sales@impactmailing.com, Web Site: www.impactmailing.com
Pres: Mark Anderson

IMPRESSIONS DIRECT
2116 59th St
Saint Louis, MO 63110-2808
Telephone: (314) 951-2100, Web Site: www.impressions-direct.com
Owner: Richie Graham
Sales Exec: John Moresi
Founded: 2000

INNOTRAC CORP
6465 E Johns Xing Ste 400
Duluth, GA 30097-1581
Telephone: (678) 584-4000, FAX: (678) 475-5840, Web Site: www.innotrac.com

INNOVATIVE INDUSTRIES INC
421 W Centennial Ave
Carthage, MO 64836-3528
Telephone: (417) 358-6891, Toll Free: (800) 344-7467, FAX: (417) 358-1849, E-Mail: info@innovativeindustries.com, Web Site: www.innovativeindustries.com
Exec Dir: Jeff Jones
HR Exec: Cammy Barton
Founded: 1969

INTEGRATED MAIL INDUSTRIES LTD
3450 W Hopkins St
Milwaukee, WI 53216-1700
Telephone: (414) 908-3500, FAX: (414) 449-2906, E-Mail: sales@integratedmail.com, Web Site: www.integratedmail.com
HR Mgr: Gail Rulle

Full-service lettershop & direct mail company offering comprehensive print, mail & data management services.

INTERACT DIRECT MARKETING INC
787 Industrial Rd
London, ON, Canada N5V 4J4

Telephone: (519) 439-6245, Web Site: www.interactdirect.com
Pres: Jeffrey B Bisset
Founded: 1992

Direct mail advertising services.

INTERNATIONAL DIRECT RESPONSE SERVICES LTD
10159 Nordel Ct
Delta, BC, Canada V4G1J8
Telephone: (604) 951-6855, Web Site: www.idrs.ca
Pres & CEO: Mark Weeks
Founded: 1989

A catalog & mail-order house.

INTERNATIONAL MAILING SOLUTIONS LLC
25 Corporate Dr (Suite 175)
Burlington, MA 01803-4243
Telephone: (718) 376-5000, Web Site: www.mailims.com
Mng Partner: Gary Hardam
Employees: 13
Founded: 1998
Gross sales or billing: $1,400,000

INTERSTATE EDP & DIRECT MAIL CENTER INC
754 4th Ave
Brooklyn, NY 11232-1414
Telephone: (718) 965-2500, FAX: (718) 965-2504, E-Mail: info@interstateedp.com, Web Site: www.interstateedp.com
Pres: Max Houss
Employees: 60
Founded: 1984
Gross sales or billing: $16,738,333

IRON MOUNTAIN FULFILLMENT SERVICES
565 Sinclair Frontage Rd
Milpitas, CA 95035
Telephone: (408) 945-1600, FAX: (408) 946-1135, E-Mail: info@comac.com, Web Site: www.ironmountain.com
Chmn: C. Richard Reese

IRRESISTIBLE INK INC
Subs. of Hallmark Cards Inc
4444 Haines Rd
Duluth, MN 55811
Telephone: (218) 336-4200, Toll Free: (800) 543-8396, Web Site: www.irresistibleink.com
Employees: 300
Founded: 1998
Gross sales or billing: $18,900,000

JC DIRECT MAIL INC
4241 Williams Rd

Groveport, OH 43125
Telephone: (614) 836-4848, FAX:
(614) 836-4847
Pres: Wayne Caltrider
HR Mgr: Mary Ritchey
Employees: 200
Founded: 1985

Direct mail advertising services.

JHL MAIL MARKETING INC

3100 Borham Ave
Stevens Point, WI 54481-5097
Telephone: (715) 341-0581, Toll Free:
(800) 236-0581, FAX: (715) 341-
9645, E-Mail: ren@jhl.com, Web
Site: www.jhl.com
Pres: Joseph Leek
Sls Exec: Jim Felhorfer
Supvr: Lorena Berry
Fin Exec: Sharon Dennis
Founded: 1985

Specializes in data processing, variable
data printing & mailing services.

JLS MAILING SERVICES INC

672 Crescent St
Brockton, MA 02302-3360
Telephone: (508) 313-1050, Toll Free:
(866) JLS-MAIL, FAX: (508) 313-
1093, E-Mail: rparkinson@jlsms.
com, Web Site: www.jlsms.com
Pres: James Clark
VP Sls: Ron Parkinson
Acct Exec: Tim Regan
Founded: 1983

Provides postal automation (presort),
data processing, database management,
lettershop & inventory management.

JENCO PRODUCTIONS INC

401 S J St
San Bernardino, CA 92410-2605
Telephone: (909) 381-9453, FAX:
(909) 383-1106, Web Site: www.
jencoproductions.com
Sls Pres: Jennifer Imbriani
Gen Mgr: Roger Imbriani
Pres: Jennifer Degorter
CFO: Hazel Walters
Founded: 1995

Provides mailing & fulfillment, bindery
& packaging services.

JOHNSON & QUIN INC

7460 N Lehigh Ave
Niles, IL 60714-4099
Telephone: (847) 588-4800, FAX:
(847) 647-6949, E-Mail: jqinfo@j-
quin.com, Web Site: www.j-quin.
com
Pres & CEO: Dave Henkel
Exec VP: Robert Arkema
VP Opers: Bob Granat
VP Sales: Andrew Henkel

Dir Mktg: Kay Wilt
Dir HR: Jean Locklund
Employees: 110
Founded: 1876
Gross sales or billing: $22,000,000

Full service direct mail production
company. Services include: pre-press,
printing, data processing, personalization, card imaging, affixing, lettershop,
and hand assembly.

JUST PACKAGING INC

450 Oak Tree Ave
South Plainfield, NJ 07080
Telephone: (908) 753-6700, FAX:
(908) 753-6709, E-Mail: sfischbein@
justpackaging.com, Web Site: www.
justpackaging.com
Pres: Stephen Fischbein
Founded: 1985

Packaging & labeling services.

KAROL MEDIA

375 Stewart Rd
Wilkes-Barre, PA 18773-7600
Telephone: (570) 822-8899, Toll Free:
(800) 526-4773, FAX: (570) 822-
8226, Web Site: www.karolmedia.
com
Owner: Mark Kincheloe
VP: Michael Kincheloe
Founded: 1976

Specializes in packaging & assembly,
digital printing & sheet-fed press services for manuals, direct mail campaigns
& promotional literature, inventory &
warehousing services & distribution of
products to schools, medical groups &
other educational organizations.

KD MAILING & FULFILLMENT SERVICE

6850 N Central Park
Lincolnwood, IL 60712-2704
Telephone: (847) 673-0186, Toll Free:
(866) 330-6245, FAX: (874) 673-
0188, E-Mail: dan@kdmailing.com,
Web Site: www.kdmailing.com
Pres: Hal Cohen
VP: Dan Goldberg
VP, Fulfillment: Jim Schwartz
Sls Assoc: Bill Heynes
Primary Market Served: Business &
Consumer
Founded: 1951

Mailing & fulfillment services.

KEY COMPUTER SERVICE OF CHELSEA

227 E 56th St Rm 403
New York, NY 10022-3775
Telephone: (212) 206-8060, FAX:
(212) 206-8398
Founded: 1991

LSC MARKETING

2207 Cantrell Rd
Little Rock, AR 72203
Telephone: (501) 374-2332, Toll Free:
(866) LSC-MKGT, FAX: (501) 372-
6570, E-Mail: sales@lscmarketing.
com, Web Site: www.lscmarketing.
com
Pres: C. Scott Schuh
Founded: 1994

THE LEAD CONNECTION INC

2300 W Morton St (Suite 131)
Denison, TX 10543
Telephone: (903) 337-1636, Toll Free:
(888) 267-3165, FAX: (903) 337-
1640, E-Mail: chriswithtlc@gmail.
com, Web Site: www.
leadconnections.com
Pres: Chris Etheridge
Primary Market Served: Business &
Consumer
Founded: 1998

Lead generation, targeted lists and in-
house mailing services company.

MBI DIRECT MAIL

710 W New Hampshire Ave
Deland, FL 32720-7231
Telephone: (386) 736-9998, Toll Free:
(800) 359-4780, FAX: (386) 736-
1100, E-Mail: sales@mbidirectmail.
com, Web Site: www.directmail-mbi.
com
Pres & CEO: Jim Grogan
COO: Mike Grogan
Founded: 1989

Services offered include marketing
analysis, concept & creative design,
data management & list rental, full col-
or offset printing, color laser personalization & letter shop mailing services.

MT&L CARD PRODUCTS & FULFILLMENT SERVICES

2911 Kraft Dr
Nashville, TN 37204-3618
Telephone: (615) 254-9471, FAX:
(615) 244-6063, E-Mail: sales@
magticket.com, Web Site: www.
mtlcard.com
Pres: Peter A Pyhrr
Founded: 1982

MVS MAILERS INC

31 Crossways E Rd
Bohemia, NY 11716-1204
Toll Free: (800) 641-7917, FAX: (631)
699-0101, E-Mail: sales@
mvsmailers.com, Web Site: www.
mvsmailers.com
CEO & Pres: Steven Muraco
Sls Exec: Rick Romero

Conducts Business: U.S.
Employees: 35
Primary Market Served: Business
Advertising/Marketing Budget Related
  to Direct Marketing: 0-25%
Direct Marketing ad budget:
Direct Mail: 95%
Magazines: 5%
Founded: 1986
Gross sales or billing: $15,000,000

Advertising, design and printing, international mailing and courier services, shareholder communication and website services.

MACKE BINDERY INC
10355 Spartan Dr
Cincinnati, OH 45215
Telephone: (513) 771-7500, FAX:
  (531) 771-3830, Web Site: www.
  mackebrothers.com
Controller: Joseph D. Macke Sr.
Pres: Bill Macke
VP: Susan Macke
Founded: 1907

MAIL ADVERTISING SERVICES INC
15711 Pagano Ln
Darnestown, MD 20874-3115
Telephone: (301) 762-9015
Pres: Richard Jurgena
Employees: 2
Founded: 1976
Gross sales or billing: $30,000

MAIL HANDLING SERVICES
7550 Corporate Way
Eden Prairie, MN 55344-2045
Telephone: (952) 975-5000, FAX:
  (952) 975-5030, Web Site: www.
  mailhandling.com
Owner: Brian Ostenso
Founded: 2009

THE MAILBOX OF ITHACA INC
1650 Hanshaw Rd
Ithaca, NY 14850-6348
Telephone: (607) 257-3865, Toll Free:
  (800) 382-6348, FAX: (607) 266-
  0508, E-Mail: mailbox@lightlink.
  com, Web Site: www.
  mailboxofithaca.com
Plant Mgr: Cindy Whittaker

MAILING SOURCE
1760 Monrovia Ave (#C1)
Costa Mesa, CA 92627
Telephone: (949) 722-9391
Owner: Cheryl Keating
Employees: 4
Founded: 1995
Gross sales or billing: $500,000

MAILING SPECIALISTS INC
1130 Garden St
Greensburg, PA 15601
Telephone: (724) 832-3840, Toll Free:
  (888) 216-1056, FAX: (724) 832-
  8419, E-Mail: sales@mailmsi.com,
  Web Site: www.mailmsi.com
Contact: David Gallatin
Pres: Bill Rosa
Founded: 1986

MAILMASTER CORP
5115 E Highland Dr
Jonesboro, AR 72401
Telephone: (870) 972-8845, Toll Free:
  (800) 551-7018, FAX: (870) 972-
  0877, E-Mail: info@mail-master.
  com, Web Site: www.mail-master.
  com
Pres: Steve Smith
Founded: 1990

MAILMEN INC
15 Enter Ln
Hauppauge, NY 11749-4897
Telephone: (631) 582-6900, FAX:
  (631) 582-6948, E-Mail: getresults@
  mailmeninc.com, Web Site: www.
  mailmeninc.com
Pres: William Vignola
Dir Sls: Michael Vignola
HR Exec: Jackie Gonzalez
Founded: 1977

MAILWAYS ENTERPRISES INC
6105 Factory Rd (Suite 1)
Crystal Lake, IL 60014-7965
Telephone: (815) 455-4850, FAX:
  (815) 455-7327, E-Mail: dave@
  mailways.com, Web Site: www.
  mailways.com
Pres: David Carson
Founded: 1963

Inkjet addressing, hand assembly & polybagging.

MARCO SALES & INCENTIVES LTD
470 Hardy Rd
Brantford, ON, Canada N3V 6T1
Telephone: (519) 751-2227, Toll Free:
  (888) 636-6161, FAX: (519) 751-
  0561, E-Mail: sales@
  themarcocorporation.com, Web Site:
  www.themarcocorporation.com
Pres: Robert Martin
Employees: 135

Major promotion management company specializing in fulfillment, contest rules and regulations, AD specialties, call centers and letter shop.

MARKET FOCUS DIRECT
aka Market Focus Distribution Services
  Inc
550 Alden Rd (Suite 207)
Markham, ON, Canada L3R 6A8
Telephone: (905) 477-0801, FAX:
  (905) 477-4473, E-Mail: info@
  market-focus.com, Web Site: www.
  market-focus.com
Pres: Paul Gaynor
Employees: 15
Founded: 1985
Gross sales or billing: $2,179,840

MARKETING COMMUNICATION RESOURCE INC
4800 E 345th St
Willoughby, OH 44094-4607
Telephone: (440) 484-3010, FAX:
  (440) 484-3020
Pres: Frank Piunno
Pres: Dominic Piunno
Founded: 1993

MATRIX MANAGER
1430 Blue Oaks Blvd (Suite 280)
Roseville, CA 95747-5156
Telephone: (916) 783-1536, Toll Free:
  (877)-258-9037, E-Mail: info@
  mymatrixmanager.com, Web Site:
  www.mymatrixmanager.com
Pres: Ann Bouchard
Founded: 2006

PJ MCNERNEY & ASSOCIATES INC
440 Northland Blvd
Cincinnati, OH 45240
Telephone: (513) 825-5547, FAX:
  (513) 825-5601, E-Mail: tim@
  pjmcnerney.com, Web Site: www.
  pjmcnerney.com
Pres: Patrick McNerney

MERCURY PRINT & MAIL CO INC
1110 Central Ave
Pawtucket, RI 02861-2262
Telephone: (401) 724-7600, FAX:
  (401) 724-9920, Web Site: www.
  mpmri.com
CEO: Peter H. Ottmar
Sls Exec: Al Ervey
Founded: 1995
Gross sales or billing: $10,800,000

MEYER FULFILLMENT
Div. of William B Meyer Inc
255 Long Beach Blvd
Stratford, CT 06615-7117

Telephone: (203) 375-5801, Toll Free: (800) 873-6393, E-Mail: vdarish@meyerfulfillment.com, Web Site: www.meyerfulfillment.com
Dir Sls: Peter Oman
Bus Devel: Christine Quinn
Founded: 1915

MID-CENTRAL PRINTING & MAILING INC
1225 Central Ave
Wilmette, IL 60091
Telephone: (847) 251-4040, FAX: (847) 251-8615, E-Mail: mcpm1910@yahoo.com, Web Site: www.mcpm.com
VP: Carrie Korzak
Founded: 1974

MIDPOINT NATIONAL INC
1263 Southwest Blvd
Kansas City, KS 66103-1901
Telephone: (913) 362-7400, Toll Free: (800) 228-4321, FAX: (913) 362-7401, E-Mail: info@midpt.com, Web Site: www.midpointorderfulfillment.com
Pres: Ronald Freund
Founded: 1988

MYSTIC LOGISTICS INC
2187 New London Tpke
South Glastonbury, CT 06073
Telephone: (860) 659-1566, Toll Free: (800) 969-1566, FAX: (860) 659-1420, Web Site: www.mysticlogistics.com
VP Opers: Joanne V. Sproull
Founded: 1989

Direct mail & marketing materials distribution company.

NATIONAL FULFILLMENT SERVICES
100 Pine Ave
Holmes, PA 19043-1444
Telephone: (610) 532-4700, Toll Free: (800) NFS-1306, FAX: (610) 586-3232, E-Mail: tkrueger@nfsrv.com, Web Site: www.nfsrv.com
Pres: Eugene C. Krueger
VP Mktg: Thomas Krueger

NORTHWEST MAILING SERVICE INC
5501 W Grand Ave
Chicago, IL 60639-2909
Telephone: (773) 237-2264, Web Site: www.nwmail.com
VP Opers: Thomas Orgler

OBERTHUR CARD SYSTEMS
Div. of De La Rue Plc

4250 Pleasant Valley Rd
Chantilly, VA 20151
Telephone: (703) 263-0100, FAX: (703) 263-0503, E-Mail: info@oberthurcs.com, Web Site: www.oberthurcs.com

ON-DEMAND MAIL SERVICES
2083 Pontiac Rd Ste B
Auburn Hills, MI 48326-2485
Toll Free: (888) 954-6245, Web Site: www.odmailservices.com
Pres: Timothy Laura
Primary Market Served: Business & Consumer

ONTIME COMPANIES
201 Crescent Ave
Chelsea, MA 02150-3072
Telephone: (617) 884-8488, Web Site: www.ontimecompanies.com
Pres: Richard Connolly
Primary Market Served: Business

ONTRAC
2501 S Price Rd (Suite 201)
Chandler, AZ 85286-7897
Telephone: (602) 333-4417, Toll Free: (800) 334-5000

THE ORDER FULFILLMENT GROUP
7313 Mayflower Park Dr
Zionsville, IN 46077-7903
Telephone: (317) 733-7755, FAX: (317) 733-8799, E-Mail: thughes@tofg.com, Web Site: www.tofg.com
Pres: Tony Hughes

PBD WORLDWIDE FULFILLMENT SERVICES
1650 Bluegrass Lakes Pkwy
Alpharetta, GA 30004-7714
Telephone: (770) 442-8633, FAX: (770) 442-9742, E-Mail: sales.marketing@pbd.com, Web Site: www.pbd.com
Chmn & CEO: James E. Dockter

PBM GRAPHICS
415 Westcliff Rd, Greensboro, NC 27409-9786-POST
415 Westcliff Rd
Greensboro, NC 27409
Telephone: (336) 664-5800, Toll Free: (800) 849-8200, FAX: (336) 931-0965, Web Site: www.pbmgraphics.com
Plant Mgr: Steve Welch

PDS INTERNATIONAL MAIL SERVICE
Div Flexible International Mail Systems
85 Corporate Dr
Hauppauge, NY 11788
Telephone: (631) 815-1750, Web Site: www.pdsmail.com; www.internationalmail.com
Pres: Joseph Saggio

PALM COAST DATA LLC
Div. of Kable Media Services
11 Commerce Blvd
Palm Coast, FL 32164-7961
Telephone: (386) 445-4662, FAX: (386) 445-2728, Web Site: www.palmcoastd.com
CEO & Pres.: Rory Burke

PENTERA INC
8650-G Commerce Park Pl
Indianapolis, IN 46268-3126
Telephone: (617) 277-5033, Web Site: www.pentera.com
Dir Consulting Svcs: Claudine Donikian

THE PIONEER GROUP
Subs. of Pioneer Group
316 W 5th St
Waterloo, IA 50701-5508
Telephone: (319) 234-8969, FAX: (319) 234-8518, E-Mail: jslife@thepioneergroup.com, Web Site: www.pioneergroup.com
CEO: James H. Slife

PITNEY BOWES INTERNATIONAL MAIL SERVICES
158 Mount Olivet Ave
Newark, NJ 07114-2114
Toll Free: (800) 521-0080, FAX: (973) 368-6301, E-Mail: marketing@pb.com, Web Site: www.intmail.com

PITTSBURGH MAILING
dba Pittsburgh Mailing Systems, Inc
4777 Streets Run Rd
Pittsburgh, PA 15236-1200
Telephone: (412) 922-8181, FAX: (412) 937-1730, E-Mail: ksmallhoover@pittsburghmailing.com, Web Site: www.pitsburghmailing.com
Pres: Kurt Smallhoover

POLARIS DIRECT
300 Technology Dr
Hooksett, NH 03106-2520
Telephone: (603) 626-5800, E-Mail: info@polarisdirect.net, Web Site: www.polarisdirect.net

Dir: Judith Maloy

POST LINX CORP
Div. of Pitney Bowes
1170 Birchmount Rd
Scarborough, ON, Canada M1P 5E3
Telephone: (416) 752-8100, FAX:
(416) 752-8239, Web Site: www.
postlinx.com
VP Bus Devel: Michael Price

POSTLINK CORP
1475 Startop Rd (Unit 8)
Ottawa, ON, Canada K1B 3W5
Telephone: (613) 741-4538, Web Site:
www.ottawamailingservices.com
CEO: Leonard Mandel
Conducts Business: Canada
Primary Market Served: Business &
Consumer

Direct mail programming and data
services company.

PREMIER DIRECT
MARKETING INC
7725 National Tpke (Unit 100)
Louisville, KY 40214-4803
Telephone: (502) 367-6441, Toll Free:
(800) 737-0205, FAX: (502) 361-
2961, E-Mail: rmeredith@
premierdm.net, Web Site: www.
premierdm.net
Gen Mgr: Rick Meredith

PRODIGY MAILING
SERVICES
389 E South Frontage Rd
Bolingbrook, IL 60440-3029
Telephone: (630) 783-9070, Web Site:
www.prodigymailing.com
Primary Market Served: Business

PROFESSIONAL MAILING
SERVICES INC
12 Commerce St
Springfield, NJ 07081-2996
Telephone: (973) 376-0607, Toll Free:
(800) 238-1316, FAX: (973) 376-
0949, E-Mail: jschobel@profmail.
com, Web Site: www.profmail.com

PROGRESSIVE
DISTRIBUTION SERVICES
INC
5505 36th St SE
Grand Rapids, MI 49512
Telephone: (616) 957-5900, Toll Free:
(800) 304-3699, FAX: (616) 957-
2990, E-Mail: sales@progressive-
commerce.com, Web Site: www.
prodist.com
Pres: John C. McGovern
Bus Devel Coord: Tracey Jobse

PROMOTION FULFILLMENT
CTR
311 21st St
Camanche, IA 52730-9699
Telephone: (563) 259-0105, Toll Free:
(800) 493-7063, FAX: (563) 259-
0110, E-Mail: info@pfcfulfills.com,
Web Site: www.pfcfulfills.com

PROMOTION SUPPORT
SERVICES INC
2832 5th St Ste 1
Rock Island, IL 61201-4027
Telephone: (309) 788-4400, FAX:
(309) 788-4465, E-Mail: dbender@
pss-inc.net, Web Site: www.pss-inc.
net
Pres & CEO: David A. Bender

PROMPT DIRECT
66 Willow Ave (Suite 1)
Staten Island, NY 10305-1848
Telephone: (718) 447-6206, FAX:
(718) 981-7333, E-Mail: info@
promptmailers.com, Web Site: www.
promptmailers.com
Pres: Richard Masucci

QUAD/GRAPHICS
N63 W23075 Hwy 74
Sussex, WI 53089-2827
Telephone: (414) 566-6000, E-Mail:
qgraphics@qg.com, Web Site: www.
QG.com
Pres & CEO: Joel Quadracci

QUANTUMDIGITAL
8702 Cross Park Dr.
Austin, TX 78754-5235
Toll Free: (800) 637-7373, Web Site:
www.quantumdigital.com
Pres & CEO: Steve Damman

RADIAL INC
935 First Ave
King of Prussia, PA 19406
Telephone: (610) 491-7000, Web Site:
www.radial.com
Pres & CEO: Dan Brutto
Pres: Tobias Hartmann
Chief Revenue Officer: Steven Birdsall
Chief Admin Officer: Paul Cataldo
Exec VP & CFO: Fred Pensotti
Conducts Business: Worldwide
Primary Market Served: Business
Founded: 2016

E-commerce company offering order
management, payment processing, order routing fulfillment & analytics
services.

A RAPID MAILING INC
8221 Preston Ct

Jessup, MD 20794-9368
Telephone: (410) 792-4000, Toll Free:
(800) US-RAPID, FAX: (301) 776-
3690, E-Mail: info@rairapid.com,
Web Site: www.rairapid.com
Pres: Neal H. Ruchman

REDI-MAIL DIRECT
MARKETING INC
Subs. of Redi-Direct Inc
5 Audrey Pl
Fairfield, NJ 07004-3401
Telephone: (973) 808-4500, FAX:
(973) 808-5511, E-Mail: sales@
redimail.com, Web Site: www.
redimail.com
Pres: Tom Buckley
Conducts Business: U.S.
Primary Market Served: Business
Founded: 1990

Direct mail, lettershop, fulfillment &
multi-channel direct marketing company.

REES ASSOCIATES INC
1800 SW 2nd St
Des Moines, IA 50315-7147
Telephone: (515) 243-2127, FAX:
(515) 243-1026, Web Site: www.
reesassociates.com
Pres: Stephen D. Lundstrom

RELIABLE MAIL SERVICE
INC
121 Fieldcrest Ave Ste C
Edison, NJ 08837-3658
Telephone: (732) 346-9779, Toll Free:
(800) 773-6338, FAX: (732) 346-
9799, E-Mail: bdobin@
reliablemailservice.com, Web Site:
www.reliablemailservice.com
Pres: Bruce Dobin

RELIANT DATA
PROCESSING
197 Alder Dr
North Aurora, IL 60542-1471
Telephone: (630) 844-4210, FAX:
(630) 844-9530, E-Mail: rdpmail@
aol.com
Pres: Joyce Bousquet

RIVERSIDE ACQUISITION
GROUP LLC
Com-Pak Presort Services Inc.
365 New Albany Rd Ste A
Moorestown, NJ 08057-1105
Telephone: (856) 802-1900, Web Site:
www.com-pak.com
VP Mktg & Bus Devel: Clif McGou-
gall
VP & Gen Mgr: Russ Stewart
Dir Client Svcs: Andrea Giordano

Mgr HR: Dionne Daniels
Provides integrated direct mail production services & fulfillment solutions for the direct mail industry.

THE JOHN ROBERTS CO
9687 E River Rd
Minneapolis, MN 55433
Telephone: (763) 755-5500, Toll Free: (800) 551-1534, FAX: (763) 755-0394, E-Mail: jfoster@johnroberts.com, Web Site: www.johnroberts.com
Pres & CEO: Michael Keene

SP EXPRESS
Div. of Integrated Distribution & Logistics Direct LLC
7855 S River Pkwy (Suite 222)
Tempe, AZ 85284
Toll Free: (866) 773-7363, E-Mail: info@spexpress.com, Web Site: www.spexpress.com
Dir: Mich A. Bayley
VP: Dave Crowder
Opers Mgr: Doug Finnie
VP Fin: Daniel Galassi
Controller: Violet McDowell
Conducts Business: U.S., Europe
Primary Market Served: Business & Consumer
Founded: 2002
Full-service e-commerce, fulfillment and marketing logistics company.

SACRED HEART LEAGUE
6050 Hwy 161 N
Walls, MS 38686-0001
Telephone: (662) 781-1360, Toll Free: (800) 232-9079, FAX: (662) 781-3340, E-Mail: comments@shl.org, Web Site: www.shl.org
Pres: Ed Savage

THE SERVICE CENTER LTD
6450 Clara St (Suite 100)
Houston, TX 77041
Telephone: (713) 690-8175, FAX: (713) 690-6844, Web Site: www.calltsc.com
Sr Sls Exec: Gale Pashia

SERVICE MAILERS & FULFILLMENT INC
2468 E 26th St
Vernon, CA 90058-1214
Telephone: (323) 292-0133, FAX: (323) 292-1038, E-Mail: dgsteinhart@gmail.com, Web Site: servicemailersandfulfillment.com
CEO: Marcy Clarke
COO: Mary Dollison
Pres: David Steinhart

Founded: 1975
Full-service mailing & fulfillment provider.

SHAKESPEARE MAILING SERVICE
3107 Central Ave
Union City, NJ 07087
Telephone: (212) 560-8958, E-Mail: support@shakespearemailing.com, Web Site: www.shakespearemailing.com
Pres: Hal Hochhauser

SHEERAN DIRECT MARKETING
71 Southgate Blvd
New Castle, DE 19720-2000
Telephone: (302) 324-0200, Toll Free: (888) 325-2101, FAX: (302) 324-0213, E-Mail: jjs@jjsheeran.com, Web Site: www.jjsheeran.com
Chmn & CEO: Joseph J. Sheeran

SILVERSTATE MARKETING SOLUTIONS
3585 E Patrick Ln (#200)
Las Vegas, NV 89120-6211
Telephone: (702) 489-2124, Web Site: www.silverstateprintmail.com
Pres & Owner: John Evans

ARLEEN SMITH MARKETING INC
60 Mayflower Ln
Stoughton, MA 02072-3024
Telephone: (781) 341-0882, FAX: (781) 344-0710, Web Site: www.arleensmithmarketing.com
Pres: Arleen Smith

SOURCE LINK
500 Park Blvd (Suite 1425)
Itasca, IL 60143-2610
Telephone: (866) 947-6872, FAX: (937) 885-8010, E-Mail: info@sourcelink.com, Web Site: www.sourcelink.com

SOUTHERN FULFILLMENT SERVICES
1650 90th Ave
Vero Beach, FL 32966
Telephone: (772) 226-3321
Primary Market Served: Business & Consumer

SOUTHWEST PUBLISHING & MAILING CORP
2600 NW Topeka Blvd
Topeka, KS 66617-1160
Telephone: (785) 233-5662, Web Site: www.swpks.com

VP: Angie McAtee

SPECIALIZED MAILING SERVICES INC
17451 Nichols Ln (Unit J)
Huntington Beach, CA 92647
Telephone: (714) 274-2284, E-Mail: info@specializedmailing.com, Web Site: www.specializedmailing.com
Pres: Alice Mishica

STAPLES INDUSTRIAL
500 Staples Dr
Framingham, MA 01702-4478
Telephone: (978) 443-9592, Toll Free: (800) 638-9899, FAX: (978) 443-2678

STRATEGIC MARKETING & MAILING
3002 N Apollo Dr, PO Box 6013
Champaign, IL 61826-6013
Telephone: (217) 355-2600, Toll Free: (800) 871-4524, Web Site: www.strategicmail.com
Founder & Pres: Jason Combs
COO: Jeff Combs
Primary Market Served: Business

SUMMIT DIRECT MAIL INC
1655 Terre Colony Ct
Dallas, TX 75212-6222
Telephone: (469) 916-5170, Toll Free: (877) 247-0993, E-Mail: info@summitdm.com, Web Site: www.summitdm.com
Pres: John Barber

SWAN PACKAGING FULFILLMENT
415 Hamburg Tpke (Suite G)
Wayne, NJ 07470-2164
Telephone: (973) 790-8417, FAX: (973) 790-0216, E-Mail: info@swanpkg.com, Web Site: www.swanpackaging.com
Pres: Timothy S. Werkley
Employees: 40
Founded: 1986
SPF provides 3rd party pick-pack fulfillment services for B2C & B2B product marketers in the e-commerce & catalog markets, specializing in books, CDs, clothing, gifts & other products. We offer electronic reports & shipping via USPS, UPS, & FedEx. Our 85,000 sq. ft. facility is located 20 miles from NYC & maintains secured client storage in flow rack, shelving & pallet storage environments. SPF also provides value-added packaging services such as kit assembly & automated packaging.

We are a USPS plant-load-approved vendor, offering bulk mailing services through our in-house post office.

TNT INTERNATIONAL EXPRESS
Div. of TNT USA Inc
68 S Service Rd (Suite 340
Melville, NY 11747-2358
Toll Free: (800) 558-5555

TAUBENPOST INC
20702 Linear Ln
Lake Forest, CA 92630
Telephone: (949) 770-3233, FAX: (949) 380-3940, E-Mail: info@taubenpost.com, Web Site: www.taubenpost.com

THINKDIRECT MARKETING GROUP
8285 Bryan Dairy Rd (Suite 150)
Largo, FL 33777-1306
Telephone: (727) 369-2700, E-Mail: info@tdmg.com, Web Site: www.tdmg.com
Chmn & CEO: Dennis A Cahill

DAVID J THOMPSON MAILING CORP
21 Naus Way
Bloomsburg, PA 17815
Telephone: (570) 759-6690, FAX: (570) 759-7160, E-Mail: sales@thompsonmailing.com, Web Site: www.thompsonmailing.com
Pres: David J. Thompson
Exec VP: Joan E. Thompson

3PL WORLDWIDE INC
500 Bic Dr
Milford, CT 06461-1734
Telephone: (203) 567-1099, Web Site: www.3plworldwide.com
Pres: Clyde Mount

THREESOURCE FULFILLMENT
655 Mulberry
Manteno, IL 60950-9219
Telephone: (815) 936-1094 x4179, Toll Free: (888) 673-4650, FAX: (815) 936-9743, Web Site: www.threesource.tv
Sls Mgr: Toby Cahilll

TRINITY ROAD LLC
PO Box 7445
Charlotte, NC 28241-7445
Telephone: (704) 940-2240

TRIPAR INTERNATIONAL INC
20 Presidential Dr
Roselle, IL 60172
Telephone: (630) 980-5100, Toll Free: (800) 222-1142, FAX: (800) 648-9015, E-Mail: sales@tripar.com, Web Site: www.tripar.com
VP Sls & Mktg: Gretchen Kroll

THE UPS STORE, INC.
6060 Cornerstone Ct W
San Diego, CA 92121-3795
Telephone: (858) 455-8800, FAX: (858) 546-7488, Web Site: www.mbe.com

UNICOR- SERVICES BUSINESS GROUP
400 1st St NW
Washington, DC 20534-0004
Telephone: (202) 305-3500, Web Site: www.unicor.gov/services

UNITED PARCEL SERVICE
dba UPS
55 Glenlake Pkwy NE
Atlanta, GA 30328
Telephone: (404) 828-6000, Toll Free: (800) 874-5877, FAX: (404) 828-6562, Web Site: www.ups.com
Chmn & CEO: D. Scott Davis

US MONITOR
86 Maple Ave
New City, NY 10956-5019
Telephone: (845) 634-1331, Toll Free: (800) 767-7967, FAX: (845) 634-9618, E-Mail: info@usmonitor.com, Web Site: www.usmonitor.com
Pres: Anita Sass

US POSTAL SERVICE- LIBRARY
Corporate Information Services, Information Systems
475 L'Enfant Plz SW
Washington, DC 20260-1540
Telephone: (202) 268-2904, FAX: (202) 268-6436, Web Site: www.usps.com

UNITED WIRE SERVICE
Div. of ChoicePoint
8512 N Allen Rd
Peoria, IL 61615-1527
Telephone: (309) 689-6160, FAX: (309) 689-6488, Web Site: www.unitedwire.net

UNIVERSAL DISTRIBUTION SERVICES
Div. of InnoTrac Inc

4910 Longley Ln (Suite 101)
Reno, NV 89502
Telephone: (775) 332-5700, FAX: (775) 332-5715, E-Mail: sales@udsi.com, Web Site: www.udsi.com

VINCENT GRAPHICS, LLC
PO Box 39, Box 386
Hilliard, OH 43026-0039
Telephone: (614) 771-5440, Toll Free: (800) 331-0517, FAX: (614) 771-5449
Pres & CEO: Ty Vincent

WELLS MAILING
4521 Troy Hwy
Montgomery, AL 36116-5121
Telephone: (334) 286-4667, FAX: (334) 286-6008, E-Mail: info@wellsprinting.com, Web Site: www.wellsprinting.com
CEO: Pat Parvin

Full service direct mail letter shop and presort service.

WIT POSTAL LOGISTICS LLC
350 N La Salle Dr (Suite 1100)
Chicago, IL 60654-5131
Telephone: (815) 215-5100, Web Site: www.witpostal.com

WOLFF/SMG
Div. of SMG Direct, Inc
1641 Commons Pkwy
Macedon, NY 14502-9190
Telephone: (315) 986-1155, FAX: (315) 986-1161, E-Mail: rdelmonte@wolff-smg.com, Web Site: www.wolff-smg.com
CEO: Ray Del Monte

WOLVERINE SOLUTIONS GROUP
1601 Clay St
Detroit, MI 48211-1902
Telephone: (313) 873-6800, FAX: (313) 873-8730, Web Site: www.wolverinemail.com
CEO: Bob Tokar

WOOD & ASSOCIATES DIRECT MARKETING SERVICES LTD
9-1410 Bayly St.
Pickering, ON, Canada L1W 3R3
Telephone: (416) 293-2511, FAX: (416) 293-2594, E-Mail: clientservices@wood-and-associates.com, Web Site: www.wood-and-associates.com
Pres: Annabelle Wood

XPO
3541 Lomita Blvd
Torrance, CA 90505-5016
Telephone: (310) 784-8485, Web Site:
www.xpomail.com
CEO: Kelly Herold-Martinez
Primary Market Served: Business &
Consumer

ZACHRY ASSOCIATES INC
500 Chestnut (Suite 2000)
Abilene, TX 79602
Telephone: (325) 677-1342, E-Mail:
bnutt@zachryinc.com, Web Site:
www.zachryinc.com
VP Mktg: Bob Nutt

ZIP MAILING SERVICES INC
6304 Sheriff Rd (Suite Z)
Landover, MD 20785-4361
Telephone: (301) 386-3633, FAX:
(301) 386-3637, E-Mail: zipmail@
zipmailing.com, Web Site: www.
zipmailing.com
Pres: Charlain L Bland

ALABAMA

ASK, 5815 Carmichael Rd, Montgomery, 36117

ARIZONA

Direct Response Enhancements LLC, 12772 E Sunnyside Dr, Scottsdale, 85259-3438

TeleDirect International Inc, 17255 N 82nd St, Scottsdale, 85255

Virido LLC, 6626 E Oberlin Way, Scottsdale, 85266-6786

ARKANSAS

The Heritage Co, 2402 Wildwood Ave (Suite 500), North Little Rock, 72120-5094

CALIFORNIA

Alorica Inc, 5 Park Plaza (Suite 1100), Irvine, 92614-8502

Ansafone Communications, 145 E Columbine Ave, Santa Ana, 92707-4401

Answering 365, 3699 Wilshire Blvd (#850), Los Angeles, 90010-2718

Direct Marketing Partners, 2045 Hallmark Dr (Suite 5), Sacramento, 95825-2224

LanguageLine Solutions, 1 Lower Ragsdale Dr (Bldg 2), Monterey, 93940-5747

LiveOps Inc, 555 Twin Dolphin Dr (Suite 400), Redwood City, 94065-2132

Lucas & Associates, 617 N Seventh St, Montebello, 90640-3536

Marketeers, PO Box 3571, Mission Viejo, 92690-1571

Omega Mobile, 350 Townsend St Ste 220, San Francisco, 94107-1671

SmartReply Inc, 6410 Oak Canyon Rd (Suite 100), Irvine, 92618-5225

Telecom Inc, 2201 Broadway (Suite 103), Oakland, 94612-3028

TollFreeForwarding.com, 9841 Airport Blvd (fl 9), Los Angeles, 90045-5421

COLORADO

Mountain West Communications Inc, 110 E Hotchkiss Ave, PO Box 216, Hotchkiss, 81419

CONNECTICUT

American Customer Care Inc, 225 N Main St, Bristol, 06010-4997

Frontier Communications Corp, 3 High Ridge Dr, Stamford, 06905-3806

Lester Inc, 19 Business Park Dr (Suite A), Branford, 06405-2936

Scholastic Direct Mktg, 90 Sherman Tpke, Danbury, 06816-0001

Technology Marketing Corp/TMC, 800 Connecticut Ave, Norwalk, 06854-1631

DISTRICT OF COLUMBIA

TRG World, 1700 Pennsylvania Ave NW (Suite 560), Washington, 20006

FLORIDA

America's Call Center, 7901 Baymeadows Way (Suite 14), Jacksonville, 32256-8535

ChoiceConnex, 13555 Automobile Blvd (Suite 530), Clearwater, 33762-3838

Global Response Corp, 777 S State Rd 7, Margate, 33068-2803

Interactive Response Technologies Inc, 4500 N State Rd Seven (Suite 301), Fort Lauderdale, 33319

Alan Morgan & Associates Inc, 2854 Lake Vista Rd, Jacksonville, 32223-7934

The Office Gurus, 10055 Seminole Blvd, Seminole, 33772-2539

One World Telecom, 2620 SW 27th Ave, Miami, 33133

Prosodie Interactive, 855 SW 78th Ave (Suite 100), Plantation, 33324-3223

Teleperformance Interactive, 1601 Washington Ave (Suite 400), Miami Beach, 33139-3166

White Point Leads Group LLC, 362 Gulf Breeze Pkwy (Suite 350), Gulf Breeze, 32561-4492

Winn Technology Group Inc, 523 Palm Harbor Blvd, Palm Harbor, 34682-0927

GEORGIA

JAK Productions, 3060 Peachtree Rd NW (Suite 875), Atlanta, 30305-2255

Teletrack Inc, 5550-A Peachtree Pkwy (Suite 600), Norcross, 30092

IDAHO

Intelesure LLC, 104 E Fairview Ave (#262), PMB 262, Meridian, 83642-1733

ILLINOIS

APAC Customer Services Inc, 2333 Waukegan Rd Ste W100, Bannockburn, 60015-1545

Afni Inc, 404 Brock Dr, Bloomington, 61701-2654

AmeriCall Group Inc, 1211 W 22nd St (Suite 804), Oak Brook, 60523-3221

CTC Teleservices, 304 N 6th St, De Kalb, 60115-3484

Consolidated Market Response, 700 W Lincoln (Suite 200), Charleston, 61920

Conversational Voice Technologies Corp, 28 N US Highway 12 Apt E, Fox Lake, 60020-1257

Creative Compliance, 900 N Franklin (Suite 706), Chicago, 60610

Edge Teleservices, Inc, 4020 W 111th St (Suite 1102), Oak Lawn, 60453-5783

FTD Group Inc, 3113 Woodcreek Dr, Downers Grove, 60515

Lieber & Associates, 3740 N Lake Shore Dr (Ste 15B-2), Chicago, 60613-4237

National Systems Corp, 414 N Orleans St (Suite 501), Chicago, 60610-4498

ORC ProTel LLC, 17233 Continental Dr, Lansing, 60438-6005

PSI Marketing Consultants Inc, 3501 Algonquin Rd (Suite 350), Rolling Meadows, 60008-3129

TTC Marketing Solutions, 3945 N Neenah Ave, Chicago, 60634-2419

Tele Business USA, 1945 Techny Rd (Suite 3), Northbrook, 60062

INDIANA

American Inbound, 241 E Winslow Rd, Bloomington, 47401-8638

TeleServices Direct, 5305 Lakeshore Pkwy South Dr, Indianapolis, 46268-4113

IOWA

Prism Marketing Group, 111 W Second St, Schaller, 51053

TMone LLC, 2937 Sierra Ct SW, Iowa City, 52240

WS Live LLC, 131 W 10th St, Dubuque, 52001

KANSAS

Blue Valley Tele-Marketing Inc, 1555 Pony Express Hwy, Home, 66438

LOUISIANA

CenturyLink, 100 Centurytel Dr, Monroe, 71203

MAINE

Innovative Marketing Solutions LLC, 121 Target Cir, Bangor, 04401-5717

MARYLAND

TeleRep, 14 Wellham Ave, Glen Burnie, 21061

MASSACHUSETTS

Aspect Softwear, 300 Apollo Dr, Chelmsford, 01824

Carroll Enterprises Inc, 554 Main St, Worcester, 01608-2014

OnBrand24, 100 Cummings Ctr (Suite 306L), Beverly, 01915-6107

Power Seminars, 53 New Ocean St (Suite 3), Swampscott, 01907-1840

Share Group Inc, 79 Chapel St, Newton, 02458-1010

MICHIGAN

Amrigon, 1815 Long Lake Shore Dr, Bloomfield Hills, 48302-1234

Demand Telemarketing Inc, 377 Fisher Rd (Suite D), Grosse Pointe, 48230-1600

DialogDirect, 300 E Big Beaver Rd (Suite 400), Troy, 48083-1266

Minacs Worldwide, 34115 W Twelve Mile Rd, Farmington Hills, 48331-3368

MINNESOTA

A Marketing Resource, 1185 Concord St N (Suite 228), South St Paul, 55075-1157

Answer America, 1600 University Ave (Suite 208), Saint Paul, 55104-3825

Arrowhead Promotion & Fulfillment, 1105 Eighth St SE, Grand Rapids, 55744-4099

CareCall Inc, 200 14th Ave E, Sartell, 56377-4500

The Connection Contact Center Services, 11351 Rupp Dr, Burnsville, 55337-1200

The Connection Outsourced Call Ctr, 11351 Rupp Dr, Burnsville, 55337-1200

CustomerLink, 11 E Superior St Ste 430, Duluth, 55802-3013

Meyer Associates Teleservices, 14 7th Ave N, Saint Cloud, 56303-4753

Tele Resources Inc, 222 W Superior St Ste 100, Duluth, 55802-1940

Time Communications, 4444 Centerville Rd (Suite 245), Saint Paul, 55127-3712

MISSOURI

Communication Solutions LLC, 1655 S Enterprise Ave (Suite B4), Springfield, 65804-1864

800 Call KC, 1616 N Corrington Ave, Kansas City, 64120

USA 800 Inc, 9808 E 66 Ter, Raytown, 64133

NEBRASKA

Affinitas Corp, PO Box 728, Boys Town, 68010-0728

CSG Interactive Messaging, 2525 N 117th Ave, Omaha, 68164-3679

CSS Direct, 3707 N 200th St, Elkhorn, 68022-2922

Call Interactive, 10910 Mill Valley Rd, Omaha, 68154-3930

Quality Contact Solutions Inc, 808 4th St, Aurora, 68818-2201

Telenational Marketing, 2918 N 72nd St, Omaha, 68134-5107

Timberline Total Solutions LLC, 8429 Blood St, Omaha, 68134-1051

US Data Corp, 17310 Wright St (Suite 100), Omaha, 68130-2405

NEW HAMPSHIRE

Marketing Connections Corp, 55 S Commercial St (Suite 101), Manchester, 03101-2606

NEW JERSEY

Centrac Inc, 759 Bloomfield Ave (#359), West Caldwell, 07006-6701

Colwell & Salmon Communications Inc, 100 Hillside Ave, Cresskill, 07626-1612

Cyber City Teleservices Marketing Inc, 401 Hackensack Ave (fl 3), Hackensack, 07601-6405

DialAmerica Marketing Inc, 960 Macarthur Blvd, Mahwah, 07430-2040

Person to Person Marketing LLC, 8 N Corporate Dr, Riverdale, 07457

Selltel Inc, 393 Mantoloking Rd, Brick, 08723

TMP Direct, PO Box 308, Budd Lake, 07828-0308

NEW YORK

Atlantic Business Products, 134 W 26th St, New York, 10001-6803

Call Compliance Inc, 90 Pratt Oval, Glen Cove, 11542-1413

ETI Sales Support, 465 Columbus Ave Ste 280, Valhalla, 10595-2301

King Teleservices, 48 Wall St Fl 23, New York, 10005-2922

Joel Linchitz Consulting Services/ Phone for Success, 2578 Broadway (Suite 135), New York, 10025

Milberg Penn International, 116 Radio Cir (Suite 206), Mount Kisco, 10549-2632

PTM Communications, 330 W 38th St (Suite 801), New York, 10018-8465

SpeechSoft Inc, 49 The Crossing, Armonk, 10504

Stratmar Systems Inc, 109 Willet Ave, Port Chester, 10573

NORTH CAROLINA

1-800-DialWord.com, 1095 E King St Box 10, Boone, 28607-4325

Walker & Associates, 7129 Old Hwy 52 N, PO Box 1029, Welcome, 27374-1029

OHIO

Incept Corp, 4150 Belden Village St NW (Suite 205), Canton, 44718-3643

Influent Inc, 565 Metro Pl S (Suite 250), Dublin, 43017-7312

InfoCision Management Corp, 325 Springside Dr, Akron, 44333-4504

National Administrative Service Co LLC, 400 Metro Pl N (Suite 360), Dublin, 43017-3318

PCCW Teleservices, 565 Metro Pl S (Suite 250), Dublin, 43017-7312

Synergy Direct Marketing Solutions LLC, 480 W Tuscarawas Ave Ste 307, Barberton, 44203-2597

Unicall International Inc, 3250 W Market St, Fairlawn, 44333

OKLAHOMA

United America Advertising Inc, 1018 West Cherry Ave, Enid, 73703

OREGON

Advanced Business Teleservices, Inc, 304 E Main St, Talent, 97540-9752

PENNSYLVANIA

Advanced Telecom Services Inc, 1150 1st Ave (Suite 105), King of Prussia, 19406-1350

AnswerNet Network, 2325 Maryland Rd (Suite 210), Willow Grove, 19090

Thomas L Cardella & Associates, 2100 Kimberton Rd, Kimberton, 19442-0816

Direct Advantage Marketing, 2100 Wharton St Ste 510, Pittsburgh, 15203-1691

Falzone & Associates LLC, 5 Narothyn Rd, Sellersville, 18960-2958

MarketMakers Group Inc, 687 W Lancaster Ave, Wayne, 19087-2545

NCO Financial Systems, 507 Prudential Rd, Horsham, 19044

OKS-Ameridial Inc, 303 Parsons Ave, Bala Cynwyd, 19004

One Call Systems Inc, 155 McCartney Ln, Baden, 15005-2827

Sykes Acquisition, 100 Brandywine Blvd, Newtown, 18940-4000

Telerx, 723 Dresher Rd, Horsham, 19044-2299

Visions Marketing Services, 425 Dolly Dr, Lancaster, 17601-3619

Yellowbook, 2201 Renaissance Blvd, King of Prussia, 19406-2766

RHODE ISLAND

Barterbing.com, 18 Chestnut Ave, Cranston, 02910-4625

Providence Journal Telemarketing, 75 Fountain St, Providence, 02902-0050

SOUTH DAKOTA

Midco Call Center Services, 4901 E 26th St, Sioux Falls, 57110-6950

TENNESSEE

Eperformax Inc, 100 Saddle Springs Blvd (Suite 100), Thompsons Station, 37179-5328

Sitel, 3102 West End Ave (Suite 1000), Two American Center, Nashville, 37203-1324

TEXAS

Aegis Communications, 8201 Ridgepoint Dr, Irving, 75063-3160

Calling Solutions, 2200 McCullough Ave, San Antonio, 78212-3751

Etech Inc, 106 N John Redditt Dr, Lufkin, 75904-2640

Integrated Alliance Limited Partnership, 5800 N Interstate 35 (Suite 200B), Denton, 76207-1438

MKS Marketing Inc, 3404 San Mateo Dr, Austin, 78733

Our Data Works Inc, 1504 Fairway Dr, Lewisville, 75057-2329

Premier Messaging LP, 9850 Sagepike Dr, Houston, 77089-3514

Skytel Communications Inc, 1720 Lakepoint Dr, Lewisville, 75057-6408

Sturner & Klein, 4301 Cambridge Rd, Fort Worth, 76155-2627

Telesystems Marketing Inc, 3600 S Gessner Rd (Suite 250), Houston, 77063

Warrantech Direct Inc, 2200 Hwy 121 (Suite 105), Bedford, 76021-5983

UTAH

Convergys Corp, 1400 W 4400 S, Ogden, 84405-3300

VIRGINIA

Access Worldwide Communications Inc, 6402 Arlington Blvd Ste 400, Falls Church, 22042-2343

Bridgewell Associates, 405 S Union St, Alexandria, 22314-3825

Neustar Inc, 21575 Ridgetop Cir, Sterling, 20166

Public Interest Communications Inc, 7700 Leesburg Pike (Suite 301), Falls Church, 22043

WASHINGTON

T-Mobile, 12920 SE 38th St, Bellevue, 98006-1350

WISCONSIN

Alta Resources (West Coast Office), 120 N Commercial St, Neenah, 54956-3006

AnSer Services, 2761 Allied St, Green Bay, 54304

Charlton, 222 W Washington Ave (Suite 200), Madison, 53703-2719

iMarketing Solutions Group Inc, 700 W Virginia St (Suite 700), Timbers Building, Milwaukee, 53204-1555

Spectrum Communication Services Inc, 125 N Executive Dr Ste 300, Brookfield, 53005-6035

Torcom Inbound Telemarketing, 25 Kessel Ct (Suite 107), Madison, 53711-6227

CANADA

British Columbia

MarCom Technologies, 337 Rio Dr S, Kelowna, V1V 2B1

Manitoba

Integrated Messaging Inc, 550 Berry St, Winnipeg, R3H 0R9

Ontario

Omega Direct Response Inc, 30 Wertheim Ct (Unit 12), Richmond Hill, L4B 1B9

Ventriloquist Voice Solutions International Inc, 5025 Orbitor Dr (Suite 300), Bldg 1, Mississauga, L4W 4Y5

Voicelogic, 662 King St W, Toronto, M5V 1M7

Quebec

Voxdata Telecom, 1155 Metcalfe St (Suite 1860), Montreal, H3B 2V6

Saskatchewan

Marketlinc, 105 21 St E (Suite 100), Saskatoon, S7K 0B3

A MARKETING RESOURCE
1185 Concord St N (Suite 228)
South St Paul, MN 55075-1157
Telephone: (651) 451-1765, Web Site:
  www.amr-advantage.com
Pres: Ed Spagnola

APAC CUSTOMER SERVICES INC
6 Parkway N, Deerfield, IL 60015-2544
2333 Waukegan Rd Ste W100
Bannockburn, IL 60015-1545
Telephone: (847) 374-4980, Toll Free:
  (800) 688-7687, FAX: (847) 236-5453, Web Site: www.
  apaccustomerservices.com

ACCESS WORLDWIDE COMMUNICATIONS INC
6402 Arlington Blvd Ste 400
Falls Church, VA 22042-2343
Telephone: (571) 384-7400, Toll Free:
  (800) 522-3447, FAX: (703) 531-0711, Web Site: www.accessww.com

ADVANCED BUSINESS TELESERVICES, INC
304 E Main St
Talent, OR 97540-9752
Telephone: (541) 535-7878, Toll Free:
  (800) 866-9225, FAX: (541) 535-6942, Web Site: www.abtc.com
Gen Mgr: Gretchen Hartrick

ADVANCED TELECOM SERVICES INC
1150 1st Ave (Suite 105)
King of Prussia, PA 19406-1350
Telephone: (610) 688-6000, Toll Free:
  (800) 247-1287, FAX: (610) 964-9117, E-Mail: sales@advancedtele.
  com, Web Site: www.advancedtele.
  com
Mktg & Sls Dir: Bob Bentz

The leader in automated telepromotion services for over a decade. Extensive industry experience in sweepstakes, contests and games; product information and public affairs; surveys and market research; couponing, sampling and lead generating; web integrated programs. Detailed call reporting, fulfillment, live operator redirect. Turnkey marketing support and unsurpassed customer service.

AEGIS COMMUNICATIONS
8201 Ridgepoint Dr
Irving, TX 75063-3160
Telephone: (972) 830-1800, Toll Free:
  (800) 332-0266, FAX: (972) 830-1801, E-Mail: info@aegisglobal.
  com, Web Site: www.
  aegiscomgroup.com
Sr Dir of Mktg: Kevin Nolan

AFFINITAS CORP
PO Box 728
Boys Town, NE 68010-0728
Telephone: (402) 397-7077, Toll Free:
  (800) 369-6495, FAX: (402) 397-7576, Web Site: www.affinitas.net
Pres: Jim Schinco
VP: Steven Gilbert

AFNI INC
404 Brock Dr
Bloomington, IL 61701-2654
Toll Free: (800) 767-2364, Web Site:
  www.afni.com

ALORICA INC
5 Park Plaza (Suite 1100)
Irvine, CA 92614-8502
Telephone: (909) 606-3600, Toll Free:
  (866) 256-7422, FAX: (909) 606-7708, E-Mail: info@alorica.com,
  Web Site: www.alorica.com
CEO & Founder: Andy Lee

ALTA RESOURCES (WEST COAST OFFICE)
120 N Commercial St
Neenah, WI 54956-3006
Telephone: (920) 751-5800, Toll Free:
  (877) 934-6377, Web Site: www.
  altaresources.com
Employees: 800
Founded: 1995

AMERICALL GROUP INC
1211 W 22nd St (Suite 804)
Oak Brook, IL 60523-3221
Telephone: (630) 955-9100, Toll Free:
  (800) 688-0078, FAX: (630) 955-9955, E-Mail: sales@americallgroup.
  com, Web Site: www.
  americallgroup.com
Chmn & CEO: George Kestler
Conducts Business: U.S.
Primary Market Served: Business &
  Consumer
Catalog available online
Advertising/Marketing Budget Related
  to Direct Marketing: 0-25%
Gross sales or billing: $317,000,000

Full-service, all line insurance agency specializing in mass marketing of insurance products to the customers of financial institutions & mortgage companies. Provide outbound telemarketing by licensed agents, database management & customer service.

AMERICAN CUSTOMER CARE INC
225 N Main St
Bristol, CT 06010-4997
Telephone: (866) 400-6886, Web Site:
  www.americancustomercare.com
VP Strategic Sales: Staci Kress

AMERICAN INBOUND
241 E Winslow Rd
Bloomington, IN 47401-8638
Toll Free: (800) 322-6445, FAX: (800)
  224-3583, Web Site: www.
  americanbound.com
Pres: Don Adams

AMERICA'S CALL CENTER
7901 Baymeadows Way (Suite 14)
Jacksonville, FL 32256-8535
Telephone: (904) 224-2000, Toll Free:
  (800) 598-2580, FAX: (904) 737-1107, E-Mail: info@webcallusa.com,
  Web Site: www.webcallusa.com
Pres: Dick Emberson
VP: Barry Krawchuk

AMRIGON
1815 Long Lake Shore Dr
Bloomfield Hills, MI 48302-1234
Telephone: (248) 332-2300, FAX:
  (248) 333-9710
Partner: Richard Smith

ANSAFONE COMMUNICATIONS
145 E Columbine Ave
Santa Ana, CA 92707-4401
Telephone: (714) 560-1000, FAX:
  (714) 560-1035, Web Site: www.
  ansafone.com
Dir Contact Ctr Sls: Stewart Wolfenson

ANSER SERVICES
2761 Allied St
Green Bay, WI 54304
Telephone: (920) 490-7000, Toll Free:
  (800) 723-0000, E-Mail: allanf@
  anser.com, Web Site: www.anser.
  com
Owner: Allan Fromm

ANSWER AMERICA
1600 University Ave (Suite 208)
Saint Paul, MN 55104-3825

Toll Free: (800) 258-2669, FAX: (651) 644-8295, E-Mail: sales@ answeramerica.com, Web Site: www. answeramerica.com

ANSWERING 365
3699 Wilshire Blvd (#850)
Los Angeles, CA 90010-2718
Telephone: (310) 854-4411, Toll Free: (800) 800-4411, FAX: (310) 854-0551, Web Site: www. concordecommunications.com
Pres: Sylviane Herzog

ANSWERNET NETWORK
2325 Maryland Rd (Suite 210)
Willow Grove, PA 19090
Toll Free: (800) 411-5777, FAX: (215) 659-6486, Web Site: www. answernetnetwork.com
CEO: Gary Pudles

ARROWHEAD PROMOTION & FULFILLMENT
1105 Eighth St SE
Grand Rapids, MN 55744-4099
Telephone: (218) 327-1165, FAX: (218) 327-2576, Web Site: www. apfco.com

ASK
5815 Carmichael Rd
Montgomery, AL 36117
Telephone: (334) 387-ASKT, FAX: (334) 387-2759, E-Mail: rburley@ asktelemarketing.com, Web Site: www.asktelemarketing.com
CEO: Rick Burley

ASPECT SOFTWEAR
300 Apollo Dr
Chelmsford, MA 01824
Telephone: (978) 250-7900, FAX: (978) 244-7410, E-Mail: info@ aspect.com, Web Site: www.aspect.com

ATLANTIC BUSINESS PRODUCTS
Ascom
134 W 26th St
New York, NY 10001-6803
Telephone: (212) 741-6400, FAX: (212) 645-1518, E-Mail: info@ tomorrowsoffice.com, Web Site: www.tomorrowsoffice.com
Pres: Larry Weiss

BARTERBING.COM
18 Chestnut Ave
Cranston, RI 02910-4625

Toll Free: (800) 345-6733, FAX: (401) 679-0326, Web Site: www. barterbing.com
Pres: Bill Rosenberg

BLUE VALLEY TELE-MARKETING INC
Subs. of Blue Valley Telephone Co
1555 Pony Express Hwy
Home, KS 66438
Telephone: (785) 799-3500, Toll Free: (800) 882-0803, FAX: (785) 799-3504, E-Mail: info@ bluevalleytelemarketing.com
Gen Mgr: Judy Zimmerling

BRIDGEWELL ASSOCIATES
405 S Union St
Alexandria, VA 22314-3825
Telephone: (703) 360-6500

CSG INTERACTIVE MESSAGING
2525 N 117th Ave
Omaha, NE 68164-3679
Telephone: (402) 398-4100, Toll Free: (800) 888-3151, FAX: (402) 398-4000, Web Site: www.prairiesys.com

CSS DIRECT
3707 N 200th St
Elkhorn, NE 68022-2922
Telephone: (402) 359-1515, FAX: (402) 359-1516, E-Mail: custserv@ cssdirect.com, Web Site: www. cssdirect.com

CTC TELESERVICES
304 N 6th St
De Kalb, IL 60115-3484
Telephone: (815) 748-4200, FAX: (630) 773-4765, Web Site: www. ctcteleservices.com
Pres: Guy J. Scarpelli

CALL COMPLIANCE INC
90 Pratt Oval
Glen Cove, NY 11542-1413
Telephone: (516) 674-4545, FAX: (516) 676-2420, E-Mail: sales@ callcompliance.com, Web Site: www.callcompliance.com
Pres: Alison Garfinkel Andrews
VP Admin: Phyllis Gorham
VP Sales & Mktg: Keith Altman
Conducts Business: U.S.
Employees: 25
Primary Market Served: Business
Direct online sales
Advertising/Marketing Budget Related to Direct Marketing: 76-100%
Direct Marketing ad budget:
Direct Mail: 45%
Magazines: 35%

Newspapers: 10%
Telephone: 10%
Founded: 2001

CALL INTERACTIVE
Subs. of First Data Corp
10910 Mill Valley Rd
Omaha, NE 68154-3930
Telephone: (402) 498-7000, FAX: (402) 498-7900, Web Site: www. callit.com

CALLING SOLUTIONS
2200 McCullough Ave
San Antonio, TX 78212-3751
Telephone: (210) 801-9630, Toll Free: (800) 683-5500, FAX: (210) 491-1777, E-Mail: marketing@ callingsolutions.com, Web Site: www.callingsolutions.com
Pres: Louis Cooper

THOMAS L CARDELLA & ASSOCIATES
2100 Kimberton Rd
Kimberton, PA 19442-0816
Telephone: (610) 933-3822, Web Site: www.tlcassociates.com

CARECALL INC
200 14th Ave E
Sartell, MN 56377-4500
Telephone: (320) 253-0800, Web Site: www.arraysg.com

CARROLL ENTERPRISES INC
554 Main St
Worcester, MA 01608-2014
Telephone: (508) 756-3513, Toll Free: (800) 548-6900, FAX: (508) 770-0528, E-Mail: info@ carrollenterprises.com, Web Site: carrollenterprises.com
Pres & COO: Brian Carroll

CENTRAC INC
759 Bloomfield Ave (#359)
West Caldwell, NJ 07006-6701
Telephone: (973) 402-0999, FAX: (973) 402-0993, Web Site: www. centrac.com

CENTURYLINK
100 Centurytel Dr
Monroe, LA 71203
Telephone: (318) 388-9000, Toll Free: (800) 201-4102, Web Site: centurytel.com

CHARLTON
222 W Washington Ave (Suite 200)
Madison, WI 53703-2719

Telephone: (608) 259-8004, FAX:
(608) 259-8061, E-Mail: jdragisic@
tcgcorp.net, Web Site: www.tcgcorp.
net
Chmn Bd: John Dragisic

CHOICECONNEX
13555 Automobile Blvd (Suite 530)
Clearwater, FL 33762-3838
Telephone: (727) 571-3302, Web Site:
www.choiceconnex.com

COLWELL & SALMON COMMUNICATIONS INC
100 Hillside Ave
Cresskill, NJ 07626-1612
Telephone: (518) 482-1596, Toll Free:
(800) 724-5318, FAX: (518) 482-
1998, E-Mail: sales@colwell-
salmon.com, Web Site: www.
colwell-salmon.com

COMMUNICATION SOLUTIONS LLC
1655 S Enterprise Ave (Suite B4)
Springfield, MO 65804-1864
Telephone: (417) 862-4567, Web Site:
www.comsolllc.com
VP: Tony Ridenour
Primary Market Served: Business

THE CONNECTION CONTACT CENTER SERVICES
11351 Rupp Dr
Burnsville, MN 55337-1200
Telephone: (952) 948-5335, Toll Free:
(800) 883-5777, FAX: (952) 948-
5498, E-Mail: sales@the-connection.
com, Web Site: www.the-connection.
com
Sls & Mktg Specialist: Erin Brooks
VP Sls & Mktg: Tim Austrums

THE CONNECTION OUTSOURCED CALL CTR
11351 Rupp Dr
Burnsville, MN 55337-1200
Toll Free: (800) 883-5777, Web Site:
www.the-connection.com
VP Sls & Mktg: Tim Austrums

CONSOLIDATED MARKET RESPONSE
A McLeod USA Company
700 W Lincoln (Suite 200)
Charleston, IL 61920
Telephone: (217) 348-7050, FAX:
(217) 348-7060
Chmn Bd: Richard A. Lumpkin

CONVERGYS CORP
1400 W 4400 S

Ogden, UT 84405-3300
Telephone: (630) 668-6174, Web Site:
www.convergys.com

CONVERSATIONAL VOICE TECHNOLOGIES CORP
28 N US Highway 12 Apt E
Fox Lake, IL 60020-1257
Telephone: (847) 265-4901, Toll Free:
(800) 994-4400, FAX: (847) 265-
4915, E-Mail: sales@conservit.com,
Web Site: www.conservit.com
Pres: Peter F. Theis

CREATIVE COMPLIANCE
900 N Franklin (Suite 706)
Chicago, IL 60610
Telephone: (916) 216-3379, E-Mail:
info@creativecompliance.com, Web
Site: www.creativecompliance.com
Conducts Business: U.S.
Primary Market Served: Business
Advertising/Marketing Budget Related
to Direct Marketing: 0-25%
Direct Marketing ad budget:
Direct Mail: 50%
Telephone: 50%
Founded: 2003

Help businesses keep current with the
continually changing legislative and
regulatory climate of the teleservices
industry.

CUSTOMERLINK
11 E Superior St Ste 430
Duluth, MN 55802-3013
Telephone: (218) 722-2800, Toll Free:
(866) 245-5569, FAX: (218) 722-
3287, E-Mail: info@
customerlinkone.com, Web Site:
www.customerlinkone.com
Conducts Business: U.S., Canada
Employees: 150
Primary Market Served: Business &
Consumer
Advertising/Marketing Budget Related
to Direct Marketing: 76-100%
Direct Marketing ad budget:
Direct Mail: 20%
Telephone: 80%
Founded: 1988

Call center services, outbound sales, inbound sales and service to the energy
industries and medical industries.

CYBER CITY TELESERVICES MARKETING INC
401 Hackensack Ave (fl 3)
Hackensack, NJ 07601-6405
Telephone: (201) 487-1616, Toll Free:
(800) 213-4144, E-Mail: info@cctll.
com, Web Site: www.cctll.com
Sr VP Bus Devel: Fred Shadding
Conducts Business: U.S.

Employees: 3,000
Primary Market Served: Business &
Consumer
Advertising/Marketing Budget Related
to Direct Marketing: 0-25%
Founded: 1999

Call center & back office processing
services.

DEMAND TELEMARKETING INC
377 Fisher Rd (Suite D)
Grosse Pointe, MI 48230-1600
Telephone: (313) 823-8598, Toll Free:
(888) 977-2256, FAX: (313) 823-
8598, E-Mail: info@create-demand.
com, Web Site: www.create-demand.
com
Pres: William Patterson
Dir Opers: Ronne Newton
Conducts Business: U.S.
Employees: 3
Primary Market Served: Business
Advertising/Marketing Budget Related
to Direct Marketing: 76-100%
Direct Marketing ad budget:
$1,500,000
Direct Mail: 35%
Magazines: 35%
Telephone: 30%
Founded: 2003
Gross sales or billing: $1,500,000

Full service direct & database marketing agency focusing on business to
business lead generation customer acquisition & retention.

DIALAMERICA MARKETING INC
960 Macarthur Blvd
Mahwah, NJ 07430-2040
Telephone: (201) 327-0200, Toll Free:
(800) 531-3131, FAX: (201) 327-
4875, Web Site: www.dialamerica.
com
Pres & CEO: Arthur Conway

DIALOGDIRECT
300 E Big Beaver Rd (Suite 400)
Troy, MI 48083-1266
Telephone: (734) 374-8400, Toll Free:
(800) 523-5867, FAX: (248) 836-
2601, Web Site: www.dialogue-
marketing.com

DIRECT ADVANTAGE MARKETING
2100 Wharton St Ste 510
Pittsburgh, PA 15203-1691
Telephone: (412) 381-2300, E-Mail:
information@dam.com, Web Site:
www.dam.com
Pres: Jay P. Fairbrother

DIRECT MARKETING PARTNERS

2045 Hallmark Dr (Suite 5)
Sacramento, CA 95825-2224
Telephone: (916) 974-6969, Toll Free:
  (800) 909-2626, FAX: (916) 920-
  5156, E-Mail: info@dirmkt.com,
  Web Site: www.
  directmarketingpartners.com
Pres: Debra Da Costa
VP Bus Devel & Strategy: Tom Judge
Conducts Business: U.S., Canada,
  Western Europe
Primary Market Served: Business
Founded: 1991
A B2B direct marketing and teleservices provider. This U.S. based call center specializes in the complex sale and provides metrics-driven refinements to achieve client goals.

DIRECT RESPONSE ENHANCEMENTS LLC

12772 E Sunnyside Dr
Scottsdale, AZ 85259-3438
Telephone: (480) 451-7384, FAX:
  (480) 661-8460, Web Site: www.
  dreteleconsultants.com
Pres: Gail K. Eberlein

ETI SALES SUPPORT

465 Columbus Ave Ste 280
Valhalla, NY 10595-2301
Telephone: (914) 747-3030, Toll Free:
  (800) 466-4384, FAX: (914) 747-
  3466, E-Mail: info@etisales.com,
  Web Site: www.etisales.com
Pres: Michael Falkson

EDGE TELESERVICES, INC

4020 W 111th St (Suite 1102)
Oak Lawn, IL 60453-5783
Telephone: (708) 857-5000, Toll Free:
  (800) 394-2323, FAX: (708) 857-
  5029, E-Mail: contactme@
  edgeteleservices.com, Web Site:
  www.edgeteleservices.com

800 CALL KC

1616 N Corrington Ave
Kansas City, MO 64120
Telephone: (816) 231-4321, Toll Free:
  (800) 722-5554, FAX: (816) 241-
  2743, E-Mail: sales@call-kc.com,
  Web Site: www.call-kc.com

EPERFORMAX INC

100 Saddle Springs Blvd (Suite 100)
Thompsons Station, TN 37179-5328
Telephone: (901) 751-4800, Toll Free:
  (888) 384-7004, FAX: (901) 751-
  4805, E-Mail: info0609@
  eperformax.com, Web Site: www.
  eperformax.com

Pres: Teresa Hartsaw

ETECH INC

106 N John Redditt Dr
Lufkin, TX 75904-2640
Telephone: (936) 633-9333, Web Site:
  www.effectiveteleservices.com
COO: Matt Rocco

FTD GROUP INC

3113 Woodcreek Dr
Downers Grove, IL 60515
Telephone: (630) 719-7800, Toll Free:
  (800) 788-9000, FAX: (630) 719-
  6170, E-Mail: ftdmemberservices@
  ftdi.com, Web Site: www.ftdi.com
CEO & Pres.: John Walden

FALZONE & ASSOCIATES LLC

5 Narothyn Rd
Sellersville, PA 18960-2958
Telephone: (215) 822-8941
Pres: Mary Ann Falzone

FRONTIER COMMUNICATIONS CORP

3 High Ridge Dr
Stamford, CT 06905-3806
Telephone: (203) 614-5600, Web Site:
  www.frontier.com
Pres & COO: Daniel McCarthy
EVP & CFO: R. Perley McBride
Founded: 1927

Telecommunications services & products.

GLOBAL RESPONSE CORP

777 S State Rd 7
Margate, FL 33068-2803
Telephone: (954) 973-7300, Toll Free:
  (800) 537-8000, FAX: (954) 968-
  9862, E-Mail: wendys@
  globalresponse.com, Web Site: www.
  globalresponse.com
Chmn & Owner: Herman Shooster
Co-CEO: Frank Shooster

THE HERITAGE CO

2402 Wildwood Ave (Suite 500)
North Little Rock, AR 72120-5094
Telephone: (501) 835-5000 x1142,
  FAX: (501) 835-5834, Web Site:
  www.theheritagecompany.com
Pres & CEO: John Braune

IMARKETING SOLUTIONS GROUP INC

700 W Virginia St (Suite 700), Timbers
  Building
Milwaukee, WI 53204-1555

Telephone: (414) 224-0701, Toll Free:
  (800) 879-0076, FAX: (414) 224-
  0943, Web Site:
  imarketingsolutionsgroup.com
Dir Opers: Wendy Wenaas
COO: Andrew Langhorne

INCEPT CORP

4150 Belden Village St NW (Suite
  205)
Canton, OH 44718-3643
Telephone: (330) 649-8000, Web Site:
  www.inceptcorp.com
Pres: Jeff White
Primary Market Served: Business &
  Consumer

INFLUENT INC

565 Metro Pl S (Suite 250)
Dublin, OH 43017-7312
Telephone: (614) 280-1600, Toll Free:
  (800) 856-6768, FAX: (614) 280-
  1610, E-Mail: info@influentinc.com,
  Web Site: www.influentinc.com
Pres & CEO: Andrew Jacobs
Conducts Business: U.S., Panama, Philippines
Employees: 1,600
Primary Market Served: Business &
  Consumer
Advertising/Marketing Budget Related
  to Direct Marketing: 0-25%
Direct Marketing ad budget:
Direct Mail: 75%
Telephone: 25%
Founded: 1992
Gross sales or billing: $30,000,000

Provides multi-lingual outsourced sales and customer service and a full service resource for inbound and outbound customer contact solutions. Industry specialization includes financial services, insurance, telecommunications, business services, and Hispanic marketing.

INFOCISION MANAGEMENT CORP

325 Springside Dr
Akron, OH 44333-4504
Telephone: (330) 668-1400, FAX:
  (330) 668-1401, E-Mail: infocision@
  infocision.com, Web Site: www.
  infocision.com
Pres: Gary Taylor

INNOVATIVE MARKETING SOLUTIONS LLC

121 Target Cir
Bangor, ME 04401-5717
Telephone: (207) 262-6233, Web Site:
  www.imsmaine.net
Pres: Vincent Wank

INTEGRATED ALLIANCE LIMITED PARTNERSHIP

5800 N Interstate 35 (Suite 200B)
Denton, TX 76207-1438
Telephone: (940) 565-9415, FAX:
(940) 383-1876, E-Mail: ryoung@
integratedalliance.com, Web Site:
www.integratedalliance.com
CEO: Randy Keylor

INTEGRATED MESSAGING INC

550 Berry St
Winnipeg, MB, Canada R3H 0R9
Telephone: (204) 786-7630, Toll Free:
(800) 561-3734, FAX: (204) 786-
7718, E-Mail: sales@imi.mb.ca, Web
Site: www.imi.mb.ca
Conducts Business: U.S., Canada
Employees: 200
Primary Market Served: Business &
Consumer
Advertising/Marketing Budget Related
to Direct Marketing: 76-100%
Direct Marketing ad budget:
Direct Mail: 5%
Magazines: 80%
Newspapers: 5%
Telephone: 10%
Founded: 1989
Gross sales or billing: $6,000,000

Twenty four seven inbound order entry
& customer service including fulfillment.

INTELESURE LLC

104 E Fairview Ave (#262), PMB 262
Meridian, ID 83642-1733
Telephone: (866) 808-7366, Web Site:
www.intelesure.com

INTERACTIVE RESPONSE TECHNOLOGIES INC

4500 N State Rd Seven (Suite 301)
Fort Lauderdale, FL 33319
Telephone: (954) 484-4973, Toll Free:
(800) 700-3033, FAX: (954) 484-
0818, E-Mail: hglass@callcenter.
com, Web Site: www.callcenter.com

JAK PRODUCTIONS

3060 Peachtree Rd NW (Suite 875)
Atlanta, GA 30305-2255
Telephone: (404) 883-2450, FAX:
(404) 883-2672, E-Mail: info@jak-
productions.com
Pres: Jack Keller

KING TELESERVICES

Div. of DF King
48 Wall St Fl 23
New York, NY 10005-2922
Telephone: (718) 361-4100, Toll Free:
(800) 817-5468, E-Mail: info@king-
teleservices.com, Web Site: www.
king-teleservices.com

LANGUAGELINE SOLUTIONS

1 Lower Ragsdale Dr (Bldg 2)
Monterey, CA 93940-5747
Toll Free: (800) 752-6096, E-Mail:
customercare@languageline.com,
Web Site: www.languageline.com

LESTER INC

19 Business Park Dr (Suite A)
Branford, CT 06405-2936
Telephone: (203) 488-5265, Toll Free:
(800) 999-5265, FAX: (203) 483-
0408, Web Site: www.lesterusa.com
Pres: Rajiv Samant

LIEBER & ASSOCIATES

3740 N Lake Shore Dr (Ste 15B-2)
Chicago, IL 60613-4237
Telephone: (773) 325-9400, FAX:
(773) 325-0621, E-Mail: info@
lieberandassociates.com, Web Site:
www.lieberandassociates.com
Pres: Mitchell A. Lieber

Consultants Enhancing Contact Rent-
ers.

JOEL LINCHITZ CONSULTING SERVICES/ PHONE FOR SUCCESS

Joel Linchitz Associates
2578 Broadway (Suite 135)
New York, NY 10025
Telephone: (212) 431-6700, FAX:
(212) 865-2008, E-Mail:
phoneforsuccess@compuserve.com,
Web Site: www.callcenter-
salestraining.com/index.php
Pres: Joel Linchitz

LIVEOPS INC

555 Twin Dolphin Dr (Suite 400)
Redwood City, CA 94065-2132
Telephone: (408) 844-2400, Web Site:
www.liveops.com
Pur Mgr: Sandy Mar

LUCAS & ASSOCIATES

617 N Seventh St
Montebello, CA 90640-3536
Telephone: (323) 728-7899
Pres: Ned Lucas

MILBERG PENN INTERNATIONAL

116 Radio Cir (Suite 206)
Mount Kisco, NY 10549-2632
Telephone: (914) 239-4300, (914) 241-
0858, E-Mail: contact@
mpioutsourcing.com, Web Site:
www.mpioutsourcing.com
Pres: Jeffrey A. Milberg
Conducts Business: U.S., Worldwide
Employees: 25
Primary Market Served: Business &
Consumer
Advertising/Marketing Budget Related
to Direct Marketing: 76-100%
Direct Marketing ad budget: $10,000
Direct Mail: 65%
Telephone: 35%
Founded: 2005

Program management company for direct marketing, call centers services.

MKS MARKETING INC

3404 San Mateo Dr
Austin, TX 78733
Telephone: (512) 263-8017, Toll Free:
(800) 544-8989, FAX: (402) 333-
9610, E-Mail: info@
telemarketingoutsource.com, Web
Site: www.telemarketingoutsource.
com
Pres: Jerry Schoemann

MARCOM TECHNOLOGIES

337 Rio Dr S
Kelowna, BC, Canada V1V 2B1
Telephone: (250) 868-9352, FAX:
(250) 868-9362
Pres: Henry Schuyler

MARKETEERS

PO Box 3571
Mission Viejo, CA 92690-1571
Telephone: (949) 364-1669, FAX:
(949) 582-0829, E-Mail: wbower@
apc.net
Co-Owner: W. Bower

MARKETING CONNECTIONS CORP

55 S Commercial St (Suite 101)
Manchester, NH 03101-2606
Telephone: (603) 472-8989, Toll Free:
(800) 472-1818, FAX: (603) 472-
9881, E-Mail: lcasey@mccnh.com,
Web Site: www.mcciq.com
Pres: Larry Casey

MARKETLINC

105 21 St E (Suite 100)
Saskatoon, SK, Canada S7K 0B3
Telephone: (306) 956-7000, FAX:
(306) 668-5812, E-Mail: info@
marketlinc.com, Web Site: www.
marketlinc.com
Gen Mgr: Donna Ghuman
Primary Market Served: Business &
Consumer

MARKETMAKERS GROUP INC

687 W Lancaster Ave
Wayne, PA 19087-2545
Telephone: (610) 254-8924, FAX:
(610) 254-9190, E-Mail: rlail@
marketmakers.com, Web Site: www.
marketmakersgroup.com
Pres: Robert Lail
HR Assoc: Karen Boyle
Conducts Business: U.S.
Employees: 70
Primary Market Served: Business
Catalog available online
Direct online sales
Advertising/Marketing Budget Related
to Direct Marketing: 76-100%
Founded: 1996
Gross sales or billing: $21,000,000
Business to business telemarketing.

MEYER ASSOCIATES TELESERVICES

aka Meyer Teleservices
14 7th Ave N
Saint Cloud, MN 56303-4753
Telephone: (320) 259-4000, Toll Free:
(800) 676-9233, FAX: (320) 259-
4044, E-Mail: info@callmeyer.com,
Web Site: www.callmeyer.com
Pres: Lawrence R Meyer
CEO: Nick Gerten

MIDCO CALL CENTER SERVICES

Subs. of Midcontinent Media
4901 E 26th St
Sioux Falls, SD 57110-6950
Telephone: (605) 330-4125, Toll Free:
(800) 843-8800, FAX: (605) 357-
5414, Web Site: www.midcocall.com
Gen Mgr: Doreen West

MINACS WORLDWIDE

34115 W Twelve Mile Rd
Farmington Hills, MI 48331-3368
Telephone: (416) 380-3800, FAX:
(416) 380-3830, E-Mail: info@
minacs.com, Web Site: www.minacs.
com
Chmn & CEO: Elaine Minac

ALAN MORGAN & ASSOCIATES INC

2854 Lake Vista Rd
Jacksonville, FL 32223-7934
Telephone: (904) 262-1316, FAX:
(904) 880-6182, E-Mail: amorgan@
alanmorgan.com, Web Site: www.
alanmorgan.com
Pres: Alan Morgan

MOUNTAIN WEST COMMUNICATIONS INC

110 E Hotchkiss Ave, PO Box 216
Hotchkiss, CO 81419
Telephone: (970) 872-2500, Toll Free:
(800) 642-9378, FAX: (970) 872-
3862, E-Mail: sales@mountainwest.
com, Web Site: www.mountainwest.
com
CEO: Kirby Clock

NCO FINANCIAL SYSTEMS

Subs of NCO Group Inc
507 Prudential Rd
Horsham, PA 19044
Telephone: (215) 441-3000, Toll Free:
(800) 220-2274, FAX: (215) 441-
3923, E-Mail: marketing@ncogroup.
com, Web Site: www.ncogroup.com
Sr VP Mktg: Lisa Hagee

NATIONAL ADMINISTRATIVE SERVICE CO LLC

400 Metro Pl N (Suite 360)
Dublin, OH 43017-3318
Telephone: (614) 358-1500
Member: Haytehm ElZayn
Primary Market Served: Business

NATIONAL SYSTEMS CORP

414 N Orleans St (Suite 501)
Chicago, IL 60610-4498
Telephone: (312) 855-1000, FAX:
(312) 222-1605, E-Mail: support@
nationalsystems.com, Web Site:
www.nationalsystems.com
Sls Mgr: Eric Beamont

NEUSTAR INC

21575 Ridgetop Cir
Sterling, VA 20166
Telephone: (571) 434-5400, Toll Free:
(877) 245-5277, E-Mail:
billingsupport@neustar.biz, Web
Site: www.neustar.biz
VP Mobile Svcs: Lisa Hook
Sr VP & CFO: Paul Lalljie
Sr VP & CMO: Steven Wolfe Pereira
Conducts Business: Worldwide
Primary Market Served: Business
Founded: 1996

A global information and analytics
services provider for the Internet, telecommunications, entertainment & marketing industries.

OKS-AMERIDIAL INC

303 Parsons Ave
Bala Cynwyd, PA 19004
Telephone: (610) 667-3000, FAX:
(610) 667-3002, E-Mail: info@
oksgroup.com, Web Site: www.
oksameridial.com

Pres & CEO: Vinit Khanna

ORC PROTEL LLC

17233 Continental Dr
Lansing, IL 60438-6005
Telephone: (708) 418-7413, FAX:
(708) 418-7457, Web Site: www.
orcprotel.com
CEO: Ruth R. Wolf
Exec VP Mktg: Allen E. Wolf

THE OFFICE GURUS

10055 Seminole Blvd
Seminole, FL 33772-2539
Telephone: (727) 803-7114, Web Site:
www.theofficegurus.com
Mng Dir: Dominic Leide

OMEGA DIRECT RESPONSE INC

30 Wertheim Ct (Unit 12)
Richmond Hill, ON, Canada L4B 1B9
Telephone: (905) 482-2340, FAX:
(905) 482-9721, E-Mail: odrsales@
omegadirect.com, Web Site: www.
omegadirect.com
Pres & CEO: Bharat Hansraj
VP & COO: Everton Thompson
CFO: Paul Pullano
Conducts Business: U.S., Canada,
Worldwide
Primary Market Served: Business &
Consumer
Founded: 1997
Gross sales or billing: $22,000,000
Telemarket for various clients.

OMEGA MOBILE

350 Townsend St Ste 220
San Francisco, CA 94107-1671
Telephone: (415) 596-6342, Web Site:
www.omegamobile.com

ONBRAND24

100 Cummings Ctr (Suite 306L)
Beverly, MA 01915-6107
Toll Free: (855) 662-7263

ONE CALL SYSTEMS INC

155 McCartney Ln
Baden, PA 15005-2827
Telephone: (412) 415-5000, Toll Free:
(800) 845-9945, FAX: (412) 415-
5023, E-Mail: jmcnamara@1-call.
com, Web Site: www.1-call.com
VP Mktg: John McNamara

1-800-DIALWORD.COM

1095 E King St Box 10
Boone, NC 28607-4325
Toll Free: (800) DIALWORD, FAX:
(877) 329-3627, Web Site: www.
1800dialword.com

Pres: Andy Owens

ONE WORLD TELECOM
2620 SW 27th Ave
Miami, FL 33133
Telephone: (786) 664-6100 x6672,
Web Site: www.nopin.us
Primary Market Served: Business &
Consumer

OUR DATA WORKS INC
1504 Fairway Dr
Lewisville, TX 75057-2329
Telephone: (469) 546-3000, Toll Free:
(800) 268-2505, FAX: (469) 546-
3013, E-Mail: info@ourdataworks.
com, Web Site: www.ourdataworks.
com
Pres: Bruce Klotzman
VP: Michelle Harris

PCCW TELESERVICES
565 Metro Pl S (Suite 250)
Dublin, OH 43017-7312
Telephone: (614) 280-1600, Web Site:
www.influentinc.com
Primary Market Served: Consumer

PSI MARKETING
CONSULTANTS INC
3501 Algonquin Rd (Suite 350)
Rolling Meadows, IL 60008-3129
Telephone: (773) 878-0800, Toll Free:
(800) 933-4774, FAX: (773) 878-
4219
Pres: Phillip S. Immergluck
VP Mktg: Mike Baker

PERSON TO PERSON
MARKETING LLC
8 N Corporate Dr
Riverdale, NJ 07457
Telephone: (973) 835-8112, FAX:
(973) 835-8525, E-Mail: sales@
persontopersondirect.com, Web Site:
www.persontopersondirect.com
Pres: Steve Alario

POWER SEMINARS
The Learning Center
53 New Ocean St (Suite 3)
Swampscott, MA 01907-1840
Telephone: (781) 595-9990, FAX:
(781) 595-0770, Web Site: www.
gailcohen.com
Pres: Gail Cohen

PREMIER MESSAGING LP
9850 Sagepike Dr
Houston, TX 77089-3514
Toll Free: (888) 405-7000, E-Mail:
sales@premiermessaging.com, Web
Site: www.premiermessaging.com

Primary Market Served: Business &
Consumer

PRISM MARKETING GROUP
111 W Second St
Schaller, IA 51053
Toll Free: (800) 862-4827, FAX: (712)
275-4855, E-Mail: cjgrothe@
schallertel.net, Web Site: www.
prismktg.com
Gen Mgr: Chris Grothe
Conducts Business: U.S.
Primary Market Served: Business &
Consumer
Founded: 1994

PROSODIE INTERACTIVE
855 SW 78th Ave (Suite 100)
Plantation, FL 33324-3223
Telephone: (954) 671-6500, Toll Free:
(866) 776-7634, FAX: (954) 915-
0567, E-Mail: info@prosodiemail.
com, Web Site: www.ivrinc.com
Dir Mktg: Ross Krisel
Conducts Business: U.S., Canada
Employees: 986
Primary Market Served: Business
Advertising/Marketing Budget Related
to Direct Marketing: 0-25%
Founded: 1986
Gross sales or billing: $264,000,000

Interactive voice response, inbound call
routing, automated call distribution, automated surveys, customer experience
enhancements.

PROVIDENCE JOURNAL
TELEMARKETING
75 Fountain St
Providence, RI 02902-0050
Telephone: (401) 277-7000, FAX:
(401) 277-8046, E-Mail: bnauman@
projo.com, Web Site: www.projo.
com
Sr Dir Consumer Mktg: Barbara Nauman

PTM COMMUNICATIONS
330 W 38th St (Suite 801)
New York, NY 10018-8465
Telephone: (212) 643-5458, FAX:
(212) 643-5486, E-Mail: info@
ptmcomm.com, Web Site: www.
ptmcomm.com
Pres: Gail Stone

PUBLIC INTEREST
COMMUNICATIONS INC
7700 Leesburg Pike (Suite 301)
Falls Church, VA 22043
Telephone: (703) 847-8300, FAX:
(703) 734-9620, Web Site: www.
pubintcom.com
Pres: Kenneth Whitaker

QUALITY CONTACT
SOLUTIONS INC
808 4th St
Aurora, NE 68818-2201
Telephone: (402) 210-2692, Toll Free:
(866) 963-2889, FAX: (402) 210-
2692, E-Mail: info@
qualitycontactsolutions.com, Web
Site: www.qualitycontactsolutions.
com
COO: Dean Garfinkel
Pres: Angela Morris
Dir Opers: Nathan Teahon
Dir Client Svcs: Melissa Hinrichs
Dir Back Office Opers: Kelsey Olsen
Conducts Business: U.S., Canada
Employees: 45
Primary Market Served: Business &
Consumer
Advertising/Marketing Budget Related
to Direct Marketing: 76-100%
Direct Marketing ad budget:
Telephone: 100%
Founded: 2007
Gross sales or billing: $4,600,000

Provides business to business telemarketing & call center solutions. Helps
clients with inbound, outbound and e-
contact strategies.

SCHOLASTIC DIRECT MKTG
Subs. of Scholastic Inc
90 Sherman Tpke
Danbury, CT 06816-0001
Telephone: (203) 797-3500, FAX:
(203) 797-3667
Pres: George Saul

SELLTEL INC
393 Mantoloking Rd
Brick, NJ 08723
Telephone: (732) 920-8700, Toll Free:
(888) 840-9481, FAX: (732) 903-
0836, E-Mail: info@
nationalprotection.com
Pres: David Gartenberg
Controller: Lucy M. Hull

SHARE GROUP INC
79 Chapel St
Newton, MA 02458-1010
Telephone: (617) 629-4500, FAX:
(617) 629-4510, E-Mail: info@
sharegroup.com, Web Site: www.
sharegroup.com
CEO: Susan Paine

SITEL
Subs. of Acticall Sitel
3102 West End Ave (Suite 1000), Two
American Center
Nashville, TN 37203-1324

Telephone: (615) 301-7100, Toll Free: (866) 95-SITEL, Web Site: www.sitel.com
Pres & CEO: Laurent Uberti
Chmn: Don Berryman
COO: Olivier Camino
CFO: Elisabeth Destailleur
CMO: Arnaud de Lacoste
Conducts Business: Worldwide
Founded: 1985

Customer experience management & business process outsourcing company.

SKYTEL COMMUNICATIONS INC

A Worldcom Company
1720 Lakepoint Dr
Lewisville, TX 75057-6408
Toll Free: (800) 759-8737, Web Site: www.skytel.com
Dir Sls: Kevin Calvey

SMARTREPLY INC

6410 Oak Canyon Rd (Suite 100)
Irvine, CA 92618-5225
Telephone: (949) 340-0700, Web Site: www.smartreply.com
Dir Mktg: Tania Eckweiler
Primary Market Served: Business & Consumer

SPECTRUM COMMUNICATION SERVICES INC

125 N Executive Dr Ste 300
Brookfield, WI 53005-6035
Telephone: (262) 821-8400, Toll Free: (800) 701-3559, FAX: (262) 821-1492, E-Mail: sales@spectrumcomm.com, Web Site: www.spectrumcomm.com
Pres: Roy Osmon

SPEECHSOFT INC

49 The Crossing
Armonk, NY 10504
Telephone: (914) 273-5560, Toll Free: (800) 878-8117, E-Mail: sales@speechsoft.com, Web Site: www.speechsoft.com
Pres: Morris Neuman

STRATMAR SYSTEMS INC

dba "Intercept" & "Stratmar Retail Svcs"
109 Willet Ave
Port Chester, NY 10573
Telephone: (914) 937-7171, Toll Free: (800) 866-2399, FAX: (914) 937-6045, E-Mail: info@stratmar.com, Web Site: www.stratmar.com
Sr VP Sls & Mktg: Clayton Zimmerman

STURNER & KLEIN

Div. of NOVI
4301 Cambridge Rd
Fort Worth, TX 76155-2627
Toll Free: (800) 678-4960, FAX: (301) 881-3745
Pres: Jerry Sturner

SYKES ACQUISITION

100 Brandywine Blvd
Newtown, PA 18940-4000
Toll Free: (800) 799-6880, Web Site: www.ictgroup.com
Chmn & CEO: John Brennan

SYNERGY DIRECT MARKETING SOLUTIONS LLC

480 W Tuscarawas Ave Ste 307
Barberton, OH 44203-2597
Telephone: (330) 869-5886, Web Site: www.synmar.biz
Pres: Alexander Stavarz
Primary Market Served: Business & Consumer

T-MOBILE

12920 SE 38th St
Bellevue, WA 98006-1350
Telephone: (425) 999-2084, Web Site: www.t-mobile.com

TMP DIRECT

PO Box 308
Budd Lake, NJ 07828-0308
Telephone: (973) 347-9400, Toll Free: (800) 328-2439, FAX: (973) 347-8773, E-Mail: ron.pearl@tmpwdirect.com, Web Site: www.tmpwdirect.com
VP: Ron Pearl
VP: Mary Ann Kerr
Pres: Daniel Collins

TRG WORLD

1700 Pennsylvania Ave NW (Suite 560)
Washington, DC 20006
Telephone: (202) 289-9898
Primary Market Served: Business & Consumer

TTC MARKETING SOLUTIONS

3945 N Neenah Ave
Chicago, IL 60634-2419
Telephone: (773) 545-0407, Toll Free: (800) 777-6348, FAX: (773) 545-4034, E-Mail: sales@ttcmarketingsolutions.com, Web Site: www.ttcmarketingsolutions.com
Pres: Mary Shanley
VP: Bob Aloisio

TECHNOLOGY MARKETING CORP/TMC

800 Connecticut Ave
Norwalk, CT 06854-1631
Telephone: (203) 852-6800, Toll Free: (800) 243-6002, FAX: (203) 953-2845, E-Mail: tmc@tmcnet.com, Web Site: www.tmcnet.com
CEO: Nadji Tehrani
Mktg Mgr: Jan Perret

TELE BUSINESS USA

1945 Techny Rd (Suite 3)
Northbrook, IL 60062
Telephone: (847) 480-1560, FAX: (847) 897-4120, Web Site: www.tbiz.com
CEO: Larry Kaplan
Pres: Jeff Levine
Exec VP: Robert Levy

Tele Business USA is the nation's premier business-to-business teleservices resource. More than just a telemarketing service bureau, we are the leading professional teleservices agency for inbound and outbound outsourced sales, lead generation and qualification, account management, appointment setting, market research, customer service, and database management.

TELE RESOURCES INC

222 W Superior St Ste 100
Duluth, MN 55802-1940
Toll Free: (888) 698-8787 X114, FAX: (218) 724-2466, E-Mail: mark.swanson@teleresources.net, Web Site: www.teleresources.net
Dir Bus Devel: Mark Swanson
Pres & CEO: Jack L. Keenan
Conducts Business: U.S.
Employees: 120
Primary Market Served: Business & Consumer
Advertising/Marketing Budget Related to Direct Marketing: 0-25%
Direct Marketing ad budget:
Direct Mail: 60%
Magazines: 40%
Founded: 1996
Gross sales or billing: $5,000,000

Tele Resources Inc., is an outbound only call center with both B to B and B to C capabilities, providing custom program management and analysis, with a hands on operating team devoted to our clients and their programs. Tele Resources Inc., places years of quality telemarketing experience into every program.

TELECOM INC

2201 Broadway (Suite 103)
Oakland, CA 94612-3028

Telephone: (510) 873-8283, Toll Free: (800) 243-3101, FAX: (510) 873-8293, Web Site: www.telecominc. com
Pres CEO & Owner: Jonathan Martin
Exec VP & Owner: William M Smith
Chief Tech Officer: Greg Haggerty
VP Mktg & Bus Devel: Hywel ap Rees

TELEDIRECT INTERNATIONAL INC
17255 N 82nd St, Scottsdale, AZ 85255-5456
17255 N 82nd St
Scottsdale, AZ 85255
Telephone: (480) 585-6464, Toll Free: (800) 531-6440, FAX: (480) 585-3373, Web Site: www.tdirect.com
Prod Mngmt Dir: Mark Moore

TELENATIONAL MARKETING
2918 N 72nd St
Omaha, NE 68134-5107
Toll Free: (800) 333-6106 X132, FAX: (402) 391-2044, Web Site: www. telenational.com
VP Mktg: Bonnie P. Powell

TELEPERFORMANCE INTERACTIVE
1601 Washington Ave (Suite 400)
Miami Beach, FL 33139-3166
Telephone: (786) 437-3300, FAX: (786) 276-8452, Web Site: www. teleperformance.com
Pres: Jeff Cohen

TELEREP
14 Wellham Ave
Glen Burnie, MD 21061
Toll Free: (800) 638-2000, FAX: (410) 761-3357, Web Site: www.telerep. com
Pres: Sandra S. Olson

TELERX
723 Dresher Rd
Horsham, PA 19044-2299
Toll Free: (800) 2TELERX, Web Site: www.telerx.com
Sr Dir Sls & Mktg: Loralee Hare
Conducts Business: Worldwide
Primary Market Served: Business
Founded: 1980
Contact center and BPO services.

TELESERVICES DIRECT
5305 Lakeshore Pkwy South Dr
Indianapolis, IN 46268-4113
Toll Free: (888) 646-6626, Web Site: www.teleservicesdirect.com
CEO & Pres: Patricia Totton

TELESYSTEMS MARKETING INC
3600 S Gessner Rd (Suite 250)
Houston, TX 77063
Telephone: (713) 784-3439, Toll Free: (800) 622-0190, FAX: (713) 780-5974, E-Mail: kimberly@nwpros. com, Web Site: www. telesystemsmarketing.com
Pres: Robin Fisher

TELETRACK INC
5550-A Peachtree Pkwy (Suite 600)
Norcross, GA 30092
Telephone: (770) 449-8809
Mktg Mgr: Katie Bryson
Primary Market Served: Business

TIMBERLINE TOTAL SOLUTIONS LLC
8429 Blood St
Omaha, NE 68134-1051
Telephone: (402) 397-6945, Toll Free: (877) 575-2255, FAX: (402) 255-5045, E-Mail: rleavitt@ timberlinesolutions.com
CEO: Russell Leavitt

Provides inbound customer service supplemented with outbound sales and service to the existing business relationship market. Has over 200 customer service professionals and 15 years experience.

TIME COMMUNICATIONS
Div. of Bell Telephone Inc
4444 Centerville Rd (Suite 245)
Saint Paul, MN 55127-3712
Toll Free: (800) 486-8581, FAX: (612) 298-1945, E-Mail: info@ timecommunications.biz, Web Site: www.timecommunications.biz
Pres: Michael Eastwood

TMONE LLC
dba Mass Markets
2937 Sierra Ct SW
Iowa City, IA 52240
Telephone: (868) 577-2461, E-Mail: info@massmarkets.com, Web Site: www.massmarkets.com
Pres: Anthony Marlowe
COO: Jason Falco
Employees: 800
Primary Market Served: Business & Consumer
Founded: 2003

Inbound & outbound contact center services company.

TOLLFREEFORWARDING. COM
9841 Airport Blvd (fl 9)

Los Angeles, CA 90045-5421
Telephone: (213) 452-1505, Web Site: www.tollfreeforwarding.com

TORCOM INBOUND TELEMARKETING
25 Kessel Ct (Suite 107)
Madison, WI 53711-6227
Toll Free: (800) 832-4939, FAX: (608) 275-6557, E-Mail: torcom@torcom. com, Web Site: www.torcom.com
Natl Sls Mgr: Elin Torvik
Dir Opers: John Poehling
Client Svcs Mgr: John Ross

UNICALL INTERNATIONAL INC
3250 W Market St
Fairlawn, OH 44333
Telephone: (330) 864-9364, FAX: (330) 864-9367, E-Mail: harrisb@ unicallinc.com, Web Site: www. unicallinc.com
Pres: Benjamin C. Harris
Conducts Business: U.S.
Employees: 150
Primary Market Served: Business & Consumer
Catalog available online
Direct online sales
Advertising/Marketing Budget Related to Direct Marketing: 76-100%
Direct Marketing ad budget:
Telephone: 100%
Founded: 1999
Gross sales or billing: $5,000,000

UNITED AMERICA ADVERTISING INC
1018 West Cherry Ave
Enid, OK 73703
Telephone: (580) 233-7200, FAX: (580) 548-8432
Pres: Tim H. Morgan

US DATA CORP
17310 Wright St (Suite 100)
Omaha, NE 68130-2405
Telephone: (402) 502-5623, Toll Free: (888) 578-3282, FAX: (402) 502-5623, E-Mail: info@ usdatacorporation.com, Web Site: www.usdatacorporation.com
Pres: Jeff Herdzina
Primary Market Served: Business & Consumer
Founded: 1979

USA 800 INC
9808 E 66 Ter
Raytown, MO 64133

Telephone: (816) 358-1303, Toll Free: (800) 821-7539, FAX: (816) 358-8845, E-Mail: dlabatt@usa-800.com, Web Site: www.usa-800.com
Pres: Tom Davis

VENTRILOQUIST VOICE SOLUTIONS INTERNATIONAL INC
5025 Orbitor Dr (Suite 300), Bldg 1
Mississauga, ON, Canada L4W 4Y5
Telephone: (866) 446-0860, E-Mail: info@ventriloquistsolutions.com, Web Site: www.ventriloquistsolutions.com
Pres & CEO: J. Hunt
Exec VP Sales & Mktg: L Dykun
VP Opers & Customer Svc: C Hunt
VP Sales & Bus Devel: M Strauss
VP Mktg: Joe Palombo
Sr VP Sales & Mktg: R Savein
Employees: 9
Founded: 1999

Leading cloud-based multi-channel service provider of voice, SMS/text, email, web, predictive dialer solutions & mobile applications. Provides proven, low cost interactive engagements throughout the full consumer lifecycle: marketing, customer care/service, payments & collections, channel preference & permission management.

VIRIDO LLC
6626 E Oberlin Way
Scottsdale, AZ 85266-6786
Telephone: (480) 419-9063, Web Site: www.virido.com
Pres & Owner: Gary Finney

VISIONS MARKETING SERVICES
425 Dolly Dr
Lancaster, PA 17601-3619
Telephone: (717) 381-2100, Toll Free: (800) 222-1577, FAX: (717) 295-8020, Web Site: www.wecloseloans.com
Pres: Allan Geller

VOICELOGIC
662 King St W
Toronto, ON, Canada M5V 1M7
Toll Free: (888) 552-8858, Web Site: www.voicelogic.com
Bus Devel Mgr: Laura Leduc

VOXDATA TELECOM
Subs. of Voxdata Telecom Inc
1155 Metcalfe St (Suite 1860)
Montreal, QC, Canada H3B 2V6
Telephone: (514) 871-1920, Toll Free: (800) 861-9599, FAX: (514) 871-0445, E-Mail: fcouture@voxdata.com, Web Site: www.voxdata.com
Pres: France Couture
Exec VP: Jason Drum

WS LIVE LLC
Sub. of Working Solutions
131 W 10th St
Dubuque, IA 52001
Telephone: (563) 582-9501, Toll Free: (800) 582-9501, FAX: (563) 582-2003, Web Site: www.wslive.com
CEO: Tim Houlne
Compliance Mgr: Jeff L. Schmitt
Founded: 1988

WALKER & ASSOCIATES
7129 Old Hwy 52 N, PO Box 1029
Welcome, NC 27374-1029
Telephone: (336) 731-6391, Toll Free: (800) WALKER-1, FAX: (336) 731-7253/6973, E-Mail: info@walkerfirst.com, Web Site: www.walkerfirst.com
CEO: Virginia Walker

WARRANTECH DIRECT INC
Subs. of Warrantech Corp
2200 Hwy 121 (Suite 105)
Bedford, TX 76021-5983
Telephone: (817) 786-1000, Toll Free: (800) 833-8801, FAX: (817) 786-1020, Web Site: www.warrantech.com
Pres & Gen Mgr: Randall San Antonio
VP: Mary Aldrich
Conducts Business: U.S.
Employees: 120
Primary Market Served: Business & Consumer
Advertising/Marketing Budget Related to Direct Marketing: 76-100%
Founded: 1990

Direct marketing of extended service contracts to consumers, businesses & wholesalers.

WHITE POINT LEADS GROUP LLC
362 Gulf Breeze Pkwy (Suite 350)
Gulf Breeze, FL 32561-4492
Telephone: (850) 934-5577, Web Site: www.whitepointleads.com
Pres: J. Glenn Goodroe
Primary Market Served: Business & Consumer

WINN TECHNOLOGY GROUP INC
523 Palm Harbor Blvd
Palm Harbor, FL 34682-0927
Telephone: (727) 789-0006, Toll Free: (800) 444-5622, FAX: (727) 789-0638, E-Mail: winn@winntech.net, Web Site: www.winntech.net
Pres: G. Swallow
Mktg Mgr: Judith Woodward

YELLOWBOOK
2201 Renaissance Blvd
King of Prussia, PA 19406-2766
Telephone: (610) 731-2335, Web Site: www.yellowbook.com
Primary Market Served: Consumer

ALABAMA

Compass Media, 175 Northshore Pl, Gulf Shores, 36542

ARIZONA

Higher Power Marketing, 2949 E Shady Spring Trail, Phoenix, 85024-6251

ARKANSAS

ChoicePoint Precision Marketing, 601 E 3rd St, Little Rock, 72201-1709

CALIFORNIA

Advanced Research Services, 31510 Anacap View Dr, Malibu, 90265-5123

Advantage Plus Marketing Group, 13 Crestview, Aliso Viejo, 92656-1818

AutoPacific Inc, 2991 Dow Ave, Tustin, 92780-7219

Broadcast Media Associates, PO Box 1233, Santa Maria, 93456-1233

Cheskin, 255 Shoreline Dr (Suite 350), Redwood Shores, 94065

Continuum Global, 431 Bryant St, San Francisco, 94107-1303

DMRA & Matchkey Corp, 201 San Antonio Cir (Suite 280), Mountain View, 94040-1256

Experian, 475 Anton Blvd, Costa Mesa, 92626-7037

Facts 'n Figures, 15301 Ventura Blvd (Bldg B, Suite 500), Garden Bldg B, Sherman Oaks, 91403-6626

First National Information Network, 3727 W Magnolia Blvd (Suite 711), Burbank, 91505-2818

Frost & Sullivan Inc, 331 E Evelyn Ave (# 100), Mountain View, 94041-1530

Kenneth Hollander Associates Inc, 45431 Greenling Cir, Mendocino, 95460-9729

House of Marketing Research, 2555 E Colorado Blvd (Suite 205), Pasadena, 91107-6637

Nielsen SiteReports, 9276 Scranton Rd (Suite 300), San Diego, 92121-7703

Nimblefish Technologies, 100 Spear St (Suite 740), San Francisco, 94105-1525

JD Power Associates, 2625 Townsgate Rd, Westlake Village, 91361-5751

Sales Portal, 13101 Diericx Dr, Mountain View, 94040-3915

The Sausalito Group, PO Box 1559, Sausalito, 94966-1559

Triggerfish Marketing, 200 Townsend St (#45), San Francisco, 94107-5703

Where 2 Get It Inc, 5101 E La Palma Ave Ste 107, Anaheim, 92807-2056

Wpromote Inc, 1700 E Walnut Ave Fl 5, El Segundo, 90245-2610

COLORADO

Paragon Media Strategies, 7550 W Yale Ave Ste B204, Denver, 80227-3460

CONNECTICUT

SHR Capital Partners, 165 Mason St, Greenwich, 06830

DELAWARE

Trellist Marketing and Technology, 117 N Market St (Suite 300), Wilmington, 19801-2538

Bill Ward Inc, 1010 Philadelphia Pike, Wilmington, 19809-2029

DISTRICT OF COLUMBIA

Guideline Washington DC, 900 17th St NW (Suite 850), Washington, 20006-2523

Hamilton Campaigns, 4201 Connecticut Ave (Suite 610), Washington, 20008-1119

National Research LLC, 4201 Connecticut Ave NW (Suite 212), Washington, 20008-1162

FLORIDA

AMD Research & Marketing LLC, 881 Harbor Hill Dr, Safety Harbor, 34695-4130

Behavioral Science Research, 2121 Ponce De Leon Blvd (Suite 250), Coral Gables, 33134-5221

Bolton Research Corp, 2709 SW 22nd Ave, Miami, 33133-3101

Catalogs.com, 2800 Glades Cir (Suite 135), Fort Lauderdale, 33327-2280

Cherry Communications Co, 227 N Bronough St (Suite 4100), Tallahassee, 32301-1329

Elephant Group Inc, 3303 W Commercial Blvd, Fort Lauderdale, 33309-3438

Franklin & Welker Direct Marketing Services, 12555 Biscayne Blvd (PMB 440), Miami, 33181-2522

Interdata Inc, 1101 Periwinkle Way (#108), Sanibel, 33957-4708

Lead Me Media, 1200 NW 17th Ave (Suite 17), Delray Beach, 33445

Mars Research, 550 W Cypress Creek Rd (Suite 310), Fort Lauderdale, 33309-6169

Take 5 Solutions LLC, 2385 NW Executive Center Dr (Suite 320), Boca Raton, 33431-8530

GEORGIA

AnalyticsIQ Inc, 115 Perimeter Center Pl NE (Suite 312), Atlanta, 30346-1244

CSM Inc, 2137 Flintstone Dr (Suite H), Tucker, 30084-5022

Fry Consultants Inc, 2000 Riveredge Pkwy NW, Atlanta, 30328-4694

Integrative Logic LLC, 2397 Huntcrest Way (Suite 200), Lawrenceville, 30043-6309

LexisNexis Risk Soulutions, 1000 Alderman Dr, Alpharetta, 30005

Message Technologies Inc, 1995 N Park Pl, Meridian (5th fl), Atlanta, 30339

Tangent Media LLC, 570 Westover Dr NW (Suite 200), Atlanta, 30305-3538

ILLINOIS

Affina, 2001 Ruppman Plaza, Peoria, 61614-7917

CompetiScan, 200 S Michigan Ave Ste 1060, Chicago, 60604-2421

Exhibitgroup/Giltspur, 200 N Gary Ave, Roselle, 60172

Global Business Information Services Inc (GLoBIS), 1820 N Lincoln Ave, Chicago, 60614-5812

Group O Inc, 4905 77th Ave, Milan, 61264-3250

BW Hill & Associates LLC, 7115 W North Ave (Suite 375), Oak Park, 60302-1002

Ifbyphone, 300 W Adams St (Suite 900), Chicago, 60606-5109

Information Resources Inc, 150 N Clinton St, Chicago, 60661-1416

Market Focus Inc, 2325 Asbury Ave, Evanston, 60201-2602

Marketing Synergy Inc, 1700 Park St (Suite 103), Naperville, 60563-2356

The McIlvaine Co, 191 Waukegan Rd (Suite 208), Northfield, 60093-2743

Mintel International, 351 W Hubbard St (fl 8), Chicago, 60654-4941

PartnerData LLC, 2119 Dewey Ave (Suite B), Evanston, 60201-3035

Strata Marketing Inc, 30 W Monroe (Suite 1900), Chicago, 60603

INDIANA

RSC The Quality Measurement Co, 110 Walnut St, Evansville, 47708

IOWA

Frank N Magid Associates Inc, One Research Ctr, Marion, 52302-5868

KANSAS

Ruf Corp, 1533 E Spruce St, Olathe, 66061

MARYLAND

GXS Corp, 9711 Washingtonian Blvd, Gaithersburg, 20878-7365

MASSACHUSETTS

Atlantic Research & Consulting Inc, 109 State St (Suite 3), Boston, 02109-2911

Boston Research Group, 1 Ash St (Suite 3), Hopkinton, 01748-1886

Market Response International, 10 Little Marsh Ln, Orleans, 02653

OTOlabs LLC, 465 Medford St (Suite 300), Charlestown, 02129-1454

RJ Olsen Inc, 41 Indian Ridge Rd, Natick, 01760-5635

Research Communications Ltd, 95 Washington St (401-357), Canton, 02021-4006

TMP Directional Marketing, 200 Berkeley St (Suite 1), Boston, 02116-5030

MICHIGAN

Editorial Code & Data Inc, 814 Wolverine Dr (Suite 2), Walled Lake, 48390-2377

ForeSee Results Inc, 2500 Green Rd (Suite 400), Ann Arbor, 48105-1573

Morpace Inc, 31700 Middlebelt Rd Ste 200, Farmington Hills, 48334-2375

W J Schroer Co, Two W Michigan Ave, Battle Creek, 49017-3609

MINNESOTA

Anderson Niebuhr & Associates Inc, 6 Pine Tree Dr (Suite 200), Northpark Corp Ctr, Arden Hills, 55112-3790

Ideas To Go Inc, One Main St SE (fl 5), Minneapolis, 55414-1027

Sight Marketing, 400 1st Ave N (Suite 100), Minneapolis, 55401-1764

MISSOURI

Magnets 4 Media, 672 Marina Dr (#209), Washington, 63090

Marketing Horizons Inc, 1001 Craig Rd (Suite 100), Saint Louis, 63146-5200

Outrider North America, 111 Westport Plaza (Suite 350), Saint Louis, 36146-3099

MONTANA

A & A Research, 690 Sunset Blvd, Kalispell, 59901-3641

NEBRASKA

The MSR Group, 1121 N 102nd Ct (Suite 100), Omaha, 68114-1947

Vente Inc, 4509 S 143rd St (Suite 9), Omaha, 68137-4521

NEVADA

Cobbey & Associates Marketing Research, PO Box 12, Carson City, 89702-0012

NEW JERSEY

Aurora Marketing Inc, 66 Witherspoon St (Suite 600), Princeton, 08542-3239

Bruno & Ridgway Research Associates Inc, 3131 Princeton Pike (Bldg 2A), Lawrenceville, 08648-2201

CMMC Market Research, PO Box 306, Mount Freedom, 07970-0306

Data Analytics Corp, 44 Hamilton Ln, Plainsboro, 08536-1126

Education Dynamics LLC, 5 Marine View Plz Ste 212, Hoboken, 07030-5722

Glickman Research Associates/GRA Focus Center, 160 Paris Ave, Northvale, 07647-0006

Industrial Marketing Associates, PO Box 481, Cranford, 07016-0481

James M Sears Associates, 375 S Washington Ave, Bergenfield, 07621-4323

Knowledge Networks/SRI, 570 South Avenue East (Bldg G), Ashley Business Park, Cranford, 07016-3200

Spectrum Research, 5000 Boardwalk (Suite 602), Ventnor City, 08406-2918

USA/DIRECT Inc, 43 Fawn Lake Rd, Stockholm, 07460

NEW YORK

ACNielsen Corp, 85 Broad St, New York, 10004-2434

Beta Research Corp, 6400 Jericho Tpke, Syosset, 11791-4497

CBSI, 550 Mamaroneck Ave (Suite 309), Harrison, 10528-1615

Claritas Express, 53 Brown Rd, Ithaca, 14850

Mark Clements Research Inc, 25 Barker St (#309), Mount Kisco, 10549-1630

Electric Media, 169 S Main St (PMB 311), New York, 10956-3353

Erdos & Morgan Inc, 6400 Jericho Turnpike (Suite 102), Syosset, 11791-4427

Experian Simmons, 1271 Avenue Of The Americas (fl 45), New York, 10020-1309

Focus Plus Inc, 462 7th Ave (fl 18), 462 Seventh Avenue, New York, 10018-7425

Friedman Marketing Svcs, 500 Mamaroneck Ave (Suite 103), Harrison, 10528-1600

GfK Custom Research LLC, 75 Ninth Ave (fl 5), New York, 10011-7076

Guideline, 315 Park Ave S, New York, 10010-3607

Guideline Research Corp, 625 Ave of the Americas (fl 2), New York, 10011-2020

Harris Interactive, 60 Corporate Woods, Rochester, 14623-1457

Norman Hecht Research Inc, 33 Queens St (Suite 301), Syosset, 11791-3063

House Party Inc, One Bridge St (Suite 3), Irvington, 10533-1553

IC International, 266A Duffy Ave, Hicksville, 11801-3605

Informed Sources Inc, 88 Sunnyside Blvd Ste 201, Plainview, 11803-1507

Ipsos America Inc, 1700 Broadway (fl 5), New York, 10019-5979

JRH Marketing Services Inc, 8319 141st St (#707), Jamaica, 11435-1622

Market Discovery Group, 302 Baltustrol Cir, Roslyn, 11576-3059

Market Probe International Inc, 805 3rd Ave (fl 11), New York, 10022-7567

Media Monitors Inc, 445 Hamilton Ave Ste 700, White Plains, 10601-1828

Mediamark Research Inc, 200 Liberty St (fl 4), New York, 10281-1033

MSW Research, 1111 Marcus Ave (Suite MZ 200), Lake Success, 11042-1034

The NPD Group Inc, 900 W Shore Rd, Port Washington, 11050

ORC Macro International, 40 Wall St (Suite 3400), New York, 10005-1325

Oxbridge Communications Inc, 186 5th Ave, New York, 10010-5202

Ruder Finn Inc, 301 E 57th St (fl 3), New York, 10022-5997

SRB Marketing Inc, 10 Caroline Way, New Paltz, 12561-1157

Synovate, 360 Park Ave S (fl 5), New York, 10010-1712

TNS Intersearch, 3 Barker Ave (#3), White Plains, 10601-1509

Tabline Data Services Inc, 625 Ave of the Americas (2nd fl), New York, 10001-2020

The Teleconference Network, 137 E Townline Rd, Nanuet, 10954

NORTH CAROLINA

Ad Facts Inc, 1251 NW Maynard Rd (Suite 358), Cary, 27513-8703

Bellomy Research Inc, 175 Sunnynoll Ct, Winston Salem, 27106-5076

Coleman Research Inc, 4020 Aerial Center Pkwy (Suite 102), Morrisville, 27560-8563

The Dialog Corp, 2250 Perimeter Park Dr (Suite 300), Morrisville, 27560-8893

Leibowitz Market Research Associates Inc, 3120 Whitehall Park Dr, Charlotte, 28273-3335

North Carolina Electric Membership Corp, 3400 Summer Blvd, Raleigh, 27616-7306

TSE Services, 3400 Summer Blvd, Raleigh, 27611-7306

OHIO

Hanson Inc, 1695 Indian Wood Cir (Suite 200), Maumee, 43537-4082

MarketVision Research Inc, 10300 Alliance Rd, Cincinnati, 45242-4734

Q Fact Marketing Research Inc & Videoconferencing Center, 9908 Carver Rd, Cincinnati, 45242-5502

Speedeon Data Corp, 5875 Landerbrook Dr (Suite 130), Cleveland, 44124

SummitQwest, 446 Windsor Park Dr, Dayton, 45459-4111

PENNSYLVANIA

Delta Market Research Inc, 333 N York Rd, Hatboro, 19040-2000

Environmental Research Associates, 414 Mill Rd, Havertown, 19083-3740

GENESYS Sampling Systems, 755 Business Center Dr (Suite 200), Horsham, 19044-3443

Impact Ratings Inc, 3402 Horton Rd, Newtown, 19073-3418

MTI Information Technologies LLC, 1 Oxford Vly (Suite 500), Langhorne, 19047-3314

Marshall Marketing & Communications Inc, 2600 Boyce Plaza Rd (Suite 210), Pittsburgh, 15241-3949

Phoenix Marketing International, 865 Easton Rd, Warrington, 18976-1838

Sindlinger & Co Inc, 405 Osborne Ln, Wallingford, 19086

Taylor Nelson Sofres Intersearch, 410 Horsham Rd Frnt, Horsham, 19044-2041

RHODE ISLAND

Horton Interpreting Inc, 225 Chapman St (Suite 303), Providence, 02905-4533

MacIntosh Survey Center, 450 Veterans Memorial Pkwy (Suite 201), East Providence, 02914-5300

Marketing & Media Services LLC, 931 Jefferson Blvd (Suite 1001), Warwick, 02886-2247

TEXAS

The Benchmark Co, 907 S Congress Ave (Suite C), Austin, 78704-1741

cbsi, 2651 S Polaris Dr, Fort Worth, 76137-4804

Consumer Focus, 6505 W Park Blvd (Suite 306-368), Plano, 75093-6212

DMS Insights, 19111 N Dallas Pkwy (Suite 350), Dallas, 75287

Decision Analyst Inc, 604 Ave "H" E, Arlington, 76011-3100

Galloway Research Service, 4751 Hamilton Wolfe Rd (Suite 100), San Antonio, 78229-3458

Innovative Marketing Services Inc, 16360 Park Ten Pl (Suite 102), Houston, 77084

Javelin Marketing Group, 7850 N Belt Line Rd, Irving, 75063-6062

NuStats Inc, PO Box 19304, Austin, 78760-9304

Relevant Insights LLC, 2508 Salmon Run Ln, Euless, 76039-6096

Who's Calling, 200 Quality Cir, College Station, 77845

VIRGINIA

Berry Best Services Ltd, 12210 Fairfax Town Center #924, Fairfax, 22033-2877

Comsearch, 19700 Janelia Farm Blvd, Janelia Technology Park, Ashburn, 20147-2405

Decision Demographics, 4312 39th St N, Arlington, 22207-4606

Faneuil ISG, 2 Eaton St (Suite 1002), Hampton, 23669-3979

Issues & Answers Network Inc, 5151 Bonney Rd (Suite 100), Virginia Beach, 23462-4384

JetSpring, 4022 Monument Ave, Richmond, 23230-3908

Magnets USA, 817 Connecticut Ave NE, Roanoke, 24012-5317

Nathan Associates Inc, 2101 Wilson Blvd Ste 1200, Arlington, 22201-3049

2ergo, 2020 N 14th St (Suite 500), Arlington, 22201-2515

Veritas Analytics Inc, 21351 Gentry Dr, Sterling, 20166-8510

WASHINGTON

Consumer Opinion Services Inc, 12825 First Ave S, Seattle, 98168-2618

CANADA

Ontario

BBM Canada Inc, 1500 Don Mills Rd (Suite 305), Don Mills, M3B 3L7

Custometrics Inc, 30 E Beaver Creek (Unit 210), Richmond Hill, L4B 1J2

D&B Canada, 6750 Century Ave (Suite 305), Mississauga, L5N 0B7

TNF, 900-2 Bloor St E, Toronto, M4W 3H8

Quebec

IRPP, 1470 Peel St (Suite 200), Montreal, H3A 1T1

Market Research (30)

A & A RESEARCH
690 Sunset Blvd
Kalispell, MT 59901-3641
Telephone: (406) 752-7857
Pres: Judith Doonan

ACNIELSEN CORP
85 Broad St
New York, NY 10004-2434
Telephone: (646) 654-5000, FAX:
(646) 654-5002, E-Mail: globalc@
nielsen.com, Web Site: www.
acnielsen.com/us
Pres Entertainment & Automotive:
Kenneth Orkin
Sec: Mary A. Dresdow
Founded: 1923

Operates as a marketing and media information company in the United States.

AD FACTS INC
1251 NW Maynard Rd (Suite 358)
Cary, NC 27513-8703
Telephone: (919) 388-3015, Toll Free:
(800) 923-3228, E-Mail: adfacts@
adfacts.com, Web Site: www.adfacts.
com
Pres: Michelle S. Dawson

Company that monitors and measures competitive advertising and publicity for business-to-business marketers.

ADVANCED RESEARCH SERVICES
31510 Anacap View Dr
Malibu, CA 90265-5123
Telephone: (310) 589-0223, Web Site:
www.tvsurveys.com
Pres: Scott V. Tallal

ADVANTAGE PLUS MARKETING GROUP
13 Crestview
Aliso Viejo, CA 92656-1818
Telephone: (714) 573-7300, Toll Free:
(800) 432-9466, FAX: (714) 573-
7301, E-Mail: info@apmg.com, Web
Site: www.apmg.com
Pres: Barry Lieberman
Conducts Business: U.S.
Employees: 15
Primary Market Served: Business &
Consumer
Direct online sales
Advertising/Marketing Budget Related
to Direct Marketing: 76-100%
Founded: 1992

Gross sales or billing: $2,000,000
We revitalize a company's marketing to create a truly measurable ROI. We bridge the gap between marketing and sales. We offer web, email, postal mail and telephone marketing services.

AFFINA
2001 Ruppman Plaza
Peoria, IL 61614-7917
Telephone: (309) 685-5901, Toll Free:
(877) 4 AFFINA, FAX: (309) 679-
4199, Web Site: www.affina.com
CEO: Donna Malone
Pres: Kathleen Hamburger
Founded: 1973

Provides customer relationship management solutions.

AMD RESEARCH & MARKETING LLC
881 Harbor Hill Dr
Safety Harbor, FL 34695-4130
Telephone: (727) 409-1087, Web Site:
www.amdresearch-marketing.com
Owner: Anna Marie Dunn
Primary Market Served: Business &
Consumer

Provides advertising and marketing services.

ANALYTICSIQ INC
115 Perimeter Center Pl NE (Suite 312)
Atlanta, GA 30346-1244
Telephone: (770) 407-8855, Toll Free:
(888) 612-4309, Web Site: www.
analytics-iq.com
Pres & CEO: David Kelly
Primary Market Served: Business &
Consumer

Innovative company with a fresh approach to developing marketing analytics and modeling.

ANDERSON NIEBUHR & ASSOCIATES INC
6 Pine Tree Dr (Suite 200), Northpark
Corp Ctr
Arden Hills, MN 55112-3790
Telephone: (651) 486-8712, Toll Free:
(800) 678-5577, FAX: (651) 486-
0536, E-Mail: info@ana-inc.com,
Web Site: www.ana-inc.com
Pres: John F. Anderson
Admin Asst: Jennifer Koper

Full-service firm offering the full range of quantitative and qualitative marketing research services.

ATLANTIC RESEARCH & CONSULTING INC
109 State St (Suite 3)
Boston, MA 02109-2911
Telephone: (617) 720-0174, FAX:
(617) 589-3731, E-Mail:
generalmailbox@guideline.com,
Web Site: www.atlanticresearch.net
Pres: Kelly Basile
VP of Admin: Elaine Becker
Founded: 1981

Marketing research firm, provides research and consulting services.

AURORA MARKETING INC
66 Witherspoon St (Suite 600)
Princeton, NJ 08542-3239
Telephone: (609) 520-8863, FAX:
(908) 359-1108, E-Mail: aurora2@
voicenet.com, Web Site: www.
auroramarketing.net
Pres & CEO: Guy Sucharczuk
VP Mktg: John Dahlquist

Provides services in the field of Public Relations Counselors.

AUTOPACIFIC INC
2991 Dow Ave
Tustin, CA 92780-7219
Telephone: (714) 838-4234, FAX:
(714) 838-4260, Web Site: www.
autopacific.com
Pres: George C. Peterson
Mktg Analyst: Deborah L. Grieb

Provide primary research and consulting services to the automotive industry.

BBM CANADA INC
1500 Don Mills Rd (Suite 305)
Don Mills, ON, Canada M3B 3L7
Telephone: (416) 445-9800, FAX:
(416) 445-8644, E-Mail: info@bbm.
ca, Web Site: www.bbm.ca
Pres & CEO: Jim MacLeod
Dir Communs: Tom Jenks
VP Finance: Anna Giagkou
SVP & CIO: Don Head

Provide broadcast measurement and consumer behavior data, as well as industry-leading intelligence to broadcasters, advertisers and agencies.

BEHAVIORAL SCIENCE RESEARCH
2121 Ponce De Leon Blvd (Suite 250)
Coral Gables, FL 33134-5221
Telephone: (305) 443-2000, Toll Free:
(800) 282-2771, FAX: (305) 448-
6825
Pres & Res Dir: Robert Ladner

Sr Res Mgr: Petra Brock-Getz
provides intelligent solutions to problems of marketing and management.

BELLOMY RESEARCH INC

175 Sunnynoll Ct
Winston Salem, NC 27106-5076
Telephone: (336) 721-1140, Toll Free:
(800) 443-7344, FAX: (336) 721-1597, E-Mail: bellomy@interpath.
com, Web Site: www.
bellomyresearch.com
Pres: John Sessions
VP Shopper Insights: Andrea Durning
CIO: Tony Eggers

A full-service marketing research company.

THE BENCHMARK CO

907 S Congress Ave (Suite C)
Austin, TX 78704-1741
Telephone: (512) 707-7500, FAX:
(512) 707-7757, E-Mail: thebenc@
earthlink.net, Web Site: www.
thebenchmarkcompany.net
Pres & CEO: Dr Robert E. Balon

Market research firm.

BERRY BEST SERVICES LTD

12210 Fairfax Town Center #924
Fairfax, VA 22033-2877
Telephone: (202) 293-4964, FAX:
(202) 293-3431, E-Mail: admin@
berrybest.com, Web Site: www.
berrybest.com
Pres: Thomas L. Berry

Communications industry's most comprehensive providers of FCC information and research services.

BETA RESEARCH CORP

6400 Jericho Tpke
Syosset, NY 11791-4497
Telephone: (516) 935-3800, FAX:
(516) 935-4092, E-Mail: beta@
nybeta.com, Web Site: www.nybeta.
com
CEO: Amy Gorelkin
Pres: Maxine Kossoff
COO: Jason Gorelkin
Founded: 1970

Operates as a market research company in the United States.

BOLTON RESEARCH CORP

2709 SW 22nd Ave
Miami, FL 33133-3101
Telephone: (305) 854-3887, FAX:
(305) 854-3807, E-Mail: brcted@aol.
com, Web Site: www.boltonresearch.
com

Pres: Ted Bolton
Helping media owners and investors grow their audience base.

BOSTON RESEARCH GROUP

1 Ash St (Suite 3)
Hopkinton, MA 01748-1886
Telephone: (508) 497-2555, FAX:
(508) 497-2592, E-Mail: BRGrep@
BostonResearchGroup.com, Web
Site: www.bostonresearchgroup.com
Partner: James Fazzio

Helping companies in a wide range of industries understand their customers and markets here and abroad.

BROADCAST MEDIA ASSOCIATES

PO Box 1233
Santa Maria, CA 93456-1233
Telephone: (805) 937-1553, E-Mail:
cliffhunter@cliffhunter.com, Web
Site: www.broadcastmediabroker.
com
Pres: Clifford M. Hunter

Consulting & media brokerage for radio & television stations.

BRUNO & RIDGWAY RESEARCH ASSOCIATES INC

3131 Princeton Pike (Bldg 2A)
Lawrenceville, NJ 08648-2201
Telephone: (609) 895-9889, FAX:
(609) 895-6665, E-Mail: info@
brunoandridgway.com, Web Site:
www.brra.com
Pres: Joseph Ridgway
CEO: Tom Kirwan

Quantitative market research and business forecasting.

CBSI

550 Mamaroneck Ave (Suite 309)
Harrison, NY 10528-1615
Telephone: (914) 381-5353, Web Site:
www.cbsiservices.com
VP: Kenneth Kraetzer
Primary Market Served: Business

Produce a select range of need-driven, quality products & services that help organizations increase loyalty, generate revenue, and stimulate usage among their existing customers & target markets.

CMMC MARKET RESEARCH

PO Box 306
Mount Freedom, NJ 07970-0306
Telephone: (973) 989-0229, FAX:
(973) 366-1185, E-Mail: dmmp@
cmmcinc.com, Web Site: www.
cmmcinc.com

Pres & CEO: Richard W. Pavely
Offers executive-level decision support, operations planning, and implementation assistance to public & private organizations desiring to consolidate and/or outsource multi-site mail service operations.

CSM INC

2137 Flintstone Dr (Suite H)
Tucker, GA 30084-5022
Telephone: (404) 892-2626, Toll Free:
(800) 849-6788, FAX: (404) 589-9779, E-Mail: info@csmresearch.
com, Web Site: www.csmresearch.
com
Pres: Derald M. Alford

Janitorial & specialty services.

CATALOGS.COM

2800 Glades Cir (Suite 135)
Fort Lauderdale, FL 33327-2280
Telephone: (954) 659-9005, FAX:
(954) 659-9007, Web Site: www.
catalogs.com
VP Bus Devel: Trish Baron

Provide shopping access via web, tablet and mobile phone platforms.

CBSI

2651 S Polaris Dr
Fort Worth, TX 76137-4804
Telephone: (817) 332-3681, FAX:
(817) 332-3686, Web Site: www.
buxtonco.com
Pres & CEO: Tom Buxton
CFO & Treas: David Glover
SVP Bus Devel: Brandon Norrell
Primary Market Served: Business & Consumer
Founded: 1994

Provides strategic decision-making information for retail site selection and targeted marketing.

CHERRY COMMUNICATIONS CO

227 N Bronough St (Suite 4100)
Tallahassee, FL 32301-1329
Telephone: (850) 561-3600, FAX:
(850) 561-1155, E-Mail: phones@
cherrycomm.com, Web Site: www.
cherrycomm.com
Pres: Linda Z. Cherry

Provides polling, voter contact, & related phone and research services to political candidates, committees, trade & advocacy groups, & non-profit organizations.

CHESKIN

255 Shoreline Dr (Suite 350)
Redwood Shores, CA 94065

Telephone: (650) 802-2100, FAX: (650) 593-1125, E-Mail: info@cheskin.com, Web Site: www.cheskin.com
Global CEO: Bart Michels

Consulting firm that guides innovation through its deep understanding of people, cultures and change.

CHOICEPOINT PRECISION MARKETING

601 E 3rd St
Little Rock, AR 72201-1709
Telephone: (978) 738-0544, Toll Free: (800) 937-4232, FAX: (978) 738-0582, Web Site: www.cp-pm.com
Pres: James N. Alvarez

CLARITAS EXPRESS

53 Brown Rd
Ithaca, NY 14850
Telephone: (607) 257-5757, Toll Free: (866) 737-7429, FAX: (607) 266-0425, E-Mail: info@claritas.com, Web Site: www.claritas.com/express
VP: Barbara Policay

MARK CLEMENTS RESEARCH INC

25 Barker St (#309)
Mount Kisco, NY 10549-1630
Telephone: (914) 241-1803, FAX: (914) 241-7763, E-Mail: mjfharvey@aol.com, Web Site: www.markclementsresearch.com
Pres: Mark Clements
VP, Dir Research Sales: Martin J Feldman

editorial research provider, working with both consumer & trade publications.

COBBEY & ASSOCIATES MARKETING RESEARCH

PO Box 12
Carson City, NV 89702-0012
Telephone: (775) 847-0321, Toll Free: (877) 433-3242, E-Mail: cobbey@cobbey.com, Web Site: www.cobbey.com
Pres: Robin Cobbey

Research firm providing services nationwide for product development and marketing.

COLEMAN RESEARCH INC

4020 Aerial Center Pkwy (Suite 102)
Morrisville, NC 27560-8563
Telephone: (919) 571-0000, FAX: (919) 571-9999, E-Mail: callcoleman@colemaninsights.com, Web Site: www.colemaninsights.com
Chmn & CEO: Jon Coleman

Pres & COO: Warren Kurtzman
Founded: 1978

Media research firm that provides a range of marketing & research services for the media industry.

COMPASS MEDIA

175 Northshore Pl
Gulf Shores, AL 36542
Telephone: (251) 968-4600, Toll Free: (800) 239-9880, E-Mail: info@compassmedia.com, Web Site: www.compassmedia.com
Consultant: Susan O'Connell

Provides leisure tourism marketing for the Southern U.S.

COMPETISCAN

200 S Michigan Ave Ste 1060
Chicago, IL 60604-2421
Telephone: (312) 546-3489, Web Site: www.competiscan.com
CEO: Richard Goldman
Primary Market Served: Business & Consumer

COMSEARCH

19700 Janelia Farm Blvd, Janelia Technology Park
Ashburn, VA 20147-2405
Telephone: (703) 726-5500, FAX: (703) 726-5600, Web Site: www.comsearch.com
Sr Mktg Mgr: Jeanette Carlisle

Provides innovative spectrum management and wireless engineering solutions to the global market for fixed, mobile, and broadband wireless applications.

CONSUMER FOCUS

6505 W Park Blvd (Suite 306-368)
Plano, TX 75093-6212
Telephone: (972) 378-9697, (214) 542-8787, E-Mail: sstewart@consumerfocusco.com, Web Site: www.consumerfocusco.com
Pres: Sue Stewart
Primary Market Served: Business & Consumer

Custom quantitative and qualitative research.

CONSUMER OPINION SERVICES INC

12825 First Ave S
Seattle, WA 98168-2618
Telephone: (206) 241-6050, FAX: (206) 241-5213, E-Mail: info@cosvc.com, Web Site: www.cosvc.com
Pres: Jerry Carter

Founded: 1960

Conducts qualitative, quantitative, and hybrid studies, with executive offices, focus group facilities and call centers located in Seattle, Portland, and Las Vegas.

CONTINUUM GLOBAL

431 Bryant St
San Francisco, CA 94107-1303
Telephone: (415) 685-3301, Web Site: www.continuumglobal.com
CEO: Suresh Mathai
Founded: 2010

CUSTOMETRICS INC

30 E Beaver Creek (Unit 210)
Richmond Hill, ON, Canada L4B 1J2
Telephone: (905) 886-9020, E-Mail: info@custometrics.ca, Web Site: www.custometrics.com
Sr Partner: David Beaton
Sr Partner: Katherine Krass
Primary Market Served: Business & Consumer

Customer & market analysis.

D&B CANADA

Subs. of Dun & Bradstreet International
6750 Century Ave (Suite 305)
Mississauga, ON, Canada L5N 0B7
Toll Free: (800) 463-6362, FAX: (800) 668-7800, Web Site: www.dnb.ca
Pres: Lawrence Franco
VP Mktg: Geoff Vincent
Founded: 1841

Provides business information for credit, marketing, and data solutions decisions worldwide.

DMRA & MATCHKEY CORP

201 San Antonio Cir (Suite 280)
Mountain View, CA 94040-1256
Telephone: (650) 856-9988, FAX: (650) 856-9986
Pres: Michael E. Green

DMS INSIGHTS

Div. of United Sample, Inc.
19111 N Dallas Pkwy (Suite 350)
Dallas, TX 75287
Toll Free: (800) 409-6262, FAX: (214) 222-6103, E-Mail: info@dmsinsights.com, Web Site: www.dmsdallas.com
Pres & CEO: Dennis E. Gonier
Founded: 1995

Offers a full suite of online sample services and solutions.

DATA ANALYTICS CORP

44 Hamilton Ln

Plainsboro, NJ 08536-1126
Telephone: (609) 936-8999, Web Site:
www.dataanalyticscorp.com
Pres: Walter Paczkowski
Primary Market Served: Business &
Consumer

Quantitative Pricing Research.

DECISION ANALYST INC
604 Ave "H" E
Arlington, TX 76011-3100
Telephone: (817) 640-6166, Toll Free:
(800) 262-5974, FAX: (817) 640-
6567, E-Mail: jthomas@
decisionanalyst.com, Web Site:
www.decisionanalyst.com
Pres & CEO: Jerry W. Thomas
Exec VP: Bonnie Kenoly

Specializing in product testing, concept
testing, advertising research, site selection & strategy research.

DECISION DEMOGRAPHICS
4312 39th St N
Arlington, VA 22207-4606
Telephone: (703) 931-9200, FAX:
(703) 527-1448, E-Mail: tordella@
decision-demographics.com, Web
Site: www.decision-demographics.
com
Pres: Stephen J Tordella

Market research & program evaluation
solutions.

DELTA MARKET RESEARCH
INC
333 N York Rd
Hatboro, PA 19040-2000
Telephone: (215) 674-1180, (267) 960-
1033, FAX: (215) 674-1271, E-Mail:
information@deltamarketresearch.
com, Web Site: www.
deltamarketresearch.com
Exec VP: Bob Norman

Market research & analysis.

THE DIALOG CORP
2250 Perimeter Park Dr (Suite 300)
Morrisville, NC 27560-8893
Telephone: (919) 804-6400, Toll Free:
(800) 3 DIALOG, FAX: (919) 804-
6410, E-Mail: customer@dialog.
com, Web Site: www.dialog.com
VP Strategic Initiatives: Libby Trudell
Founded: 1972

Provides Web-based information solutions for researchers in corporate, business, and government settings
worldwide.

EDITORIAL CODE & DATA
INC
814 Wolverine Dr (Suite 2)

Walled Lake, MI 48390-2377
Telephone: (248) 926-5187, FAX:
(248) 926-6047, E-Mail: Monique@
marketsize.com, Web Site: www.
marketsize.com
VP: Monique Darnay Magee
Founded: 1990

make reference works under contract
for publishers.

EDUCATION DYNAMICS LLC
5 Marine View Plz Ste 212
Hoboken, NJ 07030-5722
Telephone: (201) 377-3000, FAX:
(201) 377-3081, Web Site: www.
educationdynamics.com
Pres: Bruce Douglas
Founded: 2006

provides marketing information &
technology services to higher education
clients.

ELECTRIC MEDIA
169 S Main St (PMB 311)
New York, NY 10956-3353
Telephone: (201) 461-5252
Pres: Arthur Cohen

ELEPHANT GROUP INC
3303 W Commercial Blvd
Fort Lauderdale, FL 33309-3438
Telephone: (954) 657-9611, FAX:
(866) 699-5786, Web Site: www.
elephantgroup.com
CEO: Benzion Aboud
CFO & Exec VP: Michael W. Wallace
Primary Market Served: Business &
Consumer
Founded: 1997

Offers performance-based marketing
solutions.

ENVIRONMENTAL
RESEARCH ASSOCIATES
Div. of Integrated Marketing Services
414 Mill Rd
Havertown, PA 19083-3740
Telephone: (610) 449-7400
Pres: Lois Kaufman

Professional environmental counsel.

ERDOS & MORGAN INC
6400 Jericho Turnpike (Suite 102)
Syosset, NY 11791-4427
Telephone: (516) 935-6959, FAX:
(516) 935-4040, E-Mail: info@
erdosmorgan.com, Web Site: www.
erdosmorgan.com
Exec VP: David March
Contact: Jane Stiffa

International market and media research.

EXHIBITGROUP/GILTSPUR
200 N Gary Ave
Roselle, IL 60172
Telephone: (972) 538-3031, Toll Free:
(800) 843-3944, Web Site: www.e-g.
com
CEO: John Jastrem
Exec VP, COO & CFO: Bryceon J.
Sumner Jr
SVP, Strategy & Mktg: David Saef

Constructs & designs trade show, museum, & retail exhibits of all shapes,
sizes, and styles.

EXPERIAN
475 Anton Blvd
Costa Mesa, CA 92626-7037
Telephone: (714) 830-7000, Toll Free:
(888) EXPERIAN, FAX: (949) 242-
2938, Web Site: www.experian.com
CEO: Victor K. Nichols
Pres Mktg Solutions Bus Unit: Deborah
Zuccarini
Founded: 1992

Provides information, analytical &
marketing services to organizations &
consumers.

EXPERIAN SIMMONS
1271 Avenue Of The Americas (fl 45)
New York, NY 10020-1309
Telephone: (212) 749-3162, FAX:
(212) 471-2940, E-Mail: ellenr@
smrb.com, Web Site: www.smrb.com
Gen Mgr Global Res Experian Mktg
Svcs: Bill Tancer

Marketing services.

FACTS 'N FIGURES
15301 Ventura Blvd (Bldg B, Suite
500), Garden Bldg B
Sherman Oaks, CA 91403-6626
Telephone: (661) 222-2278, Toll Free:
(818) 986-6600, FAX: (661) 222-
2287, Web Site: www.
factsnfiguresinc.com
Pres: Steven Escoe
Dir Client Rels: Bob Johnson
Founded: 1969

Qualitative and quantitative full service
data collection, field management and
tabulation firm.

FANEUIL ISG
2 Eaton St (Suite 1002)
Hampton, VA 23669-3979
Telephone: (757) 722-3235, FAX: 757-
722-5293, Web Site: www.faneuil.
com
CEO: Anna Van Buren McNider
Sr VP Opers & Program Mngmt: Evelio Suarez

Conducts Business: U.S.

Provides business process outsourcing services to private and public sector customers.

FIRST NATIONAL INFORMATION NETWORK

Subs. of Bentley Communications Corp.
3727 W Magnolia Blvd (Suite 711)
Burbank, CA 91505-2818
Telephone: (855) 909-6800, Toll Free: (800) 562-1999, FAX: (818) 558-6663, E-Mail: info@fnin.com, Web Site: www.fnin.com
CEO: Mark Savoy
VP Sls & Mktg: David Kieran
Conducts Business: U.S.
Advertising/Marketing Budget Related to Direct Marketing: 26-50%
Direct Marketing ad budget:
Direct Mail: 10%
Magazines: 10%
Telephone: 80%
Founded: 1992

Provider of investor profiling, custom lead generation, internet marketing, direct response and list management services.

FOCUS PLUS INC

462 7th Ave (fl 18), 462 Seventh Avenue
New York, NY 10018-7425
Telephone: (212) 675-0142, Toll Free: (800) 340-8846, FAX: (212) 645-3171, E-Mail: info@focusplusny.com, Web Site: www.focusplusny.com
Partner: John Markham
Partner: Elizabeth Lobrano-Markham

Qualitative research.

FORESEE RESULTS INC

2500 Green Rd (Suite 400)
Ann Arbor, MI 48105-1573
Telephone: (734) 205-2600, Toll Free: (800) 621-2850, FAX: (734) 205-2601, Web Site: www.foreseeresults.com
Exec VP & Gen Mgr: Don Morrison
Sr VP Products, Mktg & Client Svcs: Jim Yang
CFO: Jeff Blackman
Conducts Business: U.S.
Primary Market Served: Business & Consumer

Provides customer satisfaction measurement solutions.

FRANKLIN & WELKER DIRECT MARKETING SERVICES

12555 Biscayne Blvd (PMB 440)
Miami, FL 33181-2522
Telephone: (305) 758-6690, FAX: (305) 758-9399
Pres: Leonard G. Franklin

Marketing and advertising firm.

FRIEDMAN MARKETING SVCS

aka GfK
500 Mamaroneck Ave (Suite 103)
Harrison, NY 10528-1600
Telephone: (914) 698-0800, FAX: (914) 698-0485, E-Mail: paula.wynne@gfk.com, Web Site: www.friedmanmktg.com
Exec VP: Ruth Roller

Management consulting service.

FROST & SULLIVAN INC

RP-NFOA
331 E Evelyn Ave (# 100)
Mountain View, CA 94041-1530
Toll Free: (877) 463-7678, (877) 690-3329, FAX: (877) 690-3329, E-Mail: myfrost@frost.com, Web Site: www.frost.com
Chmn: David Frigstad
Pres: Krishna Srinivasan
Founded: 1961

Market analysis, market research reports.

FRY CONSULTANTS INC

2000 Riveredge Pkwy NW
Atlanta, GA 30328-4694
Telephone: (770) 226-8888, FAX: (770) 226-8899, E-Mail: lynesmith@fryconsultants.com, Web Site: www.fryconsultants.com
Pres & CEO: L. Lyne Smith III

Research-based strategic consulting firm.

GXS CORP

9711 Washingtonian Blvd
Gaithersburg, MD 20878-7365
Telephone: (301) 340-4000, Toll Free: (800) 560-4347, FAX: (301) 340-5299, Web Site: www.gxs.com
CEO: Robert E E. Segert
CFO & Exec VP: Gregg Clevenger
Founded: 1967

Provides B2B integration services to supply chains worldwide.

GALLOWAY RESEARCH SERVICE

4751 Hamilton Wolfe Rd (Suite 100)

San Antonio, TX 78229-3458
Telephone: (210) 734-4346, FAX: (210) 732-4500, E-Mail: info@gallowayresearch.com, Web Site: www.gallowayresearch.com
Mgr: Janet Ayers

Provides marketing research services.

GENESYS SAMPLING SYSTEMS

755 Business Center Dr (Suite 200)
Horsham, PA 19044-3443
Telephone: (215) 653-7100, Toll Free: (800) 336-7674, FAX: (215) 653-7115, E-Mail: alambert@m-s-g.com, Web Site: www.m-s-g.com
VP Sls: Alan Lambert

Provides full service sampling capabilities for survey research.

GFK CUSTOM RESEARCH LLC

75 Ninth Ave (fl 5)
New York, NY 10011-7076
Telephone: (212) 240-5300, Toll Free: (800) 274-3577, FAX: (212) 240-5353, E-Mail: info@gfkamerica.com, Web Site: www.gfkamerica.com
CEO: Matthias Hartmann
CFO: Pamela Knapp

Source of relevant market & consumer information.

GLICKMAN RESEARCH ASSOCIATES/GRA FOCUS CENTER

160 Paris Ave
Northvale, NJ 07647-0006
Telephone: (201) 767-8888, Toll Free: (800) 334-3978, FAX: (201) 767-6933, E-Mail: j.glickman@glickmanresearch.com, Web Site: www.glickmanresearch.com
Pres: James Glickman

Specialists in communication research with extensive experience serving the health care industry.

GLOBAL BUSINESS INFORMATION SERVICES INC (GLOBIS)

1820 N Lincoln Ave
Chicago, IL 60614-5812
Telephone: (877) 456-2478, FAX: (877) 456-2478, E-Mail: info@glo-bis.com, Web Site: www.glo-bis.com
Mng Dir: Louise Kern
Conducts Business: Worldwide
Primary Market Served: Consumer
Founded: 2003

Provider of business credit reports, market intelligence and worldwide databases.

GROUP O INC

4905 77th Ave
Milan, IL 61264-3250
Telephone: (309) 736-8300, FAX:
(309) 736-8301, Web Site: www.
groupo.com
Chmn & Founder: Robert Ontiveros
CEO: Gregg Ontiveros
Pres Mktg Solutions: Charles Wetzel

provides marketing, supply chain, &
packaging solutions in North America.

GUIDELINE

315 Park Ave S
New York, NY 10010-3607
Telephone: (212) 463-6232, Toll Free:
(866) GUIDELINE, FAX: (212) 645-
7681, Web Site: www.findsvp.com
Conducts Business: U.S.
Employees: 239
Primary Market Served: Business
Advertising/Marketing Budget Related
to Direct Marketing: 0-25%
Direct Marketing ad budget:
Direct Mail: 100%
Founded: 1969
Gross sales or billing: $46,300,000

Customized business research & analysis.

GUIDELINE RESEARCH CORP

625 Ave of the Americas (fl 2)
New York, NY 10011-2020
Telephone: (212) 947-5140, FAX:
(212) 629-0061, Web Site: www.
guidelineresearch.com

GUIDELINE WASHINGTON DC

900 17th St NW (Suite 850)
Washington, DC 20006-2523
Telephone: (703) 312-6004, Toll Free:
(866) GUIDELINE, E-Mail:
fdudley@guideline.com, Web Site:
www.guideline.com
VP Mktg: Frank Dudley

HAMILTON CAMPAIGNS

4201 Connecticut Ave (Suite 610)
Washington, DC 20008-1119
Telephone: (202) 686-5900, FAX:
(202) 686-7080, E-Mail: info@
hamiltoncampaigns.com, Web Site:
www.hamiltoncampaigns.com
Pres: David Beattie

Consulting firm.

HANSON INC

1695 Indian Wood Cir (Suite 200)
Maumee, OH 43537-4082

Telephone: (419) 327-6100, FAX:
(419) 327-6101, Web Site: www.
hansoninc.com
Pres & CEO: Steve Hanson
COO: Jenny Jacob

Full-service digital agency.

HARRIS INTERACTIVE

60 Corporate Woods
Rochester, NY 14623-1457
Telephone: (585) 272-8400, Toll Free:
(800) 866-7655, FAX: (585) 272-
8680, E-Mail: info@
harrisinteractive.com, Web Site:
www.harrisinteractive.com
Chmn: Albert A. Angrisani
CFO: Eric W. Narowski
COO: Marc H. Levin
Conducts Business: U.S., Canada, UK,
France & Germany
Founded: 1956

Operates as a consultative market research company.

NORMAN HECHT RESEARCH INC

33 Queens St (Suite 301)
Syosset, NY 11791-3063
Telephone: (516) 496-8866, FAX:
(516) 496-8165, E-Mail: nhr@
normanhechtresearch.com, Web Site:
www.normanhechtresearch.com
Co-Pres & COO: Laura Greenberg
Pres: Daniel Greenberg
Founded: 1985

Provides research and business development consulting services to the media sector.

HIGHER POWER MARKETING

2949 E Shady Spring Trail
Phoenix, AZ 85024-6251
Telephone: (480) 837-3580, Toll Free:
(888) 501-5544, FAX: (480) 837-
3589, E-Mail: info@
hpowermarketing.com, Web Site:
www.hpowermarketing.com
Pres & CEO: Peter Feinstein
Bus Devel: Shaun Mahoney
Founded: 1999

Per inquiry advertising.

BW HILL & ASSOCIATES LLC

7115 W North Ave (Suite 375)
Oak Park, IL 60302-1002
Telephone: (312) 268-6361, Toll Free:
(800) 431-3183, Web Site: www.
bwhillassociates.com
Pres: Benjamin Hill

Business service.

KENNETH HOLLANDER ASSOCIATES INC

45431 Greenling Cir
Mendocino, CA 95460-9729
Telephone: (707) 962-1648, FAX:
(707) 962-1635, Web Site: www.
kharesearch.com
Pres: Ken Hollander
VP: Cheryl S. Richards

Full-service marketing research firm.

HORTON INTERPRETING INC

225 Chapman St (Suite 303)
Providence, RI 02905-4533
Telephone: (401) 331-4798, Toll Free:
(800) 345-2135, FAX: (401) 331-
2822, Web Site: www.language-link.
com
Pres & CEO: Juana I Horton

Provides professional interpretation
and translation services to businesses,
governmental agencies, law and medical professionals and many others.

HOUSE OF MARKETING RESEARCH

2555 E Colorado Blvd (Suite 205)
Pasadena, CA 91107-6637
Telephone: (626) 486-1400, FAX:
(626) 486-1404, Web Site: www.
hmr-research.com
Pres: Amy Siadak
Founded: 1975

Full service market research firm providing qualitative & quantitative insights & research data to help
businesses make better decisions.

HOUSE PARTY INC

One Bridge St (Suite 3)
Irvington, NY 10533-1553
Telephone: (720) 496-2503, Toll Free:
(888) 591-1678, FAX: (914) 591-
4561, E-Mail: help@houseparty.com,
Web Site: www.houseparty.com
CEO: Chris Maher
Founded: 2005

In-home events through which consumers & their invited guests can experience new products, television shows,
software, books etc.

IC INTERNATIONAL

266A Duffy Ave
Hicksville, NY 11801-3605
Telephone: (516) 479-2200, Toll Free:
(800) 631-0209, FAX: (516) 479-
2215, E-Mail: info@ic-mr.com, Web
Site: www.ic-mr.com

Pres: Jerry Sycoff

Provides marketing research services for clients both in the U.S. & internationally, including emerging markets.

IFBYPHONE
300 W Adams St (Suite 900)
Chicago, IL 60606-5109
Telephone: (877) 295-5100, Toll Free: (877) 387-7192, Web Site: www. ifbyphone.com
VP Fin & Admin: Jason V Pinter
VP Prod Engrng: Josh Kugler
Primary Market Served: Consumer
Founded: 2005

Voice based marketing automation platform, provides software-as-a-service voice applications.

IRPP
aka Institute for Research on Public Policy
1470 Peel St (Suite 200)
Montreal, QC, Canada H3A 1T1
Telephone: (514) 985-2461, FAX: (514) 985-2559, E-Mail: irpp@irpp. org, Web Site: www.irpp.org
Pres: Graham Fox
VP Opers: Suzanne Ostiguy McIntyre
Founded: 1972

Seeks to improve public policy in Canada by generating research, providing insight & sparking debate on current & emerging policy issues facing Canadians and their governments.

IDEAS TO GO INC
One Main St SE (fl 5)
Minneapolis, MN 55414-1027
Telephone: (612) 331-1570, FAX: (612) 331-1602, E-Mail: cebert@ ideastogo.com, Web Site: www. ideastogo.com
Innovation Process Consultant: Gregg Cobb

Ideation and innovation agency that creates concepts &solutions for Fortune 500 companies.

IMPACT RATINGS INC
RP-NFOA
3402 Horton Rd
Newtown, PA 19073-3418
Telephone: (610) 353-8311, FAX: (610) 353-8311
Chmn Bd: Mike Gerhardt

Direct mail advertising company.

INDUSTRIAL MARKETING ASSOCIATES
PO Box 481
Cranford, NJ 07016-0481

Telephone: (908) 276-4256, E-Mail: ken@industrialmarketingassociates. com, Web Site: www. industrialmarketingassociates.com
Pres: Ken S. Eisenberg

Expert consulting associates in marketing, lead generation, web design, advertising, corporate communications, social media, telephone skills training, career coaching, networking, providing a complete solution to your marketing challenges.

INFORMATION RESOURCES INC
150 N Clinton St
Chicago, IL 60661-1416
Telephone: (312) 726-1221, FAX: (312 (726-8214, Web Site: www.infores. com
Chmn Bd: Richard H. Lenny
Pres & CEO: Andrew M. Appel
Founded: 1979

Provides market & shopper information, predictive analysis, & the foresight services.

INFORMED SOURCES INC
88 Sunnyside Blvd Ste 201
Plainview, NY 11803-1507
Toll Free: (800) 201-6060, FAX: (516) 576-0249, E-Mail: info@informed-sources.com, Web Site: www. informed-sources.com
Pres: Stuart Goldberg
VP, Mktg & Sls: Robert Kasper

INNOVATIVE MARKETING SERVICES INC
16360 Park Ten Pl (Suite 102)
Houston, TX 77084
Telephone: (281) 398-0321, Toll Free: (800) 231-4678, FAX: (281) 398-0679, E-Mail: mfisher@imstcorp. com, Web Site: www.imstcorp.com
Pres & CEO: James B. Fisher

INTEGRATIVE LOGIC LLC
Subs. of Luckie & Company, LLC
2397 Huntcrest Way (Suite 200)
Lawrenceville, GA 30043-6309
Telephone: (678) 638-2600, FAX: (678) 638-2601, Web Site: www. integrativelogic.com
Pres & CEO: John Gardner
COO: Russ Riggs
Primary Market Served: Business

Provides integrated database-marketing services.

INTERDATA INC
1101 Periwinkle Way (#108)
Sanibel, FL 33957-4708

Telephone: (239) 472-2700, FAX: (941) 472-4272, E-Mail: jfisher435@ aol.com, Web Site: www.interdata. org
Pres: Joseph C. Fisher

Market Research & Analysis company.

IPSOS AMERICA INC
1700 Broadway (fl 5)
New York, NY 10019-5979
Telephone: (212) 265-3200, FAX: (212) 265-3790, E-Mail: info@ipsos-asi.com, Web Site: www.ipsos-asi. com
Chmn & CEO: James T. Smith
Pres: Thomas Riehle
CEO & Pres of Ipsos ASI Worldwide: Jim Thompson
Founded: 1975

Market research company.

ISSUES & ANSWERS NETWORK INC
5151 Bonney Rd (Suite 100)
Virginia Beach, VA 23462-4384
Telephone: (757) 456-1100, FAX: (757) 456-0377, E-Mail: info@ issans.com, Web Site: www.issans. com
Chmn: Peter Scheibemantel
Pres: Peter Guinness
CTO: Denise Dodson

Independent global marketing research firm providing scalable research services.

JRH MARKETING SERVICES INC
8319 141st St (#707)
Jamaica, NY 11435-1622
Telephone: (718) 805-7300, FAX: (718) 805-7303, E-Mail: office@ jrhmarketingservices.com, Web Site: www.jrhmarketingservices.com
Pres & Owner: J. Robert Harris II

Full-service marketing consulting & research firm.

JAMES M SEARS ASSOCIATES
375 S Washington Ave
Bergenfield, NJ 07621-4323
Telephone: (201) 501-9977, FAX: (201) 453-0833
Principal: James M. Sears

JAVELIN MARKETING GROUP
An Omnicom Group Co
7850 N Belt Line Rd
Irving, TX 75063-6062

Telephone: (972) 443-7000, FAX: (972) 443-7194, E-Mail: info@ javelin.mg, Web Site: www.javelin. mg
CEO: Pam Larrick
Pres: Mike McCartin

Operates as a customer relationship marketing agency.

JETSPRING
4022 Monument Ave
Richmond, VA 23230-3908
Toll Free: (804) 359-8295, FAX: (804) 359-1686, Web Site: www.jetspring. com
VP Program Devel: Paul Glancy
Primary Market Served: Consumer

Internet marketing services.

KNOWLEDGE NETWORKS/ SRI
570 South Avenue East (Bldg G), Ashley Business Park
Cranford, NJ 07016-3200
Telephone: (908) 497-8000, FAX: (908) 497-8001, E-Mail: mclancey@ knowledgenetworks.com, Web Site: www.knowledgenetworks.com
Co-founder & Principal: Dr. Gerald J. Glasser
Sr VP & Gen Mgr Yellow Pages Business Unit: Jane Dennison-Bauer
Founded: 1969

Engages in media research for advertisers, agencies, and media buyers and sellers.

LEAD ME MEDIA
1200 NW 17th Ave (Suite 17)
Delray Beach, FL 33445
Toll Free: (888) 445-3282, FAX: (561) 423-7890, E-Mail: info@ leadmemedia.com, Web Site: www. leadmemedia.com
CEO: Robert Clouse
Mgr: Deborah McDaniels
Primary Market Served: Business

Provider of multichannel marketing lists and database services.

LEIBOWITZ MARKET RESEARCH ASSOCIATES INC
3120 Whitehall Park Dr
Charlotte, NC 28273-3335
Telephone: (704) 357-1961, FAX: (704) 357-1965, E-Mail: info@ leibowitz-research.com, Web Site: www.leibowitz-research.com
Pres & CEO: Teri Leibowitz
Founded: 1959

Market research & analysis.

LEXISNEXIS RISK SOULUTIONS
1000 Alderman Dr
Alpharetta, GA 30005
Telephone: (678) 694-6000, Web Site: www.lexisnexis.com/risk
CEO: Mark Kelsey
Sr VP, Chief Mktg Officer: Scott Sessler
Primary Market Served: Business & Consumer

Provides risk management, fraud prevention, background checks, public records & identity management solutions.

THE MSR GROUP
1121 N 102nd Ct (Suite 100)
Omaha, NE 68114-1947
Telephone: (402) 392-0755, Toll Free: (800) 737-0755, FAX: (402) 392-1068, E-Mail: info@theMSRgroup. com, Web Site: www.theMSRgroup. com
Pres & CEO: Dick Worick

Full-service research firm.

MTI INFORMATION TECHNOLOGIES LLC
1 Oxford Vly (Suite 500)
Langhorne, PA 19047-3314
Telephone: (267) 569-2400, FAX: (215) 741-3898, Web Site: www. mtiadvantage.com
Founder: William M. Clapper
CFO: William Rymer
Chief Production Officer: Carol Anne Ritts
Founded: 1999

Develops pharmaceutical marketing products.

MACINTOSH SURVEY CENTER
450 Veterans Memorial Pkwy (Suite 201)
East Providence, RI 02914-5300
Telephone: (401) 438-8330, FAX: (401) 434-9219, E-Mail: macsurvey@aol.com
Pres: Ann MacIntosh
Dir Field Svcs: Maryann Almeida

Reviews by real people.

FRANK N MAGID ASSOCIATES INC
One Research Ctr
Marion, IA 52302-5868
Telephone: (319) 377-7345, FAX: (319) 377-5861, E-Mail: iowa@ magid.com, Web Site: www.magid. com

CEO & Pres: Brent Magid

Research-based strategic consulting firm that helps clients become profitable by solving problems & helping them take advantage of opportunities.

MAGNETS 4 MEDIA
Div. of The Magnet Group
672 Marina Dr (#209)
Washington, MO 63090
Telephone: (843) 216-6665, Toll Free: (800) 642-6384, FAX: (636) 390-5147, E-Mail: sales@ magnets4media.com, Web Site: www.magnets4media.com
CEO & Pres: Bill Korowitz
Conducts Business: U.S.
Primary Market Served: Business
Catalog available online
Advertising/Marketing Budget Related to Direct Marketing: 26-50%
Founded: 1983

Sells promotional magnets to the direct mail & printing industry.

MAGNETS USA
817 Connecticut Ave NE
Roanoke, VA 24012-5317
Telephone: (540) 857-3045, Toll Free: (800) 869-7562, FAX: (800) 788-6872, Web Site: www.magnetsusa. com
CEO: Alan Turner
Founded: 1989

Magnetic marketing products designed & produced in Roanoke VA.

MARKET DISCOVERY GROUP
302 Baltustrol Cir
Roslyn, NY 11576-3059
Telephone: (516) 365-8555, E-Mail: schiffmanl@aol.com
Pres: Leon Schiffman

MARKET FOCUS INC
2325 Asbury Ave
Evanston, IL 60201-2602
Telephone: (847) 328-2900, FAX: (847) 328-8121
Pres: Richard C. Fowler

Business services.

MARKET PROBE INTERNATIONAL INC
805 3rd Ave (fl 11)
New York, NY 10022-7567
Telephone: (212) 725-7676, FAX: (212) 725-7529, E-Mail: info@ marketprobeint.com, Web Site: www.marketprobeint.com
Pres & CEO: Alan Appelbaum

Founded: 1967

Reliable market research data, data gathering and analytical services.

MARKET RESPONSE INTERNATIONAL

10 Little Marsh Ln
Orleans, MA 02653
Telephone: (508) 240-1877, FAX: (508) 945-4010, E-Mail: rmiller@capecod.net, Web Site: www.millerinternational.com
Mng Partner: Richard N. Miller

MARKETING & MEDIA SERVICES LLC

931 Jefferson Blvd (Suite 1001)
Warwick, RI 02886-2247
Telephone: (401) 737-7730, FAX: (401) 737-6465, Web Site: www.mmsipitv.com
Pres: Sally Dickson
Exec VP: Tony Ferranti
Media Dir: Tom Wetzel
Primary Market Served: Business
Founded: 1985

Direct response industry.

MARKETING HORIZONS INC

1001 Craig Rd (Suite 100)
Saint Louis, MO 63146-5200
Telephone: (314) 432-1957, Toll Free: (800) 669-0839, FAX: (314) 432-7014, E-Mail: jkramer@mhorizons.com
Pres & CEO: Robert G. Jasper
VP Project Mngmt: Margie Reaka
Founded: 1986

Marketing research & consulting company.

MARKETING SYNERGY INC

1700 Park St (Suite 103)
Naperville, IL 60563-2356
Telephone: (630) 328-9550, FAX: (630) 328-9552, E-Mail: info@MSINetwork.com, Web Site: www.msinetwork.com
Pres: Randy Hlavac
Founded: 1990

Assisting B-2-B & B-2-C direct marketing clients in developing highly targeted, profitable programs for their products & services.

MARKETVISION RESEARCH INC

10300 Alliance Rd
Cincinnati, OH 45242-4734

Telephone: (513) 791-3100, Toll Free: (800) 232-4250, FAX: (513) 794-3500, E-Mail: jpinnell@mv-research.com, Web Site: www.marketvisionresearch.com
Pres & COO: Jonathan M. Pinnell
Sr VP: Chris Ratcliff
Founded: 1983

Provides marketing research solutions to drive client business decisions.

MARS RESEARCH

550 W Cypress Creek Rd (Suite 310)
Fort Lauderdale, FL 33309-6169
Telephone: (954) 771-7725, Toll Free: (877) 755-2805, FAX: (954) 703-4377, E-Mail: ron@marsresearch.com, Web Site: www.marsresearch.com
Pres: Ron Teblum

Provides quality market research services.

MARSHALL MARKETING & COMMUNICATIONS INC

2600 Boyce Plaza Rd (Suite 210)
Pittsburgh, PA 15241-3949
Telephone: (412) 914-0970, FAX: (412) 914-0971, Web Site: www.mm-c.com
Chmn & CEO: Craig A. Marshall
Founded: 1985

Provides marketing research & analysis to clients in the retail & media industries.

THE MCILVAINE CO

191 Waukegan Rd (Suite 208)
Northfield, IL 60093-2743
Telephone: (847) 784-0012, FAX: (847) 784-0061, E-Mail: editor@mcilvainecompany.com, Web Site: www.mcilvainecompany.com
CEO: Marilyn McIlvaine
Pres: Robert McIlvaine
Mgr: Gloria Castle

Market research & more.

MEDIA MONITORS INC

RP-NFOA
445 Hamilton Ave Ste 700
White Plains, NY 10601-1828
Telephone: (914) 428-5971, FAX: (914) 428-4541, E-Mail: jselig@mediamonitors.com, Web Site: www.mediamonitors.com
CEO & Pres: Philippe Generali
VP Sls: Frank Cammarata
VP Mktg: Dwight Douglas
Founded: 2002

Provides broadcast & cable monitoring and verification services.

MEDIAMARK RESEARCH INC

Subs. of GFK
200 Liberty St (fl 4)
New York, NY 10281-1033
Telephone: (212) 884-9200, Toll Free: (800) 310-3305, FAX: (212) 884-9339, Web Site: www.mediamark.com
CFO & Exec VP of Fin & HR: Steve Goodreds
Sr VP Res & Mktg Solutions: David Napior
Conducts Business: U.S.
Employees: 90
Founded: 1979

Syndicated media research data that includes demos, lifestyle and product data. We sell to advertising agencies, direct marketing agencies and advertisers.

MESSAGE TECHNOLOGIES INC

1995 N Park Pl, Meridian (5th fl)
Atlanta, GA 30339
Telephone: (770) 240-8000, Toll Free: (800) 868-3684, FAX: (770) 240-7474, E-Mail: info@messagetech.com, Web Site: www.messagetech.com
CEO: Mark Abramson
Pres: Darrell Knight

MINTEL INTERNATIONAL

351 W Hubbard St (fl 8)
Chicago, IL 60654-4941
Telephone: (312) 932-0500, Web Site: www.comperemedia.com
Pres: Pam McHugh
Primary Market Served: Business & Consumer

MORPACE INC

31700 Middlebelt Rd Ste 200
Farmington Hills, MI 48334-2375
Telephone: (248) 737-5300, FAX: (248) 737-5326, E-Mail: information@morpace.com, Web Site: www.morpace.com
Pres: Valerie Utley

MSW RESEARCH

Div. of MSW-McCollum Spielman Worldwide
1111 Marcus Ave (Suite MZ 200)
Lake Success, NY 11042-1034
Telephone: (516) 394-6000, FAX: (516) 394-6001, E-Mail: mail@mswresearch.com, Web Site: www.mswresearch.com
CEO: Harold Spielman

THE NPD GROUP INC

900 W Shore Rd
Port Washington, NY 11050
Telephone: (516) 625-0700, FAX:
(516) 625-2444, Web Site: www.npd.
com
VP, Corp Commun: Leslie Singer

NATHAN ASSOCIATES INC

2101 Wilson Blvd Ste 1200
Arlington, VA 22201-3049
Telephone: (703) 516-7700, FAX:
(703) 351-6162, Web Site: www.
nathaninc.com
CEO & Bd Chmn: John Beyer

NATIONAL RESEARCH LLC

4201 Connecticut Ave NW (Suite 212)
Washington, DC 20008-1162
Telephone: (202) 686-9350, FAX:
(202) 686-7163, E-Mail: survey@
nationalres.com, Web Site: www.
nationalres.com
Pres: Becky Craig

NIELSEN SITEREPORTS

9276 Scranton Rd (Suite 300)
San Diego, CA 92121-7703
Toll Free: (800) 866-6520, FAX: (858)
550-5800, Web Site: www.claritas.
com
Pres: Matt O'Grady
Primary Market Served: Business &
Consumer

Online source for US demographic information.

NIMBLEFISH TECHNOLOGIES

100 Spear St (Suite 740)
San Francisco, CA 94105-1525
Telephone: (415) 247-7000, Web Site:
www.nimblefish.com
Mktg Mgr: Catalina Garreton

NORTH CAROLINA ELECTRIC MEMBERSHIP CORP

3400 Summer Blvd
Raleigh, NC 27616-7306
Telephone: (919) 872-0800, Toll Free:
(800) 662-8835, FAX: (919) 645-
3410, E-Mail: info@ncemcs.com,
Web Site: www.ncemcs.com
Pres: J. Ronald McElheney

NUSTATS INC

PO Box 19304
Austin, TX 78760-9304
Telephone: (512) 306-9065, Toll Free:
(800) 44-STATS, FAX: (512) 306-
9065, Web Site: www.nustats.com
Pres: Carlos Arce

ORC MACRO INTERNATIONAL

Div. of Macro International
40 Wall St (Suite 3400)
New York, NY 10005-1325
Telephone: (212) 941-5555, FAX:
(212) 941-7031, E-Mail: info@icfi.
com, Web Site: www.icfi.com
Chmn: Tibor Weiss Sr

OTOLABS LLC

465 Medford St (Suite 300)
Charlestown, MA 02129-1454
Telephone: (617) 236-8400, Web Site:
www.otolabs.com
Dir Prod Mngmt: Mitchel Ahern

OUTRIDER NORTH AMERICA

111 Westport Plaza (Suite 350)
Saint Louis, MO 36146-3099
Telephone: (314) 209-1005, FAX:
(314) 209-1126, Web Site: www.
outrider.com
Sr Partner: Chris Copeland
Dir Corp Commun: Cindy Kerber
Spellman

OXBRIDGE COMMUNICATIONS INC

186 5th Ave
New York, NY 10010-5202
Telephone: (212) 741-0231, Toll Free:
(800) 955-0231, FAX: (212) 633-
2938, E-Mail: custserv@oxbridge.
com, Web Site: www.mediafinder.
com; www.oxbridge.com
CEO: Louis Hagood
Treas: Patricia Hagood
Editorial Dir: Deborah Striplin
Customer Svc & Mktg: Johanna Barwick
Primary Market Served: Business &
Consumer
Catalog available online
Direct online sales
Founded: 1961

Most comprehensive database of U.S.
and Canadian periodicals and catalogs,
in print and interactive online service.
Used by direct marketers, research,
reference and marketing to printers,
publishers, editors, etc.

PARAGON MEDIA STRATEGIES

7550 W Yale Ave Ste B204
Denver, CO 80227-3460
Telephone: (303) 922-5600, FAX:
(303) 922-1589, E-Mail: info@
paragonmediastrategies.com, Web
Site: www.paragonmediastrategies.
com
Pres: John Stevens

VP Mktg: Michele Tharp

PARTNERDATA LLC

2119 Dewey Ave (Suite B)
Evanston, IL 60201-3035
Telephone: (847) 733-0819
Dir Mktg: Lisa Henthorn

PHOENIX MARKETING INTERNATIONAL

865 Easton Rd
Warrington, PA 18976-1838
Telephone: (215) 392-0264, Web Site:
www.phoenixmi.com
Pres Response Mktg: John Schiela
Primary Market Served: Business &
Consumer

JD POWER ASSOCIATES

2625 Townsgate Rd
Westlake Village, CA 91361-5751
Telephone: (805) 418-8000, Toll Free:
(888) 537-6937, FAX: (805) 418-
8900, E-Mail: information@jdpa.
com, Web Site: www.jdpower.com
Sr Dir Bus Devel: Tom Petro
Primary Market Served: Consumer

Q FACT MARKETING RESEARCH INC & VIDEOCONFERENCING CENTER

9908 Carver Rd
Cincinnati, OH 45242-5502
Telephone: (513) 891-2271, FAX:
(513) 984-7464, E-Mail: info@qfact.
com, Web Site: www.qfact.com
VP, Res & Opers: Mary Swart

RJ OLSEN INC

41 Indian Ridge Rd
Natick, MA 01760-5635
Telephone: (508) 647-3777, FAX:
(508) 647-6777, E-Mail: dickolsen@
aol.com
Pres: Richard J. Olsen

RSC THE QUALITY MEASUREMENT CO

110 Walnut St
Evansville, IN 47708
Telephone: (812) 425-4562, FAX:
(812) 425-2844
Exec VP: Allan Kuse

RELEVANT INSIGHTS LLC

2508 Salmon Run Ln
Euless, TX 76039-6096
Telephone: (817) 545-8017
Pres: Michaela Mora
Primary Market Served: Business &
Consumer

RESEARCH COMMUNICATIONS LTD
95 Washington St (401-357)
Canton, MA 02021-4006
Telephone: (781) 341-1190, FAX:
(781) 341-1191, E-Mail: info@
researchcommunications.com
Pres: Valerie Crane

RUDER FINN INC
301 E 57th St (fl 3)
New York, NY 10022-5997
Telephone: (212) 593-6400, FAX:
(212) 715-1556, E-Mail:
rfnewyork@ruderfinn.com, Web
Site: www.ruderfinn.com
VP: Dan Carlson

RUF CORP
1533 E Spruce St
Olathe, KS 66061
Telephone: (913) 782-8544, Toll Free:
(800) 829-8544, FAX: (913) 782-
0150, E-Mail: solutions@ruf.com,
Web Site: www.ruf.com
VP, Sls & Mktg: Kurtis M. Ruf
Office Mgr: Sharon Crozier

SHR CAPITAL PARTNERS
165 Mason St
Greenwich, CT 06830
Telephone: (203) 618-1110
Primary Market Served: Business

SRB MARKETING INC
10 Caroline Way
New Paltz, NY 12561-1157
Telephone: (866) 210-1183, Web Site:
www.srbmarketing.com
Mng Dir: Perry Goldschein

SALES PORTAL
13101 Diericx Dr
Mountain View, CA 94040-3915
Telephone: (800) 634-3474, Web Site:
www.salesportal.com
Pres: Kevin Sandhu

THE SAUSALITO GROUP
PO Box 1559
Sausalito, CA 94966-1559
Telephone: (415) 332-3333, FAX:
(415) 332-6571, Web Site: www.
sausolitogroup.com
Founder & CEO: Peter Sealey Ph.D.

W J SCHROER CO
Two W Michigan Ave
Battle Creek, MI 49017-3609
Telephone: (269) 963-4874, FAX:
(269) 963-5930, E-Mail: info@
socialmarketing.org, Web Site: www.
socialmarketing.org

Pres: William J. Schroer

SIGHT MARKETING
400 1st Ave N (Suite 100)
Minneapolis, MN 55401-1764
Telephone: (651) 379-4059, Web Site:
www.sightmarketing.com
Dir Mktg: Ted Loken

SINDLINGER & CO INC
405 Osborne Ln
Wallingford, PA 19086
Telephone: (610) 565-0247, E-Mail:
nelSind@aol.com
Chmn: Nellie H. Sindlinger

SPECTRUM RESEARCH
5000 Boardwalk (Suite 602)
Ventnor City, NJ 08406-2918
Telephone: (609) 822-0056, E-Mail:
peter@spectrumresearch.com
Pres: Peter Mokover

SPEEDEON DATA CORP
5875 Landerbrook Dr (Suite 130)
Cleveland, OH 44124
Telephone: (866) 647-9219, Web Site:
www.speedeondata.com
Pres: Gerard Daher
COO: Joshua Shale
CFO: Linda Montgomery
Chief Revenue Officer: Marc Jerauld
Chief Strategy Officer: Kyle Kittleson
Conducts Business: U.S.
Primary Market Served: Business &
Consumer
Founded: 2008

Market research company specializing
in big data analytics, data processing &
direct marketing.

STRATA MARKETING INC
30 W Monroe (Suite 1900)
Chicago, IL 60603
Telephone: (312) 222-1555, FAX:
(312) 222-2510, Web Site: www.
stratag.com
Pres, Sls & Mktg: Bruce W. Johnson

SUMMITQWEST
446 Windsor Park Dr
Dayton, OH 45459-4111
Telephone: (937) 291-4333, Web Site:
www.sqinteractive.com
Interactive Mktg Svcs: Patrick Sepate

SYNOVATE
360 Park Ave S (fl 5)
New York, NY 10010-1712
Telephone: (212) 293-6100, FAX:
(212) 293-6666
CEO North America: Robert Skolnick

TMP DIRECTIONAL MARKETING
200 Berkeley St (Suite 1)
Boston, MA 02116-5030
Telephone: (212) 351-7595, Web Site:
www.tmpdm.com
VP Mktg & Strategy: Monica Ho

TNF
Div. of NFO World Group
900-2 Bloor St E
Toronto, ON, Canada M4W 3H8
Telephone: (416) 924-5751, FAX:
(416) 923-7085, Web Site: www.tnf-
cf.com
Pres: Michael LoPresti

TNS INTERSEARCH
3 Barker Ave (#3)
White Plains, NY 10601-1509
Telephone: (914) 684-6100, FAX:
(914) 684-6078, Web Site: www.tns-
global.com
VP Mktg: Brenda Edwards

TSE SERVICES
3400 Summer Blvd
Raleigh, NC 27611-7306
Telephone: (919) 875-3037, Web Site:
www.ncemcs.com
Sr Analyst: Scott Staff
Primary Market Served: Consumer
Founded: 1998

Cooperative market research organization

TABLINE DATA SERVICES INC
625 Ave of the Americas (2nd fl)
New York, NY 10001-2020
Telephone: (212) 695-4873, FAX:
(212) 629-4423
VP & Mng Dir: Arye Lubovitz

TAKE 5 SOLUTIONS LLC
2385 NW Executive Center Dr (Suite
320)
Boca Raton, FL 33431-8530
Telephone: (561) 819-5555, Toll Free:
(866) 861-8862, FAX: (561) 819-
0245, E-Mail: sales@take5s.com,
Web Site: www.take5solutions.com
COO of Data: Alex Radetich
Dir Mktg & Commun: John J Lofquist

TANGENT MEDIA LLC
570 Westover Dr NW (Suite 200)
Atlanta, GA 30305-3538
Telephone: (404) 444-2357, Web Site:
www.tangentmedia.us
CEO: Dr. Kevin McCarthy
Primary Market Served: Business

**TAYLOR NELSON SOFRES
INTERSEARCH**
410 Horsham Rd Frnt
Horsham, PA 19044-2041
Telephone: (419) 725-8560, E-Mail:
info@intersearch.tnsofres.com, Web
Site: www.intersearch.tnsofres.com
VP, Mktg: Melanie Mumper

**THE TELECONFERENCE
NETWORK**
Div. of Market Navigation Inc
137 E Townline Rd
Nanuet, NY 10954
Telephone: (845) 624-0633, FAX:
(845) 623-9394, E-Mail: nospam@
mnav.com, Web Site: www.market-
navigation.com
Pres, CEO, & Founder: George Silverman

**TRELLIST MARKETING AND
TECHNOLOGY**
117 N Market St (Suite 300)
Wilmington, DE 19801-2538
Telephone: (302) 778-1300, Web Site:
www.trellist.com
Mng Partner: David Atadan

TRIGGERFISH MARKETING
200 Townsend St (#45)
San Francisco, CA 94107-5703
Telephone: (415) 671-4699, Web Site:
www.triggerfish.com
Pres & CEO: Scott Gregory

2ERGO
2020 N 14th St (Suite 500)
Arlington, VA 22201-2515
Telephone: (703) 879-3400, Web Site:
www.2ergo.com
Dir Mktg: Lindsay Woodworth

USA/DIRECT INC
43 Fawn Lake Rd
Stockholm, NJ 07460
Telephone: (973) 222-3800, FAX:
(973) 823-8223, E-Mail: gparker@
usadirectinc.com, Web Site: www.
usadirectinc.com
CEO: Guy Parker

VENTE INC
4509 S 143rd St (Suite 9)
Omaha, NE 68137-4521
Telephone: (402) 898-6800, Toll Free:
(877) 899-9691, FAX: (402) 334-
4829, Web Site: www.venteinc.com
Mgr, Prod Mngmt: Katie Geilenkrichen

VERITAS ANALYTICS INC
21351 Gentry Dr
Sterling, VA 20166-8510

Telephone: (703) 707-5620, Web Site:
www.veritas-analytics.com
Principal Staff Analyst: Eric Qualken-
bush
Program Mgr: Roger Andrews
Primary Market Served: Business &
Consumer

BILL WARD INC
1010 Philadelphia Pike
Wilmington, DE 19809-2029
Telephone: (302) 762-6600, FAX:
(302) 397-2153, E-Mail: billward@
billwardinc.com
Pres: William F. Ward Jr

WHERE 2 GET IT INC
5101 E La Palma Ave Ste 107
Anaheim, CA 92807-2056
Toll Free: (888) 377-2767, Web Site:
www.where2getit.com
VP Mktg & Bus: Vickie McGee

WHO'S CALLING
200 Quality Cir
College Station, TX 77845
Toll Free: (866) 688-9300, FAX: (888)
821-4260, E-Mail: contact@
whoscalling.com, Web Site: www.
whoscalling.com
Mktg Mgr: Susan DeSantis
Primary Market Served: Business

WPROMOTE INC
1700 E Walnut Ave Fl 5
El Segundo, CA 90245-2610
Telephone: (310) 421-4844, Web Site:
www.wpromote.com
Dir Mktg: Jamie Lane
Primary Market Served: Business &
Consumer

Print & Alternative Media (31) — Geographic Index

ARKANSAS

Vestcom International Inc, 2800 Cantrell Rd (Suite 400), Little Rock, 72202

CALIFORNIA

Facebook Inc, 1 Hacker Way, Menlo Park, 94025

Google Inc, 1600 Amphitheatre Pkwy, Mountain View, 94043

Hoelscher Marketing Group, 1145 N Second St, El Cajon, 92021-5024

Los Angeles Times, 202 W First St, Los Angeles, 90012-4105

Money Mailer LLC, 12131 Western Ave, Garden Grove, 92841

Senior Publishers Media Group, 4141 Jutland Dr (Suite 300), San Diego, 92117-7316

Vegetarian Times, 300 N Continental Blvd (Suite 650), El Segundo, 90245

Zinio Systems Inc, 114 Sansome St (fl 4), San Francisco, 94104

COLORADO

Dex Direct Marketing, 9380 Station St, Lone Tree, 80124-6807

CONNECTICUT

Adriana Associates Ltd, 20 Church St (Apt B25), Greenwich, 06830-5658

Bayard Inc, 1 Montauk Ave (Suite 200), New London, 06320-4967

Choice Magazine, 575 Main St (Suite 300), Middletown, 06457-2845

The Hartford Courant, 285 Broad St, Hartford, 06115-2510

Madison Direct Marketing Ltd, 60 Long Ridge Rd (Suite 306), Stamford, 06902-1841

Media Dynamics LLC, 12 Choctaw Ln, Greenwich, 06831-3203

Media Horizons Management LLC, 40 Richards Ave, Norwalk, 06854-2319

Multichannel Merchant Magazine, 11 River Bend Dr S, Stamford, 06907-0242

Valassis Direct Mail Inc, 1 Targeting Ctr, Windsor, 06095-2639

DISTRICT OF COLUMBIA

Capitol Advantage/Roll Call Group, 77 K St NE (fl 8), Washington, 20002-4681

FLORIDA

AMC Publishing/Agent Media Corp, 1255 Cleveland St (Suite 200), Clearwater, 33755

Alternative Media Group, 999 Vanderbilt Beach Rd (Suite 200), Naples, 34108-3512

Catalina Marketing Corp, 200 Carillon Pkwy, Saint Petersburg, 33716

Finest LED Signs, 265 NE 44th St, Fort Lauderdale, 33334

First Marketing Co, 3300 Gateway Dr, Pompano Beach, 33069-4841

RSVP Publications, 6730 W Linebaugh Ave (Suite 201), Tampa, 33625-4914

Valpak Direct Marketing Systems Inc, 8605 Largo Lakes Dr, Largo, 33773-4912

GEORGIA

AAVIM, 220 Smithsonia Rd, Winterville, 30683-1418

Ashrae Learning Institute, 1791 Tullie Cir NE, Atlanta, 30329-2305

Morris Communications Corp, 725 Broad St, Augusta, 30901-1336

RentPath LLc, 3585 Engineering Dr (Suite 100), Norcross, 30092

ILLINOIS

Angel Sales Inc, 3336 W Lawrence Ave (Suite 301), Chicago, 60605-5212

BBS Chicago, 111 S Wacker Dr, Chicago, 60606-4301

Chicago Sun-Times, 350 N Orleans St (fl 10), Chicago, 60654-1700

Chicago Tribune, 425 N Michigan Ave (TT200), Chicago, 60611-4024

RR Donnelley & Sons Co, 111 S Wacker Dr, Chicago, 60606-4304

Fox Associates Inc, 116 W Kinzie St, Chicago, 60654-4655

RR Donnelley Response Marketing Services, 4101 Winfield Rd, Warrenville, 60555-3521

Solar Communications, 1120 Frontenac Rd, Naperville, 60563-1799

Today's Christian Woman, 465 Gundersen Dr, Carol Stream, 60188

Winfield Marketing Corp, 5724 N Palaski Rd, Chicago, 60646

KANSAS

YP Talk, 1101 Cedar Crest Dr, Pittsburg, 66762-6631

MARYLAND

Automated Graphic Systems LLC, 4590 Graphics Dr, White Plains, 20695

MASSACHUSETTS

AMI Instore, 945 Concord St, Framingham, 01701

The Christian Science Monitor, 210 Massachusetts Ave, Boston, 02115-3012

Course Technology, 1 Main St, Cambridge, 02142-1522

The MarketPlace Group Inc, 9 Jaybarry Ln, Norwood, 02062-1925

The NH Broadcaster, 491 Dutton St (Suite 1), Lowell, 01854-4292

MICHIGAN

Entertainment Publications Inc, 1414 E Maple Rd, Troy, 48083-9935

MINNESOTA

CardSource, 1286 Trapp Rd, Eagan, 55121-1217

Duplication Factory Inc, 4275 Norex Dr, Chaska, 55318-3046

Machalek Communications, 12550 W Frontage Rd (Suite 220), Burnsville, 55337

Mediaspace Solutions, 904 Mainstreet, Hopkins, 55343

Novus Media Inc, 2 Carlson Pkwy (Suite 400), Plymouth, 55447-4470

Vocational Biographies Inc, 414 S Sixth St, PO Box 31, Sauk Centre, 56378-0031

MISSOURI

Commercial Lithographing Co Inc, 1226 Chestnut Ave, Kansas City, 64127-2022

Roberts & Buchanan Inc, 513 S Travis St, Concordia, 64020-7329

MONTANA

The Missoulian, 500 S Higgins, Missoula, 59801-2736

NEBRASKA

First Cyber Services, 13624 Montclair Dr, Omaha, 68144-2438

International Gamco Inc, 9335 N 48th St, Omaha, 68152

Papillion Times Group, 604 Fort Crook Rd N, Bellevue, 68005-4557

NEW HAMPSHIRE

Choice Media, 15 Danbury Cir, Amherst, 03031-2016

NEW JERSEY

Cable Direct Marketing Inc, One Gabriel Dr, Montville, 07045

Direct Mail Strategy Group (DMSG), 300 Knickerbocker Rd, Cresskill, 07626-1350

Karaban Media Services Inc, 208 Lenox Ave (#316), Westfield, 07090-5120

Sancoa International LP, 92 Ark Rd, Lumberton, 08048-4103

We Deliver America Inc, 68 Irving Ave, Englewood Cliffs, 07632

NEW YORK

ARA Media Solutions Inc, 347 W 57th St (fl 18), New York, 10019-3173

Better Homes & Gardens, 805 3rd Ave, New York, 10022-7513

Bon Appetit Magazine, 1 World Trade Center (fl 35), New York, 10007-0090

Butler Till Media Services, 1565 Jefferson Rd Bldg 200 (Suite 280), Rochester, 14623-3178

Computer Shopper, 28 E 28th (fl 11), New York, 10016

Editorial Freelance Association, 71 W 23rd St (4th fl), New York, 10010-4181

Everyday Media, 230 Old Albany Post Rd, Garrison, 10524-3711

Family Circle Magazine Inc, 125 Park Ave, New York, 10017

GLM Communications, 242 W 27th St (Suite 1B), New York, 10001-5926

David Geller Associates, 110 W 40th St (Suite 405), New York, 10018-8567

Guidance Associates, 31 Pine View Rd, Mount Kisco, 10549

Halogen Response Media, 1675 Broadway, New York, 10019-5820

Hearst Direct Response Advertising Sales, 300 W 57th St, New York, 10019-5239

InterMedia Outdoors Inc, 512 Fashion Ave (fl 11), New York, 10018-4618

iThink Direct LLC, 2 Westchester Park Dr (Suite 208), West Harrison, 10604

List Process Direct Inc, 404 E 79th St (Suite 23G), New York, 10075

Main Street Direct, 575 Lexington Ave (fl 4), New York, 10022-6146

Marvel Entertainment Inc, 135 W 50th St (fl 7), New York, 10020-1201

Media People Inc, 122 E 42nd St (Suite 725), New York, 10168-0601

Media Resource Group Inc, 100 S Bedford Rd (Suite 320), Mount Kisco, 10549-3444

Metropolitan Newspaper Advertising Services Inc, 28 Wells Ave (fl 4), Yonkers, 10701-7045

Military Direct Marketing Inc, 1 Bushwick Rd, Poughkeepsie, 12603-3839

New York Daily News, 4 New York Plaza, New York, 10004-2413

News America Marketing, 1185 Ave of the Americas (fl 27), New York, 10036-2603

Parade Publications, 711 Third Ave, New York, 10017-4014

Iris Shokoff Associates, 130 W 42nd St (#801), New York, 10036-7804

Specialized Marketing Inc, 162 Prospect Hill Rd (Suite 203), Brewster, 10509-2374

Spectra Products LLC, 1364 Reynolds Rd, Johnson City, 13790-4837

Stanton Direct Marketing Inc, 329 Shappee St, Horseheads, 14848-1918

TVGuide.com, 11 W 42nd St (fl 16), New York, 10036

USA Weekend, 535 Madison Ave, New York, 10022

Working Mother, 2 Park Ave (fl 10), New York, 10016

ZCard North America, 39 Broadway (fl 32), New York, 10006-3047

NORTH CAROLINA

News & Record, 200 E Market St, Greensboro, 27401

OHIO

JB Dollar Stretcher Magazine, 3105 Farnham Rd, Richfield, 44286-7200

Town Money Saver, 6 E Main St, Lucas, 44843-9701

OREGON

New Customer Acquisition, 620 Franquette St, Medford, 97501-7832

PENNSYLVANIA

Clipper Magazine, 3708 Hempland Rd, Mountville, 17554-1542

H & H Graphics, 854 N Prince St, Lancaster, 17603-2752

IMC - Multi Media Marketing, 930 Fox Pavilion, Jenkintown, 19046

The Philadelphia Inquirer & Daily News, 400 N Broad St, Box 8263, Philadelphia, 19101

Target Marketing Group, 1500 Spring Garden St (Suite 1200), Philadelphia, 19130-4069

TelAmerica Media Inc, 1701 John F Kennedy Blvd (Suite 2510), Philadelphia, 19103-2876

SOUTH CAROLINA

Miller Direct Inc, 1096 Assembly Dive (Suite 316), Fort Mill, 29708

The Press & Standard, 1025 Bells Hwy, Walterboro, 29488

TENNESSEE

Alternative Concepts Inc, 10420 Jackson Oaks Way (Suite 103), Knoxville, 37922-0708

TEXAS

Dex Media, 2200 W Airfield Dr, PO Box 619810, Dallas-Fort Worth Airport, 75261

Harland Clarke Marketing Services, 15955 La Cantera Pkwy, San Antonio, 78256-2589

The Houston Chronicle, 801 Texas Ave (Suite 300), Houston, 77002-2996

CANADA

Ontario

Scott's Directories, 12 Concorde Pl (Suite 800), Toronto, M3C 4J2

Quebec

Trans Continental Inc, One Place Ville Marie (Suite 3315), Montreal, H3B 3N2

Print & Alternative Media (31)

AAVIM
220 Smithsonia Rd
Winterville, GA 30683-1418
Telephone: (706) 742-5355, Toll Free:
(800) 228-4689, FAX: (706) 742-
7005, E-Mail: gary@aavim.com,
Web Site: www.aavim.com
Dir: Gary Farmer
Bus Mgr: Kim Butler
Conducts Business: U.S.
Employees: 4
Primary Market Served: Business &
Consumer
Catalog available online
Direct online sales
Advertising/Marketing Budget Related
to Direct Marketing: 76-100%
Direct Marketing ad budget:
Magazines: 5%
Newspapers: 85%
Online: 10%
Founded: 1949
Gross sales or billing: $300,000

Develop, produce & distribute instructional materials for vocational education, including publications, videos &
computer software.

**AMC PUBLISHING/AGENT
MEDIA CORP**
1255 Cleveland St (Suite 200)
Clearwater, FL 33755
Telephone: (727) 446-1100, Toll Free:
(800) 933-9449, FAX: (727) 446-
1166, E-Mail: sales@
agentmediacorp.com, Web Site:
www.agentmediacorp.com
CEO: Roscoe Smith
COO & CFO: Steven Canan
Editor Sls Journal: Christina Pellett
Founded: 1988

Provides integrated marketing solutions
for companies in insurance & financial
services industries.

AMI INSTORE
945 Concord St
Framingham, MA 01701
Telephone: (508) 652-0200, Toll Free:
(877) 652-0200, FAX: (508) 652-
0101, E-Mail: info@
advancemarketing.com, Web Site:
www.advancemarketing.com
CEO: Joel Goodfader

National in-store marketing firm specializing in brand consumer promotions
& in-store cross-merchandising events.

ARA MEDIA SOLUTIONS INC
347 W 57th St (fl 18)
New York, NY 10019-3173
Telephone: (212) 245-6691, Web Site:
www.aramediasolutions.com
Pres: Arlene Rosen

ADRIANA ASSOCIATES LTD
20 Church St (Apt B25)
Greenwich, CT 06830-5658
Telephone: (212) 719-5952, FAX:
(212) 398-6414
Founded: 1982

**ALTERNATIVE CONCEPTS
INC**
10420 Jackson Oaks Way (Suite 103)
Knoxville, TN 37922-0708
Telephone: (865) 690-1990, FAX:
(865) 692-0072, E-Mail: support@
acmarketing.biz, Web Site: www.
acmarketing.biz
Primary Market Served: Business

Provide the tools today's small business
owners need, make it easy to use & affordable.

**ALTERNATIVE MEDIA
GROUP**
999 Vanderbilt Beach Rd (Suite 200)
Naples, FL 34108-3512
Telephone: (732) 741-0585, FAX:
(732) 741-0489, Web Site: www.
amg-global.com
Pres: James Cunningham
VP Sls & Bus Devel: Judd Bergenfeld
Founded: 1992

Provides direct marketing services utilizing newspapers; mail (product samples, package inserts, billing inserts);
billboards & mobile media & the Internet to spread its clients' marketing messages as well as providing design &
production services for direct mail &
list management services.

ANGEL SALES INC
3336 W Lawrence Ave (Suite 301)
Chicago, IL 60605-5212
Telephone: (773) 883-8858, FAX:
(773) 883-8889, E-Mail: info@
angelsales.com, Web Site: www.
angelsales.com
Pres: Robert Engel
VP: Laura Engel

Helping individuals & companies successfully bring their products to the international marketplace.

**ASHRAE LEARNING
INSTITUTE**
1791 Tullie Cir NE
Atlanta, GA 30329-2305
Telephone: (404) 636-8400, Toll Free:
(800) 527-4723, FAX: (404) 321-
5478, E-Mail: ashrae@ashrae.org,
Web Site: www.ashrae.org
Exec VP: Jeff Littleton
Outside Sls: Ed Farley
Dir Mktg: Vanita Vanita Gupta Gupa
Founded: 1894

Global society advancing human well-
being through sustainable technology
for the built environment focusing on
building systems, energy efficiency, indoor air quality, refrigeration & sustainability within the industry.

**AUTOMATED GRAPHIC
SYSTEMS LLC**
4590 Graphics Dr
White Plains, MD 20695
Toll Free: (800) 678-8760, FAX: (240)
222-3419, E-Mail: info@ags.com,
Web Site: www.ags.com
Pres: Katie Kriemelmeyer
VP Sls & Mktg: Alan Flint
VP Admin & Controller: Teresa Will-
ingham
Founded: 1975

Provides printing, programming,
graphic design & supporting ancillary
services of storage, fulfillment, finishing mailing & content creation.

BBS CHICAGO
Div of RR Donnelley
111 S Wacker Dr
Chicago, IL 60606-4301
Telephone: (312) 326-8000, Toll Free:
(800) 742-4455, Web Site: www.
rrdonnelley.com
Pres & CEO: Thomas J. Quinlan

Helps organizations communicate more
effectively by working to create, manage, produce, distribute & process content on behalf of customers.

BAYARD INC
1 Montauk Ave (Suite 200)
New London, CT 06320-4967
Telephone: (860) 437-3012, Toll Free:
(800) 321-0411, FAX: (800) 572-
0788, Web Site: www.bayard-inc.
com
Co-Dir Sls & Mktg: Kerry Moriarty
Founded: 1986

Publishes books, magazines & periodicals for children, teens, Catholics &
older adults worldwide, as well as videos for parish & catechetical use.

BETTER HOMES & GARDENS

Subs. of Meredith Corp
805 3rd Ave
New York, NY 10022-7513
Telephone: (212) 551-7097, FAX:
(212) 551-7114, E-Mail: support@
bhg.com, Web Site: www.bhg.com
Mktg: Jodi Marchiscotta

BON APPETIT MAGAZINE

Div. of Conde Nast Publications
1 World Trade Center (fl 35)
New York, NY 10007-0090
Telephone: (212) 286-2860, FAX:
(212) 286-2536, E-Mail:
paul_jowdy@bonappetit.com, Web
Site: www.bonappetit.com
Sr Food Editor: Alison Roman

BUTLER TILL MEDIA SERVICES

1565 Jefferson Rd Bldg 200 (Suite
280)
Rochester, NY 14623-3178
Telephone: (855) 472-5100, FAX:
(855) 274-5199, Web Site: www.
butlertill.com
CEO: Peter Infante
Pres: Kimberely Jones
Exec VP: Melissa Palmer
Primary Market Served: Consumer
Founded: 1998

CABLE DIRECT MARKETING INC

One Gabriel Dr
Montville, NJ 07045
Telephone: (973) 244-0010, FAX:
(973) 244-0302, E-Mail: cabledm@
aol.com
Pres: Matt Kraner
VP Mktg: David Martel

CAPITOL ADVANTAGE/ ROLL CALL GROUP

77 K St NE (fl 8)
Washington, DC 20002-4681
Telephone: (202) 6550-6500, Toll
Free: (800) 432-2250, E-Mail:
sales@cq.com, Web Site: www.
corporate.cqrollcall.com
Dir Adv & Events Mktg: Michelle Ri-
deout
Primary Market Served: Business

Provider of congressional news, legislative tracking & advocacy services,
connecting policy professionals &
opinion leaders with the information &
tools they need to understand & influ-
ence Congress.

CARDSOURCE

1286 Trapp Rd

Eagan, MN 55121-1217
Telephone: (651) 686-0660, Toll Free:
(800) 284-9194, FAX: (651) 686-
0330, Web Site: www.cardsource.
com
Founded: 1983

Develop unique data & programming
options for your plastic card programs.

CATALINA MARKETING CORP

200 Carillon Pkwy
Saint Petersburg, FL 33716
Telephone: (727) 579-5000, FAX:
(727) 556-2700, Web Site: www.
catalinamarketing.com
CEO & Dir: Jaime Egasti
Pres, US: Todd Morris
Founded: 1983

Provides personalized, digital media
solutions for the packaged goods industry.

CHICAGO SUN-TIMES

Subs. of The Sun-Times Co
350 N Orleans St (fl 10)
Chicago, IL 60654-1700
Telephone: (312) 321-3000, FAX:
(312) 321-9655, E-Mail: jmorawez@
suntimes.com, Web Site: www.
suntimes.com
CEO: Tim Knight

Offering news from international to local community news, sports & weather.

CHICAGO TRIBUNE

Subs. of Tribune Co
425 N Michigan Ave (TT200)
Chicago, IL 60611-4024
Telephone: (312) 222-3232, Toll Free:
(800) 874-2863, FAX: (312) 222-
2598, E-Mail: consumerservices@
tribune.com, Web Site: www.
chicagotribune.com
CEO & Publr: Tony W. Hunter
Founded: 1847

Multi-platform company, publishes
newspaper & a magazine.

CHOICE MAGAZINE

Div. of American Library Association
575 Main St (Suite 300)
Middletown, CT 06457-2845
Telephone: (860) 347-6933, (860) 347-
1387, FAX: (860) 346-8586, E-Mail:
adsales@ala-choice.org, Web Site:
www.ala.org/ala/acrl/acrlpubs/
choice/home.cfm
Science & Tech Editor: Cynthia
Crooker
Adv Sls Mgr: Pamela Marino

Founded: 1964

Source for reviews of academic books
& digital resources of interest to scholars & students in higher education.

CHOICE MEDIA

15 Danbury Cir
Amherst, NH 03031-2016
Telephone: (603) 672-3338, FAX:
(603) 249-9732, E-Mail:
choicemedia@comcast.net
Pres: Diane Caruso
Primary Market Served: Business
Founded: 2005

Specializing in Insert Media & Print
Media offers 25 years experience in insert media program management & insert brokerage placement.

THE CHRISTIAN SCIENCE MONITOR

The Christian Science Publishing Soci-
ety
210 Massachusetts Ave
Boston, MA 02115-3012
Telephone: (617) 450-2300, FAX:
(617) 450-2031, Web Site: www.
csmonitor.com
Mng Publr: Jonathan Wells
Chief Strategy & Mktg Officer: Susan
Paardercamp Hackney

An independent international news organization that delivers thoughtful,
global coverage.

CLIPPER MAGAZINE

3708 Hempland Rd
Mountville, PA 17554-1542
Toll Free: (888) 569-5100, FAX: (717)
569-5101, Web Site: www.
clippermagazine.com
Founder, Sec & Treas: Steven Zucker-
man
CEO: Steve Hauber
Founded: 1983

Provides direct mail advertising services in the U.S. & publishes regional &
local market edition magazines.

COMMERCIAL LITHOGRAPHING CO INC

1226 Chestnut Ave
Kansas City, MO 64127-2022
Telephone: (816) 241-2218, FAX:
(816) 241-6091, E-Mail: sjohnson@
commercial-lithographing.com, Web
Site: www.clitho.com
Chmn Bd: Bill Pfeiffer Sr.
Founded: 1923

Sheetfed commercial printing.

COMPUTER SHOPPER

Div. of Ziff Davis Publishing

28 E 28th (fl 11)
New York, NY 10016
Telephone: (646) 472-4000, FAX:
(646) 472-3912, E-Mail: feedback@
computershopper.com, Web Site:
www.computershopper.com
Editor in Chief: John Burek
Founded: 1979

Digital media company specializing in
the technology market.

COURSE TECHNOLOGY
RP-NFOA
Div. of Cengage Learning
1 Main St
Cambridge, MA 02142-1522
Telephone: (617) 225-2595, FAX:
(617) 225-7976, E-Mail: ed.moura@
cengage.com, Web Site: www.
course.com
CEO: Joe Dougherty
Founded: 1989

Publishes texts & electronic learning
solutions to help educators teach, students learn & individuals understand
emergent & current technologies.

DEX DIRECT MARKETING
Div of R.H. Donnelley
9380 Station St
Lone Tree, CO 80124-6807
Toll Free: (800) 999-4630, Web Site:
www.dexlist.com
Sls/Mktg Mgr: Linda Langhoff
Primary Market Served: Business &
Consumer

Marketing Consultant offers the fresh
telemarketing & mailing lists, updated
daily, based on geography.

DEX MEDIA
2200 W Airfield Dr, PO Box 619810
Dallas-Fort Worth Airport, TX 75261
Telephone: (972) 453-7000, Web Site:
www.dexmedia.com
Mgr Mktg Res: Joe Walsh
Exec VP & CMO: Gordon Henry
Exec VP & CFO: Paul Rouse
Chief Info Officer: Gary Shaw
Primary Market Served: Consumer
Founded: 2013

Local, social & mobile marketing solutions provider.

**DIRECT MAIL STRATEGY
GROUP (DMSG)**
Div. of Conrad Direct
300 Knickerbocker Rd
Cresskill, NJ 07626-1350
Telephone: (201) 567-3200, FAX:
(201) 567-1530, E-Mail: listinfo@
conraddirect.com, Web Site: www.
conraddirect.com
CEO: Barbara Schonwald

COO: Steven Maier
Direct Response Marketing Agency
specializing in print media planning
and buying (on-the-page and insert
space), merge/purge management, on-
the-page advertising sales, strategic
consulting, creative (copy/design) and
production (printing/mailing) management, and analytical data services.

RR DONNELLEY & SONS CO
111 S Wacker Dr
Chicago, IL 60606-4304
Telephone: (312) 326-8000, Toll Free:
(800) 742-4455, FAX: (312) 326-
7156, Web Site: www.rrdonnelly.
com
Pres, CEO & Dir: Thomas J. Quinlan
III
Conducts Business: North America,
Latin America, Asia & Europe
Employees: 60,000
Primary Market Served: Business
Founded: 1864
Gross sales or billing: $9,316,600,000

Book, catalog, magazine, direct marketing, commercial printing, fulfillment
and distribution services company.

**DUPLICATION FACTORY
INC**
4275 Norex Dr
Chaska, MN 55318-3046
Telephone: (952) 448-9912, Toll Free:
(800) 279-2009, FAX: (952) 448-
3983, E-Mail: info@
duplicationfactory.com, Web Site:
www.duplicationfactory.com
Pres: Peter McCarthy
Founded: 1984

Provides a range of CD & DVD replication services & a variety of fulfillment services as well as offering
duplication, authoring & packaging solutions.

**EDITORIAL FREELANCE
ASSOCIATION**
71 W 23rd St (4th fl)
New York, NY 10010-4181
Telephone: (212) 929-5400, Toll Free:
(866) 929-5425, FAX: (212) 929-
5439, E-Mail: office@the-efa.org,
Web Site: www.the-efa.org
Sec: Karen Williams
Founded: 1970

**ENTERTAINMENT
PUBLICATIONS INC**
Subs. of IAC/Inter Active Corporation
1414 E Maple Rd
Troy, MI 48083-9935

Telephone: (248) 404-1000, Toll Free:
(888) 231-SAVE, FAX: (248) 404-
1915, Web Site: www.entertainment.
com
CEO: Lowell Potiker
COO: Steven J. Lemberg
Founded: 1962

Provides consumer discount, promotion
& coupon products in communities in
North America.

EVERYDAY MEDIA
230 Old Albany Post Rd
Garrison, NY 10524-3711
Telephone: (845) 788-3900, FAX:
(212) 481-7800, Web Site: www.
everydaymedia.com
Pres: Lisa Martens
Founded: 1998

Small marketing consulting company.

FACEBOOK INC
1 Hacker Way
Menlo Park, CA 94025
Telephone: (650) 543-4800, Web Site:
www.facebook.com
Founder, Chmn & CEO: Mark Zucker-
berg
COO: Sheryl Sandberg
Primary Market Served: Business &
Consumer
Founded: 2004

Online social networking service.

**FAMILY CIRCLE MAGAZINE
INC**
Div. of Meredith Corp.
125 Park Ave
New York, NY 10017
Telephone: (212) 557-6600, Web Site:
www.familycircle.com
VP & Editor in Chief: Linda Fears

FINEST LED SIGNS
Div. of Finest Services Inc
265 NE 44th St
Fort Lauderdale, FL 33334
Telephone: (954) 771-5488, E-Mail:
finestservices@bellsouth.net, Web
Site: www.finestledsigns.com
Pres: Terri Effrain
Conducts Business: U.S.
Primary Market Served: Business
Founded: 1982

Marketing & advertising company specializing in LED signage.

FIRST CYBER SERVICES
13624 Montclair Dr
Omaha, NE 68144-2438

Telephone: (402) 330-3222, Toll Free: (888) 977-3222, FAX: (402) 330-3444, E-Mail: cat@1csinc.com, Web Site: www.firstcyberserv.com
Pres: Andy Fitzmorris
Founded: 1997

FIRST MARKETING CO
3300 Gateway Dr
Pompano Beach, FL 33069-4841
Telephone: (954) 979-0700, FAX: (954) 971-4707, Web Site: www.first-marketing.com
Pres & CEO: Ronald Drenning
Founded: 1972

Publishes custom newsletters for the entertainment & media-magazine industry in the U.S. as well as offering print & digital solutions.

FOX ASSOCIATES INC
116 W Kinzie St
Chicago, IL 60654-4655
Telephone: (312) 644-3888, FAX: (312) 644-8718, E-Mail: sales@foxrep.com, Web Site: www.foxrep.com
Pres: Marlys Fox

Developing an effective, strategically targeted plan for advertising across a broad spectrum of print & electronic media.

GLM COMMUNICATIONS
242 W 27th St (Suite 1B)
New York, NY 10001-5926
Telephone: (212) 929-1300, FAX: (212) 929-9574, E-Mail: info@glmcommunications.com, Web Site: www.glmcommunications.com
Pres: Gerald L. Massa
Founded: 1980

Advertising sales representation firm offering commitment to top print & digital media publishers.

DAVID GELLER ASSOCIATES
110 W 40th St (Suite 405)
New York, NY 10018-8567
Telephone: (212) 455-0100, FAX: (212) 455-0164
VP Sls: Joanne Sausto

Engaged in all facets of direct marketing.

GOOGLE INC
1600 Amphitheatre Pkwy
Mountain View, CA 94043
Telephone: (650) 253-0000, FAX: (650) 253-0001, Web Site: www.google.com
CEO & Co-Founder: Larry Page

Exec Chmn: Eric E. Schmidt
Co-Founder: Sergey Brin
Sr VP & Chief Bus Officer: Omid Kordestarni
Sr VP Corp Devel & Chief Legal Officer: David C. Drummond
Sr VP & CFO: Patrick Pichette
Primary Market Served: Business
Founded: 1998

Provider of Internet-based services and products including online advertising, search, cloud computing and software.

GUIDANCE ASSOCIATES
31 Pine View Rd
Mount Kisco, NY 10549
Telephone: (914) 666-4100, Toll Free: (800) 431-1242, FAX: (914) 666-5319, E-Mail: willg1961@gmail.com, Web Site: www.guidanceassociates.com
Pres: Will Goodman
Conducts Business: U.S., Canada, Singapore, Hong Kong, Europe
Employees: 100
Primary Market Served: Business
Catalog available online
Direct online sales
Founded: 1971

Publisher of audio-visual material & Internet software for the educational marketplace.

H & H GRAPHICS
854 N Prince St
Lancaster, PA 17603-2752
Telephone: (717) 393-3941, Toll Free: (866) 338-7569, E-Mail: info@thehandhgroup.com, Web Site: www.hhgraphicsgroup.com
Pres: Mary Kohler
Mktg Mgr: Josh Rittenhouse
Primary Market Served: Consumer

Print & marketing services provider.

HALOGEN RESPONSE MEDIA
1675 Broadway
New York, NY 10019-5820
Telephone: (212) 468-4000, Web Site: www.halogenresponse.com
Sr VP: Tom Benelli

Marketing & Advertising.

HARLAND CLARKE MARKETING SERVICES
15955 La Cantera Pkwy
San Antonio, TX 78256-2589
Telephone: (210) 697-8888, Web Site: www.harlandclarke.com
CEO: Charles T. Dawson

Primary Market Served: Consumer

Provides data-driven direct and digital marketing solutions to a complete range of vertical industries, including financial services, retail, insurance, healthcare, high-tech/software & more.

THE HARTFORD COURANT
285 Broad St
Hartford, CT 06115-2510
Telephone: (860) 241-6200, FAX: (860) 293-0178, Web Site: www.courant.com
Mng Editor: Barbara T. Roessner
Publr & Chief Exec Hartford Courand Media Group: Richard J. Daniels
Founded: 1764

Publishes daily newspaper.

HEARST DIRECT RESPONSE ADVERTISING SALES
Div. of Hearst Corp
300 W 57th St
New York, NY 10019-5239
Telephone: (212) 649-2000, Web Site: www.hearst.com
Exec VP Sls & Mktg: Jeff Hamill

Diversified media & information companies

HOELSCHER MARKETING GROUP
1145 N Second St
El Cajon, CA 92021-5024
Telephone: (619) 588-2155, FAX: (619) 588-9103, E-Mail: rvhmedia@aol.com
Pres: Russ Hoelscher

THE HOUSTON CHRONICLE
801 Texas Ave (Suite 300)
Houston, TX 77002-2996
Telephone: (713) 362-7171, FAX: (713) 362-3575, Web Site: www.houstonchronicle.com
Pres: John T. O'Loughlin
CFO & VP Fin & Planning: Michael A. Rutiedge
Primary Market Served: Business & Consumer
Founded: 1901

Publishing Company prints & publishes daily newspapers.

IMC - MULTI MEDIA MARKETING
Div. of IMC Inc
930 Fox Pavilion
Jenkintown, PA 19046
Telephone: (215) 887-5700 X107, FAX: (215) 887-7076, E-Mail: berylwolk@aol.com, Web Site: berylsworld.com

Chmn Bd: Beryl Wolk

INTERMEDIA OUTDOORS INC

512 Fashion Ave (fl 11)
New York, NY 10018-4618
Telephone: (212) 852-6641, FAX:
(212) 302-4472, Web Site:
imomages.com
VP Strategic Sls Mktg: Ted Gramkow
Primary Market Served: Business &
Consumer
Founded: 2006

Outdoor sports-oriented media group,
provides magazines & special interest
publications for sportsmen in the U.S.

INTERNATIONAL GAMCO INC

9335 N 48th St
Omaha, NE 68152
Telephone: (402) 571-2449, Toll Free:
(800) 524-2626, FAX: (402) 571-
7941, E-Mail: mark.stevens@
intlgamco.com, Web Site: www.
intlgamco.com
VP, Mktg: Mark Stevens
Founded: 1983

Manufactures & markets pull-tab ticket
products.

ITHINK DIRECT LLC

2 Westchester Park Dr (Suite 208)
West Harrison, NY 10604
Telephone: (914) 984-2109, E-Mail:
info@ithinkdirect.com, Web Site:
www.ithinkdirect.com
SVP: Fred Singer
Pres: Andrew Singer
Conducts Business: U.S.
Primary Market Served: Consumer
Founded: 2011

Direct & digital marketing agency.

JB DOLLAR STRETCHER MAGAZINE

3105 Farnham Rd
Richfield, OH 44286-7200
Telephone: (330) 659-3590, Toll Free:
(800) 673-2531, FAX: (330) 659-
6741, Web Site: www.jbdollar.com
Pres: Robert J. Minchak Jr
Asst to Pres: Pat Berganti
Founded: 1984

Publishes direct-mail advertising magazine.

KARABAN MEDIA SERVICES INC

208 Lenox Ave (#316)
Westfield, NJ 07090-5120

Telephone: (212) 840-0660, E-Mail:
gkaraban@karabanmediaservices.
com, Web Site: www.klapublishing.
com
Pres: Glenn Karaban
Founded: 1969

Independently owned & operated rep
firms in the U.S.

LIST PROCESS DIRECT INC

404 E 79th St (Suite 23G)
New York, NY 10075
Telephone: (212) 517-8550, FAX:
(212) 517-9728, E-Mail: pkranjac@
listprocessdirect.com, Web Site:
www.listprocessdirect.com
Pres & CEO: Paulette Kranjac
Conducts Business: U.S.
Primary Market Served: Business &
Consumer
Founded: 1983

Marketing company specializing in
print media, insert media and mailing
lists.

LOS ANGELES TIMES

202 W First St
Los Angeles, CA 90012-4105
Telephone: (213) 237-5000, Toll Free:
(800) 528-4637, FAX: (213) 237-
7679, E-Mail: rob.barrett@latimes.
com, Web Site: www.latimes.com
VP: Rob Barrett

MACHALEK COMMUNICATIONS

12550 W Frontage Rd (Suite 220)
Burnsville, MN 55337
Telephone: (952) 736-8000, Toll Free:
(800) 846-5520, FAX: (886) 490-
8834, E-Mail: publisher@machalek.
com, Web Site: www.machalek.com
Pres & CEO: Andrea Machalek
Founded: 1987

Help promote products & services for
companies both large & small.

MADISON DIRECT MARKETING LTD

60 Long Ridge Rd (Suite 306)
Stamford, CT 06902-1841
Telephone: (203) 653-3200, FAX:
(203) 316-0518, Web Site: www.
madisondm.com
Pres: Chris Hulse
Mktg Mgr: Michael Boccuzzi
Founded: 1984

Provides life stage database & marketing services.

MAIN STREET DIRECT

575 Lexington Ave (fl 4)
New York, NY 10022-6146

Telephone: (212) 779-3000, FAX:
(212) 779-3061, E-Mail: contact@
mainstreetdirect.com, Web Site:
www.mainstreetdirect.com
Mng Dir: Dan Kern

Develops multi-channel marketing solutions that drive consumer behavior &
help clients achieve their goals.

THE MARKETPLACE GROUP INC

9 Jaybarry Ln
Norwood, MA 02062-1925
Telephone: (781) 762-6600, FAX:
(781) 762-1300
Pres: Andrew C. Nimmo

MARVEL ENTERTAINMENT INC

135 W 50th St (fl 7)
New York, NY 10020-1201
Telephone: (212) 576-4000, FAX:
(212) 576-8506, Web Site: www.
marvel.com
CEO: Isaac Perlmutter
Founded: 1939

Operates as a character-based entertainment company.

MEDIA DYNAMICS LLC

12 Choctaw Ln
Greenwich, CT 06831-3203
Telephone: (203) 531-6600, FAX:
(203) 531-6661, E-Mail: bjann@
mediadynamx.com, Web Site: www.
Media-Dynamics.com
Pres: Bill Jann

MEDIA HORIZONS MANAGEMENT LLC

40 Richards Ave
Norwalk, CT 06854-2319
Telephone: (203) 857-0770, FAX:
(203) 857-0296, E-Mail: info@
mediahorizons.com, Web Site: www.
mediahorizons.com
Dir Digital Mktg: Kate Palmer
Mktg Communs Mgr: Katie Brown
Founded: 1988

Direct marketing agency that offers a
complete suite of services to provide
measurable marketing solutions.

MEDIA PEOPLE INC

Subs. of Media Horizons Inc
122 E 42nd St (Suite 725)
New York, NY 10168-0601
Telephone: (212) 779-7172, FAX:
(212) 779-7248, E-Mail: info@
mediapeople.com, Web Site: www.
mediapeople.com
Pres: Greg Pepe
VP & Gen Mgr: Nancy Forman

Founded: 1976
Publisher's representative firm that operates as a full-service extension of our publishing client's media sales department for both print & digital media.

MEDIA RESOURCE GROUP INC
100 S Bedford Rd (Suite 320)
Mount Kisco, NY 10549-3444
Telephone: (914) 244-4250, FAX: (914) 244-4458, Web Site: www.mrginc.com
VP: Kevin Vas
VP: Jillian Payne
Founded: 1997
Media buying firm for direct response advertisers.

MEDIASPACE SOLUTIONS
904 Mainstreet
Hopkins, MN 55343
Telephone: (612) 253-3900, Toll Free: (888) 672-2100, FAX: (612) 454-2848, E-Mail: bstcy@mediaspace.com, Web Site: www.mediaspacesolutions.com
COO: Randy Grunow
VP Bus Devel & Mktg: Brian St Cyr
Founded: 1999
Media company, assists advertisers & media agencies in planning, buying & placing media.

METROPOLITAN NEWSPAPER ADVERTISING SERVICES INC
28 Wells Ave (fl 4)
Yonkers, NY 10701-7045
Telephone: (212) 689-8200, FAX: (212) 779-9795, E-Mail: info@metrosn.com, Web Site: www.metrosn.com
Principal: Michael Baratoff
Principal: Phyllis Cavaliere
Founded: 1932
Offer a full service, comprehensive advertising resource that deals with all traditional print & digital newspaper platforms.

MILITARY DIRECT MARKETING INC
1 Bushwick Rd
Poughkeepsie, NY 12603-3839
Telephone: (845) 454-7900, FAX: (845) 454-7987, E-Mail: info@militarymedia.com
CEO: John Bradbury

Gen Mgr: Lori J. Nutting
Provide full service advertising, marketing, consumer promotions and branding strategies to target the military audience.

MILLER DIRECT INC
1096 Assembly Dive (Suite 316)
Fort Mill, SC 29708
Telephone: (803) 548-6900, FAX: (803) 548-8701
Pres: Steve Miller
Offers a full range of digital marketing services.

THE MISSOULIAN
Div. of Lee Enterprises
500 S Higgins
Missoula, MT 59801-2736
Telephone: (406) 523-5200, Toll Free: (800) 366-7102, FAX: (406) 523-5221, Web Site: www.missoulian.com
Publr: Mark Heintzelman
Editor: Sherry Devlin
Sls Mgr: Jim McGowan
List Mgr: Jackie Maunder
Mktg Mgr: Stephanie Bull
Employees: 160
Primary Market Served: Business & Consumer
Catalog available online
Direct online sales
Advertising/Marketing Budget Related to Direct Marketing: 0-25%
Founded: 1873
Newspaper covering five counties.

MONEY MAILER LLC
12131 Western Ave
Garden Grove, CA 92841
Toll Free: (800) 624-5371, Web Site: www.moneymailer.net
Chmn & CEO: Garry Mulloy
Sr VP Company Opers: Mike Hiskett
Founded: 1979
Provides advertising services through franchises & offers integrated shared mail & interactive solutions through various methods.

MORRIS COMMUNICATIONS CORP
725 Broad St
Augusta, GA 30901-1336
Telephone: (706) 724-0851, Toll Free: (800) 622-6358, Web Site: www.morris.com
Pres: Donna Kessler
Founded: 1945
Provides community, news, information, advertising, entertainment, and related content through diverse digital channels & distribution outlets.

MULTICHANNEL MERCHANT MAGAZINE
Subs. of Penton Media
11 River Bend Dr S
Stamford, CT 06907-0242
Telephone: (203) 358-4386, FAX: (203) 358-5823, E-Mail: melissa.dowling@penton.com, Web Site: www.multichannelmerchant.com
Mng Editor: Tim Parry
Sls & Mktg Exec: Elizabeth O'Connor
Reaches key decision makers responsible for commerce, management, marketing & operations at companies that sell merchandise through multiple channels, including commerce & catalog.

THE NH BROADCASTER
Div of The Sun
491 Dutton St (Suite 1)
Lowell, MA 01854-4292
Telephone: (978) 458-7100, Web Site: www.nhbroadcaster.com
Pres & Publr: Mark O'Neil
Chmn Bd: Kendall Wallace
CFO: John Habbee

NEW CUSTOMER ACQUISITION
Div. of Jon Jay Corp
620 Franquette St
Medford, OR 97501-7832
Telephone: (541) 779-9999, FAX: (541) 779-1935, E-Mail: bobk@postage-exempt.com
Pres: Bob Karl

NEW YORK DAILY NEWS
4 New York Plaza
New York, NY 10004-2413
Telephone: (212) 210-2100, FAX: (212) 643-7844, Web Site: www.nydailynews.com
Mktg Database Administrator: Irina Ratner
Largest newspaper in the New York metro market.

NEWS AMERICA MARKETING
1185 Ave of the Americas (fl 27)
New York, NY 10036-2603
Telephone: (212) 852-8000, Toll Free: (800) 462-0852, FAX: (212) 575-5845, Web Site: www.newsamerica.com
Chmn & CEO: K. Rupert Murdoch
Publisher of coupons in the U.S & Canada as well as provider of in-store marketing products & services, primarily to consumer packaged goods manufacturers.

NEWS & RECORD
Div. of Landmark Communications
200 E Market St
Greensboro, NC 27401
Telephone: (336) 373-7000, Toll Free:
(800) 553-6880
Editor & Publr: Jeff Gauger

Multimedia news, information, advertising & entertainment source for the cities of Greensboro & High Point, Guilford County & Rockingham & Randolph counties in North-Central North Carolina.

NOVUS MEDIA INC
2 Carlson Pkwy (Suite 400)
Plymouth, MN 55447-4470
Telephone: (612) 758-8600, FAX:
(612) 336-8600, Web Site: www.
npmnetwork.com
CEO: David P. Murphy
VP Media Investment: Bridgit Wallace
Founded: 1987

Provides digital & print media advertising services for direct response advertisers, retailers, entrepreneurial companies & agencies.

PAPILLION TIMES GROUP
Subs. of Omaha World Herald
604 Fort Crook Rd N
Bellevue, NE 68005-4557
Telephone: (402) 733-7300, Toll Free:
(877) 476-4237, FAX: (402) 537-
2997, E-Mail: advertising@
papilliontimes.com, Web Site: www.
papilliontimes.com
Publr: Shon Barenklau

PARADE PUBLICATIONS
Subs of Athlon Media Group
711 Third Ave
New York, NY 10017-4014
Telephone: (212) 450-7000, FAX:
(212) 450-7287, Web Site: www.
parade.com
CEO: John E. Haire
Pres & Group Publr: Wayne Powers
Founded: 1941

Publishes a weekly magazine in the U. S. distributed through various newspapers offering entertainment, living, food, health, fitness, nutrition & beauty related information.

THE PHILADELPHIA INQUIRER & DAILY NEWS
Subs of Philadelphia Newspapers LLC
400 N Broad St, Box 8263
Philadelphia, PA 19101
Telephone: (215) 854-2000, FAX:
(215) 854-4788, Web Site: www.
phil.com/inquirer
CEO: Robert J. Hall
Mng Editor & VP: Anne Gordon
Founded: 1829

Provides digital news publishing services & offers content related to Philadelphia news, sports, weather, entertainment, business, restaurants & food, living, video, classifieds & shopping categories through its digital newspapers.

THE PRESS & STANDARD
Div. of Walterboro Newspaper
1025 Bells Hwy
Walterboro, SC 29488
Telephone: (843) 549-2586, Web Site:
colletontoday.com
Publr & Adv Dir: Barry Moore
Mng Editor: Brantley Strickland
Founded: 1877

Committed to offering relevant local news & information to the residents of Colleton County.

RR DONNELLEY RESPONSE MARKETING SERVICES
4101 Winfield Rd
Warrenville, IL 60555-3521
Telephone: (630) 963-9494, Toll Free:
(800) 722-9001, FAX: (630) 322-
6270, Web Site: www.rms.rrd.com
Sr VP, Sls: Mark Gaier

RR Donnelley Response Marketing Services offers the most comprehensive single-source direct mail and marketing solutions. Services include: Direct Marketing Strategy, CRM and Database Marketing, Literature Management, List Processing, Creative Design, Direct Mail Print and Production, Postal Logistics and Project Management. We combine quality commercial and web printing with powerful imaging, for highly personalized, feature rich direct mail that delivers Outstanding Financial Results.

RSVP PUBLICATIONS
6730 W Linebaugh Ave (Suite 201)
Tampa, FL 33625-4914
Telephone: (813) 960-7787, FAX:
(866) 554-3003, Web Site: www.
MailToTheAffluent.com
Co-CEO: Lawrence Golden
Primary Market Served: Business
Founded: 1985

Direct mail advertising, design, print & mail 4-color picture postcards, advertising the more upscale local businesses to the homeowners most likely to buy.

RENTPATH LLC
3585 Engineering Dr (Suite 100)
Norcross, GA 30092
Telephone: (678) 421-3000, Toll Free:
(800) 216-1423, Web Site: www.
primedia.com
Chmn: Dean Nelson
Pres & CEO: Charles Stubbs
Sr VP & CFO: Kim Payne
Sr VP, Gen Counsel & Sec: Marlon Starr
Conducts Business: U.S., Brazil
Employees: 1,000
Primary Market Served: Business & Consumer
Catalog available online
Founded: 1975
Gross sales or billing: $73,400,000

Publisher of free print and online consumer guides such as, apartment guide, new home guide and rentals.com.

ROBERTS & BUCHANAN INC
513 S Travis St
Concordia, MO 64020-7329
Telephone: (660) 463-2192, E-Mail:
kmroberts@centurytel.net
Pres: Margaret Rose Roberts

SANCOA INTERNATIONAL LP
92 Ark Rd
Lumberton, NJ 08048-4103
Telephone: (856) 273-0700, FAX:
(856) 273-2710, E-Mail: sancoa@
sancoa.com, Web Site: sancoa.com
Pres & CEO: Joseph Saski
Founded: 1987

Designs & develops labeling & tube solutions for the manufacturers of personal care, beverage & other consumer products.

SCOTT'S DIRECTORIES
Div. of Business Information Group
12 Concorde Pl (Suite 800)
Toronto, ON, Canada M3C 4J2
Telephone: (416) 510-5131, FAX:
(416) 510-5129, E-Mail: info@
scottsinfo.com, Web Site: www.
scottsinfo.com
Mktg Dir: Jennifer Hunter

Information & Cultural Industries.

SENIOR PUBLISHERS MEDIA GROUP
Div. of Motivate Inc
4141 Jutland Dr (Suite 300)
San Diego, CA 92117-7316
Telephone: (858) 272-9023, Toll Free:
(800) 727-3646, FAX: (858) 272-
7275, E-Mail: info@spmg.com, Web
Site: www.spmg.com
CEO: Trevor Hansen

Specialist at placing targeted media messaging to the senior market.

IRIS SHOKOFF ASSOCIATES
130 W 42nd St (#801)
New York, NY 10036-7804
Telephone: (212) 295-9191, FAX:
(212) 293-3779
Pres: Iris Shokoff

Marketing Consultant.

SOLAR COMMUNICATIONS
1120 Frontenac Rd
Naperville, IL 60563-1799
Telephone: (630) 983-1400, Toll Free:
(800) 890-6906, FAX: (630) 983-
6125, Web Site: www.
solarcommunications.com
CEO & Pres: Frank Hudetz
Sr VP Sls & Mktg: John Thompson
Founded: 1961

Full-service direct mail provider, offers
marketing & production services in the
U.S.

**SPECIALIZED MARKETING
INC**
162 Prospect Hill Rd (Suite 203)
Brewster, NY 10509-2374
Telephone: (845) 278-6100, FAX:
(845) 278-6150, Web Site: www.
specialized-mktg.com
Pres: Bob Wood

Helping clients increase revenue by
creating & implementing strategiv media plans that enhance & support all of
the marketers' advertising channels.

SPECTRA PRODUCTS LLC
1364 Reynolds Rd
Johnson City, NY 13790-4837
Telephone: (607) 770-1985, FAX:
(607) 798-7771, E-Mail: info@
spectraproducts.com, Web Site:
www.spectraproducts.com
Pres: Anthony Aquino

**STANTON DIRECT
MARKETING INC**
329 Shappee St
Horseheads, NY 14848-1918
Telephone: (607) 734-1665, Toll Free:
(877) 734-1665, FAX: (607) 734-
3708, Web Site: www.stantondirect.
com
Pres: Aloysius F. Stanton

TVGUIDE.COM
Div. of CBS Interactive
11 W 42nd St (fl 16)
New York, NY 10036
Telephone: (212) 626-2500, Web Site:
www.tvguide.com
Sr VP & Gen Mgr Media Grp, CBS In-
teractive: Christy Tanner
Sr VP Natl Sls: Ian Wallin

VP & Gen Mgr: Paul Wehrley
VP Product Devel: David Singer
VP Mktg: Carrie Hoffman

Website featuring television programming news.

**TARGET MARKETING
GROUP**
1500 Spring Garden St (Suite 1200)
Philadelphia, PA 19130-4069
Telephone: (215) 238-5300, Web Site:
www.targetonline.com
Group Pres & Publishing Dir: Peggy
Hatch
Primary Market Served: Consumer

TELAMERICA MEDIA INC
1701 John F Kennedy Blvd (Suite
2510)
Philadelphia, PA 19103-2876
Telephone: (215) 568-7066, FAX:
(215) 564-5388, Web Site: www.
telamericamedia.com
VP, Direct Response Media Sls: Ivan
Silverman

**TODAY'S CHRISTIAN
WOMAN**
Div. of Christianity Today Internation-
al
465 Gundersen Dr
Carol Stream, IL 60188
Telephone: (630) 260-6200, FAX:
(630) 260-0114, E-Mail: tcwedit@
christianitytoday.com, Web Site:
www.todayschristianwoman.net
Editor in Chief & CEO: Harold B.
Smith

TOWN MONEY SAVER
6 E Main St
Lucas, OH 44843-9701
Telephone: (419) 892-1913, Web Site:
www.townmoneysaver.com
Pres: William Zirzow
Primary Market Served: Business

TRANS CONTINENTAL INC
One Place Ville Marie (Suite 3315)
Montreal, QC, Canada H3B 3N2
Telephone: (514) 954-4000, FAX:
(514) 954-4016, Web Site: www.
transcontinental-gtc.com
Pres: Remi Marcoux

USA WEEKEND
Div. of Gannett Co
535 Madison Ave
New York, NY 10022
Toll Free: (800) 487-4956, FAX: (703)
854-2122, Web Site: www.
usaweekend.com
Pres & Publr: Charles Gabrielson
Mktg Asst: Christa Hylton

VALASSIS DIRECT MAIL INC
Subs. of Valassis Communications Inc.
1 Targeting Ctr
Windsor, CT 06095-2639
Telephone: (860) 285-6100, FAX:
(203) 845-5338, Web Site: www.
valassis.com

**VALPAK DIRECT
MARKETING SYSTEMS
INC**
8605 Largo Lakes Dr
Largo, FL 33773-4912
Telephone: (727) 399-3000, Web Site:
www.valpak.com
Channel Mktg Mgr: Keith Brickell

VEGETARIAN TIMES
Div. of Active Interest Media
300 N Continental Blvd (Suite 650)
El Segundo, CA 90245
Telephone: (310) 356-4100, FAX:
(310) 356-4110, Web Site: www.
vegetariantimes.com
Group Publr Healthy Living Group:
Bill Harper

**VESTCOM INTERNATIONAL
INC**
2800 Cantrell Rd (Suite 400)
Little Rock, AR 72202
Telephone: (501) 663-0100, Toll Free:
(800) 264-0965, E-Mail: sales@
vestcom.com, Web Site: vestcom.
com
Pres: John Lawlor
COO: Shannon Palmer
COO: George Wishart
Conducts Business: Canada, U.S.
Primary Market Served: Business
Founded: 1985

Provider of customized shelf-edge
communications & marketing services
for the retail industry.

**VOCATIONAL BIOGRAPHIES
INC**
dba Project Special Education; vocbio-
sonline.com
414 S Sixth St, PO Box 31
Sauk Centre, MN 56378-0031
Telephone: (320) 352-6516, Toll Free:
(800) 255-0752, FAX: (320) 352-
5546, E-Mail: careers@vocbios.com,
Web Site: www.vocbio.com
Pres: Toby P. Behnen
Gen Mgr: Roxann Kleinschmidt
Conducts Business: U.S., Canada
Employees: 4
Primary Market Served: Business &
Consumer
Direct online sales

Advertising/Marketing Budget Related to Direct Marketing: 76-100%

Career success stories of real people in easy-to-read four page career profiles showing how real people deal with career upheavals in real life inspiring you to discover your dream career. As well as content rich special education programs using minimum prep time, no adapting non-threatening, easy to teach.

WE DELIVER AMERICA INC

68 Irving Ave
Englewood Cliffs, NJ 07632
Telephone: (201) 307-8888, FAX: (201) 307-1200, E-Mail: info@we-deliver-america.com, Web Site: www.we-deliver-america.com
CEO: Larry Tucker
Opers Mgr: Barb Keller
Customer Svc Mgr: Kim D'Aurizio
CFO: Herb Lefkowitz
CMO: Neil Boggart
Employees: 20
Primary Market Served: Business
Founded: 1994
Gross sales or billing: $10,000,000

Insert Media: Consumer Co-ops, Packages, Statements, ride-a-longs, handouts, take-ones. Take-Ones: College, post office, malls, retail, bowling alleys, fast food, hotels, motels, RV parks, tourist centers. New Mover Media: Co-op & lists 400,000 to 525,000 weekly pre movers. Sampling: Families, teens, fifty plus. Shopping malls: Sampling, take-ones, handouts. National, regional, local.

WINFIELD MARKETING CORP

RP-NFOA
5724 N Palaski Rd
Chicago, IL 60646
Telephone: (773) 743-8784, FAX: (440) 764-4871
Pres: Audrey Garrett

WORKING MOTHER

Part of The Parenting.com, Div. of Bonnier Corp
2 Park Ave (fl 10)
New York, NY 10016
Telephone: (212) 221-9595, FAX: (212) 219-7448, Web Site: www.workingmother.com
Pres: Carol Evans
Group Publr: Joan Sheridan Labarge
Editor in Chief: Suzanne Riss

YP TALK

1101 Cedar Crest Dr
Pittsburg, KS 66762-6631
Telephone: (620) 308-6434, E-Mail: info@yptalk.com, Web Site: www.yptalk.com
Publr: Kenneth Clark
Conducts Business: U.S.
Primary Market Served: Business
Direct online sales
Advertising/Marketing Budget Related to Direct Marketing: 76-100%
Founded: 2004

Industry enewsletter, recruiting & consulting.

ZCARD NORTH AMERICA

39 Broadway (fl 32)
New York, NY 10006-3047
Telephone: (212) 797-3450, Web Site: www.zcard.com
Fin Mgr: Denise Eagle

ZINIO SYSTEMS INC

114 Sansome St (fl 4)
San Francisco, CA 94104
Telephone: (415) 494-2700, FAX: (415) 494-2701, Web Site: www.zinio.com
Global Exec VP & CMO: Jeanniey Mullen Founder

ARIZONA

Whitehat Inc, 4665 S Ash Ave (Suite G-10), Tempe, 85282-6765

ARKANSAS

Windstream Communications Inc, 4001 Rodney Parham Rd, Little Rock, 72212

CALIFORNIA

Advisor Media Inc, PO Box 503350, San Diego, 92150-3350

Alan Gordon Enterprises Inc, 5625 Melrose Ave, Hollywood, 90038

Amobee, 950 Tower Ln (Suite 2000), Foster City, 94404

Bunchball, 2200 Bridge Pkwy (Suite 201), Redwood City, 94065-1187

CCI Digital, 2921 W Alameda Ave, Burbank, 91505

Catalyst Computer Services Inc, 2271 Prosser Ave, Los Angeles, 90064-2321

Caudill & Associates Inc, 1334 E Chapman Ave, Orange, 92866-2219

ClickMail Marketing Inc, 155 Bovet Rd (Suite 310), San Mateo, 94401-3135

Crossroads Films Inc, 1722 Whitley Ave, Los Angeles, 90028

Dial 800 LLC, 911 Pico Blvd (Suite 1200), Los Angeles, 90035

Disney/ABC Television Group, 500 S Buena Vista St, Burbank, 91521

E! Entertainment Television, 5750 Wilshire Blvd, Los Angeles, 90036

Electrosonic Group, 3320 N San Fernando Blvd, Burbank, 91504

Far West Media Services, 4140 Norse Way, Long Beach, 90808-1531

Golden Millennium Productions Inc, 622 E Villa St (Suite B), Pasadena, 91101-1120

Goolara LLC, 2150 Mariner Square Dr (Suite 100), Alameda, 94501-1085

Group 236, Two Jack London Sq, Oakland, 94607

Guthy-Renker Corp, 3340 Ocean Park Blvd, Santa Monica, 90405

Infomercial Solutions Inc, PO Box 1803, Agoura Hills, 91376

Ingenio LLC, 182 Howard St (Suite 826), San Francisco, 94105

It Really Works Inc, 9528 Dalegrove Dr, Beverly Hills, 90210-1711

JDS Uniphase Corp, 430 N McCarthy Blvd, Milpitas, 95035

Tylie Jones & Associates, 58 E Santa Anita Ave, Burbank, 91502

KICU-TV36, Two Jack London Sq, Oakland, 94607

Kappa Studios, 3619 W Magnolia Blvd, Burbank, 91505

Kragen & Co, 14039 Aubrey Rd, Beverly Hills, 90210

Liberman Broadcasting Inc, 1845 Empire Ave, Burbank, 91504

Lieberman Productions, 455 Ninth St, San Francisco, 94103-4410

Local Corp, 7555 Irvine Center Dr, Irvine, 92618-2930

Lyris Inc, 6401 Hollis St (Suite 125), Emeryville, 94608-1462

MundoFOX22, 4975 W Pico Blvd, Los Angeles, 90019

Marketing Solutions Group Inc, 480 St John St (Suite 150), Pleasanton, 94566-6682

MarketingWorks Inc, 6600 Sunset Blvd, Los Angeles, 90028

Media Funding Corp, 28990 W Pacific Coast Hwy (Suite 116), Malibu, 90265

Mercury Media, 520 Broadway (Suite 400), Santa Monica, 90401

Muscle Dynamics Corp, 14133 Freeway Dr, Santa Fe Springs, 90670-5813

NAGRA USA, 275 Sacramento St, San Francisco, 94111

NTN Buzztime Inc, 2231 Rutherford Rd, Carlsbad, 92008

Nor1, 3255 Scott Blvd, Bldg 7 (Suite 120), Santa Clara, 95054-3023

Online Print Solutions, 268 Bush St (Suite 4045), San Francisco, 94104-3503

Onyx Productions Direct Inc, 2355 Westwood Blvd (Suite 401), Los Angeles, 90064-2109

PM Productions, 5882 W Bowcroft St (Suite 2), Los Angeles, 90016-4907

Patriot Communications LLC, 1201 Alta Loma Rd, West Hollywood, 90069

Reputation.com, 1001 Marshall St (fl 2), Redwood City, 94063

Results Producers, 5800 Rhodes Ave, Los Angeles, 91607

Script to Screen Inc, 200 N Tustin Ave (Suite 200), Santa Ana, 92705

Smart Inventions Inc, 6421 E Alondra Blvd, Paramount, 90723

Smarthome/INSTEON, 16542 Millikan Ave, Irvine, 92606

StrongView Systems Inc, 1300 Island Dr (Suite 200), Redwood City, 94065-5171

Submit Express Inc, 315 W Verdugo Ave (Suite 101), Burbank, 91502

Vidi Emi Inc, 2450 Washington Ave (Suite 285), San Leandro, 94577

Voice Message Broadcasting Corp, 1 Columbia (Suite 250), Aliso Viejo, 92656

Walker/Fitzgibbon TV & Film Productions, 2399 Mount Olympus Dr, Los Angeles, 90046

Jordan Whitney Inc, 360 E First St (#593), Tustin, 92780

Yahoo! Inc, 701 First Ave, Sunnyvale, 94089

COLORADO

Canoe Ventures LLC, 160 Inverness Dr W (Suite 200), Englewood, 80112-5005

Intermap Technologies, 8310 S Valley Hwy (Suite 400), Englewood, 80112

Location3 Media, 1515 Arapahoe St, Tower 2 (Suite 400), Denver, 80202-2128

Net-Results, 221 Corporate Cir (Suite N), Golden, 80401

CONNECTICUT

CRN International Inc, One Circular Ave, Hamden, 06514-4002

CertainSource Inc, 338 Commerce Dr, Fairfield, 06825

Color Film Media Group LLC, 45 Keeler Ave, Norwalk, 06854-2307

Liquid Focus Direct LLC, 1335 Wood Ave (Suite 1), Bridgeport, 06604-1442

Robert Rosenheim Associates, 5 Gay St, PO Box 308, Sharon, 06069-2000

Webloyalty.com, 6 High Ridge Park, Stamford, 06905-1327

FLORIDA

Bamboo Cricket, 777 S Flagler Dr, W Tower (Suite 800), West Palm Beach, 33407-4438

Cendyn, 980 N Federal Hwy (Suite 200), Boca Raton, 33432

CityTwist, 1200 N Federal Hwy (Suite 417), Boca Raton, 33432

eTargetMedia.com Inc, 6810 Lyons Technology Cir (Suite 160), Coconut Creek, 33073-4322

Health International Corp, 1511 N West Shore Blvd (Suite 700), Tampa, 33607-4534

Home Shopping Network, One HSN Dr, Saint Petersburg, 33729

Ion Media Networks Inc, 601 Clearwater Park Rd, West Palm Beach, 33401

Jordan Direct LLC, 100 2nd Ave N, Saint Petersburg, 33701

Marcus Productions Inc, 3107 Stirling Rd (Suite 204), Fort Lauderdale, 33312-8500

MoreVisibility, 925 S Federal Hwy (Suite 750), Boca Raton, 33432

Sales Magic Inc, 2107 Corporate Dr, Boynton Beach, 33426-6645

GEORGIA

Allconnect Inc, 4 Concourse Pkwy (Suite 410), Atlanta, 30328-6199

ListK, 1200 Abernathy Rd (fl 17), Atlanta, 30328

Response Media, 3155 Medlock Bridge Rd, Norcross, 30071-1423

SilverPop, 200 Galleria Pkwy (Suite 750), Atlanta, 30339-5945

ThePort Network, 5500 N Interstate Pkwy (#550), Atlanta, 30328

Turner Broadcasting System Inc, One CNN Center, Atlanta, 30303

Turner Network Television (TNT), One CNN Center, Atlanta, 30303

The Weather Channel, 300 Interstate N Pkwy SE, Atlanta, 30339

ILLINOIS

Conversant Inc, 101 N Wacker (Floor 23), Chicago, 60606

Impact Communications Inc, 3283 RFD, Long Grove, 60047

Kelly, Scott & Madison Inc, 303 E Wacker Dr (fl 8), Chicago, 60601

Northern Lights Direct, 314 W Superior St (Suite 503), Chicago, 60654

SMY Media Inc, 625 N Michigan Ave (Suite 525), Chicago, 60611

TownNews.com, 1510 47th Ave, Moline, 61265

US Cellular, 8410 W Bryn Mawr Ave (Suite 700), Chicago, 60631-3463

INDIANA

DEFENDER Direct Inc, 3750 Priority Way S Dr (Suite 200), Indianapolis, 46240

Delivra, 9365 Counselors Row (Ste 210), Indianapolis, 46240

ExactTarget, 20 N Meridian St, Indianapolis, 46204-3023

Interactive Marketing Group LLC, 563 Heartland Ln, Brownsburg, 46112

LOUISIANA

Dukky Inc, 1200 W Causeway Approach, Mandeville, 70119

MAINE

Groff DRTV LLC, PO Box 8673, Portland, 04104

MARYLAND

Americatel Corp, 11300 Rockville Pike (Suite 900), Rockville, 20855

Blue Sky Factory, 40 E Cross St (Suite 2), Baltimore, 21230-4558

Invenda Corp, 7250 Woodmont Ave (Suite 320), Bethesda, 20814

Message Systems, 9130 Guilford Rd, Columbia, 21046

Publishers Circulation Fulfillment Inc, 502 Washington Ave (Suite 500), Towson, 21204

Startec Global Communications, 11300 Rockville Pike (Suite 900), Rockville, 20852

TLC, 1 Discovery Pl, Silver Spring, 20910

MASSACHUSETTS

Constant Contact Inc, 1601 Trapelo Rd, Reservoir Place, Waltham, 02451-7357

Fox Media Lab, 5 Rockland Terrace, Natick, 01760-5858

IMN, 200 Fifth Ave, Waltham, 02451

Masscot Internet Inc, 20 Grove St, West Yarmouth, 02673

September Productions, 15 Madaket Rd, Nantucket, 02554-2618

SmartSource Corp, 209 Burlington Rd (Suite 219), Bedford, 01730-1422

SoundBite Communications, 22 Crosby Dr, Bedford, 01730

MINNESOTA

Jump Technologies Inc, 2600 Eagan Woods Dr (Suite 350), Eagan, 55121

TopRank Online Marketing, 4032 Shoreline Dr (Suite 1), Spring Park, 55384

ValueVision Media Inc, 6740 Shady Oak Rd, Eden Prairie, 55344-3433

MISSOURI

Adknowledge, 4600 Madison Ave (fl 10), Kansas City, 64112-3042

Avatar Studios, 2675 Scott Ave (Suite G), Saint Louis, 63103

MEGA MEDIA, 5671 State Hwy DD, Reeds Spring, 65737

SEOinhouse, 5214 Cedarfield Dr, Saint Charles, 63304-8014

Schwartz & Associates Creative, 212 S Bemiston (Suite 3), Clayton, 63105

NEBRASKA

Infogroup, 1020 E 1st St, Papillion, 68046

NEVADA

The Gourley Group, PO Box 530273, Henderson, 89053-0273

Infomercial Sales Inc, 5921 Palmyra Ave, Las Vegas, 89146

Ben Kalb Productions, 5905 S Decatur Blvd (Suite 1), Las Vegas, 89118

Price Target Media, 108 Kentuck Ln, Carson City, 89706

Rapid Response Marketing, 7500 W Lake Mead Blvd (#9463), Las Vegas, 89128

NEW HAMPSHIRE

Level 5 Communications Inc, 1283 Main St, Dublin, 03444

New Hampshire Public Television, 268 Mast Rd, Durham, 03824-4601

NEW JERSEY

CNBC, 900 Sylvan Ave, Englewood Cliffs, 07632

Concepts TV Productions Inc, 328 W Main St, Boonton, 07005

Sandy Alexander Inc, 200 Entin Rd, Clifton, 07014-1423

ValCom Inc, 429 Rockaway Valley Rd, Boonton, 07005

Virgin Mobile USA LP, 10 Independence Blvd, Warren, 07059

Vonage, 23 Main St, Holmdel, 07733

NEW YORK

AOL Corp, 770 Broadway, New York, 10003

The Artists Co, 79 Mercer St (fl 2), New York, 10012-4430

Cinema World Studios, 220 Dupont St, Greenpoint, 11222

ClickSpark LLC, 530 Summit Point Dr, Rochester, 14467

The Collegebound Network, 1200 South Ave (Suite 202), Staten Island, 10314-3424

Comedy Central, 345 Hudson St, New York, 10014

Crescent Beach Productions, 3900 Veterans Memorial Hwy (Suite 271), Bohemia, 11716

Firebrand Group, 419 Park Ave S, New York, 10016

Fujisankei Communications International Inc, 150 E 52nd St (34th fl), New York, 10022-6017

iCrossing, 300 W 57th St, New York, 10019

iN DEMAND LLC, 345 Hudson St (fl 17), New York, 10014

Initiative, 1 Dag Hammarskjold Plz (fl 5), New York, 10017

Kantar Media, 11 Madison Ave (fl 12), New York, 10010

Katz Media Group, 125 W 55th St, New York, 10019-5366

LinkShare Corp, 215 Park Ave S (fl 9), New York, 10003-1622

Lionsgate Entertainment Inc, 75 Rockefeller Plaza (#1600), New York, 10019-6904

Mass Transmit, 333 Hudson St (Suite 802), New York, 10013

Media Consultants Inc, 29-15 Bell Blvd, Bayside, 11360

Mediacom Communications Corp, One Mediacom Way, Chester, 10918

NCC Media, 405 Lexington Ave (fl 6), New York, 10174

Petry Television Inc, 200 Park Ave (fl 17), New York, 10117

Rocket Direct Marketing Inc, 156 E 37th St (Suite 5A), New York, 10016

SAS Group, 220 White Plains Rd (Suite 100), Tarrytown, 10591-5823

Saatchi & Saatchi New York, 375 Hudson St, New York, 10014-3660

Syfy, 30 Rockefeller Plaza, New York, 10112

TowerData, 379 Park Ave S (fl 5), New York, 10016-8811

USA Network, 30 Rockefeller Plz (fl 27), New York, 10112

Viacom Media Networks, 1515 Broadway, New York, 10036

Video Ordnance Inc, 611 Broadway (Suite 307), New York, 10012

Visible World, 460 W 34th St (fl 14), New York, 10001

WLNY-TV 10/55, 270 S Service Rd, Melville, 11747-2399

Zeppo Marketing Inc, 423 Pacific St, Brooklyn, 11217

Zeta Interactive, 185 Madison Ave (fl 5), New York, 10016

NORTH CAROLINA

Emisare Inc, 620 Elm St (Suite 332), Greensboro, 27406-1467

INSP LLC, PO Box 7750, Charlotte, 28241

iContact LLC, 2121 RDU Center Dr (Floor 4), Morrisville, 27560

Sunbelt Media Service, 808 Beaver Dam Rd (Suite 100), PO Box 3116, Chapel Hill, 27515-3116

WCPE-FM, PO Box 897, Wake Forest, 27588

OHIO

AG Interactive, 1 American Rd, Cleveland, 44144-2301

Consolidated Technologies Group LLC, 1614 E 40th St, Cleveland, 44103-2319

List Media Inc, 251 W Garfield Rd, Aurora, 44202-8856

OREGON

Group Mojo, 800 NW Sixth Ave (Suite 313), Portland, 97209-3700

SuccessWorks Search Marketing Inc, 0650 SW Gaines St (Apt 1605), Portland, 97239-4451

PENNSYLVANIA

American Telecast Products LLC, 835 Springdale Dr (Suite 206), Exton, 19341

Comcast Corp, 1701 JFK Blvd, Philadelphia, 19103

Harmelin Media, 525 Righters Ferry Rd, Bala Cynwyd, 19004

Listrak, 529 Main St, Lititz, 17543-2121

NAPCO Media, 1500 Spring Garden St (Suite 1200), Philadelphia, 19130

QVC Inc, 1200 Wilson Dr, West Chester, 19380

Rajant Corp, 400 E King St, Malvern, 19355

Voice Systems Engineering Inc, 900 Wheeler Way (Suite A), Langhorne, 19047-1706

SOUTH DAKOTA

Bulldog Media Group Inc, 114 N Egan Ave, PO Box 463, Madison, 57042

TEXAS

AT&T Inc, 175 E Houston St, San Antonio, 78205-2233

Koeppel Direct, 16200 Dallas Pkwy (Suite 270), Dallas, 75248-6875

LinkWorth, 417 Oakbend (Suite C1), Lewisville, 75067

SUCCESS Partners Co, 200 Swisher Rd, Lake Dallas, 75065

Youtoo TV, 6565 N MacArthur Blvd (Suite 400), Irving, 75039

UTAH

Prosper Inc, 5252 N Edgewood Dr (Suite 150), Provo, 84604-5853

VERMONT

800 Response, PO Box 1049, 200 Church St, Burlington, 05402-1049

VIRGINIA

Dominion Enterprises, 150 Granby St, Norfolk, 23510

Network Solutions LLC, 13861 Sunrise Valley Dr (Suite 300), Herndon, 20171

WASHINGTON

Innovyx Inc, 1000 2nd Ave (Suite 900), Seattle, 98104

WISCONSIN

Cannella Response Television Inc, 848 Liberty Dr, Burlington, 53105-9384

The Metal Ware Corp, 1700 Monroe St, PO Box 237, Two Rivers, 54241

CANADA

Ontario

CFA Communications, 202-2 Duncan Mill Rd, Toronto, M3B 1Z4

Movie Central, 25 Dockside Dr, Corus Quay, Toronto, M5A 0B5

Protus, 2379 Holly Ln (Suite 210), Ottawa, K1V 7P2

Electronic & Broadcast Media & Services (32)

AG INTERACTIVE
Div. of American Greetings
1 American Rd
Cleveland, OH 44144-2301
Telephone: (216) 252-7300, Toll Free:
(800) 711-4474, FAX: (216) 252-
6778, Web Site: www.
americangreetings.com
Chmn Bd: Morry Weiss
Co-CEO: Zev Weiss
Co-CEO: Jeffrey Weiss
Pres & COO: John Beeder
Sr VP Creative & Mdsg: Thomas John-
ston
Primary Market Served: Business &
Consumer

Electronic greeting cards.

ADKNOWLEDGE
4600 Madison Ave (fl 10)
Kansas City, MO 64112-3042
Telephone: (816) 931-1771, Toll Free:
(866) 730-2109, Web Site: www.
adknowledge.com
Chmn Bd: Scott Lynn
CEO: Ben Legg
Pres: Marco Ilardi
CFO: Raffaele Sadun
Sr VP Corp Devel: Brett Brewer
Founded: 2004

Digital marketing company.

ADVISOR MEDIA INC
Div. of Hawkins Media LLC
PO Box 503350
San Diego, CA 92150-3350
Telephone: (858) 278-5600, FAX:
(858) 278-5600, Web Site: www.
advisor.com
Cust Svc Dir: John Hawkins
Pres: Jeanne Banfield Hawkins
Conducts Business: U.S.
Primary Market Served: Business &
Consumer
Founded: 1983

Producer of advice & how-to forums
across various industries.

ALAN GORDON
  ENTERPRISES INC
5625 Melrose Ave
Hollywood, CA 90038
Telephone: (323) 466-3561, FAX:
(323) 871-2193, E-Mail: contactus@
alangordon.com, Web Site: www.
alangordon.com
Pres: Grant Loucks
VP: Don Sahlein
VP & Gen Mgr: Wayne Loucks
Office Mgr: Stacey Sahlein

Founded: 1952
Motion picture and video support
equipment rental & sales.

ALLCONNECT INC
dba allconnect
4 Concourse Pkwy (Suite 410)
Atlanta, GA 30328-6199
Telephone: (404) 260-2200, Web Site:
www.allconnect.com
Chmn & CEO: Mark Miller
CFO: Mike Picchi
Exec VP Mktg & eCommerce: Scott
Klinger
Exec VP Sls & Svc: Rob Kocerha

Consumer services company.

AMERICAN TELECAST
PRODUCTS LLC
835 Springdale Dr (Suite 206)
Exton, PA 19341
Telephone: (610) 430-7800, FAX:
(484) 879-4046, E-Mail: info@
americantelecast.com, Web Site:
www.americantelecast.com
Pres & CEO: James E. McFadden
VP Mktg: Joseph Crowley
VP Media & Telemarketing: David
Scudder
CFO: Donald R. Kalb
Founded: 1975

Direct marketing company.

AMERICATEL CORP
Subs. of Impact Telecom
11300 Rockville Pike (Suite 900)
Rockville, MD 20855
Toll Free: (800) 221-3020, E-Mail:
customerservice@americatel.com,
Web Site: www.americatel.com
Exec VP Residential Svcs & Mktg:
Nermin Selimic

Telecommunications provider.

AMOBEE
Subs. of Singtel
950 Tower Ln (Suite 2000)
Foster City, CA 94404
Telephone: (650) 802-8871, Web Site:
www.amobee.com
VP: Kim Perell
CFO: Craig Foster
Conducts Business: Worldwide
Primary Market Served: Consumer
Founded: 2005

Global digital marketing technology
company.

AOL CORP
RP-NFOA
770 Broadway

New York, NY 10003
Telephone: (212) 206-4400, Web Site:
www.aol.com
Chmn & CEO: Tim Armstrong
Exec VP & Chief Fin & Admin Offi-
cer: Karen Dykstra
Global Head Media Sls: Jim Norton
CEO Platforms: Bob Lord
CEO Brand Grp: Susan Lyne

Mass media corporation.

THE ARTISTS CO
79 Mercer St (fl 2)
New York, NY 10012-4430
Telephone: (212) 679-7199, Web Site:
blog.theartistscompany.com
Exec Producer: Sally Antonacchio
Exec Creative Dir: Otis Mass
Bus Mgr: Christine Barbieri
Ops Mgr: Casey Cormier

Production company.

AT&T INC
175 E Houston St
San Antonio, TX 78205-2233
Telephone: (210) 821-4105, FAX:
(210) 351-2071, Web Site: www.
bellsouth.com
VP Consumer Mktg: Joey Schultz
Primary Market Served: Business &
Consumer

AVATAR STUDIOS
2675 Scott Ave (Suite G)
Saint Louis, MO 63103
Telephone: (314) 533-2242, FAX:
(314) 533-3349, Web Site: www.
avatar-studios.com
Pres: Bill Faris
Founded: 1999

Production studio.

BAMBOO CRICKET
777 S Flagler Dr, W Tower (Suite 800)
West Palm Beach, FL 33407-4438
Telephone: (561) 515-4546, Toll Free:
(800) 260-8050, FAX: (561) 653-
3990, E-Mail: info@bamboocricket.
com, Web Site: www.bamboocricket.
com
CEO: Paul Westhorpe
Pres: Barbara Westhorpe
VP Client Svcs: Susan O'Neil
Founded: 2006

Customer service company related to
inbound email response management,
live chat and email marketing.

BLUE SKY FACTORY
40 E Cross St (Suite 2)
Baltimore, MD 21230-4558

Telephone: (410) 230-0061, Web Site:
www.blueskyfactory.com
Mktg Mgr: Amy Garland

BULLDOG MEDIA GROUP INC
114 N Egan Ave, PO Box 463
Madison, SD 57042
Telephone: (866) 309-7687, E-Mail:
info@bulldogmediagroup.com, Web
Site: www.bulldogmediagroup.com
Founder & Pres: Darin Namken
Founder & CEO: Todd Knodel
Founder & Dir: Chad Ekroth
Conducts Business: U.S., Canada
Primary Market Served: Business &
Consumer
Catalog available online
Direct online sales
Founded: 2000

Online marketing services company
specializing in lead generation, data
management, email marketing and display advertising.

BUNCHBALL
2200 Bridge Pkwy (Suite 201)
Redwood City, CA 94065-1187
Telephone: (408) 985-2034, Web Site:
www.bunchball.com
CEO: Jim Scullion
Chief Product Officer: Rajat Paharia
CFO: David Overmyer
VP Mktg: Erika Blaney
VP Strategy & Corp Devel: Kenneth
Jones
Founded: 2007

Gamification solutions company.

CCI DIGITAL
2921 W Alameda Ave
Burbank, CA 91505
Telephone: (818) 562-6300, FAX:
(818) 562-8222, E-Mail: info@
ccidigital.com, Web Site: www.
ccidigital.com
Pres: Rick Morris

Full service post-production company.

CNBC
Div. of NBCUniversal
900 Sylvan Ave
Englewood Cliffs, NJ 07632
Telephone: (201) 735-2622, FAX:
(201) 735-3200, Web Site: www.
cnbc.com
Pres & CEO: Mark Hoffman
Sr VP Mktg: Thomas J. Clendenin
Sr VP Strategic Programming & Devel:
Susan Krakower
Founded: 1989

Cable business news channel.

CRN INTERNATIONAL INC
One Circular Ave
Hamden, CT 06514-4002
Telephone: (203) 288-2002, FAX:
(203) 281-3291, E-Mail: info@
crnradio.com, Web Site: www.
crnradio.com
Pres: Barry Berman
Mng Dir Strategy & Devel: Rob
O'Mara
Mktg Dir: Jim Alkon

Radio promotions & marketing company.

CANNELLA RESPONSE TELEVISION INC
848 Liberty Dr
Burlington, WI 53105-9384
Telephone: (262) 763-4810, FAX:
(262) 763-2875, Web Site: www.
drtv.com
Founder & CEO: Frank Cannella
CEO: Rob Medved
Pres: Tony Besasie
CFO: Mike Hennen

Long-form DRTV media service provider.

CANOE VENTURES LLC
160 Inverness Dr W (Suite 200)
Englewood, CO 80112-5005
Telephone: (212) 364-3600, FAX:
(212) 364 3601, Web Site: www.
canoe-ventures.com
CEO: Joel Hassell
Founded: 2008

Advertising technology company.

CATALYST COMPUTER SERVICES INC
2271 Prosser Ave
Los Angeles, CA 90064-2321
Telephone: (310) 441-4300, Toll Free:
(800) 659-2267, FAX: (310) 441-
4332, E-Mail: sales@
catalystsoftware.com, Web Site:
www.catalystsoftware.com
Pres: Richard Shaw
Founded: 1980

Computer software and services company specializing in direct response
media buying and marketing companies.

CAUDILL & ASSOCIATES INC
1334 E Chapman Ave
Orange, CA 92866-2219
Telephone: (714) 210-2585, FAX:
(714) 210-2595, E-Mail: bobc@
caudill4production.com, Web Site:
www.caudill4production.com
Pres: Robert S. Caudill

Dir Client Svcs: Susan Harper
Bus Affairs: Mary Caudill
Founded: 1986

Independent film and digital production
company.

CENDYN
980 N Federal Hwy (Suite 200)
Boca Raton, FL 33432
Toll Free: (800) 760-8152, FAX: (561)
750-6795, E-Mail: info@cendyn.
com, Web Site: www.cendyn.com
CEO: Charles Deyo
Primary Market Served: Business
Founded: 1996

Travel, hospitality & event planning
marketing agency.

CERTAINSOURCE INC
338 Commerce Dr
Fairfield, CT 06825
Telephone: (203) 254-0404, Toll Free:
(888) 655-0464, FAX: (203) 254-
0411, E-Mail: neil@certainsource.
com, Web Site: www.certainsource.
com
CEO: Neil Rosen
CTO: George Kydes
Pres: Lori Clure
Conducts Business: U.S.
Primary Market Served: Business
Founded: 2001

Email marketing and lead acquisition
technology company.

CFA COMMUNICATIONS
202-2 Duncan Mill Rd
Toronto, ON, Canada M3B 1Z4
Telephone: (416) 504-5071, FAX:
(416) 504-7390, Web Site: www.
cfacommunications.com
Pres: Andre Desroches

E-commerce video and digital media
production company.

CINEMA WORLD STUDIOS
220 Dupont St
Greenpoint, NY 11222
Telephone: (718) 389-9800, FAX:
(718) 389-9897, E-Mail:
cinemaworldfd@verizon.net, Web
Site: www.cinemaworldstudios.com
Pres & CEO: Maurice Keshner

Motion picture, network television,
commercial & music video production
studio.

CITYTWIST
1200 N Federal Hwy (Suite 417)
Boca Raton, FL 33432
Telephone: (866) 798-2489, FAX:
(561) 314-2692, Web Site: www.
citytwist.com

Founder: Lou Nobile
CEO: Ken Schwartz
Chief Tech Officer: Lyndon Griffin
VP Fin: Edward Smith
VP Opers: Jason Elston
VP Sls: Marc Lefevre
Founded: 2003

Email advertising company specializing in new customer acquisition.

CLICKMAIL MARKETING INC

155 Bovet Rd (Suite 310)
San Mateo, CA 94401-3135
Telephone: (650) 653-8055, Web Site:
   clickmail.com
CEO: Marco Marini
Chief Tech Officer: Cameron Kane
CFO: Russ Cerminaro
VP Sls: Brian Steacy
VP Strategic Svcs: Grant Johnson

CLICKSPARK LLC

530 Summit Point Dr
Rochester, NY 14467
Toll Free: (800) 878-5709, E-Mail:
   amy@clickspark.com, Web Site:
   www.clickspark.com
CEO: Brian Einhaus
Founded: 2006

Search engine marketing firm.

THE COLLEGEBOUND NETWORK

1200 South Ave (Suite 202)
Staten Island, NY 10314-3424
Telephone: (718) 761-4800, Toll Free:
   (888) 338-6960, FAX: (718) 761-
   3300, E-Mail: info@collegebound.
   net, Web Site: www.collegebound.
   net
CEO: Luciano Rammairone
COO: Mario Lupia
Primary Market Served: Consumer
Founded: 1987

Recruitment lead generation solutions company specializing in higher education.

COLOR FILM MEDIA GROUP LLC

45 Keeler Ave
Norwalk, CT 06854-2307
Telephone: (203) 202-2930, E-Mail:
   info@itownstore.com, Web Site:
   www.itownstore.com
Mgr: Brad Lareau

Communication, marketing and promotion solutions company.

COMCAST CORP

1701 JFK Blvd
Philadelphia, PA 19103

Telephone: (215) 665-1700, Web Site:
   www.comcast.com
Chmn & CEO: Brian L. Roberts
Vice Chmn & CFO: Michael J. Angelakis
Exec VP & CEO, NBCUNiversal: Stephen B. Burke
Exec VP, Pres & CEO Comcast Cable:
   Neil Smit
Primary Market Served: Consumer

Global media and technology company with two primary businesses, Comcast Cable (video, high-speed Internet & phone provider) and NBCUniversal (news & television networks, motion pictures & theme parks).

COMEDY CENTRAL

Div. of Viacom Entertainment Group
345 Hudson St
New York, NY 10014
Telephone: (212) 767-8600, Web Site:
   www.cc.com
Pres: Michele Ganeless
Pres Content Devel & Original Programming: Kent Alterman
Exec VP Programming & Multiplatform Strategy: David Bernath
Chief Mktg Officer: Walter Levitt

Cable television channel carrying comedy programming.

CONCEPTS TV PRODUCTIONS INC

328 W Main St
Boonton, NJ 07005
Telephone: (973) 331-1500, FAX:
   (973) 331-1550, E-Mail: info@
   conceptstv.com, Web Site: www.
   conceptstv.com
Pres: Collette Liantonio
VP Sls & Mktg: Kristy Pinand-Dumpert

Direct response commercial production company.

CONSOLIDATED TECHNOLOGIES GROUP LLC

1614 E 40th St
Cleveland, OH 44103-2319
Toll Free: (866) 742-0109, E-Mail:
   info@ctgconvergence.com, Web
   Site: www.ctgadvisor.com
Pres: Rick Spector
Primary Market Served: Consumer

Technology solutions company specializing in customer relationship management, marketing automation and contact segmentation & analytics.

CONSTANT CONTACT INC

A unit of Endurance International Group
1601 Trapelo Rd, Reservoir Place
Waltham, MA 02451-7357
Telephone: (781) 472-8100, FAX:
   (781) 472-8101, Web Site: www.
   constantcontact.com
Exec VP, CFO & Treas: Harpreet Grewal
Conducts Business: Worldwide
Primary Market Served: Business
Founded: 1995

Email marketing company.

CONVERSANT INC

101 N Wacker (Floor 23)
Chicago, IL 60606
Telephone: (312) 588-3671, Web Site:
   www.conversantmedia.com
Pres & CEO: Bryan Kennedy
Primary Market Served: Business
Founded: 1998

Digital marketing company.

CRESCENT BEACH PRODUCTIONS

3900 Veterans Memorial Hwy (Suite 271)
Bohemia, NY 11716
Telephone: (631) 588-6600, Toll Free:
   (888) 401-7700, FAX: (631) 918-
   5044, E-Mail: info@cbprod.com,
   Web Site: www.cbprod.com
Pres: Roy Dahl
Founded: 1996

Full-service video production company.

CROSSROADS FILMS INC

1722 Whitley Ave
Los Angeles, CA 90028
Telephone: (310) 659-6220, FAX:
   (310) 659-3105, Web Site: www.
   crossroadfilms.com
Exec Producer: Cami Taylor

Production company.

DEFENDER DIRECT INC

3750 Priority Way S Dr (Suite 200)
Indianapolis, IN 46240
Telephone: (317) 810-4720, Toll Free:
   (800) 860-0303, FAX: (317) 810-
   4723, Web Site: www.
   defenderdirect.com
Pres & CEO: David Lindsey
CFO: Bart Shroyer
COO: Jim Boyce
Chief Mktg Officer: Brad Cumings
Founded: 1998

Home security, HVAC and plumbing services provider.

DELIVRA
9365 Counselors Row (Ste 210)
Indianapolis, IN 46240
Telephone: (317) 915-9400, Toll Free:
(866) 915-9465, Web Site: www.
delivra.com
Pres & CEO: Neil Berman
Dir Opers: Kris Dougherty
Founded: 1999

Digital marketing services provider.

DIAL 800 LLC
911 Pico Blvd (Suite 1200)
Los Angeles, CA 90035
Telephone: (310) 273-9023, Toll Free:
(800) 700-1987, E-Mail: sales@
dial800.com, Web Site: www.
dial800.com
Chmn: Scott Richards
CEO: James Diorio
Sr Dir Telecom: Chris Lowe
Dir Strategic Partnerships: Eddie Treiz-
man

Provides call tracking & routing, vanity
numbers and data integration services
to optimize marketing.

DISNEY/ABC TELEVISION GROUP
500 S Buena Vista St
Burbank, CA 91521
Telephone: (818) 460-7477, Web Site:
www.disneyabctv.com
Co-Chair Disney Media Networks &
Pres: Anne Sweeney
Exec VP & CFO: Peter Seymour

The Walt Disney Company's global entertainment and news television properties, owned television stations group
and radio business.

DOMINION ENTERPRISES
150 Granby St
Norfolk, VA 23510
Telephone: (757) 351-7000, Web Site:
www.dominionenterprises.com
Pres & COO: Jack J. Ross
Exec VP & CFO: Teresa F. Blevins

Marketing services company serving
the real estate, employment, automotive and travel industries.

DUKKY INC
1200 W Causeway Approach
Mandeville, LA 70119
Toll Free: (888) 662-9096, E-Mail:
info@dukky.com, Web Site: www.
dukky.com
Sr VP: Mike Paine
Primary Market Served: Business &
Consumer

Founded: 2008
Sales, marketing & analytics technology company.

E! ENTERTAINMENT TELEVISION
Div. of NBCUniversal
5750 Wilshire Blvd
Los Angeles, CA 90036
Telephone: (323) 954-2400, FAX:
(323) 954-2665, Web Site: www.
eonline.com
Pres: Suzanne Kolb
Pres Network Strategy & E! News:
Cyndi McClellan
Exec VP & Gen Mgr Digital & Bus De-
vel: John Najarian

Cable television channel featuring entertainment & pop culture programming.

800 RESPONSE
PO Box 1049, 200 Church St
Burlington, VT 05402-1049
Telephone: (802) 860-0378, Toll Free:
(800) 639-7253, FAX: (800) 639-
6733, E-Mail: sales@800response.
com, Web Site: www.800response.
com
VP Mktg & Corp Commun: Laura
Noonan
VP Sls: Kathy Rossner
Conducts Business: U.S.
Primary Market Served: Business
Catalog available online
Founded: 1989

Provides top quality vanity 800 numbers which boost ad response for regional advertisers.

ELECTROSONIC GROUP
3320 N San Fernando Blvd
Burbank, CA 91504
Telephone: (818) 333-3600, FAX:
(818) 641-6384, E-Mail: info@
electrosonic.com, Web Site: www.
electrosonic.com
Pres: Jim Bowie
Founded: 1964

Audio-visual company that provides
systems integration, technical design,
project management & support of AV
products and systems.

EMISARE INC
620 Elm St (Suite 332)
Greensboro, NC 27406-1467
Telephone: (336) 378-0510, E-Mail:
info@emisare.com, Web Site: www.
emisare.com
Pres: Scott Williams

Founded: 2002
Marketing company that blends research, analysis & exceptional creative
into traditional and new media communications programs that build bonds between clients and customers.

ETARGETMEDIA.COM INC
6810 Lyons Technology Cir (Suite
160)
Coconut Creek, FL 33073-4322
Telephone: (954) 480-8470, Toll Free:
(888) 805-3282, FAX: (954) 480-
8489, E-Mail: info@etargetmedia.
com, Web Site: www.etargetmedia.
com
Mng Partner: Harris Kreichman

Marketing & promotion strategy company.

EXACTTARGET
A salesforce.com company
20 N Meridian St
Indianapolis, IN 46204-3023
Telephone: (317) 423-3928, FAX:
(317) 396-1592, Web Site: www.
exacttarget.com
CEO: Scott Dorsey
Pres Tech & Strategy: Scott McCorkle
COO: Andy Kofoid
Founded: 2000

Digital marketing software company.

FAR WEST MEDIA SERVICES
4140 Norse Way
Long Beach, CA 90808-1531
Telephone: (562) 496-3342, FAX:
(562) 496-4329, E-Mail: info@
farwestmedia.com, Web Site: www.
farwestmedia.com
Pres: Robert A. Ranaldi
Founded: 1988

Direct response advertising company.

FIREBRAND GROUP
419 Park Ave S
New York, NY 10016
Telephone: (866) 757-3362, E-Mail:
info@firebrandgroup.com, Web Site:
www.firebrandgroup.com
Founder & CEO: Jeremy Goldman
Creative Dir: Grant Newton
Conducts Business: U.S.
Primary Market Served: Consumer
Founded: 2012

Management consultancy specializing
in building brands through improved
marketing, communications & corporate strategy.

FOX MEDIA LAB
5 Rockland Terrace

Natick, MA 01760-5858
Telephone: (508) 655-5665, FAX:
(508) 655-2051, E-Mail:
foxmedialabs@gmail.com
CEO & Exec Producer: Joseph M. Fox
Founded: 1988

Direct response media firm.

FUJISANKEI COMMUNICATIONS INTERNATIONAL INC

Subs. of Fuji Media Holdings Inc
150 E 52nd St (34th fl)
New York, NY 10022-6017
Telephone: (212) 753-8100, FAX:
(212) 702-0420, Web Site: www.
fujisankei.com
Chmn & CEO: Takashi Hoga
Pres & COO: Makoto Wakamatsu
Founded: 1986

Japanese media company.

GOLDEN MILLENNIUM PRODUCTIONS INC

622 E Villa St (Suite B)
Pasadena, CA 91101-1120
Telephone: (818) 500-1099, FAX:
(866) 886-5802, E-Mail: info@
goldenproductions.com, Web Site:
www.goldenproductions.com
Sr Exec: Robert Hernandez

Integrated marketing services company.

GOOLARA LLC

2150 Mariner Square Dr (Suite 100)
Alameda, CA 94501-1085
Telephone: (510) 522-8000, Toll Free:
(888) 362-4575, FAX: (510) 522-
2457, E-Mail: info@goolara.com,
Web Site: www.goolara.com
CEO: Philip Thorne
Founded: 2005

Email marketing software company.

THE GOURLEY GROUP

PO Box 530273
Henderson, NV 89053-0273
Toll Free: (888) 656-1324, E-Mail:
issuestoday@yahoo.com, Web Site:
www.issuestodayradio.com
Pres: Bob Gourley

Production company for syndicated radio program, Issues Today with Bob Gourley.

GROFF DRTV LLC

PO Box 8673
Portland, ME 04104
Telephone: (207) 415-1374, FAX:
(207) 771-5320, E-Mail: regfilm@
gmail.com, Web Site: www.
groffdrtv.com

Pres: Reginald Groff
Primary Market Served: Business
Founded: 1982

Direct response television and radio production.

GROUP MOJO

800 NW Sixth Ave (Suite 313)
Portland, OR 97209-3700
Telephone: (503) 493-2242, FAX:
(503) 493-2246, E-Mail: sam@
groupmojo.com, Web Site: www.
groupmojo.com
Pres: Sam Rath
Principal: Roger Thompson
Creative Dir: Darrell Williams
Conducts Business: U.S., Canada
Primary Market Served: Consumer
Advertising/Marketing Budget Related
to Direct Marketing: 51-75%
Founded: 2003

Long form direct response, short form DR, long form content for distribution. Web and tradeshow distribution presentation sales.

GROUP 236

Subs. of Cox Media Group
Two Jack London Sq
Oakland, CA 94607
Telephone: (510) 874-0141, Web Site:
group236.com
Dir Retail Svcs: Heather Azim
Dir Res: Nicole Bergen
Dir Mktg: Steve Poitras
Dir Broadcast Design: Dylan Wilbur

Creative Services, Design, Program Services and Retail Services departments at KTVU Fox 2 and KICU/TV36 in the San Francisco Bay Area.

GUTHY-RENKER CORP

3340 Ocean Park Blvd
Santa Monica, CA 90405
Telephone: (310) 581-6250, FAX:
(310) 581-3232, Web Site: www.
guthy-renker.com
Co-Chmn: Bill Guthy
Co-Chmn: Greg Renker
Vice Chmn & CFO: Kevin Knee
CEO: Ben Van de Bunt
Chief Creative Officer: Lenny Lieberman
Founded: 1988

Direct marketing company.

HARMELIN MEDIA

525 Righters Ferry Rd
Bala Cynwyd, PA 19004
Telephone: (610) 668-7900, FAX:
(610) 668-9257, E-Mail: info@
harmelin.com, Web Site: www.
harmelin.com
CEO: Joanne Harmelin

Pres: Mary Meder
Founded: 1982

Direct response advertising services.

HEALTH INTERNATIONAL CORP

1511 N West Shore Blvd (Suite 700)
Tampa, FL 33607-4534
Toll Free: (800) 780-6744, FAX: (727)
595-6456, E-Mail: info@tonylittle.
com, Web Site: www.tonylittle.com
Owner, Pres & CEO: Tony Little

Direct response and television home shopping company.

HOME SHOPPING NETWORK

Div. of HSN Inc
One HSN Dr
Saint Petersburg, FL 33729
Telephone: (727) 872-1000, FAX:
(727) 872-7292, Web Site: www.hsn.
com
Chief Mdsg Officer: Anne Martin-Vachon
Exec VP Affiliate Rels: Peter Ruben
Founded: 1982

Shopping television network.

IMN

200 Fifth Ave
Waltham, MA 02451
Telephone: (781) 672-7000, Toll Free:
(866) 964-6397, FAX: (781) 890-
4701, E-Mail: support@imninc.com,
Web Site: www.imninc.com
Pres & CEO: Ben Levitan

Content-driven digital marketing service.

INSP LLC

Subs. of Inspiration Ministries
PO Box 7750
Charlotte, NC 28241
Telephone: (803) 578-1000, FAX:
(803) 578-1725, E-Mail: info@insp.
com, Web Site: www.insp.com
Pres: David Cerullo
Founded: 1990

Family value-based entertainment and religious programming television network.

ICONTACT LLC

2121 RDU Center Dr (Floor 4)
Morrisville, NC 27560
Telephone: (919) 820-7837, Toll Free:
(877) 820-7837, E-Mail: sales@
icontact.com, Web Site: www.
icontact.com
CEO: Geoff Alexander
VP Mktg: Nancy Vodicka
VP Sales: Eric Sternkopf

Conducts Business: Worldwide
Primary Market Served: Business &
   Consumer
Founded: 2003

Email & social media marketing services.

ICROSSING

Unit of Hearst Corp
300 W 57th St
New York, NY 10019
Telephone: (212) 649-3900, FAX:
   (646) 280-1091, Web Site: www.
   icrossing.com
Global Pres: Brian Powley
Chief Creative Officer: Patrick Stern
Exec VP, CFO: Michael J. Jackson
COO: Dave Johnson
Chief Tech Officer: Peter Randazzo
Chief Mktg Officer: Tari Haro
Employees: 750

Digital marketing agency.

IMPACT COMMUNICATIONS INC

RP-NFOA
3283 RFD
Long Grove, IL 60047
Telephone: (847) 438-4480, E-Mail:
   info@impactcommunicationsinc.
   com, Web Site: www.
   impactcommunicationsinc.com
Pres: Judith Filek

IN DEMAND LLC

345 Hudson St (fl 17)
New York, NY 10014
Telephone: (646) 638-8200, FAX:
   (646) 486-0855, Web Site: www.
   indemand.com
Pres & CEO: Robert G. Benya
Exec VP Programming: Michael Berman
Exec VP Bus Devel & CFO: Eric Petro
Exec VP & Chief Creative Officer: Stacie Gray
Founded: 1985

Distributor of transactional and subscription content.

INFOGROUP

1020 E 1st St
Papillion, NE 68046
Telephone: (402) 836-5290, E-Mail:
   contentfeedback@infogroup.com,
   Web Site: www.infogroup.com
Chmn & CEO: Michael Iaccarino
CFO: John Hoffmann
Chief Data Officer: Matt Graves
VP, Corp Commun: Ed McCormick
Primary Market Served: Business &
   Consumer

Founded: 1972

Big data, analytics and marketing services provider.

INFOMERCIAL SALES INC

5921 Palmyra Ave
Las Vegas, NV 89146
Telephone: (702) 253-0433, FAX:
   (702) 871-0759, Web Site: www.
   infomercialsalesinc.com
Pres & Owner: Jill L. Smith
Founded: 1988

Direct response television company.

INFOMERCIAL SOLUTIONS INC

PO Box 1803
Agoura Hills, CA 91376
Telephone: (818) 879-1140, FAX:
   (818) 879-1148, E-Mail: david@
   infomercialsolutions.com, Web Site:
   www.infomercialsolutions.com
Pres: David Schwartz

INGENIO LLC

182 Howard St (Suite 826)
San Francisco, CA 94105
Telephone: (877) 529-1193, Web Site:
   www.ingenio.com
Chief Product Officer: Amit Akhouri
Founded: 1999

Phone, chat & Web-based personal advice exchange.

INITIATIVE

1 Dag Hammarskjold Plz (fl 5)
New York, NY 10017
Telephone: (212) 605-7000, FAX:
   (212) 605-7200, Web Site: www.
   initiative.com
Global CEO: Jim Elms
Global Commun Dir: Christopher
   Jones
Global Chief Creative Officer: Michael
   Siegenthaler
Pres North America: Peter Mears

INNOVYX INC

Member of Omnicom Group
1000 2nd Ave (Suite 900)
Seattle, WA 98104
Telephone: (206) 674-8720, Web Site:
   www.innovyx.com
CEO: Derek Harding
Chief External Officer: Dominic Symes
Exec VP Delivery Svc: Matt Sinacori

Digital marketing solutions to advertising and marketing agencies and global 2000 enterprises.

INTERACTIVE MARKETING GROUP LLC

563 Heartland Ln

Brownsburg, IN 46112
Telephone: (317) 965-9215, Web Site:
   immarkgrp.com
Conducts Business: U.S.
Primary Market Served: Business

Web design & maintenance company.

INTERMAP TECHNOLOGIES

8310 S Valley Hwy (Suite 400)
Englewood, CO 80112
Telephone: (303) 708-0955, FAX:
   (303) 708-0952, E-Mail: info@
   intermap.com, Web Site: www.
   intermap.com
Pres & CEO: Todd Oseth
Sr VP & CFO: Richard Mohr
VP Worldwide Mktg: Kevin Burns
VP Engrng: J. Keith Tennant
Pres Dir PT ExsaMap Asia: Nigel D.
   Jackson
Primary Market Served: Business
Founded: 1996

Geospatial solutions company.

INVENDA CORP

7250 Woodmont Ave (Suite 320)
Bethesda, MD 20814
Telephone: (240) 333-6111, E-Mail:
   sales@invenda.com, Web Site:
   www.invenda.com
Chmn, CEO & Co-Founder: Kamran
   Amjadi
Pres, Chief Mktg Officer: Dadi Akhavan
CFO: Tracy Slavin
VP Client Svcs: Amori Langstaff

Digital marketing company.

ION MEDIA NETWORKS INC

601 Clearwater Park Rd
West Palm Beach, FL 33401
Telephone: (561) 659-4122, Toll Free:
   (800) 646-7296, FAX: (561) 659-
   4252, Web Site: www.ionmedia.tv
Chmn & CEO: Brandon Burgess
Sr VP Mktg: Chris Addeo
Founded: 2006

Independent, privately owned television company.

IT REALLY WORKS INC

12254 Montana Ave, Ste A, Los Angeles, CA 90049-5208
9528 Dalegrove Dr
Beverly Hills, CA 90210-1711
Telephone: (310) 888-4009, FAX:
   (310) 888-4025, E-Mail: steve@
   itreallyworks.tv, Web Site: www.
   itreallyworks.tv
Pres: Steven Dworman
Founded: 2001

Direct response television company.

JDS UNIPHASE CORP
430 N McCarthy Blvd
Milpitas, CA 95035
Telephone: (408) 546-5000, FAX:
(408) 546-4300, Web Site: www.
jdsu.com
Pres & CEO: Thomas Waechter
Exec VP & CFO: Rex Jackson

Innovates & markets diverse technologies through three business segments:
Network and Service Enablement,
Communications & Commercial Optical Products and Optical Security &
Performance Products.

TYLIE JONES & ASSOCIATES
58 E Santa Anita Ave
Burbank, CA 91502
Toll Free: (855) 955-7600, E-Mail:
email@tylie.com, Web Site: www.
tylie.com
CEO: Tylie Jones

Develops and manages customized radio & TV delivery solutions.

JORDAN DIRECT LLC
100 2nd Ave N
Saint Petersburg, FL 33701
Telephone: (727) 452-7718, E-Mail:
bruce@jordandirecttv.com, Web
Site: www.jordandirecttv.com
Co-Owner: Bruce Dworsky
VP Opers: Shannon Dworsky
Conducts Business: U.S.
Primary Market Served: Consumer
Direct online sales

Direct response television production
company.

JUMP TECHNOLOGIES INC
2600 Eagan Woods Dr (Suite 350)
Eagan, MN 55121
Telephone: (651) 287-6000, FAX:
(651) 287-6020, E-Mail: info@
jumptech.com, Web Site: www.
jumptech.com
Primary Market Served: Consumer
Founded: 1999

Supply-chain management solutions
company.

KANTAR MEDIA
Subs. of WPP plc
11 Madison Ave (fl 12)
New York, NY 10010
Telephone: (212) 991-6000, Toll Free:
(800) 497-8450, FAX: (212) 991-
6100, Web Site: kantarmedia.us
Global CEO: Terry Kent
Chief Client Officer: Richard Fielding
CFO: Amy Silverstein

Measures media impact and image.

KICU-TV36
Subs. of Cox Media Group
Two Jack London Sq
Oakland, CA 94607
Telephone: (510) 834-1212, E-Mail:
kicu.public@coxmg.com, Web Site:
www.ktvu.com/kicu/index
VP & Gen Mgr: Thomas Raponi
Gen Sls Mgr: Romeo Solomon

Independent television station serving
the San Francisco Bay Area.

BEN KALB PRODUCTIONS
RP-NFOA
5905 S Decatur Blvd (Suite 1)
Las Vegas, NV 89118
Telephone: (702) 871-8787, FAX:
(702) 597-0741, E-Mail: benkalb@
benkalbproductions.com, Web Site:
www.benkalbproductions.com
Exec Producer: Ben Kalb

Infomercial production company.

KAPPA STUDIOS
3619 W Magnolia Blvd
Burbank, CA 91505
Telephone: (818) 843-3400, FAX:
(818) 559-5684, E-Mail: info@
kappastudios.com, Web Site: www.
kappastudios.com
Pres: Paul Long

Full service television production &
post-production facility.

KATZ MEDIA GROUP
Subs. of Clear Channel Communications
125 W 55th St
New York, NY 10019-5366
Telephone: (212) 424-6000, Web Site:
www.katz-media.com
Pres & CEO Katz Television: Leo
MacCourtney
Pres & COO Katz Television: Craig
Broitman
Pres Katz Direct: Chickie Bucco
Pres Katz Radio: Mark Gray
Pres Proxi Digital: Mort Greenberg
Founded: 1988

Media representation company.

KELLY, SCOTT & MADISON INC
303 E Wacker Dr (fl 8)
Chicago, IL 60601
Telephone: (312) 977-0772, FAX:
(312) 977-0874, E-Mail: info@
ksmmedia.com, Web Site: www.
ksmmedia.com
Pres: Joni Williams
Chief Strategy Officer: Jonathan
Lichter

CFO: Mark Sloane
Independent media agency.

KOEPPEL DIRECT
16200 Dallas Pkwy (Suite 270)
Dallas, TX 75248-6875
Telephone: (972) 732-6110, FAX:
(972) 248-2759, E-Mail: pkoeppel@
koeppelinc.com, Web Site: www.
koeppeldirect.com
Pres: Peter Koeppel
Chief Media Strategist: Christena Garduno
Sr VP Bus Devel: Sean Bartyzel
Conducts Business: U.S.
Employees: 15
Primary Market Served: Business &
Consumer
Advertising/Marketing Budget Related
to Direct Marketing: 76-100%
Direct Marketing ad budget:
Magazines: 10%
TV/Radio: 90%
Founded: 1995
Gross sales or billing: $25,000,000

Direct response media-buying agency,
specializing in integrated direct response TV and online advertising campaigns, designed to maximize clients'
ROI from their marketing initiatives.

KRAGEN & CO
14039 Aubrey Rd
Beverly Hills, CA 90210
Telephone: (310) 854-4400, Toll Free:
(877) 808-0698, FAX: (310) 854-
0238, E-Mail: info@
kragenandcompany.com, Web Site:
www.kenkragen.com
Pres: Ken Kragen

Consultancy, management & production company.

LEVEL 5 COMMUNICATIONS INC
dba Desktop Engineering
1283 Main St
Dublin, NH 03444
Telephone: (603) 563-1631, FAX:
(603) 563-8912, E-Mail: de-news@
deskeng.com, Web Site: www.
deskeng.com
Publr: Steve Robbins
Mng Editor: Jaime Gooch
Art & Production Dir: Darlene Sweeney
Primary Market Served: Business &
Consumer
Catalog available online
Direct online sales

Publication for design engineering industry news, products & services.

LIBERMAN BROADCASTING INC

1845 Empire Ave
Burbank, CA 91504
Telephone: (818) 729-5300, E-Mail:
lbiinfo@lbimedia.com, Web Site:
www.lbimedia.com
Pres: Jose Liberman
Exec VP & Sec: Lenard Liberman
VP Programming: Eduardo Leon
Founded: 1987

Privately held, minority-owned Spanish language broadcaster.

LIEBERMAN PRODUCTIONS

Subs. of Guthy-Renker
455 Ninth St
San Francisco, CA 94103-4410
Telephone: (415) 955-0855, FAX:
(415) 955-0822, E-Mail: lpinfo@
lieberman.com, Web Site: www.
lieberman.com
Founder: Lenny Lieberman
Pres: Toni Beauchamp
Exec Creative Dir: Paul Allen

Direct-response TV infomercial & short-form TV spot production company.

LINKSHARE CORP

Div. of Rakuten Inc
215 Park Ave S (fl 9)
New York, NY 10003-1622
Telephone: (646) 943-8200, FAX:
(646) 943-8204, Web Site: www.
linkshare.com
CEO: Yaz Iida
COO: Liane Dietrich
CFO: Bodie Gagnon
CIO: Rohinee Mohindroo
Gen Counsel: Reginald Rasch
Founded: 1996

Online marketing services company for e-commerce businesses.

LINKWORTH

417 Oakbend (Suite C1)
Lewisville, TX 75067
Telephone: (214) 440-3900, Toll Free:
(866) 565-9784, Web Site: www.
linkworth.com
Pres: Ron Wicker

Marketing products & service company.

LIONSGATE ENTERTAINMENT INC

75 Rockefeller Plaza (#1600)
New York, NY 10019-6904
Telephone: (212) 577-2400, FAX:
(212) 962-2872, Web Site: www.
lionsgate.com
CEO: John Feltheimer

Vice Chmn: Michael Burns
Co-COO & Pres Motion Picture Grp:
Steve Beeks
Co-COO: Brian Goldsmith
Gen Counsel & Chief Strategic Officer:
Wayne Levin
CFO: James W. Barge
Primary Market Served: Business
Founded: 1997

Television distribution company & movie studio.

LIQUID FOCUS DIRECT LLC

1335 Wood Ave (Suite 1)
Bridgeport, CT 06604-1442
Telephone: (866) 892-0259, FAX:
(203) 339-0066, Web Site: www.
getliquidfocus.com
CEO: Kenneth Osborn
Founded: 2003

E-commerce & interactive marketing agency.

LIST MEDIA INC

dba admail.net
251 W Garfield Rd
Aurora, OH 44202-8856
Telephone: (330) 995-0864, FAX:
(330) 995-0873, E-Mail: sales@
admail.net, Web Site: www.admail.
net
Pres: Robert Hicks
Conducts Business: U.S., Canada
Primary Market Served: Business &
Consumer
Advertising/Marketing Budget Related
to Direct Marketing: 76-100%
Founded: 1991

Web-based marketing company offering list management & direct marketing services.

LISTK

1200 Abernathy Rd (fl 17)
Atlanta, GA 30328
Toll Free: (800) 600-3389, FAX: (770)
825-9188, E-Mail: questions@listk.
com, Web Site: www.listk.com
Dir Mktg Svcs: Nicole Lobisco
Sls Dir: Kathy Morandini
Dir Opers & Customer Svcs: Annette
Clemens
Conducts Business: U.S., Canada
Primary Market Served: Business
Founded: 2002

Email & lead generation technology company.

LISTRAK

529 Main St
Lititz, PA 17543-2121

Telephone: (717) 627-4528, Toll Free:
(877) 362-4556, E-Mail: info@
listrak.com, Web Site: www.listrak.
com
CEO: Ross Kramer
COO: Howard Kramer
Pres: Ben Smith
Founded: 1999

Integrated digital marketing platform providing omnichannel solutions for retailers.

LOCAL CORP

7555 Irvine Center Dr
Irvine, CA 92618-2930
Toll Free: (877) 784-0805, FAX: (949)
784-0880, Web Site: www.local.com
Chmn & CEO: Fred Thiel
CFO: Ken Cragun
Gen Counsel: Scott Reinke
Founded: 1999

Advertising & technology company.

LOCATION3 MEDIA

1515 Arapahoe St, Tower 2 (Suite 400)
Denver, CO 80202-2128
Telephone: (720) 881-8510, FAX:
(303) 298-1986, E-Mail: info@
location3.com, Web Site: www.
location3.com
CEO: Andrew Beckman
Pres: Alex Porter
Sr VP Digital Media: Samantha Bedford
VP Fin: Ryan Guilford

LYRIS INC

6401 Hollis St (Suite 125)
Emeryville, CA 94608-1462
Telephone: (510) 844-1551, Toll Free:
(800) 768-2929, FAX: (510) 844-
1598, E-Mail: sales@lyris.com, Web
Site: www.lyris.com
CEO: John Philpin
COO & CFO: Deborah Eudaley
Chief Mktg Officer: Alex Lustberg
Conducts Business: Worldwide
Employees: 40
Primary Market Served: Business
Catalog available online
Direct online sales
Advertising/Marketing Budget Related
to Direct Marketing: 0-25%
Founded: 1994
Gross sales or billing: $12,000,000

Develops e-mail marketing software and hosts services for medium and large sized businesses

MUNDOFOX22

KWHY Canal 22 Los Angeles
4975 W Pico Blvd
Los Angeles, CA 90019

Telephone: (213) 344-3700, E-Mail:
info@canal22.tv, Web Site: www.
mundofox22.com
Pres & COO: Otto Padron
VP & Gen Mgr: Lino Alvarez
VP & Gen Mgr: Bernarda Duarte
Spanish language television station located in Los Angeles.

MARCUS PRODUCTIONS INC
3107 Stirling Rd (Suite 204)
Fort Lauderdale, FL 33312-8500
Telephone: (954) 965-5295, E-Mail:
steve@marcusproductions.com, Web
Site: www.marcusproductions.com
Pres: Steven Marcus
Film & high def television production
company.

MARKETING SOLUTIONS GROUP INC
RP-NFOA
480 St John St (Suite 150)
Pleasanton, CA 94566-6682
Telephone: (510) 331-7625, E-Mail:
info@marketingsolutionsgroup.biz,
Web Site: marketingsolutionsgroup.
biz
Pres & CEO: Gary O. Bosley
Television advertising production company.

MARKETINGWORKS INC
PO Box 480354, Los Angeles, CA
90048-1354
6600 Sunset Blvd
Los Angeles, CA 90028
Telephone: (323) 436-2000, E-Mail:
chas@mwks.net, Web Site: www.
marketingworksagency.com
CEO: Charles Salmore
Chief Digital Officer: Aaron Moskowitz
Social media marketing company.

MASS TRANSMIT
333 Hudson St (Suite 802)
New York, NY 10013
Telephone: (646) 797-4349, E-Mail:
info@masstransmit.com, Web Site:
www.masstransmit.com
CEO: Adam Holden-Bache
Pres: Anthony Schneider

MASSCOT INTERNET INC
20 Grove St
West Yarmouth, MA 02673
Telephone: (508) 778-4500, FAX:
(888) 884-9960, E-Mail: admin@
masscot.net, Web Site:
masscothosting.com
Pres: John McDonald

Primary Market Served: Business &
Consumer
Founded: 1988
Web site design, development & hosting company.

MEDIA CONSULTANTS INC
29-15 Bell Blvd
Bayside, NY 11360
Telephone: (718) 423-6300, FAX:
(718) 428-7482, E-Mail:
mediaconsults@aol.com
Pres: Jill Albert
Advertising agency.

MEDIA FUNDING CORP
RP-NFOA
28990 W Pacific Coast Hwy (Suite
116)
Malibu, CA 90265
Telephone: (310) 457-4140, FAX:
(310) 774-1234, E-Mail: info@
mediafunding.com, Web Site:
mediafunding.com
Pres: Peter Bieler
VP Fin: Jeanne Rothman
Founded: 1999
Provides funding for television direct
response marketing.

MEDIACOM COMMUNICATIONS CORP
One Mediacom Way
Chester, NY 10918
Toll Free: (855) 633-4226, FAX: (845)
698-4100, Web Site: www.
mediacomcable.com
Chmn & CEO: Rocco B. Commisso
Exec VP & CFO: Mark E. Stephan
Exec VP Opers: John G. Pascarelli
Exec VP Programming & HR: Italia
Commisso Weinand
Sr VP Mktg & Consumer Svcs: David
M. McNaughton
Employees: 4,700
Digital cable television, high-speed Internet & phone service provider.

MEGA MEDIA
5671 State Hwy DD
Reeds Spring, MO 65737
Telephone: (405) 623-0023, E-Mail:
lisa@mega-media.biz, Web Site:
mega-media.biz
Pres: Lisa Liebl
Primary Market Served: Consumer
Founded: 2002
Strategic media relations & publicity
firm.

MERCURY MEDIA
520 Broadway (Suite 400)
Santa Monica, CA 90401

Telephone: (310) 451-2900, FAX:
(310) 451-0180, Web Site: www.
mercurymedia.com
Pres: Maria Eden
Pres Digital: Keith Kochberg
Pres Performance Guarantee: Beth
Vendice
Pres Long Form & Espanol: Ruben
Hernandez
Privately owned, full-service performance marketing agency.

MESSAGE SYSTEMS
9130 Guilford Rd
Columbia, MD 21046
Telephone: (410) 872-4910, Toll Free:
(877) 887-3031, FAX: (410) 872-
4912, E-Mail: information@
messagesystems.com, Web Site:
www.messagesystems.com
CEO: Phillip Merrick
Pres: George Schlossnagle
CFO: James Elder
Sr VP Sls for the Americas: Barry Abel
Sr VP Mktg: Steve Dille
Conducts Business: U.S., Canada, Europe & Asia
Primary Market Served: Business
Advertising/Marketing Budget Related
to Direct Marketing: 26-50%
Founded: 1997
Software developer for complex email,
text & cross-channel messaging operations.

THE METAL WARE CORP
1700 Monroe St, PO Box 237
Two Rivers, WI 54241
Telephone: (920) 793-1368, Toll Free:
(800) 288-4545, FAX: (920) 794-
3161, Web Site: www.nesco.com
Pres & CEO: Wesley Drumm
Exec VP & COO: Don Kozlowski
VP Sls & Mktg: Darlene Schmitz
Manufacturer of electric cooking appliances.

MOREVISIBILITY
925 S Federal Hwy (Suite 750)
Boca Raton, FL 33432
Telephone: (561) 620-9682, Toll Free:
(800) 787-0497, FAX: (561) 620-
9684, E-Mail: info@morevisibility.
com, Web Site: www.morevisibility.
com
Pres: Andrew Wetzler
CEO: Dennis Pushkin
Exec VP: Danielle Leitch
VP Sls & Mktg: Khrysti Nazzaro
Founded: 1999
Digital marketing agency.

MOVIE CENTRAL
Div. of Corus Entertainment

25 Dockside Dr, Corus Quay
Toronto, ON, Canada M5A 0B5
Telephone: (416) 479-6784, E-Mail:
info@moviecentral.ca, Web Site:
www.moviecentral.ca
Pres & CEO: John Cassaday
VP Television & Head Content Distr &
Pay TV: Maria Hale

Premium pay television service available in western Canada.

MUSCLE DYNAMICS CORP
14133 Freeway Dr
Santa Fe Springs, CA 90670-5813
Telephone: (562) 926-3232, Toll Free:
(888) 629-4226, FAX: (562) 926-9191, E-Mail: info@
muscledynamics.com, Web Site:
www.muscledynamics.com
Pres: Brian Lewallen

Fitness industry company.

NAGRA USA
Div. of Kudelski Group
275 Sacramento St
San Francisco, CA 94111
Telephone: (415) 962-5000, FAX:
(415) 962-5300, E-Mail: dtv@nagra.
com, Web Site: www.nagra.com
Chmn & CEO: Andre Kudelski
Exec VP & CFO: Mauro Saladini
Sr VP Grp Mktg: Ivan Verbesselt
Sr VP Sls Americas: Tom Wirth

Provider of security & multiscreen user experience solutions for the monetization of digital media.

NAPCO MEDIA
North American Publishing Co
1500 Spring Garden St (Suite 1200)
Philadelphia, PA 19130
Telephone: (215) 238-5300, FAX:
(215) 238-5412, Web Site: www.
napco.com
Pres: Ned Borowsky
Exec VP: Dave Leskusky
List Mgr: Bob Gibbons
Primary Market Served: Business &
Consumer
Founded: 1958

Full-service B2B digital media company serving the consumer technology, marketing, retail, nonprofit, printing & packaging, publishing and promotional products industries.

NCC MEDIA
405 Lexington Ave (fl 6)
New York, NY 10174
Telephone: (212) 548-3300, FAX:
(212) 519-0099, Web Site: nccmedia.
com
Pres & CEO: Greg Schaefer
COO: Ken Little

CFO: Bob Curcuruto
Sr VP Mktg & Bus Devel: Andrew Capone

Advertising sales, marketing & technology company.

NTN BUZZTIME INC
2231 Rutherford Rd
Carlsbad, CA 92008
Telephone: (760) 438-7400, Toll Free:
(877) 963-9200, FAX: (760) 438-3505, Web Site: www.
buzztimebusiness.com
Chmn: Jeff Berg
CFO: Kendra Berger
Chief Devel Officer: Vladimir Edelman
COO: Bob Cooney
Chief Revenue Officer: Kirk Nagamine
Founded: 1984

In-venue social gaming marketing & entertainment company.

NET-RESULTS
221 Corporate Cir (Suite N)
Golden, CO 80401
Telephone: (303) 771-2552, E-Mail:
info@net-results.com, Web Site:
www.net-results.com
Founder & CEO: Michael Ward
Pres: Matt Filios
Chief Architect: Dan Vande More
Founded: 2003

Marketing automation software company.

NETWORK SOLUTIONS LLC
A Web.com Co
13861 Sunrise Valley Dr (Suite 300)
Herndon, VA 20171
Toll Free: (877) 628-8686, Web Site:
www.networksolutions.com
Chmn, Pres & CEO: David L. Brown

Website services company.

NEW HAMPSHIRE PUBLIC TELEVISION
268 Mast Rd
Durham, NH 03824-4601
Telephone: (603) 868-1100, E-Mail:
themailbox@nhptv.org, Web Site:
www.nhptv.org
Pres & CEO: Peter A. Frid
Chief Content Officer: Dawn DeAngelis
Dir Corp Rels: Jeff Morris
Founded: 1959

NHPTV is New Hampshire's PBS station. In addition to serving the state, our signal and services reach metro Boston, southern Maine and eastern Vermont.

NOR1
3255 Scott Blvd, Bldg 7 (Suite 120)
Santa Clara, CA 95054-3023
Telephone: (408) 850-9937, FAX:
(408) 608-0443, E-Mail: sales@nor1.
com, Web Site: www.nor1.com
Exec Chmn: Art Norins
CEO: Jason Bryant
Chief Comml Officer: Ravneet Bhandari

Pricing and merchandising technology solutions company for the hospitality industry.

NORTHERN LIGHTS DIRECT
314 W Superior St (Suite 503)
Chicago, IL 60654
Telephone: (312) 263-8686, FAX:
(312) 600-9050, E-Mail: contact@
northernlightsdirect.com, Web Site:
www.northernlightsdirect.com
CEO: Sandy French
Pres: Ian French
COO: Luc Bourgon
Conducts Business: U.S., Canada
Employees: 32
Primary Market Served: Business
Founded: 1985

Leading brand direct response agency with offices in Toronto and Chicago. Services include strategic planning, media management, and creative and production services for direct response television (DRTV) and direct response online.

ONLINE PRINT SOLUTIONS
268 Bush St (Suite 4045)
San Francisco, CA 94104-3503
Telephone: (415) 651-4157, Toll Free:
(800) 875-7117, E-Mail: info@
onlineprintsolutions.com, Web Site:
www.onlineprintsolutions.com
CEO: Mark McGowan
Founded: 2002

Web-to-print, dynamic publishing & cross media solutions company.

ONYX PRODUCTIONS DIRECT INC
2355 Westwood Blvd (Suite 401)
Los Angeles, CA 90064-2109
Telephone: (323) 692-9830, FAX:
(323) 692-9832, E-Mail: joan@
onyxprod.com, Web Site: www.
onyxprod.com
Pres: Joan Renfrow

Production company for the direct response marketing industry.

PM PRODUCTIONS
5882 W Bowcroft St (Suite 2)
Los Angeles, CA 90016-4907

Telephone: (310) 559-3127, FAX:
    (310) 559-3168, E-Mail:
    odellmack@hotmail.com, Web Site:
    www.pmproductionsvideos.com
Producer: Odell Mack
Founded: 1985

Full service video production company.

PATRIOT
    COMMUNICATIONS LLC
Div. of US International Media LLC
1201 Alta Loma Rd
West Hollywood, CA 90069
Telephone: (888) 833-4711, FAX:
    (310) 482-6701, E-Mail:
    dlivingston@patriotllc.com, Web
    Site: www.patriotllc.com
Chmn & CEO: Dennis Holt
Pres & COO: Doug Livingston
Mng Dir Sls: David Gregitis

Provider of on-demand interactive telecommunications services, database
management and Internet solutions.

PETRY TELEVISION INC
Sub. of Petry Media Corp
200 Park Ave (fl 17)
New York, NY 10117
Telephone: (212) 230-5600, E-Mail:
    info@petrymedia.com, Web Site:
    www.petrymedia.com
Pres & CEO: Val Napolitano
Sr VP & Mng Dir: Steve Capozzoli
Dir Rsch: Alan Picozzi

Advertising sales representation firm.

PRICE TARGET MEDIA
108 Kentuck Ln
Carson City, NV 89706
Telephone: (775) 434-4451, FAX:
    (206) 888-2403, E-Mail: info@
    pricetargetmedia.com, Web Site:
    pricetargetmedia.com
Pres: Eric Stevenson
Primary Market Served: Consumer

Investor relations services agency.

PROSPER INC
5252 N Edgewood Dr (Suite 150)
Provo, UT 84604-5853
Telephone: (801) 371-0755, Toll Free:
    (800) 748-5799, FAX: (801) 374-
    2358, E-Mail: support@prospering.
    com, Web Site: www.prospering.com
Co-Founder: Ethan Willis
Co-Founder: Randy Garn
Primary Market Served: Consumer
Founded: 1999

Coaching and distance training provider.

PROTUS
Subs. of j2 Global Communications Inc

2379 Holly Ln (Suite 210)
Ottawa, ON, Canada K1V 7P2
Telephone: (613) 733-0000, Toll Free:
    (888) 733-0000, E-Mail: info@
    protus.com, Web Site: www.protus.
    com
CEO: Hemi Zucker
Pres: Scott Turicchi
VP Mktg: Mike Pugh

Software-as-a-Service communication
services & solutions provider.

PUBLISHERS CIRCULATION
    FULFILLMENT INC
502 Washington Ave (Suite 500)
Towson, MD 21204
Telephone: (410) 821-8614, E-Mail:
    sales@pcfcorp.com, Web Site: www.
    pcfcorp.com
Pres & CEO: Jerry Giordana
Founded: 1984

Provides distribution solutions to the
print media industry.

QVC INC
1200 Wilson Dr
West Chester, PA 19380
Telephone: (484) 701-1000, FAX:
    (484) 701-8500, Web Site: www.qvc.
    com
Pres & CEO: Mike George

Video & ecommerce retailer.

RAJANT CORP
400 E King St
Malvern, PA 19355
Telephone: (484) 595-0233, FAX:
    (484) 595-0244, E-Mail: support@
    rajant.com, Web Site: www.rajant.
    com
Chmn & CEO: Robert Schena
Chief Tech Officer: Paul Hellhake
COO: Scott Beer
Sr VP Bus Devel: Peter Lenard
Founded: 2001

Kinetic Mesh network technology company.

RAPID RESPONSE
    MARKETING
7500 W Lake Mead Blvd (#9463)
Las Vegas, NV 89128
Telephone: (702) 475-5235, Web Site:
    www.rapidresponseonline.com
CEO: Kevin Devincenzi
CFO: Rhianna Ross
Conducts Business: U.S., Canada
Primary Market Served: Business &
    Consumer
Catalog available online
Advertising/Marketing Budget Related
    to Direct Marketing: 51-75%

Founded: 2003
Internet marketing.

REPUTATION.COM
1001 Marshall St (fl 2)
Redwood City, CA 94063
Telephone: (877) 425-5792, E-Mail:
    info@reputation.com, Web Site:
    www.reputation.com
CEO: Michael Fertik
Pres: Shrey Bhatia
VP Res: Tom Dignan
CFO: Mark Phillips

Online reputation management (ORM)
products and services.

RESPONSE MEDIA
3155 Medlock Bridge Rd
Norcross, GA 30071-1423
Telephone: (770) 451-5478, FAX:
    (770) 451-4929, E-Mail:
    postmaster@responsemedia.com,
    Web Site: www.responsemedia.com
CEO: Joshua Perlstein
Chief Technical Officer: Keith Perl-
    stein
Chairwoman: Betty Abion
COO: Douglas Breuer
Conducts Business: Worldwide
Employees: 40
Primary Market Served: Business &
    Consumer
Advertising/Marketing Budget Related
    to Direct Marketing: 76-100%
Founded: 1978
Gross sales or billing: $18,000,000

Customer acquisition and database
management.

RESULTS PRODUCERS
5800 Rhodes Ave
Los Angeles, CA 91607
Telephone: (818) 985-9200, E-Mail:
    info@resultsproducers.com, Web
    Site: resultsproducers.com
CEO: Patrick Finn
Founded: 1989

Direct response television production
company.

ROCKET DIRECT
    MARKETING INC
156 E 37th St (Suite 5A)
New York, NY 10016
Telephone: (212) 689-5800, FAX:
    (212) 689-0635, E-Mail: info@
    rocketdirect.com, Web Site: www.
    rocketdirect.com
Pres: Jonathan Salkin
Founded: 1982

Direct response marketing of products
and services using traditional and electronic media.

ROBERT ROSENHEIM ASSOCIATES
5 Gay St, PO Box 308
Sharon, CT 06069-2000
Telephone: (860) 364-0050, FAX: (860) 364-5577, Web Site: rrallc.com
Pres: Robert Rosenheim

Media buying services.

SAS GROUP
220 White Plains Rd (Suite 100)
Tarrytown, NY 10591-5823
Telephone: (914) 332-7878, FAX: (914) 332-7859, Web Site: www.sasgroup.com
Owner: Scott Sobo

Marketing & distribution of direct response products.

SEOINHOUSE
5214 Cedarfield Dr
Saint Charles, MO 63304-8014
Telephone: (888) 899-0195, FAX: (888) 899-0195, Web Site: www.seoinhouse.com
Pres & Founder: Jessica Bowman

Search engine optimization (SEO) consultant.

SMY MEDIA INC
625 N Michigan Ave (Suite 525)
Chicago, IL 60611
Telephone: (312) 621-9600, FAX: (312) 621-0924, E-Mail: info@smymedia.com, Web Site: www.smymedia.com
Exec VP: Karen P. Sheridan
Exec VP Sls & Account Svcs: Gerald Grant
Founded: 1969

Media management company.

SAATCHI & SAATCHI NEW YORK
375 Hudson St
New York, NY 10014-3660
Telephone: (212) 463-2000, FAX: (212) 463-9856, Web Site: www.saatchiny.com
CEO: Brent Smart
Chief Creative Officer: Jay Benjamin
Founded: 1970

Flagship office of the global advertising agency.

SALES MAGIC INC
Div. of Historical Research Center
2107 Corporate Dr
Boynton Beach, FL 33426-6645
Telephone: (561) 732-5263, Toll Free: (800) 985-9956, FAX: (561) 375-9413, E-Mail: custsvc@names.com, Web Site: www.names.com

Dir: Mick Walshe

Television commercial writing & production company.

SANDY ALEXANDER INC
200 Entin Rd
Clifton, NJ 07014-1423
Telephone: (973) 470-8100, FAX: (973) 470-9269, E-Mail: sandy@sandyinc.com, Web Site: www.sandyinc.com
Pres & CEO: Michael Graff
Exec VP Mktg: Larry Westlake
Exec VP Bus Devel: Hugh Haas
Primary Market Served: Business

Marketing solutions and printing company.

SCHWARTZ & ASSOCIATES CREATIVE
212 S Bemiston (Suite 3)
Clayton, MO 63105
Telephone: (314) 531-6810, FAX: (314) 531-1448, E-Mail: info@sacreative.com, Web Site: www.sacreative.com
Pres: Elizabeth Schwartz PhD
Dir Bus Devel: Tyler Schwartz

Production services company.

SCRIPT TO SCREEN INC
200 N Tustin Ave (Suite 200)
Santa Ana, CA 92705
Telephone: (714) 558-3971, Toll Free: (800) 453-0003, FAX: (714) 558-1759, E-Mail: newbusiness@scripttoscreen.com, Web Site: www.scripttoscreen.com
Chmn & CEO: Barbara L. Kerry
Exec Producer & Creative Dir: Ken Kerry
Exec VP & Chief Strategy Officer: Alex Dinsmoor
Chief Mktg Exec: James Spencer Hall
Founded: 1986

Direct response television production agency.

SEPTEMBER PRODUCTIONS
15 Madaket Rd
Nantucket, MA 02554-2618
Telephone: (508) 332-3577, FAX: (508) 228-3853, E-Mail: info@september.com, Web Site: www.september.com
CEO: Dan Driscoll

Television commercial, documentary & short film production company.

SILVERPOP
An IBM Co
200 Galleria Pkwy (Suite 750)
Atlanta, GA 30339-5945
Telephone: (678) 247-0500, Toll Free: (866) 745-8767, FAX: (678) 247-0501, E-Mail: contactsales@silverpop.com, Web Site: www.silverpop.com
Pres & CEO: Bill Nussey
Exec VP & CFO: Jim McCormick
Sr VP Product Devel: Jeff Browning
Sr VP Sls: Todd McCormick
Mng Dir & Sr VP Intl Bus Devel: Will Schnabel
Sr VP Opers: Barry Schnur
Conducts Business: U.S., Canada
Primary Market Served: Business
Indirect online sales
Advertising/Marketing Budget Related to Direct Marketing: 76-100%
Direct Marketing ad budget:
Online: 100%
Founded: 1999

Digital marketing software company.

SMART INVENTIONS INC
6421 E Alondra Blvd
Paramount, CA 90723
Telephone: (562) 272-1416, Toll Free: (800) 275-7494, FAX: (562) 272-1423, E-Mail: customerservice@smartinventions.com, Web Site: www.smartinventions.com
CEO & Founder: Jon Nokes
Founded: 1991

Direct response marketing company.

SMARTHOME/INSTEON
Div. of SmartLabs Inc
16542 Millikan Ave
Irvine, CA 92606
Telephone: (949) 221-0037, Toll Free: (800) 762-7846, FAX: (949) 221-9240, E-Mail: feedback@smarthome.com, Web Site: www.smarthome.com
CEO: Joe Dada
Founded: 1992

Inventor, product designer, manufacturer & online retailer of home automation products.

SMARTSOURCE CORP
209 Burlington Rd (Suite 219)
Bedford, MA 01730-1422
Telephone: (781) 785-3375, Toll Free: (800) 239-0239, Web Site: www.smartsourceonline.com
Pres: Mike Curtain
VP Opers: Rich Giurleo
VP Sls: Tom Winchell
VP Devel: Gene Zylkuski
Founded: 1994

Develop, host & manage e-marketing applications.

SOUNDBITE COMMUNICATIONS
Subs. of Genesys
22 Crosby Dr
Bedford, MA 01730
Toll Free: (877) SOUNDBITE, Web
    Site: www.soundbite.com
Pres & CEO: Jim Milton
COO & CFO: Bob Leahy
Chief Tech Officer: Tim Segall
Exec VP & Gen Mgr Mobile Svcs and
    Chief Mktg & Bus Devel Officer:
    Mark Friedman

STARTEC GLOBAL COMMUNICATIONS
Subs. of Impact Telecom
11300 Rockville Pike (Suite 900)
Rockville, MD 20852
Telephone: (301) 610-4300, FAX:
    (301) 610-4301, Web Site: www.
    startec.com
Sr Dir Mktg: Anna Porteus
Founded: 1989

Telephone, Internet & communications
services company.

STRONGVIEW SYSTEMS INC
1300 Island Dr (Suite 200)
Redwood City, CA 94065-5171
Telephone: (650) 421-4200, Toll Free:
    (800) 971-0380, FAX: (650) 421-
    4201, E-Mail: info@strongview.com,
    Web Site: www.strongview.com
CEO: Bill Wagner
CFO: Bill Griffin
Chief Tech Officer: Jeremy Sterns
Sr VP Client Svcs: Tal Nathan
Sr VP Strategy: Rob Bronson
VP Worldwide Sls: Michael Heilmann
VP Mktg Svcs: Katrina Conn

Email & cross-channel marketing solutions company.

SUBMIT EXPRESS INC
315 W Verdugo Ave (Suite 101)
Burbank, CA 91502
Telephone: (818) 567-3030, Toll Free:
    (877) 737-3083, FAX: (818) 567-
    0202, E-Mail: feedbacks@
    submitexpress.com, Web Site: www.
    submitexpress.com
Pres & CEO: Pierre Zarokian
Founded: 1998

Search engine optimization (SEO) &
Website promotion company.

SUCCESS PARTNERS CO
200 Swisher Rd
Lake Dallas, TX 75065
Telephone: (940) 497-9700, Toll Free:
    (800) 752-2030, FAX: (940) 497-
    9987, Web Site: successpartners.com
CEO: Stuart Johnson

Sr VP Strategic Mktg: Paul Adams
Founded: 1987

Media, publications & communications
company.

SUCCESSWORKS SEARCH MARKETING INC
0650 SW Gaines St (Apt 1605)
Portland, OR 97239-4451
Telephone: (503) 922-3627, Web Site:
    www.seocopywriting.com
CEO: Heather Lloyd-Martin

Search engine optimization (SEO)
copywriting agency.

SUNBELT MEDIA SERVICE
PO Box 3116, Chapel Hill, NC 27515-
    3116
808 Beaver Dam Rd (Suite 100), PO
    Box 3116
Chapel Hill, NC 27515-3116
Telephone: (919) 967-7174, FAX:
    (919) 967-6050, E-Mail: jkluger@
    sunbelt-media.com, Web Site: www.
    sunbelt-media.com
Pres & Media Dir: Joel Kluger
Founded: 1985

Media services agency.

SYFY
Div. of NBCUniversal Cable
30 Rockefeller Plaza
New York, NY 10112
Telephone: (212) 664-4444, Web Site:
    www.syfy.com
Chmn NBCUniversal Cable Entertain-
    ment: Bonnie Hammer
Pres: Dave Howe
Exec VP Mktg, Digital & Global Brand
    Strategy: Michael Engleman
Exec VP Programming & Original
    Movies: Thomas P. Vitale
Exec VP Original Content: Bill McGol-
    drick
Founded: 1992

Imagination based entertainment cable
network.

TLC
Div. of Discovery Communications
    LLC
1 Discovery Pl
Silver Spring, MD 20910
Telephone: (240) 662-2000, Web Site:
    www.tlc.com
Grp Pres: Marjorie Kaplan

Cable television network.

THEPORT NETWORK
5500 N Interstate Pkwy (#550)
Atlanta, GA 30328
Telephone: (703) 431-2208

VP Mktg & Strategy: Suzanne Carawan

TOPRANK ONLINE MARKETING
4032 Shoreline Dr (Suite 1)
Spring Park, MN 55384
Telephone: (952) 400-0194, Toll Free:
    (877) 872-6628, E-Mail: winning@
    toprankmarketing.com, Web Site:
    www.toprankmarketing.com
CEO: Lee Odden

Online marketing services.

TOWERDATA
379 Park Ave S (fl 5)
New York, NY 10016-8811
Telephone: (646) 742-1771, FAX:
    (646) 365-3060, Web Site: www.
    towerdata.com
Pres: Tom Burke
Founded: 2001

Email marketing solutions company.

TOWNNEWS.COM
1510 47th Ave
Moline, IL 61265
Telephone: (309) 743-0800, Toll Free:
    (800) 293-9576, FAX: (309) 743-
    0830, E-Mail: info@townnews.com,
    Web Site: www.townnews365.com
CEO & Gen Mgr: Marc Wilson
Sr VP & Chief Tech Officer: Brad
    Ward
VP Sls: Greg Booras
Founded: 1989

Online publishing & revenue solutions
company.

TURNER BROADCASTING SYSTEM INC
Subs. of Time Warner
One CNN Center
Atlanta, GA 30303
Telephone: (404) 827-1700, Web Site:
    www.turner.com
CEO: John Martin
Pres: David Levy
Exec VP & CFO: John E. Kampfe
Exec VP, Chief Tech Officer & Chief
    Digital Strategy Officer: Scott Teiss-
    ler

Cable television & global media operator.

TURNER NETWORK TELEVISION (TNT)
Div. of Turner Broadcasting System (a
    Time Warner co.)
One CNN Center
Atlanta, GA 30303

Telephone: (404) 827-1700, E-Mail: tnt@turner.com, Web Site: www.turner.com
Pres & Head Programming: Michael Wright
Exec VP & Chief Mktg Officer: Jeff Gregor

Cable television network

US CELLULAR
Subs. of TDS Telecom
8410 W Bryn Mawr Ave (Suite 700)
Chicago, IL 60631-3463
Toll Free: (888) 944-9400, Web Site: www.uscellular.com
Pres & CEO: Kenneth R. Meyers
Exec VP Fin & CFO: Steven T. Campbell
Exec VP Sls & Customer Svc: Jay Ellison
Exec VP & Chief Tech Officer: Michael S. Irizarry
VP Brand Mktg: Grant Leech
Founded: 1983

Regional wireless communications company.

USA NETWORK
8800 W Sunset Blvd, Los Angeles, CA 90069-2117
Div. of NBCUniversal Cable
30 Rockefeller Plz (fl 27)
New York, NY 10112
Telephone: (212) 664-4444, FAX: (212) 664-6365, Web Site: www.usanetwork.com
Chmn NBCUniversal Cable Entertainment Grp: Bonnie Hammer
Pres: Chris McCumber
Exec VP Programming Acquisitions & Scheduling: Jane Blaney
Exec VP Mktg & Digital: Alexandra Shapiro
CFO: Cynthia Chu
Founded: 1971

Cable television network.

VALCOM INC
429 Rockaway Valley Rd
Boonton, NJ 07005
Telephone: (973) 588-7084, FAX: (973) 257-7216, E-Mail: info@valcom.tv, Web Site: www.valcom.tv
CEO: Anthony Barrett
VP Affiliate Sls & Mktg: Chip Harwood
Natl & Direct Response Adv Sls: Andrea Rhum
Founded: 1983

Diversified, fully integrated, independent entertainment company.

VALUEVISION MEDIA INC
dba ShopHQ

6740 Shady Oak Rd
Eden Prairie, MN 55344-3433
Telephone: (952) 943-6000, Web Site: www.shophq.com
CEO: Keith R. Stewart
Pres: G. Robert Ayd
Exec VP & CFO: William J. McGrath
COO: Carol Steinberg
Sr VP & Chief Mdsg Officer: Annette Repasch
Founded: 1990

Direct marketing company that sells and distributes products through television, the Internet & direct mail.

VIACOM MEDIA NETWORKS
Subs. of Viacom Inc
1515 Broadway
New York, NY 10036
Telephone: (212) 258-6000, Web Site: www.viacom.com
Pres & CEO: Philippe Dauman
Chmn & CEO BET Networks: Debra Lee
Pres Entertainment Grp: Doug Herzog
Pres Nickelodeon: Cyma Zarghami
Pres Music & Logo Grp: Van Toffler

Operator of various television and Internet brands including MTV, VH1, Nickelodeon, Comedy Central, TV Land, BET & others.

VIDEO ORDNANCE INC
611 Broadway (Suite 307)
New York, NY 10012
Telephone: (212) 334-3939, Toll Free: (800) 377-7773, FAX: (212) 219-1969, E-Mail: info@videoordnance.com, Web Site: www.videoordnance.com
Founded: 1985

Producer of television, video & new media programs on contemporary aerospace and defense technology.

VIDI EMI INC
2450 Washington Ave (Suite 285)
San Leandro, CA 94577
Telephone: (510) 667-9999, FAX: (510) 352-9999, E-Mail: info@vidiemi.com, Web Site: www.vidiemi.com
CEO: John Ludgey
Conducts Business: U.S.
Primary Market Served: Business
Advertising/Marketing Budget Related to Direct Marketing: 0-25%
Direct Marketing ad budget: $20,000
Magazines: 50%
Telephone: 50%
Founded: 2001

Full service integrated marketing & marketing technology agency.

VIRGIN MOBILE USA LP
Subs. of Sprint Corp
10 Independence Blvd
Warren, NJ 07059
Telephone: (908) 607-4000, Toll Free: (888) 322-1122, E-Mail: vmugeneral@sprint.com, Web Site: www.virginmobileusa.com
VP Virgin Mobile: Jeff Auman
Bus Line Dir Virgin Mobile USA: Mark Lederman
Founded: 2002

Prepaid wireless telecommunications service provider.

VISIBLE WORLD
460 W 34th St (fl 14)
New York, NY 10001
Telephone: (212) 739-1900, E-Mail: info@visibleworld.com, Web Site: www.visibleworld.com
Pres: Tara Walpert Levy
Primary Market Served: Consumer
Founded: 2000

Provider of targeted television advertisement solutions.

VOICE MESSAGE BROADCASTING CORP
dba VMBC
1 Columbia (Suite 250)
Aliso Viejo, CA 92656
Telephone: (714) 437-0600, FAX: (714) 242-1989, Web Site: www.vmbc.com
CEO: Jesse Crowe
Conducts Business: U.S.
Primary Market Served: Business & Consumer
Founded: 1997

Voice & mobile broadcasting services.

VOICE SYSTEMS ENGINEERING INC
900 Wheeler Way (Suite A)
Langhorne, PA 19047-1706
Telephone: (215) 953-8568, E-Mail: info@vseinc.com, Web Site: www.vseinc.com
Pres & CEO: Gary Baron
Chief Administrative Officer: Susan Wenitsky
Chief Bus Devel Officer: Stu Segal
Chief Mktg Officer: Samantha Liss
Dir Brand & Mktg: Maryanne Fiedler

VONAGE
23 Main St
Holmdel, NJ 07733
Telephone: (732) 528-2600, Web Site: www.vonage.com
CEO: Marc Lefar
CFO & Treas: David Pearson
Pres Consumer Svcs: Joseph Redling

Chief Mktg Officer: Barbara Goodstein

Voice over IP network & SIP company that provide telephone service over a broadband connection.

WCPE-FM

PO Box 897
Wake Forest, NC 27588
Telephone: (800) 556-5178, FAX: (919) 556-9273, Web Site: theclassicalstation.org
Gen Mgr & Chief Engineer: Deborah Proctor
Bus Devel Dir: Peter Blume
Music Dir: William Woltz
Primary Market Served: Consumer

Classical music broadcasting.

WLNY-TV 10/55

Part of CBS Television Stations Group
270 S Service Rd
Melville, NY 11747-2399
Telephone: (631) 777-8855, Web Site: newyork.cbslocal.com/station/wlny
VP & Station Mgr: Betty Ellen Berlamino
VP & News Dir: David Friend
Founded: 1985

Long Island based commercial broadcast TV station serving New York, New Jersey & Connecticut.

WALKER/FITZGIBBON TV & FILM PRODUCTIONS

2399 Mount Olympus Dr
Los Angeles, CA 90046
Telephone: (323) 469-6800, FAX: (323) 878-0600, E-Mail: mo@ walkerfitzgibbon.com, Web Site: www.walkerfitzgibbon.com
Exec Producer & Dir: Mo Fitzgibbon
Writer & Dir: Robert Walker

Television & film production company.

THE WEATHER CHANNEL

300 Interstate N Pkwy SE
Atlanta, GA 30339
Telephone: (770) 226-0000, FAX: (770) 226-2390, Web Site: www.weather.com
Chmn & CEO: David Kenny
COO: Chris Walters
Pres: David Clark
EVP Corp Commun: Shirley Powell
Exec VP & Chief Mktg Officer: Scot Safon
Founded: 1982

Cable television channel broadcasting national and local weather forecasts & news.

WEBLOYALTY.COM

Subs. of Affinion Group

6 High Ridge Park
Stamford, CT 06905-1327
Telephone: (203) 956-1000, E-Mail: info@webloyalty.com, Web Site: www.webloyalty.com
Founded: 1999

Online marketing program offering discounts, services & benefits to members.

WHITEHAT INC

4665 S Ash Ave (Suite G-10)
Tempe, AZ 85282-6765
Telephone: (480) 858-9000, FAX: (480) 858-9001, E-Mail: sales@ whitehat.com, Web Site: www.whitehat.com
Chmn: Rodney Joffe
Exec VP: Kevin Finocchiaro
VP Corp Controller: Patricia Lee Bambridge
Founded: 1983

Provides data management & data processing services to direct marketing organizations.

JORDAN WHITNEY INC

360 E First St (#593)
Tustin, CA 92780
Telephone: (714) 832-3353, FAX: (714) 832-4422, E-Mail: info@ jwgreensheet.com, Web Site: www.jwgreensheet.com
Publr: John Kogler
Pres: Clare Kogler

Research, consulting & publishing company for the direct response television industry.

WINDSTREAM COMMUNICATIONS INC

4001 Rodney Parham Rd
Little Rock, AR 72212
Telephone: (501) 748-7000, Web Site: www.windstream.com
Pres & CEO: Jeff Gardner
COO: Brent Whittington
CFO: Tony Thomas
Sr VP Enterprise & Chief Mktg Officer: Matt Preschern

Provider of advanced network communications.

YAHOO! INC

701 First Ave
Sunnyvale, CA 94089
Telephone: (408) 349-3300, Web Site: www.yahoo.com
Pres & CEO: Marissa Mayer
CFO: Ken Goldman
Chief Mktg Officer: Kathy Savitt
Chief Devel Officer: Jacqueline D. Reese
Primary Market Served: Business

Founded: 1994

Multinational Internet corporation.

YOUTOO TV

6565 N MacArthur Blvd (Suite 400)
Irving, TX 75039
Web Site: www.youtoo.com
CEO: Chris Wyatt

Social TV platform that allows viewers to participate in television programming.

ZEPPO MARKETING INC

423 Pacific St
Brooklyn, NY 11217
Telephone: (212) 308-5734, FAX: (646) 304-7364, Web Site: www.zeppomarketing.com
Pres: Harley Weber
Acct Mngmt: Olgerta Kondo
Primary Market Served: Business & Consumer
Founded: 2006

Direct marketing services company specializing in email, direct mail, lead generation, email append & mobile advertising.

ZETA INTERACTIVE

185 Madison Ave (fl 5)
New York, NY 10016
Telephone: (212) 660-2500, FAX: (212) 967-1028, E-Mail: info@ zetainteractive.com, Web Site: www.zetainteractive.com
CEO: David A. Steinberg
COO: Steven Gerber
CFO: Chris Spring
CIO: Dr. Jeffry Nimeroff
Founded: 2007

Big Data-driven marketing company that uses data, analytics & proprietary technology to acquire, engage & retain customers.

ALABAMA

The Source, 2495 Washington St, PO Box 3888, Huntsville, 35810

CALIFORNIA

CX&B United Corp, 1301 W 253rd St, Harbor City, 90710-2805

Casablanca Express, 6300 Canoga Ave (Suite 550), Woodland Hills, 91367

de Emley & Associates Inc, 33702 Calle Miramar, San Juan Capistrano, 92675-4926

Promotional Media Inc, 727 N Main St, Orange, 92868-1105

Top Year International Inc, 22425 E La Palma, Yorba Linda, 92887-3803

COLORADO

Blakar Inc, PO Box 5156, Englewood, 80155-5156

CONNECTICUT

Barker Specialty Co, 27 Realty Dr, Cheshire, 06410-1656

Gulbenkian Swim Inc, 16 Beaver Brook Rd, Danbury, 06810-6201

McWeeney Marketing, 53 Robinson Blvd, Orange, 06477-3623

John Michaels Associates Inc, 94 Holmes Rd, Newington, 06110-1708

Product Marketplace, 1128 Stratford Ave, Stratford, 06615

Putnam Group Ltd, 35 Corporate Dr Ste 1065, Trumbull, 06611-6320

Robustelli Merchandise, PO Box 17295, Stamford, 06907-7295

JM Wechter & Associates Inc, 569 Main St, Monroe, 06468-2806

FLORIDA

BIC Graphic USA, 14421 Myerlake Cir, Clearwater, 33760

King Direct Marketing Inc, 1184 Pelican Bay Dr, Daytona Beach, 32119

Nat Com Marketing, 318 NW 23rd St, Miami, 33127

Wilcox & Associates, 258 Short Ave, Longwood, 32750

GEORGIA

J&L Concepts Inc, PO Box 3716, Valdosta, 31604-3716

Ted's Promotions Inc, 144 Lake Ridge Trail, Baldwin, 30511

ILLINOIS

Creative Awards by Lane, 1713 Elmhurst Rd, Elk Grove Village, 60007-5924

Four Star Marketing Inc, 3732 W Morse Ave, Lincolnwood, 60712

Gorham's Inc, 1615 S Fifth St, Springfield, 62703

Great Ideas Inc/CSP, 1633 Ravine Ln, Highland Park, 60035

Halo Branded Solutions, 1980 Industrial Dr, Sterling, 61081

Hinda Incentives, 2440 W 34th St, Chicago, 60608

Konik & Co Inc, 7535 N Lincoln Ave, Skokie, 60076-3851

Madison Sales Group, 3029 Commercial Ave, Northbrook, 60062-1912

Marketing Incentives International Inc, 1310 N Ritchie Ct (Suite 16C), Chicago, 60610-8401

RB Toy Design Inc, 3838 Chester Dr, Glenview, 60026-1013

INDIANA

Kipp Brothers Inc, 351 W Muskegon Dr, Greenfield, 46140-3071

Special Markets Sales Co, 7435 E 86th St, Indianapolis, 46256-1207

IOWA

ITAGroup, 4600 Westown Pkwy (Suite 100), West Des Moines, 50266-1042

KANSAS

American Identity, 7500 W 110th St, Overland Park, 66210

Clayman Promotional Group, 3200 Merriam Ln, Kansas City, 66106-4618

Incentive Associates Inc, PO Box 12065, Overland Park, 66282-2065

The Promotional Resources Group of Companies, Inc, PO Box 19235, Topeka, 66619-0235

Swag Inc, 69 Via Verde, Wichita, 67230

Zouire, 4200 W 115th St (Suite 100), Leawood, 66211-2729

KENTUCKY

MPC Louisville Promotions, 4300 Produce Rd, Louisville, 40218-3062

Stonebridge Press Ltd, 7620 WH Negley Rd, Henderson, 42420-9182

LOUISIANA

Augie Leopold Advertising Specialties, 3214 Roman St, Metairie, 70001-5224

MAINE

Andersen Design, 5 Andersen Rd, PO Box 246, East Boothbay, 04544

Geiger Brothers, 70 Mount Hope Ave, Lewiston, 04240-1021

MASSACHUSETTS

All Star Premium Products Inc, 660 Main St, PO Box 980, Sturbridge Office Park, Fiskdale, 01518

Aloft Group, 26 Parker St, Newburyport, 01950

MICHIGAN

A Dean Watkins, 2395 Jolly Rd (Suite 170), Okemos, 48864

General Motivation Co, 3085 Walkent Dr NW, Grand Rapids, 49508

Morley Companies, 1 Morley Plaza, Saginaw, 48603-1305

Rohlik Specialties Co, 42505 Woodward Ave, Bloomfield Hills, 48304

Twin City Engraving/Premier Promotions, 1232 Broad St, Box 85, Saint Joseph, 49085

MINNESOTA

Cassidy & Co, 2005 Pin Oak Dr (Suite 3), Eagan, 55122-2480

Major Brands Group, 12032 Cottonwood St, NW, Minneapolis, 55448

Strategic Marketing Services, PO Box 21686, Eagan, 55121-0686

MISSOURI

Accent Advertising Inc, 1227 Clay St, North Kansas City, 64116-4026

Bowers & Associates Inc, 2025 S Brentwood Blvd (Suite 207), Saint Louis, 63144-1851

CWC Inventories Inc, 8000 Hall St, Saint Louis, 63147

Clark & Clark Inc, 13221 W Watson Rd, Saint Louis, 63127-1920

Lipic's Recognition, 10030 Big Bend Rd, Saint Louis, 63122

NEVADA

The Premium Connection, 6165 S Pecos, Las Vegas, 89120

Marty Wolf Game Co, 3601 E Wyoming Ave (SPC 107), Las Vegas, 89104-4937

NEW JERSEY

All-Ways Advertising Co, 1442 Broad St, Bloomfield, 07003

Award Marketing Services LLC, Eight Salem Park, PO Box 175, Whitehouse, 08888

BI, 535 Springfield Ave (Suite 110), Summit, 07901-2631

Business Promotion Ideas Inc, 20 Chestnut St (Suite 6A), Tenafly, 07670-1700

Ben Loeb Inc, 25 Pier Ln W, Fairfield, 07004

Porter Wallace Corp, 334 Drum Point Rd, Brick, 08723

Supreme Specialty Advertising, 34 Mulberry Ln, Mount Arlington, 07856-1383

UniServ Advertising Inc, 37 Hwy 35, Neptune City, 07753

NEW YORK

Advertising Gifts Inc, 79 Main St (Suite 302), Port Washington, 11050-2938

MJM Incentives Inc, 535 Summit Point Dr (Suite 3), Henrietta, 14467-9628

The Print Box Inc, 8802 Flatlands Ave, Brooklyn, 11236-3612

RPM Industries Inc, 26 Aurelius Ave, Auburn, 13021-0400

Standard Buying Service Ltd, 424 W 33rd St (Rm 230), New York, 10001-2656

Stromberg Brand, 12 Ford Products Rd, Valley Cottage, 10989-1238

OHIO

Associated Premium Corp, 1870 Summit Rd, Cincinnati, 45237-2804

GIE Corporation, 6663 Huntley Rd (Suite H), Columbus, 43229-1038

Kid Stuff Marketing, Inc, 7090 Whipple Ave, North Canton, 44720

Jim Mersfelder & Associates Inc, 2202 Superior Ave E Ste 1, Cleveland, 44114-4259

Partners for Incentives, 6545 Carnegie Ave, Cleveland, 44103-4619

S Group Inc, 661 W Market St, Akron, 44303

PENNSYLVANIA

Market Incentives Corp, 11 N Bacton Hill Rd, Frazer, 19355

RHODE ISLAND

Capital Design, 245 Waterman St (Suite 505), Providence, 02906

Peck Rock Associates, 28 Oyster Point, Warren, 02885

SOUTH CAROLINA

Professional Marketing Associates, PO Box 1772, Mount Pleasant, 29465-1772

TENNESSEE

American Accessories International, 550 W Main St (Suite 825), Knoxville, 37902-2542

Safe Specialties, 223 Green Acres Rd, Kingston, 37763

TEXAS

The B&F System Inc, 3920 S Walton Walker Blvd, Dallas, 75236-1510

BC Incentives, 106 Industrial Dr, Fate, 75132

Dallas Midwest, 4100 Alpha Rd, Dallas, 75244

SA-SO/Time Wise, 525 N Great Southwest Pkwy, Arlington, 76011-5422

VIRGINIA

Fiddler's Rock Communications Inc, 6841 Elm St, Box 6510, McLean, 22106

WASHINGTON

Costco Wholesale, 999 Lake Dr, Issaquah, 98027-8990

WISCONSIN

CSE Inc, 5400 S Westridge Dr, New Berlin, 53151-0941

Fire Light Group, 1035 Williamson St, Madison, 53703

William W Schwartz Associates Inc, 1907 Erie Ave, Sheboygan, 53081-3708

CANADA

Ontario

Williams Direct Marketing Inc, 1885 Clements Rd (Unit 244), Pickering, L1W 3V4

Premium Wholesalers & Agents (33)

A DEAN WATKINS
2395 Jolly Rd (Suite 170)
Okemos, MI 48864
Telephone: (517) 349-7700, FAX:
(517) 349-7748, E-Mail:
adeanwatkins@aol.com, Web Site:
www.adeanwatkins.com
Pres: Robert Watkins

ACCENT ADVERTISING INC
1227 Clay St
North Kansas City, MO 64116-4026
Telephone: (816) 842-1860, FAX:
(816) 471-4836, E-Mail:
lindaaccentadv@sbcglobal.net, Web
Site: www.accentadv.com
Pres: Paul J. Weishar Jr.

ADVERTISING GIFTS INC
79 Main St (Suite 302)
Port Washington, NY 11050-2938
Telephone: (516) 767-3577, FAX:
(516) 7673567, E-Mail: sales@
adgiftsinc.com, Web Site: www.
adgiftsinc.com
Pres: Eric Weintraub

**ALL STAR PREMIUM
PRODUCTS INC**
Subs. of All Star Incentive Marketing
660 Main St, PO Box 980, Sturbridge
Office Park
Fiskdale, MA 01518
Toll Free: (800) 526-8629, E-Mail:
info@incentiveusa.com, Web Site:
www.incentiveusa.com
Pres: Brian A. Galonek
CEO: Ed Galonek Sr

**ALL-WAYS ADVERTISING
CO**
1442 Broad St
Bloomfield, NJ 07003
Telephone: (973) 338-0700, Toll Free:
(800) 255-9291, FAX: (973) 338-
1410, Web Site: www.awadv.com
Pres: Robert Jay Lieberman

ALOFT GROUP
26 Parker St
Newburyport, MA 01950
Telephone: (978) 462-0002, E-Mail:
hello@aloftgroup.com, Web Site:
www.aloftgroup.com
Pres & CEO: Matt Bowen

**AMERICAN ACCESSORIES
INTERNATIONAL**
550 W Main St (Suite 825)
Knoxville, TN 37902-2542

Telephone: (865) 525-9100, Web Site:
www.americanaccessoriesintl.com
Pres: Eric Zeanah

AMERICAN IDENTITY
7500 W 110th St
Overland Park, KS 66210
Telephone: (913) 319-3100, Toll Free:
(800) 848-8028
Pres & CEO: David J Kumbholz

ANDERSEN DESIGN
5 Andersen Rd, PO Box 246
East Boothbay, ME 04544
Telephone: (207) 350-4016, Toll Free:
(866)711-8421, FAX: (207) 449-
1449, E-Mail: studio@
andersenstudio.com, Web Site: www.
andersenstudio.com
Other: Mackenzie Andersen

**ASSOCIATED PREMIUM
CORP**
1870 Summit Rd
Cincinnati, OH 45237-2804
Telephone: (513) 679-4444, FAX:
(513) 679-4447, E-Mail: inof@
associatedpremium.com, Web Site:
www.associatedpremium.com
Pres: Randy Ficke

**AWARD MARKETING
SERVICES LLC**
Eight Salem Park, PO Box 175
Whitehouse, NJ 08888
Telephone: (908) 534-5700, FAX:
(908) 534-0903, E-Mail: info@
awardmarketingservices.com, Web
Site: www.awardmarketingservices.
com
Pres: Gregory Canose

THE B&F SYSTEM INC
3920 S Walton Walker Blvd
Dallas, TX 75236-1510
Telephone: (214) 333-2111, FAX:
(214) 333-2137, Web Site: www.
maxam.com
Pres: John Meyer

BC INCENTIVES
106 Industrial Dr
Fate, TX 75132
Toll Free: (800) 275-1298, E-Mail:
terri@bcincentives.com, Web Site:
www.bcincentives.com
Pres: Terri L. Jones

BI
535 Springfield Ave (Suite 110)
Summit, NJ 07901-2631

Telephone: (908) 516-1393, E-Mail:
info@biworldwide.com, Web Site:
www.biworldwide.com
Mng Dir: Mike Davies

BARKER SPECIALTY CO
27 Realty Dr
Cheshire, CT 06410-1656
Telephone: (203) 272-2222, Toll Free:
(800) 227-5377, E-Mail: promo@
barkerspecialty.com, Web Site:
www.barkerspecialty.com
Pres: Gerald Barker
Dir Mktg: Bridget Ann Kingsbury
Employees: 98
Founded: 1951
Gross sales or billing: $29,545,000

BIC GRAPHIC USA
Div. of BIC Corporation
14421 Myerlake Cir
Clearwater, FL 33760
Telephone: (727) 536-7895, E-Mail:
customerservice@bicgraphic.com,
Web Site: www.bicgraphic.com
VP Sales: Rob Babb

BLAKAR INC
PO Box 5156
Englewood, CO 80155-5156
Telephone: (201) 672-0705, FAX:
(201) 673-0725, Web Site: www.
blakar.com
Chmn: Norman Somer

**BOWERS & ASSOCIATES
INC**
2025 S Brentwood Blvd (Suite 207)
Saint Louis, MO 63144-1851
Telephone: (314) 963-4477, E-Mail:
info@bowerspromotes.com
Pres & Treas: Thomas M. Bowers

**BUSINESS PROMOTION
IDEAS INC**
20 Chestnut St (Suite 6A)
Tenafly, NJ 07670-1700
Telephone: (201) 569-9777, FAX:
(201) 569-2642, E-Mail: bpi@
buspromoideas.com, Web Site:
www.buspromoideas.com
Pres: Barbara Stubbs

CSE INC
5400 S Westridge Dr
New Berlin, WI 53151-0941
Telephone: (262) 786-8400, Toll Free:
(800) 999-0001, FAX: (262) 796-
2089, E-Mail: info@csepromo.com,
Web Site: www.topideas.cseideas.
com
Pres: Tom Savio

CWC INVENTORIES INC
8000 Hall St
Saint Louis, MO 63147
Telephone: (314) 739-1311
Chmn: Frank Ginsberg

CX&B UNITED CORP
1301 W 253rd St
Harbor City, CA 90710-2805
Telephone: (310) 530-2102, Toll Free:
(800) 292-8258, FAX: (310) 530-
2513, E-Mail: sales@cxbunited.com,
Web Site: www.cxbunited.com
Pres: Fenton Mitchell
Founded: 1970

CAPITAL DESIGN
245 Waterman St (Suite 505)
Providence, RI 02906
Telephone: (401) 270-6777, E-Mail:
info@freemiums.com, Web Site:
www.freemiums.com
Pres: Judith S. Mann
Founded: 1987

CASABLANCA EXPRESS
6300 Canoga Ave (Suite 550)
Woodland Hills, CA 91367
Telephone: (818) 992-5100, Toll Free:
(800) 315-2065, Web Site: www.
casablancaexpress.com
Pres: Charles McClendon

CASSIDY & CO
2005 Pin Oak Dr (Suite 3)
Eagan, MN 55122-2480
Telephone: (651) 452-4485, FAX:
(651) 452-0561, E-Mail: sarah@
cassidycompany.com, Web Site:
www.cassidycompany.com
Owner: Bill Cassidy

CLARK & CLARK INC
11821 Adie Rd, Maryland Heights, MO
63043-3303
13221 W Watson Rd
Saint Louis, MO 63127-1920
Telephone: (314) 994-9155, FAX:
(314) 994-0573, E-Mail: jim.clark@
clark-clark.net, Web Site: clark-
clark.net
Pres & Owner: Jim Clark

**CLAYMAN PROMOTIONAL
GROUP**
3200 Merriam Ln
Kansas City, KS 66106-4618
Telephone: (913) 384-3600, FAX:
(913) 384-1227, E-Mail: jloud@
claymanpromo.com, Web Site: www.
claymanpromo.com
CEO: Jamie Loud

COSTCO WHOLESALE
999 Lake Dr
Issaquah, WA 98027-8990
Telephone: (425) 313-8647, Toll Free:
800-774-2678, E-Mail:
customerservice@contactcostco.com,
Web Site: www.costco.com
CEO: Craig Jelinek
Primary Market Served: Business &
Consumer

**CREATIVE AWARDS BY
LANE**
1713 Elmhurst Rd
Elk Grove Village, IL 60007-5924
Telephone: (847) 593-7700, FAX:
(847) 593-1155, E-Mail: info@
creativeawardsbylane.com, Web
Site: www.creativeawardsbylane.
com

DALLAS MIDWEST
4100 Alpha Rd
Dallas, TX 75244
Toll Free: (800) 527-2417, FAX: (800)
301-8314, Web Site: www.
dallasmidwest.com
Conducts Business: U.S.
Employees: 2
Primary Market Served: Business &
Consumer
Catalog available online
Direct online sales
Advertising/Marketing Budget Related
to Direct Marketing: 76-100%
Direct Marketing ad budget:
$1,000,000
Direct Mail: 100%
Founded: 1946
Gross sales or billing: $15,000,000
Direct marketing of furniture & equip-
ment to churches, schools & other insti-
tutions & businesses.

**DE EMLEY & ASSOCIATES
INC**
33702 Calle Miramar
San Juan Capistrano, CA 92675-4926
Telephone: (949) 493-5117, FAX:
(949) 493-6382
Pres: Fredi Thorndike Emley

**FIDDLER'S ROCK
COMMUNICATIONS INC**
6841 Elm St, Box 6510
McLean, VA 22106
Telephone: (703) 406-1500, E-Mail:
customerservice@frcmktg.com, Web
Site: www.frcmarketing.com
Pres: Christopher S. Paul

FIRE LIGHT GROUP
1035 Williamson St
Madison, WI 53703

Telephone: (608) 441-3473, E-Mail:
info@firelightgroup.com, Web Site:
firelightgroup.com
Pres & CEO: Sandra Daniel
Dir Opers: Anjee M. Sorge
Full service incentive marketing & corporate engagement company.

**FOUR STAR MARKETING
INC**
aka conventionbags.com
3732 W Morse Ave
Lincolnwood, IL 60712
Toll Free: (800) 888-2991, FAX: (847)
679-6449, E-Mail: cari@
fourstarmarketing.com, Web Site:
www.conventionbags.com
Mktg Exec: Carl Moss

GIE CORPORATION
6663 Huntley Rd (Suite H)
Columbus, OH 43229-1038
Telephone: (614) 888-5850, Web Site:
www.giecorporation.net
Pres: Mark Dennison

GEIGER BROTHERS
70 Mount Hope Ave
Lewiston, ME 04240-1021
Telephone: (207) 755-2000, Toll Free:
(888) 953-9340, E-Mail:
geigerorders@geiger.com, Web Site:
www.geiger.com
Pres: Eugene Geiger
Exec VP & Co-Owner: Peter Geiger

GENERAL MOTIVATION CO
3085 Walkent Dr NW
Grand Rapids, MI 49508
Telephone: (616) 647-3085, Toll Free:
(888) 664-6449, FAX: (616) 647-
5909, E-Mail: i2k@
generalmotivation.com, Web Site:
www.generalmotivation.com
Owner: Jan Bennett

GORHAM'S INC
1615 S Fifth St
Springfield, IL 62703
Telephone: (217) 544-1727, FAX:
(217) 544-1623, E-Mail: gorhams@
gorhams.com, Web Site: www.
gorhams.com
Owner: Mark Zink

GREAT IDEAS INC/CSP
1633 Ravine Ln
Highland Park, IL 60035
Toll Free: (800) 611-5515, FAX: (847)
432-8557, E-Mail: art@
greatideasinc.com, Web Site: www.
greatideasinc.com
Pres: Scott Rubin

GULBENKIAN SWIM INC

16 Beaver Brook Rd
Danbury, CT 06810-6201
Telephone: (203) 790-0800, Toll Free:
(800) 431-2586, Web Site: www.
gulbenkianswim.com
Pres & CEO: Ed Gulbenkian Jr.
Conducts Business: Worldwide
Employees: 12
Primary Market Served: Business &
Consumer
Catalog available online
Direct online sales
Advertising/Marketing Budget Related
to Direct Marketing: 0-25%
Direct Marketing ad budget: $25,000
Direct Mail: 83%
Magazines: 10%
Newspapers: 2%
Online: 1%
TV/Radio: 1%
Telephone: 3%
Founded: 1961
Gross sales or billing: $1,500,000

Lifeguard uniforms, swimsuits &
equipment. Sell to department stores,
high schools, colleges, Y's, & swim
clubs.

HALO BRANDED SOLUTIONS

1980 Industrial Dr
Sterling, IL 61081
Telephone: (815) 625-0980, Toll Free:
(866) 840-6401, Web Site: www.
halo.com
CEO & Dir: Marc S. Simon
Sr VP Mktg: Terry McGuire

HINDA INCENTIVES

2440 W 34th St
Chicago, IL 60608
Telephone: (773) 890-5900, FAX:
(773) 890-4606, E-Mail: contact@
hinda.com, Web Site: www.hinda.
com
Pres: Michael Donnelly

ITAGROUP

4600 Westown Pkwy (Suite 100)
West Des Moines, IA 50266-1042
Toll Free: (800) 257-1985, E-Mail:
drivenbyloyalty@itagroup.com, Web
Site: www.itagroup.com
Pres & COO: Tom Mahoney
Pres & COO: Brent Vander Waal

INCENTIVE ASSOCIATES INC

PO Box 12065
Overland Park, KS 66282-2065
Telephone: (913) 722-2848, E-Mail:
incentiveassociate@sbcglobal.net

J&L CONCEPTS INC

PO Box 3716
Valdosta, GA 31604-3716
Telephone: (229) 247-5731, E-Mail:
promo@jlconcepts.com, Web Site:
www.jlconcepts.com
Pres: Joyce Aigen

KID STUFF MARKETING, INC

7090 Whipple Ave
North Canton, OH 44720
Toll Free: (800) 837-5437, FAX: (330)
244-9518, Web Site: www.kidsstuff.
com
Pres: William L. Miller
Conducts Business: U.S., Canada, Europe
Employees: 40
Primary Market Served: Consumer
Catalog available online
Direct online sales
Advertising/Marketing Budget Related
to Direct Marketing: 76-100%
Founded: 1982
Gross sales or billing: $4,000,000

Perfectly Safe, Kids Club & Natural
Baby Catalogs.

KING DIRECT MARKETING INC

1184 Pelican Bay Dr
Daytona Beach, FL 32119
Telephone: (386) 788-8925
Owner: Cathy King

KIPP BROTHERS INC

Div. of Novelty Inc
351 W Muskegon Dr
Greenfield, IN 46140-3071
Toll Free: (800) 428-1153, E-Mail:
support@kippbrothers.com, Web
Site: kippbrothers.com
Pres: Todd Green

KONIK & CO INC

7535 N Lincoln Ave
Skokie, IL 60076-3851
Telephone: (847) 933-1800, E-Mail:
amy@konik.com, Web Site: www.
konik.com
Pres, Owner: Stan Konik

AUGIE LEOPOLD ADVERTISING SPECIALTIES

3214 Roman St, Metairie, LA 70001-
5224
3214 Roman St
Metairie, LA 70001-5224
Telephone: (504) 836-0525, E-Mail:
sales@augieleopold.com
CEO: Augie Leopold Jr.

LIPIC'S RECOGNITION

10030 Big Bend Rd
Saint Louis, MO 63122
Telephone: (314) 775-2500, Toll Free:
(800) 771-4640, FAX: (314) 775-
2501, E-Mail: lipic@lipic.com, Web
Site: www.lipicsengagement.com
Pres: Steve Lipic

BEN LOEB INC

25 Pier Ln W
Fairfield, NJ 07004
Telephone: (908) 788-0542, FAX:
(908) 788-6861, E-Mail: tbecker@
bsloeb.com, Web Site: www.bsloeb.
com
Pres: Ben Goldstein

MJM INCENTIVES INC

535 Summit Point Dr (Suite 3)
Henrietta, NY 14467-9628
Telephone: (585) 334-6720, Toll Free:
(888) 633-9655, E-Mail:
pmarchese@mjmincentives.com,
Web Site: www.mjmincentives.com
Pres: Sean Murphy

MPC LOUISVILLE PROMOTIONS

4300 Produce Rd
Louisville, KY 40218-3062
Toll Free: (800) 331-0989, FAX: (888)
451-8475, E-Mail: sales@
mpcpromotions.com, Web Site:
www.mpcpromotions.com
Mgr: Don Dobina

MADISON SALES GROUP

3029 Commercial Ave
Northbrook, IL 60062-1912
Telephone: (847) 480-2370, FAX:
(847) 480-7437, E-Mail: sales@
madisonsalesgroup.com, Web Site:
madisonsalesgroup.com
Pres: Marc Denenberg

MAJOR BRANDS GROUP

12032 Cottonwood St, NW
Minneapolis, MN 55448
Telephone: (763) 767-6800, FAX:
(763) 767-1264, E-Mail:
mbgcustomerservice@mrgmn.com,
Web Site: www.mrgrp.com
Pres: Mark Rue
Co-Owner: Joe Gabler

MARKET INCENTIVES CORP

11 N Bacton Hill Rd
Frazer, PA 19355
Toll Free: (800) 486-8881, E-Mail:
sales@marketincentives.com, Web
Site: www.marketincentives.com

MARKETING INCENTIVES INTERNATIONAL INC
1310 N Ritchie Ct (Suite 16C)
Chicago, IL 60610-8401
Telephone: (312) 440-3700, FAX: (312) 943-5813, E-Mail: info@ mktgincentiveintl.com, Web Site: www.mktgincentiveintl.com
Pres: Ronald A. Bernstein
Employees: 2
Founded: 1995

Value added benefit broker. See website for benefits, clubs, and premiums.

MCWEENEY MARKETING
Div. of Geiger
53 Robinson Blvd
Orange, CT 06477-3623
Toll Free: (800) 272-3440, E-Mail: gmcweeney@geiger.com, Web Site: www.mcweeneymarketing.geiger. com
Pres: George McWeeney
Founded: 1989

Offers a complete range of promotional products & apparel.

JIM MERSFELDER & ASSOCIATES INC
2202 Superior Ave E Ste 1
Cleveland, OH 44114-4259
Telephone: (216) 574-9009, Toll Free: (800) 431-1101, FAX: (216) 574-9721, Web Site: www. jmapromotions.com
Owner & Pres: Bob Walker

JOHN MICHAELS ASSOCIATES INC
94 Holmes Rd, Newington, CT 06111-1708
94 Holmes Rd
Newington, CT 06110-1708
Telephone: (860) 666-1414, Toll Free: (800) 499-2606, FAX: (860) 666-1515, E-Mail: info@jmalogos.com, Web Site: www.jmalogos.com
CEO: Sara Papa
Pres: John J. Papa

MORLEY COMPANIES
1 Morley Plaza
Saginaw, MI 48603-1305
Telephone: (989) 791-2550, Toll Free: (800) 336-5554, FAX: (800) 426-6753, Web Site: www.morleynet. com
Pres & CEO: Paul Furlo
Founded: 1863

NAT COM MARKETING
318 NW 23rd St
Miami, FL 33127
Telephone: (305) 756-8600, FAX: (786) 425-0067, E-Mail: info@ natcom-marketing.com, Web Site: www.natcom-marketing.com
Pres: Robert Rodriguez

PARTNERS FOR INCENTIVES
6545 Carnegie Ave
Cleveland, OH 44103-4619
Toll Free: (800) 292-7371, Web Site: www.pfi-awards.com
Sls & Mktg Mgr: Joy Smith

PECK ROCK ASSOCIATES
28 Oyster Point
Warren, RI 02885
Telephone: (401) 289-3757, FAX: (401) 289-3759, E-Mail: pra@aol. com, Web Site: www.peckrock.com
Pres: Katherine Waite

PORTER WALLACE CORP
334 Drum Point Rd
Brick, NJ 08723
Telephone: (732) 920-1405, FAX: (732) 920-1406, Web Site: www. porterwallace.com
Owner: Jodie Bixon

THE PREMIUM CONNECTION
6165 S Pecos
Las Vegas, NV 89120
Toll Free: (800) 683-0933, Web Site: www.premiumconnection.net
Pres: Ron Worth

THE PRINT BOX INC
Sub. of Promobrands
8802 Flatlands Ave
Brooklyn, NY 11236-3612
Telephone: (212) 741-1381, Toll Free: (800) 546-4011, FAX: (212) 463-9071, E-Mail: info@promobrands. com, Web Site: www.promobrands. com
Sls Mgr: Jeff Huvar

PRODUCT MARKETPLACE
1128 Stratford Ave
Stratford, CT 06615
Telephone: (203) 375-8371, Toll Free: (800) 286-4768, FAX: (203) 386-1203, E-Mail: rita@sabinc.com
Pres: Bruce T. Silverstone

PROFESSIONAL MARKETING ASSOCIATES
PO Box 1772
Mount Pleasant, SC 29465-1772
Telephone: (843) 971-8150, FAX: (843) 971-8159
Pres: David Mann

PROMOTIONAL MEDIA INC
727 N Main St
Orange, CA 92868-1105
Telephone: (714) 639-6590, Toll Free: (800) 346-5348, FAX: (714) 639-6270, E-Mail: contactus@ promotionalmedia.com, Web Site: www.promotionalmedia.com
Pres: Peter Bodourian

THE PROMOTIONAL RESOURCES GROUP OF COMPANIES, INC
PO Box 19235
Topeka, KS 66619-0235
Telephone: (785) 862-3707, Toll Free: (800) 467-4712, FAX: (785) 862-1424, E-Mail: info@kidstuff.com, Web Site: www.kidstuffnet.com

PUTNAM GROUP LTD
35 Corporate Dr Ste 1065
Trumbull, CT 06611-6320
Telephone: (203) 452-7270, FAX: (203) 268-8071, E-Mail: info@ putnamgroup.net, Web Site: putnamgroup.net
Pres: Terrance M. Bussen

RB TOY DESIGN INC
3838 Chester Dr
Glenview, IL 60026-1013
Telephone: (847) 577-5683, FAX: (847) 272-4034, E-Mail: info@ rbtoydesign.com, Web Site: www. rbtoy.com
Pres: Dennis Kupperman

RPM INDUSTRIES INC
26 Aurelius Ave
Auburn, NY 13021-0400
Telephone: (315) 255-1105, Toll Free: (800) 669-3676, FAX: (315) 252-1167, Web Site: www.rpmdisplays. com
VP, Sls: Roger P. Mueller

ROBUSTELLI MERCHANDISE
PO Box 17295
Stamford, CT 06907-7295
Telephone: (203) 965-0200, FAX: (203) 965-0387, Web Site: www. robustelli.com
Pres: Richard Robustelli

ROHLIK SPECIALTIES CO
42505 Woodward Ave
Bloomfield Hills, MI 48304
Telephone: (248) 858-8880, FAX: (248) 858-7323

Pres: Thomas Griesen

S GROUP INC
661 W Market St
Akron, OH 44303
Telephone: (330) 535-2103, Toll Free:
(800) 686-7435, FAX: (330) 535-
1723, E-Mail: info@s-groupinc.com,
Web Site: www.s-groupinc.com
VP: Jeff Sheeks

SAFE SPECIALTIES
223 Green Acres Rd
Kingston, TN 37763
Telephone: (865) 675-2815, Toll Free:
(800) 695-2815, FAX: (865) 717-
8249, E-Mail: black223@aol.com,
Web Site: www.safespec.com
CEO: Betty Blackburn
Primary Market Served: Business &
Consumer
Catalog available online
Direct online sales
Advertising/Marketing Budget Related
to Direct Marketing: 0-25%
Direct Marketing ad budget:
Online: 50%
Telephone: 50%
Founded: 1989

Office equipment merchant wholesalers

SA-SO/TIME WISE
525 N Great Southwest Pkwy
Arlington, TX 76011-5422
Telephone: (972) 641-4911, Toll Free:
(800) 523-8060, FAX: (972) 660-
5684, E-Mail: info@sa-so.com, Web
Site: www.sa-so.com
Customer Service: Debbie Galling
Pres: Becky Nussbaum

WILLIAM W SCHWARTZ
ASSOCIATES INC
1907 Erie Ave
Sheboygan, WI 53081-3708
Telephone: (920) 458-4661, FAX:
(920) 458-6297, E-Mail: wws1503@
excel.net, Web Site: www.
wschwartz.com
Pres: Jeff Schwartz

THE SOURCE
Div. of Wholesale Trophies
2495 Washington St, PO Box 3888
Huntsville, AL 35810
Telephone: (256) 536-7305, Toll Free:
(800) 433-2375, FAX: (256) 539-
8547, Web Site: www.thesource-wti.
com
Pres: Barry Tittsworth

SPECIAL MARKETS SALES
CO
7435 E 86th St
Indianapolis, IN 46256-1207
Telephone: (317) 595-6587, FAX:
(317) 595-9853, E-Mail: info@
specialmkts.com, Web Site: www.
specialmkts.com
Pres: Robert J. Estka

STANDARD BUYING
SERVICE LTD
424 W 33rd St (Rm 230)
New York, NY 10001-2656
Telephone: (212) 686-6800, FAX:
(212) 532-4102, E-Mail: info@
sbspromo.com, Web Site: www.
standardbuying.com
Pres: Kevin Geiger

STONEBRIDGE PRESS LTD
7620 WH Negley Rd
Henderson, KY 42420-9182
Telephone: (270) 826-0341, FAX:
(270) 826-8325
Prodn Coord: Susan Pinkston

STRATEGIC MARKETING
SERVICES
PO Box 21686
Eagan, MN 55121-0686
Telephone: (651) 456-0100, E-Mail:
sms@fishnet.com
Pres: Scott Larson

STROMBERG BRAND
12 Ford Products Rd
Valley Cottage, NY 10989-1238
Telephone: (914) 739-7410, Toll Free:
(800) 724-0996, FAX: (914) 739-
8642, E-Mail: info@stromberggroup.
com, Web Site: www.
strombergbrand.com
Pres: Helen Stromberg

SUPREME SPECIALTY
ADVERTISING
34 Mulberry Ln
Mount Arlington, NJ 07856-1383
Telephone: (973) 770-8700, FAX:
(973) 770-0808
Owner: Donald Chopoorian

SWAG INC
69 Via Verde
Wichita, KS 67230
Telephone: (316) 685-3811, FAX:
(316) 685-4422, E-Mail: swag@cox.
net, Web Site: www.swagpromos.
com
Owner: Walter Burdick

TED'S PROMOTIONS INC
144 Lake Ridge Trail
Baldwin, GA 30511
Telephone: (770) 972-8081, FAX:
(770) 573-3141, E-Mail: ted@
tedspromotions.com, Web Site:
www.tedspromotions.com
Pres: Ted Lehmen

TOP YEAR INTERNATIONAL
INC
dba Akira
22425 E La Palma
Yorba Linda, CA 92887-3803
Telephone: (714) 692-6688, Toll Free:
(800) 942-8722, FAX: (714) 692-
8691, E-Mail: sales@akirausa.com,
Web Site: www.akirausa.com
Pres: Susan Tsai

TWIN CITY ENGRAVING/
PREMIER PROMOTIONS
1232 Broad St, Box 85
Saint Joseph, MI 49085
Telephone: (616) 983-0601, Toll Free:
(800) 222-7752, FAX: (616) 983-
3571, Web Site: www.
premierpromos.com
Pres & Travel Buyer: Jerry Jones

UNISERV ADVERTISING INC
37 Hwy 35
Neptune City, NJ 07753
Telephone: (732) 774-1010, FAX:
(732) 774-3311, Web Site: www.
uniservinc.com
Pres & CEO: Glen Suchecki

JM WECHTER &
ASSOCIATES INC
569 Main St
Monroe, CT 06468-2806
Telephone: (203) 452-0063, FAX:
(203) 452-0414, Web Site: www.
wechter.com
Pres: Janet Wechter

WILCOX & ASSOCIATES
258 Short Ave
Longwood, FL 32750
Telephone: (407) 830-4808, FAX:
(407) 830-5265
Pres: Jack Wilcox

WILLIAMS DIRECT
MARKETING INC
1885 Clements Rd (Unit 244)
Pickering, ON, Canada L1W 3V4
Telephone: (416) 292-7459, FAX:
(416) 292-4635, E-Mail: info@
williamsdirectmarketing.com, Web
Site: www.williamsdirectmarketing.
com

Pres: William Sears
Conducts Business: Canada
Primary Market Served: Consumer
Founded: 1997

Wholesale distributor of cosmetics
across Canada.

MARTY WOLF GAME CO

3601 E Wyoming Ave (SPC 107)
Las Vegas, NV 89104-4937
Telephone: (702) 385-2963, FAX:
  (702) 385-6963, E-Mail: info@
  gamblersjunkyard.com, Web Site:
  www.gamblersjunkyard.com
Owner: Marty Wolf

ZOUIRE

4200 W 115th St (Suite 100)
Leawood, KS 66211-2729
Telephone: (913) 384-6888, Toll Free:
  (800) 346-8991, FAX: (913) 384-
  5757, E-Mail: info@zouire.com,
  Web Site: www.zouire.com
CEO: Houston Hale

ARIZONA

Salt River Project, 1521 N Project Dr, Tempe, 85281-1206

CALIFORNIA

Advent Software Inc, 600 Townsend (fl 5), San Francisco, 94103-4945

Auto Anything, 6602 Convoy Ct # 200, San Diego, 92111-1009

Avaya Communication, 41460 Bellerive Ct, Temecula, 92591-7942

Dataprint Corp, 1650 Borel Pl Ste 206, San Mateo, 94402-3508

HB Distributors, 21612 Marilla St, Chatsworth, 91311-4123

HD Supply, 10641 Scripps Summit Ct, San Diego, 92131-3961

IMSI/Design LLC, 25 Leveroni Ct (Suite 300), Novato, 94949-5726

Johnson Wilshire Distributors Service Corp, 11650 Burke St, Santa Fe Springs, 90670-2544

PFE Inc, 475 Goddard (Suite 150), Irvine, 92626

Parker Boiler Co, 5930 Bandini Blvd, Los Angeles, 90040-2999

Toyota Racing Development USA Inc, 335 Baker St E, Costa Mesa, 92626-4518

Vertical Communications Inc, 3940 Freedom Cr, Santa Clara, 95054-1204

COLORADO

Quark Inc, 1225 17th St (Suite 1200), Denver, 80202-5503

Stolle Machinery LLC, 6949 S Potomac St, Centennial, 80112

CONNECTICUT

A&R Mailing Machine Inc, 757 Goodwin St, East Hartford, 06108-1202

Cognitronics Corp, Corporate Dr, Danbury, 06810

Cooper-Atkins Corp, 33 Reeds Gap Rd, Middlefield, 06455-0450

Gerber Garment Technology Inc, 24 Industrial Park Rd W, Tolland, 06084-2806

HB Communications, 60 Dodge Ave, North Haven, 06473-1124

Hasler Inc, 478 Wheelers Farms Rd, Milford, 06461

Neopost USA, 478 Wheelers Farm Rd, Milford, 06461

OCE North America Inc, 100 Oakview Dr, Trumbull, 06611-4724

FLORIDA

BH Bunn Co, 2730 Drane Field Rd, Lakeland, 33811-1325

East Coast Industrial Equipment & Tire, 1330 W Beaver St, Jacksonville, 32209-7633

Modular Mailing Systems, 4913 W Laurel St, Tampa, 33607

Strong Enterprises, 11236 Satellite Blvd, Orlando, 32837-9222

GEORGIA

Apollo Technologies Inc, 1850 S Cobb Industrial Blvd SE, Smyrna, 30082

The Linton Co, 1091 Baker Ln SE, Darien, 31305

New Hermes Inc, 2200 Northmont Pkwy, Duluth, 30096

Staples Business Advantage, 2077 Convention Center Concourse Ste 125, Atlanta, 30337-4205

IDAHO

KNG Inc, 2102 E Karcher Rd, Nampa, 83687-3000

ILLINOIS

Colorworks Graphics Inc, 451 N Racine, Chicago, 60642-5841

FP Mailing Solutions, 140 N Mitchell Ct (Suite 200), Addison, 60101-5629

Global Infomercial Services Inc, 745 McClintock Dr (Suite 220), Burr Ridge, 60527-0863

Gummed Papers of America, 8740 W 50th St, Mc Cook, 60525-3149

Heyer Corp, 642 Glacier Trl, Roselle, 60172-1035

Hurletron Inc, 1820 Tempel Dr, Libertyville, 60048-9729

Jacobsen Lenticular Tool & Cylinder Engraving Technologies Co (Jacotech), PO Box 4289, Itasca, 60143-4289

Jon-Don, 400 Medinah Rd, Roselle, 60172-2329

Old World Ind, 4065 Commercial Ave, Northbrook, 60062-1828

Royal Performance Group, 2100 Western Ct (Suite 80), Lisle, 60532-1971

USG Corp, 550 W Adams St, Chicago, 60661-3665

UV Process Supply, 1229 W Cortland St, Chicago, 60614-4805

Video Jet Technologies Inc, 1500 Mittel Blvd, Wood Dale, 60191-1073

Wells Lamont Corp, 6640 W Touhy Ave, Niles, 60714-4516

Western Printing Machinery (WPM), 9229 Ivanhoe St, Schiller Park, 60176-2305

INDIANA

Merchandising Equipment Group (MEG), 502 S Green St, Cambridge City, 47327

IOWA

Business Technologies, 3350 Center Grove Dr (Suite 2), Dubuque, 52003-5200

MAINE

Shape Global Technology, 90 Community Dr, Sanford, 04073

MARYLAND

Healthy Directions LLC, 6710 Rockledge Dr (Suite 500), Bethesda, 20817-1864

925 Business Furniture, 10400 Connecticut Ave (Suite 402), Kensington, 20895-3943

MASSACHUSETTS

Data Translation Inc, 100 Locke Dr, Marlborough, 01752-7235

Durasol Corp, 1 Oakland St, Amesbury, 01913-3013

Empire Imports Inc, PO Box 2728, Amherst, 01004-2728

Titan Manufacturing, 27 Maple Ave Ste 5, Holbrook, 02343-1077

MICHIGAN

Haworth Inc, One Haworth Ctr, Holland, 49423-9570

Interior Concepts Corp, 18525 Trimble Ct, Spring Lake, 49456-9570

Jesco Industries Inc, 950 Anderson Rd, Litchfield, 49252

MINNESOTA

Buhrs Americas Inc, 2405 Xenium Ln N (Suite 100), Minneapolis, 55441-3625

Datacard Ga-Vehren Corp, 11111 Bren Rd W, Minnetonka, 55343-9015

GS Direct Inc, 6490 Carlson Dr, Eden Prairie, 55346-1729

Postmatic Inc, 9405 Holly St (Suite D), Minneapolis, 55433-5976

Streamfeeder, 103 Osborne Rd, Minneapolis, 55418-2715

TENNANT Co, 701 N Lilac Dr, Minneapolis, 55422-4687

MISSOURI

Dispensa-Matic Label Dispensers, 725 N 23rd St, Saint Louis, 63103-1533

VisiPak Inc, 123 Manufacturers Dr, Arnold, 63010-4727

NEBRASKA

Direct Tech Inc, 13259 Millard Ave Ste 306, Omaha, 68137-1782

NEW HAMPSHIRE

Perimeter Technology Inc, 540 N Commercial St, Manchester, 03101-1122

NEW JERSEY

Check Point Systems, 101 Wolf Dr, Thorofare, 08086

Flex Products, 640 Dell Rd (Suite 1), Carlstadt, 07072-2202

Opex Corp, 305 Commerce Dr, Moorestown, 08057-4234

NEW YORK

Automated Equipment Service Inc, 60 Noxon Rd, Poughkeepsie, 12603

Colonial Redi Record Co, 1225 36th St, Brooklyn, 11218-2023

DeSantis Holster & Leather Goods Co, 431 Bayview Ave, Amityville, 11701-2638

Global Computer Supplies, 11 Harbor Park Dr, Port Washington, 11050-4656

Laerdal Medical, 167 Myers Corners Rd, Wappingers Falls, 12590-3869

Mailing and Fulfillment Service Association of New York, 411 E 53 St (Suite 20B), New York, 10022

MSC Metalworking, 75 Maxess Rd, Melville, 11747-3151

OccuNomix, 585-52 Bicycle Path, Port Jefferson Station, 11776-3431

The Staplex Co, 777 Fifth Ave, Brooklyn, 11232-1626

Surchin Advanced Mailing Technologies, 80 E Jefryn Blvd (Suite C), Deer Park, 11729-5755

Thomson Reuters, 3 Times Sq, New York, 10036

Ty Pac, 7858 River Rd, Baldwinsville, 13027-9216

Ulano Corp, 110 Third Ave, Brooklyn, 11217-2305

Ward's Natural Science, 5100 W Henrietta Rd, Rochester, 14692

NORTH CAROLINA

Rochling Engineered Plastics, 903 Gastonia Technology Pkwy, Dallas, 28034-7791

OHIO

Aspen Imaging International Inc, 3830 Kelley Ave, Cleveland, 44114-4534

Hamilton Sorter Co, 3158 Production Dr, Fairfield, 45014-4228

SGD Golf LLC, 7600 Olde Eight Rd, Hudson, 44236-1057

Washington Products Inc, 1875 Harsh Ave SE, Massillon, 44646-7182

OKLAHOMA

Hilti North America, 5400 S 122nd East Ave, Tulsa, 74146-6007

Petra Industries, 2101 S Kelly Ave, Edmond, 73013-3665

OREGON

Datalogic Scanning, 959 Terry St, Eugene, 97402-9150

NTP Distribution, 27150 SW Kinsman Rd, Wilsonville, 97070-9241

PENNSYLVANIA

ATD American Co, 135 Greenwood Ave, Wyncote, 19095-1396

Calloway House Inc, 451 Richardson Dr, Lancaster, 17603-4098

Case Design Corp, 333 School Ln, Telford, 18969-2047

Decision One, 426 W Lancaster Ave, Devon, 19333

Foster Keencut, 204B Progress Dr, Montgomeryville, 18936-9616

Frank Mobility Systems Inc, 1003 International Dr, Oakdale, 15071-9226

S Morantz Inc, 9984 Gantry Rd, Philadelphia, 19115-1002

Playworld Systems, 1000 Buffalo Rd, Lewisburg, 17837-9795

Priority Systems Inc, 1201 Fulling Mill Rd (Suite 200), Middletown, 17057

Red Hill Corp, 1540 Biglerville Rd, Gettysburg, 17325-8079

Roovers Inc, 125 Butler Dr, Hazleton, 18201-7364

FL Smithe Machine Co Inc, 899 Old Rte 220 N, Duncansville, 16635-9432

Styled Packaging LLC, PO Box 30299, Philadelphia, 19103-8299

VWR International, 100 Matsonford Rd (Suite 200), Radnor Corporate Ctr Bldg 1, Radnor, 19087-4560

SOUTH DAKOTA

Fenske Media Corp, 3635 Homestead St, Rapid City, 57703-8101

TEXAS

Automated Mailing Systems Corp, 10730 Spangler Rd, Dallas, 75220-7102

Carlton Industries CP, PO Box 280, La Grange, 78945-0280

Echnologist Scrub Tech, 2701 Cameron Way, Mesquite, 75181-4405

Infinity Trading Co Inc, PO Box 9685, Spring, 77387-6685

NCH Corp, 2727 Chemsearch Blvd, Irving, 75062

Stevens International Inc, 5700 E Belknap St, Fort Worth, 76117-4139

Swords Music Co Inc, 4300 E Lancaster Ave, Fort Worth, 76103-3225

VIRGINIA

National Electrical Manufacturers Association (NEMA), 1300 N 17th St (Suite 900), Rosslyn, 22209-3806

Spectrum Systems Inc, PO Box 2265, Reston, 20195-0265

United Way Store, 85 S Bragg St Ste 600, Alexandria, 22312-2793

WISCONSIN

Bemis Co Inc, 1 Neenah Center, Neenah, 54956-3087

HK Systems Inc, 2855 S James Dr, New Berlin, 53151-3662

Windway Capital Corp, 630 Riverfront Dr (Suite 200), Sheboygan, 53082-0897

A&R MAILING MACHINE INC
757 Goodwin St
East Hartford, CT 06108-1202
Telephone: (860) 290-6640, FAX: (860) 290-6644, E-Mail: info@a-r-machine.com, Web Site: a-r-machine.com
VP: Leo Gagliardi
Exec Officer: Roman Plewa

ATD AMERICAN CO
135 Greenwood Ave
Wyncote, PA 19095-1396
Telephone: (215) 576-1380, Toll Free: (866) 283-9327, FAX: (215) 576-1827, E-Mail: janet@atd.com, Web Site: www.atdamerican.com
Pres: Janet Wischnia
Founded: 1931

ADVENT SOFTWARE INC
600 Townsend (fl 5)
San Francisco, CA 94103-4945
Telephone: (415) 543-7696, FAX: (415) 543-5070, E-Mail: info@advent.com, Web Site: www.advent.com
Sr VP & CMO: Katherine Calvert
Primary Market Served: Business

APOLLO TECHNOLOGIES INC
1850 S Cobb Industrial Blvd SE
Smyrna, GA 30082
Telephone: (770) 433-0210, Toll Free: (800) 533-3548, FAX: (770) 433-0132, E-Mail: customerservice@apolloind.com, Web Site: www.apolloind.com
Dir Tech Svcs: Bill Sabo
Pres: Pat Formica
Employees: 150
Founded: 1970

ASPEN IMAGING INTERNATIONAL INC
3830 Kelley Ave
Cleveland, OH 44114-4534
Telephone: (216) 881-5300, Toll Free: (800) 955-5555, FAX: (216) 881-8380, (800) 756-0990
Chmn Bd: Robert H. Kanner
Div Subsidiary Head: Don Lunday

AUTO ANYTHING
Div. of Motorlamb Accessories International
6602 Convoy Ct # 200
San Diego, CA 92111-1009
Telephone: (858) 569-8111, Toll Free: (800) 874-8888, FAX: (858) 569-8503, E-Mail: customerservice@autoanything.com, Web Site: www.autoanything.com
COO: David Klein
Founded: 1979

AUTOMATED EQUIPMENT SERVICE INC
60 Noxon Rd
Poughkeepsie, NY 12603
Telephone: (607) 733-2108, Toll Free: (800) 468-4068, FAX: (845) 485-8221, E-Mail: info@aesmailpro.com, Web Site: www.aesmailpro.com
C.E.O.: James T. Maine

AUTOMATED MAILING SYSTEMS CORP
10730 Spangler Rd
Dallas, TX 75220-7102
Telephone: (972) 869-2844, Toll Free: (800) 527-1668, FAX: (972) 869-2735, E-Mail: amsco@amscodallas.com
Pres: Tom Helsley

AVAYA COMMUNICATION
41460 Bellerive Ct
Temecula, CA 92591-7942
Toll Free: (866) 462-8292, Web Site: www.avaya.com
Opers Mgr, North America Mktg: Cynthia Syroka

BEMIS CO INC
1 Neenah Center
Neenah, WI 54956-3087
Telephone: (920) 727-4100, E-Mail: contact@beemis.com, Web Site: www.bemis.com
Chmn Bd: Henry J. Theisen

BUHRS AMERICAS INC
Subs. of Buhrs Holdings BB
2405 Xenium Ln N (Suite 100)
Minneapolis, MN 55441-3625
Telephone: (763) 557-9100, FAX: (763) 557-9700, Web Site: www.buhrs.com
Pres: Michael Aumann

BH BUNN CO
2730 Drane Field Rd
Lakeland, FL 33811-1325
Telephone: (863) 647-1555, Toll Free: (800) 222-2866, FAX: (863) 686-2866, E-Mail: info@bunntyco.com, Web Site: www.bunntyco.com
Pres & CEO: John R. Bunn

BUSINESS TECHNOLOGIES
R J B Enterprises Inc
3350 Center Grove Dr (Suite 2)
Dubuque, IA 52003-5200
Telephone: (563) 556-7994, Toll Free: (800) 451-0399, FAX: (563) 556-2512
Pres: Ron Bezdon
Founded: 1995

CALLOWAY HOUSE INC
451 Richardson Dr
Lancaster, PA 17603-4098
Telephone: (717) 299-5703, Toll Free: (800) 233-0290, FAX: (717) 299-6754, Web Site: www.callowayhouse.com
Dir Bus Devel: Matthew Carr
CEO: Dustin Knarr
Pres: Monica Knarr
Founded: 1968

CARLTON INDUSTRIES CP
PO Box 280
La Grange, TX 78945-0280
Telephone: (979) 242-5055, Toll Free: (800) 231-5988, FAX: (800) 231-5934, E-Mail: sales@carltonusa.com, Web Site: www.carltonusa.com
Pres: Kay Carlton

CASE DESIGN CORP
RP-NFOA
333 School Ln
Telford, PA 18969-2047
Telephone: (215) 703-0130, Toll Free: (800) 847-4176, FAX: (215) 703-0139, E-Mail: sales@casedesigncorp.com, Web Site: www.casedesigncorp.com
Pres: Roger Ernst
VP, Sls: Paul Lowman
Conducts Business: U.S.
Employees: 150
Primary Market Served: Business
Catalog available online
Indirect online sales
Advertising/Marketing Budget Related to Direct Marketing: 0-25%
Founded: 1921
Gross sales or billing: $5,000,000

Design & manufacture sample, display & video equipment cases.

CHECK POINT SYSTEMS
101 Wolf Dr
Thorofare, NJ 08086
Telephone: (856) 848-1800, Toll Free: (800) 257-5540, FAX: (856) 848-0937, Web Site: www.checkpointsystems.com
Pres & CEO: George Babich Jr

Pres & COO: Farrokh Abadi
Pres & CIO: Salvatore Dona
Pres & CSO: Per H. Levin

COGNITRONICS CORP
Corporate Dr
Danbury, CT 06810
Telephone: (203) 830-3400, Toll Free:
(888) 228-5061, FAX: (508) 624-
0289, E-Mail: info@thinkengine.
com, Web Site: www.cognitronics.
com
CEO: Brian Kelley
Founded: 2008

COLONIAL REDI RECORD CO
1225 36th St
Brooklyn, NY 11218-2023
Telephone: (718) 972-7433, Toll Free:
(800) 637-0040, FAX: (718) 972-
7438, E-Mail: redirecord@aol.com,
Web Site: www.colonialredirecord.
com
Pres: Joe Berkobits
Founded: 1990

COLORWORKS GRAPHICS INC
451 N Racine
Chicago, IL 60642-5841
Telephone: (312) 666-7642, FAX:
(312) 666-0473, E-Mail:
colorworks@ameritech.net, Web
Site: www.colorworksgraphics.com
Owner: Al Jay

COOPER-ATKINS CORP
33 Reeds Gap Rd
Middlefield, CT 06455-0450
Telephone: (860) 347-2256, Toll Free:
(800) 835-5011, FAX: (860) 347-
5135, E-Mail: info@cooper-atkins.
com, Web Site: www.cooper-atkins.
com
Dir Foodservice Distribution: Geoff
Grosz
Conducts Business: Worldwide
Employees: 105
Primary Market Served: Business
Catalog available online
Advertising/Marketing Budget Related
to Direct Marketing: 0-25%
Direct Marketing ad budget:
Direct Mail: 20%
Magazines: 80%
Founded: 1885
Sells temperature, time & humidity in-
struments for HVAC/R, foodservice,
industrial, consumer, OEM & export
markets, measuring success for 125
years!

DATA TRANSLATION INC
100 Locke Dr
Marlborough, MA 01752-7235
Telephone: (508) 481-3700, Toll Free:
(800) 525-8528, FAX: (508) 481-
8620, E-Mail: info@datatranslation.
com, Web Site: www.datatranslation.
com
Pres: Alfred Molinari

DATACARD GA-VEHREN CORP
Subs. of Datacard Group
11111 Bren Rd W
Minnetonka, MN 55343-9015
Telephone: (952) 933-1223, Toll Free:
(800) 621-6972 x6930, FAX: (952)
931-0418, E-Mail: info@datacard.
com, Web Site: www.gavehren.com
CEO & Pres: Todd G. Wilkinson
CFO: Kurt Ishaug
Founded: 1969

DATALOGIC SCANNING
959 Terry St
Eugene, OR 97402-9150
Toll Free: (800) 695-5700, FAX: (541)
345-7140, Web Site: www.scanning.
datalogic.com
Pres & CEO: Bill Parnell
VP Fin: Chet Galka
Founded: 1969

DATAPRINT CORP
1650 Borel Pl Ste 206
San Mateo, CA 94402-3508
Telephone: (650) 340-0550, Toll Free:
(800) 227-6191, FAX: (650) 340-
7028, Web Site: www.dataprint.com
Exec VP: Donna Misa

DECISION ONE
426 W Lancaster Ave
Devon, PA 19333
Telephone: (610) 296-6000, Toll Free:
(800) 767-2876, FAX: (610) 296-
2910, Web Site: www.decisionone.
com
CEO: Annand Sarnaaik
Founded: 1969

DESANTIS HOLSTER & LEATHER GOODS CO
431 Bayview Ave
Amityville, NY 11701-2638
Telephone: (631) 841-6300, Toll Free:
(800) GUNHIDE, FAX: (631) 841-
6320, E-Mail: contact@
desantisholster.com, Web Site: www.
desantisholster.com
Sec & Treas: Helen DeSantis
Founder: Gene DeSantis

DIRECT TECH INC
13259 Millard Ave Ste 306
Omaha, NE 68137-1782
Telephone: (402) 895-2100, Web Site:
www.direct-tech.com
Pres: Craig Harding
Dir Mktg & Sls: Joe Palzkil

DISPENSA-MATIC LABEL DISPENSERS
725 N 23rd St
Saint Louis, MO 63103-1533
Telephone: (314) 231-6006, Toll Free:
(800) 325-7303, FAX: (314) 621-
1602, E-Mail: info@dispensamatic.
com, Web Site: www.dispensa-matic.
com
Pres: Allen H. Oglander

DURASOL CORP
1 Oakland St
Amesbury, MA 01913-3013
Telephone: (978) 388-2020, Toll Free:
(800) 370-0683, FAX: (978) 388-
9762, Web Site: www.durasolcorp.
com
Pres: Lisa J. Israel
Owner: Walter Israel

EAST COAST INDUSTRIAL EQUIPMENT & TIRE
1330 W Beaver St
Jacksonville, FL 32209-7633
Telephone: (904) 358-5681, Toll Free:
(800) 874-1942, FAX: (904) 354-
0888
CEO: Jim Burch

ECHNOLOGIST SCRUB TECH
2701 Cameron Way
Mesquite, TX 75181-4405
Telephone: (520) 208-6314
Mgr: Keith Howe
Primary Market Served: Business &
Consumer

EMPIRE IMPORTS INC
PO Box 2728
Amherst, MA 01004-2728
Telephone: (413) 256-4917, Toll Free:
(800) 544-4744, FAX: (413) 256-
4645, E-Mail: custsvc@
empireimports.com, Web Site: www.
empireimports.com
Pres: Andy Beall
Founded: 1940

FP MAILING SOLUTIONS
140 N Mitchell Ct (Suite 200)
Addison, IL 60101-5629

Telephone: (630) 827-5500, Toll Free:
(800) 341-6052, FAX: (630) 693-
0626, E-Mail: custserv@fp-usa.com,
Web Site: www.fp-usa.com
CEO: Anthony Tony Malak
Dir Mktg: Kevin Pietras

FENSKE MEDIA CORP
aka Fenskemedia.com
3635 Homestead St
Rapid City, SD 57703-8101
Telephone: (605) 343-6070, Toll Free:
(800) 821-6343, FAX: (605) 348-
2108, E-Mail: tomf@fenskemedia.
com, Web Site: www.fenskemedia.
com
Partner: Tom Fenske

FLEX PRODUCTS
Sinclair & Rush Co
640 Dell Rd (Suite 1)
Carlstadt, NJ 07072-2202
Telephone: (636) 282-6800, Toll Free:
(800) 526-6273, FAX: (6361) 282-
6888, E-Mail: info@flex-products.
com, Web Site: www.flex-products.
com
Pres: Ed Friedhoff

FOSTER KEENCUT
204B Progress Dr
Montgomeryville, PA 18936-9616
Telephone: (267) 413-6220, Toll Free:
(800) 523-4855, FAX: (267) 413-
6227, E-Mail: information@
fostermfg.com, Web Site: www.
fostermfg.com
Pres: Ted Borowsky

**FRANK MOBILITY SYSTEMS
INC**
1003 International Dr
Oakdale, PA 15071-9226
Toll Free: (888) 426-8581, FAX: (724)
695-3710, E-Mail: info@
lfrankmobility.com, Web Site: www.
lifestandusa.com

GS DIRECT INC
6490 Carlson Dr
Eden Prairie, MN 55346-1729
Telephone: (952) 942-6115, Toll Free:
(800) 234-3729, FAX: (952) 942-
0216, Web Site: www.gsdirect.net
Conducts Business: U.S.
Primary Market Served: Business &
Consumer
Catalog available online
Indirect online sales
Advertising/Marketing Budget Related
to Direct Marketing: 51-75%
Direct Marketing ad budget:
Direct Mail: 70%
Online: 20%

Telephone: 10%
Founded: 1988
National distributor of graphic supplies
& equipment. Products include: wide
format printers, paper, media & supplies.

**GERBER GARMENT
TECHNOLOGY INC**
24 Industrial Park Rd W
Tolland, CT 06084-2806
Telephone: (800) 826-3243, FAX:
(860) 871-6007, E-Mail: info@
gerbertechnology.com, Web Site:
www.gerbertechnology.com
Pres & CEO: Michael Elia

**GLOBAL COMPUTER
SUPPLIES**
11 Harbor Park Dr
Port Washington, NY 11050-4656
Telephone: (516) 403-2800, Toll Free:
(800) 446-9662, FAX: (516) 625-
6683, Web Site: www.
globalcomputer.com
CIO: Gary Bornkamp

**GLOBAL INFOMERCIAL
SERVICES INC**
745 McClintock Dr (Suite 220)
Burr Ridge, IL 60527-0863
Telephone: (708) 229-2424, FAX:
(708) 229-2407, E-Mail: info@
giservices.tv, Web Site: www.
giservices.tv

**GUMMED PAPERS OF
AMERICA**
8740 W 50th St
Mc Cook, IL 60525-3149
Telephone: (773) 650-2020, Toll Free:
(800) 395-9000, FAX: (708) 485-
8603, (800) 395-3581, E-Mail: info@
labelexperts.com, Web Site: www.
labelexperts.com
CEO & Pres: Tom Brooker
Sr VP Sls & Mktg: Bob Niesen
Founded: 1940

HB COMMUNICATIONS
60 Dodge Ave
North Haven, CT 06473-1124
Telephone: (203) 234-9246, Toll Free:
(800) 243-4414, FAX: (203) 234-
2013, E-Mail: info@
hbcommunications.com, Web Site:
www.hbcommunications.com
CEO: Dana Barron
Founder & Pres: Mackey Barron
Founded: 1946

HB DISTRIBUTORS
21612 Marilla St

Chatsworth, CA 91311-4123
Telephone: (818) 882-0000, Toll Free:
(800) 266-3478, FAX: (818) 700-
1808, E-Mail: info@hbdistributors.
com, Web Site: www.hddistributors.
com
Mktg Mgr: Sharon McAdams
Founded: 1976

HD SUPPLY
10641 Scripps Summit Ct
San Diego, CA 92131-3961
Telephone: (877) 610-6912, FAX:
(877) 219-8526, Web Site: www.
hdsupplysolutions.com
Pres & CEO: Joseph J. DeAngelo

HK SYSTEMS INC
2855 S James Dr
New Berlin, WI 53151-3662
Telephone: (262) 860-7000, Toll Free:
(800) HK SYSTEMS, FAX: (262)
860-7010, E-Mail: hkinfo@
hksystems.com, Web Site: www.
hksystems.com

HAMILTON SORTER CO
Div. of Workstream
3158 Production Dr
Fairfield, OH 45014-4228
Telephone: (513) 870-4400, Toll Free:
(800) 503-9966, FAX: (800) 503-
9963, E-Mail: sstreight@
hamiltonsorter.com, Web Site: www.
hamiltonsorter.com
VP New Bus Devel: Steve Streight
Gen Mgr: Brad Quick
Founded: 1966

HASLER INC
Neopost USA Co
478 Wheelers Farms Rd
Milford, CT 06461
Telephone: (203) 301-3400, Toll Free:
(800) 995-2035, FAX: (203) 301-
2600, E-Mail: info@haslerinc.com,
Web Site: www.haslerinc.com
Pres & CEO: John Vavra
Founded: 1981

HAWORTH INC
One Haworth Ctr
Holland, MI 49423-9570
Telephone: (616) 393-3000, Toll Free:
(800) 344-2600, FAX: (616) 393-
1570, Web Site: www.haworth.com
CEO & Pres: Franco Bianchi
Founder: G. W. Haworth
CFO: Calvin W. Kreuze
Founded: 1948

HEALTHY DIRECTIONS LLC
6710 Rockledge Dr (Suite 500)
Bethesda, MD 20817-1864

Telephone: (301) 340-2100, FAX:
(301) 309-8516, Web Site: www.
healthydirections.com
CEO: Connie Hallquist
CFO: Ben Teicher
COO & Exec VP: Roger DiFato
Founded: 1974

HEYER CORP

642 Glacier Trl
Roselle, IL 60172-1035
Telephone: (773) 884-0815, FAX:
(708) 952-4491, E-Mail: info@
heyerco.com, Web Site: www.
heyerco.com
Founded: 1997

HILTI NORTH AMERICA

5400 S 122nd East Ave
Tulsa, OK 74146-6007
Telephone: (866) 445-8827, FAX:
(800) 879-7000, Web Site: www.
hilti.com
CEO & Pres Hilti Western Hemi-
sphere: Cary Evert
CFO: Eugene Hodel
Sr VP Mktg: Michael Gahleiter

HURLETRON INC

1820 Tempel Dr
Libertyville, IL 60048-9729
Telephone: (847) 680-7022, FAX:
(847) 680-7338, E-Mail: sales@
hurletron.com, Web Site: www.
hurletron.com
Gen Mgr: Steve J. Siler

IMSI/DESIGN LLC

25 Leveroni Ct (Suite 300)
Novato, CA 94949-5726
Telephone: (415) 483-8000, Toll Free:
(800) 833-4674, FAX: (415) 884-
9023, Web Site: www.imsidesign.
com
Chmn Bd & CEO: Royal P. Farros
Co-Founder: Robert Mayer
Founded: 1983

INFINITY TRADING CO INC

PO Box 9685
Spring, TX 77387-6685
Telephone: (281) 292-8509, FAX:
(281) 931-8139, E-Mail: sales@
infinitytradingcompany.com, Web
Site: www.infinitytradingcompany.
com
Pres & Owner: Ben Baker
Principal: Mary Baker
Founded: 2007

INTERIOR CONCEPTS CORP

18525 Trimble Ct
Spring Lake, MI 49456-9570

Telephone: (616) 842-5550, Toll Free:
(800) 678-5550, FAX: (616) 846-
3925, Web Site: www.
interiorconcepts.com
Pres: David Kendrick

JACOBSEN LENTICULAR TOOL & CYLINDER ENGRAVING TECHNOLOGIES CO (JACOTECH)

Div. of Web Communications Group,
Inc.
PO Box 4289
Itasca, IL 60143-4289
Telephone: (630) 467-0900, FAX:
(630) 467-0900, E-Mail: sales@
lenticlearlens.com, Web Site: www.
jacotech.ww.lenticlearlens.com
CEO & Pres: Gary A. Jacobsen Ph.D.
Founded: 2003

Full Service Cylinder Engraving & Optical Engineering.

JESCO INDUSTRIES INC

950 Anderson Rd
Litchfield, MI 49252
Telephone: (517) 542-2903, Toll Free:
(866) 638-8577, FAX: (517) 542-
2501, E-Mail: jesco@jescoonline.
com, Web Site: www.jescoonline.
com
Pres & CEO: Bonny DesJardin

JOHNSON WILSHIRE DISTRIBUTORS SERVICE CORP

11650 Burke St
Santa Fe Springs, CA 90670-2544
Telephone: (562) 777-0088, Toll Free:
(800) 922-2456, FAX: (562) 777-
0099, (800) 993-9699, E-Mail:
jwigloves@aol.com, Web Site:
www.johnsonwilshire.com
Pres: David Pang

JON-DON

400 Medinah Rd
Roselle, IL 60172-2329
Telephone: (630) 893-4747, Toll Free:
(800) 556-6366, FAX: (888) 344-
6878, Web Site: www.jondon.com
Mktg Mgr: Jacki Fry
Primary Market Served: Business
Founded: 1978

KNG INC

2102 E Karcher Rd
Nampa, ID 83687-3000
Telephone: (208) 318-0188, Web Site:
www.kng.com

LAERDAL MEDICAL

167 Myers Corners Rd
Wappingers Falls, NY 12590-3869
Telephone: (845) 297-7770, FAX:
(800) 227-1143, Web Site: www.
laerdal.com
CEO: Clive Patrickson
CFO: Egil Mathisen
Corp Dir Mktg: Jan Holm
Primary Market Served: Business &
Consumer
Founded: 1967

THE LINTON CO

1091 Baker Ln SE
Darien, GA 31305
Telephone: (912) 437-3193, Toll Free:
(800) 841-0200, FAX: (912) 437-
3195, E-Mail: cinfo@davientel.net,
Web Site: www.lintonlabels.com
Pres: D.B. Linton

MAILING AND FULFILLMENT SERVICE ASSOCIATION OF NEW YORK

411 E 53 St (Suite 20B)
New York, NY 10022
Telephone: (212) 217-6824, Toll Free:
(800) 394-5106, FAX: (212) 217-
6824, E-Mail: info@mfsany.com,
Web Site: www.mfsany.com
Dir: Jim Prendergast

Trade organization for professional
mailing organizations to provide an active network for participation &
growth.

MERCHANDISING EQUIPMENT GROUP (MEG)

Div. of Hirsch
502 S Green St
Cambridge City, IN 47327
Telephone: (765) 478-3141, Toll Free:
(800) 645-3315, FAX: (765) 478-
4439, E-Mail: meginfo@
megfixtures.com, Web Site: www.
megfixtures.com
Pres: Tom Hilkert

MODULAR MAILING SYSTEMS

4913 W Laurel St
Tampa, FL 33607
Telephone: (305) 826-9077, Toll Free:
(800) 881-MAIL, E-Mail: sales@
modularmailing.com, Web Site:
www.modularmailing.com
Gen Mgr: Art Wagaheim

S MORANTZ INC

9984 Gantry Rd

Philadelphia, PA 19115-1002
Telephone: (215) 969-0266, Toll Free:
(800) 695-4522, FAX: (215) 969-
0566, E-Mail: info@morantz.com,
Web Site: www.morantz.com
CEO: Stan Morantz
Controller: Heather Morantz
Pres: Lisa Morantz

Manufacturer of ultrasonic cleaning
machines.

MSC METALWORKING

75 Maxess Rd
Melville, NY 11747-3151
Telephone: (516) 812-2000, Toll Free:
(800) 521-9520, E-Mail: inquiry@
rutlandtool.com, Web Site: www.
rutlandtool.com
Pres: Andrew Verey
VP Sls: Paul Martin
VP, Pur: Rich Lawce
Employees: 207
Primary Market Served: Business &
Consumer
Founded: 1955
Gross sales or billing: $17,000,000

Distributor of metalworking and maintenance supplies to industrial customers.

NCH CORP

2727 Chemsearch Blvd
Irving, TX 75062
Telephone: (972) 438-0211, FAX:
(972) 438-0707, Web Site: www.nch.
com
Exec VP & Dir: Lester A. Levy
Exec VP & Dir: Robert M. Levy
Founded: 1919

NCH Corporation manufactures and
markets industrial and institutional
maintenance, water treatment and remediation, plumbing, pet care, and specialty industrial supplies for industrial,
commercial, and institutional customers.

NTP DISTRIBUTION

27150 SW Kinsman Rd
Wilsonville, OR 97070-9241
Telephone: (503) 570-0171, FAX:
(888) 570-0342, Web Site: www.
ntpdistribution.com
CEO: Robert Morter
Pres: Greg Boyd
COO: Steve Whitrock
VP Sls & Mktg: Mark Jenson
Primary Market Served: Business
Founded: 1962

NTP Distribution, Inc. distributes parts,
supplies, and accessories in the RV industry. It also offers benefits and mar-

keting programs, and strategic
merchandising and retail technology
solutions.

NATIONAL ELECTRICAL MANUFACTURERS ASSOCIATION (NEMA)

1300 N 17th St (Suite 900)
Rosslyn, VA 22209-3806
Telephone: (703) 841-3200, FAX:
(703) 841-5900, E-Mail:
communications@nema.org, Web
Site: www.nema.org
Pres & CEO: Evan R. Gaddis
VP & Chief Economist: Donald R.
Leavens PhD
Exec Asst: Karen Sterba-Miller
Conducts Business: Worldwide
Employees: 100
Primary Market Served: Business &
Consumer
Advertising/Marketing Budget Related
to Direct Marketing: 0-25%
Direct Marketing ad budget: $17,000
Direct Mail: 100%
Founded: 1926
Gross sales or billing: $400,000

Standard development organization for
the electrical manufacturing industry.

NEOPOST USA

478 Wheelers Farm Rd
Milford, CT 06461
Telephone: (203) 301-3400, Web Site:
www.neopostusa.com
Pres & CEO: Alain Fairise
VP Fin: Fabrice Assous
Mktg Commun Mgr: Kevin O'Connor
VP Mktg: Gerard Grossano
Conducts Business: Worldwide
Primary Market Served: Business

Digital communications, mailing solutions and shipping software supplier.

NEW HERMES INC

Subs. of Gravograph Industry International
2200 Northmont Pkwy
Duluth, GA 30096
Telephone: (770) 623-0331, Toll Free:
(800) 843-7637, FAX: (800) 533-
7637, E-Mail: sales@gravograph-
newhermes.com, Web Site: www.
gravograph.com/usa/government/
index.php
CEO: John Norris

Manufacturer of engraved metal products suitable using rotary & laser engraving systems.

925 BUSINESS FURNITURE

10400 Connecticut Ave (Suite 402)
Kensington, MD 20895-3943

Telephone: (301) 946-7288, Toll Free:
(800) 525-0302, FAX: (302) 349-
4587, E-Mail: bjfreed@erols.com,
Web Site: www.natcofurniture.com
Mktg Dir: Bernie Freed

OCCUNOMIX

585-52 Bicycle Path
Port Jefferson Station, NY 11776-3431
Telephone: (631) 791-1955, Toll Free:
(800) 466-0071, FAX: (631) 474-
0073, Web Site: www.occunomix.
com
CEO: Paul W. Russo
Primary Market Served: Business &
Consumer
Founded: 2003

OccuNomix International LLC designs
and manufactures personal safety
equipment.

OCE NORTH AMERICA INC

Sub. Canon Inc
100 Oakview Dr
Trumbull, CT 06611-4724
Telephone: (773) 714-8500, Toll Free:
(800) 523-5444, FAX: (773) 714-
4056, Web Site: www.oceusa.com
CEO: Patrick Chapuis
Pres Document Printing Systems Div
Oce North: John Reilly
Founded: 1982

Provides document management and
printing solutions for professionals.

OLD WORLD IND

4065 Commercial Ave
Northbrook, IL 60062-1828
Telephone: (847) 559-2000, FAX:
(847) 559-2266, Web Site: www.
oldworldind.com
Co-Founder: John Thomas Hurvis
Pres: Kal Mahmood
CFO: Mark Rocco
Chief Mktg Officer: Bryan Emrich
Founded: 1973

Antifreeze manufacturer, marketer and
reseller of auto parts and chemicals.

OPEX CORP

305 Commerce Dr
Moorestown, NJ 08057-4234
Telephone: (856) 727-1100, FAX:
(856) 727-1955, Web Site: www.
opex.com
CEO & Pres: David Stevens
COO: Mark Stevens
Dir of Strategic Alliances: Mark Smith
Founded: 1973

PFE INC

475 Goddard (Suite 150)
Irvine, CA 92626

Telephone: (949) 417-0330, FAX: (949) 417-0331, Web Site: www.pfeinc.com
Gen Mgr: Jonathan Garcia

PARKER BOILER CO

5930 Bandini Blvd
Los Angeles, CA 90040-2999
Telephone: (323) 727-9800, FAX: (323) 722-2848, E-Mail: mleeming@parkerboiler.com, Web Site: www.parkerboiler.com
Pres & Gen Mgr: Sid D. Danenhauer
VP Engrng Eng & Special Sls: Greg Danenhauer
Controller: Ed Marchak
Conducts Business: U.S.
Employees: 65
Primary Market Served: Business
Catalog available online
Advertising/Marketing Budget Related to Direct Marketing: 0-25%
Founded: 1946
Gross sales or billing: $20,000,000

Manufacturer & distributor of steam & hot water boilers, thermal fluid, water heaters, tanks & accessories.

PERIMETER TECHNOLOGY INC

540 N Commercial St
Manchester, NH 03101-1122
Telephone: (603) 645-1616, Toll Free: (800) 645-1650, FAX: (603) 645-1424, Web Site: www.perimetertechnology.com
Pres: Mike Dobbins
Information Tech Support Mgr: Jason Sutherland
Product Mgr: Howard Smedley
Founded: 1987

Provides contact center and enterprise Internet protocol telephony software solutions and services.

PETRA INDUSTRIES

2101 S Kelly Ave
Edmond, OK 73013-3665
Telephone: (405) 216-2100, FAX: (405) 216-2102, Web Site: www.patra.com
CEO: Bill Stewart
Pres: Tate Morgan
Exec VP: Tish Zitzow
VP Sls: Jackie Mallory
Primary Market Served: Business
Founded: 1985

Wholesale distributor of consumer electronics, and mobile audio/video and appliance connection supplies.

PLAYWORLD SYSTEMS

1000 Buffalo Rd
Lewisburg, PA 17837-9795
Telephone: (570) 522-9800, FAX: (570) 522-3030, Web Site: www.playworldsystems.com
CEO & Pres: Matt Miller
Mktg Mgr: Jan Price
Primary Market Served: Business & Consumer
Founded: 1952

Engages in the design, manufacture, and sale of commercial recreation and playground equipment.

POSTMATIC INC

9405 Holly St (Suite D)
Minneapolis, MN 55433-5976
Telephone: (763) 784-6046, Toll Free: (888) 784-6046, FAX: (763) 784-9433, E-Mail: info@postmatic.net, Web Site: www.postmatic.com
Pres: John Talbot

Provide our customers with the most efficient and cost effective solutions to their mailing, packaging and paper handling needs.

PRIORITY SYSTEMS INC

A Neopost USA company.
1201 Fulling Mill Rd (Suite 200)
Middletown, PA 17057
Telephone: (717) 939-2700, Toll Free: (800) 479-2208, FAX: (717) 939-6180, E-Mail: contactus@prioritysystems.com, Web Site: www.prioritysystems.com
Pres: Andy Orons
Primary Market Served: Business
Founded: 1986

Business communications and mailing equipment dealership.

QUARK INC

1225 17th St (Suite 1200)
Denver, CO 80202-5503
Telephone: (303) 894-8888, Web Site: www.quark.com
Pres & CEO: Raymond Schiavone
CFO: Kevin Mammel
Sr VP Sls, North America: Mark Benfer
Founded: 1981

Provides publishing software and solutions for professional designers, small and mid-sized businesses, or large organizations worldwide.

RED HILL CORP

1540 Biglerville Rd
Gettysburg, PA 17325-8079
Telephone: (717) 337-3038, Toll Free: (800) 822-4003, FAX: (717) 337-0732, E-Mail: custserv@supergrit.com, Web Site: www.supergrit.com
Pres: Arturo M. Ottolenghi
Office Mgr: Ginny Mowen

It Mgr: Laura Ripple
Conducts Business: Worldwide
Employees: 5
Primary Market Served: Business & Consumer
Catalog available online
Indirect online sales
Advertising/Marketing Budget Related to Direct Marketing: 76-100%
Direct Marketing ad budget: $100,000
Direct Mail: 50%
Magazines: 45%
Online: 5%
Founded: 1978
Gross sales or billing: $1,300,000

Sanding & polishing supplies for auto body, wood & metal working.

ROCHLING ENGINEERED PLASTICS

Subs. of Rochling Haren KG
903 Gastonia Technology Pkwy
Dallas, NC 28034-7791
Telephone: (704) 922-7814, Toll Free: (800) 541-4419, FAX: (704) 922-7651, E-Mail: rep@roechling-plastics.us, Web Site: www.roechling-plastics.us
Sr VP: Lewis Carter
Founded: 1987

Engages in the manufacture of plastic composites in the United States and Canada.

ROOVERS INC

125 Butler Dr
Hazleton, PA 18201-7364
Telephone: (570) 455-7548, FAX: (570) 454-1477
Pres: Nancy M. Andrasko

Manufacturers of metal tape embossing machines.

ROYAL PERFORMANCE GROUP

2100 Western Ct (Suite 80)
Lisle, IL 60532-1971
Telephone: (630) 353-7900, Toll Free: (888) 774-0125, FAX: (630) 353-7902, E-Mail: info@rpgglobal.com, Web Site: www.rpggiftcards.com
Gen Opers Mgr: Bryan Jendra
Gen Sls Mgr: Jim Atten
Mktg Mgr: Julie Feece

Gift card provider to businesses and organizations throughout the U.S.

SGD GOLF LLC

7600 Olde Eight Rd
Hudson, OH 44236-1057
Telephone: (234) 380-5037, Toll Free: (800) 321-3411, E-Mail: sales@sgdgolf.com, Web Site: www.sgdgolf.com

Owner: Robert Robinson
Founded: 1961

Supplier of Miniature Golf and Family Entertainment Centers in America and around the world.

SALT RIVER PROJECT

1521 N Project Dr
Tempe, AZ 85281-1206
Telephone: (602) 236-5900, FAX: (602) 236-8640, Web Site: www. srpnet.com
CEO & Gen Mgr: Mark B. Bonsall
Pres: David Rousseau
Founded: 1937

Provides electric services to residential, commercial, industrial, and agricultural power users.

SHAPE GLOBAL TECHNOLOGY

c/o Shape Inc, 90 Community Dr, Sanford, ME 04073-5810
90 Community Dr
Sanford, ME 04073
Telephone: (207) 324-5200, Toll Free: (800) 627-5836, FAX: (207) 324-0875, E-Mail: info@shapeglobal. com, Web Site: www.shapenet.com
Pres: Vincent Boragine
Mktg Officer: Sandra Mckenney
Founded: 1973

Develops and manufactures plastic injection molded media storage devices.

FL SMITHE MACHINE CO INC

899 Old Rte 220 N
Duncansville, PA 16635-9432
Telephone: (814) 695-5521, FAX: (814) 695-0860, E-Mail: info@ flsmithe.com, Web Site: www. flsmithe.com
Pres: Edgar Smithe Jr
Founded: 1904

SPECTRUM SYSTEMS INC

PO Box 2265
Reston, VA 20195-0265
Telephone: (703) 591-7400 X217, Toll Free: (800) 929-3781, FAX: (703) 591-9780, E-Mail: spectrum@ spectrum-systems.com, Web Site: www.spectrum-systems.com
CEO: Barry Culman
Co-Founder & Chmn Bd: Ronald Segal

Provides enterprise-level application lifecycle management and information assurance solutions that enable public and private organizations to develop, deploy, manage, optimize, and protect IT systems and asset.

STAPLES BUSINESS ADVANTAGE

2077 Convention Center Concourse Ste 125
Atlanta, GA 30337-4205
Telephone: (770) 997-2512, Toll Free: (877) 826-7754, FAX: (888) 387-9592, Web Site: www.staples.com
Chmn & CEO: Ronald L. Sargent

THE STAPLEX CO

777 Fifth Ave
Brooklyn, NY 11232-1626
Telephone: (718) 768-3333, Toll Free: (800) 221-0822, FAX: (718) 965-0750, E-Mail: info@staplex.com, Web Site: www.staplex.com
Sls Mgr: Doug Butler
Commun Mgr: Phil Reed
Founded: 1949

STEVENS INTERNATIONAL INC

5700 E Belknap St
Fort Worth, TX 76117-4139
Telephone: (817) 831-3911, FAX: (817) 838-4344, E-Mail: main@ stevensintl.com
Pres, COO & Dir: Richard I. Stevens
Founded: 1965

Engages in the design, manufacture, marketing, and servicing of Web-fed packaging and printing systems and related equipment.

STOLLE MACHINERY LLC

6949 S Potomac St
Centennial, CO 80112
Telephone: (303) 708-9044, Toll Free: (800) 228-4593, FAX: (303) 708-9045, E-Mail: cmd.info@ stollemachinery.com, Web Site: www.stollemachinery.com
CEO: Gus Reall
CFO: Denise Stasiak
Founded: 2003

Provides packaging solutions for beverage, food, and consumer container industries.

STREAMFEEDER

103 Osborne Rd
Minneapolis, MN 55418-2715
Telephone: (763) 502-0000, FAX: (763) 502-0100, Web Site: www. streamfeeder.com
VP Sls & Mktg: Tim Voit
Founded: 1990

STRONG ENTERPRISES

Div. of SE Inc
11236 Satellite Blvd
Orlando, FL 32837-9222
Telephone: (407) 859-9317, Toll Free: (800) 344-6319, FAX: (407) 850-6978, E-Mail: sales@ strongparachutes.com, Web Site: www.strongparachutes.com
Pres: Ted Strong

STYLED PACKAGING LLC

PO Box 30299
Philadelphia, PA 19103-8299
Telephone: (610) 529-4122, FAX: (610) 520-9662, E-Mail: bill@ styledpackaging.com, Web Site: www.styledpackaging.com
Pres: William R. Fenkel

Packaging solutions including custom packaging, slipcases, box sets and corrugated designed packaging.

SURCHIN ADVANCED MAILING TECHNOLOGIES

80 E Jefryn Blvd (Suite C)
Deer Park, NY 11729-5755
Telephone: (631) 667-0200, Toll Free: (800) 645-5240, FAX: (631) 667-0242, E-Mail: info@surchin.com, Web Site: www.surchin.com
Pres: Hyman M. Surchin

SWORDS MUSIC CO INC

4300 E Lancaster Ave
Fort Worth, TX 76103-3225
Telephone: (817) 53-MUSIC, Toll Free: (800) 522-3028, FAX: (817) 536-4293, E-Mail: daveshep4300@ sbcglobal.net, Web Site: www. swordsmusicinc.com
Pres: Logan Swords
Sls Mgr: David Sheppard
Conducts Business: U.S.
Employees: 3
Primary Market Served: Business & Consumer
Catalog available online
Direct online sales
Advertising/Marketing Budget Related to Direct Marketing: 0-25%
Direct Marketing ad budget: $5,000
Direct Mail: 30%
Newspapers: 20%
Online: 40%
TV/Radio: 10%
Founded: 1969
Gross sales or billing: $400,000

Retail sales of musical instruments to individuals, schools, churches & businesses.

TENNANT CO

701 N Lilac Dr
Minneapolis, MN 55422-4687

Telephone: (763) 540-1200, Toll Free: (800) 553-8033, FAX: (763) 513-2142, E-Mail: info@tennantco.com, Web Site: www.tennantco.com
Pres & CEO: Chris Killingstad

World leader in designing, manufacturing and marketing solutions that help create a cleaner, safer, healthier world.

THOMSON REUTERS
3 Times Sq
New York, NY 10036
Telephone: (646) 223-4000, Web Site: www.thomsonreuters.com
VP Adv Sls: Nick Johnson
Primary Market Served: Business & Consumer

Global information corporation.

TITAN MANUFACTURING
27 Maple Ave Ste 5
Holbrook, MA 02343-1077
Telephone: (781) 767-1963, Web Site: www.americantitan.com
Pres: Gregory Hill

TOYOTA RACING DEVELOPMENT USA INC
Subs. of Toyota Technocraft Co Ltd & Toyota Motor Sales USA Inc
335 Baker St E
Costa Mesa, CA 92626-4518
Telephone: (714) 444-1188, FAX: (714) 444-0339, Web Site: www.trdusa.com
Pres & Gen Mgr: David Wilson
Founded: 1979

Designs, develops, and assembles engines to support Toyota's racing programs.

TY PAC
7858 River Rd
Baldwinsville, NY 13027-9216
Telephone: (315) 638-9431, Toll Free: (800) 356-8964, FAX: (315) 638-9433, E-Mail: info@typac.com, Web Site: www.typack.com
Pres: Glenn Jaeck
Founded: 1972

USG CORP
550 W Adams St
Chicago, IL 60661-3665
Telephone: (312) 436-4000, Toll Free: (800) 621-9622, FAX: (312) 672-4093, Web Site: www.usg.com
Chmn: James S. Metcalf
CFO: Matthew F. Hilzinger
Interactive Mktg Mgr: Richard Long
COO & Exec VP: Christopher R. Griffin
Sr VP: Brendan J. Deely
Exec VP: Stanley L. Ferguson

Founded: 1901
Through subsidiaries, operates as a manufacturer and distributor of building materials worldwide.

UV PROCESS SUPPLY
1229 W Cortland St
Chicago, IL 60614-4805
Telephone: (773) 248-0099, Toll Free: (800) 621-1296, FAX: (773) 880-6647, E-Mail: info@uvps.com, Web Site: www.uvprocess.com
Pres: Stephen Siegel
Founded: 1979

Serves the complete production needs of radiation curing professionals over a wide range of industries.

ULANO CORP
Div. of Kissel & Wolf GmbH Group of Cos
110 Third Ave
Brooklyn, NY 11217-2305
Telephone: (718) 237-4700, Toll Free: (800) 221-0616, FAX: (718) 802-1119, E-Mail: ulano@ulano.com, Web Site: www.ulano.com
Pres: Alfred Guercio
Gen Mgr: Ethel Grasso

Specializes in the manufacture of stencil-making products and chemicals for screen process printing.

UNITED WAY STORE
85 S Bragg St Ste 600
Alexandria, VA 22312-2793
Telephone: (703) 212-6300, Toll Free: (800) 772-0008, FAX: (703) 212-6319, E-Mail: customerservice@unitedwaystore.com, Web Site: www.unitedwaystore.com
Pres: Edmund Cochran

VWR INTERNATIONAL
100 Matsonford Rd (Suite 200), Radnor Corporate Ctr Bldg 1
Radnor, PA 19087-4560
Telephone: (610) 386-1700, Toll Free: (800) 932-5000, FAX: (610) 431-9174, Web Site: www.vwrsp.com
CEO: Manuel A. H. Brocke-Benz
CFO & Sr VP: Gregory L. Cowan
Founded: 1986

Distributes scientific equipment, supplies, chemicals, and furniture for industrial, government, life science, education, electronics, and pharmaceutical markets worldwide.

VERTICAL COMMUNICATIONS INC
3940 Freedom Cr
Santa Clara, CA 95054-1204

Telephone: (408) 404-1600, Toll Free: (800) COMDIAL, FAX: (408) 969-9601, Web Site: www.comdial.com
Pres & CEO: Peter Bailey
Exec Chmn: William Y. Tauscher
VP Mktg: Steven De Korne

Specializes in premise-based private branch exchanges, i.e., business telephone systems.

VIDEO JET TECHNOLOGIES INC
Subs. of Danaher Corp
1500 Mittel Blvd
Wood Dale, IL 60191-1073
Telephone: (630) 860-7300, Toll Free: (800) 654-4663, FAX: (630) 616-3623, E-Mail: info@videojet.com, Web Site: www.videojet.com
CEO: Craig E. Bauer
Pres: Craig B. Purse
Founded: 1966

Develops, manufactures, and sells coding, printing, and laser marking products, fluids, and accessories for the product identification industry.

VISIPAK INC
Div. of Sinclair & Rush Inc
123 Manufacturers Dr
Arnold, MO 63010-4727
Telephone: (636) 282-6800, Toll Free: (800) 922-9391, FAX: (636) 282-6888, E-Mail: visipak@sinclair-rush.com, Web Site: www.visipak.com
President Sinclair & Rush: Bradford M. Philip

Manufactures clear plastic packaging products.

WARD'S NATURAL SCIENCE
5100 W Henrietta Rd
Rochester, NY 14692
Telephone: (585) 359-2502, Toll Free: (800) 962-2660, FAX: (585) 334-6174, E-Mail: customer_service@wardsci.com, Web Site: www.wardsci.com
CEO: Mike Colyer
Commun Dir: Noel Vache
Conducts Business: Worldwide
Employees: 400
Primary Market Served: Business & Consumer
Catalog available online
Direct online sales
Advertising/Marketing Budget Related to Direct Marketing: 76-100%
Direct Marketing ad budget:
Direct Mail: 80%
Magazines: 5%
Online: 15%
Founded: 1862

Gross sales or billing: $25,000,000
Full line of science education supplies
for grades five through college. Micro-
scope slides, lab equipment, living &
preserved specimens, microscopes,
models, AV, etc.

WASHINGTON PRODUCTS
INC
1875 Harsh Ave SE
Massillon, OH 44646-7182
Telephone: (330) 837-5101, FAX:
    (330) 837-5401
Pres: Robert Russell

WELLS LAMONT CORP
c/o John Varaljay, 8145 River Dr, Mor-
    ton Grove, IL 60053-2660
6640 W Touhy Ave
Niles, IL 60714-4516
Telephone: (847) 647-8200, Toll Free:
    (800) 247-3295, FAX: (847) 647-
    6943, Web Site: www.wellslamont.
    com
CEO: David W. Kennedy
Pres: William Trainer
CFO & VP: Tom Palzer
Founded: 1907

Manufactures leather, synthetic leather,
coated, and jersey gloves for men,
women, and kids.

WESTERN PRINTING
MACHINERY (WPM)
9229 Ivanhoe St
Schiller Park, IL 60176-2305
Telephone: (847) 678-1740, FAX:
    (847) 678-6176, E-Mail: info@wpm.
    com, Web Site: www.wpm.com
CEO: Michael K. Musgrave

Manufacturer of web inline/offline finishing and converting systems.

WINDWAY CAPITAL CORP
630 Riverfront Dr (Suite 200)
Sheboygan, WI 53082-0897
Telephone: (920) 457-8600, FAX:
    (920) 457-8599, Web Site: www.
    windway.com
CEO & Pres: Terry Kohler
Founded: 1988

Co through its subsidiaries, manufactures commercial cookware, kitchen accessories, and plastic ware for the food
service and catering industry.

Agencies: Advertising, Direct Response & Sales Promotion (35) — Geographic Index

ALABAMA

HF Direct, 950 22nd St N (Ste 700), Birmingham, 35203

Sales by Dees, PO Box 931, Montgomery, 36101-0931

ARIZONA

AmazingMail Inc, 8300 E Raintree Dr (Suite 201), Scottsdale, 85260-2598

B2BMarketing.com, 8255 E Raintree Dr (Suite 200), Scottsdale, 85260-2684

BolchalkFReY Marketing, 310 S Williams Blvd (Suite 260), Tucson, 85711-7703

IMPACT International Marketing, 349 S Lake Havasu Ave (Ste 104), Lake Havasu City, 86403

LemmonTree Marketing Group, 6220 E Thomas rd (Suite 303), Scottsdale, 85251

Revana Inc, 8123 S Hardy Dr, Tempe, 85284-1106

SHR Perceptual Branding, 2575 E Camelback Rd (Suite 450), Phoenix, 85016-9288

Shaver Direct Inc, 6430 W Bucksin, Phoenix, 85083-3447

CALIFORNIA

The Adcentive Group Inc, 3645 Ruffin Rd Ste 101, San Diego, 92123

Anderson Direct & Digital, 12650 Danielson Ct, Poway, 92064-6822

Ariago Design and Communications, 51 E Campbell Ave (Suite 126), Campbell, 95008-2055

BP Rice & Company Inc, 1205 E Grand Ave, El Segundo, 90245-4220

Beasley Direct Marketing Inc, 15227 Perry Ln, Morgan Hill, 95037-9659

BersonDeanStevens Inc, PO Box 3997, Westlake Village, 91359-3997

Bleu Marketing Solutions Inc, 3025 Fillmore St, San Francisco, 94123-4009

CCMR Global Marketing, 78 Homestead Blvd, Mill Valley, 94941

Camp + King, 87 Graham St (Ste 250), The Presidio, San Francisco, 94129

Carson & Co, 1740 E Garry Ave (Ste 231), Santa Ana, 92705

Catalyst Marketing Group, 5701 Lonetree Blvd (Ste 118), Rocklin, 95765

Celebrity Endorsement Network (CEN), 23679 Calabasas Rd (#728), Calabasas, 91302-1502

Creative Lift Inc, 115 Sansome St (Ste 600), San Francisco, 94104

CustomerMining Inc, 2901 Park Ave (Ste C4), Soquel, 95073-2831

DBM Group Inc, 5 Peters Canyon Rd (Ste 150), Irvine, 92606-1793

DMS Marketing Inc, 26035 Acero (Ste 100), Mission Viejo, 92691-7951

Direct Cinema Ltd Inc, PO Box 10003, Santa Monica, 90410-1003

Direct Partners, 4755 Alla Rd, Marina Del Rey, 90292-6311

The Directors Network, 17071 Ventura Blvd (Ste 105), Encino, 91316

Eagle Marketing Services Inc, PO Box 60666, San Diego, 92166-8666

Eleven Inc, 500 Sansome St, San Francisco, 94111

FMS Direct, 18344 Oxnard St (Ste 101), Tarzana, 91356

Front Porch Inc, 14520 Mono Way (Ste 200), Sonora, 95370-7829

Galanty & Co Inc, 1640 Fifth St (Ste 202), Santa Monica, 90401

Game Show Placements Ltd, 7011 Willoughby Ave, Hollywood, 90038-2332

Gennera Knab & Co, 11536 Sunshine Terr, Studio City, 91604

Goodman Marketing Partners Inc, 4340 Redwood Hwy (Ste B-52), San Rafael, 94903-2107

Gumas Advertising, 99 Shotwell St, San Francisco, 94103-3625

Hawthorne Direct Inc, 1201 W 5th St (Ste T230), Los Angeles, 90017

The Honey Agency, 1050 20th St (Suite 220), Sacramento, 95811

Icon Media Direct Inc, 5910 Lemona Ave, Sherman Oaks, 91411

InterMedia Advertising, 22120 Clarendon St, Woodland Hills, 91367

International Marketing Partners Ltd, 6371 W 79th St, Los Angeles, 90045-1442

interTrend Communications Inc, 555 E Ocean Blvd Ste 900, Long Beach, 90802-5056

iVisionMobile Inc, 9566 Topanga Cyn Blvd, Chatsworth, 91311

JWT Inside, 6300 Wilshire Blvd (Fl 19), Los Angeles, 90048

Jones & O'Malley, 10123 Camarillo St, Toluca Lake, 91602

KERN, 20955 Warner Center Ln, Los Angeles, 91367

LinkedIn Marketing Solutions, 2029 Stierlin Ct, Mountain View, 94043

Majestic Marketing Inc, 1160 California Ave, Corona, 92881-3324

Marchese Communications Inc, 4652 Via Marina (#104), Marina Del Rey, 90292

MARKOTS, 470 Harvest Park Dr (Suite A), Brentwood, 94513

The Marx Group, 2175 E Francisco Blvd (Suite F), San Rafael, 94901

The Miller Group, 1516 S Bundy (Suite 200), Los Angeles, 90025

Monarch Direct Response, 14724 Ventura Blvd (Suite 1200), Sherman Oaks, 91403-3512

More Media Direct Inc, 4519 Admiralty Way, Marina Del Rey, 90292

MyPoints.com Inc, 44 Montgomery St (Suite 250), San Francisco, 94104

New Day Marketing Ltd, 923 Olive St (Suite 2), Santa Barbara, 93101-1447

Nixle LLC, 594 Howard St (Suite 200), San Francisco, 94105

Nostrum Inc, 401 E Ocean Blvd (Suite M101), Long Beach, 90802-8900

Paradigm Promotions LLC, 561 34th Ave, San Francisco, 94121-2705

Pasadena Advertising Marketing & Design, 117 E Colorado Blvd (Suite 165), Pasadena, 91105

Power Direct, 23456 Madero (Suite 105), Mission Viejo, 92691

Practice Builders, 1 Technology Dr (Bldg I, Suite 829), Irvine, 92618-5320

Quigley Simpson, 11601 Wilshire Blvd (Floor 7), Los Angeles, 90025-0509

Rauxa, 275A McCormick Ave, Costa Mesa, 92626

Response FX, 2216 Corte Cicuta, Carlsbad, 92009-8713

The Response Shop Inc, 42215 Washington St (Suite A-407), Palm Desert, 92211

Revana Digital, 160 E Via Verde (Suite 100), San Dimas, 91773-3901

Ron Perrella DRS, 29632 Seriana, Laguna Niguel, 92677-7967

Russ Reid Co, 2 N Lake Ave (Suite 600), Pasadena, 91101-1868

Brody Smythe Direct Inc, 8665 Wilshire Blvd (#301), Beverly Hills, 90211

Social Reality Inc, 456 Seaton St, Los Angeles, 90013

The Spector Agency, 4600 Dietz Way (Suite 100), Fair Oaks, 95628

Starbird Creative, PO Box 1722, Sebastopol, 95473-1722

The Stone Group Inc, 120 Spring St, Pleasanton, 94566

TVA Media Group, 3950 Vantage Ave, Studio City, 91604-3613

Team One Advertising, 13031 W Jefferson Blvd, Los Angeles, 90094-7039

Technical Marketing Group, 2068 Walsh Ave (Suite B2), Santa Clara, 95050

The Testimonial Wrangler, 7486 La Jolla Blvd (Suite 164), La Jolla, 92037-5029

Thane International Inc, 2321 Rosecrans Ave (Suite 4210), El Segundo, 90245

Viant Technology LLC, 4 Park Plaza (Suite 1500), Irvine, 92614

Wikreate, 145 Vallejo St (Suite 6), San Francisco, 94111-1415

Williams Worldwide Television, 3130 Wilshire Blvd (Suite 300), Santa Monica, 90403-2300

Xpectrum Marketing Group, 1953 Ainsley Rd, San Diego, 92123

Yates Advertising, 357 Castenada Ave, San Francisco, 94116-1448

COLORADO

Booyah! Online Advertising, 3001 Brighton Blvd (Ste 236), Denver, 80216

Concepts Unlimited, 2913 Saratoga Trail, Frederick, 80516

CorCreative Group LLC, 4800 Baseline Rd (Suite E104-276), Boulder, 80303

The Creative Alliance Inc, 2675 North Park Dr, Lafayette, 80026-3483

Customer Communications Group Inc, 165 S Union Blvd (Ste 260), Lakewood, 80228-2241

Direct Marketing Designs Inc, 6565 S Dayton (Ste 2200), Greenwood Village, 80111-5386

GA Wright Sales Inc, 90 Madison St (Suite 700), Denver, 80206

Heinrich, 2228 Blake St (Ste 200), Denver, 80205-2013

Pluzynski & Associates Inc, 4800 Baseline Rd E104-276, Boulder, 80303

Point To Point Marketing Inc, 4420 Eagle Lake Dr, Fort Collins, 80524-9671

Walt Klein Advertising, 1873 S Bellaire St (#908), Denver, 80222-4356

CONNECTICUT

Adkins Design LLC, 35 Corporate Dr (Suite 1090), Trumbull, 06611-1355

Affinion Group, 6 High Ridge Park, Stamford, 06905

Charles F Beardsley Advertising, 31 E Main St, Avon, 06001-3805

Bluespire Senior Living, 29 S Main St (Suite 301), West Hartford, 06107

Catalyst Marketing Communications Inc, 2777 Summer St (Ste 301), Stamford, 06905-4310

Customer Growth Inc, 2452 Black Rock Turnpike (Ste 10), Fairfield, 06825

Customer Marketing Group LLC, 7 Hill Farm Rd, Weston, 06883-2007

FPS Marketing Communications, 91 Shelter Cove Rd, Milford, 06460-6548

Fosina Marketing Group Inc, 51-53 Kenosia Ave, Danbury, 06810

The GRI Marketing Group Inc, 35 Corporate Dr (Ste 1040), Trumbull, 06611

Gray & Graham Inc, 136 Main St (Ste 6), Westport, 06880-3304

Leverage Marketing Group, 117 S Main St, Newtown, 06470-2380

The Marlin Company, 10 Research Pkwy, Wallingford, 06492

Mason Inc, 23 Amity Rd, Bethany, 06524

Nova Marketing Services, 1 Darling Dr, Avon, 06001

One On One Advertising Inc, 584 Middletown Ave, New Haven, 06513-1011

1to1 Media, 1111 Summer St (Floor 5), Stamford, 06905-5511

Pappas MacDonnell Inc, 135 Rennell Dr, Southport, 06890-1450

PlusMedia LLC, 100 Mill Plain Rd (Floor 4), Danbury, 06811-5189

PromoWriting, 13 Frenchtown Rd, Trumbull, 06611-4729

Red Rock Branding, 760 Chapel St, New Haven, 06510

School Market Research Institute Inc, 90 Main St (Suite 212), Centerbrook, 06409-1058

Sinish Marketing Communications, 650 Hilltop Dr (Suite B), Stratford, 06614-2414

Source, 761 Main Ave (Suite 2), Norwalk, 06851-1080

Tanen Directed Advertising, 12 S Main St, Norwalk, 06854-2980

DELAWARE

ab + c Creative Intelligence, 819 N Washington St, Wilmington, 19801

DISTRICT OF COLUMBIA

JAM Communications Inc, 1156 15th St NW (Suite 1000), Washington, 20005

Meadows Design Office Inc, 3800 Yuma St NW, Washington, 20016

Wunderman DC, 1055 Thomas Jefferson St NW (Suite 200), Washington, 20007-5256

FLORIDA

Acquirgy Inc, 877 Executive Center Dr W (Suite 300), Saint Petersburg, 33702

Americana Sales Ventures Inc, 1000 Sunshine Ln, Altamonte Springs, 32714-3805

Andersen Advertising, 8550 Touchton Rd (#126), Jacksonville, 32216

Answerthink, 1001 Brickell Bay Dr (fl 30), Miami, 33131

Axia Public Relations, 222 E Forsyth St, Jacksonville, 32202

Beber Silverstein Group, 89 N E 27th St, Miami, 33137-4409

George Blake & Associates, 6015 Courtside Dr, Bradenton, 34210-4018

ByOwner.com Inc, 2200 N Federal Hwy (#203), Boca Raton, 33431

C-Suite Communications, 401 N Cattlemen Rd (Ste 308), Sarasota, 34232

Cade & Associates Advertising Inc, 1645 Metropolitan Blvd, Tallahassee, 32308-3730

Clickbooth.com LLC, 5901 N Honore Ave (Ste 210), Sarasota, 34243-2632

CO-OP Promotions, 2301 S Ocean Dr (Ste 2504), Hollywood, 33019

Crispin Porter + Bogusky, 3390 Mary St (Ste 300), Miami, 33133

DigDev Direct, 260 SW Natura Ave (fl 2), Deerfield Beach, 33441-3026

DM Communications Inc, 3236 Southgate Cir, Sarasota, 34239

GHW Associates, 13063 SW Pembroke Cir N, Lake Suzy, 34269-6914

Lois Geller Marketing Group, 3801 NE 207th St (#1003), Aventura, 33180

Integrated Advertising Inc, 6817 Southpoint Pkwy (Ste 804), Jacksonville, 32216

Interval International, 6262 Sunset Dr, South Miami, 33143-4843

Kelley Swofford Roy Inc, 50 NE 29th St, Miami, 33137-4413

Kobie Marketing Inc, 100 2nd Ave S (Suite 1000), Saint Petersburg, 33701

LMS Inc, 5728 Major Blvd (Suite 650), Orlando, 32819-7963

The Marketing Agency LLC, 2881 E Oakland Park Blvd (Suite 425), Fort Lauderdale, 33306-1813

The Media Crew, 12597 Walsingham Rd (Suite 2), Largo, 33774

Media Response Inc, 2450 Hollywood Blvd (Suite 200B), Hollywood, 33020

Myers, Myers & Adams Advertising LLC, 1616 NE 5th Ct, Fort Lauderdale, 33301-1330

NYK Rapp Enterprises LLC, 215 N Federal Hwy, Hallandale, 33009

Omni Direct Inc, 10800 Biscayne Blvd (Suite 510), Miami, 33161

Premier World Marketing LLC, 3191 Coral Way (PH 202), Miami, 33145

ProLogic Retail Services, 1625 S Congress Ave (Suite 301), Delray Beach, 33445-6304

Quaxar, 2601 S Bayshore Dr (Suite 245), SBS Tower, Miami, 33133

Ronald Erkes & Associates Inc, 3045 Regal Oaks Blvd, Palm Harbor, 34684

Sandi Brown Marketing, 4342 14th Way NE, Saint Petersburg, 33703-5349

Turkel Brands, 2871 Oak Ave, Miami, 33133

Vision Media Inc, 4544 N Hiatus Rd, Sunrise, 33351

Zimmerman Advertising, 6600 N Andrews Ave (Suite 300), Fort Lauderdale, 33309

GEORGIA

Advantage Fulfillment Services, 805 Jamerson Rd (Bldg 2), Marietta, 30066-1057

BKV Inc, 3390 Peachtree Rd (fl 10), Atlanta, 30326

BAM! Direct Inc, 3651 Peachtree Pkwy (Ste E-211), Suwanee, 30024-6034

Business Direct Marketing Associates Inc, 6825 Polo Fields Pkwy, Cumming, 30040-5731

Frank W Cawood & Associates, 103 Clover Green, Peachtree City, 30269-1672

Crawford & Co, 1001 Summit Blvd (Ste 500), Atlanta, 30319-6410

Cypress Media Group Inc, PO Box 53198, Atlanta, 30355-1198

Fitzgerald & CO, 3333 Piedmont Rd (Ste 1100), Atlanta, 30305

Grizzard Communications Group Inc, 229 Peachtree St NE (Ste 1400), Atlanta, 30303

Haynes Marketing Network Inc, 4149 Arkwright Rd (Ste A), Macon, 31210

IQ Agency, 280 Interstate N Cir SE, Atlanta, 30339

Marc G Gault Consulting, 5380 Smoke Rise Dr (Ste B), Stone Mountain, 30087-1529

MarketPower Direct Marketing, 1449 Druid Valley Dr NE (Suite C), Atlanta, 30329-2967

Moxie, 384 Northyards Blvd NW (Ste 300), Atlanta, 30313

Red Clay Interactive, 22 Buford Village Way (Suite 221), Buford, 30518

Response Mine Interactive Inc, 3390 Peachtree Rd NE (Suite 800), Atlanta, 30326-2840

Selling Solutions Inc, 3525 Piedmont Rd NE (Bldg 5, Suite 515), Atlanta, 30305-1586

Strategic Alliance Group, PO Box 88824, Atlanta, 30356-8824

Target MarkeTeam, 1200 Abernathy Rd (Suite 1600), Northpark Town Center, Atlanta, 30328-5673

22squared Inc, 1170 Peachtree St NE (Floor 15), Atlanta, 30309-7649

HAWAII

Dik & Associates Direct Marketing, 2626 Peter St, Honolulu, 96816

IMC Direct, 81 S Hotel St (Ste 315), Honolulu, 96813

MVNP, 999 Bishop St (Floor 24), Honolulu, 96813

IDAHO

Oliver Russell & Associates, 217 S 11th St, Boise, 83702-6902

ILLINOIS

AbelsonTaylor Inc, 33 W Monroe St, Chicago, 60603-5300

Adtron Inc, 1700 Morrissey Dr, Bloomington, 61704-7107

Agency 360 LLC, 1368 Briarwood Dr, Naperville, 60540

All USA Partners LLC, 2600 25th Ave (Ste T), Broadview, 60155-2819

Arends, 515 N River St (Ste 101), Batavia, 60510-2390

Aspen Marketing Services, 1240 North Ave, West Chicago, 60185-1087

Keith Bates & Associates Inc, 4319 N Lowell Ave, Chicago, 60641-2015

Benoit & Associates, 279 S Schuyler Ave, Kankakee, 60901-3809

Beyond Quota LLC, 537 King Muir Rd, Lake Forest, 60045-1640

Black Dot Group, 101 N Virginia St, Crystal Lake, 60014

Black Olive Co, 125 S Wacker Dr (Ste 300), Chicago, 60606-4421

Blast! Marketing & PR, 900 W Jackson Blvd (Suite 3E), Chicago, 60607-3746

Leo Burnett Worldwide, 35 W Wacker Dr, Chicago, 60601-1723

CPO Direct Inc, 736 N Western Ave (#147), Lake Forest, 60045-1820

Cooper Concepts Inc, 2232 N Clybourn Ave (Ste 400), Chicago, 60614

Cramer-Krasselt, 225 N Michigan Ave, Chicago, 60601-7684

Diamond Marketing Solutions, 900 Kimberly Dr, Carol Stream, 60188

The Direct Marketing Specialists Inc, 900 N Franklin (Ste 706), Chicago, 60610-3124

Dixon Direct, 1226 W Seventh St, Dixon, 61021

Dorn Marketing, 34 N Bennett St, Geneva, 60134

A Eicoff & Co, 401 N Michigan Ave (fl 4), Chicago, 60611

Esrock Partners, 14550 S 94th Ave, Orland Park, 60462-2652

Feldman & Associates Inc, 3200 Sandy Ln, Glenview, 60026

Finerty & Wolfe Advertising Inc, 2418 N Burling St, Chicago, 60614

Flair Communications Agency Inc, 214 W Erie St, Chicago, 60654

Foote, Cone & Belding, 875 N Michigan, Chicago, 60611

Fujii Communications Inc, 7369 E Prairie Rd, Lincolnwood, 60712-1039

Grove Communications, 3918 Valley View Rd, Crystal Lake, 60012

Hult Marketing, 619 SW Water St (Ste 2A), Peoria, 61602-1586

Ignition Network, 400 W Erie St (Ste 205), Chicago, 60654

InnerWorkings Inc, 600 W Chicago Ave, Chicago, 60654

Interline Creative Group Inc, 553 N North Ct (Ste 160), Palatine, 60067-8124

Jacobs & Clevenger Inc, 303 E Wacker Dr (Suite 2030), Chicago, 60601-5278

Jones & Thomas Inc, 363 S Main St, Decatur, 62523

Killian Branding, 1113 W Armitage, Chicago, 60614

Kollias & Associates, 210 N Wells St (#4108), Chicago, 60606-1352

Kryl & Co Inc, PO Box 498, Chicago, 60690

LKH&S Inc, 54 W Hubbard (Suite 100), Chicago, 60610

Laughlin Constable, 200 S Michigan Ave (Fl 17), Chicago, 60604-2460

Leapfrog Online, 807 Greenwood St, Evanston, 60201-4311

MSI, 200 E Randolph Dr (Ste 5000), Chicago, 60601

Marketing Innovators, 9701 W Higgins Rd (Suite 400), Rosemont, 60018-4717

The Marketing Store, 55 W Monroe St (Suite 1400), Chicago, 60603-5005

Media Directions Creative Group, 250 Parkway Dr (Suite 350), Lincolnshire, 60069

The Mx Group, 7020 High Grove Blvd, Burr Ridge, 60527-7595

Nova Communications Inc, 27 S 1st St, Geneva, 60134-2243

pii, 1 Hardman Dr, Bloomington, 61701-6934

Precision Dialogue Marketing LLC, 5501 W Grand Ave, Chicago, 60639

Propco Incentives, 8750 W Bryn Mawr Ave (Suite 1020), Chicago, 60631

Purohit Navigation Inc, 111 S Wacker Dr (Ste 4700), Chicago, 60606-4309

Quantum Group, 6511 Oakton St, Morton Grove, 60053-2728

Radiant 1, 824 W Superior St, Chicago, 60642-8083

Gloria Shurn Creative Services, 1633 N Burling St, Chicago, 60614

Springboard Brand & Creative Strategy Ltd, 111 W Campbell St (Suite 401), Arlington Heights, 60005

Starcom MediaVest Group, 35 W Wacker Dr (Suite 3200), Chicago, 60601-1723

Sutter Marketing Inc, 800 E Northwest Hwy (Suite 430), Palatine, 60067

Target & Response Inc, 1751 S Naperville Rd (Unit 208), Naperville, 60189

Tech Image, 330 N Wabash Ave (Suite 1900), Chicago, 60611

Temkin & Temkin, 156 Barberry, Highland Park, 60035-4420

Tobe Direct, 605 Territorial Dr, Bolingbrook, 60440

Tower Media Advertising Inc, 233 N Michigan Ave (Suite 2350), Chicago, 60601-5701

UMarketing LLC, 1 E 22nd St (Suite 200), Lombard, 60148

Unicom Marketing Group Inc, 2875 S 25th Ave, Broadview, 60155-4531

Zephyr Media Group Inc, 990 Grove St (Suite 300), Evanston, 60201-6513

INDIANA

dgs Marketing Engineers, 10100 Lantern Rd (Ste 225), Fishers, 46037

5MetaCom, 630 W Carmel Dr (Ste 180), Carmel, 46032

Interact Medical, 115 N William St, South Bend, 46601

The Jackson Group, 5804 Churchman By-Pass, Indianapolis, 46203

Techcom Inc, 7515 Company Dr (Suite A), Indianapolis, 46237

IOWA

Action-AD, 1035 Lincoln Dr (Suite 109), PO Box 810, Bettendorf, 52722-4149

Integer Group, 2633 Fleur Dr, Des Moines, 50321-1753

Meyocks, 6800 Lake Dr (Suite 150), West Des Moines, 50266

Storey Kenworthy, 1333 Ohio St, Des Moines, 50314

Strategic America, 6600 Westown Pkwy (Suite 100), West Des Moines, 50266-7708

ZLR Ignition, 303 Watson Powell Jr Way (Suite 100), Des Moines, 50309-1799

KANSAS

Associated Integrated Marketing, 330 N Mead (Ste 200), Wichita, 67202

Consolidated Printing & Stationary Co Inc, 319 S 5th St, Salina, 67401-3907

KeyPath Education, 15500 W 113th St (Suite 200), Lenexa, 66219-5106

TradeNet Publishing Inc, 1200 Energy Center Dr, Gardner, 66030-1599

Zillner, 8725 Rosehill Rd (Suite 200), Lenexa, 66215-4611

KENTUCKY

Creative Media Inc, 59 Summertree Ct, Nicholasville, 40356-9780

Hammond Communications Group Inc, 173 Trade St, Lexington, 40511

Monster Magnet, 7725 National Turnpike (Unit 100), Louisville, 40214-4813

Price Weber Marketing Communications Inc, 10701 Shelbyville Rd, Louisville, 40243-1241

LOUISIANA

Foster Marketing LLC, 3909-F Ambassador Caffery Pkwy, Lafayette, 70503

Keating Magee, 708 Phosphor Ave, Metairie, 70005

Peter A Mayer Advertising Inc, 318 Camp St, New Orleans, 70130-2804

MAINE

McCabe Duval + Associates, Box 76, 14 Main St (Suite 203B), Portland, 04011

MARYLAND

BeaconFey LLC, 1107 Kenilworth Dr (Ste 307), Baltimore, 21042

Boscobel Marketing Communications Inc, 8606 Second Ave, Silver Spring, 20910-3326

Direct Marketing Dynamics Inc, 18633 Village Fountain Dr, Germantown, 20874-2122

Doner, 25900 Northwestern Hwy, Southfield, 48075

GKV, 1500 Whetstone Way (fl 4), The Cascade Bldg, Baltimore, 21230-4768

MGP Direct Inc, PO Box 292, Clarksville, 21029-0292

New Village Media Inc, 10320 Little Patuxent Pkwy (Suite 200), Columbia, 21044

Silver Marketing Inc, 7910 Woodmont Ave (Suite 914), Bethesda, 20814-7028

Siquis Ltd, 1340 Smith Ave (Suite 300), Baltimore, 21209-3731

TBC Inc, 900 S Wolfe St, Baltimore, 21231-3514

MASSACHUSETTS

AAI, 65 Sprague St, Boston, 02136

Allied Integrated Marketing, 55 Cambridge Pkwy, Ste 200, Boston, 02142

Arnold Worldwide Boston, 10 Summer St, Boston, 02110

ARRCO Medical Advertising, 1600 Providence Hwy, Walpole, 02081-2542

BBK Worldwide, 117 Kendrick St (Ste 600), Needham Heights, 02494

CP Travel, 46 Waltham St (Fl 4), Boston, 02118

Cartera Commerce Inc, One Cranberry Hill, Lexington, 02421

DigitasLBi, 33 Arch St, Boston, 02110-1437

Direct Impact Group, 200 Highland Ave (Ste 403), Needham, 02494-3019

EMI Strategic Marketing Inc, 15 Broad St, Boston, 02109-3812

Greystone Services Inc, PO Box 482, Beverly, 01915-0482

Hill Holliday, 53 State St, Boston, 02109

Ikon Communications Consultants Inc, 554 Washington St, Wellesley, 02482

Infotrends Inc, 97 Libbey Industrial Pkwy, Weymouth, 02189

LCH Direct Inc, 74 Boynton St, Waltham, 02453-2866

MKE Enterprises, 193 Haverhill St, North Reading, 01864

MRW Communications, 6 Barker Square Dr, Pembroke, 02359

McCarthy & King Marketing Inc, 8 Esther Dr, Milford, 01757-1057

MediaConcepts Corp, 25 N Main St, Assonet, 02702-1136

MullenLowe US, 40 Broad St, Boston, 02109

O'Rourke Hospitality Marketing LLC, 7 Prince Pl, Newburyport, 01950-2644

Precision Arts Advertising Inc, 57 Fitchburg Rd, Ashburnham, 01430-1409

Publicity Inc, 39 S Main St, Mansfield, 02048-2527

Rockett Communications Inc, 11 Juniper Ridge Rd (Suite 1100), Danvers, 01923-1741

Sage Communications, 2 Watson Pl (Bldg 3), Framingham, 01701-4109

THARLER DIRECTs, 4 Cabot Rd, Wayland, 01778-3716

Trinity Marketing Inc, 82 Broad St (Suite 358), Boston, 02110

WebReply Inc, 1085 Worcester Rd, Natick, 01760-1531

MICHIGAN

Dialog Direct, 13700 Oakland St, Highland Park, 48203-3174

Doner, 25900 Northwestern Hwy, Southfield, 48075

Duffey Petrosky, 38505 Country Club Dr (Ste 110), Farmington Hills, 48331-3403

Dziurman Dzign Inc, 620 S Main St, Clawson, 48017

FATHOM Works, 1101 Broad St (Ste 316), PO Box 240, Saint Joseph, 49085-1091

GM Customer Relationship Management, 100 Renaissance Ctr, Detroit, 48265-0001

Harris Marketing Group, 102 Pierce St, Birmingham, 48009-6030

JohnsonRauhoff Inc, 2525 Lake Pines Dr, Saint Joseph, 49085

Lowe Campbell Ewald, 2000 Brush St (Ste 601), Detroit, 48226

Maxwell + Miller, 141 E Michigan Ave (Suite 500), Kalamazoo, 49007

Oneupweb, 1371 Gray Dr (Suite 100), Traverse City, 49684

SMZ Advertising, 1200 Kirts Blvd (Suite 100), Troy, 48084

MINNESOTA

Carmichael Lynch Inc, 110 N Fifth St, Minneapolis, 55403

Colle+McVoy, 400 First Ave N (Ste 400), Minneapolis, 55401

Cuneo Advertising, 1401 American Blvd East (Ste 6), Bloomington, 55425-1105

Direct Marketing Group, 7550 Corporate Way, Eden Prairie, 55344-2045

d.trio marketing group, 401 N 3rd St (Ste 480), Minneapolis, 55401-1351

Fallon, 900 Marquette Ave (Ste 2400), Minneapolis, 55402

R Falls Agency, 900 6th Ave SE (Ste 105), Minneapolis, 55414-1379

Gage, 10000 Hwy 55, Minneapolis, 55441-6300

Garritano Group, 305 Minnetonka Ave S, Wayzata, 55391

ICF Olson, 420 N 5th St, Loring Corners, Minneapolis, 55401-1348

Infinity Direct Inc, 13220 County Rd 6 (Ste 200), Plymouth, 55441-8791

The Lacek Group, 900 Second Ave S (Suite 1800), Minneapolis, 55402-1099

Lorex Inc, 19131 Industrial Blvd (Suite 1), Elk River, 55330

Markgraf & Wells Marketing, 2939 Toledo Ave S, Minneapolis, 55416-1926

Martin Williams Advertising, 60 S 6th St (Suite 2800), Minneapolis, 55402-4444

Mithun Agency, 510 Marquette Ave, Minneapolis, 55402

Periscope Inc, 921 Washington Ave S, Minneapolis, 55415-1257

Presentation Packaging, 870 Louisiana Ave S, Minneapolis, 55426

Response Marketing Inc, 6900 Shady Oak Rd, Eden Prairie, 55344-3403

Risdall Marketing Group, 550 Main St (Suite 100), New Brighton, 55112-3271

TN Marketing, 1903 Wayzata Blvd, Wayzata, 55391-2047

Visions Inc, 8801 Wyoming Ave N, Brooklyn Park, 55445

MISSISSIPPI

Maris West & Baker, 18 Northtown Dr, Jackson, 39211

MISSOURI

Ansira, 2300 Locust St, Saint Louis, 63103

Barkley, 1740 Main St, Kansas City, 64108-1311

Bernstein-Rein, 4600 Madison Ave, Kansas City, 64112-1283

Blackhawk Engagement Solutions Inc, 1400 S Highway Dr, Fenton, 63099-0001

Direct Impact Inc, 655 Craig Rd (Ste 240), Saint Louis, 63141-7170

Gragg Advertising, 450 E 4th St (Ste 100), Kansas City, 64106-1171

HughesLeahyKarlovic, 1141 S 7th St, Saint Louis, 63104

Latin-Pak, 141 Chesterfield Business Pkwy, Chesterfield, 63005-1233

Lundmark Advertising + Design Inc, 2345 Grand Blvd, Kansas City, 64018

Maritz, 1375 N Highway Dr, Fenton, 63026

Noble Communications Co, 2215 W Chesterfield Blvd, Springfield, 65807

Summit Marketing, 425 N New Ballas Rd, Saint Louis, 63141

Target Direct Marketing Inc, 510 W 5th St, Kansas City, 64105

Trozzolo Communications Group, 811 Wyandotte, Kansas City, 64105

VML Inc, 250 Richards Rd, Kansas City, 64116

Wunderman Health, 530 Maryville Centre Dr (Suite 300), Saint Louis, 63141-5825

NEBRASKA

Skar Advertising, 111 S 108th Ave, Omaha, 68154

NEVADA

VastCast Media Inc, 8820 W Russell Rd (Suite 110), Las Vegas, 89148

NEW JERSEY

ARCHES Technology, 111 River St (Ste 1230), Hoboken, 07030

Beacon Marketing Group, 325 E Jimmy Leeds Rd (Ste 7149), Smithville, 08205

Block & DeCorso, 3 Claridge Dr, Verona, 07044-3000

Bluberries Advertising Agency, 70 Outwater Ln (Suite 401), Garfield, 07026

Brushfire Inc, 2 Wing Dr, Cedar Knolls, 07927

Creative Marketing Alliance Inc, 191 Clarksville Rd, Princeton Junction, 08550

Creative Packaging Solutions, 5 W First St, Keyport, 07735-1010

D2: Direct, 54 Cedar Lake W, Bldg # 2, Denville, 07834-1704

Dentino Marketing, 515 Executive Dr, Princeton, 08540-1527

Echomax, 883 Columbus Dr, Teaneck, 07666-6612

Eclipse Marketing Services Inc, 240 Cedar Knolls Rd (Suite 100), Cedar Knolls, 07927

FocalPoint Marketing LLC, 323 Main St, Metuchen, 08840

The Fort Group, 100 Challenger Rd (fl 8), Ridgefield Park, 07660

Fractal Analytics, 803 Plaza 3 (fl 8), Jersey City, 07311

The Goldmark Group Inc, 1155 Bloomfield Ave, Clifton, 07012

Grafica Group, 67 E Park Pl (Ste 425), Morristown, 07960-7103

Harvey Associates, 63 Hoover Dr, Cresskill, 07626

Hercky-Pasqua-Herman, 324 Chestnut St, Roselle Park, 07204-1904

Innovairre Communications LLC, 2 Executive Campus (Suite 200), Cherry Hill, 08002

Intermedia Consultants Inc, 100 Overlook Center (fl 2), Princeton, 08540-7814

Lanmark360 Inc, 804 Broadway, West Long Branch, 07764

The Lifestyle Marketing Corp, 310 Gramercy Pl, Glen Rock, 07452-2226

Linett & Harrison, 219 Changebridge Rd, Montville, 07045-9514

Marketing & Promotions Group, 55 E Ridgewood Ave (Suite A), Ridgewood, 07450

Media Consultants, 205B Chubb Ave (Fl 2), Lyndhurst, 07071

The Nulman Group, 18 Commerce St, Flemington, 08822

PRM Media Group, 105 Mountain Ct, Hackettstown, 07840-2300

Panzano + Partners LLC, 304 Harper Dr (Ste 2251), Moorestown, 08057

Princeton Marketech, 2 Alice Rd, Princeton Junction, 08550-3027

Princeton Partners Inc, 205 Rockingham Row, Princeton, 08540-5759

RPM Direct LLC, 24 Arnett Ave (Suite 100), Lambertville, 08530-1500

Results Advertising Inc, 777 Terrace Ave (Suite 506), Hasbrouck Heights, 07604-3114

Safian Communications Inc, 31 Hickory Dr, Maplewood, 07040

Sawtooth Group, 141 W Front St (Suite 320), Red Bank, 07701

Scientific Marketing Services Inc, 145 E Weymouth Rd, Landisville, 08326

Source Communications, 433 Hackensack Ave, Hackensack, 07601

TRANZACT, 2200 Fletcher Ave (Floor 4), Fort Lee, 07024

NEW MEXICO

Western Data Services Inc, 513 N Canal St, Carlsbad, 88220

NEW YORK

ABI Inc, 29 Broadway, New York, 10006

Andrews Wharton Inc, 2171 Jericho Tpke (Ste 240), Commack, 11725-2900

Atmosphere Proximity, 1285 Avenue of the Americas (fl 5), New York, 10019

Austin & Williams, 125 Kennedy Dr (Suite 100), Hauppauge, 11788-4017

Avalanche Creative Services Inc, 135 W 29th St (Ste 302), New York, 10001-5187

BannerDirect, PO Box 1548, Westhampton Beach, 11978-7548

DL Blair Inc, 400 Post Ave (Ste 400), Westbury, 11590-2226

Blass Communications LLC, 17 Drowne Rd, Old Chatham, 12136-3006

Carl Bloom Associates Inc, 81 Main St (Ste 126), White Plains, 10601-1745

Bodden Partners, 102 Madison Ave (fl 8), New York, 10016

Brashe Advertising Inc, 420 Jericho Turnpike (Ste 320), Jericho, 11753

Broadford & Maloney Inc, 445 Park Ave (fl 10), New York, 10022-2606

CGT Marketing LLC, 275-B Dixon Ave, Amityville, 11701-2874

The Carnegie Hall Corp, 881 Seventh Ave (fl 7), New York, 10019-8077

Catalyst, 110 Marina Dr, Rochester, 14626-5104

Channel Neutral Marketing, 60 Peerless Dr, Oyster Bay, 11771

Charter Direct Marketing, 295 Madison Ave (#1200), New York, 10017

Chase Online Marketing Strategies Inc, 79 Pine St (#102), New York, 10005

Chief Media LLC, 875 6th Ave (Ste 1100), New York, 10001-3507

CL&B Capital Management, 7583 Hunt Ln, Fayetteville, 13066-2554

Collective[i], 130 Madison Ave (fl 3), New York, 10016-7026

Command Financial, 345 Hudson St, New York, 10014

The Computer Studio, 1280 Saw Mill River Rd, Yonkers, 10710-2738

Concept Media Partners Inc, 108 Village Sq (#307), Yorktown Heights, 10598

ConvergeDirect, 33 E 33rd St (fl 3), New York, 10016

The Cooper Group, 381 Park Ave S (Ste 801), New York, 10016-8806

Corinthian Media, 500 8th Ave (fl 5), New York, 10018-6504

CorporateRewards.com, 350 5th Ave (Ste 3920), New York, 10118

Crawford Advertising Associates Ltd, 216 Congers Rd (Ste 2C), New City, 10956-6280

DDB North America, 437 Madison Ave, New York, 10022

DeBow Communications Ltd, PO Box 5432, New York, 10185-9998

Defy Media Inc, 498 7th Ave (fl 19), New York, 10018

Design Matters Inc!, 448 W 37th St, New York, 10018

Dexposito & Partners, 875 Avenue of the Americas, New York, 10001-3507

The Direct Channels Group, 140 Broadway (fl 46), New York, 10005

Doremus & Co, 200 Varick St (fl 11), New York, 10014-4810

E+M Advertising Inc, 462 Seventh Ave (fl 8), New York, 10018

E&M Media Group Inc, 1410 Broadway (Ste 1002), New York, 10018-9359

The EGC Group, 1175 Walt Whitman Rd (Ste 200), Melville, 11747-3030

Eric Mower + Associates, 211 W Jefferson St, Syracuse, 13202

Exposed Brick, 1 Astor Pl (# 7-T), New York, 10003-6937

FCB Health, 100 W 33rd St, New York, 10001

FARM, 6350 Transit Rd, Depew, 14043-1039

Fifteen Degrees, 27 E 21st St (2nd fl), New York, 10010

First Direct Corp, 2345 Route 52 (Suite 1B), Hopewell Junction, 12533-3220

Furman Roth Advertising, 801 Second Ave, New York, 10017

Garver Advertising Service Inc, 440 E 57th St (Ste 5C), New York, 10022-3047

Karen Gedney Communications, 272 87th St, Brooklyn, 11209

Geometry Global, 636 11th Ave, The Chocolate Factory, New York, 10036

Grey Healthcare Group, 200 Fifth Ave, New York, 10010

Group M Inc, 15 N Mill St (Ste 210), Nyack, 10960-3015

GroupM Direct, 825 7th Ave, New York, 10019-6014

Havas Worldwide LLC, 200 Hudson St, New York, 10013

Holsted Marketing Inc, 112 W 34th St (Ste 1405), New York, 10120

Indros Group, 210 Richardson St (fl 2), Brooklyn, 11222

JSR Advertising Corp, 21 Astor Pl (Suite 2D), New York, 10003-6931

Jack Morton Worldwide, 909 Third Ave (Fl 11), New York, 10022

Don Jagoda Associates Inc, 100 Marcus Dr, Melville, 11747

K Public Relations LLC, 101 6th Ave (Floor 9), New York, 10013

KZSW Advertising Inc, 19 Bennetts Rd, East Setauket, 11733

The Keehn Co, 43 Cradle Rock Rd, Pound Ridge, 10576

Ketchum, 1285 Avenue of the Americas (Floor 4), New York, 10019-6029

Kirshenbaum Bond Senecal & Partners, 160 Varick St (fl 4), New York, 10013

The Linick Group Inc, Seven Putter Ln, Linick Bldg, Middle Island, 11953-1920

Lockard & Wechsler Direct, 2 Bridge St (Suite 200), Irvington, 10533

Luxe Collective Group, 49 W 27th St (Floor 6), New York, 10001-6936

MRM//McCann, 622 Third Ave, New York, 10017

Marden-Kane Inc, 195 Froehlich Farm Blvd, Woodbury, 11797

Marke Communications Inc, 45 W 45th St, New York, 10036-4602

Marketing Visions Inc, 520 White Plains Rd (Suite 500), Tarrytown, 10591-5118

MeltzerMedia Productions, 49 Nassau St, New York, 10038

MODCo Media, 102 Madison Ave (fl 10), New York, 10016

Moddern Marketing, 8 E 36th St (fl 5), New York, 10016

Morton Advertising Inc, 875 Avenue of the Americas (Suite 1111), New York, 10001

Mullen & McCaffrey Communications, 197 Hog Creek Rd, East Hampton, 11937-4307

Neo@Ogilvy, 636 11th Ave, New York, 10036

O2 Agency Inc, 149 Madison Ave (Floor 6), New York, 10016

o2kl Advertising, 3 W 18th St (Floor 4), New York, 10011-4662

OgilvyOne Worldwide, 636 11th Ave, New York, 10036

Omnicom Media Group, 195 Broadway (Floor 28), New York, 10007-3100

Parise Marketing Group, 5 Schuman Rd, Millwood, 10546

Progressive Direct Marketing, 5800 Transit Rd, Depew, 14043-2820

Publicis Worldwide North America, 950 Avenue of the Americas, New York, 10001

Rapp, 437 Madison Ave, New York, 10022-7043

Roberts Communications Inc, 64 Commercial St, Rochester, 14614

RolaKimmerling Associates, 501 Fifth Ave (3rd fl), New York, 10017-7805

Roth Advertising Inc, 5 Brewster St (Suite 212), Glen Cove, 11542

SMM Advertising, 811 W Jericho Tpke, Smithtown, 11787

Sandy Goldshein Associates Inc, 38 W 21st St (Floor 8), New York, 10010-6906

Schramm Marketing Group, 160 E 38th St (Suite 35C), New York, 10016

Smart Marketing, 23 Highland Blvd, Dix Hills, 11746

Spring O'Brien & Co, 20 W 22nd St (Suite 906), New York, 10010

The Stanford Group, 70 W 40th St (Floor 8), New York, 10018-2623

Steel Media Inc, 350 5th Ave (Floor 59), The Empire State Building, New York, 10118

Stein IAS, 432 Park Ave S (Floor 16), New York, 10016-8013

Stephan Partners Inc, 233 Spring St (Suite 801), New York, 10013

Sutherland Global Services, 1160 Pittsford-Victor Rd, Pittsford, 14534

TBWA/Chiat/Day Inc, 488 Madison Ave, New York, 10022-5727

TBWA Worldwide, 488 Madison Ave, New York, 10022

TMP Worldwide, 125 Broad St (Floor 10), New York, 10004

Tenet Partners, 122 W 27th St (fl 9), New York, 10001

Trepoint, 315 W 36th St (Fl 10), New York, 10018-6527

True North Inc, 630 3rd Ave (Floor 12), New York, 10017-6749

Underline Communications LLC, 12 W 27th St (Floor 14), New York, 10001-6903

Valmark Associates LLC, 4242 Ridge Lea Rd (Suite 5), Buffalo, 14226-5122

Vanguard Direct, 519 8th Ave (Floor 23), New York, 10018-4570

Ventura Associates International LLC, 60 E 42nd St (Suite 650), New York, 10165

The Verdi Group Inc, 190 Office Park Way, Pittsford, 14534

The Vidal Partnership, 228 E 45th St (Floor 14), New York, 10017-3303

Videoware Corp, 53 Doral Greens Dr W, Rye Brook, 10573

Wilson RMS, 345 7th Ave (Suite 1100), New York, 10001

Wunderman, 3 Columbus Cir, New York, 10019

ZenithOptimedia Direct, 299 W Houston St (Floor 11), New York, 10014

NORTH CAROLINA

Barringer & Associates Ltd, 224 Third Ave NW, PO Box 2525, Hickory, 28603-2525

The Burris Agency Inc, 1175 Revolution Mill Dr (Ste 11), Greensboro, 27405-5053

Cakuun, 28 Schenck Pkwy (Ste 200), Asheville, 28803-5088

Concinnity Marketing & Technology Inc, 1012 Glade St, Winston-Salem, 27101

FGI Research Inc, 6350 Quadrangle Dr (Ste 310), Chapel Hill, 27517

Fletcher Direct, 126 Castlewood Dr, Cary, 27511-5510

Herrmann Global LLC, 794 Buffalo Creek Rd, Lake Lure, 28746

Loyalogy, 3 Chestnut Mountain Rd, Asheville, 28803

The Signature Agency, 1784 Heritage Center Dr (Suite 101), Wake Forest, 27587-3989

Trone Brand Energy Inc, 1823 Eastchester Dr (Suite A), High Point, 27265

Wendover Associates Inc, 309 Edwardia Dr (Suite A), Greensboro, 27409

NORTH DAKOTA

Flint Communications, 101 10th St N, Fargo, 58102

Sundog, 2000 44th St SW (fl 6), Fargo, 58103-7411

OHIO

The Adcom Group, 1370 W 6th St (fl 3), Cleveland, 44113-1315

Alairis Interactive, PO Box 1758, Medina, 44258

The Berry Company, 3100 Research Blvd, Dayton, 45420

Burkholder Flint Associates, 300 Spruce St (Ste 275), Columbus, 43215-1174

Clay Creative Group LLC, 1550 Lewis Center Rd (Ste C), Lewis Center, 43035-8232

Direct Connect Group, 5501 Cass Ave, Cleveland, 44102-2121

Direct Options, 9565 Cincinnati Columbus Rd, West Chester, 45069

E3 Local Marketing Solutions, 4601 Malsbary Rd, Cincinnati, 45242-5659

Emerging Marketing, 29 W Third Ave, Columbus, 43201-3208

Fahlgren Mortine, 4030 Easton Station (Ste 300), Columbus, 43219

G&A Marketing, 1001 Ford Cir, Cincinnati, 45150

Gianfagna Strategic Marketing Inc, 1991 Crocker Rd (Ste 225), Westlake, 44145-6970

Innis Maggiore Group Inc, 4715 Whipple Ave NW, Canton, 44718

Lunar Cow, 344 W Turkeyfoot Lake Rd (Suite B), Akron, 44319

Miami Valley Marketing Group Inc, 1500 Devereux Dr, Dayton, 45419

Northlich, 720 E Pete Rose Way, Cincinnati, 45202-3579

The Ohlmann Group, 1605 N Main St, Dayton, 45405-4141

Pinnacle Direct Marketing LLC, 175 S 3rd St (Suite 200), Columbus, 43215

Resource/Ammirati, 250 S High St (Suite 400), Columbus, 43215

Richards Communications, 8350 Whispering Pines Dr, Russell, 44072-9591

SBC Advertising, 333 W Nationwide Blvd, Columbus, 43215-2311

ST&P Marketing Communications Inc, 320 Springside Dr (Suite 150), Fairlawn, 44333

Saint Gregory Group, 9435 Waterstone Blvd (Suite 180), Cincinnati, 45249

Sherman & Associates Inc, 333 Harmon NW, Warren, 44483

Stephens Direct Inc, 417 E Stroop Rd, Dayton, 45429

Stretch Multimedia LLC, PO Box 3398, Dublin, 43017

Universal Media Syndicate Inc, 3939 Everhard Rd NW, Canton, 44709-4004

Wolf Blumberg Krody Inc, 537 E Pete Rose Way (Suite 100), Cincinnati, 45202-3578

Wyse Advertising, 668 Euclid Ave, Cleveland, 44114

Yeck Brothers Co, 2222 Arbor Blvd, Dayton, 45439-1594

OKLAHOMA

Bullseye Database Marketing LLC, 5546 S 104th East Ave, Tulsa, 74146-6505

OREGON

Atomic Direct LLC, 1219 SE Lafayette St, Portland, 97202-3802

Babcock & Jenkins, 711 SW Alder St (Ste 200), Portland, 97205

Direct Marketing Solutions Inc, 8534 NE Alderwood Rd, Portland, 97220-1347

Gard Communications, 1140 SW 11th Ave (fl 3), Portland, 97205

R2C Group, 207 NW Park Ave, Portland, 97209-3316

Rosen Inc, 1631 NE Broadway (Suite 615), Portland, 97232-1425

PENNSYLVANIA

Danielle Adams Publishing Co, PO Box 100, Merion Station, 19066

Advertising Idea Stores, 37 E Lancaster Ave, Ardmore, 19003-2319

Backe Digital Brand Marketing, 100 Matsonford Rd (Bldg 3, Ste 101), Radnor Corporate Center, Radnor, 19087

The Ted Barkus Co Inc, 8017 Anderson St, Philadelphia, 19118-2936

Boyd Tamney Cross Inc, 994 Old Eagle School Rd (Suite 1015), Wayne, 19087-1802

Brunner, 11 Stanwix St, Pittsburgh, 15222

BullsEye Marketing Systems LLC, 220 W Gay St, West Chester, 19380

BusinessCreator Inc, 47 N Jefferson St, Allentown, 18102

Creative Commerce LLC, 1301 Wright's Ln E (Ste 102), West Chester, 19380

Creative Strategy Group Inc, 330 S State St, Newtown, 18940

DMW Worldwide LLC, 701 Lee Rd (Ste 103), Chesterbrook, 19087-5612

Direct Choice Inc, 480 E Swedesford Rd (Ste 210), Wayne, 19087

Direct Success Communications Inc, 308 Lynne Pl, Chester Springs, 19425

Donovan Advertising, 180 W Airport Rd, Lititz, 17543

Doran & Forgacs Inc, 1306 Barkway Dr, West Chester, 19380-5820

Dudnyk, 5 Walnut Grove Dr (Ste 300), Horsham, 19044

Fried-Cassorla Communications Inc, 7408 Woodlawn Ave, Melrose Park, 19027

Goodway Group, 261 Old York Rd (Ste 930), Jenkintown, 19046-3711

GroupLevinson, 128 Chestnut St (Ste 403), Philadelphia, 19106

Hanobik Communications, 140 Convair Dr, Coraopolis, 15108-2404

Hoff Communications Inc, 23 S Lansdowne Ave, Lansdowne, 19050

JPL Integrated Communications Inc, 471 JPL Wick Dr, Harrisburg, 17111

JVW Direct, 309 W Hutchinson Ave, Pittsburgh, 15218-1325

Kenney Marketing & Advertising Inc, 150 S Warner Rd (Suite 250), King of Prussia, 19406

LevLane Advertising, 100 Penn Square E, The Wanamaker Bldg, Philadelphia, 19107

Lorel Marketing Group, 235 S 17th St, Philadelphia, 19103

Marc USA, 225 W Station Square Dr (Suite 500), Pittsburgh, 15219-1174

Market Share Development Inc, 516 N Blakely St, Dunmore, 18512

Nova DM Agency Inc, 633 E Drinker St, Dunmore, 18512-2505

PulseCX, 211B Progress Dr, Montgomeryville, 18936-9618

Quattro Direct LLC, 200 Berwyn Park (Suite 310), Berwyn, 19312

The Radio Agency, 1400 N Providence Rd (Suite 4000), Media, 19063-2061

Robinson Direct, 6945 Wards Ln, Center Valley, 18034

SWB&R Inc, 3865 Adler Pl, Bethlehem, 18017

The Scholl Group, 316 Highland Ln, Bryn Mawr, 19010-3742

Spencer Zahn & Associates, 2015 Sansom St, Philadelphia, 19103-4416

TPG Direct Inc, 7 N Columbus Blvd, The Piers at Penns Landing, Philadelphia, 19106

Tierney Communications, 200 S Broad St (Floor 10), Philadelphia, 19102-3845

tomsheehan worldwide, 645 Penn St (Suite 301), Reading, 19601-3527

TrueSense Marketing, 155 Commerce Dr, Freedom, 15042-9202

RHODE ISLAND

Catalyst Inc, 275 Promenade St, Providence, 02908

Chaffee & Communications, 310 Maple Ave (Ste L02), Barrington, 02806

JJI International Inc, 200 1st Ave, Cranston, 02910

SOUTH CAROLINA

Chernoff Newman, 1411 Gervais St (fl 5), Columbia, 29201-3379

Ferillo & Associates Inc, 1728 Main St, Columbia, 29201

Marketing Strategies Inc, 4603 Oleander Dr (Suite 4), North Myrtle Beach, 29577-5738

Rawle Murdy, 960 Morrison Dr (Suite 300), Charleston, 29403

Richard Riccelli Inc, 23 Charlotte St, Charleston, 29403

Sweetgrass Marketing LLC, 192 E Bay St (Suite 210), Charleston, 29401

TENNESSEE

Allegiant Direct Inc, 278 Franklin Rd (Suite 290), Brentwood, 37027-3222

Archer Malmo Inc, 65 Union Ave (Suite 500), Memphis, 38103

GS&F, 209 10th Ave (Ste 222), Nashville, 37203

Good Advertising, 5100 Poplar Ave (Ste 1700), Memphis, 38137

The Hogan Co, 107 Fifth St, Knoxville, 37917

Ibis Communications Inc, 1024 17th Ave S, Nashville, 37212

Oden, 119 S Main St (Suite 300), Memphis, 38103-3677

Tigert Communications, 2815 Dogwood Pl, Nashville, 37204

White Post Media Group, PO Box 23232, Nashville, 37202

TEXAS

AdPlex, 15625 Vickery Dr (Suite 400), Houston, 77032-2570

Bigham Agency Inc, 6404 International Pkwy, Plano, 75093

Brierley & Partners, 5465 Legacy Dr (Ste 300), Dallas, 75024

Bromley Communications, 401 E Houston St, San Antonio, 78205-2615

The Company of Others, 1800 West Loop S (Suite 2100), Houston, 77027-3281

DMN3, 2190 North Loop W (Ste 200), Houston, 77018

Datamark Inc, 123 W Mills Ave (Ste 400), El Paso, 79901

Dieste, 1999 Bryan St (Ste 2700), Dallas, 75201-6817

Epsilon, 6021 Connection Dr, Irving, 75039

Farstar Inc, 7110 Main St, Frisco, 75034-4225

GSD&M, 828 W 6th St, Austin, 78703-5420

hawkeye, 2828 Routh St (Ste 300), Dallas, 75201

Hennerberg Group Inc, 5501 Willow Ln, Colleyville, 76034-5149

Internet Direct Response, Inc, PO Box 93157, Austin, 78709-3157

Ivie & Associates Inc, 601 Silveron Blvd (Ste 200), Flower Mound, 75028

The Levenson Group, 717 N Harwood (Suite 800), Dallas, 75201-6501

Lopez Negrete Communications, 3336 Richmond Ave (Suite 200), Houston, 77098-3022

Marketability Inc, 404 Reinerman St, Houston, 77007

nFusion Group LLC, 6500 River Place Blvd (Bldg 2, Suite 201, Austin, 78730

Pop Labs Inc, 7324 Southwest Freeway (Suite 1810), Houston, 77074

Richards Partners, 2801 N Central Expwy (Suite 100), Dallas, 75204-3663

The Snyder Agency, 2918 Plantation Wood, Missouri City, 77459

TaCito Direct, 14165 Proton Rd, Dallas, 75244-3604

Targetbase, 7850 N Beltline Rd, Irving, 75063-6062

TracyLocke, 1999 Bryan St (Suite 2800), Dallas, 75201

Wisdom Marketing Group, 11202 Disco Dr (Suite 100), One Kruse Plaza, San Antonio, 78216-2860

The Woodlands Marketing Agency LLC, 21 Waterway Ave (Suite 300), The Woodlands, 77380

UTAH

Access Development, 1012 W Beardsley Pl, Salt Lake City, 84119-1522

Bonneville International, 55 North 300 West, Salt Lake City, 84101-3502

Merrell Remington & Associates, 1050 East 3300 South (Suite 204), Salt Lake City, 84106

Redirect, 1336 East 1100 South, Salt Lake City, 84105

Response Agency Inc, 936 Granite Peak Dr (Suite 1100), Sandy, 84094

ThomasARTS, 240 South 200 West, Farmington, 84025-0070

VERMONT

802 Creative Partners Inc, 15 E State St, Montpelier, 05602-3015

Gaylord Communications Unlimited, PO Box 28, Bridgewater, 05034-0028

Kelliher Samets Volk, 212 Battery St, Burlington, 05401

VIRGINIA

Affinity Marketing Services Corp, 1332 Windy Hill Rd, McLean, 22102

American Target Advertising Inc, 9625 Surveyor Ct (Suite 400), Manassas, 20110-4408

BCF, 4500 Main St (Ste 600), Virginia Beach, 23462-3362

BrabenderCox, 108 South St (fl 3), Market Station, Leesburg, 20175

BrandCommand LLC, PO Box 71239, Richmond, 23255

CRC Public Relations, 2760 Eisenhower Ave (fl 4), Alexandria, 22314-4569

Cadmus Communications, 2901 Byrdhill Rd, Richmond, 23228

Creating Results LLC, 14000 Crown Ct, Woodbridge, 22193

DeBellis & Ferrara, 2136 Gallows Rd, Vienna, 22027

Eberle Associates Inc, 1420 Springhill Rd (Ste 490), McLean, 22102

Edelmann Scott Inc, 3751 Westerre Pkwy (Ste A), Richmond, 23238-4129

EdgeMark Partners Inc, 4510 Cox Rd (Ste 305), Glen Allen, 23060-6759

Edmonds Associates Inc, 8221 Old Courthouse Rd (Ste 204), Vienna, 22182-3839

Globalization Partners International, 1600 Tysons Blvd (fl 8), Mc Lean, 22102-4872

Harris Connect LLC, 1400-A Crossways Blvd, Chesapeake, 23320

IXI Services, 7927 Jones Branch Dr (Ste 400), McLean, 22102

The Lukens Company, 2800 Shirlington Rd (fl 9), Alexandria, 22206

Marketing General Inc, 625 N Washington St (Suite 450), Alexandria, 22314-1938

The Martin Agency, 1 Shockoe Plaza, Richmond, 23219-4132

Martin Thomas International, 20367 Clover Field Terrace, Sterling, 20165

Nexus Direct, 101 W Main St (Suite 400), Norfolk, 23510

OTM Partners, 5852 N Washington Blvd (Suite 6), Arlington, 22205-2925

Odell, Simms & Lynch Inc, 1593 Spring Hill Rd (Suite 450), Tysons Corner, 22182

Parmelee Associates, PO Box 5557, Arlington, 22205-0057

Response Dynamics Inc, 2070 Chain Bridge Rd (Suite 520), Vienna, 22182-2569

Response Marketing Group, 1145 Gaskins Rd (Suite 109), Richmond, 23238

Wexler Consulting Group LLC, 2121 Eisenhower Ave (Suite 101), Alexandria, 22314

White64, 8603 Westwood Center Dr (Floor 4), Vienna, 22182

WASHINGTON

Cole & Weber United, 221 Yale Ave N (Ste 600), Seattle, 98109-5490

Direct Resources Group Inc, 1221 Second Ave (Ste 300), Seattle, 98101-2986

Eenigenburg & Co, 14504 SE 47th Pl, Bellevue, 98006-3142

Firepower Marketing Inc, 1124 Fir Ave (#161), Blaine, 98230-9702

GCDirect, 911 Western Ave (Ste 509), Seattle, 98104-1047

HackerAgency Inc, 1215 4th Ave (Ste 2100), Seattle, 98161-1018

Hunt Marketing Group, 1809 7th Ave (Ste 411), Seattle, 98101-4403

WEST VIRGINIA

Mail America Inc, 89 Bridge St Plaza, Wheeling, 26003-5209

WISCONSIN

Affirm Agency, N28W23050 Roundy Dr, Pewaukee, 53072

Bader Rutter, 13845 Bishops Dr, Brookfield, 53005

Boelter + Lincoln Marketing Communications, 222 E Erie St (Ste 400), Milwaukee, 53202

DCI-Artform, 2727 W Good Hope Rd, Milwaukee, 53209

Henke & Associates Inc, 236 Hamilton Rd, Cedarburg, 53012

The Hiebing Group, 315 Wisconsin Ave, Madison, 53703

Johnson Direct LLC, 250 Bishops Way (Suite 203), Brookfield, 53005

Frank Mayer & Associates Inc, 1975 Wisconsin Ave, Grafton, 53024

MediaGraphics, PO Box 162, Eau Claire, 54702-0162

Milwaukee Direct Marketing Inc, 675 N Barker Rd (Suite 130), Brookfield, 53045

Nelson Schmidt Inc, 600 E Wisconsin Ave, Milwaukee, 53202

Pro Media Marketing Group, W127N8690 Westbrook Crossing, Menomonee Falls, 53051-3342

The Scan Group Inc, W222 N625 Cheaney Dr, Waukesha, 53186

Seroka, 200 S Executive Dr, Brookfield, 53005

Stephan & Brady Inc, 1850 Hoffman St, Madison, 53704-2594

STIR LLC, 330 W Kilbourn Ave (Suite 222), Milwaukee, 53202

WYOMING

Marquis Awards & Specialties Inc, 108 N Bent St, Powell, 82435-2712

CANADA

British Columbia

DDB Canada, 1600 - 777 Hornby St, Vancouver, V6Z 2T3

Odenza Marketing Group Inc, 4664 Lougheed Hwy, Burnaby, V5C 5T5

Traction On Demand, 2700 Production Way (Ste 500), Burnaby, V5A 0C2

Ontario

Arnold Worldwide Toronto, 473 Adelaide St W (fl 3), Toronto, M5V 1T1

Array Marketing Group Inc, 45 Progress Ave, Toronto, M1P 2Y6

BMC Group, 647 Neal Dr, Peterborough, K9J 6X7

Blue Vidalia, 1-5595 Finch Ave E, Toronto, M1B 2T9

MacLaren McCann, 10 Bay St, Toronto, M5J 2S3

Padulo Integrated, One St Clair Ave W, Padulo Bldg, Toronto, M4V 1K7

Pilot Interactive Inc, 555 Richmond St W, Toronto, M5V 3B1

RI Direct + Digital, 256 Adelaide St E, Toronto, M5A 1N1

Teleperformance Canada, 75 Eglinton Ave E, Toronto, M4P 3A4

Valassis Canada, 47 Jutland Rd, Toronto, M8Z 2G6

WSI, 1660 Tech Ave (Unit 2), Mississauga, L4W 5S9

WiredPente Inc, 21 Wales Ave, Markham, L3P 2C2

Quebec

Aimia Inc, 525 Viger Ave W (Ste 1000), Montreal, H2Z 0B2

Baker-Blais Marketing Inc, 295 Hymus Blvd, Pointe-Claire, H9R 6A5

Cossette, 300 St-Paul St (fl 3), Quebec, G1K 7R1

TC Transcontinental, 1 Place Ville Marie (Suite 3315), Montreal, H3B 3N2

Agencies: Advertising, Direct Response & Sales Promotion (35)

AAI
Div. of Marketing Assistance Inc
65 Sprague St
Boston, MA 02136
Telephone: (508) 544-1250, Toll Free:
(877) 866-8500, FAX: (508) 544-
1253, E-Mail: info@aai-agency.com,
Web Site: www.aai-agency.com
Exec VP: Mark Hersum

AB + C CREATIVE INTELLIGENCE
819 N Washington St
Wilmington, DE 19801
Telephone: (302) 655-1552, Toll Free:
(800) 848-1552, FAX: (302) 655-
3105, Web Site: www.a-b-c.com
Pres & CEO: John Hawkins
Founded: 1971

Advertising agency.

ABI INC
29 Broadway
New York, NY 10006
Telephone: (212) 529-4500, FAX:
(212) 529-4442, E-Mail: info@abipr.
com, Web Site: www.abipr.com
CEO: Alan Isacson
Exec Dir: Nicole Zampino
Founded: 1980

Global marketing public relations
agency.

ABELSONTAYLOR INC
33 W Monroe St
Chicago, IL 60603-5300
Telephone: (312) 894-5500, FAX:
(312) 894-5526, E-Mail: info@
abelsontaylor.com, Web Site: www.
abelsontaylor.com
Chmn & CEO: Dale Taylor
Founded: 1981

ACCESS DEVELOPMENT
1012 W Beardsley Pl
Salt Lake City, UT 84119-1522
Telephone: (801) 656-1529, Toll Free:
(800) 840-0032, Web Site: www.
accessdevelopment.com
Founder & CEO: Larry Maxfield
Founded: 1984

ACQUIRGY INC
877 Executive Center Dr W (Suite 300)
Saint Petersburg, FL 33702
Telephone: (727) 576-6630, FAX:
(727) 576-4864, Web Site: www.
sendtec.com
CEO: Paul Soltoff

Pres: Steven Morvay
Conducts Business: U.S.
Primary Market Served: Business

Acquisition marketing agency that develops and executes marketing programs across digital & traditional
platforms.

ACTION-AD
1035 Lincoln Dr (Suite 109), PO Box
810
Bettendorf, IA 52722-4149
Telephone: (563) 355-9581, FAX:
(563) 355-9586
Pres: Roger Enke

DANIELLE ADAMS PUBLISHING CO
PO Box 100
Merion Station, PA 19066
Telephone: (610) 642-1000, E-Mail:
jeff@dobkin.com, Web Site: www.
danielleadams.com
Pres: Jeffrey Dobkin

THE ADCENTIVE GROUP INC
Div of Brown & Bigelow
3645 Ruffin Rd Ste 101
San Diego, CA 92123
Telephone: (858) 278-9200, FAX:
(858) 571-2832, Web Site: www.
brownandbigelow.com
Reg VP: Beverly Walter
Reg Opers Mgr: Jim Ellis
Founded: 1980

THE ADCOM GROUP
1370 W 6th St (fl 3)
Cleveland, OH 44113-1315
Telephone: (216) 574-9100, FAX:
(216) 574-6131, Web Site: www.
theadcomgroup.com
Pres: Joe Kubic
Chief Creative Officer: Mark Nuss
Founded: 1990

ADKINS DESIGN LLC
35 Corporate Dr (Suite 1090)
Trumbull, CT 06611-1355
Telephone: (203) 880-9517, E-Mail:
tom@adkins-design.com, Web Site:
www.sabinc.com
Art Dir: Thomas Adkins
Founded: 1985

Marketing communications agency.

ADPLEX
15625 Vickery Dr (Suite 400)

Houston, TX 77032-2570
Telephone: (281) 821-5522, FAX:
(281) 443-1040, Web Site: www.
adplex.com
CEO: Ed Raine

ADTRON INC
1700 Morrissey Dr
Bloomington, IL 61704-7107
Telephone: (309) 662-1221, FAX:
(309) 663-6691
Mgr: Andrea Owen Beyer
Founded: 1992

ADVANTAGE FULFILLMENT SERVICES
805 Jamerson Rd (Bldg 2)
Marietta, GA 30066-1057
Telephone: (678) 921-2134, FAX:
(770) 592-0204, Web Site: www.
atlantamailervices.com
Owner: Eric Tatum
Founded: 1995

ADVERTISING IDEA STORES
37 E Lancaster Ave
Ardmore, PA 19003-2319
Telephone: (484) 416-0004, E-Mail:
marc@uniongoods.com, Web Site:
www.uniongoods.com
VP Sls: Marc S. Goldberg
Founded: 1968

AFFINION GROUP
6 High Ridge Park
Stamford, CT 06905
Telephone: (203) 956-1000, Toll Free:
(800) 282-3315, Web Site: www.
affinion.com
CEO: Todd H. Siegel
Exec VP & CFO: Greg Miller
COO: Bob Lyons
Pres & Mng Dir: Michele Conforti

AFFINITY MARKETING SERVICES CORP
1332 Windy Hill Rd
McLean, VA 22102
Telephone: (703) 917-9822, FAX:
(703) 917-9804, E-Mail: serota@
affinitymarketingservicescorp.com,
Web Site: www.
affinitymarketingservicescorp.com
Pres: Gary Serota

AFFIRM AGENCY
N28W23050 Roundy Dr
Pewaukee, WI 53072

Telephone: (262) 650-9900, E-Mail: info@affirmagency.com, Web Site: affirmagency.com
Principal & Mktg Dir: Danny Mager
Principal & Creative Dir: Steve Stocker
VP Client Svcs & Pub Rels: Laura Monagle
Founded: 1985

Full-service advertising, marketing & public relations agency.

AGENCY 360 LLC
1368 Briarwood Dr
Naperville, IL 60540
Telephone: (312) 316-7070, (312) 371-4104, E-Mail: mail@ agencythreesixty.com, Web Site: agencythreesixty.com
Partner: Bill Bracken
Partner: Dakota Shultz
Founded: 2007

Full-service marketing communications and development firm.

AIMIA INC
525 Viger Ave W (Ste 1000)
Montreal, QC, Canada H2Z 0B2
Web Site: www.aimia.com
Grp CEO: Rupert Duchesne
Exec VP & CFO: David L. Adams
Founded: 1984

ALAIRIS INTERACTIVE
PO Box 1758
Medina, OH 44258
Telephone: (877) 770-0350, E-Mail: info@alairis.com, Web Site: www. alairis.com
Pres: Jason Valore
Founded: 2008

Marketing, multimedia production and creative consulting agency that provides advertising & graphic design, website & custom application development, email & social media marketing, videography and Web IT solutions.

ALL USA PARTNERS LLC
2600 25th Ave (Ste T)
Broadview, IL 60155-2819
Toll Free: (800) 861-4116, Web Site: allusa.net

ALLEGIANT DIRECT INC
278 Franklin Rd (Suite 290)
Brentwood, TN 37027-3222
Telephone: (615) 373-2042, FAX: (615) 373-2099, E-Mail: welcome@ allegiantdirect.com, Web Site: www. allegiantdirect.com
Pres & Creative Dir: Wayne Gurley
Founded: 1984

ALLIED INTEGRATED MARKETING
55 Cambridge Pkwy, Ste 200
Boston, MA 02142
Telephone: (617) 859-4800, E-Mail: alliedimsocial@alliedim.com, Web Site: alliedim.com
Pres: Clint Kendall
COO: Kymn Goldstein
CFO: Adam Cinque
Chief Digital Officer: Adam Cunningham
Founded: 1985

Full service entertainment & consumer marketing services company.

AMAZINGMAIL INC
8300 E Raintree Dr (Suite 201)
Scottsdale, AZ 85260-2598
Telephone: (480) 281-4800, E-Mail: customersupport@amazingmail.com, Web Site: www.amazingmail.com
Pres & CEO: Bob Blackman
Founded: 1999

AMERICAN TARGET ADVERTISING INC
Sub. of The Viguerie Company
9625 Surveyor Ct (Suite 400)
Manassas, VA 20110-4408
Telephone: (703) 392-7676, FAX: (703) 392-7654, E-Mail: info@ americantarget.com, Web Site: americantarget.com
Chmn: Richard A. Viguerie
Pres & CEO: Kathleen Pattern
Sr VP Mktg & Devel: Gary Meredith
VP Admin: Viola Shields

AMERICANA SALES VENTURES INC
1000 Sunshine Ln
Altamonte Springs, FL 32714-3805
Telephone: (407) 862-8388, Toll Free: (800) 445-4302, FAX: (407) 862-6535, Web Site: www. americanashopper.com
Pres: Timothy Randolph
VP: Kim Seamens

ANDERSEN ADVERTISING
8550 Touchton Rd (#126)
Jacksonville, FL 32216
Telephone: (904) 859-8165, E-Mail: bob@andersenadvertising.com, Web Site: www.andersenadvertising.com
Creative Dir: Bob Andersen

ANDERSON DIRECT & DIGITAL
12650 Danielson Ct
Poway, CA 92064-6822
Toll Free: (888) 694-5094, Web Site: www.andersondd.com

CEO: Ted Tietge
Pres: Randy Dale
Exec VP: Scott Hopkins
VP Client Strategy: Michael Campbell
Mktg Mgr: Danielle Nelson
Founded: 1985

ANDREWS WHARTON INC
2171 Jericho Tpke (Ste 240)
Commack, NY 11725-2900
Telephone: (631) 470-4546, Toll Free: (631) 470-5683, E-Mail: info@ andrewswharton.com, Web Site: andrewswharton.com
Pres & CEO: Jack Lee
VP Sls & Mktg: Rob Brickley

ANSIRA
2300 Locust St
Saint Louis, MO 63103
Telephone: (314) 783-2300, FAX: (314) 783-2301, E-Mail: dl-newbusiness@ansira.com, Web Site: ansira.com
Pres & CEO: Martin Reidy
Exec VP, CFO: Gary Weller
Exec VP, Chief Mktg Officer: Judge Graham
Founded: 1919

Digital and direct marketing agency.

ANSWERTHINK
Div of The Hackett Group
1001 Brickell Bay Dr (fl 30)
Miami, FL 33131
Telephone: (305) 375-8005, Toll Free: (866) 844-6514, FAX: (305) 379-8810, Web Site: www.answerthink. com
Chm & CEO: Ted A. Fernandez
Exec VP & CFO: Robert A. Ramirez
COO & Dir: David N. Dungan
Founded: 1997

ARCHER MALMO INC
65 Union Ave (Suite 500)
Memphis, TN 38103
Telephone: (901) 523-2000, FAX: (901) 524-5578, Web Site: www. archermalmo.com
CEO: Russ Williams
Chief Creative & Strategy Officer: Yvonne Tocquigny
Sr VP, Grp Acct Dir: Jay Cooper
Pres TMB Mktg: Tom Barzizza
Sr VP & Chief Digital Officer: Ken Rohman
Founded: 1952

Advertising & marketing communications firm.

ARCHES TECHNOLOGY
111 River St (Ste 1230)
Hoboken, NJ 07030

Telephone: (973) 882-0900, E-Mail: info@archestechnology.com, Web Site: www.archestechnology.com
Founder & CEO: Daniella Koren
Founded: 2013

ARENDS
515 N River St (Ste 101)
Batavia, IL 60510-2390
Telephone: (630) 990-0220, FAX: (630) 990-2556, Web Site: www.arends-inc.com
CEO & Pres: John Arends
VP & Brand Mgr: Jim McMillen
Digital Media: Iwona Ponze
Founded: 1958

ARIAGO DESIGN AND COMMUNICATIONS
51 E Campbell Ave (Suite 126)
Campbell, CA 95008-2055
Telephone: (408) 668-0400, FAX: (408) 688-0401, E-Mail: ddahart@ariago.com, Web Site: www.ariago.com
Founder & Pres: Denise Dahart
Founded: 1996

ARNOLD WORLDWIDE BOSTON
10 Summer St
Boston, MA 02110
Telephone: (617) 587-8000, FAX: (617) 587-8004, Web Site: www.arn.com
Global Pres: Pam Hamlin
Chief Marketing Officer: Lisa Unsworth

ARNOLD WORLDWIDE TORONTO
473 Adelaide St W (fl 3)
Toronto, ON, Canada M5V 1T1
Telephone: (416) 355-5009, E-Mail: bsharp@arnoldworldwide.ca, Web Site: arn.com
Chmn: Bill Sharpe

ARRAY MARKETING GROUP INC
45 Progress Ave
Toronto, ON, Canada M1P 2Y6
Telephone: (416) 299-4865, FAX: (416) 292-9759, E-Mail: inquiry@arraymarketing.com, Web Site: arraymarketing.com
CEO: Tom Hendren
CFO: Kevin Patrick
VP Design Innovation: James Della Rossa
VP Sls: Robert Thiry
Founded: 1981

ARRCO MEDICAL ADVERTISING
1600 Providence Hwy
Walpole, MA 02081-2542
Telephone: (508) 404-1105, FAX: (508) 404-1106, E-Mail: info@arrco.com, Web Site: www.arrco.com
Pres: Jerome Reicher
Sr VP: Jayne Talmage

ASPEN MARKETING SERVICES
Div of Epsilon
1240 North Ave
West Chicago, IL 60185-1087
Toll Free: (800) 848-0212, FAX: (630) 293-7584, Web Site: www.aspenms.com
Pres & CEO: Patrick J. O'Rahilly

ASSOCIATED INTEGRATED MARKETING
330 N Mead (Ste 200)
Wichita, KS 67202
Telephone: (316) 683-4691, E-Mail: info@meetassociated.com, Web Site: www.meetassociated.com
VP & Exec Creative Dir: Dave Stewart
VP Client Svcs & Pub Rels: Shawn Steward
VP Fin & HR: Kim Weprin

ATMOSPHERE PROXIMITY
Member of Omnicom Group
1285 Avenue of the Americas (fl 5)
New York, NY 10019
Telephone: (212) 827-2500, FAX: (212) 827-2525, E-Mail: andreas.combuechen@atmospeherebbdo.com, Web Site: www.atmosphereproximity.com
Chmn, CEO & Chief Creative Officer: Andreas Combuchen
Mng Dir: Garrett Franklin
Exec VP & Exec Creative Dir: Stewart Krull
Founded: 1999

ATOMIC DIRECT LLC
1219 SE Lafayette St
Portland, OR 97202-3802
Telephone: (503) 296-6131, FAX: (503) 296-9890, Web Site: www.atomicdirect.com
Founder & CEO: Doug Garnett
Exec Producer: John Gurney
CFO: Dave Fallon

AUSTIN & WILLIAMS
125 Kennedy Dr (Suite 100)
Hauppauge, NY 11788-4017
Telephone: (631) 938-2279, FAX: (212) 434-7022, E-Mail: info@austin-williams.com, Web Site: www.austin-williams.com
Pres CEO: Rick Chiorando
Pres: Eva Lamere
VP, Mng Dir: Lisa Liebman
Opers Dir: Sallianne Nichols
Creative Dir: Bryan Hynes
Primary Market Served: Business
Founded: 1992

Full service advertising & marketing company specializing in healthcare, higher education, financial services & professional services.

AVALANCHE CREATIVE SERVICES INC
135 W 29th St (Ste 302)
New York, NY 10001-5187
Telephone: (212) 206-9335, FAX: (212) 206-1538, E-Mail: info@avalanchecreative.tv, Web Site: www.avalanchecreative.tv
Pres: Ava Seavey
Creative Dir & Sr Copywriter: Neil Brownlee
Creative Dir & Sr Art Dir: George Brianka

AXIA PUBLIC RELATIONS
222 E Forsyth St
Jacksonville, FL 32202
Telephone: (904) 425-1500, Toll Free: (866) 773-4768, Web Site: www.axiapr.com
CEO & Pres: Jason Mudd
Pub Rels Account Mgr: Marjorie A. Comer

B2BMARKETING.COM
8255 E Raintree Dr (Suite 200)
Scottsdale, AZ 85260-2684
Telephone: (602) 402-6588, Web Site: www.b2bmarketing.com
Co-Founder & Principal: John M. Coe
Co-Founder & Principal: Jim Wheaton
Principal: Leo G. Sterk
Principal: Boris Gendelev
Founded: 2010

Business-to-business marketing consulting, data services, education and training company.

BBK WORLDWIDE
117 Kendrick St (Ste 600)
Needham Heights, MA 02494
Telephone: (617) 630-4477, FAX: (617) 630-5090, E-Mail: info@bbkworldwide.com, Web Site: www.bbkworldwide.com
Creative & Media Strategy: Matthew Stumm
Founded: 1983

BCF
4500 Main St (Ste 600)
Virginia Beach, VA 23462-3362
Telephone: (757) 497-4811, FAX:
(757) 497-3684, Web Site: www.
bcfagency.com
Pres: Art Webb
New Bus Dir: John Runberg
Founded: 1979

BKV INC
3390 Peachtree Rd (fl 10)
Atlanta, GA 30326
Telephone: (404) 233-0332, E-Mail:
rina.cook@bkv.com, Web Site:
www.bkv.com
Pres: Maribett Varner
Vice Chmn: Brent Kuhn
Dir Bus Devel: Rina Cook
Founded: 1981

BMC GROUP
647 Neal Dr
Peterborough, ON, Canada K9J 6X7
Telephone: (705) 745-4766, Toll Free:
(866) 311-7711, FAX: (705) 745-
0177, E-Mail: hello@bmcgroup.ca,
Web Site: bmcgroup.ca
Pres: Ted Cooney

Integrated promotional marketing company.

BP RICE & COMPANY INC
1205 E Grand Ave
El Segundo, CA 90245-4220
Telephone: (310) 322-2210, FAX:
(310) 322-0617, E-Mail: stephanie@
bprco.com, Web Site: www.bprco.
com
Pres & Creative Dir: Stephanie Lesko
Founded: 1979

Advertising, public relations and marketing services agency.

BABCOCK & JENKINS
711 SW Alder St (Ste 200)
Portland, OR 97205
Telephone: (503) 382-8500, E-Mail:
laureng@bnj.com, Web Site: www.
bnj.com
Pres: Denise Barnes
VP Strategy & Partnerships: Lauren
Goldstein

**BACKE DIGITAL BRAND
MARKETING**
100 Matsonford Rd (Bldg 3, Ste 101),
Radnor Corporate Center
Radnor, PA 19087
Telephone: (610) 947-6901, E-Mail:
jbacke@backemarketing.com, Web
Site: www.backemarketing.com
CEO: John Backe

Sr VP & Dir Client Svcs: Malcolm
Brown
Sr VP Interactive: Boyd Maits
VP & Chief Creative Officer: Zeke
Kisling

BADER RUTTER
13845 Bishops Dr
Brookfield, WI 53005
Telephone: (262) 784-7200, FAX:
(262) 938-5595, Web Site: www.
baderrutter.com
Chief Mktg Officer: Ryann Greve

**BAKER-BLAIS MARKETING
INC**
295 Hymus Blvd
Pointe-Claire, QC, Canada H9R 6A5
Telephone: (514) 693-9900, FAX:
(514) 693-9960, E-Mail: donbaker@
bakerblais.com, Web Site: www.
bakerblais.com
Pres: Don Baker

BAM! DIRECT INC
3651 Peachtree Pkwy (Ste E-211)
Suwanee, GA 30024-6034
Telephone: (678) 947-1943, FAX:
(678) 947-3562, Web Site: www.
bamdirect.com
Prin: Tom Vonderschmidt
Prin: Kim McGill
Primary Market Served: Business &
Consumer

BANNERDIRECT
Div. of MM Batch LLC
PO Box 1548
Westhampton Beach, NY 11978-7548
Telephone: (212) 858-9883, E-Mail:
info@bannerdirect.com, Web Site:
www.bannerdirect.com
Pres: Christine Fontana
VP Bus Devel & Client Svcs: Bill Lawrence
Founded: 1990

Direct response marketing agency.

BARKLEY
1740 Main St
Kansas City, MO 64108-1311
Telephone: (816) 842-1500, E-Mail:
411@barkleyus.com, Web Site:
www.barkleyus.com
CEO: Jeff King
Pres & COO: Dave Fromm
Exec VP & Mng Dir: Jason Parks

THE TED BARKUS CO INC
8017 Anderson St
Philadelphia, PA 19118-2936
Telephone: (215) 545-0616, FAX:
(215) 242-8814, E-Mail: a.barkus-
tbc@att.net

Pres: Allen Barkus
Employees: 76
Founded: 1958

Independent advertising & marketing
agency.

**BARRINGER & ASSOCIATES
LTD**
224 Third Ave NW, PO Box 2525
Hickory, NC 28603-2525
Telephone: (828) 322-5550, FAX:
(828) 327-8440, E-Mail: barringer@
barringeragency.com, Web Site:
www.barringeragency.com
Pres: Phil Barringer

**KEITH BATES &
ASSOCIATES INC**
4319 N Lowell Ave
Chicago, IL 60641-2015
Telephone: (773) 205-7992, FAX:
(773) 205-7988, E-Mail: keithbates@
kbates.com, Web Site: www.kbates.
com
Pres: Keith Bates

**BEACON MARKETING
GROUP**
325 E Jimmy Leeds Rd (Ste 7149)
Smithville, NJ 08205
Telephone: (609) 677-1776, FAX:
(609) 677-1777, Web Site: www.
beaconmktg.com
Prin: Phillip Kening
Sr VP Bus Devel: George Latella
Founded: 1993

BEACONFEY LLC
1107 Kenilworth Dr (Ste 307)
Baltimore, MD 21042
Telephone: (410) 583-1203, FAX:
(410) 583-1506, E-Mail: info@
beaconfey.com, Web Site: www.
beaconfey.com
Prin: Paul J. Wingate
Prin: Robert A. Fey

**CHARLES F BEARDSLEY
ADVERTISING**
31 E Main St
Avon, CT 06001-3805
Telephone: (860) 676-0256, FAX:
(860) 674-1917
Owner: David Ketchiff
Partner: Nancy Ketchiff

**BEASLEY DIRECT
MARKETING INC**
15227 Perry Ln
Morgan Hill, CA 95037-9659

Telephone: (408) 782-0046, FAX:
(408) 782-9604, E-Mail: lbeasley@
beasleydirect.com, Web Site: www.
beasleydirect.com
Pres: Laurie Beasley
VP Online Mktg: David Beasley

BEBER SILVERSTEIN
GROUP
89 N E 27th St
Miami, FL 33137-4409
Telephone: (305) 856-9800, FAX:
(305) 854-7686, E-Mail: jennifer@
thinkbsg.com, Web Site: www.
thinkbsg.com
Pres: Jennifer Beber
VP Brand Devel: Ann Marie Drozd
Founded: 1972

BENOIT & ASSOCIATES
279 S Schuyler Ave
Kankakee, IL 60901-3809
Telephone: (815) 932-2582, FAX:
(815) 932-2582, E-Mail: mbenoit@
benoit-associates.com, Web Site:
www.benoit-associates.com
Pres: Michael J. Benoit

BERNSTEIN-REIN
4600 Madison Ave
Kansas City, MO 64112-1283
Telephone: (816) 756-0640, FAX:
(816) 399-6000, E-Mail: general@b-
r.com, Web Site: www.b-r.com
Pres: Steve Berstein

THE BERRY COMPANY
3100 Research Blvd
Dayton, OH 45420
Telephone: (937) 610-4100, Toll Free:
(800) 877-0475, Web Site: www.
theberrycompany.com
Exec Chmn Bd: James Continenza
VP Mktg: Laura Cole

BERSONDEANSTEVENS INC
PO Box 3997
Westlake Village, CA 91359-3997
Telephone: (818) 713-0134, Toll Free:
(877) 447-0134, E-Mail: info@
bersondeanstevens.com, Web Site:
www.bersondeanstevens.com
Pres: Lori Berson

BEYOND QUOTA LLC
537 King Muir Rd
Lake Forest, IL 60045-1640
Telephone: (847) 234-9475, FAX:
(847) 234-5260, E-Mail:
megrinnell@beyondquota.com, Web
Site: www.beyondquota.com
Principal: Maureen Eddy Grinnell
Principal: Dave C. Grinnell

BIGHAM AGENCY INC
6404 International Pkwy
Plano, TX 75093
Telephone: (972) 801-2600, FAX:
(972) 801-2649, E-Mail: info@
bighamagency.com, Web Site: www.
bighamagency.com
Pres: Paul Bigham
Exec Creative Dir: Kevin Breeding
Conducts Business: Worldwide
Employees: 10
Primary Market Served: Business &
Consumer
Catalog available online
Indirect online sales
Advertising/Marketing Budget Related
to Direct Marketing: 51-75%
Direct Marketing ad budget:
Direct Mail: 80%
Magazines: 15%
TV/Radio: 5%
Founded: 1983
Gross sales or billing: $10,000,000

Direct response, online/off-line creative
and strategy, business/corporate consultant.

BLACK DOT GROUP
101 N Virginia St
Crystal Lake, IL 60014
Telephone: (815) 893-8799, E-Mail:
pkelley@blackdot.com, Web Site:
www.blackdot.com
Pres: Jim Bossemeyer
Dir Digital Pub: Paul Kelley
VP Sls: Jim Kowalczyk
Conducts Business: U.S.
Employees: 1,700
Primary Market Served: Business &
Consumer
Advertising/Marketing Budget Related
to Direct Marketing: 0-25%
Founded: 1963

Provides turnkey catalog services, marketing consultation, creative, page layout, production, photography, color
correction and prepress services.

BLACK OLIVE CO
125 S Wacker Dr (Ste 300)
Chicago, IL 60606-4421
Telephone: (312) 893-5454, FAX:
(312) 276-8636, E-Mail: info@
blackoliveco.com, Web Site: www.
blackoliveco.com
Pres: Karen Pittenger
Conducts Business: U.S.
Employees: 10
Primary Market Served: Business &
Consumer
Indirect online sales
Advertising/Marketing Budget Related
to Direct Marketing: 26-50%
Direct Marketing ad budget:
Direct Mail: 50%

Online: 40%
TV/Radio: 5%
Telephone: 5%
Founded: 2003
Gross sales or billing: $2,000,000

Strategic & creative development for
B2B & multichannel advertisers focused on brand, ROI & direct marketing.

BLACKHAWK
ENGAGEMENT SOLUTIONS
INC
1400 S Highway Dr
Fenton, MO 63099-0001
Telephone: (636) 226-2000, Web Site:
www.bhengagement.com
Sr VP & Gen Mgr: Juli Spottiswood
Global VP Mktg: Rodney Mason

DL BLAIR INC
400 Post Ave (Ste 400)
Westbury, NY 11590-2226
Telephone: (516) 746-3700, FAX:
(516) 746-3889, Web Site: www.
dlblair.com
Chmn: T.J. Conlon
Vice Chmn & CEO: Brian T. Conlon
Pres & COO: Sandy M. Reichard
Founded: 1959

GEORGE BLAKE &
ASSOCIATES
6015 Courtside Dr
Bradenton, FL 34210-4018
Telephone: (941) 755-8637, E-Mail:
single14all@verizon.net
Pres: George Blake

BLASS COMMUNICATIONS
LLC
17 Drowne Rd
Old Chatham, NY 12136-3006
Telephone: (518) 766-2222, FAX:
(518) 766-2445, E-Mail:
brandthink@blasscommunications.
com, Web Site: www.blasscom.com
Pres: Kenneth L. Blass
Exec VP: Kathy Weiss
Founded: 1969

BLAST! MARKETING & PR
900 W Jackson Blvd (Suite 3E)
Chicago, IL 60607-3746
Web Site: blastmarketing.net
Pres: John McCartney
Founded: 2003

Full-service public relations & marketing firm.

BLEU MARKETING
SOLUTIONS INC
3025 Fillmore St

San Francisco, CA 94123-4009
Telephone: (415) 345-3300, FAX:
(415) 353-0299, E-Mail: helpdesk@
bleumarketing.com, Web Site:
bleumarketing.com
CEO & Dir New Bus Solutions: Laura
van Galen
Conducts Business: U.S., Canada,
Worldwide
Employees: 20
Primary Market Served: Business
Founded: 2001
Gross sales or billing: $3,000,000

Direct marketing, consulting and services.

BLOCK & DECORSO
3 Claridge Dr
Verona, NJ 07044-3000
Telephone: (973) 857-3900, FAX:
(973) 857-4041, E-Mail: bdecorso@
blockdecorso.com, Web Site: www.
blockdecorso.com
Pres & Creative Dir: Bill DeCorso
Ptnr & VP Acct Svcs: Carla Pugliese
Dean

CARL BLOOM ASSOCIATES INC
81 Main St (Ste 126)
White Plains, NY 10601-1745
Telephone: (914) 761-2800, FAX:
(914) 761-2744, E-Mail: info@
carlbloom.com, Web Site: www.
carlbloom.com
Chmn: Carl Bloom
Pres & Dir Electronic Mktg: Rob
Bloom
VP Gen Mgr: Brooke Coneys
Conducts Business: U.S.
Employees: 14
Primary Market Served: Business
Catalog available online
Indirect online sales
Advertising/Marketing Budget Related
to Direct Marketing: 76-100%
Direct Marketing ad budget:
Online: 100%
Founded: 1976
Gross sales or billing: $7,604,457

Direct marketing full service direct response fundraising agency.

BLUBERRIES ADVERTISING AGENCY
70 Outwater Ln (Suite 401)
Garfield, NJ 07026
Telephone: (973) 478-2200, FAX:
(973) 478-9662, E-Mail: mail@
bluberries.com, Web Site: www.
bluberries.com
Co-Founder: Nick Sadowski
Co-Founder: Bart Sadowski
Co-Founder: Chris Sadowski

Founded: 2002
Full-service advertising agency providing advertising, marketing, design & commercial photography services.

BLUE VIDALIA
1-5595 Finch Ave E
Toronto, ON, Canada M1B 2T9
Telephone: (416) 572-5222, FAX:
(416) 609-0670, E-Mail: info@
bluevidalia.ca, Web Site: www.
bluevidalia.ca
Sls: Burl Mathias
Primary Market Served: Business

BLUESPIRE SENIOR LIVING
29 S Main St (Suite 301)
West Hartford, CT 06107
Telephone: (888) 818-4715, Web Site:
www.bluespireseniorliving.com
Pres: Jay Hibbard
Chief Creative Officer: David Martino
Founded: 1980

Full-service retirement community marketing agency that integrates marketing & sales with technology.

BODDEN PARTNERS
102 Madison Ave (fl 8)
New York, NY 10016
Telephone: (212) 328-1111, E-Mail:
info@boddenpartners.com, Web
Site: www.boddenpartners.com
Pres & Exec Creative Dir: Chris Bodden

BOELTER + LINCOLN MARKETING COMMUNICATIONS
222 E Erie St (Ste 400)
Milwaukee, WI 53202
Telephone: (414) 271-0101, FAX:
(414) 271-1436, E-Mail: jbrzeski@
boelterlincoln.com, Web Site:
boelterlincoln.com
Pres & CEO: Jill Brzeski
VP & COO: Dawn Agacki
VP & Dir Pub Rels: Andy Larson
Dir Fin Svcs: Wendy Appelbaum

BOLCHALKFREY MARKETING
310 S Williams Blvd (Suite 260)
Tucson, AZ 85711-7703
Telephone: (520) 745-8221, FAX:
(520) 745-5540, E-Mail: info-mb@
adwiz.com, Web Site: www.adwiz.
com
Pres & Creative Dir: Robyn Frey
Mktg Svcs: Michael Bolchalk
Sr Dir Mktg Svcs: Paul O'Rourke
Founded: 1964

BONNEVILLE INTERNATIONAL
55 North 300 West
Salt Lake City, UT 84101-3502
Telephone: (801) 575-7500, FAX:
(801) 575-5820, E-Mail:
bonneville@bonneville.com, Web
Site: www.bonneville.com
Pres: Darrell Brown
VP & CFO: Kent Nate
VP Bus Affairs & Gen Counsel: Mike
Dowdle
Founded: 1964

BOOYAH! ONLINE ADVERTISING
3001 Brighton Blvd (Ste 236)
Denver, CO 80216
Telephone: (303) 345-6100, FAX:
(303) 345-6700, E-Mail: info@
booyahadvertising.ocm, Web Site:
www.booyahadvertising.com
Pres: Troy Lemer
Exec VP: Dan Gallagher
VP Bus Devel: Jeff Stever
Conducts Business: U.S.
Employees: 27
Primary Market Served: Business
Founded: 2001

Online advertising company featuring search engine marketing capabilities and broadband video.

BOSCOBEL MARKETING COMMUNICATIONS INC
8606 Second Ave
Silver Spring, MD 20910-3326
Telephone: (301) 588-2900, E-Mail:
info@boscobel.com, Web Site:
www.boscobel.com
Pres: Joyce L. Bosc
Sr Mktg & Brand Devel Strategist:
Alex Zavistovich
VP Pub Rels: Michael Rudd

BOYD TAMNEY CROSS INC
994 Old Eagle School Rd (Suite 1015)
Wayne, PA 19087-1802
Telephone: (610) 293-0500, FAX:
(610) 687-8199, E-Mail: info@
btcmarketing.com, Web Site: www.
boydtamneycross.com
CEO: Joseph Tamney
Pres: Thomas Cancelmo

BRABENDERCOX
c/o Brabender Cox Mihalke, 1 Station
Sq, Ste 315, Pittsburgh, PA 15219-
1122
108 South St (fl 3), Market Station
Leesburg, VA 20175
Telephone: (703) 896-5300, FAX:
(703) 896-5315, Web Site: www.
brabendercox.com

Pres: John Brabender

BRANDCOMMAND LLC
PO Box 71239
Richmond, VA 23255
Telephone: (804) 708-7100, E-Mail:
  cthurston@brandcommand.com,
  Web Site: www.brandcommand.com
Pres & CEO: Chris Thurston
Founded: 2011

Brand management, digital strategy &
marketing services agency.

BRASHE ADVERTISING INC
420 Jericho Turnpike (Ste 320)
Jericho, NY 11753
Telephone: (516) 935-5544, FAX:
  (516) 932-7264, E-Mail: info@
  brasheadv.com, Web Site: brashe.
  com
Pres: Jeff Cherkis
Founded: 1977

BRIERLEY & PARTNERS
5465 Legacy Dr (Ste 300)
Dallas, TX 75024
Telephone: (214) 760-8700, FAX:
  (214) 743-5511, E-Mail: bpayton@
  brierley.com, Web Site: www.
  brierley.com
Chmn, Founder & Chief Loyalty Archi-
  tect: Harold M. Brierley
Pres & CEO: Jim Sturm
Pres, Retail Practice: Billy Payton
Sr VP Sls, Mktg & Alliances: Kristen
  Dearing
Founded: 1985

BROADFORD & MALONEY
INC
445 Park Ave (fl 10)
New York, NY 10022-2606
Telephone: (212) 836-4710, FAX:
  (917) 322-2105, E-Mail: m.
  maloney@bmcorp.com, Web Site:
  bmcorp.com
Chmn: Martin J. Maloney

BROMLEY
COMMUNICATIONS
401 E Houston St
San Antonio, TX 78205-2615
Telephone: (210) 244-2000, E-Mail:
  ernest.bromley@bromley.biz, Web
  Site: bromley.biz
CEO: Ernest Bromley
CFO: Edith Ramirez
VP & Creative Dir: Ron Landreth
VP & Dir Acct Planning: Paul Bryan
Founded: 1981

BRUNNER
11 Stanwix St
Pittsburgh, PA 15222

Telephone: (412) 995-9500, FAX:
  (412) 995-9501, Web Site: www.
  brunnerworks.com
CEO: Michael Brunner
Pres: Scott Morgan
Partner: Mary Kay Modaffari
Chief Growth Officer: Dan Wald

BRUSHFIRE INC
2 Wing Dr
Cedar Knolls, NJ 07927
Telephone: (973) 871-1700, FAX:
  (973) 871-1717, E-Mail: vwarner@
  brushfireinc.com, Web Site: www.
  brushfireinc.com
Owner: Monica C. Smith
Pres: Joan Mueller
Exec VP: Jon Renner
Sr VP & Grp Dir: Valerie Warner

BULLSEYE DATABASE
MARKETING LLC
5546 S 104th East Ave
Tulsa, OK 74146-6505
Telephone: (918) 587-1731, FAX:
  (918) 587-0450, E-Mail: inquiries@
  bullseyedm.com, Web Site: www.
  bullseyedm.com
Pres: Mark Jennemann
Founded: 1988

BULLSEYE MARKETING
SYSTEMS LLC
220 W Gay St
West Chester, PA 19380
Telephone: (484) 356-2240, E-Mail:
  info@bullseyemarketingsystems.
  com, Web Site:
  bullseyemarketingsystems.com
Mng Partner: Stephen F. Horstmann
Primary Market Served: Consumer
Founded: 2005

BURKHOLDER FLINT
ASSOCIATES
300 Spruce St (Ste 275)
Columbus, OH 43215-1174
Telephone: (614) 228-2425, FAX:
  (614) 228-0631, E-Mail: easterday@
  burkholderflint.com, Web Site:
  www.burkholderflint.com
Pres: Bob Wiseman
VP Acct Svcs: Vickie Easterday
Founded: 1959

LEO BURNETT WORLDWIDE
35 W Wacker Dr
Chicago, IL 60601-1723
Telephone: (312) 220-5959, Web Site:
  leoburnett.com
CEO: Rich Stoddart
Chmn: Tom Bernardin
Chief Creative Officer: Mark Tutssel

Founded: 1935
Globally active advertising agency.

THE BURRIS AGENCY INC
1175 Revolution Mill Dr (Ste 11)
Greensboro, NC 27405-5053
Telephone: (336) 378-1221, FAX:
  (336) 378-1221, E-Mail: info@
  burris.com, Web Site: www.burris.
  com
Project Leader: Lyn Rollins
Creative Dir: Dean Wagner
Design Dir: Anne Cassity
Strategy Leader: Jack Burris
Digital Dir: Jesse Cummings
Founded: 1985

BUSINESS DIRECT
MARKETING ASSOCIATES
INC
6825 Polo Fields Pkwy
Cumming, GA 30040-5731
Telephone: (770) 888-8300, FAX:
  (770) 888-6482, E-Mail: joes@
  bdmainc.com, Web Site: www.
  bdmainc.com
Pres: Joe A. Staffieri Jr
Founded: 1985

BUSINESSCREATOR INC
47 N Jefferson St
Allentown, PA 18102
Telephone: (610) 437-8822, Toll Free:
  (855) 943-8736, FAX: (484) 709-
  1851, E-Mail: marketing@
  businesscreatorplus.com, Web Site:
  www.businesscreatorplus.com
Pres: Dr. Edward Kundahl
Employees: 15
Primary Market Served: Business &
  Consumer
Founded: 1994

BYOWNER.COM INC
A service of Wild Wild West Group
  LLC.
2200 N Federal Hwy (#203)
Boca Raton, FL 33431
Toll Free: (800) BY-OWNER, Web
  Site: www.byowner.com
Pres: Greg Sullivan
Founded: 1996

C-SUITE COMMUNICATIONS
401 N Cattlemen Rd (Ste 308)
Sarasota, FL 34232
Telephone: (941) 365-2710, E-Mail:
  info@c-suitecomms.com, Web Site:
  www.c-suitecomms.com
Pres & CEO: Patricia Courtois

CCMR GLOBAL MARKETING
78 Homestead Blvd
Mill Valley, CA 94941
Telephone: (415) 847-1239, E-Mail: globalmarketing1@aol.com, Web Site: www.gotoccmr.com
Mng Dir: Frank Rocco
VP, Acct Supvr & Mktg Strategist: Joan Schuman

CGT MARKETING LLC
275-B Dixon Ave
Amityville, NY 11701-2874
Telephone: (631) 842-4600, E-Mail: info@cgtmarketing.com, Web Site: www.cgtmarketing.com
Partner: Mitch Tobol
Partner: Fred Candiotti
Partner: Vince Grucci
Founded: 1981

Full-service advertising & digital marketing agency.

CP TRAVEL
Div. of Connelly Partners
46 Waltham St (Fl 4)
Boston, MA 02118
Telephone: (617) 521-5400, Web Site: travel.connellypartners.com
Pres: Gary Leopold
Mng Dir: Courtney Doyle
Founded: 1984

Travel & tourism marketing firm.

CPO DIRECT INC
736 N Western Ave (#147)
Lake Forest, IL 60045-1820
Telephone: (847) 735-7365, FAX: (847) 735-9825, E-Mail: ngoldring@cpodirect.com, Web Site: www.cpodirect.com
CEO: Norm Goldring
Conducts Business: U.S., Canada
Primary Market Served: Consumer
Founded: 1980

Direct response agency services to consumer marketers.

CRC PUBLIC RELATIONS
2760 Eisenhower Ave (fl 4)
Alexandria, VA 22314-4569
Telephone: (703) 683-5004, FAX: (703) 683-1703, E-Mail: crc@crcpublicrelations.com, Web Site: www.crcpublicrelations.com
Chmn: Leif E. Noren
Pres: Greg Mueller

CADE & ASSOCIATES ADVERTISING INC
1645 Metropolitan Blvd
Tallahassee, FL 32308-3730
Telephone: (850) 385-0300, Toll Free: (800) 715-CADE, FAX: (850) 385-1165, E-Mail: webmaster@cade1.com, Web Site: www.cade1.com
Partner & Acct Supvr: Laura Frandsen
Pres & Mktg Dir: Rick Shapley
Partner: John Cade
Founded: 1993

CADMUS COMMUNICATIONS
Subs. of Cenveo Inc.
2901 Byrdhill Rd
Richmond, VA 23228
Telephone: (804) 261-3000, Toll Free: (800) 888-2973, Web Site: www.cenveo.com
Exec VP: Andy Johnson

CAKUUN
28 Schenck Pkwy (Ste 200)
Asheville, NC 28803-5088
Telephone: (828) 771-0820, Web Site: acreativecompany.com
CEO: David Anderson

CAMP + KING
87 Graham St (Ste 250), The Presidio
San Francisco, CA 94129
Telephone: (415) 345-6680, Web Site: www.camp-king.com
Partner & Chief Creative Officer: Roger Camp
Partner & CEO: Jaime King
Founded: 2011

CARMICHAEL LYNCH INC
110 N Fifth St
Minneapolis, MN 55403
Telephone: (612) 334-6000, FAX: (612) 334-6101, E-Mail: inquiry@clynch.com, Web Site: www.carmichaellynch.com
Pres & Chief Strategy Officer: Marcus Fischer

THE CARNEGIE HALL CORP
881 Seventh Ave (fl 7)
New York, NY 10019-8077
Telephone: (212) 903-9600, E-Mail: feedback@carnegiehall.org, Web Site: www.carnegiehall.org
Dir Mktg & Visitor Svcs: David Wyeth

CARSON & CO
1740 E Garry Ave, Ste 231, Santa Ana, CA 92705-5844
1740 E Garry Ave (Ste 231)
Santa Ana, CA 92705
Telephone: (949) 477-9400, E-Mail: gcarson@carsonandcompany.com, Web Site: carsonpr.com
Pres: George Carson

CARTERA COMMERCE INC
One Cranberry Hill
Lexington, MA 02421
Telephone: (781) 541-6800, Toll Free: (888) 456-6255, FAX: (781) 541-6801, E-Mail: info@cartera.com, Web Site: www.cartera.com
Pres & CEO: Tom Beecher
Sr VP Mktg: Erin Warren
Sr VP Partnerships: Marc Mazzone
Founded: 2000

Leading provider of card-linked marketing solutions for merchants, banks & loyalty programs.

CATALYST
110 Marina Dr
Rochester, NY 14626-5104
Telephone: (585) 453-8300, Toll Free: (800) 836-7720, FAX: (585) 453-8360, E-Mail: info@catalystinc.com, Web Site: www.catalystinc.com
Mng Dir: Michael Osborn
Mng Dir: Jeff Cleary
Exec Creative Dir: Ken Fitzgerald
Conducts Business: U.S. Canada
Primary Market Served: Business & Consumer
Advertising/Marketing Budget Related to Direct Marketing: 76-100%
Founded: 1990

A direct & digital marketing agency that helps clients acquire, retain & develop long term relationships with their customers. The agency takes the guesswork out of marketing decisions by combining intellectual curiosity with hard-core analytics, deep customer insight & a measurement mindset.

CATALYST INC
275 Promenade St
Providence, RI 02908
Telephone: (401) 732-1886, FAX: (401) 732-5528, Web Site: www.catalystb2b.com
Pres: Brian Odell
Chief Activation Officer: Tom Hamlin
Chief Creative Officer: Michael Friend
Chief Brand Architect: Greg Dobos
Founded: 1991

Brand strategy & activation agency.

CATALYST MARKETING COMMUNICATIONS INC
2777 Summer St (Ste 301)
Stamford, CT 06905-4310
Telephone: (203) 348-7541, FAX: (203) 348-5688, E-Mail: b2b@catalystmc.com, Web Site: www.catalystmc.com
Owner & Pres: Charles Wintrub
VP & Pub Rels: Melissa A. LoParco

CATALYST MARKETING GROUP

5701 Lonetree Blvd (Ste 118)
Rocklin, CA 95765
Telephone: (916) 218-6066, E-Mail:
info@catalystmarketinggroup.com,
Web Site: www.
catalystmarketinggroup.com
CEO: Keri LaRue
Creative Dir: Abbe Lyle

FRANK W CAWOOD & ASSOCIATES

103 Clover Green
Peachtree City, GA 30269-1672
Telephone: (770) 487-6307, Web Site:
www.fca.com
Creative Dir: Anne Kaufmann
Founded: 1969

CELEBRITY ENDORSEMENT NETWORK (CEN)

23679 Calabasas Rd (#728)
Calabasas, CA 91302-1502
Telephone: (818) 225-7090, FAX:
(818) 880-0898, E-Mail: info@
celebrityendorsement.com, Web Site:
www.celebrityendorsement.com
Pres: Noreen S. Jenney Laffey

CHAFFEE & COMMUNICATIONS

310 Maple Ave (Ste L02)
Barrington, RI 02806
Telephone: (401) 247-2300, FAX:
(401) 247-2002, E-Mail: dchaffee@
fullchannel.net, Web Site: www.
chaffeecommunications.com
CEO: David S. Chaffee
VP: Carolyn Crook

CHANNEL NEUTRAL MARKETING

60 Peerless Dr
Oyster Bay, NY 11771
Telephone: (516) 992-7777, E-Mail:
deb_kennedy1127@yahoo.com
Pres: Deborah Kennedy

CHARTER DIRECT MARKETING

Div. of The Charter Group
295 Madison Ave (#1200)
New York, NY 10017
Telephone: (212) 717-2770, FAX:
(561) 750-2150, E-Mail:
terrykollman@
charterdirectmarketing.com, Web
Site: www.charterdirectmarketing.
com
Pres & CEO: Terry Kollman
Founded: 1986

CHASE ONLINE MARKETING STRATEGIES INC

79 Pine St (#102)
New York, NY 10005
Telephone: (646) 535-8160, Web Site:
www.wdfm.com
Pres: Larry Chase
Founded: 1993

CHERNOFF NEWMAN

1411 Gervais St (fl 5)
Columbia, SC 29201-3379
Telephone: (803) 254-8158, FAX:
(803) 252-2016, E-Mail: columbia@
chernoffnewman.com, Web Site:
www.chernoffnewman.com
Pres & COO: David Campbell

CHIEF MEDIA LLC

875 6th Ave (Ste 1100)
New York, NY 10001-3507
Telephone: (212) 300-8487, FAX:
(212) 629-9505, E-Mail: info@
chiefmedia.com, Web Site: www.
chiefmedia.com
Pres & Founder: Scott J. Paternoster
Exec VP: Vic Golio
Founded: 2001

CL&B CAPITAL MANAGEMENT

7583 Hunt Ln
Fayetteville, NY 13066-2554
Telephone: (315) 637-0915, FAX:
(815) 642-9396, E-Mail:
webinquiry@clbcm.com, Web Site:
www.clbcm.com
Owner: Rick Labs

CLAY CREATIVE GROUP LLC

1550 Lewis Center Rd (Ste C)
Lewis Center, OH 43035-8232
Telephone: (740) 548-0307, FAX:
(740) 548-0898, E-Mail: marketing@
claycreativeresults.com, Web Site:
www.claycreativeresults.com
Dir Client Svcs: Franklin Clay
Dir Creative Svcs: Jessica Clay
Conducts Business: U.S.
Primary Market Served: Business &
Consumer
Founded: 1977

Branding, advertising, sales promotion,
creative design, direct marketing, trade
show, interactive and social media.

CLICKBOOTH.COM LLC

5901 N Honore Ave (Ste 210)
Sarasota, FL 34243-2632
Telephone: (941) 483-4188, Web Site:
www.clickbooth.com
CEO: Erin Cigich

CFO: David Fairey
Chief Tech Officer: Dzenis Softic

CO-OP PROMOTIONS

2301 S Ocean Dr (Ste 2504)
Hollywood, FL 33019
Telephone: (954) 922-2323, FAX:
(954) 922-2071, E-Mail: art@co-
oppromotions.com, Web Site: www.
co-oppromotions.com
Pres: Arthur Averbook

COLE & WEBER UNITED

221 Yale Ave N (Ste 600)
Seattle, WA 98109-5490
Telephone: (206) 447-9595, FAX:
(206) 233-0178, E-Mail: info@
cwunited.com, Web Site: www.
cwunited.com
Pres: Mike Doherty
Exec Creative Dir: Pat McKay
Mng Dir: Elizabeth Rowny
Primary Market Served: Business

COLLE+MCVOY

400 First Ave N (Ste 400)
Minneapolis, MN 55401
Telephone: (612) 305-6000, FAX:
(612) 305-6500, E-Mail: info@
collemcvoy.com, Web Site: www.
collemcvoy.com
Pres: Christine Fruechte
Chief Creative Officer: Mike Caguin
COO: Phil Johnson
CFO: Lisa Miller

COLLECTIVE[I]

130 Madison Ave (fl 3)
New York, NY 10016-7026
Toll Free: (888) 890-0020, Web Site:
www.collectivei.com
CEO: Tad Martin
Chmn: Heidi Messer
Vice Chmn: Stephen Messer

COMMAND FINANCIAL

345 Hudson St
New York, NY 10014
Telephone: (212) 274-0070, FAX:
(212) 274-8262, E-Mail: csd@
commandfinancial.com, Web Site:
www.commandfinancial.com
CEO & Pres: Jim Penders
Founded: 1990

Financial printing company.

THE COMPANY OF OTHERS

1800 West Loop S (Suite 2100)
Houston, TX 77027-3281
Toll Free: (800) 994-1681, E-Mail:
inquiry@thecompany.com, Web
Site: www.thecompany.com
CEO: Jose Lozano

Founded: 1980
Media buying & advertising consulting services company.

THE COMPUTER STUDIO
1280 Saw Mill River Rd
Yonkers, NY 10710-2738
Telephone: (914) 968-1212, FAX: (914) 968-1228, E-Mail: connect@webbusconnect.com, Web Site: www.webbusconnect.com
Pres: Alan J. Goldstein
Founded: 1986

CONCEPT MEDIA PARTNERS INC
108 Village Sq (#307)
Yorktown Heights, NY 10598
Telephone: (914) 767-0032, FAX: (914) 514-1711, E-Mail: karen@conceptmediapartners.com, Web Site: www.conceptmediapartners.com
Pres: Karen Capalbo
VP: Margie Gornnert

CONCEPTS UNLIMITED
2913 Saratoga Trail
Frederick, CO 80516
Telephone: (303) 918-9416, E-Mail: conceptsunlimited@estreet.com, Web Site: www.conceptsunlimitedinc.com
Principal & Owner: Pam McKinnie
Founded: 1982

CONCINNITY MARKETING & TECHNOLOGY INC
1012 Glade St
Winston-Salem, NC 27101
Telephone: (336) 245-4561, E-Mail: chris@concinnitymarketing.com, Web Site: www.concinnitymarketing.com
CEO: Chris Gunzenhauser
Partner & Chief Client Officer: Neil Linnell
Primary Market Served: Consumer

CONSOLIDATED PRINTING & STATIONARY CO INC
319 S 5th St
Salina, KS 67401-3907
Telephone: (785) 825-5426, Toll Free: (800) 432-0266, FAX: (785) 825-6536, Web Site: www.consolidatedprinting.com
Owner & Pres: Don Vandegrift
Gen Mgr: Don Commerford
Founded: 1916

CONVERGEDIRECT
33 E 33rd St (fl 3)

New York, NY 10016
Telephone: (212) 213-0111, E-Mail: info@convergedirect.com, Web Site: www.convergedirect.com
Pres: Thomas Marianacci
Exec VP New Bus Devel: Robin Bender
Exec VP & Mng Dir: Maarten Terry
Primary Market Served: Consumer

COOPER CONCEPTS INC
2232 N Clybourn Ave (Ste 400)
Chicago, IL 60614
Telephone: (872) 206-8145, E-Mail: contact.hr@cooperconcepts.com, Web Site: www.cooperconcepts-inc.com
Pres: Apryl Christensen

THE COOPER GROUP
Unit of EdgeCore
381 Park Ave S (Ste 801)
New York, NY 10016-8806
Telephone: (212) 696-2512, Web Site: www.thecoopergroup.com
CEO & Principal: Harold Cooper
COO & Principal: Tom Cooper
Founded: 1985

CORCREATIVE GROUP LLC
4800 Baseline Rd (Suite E104-276)
Boulder, CO 80303
Telephone: (917) 971-4847, E-Mail: ccginfo@corcreativegroup.com, Web Site: corcreativegroup.com
Pres: Scott Pluzynski
Founded: 2010
Branding & advertising agency specializing in the design & execution of brand conscious catalogs and collateral.

CORINTHIAN MEDIA
500 8th Ave (fl 5)
New York, NY 10018-6504
Telephone: (212) 279-5700, FAX: (212) 239-1772, E-Mail: info@mediabuying.com, Web Site: www.mediabuying.com
Owner & Pres: Larry Miller
Exec VP Acct Svcs: Ellen Carry
Exec VP Buying: Tina Snitzer
Exec VP Direct Response: Larry Schneiderman
Exec VP New Bus & Trade: Bob Klein
Founded: 1974
Media buying and planning company.

CORPORATEREWARDS.COM
350 5th Ave (Ste 3920)
New York, NY 10118
Telephone: (212) 689-1200, Web Site: www.corporaterewards.com
CEO: Jim Hemmer
Exec VP Sls & Mktg: Tom Silk

Chief Tech Officer: Marc Hollander

COSSETTE
Div. of Vision7 International
300 St-Paul St (fl 3)
Quebec, QC, Canada G1K 7R1
Telephone: (418) 647-2727, FAX: (418) 647-2564, E-Mail: info@cossette.com, Web Site: www.cossette.com
CEO: Brett Marchand
Pres: Melanie Dunn
Founded: 1972

CRAMER-KRASSELT
225 N Michigan Ave
Chicago, IL 60601-7684
Telephone: (312) 616-9600, FAX: (312) 616-3839, E-Mail: pkrivkov@c-k.com, Web Site: c-k.com
Pres & CEO: Peter Krivkovich
Pres & COO: Karen Seaman
Vice Chmn & Chief Creative Officer: Marshall Ross

CRAWFORD ADVERTISING ASSOCIATES LTD
216 Congers Rd (Ste 2C)
New City, NY 10956-6280
Telephone: (914) 946-2444, FAX: (914) 946-9236, E-Mail: crawads@aol.com, Web Site: www.crawfordadv.com
Pres: Howard A. Wolfe
Founded: 1992

CRAWFORD & CO
RP-NFOA
1001 Summit Blvd (Ste 500)
Atlanta, GA 30319-6410
Telephone: (404) 300-1000, Toll Free: (800) 241-2541, FAX: (404) 300-1905, E-Mail: info@us.crawco.com, Web Site: us.crawfordandcompany.com
Chmn: Jesse C. Crawford
Pres & CEO: Jeffrey T. Bowman
VP Corp Commun: Kara Pardini

CREATING RESULTS LLC
14000 Crown Ct
Woodbridge, VA 22193
Telephone: (703) 494-7888, Toll Free: (888) 205-8899, Web Site: www.creatingresults.com
CEO: Judy Harff
Pres: Todd Harff
Dir Bus Devel: Beth Spohn
Dir Strategic Planning: Erin Read
Mktg Coord: Allison Lloyd
Conducts Business: U.S.
Primary Market Served: Consumer

Founded: 1993

Strategic marketing, communications & advertising that drives demand for life style products & services; Special expertise in reaching the fifty plus consumer.

THE CREATIVE ALLIANCE INC

2675 North Park Dr
Lafayette, CO 80026-3483
Telephone: (303) 665-8101, FAX: (303) 665-3136, E-Mail: info@ thecreativealliance.com, Web Site: www.thecreativealliance.com
Founder & CEO: T. Robert Taylor
Pres & Creative Dir: David Heitman
Dir Creative Svcs: Jodee Goodwin
Founded: 1991

CREATIVE COMMERCE LLC

1301 Wright's Ln E (Ste 102)
West Chester, PA 19380
Telephone: (610) 918-8800, FAX: (610) 918-1349, E-Mail: info@ creativecommerce.com, Web Site: creativecommerce.com
CEO: Edwin Garrubbo
Pres: Angus Grover Wilson
Creative & Technical Dir: Francisco Lewis
Creative Dir: Chris Harris

CREATIVE LIFT INC

115 Sansome St (Ste 600)
San Francisco, CA 94104
Telephone: (415) 248-3170, E-Mail: hello@creativelift.net, Web Site: www.creativelift.net
Founder: Tim Carr
Acct Dir: Marisa Badovinus
Dir Tech: Tim Stephenson
Founded: 2003

CREATIVE MARKETING ALLIANCE INC

191 Clarksville Rd
Princeton Junction, NJ 08550
Telephone: (609) 297-2235, FAX: (609) 799-7032, E-Mail: info@ cmasolutions.com, Web Site: www. gotocma.com
Pres & CEO: Jeffrey E. Barnhart
Controller: Joanne Trautwein
Dir Mktg Svcs: Erin Klebaur
Founded: 1987

CREATIVE MEDIA INC

59 Summertree Ct
Nicholasville, KY 40356-9780
Telephone: (859) 227-6513
Founder & Pres: Gene Doyle
Founded: 1982

CREATIVE PACKAGING SOLUTIONS

5 W First St
Keyport, NJ 07735-1010
Telephone: (732) 335-3700, Toll Free: (888) 826-1646, FAX: (732) 264-9313, E-Mail: info@packaging-usa. com, Web Site: www.packaging-usa. com
Pres: Coni Lefferts

Wholesale distributor and factory representative in package containers.

CREATIVE STRATEGY GROUP INC

5454 Wisconsin Ave, #1655, Chevy Chase, MD 20815-6901
330 S State St
Newtown, PA 18940
Telephone: (215) 860-3045, FAX: (215) 860-3129, E-Mail: info@ csgmarketing.com, Web Site: www. csg-design.com
Founder, Pres & CEO: Evan Connolly
Founded: 1999

CRISPIN PORTER + BOGUSKY

3390 Mary St (Ste 300)
Miami, FL 33133
Telephone: (305) 859-2070, FAX: (305) 854-3419, E-Mail: info@ cpbgroup.com, Web Site: www. cpbgroup.com
Partner & Chmn: Chuck Porter
Partner & Vice Chmn: Jeff Steinhour
Global Mng Dir: Spence Kramer
Exec Creative Dir: Gustavo Sarkis
Exec VP & Dir Production Svcs: Sara Gennett
VP & Chief Talent Officer: Marlene Root
Founded: 1988

CUNEO ADVERTISING

1401 American Blvd East (Ste 6)
Bloomington, MN 55425-1105
Telephone: (952) 707-1212, FAX: (952) 707-1295, E-Mail: agency@ cuneocom.com, Web Site: cuneocom.com
CEO: Laurence A. Cuneo
Pres & COO: Darrell Schmidt
Creative Dir: Mike Sorenson

CUSTOMER COMMUNICATIONS GROUP INC

165 S Union Blvd (Ste 260)
Lakewood, CO 80228-2241
Telephone: (303) 525-0313, E-Mail: info@customer.com, Web Site: www.customer.com
Pres & CEO: Sandra Gudat

Sr VP Strategic Consulting & Acct Mngmt: Lane Ware
Sr VP & Strategist: Greg Sultan
Founded: 1977

Full service customer relationship marketing agency.

CUSTOMER GROWTH INC

2452 Black Rock Turnpike (Ste 10)
Fairfield, CT 06825
Telephone: (203) 226-8795, FAX: (203) 286-1049, E-Mail: info@ customer-growth.com, Web Site: www.customer-growth.com
Mng Partner: Joshua Moritz
Mng Partner: Peter Blau
Mng Partner: David Klang
Conducts Business: U.S.
Employees: 20
Primary Market Served: Business & Consumer
Direct online sales
Founded: 2001
Gross sales or billing: $20,000,000

Direct and Interactive Advertising.

CUSTOMER MARKETING GROUP LLC

7 Hill Farm Rd
Weston, CT 06883-2007
Telephone: (203) 226-9845, FAX: (203) 226-9837, E-Mail: bill@4cmg. com, Web Site: www.4cmg.com
Pres: William E. McKinney
Info Architect: Lori J. Monnett

CUSTOMERMINING INC

2901 Park Ave (Ste C4)
Soquel, CA 95073-2831
Telephone: (831) 465-0898, FAX: (831) 465-1186, E-Mail: biz@ customermining.com, Web Site: www.customermining.com
Pres: Beverly Capwell
Founded: 2001

CYPRESS MEDIA GROUP INC

PO Box 53198
Atlanta, GA 30355-1198
Telephone: (770) 640-9918, E-Mail: info@cypressmedia.net, Web Site: www.cypressmedia.net
Pres: Randall P. Whatley
Founded: 1978

D2: DIRECT

54 Cedar Lake W, Bldg # 2
Denville, NJ 07834-1704
Telephone: (973) 627-4410, FAX: (973) 627-3703, E-Mail: info@ d2direct.com, Web Site: www. d2direct.com
Pres & Brdcst Spot Dir: Peter Marshall

VP & Dir Media Svcs: Maxeen Schon-
feld
VP & Dir Creative Svcs: Neil Callari
CFO: Cathy Marshall
Conducts Business: U.S.
Primary Market Served: Business &
Consumer
Founded: 1995

Direct response advertising agency.

DBM GROUP INC
5 Peters Canyon Rd (Ste 150)
Irvine, CA 92606-1793
Telephone: (714) 727-0825, FAX:
(714) 838-0327, E-Mail: sales@
dbmgroup.com, Web Site: www.
dbmgroup.com
CEO: John Engstrom
Primary Market Served: Business &
Consumer
Founded: 1991

DCI-ARTFORM
A Marmon/Berkshire Hathaway Co
2727 W Good Hope Rd
Milwaukee, WI 53209
Telephone: (414) 228-7000, Web Site:
www.dci-artform.com
CEO: Mike Doody
COO: Scott Feldner

DDB CANADA
1600 - 777 Hornby St
Vancouver, BC, Canada V6Z 2T3
Telephone: (604) 687-7911, FAX:
(604) 640-4343, E-Mail: vancouver.
info@ddbcanada.com, Web Site:
www.ddbcanada.com
Chmn & CEO: Frank Palmer
Exec VP & Co-Mng Dir: Patty Jones
Exec VP & Co-Mng Dir: Michelle
Kitchen
Primary Market Served: Business &
Consumer

DDB NORTH AMERICA
437 Madison Ave
New York, NY 10022
Telephone: (212) 415-2000, FAX:
(212) 415-3550, Web Site:
ddbnorthamerica.com
Pres: Mark O'Brien
Dir Corp Commun & North American
Pub Rels: Christie Giera
Founded: 1949

DGS MARKETING
ENGINEERS
10100 Lantern Rd (Ste 225)
Fishers, IN 46037

Telephone: (317) 813-2222, FAX:
(317) 813-2233, E-Mail: info@
dgsmarketingengineers.com, Web
Site: www.dgsmarketingengineers.
com
Pres & CEO: Marc Diebold
Exec VP & Chief Mktg Officer: Leslie
Galbreath

DMN3
2190 North Loop W (Ste 200)
Houston, TX 77018
Telephone: (713) 893-4275, Toll Free:
(888) 721-0377, E-Mail: sales@
dmn3.com, Web Site: www.dmn3.
com
Founder & CEO: Pamela Lockard
COO: John LaCour
Primary Market Served: Business &
Consumer
Indirect online sales
Founded: 1992

DMN is a full-service direct response
marketing agency that delivers results
to businesses and consumers through
offline and online solutions.

DMS MARKETING INC
26035 Acero (Ste 100)
Mission Viejo, CA 92691-7951
Telephone: (888) 794-1777, E-Mail:
inquiries@dms-marketing.com, Web
Site: www.dms-marketing.com
Pres & CEO: Lucy Belcher

DMW WORLDWIDE LLC
701 Lee Rd (Ste 103)
Chesterbrook, PA 19087-5612
Telephone: (610) 407-0407, Toll Free:
(877) 744-3699, FAX: (610) 407-
9201, E-Mail: info@dmwdirect.com,
Web Site: www.dmwdirect.com
Chmn: Warren Hunter
Pres & CEO: Mark Mandia
Exec VP & COO: Gina Kneib
Exec VP & Chief Creative Officer: Bill
Spink
Exec VP & Practice Leader: Linda
Armstrong
Conducts Business: U.S. & Canada
Primary Market Served: Business &
Consumer
Advertising/Marketing Budget Related
to Direct Marketing: 76-100%
Founded: 1984

Full service direct response advertising
agency providing direct marketing
services, insurance, healthcare, financial services, fund raising, consumer &
B-to-B, and non-profit industries building market-driven programs grounded
in consumer intelligence & delivered
through multimedia, multichannel integration.

DATAMARK INC
123 W Mills Ave (Ste 400)
El Paso, TX 79901
Toll Free: (800) 477-1944, E-Mail:
info@datamark.net, Web Site: www.
datamark.net
Pres: Bill Randag
Sr VP: John Holmes
Dir Sls & Mktg: Stephen Darling
Founded: 1989

DEBELLIS & FERRARA
2136 Gallows Rd
Vienna, VA 22027
Toll Free: (888) 748-2133, FAX: (888)
979-6345, E-Mail: info@debellis-
ferrara.com, Web Site: www.
debellis-ferrara.com
Pres: Gail E. Donohue

DEBOW COMMUNICATIONS
LTD
PO Box 5432
New York, NY 10185-9998
Telephone: (212) 977-8815, FAX:
(212) 977-8376, E-Mail: info@
debow.com, Web Site: www.debow.
com
Owner: Tom DeBow
Pres: Suzanne Hayat DeBow
Founded: 1976

DEFY MEDIA INC
498 7th Ave (fl 19)
New York, NY 10018
E-Mail: info@defymedia.com, Web
Site: www.defymedia.com
CEO: Matthew C Diamond
Pres: Keith Richman
Exec VP Mktg: Andy Tu

DENTINO MARKETING
515 Executive Dr
Princeton, NJ 08540-1527
Telephone: (609) 454-3202, FAX:
(609) 454-3239, E-Mail: karl@
dentinomarketing.com, Web Site:
www.dentinomarketing.com
Pres: Karl Dentino
Sr Creative Dir: Joel Rubinstein
Creative Dir: Rosalba De Meo
Mngmt Supvr: Richard Skolits

Full service direct marketing agency:
Strategy, planning, database management, creative, production, fulfillment,
interactive media and web, testing, results analysis internal & investor communications.

DESIGN MATTERS INC!
448 W 37th St
New York, NY 10018

Telephone: (212) 560-0681, FAX:
(646) 478-9149, E-Mail: stephen@
designmattersinc.com, Web Site:
www.designmattersinc.com
Creative Dir & CEO: Stephen McAllister
Founded: 1990

DEXPOSITO & PARTNERS
The New American Agency
875 Avenue of the Americas
New York, NY 10001-3507
Telephone: (646) 747-8800, Web Site:
newamericanagency.com
Chmn & CEO: Daisy Exposito-Ulla
Partner & Chief Ideation Officer: Jorge
Ulla
Partner & Chief Activation Officer:
Gloria Constanza
Partner & CFO: John Ross
Partner & Chief Client Officer: Fernando Fernandez
Partner & Mng Dir: Louis Maldonado
Partner & Chief Creative Officer:
Mauricio Galvan
Partner & Bus Devel & Integration Officer: Leo Olper
Dir Media Svcs: Don Davis
Primary Market Served: Consumer
Founded: 2005

DIALOG DIRECT
13700 Oakland St
Highland Park, MI 48203-3174
Toll Free: (800) 523-5867, E-Mail:
sales@dialog-direct.com, Web Site:
www.dialog-direct.com
Pres: Doug Kearney

DIAMOND MARKETING SOLUTIONS
900 Kimberly Dr
Carol Stream, IL 60188
Telephone: (630) 597-9100, E-Mail:
info@dmsolutions.com, Web Site:
www.dmsolutions.com
Pres & CEO: Mark Peterson
Pres West Coast Opers: Mark Selland
Pres Midwest Opers & COO: Greg
Waite
Sr VP Strategic Solutions: Cyndi
Greenglass
Primary Market Served: Business &
Consumer
Advertising/Marketing Budget Related
to Direct Marketing: 76-100%
Founded: 1975

A full service direct marketing firm
providing targeted & strategic services
from database through creative to fulfillment & direct mail production.

DIESTE
1999 Bryan St (Ste 2700)
Dallas, TX 75201-6817

Telephone: (214) 259-8000, FAX:
(214) 259-8040, E-Mail: contact@
dieste.com, Web Site: www.dieste.
com
CEO: Greg Knipp
Chmn: Tony Dieste
Chief Creative Officer: Paco Olavarrieta
Chief Mktg Officer: Carla Eboli
Conducts Business: U.S., Latin America
Primary Market Served: Consumer
Advertising/Marketing Budget Related
to Direct Marketing: 0-25%
Founded: 1995

Hispanic advertising & direct marketing agency.

DIGDEV DIRECT
260 SW Natura Ave (fl 2)
Deerfield Beach, FL 33441-3026
Telephone: (954) 949-9500, Toll Free:
(800) 873-5137, FAX: (954) 337-
0251, E-Mail: info@digdev.com,
Web Site: www.digdevdirect.com
CEO: Michael Richmond
COO: Shawn McNamara
CFO: James Salerno
VP Devel: Rebecca Noble
Primary Market Served: Business &
Consumer
Founded: 2008

DIGITASLBI
33 Arch St
Boston, MA 02110-1437
Telephone: (617) 867-1000, E-Mail:
newbusiness@digitas.com, Web Site:
www.digitaslbi.com
Global CEO: Luke Taylor
CEO The Americas: Tony Weisman
Chief Mktg Officer: Kenneth Parks
CFO North America: Thomas Meisner
Chief Creative Officer North America:
Ronald Ng

Global marketing and technology
agency.

DIK & ASSOCIATES DIRECT MARKETING
2626 Peter St
Honolulu, HI 96816
Telephone: (808) 734-8868, FAX:
(808) 734-8868, E-Mail: susandik@
gmail.com
Owner & Pres: Susan Dik

THE DIRECT CHANNELS GROUP
140 Broadway (fl 46)
New York, NY 10005

Telephone: (212) 208-1479, FAX:
(631) 514-8716, E-Mail: info@
directchannelsgroup.com, Web Site:
www.directchannelsgroup.com
Owner & CEO: Melody Medina
VP Strategic Opers & Execution: T.J.
Johnson
Founded: 2008

DIRECT CHOICE INC
480 E Swedesford Rd (Ste 210)
Wayne, PA 19087
Telephone: (610) 995-8201, Toll Free:
(866) 995-2111, E-Mail: hello@
directchoice.com, Web Site: www.
directchoiceinc.com
CEO: Nickolas Lanzi
Founded: 1995

DIRECT CINEMA LTD INC
PO Box 10003
Santa Monica, CA 90410-1003
Telephone: (310) 636-8200, FAX:
(310) 636-8228, E-Mail: dclvideo@
aol.com, Web Site: www.
directcinema.com
Pres: Mitchell W. Block
Founded: 1974

DIRECT CONNECT GROUP
5501 Cass Ave
Cleveland, OH 44102-2121
Telephone: (216) 651-9500, Web Site:
www.directconnectgroup.com
Dir Mktg Svcs: Ben Allen
Dir Online Mktg: Catherine Fonk
Creative Dir: Matt Kling
Dir Strategy: Andy Lueck

DIRECT IMPACT GROUP
200 Highland Ave (Ste 403)
Needham, MA 02494-3019
Telephone: (781) 453-2200, FAX:
(781) 453-1200, E-Mail: info@
directimpactgroup.com, Web Site:
www.directimpactgroup.com
Founder & Pres: Andrew Gordon
Primary Market Served: Business &
Consumer

Full-service direct marketing firm specializing in results-oriented television,
radio, direct mail, print & electronic
marketing.

DIRECT IMPACT INC
655 Craig Rd (Ste 240)
Saint Louis, MO 63141-7170
Telephone: (314) 336-1300, FAX:
(314) 336-0013, E-Mail: info@
directimpactinc.com, Web Site:
www.directimpactinc.com
Pres: George Snyder
Founded: 1995

DIRECT MARKETING DESIGNS INC

6565 S Dayton (Ste 2200)
Greenwood Village, CO 80111-5386
Telephone: (303) 649-9888, FAX:
(303) 649-1917, E-Mail: info@
directmarketingdesigns.com, Web
Site: www.directmarketingdesigns.
com
Pres: James Morris
Founded: 1990

DIRECT MARKETING DYNAMICS INC

18633 Village Fountain Dr
Germantown, MD 20874-2122
Telephone: (301) 916-3900, FAX:
(301) 515-0404, E-Mail: jim@
directmarketingdynamics.com, Web
Site: www.directmarketingdynamics.
com
Pres: James Gribble
Founded: 1995

DIRECT MARKETING GROUP

7550 Corporate Way
Eden Prairie, MN 55344-2045
Telephone: (952) 975-5060, Toll Free:
(888) 397-5060, FAX: (952) 906-
0608, Web Site: www.directmg.com
Pres: Gregg Smith
COO: Brian Ostenso
VP Lead Generation: Cris Jerden
Dir Bus Devel: Melanie Anderson

DIRECT MARKETING SOLUTIONS INC

8534 NE Alderwood Rd
Portland, OR 97220-1347
Telephone: (503) 281-1400, FAX:
(503) 249-5120, Web Site: www.
teamdms.com
CEO: Mike Sherman
Pres: Steve Sherman

THE DIRECT MARKETING SPECIALISTS INC

900 N Franklin (Ste 706)
Chicago, IL 60610-3124
Telephone: (312) 266-7906, FAX:
(312) 266-9230, E-Mail: rwinedms@
networkgci.com, Web Site:
thedirectmarketingspecialists.com
Pres: Randi Wine
Founded: 1983
Full-service advertising agency special-
izing in direct marketing.

DIRECT OPTIONS

9565 Cincinnati Columbus Rd
West Chester, OH 45069
Telephone: (513) 779-4416, Toll Free:
(800) 749-3678, FAX: (513) 779-
4426, E-Mail: info@directoptions.
com, Web Site: www.directoptions.
com
Pres: Jan S. Moore
Founded: 1991

DIRECT PARTNERS

4755 Alla Rd
Marina Del Rey, CA 90292-6311
Telephone: (310) 482-4200, FAX:
(310) 482-4201, Web Site: www.
directpartners.com
Founder & CEO: Skip Reed
Founder & Pres: Jerry McRuer
Founded: 1994

DIRECT RESOURCES GROUP INC

1221 Second Ave (Ste 300)
Seattle, WA 98101-2986
Telephone: (206) 455-6157, FAX:
(206) 749-0005, E-Mail: results@
drg.com, Web Site: www.drg.com
Co-Founder & Pres: Stephan Jensen
Co-Founder & Mng Partner: Scott Zorn
VP Client Svcs: Brad Douglas
Conducts Business: U.S., Canada
Primary Market Served: Business &
Consumer
Founded: 1993

Direct marketing - outsourcing of strategy, program development, production,
mail printing & personalization & response analysis - usually on a project
basis.

DIRECT SUCCESS COMMUNICATIONS INC

308 Lynne Pl
Chester Springs, PA 19425
Telephone: (610) 321-0321, FAX:
(610) 321-0322
Pres: Stephanie G. Schmidt
Founded: 1985

THE DIRECTORS NETWORK

aka TDN
17071 Ventura Blvd (Ste 105)
Encino, CA 91316
Telephone: (818) 906-0006, E-Mail:
info@tdnartists.com, Web Site:
www.tdnartists.com
Pres & Agent: Jeff Lewis
Agent: Rae Lucas
Consultant: Steve Lewis
Founded: 1985

DIXON DIRECT

Subs. of Visant
1226 W Seventh St
Dixon, IL 61021
Telephone: (815) 284-2211, FAX:
(630) 810-1934, E-Mail: info@
dixondirect.com, Web Site:
dixondirect.com
VP & Gen Mgr: Rich Boysen
Full-service, in-line direct marketing
company.

DM COMMUNICATIONS INC

3236 Southgate Cir
Sarasota, FL 34239
Telephone: (617) 482-5900, E-Mail:
cmay@dmcommunications.com,
Web Site: www.dmcommunications.
com
Pres: Christy May
Founded: 1982
Strategic planning, marketing, scouting
& sales agency.

DONER

25900 Northwestern Hwy
Southfield, MI 48075
Telephone: (248) 354-9700, FAX:
(248) 827-0880, Web Site: www.
doner.com
Pres: David DeMuth
Primary Market Served: Business &
Consumer
Founded: 1937
Independent, creative and advertising
agency.

DONOVAN ADVERTISING

180 W Airport Rd
Lititz, PA 17543
Telephone: (717) 560-1333, FAX:
(717) 560-2034, Web Site: www.
donovanadv.com
Pres & CEO: William Donovan Jr.

DORAN & FORGACS INC

1306 Barkway Dr
West Chester, PA 19380-5820
Telephone: (610) 344-0570, FAX:
(610) 344-7203, E-Mail: bdoran@
doranforgacs.com, Web Site: www.
doranforgacs.com
Principal: Barbara H. Doran
Principal: Frank Forgacs

DOREMUS & CO

Div. of Omnicom Group Inc
200 Varick St (fl 11)
New York, NY 10014-4810
Telephone: (212) 366-3000, FAX:
(212) 366-3060, E-Mail: mbroom@
doremus.com, Web Site: www.
doremus.com
Pres & CEO: Howard Sherman
Pres Intl: Matt Broom
COO & CFO: Vera Trulby

DORN MARKETING

34 N Bennett St
Geneva, IL 60134
Telephone: (630) 232-2010, FAX:
(630) 232-2033, E-Mail: info@
dornmarketing.com, Web Site: www.
dornmarketing.com
Pres: Brian Dorn
VP: Elizabeth Dorn
Sr VP Strategy & Insights: Dan Roglin
Founded: 1976

D.TRIO MARKETING GROUP

401 N 3rd St (Ste 480)
Minneapolis, MN 55401-1351
Telephone: (612) 787-3333, FAX:
(612) 436-0324, E-Mail: greatideas@
dtrio.com, Web Site: www.dtrio.com
Partner: Megan Devine
Partner: Maureen Dyvig
Partner: Fred Driver
Founded: 2000

Full-service marketing agency.

DUDNYK

5 Walnut Grove Dr (Ste 300)
Horsham, PA 19044
Telephone: (215) 443-9406, Toll Free:
(800) 438-3695, E-Mail: fpowers@
dudnyk.com, Web Site: dudnyk.com
Pres: Frank Powers
Exec VP & Mng Dir: Christopher To-
bias PhD
VP HR: Kathie Carnes

Healthcare industry advertising agency.

DUFFEY PETROSKY

38505 Country Club Dr (Ste 110)
Farmington Hills, MI 48331-3403
Telephone: (248) 489-8300, FAX:
(248) 994-1600, Web Site: www.
duffeypetrosky.com
Co-Founder & CEO: Mark Petrosky
Pres: Jeff Scott
Exec VP & Chief Creative Officer: Bill
Hyde
Exec VP, Chief Integration Officer &
Bus Intelligence: Andy Prakken
Founded: 1997

Full-service marketing communications
agency.

DZIURMAN DZIGN INC

620 S Main St
Clawson, MI 48017
Telephone: (248) 288-8800, FAX:
(248) 288-8804, E-Mail: dziurman@
dzdzign.com, Web Site: www.
dzdzign.com
Pres: Mark Dziurman
Sr Creative Assoc: Kevin Beals

E+M ADVERTISING INC

462 Seventh Ave (fl 8)
New York, NY 10018
Telephone: (212) 981-5900, E-Mail:
jtarsitano@emadv.com, Web Site:
www.emadv.com
CEO: Michael L. Medico
Pres: Anthony Medico
VP Mktg: Jennifer Tarsitano
Founded: 1981

E&M MEDIA GROUP INC

1410 Broadway (Ste 1002)
New York, NY 10018-9359
Telephone: (212) 455-0177, FAX:
(212) 455-0176, Web Site: www.
emtvsales.com
Pres: Bonnie Schalle
Founded: 1995

E3 LOCAL MARKETING
SOLUTIONS

4601 Malsbary Rd
Cincinnati, OH 45242-5659
Telephone: (513) 699-3300, Toll Free:
(888) 878-2768, FAX: (513) 699-
3310, Web Site: e3local.com
Owner & CEO: Kevin Slattery
Pres: Terry McKiernan
Primary Market Served: Consumer

Targeted local marketing solutions
company.

THE EGC GROUP

1175 Walt Whitman Rd (Ste 200)
Melville, NY 11747-3030
Telephone: (516) 935-4944, FAX:
(516) 935-7030, E-Mail: contact@
egcgroup.com, Web Site: www.
egcgroup.com
Pres: Ernest Canadeo
Mng Ptnr: Nicole Larrauri
Creative Dir: Rich DeSimone

EMI STRATEGIC
MARKETING INC

15 Broad St
Boston, MA 02109-3812
Telephone: (617) 224-1101, E-Mail:
info@emiboston.com, Web Site:
emiboston.com
Pres: Campbell Edlund
Exec VP Investments Practice: An-
thony Nygren
Chief Tech Officer: Ken Lubar
Exec Creative Dir: Mark Malloy
Founded: 1989

EAGLE MARKETING
SERVICES INC

PO Box 60666
San Diego, CA 92166-8666
Telephone: (619) 223-1273, E-Mail:
info@eaglemarketing.com, Web
Site: www.eaglemarketing.com
Pres: Amy Blum

Founded: 1980

EBERLE ASSOCIATES INC

Subs. of Eberle Communications
Group
1420 Springhill Rd (Ste 490)
McLean, VA 22102
Telephone: (703) 821-1550, FAX:
(703) 821-0920, Web Site: www.
eberleassociates.com
Chmn: Bruce Eberle
Pres & CEO: Tammy Lyles Cali

ECHOMAX

883 Columbus Dr
Teaneck, NJ 07666-6612
Telephone: (201) 837-1371, FAX:
(201) 837-6142
Sr Partner: Robert DeStefano

ECLIPSE MARKETING
SERVICES INC

240 Cedar Knolls Rd (Suite 100)
Cedar Knolls, NJ 07927
Toll Free: (800) 837-4648, E-Mail:
hello@eclipse2.com, Web Site:
www.eclipsemarketingservices.com
Founder & Pres: Margaret Boller
SVP Mktg & Client Svcs: Chris Bach-
ler
Primary Market Served: Consumer
Founded: 1992

Creative marketing services agency
and entertainment & technology industry growth expert.

EDELMANN SCOTT INC

3751 Westerre Pkwy (Ste A)
Richmond, VA 23238-4129
Telephone: (804) 643-1931, FAX:
(804) 643-1934
Pres & CEO: Richard Scott
CFO: Bob Judge

EDGEMARK PARTNERS INC

4510 Cox Rd (Ste 305)
Glen Allen, VA 23060-6759
Telephone: (804) 967-2000, Toll Free:
(800) 488-0289, FAX: (804) 967-
2111, E-Mail: info@
edgemarkpartners.com, Web Site:
www.edgemarkpartners.com
Pres & CFO: Rick Glasco
Exec VP: Doug Glasco
VP: Jerry Glover

EDMONDS ASSOCIATES INC

8221 Old Courthouse Rd (Ste 204)
Vienna, VA 22182-3839
Telephone: (703) 448-8000, E-Mail:
tedmonds@edmondsassociates.com,
Web Site: www.edmondsassociates.
com
Pres: Thomas Edmonds

EENIGENBURG & CO
14504 SE 47th Pl
Bellevue, WA 98006-3142
Telephone: (425) 649-0777, FAX:
  (425) 649-0719
Pres: Jill Eenigenburg

A EICOFF & CO
Div. of Ogilvy & Mather
401 N Michigan Ave (fl 4)
Chicago, IL 60611
Telephone: (312) 527-7183, Toll Free:
  (800) 333-6605, FAX: (312) 527-
  7192, E-Mail: bill.mccabe@eicoff.
  com, Web Site: www.eicoff.com
Chmn: Ronald Bliwas
Pres & CEO: Bill McCabe
Sr VP & Exec Creative Dir: Mike Po-
  well

**802 CREATIVE PARTNERS
  INC**
15 E State St
Montpelier, VT 05602-3015
Telephone: (802) 234-9755, FAX:
  (802) 732-9056, E-Mail: info@
  802creative.com, Web Site: www.
  802creative.com
Pres: Michael Hickey
Media Buyer & Office Mgr: Linda
  Trask

ELEVEN INC
500 Sansome St
San Francisco, CA 94111
Telephone: (415) 707-1111, Web Site:
  www.eleveninc.com
CEO: Courtney Buechert
Partner & Chief Strategy Officer: Jarett
  Hausske
Partner & Chief Activation Officer:
  Alison Mori Fowler
Partner & CFO: Ken Kula
Founded: 1999

EMERGING MARKETING
29 W Third Ave
Columbus, OH 43201-3208
Telephone: (614) 923-6000, FAX:
  (614) 424-6200, E-Mail: info@
  emergingmarketing.com, Web Site:
  www.emergingmarketing.com
Pres: Chris McGovern

EPSILON
Epsilon Data Management LLC
6021 Connection Dr
Irving, TX 75039
Telephone: (469) 262-0600, Web Site:
  www.epsilon.com
Chief Exec: Bryan Kennedy
CEO: Andy Frawley

Founded: 1969
Full-service global marketing company.

**ERIC MOWER +
  ASSOCIATES**
211 W Jefferson St
Syracuse, NY 13202
Telephone: (315) 466-1000, Web Site:
  www.mower.com
Chmn & CEO: Eric Mower
Founded: 1968

Full-service integrated marketing services agency.

ESROCK PARTNERS
14550 S 94th Ave
Orland Park, IL 60462-2652
Telephone: (708) 349-8400, Toll Free:
  (888) ESROCKS, FAX: (708) 349-
  8471, E-Mail: kwilson@esrock.com,
  Web Site: www.esrock.com
Partner & CEO: Jack Coughlin
Partner & Pres: Kevin Wilson
Founded: 1978

Full-service marketing, advertising &
public relations agency.

EXPOSED BRICK
1 Astor Pl (# 7-T)
New York, NY 10003-6937
Telephone: (646) 454-0880, E-Mail:
  andrewc@exposedbrick.com, Web
  Site: www.exposedbrick.com
Pres: Andrew Cohen

FCB HEALTH
A unit of FCB
100 W 33rd St
New York, NY 10001
Telephone: (212) 672-2300, FAX:
  (212) 672-2301, E-Mail: hello@
  fcbhealthcare.com, Web Site:
  fcbhealthcare.com
Pres & CEO: Dana Maiman
Exec VP & Grp Mngmt Dir: Kerry Ann
  Dwyer
Founded: 1977

FGI RESEARCH INC
6350 Quadrangle Dr (Ste 310)
Chapel Hill, NC 27517
Telephone: (919) 929-7759, FAX:
  (919) 932-8829, E-Mail: info@
  fgiresearch.com, Web Site: www.
  fgiresearch.com
CEO: David Wilson
VP Sls & Mktg: Steve Wall
Dir Consulting Svcs: Philip Atkins
Chief Scientific Officer: Dino Fire
Founded: 1980

FMS DIRECT
18344 Oxnard St (Ste 101)
Tarzana, CA 91356
Telephone: (818) 708-7814, FAX:
  (818) 708-7842, E-Mail: info@
  fmsdirect.com, Web Site: www.
  fmsdirect.com
Pres: Rodney H. Buchser
Creative Dir: Walter Burch
Founded: 1983

**FPS MARKETING
  COMMUNICATIONS**
91 Shelter Cove Rd
Milford, CT 06460-6548
Telephone: (203) 783-1940, FAX:
  (203) 685-1940, E-Mail: info@
  fpsmarketing.com, Web Site: www.
  fpsmarketing.com
Pres: Thomas Cabeen
Founded: 1987

FAHLGREN MORTINE
4030 Easton Station (Ste 300)
Columbus, OH 43219
Toll Free: (800) 731-8927, E-Mail:
  info@fahlgren.com, Web Site: www.
  fahlgrenmortine.com
Pres & CEO: Neil Mortine
Chief Creative Officer: Dave Bowers

FALLON
900 Marquette Ave (Ste 2400)
Minneapolis, MN 55402
Telephone: (612) 758-2345, FAX:
  (612) 758-2346, E-Mail: info@
  fallon.com, Web Site: www.fallon.
  com
CEO: Mike Buchner
Chief Creative Officer: Jeff Kling
Chief Mktg Officer: John King
Mng Dir: Rocky Novak

R FALLS AGENCY
900 6th Ave SE (Ste 105)
Minneapolis, MN 55414-1379
Telephone: (612) 872-6372, Toll Free:
  (800) 339-1119, FAX: (612) 872-
  1018, E-Mail: info@fallsagency.
  com, Web Site: fallsagency.com
VP & CFO: Toni Baraga
Partner: Sharon Lund

FARM
5166 Main St, Buffalo, NY 14221-
  5246
6350 Transit Rd
Depew, NY 14043-1039
Telephone: (716) 989-3200, FAX:
  (716) 989-3220, E-Mail: bizdev@
  farmbuffalo.com, Web Site: www.
  growwiththefarm.com
Pres & CEO: Larry Robb
COO: Bryan LeFauve

Founded: 1986
Full-service advertising agency.

FARSTAR INC
7110 Main St
Frisco, TX 75034-4225
Telephone: (214) 649-0422, E-Mail:
    realhuman@wedontplay.com, Web
    Site: blog.wedontplayfair.com
Founder & CEO: Kevin Lofgren
Primary Market Served: Consumer
Founded: 2002

FATHOM WORKS
1101 Broad St (Ste 316), PO Box 240
Saint Joseph, MI 49085-1091
Telephone: (269) 932-3623, Toll Free:
    (800) 800-9547, Web Site: fathom-
    works.com
Pres: Gary Tipton

FELDMAN & ASSOCIATES INC
3200 Sandy Ln
Glenview, IL 60026
Telephone: (630) 684-0404, FAX:
    (847) 272-0664, E-Mail: rfeldman@
    feldmans.net, Web Site: www.
    feldmans.net
Pres: Roger S. Feldman
Founded: 1984

FERILLO & ASSOCIATES INC
1728 Main St
Columbia, SC 29201
Telephone: (803) 771-6106, FAX:
    (803) 799-8019
Pres: Charles Ferillo
Founded: 1987

FIFTEEN DEGREES
27 E 21st St (2nd fl)
New York, NY 10010
Telephone: (212) 545-7400, FAX:
    (212) 545-7433, E-Mail: hello@
    fifteendegrees.com, Web Site:
    fifteendegrees.com
Co-Founder & Dir Acct Svcs: Richard
    A. Clarke
Co-Founder & Creative Chief: Mac
    McLaurin
Founded: 1965

FINERTY & WOLFE ADVERTISING INC
2418 N Burling St
Chicago, IL 60614
Telephone: (773) 348-3918, FAX:
    (773) 348-5873
Pres: Judith E. Finerty

FIREPOWER MARKETING INC
1124 Fir Ave (#161)
Blaine, WA 98230-9702
Telephone: (888) 353-5012, FAX:
    (800) 253-1633, Web Site: www.
    firepowermarketing.com
Pres: Rory Fatt

FIRST DIRECT CORP
2345 Route 52 (Suite 1B)
Hopewell Junction, NY 12533-3220
Telephone: (845) 221-3800, Toll Free:
    (800) 935-4386, E-Mail: info@
    1stdirect.com, Web Site: www.
    1stdirect.com
Pres: Robert Ritter

FITZGERALD & CO
Div. of Interpublic Group
3333 Piedmont Rd (Ste 1100)
Atlanta, GA 30305
Telephone: (404) 504-6900, FAX:
    (404) 239-0548, E-Mail: dave.
    fitzgerald@fitzco.com, Web Site:
    www.fitzco.com
Pres & CEO: David Fitzgerald
Mng Dir: Lisa Galanti
Chief Creative Officer: Noel Cottrell

5METACOM
630 W Carmel Dr (Ste 180)
Carmel, IN 46032
Telephone: (317) 580-7540, FAX:
    (317) 580-7550, E-Mail: mail@
    5metacom.com, Web Site: www.
    5metacom.com
CEO: Chris Wirthwein
VP Bus Svcs: Eric DeWitt
Founded: 1977

FLAIR COMMUNICATIONS AGENCY INC
214 W Erie St
Chicago, IL 60654
Telephone: (312) 943-5959, Toll Free:
    (800) 621-8317, FAX: (312) 943-
    0881, E-Mail: lflaherty@flairagency.
    com, Web Site: www.flairpromo.com
Chmn & CEO: Lee F. Flaherty
Founded: 1964

FLETCHER DIRECT
126 Castlewood Dr
Cary, NC 27511-5510
Telephone: (919) 880-5301, FAX:
    (919) 459-6816, E-Mail: billf@
    fletcherdirect.com, Web Site: www.
    fletcherdirect.com
Pres: William U. Fletcher

FLINT COMMUNICATIONS
101 10th St N
Fargo, ND 58102

Telephone: (701) 237-4850, FAX:
    (701) 234-9680, Web Site: www.
    flintcom.com
Pres & CEO: Roger Reierson

FOCALPOINT MARKETING LLC
323 Main St
Metuchen, NJ 08840
Toll Free: (877) 252-4305, Web Site:
    www.focalpoint-emarketing.com
Pres: Fred Ey
Founded: 2003

FOOTE, CONE & BELDING
Div. of Interpublic Group
875 N Michigan
Chicago, IL 60611
Telephone: (312) 425-5000, FAX:
    (312) 425-5010, E-Mail: chicago@
    fcb.com, Web Site: www.fcb.com
CEO & Pres: Michael Fassnacht
Chief Creative Officer: Todd Tilford
Sr VP & Bus Devel Dir: Sue Redington

THE FORT GROUP
100 Challenger Rd (fl 8)
Ridgefield Park, NJ 07660
Telephone: (201) 445-0202, FAX:
    (201) 445-0626, E-Mail: info@
    fortgroupinc.com, Web Site: www.
    fortgroupinc.com
Pres & CEO: Frank Digioia
COO: Ron Schutte
Exec VP: Steven A. Laux
Chief Mktg Officer: Jeff Wolfson
Founded: 1989

Fully integrated marketing services
company.

FOSINA MARKETING GROUP INC
51-53 Kenosia Ave
Danbury, CT 06810
Telephone: (203) 790-0013, E-Mail:
    info@fosinamarketing.com, Web
    Site: fosinamarketinggroup.com
Founder & CEO: Jim Fosina
CFO: Ron Lichwalla
Exec VP Client Svcs: Diane Petruzzelli
Chief Mktg Officer: George Saul
Chief Tech Officer: Kenneth Sciuto

Full-service online marketing company.

FOSTER MARKETING LLC
3909-F Ambassador Caffery Pkwy
Lafayette, LA 70503
Telephone: (337) 235-1848, FAX:
    (337) 237-7246, E-Mail: gfoster@
    fostermarketing.com, Web Site:
    fostermarketing.com
CEO: George Foster
Pres: Tiffany Harris

Mktg Dir: Rachel Bonnette

FRACTAL ANALYTICS
803 Plaza 3 (fl 8)
Jersey City, NJ 07311
Telephone: (201) 469-0600, Web Site:
  www.fractalanalytics.com
CEO: Srikanth Velamakanni
Sr VP & Chief Mktg Officer: Careen
  Foster
Primary Market Served: Consumer

FRIED-CASSORLA COMMUNICATIONS INC
7408 Woodlawn Ave
Melrose Park, PA 19027
Telephone: (215) 635-5189, FAX:
  (215) 635-0461, E-Mail: albert@
  fried-cas.com, Web Site: www.fried-
  cas.com
Pres: Albert Fried-Cassorla

FRONT PORCH INC
14520 Mono Way (Ste 200)
Sonora, CA 95370-7829
Telephone: (209) 288-5500, Toll Free:
  (800) 728-1464, Web Site: www.
  frontporch.com
CEO: Zach Britton
Founder: Derek Maxson
Pres & CFO: Bob Hohne
Chief Tech Officer: Carlos Vazquez
VP Sls: Carl Daly

FUJII COMMUNICATIONS INC
7369 E Prairie Rd
Lincolnwood, IL 60712-1039
Telephone: (847) 677-0542, FAX:
  (847) 677-0523, E-Mail: fci@
  fujiicommunications.com, Web Site:
  www.fujiicommunications.com
Partner: Laurie Fujii Falcone
Partner: Marcello Falcone
Founded: 1987

FURMAN ROTH ADVERTISING
801 Second Ave
New York, NY 10017
Telephone: (212) 687-2300, FAX:
  (212) 687-0858, E-Mail: eroth@
  furmanroth.com, Web Site: www.
  furmanroth.com
Pres & CEO: Ernie M. Roth
Exec VP, Partner & Media Dir: Mark
  Lefkowitz
Sr VP, Partner & Dir Acct Svcs: Jacki
  Friedman

G&A MARKETING
1001 Ford Cir
Cincinnati, OH 45150

Toll Free: (800) 688-1370, FAX: (513)
  688-1570, E-Mail: info@
  gamarketing.com, Web Site: www.
  gamarketing.com
Pres & CEO: Pat Gunning
Founded: 1994

GHW ASSOCIATES
13063 SW Pembroke Cir N
Lake Suzy, FL 34269-6914
Telephone: (941) 625-4293, E-Mail:
  info@ghw-associates.com, Web Site:
  www.ghw-associates.com
Principal: George H. Wojtkiewicz
Founded: 1974

GKV
1500 Whetstone Way (fl 4), The Cas-
  cade Bldg
Baltimore, MD 21230-4768
Telephone: (410) 539-5400, FAX:
  (410) 234-2441, E-Mail:
  newbusiness@gkv.com, Web Site:
  gvk.com
Partner & CEO: Roger Gray
Partner & Chief Creative Officer: Jeff
  Millman
Partner & Exec VP Direct & Interactive
  Mktg: Garry Raim
Partner & Exec VP Pub Rels & Grass-
  roots Outreach: Kevin Kempske

GM CUSTOMER RELATIONSHIP MANAGEMENT
100 Renaissance Ctr
Detroit, MI 48265-0001
Telephone: (313) 665-6605, Web Site:
  www.gm.com
Gen Dir Consumer Websites, CRM
  Mktg Opers & Dealer Systems: Ed
  Vogt
Gen Dir Customer & Relationship
  Svcs: Jim Maloney
Primary Market Served: Business &
  Consumer

THE GRI MARKETING GROUP INC
35 Corporate Dr (Ste 1040)
Trumbull, CT 06611
Telephone: (203) 261-3337, FAX:
  (203) 261-1113, E-Mail: bsnider@
  gridirect.com, Web Site: www.
  gridirect.com
Pres: Brian S. Snider

GS&F
209 10th Ave (Ste 222)
Nashville, TN 37203
Telephone: (615) 385-1100, Toll Free:
  (800) 241-3325, FAX: (615) 783-
  0500, E-Mail: biz@gsandf.com, Web
  Site: www.gsandf.com

Founder: Hank Sherwood
CEO & Owner: Jeff Lipscomb
Chief Creative Officer & Owner: Ro-
  land Gibbons
Exec VP, Mng Dir & Exec Creative
  Dir: Gregg Boling
Founded: 1978

GSD&M
828 W 6th St
Austin, TX 78703-5420
Telephone: (512) 242-4736, Web Site:
  www.gsdm.com
CEO: Duff Stewart
Pres: Marianne Malina
Chief Creative Officer: Jay Russell
Sr VP & Chief Mktg Officer: J.B. Raf-
  tus

GA WRIGHT SALES INC
90 Madison St (Suite 700)
Denver, CO 80206
Telephone: (303) 333-4453, FAX:
  (303) 393-5320, E-Mail: info@
  gawright.com, Web Site: www.
  gawrightsales.com
CEO: Gary A Wright

Retail sales promotion & exit strategies
company.

GAGE
10000 Hwy 55
Minneapolis, MN 55441-6300
Telephone: (763) 595-3800, FAX:
  (763) 595-5845, Web Site: www.
  gage.com
Sr VP: Jane Blanco
Founded: 1992

Full-service marketing agency.

GALANTY & CO INC
1640 Fifth St (Ste 202)
Santa Monica, CA 90401
Telephone: (310) 451-2525, FAX:
  (310) 451-5020, Web Site: www.
  galanty.com
Principal & Exec Producer: Mark Galanty
Founded: 1987

GAME SHOW PLACEMENTS LTD
7011 Willoughby Ave
Hollywood, CA 90038-2332
Telephone: (323) 874-7818, E-Mail:
  gsp@ix.netcom.com, Web Site:
  www.gameshowplacements.com
Pres: Ben Robertson

GARD COMMUNICATIONS
1140 SW 11th Ave (fl 3)
Portland, OR 97205

Telephone: (503) 221-0100, Toll Free: (800) 800-7132, E-Mail: lfuller@gardcommunications.com, Web Site: gardcommunications.com
Pres: Brian Gard
Mng Dir: Liz Fuller
Dir Fin & Opers: Valerie Grudier Edwards

GARRITANO GROUP
305 Minnetonka Ave S
Wayzata, MN 55391
Telephone: (612) 333-3775, FAX: (612) 333-3778, Web Site: garritanogroup.com
Pres: Joe Garritano
Conducts Business: U.S., Canada
Primary Market Served: Business & Consumer
Founded: 1999

Full spectrum of traditional & digital marketing.

GARVER ADVERTISING SERVICE INC
440 E 57th St (Ste 5C)
New York, NY 10022-3047
Telephone: (212) 371-3325, E-Mail: garverads@aol.com
Pres: Arthur Ball

GAYLORD COMMUNICATIONS UNLIMITED
PO Box 28
Bridgewater, VT 05034-0028
Telephone: (802) 672-6200, FAX: (802) 672-6226
Partner: Jeremy P. Gaylord
Founded: 1996

GCDIRECT
911 Western Ave (Ste 509)
Seattle, WA 98104-1047
Telephone: (206) 262-1999, E-Mail: info@gcdirect.com, Web Site: www.gcdirect.com
Partner: Mike Gilbert
Partner: Cynthia Cruver

KAREN GEDNEY COMMUNICATIONS
272 87th St
Brooklyn, NY 11209
Telephone: (718) 680-1627, FAX: (917) 591-5547
Owner & Pres: Karen Gedney
Founded: 1987

LOIS GELLER MARKETING GROUP
3801 NE 207th St (#1003)
Aventura, FL 33180
Telephone: (646) 723-3231, E-Mail: info2@loisgellermarketinggroup.com, Web Site: www.loisgellermarketinggroup.com
Pres & Owner: Lois Geller
VP: Mike McCormick
Art Dir: James Pepper Huff
Conducts Business: U.S., Can., S. America, Europe
Primary Market Served: Business
Founded: 1997

Strategic direct marketing agency providing complete planning through implementation. Expertise with publishing, banking, insurance, catalogs, business to business, collectibles and travel clients.

GENNERA KNAB & CO
11536 Sunshine Terr
Studio City, CA 91604
CEO: Michael Knab
Founded: 1980

Advertising & marketing communications company.

GEOMETRY GLOBAL
Unit of WPP
636 11th Ave, The Chocolate Factory
New York, NY 10036
Telephone: (212) 537-3700, E-Mail: press@geometry.com, Web Site: www.geometry.com
Chmn: Toby Hoare
Global CEO: Steve Harding
CEO North America: Carl Hartman
Global Chief Creative Officer: Jon Hamm
Global Dir Corp Commun: Selinde Dulckeit
Primary Market Served: Business & Consumer

GIANFAGNA STRATEGIC MARKETING INC
1991 Crocker Rd (Ste 225)
Westlake, OH 44145-6970
Telephone: (440) 808-4700, FAX: (440) 808-4707, E-Mail: tellmemore@gianfagnamarketing.com, Web Site: www.gianfagnamarketing.com
Pres: Jean M. Gianfagna
VP Opers: Jim Gianfagna
Art Dir: Mark Wilcox
Founded: 1992

GLOBALIZATION PARTNERS INTERNATIONAL
1600 Tysons Blvd (fl 8)
Mc Lean, VA 22102-4872
Telephone: (703) 268-2193, Toll Free: (866) 272-5874, FAX: (202) 478-0956, E-Mail: info@globalizationpartners.com, Web Site: www.globalizationpartners.com
Founder & Mng Partner: Martin Spethman
Primary Market Served: Consumer
Founded: 2001

THE GOLDMARK GROUP INC
1155 Bloomfield Ave
Clifton, NJ 07012
Telephone: (973) 777-5720, Toll Free: (800) 632-9632, FAX: (973) 777-2390, E-Mail: info@goldmarkgroup.com, Web Site: www.goldmarkgroup.com
Principal: Joseph Goldbrenner
Principal: Eugene Markowitz
Founded: 1974

GOOD ADVERTISING
5100 Poplar Ave (Ste 1700)
Memphis, TN 38137
Telephone: (901) 761-0741, Toll Free: (800) 325-9857, FAX: (901) 682-2568, E-Mail: info@goodadvertising.com, Web Site: www.goodadvertising.com
Pres: Dale Cox
Exec VP & Creative Dir: Ellen Isaacman

GOODMAN MARKETING PARTNERS INC
4340 Redwood Hwy (Ste B-52)
San Rafael, CA 94903-2107
Telephone: (415) 507-9060, FAX: (415) 507-9067, E-Mail: info@goodmanmarketing.com, Web Site: www.goodmanmarketing.com
Pres & Creative Dir: Carolyn Goodman
Dir Strategic Mktg & New Bus Devel: Denise Williams
Conducts Business: U.S., Canada, Worldwide
Primary Market Served: Business & Consumer
Founded: 2002

Full-service direct marketing agency.

GOODWAY GROUP
261 Old York Rd (Ste 930)
Jenkintown, PA 19046-3711
Telephone: (626) 355-7800, E-Mail: info@goodwaygroup.com, Web Site: goodwaygroup.com
Pres: David Wolk
Exec VP Sls: Dan Mauch
COO: Jay Friedman
Founded: 1929

GRAFICA GROUP
67 E Park Pl (Ste 425)
Morristown, NJ 07960-7103
Telephone: (973) 309-7500, FAX:
(973) 309-7501, E-Mail:
information@grafica.com, Web Site:
www.grafica.com
Founder, Pres & CEO: Debra Taeschler
Co-Founder & VP Creative: John Pu-
glionisi
CFO: Ed Miller
VP Acct Mngmt: Cheryle Barnett
Conducts Business: U.S.
Primary Market Served: Business &
Consumer
Founded: 1986

Multi-channel, integrated direct marketing, advertising, web site design and
public relations.

GRAGG ADVERTISING
450 E 4th St (Ste 100)
Kansas City, MO 64106-1171
Toll Free: (877) GRAGGADV, FAX:
(816) 931-2227, E-Mail: contact@
graggadv.com, Web Site: www.
graggadv.com
Chmn, CEO & Partner: Greg Gragg
Pres, COO & Partner: Darryl Mattox
Chief Info Officer & Partner: Michael
Schuler
Lever 1 Pres & Partner: Erica Brune
Primary Market Served: Consumer
Founded: 1992

GRAY & GRAHAM INC
136 Main St (Ste 6)
Westport, CT 06880-3304
Telephone: (203) 227-3900, FAX:
(203) 227-3593, E-Mail: info@
graygraham.com, Web Site: www.
graygraham.com
Pres: Jeff R. Gray
Founded: 1991

GREY HEALTHCARE GROUP
200 Fifth Ave
New York, NY 10010
Telephone: (212) 886-3000, FAX:
(212) 886-3297, E-Mail: info@
ghgroup.com, Web Site: www.
ghgroup.com
CEO: Lynn O'Connor-Vos

Full-service, global, integrated communications agency.

GREYSTONE SERVICES INC
PO Box 482
Beverly, MA 01915-0482
Telephone: (978) 535-9185, FAX:
(978) 535-7826, E-Mail: lee@gstone.
biz, Web Site: www.gstone.biz
Pres: Lee Yaffa

GRIZZARD COMMUNICATIONS GROUP INC
An OMNICOM Co
229 Peachtree St NE (Ste 1400)
Atlanta, GA 30303
Telephone: (404) 522-8330, Toll Free:
(800) 241-9351, Web Site: www.
grizzard.com
CEO: Chip Grizzard
Pres: Debbi Barber
Chief Info Officer & COO: Chris Joos

GROUP M INC
15 N Mill St (Ste 210)
Nyack, NY 10960-3015
Telephone: (845) 535-3453, E-Mail:
gmi.prm@gmail.com, Web Site:
www.groupm.org
Pres & CEO: Rosemarie Monaco
Conducts Business: Worldwide
Employees: 6
Primary Market Served: Business
Founded: 1990

Integrated public relations and direct
marketing company to boost effectiveness of direct marketing efforts.

GROUPLEVINSON
128 Chestnut St (Ste 403)
Philadelphia, PA 19106
Telephone: (215) 627-3030, Web Site:
grouplevinson.com
CEO: Leo Levinson

Full-service advertising, public relations, Internet, Website & marketing
agency.

GROUPM DIRECT
825 7th Ave
New York, NY 10019-6014
Telephone: (212) 474-0830, Web Site:
www.groupm.com
Pres: Marion Murphy

GROVE COMMUNICATIONS
3918 Valley View Rd
Crystal Lake, IL 60012
Telephone: (815) 459-4552, FAX:
(815) 459-4553, E-Mail: bobg@
grovecommunications.com, Web
Site: www.grovecommunications.
com
Pres: Robert Grzelewski

Graphic communications provider.

GUMAS ADVERTISING
99 Shotwell St
San Francisco, CA 94103-3625
Telephone: (415) 621-7575, FAX:
(415) 255-8804, E-Mail: jgumas@
gumas.com, Web Site: www.gumas.
com

Pres: John Gumas

HF DIRECT
950 22nd St N (Ste 700)
Birmingham, AL 35203
Telephone: (205) 458-8200, FAX:
(205) 458-8206, E-Mail: info@
hfdirect.com, Web Site: www.
hfdirect.com
Pres: Ray Fagan
Sr VP: David Johnson
Client Svcs: Kim Twitchell
Creative Dir: Ray Brooks
Primary Market Served: Business &
Consumer

Full-service direct marketing agency.

HACKERAGENCY INC
1215 4th Ave (Ste 2100)
Seattle, WA 98161-1018
Telephone: (206) 805-1500, Web Site:
www.hal2l.com
Pres & CEO: Spyro Kourtis
Mng Dir Bus Devel: Kristin Flor
Gen Mgr: Matt Witter
Founded: 1986

HAMMOND COMMUNICATIONS GROUP INC
173 Trade St
Lexington, KY 40511
Telephone: (859) 254-1878, Toll Free:
(888) 424-1878, FAX: (859) 254-
4290, E-Mail: info@hammondcg.
com, Web Site: www.hammondcg.
com
Founder & Pres: Ron Mossotti
Founder & Consultant: Tom Hammond

HANOBIK COMMUNICATIONS
140 Convair Dr
Coraopolis, PA 15108-2404
Telephone: (412) 264-3077, FAX:
(412) 264-0321
Pres & Owner: Raymond G. Hanobik

HARRIS CONNECT LLC
1400-A Crossways Blvd
Chesapeake, VA 23320
Toll Free: (800) 877-6554, E-Mail:
moreinfo@harrisconnect.com, Web
Site: www.harrisconnect.com
Sr VP Opers & Admin: Susan D'Agos-
tino
Natl Sls Dir: Hardeep Avery

HARRIS MARKETING GROUP
102 Pierce St
Birmingham, MI 48009-6030

Telephone: (248) 723-6300, FAX:
(248) 723-6301, E-Mail: info@
harris-hmg.com, Web Site: www.
harris-hmg.com
Founder & CEO: Janice Rosenhaus
Founded: 1978

HARVEY ASSOCIATES
63 Hoover Dr
Cresskill, NJ 07626
Telephone: (201) 962-8463, E-Mail:
harveyfnj@optonline.net, Web Site:
harveyfeldmanassociates.com
Pres: Harvey A. Feldman
Founded: 1986

Marketing consulting & creative
agency.

HAVAS WORLDWIDE LLC
200 Hudson St
New York, NY 10013
Telephone: (212) 886-2000, FAX:
(212) 886-5013, Web Site: www.
havasworldwide.com
Chmn & CEO: Yannick Bollore
Global CEO: Andrew Benett
Global Chief Mktg Officer: Matt Weiss
Global Commun Dir: Yvonne Bond
Founded: 1991

HAWKEYE
2828 Routh St (Ste 300)
Dallas, TX 75201
Telephone: (214) 749-0080, E-Mail:
sdapper@hawkeyeww.com, Web
Site: www.hawkeyeww.com
Chmn & Founder: Steve Dapper

Integrated digital marketing agency.

HAWTHORNE DIRECT INC
1201 W 5th St (Ste T230)
Los Angeles, CA 90017
Telephone: (301) 248-3972, E-Mail:
inquiries@hawthornedirect.com,
Web Site: www.hawthornedirect.com
Founder: Timothy R. Hawthorne
Owner, Chmn & CEO: Thomas Kelly
Chief Mktg & Creative Officer: John
Pucci
Dir Bus Devel & Corp Rels: Karla
Crawford Kerr

Brand response agency.

HAYNES MARKETING
NETWORK INC
4149 Arkwright Rd (Ste A)
Macon, GA 31210
Telephone: (912) 742-5266, Web Site:
www.haynesmarketing.com
Pres: Phil Haynes
Principal: Amelia Haynes

Founded: 1976
Full-service advertising and marketing
agency.

HEINRICH
2228 Blake St (Ste 200)
Denver, CO 80205-2013
Telephone: (303) 233-8660, Toll Free:
(800) 356-5036, FAX: (303) 239-
5352, E-Mail: info@heinrich.com,
Web Site: www.heinrich.com
Pres: George Eddy
VP Digital Mktg: Erin Iwata
Creative Dir: Robert Mason

HENKE & ASSOCIATES INC
236 Hamilton Rd
Cedarburg, WI 53012
Telephone: (262) 375-9090, FAX:
(262) 375-2262, E-Mail: info@
henkeinc.com, Web Site: www.
henkeinc.com
CEO: Bill Henke
Pres & Creative Dir: Jack Henke

HENNERBERG GROUP INC
5501 Willow Ln
Colleyville, TX 76034-5149
Telephone: (817) 318-8100, E-Mail:
gary@hennerberg.com, Web Site:
hennerberg.com
Direct Mktg Consultant: Gary Henner-
berg
Bus & Mktg Strategist & Designer:
Perry Alexander

HERCKY-PASQUA-HERMAN
324 Chestnut St
Roselle Park, NJ 07204-1904
Telephone: (908) 241-9474, FAX:
(908) 241-8961, E-Mail: hercky@
hph-comm.com, Web Site: www.
hph-comm.com
Pres: Peter Hercky

HERRMANN GLOBAL LLC
dba Herrmann International
794 Buffalo Creek Rd
Lake Lure, NC 28746
Telephone: (828) 625-9153, Toll Free:
(800) 432-4234, E-Mail: info@hbdi.
com, Web Site: www.
herrmannsolutions.com
CEO: Ann Herrmann-Nehdi
Pres: John Graves
Mktg Dir: Betsy Summers
Dir Opers: Dorothy Roche

THE HIEBING GROUP
315 Wisconsin Ave
Madison, WI 53703

Telephone: (608) 256-6357, FAX:
(608) 256-0693, E-Mail: ideas@
hiebing.com, Web Site: www.
hiebing.com
Pres: Dave Florin
VP & Creative Dir: Sean Mullen
Bus Devel: Ted Jun
Founded: 1981

HILL HOLLIDAY
53 State St
Boston, MA 02109
Telephone: (617) 366-4000, Web Site:
www.hhcc.com
Chmn & CEO: Karen Kaplan
Exec VP & Chief Creative Officer:
Lance Jensen
Exec VP & Chief Growth Officer:
Chris Wallrapp
Exec VP & Mng Dir: Leslee Kiley
Exec VP & Mng Dir: Kerry Benson

HOFF COMMUNICATIONS
INC
23 S Lansdowne Ave
Lansdowne, PA 19050
Telephone: (610) 623-2091, FAX:
(610) 623-2041, E-Mail: service@
hoffcomm.com, Web Site:
hoffcomm.com
Pres: Jennifer Hoff
Founded: 1988

THE HOGAN CO
107 Fifth Ave
Knoxville, TN 37917
Telephone: (865) 546-7661, FAX:
(865) 523-7300
Pres & CEO: Douglas W. Hogan

HOLSTED MARKETING INC
112 W 34th St (Ste 1405)
New York, NY 10120
Telephone: (212) 686-8537, FAX:
(212) 481-0415, E-Mail: preulbach@
holstedmarketing.com, Web Site:
www.holstedmarketing.com
CEO & Chmn: Victor N. Benson
Sr VP Sls & Bus Devel: Paul Reulbach
Sr VP Mktg & Adv: Carolyn Kraft
Founded: 1971

THE HONEY AGENCY
1050 20th St (Suite 220)
Sacramento, CA 95811
Telephone: (916) 444-0203, E-Mail:
buzz@honeyagency.com, Web Site:
honeyagency.com
Co-Founder: Meghan Phillips
Co-Founder: Rebecca Parker
Founded: 2008

Marketing agency specializing in brand
building & creative design for the food,
wine & lifestyle industries.

HUGHESLEAHYKARLOVIC

1141 S 7th St
Saint Louis, MO 63104
Telephone: (314) 571-6300, FAX:
(314) 862-1616, E-Mail: hello@
hlkagency.com, Web Site:
hlkagency.com
Mng Ptnr: Bill Hughes
Partner: Joe Leahy
Partner: Eric Karlovic

Full-service digital agency.

HULT MARKETING

619 SW Water St (Ste 2A)
Peoria, IL 61602-1586
Telephone: (309) 673-8191, FAX:
(309) 674-5530, E-Mail: jflynn@
hultmarketing.com, Web Site: www.
hultmarketing.com
Pres & CEO: Jim Flynn
Founded: 1956

HUNT MARKETING GROUP

1809 7th Ave (Ste 411)
Seattle, WA 98101-4403
Telephone: (206) 447-5665, FAX:
(206) 447-5789, E-Mail: info@
hmgseattle.com, Web Site: www.
hmgseattle.com
Pres: Brian Hunt
Dir Client Svcs: Natalie Gossett
Sr Copywriter: Matt Hunt
Dir Agency Svcs: Corey Moran

ICF OLSON

An ICF International Co.
420 N 5th St, Loring Corners
Minneapolis, MN 55401-1348
Telephone: (612) 215-9800, FAX:
(612) 215-9801, E-Mail: info@olson.
com, Web Site: www.olson.com
Grp Lead: Louise Clements
Pres & COO: Margaret Murphy
Exec VP & Gen Mgr: Tanya Bennett
Founded: 1992

Creative agency.

IMC DIRECT

81 S Hotel St (Ste 315)
Honolulu, HI 96813
Telephone: (808) 545-1680, FAX:
(808) 528-4293, E-Mail: vfujita@
imcdm.com
Owner: Victor Fujita

IQ AGENCY

280 Interstate N Cir SE
Atlanta, GA 30339
Telephone: (404) 255-3550, E-Mail:
newbiz@iqagency.com, Web Site:
iqagency.com
Pres & CEO: Tony Quin
Conducts Business: U.S.
Primary Market Served: Business

Founded: 1995
Integrated, digital advertising agency.

IBIS COMMUNICATIONS INC

1024 17th Ave S
Nashville, TN 37212
Telephone: (615) 777-1900, FAX:
(615) 777-1906, E-Mail:
mhowland@ibiscommunications.
com, Web Site: www.
ibiscommunications.com
Pres & CEO: MaryAnne Howland

ICON MEDIA DIRECT INC

5910 Lemona Ave
Sherman Oaks, CA 91411
Telephone: (818) 995-6400, FAX:
(818) 995-6405, E-Mail: info@
iconmediadirect.com, Web Site:
www.iconmediadirect.com
Pres & CEO: Nancy Lazkani
Dir Media & Mktg: Rebecca Rodriguez

IGNITION NETWORK

400 W Erie St (Ste 205)
Chicago, IL 60654
Telephone: (312) 893-5000, E-Mail:
inquiries@ignitionnetwork.com,
Web Site: www.ignitionnetwork.com
Gen Mgr: Brian Opyd
Mktg Mgr: Michael Olsen
Dir Client Svcs: Brent Gross
Founded: 2006

Shopper marketing company.

IKON COMMUNICATIONS CONSULTANTS INC

554 Washington St
Wellesley, MA 02482
Telephone: (781) 237-6060, FAX:
(781) 235-3504, E-Mail: info@
ikoncommunications.com, Web Site:
www.ikoncommunications.com
Founder & CEO: Daniel F. Sweeney
Pres & COO: Gregg M. Sweeney

IMPACT INTERNATIONAL MARKETING

349 S Lake Havasu Ave (Ste 104)
Lake Havasu City, AZ 86403
Telephone: (866) 389-9798, E-Mail:
sales@iimgroup.com, Web Site:
iimgroup.com
Pres: Kathryn Felke

INDROS GROUP

210 Richardson St (fl 2)
Brooklyn, NY 11222
Toll Free: (866) 463-7671, E-Mail:
info@indrosgroup.com, Web Site:
www.indrosgroup.com
Pres: Tej Kohli
Primary Market Served: Consumer

Founded: 2002

INFINITY DIRECT INC

13220 County Rd 6 (Ste 200)
Plymouth, MN 55441-8791
Telephone: (763) 559-1111, Web Site:
www.infinitydirect.com
CEO: Tom Harding
Exec VP: Shawn Harding
Founded: 1991

Direct marketing agency.

INFOTRENDS INC

A Questex Co.
97 Libbey Industrial Pkwy
Weymouth, MA 02189
Telephone: (781) 616-2100, FAX:
(781) 616-2121, E-Mail: info@
infotrends.com, Web Site: www.
infotrends.com
Sls: Scott Phinney
Office & Production Print & Media:
Keith LaVangie
Consumer & Pro Imaging: Matt
O'Keefe
Media Rels: Donna O'Malley

INNERWORKINGS INC

600 W Chicago Ave
Chicago, IL 60654
Telephone: (317) 642-3700, Toll Free:
(866) 766-5176, E-Mail: info@inwk.
com, Web Site: www.inwk.com
Pres & CEO: Eric D. Belcher
COO: John Eisel
Chief Mktg Officer: Leigh Segall
Founded: 2002

Global brand delivery service.

INNIS MAGGIORE GROUP INC

4715 Whipple Ave NW
Canton, OH 44718
Telephone: (330) 492-5500, Toll Free:
(800) 460-4111, FAX: (330) 492-
5568, E-Mail: dick@innismaggiore.
com, Web Site: www.innismaggiore.
com
Pres & CEO: Dick Maggiore

INNOVAIRRE COMMUNICATIONS LLC

2 Executive Campus (Suite 200)
Cherry Hill, NJ 08002
Telephone: (856) 663-2500, E-Mail:
info@innovairre.com, Web Site:
www.innovairre.com
Pres & Chief Growth Officer: Don
McKenzie
Pres & COO: John Hartwell
CFO: Rebecca Sijl-Gacel
Acct Exec: Matt Graham

Founded: 2014

Marketing company specializing in fundraising, supporting partner agencies & nonprofit organizations.

INTEGER GROUP

Part of Omnicom Group Inc.
2633 Fleur Dr
Des Moines, IA 50321-1753
Telephone: (515) 288-7910, FAX: (515) 288-8439, E-Mail: fmaher@ integermidwest.com, Web Site: www.integer.com
Group Pres & COO: Frank Maher
Dir Customer Relationship Mktg: David Ausley

INTEGRATED ADVERTISING INC

6817 Southpoint Pkwy (Ste 804)
Jacksonville, FL 32216
Telephone: (904) 296-2585, FAX: (904) 296-2586, E-Mail: mary@ intadvertising.com, Web Site: www.intadvertising.com
Pres: Mary T. Lopez Huston

INTERACT MEDICAL

115 N William St
South Bend, IN 46601
Telephone: (415) 354-1777, Web Site: www.interactmedical.com
Pres: Steve Colucci
Founded: 1993

INTERLINE CREATIVE GROUP INC

553 N North Ct (Ste 160)
Palatine, IL 60067-8124
Telephone: (847) 358-4848, FAX: (847) 358-8089, E-Mail: info@ interlinegroup.com, Web Site: www.interlinegroup.com
Pres: James A. Nowakowski

INTERMEDIA ADVERTISING

22120 Clarendon St
Woodland Hills, CA 91367
Telephone: (818) 995-1455, Toll Free: (800) 846-3289, FAX: (818) 719-9977, E-Mail: sales@intermedia-advertising.com, Web Site: www.intermedia-advertising.com
Pres: Robert Yallen
Sr VP & Chief Info Officer: Joseph Poulose
Sr VP & CFO: Tim Gerrity
Founded: 1974

INTERMEDIA CONSULTANTS INC

100 Overlook Center (fl 2)
Princeton, NJ 08540-7814

Telephone: (609) 430-8460, Web Site: www.interprintmedia.com
Pres: Darr Kartychak
Employees: 4
Founded: 1980

Provide end-to-end print media production, using new & emerging technologies. We can expertly design, print, finish, kit, store, direct mail & distribute nationwide almost any product . Over 50+ printed & promotional product categories, as well as apparel, across many industries.

INTERNATIONAL MARKETING PARTNERS LTD

6371 W 79th St
Los Angeles, CA 90045-1442
Telephone: (310) 665-1155, FAX: (310) 665-1155, E-Mail: info@ intermarketingonline.com, Web Site: www.intermarketingonline.com
Founder & CEO: Allyson Stewart-Allen

INTERNET DIRECT RESPONSE, INC

PO Box 93157
Austin, TX 78709-3157
Telephone: (512) 551-8417, FAX: (888) 763-5177, E-Mail: tbroderick@internet-direct-response.com, Web Site: www.internet-direct-response.com
Pres: Tom Broderick

INTERTREND COMMUNICATIONS INC

555 E Ocean Blvd Ste 900
Long Beach, CA 90802-5056
Telephone: (562) 733-1888, E-Mail: info@intertrend.com, Web Site: www.intertrend.com
CEO: Julia Huang
CFO: Susanna Jue
VP: Jon Yokogawa

INTERVAL INTERNATIONAL

6262 Sunset Dr
South Miami, FL 33143-4843
Telephone: (305) 666-1884, Toll Free: (800) 468-3782, FAX: (305) 667-5321, Web Site: www.intervalworld.com
CEO: Craig M. Nash
COO: Jeanette E. Marbert
CFO: William L. Harvey
Chief Acctg Officer: John A. Galea
Founded: 1976

Operator of membership programs for vacationers.

IVIE & ASSOCIATES INC

601 Silveron Blvd (Ste 200)
Flower Mound, TX 75028
Telephone: (972) 899-5000, FAX: (972) 899-5050, Web Site: www.ivieinc.com
Founder & CEO: Warren Ivie
Exec VP: Kay Ivie
Pres: Brandon Ivie
Exec VP & Chief Mktg Officer: Buddy Martensen
Primary Market Served: Consumer
Founded: 1993

Full-service marketing company.

IVISIONMOBILE INC

9566 Topanga Cyn Blvd
Chatsworth, CA 91311
Telephone: (866) 655-5302, FAX: (818) 812-6126, E-Mail: sales@ ivisionmobile.com, Web Site: www.ivisionmobile.com
CEO & Co-Founder: Omer Samiri
CTO & Co-Founder: Derek Simms
Lead Software Engr: Paddy Ordway
Founded: 2003

Mobile marketing & communications company.

IXI SERVICES

Div. of Equifax
7927 Jones Branch Dr (Ste 400)
McLean, VA 22102
Telephone: (703) 848-3800, FAX: (703) 848-3868, E-Mail: info.ixiservices@equifax.com, Web Site: www.ixicorp.com
Gen Mgr: Isio Nelson

JJI INTERNATIONAL INC

RP-NFOA
200 1st Ave
Cranston, RI 02910
Telephone: (401) 780-8668
Pres: Lisa Weingeroff
Employees: 14

Premiums, confined goods & logo merchandise.

JPL INTEGRATED COMMUNICATIONS INC

471 JPL Wick Dr
Harrisburg, PA 17111
Telephone: (717) 558-8048, E-Mail: jpl@jplcreative.com, Web Site: www.jplcreative.com
List Sls Mgr: Luke Kempski
Dir: Mary Pedersen
Conducts Business: Worldwide
Primary Market Served: Business & Consumer
Founded: 1989

Full-service, integrated marketing agency.

JSR ADVERTISING CORP

The Quant Method
21 Astor Pl (Suite 2D)
New York, NY 10003-6931
Telephone: (212) 995-1661, E-Mail:
jay@tqm1.com, Web Site: www.
quantmethod.com
Pres: Jay Rosenberg

Personality-based direct marketing
company.

JVW DIRECT

309 W Hutchinson Ave
Pittsburgh, PA 15218-1325
Telephone: (412) 241-5920, FAX:
(412) 241-5850, E-Mail: john@
jvwdirect.com
Pres: Jay van Wagenen
Partner: John C. O'Connor

JWT INSIDE

Subs. of J Walter Thompson
6300 Wilshire Blvd (Fl 19)
Los Angeles, CA 90048
Telephone: (310) 309-8282, Toll Free:
(877) 665-8768, FAX: (310) 309-
8283, E-Mail: conversations@
jwtinside.com, Web Site: www.
jwtinside.com
CEO: John Windolph
CFO: Jeff Press
Creative Dir: Bruce Carey

Full service recruitment, advertising
and employment communications
agency.

JACK MORTON
WORLDWIDE

Subs. of Interpublic Group
909 Third Ave (Fl 11)
New York, NY 10022
Telephone: (212) 401-7000, (212) 401-
7121, E-Mail: experience@
jackmorton.com, Web Site: www.
jackmorton.com
CEO: Josh McCall
COO & CFO: Bill Davies
Chief Creative Officer: Bruce Hender-
son
Pres: Rob McQueen
Founded: 1939

THE JACKSON GROUP

An RR Donnelley Co
5804 Churchman By-Pass
Indianapolis, IN 46203
Telephone: (317) 791-9000, Toll Free:
(888) 522-5766, FAX: (317) 791-
9800, Web Site: www.jacksongroup.
com
Pres: Mark Leggio

Printing, mailing, fulfillment, telemarketing & technological services company.

JACOBS & CLEVENGER INC

303 E Wacker Dr (Suite 2030)
Chicago, IL 60601-5278
Telephone: (312) 894-3000, FAX:
(312) 645-9825, E-Mail: mail2350@
jacobsclevenger.com, Web Site:
www.jacobsclevenger.com
Pres: Ron Jacobs
VP & Creative Dir: Kim Redlin

Digital direct marketing agency.

DON JAGODA ASSOCIATES
INC

100 Marcus Dr
Melville, NY 11747
Telephone: (631) 454-1800, FAX:
(631) 454-1834, E-Mail:
information@dja.com, Web Site:
www.dja.com
Pres: Don Jagoda
Exec VP: Bruce Hollander

JAM COMMUNICATIONS
INC

1156 15th St NW (Suite 1000)
Washington, DC 20005
Telephone: (202) 986-4750, FAX:
(202) 232-9146, E-Mail: neil@
jamagency.com, Web Site: www.
jamagency.com
Pres: Neil Griffin
Founded: 1992

Direct marketing & creative services
agency.

JOHNSON DIRECT LLC

250 Bishops Way (Suite 203)
Brookfield, WI 53005
Telephone: (262) 782-2750, Toll Free:
(800) 710-2750, FAX: (262) 782-
2751, E-Mail: info@responsory.com,
Web Site: www.johnsondirect.com
Pres: Grant A. Johnson

Multichannel marketing communications agency.

JOHNSONRAUHOFF INC

2525 Lake Pines Dr
Saint Joseph, MI 49085
Telephone: (269) 428-3377, Toll Free:
(800) 572-3996, FAX: (269) 428-
3312, E-Mail: questions@johnson-
rauhoff.com, Web Site: www.
johnsonrauhoff.com
Founder & CEO: Don Johnson
Pres: Jackie Hui

JONES & O'MALLEY

10123 Camarillo St
Toluca Lake, CA 91602
Telephone: (818) 762-8353, FAX:
(818) 762-6736, Web Site: www.
jonesomalley.com

CEO & Head Publicist: Jana O. Collins
Founded: 1985

Public relations & product placement
firm.

JONES & THOMAS INC

363 S Main St
Decatur, IL 62523
Telephone: (217) 423-1889, FAX:
(217) 425-0680, E-Mail: corp@
jonesthomas.com, Web Site: www.
jonesthomas.com
Pres: Bill Lehmann

Integrated marketing communications
and advertising firm.

K PUBLIC RELATIONS LLC

101 6th Ave (Floor 9)
New York, NY 10013
Telephone: (646) 756-4217, FAX:
(646) 688-3017, Web Site: www.kpr-
nyc.com
Founder & Pres: Kira Kohrherr
Founded: 2007

Full-service public relations firm.

KZSW ADVERTISING INC

19 Bennetts Rd
East Setauket, NY 11733
Telephone: (631) 348-1440, FAX:
(631) 348-1449, E-Mail: contact@
kzswadvertising.com, Web Site:
kzsadvertising.com
Owner & Creative Dir: Ken Kopf
Owner: Jack Schultheis
Founded: 1980

KEATING MAGEE

708 Phosphor Ave
Metairie, LA 70005
Telephone: (504) 299-8000, FAX:
(504) 525-6647, E-Mail: info@
keatingmagee.com, Web Site: www.
keatingmagee.com
CEO: Jennifer Keating Magee

Marketing communications company.

THE KEEHN CO

43 Cradle Rock Rd
Pound Ridge, NY 10576
Telephone: (914) 764-8591, FAX:
(914) 764-5388, E-Mail: dkeehnco@
optonline.net
Pres: Dennis Keehn

KELLEY SWOFFORD ROY
INC

50 NE 29th St
Miami, FL 33137-4413
Telephone: (305) 444-0004, Toll Free:
(800) 537-5565, FAX: (305) 444-
9057, E-Mail: info@ksrteam.com,
Web Site: www.ksrteam.com

Chairwoman & CEO: Susan Kelley
Sr Partner: William R Roy PhD

Advertising, marketing communications & public relations firm.

KELLIHER SAMETS VOLK
212 Battery St
Burlington, VT 05401
Telephone: (802) 862-8261, FAX:
  (802) 863-4724, E-Mail: info@ksvc.
  com, Web Site: www.ksvc.com
Chief Creative Officer: Linda Kelliher
Mng Dir: Yoram Samets

Independent, full-service advertising agency.

KENNEY MARKETING & ADVERTISING INC
150 S Warner Rd (Suite 250)
King of Prussia, PA 19406
Telephone: (610) 341-0430, FAX:
  (610) 341-0480, E-Mail: info@
  kenneymarketing.com, Web Site:
  www.kmaphl.com
Pres & CEO: Robert Kenney
VP: Matthew Gaskins

KERN
An Omnicom Agency
20955 Warner Center Ln
Los Angeles, CA 91367
Telephone: (818) 703-8775, FAX:
  (818) 703-8458, E-Mail: info@
  kernagency.com, Web Site:
  kernagency.com
Pres: Russell Kern
Exec Creative Dir: Nobbie Kim

Direct response marketing company.

KETCHUM
1285 Avenue of the Americas (Floor 4)
New York, NY 10019-6029
Telephone: (646) 935-3900, Web Site:
  www.ketchum.com
CEO & Pres: Rob Flaherty
CEO, North America: Barri Friedman
  Rafferty

Public relations & marketing agency.

KEYPATH EDUCATION
15500 W 113th St (Suite 200)
Lenexa, KS 66219-5106
Telephone: (913) 254-6000, Web Site:
  keypathedu.com
CEO: Steve Fireng
Group Pres: Mike McHugh
Sr VP Mktg: Lori Turec
Primary Market Served: Business
Catalog available online
Founded: 1989

Higher education marketing agency.

KILLIAN BRANDING
1113 W Armitage
Chicago, IL 60614
Telephone: (312) 836-0050, E-Mail:
  info@killianbranding.com, Web Site:
  www.killianbranding.com
Pres: Bob Killian
Founded: 1987

Branding agency.

KIRSHENBAUM BOND SENECAL & PARTNERS
160 Varick St (fl 4)
New York, NY 10013
Telephone: (212) 633-0080, FAX:
  (212) 463-8643, E-Mail: press@
  kbsp.com, Web Site: www.kbsp.com
Chmn & CEO: Lori Senecal
Global Chief Mktg Officer: Jennifer
  Hohman
Founded: 1987

Full-service, global advertising company.

KOBIE MARKETING INC
100 2nd Ave S (Suite 1000)
Saint Petersburg, FL 33701
Telephone: (727) 822-5353, Toll Free:
  (800) 821-7892, FAX: (727) 822-
  5265, E-Mail: info@kobie.com, Web
  Site: www.kobie.com
CEO: Bram Hechtkopf

Customer loyalty marketing & retention agency.

KOLLIAS & ASSOCIATES
210 N Wells St (#4108)
Chicago, IL 60606-1352
Telephone: (312) 857-7707
Pres & CEO: George Kollias

KRYL & CO INC
PO Box 498
Chicago, IL 60690
Telephone: (312) 961-0928, E-Mail:
  info@krylandco.com, Web Site:
  www.krylandco.com
Pres: Susan Kryl

Full-service marketing company.

LCH DIRECT INC
74 Boynton St
Waltham, MA 02453-2866
Telephone: (978) 664-2900, FAX:
  (978) 664-4812, E-Mail: info@
  lchdirect.com, Web Site: www.
  lchdirect.com
Pres: Bill Licata
Conducts Business: U.S.
Primary Market Served: Business
Founded: 1988

Full service, direct response marketing and digital agency.

LKH&S INC
54 W Hubbard (Suite 100)
Chicago, IL 60610
Telephone: (312) 595-0200, FAX:
  (312) 595-0300, E-Mail: lkhs@lkhs.
  com, Web Site: www.lkhs.com
Mng Dir: Stanton Lewin

LMS INC
List Management Services, Inc.
5728 Major Blvd (Suite 650)
Orlando, FL 32819-7963
Telephone: (407) 876-5544, Toll Free:
  (800) 257-5902, Web Site:
  lmsonline.com
CEO: Steve Cohen
Founded: 1995

Direct response marketing agency.

THE LACEK GROUP
Specialty agency of Ogilvy & Mather
900 Second Ave S (Suite 1800)
Minneapolis, MN 55402-1099
Telephone: (612) 359-3700, FAX:
  (612) 359-9395, E-Mail: info@lacek.
  com, Web Site: www.lacek.com
Pres: William Baker
Exec VP Client Svcs: Dan Knudsen
Exec VP & Chief Creative Officer:
  John Jarvis

Retention marketing & loyalty programs practice.

LANMARK360 INC
804 Broadway
West Long Branch, NJ 07764
Telephone: (732) 389-4500, Web Site:
  www.lanmark360.com
Pres: Howard Klein

Fully-integrated healthcare marketing agency.

LATIN-PAK
141 Chesterfield Business Pkwy
Chesterfield, MO 63005-1233
Telephone: (636) 536-5344, Toll Free:
  (800) 625-4283, FAX: (636) 536-
  9456, E-Mail: latinpak@latinpak.
  com, Web Site: www.latinpak.com
Pres & CEO: Vincent Andaloro
Founded: 1996

Hispanic digital direct marketing agency.

LAUGHLIN CONSTABLE
200 S Michigan Ave (Fl 17)
Chicago, IL 60604-2460
Telephone: (312) 422-5900, FAX:
  (312) 422-5901, Web Site: www.
  laughlin.com
Founder: Steve Laughlin
Chief Mktg Officer: Michael Baer

Primary Market Served: Business & Consumer
Founded: 1976
Creative, full-service advertising agency.

LEAPFROG ONLINE
807 Greenwood St
Evanston, IL 60201-4311
Telephone: (847) 492-1968, Web Site: www.leapfrogonline.com
CEO: Dave Husain
Pres: Scott Epskamp
Exec VP: Jason Wadler
Founded: 1995
Digital marketing company.

LEMMONTREE MARKETING GROUP
6220 E Thomas rd (Suite 303)
Scottsdale, AZ 85251
Telephone: (480) 967-1405, Toll Free: (888) 536-6243, FAX: (480) 967-1407, E-Mail: 7solutions@lemmontree.com, Web Site: www.lemmontree.com
Pres: Nicolette Lemmon
VP: Dennis Koepke
Founded: 1984
Full-service marketing agency.

THE LEVENSON GROUP
717 N Harwood (Suite 800)
Dallas, TX 75201-6501
Telephone: (214) 932-6000, E-Mail: hello@levensongroup.com, Web Site: levensongroup.com
Pres & CEO: Andy Harmon
Chief Mktg Officer: Robert McEnany
Founded: 1984
Independent, integrated advertising company.

LEVERAGE MARKETING GROUP
117 S Main St
Newtown, CT 06470-2380
Telephone: (203) 270-6699, E-Mail: info@lev-mg.com, Web Site: www.leverage-marketing.com
CEO & Gen Mgr: Tom Marks
Marketing communications & promotional marketing agency.

LEVLANE ADVERTISING
100 Penn Square E, The Wanamaker Bldg
Philadelphia, PA 19107
Telephone: (215) 825-9600, FAX: (215) 825-9601, Web Site: www.levlane.com
Full-service advertising agency.

THE LIFESTYLE MARKETING CORP
310 Gramercy Pl
Glen Rock, NJ 07452-2226
Telephone: (201) 670-7985, FAX: (201) 251-2443
Pres: Jim Kapotes
Founded: 1992

LINETT & HARRISON
219 Changebridge Rd
Montville, NJ 07045-9514
Telephone: (908) 686-0606, FAX: (908) 686-0623, E-Mail: sharrison@linettandharrison.com, Web Site: www.linettandharrison.com
Pres & COO: Sam Harrison
Full-service advertising & branding agency.

THE LINICK GROUP INC
Seven Putter Ln, Linick Bldg
Middle Island, NY 11953-1920
Telephone: (631) 924-3888, FAX: (631) 924-8555, E-Mail: andrew@linick.com, Web Site: www.andrewlinickdirectmarketing.com
Chmn & CEO: Andrew S. Linick Ph.D.
Founded: 1967
Direct response advertising & public relations agency.

LINKEDIN MARKETING SOLUTIONS
2029 Stierlin Ct
Mountain View, CA 94043
Telephone: (650) 687-3600, Web Site: business.linkedin.com/biz
VP Mktg: Nick Besbeas

LOCKARD & WECHSLER DIRECT
2 Bridge St (Suite 200)
Irvington, NY 10533
Telephone: (914) 250-0241, E-Mail: info@lwdirect.com, Web Site: www.lwdirect.com
CEO: Richard Wechsler
Pres: Asieya Pine
Founded: 1967
Full-service direct marketing agency.

LOPEZ NEGRETE COMMUNICATIONS
3336 Richmond Ave (Suite 200)
Houston, TX 77098-3022
Telephone: (713) 877-8777, FAX: (713) 877-8796, Web Site: lopeznegrete.com
Pres & CEO: Alex Lopez Negrete
Exec VP, CFO & COO: Cathy Lopez Negrete
Primary Market Served: Consumer

Founded: 1985
Full-service advertising agency.

LOREL MARKETING GROUP
235 S 17th St
Philadelphia, PA 19103
Telephone: (610) 337-2343, FAX: (610) 768-9511, E-Mail: info@lorel.com, Web Site: www.lorel.com
Pres: Sebastian Pistritto

LOREX INC
19131 Industrial Blvd (Suite 1)
Elk River, MN 55330
Telephone: (763) 441-0055, Toll Free: (800) 792-8812, E-Mail: customerservice@lorexinc.com, Web Site: www.lorexinc.com
Pres: Ken Janc
Founded: 1996
Brand management and direct marketing agency.

LOWE CAMPBELL EWALD
2000 Brush St (Ste 601)
Detroit, MI 48226
Telephone: (586) 574-3400, E-Mail: lowecampbellewald@lowe-ce.com, Web Site: www.lowecampbellewald.com
CEO: Jim Palmer
COO & CFO: Jarilyn Auger
Chief Creative Officer: Mark Simon
Pres & Chief Mktg Officer: Angela Zepeda
Full service, fully integrated advertising and marketing communications agency.

LOYALOGY
3 Chestnut Mountain Rd
Asheville, NC 28803
Telephone: (828) 333-5860, Web Site: loyalogy.com
CEO: Dennis Duffy
Conducts Business: U.S.
Primary Market Served: Business
Advertising/Marketing Budget Related to Direct Marketing: 76-100%
Founded: 2009
Loyalty marketing, data analysis and research services to consumer marketing companies.

THE LUKENS COMPANY
2800 Shirlington Rd (fl 9)
Alexandria, VA 22206
Telephone: (703) 845-8484, FAX: (703) 845-9655, Web Site: www.thelukenscompany.com
Founder & Pres: Walter G. Lukens III
Pres, The Morey Group: John Morey
COO: Bruce Stuck

LUNAR COW
344 W Turkeyfoot Lake Rd (Suite B)
Akron, OH 44319
Telephone: (330) 253-9000, Toll Free:
(800) 594-9620, FAX: (330) 253-
9001, E-Mail: info@lunarcow.com,
Web Site: www.lunarcow.com
Pres: Benjamin Harris
Sr Designer: John Cooper
Conducts Business: U.S., Canada
Direct online sales
Advertising/Marketing Budget Related
to Direct Marketing: 26-50%
Direct Marketing ad budget:
Direct Mail: 10%
Online: 30%
Telephone: 60%
Founded: 1999

Destination marketing & advertising
company.

LUNDMARK ADVERTISING + DESIGN INC
2345 Grand Blvd
Kansas City, MO 64018
Telephone: (816) 842-5236, Web Site:
lundmarkadvertising.com
Pres: Brandon Myers
Creative Dir: Kia Hunt
Design Dir: Nick Ogden
Founded: 1947

Design, brand building & marketing
agency.

LUXE COLLECTIVE GROUP
49 W 27th St (Floor 6)
New York, NY 10001-6936
Telephone: (212) 627-3300, FAX:
(212) 627-3388, E-Mail: info@
luxecg.com, Web Site: luxecg.com
CEO: Walter Coyle
Pres: Alyce Panico
Founded: 2015

Media planning and buying agency for
luxury and premium brands.

MGP DIRECT INC
PO Box 292
Clarksville, MD 21029-0292
Telephone: (410) 531-0383, FAX:
(410) 531-8142, E-Mail: roberta@
mgpdirect.com, Web Site: www.
mgpdirect.com
Pres & CEO: Roberta Rosenberg
Founded: 1987

Direct marketing consultancy.

MKE ENTERPRISES
193 Haverhill St
North Reading, MA 01864
Telephone: (978) 664-3877, FAX:
(978) 664-2835, E-Mail: e.marilyn@
mke-enterprises.com, Web Site:
www.mke-enterprises.com

Pres: Marilyn Ewer
Founded: 1982
Direct marketing agency.

MRM//MCCANN
Part of Interpublic Group
622 Third Ave
New York, NY 10017
Telephone: (646) 865-6230, E-Mail:
gbc@mrm-mccann.com, Web Site:
mrm-mccann.com
CEO: Michael McLaren
Pres: Lori Feld
Exec VP & Global Chief Growth Offi-
cer: Marcy Samet
Founded: 1982

Marketing services company specializing in digital marketing & relationship
management.

MRW COMMUNICATIONS
6 Barker Square Dr
Pembroke, MA 02359
Telephone: (781) 924-5282, FAX:
(718) 926-0371, E-Mail: jim@
mrwinc.com, Web Site: www.
mrwinc.com
Creative Dir: Tom Matzell
Dir Acct Svcs: Jim Watts
Creative Dir: Kristen Balunas

Integrated marketing communications
company.

MSI
200 E Randolph Dr (Ste 5000)
Chicago, IL 60601
Telephone: (312) 565-0044, FAX:
(312) 946-6100, E-Mail: info@
agencymsi.com, Web Site:
agencymsi.com
Exec VP Strategy & Devel: Dave Gaston

MVNP
999 Bishop St (Floor 24)
Honolulu, HI 96813
Telephone: (808) 536-0881, FAX:
(808) 529-6208, E-Mail: ideas@
mvnp.com, Web Site: www.mvnp.
com
Pres: Markus Staib
Exec Creative Dir: Vince Soliven
Founded: 1946

Integrated advertising agency.

MACLAREN MCCANN
Subs. of Interpublic Group of Companies, Inc.
10 Bay St
Toronto, ON, Canada M5J 2S3
Telephone: (416) 594-6000, FAX:
(416) 643-7026, Web Site: www.
maclaren.com
CEO: David Leonard

Pres: Jay Miles
Chief Creative Officer: Darren Clark
Founded: 1922

Multi-disciplined integrated advertising
agency.

MAIL AMERICA INC
89 Bridge St Plaza
Wheeling, WV 26003-5209
Telephone: (304) 242-8081, Toll Free:
(800) 421-2150, FAX: (304) 242-
8082, E-Mail: sales@mailamerica.
com, Web Site: www.mailamerica.
com
Pres: Richard Dlesk Sr.
Sr VP: Leo Bartsch
Founded: 1993

Direct marketing company specializing
in direct mail & email advertising, layout & design, traditional & digital
printing and bindery & mailing services.

MAJESTIC MARKETING INC
1160 California Ave
Corona, CA 92881-3324
Telephone: (951) 280-2400, Toll Free:
(800) 843-2247, FAX: (951) 280-
2410, E-Mail: sales@bagmasters.
com, Web Site: www.bagmasters.
com
Pres: Richard Whittier
Catalog available online
Founded: 1922

Marketing firm specializing in the manufacture of promotional tote bags.

MARC G GAULT CONSULTING
5380 Smoke Rise Dr (Ste B)
Stone Mountain, GA 30087-1529
Telephone: (770) 938-0781
Adv & Mktg Consultant: Marc G.
Gault

MARC USA
An Eastport Holdings company
225 W Station Square Dr (Suite 500)
Pittsburgh, PA 15219-1174
Telephone: (412) 562-2000, FAX:
(412) 562-2022, E-Mail: pittsburgh@
marcusa.com, Web Site: www.
marcusa.com
Chmn: Tony Bucci
Pres & CEO: Michele Fabrizi
Founded: 1955

Full-service integrated marketing communications firm.

MARCHESE COMMUNICATIONS INC
4652 Via Marina (#104)
Marina Del Rey, CA 90292

Toll Free: (866) 441-8086, E-Mail: david@marchesecommunications.com, Web Site: www.marchesecommunications.com
Pres: David Marchese
Employees: 5
Founded: 1986

Specializing in generating superior response-acquisition, retention, and conversion through the integration of DRTV, online marketing, and sales promotion.

MARDEN-KANE INC
195 Froehlich Farm Blvd
Woodbury, NY 11797
Telephone: (516) 365-3999, FAX: (516) 365-5250, E-Mail: expert@mardenkane.com, Web Site: www.mardenkane.com
CFO & Gen Mgr: Alan Richter
Chief Prod Officer: Martin Glovin
Sr VP: Fae Savignano
Founded: 1957

Full-service promotion marketing agency.

MARIS WEST & BAKER
18 Northtown Dr
Jackson, MS 39211
Telephone: (601) 977-9200, FAX: (601) 977-9257, Web Site: www.mwb.com
Pres: Peter Marks
CFO: Mike Booth
Founded: 1970

Full-service marketing, web design and advertising agency.

MARITZ
1375 N Highway Dr
Fenton, MO 63026
Telephone: (636) 827-4000, Web Site: www.maritz.com
Chmn & CEO: Steve Maritz
Pres: Dennis Hummel
Founded: 1894

Sales and marketing services company specializing in incentive, rewards and customer loyalty programs.

MARKE COMMUNICATIONS INC
45 W 45th St
New York, NY 10036-4602
Telephone: (212) 201-0600, Toll Free: (800) 716-2753, FAX: (212) 213-0785, Web Site: www.marke.com
Exec VP: Allen G. Rosenberg
Founded: 1979

Full-service advertising, direct response & catalog agency.

MARKET SHARE DEVELOPMENT INC
516 N Blakely St
Dunmore, PA 18512
Telephone: (570) 961-3762, FAX: (570) 941-0508, E-Mail: jmahon@market-shareinc.com, Web Site: www.market-shareinc.com
Pres: Jerry Mahon
Conducts Business: U.S.
Primary Market Served: Business & Consumer
Founded: 1986

Strategic branding and marketing firm.

MARKETABILITY INC
404 Reinerman St
Houston, TX 77007
Telephone: (713) 462-6000, FAX: (713) 481-8465, E-Mail: mickey@marketabilityinc.com, Web Site: www.marketabilityinc.com
Owner: Mickey Blake

Full-service promotions company.

THE MARKETING AGENCY LLC
2881 E Oakland Park Blvd (Suite 425)
Fort Lauderdale, FL 33306-1813
Telephone: (954) 771-1177, FAX: (866) 379-5788, E-Mail: marketing@themarketingagency.com, Web Site: www.themarketingagency.com

Sweepstakes, contests & promotions management company.

MARKETING & PROMOTIONS GROUP
55 E Ridgewood Ave (Suite A)
Ridgewood, NJ 07450
Telephone: (201) 251-8339, FAX: (201) 251-8340, E-Mail: michael@promowaves.com, Web Site: www.promowaves.com
Pres: Michael W. Gray
Founded: 1993

Marketing & promotional products company.

MARKETING GENERAL INC
625 N Washington St (Suite 450)
Alexandria, VA 22314-1938
Telephone: (703) 739-1000, Toll Free: (800) 644-6646, FAX: (703) 549-6057, E-Mail: info@marketinggeneral.com, Web Site: www.marketinggeneral.com
Pres: Rick Whelan
Sr VP & COO: Raylene Woods
Sr VP: Tony Rossell
VP: Tom Beauchamp
Primary Market Served: Business

Founded: 1978
Member marketing & association membership solutions company.

MARKETING INNOVATORS
9701 W Higgins Rd (Suite 400)
Rosemont, IL 60018-4717
Telephone: (847) 696-1111, Toll Free: (800) 543-7373, FAX: (847) 696-3194, E-Mail: info@marketinginnovators.com, Web Site: www.marketinginnovators.com
Chmn & CEO: Lois M. LeMenager
Pres: Richard A. Blabolil
Founded: 1978

Full-service people performance management and measurement company.

THE MARKETING STORE
A HAVI Group, LP company
55 W Monroe St (Suite 1400)
Chicago, IL 60603-5005
Telephone: (312) 614-1400, Web Site: www.tmsw.com
Pres: Mark Landolt
Founded: 1986

Integrated brand activation agency.

MARKETING STRATEGIES INC
4603 Oleander Dr (Suite 4)
North Myrtle Beach, SC 29577-5738
Telephone: (843) 692-9662, FAX: (843) 692-0558, E-Mail: pr@marketingstrategiesinc.com, Web Site: marketingstrategiesinc.com
Pres & CEO: Denise Blackburn-Gay
Founded: 1997

Full-service marketing & public relations firm.

MARKETING VISIONS INC
520 White Plains Rd (Suite 500)
Tarrytown, NY 10591-5118
Telephone: (914) 631-3900, FAX: (914) 693-8338, E-Mail: jsloofman@marketingvisions.com, Web Site: www.marketingvisions.com
Pres: Jay Sloofman

Strategic marketing solutions company.

MARKETPOWER DIRECT MARKETING
1449 Druid Valley Dr NE (Suite C)
Atlanta, GA 30329-2967
Telephone: (435) 565-1889, E-Mail: joelalpert123@gmail.com, Web Site: www.marketpoweronline.com
Pres: Joel Alpert
Founded: 1990

Integrated marketing consultancy.

MARKGRAF & WELLS MARKETING

2939 Toledo Ave S
Minneapolis, MN 55416-1926
Telephone: (612) 870-8550
Pres: Richard J. Markgraf

Specializing in segment isolation & description of metrics & demographics. Commercial, industrial, consumer, nonprofit & government.

MARKOTS

470 Harvest Park Dr (Suite A)
Brentwood, CA 94513
Telephone: (925) 240-0093, Toll Free: (877) 946-7253, FAX: (925) 240-0097, E-Mail: info@markots.com, Web Site: www.markots.com
CEO: Ray Gulam
Founded: 2002

Direct mail & direct-to-door advertising service company.

THE MARLIN COMPANY

10 Research Pkwy
Wallingford, CT 06492
Toll Free: (877) 890-9116, Web Site: www.themarlincompany.com
CEO & Pres: Frank Kenna III
VP Editorial: Edward LaFreniere
VP Fin: David Thibault
Dir Mktg: Jude Carter
Conducts Business: U.S., Canada
Primary Market Served: Business

Digital signage provider.

MARQUIS AWARDS & SPECIALTIES INC

108 N Bent St
Powell, WY 82435-2712
Telephone: (307) 754-2272, Toll Free: (800) 327-2446, FAX: (307) 754-9577, E-Mail: marquisawards@bresnan.net, Web Site: www.rushawards.com
Pres: John Collins
Founded: 1983

Manufacturer of high quality awards & distributor of promotional products.

THE MARTIN AGENCY

1 Shockoe Plaza
Richmond, VA 23219-4132
Telephone: (804) 698-8000, FAX: (804) 698-8001, Web Site: www.martinagency.com
Chmn: John Adams
CEO: Matt Williams
Chief Creative Officer: Joe Alexander
Pres: Beth Rilee-Kelley

Founded: 1965

Full-service agency with capabilities in advertising, strategic planning, direct response, digital, data analytics, design & branded content.

MARTIN THOMAS INTERNATIONAL

20367 Clover Field Terrace
Sterling, VA 20165
Telephone: (401) 225-3905, E-Mail: mpottle@martinthomas.com, Web Site: www.martinthomas.com
Pres: Martin K. Pottle
Founded: 1987

Business to business marketing firm helping businesses grow & prosper using cost effective modeling tools.

MARTIN WILLIAMS ADVERTISING

60 S 6th St (Suite 2800)
Minneapolis, MN 55402-4444
Telephone: (612) 342-9739, FAX: (612) 342-9700, Web Site: www.martinwilliams.com
Chmn & CFO: Tim Frojd
Mgr: Jennifer Hahs

THE MARX GROUP

2175 E Francisco Blvd (Suite F)
San Rafael, CA 94901
Telephone: (415) 453-0844, FAX: (415) 451-0166, E-Mail: info@themarxgrp.com, Web Site: www.themarxgrp.com
Chmn & Co-CEO: Tom Marx
Pres & Co-CEO: Devin Hart
VP Mktg & Creative Svcs: Kerri Petersen
Founded: 1982

Full-service business strategy & marketing communications firm.

MASON INC

23 Amity Rd
Bethany, CT 06524
Telephone: (203) 393-1101, Web Site: mason23.com
CEO: Charlie Mason
VP & Creative Dir: Richard Gamer
Founded: 1951

Brand development & integrated marketing firm.

MAXWELL + MILLER

141 E Michigan Ave (Suite 500)
Kalamazoo, MI 49007
Telephone: (269) 382-4060, FAX: (269) 382-0504, E-Mail: info@maxwellandmiller.com, Web Site: www.maxwellandmiller.com
Pres & Creative Dir: Greg Miller

Acct Dir: Lisa Hall

Branding, content marketing and advertising agency.

FRANK MAYER & ASSOCIATES INC

1975 Wisconsin Ave
Grafton, WI 53024
Telephone: (855) 294-2875, FAX: (262) 377-3449, E-Mail: info@frankmayer.com, Web Site: www.frankmayer.com
Pres: Mike Mayer
Founded: 1931

Branded in-store merchandising & point-of-purchase design & production company.

PETER A MAYER ADVERTISING INC

318 Camp St
New Orleans, LA 70130-2804
Telephone: (504) 581-7191, FAX: (504) 581-3009, E-Mail: contact@petermayer.com, Web Site: www.peteramayer.com
Pres: Mark Mayer
Chief Creative Officer: Josh Mayer
Chief Strategy Officer: Michelle Edelman
Founded: 1967

Full-service advertising, marketing & public relations agency.

MCCABE DUVAL + ASSOCIATES

Box 76, 14 Main St (Suite 203B)
Portland, ME 04011
Telephone: (207) 347-8614, FAX: (207) 773-7245, E-Mail: cduval@mccabe-duval.com, Web Site: www.mccabe-duval.com
Pres: Christopher Duval
Founded: 1988

Full-service marketing, advertising & design firm.

MCCARTHY & KING MARKETING INC

8 Esther Dr
Milford, MA 01757-1057
Telephone: (508) 473-8643, FAX: (508) 473-7294, E-Mail: bob@mccarthyandking.com, Web Site: www.mccarthyandking.com
Pres: Robert McCarthy
Founded: 1990

Marketing firm specializing in lead generation, direct marketing & creative communications.

MEADOWS DESIGN OFFICE INC

3800 Yuma St NW
Washington, DC 20016
Telephone: (202) 966-6007, FAX:
 (202) 966-6733, E-Mail:
 postmaster@mdomedia.com, Web
 Site: www.mdomedia.com
Creative Dir: Marc Meadows
Founded: 1981

Graphic design firm specializing in
books & print media.

MEDIA CONSULTANTS

Div. of Digital Dimensions3 Inc
205B Chubb Ave (Fl 2)
Lyndhurst, NJ 07071
Telephone: (201) 933-2015, FAX:
 (201) 933-6314, E-Mail: info@
 mediaconsultants.net, Web Site:
 mediaconsultants.net
Pres: Harvey Hirsch

Full-service direct marketing agency.

THE MEDIA CREW

12597 Walsingham Rd (Suite 2)
Largo, FL 33774
Telephone: (813) 551-0902, E-Mail:
 marketing@themediacrew.com, Web
 Site: www.themediacrew.com
Pres/Gen Mgr: Nick Foley
Founded: 1999

Full-service, performance based marketing agency specializing in online advertising.

MEDIA DIRECTIONS CREATIVE GROUP

250 Parkway Dr (Suite 350)
Lincolnshire, IL 60069
Telephone: (847) 948-0099, E-Mail:
 info@mdcreativegroup.com, Web
 Site: www.mdcreativegroup.com
Pres: Marv Kogan
VP: Lindsay Kogan
Creative Dir: Joel Wolter
Conducts Business: U.S.
Primary Market Served: Business &
 Consumer

Full-service creative agency.

MEDIA RESPONSE INC

2450 Hollywood Blvd (Suite 200B)
Hollywood, FL 33020
Telephone: (954) 967-9899, E-Mail:
 info@media-response.com, Web
 Site: www.media-response.com
Pres: Ellis Kahn
Founded: 1989

Direct response advertising agency.

MEDIACONCEPTS CORP

25 N Main St

Assonet, MA 02702-1136
Telephone: (508) 644-3131, FAX:
 (508) 644-5201, E-Mail: at3@
 mediaconceptscorp.com, Web Site:
 www.mediaconceptscorp.com
Owner & Pres: Paul Beaulieu
Founded: 1968

Full-service marketing communications
firm specializing in corporate & product branding.

MEDIAGRAPHICS

Subs. of Dev. Kinney/MediaGraphics
PO Box 162
Eau Claire, WI 54702-0162
Telephone: (751) 590-4488, Toll Free:
 (866) 324-1658, E-Mail:
 mediagraphics@devkinney.com,
 Web Site: www.devkinney.com
Owner & CEO: J.D. Kinney
Founded: 1973

Direct response marketing agency.

MELTZERMEDIA PRODUCTIONS

49 Nassau St
New York, NY 10038
Telephone: (212) 868-4600, E-Mail:
 contact@meltzermedia.com, Web
 Site: www.meltzermedia.com
Pres: Jeff Meltzer
Founded: 1985

Fully integrated multi-media marketing
company.

MERRELL REMINGTON & ASSOCIATES

1050 East 3300 South (Suite 204)
Salt Lake City, UT 84106
Telephone: (801) 975-0109, FAX:
 (801) 975-0107, E-Mail: kent@
 mrdirect.com, Web Site: www.
 merrellremington.com
CEO: A. Kent Merrell
Founded: 1992

Direct response marketing & advertising firm.

MEYOCKS

6800 Lake Dr (Suite 150)
West Des Moines, IA 50266
Telephone: (515) 225-1200, FAX:
 (515) 225-6400, E-Mail:
 meanmore@meyocks.com, Web
 Site: www.meyocks.com
Pres: Doug Jeske
Founded: 1984

Full-service advertising agency focused
on food, agriculture health & mentor
brands.

MIAMI VALLEY MARKETING GROUP INC

1500 Devereux Dr
Dayton, OH 45419
Telephone: (937) 299-1825, FAX:
 (937) 299-9967, E-Mail:
 tomnorwalk@aol.com
Pres: Thomas S. Norwalk
Founded: 1981

Web design, development & marketing
services provider.

THE MILLER GROUP

Marketing and Digital Advertising
 Agency
1516 S Bundy (Suite 200)
Los Angeles, CA 90025
Telephone: (310) 442-0101, FAX:
 (310) 442-0107, E-Mail: info@
 millergroupmarketing.com, Web
 Site: www.millergroupmarketing.
 com
Pres & Exec Creative Dir: Renee Mill-
 er
Founded: 1990

Digital marketing & advertising company specializing in new product
launches and brand revitalization.

MILWAUKEE DIRECT MARKETING INC

675 N Barker Rd (Suite 130)
Brookfield, WI 53045
Telephone: (262) 789-2240, FAX:
 (262) 789-2250, E-Mail: info@
 milwaukeedirect.com, Web Site:
 milwaukeedirect.com
Pres: Ron Davis

Direct response fundraising for rescue
missions & nonprofits.

MITHUN AGENCY

510 Marquette Ave
Minneapolis, MN 55402
Telephone: (612) 347-1000, FAX:
 (612) 347-1515, Web Site: www.
 everythingtalks.com
CEO: Rob Buchner
Chief Creative Officer: David Carter
Dir Acct Leadership & Growth: Denis
 Budniewski
Dir HR: Debbie Fischer
Employees: 700
Founded: 1933

Mithun is a full-service national advertising & marketing communications
agency.

MODCO MEDIA

102 Madison Ave (fl 10)
New York, NY 10016

Telephone: (212) 686-0006, FAX: (212) 686-6991, Web Site: modcomedia.com
CEO: Erik Dochtermann
Pres: Eileidh Bamford

Strategy, research, media & analytics company.

MODDERN MARKETING
8 E 36th St (fl 5)
New York, NY 10016
Telephone: (212) 334-9800, E-Mail: mark@moddern.com, Web Site: www.moddern.com
Partner Mngmt: Mark Kolier
Partner Media: David Adelman
Partner Creative: Nader Ashway
Conducts Business: U.S., Canada
Primary Market Served: Business

MONARCH DIRECT RESPONSE
14724 Ventura Blvd (Suite 1200)
Sherman Oaks, CA 91403-3512
Telephone: (818) 817-8000, Web Site: www.monarchdr.com
Pres: Eitan Cohen
Founded: 2007

Full-service direct-response marketing firm.

MONSTER MAGNET
7725 National Turnpike (Unit 100)
Louisville, KY 40214-4813
Toll Free: (866) 259-6554, E-Mail: joe@monstermagnet.com, Web Site: www.monstermagnet.com
Pres & CEO: Joe Martin

Manufacturer of magnetic, direct mail marketing products.

MORE MEDIA DIRECT INC
4519 Admiralty Way
Marina Del Rey, CA 90292
Telephone: (310) 577-2025, E-Mail: info@moremediadirect.com, Web Site: www.moremediadirect.com
Pres & CEO: Mickey Silverman
Sr VP Mktg & Bus Devel: Richard Sangerman
Founded: 1997

Full-service media, product placement, retail innovation & public relations company.

MORTON ADVERTISING INC
875 Avenue of the Americas (Suite 1111)
New York, NY 10001
Telephone: (212) 465-2250, FAX: (212) 465-1575, E-Mail: info@mortonad.com, Web Site: www.mortonad.com

Pres: Donald Reisfeld
Founded: 1961

Full-service advertising agency.

MOXIE
Owned by Zenith Optimedia, part of Publicis Groupe
384 Northyards Blvd NW (Ste 300)
Atlanta, GA 30313
Telephone: (678) 916-4500, E-Mail: info@moxieusa.com, Web Site: moxieusa.com
CEO: Suzy Deering
Chief Tech Officer: Matt Fleischman
Chief Creative Officer: Anthony Reeves
CFO: Chris Walker
COO: Solange Claudio

MULLEN & MCCAFFREY COMMUNICATIONS
197 Hog Creek Rd
East Hampton, NY 11937-4307
Telephone: (631) 324-4265, FAX: (631) 324-2135, E-Mail: mullenmccaffrey@aol.com, Web Site: www.mullenandmccaffrey.com
Partner: Mary Ann McCaffrey
Partner: John J. Mullen
Founded: 1984

Full-service advertising & communications company.

MULLENLOWE US
RP-NFOA
40 Broad St
Boston, MA 02109
Telephone: (617) 226-9000, FAX: (617) 226-9100, Web Site: us.mullenlowe.com
CEO: Lee Newman
Chief Creative Officer: Mark Wenneker
Pres: Kristen Cavallo

Integrated marketing communications agency.

THE MX GROUP
7020 High Grove Blvd
Burr Ridge, IL 60527-7595
Telephone: (800) 827-0170, FAX: (630) 654-0302, Web Site: www.themxgroup.com
Co-Founder & CEO: Andy Mahler
Co-Founder & Principal: Pete Wroblewski
Founded: 2013

Digital & demand generation company.

MYERS, MYERS & ADAMS ADVERTISING LLC
1616 NE 5th Ct
Fort Lauderdale, FL 33301-1330

Telephone: (954) 523-6262, FAX: (954) 523-3517, E-Mail: pete@mmanda.com, Web Site: www.mmanda.com
Pres: Peter Myers
Founded: 1986

Full-service advertising, marketing & public relations agency.

MYPOINTS.COM INC
Subs. of United Online, Inc.
44 Montgomery St (Suite 250)
San Francisco, CA 94104
Telephone: (415) 856-0877, FAX: (415) 615-1122, E-Mail: memberservices@mypoints.com, Web Site: www.mypoints.com
Pres: Sha Fakiri
Founded: 1996

Direct marketing company specializing in customer retention & rewards programs.

NYK RAPP ENTERPRISES LLC
215 N Federal Hwy
Hallandale, FL 33009
Telephone: (954) 457-9100, FAX: (954) 457-9015, Web Site: nykrapp.com
CEO: Arie Kaduri
Pres: Howard Rapp
VP: Alison Chaplin
VP: Arnold Graham
Founded: 2007

Entertainment management company.

NELSON SCHMIDT INC
600 E Wisconsin Ave
Milwaukee, WI 53202
Telephone: (414) 224-0210, FAX: (414) 224-9463, Web Site: nelsonschmidt.com
Pres & CEO: Daniel H. Nelson Jr
Chief Mktg Officer: Christopher Vitrano
COO: Cody Pearce
Founded: 1971

Full-service marketing & communications agency specializing in considered purchases.

NEO@OGILVY
Div. of Ogilvy & Mather
636 11th Ave
New York, NY 10036
Telephone: (212) 259-5200, Web Site: www.neoogilvy.com
CEO Worldwide: Nasreen Madhany
CEO North America: Sean Muzzy
COO North America: Bradley Rogers
Global Mng Dir: Patty Sachs

Digital, direct response and search marketing media division.

NEW DAY MARKETING LTD
923 Olive St (Suite 2)
Santa Barbara, CA 93101-1447
Telephone: (805) 965-7833, FAX:
(805) 965-1284, E-Mail: robert@
ndm.tv, Web Site: www.
newdaymarketing.com
Pres: Robert Hunt
VP: Jeff Thomson
Founded: 1987

Direct response agency focused on
long form media buying & management experience.

NEW VILLAGE MEDIA INC
10320 Little Patuxent Pkwy (Suite 200)
Columbia, MD 21044
Telephone: (443) 832-4007, E-Mail:
jskillington@newvillagemedia.com,
Web Site: www.newvillagemedia.
com
Pres & CEO: James Skillington
Founded: 1999

Full-service online marketing agency.

NEXUS DIRECT
101 W Main St (Suite 400)
Norfolk, VA 23510
Telephone: (757) 340-5960, Toll Free:
(800) 965-0577, FAX: (757) 340-
5980, E-Mail: hello@nexusdirect.
com, Web Site: www.nexusdirect.
com
CEO: Suzanne Cole Nowers
Primary Market Served: Business &
Consumer
Founded: 2004

Full-service direct response marketing
company.

NFUSION GROUP LLC
6500 River Place Blvd (Bldg 2, Suite
201
Austin, TX 78730
Telephone: (512) 716-7000, FAX:
(512) 716-7001, E-Mail: info@
nfusion.com, Web Site: nfusion.com
CEO: John Ellett
Mng Dir: Matt Huser
Conducts Business: U.S., Canada,
Worldwide
Primary Market Served: Business &
Consumer
Advertising/Marketing Budget Related
to Direct Marketing: 26-50%
Direct Marketing ad budget:
$4,734,000
Direct Mail: 36%
Magazines: 64%
Founded: 2001

A results-oriented integrated marketing
agency that applies a unique methodology to developing strategy-driven pro-

grams, executed with insightful
creative & supported by the most effective marketing technologies.

NIXLE LLC
Div. of Everbridge, Inc.
594 Howard St (Suite 200)
San Francisco, CA 94105
Toll Free: (877) 649-5362, E-Mail:
support@nixle.com, Web Site: www.
nixle.com
CEO: Eric Liu
Primary Market Served: Business &
Consumer
Founded: 2007

Open communications company connecting public safety agencies, municipalities, schools, businesses and the
communities they serve.

**NOBLE COMMUNICATIONS
CO**
2215 W Chesterfield Blvd
Springfield, MO 65807
Telephone: (417) 875-5015, Web Site:
www.noble.net
Founder & Chmn: Bob Noble
CEO: Keith Acuff
Pres & COO: David Nehmer
Founded: 1969

Full-service advertising agency specializing in the food, shelter & service industries.

NORTHLICH
720 E Pete Rose Way
Cincinnati, OH 45202-3579
Telephone: (513) 762-1717, FAX:
(513) 421-8840, E-Mail: northlich@
northlich.com, Web Site: www.
northlich.com
Owner & CEO: Kathy Selker
Founded: 1949

Full-service strategic communications
agency.

NOSTRUM INC
401 E Ocean Blvd (Suite M101)
Long Beach, CA 90802-8900
Telephone: (562) 437-2200, Web Site:
www.nostruminc.com
Pres & CEO: Susan Collida
Acct Svcs Dir: Abby Holpp
Creative Dir: Susan Chew
Conducts Business: U.S.
Primary Market Served: Business &
Consumer
Direct online sales
Founded: 1980

Full-service advertising agency specializing in customizable web to print direct mail products.

**NOVA COMMUNICATIONS
INC**
27 S 1st St
Geneva, IL 60134-2243
Telephone: (630) 377-1889, Toll Free:
(800) 816-6682, FAX: (630) 377-
1899, E-Mail: jim@novacominc.
com, Web Site: www.novacominc.
com
Pres: James P. Emma
Founded: 1981

Service oriented voice/data company.

NOVA DM AGENCY INC
633 E Drinker St
Dunmore, PA 18512-2505
Telephone: (570) 342-8668, FAX:
(570) 342-8666, E-Mail: info@
novadmagency.com, Web Site:
www.novadmagency.com
VP: John McNeff
Primary Market Served: Business &
Consumer
Founded: 1993

Direct response advertising agency focused on the delivery of creative marketing solutions in both print & online
media.

**NOVA MARKETING
SERVICES**
1 Darling Dr
Avon, CT 06001
Toll Free: (800) 879-0288, Web Site:
www.nova-marketing.com
Mng Partner: Jeff Grindrod
VP Mktg & Commun: Liz Benyon

Beverage alcohol trade marketing &
communications agency.

THE NULMAN GROUP
18 Commerce St
Flemington, NJ 08822
Telephone: (908) 751-5299, Toll Free:
(888) 440-3367, FAX: (908) 751-
5621, E-Mail: info@nulmangroup.
com, Web Site: www.nulmangroup.
com
CEO & Creative Dir: Philip R. Nulman
Gen Mgr: Claire L. Curry

Marketing strategies and communications programs company.

O2 AGENCY INC
149 Madison Ave (Floor 6)
New York, NY 10016
Telephone: (212) 675-7334, E-Mail:
newbiz@o2agency.com, Web Site:
o2agency.strikingly.com
Mng Member: James Heathman
VP Media: Anthony Whetzel
Conducts Business: U.S.

Primary Market Served: Business & Consumer
Founded: 2000

Digital & print creative agency specializing in advertising, promotions, branding and direct response.

O2KL ADVERTISING

3 W 18th St (Floor 4)
New York, NY 10011-4662
Telephone: (646) 839-6236, E-Mail: towens@o2kl.com, Web Site: www. o2k1.com
Pres: Tracey Owens
Founded: 2004

Boutique full-service advertising agency.

OTM PARTNERS

5852 N Washington Blvd (Suite 6)
Arlington, VA 22205-2925
Toll Free: (800) 759-2244, Web Site: otmpartners.com
Pres: Read deButts
COO: Doug Anderson
Chief Mktg Officer: Regan Lamb
Founded: 1995

Branded communications development & management company focused on corporate social responsibility.

ODELL, SIMMS & LYNCH INC

1593 Spring Hill Rd (Suite 450)
Tysons Corner, VA 22182
Telephone: (703) 903-9797, FAX: (703) 903-8850, Web Site: odellsimms.com
Pres & CEO: John M. Simms
Pres Direct Mktg Division: George Waldmann
Founded: 1974

Marketing & communications programs company focused on fundraising & sponsorship, direct marketing and economic development.

ODEN

119 S Main St (Suite 300)
Memphis, TN 38103-3677
Telephone: (901) 578-8055, Toll Free: (800) 371-6233, FAX: (901) 578-1911, Web Site: www.oden.com
Principal/CEO: Bill Carkeet
Principal/COO: Bret Terwilleger
Principal/Exec VP: Tina Lazarini Niclosi
Founded: 1971

Marketing communications firm specializing in B2B strategy, content development, design & technology.

ODENZA MARKETING GROUP INC

4664 Lougheed Hwy
Burnaby, BC, Canada V5C 5T5
Toll Free: (800) 515-5371, Web Site: www.odenza.com
VP & Dir Mktg: Pav Sangha
Primary Market Served: Business & Consumer
Founded: 1998

Travel incentives, marketing solutions and digital marketing company.

OGILVYONE WORLDWIDE

Div of Ogilvy & Mather
636 11th Ave
New York, NY 10036
Telephone: (212) 237-4000, Web Site: www.ogilvy.com
Chmn & CEO: Brian Fetherstonhaugh
Pres & COO: Gunther Schumacher

Leading customer engagement agency.

THE OHLMANN GROUP

1605 N Main St
Dayton, OH 45405-4141
Telephone: (937) 278-0681, FAX: (937) 277-1723, E-Mail: info@ohlmanngroup.com, Web Site: ohlmanngroup.com
CEO & Media Dir: Linda Kahn
Pres: David E. Bowman
Founded: 1949

Full-service marketing solutions firm.

OLIVER RUSSELL & ASSOCIATES

217 S 11th St
Boise, ID 83702-6902
Telephone: (208) 344-1734, E-Mail: info@oliverrussell.com, Web Site: www.oliverrussell.com
Pres & Founder: Russ Stoddard
Creative Dir: David Cook
Conducts Business: U.S.
Primary Market Served: Business & Consumer
Founded: 1991

Direct & engagement marketing agency.

OMNI DIRECT INC

10800 Biscayne Blvd (Suite 510)
Miami, FL 33161
Toll Free: (800) 459-4034, Web Site: www.omnidirect.tv
Pres: Alex Agurcia
COO: Denira Borrero
Founded: 1999

Direct response marketing agency targeting the Hispanic market.

OMNICOM MEDIA GROUP

Div. of Omnicom Group Inc.
195 Broadway (Floor 28)
New York, NY 10007-3100
Telephone: (212) 590-7020, E-Mail: info@omnicommediagroup.com, Web Site: www. omnicommediagroup.com
Chmn & CEO: Daryl Simms
CEO North America: Page Thompson

Media services division of global advertising, marketing and corporate communications company Omnicom Group.

ONE ON ONE ADVERTISING INC

584 Middletown Ave
New Haven, CT 06513-1011
Telephone: (203) 562-6259, (203) 671-2339, E-Mail: snevard@comcast.net, Web Site: snevard.wix.com/portfolio
Pres: Stephen Nevard
Founded: 1989

Direct response & consumer advertising consultancy.

1TO1 MEDIA

c/o Peppers & Rogers Group, 20 Glover Ave, Norwalk, CT 06850-1202
Div. of Peppers & Rogers Group
1111 Summer St (Floor 5)
Stamford, CT 06905-5511
Telephone: (203) 989-2200, Web Site: www.1to1media.com
Editor-in-Chief: Mila D'Antonio
Grp Publr: Michael Dandrea
Sr Mktg Mgr: Vanessa Saulsberry
Founded: 1993

Customer experience content production company.

ONEUPWEB

1371 Gray Dr (Suite 100)
Traverse City, MI 49684
Telephone: (231) 922-9977, Toll Free: (877) 568-7477, E-Mail: info@oneupweb.com, Web Site: www. oneupweb.com
CEO: Fernando Meza
Founded: 1996

Full-service digital marketing agency specializing in education, healthcare, specialty e-commerce & franchise businesses.

O'ROURKE HOSPITALITY MARKETING LLC

7 Prince Pl
Newburyport, MA 01950-2644
Telephone: (978) 465-5955, E-Mail: hello@orourkehospitality.com, Web Site: www.orourkehospitality.com

Pres & CEO: Tom O'Rourke
CCO & Exec Creative Dir: Susan O'Rourke
Founded: 2001

Hotel marketing firm specializing in Internet marketing strategies, website design & optimization and hotel print design.

PII
Progressive Impressions International
1 Hardman Dr
Bloomington, IL 61701-6934
Telephone: (800) 664-0444, FAX: (309) 662-2055, E-Mail: sales@whateverittakes.com, Web Site: www.whateverittakes.com
Pres: Jamie Huff
VP Sls & Mktg: Ron Drenning
Founded: 1993

Full-service direct marketing service provider for companies in insurance, financial services, healthcare & education.

PRM MEDIA GROUP
105 Mountain Ct
Hackettstown, NJ 07840-2300
Telephone: (973) 765-9600, Toll Free: (877) 588-9552, FAX: (973) 765-0004, E-Mail: paul.morgan@prmmediagroup.com, Web Site: www.prmmediagroup.com
Pres: Paul Morgan

Yellow Pages, Internet & direct mail services management company.

PADULO INTEGRATED
One St Clair Ave W, Padulo Bldg
Toronto, ON, Canada M4V 1K7
Telephone: (416) 966-4000, Toll Free: (800) 454-5321, FAX: (416) 966-4012, E-Mail: info@padulo.ca, Web Site: www.padulo.ca
Chmn & CEO: Richard Padulo
CFO: Kamel Mikhael
VP & Creative Dir/Strategist: Chris Stavenjord
Founded: 1985

Multi medium retail communications company.

PANZANO + PARTNERS LLC
304 Harper Dr (Ste 2251)
Moorestown, NJ 08057
Telephone: (856) 866-5500, E-Mail: info@p2site.com, Web Site: panzanoandpartners.com
Pres: Michael Panzano
CEO: Joan Massaro
Conducts Business: Worldwide
Primary Market Served: Consumer

Founded: 1972

Brand advertising & marketing company utilizing traditional & social media, digital executions and guerrilla marketing.

PAPPAS MACDONNELL INC
135 Rennell Dr
Southport, CT 06890-1450
Telephone: (203) 254-1944, FAX: (203) 256-8232, E-Mail: info@pappasmacdonnell.com, Web Site: www.pappasmacdonnell.com
Principal: Kyle MacDonnell
Founded: 1977

Marketing and communications agency specializing in the financial services, insurance, healthcare and business services industries.

PARADIGM PROMOTIONS LLC
561 34th Ave
San Francisco, CA 94121-2705
Telephone: (415) 387-2158, FAX: (415) 387-2185, E-Mail: brian@brianharris.com, Web Site: www.paradigmpromotions.com
Mng Dir: Brian Harris
Founded: 2008

Full-service promotional products company.

PARISE MARKETING GROUP
5 Schuman Rd
Millwood, NY 10546
Telephone: (914) 941-7467, FAX: (914) 941-7931, Web Site: www.parise.com
Principal: Chip Williams
Principal: Adele Santomassimo
Founded: 1993

Diversified, full-service marketing & creative firm.

PARMELEE ASSOCIATES
PO Box 5557
Arlington, VA 22205-0057
Telephone: (703) 502-0161, E-Mail: jtparmlee@aol.com
Pres: James Parmelee

PASADENA ADVERTISING MARKETING & DESIGN
117 E Colorado Blvd (Suite 165)
Pasadena, CA 91105
Telephone: (626) 584-0011, FAX: (626) 584-0907, Web Site: www.pasadenaadv.com
Pres & CEO: Suzanne Marks
Sr Creative, Mktg & Adv Strategist: Tony Nino

Founded: 1986

Design, marketing & advertising company.

PERISCOPE INC
921 Washington Ave S
Minneapolis, MN 55415-1257
Telephone: (612) 339-0500, FAX: (612) 339-0600, E-Mail: info@periscope.com, Web Site: www.periscope.com
Chmn: Bill Simpson
Pres & CEO: Elizabeth Ross
Chief Creative Officer: Peter Nicholson
Founded: 1994

Independent, full-service marketing services agency.

PILOT INTERACTIVE INC
555 Richmond St W
Toronto, ON, Canada M5V 3B1
Telephone: (416) 840-6438, E-Mail: hello@pilotinteractive.ca, Web Site: pilotinteractive.ca
Co-founder & Dir: David Di Biase
Founded: 2009

Interactive design & branding agency.

PINNACLE DIRECT MARKETING LLC
175 S 3rd St (Suite 200)
Columbus, OH 43215
Telephone: (800) 716-0173, FAX: (888) 754-4511, Web Site: www.pinnacledirectonline.com
Pres & CEO: Craig Childs
Founded: 2003

Full-service direct response marketing agency.

PLUSMEDIA LLC
100 Mill Plain Rd (Floor 4)
Danbury, CT 06811-5189
Telephone: (203) 748-6500, FAX: (203) 748-6600, E-Mail: contact@plusme.com, Web Site: www.plusme.com
Pres: Sherry Scapperotti
Pres Digital: Paul Thau
CFO: Elise Nathan
Conducts Business: U.S., Canada
Primary Market Served: Business
Indirect online sales
Founded: 1998

Full-service media agency specializing in multi-channel direct response marketing and list & media management.

PLUZYNSKI & ASSOCIATES INC
4800 Baseline Rd E104-276
Boulder, CO 80303

Telephone: (646) 434-8785, E-Mail: info@pluzynski.com, Web Site: www.pluzynski.com
Pres: Scott Pluzynski

Full-service catalog creative and marketing agency.

POINT TO POINT MARKETING INC
4420 Eagle Lake Dr
Fort Collins, CO 80524-9671
Telephone: (513) 231-0344, E-Mail: info@ptpmarketing.com, Web Site: ptpmarketing.com
Pres & Owner: Tim Bronsil
COO: Mark Heiden
Founded: 1998

Full-service, marketing strategies agency.

POP LABS INC
7324 Southwest Freeway (Suite 1810)
Houston, TX 77074
Telephone: (877) 500-1399, FAX: (877) 850-2420, Web Site: www.poplabs.com
Pres: Gene McCubbin
Primary Market Served: Business & Consumer
Founded: 2001

Full-service interactive marketing agency.

POWER DIRECT
23456 Madero (Suite 105)
Mission Viejo, CA 92691
Telephone: (877) 737-8977, FAX: (949) 253-3458, E-Mail: info@powerdirect.net, Web Site: www.powerdirect.net
COO & Partner: Ann Marie Griffith
VP Bus Devel & Partner: Ed Dryden
VP Bus Devel & Partner: Scott Grier
Partner: Tom Ling
Founded: 2002

Front-door media, door hanger & marketing services company.

PRACTICE BUILDERS
1 Technology Dr (Bldg I, Suite 829)
Irvine, CA 92618-5320
Telephone: (800) 679-1262, FAX: (714) 751-7801, E-Mail: info@practicebuilders.com, Web Site: www.practicebuilders.com
CEO: Parham Javaherian
VP Client Svcs: Nina Grant
Sr Dir Creative Svcs: Howard Edgar
Founded: 1979

Private healthcare practice marketing company.

PRECISION ARTS ADVERTISING INC
57 Fitchburg Rd
Ashburnham, MA 01430-1409
Telephone: (978) 855-7648, E-Mail: info@precisionarts.com, Web Site: www.precisionarts.com
Pres & Owner: Terri Adams
Founded: 1985

Provides professional advertising services to small businesses, industrial manufacturers & distributors.

PRECISION DIALOGUE MARKETING LLC
5501 W Grand Ave
Chicago, IL 60639
Telephone: (440) 471-6001, Web Site: www.precisiondialogue.com
Pres & CEO: Tom Ragen
Founded: 2009

Analytical, multi-channel customer engagement firm.

PREMIER WORLD MARKETING LLC
3191 Coral Way (PH 202)
Miami, FL 33145
Telephone: (305) 445-1077, FAX: (305) 445-1075, Web Site: pwmktg.com
VP Sls & Mktg: Rienk de Jong
Primary Market Served: Business & Consumer

Innovative, full-service sales & marketing agency specializing in the hospitality industry.

PRESENTATION PACKAGING
A Liberty Diversified International Co.
870 Louisiana Ave S
Minneapolis, MN 55426
Telephone: (763) 540-9544, Toll Free: (800) 818-2698, FAX: (763) 540-9522, E-Mail: customerservice@presentationpackaging.com, Web Site: www.presentationpackaging.com
Chmn & CEO: Mike Fiterman
Pres & COO: Mark S. Schumacher

Full-service packaging agency.

PRICE WEBER MARKETING COMMUNICATIONS INC
10701 Shelbyville Rd
Louisville, KY 40243-1241
Telephone: (502) 499-9220, FAX: (502) 491-5593, E-Mail: info@priceweber.com, Web Site: www.priceweber.com
CEO: Fred Davis

Pres & Chief Creative Officer: Tony Beard
Chief Mktg Officer: Mike Nickerson
Founded: 1968

Independent digital and full-service creative agency.

PRINCETON MARKETECH
2 Alice Rd
Princeton Junction, NJ 08550-3027
Telephone: (609) 936-0021, FAX: (609) 936-0015, E-Mail: bzyontz@princetonmarketech.com, Web Site: www.princetonmarketech.com
Pres: Robert Zyontz
Founded: 1987

Creative marketing consultancy that specializes in business-to-business and financial services marketing.

PRINCETON PARTNERS INC
205 Rockingham Row
Princeton, NJ 08540-5759
Telephone: (609) 452-8500, FAX: (609) 452-7212, E-Mail: moreinfo@princetonpartners.com, Web Site: www.princetonpartners.com
CEO: Thomas Sullivan
Pres: Jeff Chesebro
Creative Dir: Paul Federico
Founded: 1965

Integrated brand marketing agency.

PRO MEDIA MARKETING GROUP
W127N8690 Westbrook Crossing
Menomonee Falls, WI 53051-3342
Telephone: (800) 328-0439, FAX: (262) 532-4147, E-Mail: sales@promediaus.com, Web Site: www.promediaus.com
Principal: Rick Stolowski
Gen Mgr: Christine Plewa
Founded: 1984

Full-service promotional products and incentive company.

PROGRESSIVE DIRECT MARKETING
3242 Union Rd, Buffalo, NY 14227-1044-POST
5800 Transit Rd
Depew, NY 14043-2820
Telephone: (716) 681-6848, Toll Free: (800) 344-7593, FAX: (716) 681-9173, E-Mail: info@pdmny.com, Web Site: www.pdmny.com
Pres & Owner: Tommaso Occhiuto
Founded: 1979

Full-service, single-source direct mail agency.

PROLOGIC RETAIL SERVICES

1625 S Congress Ave (Suite 301)
Delray Beach, FL 33445-6304
E-Mail: info@prologicretail.com, Web
  Site: www.prologicretail.com
Pres & CEO: Ross Ely
Sr VP Sls & Mktg: Guy Keller
Sr VP Opers: Al Smith
VP Fin: Estela Santiago
Founded: 2012

Loyalty and customer relationship marketing services provider for the grocery industry.

PROMOWRITING

13 Frenchtown Rd
Trumbull, CT 06611-4729
Telephone: (203) 371-0654, E-Mail:
  shira@promowriting.com, Web Site:
  promowriting.com
Copywriter & Creative Consultant:
  Shira Linden
Founded: 1990

Direct mail copywriting consultancy.

PROPCO INCENTIVES

8750 W Bryn Mawr Ave (Suite 1020)
Chicago, IL 60631
Telephone: (773) 463-9193, FAX:
  (773) 463-6673, E-Mail: sales@
  propco.com, Web Site: www.propco.
  com
Owner, Pres: Dennis Propp
Founded: 1980

Loyalty and incentive programs company.

PUBLICIS WORLDWIDE NORTH AMERICA

3500 Maple Ave #Fl4, Dallas, TX
  75219-3931
Div. of Publicis Groupe
950 Avenue of the Americas
New York, NY 10001
Telephone: (212) 279-5550, E-Mail:
  andrew.bruce@publicisna.com, Web
  Site: publicisna.com
Chmn: Susan Gianinno
CEO: Andrew Bruce
Chief Digital Officer: Dawn Winchester
Chief Talent Officer: Patty Enright
CFO: Kevin Sweeney
Chief Creative Officer: Andy Bird
COO: Nathalie Fagnan
Founded: 1926

Full-service advertising agency.

PUBLICITY INC

39 S Main St
Mansfield, MA 02048-2527
Telephone: (617) 367-3555, FAX:
  (617) 367-3557
Chmn & CEO: Al Longo

PULSECX

211B Progress Dr
Montgomeryville, PA 18936-9618
Telephone: (215) 699-9200, FAX:
  (215) 699-9240, Web Site: www.
  pulsecx.com
CEO: Jay Bolling
Pres: David Zaritsky
Founded: 1981

Healthcare marketing agency specializing in optimizing the customer experience for pharmaceutical brands, medical devices, and OTC products.

PUROHIT NAVIGATION INC

111 S Wacker Dr (Ste 4700)
Chicago, IL 60606-4309
Telephone: (312) 341-8100, FAX:
  (312) 341-8119, E-Mail: purohit@
  purohitnavigation.com, Web Site:
  www.purohitnavigation.com
Pres & CEO: Ahnal Purohit
Exec VP Strategic Devel: Anshal Purohit
Exec VP Creative: Monica Noce Kanarek
Founded: 1985

QUANTUM GROUP

6511 Oakton St
Morton Grove, IL 60053-2728
Telephone: (847) 967-3600, FAX:
  (847) 967-3610, Web Site: www.
  quantumgroup.com
CEO: Bill White
Exec VP Sales: Betsy Davis
Founded: 1992

Marketing & printing services company.

QUATTRO DIRECT LLC

200 Berwyn Park (Suite 310)
Berwyn, PA 19312
Telephone: (610) 993-0070, Web Site:
  www.quattrodirect.com
Mng Dir & Partner: Dan Boerger
Mng Dir & Partner: Scott Cohen
Mng Dir & Partner: Tom McNamara
Mng Dir & Partner: Tom Pitcherella
Founded: 2004

Marketing & advertising company specializing in effective, multi-channel marketing programs.

QUAXAR

2601 S Bayshore Dr (Suite 245), SBS
  Tower
Miami, FL 33133
Telephone: (305) 350-9520, Web Site:
  www.quaxar.com
CEO: Leonel Azuela
VP Sls & Mktg: Carlos Baruki
Founded: 2000

Loyalty and digital marketing firm.

QUIGLEY SIMPSON

11601 Wilshire Blvd (Floor 7)
Los Angeles, CA 90025-0509
Telephone: (310) 996-5800, E-Mail:
  info@quigleysimpson.com, Web
  Site: www.quigleysimpson.com
CEO: Angela Zepeda
Founded: 2002

Full-service advertising agency specializing in strategic planning, marketing media planning & buying, brand building, creative development, production and multi-cultural advertising.

R2C GROUP

207 NW Park Ave
Portland, OR 97209-3316
Telephone: (866) 402-1124, E-Mail:
  getintouch@r2cgroup.com, Web
  Site: www.r2cgroup.com
Co-Founder & CEO: Michelle Cardinal
Chmn: Tim O'Leary
Chief Mktg Officer: Mark Toner
Pres & COO: Jane Crisan
Founded: 1998

Creative and media agency with end-to-end direct response marketing capabilities.

RI DIRECT + DIGITAL

Response Innovations Corp.
256 Adelaide St E
Toronto, ON, Canada M5A 1N1
Telephone: (416) 368-6211, E-Mail:
  info@responseinnovations.com, Web
  Site: www.responseinnovations.com
Pres: Stephen Forchon
Founded: 1997

Full-service direct response marketing company.

RPM DIRECT LLC

An EXL Company
24 Arnett Ave (Suite 100)
Lambertville, NJ 08530-1500
Telephone: (609) 566-7150, FAX:
  (609) 566-7155, E-Mail: jimarslan@
  rpmdirectllc.com, Web Site: www.
  rpmdirectllc.com
CEO: David Denaci
Pres Data Solutions: Jim Arslan
Pres Diversified Strategies: Shawn
  Morris
COO: Thomas Murray

Database and diversified media services provider.

RADIANT 1

824 W Superior St
Chicago, IL 60642-8083
Telephone: (312) 933-7764, E-Mail:
   amaites@radiant-1.com, Web Site:
   www.radiant-1.com
Pres: Alan Maites
Founded: 2013

Marketing agency.

THE RADIO AGENCY

1400 N Providence Rd (Suite 4000)
Media, PA 19063-2061
Telephone: (610) 892-7300, Toll Free:
   (800) 969-2636, FAX: (610) 892-
   1899, E-Mail: contact@
   theradioagency.com, Web Site:
   www.radiodirect.com
Pres & CEO: Mark Lipsky
Founded: 1993

Radio advertising agency.

RAPP

An Omnicom Company
437 Madison Ave
New York, NY 10022-7043
Telephone: (212) 817-6800, FAX:
   (212) 686-7047, E-Mail: rick.doerr@
   rapp.com, Web Site: www.rapp.com
CEO: Alexei Orlov
CFO & COO: Matt Hafkin
Mng Dir, NY: Rick Doerr
Founded: 1965

Marketing & advertising agency connecting people to brands.

RAUXA

275A McCormick Ave
Costa Mesa, CA 92626
Telephone: (714) 427-1271, E-Mail:
   newbiz@rauxa.com, Web Site:
   www.rauxa.com
Founder: Jill Gwaltney
Pres & CEO: Gina Alshuler
Chief Strategy Officer: Ian Baer
Founded: 1999

Independent, full-service marketing
agency.

RAWLE MURDY

960 Morrison Dr (Suite 300)
Charleston, SC 29403
Telephone: (843) 577-7327, E-Mail:
   contact@rawlemurdy.com, Web Site:
   www.rawlemurdy.com
Pres: Bruce Murdy
VP & Dir Mktg & Opers: Michele
   Crull
VP & Dir Brand Leadership: John
   Kautz
Founded: 1975

Integrated brand and advertising
agency.

RED CLAY INTERACTIVE

22 Buford Village Way (Suite 221)
Buford, GA 30518
Telephone: (770) 297-2430, Toll Free:
   (866) 251-2800, E-Mail: hello@
   redclayinteractive.com, Web Site:
   www.redclayinteractive.com
Pres & COO: Lance Compton
Exec VP & COO: Scott Atkinson
VP & Creative Dir: Brett Compton
Primary Market Served: Consumer
Founded: 2000

Interactive advertising and marketing
agency.

RED ROCK BRANDING

760 Chapel St
New Haven, CT 06510
Telephone: (203) 295-4882, E-Mail:
   glen@redrockbranding.com, Web
   Site: www.redrockbranding.com
Founder & Creative Dir: Glen McDer-
   mott
Founded: 2008

Branding, marketing, advertising and
creative agency.

REDIRECT

1336 East 1100 South
Salt Lake City, UT 84105
Telephone: (801) 453-0100, E-Mail:
   hello@redirectdigital.com, Web Site:
   redirectdigital.com
Mng Partner: James Roberts
Mng Partner: Wendy Jackson
Founded: 2004

Digital and direct marketing agency.

RESOURCE/AMMIRATI

An IBM Co.
250 S High St (Suite 400)
Columbus, OH 43215
Telephone: (614) 621-2888, FAX:
   (614) 621-2873, E-Mail:
   businessdevelopment@
   resourceammirati.com, Web Site:
   www.resourceammirati.com
Founder & Chmn: Nancy Kramer
Dir New Bus: Kelly Mooney
Exec Dir: John Kadlic
Chief Creative Officer: Dennis Bajec
Founded: 1981

Digital creative agency.

RESPONSE AGENCY INC

936 Granite Peak Dr (Suite 1100)
Sandy, UT 84094
Telephone: (801) 352-9100, E-Mail:
   info@responseagency.com, Web
   Site: www.responseagency.com
Agency Head: Steve Cuno
Founded: 1994

Direct response marketing & advertising firm.

RESPONSE DYNAMICS INC

2070 Chain Bridge Rd (Suite 520)
Vienna, VA 22182-2569
Telephone: (703) 442-7595, FAX:
   (703) 442-4565, E-Mail: info@
   responsedynamicsinc.com, Web Site:
   www.responsedynamicsinc.com
Pres: Ronald Kanfer
Founded: 1981

Direct response marketing company
specializing in political fundraising.

RESPONSE FX

Div. of Strategic Marketing and Adver-
   tising Inc
2216 Corte Cicuta
Carlsbad, CA 92009-8713
Telephone: (760) 479-0012, E-Mail:
   services@responsefx.com, Web Site:
   www.responsefx.com
Content Writer & Copywriter: Karen J
   Marchetti
Web Programmer & Developer: Doug
   Baird
Founded: 1991

Online & direct marketing agency.

RESPONSE MARKETING GROUP

1145 Gaskins Rd (Suite 109)
Richmond, VA 23238
Toll Free: (866) 574-7665, E-Mail:
   info@rmg-info.com, Web Site: rmg-
   usa.com
Founder & Principal: Stuart Holt
Pres, CEO & Principal: Jim Harenchar
Creative Dir & Principal: Scott Highfill

Integrated marketing communications
company.

RESPONSE MARKETING INC

6900 Shady Oak Rd
Eden Prairie, MN 55344-3403
Telephone: (952) 949-4913
CEO: Judith J. Swenson

RESPONSE MINE INTERACTIVE INC

3390 Peachtree Rd NE (Suite 800)
Atlanta, GA 30326-2840
Telephone: (404) 233-0370, Web Site:
   www.responsemine.com
Founder & CEO: Ken Robbins
Sr VP & Division Head, Customer Ac-
   quisition Partnerships: Brent Wheeler
Sr VP & Division Head, Agency Svcs:
   Ryan Woolley
Founded: 2001

Full-service digital marketing agency
specializing in the health, multi-channel retail, travel and home services
markets.

THE RESPONSE SHOP INC
42215 Washington St (Suite A-407)
Palm Desert, CA 92211
Telephone: (858) 735-7646, FAX:
    (858) 777-5418, E-Mail: marla@
    responseshop.com, Web Site: www.
    responseshop.com
Pres: Marla Hoskins
Conducts Business: U.S.
Primary Market Served: Business &
    Consumer
Founded: 1997

Full-service agency specializing in direct response TV and radio.

RESULTS ADVERTISING INC
777 Terrace Ave (Suite 506)
Hasbrouck Heights, NJ 07604-3114
Telephone: (201) 288-7888, FAX:
    (201) 288-5112, E-Mail: info@
    resultsinc.com, Web Site: www.
    resultsinc.com
Pres & CEO: David I. Green
Exec VP & Creative Dir: Jeff Rubin
Founded: 1982

Full-service, integrated advertising and branding agency specializing in consumer products, financial, real estate, sports and entertainment.

REVANA DIGITAL
A Revana Growth Services company
160 E Via Verde (Suite 100)
San Dimas, CA 91773-3901
Telephone: (909) 599-8885, Toll Free:
    (866) 922-4632, Web Site: www.
    revanadigital.com
Pres: Judi Hand
Chief Tech Officer: Martin Longo
Sr VP Bus Devel & Mktg Svcs: Jonathan Gray
Founded: 1995

Digital marketing and sales solutions company.

REVANA INC
A Tele Tech Holdings Inc company
8123 S Hardy Dr
Tempe, AZ 85284-1106
Telephone: (408) 902-5900, Toll Free:
    (800) 535-0343, Web Site: www.
    revana.com
Pres & CEO: Judi Hand
CFO: Marc Arseneau
Sr VP Bus Devel & Mktg Svcs: Jonathon Gray
Primary Market Served: Business
Founded: 1993

Technology-enabled revenue generation solutions company.

RICHARD RICCELLI INC
23 Charlotte St
Charleston, SC 29403
Telephone: (843) 727-0183, FAX:
    (843) 727-0184, E-Mail: richard@
    riccelli.com, Web Site: riccelli.com
Pres: Richard Riccelli
Founded: 1987

Direct response advertising agency.

RICHARDS COMMUNICATIONS
8350 Whispering Pines Dr
Russell, OH 44072-9591
Telephone: (216) 514-7800, FAX:
    (216) 514-7801, E-Mail: jrichards@
    richardsgo.com, Web Site: www.
    richardsgo.com
Pres & CEO: John Richards
VP: Jared Richards
Founded: 1981

Full-service marketing and communications agency.

RICHARDS PARTNERS
Div. of Richards Group
2801 N Central Expwy (Suite 100)
Dallas, TX 75204-3663
Telephone: (214) 891-5700, FAX:
    (214) 891-3515, E-Mail:
    ruth_fitzgibbons@richards.com, Web
    Site: richardspartners.com
Principal: Stacie Barnett
Principal: Ruth Fitzgibbons
Principal: George McCane
Founded: 1976

Independent branding agency.

RISDALL MARKETING GROUP
550 Main St (Suite 100)
New Brighton, MN 55112-3271
Telephone: (651) 286-6700, Toll Free:
    (888) 747-3255, FAX: (651) 631-
    2561, E-Mail: info@risdall.com,
    Web Site: www.risdall.com
Founding Chmn: John Risdall
Chmn & CEO: Ted Risdall
COO: Jennifer Risdall
Founded: 1972

Independent, full-service advertising agency.

ROBERTS COMMUNICATIONS INC
64 Commercial St
Rochester, NY 14614
Telephone: (716) 325-6000, FAX:
    (716) 325-6001, Web Site: www.
    robertscomm.com
CEO: Bill Murtha
Pres: Katrina Busch

Founded: 1971
Full-service marketing communications firm with specific focus in financial services, healthcare, industrial and technology markets.

ROBINSON DIRECT
6945 Wards Ln
Center Valley, PA 18034
Telephone: (610) 838-5589, FAX:
    (610) 838-5589, E-Mail: carole@
    robinson-direct.com, Web Site:
    www.robinson-direct.com
Pres: Carole Robinson

Advertising and graphic design company.

ROCKETT COMMUNICATIONS INC
11 Juniper Ridge Rd (Suite 1100)
Danvers, MA 01923-1741
Telephone: (978) 774-1780, E-Mail:
    rockett.comm@verizon.net, Web
    Site: www.rockett.us
Pres: Brian Rockett
Founded: 1996

Business development, marketing and management consulting firm.

ROLAKIMMERLING ASSOCIATES
501 Fifth Ave (3rd fl)
New York, NY 10017-7805
Telephone: (646) 367-4815, FAX:
    (646) 367-4901
Partner: Fernando E. Rola
Partner: Pamela Kimmerling Hoveling
Founded: 1986

Culturally relevant, data-driven advertising & marketing agency.

RON PERRELLA DRS
29632 Seriana
Laguna Niguel, CA 92677-7967
Telephone: (949) 495-7661, FAX:
    (949) 495-7660, E-Mail: rperrdrs@
    aol.com, Web Site: www.
    ronperrelladrs.com
Pres: Ronald Perrella
Conducts Business: U.S.
Primary Market Served: Business &
    Consumer
Founded: 1994

Direct response advertising & marketing consultancy.

RONALD ERKES & ASSOCIATES INC
3045 Regal Oaks Blvd
Palm Harbor, FL 34684
Principal: Ronald D. Erkes

ROSEN INC

Rosen Convergence Marketing
1631 NE Broadway (Suite 615)
Portland, OR 97232-1425
Telephone: (503) 224-9811, Web Site:
   rosenconvergence.com
Pres & CEO: Richard G. Rosen
Partner & Chief Creative Officer: Jane
   C. Rosen
Conducts Business: U.S.
Employees: 15
Primary Market Served: Business &
   Consumer
Advertising/Marketing Budget Related
   to Direct Marketing: 26-50%
Founded: 1990

Marketing and advertising agency.

ROTH ADVERTISING INC

5 Brewster St (Suite 212)
Glen Cove, NY 11542
Telephone: (516) 674-8603, FAX:
   (516) 368-3885, E-Mail: charles@
   rothadvertising.com, Web Site:
   www.rothadvertising.com
Pres: Daniel J. Roth
Founder: Charles A. Roth

Advertising and marketing agency specializing in promoting book sales.

RUSS REID CO

2 N Lake Ave (Suite 600)
Pasadena, CA 91101-1868
Telephone: (626) 449-6100, FAX:
   (626) 449-6190, E-Mail: info@
   russreid.com, Web Site: www.
   russreid.com
Pres & CEO: Alan Hall
Chief Marketing Officer: Lisa Scott
   Benson
COO: Don Haggstrom
Sr VP Client Svcs: Steve Harrison
Founded: 1964

Full-service advertising agency specializing in the non-profit sector.

SBC ADVERTISING

333 W Nationwide Blvd
Columbus, OH 43215-2311
Telephone: (614) 255-2333, Web Site:
   www.sbcadvertising.com
Pres & CEO: Scott Wolfe
COO & Gen Mgr: Matt Wilson
Founded: 1969

Full-service advertising and marketing services company.

SHR PERCEPTUAL BRANDING

2575 E Camelback Rd (Suite 450)
Phoenix, AZ 85016-9288

Telephone: (480) 483-3700, FAX:
   (480) 483-9675, E-Mail: info@
   shrbranding.com, Web Site: www.
   shrbranding.com
Principal: Will Rodgers
Founded: 1970

Brand strategy, analysis & performance company.

SMM ADVERTISING

Sanna Mattson MacLeod
811 W Jericho Tpke
Smithtown, NY 11787
Telephone: (631) 265-5160, FAX:
   (631) 265-5185, E-Mail: marketing@
   smmadvertising.com, Web Site:
   smmadvertising.com
Pres: Charles MacLeod
Creative Dir: Robert Mattson
Founded: 1985

Full-service advertising and digital marketing agency.

ST&P MARKETING COMMUNICATIONS INC

320 Springside Dr (Suite 150)
Fairlawn, OH 44333
Telephone: (330) 668-1932, FAX:
   (330) 668-2078, Web Site: stpinc.
   com
COO: Rick Kenney
Creative Dir: Russ Kern
Founded: 1992

Full-service promotion agency.

SWB&R INC

3865 Adler Pl
Bethlehem, PA 18017
Telephone: (610) 866-0611, Toll Free:
   (877) 377-9286, FAX: (610) 866-
   8650, E-Mail: swbr@swbrinc.com,
   Web Site: www.swbrinc.com
CEO: Ernie Steigler
Pres & COO: Scott Friedman
Founded: 1969

Advertising, public relations & marketing communications agency.

SAFIAN COMMUNICATIONS INC

31 Hickory Dr
Maplewood, NJ 07040
Telephone: (973) 378-3672, FAX:
   (973) 378-2456, E-Mail: gail.
   safian@safianhealth.com, Web Site:
   safianhealth.com
Pres: Shelley Gail

Public relations, marketing and communications agency specializing in the health care industry.

SAGE COMMUNICATIONS

2 Watson Pl (Bldg 3)

Framingham, MA 01701-4109
Telephone: (508) 309-6678, FAX:
   (508) 309-6372, E-Mail: info@
   sagecommunications.com, Web Site:
   www.sagecommunications.com
Creative Dir & Founding Partner: Josef
   Kottler
Pres & Founding Partner: Anne Kottler
Conducts Business: U.S.
Primary Market Served: Business &
   Consumer
Founded: 1998

Ad agency specializing in direct mail and circulation promotions.

SAINT GREGORY GROUP

9435 Waterstone Blvd (Suite 180)
Cincinnati, OH 45249
Telephone: (513) 769-8440, FAX:
   (513) 769-1640, E-Mail: info@
   stgregory.com, Web Site: www.
   stgregory.com
CEO: Patrick C. Martin
Creative Dir: Lori Martin
Creative Dir: Timothy Holland

Full-service advertising agency.

SALES BY DEES

dba sbdees
PO Box 931
Montgomery, AL 36101-0931
Telephone: (334) 333-1567, E-Mail:
   dees@sbdees.com, Web Site: www.
   sbdees.com
Owner: John Allen Dees Jr
Founded: 2013

SANDI BROWN MARKETING

4342 14th Way NE
Saint Petersburg, FL 33703-5349
Telephone: (727) 528-6980, FAX:
   (703) 960-4492
Pres: Sandi Brown
Founded: 1988

SANDY GOLDSHEIN ASSOCIATES INC

38 W 21st St (Floor 8)
New York, NY 10010-6906
Telephone: (212) 366-5105, E-Mail:
   info@sgany.com, Web Site: www.
   sgany.com
Pres: Sandy Goldshein
Founded: 1995

Direct marketing agency offering creative services, marketing support & production management.

SAWTOOTH GROUP

141 W Front St (Suite 320)
Red Bank, NJ 07701
Telephone: (732) 945-1004, Web Site:
   www.sawtoothgroup.com
Pres: Kristi Bridges

Founded: 1988

Brand building and product marketing agency.

THE SCAN GROUP INC
W222 N625 Cheaney Dr
Waukesha, WI 53186
Telephone: (262) 521-1365, FAX: (262) 521-3265, Web Site: www. scangroup.net
Pres: Dave Patzer
Founded: 1983

Commercial print, pre-press, photography, digital asset management & marketing services company.

THE SCHOLL GROUP
316 Highland Ln
Bryn Mawr, PA 19010-3742
Telephone: (610) 527-7310, FAX: (610) 527-7323, E-Mail: rscholl@ theschollgroup.com, Web Site: www. theschollgroup.com
Pres & Creative Dir: Richard J. Scholl

Advertising and marketing agency.

SCHOOL MARKET RESEARCH INSTITUTE INC
90 Main St (Suite 212)
Centerbrook, CT 06409-1058
Toll Free: (800) 838-3444, FAX: (860) 581-8549, E-Mail: info@smriinc. com, Web Site: www.smriinc.com
Pres: Bob Stimolo
CFO: Lynn Stimolo
Gen Mgr: Kathleen Bill
Founded: 1980

Full-service direct marketing agency & consulting service specializing in the school market.

SCHRAMM MARKETING GROUP
160 E 38th St (Suite 35C)
New York, NY 10016
Telephone: (212) 983-0219, E-Mail: info@schrammnyc.com, Web Site: www.schrammnyc.com
Founder & Sr Partner: Joseph F. Schramm
Partner: Rafael Eli

Multicultural marketing services company.

SCIENTIFIC MARKETING SERVICES INC
145 E Weymouth Rd
Landisville, NJ 08326
Telephone: (856) 697-1257, FAX: (856) 697-9639, E-Mail: info@ smsmktg.com, Web Site: www. smsmktg.com
Pres: Robert W. Norton

Founded: 1979

Full-service B2B marketing, branding, digital and public relations agency.

SELLING SOLUTIONS INC
3525 Piedmont Rd NE (Bldg 5, Suite 515)
Atlanta, GA 30305-1586
Telephone: (404) 261-4966, FAX: (404) 264-1767, E-Mail: information@selsol.com, Web Site: www.selsol.com
Pres & Founder: William Paullin
VP Communications & Sls Motivation: James Paullin

Marketing strategy and sales improvement agency.

SEROKA
200 S Executive Dr
Brookfield, WI 53005
Telephone: (866) 379-0400, E-Mail: information@seroka.com, Web Site: www.seroka.com
CEO: Patrick H. Seroka
Founded: 1987

Brand development and marketing communications company.

SHAVER DIRECT INC
6430 W Bucksin
Phoenix, AZ 85083-3447
Telephone: (623) 594-3076, (857) 498-1853, E-Mail: dshaver934@aol.com

Advanced database marketing consultancy.

SHERMAN & ASSOCIATES INC
333 Harmon NW
Warren, OH 44483
Telephone: (330) 399-4500, FAX: (330) 399-6747, E-Mail: info@ shermanexperience.com, Web Site: www.shermanexperience.com
Pres: Jonathan Sherman
Founded: 1984

Marketing & advertising consultancy.

GLORIA SHURN CREATIVE SERVICES
1633 N Burling St
Chicago, IL 60614
Telephone: (312) 337-0032, FAX: (312) 337-3958
Owner: Gloria J. Shurn

Writing & editing consultancy.

THE SIGNATURE AGENCY
1784 Heritage Center Dr (Suite 101)
Wake Forest, NC 27587-3989

Telephone: (919) 878-8989, Toll Free: (800) 870-8700, FAX: (919) 878-3939, E-Mail: info@ signatureagency.com, Web Site: www.signatureagency.com
Pres: Sidney Reynolds
Founded: 1987

Direct response advertising, public relations & digital marketing agency specializing in health & beauty & life sciences.

SILVER MARKETING INC
7910 Woodmont Ave (Suite 914)
Bethesda, MD 20814-7028
Telephone: (301) 951-3505, FAX: (301) 652-3691, E-Mail: psilver@ silvermktg.com, Web Site: www. silvermarketing.com
Pres: Patricia Silver
Founded: 1984

Full-service marketing agency.

SINISH MARKETING COMMUNICATIONS
650 Hilltop Dr (Suite B)
Stratford, CT 06614-2414
Telephone: (203) 375-1919, E-Mail: jon@sinishmarketing.com, Web Site: www.sinishmarketing.com
Pres: Jon Sinish

Advertising and marketing services provider.

SIQUIS LTD
1340 Smith Ave (Suite 300)
Baltimore, MD 21209-3731
Telephone: (410) 323-4800, FAX: (410) 323-4113, Web Site: www. siquis.com
Pres: Anita Kaplan
Founded: 1986

Full-service advertising, design and new media agency.

SKAR ADVERTISING
111 S 108th Ave
Omaha, NE 68154
Telephone: (402) 330-0110, Toll Free: (866) 330-0112, FAX: (402) 330-8791, E-Mail: skar@skar.com, Web Site: skar.com
Pres & Dir Pub Rels: Joleen David
Sr VP Mktg Svcs: Mike Collins
VP & Co-Creative Dir: Greg Ahrens
VP & Co-Creative Dir: Mike Duman
Direct online sales
Founded: 1962

Full-service advertising agency with expertise in the healthcare, financial and retail industries.

SMART MARKETING

23 Highland Blvd
Dix Hills, NY 11746
Telephone: (631) 254-5259, FAX:
(631) 254-4814, E-Mail: info@
smartmarketing.com, Web Site:
www.smartmarketing.com
Pres: Bruce Levine
Founded: 1985

Full-service marketing and advertising
company.

BRODY SMYTHE DIRECT INC

8665 Wilshire Blvd (#301)
Beverly Hills, CA 90211
Telephone: (310) 779-9682, FAX:
(310) 550-1659, E-Mail: rsollish@
brodysmythe.com, Web Site: www.
brodysmythe.com
CEO & Creative Dir: Rochelle Sollish
Conducts Business: U.S.
Founded: 1996

Full-service direct response, marketing
communications & advertising agency.

SMZ ADVERTISING

Simons Michelson Zieve Inc
1200 Kirts Blvd (Suite 100)
Troy, MI 48084
Telephone: (248) 362-4242, FAX:
(248) 362-2014, E-Mail: info@smz.
com, Web Site: www.smz.com
Chmn: James A. Michelson
Pres & CEO: Jaime Michelson
Exec Creative Dir: Michael Corbeille

Full-service advertising agency.

THE SNYDER AGENCY

2918 Plantation Wood
Missouri City, TX 77459
Telephone: (281) 437-9200, FAX:
(832) 460-3022, E-Mail: info@
snyderagency.com, Web Site:
snyderagency.com
CEO: Philip R. Snyder
Founded: 1979

Full-service marketing, advertising,
public relations, web design and media
planning agency.

SOCIAL REALITY INC

456 Seaton St
Los Angeles, CA 90013
Telephone: (323) 694-9800, Web Site:
www.socialreality.com
Founder & CEO: Chris Miglino
Founder & Chief Innovations Officer:
Erin DeRuggiero
Pres: Richard Steel
Founded: 2010

Internet advertising and marketing
technology company.

SOURCE

An MDC Partners company
761 Main Ave (Suite 2)
Norwalk, CT 06851-1080
Telephone: (203) 291-4000, FAX:
(203) 291-4010, E-Mail: info@
sourcecxm.com, Web Site: www.
sourcecxm.com
Mng Partner: Rich Feldman
Pres: Kersten Mitton Rivas
Sr VP & Exec Creative Dir: Chris Healey
Founded: 1989

Consumer experience marketing company.

SOURCE COMMUNICATIONS

433 Hackensack Ave
Hackensack, NJ 07601
Telephone: (201) 343-5222, E-Mail:
admin@sourcead.com, Web Site:
sourcead.com
Pres & Mng Partner: Larry Rothstein
COO & Mng Partner: Barry Bluestein
Exec Creative Dir & Partner: Dennis
Koye
Exec VP & Chief Mktg Officer: Marcia
Wasser
Conducts Business: U.S., Canada
Primary Market Served: Business &
Consumer
Founded: 1983

Full-service integrated advertising
agency.

THE SPECTOR AGENCY

4600 Dietz Way (Suite 100)
Fair Oaks, CA 95628
Telephone: (916) 966-1605, FAX:
(916) 966-1609, Web Site: www.
spectoragency.com
Pres: Paul Spector
Founded: 1986

Full-service advertising and marketing
agency.

SPENCER ZAHN & ASSOCIATES

2015 Sansom St
Philadelphia, PA 19103-4416
Telephone: (215) 564-5979, FAX:
(215) 564-6285, E-Mail: szahn@
erols.com, Web Site: www.
spencerzahn.com
Pres: Spencer Zahn
Employees: 5
Founded: 1970

Market and communications consultancy specializing in the entertainment,
hospitality, automotive, financial &
service industries.

SPRING O'BRIEN & CO

20 W 22nd St (Suite 906)

New York, NY 10010
Telephone: (212) 620-7100, FAX:
(212) 620-7166, E-Mail: info@
spring-obrien.com, Web Site: www.
spring-obrien.com
Pres: Christopher Spring
Sr VP: Lauren Kaufman
Founded: 1982

Integrated marketing solutions agency
specializing in travel & tourism communications, B2B & economic development.

SPRINGBOARD BRAND & CREATIVE STRATEGY LTD

111 W Campbell St (Suite 401)
Arlington Heights, IL 60005
Telephone: (847) 398-4920, FAX:
(847) 398-4921, E-Mail:
springboard@springboardbrand.com,
Web Site: www.springboardbrand.
com
Pres: Robert Rosenberg
Founded: 2002

Brand development and communications company.

THE STANFORD GROUP

70 W 40th St (Floor 8)
New York, NY 10018-2623
Telephone: (212) 333-5514, E-Mail:
info@stanfordgroupinc.com, Web
Site: www.stanfordgroupinc.com
Pres: Sheila Stanford

Direct marketing agency specializing
in nonprofit organizations.

STARBIRD CREATIVE

PO Box 1722
Sebastopol, CA 95473-1722
Telephone: (707) 829-0277, E-Mail:
susan@starbirdcreative.com, Web
Site: www.starbirdcreative.com
Owner: Susan Starbird
Founded: 1987

Marketing consultancy specializing in
the health, environmental & social justice sectors.

STARCOM MEDIAVEST GROUP

Div. of Publicis Groupe operating unit
Vivaki
35 W Wacker Dr (Suite 3200)
Chicago, IL 60601-1723
Telephone: (312) 220-3535, Web Site:
smvgroup.com
CEO: Laura Desmond

Precision marketing, content and technology solutions company.

STEEL MEDIA INC
350 5th Ave (Floor 59), The Empire
    State Building
New York, NY 10118
Telephone: (212) 601-2840, E-Mail:
    info@steelmediainc.com, Web Site:
    www.steelmediainc.com
Pres: Chad Holsinger
Founded: 1999

Full-service digital advertising company.

STEIN IAS
432 Park Ave S (Floor 16)
New York, NY 10016-8013
Telephone: (212) 213-1112, Web Site:
    www.steinias.com
Chmn & Chief Client Officer: Thomas
    Stein
VP & Dir Acct Svcs: Susan Guerrero
Chief Content Strategist: Mike Azzara
Founded: 2013

Global digital and integrated marketing
agency.

STEPHAN & BRADY INC
1850 Hoffman St
Madison, WI 53704-2594
Telephone: (608) 241-4141, FAX:
    (608) 241-4246, E-Mail: gwhitely@
    stephanbrady.com, Web Site: www.
    stephanbrady.com
Pres & CEO: George Whitely
Exec VP & COO: Daniel Hearn
Founded: 1952

Full-service advertising agency offering advertising, public relations & digital solutions.

STEPHAN PARTNERS INC
233 Spring St (Suite 801)
New York, NY 10013
Telephone: (212) 524-8583, E-Mail:
    george@stephenpartners.com, Web
    Site: www.stephanpartners.com
Mng Dir: George N. Stephan
Mgr: Brian Hack
Creative Dir: Bob Feinberg
Creative Dir: Jeff Bretl
Creative Dir: Carol Bokuniewicz
Creative Dir: Jim Parry
Creative Dir: Steve Meltzer
Founded: 2000

Branding & digital marketing agency.

STEPHENS DIRECT INC
417 E Stroop Rd
Dayton, OH 45429
Telephone: (937) 299-4993, E-Mail:
    info@stephensdirect.com, Web Site:
    www.stephensdirect.com
Pres: Phil Stephens

Full-service marketing communications
agency.

STIR LLC
330 W Kilbourn Ave (Suite 222)
Milwaukee, WI 53202
Telephone: (414) 278-0040, FAX:
    (414) 278-0390, E-Mail: info@
    stirstuff.com, Web Site: www.
    stirstuff.com
Owner, Strategic Planning: Brian Ben-
    nett
Partner & Exec Creative Dir: Bill
    Kresse
Founded: 2000

Full-service marketing and advertising
agency.

THE STONE GROUP INC
120 Spring St
Pleasanton, CA 94566
Telephone: (925) 846-4432, FAX:
    (925) 846-2767, E-Mail: kbutler@
    stonegroupinc.com, Web Site:
    stonegroupinc.com
Pres: Kathleen Butler
Founded: 2011

Full-service marketing, advertising, design & public relations agency.

STOREY KENWORTHY
1333 Ohio St
Des Moines, IA 50314
Telephone: (515) 288-3243, Toll Free:
    (800) 622-4536, FAX: (515) 288-
    9807, E-Mail: info@
    storeykenworthy.com, Web Site:
    www.storeykenworthy.com
Pres: John Kenworthy

Promotional & branded products company.

**STRATEGIC ALLIANCE
GROUP**
PO Box 88824
Atlanta, GA 30356-8824
Telephone: (404) 275-1077, E-Mail:
    pete@sagpromo.com, Web Site:
    www.sagpromo.com
Pres: Pete Severens
Founded: 1992

STRATEGIC AMERICA
6600 Westown Pkwy (Suite 100)
West Des Moines, IA 50266-7708
Telephone: (515) 453-2000, Toll Free:
    (888) 898-6400, FAX: (515) 224-
    4181, Web Site: www.
    strategicamerica.com
CEO: Mike Schreurs
Pres & COO: John Schreurs
Founded: 1980

Full-service integrated advertising
agency specializing in public relations,
digital, traditional, direct response &
creative solutions.

STRETCH MULTIMEDIA LLC
PO Box 3398
Dublin, OH 43017
Telephone: (614) 363-4444, FAX:
    (614) 363-3772, E-Mail: dougj@
    stretch-multimedia.com, Web Site:
    www.stretch-multimedia.com
Principal: Doug Jones
Founded: 2015

Marketing & communications agency.

SUMMIT MARKETING
425 N New Ballas Rd
Saint Louis, MO 63141
Telephone: (844) 792-2013, Toll Free:
    (800) 843-7347, E-Mail: info@
    summitmarketing.com, Web Site:
    www.summitmarketing.com
CEO: Daniel Renz
Founded: 1996

Fully integrated marketing communications firm serving the commercial, government & nonprofit markets.

SUNDOG
2000 44th St SW (fl 6)
Fargo, ND 58103-7411
Telephone: (701) 235-5525, Toll Free:
    (888) 9-SUNDOG, FAX: (701) 235-
    8941, E-Mail: info@
    sundoginteractive.com, Web Site:
    www.sundoginteractive.com
CEO: Brent Teiken
Chief Tech Officer: Johnathon Rade-
    macher
Chief Strategy Officer: Eric Dukart
Founded: 1995

Marketing & technology company.

**SUTHERLAND GLOBAL
SERVICES**
1160 Pittsford-Victor Rd
Pittsford, NY 14534
Telephone: (585) 586-5757, Toll Free:
    (800) 388-4557, Web Site: www.
    sutherlandglobal.com
CEO: Dilip R. Vellodi
Founded: 1986

Global provider of business process
and technology management services.

SUTTER MARKETING INC
800 E Northwest Hwy (Suite 430)
Palatine, IL 60067
Telephone: (847) 358-3100, Web Site:
    www.suttermarketing.com
Pres: Lynn R. Sutter
Founded: 1976

Full-service marketing and advertising
services provider.

SWEETGRASS MARKETING LLC
192 E Bay St (Suite 210)
Charleston, SC 29401
Telephone: (843) 834-1884, Web Site: sweetgrassmarketing.net
Owner & Pres: John P De La Cruz
Founded: 2011

Full-service inbound marketing and website development company.

TBC INC
900 S Wolfe St
Baltimore, MD 21231-3514
Telephone: (410) 347-7500, FAX: (410) 986-1299, E-Mail: info@tbc.us, Web Site: www.tbc.us
Chmn & Chief Creative Officer: Allan Charles
Vice Chmn: Tom Burden
Pres: Nichole Baccala Ward
Pres: Howe Burch
Founded: 1974

Full-service advertising agency with in-house branding, direct marketing, public relations, media, interactive, broadcast production & digital production expertise.

TBWA/CHIAT/DAY INC
488 Madison Ave Fl 6, New York, NY 10022-5702-POST
Part of Omnicom Group Inc.
488 Madison Ave
New York, NY 10022-5727
Telephone: (212) 804-1000, FAX: (212) 804-1200, Web Site: www.tbwachiatdayny.com
CEO: Rob Schwartz
Chief Creative Officer: Chris Garbutt
Dir Bus Devel: Kyla Jacobs
CFO: Brian Carr
Founded: 1970

Global advertising company.

TBWA WORLDWIDE
Part of Omnicom Group Inc.
488 Madison Ave
New York, NY 10022
Telephone: (212) 804-1300, E-Mail: info@tbwa.com, Web Site: www.tbwa.com
Pres & CEO: Troy Ruhanen
Founded: 1970

Global advertising company.

TC TRANSCONTINENTAL
1 Place Ville Marie (Suite 3315)
Montreal, QC, Canada H3B 3N2
Telephone: (514) 954-4000, FAX: (514) 954-4016, Web Site: tctranscontinental.com
Pres & CEO: Francois Olivier
Pres: Brian Reid

Primary Market Served: Business
Founded: 1976

Publishing, media & marketing company.

TMP WORLDWIDE
125 Broad St (Floor 10)
New York, NY 10004
Toll Free: (800) 867-2001, E-Mail: wecanhelp@tmp.com, Web Site: www.tmp.com
Pres & CEO: Michelle Abbey
Founded: 2006

Advertising & marketing agency.

TN MARKETING
1903 Wayzata Blvd
Wayzata, MN 55391-2047
Telephone: (763) 577-1200, Web Site: www.tnmarketing.com
CEO: Cal Franklin

Full-service content, marketing and customer support solutions company.

TPG DIRECT INC
7 N Columbus Blvd, The Piers at Penns Landing
Philadelphia, PA 19106
Telephone: (215) 592-8381, FAX: (215) 574-8316, E-Mail: slongley@tpgdirect.com, Web Site: www.tpgdirect.com
CEO: Steve Longley
Co-Pres: Alison Denis
Exec Creative Dir: Miguel Ferry
Founded: 1992

Digital & direct insurance marketing agency.

TVA MEDIA GROUP
3950 Vantage Ave
Studio City, CA 91604-3613
Telephone: (818) 505-8300, Toll Free: (888) 322-4296, FAX: (818) 505-8370, E-Mail: info@tvamediagroup.com, Web Site: www.tvamediagroup.com
Founder, CEO & Exec Producer: Jeffrey Goddard
Partner, CFO & Exec Producer: Laura Wu
Exec Creative Dir: Bruce Somers Jr.
Conducts Business: Worldwide
Primary Market Served: Business & Consumer
Founded: 1987

Full-service direct response television advertising agency.

TACITO DIRECT
14165 Proton Rd
Dallas, TX 75244-3604

Telephone: (800) 621-2225, FAX: (972) 490-6520, E-Mail: contact@tacito.com, Web Site: www.tacito.com
Chmn & CEO: Anthony J. Tacito
Pres: Gerard Luisi

Direct marketing agency specializing in the automotive industry.

TANEN DIRECTED ADVERTISING
12 S Main St
Norwalk, CT 06854-2980
Telephone: (203) 855-5855, FAX: (203) 855-5865, E-Mail: ilene@tanendirected.com, Web Site: www.tanendirected.com
Pres: Ilene Tanen
Founded: 1985

Full-service advertising and direct marketing agency.

TARGET & RESPONSE INC
1751 S Naperville Rd (Unit 208)
Naperville, IL 60189
Telephone: (312) 321-0500, FAX: (312) 321-0051, Web Site: www.target-response.com
Pres: Mike Battisto
Founded: 1987

Direct response agency specializing in pay-per-lead advertising.

TARGET DIRECT MARKETING INC
510 W 5th St
Kansas City, MO 64105
Telephone: (815) 558-0919, Web Site: www.targetdirectmarketing.com
Pres: John Pirroni
Founded: 1993

Full-service digital marketing, direct mail, Internet inquiry & response technology agency.

TARGET MARKETEAM
1200 Abernathy Rd (Suite 1600), Northpark Town Center
Atlanta, GA 30328-5673
Telephone: (770) 274-3700, FAX: (770) 274-3730, E-Mail: inquiries@tmtinc.com, Web Site: www.tmtinc.com
Founder & Mng Partner: Ron Bell
Exec VP & Mng Creative Dir: Ann Hattaway
Primary Market Served: Consumer
Founded: 1987

Full-service advertising agency specializing in fundraising for nonprofit organizations.

TARGETBASE
An Omnicom Group Inc. company
7850 N Beltline Rd
Irving, TX 75063-6062
Telephone: (972) 506-3400, E-Mail:
info@targetbase.com, Web Site:
targetbase.com
Pres & CEO: Mark Wright
Mng Dir: Robin Rettew
Founded: 1979

Data-driven, strategic communications
agency that provides clients with market technology, business intelligence,
analytics and creative services.

TEAM ONE ADVERTISING
Div. of Saatchi & Saatchi North America Inc.
13031 W Jefferson Blvd
Los Angeles, CA 90094-7039
Telephone: (310) 437-2500, Web Site:
www.teamone-usa.com
Chmn & CEO: Kurt Ritter
Pres: Julie Michael
Chief Creative Officer: Chris Graves
Founded: 1987

Fully integrated advertising agency
specializing in premium, luxury and aspirational brands.

TECH IMAGE
Subs. of SmithBucklin
330 N Wabash Ave (Suite 1900)
Chicago, IL 60611
Telephone: (847) 279-0022, Toll Free:
(888) 483-2477, FAX: (847) 279-
8922, E-Mail: info@techimage.com,
Web Site: www.techimage.com
Pres: Dan O'Brien
VP Acct. Svcs.: Philip Anast
Founded: 1993

Digital public relations company.

TECHCOM INC
7515 Company Dr (Suite A)
Indianapolis, IN 46237
Telephone: (317) 865-2530, FAX:
(317) 865-2540, E-Mail: info@
techcom.com, Web Site: www.
techcom.com
Pres: Ilene Adams

Producer of product cutaways, technical manuals, trade show exhibits, technical graphics, custom software &
electronic simulators.

**TECHNICAL MARKETING
GROUP**
2068 Walsh Ave (Suite B2)
Santa Clara, CA 95050
Toll Free: (888) 554-0256, Web Site:
www.technicalmarketing.org

Founded: 2007
Provider of fast, focused and high quality technical marketing data.

**TELEPERFORMANCE
CANADA**
75 Eglinton Ave E
Toronto, ON, Canada M4P 3A4
Telephone: (416) 922-8240, E-Mail:
canada@teleperformance.com, Web
Site: www.teleperformance.com
CEO: Terry Rybolt
Founded: 1996

Customer experience services & management company.

TEMKIN & TEMKIN
156 Barberry
Highland Park, IL 60035-4420
Telephone: (847) 831-0237, FAX:
(847) 851-0409, E-Mail: t2@temkin.
com, Web Site: temkin.com
Pres: Steve Temkin
Founded: 1982

Full-service advertising and marketing
communications agency.

TENET PARTNERS
122 W 27th St (fl 9)
New York, NY 10001
Telephone: (212) 329-3030, FAX:
(212) 329-3031, Web Site:
tenetpartners.com
Chmn & Founder: James Gregory
CEO & Mng Partner: Hampton Bridwell
COO: Russ Napolitano
Mgr Bus Devel & Mktg: Jessica McHie

**THE TESTIMONIAL
WRANGLER**
7486 La Jolla Blvd (Suite 164)
La Jolla, CA 92037-5029
Telephone: (858) 735-7646, FAX:
(858) 777-5418
Pres: Marla Hoslins

Television testimonial production and
consulting company.

**THANE INTERNATIONAL
INC**
2321 Rosecrans Ave (Suite 4210)
El Segundo, CA 90245
Telephone: (310) 531-1956, FAX:
(310) 531-1957, E-Mail: info@
thaneinc.com, Web Site: www.
thaneinc.com
CEO: Amir Tukulj
Founded: 1990

Global, multi-channel consumer products direct marketing company.

THARLER DIRECTS
4 Cabot Rd
Wayland, MA 01778-3716
Telephone: (508) 358-3554, FAX:
(508) 358-5623, E-Mail: steve@
tharlerdirects.com, Web Site: www.
tharlerdirects.com
Chief Guide: Steven R. Tharler

Full-service direct marketing firm.

THOMASARTS
240 South 200 West
Farmington, UT 84025-0070
Telephone: (801) 451-5365, E-Mail:
welcome@thomasarts.com, Web
Site: thomasarts.com
CEO: Dave Thomas
Founded: 2003

Full-service marketing communications
firm and advertising agency.

**TIERNEY
COMMUNICATIONS**
Div. of Interpublic Group
200 S Broad St (Floor 10)
Philadelphia, PA 19102-3845
Telephone: (215) 790-4100, FAX:
(215) 790-4363, Web Site: www.
tierneyagency.com
Pres & CEO: Mary Stengel Austen
Exec Creative Dir: Patrick Hardy

Full-service advertising, public relations, interactive and media agency.

TIGERT COMMUNICATIONS
2815 Dogwood Pl
Nashville, TN 37204
Telephone: (615) 298-9957
Owner, Pres & Mktg Dir: Bob Tigert

Video production company.

TOBE DIRECT
A Vision Integrated Graphics Group
company
605 Territorial Dr
Bolingbrook, IL 60440
Telephone: (630) 910-7080, FAX:
(630) 910-3670, E-Mail: sales@
tobedirect.com, Web Site: www.
tobedirect.com
Pres: John Tobe
VP Sls & Mktg: Rob Baraban

Targeted direct mail solutions provider.

TOMSHEEHAN WORLDWIDE
645 Penn St (Suite 301)
Reading, PA 19601-3527
Telephone: (610) 478-8448, FAX:
(610) 478-8449, E-Mail:
tomsheehan@tomsheehan.com, Web
Site: www.tomsheehan.com
Principal & Creative Dir: Tom Sheehan

Founded: 1989

Advertising agency specializing in healthcare & B2B branding, marketing, advertising and strategic communications.

TOWER MEDIA ADVERTISING INC

233 N Michigan Ave (Suite 2350)
Chicago, IL 60601-5701
Telephone: (312) 856-9200, FAX: (312) 856-1300, E-Mail: info@ towermedia.com, Web Site: www. towermedia.com
Pres: Phil Rozansky
Dir Client Svcs: Sheeri Weyers

Full-service direct response media buying agency.

TRACTION ON DEMAND

2700 Production Way (Ste 500)
Burnaby, BC, Canada V5A 0C2
Telephone: (604) 620-6040, Web Site: www.tractionondemand.com
CEO: Greg Malpass
COO: Mike Winterfield
Exec VP: Andrew Buckley
VP Data Driven Mktg: Dave Jenkins
Founded: 2006

Sales & marketing consulting firm.

TRACYLOCKE

An Omnicom Group company.
1999 Bryan St (Suite 2800)
Dallas, TX 75201
Telephone: (214) 969-9000, FAX: (214) 259-3550, E-Mail: parker. harrison@tracylocke.com, Web Site: tracylocke.com
Pres & CEO: Hugh Boyle
Pres & Chief Creative Officer: Michael Lovegrove
Founded: 1913

Global communications agency.

TRADENET PUBLISHING INC

1200 Energy Center Dr
Gardner, KS 66030-1599
Toll Free: (800) 884-7301, Web Site: www.tradenetonline.com
Pres & CEO: Tom Mertz
Primary Market Served: Business
Founded: 1986

Supplier of consumer items used in specialty advertising.

TRANZACT

2200 Fletcher Ave (Floor 4)
Fort Lee, NJ 07024
Telephone: (201) 461-5665, E-Mail: info@tranzact.net, Web Site: www. tranzact.net
Pres & CEO: David Graf

Exec VP: Mercer Carlin
Exec VP: Mitchell Ginzburg
Exec VP: Andy Nelson

Marketer & seller of insurance to consumers and major insurers.

TREPOINT

315 W 36th St (Fl 10)
New York, NY 10018-6527
Telephone: (646) 867-2252, E-Mail: challengeus@trepoint.com, Web Site: www.trepoint.com
CEO: Bill Carmody
Pres: Len Devanna
Founded: 2005

Strategic marketing services and consulting provider for challenger brands.

TRINITY MARKETING INC

82 Broad St (Suite 358)
Boston, MA 02110
Telephone: (617) 292-7399, E-Mail: info@trinitynet.com, Web Site: www.trinitynet.com
Founder & Mng Partner: Dan Logan

Marketing communications & consulting agency specializing in advertising, marketing, branding, design & interactive.

TRONE BRAND ENERGY INC

1823 Eastchester Dr (Suite A)
High Point, NC 27265
Telephone: (336) 886-1622, E-Mail: info@trone.com, Web Site: www. tronebrandenergy.com
Pres: Doug Barton
CFO: Rick Morgan
Founded: 1982

Marketing, advertising & brand communications agency.

TROZZOLO COMMUNICATIONS GROUP

811 Wyandotte
Kansas City, MO 64105
Telephone: (816) 842-8111, Web Site: www.trozzolo.com
Pres & CEO: Angelo Trozzolo
Exec Creative Dir: Paul Behnen
Founded: 1989

Full-service, omni-directional integrated marketing services provider.

TRUE NORTH INC

630 3rd Ave (Floor 12)
New York, NY 10017-6749
Telephone: (212) 557-4202, Web Site: truenorthinc.com
CEO: Steve Fuchs
Chief Creative Officer: Tom Goosman
COO: Tim Taylor

Founded: 1994

Independent advertising agency offering creative, media & technology services.

TRUESENSE MARKETING

155 Commerce Dr
Freedom, PA 15042-9202
Toll Free: (877) 878-6584, Web Site: www.truesense.com
Principal: Steven Bushee
SVP: Jeff Nickel
Founded: 2008

Full-service direct marketing agency specializing in fundraising.

TURKEL BRANDS

2871 Oak Ave
Miami, FL 33133
Telephone: (305) 445-9111, FAX: (305) 448-6691, E-Mail: speaking@ turkelbrands.com, Web Site: turkelbrands.com
CEO & Exec Creative Dir: Bruce Turkel
Founded: 1983

Full-service multicultural brand management firm.

22SQUARED INC

1170 Peachtree St NE (Floor 15)
Atlanta, GA 30309-7649
Telephone: (404) 347-8700, FAX: (404) 347-8800, Web Site: www. 22squared.com
Pres & CEO: Richard Ward
Exec VP & Chief Creative Officer: John Stapleton
Founded: 1922

Full-service, fully-integrated advertising agency.

UMARKETING LLC

1 E 22nd St (Suite 200)
Lombard, IL 60148
Telephone: (630) 916-1717, Web Site: www.umarketing.com
CEO: George Wiedemann
Founded: 2007

Data-driven, full-service direct marketing agency.

UNDERLINE COMMUNICATIONS LLC

12 W 27th St (Floor 14)
New York, NY 10001-6903
Telephone: (212) 994-4340, FAX: (212) 686-8234, E-Mail: inquiries@ underline.com, Web Site: www. underlinecom.com
Principal & Mng Dir: Susan Berman
Principal & Creative Dir: Luke Daigle
Primary Market Served: Consumer

Founded: 2001

Relationship marketing agency that connects businesses with customers through multi-channel communication programs.

UNICOM MARKETING GROUP INC

1526 W Monroe St, Chicago, IL 60607-2408
2875 S 25th Ave
Broadview, IL 60155-4531
Telephone: (312) 738-1404, FAX: (312) 738-1405
Pres: Joe Iazzetto

Marketing & advertising consultancy.

UNIVERSAL MEDIA SYNDICATE INC

An Arthur Middleton Capital Holdings Inc company
3939 Everhard Rd NW
Canton, OH 44709-4004
Telephone: (330) 966-9000, E-Mail: lfish@uni-syn.com, Web Site: www. universalmediasyndicate.com
Dir New Bus Devel: Laura Fish

Full-service media agency specializing in advertising & promotions, buying media and placing advertisements.

VML INC

250 Richards Rd
Kansas City, MO 64116
Telephone: (816) 283-0700, FAX: (816) 283-0954, E-Mail: dl-vmlcommarketing@vml.com, Web Site: www.vml.com
CEO: Jon Cook
Pres: Eric Campbell
Chief Mktg Officer: Beth Wade
Chief Strategy Officer: Amy Winger
Founding Ptnr & Chief Vision Officer: Scott McCormick
Employees: 80

VALASSIS CANADA

47 Jutland Rd
Toronto, ON, Canada M8Z 2G6
Telephone: (416) 259-3600, Toll Free: (866) 333-2386, Web Site: www. valassis.com
Pres: Mark McHugh
Founded: 1970

Media and marketing services company.

VALMARK ASSOCIATES LLC

4242 Ridge Lea Rd (Suite 5)
Buffalo, NY 14226-5122

Telephone: (716) 836-3414, FAX: (716) 836-3415, E-Mail: joe@ valmarkassociates.com, Web Site: www.valmarkassociates.com
Pres: Joseph Lojacono
Founded: 2006

Marketing communications and resource consultancy .

VANGUARD DIRECT

519 8th Ave (Floor 23)
New York, NY 10018-4570
Telephone: (212) 736-0770, FAX: (212) 736-8305, Web Site: www. vanguarddirect.com
Pres: Robert O'Connell
COO: Ralph Fucci
Exec Creative Dir: Thomas Miller
Dir Creative Svcs: Kevin Green
Founded: 1976

Direct marketing agency specializing in the business, government, education & healthcare sectors.

VASTCAST MEDIA INC

8820 W Russell Rd (Suite 110)
Las Vegas, NV 89148
Telephone: (702) 221-8261, Toll Free: (800) 946-7112, FAX: (702) 666-8553, E-Mail: support@vastcast. com, Web Site: www.vastcastmedia. com
CEO: Jared Dingwerth
Founded: 2001

Specialized interactive marketing agency.

VENTURA ASSOCIATES INTERNATIONAL LLC

60 E 42nd St (Suite 650)
New York, NY 10165
Telephone: (212) 302-8277, FAX: (212) 302-2587, E-Mail: info@ sweepspros.com, Web Site: www. sweepspros.com
CEO: Marla Altberg
Pres: Al B. Wester III
Exec VP & Chief Mktg Officer: Lisa Manhart
Founded: 1971

Marketing and sales promotion agency that creates, manages & administers corporate sweepstakes.

THE VERDI GROUP INC

190 Office Park Way
Pittsford, NY 14534
Telephone: (585) 381-4275, FAX: (585) 381-4293, E-Mail: info@ theverdigroup.com, Web Site: www. theverdigroup.com
Pres: Robert A. Green Jr.
Dir Client Svcs: Mary Bonaccio

Founded: 1995

Integrated marketing communications agency that creates & produces print, broadcast, direct mail, Web, email, exhibit and promotional content.

VIANT TECHNOLOGY LLC

Subs. of Time Inc.
4 Park Plaza (Suite 1500)
Irvine, CA 92614
Telephone: (949) 861-8888, E-Mail: info@viantinc.com, Web Site: viantinc.com
CEO: Tim Vanderhook
COO: Chris Vanderhook
Sr VP: Russ Vanderhook
Primary Market Served: Business
Direct online sales
Founded: 1999

Advertising technology & marketing services company.

THE VIDAL PARTNERSHIP

228 E 45th St (Floor 14)
New York, NY 10017-3303
Telephone: (212) 867-5185, FAX: (212) 661-7650, Web Site: www. vidalpartnership.com
Pres & CEO: Manny Vidal
Founded: 1999

Multicultural advertising & marketing communications agency.

VIDEOWARE CORP

RP-NFOA
53 Doral Greens Dr W
Rye Brook, NY 10573
Telephone: (914) 937-6007, FAX: (914) 937-6414, E-Mail: info@ videoware.com, Web Site: videoware.com
Chmn & CEO: Dick Hubert
Founded: 1984

Video content development, production & distribution company.

VISION MEDIA INC

4544 N Hiatus Rd
Sunrise, FL 33351
Toll Free: (877) 877-2047, Web Site: www.visionmediainc.com
Pres: Jay Juliano
VP: Donna Juliano
Founded: 2003

Radio and television commercial production company specializing in automotive & retail promotional advertising.

VISIONS INC

8801 Wyoming Ave N
Brooklyn Park, MN 55445

Telephone: (763) 425-4251, FAX: (763) 425-4614, E-Mail: general@ visionsfirst.com, Web Site: www. visionsfirst.com
CEO: John Otto
Pres: Rick Hansen
Founded: 1985

Full-service, integrated marketing services provider.

WSI
1660 Tech Ave (Unit 2)
Mississauga, ON, Canada L4W 5S9
Telephone: (905) 678-7588, Toll Free: (888) 678-7588, FAX: (905) 678-7242, E-Mail: contact@wsiworld. com, Web Site: www.wsiworld.com
Co-Founder & CEO: Mark Dobson
Exec VP Global Opers: Valerie Brown-Dufour
VP Info Tech: Shaunak Dave
VP Prof Svcs: Justin Jones
Primary Market Served: Business
Founded: 1995

Digital marketing company.

WALT KLEIN ADVERTISING
1873 S Bellaire St (#908)
Denver, CO 80222-4356
Telephone: (303) 298-8015, FAX: (303) 298-8194, Web Site: www. wka.com
Owner: Walt Klein
Owner: Susan Klein

Full-service advertising agency.

WEBREPLY INC
1085 Worcester Rd
Natick, MA 01760-1531
Telephone: (508) 318-4600, E-Mail: info@webreply.com, Web Site: www.webreply.com
CEO: Henry Haugland
Founded: 1999

Marketing company utilizing a proprietary suite of technologies to generate demand and nurture sales leads.

WENDOVER ASSOCIATES INC
309 Edwardia Dr (Suite A)
Greensboro, NC 27409
Telephone: (336) 299-6611, FAX: (336) 292-4261, E-Mail: wendover@ wendoverassociates.com, Web Site: www.wendoverassociates.com
Owner & Pres: Betty Hooker
Client Svcs Mgr: Robin Rogers

Full-service advertising & design agency.

WESTERN DATA SERVICES INC
513 N Canal St
Carlsbad, NM 88220
Telephone: (575) 628-8318, Toll Free: (877) 870-5566, FAX: (575) 628-8917, E-Mail: directmail@wdsi.net, Web Site: www.wdsi.net

Personalized direct mailing and banking solutions provider.

WEXLER CONSULTING GROUP LLC
2121 Eisenhower Ave (Suite 101)
Alexandria, VA 22314
Telephone: (202) 573-9355, E-Mail: welcome@wexlerllc.com, Web Site: wexlerconsultinggroup.com
CEO: Zeev Wexler
Dir Opers: Mike Bobrowski
VP Mktg: Monica Quintero
Founded: 2012

Sales, marketing and business development consulting firm specializing in small to medium size businesses and government contractors.

WHITE POST MEDIA GROUP
PO Box 23232
Nashville, TN 37202
Telephone: (615) 469-4409, Web Site: whitepostmedia.com
Owner & Partner: Chuck Merritt
Primary Market Served: Consumer
Founded: 2001

Strategic communications, content marketing & advertising agency.

WHITE64
13665 Dulles Technology Dr #150, Herndon, VA 20171-4607-POST
8603 Westwood Center Dr (Floor 4)
Vienna, VA 22182
Telephone: (703) 793-3000, E-Mail: info@white64.com, Web Site: white64.com
Chmn & CEO: Matthew C. White
Pres: Carrie Edwards
Exec Creative Dir: Kipp Monroe
Chief Mktg Officer: Jose Banzon
Founded: 1964

Independent advertising and communications agency.

WIKREATE
145 Vallejo St (Suite 6)
San Francisco, CA 94111-1415
Telephone: (415) 362-0440, FAX: (415) 362-0430, E-Mail: ezequieltrivino@wikreate.com, Web Site: www.wikreate.com
Founder & Principal: Ezequiel Trivino
Co-Founder & COO: Elena Castanon

Founded: 2007

Advertising & communications agency structured as a social network of skilled professionals and partner agencies.

WILLIAMS WORLDWIDE TELEVISION
3130 Wilshire Blvd (Suite 300)
Santa Monica, CA 90403-2300
Telephone: (310) 449-4506, FAX: (310) 449-4556, E-Mail: curious@ williamsworldwidetv.com, Web Site: www.williamsworldwidetv.com
Pres & CEO: Alain Bransford
Exec VP: Sylvia Morales
Founded: 1987

Direct response television marketing agency.

WILSON RMS
Wilson Relationship Marketing Services
345 7th Ave (Suite 1100)
New York, NY 10001
Telephone: (212) 473-6900, Web Site: www.wilsonrms.com
CEO: David Wilson
Gen Mgr: Michael Asaro
Founded: 2001

Marketing agency specializing in the finance, insurance, telecom & wellness sectors.

WIREDPENTE INC
21 Wales Ave
Markham, ON, Canada L3P 2C2
Telephone: (416) 399-8458, Web Site: wiredpente.com
Chief Strategist & Creative Dir: Bob Pente
Founded: 2008

Data-driven, variable communication direct marketing agency.

WISDOM MARKETING GROUP
Div. of Kruse Asset Management
11202 Disco Dr (Suite 100), One Kruse Plaza
San Antonio, TX 78216-2860
Telephone: (210) 499-0777, Toll Free: (800) 952-1973, FAX: (210) 499-4217, E-Mail: sales@kruseasset.com, Web Site: www.kruseasset.com
Pres: John A. Aguillard

Marketing, advertising, public relations and mass media company.

WOLF BLUMBERG KRODY INC
537 E Pete Rose Way (Suite 100)
Cincinnati, OH 45202-3578

Telephone: (513) 784-0066, FAX:
(513) 784-0986, E-Mail: sklein@
wbk.com, Web Site: www.wbk.com
Pres: Steve Klein

THE WOODLANDS MARKETING AGENCY LLC

21 Waterway Ave (Suite 300)
The Woodlands, TX 77380
Telephone: (281) 318-1601, Web Site:
thewoodlandsagency.com
Pres & CEO: Lance O'Bleness
Founded: 2010

Full-service marketing agency.

WUNDERMAN

A member of Young & Rubicam Group
and WPP
3 Columbus Cir
New York, NY 10019
Telephone: (212) 941-3000, Web Site:
www.wunderman.com
Global CEO: Mark Read
Global Chief Creative Officer: Lincoln
Bjorkman
Global Chief Mktg Officer: Jaime Gut-
freud
CEO North America: Seth Solomons
Conducts Business: Worldwide
Primary Market Served: Business &
Consumer
Founded: 1958

Global network of digital, marketing
communications & advertising agencies.

WUNDERMAN DC

A Wunderman network agency, part of
WPP
1055 Thomas Jefferson St NW (Suite
200)
Washington, DC 20007-5256
Telephone: (202) 625-2111, FAX:
(202) 424-7900, E-Mail: anne.
wolek@wundermandc.com, Web
Site: wundermandc.com
Pres & CEO: Jeffrey Ross
Sr VP Mktg & Bus Devel: Anne Wolek

Full-service relationship marketing
agency.

WUNDERMAN HEALTH

Div. of Wunderman, a member of
Young & Rubicam Group & WPP
530 Maryville Centre Dr (Suite 300)
Saint Louis, MO 63141-5825
Telephone: (314) 590-8300, FAX:
(314) 590-8383, Web Site: www.
wunderman.com/health
Pres: Becky Chidester
Founded: 1997

Marketing services company specializing in the healthcare and insurance industries.

WYSE ADVERTISING

668 Euclid Ave
Cleveland, OH 44114
Telephone: (216) 696-2424, E-Mail:
info@wyseadv.com, Web Site: www.
wyseadv.com
CEO: Michael Marino
Creative Dir: Lane Strauss
Founded: 1951

Full-service marketing, branding and
advertising agency

XPECTRUM MARKETING GROUP

1953 Ainsley Rd
San Diego, CA 92123
Telephone: (858) 277-0079, FAX:
(858) 277-0076, E-Mail: info@
xpectrummg.com, Web Site: www.
xpectrummg.com
CEO: William Lopez

Marketing communications agency.

YATES ADVERTISING

357 Castenada Ave
San Francisco, CA 94116-1448
Telephone: (415) 887-9545, FAX:
(415) 887-9549
Founder & Pres: Susan Yates
Founded: 1991

Full-service advertising agency.

YECK BROTHERS CO

2222 Arbor Blvd
Dayton, OH 45439-1594
Telephone: (937) 294-4000, Toll Free:
(800) 417-2767, FAX: (937) 294-
6985, E-Mail: byeck@yeck.com,
Web Site: www.yeck.com
Pres: Robert Yeck
Dir Mktg & Creative Svcs: Sherry
Hang
Founded: 1938

Full-service direct mail and related
marketing company.

ZLR IGNITION

303 Watson Powell Jr Way (Suite 100)
Des Moines, IA 50309-1799
Telephone: (515) 244-4456, FAX:
(515) 244-5749, Web Site: www.
zlrignition.com
Pres & Owner: Louie Laurent
Founded: 1987

Full-service marketing communications
firm.

ZENITHOPTIMEDIA DIRECT

The ROI Agency
299 W Houston St (Floor 11)
New York, NY 10014

Telephone: (212) 859-5100, FAX:
(212) 757-9495, Web Site: www.
zenithoptimedia.com
CEO: Tim Jones
Pres: Josh Martin

Media communications agency.

ZEPHYR MEDIA GROUP INC

990 Grove St (Suite 300)
Evanston, IL 60201-6513
Telephone: (847) 328-1519, FAX:
(847) 328-3518, Web Site: www.
zephyr-media.com
Pres: Daniel Zefkin
Founded: 1991

Infomercial direct response agency
whose core business is buying & selling media time.

ZILLNER

8725 Rosehill Rd (Suite 200)
Lenexa, KS 66215-4611
Telephone: (913) 599-3230, Web Site:
zillner.com
Founder & CEO: Ronda Shea Zillner
Founded: 1992

Advertising, marketing & strategy
agency specializing in CCRC, retirement communities & seniors

ZIMMERMAN ADVERTISING

Div. of Omnicom Group
6600 N Andrews Ave (Suite 300)
Fort Lauderdale, FL 33309
Telephone: (954) 644-4000, E-Mail:
contact@zadv.com, Web Site: www.
zadv.com
CEO: Michael Goldberg
Pres: David Kissell
Exec VP & Chief Creative Officer: Da-
vid Nathanson
Founded: 1984

Advertising agency specializing in retail brands.

Art Services (36) — Geographic Index

ARIZONA

Asciutto Art Representatives Inc, 1712 E Butler Cir, Chandler, 85225-5786

CALIFORNIA

Crawshaw Design, 120 Bayview Dr, San Rafael, 94901-2502

Jack Lucey Art & Illustration, 84 Crestwood Dr, San Rafael, 94901

Jim M'Guinness Design, 1122 Golden Way, Los Altos, 94024-5059

Stuart Karten Design, 4204 Glencoe Ave, Marina Del Rey, 90292

Edward Weston Fine Art & Photography, PO Box 3098, Chatsworth, 91311

Greg Zerovnik, 1805 N First Ave, Upland, 91784-1623

FLORIDA

American Writers & Artists Inc, 245 NE 4th Ave (Suite 102), Delray Beach, 33483-4568

ILLINOIS

AMD Industries Inc, 4620 W 19th St, Cicero, 60804-2502

BN Creative Advertising, 1100 W Northwest Hwy (#201), Mount Prospect, 60056-2273

Graphic Converting Inc, 877 N Larch Ave, Elmhurst, 60126

Ion Exhibits, 700 District Dr, Itasca, 60143-1320

Swimmer Design Associates, 4 Piper Ln (Suite F), Prospect Heights, 60070-1741

KANSAS

Pat Friesen & Co LLC, 9636 Meadow Ln, Leawood, 66206-2259

KENTUCKY

Beau Graphics Ltd Inc, 1910 Harrodsburg Rd, Lexington, 40503-1247

MARYLAND

EPI Colorspace, 8435 Helgerman Ct, Gaithersburg, 20877

MASSACHUSETTS

Rodelinde Graphic Design, PO Box 444, Lenox Dale, 01242-0444

MICHIGAN

Pangborn Design Ltd, 275 Iron St, Detroit, 48207-4305

Presence II Productions, 3810 Mystic Valley Dr, Bloomfield Hills, 48302-1437

NEW JERSEY

Miller Advertising Inc, 24 Nottingham Rd, Edison, 08820

Robert Burger Illustration, 145 Kingwood Stockton Rd, Stockton, 08559

NEW YORK

Blakeney Design, 61 Horatio St, New York, 10014-1505

Cecile Brunswick, 127 W 96th St (Suite 15D), New York, 10025-6482

Karen Levy Calligraphy, 370 E 76th St, New York, 10021

Nostradamus Advertising, 884 W End Ave (Suite 2), New York, 10025

Paul Chevannes, 445A 5th St, Brooklyn, 11215-3401

Synergy Arts Interactive, 222 Bloomingdale Rd (#310), White Plains, 10605-1513

Carl Waltzer Digital Service Bureau, 873 Broadway (Rm 412), New York, 10003

Westbeth Gallery, 55 Bethane St (#219), New York, 10014

OREGON

Skies America International Publishing & Communications, 9655 SW Sunshine Ct (Suite 500), Beaverton, 97005

PENNSYLVANIA

Inkwell Inc, 2256 High Rd, Cresco, 18326

Interdisciplinary Design Team, 75 Toll Dr, Southhampton, 18966-3074

Sargeant House Design Studio, 1433 Johnny's Way, Westchester, 19382-7857

TEXAS

Olivette Hubler Graphics Inc, 1568 Bar Harbor Dr, Dallas, 75232-3016

VIRGINIA

Gramma's Graphics Inc, 49 Starview Pl, Lancaster, 22503

WISCONSIN

Communicor, 629 E Keefe Ave, Milwaukee, 53212-1612

AMD INDUSTRIES INC
4620 W 19th St
Cicero, IL 60804-2502
Telephone: (708) 863-8900, Toll Free:
(800) 367-9999, FAX: (708) 863-
2065, Web Site: www.amdpop.com
Pres & CEO: David E. Allen
Founded: 1989

Window & lobby displays & cutouts.

AMERICAN WRITERS &
ARTISTS INC
245 NE 4th Ave (Suite 102)
Delray Beach, FL 33483-4568
Telephone: (561) 278-5557, Web Site:
www.awaionline.com
Exec Dir: Kate Yeakle

ASCIUTTO ART
REPRESENTATIVES INC
1712 E Butler Cir
Chandler, AZ 85225-5786
Telephone: (480) 814-8010, E-Mail:
aartreps@cox.net, Web Site:
wwwaartreps.com
Art Rep: Mary Anne Asciutto
Founded: 1980

Represents professional artists for quality children's book illustrations.

BN CREATIVE
ADVERTISING
1100 W Northwest Hwy (#201)
Mount Prospect, IL 60056-2273
Telephone: (847) 577-1300, FAX:
(847) 577-2101
Pres: James M. Bataille

BEAU GRAPHICS LTD INC
RP-NFOA
1910 Harrodsburg Rd
Lexington, KY 40503-1247
Telephone: (859) 277-2328, Toll Free:
(877) 279-2328, FAX: (859) 278-
6193, Web Site: www.beaugraphics.
com
Owner: H. Duncan Veach
Founded: 1980

Photoengraving.

BLAKENEY DESIGN
61 Horatio St
New York, NY 10014-1505
Telephone: (212) 243-0109, FAX:
(212) 243-0109
Pres: Leslie Blakeney

CECILE BRUNSWICK
127 W 96th St (Suite 15D)
New York, NY 10025-6482

Telephone: (212) 222-2088, E-Mail:
cbrunswick@nyc.rr.com, Web Site:
www.cecilebrunswicknyc.com
Owner: Cecile Brunswick

Original colorful oil abstract paintings
are available.

COMMUNICOR
629 E Keefe Ave
Milwaukee, WI 53212-1612
Telephone: (414) 961-5999, FAX:
(414) 961-5990, Web Site: www.
communicor.com
Pres: Robert Jarr
Founded: 1989

CRAWSHAW DESIGN
120 Bayview Dr
San Rafael, CA 94901-2502
Telephone: (415) 456-5544, FAX:
(415) 456-4319, E-Mail:
crawshawdesign@earthlink.net, Web
Site: www.crawshawdesign.com
Owner & Pres: Todd Crawshaw

EPI COLORSPACE
8435 Helgerman Ct
Gaithersburg, MD 20877
Telephone: (301) 230-2023, FAX:
(301) 990-7890, E-Mail: jcriscuoli@
epicolorspace.com, Web Site: www.
epicolorspace.com
VP, Corp Communs: Joseph Criscuoli

A full-service graphics production
company.

PAT FRIESEN & CO LLC
9636 Meadow Ln
Leawood, KS 66206-2259
Telephone: (913) 341-1211, FAX:
(913) 341-4343, Web Site: www.
patfriesen.com
Pres: Patricia Friesen
Founded: 1995

Marketing Consultants.

GRAMMA'S GRAPHICS INC
49 Starview Pl
Lancaster, VA 22503
Telephone: (804) 462-0884, FAX:
(804) 462-0884, E-Mail: sunprints@
grandloving.com, Web Site: www.
bubblink.com/donnelly
Pres: Susan Johnson
Sec & Treas: F.B. Johnson
Conducts Business: U.S.; Canada
Primary Market Served: Business &
Consumer
Catalog available online
Indirect online sales
Advertising/Marketing Budget Related
to Direct Marketing: 0-25%

Founded: 1980

Sun print kits for blueprinting photos or
opaque objects onto fabric. Also sun
print kits for sun printing note cards in
three colors. Sell unconditionally guaranteed kits to quilters, crafters, craft
clubs, schools, retailers & wholesalers.
For information send $1 & legal self
addressed stamped envelope.

GRAPHIC CONVERTING INC
877 N Larch Ave
Elmhurst, IL 60126
Telephone: (630) 758-4100, Toll Free:
(800) 447-1935, FAX: (630) 833-
1058, E-Mail: sales@
graphicconverting.com, Web Site:
www.graphicconverting.com
Pres & Owner: John Tinnon
Partner, CEO & Exec VP: Steve Skal-
ski
Partner & CFO: Joe Yaney
Partner & Pres: Tom Burnight
Founded: 1976

Provides a range of converting & distribution services to trading & collectible
game cards, greeting cards & publishing, packaging & industrial packaging
companies

OLIVETTE HUBLER
GRAPHICS INC
1568 Bar Harbor Dr
Dallas, TX 75232-3016
Telephone: (214) 941-9444
Pres: Olivette Hubler
Founded: 1989

Provides graphic services.

INKWELL INC
2256 High Rd
Cresco, PA 18326
Telephone: (570) 595-3344, E-Mail:
philip@inkwellinc.com
Pres: Philip Gruber

INTERDISCIPLINARY
DESIGN TEAM
75 Toll Dr
Southhampton, PA 18966-3074
Telephone: (215) 364-5608, FAX:
(215) 364-6509, E-Mail: rich.
bomze@gmail.com
Graphic Designer, Creative Dir & Con-
sultant IDT: Rich Bomze
Founded: 1985

ION EXHIBITS
700 District Dr
Itasca, IL 60143-1320

Telephone: (877) 499-6197, FAX:
(630) 235-9501, E-Mail: info@
ionexhibits.com, Web Site: www.
ionexhibits.com
Pres: Michael Levi
IT Exec: Ken Callaway
Fin Exec: Dennis Stock
Mktg: Mary Levi
Founded: 1996

Provides a complete selection of event
marketing & trade show exhibit solutions.

KAREN LEVY CALLIGRAPHY
370 E 76th St
New York, NY 10021
Telephone: (212) 472-1669
Owner: Karen Levy
Founded: 1980

JACK LUCEY ART & ILLUSTRATION
84 Crestwood Dr
San Rafael, CA 94901
Telephone: (415) 453-3172, E-Mail:
clucey1@sbcglobal.net
Artist: Jack Lucey

JIM M'GUINNESS DESIGN
1122 Golden Way
Los Altos, CA 94024-5059
Telephone: (650) 967-3811
Pres: Jim M'Guinness
Founded: 1979

MILLER ADVERTISING INC
24 Nottingham Rd
Edison, NJ 08820
Telephone: (732) 494-5611, FAX:
(732) 494-6075
Owner: Roseann Miller
Founded: 1971

NOSTRADAMUS ADVERTISING
Div. of Advocate Enterprises Inc
884 W End Ave (Suite 2)
New York, NY 10025
Telephone: (212) 581-1362, E-Mail:
nos@nostradamus.net, Web Site:
www.nostradamus.net
Pres: Barry Sher
Founded: 1974

PANGBORN DESIGN LTD
275 Iron St
Detroit, MI 48207-4305
Telephone: (313) 259-3400, FAX:
(313) 259-5690, E-Mail: info@
pangborndesign.com, Web Site:
www.pangborndesign.com
Pres: Dominic Pangborn

Founded: 1979
Commercial Art & Graphic Design.

PAUL CHEVANNES
445A 5th St
Brooklyn, NY 11215-3401
Telephone: (718) 788-3550
Pres: Paul Chevannes
Founded: 2003
Commercial Art/Graphic Design.

PRESENCE II PRODUCTIONS
3810 Mystic Valley Dr
Bloomfield Hills, MI 48302-1437
Telephone: (248) 723-9770, E-Mail:
leslie@presenceiiproductiions.com,
Web Site: www.
presenceiiproductions.com
CEO: Leslie Ann Pilling
Founded: 1989

Innovative design, high impact production & experiential public relations.

ROBERT BURGER ILLUSTRATION
145 Kingwood Stockton Rd
Stockton, NJ 08559
Telephone: (609) 397-3737, E-Mail:
burgerbobz@aol.com
Pres: Robert Burger

RODELINDE GRAPHIC DESIGN
PO Box 444
Lenox Dale, MA 01242-0444
Telephone: (413) 243-4350, FAX:
(413) 243-3066, E-Mail: rodelinde@
earthlink.net
Pres & Owner: Rodelinde Albrecht
Graphic Design Services.

SARGEANT HOUSE DESIGN STUDIO
1433 Johnny's Way
Westchester, PA 19382-7857
Telephone: (610) 399-1983, E-Mail:
sargeant house @verizon.net, Web
Site: www.sargeanthouse.com
Pres: Lisa Balch

SKIES AMERICA INTERNATIONAL PUBLISHING & COMMUNICATIONS
9655 SW Sunshine Ct (Suite 500)
Beaverton, OR 97005
Telephone: (503) 520-1955, FAX:
(503) 520-1275, E-Mail: skies@
skies.com, Web Site: www.skies.com
Owner: Jim Rullo
Sr VP: Sheri Cunningham
Founded: 1996

STUART KARTEN DESIGN
4204 Glencoe Ave
Marina Del Rey, CA 90292
Telephone: (310) 827-8722, FAX:
(310) 821-4492, Web Site: www.
kartendesign.com
Pres: Stuart Karten
Founded: 1984

A full-service product innovation consultancy.

SWIMMER DESIGN ASSOCIATES
4 Piper Ln (Suite F)
Prospect Heights, IL 60070-1741
Telephone: (847) 215-0900, FAX:
(847) 215-9821, E-Mail: mail@
swimmerdesign.com, Web Site:
www.swimmerdesign.com
Owner: Mark Swimmer

A graphic design, marketing & web development firm.

SYNERGY ARTS INTERACTIVE
222 Bloomingdale Rd (#310)
White Plains, NY 10605-1513
Telephone: (914) 997-7222, FAX:
(914) 997-8893, E-Mail: bgeorge@
synergyarts.com, Web Site: www.
synergyarts.com
Pres: Bill George
Founded: 1996

Commercial Art & Graphic Design.

CARL WALTZER DIGITAL SERVICE BUREAU
Affiliate of Waltzer Photography Studio
873 Broadway (Rm 412)
New York, NY 10003
Telephone: (212) 475-7848, FAX:
(212) 475-9359, E-Mail: cwdigital@
aol.com, Web Site: www.waltzer.
com
Pres: Carl Waltzer

WESTBETH GALLERY
55 Bethane St (#219)
New York, NY 10014
Telephone: (212) 989-4650
Dir: Jack Dowling

EDWARD WESTON FINE ART & PHOTOGRAPHY
Subs. of Edward Weston Graphics Inc
PO Box 3098
Chatsworth, CA 91311
Telephone: (818) 885-1044, FAX:
(818) 885-1021, E-Mail:
edwardweston@westoncollection.
com, Web Site: edward-weston.com
Pres: Ann Weston

GREG ZEROVNIK
1805 N First Ave
Upland, CA 91784-1623
Telephone: (909) 982-3787, FAX:
  (909) 931-2402
Pres: Greg Zerovnik
Founded: 1984

Photographers (37) — Geographic Index

CALIFORNIA

The Icon, 5450 Wilshire Blvd, Los Angeles, 90036

CONNECTICUT

Peter Glass Photography, 15 Oakwood St, East Hartford, 06108

The Lakeville Journal LLC, PO Box 1688, 33 Bissell St, Lakeville, 06039-1688

FLORIDA

Christopher Morrow Photography, 522 NW Blue Lake Dr, Port Saint Lucie, 34986-2650

ILLINOIS

Dennis Jourdan Photography Inc, 1417 Rose Blvd, Buffalo Grove, 60089-3263

Hodes Photography, 352 Lexington Dr., Buffalo Grove, 60089

William Koechling Photography, 1307 E Harrison Ave, Wheaton, 60187

Omega Studios, 168 E Highland Ave, Elgin, 60120-5564

MASSACHUSETTS

Frank Siteman Photography, 136 Pond St, Winchester, 01890

Sarah Putnam, 320 Brookline St, Cambridge, 02139

MICHIGAN

Photographix, 915 Lutz Ave, Ann Arbor, 48103

MISSOURI

Mom365, 3613 Mueller Rd, Saint Charles, 63301

MONTANA

Laurance Aiuppy, 522 W Chinook St, Livingston, 59047-0026

NEW MEXICO

Eduardo Fuss, 2462 Camino Capitan, Santa Fe, 87505-6464

NEW YORK

Ann Chwatsky Photography, 29 E 22nd St (#3N), New York, 10010

Henry Grossman, 604 Riverside Dr, New York, 10031-7800

E Trina Lipton, 60 E Eighth St (#15F), New York, 10003

Shelly Rusten, PO Box 120, Hankins, 12741-0120

Walter Weissman Photo Studio, 463 West St (Suite B-332), New York, 10014-2031

NORTH CAROLINA

Alderman Co, 325 Model Farm Rd, High Point, 27263

Photo Shuttle Japan, 1501 Ford Rd Lot 37, Chapel Hill, 27516-5749

OHIO

Michael Wilson Photographer, 1604 Manss Ave, Cincinnati, 45205

PENNSYLVANIA

David K Horowitz Studio Inc, 915 N 28th St, Philadelphia, 19130

TENNESSEE

Borum Photographics Inc, 625 Fogg St, Nashville, 37203-4605

VIRGINIA

Michael Carpenter Photography, 7704 Carrleigh Pkwy, Springfield, 22152-1304

Photographers (37)

LAURANCE AIUPPY
522 W Chinook St
Livingston, MT 59047-0026
Telephone: (406) 222-7308, FAX:
(406) 222-7308, E-Mail: aiuppix@
wispwest.net, Web Site: www.agpix.
com/aiuppy
Bus Mgr: Janis M. Aiuppy
Owner: Laurance B. Aiuppy
Founded: 1979

Commercial Photography.

ALDERMAN CO
325 Model Farm Rd
High Point, NC 27263
Telephone: (336) 889-6121, FAX:
(336) 889-7717, E-Mail: sales@
aldermancompany.com, Web Site:
www.aldermancompany.com
Pres: Jeff Williams
Chmn: Pete Williams
Founded: 1898

Provides commercial photography
services for advertising agencies, publishers, & other industrial users.

**BORUM PHOTOGRAPHICS
INC**
dba Chromatics
625 Fogg St
Nashville, TN 37203-4605
Telephone: (615) 254-0063, Toll Free:
(888) 254-0063, FAX: (615) 242-
2334, Web Site: www.chromatics.
com
Pres: Michael Borum
Founded: 1970

**MICHAEL CARPENTER
PHOTOGRAPHY**
7704 Carrleigh Pkwy
Springfield, VA 22152-1304
Telephone: (703) 644-9666
Owner: Michael Carpenter

**ANN CHWATSKY
PHOTOGRAPHY**
29 E 22nd St (#3N)
New York, NY 10010
Telephone: (212) 673-5689, FAX:
(212) 673-5689, E-Mail:
annphotog@aol.com, Web Site:
www.annchwatskyphoto.com
Owner: Ann Chwatsky
Founded: 1977

Commercial photographer.

**DENNIS JOURDAN
PHOTOGRAPHY INC**
1417 Rose Blvd
Buffalo Grove, IL 60089-3263

Telephone: (847) 564-2570, FAX:
(847) 255-5976, E-Mail: info@
djphoto.com, Web Site: www.
djphoto.com
Pres: Dennis Jourdan

Photography for advertising including
brochures, websites, annual reports,
trade shows, packaging, banners, corporate events & portraits.

**FRANK SITEMAN
PHOTOGRAPHY**
136 Pond St
Winchester, MA 01890
Telephone: (781) 729-3747, E-Mail:
frank@franksiteman.com, Web Site:
www.franksiteman.com
Owner: Frank Siteman
Employees: 1
Founded: 1985
Gross sales or billing: $200,000

Photography of people & products for
brochures, annual reports for website
use & images used for advertising.

EDUARDO FUSS
2462 Camino Capitan
Santa Fe, NM 87505-6464
Telephone: (505) 424-0304, FAX:
(505) 424-0602
Owner: Eduardo Fuss

**PETER GLASS
PHOTOGRAPHY**
15 Oakwood St
East Hartford, CT 06108
Telephone: (860) 528-8559, E-Mail:
peter@peterglass.com, Web Site:
www.peterglass.com
Owner: Peter Glass

HENRY GROSSMAN
604 Riverside Dr
New York, NY 10031-7800
Telephone: (212) 580-7751, E-Mail:
info.grossmanenterprises@gmail.
com
Owner: Henry Grossman

HODES PHOTOGRAPHY
Subs. of Close Encounter Productions
352 Lexington Dr.
Buffalo Grove, IL 60089
Telephone: (847) 215-3939, E-Mail:
hodesphotography@comcast.net,
Web Site: www.hodesphotography.
com
Dir: Chuck Hodes
Founded: 1979

**DAVID K HOROWITZ
STUDIO INC**
915 N 28th St
Philadelphia, PA 19130
Telephone: (215) 765-3600, FAX:
(215) 763-1056
Founded: 1966

THE ICON
5450 Wilshire Blvd
Los Angeles, CA 90036
Telephone: (323) 933-1666, E-Mail:
icon@iconia.com, Web Site: www.
iconia.com

Scanning, printing & restoration services for digital media & film.

**WILLIAM KOECHLING
PHOTOGRAPHY**
1307 E Harrison Ave
Wheaton, IL 60187
Telephone: (630) 665-4379, Web Site:
www.koechlingphoto.com
Owner: William Koechling

**THE LAKEVILLE JOURNAL
LLC**
PO Box 1688, 33 Bissell St
Lakeville, CT 06039-1688
Telephone: (860) 435-9873, FAX:
(860) 435-4802
Publr & Ed-in-Chief: Janet Manko

E TRINA LIPTON
60 E Eighth St (#15F)
New York, NY 10003
Telephone: (212) 674-5558, (917) 327-
6886, FAX: (212) 674-3523, E-Mail:
trinalipton@hotmail.com
Dir: E. Trina Lipton
Founded: 1970

MOM365
3613 Mueller Rd
Saint Charles, MO 63301
Telephone: (636) 946-5136, Web Site:
www.growingfamily.com

**CHRISTOPHER MORROW
PHOTOGRAPHY**
522 NW Blue Lake Dr
Port Saint Lucie, FL 34986-2650
Telephone: (845) 325-1233, E-Mail:
chris@chrismorrow.com, Web Site:
www.chrismorrow.com
Owner: Christopher Morrow

OMEGA STUDIOS
168 E Highland Ave
Elgin, IL 60120-5564

Telephone: (972) 444-8556, FAX:
(972) 444-8559, E-Mail:
omegastudios@rrd.com, Web Site:
www.omega-studios.com

Commercial printing.

PHOTO SHUTTLE JAPAN
1501 Ford Rd Lot 37
Chapel Hill, NC 27516-5749
Telephone: (919) 967-1585, E-Mail:
sonia@photoshuttle.com, Web Site:
www.photoshuttle.com
Dir: Sonia Katchian
Founded: 1984

Commercial Photographers.

PHOTOGRAPHIX
915 Lutz Ave
Ann Arbor, MI 48103
Telephone: (734) 769-6756, FAX:
(734) 476-2068, E-Mail:
lkburghardt@comcast.net
Owner: Lance Burghardt
Founded: 1973

Commercial photographers.

SHELLY RUSTEN
PO Box 120
Hankins, NY 12741-0120
Telephone: (917) 421-0980, Toll Free:
(845) 887-5662, E-Mail: srusten@
msn.com, Web Site: www.
shellyrusten.com
Pres: Shelly Rusten

Editorial photography.

SARAH PUTNAM
320 Brookline St
Cambridge, MA 02139
Telephone: (617) 547-3758, E-Mail:
sarah@sarahputnam.com, Web Site:
www.sarahputnam.com
Pres: Sarah Putnam
Founded: 2010

Videographer.

WALTER WEISSMAN PHOTO
STUDIO
463 West St (Suite B-332)
New York, NY 10014-2031
Telephone: (212) 989-9694, FAX:
(212) 989-9694, E-Mail:
wweissmanphoto@nyc.rr.com, Web
Site: www.weissmanphoto.com
Pres: Walter Weissman

MICHAEL WILSON
PHOTOGRAPHER
1604 Manss Ave
Cincinnati, OH 45205

Telephone: (513) 921-1749, E-Mail:
michaelwilson@fuse.net, Web Site:
www.michaelwilsonphotographer.
com
Owner: Michael Wilson
Founded: 1987

Videographer.

Stock Photo Agencies (38) — Geographic Index

ARIZONA

The Source Stock Footage Library Inc, 140 S Camino Seco (Suite 308), Tucson, 85710-4473

CALIFORNIA

Animal Fund, Fort Mason Center (East Room 205), San Francisco, 94123-1313

Biological Photo Service & Terraphotographics, 80 Eureka Sq (Suite 146), Pacifica, 94044-2676

eFootage, 87 N Raymond Ave (Suite 850), Pasadena, 91103-3968

Foster Travel Publishing, 1623 Martin Luther King Jr Way, Berkeley, 94709

Jeroboam, 120 27th St, San Francisco, 94110-4313

Minden Pictures, 558 Main St, Watsonville, 95076-4318

PhotoEdit Inc, 3505 Cadillac Ave (Suite P101), Costa Mesa, 92626-1434

Shooting Star International, 1441 N McCadden, Hollywood, 90028

Underwood Photo Archives Inc, 143 Alta Vista Rd, Woodside, 94062

University of Southern California, University Library, Dept of Special Collections, Los Angeles, 90089-0189

COLORADO

Viesti Associates Inc, 434 Turner Dr, Durango, 81303

CONNECTICUT

New England Stock Photo, 2389 Main St (Suite 303), Glastonbury, 06033-6399

FLORIDA

Tom Stack & Associates Inc, 154 Tequesta St, Tavernier, 33070

Superstock Inc, 6622 Southpoint Dr S Ste 230, Jacksonville, 32216-6171

IDAHO

David R Frazier Photolibrary Inc, 1921 Cataldo Dr, Boise, 83705

ILLINOIS

Stock Montage Inc, 1817 N Mulligan Ave, Chicago, 60639

Tony Stone Images, 122 S Michigan Ave (Suite 900), Chicago, 60603

INDIANA

Trends International LLC, 5188 W 74th St, Indianapolis, 46268

LOUISIANA

DDB Stock Photography LLC, 4845 Newcomb Dr, Baton Rouge, 70808-4747

MAINE

North Wind Picture Archives, 12 Waterboro Rd, Alfred, 04002-3243

MARYLAND

US Naval Institute, 291 Wood Rd, Annapolis, 21402

MASSACHUSETTS

Anthro Photo File, 33 Hurlbut St, Cambridge, 02138-1603

Davis Art Images, 50 Portland St, Worcester, 01608-2013

Image Photos/Clemens Kalischer, 34 Main St, Stockbridge, 01262

LLR/Research, 21 Wingate St, Haverhill, 01832

Stock Boston Inc, 258 Harvard St (#355), Brookline, 02446

MICHIGAN

ChinaStock/WorldViews, 2506 Country Village, Ann Arbor, 48103-6500

MINNESOTA

Chip Peterson Photos, 1711 Lincoln Ave, Saint Paul, 55105-1952

Scenic Photo!, 9208 32nd Ave N, Minneapolis, 55427-2325

NEW JERSEY

Bergman Medical/Scientific/Technical Collection, PO Box AG, Princeton, 08542-0872

NEW YORK

AP Images, 450 W 33rd St, New York, 10001

American Heritage Picture Library, 90 Fifth Ave, New York, 10011-7629

Animals Animals/Earth Scenes, 17 Railroad Ave, Chatham, 12037-1117

Art Resource Inc, 536 Broadway (fl 5), New York, 10012-3915

Black Star Publishing Co, 333 Mamaroneck Ave, White Plains, 10605

Corbis Images, 250 Hudson St (fl 5), New York, 10013

Culver Pictures Inc, 5102 21st St, Long Island City, 11101-5838

Esto Photographics Inc, 222 Valley Pl, Mamaroneck, 10543

eStock Photo, 27-28 Thomson Ave (Suite 628), Long Island City, 11101

Fundamental Photographs, 210 Forsyth St (#2), New York, 10002

Globe Photos Inc, 24 Edmore Ln S, West Islip, 11795-4016

Joel Gordon Photography, 112 Fourth Ave (4th fl), New York, 10003-5421

The Granger Collection, 381 Park Ave S (# 901), New York, 10016

Al Grotell, Underwater Photography, 170 Park Row (#15D), New York, 10038-1154

The Image Bank, 75 Varick St (fl 5), New York, 10013

The Image Works Inc, PO Box 443, Woodstock, 12498

Magnum Photos Inc, 12 W 31st St (fl 11), New York, 10001-7204

The New York Times Agency - Photo, 620 8th Ave, New York, 10018

Photo Researchers Inc, 307 5th Ave Fl 3, New York, 10016-6517

Photofest, 32 E 31st St (5th fl), New York, 10016-6881

Phototake/The Creative Link, 224 W 29th St (fl 9), New York, 10001

Sipa Press, 307 Seventh Ave (Suite 807), New York, 10001-6066

NORTH CAROLINA

Billy E Barnes, 313 Severin St, Chapel Hill, 27516-1512

OHIO

Lincoln Picture Studio, 225 Lookout Dr, Dayton, 45419-3813

PENNSYLVANIA

Brown Brothers, 100 Bortree Rd, Sterling, 18463-0050

Grant Heilman Photography Inc, 506 W Lincoln Ave, PO Box 317, Lititz, 17543-8707

H Armstrong Roberts Inc, 4203 Locust St, Philadelphia, 19104

Roberts Stock/Classic Stock, 4203 Locust St, Philadelphia, 19104-5228

RHODE ISLAND

Envision, 27 Hoppin Rd, Newport, 02840

UTAH

The Stock Solution Inc, 6640 S 2200 W, West Jordan, 84084-2203

VIRGINIA

Photri Images LLC, 9653 Sherman Oaks Ct, Fairfax, 22032-2816

WASHINGTON

Getty Images, 605 Fifth Ave S (Suite 400), Seattle, 98104

WEST VIRGINIA

AppaLight, 230 Griffith Run Rd, Spencer, 25276-6809

WISCONSIN

PhotoSource International, 1910 35th Rd, Pine Lake Farm, Osceola, 54020-5602

CANADA

Quebec

Keystone Press Agency Inc, 664 Grosvenor Ave, Montreal, H3Y 2S8

Stock Photo Agencies (38)

AP IMAGES
Subs. of The Associated Press
450 W 33rd St
New York, NY 10001
FAX: (212) 621-1679, E-Mail:
apimages_us@ap.org, Web Site:
www.apimages.com
Bureau Chief: Howard Goldberg

**AMERICAN HERITAGE
PICTURE LIBRARY**
Forbes Inc
90 Fifth Ave
New York, NY 10011-7629
Telephone: (212) 206-5107, Toll Free:
(800) 777-1222, FAX: (212) 367-
3151, Web Site: www.
americanheritage.com
Editor: Joshua Zeitz

ANIMAL FUND
Fort Mason Center (East Room 205)
San Francisco, CA 94123-1313
Telephone: (415) 775-4636, E-Mail:
delphinus@aol.com, Web Site:
www.animalfund.org
Exec Dir: Stanley Minasian
Founded: 1972

**ANIMALS ANIMALS/EARTH
SCENES**
17 Railroad Ave
Chatham, NY 12037-1117
Telephone: (518) 392-5500, Toll Free:
(800) 392-5503, FAX: (518) 392-
5550, E-Mail: info@animalsanimals.
com, Web Site: www.
animalsanimals.com
Exec VP: Nancy Carrizales

Agency specializes in natural history
imagery. Includes subjects such as
wildlife, domestic animals, scenics,
botany, geology, weather, travel &
sports.

ANTHRO PHOTO FILE
33 Hurlbut St
Cambridge, MA 02138-1603
Telephone: (617) 497-7227, FAX:
(617) 484-6428, Web Site: www.
anthrophoto.com
Pres: Irven DeVore

APPALIGHT
230 Griffith Run Rd
Spencer, WV 25276-6809
Telephone: (304) 927-2978, E-Mail:
wyro@appalight.com, Web Site:
www.appalight.com
Owner: Chuck Wyrostok

Founded: 2009
Provides photo assignment coverage in
the Charleston WV region & a wide array of stock images from Appalachia.

ART RESOURCE INC
536 Broadway (fl 5)
New York, NY 10012-3915
Telephone: (212) 505-8700, FAX:
(212) 505-2053, E-Mail: requests@
artres.com, Web Site: www.artres.
com
Pres: Teodore Feder
Founded: 1968

**BERGMAN MEDICAL/
SCIENTIFIC/TECHNICAL
COLLECTION**
Div. of Project Masters Inc
PO Box AG
Princeton, NJ 08542-0872
Telephone: (609) 921-0749, E-Mail:
information@pmiprinceton.com,
Web Site: www.pmiprinceton.com
Pres: Richard L. Bergman
VP: Victoria Bergman

BILLY E BARNES
313 Severin St
Chapel Hill, NC 27516-1512
Telephone: (919) 942-6350, FAX:
(919) 942-6350, E-Mail:
bbarnes218@aol.com, Web Site:
www.billybarnes.com
Pres: Billy E. Barnes
Founded: 1969

**BIOLOGICAL PHOTO
SERVICE &
TERRAPHOTOGRAPHICS**
80 Eureka Sq (Suite 146)
Pacifica, CA 94044-2676
Telephone: (650) 359-6219, FAX:
(650) 359-6219, E-Mail: bpsterra@
pacbell.net, Web Site: www.agpix.
com/biologicalphoto
Owner: Carl W. May
Founded: 1980

**BLACK STAR PUBLISHING
CO**
333 Mamaroneck Ave
White Plains, NY 10605
Telephone: (212) 679-3288, FAX:
(212) 889-2052, Web Site: www.
blackstar.com
Pres & Mktg Dir: Benjamin J. Chadnick

Founded: 1935
Photographers for corporate assignment
photography, photojournalism & stock
photography.

BROWN BROTHERS
100 Bortree Rd
Sterling, PA 18463-0050
Telephone: (570) 689-9688, FAX:
(570) 689-7873, E-Mail: info@
brownbrotherusa.com, Web Site:
www.brownbrothersusa.com
Pres: Raymond A. Collins
Founded: 1904

Art copy, publishing & printing.

CHINASTOCK/WORLDVIEWS
Subs. of Dennis Cox LLC
2506 Country Village
Ann Arbor, MI 48103-6500
Telephone: (734) 996-1440, Toll Free:
(800) 315-4462, FAX: (734) 996-
1481, E-Mail: decoxphoto@aol.com,
Web Site: www.denniscox.com
Pres: Dennis Cox

CHIP PETERSON PHOTOS
1711 Lincoln Ave
Saint Paul, MN 55105-1952
Telephone: (651) 699-4286, FAX:
(651) 698-7667
Mktg Dir: Rosa Maria de la Cueva-Peterson

CORBIS IMAGES
Div. of Corbis
250 Hudson St (fl 5)
New York, NY 10013
Telephone: (212) 777-6200, FAX:
(212) 375-7700, Web Site: www.
corbis.com
Pres: Leslie Hughes
Founded: 1989

CULVER PICTURES INC
5102 21st St
Long Island City, NY 11101-5838
Telephone: (718) 752-9393, FAX:
(718) 752-9394, Web Site: www.
culverpictures.com
Pres: Harriet L Culver
Founded: 1926
Stock Photo Agency Specializing In
Historical Pictures.

**DDB STOCK PHOTOGRAPHY
LLC**
4845 Newcomb Dr
Baton Rouge, LA 70808-4747

Telephone: (225) 763-6235, FAX: (225) 763-6894, E-Mail: info@ddbstock.com, Web Site: www.ddbstock.com
Pres: Douglas Donne Bryant
Founded: 1970

Specializes exclusively in photographic coverage of Latin America & the Caribbean.

DAVIS ART IMAGES

Div. of Davis Publications Inc
50 Portland St
Worcester, MA 01608-2013
Telephone: (508) 754-7201, Toll Free: (800) 533-2847, FAX: (508) 831-9260, (508) 753-3834, E-Mail: lkeenekendrick@davisart.com, Web Site: www.davisartimages.com
Mktg Coord: Lydia Keene-Kendrick
Pres: Wyatt Wade

EFOOTAGE

87 N Raymond Ave (Suite 850)
Pasadena, CA 91103-3968
Telephone: (626) 395-9593, FAX: (626) 395-5394, E-Mail: info@efootage.com, Web Site: www.efootage.com
VP: Lawrence Faso
Owner: Paul Lisy
Founded: 2003

Motion picture & tape distribution.

ENVISION

27 Hoppin Rd
Newport, RI 02840
Telephone: (401) 619-1500, Toll Free: (800) 524-8238, FAX: (401) 619-0130, E-Mail: envision@att.net, Web Site: www.envision-stock.com
Pres: Sue Pashko
Founded: 2005

Photo Enlargement Services.

ESTO PHOTOGRAPHICS INC

222 Valley Pl
Mamaroneck, NY 10543
Telephone: (914) 698-4060, FAX: (914) 698-1033, E-Mail: esto@esto.com, Web Site: www.esto.com
Pres: Erica Stoller
Gen Mgr: Christine Cordazzo
Founded: 1986

ESTOCK PHOTO

27-28 Thomson Ave (Suite 628)
Long Island City, NY 11101
Telephone: (718) 433-4295, Toll Free: (800) 284-3399, E-Mail: sales@estockphoto.com, Web Site: www.estockphoto.com
Mgr: Michael Brennen
Founded: 2008

FOSTER TRAVEL PUBLISHING

1623 Martin Luther King Jr Way
Berkeley, CA 94709
Telephone: (510) 549-2202, FAX: (510) 549-1131, E-Mail: lee@fostertravel.com, Web Site: www.fostertravel.com
Pres: Lee Foster
Founded: 1972

Travel Writing Photography Publishing.

DAVID R FRAZIER PHOTOLIBRARY INC

1921 Cataldo Dr
Boise, ID 83705
Telephone: (208) 342-9250, Toll Free: (800) 342-3283, FAX: (208) 342-2307, E-Mail: dave@drfphoto.com, Web Site: www.drfphoto.com
Pres & Mktg Mgr: David R. Frazier
Founded: 1987

Photo portrait studio commercial photography.

FUNDAMENTAL PHOTOGRAPHS

210 Forsyth St (#2)
New York, NY 10002
Telephone: (212) 473-5770, FAX: (212) 228-5059, E-Mail: mail@fphoto.com, Web Site: www.fphoto.com
Dir: Richard Megna
Founded: 1979

A photographic studio that transforms difficult science specs into visual illustrations.

GETTY IMAGES

605 Fifth Ave S (Suite 400)
Seattle, WA 98104
Telephone: (206) 925-5000, Toll Free: (888) 888-5889, Web Site: www.gettyimages.com
Co-Founder, Chmn: Mark Getty
Co-Founder & CEO: Jonathan Klein
Sr VP Bus Devel, Product & Content: Craig Peters

GLOBE PHOTOS INC

24 Edmore Ln S
West Islip, NY 11795-4016
Telephone: (631) 661-3131
COO & Mktg Dir: Raymond F. Whelan
Founded: 2006

Commercial photography.

JOEL GORDON PHOTOGRAPHY

112 Fourth Ave (4th fl)
New York, NY 10003-5421

Telephone: (212) 254-1688, E-Mail: joel.gordon@verizon.net, Web Site: www.joelgordonphotography.com
Pres: Joel Gordon
Founded: 1972

Studio photography, location photography, portrait photography, digital photography, editorial & documentary photography.

THE GRANGER COLLECTION

381 Park Ave S (# 901)
New York, NY 10016
Telephone: (212) 447-1789, FAX: (212) 447-1492, Web Site: www.granger.com
Exec Dir: William Glover
Mng Dir: Lila Dlaboha
Founded: 1964

The Granger collection is an historical picture library encompassing people, places, things and events of the world from prehistoric times through the mid-20th century.

AL GROTELL, UNDERWATER PHOTOGRAPHY

170 Park Row (#15D)
New York, NY 10038-1154
Telephone: (212) 349-3165, FAX: (212) 349-4363
Owner: Al Grotell

GRANT HEILMAN PHOTOGRAPHY INC

506 W Lincoln Ave, PO Box 317
Lititz, PA 17543-8707
Telephone: (717) 626-0296, Toll Free: (800) 622-2046, FAX: (717) 626-0971, E-Mail: info@heilmanphoto.com, Web Site: www.heilmanphoto.com
Pres: Sonia Shaner Wasco

Collection of images from professional photographers containing the finest agriculture, natural science, horticulture, wildlife, travel & lifestyle imagery.

THE IMAGE BANK

75 Varick St (fl 5)
New York, NY 10013
Telephone: (646) 613-4000, FAX: (646) 613-4601, Web Site: www.gettyimages.com
Pres: Mark Getty

IMAGE PHOTOS/CLEMENS KALISCHER

34 Main St
Stockbridge, MA 01262

Telephone: (413) 298-5500, FAX:
(413) 298-5500, E-Mail: inform@
bcn.net
Dir & Owner: Clemens Kalischer
Founded: 1951

THE IMAGE WORKS INC
PO Box 443
Woodstock, NY 12498
Telephone: (845) 679-8500, Toll Free:
(800) 475-8801, FAX: (845) 679-
0606, E-Mail: info@theimageworks.
com, Web Site: www.
theimageworks.com
Pres: Mark Antman
Founded: 1983

JEROBOAM
120 27th St
San Francisco, CA 94110-4313
Telephone: (415) 824-8085 cell,
E-Mail: jeroboamster@gmail.com
Owner & Pres: Ellen Bunning
Founded: 1972

KEYSTONE PRESS AGENCY INC
664 Grosvenor Ave
Montreal, QC, Canada H3Y 2S8
Telephone: (514) 482-5312, Toll Free:
(877) 482-5312, FAX: (514) 483-
9005, E-Mail: pictures@
keystonepressagency.com, Web Site:
www.ketstonepressagency.com
Founder: Bob Moynier
Founded: 1960

LLR/RESEARCH
21 Wingate St
Haverhill, MA 01832
Telephone: (978) 374-0931, FAX:
(978) 374-1008
Owner: Linda L. Rill

LINCOLN PICTURE STUDIO
225 Lookout Dr
Dayton, OH 45419-3813
Telephone: (937) 439-9633
Owner: Dan Ostendorf
Lincoln & civil war photographs, original art.

MAGNUM PHOTOS INC
12 W 31st St (fl 11)
New York, NY 10001-7204
Telephone: (212) 929-6000, FAX:
(212) 929-9325, E-Mail:
photography@magnumphotos.com,
Web Site: www.magnumphotos.com
Mng Dir: Mark Lubell
Founded: 1947

MINDEN PICTURES
558 Main St
Watsonville, CA 95076-4318
Telephone: (831) 761-3600, Toll Free:
(888) 825-0641, FAX: (831) 761-
3233, E-Mail: info@mindenpictures.
com, Web Site: www.
mindenpictures.com
Pres: Larry Minden
A wildlife & nature stock photo agency.

NEW ENGLAND STOCK PHOTO
2389 Main St (Suite 303)
Glastonbury, CT 06033-6399
Telephone: (860) 659-4949, FAX:
(860) 659-3235
Owner: Rich James

THE NEW YORK TIMES AGENCY - PHOTO
Div. of The New York Times
620 8th Ave
New York, NY 10018
Telephone: (212) 556-4939, Toll Free:
(888) NYT-PHOTO, FAX: (212)
556-5257, E-Mail: photosales@
nytimes.com, Web Site: www.
nytimesagency.com

NORTH WIND PICTURE ARCHIVES
12 Waterboro Rd
Alfred, ME 04002-3243
Telephone: (207) 490-1940, Toll Free:
(800) 952-0703, FAX: (207) 490-
3627, E-Mail: mail@
northwindpictures.com, Web Site:
www.northwindpictures.com
Dir: Nancy L. Carter
Founded: 1986
Stock picture agency specializing in history. Images portray world history from classical civilizations to about 1900.

PHOTO RESEARCHERS INC
307 5th Ave Fl 3
New York, NY 10016-6517
Telephone: (212) 758-3420, Toll Free:
(800) 833-9033, FAX: (212) 355-
0731, E-Mail: info@
photoresearchers.com, Web Site:
www.photoresearchers.com
Pres: Robert L. Zentmaier
Source of healthcare, medicine, technology, animals & nature images using specialist photography techniques.

PHOTOEDIT INC
3505 Cadillac Ave (Suite P101)
Costa Mesa, CA 92626-1434

Toll Free: (800) 860-2098, FAX: (800)
804-3707, E-Mail: sales@
photoeditinc.com, Web Site: www.
photoeditinc.com
Pres: Leslye Borden
Founded: 1985
Stock photography & stock illustration agency specializing in pictures of diversity, education & careers.

PHOTOFEST
32 E 31st St (5th fl)
New York, NY 10016-6881
Telephone: (212) 633-6330, FAX:
(212) 366-9062, E-Mail: requests@
photofestnyc.com
Pres: Howard Mandelbaum
An agency & archive which specializes in entertainment stock photography.

PHOTOSOURCE INTERNATIONAL
1910 35th Rd, Pine Lake Farm
Osceola, WI 54020-5602
Telephone: (715) 248-3800, X27, Toll
Free: (800) 223-3860, FAX: (715)
248-3800, E-Mail: info@
photosource.com, Web Site: www.
photosource.com
Editor: Lela LaBree

PHOTOTAKE/THE CREATIVE LINK
224 W 29th St (fl 9)
New York, NY 10001
Telephone: (212) 736-2525, Toll Free:
(800) 542-3686, FAX: (212) 736-
1919, E-Mail: photoinfo@
phototakeusa.com, Web Site: www.
phototakeusa.com
Pres & CEO: Yoav Levy
Founded: 2010
Photofinishing Laboratory.

PHOTRI IMAGES LLC
9653 Sherman Oaks Ct
Fairfax, VA 22032-2816
Telephone: (703) 978-0129, E-Mail:
info@photriimages.com, Web Site:
www.photriimages.com
Owner: Gail Schooefield
Owner: Sharon Dupuis
Founded: 2008

H ARMSTRONG ROBERTS INC
4203 Locust St
Philadelphia, PA 19104
Telephone: (212) 685-3870, Toll Free:
(800) 786-6300, FAX: (800) 786-
1920, E-Mail: info@robertstock.com,
Web Site: www.robertstock.com
Pres: Bob Roberts

Mktg Exec: Lisa Giokas
Founded: 1920

ROBERTS STOCK/CLASSIC STOCK

3460 Wilshire Blvd, Ste #304, Los Angeles, CA 90010-2231
4203 Locust St
Philadelphia, PA 19104-5228
Telephone: (213) 386-4600, Toll Free: (800) 786-6300, FAX: (213) 365-7171, E-Mail: aspstockpix@earthlink.net, Web Site: www.americanstockphotos.com
Pres: Christopher C. Johnson

SCENIC PHOTO!

9208 32nd Ave N
Minneapolis, MN 55427-2325
Telephone: (612) 810-0797, E-Mail: manager@scenicphoto.com, Web Site: www.scenicphoto.com
Owner: Conrad Bloomquist
Founded: 1986

SHOOTING STAR INTERNATIONAL

Div. of Shooting Star International Photo Agency
1441 N McCadden
Hollywood, CA 90028
Telephone: (323) 469-2020, FAX: (323) 464-0880, Web Site: www.shootingstaragency.com
Pres: Yoram Kahana
Founded: 1980

Celebrity photos.

SIPA PRESS

307 Seventh Ave (Suite 807)
New York, NY 10001-6066
Telephone: (212) 463-0150, FAX: (212) 463-0160, E-Mail: sipa@usa.com, Web Site: www.sipa.com
Mgr: Jonathan Wells
Founded: 1984

THE SOURCE STOCK FOOTAGE LIBRARY INC

140 S Camino Seco (Suite 308)
Tucson, AZ 85710-4473
Telephone: (520) 298-4810, FAX: (520) 290-8831, E-Mail: requests@sourcefootage.com, Web Site: www.sourcefootage.com
Pres: Bill Briggs
Library Mgr: Don French
Founded: 1982

TOM STACK & ASSOCIATES INC

c/o Tom Stack, 98310 Overseas Hwy, Key Largo, FL 33037-2370
154 Tequesta St
Tavernier, FL 33070
Telephone: (305) 852-5520, E-Mail: tomstack@earthlink.net, Web Site: www.tomstackassociatesphotoshelter.com
VP: Thomas Stack
Founded: 1965

Photography brokers.

STOCK BOSTON INC

258 Harvard St (#355)
Brookline, MA 02446
Telephone: (617) 266-2300, FAX: (617) 277-0502, E-Mail: info@stockboston.com, Web Site: www.stockboston.com
Pres: Michael Mazzaschi

STOCK MONTAGE INC

1817 N Mulligan Ave
Chicago, IL 60639
Telephone: (773) 637-9790, Toll Free: (800) 404-0425, FAX: (773) 637-9794, E-Mail: mail@stockmontage.com, Web Site: www.stockmontage.com
Pres: Shirley Neiman
Founded: 1992

Stock picture service.

THE STOCK SOLUTION INC

6640 S 2200 W
West Jordan, UT 84084-2203
Telephone: (801) 566-8684, Toll Free: (888) 366-0430, FAX: (801) 961-8030, E-Mail: info@tssphoto.com, Web Site: www.tssphoto.com
Pres: Royce Bair
Employees: 5
Founded: 1976

SUPERSTOCK INC

6622 Southpoint Dr S Ste 230
Jacksonville, FL 32216-6171
Telephone: (904) 565-0066, Toll Free: (800) 828-4545, FAX: (904) 641-4480, E-Mail: yourfriends@superstock.com, Web Site: www.superstockimages.com
CEO: Thomas V. Butta
Founded: 2004

TONY STONE IMAGES

Subs. of Getty Images (London)
122 S Michigan Ave (Suite 900)
Chicago, IL 60603
Toll Free: (800) 234-7880, FAX: (312) 922-9075, Web Site: www.getty-images.com
Pres: Andrew Duncomb

TRENDS INTERNATIONAL LLC

5188 W 74th St
Indianapolis, IN 46268
Telephone: (317) 388-1212, Toll Free: (800) 354-4639, FAX: (317) 388-1414, E-Mail: info@trendsinternational.com, Web Site: www.trendsinternational.com
Dir: Steve Patterson
Pres: Phil Jean
Mgr: Jay Myers
Founded: 2001

UNDERWOOD PHOTO ARCHIVES INC

143 Alta Vista Rd
Woodside, CA 94062
Telephone: (650) 851-5190, FAX: (650) 851-5193, E-Mail: ray@underwoodarchives.com, Web Site: www.underwoodarchives.com
Pres: Raymond Chipault

US NAVAL INSTITUTE

291 Wood Rd
Annapolis, MD 21402
Telephone: (410) 268-6110, Toll Free: (800) 233-8764, FAX: (410) 571-1703, E-Mail: customer@usni.org, Web Site: www.usni.org
CEO: Peter Daly
COO & CFO: Robert Johnson
Publr: William M. Miller III
Exec VP Membership & Mktg: W. Scott Gureck
Founded: 2011

Independent, non-profit, non-partisan professional military association.

UNIVERSITY OF SOUTHERN CALIFORNIA

University Library, Dept of Special Collections
Los Angeles, CA 90089-0189
Telephone: (213) 821-2366, FAX: (213) 740-2343, E-Mail: taube@usc.edu, Web Site: www.usc.edu
Reg History Collection Librarian: Dace Taube
Library Mgr: Rachelle Smith

VIESTI ASSOCIATES INC

434 Turner Dr
Durango, CO 81303
Telephone: (970) 382-2600, FAX: (970) 382-2700, E-Mail: photos@viestiphoto.com, Web Site: www.viestiassociates.com
Pres: Joe Viesti
Employees: 5
Founded: 1990

CALIFORNIA

Carnival Creations, 126 Agostino, Irvine, 92614-8420

Catalyst Creative Services, 619 Marion Pl, Palo Alto, 94301-4251

The Marketing Machine, 4790 Irvine Blvd (Suite 105), Irvine, 92620-1998

Mayne Associates, PO Box 48, Lafayette, 94549

McNamara & Associates, 6647 Peach Ave, Van Nuys, 91406

Lea Pierce Direct Response Strategy & Execution, 1007B W College Ave (#190), Santa Rosa, 95401-5029

COLORADO

The Write Direction, 948 North St (#12), Boulder, 80304-3386

CONNECTICUT

Al Bredenberg Creative Services, 56 Natureview Trail, Bethel, 06801

Jane Corcillo, 17 Karen Dr, Norwalk, 06851-6012

O'Halloran Advertising, 270 Saugatuck Ave, Westport, 06880-6431

FLORIDA

Creative Freelancers Inc, 7133 W Country Club Dr N Apt 150, Sarasota, 34243-3519

Jim Kerwin Freelance Copywriter, 12013 Covent Garden Ct (#2902), Naples, 34120-4689

Lewis Enterprises, 451 Heritage Dr (Suite 215), Pompano Beach, 33060-7778

Richard K Neukranz Associates, 4569 Glen Kernan Pkwy E, Jacksonville, 32224-5628

Galen Stilson Copywriter, 1338 Kinsmore Dr, Trinity, 34655

ILLINOIS

Across The Board Marketing Inc, 1636 N Wells St (#2515), Chicago, 60614-6037

Bauer Associates, 301 N Water St, Batavia, 60510

Paul Connors Creative, 213 Surrey Ln, Lake Forest, 60045-3488

Creative Copywriting, 4300 Glenlow Dr, Plainfield, 60586-7813

Bill Gershon Marketing Communications, 9828 Crawford Ave, Skokie, 60076-1107

Steve A Glaser Communications Services, 1903 Southwood Dr, Champaign, 61821-5428

Holden Copywriting, PO Box 5, Deerfield, 60015-0005

JSA Creative Services LLC, 2525 N Talman Ave, Chicago, 60647

Kevin J Shea & Associates, 311 N Hickory Ave, Arlington Heights, 60004-6210

MAINE

John Lovell Communication Services, 59 Richardson St, Portland, 04103-2518

MARYLAND

Daly Direct Marketing, 8911 Bradley Blvd, Potomac, 20854-4602

Frank Joseph, 5617 Warwick Pl, Chevy Chase, 20815-5503

J Stack & Associates, 4402 Wickford Rd, Baltimore, 21210

MASSACHUSETTS

Brian Turley & Co, 61 Sheffield Rd, Melrose, 02176

MICHIGAN

Barbara S Anderson, 706 W Davis Ave, Ann Arbor, 48103-4855

Susan K Jones & Associates, 251 Plymouth Ave SE, Grand Rapids, 49506-1755

MINNESOTA

S Connelly & Co Inc, 9687 Jeske Ave NW, Annandale, 55302-2936

Wonderful Writer LLC, 13615 61st Ave N, Minneapolis, 55446-3503

NEW HAMPSHIRE

Duncan Direct Associates, 16 Elm St, Peterborough, 03458

NEW JERSEY

Bob Bly, 590 Delcina Dr, River Vale, 07675-6111

The Copy Pro, 684 Park Ave, Oradell, 07649-2008

The Copy Shoppe, 186 Mendham Rd E, Mendham, 07945-3012

The Wordstation, 526 Main St Ste 2, Avon By The Sea, 07717-1061

NEW MEXICO

John Nicksic, 707 E Palace Ave (#2), Santa Fe, 87501

Open Horizons, 324 Ranchos De Rd, Taos, 87571

NEW YORK

B-T-B Internet Marketing Solutions, 7 Putter Ln, Linick Bldg, Middle Island, 11953-1920

Backman Writing & Communications, 32 Hillview Ave, Rensselaer, 12144-3513

Monte Brick, Wordsmith, Six Inwood Pl, Melville, 11747

Copywriter's Council of America - (Freelancers), 7 Putter Ln, Middle Island, 11953-1920

Samuel Feldman, 165 West End Ave (Suite 10H), New York, 10023

Diane Gallo Associates, PO Box 106, Gilbertsville, 13776-0106

Jack Galub, 1339 York Ave, New York, 10021-4707

Max Lent Communications, 812 Coventry Dr, Webster, 14580

Lerose Copywriting, 628 Meadowbrook Rd, Uniondale, 11553-2620

Robert Lerose, 628 Meadowbrook Rd, Uniondale, 11553-2620

Martin Gross & Friends, 145 E 27th St (Penthouse C), New York, 10016-9039

Geraldine Newman Communications, 315 E 72nd St (Suite 5K), New York, 10021

Tom Pelletier, 204 Bay Ave, Patchogue, 11772-4006

Richard Silverman, 83-33 Austin St, Kew Gardens, 11415-1814

GJ Whalen & Co Inc, 451 High Cliffe Ln, Tarrytown, 10591

NORTH CAROLINA

Charlie Browne Communications, 3002 Atando Ct, Apex, 27502-4150

Clausen Enterprises, 128A Main St, Hendersonville, 28792-5065

Creative Direct Marketing, 402 Whitehead Cir, Chapel Hill, 27514-4833

OHIO

Direct Creative, 701 Lookout Ridge Dr, Westerville, 43082-8601

Don Pendell & Associates, 2622 Wayland Ave, Dayton, 45420

Profit Boosters Copywriting, 525 Club Dr, Aurora, 44202

PENNSYLVANIA

Barcia Direct Marketing, 19 Oxford Dr, Langhorne, 19047-2056

CoreMessagink, 334 Valleybrook Dr, Lancaster, 17601-4633

Hebden Direct, 634 Spruce St, Philadelphia, 19106

TEXAS

Luther Brock PhD, The Letter Doctor, 2911 Nottingham Dr, Denton, 76209-1352

UTAH

Stephen Kimball DM Copywriting, 9489 N Canyon Heights Dr, Pleasant Grove, 84062-8812

Copywriters (39)

ACROSS THE BOARD MARKETING INC
c/o Anne E. Aldrich, 1636 N Wells St
  Apt 2515, Chicago, IL 60614-6022
1636 N Wells St (#2515)
Chicago, IL 60614-6037
Telephone: (312) 787-1642, FAX:
  (312) 787-1645, E-Mail: info@
  acrosstheboardmarketing.com, Web
  Site: www.acrosstheboardmarketing.
  com
Pres: Anne Aldrich
Founded: 1998

Marketing consultants.

BARBARA S ANDERSON
706 W Davis Ave
Ann Arbor, MI 48103-4855
Telephone: (734) 995-0125, FAX:
  (734) 994-5207
Copywriter & Graphic Artist: Barbara
  Anderson
Employees: 2
Founded: 1987

B-T-B INTERNET MARKETING SOLUTIONS
Div. of The Linick Group Inc
7 Putter Ln, Linick Bldg
Middle Island, NY 11953-1920
Telephone: (631) 924-3888, E-Mail:
  linickgroup@gmail.com, Web Site:
  www.linick.net; 222.asklinick.com
Pres: Gaylen Andrews
Exec VP: Shane Clarke
VP: Roger Dexter

BACKMAN WRITING & COMMUNICATIONS
32 Hillview Ave
Rensselaer, NY 12144-3513
Telephone: (518) 449-4985, FAX:
  (518) 449-7273, E-Mail: johnb@
  backwrite.com, Web Site: www.
  backwrite.com
Principal: John Backman
Founded: 1996

BARCIA DIRECT MARKETING
19 Oxford Dr
Langhorne, PA 19047-2056
Telephone: (215) 757-5785, FAX:
  (215) 757-5785, E-Mail: j.
  barciadirect@comcast.net
Pres: Joseph A. Barcia
Employees: 3
Founded: 1992

BAUER ASSOCIATES
301 N Water St

Batavia, IL 60510
Telephone: (630) 406-8595, FAX:
  (630) 406-8596, E-Mail: lbauer@
  bauerassoc.net, Web Site: www.
  bauerassoc.net
Owner: Larry Bauer
Founded: 1996

Marketing consultants.

BOB BLY
590 Delcina Dr
River Vale, NJ 07675-6111
Telephone: (201) 505-9451, FAX:
  (201) 573-4094, E-Mail: rwbly@bly.
  com, Web Site: www.bly.com
Copywriter: Bob Bly

AL BREDENBERG CREATIVE SERVICES
Div. of Bredenberg Associates Inc
RP-NFOA
56 Natureview Trail
Bethel, CT 06801
Telephone: (203) 791-8204, E-Mail:
  ab@copywriter.com, Web Site:
  www.copywriter.com
Pres: Al Bredenberg

MONTE BRICK, WORDSMITH
Six Inwood Pl
Melville, NY 11747
Telephone: (631) 549-9640, FAX:
  (631) 549-9640
Pres: Monte Brick

LUTHER BROCK PHD, THE LETTER DOCTOR
2911 Nottingham Dr
Denton, TX 76209-1352
Telephone: (940) 387-8058
Pres: Luther A. Brock Jr

CHARLIE BROWNE COMMUNICATIONS
3002 Atando Ct
Apex, NC 27502-4150
Telephone: (919) 267-9271, FAX:
  (919) 267-9271, E-Mail:
  cbrownecom@sbcglobal.net
Pres: Charlie Browne
Employees: 2
Founded: 2011

CARNIVAL CREATIONS
126 Agostino
Irvine, CA 92614-8420
Telephone: (949) 833-9370, FAX:
  (949) 955-2078
VP & Creative Dir: Steven Finkelstein
Employees: 4

Founded: 2001
Advertising-Art Layout and Production
Services.

CATALYST CREATIVE SERVICES
619 Marion Pl
Palo Alto, CA 94301-4251
Telephone: (650) 325-1500, E-Mail:
  chief@catalystcreative.us, Web Site:
  www.catalystcreative.us
Owner: Dennis Briskin

CLAUSEN ENTERPRISES
dba copy-design.com
128A Main St
Hendersonville, NC 28792-5065
Telephone: (828) 692-8535, E-Mail:
  jhclausen@mchsi.com, Web Site:
  www.copy-design.com
Owner: John Clausen
Founded: 1985

Marketing Consultants.

S CONNELLY & CO INC
9687 Jeske Ave NW
Annandale, MN 55302-2936
Telephone: (320) 274-7054, E-Mail:
  sconco@aol.com
Pres: Stephen P. Connelly
Employees: 3
Founded: 1987

Direct Mail Advertising.

PAUL CONNORS CREATIVE
213 Surrey Ln
Lake Forest, IL 60045-3488
Telephone: (847) 295-8746
Pres: Paul F. Connors

THE COPY PRO
684 Park Ave
Oradell, NJ 07649-2008
Telephone: (201) 986-1080, FAX:
  (201) 986-1170, E-Mail:
  thecopypro@aol.com, Web Site:
  www.thecopypronj.com
Owner & Copywriter: Kristina Elliot
Founded: 1992

THE COPY SHOPPE
Div. of CataLogistics Inc
186 Mendham Rd E
Mendham, NJ 07945-3012
Telephone: (973) 543-2679, FAX:
  (973) 543-2679, E-Mail:
  catalogistics@juno.com, Web Site:
  www.catalogistics.com
Pres: Jack Schrier

Marketing Programs & Services.

COPYWRITER'S COUNCIL OF AMERICA - (FREELANCERS)

Div. of The Linick Group Inc. aka CCA
7 Putter Ln
Middle Island, NY 11953-1920
Telephone: (631) 924-3888, FAX:
   (631) 924-8555, E-Mail:
   cca4dmcopy@gmail.com, Web Site:
   www.linick.net; www.
   andrewlinickdirectmarketing.com
Exec VP: Roger Dexter
Pres: Gaylen Andrews

COREMESSAGINK

334 Valleybrook Dr
Lancaster, PA 17601-4633
Telephone: (717) 207-0212, Web Site:
   www.cormessagink.com
Pres & Co-Founder: Lindy Litrides
Conducts Business: U.S.
Primary Market Served: Business &
   Consumer
Founded: 2007

Inspired creative messaging to attract, maintain and advance your donor relationships.

CREATIVE COPYWRITING

4300 Glenlow Dr
Plainfield, IL 60586-7813
Telephone: (815) 439-9160, FAX:
   (815) 439-9158
Pres: John M. Mora
Founded: 1991

Advertising copywriting.

CREATIVE DIRECT MARKETING

402 Whitehead Cir
Chapel Hill, NC 27514-4833
Telephone: (919) 929-5757, E-Mail:
   jeffb.cdm@mindspring.com
Principal: Jeff D. Bryant
Founded: 1989

Management Consulting Services.

CREATIVE FREELANCERS INC

7133 W Country Club Dr N Apt 150
Sarasota, FL 34243-3519
Telephone: (203) 532-2924, Toll Free:
   (800) 398-9544, E-Mail: cfonline@
   freelancers.com, Web Site: www.
   freelancers.com
Pres: Marilyn Howard

DALY DIRECT MARKETING

8911 Bradley Blvd
Potomac, MD 20854-4602
Telephone: (301) 365-3201, FAX:
   (301) 365-7514
Pres: M. Virginia Daly
Employees: 5
Marketing Programs & Services.

DIRECT CREATIVE

701 Lookout Ridge Dr
Westerville, OH 43082-8601
Telephone: (614) 882-8823, E-Mail:
   dean@directcreative.com, Web Site:
   www.directcreative.com
Pres: Dean Rieck
Founded: 1991

DUNCAN DIRECT ASSOCIATES

16 Elm St
Peterborough, NH 03458
Telephone: (603) 924-3121, FAX:
   (603) 924-8511, E-Mail:
   duncandirect@pobox.com, Web Site:
   www.duncandirect.com
Pres: George Duncan
Founded: 1976

SAMUEL FELDMAN

165 West End Ave (Suite 10H)
New York, NY 10023
Telephone: (212) 362-9517, E-Mail:
   samuelfeldman@verizon.net
Pres: Samuel Feldman

FRANK JOSEPH

5617 Warwick Pl
Chevy Chase, MD 20815-5503
Telephone: (301) 656-8753, E-Mail:
   mr.dm@verizon.net
Pres: Frank Joseph

DIANE GALLO ASSOCIATES

PO Box 106
Gilbertsville, NY 13776-0106
Telephone: (607) 783-2386, E-Mail:
   dgallo@stny.rr.com, Web Site: www.
   dianegallo.com
Owner: Diane Gallo

JACK GALUB

1339 York Ave
New York, NY 10021-4707
Telephone: (212) 737-9013
Pres: Jack Galub

BILL GERSHON MARKETING COMMUNICATIONS

9828 Crawford Ave
Skokie, IL 60076-1107
Telephone: (847) 676-9452, FAX:
   (847) 674-7205, E-Mail: gershcom@
   yahoo.com
Owner & Creative Dir: Bill Gershon

Advertising Agency & Marketing Consultant.

STEVE A GLASER COMMUNICATIONS SERVICES

1903 Southwood Dr
Champaign, IL 61821-5428
Telephone: (217) 351-0981, FAX:
   (217) 351-0981, E-Mail: steve@
   sagcs.net, Web Site: www.sags.net
Pres: Steve A. Glaser

HEBDEN DIRECT

634 Spruce St
Philadelphia, PA 19106
Telephone: (215) 923-3891, E-Mail:
   hebdendirect@comcast.net
Pres & Partner: William Hebden
Founded: 1986

HOLDEN COPYWRITING

PO Box 5
Deerfield, IL 60015-0005
Telephone: (847) 236-0669, E-Mail:
   holdendm@aol.com
Pres: Stan Holden

JSA CREATIVE SERVICES LLC

2525 N Talman Ave
Chicago, IL 60647
Telephone: (773) 772-3445, FAX:
   (773) 772-3446, E-Mail:
   jsacreative@comcast.net, Web Site:
   www.jsacreative.com
Pres: Jill Shtulman
Founded: 2010

JANE CORCILLO

17 Karen Dr
Norwalk, CT 06851-6012
Telephone: (203) 866-2008, FAX:
   (203) 299-0844, E-Mail: queries@
   corcillodirect.com, Web Site: www.
   corcillodirect.com
Pres: Jane Corcillo

SUSAN K JONES & ASSOCIATES

251 Plymouth Ave SE
Grand Rapids, MI 49506-1755
Telephone: (616) 458-0305, E-Mail:
   sjones9200@aol.com
Owner: Susan K. Jones
Founded: 1980

JIM KERWIN FREELANCE COPYWRITER

12013 Covent Garden Ct (#2902)
Naples, FL 34120-4689
Telephone: (239) 597-4445, E-Mail:
   jwkerwin@mac.com
Owner: Jim Kerwin

**KEVIN J SHEA &
ASSOCIATES**
311 N Hickory Ave
Arlington Heights, IL 60004-6210
Telephone: (847) 392-2713
Owner & Pres: Kevin J. Shea
Founded: 1987

**STEPHEN KIMBALL DM
COPYWRITING**
9489 N Canyon Heights Dr
Pleasant Grove, UT 84062-8812
Telephone: (801) 796-7234, FAX:
(801) 796-5799, E-Mail: stephen@
skcopywriting.com, Web Site: www.
skcopywriting.com
Owner: Stephen Kimball
Conducts Business: U.S. & Canada
Employees: 1
Primary Market Served: Business
Founded: 2005
Gross sales or billing: $500,000
Direct response copywriting.

**MAX LENT
COMMUNICATIONS**
812 Coventry Dr
Webster, NY 14580
Telephone: (585) 670-9322, E-Mail:
max@maxlent.com, Web Site: www.
maxlent.com
Dir: Max Lent
Founded: 2005

LEROSE COPYWRITING
628 Meadowbrook Rd
Uniondale, NY 11553-2620
Telephone: (516) 486-0472, FAX:
(516) 486-0386, E-Mail: robertler@
optonline.net, Web Site: www.
robertlerose.com
Pres: Robert Lerose

ROBERT LEROSE
628 Meadowbrook Rd
Uniondale, NY 11553-2620
Telephone: (516) 486-0472, FAX:
(516) 486-0386, E-Mail: robertler@
optonline.net, Web Site: www.
robertlerose.com
Pres: Robert Lerose
Conducts Business: U.S.
Employees: 1
Primary Market Served: Business
Advertising/Marketing Budget Related
to Direct Marketing: 26-50%
Founded: 1994

Provides marketing and corporate communications copywriting to business-
to-business and consumer marketers.

LEWIS ENTERPRISES
451 Heritage Dr (Suite 215)

Pompano Beach, FL 33060-7778
Telephone: (954) 782-1750, FAX:
(954) 785-3391, E-Mail: hglewis1@
aol.com; hgl@herschellgordonlewis.
com, Web Site: www.
herschellgordonlewis.com
Author: Herschell Gordon Lewis
Partner: Margo E Lewis
Primary Market Served: Business &
Consumer
Catalog available online
Founded: 1997

3rd edition, On the Art of Writing
Copy, ISBN: 0-9704515-4-7. 4th edition 2011: Internet marketing tips,
tricks & tactics. Marketing mayhem.

**JOHN LOVELL
COMMUNICATION
SERVICES**
59 Richardson St
Portland, ME 04103-2518
Telephone: (207) 774-0232, FAX:
(207) 774-0232
Dir: John Lovell
Founded: 2001

THE MARKETING MACHINE
4790 Irvine Blvd (Suite 105)
Irvine, CA 92620-1998
Telephone: (949) 733-1778, (949) 733-
3778, FAX: (949) 559-6993, E-Mail:
request@the-marketing-machine.
com, Web Site: www.mktgmach.com
Pres: Virginia Nicols
Founded: 1981

MARTIN GROSS & FRIENDS
145 E 27th St (Penthouse C)
New York, NY 10016-9039
Telephone: (212) 689-0772, FAX:
(212) 481-0552, E-Mail:
grossdirect@aol.com
Pres: Martin Gross

MAYNE ASSOCIATES
PO Box 48
Lafayette, CA 94549
Telephone: (925) 284-8500, FAX:
(925) 284-8502
Owner: Clifton P. Mayne
Founded: 1988

MCNAMARA & ASSOCIATES
6647 Peach Ave
Van Nuys, CA 91406
Telephone: (818) 907-6212, E-Mail:
jim@mcdrtv.com, Web Site: www.
mcdrtv.com
Owner & Pres: Jim McNamara
Founded: 2000

**RICHARD K NEUKRANZ
ASSOCIATES**
4569 Glen Kernan Pkwy E
Jacksonville, FL 32224-5628
Telephone: (904) 998-1201, FAX:
(904) 998-1579, E-Mail: rneukranz@
bellsouth.net
Pres: Richard K. Neukranz

**GERALDINE NEWMAN
COMMUNICATIONS**
315 E 72nd St (Suite 5K)
New York, NY 10021
Telephone: (212) 988-3395, FAX:
(212) 988-3407, E-Mail: ger@
newthynk.com, Web Site: www.
newthynk.com
Owner: Geraldine Newman
Employees: 2
Founded: 2010

JOHN NICKSIC
707 E Palace Ave (#2)
Santa Fe, NM 87501
Telephone: (505) 983-7656, FAX:
(505) 983-7159, E-Mail: nicksic@
mindspring.com
Pres: John Nicksic
Founded: 1969

O'HALLORAN ADVERTISING
270 Saugatuck Ave
Westport, CT 06880-6431
Telephone: (203) 341-9400
CEO: James O'Halloran
VP: Ken Gary
Sales Exec: Rose Hebeler
Fin Exec: Kevin O'Halloran
Oper Exec: George Ramirez
Dir: Aron Caruso
Primary Market Served: Consumer
Founded: 1971

A full service agency specializing in D/
R, Directory (YP) advertising & local
searches as well as general advertising
for regional & national clients.

OPEN HORIZONS
Div. of Open Horizons
324 Ranchos De Rd
Taos, NM 87571
Telephone: (575) 751-3398, FAX:
(575) 751-3100, E-Mail: info@
bookmarket.com, Web Site: www.
bookmarket.com
Pres: John Kremer
Founded: 1982

TOM PELLETIER
204 Bay Ave
Patchogue, NY 11772-4006

Telephone: (631) 569-5552, FAX:
(413) 825-7968, E-Mail: tom@
tompelletier.com, Web Site: www.
tompelletier.com
Owner & Writer: Tom Pelletier

DON PENDELL & ASSOCIATES

2622 Wayland Ave
Dayton, OH 45420
Telephone: (937) 254-4210
Pres: Donald Pendell
Founded: 1985

Management Consulting Services.

LEA PIERCE DIRECT RESPONSE STRATEGY & EXECUTION

1007B W College Ave (#190)
Santa Rosa, CA 95401-5029
Telephone: (707) 571-1586, Toll Free:
(800) 932-4748, E-Mail: info@
leapierce.com, Web Site: www.
leapierce.com
Owner: Lea Pierce
Founded: 1985

PROFIT BOOSTERS COPYWRITING

525 Club Dr
Aurora, OH 44202
Telephone: (330) 963-0330, FAX:
(330) 562-2446, E-Mail:
mikepavlish@profitboosterscopy.
com, Web Site: www.
profitboosterscopy.com
Pres: Michael Pavlish
Founded: 1995

Copywriting - Headlines And Book Titles.

RICHARD SILVERMAN

83-33 Austin St
Kew Gardens, NY 11415-1814
Telephone: (718) 441-5358, FAX:
(718) 441-5358, E-Mail: vze268ci@
verizon.net
Owner: Richard Silverman

J STACK & ASSOCIATES

4402 Wickford Rd
Baltimore, MD 21210
Telephone: (410) 889-3327, FAX:
(410) 889-9039
Owner: John Stack

GALEN STILSON COPYWRITER

1338 Kinsmore Dr
Trinity, FL 34655
Telephone: (727) 372-2032, E-Mail:
galen@galenstilson.com, Web Site:
www.galenstilson.com

Pres: Galen Stilson

BRIAN TURLEY & CO

61 Sheffield Rd
Melrose, MA 02176
Telephone: (781) 662-8538, FAX:
(781) 662-5590, E-Mail: turley@
shore.net
Pres: Brian C. Turley
Employees: 1
Founded: 1981

Direct Retail Sales.

GJ WHALEN & CO INC

451 High Cliffe Ln
Tarrytown, NY 10591
Telephone: (914) 333-0085, E-Mail:
george@gjwhalen.com
Pres: George J. Whalen

Technology & business writing contractor.

WONDERFUL WRITER LLC

13615 61st Ave N
Minneapolis, MN 55446-3503
Telephone: (763) 557-7116, Toll Free:
(888) 557-7116, FAX: (763) 551-
4831, E-Mail: colleen@
wonderfulwriter.com, Web Site:
www.wonderfulwriter.com
Owner & Pres: Colleen Szot

Direct response television writer.

THE WORDSTATION

526 Main St Ste 2
Avon By The Sea, NJ 07717-1061
Telephone: (732) 774-4831, FAX:
(732) 869-1822, E-Mail:
pattyshannone@optonline.net
Owner: Patty Shannon
Founded: 1990

THE WRITE DIRECTION

948 North St (#12)
Boulder, CO 80304-3386
Toll Free: (808) 635-8031, E-Mail:
debra@writedirection.com, Web
Site: www.writedirection.com
Owner & Copywriter: Debra Jason
Founded: 1989

Direct-response copywriter.

Direct Marketing Associations, Clubs & Organizations (40)

Listed in this section are associations, clubs and membership organizations related to all areas of the direct marketing industry.

ADVERTISING RESEARCH FOUNDATION

432 Park Ave S (fl 6)
New York, NY 10016-8013
Telephone: (212) 751-5656, FAX:
(212) 319-5265, E-Mail: info@
thearf.org, Web Site: www.thearf.org
Pres & CEO: Gayle Fuguitt
Membership Svcs: Jacqueline
McLoughlin
Sr VP, Opers: Carole White
Conducts Business: Worldwide
Employees: 18
Primary Market Served: Business &
Consumer

Non-profit professional association devoted to advertising research.

ALLIANCE OF NONPROFIT MAILERS

1211 Connecticut Ave NW (Suite 610)
Washington, DC 20036-2705
Telephone: (202) 462-5132, FAX:
(202) 462-0423, E-Mail: alliance@
nonprofitmailers.org, Web Site:
www.nonprofitmailers.org
Exec Dir: Neal Denton
Exec Dir: Anthony W. Conway
Asst Dir: Heidi Kurtz
Policy & Program Asst: Melissa Simonich
Conducts Business: U.S.
Employees: 3
Primary Market Served: Business
Catalog available online
Advertising/Marketing Budget Related
to Direct Marketing: 0-25%
Founded: 1980

Represent non-profit mailers before the
U.S. Congress, U.S. Postal Service &
Postal Rate Commission.

AMERICAN ASSOCIATION OF ADVERTISING AGENCIES

1065 Avenue Of The Americas Fl 16
New York, NY 10018-0174
Telephone: (212) 682-2500, FAX:
(212) 682-8391, Web Site: www.
aaaa.org
Pres & CEO: O. Burtch Drake

Exec VP & CFO: James Martucci
Exec VP: Michael D. Donahue
Sr VP: Marsha Appel
Bd Sec: Michele Adams
Conducts Business: U.S.
Employees: 95
Primary Market Served: Business
Catalog available online
Founded: 1917

Advertising trade association of full
service advertising agency members.

AMERICAN INSTITUTE OF GRAPHIC ARTS (AIGA)

164 Fifth Ave
New York, NY 10010-5901
Telephone: (212) 807-1990, FAX:
(212) 807-1799, E-Mail: grefe@aiga.
org, Web Site: www.aiga.org
Exec Dir: Richard Grefe
Founded: 1914
Gross sales or billing: $5,400,000

National non-profit organization for the
graphic design profession.

AMERICAN ISRAEL PUBLIC AFFAIRS COMMITTEE

251 H St NW
Washington, DC 20001-2604
Telephone: (202) 639-5226, Web Site:
www.aipac.org
Primary Market Served: Business &
Consumer

AMERICAN MARKETING ASSOCIATION

311 S Wacker Dr (Suite 5800)
Chicago, IL 60606-6629
Telephone: (312) 542-9000, Toll Free:
(800) AMA-1150, FAX: (312) 542-
9001, Web Site: www.
marketingpower.com
CEO: Dennis Dunlap
Chief Mktg Officer: Nancy Costopulos
Employees: 63
Primary Market Served: Business
Catalog available online
Advertising/Marketing Budget Related
to Direct Marketing: 0-25%
Direct Marketing ad budget:
$7,600,000

Founded: 1937
Professional society of marketing &
marketing research executives, sales &
promotion managers, advertising specialists, academics & others interested
in marketing. Foster research, sponsors
& seminars & provide educational
placement.

AMERICAN MARKETING ASSOCIATION/NEW YORK CHAPTER

116 E 27th St (Floor 6)
New York, NY 10016-8942
Telephone: (212) 687-3280, FAX:
(212) 557-9242, E-Mail: mlkeane@
nyama.org, Web Site: www.nyama.
org
Exec Dir: Marylee Keane
Mktg Dir: Bart Lewin
Conducts Business: U.S.
Primary Market Served: Business
Catalog available online
Direct online sales

Association of marketing & market research professionals with international
headquarters in Chicago, IL. Branch offices nationwide.

AMERICAN SOCIETY OF MEDIA PHOTOGRAPHERS (ASMP)

150 N Second St
Philadelphia, PA 19106-1912
Telephone: (215) 451-ASMP, FAX:
(215) 451-0880, Web Site: www.
asmp.org
Exec Dir: Eugene Mopsik
Gen Counsel: Victor Perlman
Gen Mgr: Elena Goertz
Bookkeeper: Chris Chandler
Dir Commun: Peter Dyson
Employees: 7
Primary Market Served: Business
Catalog available online
Indirect online sales
Founded: 1944

Maintain & promote high ethics in photography; cultivate mutual understanding among photographers; protect &
promote photographer's interests.

AMERICAN TELESERVICES ASSOCIATION

8500 Keystone Crossing (Suite 480)
Indianapolis, IN 46240-2460
Telephone: (317) 816-9336, Toll Free:
(877) 779-3974, FAX: (317) 218-
0323, Web Site: www.ataconnect.org
Exec VP Bus Devel: Tom Chandler
Pres & CEO: Phil Grudzinski
Dir, Fin: Bill Morris
Dir Digital Mktg: Tom Deeter
Mgr, Admin Svcs: Ken Hennenfent
Conducts Business: U.S., Canada, Aus-
tralia, Japan, Europe, Mexico, South
America
Employees: 12
Primary Market Served: Business
Catalog available online
Indirect online sales
Advertising/Marketing Budget Related
to Direct Marketing: 0-25%
Direct Marketing ad budget:
Direct Mail: 20%
Telephone: 80%
Founded: 1983

Provide education & leadership in the
ethical use of the telephone in commerce & advocacy in relevant legislative affairs.

THE ARIZONA DIRECT MARKETING ASSOCIATION

2107 N 69th Pl
Scottsdale, AZ 85257-2630
Telephone: (480) 970-8643, FAX:
(480) 893-1157, E-Mail: julie@
brownies.com, Web Site: www.
azdma.org
Administrator: Julie Gaffney
Conducts Business: U.S.
Employees: 280
Primary Market Served: Business &
Consumer
Advertising/Marketing Budget Related
to Direct Marketing: 76-100%
Founded: 1979

Statewide direct marketing association.

ASSOCIATION FOR AUDIENCE MARKETING PROFESSIONALS (AAMP)

PO Box 15281
North Hollywood, CA 91615-5281
Telephone: (310) 323-7220, FAX:
(310) 323-7231, E-Mail: mjordan@
espcomp.com, Web Site: www.
wfma.org
Pres: John Brooks
VP Mktg: Eric Holden
VP Membership: Meg Clark
VP Programming: Nicole Fromm
VP Sponsorship: Melanie Russell
Primary Market Served: Business

Catalog available online

ASSOCIATION FOR POSTAL COMMERCE

RP-NFOA
1800 Diagonal Rd (Suite 320)
Alexandria, VA 22314-2862
Telephone: (703) 524-0096, FAX:
(703) 524-1871, Web Site: www.
postcom.org
Pres: Gene A. Del Polito
VP: Anthony Gallo
Admin Dir: Donna Hoffman
Conducts Business: U.S.
Employees: 4
Catalog available online
Advertising/Marketing Budget Related
to Direct Marketing: 76-100%
Direct Marketing ad budget: $20,000
Direct Mail: 100%
Founded: 1947
Gross sales or billing: $1,200,000

Interested in all legislation pertaining
to postal laws & regulations. Keep
members informed about happenings in
Congress, the U.S. Postal Service & the
Postal Rate Commission.

ASSOCIATION OF COUPON PROFESSIONALS

1051 Pontiac Rd
Drexel Hill, PA 19026-4816
Telephone: (610) 789-1478, FAX:
(610) 789-5309, E-Mail: john.
morgan@acp-hq.org, Web Site:
www.couponpros.org
Exec Dir: John Morgan
Primary Market Served: Business
Catalog available online
Direct online sales

Represent companies in the coupon industry, including manufacturers, retailers, processors & suppliers.
Membership is limited to corporations
paying annual membership dues.

ASSOCIATION OF ENERGY ENGINEERS

4025 Pleasantdale Rd (Suite 420)
Atlanta, GA 30340-4264
Telephone: (770) 447-5083 x210,
FAX: (770) 446-3969, E-Mail:
info@aeecenter.org, Web Site: www.
aeecenter.org
Dir: Brian Douglas
Dir Info Sys: Ruth Marie
Exec Dir: Albert Thumann
Exec Admin: Ruth Whitlock
Conducts Business: Worldwide
Employees: 12
Primary Market Served: Business
Catalog available online
Direct online sales

Founded: 1977
Technical conferences, seminars, exhibitions, certification & book programs
for energy engineers.

ASSOCIATION OF MARKETING SERVICE PROVIDERS

1800 Diagonal Rd (Suite 320)
Alexandria, VA 22314-2806
Telephone: (703) 836-9200, Toll Free:
(800) 333-6272, FAX: (703) 548-
8204, E-Mail: mfsa-mail@mfsanet.
org, Web Site: www.mfsanet.org
Pres & CEO: Kenneth Garner
VP Postal & Member Rels: Leo Ray-
mond
Asst Dir Mktg/Commun: Brittney
Brown
Dir Mktg/Commun: Michelle Raymone
Conducts Business: U.S., U.K., Cana-
da, Japan, Australia, Germany
Employees: 10
Primary Market Served: Business
Catalog available online
Indirect online sales
Advertising/Marketing Budget Related
to Direct Marketing: 76-100%
Direct Marketing ad budget: $100,000
Direct Mail: 75%
Magazines: 5%
Online: 20%
Founded: 1920
Gross sales or billing: $2,000,000

Trade association to mailing and fulfillment industry. Approximately 700
member companies-consisting primarily of mailing service companies.

ASSOCIATION OF NATIONAL ADVERTISERS INC

708 3rd Ave (Floor 33)
New York, NY 10017-4201
Telephone: (212) 697-5950, FAX:
(212) 687-7310, Web Site: www.ana.
net
COO: Christina Manna
Pres & CEO: Robert Liodice
Sr Dir: Brian Davidson
Sr VP Mktg: Nick Primola
Sr VP Info Svcs: Kathleen Hunter
Conducts Business: U.S.
Employees: 25
Primary Market Served: Business
Catalog available online
Direct online sales
Founded: 1910
Gross sales or billing: $16,000,000

Organization exclusively dedicated to
serving the interests of corporations
that advertise either regionally or nationally. Membership is a cross section
of American industry, consisting of

manufacturers, retailers, service providers, & financial institutions. Markets to consumers & other companies.

BUSINESS MARKETING ASSOCIATION

1833 Center Point Cir (Suite 123)
Naperville, IL 60563-4848
Telephone: (630) 544-5054, FAX: (630) 544-5055, E-Mail: info@marketing.org, Web Site: www.marketing.org
Exec Dir: Al Maag
Events Mgr: Kriston Ewoldt
Bus Devel Mgr: Michael Greskiewicz
Commun Mgr: Ryan Foster
Opers Mgr: Sarah Washburn
Conducts Business: U.S., Canada, Europe, Asia, S. America
Employees: 4
Primary Market Served: Business
Catalog available online
Direct online sales
Advertising/Marketing Budget Related to Direct Marketing: 0-25%
Founded: 1922

Association with over 4000 members involved in business marketing & marketing communications.

CANADIAN MARKETING ASSOCIATION

1 Concorde Gate (Suite 607)
Don Mills, ON, Canada M3C 3N6
Telephone: (416) 391-2362, Toll Free: (800) 267-8805, FAX: (416) 441-4062, E-Mail: info@the-cma.org, Web Site: www.the-cma.org
Pres & CEO: Doug Brooks
Conducts Business: Canada
Primary Market Served: Business & Consumer
Catalog available online
Founded: 1967

The Canadian Marketing Association (CMA) embraces Canadaï¿1/2s major business sectors and all marketing disciplines, channels and technologies. Its corporate members encompass all facets of marketing and represent consumer and business-to-business marketers plus agencies. These organizations make a major contribution to the economy, driving commerce, investments in media and new marketing technologies while providing employment for millions of Canadians.

CHICAGO ASSOCIATION OF DIRECT MARKETING

PO Box 578
Westmont, IL 60559-0578

Telephone: (312) 849-2236, FAX: (312) 849-2239, E-Mail: info@cadm.org, Web Site: www.cadm.org
Pres: Joe DeCosmo
VP: Michelle Blechman
Conducts Business: U.S.
Primary Market Served: Business
Catalog available online

Hold monthly meetings, workshops, seminars & an annual two day conference in February to advance new ideas, current trends & future prospects in the direct response industry.

CHILDREN'S MIRACLE NETWORK

205 W 700 S
Salt Lake City, UT 84101-2726
Toll Free: (801) 214-7400, Web Site: www.cmn.org
Sr VP: Robert Banner
Primary Market Served: Consumer

Raises funds for children's hospitals across North America.

CROSSBOW GROUP

991 Post Rd E, Westport, CT 06880-5343
136 Main St Ste 5
Westport, CT 06880-3304
Telephone: (203) 222-2244, FAX: (203) 226-7838, E-Mail: info@crossbowgroup.com, Web Site: www.crossbowgroup.com
Founder: H.W. Mirbach
Pres & CEO: Jay Bower
COO: Mary Plamieniak
Primary Market Served: Business & Consumer
Founded: 1984
Gross sales or billing: $1,250,000

Help companies quickly & efficiently acquire & retain new customers using traditional & digital media.

DMG DIRECT INC

c/o Greg Bassine, 13335 SW Chimney Ridge Ct, Tigard, OR 97223-1849
13335 SW Chimney Ridge Ct
Tigard, OR 97223-1849
Telephone: (503) 579-5609, Toll Free: (888) 282-2122, FAX: (503) 579-4919, E-Mail: dmg@dirmarketing.com, Web Site: www.dirmarketing.com/dmginc
Pres: Greg Bassine
Employees: 3
Primary Market Served: Business & Consumer
Founded: 1984
Gross sales or billing: $71,000

Provides the direct marketing community with an ongoing source of awareness, education, information &

networking through the interaction of direct marketing professionals while maintaining the highest levels of ethics & standards within the direct marketing industry.

DMSA INC

One Enterprise Dr (Bldg H)
Newfoundland, PA 18445-0080
Telephone: (570) 676-6000
Mng Dir: Gerry Pike

DATADIRECT

American Marketing Association
2707 Peach Tree Sq
Atlanta, GA 30360-2634
Telephone: (678) 530-0034, FAX: (678) 530-9563, E-Mail: info@ddirect.com, Web Site: www.ddirect.com
Pres: Tom Coggin
Exec VP, Bus Intelligence: Scott Coggin
VP Bus Devel: Melanie Jones
VP Mktg Tech: Bert Garris
Dir Opers: Behrange Derakhshan
Conducts Business: U.S.
Employees: 20
Primary Market Served: Business & Consumer

Regional direct marketing association.

DIRECT MARKETING ASSOCIATION OF DETROIT

PO Box 70
Royal Oak, MI 48068-0070
Telephone: (248) 478-4888, FAX: (248) 478-6437, E-Mail: dmad@ameritech.net, Web Site: www.dmad.org
Pres: Dan Chester
Treas: Bruce Moyer
Sec: Alex Della Torre
Dir: Terry Burnett
Dir: Dan Dembicki
Conducts Business: U.S.
Employees: 500
Primary Market Served: Business & Consumer
Founded: 1958

Hold monthly meetings & a "Direct Marketing Day" in the fall of each year. Also, monthly meetings first Thursday of each month, September through June.

DIRECT MARKETING ASSOCIATION OF NORTHERN CALIFORNIA

Sub. of www.the-dma.org
Div. of www.the-dma.org
15227 Perry Ln
Morgan Hill, CA 95037-9659

Toll Free: (800) 613-9266, FAX: (800) 613-8819, E-Mail: lbeasley@ beasleydirect.com, Web Site: www. dmanc.org
Pres: Laurie Beasley
Primary Market Served: Business & Consumer

DIRECT MARKETING ASSOCIATION OF SAINT LOUIS

PO Box 1005
Washington, MO 63090-8005
Toll Free: (866) 516-0121, FAX: (636) 239-2324, E-Mail: mparisien@mac. com, Web Site: www.dmastl.org
Exec Dir: Sue Cullinane
VP: George Snyder
Pres: Maurice R. Parisien
Sec & Treas: Glenna Phillips
Conducts Business: U.S.
Primary Market Served: Business
Founded: 1975

A not-for-profit professional business association of users & suppliers of direct marketing media.

DIRECT MARKETING ASSOCIATION OF SOUTHERN CALIFORNIA

1800 Hillcrest Dr (#297)
Newbury Park, CA 91320
Telephone: (818) 541-1152, FAX: (818) 541-1959, Web Site: www. ladma.org
Pres: Steve Stullman
Exec Dir: Bob Hughes
Conducts Business: U.S.
Primary Market Served: Business & Consumer
Catalog available online
Direct online sales
Founded: 1980

Non-profit trade association of diners.

DIRECT MARKETING ASSOCIATION OF TORONTO

75 Superior Blvd
Toronto, ON, Canada L5T 2X9
Telephone: (905) 564-0150 X108, FAX: (905) 564-6621, E-Mail: pete@themose.ca, Web Site: www. dmatoronto.org
Pres: Alan Brodeur
Conducts Business: Canada
Primary Market Served: Business & Consumer
Founded: 1962

Direct marketing association. Networking & ideas exchange form for Direct Marketing professionals.

DIRECT MARKETING ASSOCIATION OF WASHINGTON

11709 Bowman Green Dr
Reston, VA 20190
Telephone: (703) 689-DMAW, FAX: (703) 481-DMAW, E-Mail: info@ dmaw.org, Web Site: www.dmaw. org
Exec Dir: Donna Tschiffely
Conducts Business: U.S.
Primary Market Served: Business
Founded: 1955

Professional association for 1500 DM professionals in the Washington metro area, with chapters in Central Virginia & Baltimore. Comprehensive schedule of seminars, monthly meetings & in-house training. Annual Conference & Expo is The Bridge Conference, co-hosted with Assn. of Fundraising Professionals, DC Metro Chapter and attended by more than 1500. Monthly newsletter & annual directory of members.

DIRECT SELLING ASSOCIATION

1667 K St NW (Suite 1100)
Washington, DC 20006-1660
Telephone: (202) 452-8866, FAX: (202) 452-9010, E-Mail: info@dsa. org, Web Site: www.dsa.org
Pres: Joseph Mariano
Dir Mktg & Publications Svcs: Karen Garrett
Exec VP: Adolfo Franco
VP & CMO: Amy Robinson
VP, Education & Meeting: Melissa Brunton
Dir Opers: Jennifer Dunleavey
Conducts Business: US
Employees: 20
Primary Market Served: Business
Advertising/Marketing Budget Related to Direct Marketing: 0-25%
Direct Marketing ad budget: $150,000
Founded: 1910
Gross sales or billing: $6,000,000

Represents manufacturers & distributors selling consumer products door-to-door, by appointment & through home-party plans.

DIRECT SELLING EDUCATION FOUNDATION

1667 K St (Suite 1100)
Washington, DC 20006-1660
Telephone: (202) 452-8866, FAX: (202) 452-9015, E-Mail: info@dsef. org, Web Site: www.dsef.org
Exec Dir: Charles L Orr
Chief Mktg & Devel Officer: Nancy J Laichas
Employees: 6

Primary Market Served: Consumer
Catalog available online
Advertising/Marketing Budget Related to Direct Marketing: 0-25%
Direct Marketing ad budget: $450,000
Founded: 1973

Advocates of marketplace ethics, consumer knowledge & consumer satisfaction.

DISCMAIL DIRECT COALITION

39 North Bayles Ave
Port Washington, NY 11050-2930
Telephone: (516) 757-6720, Web Site: http://mesalliance.org/
Primary Market Served: Consumer

FLORIDA DIRECT MARKETING ASSOCIATION

7154 N University Dr (# 241)
Tamarac, FL 33321
Telephone: (786) 357-3275, E-Mail: president@fdma.org, Web Site: www.fdma.org
Pres: Keith Fletcher
Employees: 1
Primary Market Served: Business & Consumer
Founded: 1977

A 500 member direct marketing association dedicated to the networking & education of direct marketers. In addition to monthly meetings, the association's annual convention DM Summit is held annually. Call for more information. Governor of the state of Florida proclaims that week as "Direct Market Industry Week."

FOOD MARKETING INSTITUTE (FMI)

2345 Crystal Dr (Suite 800)
Arlington, VA 22202
Telephone: (202) 452-8444, FAX: (202) 429-4519, E-Mail: fmi@fmi. org, Web Site: www.fmi.org
Pres & CEO: Tim Hammonds
Employees: 70
Primary Market Served: Business
Founded: 1971

A non-profit trade association representing the supermarket industry, both retail & wholesale.

GREENPEACE USA

702 H St NW (Suite 300)
Washington, DC 20001
Telephone: (202) 462-1177, Web Site: www.greenpeace.org
Primary Market Served: Business & Consumer

HOUSTON DIRECT MARKETING ASSOCIATION

Box 2382
Houston, TX 77252-2382
Telephone: (281) 931-8883, FAX: (281) 820-4023, Web Site: www. houstondma.org
Pres: Dan Singer
VP Programs Chair: Deborah Hayden
Sec: Kent Guida
Treas: Art Fallon
Arrangements: Barbara Kilawee
Past Pres Membership: Steve Fowler
Newsletter: Harry Romberg
Direct Mktg Day Programs Chair: Gem Smith
Sponsorships: James Helsley
July Social Mixer: Jim Richards
Direct Mktg Day Facilities: Tom Filla
Member at Large: Barbara Hicks
Member at Large: Elroy Forbes
Member at Large: Jennifer Hoff
Primary Market Served: Business & Consumer
Founded: 1953

Purpose is: to eliminate trade abuse, upgrade the image of the direct marketing industry, improve operations & self-promotion methods, establish better industry communications, maintain a code of ethics among all direct marketers, foster friendship among those in the industry, conduct a conference for all direct marketers & promote Houston's direct marketing community.

HUMAN RIGHTS CAMPAIGN

1640 Rhode Island Ave NW
Washington, DC 20036-3200
Telephone: (202) 216-1500, Toll Free: (800) 777-4723, Web Site: www.hrc. org
Pres: Chad Griffin
Mgr Dir: Sussanne J Salkind
Primary Market Served: Business & Consumer

IDEALLIANCE

SIG of Printing Industries of America
6600 Duke St (Suite 420)
Alexandria, VA 22314-2805
Telephone: (703) 837-1070, FAX: (703) 837-1072
Pres & CEO: David J. Steinhardt
Conducts Business: Worldwide
Employees: 21
Primary Market Served: Business
Catalog available online
Founded: 1966

Volunteer, non-profit membership association for the printing & publishing industry. The purpose is to bring about the coordination among industry segments necessary to apply technologies & in other ways increase productivity & market responsiveness in the addressing & distribution of print & information products.

INCENTIVE MANUFACTURERS REPRESENTATIVES ASSOCIATION (IMRA)

Subs. of Incentive Marketing Assoc
1601 N Bond St (Suite 303)
Naperville, IL 60563-3801
Telephone: (630) 369-7786, FAX: (630) 369-3773, E-Mail: nicole@ incentivemarketing.org, Web Site: www.imraonline.org
Exec Dir: Karen Renk
Administrative Dir: Nicole Sweigart
Primary Market Served: Business & Consumer
Founded: 1963

An independent representative & supplier of products to the premium & incentive industry.

INTERNATIONAL PREPAID COMMUNICATIONS ASSOCIATION

904 Massachusetts Ave NE
Washington, DC 20002
Telephone: (202) 544-4448, Toll Free: (800) 333-3513, FAX: (202) 547-7417
Exec Dir: Howard Segermark
Employees: 6
Primary Market Served: Business
Founded: 1995
Gross sales or billing: $400,000

The trade association for the pre-paid phone card industry.

THE INTERNET ALLIANCE

1615 L St NW (Suite 1100)
Washington, DC 20036-5624
Telephone: (202) 861-2476, FAX: (202) 955-8081, E-Mail: info@ internetalliance.org, Web Site: www. internetalliance.org
Exec Dir: Tammy Cota
Conducts Business: U.S., Canada
Employees: 1
Primary Market Served: Business
Advertising/Marketing Budget Related to Direct Marketing: 0-25%
Founded: 1981

Trade association for interactive telecommunications services.

KANSAS CITY DIRECT MARKETING ASSOCIATION

638 W 39th St, PO Box 419264
Kansas City, MO 64141
Telephone: (816) 561-5323, FAX: (816) 561-1991, E-Mail: info@ kcdma.org, Web Site: www.kcdma. org
Exec Dir: Jane Male
Pres: Sandy Pennington
Conducts Business: U.S.
Employees: 450
Primary Market Served: Business
Founded: 1948

Association of direct marketers in Greater Kansas City. Hold monthly meetings (2nd Tuesday of every month), an annual direct marketing day in March & an annual awards program. Provide scholarships through the KCDMA educational foundation.

LANGEVIN LEARNING SERVICES

38 Antares Dr (Suite 1200)
Ottawa, ON, Canada K2E 7V2
Telephone: (613) 288-3064, Toll Free: (800) 223-2209, Web Site: www. langevin.com
Pres: Erin Langevin
Primary Market Served: Business

LICENSING INDUSTRY MERCHANDISERS' ASSOCIATION (LIMA)

350 Fifth Ave (Suite 1419)
New York, NY 10118-0110
Telephone: (212) 244-1944, FAX: (212) 563-6552, E-Mail: info@ licensing.org, Web Site: www. licensing.org
Pres: Charles M. Riotto
Admin Dir: Janet Lawlor
Conducts Business: U.S., U.K., Germany, Japan
Employees: 5
Primary Market Served: Business
Catalog available online
Indirect online sales
Advertising/Marketing Budget Related to Direct Marketing: 0-25%
Founded: 1985
Gross sales or billing: $1,500,000

The International Trade Association for the advancement of professionalism in licensing.

LOUISVILLE DIRECT MARKETING ASSOCIATION

PO Box 36034
Louisville, KY 40233-6034
Toll Free: (888) 392-1941, E-Mail: ldmacontact@ldma.org, Web Site: www.ldma.org
Pres: Al Klein
Treas: Jo Holt
Primary Market Served: Business

Advertising/Marketing Budget Related
to Direct Marketing: 51-75%
Founded: 1983

Educational & social association dedicated to educating members in direct
marketing.

MARKETING AGENCIES ASSOCIATION WORLDWIDE

89 Woodland Cr
Edina, MN 55424-1454
Telephone: (952) 922-0130, FAX:
(203) 969-1499, E-Mail: keith.
mccracker@maaw.org, Web Site:
www.maaw.org
VP, Global Opers: Brad Byen
Pres: Kieran Kileen
Sec: Rico Di Giovanni
Treas: Rich Butwinick
Conducts Business: Worldwide
Primary Market Served: Business
Founded: 1961

Provide support to agencies in the promotion & marketing field, concentrating on the development & growth of
agencies.

MARKETING RESEARCH ASSOCIATION

1156 15th St NW Ste 302
Washington, DC 20005-1745
Telephone: (860) 682-1000, Toll Free:
(202) 800-2545, FAX: (860) 682-
1010, (888) 512-1050, E-Mail:
membership@marketingresearch.org,
Web Site: www.mra-net.org
COO: Kristen Darby
CEO: David Almy
CFO: Tasha Jackson
Dir: Bruce Mendelsohn
Dir: Lucy Haydu
Membership Mgr: Lisa Lockwood
Conducts Business: Latin America, Europe, Asia, Middle East, South America
Employees: 12
Primary Market Served: Business &
Consumer
Catalog available online
Indirect online sales
Founded: 1954

Not-for-profit association dedicated to
promoting excellence in marketing &
opinion research members, includes
more than 3,000 full service research
companies, data collectors, end users &
more.

MID AMERICA DIRECT MARKETING ASSOCIATION

Subs. of NATIL DMA
1620 Dodge St

Omaha, NE 68197
Telephone: (402) 965-4318, FAX:
(402) 964-8484, Web Site: www.
madma.org
Pres: Matt Smolsky
VP: Jim Svoboda
VP: Mary Vorthmann
Primary Market Served: Business
Catalog available online
Indirect online sales

Professional organization of individual
members who share a common interest
in direct marketing.

MIDWEST DIRECT MARKETING ASSOCIATION INC

1821 University Ave W (Suite S-256)
Saint Paul, MN 55104
Telephone: (651) 999-5351, FAX:
(651) 917-1835, E-Mail: mdma@
mdma.org, Web Site: www.mdma.
org
Pres: Joan Forde
Conducts Business: U.S.
Employees: 1
Primary Market Served: Business
Advertising/Marketing Budget Related
to Direct Marketing: 76-100%
Founded: 1960

Members meet regularly to exchange
ideas & information about the direct
marketing field. Monthly newsletters,
monthly meetings, a direct marketing
conference in the spring, & an annual
awards competition recognizing excellence in Midwest direct marketing.

MODERNAD MEDIA LLC

2200 SW 10th St
Deerfield Beach, FL 33442-7622
Telephone: (954) 312-4700, FAX:
(954) 312-4853, Web Site: www.
modernad.com
Pres & CEO: Kevin Collins
Chief Mktg Officer: Tony Provenzano
Founded: 2007

NATIONAL CABLE & TELECOMMUNICATIONS ASSOCIATION

25 Massachusetts Ave NW (Suite 400)
Washington, DC 20001
Telephone: (202) 222-2300, FAX:
(202) 775-3675, Web Site: www.
ncta.com
Pres & CEO: Kyle McSlasrow
Sr VP: Eleanor Winites
Catalog available online
Advertising/Marketing Budget Related
to Direct Marketing: 0-25%
Founded: 1952
Gross sales or billing: $6,600,000
Represent the cable television industry.

NATIONAL MAIL ORDER ASSOCIATION (NMOA)

2807 Polk St NE
Minneapolis, MN 55418-2954
Telephone: (612) 788-1673, E-Mail:
info@nmoa.org, Web Site: www.
nmoa.org
Pres: John D. Schulte
Editor: Brad Lee
Conducts Business: Worldwide
Primary Market Served: Business
Catalog available online
Direct online sales
Advertising/Marketing Budget Related
to Direct Marketing: 76-100%
Direct Marketing ad budget:
Direct Mail: 75%
Magazines: 25%
Founded: 1972

Helps small & medium firms
(50,000,000 & under) in the area of
mail order & direct mail marketing.
Publishers of Mail Order Digest &
Washington Newsletter. Operates "The
Mail Order Connection" website. Also
operates the mail order trade show on
www.nmoadirect.com & marketingdemographics.com; a connecting spot for
manufacturers & merchandise buyers.

NETWEB/OMNI LLC

PO Box 1298
Ellicott City, MD 21041-1298
Telephone: (410) 591-1900, E-Mail:
barry@netwebomni.com, Web Site:
www.netwebomni.com
Pres: Barry Dennis
Webmaster: Daniel Dennis
Conducts Business: Worldwide
Employees: 15
Primary Market Served: Business &
Consumer
Catalog available online
Indirect online sales
Advertising/Marketing Budget Related
to Direct Marketing: 76-100%
Direct Marketing ad budget: $100,000
Direct Mail: 25%
Magazines: 20%
Newspapers: 25%
Online: 20%
Telephone: 10%
Founded: 1997

Online internet marketing consulting.
Review, design & monitor online &
offline marketing programs. Design &
recommend marketing programs that
maximize response to client websites &
offline marketing.

NETWORKING ALTERNATIVES FOR PUBLISHERS, RETAILERS & ARTISTS, INC

PO Box 9

Eastsound, WA 98245-0009
Telephone: (360) 376-2702, Toll Free:
(800) 367-1907, FAX: (360) 376-
2704, E-Mail: futureweb@
rockisland.com
Exec Dir Membership & Trade Shows:
Suzanne Homes
Dir: Marilyn McGuire
Mng Ed Napra Review: Michael Wea-
ver
Employees: 12
Primary Market Served: Business
Catalog available online
Advertising/Marketing Budget Related
to Direct Marketing: 26-50%
Founded: 1986
Gross sales or billing: $1,000,000
Education, networking, bimonthly jour-
nal, trade show representation, mem-
bership gatherings.

NEW ENGLAND DIRECT MARKETING ASSOCIATION

396 Washington St
Wellesley Hills, MA 02481-6209
Telephone: (781) 237-1366, FAX:
(781) 431-8118, E-Mail: info@
nedma.com, Web Site: www.nedma.
com
VP Conference: Gary Lubarsky
Pres: Mariah Hunt
VP Awards: Erin Daly
VP Education: Christine J. Erna
VP Membership: Theresa Coultier
Conducts Business: U.S.
Employees: 725
Primary Market Served: Business &
Consumer

Regional association of more than 900
firms & individuals using & supplying
direct marketing services - mail order,
direct mail or direct response. Meets
monthly; features direct marketing day
annually in the spring, plus awards
competition & special events.

NEW ENGLAND MAIL ORDER ASSOCIATION

PO Box 658
Scarborough, ME 04070-0658
Telephone: (207) 885-0090, Toll Free:
(860) 691-1260, FAX: (207) 885-
0097, Web Site: www.nemoa.org
Pres: Jean Giesmann
VP: Margot Murphy Moore
Exec Dir: Janie Downey
Treas: Marlies Duke
Conducts Business: U.S.
Employees: 1
Primary Market Served: Business &
Consumer

Founded: 1947
Organization of over 250 members in
the catalog industry. Dedicated to information exchange. Holds conferences
in March & September.

NEWS & OBSERVER DIRECT MARKETING

215 S McDowell St
Raleigh, NC 27601-1331
Telephone: (919) 836-5658, Toll Free:
(800) 522-4205
Direct Mktg Mgr: Doug Rogers
Primary Market Served: Consumer

POPAI-THE GLOBAL ASSOCIATION FOR MARKETING AT RETAIL

440 N Wells St (Suite 740)
Chicago, IL 60654
Telephone: (312) 863-2900, FAX:
(312) 229-1152, Web Site: www.
popai.com
Pres: Richard Winter
Primary Market Served: Business
Founded: 1936

Provides its members with a variety of
benefits designed to promote, protect &
advance the broader issues of point-of-
purchase advertising.

PHOTOGRAPHIC SOCIETY OF AMERICA INC (PSA)

3000 United Founders Blvd (Suite 103)
Oklahoma City, OK 73112-4294
Telephone: (405) 843-1437, Toll Free:
(855) 772-4636, FAX: (405) 843-
1438, E-Mail: HQ@psa-photo.org,
Web Site: www.psa-photo.org
Pres: John Davis
Membership VP: Donald Brown
Conducts Business: Worldwide
Employees: 3
Primary Market Served: Consumer
Catalog available online
Founded: 1934

Sponsor workshops & awards for members.

PROMOTIONAL PRODUCTS ASSOCIATION INTERNATIONAL

3125 Skyway Cir N
Irving, TX 75038-3526
Telephone: (972) 252-0404, FAX:
(972) 258-3004, (800) I-AM-PPAI,
E-Mail: membership@ppa.org, Web
Site: www.ppa.org
Dir: Rick Merrill
Pres & CEO: Paul Bellantone
Dir: Gary Slavonic
Exec Office Mgr: Lisa Beck
Exec VP: Bob McLean

Conducts Business: Worldwide
Employees: 56
Primary Market Served: Business
Catalog available online
Indirect online sales
Advertising/Marketing Budget Related
to Direct Marketing: 26-50%
Direct Marketing ad budget:
Direct Mail: $100,000
Magazines: $20,000
Founded: 1904
Gross sales or billing: $10,000,000

Membership trade association representing the manufacturers & distributors of promotional products,
incentives, gifts, awards & premiums.

PUBLISHERS MARKETING ASSOCIATION (PMA)

627 Aviation Way
Manhattan Beach, CA 90266-7107
Telephone: (310) 372-2732, FAX:
(310) 374-3342, E-Mail: info@pma-
online.org, Web Site: www.pma-
online.org
Pres: Florrie Binford Kichler
Principal: David Bates
Mktg Dir: Amanda Ballard
Conducts Business: U.S., Germany, Ja-
pan, Mexico, U.K., New Zealand,
Canada
Employees: 6
Primary Market Served: Business
Catalog available online
Direct online sales
Advertising/Marketing Budget Related
to Direct Marketing: 26-50%
Direct Marketing ad budget:
Direct Mail: 60%
Magazines: 40%
Founded: 1983

A national non-profit publishers' co-operative which coordinates discounted
participation in major book & library
exhibits & trade shows throughout the
country, as well as ad placement in major publications & direct mail programs.

Q INTERACTIVE

1 N Dearborn St (12th fl)
Chicago, IL 60602-4337
Telephone: (312) 977-0390, Toll Free:
(888) 729-6465, FAX: (312) 224-
5001, E-Mail: solutions@
qinteractive.com, Web Site: www.
qinteractive.com
Pres & CEO: Matthew Moog
Sr VP, Sls: Christine McNicholas
VP Mktg: Melissa Lederer
Sr VP Mktg Prod Mngmt: Matt Wise
Employees: 135
Primary Market Served: Business &
Consumer
Indirect online sales

Primary Market Served: Business & Consumer
Catalog available online
Founded: 1989

DIRECT RESPONSE ACADEMY

140 Lotus Cir
Austin, TX 78737-8728
Telephone: (512) 301-5900, FAX: (512) 301-7900, Web Site: www.directresponseacademy.com
CEO: Greg Sarnow
Conducts Business: US, Canada, Europe
Employees: 3
Catalog available online
Founded: 2000

Courses & seminars on direct response marketing.

FLAGG MANAGEMENT INC

353 Lexington Ave Rm 1002
New York, NY 10016-0031
Telephone: (212) 286-0333, FAX: (212) 286-0086, E-Mail: flaggmgmt@msn.com, Web Site: www.flaggmgmt.com
Pres: Russell E. Flagg
Conducts Business: U.S.
Employees: 6
Primary Market Served: Business
Founded: 1983

Business-to-business market expositions & conferences.

FORDHAM UNIVERSITY GRADUATE SCHOOL OF BUSINESS ADMINISTRATION

113 W 60th St (Lowenstein Suite 616)
New York, NY 10023
Telephone: (212) 636-6200, Toll Free: (800) 825-4422, FAX: (212) 636-7076, Web Site: www.fordham.edu
Dean: David A. Gautschi
Conducts Business: U.S.
Primary Market Served: Business & Consumer
Founded: 1841

FORT HAYS STATE UNIVERSITY

Dept of Business Administration
600 Park St
Hays, KS 67601-4099
Telephone: (785) 628-FHSU, FAX: (785) 628-4046, Web Site: www.fhsu.edu
Pres: Edward H. Hammond
Controller: Phil Toepfer
Dept Chair: Dr Gregory Weisenborn

Catalog available online
Course titled: Services Marketing.

GLOBAL VILLAGE MARKETING & DATA SERVICES INC

2710 Thomes Ave (Suite 547)
Cheyenne, WY 82001-3029
Telephone: (307) 222-4135, E-Mail: sales@globalvillagemktg.com, Web Site: www.globalvillagemktg.com

HAROLD WALTER SIEBENS SCHOOL OF BUSINESS

Buena Vista University
610 W Fourth St
Storm Lake, IA 50588-1713
Telephone: (712) 749-2410, Toll Free: (800) 383-2821, FAX: (712) 749-2037, Web Site: www2.bvu.edu/academics/business
Prof Mktg: Dr Steven J. Remington
Assoc Prof Mktg: Scott Anderson
Conducts Business: U.S.
Primary Market Served: Business & Consumer
Founded: 1891

Harold Walter Siebens Sch of Bus - Educational institution offering a major in marketing.

HAWORTH COLLEGE OF BUSINESS

Western Michigan University
3120 Schneider Hall
Kalamazoo, MI 49008-3812
Telephone: (616) 387-5050, FAX: (616) 387-5710, E-Mail: jessica.pelkey@wmich.edu, Web Site: www.wmich.edu/business
Dean: Dr. Kay Palan
Chmn: Dr. Mushtaq Luqmani
Conducts Business: U.S.
Primary Market Served: Business & Consumer
Founded: 1903

WALTER E HELLER COLLEGE OF BUSINESS ADMINISTRATION

Subs. of Roosevelt University
18 S Michigan Ave (Room 400)
Chicago, IL 60603
Telephone: (312) 281-3293, FAX: (312) 281-3290, Web Site: www.roosevelt.edu
Chmn & Professor Mktg: Paul Wellen
Professor Mktg: Sumaria Mohan-Neill
Professor Mktg: Gordon Patzer
Professor Mktg: Carl Witte
Conducts Business: U.S.
Primary Market Served: Business & Consumer
Catalog available online

Founded: 1945

HOFSTRA UNIVERSITY

Div. of Professional Development: Business Studies
Univ College for Continuing Educ, 250 Hofstra Univ
Hempstead, NY 11549-2500
Telephone: (516) 463-7200, FAX: (516) 463-4833, E-Mail: ce@hofstra.edu, Web Site: www.hofstra.edu/Academics/CE
Sr Assoc Dean, Continuing Education: Colleen Slattery
Sr Dir, Fin & Admin: Maryanne Langro
Sr Dir, Mktg & Commun: Debbi Hanorof
Conducts Business: U.S.
Employees: 2,000
Primary Market Served: Business & Consumer
Catalog available online
Founded: 1935
Gross sales or billing: $317,000,000

Marketing courses.

INTERACTIVE MARKETING INSTITUTE

Div. of Virginia Commonwealth University
901 W Main St, PO Box 84-2034
Richmond, VA 23284
Toll Free: (800) 925-5308, Web Site: www.imi.vcu.edu
Exec Dir: Pamela Kiecker
Mng Dir: Anne A. Schaeffer
Conducts Business: U.S.
Primary Market Served: Business & Consumer
Catalog available online
Direct online sales
Advertising/Marketing Budget Related to Direct Marketing: 76-100%
Founded: 1996

Specializes in education-professional certificate program (certified direct marketer) direct and interactive marketing, consulting, and research.

JOHNSON & WALES UNIVERSITY

8 Abbott Park Pl
Providence, RI 02903-3703
Telephone: (401) 598-1000, Toll Free: (800) DIAL-JWU, FAX: (401) 598-1833, Web Site: www.jwu.edu
Chancellor: John J. Bowen
Dean: Richard L. Brush
Dept Chmn Mktg: Patricia Fisher
Conducts Business: U.S.
Employees: 1,027
Primary Market Served: Business & Consumer
Catalog available online

KENNESAW STATE UNIVERSITY

Coles College of Business
1000 Chastain Rd (Mail Stop 0406)
Kennesaw, GA 30144-5588
Telephone: (770) 423-6060, FAX:
(770) 499-3261, Web Site: www.
kennesaw.edu
Dept Chair: Dr. Keith Tudor
Asst Dean, Graduate Bus & Exec Programs: Mandy T. Brooks
Conducts Business: U.S.
Employees: 500
Catalog available online
Founded: 1963

MERRIMACK COLLEGE

Office of Admission
315 Turnpike Dr (Mailstop 07)
North Andover, MA 01845
Telephone: (978) 837-5000, E-Mail:
denise.tuccelli@merrimack.edu, Web
Site: www.merrimack.edu
Chmn, Mktg Dept & Assoc Professor:
Catherin Rich-Duval
Employees: 6
Primary Market Served: Business &
Consumer
Direct online sales
Founded: 1993

Courses offered at Merrimack College.

NASSAU COMMUNITY COLLEGE

1 Education Dr
Garden City, NY 11530-6793
Telephone: (516) 572-7501, FAX:
(516) 572-7497, E-Mail: marketing-
communications@ncc.edu, Web Site:
www.ncc.edu
Acting Pres: Dr. Kenneth Saunders
Exec VP: Maria Conzatti
VP, Fin & CFO: James Behrens Jr.
Conducts Business: U.S.
Catalog available online

Course offered through college's Marketing-Retailing Department.

NEW MEXICO STATE UNIVERSITY

Marketing Department
PO Box 30001, MSC 5280
Las Cruces, NM 88003-8001
Telephone: (505) 646-3341, (575) 646-
0111, FAX: (505) 646-1498, Web
Site: www.nmsu.edu
Dean & VP, Economic Devel: Garrey
E. Carruthers
Dept Head: Elise Sautter
Conducts Business: U.S.
Employees: 12
Primary Market Served: Business &
Consumer

NEW YORK UNIVERSITY/ CENTER FOR MARKETING

44 W 4th St (Suite 9-170), Henry Kaufman Management Ctr
New York, NY 10012-1106
Telephone: (212) 998-0100, FAX:
(212) 995-4006, E-Mail: mkt@stern.
nyu.edu, Web Site: www.stern.nyu.
edu/marketing
Dir, Doctoral Prog, Mktg: Priya Raghubir
Conducts Business: U.S., Asia, Europe,
South America
Employees: 25
Primary Market Served: Business &
Consumer
Catalog available online
Direct online sales
Advertising/Marketing Budget Related
to Direct Marketing: 26-50%
Founded: 1934

NEWHOUSE SCHOOL OF PUBLIC COMMUNICATIONS

Div. of Syracuse University
215 University Pl
Syracuse, NY 13244-2100
Telephone: (315) 443-3611, FAX:
(315) 443-4426, Web Site:
newhouse.syr.edu
Chmn Advisory Bd: Larry Kramer
Dean: Lorraine Branham
Conducts Business: U.S.
Employees: 50
Catalog available online

Advanced advertising instruction.

NON-PROFIT MANAGEMENT PROGRAM/MILANO - THE NEW SCHOOL OF MANAGEMENT & URBAN POLICY

Div. of New School for Social Research
72 Fifth Ave
New York, NY 10011
Telephone: (212) 229-5400, E-Mail:
milanocommunications@newschool.
edu, Web Site: www.newschool.edu/
milano
Dean: Lisa J. Servon
Conducts Business: U.S.
Primary Market Served: Consumer

NORTHERN KENTUCKY UNIVERSITY

Nunn Dr
Highland Heights, KY 41099
Telephone: (859) 572-5220, Toll Free:
(800) 637-9948, FAX: (859) 572-
6177, Web Site: www.nku.edu
Pres: Geoffrey S. Mearns
VP & Provost: Dr. Gail W. Wells

Dean: Dr. Rick Kolbe
Conducts Business: U.S.
Employees: 15
Primary Market Served: Business &
Consumer
Catalog available online
Founded: 1968

NORTHWESTERN UNIVERSITY

Integrated Mktg Communications Dept
Medill School of Journalism
633 Clark St
Evanston, IL 60208-2980
Telephone: (847) 491-5665, FAX:
(847) 491-5925, E-Mail: jimc@
northwestern.edu, Web Site: www.
northwestern.edu
Pres: Morton Schapiro
VP & General Counsel: Thomas Cline
Provost: Daniel H. Linzer
Dept Head: Francis Mulhern
Conducts Business: U.S., Europe, Asia,
South America
Catalog available online
Founded: 1950

Master's degree program in integrated
marketing & communications.

OAKTON COMMUNITY COLLEGE

1600 E Golf Rd
Des Plaines, IL 60016-1234
Telephone: (847) 635-1600, FAX:
(847) 635-1706, Web Site: www.
oakton.edu
Pres: Margaret B. Lee
Interim Chair, Bus, Fin, Global Bus,
Mngmt & Supvr & Mktg: Jay Cohen
Conducts Business: U.S.
Catalog available online
Founded: 1969

Courses in direct marketing leading to
certificate & degree.

PARSONS SCHOOL OF DESIGN HUMAN RESOURCE DEPT

Div. of The New School for Social Research
79 Fifth Ave (5th fl)
New York, NY 10003
Telephone: (212) 229-5671, FAX:
(212) 229-8975, E-Mail:
communications@newschool.edu,
Web Site: www.newschool.edu/
parsons/
Sr VP HR & Labor Rels: Carol S. Cantrell
Asst VP, HR: Irwin Kroot
Dir Labor Rels: Stephanie Basta
Conducts Business: U.S.
Primary Market Served: Business &
Consumer

Catalog available online
Indirect online sales
Founded: 1896

Continuing education offering day,
evening & Saturday classes for New
York metropolitan students.

POST UNIVERSITY

School of Business
800 Country Club Rd
Waterbury, CT 06708-3240
Telephone: (203) 596-4520, Toll Free:
(800) 345-2562, E-Mail:
admissions@post.edu, Web Site:
www.post.edu
Pres & CEO: Tom Samph
Conducts Business: U.S.
Primary Market Served: Business &
Consumer
Catalog available online
Founded: 1890

QUEENS COLLEGE/CUNY PROFESSIONAL AND CONTINUING STUDIES (PCS)

City University of New York
65-30 Kissena Blvd (Queens Hall 105)
Flushing, NY 11367-1575
Telephone: (718) 997-5700, FAX:
(718) 997-5723, E-Mail: pcs@qc.
cuny.edu, Web Site: www.qc.cuny.
edu/pcs
Pres: James L. Muyskens
Exec Dir Professional & Continuing
Studies: Douglas A Boethner
Dir Fin & Budget (PCS): Selena Chu
Conducts Business: U.S., China
Primary Market Served: Business &
Consumer
Catalog available online
Direct online sales

Offer non-credit certificate & certificate courses & seminars to general public, business & industry.

QUINNIPIAC COLLEGE

Dept. of Marketing & Advertising
275 Mount Carmel Ave
Hamden, CT 06518-1908
Telephone: (203) 582-8200, (203) 582-
8600, Toll Free: (800) 462-1944,
FAX: (203) 281-8664, Web Site:
www.quinnipiac.edu
Pres: John L. Lahey
Sr VP, Fin: Patrick Healy
Sr VP Academic Affairs: Mark Thomp-
son
Conducts Business: U.S.
Employees: 750
Primary Market Served: Consumer
Catalog available online
Founded: 1929

Course titled: Direct marketing.

SAMFORD UNIVERSITY

800 Lakeshore Dr
Birmingham, AL 35229
Telephone: (205) 726-2011, Web Site:
www.samford.edu
Assoc Dean: Charles Carson
Conducts Business: U.S.
Primary Market Served: Business &
Consumer

SAN FRANCISCO STATE UNIVERSITY

1600 Holloway Ave
San Francisco, CA 94132
Telephone: (415) 338-1111, FAX:
(415) 338-0501, Web Site: www.
sfsu.edu
Pres: Leslie E. Wong
VP, Student Affairs & Enrollment
Mngmnt: Dr. Jo Volkert
Dean, College of Bus: Linda Oubre
Conducts Business: U.S.
Primary Market Served: Business &
Consumer
Catalog available online

SCHOOL OF BUSINESS & ECONOMICS

California State University Los An-
geles Small Business Institute
5151 State University Dr
Los Angeles, CA 90032-4226
Telephone: (323) 343-2800, FAX:
(323) 343-2813, Web Site: cbe.
calstatela.edu
Mktg Prof: Jens D. Biermeier
Mktg Prof: Tyrone W. Jackson
Mktg Prof: H. Rika Houston
Mktg Prof: Ik-suk Kim
Mktg Prof: Richard H. Kao
Mktg Prof: Freddy S. Lee
Mktg Prof: Shirley M. Stretch-Stephen-
son
Conducts Business: U.S.
Primary Market Served: Business &
Consumer
Catalog available online

SCHOOL OF BUSINESS ADMINISTRATION

Portland State University
631 SW Harrison St
Portland, OR 97201-3548
Telephone: (503) 725-3712, FAX:
(503) 725-5850, E-Mail: info@sba.
pdx.edu, Web Site: www.sba.pdx.edu
Dean: Scott Dawson
Asst Dir, Devel: Kristin Mihalko
Primary Market Served: Business &
Consumer
Founded: 1946

SCHOOL OF MANAGEMENT

New York Institute of Technology,
Wisser Library, Northern Blvd
Old Westbury, NY 11568-8000
Telephone: (516) 686-1000, Toll Free:
(800) 345-NYIT, (800) 345-6948,
E-Mail: asknyit@nyit.edu, Web Site:
www.nyit.edu
Pres & CEO: Edward Guiliano
Mktg Dir: Paul Kutasovic
Mktg & Mngmt Professor: Donald Na-
gourney
Mktg & Mngmt Professor: Abram
Proctzer
Conducts Business: U.S.
Employees: 303
Primary Market Served: Business &
Consumer
Catalog available online
Direct online sales
Founded: 1961
Gross sales or billing: $171,100,000

Course titled: Direct Response Marketing.

STATE UNIVERSITY OF NEW YORK-COLLEGE OF PLATTSBURGH

School of Business & Economics
101 Broad St
Plattsburgh, NY 12901-2637
Telephone: (518) 564-2000, FAX:
(518) 564-3183, E-Mail: nancy.
church@plattsburgh.edu, Web Site:
www.plattsburgh.edu
Professor & Chmn, Dept Mktg & En-
trepreneurship: Dr. Nancy J. Church
Professor: Dr. Lise Heroux
Professor: Dr. James Csipak
Conducts Business: U.S.
Primary Market Served: Consumer
Catalog available online
Founded: 1889

Courses MKE401-Interactive Marketing and ECommerce.

STETSON UNIVERSITY

School of Business Administration
421 N Woodland Blvd, Campus Box
8398
Deland, FL 32723
Telephone: (904) 822-7405/7406,
FAX: (904) 822-7430, Web Site:
www.stetson.edu
Chmn Mktg Dept: Michelle DeMoss
Conducts Business: U.S.
Primary Market Served: Business &
Consumer
Founded: 1883

Two courses titled Channels & Global
Internet Marketing.

TEMPLE UNIVERSITY

Small Business Development Center

1816 Chestnut St
Philadelphia, PA 19103-4902
Telephone: (215) 204-7282, FAX:
(215) 204-4554, Web Site: www.
sbm.temple.edu
Pres: Ann Weaver Hart
Dir: Eustace Kangaju
Conducts Business: U.S.
Employees: 15
Catalog available online
Gross sales or billing: $1,800,000,000

Courses in marketing, management, entrepreneurial development & free consulting for small businesses.

THE PETER A TOBIN COLLEGE OF BUSINESS

Div. of St John's University
8000 Utopia Pkwy
Jamaica, NY 11439
Telephone: (718) 990-2600, FAX:
(718) 990-1868, Web Site: www.
stjohns.edu
Dean: Steven D. Papamarcos Ph.D.
Asst Dean Staten Island Campus: Susan
V. Bradley
Asst Dean Queens Campus: Nicole
Bryan
Dir Mktg: Maureen Furlong-Weber
Asst Dean Queens Campus: Susan
McCall
Conducts Business: U.S.
Primary Market Served: Business &
Consumer
Catalog available online
Advertising/Marketing Budget Related
to Direct Marketing: 0-25%
Founded: 1872

Course titled: Direct Marketing.

UF COLLEGE OF ADVERTISING, JOURNALISM, & COMMUNICATIONS

University of Florida
2086 Weimer Hall
Gainesville, FL 32611
Telephone: (352) 392-4046, FAX:
(352) 392-3919, Web Site: www.jou.
ufl.edu
Sec: Christina Barnes
Adv Dept Chmn: John Sutherland PhD
Conducts Business: Florida
Primary Market Served: Business &
Consumer
Catalog available online
Indirect online sales
Founded: 1925

Course title: Direct Response Advertising & Promotional Writing. Special
Study in Advertising.

UNIVERSITY OF MISSOURI

School of Journalism

321 University Hall
Columbia, MO 65211-3020
Telephone: (573) 882-6333, Toll Free:
(800) 856-2181, FAX: (573) 882-
2721, E-Mail: visitus@missouri.edu,
Web Site: www.missouri.edu
Pres: Elson S. Floyd
VP, Fin & Admin: Natalie R. Krawitz
VP, IT: Gary K. Allen
VP, HR: R. Kenneth Hutchinson
Conducts Business: U.S.
Primary Market Served: Business &
Consumer
Catalog available online
Founded: 1908

Offers Direct & Mail Order Advertising Class (Journalism/327).

UNIVERSITY OF MISSOURI/ KANSAS CITY

Henry W Bloch School of Business &
Public Administration
5110 Cherry St (Rm 115)
Kansas City, MO 64110
Telephone: (816) 235-2215, FAX:
(816) 235-2312, Web Site: www.
umkc.edu
Chmn: Richard Hamilton
Professor: Gene Brown
Conducts Business: U.S.
Primary Market Served: Business
Catalog available online
Advertising/Marketing Budget Related
to Direct Marketing: 76-100%
Founded: 1985

Offer M.B.A. degree programs in direct
marketing. Also, continuing education
courses in direct marketing, including
professional certification and in-house
training & seminars.

UNIVERSITY OF PITTSBURGH AT BRADFORD

300 Campus Dr
Bradford, PA 16701-2812
Telephone: (814) 362-7500, FAX:
(814) 362-5150, E-Mail:
admissions@www.upb.pitt.edu, Web
Site: www.upd.pitt.edu
Pres: Dr. Livingston Alexander
Dept Chair: Alberto Cardello
Dept Chair: Lisa Fiorentino
Asst Dean: James L. Baldwin
Assoc Professor: David Blackmore
Conducts Business: U.S.
Catalog available online
Direct Marketing ad budget:
Direct Mail: $30,000
Telephone: $5,000
Course title: Direct Marketing.

USC MARSHALL SCHOOL OF BUSINESS DEPT OF MARKETING

Marshall School of Business
3660 Trousdale Pkwy, ACC 306E
Los Angeles, CA 90089-0443
Telephone: (213) 740-5033, FAX:
(213) 740-7828, E-Mail: dennis.
rook@marshall.usc.edu
Professor: Gary Frazier
Chmn Mktg Dept: Valerie Folks
Conducts Business: Worldwide
Course titled: Direct Response Mktg.

VALPAK OF NEW YORK

875 Avenue of the Americas (Ste 910)
New York, NY 10001-3578
Telephone: (212) 560-9400, Web Site:
www.valpaknewyork.com
Primary Market Served: Consumer

WEST VIRGINIA UNIVERSITY

School of Journalism
Martin Hall
Morgantown, WV 26506
Telephone: (304) 293-3505, FAX:
(304) 293-3072, E-Mail:
wvuwebmaster@mail.wvu.edu, Web
Site: www.wvu.edu
Dean & Professor: Kristina M. Martin
IMC Coord & Asst Professor: Robyn
Blakeman
Asst Professor: Kurt Schimmel
Conducts Business: U.S.
Employees: 5
Founded: 1939

School of Journalism offering courses
in advertising, public relations, broadcast news & print journalism. Direct
marketing courses offered through the
advertising department.

WESTERN CONNECTICUT STATE UNIVERSITY

Ancell School of Business
181 White St
Danbury, CT 06810
Telephone: (203) 837-8200, FAX:
(203) 837-8527, E-Mail: hills@wcsu.
edu, Web Site: www.wcsu.edu
Co-Chmn, Mktg Dept: John Kakalik
Co-Chmn, Mktg Dept: Ronald Droz-
denko
Conducts Business: U.S.
Primary Market Served: Consumer
Founded: 1903

Course titled: Direct Response Marketing (327).

WRIGHT STATE UNIVERSITY

Dept of Marketing, Raj Soin College of Business
3640 Colonel Glen Hwy, 266 Rike Hall
Dayton, OH 45435
Telephone: (937) 775-3047, FAX: (513) 775-3952, E-Mail: teresa. stelmat@wright.edu, Web Site: www.wright.edu/business/acad/ marketing
Chair: Dr. James Munch
Conducts Business: U.S.
Employees: 14
Primary Market Served: Business & Consumer
Catalog available online
Indirect online sales
Founded: 1964

Courses titled: Integrated Mktg Communs; Technologies in Mktg; Database Mktg; Internet Mktg.

YOUNGSTOWN STATE UNIVERSITY

Williamson College of Business Administration
One University Plaza
Youngstown, OH 44555
Telephone: (330) 742-3064, Web Site: www.ysu.edu
Chmn, Mktg Dept: Dr James Kohut
Conducts Business: U.S.
Employees: 10
Primary Market Served: Business & Consumer
Founded: 1906

Advertising, public relations/direct mail advertising & direct marketing.

AMA ANNUAL CONFERENCE
American Marketing Association
130 E Randolph St (fl 22)
Chicago, IL 60601
Telephone: (312) 542-9000, Toll Free:
(800) 262-1150, Web Site: www.
ama.org
CEO: Russ Klein
Primary Market Served: Business
Catalog available online
Indirect online sales
Founded: 1932

Provides a forum where marketing educators can share ideas, explore findings, discuss issues and trends, and network with colleagues.

ANA/BMA NATIONAL CONFERENCES
Business Marketing Association, div.
of Association of National Advertisers
708 Third Ave
New York, NY 10017
Telephone: (212) 697-5950, FAX:
(212) 687-7310, E-Mail: info@
marketing.net, Web Site: www.
marketing.org
Exec Dir: Michael Palmer
Primary Market Served: Business
Founded: 1922

ARF EVENTS
Advertising Research Foundation
432 Park Ave S
New York, NY 10016
Telephone: (212) 751-5656, FAX:
(212) 319-5265, E-Mail: info@
theARF.org, Web Site: theARF.org
Pres & CEO: Gayle Fuguitt
Chmn: David Poltrack
Founded: 1936

AMERICASMART ATLANTA
240 Peachtree St NW (Suite 2200)
Atlanta, GA 30303-1327
Telephone: (404) 220-3000, FAX:
(404) 220-3030, Web Site: www.
americasmart.com
Chmn, CEO & Dir: John Portman Jr
Conducts Business: Worldwide
Primary Market Served: Business &
Consumer
Founded: 1961

Provides an opportunity for manufacturers & retailers of gifts & related products to meet together, on an international level, for order-writing purposes.

BOSTON GIFT SHOW
Urban Exposition
1090 Roberts Blvd NW (Suite 111)
Kennesaw, GA 30144
Telephone: (678) 285-3976, FAX:
(678) 285-7469, Web Site: www.
bostongiftshow.com
Pres & CEO: Doug Miller
Partner & COO: Timothy C Von Gal
Primary Market Served: Business
Catalog available online

Regional gift show for New England, Northeastern & Canadian markets. Semi-annual show is attended by gift & department stores, jewelers, mail order & catalog houses, antique & craft shops, boutiques & resort shops. Markets represented are gifts, stationery, souvenirs, traditional & New England crafts, novelties, toys, decorative & personal accessories & other items.

CMA AWARDS
Canadian Marketing Association
One Concorde Gate (Suite 607)
Don Mills, ON, Canada M3C 3N6
Telephone: (416) 391-2362, FAX:
(416) 441-4062, E-Mail: info@the-cma.org, Web Site: www.the-cma.org/awards
VP Learning & Events: Gabriele Janes
Primary Market Served: Business &
Consumer
Founded: 1967

Marketers gather to pay tribute to the best marketing campaigns of the year. The awards recognize outstanding achievements in all facets of marketing, from concept & execution to final results.

CMA EVENTS & EDUCATION
Canadian Marketing Association
One Concorde Gate (Suite 607)
Don Mills, ON, Canada M3C 3N6
Telephone: (416) 391-2362, FAX:
(416) 441-4062, E-Mail: info@the-cma.org, Web Site: www.the-cma.org
VP Learning & Events: Gabriele Janes
Primary Market Served: Business

Marketplace for financial institutions, publishers, cataloguers & charities to contact suppliers to the industry.

CUES EVENTS, TRAINING & EDUCATION
Credit Union Executives Society, Inc
5510 Research Park Dr
Madison, WI 53711-0167
Telephone: (608) 271-2664, Toll Free:
(800) 252-2664, FAX: (608) 271-2303, E-Mail: cues@cues.org, Web
Site: www.cues.org

Pres & CEO: John Pembroke
VP Exec Education & Meetings: Joette
Mitchell
Primary Market Served: Business
Catalog available online
Direct online sales
Founded: 1962

Immersion learning for marketing, technology & operations leaders.

DMA ANNUAL MARKETING CONFERENCE
Direct Marketing Association
1333 Broadway (Suite 301)
New York, NY 10018
Telephone: (212) 768-7277, Web Site:
thedma.org
CEO: Thomas Benton
Primary Market Served: Business
Founded: 1917

Annual conference for professionals in the data-driven industry of direct marketing.

ERA D2C CONVENTION
Electronic Retailing Association
607 14th St NW Ste 530
Washington, DC 20005-2018
Telephone: (703) 841-1751, Toll Free:
(800) 987-6462, FAX: (425) 977-1036, E-Mail: webadmin@retailing.org, Web Site: retailing.org/d2c
Exec Dir: Chris Reinmuth
Conducts Business: Worldwide
Employees: 15
Primary Market Served: Business &
Consumer
Catalog available online
Direct online sales
Founded: 1990

Annual convention of the ERA that brings together leaders and professionals from the direct-to-consumer industry.

IAEE EXPO! EXPO! ANNUAL MEETING AND EXHIBITION
International Association of Exhibitions and Events
12700 Park Central Dr (Suite 308)
Dallas, TX 75251-1526
Telephone: (972) 458-8002, FAX:
(972) 458-8119, E-Mail: info@iaee.com, Web Site: www.iaee.com
Pres & CEO: David DuBois
VP Exhibitions & Events: Scott Craighead
Primary Market Served: Business
Catalog available online

Founded: 1928

Annual meeting of the IAEE that brings together industry professionals that represent the interests of tradeshows and expositions.

IDG WORLD EXPO

International Data Group
492 Old Connecticut Path (Suite 420)
Framingham, MA 01701
Telephone: (508) 879-0700, E-Mail: info@idgworldexpo.com, Web Site: www.idgworldexpo.com
CEO: Mary Dolaher
Sr VP Strategic Commun & Event Devel: Carolyn Rauch

Producer of tradeshows and events for professionals and consumers seeking world-class education, strategic business relationships and access to industry-leading products and services.

IMA EXECUTIVE SUMMIT

Incentive Marketing Association
4248 Park Glen Rd
Minneapolis, MN 55416
Telephone: (952) 928-4649, E-Mail: info@incentivemarketing.com, Web Site: www.incentivemarketing.com
Exec Dir: Kim Wesloh
Primary Market Served: Business
Catalog available online

Annual meeting for professionals in the promotion & incentive marketing industry.

INTX - THE INTERNET & TELEVISON EXPO

National Cable & Telecommunications Association
25 Massachusetts Ave (Suite 100)
Washington, DC 20001
Telephone: (202) 222-2430, FAX: (202) 222-2431, E-Mail: infointx@ncta.com, Web Site: www.intxshow.com
Pres & CEO: Michael Powell
VP Communications & Digital Strategy: Brian Dietz
Primary Market Served: Business
Founded: 1979

Annual conference of NCTA that brings together the people, companies and ideas behind the multi-billion dollar digital and communications marketplace.

ISA INTERNATIONAL SIGN EXPO

International Sign Association
1001 N Fairfax St (Suite 301)
Alexandria, VA 22314-1587

Telephone: (703) 836-4012, FAX: (703) 836-8353, Web Site: signexpo.org
VP Meetings & Events: Iain Mackenzie
Dir Meetings & Conferences: Kelly Maguire
Primary Market Served: Business
Catalog available online
Indirect online sales
Founded: 1944

Exhibit lighting products & other products & services used in sign manufacturing.

INCOMPAS SHOW

Competitive Telecommunications Association
1200 G St NW (Suite 350)
Washington, DC 20005
Telephone: (202) 296-6650, FAX: (202) 296-7585, Web Site: show.incompas.org
CEO: Chip Pickering
Sr Dir Event Svcs: Megan McDonald Paulson
Primary Market Served: Business
Catalog available online
Founded: 1981

Exhibits products & services regarding network management systems, voice & data communications, electronic mail & teleconferencing services.

INVENTHELP'S INPEX

Invention & New Product Exposition
217 Ninth St
Pittsburgh, PA 15222-3506
Telephone: (412) 288-1343, Toll Free: (888) 544-6739, FAX: (412) 288-4546, E-Mail: info@inpex.com, Web Site: www.inpex.com
Trade Show Mgr: Susan Rich
Dir Corp Commun Trade Show & Intl Rels: Nicole Lininger
Conducts Business: Worldwide
Primary Market Served: Business & Consumer
Catalog available online
Indirect online sales
Founded: 1984

Annual invention, new product & innovation trade show where inventors can meet with companies interested in licensing, marketing or manufacturing new product ideas.

THE MERCHANDISE MART

A Vornado property
222 Merchandise Mart Plaza (Suite 470)
Chicago, IL 60654
Toll Free: (800) 677-6278, Web Site: www.merchandisemart.com

COO: Myron Maurer

Commercial building, design center and international business location that hosts various trade shows and consumer events.

NAB SHOW

National Association Broadcasters
1771 "N" St NW
Washington, DC 20036
Telephone: (202) 429-5300, Toll Free: (800) 622-3976, FAX: (202) 429-4199, E-Mail: nab@nab.org, Web Site: www.nabshow.com
Pres & CEO: Gordon Smith
Exec VP Commun: Dennis Wharton
Primary Market Served: Business
Founded: 1923

Exhibits of radio & television broadcasting equipment, computer software, post/television production equipment, radio & audio services & internet streaming.

NAMA AGRI-MARKETING CONFERENCE

National Agri Marketing Association
11020 King St (Suite 205)
Overland Park, KS 66210
Telephone: (913) 491-6500, FAX: (913) 491-6502, E-Mail: agrimktg@nama.org, Web Site: www.nama.org
COO & Dir, Commun & Admin: Jenny Picket

NY NOW

Emerald Expositions LLC
1133 Westchester Ave (Suite N136)
White Plains, NY 10604-3547
Toll Free: (800) 272-7469, Web Site: www.nynow.com
VP & Show Dir: Scott Kramer
VP & Show Dir: Randi Mohr
Primary Market Served: Business
Catalog available online

Provides a gift & decorative accessories market in the U.S. Held twice a year, it houses ten major merchandise sections at the Jacob K. Javits Convention Center & the Passenger Ship Terminal. Handmade in the U.S., a wholesale craft market juried section is held biannually in conjunction with the January Gift Fair.

NATIONAL HARDWARE SHOW

National Retail Hardware Association
Reed Exhibitions
383 Main Ave
Norwalk, CT 06851

Telephone: (203) 840-5622, Toll Free: (888) 425-9377, FAX: (203) 840-9622, E-Mail: inquiry@hardware. reedexpo.com, Web Site: www. nationalhardwareshow.com
Sales Dir: Juliana Sherwood

NATIONAL POSTAL FORUM
3998 Fair Ridge Dr (Suite 150)
Fairfax, VA 22033-2920
Telephone: (703) 218-5015, FAX: (703) 218-5020, E-Mail: info@npf. org, Web Site: www.npf.org
Exec Dir: Maureen Goodson
Dir, Mktg & Exhibits: Mary Guthrie
Employees: 12
Primary Market Served: Business
Catalog available online
Direct online sales
Advertising/Marketing Budget Related to Direct Marketing: 51-75%
Founded: 1968

Brings together business mailers, postal equipment, service providers & the U. S. Postal Service. It features more than 100 informative sessions on postal developments & an exhibition of mailing, sorting, addressing, printing & more.

NATIONAL STATIONERY SHOW
Emerald Expositions LLC
1133 Westchester Ave (Suite N136)
White Plains, NY 10604-3547
Telephone: (914) 421-3394, Web Site: www.nationalstationeryshow.com
VP, Show Dir: Patti Stracher
Primary Market Served: Business
Founded: 1924

Provides an annual domestic & international marketplace for greeting cards, postcards, note paper, social stationery, gift wrappings & related products such as rubber stamps, picture frames, games, toys, calendars, party goods, desk accessories, writing instruments, small leather goods, prints & posters, balloons, baby & wedding gifts, back-to-school & holiday merchandise.

PPAI EXPO
Promotional Products Association International
3125 Skyway Cir N
Irving, TX 75038
Telephone: (972) 252-0404, Toll Free: (888) 426-7724, FAX: (972) 258-3004, E-Mail: expo@ppai.org, Web Site: expo.ppai.org
Pres & CEO: Paul Bellantone
Expositions Dir: Darel Cook
Conducts Business: Worldwide

Primary Market Served: Business
International promotional products tradeshow that connects marketers, suppliers and distributors.

SHSMD ANNUAL CONFERENCE
Society for Healthcare Strategy & Market Development
155 N Wacker Dr (Suite 400)
Chicago, IL 60606
Telephone: (312) 422-3888, FAX: (312) 278-0883, E-Mail: shsmd@ aha.org, Web Site: www.shsmd.org
Exhibits Mgmt: Linda Griffin
Event Planner: Anne Marie Bell
Primary Market Served: Business
Catalog available online
Direct online sales
Founded: 1996

Exhibits of audiovisual, communications, printing & computer equipment. Services for health care profession include strategic planning, public relations & fund-raising consulting.

TMC INTERNET TELEPHONY & EXPO
Technology Marketing Corp
800 Connecticut Ave (Floor 1 E)
Norwalk, CT 06854
Telephone: (203) 852-6800, Toll Free: (800) 243-6002, FAX: (203) 866-3326, E-Mail: tmc@tmcnet.com, Web Site: www.tmcnet.com
Chmn: Nadji Tehrani
CEO: Rich Tehrani
Pres: David Rodriguez
Conducts Business: U.S., Canada
Primary Market Served: Business & Consumer
Catalog available online
Direct online sales
Founded: 1972

TMC's two major bi-annual trade shows.

Direct Marketing Books & Periodicals (43)

**ACADEMY OF MARKETING
SCIENCE JOURNAL**
Sage Publications Inc
2455 Teller Rd
Thousand Oaks, CA 91320-9924
Telephone: (800) 818-7243, FAX:
 (800) 583-2665, E-Mail: journals@
 sagepub.com, Web Site: www.
 sagepub.com
Pres & CEO: Blaise R. Simqu
Exec VP & COO: Tracey A. Ozmina
Sr VP & CFO: Chris Hickok
Conducts Business: US, London, India
Primary Market Served: Business
Catalog available online
Advertising/Marketing Budget Related
 to Direct Marketing: 51-75%

Scholarly research academic journal.
Quarterly.

ADVERTISING AGE
Div. of Crain Communications
685 Third Ave
New York, NY 10017-4024
Telephone: (212) 210-0100, FAX:
 (212) 210-0111, Web Site: www.
 crain.com
VP/Publr: Allison Arden
Mktg Svcs Mgr: Emily Chiang
Conducts Business: Worldwide
Employees: 100
Primary Market Served: Business
Advertising/Marketing Budget Related
 to Direct Marketing: 51-75%
Direct Marketing ad budget:
 $3,000,000
Direct Mail: 70%
Magazines: 30%
Founded: 1930
Gross sales or billing: $40,000,000

Weekly magazine serving advertising
& marketing executives with news &
feature material, $3.

ALL-IN-ONE DIRECTORY
Gebbie Press
Box 1000
New Paltz, NY 12561-0017
Telephone: (845) 255-7560, FAX:
 (888) 345-2790, E-Mail:
 gebbiepress@pipeline.com, Web
 Site: www.gebbieinc.com
Publr & Ed: Mark Gebbie
Assoc Ed: Barbara Edelman
Conducts Business: Worldwide

Employees: 2
Primary Market Served: Business
Catalog available online
Direct online sales
Advertising/Marketing Budget Related
 to Direct Marketing: 51-75%
Founded: 1955

Listings for 24,000+ public relations
outlets in all media. Also available on
excel spreadsheet, PR Pro online app.

**AMERICAN BUSINESS
DIRECTORIES**
Div. of info USA Inc
5711 S 86th Cir
Omaha, NE 68127
Telephone: (402) 593-4600, Toll Free:
 (800) 555-6124, FAX: (402) 596-
 0475, Web Site: www.infousa.com
Pres: Vin Gupta
VP: Bill Mattern
Mktg Mgr: Jan Wilson
Conducts Business: U.S., Canada
Employees: 1,000
Primary Market Served: Business &
 Consumer
Catalog available online
Direct online sales
Advertising/Marketing Budget Related
 to Direct Marketing: 76-100%
Direct Marketing ad budget:
Direct Mail: 95%
Telephone: 5%
Founded: 1972

Print business directories that are used
as a source of suppliers & a sales prospecting tool.

**AMERICAN SOCIETY OF
JOURNALISTS & AUTHORS
DIRECTORY**
American Society of Journalists & Au-
thors
1501 Broadway (Suite 403)
New York, NY 10036-5505
Telephone: (212) 997-0947, FAX:
 (212) 768-7414, E-Mail: asjany@
 ibm.net
Exec Dir: Alexandra Owens
Admin Asst: Heather Van Arsdel
Employees: 2
Primary Market Served: Business &
 Consumer

Founded: 1948

Lists more than 1000 freelance writers,
cross-indexed by geographic location,
pseudonym, media expertise & over
100 subject specialties. Annual.

AUDIENCE DEVELOPMENT
10 Norden Pl
Norwalk, CT 06855-1452
Telephone: (203) 854-6730, FAX:
 (203) 854-6735, E-Mail: inolan@
 red7media.com, Web Site: www.
 audiencedevelopment.com
Editor & Publr: Tony Silber
Mng Editor: Bill Mickey
Mktg Mgr: Irene Nolan
Audience Devel Mgr: Jeff Hartford
Conducts Business: U.S.
Primary Market Served: Business
Advertising/Marketing Budget Related
 to Direct Marketing: 51-75%

Comprehensive source on strategic
trends and ongoing developments affecting circulation management, as
well as in-depth, practical advice on
every aspect of circulation management
and marketing.

BOOK NEWS INC
5739 NE Sumner St
Portland, OR 97218-2642
Telephone: (503) 281-9230, FAX:
 (503) 287-4485, E-Mail: info@
 booknews.com
Pres: Fred Gullette
Editor: Eithne O'Leyne
Employees: 6
Primary Market Served: Business &
 Consumer
Founded: 1971

Paid advertising, news & information
pertinent to mail order book sales. $3
an issue, three publications per year.

CISION US INC
332 S Michigan Ave (Suite 900)
Chicago, IL 60604-4393
Telephone: (312) 922-2400, Toll Free:
 (866) 639-5087, FAX: (312) 922-
 3126, E-Mail: info.us@cision.com,
 Web Site: us.cision.com
CEO & Pres.: Peter Granat
CFO: Jim Franke
COO: Dawn . Conway

Employees: 550
Primary Market Served: Business
Catalog available online
Advertising/Marketing Budget Related
  to Direct Marketing: 26-50%
Founded: 1932

COASTAL LIVING

Imprint of Southern Progress Corp;
  Subs of Time, Inc.
2100 Lakeshore Dr
Birmingham, AL 35209
Telephone: (205) 445-6000, FAX:
  (205) 445-7263, E-Mail:
  coastalliving@customersvc.com,
  Web Site: www.coastalliving.com
Publr: Greg Keyes
Assoc Publr: Julie Arkin
Exec Dir Mktg: Jennel O'Brien
Production Mgr: Jamie Elliott
Conducts Business: U.S.
Founded: 1997

Magazine emphasizing home design,
architecture, coastal lifestyles & topics.

COMMERCIAL ATLAS & MARKETING GUIDE

Published by Rand McNally & Co
9855 Woods Dr
Skokie, IL 60077
Telephone: (847) 329-8100, Toll Free:
  (800) 678-7263, FAX: (800) 934-
  3479, E-Mail: store@randmcnally.
  com, Web Site: www.randmcnally.
  com
Editor: David Zapenski
Employees: 636
Primary Market Served: Business &
  Consumer
Catalog available online
Direct online sales
Founded: 1857

DM NEWS

Div. of Courtenay Communications
114 W 26th St (Fl 4)
New York, NY 10001-6812
Telephone: (646) 638-6000, Toll Free:
  (800) 558-1703, FAX: (212) 925-
  8752, E-Mail: dmnewssubs@
  haymarketmedia.com, Web Site:
  www.dmnews.com
Chmn & CEO: Lee Maniscalco
Exec VP: Julia Hood
Ed-in-Chief: Ginger Conlon
Sr Editor: Al Urbanski
Conducts Business: U.S., Canada, Eu-
  rope, Asia
Employees: 50
Primary Market Served: Business
Catalog available online
Direct online sales
Advertising/Marketing Budget Related
  to Direct Marketing: 51-75%
Direct Marketing ad budget: $200,000

Direct Mail: 50%
Newspapers: 50%
Founded: 1979

As a weekly newspaper serving a BPA
audited circulation of 40,000 direct
marketers, DM News provides news
coverage of new direct marketing campaigns, postal rate changes & delivery
problems, sales tax disputes, new lists
& databases & many other topics of interest to the people & firms involved in
direct marketing. Staff reported news
coverage is supplemented with columns & articles by industry experts,
special reports, regular departments &
op/ed pieces. ISSN# 0914-3588; 48 issues, $49. (Canada $99 & Mexico
$149). (Europe) by written request
only.

DMA STATISTICAL FACT BOOK

Direct Marketing Association
1333 Broadway (Suite 301)
New York, NY 10018
Telephone: (212) 768-7277, Web Site:
  thedma.org
Primary Market Served: Business &
  Consumer
Catalog available online
Direct online sales
Founded: 1917

Covers many aspects of direct marketing including: media & market growth
& usage trends, consumer & business
attitudes, buying habits, expectations &
outlooks, production & operating cost
figures & environmental issues concerns.

DIANE PUBLISHING CO

PO Box 617
Darby, PA 19023-0617
Telephone: (610) 461-6200, E-Mail:
  hbaron@dianepublishing.net, Web
  Site: www.dianepublishing.net
Pres & Publr: Herman Baron
Conducts Business: Worldwide
Employees: 6
Primary Market Served: Business
Catalog available online
Direct online sales
Advertising/Marketing Budget Related
  to Direct Marketing: 0-25%
Founded: 1987

Books, reports & documents primarily
from government sources, sold to businesses, libraries & governments & distributes hard to find remainder books.

DICTIONARY OF MARKETING TERMS

Barron's Education Series Inc
250 Wireless Blvd

Hauppauge, NY 11788-3924
Telephone: (631) 434-3311, Toll Free:
  (800) 645-3476, FAX: (631) 434-
  3723, E-Mail: barrons@barronseduc.
  com, Web Site: www.barronseduc.
  com
Dir Mktg: Lonny Stein
Conducts Business: Worldwide
Primary Market Served: Business &
  Consumer
Catalog available online
Direct online sales
Advertising/Marketing Budget Related
  to Direct Marketing: 0-25%
Direct Marketing ad budget:
Online: 100%
Founded: 1941

Publishes test preparation manuals including SAT, ACT & Regent's exam,
Profiles of American Colleges, business & financial books & audio & video learning materials.

DIRECT MARKETING DIGEST

Div. of National Mail Order Associa-
  tion LLC
2807 Polk St NE
Minneapolis, MN 55418
Telephone: (612) 788-1673, E-Mail:
  info@nmoa.org, Web Site: www.
  nmoa.org
Pres: John Schulte
Conducts Business: Worldwide
Primary Market Served: Business
Catalog available online
Direct online sales
Advertising/Marketing Budget Related
  to Direct Marketing: 76-100%
Founded: 1972

Publication for direct marketers & mail
order sellers

DIRECT MARKETING MARKET PLACE

NRP Direct
430 Mountain Ave (Suite 403)
New Providence, NJ 07974
Telephone: (908) 517-0780, Toll Free:
  (844) 592-4197, FAX: (908) 608-
  3012, Web Site: www.dirmktgplace.
  com
Publr: Robert Docherty
Sls Mgr: Gina Marie Delia

Reference & mailing list source designed to enable direct marketing professionals to find new business, locate
service & supply sources (printers, lettershop, list brokers, managers & computer services), find advertising
agencies, consultants, design studios,
freelance artists, writers & locate key
executives & companies. Includes 43
categories of information & more than
25,000 key organizations & executives.

DIRECT MARKETING NEWS

Div. of Lloydmedia Inc
302-137 Main St N
Markham, ON, Canada L3P 1Y2
Telephone: (905) 201-6600, Toll Free:
   (800) 668-1838, FAX: (905) 201-
   6601, E-Mail: home@dmn.ca, Web
   Site: www.dmn.ca
Editor: Amy Bostock
Production: Mike Demi
Pres: Steve Lloyd
Conducts Business: U.S., Canada
Primary Market Served: Business
Catalog available online
Direct Marketing ad budget:
Direct Mail: 70%
Magazines: 20%
Telephone: 10%
Founded: 1988

Canadian publication for direct marketers. Also provide conferences & seminars for advertising & marketing
executives. 12 issues: $60-U.S., $48-
Canada.

DIRECT MARKETING STRATEGY, PLANNING & EXECUTION

McGraw-Hill Publishers
PO Box 545
Blacklick, OH 43004-0545
Telephone: (614) 755-4152, Toll Free:
   (800) 722-4726, Web Site: www.
   mcgraw-hill.com
Author: Edward Nash
Primary Market Served: Business &
   Consumer

Comprehensive "how to" publication
used worldwide in schools & for company training.

DIRECT MARKETING TOOL KIT FOR SMALL BUSINESS

Div. of Marketing Logistics Inc
2807 Polk St NE
Minneapolis, MN 55418-2954
Telephone: (612) 788-1673, E-Mail:
   info@nmoa.org, Web Site: www.
   nmoa.org/directmarketingtoolkit
Pres & Chmn: John Schulte
Primary Market Served: Business &
   Consumer

THE DIRECTORY OF BUSINESS INFORMATION RESOURCES

Grey House Publishing
4919 Route 22
Amenia, NY 12501
Toll Free: (845) 373-8263, E-Mail:
   cstupak@greyhouse.com, Web Site:
   www.greyhouse.com
Publr: Leslie MacKenzie
Pres: Richard Gottlieb

VP Mktg: Jessica Moody
Primary Market Served: Business
Catalog available online
Direct online sales
Founded: 1979

DIRECTORY OF MAIL ORDER CATALOGS

Grey House Publishing
4919 Route 22
Amenia, NY 12501
Telephone: (518) 789-8700, Toll Free:
   (800) 562-2139, FAX: (518) 789-
   0556, E-Mail: cstupak@greyhouse.
   com, Web Site: www.greyhouse.com
Pres: Richard Gottlieb
Publr: Leslie MacKenzie
VP Mktg: Jessica Moody
Mkgt Asst: Caitlin Stupak
Primary Market Served: Business
Catalog available online
Direct online sales
Founded: 1979

Complete coverage of the consumer
mail order industry for sales & marketing managers. Published annually in
December. Available in print and online.

DIRECTORY OF MAIL ORDER CATALOGS

National Mail Order Association
2807 Polk St NE
Minneapolis, MN 55418-2954
Telephone: (612) 788-1673, E-Mail:
   info@nmoa.org, Web Site: www.
   nmoa.org
Pres: John Schulte
Primary Market Served: Business &
   Consumer
Catalog available online
Direct online sales

Annual information base directory of
all mail order businesses with sales of
$5MM or more & all mail order subsid-
iaries. 2000 directory listings, including
sales data.

DIRECTORY OF MAJOR MAILERS & WHAT THEY MAIL

Div. of North American Publishing Co
1500 Spring Garden St (Suite 1200),
   North American Publishing Co
Philadelphia, PA 19130-4094
Telephone: (215) 238-5300, Toll Free:
   (800) 777-8074, FAX: (215) 238-
   5412, E-Mail: customerservice@
   napco.com, Web Site: www.
   majormailers.com
VP Mktg: Patty Perkins
Ed: Tiffini Weddle
Conducts Business: Worldwide
Primary Market Served: Business

Catalog available online
Indirect online sales
Advertising/Marketing Budget Related
   to Direct Marketing: 51-75%

A single volume, listing over 6000 top
direct mail users, including the names,
addresses, phone & fax numbers of key
personnel. Also shows if mailers are using color, carrier sorting, the dimensions & number of pages of their latest
mailings, size of their house files &
more. Subscribers also gain access to
the Who's Mailing What! Archive, a library of over 150,000 samples of direct
mail packages. Published annually.
$395 printed; $645 CD ROM.

DIRECTORY OF PREMIUM, INCENTIVE & TRAVEL BUYERS

Div. of The Salesman's Guide A Unit
   of Douglas Publications Inc
2807 N Parham Rd (Suite 200)
Richmond, VA 23294
Telephone: (804) 762-4455, Toll Free:
   (800) 223-1797, FAX: (804) 935-
   0271, E-Mail: amdouglas4@aol.com,
   Web Site: www.douglaspublications.
   com
Edit Dir: Keith Cavedo
Mktg Dir: Rusty Hopkins
Sls Dir: Jim Desborough
Employees: 50
Primary Market Served: Business &
   Consumer
Catalog available online
Indirect online sales
Founded: 1985

Provides information on premium & incentive & travel usage & dollar
amounts spent during the past year. In-
dicates names of premium incentive &
travel buyers.

DO IT YOURSELF DIRECT MARKETING

John Wiley & Sons Inc
111 River St
Hoboken, NJ 07030-5774
Telephone: (201) 748-6000, FAX:
   (201) 748-6088, E-Mail: info@wiley.
   com, Web Site: www.wiley.com
Chmn Bd: Peter B. Wiley
Pres & CEO: Stephen M. Smith
Sr VP, Chief Mktg Officer: Clay Sto-
   baugh
Employees: 4,900
Primary Market Served: Business &
   Consumer
Catalog available online
Direct online sales
Founded: 1807

Gross sales or billing: $1,100,000,000

Subtitled Secrets for a Small Business. This book provides information for anyone initiating or enhancing a direct marketing program. 304 pages. ISBN: 0471163848; $19.95 paperback.

FRAUD & THEFT INFORMATION BUREAU

9770 S Military Trail (Suite 380)
Boynton Beach, FL 33436-3207
Telephone: (561) 737-8700, FAX: (561) 737-5800, E-Mail: sales@ fraudandtheft.com, Web Site: www. fraudandtheftinfo.com
Pres & Publr: Larry Schwartz
VP: Pearl Sax
Employees: 8
Primary Market Served: Business
Catalog available online
Direct online sales
Advertising/Marketing Budget Related to Direct Marketing: 51-75%
Direct Marketing ad budget:
Direct Mail: 20%
Magazines: 20%
Online: 20%
Telephone: 40%
Founded: 1982
Gross sales or billing: $4,000,000

Publishers of credit card, check fraud control, loss prevention manuals and databases.

FRIDAY REPORT

Div. of Hoke Communications
54 Adams St
Garden City, NY 11530-3918
Telephone: (516) 746-6700, FAX: (516) 294-8141
Ed: George Reis
Employees: 40
Primary Market Served: Business
Founded: 1938

Newsletter covering the direct marketing industry. $165 (52 issues).

FRM WEEKLY

Div. of Hoke Communications
54 Adams St
Garden City, NY 11530-3918
Telephone: (516) 746-6700, FAX: (516) 294-8141
Ed: George Reis
Pres & Publ: Henry Hoke
Conducts Business: U.S., Canada
Employees: 40
Primary Market Served: Business
Advertising/Marketing Budget Related to Direct Marketing: 76-100%
Direct Marketing ad budget:
Direct Mail: 40%
Magazines: 40%
Telephone: 20%

Founded: 1938

Weekly magazine serving the informational needs of decision makers in non-profit organizations. Paid circulation. $58 annually.

GREENBOOK WORLDWIDE DIRECTORY OF MARKETING RESEARCH COMPANIES & SERVICES

American Marketing Association (New York)
4301 32nd St W (Suite E-11)
Bradenton, FL 34208
Telephone: (212) 849-2752, Toll Free: (800) 792-9202, FAX: (212) 202-7920, E-Mail: info@greenbrook.org, Web Site: www.greenbook.org
Publr: Camille Crifasi
Coord: Penny Guerrero
Employees: 9
Primary Market Served: Business
Catalog available online
Indirect online sales
Advertising/Marketing Budget Related to Direct Marketing: 0-25%
Direct Marketing ad budget:
Direct Mail: 90%
Magazines: 10%
Founded: 1962

Lists over 2,000 marketing research companies & research services from 50 countries.

GREY HOUSE PUBLISHING

4919 Rte 22
Amenia, NY 12501
Telephone: (518) 789-8700, Toll Free: (800) 562-2139, FAX: (518) 789-0556, E-Mail: books@greyhouse. com, Web Site: www.greyhouse.com
Publr, VP: Leslie MacKenzie
Pres: Richard Gottlieb
VP, Mktg: Jessica Moody
Mktg Asst: Caitlin Stupak
Conducts Business: Worldwide
Employees: 84
Primary Market Served: Business
Catalog available online
Direct online sales
Founded: 1979
Gross sales or billing: $7,300,000

GUIDE TO AMERICAN & INTERNATIONAL DIRECTORIES

B Klein Publications
6037 W Atlantic Ave
Delray Beach, FL 33484-8408
Telephone: (561) 496-3316, FAX: (561) 451-0803, E-Mail: bkleinpub@ aol.com
Pres & Ed: Bernard Klein

Primary Market Served: Business & Consumer
Catalog available online
Founded: 1946

HOW I GROSSED MORE THAN $1 MILLION IN DIRECT MAIL ORDER STARTING WITH LITTLE CASH & LESS KNOW HOW

International Wealth Success Inc
24 Canterbury Rd
Rockville Centre, NY 11570-1310
Telephone: (516) 766-5850, Toll Free: (800) 323-0548, FAX: (516) 766-5919, E-Mail: admin@iwsmony. com, Web Site: www.iwsmoney.com
Pres: Tyler G. Hicks
Employees: 1
Primary Market Served: Business & Consumer
Catalog available online
Indirect online sales
Founded: 1967

INSIDE DIRECT MAIL

Div. of North American Publishing Co
1500 Spring Green St (Suite 1200)
Philadelphia, PA 19130-4069
Telephone: (215) 238-5300, Toll Free: (800) 777-8074, FAX: (215) 238-5412, E-Mail: customservice@ napco.com, Web Site: www. insidedirectmail.com
Mktg Mgr & Circ Dir: Patty Perkins
Editor-in-Chief: Hallie Mummert
Editor: Ethan Boldt
Copy Editor: Mavis Linnemann
Conducts Business: Worldwide
Primary Market Served: Business
Catalog available online
Direct online sales
Advertising/Marketing Budget Related to Direct Marketing: 51-75%
Founded: 1974

Monthly newsletter: Analysis & Record of Direct Mail in America. In-depth features and articles on all facets of direct marketing: consumer, business, fund-raising & catalogs. Detailed log of more than 1500 mailings received the prior month, plus subscribers can receive photocopies of mailings from the Who's Mailing What! Archive, a library of more than 150,000 mailings in over 200 categories. Also publisher of: The Directory of Major Mailers & What They Mail. $165 annual, 12 monthly issues.

JOURNAL OF MARKETING RESEARCH

American Marketing Association
311 S Wacker Dr (Suite 5800)

Chicago, IL 60606
Telephone: (312) 542-9000, Toll Free:
(800) AMA-1150, FAX: (312) 542-
9001, E-Mail: info@ama.org, Web
Site: www.marketingpower.org
Ed: Robert Meyer
Dir HR: Rebecca Youngberg
Primary Market Served: Business &
Consumer
Catalog available online
Direct online sales
Advertising/Marketing Budget Related
to Direct Marketing: 0-25%
Founded: 1936

Marketing research. ISSN# 0022437;
$200 library. Published quarterly.

LITERARY MARKET PLACE

Information Today Inc
143 Old Marlton Pike
Medford, NJ 08055-8750
Telephone: (609) 654-6266, FAX:
(609) 654-4309, E-Mail: custserv@
infotoday.com, Web Site: www.
literarymarketplace.com
Publr & Pres: Thomas H. Hogan
Primary Market Served: Business &
Consumer
Catalog available online

Directory of over 28,000 companies &
individuals in U.S. & Canadian publishing. Areas covered include book
publishers, associations, book trade
events, courses, conferences & contests; agents & agencies, services &
suppliers, book manufacturers, direct
mail promotion, sales & distribution,
magazines & reference books for the
trade. Indexes. Annual.

MAIL ORDER BUSINESS

Subs. of Kendall Hunt Publishing Co
4050 Westmark Dr
Dubuque, IA 52002
Telephone: (319) 589-1000 X1076,
Toll Free: (800) 228-0810, FAX:
(319) 589-1046, Web Site: www.
kendallhunt.com
Pres & COO: Chad Chandlee
Sr Editor: David M. Mattaliano
Primary Market Served: Consumer
Advertising/Marketing Budget Related
to Direct Marketing: 0-25%

MAIL ORDER BUSINESS
DIRECTORY

B Klein Publications
6037 W Atlantic Ave
Delray Beach, FL 33484
Telephone: (561) 496-3316, E-Mail:
bkleinpub@aol.com
Pres: Bernard Klein
Conducts Business: Worldwide

Primary Market Served: Business &
Consumer

Contains the names of the 5,000 most
active mail order houses, listed geo-
graphically with indexes. Annual.

MARKETING ADVENTS

Direct Marketing Association of Wash-
ington
1615 L St NW (Suite 1100)
Washington, DC 20036
Telephone: (202) 955-5030, FAX:
(202) 955-0085, E-Mail: info@
dmaw.org, Web Site: www.dmaw.
org
Mgr Programs & Mktg: Eerik Kreek
Exec Dir: Donna Tschiffely
Conducts Business: U.S.
Employees: 4
Primary Market Served: Business
Direct online sales
Founded: 1955

Covers news of the DMAW's events &
information of professional interest to
members, including postal related
news. Free with $175 membership.

MARKETING NEWS

American Marketing Association
311 S Wacker Dr (Suite 5800)
Chicago, IL 60606
Telephone: (312) 542-9000, Toll Free:
(800) 262-1150, FAX: (312) 542-
9001, E-Mail: news@ama.org, Web
Site: www.ama.org
Chmn: Michael Lotti
Publr: Jack Hollfelder
Primary Market Served: Business
Catalog available online
Direct online sales
Advertising/Marketing Budget Related
to Direct Marketing: 0-25%
Founded: 1936

Reports on marketing & its association.
ISSN# 00253790; membership-no additional fee: $100 non-member; $130
library, $130 institution. Published bi-
weekly.

MARKETING SCIENCE
INSTITUTE REVIEW

Marketing Science Institute
1000 Massachusetts Ave
Cambridge, MA 02138-5396
Telephone: (617) 491-2060, FAX:
(617) 491-2065, E-Mail: msi@msi.
org, Web Site: www.msi.org
COO: Marni Z. Clippinger
Chief Mktg Officer: Earl Taylor
Exec Dir: Kevin Lane Keller
Employees: 10
Primary Market Served: Business &
Consumer

Founded: 1961

Covers events, research findings, conferences & membership of the institute,
a research center whose purpose is to
advance marketing practice & knowledge. Free; published semi-annually.

O'DWYERS DIRECTORY OF
PUBLIC RELATIONS
FIRMS

JR O'Dwyer Co
271 Madison Ave (Suite 600)
New York, NY 10016-1013
Telephone: (212) 683-2750, Toll Free:
(866) 395-7710, FAX: (212) 683-
2750, E-Mail: john@odwyerpr.com,
Web Site: www.odwyerpr.com
Publr & Editor-in-Chief: Jack O'Dwyer
Conducts Business: Worldwide
Employees: 10
Primary Market Served: Business &
Consumer
Catalog available online
Founded: 1968

1001 WAYS TO MARKET
YOUR BOOKS

Open Horizons Publishing Co
PO Box 2887
Taos, NM 87571
Telephone: (575) 751-3398, FAX:
(575) 751-3100, E-Mail: info@
bookmarket.com, Web Site: www.
bookmarket.com
Publr: John Kremer
Conducts Business: Worldwide
Primary Market Served: Business &
Consumer
Catalog available online
Indirect online sales
Advertising/Marketing Budget Related
to Direct Marketing: 0-25%
Founded: 1986

A comprehensive introduction to marketing your books. Contains practical,
easy-to-use information designed to
help anyone develop a successful marketing program. $27.95.

PHOTOGRAPHER'S MARKET

Div. of Writer's Digest Books / F & W
Publications
10151 Carver Rd (Suite 200)
Blue Ash, OH 45242-4760
Telephone: (513) 531-2690, FAX:
(513) 531-2686, E-Mail:
photomarket@fwpubs.com, Web
Site: www.photographersmarket.com
Mktg Mgr: Scott Francis
Market Books Dept: Alice Pope
Employees: 1
Primary Market Served: Business
Catalog available online
Indirect online sales

Founded: 1977

More than 2000 listings of photo buyers with complete contact information; for freelance & stock photographers. Annual publication; $24.99.

RESPONSE MAGAZINE

Div. of Questex Media Group Inc
6 Hutton Centre Dr (Fl 6)
Santa Ana, CA 92707
Telephone: (714) 513-8624, Toll Free: (800) 371-6897, FAX: (714) 338-6710, Web Site: www. responsemagazine.com
Publr: John Yarrington
Mktg Devel: Ilene Schwartz
Conducts Business: U.S., Canada
Primary Market Served: Business
Advertising/Marketing Budget Related to Direct Marketing: 26-50%
Founded: 1992

Published monthly. Covers all aspects of the direct response marketing industry. From the 30-second spot, to the infomercial, to online & internet programming for the marketing, advertising & television executive. ISSN# 1077-5439.

STANDARD DIRECTORY OF ADVERTISING AGENCIES

Advertising Red Books A Member of the LexisNexis Group
PO Box 1514
Summit, NJ 07902
Toll Free: (800) 908-5395
CEO: Mike Walsh

SUCCESS MAGAZINE

RP-NFOA
200 Swisher Rd
Lake Dallas, TX 75065
Toll Free: (877) 243-8383, E-Mail: editor@success.com, Web Site: www.successmagazine.com
Publ & Founding Editor: Darren Hardy
Sr. VP Creative Svcs: Deborah Heisz
Conducts Business: Worldwide
Employees: 3
Primary Market Served: Business & Consumer
Founded: 2006

Entrepreneurial Magazine.

TARGET MARKETING MAGAZINE

North American Publishing Co
1500 Spring Garden St (12th fl)
Philadelphia, PA 19130-4094
Telephone: (215) 238-5300, Toll Free: (800) 777-8074, FAX: (215) 238-5270, Web Site: www. targetmarketingmag.com
Pres & Grp Publr: Peggy Hatch

Publr: Drew James
Primary Market Served: Business

The monthly magazine of how-to, hands-on, information for direct marketers. $65 annually; Free to qualified subscribers.

TELEPHONE SELLING REPORT

Div. of Business By Phone Inc
14005 E Cholla Dr
Scottsdale, AZ 85259-4619
Telephone: (402) 895-9399, FAX: (402) 896-3353, E-Mail: arts@ businessbyphone.com, Web Site: www.businessbyphone.com
Pres & Publr: Art Sobczak
Conducts Business: Worldwide
Employees: 3
Primary Market Served: Business
Catalog available online
Direct online sales
Advertising/Marketing Budget Related to Direct Marketing: 76-100%
Founded: 1983

Monthly "how-to" newsletter providing proven ideas & techniques for sales reps who use the phone to prospect, qualify, set appointments & sell by telephone. Also have catalog of telesales training audio tapes, videos, books & other how-to resources. Provide training seminars.

WEIDER HISTORY GROUP

350 Bennetts Farm Rd
Ridgefield, CT 06877
Telephone: (203) 273-1092

WHO'S WHO - THE MFSA BUYERS' GUIDE TO BLUE RIBBON MAILING SERVICES

Mailing & Fulfillment Service Association
1421 Prince St (Suite 410)
Alexandria, VA 22314-2805
Telephone: (703) 836-9200, FAX: (703) 548-8204, E-Mail: masa-mail@masa.org, Web Site: www. mfsanet.org
Pres: J Kenneth Garner
Dir Mktg & Programs: Bill Stevenson
Dir Membership: Tyler Keeney
Employees: 11
Catalog available online
Founded: 1920

Lists over 750 mailhouses, fulfillment lettershops & direct mail agencies. Latest edition, 2002. No charge to buyers of mailing services.

Alphabetical Index to Companies & Individuals

This alphabetical index interfiles the companies and individuals found within all sections of DMMP.

A

A & A Research, Kalispell, MT. Tel: (406) 752-7857 (30)

A&B Equipment Co, Fort Worth, TX. Tel: (817) 332-8361, (800) 426-0683, FAX: (817) 332-8430 (16)

A&E Promotions LLC, Atlantic Highlands, NJ. Tel: (732) 275-1520, FAX: (732) 275-1147, E-Mail: eveltri@aepromo.com, Web Site: www.promoplace.com (27)

A&H Lithoprint Inc, Broadview, IL. Tel: (708) 345-1196, FAX: (708) 345-1225, Web Site: www.ahlithoprint.com (27)

A&M Direct Mail Service Inc, San Dimas, CA. Tel: (909) 599-3905, (909) 579-0111, (800) 735-3905, FAX: (909) 599-3516, E-Mail: mail@amdirectmail.com (28)

A&P, Montvale, NJ. Tel: (201) 573-9700, (866) 44 FRESH, FAX: (201) 505-3054, E-Mail: apcustomerrel@aptea.com, Web Site: www.aptea.com (16)

A&R Mailing Machine Inc, East Hartford, CT. Tel: (860) 290-6640, FAX: (860) 290-6644, E-Mail: info@a-r-machine.com, Web Site: a-r-machine.com (34)

A Dean Watkins, Okemos, MI. Tel: (517) 349-7700, FAX: (517) 349-7748, E-Mail: adeanwatkins@aol.com, Web Site: www.adeanwatkins.com (33)

A La Carte, Chicago, IL. Tel: (773) 745-5900, (800) 723-2370, FAX: (773) 237-3075, E-Mail: service@alacarteline.com, Web Site: www.alacarteline.com (16)

A La Mode Inc, Oklahoma City, OK. Tel: (405) 359-6587, (800) ALAMODE, FAX: (405) 359-8612, Web Site: www.alamode.com (22)

A-Mark Inc, Dresher, PA. Tel: (215) 886-4740, FAX: (215) 886-4749 (15)

A Marketing Resource, South St Paul, MN. Tel: (651) 451-1765, Web Site: www.amr-advantage.com (29)

A-1 Direct Mail Marketing Inc, Miami, FL. Tel: (305) 251-3187 (28)

A+ Letter Service, Lakewood, NJ. Tel: (732) 905-2010, FAX: (732) 905-4662, E-Mail: aplus@aplusletter.com, Web Site: www.aplusletters.com (28)

A Plus Marketing Ltd, Buffalo Grove, IL. Tel: (847) 537-1166, FAX: (847) 537-5611, Web Site: www.aplusmarketing.com (20)

A-T Surgical Manufacturing Co, Holyoke, MA. Tel: (413) 532-4551, (800) 225-2023, FAX: (413) 532-0826, Web Site: www.atsurgical.com (2)

AAA Auto Club South, Tampa, FL. Tel: (813) 289-5800, FAX: (813) 289-1475, Web Site: www.aaa.com (1)

AAA-Chicago Motor Club, Aurora, IL. Tel: (630) 328-7000, FAX: (630) 499-8200, Web Site: www.aaa.com (1)

AAA Mid-Atlantic Insurance Groups, Wilmington, DE. Tel: (302) 299-4700, (800) 451-5921, FAX: (215) 864-5486, Web Site: www.aaamidatlantic.com (15)

AAA Southern New England, Providence, RI. Tel: (401) 868-2045, FAX: (401) 868-2088, Web Site: www.aaa.com (1)

AAA Umbrella Co Inc, Northvale, NJ. Tel: (201) 784-3242, (800) 426-7446, FAX: (201) 226-0041, E-Mail: sales@aaaumbrella.com, Web Site: www.aaaumbrella.com (16)

AAAS/Science, Washington, DC. Tel: (202) 326-6400, FAX: (202) 371-9526, E-Mail: membership@aaas.org, Web Site: www.aaas.org (1)

AAFES, Dallas, TX. Tel: (214) 312-2011, (800) 527-2345, FAX: (800) 446-0163, Web Site: www.aafes.com (5)

AAI, Boston, MA. Tel: (508) 544-1250, (877) 866-8500, FAX: (508) 544-1253, E-Mail: info@aai-agency.com, Web Site: www.aai-agency.com (35)

AARP, Washington, DC. Tel: (202) 434-2277, FAX: (202) 434-2525, Web Site: www.aarp.org (1)

AAVIM, Winterville, GA. Tel: (706) 742-5355, (800) 228-4689, FAX: (706) 742-7005, E-Mail: gary@aavim.com, Web Site: www.aavim.com (31)

ab + c Creative Intelligence, Wilmington, DE. Tel: (302) 655-1552, (800) 848-1552, FAX: (302) 655-3105, Web Site: www.a-b-c.com (35)

AB Data Ltd, Milwaukee, WI. Tel: (414) 963-7800, FAX: (414) 963-7899, E-Mail: dmservices@abdata.com, Web Site: dms.abdata.com (21)

ABC Carpet & Home, New York, NY. Tel: (212) 473-3000, Web Site: www.abccarpet.com (8)

ABC Clio, Santa Barbara, CA. Tel: (805) 968-1911, FAX: (805) 685-9685, E-Mail: elott@abc-clio.com, Web Site: www.abc-clio.com (17)

ABCO Inc, Dallas, TX. Tel: (214) 565-1191, Web Site: www.abcoinc.com (20)

ABDI, Inc Global Order Fulfillment, Leetsdale, PA. Tel: (412) 741-1142, (800) 796-6471, FAX: (412) 741-4161, E-Mail: info@abdintl.com, Web Site: www.abdintl.com (28)

ABI Inc, New York, NY. Tel: (212) 529-4500, FAX: (212) 529-4442, E-Mail: info@abipr.com, Web Site: www.abipr.com (35)

ABR Employment Services, Madison, WI. Tel: (608) 244-3526, FAX: (608) 244-8279, E-Mail: info@abrjobs.com, Web Site: www.abrjobs.com (20)

ABS Graphics, Addison, IL. Tel: (630) 495-2400, FAX: (630) 495-0728, E-Mail: info@absinet.com, Web Site: www.absinet.com (27)

AC Pedreiro, Morganville, NJ. Tel: (732) 598-6766 (27)

ACBL, Horn Lake, MS. Tel: (662) 253-3100, FAX: (662) 253-3187, E-Mail: service@acbl.org, Web Site: www.acbl.org (1)

ACCO Brands Corp, Lake Zurich, IL. Tel: (800) 222-6462, FAX: (800) 247-1317, Web Site: www.accobrands.com (16)

ACG/Computech Direct, Hoffman Estates, IL. Tel: (847) 843-3200, FAX: (847) 843-8060, E-Mail: info@acg-computech-direct.com, Web Site: www.acg-computech-direct.com (22)

ACN USA, Brooklyn, NY. Tel: (718) 609-0939, (800) 628-6333, FAX: (718) 609-0938, Web Site: www.churchineed.org (1)

ACP Medicine, Hamilton, ON Canada. Tel: (905) 522-8526, (855) 647-6511, FAX: (905) 522-9273, E-Mail: acpmedicine@deckerpublishing.com, Web Site: acpmedicine.com (17)

ADM Marketing, Burbank, CA. Tel: (888) 800-1001 (20)

ADM Productions Inc, Port Washington, NY. Tel: (516) 484-6900, (800) ADM-DIAL, FAX: (516) 621-2531, Web Site: www.admpro.com (16)

ADP Inc, Roseland, NJ. Tel: (973) 974-5000, (800) 225-5237, FAX: (973) 974-3334, Web Site: www.adp.com (16)

ADRA International, Silver Spring, MD. Tel: (301) 680-6373, (800) 424-2372, Web Site: www.adra.org (1)

ADRFCO, Washington, DC. Tel: (202) 293-9640, FAX: (202) 463-7980, E-Mail: adrfco@msn.com, Web Site: www.adrfco.org (1)

ADS Media Group Inc, San Antonio, TX. Tel: (210) 655-6613, FAX: (210) 655-6269, Web Site: www.adsmediagroup.com (27)

ADT LLC, Boca Raton, FL. Tel: (561) 988-3600, FAX: (561) 988-3673, Web Site: www.adt.com (16)

AESU Inc, Baltimore, MD. Tel: (410) 366-5494, (800) 638-7640, FAX: (410) 366-6999, E-Mail: res@aesu.com, Web Site: www.aesu.com (19)

AFA Service Corp, Atlanta, GA. Tel: (404) 237-2964, (404) 262-2729, Web Site: www.arbys.com (16)

AFL-CIO, Washington, DC. Tel: (202) 637-5000, FAX: (202) 637-5323, (202) 637-5058, Web Site: www.aflcio.org (1)

AFLAC, Columbus, GA. Tel: (706) 243-5428, Web Site: www.aflac.com (15)

AG Interactive, Cleveland, OH. Tel: (216) 252-7300, (800) 711-4474, FAX: (216) 252-6778, Web Site: www.americangreetings.com (32)

AGCO Inc, Norcross, GA. Tel: (770) 447-6990, FAX: (770) 446-2102, Web Site: www.agcomarble.com (9)

AGIA Insurance Services, Carpinteria, CA. Tel: (805) 566-9191, FAX: (805) 566-1887, Web Site: www.agia.com (15)

AIDC (American International Distribution Corp), Williston, VT. Tel: (800) 678-2432, FAX: (802) 864-7749, E-Mail: jmacon@aidcvt.com, Web Site: www.aidcvt.com (22)

AIFS, Stamford, CT. Tel: (203) 399-5000, (866) 906-2437, FAX: (203) 599-5590, E-Mail: info@aifs.com, Web Site: www.aifs.com (19)

AIG Accident & Health, New York, NY. Tel: (212) 770-7000, (877) 638-4244, FAX: (212) 509-9705, Web Site: www.aig.com (15)

AIG Marketing, New York, NY. Tel: (212) 770-7000, (212) 770-2237, Web Site: www.agac.com (15)

AIIM International, Silver Spring, MD. Tel: (301) 587-8202, (800) 477-2446, FAX: (301) 587-2711, E-Mail: aiim@aiim.org, Web Site: www.aiim.org (1)

AIN Plastics Inc, Yonkers, NY. Tel: (914) 668-6800, (800) 431-2451, FAX: (914) 668-8820, Web Site: www.ainplastics.com (16)

AKA Direct, Portland, OR. Tel: (503) 467-2200, (800) 647-8587, FAX: (503) 445-0064, Web Site: www.akadirect.com (27)

AKS Marketing & Media, Chapel Hill, NC. Tel: (919) 240-5496 (20)

ALC Inc, Princeton, NJ. Tel: (609) 580-2800, (800) 252-5478, FAX: (609) 580-2888, E-Mail: info@alc.com, Web Site: www.alc.com (23)

ALSAC - St Jude, Memphis, TN. Tel: (901) 495-3300, (800) 278-5833, FAX: (901) 495-3966, Web Site: www.stjude.org (1)

AMA Annual Conference, Chicago, IL. Tel: (312) 542-9000, (800) 262-1150, Web Site: www.ama.org (42)

AMA Insurance Agency Inc, Chicago, IL. Tel: (312) 464-2425, (800) 458-5736, FAX: (312) 419-5096, Web Site: www.amainsure.com (15)

AMC Inc, Atlanta, GA. Tel: (404) 220-2000, FAX: (404) 220-3030 (2)

AMC Publishing/Agent Media Corp, Clearwater, FL. Tel: (727) 446-1100, (800) 933-9449, FAX: (727) 446-1166, E-Mail: sales@agentmediacorp.com, Web Site: www.agentmediacorp.com (31)

AMD Industries Inc, Cicero, IL. Tel: (708) 863-8900, (800) 367-9999, FAX: (708) 863-2065, Web Site: www.amdpop.com (36)

AMI Instore, Framingham, MA. Tel: (508) 652-0200, (877) 652-0200, FAX: (508) 652-0101, E-Mail: info@advancemarketing.com, Web Site: www.advancemarketing.com (31)

Ampac Holdings LLC, Cincinnati, OH. Tel: (513) 671-1777, (800) 543-7030, FAX: (513) 671-2920, Web Site: www.ampaconline.com (27)

AMVETS National Service Foundation, Lanham, MD. Tel: (301) 459-6181, (800) 810-7148, FAX: (301) 459-5578, Web Site: www.amvetsnsf.org (1)

ANA/BMA National Conferences, New York, NY. Tel: (212) 697-5950, FAX: (212) 687-7310, E-Mail: info@marketing.net, Web Site: www.marketing.org (42)

AON Center, Chicago, IL. Tel: (312) 381-1000, FAX: (312) 381-6032, Web Site: www.aon.com (15)

Aon Consulting New York, New York, NY. Tel: (212) 792-9700, (212) 792-9759, (212) 441-2000, FAX: (212) 792-9720, E-Mail: garry_sullivan@aoncons.com (15)

Aon Innovative Solutions, Chicago, IL. Tel: (312) 381-1000, Web Site: www.aon.com (16)

AP Images, New York, NY. FAX: (212) 621-1679, E-Mail: apimages_us@ap.org, Web Site: www.apimages.com (38)

APAC Customer Services Inc, Bannockburn, IL. Tel: (847) 374-4980, (800) 688-7687, FAX: (847) 236-5453, Web Site: www.apaccustomerservices.com (29)

APC by Schneider Electric, West Kingston, RI. Tel: (800) 555-7927, FAX: (401) 789-3710, E-Mail: public.relations@apcc.com, Web Site: www.apcc.com (3)

APSCO, Davenport Center, NY. Tel: (607) 278-6218, FAX: (607) 278-6218, E-Mail: webmaster@antiquephono.com, Web Site: www.antiquephono.com (11)

APW-Wright Line, Worcester, MA. Tel: (508) 852-4300, (800) 225-7348, FAX: (508) 852-3060, Web Site: www.wrightline.com (16)

ARA Media Solutions Inc, New York, NY. Tel: (212) 245-6691, Web Site: www.aramediasolutions.com (31)

ARAG, Des Moines, IA. Tel: (800) 247-4184, FAX: (515) 246-8710, E-Mail: service@ARAGgroup.com, Web Site: www.araggroup.com (15)

ARE Press, Virginia Beach, VA. Tel: (757) 428-3588, (800) 333-4499, FAX: (757) 491-0689, Web Site: www.arepress.com (1)

ARF Events, New York, NY. Tel: (212) 751-5656, FAX: (212) 319-5265, E-Mail: info@theARF.org, Web Site: www.theARF.org (42)

ARI, Orchard Hill, GA. Tel: (770) 227-8222, (800) 241-5064, FAX: (770) 227-9190, Web Site: www.halt.com (16)

ASE Technologies Inc, Wilmington, MA. Tel: (978) 658-0009, FAX: (978) 658-9990, E-Mail: info@ase-tech.com, Web Site: www.ase-tech.com (16)

ASH Recruitment Solutions, Exeter, NH. Tel: (603) 778-8888, E-Mail: t.hall@ashrecruit.com, Web Site: www.ashrecruit.com (20)

ASL Marketing Inc, Farmingdale, NY. Tel: (516) 248-6100, FAX: (516) 248-6364, E-Mail: info@aslmarketing.com, Web Site: www.aslmarketing.com (23)

ASM International, Materials Park, OH. Tel: (440) 338-5151, (800) 336-5152, FAX: (440) 338-4634, E-Mail: customerservice@asminternational.org, Web Site: www.asminternational.org (1)

ASM Press, Washington, DC. Tel: (202) 737-3600, (800) 546-2416, FAX: (202) 942-9342, E-Mail: books@asmusa.org, Web Site: www.asmpress.org (17)

ASPCA, New York, NY. Tel: (212) 876-7700, Web Site: www.aspca.org (1)

ASTM International, West Conshohocken, PA. Tel: (610) 832-9500, FAX: (610) 832-9555, E-Mail: service@astm.org, Web Site: www.astm.org (1)

AT&T Inc, Dallas, TX. Tel: (210) 821-4105, Web Site: www.att.com (16)

ATD American Co, Wyncote, PA. Tel: (215) 576-1380, (866) 283-9327, FAX: (215) 576-1827, E-Mail: janet@atd.com, Web Site: www.atdamerican.com (34)

AVD Marketing, Hollywood, FL. Tel: (954) 410-9000, Web Site: www.avdmarketing.com (20)

AW Direct Inc, Madison, WI. Tel: (860) 828-7800, (800) 243-3194, FAX: (800) 828-9678, E-Mail: contactus@awdirect.com, Web Site: www.awdirect.com (12)

AXA Equitable, New York, NY. Tel: (212) 554-1234, (212) 314-2956, Web Site: www.axaonline.com (15)

A+E Television Networks LLC, New York, NY. Tel: (212) 210-1400, FAX: (212) 210-1326, E-Mail: aefeedback@aenetworks.com, Web Site: www.aenetworks.com (16)

Aardvark Enterprises, Calgary, AB Canada. Tel: (360) 779-5374 (17)

Aaron, M., Brim Electronics Inc, Lodi, NJ. Tel: (201) 796-2886, FAX: (973) 778-2792, E-Mail: info@brimelectronics.com, Web Site: www.brimelectronics.com (3)

Aaronson, Lawrence, Craig Envelope Corp, Long Island City, NY. Tel: (718) 786-4277, (888) 272-4436, FAX: (718) 937-8178, E-Mail: info@craigenvelope.com, Web Site: www.craigenvelope.com (26)

Abadi, Farrokh, Check Point Systems, Thorofare, NJ. Tel: (856) 848-1800, (800) 257-5540, FAX: (856) 848-0937, Web Site: www.checkpointsystems.com (34)

Abbate, Guy, Sherman Specialty Toy Co Inc, Jericho, NY. Tel: (516) 861-6420, (516) 546-7400, (800) 645-6513, FAX: (516) 861-1033, (800) 853-8697, E-Mail: orders@shermanspecialty.com, Web Site: www.shermanspecialty.com (16)

Abbattista, Denise, AccuData Integrated Marketing, Fort Myers, FL. Tel: (239) 425-4400, (800) 732-3440, FAX: (239) 425-4401, E-Mail: info@accudata.com, Web Site: www.accudata.com (23)

Abbeon Cal Inc, Santa Barbara, CA. Tel: (805) 966-0810, (800) 922-0977, FAX: (805) 966-7659, E-Mail: abbeoncal@abbeon.com, Web Site: www.abbeon.com (9)

Abbey of Gethsemani, Trappist, KY. Tel: (502) 549-4133, FAX: (502) 549-4124, E-Mail: reservations@monks.org, Web Site: www.monks.org (1)

Abbey Press, Saint Meinrad, IN. Tel: (812) 357-8368, FAX: (812) 357-8388, Web Site: www.abbeypress.com (1)

Abbey, Michelle, TMP Worldwide, New York, NY. Tel: (800) 867-2001, E-Mail: wecanhelp@tmp.com, Web Site: www.tmp.com (35)

Abbot, Jonathan C., WGBH Educational Foundation, Brighton, MA. Tel: (617) 300-2000, FAX: (617) 300-1026, Web Site: www.wgbh.org (1)

Abbott, Abbott Park, IL. Tel: (224) 667-6100, FAX: (847) 937-9555, Web Site: www.abbott.com (7)

Abbott Products, Weymouth, MA. Tel: (781) 331-2030, (800) 392-7700, FAX: (781) 331-2030, E-Mail: abbottproducts@comcast.net, Web Site: abbottbingoproducts.com (16)

Abbott, Andrea, The New Yorker Magazine, New York, NY. Tel: (212) 286-2860, FAX: (212) 286-4168, Web Site: www.newyorker.com (17)

Abbott, Bruce, Continental Supply Inc, Cleveland, OH. Tel: (440) 864-6231, (800) 672-0321, FAX: (888) 672-9808 (9)

Abbott, George, American Foundation for the Blind Inc, New York, NY. Tel: (212) 502-7600, FAX: (212) 502-7777, E-Mail: afbinfo@afb.org, Web Site: www.afb.org (1)

Abbott, James Cooper, Eagle Asset Management Inc, Saint Petersburg, FL. Tel: (727) 573-2453, FAX: (727) 573-8655, Web Site: www.eagleasset.com (14)

Abbott, James, Westlake Plastics Co, Lenni, PA. Tel: (610) 459-1000, (800) 999-1700, FAX: (610) 459-1084, Web Site: www.westlakeplastics.com (16)

Abbruzzese, Chris, Maui Jim Inc, Peoria, IL. Tel: (309) 691-3700, FAX: (309) 683-2202, Web Site: www.mauijim.com (16)

Abel, Barry, Message Systems, Columbia, MD. Tel: (410) 872-4910, (877) 887-3031, FAX: (410) 872-4912, E-Mail: information@messagesystems.com, Web Site: www.messagesystems.com (32)

Abele, Jr. James A., Robert James Co Inc, Moody, AL. Tel: (205) 640-7081, (800) 633-8296, FAX: (205) 640-7087 (10)

Abeles, David, National Golf Foundation, Jupiter, FL. Tel: (561) 744-6006, FAX: (561) 744-6107, E-Mail: ngf@ngf.org, Web Site: www.ngf.org (1)

Abell, Sherri, Mohawk Lifts, Amsterdam, NY. Tel: (518) 842-1431, (800) 833-2006, FAX: (518) 842-1289, E-Mail: rwells@mohawklifts.com, Web Site: www.mohawklifts.com (9)

Abeloe, Dave, Patagonia Mail Order Inc, Reno, NV. Tel: (775) 747-1992, (800) 638-6464, FAX: (775) 747-6159, Web Site: www.patagonia.com (2)

Abelove, David, Associated Textile Rental Services, Rochester, NY. Tel: (585) 454-5988, (800) 639-4624, Web Site: www.associatedtextile.com (16)

Abelow, Justin, New York Landmarks Conservancy, New York, NY. Tel: (212) 995-5260, FAX: (212) 995-5268, Web Site: www.nylandmarks.org (1)

Abels, Stephen, Mutual of Omaha, Omaha, NE. Tel: (402) 342-7600, (800) 775-6000, FAX: (402) 351-2775, Web Site: www.mutualofomaha.com (15)

AbelsonTaylor Inc, Chicago, IL. Tel: (312) 894-5500, FAX: (312) 894-5526, E-Mail: info@abelsontaylor.com, Web Site: www.abelsontaylor.com (35)

Abend, Sarah, Wyandotte West Communications Inc, Kansas City, KS. Tel: (913) 788-5565, FAX: (913) 788-9812, E-Mail: news@wyandottewest.com, Web Site: www.wyandottewest.com (17)

Aberle, Craig, Microbiz Corp, Menlo Park, CA. Tel: (702) 749-5353, (800) 726-3282, FAX: (650) 440-4870, E-Mail: info@microbiz.com, Web Site: www.microbiz.com (3)

Abernathy, Robert E., Kimberly-Clark Corp, Neenah, WI. Tel: (920) 721-2000, (888) 525-8388, FAX: (920) 721-7722, Web Site: www.kimberly-clark. com (16)

Abeyta, Joseph, McMurry Inc, Phoenix, AZ. Tel: (602) 395-5850, Web Site: www.mcmurry.com (17)

Abi-Karam, Leslie, Pitney Bowes, Stamford, CT. Tel: (203) 356-5000, (800) MR-BOWES, Web Site: www.pitneybowes.com (10)

Ability Commerce, Delray Beach, FL. Tel: (561) 330-3151, Web Site: www.abilitycommerce.com (20)

Abion, Betty, Response Media, Norcross, GA. Tel: (770) 451-5478, FAX: (770) 451-4929, E-Mail: postmaster@responsemedia.com, Web Site: www. responsemedia.com (32)

Abney, Wendy, Brigade Quartermasters Ltd, Providence, RI. Tel: (770) 428-1248, (800) 338-4327, FAX: (800) 892-2992, Web Site: www.actiongear. com (11)

Aboid, Joe, The Professional Putters Association, Winston Salem, NC. Tel: (866) 788-8788, Web Site: www.proputters.com (1)

Aboud, Benzion, Elephant Group Inc, Fort Lauderdale, FL. Tel: (954) 657-9611, FAX: (866) 699-5786, Web Site: www.elephantgroup.com (30)

About Books Inc, Colorado Springs, CO. Tel: (719) 632-8226, FAX: (719) 471-2182, E-Mail: infoabi2@ about-books.com, Web Site: www.about-books.com (20)

Abraham, Dan, Pennstreet Bakery, Grand Rapids, MI. Tel: (616) 241-2583, (800) 84-CAKES, FAX: (616) 241-6332, Web Site: www.pennstreet.com (16)

Abraham, Kelsha, Ashworth College, Norcross, GA. Tel: (770) 729-8400, (800) 957-5412, FAX: (770) 729-9294, Web Site: www.ashworthcollege.edu (13)

Abrahams, Mark, DelStar Technologies Inc, Middletown, DE. Tel: (302) 378-8888, (800) 521-6713, FAX: (302) 378-4482, Web Site: www.delstarinc. com (16)

Abrahamson, Kathy, Rose Resnick Lighthouse for the Blind & Visually Impaired, San Francisco, CA. Tel: (415) 431-1481, FAX: (415) 863-7568, E-Mail: executive@lighthouse-sf.org, Web Site: www. lighthouse-sf.org (1)

Harry N Abrams Inc, New York, NY. Tel: (212) 206-7715, FAX: (212) 645-8437, Web Site: www. hnabooks.com (17)

Abrams, Leonard, Paul Fredrick Menstyle, Fleetwood, PA. Tel: (610) 944-0909, (800) 247-1417, FAX: (610) 944-6452, E-Mail: custserv@menstyle.com, Web Site: www.paulfredricks.com (2)

Abrams, Marjory, Boardroom Inc, Stamford, CT. Tel: (203) 973-5900, FAX: (203) 967-3086, Web Site: www.bottomlinepublications.com (17)

Abrams, Martin E, Center For Information Policy Leadership, Washington, DC. Tel: (202) 778-2264, FAX: (202) 778-2201, Web Site: www.policyleaders.com (20)

Abrams, Mike, Iowa Medical Society, Des Moines, IA. Tel: (515) 223-1401, (800) 747-3070, FAX: (515) 223-0590, Web Site: www.iowamedical.org (1)

Abrams, Neal, Pilgrim Printed Promotional Plastics, Brockton, MA. Tel: (508) 436-6300, (800) 343-7810, FAX: (508) 580-3542, E-Mail: pilgrimsales@ pilgrimplastics.com, Web Site: www.pilgrimplastics. com (27)

Abrams, Paul, Roto-Rooter Services Co, Cincinnati, OH. Tel: (513) 762-6690, FAX: (513) 762-6590, Web Site: www.rotorooter.com (16)

Abrams, Ralph, Lea & Perrins Inc, Fair Lawn, NJ. Tel: (201) 791-1600, FAX: (201) 791-8945, Web Site: www.leaperrins.com (16)

Abrams, Richard, Tom Snyder Productions, Watertown, MA. Tel: (617) 926-6000, (800) 342-0236, FAX: (800) 304-1254, E-Mail: ask@tomsnyder.com, Web Site: www.tomsnyder.com (16)

Abramson, Betty, Starcrest Products of California Inc, Perris, CA. Tel: (909) 943-2011, FAX: (909) 943-2971, E-Mail: tmc@tstonramp.com (16)

Abramson, Howard, TT Publishing, Arlington, VA. Tel: (703) 838-1770, FAX: (703) 838-0285, Web Site: www.ttnews.com (17)

Abramson, Jill, The New York Times Co, New York, NY. Tel: (212) 556-1234, Web Site: www.nytimes. com (17)

Abramson, Karen, CCH Inc, Riverwoods, IL. Tel: (847) 267-7000, (888) 224-7377, Web Site: www. cchgroup.com (17)

Abramson, Mark, Message Technologies Inc, Atlanta, GA. Tel: (770) 240-8000, (800) 868-3684, FAX: (770) 240-7474, E-Mail: info@messagetech.com, Web Site: www.messagetech.com (30)

Abramson, Robert, House of Oldies, New York, NY. Tel: (212) 243-0500, FAX: (212) 989-1697, E-Mail: rabramson@houseofoldies.com, Web Site: www. houseofoldies.com (6)

Abrei, Cybell, Hy Cite Corp, Madison, WI. Tel: (608) 273-3373, (877) 494-2289, FAX: (608) 273-0936, Web Site: www.hycite.com (16)

Abruzzese, Joe, Discovery Communications Inc, Silver Spring, MD. Tel: (240) 662-2000, FAX: (240) 662-1868, Web Site: corporate.discovery.com (16)

Absolute Reservation Center Inc, Longwood, FL. Tel: (407) 660-9995, Web Site: www.arcfun.com (19)

Abusow, Kathy, Sustainable Forestry Initiative Inc, Washington, DC. Tel: (202) 596-3450, FAX: (202) 596-3451, E-Mail: info@sfiprogram.org, Web Site: www.sfiprogram.org (1)

Academic Management Services, Swansea, MA. Tel: (508) 235-2870, (800) 891-4203, FAX: (508) 235-2991, E-Mail: info@amsweb.com, Web Site: www. amsweb.com (14)

Academic Travel Abroad Inc, Washington, DC. Tel: (202) 785-9000, (800) 556-7896, FAX: (202) 342-0317, Web Site: www.academictravel.com (19)

Academy of Marketing Science Journal, Thousand Oaks, CA. Tel: (800) 818-7243, FAX: (800) 583-2665, E-Mail: journals@sagepub.com, Web Site: www.sagepub.com (43)

Accelerated Learning Foundation, Fairfield. IA. Tel: (641) 954-5443, (800) 289-2377, FAX: (641) 954-5851, E-Mail: info@gamesforthinkers.org, Web Site: www.gamesforthinkers.org (17)

Accellos Inc, Colorado Springs, CO. Tel: (719) 433-7000, Web Site: www.accellos.com (12)

Accent Advertising Inc, North Kansas City, MO. Tel: (816) 842-1860, FAX: (816) 471-4836, E-Mail: lindaaccentadv@sbcglobal.net, Web Site: www. accentadv.com (33)

ACCENT Marketing Services LLC, Jeffersonville, IN. Tel: (812) 206-6200, Web Site: www.accentonline. com (20)

Accenture, Boston, MA. Tel: (617) 488-4000, FAX: (617) 488-4001, Web Site: www.accenture.com (20)

Access Business Communications Inc, Huntington Beach, CA. Tel: (800) 675-2415, Web Site: www. abcimarketing.com (20)

Access Development, Salt Lake City, UT. Tel: (801) 656-1529, (800) 840-0032, Web Site: www. accessdevelopment.com (35)

Access Direct Systems Inc, Farmingdale, NY. Tel: (631) 420-0700, Web Site: www.accessdirect.com (28)

Access International, Cambridge, MA. Tel: (617) 218-5000, (877) 433-9097, FAX: (617) 494-8404, E-Mail: info@accessint.com, Web Site: www. accessint.com (22)

Access Worldwide Communications Inc, Falls Church, VA. Tel: (571) 384-7400, (800) 522-3447, FAX: (703) 531-0711, Web Site: www.accessww.com (29)

Accinno, Nancy, Racer's Equipment Warehouse, Warwick, RI. Tel: (401) 348-6010, (800) 556-2864, FAX: (401) 348-6023, E-Mail: scott@racers-eq. com, Web Site: www.racers-eq.com (16)

Accinno, Peter, Racer's Equipment Warehouse, Warwick, RI. Tel: (401) 348-6010, (800) 556-2864, FAX: (401) 348-6023, E-Mail: scott@racers-eq. com, Web Site: www.racers-eq.com (16)

Accinno, Ralph, Racer's Equipment Warehouse, Warwick, RI. Tel: (401) 348-6010, (800) 556-2864, FAX: (401) 348-6023, E-Mail: scott@racers-eq. com, Web Site: www.racers-eq.com (16)

Accoona Corp, Jersey City, NJ. Tel: (201) 557-9388, Web Site: www.accoona.com (16)

Accountants Education Group, Dallas, TX. Tel: (214) 373-3486, (800) 627-7310, FAX: (800) 627-7310, E-Mail: customerservice@accountantsed.com, Web Site: www.accountantsed.com (10)

Accountants' Supply House, Lancaster, CA. Tel: (856) 384-1144, (800) 342-5274, FAX: (800) 468-4446, Web Site: www.rapidforms.com (10)

Accountemps, Menlo Park, CA. Tel: (650) 234-6000, (800) 803-8367, FAX: (650) 234-6998, Web Site: www.accountemps.com (16)

Accounting with Debits and Credits with Coates & Hutchinson PC, Odenton, MD. Tel: (410) 672-6339, (800) 833-5933, FAX: (301) 912-3364, E-Mail: info@awdc.org (14)

AccountMate Software Corp, Petaluma, CA. Tel: (707) 774-7500, FAX: (707) 774-7590, E-Mail: information@accountmate.com, Web Site: www. accountmate.com (22)

AccuData Integrated Marketing, Fort Myers, FL. Tel: (239) 425-4400, (800) 732-3440, FAX: (239) 425-4401, E-Mail: info@accudata.com, Web Site: www. accudata.com (23)

AccuDirect Response, Portland, OR. Tel: (503) 223-2076, Web Site: accdirectnw.com (22)

AccuList Inc, San Antonio, TX. Tel: (210) 807-9940, (877) 505-8747, FAX: (210) 494-5478, E-Mail: sales@acculistusa.com, Web Site: www.acculistusa. com (23)

Accuracy in Media Inc, Bethesda, MD. Tel: (202) 364-4401, FAX: (202) 364-4098, E-Mail: info@aim.org, Web Site: www.aim.org (1)

Accurate Marketing Systems, River Edge, NJ. Tel: (201) 265-5198 (22)

ACCUSPLIT Inc, Livermore, CA. Tel: (925) 226-0888, (800) 935-1996, FAX: (925) 463-0147, E-Mail: sales@accusplit.com, Web Site: www.accusplit.com (16)

AccuTrade Inc, Bellevue, NE. Tel: (402) 970-7400, (800) 882-4887, FAX: (816) 243-3762, E-Mail: info@accutrade.com (14)

Accutrend Data Corp, Greenwood Village, CO. Tel: (303) 488-0011, FAX: (303) 488-0133, E-Mail: info@accutrend.com, Web Site: www.accutrend. com (24)

Ace Hardware Corp, Oak Brook, IL. Tel: (630) 990-6600, FAX: (630) 990-6838, Web Site: www. acehardware.com (16)

Achieve Global, Tampa, FL. Tel: (813) 631-5500, (800) 566-0630, FAX: (813) 631-5796, Web Site: www. achieveglobal.com (16)

Acker, David, Sleepy's Inc, Hicksville, NY. Tel: (516) 844-8800, (800) sleepys, FAX: (516) 844-8847, Web Site: www.sleepys.com (16)

Ackerman, Jason, FreshDirect, Long Island City, NY. Tel: (212) 796-8002 (5)

Ackerman, Steve, AHC Media, Atlanta, GA. Tel: (404) 262-7436, FAX: (404) 262-7837 (17)

Ackerman, Steve, Thompson Publishing Group Inc, Washington, DC. Tel: (202) 872-4000, (800) 677-3789, FAX: (800) 999-5661, E-Mail: service@thompson.com, Web Site: www.thompson.com (17)

Ackford, Rob, Ideal Industries (Canada) Corp, Ajax, ON Canada. Tel: (905) 683-3400, (800) 824-3325, FAX: (905) 683-0209, E-Mail: nick.shkordoff@idealindustries.com, Web Site: www.idealindustries.com (9)

Acme Tools, Grand Forks, ND. Tel: (701) 746-6481, (800) 732-4287, FAX: (701) 746-2857, Web Site: www.acmetools.com (8)

ACNielsen Corp, New York, NY. Tel: (646) 654-5000, FAX: (646) 654-5002, E-Mail: globalc@nielsen.com, Web Site: www.acnielsen.com/us (30)

AcquireWEB Inc, Foster City, CA. Tel: (650) 212-2233, FAX: (650) 212-2234, E-Mail: sales@aquireweb.com, Web Site: www.acquireWEB.com (22)

Acquirgy Inc, Saint Petersburg, FL. Tel: (727) 576-6630, FAX: (727) 576-4864, Web Site: www.sendtec.com (35)

Across The Board Marketing Inc, Chicago, IL. Tel: (312) 787-1642, FAX: (312) 787-1645, E-Mail: info@acrosstheboardmarketing.com, Web Site: www.acrosstheboardmarketing.com (39)

Act One Lists, Marblehead, MA. Tel: (781) 639-1919, (800) 228-5478, FAX: (781) 639-2733, E-Mail: info@act1lists.com, Web Site: www.actonelists.com (23)

Action-AD, Bettendorf, IA. Tel: (563) 355-9581, FAX: (563) 355-9586 (35)

Action Direct Inc, Miami, FL. Tel: (305) 969-0056, E-Mail: info@action-direct.com, Web Site: www.action-direct.com (11)

Action Mailers Inc, Aston, PA. Tel: (610) 859-0500, (800) 258-5992, FAX: (610) 859-0505, Web Site: www.actionmailer.com (27)

ActionAid, Washington, DC. Tel: (202) 835-1240, E-Mail: info@actionaid.org, Web Site: www.actionaidusa.org (1)

Active Graphics Inc, Cicero, IL. Tel: (708) 656-8900, FAX: (708) 656-2176, E-Mail: support@active-us.com, Web Site: www.active-us.com (21)

ACTIVE Network LLC, Dallas, TX. Tel: (858) 964-6064, (877) 228-4808, Web Site: www.activenetwork.com (22)

Active Parenting, Marietta, GA. Tel: (770) 429-0565, (800) 825-0060, (800) 235-7755, FAX: (770) 429-0334, E-Mail: cservice@activeparenting.com, Web Site: www.activeparenting.com (17)

Active Voice, San Francisco, CA. Tel: (415) 487-2000, FAX: (415) 487-2260, E-Mail: info@activevoice.net, Web Site: www.activevoice.net (21)

Active Web Group, Hauppauge, NY. Tel: (800) 978-3417, FAX: (800) 719-4402, E-Mail: info@activewebgroup.com, Web Site: www.activewebgroup.com (9)

ActiveCampaign Inc, Chicago, IL. Tel: (800) 357-0402, E-Mail: help@activecampaign.com, Web Site: www.activecampaign.com (24)

Activision Value, Eden Prairie, MN. Tel: (952) 918-9400, FAX: (952) 918-9560 (16)

ActivStyle, Minneapolis, MN. Tel: (612) 520-9333, (800) 651-6223, FAX: (612) 520-9300, Web Site: www.activstyle.com (16)

ACTON International Ltd, Lincoln, NE. Tel: (402) 905-9566, E-Mail: info@acton.com, Web Site: www.acton.com (23)

Acton, Randy, US Cavalry, Radcliff, KY. Tel: (270) 351-1164, (800) 777-7172, FAX: (270) 352-0266, E-Mail: hq@uscavalry.com, Web Site: www.uscavalry.com (6)

Actuarial Enterprises Ltd, Chicago, IL. Tel: (312) 397-0099, E-Mail: jay@actentltd.com (20)

Acuff, Keith, Noble Communications Co, Springfield, MO. Tel: (417) 875-5015, Web Site: www.noble.net (35)

Acurian, Horsham, PA. Tel: (215) 323-9000, (866) 566-5966, FAX: (215) 323-9001, Web Site: www.acurian.com (7)

AcuSport Corp, Bellefontaine, OH. Tel: (937) 593-7010, FAX: (937) 592-5625, E-Mail: mwsales@acusport.com, Web Site: www.acusport.com (11)

Acxiom Corp, Little Rock, AR. Tel: (501) 342-1000, FAX: (501) 342-3913, Web Site: www.acxiom.com (22)

Ad Facts Inc, Cary, NC. Tel: (919) 388-3015, (800) 923-3228, E-Mail: adfacts@adfacts.com, Web Site: www.adfacts.com (30)

The Ad Farm, Ottawa Hills, OH. Tel: (419) 720-5676, Web Site: www.theadfarm.com (20)

Ad Hoc Marketing Resources Inc, New York, NY. Tel: (212) 595-1800, FAX: (212) 656-1860, E-Mail: adhocmrktg@aol.com, Web Site: www.members.aol.com/adhocmrktg (20)

Ad Infinitum Books, Mount Vernon, NY. Tel: (914) 664-5930, (800) 697-0402, FAX: (914) 664-2642, E-Mail: aibservice@adinfinitumbooks.com, Web Site: www.adinfinitumbooks.com (16)

Ad-Lib Advertising Inc, Old Bridge, NJ. Tel: (732) 679-9226, (800) 622-3542, FAX: (732) 679-9511, E-Mail: info@adlibadvertising.com, Web Site: www.adlibadvertising.com (10)

AD-Vantage Marketing, Santa Rosa, CA. Tel: (707) 578-8700, FAX: (707) 578-0258, E-Mail: info@ad-vantagemarketing.com, Web Site: ad-vantagemarketing.com (28)

Adair, Karen, Oklahoma Dept of Commerce, Oklahoma City, OK. Tel: (405) 815-6552, (800) 879-6552, FAX: (405) 815-5344, Web Site: www.okcommerce.com (1)

Adam, Bill, Alliant, Brewster, NY. Tel: (845) 276-2600, FAX: (845) 276-2605, Web Site: www.alliantdata.com (22)

Adames, Fermin, Tempco Electric Heater Corp, Wood Dale, IL. Tel: (630) 350-2252, (800) 323-6859, FAX: (630) 350-0232, E-Mail: dpadlo@tempco.com, Web Site: www.tempco.com (9)

Adamo, John, Random House Children's Books, New York, NY. Tel: (212) 782-9000, (800) 726-0600, E-Mail: rhkidspublicity@randomhouse.com, Web Site: www.randomhousekids.com (13)

Danielle Adams Publishing Co, Merion Station, PA. Tel: (610) 642-1000, E-Mail: jeff@dobkin.com, Web Site: www.danielleadams.com (35)

Adams Manufacturing Co, Cleveland, OH. Tel: (216) 587-6801, FAX: (216) 587-6807, E-Mail: adamsx@att.net, Web Site: www.adamsmanufacturing.com (9)

Adams, Allison, Institutional Investor Inc, New York, NY. Tel: (212) 224-3300, FAX: (212) 224-3592, Web Site: www.institutionalinvestor.com (17)

Adams, Bart, Daily Record & Dispatch Co, Dunn, NC. Tel: (910) 891-1234, FAX: (910) 891-5253, Web Site: www.mydailyrecord.com (17)

Adams, Bob, Hampden Papers Inc, Holyoke, MA. Tel: (413) 536-1000, FAX: (413) 532-9161, Web Site: www.hampdenpapers.com (25)

Adams, Carl, Tidbits Media, Montgomery, AL. Tel: (334) 290-0225, (800) 523-3096, FAX: (334) 386-0302, E-Mail: editors@tidbitsweekly.com, Web Site: www.tidbitsweekly.com (17)

Adams, David L., Aimia Inc, Montreal, QC Canada. Web Site: www.aimia.com (35)

Adams, Don, American Inbound, Bloomington, IN. Tel: (800) 322-6445, FAX: (800) 224-3583, Web Site: www.americanbound.com (29)

Adams, Dr Virginia, National League for Nursing, Washington, DC. Tel: (212) 363-5555, (800) 669-1656, FAX: (212) 812-0391, E-Mail: generalinfo@nln.org, Web Site: www.nln.org (1)

Adams, Greg, Chapman Cubine Adams & Hussey, Arlington, VA. Tel: (703) 248-0025, Web Site: www.ahadirect.com (20)

Adams, Guy, Christian Appalachian Project, Paintsville, KY. Tel: (866) 270-4227, (866) 270-4CAP, FAX: (859) 792-6560, E-Mail: capinfo@chrisapp.org, Web Site: www.christianapp.org (1)

Adams, Ilene, Techcom Inc, Indianapolis, IN. Tel: (317) 865-2530, FAX: (317) 865-2540, E-Mail: info@techcom.com, Web Site: www.techcom.com (35)

Adams, John, The Martin Agency, Richmond, VA. Tel: (804) 698-8000, FAX: (804) 698-8001, Web Site: www.martinagency.com (35)

Adams, Leslie, Checks by Phone/Checks by Web, Boynton Beach, FL. Tel: (561) 737-8700, FAX: (561) 737-5800, E-Mail: LarrySchwartz@checksbyphone.com, Web Site: www.checksbyphone.com (14)

Adams, Marv, TD Ameritrade Holding Corp, Omaha, NE. Tel: (800) 237-8692, Web Site: www.amtd.com (16)

Adams, Marvin, Fidelity Investments, Boston, MA. Tel: (617) 563-7000, (800) 343-3548, FAX: (617) 476-6150, Web Site: www.fidelity.com (14)

Adams, Michele, American Association of Advertising Agencies, New York, NY. Tel: (212) 682-2500, FAX: (212) 682-8391, Web Site: www.aaaa.org (40)

Adams, Mike, CTRAC Information Solutions, Strongsville, OH. Tel: (440) 572-1000, FAX: (440) 572-3330, E-Mail: ctrac@ctrac.com, Web Site: www.ctrac.com (22)

Adams, Paul, SUCCESS Partners Co, Lake Dallas, TX. Tel: (940) 497-9700, (800) 752-2030, FAX: (940) 497-9987, Web Site: successpartners.com (32)

Adams, Sharon, Christian Appalachian Project, Paintsville, KY. Tel: (866) 270-4227, (866) 270-4CAP, FAX: (859) 792-6560, E-Mail: capinfo@chrisapp.org, Web Site: www.christianapp.org (1)

Adams, Stephen, American Institute for Economic Research, Great Barrington, MA. Tel: (413) 528-1216, (888) 528-1216, FAX: (413) 528-0103, E-Mail: info@aier.org, Web Site: www.aier.org (1)

Adams, Stephen, Woodall Publishing Co LP, Ventura, CA. Tel: (805) 667-4100, (800) 323-9076, FAX: (805) 667-4468, Web Site: www.woodalls.com (17)

Adams, Synthia, MGM Grand Detroit, Detroit, MI. Tel: (877) 888-2121, Web Site: www.mgmgrand.com/det (16)

Adams, Terri, Precision Arts Advertising Inc, Ashburnham, MA. Tel: (978) 855-7648, E-Mail: info@precisionarts.com, Web Site: www.precisionarts.com (35)

Adams, Tim, Time Customer Service Inc, Tampa, FL. Tel: (813) 878-6100, (800) 723-NCOA, FAX: (813) 878-6452, Web Site: www.timecustomerservice.com (22)

Adamson, Lori, Kelco Supply Co, Big Lake, MN. Tel: (763) 493-1260, (800) 328-7720, FAX: (763) 493-1261, E-Mail: info@kelcosupply.com, Web Site: www.kelcosupply.com (16)

Adamson, Terrence B., National Geographic Society, Washington, DC. Tel: (202) 862-8638, (800) 373-1717, Web Site: www.nationalgeographic.com (17)

Adanuncio, James, Connex International Inc, Danbury, CT. Tel: (203) 731-5400, (800) 426-6639, FAX: (203) 730-9060, E-Mail: marketing@connexintl.com, Web Site: www.connexintl.com (22)

The Adcentive Group Inc, San Diego, CA. Tel: (858) 278-9200, FAX: (858) 571-2832, Web Site: www.brownandbigelow.com (35)

The Adcom Group, Cleveland, OH. Tel: (216) 574-9100, FAX: (216) 574-6131, Web Site: www.theadcomgroup.com (35)

Adcox, Jack, Health Sciences Consortium, Chapel Hill, NC. Tel: (919) 942-8731, FAX: (919) 942-3689, E-Mail: tony.penta@edtsi.com, Web Site: www.healthsciencesconsortium.org (17)

The Added Touch, Oakville, ON Canada. Tel: (905) 828-4041, (888) AD-TOUCH, FAX: (905) 338-1486, E-Mail: addedtouch@gmail.com, Web Site: www.addedtouch.com (28)

Addeo, Chris, Ion Media Networks Inc, West Palm Beach, FL. Tel: (561) 659-4122, (800) 646-7296, FAX: (561) 659-4252, Web Site: www.ionmedia.tv (32)

Addicks, Mark W., The Pillsbury Co, Minneapolis, MN. Tel: (763) 764-7600, (800) 248-7310, FAX: (763) 764-8330, Web Site: www.pillsbury.com (16)

Addington, Kim, Web Decisions, Greensboro, NC. Tel: (336) 545-7817 x100 (22)

Adecco Employment Services, Melville, NY. Tel: (631) 844-7800, Web Site: www.adecco.com (20)

Adelman, David, Moddern Marketing, New York, NY. Tel: (212) 334-9800, E-Mail: mark@moddern.com, Web Site: www.moddern.com (35)

Adelson, Scott J., Houlihan Lokey Howard & Zukin, Los Angeles, CA. Tel: (310) 553-8871, (800) 788-5300, FAX: (310) 553-2173, Web Site: www.hlhz.com (14)

Ades, Abraham, Anything Goes, Allenhurst, NJ. Tel: (732) 531-8040, Web Site: www.heavenlytreasures.com (6)

Ades, Michael, Anything Goes, Allenhurst, NJ. Tel: (732) 531-8040, Web Site: www.heavenlytreasures.com (6)

Adey, W. Richard, Analytical Measurements, Chester, NJ. Tel: (800) 635-5580, FAX: (973) 399-1446, E-Mail: phmeter@bellatlantic.net, Web Site: www.analyticalmeasurements.com (9)

Adirondack Direct, Long Island City, NY. Tel: (718) 932-4003, (800) 221-2444, FAX: (800) 477-1330, E-Mail: info@adirondackdirect.com, Web Site: www.adirondackdirect.com (10)

Adkins Design LLC, Trumbull, CT. Tel: (203) 880-9517, E-Mail: tom@adkins-design.com, Web Site: www.sabinc.com (35)

Adkins, Jennifer, Scott Sign Systems Inc, Sarasota, FL. Tel: (941) 355-5171, (800) 237-9447, FAX: (941) 351-1787, E-Mail: mail@scottsigns.com, Web Site: www.scottsigns.com (16)

Adkins, John, Intromark Inc, Pittsburgh, PA. Tel: (412) 288-1300, (800) 851-6030 X1368, FAX: (412) 338-0497, E-Mail: licensing@intromark.com (16)

Adkins, Thomas, Adkins Design LLC, Trumbull, CT. Tel: (203) 880-9517, E-Mail: tom@adkins-design.com, Web Site: www.sabinc.com (35)

Adkins-Green, Sheryl, Mary Kay Cosmetics Inc, Addison, TX. Tel: (972) 687-6300, (800) MARY KAY, FAX: (972) 687-1611, Web Site: www.marykay.com (16)

Adknowledge, Kansas City, MO. Tel: (816) 931-1771, (866) 730-2109, Web Site: www.adknowledge.com (32)

Adler, Allan, Association of American Publishers, Washington, DC. Tel: (202) 347-3375, FAX: (202) 347-3690, E-Mail: info@publishers.org, Web Site: www.publishers.org (1)

Adler, George, Four Wheel Drive Hardware LLC, Columbiana, OH. Tel: (330) 482-4924, FAX: (330) 482-5035, E-Mail: info@4wd.com, Web Site: www.4wd.com (12)

Adler, Jim, Myron Corp, Maywood, NJ. Tel: (201) 843-6464, (877) 803-3358, FAX: (201) 843-8390, Web Site: www.myron.com (16)

Adler-Kravecas, Marie, Myron Corp, Maywood, NJ. Tel: (201) 843-6464, (877) 803-3358, FAX: (201) 843-8390, Web Site: www.myron.com (16)

Admiral Packaging Inc, Providence, RI. Tel: (401) 274-7000, (800) 262-0027, FAX: (401) 331-1910, Web Site: www.admiralpkg.com (26)

Admore Inc, Macomb, MI. Tel: (810) 949-8200, (800) 523-6673, FAX: (800) 215-2664, Web Site: www.admoreonline.com (10)

Adobe Systems Inc, San Jose, CA. Tel: (408) 536-6000, (800) 833-6687, FAX: (408) 537-6000, Web Site: www.adobe.com (22)

AdPlex, Houston, TX. Tel: (281) 821-5522, FAX: (281) 443-1040, Web Site: www.adplex.com (35)

Adpress Inc, New York, NY. Tel: (212) 679-1710, FAX: (212) 532-9508, E-Mail: adpressinc@aol.com, Web Site: www.adpressinc.com (23)

Adrea Rubin Marketing Inc, New York, NY. Tel: (212) 983-0020, FAX: (212) 983-1057, E-Mail: info@adrearubin.com, Web Site: www.adrearubin.com (21)

Adriana Associates Ltd, Greenwich, CT. Tel: (212) 719-5952, FAX: (212) 398-6414 (31)

AdSell Companies, Saint Louis, MO. Tel: (314) 773-0500, FAX: (314) 773-0555, E-Mail: marks@adsell.com, Web Site: www.adsell.com (21)

Adtron Inc, Bloomington, IL. Tel: (309) 662-1221, FAX: (309) 663-6691 (35)

Advance Mailing Services Inc, West Chicago, IL. Tel: (630) 293-0707, FAX: (630) 293-9268 (28)

Advanced Business Teleservices, Inc, Talent, OR. Tel: (541) 535-7878, (800) 866-9225, FAX: (541) 535-6942, Web Site: www.abtc.com (29)

Advanced Concepts Inc, Milwaukee, WI. Tel: (414) 362-9640, FAX: (414) 362-9646, E-Mail: info@advanced-concepts.com, Web Site: www.advanced-concepts.com (22)

Advanced Direct, Greensboro, NC. Tel: (336) 299-0800, (800) 786-2812, FAX: (336) 299-2619, E-Mail: info@advdirectinc.com, Web Site: www.advdirectinc.com (21)

Advanced Direct Marketing Inc, Loveland, CO. Tel: (970) 669-9800, FAX: (970) 669-1920, E-Mail: sales@admimail.com, Web Site: www.admimail.com (21)

Advanced Financial Services, Middletown, RI. Tel: (401) 849-0892, (800) 620-6292, FAX: (401) 851-5621, Web Site: www.embracehomeloans.com (14)

Advanced Image Direct, Fullerton, CA. Tel: (714) 502-3900, (800) 540-3848, FAX: (714) 502-3901, Web Site: www.advancedimagedirect.com (28)

Advanced Machinery, New Castle, DE. Tel: (302) 322-2226, (800) 727-6553, FAX: (866) 686-1615, E-Mail: jean@advmachinery.com, Web Site: www.advmachinery.com (9)

Advanced Mail Inc, Eau Claire, WI. Tel: (715) 839-8801, 888-624-5255, FAX: (715) 839-8906, Web Site: www.amailinc.com (28)

Advanced Marketing Direct, Buffalo, NY. Tel: (800) 696-7567, FAX: 716-821-5300, Web Site: www.amdirect.com (28)

Advanced Medical Nutrition Inc, Pittsburgh, PA. Tel: (412) 494-0100, (800) 437-8888, (800) 879-2664, FAX: (888) 245-4440, Web Site: www.douglaslabs.com (7)

Advanced Research Services, Malibu, CA. Tel: (310) 589-0223, Web Site: www.tvsurveys.com (30)

Advanced Software Applications Corp, Morgan, PA. Tel: (412) 220-9300, FAX: (412) 220-3878, E-Mail: asa@asacorp.com, Web Site: www.asacorp.com (22)

Advanced Telecom Services Inc, King of Prussia, PA. Tel: (610) 688-6000, (800) 247-1287, FAX: (610) 964-9117, E-Mail: sales@advancedtele.com, Web Site: www.advancedtele.com (29)

AdvanceMe Inc, Kennesaw, GA. Tel: (888) 700-8181, Web Site: www.advanceme.com (14)

Advanstar Communications Inc, North Olmstead, OH. Tel: (440) 243-8100, (800) 225-4569, FAX: (440) 891-2651, E-Mail: info@advanstar.com, Web Site: www.advanstarlists.com (17)

Advanta Corp, Conshohocken, PA. Tel: (215) 657-4000, (800) 255-0022, Web Site: www.advanta.com (14)

Advantage Fulfillment Services, Marietta, GA. Tel: (678) 921-2134, FAX: (770) 592-0204, Web Site: www.atlantamailervices.com (35)

Advantage List Marketing Inc, Holliston, MA. Tel: (508) 429-4400, FAX: (508) 429-7117, E-Mail: markm@advantagelist.com, Web Site: www.advantagelist.com (23)

Advantage Mailing Inc, Anaheim, CA. Tel: (714) 538-3881, (888) 909-6245, FAX: (714) 282-3903, Web Site: www.advantagemailinginc.com (28)

Advantage Marketing Group, Elk Grove Village, IL. Tel: (847) 952-2100, FAX: (847) 952-3348, Web Site: www.goamg.com (28)

Advantage Plus Marketing Group, Aliso Viejo, CA. Tel: (714) 573-7300, (800) 432-9466, FAX: (714) 573-7301, E-Mail: info@apmg.com, Web Site: www.apmg.com (30)

Advent Software Inc, San Francisco, CA. Tel: (415) 543-7696, FAX: (415) 543-5070, E-Mail: info@advent.com, Web Site: www.advent.com (34)

Adventure Creations Inc, Costa Mesa, CA. Tel: (949) 515-3600, FAX: (949) 515-3933, E-Mail: sales@adv-creations.com, Web Site: www.adv-creations.com (16)

Advertising Age, New York, NY. Tel: (212) 210-0100, FAX: (212) 210-0111, Web Site: www.crain.com (43)

The Advertising Council Inc, New York, NY. Tel: (212) 922-1500, FAX: (212) 922-1676, E-Mail: info@adcouncil.org, Web Site: www.adcouncil.org (1)

Advertising Distributors of America Inc, Ronkonkoma, NY. Tel: (631) 231-5700, FAX: (631) 434-1063 (21)

Advertising Gifts Inc, Port Washington, NY. Tel: (516) 767-3577, FAX: (516) 7673567, E-Mail: sales@adgiftsinc.com, Web Site: www.adgiftsinc.com (33)

Advertising Idea Stores, Ardmore, PA. Tel: (484) 416-0004, E-Mail: marc@uniongoods.com, Web Site: www.uniongoods.com (35)

Advertising Mailers Inc, Edison, NJ. Tel: (732) 225-3404, (800) 427-8513, FAX: (732) 225-7429, E-Mail: admailers@aol.com (28)

Advertising Network Solutions, Oxford, MI. Tel: (248) 475-7845, Web Site: www.adnetworksolutions.com (20)

Advertising Research Foundation, New York, NY. Tel: (212) 751-5656, FAX: (212) 319-5265, E-Mail: info@thearf.org, Web Site: www.thearf.org (40)

Advertising That Works, Bloomfield Hills, MI. Tel: (248) 757-2878, FAX: (248) 626-2264, Web Site: www.advthatworks.com (23)

Advisor Media Inc, San Diego, CA. Tel: (858) 278-5600, FAX: (858) 278-5600, Web Site: www.advisor.com (32)

Adwest Mailers Inc, Northridge, CA. Tel: (818) 982-3720, FAX: (818) 982-3786, E-Mail: sales@adwest.com, Web Site: www.adwest.com (28)

Aegis Communications, Irving, TX. Tel: (972) 830-1800, (800) 332-0266, FAX: (972) 830-1801, E-Mail: info@aegisglobal.com, Web Site: www.aegiscomgroup.com (29)

Aegon Direct Marketing Services Inc, Baltimore, MD. Tel: (410) 209-5617, FAX: (410) 209-5932, Web Site: www.aegondms.com (15)

Aegon USA Investment Management, Inc, Cedar Rapids, IA. Tel: (502) 560-2000, FAX: (502) 560-2030, Web Site: www.aegonins.com (14)

Aeling, Jim, CMI Direct, Pasadena, CA. Tel: (951) 300-1700, FAX: (866) 723-5433, Web Site: www.cmidirect.net (15)

Aeppli, Matt, Pernod Ricard USA, Purchase, NY. Tel: (914) 848-4800, Web Site: www.pernod-ricard-usa.com (16)

Aerosoles, Edison, NJ. Tel: 732-985-6900, (800)798-9478, FAX: (732) 985-3697, Web Site: www.aerosoles.com (2)

Aerovox Inc, New Bedford, MA. Tel: (508) 994-9661, (888) AEROVOX, FAX: (508) 995-3000, E-Mail: sales1@aerovox.com, Web Site: www.aerovox.com (16)

AETNA - Marketing Product & Communication, Hartford, CT. Tel: (860) 273-0123, (800) 872-3862, FAX: (860) 273-3971, Web Site: www.aetna.com (14)

Affina, Peoria, IL. Tel: (309) 685-5901, (877) 4 AFFINA, FAX: (309) 679-4199, Web Site: www.affina.com (30)

Affinion Group, Stamford, CT. Tel: (203) 956-1000, (800) 282-3315, Web Site: www.affinion.com (35)

Affinion Group, Stamford, CT. Tel: (203) 956-1000, (800) 251-2148, Web Site: www.affiniongroup.com (16)

Affinitas Corp, Boys Town, NE. Tel: (402) 397-7077, (800) 369-6495, FAX: (402) 397-7576, Web Site: www.affinitas.net (29)

Affinity Express, Elgin, IL. Tel: (847) 930-3200, FAX: (847) 930-3299, E-Mail: kellyg@affinityexpress.com, Web Site: www.affinityexpress.com (16)

Affinity Federal Credit Union, Basking Ridge, NJ. Tel: (908) 860-7300, FAX: (908) 860-3883, Web Site: www.affinityfcu.org (1)

Affinity4, Norfolk, VA. Tel: (757) 465-4602, Web Site: www.affinity4.com (16)

Affinity Marketing Services Corp, McLean, VA. Tel: (703) 917-9822, FAX: (703) 917-9804, E-Mail: serota@affinitymarketingservicescorp.com, Web Site: www.affinitymarketingservicescorp.com (35)

Affirm Agency, Pewaukee, WI. Tel: (262) 650-9900, E-Mail: info@affirmagency.com, Web Site: affirmagency.com (35)

Affrunti, Tamara L., The Allant Group, Naperville, IL. Tel: (800) 367-7311, FAX: (630) 355-3090, E-Mail: dirwin@allantgroup.com, Web Site: www.allantgroup.com (22)

Afni Inc, Bloomington, IL. Tel: (800) 767-2364, Web Site: www.afni.com (29)

African Wildlife Foundation, Washington, DC. Tel: (202) 939-3333, (888) 494-5354, FAX: (202) 939-3332, Web Site: www.awf.org (1)

Afzal, Zahid, Huntington Bancshares, Columbus, OH. Tel: (614) 480-5160, (800) 480-BANK, FAX: (614) 480-5284, Web Site: www.huntington.com (14)

Agacki, Dawn, Boelter + Lincoln Marketing Communications, Milwaukee, WI. Tel: (414) 271-0101, FAX: (414) 271-1436, E-Mail: jbrzeski@boelterlincoln.com, Web Site: boelterlincoln.com (35)

Agar, Gideon, Scan Optics Inc, Manchester, CT. Tel: (860) 645-7878, (800) 745-6001, FAX: (860) 645-7995, E-Mail: info@scanoptics.com, Web Site: www.scanoptics.com (16)

Agate Publishing, Evanston, IL. Tel: (847) 475-4457, (800) 326-4430, FAX: (312) 751-7334, Web Site: www.surreybooks.com (17)

Agco Spra-Coup, Duluth, GA. Tel: (320) 231-9400, FAX: (320) 231-9413, Web Site: www.agcocorp.com (16)

Agency.com, New York, NY. Tel: (212) 358-2600, FAX: (212) 358-2604, Web Site: www.agency.com (20)

Agency 360 LLC, Naperville, IL. Tel: (312) 316-7070, (312) 371-4104, E-Mail: mail@agencythreesixty.com, Web Site: agencythreesixty.com (35)

Aggarwal, Bharat, Pilani's Live in Style, Egg Harbor Township, NJ. Tel: (609) 927-4686, (800) 537-1832, FAX: (609) 927-5686, E-Mail: sihart@aol.com (2)

Aggarwal, Sanjay, Pilani's Live in Style, Egg Harbor Township, NJ. Tel: (609) 927-4686, (800) 537-1832, FAX: (609) 927-5686, E-Mail: sihart@aol.com (2)

Agile Education Marketing LLC, Denver, CO. Tel: (866) 783-0241, E-Mail: info@agile-ed.com, Web Site: www.agile-ed.com (24)

Agilis Co, Albert Lea, MN. Tel: (507) 377-5028 (14)

Agiropolous, Kathleen O., Airlines Reporting Corp, Arlington, VA. Tel: (703) 816-8135, FAX: (703) 816-8104, E-Mail: corpcom@arccorp.com, Web Site: www.arccorp.com (17)

Agnes, Bob, Tektronix Inc, Beaverton, OR. Tel: (503) 627-7111, (800) 833-9200, FAX: (503) 627-3247, Web Site: www.tektronix.com (16)

Agnihotri, Anu, Nuclear Plant Journal, Downers Grove, IL. Tel: (630) 858-6161, FAX: (630) 852-8787, Web Site: www.nuclearplantjournal.com (17)

Agnihotri, Newal, Nuclear Plant Journal, Downers Grove, IL. Tel: (630) 858-6161, FAX: (630) 852-8787, Web Site: www.nuclearplantjournal.com (17)

Agno, John, Signature Inc, Ann Arbor, MI. Tel: (734) 426-2000, FAX: (734) 426-2109, E-Mail: johnagno@signatureseries.com, Web Site: www.mentoringandcoaching.com (20)

Agona, Lisa, LexisNexis Matthew Bender, Albany, NY. Tel: (518) 487-3000, (800) 424-4200, E-Mail: lexisnexis@matthewbender, Web Site: www.bender.lexisnexis.com (17)

Agona, Lisa, Martindale-Hubbell, New Providence, NJ. Tel: (908) 771-7777, (800) 526-4902, FAX: (908) 771-8704, Web Site: www.martindale.com (17)

AGORA Inc, Baltimore, MD. Tel: (410) 783-8499, FAX: (410) 783-8414, E-Mail: csteam@agorapublishinggroup.com, Web Site: www.agora-inc.com (17)

Agri Drain Corp. Adair, IA. Tel: (641) 742-5211, (800) 232-4742, FAX: (800) 282-3353, (641) 742-5222, E-Mail: info@agridrain.com, Web Site: www.agridrain.com (9)

Aguillard, John A., Wisdom Marketing Group, San Antonio, TX. Tel: (210) 499-0777, (800) 952-1973, FAX: (210) 499-4217, E-Mail: sales@kruseasset.com, Web Site: www.kruseasset.com (35)

Agurcia, Alex, Omni Direct Inc, Miami, FL. Tel: (800) 459-4034, Web Site: www.omnidirect.tv (35)

Ahad, Edward, Promotional Product Professionals of Canada, Dorval, QC Canada. Tel: (514) 489-5359, FAX: (800) 489-8741, (514) 489-7760, E-Mail: gladys@pppc.ca, Web Site: www.pppc.ca (1)

AHC Media, Atlanta, GA. Tel: (404) 262-7436, FAX: (404) 262-7837 (17)

Ahern, Mitchel, OTOlabs LLC, Charlestown, MA. Tel: (617) 236-8400, Web Site: www.otolabs.com (30)

Ahmad, Mush, Involve Social, Fremont, CA. Tel: (510) 396-3941, Web Site: www.involvesocial.com (1)

Ahn, Henry, Scripps Networks Interactive Inc, Knoxville, TN. Tel: (865) 560-2700, Web Site: scrippsnetworksinteractive.com (17)

Ahrens, Greg, Skar Advertising, Omaha, NE. Tel: (402) 330-0110, (866) 330-0112, FAX: (402) 330-8791, E-Mail: skar@skar.com, Web Site: skar.com (35)

Ahrens, John E., Veratad Technologies LLC, Teaneck, NJ. Tel: (201) 510-6000, FAX: (201) 510-6036, Web Site: www.veratad.com (22)

Ahrensdorf & Associates, Saint Davids, PA. Tel: (610) 971-0500, FAX: (610) 971-9530, E-Mail: leeahrensdorf@att.net (16)

Ahrensdorf, Lee, Ahrensdorf & Associates, Saint Davids, PA. Tel: (610) 971-0500, FAX: (610) 971-9530, E-Mail: leeahrensdorf@att.net (16)

Aigen, Joyce, J&L Concepts Inc, Valdosta, GA. Tel: (229) 247-5731, E-Mail: promo@jlconcepts.com, Web Site: www.jlconcepts.com (33)

Aigner, Hans, DataLab USA, Germantown, MD. Tel: (301) 972-1430, (800) 972-1430, E-Mail: information@datalabusa.com, Web Site: datalabusa.com (21)

Aigner, Olga, DataLab USA, Germantown, MD. Tel: (301) 972-1430, (800) 972-1430, E-Mail: information@datalabusa.com, Web Site: datalabusa.com (21)

Aiken, Karen, The Animal Medical Center, New York, NY. Tel: (212) 838-8100, FAX: (212) 832-9630, Web Site: www.amcny.org (16)

Aimia Inc, Montreal, QC Canada. Web Site: www.aimia.com (35)

Ainsworth, Doug, Modern Mail, Bear, DE. Tel: (302) 391-1200, Web Site: www.triggermarketing.com (20)

Ainsworth, Earl, Farm Journal Inc, Philadelphia, PA. Tel: (215) 557-8937, FAX: (215) 568-4238 (17)

Air Ambulance Network Inc, Palm Harbor, FL. Tel: (727) 934-3999, (800) 327-1966, FAX: (727) 937-0276, Web Site: www.airambulancenetwork.com (16)

Air Chek Inc, Naples, NC. Tel: (828) 684-0893, (800) AIR-CHEK, FAX: (828) 684-8498, Web Site: www.radon.com (9)

Air Force Sergeants Association, Suitland, MD. Tel: (301) 899-3500, (800) 638-0594, FAX: (301) 899-8136, E-Mail: staff@hqafsa.org, Web Site: www.hqafsa.org (1)

Air France, New York, NY. Tel: (212) 830-4000, FAX: (212) 830-4244, Web Site: www.airfrance.us (16)

Air-Lec Industries Inc, Madison, WI. Tel: (608) 244-4754, FAX: (608) 246-7676, E-Mail: info@air-lec.com, Web Site: www.air-lec.com (16)

Air Power USA, Los Angeles, CA. Tel: (310) 641-0830, (888) 888-8231, FAX: (310) 641-8515, Web Site: www.airpowerusa.com (12)

Air-Scent International, Pittsburgh, PA. Tel: (800) 247-0770, FAX: (412) 252-2000, E-Mail: laura@aromaresource.com, Web Site: www.airscent.com (16)

Aircraft Owners & Pilots Association, Frederick, MD. Tel: (301) 695-2000, (800) 872-2672, FAX: (301) 695-2375, E-Mail: aopahq@aopa.org, Web Site: www.aopa.org (1)

Aircraft Spruce & Specialty Co, Corona, CA. Tel: (909) 372-9555, (877) 4-Spruce, FAX: (909) 372-0555, E-Mail: info@aircraft-spruce.com, Web Site: www.aircraft-spruce.com (12)

Airlines Reporting Corp, Arlington, VA. Tel: (703) 816-8135, FAX: (703) 816-8104, E-Mail: corpcom@arccorp.com, Web Site: www.arccorp.com (16)

Airomat Corp, Fort Wayne, IN. Tel: (260) 747-7408, (800) 348-4905, FAX: (260) 747-7409, E-Mail: airomat@airomat.com, Web Site: www.mymatting.com (16)

Airs Inc, Douglasville, GA. Tel: (770) 949-0133, FAX: (770) 949-2773, E-Mail: estacks@aol.com (22)

AirTran Airways, Atlanta, GA. Tel: (678) 254-7999, (800) 247-8726, Web Site: www.airtran.com (19)

Aitken, Stuart, Michael's, Irving, TX. Tel: (972) 409-1300, FAX: (972) 409-1551, Web Site: www.michaels.com (11)

Laurance Aiuppy, Livingston, MT. Tel: (406) 222-7308, FAX: (406) 222-7308, E-Mail: aiuppix@wispwest.net, Web Site: www.agpix.com/aiuppy (37)

Aiuppy, Janis M., Laurance Aiuppy, Livingston, MT. Tel: (406) 222-7308, FAX: (406) 222-7308, E-Mail: aiuppix@wispwest.net, Web Site: www.agpix.com/aiuppy (37)

Aiuppy, Laurance B., Laurance Aiuppy, Livingston, MT. Tel: (406) 222-7308, FAX: (406) 222-7308, E-Mail: aiuppix@wispwest.net, Web Site: www.agpix.com/aiuppy (37)

Aizikowitz, Dr Jacob, XMPIE Inc, New York, NY. Tel: (212) 479-5166, FAX: (212) 888-2061, Web Site: www.xmpie.com (22)

Ajeska, Craig, West Marine Inc, Watsonville, CA. Tel: (831) 728-2700, (800) 262-8464, (800) BOATING, FAX: (831) 768-5000, E-Mail: customercare@westmarine.com, Web Site: www.westmarine.com (11)

The Akadine Press Inc, White Plains, NY. Tel: (914) 747-0777, FAX: (914) 747-0778, Web Site: www.commonreader.com (16)

Akers Ski Inc, Andover, ME. Tel: (207) 392-4582, FAX: (207) 392-1225, E-Mail: sales@akers-ski.com, Web Site: www.akers-ski.com (11)

Akers, Jennifer, Sara Lee Direct Home Shopping, Winston-Salem, NC. Tel: (336) 519-4400, (800) 671-5056, E-Mail: ohp.manager@onehanesplace.com, Web Site: www.onehanesplace.com (2)

Akers, Leon, Akers Ski Inc, Andover, ME. Tel: (207) 392-4582, FAX: (207) 392-1225, E-Mail: sales@akers-ski.com, Web Site: www.akers-ski.com (11)

Akhavan, Dadi, Invenda Corp, Bethesda, MD. Tel: (240) 333-6111, E-Mail: sales@invenda.com, Web Site: www.invenda.com (32)

Akhouri, Amit, Ingenio LLC, San Francisco, CA. Tel: (877) 529-1193, Web Site: www.ingenio.com (32)

Akin, Bruce, Southern Progress Corp, Birmingham, AL. Tel: (205) 877-6000, FAX: (205) 877-6283, Web Site: www.southernprogress.com (17)

Al-Roumi, Rasha A., Kuwait Airways Corp, Fort Lee, NJ. Tel: (201) 582-9222, (800) 4-KUWAIT, FAX: (212) 947-8113, E-Mail: nyc@kuwait-airways.com, Web Site: www.kuwait-airways.com (19)

Alabama State University/College of Business Administration, Montgomery, AL. Tel: (334) 229-4124, FAX: (334) 229-4870, Web Site: coba.alasu.edu (41)

Alaimo, Ross, Paul Fredrick Menstyle, Fleetwood, PA. Tel: (610) 944-0909, (800) 247-1417, FAX: (610) 944-6452, E-Mail: custserv@menstyle.com, Web Site: www.paulfredricks.com (2)

Alairis Interactive, Medina, OH. Tel: (877) 770-0350, E-Mail: info@alairis.com, Web Site: www.alairis.com (35)

Alameida, Jose, Baxter Healthcare, Renal Division, Deerfield, IL. Tel: (800) 284-4060, Web Site: www.baxter.com (7)

Alamo Mailing, San Antonio, TX. Tel: (210) 637-0404, FAX: (210) 637-0081 (28)

Alamo Rent A Car, Saint Louis, MO. Tel: (314) 512-2880, Web Site: www.alamo.com (16)

Alan Gordon Enterprises Inc, Hollywood, CA. Tel: (323) 466-3561, FAX: (323) 871-2193, E-Mail: contactus@alangordon.com, Web Site: www.alangordon.com (32)

AlanizMetroGroup, Mount Pleasant, IA. Tel: (319) 385-7259, FAX: (319) 385-2825, E-Mail: info@alanizdirect.com, Web Site: www.alanizdirect.com (28)

Alar, MIC Father Chris, Marian Helpers Center, Stockbridge, MA. Tel: (413) 298-3691, (800) 462-7426, FAX: (413) 298-3583, Web Site: www.marian.org (1)

Alarie, Dave, Plas-Tanks Industries Inc, Hamilton, OH. Tel: (513) 942-3800, FAX: (513) 942-3993, E-Mail: info@plastanks.com, Web Site: www.plastanks.com (9)

Alario, Steve, Person to Person Marketing LLC, Riverdale, NJ. Tel: (973) 835-8112, FAX: (973) 835-8525, E-Mail: sales@persontopersondirect.com, Web Site: www.persontopersondirect.com (29)

AlarmingYou.com, Boca Raton, FL. Tel: (714) 981-2900, Web Site: www.alarmingyou.com (16)

Alber, Laura J, Williams-Sonoma Inc, San Francisco, CA. Tel: (415) 421-7900, (800) 840-2591, Web Site: www.williams-sonomainc.com (8)

Albergetis, Charlotte, KPBS FM/TV, San Diego, CA. Tel: (619) 594-1515, Web Site: www.kpbs.org (1)

Albert, Andrew B., Svoboda Collins LLC, Chicago, IL. Tel: (312) 267-8750, FAX: (312) 267-6025, E-Mail: info@svoco.com, Web Site: www.svoco.com (5)

Albert, Diane, TVC Enterprises and the TV Collector Magazine, Las Vegas, NV. Tel: (760) 495-7956, E-Mail: tvcinquiries@happyretrogirl.com, Web Site: www.angelfire.com/ma/tvcollector/home.html (6)

Albert, Jill, Media Consultants Inc, Bayside, NY. Tel: (718) 423-6300, FAX: (718) 428-7482, E-Mail: mediaconsults@aol.com (32)

Alberts, Greg, A Plus Marketing Ltd, Buffalo Grove, IL. Tel: (847) 537-1166, FAX: (847) 537-5611, Web Site: www.aplusmarketing.com (20)

Alberts, JoAnn, Crosslists Cross & Co, Lone Jack, MO. Tel: (816) 697-3306, FAX: (816) 697-3317, E-Mail: info@crosscompany.com, Web Site: www.crosscompany.com (23)

Alboushi, Nicole, Imperial Supplies, Green Bay, WI. Tel: (920) 494-5403, (800) 558-2808, FAX: (800) 553-8769, Web Site: www.imperialsupplies.com (16)

Albrecht, Chris, Starz Entertainment LLC, Englewood, CO. Tel: (855) 807-2929, Web Site: www.starz.com (16)

Albrecht, Chuck, Northern Tool & Equipment Inc, Burnsville, MN. Tel: (952) 894-9510, (800) 221-0516, FAX: (952) 894-1020, Web Site: www.northerntool.com (16)

Albrecht, Rodelinde, Rodelinde Graphic Design, Lenox Dale, MA. Tel: (413) 243-4350, FAX: (413) 243-3066, E-Mail: rodelinde@earthlink.net (36)

Alcom, Harleysville, PA. Tel: (215) 513-1600, E-Mail: stucker@alcomprinting.com, Web Site: www.alcomprinting.com (21)

John Alden Life Insurance Co/North Star Marketing, Duluth, GA. Tel: (678) 473-1211, (800) 768-6288, FAX: (678) 473-9573, Web Site: www.nstarmarketing.com (15)

Alden, Robert, RayPress Corp, Birmingham, AL. Tel: (205) 989-3731, FAX: (205) 989-7203, Web Site: www.raypress.com (27)

Alder, Rob, Prestone Printing Co Inc, Long Island City, NY. Tel: (347) 468-7900, FAX: (347) 468-7885, E-Mail: info@prestoneprint.com, Web Site: www.prestoneprinting.com (25)

Alderman Co, High Point, NC. Tel: (336) 889-6121, FAX: (336) 889-7717, E-Mail: sales@aldermancompany.com, Web Site: www.aldermancompany.com (37)

Aldred, Duncan, Buick, Detroit, MI. Tel: (313) 556-5000, (800) 521-7300, FAX: (313) 556-5108, Web Site: www.buick.com (16)

The Aldrich Group, Woodbury, CT. Tel: (860) 274-7693, (203) 263-5505, FAX: (203) 263-5572, E-Mail: jeff.aldrich@aldrichsearch.com, Web Site: www.aldrichsearch.com (20)

Aldrich, Anne, Across The Board Marketing Inc, Chicago, IL. Tel: (312) 787-1642, FAX: (312) 787-1645, E-Mail: info@acrosstheboardmarketing.com, Web Site: www.acrosstheboardmarketing.com (39)

Aldrich, Brenda, Harman's Cheese & Country Store Inc, Sugar Hill, NH. Tel: (603) 823-8000, E-Mail: cheese@harmanscheese.com, Web Site: www.HarmansCheese.com (4)

Aldrich, Jeff, The Aldrich Group, Woodbury, CT. Tel: (860) 274-7693, (203) 263-5505, FAX: (203) 263-5572, E-Mail: jeff.aldrich@aldrichsearch.com, Web Site: www.aldrichsearch.com (20)

Aldrich, Mary, Warrantech Direct Inc, Bedford, TX. Tel: (817) 786-1000, (800) 833-8801, FAX: (817) 786-1020, Web Site: www.warrantech.com (29)

Aldrich, Maxine, Harman's Cheese & Country Store Inc, Sugar Hill, NH. Tel: (603) 823-8000, E-Mail: cheese@harmanscheese.com, Web Site: www.HarmansCheese.com (4)

Aldridge, Pauline, LISTS Inc, Jacksonville, FL. Tel: (904) 733-6106, (800) 805-5478, FAX: (904) 730-7540, E-Mail: info@lists-inc.com, Web Site: www.lists-inc.com (23)

Aleksov, Marin, Rosland Capital LLC, Santa Monica, CA. Tel: (800) 891-2341, Web Site: www.roslandcapital.com (14)

Alert Marketing, Lyndhurst, NJ. Web Site: www.alertmarketing.com (28)

Alerus Financial National Assoc, Grand Forks, ND. Tel: (701) 795-3200, (800) 279-3200, Web Site: www2.alerusfinancial.com (14)

Alesco Data Group LLC, Fort Myers, FL. Tel: (239) 275-5006, (800) 701-6531, FAX: (239) 275-7737, E-Mail: lists@alescodata.com, Web Site: www.alescodata.com (23)

Alesio, Steven W., D&B Sales and Marketing Solutions, Waltham, MA. Tel: (781) 672-9200, (800) 590-0065, FAX: (781) 672-9290, Web Site: www.b2bsalesandmarketing.com (22)

Alexander & Co LLC, Stonington, CT. Tel: (860) 535-9160, FAX: (860) 535-9161, E-Mail: jraandco@aol.com (20)

Alexander + Roberts, Keene, NH. Tel: (603) 357-5033, (800) 221-2216, FAX: (603) 357-4548, E-Mail: info@generaltours.com, Web Site: www.generaltours.com (19)

Alexander, Dr. Livingston, University of Pittsburgh at Bradford, Bradford, PA. Tel: (814) 362-7500, FAX: (814) 362-5150, E-Mail: admissions@www.upb.pitt.edu, Web Site: www.upd.pitt.edu (41)

Alexander, Geoff, iContact LLC, Morrisville, NC. Tel: (919) 820-7837, (877) 820-7837, E-Mail: sales@icontact.com, Web Site: www.icontact.com (32)

Alexander, James R., Alexander & Co LLC, Stonington, CT. Tel: (860) 535-9160, FAX: (860) 535-9161, E-Mail: jraandco@aol.com (20)

Alexander, Jennifer, Manchester Farms Inc, Columbia, SC. Tel: (803) 845-0421, FAX: (803) 227-3103, E-Mail: customerservice@manchesterfarms.com, Web Site: www.manchesterfarms.com (4)

Alexander, Joe, The Martin Agency, Richmond, VA. Tel: (804) 698-8000, FAX: (804) 698-8001, Web Site: www.martinagency.com (35)

Alexander, John, Sturbridge Yankee Workshop Inc, Portland, ME. Tel: (207) 774-9045, (800) 343-1144, FAX: (207) 774-2561, Web Site: www.sturbridgeyankee.com (16)

Alexander, Neil, The United Methodist Publishing House, Nashville, TN. Tel: (615) 749-6000, (800) 672-1789, FAX: (615) 749-6417, E-Mail: productsandservices@umpublishing.com, Web Site: www.umpublishing.com (17)

Alexander, Patrick H., Pennsylvania State University Press, University Park, PA. Tel: (814) 865-1327, (800) 326-9180, FAX: (814) 863-1408, Web Site: www.psupress.org (17)

Alexander, Perry, Hennerberg Group Inc, Colleyville, TX. Tel: (817) 318-8100, E-Mail: gary@hennerberg.com, Web Site: hennerberg.com (35)

Alexander, S. Tyrone, Highmark Blue Cross Blue Shield, Pittsburgh, PA. Tel: (412) 544-7000, FAX: (412) 544-5350, Web Site: www.highmark.com (15)

Alexander, Steven H., Star Tribune Media Co, Minneapolis, MN. Tel: (612) 673-4000, FAX: (612) 673-4359, Web Site: www.startribunecompany.com (17)

Alexian Brothers Bonaventure House, Chicago, IL. Tel: (773) 327-9921, FAX: (773) 327-9113, E-Mail: info@abam.org, Web Site: www.bonaventurehouse.org (1)

Alfa Aesar-A Johnson Matthey Co, Ward Hill, MA. Tel: (800) 343-0660, FAX: (800) 322-4757, E-Mail: info@alfa.com, Web Site: www.alfa.com (9)

Alfa CTP Systems, Tewksbury, MA. Tel: (603) 689-1101, FAX: (603) 689-1197, Web Site: www.alfactp.com (10)

Alfa Insurance, Montgomery, AL. Tel: (334) 288-3900, Web Site: www.alfains.com (15)

Alfano, Diane, Institutional Investor Inc, New York, NY. Tel: (212) 224-3300, FAX: (212) 224-3592, Web Site: www.institutionalinvestor.com (17)

Alford, Derald M., CSM Inc, Tucker, GA. Tel: (404) 892-2626, (800) 849-6788, FAX: (404) 589-9779, E-Mail: info@csmresearch.com, Web Site: www.csmresearch.com (30)

Alford, Karron, Baton Rouge Conventions & Visitors Bureau, Baton Rouge, LA. Tel: (225) 383-1825, (800) LA-ROUGE, FAX: (225) 346-1253, E-Mail: karron@visitbatonrouge.com, Web Site: www.bracvb.com (1)

Alfred Publishing Co Inc, Van Nuys, CA. Tel: (818) 891-5999, (800) 292-6122, FAX: (818) 893-5560, E-Mail: sales@alfred.com, Web Site: www.alfred.com (17)

Alguire, MD Patrick, American College of Physicians, Philadelphia, PA. Tel: (215) 351-2600, (800) 523-1546, FAX: (215) 351-2686, Web Site: www.acponline.org (17)

Ali, Mohamad, Hewlett-Packard Co, Palo Alto, CA. Tel: (650) 857-1501, (800) 752-0900, FAX: (650) 857-5518, Web Site: www.hp.com (16)

AliMed Inc, Dedham, MA. Tel: (781) 329-2900, (800) 225-2610, FAX: (800) 437-2966, (781) 329-8392, E-Mail: info@alimed.com, Web Site: www.alimed.com (7)

Alkinburgh, Scott, Pete Rickard Inc, Cobleskill, NY. Tel: (518) 234-2731, (800) 282-5663, FAX: (518) 234-2454, E-Mail: info@peterickard.com, Web Site: www.peterickard.com (11)

Alkon, Jim, CRN International Inc, Hamden, CT. Tel: (203) 288-2002, FAX: (203) 281-3291, E-Mail: info@crnradio.com, Web Site: www.crnradio.com (32)

All American List Corp, Upper Marlboro, MD. Tel: (301) 420-5760, (888) 690-2252, FAX: (301) 420-5765, E-Mail: info@allamericanlist.com, Web Site: www.allamericanlist.com (23)

All-In-One Directory, New Paltz, NY. Tel: (845) 255-7560, FAX: (888) 345-2790, E-Mail: gebbiepress@pipeline.com, Web Site: www.gebbieinc.com (43)

All-n-One List Marketing Inc, Fishersville, VA. Tel: (703) 717-5621, FAX: (703) 286-5418, E-Mail: info@allinonelistmarketing.com, Web Site: www.allinonelistmarketing.com (23)

All Star Carts & Vehicles, Bay Shore, NY. Tel: (631) 666-5252, (800) 831-3166, FAX: (631) 666-1319, Web Site: www.allstarcarts.com (16)

All Star Directories, Seattle, WA. Tel: (888) 404-8043, FAX: (707) 667-1524, Web Site: www.allstardirectories.com (17)

All Star Premium Products Inc, Fiskdale, MA. Tel: (800) 526-8629, E-Mail: info@incentiveusa.com, Web Site: www.incentiveusa.com (33)

All-State Legal, Cranford, NJ. Tel: (908) 272-0800, (800) 222-0510, FAX: (800) 634-5184, E-Mail: sjacobs@aslegal.com, Web Site: www.aslegal.com (16)

All USA Partners LLC, Broadview, IL. Tel: (800) 861-4116, Web Site: allusa.net (35)

All-Ways Advertising Co, Bloomfield, NJ. Tel: (973) 338-0700, (800) 255-9291, FAX: (973) 338-1410, Web Site: www.awadv.com (33)

Allaman, Marlana, Emfluence, Kansas City, MO. Tel: (816) 472-4455, (877) 81-EMAIL, FAX: (816) 472-8855, E-Mail: expert@emfluence.com, Web Site: www.emfluence.com (21)

Allan, Elyse, GE Canada, Mississauga, ON Canada. Tel: (905) 858-5100, Web Site: www.ge.com/canada (9)

The Allant Group, Naperville, IL. Tel: (800) 367-7311, FAX: (630) 355-3090, E-Mail: dirwin@allantgroup.com, Web Site: www.allantgroup.com (22)

AllBrands.com Sewing Machine Superstore, Baton Rouge, LA. Tel: (225) 923-1285, (866) 255-2726, FAX: (225) 923-1261, E-Mail: info@allbrands.com, Web Site: www.allbrands.com (11)

Allconnect Inc, Atlanta, GA. Tel: (404) 260-2200, Web Site: www.allconnect.com (32)

Allegiant Direct Inc, Brentwood, TN. Tel: (615) 373-2042, FAX: (615) 373-2099, E-Mail: welcome@allegiantdirect.com, Web Site: www.allegiantdirect.com (35)

Allegra Marketing Services, Louisville, KY. Tel: (502) 895-1530, FAX: (502) 895-1624, Web Site: www.allegra-east.com (27)

Allegra Network, LLC, Plymouth, MI. Tel: (248) 596-8600, FAX: (248) 596-8601, Web Site: www2.allegranetwork.com (27)

Allen Consulting, Holmdel, NJ. Tel: (732) 946-2711, FAX: (732) 946-8032, E-Mail: sylvia@allenconsulting.com, Web Site: www.allenconsulting.com (20)

Fred E Allen Inc, Mount Pleasant, TX. Tel: (903) 572-1701, FAX: (903) 572-1703 (23)

Allen, Matkins, Leck, Gamble & Mallory, Los Angeles, CA. Tel: (213) 622-5555, FAX: (213) 620-8816, E-Mail: communications@allenmatkins.com, Web Site: www.allenmatkins.com (20)

Allen Wood, Danita, Missouri Life Inc, Boonville, MO. Tel: (660) 882-9898, (800) 492-2593, FAX: (660) 882-9899, E-Mail: info@missourilife.com, Web Site: www.missourilife.com (17)

Allen, Ben, Direct Connect Group, Cleveland, OH. Tel: (216) 651-9500, Web Site: www.directconnectgroup.com (35)

Allen, Carole Ward, San Francisco Bay Area Rapid Transit District (BART), Oakland, CA. Tel: (510) 464-6000, FAX: (510) 464-7103, Web Site: www.bart.gov (16)

Allen, Chy, American Meadows Inc & Vermont Wild Flowers Farm, Shelburne, VT. Tel: (877) 309-7333, FAX: (802) 951-9089, E-Mail: customerservice@americanmeadows.com, Web Site: www.americanmeadows.com (8)

Allen, David E., AMD Industries Inc, Cicero, IL. Tel: (708) 863-8900, (800) 367-9999, FAX: (708) 863-2065, Web Site: www.amdpop.com (36)

Allen, David, Gems Sensors & Controls, Plainville, CT. Tel: (860) 747-3000, (800) 378-1600, FAX: (860) 747-4244, E-Mail: info@gemssensors.com, Web Site: www.gemssensors.com (9)

Allen, David, Tetley USA Inc, Montvale, NJ. Tel: (201) 571-0300, Web Site: www.tetleyusa.com (16)

Allen, Don, Center for Science in the Public Interest, Washington, DC. Tel: (202) 332-9110, FAX: (202) 265-4954, E-Mail: circ@cspinet.org, Web Site: www.cspinet.org (1)

Allen, Fred, Fred E Allen Inc, Mount Pleasant, TX. Tel: (903) 572-1701, FAX: (903) 572-1703 (23)

Allen, Gary K., University of Missouri, Columbia, MO. Tel: (573) 882-6333, (800) 856-2181, FAX: (573) 882-2721, E-Mail: visitus@missouri.edu, Web Site: www.missouri.edu (41)

Allen, Gordie, Leads-Plus Inc, Killarney, FL. Tel: (800) 548-4571, E-Mail: eurekaman43@hotmail.com, Web Site: www.salesprospectingexpert.com (20)

Allen, Jack, Navistar, Lisle, IL. Tel: (331) 332-5000, Web Site: www.navistar.com (16)

Allen, Jenny, Chapman Cubine Adams & Hussey, Arlington, VA. Tel: (703) 248-0025, Web Site: www.ahadirect.com (20)

Allen, Kathleen, Millipore Corp, Bedford, MA. Tel: (781) 869-5141, FAX: (781) 533-3110, Web Site: www.millipore.com (9)

Allen, Kim, Butler Schein Animal Health, Dublin, OH. Tel: (614) 761-9095, (888) 691-2724, FAX: (888) 329-3861, Web Site: www.butlerschein.com (16)

Allen, Kim, Eggs by Byrd, Wappapello, MO. Tel: (573) 222-7999, (800) 235-EGGS, FAX: (573) 222-8009, E-Mail: eggsbybyrd@dishmail.net (10)

Allen, Layman G., Accelerated Learning Foundation, Fairfield, IA. Tel: (641) 954-5443, (800) 289-2377, FAX: (641) 954-5851, E-Mail: info@ gamesforthinkers.org, Web Site: www. gamesforthinkers.org (17)

Allen, Matt, Markwins International Corp, City of Industry, CA. Tel: (909) 595-8898, FAX: (909) 595-8820, Web Site: www.markwins.com (16)

Allen, Nicole, Direct Marketers On Call Inc (DMOC), New York, NY. Tel: (212) 691-1942, FAX: (212) 924-1331, E-Mail: info@dmoc-inc.com, Web Site: www.dmoc-inc.com (20)

Allen, Paul, Lieberman Productions, San Francisco, CA. Tel: (415) 955-0855, FAX: (415) 955-0822, E-Mail: lpinfo@lieberman.com, Web Site: www.lieberman. com (32)

Allen, Quincy, Unisys, Blue Bell, PA. Tel: (215) 986-4011, (800) 874-8647, FAX: (215) 986-2312, Web Site: www.unisys.com (16)

Allen, Ray, American Meadows Inc & Vermont Wild Flowers Farm, Shelburne, VT. Tel: (877) 309-7333, FAX: (802) 951-9089, E-Mail: customerservice@ americanmeadows.com, Web Site: www. americanmeadows.com (8)

Allen, Samuel R., Deere & Co, Moline, IL. Tel: (309) 765-8000, FAX: (309) 748-0114, Web Site: www. deere.com (16)

Allen, Scott, Ames Specialty Packaging & Digital Print, Somerville, MA. Tel: (617) 684-1000, (800) 521-2637, FAX: (617) 684-1264, E-Mail: info@ amespage.com, Web Site: www.amespage.com (26)

Allen, Sylvia, Allen Consulting, Holmdel, NJ. Tel: (732) 946-2711, FAX: (732) 946-8032, E-Mail: sylvia@allenconsulting.com, Web Site: www. allenconsulting.com (20)

Allen, Terry, Orbit Manufacturing Co, Perkasie, PA. Tel: (215) 257-0727, (888) 895-0958, FAX: (215) 257-7399, Web Site: www.orbitmfg.com (9)

Allen, Tom, Association of American Publishers, Washington, DC. Tel: (202) 347-3375, FAX: (202) 347-3690, E-Mail: info@publishers.org, Web Site: www. publishers.org (1)

Allergan Inc, Irvine, CA. Tel: (714) 246-4500, (800) 347-4500, FAX: (714) 246-6987, Web Site: www. allergan.com (16)

Alliance Bernstein, New York, NY. Tel: (212) 969-1000, (800) 962-2134, FAX: (212) 969-2293, Web Site: www.alliancebernstein.com (14)

Alliance Data, Plano, TX. Tel: (972) 348-5100, E-Mail: info@thealliedgrp.com, Web Site: www. alliancedata.com (22)

Alliance Defense Fund, Scottsdale, AZ. Tel: (480) 444-0020, Web Site: www.telladf.org (1)

Alliance Direct Marketing Solutions LLC, Jersey City, NJ. Tel: (201) 863-1360, (888) 455-2367, FAX: (201) 863-3910, E-Mail: vteran@alliancedirectleads. com, Web Site: www.alliancedirectleads.com (20)

Alliance of Area Business Publications, Redondo Beach, CA. Tel: (310) 379-8261, FAX: (310) 379-8283, E-Mail: info@bizpubs.org, Web Site: www. bizpubs.org (1)

Alliance of Nonprofit Mailers, Washington, DC. Tel: (202) 462-5132, FAX: (202) 462-0423, E-Mail: alliance@nonprofitmailers.org, Web Site: www. nonprofitmailers.org (40)

Alliance Strategies Group Inc, Boca Raton, FL. Tel: (561) 499-3201, E-Mail: info@asgroupinc.com, Web Site: www.asgroupinc.com (23)

Alliant, Brewster, NY. Tel: (845) 276-2600, FAX: (845) 276-2605, Web Site: www.alliantdata.com (22)

Allianz Life Insurance Co of North America, Minneapolis, MN. Tel: (763) 765-6500, (800) 950-5872, Web Site: www.allianzlife.com (15)

The Allied Group, Cranston, RI. Tel: (401) 946-6100, Web Site: www.thealliedgrp.com (28)

Allied Integrated Marketing, Boston, MA. Tel: (617) 859-4800, E-Mail: alliedimsocial@alliedim.com, Web Site: alliedim.com (35)

Allied Printing Services Inc, Manchester, CT. Tel: (860) 643-1101, (800) 225-8777, (800) 224-8894, FAX: (860) 646-7954, E-Mail: allied@alliedprinting.com, Web Site: www.alliedprinting.com (27)

Allison, A. Reid, Remington College, Heathrow, FL. Tel: (407) 562-5691, (800) 560-6192, Web Site: www.remingtoncollege.edu (13)

Allison, Joel T., Baylor Health Care System, Dallas, TX. Tel: (214) 820-4901, (800) 4Baylor, FAX: (214) 820-7499, Web Site: www.baylorhealth.com (16)

Allison, Scott, Driasi, Chanhassen, MN. Tel: (952) 556-5600, (800) 688-0760, FAX: (952) 556-8200, E-Mail: tpa@driasi.com, Web Site: www.driasi.com (21)

Allison, Steve, Lion Apparel, Dayton, OH. Tel: (937) 898-1949, (800) 548-6614, FAX: (937) 913-5667, Web Site: www.lionprotects.com (2)

Allman, George P, NEBS, Groton, MA. Tel: (978) 448-6111, (800) 225-6380, (888) 823-6327, FAX: (978) 448-3653, (800) 234-4324. E-Mail: customerservice@nebs.com, Web Site: www.nebs. com (10)

Allmark, David, Fisher-Price, East Aurora, NY. Tel: (716) 687-3000, FAX: (716) 687-3636, Web Site: www.fisherprice.com (16)

AllMedia Inc, Plano, TX. Tel: (469) 467-9100, FAX: (214) 291-5431, E-Mail: brokerage@allmediainc. com, Web Site: www.allmediainc.com (23)

Alloyd Brands, Dekalb, IL. Tel: (815) 756-8451, (800) 756-7639, FAX: (815) 756-5187/9192, Web Site: www.alloyd.com (16)

Allpro Direct Marketing, Odessa, FL. Tel: (888) 679-0255, (727) 375-1502, (866) 472-3982, FAX: (727) 499-7999, Web Site: www.allprodirectmarketing. com (20)

Allred, Betty, National Wholesale Co Inc, Lexington, NC. Tel: (336) 248-5904, (800) 480-4673, FAX: (336) 248-2880, E-Mail: customerservice@ shopnational.com, Web Site: www.shopnational. com (2)

Allsop, Joseph W., Progress Software Corp, Bedford, MA. Tel: (781) 280-4000, (800) 477-6473, FAX: (781) 280-4095, Web Site: www.progress.com (16)

Allstate Motor Club Inc, Arlington Heights, IL. Tel: (847) 551-2300, (800) 998-8697 (13)

Alltel Publishing Corp, Hudson, OH. Tel: (330) 650-7100, FAX: (330) 650-7883, Web Site: www.alltel. com (22)

Allyn & Bacon, Upper Saddle River, NJ. Tel: (617) 848-7216, FAX: (781) 455-1220 (17)

Allyn, David, Welch Allyn, Inc, Skaneateles Falls, NY. Tel: (315) 685-4100, Web Site: www.welchallyn. com (19)

Almeida, Gil, Advanced Financial Services, Middletown, RI. Tel: (401) 849-0892, (800) 620-6292, FAX: (401) 851-5621, Web Site: www. embracehomeloans.com (14)

Almeida, Maryann, MacIntosh Survey Center, East Providence, RI. Tel: (401) 438-8330, FAX: (401) 434-9219, E-Mail: macsurvey@aol.com (30)

Almon, Robert C., Pace University, New York, NY. Tel: (212) 346-1781, (866) 722-3338, FAX: (212) 346-1821, Web Site: www.pace.edu (16)

Almore International Inc, Beaverton, OR. Tel: (503) 643-6633, (800) 547-1511, FAX: (503) 643-9748, E-Mail: info@almore.com, Web Site: www.almore. com (7)

Almost Heaven Group, Renick, WV. Tel: (304) 645-2310, FAX: (304) 497-2698, E-Mail: art@ almostheaven.net, Web Site: www.almostheaven.net (16)

CM Almy & Son Inc, Armonk, NY. Tel: (800) 225-2569, FAX: (800) 426-2569, E-Mail: almyaccess@ almy.com, Web Site: www.almy.com (5)

Almy, David, Marketing Research Association, Washington, DC. Tel: (860) 682-1000, (202) 800-2545, FAX: (860) 682-1010, (888) 512-1050. E-Mail: membership@marketingresearch.org, Web Site: www.mra-net.org (40)

Aloft Group, Newburyport, MA. Tel: (978) 462-0002, E-Mail: hello@aloftgroup.com, Web Site: www. aloftgroup.com (33)

Aloisio, Bob, TTC Marketing Solutions, Chicago, IL. Tel: (773) 545-0407, (800) 777-6348, FAX: (773) 545-4034, E-Mail: sales@ttcmarketingsolutions. com, Web Site: www.ttcmarketingsolutions.com (29)

Alorica Inc, Irvine, CA. Tel: (909) 606-3600, (866) 256-7422, FAX: (909) 606-7708, E-Mail: info@alorica. com, Web Site: www.alorica.com (29)

Alperson, Joel, Omaha Fixture International, Omaha, NE. Tel: (402) 592-3720, (800) 637-2257, FAX: (402) 593-5716, (800) 531-6627, E-Mail: sales@ omahafixture.com, Web Site: www.omahafixture. com (8)

Alpert, Joel, MarketPower Direct Marketing, Atlanta, GA. Tel: (435) 565-1889, E-Mail: joelalpert123@ gmail.com, Web Site: www.marketpoweronline.com (35)

Alpert-Romm, Adria, Discovery Communications Inc, Silver Spring, MD. Tel: (240) 662-2000, FAX: (240) 662-1868, Web Site: corporate.discovery.com (16)

Alpha Dog Marketing Inc, Lincoln, NE. Tel: (402) 486-0668, Web Site: www.alphadogmktg.com (1)

Alpha List Marketing Inc, Marietta, GA. Tel: (404) 995-7049, FAX: (404) 601-0826 (23)

Alpha Supply Inc, Bremerton, WA. Tel: (360) 373-3302, (800) 257-4211, FAX: (360) 379-9235 (16)

AlphaGraphics World Headquarters, Salt Lake City, UT. Tel: (801) 595-7270, (800) 955-6246, FAX: (801) 595-7271, E-Mail: contactus@alphagraphics. com, Web Site: www.alphagraphics.com (27)

Alshuler, Gina, Rauxa, Costa Mesa, CA. Tel: (714) 427-1271, E-Mail: newbiz@rauxa.com, Web Site: www. rauxa.com (35)

ALSTOM Signaling Inc, West Henrietta, NY. Tel: (585) 279-2228, Web Site: www. alstomsignalingsolutions.com (16)

Alta Resources (West Coast Office), Neenah, WI. Tel: (920) 751-5800, (877) 934-6377, Web Site: www. altaresources.com (29)

Altair Customer Intelligence, Franklin, TN. Tel: (615) 468-6800, (800) 241-6631, FAX: (615) 468-6878, E-Mail: asales@altairci.com, Web Site: www. altairci.com (23)

Altberg, Marla, Ventura Associates International LLC, New York, NY. Tel: (212) 302-8277, FAX: (212) 302-2587, E-Mail: info@sweepspros.com, Web Site: www.sweepspros.com (35)

Altebrando, Jim, Printing Spectrum, East Setauket, NY. Tel: (631) 689-1010, Web Site: www. printingspectrum.com (27)

Altenpohl, Kathy, Laser Label Technologies Inc, Stow, OH. Tel: (800) 882-4050, FAX: (800) 395-4721, E-Mail: sales@lltproducts.com, Web Site: www.lltproducts.com (10)

Alter, Dennis, Advanta Corp, Conshohocken, PA. Tel: (215) 657-4000, (800) 255-0022, Web Site: www.advanta.com (14)

Alter, Sy, Spectrum eCommerce, Mission Viejo, CA. Tel: (949) 600-7900, Web Site: elifemarketers.com (15)

Alterian, Chicago, IL. Tel: (312) 704-1700, FAX: (312) 704-1701, Web Site: www.alterian.com (22)

Alterman, Kent, Comedy Central, New York, NY. Tel: (212) 767-8600, Web Site: www.cc.com (32)

Alternate Marketing Networks Inc, Hudsonville, MI. Tel: (616) 662-6420, FAX: (616) 662-6422, Web Site: www.altmarknet.com (28)

Alternative Concepts Inc, Knoxville, TN. Tel: (865) 690-1990, FAX: (865) 692-0072, E-Mail: support@acmarketing.biz, Web Site: www.acmarketing.biz (31)

Alternative Media Group, Naples, FL. Tel: (732) 741-0585, FAX: (732) 741-0489, Web Site: www.amg-global.com (31)

Alteslane, Al, Global Turnkey Systems Inc, Parsippany, NJ. Tel: (973) 331-1010, FAX: (973) 331-0042, E-Mail: sales@gtsystems.com, Web Site: www.gtsystems.com (22)

Althen, Marc, Penske Logistics, Reading, PA. Tel: (800) 529-6531, FAX: (610) 775-2449, E-Mail: info.penskelogistics@penske.com, Web Site: www.penskelogistics.com (16)

Altiris, Lindon, UT. Tel: (801) 226-8500, (888) 252-5551, FAX: (801) 226-8506, Web Site: www.symantec.com (16)

Altman Dedicated Direct, Rural Hall, NC. Tel: (336) 969-9538, FAX: (336) 969-0187, E-Mail: saltman@AltmanDedicatedDirect.com, Web Site: www.altmandedicateddirect.com (20)

Altman, Allan, Video Artists International, Pleasantville, NY. Tel: (914) 769-3691, (800) 477-7146, FAX: (914) 769-5407, E-Mail: orders@vaimusic.com, Web Site: www.vaimusic.com (3)

Altman, Dan, World Publications Inc, Winter Park, FL. Tel: (407) 628-4802, FAX: (407) 628-7061, Web Site: www.worldpub.net (17)

Altman, Dara, SiriusXM Radio Inc, New York, NY. Tel: (212) 584-5100, Web Site: www.siriusxm.com (16)

Altman, David G., Center for Creative Leadership, Greensboro, NC. Tel: (336) 545-2810, FAX: (336) 282-3284, E-Mail: info@ccl.org, Web Site: www.ccl.org (14)

Altman, Keith, Call Compliance Inc, Glen Cove, NY. Tel: (516) 674-4545, FAX: (516) 676-2420, E-Mail: sales@callcompliance.com, Web Site: www.callcompliance.com (29)

Altman, Shari, Altman Dedicated Direct, Rural Hall, NC. Tel: (336) 969-9538, FAX: (336) 969-0187, E-Mail: saltman@AltmanDedicatedDirect.com, Web Site: www.altmandedicateddirect.com (20)

Altschul, Alfred, Airlines Reporting Corp, Arlington, VA. Tel: (703) 816-8135, FAX: (703) 816-8104, E-Mail: corpcom@arccorp.com, Web Site: www.arccorp.com (16)

Altstadt, Manfred, Mutual of America Life Insurance Co, New York, NY. Tel: (212) 224-1600, (800) 468-3785, FAX: (212) 207-3001, Web Site: www.mutualofamerica.com (14)

Alty, Julia, Beemak Plastics Inc, La Mirada, CA. Tel: (310) 886-5880, (800) 421-4393, FAX: (310) 764-0330, E-Mail: info@beemak.com, Web Site: www.beemak.com (16)

Alvarez, James N., ChoicePoint Precision Marketing, Little Rock, AR. Tel: (978) 738-0544, (800) 937-4232, FAX: (978) 738-0582, Web Site: www.cp-pm.com (30)

Alvarez, Lino, MundoFOX22, Los Angeles, CA. Tel: (213) 344-3700, E-Mail: info@canal22.tv, Web Site: www.mundofox22.com (32)

Alverson, Amelia J., Columbia University, Annual Fund Programs, New York, NY. E-Mail: donorrelations@columbia.edu, Web Site: http://giving.columbia.edu (5)

Alvion LLC, Cape Coral, FL. Tel: (239) 574-8600, (877) 528-7800, FAX: (239) 574-8551, Web Site: www.alvion.com (22)

Alzheimer Society of Canada, Toronto, ON Canada. Tel: (416) 488-8772, (800) 616-8816, FAX: (416) 488-3778, E-Mail: gpage@alzheimer.ca, Web Site: www.alzheimer.ca (1)

Alzheimer's Association, Chicago, IL. Tel: (312) 335-8700, (800) 272-3900, Web Site: www.alz.org (1)

AM Solutions, Edgerton, WI. Tel: (800) 410-6245, E-Mail: fschulze@amsolutionswi.com, Web Site: www.amsolutionswi.com (21)

Amabili, Bridget, Data Services Inc, Salisbury, MD. Tel: (410) 546-2206, (800) 432-4066, FAX: (410) 546-2274, Web Site: www.dataservicesinc.com (22)

Amacom Books, New York, NY. Tel: (212) 903-8376, FAX: (212) 903-8083, E-Mail: customerservice@amanet.org, Web Site: www.amacombooks.org (17)

Amanet, Canoga Park, CA. Tel: (818) 786-1113, FAX: (818) 786-5736, E-Mail: info@amanet-usa.com, Web Site: www.amanet.com (16)

Amaryllis Inc, Baton Rouge, LA. Tel: (225) 924-5560 (8)

Amateur Electronic Supply LLC, Milwaukee, WI. Tel: (414) 558-0333, (800) 558-0411, FAX: (414) 358-3337, Web Site: www.aesham.com (16)

Amato, Sheri L., Hobby Surplus Sales, New Britain, CT. Tel: (860) 223-0600, (800) 233-0872, FAX: (860) 225-5316, E-Mail: amatohobby@sbcglobal.net, Web Site: www.hobbysurplus.com (11)

Amato, Steven, Hobby Surplus Sales, New Britain, CT. Tel: (860) 223-0600, (800) 233-0872, FAX: (860) 225-5316, E-Mail: amatohobby@sbcglobal.net, Web Site: www.hobbysurplus.com (11)

Amato, Vincent, Hobby Surplus Sales, New Britain, CT. Tel: (860) 223-0600, (800) 233-0872, FAX: (860) 225-5316, E-Mail: amatohobby@sbcglobal.net, Web Site: www.hobbysurplus.com (11)

AmazingMail Inc, Scottsdale, AZ. Tel: (480) 281-4800, E-Mail: customersupport@amazingmail.com, Web Site: www.amazingmail.com (35)

Amazon.com, Seattle, WA. Tel: (206) 266-1000, Web Site: www.amazon.com (16)

Amazon Drygoods, Osgood, IN. FAX: (812)852-1780, Web Site: www.amazondrygoods.com (2)

Ambassador Press, Minneapolis, MN. Tel: (612) 521-0123, (800) 544-9112, FAX: (612) 521-4587, E-Mail: info@ambpress.com, Web Site: www.ambpress.com (27)

Ambassador Programs, Spokane, WA. Tel: (509) 568-7800, (800) 669-7882, FAX: (877) 284-4517, Web Site: www.peopletopeople.com (19)

Ambient Shapes Inc, Hickory, NC. Tel: (800) 438-2244, FAX: (800) 872-2005, E-Mail: sales@ambientshapes.com, Web Site: www.ambientshapes.com (7)

Ambio, Jeff, Bowers & Merena Auctions, Irvine, CA. Tel: (949) 253-0916, (800) 458-4646, FAX: (949) 253-4091, E-Mail: auction@bowersandmerena.com, Web Site: www.bowersandmerena.com (16)

Amboian, John P., Nuveen Investments, Chicago, IL. Tel: (312) 917-7700, (800) 257-8787, FAX: (312) 917-8049, Web Site: www.nuveen.com (14)

Ambrose, Paul, George W Park Seed Co Inc, Hodges, SC. Tel: (864) 330-2003, (800) 845-3369, E-Mail: info@parkseed.com, Web Site: www.parkseed.com (8)

Amburgey, Doug, Fetter Printing Company Inc, Louisville, KY. Tel: (502) 634-4771, (800) 234-4771, FAX: (502) 634-3587, E-Mail: info@fettergroup.com (27)

Amcat TeleProfit Inc, Oklahoma City, OK. Tel: (405) 216-8080, (800) 364-5518, FAX: (405) 216-8063, E-Mail: smart@amcat.com, Web Site: www.amcat.com (16)

AMD Research & Marketing LLC, Safety Harbor, FL. Tel: (727) 409-1087, Web Site: www.amdresearch-marketing.com (30)

Amedio, Steve, Technekes LLC, Charlotte, NC. Tel: (704) 342-2900, FAX: (704) 342-2975, Web Site: www.technekes.com (22)

Amergent, Peabody, MA. Tel: (800) 370-7500, FAX: (978) 531-0400, Web Site: www.amergent.com (1)

America Direct Book Service Custom Publishing, Ossining, NY. Tel: (914) 271-3640, FAX: (914) 271-3641, E-Mail: info@americadirectbook.com, Web Site: www.americadirectbook.com (17)

AmeriCall Group Inc, Oak Brook, IL. Tel: (630) 955-9100, (800) 688-0078, FAX: (630) 955-9955, E-Mail: sales@americallgroup.com, Web Site: www.americallgroup.com (29)

American Academy of Neurology, Minneapolis, MN. Tel: (651) 695-2793, 800 (879)-1960, FAX: (612) 454-2746, E-Mail: memberservices@aan.com, Web Site: www.aan.com (1)

American Accessories International, Knoxville, TN. Tel: (865) 525-9100, Web Site: www.americanaccessoriesintl.com (33)

American Airlines, Fort Worth, TX. Tel: (817) 963-1234 (12)

American Airlines Inc, Fort Worth, TX. Tel: (817) 963-1234, FAX: (817) 967-2841, Web Site: www.aa.com (19)

American Appraisal Associates, Milwaukee, WI. Tel: (414) 271-7240, (800) 558-8650, FAX: (414) 221-7065, Web Site: www.american-appraisal.com (14)

American Arbitration Association, New York, NY. Tel: (212) 716-5800, (800) 778-7879, FAX: (212) 716-5905, E-Mail: kesslerw@adr.org, Web Site: www.adr.org (1)

American Association for Justice, Washington, DC. Tel: (202) 965-3500, (800) 424-2725, FAX: (202) 625-7313, E-Mail: membership@justice.org, Web Site: www.justice.org (1)

American Association of Advertising Agencies, New York, NY. Tel: (212) 682-2500, FAX: (212) 682-8391, Web Site: www.aaaa.org (40)

American Association of Critical-Care Nurses, Aliso Viejo, CA. Tel: (949) 362-2000, (800) 809-CARE, FAX: (949) 362-2020, E-Mail: info@aacn.com, Web Site: www.aacn.org (1)

American Association of Individual Investors, Chicago, IL. Tel: (312) 280-0170, FAX: (312) 280-9883, E-Mail: adam@aaii.com, Web Site: www.aaii.com (1)

American Association of University Women, Washington, DC. Tel: (202) 785-7700, FAX: (202) 872-1425, E-Mail: connect@aauw.org, Web Site: www.aauw.org (1)

American Automobile Association, Heathrow, FL. Tel: (407) 444-8000, Web Site: www.aaa.com (16)

American Bankers Association, Washington, DC. Tel: (202) 663-5000, (800) 226-5377, FAX: (202) 663-7543, Web Site: www.aba.com (1)

American Bar Association, Chicago, IL. Tel: (312) 988-5000, (800) 285-2221, FAX: (312) 988-5177, Web Site: www.abanet.org (1)

American Baseball Coaches Association, Greensboro, NC. Tel: (336) 821-3140, FAX: (336) 886-0000, E-Mail: abca@abca.org, Web Site: www.abca.org (1)

American Bible Society, New York, NY. Tel: (212) 408-1200, FAX: (212) 408-1264, Web Site: www.americanbible.org (1)

American Biographical Institute Inc, Raleigh, NC. Tel: (919) 781-8710, FAX: (919) 781-8712 (17)

American Breast Cancer Foundation, Columbia, MD. Tel: (410) 730-5105, E-Mail: info@abcf.org, Web Site: www.abcf.org (1)

American Bronzing Co, Columbus, OH. Tel: (614) 252-7388, (800) 423-5678, FAX: (614) 252-4602, E-Mail: bronzeinfo@bronshoe.com, Web Site: www.abcbronze.com (16)

American Business Directories, Omaha, NE. Tel: (402) 593-4600, (800) 555-6124, FAX: (402) 596-0475, Web Site: www.infousa.com (43)

American Cancer Society, Atlanta, GA. Tel: (404) 320-3333, (800) ACS-2345, FAX: (404) 329-5787, Web Site: www.cancer.org (1)

American Capital, Bethesda, MD. Tel: (301) 951-6122, FAX: (301) 654-6714, E-Mail: info@americancapital.com, Web Site: www.americancapital.com (15)

American Catalog Mailers Association, Providence, RI. Tel: (800) 509-9514, E-Mail: info@catalogmailers.org, Web Site: www.catalogmailers.org (1)

American Catalog Partnerships LLC, Summit, NJ. Tel: (908) 598-1947 (20)

American Century Investments, Kansas City, MO. Tel: (816) 531-5575, (800) 345-2021, FAX: (816) 340-4964, Web Site: www.americancentury.com (14)

American Chemical Society, Washington, DC. Tel: (202) 872-4600, (800) 227-5558, FAX: (202) 452-8913, E-Mail: service@acs.org, Web Site: www.acs.org (1)

American Church Inc, Youngstown, OH. Tel: (330) 758-4545, (800) 250-7112, FAX: (800) 763-8772, E-Mail: sales@americanchurch.com, Web Site: www.americanchurch.com (26)

American Civil Defense Association, Draper, UT. Tel: (801) 501-0077, (800) 425-5397, FAX: (888) 425-5339, E-Mail: info@tacda.org, Web Site: www.tacda.org (16)

American Civil Liberties Union Foundation, New York, NY. Tel: (212) 549-2500, Web Site: www.aclu.org (1)

American Clearinghouse Inc, Louisville, KY. Tel: (502) 499-4185, (800) 944-6361 (23)

American College of Cardiology, Washington, DC. Tel: (202) 375-6000, FAX: (202) 375-7000, E-Mail: resource@acc.org, Web Site: www.acc.org (1)

American College of Emergency Physicians, Irving, TX. Tel: (972) 550-0911, (800) 798-1822, FAX: (972) 580-2816, Web Site: www.acep.org (1)

American College of Physician Executives, Tampa, FL. Tel: (813) 287-2000, (800) 562-8088, FAX: (813) 287-8993, E-Mail: acpe@acpe.org, Web Site: www.acpe.org (1)

American College of Physicians, Philadelphia, PA. Tel: (215) 351-2600, (800) 523-1546, FAX: (215) 351-2686, Web Site: www.acponline.org (17)

American Color, Irving, TX. Tel: (602) 333-1000, FAX: (602) 333-1099, Web Site: www.amcolor.com (27)

American Council on Exercise, San Diego, CA. Tel: (858) 576-6500, (888) 825-3636, FAX: (858) 576-6564, Web Site: www.acefitness.org (1)

American Counseling Association, Broken Arrow, OK. Tel: (918) 994-4413, FAX: (918) 663-7058, E-Mail: webmaster@counseling.org, Web Site: www.counseling.org (1)

American Craft Council, Minneapolis, MN. Tel: (212) 274-0630, FAX: (212) 274-0650, E-Mail: council@craftcouncil.org, Web Site: www.craftcouncil.org (17)

American Crane & Equipment Corp, Douglassville, PA. Tel: (610) 385-4876, (877) 877-6778, FAX: (610) 385-3191, E-Mail: info@americancrane.com, Web Site: www.americancrane.com (16)

American Customer Care Inc, Bristol, CT. Tel: (866) 400-6886, Web Site: www.americancustomercare.com (29)

American Database Marketing Inc, Jacksonville, FL. Tel: (888) 565-7724, FAX: (888) 270-4338, E-Mail: admdun@cs.com, Web Site: www.admlists.com (23)

American Dermatological Corp, Miami, FL. Tel: (305) 573-0763, (888) 573-0763, FAX: (305) 573-1704, E-Mail: info@dermatique.com, Web Site: www.dermatique.com (16)

American Diabetes Association, Alexandria, VA. Tel: (703) 549-1500, (800) 342-2383, Web Site: www.diabetes.org (1)

American Direct Marketing Resources Inc, Chesterfield, MO. Tel: (636) 532-7703, FAX: (636) 532-2427, E-Mail: admr@admr.com, Web Site: www.americandirectmarketing.com (21)

American Direct Marketing Services Inc, Dallas, TX. Tel: (214) 634-2361, (800) 527-5080, FAX: (214) 905-3829, Web Site: www.dmlist.com (23)

American Eagle Outfitters, Pittsburgh, PA. Tel: (412) 432-3382, Web Site: www.ae.com (2)

American Express Co, New York, NY. Tel: (212) 640-2000, FAX: (212) 619-9802, Web Site: www.americanexpress.com (14)

American Express Publishing Corp, New York, NY. Tel: (212) 382-5600, (888) 461-6180, FAX: (212) 827-6496, E-Mail: aepc@custmersvc.com, Web Site: www.amexpub.com (17)

American Family Insurance Group, Madison, WI. Tel: (608) 249-2111, FAX: (608) 243-6525, E-Mail: akin1@amfam.com, Web Site: www.amfam.com (15)

American Family Life Assurance Co of Columbus (AFLAC), Columbus, GA. Tel: (706) 323-3431, (800) 992-3522, FAX: (706) 660-7446, Web Site: www.aflac.com (15)

American Federation of Astrologers, Tempe, AZ. Tel: (480) 838-1751, (888) 301-7630, FAX: (480) 838-8293, E-Mail: afa@msn.com, Web Site: www.astrologers.com (1)

American Fidelity Assurance Co, Oklahoma City, OK. Tel: (405) 525-6900, FAX: (405) 523-5215, Web Site: www.afadvantage.com (15)

The American Film Institute, Los Angeles, CA. Tel: (323) 856-7600, FAX: (323) 467-4578, Web Site: www.afi.com (1)

American Fine Paper Co, Appleton, WI. Tel: (920) 733-6100, (800) 458-5446, FAX: (920) 380-8711, E-Mail: found@americanfinepaper.com, Web Site: www.americanfinepaper.com (25)

American Forests, Washington, DC. Tel: (202) 737-1944, FAX: (202) 737-2457, E-Mail: info@amfor.org, Web Site: www.americanforests.org (1)

American Foundation for the Blind Inc, New York, NY. Tel: (212) 502-7600, FAX: (212) 502-7777, E-Mail: afbinfo@afb.org, Web Site: www.afb.org (1)

American General Co, Neptune, NJ. Tel: (732) 922-7000, FAX: (732) 922-7595 (15)

American General Life & Accident Insurance, Nashville, TN. Tel: (615) 749-1000, (800) 888-2452, Web Site: www.agla.com (15)

American General Life Insurance Co, Houston, TX. Tel: (713) 522-1111, FAX: (713) 522-8531, Web Site: www.aglife.com (15)

American Girl Brands LLC, Middleton, WI. Tel: (608) 836-4848, Web Site: www.americangirl.com (6)

American Graphics Network Inc, Glenview, IL. Tel: (847) 729-7220, FAX: (847) 724-5080, E-Mail: info@agninc.com, Web Site: www.agninc.com (27)

American Greetings Corp, Cleveland, OH. Tel: (216) 252-7300, FAX: (216) 252-6778, Web Site: www.americangreetings.com (16)

American Health & Life Insurance Co, Fort Worth, TX. Tel: (817) 348-7500, (800) 995-2274, FAX: (817) 348-7553, Web Site: www.citifinancial.com (15)

American Health & Safety Inc, Stoughton, WI. Tel: (630) 413-5662, (800) 522-7554, FAX: (800) 326-3245, Web Site: www.ahsafety.com (16)

American Health Information Management Association, Chicago, IL. Tel: (312) 233-1100, (800) 335-5535, FAX: (312) 233-1090, E-Mail: info@ahima.org, Web Site: www.ahima.org (1)

American Healthways, Franklin, TN. Tel: (615) 665-7716, FAX: (615) 665-7697, Web Site: www.americanhealthways.com (16)

American Heart Association, Dallas, TX. Tel: (214) 373-6300, (800) AHA-USA-1, FAX: (214) 373-3406, Web Site: www.americanheart.org (1)

American Heritage Picture Library, New York, NY. Tel: (212) 206-5107, (800) 777-1222, FAX: (212) 367-3151, Web Site: www.americanheritage.com (38)

American Historic Inns Inc, Dana Point, CA. Tel: (949) 497-2232, (800) 397-4667, FAX: (949) 497-9228, E-Mail: comments@iloveinns.com, Web Site: www.iloveinns.com (17)

American Horse Products, San Juan Capistrano, CA. Tel: (949) 248-5300, (800) 500-0799, FAX: (949) 248-5305, E-Mail: zjim@sbcglobal.net, Web Site: www.americanhorseproducts.com (11)

American Hotel Register Co, Vernon Hills, IL. Tel: (708) 743-4163, FAX: (708) 564-5797, Web Site: www.americanhotel.com (23)

American Humane Association, Washington, DC. Tel: (303) 925-9497, Web Site: www.americanhumane.org (1)

American Identity, Overland Park, KS. Tel: (913) 319-3100, (800) 848-8028 (33)

American Inbound, Bloomington, IN. Tel: (800) 322-6445, FAX: (800) 224-3583, Web Site: www.americanbound.com (29)

American Indian College Fund, Denver, CO. Tel: (303) 426-8900, (800) 776-3863, FAX: (303) 426-1200, Web Site: www.collegefund.org (1)

American Institute for Cancer Research, Washington, DC. Tel: (202) 328-7744, (800) 843-8114, FAX: (202) 328-7226, E-Mail: aicrweb@aicr.org, Web Site: www.aicr.org (1)

American Institute for Economic Research, Great Barrington, MA. Tel: (413) 528-1216, (888) 528-1216, FAX: (413) 528-0103, E-Mail: info@aier.org, Web Site: www.aier.org (1)

American Institute of Chemical Engineers, New York, NY. Tel: (203) 702-7660, (800) 242-4363, FAX: (203) 775-5177, E-Mail: xpress@aiche.org, Web Site: www.aiche.org (1)

American Institute of CPAs, New York, NY. Tel: (212) 596-6200, (888) 777-7077, FAX: (212) 596-6213, Web Site: www.aicpa.org (1)

American Institute of Graphic Arts (AIGA), New York, NY. Tel: (212) 807-1990, FAX: (212) 807-1799, E-Mail: grefe@aiga.org, Web Site: www.aiga.org (40)

American Institute of Physics, Melville, NY. Tel: (516) 576-2200, (800) 892-8259, FAX: (516) 576-2374, E-Mail: aipinfo@aip.org, Web Site: www.aip.org (17)

American Insurance Administrators Inc, Columbus, OH. Tel: (614) 486-5388, FAX: (614) 486-2728 (15)

American International Group, New York, NY. Tel: (212) 770-7000, (877) 638-4244, FAX: (212) 742-8692, Web Site: www.aig.com (15)

American Israel Public Affairs Committee, Washington, DC. Tel: (202) 639-5226, Web Site: www.aipac.org (40)

American Kennel Club, New York, NY. Tel: (212) 696-8200, FAX: (212) 696-8217, (212) 696-8299, Web Site: www.akc.org (17)

American Kidney Fund, Rockville, MD. Tel: (301) 881-3052, (800) 638-8299, FAX: (301) 881-0898, Web Site: www.kidneyfund.org (1)

The American Legion National Headquarters, Indianapolis, IN. Tel: (317) 860-3100, (800) 433-2700, FAX: (317) 860-3001, Web Site: www.legion.org (1)

American Library Association-Publishing Services, Chicago, IL. Tel: (312) 944-6780, (800) 545-2433, FAX: (312) 440-9374, Web Site: www.ala.org (1)

American Locker Security Systems Inc, Coppell, TX. Tel: (817) 329-1600, (800) 828-9118, E-Mail: info@americanlocker.com, Web Site: www.americanlocker.com (16)

American Lung Association, Chicago, IL. Tel: (212) 889-3370, (800) 548-8252, FAX: (212) 889-3375, E-Mail: info@alany.org, Web Site: www.lungusa.org (1)

American Mail-Well Envelope Co/St Louis Div, Eureka, MO. Tel: (314) 966-2000, (800) 800-8845, FAX: (314) 966-4725, E-Mail: info@cenveo.com, Web Site: www.mail-well.com (26)

American Mailing Lists Corp, Manassas, VA. Tel: (571) 292-5806, FAX: (571) 292-5807, E-Mail: dorothy@amlc.info, Web Site: amlc.info.575elmp01.blackmesh.com (23)

American Mailing Service Inc, Ashland, KY. Tel: (606) 329-2741, (800) 678-8384, FAX: (606) 325-8558, Web Site: www.thegallahergroup.com (28)

American Management Association, New York, NY. Tel: (212) 586-8100, FAX: (212) 903-8186, Web Site: www.amanet.org (1)

American Management Association International, New York, NY. Tel: (212) 586-8100, (877) 566-9441, FAX: (212) 903-8168, Web Site: www.amanet.org (41)

American Marketing & Communication Corp, Hagerstown, MD. Tel: (240) 625-9225, FAX: (240) 625-9235, E-Mail: info@amcc1.com, Web Site: www.americanmarketingcc.com (20)

American Marketing Association, Chicago, IL. Tel: (312) 542-9000, (800) AMA-1150, FAX: (312) 542-9001, Web Site: www.marketingpower.com (40)

American Marketing Association/New York Chapter, New York, NY. Tel: (212) 687-3280, FAX: (212) 557-9242, E-Mail: mlkeane@nyama.org, Web Site: www.nyama.org (40)

American Mathematical Society, Providence, RI. Tel: (401) 455-4000, (800) 321-4267, FAX: (401) 331-3842, E-Mail: ams@ams.org, Web Site: www.ams.org (17)

American Meadows Inc & Vermont Wild Flowers Farm, Shelburne, VT. Tel: (877) 309-7333, FAX: (802) 951-9089, E-Mail: customerservice@americanmeadows.com, Web Site: www.americanmeadows.com (8)

American Medical Association, Chicago, IL. Tel: (312) 464-5000, (800) 621-8335, FAX: (312) 464-4184, Web Site: www.ama-assn.org (1)

American Megatrends Inc, Norcross, GA. Tel: (770) 246-8600, (800) 828-9264, FAX: (770) 246-8790, Web Site: www.ami.com (3)

American Mint LLC, Mechanicsburg, PA. Tel: (717) 458-9200, (877) 807-MINT, FAX: (717) 458-9211, E-Mail: contact@americanmint.com, Web Site: www.americanmint.com (6)

American Modern Insurance Group, Amelia, OH. Tel: (513) 943-7200, (800) 759-9008, FAX: (513) 947-4779, (800) 217-5150, E-Mail: customer_care@amig.com, Web Site: www.amig.com (15)

American Movie Classics Holding Corp, Jericho, NY. Tel: (516) 803-3000, FAX: (516) 803-3003, Web Site: www.amctv.com (16)

American Name Services Inc, Orem, UT. Tel: (801) 235-8061, (800) 434-1851, FAX: (801) 764-0613, E-Mail: sales@americannameservices.com, Web Site: www.americannameservices.com (23)

American National Standards Institute, New York, NY. Tel: (212) 642-4900, FAX: (212) 398-0023, Web Site: www.ansi.org (1)

American Nicaraguan Foundation, Miami, FL. Tel: (305) 374-3391, FAX: (305) 374-5993, Web Site: www.aidnicaragua.org (1)

American Numismatic Association, Colorado Springs, CO. Tel: (719) 632-2646, Web Site: www.money.org (1)

American Nurses' Association, Silver Spring, MD. Tel: (301) 628-5000, (800) 274-4262, (800) 284-2378, FAX: (301) 628-5001, Web Site: www.nursingworld.org (1)

American Ostomy Supply, Earth City, MO. Tel: (314) 291-2900, (800) 858-5858, FAX: (800) 545-0065 (16)

American Period Lighting Inc, Lancaster, PA. Tel: (717) 392-5649, FAX: (717) 509-3127, E-Mail: info@americanperiodlighting.com, Web Site: www.americanperiodlighting.com (8)

The American Phytopathological Society, Saint Paul, MN. Tel: (651) 454-7250, FAX: (651) 454-0766, E-Mail: apsheadquarters@scisoc.org, Web Site: www.apsnet.org (1)

American Preferred Reader's Service Inc, Fort Lauderdale, FL. Tel: (954) 767-6022, (888) 482-2443, FAX: (954) 767-6065, E-Mail: jfarrell@amerpref.com, Web Site: www.amerpref.com (18)

American Printing House for the Blind, Louisville, KY. Tel: (502) 895-2405, (800) 223-1839, FAX: (502) 899-2274, E-Mail: info@aph.org, Web Site: www.aph.org (7)

American Psychological Association, Washington, DC. Tel: (202) 336-5500, (800) 374-2721, FAX: (202) 336-5568, E-Mail: order@apa.org, Web Site: www.apa.org (1)

American Radio Relay League, Newington, CT. Tel: (860) 594-0200, FAX: (860) 594-0259, Web Site: www.arrl.org (1)

American Recreation Products Inc, Saint Louis, MO. Tel: (314) 576-8000, FAX: (314) 576-8072 (11)

American Red Cross, Washington, DC. Tel: (202) 303-5214, (800) RED-CROSS, FAX: (202) 303-6604, Web Site: www.redcross.org (1)

American Running Association, Bethesda, MD. Tel: (301) 913-9517, (800) 776-2732, FAX: (301) 913-9520, E-Mail: run@americanrunning.org, Web Site: www.americanrunning.org (1)

American Science & Surplus, Niles, IL. Tel: (847) 647-0020, (888) SCI-PLUS, FAX: (847) 647-5010, E-Mail: info@sciplus.com, Web Site: www.sciplus.com (9)

American Securities Capital Partners, New York, NY. Tel: (212) 476-8000, Web Site: www.american-securities.com (15)

American Slide-Chart Corp, Carol Stream, IL. Tel: (630) 665-3333, (800) 323-4433, FAX: (630) 665-3491, E-Mail: info2@americanslidechart.com, Web Site: www.americanslidechart.com (27)

American Society for Quality, Milwaukee, WI. Tel: (414) 272-8575, (800) 248-1946, FAX: (414) 272-1734, E-Mail: help@asq.org, Web Site: www.asq.org (1)

American Society of Civil Engineers, Reston, VA. Tel: (703) 295-6000, (800) 548-2723, FAX: (703) 295-6343, Web Site: www.asce.org (1)

American Society of Interior Designers, Washington, DC. Tel: (202) 546-3480, FAX: (202) 546-3240, E-Mail: membership@asid.org, Web Site: www.asid.org (1)

American Society of Journalists & Authors Directory, New York, NY. Tel: (212) 997-0947, FAX: (212) 768-7414, E-Mail: asjany@ibm.net (43)

American Society of Mechanical Engineers, New York, NY. Tel: (973) 882-1167, (800) 843-2763, FAX: (973) 882-1717, E-Mail: infocentral@asme.org, Web Site: www.asme.org (25)

American Society of Media Photographers (ASMP), Philadelphia, PA. Tel: (215) 451-ASMP, FAX: (215) 451-0880, Web Site: www.asmp.org (40)

American Society of Radiologic Technologists, Albuquerque, NM. Tel: (505) 298-4500, FAX: (505) 298-5063, Web Site: www.asrt.org (1)

American Society on Aging, San Francisco, CA. Tel: (415) 974-9600, (800) 537-9728, FAX: (415) 974-0300, E-Mail: info@asaging.org, Web Site: www.asaging.org (1)

American Solutions for Business, Glenwood, MN. Tel: (320) 634-5471, FAX: (320) 634-5265, Web Site: www.americanbus.com (1)

American Speech-Language-Hearing Association, Rockville, MD. Tel: (301) 897-5700, (800) 638-8255, FAX: (301) 296-8580, E-Mail: productsales@asha.org, Web Site: www.asha.org (1)

American Spirit Graphics Corp, Minneapolis, MN. Tel: (612) 623-3333, FAX: (612) 623-9314, E-Mail: asgc@asgc.com, Web Site: www.asgc.com (27)

American Spirit Mailing, Howard Lake, MN. Tel: (320) 543-3737, FAX: (320) 543-3228, E-Mail: asgc@asgc-mail.com, Web Site: www.asgc.com (28)

American Stationery Co Inc, Peru, IN. Tel: (765) 473-4438, (800) 822-2577, FAX: (800) 253-9054, Web Site: www.americanstationery.com (10)

American Student Assistance, Boston, MA. Tel: (800) 999-9080, Web Site: www.asa.com (1)

American Student Marketing LLC, Highland Park, IL. Tel: (847) 432-4329, FAX: (847) 432-4811, E-Mail: admin@asmdm.com, Web Site: www.asmdm.com (23)

American Target Advertising Inc, Manassas, VA. Tel: (703) 392-7676, FAX: (703) 392-7654, E-Mail: info@americantarget.com, Web Site: americantarget.com (35)

American Tax Associates Inc, Columbus, OH. Tel: (614) 443-5343, FAX: (614) 443-0279 (20)

American Technical Publishers Inc, Orland Park, IL. Tel: (708) 957-1100, (800) 323-3471, FAX: (708) 957-1101, E-Mail: service@americantech.net, Web Site: www.atplearning.com (17)

American Telecast Products LLC, Exton, PA. Tel: (610) 430-7800, FAX: (484) 879-4046, E-Mail: info@ americantelecast.com, Web Site: www. americantelecast.com (32)

American Teleservices Association, Indianapolis, IN. Tel: (317) 816-9336, (877) 779-3974, FAX: (317) 218-0323, Web Site: www.ataconnect.org (40)

American Thermoplastic Co, Pittsburgh, PA. Tel: (412) 967-0900, (800) 245-6600, FAX: (412) 967-9990, E-Mail: atc@binders.com, Web Site: www.binders. com (27)

American 3B Scientific, Tucker, GA. Tel: (770) 492-9111, Web Site: www.a3bs.com (16)

American Tourister, Mansfield, MA. Tel: (800) 765-2247, Web Site: www.americantourister.com (16)

American Trim, Lima, OH. Tel: (419) 228-1145, FAX: (419) 996-4850, E-Mail: sales@amtrim.com, Web Site: www.amtrim.com (9)

American Trucking Association, Arlington, VA. Tel: (703) 838-1700, FAX: (800) 254-2571, E-Mail: atamembership@trucking.org, Web Site: www. trucking.org (1)

The American Vintage Library, Los Angeles, CA. Tel: (310) 552-3176, (800) 235-1919, Web Site: www. vintagelibrary.com (17)

American Writers & Artists Inc, Delray Beach, FL. Tel: (561) 278-5557, Web Site: www.awaionline.com (36)

Americana Sales Ventures Inc, Altamonte Springs, FL. Tel: (407) 862-8388, (800) 445-4302, FAX: (407) 862-6535, Web Site: www.americanashopper.com (35)

Americans for Peace Now, Washington, DC. Tel: (202) 408-9898, FAX: (202) 408-9899, E-Mail: apndc@ peacenow.org, Web Site: www.peacenow.org (1)

AmeriCares, Stamford, CT. Tel: (203) 658-9500, (800) 486-4357, E-Mail: info@americares.org, Web Site: www.americares.org (1)

America's Call Center, Jacksonville, FL. Tel: (904) 224-2000, (800) 598-2580, FAX: (904) 737-1107, E-Mail: info@webcallusa.com, Web Site: www. webcallusa.com (29)

America's Finest Pet Doors, San Luis Obispo, CA. Tel: (805) 781-7700 X201, (800) 826-2871, FAX: (805) 781-9734, E-Mail: alan@petdoors.com, Web Site: www.petdoors.com (16)

AmericasMart Atlanta, Atlanta, GA. Tel: (404) 220-3000, FAX: (404) 220-3030, Web Site: www. americasmart.com (42)

Americatel Corp, Rockville, MD. Tel: (800) 221-3020, E-Mail: customerservice@americatel.com, Web Site: www.americatel.com (32)

Americraft - The Gift Brokers Inc, Wendell, MA. Tel: (978) 544-7330, (800) 866-2723, FAX: (978) 544-2771, E-Mail: info@americraft.us, Web Site: www. americraft.us (16)

Amerikal Products, Waukegan, IL. Tel: (847) 244-3600, FAX: (847) 244-2860, E-Mail: info@amerikal.com, Web Site: www.amerikal.com (25)

AmeriList Inc, Orangeburg, NY. Tel: (845) 362-6737, (800) 457-2899, FAX: (845) 362-6433, E-Mail: info@amerilist.com, Web Site: www.amerilist.com (23)

AmeriMark Direct LLC, Middleburg Heights, OH. Tel: (440) 325-2000, FAX: (440) 234-8925, E-Mail: affiliate@amerimark.com, Web Site: www. amerimark.com (2)

Ameriprise Financial Services Inc, Minneapolis, MN. Tel: (612) 671-3131, (651) 671-3434, (800) 386-2042, FAX: (612) 547-2736, Web Site: www. ameriprise.com (14)

AmerisourceBergen, Chesterbrook, PA. Tel: (610) 727-7000, (800) 829-3132, E-Mail: solutions@ amerisourcebergan.com, Web Site: www. amerisourcebergan.com (7)

Ameristar Casinos Inc, Las Vegas, NV. Tel: (702) 567-7000, FAX: (702) 369-8860, Web Site: www. ameristarcasinos.com (19)

Amerisure Insurance Cos, Farmington Hills, MI. Tel: (248) 615-9000, (800) 257-1900, FAX: (248) 615-8224, Web Site: www.amerisure.com (15)

Amerson, Ken, Oblate Missions, San Antonio, TX. Tel: (210) 736-1685, FAX: (210) 736-1314, E-Mail: contact@oblatemissions.org, Web Site: www. oblatemissions.org (1)

Ames Specialty Packaging & Digital Print, Somerville, MA. Tel: (617) 684-1000, (800) 521-2637, FAX: (617) 684-1264, E-Mail: info@amespage.com, Web Site: www.amespage.com (26)

Ames Taping Tool System Inc, Stone Mountain, GA. Tel: (770) 243-2647, (800) 303-1827, FAX: (770) 243-2658, Web Site: www.amestools.com (9)

Ames-Tru-Temper, Camp Hill, PA. Tel: (800) 393-1846, Web Site: ames.com (8)

Ames-Johnson, Jere, McCormick-Armstrong Co Inc, Wichita, KS. Tel: (316) 264-1363, (800) 733-1363, FAX: (316) 263-4511, E-Mail: sales@ mccormickarmstrong.com, Web Site: www. mccormickarmstrong.com (27)

Amica Insurance, Lincoln, RI. Tel: (401) 334-6000, (800) 652-6422, FAX: (401) 334-4241, Web Site: www.amica.com (15)

Amigo Mobility International Inc, Bridgeport, MI. Tel: (989) 777-0910, (800) 692-6446, FAX: (989) 777-8184, E-Mail: info@myamigo.com, Web Site: www.myamigo.com (16)

Amiral, Tracy, Making It Big, Cotati, CA. Tel: (707) 795-1997, (877) 644-1995, FAX: (707) 795-4874, E-Mail: mib@makingitbig.com, Web Site: www. makingitbig.com (2)

Amjadi, Kamran, Invenda Corp, Bethesda, MD. Tel: (240) 333-6111, E-Mail: sales@invenda.com, Web Site: www.invenda.com (32)

Ammann, Dieter, Fulfillment Express Inc, Pico Rivera, CA. Tel: (562) 948-4400, (800) 700-9295, FAX: (562) 948-4459, E-Mail: information@fex.com, Web Site: www.fex.com (28)

AmMed Direct, Parsons, TN. Tel: (615) 941-3900, (800) 282-3524, Web Site: www.arrivamedical.com (7)

Ammendola, John, Response Insurance, Scranton, PA. Tel: (203) 634-7255, (800) 518-2984, FAX: (203) 634-7319, E-Mail: webcs@response.com, Web Site: www.response.com (15)

Ammiano, Tom, Golden Gate Transportation District, San Rafael, CA. Tel: (415) 921-5858, FAX: (415) 923-2014, Web Site: www.goldengate.org (16)

Amnesty International USA, New York, NY. Tel: (212) 807-8400, FAX: (212) 627-1451, Web Site: www. amnestyusa.org (1)

Amobee, Foster City, CA. Tel: (650) 802-8871, Web Site: www.amobee.com (32)

Amorin, Jim, Appraisal Institute, Chicago, IL. Tel: (312) 335-4100, (888) 756-4624, FAX: (312) 335-4400, E-Mail: aiservice@appraisalinstitute.org, Web Site: www.appraisalinstitute.org (1)

Amos Press, Inc, Sidney, OH. Tel: (937) 498-2111, FAX: (937) 498-0876, Web Site: www.amospress. com (17)

Amos, Daniel P., American Family Life Assurance Co of Columbus (AFLAC), Columbus, GA. Tel: (706) 323-3431, (800) 992-3522, FAX: (706) 660-7446, Web Site: www.aflac.com (15)

Ampersand Press, Port Townsend, WA. Tel: (360) 379-5187, (800) 624-4263, FAX: (360) 379-0324, E-Mail: info@ampersandpress.com, Web Site: www.ampersandpress.com (11)

Amplify Federal Credit Union, Austin, TX. Tel: (512) 836-5901, Web Site: www.goamplify.com (1)

Amref Health Africa in the USA, New York, NY. Tel: (212) 768-2440, FAX: (212) 768-4230, Web Site: www.amrefusa.org (1)

Amrel, El Monte, CA. Tel: (626) 443-6818, (800) 654-9838, FAX: (626) 443-8600, E-Mail: amrel@amrel. com, Web Site: www.amrel.com (16)

Amrigon, Bloomfield Hills, MI. Tel: (248) 332-2300, FAX: (248) 333-9710 (29)

Amsterdam Printing, Amsterdam, NY. Tel: (518) 842-6000, (800) 203-9917, FAX: (518) 843-5204, E-Mail: customerservice@amsterdamprinting.com, Web Site: www.amsterdamprinting.com (16)

Amsterdam Printing, Amsterdam, NY. Tel: (800) 846-6600, FAX: (518) 770-7018, Web Site: www. amsterdamprinting.com (5)

Amtelco, McFarland, WI. Tel: (608) 838-4194, (800) 356-9148, FAX: (608) 838-8998, E-Mail: info@ amtelco.com, Web Site: www.amtelco.com (16)

Amtower & Co Federal Direct, Highland, MD. Tel: (240) 882-9546, E-Mail: markamtower@gmail.com, Web Site: www.federaldirect.net (20)

Amtower, Mark, Amtower & Co Federal Direct, Highland, MD. Tel: (240) 882-9546, E-Mail: markamtower@gmail.com, Web Site: www. federaldirect.net (20)

Amvac Chemical Corp, Los Angeles, CA. Tel: (323) 264-3910, (888) 462-6822, Web Site: www.amvac-chemical.com (8)

Anagnost, Andrew, Autodesk Inc, San Rafael, CA. Tel: (415) 507-5000, FAX: (415) 507-5100, Web Site: www.autodesk.com (16)

Analytic Recruiting Inc, New York, NY. Tel: (212) 545-8511, FAX: (212) 545-8520, E-Mail: rita@ analyticrecruiting.com, Web Site: www. analyticrecruiting.com (20)

Analytical Measurements, Chester, NJ. Tel: (800) 635-5580, FAX: (973) 399-1446, E-Mail: phmeter@ bellatlantic.net, Web Site: www. analyticalmeasurements.com (9)

AnalyticsIQ Inc, Atlanta, GA. Tel: (770) 407-8855, (888) 612-4309, Web Site: www.analytics-iq.com (30)

Anand, Kandy, Molson Coors Brewing Co, Denver, CO. Tel: (303) 927-2337, (800) 665-7661, Web Site: www.molsoncoors.com (16)

Anast, Philip, Tech Image, Chicago, IL. Tel: (847) 279-0022, (888) 483-2477, FAX: (847) 279-8922, E-Mail: info@techimage.com, Web Site: www. techimage.com (35)

Anastassov, Stassi, Duracell, Bethel, CT. Tel: (800) 551-2355, Web Site: www.duracell.com (16)

Anatomical Chart Co, Riverwoods, IL. Tel: (847) 580-5000, (800) 621-7500, FAX: (847) 674-0211, E-Mail: service@anatomical.com, Web Site: www.anatomical.com (7)

Anchor Computer Inc, Farmingdale, NY. Tel: (631) 293-6100, FAX: (631) 293-0891, Web Site: www.anchorcomputer.com (22)

Ancient Circles, Willits, CA. Tel: (800) 726-8032, FAX: (707) 459-0261, E-Mail: ancient@pacific.net, Web Site: www.ancientcircles.com (6)

ANCOR, Troy, MI. Tel: (248) 740-8866, (800) 229-3860, FAX: (248) 740-9025, Web Site: www.anchorinfo.com (22)

Anda Inc, Parsippany, NJ. Tel: (954) 217-4500, (800) 331-2632, FAX: (866) 600-3860, Web Site: www.andanet.com (7)

Andaloro, Vincent, Latin-Pak, Chesterfield, MO. Tel: (636) 536-5344, (800) 625-4283, FAX: (636) 536-9456, E-Mail: latinpak@latinpak.com, Web Site: www.latinpak.com (35)

Andell Packaging Corp, Manhasset, NY. Tel: (718) 937-6500, FAX: (718) 482-9416 (27)

Anderberg-Lund Printing, Saint Louis Park, MN. Tel: (952) 920-9720, (800) 231-9777, FAX: (952) 920-1103, E-Mail: sales@anderberglund.com, Web Site: www.anderberglund.com (27)

Anderberg, Jack, Anderberg-Lund Printing, Saint Louis Park, MN. Tel: (952) 920-9720, (800) 231-9777, FAX: (952) 920-1103, E-Mail: sales@anderberglund.com, Web Site: www.anderberglund.com (27)

Andersen Advertising, Jacksonville, FL. Tel: (904) 859-8165, E-Mail: bob@andersenadvertising.com, Web Site: www.andersenadvertising.com (35)

Andersen Design, East Boothbay, ME. Tel: (207) 350-4016, (866)711-8421, FAX: (207) 449-1449, E-Mail: studio@andersenstudio.com, Web Site: www.andersenstudio.com (33)

Andersen, Bob, Andersen Advertising, Jacksonville, FL. Tel: (904) 859-8165, E-Mail: bob@andersenadvertising.com, Web Site: www.andersenadvertising.com (35)

Andersen, Jean, Taylor Corp, North Mankato, MN. Tel: (507) 625-2828, FAX: (507) 625-3388 (16)

Andersen, Jean, The Occasions Group, North Mankato, MN. Tel: (507) 625-6464 (16)

Andersen, John, Admore Inc, Macomb, MI. Tel: (810) 949-8200, (800) 523-6673, FAX: (800) 215-2664, Web Site: www.admoreonline.com (10)

Andersen, Mackenzie, Andersen Design, East Boothbay, ME. Tel: (207) 350-4016, (866)711-8421, FAX: (207) 449-1449, E-Mail: studio@andersenstudio.com, Web Site: www.andersenstudio.com (33)

Andersen, Paul, Current USA Inc, Colorado Springs, CO. Tel: (719) 594-4100, (877) 665-4458, FAX: (719) 531-2283, Web Site: www.currentinc.com (6)

Barbara S Anderson, Ann Arbor, MI. Tel: (734) 995-0125, FAX: (734) 994-5207 (39)

Anderson Direct & Digital, Poway, CA. Tel: (888) 694-5094, Web Site: www.andersndd.com (35)

MD Anderson Cancer Center - Children's Art Project, Houston, TX. Tel: (713) 745-2575, (800) 231-1580, FAX: (713) 794-1950, E-Mail: krenner@mdanderson.org, Web Site: www.childrensart.org (1)

Anderson Niebuhr & Associates Inc, Arden Hills, MN. Tel: (651) 486-8712, (800) 678-5577, FAX: (651) 486-0536, E-Mail: info@ana-inc.com, Web Site: www.ana-inc.com (30)

Anderson/Skow, San Francisco, CA. Tel: (888) 983-0880, Web Site: www.andersonskow.com (20)

Anderson, A., Dreis & Krump Manufacturing Co, Peotone, IL. Tel: (708) 258-1200, FAX: (708) 258-9682, E-Mail: chicago@dreis-krump.com, Web Site: www.dreis-krump.com (16)

Anderson, Al, Minnesota Public Radio, Saint Paul, MN. Tel: (651) 290-1500, (800) 228-7123, FAX: (651) 290-1260, E-Mail: mail@mpr.org, Web Site: www.mpr.org (1)

Anderson, Barbara, Barbara S Anderson, Ann Arbor, MI. Tel: (734) 995-0125, FAX: (734) 994-5207 (39)

Anderson, Bob, Butler Schein Animal Health, Dublin, OH. Tel: (614) 761-9095, (888) 691-2724, FAX: (888) 329-3861, Web Site: www.butlerschein.com (16)

Anderson, Carole A, American Society on Aging, San Francisco, CA. Tel: (415) 974-9600, (800) 537-9728, FAX: (415) 974-0300, E-Mail: info@asaging.org, Web Site: www.asaging.org (1)

Anderson, Connie, Minnesota Multi Housing Association, Bloomington, MN. Tel: (952) 854-8500, FAX: (952) 854-3810, E-Mail: mha@mmha.com, Web Site: www.mmha.com (1)

Anderson, Dagmar, International Academy - Compounding Pharmacists, Missouri City, TX. Tel: (281) 933-8400, Web Site: www.iacprx.org (1)

Anderson, David, Cakuun, Asheville, NC. Tel: (828) 771-0820, Web Site: acreativecompany.com (35)

Anderson, Doug, OTM Partners, Arlington, VA. Tel: (800) 759-2244, Web Site: otmpartners.com (35)

Anderson, Frances, List Marketing Group Inc, Cleveland, OH. Tel: (216) 990-2000, E-Mail: fran@listmarketinggroup.com, Web Site: www.listmarketinggroup.com (23)

Anderson, Holly, Eventful Inc, San Diego, CA. Tel: (858) 882-0360, FAX: (858) 964-4640, Web Site: www.eventful.com (19)

Anderson, Jason, Modern Postcard, Carlsbad, CA. Tel: (800) 959-8365, Web Site: www.modernpostcard.com (10)

Anderson, Jim, IWCO Direct, Chanhassen, MN. Tel: (952) 474-0961, FAX: (952) 474-6467, Web Site: www.iwco.com (21)

Anderson, John F., Anderson Niebuhr & Associates Inc, Arden Hills, MN. Tel: (651) 486-8712, (800) 678-5577, FAX: (651) 486-0536, E-Mail: info@ana-inc.com, Web Site: www.ana-inc.com (30)

Anderson, Jon, Random Lengths Publications Inc, Eugene, OR. Tel: (541) 686-9925, (888) 686-9925, FAX: (541) 686-9629, (800) 874-7979, E-Mail: rlmail@rlpi.com, Web Site: www.randomlengths.com (17)

Anderson, Joy M., Journal Star, Peoria, IL. Tel: (309) 686-3026, FAX: (309) 686-3265, Web Site: www.pjstar.com (17)

Anderson, Karen, Mi-T-M Corp, Peosta, IA. Tel: (563) 556-7484, Web Site: www.mitm.com (9)

Anderson, Lars C., Comerica Inc, Dallas, TX. Tel: (800) 521-1190, FAX: (925) 941-1999, Web Site: www.comerica.com (14)

Anderson, Lori, International Sign Association, Alexandria, VA. Tel: (703) 836-4012, FAX: (703) 836-8353, E-Mail: info@signs.org, Web Site: www.signs.org (1)

Anderson, Mark, Demco Inc, Madison, WI. Tel: (608) 241-1201, (800) 356-1200, FAX: (608) 241-1799, E-Mail: custserv@demco.com, Web Site: www.demco.com (10)

Anderson, Mark, Impact Mailing, Minneapolis, MN. Tel: (612) 521-6245, FAX: (612) 521-1349, E-Mail: sales@impactmailing.com, Web Site: www.impactmailing.com (28)

Anderson, Melanie, Direct Marketing Group, Eden Prairie, MN. Tel: (952) 975-5060, (888) 397-5060, FAX: (952) 906-0608, Web Site: www.directmg.com (35)

Anderson, Michael J, SpencerStuart, Chicago, IL. Tel: (312) 822-0088, FAX: (312) 822-0116, Web Site: www.spencerstuart.com (20)

Anderson, Peggy, Concordia Publishing House, Saint Louis, MO. Tel: (314) 268-1000, (800) 325-3040, FAX: (314) 268-1329, E-Mail: order@cph.org, Web Site: www.cph.org (17)

Anderson, Price, DirectMail.com, Prince Frederick, MD. Tel: (888) 690-2252, FAX: (301) 855-9810, Web Site: www.directmail.com (28)

Anderson, R., The Doctor's Co, Napa, CA. Tel: (707) 226-0176, E-Mail: info@thedoctors.com, Web Site: www.thedoctors.com (15)

Anderson, Robert D., Winmill & Co, New York, NY. Tel: (212) 785-0900, (800) 400-MIDAS 6432, FAX: (212) 363-1100, E-Mail: info@midasfunds.com, Web Site: www.midasfunds.com (14)

Anderson, Scott, Harold Walter Siebens School of Business, Storm Lake, IA. Tel: (712) 749-2410, (800) 383-2821, FAX: (712) 749-2037, Web Site: www2.bvu.edu/academics/business (41)

Anderson, Scott P, Patterson Dental, Saint Paul, MN. Tel: (651) 686-1600, (800) 328-5536, FAX: (651) 686-9331, Web Site: www.pattersondental.com (10)

Anderson, Terry, Sensient Technologies, Saint Louis, MO. Tel: (314) 889-7600, (800) 325-8110, FAX: (314) 658-7318, Web Site: www.sensient-tech.com (16)

Anderson, Terry, White Cap Wholesale Contractors Supplies, Costa Mesa, CA. Tel: (800) 944-8322, FAX: (866) 791-8396, E-Mail: customerservice@whitecap.com, Web Site: www.whitecapdirect.com (16)

Hanna Andersson Corp, Portland, OR. Tel: (503) 242-0920, (800) 222-0544, FAX: (503) 321-5289, Web Site: www.hannaandersson.com (2)

Andrasko, Nancy M., Roovers Inc, Hazleton, PA. Tel: (570) 455-7548, FAX: (570) 454-1477 (34)

Andre, Julie, Starmount Life Insurance Co, Baton Rouge, LA. Tel: (225) 926-2888, (888) 729-5433, (888) 729-7827, E-Mail: info@starmountlife.com, Web Site: www.starmountlife.com (15)

Andrea Electronics Corp, Bohemia, NY. Tel: (631) 719-1800, (800) 442-7787, FAX: (631) 719-1950, Web Site: www.andreaelectronics.com (16)

Andrea Jr, Frank A.D., Andrea Electronics Corp, Bohemia, NY. Tel: (631) 719-1800, (800) 442-7787, FAX: (631) 719-1950, Web Site: www.andreaelectronics.com (16)

Andrea, Douglas, Andrea Electronics Corp, Bohemia, NY. Tel: (631) 719-1800, (800) 442-7787, FAX: (631) 719-1950, Web Site: www.andreaelectronics.com (16)

Andrea, John, Andrea Electronics Corp, Bohemia, NY. Tel: (631) 719-1800, (800) 442-7787, FAX: (631) 719-1950, Web Site: www.andreaelectronics.com (16)

Andreotti, Lamberto, Bristol-Myers Squibb Co, New York, NY. Tel: (212) 546-4000, FAX: (212) 546-9544, Web Site: www.bms.com (16)

Andrew Associates Inc, Enfield, CT. Tel: (860) 253-0000, FAX: (860) 253-0007, Web Site: www.andrewdm.com (23)

Andrews Wharton Inc, Commack, NY. Tel: (631) 470-4546, (631) 470-5683, E-Mail: info@andrewswharton.com, Web Site: andrewswharton.com (35)

Andrews, Chris, Mitchell International, San Diego, CA. Tel: (858) 368-7000, FAX: (858) 238-9111, Web Site: www.mitchell.com (17)

Andrews, Gaylen, B-T-B Internet Marketing Solutions, Middle Island, NY. Tel: (631) 924-3888, E-Mail: linickgroup@gmail.com, Web Site: www.linick.net; 222.asklinick.com (39)

Andrews, Gaylen, Copywriter's Council of America - (Freelancers), Middle Island, NY. Tel: (631) 924-3888, FAX: (631) 924-8555, E-Mail: cca4dmcopy@gmail.com, Web Site: www.linick.net; www.andrewlinickdirectmarketing.com (39)

Andrews, Patricia, Gamma Photo Labs LLC, Chicago, IL. Tel: (312) 337-0022, FAX: (312) 337-3753, Web Site: www.photobition.com (16)

Andrews, Roger, Veritas Analytics Inc, Sterling, VA. Tel: (703) 707-5620, Web Site: www.veritas-analytics.com (30)

Andrzejewski, Steve, King Pharmaceuticals, Inc, Tenafly, NJ. Tel: (972) 885-0929, (888) 840-5370, E-Mail: igal@navehpharma.com, Web Site: www.kingpharma.com (7)

Andsor Research Inc, Etobicoke, ON Canada. Tel: (416) 245-8073, FAX: (416) 240-8473 (22)

aNETorder/American Mailers, Naperville, IL. Tel: (630) 579-8800, Web Site: www.anetorder.com (28)

Angel Sales Inc, Chicago, IL. Tel: (773) 883-8858, FAX: (773) 883-8889, E-Mail: info@angelsales.com, Web Site: www.angelsales.com (31)

Angel, Myron, American Spirit Graphics Corp, Minneapolis, MN. Tel: (612) 623-3333, FAX: (612) 623-9314, E-Mail: asgc@asgc.com, Web Site: www.asgc.com (27)

Angelakis, Michael J., Comcast Corp, Philadelphia, PA. Tel: (215) 665-1700, Web Site: www.comcast.com (32)

Angelica Image Apparel, Saint Louis, MO. Tel: (314) 854-3800, (800) 235-8410, Web Site: www.angelica.com (16)

Angelillo, Tom K., Southern Progress Corp, Birmingham, AL. Tel: (205) 877-6000, FAX: (205) 877-6283, Web Site: www.southernprogress.com (17)

Angell, Marsha, New England Journal of Medicine, Waltham, MA. Tel: (781) 893-3800, FAX: (781) 893-7729, Web Site: www.nejm.org (17)

Angelsom, Mark A., Veriad, Brea, CA. Tel: (714) 990-2700, (800) 962-0658, FAX: (800) 962-0658, E-Mail: info@veriad.com, Web Site: www.veriad.com (16)

Angler's Catalog Co, Eagle, ID. Tel: (208) 378-9536, (800) 657-8040, FAX: (208) 735-8758, E-Mail: sales@anglers-catalog.com, Web Site: www.anglers-catalog.com (11)

The Angler's Den, Pawling, NY. Tel: (845) 855-5182, E-Mail: flyfish@anglersden.net, Web Site: www.anglersden.net (11)

Anglicans United & Latimer Press, Cedar Hill, TX. Tel: (972) 293-7443, (800) 553-3645, FAX: (972) 293-7559, E-Mail: anglicansunited@sbcglobal.net, Web Site: www.anglicansunited.com, www.latimerpress.com (1)

Angood, Peter, American College of Physician Executives, Tampa, FL. Tel: (813) 287-2000, (800) 562-8088, FAX: (813) 287-8993, E-Mail: acpe@acpe.org, Web Site: www.acpe.org (1)

Angrisani, Albert A., Harris Interactive, Rochester, NY. Tel: (585) 272-8400, (800) 866-7655, FAX: (585) 272-8680, E-Mail: info@harrisinteractive.com, Web Site: www.harrisinteractive.com (30)

Angstadt, Edward, ActiveCampaign Inc, Chicago, IL. Tel: (800) 357-0402, E-Mail: help@activecampaign.com, Web Site: www.activecampaign.com (24)

Angstrom Graphics, Cleveland, OH. Tel: (216) 271-5300, FAX: (216) 271-7650, E-Mail: wayne.angstrom@st-ives-usa.com, Web Site: www.angstromgraphics.com (27)

Angstrom, Wayne, Angstrom Graphics, Cleveland, OH. Tel: (216) 271-5300, FAX: (216) 271-7650, E-Mail: wayne.angstrom@st-ives-usa.com, Web Site: www.angstromgraphics.com (27)

Angus, Mark A, Tandy Leather Co, Fort Worth, TX. Tel: (817) 872-3200, FAX: (817) 496-7859, E-Mail: tlfhelp@tandyleather.com, Web Site: www.tandyleatherfactory.com (11)

Anheuser-Busch Inc Promotional Products Group, Shelton, CT. Tel: (800) 742-5283, Web Site: www.budshop.com (6)

Animal Fund, San Francisco, CA. Tel: (415) 775-4636, E-Mail: delphinus@aol.com, Web Site: www.animalfund.org (38)

Animal Health Express, Inc, Tucson, AZ. Tel: (520) 888-0294, (800) 533-8115, FAX: (520) 888-0297, (800) 437-9898, E-Mail: info@animalhealthexpress.com, Web Site: www.animalhealthexpress.com (5)

The Animal Medical Center, New York, NY. Tel: (212) 838-8100, FAX: (212) 832-9630, Web Site: www.amcny.org (16)

Animals Animals/Earth Scenes, Chatham, NY. Tel: (518) 392-5500, (800) 392-5503, FAX: (518) 392-5550, E-Mail: info@animalsanimals.com, Web Site: www.animalsanimals.com (38)

Ann Inc, New York, NY. Tel: (212) 541-3300, (800) 342-5266, FAX: (866) 232-9266, Web Site: www.anninc.com (2)

Anne Klein, New York, NY. Web Site: www.anneklein.com (16)

Annie's Attic LLC, Big Sandy, TX. Tel: (903) 636-4303, (800) 282-6643, FAX: (903) 636-4088, Web Site: www.anniesattic.com (11)

Annunzio, Susan Lucia, University of Chicago GSB, Chicago, IL. Tel: (312) 464-8733, E-Mail: exec.ed@chicagobooth.edu, Web Site: www.chicagobooth.edu (1)

Anritsu Co, Morgan Hill, CA. Tel: (408) 778-2000, (800) 267-4878, FAX: (408) 776-1744, Web Site: www.us.anritsu.com (16)

Ansafone Communications, Santa Ana, CA. Tel: (714) 560-1000, FAX: (714) 560-1035, Web Site: www.ansafone.com (29)

Ansar Inc, Thompsons Station, TN. Tel: (615) 368-2025, Web Site: www.ansarinc.com (1)

Anschutz, Philip F., Los Angeles Kings, Los Angeles, CA. Tel: (213) 742-7100, (888) KINGS-LA, FAX: (213) 742-7296, Web Site: kings.nhl.com (16)

AnSer Services, Green Bay, WI. Tel: (920) 490-7000, (800) 723-0000, E-Mail: allanf@anser.com, Web Site: www.anser.com (29)

Ansira, Saint Louis, MO. Tel: (314) 783-2300, FAX: (314) 783-2301, E-Mail: dl-newbusiness@ansira.com, Web Site: ansira.com (35)

Anstrand, Susan, Names in the News, Oakland, CA. Tel: (415) 989-3350, FAX: (415) 433-7796, E-Mail: susananstrand@nincal.com, Web Site: www.nincal.com (23)

Answer America, Saint Paul, MN. Tel: (800) 258-2669, FAX: (651) 644-8295, E-Mail: sales@answeramerica.com, Web Site: www.answeramerica.com (29)

Answering 365, Los Angeles, CA. Tel: (310) 854-4411, (800) 800-4441, FAX: (310) 854-0551, Web Site: www.concordecommunications.com (29)

AnswerNet Network, Willow Grove, PA. Tel: (800) 411-5777, FAX: (215) 659-6486, Web Site: www.answernetnetwork.com (29)

Answerthink, Miami, FL. Tel: (305) 375-8005, (866) 844-6514, FAX: (305) 379-8810, Web Site: www.answerthink.com (35)

Anthem Blue Cross, Westlake Village, CA. Tel: (805) 557-6655, (800) 333-0912, FAX: (800) 557-6872, Web Site: www.bluecrossca.com (15)

Anthem Blue Cross Blue Shield, Saint Louis, MO. Tel: (314) 923-4444, (888) 877-9125, FAX: (314) 923-5151, E-Mail: moreinfo@bcbsmo.com, Web Site: www.bcbsmo.com (15)

Anthem Blue Cross Blue Shield, North Haven, CT. Tel: (203) 239-8381, (800) 545-0948, FAX: (203) 985-7918, Web Site: www.anthem.com (15)

Anthem Corporate Communications, Indianapolis, IN. Tel: (207) 822-7000, FAX: (207) 822-7741, Web Site: www.anthem.com (15)

Anthem Inc, Indianapolis, IN. Tel: (317) 488-6000, Web Site: www.antheminc.com (7)

Anthem Marketing, Chicago, IL. Tel: (312) 441-0382 (22)

Anthony, John, Cosco Industries Inc, Chicago, IL. Tel: (708) 867-5800, (800) 323-0253, FAX: (800) 323-0275 (16)

Anthony, Michael F., Things Remembered, Highland Heights, OH. Tel: (440) 473-2000, (866) 902-4438, FAX: (440) 473-2018, E-Mail: customerservice@thingsremembered.com, Web Site: www.thingsremembered.com (6)

Anthro Photo File, Cambridge, MA. Tel: (617) 497-7227, FAX: (617) 484-6428, Web Site: www.anthrophoto.com (38)

Anti-Defamation League, New York, NY. Tel: (212) 885-7700, Web Site: www.adl.org (1)

Antik, Kandal, DB Consulting, Harrison, NY. Tel: (914) 698-2008, E-Mail: darcybev@yahoo.com (20)

Antinetto, Anthony, Tucker Printers, Henrietta, NY. Tel: (585) 359-3030, Web Site: www.tuckerprinters.com (27)

Antiquarian Booksellers Association of America Inc, New York, NY. Tel: (212) 944-8291, FAX: (212) 944-8293, E-Mail: sbenne@abaa.org, Web Site: www.abaa.org (1)

Antique & Collectible Tools Inc, Pownal, ME. Tel: (207) 688-4962, FAX: (207) 688-4831, E-Mail: ceb@finetoolj.com, Web Site: www.finetoolj.com (11)

Antique Electronic Supply, Tempe, AZ. Tel: (480) 820-5411, (800) 706-6789, FAX: (480) 820-4643, E-Mail: info@tubesandmore.com, Web Site: www.tubesandmore.com (3)

Antique Rose Emporium, Brenham, TX. Tel: (979) 836-9051, (800) 441-0002, FAX: (979) 836-0928, E-Mail: roses@weareroses.com, Web Site: antiqueroseemporium .com (8)

Antman, Dan, Warren, Gorham & Lamont Inc, New York, NY. Tel: (617) 423-2020, Web Site: ria.thomsonreuters.com (17)

Antman, Mark, The Image Works Inc, Woodstock, NY. Tel: (845) 679-8500, (800) 475-8801, FAX: (845) 679-0606, E-Mail: info@theimageworks.com, Web Site: www.theimageworks.com (38)

Anton, Frank, Hanley Wood LLC, Washington, DC. Tel: (202) 452-0800, FAX: (202) 785-1974, Web Site: www.hanleywood.com (16)

Antonacchio, Sally, The Artists Co, New York, NY. Tel: (212) 679-7199, Web Site: blog. theartistscompany.com (32)

Antoniuk, David J., Champion, Quincy, IL. Tel: (217) 222-5400, FAX: (217) 228-8260, Web Site: www. championpneumatic.com (16)

Antunez, Caroline, MxEnergy Inc, Stamford, CT. Tel: (203) 356-1318, Web Site: www.mxenergy.com (16)

Anything Goes, Allenhurst, NJ. Tel: (732) 531-8040, Web Site: www.heavenlytreasures.com (6)

AOL Corp, New York, NY. Tel: (212) 206-4400, Web Site: www.aol.com (32)

Aon's Affinity Insurance Services Inc, Hatboro, PA. Tel: (215) 773-4600, Web Site: www.aon.com (15)

Apatoff, Robert S., FTD Companies Inc, Downers Grove, IL. Tel: (630) 719-7800, Web Site: www. ftdcompanies.com (16)

Apollo Technologies Inc, Smyrna, GA. Tel: (770) 433-0210, (800) 533-3548, FAX: (770) 433-0132, E-Mail: customerservice@apolloind.com, Web Site: www.apolloind.com (34)

Aponte Jr, Hiram, Hi-C Production, New Hyde Park, NY. Tel: (516) 746-2142, FAX: (516) 294-1964, E-Mail: haponte435@aol.com (27)

Apostolou, Theana, American Movie Classics Holding Corp, Jericho, NY. Tel: (516) 803-3000, FAX: (516) 803-3003, Web Site: www.amctv.com (16)

Apothecary Products Inc, Burnsville, MN. Tel: (952) 890-1940, (800) 328-2742, FAX: (800) 328-1584, E-Mail: info@apothecaryproducts.com, Web Site: www.apothecaryproducts.com (7)

Appalachian Mountain Club, Boston, MA. Tel: (617) 523-0655, FAX: (617) 523-0722, Web Site: www. outdoors.com (1)

AppaLight, Spencer, WV. Tel: (304) 927-2978, E-Mail: wyro@appalight.com, Web Site: www.appalight. com (38)

Appel, Andrew M., Information Resources Inc, Chicago, IL. Tel: (312) 726-1221, FAX: (312(726-8214, Web Site: www.infores.com (30)

Appel, Marsha, American Association of Advertising Agencies, New York, NY. Tel: (212) 682-2500, FAX: (212) 682-8391, Web Site: www.aaaa.org (40)

Appelbaum, Alan, Market Probe International Inc, New York, NY. Tel: (212) 725-7676, FAX: (212) 725-7529, E-Mail: info@marketprobeint.com, Web Site: www.marketprobeint.com (30)

Appelbaum, Bob, Cadie Products Corp, Paterson, NJ. Tel: (973) 278-8300, FAX: (973) 278-0303, E-Mail: emeyers@cadie.com, Web Site: www. cadieproducts.com (16)

Appelbaum, Wendy, Boelter + Lincoln Marketing Communications, Milwaukee, WI. Tel: (414) 271-0101, FAX: (414) 271-1436, E-Mail: jbrzeski@ boelterlincoln.com, Web Site: boelterlincoln.com (35)

Appell, Louis J., Pfaltzgraff Co, York, PA. Tel: (800) 999-2811, FAX: (800) 757-6872, E-Mail: service@ pfaltzgraff.com, Web Site: www.pfaltzgraff.com (8)

Apperson Inc, Cerritos, CA. Tel: (562) 356-3333, (800) 877-2341, FAX: (562) 356-3310, E-Mail: sales@ appersonprint.com, Web Site: www.appersonprint. com (27)

Apperson, R.P., Apperson Inc, Cerritos, CA. Tel: (562) 356-3333, (800) 877-2341, FAX: (562) 356-3310, E-Mail: sales@appersonprint.com, Web Site: www. appersonprint.com (27)

Apple Inc, Cupertino, CA. Tel: (408) 996-1010, FAX: (408) 996-0275, Web Site: www.apple.com (16)

Appleton Coated LLC, Combined Locks, WI. Tel: (920) 788-3550, FAX: (920) 687-3420, Web Site: www. appletoncoated.com (25)

Appleton, Stefanie, Oklahoma Dept of Commerce, Oklahoma City, OK. Tel: (405) 815-6552, (800) 879-6552, FAX: (405) 815-5344, Web Site: www. okcommerce.com (1)

Applications Development Corp, Dekalb, IL. Tel: (815) 754-7432, Web Site: www.appdevcorp.com (20)

Applied Info Group, Kenilworth, NJ. Tel: (908) 241-7007, FAX: (9080 241-7088, Web Site: www. appliedinfogroup.com (22)

Applied Printing Technologies, Moonachie, NJ. Tel: (201) 896-6600, (888) 282-4141, FAX: (201) 896-6839, E-Mail: vpsales@appliedprinting.com, Web Site: www.appliedprinting.com (27)

Appraisal Institute, Chicago, IL. Tel: (312) 335-4100, (888) 756-4624, FAX: (312) 335-4400, E-Mail: aiservice@appraisalinstitute.org, Web Site: www. appraisalinstitute.org (1)

Apprendi, Joe, Collective - The Audience Engine, New York, NY. Tel: (646) 722-8550, FAX: (646) 442-6529, Web Site: www.collective.com (22)

Aptara, Inc, Falls Church, VA. Tel: (703) 352-0001, FAX: (703) 352-8862, E-Mail: info@aptaracorp. com, Web Site: www.aptaracorp.com (27)

Aptimus, San Francisco, CA. Tel: (415) 896-2123, FAX: (415) 896-2561 (22)

Aquino, Anthony, Spectra Products LLC, Johnson City, NY. Tel: (607) 770-1985, FAX: (607) 798-7771, E-Mail: info@spectraproducts.com, Web Site: www.spectraproducts.com (31)

Aradi, Theresa, Commemorative Brands Inc, Austin, TX. Tel: (512) 444-0571, FAX: (512) 444-0065 (16)

Aradius Group, Omaha, NE. Tel: (402) 734-4400, (800) 369-0033, FAX: (402) 734-7492, E-Mail: info@ aradiusgroup.com, Web Site: www.aradiusgroup. com (21)

Aragon, Marilyn, Jeppesen, Englewood, CO. Tel: (303) 799-9090, (800) 353-2107, Web Site: www. jeppesen.com (22)

Aramark Uniform Services, Burbank, CA. Tel: (800) 272-6275, Web Site: www.aramark-uniform.com (2)

Arandell Corp, Menomonee Falls, WI. Tel: (262) 255-4400, (800) 558-8724, FAX: (262) 253-3162, E-Mail: jft@arandell.com, Web Site: www.arandell. com (27)

Arbill Safety Products, Philadelphia, PA. Tel: (215) 632-2000, (800) 523-5367, FAX: (800) 426-5808, E-Mail: orders@arbill.com, Web Site: www.arbill. com (19)

Arbor Capital 1, Omaha, NE. Tel: (402) 991-4962 (14)

Arbor Commercial Mortgage, Uniondale, NY. Tel: (516) 229-6615, Web Site: www.thearbornet.com (14)

Arbor Day Foundation, Nebraska City, NE. Tel: (402) 474-5655, (888) 448-7337, Web Site: www. arborday.org (1)

Arbus Capital Ltd, Schaumburg, IL. Tel: (847) 290-9600, FAX: (847) 290-9601 (16)

Arcade Marketing, Inc, Chattanooga, TN. Tel: (423) 624-3301, FAX: (423) 622-4635, E-Mail: resumes@ arcadeinc.com (27)

Arce, Carlos, NuStats Inc, Austin, TX. Tel: (512) 306-9065, (800) 44-STATS, FAX: (512) 306-9065, Web Site: www.nustats.com (30)

Arce, Maria, Battery Pros Inc, Horseshoe Beach, FL. Tel: (352) 498-2662, (800) 451-7171, FAX: (352) 498-2482, E-Mail: sales@probattery.com, Web Site: www.probattery.com (9)

ArcelorMittal, Chicago, IL. Tel: (312) 899-3440, FAX: (312) 899-3504, Web Site: www.mittalsteel.com (16)

ArcelorMittal, Coatesville, PA. Tel: (610) 383-2000, FAX: (610) 383-5036, Web Site: www. arcelormittal.com (16)

Arch Telecom Inc, Austin, TX. Tel: (512) 492-0735, (800) 890-7575, FAX: (512) 495-7101, Web Site: www.archtelecom.com (16)

Arch, John, Father Flanagan's Boy's Home, Boys Town, NE. Tel: (402) 498-1111, FAX: (402) 498-1969, Web Site: www.boystown.org (1)

Archaeology Magazine, Long Island City, NY. Tel: (718) 472-3050, FAX: (718) 472-3051, E-Mail: production@archaeology.org, Web Site: www. archaeology.org (17)

Archer Malmo Inc, Memphis, TN. Tel: (901) 523-2000, FAX: (901) 524-5578, Web Site: www. archermalmo.com (35)

ARCHES Technology, Hoboken, NJ. Tel: (973) 882-0900, E-Mail: info@archestechnology.com, Web Site: www.archestechnology.com (35)

Archway Marketing Services, Rogers, MN. Tel: (763) 428-3300, (866) 779-9855 X1933, FAX: (763) 488-6803, E-Mail: info@archway.com, Web Site: www. archway.com (28)

Arctic Trading Co Inc, Churchill, MB Canada. Tel: (204) 675-8804, (800) 665-0431, FAX: (204) 675-2164, E-Mail: atcpenny@mts.net, Web Site: www. arctictradingco.com (6)

Elizabeth Arden Spas LLC, Stamford, CT. Tel: (203) 905-1700, FAX: (203) 905-1716, Web Site: www. reddoorspas.com (19)

Arden, Allison, Advertising Age, New York, NY. Tel: (212) 210-0100, FAX: (212) 210-0111, Web Site: www.crain.com (43)

Arden, Patricia, Physicians Planning Association Services, Deerfield Beach, FL. Tel: (954) 571-1877, (800) 221-2168, FAX: (954) 571-8582, E-Mail: insurance@assnservices.com, Web Site: www. physiciansplanning.com (16)

Ardoff, Chad, Crest Healthcare Supply, Dassel, MN. Tel: (800) 328-8908, (800) 369-9207, Web Site: www.cresthealthcare.com (16)

Arends, Batavia, IL. Tel: (630) 990-0220, FAX: (630) 990-2556, Web Site: www.arends-inc.com (35)

Arends, John, Arends, Batavia, IL. Tel: (630) 990-0220, FAX: (630) 990-2556, Web Site: www.arends-inc. com (35)

Arent Fox LLP, Washington, DC. Tel: (202) 715-8582, Web Site: www.arentfox.com (9)

Argent Trading LLC, New York, NY. Tel: (212) 697-8800, FAX: (212) 697-8606, Web Site: www. Argenttrading.com (16)

Argentine, Jan, Cold Spring Harbor Lab Press, Woodbury, NY. Tel: (516) 422-4100, (800) 843-4388, FAX: (516) 422-4097. E-Mail: cshpress@cshl.edu. Web Site: www.cshlpress.com (17)

Argentine, Peter, Nestle USA, Glendale, CA. Tel: (818) 549-6000, (800) 225-2270, FAX: (818) 553-3547, Web Site: www.nestleusa.com (4)

Arguilla, Richard, Roto-Rooter Services Co, Cincinnati, OH. Tel: (513) 762-6690, FAX: (513) 762-6590, Web Site: www.rotorooter.com (16)

Argyropoulos, Antoinette, Golden Fleece Designs Inc, Burbank, CA. Tel: (818) 848-7724. FAX: (818) 566-7100, Web Site: www.mandonia.com (16)

Argyropoulos, Maria, Golden Fleece Designs Inc, Burbank, CA. Tel: (818) 848-7724, FAX: (818) 566-7100, Web Site: www.mandonia.com (16)

Argyropoulos, Symeon D., Golden Fleece Designs Inc, Burbank, CA. Tel: (818) 848-7724, FAX: (818) 566-7100, Web Site: www.mandonia.com (16)

Ariagno, William G., Direct One Inc, Winter Park, FL. Tel: (407) 673-4500, FAX: (407) 673-4501, E-Mail: wariagno@directoneinc.com, Web Site: www.directoneinc.com (28)

Ariago Design and Communications, Campbell, CA. Tel: (408) 668-0400, FAX: (408) 688-0401, E-Mail: ddahart@ariago.com, Web Site: www.ariago.com (35)

Arich Corp, New York, NY. Tel: (212) 247-1800, FAX: (212) 247-2231, Web Site: www.arichinc.com (20)

Arison, Micky, Carnival Cruise Lines, Miami, FL. Tel: (212) 599-2600, Web Site: www.carnival.com (19)

Aristokraft Inc, Jasper, IN. Tel: (812) 482-2527, FAX: (812) 482-9872, Web Site: www.aristokraft.com (16)

The Arizona Direct Marketing Association, Scottsdale, AZ. Tel: (480) 970-8643, FAX: (480) 893-1157, E-Mail: julie@brownies.com, Web Site: www.azdma.org (40)

Arizona Highways Magazine, Phoenix, AZ. Tel: (602) 712-2200, FAX: (602) 254-4505, E-Mail: editor@arizonahighways.com, Web Site: www.arizonahighways.com (17)

The Arizona Republic, Phoenix, AZ. Tel: (602) 444-8000, Web Site: www.azcentral.com (17)

Arkema, Robert, Johnson & Quin Inc, Niles, IL. Tel: (847) 588-4800, FAX: (847) 647-6949, E-Mail: jqinfo@j-quin.com, Web Site: www.j-quin.com (28)

Arkin, Julie, Coastal Living, Birmingham, AL. Tel: (205) 445-6000, FAX: (205) 445-7263, E-Mail: coastalliving@customersvc.com, Web Site: www.coastalliving.com (43)

Arlen Communications Inc, Bethesda, MD. Tel: (301) 656-7940, E-Mail: info@arlencom.com, Web Site: www.arlencom.com (20)

Arlen, Gary, Arlen Communications Inc, Bethesda, MD. Tel: (301) 656-7940, E-Mail: info@arlencom.com, Web Site: www.arlencom.com (20)

Arlen, John, Thetford Corp, Ann Arbor, MI. Tel: (734) 769-6000, (800) 543-1219, FAX: (734) 769-2023, Web Site: www.thetford.com (16)

Arleth, John, Artful Dragon Press Inc, Minnetonka, MN. Tel: (612) 221-8908, Web Site: www.artfuldragon.com (22)

Armata, Kevin, Windsor House, Windsor Locks, CT. Tel: (860) 627-5927, FAX: (860) 627-0252, E-Mail: ahalley@windsormarketing.com, Web Site: windsormarketing.com (20)

Armault, Bernard, Christian Dior Perfumes, New York, NY. Tel: (877) 903-4671, (800) 929-3467, FAX: (212) 931-2954, Web Site: www.dior.com (7)

Armbrust Paper Tubes Inc, Chicago, IL. Tel: (773) 586-3232, FAX: (773) 586-8997, E-Mail: tubesrus@corecomm.net, Web Site: www.tubesrus.com (10)

Armbrust, Bernerd, Armbrust Paper Tubes Inc, Chicago, IL. Tel: (773) 586-3232, FAX: (773) 586-8997, E-Mail: tubesrus@corecomm.net, Web Site: www.tubesrus.com (10)

Armbrust, Chris, Armbrust Paper Tubes Inc, Chicago, IL. Tel: (773) 586-3232, FAX: (773) 586-8997, E-Mail: tubesrus@corecomm.net, Web Site: www.tubesrus.com (10)

Armbrust, Marc, Armbrust Paper Tubes Inc, Chicago, IL. Tel: (773) 586-3232, FAX: (773) 586-8997, E-Mail: tubesrus@corecomm.net, Web Site: www.tubesrus.com (10)

Armento Inc, Buffalo, NY. Tel: (716) 875-2423, (866) 276-3686, FAX: (716) 875-8011, E-Mail: info@armento.com, Web Site: www.armento-columbarium.com (5)

Armes, Roy V., Cooper Tire & Rubber Co Inc, Findlay, OH. Tel: (419) 423-1321, (800) 537-9523, FAX: (419) 424-4212, E-Mail: cooperinfo@coopertire.com, Web Site: www.coopertire.com (16)

Armijo, Micah, Creel Printing of California, Costa Mesa, CA. Tel: (714) 540-7005, FAX: (714) 979-1496, Web Site: www.creelprint.com (27)

Armstrong, Darryl, Interex, Amesbury, MA. Tel: (978) 388-8755, (800) INTEREX, FAX: (978) 388-8747, Web Site: www.interexexhibits.com (17)

Armstrong, Durrell, Player Piano Co Inc, Wichita, KS. Tel: (316) 263-3241, FAX: (316) 263-5480, Web Site: www.playerpianocompany.com (11)

Armstrong, John, USX, Pittsburgh, PA. Tel: (412) 433-1121, E-Mail: webmaster@usx.com, Web Site: www.usx.com (16)

Armstrong, Linda, DMW Worldwide LLC, Chesterbrook, PA. Tel: (610) 407-0407, (877) 744-3699, FAX: (610) 407-9201, E-Mail: info@dmwdirect.com, Web Site: www.dmwdirect.com (35)

Armstrong, Steve, MSC Industrial Supply Co, Melville, NY. Tel: (516) 812-2000, (800) 645-7270, FAX: (800) 255-5067, E-Mail: executive@mscdirect.com, Web Site: www.mscdirect.com (9)

Armstrong, Tim, AOL Corp, New York, NY. Tel: (212) 206-4400, Web Site: www.aol.com (32)

Army Times Publishing Co, Springfield, VA. Tel: (703) 750-9000, (800) 336-4590, FAX: (703) 750-8129, E-Mail: cust-svc@atpco.com, Web Site: www.armytimes.com (17)

Arnaud's, New Orleans, LA. Tel: (504) 523-0611, (866) 230-8895, FAX: (504) 581-7908, Web Site: www.arnauds.com (16)

Arnet Pharmaceutical, Davie, FL. Tel: (954) 236-9053, (800) 968-6673, FAX: (954) 370-2508, E-Mail: arnet@arnetusa.com, Web Site: www.arnetusa.com (7)

Arnett, Gail R., Zig Ziglar Corp, Plano, TX. Tel: (972) 233-9191, (800) 527-0306, FAX: (469) 321-7556, E-Mail: info@ziglar.com, Web Site: www.zigziglar.com (16)

Arnett, Mark F., New Track Media LLC, Cincinnati, OH. Tel: (513) 421-6500, FAX: (513) 421-1244, E-Mail: lriggs@newtrackmedia.com, Web Site: www.newtrackmedia.com (17)

Arnold Worldwide Boston, Boston, MA. Tel: (617) 587-8000, FAX: (617) 587-8004, Web Site: www.arn.com (35)

Arnold Worldwide Toronto, Toronto, ON Canada. Tel: (416) 355-5009, E-Mail: bsharp@arnoldworldwide.ca, Web Site: arn.com (35)

Arnold, Bill, EMED Co Inc, Buffalo, NY. Tel: (716) 626-1616, (800) 442-3633, FAX: (716) 626-1630, E-Mail: customerservice@emedco.com, Web Site: www.emedco.com (16)

Arnold, Carol Christopher, ListAbility Inc, Venice, FL. Tel: (866) 446-2055, E-Mail: info@listability.com, Web Site: www.listability.com (23)

Arnold, Craig, Eaton Corp, Raleigh, NC. Tel: (216) 523-4400, (800) 356-5794, FAX: (216) 523-4787, Web Site: www.eaton.com (16)

Arnold, Dorothy, Universal Tea Co Inc, Tigard, OR. Tel: (503) 684-4482, (800) 547-1514, FAX: (503) 684-4424, E-Mail: stash@stashtea.com, Web Site: www.stashtea.com (4)

Arnold, Martha G., International Manufacturing Co, Whitesburg, GA. Tel: (770) 834-2094, FAX: (770) 834-2096, E-Mail: textilenterprise@aol.net (8)

Arnold, Mary, ChildFund International, Richmond, VA. Tel: (804) 756-2700, Web Site: www.ChildFund.org (1)

Arnold, Mary, ChildFund International, Richmond, VA. Tel: (804) 756-2700, (800) 776-6767, FAX: (804) 756-2718, Web Site: www.christianchildrensfund.org (1)

Arnold, Michael, General Nutrition Corp, Pittsburgh, PA. Tel: (412) 288-4600, (877) 462-4700, FAX: (412) 402-7218, Web Site: www.gnc.com (7)

Arnold, Travis, Feed the Children, Oklahoma City, OK. Tel: (800) 627-4556, Web Site: www.feedthechildren.org (1)

Arnowitz, Dan, LOG-ON, New York, NY. Tel: (212) 279-4567, E-Mail: sales@log-on.org, Web Site: www.log-on.org (21)

Arnsdorff, Ashley, Atlantic Publication Group LLC, Charleston, SC. Tel: (843) 747-0025, FAX: (843) 744-0816, E-Mail: info@atlanticpublicationgrp.com, Web Site: www.atlanticpublicationgrp.com (17)

Aronson, Risa, The New Yorker Magazine, New York, NY. Tel: (212) 286-2860, FAX: (212) 286-4168, Web Site: www.newyorker.com (17)

Arora, Arun, Sears Home Improvement Products & Services, Hoffman Estates, IL. Tel: (800) 424-2047, Web Site: www.searshomeservices.com (16)

Arquest Inc, Millstone Twp, NJ. Tel: (609) 395-9500, (888) 270-8378, (888) ARQUEST, FAX: (609) 395-9778, Web Site: www.arquest.com (16)

Array Marketing Group Inc, Toronto, ON Canada. Tel: (416) 299-4865, FAX: (416) 292-9759, E-Mail: inquiry@arraymarketing.com, Web Site: arraymarketing.com (35)

ARRCO Medical Advertising, Walpole, MA. Tel: (508) 404-1105, FAX: (508) 404-1106, E-Mail: info@arrco.com, Web Site: www.arrco.com (35)

Arredia, Phil, BrownCor International, Milwaukee, WI. Tel: (800) 327-2278, Web Site: www.bcadvantage.com (5)

Arrigo, Paul J., Baton Rouge Conventions & Visitors Bureau, Baton Rouge, LA. Tel: (225) 383-1825, (800) LA-ROUGE, FAX: (225) 346-1253, E-Mail: karron@visitbatonrouge.com, Web Site: www.bracvb.com (1)

Arrington, Don, Aircraft Spruce & Specialty Co, Corona, CA. Tel: (909) 372-9555, (877) 4-Spruce, FAX: (909) 372-0555, E-Mail: info@aircraft-spruce.com, Web Site: www.aircraft-spruce.com (12)

Arriola, Dennis, Southern California Gas Co, Anaheim, CA. Tel: (714) 634-3054, (877) 238-0092, FAX: (714) 937-7712, E-Mail: Tjavid@socalgas.com, Web Site: www.socalgas.com (1)

Arrow Co, Indianapolis, IN. Tel: (317) 692-6666, FAX: (317) 692-6769, Web Site: www.aearo.com (16)

Arrow Companies, LLC, Delavan, WI. Tel: (262) 724-8822, FAX: (262) 724-8824, Web Site: www.arrowcompanies.com (22)

Arrow Electronics Inc, Englewood, CO. Tel: (952) 828-5350, (800) 833-3557, FAX: (952) 828-5399, Web Site: www.arrow.com (3)

Arrow Mailing Services II Inc, Hawthorne, CA. Tel: (310) 219-7740, FAX: (310) 219-3335 (28)

Arrowhead Mountain Spring Water, Wilkes Barre, PA. Tel: (800) 873-7775, Web Site: www.arrowheadwater.com (16)

Arrowhead Promotion & Fulfillment, Grand Rapids, MN. Tel: (218) 327-1165, FAX: (218) 327-2576, Web Site: www.apfco.com (29)

ArrowMail Canada, Windsor, ON Canada. Tel: (313) 961-8334, FAX: (313) 961-7849, E-Mail: info@mailingcanada.com, Web Site: www.mailingcanada.com (28)

Arsenault, Lisa, McArdle Printing Co Inc, Upper Marlboro, MD. Tel: (301) 390-8500, FAX: (301) 390-8052, Web Site: www.mcardleprinting.com (27)

Arseneau, Marc, Revana Inc, Tempe, AZ. Tel: (408) 902-5900, (800) 535-0343, Web Site: www.revana.com (35)

Arslan, Jim, RPM Direct LLC, Lambertville, NJ. Tel: (609) 566-7150, FAX: (609) 566-7155, E-Mail: jimarslan@rpmdirectllc.com, Web Site: www.rpmdirectllc.com (35)

Art.com, Emeryville, CA. Tel: (510) 879-4700, (800) 952-5592, FAX: (510) 588-3915, E-Mail: support@art.com, Web Site: www.art.com (8)

Art Instruction Schools, Minneapolis, MN. Tel: (612) 362-5075, (800) 801-6940, FAX: (612) 362-5260, Web Site: www.artinstructionschools.edu (13)

Art News Magazine, New York, NY. Tel: (212) 398-1690, FAX: (212) 819-0394, E-Mail: info@artnews.com, Web Site: www.artnews.com (17)

The Art of Self Promotion, Hoboken, NJ. Tel: (201) 653-0783, FAX: (201) 222-2494, E-Mail: ilise@marketing-mentor.com, Web Site: www.artofselfpromotion.com (17)

Art Resource Inc, New York, NY. Tel: (212) 505-8700, FAX: (212) 505-2053, E-Mail: requests@artres.com, Web Site: www.artres.com (38)

Artech House, Norwood, MA. Tel: (781) 769-9750, FAX: (781) 769-6334, E-Mail: artech@artechhouse.com, Web Site: www.artechhouse.com (17)

Artemis International Solutions Corp, Austin, TX. Tel: (512) 201-8222, FAX: (512) 874-8900, Web Site: www.aisc.com (22)

Artful Dragon Press Inc, Minnetonka, MN. Tel: (612) 221-8908, Web Site: www.artfuldragon.com (22)

Artful Home, Tel: (608) 257-2590, (877) 233-4600, FAX: (608) 257-2690, E-Mail: info@artfulhome.com, Web Site: www.artfulhome.com (8)

Arthritis Foundation, Atlanta, GA. Tel: (404) 872-7100, FAX: (404) 872-0457, Web Site: www.arthritis.org (1)

Arthur, Charlie, Atlanta Offset, Atlanta, GA. Tel: (404) 699-6200, FAX: (404) 699-1393, Web Site: www.gannett.com/about/map/offset.htm (27)

The Artists Co, New York, NY. Tel: (212) 679-7199, Web Site: blog.theartistscompany.com (32)

Arum, Herbert R., Stock Drive Products, New Hyde Park, NY. Tel: (516) 328-3300, (800) 819-8900, FAX: (516) 326-8827, E-Mail: sdp-sisupport@sdp-si.com, Web Site: www.sdp.si.com (5)

Arvidson, Andy, Imagine Fulfillment Services, La Mirada, CA. Tel: (310) 217-4610, FAX: (310) 217-9632, E-Mail: andya@imaginefulfillment.com, Web Site: www.imaginefulfillment.com (28)

Aryai, Sean, Global Equipment Co Inc, Port Washington, NY. Tel: (516) 484-3100, (888) 381-2861, FAX: (516) 608-7111, E-Mail: sales@globalindustrial.com, Web Site: www.globalindustrial.com (9)

Arzbacher, Bob, Enerpac, Menomonee Falls, WI. Tel: (262) 781-6600, (800) 433-2766, FAX: (262) 781-1028, Web Site: www.enerpac.com (16)

AS Kleeman & Associates, Duluth, GA. Tel: (770) 752-0500, FAX: (770) 752-0066 (20)

As We Change, Oshkosh, WI. Tel: (619) 213-2200, (855) 202-7392, (800) 699-6993, FAX: (888) 534-8469, E-Mail: help@aswechange.com, Web Site: www.aswechange.com (7)

Asaro, Michael, Wilson RMS, New York, NY. Tel: (212) 473-6900, Web Site: www.wilsonrms.com (35)

Asciolla, Brittany, ThomasNet RPM, New York, NY. Tel: (844) 851-8715, Web Site: rpm.thomasnet.com (24)

Asciutto Art Representatives Inc, Chandler, AZ. Tel: (480) 814-8010, E-Mail: aartreps@cox.net, Web Site: wwwaartreps.com (36)

Asciutto, Mary Anne, Asciutto Art Representatives Inc, Chandler, AZ. Tel: (480) 814-8010, E-Mail: aartreps@cox.net, Web Site: wwwaartreps.com (36)

Ash, Paul J., Sam Ash Music Direct, Hicksville, NY. Tel: (800) 472-6274, E-Mail: sales@samash.com, Web Site: www.samash.com (5)

Ashburn, Bill, Accellos Inc, Colorado Springs, CO. Tel: (719) 433-7000, Web Site: www.accellos.com (12)

Ashby, Carol, Children's Hospital of Pittsburgh, Pittsburgh, PA. Tel: (412) 692-5325, FAX: (412) 692-7140, Web Site: www.chp.edu (1)

Ashby, Joan, Pango Pango Swimwear Corp, Pompano Beach, FL. Tel: (954) 786-0255, (800) 858-9431, FAX: (954) 786-7745, E-Mail: pango_swimwear@bellsouth.net, Web Site: www.pango-pangoswimwear.com (2)

Ashby, Scott, Web Decisions, Greensboro, NC. Tel: (336) 545-7817 x100 (22)

Ashe, Peter, Premier Packaging Corp, Victor, NY. Tel: (877) 924-8460, FAX: (585) 924-8753, E-Mail: info@premiercustompkg.com, Web Site: www.premiercustompkg.com (16)

Asher, James M., The Hearst Corp, New York, NY. Tel: (212) 649-2000, FAX: (212) 649-2108, Web Site: www.hearst.com/magazines/ (17)

Asher, Paula, C&S Sales Inc, Wheeling, IL. Tel: (847) 541-0710, (800) 292-7711, FAX: (847) 541-9904, E-Mail: sales@cs-sales.com, Web Site: www.cs_sales.com (9)

Asher, S., Baxter Bros Inc, Greenwich, CT. Tel: (203) 637-4559, (866) 280-1924, FAX: (203) 637-4550, E-Mail: info@baxterinvestment.com, Web Site: www.baxterinvestment.com (17)

Asheville Compassionate Communication Center, Asheville, NC. Tel: (828) 252-0538, E-Mail: jerry@ashevilleccc.com, Web Site: ashevilleccc.com (13)

Ashken, Ian G., Jarden Corp, Boca Raton, FL. Tel: (561) 912-4395, Web Site: www.jarden.com (16)

Ashkin, Barbara S, Cablexpress Technologies, Syracuse, NY. Tel: (315) 476-3000, (800) 913-9467, FAX: (315) 455-1800, E-Mail: info@cablexpress.com, Web Site: www.CXTec.com (10)

Ashland Inc, Covington, KY. Tel: (859) 815-3333, Web Site: www.ashland.com (16)

Ashley, David, A&H Lithoprint Inc, Broadview, IL. Tel: (708) 345-1196, FAX: (708) 345-1225, Web Site: www.ahlithoprint.com (27)

Ashley, Judy, Names in the Mail Inc, Dallas, TX. Tel: (972) 681-5701, (800) 688-5701, FAX: (972) 681-5786, E-Mail: nimnames@att.net (23)

Ashley, Richard W., Abbott, Abbott Park, IL. Tel: (224) 667-6100, FAX: (847) 937-9555, Web Site: www.abbott.com (7)

Ashman, Greg, Professional Training Associates Inc, Duquesne, PA. Tel: (412) 460-0266, FAX: (412) 460-0269, E-Mail: info@ptainc.com, Web Site: www.ptainc.com (17)

Ashrae Learning Institute, Atlanta, GA. Tel: (404) 636-8400, (800) 527-4723, FAX: (404) 321-5478, E-Mail: ashrae@ashrae.org, Web Site: www.ashrae.org (31)

Ashway, Nader, Moddern Marketing, New York, NY. Tel: (212) 334-9800, E-Mail: mark@moddern.com, Web Site: www.moddern.com (35)

Ashworth College, Norcross, GA. Tel: (770) 729-8400, (800) 957-5412, FAX: (770) 729-9294, Web Site: www.ashworthcollege.edu (13)

AsiaEXP, Miami, FL. Tel: (305) 675-5969, Web Site: www.asiaexp.com (16)

ASK, Montgomery, AL. Tel: (334) 387-ASKT, FAX: (334) 387-2759, E-Mail: rburley@asktelemarketing.com, Web Site: www.asktelemarketing.com (29)

Aslett, Michael, Real Media Solutions, Wayne, NJ. Tel: (973) 835-7060, Web Site: www.get-realmedia.com (27)

Aspect Softwear, Chelmsford, MA. Tel: (978) 250-7900, FAX: (978) 244-7410, E-Mail: info@aspect.com, Web Site: www.aspect.com (29)

Aspen Imaging International Inc, Cleveland, OH. Tel: (216) 881-5300, (800) 955-5555, FAX: (216) 881-8380, (800) 756-0990 (34)

Aspen Marketing Services, West Chicago, IL. Tel: (800) 848-0212, FAX: (630) 293-7584, Web Site: www.aspenms.com (35)

Aspen Packaging Corp, Cicero, IL. Tel: (708) 652-6444, (800) 367-5493, FAX: (708) 652-6444, E-Mail: sales@aspenpkg.com, Web Site: www.aspenpkg.com (27)

Aspen Publishers Inc, New York, NY. Tel: (212) 771-0600, (800) 638-8437, Web Site: www.aspenpublishers.com (17)

Asset Marketing Services Inc, Burnsville, MN. Tel: (952) 707-7000, Web Site: www.amsi-corp.com (16)

Assinin, Ferdinando L., The Bil-Ray Aluminum Siding Corp of Queens Inc, New Hyde Park, NY. Tel: (516) 616-4200, (800) 474-4415, FAX: (516) 616-4030, Web Site: www.homeclub.com (15)

Associated Bag Co, Milwaukee, WI. Tel: (414) 769-1000, (800) 926-6100, FAX: (800) 926-4610, E-Mail: customerservice@associatedbag.com, Web Site: www.associatedbag.com (10)

Associated Construction Publications, Indianapolis, IN. Tel: (317) 423-7080, FAX: (317) 423-7094, Web Site: www.acppubs.com (17)

Associated Integrated Marketing, Wichita, KS. Tel: (316) 683-4691, E-Mail: info@meetassociated.com, Web Site: www.meetassociated.com (35)

Associated Materials, Cuyahoga Falls, OH. Tel: (330) 922-2182, Web Site: www.alside.com (8)

Associated Photo, Erlanger, KY. Tel: (859) 344-1460, (800) 727-2580, FAX: (859) 282-0032 (16)

Associated Premium Corp, Cincinnati, OH. Tel: (513) 679-4444, FAX: (513) 679-4447, E-Mail: inof@associatedpremium.com, Web Site: www.associatedpremium.com (33)

Associated Textile Rental Services, Rochester, NY. Tel: (585) 454-5988, (800) 639-4624, Web Site: www.associatedtextile.com (16)

Association for Audience Marketing Professionals (AAMP), North Hollywood, CA. Tel: (310) 323-7220, FAX: (310) 323-7231, E-Mail: mjordan@espcomp.com, Web Site: www.wfma.org (40)

Association for Computing Machinery, New York, NY. Tel: (212) 626-0500, (800) 342-6626, FAX: (212) 944-1318, Web Site: www.acm.org (1)

Association for Facilities Engineering, McLean, VA. Tel: (571) 203-7171, FAX: (571) 766-2142, E-Mail: info@afe.org, Web Site: www.afe.org (1)

Association for Financial Professionals, Bethesda, MD. Tel: (301) 907-2862, FAX: (301) 907-2864, Web Site: www.afponline.org (14)

Association for Postal Commerce, Alexandria, VA. Tel: (703) 524-0096, FAX: (703) 524-1871, Web Site: www.postcom.org (40)

Association for Talent Development, Alexandria, VA. Tel: (703) 683-8100, (800) 628-2783, FAX: (703) 683-8103, E-Mail: customercare@td.org (1)

Association of American Publishers, Washington, DC. Tel: (202) 347-3375, FAX: (202) 347-3690, E-Mail: info@publishers.org, Web Site: www.publishers.org (1)

Association of Bridal Consultants, New Milford, CT. Tel: (860) 355-0464, FAX: (860) 354-1404, E-Mail: office@bridalassn.com, Web Site: www.bridalassn.com (1)

Association of Coupon Professionals, Drexel Hill, PA. Tel: (610) 789-1478, FAX: (610) 789-5309, E-Mail: john.morgan@acp-hq.org, Web Site: www.couponpros.org (40)

Association of Energy Engineers, Atlanta, GA. Tel: (770) 447-5083 x210, FAX: (770) 446-3969, E-Mail: info@aeecenter.org, Web Site: www.aeecenter.org (40)

Association of Fundraising Professionals, Arlington, VA. Tel: (703) 684-0410, (800) 666-3863, FAX: (703) 684-0540, Web Site: www.afpnet.org (1)

Association of Marian Helpers, Stockbridge, MA. Tel: (413) 298-3931, (800) 462-7426, Web Site: www.marian.org (1)

Association of Marketing Service Providers, Alexandria, VA. Tel: (703) 836-9200, (800) 333-6272, FAX: (703) 548-8204, E-Mail: mfsa-mail@mfsanet.org, Web Site: www.mfsanet.org (40)

Association of National Advertisers Inc, New York, NY. Tel: (212) 697-5950, FAX: (212) 687-7310, Web Site: www.ana.net (40)

Association of the Miraculous Medal, Perryville, MO. Tel: (573) 547-8343, (800) 264-6279, FAX: (573) 547-1389, E-Mail: amm1@amm.org, Web Site: www.amm.org (1)

Assous, Fabrice, Neopost USA, Milford, CT. Tel: (203) 301-3400, Web Site: www.neopostusa.com (34)

Assurant Group, New York, NY. Tel: (305) 253-2244, FAX: (305) 252-6987, Web Site: www.assurant.com (15)

Assurant Health, Milwaukee, WI. Tel: (414) 244-0658, (800) 800-1212, FAX: (414) 224-0472, Web Site: www.assuranthealth.com (15)

Assurant Solutions Preneed Division, Atlanta, GA. Tel: (770) 763-1000, (800) PRE NEED, FAX: (770) 859-4325, Web Site: www.assurantpreneed.com (15)

Astarita, Anthony, Rodale Inc, Emmaus, PA. Tel: (610) 967-5171, FAX: (610) 967-8963, Web Site: www.rodaleinc.com (17)

Astoria Federal Savings, Lake Success, NY. Tel: (516) 327-7000, Web Site: www.astoriafederal.com (14)

Astral Brands LLC, Atlanta, GA. Tel: (678) 303-3088, Web Site: www.astralbrands.com (7)

AstraZeneca, Wilmington, DE. Tel: (302) 866-1482, Web Site: www.astrazeneca-us.com (7)

Astro Air, LP, Jacksonville, TX. Tel: (903) 586-3691, FAX: (903) 589-8094, E-Mail: sales@astroair.com, Web Site: www.astroair.com (9)

Astrologer's Fund Inc, Brooklyn, NY. Tel: (212) 949-7275, FAX: (212) 608-6964, E-Mail: books@afund.com, Web Site: www.afund.com (16)

Astronomical Society of the Pacific, San Francisco, CA. Tel: (415) 337-1100, (800) 335-2624, FAX: (415) 337-5205, E-Mail: service@astrosociety.org, Web Site: www.astrosociety.org (1)

AT&T Inc, San Antonio, TX. Tel: (210) 821-4105, FAX: (210) 351-2071, Web Site: www.bellsouth.com (32)

At Last Naturals, North Salem, NY. Tel: (914) 747-3599, (800) 527-8123, FAX: (914) 747-3791, E-Mail: info@atlastnaturals.com, Web Site: www.atlastnaturals.com (7)

Atadan, David, Trellist Marketing and Technology, Wilmington, DE. Tel: (302) 778-1300, Web Site: www.trellist.com (30)

Atchison, Rebecca Lynn, HomeAway.com Inc, Austin, TX. Tel: (512) 684-1100, (877) 228-3145, Web Site: www.homeaway.com (19)

Atkins, Clint, Tower Hobbies/Hobbico, Champaign, IL. Tel: (217) 398-3636, (800) 637-6050, FAX: (217) 398-1104, Web Site: www.towerhobbies.com (11)

Atkins, Dee, Mercy Home for Boys & Girls, Chicago, IL. Tel: (312) 738-7560, (888) 981-4682, Web Site: www.mercyhome.org (1)

Atkins, Philip, FGI Research Inc, Chapel Hill, NC. Tel: (919) 929-7759, FAX: (919) 932-8829, E-Mail: info@fgiresearch.com, Web Site: www.fgiresearch.com (35)

Atkinson, Jeff, Burden Sales Co, Lincoln, NE. Tel: (402) 474-4055, (800) 488-3407, FAX: (402) 474-5198, Web Site: www.burdensales.com (9)

Atkinson, Jeff, Surplus Center, Lincoln, NE. Tel: (402) 474-4055, (800) 488-3407, FAX: (402) 474-5198, E-Mail: customerservice@surpluscenter.com, Web Site: www.surpluscenter.com (9)

Atkinson, Mesonga, Oomingmak Musk Ox Producers Cooperative, Anchorage, AK. Tel: (907) 272-9225, (888) 360-9665, FAX: (907) 258-4225, E-Mail: oomingmak@qiviut.com, Web Site: www.qiviut.com (6)

Atkinson, Noel J., The Keystone Equities Group, Oaks, PA. Tel: (610) 415-6300, (800) 715-9905, FAX: (610) 415-6328, Web Site: www.keystoneequities.com (20)

Atkinson, Ron, American Society for Quality, Milwaukee, WI. Tel: (414) 272-8575, (800) 248-1946, FAX: (414) 272-1734, E-Mail: help@asq.org, Web Site: www.asq.org (1)

Atkinson, Scott, Red Clay Interactive, Buford, GA. Tel: (770) 297-2430, (866) 251-2800, E-Mail: hello@redclayinteractive.com, Web Site: www.redclayinteractive.com (35)

Atlanta Cutlery Corp, Conyers, GA. Tel: (770) 922-3700, (800) 833-8838, FAX: (770) 760-8993, E-Mail: webmaster@atlantacutlery.com, Web Site: www.atlantacutlery.com (11)

Atlanta Journal & Constitution, Atlanta, GA. Tel: (404) 526-5151, Web Site: www.ajc.com (17)

Atlanta Offset, Atlanta, GA. Tel: (404) 699-6200, FAX: (404) 699-1393, Web Site: www.gannett.com/about/map/offset.htm (27)

AtlantaPrintAndMail.com Inc, Atlanta, GA. Tel: (404) 321-6222, E-Mail: info@mymailingservice.com, Web Site: www.mymailingservice.com (21)

Atlantic-ACM, Boston, MA. Tel: (617) 720-3700, FAX: (617) 720-1077, E-Mail: atlantic@atlantic-acm.com, Web Site: www.atlantic-acm.com (20)

Atlantic Business Products, New York, NY. Tel: (212) 741-6400, FAX: (212) 645-1518, E-Mail: info@tomorrowsoffice.com, Web Site: www.tomorrowsoffice.com (29)

Atlantic List Company Inc, Arlington, VA. Tel: (703) 528-7482, FAX: (703) 528-7492, E-Mail: ingridloukota@atlanticlist.com, Web Site: www.atlanticlist.com (23)

The Atlantic Monthly, Washington, DC. Tel: (202) 266-6000, (800) 234-2411, FAX: (202) 266-6001, Web Site: www.theatlantic.com (17)

Atlantic Publication Group LLC, Charleston, SC. Tel: (843) 747-0025, FAX: (843) 744-0816, E-Mail: info@atlanticpublicationgrp.com, Web Site: www.atlanticpublicationgrp.com (17)

Atlantic Research & Consulting Inc, Boston, MA. Tel: (617) 720-0174, FAX: (617) 589-3731, E-Mail: generalmailbox@guideline.com, Web Site: www.atlanticresearch.net (30)

Atlantic Spice Co, North Truro, MA. Tel: (508) 487-6100, (800) 316-7965, FAX: (508) 487-2550, E-Mail: weborders@atlanticspice.com, Web Site: www.atlanticspice.com (4)

Atmosphere Proximity, New York, NY. Tel: (212) 827-2500, FAX: (212) 827-2525, E-Mail: andreas.combuechen@atmospeherebbdo.com, Web Site: www.atmosphereproximity.com (35)

Atomic Direct LLC, Portland, OR. Tel: (503) 296-6131, FAX: (503) 296-9890, Web Site: www.atomicdirect.com (35)

Attard, Jerry, Guiding Eyes for the Blind, Yorktown Heights, NY. Tel: (914) 245-4042, (800) 942-0149, FAX: (914) 245-1609, Web Site: www.guidingeyes.org (16)

Attayek, John, York Label, York, PA. Tel: (717) 266-9675, FAX: (717) 266-9834, Web Site: www.yorklabel.com (27)

Atten, Jim, Royal Performance Group, Lisle, IL. Tel: (630) 353-7900, (888) 774-0125, FAX: (630) 353-7902, E-Mail: info@rpgglobal.com, Web Site: www.rpggiftcards.com (34)

Atterbury, Rick R, Merrill Corp, Saint Cloud, MN. Tel: (320) 656-5000, FAX: (320) 656-5163 (18)

Attfield, Mary, Stephen Thomas, Toronto, ON Canada. Tel: (416) 690-8801, FAX: (416) 690-7256, E-Mail: mail@stephenthomas.ca, Web Site: www.stephenthomas.ca (1)

Atwood, Nancy, Anchor Computer Inc, Farmingdale, NY. Tel: (631) 293-6100, FAX: (631) 293-0891, Web Site: www.anchorcomputer.com (22)

Auburn University at Montgomery, Montgomery, AL. Tel: (334) 244-3621, (800) 227-2649, FAX: (334) 244-3826, Web Site: www.aum.edu (41)

Auburn, Susan, Chartifacts, Richmond, VA. Tel: (804) 272-7120 (6)

Audience Development, Norwalk, CT. Tel: (203) 854-6730, FAX: (203) 854-6735, E-Mail: inolan@red7media.com, Web Site: www.audiencedevelopment.com (43)

Audience Identification Inc, Lisle, IL. Tel: (630) 435-0460, FAX: (630) 435-0470, E-Mail: rmarsh@audienceid.com (22)

Audience Research & Development, Fort Worth, TX. Tel: (817) 924-6922, FAX: (817) 924-7539, E-Mail: jgumbert@ar-d.com, Web Site: www.ar-d.com (20)

Audio & Video Labs Inc, Pennsauken, NJ. Tel: (856) 663-9030, (800) 468-9353, FAX: (856) 661-3450, E-Mail: info@discmakers.com, Web Site: www.discmakers.com (16)

Audio Classics Ltd, Vestal, NY. Tel: (607) 766-3501, FAX: (607) 766-3502, E-Mail: steve@audioclassics.com, Web Site: www.audioclassics.com (3)

Audio-Digest Foundation, Glendale, CA. Tel: (818) 240-7500, (800) 423-2308, FAX: (818) 240-7379, Web Site: www.audio-digest.org (1)

Audio Editions Books-on-Cassette & CD, Auburn, CA. Tel: (800) 231-4261, FAX: (800) 882-1840, E-Mail: info@audioeditions.com, Web Site: www.audioeditions.com (3)

Audiovox, Hauppauge, NY. Tel: (631) 436-6550, FAX: (631) 273-5939, Web Site: www.voxxintl.com (16)

Auerbach, Carolyn, Kellyco Metal Detector Distributors, Winter Springs, FL. Tel: (407) 699-8700, (800) 327-9697, FAX: (407) 695-6671, E-Mail: customerservice@kellycodetectors.com, Web Site: www.kellycodetectors.com (11)

Auerbach, Karen, Kensington Publishing Corp, New York, NY. Tel: (212) 407-1500, (800) 221-2647, FAX: (212) 407-1590, Web Site: www.kensingtonbooks.com (17)

Auerbach, Robert D, Cooper Surgical Inc, Trumbull, CT. Tel: (203) 601-5202, (800) 243-2974, FAX: (203) 601-1007, E-Mail: orders@coopersurgical.com, Web Site: www.coopersurgical.com (7)

Auerbach, Stuart, Kellyco Metal Detector Distributors, Winter Springs, FL. Tel: (407) 699-8700, (800) 327-9697, FAX: (407) 695-6671, E-Mail: customerservice@kellycodetectors.com, Web Site: www.kellycodetectors.com (11)

Auger, Jarilyn, Lowe Campbell Ewald, Detroit, MI. Tel: (586) 574-3400, E-Mail: lowecampbellewald@lowe-ce.com, Web Site: www.lowecampbellewald.com (35)

Augsburg Fortress Publishers, Minneapolis, MN. Tel: (612) 330-3300, (800) 426-0115, FAX: (612) 330-3455, E-Mail: info@augsburgfortress.org, Web Site: www.augsburgfortress.org (17)

Auguin, Philippe, Washington National Opera, Washington, DC. Tel: (202) 467-4600, (800) 444-1324, Web Site: www.kennedy-center.org/wno (16)

August Home Publishing Co, Des Moines, IA. Tel: (515) 875-7000, FAX: (515) 333-5441, Web Site: www.augusthome.com (17)

August Marketing, Tampa, FL. Tel: (561) 747-1325, (866) 242-4414, E-Mail: sbarret@augustmktg.com, Web Site: www.augustmktg.com (22)

Wendell August Forge Inc, Grove City, PA. Tel: (724) 458-8360, (800) 923-1390, FAX: (724) 458-0906, E-Mail: info@wendell.com, Web Site: www.wendellaugust.com (6)

Augusto, Carl, American Foundation for the Blind Inc, New York, NY. Tel: (212) 502-7600, FAX: (212) 502-7777, E-Mail: afbinfo@afb.org, Web Site: www.afb.org (1)

Augustyn, John, PTI Pyramid Technologies LLC, Meriden, CT. Tel: (203) 238-0550, (888) 479-7264, FAX: (203) 634-1696, Web Site: www.pyramid-technologies.com (10)

Auman, Jeff, Virgin Mobile USA LP, Warren, NJ. Tel: (908) 607-4000, (888) 322-1122, E-Mail: vmugeneral@sprint.com, Web Site: www.virginmobileusa.com (32)

Aumann, Michael, Buhrs Americas Inc, Minneapolis, MN. Tel: (763) 557-9100, FAX: (763) 557-9700, Web Site: www.buhrs.com (34)

Aurand, Layne, No Load Fund Investor, Brentwood, TN. Tel: (800) 706-6364, FAX: (800) 785-9212, E-Mail: NoLoad@mleesmith.com, Web Site: www.noloadfundinvestor.com (14)

Auriemma Consulting Group, New York, NY. Tel: (516) 333-4800, FAX: (516) 333-4815, E-Mail: info@acg.net, Web Site: www.acg.net (20)

Auriemma, Michael, Auriemma Consulting Group, New York, NY. Tel: (516) 333-4800, FAX: (516) 333-4815, E-Mail: info@acg.net, Web Site: www.acg.net (20)

Aurora Marketing Inc, Princeton, NJ. Tel: (609) 520-8863, FAX: (908) 359-1108, E-Mail: aurora2@voicenet.com, Web Site: www.auroramarketing.net (30)

Ausenda, Marco, Rizzoli International Publications Inc, New York, NY. Tel: (212) 387-3400, FAX: (212) 387-3535 (17)

Ausick, Richard M., Brown Shoe Co, Saint Louis, MO. Tel: (314) 854-4000, FAX: (314) 854-4274, Web Site: www.brownshoe.com (16)

Ausley, David, Integer Group, Des Moines, IA. Tel: (515) 288-7910, FAX: (515) 288-8439, E-Mail: fmaher@integermidwest.com, Web Site: www.integer.com (35)

Austen, Heather, (C) Systems LLC, Edison, NJ. Tel: (732) 548-6100, FAX: (732) 548-3883, Web Site: www.csysemsllc.net (22)

Austen, Mary Stengel, Tierney Communications, Philadelphia, PA. Tel: (215) 790-4100, FAX: (215) 790-4363, Web Site: www.tierneyagency.com (35)

Austin & Williams, Hauppauge, NY. Tel: (631) 938-2279, FAX: (212) 434-7022, E-Mail: info@austin-williams.com, Web Site: www.austin-williams.com (35)

Austin, Bill, Coyne American Institute, Chicago, IL. Tel: (773) 935-2520, (800) 999-5220, FAX: (773) 935-2920, Web Site: www.coyneamerican.edu (16)

Austin, Daryl, Phillips Kiln Service LTD, South Sioux City, NE. Tel: (402) 494-6837, (800) 831-0876, FAX: (402) 494-6858, E-Mail: info@kilm.com, Web Site: www.kiln.com (16)

Austin, Sarah, Veridian Credit Union, Waterloo, IA. Tel: (319) 236-5692, (800) 235-3228, FAX: (319) 833-1185, E-Mail: sarahma@veridiancu.org, Web Site: www.veridiancu.org (1)

Australian Tourist Commission, Los Angeles, CA. Tel: (310) 695-3200, Web Site: www.australia.com (19)

Austrums, Tim, The Connection Contact Center Services, Burnsville, MN. Tel: (952) 948-5335, (800) 883-5777, FAX: (952) 948-5498, E-Mail: sales@the-connection.com, Web Site: www.the-connection.com (29)

Austrums, Tim, The Connection Outsourced Call Ctr, Burnsville, MN. Tel: (800) 883-5777, Web Site: www.the-connection.com (29)

Authentic Designs, West Rupert, VT. Tel: (802) 394-7713, (800) 844-9416, E-Mail: lighting@authenticdesigns.com, Web Site: www.authenticdesigns.com (8)

Auto Anything, San Diego, CA. Tel: (858) 569-8111, (800) 874-8888, FAX: (858) 569-8503, E-Mail: customerservice@autoanything.com, Web Site: www.autoanything.com (34)

Autobytel Inc, Irvine, CA. Tel: (949) 225-4500, E-Mail: consumercareabtl@autobytel.com, Web Site: www.autobytel.com (12)

Autodesk Inc, San Rafael, CA. Tel: (415) 507-5000, FAX: (415) 507-5100, Web Site: www.autodesk.com (16)

Automated Equipment Service Inc, Poughkeepsie, NY. Tel: (607) 733-2108, (800) 468-4068, FAX: (845) 485-8221, E-Mail: info@aesmailpro.com, Web Site: www.aesmailpro.com (34)

Automated Graphic Systems LLC, White Plains, MD. Tel: (800) 678-8760, FAX: (240) 222-3419, E-Mail: info@ags.com, Web Site: www.ags.com (31)

Automated Mailing Systems Corp, Dallas, TX. Tel: (972) 869-2844, (800) 527-1668, FAX: (972) 869-2735, E-Mail: amsco@amscodallas.com (34)

Automation Control Products, Alpharetta, GA. Tel: (678) 990-0945, FAX: (678) 990-0951, E-Mail: info@thinmanager.com, Web Site: www.thinmanager.com (16)

Automation Mailing & Shipping Solutions Inc, Cleveland, OH. Tel: (216) 241-4487, (800) 883-7935, FAX: (216) 241-5918, E-Mail: service@mailshipsolutions.com, Web Site: www.mailshipsolutions.com (16)

Automod, Atlanta, GA. Tel: (770) 457-9663, (800) 241-1832, FAX: (770) 457-6089, E-Mail: info@automod.fdn.com, Web Site: www.automod.net (12)

Automotive Headphones, Sterling Heights, MI. Tel: (586) 292-6166 (16)

AutoPacific Inc, Tustin, CA. Tel: (714) 838-4234, FAX: (714) 838-4260, Web Site: www.autopacific.com (30)

Avalanche Creative Services Inc, New York, NY. Tel: (212) 206-9335, FAX: (212) 206-1538, E-Mail: info@avalanchecreative.tv, Web Site: www.avalanchecreative.tv (35)

Avantus, Maryland Heights, MO. Tel: (314) 994-3449, Web Site: www.avantus.com (20)

Avary, Robert, Wagner Hines & Avary Inc, Alexandria, VA. Tel: (703) 684-7740, FAX: (703) 548-3721 (20)

Avatar Studios, Saint Louis, MO. Tel: (314) 533-2242, FAX: (314) 533-3349, Web Site: www.avatar-studios.com (32)

Avaya Communication, Temecula, CA. Tel: (866) 462-8292, Web Site: www.avaya.com (34)

Aveda Corp, Blaine, MN. Tel: (763) 951-4201, (800) 644-4831, Web Site: www.aveda.com (7)

Averbook, Arthur, CO-OP Promotions, Hollywood, FL. Tel: (954) 922-2323, FAX: (954) 922-2071, E-Mail: art@co-oppromotions.com, Web Site: www.co-oppromotions.com (35)

Averill, Howard M., Time Inc, New York, NY. Tel: (212) 522-1212, Web Site: www.timeinc.com (17)

Averill, Howard M., Time Warner Inc, New York, NY. Tel: (212) 484-8000, Web Site: www.timewarner.com (16)

Avery Dennison Corp, Brea, CA. Tel: (714) 674-8500, (800) 462-8379, FAX: (714) 674-6929, Web Site: www.avery.com (10)

Avery, Hardeep, Harris Connect LLC, Chesapeake, VA. Tel: (800) 877-6554, E-Mail: moreinfo@harrisconnect.com, Web Site: www.harrisconnect.com (35)

Avery, Sharon, UNICEF Canada, Toronto, ON Canada. Tel: (416) 482-4444, (800) 567-4483, FAX: (416) 487-8875, E-Mail: on.secretary@unicef.ca, Web Site: www.unicef.ca (1)

Avery, William J., Lincoln Financial Group, Radnor, PA. Tel: (215) 448-1400, (877) 275-5462, FAX: (215) 448-3962, Web Site: www.lfg.com (15)

Aviation Book Co, Seattle, WA. Tel: (206) 767-5232, FAX: (206) 763-3428, E-Mail: sales@aviationbook.com, Web Site: www.aviationbook.com (17)

Avis World Headquarters, Parsippany, NJ. Tel: (973) 496-3500, Web Site: www.avis.com (19)

Aviv, Diana, FEEDING AMERICA, Chicago, IL. Tel: (312) 263-2303, FAX: (312) 263-5626, Web Site: www.secondharvest.org (1)

Aviva USA Corp, Des Moines, IA. Tel: (515) 362-3600, FAX: (800) 531-0038, Web Site: www.avivausa.com (14)

AvMed Health Plan Inc, Miami, FL. Tel: (305) 671-5437, FAX: (305) 671-4782, Web Site: www.avmed.org (1)

Avnet Inc, Phoenix, AZ. Tel: (480) 643-2000, FAX: (480) 643-7240, Web Site: www.avnet.com (16)

Avon Products Inc, New York, NY. Tel: (212) 282-7000, (800) 367-2866, FAX: (212) 282-6225, Web Site: www.avon.com (7)

Avrick Direct Inc, Goleta, CA. Tel: (805) 683-6551, FAX: (805) 683-6553, E-Mail: doreen@avrick.com, Web Site: avrickdirect.com (23)

Avrick, Adam, Design Distributors, Inc. Deer Park, NY. Tel: (631) 242-2000, FAX: (631) 242-7367, E-Mail: info@designdistributors.com, Web Site: www.designdistributors.com (21)

Avril, Alisha, Georgetown University Law Center, Washington, DC. Tel: (202) 662-9890, FAX: (202) 662-9891, E-Mail: cle@law.georgetown.edu, Web Site: www.law.georgetown.edu (13)

Award Co of America, Tuscaloosa, AL. Tel: (205) 349-2990, (800) 633-5953, FAX: (205) 752-0930, Web Site: www.randallpub.com (6)

Award Marketing Services LLC, Whitehouse, NJ. Tel: (908) 534-5700, FAX: (908) 534-0903, E-Mail: info@awardmarketingservices.com, Web Site: www.awardmarketingservices.com (33)

AWeber Communications, Chalfont, PA. Tel: (877) 293-2371, Web Site: www.aweber.com (24)

Axia Public Relations, Jacksonville, FL. Tel: (904) 425-1500, (866) 773-4768, Web Site: www.axiapr.com (35)

Axis Capital, New York, NY. Tel: (212) 500-7743 (14)

Axmacher, Thomas, Global Equipment Co Inc, Port Washington, NY. Tel: (516) 484-3100, (888) 381-2861, FAX: (516) 608-7111, E-Mail: sales@globalindustrial.com, Web Site: www.globalindustrial.com (9)

Ayan, Jordan, SubscriberMail LLC, Lisle, IL. Tel: (630) 303-5000, FAX: (630) 303-5100, Web Site: www.subscribermail.com (22)

Aycock, Thomas, United Investors Life Insurance Co, Birmingham, AL. Tel: (205) 325-4300, (800) 288-2722, FAX: (205) 325-4157, Web Site: www.uilic.com (15)

Ayd, G. Robert, ValueVision Media Inc, Eden Prairie, MN. Tel: (952) 943-6000, Web Site: www.shophq.com (32)

Ayer, Ramani, The Hartford Financial Services Inc, Southington, CT. Tel: (860) 547-5000, (860) 843-8070, FAX: (860) 547-2680, Web Site: www.thehartford.com (15)

Ayers, Borden, The Diversified Services Group Inc, Wayne, PA. Tel: (610) 989-1710, FAX: (610) 989-1730, E-Mail: rfgrieb@dsg-network.com, Web Site: www.dsg-network.com (20)

Ayers, Janet, Galloway Research Service, San Antonio, TX. Tel: (210) 734-4346, FAX: (210) 732-4500, E-Mail: info@gallowayresearch.com, Web Site: www.gallowayresearch.com (30)

Ayers, Scott, Beckmann Converting Inc, Amsterdam, NY. Tel: (518) 842-0073, FAX: (518) 842-0282, E-Mail: ppiusz@beckmannconverting.com, Web Site: www.beckmannconverting.com (16)

Ayers, Teresa W., Gambro Inc, Lakewood, CO. Tel: (303) 232-6800, (800) 525-2623, FAX: (303) 222-6810, Web Site: www.gambro.com (16)

The Ayn Rand Institute, Irvine, CA. Tel: (949) 222-6550, FAX: (949) 222-6558, E-Mail: archives@aynrand.org, Web Site: www.aynrand.org (1)

Ayvazian, Berge, The Yankee Group, Boston, MA. Tel: (617) 598-7200, E-Mail: info@yankeegroup.com, Web Site: www.yankeegroup.com (1)

Azim, Heather, Group 236, Oakland, CA. Tel: (510) 874-0141, Web Site: group236.com (32)

Azuela, Leonel, Quaxar, Miami, FL. Tel: (305) 350-9520, Web Site: www.quaxar.com (35)

Azzara, Mike, Stein IAS, New York, NY. Tel: (212) 213-1112, Web Site: www.steinias.com (35)

B

The B&F System Inc, Dallas, TX. Tel: (214) 333-2111, FAX: (214) 333-2137, Web Site: www.maxam.com (33)

B&G Lieberman Co Inc, Charlotte, NC. Tel: (704) 376-0717, (800) 438-0346, FAX: (800) 248-2696, E-Mail: bgl@bglieberman.com, Web Site: www.bglieberman.com (16)

B&W Press Inc, Georgetown, MA. Tel: (978) 352-6100, (877) 246-3467, FAX: (978) 352-5955, E-Mail: csr@bwpress.com, Web Site: www.bwpress.com (21)

B Bunch Co Inc, Phoenix, AZ. Tel: (602) 997-6452, FAX: (602) 997-7266, E-Mail: sales@bbunch.com, Web Site: www.bbunch.com (16)

B-T-B Internet Marketing Solutions, Middle Island, NY. Tel: (631) 924-3888, E-Mail: linickgroup@gmail.com, Web Site: www.linick.net; 222.asklinick.com (39)

B2BMarketing.com, Scottsdale, AZ. Tel: (602) 402-6588, Web Site: www.b2bmarketing.com (35)

BAI, Chicago, IL. Tel: (312) 683-2464, FAX: (312) 683-2373, E-Mail: info@bai.org, Web Site: www.bai.org (17)

BBC Direct Mktg Svcs, Shamong, NJ. Tel: (609) 268-9919, (877) 786-4389, FAX: (609) 268-9939, E-Mail: csr@bbcglobal.com, Web Site: www.bbcglobal.com (20)

BBC Worldwide Americas Inc, New York, NY. Tel: (212) 705-9300, (800) 898-4921, FAX: (212) 888-0576, Web Site: www.bbcamerica.com (3)

BBF Integrated Solutions, Largo, FL. Tel: (727) 545-8703, (800) 666-8082, Web Site: www.bbfprinting.com (27)

BBK Worldwide, Needham Heights, MA. Tel: (617) 630-4477, FAX: (617) 630-5090, E-Mail: info@bbkworldwide.com, Web Site: www.bbkworldwide.com (35)

BBM Canada Inc, Don Mills, ON Canada. Tel: (416) 445-9800, FAX: (416) 445-8644, E-Mail: info@bbm.ca, Web Site: www.bbm.ca (30)

BBS & Associates, Akron, OH. Tel: (330) 665-5227, E-Mail: contactus@servantheart.com, Web Site: www.servantheart.com (1)

BBS Chicago, Chicago, IL. Tel: (312) 326-8000, (800) 742-4455, Web Site: www.rrdonnelley.com (31)

BC Incentives, Fate, TX. Tel: (800) 275-1298, E-Mail: terri@bcincentives.com, Web Site: www.bcincentives.com (33)

BCC Software Inc, Rochester, NY. Tel: (585) 272-9130, (800) 453-3130, FAX: (585) 272-9141, Web Site: www.bccsoftware.com (22)

BCF, Virginia Beach, VA. Tel: (757) 497-4811, FAX: (757) 497-3684, Web Site: www.bcfagency.com (35)

BCR Enterprises Inc, Downers Grove, IL. Tel: (630) 986-1432, (800) 227-1234, FAX: (630) 323-5324, Web Site: www.bcr.com (17)

BFC, Batavia, IL. Tel: (630) 879-9240, Web Site: www.bfcprint.com (28)

BFS Credit Services Co, Brook Park, OH. Tel: (216) 362-5094, FAX: (216) 362-5236, E-Mail: lupinettijim@bfsusa.com (16)

BGE Home Products & Services Inc, Baltimore, MD. Tel: (888) 243-4663, Web Site: www.bgehome.com (16)

BI, Summit, NJ. Tel: (908) 516-1393, E-Mail: info@biworldwide.com, Web Site: www.biworldwide.com (33)

BJ's Wholesale Club Inc, Westborough, MA. Tel: (508) 651-7400, FAX: (508) 651-6167, Web Site: www.bjs.com (13)

BJT Management Group, Ada, MI. Tel: (616) 682-0369, Web Site: www.bjtmgt.com (20)

BJU Press, Greenville, SC. Tel: (864) 242-5100, (800) 845-5731, FAX: (864) 271-8151, (800) 525-8398, E-Mail: bjupinfo@bjupress.com, Web Site: www.bjupress.com (17)

BKV Inc, Atlanta, GA. Tel: (404) 233-0332, E-Mail: rina.cook@bkv.com, Web Site: www.bkv.com (35)

BLS Inc, Wilmington, DE. Tel: (302) 631-1616, (800) 545-7766, FAX: (302) 631-1619, E-Mail: bls@tutorsystems.com, Web Site: www.tutorsystems.com (17)

BMC Group, Peterborough, ON Canada. Tel: (705) 745-4766, (866) 311-7711, FAX: (705) 745-0177, E-Mail: hello@bmcgroup.ca, Web Site: bmcgroup.ca (35)

BMG Columbia House, New York, NY. Tel: (212) 287-0081, E-Mail: cs1@bmgmusicservice.com (13)

BMI, Nashville, TN. Tel: (615) 401-2000, (800) 925-8451, FAX: (615) 401-2812, E-Mail: nashville@bmi.com, Web Site: www.bmi.com (1)

BMI Fulfillment Services, Danbury, CT. Tel: (203) 546-5580, FAX: (203) 546-5575, E-Mail: barry@bmigroup.com, Web Site: www.bmigroup.com (28)

BMI Home Decorating, Spring Grove, IL. Tel: (815) 675-3703, FAX: (815) 675-3703, E-Mail: bmigroup@aol.com (16)

BN Creative Advertising, Mount Prospect, IL. Tel: (847) 577-1300, FAX: (847) 577-2101 (36)

BNY Mellon, New York, NY. Tel: (412) 234-5000, (212) 495-1784, FAX: (412) 635-1799, Web Site: www.bnymellon.com (14)

BOC Gases, Murray Hill, NJ. Tel: (908) 464-8100, (800) 262-4273, FAX: (410) 749-4073, E-Mail: info@linde.com, Web Site: www.boc-gases.com (16)

BP, Warrenville, IL. Tel: (630) 821-3000, (800) 638-5672, Web Site: www.bp.com (16)

BP Rice & Company Inc, El Segundo, CA. Tel: (310) 322-2210, FAX: (310) 322-0617, E-Mail: stephanie@bprco.com, Web Site: www.bprco.com (35)

BT Americas, Irving, TX. Tel: (972) 830-8169, FAX: (703) 755-6740, Web Site: www.btglobalservices.com (22)

BWB Marketing Services, Ankeny, IA. Tel: (515) 986-1992, Web Site: www.bwbmarketing.com (22)

BYK-Gardner USA, Columbia, MD. Tel: (310) 483-6500, Web Site: www.byk.com (16)

B2E Direct Marketing Inc, Grimes, IA. Tel: (515) 986-1992, Web Site: www.bwbmarketing.com (22)

Babb, Jr. Ralph W., Comerica Inc, Dallas, TX. Tel: (800) 521-1190, FAX: (925) 941-1999, Web Site: www.comerica.com (14)

Babb, Rob, BIC Graphic USA, Clearwater, FL. Tel: (727) 536-7895, E-Mail: customerservice@bicgraphic.com, Web Site: www.bicgraphic.com (33)

Babcock & Jenkins, Portland, OR. Tel: (503) 382-8500, E-Mail: laureng@bnj.com, Web Site: www.bnj.com (35)

Babcox Publications LLC, Akron, OH. Tel: (330) 670-1234, FAX: (330) 670-0874, E-Mail: bbabcox@babcox.com, Web Site: www.babcox.com (17)

Babcox, Bill, Babcox Publications LLC, Akron, OH. Tel: (330) 670-1234, FAX: (330) 670-0874, E-Mail: bbabcox@babcox.com, Web Site: www.babcox.com (17)

Baber Direct Marketing, Memphis, TN. Tel: (901) 332-6300, (800) 847-7040, FAX: (901) 332-6441, E-Mail: info@baberweb.com, Web Site: www.baberweb.com (21)

Baber, Michael, Baber Direct Marketing, Memphis, TN. Tel: (901) 332-6300, (800) 847-7040, FAX: (901) 332-6441, E-Mail: info@baberweb.com, Web Site: www.baberweb.com (21)

Babiak, Jennifer, Miracle of Aloe, Dallas, TX. Tel: (800) 966-2563, FAX: (800) 859-9881, E-Mail: LJohnson@miracleofaloe.com, Web Site: www.miracleofaloe.com (7)

Babich, Jr George, Check Point Systems, Thorofare, NJ. Tel: (856) 848-1800, (800) 257-5540, FAX: (856) 848-0937, Web Site: www.checkpointsystems.com (34)

Babyshoe.com, Hendersonville, NC. Tel: (828) 697-5811, (800) 543-8566, FAX: (828) 697-5815, E-Mail: info@babyshoe.com, Web Site: www.babyshoe.com (6)

Baccala Ward, Nichole, TBC Inc, Baltimore, MD. Tel: (410) 347-7500, FAX: (410) 986-1299, E-Mail: info@tbc.us, Web Site: www.tbc.us (35)

Bachler, Chris, Eclipse Marketing Services Inc, Cedar Knolls, NJ. Tel: (800) 837-4648, E-Mail: hello@eclipse2.com, Web Site: www.eclipsemarketingservices.com (35)

Bachrach Clothing Inc, New York, NY. Web Site: www.bachrach.com (2)

Bachus, Dan, Grand Canyon University, Phoenix, AZ. Tel: (602) 639-7500, (877) 860-3951, Web Site: www.gcu.edu (13)

Bacic, Bill, Deloitte & Touche, Boston, MA. Tel: (617) 437-2000, FAX: (617) 437-2111, Web Site: www.deloitte.com (14)

Back Designs Inc, Novato, CA. Tel: (415) 883-4683, (800) 466-1341, FAX: (707) 557-2225, E-Mail: info@backdesigns.com, Web Site: www.backdesigns.com (7)

Back to the Bible, Lincoln, NE. Tel: (402) 464-7200, (800) 759-2425, FAX: (402) 464-7474, E-Mail: info@backtothebible.org, Web Site: www.backtothebible.org (5)

Backe Digital Brand Marketing, Radnor, PA. Tel: (610) 947-6901, E-Mail: jbacke@backemarketing.com, Web Site: www.backemarketing.com (35)

Backe, John, Backe Digital Brand Marketing, Radnor, PA. Tel: (610) 947-6901, E-Mail: jbacke@backemarketing.com, Web Site: www.backemarketing.com (35)

Backman Writing & Communications, Rensselaer, NY. Tel: (518) 449-4985, FAX: (518) 449-7273, E-Mail: johnb@backwrite.com, Web Site: www.backwrite.com (39)

Backman, John, Backman Writing & Communications, Rensselaer, NY. Tel: (518) 449-4985, FAX: (518) 449-7273, E-Mail: johnb@backwrite.com, Web Site: www.backwrite.com (39)

Backus, Richard, Mother Earth News Magazine, Topeka, KS. Tel: (785) 274-4300, (800) 678-5779, FAX: (785) 274-4305, E-Mail: bwelch@ogdenpubs.com, Web Site: www.cappers.com (17)

Bacompt Systems Inc, Carmel, IN. Tel: (317) 574-7474, (800) 533-7109, FAX: (317) 574-7475, E-Mail: customer.service@bacompt.com, Web Site: www.bacompt.com (21)

Bacon, Donald, Lockhart Industries Inc, Dallas, TX. Tel: (214) 348-1422, Web Site: www.lockhartadvantage.com (9)

Bacon, Laura B, Tridium Inc, Richmond, VA. Tel: (804) 525-1648, Web Site: www.tridium.com (9)

Bacon, Leslie, Promo Magazine, New York, NY. Tel: (203) 358-9900, (800) 927-5007, FAX: (203) 358-5816, E-Mail: larry.jaffee@penton.com, Web Site: www.promomagazine.com (17)

Baden, Erik, American General Life Insurance Co, Houston, TX. Tel: (713) 522-1111, FAX: (713) 522-8531, Web Site: www.aglife.com (15)

Bader Rutter, Brookfield, WI. Tel: (262) 784-7200, FAX: (262) 938-5595, Web Site: www.baderrutter.com (35)

Badge-A-Minit, Oglesby, IL. Tel: (815) 883-8822, (800) 223-4103, FAX: (815) 883-9696, Web Site: www.badgeaminit.com (16)

Badger Press Inc, Grayslake, IL. Tel: (847) 996-1190, E-Mail: info@badgerpressinc.com, Web Site: www.badgerpressinc.com (27)

Badger Press/Photographics Inc, Kenosha, WI. Tel: (262) 658-1628, (800) 635-9773, FAX: (262) 658-0307 (27)

Badger, Bill, Guiding Eyes for the Blind, Yorktown Heights, NY. Tel: (914) 245-4042, (800) 942-0149, FAX: (914) 245-1609, Web Site: www.guidingeyes.org (16)

Badgett, III Guy M., Vulcan Materials Co, Birmingham, AL. Tel: (205) 298-3000, FAX: (205) 298-2960, Web Site: www.vulcanmaterials.com (16)

Badillo, Juan, LaPreferida Inc, Chicago, IL. Tel: (773) 254-7200, (800) 621-5422, FAX: (773) 254-8546, Web Site: www.lapreferida.com (4)

Maurice Badler Fine Jewelry Ltd, New York, NY. Tel: (212) 575-9632, (800) M-BADLER, FAX: (212) 575-9205, E-Mail: info@badler.com, Web Site: www.badler.com (2)

Badler, Jeffrey P., Maurice Badler Fine Jewelry Ltd, New York, NY. Tel: (212) 575-9632, (800) M-BADLER, FAX: (212) 575-9205, E-Mail: info@badler.com, Web Site: www.badler.com (2)

Badman, Jeremy, Oliver Wyman, New York, NY. Tel: (212) 345-8000, (212) 541-8100, Web Site: www.oliverwyman.com (14)

Badovinus, Marisa, Creative Lift Inc, San Francisco, CA. Tel: (415) 248-3170, E-Mail: hello@creativelift.net, Web Site: www.creativelift.net (35)

Baer, D. Richard, Hollywood Film Archive, Los Angeles, CA. Tel: (323) 655-4968, Web Site: www.hfarchive.com (17)

Baer, Dave, Simplex Grinnell, Westminster, MA. Tel: (978) 731-2500, (800) SIMPLEX, FAX: (978) 731-7856, Web Site: www.simplexgrinnel.com (16)

Baer, Ian, Rauxa, Costa Mesa, CA. Tel: (714) 427-1271, E-Mail: newbiz@rauxa.com, Web Site: www.rauxa.com (35)

Baer, J., Muldoon & Baer Inc, Palm Beach Gardens, FL. Tel: (561) 630-0999, FAX: (561) 630-9466, Web Site: www.muldoonandbaer.com (20)

Baer, Michael, Laughlin Constable, Chicago, IL. Tel: (312) 422-5900, FAX: (312) 422-5901, Web Site: www.laughlin.com (35)

Baer, Timothy, Target Corp, Minneapolis, MN. Tel: (612) 304-6073, Web Site: www.target.com (16)

Baert, Bernard, Poly One Corp, Avon Lake, OH. Tel: (440) 930-1000, (866) POLY-ONE, FAX: (440) 930-1428, Web Site: www.polyone.com (16)

Baez, Lisa, Travel Planners Inc, New York, NY. Tel: (212) 532-1660, (800) 221-3531, FAX: (212) 532-1556, Web Site: www.tphousing.com (20)

Baeza, Cesar, Brotherhood America's Oldest Winery Ltd, Washingtonville, NY. Tel: (845) 496-3661, FAX: (845) 496-8720, E-Mail: contact@brotherhoodwinery.net, Web Site: www.brotherhoodwinery.net (19)

Bafaro, Tami, Anheuser-Busch Inc Promotional Products Group, Shelton, CT. Tel: (800) 742-5283, Web Site: www.budshop.com (6)

Baggett, Sandy, ITW Vortec, Cincinnati, OH. Tel: (513) 891-7474, (800) 441-7475, FAX: (513) 891-4092, E-Mail: techsupport@vortec.com, Web Site: www.vortec.com (16)

Bahamas Ministry of Tourism, Fort Lauderdale, FL. Tel: (954) 236-9292, (800) 422-4262, Web Site: www.bahamas.com (19)

Bahler, Gary M., Champs Corp, Bradenton, FL. Tel: (941) 748-0577, (800) 991-6813, E-Mail: customer_service@champssports.com, Web Site: www.champssports.com (11)

Baia, Paul E., Datum Timing, Test & Measurement, Beverly, MA. Tel: (978) 927-8220, FAX: (978) 927-4099, E-Mail: wriley@datum.com, Web Site: www.datum.com (9)

Baiamonte, Geno, PremierIMS Inc, Houston, TX. Tel: (832) 608-6400, FAX: (832) 608-6420, E-Mail: contact@mailplex.com, Web Site: www.premiercompany.com (21)

Baier Stein Direct, Bernardsville, NJ. Tel: (908) 781-7849, Web Site: www.directcopy.com (20)

Baier Stein, Donna, Baier Stein Direct, Bernardsville, NJ. Tel: (908) 781-7849, Web Site: www.directcopy.com (20)

Bailey, A. Robert, Anda Inc, Parsippany, NJ. Tel: (954) 217-4500, (800) 331-2632, FAX: (866) 600-3860, Web Site: www.andanet.com (7)

Bailey, Anne, Collector's Teapot, Kingston, NY. Tel: (845) 339-1109, (800) 724-3306, FAX: (845) 339-5530, Web Site: www.collectorsteapot.com (6)

Bailey, Christopher, Burberry, New York, NY. Tel: (877) 217-4085, E-Mail: us.customerservice@burberry.com, Web Site: www.burberry.com (2)

Bailey, Hal, Family Christian Stores, Grand Rapids, MI. Tel: (888) 887-6555, E-Mail: customerservice@familychristian.com, Web Site: www.familychristian.com (5)

Bailey, Jim, Collector's Teapot, Kingston, NY. Tel: (845) 339-1109, (800) 724-3306, FAX: (845) 339-5530, Web Site: www.collectorsteapot.com (6)

Bailey, Michael, Jostens, Inc, Minneapolis, MN. Tel: (952) 830-3300, FAX: (952) 830-3293, Web Site: www.jostens.com (16)

Bailey, Mike, Reb Storage Systems International, Chicago, IL. Tel: (773) 252-0400, (800) 252-5955, FAX: (773) 252-0303, E-Mail: sales@rebsteel.com, Web Site: www.industrialebuy.com (9)

Bailey, Nik, Bailey's Inc, Woodland, CA. Tel: (800) 322-4539, FAX: (530) 406-0895, E-Mail: baileys@bbaileys.com, Web Site: www.baileys-online.com (9)

Bailey, Peter, Vertical Communications Inc, Santa Clara, CA. Tel: (408) 404-1600, (800) COMDIAL, FAX: (408) 969-9601, Web Site: www.comdial.com (34)

Bailey, Victoria, Theatre Development Fund Inc, New York, NY. Tel: (212) 912-9770, E-Mail: info@tdf.org, Web Site: www.tdf.org (1)

Bailey's Inc, Woodland, CA. Tel: (800) 322-4539, FAX: (530) 406-0895, E-Mail: baileys@bbaileys.com, Web Site: www.baileys-online.com (9)

Bailon, Gilbert, St Louis Post-Dispatch, Saint Louis, MO. Tel: (314) 340-8000, (800) 365-0820, FAX: (314) 340-3140, Web Site: www.stltoday.com (17)

Bain, Judith S., Epson America, Long Beach, CA. Tel: (562) 981-3840, (800) 873-7766, FAX: (562) 290-5220, Web Site: www.epson.com (10)

Baione, Liz, Mardevdm2, Oak Brook, IL. Tel: (800) 323-4958, FAX: (303) 265-5457, E-Mail: info@mardevdm2.com, Web Site: www.mardevdm2.com (24)

Bair, Royce, The Stock Solution Inc, West Jordan, UT. Tel: (801) 566-8684, (888) 366-0430, FAX: (801) 961-8030, E-Mail: info@tssphoto.com, Web Site: www.tssphoto.com (38)

Baird, Amy, Peter Li Education Group, Dayton, OH. Tel: (937) 293-1415, (800) 523-4625, FAX: (937) 293-1310, Web Site: www.peterli.com (17)

Baird, Doug, Response FX, Carlsbad, CA. Tel: (760) 479-0012, E-Mail: services@responsefx.com, Web Site: www.responsefx.com (35)

Baird, Pat, Life Investors Insurance Co of America, Cedar Rapids, IA. Tel: (319) 398-8511, (800) 231-7220, FAX: (319) 369-2188, Web Site: www.lifeinvestors.com (14)

Bajec, Dennis, Resource/Ammirati, Columbus, OH. Tel: (614) 621-2888, FAX: (614) 621-2873, E-Mail: businessdevelopment@resourceammirati.com, Web Site: www.resourceammirati.com (35)

Bak, Jeff, HealthPlan Services, Tampa, FL. Tel: (813) 289-1000, (800) 545-6441, Web Site: www.healthplan.com (15)

Bakehorn, Michael, American Stationery Co Inc, Peru, IN. Tel: (765) 473-4438, (800) 822-2577, FAX: (800) 253-9054, Web Site: www.americanstationery.com (10)

Bakehorn, Mike, The RYTEX Co, Peru, IN. Tel: (317) 872-8553, (800) 277-5458, FAX: (317) 872-8535, (800) 329-1669, Web Site: www.rytex.com (10)

Baker & Hostetler LLP, Washington, DC. Tel: (202) 861-1500, FAX: (202) 861-1783, E-Mail: wschweitzer@bakerlaw.com, Web Site: www.bakerlaw.com (20)

Baker & Taylor Inc, Charlotte, NC. Tel: (704) 998-3100, (800) 775-1800, FAX: (704) 998-3316, E-Mail: btinfo@btol.com, Web Site: www.btol.com (16)

Baker-Blais Marketing Inc, Pointe-Claire, QC Canada. Tel: (514) 693-9900, FAX: (514) 693-9960, E-Mail: donbaker@bakerblais.com, Web Site: www.bakerblais.com (35)

Baker Corp, Seal Beach, CA. Tel: (562) 430-6262 (16)

Baker, Ben, Infinity Trading Co Inc, Spring, TX. Tel: (281) 292-8509, FAX: (281) 931-8139, E-Mail: sales@infinitytradingcompany.com, Web Site: www.infinitytradingcompany.com (34)

Baker, Constance, Edo Interactive, Nashville, TN. Tel: (615) 297-6080, Web Site: www.edointeractive.com (16)

Baker, Craig A., Domestic Bank, Providence, RI. Tel: (401) 943-1600, (800) 566-6600, FAX: (401) 943-6708, Web Site: www.domesticbank.com (14)

Baker, Daniel, The Library of America, New York, NY. Tel: (212) 308-3360, (800) 964-5778, FAX: (212) 750-8352, E-Mail: info@loa.org, Web Site: www.loa.org (13)

Baker, Dave, Dome Printing, Sacramento, CA. Tel: (800) 343-3139 (27)

Baker, David, Sterling Fluid Systems, Indianapolis, IN. Tel: (317) 925-9661, (800) 879-0182, FAX: (317) 924-7388, Web Site: www.peerlesspump.com (16)

Baker, Dean, Intelligencer Printing Co, Lancaster, PA. Tel: (717) 291-3100, (800) 233-0107, FAX: (717) 569-2643, Web Site: www.intellprinting.com (27)

Baker, Don, Baker-Blais Marketing Inc, Pointe-Claire, QC Canada. Tel: (514) 693-9900, FAX: (514) 693-9960, E-Mail: donbaker@bakerblais.com, Web Site: www.bakerblais.com (35)

Baker, Heather, BennettBaker Ltd, Chicago, IL. Tel: (312) 252-8883, FAX: (312) 252-8209, E-Mail: nbennett@bennettwheelless.com, Web Site: www.bennettbaker.com (20)

Baker, Jeff, Domestic Bank, Providence, RI. Tel: (401) 943-1600, (800) 566-6600, FAX: (401) 943-6708, Web Site: www.domesticbank.com (14)

Baker, Jeffrey R., Hormel Foods Corp, Austin, MN. Tel: (507) 437-5611, (800) 523-4635, FAX: (507) 437-5158, Web Site: www.hormelfoods.com (16)

Baker, Jonathan, Remington College, Heathrow, FL. Tel: (407) 562-5691, (800) 560-6192, Web Site: www.remingtoncollege.edu (13)

Baker, Mark A., Steelcase Inc, Grand Rapids, MI. Tel: (616) 247-2710, FAX: (616) 475-2270, Web Site: www.steelcase.com (16)

Baker, Mary, Infinity Trading Co Inc, Spring, TX. Tel: (281) 292-8509, FAX: (281) 931-8139, E-Mail: sales@infinitytradingcompany.com, Web Site: www.infinitytradingcompany.com (34)

Baker, Mike, PSI Marketing Consultants Inc, Rolling Meadows, IL. Tel: (773) 878-0800, (800) 933-4774, FAX: (773) 878-4219 (29)

Baker, Nathaniel, Domestic Bank, Providence, RI. Tel: (401) 943-1600, (800) 566-6600, FAX: (401) 943-6708, Web Site: www.domesticbank.com (14)

Baker, Oleda, Oleda & Co Inc, Fort Worth, TX. Tel: (817) 731-1147, (800) 731-4247, FAX: (817) 731-1149, E-Mail: oleda@oleda.com, Web Site: www.oleda.com (16)

Baker, Tim, Shield Healthcare, Valencia, CA. Tel: (661) 294-4200, (800) 765-8775, FAX: (661) 294-1043, (800) 748-0713, Web Site: www.shieldhealthcare.com (7)

Baker, William C., Chesapeake Bay Foundation, Annapolis, MD. Tel: (410) 268-8816, Web Site: www.savethebay.cbf.org (1)

Baker, William F., Channel 13 WNET Catalog Division, New York, NY. Tel: (212) 560-1313, FAX: (212) 560-1314, E-Mail: programming@thirteen.org, Web Site: www.thirteen.org (5)

Baker, William, The Lacek Group, Minneapolis, MN. Tel: (612) 359-3700, FAX: (612) 359-9395, E-Mail: info@lacek.com, Web Site: www.lacek.com (35)

Balas, Jim, CoreLogic Inc, Irvine, CA. Tel: (949) 214-1000, (800) 426-1466, Web Site: www.corelogic.com (22)

Balboa Life & Casualty, Irvine, CA. Tel: (949) 222-8000, (800) 854-6115, FAX: (949) 222-8777, Web Site: www.balboainsurance.com (15)

Balch, Lisa, Sargeant House Design Studio, Westchester, PA. Tel: (610) 399-1983, E-Mail: sargeant house @verizon.net, Web Site: www.sargeanthouse.com (36)

Baldelli, Steven, Direct SAT TV LLC, Southern Pines, NC. Tel: (910) 693-3042, (800) 595-4101, FAX: (866) 935-4097, Web Site: www.directsattv.com (3)

Baldridge, Sally, Jazzercise Inc, Carlsbad, CA. Tel: (760) 476-1750, FAX: (760) 602-7180, E-Mail: customercare@jazzercise.com, Web Site: www.jazzercise.com (2)

Balducci Enterprises Inc, Germantown, MD. Tel: (240) 403-2440, FAX: (240) 403-2520 (16)

Baldwin Filters, Kearney, NE. Tel: (308) 234-1951, (800) 822-5394, FAX: (800) 828-4453, E-Mail: info@baldwinfilter.com, Web Site: www.baldwinfilter.com (16)

Baldwin, Anita S., Rose Resnick Lighthouse for the Blind & Visually Impaired, San Francisco, CA. Tel: (415) 431-1481, FAX: (415) 863-7568, E-Mail: executive@lighthouse-sf.org, Web Site: www.lighthouse-sf.org (1)

Baldwin, Barbara, American Running Association, Bethesda, MD. Tel: (301) 913-9517, (800) 776-2732, FAX: (301) 913-9520, E-Mail: run@americanrunning.org, Web Site: www.americanrunning.org (1)

Baldwin, James L., University of Pittsburgh at Bradford, Bradford, PA. Tel: (814) 362-7500, FAX: (814) 362-5150, E-Mail: admissions@www.upb.pitt.edu, Web Site: www.upd.pitt.edu (41)

Baldwin, Jess, Majestic Products Co, Paris, KY. Tel: (859) 987-0740, Web Site: majesticproducts.com (16)

Baldwin, Michael, Oppenheimer Funds, New York, NY. Tel: (212) 323-0200, FAX: (212) 323-4070, Web Site: www.oppenheimerfunds.com (14)

Bale Co, Providence, RI. Tel: (800) 822-5350, FAX: (401) 831-5500, Web Site: www.bale.com (16)

Baler, Susan, Rich Brands, Phoenix, AZ. Tel: (602) 889-4800, (877) 856-1753, FAX: (602) 889-4830, E-Mail: sales@esscentualbrands.com, Web Site: esscentualbrands.com (16)

Balfour, Austin, TX. Tel: (512) 444-0571, FAX: (512) 440-1138, Web Site: www.artcarved.com (16)

Ball Publishing, West Chicago, IL. Tel: (630) 231-3675, FAX: (630) 231-5254, E-Mail: info@ballpublishing.com, Web Site: www.ballpublishing.com (17)

Ball, Arthur, Garver Advertising Service Inc, New York, NY. Tel: (212) 371-3325, E-Mail: garverads@aol.com (35)

Ball, George, W Atlee Burpee Co, Warminster, PA. Tel: (215) 674-4900, (800) 888-1447, FAX: (215) 674-4170, Web Site: www.burpee.com (8)

Ball, John, KXEN Inc, San Francisco, CA. Tel: (415) 904-4160, FAX: (415) 904-9041, Web Site: www.kxen.com (22)

Ball, Les, Miller Stockman, Denver, CO. Tel: (303) 428-5696, FAX: (303) 430-1130 (2)

Ball, Shirley, Donihe Graphics Inc, Kingsport, TN. Tel: (423) 246-2800, (800) 251-0337, FAX: (423) 246-7297, Web Site: www.donihe.com (27)

Balland, Nerissa, National Parkinson Foundation, Miami, FL. Tel: (305) 243-6666, (800) 937-4545, FAX: (305) 243-6073, E-Mail: contact@parkinson.org, Web Site: www.parkinson.org (1)

The Ballantine Corp, Wayne, NJ. Tel: (973) 305-1500, E-Mail: connect@ballantine.com, Web Site: www.ballantine.com (27)

Ballard Designs, Atlanta, GA. Tel: (404) 603-7033, (800) 536-7551, FAX: (800) 989-4510, Web Site: www.ballarddesigns.com (8)

Ballard, Amanda, Publishers Marketing Association (PMA), Manhattan Beach, CA. Tel: (310) 372-2732, FAX: (310) 374-3342, E-Mail: info@pma-online.org, Web Site: www.pma-online.org (40)

Ballard, Monica V., RBC Funds, Milwaukee, WI. Tel: (800) 422-2766, Web Site: us.rbcgam.com (14)

Ballen, Morris, Audio & Video Labs Inc, Pennsauken, NJ. Tel: (856) 663-9030, (800) 468-9353, FAX: (856) 661-3450, E-Mail: info@discmakers.com, Web Site: www.discmakers.com (16)

Balon, Dr Robert E., The Benchmark Co, Austin, TX. Tel: (512) 707-7500, FAX: (512) 707-7757, E-Mail: thebenc@earthlink.net, Web Site: www.thebenchmarkcompany.net (30)

Balshaugh, Tod, Virginia Home For Boys & Girls, Richmond, VA. Tel: (804) 270-6566, FAX: (804) 270-6574, E-Mail: info@vhbg.org, Web Site: www.vhbg.org (1)

Baltimore Magazine, Baltimore, MD. Tel: (410) 752-4200, (800) 935-0838, FAX: (410) 625-0280, E-Mail: blori@baltimoremagazine.net, Web Site: www.baltimoremagazine.net (17)

Balunas, Kristen, MRW Communications, Pembroke, MA. Tel: (781) 924-5282, FAX: (718) 926-0371, E-Mail: jim@mrwinc.com, Web Site: www.mrwinc.com (35)

BAM! Direct Inc, Suwanee, GA. Tel: (678) 947-1943, FAX: (678) 947-3562, Web Site: www.bamdirect.com (14)

Bambace, Amy, Chase Media Group, Yorktown Heights, NY. Tel: (914) 962-3871, FAX: (914) 962-2040, Web Site: www.chasemultimedia.com (27)

Bamber, Dennis, Woodwind & Brasswind Inc, Westlake Village, CA. Tel: (574) 251-3500, (800) 348-5003, FAX: (800) 266-5962, Web Site: www.wwbw.com (5)

Bamboo Cricket, West Palm Beach, FL. Tel: (561) 515-4546, (800) 260-8050, FAX: (561) 653-3990, E-Mail: info@bamboocricket.com, Web Site: www.bamboocricket.com (32)

Bamboo Sourcery, Sebastopol, CA. Tel: (707) 823-5866, FAX: (707) 829-8106, Web Site: www.bamboosourcery.com (8)

Bambridge, Patricia Lee, Whitehat Inc, Tempe, AZ. Tel: (480) 858-9000, FAX: (480) 858-9001, E-Mail: sales@whitehat.com, Web Site: www.whitehat.com (32)

Bamford, Eileidh, MODCo Media, New York, NY. Tel: (212) 686-0006, FAX: (212) 686-6991, Web Site: modcomedia.com (35)

Banana Republic, San Francisco, CA. Tel: (650) 952-4400, (888) 277-8953, Web Site: www.bananarepublic.com (2)

Bancroft, Charles, Bristol-Myers Squibb Co, New York, NY. Tel: (212) 546-4000, FAX: (212) 546-9544, Web Site: www.bms.com (16)

Banfield Hawkins, Jeanne, Advisor Media Inc, San Diego, CA. Tel: (858) 278-5600, FAX: (858) 278-5600, Web Site: www.advisor.com (32)

Banfill, Stephanie, IMPACT Publishing Inc, Bradenton, FL. Tel: (941) 739-2611, (800) 4-A-NEW-ME, FAX: (941) 756-0315, Web Site: www.potentialsunlimited.com (17)

Banga, Ajay, MasterCard Worldwide, Purchase, NY. Tel: (914) 249-2000, (800) 622-7747, FAX: (914) 249-4220, Web Site: www.mastercard.com (14)

Banikarim, Maryam, Gannett Co Inc, Mc Lean, VA. Tel: (703) 854-6000, FAX: (703) 854-2046, Web Site: www.gannett.com (16)

Bank Boston, Boston, MA. Tel: (617) 434-2200, FAX: (617) 434-7547, Web Site: www.bankboston.com (14)

Joseph A Bank Clothiers Inc, Hampstead, MD. Tel: (410) 239-2700, (800) 285-2265, FAX: (410) 239-5911, E-Mail: service@jos-a-bank.com, Web Site: www.josbank.com (2)

Bank of America, Charlotte, NC. Tel: (704) 386-5681, (800) 841-4000, FAX: (704) 386-6699, Web Site: www.bankofamerica.com (14)

Bank of Hawaii, Honolulu, HI. Tel: (808) 537-8398, FAX: (808) 536-9433, Web Site: www.boh.com (14)

The Bank of New York/Delaware, Newark, DE. Tel: (302) 451-2500, (800) 942-1977, FAX: (302) 451-2537, Web Site: www.bankofny.com (14)

Bank of the West, Los Angeles, CA. Tel: (509) 736-0131, Web Site: www.bankofthewest.com (14)

Bank One, Chicago, IL. Tel: (888) 963-4000, (800) 452-3141, (866) 265-1727, FAX: (614) 248-5624, Web Site: www.bankone.com (14)

Bank, Joe, I-Behavior Inc, Louisville, CO. Tel: (303) 228-5000, E-Mail: ib-sales@i-behavior.com, Web Site: www.i-behavior.com (23)

Banker & Tradesman, Boston, MA. Tel: (617) 428-5100, FAX: (617) 428-5119, Web Site: www.bankerandtradesman.com (17)

Bankers Life & Casualty Co, Chicago, IL. Tel: (312) 396-6000, (800) 231-9150, Web Site: www.bankerslife.com (15)

Bankers Warranty Group, Saint Petersburg, FL. Tel: (800) 431-5843, E-Mail: info@bankerswarrantygroup.com, Web Site: www.bankerswarrantygroup.com (16)

Banks, David, Zurich, Schaumburg, IL. Tel: (847) 605-3712, (800) 382-2150, FAX: (847) 605-6403, Web Site: www.zurichna.com (15)

Banner, Robert, Children's Miracle Network, Salt Lake City, UT. Tel: (801) 214-7400, Web Site: www.cmn.org (40)

BannerDirect, Westhampton Beach, NY. Tel: (212) 858-9883, E-Mail: info@bannerdirect.com, Web Site: www.bannerdirect.com (16)

Bannigan, Patrick Thomas, American Century Investments, Kansas City, MO. Tel: (816) 531-5575, (800) 345-2021, FAX: (816) 340-4964, Web Site: www.americancentury.com (14)

Banninger, Peter, Davidoff of Geneva Inc, Pinellas Park, FL. Tel: (727) 828-5400, (800) 328-4365, FAX: (203) 975-0090 (6)

Bannister, Dan, Saunders Military Insignia, Naples, FL. Tel: (239) 298-8228, (800) 442-3133, FAX: (239) 774-3323, E-Mail: info@saundersinsignia.com, Web Site: www.saundersinsignia.com (6)

Bantam Dell Publishing Group Inc, New York, NY. Tel: (212) 782-9000, FAX: (212) 940-7381, Web Site: www.bantam-dell.atrandom.com (17)

Bantivoglio, Barbara, Channel 13 WNET Catalog Division, New York, NY. Tel: (212) 560-1313, FAX: (212) 560-1314, E-Mail: programming@thirteen.org, Web Site: www.thirteen.org (5)

Banzon, Jose, White64, Vienna, VA. Tel: (703) 793-3000, E-Mail: info@white64.com, Web Site: white64.com (35)

Baraban, Rob, Tobe Direct, Bolingbrook, IL. Tel: (630) 910-7080, FAX: (630) 910-3670, E-Mail: sales@tobedirect.com, Web Site: www.tobedirect.com (16)

Baraga, Anthony R., University of Minnesota Alumni Association, Minneapolis, MN. Tel: (612) 624-2323, (800) 862-5867, FAX: (612) 626-8167, E-Mail: umalumni@umn.edu, Web Site: www.minnesotaalumni.org (1)

Baraga, Toni, R Falls Agency, Minneapolis, MN. Tel: (612) 872-6372, (800) 339-1119, FAX: (612) 872-1018, E-Mail: info@fallsagency.com, Web Site: fallsagency.com (35)

Baranski, Dennis A., Northern Cross, Lecompton, KS. Tel: (785) 887-6010, (800) 625-7233, FAX: (785) 887-6263 (16)

Baratoff, Michael, Metropolitan Newspaper Advertising Services Inc, Yonkers, NY. Tel: (212) 689-8200, FAX: (212) 779-9795, E-Mail: info@metrosn.com, Web Site: www.metrosn.com (31)

Barbato, Anthony, Associated Textile Rental Services, Rochester, NY. Tel: (585) 454-5988, (800) 639-4624, Web Site: www.associatedtextile.com (16)

Barbeau, Ed, Global-Z International Inc, Bennington, VT. Tel: (802) 445-1011, FAX: (802) 445-1016, E-Mail: info@globalz.com, Web Site: www.globalz.com (22)

Barbello, Kelly, Denver Metro Convention & Visitors Bureau, Denver, CO. Tel: (303) 892-1112, (800) 233-6837, FAX: (303) 892-1636, Web Site: www.denver.org (1)

Barbeosch, George T., United States Bronze Sign Co Inc, New Hyde Park, NY. Tel: (516) 352-5155, (800) 872-5155, FAX: (516) 253-2328, E-Mail: peter@usbronze.com, Web Site: www.usbronze.com (1)

Barber, Bob, Advanced Financial Services, Middletown, RI. Tel: (401) 849-0892, (800) 620-6292, FAX: (401) 851-5621, Web Site: www.embracehomeloans.com (14)

Barber, Dar, Biomerica Inc, Irvine, CA. Tel: (949) 645-2111, (800) 854-3002, FAX: (949) 553-1231, E-Mail: info@biomerica.com, Web Site: www.biomerica.com (14)

Barber, Debbi, Grizzard Communications Group Inc, Atlanta, GA. Tel: (404) 522-8330, (800) 241-9351, Web Site: www.grizzard.com (35)

Barber, Howard, Shelby Insurance Companies, Birmingham, AL. Tel: (800) 443-1573, FAX: (877) 837-8203, Web Site: www.vesta.com (14)

Barber, John, Summit Direct Mail Inc, Dallas, TX. Tel: (469) 916-5170, (877) 247-0993, E-Mail: info@summitdm.com, Web Site: www.summitdm.com (28)

Barber, Lionel, The Financial Times Group, New York, NY. Tel: (212) 641-6500, Web Site: www.ft.com (17)

Barber, Michael J., Biosciences-Amersham, Piscataway, NJ. Tel: (732) 457-8000, FAX: (732) 457-0557, Web Site: www.amersham.com (16)

Barbieri, Christine, The Artists Co, New York, NY. Tel: (212) 679-7199, Web Site: blog.theartistscompany.com (32)

Barbo, Gary, Starchtech, Golden Valley, MN. Tel: (763) 545-5400, (800) 597-7225, FAX: (763) 545-9450, Web Site: www.starchtech.com (16)

Barbour Publishing Inc, Uhrichsville, OH. Tel: (740) 922-6045, FAX: (740) 922-5948, (800) 220-5948, E-Mail: info@barbourbooks.com, Web Site: www.barbourbooks.com (17)

Barbour, Matthew, Omnigraphics Inc, Aston, PA. Tel: (610) 461-3548, (800) 234-1340, FAX: (800) 875-1340, E-Mail: info@omnigraphics.com, Web Site: www.omnigraphics.com (17)

Barcia Direct Marketing, Langhorne, PA. Tel: (215) 757-5785, FAX: (215) 757-5785, E-Mail: j.barciadirect@comcast.net (39)

Barcia, Joseph A., Barcia Direct Marketing, Langhorne, PA. Tel: (215) 757-5785, FAX: (215) 757-5785, E-Mail: j.barciadirect@comcast.net (39)

Barclay, Marty, Center for eBusiness & Advanced IT, Erie, PA. Tel: (814) 898-6500, FAX: (814) 898-6534, Web Site: www.ebizitpa.org (1)

Barcoding Inc, Baltimore, MD. Tel: (410) 385-8532, (888) 860-SCAN, (888) 860-7226, FAX: (410) 385-8559, E-Mail: info@barcoding.com, Web Site: www.barcoding.com (22)

Bard, Alex, Campaign Monitor, San Francisco, CA. Tel: (888) 533-8098, E-Mail: info@campaignmonitor.com, Web Site: www.campaignmonitor.com (24)

Bardenheier, Jr. George, Partners Marketing Inc, Saint Charles, IL. Tel: (630) 524-9901, FAX: (630) 524-9909, E-Mail: georgeb@partnersmarketing.com, Web Site: www.partnersmarketing.com (22)

Bardin, Dan R., Conseco Inc, Carmel, IN. Tel: (317) 817-6100, FAX: (317) 817-2847, Web Site: www.conseco.com (15)

Barefoot, Glenn P, Strongwell, Bristol, VA. Tel: (276) 645-8000, FAX: (276) 645-8132, E-Mail: gbarefoot@strongwell.com, Web Site: www.strongwell.com (9)

Barela, Jeff, Dovetail, Littleton, CO. Tel: (303) 904-4771, FAX: (303) 904-4776, E-Mail: welcome@dovetailnet.com, Web Site: www.dovetailnet.com (22)

Barely Nothings Lingerie, Nipomo, CA. Tel: (805) 489-5591, (800) 422-7359, FAX: (888) 489-5987, E-Mail: lingerie@barelynothings.com, Web Site: www.getpassionhere.com (2)

Barenklau, Shon, Papillion Times Group, Bellevue, NE. Tel: (402) 733-7300, (877) 476-4237, FAX: (402) 537-2997, E-Mail: advertising@papilliontimes.com, Web Site: www.papilliontimes.com (31)

Bargas, Michael, Things Remembered, Highland Heights, OH. Tel: (440) 473-2000, (866) 902-4438, FAX: (440) 473-2018, E-Mail: customerservice@thingsremembered.com, Web Site: www.thingsremembered.com (6)

Barge, James W., Lionsgate Entertainment Inc, New York, NY. Tel: (212) 577-2400, FAX: (212) 962-2872, Web Site: www.lionsgate.com (32)

Barge, James W., Lionsgate Television Corp, Santa Monica, CA. Tel: (310) 449-9200, FAX: (310) 255-3870, Web Site: www.lionsgate.com (16)

Bargerhuff, Rita E., Rent-A-Center Inc, Plano, TX. Tel: (972) 801-1100, (800) 275-2996, FAX: (972) 943-0113, Web Site: www.rentacenter.com (16)

Barham, Blaine, The Union Labor Life Insurance Co, Silver Spring, MD. Tel: (202) 962-2945, FAX: (202) 962-8429, E-Mail: info@ullico.com, Web Site: www.unioncare.com (15)

Barile, Giovanni, ListGIANT, Westlake Village, CA. Tel: (800) 383-1381, E-Mail: contact@listgiant.com, Web Site: www.listgiant.com (23)

Baritz, Leonard, Eyeglass Service Industries, Lynbrook, NY. Tel: (516) 599-1135, FAX: (516) 599-4825 (2)

Bob Barker Co Inc, Fuquay Varina, NC. Tel: (800) 334-9880, FAX: (800) 322-7537, Web Site: www.bobbarker.com (5)

Barker Specialty Co, Cheshire, CT. Tel: (203) 272-2222, (800) 227-5377, E-Mail: promo@barkerspecialty.com, Web Site: www.barkerspecialty.com (33)

Barker, Gerald, Barker Specialty Co, Cheshire, CT. Tel: (203) 272-2222, (800) 227-5377, E-Mail: promo@barkerspecialty.com, Web Site: www.barkerspecialty.com (33)

Barker, Lee, The Interprovincial Group, Scarborough, ON Canada. Tel: (416) 283-5555, FAX: (416) 283-6643, E-Mail: info@interprovincialgroup.com, Web Site: www.interprovincialgroup.com (21)

Barker, Robert, Bob Barker Co Inc, Fuquay Varina, NC. Tel: (800) 334-9880, FAX: (800) 322-7537, Web Site: www.bobbarker.com (5)

Barker, Scott, Bullseye Marketing Inc, Canoga Park, CA. Tel: (818) 888-8700, Web Site: www.bullseyeb2b.com (28)

Barker, William R., Taylor-Stiles Division, Florence, KY. Tel: (859) 525-7600, (800) 365-8555, FAX: (859) 525-1446, E-Mail: sales@littleford.com, Web Site: www.littleford.com (16)

Barkley, Kansas City, MO. Tel: (816) 842-1500, E-Mail: 411@barkleyus.com, Web Site: www.barkleyus.com (35)

The Ted Barkus Co Inc, Philadelphia, PA. Tel: (215) 545-0616, FAX: (215) 242-8814, E-Mail: a.barkus-tbc@att.net (35)

Barkus, Allen, The Ted Barkus Co Inc, Philadelphia, PA. Tel: (215) 545-0616, FAX: (215) 242-8814, E-Mail: a.barkus-tbc@att.net (35)

Barkyoumb, Francis, Direct Dynamics LLC, Killingworth, CT. Tel: (860) 614-4816, E-Mail: info@direct-dynamics.com, Web Site: direct-dynamics.com (20)

Barlik, Len, Cox Communications Inc, Atlanta, GA. Tel: (404) 843-5000, (888) 566-7751, FAX: (404) 269-2243, Web Site: www.cox.com (16)

Barlow, Deborah, Forestry Suppliers Inc, Jackson, MS. Tel: (601) 354-3565, (800) 647-5368, FAX: (601) 292-0165, E-Mail: fsi@forestry-suppliers.com, Web Site: www.forestry-suppliers.com (9)

Barlow, Greg, Encyclopaedia Britannica Inc, Chicago, IL. Tel: (312) 347-7159, (800) 323-1229, FAX: (312) 294-2104, Web Site: www.britannica.com (17)

Barlow, Turalee, Prakken Publications Inc, Ann Arbor, MI. Tel: (734) 975-2800, (800) 530-9673, FAX: (734) 975-2787, Web Site: www.techdirections.com; www.eddigest.com (17)

Barn, Franklin, Vulcan Information Packaging. Vincent, AL. Tel: (205) 672-2241, (800) 633-4526, FAX: (205) 672-1276, Web Site: www.vulcan-online.com (16)

Barna, Michelle, Slifter, New York, NY. Tel: (212) 488-2222, Web Site: www.slifter.com (16)

Barnaby, Paul, Delta Tech Industries, Ontario, CA. Tel: (714) 577-8028, FAX: (714) 577-0140, E-Mail: sales@deltatechindustries.com, Web Site: www.deltatechindustries.com (12)

Barnard, John, Vita-Mix Corp, Cleveland, OH. Tel: (440) 235-4840, (800) VITA-MIX, FAX: (440) 235-3726, E-Mail: service@vitamix.com, Web Site: www.vitamix.com (16)

Barnard, W. G., Vita-Mix Corp, Cleveland, OH. Tel: (440) 235-4840, (800) VITA-MIX, FAX: (440) 235-3726, E-Mail: service@vitamix.com, Web Site: www.vitamix.com (16)

Barnes, Billy E., Billy E Barnes, Chapel Hill, NC. Tel: (919) 942-6350, FAX: (919) 942-6350, E-Mail: bbarnes218@aol.com, Web Site: www.billybarnes.com (38)

Barnes, Christina, UF College of Advertising, Journalism, & Communications, Gainesville, FL. Tel: (352) 392-4046, FAX: (352) 392-3919, Web Site: www.jou.ufl.edu (41)

Barnes, Christopher, DS Direct Response, Torrance, CA. Tel: (310) 251-1830, E-Mail: info@dsdirectresponse.com, Web Site: dsdirectresponse.com (23)

Barnes, David, Fresno Oxygen, Fresno, CA. Tel: (559) 233-6684, (800) 404-9353, FAX: (559) 233-4206, E-Mail: info@fresnooxygen.com, Web Site: www.fresnooxygen.com (9)

Barnes, Denise, Babcock & Jenkins, Portland, OR. Tel: (503) 382-8500, E-Mail: laureng@bnj.com, Web Site: www.bnj.com (35)

Barnes, Fred, Hammacher Schlemmer & Co Inc, Niles, IL. Tel: (847) 581-8600, (800) 233-4800, FAX: (847) 581-8616, Web Site: www.hammacher.com (16)

Barnes, Greg, Holiday Vacations, Eau Claire, WI. Tel: (715) 834-5555, (800) 826-2266, FAX: (715) 834-8554, E-Mail: info@holidayvacations.net, Web Site: www.holidayvacations.net (19)

Barnes, Jim, General Physics Corp, Elkridge, MD. Tel: (410) 379-3600, (800) 727-6677, FAX: (410) 540-5302, E-Mail: info@gpworldwide.com, Web Site: www.gpworldwide.com (16)

Barnes, John, Infutor Data Solutions, Oakbrook Terrace, IL. Tel: (312) 348-7900, E-Mail: sales@infutor.com, Web Site: www.infutor.com (23)

Barnes, Karen, Beauty Naturally, Burlingame, CA. Tel: (650) 596-5742, (800) 432-4323, FAX: (650) 596-5742, E-Mail: sales@beautynaturally.com, Web Site: www.beautynaturally.com (7)

Barnes, Mark, Volkswagen Group of America Inc, Herndon, VA. Tel: (248) 754-5000, Web Site: www.volkswagengroupamerica.com (16)

Barnes, Mike, Fresno Oxygen, Fresno, CA. Tel: (559) 233-6684, (800) 404-9353, FAX: (559) 233-4206, E-Mail: info@fresnooxygen.com, Web Site: www.fresnooxygen.com (9)

Barnes, Nancy, Star Tribune Media Co, Minneapolis, MN. Tel: (612) 673-4000, FAX: (612) 673-4359, Web Site: www.startribunecompany.com (17)

Barnes, Red, Fresno Oxygen, Fresno, CA. Tel: (559) 233-6684, (800) 404-9353, FAX: (559) 233-4206, E-Mail: info@fresnooxygen.com, Web Site: www.fresnooxygen.com (9)

Barnes, Scott, The Psychological Corp, San Antonio, TX. Tel: (800) 211-8378, FAX: (800) 232-1223, Web Site: www.psychcorp.com (17)

Barnes, Trevor, Markson Scientific LLC, Henderson, NC. Tel: (808) 791-0490, (800) 528-5114, FAX: (800) 858-2243, E-Mail: sales@markson.com, Web Site: www.markson.com (9)

BarnesandNoble.com, New York, NY. Tel: (212) 414-6000, (800) THE-BOOK, FAX: (212) 414-6140, E-Mail: service@barnesandnoble.com, Web Site: www.barnesandnoble.com (16)

Barnett, Bob, Telebrands Corp, Fairfield, NJ. Tel: (973) 247-8777, Web Site: www.telebrands.com (21)

Barnett, Cheryle, Grafica Group, Morristown, NJ. Tel: (973) 309-7500, FAX: (973) 309-7501, E-Mail: information@grafica.com, Web Site: www.grafica.com (35)

Barnett, George, Teva Pharmaceuticals USA, North Wales, PA. Tel: (215) 591-3000, (888) 838-2872, FAX: (215) 591-8600, Web Site: www.tevausa.com (7)

Barnett, Stacie, Richards Partners, Dallas, TX. Tel: (214) 891-5700, FAX: (214) 891-3515, E-Mail: ruth_fitzgibbons@richards.com, Web Site: richardspartners.com (35)

Barney, Jeff, Aerosoles, Edison, NJ. Tel: 732-985-6900, (800) 798-9478, FAX: (732) 985-3697, Web Site: www.aerosoles.com (2)

Barnhart, Jeffrey E., Creative Marketing Alliance Inc, Princeton Junction, NJ. Tel: (609) 297-2235, FAX: (609) 799-7032, E-Mail: info@cmasolutions.com, Web Site: www.gotocma.com (35)

Barnhill, Chris, Better Tools For Industry, Santee, CA. Tel: (619) 562-3071, FAX: (619) 562-0592, Web Site: www.bti-tool.com (9)

Barnhill, Jim, Better Tools For Industry, Santee, CA. Tel: (619) 562-3071, FAX: (619) 562-0592, Web Site: www.bti-tool.com (9)

Barnhill, Jr. Robert B., Tessco Inc, Hunt Valley, MD. Tel: (410) 229-1000, (800) 508-5444, FAX: (410) 527-0005, E-Mail: webhelp@tessco.com, Web Site: www.tessco.com (16)

Barnum, Lois, PAL Health Technologies, Pekin, IL. Tel: (309) 347-8785, (800) 223-2957, FAX: (309) 477-4456, Web Site: www.palhealth.com (16)

Baron/Barclay Bridge Supplies, Louisville, KY. Tel: (502) 426-0410, (800) 274-2221, FAX: (502) 426-2044, E-Mail: baronbarclay@baronbarclay.com, Web Site: www.baronbarclay.com (11)

Baron, Gary, Voice Systems Engineering Inc, Langhorne, PA. Tel: (215) 953-8568, E-Mail: info@vseinc.com, Web Site: www.vseinc.com (32)

Baron, Herman, Diane Publishing Co, Darby, PA. Tel: (610) 461-6200, E-Mail: hbaron@dianepublishing.net, Web Site: www.dianepublishing.net (43)

Baron, Mary, Baron/Barclay Bridge Supplies, Louisville, KY. Tel: (502) 426-0410, (800) 274-2221, FAX: (502) 426-2044, E-Mail: baronbarclay@baronbarclay.com, Web Site: www.baronbarclay.com (11)

Baron, Randall, Baron/Barclay Bridge Supplies, Louisville, KY. Tel: (502) 426-0410, (800) 274-2221, FAX: (502) 426-2044, E-Mail: baronbarclay@baronbarclay.com, Web Site: www.baronbarclay.com (11)

Baron, Rob, Finch Paper, Glens Falls, NY. Tel: (518) 793-2541, (800) 833-9983, FAX: (518) 793-7364, E-Mail: info@finchpaper.com, Web Site: www.finchpaper.com (25)

Baron, Trish, Catalogs.com, Fort Lauderdale, FL. Tel: (954) 659-9005, FAX: (954) 659-9007, Web Site: www.catalogs.com (30)

Barozzini, Brenda, Admore Inc, Macomb, MI. Tel: (810) 949-8200, (800) 523-6673, FAX: (800) 215-2664, Web Site: www.admoreonline.com (10)

Barr, Bob, A+ Letter Service, Lakewood, NJ. Tel: (732) 905-2010, FAX: (732) 905-4662, E-Mail: aplus@aplusletter.com, Web Site: www.aplusletters.com (28)

Barr, Chris, Taradel LLC, Glen Allen, VA. Tel: (804) 364-8444, (800) 481-1656, FAX: (888) 241-3023, E-Mail: info@taradel.com, Web Site: www.taradel.com (21)

Barr, Jim, Christian Broadcasting Network Inc, Virginia Beach, VA. Tel: (757) 226-7000, FAX: (757) 226-2017, Web Site: www.cbn.com (1)

Barr, MD Michael S, American College of Physicians, Philadelphia, PA. Tel: (215) 351-2600, (800) 523-1546, FAX: (215) 351-2686, Web Site: www.acponline.org (17)

Barragan, Napoleon, 1-800-Mattress.com, Hicksville, NY. Tel: (800) 327-7720, Web Site: www.1800mattress.com (17)

Barrett, Anthony, ValCom Inc, Boonton, NJ. Tel: (973) 588-7084, FAX: (973) 257-7216, E-Mail: info@valcom.tv, Web Site: www.valcom.tv (32)

Barrett, David, Mel Bay Publications Inc, Pacific, MO. Tel: (800) 8-MELBAY, FAX: (636) 257-5062, E-Mail: email@melbay.com, Web Site: www.melbay.com (17)

Barrett, Donna, Newspaper Association of America, Arlington, VA. Tel: (571) 366-1000, FAX: (571) 366-1195, Web Site: www.naa.org (1)

Barrett, Edward V., Direct Logic Solutions, Peoria, IL. Tel: (309) 688-5500, FAX: (309) 688-5502, E-Mail: nedbarrett@direct-logic.com, Web Site: www.direct-logic.com (22)

Barrett, James, Sterling Name Tape Inc, Winsted, CT. Tel: (860) 379-5142, (800) 654-5210, FAX: (860) 379-0394, E-Mail: postman@sterlingtape.com, Web Site: www.sterlingtape.com (16)

Barrett, Mark, LinguiSystems, East Moline, IL. Tel: (309) 755-2300, (800) 776-4332, FAX: (800) 577-4555, E-Mail: service@linguisystems.com, Web Site: www.linguisystems.com (17)

Barrett, Rob, Los Angeles Times, Los Angeles, CA. Tel: (213) 237-5000, (800) 528-4637, FAX: (213) 237-7679, E-Mail: rob.barrett@latimes.com, Web Site: www.latimes.com (31)

Barrett, Scott, Eastern Mountain Sports, Peterborough, NH. Tel: (603) 924-9571, (888) 463-6367, FAX: (603) 924-4320, Web Site: www.ems.com (16)

Barrie, Bruner, Sculpture House Inc, Skillman, NJ. Tel: (609) 466-2986, FAX: (888) 529-1980, E-Mail: customercare@sculpturehouse.com, Web Site: www.sculpturehouse.com (16)

Barringer & Associates Ltd, Hickory, NC. Tel: (828) 322-5550, FAX: (828) 327-8440, E-Mail: barringer@barringeragency.com, Web Site: www.barringeragency.com (35)

Barringer, Phil, Barringer & Associates Ltd, Hickory, NC. Tel: (828) 322-5550, FAX: (828) 327-8440, E-Mail: barringer@barringeragency.com, Web Site: www.barringeragency.com (35)

Barrington, Allyson, Suntrust Banks Inc, Atlanta, GA. Tel: (404) 588-7914, (800) 786-8787, FAX: (404) 532-0550, E-Mail: emmett.harmon@suntrust.com, Web Site: www.suntrust.com (14)

Barrington, Liz, Recognition Systems (Dot Works), Port Washington, NY. Tel: (516) 625-5000, FAX: (516) 625-1507, E-Mail: wade@dotworks.com, Web Site: www.dotworks.com (16)

Barron, Dana, HB Communications, North Haven, CT. Tel: (203) 234-9246, (800) 243-4414, FAX: (203) 234-2013, E-Mail: info@hbcommunications.com, Web Site: www.hbcommunications.com (34)

Barron, Mackey, HB Communications, North Haven, CT. Tel: (203) 234-9246, (800) 243-4414, FAX: (203) 234-2013, E-Mail: info@hbcommunications.com, Web Site: www.hbcommunications.com (34)

Barron, Robert, 20th Century Fox Television, Los Angeles, CA. Tel: (310) 369-4636, FAX: (310) 969-0468, Web Site: www.foxstudios.com (16)

Barros, Glenn, Hear Music, Beverly Hills, CA. Tel: (425) 452-5534, E-Mail: gail@hearmusic.com, Web Site: www.hearmusic.com (14)

Barrow, Bob, Brotherhood America's Oldest Winery Ltd, Washingtonville, NY. Tel: (845) 496-3661, FAX: (845) 496-8720, E-Mail: contact@brotherhoodwinery.net, Web Site: www.brotherhoodwinery.net (19)

Barrows, Cliff, Billy Graham Evangelistic Association, Charlotte, NC. Tel: (704) 401-2432, (877) 247-2426, Web Site: www.billygraham.org (1)

Barrs, Craig, Georgia Power, Atlanta, GA. Tel: (404) 506-3440 (16)

F Curtis Barry & Co, Henrico, VA. Tel: (804) 740-8743, FAX: (804) 740-6179, E-Mail: cbarry@fcbco.com, Web Site: www.fcbco.com (20)

RG Barry Corp, Pickerington, OH. Tel: (614) 864-6400, (800) 848-7560, FAX: (614) 866-9787, E-Mail: sales@rgbarry.com, Web Site: www.rgbarry.com (2)

Barry, Connie, Pharmavite Corp LLC (HQ), Northridge, CA. Tel: (818) 221-6200, (800) 423-2405, FAX: (818) 221-6618, Web Site: www.pharmavite.com (16)

Barry, Curt, F Curtis Barry & Co, Henrico, VA. Tel: (804) 740-8743, FAX: (804) 740-6179, E-Mail: cbarry@fcbco.com, Web Site: www.fcbco.com (20)

Barry, Kaitlin, ADRFCO, Washington, DC. Tel: (202) 293-9640, FAX: (202) 463-7980, E-Mail: adrfco@msn.com, Web Site: www.adrfco.org (1)

Barry, Richard, Atlantic Publication Group LLC, Charleston, SC. Tel: (843) 747-0025, FAX: (843) 744-0816, E-Mail: info@atlanticpublicationgrp.com, Web Site: www.atlanticpublicationgrp.com (17)

Bartash Media Group, Philadelphia, PA. Tel: (215) 724-1700, (800) 599-9792, FAX: (215) 724-3313, Web Site: www.bartash.com (27)

Bartels, Dean, Starchtech, Golden Valley, MN. Tel: (763) 545-5400, (800) 597-7225, FAX: (763) 545-9450, Web Site: www.starchtech.com (16)

Barterbing.com, Cranston, RI. Tel: (800) 345-6733, FAX: (401) 679-0326, Web Site: www.barterbing.com (29)

BarterNews, Laguna Niguel, CA. Tel: (949) 831-0607, FAX: (949) 831-9378, E-Mail: bmeyer@barternews.com, Web Site: www.barternews.com (17)

Barth, John, Walter Karl Inc, Pearl River, NY. Tel: (845) 620-0700, FAX: (845) 620-1885, E-Mail: info@walterkarl.infousa.com, Web Site: www.walterkarl.com (22)

Bartles, Dean L., Society of Manufacturing Engineers, Dearborn, MI. Tel: (313) 425-3000, (800) 733-4763, FAX: (313) 425-3400, E-Mail: communications@sme.org, Web Site: www.sme.org (1)

Bartlett, Bob, John Alden Life Insurance Co/North Star Marketing, Duluth, GA. Tel: (678) 473-1211, (800) 768-6288, FAX: (678) 473-9573, Web Site: www.nstarmarketing.com (15)

Bartlett, Marie, Lake Shore Industries, Erie, PA. Tel: (800) 458-0463, FAX: (814) 453-4293, E-Mail: info@lsisigns.com, Web Site: www.lsisigns.com (16)

Bartley, Steven, Advertising That Works, Bloomfield Hills, MI. Tel: (248) 757-2878, FAX: (248) 626-2264, Web Site: www.advthatworks.com (23)

Bartolotta, Joe, Eastern Bank, Boston, MA. Tel: (617) 897-1008, (800) EASTERN, FAX: (617) 897-1105, Web Site: www.easternbank.com (14)

Barton & Cooney, Burlington, NJ. Tel: (609) 747-9300, FAX: (609) 747-9700, E-Mail: pmdoyle@bartoncooney.com, Web Site: www.bartoncooney.com (28)

Barton-Cotton, Baltimore, MD. Tel: (410) 247-4800, (800) 348-1102, FAX: (410) 536-0491, E-Mail: info@bartoncotton.com, Web Site: www.bartoncotton.com (16)

Barton, Cammy, Innovative Industries Inc, Carthage, MO. Tel: (417) 358-6891, (800) 344-7467, FAX: (417) 358-1849, E-Mail: info@innovativeindustries.com, Web Site: www.innovativeindustries.com (28)

Barton, Doug, Trone Brand Energy Inc, High Point, NC. Tel: (336) 886-1622, E-Mail: info@trone.com, Web Site: www.tronebrandenergy.com (35)

Barton, J. Gary, State Mutual Insurance Co, Rome, GA. Tel: (706) 291-1054, FAX: (706) 291-9459 (15)

Barton, John, Nomadics Tipi Makers, Bend, OR. Tel: (541) 389-3980, FAX: (541) 389-3980, Web Site: www.tipi.com (11)

Barton, Rick, BUYSEASONS Inc, New Berlin, WI. Tel: (262) 901-2000, FAX: (262) 901-2315, Web Site: www.buyseasons.com (5)

Bartruff, Lori, Nancy's Notions LLC, Beaver Dam, WI. Tel: (920) 887-0321, (800) 833-0690, FAX: (800) 255-8119, E-Mail: comments@nancysnotions.com, Web Site: www.nancysnotions.com (11)

Bart's Watersports, North Webster, IN. Tel: (574) 834-7666, (800) 348-5016, FAX: (574) 834-4246, E-Mail: info@barts.com, Web Site: www.bartswatersports.com (11)

Bartsch, Leo, Mail America Inc, Wheeling, WV. Tel: (304) 242-8081, (800) 421-2150, FAX: (304) 242-8082, E-Mail: sales@mailamerica.com, Web Site: www.mailamerica.com (35)

Bartsch, Tom, Krause Publications Inc, Iola, WI. Tel: (715) 445-2214, FAX: (715) 445-4087, Web Site: www.krausebooks.com (17)

Bartyzel, Sean, Koeppel Direct, Dallas, TX. Tel: (972) 732-6110, FAX: (972) 248-2759, E-Mail: pkoeppel@koeppelinc.com, Web Site: www.koeppeldirect.com (32)

Bartz, John D., Sage Software Inc, Irvine, CA. Tel: (949) 753-1222, (800) 854-3415, FAX: (949) 753-0374, Web Site: www.sagesoftware.com (16)

Baruch College - Dept of Mktg & International Bus, New York, NY. Tel: (646) 312-3270, FAX: (646) 312-3271, E-Mail: mktIB@baruch.cuny.edu, Web Site: www.baruch.cuny.edu (41)

Baruki, Carlos, Quaxar, Miami, FL. Tel: (305) 350-9520, Web Site: www.quaxar.com (35)

Barwick, Johanna, Oxbridge Communications Inc, New York, NY. Tel: (212) 741-0231, (800) 955-0231, FAX: (212) 633-2938, E-Mail: custserv@oxbridge.com, Web Site: www.mediafinder.com; www.oxbridge.com (30)

Barzizza, Tom, Archer Malmo Inc, Memphis, TN. Tel: (901) 523-2000, FAX: (901) 524-5578, Web Site: www.archermalmo.com (35)

Basan, Edward J., Carefirst Blue Cross Blue Shield, Washington, DC. Tel: (202) 479-8000, FAX: (301) 470-8049, Web Site: www.carefirst.com (15)

Basch, Jeffrey W., The Progressive Corp, Mayfield Village, OH. Tel: (440) 461-5000, (800) PROGRESSIVE, (800) 776-4737, FAX: (800) 456-6590, Web Site: www.progressive.com (15)

Baseline FT, Los Angeles, CA. Tel: (212) 254-8235, (310) 393-9999, (800) 242-7546, FAX: (212) 529-3330, E-Mail: info@baseline.hollywood.com, Web Site: www.baseline.hollywood.com (17)

Basham, Barbara, Celtic Life Insurance Co, Chicago, IL. Tel: (312) 332-5401, FAX: (312) 441-0341, E-Mail: info@celtic-net.com, Web Site: www.celtic-net.com (15)

Basic Adhesives Inc, Clifton, NJ. Tel: (800) 394-9310, FAX: (973) 614-9099, E-Mail: info@basicadhesives.com, Web Site: www.basicadhesives.com (9)

Basic Research, Salt Lake City, UT. Tel: (801) 530-2911, (888) 865-5326, E-Mail: customerservice@basicresearch.com, Web Site: www.silversage.com (7)

Basile, Kelly, Atlantic Research & Consulting Inc, Boston, MA. Tel: (617) 720-0174, FAX: (617) 589-3731, E-Mail: generalmailbox@guideline.com, Web Site: www.atlanticresearch.net (30)

Baskies, Jeff, Lawyer's Weekly Publications, Boston, MA. Tel: (617) 451-7300, FAX: (617) 451-0132, Web Site: www.lawyersweekly.com (17)

Basoco, Richard, Baltimore Magazine, Baltimore, MD. Tel: (410) 752-4200, (800) 935-0838, FAX: (410) 625-0280, E-Mail: blori@baltimoremagazine.net, Web Site: www.baltimoremagazine.net (17)

Bass Pro Shops, Springfield, MO. Tel: (417) 887-7334, FAX: (417) 873-5882, Web Site: www.basspro.com (11)

Bass, Bill, Charming Shoppes Inc., Bensalem, PA. Tel: (215) 245-9100, Web Site: www.charmingshoppers.com (2)

Bass, Bill, Fair Indigo, Madison, WI. Tel: (608) 824-8974, (800) 520-1806, E-Mail: service@fairindigo.com, Web Site: www.fairindigo.com (2)

Bass, Carl, Autodesk Inc, San Rafael, CA. Tel: (415) 507-5000, FAX: (415) 507-5100, Web Site: www.autodesk.com (16)

Bass, James K., The New Piper Aircraft Inc, Vero Beach, FL. Tel: (772) 567-4361, FAX: (772) 978-6573, E-Mail: marketing@piper.com, Web Site: www.newpiper.com (16)

Bassett, David, Midwest Center for Stress & Anxiety Inc, Oak Harbor, OH. Tel: (419) 898-4357, (877) 989-8229, FAX: (419) 898-0669, Web Site: www.stresscenter.com (7)

Bassett, Lucinda, Midwest Center for Stress & Anxiety Inc, Oak Harbor, OH. Tel: (419) 898-4357, (877) 989-8229, FAX: (419) 898-0669, Web Site: www.stresscenter.com (7)

Bassick, Katherine, Cross Country Automotive Services, Medford, MA. Tel: (781) 393-9300, Web Site: www.cchs.com (16)

Bassine, Greg, DMG Direct Inc, Tigard, OR. Tel: (503) 579-5609, (888) 282-2122, FAX: (503) 579-4919, E-Mail: dmg@dirmarketing.com, Web Site: www.dirmarketing.com/dmginc (40)

Bassoul, Selim A., The Middleby Corp, Elgin, IL. Tel: (847) 741-3300, FAX: (847) 741-0015, E-Mail: sales@middleby.com, Web Site: www.middleby.com (16)

Basta, Stephanie, Parsons School of Design Human Resource Dept, New York, NY. Tel: (212) 229-5671, FAX: (212) 229-8975, E-Mail: communications@newschool.edu, Web Site: www.newschool.edu/parsons/ (41)

Bastian, Matthew, ICS Corp, West Deptford, NJ. Tel: (215) 427-3355, E-Mail: mefstathios@ics-corporation.com, Web Site: www.ics-corporation.com (21)

Bastien, Ernest, Toyota Motor Sales USA Inc, Torrance, CA. Tel: (310) 468-4000, (800) 331-4331, FAX: (310) 468-7841, Web Site: www.toyota.com (16)

Bataille, James M., BN Creative Advertising, Mount Prospect, IL. Tel: (847) 577-1300, FAX: (847) 577-2101 (36)

Keith Bates & Associates Inc, Chicago, IL. Tel: (773) 205-7992, FAX: (773) 205-7988, E-Mail: keithbates@kbates.com, Web Site: www.kbates.com (35)

Bates, David, Publishers Marketing Association (PMA), Manhattan Beach, CA. Tel: (310) 372-2732, FAX: (310) 374-3342, E-Mail: info@pma-online.org, Web Site: www.pma-online.org (40)

Bates, Keith, Keith Bates & Associates Inc, Chicago, IL. Tel: (773) 205-7992, FAX: (773) 205-7988, E-Mail: keithbates@kbates.com, Web Site: www.kbates.com (35)

Bathroom Machineries, Murphys, CA. Tel: (209) 728-2031, (800) 255-4426, FAX: (209) 728-2320, Web Site: www.deabath.com (8)

Baton Rouge Conventions & Visitors Bureau, Baton Rouge, LA. Tel: (225) 383-1825, (800) LA-ROUGE, FAX: (225) 346-1253, E-Mail: karron@visitbatonrouge.com, Web Site: www.bracvb.com (1)

Batson, Paula, BMG Columbia House, New York, NY. Tel: (212) 287-0081, E-Mail: cs1@bmgmusicservice.com (13)

Battaglia, Christopher, Pensions & Investments, New York, NY. Tel: (212) 210-0100, FAX: (212) 210-0117, Web Site: www.pionline.com (17)

Battery Pros Inc, Horseshoe Beach, FL. Tel: (352) 498-2662, (800) 451-7171, FAX: (352) 498-2482, E-Mail: sales@probattery.com, Web Site: www.probattery.com (9)

Battisto, Mike, Target & Response Inc, Naperville, IL. Tel: (312) 321-0500, FAX: (312) 321-0051, Web Site: www.target-response.com (35)

Battle, Craig L., Tucker Capital Corp, Princeton, NJ. Tel: (609) 924-5710, FAX: (609) 924-5027, E-Mail: info@tuckercapital.com, Web Site: www.tuckercapital.com (20)

Battleground Antiques Inc, New Bern, NC. Tel: (252) 636-3039, FAX: (252) 637-1862, E-Mail: tarheelrebel2000@aol.com, Web Site: www.civilwarantiques.com (6)

Batts, Ron, Things Remembered, Highland Heights, OH. Tel: (440) 473-2000, (866) 902-4438, FAX: (440) 473-2018, E-Mail: customerservice@thingsremembered.com, Web Site: www.thingsremembered.com (6)

Diana Baty, Moraga, CA. Tel: (202) 689-5332 (20)

Baudot, L. Craig, Blanchard & Co Inc, New Orleans, LA. Tel: (504) 837-3010, (800) 880-4653, FAX: (504) 837-4884, Web Site: www.blanchardonline.com (14)

Baudville Inc, Grand Rapids, MI. Tel: (616) 698-0889, (800) 728-0888, FAX: (616) 698-0554, E-Mail: service@baudville.com, Web Site: www.baudville.com (16)

Bauer Associates, Batavia, IL. Tel: (630) 406-8595, FAX: (630) 406-8596, E-Mail: lbauer@bauerassoc.net, Web Site: www.bauerassoc.net (39)

Eddie Bauer Groveport Service Center, Groveport, OH. Tel: (614) 497-1083, E-Mail: gpsrecruiting@eddiebauer.com, Web Site: www.eddiebauer.com (2)

Bauer Publishing Co, Englewood Cliffs, NJ. Tel: (201) 569-6699, FAX: (201) 569-5303, Web Site: www.bauerpublishing.com (17)

Richard Bauer & Co Inc, Teaneck, NJ. Tel: (201) 692-1005, (800) 995-7881, FAX: (201) 692-8626, E-Mail: info@richardbauer.com, Web Site: www.richardbauer.com (25)

Bauer, Craig E., Video Jet Technologies Inc, Wood Dale, IL. Tel: (630) 860-7300, (800) 654-4663, FAX: (630) 616-3623, E-Mail: info@videojet.com, Web Site: www.videojet.com (34)

Bauer, Gerhard, Bausch & Lomb Inc, Rochester, NY. Tel: (585) 338-6000, (800) 344-8815, FAX: (585) 338-6007, Web Site: www.bausch.com (16)

Bauer, Joanne B., Kimberly-Clark Corp, Neenah, WI. Tel: (920) 721-2000, (888) 525-8388, FAX: (920) 721-7722, Web Site: www.kimberly-clark.com (16)

Bauer, Larry, Bacompt Systems Inc, Carmel, IN. Tel: (317) 574-7474, (800) 533-7109, FAX: (317) 574-7475, E-Mail: customer.service@bacompt.com, Web Site: www.bacompt.com (21)

Bauer, Larry, Bauer Associates, Batavia, IL. Tel: (630) 406-8595, FAX: (630) 406-8596, E-Mail: lbauer@bauerassoc.net, Web Site: www.bauerassoc.net (39)

Bauer, Richard, Asset Marketing Services Inc, Burnsville, MN. Tel: (952) 707-7000, Web Site: www.amsi-corp.com (16)

Bauer, Robert, Liebert Corp, Columbus, OH. Tel: (614) 841-6700, (800) LIEBERT, FAX: (614) 841-6022, Web Site: www.liebert.com (16)

Baum, J. Robert, Highmark Blue Cross Blue Shield, Pittsburgh, PA. Tel: (412) 544-7000, FAX: (412) 544-5350, Web Site: www.highmark.com (15)

Baum, Jonathan Russell, The Dreyfus Corp, New York, NY. Tel: (212) 922-6000, FAX: (212) 922-6880, Web Site: www.dreyfus.com (14)

The Bauman Group, Ashland, MA. Tel: (508) 879-3009, (800) 876-3009, FAX: (508) 875-3751, E-Mail: info@bauman.com, Web Site: bauman.com (14)

Bauman, George, Mapping Analytics, Rochester, NY. Tel: (585) 271-6490, (877) 893-6490, FAX: (585) 271-1132, E-Mail: sales@mappinganalytics.com, Web Site: www.mappinganalytics.com (20)

Bauman, Marcia, The Bauman Group, Ashland, MA. Tel: (508) 879-3009, (800) 876-3009, FAX: (508) 875-3751, E-Mail: info@bauman.com, Web Site: www.bauman.com (14)

Bauman, Phil, FCL Graphics Inc, Harwood Heights, IL. Tel: (708) 867-5500, (800) 274-3380, FAX: (708) 867-7768, Web Site: www.fclgraphics.com (27)

Baumann, Angela, Liguori Publications, Liguori, MO. Tel: (636) 464-2500, (800) 325-9521, FAX: (800) 325-9526, E-Mail: liguori@liguori.org, Web Site: www.liguori.org (17)

Baumann, John, Ampac Holdings LLC, Cincinnati, OH. Tel: (513) 671-1777, (800) 543-7030, FAX: (513) 671-2920, Web Site: www.ampaconline.com (27)

Baumann, John, The Swiss Colony Inc, Monroe, WI. Tel: (608) 324-4603, FAX: (608) 328-8735, Web Site: www.swisscolony.com (4)

Baumann, Michael, Orchard Supply Hardware, San Jose, CA. Tel: (408) 281-3500, FAX: (408) 225-0388, Web Site: www.osh.com (16)

Baumgarten, Ed, Mid America Designs Inc, Effingham, IL. Tel: (217) 540-4200, (800) 350-4543, FAX: (217) 540-4800, E-Mail: mail@mamotorworks.com, Web Site: www.mamotorworks.com (12)

Baumgarten, Jay, ASE Technologies Inc, Wilmington, MA. Tel: (978) 658-0009, FAX: (978) 658-9990, E-Mail: info@ase-tech.com, Web Site: www.ase-tech.com (16)

Baumgartner, Garry, The National Underwriter Co, Erlanger, KY. Tel: (800) 543-0874, FAX: (856) 692-2246, E-Mail: customerservice@nuco.com, Web Site: www.nuco.com (17)

Baurenfeind, Eva, Davidoff of Geneva Inc, Pinellas Park, FL. Tel: (727) 828-5400, (800) 328-4365, FAX: (203) 975-0090 (6)

Bausch & Lomb Inc, Rochester, NY. Tel: (585) 338-6000, (800) 344-8815, FAX: (585) 338-6007, Web Site: www.bausch.com (16)

Bavaro, Anthony F., Herbert L Jamison & Co LLC, West Orange, NJ. Tel: (973) 731-0806, (800) 526-4766, (800) JAMISON, FAX: (973) 731-3035, Web Site: www.jamisongroup.com (15)

Baxter Bros Inc, Greenwich, CT. Tel: (203) 637-4559, (866) 280-1924, FAX: (203) 637-4550, E-Mail: info@baxterinvestment.com, Web Site: www.baxterinvestment.com (17)

Baxter Healthcare, Renal Division, Deerfield, IL. Tel: (800) 284-4060, Web Site: www.baxter.com (7)

Baxter, Jr. William J., Baxter Bros Inc, Greenwich, CT. Tel: (203) 637-4559, (866) 280-1924, FAX: (203) 637-4550, E-Mail: info@baxterinvestment.com, Web Site: www.baxterinvestment.com (17)

Bay Manufacturing, Milan, OH. Tel: (419) 499-4602, FAX: (419) 499-4603, Web Site: www.baymfg.com (16)

Mel Bay Publications Inc, Pacific, MO. Tel: (800) 8-MELBAY, FAX: (636) 257-5062, E-Mail: email@melbay.com, Web Site: www.melbay.com (17)

Bay, Bryndon, Mel Bay Publications Inc, Pacific, MO. Tel: (800) 8-MELBAY, FAX: (636) 257-5062, E-Mail: email@melbay.com, Web Site: www.melbay.com (17)

Bay, William, Mel Bay Publications Inc, Pacific, MO. Tel: (800) 8-MELBAY, FAX: (636) 257-5062, E-Mail: email@melbay.com, Web Site: www.melbay.com (17)

Bayard Inc, New London, CT. Tel: (860) 437-3012, (800) 321-0411, FAX: (800) 572-0788, Web Site: www.bayard-inc.com (31)

Bayer Corp Consumer Care Division, Whippany, NJ. Tel: (862) 404-3000, Web Site: www.consumercare.bayer.com (16)

Bayer, Greg, Sportime International, Norcross, GA. Tel: (770) 449-5700, (800) 283-5700, FAX: (770) 510-7290, E-Mail: orders@sportime.com, Web Site: www.sportime.com (11)

Bayley, Mich A., SP Express, Tempe, AZ. Tel: (866) 773-7363, E-Mail: info@spexpress.com, Web Site: www.spexpress.com (28)

Bayley, Michael W., Royal Caribbean International Ltd, Miami, FL. Tel: (305) 539-6000, FAX: (305) 374-7354, Web Site: www.royalcaribbean.com (19)

Baylor Health Care System, Dallas, TX. Tel: (214) 820-4901, (800) 4Baylor, FAX: (214) 820-7499, Web Site: www.baylorhealth.com (16)

Bayne, Lisa, Artful Home, Tel: (608) 257-2590, (877) 233-4600, FAX: (608) 257-2690, E-Mail: info@artfulhome.com, Web Site: www.artfulhome.com (8)

Bazarian, Graeme, Andrew Associates Inc, Enfield, CT. Tel: (860) 253-0000, FAX: (860) 253-0007, Web Site: www.andrewdm.com (23)

BB Direct Inc, Cape Coral, FL. Tel: (866) 501-6273, FAX: (239) 573-8764, E-Mail: info@bbdirect.com, Web Site: www.bbdirect.com (23)

Beach List Direct Inc, Nashville, TN. Tel: (615) 356-1100, E-Mail: cbeach@beachlistdirect.com, Web Site: www.beachlistdirect.com (23)

Beach, Clay, Beach List Direct Inc, Nashville, TN. Tel: (615) 356-1100, E-Mail: cbeach@beachlistdirect.com, Web Site: www.beachlistdirect.com (23)

Beach, David, Education Direct, Scranton, PA. Tel: (570) 342-7701, FAX: (570) 961-4851, Web Site: www.educationdirect.com (16)

Beachler, Tom, Redfield & Co Inc, Omaha, NE. Tel: (402) 341-0364, FAX: (402) 341-1454, Web Site: www.redfieldandcompany.com (27)

Beacon Marketing Group, Smithville, NJ. Tel: (609) 677-1776, FAX: (609) 677-1777, Web Site: www.beaconmktg.com (35)

Beacon Printing & Graphics Inc, Valdosta, GA. Tel: (912) 244-5634, (800) 227-7377, FAX: (912) 247-4405, E-Mail: sls@uspress.com, Web Site: www.uspress.com (27)

Beacon Shoe Co Inc, Maryland Heights, MO. Tel: (636) 488-5444, FAX: (636) 488-3103 (16)

BeaconFey LLC, Baltimore, MD. Tel: (410) 583-1203, FAX: (410) 583-1506, E-Mail: info@beaconfey.com, Web Site: www.beaconfey.com (35)

Beaham, David G., Faultless Starch/Bon Ami Co, Kansas City, MO. Tel: (816) 842-1230, FAX: (816) 842-3417, E-Mail: info@faultless.com, Web Site: www.faultless.com (16)

Beaham, III Gordon T., Faultless Starch/Bon Ami Co, Kansas City, MO. Tel: (816) 842-1230, FAX: (816) 842-3417, E-Mail: info@faultless.com, Web Site: www.faultless.com (16)

Beaham, Robert B., Faultless Starch/Bon Ami Co, Kansas City, MO. Tel: (816) 842-1230, FAX: (816) 842-3417, E-Mail: info@faultless.com, Web Site: www.faultless.com (16)

Beal, Graham W., The Detroit Institute of Arts, Detroit, MI. Tel: (313) 833-7900, FAX: (313) 833-1390, Web Site: www.dia.org (16)

Beal, Rocky, IDM Inc, Reston, VA. Tel: (703) 547-4961, E-Mail: info@integrated-dm.com, Web Site: www.idm.us.com (23)

Beall, Andy, Empire Imports Inc, Amherst, MA. Tel: (413) 256-4917, (800) 544-4744, FAX: (413) 256-4645, E-Mail: custsvc@empireimports.com, Web Site: www.empireimports.com (34)

Bealor, Timothy, Broadcast Electronics Inc, Quincy, IL. Tel: (217) 224-9600, FAX: (217) 224-9607, E-Mail: bdcast@bdcast.com, Web Site: www.bdcast.com (3)

Beals, Kevin, Dziurman Dzign Inc, Clawson, MI. Tel: (248) 288-8800, FAX: (248) 288-8804, E-Mail: dziurman@dzdzign.com, Web Site: www.dzdzign.com (35)

The Beam Group, Gladwyne, PA. Tel: (215) 988-2100, FAX: (215) 988-1558, Web Site: www.beamgroup.com (20)

Beamont, Eric, National Systems Corp, Chicago, IL. Tel: (312) 855-1000, FAX: (312) 222-1605, E-Mail: support@nationalsystems.com, Web Site: www.nationalsystems.com (29)

LL Bean Inc, Freeport, ME. Tel: (207) 865-4761, (800) 441-5713, FAX: (207) 552-3080, Web Site: www.llbean.com (2)

Bean, Dan, Colarelli Meyer & Associates Inc, Saint Louis, MO. Tel: (314) 721-1860, (800) 459-4548, FAX: (314) 721-1992, E-Mail: cmaconsult@cmaconsult.com, Web Site: www.cmaconsult.com (20)

Bean, Danielle, Catholic Digest, New London, CT. Tel: (800) 321-0411, E-Mail: catholicdigest@bayardinc.com, Web Site: www.catholicdigest.com (17)

Bear Computer Systems Inc, Dallas, TX. Tel: (818) 509-0459, (800) 252-1691, FAX: (818) 769-3055, E-Mail: info@bearcom.com, Web Site: www.bearcom.com (16)

Bear Woods Supply Co Inc, Cornwallis, NS Canada. Tel: (902) 638-8622, (800) 565-5066, FAX: (902) 638-8637, Web Site: www.bearwood.com, www.woodparts.ca (11)

Beard, Jeff, Infutor Data Solutions, Oakbrook Terrace, IL. Tel: (312) 348-7900, E-Mail: sales@infutor.com, Web Site: www.infutor.com (23)

Beard, Mike, DirectSmile LLC, Bloomfield, NJ. Tel: (973) 338-9368, Web Site: www.directsmile.com (22)

Beard, Tony, Price Weber Marketing Communications Inc, Louisville, KY. Tel: (502) 499-9220, FAX: (502) 491-5593, E-Mail: info@priceweber.com, Web Site: www.priceweber.com (35)

Beardon, Blanche, Long's Electronics Inc, Irondale, AL. Tel: (205) 956-6767, (800) 633-3410, FAX: (800) 633-2530, E-Mail: info@longselectronics.com, Web Site: www.longselectronics.com (3)

Charles F Beardsley Advertising, Avon, CT. Tel: (860) 676-0256, FAX: (860) 674-1917 (35)

Beardsley, David, Satisfaction Software Inc, Jamaica, NY. Tel: (732) 382-8736, FAX: (732) 382-8736, E-Mail: db@biink.com (20)

Beardsley, Nichelle, LibertyTree Press, Oakland, CA. Tel: (510) 632-1366, (800) 927-8733, FAX: (510) 568-6040, E-Mail: info@liberty-tree.com, Web Site: www.independent.org (5)

Beardsley, Sarah, Bearingpoint Inc, Dallas, TX. Tel: (703) 747-3000, FAX: (703) 747-3215, Web Site: www.bearingpoint.com (14)

Bearingpoint Inc, Dallas, TX. Tel: (703) 747-3000, FAX: (703) 747-3215, Web Site: www.bearingpoint.com (14)

Beasley Direct Marketing Inc, Morgan Hill, CA. Tel: (408) 782-0046, FAX: (408) 782-9604, E-Mail: lbeasley@beasleydirect.com, Web Site: www.beasleydirect.com (35)

Beasley, David, Beasley Direct Marketing Inc, Morgan Hill, CA. Tel: (408) 782-0046, FAX: (408) 782-9604, E-Mail: lbeasley@beasleydirect.com, Web Site: www.beasleydirect.com (35)

Beasley, Larry J., Cathedral Corp, Rome, NY. Tel: (315) 338-0021, (800) 698-0299, FAX: (315) 338-5874, E-Mail: sales@cathedralstewardship.com, Web Site: www.cathedralcorporation.com (21)

Beasley, Laurie, Beasley Direct Marketing Inc, Morgan Hill, CA. Tel: (408) 782-0046, FAX: (408) 782-9604, E-Mail: lbeasley@beasleydirect.com, Web Site: www.beasleydirect.com (35)

Beasley, Laurie, Direct Marketing Association of Northern California, Morgan Hill, CA. Tel: (800) 613-9266, FAX: (800) 613-8819, E-Mail: lbeasley@beasleydirect.com, Web Site: www.dmanc.org (40)

Beasley, W.B. Rogers, Keeneland Association Inc, Lexington, KY. Tel: (859) 254-3412, (800) 456-3412, FAX: (859) 255-2484, Web Site: www.keeneland.com (16)

Beaton, David, Custometrics Inc, Richmond Hill, ON Canada. Tel: (905) 886-9020, E-Mail: info@custometrics.ca, Web Site: www.custometrics.com (30)

Beattie, David, Hamilton Campaigns, Washington, DC. Tel: (202) 686-5900, FAX: (202) 686-7080, E-Mail: info@hamiltoncampaigns.com, Web Site: www.hamiltoncampaigns.com (30)

Beaty, Wilma E., Caraustar, Austell, GA. Tel: (770) 948-3101, E-Mail: info@caraustar.com, Web Site: www.caraustar.com (16)

Beau Graphics Ltd Inc, Lexington, KY. Tel: (859) 277-2328, (877) 279-2328, FAX: (859) 278-6193, Web Site: www.beaugraphics.com (36)

Beau Rivage Resort & Casino, Biloxi, MS. Tel: (228) 386-7111, FAX: (228) 386-7730, Web Site: www.beaurivage.com (19)

Beauchamp, Toni, Lieberman Productions, San Francisco, CA. Tel: (415) 955-0855, FAX: (415) 955-0822, E-Mail: lpinfo@lieberman.com, Web Site: www.lieberman.com (32)

Beauchemin, Ken, Voyageur Inc, Easley, SC. Tel: (802) 496-3127, (800) 311-7245, FAX: (802) 496-6247 (11)

Beauchesne, Norm, Herrington, Londonderry, NH. Tel: (603) 437-1600, (800) 903-2878, FAX: (603) 437-1340, (603) 437-3492, E-Mail: customerservice@herringtoncatalog.com, Web Site: www.herringtoncatalog.com (16)

Beaudoin, Joseph A., National Active & Retired Federal Employees Association, Alexandria, VA. Tel: (703) 838-7760, (800) 456-8410, FAX: (703) 838-7785, Web Site: www.narfe.org (1)

Beaudreau, Thomas, DirecTech Holding Company Inc, Maysville, KY. Tel: (866) 550-5030, E-Mail: ceo@directech.com, Web Site: www.directech.com (22)

Beaulieu, Paul, MediaConcepts Corp, Assonet, MA. Tel: (508) 644-3131, FAX: (508) 644-5201, E-Mail: at3@mediaconceptscorp.com, Web Site: www.mediaconceptscorp.com (35)

Beaumont, Sarah, StatSoft Inc, Tulsa, OK. Tel: (918) 749-1119, FAX: (918) 749-2217, E-Mail: info@statsoft.com, Web Site: www.statsoft.com (9)

Beauregard, Alain, MFE Instruments, Salem, NH. Tel: (603) 893-8778, (800) 843-8011, FAX: (603) 893-8851, Web Site: www.stockeryale.com (9)

Beauticontrol Cosmetics Inc, Carrollton, TX. Tel: (972) 458-0601, (800) BEAUTI-1, FAX: (972) 458-6904, E-Mail: clientservices@beauticontrol.com, Web Site: www.beauticontrol.com (7)

Beauty Naturally, Burlingame, CA. Tel: (650) 596-5742, (800) 432-4323, FAX: (650) 596-5742, E-Mail: sales@beautynaturally.com, Web Site: www.beautynaturally.com (7)

Beaver, Brenda, Otto Environmental Systems of North America, Charlotte, NC. Tel: (704) 588-9191, (800) 227-5885, FAX: (704) 588-5250, E-Mail: info@otto-usa.com, Web Site: www.otto-usa.com (16)

Beaver, John, The Great Amarillo Directory, Amarillo, TX. Tel: (806) 353-5155, FAX: (806) 359-2974, Web Site: www.worldpages.com (17)

Beavin, William, American Printing House for the Blind, Louisville, KY. Tel: (502) 895-2405, (800) 223-1839, FAX: (502) 899-2274, E-Mail: info@aph.org, Web Site: www.aph.org (7)

Bebell, Garrett, Torqmaster International, Stamford, CT. Tel: (203) 326-5945, (888) 414-4643, FAX: (203) 326-5944, E-Mail: info@torqmaster.com, Web Site: www.torqmaster.com (9)

Beber Silverstein Group, Miami, FL. Tel: (305) 856-9800, FAX: (305) 854-7686, E-Mail: jennifer@thinkbsg.com, Web Site: www.thinkbsg.com (35)

Beber, Jennifer, Beber Silverstein Group, Miami, FL. Tel: (305) 856-9800, FAX: (305) 854-7686, E-Mail: jennifer@thinkbsg.com, Web Site: www.thinkbsg.com (35)

Bechard, Doreen, Grand Pacific Resorts, Carlsbad, CA. Tel: (760) 827-4100, (800) 374-7779, Web Site: www.grandpacificresorts.com (19)

Becht, Ron, Hello Direct, Nashua, NH. Tel: (408) 972-1990, (800) 435-5634, FAX: (408) 972-8155, Web Site: www.hello-direct.com (16)

Beck, Asa, Financial Executives International, Morristown, NJ. Tel: (973) 765-1000, FAX: (973) 765-1018, Web Site: www.financialexecutives.org (1)

Beck, David A., The Clark Grave Vault Co, Columbus, OH. Tel: (614) 294-3761, FAX: (614) 299-2324, Web Site: www.clarkvault.com (16)

Beck, Douglas, The Clark Grave Vault Co, Columbus, OH. Tel: (614) 294-3761, FAX: (614) 299-2324, Web Site: www.clarkvault.com (16)

Beck, Lisa, Promotional Products Association International, Irving, TX. Tel: (972) 252-0404, FAX: (972) 258-3004, (800) I-AM-PPAI, E-Mail: membership@ppa.org, Web Site: www.ppa.org (40)

Beck, Mark A., The Clark Grave Vault Co, Columbus, OH. Tel: (614) 294-3761, FAX: (614) 299-2324, Web Site: www.clarkvault.com (16)

Beck, Tamara, Clean Lists Associates Inc, New York, NY. Tel: (212) 551-1013, FAX: (212) 551-1107, E-Mail: cleanlists@mindspring.com (27)

Beck, W Douglas, DWS Investments Service Co, Kansas City, MO. Tel: (800) 543-5776, Web Site: www.dws-investments.com (14)

Beckel, Helen, Harland Financial Solutions Inc, Lake Mary, FL. Tel: (407) 804-6600, (800) 815-5592, FAX: (407) 829-6702, Web Site: www.harlandfinancialsolutions.com (16)

Beckemeyer, William, Kurt Salmon Associates Inc, Atlanta, GA. Tel: (404) 892-0321, FAX: (404) 898-9590, E-Mail: infoksaweb@kurtsalmon.com, Web Site: www.kurtsalmon.com (20)

Rich Becker & Associates/Pump-Em-Up Publishing, In Public Relations, Lenexa, KS. Tel: (913) 894-9530, FAX: (913) 894-9530, E-Mail: rbecker@kc.rr.com (20)

Becker, Brian, Blethen Maine Newspapers Inc, Portland, ME. Tel: (207) 791-6650, FAX: (207) 791-6925, Web Site: www.mainetoday.com (17)

Becker, Chuck, Pasternack Enterprises Inc, Irvine, CA. Tel: (949) 261-1920, Web Site: www.pasternack.com (16)

Becker, Elaine, Atlantic Research & Consulting Inc, Boston, MA. Tel: (617) 720-0174, FAX: (617) 589-3731, E-Mail: generalmailbox@guideline.com, Web Site: www.atlanticresearch.net (30)

Becker, Jeffrey, Clients First, Westfield, NJ. Tel: (908) 232-1200, (800) 634-0040, FAX: (908) 233-8833, E-Mail: info@clientsfirst.com, Web Site: www.clientsfirst.com (27)

Becker, Michael, iLoop Mobile Inc, San Jose, CA. Tel: (408) 907-3360, Web Site: www.iloopmobile.com (16)

Becker, Mike, National Association of Professional Insurance Agents, Alexandria, VA. Tel: (703) 836-9340, FAX: (703) 836-1279, E-Mail: web@pianet.org, Web Site: www.pianet.com (1)

Becker, Paul C., Cosco Industries Inc, Chicago, IL. Tel: (708) 867-5800, (800) 323-0253, FAX: (800) 323-0275 (16)

Becker, Rich, Rich Becker & Associates/Pump-Em-Up Publishing, In Public Relations, Lenexa, KS. Tel: (913) 894-9530, FAX: (913) 894-9530, E-Mail: rbecker@kc.rr.com (20)

Becker, Rick, AllMedia Inc, Plano, TX. Tel: (469) 467-9100, FAX: (214) 291-5431, E-Mail: brokerage@allmediainc.com, Web Site: www.allmediainc.com (23)

Becker, Robert, Telecommunications Reports International Inc, Washington, DC. Tel: (202) 312-6060, (800) 234-1660, FAX: (202) 312-6111, E-Mail: bhammond@tr.com, Web Site: www.tr.com (17)

Beckham, Ed, Amaryllis Inc, Baton Rouge, LA. Tel: (225) 924-5560 (8)

Beckler, Robert K, Mead Westvaco Consumer & Office Products, Richmond, VA. Tel: (937) 222-6323, (804) 444-1000, FAX: (937) 495-3192, Web Site: www.meadwestvaco.com (10)

Beckman Coulter Inc, Brea, CA. Tel: (714) 993-5321, (800) 526-3821, FAX: (800) 232-3828, Web Site: www.beckmancoulter.com (16)

Beckman, Andrew, Location3 Media, Denver, CO. Tel: (720) 881-8510, FAX: (303) 298-1986, E-Mail: info@location3.com, Web Site: www.location3.com (32)

Beckman, Stephanie, Response ADvantage, Playa Del Rey, CA. Tel: (310) 577-0389, Web Site: www.responseadvantage.com (20)

Beckmann Converting Inc, Amsterdam, NY. Tel: (518) 842-0073, FAX: (518) 842-0282, E-Mail: ppiusz@beckmannconverting.com, Web Site: www.beckmannconverting.com (16)

Beckmann, Klaus, Beckmann Converting Inc, Amsterdam, NY. Tel: (518) 842-0073, FAX: (518) 842-0282, E-Mail: ppiusz@beckmannconverting.com, Web Site: www.beckmannconverting.com (16)

Bed Bath & Beyond, Union, NJ. Tel: (631) 420-7050, (800) 462-3966, Web Site: bedbathandbeyond.com (8)

Bedard, Tony, Frontier Natural Products Co-op, Norway, IA. Tel: (800) 669-3275, FAX: (800) 717-4372, E-Mail: info@frontiercoop.com, Web Site: www.frontiercoop.com (7)

Beddor, Mike, Japs-Olson Co, Saint Louis Park, MN. Tel: (952) 932-9393, (800) 548-2897, FAX: (612) 912-1900, Web Site: www.japsolson.com (27)

BeDell, Suzanne, Morgan Kaufmann Publishers Inc, Burlington, MA. Tel: (781) 313-4700, E-Mail: order@mkp.com, Web Site: www.mkp.com (17)

Bedford/St Martin's, Boston, MA. Tel: (617) 426-7440, FAX: (617) 426-8582, Web Site: www.bedfordstmartins.com (17)

Bedford, Samantha, Location3 Media, Denver, CO. Tel: (720) 881-8510, FAX: (303) 298-1986, E-Mail: info@location3.com, Web Site: www.location3.com (32)

Bedford, Stacie, Gazette Communications Inc, Cedar Rapids, IA. Tel: (319) 398-8211, (800) 397-8211, FAX: (319) 368-8834, Web Site: www.gazettecommunications.com (17)

Bedikian, Von, GBH Communications, Monrovia, CA. Tel: (818) 246-9900, (800) 222-5424, FAX: (818) 246-5850, E-Mail: customerservice@gbh.com, Web Site: www.gbh.com (3)

Bednar, R. Craig, Seattle Magazine, Seattle, WA. Tel: (206) 284-1750, (800) 637-0334, FAX: (206) 284-2550, E-Mail: customerservice@seattlemag.com, Web Site: www.seattlemag.com (17)

Bednar, Randall S., AO Smith Corp, Milwaukee, WI. Tel: (414) 359-4000, FAX: (414) 359-4064, Web Site: www.aosmith.com (16)

Bednarz, Ph.D. Shirley, Majorium, Stevens Point, WI. Tel: (715) 342-1018, (800) 654-4935, FAX: (715) 342-1118, E-Mail: sales@majorium.com, Web Site: www.letstalkselling.com (17)

Bednarz, Ph.D. Timothy, Majorium, Stevens Point, WI. Tel: (715) 342-1018, (800) 654-4935, FAX: (715) 342-1118, E-Mail: sales@majorium.com, Web Site: www.letstalkselling.com (17)

Bednoff, Mitchell E., Sage Financial Group, West Conshohocken, PA. Tel: (484) 342-4400, FAX: (484) 537-0550, E-Mail: sage@sagefinancial.com, Web Site: www.sagefinancial.com (14)

Bedwell, Judy, Sweet Tooth Candies, Newport, KY. Tel: (859) 581-4663, (877) 581-5132, FAX: (859) 581-1979 (4)

Beecher, John B., Sales Leads, Jupiter, FL. Tel: (866) 725-3753, FAX: (866) 702-5558, E-Mail: info@salesleadsinc.com, Web Site: www.salesleadsinc.com (17)

Beecher, La Verne, Sales Leads, Jupiter, FL. Tel: (866) 725-3753, FAX: (866) 702-5558, E-Mail: info@salesleadsinc.com, Web Site: www.salesleadsinc.com (17)

Beecher, Michael, Sales Leads, Jupiter, FL. Tel: (866) 725-3753, FAX: (866) 702-5558, E-Mail: info@salesleadsinc.com, Web Site: www.salesleadsinc.com (17)

Beecher, Tom, Cartera Commerce Inc, Lexington, MA. Tel: (781) 541-6800, (888) 456-6255, FAX: (781) 541-6801, E-Mail: info@cartera.com, Web Site: www.cartera.com (35)

Beechtree Assoc Inc, Cary, NC. Tel: (919) 852-1800, FAX: (919) 852-4400, E-Mail: jfoliano@aol.com (20)

Beeder, John, AG Interactive, Cleveland, OH. Tel: (216) 252-7300, (800) 711-4474, FAX: (216) 252-6778, Web Site: www.americangreetings.com (32)

Beegan, Paul, B&W Press Inc, Georgetown, MA. Tel: (978) 352-6100, (877) 246-3467, FAX: (978) 352-5955, E-Mail: csr@bwpress.com, Web Site: www.bwpress.com (21)

Beeks, Steve, Lionsgate Entertainment Inc, New York, NY. Tel: (212) 577-2400, FAX: (212) 962-2872, Web Site: www.lionsgate.com (32)

Beeks, Steve, Lionsgate Television Corp, Santa Monica, CA. Tel: (310) 449-9200, FAX: (310) 255-3870, Web Site: www.lionsgate.com (16)

Beemak Plastics Inc, La Mirada, CA. Tel: (310) 886-5880, (800) 421-4393, FAX: (310) 764-0330, E-Mail: info@beemak.com, Web Site: www.beemak.com (16)

Beeman Precision Airguns, Santa Fe Springs, CA. Tel: (562) 968-5891, (800) 227-2744, FAX: (562) 968-5823, E-Mail: sales@beeman.com, Web Site: www.beeman.com (11)

Beeman, John, Gallup Inter-Tribal Indian Ceremonial, Gallup, NM. Tel: (505) 863-3896, E-Mail: cermonial@qwestoffice.net, Web Site: www.theceremonial.com (1)

Beene, Jeff, PI Inc, Athens, TN. Tel: (423) 745-6213, FAX: (423) 745-7039, Web Site: www.pi-inc.com (16)

Beer, Mike, The Principal Financial Group, Des Moines, IA. Tel: (515) 247-5111, (800) 986-3343, FAX: (515) 246-5475, Web Site: www.principal.com (15)

Beer, Scott, Rajant Corp, Malvern, PA. Tel: (484) 595-0233, FAX: (484) 595-0244, E-Mail: support@rajant.com, Web Site: www.rajant.com (32)

Beerman, David, Moby Wrap Inc, Chico, CA. Tel: (530) 898-8201, E-Mail: info@mobywrap.com (2)

Beesley, Brian, West Bend, West Bend, WI. Tel: (262) 334-5107, (866) 290-1851, FAX: (262) 334-6800, Web Site: www.focuselectrics.com (16)

Beever, Bob, David C Cook, Colorado Springs, CO. Tel: (719) 536-0100, (800) 323-7543, FAX: (719) 536-3232, Web Site: www.davidccook.com (17)

Beffa-Negrini, David, PC Connection, Merrimack, NH. Tel: (603) 683-2167, (800) 800-0014, FAX: (603) 683-5773, E-Mail: pr@pcconnection.com, Web Site: www.pcconnection.com, macconnection.com (22)

Behavioral Science Research, Coral Gables, FL. Tel: (305) 443-2000, (800) 282-2771, FAX: (305) 448-6825 (30)

Behlen Manufacturing Co, Columbus, NE. Tel: (402) 564-3111, FAX: (402) 563-7405, E-Mail: behlen@megavision.com, Web Site: www.behlenmfg.com (16)

Behnen, Paul, Trozzolo Communications Group, Kansas City, MO. Tel: (816) 842-8111, Web Site: www.trozzolo.com (35)

Behnen, Toby P., Vocational Biographies Inc, Sauk Centre, MN. Tel: (320) 352-6516, (800) 255-0752, FAX: (320) 352-5546, E-Mail: careers@vocbios.com, Web Site: www.vocbio.com (31)

Behnke, Rob, Fair Indigo, Madison, WI. Tel: (608) 824-8974, (800) 520-1806, E-Mail: service@fairindigo.com, Web Site: www.fairindigo.com (2)

Behrens, Jr. James, Nassau Community College, Garden City, NY. Tel: (516) 572-7501, FAX: (516) 572-7497, E-Mail: marketing-communications@ncc.edu, Web Site: www.ncc.edu (41)

Behrens, Thomas, Masterworks, Poulsbo, WA. Tel: (360) 394-4300, Web Site: www.masterworks.com (1)

Behring, Alexandre, The Kraft Heinz Co, Pittsburgh, PA. Tel: (412) 456-5700, Web Site: www.kraftheinzcompany.com (4)

Beilman, Chris, CD Universe, Wallingford, CT. Tel: (203) 294-1648, (800) 231-7937, FAX: (203) 294-0391, Web Site: www.cduniverse.com (16)

Bein, Arlene, Practicing Law Institute, New York, NY. Tel: (212) 824-5700, (800) 260 4PLI, FAX: (800) 321-0093, E-Mail: info@pli.edu, Web Site: www.pli.edu (16)

Beiser, Scott L., Houlihan Lokey Howard & Zukin, Los Angeles, CA. Tel: (310) 553-8871, (800) 788-5300, FAX: (310) 553-2173, Web Site: www.hlhz.com (14)

Beitcher, Bob, Motion Picture & Television Fund, Woodland Hills, CA. Tel: (855) 760-6783, E-Mail: info@mptf.com, Web Site: www.mptf.com (1)

Belanger, David, Community Coffee Co, Baton Rouge, LA. Tel: (225) 291-3900, (800) 884-5282, FAX: (800) 643-8199, E-Mail: customerservice@communitycoffee.com, Web Site: www.communitycoffee.com (4)

Belardi, Donna, Belardi/Ostroy, New York, NY. Tel: (212) 924-1300, FAX: (212) 381-1745, E-Mail: katel@belardiostroy.com, Web Site: belardiostroy.com (23)

Belardi/Ostroy, New York, NY. Tel: (212) 924-1300, FAX: (212) 381-1745, E-Mail: katel@belardiostroy.com, Web Site: belardiostroy.com (23)

Belcaro Group Inc, Greenwood Village, CO. Tel: (303) 843-0302, Web Site: www.shopathome.com (17)

Belcher, Donald D., Boys' Life & Scouting Magazines, Irving, TX. Tel: (972) 580-2000, (866) 584-6589, FAX: (972) 580-2079, Web Site: www.boyslife.org (17)

Belcher, Eric D., InnerWorkings Inc, Chicago, IL. Tel: (317) 642-3700, (866) 766-5176, E-Mail: info@inwk.com, Web Site: www.inwk.com (35)

Belcher, Lucy, DMS Marketing Inc, Mission Viejo, CA. Tel: (888) 794-1777, E-Mail: inquiries@dms-marketing.com, Web Site: www.dms-marketing.com (35)

Belk Stores Services Inc, Charlotte, NC. Tel: (704) 357-1000, FAX: (704) 357-1782, Web Site: www.belk.com (16)

Belk, H. McKay, Belk Stores Services Inc, Charlotte, NC. Tel: (704) 357-1000, FAX: (704) 357-1782, Web Site: www.belk.com (16)

Belk, John M., Belk Stores Services Inc, Charlotte, NC. Tel: (704) 357-1000, FAX: (704) 357-1782, Web Site: www.belk.com (16)

Bell & Howell Ltd, North York, ON Canada. Tel: (416) 746-2200, FAX: (416) 228-2439, Web Site: www.bellhowell.com (9)

The Bell Group Rio Grande, Albuquerque, NM. Tel: (505) 839-3000, Web Site: www.riogrande.com (5)

Bell Performance Inc, Longwood, FL. Tel: (407) 834-3690, (800) 659-2355, FAX: (407) 767-8685, E-Mail: info@bellperformance.net, Web Site: www.bellperformance.net (9)

Bell, Alan, The Bell Group Rio Grande, Albuquerque, NM. Tel: (505) 839-3000, Web Site: www.riogrande.com (5)

Bell, Allison, Donna Salyers' Fabulous-Bridal Inc, Covington, KY. Tel: (859) 291-3300, (800) 848-4650, E-Mail: abell@fabulousfurs.com, Web Site: fabulousfurs.com (2)

Bell, Anne Marie, SHSMD Annual Conference, Chicago, IL. Tel: (312) 422-3888, FAX: (312) 278-0883, E-Mail: shsmd@aha.org, Web Site: www.shsmd.org (42)

Bell, Frederick, Touch of Class Catalog, Huntingburg, IN. Tel: (800) 457-7456, FAX: (812) 683-5921, E-Mail: customerservice@touchofclass.com, Web Site: www.touchofclass.com (8)

Bell, Gordon, LucidView, Oak Ridge, TN. Tel: (888) 582-4384, Web Site: www.lucidview.com (20)

Bell, Hugh, Rio Grande, Albuquerque, NM. Tel: (505) 839-3000, (800) 545-6566, FAX: (800) 965-2329, E-Mail: info@riogrande.com, Web Site: www.riogrande.com (16)

Bell, John, MMI Direct LLC, Columbia, MD. Tel: (410) 561-1500, FAX: (410) 561-0833, Web Site: www.mmidirect.com (22)

Bell, Kevin, Lincoln Park Zoo, Chicago, IL. Tel: (312) 742-2000, FAX: (312) 742-2137, E-Mail: webmaster@lpzoo.com, Web Site: www.lpzoo.com (1)

Bell, Linda, Kendall Products/Dri-Dek, Naples, FL. Tel: (239) 643-2244, (800) 348-2398, FAX: (800) 828-4248, E-Mail: info@dri-dek.com, Web Site: www.dri-dek.com (16)

Bell, Michael W.. CIGNA International, Philadelphia, PA. Tel: (215) 761-1741, FAX: (215) 761-5515, Web Site: www.cigna.com (15)

Bell, Raymond E., Classic Color, Broadview, IL. Tel: (708) 484-0000, FAX: (708) 344-2233, E-Mail: info@classic-color.com, Web Site: www.classic-color.com (27)

Bell, Robert, Music Barn Inc, Niagara Falls, NY. Tel: (800) 984-0047, FAX: (905) 513-6918, E-Mail: info@themusicbarn.com, Web Site: www.themusicbarn.com (6)

Bell, Ron, Target MarkeTeam, Atlanta, GA. Tel: (770) 274-3700, FAX: (770) 274-3730, E-Mail: inquiries@tmtinc.com, Web Site: www.tmtinc.com (35)

Bellacor, Minneapolis, MN. Tel: (877) 723-5522, FAX: (651) 294-2595, E-Mail: customerservice@bellacor. com, Web Site: www.bellacor.com (8)

Bellak Color Corp, Miami, FL. Tel: (305) 854-8525, FAX: (305) 858-8783, Web Site: www.foilmania. com (27)

Bellamy, Cameron, GrayHair Software, Mount Laurel, NJ. Tel: (856) 727-9372, FAX: (856) 727-1315, Web Site: www.grayhairsoftware.com (22)

Belland, Chuck, PGI Companies Inc, Minnetonka, MN. Tel: (952) 933-5745, FAX: (952) 933-5864, E-Mail: ddallum@pgicompanies.com, Web Site: www. pgicompanies.com (27)

Bellantone, Paul, PPAI Expo, Irving, TX. Tel: (972) 252-0404, (888) 426-7724, FAX: (972) 258-3004, E-Mail: expo@ppai.org, Web Site: expo.ppai.org (42)

Bellantone, Paul, Promotional Products Association International, Irving, TX. Tel: (972) 252-0404, FAX: (972) 258-3004, (800) I-AM-PPAI, E-Mail: membership@ppa.org, Web Site: www.ppa.org (40)

Bellomy Research Inc, Winston Salem, NC. Tel: (336) 721-1140, (800) 443-7344, FAX: (336) 721-1597, E-Mail: bellomy@interpath.com, Web Site: www. bellomyresearch.com (30)

Bellsey, Lisa, March of Dimes Foundation, White Plains, NY. Tel: (914) 997-4488, Web Site: www. marchofdimes.org (1)

BellTower Technologies LLC, Richardson, TX. Tel: (214) 220-8000, Web Site: www.belltowertech.com (18)

Bellusci, Adam, HubCast Inc, Wakefield, MA. Tel: (781) 221-7200, FAX: (781) 221-7223, Web Site: www.hubeast.com (27)

Belmont University, Nashville, TN. Tel: (615) 460-6000, FAX: (615) 460-6455, Web Site: www. belmont.edu (41)

Belmont, J.F., Cosmo International, Deerfield Beach, FL. Tel: (954) 798-4500, FAX: (954) 798-4514 (16)

Belth, Andrew, ASL Marketing Inc, Farmingdale, NY. Tel: (516) 248-6100, FAX: (516) 248-6364, E-Mail: info@aslmarketing.com, Web Site: www. aslmarketing.com (23)

Belton, Y. Marc, The Pillsbury Co, Minneapolis, MN. Tel: (763) 764-7600, (800) 248-7310, FAX: (763) 764-8330, Web Site: www.pillsbury.com (16)

Beltone Corp, Glenview, IL. Tel: (800) 235-8663, FAX: (847) 832-3300, E-Mail: info@beltone.com, Web Site: www.beltone.com (3)

Beluga Bar by Caviarteria, New York, NY. Tel: (212) 759-7410, (800) 422-8427, FAX: (212) 750-0358, E-Mail: info@caviarteria.com, Web Site: www. caviarteria.com (4)

Belvoir Media Group LLC, Norwalk, CT. Tel: (203) 857-3100, FAX: (203) 857-3103, E-Mail: customer_service@belvoir.com, Web Site: www. belvoir.com (17)

Belyea, Peter, Cablexpress Technologies, Syracuse, NY. Tel: (315) 476-3000, (800) 913-9467, FAX: (315) 455-1800, E-Mail: info@cablexpress.com, Web Site: www.CXTec.com (10)

Bemis Co Inc, Neenah, WI. Tel: (920) 727-4100, E-Mail: contact@beemis.com, Web Site: www. bemis.com (34)

Bench, Gerald, Hadley Fruit Orchards Inc, Cabazon, CA. Tel: (951) 849-5255, FAX: (951) 849-5255, Web Site: www.hadleys.com (4)

Benchmark Brands Inc, Norcross, GA. Tel: (770) 242-1254, FAX: (770) 242-1962, Web Site: www. footsmart.com (5)

The Benchmark Co, Austin, TX. Tel: (512) 707-7500, FAX: (512) 707-7757, E-Mail: thebenc@earthlink. net, Web Site: www.thebenchmarkcompany.net (30)

Benchmark Imaging & Display, Elk Grove Village, IL. Tel: (847) 290-0002, FAX: (847) 290-8608, Web Site: www.benchmarkimaging.com (27)

Richard L Bencin & Associates, Brecksville, OH. Tel: (440) 526-6726, FAX: (440) 546-1623, E-Mail: rlbencin@netzero.net, Web Site: www.rlbencin.com (20)

Bencin, Richard L., Richard L Bencin & Associates, Brecksville, OH. Tel: (440) 526-6726, FAX: (440) 546-1623, E-Mail: rlbencin@netzero.net, Web Site: www.rlbencin.com (20)

Bencone Uniform Connection, Winston Salem, NC. Tel: (800) 326-3261, FAX: (866) 311-8254, E-Mail: bencone1@bellsouth.net, Web Site: www.bencone. com (2)

Bendel, Jr Charles W., Center for Professional Advancement, East Brunswick, NJ. Tel: (732) 238-1600, FAX: (732) 238-9113, E-Mail: info@cfpa.com, Web Site: www.cfpa.com (13)

The Bender Group, Reno, NV. Tel: (775) 788-8800, (800) 621-9402, FAX: (775) 788-8811, E-Mail: salesinfo@benderwhs.com, Web Site: www. bendergroup.com (28)

Bender, Chris N. The Bender Group, Reno, NV. Tel: (775) 788-8800, (800) 621-9402, FAX: (775) 788-8811, E-Mail: salesinfo@benderwhs.com, Web Site: www.bendergroup.com (28)

Bender, David A., Promotion Support Services Inc, Rock Island, IL. Tel: (309) 788-4400, FAX: (309) 788-4465, E-Mail: dbender@pss-inc.net, Web Site: www.pss-inc.net (28)

Bender, John, Recognition Systems (Dot Works), Port Washington, NY. Tel: (516) 625-5000, FAX: (516) 625-1507, E-Mail: wade@dotworks.com, Web Site: www.dotworks.com (16)

Bender, Robin, ConvergeDirect, New York, NY. Tel: (212) 213-0111, E-Mail: info@convergedirect.com, Web Site: www.convergedirect.com (35)

Bender, Roman, Wrisco Industries Inc, Palm Beach Gardens, FL. Tel: (561) 626-5700, (800) 627-2646, FAX: (561) 627-3574, Web Site: www.wrisco.com (8)

Bender, Thomas, SW Caging Corp, Topeka, KS. Tel: (785) 232-0061, Web Site: www.swcaging.com (14)

Benditt, John, Technology Review, Cambridge, MA. Tel: (617) 475-8000, FAX: (617) 258-5850, Web Site: www.technologyreview.com (17)

Bendix, Jeffrey, Medical Economics Magazine, North Olmsted, OH. Tel: (440) 243-8100, FAX: (440) 891-2735, Web Site: medicaleconomics. modernmedicine.com/about (17)

Benedetto, Tony, NASW Assurance Services Inc, Frederick, MD. Tel: (800) 668-4274, E-Mail: zxi@ naswasi.org, Web Site: www.naswinsurancetrust.org (1)

Benedict, Kennette, Bulletin of the Atomic Scientists, Chicago, IL. Tel: (773) 702-6301, FAX: (773) 980-6932, E-Mail: admin@thebulletin.org, Web Site: www.thebulletin.org (1)

Benedict, Todd, Collective - The Audience Engine, New York, NY. Tel: (646) 722-8550, FAX: (646) 442-6529, Web Site: www.collective.com (22)

Beneducci, Joseph J., Fireman's Fund Insurance Co, Novato, CA. Tel: (415) 899-2000, FAX: (415) 899-3600, Web Site: www.firemansfund.com (14)

BenefitMall, Dallas, TX. Tel: (469) 791-3355, Web Site: www.benefitmall.com (15)

Benelli, Tom, Halogen Response Media, New York, NY. Tel: (212) 468-4000, Web Site: www. halogenresponse.com (31)

Benet Academy, Lisle, IL. Tel: (630) 719-2794, Web Site: www.benet.org (1)

Benett, Andrew, Havas Worldwide LLC, New York, NY. Tel: (212) 886-2000, FAX: (212) 886-5013, Web Site: www.havasworldwide.com (35)

Benetton USA, New York, NY. Tel: (212) 593-0290, (800) 274-7192, FAX: (212) 371-1438, E-Mail: mtaylor@bennettonusa.com, Web Site: www. benetton.com (2)

Benevilla, Surprise, AZ. Tel: (623) 584-4999, FAX: (623) 546-1589, Web Site: www. interfaithcommunitycare.org (1)

Benfer, Mark, Quark Inc, Denver, CO. Tel: (303) 894-8888, Web Site: www.quark.com (34)

Benik, Tina C., A T Cross Co, Lincoln, RI. Tel: (401) 333-1200, (800) 282-7677, FAX: (401) 334-2861, Web Site: www.cross.com (16)

Benjamin, Earl, Soitenly Stooges, Glendale, CA. Tel: (818) 543-0778, (800) 543-0778, FAX: (818) 543-0779, E-Mail: custserv@threestooges.com, Web Site: www.soitenlystooges.com (6)

Benjamin, Gerald A., Henry Schein Inc, Melville, NY. Tel: (631) 843-5500, (800) 472-4346, FAX: (631) 843-5658, E-Mail: custserv@henryschein.com, Web Site: www.henryschein.com (16)

Benjamin, Heather, Transamerican Mailing, Escondido, CA. Tel: (760) 745-5343, Web Site: www. transdirect.com (20)

Benjamin, Jay, Saatchi & Saatchi New York, New York, NY. Tel: (212) 463-2000, FAX: (212) 463-9856, Web Site: www.saatchiny.com (32)

Benjamin, Jeff, Avon Products Inc, New York, NY. Tel: (212) 282-7000, (800) 367-2866, FAX: (212) 282-6225, Web Site: www.avon.com (7)

Benjamin, Margie, Envelope Manufacturers Association, Alexandria, VA. Tel: (703) 739-2200, FAX: (703) 739-2209, Web Site: www.envelope.org (1)

Benjamin, Maynard H., Envelope Manufacturers Association, Alexandria, VA. Tel: (703) 739-2200, FAX: (703) 739-2209, Web Site: www.envelope.org (1)

Benmosche, Bob, American International Group, New York, NY. Tel: (212) 770-7000, (877) 638-4244, FAX: (212) 742-8692, Web Site: www.aig.com (15)

Bennack, Jr Frank A., The Hearst Corp, New York, NY. Tel: (212) 649-2000, FAX: (212) 649-2108, Web Site: www.hearst.com/magazines/ (17)

Benne, Susan, Antiquarian Booksellers Association of America Inc, New York, NY. Tel: (212) 944-8291, FAX: (212) 944-8293, E-Mail: sbenne@abaa.org, Web Site: www.abaa.org (1)

Bennett Marine Video, Venice, CA. Tel: (310) 827-8064, (800) 733-8862, FAX: (310) 827-8074, E-Mail: questions@bennettmarine.com, Web Site: www.bennettmarine.com (3)

Bennett, Alan, H&R Block Inc, Kansas City, MO. Tel: (816) 854-3000, (800) 472-5625, FAX: (816) 854-8500, Web Site: www.hrblock.com (14)

Bennett, Bill, Computer Business Services Inc, Americus, GA. Tel: (229) 924-4408, (866) 924-4408, FAX: (229) 924-3644, E-Mail: nelson@combusser. com, Web Site: www.combusser.com (22)

Bennett, Brian, STIR LLC, Milwaukee, WI. Tel: (414) 278-0040, FAX: (414) 278-0390, E-Mail: info@ stirstuff.com, Web Site: www.stirstuff.com (35)

Bennett, Cassandra, Pursuant Group, Dallas, TX. Tel: (214) 866-7700, E-Mail: info@pursuant.com, Web Site: www.pursuant.com (20)

Bennett, Frank, Clegg Industries Inc, Gardena, CA. Tel: (310) 225-3800, FAX: (800) 250-9851, E-Mail: sales@clegg.xo.com, Web Site: www.cleggonline.com (16)

Bennett, Jan, General Motivation Co, Grand Rapids, MI. Tel: (616) 647-3085, (888) 664-6449, FAX: (616) 647-5909, E-Mail: i2k@generalmotivation.com, Web Site: www.generalmotivation.com (33)

Bennett, M. Vaneeda, Epilepsy Foundation, Landover, MD. Tel: (800) 332-1000, E-Mail: contactus@efa.org, Web Site: www.efa.org (1)

Bennett, Mark D., Total Training Solutions LLC, Waunakee, WI. Tel: (608) 849-5563, (800) 831-0678, FAX: (608) 849-5605, (800) 831-3776, E-Mail: kbennett@ttstrain.com, Web Site: www.ttstrain.com (5)

Bennett, Michael, Bennett Marine Video, Venice, CA. Tel: (310) 827-8064, (800) 733-8862, FAX: (310) 827-8074, E-Mail: questions@bennettmarine.com, Web Site: www.bennettmarine.com (3)

Bennett, Neysa, BennettBaker Ltd, Chicago, IL. Tel: (312) 252-8883, FAX: (312) 252-8209, E-Mail: nbennett@bennettwheelless.com, Web Site: www.bennettbaker.com (20)

Bennett, Paula, J Jill Group, Inc, Quincy, MA. Tel: (617) 376-4300, (800) 642-9989, FAX: (617) 769-0177, Web Site: www.jjillgroup.com (2)

Bennett, Paula, The Tog Shop Inc, Beverly, MA. Tel: (800) 262-8888, FAX: (800) 755-7557, Web Site: www.togshop.com (2)

Bennett, Rodney D., University of Southern Mississippi, Hattiesburg, MS. Tel: (601) 266-1000, Web Site: www.usm.edu (1)

Bennett, Tanya, ICF Olson, Minneapolis, MN. Tel: (612) 215-9800, FAX: (612) 215-9801, E-Mail: info@olson.com, Web Site: www.olson.com (35)

Bennett, Tiffany, Classic Thermographers, North Mankato, MN. Tel: (623) 582-0002, (800) 727-4200, FAX: (800) 727-4202 (10)

BennettBaker Ltd, Chicago, IL. Tel: (312) 252-8883, FAX: (312) 252-8209, E-Mail: nbennett@bennettwheelless.com, Web Site: www.bennettbaker.com (20)

Benoit & Associates, Kankakee, IL. Tel: (815) 932-2582, FAX: (815) 932-2582, E-Mail: mbenoit@benoit-associates.com, Web Site: www.benoit-associates.com (35)

Benoit, Michael J., Benoit & Associates, Kankakee, IL. Tel: (815) 932-2582, FAX: (815) 932-2582, E-Mail: mbenoit@benoit-associates.com, Web Site: www.benoit-associates.com (35)

Bensinger, Steven J., AIG Accident & Health, New York, NY. Tel: (212) 770-7000, (877) 638-4244, FAX: (212) 509-9705, Web Site: www.aig.com (15)

Benson, Chris, Audio Editions Books-on-Cassette & CD, Auburn, CA. Tel: (800) 231-4261, FAX: (800) 882-1840, E-Mail: info@audioeditions.com, Web Site: www.audioeditions.com (3)

Benson, Janet, Audio Editions Books-on-Cassette & CD, Auburn, CA. Tel: (800) 231-4261, FAX: (800) 882-1840, E-Mail: info@audioeditions.com, Web Site: www.audioeditions.com (3)

Benson, Kerry, Hill Holliday, Boston, MA. Tel: (617) 366-4000, Web Site: www.hhcc.com (35)

Benson, Victor N., Holsted Marketing Inc, New York, NY. Tel: (212) 686-8537, FAX: (212) 481-0415, E-Mail: preulbach@holstedmarketing.com, Web Site: www.holstedmarketing.com (35)

Bentele, Barb, Profit Potentials Inc, Hull, IA. Tel: (712) 439-1496, (800) 543-5480, FAX: (712) 439-1434, Web Site: www.profitpotentials.com (1)

Bentley University, Waltham, MA. Tel: (781) 891-2473, E-Mail: execed@bentley.edu, Web Site: www.bentley.edu (13)

Benton Announcements Inc, Buffalo, NY. Tel: (716) 836-4100, FAX: (716) 836-4161 (27)

Benton, Darrell, Diversified Photo Supply Corp, Gardena, CA. Tel: (310) 328-8577, (800) 544-1609, FAX: (310) 328-8518, Web Site: www.diversifiedphoto.com (10)

Benton, Thomas, DMA Annual Marketing Conference, New York, NY. Tel: (212) 768-7277, Web Site: thedma.org (42)

Benton, Thomas J., The Direct Marketing Association, New York, NY. Tel: (212) 768-7277, E-Mail: info@the-dma.org, Web Site: thedma.org (1)

Bentz, Bob, Advanced Telecom Services Inc, King of Prussia, PA. Tel: (610) 688-6000, (800) 247-1287, FAX: (610) 964-9117, E-Mail: sales@advancedtele.com, Web Site: www.advancedtele.com (29)

Bentz, Steve, The Orange County Register, Santa Ana, CA. Tel: (877) 469-7344, E-Mail: customerservice@ocregister.com, Web Site: www.ocregister.com (17)

Benun, Ilise, The Art of Self Promotion, Hoboken, NJ. Tel: (201) 653-0783, FAX: (201) 222-2494, E-Mail: ilise@marketing-mentor.com, Web Site: www.artofselfpromotion.com (17)

Benya, Robert G., iN DEMAND LLC, New York, NY. Tel: (646) 638-8200, FAX: (646) 486-0855, Web Site: www.indemand.com (32)

Benyon, Liz, Nova Marketing Services, Avon, CT. Tel: (800) 879-0288, Web Site: www.nova-marketing.com (35)

Benz, Jr, MD Edward J., Dana-Farber Cancer Institute, Boston, MA. Tel: (617) 632-3000, (866) 408-3324, FAX: (617) 632-4070, E-Mail: suzanne_fountain@dfci.harvard.edu, Web Site: www.dana-farber.org (1)

Berard, Rosalie, Alfa Aesar-A Johnson Matthey Co, Ward Hill, MA. Tel: (800) 343-0660, FAX: (800) 322-4757, E-Mail: info@alfa.com, Web Site: www.alfa.com (9)

Berarducci, James, Kurt Salmon Associates Inc, Atlanta, GA. Tel: (404) 892-0321, FAX: (404) 898-9590, E-Mail: infoksaweb@kurtsalmon.com, Web Site: www.kurtsalmon.com (20)

Berg, Brian, BB Direct Inc, Cape Coral, FL. Tel: (866) 501-6273, FAX: (239) 573-8764, E-Mail: info@bbdirect.com, Web Site: www.bbdirect.com (23)

Berg, David E, NEBS, Groton, MA. Tel: (978) 448-6111, (800) 225-6380, (888) 823-6327, FAX: (978) 448-3653, (800) 234-4324, E-Mail: customerservice@nebs.com, Web Site: www.nebs.com (10)

Berg, Jeff, NTN Buzztime Inc, Carlsbad, CA. Tel: (760) 438-7400, (877) 963-9200, FAX: (760) 438-3505, Web Site: www.buzztimebusiness.com (32)

Berg, Ron, Independent Insurance Agents & Brokers of America, Alexandria, VA. Tel: (703) 683-4422, (800) 221-7917, FAX: (703) 683-7556, E-Mail: info@iiaba.org, Web Site: www.iiaba.org (1)

Berganti, Pat, JB Dollar Stretcher Magazine, Richfield, OH. Tel: (330) 659-3590, (800) 673-2531, FAX: (330) 659-6741, Web Site: www.jbdollar.com (31)

Bergdorf Goodman, New York, NY. Tel: (646) 735-5200, (800) 967-3788, (800) 218-4918, FAX: (212) 872-8677, E-Mail: clientservices@bergdorfgoodman.com, Web Site: www.bergdorfgoodman.com (2)

J&H Berge/The Lab Mart, South Plainfield, NJ. Tel: (908) 561-3002, (800) 684-1234, FAX: (908) 561-3002, E-Mail: info@jhberge.com, Web Site: www.jhberge.com (7)

Bergen, Nicole, Group 236, Oakland, CA. Tel: (510) 874-0141, Web Site: group236.com (32)

Bergen, Scott, Pizza Hut Inc, Plano, TX. Tel: (972) 338-7700, (866) 298-6986, FAX: (972) 338-6869, Web Site: www.pizzahut.com (16)

Bergenfeld, Judd, Alternative Media Group, Naples, FL. Tel: (732) 741-0585, FAX: (732) 741-0489, Web Site: www.amg-global.com (31)

Bergenholtz, Thomas, Viatech Publishing Solutions Inc, Bay Shore, NY. Tel: (631) 968-8500, (800) 645-8558, FAX: (631) 968-0830, Web Site: www.viatechpub.com (16)

Berger, Dave, Berger's Table Pad Co, Indianapolis, IN. Tel: (800) 305-7237, Web Site: tablepads.com (8)

Berger, Ellie, Scholastic Inc, New York, NY. Tel: (212) 343-6100, (800) SCHOLASTIC, FAX: (212) 343-6484, Web Site: www.scholastic.com (17)

Berger, Joshua, American Movie Classics Holding Corp, Jericho, NY. Tel: (516) 803-3000, FAX: (516) 803-3003, Web Site: www.amctv.com (16)

Berger, Kendra, NTN Buzztime Inc, Carlsbad, CA. Tel: (760) 438-7400, (877) 963-9200, FAX: (760) 438-3505, Web Site: www.buzztimebusiness.com (32)

Berger, Lori, Redbook Magazine, New York, NY. Tel: (212) 649-2000, (800) 888-0008, FAX: (212) 581-7605, Web Site: www.redbookmag.com (17)

Berger, Mary, University of Pennsylvania - Veterinary Medicine (Development), Philadelphia, PA. Tel: (215) 898-8841, E-Mail: vetdean@vet.upenn.edu, Web Site: www.vet.upenn.edu (1)

Berger, Morry, Anthem Blue Cross Blue Shield, Saint Louis, MO. Tel: (314) 923-4444, (888) 877-9125, FAX: (314) 923-5151, E-Mail: moreinfo@bcbsmo.com, Web Site: www.bcbsmo.com (15)

Berger, Ralph, CenterCore Group Inc, Marked Tree, AR. Tel: (800) 686-0821, FAX: (870) 358-3330, Web Site: www.centercoregroup.com (16)

Berger, Stacie, F&W Media Inc, Blue Ash, OH. Tel: (513) 531-2690, FAX: (513) 531-0293, Web Site: www.fwmedia.com (17)

Berger, Thomas, Cross Country Computer Corp, Central Islip, NY. Tel: (631) 334-1810, E-Mail: inquiry@crosscountrycomputer.com, Web Site: www.crosscountrycomputer.com (22)

Berger, Tim, WordCom Inc, Ellington, CT. Tel: (860) 875-7373, (800) 822-0622, FAX: (860) 872-2713, E-Mail: sales@wordcom-inc.com, Web Site: www.wordcom-inc.com (21)

Berger's Table Pad Co, Indianapolis, IN. Tel: (800) 305-7237, Web Site: tablepads.com (8)

Bergh, Chip, Levi Strauss & Co, San Francisco, CA. Tel: (415) 501-6000, FAX: (415) 501-7112, Web Site: www.levistrauss.com (16)

Bergin, Laura, Rhythm Band Inc, Fort Worth, TX. Tel: (817) 335-2561, (800) 424-4724, FAX: (800) 784-9401, E-Mail: sales@rhythmband.com, Web Site: www.rhythmband.com (11)

Bergman Medical/Scientific/Technical Collection, Princeton, NJ. Tel: (609) 921-0749, E-Mail: information@pmiprinceton.com, Web Site: www.pmiprinceton.com (38)

Bergman, Burton, Butler Specialty Co, Chicago, IL. Tel: (773) 221-1200, (800) 799-2857, FAX: (773) 221-5892, Web Site: www.butlerspecialty.net (16)

Bergman, David, Butler Specialty Co, Chicago, IL. Tel: (773) 221-1200, (800) 799-2857, FAX: (773) 221-5892, Web Site: www.butlerspecialty.net (16)

Bergman, Richard L., Bergman Medical/Scientific/ Technical Collection, Princeton, NJ. Tel: (609) 921-0749, E-Mail: information@pmiprinceton.com, Web Site: www.pmiprinceton.com (38)

Bergman, Stanley, Henry Schein Inc, Melville, NY. Tel: (631) 843-5500, (800) 472-4346, FAX: (631) 843-5658, E-Mail: custserv@henryschein.com, Web Site: www.henryschein.com (16)

Bergman, Victoria, Bergman Medical/Scientific/Technical Collection, Princeton, NJ. Tel: (609) 921-0749, E-Mail: information@pmiprinceton.com, Web Site: www.pmiprinceton.com (38)

Bergstrom, Keith, Prestwick House Inc, Clayton, DE. Tel: (302) 659-2070, Web Site: www. prestwickhouse.com (17)

Berisford, John, The McGraw-Hill Financial, New York, NY. Tel: (212) 904-2000, Web Site: www. mhfi.com (17)

Berk, II James L., First Media Communications Inc, Brentwood, TN. Tel: (615) 661-0826, FAX: (615) 661-4084, Web Site: www.first-media.com (16)

Berkeley College, West Paterson, NJ. Tel: (973) 278-5400, (800) 446-5400, FAX: (973) 278-6243, E-Mail: info@berkeleycollege.edu, Web Site: www. berkeleycollege.edu (13)

Berkey, Mark, Angstrom Graphics, Cleveland, OH. Tel: (216) 271-5300, FAX: (216) 271-7650, E-Mail: wayne.angstrom@st-ives-usa.com, Web Site: www. angstromgraphics.com (27)

Berkley, William, Tension Corp, Kansas City, MO. Tel: (816) 471-3400, FAX: (816) 283-1498, E-Mail: info@tensioncorp.com, Web Site: www.tension.com (26)

Berko, Paul, Time Products International, Del Rio, TX. Tel: (847) 459-8885, FAX: (847) 459-8111, E-Mail: cttpi@aol.com, Web Site: www.tpi2000.com (16)

Berkobits, Joe, Colonial Redi Record Co, Brooklyn, NY. Tel: (718) 972-7433, (800) 637-0040, FAX: (718) 972-7438, E-Mail: redirecord@aol.com, Web Site: www.colonialredirecord.com (34)

Berkobits, Joe, Colonial Redi-Record Corp, Brooklyn, NY. Tel: (718) 972-7433, (800) 637-0040, FAX: (718) 972-7438, Web Site: www.asisupplier.com/ 81110 (10)

Berkowitz, David, Gould Paper Corp, New York, NY. Tel: (212) 301-0001, (800) 221-3043, FAX: (212) 481-0392, Web Site: www.gouldpaper.com (25)

Berkowitz, Roger, Legal Sea Foods Inc, Boston, MA. Tel: (617) 530-9000, (800) 343-5804, FAX: (617) 530-9649, Web Site: www.legalseafoods.com (4)

Berks, David, Executive Enterprises Inc, Hawthorne, NY. Tel: (860) 701-5900, (800) 831-8333, FAX: (860) 701-5909, (800) 250-3861, E-Mail: info@ eeiconferences.com, Web Site: www. eeiconferences.com (16)

Berkshire Direct Inc, Williamstown, MA. Tel: (413) 458-1721, FAX: (413) 458-1727, E-Mail: info@ berkshiredirect.com, Web Site: www. berkshiredirect.com (17)

Berkshire Record Outlet Inc, Lee, MA. Tel: (413) 243-4080, FAX: (413) 243-4340, E-Mail: broinc@ berkshirerecordoutlet.com, Web Site: www2.broinc. com (3)

Berlamino, Betty Ellen, WLNY-TV 10/55, Melville, NY. Tel: (631) 777-8855, Web Site: newyork. cbslocal.com/station/wlny (32)

Berlin, Jay, Northern Tool & Equipment Inc, Burnsville, MN. Tel: (952) 894-9510, (800) 221-0516, FAX: (952) 894-1020, Web Site: www.northerntool.com (16)

Berliner, Jay, MJA International, Dix Hills, NY. Tel: (516) 676-5990, FAX: (516) 674-3309 (7)

Berliner, Jay, Unitron Ltd, Commack, NY. Tel: (631) 589-6666, FAX: (631) 589-6795, E-Mail: johnc@ unitronusa.com, Web Site: www.unitronusa.com (9)

Berlowe, Kathy, Bert Davis Executive Search, New York, NY. Tel: (212) 838-4000, FAX: (212) 935-3291, E-Mail: info@bertdavis.com, Web Site: www. bertdavis.com (20)

Berman Group, Newton Center, MA. Tel: (617) 426-0870, FAX: (617) 719-1505, E-Mail: rob@ bermanusa.com, Web Site: www.bermanusa.com (16)

Berman, Barry, CRN International Inc, Hamden, CT. Tel: (203) 288-2002, FAX: (203) 281-3291, E-Mail: info@crnradio.com, Web Site: www.crnradio.com (32)

Berman, Frank, Bloomingdale's Direct, New York, NY. Tel: (212) 705-2000, (800) 777-0000, FAX: (212) 705-2805, Web Site: www.bloomingdales.com (16)

Berman, Jeff, Warren Communications News, Washington, DC. Tel: (202) 872-9200, (800) 771-9202, FAX: (202) 318-8350, E-Mail: info@warren-news. com, Web Site: www.warren-news.com (17)

Berman, Michael, General Growth Properties, Chicago, IL. Tel: (312) 960-5000, Web Site: www. generalgrowth.com (5)

Berman, Michael, iN DEMAND LLC, New York, NY. Tel: (646) 638-8200, FAX: (646) 486-0855, Web Site: www.indemand.com (32)

Berman, Mimi, Independent Living Aids, Buffalo, NY. Tel: (516) 450-3829, (800) 537-2118, FAX: (516) 937-3906, E-Mail: techsupport@independentliving. com, Web Site: www.independentliving.com (7)

Berman, Neil, Delivra, Indianapolis, IN. Tel: (317) 915-9400, (866) 915-9465, Web Site: www.delivra.com (32)

Berman, Robert S., Berman Group, Newton Center, MA. Tel: (617) 426-0870, FAX: (617) 719-1505, E-Mail: rob@bermanusa.com, Web Site: www. bermanusa.com (16)

Berman, Susan, Underline Communications LLC, New York, NY. Tel: (212) 994-4340, FAX: (212) 686-8234, E-Mail: inquiries@underline.com, Web Site: www.underlinecom.com (35)

Bermudez, Barry, Cornell Lab of Ornithology, Ithaca, NY. Tel: (607) 254-2157, (800) 843-2473, FAX: (607) 254-2415, E-Mail: birdslides@cornell.edu, Web Site: www.birds.cornell.edu (1)

Bernacki, Adam, Leadership Directories Inc, New York, NY. Tel: (212) 627-4140, FAX: (212) 645-0931, E-Mail: info@leadershipdirectories.com, Web Site: www.leadershipdirectories.com (17)

Bernard, Edward C., T Rowe Price Associates Inc, Baltimore, MD. Tel: (410) 345-2000, (800) 638-7890, FAX: (410) 986-3618, E-Mail: info@troweprice. com, Web Site: www.troweprice.com (14)

Bernard, Jim, Star Tribune Media Co, Minneapolis, MN. Tel: (612) 673-4000, FAX: (612) 673-4359, Web Site: www.startribunecompany.com (17)

Bernard, Ted, Savicom, San Francisco, CA. Tel: (415) 983-0990, FAX: (415) 445-9999, E-Mail: sales@ savicom.net, Web Site: www.savicom.net (22)

Bernardin, Tom, Leo Burnett Worldwide, Chicago, IL. Tel: (312) 220-5959, Web Site: leoburnett.com (35)

Bernath, David, Comedy Central, New York, NY. Tel: (212) 767-8600, Web Site: www.cc.com (32)

Berner, Mary, Magazine Publishers of America, New York, NY. Tel: (212) 872-3700, FAX: (212) 888-4217, E-Mail: mpa@magazine.org, Web Site: www. magazine.org (17)

Bernhard, Jean, Vanderbilt Advertising, New York, NY. Tel: (212) 907-1500, FAX: (212) 907-1914, Web Site: www.valueline.com (14)

Bernheimer Associates, Wellesley, MA. Tel: (781) 237-8910, FAX: (781) 239-2932, E-Mail: wsbii@ hotmail.com, Web Site: bernheimer.com (20)

Bernheimer, II Walter, Bernheimer Associates, Wellesley, MA. Tel: (781) 237-8910, FAX: (781) 239-2932, E-Mail: wsbii@hotmail.com, Web Site: bernheimer.com (20)

Bernier, John E., Cape Cod Cupola Co Inc, North Dartmouth, MA. Tel: (508) 994-2119, FAX: (508) 997-2511, E-Mail: capecodcupola@gmail.com, Web Site: www.capcodcupola.com (8)

Bernstein-Rein, Kansas City, MO. Tel: (816) 756-0640, FAX: (816) 399-6000, E-Mail: general@b-r.com, Web Site: www.b-r.com (35)

Bernstein, Amy, Harvard Business Review, Boston, MA. Tel: (617) 783-7410, FAX: (617) 783-7493, Web Site: hbr.org (17)

Bernstein, David, Idearc Media Corp, Dallas, TX. Tel: (972) 453-7797 (16)

Bernstein, Ralph, Gelco Information Network, Eden Prairie, MN. Tel: (952) 947-1500, (800) 444-6588, FAX: (952) 947-1525, Web Site: www.gelco.com (16)

Bernstein, Ronald A., Cross Marketing USA, Chicago, IL. Tel: (312) 440-3700, (866) 440-3700, FAX: (312) 943-5813, E-Mail: ronbernstein@ crossmarketing.us, Web Site: www.crossmarketing. us (23)

Bernstein, Ronald A., Marketing Incentives International Inc, Chicago, IL. Tel: (312) 440-3700, FAX: (312) 943-5813, E-Mail: info@mktgincentiveintl. com, Web Site: www.mktgincentiveintl.com (33)

Berry Best Services Ltd. Fairfax, VA. Tel: (202) 293-4964, FAX: (202) 293-3431, E-Mail: admin@ berrybest.com, Web Site: www.berrybest.com (30)

The Berry Company, Dayton, OH. Tel: (937) 610-4100, (800) 877-0475, Web Site: www.theberrycompany. com (35)

Berry Hill Ltd, Saint Thomas, ON Canada. Tel: (519) 631-0480, (800) 668-3072, FAX: (519) 631-8935, E-Mail: customerservice@berryhill.ca, Web Site: www.berryhilllimited.com (8)

Berry, Brigid, Data Partners Inc, Fort Myers, FL. Tel: (239) 267-8762, (866) 423-1818, FAX: (239) 267-9043, E-Mail: info@data-partners.com, Web Site: www.datapartners.com (22)

Berry, Dennis, AmMed Direct, Parsons, TN. Tel: (615) 941-3900, (800) 282-3524, Web Site: www. arrivamedical.com (7)

Berry, Emory, Concurrent Computer Corp, Duluth, GA. Tel: (678) 228-4000, (877) 978-7363, FAX: (954) 977-5580, Web Site: www.ccur.com (3)

Berry, Jake, Simmons College, Boston, MA. Tel: (617) 521-2000, Web Site: www.simmons.edu (1)

Berry, Lorena, JHL Mail Marketing Inc, Stevens Point, WI. Tel: (715) 341-0581, (800) 236-0581, FAX: (715) 341-9645, E-Mail: ren@jhl.com, Web Site: www.jhl.com (28)

Berry, Lorna, August Marketing, Tampa, FL. Tel: (561) 747-1325, (866) 242-4414, E-Mail: sbarret@ augustmktg.com, Web Site: www.augustmktg.com (22)

Berry, Thomas L., Berry Best Services Ltd, Fairfax, VA. Tel: (202) 293-4964, FAX: (202) 293-3431, E-Mail: admin@berrybest.com, Web Site: www. berrybest.com (30)

Berryman, Patrick, National Community Pharmacists Association, Alexandria, VA. Tel: (703) 683-8200, (800) 544-7447, FAX: (703) 683-3619, E-Mail: info@ncpanet.org, Web Site: www.ncpanet.org (1)

Berson, Lori, BersonDeanStevens Inc, Westlake Village, CA. Tel: (818) 713-0134, (877) 447-0134, E-Mail: info@bersondeanstevens.com, Web Site: www.bersondeanstevens.com (35)

BersonDeanStevens Inc, Westlake Village, CA. Tel: (818) 713-0134, (877) 447-0134, E-Mail: info@bersondeanstevens.com, Web Site: www.bersondeanstevens.com (35)

Berstein, Steve, Bernstein-Rein, Kansas City, MO. Tel: (816) 756-0640, FAX: (816) 399-6000, E-Mail: general@b-r.com, Web Site: www.b-r.com (35)

Bertalli, Frank, ETTSI Premiums & Incentives, Daytona Beach, FL. Tel: (386) 271-0204, Web Site: www.ettsi.com (16)

Berthiaume, Dennis, Standard Life, Montreal, QC Canada. Tel: (514) 499-8855, (877) 499-9555, FAX: (514) 499-4908, Web Site: www.standardlife.ca (15)

Berthiaume, Douglas A., Waters Corp, Milford, MA. Tel: (508) 482-2000, (800) 252-4752, FAX: (508) 872-1990, Web Site: www.waters.com (16)

Bertness, Eric, Phillips Kiln Service LTD, South Sioux City, NE. Tel: (402) 494-6837, (800) 831-0876, FAX: (402) 494-6858, E-Mail: info@kilm.com, Web Site: www.kiln.com (16)

Bertoli, Gina, Windsor Vineyards, Santa Rosa, CA. Tel: (800) 289-9463, (800) 741-6070, E-Mail: webmaster@windsorvineyards.com, Web Site: www.windsorvineyards.com (16)

Bertolini, Mark T., AETNA - Marketing Product & Communication, Hartford, CT. Tel: (860) 273-0123, (800) 872-3862, FAX: (860) 273-3971, Web Site: www.aetna.com (14)

Bertram, Heinz-Jurgen, Symrise, Teterboro, NJ. Tel: (201) 288-3200, FAX: (201) 462-2200, Web Site: www.symrise.com (7)

Bertrand, Robert, Commonwealth Business Media Inc, Newark, NJ. Tel: (609) 371-7700, (800) 221-5488, FAX: (609) 371-7879, Web Site: www.cbizmedia.com (17)

Berway Visual Products Inc, Wilmington, MA. Tel: (978) 694-9195, (800) 452-0410, FAX: (978) 694-9212, E-Mail: sales@berway.com, Web Site: www.berway.com (3)

Besasie, Tony, Cannella Response Television Inc, Burlington, WI. Tel: (262) 763-4810, FAX: (262) 763-2875, Web Site: www.drtv.com (32)

Besbeas, Nick, LinkedIn Marketing Solutions, Mountain View, CA. Tel: (650) 687-3600, Web Site: business.linkedin.com/biz (35)

Besser, Barbara, Yoga Journal / Active Interest Media, San Francisco, CA. Tel: (415) 591-0555, Web Site: www.yogajournal.com (17)

Best Buy, Richfield, MN. Tel: (612) 291-1000, Web Site: www.bestbuy.com (3)

Best Friends Animal Society, Kanab, UT. Tel: (435) 644-2001, E-Mail: info@bestfriends.org, Web Site: www.bestfriends.org (1)

Best Mailing Lists Inc, Tucson, AZ. Tel: (520) 885-0400, (800) 692-2378, FAX: (520) 885-3100, E-Mail: best@bestmailing.com, Web Site: www.bestmailing.com (23)

Best ROI Lists, Boca Raton, FL. Tel: (877) 301-5478, E-Mail: info@bestroilists.com, Web Site: www.bestroilists.com (24)

Best Western International, Phoenix, AZ. Tel: (602) 957-4200, FAX: (623) 780-6199, Web Site: www.bestwestern.com (19)

Best, Ellen, Eire Direct, Chicago, IL. Tel: (312) 640-4000, FAX: (312) 640-0324, E-Mail: info@eiredirect.com, Web Site: www.eiredirect.com (16)

Beta Research Corp, Syosset, NY. Tel: (516) 935-3800, FAX: (516) 935-4092, E-Mail: beta@nybeta.com, Web Site: www.nybeta.com (30)

Channing L Bete Co Inc, South Deerfield, MA. Tel: (800) 477-4776, FAX: (800) 499-6464, E-Mail: custscvs@channing.bete.com, Web Site: www.channing-bete.com (17)

Bete, Michael, Channing L Bete Co Inc, South Deerfield, MA. Tel: (800) 477-4776, FAX: (800) 499-6464, E-Mail: custscvs@channing.bete.com, Web Site: www.channing-bete.com (17)

Betesh, Elliot, Dr Jays, San Diego, CA. Tel: (212) 334-7999, Web Site: drjays.com (2)

Bethel, Nalini, Bahamas Ministry of Tourism, Fort Lauderdale, FL. Tel: (954) 236-9292, (800) 422-4262, Web Site: www.bahamas.com (19)

Bethers, Brian W., 1-800-Contacts, Draper, UT. Tel: (800) 266-8228, FAX: (801) 924-9000, Web Site: www.1800contacts.com (7)

Bethesda Hospital Foundation, Boynton Beach, FL. Tel: (561) 737-7733, FAX: (561) 735-7942 (1)

Bethesda List Center Inc, Bethesda, MD. Tel: (301) 986-1455, FAX: (301) 907-4870, E-Mail: info@bethesda-list.com, Web Site: www.bethesda-list.com (24)

Better Health Fitness, Brooklyn, NY. Tel: (718) 436-4693, FAX: (718) 854-3381, Web Site: www.betterhealthfitness.com (11)

Better Homes & Gardens, New York, NY. Tel: (212) 551-7097, FAX: (212) 551-7114, E-Mail: support@bhg.com, Web Site: www.bhg.com (31)

Better Lists Inc, Stamford, CT. Tel: (203) 324-4171, FAX: (203) 358-0384, Web Site: www.betterlists.com (28)

Better Tools For Industry, Santee, CA. Tel: (619) 562-3071, FAX: (619) 562-0592, Web Site: www.bti-tool.com (9)

Betterway Books, Blue Ash, OH. Tel: (513) 531-2222, (800) 289-0963, FAX: (513) 531-4744, Web Site: www.fwpublications.com/books.asp (17)

Bettinger, II Walter W., Charles Schwab & Co Inc, San Francisco, CA. Tel: (415) 627-7000, (800) 648-5300, FAX: (415) 627-8538, Web Site: www.schwab.com (14)

Bettinger, Jim. Quality Park Products, Minneapolis, MN. Tel: (800) 828-7323, (800) 547-4252, FAX: (800) 398-9835, E-Mail: mktg@qualitypark.com, Web Site: www.qualitypark.com (26)

Betz Jr, William P., Penn Herb Co Ltd, Philadelphia, PA. Tel: (215) 632-6100, (800) 523-9971, FAX: (215) 632-7945, E-Mail: information@pennherb.com, Web Site: www.pennherb.com (7)

Betz, Ronald, Penn Herb Co Ltd, Philadelphia, PA. Tel: (215) 632-6100, (800) 523-9971, FAX: (215) 632-7945, E-Mail: information@pennherb.com, Web Site: www.pennherb.com (7)

Bevelacqua, Darcy, DB Consulting, Harrison, NY. Tel: (914) 698-2008, E-Mail: darcybev@yahoo.com (20)

Bevevino, Rita, Whirley Drink Works, Warren, PA. Tel: (814) 723-7600, (800) 825-5575, FAX: (814) 723-3245, E-Mail: info@whirleydrinkworks.com, Web Site: www.whirleydrinkworks.com (5)

Bewkes, Jeffrey L., Time Warner Inc, New York, NY. Tel: (212) 484-8000, Web Site: www.timewarner.com (16)

Beychok, Alan, Benchmark Brands Inc, Norcross, GA. Tel: (770) 242-1254, FAX: (770) 242-1962, Web Site: www.footsmart.com (5)

Beyer, John, Nathan Associates Inc, Arlington, VA. Tel: (703) 516-7700, FAX: (703) 351-6162, Web Site: www.nathaninc.com (30)

Beyond Quota LLC, Lake Forest, IL. Tel: (847) 234-9475, FAX: (847) 234-5260, E-Mail: megrinnell@beyondquota.com, Web Site: www.beyondquota.com (35)

Bezdon, Ron, Business Technologies, Dubuque, IA. Tel: (563) 556-7994, (800) 451-0399, FAX: (563) 556-2512 (34)

Bezos, Jeffrey, Amazon.com, Seattle, WA. Tel: (206) 266-1000, Web Site: www.amazon.com (16)

Bhagat, Vinay K., Convio Inc, Austin, TX. Tel: (512) 652-2600, (888) 528-9501, FAX: (512) 652-2699, Web Site: www.convio.com (22)

Bhalerao, Satish, Logical Computer Selections, Short Hills, NJ. Tel: (212) 949-2290, (800) 949-2701, FAX: (212) 697-5786, E-Mail: info@logicomputer.com, Web Site: www.logicomputer.com (16)

Bhandari, Ravneet, Nor1, Santa Clara, CA. Tel: (408) 850-9937, FAX: (408) 608-0443, E-Mail: sales@nor1.com, Web Site: www.nor1.com (32)

Bharara, Vinit, Diapers.com, Jersey City, NJ. Tel: (800) 342-7377, E-Mail: customercare@diapers.com, Web Site: www.diapers.com (5)

Bhatia, Donna, USAA Alliance Services Marketing, San Antonio, TX. Tel: (210) 456-9857, FAX: (210) 498-4542, Web Site: www.usaa.com (14)

Bhatia, Shrey, Reputation.com, Redwood City, CA. Tel: (877) 425-5792, E-Mail: info@reputation.com, Web Site: www.reputation.com (32)

Bhojwani, Gary C., Allianz Life Insurance Co of North America, Minneapolis, MN. Tel: (763) 765-6500, (800) 950-5872, Web Site: www.allianzlife.com (15)

Bhojwani, Gary C., Fireman's Fund Insurance Co, Novato, CA. Tel: (415) 899-2000, FAX: (415) 899-3600, Web Site: www.firemansfund.com (14)

Biagini, John F., HCI Direct, Bensalem, PA. Tel: (215) 244-9600, (888) 765-0062, FAX: (215) 244-0328, Web Site: www.silkies.com (16)

Bianchi, Franco, Haworth Inc, Holland, MI. Tel: (616) 393-3000, (800) 344-2600, FAX: (616) 393-1570, Web Site: www.haworth.com (34)

Bianco, Angelo, Telebrands Corp, Fairfield, NJ. Tel: (973) 247-8777, Web Site: www.telebrands.com (21)

Bianucci, Deborah, BAI, Chicago, IL. Tel: (312) 683-2464, FAX: (312) 683-2373, E-Mail: info@bai.org, Web Site: www.bai.org (17)

Bibler, Dean, PPC, Johnston, IA. Tel: (515) 986-5070, E-Mail: sales@ppcbest.com, Web Site: www.ppcbest.com (9)

BIC Corp, Shelton, CT. Tel: (203) 783-2000, FAX: (203) 783-2081, Web Site: www.bicworld.com (16)

BIC Graphic USA, Clearwater, FL. Tel: (727) 536-7895, E-Mail: customerservice@bicgraphic.com, Web Site: www.bicgraphic.com (33)

Bick International, Van Nuys, CA. Tel: (818) 997-6496, FAX: (818) 988-4337, E-Mail: iibick@sbcglobal.net, Web Site: www.bickinternational.com (6)

Bick, Israel, Bick International, Van Nuys, CA. Tel: (818) 997-6496, FAX: (818) 988-4337, E-Mail: iibick@sbcglobal.net, Web Site: www.bickinternational.com (6)

Bickham, John, Charter Communications, Stamford, CT. Tel: (203) 905-7801, Web Site: www.charter.com (16)

Bickley, Colin, Donor Services Group, Los Angeles, CA. Tel: (310) 788-9000, (888) 474-1900, Web Site: www.donorservicesgroup.com (1)

Bickman Copeland, Julie, Arbill Safety Products, Philadelphia, PA. Tel: (215) 632-2000, (800) 523-5367, FAX: (800) 426-5808, E-Mail: orders@arbill.com, Web Site: www.arbill.com (9)

Bickman, Barry, Arbill Safety Products, Philadelphia, PA. Tel: (215) 632-2000, (800) 523-5367, FAX: (800) 426-5808, E-Mail: orders@arbill.com, Web Site: www.arbill.com (9)

Biddle, Rick, Schultz & Williams Inc, Philadelphia, PA. Tel: (215) 625-9955, FAX: (215) 625-2701, E-Mail: mail@schultzwilliams.com, Web Site: www.sw-inc.com (1)

Bidwell, Tim, Moore Medical LLC, Farmington, CT. Tel: (860) 826-3600, FAX: (860) 223-2382, E-Mail: e-support@mooremedical.com, Web Site: www.mooremedical.com (7)

Biedrzycki, John A., Veterans of Foreign Wars of the US, Kansas City, MO. Tel: (816) 756-3390, FAX: (816) 968-1149, E-Mail: info@vfw.org, Web Site: www.vfw.org (1)

Biegel, Bruce, Winterberry Group, New York, NY. Tel: (212) 842-6000, FAX: (212) 842-6010, E-Mail: info@winterberrygroup.com, Web Site: www.winterberrygroup.com (20)

Biehn, Doug, Blue Shield of California, San Francisco, CA. Tel: (415) 229-5000, FAX: (415) 229-5056, Web Site: www.blueshieldca.com (15)

Bielen, Richard J., Protective Life Corp, Deerfield, IL. Tel: (847) 948-8988, (800) 323-5771, FAX: (847) 948-1156, Web Site: www.protective.com (15)

Bieler, Peter, Media Funding Corp, Malibu, CA. Tel: (310) 457-4140, FAX: (310) 774-1234, E-Mail: info@mediafunding.com, Web Site: mediafunding.com (32)

Bienenstock, George, Fluid Metering Inc, Syosset, NY. Tel: (516) 922-6050, (800) 223-3388, FAX: (516) 624-8261, E-Mail: pumps@fmipump.com, Web Site: www.fmipump.com (16)

Bierman, Rich, Wisconsin Converting Inc, Green Bay, WI. Tel: (920) 437-6400, (800) 544-1935, FAX: (920) 436-4964, E-Mail: wci@wisconsinconverting.com, Web Site: www.wisconsinconverting.com (26)

Biermeier, Jens D., School of Business & Economics, Los Angeles, CA. Tel: (323) 343-2800, FAX: (323) 343-2813, Web Site: cbe.calstatela.edu (41)

Biese, David, J Jill Group, Inc, Quincy, MA. Tel: (617) 376-4300, (800) 642-9989, FAX: (617) 769-0177, Web Site: www.jjillgroup.com (2)

Biesel, Becky, Party Kits & Equestrian Gifts, Louisville, KY. Tel: (502) 425-2126, (800) 99-DERBY, FAX: (502) 425-5230, E-Mail: info@partykits.com, Web Site: www.derbygifts.com (6)

Big Brothers Big Sisters of Greater Kansas City, Kansas City, MO. Tel: (816) 561-5269, FAX: (816) 561-5273, Web Site: www.bigbrothersbigsisterskc.org (1)

Bigelow Electronics, Bluffton, OH. Tel: (419) 358-7851 (3)

RC Bigelow Inc, Fairfield, CT. Tel: (203) 334-1212, Web Site: www.bigelowtea.com (4)

Bigelow, Chandler, Tribune Co, Chicago, IL. Tel: (312) 222-9100, FAX: (312) 222-1573, Web Site: www.tribune.com (17)

Bigelow, Clarence, Bigelow Electronics, Bluffton, OH. Tel: (419) 358-7851 (3)

Biggerstaff, Patricia, Sales Development Associates Inc, Saint Louis, MO. Tel: (314) 862-8828, FAX: (314) 862-8829, E-Mail: patb@sdastl.com, Web Site: www.sdastl.com (21)

Bigham Agency Inc, Plano, TX. Tel: (972) 801-2600, FAX: (972) 801-2649, E-Mail: info@bighamagency.com, Web Site: www.bighamagency.com (35)

Bigham, Paul, Bigham Agency Inc, Plano, TX. Tel: (972) 801-2600, FAX: (972) 801-2649, E-Mail: info@bighamagency.com, Web Site: www.bighamagency.com (35)

Bijoux Terner, Miami, FL. Tel: (305) 500-7500, (800) 262-3614, FAX: (305) 262-9286, E-Mail: customerservice@bijouxterner.com, Web Site: www.bijouxterner.com (16)

Bike Nashbar, Crab Orchard, WV. Tel: (800) NAS-HBAR, FAX: (877) 778-9456, E-Mail: custserv@nashbar.com, Web Site: www.bikenashbar.com (11)

The Bil-Ray Aluminum Siding Corp of Queens Inc, New Hyde Park, NY. Tel: (516) 616-4200, (800) 474-4415, FAX: (516) 616-4030, Web Site: www.homeclub.com (16)

Bilbrey, George, Return Path Inc, New York, NY. Tel: (212) 905-5500, FAX: (212) 905-5501, Web Site: www.returnpath.biz (22)

Bilbrey, John P. (J.P.), Hershey Park, Hershey, PA. Tel: (717) 534-3149, (800) HERSHEY, E-Mail: info@hersheypa.com, Web Site: www.hersheypark.com (19)

Bilbrey, John P., The Hershey Co, Hershey, PA. Tel: (717) 534-4200, (800) 454-7737, FAX: (717) 534-5204, Web Site: www.hersheygifts.com (4)

Bilby, Manda, MLS Data Management Solutions, Fort Worth, TX. Tel: (817) 989-3800, FAX: (817) 989-3899, Web Site: www.mlsc.com (22)

Biles, Steve, Invacare Supply Group, Milford, MA. Tel: (508) 429-1000, (800) 225-4792, FAX: (508) 429-1581, E-Mail: service.isg@invacare.com, Web Site: www.invacaresupplygroup.com (16)

Bilich, Georgeann, Society of Petroleum Engineers, Richardson, TX. Tel: (972) 952-9393, (800) 456-6863, FAX: (972) 952-9435, E-Mail: spedal@spe.org, Web Site: www.spe.org (1)

Bilisky, Mark, Americans for Peace Now, Washington, DC. Tel: (202) 408-9898, FAX: (202) 408-9899, E-Mail: apndc@peacenow.org, Web Site: www.peacenow.org (1)

Bilitardo, Kiril, Merchant E-Solutions, Redwood City, CA. Tel: (509) 232-5639, (866) 663-6132, FAX: (509) 232-5625, E-Mail: help@merchante-solutions.com, Web Site: www.merchante-solutions.com (14)

Bilitz, Paula, Minnesota Life, Saint Paul, MN. Tel: (651) 665-3500, (888) 237-1838, FAX: (651) 665-4488, Web Site: www.minnesotalife.com; www.securian.com (15)

Bill Me Later Inc, Timonium, MD. Tel: (443) 921-1900, FAX: (443) 921-1985, Web Site: www.billmelater.com (14)

Bill, Kathleen, School Market Research Institute Inc, Centerbrook, CT. Tel: (800) 838-3444, FAX: (860) 581-8549, E-Mail: info@smriinc.com, Web Site: www.smriinc.com (35)

Billin Medina-Warren, Scottsdale, AZ. Tel: (972) 951-7291 (20)

Bills, David, E I DuPont De Nemours & Co, Wilmington, DE. Tel: (302) 774-1000, (800) 441-7515, FAX: (302) 774-7321, Web Site: www.dupont.com (16)

Billue, Stan, Mr Fantastic LLC, Astor, FL. Tel: (407) 719-2020, E-Mail: sbillue@usa2net.net, Web Site: www.stanbillue.com (20)

Billy E Barnes, Chapel Hill, NC. Tel: (919) 942-6350, FAX: (919) 942-6350, E-Mail: bbarnes218@aol.com, Web Site: www.billybarnes.com (38)

Bilodeau, Sebastien, Synapse Group Inc, Stamford, CT. Tel: (203) 595-8255, FAX: (203) 329-8237, E-Mail: webmaster@synapsemail.com, Web Site: www.synapsegroupinc.com (18)

Bilstrom, Jon W., Comerica Inc, Dallas, TX. Tel: (800) 521-1190, FAX: (925) 941-1999, Web Site: www.comerica.com (14)

Binkley, Gregory R., The Sportsman's Guide Inc, South Saint Paul, MN. Tel: (651) 451-3030, (800) 882-2962, FAX: (651) 450-6130, E-Mail: custserv@sportsmansguide.com, Web Site: www.sportsmansguide.com (11)

Binnie, Ross, The Cleveland Orchestra, Cleveland, OH. Tel: (216) 231-7300, FAX: (216) 231-4038, Web Site: www.clevelandorchestra.com (1)

Binnie, Thomas, Sturbridge Yankee Workshop Inc, Portland, ME. Tel: (207) 774-9045, (800) 343-1144, FAX: (207) 774-2561, Web Site: www.sturbridgeyankee.com (16)

Biochlini, Brian, PennWell Publishing, Tulsa, OK. Tel: (918) 835-3161, (800) 331-4463, E-Mail: headquarters@pennwell.com, Web Site: www.pennwell.com (17)

Biological Photo Service & Terraphotographics, Pacifica, CA. Tel: (650) 359-6219, FAX: (650) 359-6219, E-Mail: bpsterra@pacbell.net, Web Site: www.agpix.com/biologicalphoto (38)

Biomerica Inc, Irvine, CA. Tel: (949) 645-2111, (800) 854-3002, FAX: (949) 553-1231, E-Mail: info@biomerica.com, Web Site: www.biomerica.com (7)

Biosciences-Amersham, Piscataway, NJ. Tel: (732) 457-8000, FAX: (732) 457-0557, Web Site: www.amersham.com (16)

Bird, Amanda, Sculptz, Feasterville Trevose, PA. Tel: (215) 494-2900, E-Mail: sdudek@sculptz.com, Web Site: www.silkies.com (2)

Bird, Andy, Publicis Worldwide North America, New York, NY. Tel: (212) 279-5550, E-Mail: andrew.bruce@publicisna.com, Web Site: publicisna.com (35)

Bird, Laura, Community Food Bank, Tucson, AZ. Tel: (520) 622-0525, FAX: (520) 624-6349, Web Site: www.communityfoodbank.org (1)

Bird, Michael C, NetProspex Inc, Waltham, MA. Tel: (888) 826-4877, E-Mail: sales@netprospex.com, Web Site: www.netprospex.com (22)

Bird, Shelley, Fluke Biomedical, Everett, WA. Tel: (425) 347-6100, (800) 850-4608, FAX: (425) 446-5116, Web Site: www.flukebiomedical.com (16)

Birdsall, Steven, Radial Inc, King of Prussia, PA. Tel: (610) 491-7000, Web Site: www.radial.com (28)

Birnbaum, Steven, SofTrek Corp, Amherst, NY. Tel: (716) 691-2800, (800) 442-9211, FAX: (716) 691-2828, Web Site: www.softrek.com (22)

Birney, Lori, Baltimore Magazine, Baltimore, MD. Tel: (410) 752-4200, (800) 935-0838, FAX: (410) 625-0280, E-Mail: blori@baltimoremagazine.net, Web Site: www.baltimoremagazine.net (17)

Birsh, Hope, The Maryland Saddlery Inc, Butler, MD. Tel: (410) 771-4135, (800) 428-5077, FAX: (410) 472-9722, E-Mail: mdsaddle@aol.com, Web Site: www.marylandsaddlery.com (11)

Birthday Express Inc, Kirkland, WA. Tel: (425) 250-1064, (800) 247-8432, FAX: (425) 641-2028, Web Site: www.birthdayexpress.com (5)

Birthday Keepsakes, Loveland, CO. Tel: (970) 669-5506, Web Site: www.bkeepsakes.com (6)

Bischoff, Tim, KET, Lexington, KY. Tel: (859) 258-7000, (800) 432-0951, FAX: (606) 258-7396, E-Mail: rgriffin@ket.org, Web Site: www.ket.org (17)

Bishop, Cameron, Telephony, Chicago, IL. Tel: (312) 595-1080, (800) 458-0479, FAX: (312) 595-0295, Web Site: www.internettelephony.com (17)

Bishop, Joanne, Patient News, Niagara Falls, NY. Tel: (705) 457-4030, (800) 667-0268, FAX: (705) 457-4067, E-Mail: jbishop@patientnews.com, Web Site: www.patientnews.com (17)

Bishop, Paul, Tuttle Printing & Engraving, Rutland, VT. Tel: (802) 773-9171, (800) 776-7682, FAX: (802) 773-5785, E-Mail: info@tuttleprinting.com, Web Site: www.tuttleprinting.com (10)

Bisnaire, Jean-Paul, John Hancock Financial Services Inc, Boston, MA. Tel: (617) 572-6000, (800) 732-5543, FAX: (617) 572-6451, Web Site: www.johnhancock.com (15)

Bisset, Jeffrey B, Interact Direct Marketing Inc, London, ON Canada. Tel: (519) 439-6245, Web Site: www.interactdirect.com (28)

Bissinger French Confections, Saint Louis, MO. Tel: (314) 615-2436, (800) 325-8881, Web Site: www.bissingers.com (4)

Bisson, William T., Pensions & Investments, New York, NY. Tel: (212) 210-0100, FAX: (212) 210-0117, Web Site: www.pionline.com (17)

Biswas, Michael, PhotoStamps.com, El Segundo, CA. Tel: (310) 482-5800, Web Site: www.photostamps.com (5)

Bits & Pieces Inc, Lawrenceburg, IN. Tel: (866) 503-6395, FAX: (513) 354-1290, Web Site: www.bitsandpieces.com (11)

Bitstream Inc, Marlborough, MA. Tel: (617) 497-6222, FAX: (617) 868-0784, Web Site: www.bitstream.com (22)

Bivins, Jackie, Executive Connections LLC, Sarasota, FL. Tel: (941) 323-8300, Web Site: www.executiveconnectionsllc.com (20)

Bixon, Jodie, Porter Wallace Corp, Brick, NJ. Tel: (732) 920-1405, FAX: (732) 920-1406, Web Site: www.porterwallace.com (33)

Bize, Pierre, Civil Service Employees Insurance Group, Walnut Creek, CA. Tel: (415) 274-7803, (925) 817-6300, (800) 282-6848, Web Site: www.cseinsurance.com (15)

Bizzaro Rubber Stamps, Greenville, RI. Tel: (401) 231-8777, FAX: (401) 231-4770, E-Mail: bizzaroinc@earthlink.net, Web Site: www.bizzaro.com (6)

Bjorkman, Lincoln, Wunderman, New York, NY. Tel: (212) 941-3000, Web Site: www.wunderman.com (35)

Bjornstad, Erik, Bell Performance Inc, Longwood, FL. Tel: (407) 834-3690, (800) 659-2355, FAX: (407) 767-8685, E-Mail: info@bellperformance.net, Web Site: www.bellperformance.net (9)

Blabolil, Richard A., Marketing Innovators, Rosemont, IL. Tel: (847) 696-1111, (800) 543-7373, FAX: (847) 696-3194, E-Mail: info@marketinginnovators.com, Web Site: www.marketinginnovators.com (35)

Black & Co, New York, NY. Tel: (212) 867-5533, FAX: (212) 447-0785, E-Mail: wblack6340@aol.com (20)

Stanley Black & Decker Inc, New Britain, CT. Tel: (860) 225-5111, Web Site: www.stanleyblackanddecker.com (16)

Black Box Corp, Lawrence, PA. Tel: (724) 746-5500, (877) 877-2269, FAX: (800) 321-0746, E-Mail: brian.kutchma@blackbox.com, Web Site: www.blackbox.com (3)

The Black Dog Tavern Co Inc, Vineyard Haven, MA. Tel: (800) 626-1991, E-Mail: contactus@theblackdog.com, Web Site: www.theblackdog.com; www.theblackdogtshirt.com (2)

Black Dot Group, Crystal Lake, IL. Tel: (815) 893-8799, E-Mail: pkelley@blackdot.com, Web Site: www.blackdot.com (35)

Black Enterprise Magazine, New York, NY. Tel: (212) 242-8000, FAX: (212) 886-9618, Web Site: www.blackenterprise.com (17)

Black Entertainment Television Inc, Washington, DC. Tel: (202) 608-2000, Web Site: www.bet.com (16)

Black Olive Co, Chicago, IL. Tel: (312) 893-5454, FAX: (312) 276-8636, E-Mail: info@blackoliveco.com, Web Site: www.blackoliveco.com (35)

Black Star Publishing Co, White Plains, NY. Tel: (212) 679-3288, FAX: (212) 889-2052, Web Site: www.blackstar.com (38)

Black, Eli, Decision Software Inc, Hyattsville, MD. Tel: (301) 459-9000, FAX: (301) 459-3072, E-Mail: info@dsoftware.biz, Web Site: www.dsimarketingservices.com (22)

Black, Jerry T., Kurt Salmon Associates Inc, Atlanta, GA. Tel: (404) 892-0321, FAX: (404) 898-9590, E-Mail: infoksaweb@kurtsalmon.com, Web Site: www.kurtsalmon.com (20)

Black, Kathy, Tennessee Valley Authority, Knoxville, TN. Tel: (865) 632-2101, Web Site: www.tva.gov (16)

Black, Paul, Ball Publishing, West Chicago, IL. Tel: (630) 231-3675, FAX: (630) 231-5254, E-Mail: info@ballpublishing.com, Web Site: www.ballpublishing.com (17)

Black, R. Neal, Jos A Bank Clothiers Inc, Hampstead, MD. Tel: (410) 239-2700, Web Site: www.josbank.com (2)

Black, Randy, Airlines Reporting Corp, Arlington, VA. Tel: (703) 816-8135, FAX: (703) 816-8104, E-Mail: corpcom@arccorp.com, Web Site: www.arccorp.com (16)

Black, Wahleyah, Nowetah's American Indian Store & Museum, New Portland, ME. Tel: (207) 628-4981, Web Site: www.nowetahs.webs.com (6)

Black, William, Black & Co, New York, NY. Tel: (212) 867-5533, FAX: (212) 447-0785, E-Mail: wblack6340@aol.com (20)

Blackall, Pamela, Business Automation Systems Inc, Nashville, TN. Tel: (615) 329-4585, FAX: (615) 320-0206, Web Site: www.bas-solutions.com (16)

Blackbaud Inc, Charleston, SC. Tel: (843) 216-6200, (800) 443-9441, FAX: (843) 216-6100, Web Site: www.blackbaud.com (22)

Blackburn, Betty, Safe Specialties, Kingston, TN. Tel: (865) 675-2815, (800) 695-2815, FAX: (865) 717-8249, E-Mail: black223@aol.com, Web Site: www.safespec.com (33)

Blackburn, Jeffrey M., Amazon.com, Seattle, WA. Tel: (206) 266-1000, Web Site: www.amazon.com (16)

Blackburn-Gay, Denise, Marketing Strategies Inc, North Myrtle Beach, SC. Tel: (843) 692-9662, FAX: (843) 692-0558, E-Mail: pr@marketingstrategiesinc.com, Web Site: marketingstrategiesinc.com (35)

Blackhawk Engagement Solutions Inc, Fenton, MO. Tel: (636) 226-2000, Web Site: www.bhengagement.com (35)

Blackman, Bob, AmazingMail Inc, Scottsdale, AZ. Tel: (480) 281-4800, E-Mail: customersupport@amazingmail.com, Web Site: www.amazingmail.com (35)

Blackman, Jeff, ForeSee Results Inc, Ann Arbor, MI. Tel: (734) 205-2600, (800) 621-2850, FAX: (734) 205-2601, Web Site: www.foreseeresults.com (30)

Blackman, Larry, Blue Cross Blue Shield of Louisiana, Baton Rouge, LA. Tel: (225) 295-3307, (800) 599-2583, FAX: (225) 295-2054, E-Mail: help@bcbsla.com, Web Site: www.bcbsla.com (15)

Blackmore, David, University of Pittsburgh at Bradford, Bradford, PA. Tel: (814) 362-7500, FAX: (814) 362-5150, E-Mail: admissions@www.upb.pitt.edu, Web Site: www.upd.pitt.edu (41)

Blagman Creative/Direct Response, Gainesville, VA. Tel: (703) 743-2493, E-Mail: jackbee21@comcast.net (20)

Blagman, Jack, Blagman Creative/Direct Response, Gainesville, VA. Tel: (703) 743-2493, E-Mail: jackbee21@comcast.net (20)

Blaha, Karen, Medco Supply Co Inc, Tonawanda, NY. Tel: (716) 743-8400, (800) 556-3326, FAX: (800) 222-1934, E-Mail: sales@medcosupply.com, Web Site: www.medcosupply.com (7)

Blaine Window Hardware Inc, Hagerstown, MD. Tel: (301) 797-6500, (800) 678-1919, FAX: (888) 250-3960, E-Mail: info@blainewindow.com, Web Site: www.blainewindow.com (9)

Blaine, Margaret, Blaine Window Hardware Inc, Hagerstown, MD. Tel: (301) 797-6500, (800) 678-1919, FAX: (888) 250-3960, E-Mail: info@blainewindow.com, Web Site: www.blainewindow.com (9)

Blair Corp, Warren, PA. Tel: (814) 723-3600, (800) 458-6057, FAX: (814) 726-6123, E-Mail: blair@blair.com, Web Site: www.blair.com (2)

DL Blair Inc, Westbury, NY. Tel: (516) 746-3700, FAX: (516) 746-3889, Web Site: www.dlblair.com (35)

William Blair & Co LLC, Chicago, IL. Tel: (312) 236-1600, (800) 621-0687, FAX: (312) 368-9418, E-Mail: info@williamblair.com, Web Site: www.williamblair.com (14)

Blair, Donald W., Nike Inc, Beaverton, OR. Tel: (503) 671-4565, (800) 344-6543, FAX: (503) 671-6300, Web Site: www.nike.com (2)

Blair, Greg, Escort Inc, West Chester, OH. Tel: (513) 870-8500, (800) 964-3138, FAX: (513) 870-8509, E-Mail: sales@escortradar.com, Web Site: www.escortradar.com (16)

Blakar Inc, Englewood, CO. Tel: (201) 672-0705, FAX: (201) 673-0725, Web Site: www.blakar.com (33)

George Blake & Associates, Bradenton, FL. Tel: (941) 755-8637, E-Mail: single14all@verizon.net (35)

Blake, Francis C., The Home Depot Inc, Atlanta, GA. Tel: (770) 433-8211, (800) 466-3337, FAX: (770) 384-2356, Web Site: www.homedepot.com (16)

Blake, George, George Blake & Associates, Bradenton, FL. Tel: (941) 755-8637, E-Mail: single14all@verizon.net (35)

Blake, Mickey, Marketability Inc, Houston, TX. Tel: (713) 462-6000, FAX: (713) 481-8465, E-Mail: mickey@marketabilityinc.com, Web Site: www.marketabilityinc.com (35)

Blakeman, Robyn, West Virginia University, Morgantown, WV. Tel: (304) 293-3505, FAX: (304) 293-3072, E-Mail: wvuwebmaster@mail.wvu.edu, Web Site: www.wvu.edu (41)

Blakeney Design, New York, NY. Tel: (212) 243-0109, FAX: (212) 243-0109 (36)

Blakeney, Leslie, Blakeney Design, New York, NY. Tel: (212) 243-0109, FAX: (212) 243-0109 (36)

Blakenship, Storme, Fiorella's Jack Stack Barbecue, Kansas City, MO. Tel: (816) 942-9141, Web Site: www.jackstackbbq.com (4)

Blanchard & Co Inc, New Orleans, LA. Tel: (504) 837-3010, (800) 880-4653, FAX: (504) 837-4884, Web Site: www.blanchardonline.com (16)

Blanchard, Clarence, Antique & Collectible Tools Inc, Pownal, ME. Tel: (207) 688-4962, FAX: (207) 688-4831, E-Mail: ceb@finetoolj.com, Web Site: www.finetoolj.com (11)

Blanchard, Karen, AccuData Integrated Marketing, Fort Myers, FL. Tel: (239) 425-4400, (800) 732-3440, FAX: (239) 425-4401, E-Mail: info@accudata.com, Web Site: www.accudata.com (23)

Blanchard, Ron, Standard Communications Corp, San Diego, CA. Tel: (858) 546-5300, (800) 745-2445, FAX: (858) 546-5301, E-Mail: satcommsales@stdcom.com, Web Site: www.standardcomm.com (16)

Blanco, Jane, Gage, Minneapolis, MN. Tel: (763) 595-3800, FAX: (763) 595-5845, Web Site: www.gage.com (35)

Bland Farms, Glennville, GA. Tel: (912) 654-1300, Web Site: www.blandfarms.com (4)

Bland, Charlain L, ZIP Mailing Services Inc, Landover, MD. Tel: (301) 386-3633, FAX: (301) 386-3637, E-Mail: zipmail@zipmailing.com, Web Site: www.zipmailing.com (28)

Bland, Dorothy, Florida A&M University, Tallahassee, FL. Tel: (850) 599-3379, E-Mail: sjgc@famu.edu, Web Site: sjgc.famu.edu (16)

Bland, Greg G., Optronics, Muskogee, OK. Tel: (918) 683-9514, (800) 364-5483, FAX: (918) 683-9517, E-Mail: sales@optronicsinc.com, Web Site: www.optronicsinc.com (11)

Bland, Murrel W., Wyandotte West Communications Inc, Kansas City, KS. Tel: (913) 788-5565, FAX: (913) 788-9812, E-Mail: news@wyandottewest.com, Web Site: www.wyandottewest.com (17)

Blaney, Erika, Bunchball, Redwood City, CA. Tel: (408) 985-2034, Web Site: www.bunchball.com (32)

Blaney, Jane, USA Network, New York, NY. Tel: (212) 664-4444, FAX: (212) 664-6365, Web Site: www.usanetwork.com (32)

Arthur Blank & Co Inc, Boston, MA. Tel: (617) 325-9600, (800) 776-7333, FAX: (617) 327-1235, E-Mail: abco@abco.com, Web Site: www.arthurblank.com (27)

Blank, Matthew, Showtime Networks Inc, New York, NY. Tel: (212) 708-1600, FAX: (212) 708-1450, Web Site: www.sho.com (16)

Blankman, Patrick, GE Money, Alpharetta, GA. Tel: (678) 518-2403 (14)

Blansfield, David, F&W Media Inc, Blue Ash, OH. Tel: (513) 531-2690, FAX: (513) 531-0293, Web Site: www.fwmedia.com (17)

Blase, Mary, Cole-Parmer Instrument Co, Vernon Hills, IL. Tel: (847) 549-7600, (800) 323-4340, FAX: (847) 247-2929, E-Mail: info@coleparmer.com, Web Site: www.coleparmer.com (16)

Blasingame, David T., Washington University, Saint Louis, MO. Tel: (314) 935-5000, Web Site: www.wustl.edu (1)

Blass Communications LLC, Old Chatham, NY. Tel: (518) 766-2222, FAX: (518) 766-2445, E-Mail: brandthink@blasscommunications.com, Web Site: www.blasscom.com (35)

Blass, Kenneth L., Blass Communications LLC, Old Chatham, NY. Tel: (518) 766-2222, FAX: (518) 766-2445, E-Mail: brandthink@blasscommunications.com, Web Site: www.blasscom.com (35)

Blast! Marketing & PR, Chicago, IL. Web Site: blastmarketing.net (35)

Blatt, Jeff, Synapse Group Inc, Stamford, CT. Tel: (203) 595-8255, FAX: (203) 329-8237, E-Mail: webmaster@synapsemail.com, Web Site: www.synapsegroupinc.com (18)

Blatteis Communications, San Jose, CA. Tel: (901) 356-0090, Web Site: www.blatteis.com (20)

Blatteis, Beatrice, Blatteis Communications, San Jose, CA. Tel: (901) 356-0090, Web Site: www.blatteis.com (20)

Blattman, Jim, Fairfield Industries Inc, Sugar Land, TX. Tel: (281) 275-7500, (800) 231-9809, FAX: (281) 275-7550, E-Mail: jblattman@fairfield.com, Web Site: www.fairfield.com (16)

Blatz, Cory, Lancer Label, Omaha, NE. Tel: (402) 390-9119, (800) 228-7074, FAX: (800) 344-9456, E-Mail: customerservice@lancerlabel.com, Web Site: www.lancerlabel.com (27)

Blau, Peter, Customer Growth Inc, Fairfield, CT. Tel: (203) 226-8795, FAX: (203) 286-1049, E-Mail: info@customer-growth.com, Web Site: www.customer-growth.com (35)

Blausey, Jr. William W., Eaton Corp, Raleigh, NC. Tel: (216) 523-4400, (800) 356-5794, FAX: (216) 523-4787, Web Site: www.eaton.com (16)

Blautenbach, Marc, Pitney Bowes Software Systems, Stamford, CT. Tel: (203) 356-5000, (800) 624-5377, FAX: (203) 351-7336, Web Site: www.pitneybowes.com (22)

Blauvelt, Eric, Global Specialties, Wallingford, CT. Tel: (203) 272-3285, FAX: (203) 272-4330, Web Site: www.globalspecialties.com (16)

Blazevich, Chuck, Premier Print and Services Group Inc, Chicago, IL. Tel: (312) 648-2266, (800) 648-3677, FAX: (312) 648-1361, Web Site: www.premierprint.com (21)

Blazucki, Dr. Joan Warfield, MARCOR Remediation Inc, Halethorpe, MD. Tel: (410) 785-0001, (800) 547-0128, FAX: (410) 771-0348, E-Mail: info@marcor.com, Web Site: www.marcor.com (16)

Blease, Rochelle, Wolters Kluwer Financial Services, Minneapolis, MN. Tel: (612) 656-7700, (800) 552-9408, Web Site: www.wolterskluwerfs.com (14)

Blechman, Michelle, Chicago Association of Direct Marketing, Westmont, IL. Tel: (312) 849-2236, FAX: (312) 849-2239, E-Mail: info@cadm.org, Web Site: www.cadm.org (40)

Blehm, Jake, Spalding Laboratories Inc, Reno, NV. Tel: (888) 562-5696, (888) 880-1579, FAX: (866) 738-9632, Web Site: www.spalding-labs.com (7)

Blethen Maine Newspapers Inc, Portland, ME. Tel: (207) 791-6650, FAX: (207) 791-6925, Web Site: www.mainetoday.com (17)

Bleu Marketing Solutions Inc, San Francisco, CA. Tel: (415) 345-3300, FAX: (415) 353-0299, E-Mail: helpdesk@bleumarketing.com, Web Site: bleumarketing.com (35)

Bleuel, Breonna, NewsNotes LLC, Middleton, WI. Tel: (608) 831-9600, (800) 676-9665, FAX: (608) 831-9665, E-Mail: sales@nastar-inc.com, Web Site: www.news-notes.com (27)

Blevins, Teresa F., Dominion Enterprises, Norfolk, VA. Tel: (757) 351-7000, Web Site: www.dominionenterprises.com (32)

Blevins, Tim, Augsburg Fortress Publishers, Minneapolis, MN. Tel: (612) 330-3300, (800) 426-0115, FAX: (612) 330-3455, E-Mail: info@augsburgfortress.org, Web Site: www.augsburgfortress.org (17)

Blexrud Direct, Spartanburg, SC. Tel: (864) 583-7399, FAX: (864) 583-7399, E-Mail: blexrud@bellsouth.net (20)

Blexrud, Tom, Blexrud Direct, Spartanburg, SC. Tel: (864) 583-7399, FAX: (864) 583-7399, E-Mail: blexrud@bellsouth.net (20)

Dick Blick Holdings Inc, Galesburg, IL. Tel: (309) 343-6181, FAX: (309) 343-5785, E-Mail: admin@dickblick.com, Web Site: www.dickblick.com (16)

Bliss World LLC, New York, NY. Tel: (212) 931-6383, (888) 243-8825, Web Site: www.blissworld.com (5)

Bliss, Austin, FreshAddress Inc, Newton, MA. Tel: (617) 965-4500, (800) 321-3009, FAX: (617) 965-4551, Web Site: www.freshaddress.com (22)

Bliss, Mark, Cornhusker Press, Hastings, NE. Tel: (402) 462-4141, FAX: (402) 460-4612, E-Mail: dlsales@dutton-lainson.com, Web Site: www.dutton-lainson.com (17)

Blissliving Home, Rockville, MD. Tel: (240) 485-3492, Web Site: www.blisslivinghome.com (8)

Blitman, Joan, JRB Marketing Group, East Windsor, NJ. Tel: (301) 758-2334, FAX: (302) 348-2490, E-Mail: jrblitman@gmail.com (20)

Bliwas, Ronald, A Eicoff & Co, Chicago, IL. Tel: (312) 527-7183, (800) 333-6605, FAX: (312) 527-7192, E-Mail: bill.mccabe@eicoff.com, Web Site: www.eicoff.com (35)

Bloch, Christopher, SWAT Marketing Team, Grove City, PA. Tel: (412) 851-9700, FAX: (412) 291-1155, E-Mail: cdbloch@swatmarketingteam.com, Web Site: swatmarketingteam.com (23)

Bloch, Henry W., H&R Block Inc, Kansas City, MO. Tel: (816) 854-3000, (800) 472-5625, FAX: (816) 854-8500, Web Site: www.hrblock.com (14)

Bloch, Paul, Data Direct Networks, Chatsworth, CA. Tel: (818) 700-7607, (800) 837-2298, FAX: (818) 700-7601, E-Mail: info@ddn.com, Web Site: www.datadirectnet.com (3)

Block & DeCorso, Verona, NJ. Tel: (973) 857-3900, FAX: (973) 857-4041, E-Mail: bdecorso@blockdecorso.com, Web Site: www.blockdecorso.com (35)

Block, Janice L., Kaplan Inc, Fort Lauderdale, FL. Tel: (954) 515-3993, Web Site: www.kaplan.com (16)

Block, Michael, SECO-LARM USA Inc, Irvine, CA. Tel: (949) 261-2999, (800) 662-0800, FAX: (949) 261-7326, E-Mail: info@seco-larm.com, Web Site: www.seco-larm.com (16)

Block, Mitchell W., Direct Cinema Ltd Inc, Santa Monica, CA. Tel: (310) 636-8200, FAX: (310) 636-8228, E-Mail: dclvideo@aol.com, Web Site: www.directcinema.com (16)

Block, Myrna, Basic Adhesives Inc, Clifton, NJ. Tel: (800) 394-9310, FAX: (973) 614-9099, E-Mail: info@basicadhesives.com, Web Site: www.basicadhesives.com (9)

Block, Paul, Times Union, Albany, NY. Tel: (518) 454-5694, FAX: (518) 454-5628, Web Site: www.timesunion.com (18)

Block, Yale, Basic Adhesives Inc, Clifton, NJ. Tel: (800) 394-9310, FAX: (973) 614-9099, E-Mail: info@basicadhesives.com, Web Site: www.basicadhesives.com (9)

Blodgett, Lynn, Xerox Corp, Norwalk, CT. Tel: (800) 275-9376, Web Site: www.xerox.com (16)

Blodgett, Lynn, Xerox Services, Dallas, TX. Tel: (214) 841-6111, (800) 275-9376, Web Site: www.acs-inc.com (22)

Blodgett, M.W., MFE Instruments, Salem, NH. Tel: (603) 893-8778, (800) 843-8011, FAX: (603) 893-8851, Web Site: www.stockeryale.com (9)

Bloodworth, Scott, Rhode Island Novelty, Cumberland, RI. Tel: (401) 335-3300, (800) 528-5599, FAX: (800) 448-1775, E-Mail: info@rinovelty.com, Web Site: www.rinovelty.com (16)

Carl Bloom Associates Inc, White Plains, NY. Tel: (914) 761-2800, FAX: (914) 761-2744, E-Mail: info@carlbloom.com, Web Site: www.carlbloom.com (35)

Bloom, Hergott, Diemer, Rosenthal and Laviolette LLP, Beverly Hills, CA. Tel: (310) 859-6800, FAX: (310) 860-6820, E-Mail: sfb@bhdrl.com (20)

Bloom, Carl, Carl Bloom Associates Inc, White Plains, NY. Tel: (914) 761-2800, FAX: (914) 761-2744, E-Mail: info@carlbloom.com, Web Site: www.carlbloom.com (35)

Bloom, Rob, Carl Bloom Associates Inc, White Plains, NY. Tel: (914) 761-2800, FAX: (914) 761-2744, E-Mail: info@carlbloom.com, Web Site: www.carlbloom.com (35)

Bloom, Robert, Business Development Solutions Inc, Cherry Hill, NJ. Tel: (856) 787-1500, E-Mail: info@hdsdatabase.com, Web Site: www.bdsdatabase.com (22)

Bloomer, Paul, Redleaf Press, Saint Paul, MN. Tel: (651) 641-6621, (800) 423-8309, FAX: (800) 641-0115, E-Mail: jvoltz@redleafpress.org, Web Site: www.redleafpress.org (17)

Bloomin Promotions, Boulder, CO. Tel: (303) 443-3591, E-Mail: flowers@bloomin.com, Web Site: www.bloominpromotions.com (25)

Bloomingdale's Direct, New York, NY. Tel: (212) 705-2000, (800) 777-0000, FAX: (212) 705-2805, Web Site: www.bloomingdales.com (16)

Bloomquist, Conrad, Scenic Photo!, Minneapolis, MN. Tel: (612) 810-0797, E-Mail: manager@scenicphoto.com, Web Site: www.scenicphoto.com (38)

Bluberries Advertising Agency, Garfield, NJ. Tel: (973) 478-2200, FAX: (973) 478-9662, E-Mail: mail@bluberries.com, Web Site: www.bluberries.com (35)

BluBlocker Corp, Las Vegas, NV. Tel: (702) 597-2000, (800) BLUBLOCKER, FAX: (702) 597-2002, Web Site: www.blublocker.com (2)

The Blue Book Building & Construction Network, Jefferson Valley, NY. Tel: (800) 431-2584, FAX: (914) 243-0287, E-Mail: info@thebluebook.com, Web Site: www.thebluebook.com (17)

Blue Coral Slick 50, Houston, TX. Tel: (713) 241-6161, (800) 416-1600, FAX: (713) 241-4044, E-Mail: SCD-ConsumerSolutions@Shell.com, Web Site: www.bluecoral.com (16)

Blue Cross Blue Shield of Florida, Jacksonville, FL. Tel: (904) 791-6111, (800) 477-3736, FAX: (904) 905-6638, E-Mail: katie.magee@bcbsfl.com, Web Site: www.bcbsfl.com (15)

Blue Cross Blue Shield of Illinois, Chicago, IL. Tel: (312) 938-6000, FAX: (312) 938-5722, Web Site: www.bcbsil.com (15)

Blue Cross Blue Shield of Louisiana, Baton Rouge, LA. Tel: (225) 295-3307, (800) 599-2583, FAX: (225) 295-2054, E-Mail: help@bcbsla.com, Web Site: www.bcbsla.com (15)

Blue Cross Blue Shield of North Carolina, Durham, NC. Tel: (800) 250-3630, Web Site: www.bcbsnc.com (15)

Blue Cross Blue Shield of Oklahoma, Tulsa, OK. Tel: (918) 560-3500, (800) 942-5837, E-Mail: info@bcbsok.com, Web Site: www.bcbsok.com (15)

Blue Cross Blue Shield of South Carolina, Columbia, SC. Tel: (803) 788-0222, (800) 288-2227, FAX: (803) 736-4516, Web Site: www.bcbssc.com (15)

Blue Grass Mailing, Data & Fulfillment Services, Lexington, KY. Tel: (859) 231-7272, (800) 928-6245, FAX: (859) 259-1214, E-Mail: info@bgmailing.com, Web Site: www.bgmailing.com (28)

Blue Hill Marketing Solutions Inc, Pearl River, NY. Tel: (845) 627-6600, FAX: (845) 735-3985, E-Mail: sales@liftengine.com, Web Site: www.liftengine.com (22)

Blue Raven Technology, Wilmington, MA. Tel: ((978) 658-4676, (800) 274-5343, (800) 20RAVEN, FAX: (781) 778-4848, E-Mail: sales@blueraven.com, Web Site: www.blueraven.com (3)

Blue Shield Life, San Francisco, CA. Tel: (888) 800-2742, FAX: (800) 329-2742, Web Site: www.blueshieldca.com (15)

Blue Shield of California, San Francisco, CA. Tel: (415) 229-5000, FAX: (415) 229-5056, Web Site: www.blueshieldca.com (15)

Blue Sky Factory, Baltimore, MD. Tel: (410) 230-0061, Web Site: www.blueskyfactory.com (32)

Blue Strawberry Resorts LLC, Miami, FL. Tel: (756) 513-1456, (800) 873-1440, Web Site: www.bluestrawberry-resorts.com (19)

Blue Valley Tele-Marketing Inc, Home, KS. Tel: (785) 799-3500, (800) 882-0803, FAX: (785) 799-3504, E-Mail: info@bluevalleytelemarketing.com (29)

Blue Vidalia, Toronto, ON Canada. Tel: (416) 572-5222, FAX: (416) 609-0670, E-Mail: info@bluevidalia.ca, Web Site: www.bluevidalia.ca (35)

Blue, Laurie. Mini City Ltd, Webster, NY. Tel: (585) 872-6560, FAX: (716) 872-4094, E-Mail: minicityus@aol.com, Web Site: www.minicityltd.com (12)

Bluespire Senior Living, West Hartford, CT. Tel: (888) 818-4715, Web Site: www.bluespireseniorliving.com (35)

Bluestein, Barry, Source Communications, Hackensack, NJ. Tel: (201) 343-5222, E-Mail: admin@sourcead.com, Web Site: www.sourcead.com (35)

Bluestein, Clara, Captan Associates Inc, Brick, NJ. Tel: (732) 840-1244, FAX: (732) 840-1211 (17)

Bluestem Brands, Eden Prairie, MN. Tel: (952) 656-3700, Web Site: www.fingerhut.com (16)

Bluestone Perennials Inc, Madison, OH. Tel: (800) 852-5243, FAX: (800) 852-5243, E-Mail: service@bluestoneperennials.com, Web Site: www.bluestoneperennials.com (8)

Bluewater Yachts, Mora, MN. Tel: (320) 679-3811, FAX: (320) 679-3820, E-Mail: bluewater@ncis.com, Web Site: www.bluewateryacht.com (16)

Blum & Co LLC, Fairfield, CT. Tel: (203) 255-4813, FAX: (203) 255-3936, E-Mail: e-blum@att.net, Web Site: www.blumdirect.com (20)

Blum, Amy, Eagle Marketing Services Inc, San Diego, CA. Tel: (619) 223-1273, E-Mail: info@eaglemarketing.com, Web Site: www.eaglemarketing.com (35)

Blum. Jennifer, Salesian Missions, New Rochelle, NY. Tel: (914) 633-8344, FAX: (914) 633-7404, E-Mail: info@salesianmissions.org, Web Site: www.salesianmissions.org. (1)

Blum, Sandra J., Blum & Co LLC, Fairfield, CT. Tel: (203) 255-4813, FAX: (203) 255-3936, E-Mail: e-blum@att.net, Web Site: www.blumdirect.com (20)

Blum, Sherry, SofTrek Corp, Amherst, NY. Tel: (716) 691-2800, (800) 442-9211, FAX: (716) 691-2828, Web Site: www.softrek.com (22)

Blumberg, Matthew, Return Path Inc, New York, NY. Tel: (212) 905-5500, FAX: (212) 905-5501, Web Site: www.returnpath.biz (22)

Blumberg, Warren, Kelsey National Corp, Los Angeles, CA. Tel: (310) 390-1000, (800) 366-5656, FAX: (310) 390-3158, E-Mail: info@kelsey.com, Web Site: www.kelsey.com (15)

Blume, Aron, HubCast Inc, Wakefield, MA. Tel: (781) 221-7200, FAX: (781) 221-7223, Web Site: www.hubeast.com (22)

Blume, Peter, WCPE-FM, Wake Forest, NC. Tel: (800) 556-5178, FAX: (919) 556-9273, Web Site: theclassicalstation.org (32)

Blumenfeld, Joshua, CoverClicks Media Inc, New York, NY. Tel: (646) 434-1413, E-Mail: info@coverclicksmail.com, Web Site: www.coverclicks.com (23)

Blumenfield, Arthur, BMI Fulfillment Services, Danbury, CT. Tel: (203) 546-5580, FAX: (203) 546-5575, E-Mail: barry@bmigroup.com, Web Site: www.bmigroup.com (28)

Blumenfield, Arthur, The Direct Marketing Club of New York Inc, Garden City, NY. Tel: (516) 746-6700, FAX: (516) 294-8141, E-Mail: info@dmcny.org, Web Site: www.dmcny.org (1)

Blumenfield, Barry, BMI Fulfillment Services, Danbury, CT. Tel: (203) 546-5580, FAX: (203) 546-5575, E-Mail: barry@bmigroup.com, Web Site: www.bmigroup.com (28)

Blumental, Tom, Geary's of Beverly Hills, Beverly Hills, CA. Tel: (310) 273-4741, (800) 793-6670, FAX: (310) 858-7555, Web Site: www.gearys.com (6)

Blunt, Kenyon, SIGMA Marketing Group LLC, Rochester, NY. Tel: (585) 473-7300, (888) 277-9837, FAX: (585) 473-0332, E-Mail: mbush@sigmamarketing.com, Web Site: www.sigmamarketing.com; www.jthgearanalytics.com (Blog) (20)

Blunt, Rebecca, Graphic Arts Information Network (GAIN), Sewickley, PA. Tel: (412) 741-6860, (800) 910-4283, FAX: (412) 741-2311, E-Mail: printing@printing.org, Web Site: www.gain.net (27)

Blusk, Gloria, Spectronics Corp, Westbury, NY. Tel: (516) 333-4840, (800) 274-8888, FAX: (800) 491-6868, E-Mail: vscherer@spectroline.com, Web Site: www.spectroline.com (9)

Blust, Ed, Adecco Employment Services, Melville, NY. Tel: (631) 844-7800, Web Site: www.adecco.com (20)

Bob Bly, River Vale, NJ. Tel: (201) 505-9451, FAX: (201) 573-4094, E-Mail: rwbly@bly.com, Web Site: www.bly.com (39)

Bly, Bob, Bob Bly, River Vale, NJ. Tel: (201) 505-9451, FAX: (201) 573-4094, E-Mail: rwbly@bly.com, Web Site: www.bly.com (39)

B'nai B'rith International, Washington, DC. Tel: (202) 857-6600, (888) 388-4224, FAX: (202) 857-6609, E-Mail: info@bnaibrith.org, Web Site: www.bnaibrith.org (1)

Boardman, Joseph H., National Railroad Passenger Corp, Washington, DC. Tel: (202) 906-3000, (800) USA-RAIL, FAX: (202) 906-3306, Web Site: www.amtrak.com (16)

Boardman, Michael, International Coins & Currency Inc, Montpelier, VT. Tel: (802) 223-6331, (800) 451-4463, FAX: (800) 229-3239, E-Mail: info@iccoin.org, Web Site: www.iccoin.com (6)

Boardroom Inc, Stamford, CT. Tel: (203) 973-5900, FAX: (203) 967-3086, Web Site: www.bottomlinepublications.com (17)

Boba, Denise, Country Sampler Group, Saint Charles, IL. Tel: (630) 377-8000, FAX: (630) 377-8194, Web Site: www.sampler.com (17)

Bobb. Stevan B., Burlington Northern & Santa Fe LLC, Fort Worth, TX. Tel: (817) 878-2000, (800) 795-2673, FAX: (817) 333-7593, Web Site: www.bnsf.com (16)

Bobcat Co, West Fargo, ND. Tel: (701) 241-8700, FAX: (701) 241-8704, Web Site: www.bobcat.com (16)

Bobley-Harmann Corp, Ronkonkoma, NY. Tel: (516) 364-1800, (800) 323-1692, FAX: (516) 364-1899, E-Mail: info.giftvalues@gmail.com, Web Site: www.giftvalues.com (5)

Bobley, Mark, Bobley-Harmann Corp, Ronkonkoma, NY. Tel: (516) 364-1800, (800) 323-1692, FAX: (516) 364-1899, E-Mail: info.giftvalues@gmail.com, Web Site: www.giftvalues.com (5)

Bobrowski, Mike, Wexler Consulting Group LLC, Alexandria, VA. Tel: (202) 573-9355, E-Mail: welcome@wexlerllc.com, Web Site: wexlerconsultinggroup.com (35)

Boca Java, Miami, FL. Tel: (954) 949-2010, (888) 262-2528, Web Site: www.bocajava.com (4)

Boccuzzi, Michael, Madison Direct Marketing Ltd, Stamford, CT. Tel: (203) 653-3200, FAX: (203) 316-0518, Web Site: www.madisondm.com (31)

Bock, David, Stagestep Inc, Philadelphia, PA. Tel: (215) 636-9000, (800) 523-0960, FAX: (267) 672-2912, E-Mail: stagestep@stagestep.com, Web Site: www.stagestep.com (5)

Bodden Partners, New York, NY. Tel: (212) 328-1111, E-Mail: info@boddenpartners.com, Web Site: www.boddenpartners.com (35)

Bodden, Chris, Bodden Partners, New York, NY. Tel: (212) 328-1111, E-Mail: info@boddenpartners.com, Web Site: www.boddenpartners.com (35)

Bodourian, Peter, Promotional Media Inc, Orange, CA. Tel: (714) 639-6590, (800) 346-5348, FAX: (714) 639-6270, E-Mail: contactus@promotionalmedia.com, Web Site: www.promotionalmedia.com (33)

Bodrato, Kathleen, Tri-Chem Inc, Belleville, NJ. Tel: (973) 751-9200, FAX: (973) 450-1260, (973) 450-1057, E-Mail: paints@trichem.com, Web Site: www.trichem.com (16)

Body by Jake Global LLC, Los Angeles, CA. Tel: (310) 571-7101, FAX: (310) 571-7107, E-Mail: info@bodybyjake.com, Web Site: www.bodybyjake.com (16)

The Body Shop Inc, New York, NY. Tel: (919) 554-4900, (800) 263-9746, FAX: (919) 554-4361, Web Site: www.thebodyshop.com (3)

Boehle, Hubert, Bauer Publishing Co, Englewood Cliffs, NJ. Tel: (201) 569-6699, FAX: (201) 569-5303, Web Site: www.bauerpublishing.com (17)

Boehler, Brenda, Bellacor, Minneapolis, MN. Tel: (877) 723-5522, FAX: (651) 294-2595, E-Mail: customerservice@bellacor.com, Web Site: www.bellacor.com (8)

Boehmer, Ed, Starchtech, Golden Valley, MN. Tel: (763) 545-5400, (800) 597-7225, FAX: (763) 545-9450, Web Site: www.starchtech.com (16)

Boeing Co, Chicago, IL. Tel: (312) 544-2000, FAX: (312) 544-2082, Web Site: www.boeing.com (16)

Boelter + Lincoln Marketing Communications, Milwaukee, WI. Tel: (414) 271-0101, FAX: (414) 271-1436, E-Mail: jbrzeski@boelterlincoln.com, Web Site: boelterlincoln.com (35)

Boerger, Dan, Quattro Direct LLC, Berwyn, PA. Tel: (610) 993-0070, Web Site: www.quattrodirect.com (35)

Boes, Rev. Steven E., Father Flanagan's Boy's Home, Boys Town, NE. Tel: (402) 498-1111, FAX: (402) 498-1969, Web Site: www.boystown.org (1)

Boethner, Douglas A, Queens College/CUNY Professional and Continuing Studies (PCS), Flushing, NY. Tel: (718) 997-5700, FAX: (718) 997-5723, E-Mail: pcs@qc.cuny.edu, Web Site: www.qc.cuny.edu/pcs (41)

Bogdanovic, George, Jet LithoColor Inc, Downers Grove, IL. Tel: (630) 932-9000, (800) 932-1538, (800) 932-1JET, FAX: (630) 932-9101, E-Mail: sales@jetlitho.com, Web Site: www.jetlitho.com (27)

Boggart, Neil, We Deliver America Inc, Englewood Cliffs, NJ. Tel: (201) 307-8888, FAX: (201) 307-1200, E-Mail: info@we-deliver-america.com, Web Site: www.we-deliver-america.com (31)

Boghjalian, Sarkis. ACN USA, Brooklyn, NY. Tel: (718) 609-0939, (800) 628-6333, FAX: (718) 609-0938, Web Site: www.churchinneed.org (1)

Bogie, Patty, Magazine Publishers of America, New York, NY. Tel: (212) 872-3700, FAX: (212) 888-4217, E-Mail: mpa@magazine.org, Web Site: www.magazine.org (17)

Bogle, Jack, Access Business Communications Inc, Huntington Beach, CA. Tel: (800) 675-2415, Web Site: www.abcimarketing.com (20)

Bograkos, Theresa, Mastermailer Inc, Hollywood, FL. Tel: (954) 921-0000, (800) 771-5478, FAX: (954) 925-7900, Web Site: www.mastermailer.com (23)

Bohn, Joyce, Mott Media LLC, Fenton, MI. Tel: (810) 714-4280, FAX: (810) 714-2077, E-Mail: info@mottmedia.com, Web Site: www.mottmedia.com (17)

Bohr, Marianne, The Vestal Press Ltd, Lanham, MD. Tel: (301) 459-3366, (800) 462-6420, FAX: (301) 429-5746, E-Mail: sburnett@rowman.com, Web Site: www.nbnbooks.com (17)

Bohyer, Phoebe, Children's Aid Society, New York, NY. Tel: (212) 949-4800, Web Site: www.childrensaidsociety.org (1)

Boire, Ronald D., Sears, Roebuck & Co, Hoffman Estates, IL. Tel: (847) 286-2500, FAX: (847) 286-7829, Web Site: www.sears.com (16)

Boise Cascade Holdings LLC, Boise, ID. Tel: (208) 384-6451, FAX: (208) 384-7189, E-Mail: mediarelations@bc.com, Web Site: www.bc.com (16)

Boisset, Jean-Charles, Buena Vista Winery, Sonoma, CA. Tel: (707) 252-7117, (800) 678-8504, FAX: (707) 252-0392, Web Site: www.buenavistawinery.com (16)

Boisson, Robert, Reno Gazette Journal, Reno, NV. Tel: (775) 788-6200, FAX: (775) 788-6563 (17)

Boisvert, Gary, Sturbridge Yankee Workshop Inc, Portland, ME. Tel: (207) 774-9045, (800) 343-1144, FAX: (207) 774-2561, Web Site: www.sturbridgeyankee.com (16)

Boklage, Julia, Hammock Publishing Inc, Nashville, TN. Tel: (615) 690-3400, FAX: (615) 690-3401, E-Mail: info@hammock.com, Web Site: www.hammock.com (17)

Bokuniewicz, Carol, Stephan Partners Inc, New York, NY. Tel: (212) 524-8583, E-Mail: george@stephenpartners.com, Web Site: www.stephanpartners.com (35)

Bolchalk, Michael, BolchalkFReY Marketing, Tucson, AZ. Tel: (520) 745-8221, FAX: (520) 745-5540, E-Mail: info-mb@adwiz.com, Web Site: www.adwiz.com (35)

BolchalkFReY Marketing, Tucson, AZ. Tel: (520) 745-8221, FAX: (520) 745-5540, E-Mail: info-mb@adwiz.com, Web Site: www.adwiz.com (35)

Boldt, Ethan, Inside Direct Mail, Philadelphia, PA. Tel: (215) 238-5300, (800) 777-8074, FAX: (215) 238-5412, E-Mail: customservice@napco.com, Web Site: www.insidedirectmail.com (43)

Bolgioni, Deva M., Tuttle Printing & Engraving, Rutland, VT. Tel: (802) 773-9171, (800) 776-7682, FAX: (802) 773-5785, E-Mail: info@tuttleprinting.com, Web Site: www.tuttleprinting.com (10)

Bolind Inc, Boulder, CO. Tel: (303) 443-3142, FAX: (303) 443-9889, Web Site: www.bolind.com (16)

Bolinder, Scott, Zondervan Corp, Grand Rapids, MI. Tel: (616) 698-6900, (800) 727-3060, FAX: (616) 698-3235, Web Site: www.zondervan.com (17)

Boling, Angela, BCR Enterprises Inc, Downers Grove, IL. Tel: (630) 986-1432, (800) 227-1234, FAX: (630) 323-5324, Web Site: www.bcr.com (17)

Boling, Gregg, GS&F, Nashville, TN. Tel: (615) 385-1100, (800) 241-3325, FAX: (615) 783-0500, E-Mail: biz@gsandf.com, Web Site: www.gsandf.com (35)

Boling, Patricia, Replogle Globes Inc, Broadview, IL. Tel: (708) 343-0900, FAX: (708) 343-0923, E-Mail: info@replogleglobes.com, Web Site: www.replogleglobes.com (16)

Boller, Margaret, Eclipse Marketing Services Inc, Cedar Knolls, NJ. Tel: (800) 837-4648, E-Mail: hello@eclipse2.com, Web Site: www.eclipsemarketingservices.com (35)

Bolling, Jay, PulseCX, Montgomeryville, PA. Tel: (215) 699-9200, FAX: (215) 699-9240, Web Site: www.pulsecx.com (35)

Bollore, Yannick, Havas Worldwide LLC, New York, NY. Tel: (212) 886-2000, FAX: (212) 886-5013, Web Site: www.havasworldwide.com (35)

Bolton Research Corp, Miami, FL. Tel: (305) 854-3887, FAX: (305) 854-3807, E-Mail: brcted@aol.com, Web Site: www.boltonresearch.com (30)

Bolton, Jeffrey W., Mayo Clinic, Rochester, MN. Tel: (507) 284-2511, Web Site: www.mayoclinic.org (17)

Bolton, Ted, Bolton Research Corp, Miami, FL. Tel: (305) 854-3887, FAX: (305) 854-3807, E-Mail: brcted@aol.com, Web Site: www.boltonresearch.com (30)

The Bombay Co, Toronto, ON Canada. Tel: (514) 428-9399, (877) 326-6229, E-Mail: customerservice@bombay.ca, Web Site: bombay.ca (8)

Bomberger, Brian D., MackayMitchell Envelope Co, Minneapolis, MN. Tel: (612) 331-9311, (800) 622-5299, FAX: (612) 331-3460, Web Site: www.mackayenvelope.com (26)

Bommarito, Bruce C., Nevada Commission on Tourism, Carson City, NV. Tel: (775) 687-4322, (800) NEVADA 8, FAX: (775) 687-6779, Web Site: www.travelnevada.com (1)

Bomze, Rich, Interdisciplinary Design Team, Southampton, PA. Tel: (215) 364-5608, FAX: (215) 364-6509, E-Mail: rich.bomze@gmail.com (36)

Bon Appetit Magazine, New York, NY. Tel: (212) 286-2860, FAX: (212) 286-2536, E-Mail: paul_jowdy@bonappetit.com, Web Site: www.bonappetit.com (31)

Bonaccio, Mary, The Verdi Group Inc, Pittsford, NY. Tel: (585) 381-4275, FAX: (585) 381-4293, E-Mail: info@theverdigroup.com, Web Site: www.theverdigroup.com (35)

Bonaiuto, Paul, Cygnus Business Media, Fort Atkinson, WI. Tel: (203) 227-4037, (800) 547-7377, FAX: (203) 227-4245, Web Site: www.cygnus.com (17)

Bonanno, Chris, Tristar Products, Fairfield, NJ. Tel: (973) 575-5400, FAX: (973) 683-6708, E-Mail: infotp@tristarproductsinc.com, Web Site: www.tristarproductsinc.com (16)

Boncato, Joyce, Dynamic Engineering, Santa Cruz, CA. Tel: (831) 457-8891, FAX: (831) 457-4793, E-Mail: sales@dyneng.com, Web Site: www.dyneng.com (3)

Carol Bond Health Foods, Liberty, TX. Tel: (800) 833-8282, E-Mail: customerservice@carolbond.com, Web Site: www.carolbond.com (7)

Bond, Bill, Environmental Defense Fund, Washington, DC. Tel: (202) 387-3500, (800) 684- (1)

Bond, Carol, Carol Bond Health Foods, Liberty, TX. Tel: (800) 833-8282, E-Mail: customerservice@carolbond.com, Web Site: www.carolbond.com (7)

Bond, Scott S., Bulkley Dunton Publishing Group, New York, NY. Tel: (212) 863-1800, FAX: (212) 863-1870, Web Site: www.internationalpaper.com (25)

Bond, Yvonne, Havas Worldwide LLC, New York, NY. Tel: (212) 886-2000, FAX: (212) 886-5013, Web Site: www.havasworldwide.com (35)

Bonderson, Jr. Paul R., Ducks Unlimited, Memphis, TN. Tel: (901) 758-3825, (800) 45DUCKS, FAX: (901) 758-3850, Web Site: www.ducks.org (1)

Bonelli, Anne, Gambro Inc, Lakewood, CO. Tel: (303) 232-6800, (800) 525-2623, FAX: (303) 222-6810, Web Site: www.gambro.com (16)

Boney, Ret, Clarity Group LLC, Chapel Hill, NC. Tel: (919) 932-6036, Web Site: www.claritygroupinc. com (20)

Bongiolatti, Lee, Westgroup, Eagan, MN. Tel: (800) 344-5008, Web Site: www.westgroup.com (17)

Bonnell, Tom, O'Brien Manufacturing, Marietta, OH. Tel: (740) 374-2306, (800) 638-1901, FAX: (740) 374-5447, Web Site: www.obrienmfg.com (9)

Bonner, Brian, Dalrada Financial Corp, San Diego, CA. Tel: (858) 791-6200, (877) 325-7232, FAX: (858) 277-3448, E-Mail: inquiries@dalrada.com, Web Site: www.dalrada.com (14)

Bonner, Dave, Capgemini Americas Outsourcing, New York, NY. Tel: (212) 314-8000, FAX: (212) 314-8001 (20)

Bonner, William, AGORA Inc, Baltimore. MD. Tel: (410) 783-8499, FAX: (410) 783-8414, E-Mail: csteam@agorapublishinggroup.com, Web Site: www.agora-inc.com (17)

Bonnette, Rachel, Foster Marketing LLC, Lafayette, LA. Tel: (337) 235-1848, FAX: (337) 237-7246, E-Mail: gfoster@fostermarketing.com, Web Site: fostermarketing.com (35)

Bonneville International, Salt Lake City, UT. Tel: (801) 575-7500, FAX: (801) 575-5820, E-Mail: bonneville@bonneville.com, Web Site: www. bonneville.com (35)

Bonney, Mark J., MRV Communications, Chatsworth, CA. Tel: (818) 773-0900, FAX: (818) 773-0906, Web Site: www.mrv.com (3)

Bonney, Rev. Cynthia, Diakon Lutheran Social Ministries, Allentown, PA. Tel: (877) 342-5667, FAX: (610) 682-1559, E-Mail: swangerb@diakon.org, Web Site: www.diakon.org (1)

Bonney, Rick, Cornell Lab of Ornithology, Ithaca, NY. Tel: (607) 254-2157, (800) 843-2473, FAX: (607) 254-2415, E-Mail: birdslides@cornell.edu, Web Site: www.birds.cornell.edu (1)

Bonnier, Jonas, World Publications Inc, Winter Park, FL. Tel: (407) 628-4802, FAX: (407) 628-7061, Web Site: www.worldpub.net (17)

Bonsall, Mark B., Salt River Project, Tempe, AZ. Tel: (602) 236-5900, FAX: (602) 236-8640, Web Site: www.srpnet.com (34)

Bontex, Honolulu, HI. Tel: (540) 261-2181, FAX: (540) 261-3784, E-Mail: bontex@bontex.com, Web Site: www.bontex.com (16)

Book News Inc, Portland, OR. Tel: (503) 281-9230, FAX: (503) 287-4485, E-Mail: info@booknews.com (43)

The Book of Lists, Charlotte, NC. Tel: (800) 433-4565, Web Site: www.bizjournals.com/bizbooks (23)

Book Passage Cafe, Corte Madera, CA. Tel: (415) 927-0960, (800) 999-7909, FAX: (415) 924-3838, Web Site: www.BookPassage.com (17)

Book Publishing Information Kit, Santa Barbara, CA. Tel: (805) 968-7277, (800) PARAPUB, FAX: (805) 968-1379, E-Mail: danpoynter@parapublishing. com, Web Site: www.parapublishing.com (17)

Books on Tape, Westminster, MD. Tel: (800) 733-3000, Web Site: www.booksontape.com (17)

Bookspan, New York, NY. Tel: (516) 490-4561, FAX: (516) 490-4856, E-Mail: info@directbrands.com, Web Site: bookspan.com (13)

Boone, Ken, Tidewater Direct LLC, Centreville, MD. Tel: (410) 758-1500, FAX: (410) 758-2478, Web Site: www.tidewaterdirect.com (27)

Boone, Xenia, The Direct Marketing Association, New York, NY. Tel: (212) 768-7277, E-Mail: info@the-dma.org, Web Site: thedma.org (1)

Boonstra, Sarah, Bluestone Perennials Inc, Madison, OH. Tel: (800) 852-5243, FAX: (800) 852-5243, E-Mail: service@bluestoneperennials.com, Web Site: www.bluestoneperennials.com (8)

Boonstra, William N., Bluestone Perennials Inc, Madison, OH. Tel: (800) 852-5243, FAX: (800) 852-5243, E-Mail: service@bluestoneperennials.com, Web Site: www.bluestoneperennials.com (8)

Booras, Greg, TownNews.com, Moline, IL. Tel: (309) 743-0800, (800) 293-9576, FAX: (309) 743-0830, E-Mail: info@townnews.com, Web Site: www. townnews365.com (32)

Booth Michigan, Grand Rapids, MI. Tel: (616) 222-5824, FAX: (616) 222-5318, Web Site: www. boothnewspapers.com (17)

Booth, Le-Quita R., Alabama State University/College of Business Administration, Montgomery, AL. Tel: (334) 229-4124, FAX: (334) 229-4870, Web Site: coba.alasu.edu (41)

Booth, Mike, Maris West & Baker, Jackson, MS. Tel: (601) 977-9200, FAX: (601) 977-9257, Web Site: www.mwb.com (35)

Boothe, Georgia, Children's Aid Society, New York, NY. Tel: (212) 949-4800, Web Site: www. childrensaidsociety.org (1)

Boothe, Paul, Ideal Industries (Canada) Corp, Ajax, ON Canada. Tel: (905) 683-3400, (800) 824-3325, FAX: (905) 683-0209, E-Mail: nick.shkordoff@ idealindustries.com, Web Site: www.idealindustries. com (9)

Booyah! Online Advertising, Denver, CO. Tel: (303) 345-6100, FAX: (303) 345-6700, E-Mail: info@ booyahadvertising.ocm, Web Site: www. booyahadvertising (35)

Boppe, Larry, Toter Inc, Statesville, NC. Tel: (704) 872-8171, (800) 424-0422, FAX: (704) 878-0734, E-Mail: info@toter.com, Web Site: www.toter.com (16)

Boragine, Vincent, Shape Global Technology, Sanford, ME. Tel: (207) 324-5200, (800) 627-5836, FAX: (207) 324-0875, E-Mail: info@shapeglobal.com, Web Site: www.shapenet.com (34)

Borchard, Peter, Companion Plants, Athens, OH. Tel: (740) 592-4643, FAX: (740) 593-3092, E-Mail: peter@companionplants.com, Web Site: www. companionplants.com (8)

Bordas, Theresa, Intelligent Direct, Wellsboro, PA. Tel: (570) 724-7355, Web Site: www.marketmaps.com (9)

Bordeleau, Lise, Desjardins Financial Securities, Levis, QC Canada. Tel: (418) 838-7870, FAX: (418) 833-5985, Web Site: www.desjardinsfinancialsecurity. com (15)

Borden, Fran, Association of Marian Helpers, Stockbridge, MA. Tel: (413) 298-3931, (800) 462-7426, Web Site: www.marian.org (1)

Borden, Leslye, PhotoEdit Inc, Costa Mesa, CA. Tel: (800) 860-2098, FAX: (800) 804-3707, E-Mail: sales@photoeditinc.com, Web Site: www. photoeditinc.com (38)

Border, Craig, Marketing Results Inc, Sicklerville, NJ. Tel: (856) 740-3334, FAX: (856) 740-3335, Web Site: www.marketingresults.net (16)

Border, Gary A., Marketing Results Inc, Sicklerville, NJ. Tel: (856) 740-3334, FAX: (856) 740-3335, Web Site: www.marketingresults.net (16)

Borelli Direct Marketing Inc, Kendall Park, NJ. Tel: (732) 940-1500, E-Mail: joe@borellidirect.com, Web Site: www.borellidirect.com (23)

Borelli, Joe, Borelli Direct Marketing Inc, Kendall Park, NJ. Tel: (732) 940-1500, E-Mail: joe@borellidirect. com, Web Site: www.borellidirect.com (23)

Boren, Judi, Posh Papers, Riverside, RI. Tel: (401) 331-9873, FAX: (401) 331-2229, E-Mail: info@ poshpapersonline.com, Web Site: www. poshpapersonline.com (6)

Boren, Kimberly, Autobytel Inc, Irvine, CA. Tel: (949) 225-4500, E-Mail: consumercareabtl@autobytel. com, Web Site: www.autobytel.com (12)

Boreyko, B.K., Vemma Nutrition Co, Tempe, AZ. Tel: (480) 927-8999, (800) 577-0777, FAX: (888) 314-9827, E-Mail: ms@vemma.com, Web Site: www. vemma.com (7)

Boreyko, Jason, Vemma Nutrition Co, Tempe, AZ. Tel: (480) 927-8999, (800) 577-0777, FAX: (888) 314-9827, E-Mail: ms@vemma.com, Web Site: www. vemma.com (7)

Borgelt, Andrea, Gerber Life Insurance Co, White Plains, NY. Tel: (914) 272-4000, (800) 704-2180, FAX: (914) 272-4099, Web Site: www.gerberlife. com (15)

Borgnine, Tova, Tova Corp, West Chester, PA. Tel: (800) 852-9999, Web Site: www.beautybytova.com (7)

Boring, Troy, Thermal Product Solutions, White Deer, PA. Tel: (570) 538-7200, (800) 586-2473 (16)

Boris, John, Shutterfly, Redwood City, CA. Tel: (650) 610-5200, Web Site: www.shutterfly.com (27)

Bork, Deacon Paul, Maryknoll Fathers & Brothers, Ossining, NY. Tel: (914) 941-7590, (888) 627-9566, FAX: (914) 944-3613, E-Mail: mkweb@maryknoll. org, Web Site: www.maryknoll.org (1)

Borkowski, James, Stellar Technology Inc, Amherst, NY. Tel: (716) 250-1900, (800) 274-1846, FAX: (716) 250-1909, E-Mail: info@stellartech.com, Web Site: www.stellartech.com (9)

Born Free USA, Washington, DC. Tel: (202) 450-3168, (800) 348-7387, FAX: (202) 450-3581, E-Mail: info@bornfreeusa.org, Web Site: www.bornfreeusa. org (1)

Born, David, Eagle:xm, Denver, CO. Tel: (303) 320-5411, (800) 426-5376, FAX: (303) 393-6584, E-Mail: extendedmedia@eaglexm.com, Web Site: www.eaglexm.com (21)

Bornhorst, Mike, DirectBuy Inc, Merrillville, IN. Tel: (219) 736-1100, FAX: (219) 755-6279, Web Site: www.ucctotalhome.com (1)

Bornkamp, Gary, Global Computer Supplies, Port Washington, NY. Tel: (516) 403-2800, (800) 446-9662, FAX: (516) 625-6683, Web Site: www. globalcomputer.com (34)

Bornstein, Jeffrey S., General Electric Co, Fairfield, CT. Tel: (203) 373-2211, FAX: (203) 373-3131, Web Site: www.ge.com (16)

Boro, Albert J., Golden Gate Transportation District, San Rafael, CA. Tel: (415) 921-5858, FAX: (415) 923-2014, Web Site: www.goldengate.org (16)

Boro, Seth J., Thoma Cressey Bravo, Chicago, IL. Tel: (312) 777-4444, FAX: (312) 777-4445. Web Site: www.tcb.com (14)

Borowsky, Ned, NAPCO Media, Philadelphia, PA. Tel: (215) 238-5300, FAX: (215) 238-5412, Web Site: www.napco.com (32)

Borowsky, Scott C., Spectrum Retail Associates, Ardmore, PA. Tel: (610) 645-9520, (800) 570-6565, FAX: (610) 645-9524 (20)

Borowsky, Ted, Foster Keencut, Montgomeryville, PA. Tel: (267) 413-6220, (800) 523-4855, FAX: (267) 413-6227, E-Mail: information@fostermfg.com, Web Site: www.fostermfg.com (34)

Borrero, Denira, Omni Direct Inc, Miami, FL. Tel: (800) 459-4034, Web Site: www.omnidirect.tv (35)

Borst, Margaret, Country Sampler Group, Saint Charles, IL. Tel: (630) 377-8000, FAX: (630) 377-8194, Web Site: www.sampler.com (17)

Borst, Walter G., Navistar, Lisle, IL. Tel: (331) 332-5000, Web Site: www.navistar.com (16)

Borthwick, Sandie, Capital Insurance Group (CIG), Monterey, CA. Tel: (831) 233-5500, Web Site: www.ciginsurance.com (15)

Bortnak, James M., PhotoStamps.com, El Segundo, CA. Tel: (310) 482-5800, Web Site: www.photostamps.com (5)

Boruff, Chris, Morningstar Inc, Chicago, IL. Tel: (312) 696-6000, Web Site: www.morningstar.com (14)

Borum Photographics Inc, Nashville, TN. Tel: (615) 254-0063, (888) 254-0063, FAX: (615) 242-2334, Web Site: www.chromatics.com (37)

Borum, Michael, Borum Photographics Inc, Nashville, TN. Tel: (615) 254-0063, (888) 254-0063, FAX: (615) 242-2334, Web Site: www.chromatics.com (37)

Borysiewicz, Jeff, Corona Cigar Co, Orlando, FL. Tel: (407) 248-1212, (888) 702-4427, FAX: (407) 248-1211, E-Mail: info@coronacigar.com, Web Site: www.coronacigar.com (5)

Bosanko, William J., National Archives & Records Administration, Washington, DC. Tel: (202) 357-5000, (866) 325-7208, Web Site: www.archives.gov (17)

Bosc, Joyce L., Boscobel Marketing Communications Inc, Silver Spring, MD. Tel: (301) 588-2900, E-Mail: info@boscobel.com, Web Site: www.boscobel.com (35)

Boscobel Marketing Communications Inc, Silver Spring, MD. Tel: (301) 588-2900, E-Mail: info@boscobel.com, Web Site: www.boscobel.com (35)

Bose Corp, Framingham, MA. Tel: (508) 879-7330, (800) 379-2703, FAX: (508) 766-7543, Web Site: www.bose.com (3)

Bose, Pertha, Oliver Wyman, New York, NY. Tel: (212) 345-8000, (212) 541-8100, Web Site: www.oliverwyman.com (14)

Bose, Susan, American National Standards Institute, New York, NY. Tel: (212) 642-4900, FAX: (212) 398-0023, Web Site: www.ansi.org (1)

Boshart, Joseph A., Cross Country Travcorps, Boca Raton, FL. Tel: (800) 530-6125, FAX: (561) 998-8533, Web Site: www.crosscountrytravcorps.com (16)

Boshaw, Jim, PAC Worldwide, Redmond, WA. Tel: (425) 202-4000, (800) 535-0039, FAX: (425) 885-2934, Web Site: www.pac.com (26)

Boshoven, Steve, Foremost Insurance Group, Grand Rapids, MI. Tel: (616) 956-8241, (800) 527-3905, FAX: (800) 325-1507, Web Site: www.foremost.com (15)

Bosley, Gary O., Marketing Solutions Group Inc, Pleasanton, CA. Tel: (510) 331-7625, E-Mail: info@marketingsolutionsgroup.biz, Web Site: marketingsolutionsgroup.biz (32)

Bosom Buddy Breast Forms, Boise, ID. Tel: (208) 343-9696, (800) 262-2789, FAX: (208) 343-9266, E-Mail: custserv@bosombuddy.com, Web Site: www.bosombuddy.com (7)

Bossemeyer, Jim, Black Dot Group, Crystal Lake, IL. Tel: (815) 893-8799, E-Mail: pkelley@blackdot.com, Web Site: www.blackdot.com (35)

Boster, Kari, Bluewater Yachts, Mora, MN. Tel: (320) 679-3811, FAX: (320) 679-3820, E-Mail: bluewater@ncis.com, Web Site: www.bluewateryacht.com (16)

Bostic, Terence, Colarelli Meyer & Associates Inc, Saint Louis, MO. Tel: (314) 721-1860, (800) 459-4548, FAX: (314) 721-1992, E-Mail: cmaconsult@cmaconsult.com, Web Site: www.cmaconsult.com (20)

Bostock, Amy, Direct Marketing News, Markham, ON Canada. Tel: (905) 201-6600, (800) 668-1838, FAX: (905) 201-6601, E-Mail: home@dmn.ca, Web Site: www.dmn.ca (43)

The Boston Co Asset Management LLC, Boston, MA. Tel: (617) 722-7029, FAX: (617) 722-3928, Web Site: www.thebostoncompany.com (14)

Boston Color Graphics, Billerica, MA. Tel: (978) 528-7999, (800) 767-0067, FAX: (978) 528-7609, E-Mail: sales@bostoncolorgraphics.com, Web Site: www.bostoncolorgraphics.com (27)

The Boston Consulting Group, New York, NY. Tel: (212) 446-2800 (20)

Boston Gift Show, Kennesaw, GA. Tel: (678) 285-3976, FAX: (678) 285-7469, Web Site: www.bostongiftshow.com (42)

The Boston Globe, Boston, MA. Tel: (617) 929-2000, (888) MY-GLOBE, FAX: (617) 929-2606, Web Site: www.bostonglobe.com (17)

Boston Research Group, Hopkinton, MA. Tel: (508) 497-2555, FAX: (508) 497-2592, E-Mail: BRGrep@BostonResearchGroup.com, Web Site: www.bostonresearchgroup.com (30)

Bostwick, Brent, Draper's & Damon's, Irvine, CA. Tel: (949) 784-3000, (800) 843-1174, FAX: (949) 784-3400, E-Mail: jilld@drapers.com, Web Site: www.drapers.com (2)

Boswell, Ed, The Forum Corp, Boston, MA. Tel: (617) 523-7300, (800) 367-8611, FAX: (617) 371-3300, E-Mail: forum@forum.com, Web Site: www.forum.com (20)

Botkin, Sanford, Tax Reduction Institute, Germantown, MD. Tel: (301) 972-3600, (800) TRI-0-TAX, FAX: (301) 972-0819, E-Mail: info@taxreductioninstitute.com, Web Site: www.taxreductioninstitute.com (14)

Bott, Andrew, BBC Worldwide Americas Inc, New York, NY. Tel: (212) 705-9300, (800) 898-4921, FAX: (212) 888-0576, Web Site: www.bbcamerica.com (3)

Botthof, Rick, ACG/Computech Direct, Hoffman Estates, IL. Tel: (847) 843-3200, FAX: (847) 843-8060, E-Mail: info@acg-computech-direct.com, Web Site: www.acg-computech-direct.com (22)

Botway, Jill R., Collective - The Audience Engine, New York, NY. Tel: (646) 722-8550, FAX: (646) 442-6529, Web Site: www.collective.com (22)

Bouchard, Ann, Matrix Manager, Roseville, CA. Tel: (916) 783-1536, (877)-258-9037, E-Mail: info@mymatrixmanager.com, Web Site: www.mymatrixmanager.com (28)

Bouchard, Sara, Center for Book Arts, New York, NY. Tel: (212) 481-0295, FAX: (866) 708-8994, E-Mail: info@centerforbookarts.org, Web Site: www.centerforbookarts.org (27)

Boucher, M. Adam, Wilsons Leather, Brooklyn Park, MN. Tel: (763) 391-4000, (866) 305-4704, FAX: (763) 391-4906, E-Mail: customercare@wilsonsleather.com, Web Site: www.wilsonsleather.com (2)

Bouclin, Ed, Scorecards USA, North Kingstown, RI. Tel: (401) 294-4049, (800) 553-4154, FAX: (401) 294-4076, E-Mail: sales@scorecardsusa.com, Web Site: www.scorecardsusa.com (16)

Boughner, Robert L., Boyd Gaming Corp, Las Vegas, NV. Tel: (702) 792-7200, FAX: (702) 792-7313, Web Site: www.boydgaming.com (16)

Boundless Corp, Phelps, NY. Tel: (631) 962-1500, (800) 231-5445, FAX: (631) 962-1505, E-Mail: sales@boundless.com, Web Site: www.boundless.com (16)

Bountiful Gardens, Willits, CA. Tel: (707) 459-6410, FAX: (707) 459-1925, E-Mail: bountiful@sonic.net, Web Site: www.bountifulgardens.org (8)

Bourgon, Luc, Northern Lights Direct, Chicago, IL. Tel: (312) 263-8686, FAX: (312) 600-9050, E-Mail: contact@northernlightsdirect.com, Web Site: www.northernlightsdirect.com (32)

Bourque, Paul, Catholic Digest, New London, CT. Tel: (800) 321-0411, E-Mail: catholicdigest@bayardinc.com, Web Site: www.catholicdigest.com (17)

Bousquet, Joyce, Reliant Data Processing, North Aurora, IL. Tel: (630) 844-4210, FAX: (630) 844-9530, E-Mail: rdpmail@aol.com (28)

Boutcher, Ann M., Audiovox, Hauppauge, NY. Tel: (631) 436-6550, FAX: (631) 273-5939, Web Site: www.voxxintl.com (16)

Boutelle, Mark, Paslode, Vernon Hills, IL. Tel: (847) 634-1900, (800) 222-6990, FAX: (847) 634-6602, E-Mail: tech@paslode.com, Web Site: www.paslode.com (16)

Bouzari, Alex, Data Direct Networks, Chatsworth, CA. Tel: (818) 700-7607, (800) 837-2298, FAX: (818) 700-7601, E-Mail: info@ddn.com, Web Site: www.datadirectnet.com (3)

Bovasso, Robert M, Real Media Solutions, Wayne, NJ. Tel: (973) 835-7060, Web Site: www.get-realmedia.com (27)

Bow, Frank, American Mail-Well Envelope Co/St Louis Div, Eureka, MO. Tel: (314) 966-2000, (800) 800-8845, FAX: (314) 966-4725, E-Mail: info@cenveo.com, Web Site: www.mail-well.com (26)

Bowater America Inc, Greenville, SC. Tel: (864) 271-7733, (800) 921-3244, FAX: (864) 282-9320, E-Mail: hrsc@abitibibowater.com, Web Site: www.bowater.com (25)

Bowcut, Michael, Recreational Equipment Inc, Kent, WA. Tel: (253) 395-4803, Web Site: www.rei.com (11)

Bowden, Al, Sencore Inc, Sioux Falls, SD. Tel: (605) 339-0100, (800) SEN-CORE, FAX: (605) 339-0317, E-Mail: sales@sencore.com, Web Site: www.sencore.com (16)

Bowden, Doug, Sencore Inc, Sioux Falls, SD. Tel: (605) 339-0100, (800) SEN-CORE, FAX: (605) 339-0317, E-Mail: sales@sencore.com, Web Site: www.sencore.com (16)

Bowden, Steven, Old Vine Marketing, Napa, CA. Tel: (707) 694-9647, E-Mail: info@oldvinemarketing.com, Web Site: www.oldvinemarketing.com (22)

Bowen, Craig, Gift Services Inc, Vancouver, WA. Tel: (800) 379-4065, FAX: (360) 699-0597, E-Mail: corpsales@gifttree.com, Web Site: www.gifttree.com (6)

Bowen, John J., Johnson & Wales University, Providence, RI. Tel: (401) 598-1000, (800) DIAL-JWU, FAX: (401) 598-1833, Web Site: www.jwu.edu (41)

Bowen, Matt, Aloft Group, Newburyport, MA. Tel: (978) 462-0002, E-Mail: hello@aloftgroup.com, Web Site: www.aloftgroup.com (33)

Bowen, Rebecca, The Nature Conservancy, Arlington, VA. Tel: (703) 841-5300, (800) 628-6860, FAX: (703) 841-1283, Web Site: www.nature.org (1)

Bower, Jay, Crossbow Group, Westport, CT. Tel: (203) 222-2244, FAX: (203) 226-7838, E-Mail: info@crossbowgroup.com, Web Site: www.crossbowgroup.com (40)

Bower, W., Marketeers, Mission Viejo, CA. Tel: (949) 364-1669, FAX: (949) 582-0829, E-Mail: wbower@apc.net (29)

Bowers & Associates Inc, Saint Louis, MO. Tel: (314) 963-4477, E-Mail: info@bowerspromotes.com (33)

Bowers & Merena Auctions, Irvine, CA. Tel: (949) 253-0916, (800) 458-4646, FAX: (949) 253-4091, E-Mail: auction@bowersandmerena.com, Web Site: www.bowersandmerena.com (16)

Bowers Envelope Co, Indianapolis, IN. Tel: (317) 253-4321, FAX: (317) 254-2231, Web Site: www.bowersenvelope.com (26)

Bowers, Allen, Career Blazers, New York, NY. Tel: (212) 719-3232, FAX: (212) 221-0452 (20)

Bowers, Dave, Fahlgren Mortine, Columbus, OH. Tel: (800) 731-8927, E-Mail: info@fahlgren.com, Web Site: www.fahlgrenmortine.com (35)

Bowers, Dave, WPG Americas Inc, San Jose, CA. Tel: (408) 392-8100, FAX: (408) 436-9551, E-Mail: notherncalifornia.sales@wpgamericas.com, Web Site: www.wpgamericas.com (20)

Bowers, David, Society of American Magicians Inc, Littleton, CO. Tel: (303) 362-0575, E-Mail: samadministrator@magicsam.com, Web Site: www.magicsam.com (1)

Bowers, Linda, LinguiSystems, East Moline, IL. Tel: (309) 755-2300, (800) 776-4332, FAX: (800) 577-4555, E-Mail: service@linguisystems.com, Web Site: www.linguisystems.com (17)

Bowers, Lois A., Medical Economics Magazine, North Olmsted, OH. Tel: (440) 243-8100, FAX: (440) 891-2735, Web Site: medicaleconomics.modernmedicine.com/about (17)

Bowers, Marcia, Hyatt Legal Plans Inc, Cleveland, OH. Tel: (216) 241-0022, FAX: (216) 694-4305, Web Site: www.legalplans.com (16)

Bowers, Paul, Georgia Power, Atlanta, GA. Tel: (404) 506-3440 (16)

Bowers, Scott, Ghent Manufacturing Inc, Lebanon, OH. Tel: (513) 932-3445, (800) 543-0550, FAX: (513) 932-9252, E-Mail: customer_service@ghent.com, Web Site: www.ghent.com (10)

Bowers, Thomas M., Bowers & Associates Inc, Saint Louis, MO. Tel: (314) 963-4477, E-Mail: info@bowerspromotes.com (33)

The Bowery Mission, New York, NY. Tel: (212) 684-2800, Web Site: www.bowery.org (1)

Bowes, John, Behlen Manufacturing Co, Columbus, NE. Tel: (402) 564-3111, FAX: (402) 563-7405, E-Mail: behlen@megavision.com, Web Site: www.behlenmfg.com (16)

Bowie, Jim, Electrosonic Group, Burbank, CA. Tel: (818) 333-3600, FAX: (818) 641-6384, E-Mail: info@electrosonic.com, Web Site: www.electrosonic.com (32)

R R Bowker, New Providence, NJ. Tel: (888) BOWKER-2 (269-5372), FAX: (908) 771-8699, Web Site: www.bowker.com (17)

Bowles, Susie, Universal Security Instruments Inc, Owings Mills, MD. Tel: (410) 363-3000, FAX: (410) 363-2218, E-Mail: sales@universalsecurity.com, Web Site: www.universalsecurity.com (16)

Bowman & Partners, Roanoke, TX. Tel: (888) 817-1948, E-Mail: info@bowman-partners.com, Web Site: www.bowman-partners.com (22)

Bowman Circulation Marketing, Greenwich, CT. Tel: (917) 913-6172, E-Mail: nicole@nicolebowman.com, Web Site: www.nicolebowman.com (20)

Bowman, Allyson, Merastar Insurance Co, Chattanooga, TN. Tel: (800) 637-2782, FAX: (800) 369-1430, E-Mail: merastar.assist.team@unitrindirect.com, Web Site: www.merastar.com (15)

Bowman, Bruce, Harwil Corp, Oxnard, CA. Tel: (805) 988-6800, (800) 562-2447, FAX: (805) 988-6804, E-Mail: harwil@harwil.com, Web Site: www.harwil.com (9)

Bowman, David E., The Ohlmann Group, Dayton, OH. Tel: (937) 278-0681, FAX: (937) 277-1723, E-Mail: info@ohlmanngroup.com, Web Site: ohlmanngroup.com (35)

Bowman, James, International Fulfillment Inc, Philadelphia, PA. Tel: (215) 638-8060, (800) 962-8080, FAX: (215) 638-8091, Web Site: www.ifionline.net (27)

Bowman, Jeffrey T., Crawford & Co, Atlanta, GA. Tel: (404) 300-1000, (800) 241-2541, FAX: (404) 300-1905, E-Mail: info@us.crawco.com, Web Site: us.crawfordandcompany.com (35)

Bowman, Jessica, SEOinhouse, Saint Charles, MO. Tel: (888) 899-0195, FAX: (888) 899-0195, Web Site: www.seoinhouse.com (32)

Bowman, Karoline, AESU Inc, Baltimore, MD. Tel: (410) 366-5494, (800) 638-7640, FAX: (410) 366-6999, E-Mail: res@aesu.com, Web Site: www.aesu.com (19)

Bowman, Lisa, United Way Worldwide, Alexandria, VA. Tel: (703) 836-7112, Web Site: www.unitedway.org (1)

Bowman, Lynn A., Harvard Pilgrim Health Care, Wellesley, MA. Tel: (617) 509-1000, (888) 888-4742, FAX: (617) 509-7590, Web Site: www.harvardpilgrim.org (7)

Bowman, Nicole, Bowman Circulation Marketing, Greenwich, CT. Tel: (917) 913-6172, E-Mail: nicole@nicolebowman.com, Web Site: www.nicolebowman.com (20)

Bowman, Paul, Bowman & Partners, Roanoke, TX. Tel: (888) 817-1948, E-Mail: info@bowman-partners.com, Web Site: www.bowman-partners.com (22)

Bowne, William, A-1 Direct Mail Marketing Inc, Miami, FL. Tel: (305) 251-3187 (28)

BowTie Inc, Irvine, CA. Tel: (949) 855-8822, FAX: (949) 855-1850, E-Mail: mevans@bowtieinc.com, Web Site: www.animalnetwork.com (1)

Boxer, Mark, Anthem Blue Cross Blue Shield, Saint Louis, MO. Tel: (314) 923-4444, (888) 877-9125, FAX: (314) 923-5151, E-Mail: moreinfo@bcbsmo.com, Web Site: www.bcbsmo.com (15)

Boy Scouts of America/National Supply Group, Charlotte, NC. Tel: (800) 323-0736, FAX: (704) 588-5822, E-Mail: customerservice@scoutstuff.org, Web Site: www.scoutstuff.org (1)

Boyce, Jane, Society of Petroleum Engineers, Richardson, TX. Tel: (972) 952-9393, (800) 456-6863, FAX: (972) 952-9435, E-Mail: spedal@spe.org, Web Site: www.spe.org (2)

Boyce, Jim, DEFENDER Direct Inc, Indianapolis, IN. Tel: (317) 810-4720, (800) 860-0303, FAX: (317) 810-4723, Web Site: www.defenderdirect.com (32)

Boyd Gaming Corp, Las Vegas, NV. Tel: (702) 792-7200, FAX: (702) 792-7313, Web Site: www.boydgaming.com (16)

Boyd Tamney Cross Inc, Wayne, PA. Tel: (610) 293-0500, FAX: (610) 687-8199, E-Mail: info@btcmarketing.com, Web Site: www.boydtamneycross.com (35)

Boyd, Greg, NTP Distribution, Wilsonville, OR. Tel: (503) 570-0171, FAX: (888) 570-0342, Web Site: www.ntpdistribution.com (34)

Boyd, Ron, Quick Draw Clip Systems Inc, Ventura, CA. Tel: (805) 644-6888, (888) 254-7797, FAX: (805) 644-7320, E-Mail: ron@clipsystems.com, Web Site: www.clipsystems.com (9)

Boyd, William S., Boyd Gaming Corp, Las Vegas, NV. Tel: (702) 792-7200, FAX: (702) 792-7313, Web Site: www.boydgaming.com (16)

Boyden Global Executive Search, Purchase, NY. Tel: (914) 747-0093, E-Mail: inquiry@boyden.com, Web Site: www.boyden.com (20)

Boydston, Billy, List Partners Inc, Atlanta, GA. Tel: (404) 350-0600, (800) 941-6562, E-Mail: contact@thelistinc.com, Web Site: listpartnersinc.com (24)

Boyer, Aurelia G., New York-Presbyterian/Columbia University Medical Center, New York, NY. Tel: (212) 305-2500, FAX: (212) 305-8023, Web Site: www.nyp.org (16)

Boyer, Matthew, American Forests, Washington, DC. Tel: (202) 737-1944, FAX: (202) 737-2457, E-Mail: info@amfor.org, Web Site: www.americanforests.org (1)

Boylan, Philip, Touch-Base Computing, Silver Creek, GA. Tel: (706) 378-0964, E-Mail: sales@touchbase.com, Web Site: www.touchbase.com (22)

Boyle, Doug, Blue Coral Slick 50, Houston, TX. Tel: (713) 241-6161, (800) 416-1600, FAX: (713) 241-4044, E-Mail: SCD-ConsumerSolutions@Shell.com, Web Site: www.bluecoral.com (16)

Boyle, Gert, Columbia Sportswear, Portland, OR. Tel: (503) 985-4203, (800) 622-6953, Web Site: www.columbia.com (2)

Boyle, Hugh, TracyLocke, Dallas, TX. Tel: (214) 969-9000, FAX: (214) 259-3550, E-Mail: parker.harrison@tracylocke.com, Web Site: tracylocke.com (35)

Boyle, Karen, MarketMakers Group Inc, Wayne, PA. Tel: (610) 254-8924, FAX: (610) 254-9190, E-Mail: rlail@marketmakers.com, Web Site: www.marketmakersgroup.com (29)

Boyle, Lisa C., American Marketing & Communication Corp, Hagerstown, MD. Tel: (240) 625-9225, FAX: (240) 625-9235, E-Mail: info@amcc1.com, Web Site: www.americanmarketingcc.com (20)

Boyle, Lois, J Schmid & Associates Inc, Mission, KS. Tel: (913) 236-8988, FAX: (913) 236-8987, E-Mail: info@jschmid.com, Web Site: www.jschmid.com (20)

Boyle, Lynne, Winterthur Museum & Country Estate, Wilmington, DE. Tel: (302) 888-4600, (800) 448-3883, FAX: (302) 888-4730, E-Mail: tourinfo@winterthur.org, Web Site: www.winterthur.org (6)

Boyle, Tim, Columbia Sportswear, Portland, OR. Tel: (503) 985-4203, (800) 622-6953, Web Site: www.columbia.com (2)

Boyles, Paul A., Merastar Insurance Co, Chattanooga, TN. Tel: (800) 637-2782, FAX: (800) 369-1430, E-Mail: merastar.assist.team@unitrindirect.com, Web Site: www.merastar.com (15)

Boys & Girls Clubs of America National Headquarters, Atlanta, GA. Tel: (404) 487-5700, FAX: (404) 815-5757, (404) 487-5757, E-Mail: info@bgca.org, Web Site: www.bgca.org (1)

Boys' Life & Scouting Magazines, Irving, TX. Tel: (972) 580-2000, (866) 584-6589, FAX: (972) 580-2079, Web Site: www.boyslife.org (17)

Boysen, III Stuart W., Hoke Communications Inc, Garden City, NY. Tel: (516) 746-6700, FAX: (516) 294-8141 (17)

Boysen, Rich, Dixon Direct, Dixon, IL. Tel: (815) 284-2211, FAX: (630) 810-1934, E-Mail: info@dixondirect.com, Web Site: dixondirect.com (35)

Bozeman, David P., Caterpillar Inc, Peoria, IL. Tel: (309) 675-0545, Web Site: www.cat.com (16)

Brabender, John, BrabenderCox, Leesburg, VA. Tel: (703) 896-5300, FAX: (703) 896-5315, Web Site: www.brabendercox.com (35)

BrabenderCox, Leesburg, VA. Tel: (703) 896-5300, FAX: (703) 896-5315, Web Site: www.brabendercox.com (35)

Brach, Abe, DPC Computers, Monsey, NY. Tel: (845) 426-3790, (866) 513-CORP, FAX: (845) 426-6275, E-Mail: learnmore@salestax.com, Web Site: www.salestax.com (16)

Brachfeld, Paul, National Archives & Records Administration, Washington, DC. Tel: (202) 357-5000, (866) 325-7208, Web Site: www.archives.gov (17)

Bracken, Bill, Agency 360 LLC, Naperville, IL. Tel: (312) 316-7070, (312) 371-4104, E-Mail: mail@agencythreesixty.com, Web Site: agencythreesixty.com (16)

Bracken, Lee, HR Direct, Sunrise, FL. Tel: (800) 346-1231, FAX: (800) 350-7760, Web Site: www.hrdirect.com (10)

Bradbury, Jason, Direct Response Media Group, Oakville, ON Canada. Tel: (905) 465-1233, (866) 993-0600, FAX: (905) 465-1228, E-Mail: info@drmg.ca, Web Site: www.drmg.com (21)

Bradbury, John, Military Direct Marketing Inc, Poughkeepsie, NY. Tel: (845) 454-7900, FAX: (845) 454-7987, E-Mail: info@militarymedia.com (31)

Braddon, Cynthia, The McGraw-Hill Financial, New York, NY. Tel: (212) 904-2000, Web Site: www.mhfi.com (17)

The Bradford Group, Niles, IL. Tel: (847) 966-2770, FAX: (847) 581-8630, Web Site: www.collectiblestoday.com (16)

Bradford Health Services, Birmingham, AL. Tel: (205) 251-7753, (800) 217-2849, Web Site: www.bradfordhealth.com (16)

Bradford, Gregory R., CACI International Inc, Arlington, VA. Tel: (703) 841-7800, FAX: (703) 841-7882, Web Site: www.caci.com (22)

Vera Bradley, Roanoke, IN. Tel: (800) 823-8372, Web Site: www.verabradley.com (2)

Bradley, Billie, National Mail Graphics Corp, Exton, PA. Tel: (610) 524-1600, FAX: (610) 524-7638, E-Mail: jsikorski@nmgcorp.com, Web Site: www.nmgcorp.com (27)

Bradley, Christopher W., Cuddledown Inc, Yarmouth, ME. Tel: (800) 323-6793, FAX: (207) 761-1948, Web Site: www.cuddledown.com (8)

Bradley, David, The Atlantic Monthly, Washington, DC. Tel: (202) 266-6000, (800) 234-2411, FAX: (202) 266-6001, Web Site: www.theatlantic.com (17)

Bradley, Denny, CCI Solutions, Olympia, WA. Tel: (360) 943-5378, (800) 426-8664, FAX: (360) 754-1566, (800) 339-TAPE, E-Mail: info@ccisolutions.com, Web Site: www.ccisolutions.com (16)

Bradley, Jeff, Cuba Cheese Shoppe, Cuba, NY. Tel: (585) 968-3949, FAX: (716) 968-1746, Web Site: www.cubacheese.com (4)

Bradley, John F., JP Morgan Chase & Co, New York, NY. Tel: (212) 270-6000, E-Mail: jpmcinvestorrelations@jpmchase.com, Web Site: www.jpmorgan.com (14)

Bradley, Susan V., The Peter A Tobin College of Business, Jamaica, NY. Tel: (718) 990-2600, FAX: (718) 990-1868, Web Site: www.stjohns.edu (41)

Bradley, Tom, TD Ameritrade Holding Corp, Omaha, NE. Tel: (800) 237-8692, Web Site: www.amtd.com (16)

Bradshaw, Chris, Autodesk Inc, San Rafael, CA. Tel: (415) 507-5000, FAX: (415) 507-5100, Web Site: www.autodesk.com (16)

Brady Corp, Milwaukee, WI. Tel: (414) 358-6600, (800) 541-1686, FAX: (800) 292-2289, Web Site: www.bradycorp.com (16)

Brady Marketing Co Inc, Walnut Creek, CA. Tel: (925) 676-1300, (800) 326-6080, FAX: (925) 676-3082, E-Mail: info@bradymarketing.com, Web Site: www.bradymarketing.com (16)

Reggie Brady Marketing Solutions LLC, Norwalk, CT. Tel: (203) 838-8138, Web Site: www.reggiebrady.com (20)

Brady, Frank, Brady Marketing Co Inc, Walnut Creek, CA. Tel: (925) 676-1300, (800) 326-6080, FAX: (925) 676-3082, E-Mail: info@bradymarketing.com, Web Site: www.bradymarketing.com (16)

Brady, Lorraine, Brady Marketing Co Inc, Walnut Creek, CA. Tel: (925) 676-1300, (800) 326-6080, FAX: (925) 676-3082. E-Mail: info@bradymarketing.com, Web Site: www.bradymarketing.com (16)

Brady, Regina, Reggie Brady Marketing Solutions LLC, Norwalk, CT. Tel: (203) 838-8138, Web Site: www.reggiebrady.com (20)

Bragdon, David, TransitCenter Inc, New York, NY. Tel: (646) 395-9555, E-Mail: info@transitcenter.org, Web Site: www.transitcenter.org (1)

Brahmam, Maya, The World Bank, Washington, DC. Tel: (202) 473-1000, FAX: (202) 477-6391, Web Site: www.worldbank.org (17)

Brahmin Leather Works, Fairhaven, MA. Tel: (508) 994-4000, (800) 229-2428, FAX: (508) 994-4153, Web Site: www.brahminusa.com (16)

Braillard, II Walter H., Domestic Bank, Providence, RI. Tel: (401) 943-1600, (800) 566-6600, FAX: (401) 943-6708, Web Site: www.domesticbank.com (14)

Braintree Payment Solutions LLC, Chicago, IL. Tel: (773) 489-9539, Web Site: www.braintreepaymentsolutions.com (14)

Brake, Ben, Epic Research LLC, Greenville, DE. Tel: (302) 467-5445, Web Site: www.epicresearch.net (20)

Brake, Pam, Professional Creations, New Castle, IN. Tel: (765) 529-1590, (800) 428-8855. E-Mail: sales@professionaldesignllc.com, Web Site: professionaldesignllc.com (5)

Brancaccio, Lou, The Columbian, Vancouver, WA. Tel: (360) 694-3391, FAX: (360) 735-4503, Web Site: www.columbian.com (17)

Branch Banking & Trust Co, Winston-Salem, NC. Tel: (336) 733-2000, FAX: (336) 733-2189, Web Site: www.bbt.com (14)

Branch, Greg, Luxottica Retail, Mason, OH. Tel: (513) 765-6956, Web Site: www.luxottica.com (2)

Brancheau, Jon, Nissan North America Inc, Franklin, TN. Tel: (615) 725-1000, Web Site: www.nissanusa.com (16)

Brand New Products LLC, Chicago, IL. Tel: (773) 486-8813, Web Site: www.brandnewllc.com (4)

Brand, Patrick, Pitney Bowes, Stamford, CT. Tel: (203) 356-5000, (800) MR-BOWES, Web Site: www.pitneybowes.com (10)

BrandCommand LLC, Richmond, VA. Tel: (804) 708-7100, E-Mail: cthurston@brandcommand.com, Web Site: www.brandcommand.com (16)

Brandeis, Peter, A I Friedman Inc, New York, NY. Tel: (212) 243-9000, (800) 204-6352, FAX: (212) 929-7320, Web Site: www.aifriedman.com (10)

Brandes, Richard, M2Media 360, Park Ridge, IL. Tel: (760) 318-7000, E-Mail: cnaughton@m2media360.com, Web Site: www.m2media360.com (17)

JoAnna Brandi & Co Inc, Boca Raton, FL. Tel: (561) 279-0027, E-Mail: joanna@returnonhappiness.com, Web Site: www.returnonhappiness.com (20)

Brandi, JoAnna, JoAnna Brandi & Co Inc, Boca Raton, FL. Tel: (561) 279-0027, E-Mail: joanna@returnonhappiness.com, Web Site: www.returnonhappiness.com (20)

Brandon, Mark, Diamond Machining Technology, Marlborough, MA. Tel: (508) 481-5944, (800) 666-4368, FAX: (508) 485-3924, Web Site: www.dmtsharp.com (9)

Brandon, Michael, SF Global Sourcing Inc, San Francisco, CA. Tel: (415) 288-9400, (800) 545-5865, FAX: (415) 288-9410, E-Mail: selfservice@sfvideo.com, Web Site: www.sfvideo.com (3)

Brandon, William, Ad Infinitum Books, Mount Vernon, NY. Tel: (914) 664-5930, (800) 697-0402, FAX: (914) 664-2642, E-Mail: aibservice@adinfinitumbooks.com, Web Site: www.adinfinitumbooks.com (16)

Brandt, David N., Cornhusker Press, Hastings, NE. Tel: (402) 462-4141, FAX: (402) 460-4612, E-Mail: dlsales@dutton-lainson.com, Web Site: www.dutton-lainson.com (17)

brandUNITY Inc, Rollingbay, WA. Tel: (206) 842-4948, FAX: (206) 842-4958, E-Mail: admin@brandunity.com, Web Site: www.brandunity.com (20)

Brandwein, Mark, Freestyle Solutions, Parsippany, NJ. Tel: (973) 237-9415, (800) 858-3666, FAX: (973) 237-9043, E-Mail: sales@dydacomp.com, Web Site: www.dydacomp.com (22)

Brandywine Consulting Group Inc, West Chester, PA. Tel: (610) 696-5872, FAX: (610) 429-1954, Web Site: www.brandywineconsulting.com (20)

Branham, Lorraine, Newhouse School of Public Communications, Syracuse, NY. Tel: (315) 443-3611, FAX: (315) 443-4426, Web Site: newhouse.syr.edu (41)

Brannon, Jim, Raycom Sports, Charlotte, NC. Tel: (704) 378-4456/4400, FAX: (704) 378-4465, E-Mail: whicks@raycomsports.com, Web Site: raycomsports.com (16)

Bransfield, M. Declan, Eberle & Associates Inc, McLean, VA. Tel: (703) 821-1550, FAX: (703) 821-0920, E-Mail: info@eberle1.com, Web Site: www.eberleassociates.com (1)

Bransford, Alain, Williams Worldwide Television, Santa Monica, CA. Tel: (310) 449-4506, FAX: (310) 449-4556, E-Mail: curious@williamsworldwidetv.com, Web Site: www.williamsworldwidetv.com (35)

Branstetter, Greg, Hippo Direct, Solon, OH. Tel: (440) 519-0730, FAX: (440) 519-0727, E-Mail: rapidresponse@hippodirect.com, Web Site: www.hippodirect.com (23)

Brant Publications Inc, New York, NY. Tel: (212) 941-2800, FAX: (212) 941-2885, Web Site: www.interviewmagazine.com (17)

Brant, Sandra J., Brant Publications Inc, New York, NY. Tel: (212) 941-2800, FAX: (212) 941-2885, Web Site: www.interviewmagazine.com (17)

Bras-Jorge, Muriel, Gems Sensors & Controls, Plainville, CT. Tel: (860) 747-3000, (800) 378-1600, FAX: (860) 747-4244, E-Mail: info@gemssensors.com, Web Site: www.gemssensors.com (9)

Brashe Advertising Inc, Jericho, NY. Tel: (516) 935-5544, FAX: (516) 932-7264, E-Mail: info@brasheadv.com, Web Site: brashe.com (35)

Brasher, Robert P., American Printing House for the Blind, Louisville, KY. Tel: (502) 895-2405, (800) 223-1839, FAX: (502) 899-2274, E-Mail: info@aph.org, Web Site: www.aph.org (7)

Braun, Axel J., Safe Publications Inc, Doylestown, PA. Tel: (215) 357-9049, FAX: (215) 357-5202, E-Mail: sales@safepub.com, Web Site: www.safepub.com (11)

Braun, Chris, Beemak Plastics Inc, La Mirada, CA. Tel: (310) 886-5880, (800) 421-4393, FAX: (310) 764-0330, E-Mail: info@beemak.com, Web Site: www.beemak.com (16)

Braun, Doug, Herbalife International of America Inc, Los Angeles, CA. Tel: (310) 216-9661, (866) 866-4744, FAX: (310) 258-7019, Web Site: www.herbalife.com (7)

Braun, S. Tracy, National Pension Service Inc, Burlington, VT. Tel: (802) 862-3994, FAX: (802) 865-2861, E-Mail: retirementservices@people.com, Web Site: www.peoples.com/retirementservices/ (14)

Braune, Brenda, Texas Parks & Wildlife Dept, Austin, TX. Tel: (512) 389-4800, (800) 792-1112, FAX: (512) 389-8029, Web Site: www.tpwd.state.tx.us (1)

Braune, John, The Heritage Co, North Little Rock, AR. Tel: (501) 835-5000 x1142, FAX: (501) 835-5834, Web Site: www.theheritagecompany.com (29)

Braunstein, Claudia, Belcaro Group Inc, Greenwood Village, CO. Tel: (303) 843-0302, Web Site: www.shopathome.com (17)

Braunstein, Marc, Belcaro Group Inc, Greenwood Village, CO. Tel: (303) 843-0302, Web Site: www.shopathome.com (17)

Braunstein, Max, Markertek Video Supply, Saugerties, NY. Tel: (845) 246-3036, (800) 522-2025, FAX: (845) 246-1757, E-Mail: sales@markertek.com, Web Site: www.markertek.com (3)

Brayer, David, Cartouche Ltd, Alexandria, VA. Tel: (703) 823-7904, (800) AT-EGYPT, FAX: (888) 283-4978, E-Mail: sales@egyptianimports.com, Web Site: www.egyptianimports.com (6)

Brazaitis, Greg, Sunoco Inc, Philadelphia, PA. Tel: (215) 977-3000, FAX: (215) 977-3409, Web Site: www.sunocoinc.com (16)

Brazelton, Rhonda, Clients & Profits Worldwide, Oceanside, CA. Tel: (760) 945-4334, Web Site: www.clientsandprofits.com (14)

Breard, Jack H., EBSCO Reception Room Subscription Services, Birmingham, AL. Tel: (205) 991-1409, (800) 527-5901, FAX: (205) 995-1621, E-Mail: www.ebsco.com/errss (18)

Breashears, Vicki, National Catholic Reporter Publishing Co Inc, Kansas City, MO. Tel: (816) 531-0538, (800) 444-8910, FAX: (816) 968-2268, Web Site: www.ncronline.org (17)

Breau, Shela, Bear Woods Supply Co Inc, Cornwallis, NS Canada. Tel: (902) 638-8622, (800) 565-5066, FAX: (902) 638-8637, Web Site: www.bearwood.com, www.woodparts.ca (11)

Breazeale, Deborah, Blue Coral Slick 50, Houston, TX. Tel: (713) 241-6161, (800) 416-1600, FAX: (713) 241-4044, E-Mail: SCD-ConsumerSolutions@Shell.com, Web Site: www.bluecoral.com (16)

Brecher, Bernard, Institutional Advancement Programs Inc, Tuckahoe, NY. Tel: (914) 779-4092, FAX: (914) 961-4202 (1)

Brecher, Melissa, Fairchild Fashion Media, New York, NY. Tel: (212) 286-2860, Web Site: www.condenast.com/fairchild (17)

Breck's Bulbs, Guilford, IN. Tel: (513) 354-1512, FAX: (513) 354-1505, E-Mail: service@brecks.com, Web Site: brecks.com (8)

Al Bredenberg Creative Services, Bethel, CT. Tel: (203) 791-8204, E-Mail: ab@copywriter.com, Web Site: www.copywriter.com (39)

Bredenberg, Al, Al Bredenberg Creative Services, Bethel, CT. Tel: (203) 791-8204, E-Mail: ab@copywriter.com, Web Site: www.copywriter.com (39)

Breeding, Kevin, Bigham Agency Inc, Plano, TX. Tel: (972) 801-2600, FAX: (972) 801-2649, E-Mail: info@bighamagency.com, Web Site: www.bighamagency.com (35)

Breen, Edward D., Pioneer Hi-Bred International Inc, Johnston, IA. Tel: (515) 535-3200, FAX: (515) 535-4415, E-Mail: web.editor@pioneer.com, Web Site: www.pioneer.com (4)

Breen, Edward D., Tyco Valves & Controls, Houston, TX. Tel: (713) 986-4665, (800) 343-0990, FAX: (713) 937-5466, Web Site: www.tycovalves.com (16)

Breen, Justin, Rapid City Journal, Rapid City, SD. Tel: (605) 394-8300, FAX: (605) 394-8462, E-Mail: classifieds@rapidcityjournal.com, Web Site: www.rapidcityjournal.com (18)

Breen, Peg, New York Landmarks Conservancy, New York, NY. Tel: (212) 995-5260, FAX: (212) 995-5268, Web Site: www.nylandmarks.org (1)

Bregel, Larry, Strang Communications Co, Lake Mary, FL. Tel: (407) 333-0600, FAX: (407) 333-7100, E-Mail: magcustsvc@strang.com, Web Site: www.strang.com (17)

Breimer, Stephen F., Bloom, Hergott, Diemer, Rosenthal and Laviolette LLP, Beverly Hills, CA. Tel: (310) 859-6800, FAX: (310) 860-6820, E-Mail: sfb@bhdrl.com (20)

Breisinger, James R., Kennametal Inc, Latrobe, PA. Tel: (800) 222-9327, FAX: (800) 521-3319, E-Mail: mcs-na.service@kennmetal.com, Web Site: www.kennametal.com (16)

Breitfeller, John R., Educational First Steps, Dallas, TX. Tel: (214) 824-7940), FAX: (214) 824-7428, Web Site: educationalfirststeps.org (1)

Brekhus, Melvin G., Texas Industries Inc, Dallas, TX. Tel: (972) 647-6700, FAX: (972) 647-3878, Web Site: www.txi.com (16)

Brekke, Bruce, Heartland America, Chaska, MN. Tel: (952) 361-3640, (800) 229-2901, FAX: (952) 368-3452, E-Mail: info@heartlandamerica.com, Web Site: www.heartlandamerica.com (3)

Brelsford, Dawn, Barton-Cotton, Baltimore, MD. Tel: (410) 247-4800, (800) 348-1102, FAX: (410) 536-0491, E-Mail: info@bartoncotton.com, Web Site: www.bartoncotton.com (16)

Beverly Bremer Silver Shop, Atlanta, GA. Tel: (404) 261-4009, (800) 270-4009, E-Mail: sterlingsilver@worldnet.att.net, Web Site: www.beverlybremer.com (6)

Bremer, Beverly H., Beverly Bremer Silver Shop, Atlanta, GA. Tel: (404) 261-4009, (800) 270-4009, E-Mail: sterlingsilver@worldnet.att.net, Web Site: www.beverlybremer.com (6)

Bremser, George, TomTom North American, Lebanon, NH. Tel: (603) 643-0330, (800) 331-7881, FAX: (603) 653-0249, Web Site: www.tomtom.com (22)

Brengle, George, The Sailing Co, Palm Coast, FL. Tel: (866) 436-2460, FAX: (401) 848-5048, Web Site: www.sailingworld.com (17)

Brennan, Chris, National Basketball Association, New York, NY. Tel: (212) 407-8000, FAX: (212) 826-0579, Web Site: www.nba.com (1)

Brennan, John J., Vanguard, Malvern, PA. Tel: (610) 669-1000, FAX: (610) 669-6600, Web Site: www.vanguard.com (14)

Brennan, John, Sykes Acquisition, Newtown, PA. Tel: (800) 799-6880, Web Site: www.ictgroup.com (29)

Brennan, Karen, Consolidated Mailing Corp, Shawnee Mission, KS. Tel: (913) 262-4400, (800) 706-6245, FAX: (913) 262-7801, E-Mail: cmcmail@swbell.net, Web Site: www.consolidatedmailing.com (28)

Brennan, Kelly, McKinsey & Co, New York, NY. Tel: (212) 446-7000, FAX: (212) 446-8575, Web Site: www.mckinsey.com (20)

Brennan, William, Conclusive Analytics, Inc, Huntersville, NC. Tel: (704) 887-5600, FAX: (704) 887-5601, E-Mail: info@conclusivemarketing.com, Web Site: www.conclusiveanalytics.com (1)

Brennan, William J., American Society of Radiologic Technologists, Albuquerque, NM. Tel: (505) 298-4500, FAX: (505) 298-5063, Web Site: www.asrt.org (1)

Brennen, Michael, eStock Photo, Long Island City, NY. Tel: (718) 433-4295, (800) 284-3399, E-Mail: sales@estockphoto.com, Web Site: www.estockphoto.com (38)

Brennen, Steve, Journal of Commerce Group, Newark, NJ. Tel: (973) 848-7000, FAX: (973) 848-7004, Web Site: www.joc.com (17)

Brenner, Rick, Prime, Bridgeport, CT. Tel: (203) 331-9100, (800) 873-7746, FAX: (203) 330-0123, Web Site: www.primeline.com (16)

Brenner, Stuart, SKO-Brenner-American, Baldwin, NY. Tel: (516) 771-4400, (800) 645-3390, FAX: (516) 771-7810, E-Mail: collect@skobrenner.com, Web Site: www.skobrenner.com (20)

Brent, Douglas, DB Alex Brown Inc, Baltimore, MD. Tel: (410) 727-1700, (800) 638-2956, Web Site: www.dbalexbrown.com (14)

Brentwood Benson Music Publishing, Brentwood, TN. Tel: (615) 261-3400, (800) 846-7664, FAX: (615) 261-3381, E-Mail: choral@brentwoodbensonmusic.com, Web Site: www.brentwoodbenson.com (17)

Bresch, Heather, Mylan NV, Canonsburg, PA. Tel: (724) 514-1800, (800) 231-3052, FAX: (281) 240-0002, E-Mail: communications@mylan.com, Web Site: www.mylan.com (7)

Breslawski, James P., Henry Schein Inc, Melville, NY. Tel: (631) 843-5500, (800) 472-4346, FAX: (631) 843-5658, E-Mail: custserv@henryschein.com, Web Site: www.henryschein.com (16)

Bresloff, Charles W., Recognition Products International, Easton, MD. Tel: (410) 820-0022, (800) 292-7354, FAX: (410) 820-5044, E-Mail: info@recognitionproducts.com, Web Site: www.shoprecognitionproducts.com (16)

Bretl, Jeff, Stephan Partners Inc, New York, NY. Tel: (212) 524-8583, E-Mail: george@stephenpartners.com, Web Site: www.stephanpartners.com (35)

Brett, James, Prudential Financial, Newark, NJ. Tel: (973) 802-2195, Web Site: www.prudential.com (14)

Bretz, Darcy, The Middleby Corp, Elgin, IL. Tel: (847) 741-3300, FAX: (847) 741-0015, E-Mail: sales@middleby.com, Web Site: www.middleby.com (16)

Breuer, Douglas, Response Media, Norcross, GA. Tel: (770) 451-5478, FAX: (770) 451-4929, E-Mail: postmaster@responsemedia.com, Web Site: www.responsemedia.com (32)

Breukink, Henk, ING, Minneapolis, MN. Tel: (612) 342-7061, (800) 333-6965, FAX: (612) 372-5339, Web Site: www.ing.com (15)

Breunig, Kevin, Appalachian Mountain Club, Boston, MA. Tel: (617) 523-0655, FAX: (617) 523-0722, Web Site: www.outdoors.com (1)

Brewer, Al, GG Direct, Portland, ME. Tel: (207) 772-0414, FAX: (207) 871-1444, E-Mail: data@ggdirect.com, Web Site: www.ggdirect.com (21)

Brewer, Brett, Adknowledge, Kansas City, MO. Tel: (816) 931-1771, (866) 730-2109, Web Site: www.adknowledge.com (32)

Brewer, Flora, Rhythm Band Inc, Fort Worth, TX. Tel: (817) 335-2561, (800) 424-4724, FAX: (800) 784-9401, E-Mail: sales@rhythmband.com, Web Site: www.rhythmband.com (11)

Brewster, James, Venus Fashion, Inc, Jacksonville, FL. Tel: (904) 645-6000, Web Site: www.venus.com (2)

Brianka, George, Avalanche Creative Services Inc, New York, NY. Tel: (212) 206-9335, FAX: (212) 206-1538, E-Mail: info@avalanchecreative.tv, Web Site: www.avalanchecreative.tv (35)

Monte Brick, Wordsmith, Melville, NY. Tel: (631) 549-9640, FAX: (631) 549-9640 (39)

Brick, Monte, Monte Brick, Wordsmith, Melville, NY. Tel: (631) 549-9640, FAX: (631) 549-9640 (39)

Brickell, Keith, Valpak Direct Marketing Systems Inc, Largo, FL. Tel: (727) 399-3000, Web Site: www.valpak.com (31)

Bricker, Mindy Kay, Bulletin of the Atomic Scientists, Chicago, IL. Tel: (773) 702-6301, FAX: (773) 980-6932, E-Mail: admin@thebulletin.org, Web Site: www.thebulletin.org (17)

Brickley, Rob, Andrews Wharton Inc, Commack, NY. Tel: (631) 470-4546, (631) 470-5683, E-Mail: info@andrewswharton.com, Web Site: andrewswharton.com (35)

Brickman, Christian A., Sally Beauty Supply LLC, Denton, TX. Tel: (940) 898-7500, (866) 234-9442, Web Site: www.sallybeauty.com (7)

Brickman, Nancy, HighScope Educational Research Foundation, Ypsilanti, MI. Tel: (800) 587-5639, FAX: (734) 485-0704, E-Mail: info@highscope.org, Web Site: www.highscope.org (17)

Bridge City Tool Works Inc, Portland, OR. Tel: (503) 282-6997, (800) 253-3332, FAX: (503) 287-1085, E-Mail: jjeconomaki@comcast.net, Web Site: www.bridgecitytools.com (9)

Bridge, Ross, Stock Yards Packing Co Inc, Medford, OR. Tel: (312) 733-6050, (888) 842-6111, FAX: (888) 700-9919, E-Mail: customerservice@stockyards.com, Web Site: www.stockyards.com (4)

Bridgeford, Gregory M., Lowe's Companies Inc, Mooresville, NC. Tel: (704) 758-1000, (800) 445-6937, Web Site: www.lowes.com (8)

Bridges, Kristi, Sawtooth Group, Red Bank, NJ. Tel: (732) 945-1004, Web Site: www.sawtoothgroup.com (35)

Bridgestone Americas Inc, Nashville, TN. Tel: (615) 937-1000, (800) 543-7522, FAX: (615) 937-3721, Web Site: www.bridgestonetire.com (16)

Bridgewell Associates, Alexandria, VA. Tel: (703) 360-6500 (29)

Bridson, Linda, Key Marketing Advantage LLC, Newtown, CT. Tel: (203) 491-2200, FAX: (203) 491-2201, E-Mail: info@keymarketingadvantage.com, Web Site: keymarketingcorp.com (23)

Bridwell, Hampton, Tenet Partners, New York, NY. Tel: (212) 329-3030, FAX: (212) 329-3031, Web Site: tenetpartners.com (35)

Brierley & Partners, Dallas, TX. Tel: (214) 760-8700, FAX: (214) 743-5511, E-Mail: bpayton@brierley.com, Web Site: www.brierley.com (35)

Brierley, Harold M., Brierley & Partners, Dallas, TX. Tel: (214) 760-8700, FAX: (214) 743-5511, E-Mail: bpayton@brierley.com, Web Site: www.brierley.com (35)

Brigade Quartermasters Ltd, Providence, RI. Tel: (770) 428-1248, (800) 338-4327, FAX: (800) 892-2992, Web Site: www.actiongear.com (11)

Brigar Xpress Solutions, Inc, Albany, NY. Tel: (518) 438-7817, (877) 437-7817, FAX: (518) 438-0224, E-Mail: general@brigarxpress.com, Web Site: www.brigarxpress.com (28)

Briggs, Anna C., National Humane Education Society, Charles Town, WV. Tel: (304) 725-0506, FAX: (304) 725-1523, E-Mail: information@nhes.org, Web Site: www.nhes.org (1)

Briggs, Bill, The Source Stock Footage Library Inc, Tucson, AZ. Tel: (520) 298-4810, FAX: (520) 290-8831, E-Mail: requests@sourcefootage.com, Web Site: www.sourcefootage.com (38)

Briggs, David, Datum Timing, Test & Measurement, Beverly, MA. Tel: (978) 927-8220, FAX: (978) 927-4099, E-Mail: wriley@datum.com, Web Site: www.datum.com (9)

Briggs, Kendice, Playboy Enterprises Inc, Beverly Hills, CA. Tel: (310) 860-1215, Web Site: www.playboyenterprises.com (17)

Briggs, Mark, Saks Fifth Avenue, New York, NY. Tel: (212) 940-5195, FAX: (212) 940-5339, Web Site: www.saksfifthavenue.com (16)

Briggs, Maudie, Morrison Printing Co, Morristown, TN. Tel: (423) 586-4812, (800) 251-0975, FAX: (423) 586-0322, E-Mail: info@morrcom.com, Web Site: www.morrcom.com (27)

Bright, Stacey, Fleet One LLC, Antioch, TN. Tel: (615) 523-6465, Web Site: www.fleetone.com (14)

Bright, Thomas R., Hitchcock Shoes Inc, Hingham, MA. Tel: (781) 749-3571, (888) 599-9433, FAX: (781) 749-3576, E-Mail: hitchcock@wideshoes.com, Web Site: www.wideshoes.com (2)

BrightFocus Foundation, Clarksburg, MD. Tel: (301) 948-3224, (800) 437-2423, FAX: (301) 358-9454, E-Mail: info@brightfocus.org, Web Site: www.brightfocus.org (1)

BrightKey, Annapolis Junction, MD. Tel: (301) 604-3305 (28)

Brighton, Scott, Artemis International Solutions Corp, Austin, TX. Tel: (512) 201-8222, FAX: (512) 874-8900, Web Site: www.aisc.com (22)

Brill, L Chip, Peter Glenn Publications, Delray Beach, FL. Tel: (561) 404-4290, (888) 332-6700, FAX: (561) 892-5786, E-Mail: gregjames@pgdirect.com, Web Site: www.pgdirect.com (17)

Brim Electronics Inc, Lodi, NJ. Tel: (201) 796-2886, FAX: (973) 778-2792, E-Mail: info@brimelectronics.com, Web Site: www.brimelectronics.com (3)

Brim, Alea, TransFirst Holdings Inc, Dallas, TX. Tel: (214) 453-7700, (888) 254-4137, FAX: (214) 453-7739, Web Site: www.transfirst.com (14)

Brin, Sergey, Google Inc, Mountain View, CA. Tel: (650) 253-0000, FAX: (650) 253-0001, Web Site: www.google.com (31)

Bringham, Jr. William T., WTB Associates Inc, Wilmette, IL. Tel: (847) 251-4188 (20)

Bringham, Sr. William T., WTB Associates Inc, Wilmette, IL. Tel: (847) 251-4188 (20)

Bringham, Tony, Association for Talent Development, Alexandria, VA. Tel: (703) 683-8100, (800) 628-2783, FAX: (703) 683-8103, E-Mail: customercare@td.org (1)

Brinker, Dave, Civil Service Employees Insurance Group, Walnut Creek, CA. Tel: (415) 274-7803, (925) 817-6300, (800) 282-6848, Web Site: www.cseinsurance.com (15)

Brinkerhoff, Peter, Polestar Group, West Simsbury, CT. Tel: (860) 658-4992 (20)

Brinkley, Cary, Allianz Life Insurance Co of North America, Minneapolis, MN. Tel: (763) 765-6500, (800) 950-5872, Web Site: www.allianzlife.com (15)

Briones, Andrew, Interface Engineering, Portland, OR. Tel: (503) 382-2266, FAX: (503) 382-2262, E-Mail: solutions@interfaceengineering.com, Web Site: www.ieice.com (20)

Briskin, Dennis, Catalyst Creative Services, Palo Alto, CA. Tel: (650) 325-1500, E-Mail: chief@catalystcreative.us, Web Site: www.catalystcreative.us (39)

Bristol Associates Inc, Los Angeles, CA. Tel: (310) 670-0525, FAX: (310) 670-4075, E-Mail: lfarber@bristolassoc.com, Web Site: www.bristolassoc.com (20)

Bristol-Myers Squibb Co, New York, NY. Tel: (212) 546-4000, FAX: (212) 546-9544, Web Site: www.bms.com (16)

Britanik, Thomas P., The Clorox Co, Oakland, CA. Tel: (510) 271-7000, FAX: (510) 832-1463, Web Site: www.thecloroxcompany.com (16)

British Columbia Automobile Association, Burnaby, BC Canada. Tel: (604) 268-5000, (800) 564-6222, FAX: (604) 268-5585, Web Site: www.bcaa.com (15)

Britton, Peter, The Write Answers Copywriting & Consulting, Blaine, WA. Tel: (888) 331-0322, Web Site: www.thewriteanswers.com (20)

Britton, Zach, Front Porch Inc, Sonora, CA. Tel: (209) 288-5500, (800) 728-1464, Web Site: www.frontporch.com (35)

Britts, Bill, Quantum Color, Morton Grove, IL. Tel: (847) 967-3600, FAX: (847) 967-3610, Web Site: www.cpipress.com (27)

Broadbear, Bob, Tension Corp, Kansas City, MO. Tel: (816) 471-3800, FAX: (816) 283-1498, E-Mail: info@tensioncorp.com, Web Site: www.tension.com (26)

Broadbent, Dave, Bushnell Outdoor Products, Overland Park, KS. Tel: (913) 752-3400, (800) 423-3537, FAX: (913) 752-3550, Web Site: www.bushnell.com (16)

Broadcast Electronics Inc, Quincy, IL. Tel: (217) 224-9600, FAX: (217) 224-9607, E-Mail: bdcast@bdcast.com, Web Site: www.bdcast.com (3)

Broadcast Media Associates, Santa Maria, CA. Tel: (805) 937-1553, E-Mail: cliffhunter.com, Web Site: www.broadcastmediabroker.com (30)

Broadford & Maloney Inc, New York, NY. Tel: (212) 836-4710, FAX: (917) 322-2105, E-Mail: m.maloney@bmcorp.com, Web Site: bmcorp.com (35)

Broadhead, Robert, Elizabeth Arden Spas LLC, Stamford, CT. Tel: (203) 905-1700, FAX: (203) 905-1716, Web Site: www.reddoorspas.com (19)

Broadhead, Tim, Accountants' Supply House, Lancaster, CA. Tel: (856) 384-1144, (800) 342-5274, FAX: (800) 468-4446, Web Site: www.rapidforms.com (10)

Broadhead, Tim, Amsterdam Printing, Amsterdam, NY. Tel: (800) 846-6600, FAX: (518) 770-7018, Web Site: www.amsterdamprinting.com (5)

Broadhead, Tim, Safeguard Business Systems Inc, Dallas, TX. Tel: (214) 905-3935, (800) 523-2422, FAX: (800) 439-8423, Web Site: www.gosafeguard.com (16)

Broadmoor Hotel Inc, Colorado Springs, CO. Tel: (719) 623-5112, (866) 837-9520, FAX: (719) 577-5738, Web Site: www.broadmoor.com (19)

BroadVision Inc, Redwood City, CA. Tel: (650) 295-0716, (866) 246-4887, FAX: (650) 364-3425, E-Mail: sales@broadvision.com, Web Site: www.broadvision.com (16)

Broadway Books, New York, NY. Tel: (212) 782-9644, FAX: (212) 782-8338, E-Mail: bwaypub@randomhouse.com, Web Site: www.randomhouse.com/broadway (17)

Broadway Play Publishing Inc, New York, NY. Tel: (212) 772-8334, FAX: (212) 772-8358, E-Mail: sara@broadwayplaypubl.com, Web Site: www.broadwayplaypubl.com (17)

Brocade Communications Systems Inc, San Jose, CA. Tel: (408) 333-8000, FAX: (408) 333-8101, E-Mail: info@brocade.com, Web Site: www.brocade.com (16)

Luther Brock PhD, The Letter Doctor, Denton, TX. Tel: (940) 387-8058 (39)

Brock, Gary D., Baylor Health Care System, Dallas, TX. Tel: (214) 820-4901, (800) 4Baylor, FAX: (214) 820-7499, Web Site: www.baylorhealth.com (16)

Brock, Jr Luther A., Luther Brock PhD, The Letter Doctor, Denton, TX. Tel: (940) 387-8058 (39)

Brock, Richard, First Wave Technologies Inc, Atlanta, GA. Tel: (678) 672-3100, Web Site: www.firstwave.com (22)

Brock, Wayne, Boy Scouts of America/National Supply Group, Charlotte, NC. Tel: (800) 323-0736, FAX: (704) 588-5822, E-Mail: customerservice@scoutstuff.org, Web Site: www.scoutstuff.org (1)

Brock-Getz, Petra, Behavioral Science Research, Coral Gables, FL. Tel: (305) 443-2000, (800) 282-2771, FAX: (305) 448-6825 (30)

Brocke-Benz, Manuel A. H., VWR International, Radnor, PA. Tel: (610) 386-1700, (800) 932-5000, FAX: (610) 431-9174, Web Site: www.vwrsp.com (34)

Brockman, Robert, Reynolds & Reynolds Co, Kettering, OH. Tel: (937) 485-2000, (800) 883-3031, FAX: (866) 268-5407, Web Site: www.reyrey.com (22)

Brockman, Tim, Event 360 Inc, Chicago, IL. Tel: (773) 247-5360, Web Site: www.event360.com (1)

Brockway, Kim, PlusNetMarketing Inc, Exton, PA. Tel: (610) 458-0707, E-Mail: info@pnmarketing.com, Web Site: www.plusnetmarketing.com (21)

Broderick, Tom, Internet Direct Response, Inc, Austin, TX. Tel: (512) 551-8417, FAX: (888) 763-5177, E-Mail: tbroderick@internet-direct-response.com, Web Site: www.internet-direct-response.com (35)

Brodeur, Alan, Direct Marketing Association of Toronto, Toronto, ON Canada. Tel: (905) 564-0150 X108, FAX: (905) 564-6621, E-Mail: pete@themose.ca, Web Site: www.dmatoronto.org (40)

Brodeur, Maurice, Peter Pan Bus Lines Inc, Springfield, MA. Tel: (413) 781-3320, (800) 343-9999, FAX: (413) 747-7626, E-Mail: info@peterpanbus.com, Web Site: www.peterpanbus.com (19)

Brody, Megan, UGL Equis Corp, Chicago, IL. Tel: (312) 424-8000, FAX: (312) 424-8080, Web Site: www.equiscorp.com (16)

Broering, James A., AcuSport Corp, Bellefontaine, OH. Tel: (937) 593-7010, FAX: (937) 592-5625, E-Mail: mwsales@acusport.com, Web Site: www.acusport.com (11)

Brogan, John, Global IntelliSystems, Evergreen, CO. Tel: (970) 315-3637, (800) 707-7074, FAX: (970) 432-7190, Web Site: www.globalintellisystems.com (22)

Brogan, Timothy, Pharmaceutical Care Management Association, Washington, DC. Tel: (202) 756-7210, FAX: (202) 207-3623, E-Mail: info@pcmanet.org, Web Site: www.pcmanet.org (1)

Broitman, Craig, Katz Media Group, New York, NY. Tel: (212) 424-6000, Web Site: www.katz-media.com (32)

Brokers/Consultants Inc, Flossmoor, IL. Tel: (708) 957-2900, FAX: (708) 957-4155 (15)

Brokers International Ltd, Panora, IA. Tel: (641) 755-2775, FAX: (641) 755-4201 (20)

Bromley Communications, San Antonio, TX. Tel: (210) 244-2000, E-Mail: ernest.bromley@bromley.biz, Web Site: bromley.biz (35)

Bromley, Ernest, Bromley Communications, San Antonio, TX. Tel: (210) 244-2000, E-Mail: ernest.bromley@bromley.biz, Web Site: bromley.biz (35)

Brommers, Craig, Warnaco Swimwear Inc, Los Angeles, CA. Tel: (323) 726-1262, FAX: (323) 724-6931, Web Site: www.speedo.com (16)

Bronner, Wayne, Bronner's Christmas Wonderland, Frankenmuth, MI. Tel: (989) 652-9931, Web Site: www.bronners.com (6)

Bronner's Christmas Wonderland, Frankenmuth, MI. Tel: (989) 652-9931, Web Site: www.bronners.com (6)

Bronsil, Tim, Point To Point Marketing Inc, Fort Collins, CO. Tel: (513) 231-0344, E-Mail: info@ptpmarketing.com, Web Site: ptpmarketing.com (35)

Bronson Nutritionals LLC, Hauppauge, NY. Tel: (631) 750-0000, Web Site: www.bronsonnutritionals.com (7)

Bronson, Rob, StrongView Systems Inc, Redwood City, CA. Tel: (650) 421-4200, (800) 971-0380, FAX: (650) 421-4201, E-Mail: info@strongview.com, Web Site: www.strongview.com (32)

Bronx Council on the Arts, Bronx, NY. Tel: (718) 931-9500, FAX: (718) 409-6445, E-Mail: info@bronxarts.org, Web Site: www.bronxarts.org (1)

Brook, Dan, Golden Trophy, Chicago, IL. Tel: (773) 282-2900, (800) 821-3882, FAX: (800) 835-6601, E-Mail: goldentrophy@bruss.com, Web Site: www.giftsteaksonline.com (4)

Brook, Yaron, Second Renaissance Books, Irvine, CA. Tel: (860) 354-5448, (800) 729-6149, FAX: (860) 355-7161, Web Site: www.aynrandbookstore.com (17)

Brook, Yaron, The Ayn Rand Institute, Irvine, CA. Tel: (949) 222-6550, FAX: (949) 222-6558, E-Mail: archives@aynrand.org, Web Site: www.aynrand.org (1)

Brooke Distributors Inc, Miami, FL. Tel: (305) 624-9752, (800) 275-8792, FAX: (305) 620-3988, E-Mail: sales@brookedms.com, Web Site: www.brookedist.com (3)

Brooker, Tom, Gummed Papers of America, Mc Cook, IL. Tel: (773) 650-2020, (800) 395-9000, FAX: (708) 485-8603, (800) 395-3581, E-Mail: info@labelexperts.com, Web Site: www.labelexperts.com (34)

Brookfield Office Properties, New York, NY. Tel: (212) 417-7000, FAX: (212) 417-7214, Web Site: brookfieldofficeproperties.com (16)

Brookfield Zoo, Brookfield, IL. Tel: (708) 485-0263, (800) 201-0784, FAX: (708) 485-3532, Web Site: www.brookfieldzoo.org (1)

Brookhollow Cards, Rexburg, ID. Tel: (800) 822-0256, FAX: (800) 443-8847, E-Mail: service@brookhollowcards.com, Web Site: www.brookhollowcards.com (10)

Brookhurst, Bruce, Atlanta Cutlery Corp, Conyers, GA. Tel: (770) 922-3700, (800) 833-8838, FAX: (770) 760-8993, E-Mail: webmaster@atlantacutlery.com, Web Site: www.atlantacutlery.com (11)

Brooks Brothers, New York, NY. Tel: (212) 682-8800, (800) 274-1815, FAX: (212) 309-7273, Web Site: www.brooksbrothers.com (2)

Brooks Equipment Co, Charlotte, NC. Tel: (704) 596-9438, (800) 826-3473, FAX: (704) 596-1096, Web Site: www.brooksequipment.com (9)

Brooks Sports Inc, Seattle, WA. Tel: (425) 402-1632, (800) 227-6657, FAX: (425) 489-1975, Web Site: www.brooksrunning.com (16)

Brooks, Amy, National Basketball Association, New York, NY. Tel: (212) 407-8000, FAX: (212) 826-0579, Web Site: www.nba.com (1)

Brooks, Doug, Canadian Marketing Association, Don Mills, ON Canada. Tel: (416) 391-2362, (800) 267-8805, FAX: (416) 441-4062, E-Mail: info@the-cma.org, Web Site: www.the-cma.org (40)

Brooks, Erin, The Connection Contact Center Services, Burnsville, MN. Tel: (952) 948-5335, (800) 883-5777, FAX: (952) 948-5498, E-Mail: sales@the-connection.com, Web Site: www.the-connection.com (29)

Brooks, John, Association for Audience Marketing Professionals (AAMP), North Hollywood, CA. Tel: (310) 323-7220, FAX: (310) 323-7231, E-Mail: mjordan@espcomp.com, Web Site: www.wfma.org (40)

Brooks, Jonathan, Triax Data Inc, Knoxville, TN. Tel: (865) 971-4333, (888) 241-9559, FAX: (865) 971-4333, E-Mail: info@triaxdata.com, Web Site: www.triaxdata.com (23)

Brooks, Lane, Food & Water Watch, Washington, DC. Tel: (202) 683-2500, E-Mail: info@fwwatch.org, Web Site: www.foodandwaterwatch.org (1)

Brooks, Mandy T., Kennesaw State University, Kennesaw, GA. Tel: (770) 423-6060, FAX: (770) 499-3261, Web Site: www.kennesaw.edu (41)

Brooks, Ray, HF Direct, Birmingham, AL. Tel: (205) 458-8200, FAX: (205) 458-8206, E-Mail: info@hfdirect.com, Web Site: www.hfdirect.com (35)

Brooks, Rod, PEMCO Insurance Cos, Seattle, WA. Tel: (206) 628-4000, (800) 467-3626, FAX: (206) 628-5886, Web Site: www.pemco.com (15)

Brooks, Ronald E., The American Legion National Headquarters, Indianapolis, IN. Tel: (317) 860-3100, (800) 433-2700, FAX: (317) 860-3001, Web Site: www.legion.org (1)

Brooks, Scott, Agile Education Marketing LLC, Denver, CO. Tel: (866) 783-0241, E-Mail: info@agile-ed.com, Web Site: www.agile-ed.com (24)

Brooks, William H., Hyatt Legal Plans Inc, Cleveland, OH. Tel: (216) 241-0022, FAX: (216) 694-4305, Web Site: www.legalplans.com (16)

Brookstone Co, Merrimack, NH. Tel: (603) 880-9500, (800) 846-3000, FAX: (603) 577-8005, E-Mail: customerservice@brookstone.com, Web Site: www.brookstone.com (3)

Broom, Matt, Doremus & Co, New York, NY. Tel: (212) 366-3000, FAX: (212) 366-3060, E-Mail: mbroom@doremus.com, Web Site: www.doremus.com (35)

Brostoff, Michael, Strategic Data Intelligence LLC, Northbrook, IL. Tel: (847) 897-5707, FAX: (847) 897-5715, E-Mail: info@sdintelligence.com, Web Site: www.sdintelligence.com (22)

Brotherhood America's Oldest Winery Ltd, Washingtonville, NY. Tel: (845) 496-3661, FAX: (845) 496-8720, E-Mail: contact@brotherhoodwinery.net, Web Site: www.brotherhoodwinery.net (19)

Brothers & Thompson PC, Chicago, IL. Tel: (312) 372-2909, FAX: (312) 704-6693, E-Mail: hthompson@brothersthompson.net, Web Site: www.brothersthompson.net (20)

Brothers, Alan W., Brothers & Thompson PC, Chicago, IL. Tel: (312) 372-2909, FAX: (312) 704-6693, E-Mail: hthompson@brothersthompson.net, Web Site: www.brothersthompson.net (20)

Brotherson, Gaylen M., Mechanical Breakdown Administrators Inc, Scottsdale, AZ. Tel: (480) 860-2288, FAX: (480) 860-0867, E-Mail: gaylenb@mbadirect.com, Web Site: www.mbadirect.com (14)

Brotherson, Judy K., Mechanical Breakdown Administrators Inc, Scottsdale, AZ. Tel: (480) 860-2288, FAX: (480) 860-0867, E-Mail: gaylenb@mbadirect.com, Web Site: www.mbadirect.com (14)

Brougher, Heather, Jenny Products Inc, Somerset, PA. Tel: (814) 445-3400, FAX: (814) 445-2280, Web Site: www.jennyproducts.com (16)

Broussard, Bruce D., Humana Inc, Louisville, KY. Tel: (502) 580-5005, (800) 486-2620, FAX: (502) 580-3141, Web Site: www.humana.com (7)

Broussard, Linda, Special Libraries Association (SLA), Alexandria, VA. Tel: (703) 647-4900, FAX: (703) 647-4901, E-Mail: sla@sla.org, Web Site: www.sla.org (40)

Broward, Douglas, AMC Inc, Atlanta, GA. Tel: (404) 220-2000, FAX: (404) 220-3030 (2)

Brower, Nike, KET, Lexington, KY. Tel: (859) 258-7000, (800) 432-0951, FAX: (606) 258-7396, E-Mail: rgriffin@ket.org, Web Site: www.ket.org (17)

Brown & Co, Blaine, WA. Tel: (360) 371-2489 (8)

Brown & Jenkins Trading Co, Jeffersonville, VT. Tel: (802) 644-8300, (800) 456-JAVA, Web Site: www.brownjenkins.com (4)

Arthur Brown & Bro Inc, New York, NY. Tel: (212) 575-5555, (800) 772-PENS, FAX: (212) 575-5825, E-Mail: penshop@artbrown.com, Web Site: www.artbrown.com (10)

Brown Brothers, Sterling, PA. Tel: (570) 689-9688, FAX: (570) 689-7873, E-Mail: info@brownbrotherusa.com, Web Site: www.brownbrothersusa.com (38)

Brown-Forman Corp, Louisville, KY. Tel: (502) 585-1100, FAX: (502) 774-7876, E-Mail: brown-forman@b-f.com, Web Site: www.brown-forman.com (16)

Matt Brown & Associates Inc, Dayton, OH. Tel: (937) 434-3949, (800) 233-3949, FAX: (937) 434-6272, E-Mail: mba@mbalists.com, Web Site: www.mbalists.com (23)

Brown Shoe Co, Saint Louis, MO. Tel: (314) 854-4000, FAX: (314) 854-4274, Web Site: www.brownshoe.com (16)

Tony Brown Productions, New York, NY. Tel: (718) 264-2226, FAX: (718) 264-1914, E-Mail: mail@tbol.net, Web Site: www.tonybrown.com (16)

Brown, Van Remmen, Kanuit, Inc, El Segundo, CA. Tel: (310) 640-0777, FAX: (310) 640-0606, E-Mail: info@bvksearch.com, Web Site: www.bvksearch.com (20)

Brown, Alex, Printmark, East Montpelier, VT. Tel: (802) 229-9743, FAX: (802) 229-9746, E-Mail: alex@printmark.net, Web Site: www.printmark.net (20)

Brown, B., Brim Electronics Inc, Lodi, NJ. Tel: (201) 796-2886, FAX: (973) 778-2792, E-Mail: info@brimelectronics.com, Web Site: www.brimelectronics.com (3)

Brown, B. Warren, Arthur Brown & Bro Inc, New York, NY. Tel: (212) 575-5555, (800) 772-PENS, FAX: (212) 575-5825, E-Mail: penshop@artbrown.com, Web Site: www.artbrown.com (10)

Brown, Barbara, Brown & Co, Blaine, WA. Tel: (360) 371-2489 (8)

Brown, Bart R., Gateway Inc, Irvine, CA. Tel: (949) 471-7000, (800) 369-1409, FAX: (949) 471-7041, Web Site: www.gateway.com (3)

Brown, Bob, Las Vegas Review Journal, Las Vegas, NV. Tel: (702) 383-0211, FAX: (702) 383-4646, Web Site: www.lvrj.com (17)

Brown, Brittney, Association of Marketing Service Providers, Alexandria, VA. Tel: (703) 836-9200, (800) 333-6272, FAX: (703) 548-8204, E-Mail: mfsamail@mfsanet.org, Web Site: www.mfsanet.org (40)

Brown, Brother Anselm, Abbey of Gethsemani, Trappist, KY. Tel: (502) 549-4133, FAX: (502) 549-4124, E-Mail: reservations@monks.org, Web Site: www.monks.org (1)

Brown, Cameron, Stark Brothers Nurseries & Orchards, Louisiana, MO. Tel: (573) 754-8800, (800) 325-4180, E-Mail: info@starkbros.com, Web Site: www.starkbros.com (8)

Brown, Chris, C&T Bridge Supplies, Los Alamitos, CA. Tel: (562) 598-7010, (800) 525-4718, FAX: (562) 430-8309, E-Mail: tedinlosal@aol.com (11)

Brown, Colby R., H&R Block Inc, Kansas City, MO. Tel: (816) 854-3000, (800) 472-5625, FAX: (816) 854-8500, Web Site: www.hrblock.com (14)

Brown, Courtenay, ASM Press, Washington. DC. Tel: (202) 737-3600, (800) 546-2416, FAX: (202) 942-9342, E-Mail: books@asmusa.org, Web Site: www.asmpress.org (17)

Brown, Darrell, Bonneville International, Salt Lake City, UT. Tel: (801) 575-7500, FAX: (801) 575-5820, E-Mail: bonneville@bonneville.com, Web Site: www.bonneville.com (35)

Brown, David, Astral Brands LLC, Atlanta, GA. Tel: (678) 303-3088, Web Site: www.astralbrands.com (7)

Brown, David J., National Trust for Historic Preservation, Washington, DC. Tel: (202) 588-6000, (800) 944-6847, E-Mail: info@savingplaces.org, Web Site: www.preservationnation.org (1)

Brown, David L., Network Solutions LLC, Herndon, VA. Tel: (877) 628-8686, Web Site: www.networksolutions.com (32)

Brown, Deena E., Goodman Media Group Inc, New York, NY. Tel: (212) 262-2247, FAX: (212) 262-2278, E-Mail: jgoodman@gmgpub.com, Web Site: www.goodmanmediagroup.dev.hotresponse.com (17)

Brown, Dennis, World Kitchen Inc, Corning, NY. Tel: (607) 377-8000, (800) 999-3436, FAX: (607) 377-8946, Web Site: www.worldkitchen.com (16)

Brown, Donald, Photographic Society of America Inc (PSA), Oklahoma City, OK. Tel: (405) 843-1437, (855) 772-4636, FAX: (405) 843-1438, E-Mail: HQ@psa-photo.org, Web Site: www.psa-photo.org (40)

Brown, Doug, All Star Directories, Seattle, WA. Tel: (888) 404-8043, FAX: (707) 667-1524, Web Site: www.allstardirectories.com (17)

Brown, Doug, Life Works Inc, Hollywood, FL. Tel: (954) 929-8428, (888) 780-9400, FAX: (954) 925-3365, Web Site: www.healthwagon.com (20)

Brown, Douglas, Calbiochem-Novabiochem Corp, San Diego, CA. Tel: (858) 450-9600, (800) 854-3417, FAX: (858) 453-3552, E-Mail: customerservice@emdbioscience.com, Web Site: www.calbiochem.com (9)

Brown, Ed, Brown & Co, Blaine, WA. Tel: (360) 371-2489 (8)

Brown, Edward Graham, Millipore Corp, Bedford, MA. Tel: (781) 869-5141, FAX: (781) 533-3110, Web Site: www.millipore.com (9)

Brown, Evan, Duggan & Brown Inc, Barrington, IL. Tel: (847) 381-8484, FAX: (847) 381-8499, E-Mail: evan@dugganandbrown.com, Web Site: www.dugganandbrown.com (20)

Brown, G. Mark, Brookfield Office Properties, New York, NY. Tel: (212) 417-7000, FAX: (212) 417-7214, Web Site: brookfieldofficeproperties.com (16)

Brown, Gene, University of Missouri/Kansas City, Kansas City, MO. Tel: (816) 235-2215, FAX: (816) 235-2312, Web Site: www.umkc.edu (41)

Brown, Greg, Mailer's Software, Rancho Santa Margarita, CA. Tel: (949) 858-3000, (800) 635-4772, (949) 589-5211, E-Mail: info@melissadata.com, Web Site: www.mailerssoftware.com (22)

Brown, J. Powell, Arthur Brown & Bro Inc, New York, NY. Tel: (212) 575-5555, (800) 772-PENS, FAX: (212) 575-5825, E-Mail: penshop@artbrown.com, Web Site: www.artbrown.com (10)

Brown, Janet, No Load FundX, San Francisco, CA. Tel: (415) 986-7979, (800) 763-8639, FAX: (415) 986-1595, Web Site: www.noloadfundx.com (14)

Brown, Jeffrey, National Emblem Sales, Indianapolis, IN. Tel: (317) 630-1247, (888) 453-1466, FAX: (317) 630-1381, E-Mail: emblem@legion.org, Web Site: www.emblem.legion.org (16)

Brown, Jeffrey, The American Legion National Headquarters, Indianapolis, IN. Tel: (317) 860-3100, (800) 433-2700, FAX: (317) 860-3001, Web Site: www.legion.org (1)

Brown, Jim D, Brown's Omaha Plant Farms, Omaha, TX. Tel: (903) 884-2421, FAX: (903) 884-2423, E-Mail: mail@bopf.com, Web Site: www.bopf.com (8)

Brown, Jim, Moto Franchise Corp, Dayton, OH. Tel: (937) 291-1900, (800) 733-6686, FAX: (937) 291-2005, E-Mail: expert@motophoto.com, Web Site: www.motophoto.com; www.portraitavenue.com (3)

Brown, Jody A., CACI International Inc, Arlington, VA. Tel: (703) 841-7800, FAX: (703) 841-7882, Web Site: www.caci.com (22)

Brown, Joe, L&L Management, Pasadena, CA. Tel: (626) 568-0338, FAX: (626) 568-9165 (16)

Brown, John, Fred Pryor Seminars, Mission, KS. Tel: (913) 967-8518, (800) 780-8476, FAX: (913) 967-8849, E-Mail: customerservice@pryor.com, Web Site: www.pryor.com (16)

Brown, Jr. Harold C., Golden Gate Transportation District, San Rafael, CA. Tel: (415) 921-5858, FAX: (415) 923-2014, Web Site: www.goldengate.org (16)

Brown, Katie, Media Horizons Management LLC, Norwalk, CT. Tel: (203) 857-0770, FAX: (203) 857-0296, E-Mail: info@mediahorizons.com, Web Site: www.mediahorizons.com (31)

Brown, Kelly, Communication Resources Inc, Beaufort, SC. Tel: (330) 266-1489, (800) 992-2144, FAX: (330) 493-3158, E-Mail: service@comresources.com, Web Site: www.comresources.com (18)

Brown, Kim, Booth Michigan, Grand Rapids, MI. Tel: (616) 222-5824, FAX: (616) 222-5318, Web Site: www.boothnewspapers.com (17)

Brown, Malcolm, Backe Digital Brand Marketing, Radnor, PA. Tel: (610) 947-6901, E-Mail: jbacke@backemarketing.com, Web Site: www.backemarketing.com (35)

Brown, Malinda L., Lee's Nursery, McMinnville, TN. Tel: (931) 668-4870 (8)

Brown, Marilyn, Arthur Brown & Bro Inc, New York, NY. Tel: (212) 575-5555, (800) 772-PENS, FAX: (212) 575-5825, E-Mail: penshop@artbrown.com, Web Site: www.artbrown.com (10)

Brown, Mary Lou, MLB Associates, Lake Placid, NY. Tel: (518) 523-2371, FAX: (518) 523-9011, E-Mail: mlbassoc@aol.com, Web Site: www.mlbassociates.com (20)

Brown, Matt, Nevada Magazine, Carson City, NV. Tel: (775) 687-5416, FAX: (775) 687-6159, E-Mail: editor@nevadamagazine.com, Web Site: www.nevadamagazine.com (17)

Brown, Melanie, Jason Natural Personal Care Products, Boulder, CO. Tel: (88) 659-7730, Web Site: www.jason-natural.com (7)

Brown, Michael, Symantec, Mountain View, CA. Tel: (408) 517-8000, FAX: (408) 517-8186, Web Site: www.symantec.com (16)

Brown, Michelle, Compass Ventures, Lincoln, NE. Tel: (402) 438-3222, FAX: (402) 438-3439, E-Mail: info@compassventures.com, Web Site: www.compassventures.com (23)

Brown, Nancy, American Heart Association, Dallas, TX. Tel: (214) 373-6300, (800) AHA-USA-1, FAX: (214) 373-3406, Web Site: www.americanheart.org (1)

Brown, Paulette, American Bar Association, Chicago, IL. Tel: (312) 988-5000, (800) 285-2221, FAX: (312) 988-5177, Web Site: www.abanet.org (1)

Brown, Peter D., Champs Corp, Bradenton, FL. Tel: (941) 748-0577, (800) 991-6813, E-Mail: customer_service@champssports.com, Web Site: www.champssports.com (11)

Brown, Peter G., Natural History Magazine, Durham, NC. Tel: (646) 356-6500, FAX: (646) 356-6511, E-Mail: nhmag@naturalhistorymag.com, Web Site: www.naturalhistorymag.com (17)

Brown, Peter, Lamkin Corp, San Diego, CA. Tel: (619) 661-7090, (800) 642-7755, FAX: (619) 661-0014, E-Mail: info@lamkingrips.com, Web Site: www.lamkingrips.com (11)

Brown, Rob, AliMed Inc, Dedham, MA. Tel: (781) 329-2900, (800) 225-2610, FAX: (800) 437-2966, (781) 329-8392, E-Mail: info@alimed.com, Web Site: www.alimed.com (7)

Brown, Russell, Triax Data Inc, Knoxville, TN. Tel: (865) 971-4333, (888) 241-9559, FAX: (865) 971-4333, E-Mail: info@triaxdata.com, Web Site: www.triaxdata.com (23)

Brown, Sandi, Sandi Brown Marketing, Saint Petersburg, FL. Tel: (727) 528-6980, FAX: (703) 960-4492 (35)

Brown, Sandra L., Grandma Brown's Beans Inc, Mexico, NY. Tel: (315) 963-7221, FAX: (315) 963-4072 (4)

Brown, Sharon, DM Assistance Inc, Portsmouth, NH. Tel: (603) 964-6156 (20)

Brown, Timothy J., Princess House Inc, Taunton, MA. Tel: (508) 823-0711, (508) 832-6800, (800) 622-0039, FAX: (508) 823-5182, Web Site: www.princesshouse.com (16)

Brown, Tony, Tony Brown Productions, New York, NY. Tel: (718) 264-2226, FAX: (718) 264-1914, E-Mail: mail@tbol.net, Web Site: www.tonybrown.com (16)

Brown, William M., Harris Corp, Melbourne, FL. Tel: (321) 727-9100, (800) 442-7747, E-Mail: webmaster@harris.com, Web Site: harris.com (16)

Brown-Dufour, Valerie, WSI, Mississauga, ON Canada. Tel: (905) 678-7588, (888) 678-7588, FAX: (905) 678-7242, E-Mail: contact@wsiworld.com, Web Site: www.wsiworld.com (35)

BrownCor International, Milwaukee, WI. Tel: (800) 327-2278, Web Site: www.bcadvantage.com (5)

Charlie Browne Communications, Apex, NC. Tel: (919) 267-9271, FAX: (919) 267-9271, E-Mail: cbrownecom@sbcglobal.net (39)

Browne, Charlie, Charlie Browne Communications, Apex, NC. Tel: (919) 267-9271, FAX: (919) 267-9271, E-Mail: cbrownecom@sbcglobal.net (39)

Browne, Philip M., Advanta Corp, Conshohocken, PA. Tel: (215) 657-4000, (800) 255-0022, Web Site: www.advanta.com (14)

Brownell Holly Farms, Oregon City, OR. Tel: (503) 631-7475, FAX: (503) 631-7481, E-Mail: sales@brownellhollyfarms.com, Web Site: www.brownellhollyfarms.com (6)

Browning, Jacobson & Klein LLP, Beverly Hills, CA. Tel: (310) 247-8777, FAX: (310) 247-1827 (20)

Browning, Bruce, Magjak Printing Corp, Port Chester, NY. Tel: (914) 939-8800, Web Site: www.magjak.com (27)

Browning, Jeff, SilverPop, Atlanta, GA. Tel: (678) 247-0500, (866) 745-8767, FAX: (678) 247-0501, E-Mail: contactsales@silverpop.com, Web Site: www.silverpop.com (32)

Browning, Jim, Image Checks, Bel Air, MD. Tel: (800) 562-8768, FAX: (410) 676-8269, Web Site: www.imagechecks.com (27)

Browning, Kelly B., American Institute for Cancer Research, Washington, DC. Tel: (202) 328-7744, (800) 843-8114, FAX: (202) 328-7226, E-Mail: aicrweb@aicr.org, Web Site: www.aicr.org (1)

Browning, Kenneth L., Browning, Jacobson & Klein LLP, Beverly Hills, CA. Tel: (310) 247-8777, FAX: (310) 247-1827 (20)

Brownlee, David, Paradise Galleries, Laguna Hills, CA. Tel: (858) 793-4050, (800) 67-DOLLS, FAX: (949) 743-8974, E-Mail: omancinelli@paradisegalleries.com, Web Site: www.paradisegalleries.com (27)

Brownlee, Neil, Avalanche Creative Services Inc, New York, NY. Tel: (212) 206-9335, FAX: (212) 206-1538, E-Mail: info@avalanchecreative.tv, Web Site: www.avalanchecreative.tv (35)

Brownrigg, Geoff, Improvements, West Chester, OH. Tel: (800) 634-9484, Web Site: www.improvementscatalog.com (8)

Brown's Omaha Plant Farms, Omaha, TX. Tel: (903) 884-2421, FAX: (903) 884-2423, E-Mail: mail@bopf.com, Web Site: www.bopf.com (8)

Bruce Medical Supply, Waltham, MA. Tel: (781) 894-6262, (800) 225-8446, FAX: (781) 894-9519, E-Mail: sales@brucemedial.com, Web Site: www.brucemedical.com (7)

Bruce, Andrew, Publicis Worldwide North America, New York, NY. Tel: (212) 279-5550, E-Mail: andrew.bruce@publicisna.com, Web Site: publicisna.com (35)

Bruce, Ben F., Trinity Technical Group, Inc, Arlington, TX. Tel: (817) 879-7907, E-Mail: info@trinitytechnicalgroup.com, Web Site: www.trinitytechnicalgroup.com (22)

Bruck, David, Wendell August Forge Inc, Grove City, PA. Tel: (724) 458-8360, (800) 923-1390, FAX: (724) 458-0906, E-Mail: info@wendell.com, Web Site: www.wendellaugust.com (6)

Brucker, Randy, Cooper Communities Inc, Rogers, AR. Tel: (479) 246-6500, (800) 648-6401, FAX: (479) 855-6256, E-Mail: coopernet@ccias.com, Web Site: www.cooper-communities.com (16)

Brueckner, Renee, Association of the Miraculous Medal, Perryville, MO. Tel: (573) 547-8343, (800) 264-6279, FAX: (573) 547-1389, E-Mail: amm1@amm.org, Web Site: www.amm.org (1)

Bruffey, Teresa, Outdoor Research, Seattle, WA. Tel: (206) 467-1496, (888) 467-4327, FAX: (206) 467-0374, Web Site: www.outdoorresearch.com (11)

Brugger, Christy, Custom Toll Free, Los Angeles, CA. Tel: (800) 933-3030, E-Mail: service@customtollfree.com, Web Site: www.customtollfree.com (5)

Brugh, Ken, Golfsmith International Inc, Austin, TX. Tel: (512) 821-4050, (800) 813-6897, FAX: (512) 837-9347, E-Mail: comments@golfsmith.com, Web Site: www.golfsmith.com (11)

Brun, Tom, National Association of Publishers Representatives, Hoffman Estates, IL. Tel: (877) 263-9640, FAX: (847) 885-8393, E-Mail: info@napronline.com, Web Site: www.napronline.com (1)

Brune, Erica, Gragg Advertising, Kansas City, MO. Tel: (877) GRAGGADV, FAX: (816) 931-2227, E-Mail: contact@graggadv.com, Web Site: www.graggadv.com (35)

Bruneau, Bill, Bountiful Gardens, Willits, CA. Tel: (707) 459-6410, FAX: (707) 459-1925, E-Mail: bountiful@sonic.net, Web Site: www.bountifulgardens.org (8)

Brunn, Tim, Merastar Insurance Co, Chattanooga, TN. Tel: (800) 637-2782, FAX: (800) 369-1430, E-Mail: merastar.assist.team@unitrindirect.com, Web Site: www.merastar.com (15)

Brunner, Pittsburgh, PA. Tel: (412) 995-9500, FAX: (412) 995-9501, Web Site: www.brunnerworks.com (35)

Brunner, James E., Consumer's Energy, Jackson, MI. Tel: (517) 788-0550, (800) 805-0490, FAX: (517) 788-1859, E-Mail: businesscenter@consumerenergy.com, Web Site: www.consumersenergy.com (16)

Brunner, Michael, Brunner, Pittsburgh, PA. Tel: (412) 995-9500, FAX: (412) 995-9501, Web Site: www.brunnerworks.com (35)

Bruno & Ridgway Research Associates Inc, Lawrenceville, NJ. Tel: (609) 895-9889, FAX: (609) 895-6665, E-Mail: info@brunoandridgway.com, Web Site: www.brra.com (30)

Bruno, John G., NCR Corp, Duluth, GA. Tel: (937) 445-1936, (800) CALL-NCR, FAX: (937) 445-1682, Web Site: www.ncr.com (16)

Bruno, Leo, Lake Shore Industries, Erie, PA. Tel: (800) 458-0463, FAX: (814) 453-4293, E-Mail: info@lsisigns.com, Web Site: www.lsisigns.com (16)

Bruno, Mike, Loctite Corp, Rocky Hill, CT. Tel: (860) 571-5100, (800) 562-8483, (800) LOCTITE, FAX: (860) 571-5465, Web Site: www.loctite.com (16)

Bruno, Robert, Microfluidics Corp, Westwood, MA. Tel: (617) 969-5452, (800) 370-5452, FAX: (617) 965-1213, E-Mail: info@mfics.com, Web Site: www.microfluidicscorp.com (16)

Bruno, Shirley, Lake Shore Industries, Erie, PA. Tel: (800) 458-0463, FAX: (814) 453-4293, E-Mail: info@lsisigns.com, Web Site: www.lsisigns.com (16)

Bruno, Vincent, Vcom International Multi-Media Corp, South Hackensack, NJ. Tel: (201) 229-9800, (800) 572-6373, FAX: (973) 439-1522, E-Mail: info@vcomimc.com, Web Site: www.vcomimc.com (3)

Bruns, Margie, Amos Press, Inc, Sidney, OH. Tel: (937) 498-2111, FAX: (937) 498-0876, Web Site: www.amospress.com (17)

Cecile Brunswick, New York, NY. Tel: (212) 222-2088, E-Mail: cbrunswick@nyc.rr.com, Web Site: www.cecilebrunswicknyc.com (36)

Brunswick, Cecile, Cecile Brunswick, New York, NY. Tel: (212) 222-2088, E-Mail: cbrunswick@nyc.rr.com, Web Site: www.cecilebrunswicknyc.com (36)

Brunton, Melissa, Direct Selling Association, Washington, DC. Tel: (202) 452-8866, FAX: (202) 452-9010, E-Mail: info@dsa.org, Web Site: www.dsa.org (40)

Bruscato, Nick, Bunker Hill Auctions, Millbrook, IL. Tel: (630) 553-8968, E-Mail: bunkerhillauctions@joimail.com, Web Site: www.bunkerhillauctions.com (6)

Brusco, Giorgio, Gates Corp, Denver, CO. Tel: (303) 744-1911, FAX: (303) 744-4000, Web Site: www.gates.com (9)

Brush, Richard L., Johnson & Wales University, Providence, RI. Tel: (401) 598-1000, (800) DIAL-JWU, FAX: (401) 598-1833, Web Site: www.jwu.edu (41)

Brushfire Inc, Cedar Knolls, NJ. Tel: (973) 871-1700, FAX: (973) 871-1717, E-Mail: vwarner@brushfireinc.com, Web Site: www.brushfireinc.com (35)

Bruu, Alyson, David C Cook, Colorado Springs, CO. Tel: (719) 536-0100, (800) 323-7543, FAX: (719) 536-3232, Web Site: www.davidccook.com (17)

Bryan, Daniel Keith, Hale Indian River Groves Inc, Vero Beach, FL. Tel: (800) 356-7264, FAX: (877) 329-4253, E-Mail: marketing@halegroves.com, Web Site: www.hales.com (16)

Bryan, Karen, John Wiley & Sons Canada Ltd, Etobicoke, ON Canada. Tel: (416) 236-4433, FAX: (416) 236-4448, Web Site: www.wiley.com (17)

Bryan, Nicole, The Peter A Tobin College of Business, Jamaica, NY. Tel: (718) 990-2600, FAX: (718) 990-1868, Web Site: www.stjohns.edu (41)

Bryan, Paul, Bromley Communications, San Antonio, TX. Tel: (210) 244-2000, E-Mail: ernest.bromley@bromley.biz, Web Site: bromley.biz (35)

Bryant, Andy D., Intel Corp, Santa Clara, CA. Tel: (408) 765-8080, (800) 548-4725, FAX: (408) 765-6187, Web Site: www.intel.com (16)

Bryant, Dan, Jobscope Corp, Greenville, SC. Tel: (864) 458-3143, (800) 443-5794, FAX: (864) 234-4852, E-Mail: marketing@jobscope.com, Web Site: www.jobscope.com (22)

Bryant, Douglas Donne, DDB Stock Photography LLC, Baton Rouge, LA. Tel: (225) 763-6235, FAX: (225) 763-6894, E-Mail: info@ddbstock.com, Web Site: www.ddbstock.com (38)

Bryant, Erin, Phoenix Learning Group Inc, Maryland Heights, MO. Tel: (314) 569-0211, (800) 221-1274, FAX: (314) 569-2834, E-Mail: dealersales@phoenixlearninggroup.com, Web Site: www.phoenixlearninggroup.com (16)

Bryant, Jason, Nor1, Santa Clara, CA. Tel: (408) 850-9937, FAX: (408) 608-0443, E-Mail: sales@nor1.com, Web Site: www.nor1.com (32)

Bryant, Jeff D., Creative Direct Marketing, Chapel Hill, NC. Tel: (919) 929-5757, E-Mail: jeffb.cdm@mindspring.com (39)

Brylane, Taunton, MA. Tel: (800) 544-3793, Web Site: www.brylanehome.com (2)

Bryson, Craig, Christian Resource Management, Orange, CA. Tel: (714) 974-0754, FAX: (714) 974-7845, E-Mail: CRMOrange@aol.com, Web Site: www.crmorange.com (22)

Bryson, Destiny, Mac Murray Petersen & Shuster LLP, New Albany, OH. Tel: (614) 939-9955, FAX: (614) 939-9955, E-Mail: dbryson@mpslawyers.com, Web Site: www.mpslawyers.com (20)

Bryson, Katie, Teletrack Inc, Norcross, GA. Tel: (770) 449-8809 (29)

Brzeski, Jill, Boelter + Lincoln Marketing Communications, Milwaukee, WI. Tel: (414) 271-0101, FAX: (414) 271-1436, E-Mail: jbrzeski@boelterlincoln.com, Web Site: boelterlincoln.com (35)

Brzezinski, Daniel, GetResponse Services Inc, Wilmington, DE. Tel: (877) 362-4547. Web Site: www.getresponse.com (24)

B2BAdvantage, Papillion, NE. Tel: (402) 836-5683, E-Mail: info@b2b-advantage.com, Web Site: www.b2b-advantage.com (23)

Bucci, Tony, Marc USA, Pittsburgh, PA. Tel: (412) 562-2000, FAX: (412) 562-2022, E-Mail: pittsburgh@marcusa.com, Web Site: www.marcusa.com (34)

Bucco, Chickie, Katz Media Group, New York, NY. Tel: (212) 424-6000, Web Site: www.katz-media.com (32)

Buchert, Richard, Bauer Publishing Co, Englewood Cliffs, NJ. Tel: (201) 569-6699, FAX: (201) 569-5303, Web Site: www.bauerpublishing.com (17)

Buchner, Mike, Fallon, Minneapolis, MN. Tel: (612) 758-2345, FAX: (612) 758-2346, E-Mail: info@fallon.com, Web Site: www.fallon.com (35)

Buchner, Rob, Mithun Agency, Minneapolis, MN. Tel: (612) 347-1000, FAX: (612) 347-1515, Web Site: www.everythingtalks.com (35)

Buchsbaum, Bob, Dick Blick Holdings Inc, Galesburg, IL. Tel: (309) 343-6181, FAX: (309) 343-5785, E-Mail: admin@dickblick.com, Web Site: www.dickblick.com (16)

Buchsbaum, Judy, Marmelstein Inc, Philadelphia, PA. Tel: (215) 925-9862, FAX: (215) 925-3889 (16)

Buchser, Rodney H., FMS Direct, Tarzana, CA. Tel: (818) 708-7814, FAX: (818) 708-7842, E-Mail: info@fmsdirect.com, Web Site: www.fmsdirect.com (35)

Buchweitz, Larry, MCH Strategic Data, Sweet Springs, MO. Tel: (660) 335-6373, (800) 776-6373, FAX: (660) 335-4157, E-Mail: sales@mchdata.com, Web Site: mchdata.com (23)

Buchwitz, Melody, PacNet Services Ltd. Vancouver, BC Canada. Tel: (604) 689-0399, FAX: (604) 689-0313, E-Mail: info@pacnetservices.com, Web Site: www.pacnetservices.com (14)

Buckalew, Michelle, Great-West Life, Greenwood Village, CO. Tel: (800) 537-2033, Web Site: www.greatwest.com (15)

Buckingham, Madeleine, Mother Jones Magazine, San Francisco, CA. Tel: (415) 321-1700, Web Site: www.motherjones.com (17)

Buckles, John, Marketing Consulting Services, Kingsport, TN. Tel: (423) 288-5866, FAX: (423) 288-5576 (20)

Buckley, Andrew, Traction On Demand. Burnaby, BC Canada. Tel: (604) 620-6040, Web Site: www.tractionondemand.com (35)

Buckley, Cali, Pennsylvania State University Press, University Park, PA. Tel: (814) 865-1327, (800) 326-9180, FAX: (814) 863-1408, Web Site: www.psupress.org (17)

Buckley, Heidi, Marketing Solutions Unlimited LLC, West Hartford, CT. Tel: (860) 523-0670, FAX: (860) 523-0675, E-Mail: info@msuprint.com, Web Site: msuprint.com (21)

Buckley, Jon, AccuList Inc, San Antonio, TX. Tel: (210) 807-9940, (877) 505-8747, FAX: (210) 494-5478, E-Mail: sales@acculistusa.com, Web Site: www.acculistusa.com (23)

Buckley, Michael J., Bankers Life & Casualty Co, Chicago, IL. Tel: (312) 396-6000, (800) 231-9150, Web Site: www.bankerslife.com (15)

Buckley, Tom, Redi-Data Inc, Fairfield, NJ. Tel: (973) 227-4380, (800) 635-5833, FAX: (973) 808-5511, E-Mail: sales@redidata.com, Web Site: www.redidata.com (23)

Buckley, Tom, Splashnet Inc, Fairfield, NJ. Tel: (877) 244-9362, E-Mail: contactus@splashnet.com, Web Site: www.splashnet.com (23)

Buckman, Elizabeth, Chesapeake Bay Foundation, Annapolis, MD. Tel: (410) 268-8816, Web Site: www.savethebay.cbf.org (1)

Buckredan, Ravi, AmeriList Inc, Orangeburg, NY. Tel: (845) 362-6737, (800) 457-2899, FAX: (845) 362-6433, E-Mail: info@amerilist.com, Web Site: www.amerilist.com (23)

Buda, James B., Caterpillar Inc, Peoria, IL. Tel: (309) 675-0545, Web Site: www.cat.com (16)

Budd, Scott, National Review, New York, NY. Tel: (212) 679-7330, FAX: (212) 849-2852, Web Site: www.nationalreview.com (17)

Budlong, Morrison J., King Computer Services Inc, La Crescenta, CA. Tel: (818) 951-5240, E-Mail: kingsoftware@aol.com, Web Site: www.kingcomputerservices.com (22)

Budniewski, Denis, Mithun Agency, Minneapolis, MN. Tel: (612) 347-1000, FAX: (612) 347-1515, Web Site: www.everythingtalks.com (35)

Budowski, Rob, Ghirardelli Chocolate Co, San Leandro, CA. Tel: (510) 483-6970, (800) 877-9338, FAX: (510) 297-2649, Web Site: www.ghirardelli.com (16)

Buechert, Courtney, Eleven Inc, San Francisco, CA. Tel: (415) 707-1111, Web Site: www.eleveninc.com (35)

Buena Vista Home Entertainment, Burbank, CA. Tel: (818) 560-1000, FAX: (818) 845-8728, Web Site: www.bvhe.com (3)

Buena Vista Winery, Sonoma, CA. Tel: (707) 252-7117, (800) 678-8504, FAX: (707) 252-0392, Web Site: www.buenavistawinery.com (16)

Buescher, Kent A., Beacon Printing & Graphics Inc, Valdosta, GA. Tel: (912) 244-5634, (800) 227-7377, FAX: (912) 247-4405, E-Mail: sls@uspress.com, Web Site: www.uspress.com (27)

Buffa, Vincent, Crane Pumps & Systems Inc, Piqua, OH. Tel: (937) 773-2442, FAX: (937) 773-2238, E-Mail: cranepumps@cranepumps.com, Web Site: www.cranepumps.com (16)

The Buffkin Group LLC, Brentwood, TN. Tel: (615) 988-2582, E-Mail: info@thebuffkingroup.com, Web Site: www.thebuffkingroup.com (20)

Buffkin, Craig, The Buffkin Group LLC, Brentwood, TN. Tel: (615) 988-2582, E-Mail: info@thebuffkingroup.com, Web Site: www.thebuffkingroup.com (20)

Buford, Jay, Conclusive Analytics, Inc, Huntersville, NC. Tel: (704) 887-5600, FAX: (704) 887-5601, E-Mail: info@conclusivemarketing.com, Web Site: www.conclusiveanalytics.com (22)

Buggies Unlimited, Jacksonville, FL. Tel: (888) 444-6364, E-Mail: support@buggiesunlimited.com, Web Site: www.buggiesunlimited.com (12)

Buhler, Brian K., Kelsey National Corp, Los Angeles, CA. Tel: (310) 390-1000, (800) 366-5656, FAX: (310) 390-3158, E-Mail: info@kelsey.com, Web Site: www.kelsey.com (15)

Buhr, Joel, First Direct Inc, Bellevue, NE. Tel: (402) 403-0000, (866) 363-9575, FAX: (402) 403-0001, E-Mail: sales@firstdirectmarketing.com, Web Site: www.firstdirectmarketing.com (23)

Buhrow, Victoria, New York Life Insurance Co/AARP, Tampa, FL. Tel: (813) 288-5500, FAX: (813) 288-5256, Web Site: www.nylaarp.com (15)

Buhrs Americas Inc, Minneapolis, MN. Tel: (763) 557-9100, FAX: (763) 557-9700, Web Site: www.buhrs.com (34)

Buick, Detroit, MI. Tel: (313) 556-5000, (800) 521-7300, FAX: (313) 556-5108, Web Site: www.buick.com (16)

Buijs, Peter, CARE USA, Atlanta, GA. Tel: (404) 681-2552, (800) 422-7385, FAX: (404) 589-2600, E-Mail: info@care.org, Web Site: www.careusa.org (1)

Buisson, Gilles, Domino Amjet Inc, Gurnee, IL. Tel: (847) 244-2501, FAX: (847) 244-1421, Web Site: www.dominoamjet.com (27)

Bulkley Dunton Publishing Group, New York, NY. Tel: (212) 863-1800, FAX: (212) 863-1870, Web Site: www.internationalpaper.com (25)

Bull Dog Media Group Inc, Madison, SD. Tel: (605) 256-9103, Web Site: www.commissionsoup.com (20)

Bull HN Information Systems, Chelmsford, MA. Tel: (978) 294-6000, FAX: (978) 294-7999, Web Site: www.bull.com/us (16)

Bull, Stephanie, The Missoulian, Missoula, MT. Tel: (406) 523-5200, (800) 366-7102, FAX: (406) 523-5221, Web Site: www.missoulian.com (31)

Bulldog Media Group Inc, Madison, SD. Tel: (866) 309-7687, E-Mail: info@bulldogmediagroup.com, Web Site: www.bulldogmediagroup.com (32)

Bullen, Bruce M., Harvard Pilgrim Health Care, Wellesley, MA. Tel: (617) 509-1000, (888) 888-4742, FAX: (617) 509-7590, Web Site: www.harvardpilgrim.org (7)

Bulletin of the Atomic Scientists, Chicago, IL. Tel: (773) 702-6301, FAX: (773) 980-6932, E-Mail: admin@thebulletin.org, Web Site: www.thebulletin.org (17)

Bullis, William, British Columbia Automobile Association, Burnaby, BC Canada. Tel: (604) 268-5000, (800) 564-6222, FAX: (604) 268-5585, Web Site: www.bcaa.com (15)

Bullseye Database Marketing LLC, Tulsa, OK. Tel: (918) 587-1731, FAX: (918) 587-0450, E-Mail: inquiries@bullseyedm.com, Web Site: www.bullseyedm.com (35)

Bullseye Marketing Inc, Canoga Park, CA. Tel: (818) 888-8700, Web Site: www.bullseyeb2b.com (28)

BullsEye Marketing Systems LLC, West Chester, PA. Tel: (484) 356-2240, E-Mail: info@bullseyemarketingsystems.com, Web Site: bullseyemarketingsystems.com (35)

Bulver, Thomas, Heartland America, Chaska, MN. Tel: (952) 361-3640, (800) 229-2901, FAX: (952) 368-3452, E-Mail: info@heartlandamerica.com, Web Site: www.heartlandamerica.com (3)

Bumann, Kelly, Starz Entertainment LLC, Englewood, CO. Tel: (855) 807-2929, Web Site: www.starz.com (16)

Bunch, Ed, B Bunch Co Inc, Phoenix, AZ. Tel: (602) 997-6452, FAX: (602) 997-7266, E-Mail: sales@bbunch.com, Web Site: www.bbunch.com (16)

Bunch, Janet Boutin, Montag & Caldwell Inc, Atlanta, GA. Tel: (404) 836-7100, (800) 458-5868, FAX: (404) 836-7168, Web Site: www.montag.com (14)

Bunch, Max, RobbinsKersten Direct, Richardson, TX. Tel: (800) 222-6070, E-Mail: connect@robbinskersten.com, Web Site: www.robbinskersten.com (1)

Bunchball, Redwood City, CA. Tel: (408) 985-2034, Web Site: www.bunchball.com (32)

Bundies, Todd, Badger Press/Photographics Inc, Kenosha, WI. Tel: (262) 658-1628, (800) 635-9773, FAX: (262) 658-0307 (27)

Bungart, Lutz, The Instrument Workshop, Ashland, OR. Tel: (541) 552-0989, (800) 442-6038, FAX: (541) 488-5846, E-Mail: shop77@fortepiano.com, Web Site: www.fortepiano.com (16)

Bungart, Martha, The Instrument Workshop, Ashland, OR. Tel: (541) 552-0989, (800) 442-6038, FAX: (541) 488-5846, E-Mail: shop77@fortepiano.com, Web Site: www.fortepiano.com (16)

Bunka, Susie, Arctic Trading Co Inc, Churchill, MB Canada. Tel: (204) 675-8804, (800) 665-0431, FAX: (204) 675-2164, E-Mail: atcpenny@mts.net, Web Site: www.arctictradingco.com (6)

Bunker Hill Auctions, Millbrook, IL. Tel: (630) 553-8968, E-Mail: bunkerhillauctions@joimail.com, Web Site: www.bunkerhillauctions.com (6)

Bunker, Steven, United Envelope, Ridgefield, NJ. Tel: (201) 699-5800, (800) 752-4012, FAX: (201) 313-7177, Web Site: www.unitedenvelope.com (26)

BH Bunn Co, Lakeland, FL. Tel: (863) 647-1555, (800) 222-2866, FAX: (863) 686-2866, E-Mail: info@bunntyco.com, Web Site: www.bunntyco.com (34)

Bunn-O-Matic Corp, Springfield, IL. Tel: (217) 529-6601, FAX: (217) 529-6622, E-Mail: bunn@bunn.com, Web Site: www.bunn.com (16)

Bunn, John R., BH Bunn Co, Lakeland, FL. Tel: (863) 647-1555, (800) 222-2866, FAX: (863) 686-2866, E-Mail: info@bunntyco.com, Web Site: www.bunntyco.com (34)

Bunn, Thomas W., Key Bank National Association, Albany, NY. Tel: (518) 434-4871, (800) 539-2968, Web Site: www.keybank.com (14)

Bunning, Ellen, Jeroboam, San Francisco, CA. Tel: (415) 824-8085 cell, E-Mail: jeroboamster@gmail.com (38)

Bunting, Paula, Collector Books & American Quilters Society, Paducah, KY. Tel: (270) 898-6211, (800) 626-5420, FAX: (270) 898-8890, E-Mail: info@collectorbooks.com, Web Site: www.collectorbooks.com (17)

Bunzl Distribution USA, Inc, Saint Louis, MO. Tel: (314) 997-5959, (888) 997-5959, FAX: (314) 997-1405, Web Site: www.bunzldistribution.com (16)

Buonaiuto, Jacqueline, Fulfillment Plus Inc, Holtsville, NY. Tel: (631) 758-8300, FAX: (631) 758-8360, E-Mail: jeff.ehrlich@fulfillmentplusny.com, Web Site: www.fulfillmentplusny.com (28)

Burak, Larry, Warnaco Swimwear Inc, Los Angeles, CA. Tel: (323) 726-1262, FAX: (323) 724-6931, Web Site: www.speedo.com (16)

Burbank, Dawn, Whitman Publishing LLC, Atlanta, GA. Tel: (800) 546-2995, FAX: (256) 246-1116, E-Mail: info@whitmanbooks.com, Web Site: www.whitmanbooks.com (16)

Burberry, New York, NY. Tel: (877) 217-4085, E-Mail: us.customerservice@burberry.com, Web Site: www.burberry.com (2)

Burch, David, Volunteers of America, Alexandria, VA. Tel: (703) 341-5000, (800) 899-0089, FAX: (703) 341-7000, E-Mail: info@voa.org, Web Site: www.voa.org (1)

Burch, Howe, TBC Inc, Baltimore, MD. Tel: (410) 347-7500, FAX: (410) 986-1299, E-Mail: info@tbc.us, Web Site: www.tbc.us (35)

Burch, Jim, East Coast Industrial Equipment & Tire, Jacksonville, FL. Tel: (904) 358-5681, (800) 874-1942, FAX: (904) 354-0888 (34)

Burch, Walter, FMS Direct, Tarzana, CA. Tel: (818) 708-7814, FAX: (818) 708-7842, E-Mail: info@fmsdirect.com, Web Site: www.fmsdirect.com (35)

Burchett, Chet, Reed Exhibitions, Norwalk, CT. Tel: (203) 840-4800, (888) 745-7644, FAX: (203) 840-5805, E-Mail: inquiry@reedexpo.com, Web Site: www.reedexpo.com (16)

Burd, Carolyn, Experience In Software Inc, Berkeley, CA. Tel: (510) 644-0694, (800) 678-7008, FAX: (510) 644-3823, Web Site: www.projectkickstart.com (16)

Burd, Loretta M., CUNA Mutual Group, Madison, WI. Tel: (608) 238-5851, (800) 356-2644, FAX: (608) 231-8839, Web Site: www.cunamutual.com (15)

Burden Sales Co, Lincoln, NE. Tel: (402) 474-4055, (800) 488-3407, FAX: (402) 474-5198, Web Site: www.burdensales.com (9)

Burden, David, Burden Sales Co, Lincoln, NE. Tel: (402) 474-4055, (800) 488-3407, FAX: (402) 474-5198, Web Site: www.burdensales.com (9)

Burden, David, Surplus Center, Lincoln, NE. Tel: (402) 474-4055, (800) 488-3407, FAX: (402) 474-5198, E-Mail: customerservice@surpluscenter.com, Web Site: www.surpluscenter.com (9)

Burden, Tom, TBC Inc, Baltimore, MD. Tel: (410) 347-7500, FAX: (410) 986-1299, E-Mail: info@tbc.us, Web Site: www.tbc.us (35)

Burdette, Dawn, Butler Schein Animal Health, Dublin, OH. Tel: (614) 761-9095, (888) 691-2724, FAX: (888) 329-3861, Web Site: www.butlerschein.com (16)

Burdick, Amy, Valdawn Watch Co, Long Island City, NY. Tel: (201) 807-1110, FAX: (201) 807-0228 (16)

Burdick, James R., Gateway Inc, Irvine, CA. Tel: (949) 471-7000, (800) 369-1409, FAX: (949) 471-7041, Web Site: www.gateway.com (3)

Burdick, Walter, Swag Inc, Wichita, KS. Tel: (316) 685-3811, FAX: (316) 685-4422, E-Mail: swag@cox.net, Web Site: www.swagpromos.com (33)

The Bureau Inc, Stuart, FL. Tel: (772) 283-8850, Web Site: www.bureauinc.com (28)

The Bureau of National Affairs, Inc, Arlington, VA. Tel: (703) 341-3000, (800) 372-1033, FAX: (703) 341-1688, Web Site: www.bna.com (17)

Bureau Van Dijk, New York, NY. Tel: (212) 797-3550, FAX: (212) 797-3555, E-Mail: newyork@bvdinfo.com, Web Site: www.bvdinfo.com (22)

Burek, John, Computer Shopper, New York, NY. Tel: (646) 472-4000, FAX: (646) 472-3912, E-Mail: feedback@computershopper.com, Web Site: www.computershopper.com (31)

Burgdoerfer, Stuart, L Brands Inc, Columbus, OH. Tel: (614) 415-7000, FAX: (614) 415-7440, Web Site: www.lb.com (16)

Burger, Kent, Cooper Communities Inc, Rogers, AR. Tel: (479) 246-6500, (800) 648-6401, FAX: (479) 855-6256, E-Mail: coopernet@ccias.com, Web Site: www.cooper-communities.com (16)

Burger, Nick, Windstar Cruises, Seattle, WA. Tel: (206) 292-9606, (800) 258-SAIL, FAX: (206) 340-0975, E-Mail: info@windstarcruises.com, Web Site: www.windstarcruises.com (19)

Burger, Robert, Robert Burger Illustration, Stockton, NJ. Tel: (609) 397-3737, E-Mail: burgerbobz@aol.com (36)

Burger, Steve, Burger's Ozark Country Cured Hams Inc, California, MO. Tel: (573) 796-4111, (800) 345-5185, FAX: (573) 796-3137, E-Mail: burgers@smokehouse.com, Web Site: www.smokehouse.com (4)

Burger's Ozark Country Cured Hams Inc, California, MO. Tel: (573) 796-4111, (800) 345-5185, FAX: (573) 796-3137, E-Mail: burgers@smokehouse.com, Web Site: www.smokehouse.com (4)

Burgess, Brandon, Ion Media Networks Inc, West Palm Beach, FL. Tel: (561) 659-4122, (800) 646-7296, FAX: (561) 659-4252, Web Site: www.ionmedia.tv (32)

Burgess, Mark, BBF Integrated Solutions, Largo, FL. Tel: (727) 545-8703, (800) 666-8082, Web Site: www.bbfprinting.com (27)

Burgess, Michael, Nightingale-Conant Corp, Niles, IL. Tel: (847) 647-0300, (800) 557-1660, FAX: (847) 647-7145, Web Site: www.nightingale.com (17)

Burgess, Peter S., Symetra Financial, Bellevue, WA. Tel: (425) 256-8000, (800) 426-7355, FAX: (425) 256-5737, Web Site: www.symetra.com (15)

Burghardt, Lance, Photographix, Ann Arbor, MI. Tel: (734) 769-6756, FAX: (734) 476-2068, E-Mail: lkburghardt@comcast.net (37)

Burgoon, Tracey, Disabled American Veterans, Cincinnati, OH. Tel: (859) 441-7300, FAX: (859) 442-2084, E-Mail: feedback@davmail.org, Web Site: www.dav.org (1)

Burk, Doreen Ellen, Avrick Direct Inc, Goleta, CA. Tel: (805) 683-6551, FAX: (805) 683-6553, E-Mail: doreen@avrick.com, Web Site: avrickdirect.com (23)

Burk, Doreen Ellen, HomeData, Goleta, CA. Tel: (805) 683-6551, FAX: (805) 683-6553, E-Mail: doreen@avrick.com, Web Site: avrickdirect.com/homedata (24)

Burkarel, Rev. Msgr Paul J.E., Our Lady of Victory Homes of Charity, Lackawanna, NY. Tel: (716) 828-9648, FAX: (716) 828-9643, E-Mail: rheist@olv-bvs.org, Web Site: www.ourladyofvictory.org (1)

Burke, Allison, Telefonix Inc, Waukegan, IL. Tel: (847) 244-4500, Web Site: www.telefonixinc.com (16)

Burke, Michael, The Flexi Group Inc, Bronx, NY. Tel: (718) 543-8699, (800) 665-8053, FAX: (718) 543-8609, E-Mail: info@flexigroup.com, Web Site: www.flexigroup.com (27)

Burke, Paula, Elderhostel Inc, Lowell, MA. Tel: (978) 323-4291, (800) 454-5678, FAX: (617) 426-2166, Web Site: www.elderhostel.org (1)

Burke, Peter, FLM Graphics Corp, Fairfield, NJ. Tel: (973) 575-9450, E-Mail: info@flmgraphics.com, Web Site: www.flmgraphics.com (16)

Burke, Rory, Palm Coast Data LLC, Palm Coast, FL. Tel: (386) 445-4662, FAX: (386) 445-2728, Web Site: www.palmcoastd.com (28)

Burke, Stephen B., Comcast Corp. Philadelphia, PA. Tel: (215) 665-1700, Web Site: www.comcast.com (32)

Burke, Stephen B., Universal Studios Inc, Universal City, CA. Tel: (818) 777-1000, FAX: (818) 866-3330, Web Site: www.universalstudios.com (3)

Burke, Timothy J., Jones International Ltd, Centennial, CO. Tel: (303) 792-3111, (800) 525-7002, FAX: (303) 784-8508, E-Mail: publicrelations@jones.com, Web Site: www.jones.com (16)

Burke, Tom, TowerData, New York, NY. Tel: (646) 742-1771, FAX: (646) 365-3060, Web Site: www.towerdata.com (32)

Burkett, Jeff, Advanced Direct, Greensboro, NC. Tel: (336) 299-0800, (800) 786-2812, FAX: (336) 299-2619, E-Mail: info@advdirectinc.com, Web Site: www.advdirectinc.com (21)

Burkhardt, Jill, North Shore Animal League America Inc, Port Washington, NY. Tel: (516) 883-7575, Web Site: www.animalleague.org (1)

Burkhart, Megan D., Comerica Inc, Dallas, TX. Tel: (800) 521-1190, FAX: (925) 941-1999, Web Site: www.comerica.com (14)

Burkholder Flint Associates, Columbus, OH. Tel: (614) 228-2425, FAX: (614) 228-0631, E-Mail: easterday@burkholderflint.com, Web Site: www.burkholderflint.com (35)

Burkley Envelope Co, Wahoo, NE. Tel: (402) 443-3010, FAX: (402) 443-4029, E-Mail: info@burkley.com, Web Site: www.burkley.com (26)

Burkley, Robert W., Burkley Envelope Co, Wahoo, NE. Tel: (402) 443-3010, FAX: (402) 443-4029, E-Mail: info@burkley.com, Web Site: www.burkley.com (26)

Burleson, John Eric, KTM Sportmotorcycle USA Inc, Amherst, OH. Tel: (440) 985-3553, FAX: (440) 985-3060, Web Site: www.ktmusa.com (16)

Burley, Mark L., Fidelity Security Life Insurance Co, Kansas City, MO. Tel: (816) 756-1060, (800) 648-8624, FAX: (816) 968-0580, E-Mail: info@fslins.com, Web Site: www.fslins.com (15)

Burley, Rick, ASK, Montgomery, AL. Tel: (334) 387-ASKT, FAX: (334) 387-2759, E-Mail: rburley@asktelemarketing.com, Web Site: www.asktelemarketing.com (29)

Burlington Coat Factory, Burlington, NJ. Tel: (609) 387-7800, FAX: (609) 387-7071, Web Site: www.burlingtoncoatfactory.com (16)

Burlington Industries Inc, Greensboro, NC. Tel: (336) 379-2000, FAX: (336) 379-2498, Web Site: www.burlington.com (16)

Burlington Northern & Santa Fe LLC, Fort Worth, TX. Tel: (817) 878-2000, (800) 795-2673, FAX: (817) 333-7593, Web Site: www.bnsf.com (16)

Burman, Jeff, Guarantee Trust Life Insurance Co, Glenview, IL. Tel: (847) 298-0670, FAX: (847) 298-1215, E-Mail: pr@gtlic.com, Web Site: www.gtlic.com (15)

Burman, Terry, Sterling Jewelers Inc, Akron, OH. Tel: (330) 668-5000, FAX: (330) 668-5052, E-Mail: webmaster@jewels.com, Web Site: www.sterlingjewelers.com (16)

Leo Burnett Worldwide, Chicago, IL. Tel: (312) 220-5959, Web Site: leoburnett.com (35)

Burnett, Terry, Direct Marketing Association of Detroit, Royal Oak, MI. Tel: (248) 478-4888, FAX: (248) 478-6437, E-Mail: dmad@ameritech.net, Web Site: www.dmad.org (40)

Burnham, William, Soundprints, Norwalk, CT. Tel: (203) 846-2274, (800) 228-7839, FAX: (203) 846-1776, E-Mail: soundprints@soundprints.com, Web Site: www.soundprints.com (6)

Burnight, Tom, Graphic Converting Inc, Elmhurst, IL. Tel: (630) 758-4100, (800) 447-1935, FAX: (630) 833-1058, E-Mail: sales@graphicconverting.com, Web Site: www.graphicconverting.com (36)

Burns Inc, Fall River, MA. Tel: (508) 675-0381, (800) 341-2200, FAX: (508) 677-1300, Web Site: www.burnstools.com (16)

Burns, Chris, DWS Investments Service Co, Kansas City, MO. Tel: (800) 543-5776, Web Site: www.dws-investments.com (14)

Burns, David, Magna Publications Inc, Madison, WI. Tel: (608) 246-3590, FAX: (608) 246-3597, Web Site: www.magnapubs.com (17)

Burns, Jeffery M., Burns Inc, Fall River, MA. Tel: (508) 675-0381, (800) 341-2200, FAX: (508) 677-1300, Web Site: www.burnstools.com (16)

Burns, Josh, Resource Publications Inc, San Jose, CA. Tel: (408) 286-8505, (888) 273-7782, FAX: (408) 287-8748, E-Mail: info@rpinet.com, Web Site: www.rpinet.com (17)

Burns, Kathryn, Heartland Boating Magazine, Saint Louis, MO. Tel: (314) 241-4310, (800) 366-9630, FAX: (314) 241-4207, E-Mail: info@heartlandboating.com, Web Site: www.heartlandboating.com (17)

Burns, Kevin, Intermap Technologies, Englewood, CO. Tel: (303) 708-0955, FAX: (303) 708-0952, E-Mail: info@intermap.com, Web Site: www.intermap.com (32)

Burns, Mary, Barbour Publishing Inc, Uhrichsville, OH. Tel: (740) 922-6045, FAX: (740) 922-5948, (800) 220-5948, E-Mail: info@barbourbooks.com, Web Site: www.barbourbooks.com (17)

Burns, Michael, Lionsgate Entertainment Inc, New York, NY, Tel: (212) 577-2400, FAX: (212) 962-2872, Web Site: www.lionsgate.com (32)

Burns, Michael, Lionsgate Television Corp, Santa Monica, CA. Tel: (310) 449-9200, FAX: (310) 255-3870, Web Site: www.lionsgate.com (16)

Burns, Sr. John M., Burns Inc, Fall River, MA. Tel: (508) 675-0381, (800) 341-2200, FAX: (508) 677-1300, Web Site: www.burnstools.com (16)

Burns, Steve, Nahan Printing Inc, Saint Cloud, MN. Tel: (320) 251-7611, E-Mail: info@nahan.com, Web Site: www.nahan.com (27)

Burns, Tom, Allianz Life Insurance Co of North America, Minneapolis, MN. Tel: (763) 765-6500, (800) 950-5872, Web Site: www.allianzlife.com (15)

Burns, Ursula M. Burns M., Xerox Services, Dallas, TX. Tel: (214) 841-6111, (800) 275-9376, Web Site: www.acs-inc.com (22)

Burns, Ursula M., Xerox Corp, Norwalk, CT. Tel: (800) 275-9376, Web Site: www.xerox.com (16)

Burns, William, Resource Publications Inc, San Jose, CA. Tel: (408) 286-8505, (888) 273-7782, FAX: (408) 287-8748, E-Mail: info@rpinet.com, Web Site: www.rpinet.com (17)

W Atlee Burpee Co, Warminster, PA. Tel: (215) 674-4900, (800) 888-1447, FAX: (215) 674-4170, Web Site: www.burpee.com (8)

Burr, John, Visual Reference Publications, New York, NY. Tel: (212) 279-7000, (800) 251-4545, FAX: (212) 279-7014 (17)

DV Burrell Seed Growers Co, Rocky Ford, CO. Tel: (719) 254-3318, (844) 254-7333, FAX: (719) 254-3319, E-Mail: burrellseeds@gmail.com, Web Site: www.burrellseeds.us (8)

Burrell, Bill, DV Burrell Seed Growers Co, Rocky Ford, CO. Tel: (719) 254-3318, (844) 254-7333, FAX: (719) 254-3319, E-Mail: burrellseeds@gmail.com, Web Site: www.burrellseeds.us (8)

Burrell, Chet, Carefirst Blue Cross Blue Shield, Washington, DC. Tel: (202) 479-8000, FAX: (301) 470-8049, Web Site: www.carefirst.com (15)

The Burris Agency Inc, Greensboro, NC. Tel: (336) 378-1221, FAX: (336) 378-1221, E-Mail: info@burris.com, Web Site: www.burris.com (35)

Burris, Jack, The Burris Agency Inc, Greensboro, NC. Tel: (336) 378-1221, FAX: (336) 378-1221, E-Mail: info@burris.com, Web Site: www.burris.com (35)

Burt, Chris, Belvoir Media Group LLC, Norwalk, CT. Tel: (203) 857-3100, FAX: (203) 857-3103, E-Mail: customer_service@belvoir.com, Web Site: www.belvoir.com (17)

Burtch Works LLC, Evanston, IL. Tel: (847) 440-8550, FAX: (847) 440-8556, Web Site: www.burtchworks.com (20)

Burton, Jeremy, EMC Corp, Hopkinton, MA. Tel: (888) 438-3622, Web Site: www.emc.com (17)

Burton, Jr. Rob G., Cenveo Inc, Stamford, CT. Tel: (410) 633-4200, (800) 638-2850, FAX: (410) 633-1202, Web Site: www.cenveo.com (27)

Burton, Mike, Cenveo Inc, Stamford, CT. Tel: (410) 633-4200, (800) 638-2850, FAX: (410) 633-1202, Web Site: www.cenveo.com (27)

Burton, Nigel B., Colgate-Palmolive Co, New York, NY. Tel: (212) 310-2000, (800) 468-6502, FAX: (212) 310-2475, Web Site: www.colgate.com (16)

Burton, Sr. Robert G., Cenveo Inc, Stamford, CT. Tel: (410) 633-4200, (800) 638-2850, FAX: (410) 633-1202, Web Site: www.cenveo.com (27)

Busby, Roy, University of North Texas, Denton, TX. Tel: (940) 565-2000, Web Site: www.unt.edu (1)

Busby, Scott, V12 Data, Wesley Chapel, FL. Tel: (813) 960-7800, FAX: (813) 960-7811, E-Mail: info@v12data.com, Web Site: www.v12data.com (22)

Buscaglia, Joseph S., ESL Federal Credit Union, Rochester, NY. Tel: (585) 336-1000, (800) 848-2265, FAX: (585) 336-1138, Web Site: www.esl.org (14)

Busch, John, Lorman Education Services, Eau Claire, WI. Tel: (715) 833-3940 (1)

Busch, Katrina, Roberts Communications Inc, Rochester, NY. Tel: (716) 325-6000, FAX: (716) 325-6001, Web Site: www.robertscomm.com (35)

Busch, Robert, All-State Legal, Cranford, NJ. Tel: (908) 272-0800, (800) 222-0510, FAX: (800) 634-5184, E-Mail: sjacobs@aslegal.com, Web Site: www.aslegal.com (16)

Bush, Martha, SIGMA Marketing Group LLC, Rochester, NY. Tel: (585) 473-7300, (888) 277-9837, FAX: (585) 473-0332, E-Mail: mbush@sigmamarketing.com, Web Site: www.sigmamarketing.com; www.jthgearanalytics.com (Blog) (20)

Bush, Nora, Specialists Marketing Services Inc, Hasbrouck Heights, NJ. Tel: (201) 865-5800, FAX: (201) 288-4295, E-Mail: info@sms-inc.com, Web Site: www.sms-inc.com (23)

Bushee, III Richard E., MSP Inc, Freedom, PA. Tel: (724) 774-3244, (800) 876-3211, FAX: (724) 774-6996, E-Mail: info@msp-pgh.com, Web Site: www.msp-pgh.com (21)

Bushee, Steven, TrueSense Marketing, Freedom, PA. Tel: (877) 878-6584, Web Site: www.truesense.com (35)

Bushee, Ward H., San Francisco Chronicle, San Francisco, CA. Tel: (415) 777-1111, FAX: (415) 536-5178, Web Site: www.sfgate.com (17)

Bushkie, Scott, Cornerstone Business Services Inc, Green Bay, WI. Tel: (920) 436-9890, FAX: (920) 436-9894, E-Mail: sbushkie@cornerstone-business.com, Web Site: www.cornerstone-business.com (14)

Bushnel, A.C., General Vitamin Corp, Raleigh, NC. Tel: (919) 929-5785, (800) 323-8432, FAX: (919) 929-2458, E-Mail: support@generalvitamin.com, Web Site: www.generalvitamin.com (16)

Bushnell Corporation, Overland Park, KS. Tel: (913) 752-3400, (800) 423-3537, FAX: (913) 752-3561, Web Site: www.bushnell.com (11)

Bushnell Outdoor Products, Overland Park, KS. Tel: (913) 752-3400, (800) 423-3537, FAX: (913) 752-3550, Web Site: www.bushnell.com (16)

Business Automation Systems Inc, Nashville, TN. Tel: (615) 329-4585, FAX: (615) 320-0206, Web Site: www.bas-solutions.com (16)

Business Development Solutions Inc, Cherry Hill, NJ. Tel: (856) 787-1500, E-Mail: info@hdsdatabase.com, Web Site: www.bdsdatabase.com (22)

Business Direct Marketing Associates Inc, Cumming, GA. Tel: (770) 888-8300, FAX: (770) 888-6482, E-Mail: joes@bdmainc.com, Web Site: www.bdmainc.com (35)

Business Extension Bureau, Houston, TX. Tel: (713) 528-5568, (800) 969-5568, FAX: (713) 528-1648, E-Mail: ronr@bebtexas.com, Web Site: bebtexas.com (23)

Business Graphics Inc, Elmhurst, IL. Tel: (815) 338-8222, (800) 435-4874, FAX: (815) 338-2652, E-Mail: busgraph@mc.net, Web Site: www.businessgraphics.com (16)

Business Marketing Association, Naperville, IL. Tel: (630) 544-5054, FAX: (630) 544-5055, E-Mail: info@marketing.org, Web Site: www.marketing.org (40)

Business Objects Americas, Inc, San Jose, CA. Tel: (408) 953-6000, FAX: (408) 953-6001, Web Site: www.businessobjects.com (22)

Business Planners & Consultants Inc, New York, NY. Tel: (212) 972-1970, FAX: (212) 972-1126 (15)

Business Promotion Ideas Inc, Tenafly, NJ. Tel: (201) 569-9777, FAX: (201) 569-2642, E-Mail: bpi@buspromoideas.com, Web Site: www.buspromoideas.com (33)

Business Publishers Inc, Durham, NC. Tel: (800) 223-8720, FAX: (800) 508-2592, E-Mail: custserv@bpinews.com, Web Site: www.bpinews.com (17)

Business Services Network, San Francisco, CA. Tel: (415) 282-8161, FAX: (415) 282-8176, E-Mail: sales@bsnc.com, Web Site: www.bsnc.com (28)

Business Technologies, Dubuque, IA. Tel: (563) 556-7994, (800) 451-0399, FAX: (563) 556-2512 (34)

BusinessCreator Inc, Allentown, PA. Tel: (610) 437-8822, (855) 943-8736, FAX: (484) 709-1851, E-Mail: marketing@businesscreatorplus.com, Web Site: www.businesscreatorplus.com (35)

BusinessOnline, San Diego, CA. Tel: (619) 699-0767, Web Site: www.businessol.com (16)

Busse, Erik, American Family Insurance Group, Madison, WI. Tel: (608) 249-2111, FAX: (608) 243-6525, E-Mail: akin1@amfam.com, Web Site: www.amfam.com (15)

Bussen, Terrance M., Putnam Group Ltd, Trumbull, CT. Tel: (203) 452-7270, FAX: (203) 268-8071, E-Mail: info@putnamgroup.net, Web Site: putnamgroup.net (33)

Bussert, Rosemary, Datamart Direct Inc, Bloomingdale, IL. Tel: (630) 307-7100, FAX: (630) 307-8059, E-Mail: info@datamartdirect.com, Web Site: www.datamartdirect.com (27)

Bustillo, James, Blue Cross Blue Shield of Louisiana, Baton Rouge, LA. Tel: (225) 295-3307, (800) 599-2583, FAX: (225) 295-2054, E-Mail: help@bcbsla.com, Web Site: www.bcbsla.com (15)

Butcher, Andy, Strang Communications Co, Lake Mary, FL. Tel: (407) 333-0600, FAX: (407) 333-7100, E-Mail: magcustsvc@strang.com, Web Site: www.strang.com (17)

Butcher, Jane, Mother Jones Magazine, San Francisco, CA. Tel: (415) 321-1700, Web Site: www.motherjones.com (17)

Butcher, Quentin, Vietnam Veterans of America, Silver Spring, MD. Tel: (301) 585-4000, (800) 882-1316, FAX: (301) 585-0519, Web Site: www.vva.org (1)

Butera, Jay, Cedar Fresh Products, Coral Gables, FL. Tel: (305) 870-9390, Web Site: www.cedarfresh.com (16)

Buthman, Mark A., Kimberly-Clark Corp, Neenah, WI. Tel: (920) 721-2000, (888) 525-8388, FAX: (920) 721-7722, Web Site: www.kimberly-clark.com (16)

Butler Distributing Co, Kenilworth, NJ. Tel: (908) 241-3060, FAX: (908) 298-9248, E-Mail: bwprinting@worldnet.att.net, Web Site: www.bwprinting.com (3)

Butler Schein Animal Health, Dublin, OH. Tel: (614) 761-9095, (888) 691-2724, FAX: (888) 329-3861, Web Site: www.butlerschein.com (16)

Butler Specialty Co, Chicago, IL. Tel: (773) 221-1200, (800) 799-2857, FAX: (773) 221-5892, Web Site: www.butlerspecialty.net (16)

Butler Till Media Services, Rochester, NY. Tel: (855) 472-5100, FAX: (855) 274-5199, Web Site: www.butlertill.com (31)

Butler, Bob, Merchant E-Solutions, Redwood City, CA. Tel: (509) 232-5639, (866) 663-6132, FAX: (509) 232-5625, E-Mail: help@merchante-solutions.com, Web Site: www.merchante-solutions.com (14)

Butler, C. Marion, Premera Blue Cross, Spokane, WA. Tel: (425) 670-4000, (800) 422-0032, FAX: (425) 670-5853, Web Site: www.premera.com (15)

Butler, David, Consumers Union, Yonkers, NY. Tel: (914) 378-2000, FAX: (914) 378-2906, Web Site: www.consumersunion.org (17)

Butler, David, San Jose Mercury News, San Jose, CA. Tel: (408) 920-5000, FAX: (408) 288-8060, Web Site: www.mercurynews.com (17)

Butler, Doug, The Staplex Co, Brooklyn, NY. Tel: (718) 768-3333, (800) 221-0822, FAX: (718) 965-0750, E-Mail: info@staplex.com, Web Site: www.staplex.com (34)

Butler, Gary L., Butler Distributing Co, Kenilworth, NJ. Tel: (908) 241-3060, FAX: (908) 298-9248, E-Mail: bwprinting@worldnet.att.net, Web Site: www.bwprinting.com (3)

Butler, Gary P., Boy Scouts of America/National Supply Group, Charlotte, NC. Tel: (800) 323-0736, FAX: (704) 588-5822, E-Mail: customerservice@scoutstuff.org, Web Site: www.scoutstuff.org (1)

Butler, Jason, Goldleaf Data Inc, Suwanee, GA. Tel: (888) 936-3282, E-Mail: info@goldleafdata.com, Web Site: goldleafdata.com (23)

Butler, John M., Consumer's Energy, Jackson, MI. Tel: (517) 788-0550, (800) 805-0490, FAX: (517) 788-1859, E-Mail: businesscenter@consumerenergy.com, Web Site: www.consumersenergy.com (16)

Butler, Kathleen, The Stone Group Inc, Pleasanton, CA. Tel: (925) 846-4432, FAX: (925) 846-2767, E-Mail: kbutler@stonegroupinc.com, Web Site: stonegroupinc.com (35)

Butler, Kim, AAVIM, Winterville, GA. Tel: (706) 742-5355, (800) 228-4689, FAX: (706) 742-7005, E-Mail: gary@aavim.com, Web Site: www.aavim.com (31)

Butler, Steven, Ideagroup Mail Service, Saint Paul, MN. Tel: (651) 490-2903, FAX: (651) 490-0728, E-Mail: ideagroup@visi.com (28)

H E Butt Grocery Co, San Antonio, TX. Tel: (210) 938-8357, (800) 432-3113, FAX: (210) 938-7511, Web Site: www.heb.com (16)

Butt, Charles, H E Butt Grocery Co, San Antonio, TX. Tel: (210) 938-8357, (800) 432-3113, FAX: (210) 938-7511, Web Site: www.heb.com (16)

Butta, Thomas V., Superstock Inc, Jacksonville, FL. Tel: (904) 565-0066, (800) 828-4545, FAX: (904) 641-4480, E-Mail: yourfriends@superstock.com, Web Site: www.superstockimages.com (38)

Button, Darryl D., Transamerica Life Insurance Co, Cedar Rapids, IA. Tel: (319) 398-8511, (800) 558-9011, FAX: (319) 369-2825, Web Site: www.transamerica.com (15)

Butts, Jim, C H Robinson Worldwide Inc, Eden Prairie, MN. Tel: (952) 937-8500, FAX: (952) 937-6740, E-Mail: info@chrobinson.com, Web Site: www.chrobinson.com (16)

Butwinick, Rich, Marketing Agencies Association Worldwide, Edina, MN. Tel: (952) 922-0130, FAX: (203) 969-1499, E-Mail: keith.mccracker@maaw. org, Web Site: www.maaw.org (40)

Butz, Theodore H., FMC Corp, Philadelphia, PA. Tel: (215) 299-6000, FAX: (215) 299-5998, Web Site: www.fmc.com (16)

Buxton, Tom, cbsi, Fort Worth, TX. Tel: (817) 332-3681, FAX: (817) 332-3686, Web Site: www. buxtonco.com (30)

BuyFilters.com LLC, Silverhill, AL. Tel: (866) 863-1262, E-Mail: customerservice@buyfilters.com, Web Site: www.buyfilters.com (5)

BUYSEASONS Inc, New Berlin, WI. Tel: (262) 901-2000, FAX: (262) 901-2315, Web Site: www. buyseasons.com (5)

Buzzeo, Diane, Ability Commerce, Delray Beach, FL. Tel: (561) 330-3151, Web Site: www. abilitycommerce.com (20)

Byen, Brad, Marketing Agencies Association World-wide, Edina, MN. Tel: (952) 922-0130, FAX: (203) 969-1499, E-Mail: keith.mccracker@maaw.org, Web Site: www.maaw.org (40)

Byerly, Tony, Diebold Inc, North Canton, OH. Tel: (330) 490-4000, (800) DIEBOLD, Web Site: www. diebold.com (16)

Byers, Sharon, American Cancer Society, Atlanta, GA. Tel: (404) 320-3333, (800) ACS-2345, FAX: (404) 329-5787, Web Site: www.cancer.org (1)

Byham, William C., Development Dimensions Interna-tional, Bridgeville, PA. Tel: (412) 257-0600, (800) 933-4463, FAX: (412) 220-2942, E-Mail: info@ddiworld.com, Web Site: www.ddiworld.com (16)

Byington, Melissa, CHG, Salt Lake City, UT. Tel: (866) 615-5536, (800) 453-3030, Web Site: www. comphealth.com (7)

Bylsma, Greg, Herman Miller Inc, Zeeland, MI. Tel: (616) 654-3000, FAX: (616) 654-5234, E-Mail: investor@hermanmiller.com, Web Site: www. hermanmiller.com (16)

Bylsma, PhD Wayne H, American College of Physi-cians, Philadelphia, PA. Tel: (215) 351-2600, (800) 523-1546, FAX: (215) 351-2686, Web Site: www. acponline.org (17)

Byndon, Leah, American Speech-Language-Hearing Association, Rockville, MD. Tel: (301) 897-5700, (800) 638-8255, FAX: (301) 296-8580, E-Mail: productsales@asha.org, Web Site: www.asha.org (1)

ByOwner.com Inc, Boca Raton, FL. Tel: (800) BY-OWNER, Web Site: www.byowner.com (35)

Byrne, Jane, Bale Co, Providence, RI. Tel: (800) 822-5350, FAX: (401) 831-5500, Web Site: www.bale. com (16)

Byron Plantation, Vidalia, GA. Tel: (800) 356-0171, FAX: (912) 538-8043, E-Mail: greenlinebyron@bellsouth.net, Web Site: www.byronplantation.com (4)

Byrum & Fleming, San Anselmo, CA. Tel: (415) 457-1700, (800) 850-1711, E-Mail: hilary@byrumfleming.com, Web Site: www.byrumfleming. com (23)

Byun, Hayrim, New York Easter Seal Society, New York, NY. Tel: (212) 220-2290, FAX: (212) 695-4807, Web Site: ny.easterseals.com (1)

C

C&H Distributors LLC, Milwaukee, WI. Tel: (414) 443-1700, (888) 316-2223, FAX: (414) 443-9213, E-Mail: customerservice@chdist.com, Web Site: www.chdist.com (9)

C & J Clark America Inc, Newton Upper Falls, MA. Tel: (617) 964-1222, (800) 925-4315, FAX: (617) 243-4213, Web Site: www.clarks.com (16)

C&S Sales Inc, Wheeling, IL. Tel: (847) 541-0710, (800) 292-7711, FAX: (847) 541-9904, E-Mail: sales@cs-sales.com, Web Site: www.cs_sales.com (9)

C&T Bridge Supplies, Los Alamitos, CA. Tel: (562) 598-7010, (800) 525-4718, FAX: (562) 430-8309, E-Mail: tedinlosal@aol.com (11)

C-Suite Communications, Sarasota, FL. Tel: (941) 365-2710, E-Mail: info@c-suitecomms.com, Web Site: www.c-suitecomms.com (35)

(C) Systems LLC, Edison, NJ. Tel: (732) 548-6100, FAX: (732) 548-3883, Web Site: www.csystemsllc. net (22)

C2G, Moraine, OH. Tel: (937) 224-8646, (800) 506-9607, FAX: (937) 496-2666, (800) 331-2841, Web Site: www.cablestogo.com (3)

CA Inc, Islandia, NY. Tel: (800) 225-5224, FAX: (631) 342-3300, E-Mail: info@ca.com, Web Site: www. ca.com (16)

CAA Auto Club & Travel Agency Inc, Thornhill, ON Canada. Tel: (905) 371-3000, (866) 988-, FAX: (905) 371-3101, E-Mail: membership@caasco.ca, Web Site: www.central.on.caa.ca (1)

CACI International Inc, Arlington, VA. Tel: (703) 841-7800, FAX: (703) 841-7882, Web Site: www.caci. com (22)

CAIG Laboratories Inc, Poway, CA. Tel: (858) 486-8388, FAX: (858) 486-8398, E-Mail: caig123@caig. com, Web Site: www.caig.com (9)

CAM Commerce Solutions, Fountain Valley, CA. Tel: (714) 241-9241, FAX: (714) 241-9893, Web Site: www.camcommerce.com (22)

CAS Inc, Omaha, NE. Tel: (402) 964-9998, (866) 461-4693, FAX: (402) 963-2103, E-Mail: sales@cas-online.com, Web Site: www.cas-online.com (23)

CBSI, Harrison, NY. Tel: (914) 381-5353, Web Site: www.cbsiservices.com (30)

CBT Direct, Tarpon Springs, FL. Tel: (727) 724-8994, (877) 872-4646, FAX: (727) 797-9143, Web Site: www.cbtdirect.com (16)

CCA Global Partners, Manchester, NH. Tel: (603) 626-0333, Web Site: www.ccaglobal.com (16)

CCC of America, Irving, TX. Tel: (214) 206-3130, (800) 935-2222, FAX: (214) 206-3134, Web Site: www.cccofamerica.com (16)

CCG Marketing Solutions, West Caldwell, NJ. Tel: (973) 808-0009, (866) 902-2807, FAX: (973) 808-9740, E-Mail: info@corpcomm.com, Web Site: home.corpcomm.com (21)

CCH Inc, Riverwoods, IL. Tel: (847) 267-7000, (888) 224-7377, Web Site: www.cchgroup.com (17)

CCI Digital, Burbank, CA. Tel: (818) 562-6300, FAX: (818) 562-8222, E-Mail: info@ccidigital.com, Web Site: www.ccidigital.com (32)

CCI Solutions, Olympia, WA. Tel: (360) 943-5378, (800) 426-8664, FAX: (360) 754-1566, (800) 339-TAPE, E-Mail: info@ccisolutions.com, Web Site: www.ccisolutions.com (16)

CCIM Institute, Chicago, IL. Tel: (312) 321-4460, (800) 621-7027, FAX: (312) 321-4530, Web Site: www. ccim.com (1)

CCL Label, Cold Spring, KY. Tel: (859) 781-6161, (800) 422-6633, FAX: (859) 781-6339 (27)

CCMR Global Marketing, Mill Valley, CA. Tel: (415) 847-1239, E-Mail: globalmarketing1@aol.com, Web Site: www.gotoccmr.com (35)

CD Universe, Wallingford, CT. Tel: (203) 294-1648, (800) 231-7937, FAX: (203) 294-0391, Web Site: www.cduniverse.com (16)

CDI Network Inc, Naperville, IL. Tel: (708) 409-8585, FAX: (708) 409-8589, Web Site: www.cdinet.biz (27)

CDMC/Carefree Direct Marketing Corp, Carefree, AZ. Tel: (480) 488-4227, FAX: (480) 488-2841 (20)

CDMI Inc, Huntington Beach, CA. Tel: (714) 969-4064 (1)

CDMO Inc, Deer Park, NY. Tel: (631) 242-8820, FAX: (631) 242-5761, E-Mail: cdsales@cdmo.com, Web Site: www.cdmo.com (16)

CDR Fundraising Group, Bowie, MD. Tel: (301) 858-1500, FAX: (301) 858-0107, Web Site: www.cdr-nfl.com (1)

CDS Global, Des Moines, IA. Tel: (515) 246-6837, FAX: (515) 246-6687, E-Mail: dluther@cdsfulfillment.com, Web Site: www.cdsglobal.com (22)

CDW Corp, Vernon Hills, IL. Tel: (847) 465-6000, (847) 371-6090, Web Site: www.cdw.com (16)

CGT Marketing LLC, Amityville, NY. Tel: (631) 842-4600, E-Mail: info@cgtmarketing.com, Web Site: www.cgtmarketing.com (35)

CHG, Salt Lake City, UT. Tel: (866) 615-5536, (800) 453-3030, Web Site: www.comphealth.com (7)

CIT, Livingston, NJ. Tel: (973) 740-5000, FAX: (973) 740-5383, Web Site: www.cit.com (14)

CJ Hummul Co, Nescopeck, PA. Tel: (570) 752-0936, (800) 762-0235, FAX: (570) 752-0938, E-Mail: mail@hummul.com, Web Site: www.hummul.com (11)

CM Consulting Services, Marshfield, MA. Tel: (781) 749-5000, FAX: (801) 749-5009, E-Mail: cmcalpine3@gmail.com (27)

CMA Awards, Don Mills, ON Canada. Tel: (416) 391-2362, FAX: (416) 441-4062, E-Mail: info@the-cma. org, Web Site: www.the-cma.org/awards (42)

CMA Events & Education, Don Mills, ON Canada. Tel: (416) 391-2362, FAX: (416) 441-4062, E-Mail: info@the-cma.org, Web Site: www.the-cma.org (42)

CMEinfo.com, Birmingham, AL. Tel: (205) 991-9188, (800) 284-8433, FAX: (800) 284-5964, Web Site: www.cmeinfo.com (16)

CMI Direct, Pasadena, CA. Tel: (951) 300-1700, FAX: (866) 723-5433, Web Site: www.cmidirect.net (15)

CMMC Market Research, Mount Freedom, NJ. Tel: (973) 989-0229, FAX: (973) 366-1185, E-Mail: dmmp@cmmcinc.com, Web Site: www.cmmcinc. com (30)

CMS Inc, Winston Salem, NC. Tel: (336) 631-2500, FAX: (336) 631-2903, Web Site: www. promotionslogistics.com (14)

CMS LLC, Reston, VA. Tel: (703) 258-0000, Web Site: www.craveronline.com (1)

CNA, Chicago, IL. Tel: (312) 822-5000, (800) 262-2000, E-Mail: cna_help@cna.com, Web Site: www. cna.com (15)

CNBC, Englewood Cliffs, NJ. Tel: (201) 735-2622, FAX: (201) 735-3200, Web Site: www.cnbc.com (32)

CNY Awards & Apparel Inc, New Hartford, NY. Tel: (315) 733-0931, FAX: (800) 732-3617, Web Site: www.cnyapprel.com (5)

COSE, Cleveland, OH. Tel: (216) 592-2222, (866) 553-5427, E-Mail: memberservices@cose.org, Web Site: www.cose.org (1)

CP Travel, Boston, MA. Tel: (617) 521-5400, Web Site: travel.connellypartners.com (35)

CPI Card Group, Littleton, CO. Tel: (303) 973-9311, FAX: (303) 973-8420, E-Mail: mbarber@cpicardgroup.com, Web Site: www.cpicardgroup. com (27)

CPM Delta 1, Inc, Dallas, TX. Tel: (214) 349-6886, (800) 627-0252, FAX: (214) 503-1557, Web Site: www.cpmdelta1.com (11)

CPO Direct Inc, Lake Forest, IL. Tel: (847) 735-7365, FAX: (847) 735-9825, E-Mail: ngoldring@cpodirect.com, Web Site: www.cpodirect.com (35)

The CPW Group, Ronkonkoma, NY. Tel: (888) 641-7901 (28)

CRB, Chicago, IL. Tel: (312) 554-8456, (800) 621-5271, FAX: (312) 939-4135, E-Mail: info@crbtrader.com, Web Site: www.crbtrader.com (17)

CRC Data Systems, Long Island City, NY. Tel: (718) 729-2622, E-Mail: jrafael@opinionaccess.com, Web Site: www.opinionaccess.com (22)

CRC Public Relations, Alexandria, VA. Tel: (703) 683-5004, FAX: (703) 683-1703, E-Mail: crc@crcpublicrelations.com, Web Site: www.crcpublicrelations.com (35)

CRK Computer Services, Bloomfield Hills, MI. Tel: (248) 569-3050, FAX: (248) 569-5259, E-Mail: information@crkusa.com, Web Site: www.crkusa.com (22)

CRM Learning, Carlsbad, CA. Tel: (760) 431-9800, (800) 421-0833, FAX: (760) 931-5792, E-Mail: sales@crmlearning.com, Web Site: www.crmlearning.com (16)

CRN International Inc, Hamden, CT. Tel: (203) 288-2002, FAX: (203) 281-3291, E-Mail: info@crnradio.com, Web Site: www.crnradio.com (32)

CRW Graphics, Pennsauken, NJ. Tel: (856) 662-9111, (800) 820-3000, FAX: (856) 665-1789, E-Mail: service@crwgraphics.com, Web Site: www.crwgraphics.com (27)

CSE Inc, New Berlin, WI. Tel: (262) 786-8400, (800) 999-0001, FAX: (262) 796-2089, E-Mail: info@csepromo.com, Web Site: www.topideas.cseideas.com (33)

CSG Interactive Messaging, Omaha, NE. Tel: (402) 398-4100, (800) 888-3151, FAX: (402) 398-4000, Web Site: www.prairiesys.com (29)

CSI, Conklin, NY. Tel: (607) 775-7905, Web Site: www.cleanersupply.com (16)

CSM Inc, Tucker, GA. Tel: (404) 892-2626, (800) 849-6788, FAX: (404) 589-9779, E-Mail: info@csmresearch.com, Web Site: www.csmresearch.com (30)

CSPI/Nutrition Action Health Letter, Washington, DC. Tel: (202) 332-9110, FAX: (202) 265-4954, E-Mail: cspi@cspinet.org, Web Site: www.cspinet.org (17)

CSS Direct, Elkhorn, NE. Tel: (402) 359-1515, FAX: (402) 359-1516, E-Mail: custserv@cssdirect.com, Web Site: www.cssdirect.com (29)

CTA Inc, Fenton, MO. Tel: (636) 305-3100, (800) 999-1874, FAX: (800) 315-8713, Web Site: www.ctainc.com (5)

CTB/McGraw-Hill LLC, Monterey, CA. Tel: (800) 538-9547, FAX: (800) 282-0266, E-Mail: customer_service_ind@ctb.com, Web Site: www.ctb.com (16)

CTC Corp, Bennington, VT. Tel: (802) 442-6371, FAX: (802) 442-8526 (16)

CTC Teleservices, De Kalb, IL. Tel: (815) 748-4200, FAX: (630) 773-4765, Web Site: www.ctcteleservices.com (29)

CTRAC Information Solutions, Strongsville, OH. Tel: (440) 572-1000, FAX: (440) 572-3330, E-Mail: ctrac@ctrac.com, Web Site: www.ctrac.com (22)

CUES Events, Training & Education, Madison, WI. Tel: (608) 271-2664, (800) 252-2664, FAX: (608) 271-2303, E-Mail: cues@cues.org, Web Site: www.cues.org (42)

CVS Caremark, Woonsocket, RI. Tel: (401) 765-1500, FAX: (401) 769-4488, Web Site: www.cvs.com (7)

CVT Production Inc, Granger, IN. Tel: (574) 247-0647, Web Site: www.destinationfitness.com (16)

CWC Inventories Inc, Saint Louis, MO. Tel: (314) 739-1311 (13)

CX&B United Corp, Harbor City, CA. Tel: (310) 530-2102, (800) 292-8258, FAX: (310) 530-2513, E-Mail: sales@cxbunited.com, Web Site: www.cxbunited.com (33)

CYRO Industries, Parsippany, NJ. Tel: (973) 541-8000, (800) 631-5384, FAX: (973) 442-6117, (973) 442-6135, Web Site: www.cyro.com (16)

Caballero, Tony, Westlake Plastics Co, Lenni, PA. Tel: (610) 459-1000, (800) 999-1700, FAX: (610) 459-1084, Web Site: www.westlakeplastics.com (16)

Cabeen, Thomas, FPS Marketing Communications, Milford, CT. Tel: (203) 783-1940, FAX: (203) 685-1940, E-Mail: info@fpsmarketing.com, Web Site: www.fpsmarketing.com (35)

Cabela, James, Cabela's Inc, Sidney, NE. Tel: (308) 254-5505, (800) 237-4444, FAX: (308) 254-4800, Web Site: www.cabelas.com (11)

Cabela, Richard, Cabela's Inc, Sidney, NE. Tel: (308) 254-5505, (800) 237-4444, FAX: (308) 254-4800, Web Site: www.cabelas.com (11)

Cabela's Inc, Sidney, NE. Tel: (308) 254-5505, (800) 237-4444, FAX: (308) 254-4800, Web Site: www.cabelas.com (11)

Cable Car Clothiers/Robert Kirk Ltd, San Francisco, CA. Tel: (415) 397-4740, FAX: (415) 616-8998, E-Mail: info@cablecarclothiers.com, Web Site: www.cablecarclothiers.com (2)

Cable Connection, Fremont, CA. Tel: (510) 249-9000, E-Mail: cables4u@cable-connection.com, Web Site: www.cable-connection.com (3)

Cable Direct Marketing Inc, Montville, NJ. Tel: (973) 244-0010, FAX: (973) 244-0302, E-Mail: cabledm@aol.com (31)

Cable Shopping Network, Scottsdale, AZ. Tel: (480) 624-4446, Web Site: www.shopcsntv.com (16)

Cable, Philip E., American Science & Surplus, Niles, IL. Tel: (847) 647-0020, (888) SCI-PLUS, FAX: (847) 647-5010, E-Mail: info@sciplus.com, Web Site: www.sciplus.com (9)

Cablevision Systems Corp, Bethpage, NY. Tel: (516) 803-2300, FAX: (516) 803-3134, Web Site: www.cablevision.com (16)

Cablexpress Technologies, Syracuse, NY. Tel: (315) 476-3000, (800) 913-9467, FAX: (315) 455-1800, E-Mail: info@cablexpress.com, Web Site: www.CXTec.com (10)

Cabral, Jr Robert M., Americraft - The Gift Brokers Inc, Wendell, MA. Tel: (978) 544-7330, (800) 866-2723, FAX: (978) 544-2771, E-Mail: info@americraft.us, Web Site: www.americraft.us (16)

Caccavale, Michael, Pluris Inc, Framingham, MA. Tel: (508) 663-1100, FAX: (508) 663-1060, E-Mail: info@plurismarketing.com, Web Site: www.plurismarketing.com (22)

Caccini, Gianpaolo, CertainTeed Corp, Valley Forge, PA. Tel: (610) 341-7000/7739, (800) 233-8990, FAX: (610) 341-7777, Web Site: www.certainteed.com (16)

Cacioppo, Chris, Emfluence, Kansas City, MO. Tel: (816) 472-4455, (877) 81-EMAIL, FAX: (816) 472-8855, E-Mail: expert@emfluence.com, Web Site: www.emfluence.com (21)

Cacioppo, David, Emfluence, Kansas City, MO. Tel: (816) 472-4455, (877) 81-EMAIL, FAX: (816) 472-8855, E-Mail: expert@emfluence.com, Web Site: www.emfluence.com (21)

Cactus Mailing Company, Scottsdale, AZ. Tel: (480) 443-1442, (888) 632-5282, FAX: (866) 828-7794, E-Mail: info@cactusmailing.com, Web Site: www.cactusmailing.com (21)

Cade & Associates Advertising Inc, Tallahassee, FL. Tel: (850) 385-0300, (800) 715-CADE, FAX: (850) 385-1165, E-Mail: webmaster@cade1.com, Web Site: www.cade1.com (35)

Cade, John, Cade & Associates Advertising Inc, Tallahassee, FL. Tel: (850) 385-0300, (800) 715-CADE, FAX: (850) 385-1165, E-Mail: webmaster@cade1.com, Web Site: www.cade1.com (35)

Cadie Products Corp, Paterson, NJ. Tel: (973) 278-8300, FAX: (973) 278-0303, E-Mail: emeyers@cadie.com, Web Site: www.cadieproducts.com (16)

Cadieux, Dan, InfoCanada, Mississauga, ON Canada. Tel: (800) 565-7224, FAX: (905) 803-7195, E-Mail: info@infocanada.ca, Web Site: infogroup.infocanada.ca (23)

Cadmus Communications, Richmond, VA. Tel: (804) 261-3000, (800) 888-2973, Web Site: www.cenveo.com (35)

Cady, Phillip, Magna Visual Inc, Saint Louis, MO. Tel: (314) 843-9000, (800) 843-3399, FAX: (314) 843-0000, E-Mail: magna@magnavisual.com, Web Site: www.magnavisual.com (9)

Cady, William R., Magna Visual Inc, Saint Louis, MO. Tel: (314) 843-9000, (800) 843-3399, FAX: (314) 843-0000, E-Mail: magna@magnavisual.com, Web Site: www.magnavisual.com (9)

Caesars Entertainment Corp, Las Vegas, NV. Tel: (702) 407-6000, (800) 634-6001, FAX: (702) 407-6037, Web Site: www.caesars.com (16)

Cafe Lango, Sharon Springs, NY. Tel: (203) 453-1456, (800) 243-1234, FAX: (203) 453-5110, E-Mail: mail@cafelango.com, Web Site: www.audioforum.com (16)

Caforio, MD Giovanni, Bristol-Myers Squibb Co, New York, NY. Tel: (212) 546-4000, FAX: (212) 546-9544, Web Site: www.bms.com (16)

Cagan, Dennis J., TWL Knowledge Group, Carrollton, TX. Tel: (972) 309-4000, (800) 624-2272, FAX: (972) 309-5105, Web Site: www.twlk.com (3)

Cage, Lynn, Tucker Electronics Co, Garland, TX. Tel: (214) 348-8800. (887) 667-6044, FAX: (214) 348-0367, E-Mail: sales@tucker.com, Web Site: www.tucker.com (3)

Caguin, Mike, Colle+McVoy, Minneapolis, MN. Tel: (612) 305-6000, FAX: (612) 305-6500, E-Mail: info@collemcvoy.com, Web Site: www.collemcvoy.com (35)

Cahiliane, Steve, NBTY Inc, Ronkonkoma, NY. Tel: (631) 200-2000, FAX: (631) 567-7148, Web Site: www.nbty.com (7)

Cahill, Dennis A, ThinkDirect Marketing Group, Largo, FL. Tel: (727) 369-2700, E-Mail: info@tdmg.com, Web Site: www.tdmg.com (28)

Cahill, Rose, Savings Bank Life Insurance Co of MA (SBLI), Woburn, MA. Tel: (781) 938-3500, Web Site: www.sbli.com (15)

Cahilll, Toby, ThreeSource Fulfillment, Manteno, IL. Tel: (815) 936-1094 x4179, (888) 673-4650, FAX: (815) 936-9743, Web Site: www.threesource.tv (28)

Cahn, Eric, The Pin Man, Tulsa, OK. Tel: (918) 587-2405, FAX: (918) 745-2162, Web Site: www.positivepin.com (16)

Cain, Brittany, Georgetown University Law Center, Washington, DC. Tel: (202) 662-9890, FAX: (202) 662-9891, E-Mail: cle@law.georgetown.edu, Web Site: www.law.georgetown.edu (13)

Cain, Cathy, Pacific Sportswear Co Inc, San Diego, CA. Tel: (619) 281-6688, (800) USA-8778, FAX: (619) 281-6687, E-Mail: info@pacsport.com, Web Site: www.pacsport.com (5)

Cain, Jim, Yankelovich Inc, Chapel Hill, NC. Tel: (919) 932-8600, FAX: (919) 932-8629, Web Site: www.yankelovich.com (22)

Cain, John, Priests of the Sacred Heart, Hales Corners, WI. Tel: (414) 425-3383, FAX: (414) 425-5719, Web Site: www.poshusa.org (1)

Cain, Tim, The Herald & Review, Decatur, IL. Tel: (217) 429-5151, FAX: (217) 421-6913, E-Mail: hrdirect@herald-review.com, Web Site: www.herald-review.com (17)

Caine, Paul T., The Cracker Box Inc, Blooming Glen, PA. Tel: (215) 443-7777, FAX: (215) 443-7777, E-Mail: walter@crackerboxkits.com, Web Site: www.crackerboxkits.com (16)

Caine, Tim, Automation Control Products, Alpharetta, GA. Tel: (678) 990-0945, FAX: (678) 990-0951, E-Mail: info@thinmanager.com, Web Site: www.thinmanager.com (16)

Caitlin, Ken, Renaissance Greeting Cards Inc, Downers Grove, IL. Tel: (800) 736-3383, Web Site: www.ftd.com (5)

Caito, Christopher, Admiral Packaging Inc, Providence, RI. Tel: (401) 274-7000, (800) 262-0027, FAX: (401) 331-1910, Web Site: www.admiralpkg.com (26)

CakeMail Inc, Montreal, QC Canada. Tel: (514) 316-1550, Web Site: www.cakemail.com (20)

Cakuun, Asheville, NC. Tel: (828) 771-0820, Web Site: acreativecompany.com (35)

Calabrese, Gerald, Marketing and Product Strategy, Peabody, MA. Tel: (978) 977-2000, (800) 825-5897, FAX: (781) 238-0986, Web Site: www.lhsl.com (16)

Calandra, T.M., Starcrest Products of California Inc, Perris, CA. Tel: (909) 943-2011, FAX: (909) 943-2971, E-Mail: tmc@tstonramp.com (16)

Calbiochem-Novabiochem Corp, San Diego, CA. Tel: (858) 450-9600, (800) 854-3417, FAX: (858) 453-3552, E-Mail: customerservice@emdbioscience.com, Web Site: www.calbiochem.com (9)

Calcott, C. Reid, Educational Insights, Inc, Gardena, CA. Tel: (310) 884-2000, (888) 591-9334, FAX: (310) 886-8850, E-Mail: service@edin.com, Web Site: www.educationalinsights.com (16)

Calderbank, Kathy, American Stationery Co Inc, Peru, IN. Tel: (765) 473-4438, (800) 822-2577, FAX: (800) 253-9054, Web Site: www.americanstationery.com (10)

A Caldwell List Co Inc, Norcross, GA. Tel: (770) 662-0255, (800) 241-7425, FAX: (770) 662-0351, E-Mail: guidance@caldwell-list.com, Web Site: www.caldwell-list.com (23)

Caldwell, Doug, AstraZeneca, Wilmington, DE. Tel: (302) 866-1482, Web Site: www.astrazeneca-us.com (7)

Caldwell, Joseph, Sunrise Business Products, Mineola, NY. Tel: (800) 222-7367, FAX: (631) 588-3900 (10)

Calendar Marketing Association, Wheaton, IL. Tel: (630) 510-4564, FAX: (630) 510-4501, E-Mail: info@calendarassociation.org, Web Site: www.calendarassociation.org (1)

Calhoun, Arlene, American Biographical Institute Inc, Raleigh, NC. Tel: (919) 781-8710, FAX: (919) 781-8712 (17)

Calhoun, David, The Nielsen Co, New York, NY. Tel: (800) 864-1224, Web Site: www.nielsen.com (17)

Calhoun, Jim, Daystar Data Group Inc, Schaumburg, IL. Tel: (847) 202-0100, FAX: (847) 202-0107, E-Mail: sales@daystardg.com, Web Site: www.daystardg.com (22)

Cali, Tammy Lyles, Eberle Associates Inc, McLean, VA. Tel: (703) 821-1550, FAX: (703) 821-0920, Web Site: www.eberleassociates.com (35)

Calibre Press Inc, San Francisco, CA. Tel: (214) 545-3060, (800) 323-0037, FAX: (866) 225-4273, Web Site: www.calibrepress.com (17)

Calico Corners, Kennett Square, PA. Tel: (610) 444-9700, (800) 213-6366, FAX: (610) 444-1221, Web Site: www.calicocorners.com (16)

California Chamber of Commerce, Sacramento, CA. Tel: (800) 649-4921, FAX: (916) 325-1272, E-Mail: techsupport@calchamber.com, Web Site: www.calbizcentral.com (1)

California Institute of Technology, Pasadena, CA. Tel: (626) 395-3746, FAX: (626) 795-7174, E-Mail: execedu@caltech.edu, Web Site: www.irc.caltech.edu (16)

California Mustang Parts & Accessories, City of Industry, CA. Tel: (909) 598-3383, (800) 775-0101, FAX: (909) 598-5611, E-Mail: csmustang@cal-mustang.com, Web Site: www.cal-mustang.com (16)

California Offset Printers, Glendale, CA. Tel: (818) 291-1100, (800) 280-6446, FAX: (818) 291-1190, E-Mail: info@copprints.com, Web Site: www.copprints.com (27)

California Pacific Research & New Generation, Reno, NV. Tel: (775) 829-5600, (800) 745-5642, FAX: (775) 829-5619, E-Mail: sales@newgen2000.com, Web Site: www.newgen2000.com (7)

California Society of CPA's, San Mateo, CA. Tel: (800) 922-5272, FAX: (650) 522-3009, E-Mail: info@culcpa.org, Web Site: www.calcpa.org (1)

California State University at Fresno, Fresno, CA. Tel: (559) 278-7830, FAX: (559) 278-8577, Web Site: www.csufresno.edu (41)

Call Compliance Inc, Glen Cove, NY. Tel: (516) 674-4545, FAX: (516) 676-2420, E-Mail: sales@callcompliance.com, Web Site: www.callcompliance.com (29)

Call Interactive, Omaha, NE. Tel: (402) 498-7000, FAX: (402) 498-7900, Web Site: www.callit.com (29)

Callahan, David, Putt Putt Fun Centers, Winston-Salem, NC. Tel: (336) 714-3950, (866) PUTT-PUTT, FAX: (336) 714-3955, Web Site: www.puttputt.com (16)

Callahan, Emily, ALSAC - St Jude, Memphis, TN. Tel: (901) 495-3300, (800) 278-5833, FAX: (901) 495-3966, Web Site: www.stjude.org (1)

Callahan, Jack F., The McGraw-Hill Financial, New York, NY. Tel: (212) 904-2000, Web Site: www.mhfi.com (17)

Callahan, Kevin, Service Net Warranty LLC, Jeffersonville, IN. Tel: (812) 258-4700, (812) 258-4722, FAX: (812) 258-4693, Web Site: www.servicenet.com (22)

Callahan, Laurie, New Directions Publishing Corp, New York, NY. Tel: (212) 255-0230, FAX: (212) 255-0231, E-Mail: editorial@ndbooks.com, Web Site: www.ndbooks.com (17)

Callahan, Michael, Cabela's Inc, Sidney, NE. Tel: (308) 254-5505, (800) 237-4444, FAX: (308) 254-4800, Web Site: www.cabelas.com (11)

Callari, Neil, D2: Direct, Denville, NJ. Tel: (973) 627-4410, FAX: (973) 627-3703, E-Mail: info@d2direct.com, Web Site: www.d2direct.com (35)

Callaway Gardens, Pine Mountain, GA. Tel: (706) 663-2281, (800) CALLAWAY, FAX: (706) 663-6812, E-Mail: info@callawaygardens.com, Web Site: www.callawaygardens.com/where-to-stay (19)

Callaway, Ken, Ion Exhibits, Itasca, IL. Tel: (877) 499-6197, FAX: (630) 235-9501, E-Mail: info@ionexhibits.com, Web Site: www.ionexhibits.com (36)

Callendary, Steve, Resorts Casino Hotel, Atlantic City, NJ. Tel: (609) 334-6000, (800) 336-6378, FAX: (609) 340-6349, Web Site: www.resortsac.com (19)

Calling Solutions, San Antonio, TX. Tel: (210) 801-9630, (800) 683-5500, FAX: (210) 491-1777, E-Mail: marketing@callingsolutions.com, Web Site: www.callingsolutions.com (29)

Calloway House Inc, Lancaster, PA. Tel: (717) 299-5703, (800) 233-0290, FAX: (717) 299-6754, Web Site: www.callowayhouse.com (16)

Calloway, Kevin, IJHANA, Los Angeles, CA. Tel: (213) 268-4283, (888) 421-9222, E-Mail: info@ijhana.com, Web Site: www.ijhana.com (20)

Calmark Inc, Chicago, IL. Tel: (773) 247-7200, FAX: (773) 247-3199, E-Mail: ljakobi@calmark-inc.com, Web Site: www.clamark-inc.com (28)

Caltrider, Wayne, JC Direct Mail Inc, Groveport, OH. Tel: (614) 836-4848, FAX: (614) 836-4847 (28)

Calvert, Katherine, Advent Software Inc, San Francisco, CA. Tel: (415) 543-7696, FAX: (415) 543-5070, E-Mail: info@advent.com, Web Site: www.advent.com (34)

Calvert, Lorelei, Texas Monthly, Austin, TX. Tel: (512) 320-6900, (800) 759-2000, FAX: (512) 476-9007, E-Mail: info@texasmonthly.com, Web Site: www.texasmonthly.com (17)

Calvey, Kevin, Skytel Communications Inc, Lewisville, TX. Tel: (800) 759-8737, Web Site: www.skytel.com (29)

Calvimontes, Andrew, The Envelope Connection Inc, Chicago, IL. Tel: (773) 774-4600, FAX: (773) 774-4601, E-Mail: sales@envelopeconnection.com, Web Site: envelopeconnection.com (28)

Calvin, Kathy, United Nations Foundation, Washington, DC. Tel: (202) 887-9040, FAX: (202) 887-9021, Web Site: www.unfoundation.org (1)

Cambey & West Inc, Congers, NY. Tel: (845) 267-3006, FAX: (845) 267-3503, E-Mail: info@cambeywest.com, Web Site: www.cambeywest.com (22)

Cambridge Educational, New York, NY. Tel: (800) 257-5126, FAX: (917) 339-0325, Web Site: www.filmsmediagroup.com (12)

Camellia Forest Nursery, Chapel Hill, NC. Tel: (919) 968-0504, FAX: (919) 929-8971, E-Mail: camelliaforest@gmail.com, Web Site: www.camforest.com (8)

Camelot Enterprises, Bristol, WI. Tel: (262) 857-2695 (9)

Cameron & Co, Toronto, ON Canada. Tel: (416) 268-2326 (20)

Cameron, Bill, American Fidelity Assurance Co, Oklahoma City, OK. Tel: (405) 525-6900, FAX: (405) 523-5215, Web Site: www.afadvantage.com (15)

Cameron, Diane, Relaxo-Bak Inc, Anderson, IN. Tel: (765) 643-2934, (866) 369-6914, FAX: (765) 641-7448, Web Site: www.relaxobak.com (7)

Cameron, Peter, Dansk, Bristol, PA. Tel: (914) 697-6400, (800) 326-7528, FAX: (914) 697-6464, Web Site: www.dansk.com (16)

Cameron, Wade, Cameron & Co, Toronto, ON Canada. Tel: (416) 268-2326 (20)

Camille, Keith, Touch-Base Computing, Silver Creek, GA. Tel: (706) 378-0964, E-Mail: sales@touchbase. com, Web Site: www.touchbase.com (22)

Camilly, Lisa, The Akadine Press Inc, White Plains, NY. Tel: (914) 747-0777, FAX: (914) 747-0778, Web Site: www.commonreader.com (16)

Camino, Olivier, Sitel, Nashville, TN. Tel: (615) 301-7100, (866) 95-SITEL, Web Site: www.sitel.com (29)

Camm, Robert J., Quadra Graphics Inc, Cherry Hill, NJ. Tel: (856) 665-4060, FAX: (856) 665-7324, E-Mail: richard.nixon@qgi.com (27)

Cammarata, Frank, Media Monitors Inc, White Plains, NY. Tel: (914) 428-5971, FAX: (914) 428-4541, E-Mail: jselig@mediamonitors.com, Web Site: www.mediamonitors.com (30)

Camp + King, San Francisco, CA. Tel: (415) 345-6680, Web Site: www.camp-king.com (35)

Camp, Roger, Camp + King, San Francisco, CA. Tel: (415) 345-6680, Web Site: www.camp-king.com (35)

Campaign Monitor, San Francisco, CA. Tel: (888) 533-8098, E-Mail: info@campaignmonitor.com, Web Site: www.campaignmonitor.com (24)

Campaigns & Elections Magazine, Arlington, VA. Tel: (703) 778-4028, (800) 771-8252, FAX: (703) 778-4024, Web Site: www.campaignsandelections.com (17)

Campanaro, Sal, Modern Graphic Arts, Saint Petersburg, FL. Tel: (727) 579-1527, FAX: (727) 579-1528, Web Site: www.sandyinc.com (27)

Campanella, Constance, Stateside Associates, Arlington, VA. Tel: (703) 525-7466 X228 (20)

Campanella, Joseph A., ClearOne Advantage, Baltimore, MD. Tel: (888) 785-5376, FAX: (888) 785-5365, Web Site: www.clearoneadvantage.com (14)

Campbell Soup Co, Camden, NJ. Tel: (856) 342-4800, (800) 257-8443, FAX: (856) 342-3878, Web Site: www.campbellsoupcompany.com (16)

Campbell Tools Co, Springfield, OH. Tel: (937) 882-6716, FAX: (937) 882-6648, E-Mail: campbell@campbelltools.com, Web Site: www.campbelltools.com (9)

Campbell, Anne, California Institute of Technology, Pasadena, CA. Tel: (626) 395-3746, FAX: (626) 795-7174, E-Mail: execedu@caltech.edu, Web Site: www.irc.caltech.edu (16)

Campbell, Arthur, Thermal Product Solutions, White Deer, PA. Tel: (570) 538-7200, (800) 586-2473 (16)

Campbell, Casey, Teraco Inc, Midland, TX. Tel: (888) 837-2261, Web Site: www.teraco.com (27)

Campbell, Chris, Bankers Life & Casualty Co, Chicago, IL. Tel: (312) 396-6000, (800) 231-9150, Web Site: www.bankerslife.com (15)

Campbell, Dave, Projection Video Services, Springfield, VA. Tel: (703) 912-1334, (800) 377-7650, FAX: (703) 912-1350, Web Site: www.projection.com (16)

Campbell, David, Chernoff Newman, Columbia, SC. Tel: (803) 254-8158, FAX: (803) 252-2016. E-Mail: columbia@chernoffnewman.com, Web Site: www.chernoffnewman.com (35)

Campbell, Eric, VML Inc, Kansas City, MO. Tel: (816) 283-0700, FAX: (816) 283-0954, E-Mail: dl-vmlcommarketing@vml.com, Web Site: www.vml.com (35)

Campbell, Jack, Gerstner Woodworks, Dayton, OH. Tel: (937) 228-1662, FAX: (937) 228-8557, E-Mail: info@gerstnerusa.com, Web Site: www.gerstnerusa.com (6)

Campbell, Jeffrey C., McKesson Corp, San Francisco, CA. Tel: (415) 983-8300, FAX: (415) 983-7160, Web Site: www.mckesson.com (7)

Campbell, Jerry, Squadron Mail Order, Carrollton, TX. Tel: (972) 242-8663, (877) 414-0434, FAX: (972) 242-3775, E-Mail: mailorder@squadron.com, Web Site: www.squadron.com (16)

Campbell, Jill, Cox Communications Inc, Atlanta, GA. Tel: (404) 843-5000, (888) 566-7751, FAX: (404) 269-2243, Web Site: www.cox.com (16)

Campbell, John, The American Film Institute, Los Angeles, CA. Tel: (323) 856-7600, FAX: (323) 467-4578, Web Site: www.afi.com (1)

Campbell, Michael, Anderson Direct & Digital, Poway, CA. Tel: (888) 694-5094, Web Site: www.andersondd.com (35)

Campbell, Neal J., CDW Corp, Vernon Hills, IL. Tel: (847) 465-6000, (847) 371-6090, Web Site: www.cdw.com (16)

Campbell, Nicole, FreshAddress Inc, Newton, MA. Tel: (617) 965-4500, (800) 321-3009, FAX: (617) 965-4551, Web Site: www.freshaddress.com (22)

Campbell, Phillip, Nature Publishing Group, New York, NY. Tel: (212) 726-9200, FAX: (212) 696-9006, Web Site: www.nature.com (17)

Campbell, Scott, The Columbian, Vancouver, WA. Tel: (360) 694-3391, FAX: (360) 735-4503, Web Site: www.columbian.com (17)

Campbell, Steven T., US Cellular, Chicago, IL. Tel: (888) 944-9400, Web Site: www.uscellular.com (32)

Campbell, William A., Glenview State Bank, Glenview, IL. Tel: (847) 729-1900, FAX: (847) 729-5847, E-Mail: info@gsb.com, Web Site: www.glenviewstatebank.com (14)

Camping World Inc, Bowling Green, KY. Tel: (270) 781-2718, (800) 626-6189, FAX: (270) 796-8991, Web Site: www.campingworld.com (11)

Campmor Inc, Mahwah, NJ. Tel: (201) 335-9064, (800) 525-4784, FAX: (201) 236-3601, Web Site: www.campmor.com (17)

Campos, Alexander, Center for Book Arts, New York, NY. Tel: (212) 481-0295, FAX: (866) 708-8994, E-Mail: info@centerforbookarts.org, Web Site: www.centerforbookarts.org (27)

Canada Brokerlink Insurance, Edmonton, AB Canada. Tel: (780) 474-8911, FAX: (780) 479-0573, Web Site: www.brokerlink.ca (15)

Canadeo, Ernest, The EGC Group, Melville, NY. Tel: (516) 935-4944, FAX: (516) 935-7030, E-Mail: contact@egcgroup.com, Web Site: www.egcgroup.com (35)

Canadian Blood Services, Ottawa, ON Canada. Tel: (613) 739-2300, Web Site: www.blood.ca (1)

Canadian Business, Toronto, ON Canada. Tel: (416) 596-5100, FAX: (416) 764-1200, Web Site: www.canadianbusiness.com (17)

Canadian Institute of Chartered Accountants, Toronto, ON Canada. Tel: (416) 977-3222, FAX: (416) 977-8585, Web Site: www.cica.ca (1)

Canadian Marketing Association, Don Mills, ON Canada. Tel: (416) 391-2362, (800) 267-8805, FAX: (416) 441-4062, E-Mail: info@the-cma.org, Web Site: www.the-cma.org (40)

Canan, Steven, AMC Publishing/Agent Media Corp, Clearwater, FL. Tel: (727) 446-1100, (800) 933-9449, FAX: (727) 446-1166, E-Mail: sales@agentmediacorp.com, Web Site: www.agentmediacorp.com (31)

Cancelmo, Thomas, Boyd Tamney Cross Inc, Wayne, PA. Tel: (610) 293-0500, FAX: (610) 687-8199, E-Mail: info@btcmarketing.com, Web Site: www.boydtamneycross.com (35)

Cancer Research Society, Montreal, QC Canada. Tel: (514) 861-9227, (888) 766-2262, FAX: (514) 861-9220, E-Mail: info@crs-src.ca, Web Site: www.cancerresearchsociety.ca (1)

Candiotti. Fred, CGT Marketing LLC, Amityville, NY. Tel: (631) 842-4600, E-Mail: info@cgtmarketing.com, Web Site: www.cgtmarketing.com (35)

Cane & Basket Supply Co, Los Angeles, CA. Tel: (323) 939-9644, FAX: (323) 939-7237, E-Mail: info@caneandbasket.com, Web Site: www.caneandbasket.com (8)

Canestri, Donna J., Champion America Inc, Branford, CT. Tel: (203) 315-1181, (877) 242-6709, FAX: (800) 336-3707, E-Mail: teamca@champion-america.com, Web Site: www.champion-america.com (10)

Canestri, Donna J., Tricor Direct Inc, Branford, CT. Tel: (203) 488-8059, (800) 243-6624, FAX: (800) 571-2596, E-Mail: custsvc_setonus@seton.com, Web Site: www.seton.com (9)

Cangelose, Jacques, Texas Graphic Resource, Dallas, TX. Tel: (214) 630-2800, FAX: (214) 630-0713 (27)

Cangero, Syl, Adirondack Direct, Long Island City, NY. Tel: (718) 932-4003, (800) 221-2444, FAX: (800) 477-1330, E-Mail: info@adirondackdirect.com, Web Site: www.adirondackdirect.com (10)

Canine Companions for Independence, Santa Rosa, CA. Tel: (707) 577-1700, (800) 572-2275, FAX: (707) 577-1711, E-Mail: info@cci.org, Web Site: www.caninecompanions.org (16)

The Caning Shop, Berkeley, CA. Tel: (510) 527-5010, (800) 544-3373, FAX: (510) 527-7718, Web Site: www.caning.com (11)

Canino, Jose, Argent Trading LLC, New York, NY. Tel: (212) 697-8800, FAX: (212) 697-8606, Web Site: www.Argenttrading.com (16)

Cannaday, Jim, Tony Brown Productions, New York, NY. Tel: (718) 264-2226, FAX: (718) 264-1914, E-Mail: mail@tbol.net, Web Site: www.tonybrown.com (16)

Cannella Response Television Inc, Burlington, WI. Tel: (262) 763-4810, FAX: (262) 763-2875, Web Site: www.drtv.com (32)

Cannella, Frank, Cannella Response Television Inc, Burlington, WI. Tel: (262) 763-4810, FAX: (262) 763-2875, Web Site: www.drtv.com (32)

Canning Brown, Barbara, Toys "R" Us, Wayne, NJ. Tel: (973) 617-5879, FAX: (973) 617-4006, Web Site: www.toysrus.com (11)

Canning, Kathie, Orlando/ Orange County Convention & Visitor's Bureau, Orlando, FL. Tel: (407) 354-5568, Web Site: visitorlando.com (19)

Canning, Marilyn, Martindale-Hubbell, New Providence, NJ. Tel: (908) 771-7777, (800) 526-4902. FAX: (908) 771-8704, Web Site: www.martindale.com (17)

Canoe Ventures LLC, Englewood, CO. Tel: (212) 364-3600, FAX: (212) 364 3601, Web Site: www.canoe-ventures.com (32)

Canose, Gregory, Award Marketing Services LLC, Whitehouse, NJ. Tel: (908) 534-5700, FAX: (908) 534-0903, E-Mail: info@awardmarketingservices.com, Web Site: www.awardmarketingservices.com (33)

Cantelmo, Dan, LOG-ON, New York, NY. Tel: (212) 279-4567, E-Mail: sales@log-on.org, Web Site: www.log-on.org (21)

Canter, Jeff, Innovative Systems Inc, Pittsburgh, PA. Tel: (412) 937-9300, (800) 622-6390, FAX: (412) 937-9309, E-Mail: info@innovativesystems.com, Web Site: www.innovativesystems.com (22)

Cantler, Jan, Brooks Brothers, New York, NY. Tel: (212) 682-8800, (800) 274-1815, FAX: (212) 309-7273, Web Site: www.brooksbrothers.com (2)

Canto, Adrian, UndercoverWear Inc, Tewksbury, MA. Tel: (978) 851-8580, (800) 733-0007, FAX: (978) 640-2882, E-Mail: service@undercoverwear.com, Web Site: www.undercoverwear.com (2)

Cantrall, Eric, McKenzie Taxidermy Supply, Granite Quarry, NC. Tel: (704) 279-7985, (800) 279-7985, Web Site: www.mckenziesp.com (16)

Cantrell, Carol S., Parsons School of Design Human Resource Dept, New York, NY. Tel: (212) 229-5671, FAX: (212) 229-8975, E-Mail: communications@newschool.edu, Web Site: www.newschool.edu/parsons/ (41)

Cantrell, Christy, Alfa Insurance, Montgomery, AL. Tel: (334) 288-3900, Web Site: www.alfains.com (15)

Cantrell, Joan, Glenview State Bank, Glenview, IL. Tel: (847) 729-1900, FAX: (847) 729-5847, E-Mail: info@gsb.com, Web Site: www.glenviewstatebank.com (14)

Cantu, Elsa, Megger, Dallas, TX. Tel: (214) 330-3539, Web Site: www.megger.com (16)

Canyon Marketing, Hicksville, NY(7)

Canzonetta, Gina, DMB Realty Network, Scottsdale, AZ. Tel: (480) 515-0148, Web Site: www.dmbrealty.com (16)

Capalbo, Karen, Concept Media Partners Inc, Yorktown Heights, NY. Tel: (914) 767-0032, FAX: (914) 514-1711, E-Mail: karen@conceptmediapartners.com, Web Site: www.conceptmediapartners.com (35)

Cape Cod Cupola Co Inc, North Dartmouth, MA. Tel: (508) 994-2119, FAX: (508) 997-2511, E-Mail: capecodcupola@gmail.com, Web Site: www.capcodcupola.com (8)

Cape, Mike, xpedx Stores Division, Chicago, IL. Tel: (773) 442-6200, (800) 600-0064, FAX: (630) 628-6310, Web Site: www.epedxstores.com (25)

Capell & Associates, Barnegat Light, NJ. Tel: (201) 572-8774, FAX: (609) 494-7369, E-Mail: contact@capellandassociates.com, Web Site: www.capell&associates.com (20)

Capell, E Daniel, Capell & Associates, Barnegat Light, NJ. Tel: (201) 572-8774, FAX: (609) 494-7369, E-Mail: contact@capellandassociates.com, Web Site: www.capell&associates.com (20)

Capetanakis, Mike, MCDM Strategic Direct Marketing, Plainfield, IL. Tel: (815) 436-5194, FAX: (815) 439-5941 (20)

Capezio Ballet Makers Inc, Totowa, NJ. Tel: (973) 595-9000, (800) 533-1887, FAX: (800) 595-9120, E-Mail: info@capezio.com, Web Site: www.capezio.com (16)

Capezza, Joseph C., Harvard Pilgrim Health Care, Wellesley, MA. Tel: (617) 509-1000, (888) 888-4742, FAX: (617) 509-7590, Web Site: www.harvardpilgrim.org (7)

Capgemini Americas Outsourcing, New York, NY. Tel: (212) 314-8000, FAX: (212) 314-8001 (20)

Capiraso, Michael, New York Road Runners, New York, NY. Tel: (855) 5MY-NYRR, E-Mail: mynyrr@nyrr.org, Web Site: www.nyrr.org (13)

Capital Design, Providence, RI. Tel: (401) 270-6777, E-Mail: info@freemiums.com, Web Site: www.freemiums.com (33)

Capital Insurance Group (CIG), Monterey, CA. Tel: (831) 233-5500, Web Site: www.ciginsurance.com (15)

Capitani, Randy, Vermont Media Publishing Co, West Dover, VT. Tel: (802) 464-3388, FAX: (802) 464-7255, E-Mail: publisher@vermontmedia.com, Web Site: www.dvalnews.com (17)

Capitani, Victoria, Vermont Media Publishing Co, West Dover, VT. Tel: (802) 464-3388, FAX: (802) 464-7255, E-Mail: publisher@vermontmedia.com, Web Site: www.dvalnews.com (17)

Capitanio, Francis, Biomerica Inc, Irvine, CA. Tel: (949) 645-2111, (800) 854-3002, FAX: (949) 553-1231, E-Mail: info@biomerica.com, Web Site: www.biomerica.com (7)

Capitol Advantage/Roll Call Group, Washington, DC. Tel: (202) 6550-6500, (800) 432-2250, E-Mail: sales@cq.com, Web Site: www.corporate.cqrollcall.com (31)

Capitol Concierge Inc, Washington, DC. Tel: (202) 223-4765, FAX: (202) 833-2287, E-Mail: onlineconcierge@capitolconcierge.com, Web Site: www.capitolconcierge.com (16)

Capitol Hill Lists LLC, Statham, GA. Tel: (770) 725-9596, E-Mail: grant@capitolhilllists.com, Web Site: capitolhilllists.com (23)

Caplan, Gordon M., Marvin Envelope & Paper Co, Chicago, IL. Tel: (773) 489-3300, (800) 227-0011, FAX: (773) 489-4783, E-Mail: marvinenvelope@aol.com (27)

Capobianco, Louis R., Avantus, Maryland Heights, MO. Tel: (314) 994-3449, Web Site: www.avantus.com (20)

Capone, Andrew, NCC Media, New York, NY. Tel: (212) 548-3300, FAX: (212) 519-0099, Web Site: nccmedia.com (32)

Capone, William J., Merastar Insurance Co, Chattanooga, TN. Tel: (800) 637-2782, FAX: (800) 369-1430, E-Mail: merastar.assist.team@unitrindirect.com, Web Site: www.merastar.com (15)

Caporale, Ronald L., LifeScript, Newport Beach, CA. Tel: (949) 454-0422, (800) 637-9382, Web Site: www.lifescript.com (7)

Caporilli, Peter, Tidewater Workshop, Galloway, NJ. Tel: (800) 666-8433, E-Mail: help@tidewaterworkshop.com, Web Site: www.tidewaterworkshop.net (8)

Capozzoli, Steve, Petry Television Inc, New York, NY. Tel: (212) 230-5600, E-Mail: info@petrymedia.com, Web Site: www.petrymedia.com (32)

Cappaert, Steven M., Meredith Corp, Des Moines, IA. Tel: (515) 284-3000, FAX: (515) 284-2700, Web Site: www.meredith.com (17)

Cappuccio, Paul T., Time Warner Inc, New York, NY. Tel: (212) 484-8000, Web Site: www.timewarner.com (16)

Cappy, John, Outlook Group Corp, Neenah, WI. Tel: (920) 727-7999, FAX: (920) 727-8529, E-Mail: info@outlookgroup.com, Web Site: www.outlookgroup.com (27)

Captan Associates Inc, Brick, NJ. Tel: (732) 840-1244, FAX: (732) 840-1211 (17)

Caputo, Roland, The New York Times Co, New York, NY. Tel: (212) 556-1234, Web Site: www.nytimes.com (17)

Caputo, Steve, Chanel Inc, New York, NY. Tel: (212) 688-5055, (800) 550-0005, FAX: (212) 752-1851, Web Site: www.chanel.com (16)

Capwell, Beverly, CustomerMining Inc, Soquel, CA. Tel: (831) 465-0898, FAX: (831) 465-1186, E-Mail: biz@customermining.com, Web Site: customermining.com (35)

Carabella Collection, Irvine, CA. Tel: (949) 263-2300, (800) 227-2235, FAX: (949) 263-2323, Web Site: www.carabella.com (2)

Carabini, Christina, Monex Deposit Co, Newport Beach, CA. Tel: (949) 752-1400, (800) 444-8317, FAX: (949) 752-7214, E-Mail: info@monex.com, Web Site: www.monex.com (14)

Carabini, Louis E., Monex Deposit Co, Newport Beach, CA. Tel: (949) 752-1400, (800) 444-8317, FAX: (949) 752-7214, E-Mail: info@monex.com, Web Site: www.monex.com (14)

Carabini, Michael, Monex Deposit Co, Newport Beach, CA. Tel: (949) 752-1400, (800) 444-8317, FAX: (949) 752-7214, E-Mail: info@monex.com, Web Site: www.monex.com (14)

Caraustar, Austell, GA. Tel: (770) 948-3101, E-Mail: info@caraustar.com, Web Site: www.caraustar.com (16)

Caraustar Ashland Carton Plant, Ashland, OH. Tel: (419) 289-2666, FAX: (419) 281-5415, Web Site: www.caraustar.com (27)

Caraveo, Suzanne, FAFCO Inc, Chico, CA. Tel: (530) 332-2100, (800) 994-7652, FAX: (530) 332-2109, Web Site: www.fafco.com (16)

Carawan, Suzanne, ThePort Network, Atlanta, GA. Tel: (703) 431-2208 (32)

Carbone, Becky, Book Publishing Information Kit, Santa Barbara, CA. Tel: (805) 968-7277, (800) PARA-PUB, FAX: (805) 968-1379, E-Mail: danpoynter@parapublishing.com, Web Site: www.parapublishing.com (17)

Carbone, Becky, Para Publishing, Santa Barbara, CA. Tel: (805) 968-7277, (800) PARAPUB, FAX: (805) 986-1379, E-Mail: danpoynter@parapublishing.com, Web Site: www.parapublishing.com (17)

Card Sterling, Cathy, Schultz & Williams Inc, Philadelphia, PA. Tel: (215) 625-9955, FAX: (215) 625-2701, E-Mail: mail@schultzwilliams.com, Web Site: www.sw-inc.com (1)

Card Technology Inc, Hopkins, MN. Tel: (201) 845-7373, FAX: (201) 845-3337, E-Mail: info@nbstech.com, Web Site: www.nbstech.com (16)

Card, Richard, Mastergrip Inc, Irving, TX. Tel: (972) 554-4450, (800) 275-1100, FAX: (972) 554-1109, Web Site: www.mastergrip.com (11)

Thomas L Cardella & Associates, Kimberton, PA. Tel: (610) 933-3822, Web Site: www.tlcassociates.com (29)

Cardello, Alberto, University of Pittsburgh at Bradford, Bradford, PA. Tel: (814) 362-7500, FAX: (814) 362-5150, E-Mail: admissions@www.upb.pitt.edu, Web Site: www.upd.pitt.edu (41)

Cardenas-Nolazsco, Armando, The Wedding Pages, New York, NY. Tel: (212) 219-8555, (800) 843-4983, FAX: (212) 219-1929, Web Site: www.theknot.com (16)

Cardflex Financial Services, Costa Mesa, CA. Tel: (714) 361-1900, E-Mail: aphillips@cliq.com, Web Site: www.flex1.com (14)

Cardinal Mailing Services Ltd, Honolulu, HI. Tel: (808) 538-3884, FAX: (808) 521-1419, E-Mail: mail@cardinalservicesltd.com, Web Site: www.cardinalservicesltd.com (28)

Cardinal, Michelle, R2C Group, Portland, OR. Tel: (866) 402-1124, E-Mail: getintouch@r2cgroup.com, Web Site: www.r2cgroup.com (35)

Cardinale, Kim, CBT Direct, Tarpon Springs, FL. Tel: (727) 724-8994, (877) 872-4646, FAX: (727) 797-9143, Web Site: www.cbtdirect.com (16)

Cardona, Edward, Video Artists International, Pleasantville, NY. Tel: (914) 769-3691, (800) 477-7146, FAX: (914) 769-5407, E-Mail: orders@vaimusic.com, Web Site: www.vaimusic.com (3)

Cardona, John Charles, The Dreyfus Corp, New York, NY. Tel: (212) 922-6000, FAX: (212) 922-6880, Web Site: www.dreyfus.com (14)

Cardone, Anthony, Standard Life, Montreal, QC Canada. Tel: (514) 499-8855, (877) 499-9555, FAX: (514) 499-4908, Web Site: www.standardlife.ca (15)

Cardoso, Carlos M., Kennametal Inc, Latrobe, PA. Tel: (800) 222-9327, FAX: (800) 521-3319, E-Mail: mcs-na.service@kennmetal.com, Web Site: www.kennametal.com (16)

CardSource, Eagan, MN. Tel: (651) 686-0660, (800) 284-9194, FAX: (651) 686-0330, Web Site: www.cardsource.com (31)

Care2, Washington, DC. Tel: (650) 622-0860, Web Site: www.care2.com (1)

CARE USA, Atlanta, GA. Tel: (404) 681-2552, (800) 422-7385, FAX: (404) 589-2600, E-Mail: info@care.org, Web Site: www.careusa.org (1)

CareCall Inc, Sartell, MN. Tel: (320) 253-0800, Web Site: www.arraysg.com (29)

Career Blazers, New York, NY. Tel: (212) 719-3232, FAX: (212) 221-0452 (20)

Career Education Corp, Schaumburg, IL. Tel: (847) 781-3600, E-Mail: inquiries@careered.com, Web Site: www.careered.com (1)

Carefirst Blue Cross Blue Shield, Washington, DC. Tel: (202) 479-8000, FAX: (301) 470-8049, Web Site: www.carefirst.com (15)

Careington International, Frisco, TX. Tel: (972) 335-6970, (800) 441-0380, Web Site: www.careington.com (17)

Carendi, John, Fireman's Fund Insurance Co, Novato, CA. Tel: (415) 899-2000, FAX: (415) 899-3600, Web Site: www.firemansfund.com (14)

Carestream Health Inc, Rochester, NY. Tel: (585) 627-1800, (888) 777-2072, E-Mail: corporatesecurity@carestream.com, Web Site: www.carestreamhealth.com (7)

Carew, Paul H., National Active & Retired Federal Employees Association, Alexandria, VA. Tel: (703) 838-7760, (800) 456-8410, FAX: (703) 838-7785, Web Site: www.narfe.org (1)

Peter N Carey & Associates Inc, Oak Brook, IL. Tel: (630) 573-4260, (877) PNCAREY, FAX: (630) 573-0529, E-Mail: pncarey1@sbcglobal.net (20)

Carey, Bruce, JWT Inside, Los Angeles, CA. Tel: (310) 309-8282, (877) 665-8768, FAX: (310) 309-8283, E-Mail: conversations@jwtinside.com, Web Site: www.jwtinside.com (35)

Carey, David, Hearst Magazines, New York, NY. Tel: (212) 649-2824, FAX: (212) 765-3528, Web Site: www.hearst.com/magazines (17)

Carey, Jaime, BarnesandNoble.com, New York, NY. Tel: (212) 414-6000, (800) THE-BOOK, FAX: (212) 414-6140, E-Mail: service@barnesandnoble.com, Web Site: www.barnesandnoble.com (16)

Carey, Peter N., Peter N Carey & Associates Inc, Oak Brook, IL. Tel: (630) 573-4260, (877) PNCAREY, FAX: (630) 573-0529, E-Mail: pncarey1@sbcglobal.net (20)

CARFAX Inc, Centreville, VA. Tel: (703) 934-2664, Web Site: www.carfax.com (12)

Carhill Enterprises Inc, Saint Louis, MO. Tel: (314) 621-7646, Web Site: www.cahillinsight.com (15)

Caribe Direct Inc, San Juan, PR. Tel: (787) 722-5188, FAX: (787) 723-6165, E-Mail: islaonline@prw.net, Web Site: www.islaonline.com (6)

Carino, Bill, 89 Degrees, Burlington, MA. Tel: (781) 221-5400, Web Site: www.89degrees.com (9)

Carino, Giselle, International Planned Parenthood Federation Western Hemisphere Region Inc, New York, NY. Tel: (212) 248-6400, (866) IPPFWHR, FAX: (212) 248-4221, E-Mail: info@ippfwhr.org, Web Site: www.ippfwhr.org (1)

Carioscia, Ursula, McGaw Graphics, Manchester Center, VT. Tel: (845) 353-8600, (888) 4BMCGAW, FAX: (845) 353-3155, E-Mail: sales@bmcgaw.com, Web Site: www.bmcgaw.com (6)

Carkeet, Bill, Oden, Memphis, TN. Tel: (901) 578-8055, (800) 371-6233, FAX: (901) 578-1911, Web Site: www.oden.com (35)

Carkhuff, Gregory, Human Resource Development Press, Amherst, MA. Tel: (413) 253-3488, (800) 822-2801, FAX: (413) 253-3490, E-Mail: info@hrdpress.com, Web Site: www.hrdpress.com (17)

Carkhuff, Robert, Human Resource Development Press, Amherst, MA. Tel: (413) 253-3488, (800) 822-2801, FAX: (413) 253-3490, E-Mail: info@hrdpress.com, Web Site: www.hrdpress.com (17)

Carle, Eric, Dome Printing, Sacramento, CA. Tel: (800) 343-3139 (27)

Carlgren, Kendi, MarketAide Services Inc, Hutchinson, KS. Tel: (785) 825-7161, (800) 204-2433, FAX: (785) 825-4697, E-Mail: creative@marketaide.com, Web Site: www.marketaide.com (21)

Carlier, Joe, Penske Logistics, Reading, PA. Tel: (800) 529-6531, FAX: (610) 775-2449, E-Mail: info.penskelogistics@penske.com, Web Site: www.penskelogistics.com (16)

Carlile, Doug, Professional Print & Mail Inc, Fresno, CA. Tel: (559) 237-7468, (800) 654-7468, FAX: (559) 237-4929, E-Mail: info@printfresno.com, Web Site: www.printfresno.com (21)

Carlile, Thomas E., Boise Cascade Holdings LLC, Boise, ID. Tel: (208) 384-6451, FAX: (208) 384-7189, E-Mail: mediarelations@bc.com, Web Site: www.bc.com (16)

Carlin, Mercer, TRANZACT, Fort Lee, NJ. Tel: (201) 461-5665, E-Mail: info@tranzact.net, Web Site: www.tranzact.net (35)

Carline, Lauren, Mac Direct, Colmar, PA. Tel: (215) 822-5775, (800) 278-1154, FAX: (215) 822-7977, E-Mail: info@macdirect.com, Web Site: www.macdirect.com (22)

Carlisle, Jeanette, Comsearch, Ashburn, VA. Tel: (703) 726-5500, FAX: (703) 726-5600, Web Site: www.comsearch.com (30)

Carlisle, Jr. Rex T., Deseret Book, Salt Lake City, UT. Tel: (801) 534-1515, (800) 453-4532, FAX: (801) 517-3392, Web Site: www.deseretbook.com (16)

Carlisle, Rex T., Fire Mountain Gems, Grants Pass, OR. Tel: (541) 956-7890, (800) 355-2137, (800) 423-2319, FAX: (541) 470-GEMS, E-Mail: questions@firemtn.com, Web Site: www.firemtn.com (16)

Carll, Rob, DME Holdings, Daytona Beach, FL. Tel: (877) 720-0082, E-Mail: info@dmedelivers.com, Web Site: www.dmedelivers.com (21)

Carlough, Rosemary, American Management Association, New York, NY. Tel: (212) 586-8100, FAX: (212) 903-8186, Web Site: www.amanet.org (1)

Carlson, A. Oscar, American Spirit Graphics Corp, Minneapolis, MN. Tel: (612) 623-3333, FAX: (612) 623-9314, E-Mail: asgc@asgc.com, Web Site: www.asgc.com (27)

Carlson, Bonnie J., Promotion Marketing Association (PMA) Inc, New York, NY. Tel: (212) 420-1100, FAX: (212) 533-7622, E-Mail: pma@pmalink.org, Web Site: www.pmalink.org (1)

Carlson, Bradley S., IDC, Ltd, Henderson, NV. Tel: (702) 450-1000, FAX: (702) 450-1020, E-Mail: info@goidc.com, Web Site: www.goidc.com (1)

Carlson, Charles, Dow Theory Forecasts, Hammond, IN. Tel: (219) 931-6480, (800) 233-5922, FAX: (219) 931-6487, E-Mail: custserv@horizonpublishing.com, Web Site: www.dowtheory.com (17)

Carlson, Dan, Ruder Finn Inc, New York, NY. Tel: (212) 593-6400, FAX: (212) 715-1556, E-Mail: rfnewyork@ruderfinn.com, Web Site: www.ruderfinn.com (30)

Carlson, Darren, American Spirit Graphics Corp, Minneapolis, MN. Tel: (612) 623-3333, FAX: (612) 623-9314, E-Mail: asgc@asgc.com, Web Site: www.asgc.com (27)

Carlson, David, Consumer Benefit Services Inc, Naperville, IL. Tel: (630) 420-6200, (800) 657-8309, FAX: (630) 420-2294, E-Mail: dcarlson@consumerbenefit.com, Web Site: www.consumerbenefit.com (16)

Carlson, Eric Anthony, Alerus Financial National Assoc, Grand Forks, ND. Tel: (701) 795-3200, (800) 279-3200, Web Site: www2.alerusfinancial.com (14)

Carlson, Julie, Heartstrings Press, Lancaster, VA. Tel: (804) 462-0884, (800) 462-0884, FAX: (716) 462-0884, E-Mail: sue@grandloving.com, Web Site: www.grandloving.com (17)

Carlson, Lynn, Harper's Magazine, New York, NY. Tel: (212) 420-5720, FAX: (212) 228-5889, Web Site: www.harpers.org (17)

Carlson, William, Choice Hotels International, Rockville, MD. Tel: (301) 592-5000, Web Site: www.choicehotels.com (16)

Carlton Industries CP, La Grange, TX. Tel: (979) 242-5055, (800) 231-5988, FAX: (800) 231-5934, E-Mail: sales@carltonusa.com, Web Site: www.carltonusa.com (34)

Carlton, Kay, Carlton Industries CP, La Grange, TX. Tel: (979) 242-5055, (800) 231-5988, FAX: (800) 231-5934, E-Mail: sales@carltonusa.com, Web Site: www.carltonusa.com (34)

Carlyle, Rosemarie, Barton-Cotton, Baltimore, MD. Tel: (410) 247-4800, (800) 348-1102, FAX: (410) 536-0491, E-Mail: info@bartoncotton.com, Web Site: www.bartoncotton.com (17)

Carmel, Douglas, Flaghouse Inc, Hasbrouck Heights, NJ. Tel: (201) 288-7600, (800) 793-7900, FAX: (800) 793-7922, E-Mail: sales@flaghouse.com, Web Site: www.flaghouse.com (5)

Carmel, George, Flaghouse Inc, Hasbrouck Heights, NJ. Tel: (201) 288-7600, (800) 793-7900, FAX: (800) 793-7922, E-Mail: sales@flaghouse.com, Web Site: www.flaghouse.com (5)

Carmichael Lynch Inc, Minneapolis, MN. Tel: (612) 334-6000, FAX: (612) 334-6101, E-Mail: inquiry@clynch.com, Web Site: www.carmichaellynch.com (35)

Carmichael, Greg D., Fifth Third Bank, Cincinnati, OH. Tel: (800) 972-3030, FAX: (231) 922-4060, Web Site: www.53.com (14)

Carmody, Bill, Trepoint, New York, NY. Tel: (646) 867-2252, E-Mail: challengeus@trepoint.com, Web Site: www.trepoint.com (35)

Carmody, Daniel C., Channing L Bete Co Inc, South Deerfield, MA. Tel: (800) 477-4776, FAX: (800) 499-6464, E-Mail: custscvs@channing.bete.com, Web Site: www.channing-bete.com (17)

Carneal, Jeffrey J., Eagle Publishing, Washington, DC. Tel: (202) 216-0600, FAX: (202) 216-0612, Web Site: www.eaglepub.com (17)

The Carnegie Hall Corp, New York, NY. Tel: (212) 903-9600, E-Mail: feedback@carnegiehall.org, Web Site: www.carnegiehall.org (35)

Carnes, Kathie, Dudnyk, Horsham, PA. Tel: (215) 443-9406, (800) 438-3695, E-Mail: fpowers@dudnyk.com, Web Site: dudnyk.com (35)

Carney Direct Marketing, Irvine, CA. Tel: (949) 581-5100, (800) 240-3349, E-Mail: pete@carneydirect.com, Web Site: www.carneydirect.com (23)

Carney, Lloyd, Brocade Communications Systems Inc, San Jose, CA. Tel: (408) 333-8000, FAX: (408) 333-8101, E-Mail: info@brocade.com, Web Site: www.brocade.com (16)

Carney, Pete, Carney Direct Marketing, Irvine, CA. Tel: (949) 581-5100, (800) 240-3349, E-Mail: pete@carneydirect.com, Web Site: www.carneydirect.com (23)

Carney, Thomas J., EF Maloney Inc, Mamaroneck, NY. Tel: (718) 549-7000, FAX: (718) 549-6320, E-Mail: efmaloney@aol.com, Web Site: www.efmaloney.com (16)

Carnival Creations, Irvine, CA. Tel: (949) 833-9370, FAX: (949) 955-2078 (39)

Carnival Cruise Lines, Miami, FL. Tel: (212) 599-2600, Web Site: www.carnival.com (19)

Carnwath, Alison J., PACCAR Inc, Bellevue, WA. Tel: (425) 468-7400, FAX: (425) 468-8216, Web Site: www.paccar.com (16)

Carolan, Mary, Universal Training, Lake Forest, IL. Tel: (847) 235-2170, E-Mail: information@universaltraining.com, Web Site: www.universaltraining.com (16)

Carolan, Trish, DMB Financial, Beverly, MA. Tel: (866) 810-3210, FAX: (978) 338-2347, E-Mail: help@dmbfinancial.com, Web Site: www.dmbfinancial.com (14)

Caroli, Connie, TeleManagement Search, Port Washington, NY. Tel: (516) 767-6990, FAX: (516) 767-6980, E-Mail: connie@tmrecruiters.com, Web Site: www.tmrecruiters.com (20)

Carolina Biological Supply Co, Burlington, NC. Tel: (800) 334-5551, (800) 222-7112, E-Mail: carolina@carolina.com, Web Site: www.carolina.com (9)

Caroll, John, Tom Snyder Productions, Watertown, MA. Tel: (617) 926-6000, (800) 342-0236, FAX: (800) 304-1254, E-Mail: ask@tomsnyder.com, Web Site: www.tomsnyder.com (16)

Carollo, Anthony, Syntellect, Phoenix, AZ. Tel: (602) 789-2800, (800) 788-9733, FAX: (602) 789-2899, Web Site: www.syntellect.com (16)

Carone, Christa, Xerox Services, Dallas, TX. Tel: (214) 841-6111, (800) 275-9376, Web Site: www.acs-inc.com (22)

Carothers, Leslie, Environmental Law Institute, Washington, DC. Tel: (202) 939-3800, FAX: (202) 939-3868, E-Mail: law@eli.org, Web Site: www.eli.org (17)

ER Carpenter, Taylor, TX. Tel: (512) 365-5833, (800) 234-9105, FAX: (512) 352-6025, Web Site: www.carpenter.com (16)

Michael Carpenter Photography, Springfield, VA. Tel: (703) 644-9666 (37)

Carpenter, Dave, Innovation Printing Inc, Philadelphia, PA. Tel: (215) 969-4600, FAX: (215) 464-7664, Web Site: www.innovationprinting.com (27)

Carpenter, Eleanor, Emperor Clock LLC, Amherst, VA. Tel: (800) 642-0011, FAX: (434) 946-1420, E-Mail: emperor@emperorclock.com, Web Site: www.emperorclock.com (16)

Carpenter, Judie, ER Carpenter, Taylor, TX. Tel: (512) 365-5833, (800) 234-9105, FAX: (512) 352-6025, Web Site: www.carpenter.com (16)

Carpenter, Kelly, National 4-H Supply Service, Chevy Chase, MD. Tel: (301) 961-2959, FAX: (301) 961-2937, E-Mail: 4hsupply@fourhcouncil.edu, Web Site: www.fourhcouncil.edu (16)

Carpenter, Lorelle, Dover Saddlery, Littleton, MA. Tel: (978) 952-8062, (800) 406-8204, Web Site: www.doversaddlery.com (11)

Carpenter, Michael, Michael Carpenter Photography, Springfield, VA. Tel: (703) 644-9666 (37)

Carpenter, Mike, West Bend, West Bend, WI. Tel: (262) 334-5107, (866) 290-1851, FAX: (262) 334-6800, Web Site: www.focuselectrics.com (16)

Carpenter, Nancy, KET, Lexington, KY. Tel: (859) 258-7000, (800) 432-0951, FAX: (606) 258-7396, E-Mail: rgriffin@ket.org, Web Site: www.ket.org (17)

Carqueville Graphics Inc, Streamwood, IL. Tel: (630) 837-4500, FAX: (630) 837-4510, Web Site: www.carqueville.com (27)

Carr, Adam, Emerson Ecologics, Manchester, NH. Tel: (603) 656-9778, (800) 654-4432, FAX: (603) 656-9797, (800) 718-7238, E-Mail: cs@emersonecologics.com (7)

Carr, Alicia, Kelco Supply Co, Big Lake, MN. Tel: (763) 493-1260, (800) 328-7720, FAX: (763) 493-1261, E-Mail: info@kelcosupply.com, Web Site: www.kelcosupply.com (16)

Carr, Brian, TBWA/Chiat/Day Inc, New York, NY. Tel: (212) 804-1000, FAX: (212) 804-1200, Web Site: www.tbwachiatdayny.com (35)

Carr, J. Robert, Society for Human Resource Management, Alexandria, VA. Tel: (703) 548-3440, (800) 283-7476, FAX: (703) 535-6490, E-Mail: shrmstore@shrm.org, Web Site: www.shrm.org (1)

Carr, John, Solo Printing, Miami, FL. Tel: (305) 594-8699, FAX: (305) 599-5245, Web Site: www.soloprinting.com (27)

Carr, Matthew, Calloway House Inc, Lancaster, PA. Tel: (717) 299-5703, (800) 233-0290, FAX: (717) 299-6754, Web Site: www.callowayhouse.com (34)

Carr, Mike, Strongwell, Bristol, VA. Tel: (276) 645-8000, FAX: (276) 645-8132, E-Mail: gbarefoot@strongwell.com, Web Site: www.strongwell.com (9)

Carr, Tim, Creative Lift Inc, San Francisco, CA. Tel: (415) 248-3170, E-Mail: hello@creativelift.net, Web Site: www.creativelift.net (35)

Carraher, Amy, Focus USA Inc, Paramus, NJ. Tel: (201) 489-2525, FAX: (201) 489-4499, E-Mail: info@focus-usa-l.com, Web Site: www.focus-usa-l.com (23)

Carrasco, Jim, Crystek Corp, Fort Myers, FL. Tel: (239) 561-3311, (800) 237-3061, FAX: (239) 561-1025, E-Mail: sales@crystek.com, Web Site: www.crystek.com (9)

Carrigan, Robert, Hoover's Inc, Austin, TX. Tel: (512) 374-4500, FAX: (512) 374-4051, Web Site: www.hoovers.com (22)

Carrizales, Nancy, Animals Animals/Earth Scenes, Chatham, NY. Tel: (518) 392-5500, (800) 392-5503, FAX: (518) 392-5550, E-Mail: info@animalsanimals.com, Web Site: www.animalsanimals.com (38)

Carroll Enterprises Inc, Worcester, MA. Tel: (508) 756-3513, (800) 548-6900, FAX: (508) 770-0528, E-Mail: info@carrollenterprises.com, Web Site: carrollenterprises.com (29)

Carroll Publishing, Bethesda, MD. Tel: (301) 263-9800, (800) 336-4240, FAX: (301) 263-9801, E-Mail: info@carrollpub.com, Web Site: www.carrollpub.com (17)

Carroll, Brian, Carroll Enterprises Inc, Worcester, MA. Tel: (508) 756-3513, (800) 548-6900, FAX: (508) 770-0528, E-Mail: info@carrollenterprises.com, Web Site: carrollenterprises.com (29)

Carroll, Christopher N., Anthem Marketing, Chicago, IL. Tel: (312) 441-0382 (22)

Carroll, David, Gates Corp, Denver, CO. Tel: (303) 744-1911, FAX: (303) 744-4000, Web Site: www.gates.com (9)

Carroll, Ed, American Movie Classics Holding Corp, Jericho, NY. Tel: (516) 803-3000, FAX: (516) 803-3003, Web Site: www.amctv.com (16)

Carroll, Francis R., Small Business Service Bureau Inc, Worcester, MA. Tel: (508) 756-3513, (800) 343-0939, FAX: (508) 770-0528, E-Mail: info@sbsb.com, Web Site: www.sbsb.com (1)

Carroll, John, Celestial Seasonings, Boulder, CO. Tel: (303) 530-5300, (800) 351-8175, FAX: (303) 581-1249, Web Site: www.celestialseasonings.com (16)

Carroll, John, Hain Celestial Group Inc, Boulder, CO. Tel: (800) 434-4246, Web Site: www.hain-celestial.com (16)

Carroll, John, Jason Natural Personal Care Products, Boulder, CO. Tel: (88) 659-7730, Web Site: www.jason-natural.com (7)

Carroll, Mike, American Fidelity Assurance Co, Oklahoma City, OK. Tel: (405) 525-6900, FAX: (405) 523-5215, Web Site: www.afadvantage.com (15)

Carroll, Nicole, The Arizona Republic, Phoenix, AZ. Tel: (602) 444-8000, Web Site: www.azcentral.com (17)

Carroll, Ricki, New England Cheesemaking Supply Co, South Deerfield, MA. Tel: (413) 397-2012, FAX: (413) 397-2014, E-Mail: info@cheesemaking.com, Web Site: www.cheesemaking.com (4)

Carroll, Ruth Ann, Albert S Smyth Co Inc, Timonium, MD. Tel: (410) 252-6666, (800) 638-3333, FAX: (410) 252-2355, E-Mail: smyth@albertsmyth.com, Web Site: www.albertsmyth.com (6)

Carroll, Thomas E., Carroll Publishing, Bethesda, MD. Tel: (301) 263-9800, (800) 336-4240, FAX: (301) 263-9801, E-Mail: info@carrollpub.com, Web Site: www.carrollpub.com (17)

Carron, Dr Andrew, National Economic Research Associates Inc, Washington, DC. Tel: (202) 466-3510, FAX: (202) 466-3605, E-Mail: andrew.carron@nera.com, Web Site: www.nera.com (20)

Carrot-Top Industries Inc, Hillsborough, NC. Tel: (919) 732-6200, (800) 628-3524, FAX: (919) 732-5526, E-Mail: service@carrot-top.com, Web Site: www.carrot-top.com (16)

Carruthers, Albert, Memphis Net & Twine Co Inc, Memphis, TN. Tel: (901) 458-2656, (888) 674-7638, FAX: (901) 458-1601, E-Mail: fishinfo@memphisnet.net, Web Site: www.memphisnet.net (11)

Carruthers, Court, Grainger Industrial Supply, North Brook, IL. Tel: (847) 498-5900, FAX: (847) 498-3402, Web Site: www.grainger.com (16)

Carruthers, Court, WW Grainger Inc, Lake Forest, IL. Tel: (847) 535-1000, (800) 472-4643, FAX: (847) 535-9122, Web Site: www.grainger.com (9)

Carruthers, Garrey E., New Mexico State University, Las Cruces, NM. Tel: (505) 646-3341, (575) 646-0111, FAX: (505) 646-1498, Web Site: www.nmsu.edu (41)

Carruthers, Kevin, National Emblem Sales, Indianapolis, IN. Tel: (317) 630-1247, (888) 453-4466, FAX: (317) 630-1381, E-Mail: emblem@legion.org, Web Site: www.emblem.legion.org (16)

Carry, Ellen, Corinthian Media, New York, NY. Tel: (212) 279-5700, FAX: (212) 239-1772, E-Mail: info@mediabuying.com, Web Site: www. mediabuying.com (35)

Carscaddon, Mike, Habitat For Humanity International, Americus, GA. Tel: (229) 924-6935, (800) HABI-TAT, FAX: (229) 924-6541, Web Site: www. habitat.org (1)

Carson & Co, Santa Ana, CA. Tel: (949) 477-9400, E-Mail: gcarson@carsonandcompany.com, Web Site: carsonpr.com (35)

Carson, Ann, Lincoln Park Zoo, Chicago, IL. Tel: (312) 742-2000, FAX: (312) 742-2137, E-Mail: webmaster@lpzoo.com, Web Site: www.lpzoo.com (1)

Carson, Charles, Samford University, Birmingham, AL. Tel: (205) 726-2011, Web Site: www.samford.edu (41)

Carson, Dava, American Health & Life Insurance Co, Fort Worth, TX. Tel: (817) 348-7500, (800) 995-2274, FAX: (817) 348-7553, Web Site: www. citifinancial.com (15)

Carson, David, Mailways Enterprises Inc, Crystal Lake, IL. Tel: (815) 455-4850, FAX: (815) 455-7327, E-Mail: dave@mailways.com, Web Site: www. mailways.com (28)

Carson, George, Carson & Co, Santa Ana, CA. Tel: (949) 477-9400, E-Mail: gcarson@ carsonandcompany.com, Web Site: carsonpr.com (35)

Carson, Michael, Alzheimer's Association, Chicago, IL. Tel: (312) 335-8700, (800) 272-3900, Web Site: www.alz.org (1)

Carson's, Milwaukee, WI. Tel: (414) 347-1152, FAX: (414) 278-5748, Web Site: www.carsons.com (16)

Carter & Holmes Inc, Newberry, SC. Tel: (803) 276-0579, FAX: (803) 276-0588, E-Mail: orchids@ carterandholmes.com, Web Site: www. carterandholmes.com (8)

Harriet Carter Gifts Inc, Montgomeryville, PA. Tel: (215) 361-5100, FAX: (215) 361-1127, Web Site: www.harrietcarter.com (6)

Carter, Brent, MoneyGram International, Dallas, TX. Tel: (800) 666-3947, Web Site: www.moneygram. com (14)

Carter, Cindy, FDAnews, Falls Church, VA. Tel: (703) 538-7600, (888) 838-5578, FAX: (703) 538-7676, E-Mail: customerservice@fdanews.com, Web Site: www.fdanews.com (17)

Carter, David, Mithun Agency, Minneapolis, MN. Tel: (612) 347-1000, FAX: (612) 347-1515, Web Site: www.everythingtalks.com (35)

Carter, Deborah, New Jersey Monthly, Morristown, NJ. Tel: (973) 539-8230, FAX: (973) 538-2953, E-Mail: research@njmonthly.com, Web Site: www. njmonthly.com (17)

Carter, Diane, American Horse Products, San Juan Capistrano, CA. Tel: (949) 248-5300, (800) 500-0799, FAX: (949) 248-5305, E-Mail: zjim@sbcglobal.net, Web Site: www.americanhorseproducts.com (11)

Carter, Ian R., Hilton Hotels Corp, Mc Lean, VA. Tel: (703) 883-1000, (800) HILTONS, FAX: (310) 205-3670, Web Site: www.hilton.com (19)

Carter, James, American Horse Products, San Juan Capistrano, CA. Tel: (949) 248-5300, (800) 500-0799, FAX: (949) 248-5305, E-Mail: zjim@sbcglobal.net, Web Site: www.americanhorseproducts.com (11)

Carter, Jerry, Consumer Opinion Services Inc, Seattle, WA. Tel: (206) 241-6050, FAX: (206) 241-5213, E-Mail: info@cosvc.com, Web Site: www.cosvc. com (30)

Carter, Jude, The Marlin Company, Wallingford, CT. Tel: (877) 890-9116, Web Site: www. themarlincompany.com (35)

Carter, Lewis, Rochling Engineered Plastics, Dallas, NC. Tel: (704) 922-7814, (800) 541-4419, FAX: (704) 922-7651, E-Mail: rep@roechling-plastics.us, Web Site: www.roechling-plastics.us (34)

Carter, Nancy L., North Wind Picture Archives, Alfred, ME. Tel: (207) 490-1940, (800) 952-0703, FAX: (207) 490-3627, E-Mail: mail@northwindpictures. com, Web Site: www.northwindpictures.com (38)

Carter, Natasha, Banker & Tradesman, Boston, MA. Tel: (617) 428-5100, FAX: (617) 428-5119, Web Site: www.bankerandtradesman.com (17)

Carter, Pete, Chapman Cubine Adams & Hussey, Arlington, VA. Tel: (703) 248-0025, Web Site: www. ahadirect.com (20)

Carter, Robert, Communications Unlimited Inc, Richmond, VA. Tel: (804) 754-7242, E-Mail: communicationsunlimited@verizon.net (20)

Carter, Robert W., Uniway Management Corp, Forest Park, GA. Tel: (404) 363-6200, (888) 386-4929, FAX: (404) 363-8848, E-Mail: uniway@bellsouth. net, Web Site: www.uniway.com (16)

Carter, Warrick L., Columbia College Chicago, Chicago, IL. Tel: (312) 663-1600, FAX: (312) 344-0869, Web Site: www.colum.edu (41)

Cartera Commerce Inc, Lexington, MA. Tel: (781) 541-6800, (888) 456-6255, FAX: (781) 541-6801, E-Mail: info@cartera.com, Web Site: www.cartera. com (35)

Cartouche Ltd, Alexandria, VA. Tel: (703) 823-7904, (800) AT-EGYPT, FAX: (888) 283-4978, E-Mail: sales@egyptianimports.com, Web Site: www. egyptianimports.com (6)

Carus, Andre, The Cricket Magazine Group, Chicago, IL. Tel: (603) 924-7209, (800) 821-0115, FAX: (815) 224-6615, E-Mail: customerservice@ caruspub.com, Web Site: www.cricketmag.com (17)

Carus, Marianne, The Cricket Magazine Group, Chicago, IL. Tel: (603) 924-7209, (800) 821-0115, FAX: (815) 224-6615, E-Mail: customerservice@ caruspub.com, Web Site: www.cricketmag.com (17)

Caruso, Aron, O'Halloran Advertising, Westport, CT. Tel: (203) 341-9400 (39)

Caruso, Bob, Titan List & Mailing Services Inc, Deerfield Beach, FL. Tel: (888) 345-7179, E-Mail: titanlms@bellsouth.net, Web Site: www.titanlists. com (24)

Caruso, Diane, Choice Media, Amherst, NH. Tel: (603) 672-3338, FAX: (603) 249-9732, E-Mail: choicemedia@comcast.net (31)

Caruso, Dominic J., Johnson & Johnson, New Brunswick, NJ. Tel: (732) 524-0400, FAX: (732) 214-0332, Web Site: www.jnj.com (16)

Caruso, Michael, Smithsonian Enterprises, New York, NY. Tel: (212) 916-1300, (800) 766-2149, FAX: (212) 490-0058, Web Site: www.smithsonianmag. com (17)

Carvel Corp, Atlanta, GA. Tel: (404) 255-3250, (800) 227-8353, FAX: (404) 255-4978, Web Site: www. carvel.com (4)

Casablanca Express, Woodland Hills, CA. Tel: (818) 992-5100, (800) 315-2065, Web Site: www. casablancaexpress.com (33)

Casabonne, Richard J., Steck-Vaughn, Austin, TX. Tel: (512) 343-8227, (800) 531-5015, (877) 866-2586, FAX: (512) 795-3617, (877) 265-2730, E-Mail: info@steck-vaughn.com, Web Site: www.steck-vaughn.com (17)

Casalaina, Marco, KXEN Inc, San Francisco, CA. Tel: (415) 904-4160, FAX: (415) 904-9041, Web Site: www.kxen.com (22)

Casaletto, Mark, Daily Commercial News & Construction Record, Markham, ON Canada. Tel: (905) 752-5408, (800) 465-6475, FAX: (905) 752-5450, (888) 396-9413, E-Mail: dcnonl@reedbusiness.com, Web Site: www.dcnonl.com (17)

Casbarian, Archie, Arnaud's, New Orleans, LA. Tel: (504) 523-0611, (866) 230-8895, FAX: (504) 581-7908, Web Site: www.arnauds.com (16)

Casbarian, Jane, Arnaud's, New Orleans, LA. Tel: (504) 523-0611, (866) 230-8895, FAX: (504) 581-7908, Web Site: www.arnauds.com (16)

Cascade Outfitters, Boise, ID. Tel: (208) 322-4411, (800) 223-7328, FAX: (208) 322-5016, E-Mail: mail@cascadeoutfitters.com, Web Site: www. cascadeoutfitters.com (11)

Casciano, Dan, Elite Sportswear LP, Reading, PA. Tel: (610) 921-1469, (800) 345-4087, FAX: (610) 921-0208, E-Mail: gkelite@gkelite.com, Web Site: www.gk-elitesportswear.com (2)

Cascioli, Terry, Times Publishing Co, Erie, PA. Tel: (814) 870-1600, FAX: (814) 870-1808, E-Mail: terry.cascioli@timesnews.com (18)

Case Design Corp, Telford, PA. Tel: (215) 703-0130, (800) 847-4176, FAX: (215) 703-0139, E-Mail: sales@casedesigncorp.com, Web Site: www. casedesigncorp.com (34)

Case, Cynthia, The World Bank, Washington, DC. Tel: (202) 473-1000, FAX: (202) 477-6391, Web Site: www.worldbank.org (17)

Case, Greg, AON Center, Chicago, IL. Tel: (312) 381-1000, FAX: (312) 381-6032, Web Site: www.aon. com (15)

Case, Gregory C., Aon Innovative Solutions, Chicago, IL. Tel: (312) 381-1000, Web Site: www.aon.com (16)

Casey, Daniel P., Caraustar Ashland Carton Plant, Ashland, OH. Tel: (419) 289-2666, FAX: (419) 281-5415, Web Site: www.caraustar.com (27)

Casey, Joseph, US Gas & Electric, White Plains, NY. Tel: (888) 947-7880, FAX: (888) 400-1230, E-Mail: salesinfo@usgande.com, Web Site: www.usgande. com (14)

Casey, Larry, Marketing Connections Corp, Manchester, NH. Tel: (603) 472-8989, (800) 472-1818, FAX: (603) 472-9881, E-Mail: lcasey@mccnh.com, Web Site: www.mcciq.com (29)

Casey, Terry, Tridium Inc, Richmond, VA. Tel: (804) 525-1648, Web Site: www.tridium.com (9)

Cash, Debra L., Blanchard & Co Inc, New Orleans, LA. Tel: (504) 837-3010, (800) 880-4653, FAX: (504) 837-4884, Web Site: www.blanchardonline.com (16)

CashNetUSA II LLC, Chicago, IL. Tel: (312) 568-4200, (888) 801-9075, FAX: (866) 326-5265, Web Site: www.cashnetusa.com (14)

Casillas, Pete, San Jose Mercury News, San Jose, CA. Tel: (408) 920-5000, FAX: (408) 288-8060, Web Site: www.mercurynews.com (17)

Caskey, Joan, Stonwurks, Eden Prairie, MN. Tel: (785) 526-7847, (888) 884-7881, FAX: (785) 526-7841, E-Mail: stonwurks@stonwurks.com, Web Site: www.stonwurks.com (16)

Casler, John M., The Sportsman's Guide Inc, South Saint Paul, MN. Tel: (651) 451-3030, (800) 882-2962, FAX: (651) 450-6130, E-Mail: custserv@ sportsmansguide.com, Web Site: www. sportsmansguide.com (11)

Caso, Adolph, Dante University Press, Wellesley, MA. Tel: (781) 790-1059, FAX: (781) 790-1056, E-Mail: dante@danteuniversity.org, Web Site: www.danteuniversity.org (17)

Casper, Chad, Gun Video Catalog/LMP, San Diego, CA. Tel: (858) 569-4000, (800) 942-8273, FAX: (858) 569-0505, Web Site: www.gunvideo.com; www.glockstore.com (11)

Casper, Gol, Pace Communications Inc, Greensboro, NC. Tel: (336) 378-6065, FAX: (336) 275-2864, Web Site: www.pacecommunications.com (17)

Casper, Marc C, Thermo Fisher Scientific Inc, Waltham, MA. Tel: (781) 622-1000, (800) 678-5599, FAX: (781) 622-1207, Web Site: www.thermofisher.com (9)

Caspersen, Daniel, Toys "R" Us, Wayne, NJ. Tel: (973) 617-5879, FAX: (973) 617-4006, Web Site: www.toysrus.com (11)

Cassaday, John M., John Hancock Financial Services Inc, Boston, MA. Tel: (617) 572-6000, (800) 732-5543, FAX: (617) 572-6451, Web Site: www.johnhancock.com (15)

Cassaday, John, Movie Central, Toronto, ON Canada. Tel: (416) 479-6784, E-Mail: info@moviecentral.ca, Web Site: www.moviecentral.ca (32)

Cassar, Ed, LexisNexis, New York, NY. Tel: (212) 309-8100, FAX: (800) 437-8674, Web Site: www.lexisnexis.com (16)

Cassidy & Co, Eagan, MN. Tel: (651) 452-4485, FAX: (651) 452-0561, E-Mail: sarah@cassidycompany.com, Web Site: www.cassidycompany.com (33)

Cassidy, Bill, Cassidy & Co, Eagan, MN. Tel: (651) 452-4485, FAX: (651) 452-0561, E-Mail: sarah@cassidycompany.com, Web Site: www.cassidycompany.com (33)

Cassidy, Joseph, The Orvis Co Inc, Manchester, VT. Tel: (802) 362-3622, FAX: (802) 362-3525, Web Site: www.orvis.com (11)

Cassity, Anne, The Burris Agency Inc, Greensboro, NC. Tel: (336) 378-1221, FAX: (336) 378-1221, E-Mail: info@burris.com, Web Site: www.burris.com (35)

Casson, Mike, American Direct Marketing Services Inc, Dallas, TX. Tel: (214) 634-2361, (800) 527-5080, FAX: (214) 905-3829, Web Site: www.dmlist.com (23)

Casson, Scott, American Direct Marketing Services Inc, Dallas, TX. Tel: (214) 634-2361, (800) 527-5080, FAX: (214) 905-3829, Web Site: www.dmlist.com (23)

Castaldo, John, Music Sales Corp, New York, NY. Tel: (212) 254-2100, FAX: (212) 254-2013, E-Mail: info@musicsales.com, Web Site: www.musicsales.com (17)

Castanon, Elena, Wikreate, San Francisco, CA. Tel: (415) 362-0440, FAX: (415) 362-0430, E-Mail: ezequieltrivino@wikreate.com, Web Site: www.wikreate.com (35)

Castator, Jeff, James Medical Rents & Sales Inc, Fort Wayne, IN. Tel: (260) 739-0874, E-Mail: sales@jamesmedical.com, Web Site: www.jamesmedical.net (7)

Castle, Alan, Polyair Packaging, Chicago, IL. Tel: (773) 995-1818, (888) POLYAIR X444, FAX: (773) 995-7725, E-Mail: marketing@polyair.com, Web Site: www.polyair.com (9)

Castle, Cary, United Spinal Association, Kew Gardens, NY. Tel: (718) 803-3782, (800) 404-2898, FAX: (718) 803-0414, E-Mail: info@unitedspinal.org, Web Site: www.unitedspinal.org (1)

Castle, Gloria, The McIlvaine Co, Northfield, IL. Tel: (847) 784-0012, FAX: (847) 784-0061, E-Mail: editor@mcilvainecompany.com, Web Site: www.mcilvainecompany.com (30)

Castle, Randy, The Miller Group, Dupo, IL. Tel: (800) 325-3350, FAX: (618) 286-6202, E-Mail: info@miller-group.com, Web Site: www.multiplexdisplays.com (5)

Castleberry, John, FotoBed.com, Birmingham, AL. Tel: (888) 368-6233, E-Mail: service@fotobed.com, Web Site: www.fotobed.com (20)

Castleman, Jill C., Georgetown University Law Center, Washington, DC. Tel: (202) 662-9890, FAX: (202) 662-9891, E-Mail: cle@law.georgetown.edu, Web Site: www.law.georgetown.edu (13)

Castro, John W, Merrill Corp, Saint Cloud, MN. Tel: (320) 656-5000, FAX: (320) 656-5163 (18)

Casual Male Retail Group, Canton, MA. Tel: (781) 828-9300, (800) 767-0319, E-Mail: info@casualmale.com, Web Site: www.casualmale.com (2)

Caswell-Massey Co Ltd, Edison, NJ. Tel: (732) 225-2181, (800) 326-0500, FAX: (800) 868-4407, E-Mail: info@caswellmasseyltd.com, Web Site: www.caswellmassey.com (7)

Catalano, Jim, Boundless Corp, Phelps, NY. Tel: (631) 962-1500, (800) 231-5445, FAX: (631) 962-1505, E-Mail: sales@boundless.com, Web Site: www.boundless.com (16)

Cataldo, Paul. Radial Inc, King of Prussia, PA. Tel: (610) 491-7000, Web Site: www.radial.com (28)

Catalina Marketing Corp, Saint Petersburg, FL. Tel: (727) 579-5000, FAX: (727) 556-2700, Web Site: www.catalinamarketing.com (31)

The Catalog Consultancy, Vero Beach, FL. Tel: (772) 226-7740, FAX: (772) 226-7740, E-Mail: catalog321@aol.com, Web Site: www.catalogconsultant.com (20)

Catalog Design Studios, Providence, RI. Tel: (866) 849-4264, E-Mail: sfletcher@catalogdesignstudios.com, Web Site: www.catalogdesignstudios.com (21)

Catalog Marketing Group, Evanston, IL. Tel: (847) 864-8089 (20)

Catalog Music Corp, Nashville, TN. Tel: (615) 298-4338, (800) 744-8204, FAX: (615) 298-4628, Web Site: www.catalogmusic.com (3)

Catalogs America, Gordonsville, VA. Tel: (540) 832-2253, (800) 283-4666, FAX: (540) 832-7253, E-Mail: dsayin@catalogsamerica.com, Web Site: www.catalogsamerica.com (27)

Catalogs.com, Fort Lauderdale, FL. Tel: (954) 659-9005, FAX: (954) 659-9007, Web Site: www.catalogs.com (30)

Catalyst, Rochester, NY. Tel: (585) 453-8300, (800) 836-7720, FAX: (585) 453-8360, E-Mail: info@catalystinc.com, Web Site: www.catalystinc.com (35)

Catalyst Computer Services Inc, Los Angeles, CA. Tel: (310) 441-4300, (800) 659-2267, FAX: (310) 441-4332, E-Mail: sales@catalystsoftware.com, Web Site: www.catalystsoftware.com (32)

Catalyst Creative Services, Palo Alto, CA. Tel: (650) 325-1500, E-Mail: chief@catalystcreative.us, Web Site: www.catalystcreative.us (39)

Catalyst Inc, Providence, RI. Tel: (401) 732-1886, FAX: (401) 732-5528, Web Site: www.catalystb2b.com (35)

Catalyst Marketing Communications Inc. Stamford, CT. Tel: (203) 348-7541, FAX: (203) 348-5688, E-Mail: b2b@catalystmc.com, Web Site: www.catalystmc.com (35)

Catalyst Marketing Group, Rocklin, CA. Tel: (916) 218-6066, E-Mail: info@catalystmarketinggroup.com, Web Site: www.catalystmarketinggroup.com (35)

Catanese, Samuel R., Infomercial Monitoring Service Inc, West Chester, PA. Tel: (610) 328-6902, FAX: (610) 328-6791, E-Mail: catanese@imstv.com, Web Site: www.imstv.com (20)

Catch The Wind Kite Shop, Lincoln City, OR. Tel: (541) 994-9500, (800) 227-7878, FAX: (541) 994-4766, E-Mail: catchthewindkites@yahoo.com, Web Site: www.catchthewind.com (11)

Cate, Chris, Cox Target Media Inc, St. Petersburg, FL. Tel: (727) 399-3000, (800) 678-2743, FAX: (727) 399-3061, E-Mail: info@coxtarget.com, Web Site: www.coxtarget.com (21)

Cater, Charles B., Thomson West, Eagan, MN. Tel: (651) 687-7000, (800) 328-9378, FAX: (651) 687-7849, E-Mail: jeff.patrios@thomsonreuters.com, Web Site: www.thomson.com (17)

Caterpillar Inc, Peoria, IL. Tel: (309) 675-0545, Web Site: www.cat.com (16)

Caterpillar Insurance Services Corp, Nashville, TN. Tel: (615) 386-5800, Web Site: www.cat.com (15)

Cathedral Corp, Rome, NY. Tel: (315) 338-0021, (800) 698-0299, FAX: (315) 338-5874, E-Mail: sales@cathedralstewardship.com, Web Site: www.cathedralcorporation.com (21)

Catholic Charities - Brooklyn & Queens, Brooklyn, NY. Tel: (718) 722-6001, Web Site: www.ccbq.org (1)

Catholic Church Extension Society, Chicago, IL. Tel: (312) 795-5109, (800) 842-7804, FAX: (312) 236-5276, E-Mail: info@catholicextension.org, Web Site: www.catholicextension.org (1)

Catholic Digest, New London, CT. Tel: (800) 321-0411, E-Mail: catholicdigest@bayardinc.com, Web Site: www.catholicdigest.com (17)

Catholic Relief Services, Baltimore, MD. Tel: (877) 435-7277, (888) 277-7575, Web Site: www.catholicrelief.org (1)

The Catholic University of America Press, Washington, DC. Tel: (202) 319-5052, FAX: (202) 319-4985, E-Mail: cua-press@cua.edu, Web Site: cuapress.cua.edu (17)

Cattle Kate, Boise, ID. Tel: (208) 377-5283, (800) 332-5283, FAX: (208) 375-3827, E-Mail: cattlekate@rmisp.com, Web Site: www.cattlekate.com (2)

Catz, Safra A., Oracle Corp, Redwood Shores, CA. Tel: (650) 506-7000, (800) 633-0738, FAX: (650) 506-7200, Web Site: www.oracle.com (16)

Caudill & Associates Inc, Orange, CA. Tel: (714) 210-2585, FAX: (714) 210-2595, E-Mail: bobc@caudill4production.com, Web Site: www.caudill4production.com (32)

Caudill, Mary, Caudill & Associates Inc, Orange, CA. Tel: (714) 210-2585, FAX: (714) 210-2595, E-Mail: bobc@caudill4production.com, Web Site: www.caudill4production.com (32)

Caudill, Robert S., Caudill & Associates Inc, Orange, CA. Tel: (714) 210-2585, FAX: (714) 210-2595, E-Mail: bobc@caudill4production.com, Web Site: www.caudill4production.com (32)

Caugherty Hahn Communications, Glen Rock, NJ. Tel: (201) 251-7778, FAX: (201) 251-7779, Web Site: www.chcomm.com (20)

Caulder, Lindy, CRM Learning, Carlsbad, CA. Tel: (760) 431-9800, (800) 421-0833, FAX: (760) 931-5792, E-Mail: sales@crmlearning.com, Web Site: www.crmlearning.com (16)

Andrea B Cautela, New York, NY. Tel: (212) 577-5920 (20)

Cauz, Jorge, Encyclopaedia Britannica Inc, Chicago, IL. Tel: (312) 347-7159, (800) 323-1229, FAX: (312) 294-2104, Web Site: www.britannica.com (17)

Cavaliere, Phyllis, Metropolitan Newspaper Advertising Services Inc, Yonkers, NY. Tel: (212) 689-8200, FAX: (212) 779-9795, E-Mail: info@metrosn.com, Web Site: www.metrosn.com (31)

Cavallo, Kristen, MullenLowe US, Boston, MA. Tel: (617) 226-9000, FAX: (617) 226-9100, Web Site: us.mullenlowe.com (35)

Cavanaugh, Colby, Emma, Nashville, TN. Tel: (800) 595-4401, E-Mail: hi@myemma.com, Web Site: myemma.com (24)

Cavedo, Keith, Directory of Premium, Incentive & Travel Buyers, Richmond, VA. Tel: (804) 762-4455, (800) 223-1797, FAX: (804) 935-0271, E-Mail: amdouglas4@aol.com, Web Site: www. douglaspublications.com (43)

Marshall Cavendish Corp, Tarrytown, NY. Tel: (914) 332-8888, (800) 821-9881, FAX: (914) 332-1888, Web Site: www.marshallcavendish.com (17)

Frank W Cawood & Associates, Peachtree City, GA. Tel: (770) 487-6307, Web Site: www.fca.com (35)

Caz, Ed, Professional Print & Mail Inc, Fresno, CA. Tel: (559) 237-7468, (800) 654-7468, FAX: (559) 237-4929, E-Mail: info@printfresno.com, Web Site: www.printfresno.com (21)

cbsi, Fort Worth, TX. Tel: (817) 332-3681, FAX: (817) 332-3686, Web Site: www.buxtonco.com (30)

CCI Direct Mail, Carlstadt, NJ. Tel: (201) 507-5200, E-Mail: sales@ccidirectmail.com, Web Site: ccidirectmail.com (21)

Cecchin, James, C&S Sales Inc, Wheeling, IL. Tel: (847) 541-0710, (800) 292-7711, FAX: (847) 541-9904, E-Mail: sales@cs-sales.com, Web Site: www. cs_sales.com (16)

Brad Cecil & Associates, Arlington, TX. Tel: (817) 795-8808, FAX: (817) 795-8898 (1)

Cecil, Brad, Brad Cecil & Associates, Arlington, TX. Tel: (817) 795-8808, FAX: (817) 795-8898 (1)

Cecil, Mark A, Conseco Inc, Carmel, IN. Tel: (317) 817-6100, FAX: (317) 817-2847, Web Site: www. conseco.com (15)

Cedar Fresh Products, Coral Gables, FL. Tel: (305) 870-9390, Web Site: www.cedarfresh.com (16)

Cedrone, Carl, Glens Falls Hospital Foundation, Glens Falls, NY. Tel: (518) 926-5960, FAX: (518) 926-7012, Web Site: www.glensfallshospital.org (1)

Cejvanovic, Amela, Veridian Credit Union, Waterloo, IA. Tel: (319) 236-5692, (800) 235-3228, FAX: (319) 833-1185, E-Mail: sarahma@veridiancu.org, Web Site: www.veridiancu.org (1)

Celebrity Endorsement Network (CEN), Calabasas, CA. Tel: (818) 225-7090, FAX: (818) 880-0898, E-Mail: info@celebrityendorsement.com, Web Site: celebrityendorsement.com (35)

Celestial Seasonings, Boulder, CO. Tel: (303) 530-5300, (800) 351-8175, FAX: (303) 581-1249, Web Site: www.celestialseasonings.com (16)

Celtic Life Insurance Co, Chicago, IL. Tel: (312) 332-5401, FAX: (312) 441-0341, E-Mail: info@celtic-net.com, Web Site: www.celtic-net.com (15)

Cembalest, Robin, Art News Magazine, New York, NY. Tel: (212) 398-1690, FAX: (212) 819-0394, E-Mail: info@artnews.com, Web Site: www.artnews.com (17)

Cendrowska, Teresa, ASTM International, West Conshohocken, PA. Tel: (610) 832-9500, FAX: (610) 832-9555, E-Mail: service@astm.org, Web Site: www.astm.org (1)

Cendyn, Boca Raton, FL. Tel: (800) 760-8152, FAX: (561) 750-6795, E-Mail: info@cendyn.com, Web Site: www.cendyn.com (32)

Cengage Learning, Independence, KY. Tel: (800) 354-9706, FAX: (800) 487-8488, Web Site: www. delmar.com (17)

Cenk, William E., WESCO, Pittsburgh, PA. Tel: (412) 454-2200, (800) 343-1201, E-Mail: info@wesco. com, Web Site: www.wescodist.com (16)

Centanni, Ross J., Champion, Quincy, IL. Tel: (217) 222-5400, FAX: (217) 228-8260, Web Site: www. championpneumatic.com (16)

Centaur Forge LLC, Burlington, WI. Tel: (262) 763-9175, (800) 666-9175, FAX: (262) 763-8350, E-Mail: info@centaurforge.com, Web Site: www. centaurforge.com (9)

Center for Book Arts, New York, NY. Tel: (212) 481-0295, FAX: (866) 708-8994, E-Mail: info@ centerforbookarts.org, Web Site: www. centerforbookarts.org (27)

Center for Creative Leadership, Greensboro, NC. Tel: (336) 545-2810, FAX: (336) 282-3284, E-Mail: info@ccl.org, Web Site: www.ccl.org (16)

Center for eBusiness & Advanced IT, Erie, PA. Tel: (814) 898-6500, FAX: (814) 898-6534, Web Site: www.ebizitpa.org (1)

Center For Information Policy Leadership, Washington, DC. Tel: (202) 778-2264, FAX: (202) 778-2201, Web Site: www.policyleaders.com (20)

Center for International Earth Science Information Network, Palisades, NY. Tel: (845) 365-8988, FAX: (845) 365-8922, E-Mail: ciesin.info@ciesin. columbia.edu, Web Site: www.ciesin.org (22)

Center for Professional Advancement, East Brunswick, NJ. Tel: (732) 238-1600, FAX: (732) 238-9113, E-Mail: info@cfpa.com, Web Site: www.cfpa.com (13)

Center for Professional Development, Tallahassee, FL. Tel: (850) 487-1691, (850) 644-8004, FAX: (850) 644-2589, Web Site: www.Learningforlife.fsu.com (16)

Center for Science in the Public Interest, Washington, DC. Tel: (202) 332-9110, FAX: (202) 265-4954, E-Mail: circ@cspinet.org, Web Site: www.cspinet. org (1)

Center, Lawrence J., Georgetown University Law Center, Washington, DC. Tel: (202) 662-9890, FAX: (202) 662-9891, E-Mail: cle@law.georgetown.edu, Web Site: www.law.georgetown.edu (13)

CenterCore Group Inc, Marked Tree, AR. Tel: (800) 686-0821, FAX: (870) 358-3330, Web Site: www. centercoregroup.com (16)

Centerpoint Energy, Minneapolis, MN. Tel: (612) 372-4664, FAX: (612) 321-4873, E-Mail: mgc-businessinformation@centerpointenergy.com, Web Site: www.minnegasco.centerpointenergy.com (16)

Centrac Inc, West Caldwell, NJ. Tel: (973) 402-0999, FAX: (973) 402-0993, Web Site: www.centrac.com (29)

Central Lewmar, Clifton, NJ. Tel: (973) 622-6377, (800) 772-7301, FAX: (973) 623-4323, E-Mail: dan. watkoske@expedx.com, Web Site: www. centrallewmar.com (2)

Central National-Gottesman Inc, Purchase, NY. Tel: (914) 696-9000, FAX: (914) 696-1066, E-Mail: purchase@cng-inc.com, Web Site: www.cng-inc. com (25)

Central Pacific Bank, Honolulu, HI. Tel: (808) 544-0500, (800) 544-0500, (800) 342-8422, FAX: (808) 531-2875, Web Site: www.centralpacificbank.com (14)

Central Shippee Inc, Bloomingdale, NJ. Tel: (973) 838-1100, (800) 631-8968, FAX: (973) 838-8273, Web Site: www.centralshippee.com (16)

Central States Health & Life Co of Omaha, Omaha, NE. Tel: (402) 397-1111, (800) 826-6587, FAX: (402) 391-3772, Web Site: www.cso.com (15)

Central States Indemnity, Omaha, NE. Tel: (402) 997-8000, (402) 397-1111, (800) 445-6500, Web Site: www.csi-omaha.com (15)

Centric Communications, Norfolk, VA. Tel: (757) 622-2724, E-Mail: info@centriccommunications.net, Web Site: centriccommunications.net (28)

Century Direct, Long Island City, NY. Tel: (212) 349-0600, FAX: (718) 349-9528, E-Mail: info@ centurydirect.net, Web Site: www.centurydirect.net (28)

Century Photo, Newtown, CT. Tel: (800) 767-0777, FAX: (714) 441-4550, Web Site: www. centuryphoto.com (10)

CenturyLink, Monroe, LA. Tel: (318) 388-9000, (800) 201-4102, Web Site: centurytel.com (29)

Cenveo Color Art Inc, Saint Louis, MO. Tel: (314) 966-2000, FAX: (314) 966-4725, E-Mail: mikedenny@ cenveo.com, Web Site: www.colorart.com (17)

Cenveo Commercial Envelope Group, Seattle, WA. Tel: (206) 682-7171, (800) 347-6989, FAX: (206) 329-2017, E-Mail: info@cenveo.com, Web Site: www. cenveo.com (26)

Cenveo Inc, Stamford, CT. Tel: (410) 633-4200, (800) 638-2850, FAX: (410) 633-1202, Web Site: www. cenveo.com (27)

Cerda, Adrian, Alexian Brothers Bonaventure House, Chicago, IL. Tel: (773) 327-9921, FAX: (773) 327-9113, E-Mail: info@abam.org, Web Site: www. bonaventurehouse.org (1)

Cerminaro, Russ, ClickMail Marketing Inc, San Mateo, CA. Tel: (650) 653-8055, Web Site: clickmail.com (32)

Cerrone, Barbara L., Ruskin, Moscou, Faltischek, PC, Uniondale, NY. Tel: (516) 663-6600, FAX: (516) 663-6601, E-Mail: info@rmfpc.com, Web Site: www.rmfpc.com (16)

CertainSource Inc, Fairfield, CT. Tel: (203) 254-0404, (888) 655-0464, FAX: (203) 254-0411, E-Mail: neil@certainsource.com, Web Site: www. certainsource.com (32)

CertainTeed Corp, Valley Forge, PA. Tel: (610) 341-7000/7739, (800) 233-8990, FAX: (610) 341-7777, Web Site: www.certainteed.com (16)

Cerullo, David, INSP LLC, Charlotte, NC. Tel: (803) 578-1000, FAX: (803) 578-1725, E-Mail: info@ insp.com, Web Site: www.insp.com (32)

Cerullo, David, The Inspiration Networks, Charlotte, NC. Tel: (704) 561-7872, (803) 578-1000, FAX: (803) 578-1735, Web Site: www.insptoday.com (1)

Ceruolo, Stephanie, Infogroup Media Solutions, Papillion, NE. Tel: (800) 223-2194, E-Mail: infogroupmediasolutions@infogroup.com, Web Site: www.infogroupmediasolutions.com (23)

Ceryanec, Joseph H., Meredith Corp, Des Moines, IA. Tel: (515) 284-3000, FAX: (515) 284-2700, Web Site: www.meredith.com (17)

Cescau, Patrick, InterContinental Hotels Group, Atlanta, GA. Tel: (800) 621-0555, FAX: (801) 975-1846, Web Site: www.ichotelsgroup.com (19)

Cessna Aircraft Co, Wichita, KS. Tel: (316) 517-6000, (800) 4-CESSNA, FAX: (316) 517-6640, Web Site: www.cessna.com (16)

CFA Communications, Toronto, ON Canada. Tel: (416) 504-5071, FAX: (416) 504-7390, Web Site: www. cfacommunications.com (32)

Chabin Concepts, Chico, CA. Tel: (530) 345-0364, FAX: (530) 345-6417, E-Mail: chabininc@aol.com (16)

Chabot, Andy, Cancer Research Society, Montreal, QC Canada. Tel: (514) 861-9227, (888) 766-2262, FAX: (514) 861-9220, E-Mail: info@crs-src.ca, Web Site: www.cancerresearchsociety.ca (1)

Chabot, Brian, Cape Cod Cupola Co Inc, North Dartmouth, MA. Tel: (508) 994-2119, FAX: (508) 997-2511, E-Mail: capecodcupola@gmail.com, Web Site: www.capcodcupola.com (8)

Chabot, Christian, Tableau Software, Seattle, WA. Tel: (206) 633-3400, FAX: (206) 633-3004, Web Site: www.tableausoftware.com (22)

Chace, Sharon A., Insurance Publications Inc, Overland Park, KS. Tel: (913) 383-9191, (800) 762-3387, FAX: (913) 383-1247, E-Mail: brokerwrld@primary.net, Web Site: www.brokerworldmag.com (17)

ChaCha Mobile Answers, Carmel, IN. Tel: (317) 660-6680, Web Site: partners.chacha.com (20)

Chadda, Sanjay, Petsky Prunier LLC, New York, NY. Tel: (212) 842-6001, FAX: (212) 842-6039, Web Site: www.petskyprunier.com (14)

Chadha, Deepa, Ashworth College, Norcross, GA. Tel: (770) 729-8400, (800) 957-5412, FAX: (770) 729-9294, Web Site: www.ashworthcollege.edu (13)

Chadnick, Benjamin J., Black Star Publishing Co, White Plains, NY. Tel: (212) 679-3288, FAX: (212) 889-2052, Web Site: www.blackstar.com (38)

Chadsworth's 1-800-Columns, Wilmington, NC. Tel: (910) 763-7600, (800) 265-8667, FAX: (910) 763-3191, E-Mail: sales@columns.com, Web Site: shop.columns.com (8)

Chadwick's of Boston Inc, Milford, CT. Tel: (877) 330-3393, E-Mail: service@cs.chadwicks.com, Web Site: www.chadwicks.com (2)

Chaffee & Communications, Barrington, RI. Tel: (401) 247-2300, FAX: (401) 247-2002, E-Mail: dchaffee@fullchannel.net, Web Site: www.chaffeecommunications.com (35)

Chaffee, David S., Chaffee & Communications, Barrington, RI. Tel: (401) 247-2300, FAX: (401) 247-2002, E-Mail: dchaffee@fullchannel.net, Web Site: www.chaffeecommunications.com (35)

Chaido, Lawrence J, Transglobal Consultants Inc, Canton, OH. Tel: (330) 477-6450, E-Mail: transglobal@earthlink.net (20)

Chaille, Susan, Arrow Co, Indianapolis, IN. Tel: (317) 692-6666, FAX: (317) 692-6769, Web Site: www.aearo.com (16)

Chaimson, David, Sony Creative Software, Middleton, WI. Tel: (608) 256-3133 (3)

Chain Store Guide, Tampa, FL. Tel: (800) 927-9292, FAX: (813) 627-6882, E-Mail: info@csgis.com, Web Site: www.csgis.com (17)

Chairman's Marketing Group LLC, Princeton, NJ. Tel: (732) 745-4700 (15)

Chait, Manya, VistaPrint USA Inc, Lexington, MA. Tel: (800) 961-2075, Web Site: www.vistaprint.com (27)

Chakmak, Paul J., Boyd Gaming Corp, Las Vegas, NV. Tel: (702) 792-7200, FAX: (702) 792-7313, Web Site: www.boydgaming.com (16)

Challenge Industries Inc, Ithaca, NY. Tel: (607) 272-8990, FAX: (607) 277-7865, E-Mail: info@aboutchallenge.org, Web Site: www.aboutchallenge.org (28)

Chalon, Jonathan, Simmons-Boardman Publishing Corp, New York, NY. Tel: (212) 620-7200, (800) 257-5091, Web Site: www.simmonsboardman.com (17)

Chaloux, Beverly, Circulation Specialists Inc. Shelton, CT. Tel: (888) 315-2472. FAX: (888) 315-2507 (20)

Chamberlain, Chris, Idea Art Inc, Colorado Springs, CO. Tel: (719) 594-4100, (800) 433-2278, FAX: (719) 534-6313, E-Mail: customerservice@ideaart.com, Web Site: www.ideaart.com (25)

Chambers, Charles, Sara Lee Direct Home Shopping, Winston-Salem, NC. Tel: (336) 519-4400, (800) 671-5056, E-Mail: ohp.manager@onehanesplace.com, Web Site: www.onehanesplace.com (2)

Chambers, James R., Weight Watchers International, New York, NY. Tel: (516) 390-1400, FAX: (516) 390-1302, Web Site: www.weight-watchers.com (16)

Chambers, John T., Cisco Systems Inc, San Jose, CA. Tel: (408) 526-4000, (800) 553-NETS, FAX: (408) 526-4100, Web Site: www.cisco.com (22)

Chambers, Lamar M., Ashland Inc, Covington, KY. Tel: (859) 815-3333, Web Site: www.ashland.com (16)

Chambers, Steve, Nuance Speech Solutions, Burlington, MA. Tel: (781) 565-5000, FAX: (781) 565-5001, E-Mail: sales@speechworks.com, Web Site: www.nuance.com (16)

Champion, Quincy, IL. Tel: (217) 222-5400, FAX: (217) 228-8260, Web Site: www.championpneumatic.com (16)

Champion America Inc, Branford, CT. Tel: (203) 315-1181, (877) 242-6709, FAX: (800) 336-3707, E-Mail: teamca@champion-america.com, Web Site: www.champion-america.com (10)

Champion Printing Inc. Cincinnati, OH. Tel: (513) 541-1100, (800) 543-1957, FAX: (513) 541-9398, E-Mail: cpi@championprintinginc.com, Web Site: www.championprintinginc.com (27)

Champs Corp, Bradenton, FL. Tel: (941) 748-0577, (800) 991-6813, E-Mail: customer_service@champssports.com, Web Site: www.champssports.com (11)

Champs Software Inc, Crystal River, FL. Tel: (352) 795-2362, FAX: (352) 795-9100, E-Mail: champs@champsinc.com, Web Site: www.champsinc.com (3)

Chandlee, Chad, Mail Order Business, Dubuque, IA. Tel: (319) 589-1000 X1076, (800) 228-0810, FAX: (319) 589-1046, Web Site: www.kendallhunt.com (43)

Chandler, Chris, American Society of Media Photographers (ASMP), Philadelphia, PA. Tel: (215) 451-ASMP, FAX: (215) 451-0880, Web Site: www.asmp.org (40)

Chandler, Eric D., Xpressdocs, Fort Worth, TX. Tel: (817) 870-4601, (866) 977-3627, FAX: (817) 870-1205, Web Site: www.xpressdocs.com (27)

Chandler, Jim, Ingram Book Group, La Vergne, TN. Tel: (615) 793-5000, (800) 937-8000, FAX: (800) 876-0186, Web Site: www.ipage.ingrambook.com (16)

Chandler, Tom, American Teleservices Association, Indianapolis, IN. Tel: (317) 816-9336, (877) 779-3974, FAX: (317) 218-0323, Web Site: www.ataconnect.org (40)

Chandronnait, Al, Custom Miniatures, Hudson, NH. Tel: (603) 882-6392 (6)

Chane, Andrew, Tools for Wellness, Austin, TX. Tel: (800) 456-9887, FAX: (818) 532-1775, E-Mail: info@toolsforwellness.com, Web Site: www.toolsforwellness.com (7)

Chanel Inc, New York, NY. Tel: (212) 688-5055, (800) 550-0005, FAX: (212) 752-1851, Web Site: www.chanel.com (16)

Chang, Alice, Amrel, El Monte, CA. Tel: (626) 443-6818, (800) 654-9838, FAX: (626) 443-8600, E-Mail: amrel@amrel.com, Web Site: www.amrel.com (16)

Channel Neutral Marketing, Oyster Bay, NY. Tel: (516) 992-7777, E-Mail: deb_kennedy1127@yahoo.com (35)

Channel 13 WNET Catalog Division, New York, NY. Tel: (212) 560-1313, FAX: (212) 560-1314, E-Mail: programming@thirteen.org, Web Site: www.thirteen.org (5)

Chapel, Gary, Nightingale-Conant Corp, Niles, IL. Tel: (847) 647-0300, (800) 557-1660, FAX: (847) 647-7145, Web Site: www.nightingale.com (17)

Chapin, Aldus, Chadwick's of Boston Inc, Milford, CT. Tel: (877) 330-3393, E-Mail: service@cs.chadwicks.com, Web Site: www.chadwicks.com (2)

Chapin, Bill, Kansas City Chiefs, Kansas City, MO. Tel: (816) 920-9300, (888) 99-CHIEFS, FAX: (816) 923-4719, Web Site: www.kcchiefs.com (16)

Chapin, Carrie, McIntyre Direct Group LLC, Portland, OR. Tel: (503) 516-4592, FAX: (503) 286-7622, E-Mail: marcia@mcintyredirectgroup.com, Web Site: mcintyredirectgroup.com (21)

Chaplin, Alison, NYK Rapp Enterprises LLC, Hallandale, FL. Tel: (954) 457-9100, FAX: (954) 457-9015, Web Site: nykrapp.com (35)

Chapman Cubine Adams & Hussey, Arlington, VA. Tel: (703) 248-0025, Web Site: www.ahadirect.com (20)

Chapman, Lon-Given, Chapman Cubine Adams & Hussey, Arlington, VA. Tel: (703) 248-0025, Web Site: www.ahadirect.com (20)

Chapman, Stephen, ANCOR, Troy, MI. Tel: (248) 740-8866, (800) 229-3860, FAX: (248) 740-9025, Web Site: www.anchorinfo.com (22)

Chappell, Robert E., Penn Mutual, Horsham, PA. Tel: (215) 956-8083, FAX: (215) 956-8368, Web Site: www.pennmutual.com (15)

Chapuis, Patrick, OCE North America Inc, Trumbull, CT. Tel: (773) 714-8500, (800) 523-5444, FAX: (773) 714-4056, Web Site: www.oceusa.com (34)

Char-Broil, Columbus, GA. Tel: (706) 571-7000, Web Site: www.charbroil.com (16)

Char-Broil Grill Lover's Catalog, Columbus, GA. Tel: (866) 241-7548, Web Site: charbroil.com (8)

Charisma Brands LLC, Laguna Hills, CA. Tel: (949) 788-8803, (800) 779-5335, Web Site: www.charismabrands.com (6)

Charity Dynamics, Austin, TX. Tel: (512) 241-0561, FAX: (512) 532-6037, Web Site: www.charitydynamics.com (1)

Charles, Allan, TBC Inc, Baltimore, MD. Tel: (410) 347-7500, FAX: (410) 986-1299, E-Mail: info@tbc.us, Web Site: www.tbc.us (35)

Charles, Jan, Investors Marketing Services, Danvers, MA. Tel: (978) 774-2990, (800) 462-2551, FAX: (978) 774-4249, Web Site: www.investorsmarketing.com (14)

Charles, Vignetta, ETR Associates, Scotts Valley, CA. Tel: (800) 321-4407, E-Mail: customerservice@etr.org, Web Site: www.etr.org (7)

Charleston, Ayana, Arthritis Foundation, Atlanta, GA. Tel: (404) 872-7100, FAX: (404) 872-0457, Web Site: www.arthritis.org (1)

Charlotte Chamber of Commerce, Charlotte, NC. Tel: (704) 378-1300, Web Site: www.boomcharlotte.com (1)

Charlotte Ford Trunks, Dumas, TX. Tel: (806) 934-8477, (800) 659-5614, FAX: (806) 372-3061, E-Mail: charolette@charolettefordtrunks.com, Web Site: www.charolettefordtrunks.com (11)

Charlton, Madison, WI. Tel: (608) 259-8004, FAX: (608) 259-8061, E-Mail: jdragisic@tcgcorp.net, Web Site: www.tcgcorp.net (29)

Charmaster, Grand Rapids, MN. Tel: (218) 326-6786, FAX: (218) 326-1065, E-Mail: info@charmaster. com, Web Site: www.charmaster.com (8)

Charming Shoppes Inc., Bensalem, PA. Tel: (215) 245-9100, Web Site: www.charmingshoppers.com (2)

Charnstrom, Shakopee, MN. Tel: (952) 403-0303, (800) 328-2962, FAX: (800) 916-3215, E-Mail: customerservice@charnstrom.com, Web Site: www. charnstrom.com (28)

Charter Communications, Stamford, CT. Tel: (203) 905-7801, Web Site: www.charter.com (16)

Charter Direct Marketing, New York, NY. Tel: (212) 717-2770, FAX: (561) 750-2150, E-Mail: terrykollman@charterdirectmarketing.com, Web Site: www.charterdirectmarketing.com (35)

Charter One Bank, Cleveland, OH. Tel: (216) 566-5300, (877) CHARTER, (877) 242-7837, FAX: (216) 664-1481, Web Site: www.charterone.com (14)

Chartifacts, Richmond, VA. Tel: (804) 272-7120 (6)

Chartis, New York, NY. Tel: (212) 770-8013, Web Site: www.chartisinsurance.com/pcg (15)

Chasan, Alice, World Press Review, New York, NY. Tel: (212) 982-8880, Web Site: www. worldpressreview.com (18)

Chase Industries, Inc, Cincinnati, OH. Tel: (513) 860-5565, (800) 543-4455, FAX: (800) 245-7045, Web Site: www.chasedoors.com (5)

Chase Media Group, Yorktown Heights, NY. Tel: (914) 962-3871, FAX: (914) 962-2040, Web Site: www. chasemultimedia.com (27)

Chase Online Marketing Strategies Inc, New York, NY. Tel: (646) 535-8160, Web Site: www.wdfm.com (35)

Chase, Carla, Chase Media Group, Yorktown Heights, NY. Tel: (914) 962-3871, FAX: (914) 962-2040, Web Site: www.chasemultimedia.com (27)

Chase, Larry, Chase Online Marketing Strategies Inc, New York, NY. Tel: (646) 535-8160, Web Site: www.wdfm.com (35)

Chase, Reni, Longevity Pure Medicine, Los Angeles, CA. Tel: (800) 919-2090, FAX: (760) 329-3651, E-Mail: info@longevitypuremedicine.com, Web Site: www.longevitypuremedicine.com (7)

Chateau Le Combe, Edmonton, AB Canada. Tel: (780) 428-6611, (800) 661-8801, FAX: (780) 425-6564, E-Mail: info@chateaulecombe.com, Web Site: www.chateaulecombe.com (19)

Chatelain, Elizabeth, MVI Marketing Ltd, San Luis Obispo, CA. Tel: (805) 239-2994, (805) 459-4455, FAX: (805) 239-2947, E-Mail: info@mvimarketing. com, Web Site: www.mvimarketing.com (20)

Chatham, Donald, American Library Association-Publishing Services, Chicago, IL. Tel: (312) 944-6780, (800) 545-2433, FAX: (312) 440-9374, Web Site: www.ala.org (1)

Chatman, Monique, MISSCO Corp, Flowood, MS. Tel: (601) 948-8600, (800) 647-5333, FAX: (601) 987-3038 (16)

Chattanooga Shooting Supplies Inc, Chattanooga, TN. Tel: (423) 894-3007, (800) 251-4808, FAX: (423) 855-5513, Web Site: www.chattanoogashooting.com (16)

Chaturvedi, Dr Anil, Suman Inc, Potomac, MD. Tel: (301) 461-7625, E-Mail: anil.chaturvedi@sumaninc. com, Web Site: www.sumaninc.com (21)

Chaudhry-Ekinci, Lorraine, The CPW Group, Ronkonkoma, NY. Tel: (888) 641-7901 (28)

Chauduri, Robin, Atlanta Cutlery Corp, Conyers, GA. Tel: (770) 922-3700, (800) 833-8838, FAX: (770) 760-8993, E-Mail: webmaster@atlantacutlery.com, Web Site: www.atlantacutlery.com (11)

Chavannes, Danielle, Professional Photographer Magazine, Atlanta, GA. Tel: (404) 522-8600, (800) 786-6277, FAX: (404) 614-6405, E-Mail: csc@ppa.com, Web Site: www.ppa.com (17)

Chavez, Anna Maria, Girl Scouts of the USA, New York, NY. Tel: (212) 852-8000, (800) 478-7248, Web Site: www.girlscouts.org (1)

Chavez, Ryan, Drug Policy Alliance, New York, NY. Tel: (212) 613-8020, FAX: (212) 613-8021, E-Mail: nyc@drugpolicy.org, Web Site: www.drugpolicy. org (1)

Cheak, Spencer, GameTime Inc, Fort Payne, AL. Tel: (256) 845-5610, (800) 235-2440, FAX: (256) 845-9361/2649, Web Site: www.gametime.com (11)

Cheatham, Micah, National Archives & Records Administration, Washington, DC. Tel: (202) 357-5000, (866) 325-7208, Web Site: www.archives.gov (17)

Cheatham, Scot, EOS International Inc, Carlsbad, CA. Tel: (760) 431-8400, (800) 876-5484, FAX: (760) 431-8448, Web Site: www.eosintl.com (5)

Check Point Systems, Thorofare, NJ. Tel: (856) 848-1800, (800) 257-5540, FAX: (856) 848-0937, Web Site: www.checkpointsystems.com (34)

CheckMark Communications, Saint Louis, MO. Tel: (314) 982-1000, FAX: (314) 982-3580, Web Site: www.purina.com (4)

Checks by Phone/Checks by Web, Boynton Beach, FL. Tel: (561) 737-8700, FAX: (561) 737-5800, E-Mail: LarrySchwartz@checksbyphone.com, Web Site: www.checksbyphone.com (14)

CheckVantage, Austin, TX. Tel: (512) 970-4958, (877) 243-2501, FAX: (512) 442-5515, E-Mail: marya@ checkvantage.com, Web Site: www.checkvantage. com (14)

Chee Wah, Immee, Rogers Publishing Ltd, Toronto, ON Canada. Tel: (416) 935-7777, FAX: (416) 935-3597, Web Site: www.rogerspublishing.ca (17)

Cheeseman, Rosanne, Times Publishing Co, Erie, PA. Tel: (814) 870-1600, FAX: (814) 870-1808, E-Mail: terry.cascioli@timesnews.com (18)

Cheever, Meg, Pittsburgh Parks Conservancy, Pittsburgh, PA. Tel: (412) 682-7275, Web Site: www. pittsburghparks.org (1)

Chelsea Clock Co Inc, Chelsea, MA. Tel: (617) 884-0250, (866) 899-2805, FAX: (617) 830-0599, Web Site: www.chelseaclock.com (6)

Chem-Tainer Industries Inc, North Babylon, NY. Tel: (631) 661-8300, (800) 275-2436, (800) ASK-CHEM, FAX: (631) 661-8209, E-Mail: sales@ chemtainer.com, Web Site: www.chemtainer.com (9)

Chemical Week, New York, NY. Tel: (212) 621-4900, FAX: (212) 621-4800, E-Mail: clientservices@ chemweek.com, Web Site: www.chemweek.com (17)

Chen, Dennis, Enterprex International Corp, Arcadia, CA. Tel: (626) 256-1444, FAX: (626) 256-1404, E-Mail: premium@enterprex.com, Web Site: www. enterprex.com (16)

Chen, Dr. Pehong, BroadVision Inc, Redwood City, CA. Tel: (650) 295-0716, (866) 246-4887, FAX: (650) 364-3425, E-Mail: sales@broadvision.com, Web Site: www.broadvision.com (16)

Chen, Edgar, MPS Multimedia Inc, San Mateo, CA. Tel: (650) 872-7100, FAX: (650) 872-7133, E-Mail: sales@gospg.com, Web Site: www.selectmedia.com (16)

Chen, Edward, Amrel, El Monte, CA. Tel: (626) 443-6818, (800) 654-9838, FAX: (626) 443-8600, E-Mail: amrel@amrel.com, Web Site: www.amrel. com (16)

Chen, Eric, Markwins International Corp, City of Industry, CA. Tel: (909) 595-8898, FAX: (909) 595-8820, Web Site: www.markwins.com (16)

Chen, Peng, Morningstar Inc, Chicago, IL. Tel: (312) 696-6000, Web Site: www.morningstar.com (14)

Chen, Robert S., Center for International Earth Science Information Network, Palisades, NY. Tel: (845) 365-8988, FAX: (845) 365-8922, E-Mail: ciesin. info@ciesin.columbia.edu, Web Site: www.ciesin. org (22)

Chen, Steve, MPS Multimedia Inc, San Mateo, CA. Tel: (650) 872-7100, FAX: (650) 872-7133, E-Mail: sales@gospg.com, Web Site: www.selectmedia.com (16)

Chenault, Kenneth I., American Express Co, New York, NY. Tel: (212) 640-2000, FAX: (212) 619-9802, Web Site: www.americanexpress.com (14)

Cheney, Kim, Redbook Magazine, New York, NY. Tel: (212) 649-2000, (800) 888-0008, FAX: (212) 581-7605, Web Site: www.redbookmag.com (17)

Cheng, Ken, Brocade Communications Systems Inc, San Jose, CA. Tel: (408) 333-8000, FAX: (408) 333-8101, E-Mail: info@brocade.com, Web Site: www. brocade.com (16)

Cheng, Xiangi, Boundless Corp, Phelps, NY. Tel: (631) 962-1500, (800) 231-5445, FAX: (631) 962-1505, E-Mail: sales@boundless.com, Web Site: www. boundless.com (16)

Cheny, Barbara, The Hyiad Group, Garden City, NY. Tel: (516) 433-3800, FAX: (516) 822-6670, Web Site: www.thehyaidgroup.com (22)

Cherkis, Jeff, Brashe Advertising Inc, Jericho, NY. Tel: (516) 935-5544, FAX: (516) 932-7264, E-Mail: info@brasheadv.com, Web Site: brashe.com (35)

Chernoff Newman, Columbia, SC. Tel: (803) 254-8158, FAX: (803) 252-2016, E-Mail: columbia@ chernoffnewman.com, Web Site: www. chernoffnewman.com (35)

Cherry Brothers LLC/Cherrydale, Lansdale, PA. Tel: (800) 333-4525, Web Site: www.cherrydale.com (1)

Cherry Communications Co, Tallahassee, FL. Tel: (850) 561-3600, FAX: (850) 561-1155, E-Mail: phones@ cherrycomm.com, Web Site: www.cherrycomm. com (30)

Cherry Tree Toys Inc, Beloit, WI. Tel: (608) 314-3090, (800) 848-4363, FAX: (608) 314-3097, E-Mail: sales@cherrytreetoys.com, Web Site: www. cherrytreetoys.com (11)

Cherry, Linda Z., Cherry Communications Co, Tallahassee, FL. Tel: (850) 561-3600, FAX: (850) 561-1155, E-Mail: phones@cherrycomm.com, Web Site: www.cherrycomm.com (30)

Cherry, Tom, Coptech Inc, Saugus, MA. Tel: (781) 935-2679, (800) 934-1560, FAX: (781) 935-7673, Web Site: www.coptechinc.com (16)

Cherubini, Julian, AliMed Inc, Dedham, MA. Tel: (781) 329-2900, (800) 225-2610, FAX: (800) 437-2966, (781) 329-8392, E-Mail: info@alimed.com, Web Site: www.alimed.com (7)

Chesapeake Bay Foundation, Annapolis, MD. Tel: (410) 268-8816, Web Site: www.savethebay.cbf.org (1)

Chesebro, Jeff, Princeton Partners Inc, Princeton, NJ. Tel: (609) 452-8500, FAX: (609) 452-7212, E-Mail: moreinfo@princetonpartners.com, Web Site: www. princetonpartners.com (35)

Cheskin, Redwood Shores, CA. Tel: (650) 802-2100, FAX: (650) 593-1125, E-Mail: info@cheskin.com, Web Site: www.cheskin.com (30)

Chesley, David, Interface Engineering, Portland, OR. Tel: (503) 382-2266, FAX: (503) 382-2262, E-Mail: solutions@interfaceengineering.com, Web Site: www.ieice.com (20)

Chessari, Jenna, Remedy Magazine, New York, NY. Tel: (212) 695-2223, FAX: (212) 695-2936, E-Mail: info@rmedizine.com, Web Site: www.medizine.com (17)

Chester, Dan, Direct Marketing Association of Detroit, Royal Oak, MI. Tel: (248) 478-4888, FAX: (248) 478-6437, E-Mail: dmad@ameritech.net, Web Site: www.dmad.org (40)

Chestnut, Ben, MailChimp, Atlanta, GA. Tel: (678) 999-0141, Web Site: mailchimp.com (24)

Chestnut, Mark, Laplink Software Inc, Bellevue, WA. Tel: (425) 952-6000, (800) 527-5465, FAX: (425) 952-6002, E-Mail: marketing@laplink.com, Web Site: www.laplink.com (3)

Cheteyan, II Michael D., ABDI, Inc Global Order Fulfillment, Leetsdale, PA. Tel: (412) 741-1142, (800) 796-6471, FAX: (412) 741-4161, E-Mail: info@abdintl.com, Web Site: www.abdintl.com (28)

Cheteyan, Judy G., ABDI, Inc Global Order Fulfillment, Leetsdale, PA. Tel: (412) 741-1142, (800) 796-6471, FAX: (412) 741-4161, E-Mail: info@abdintl.com, Web Site: www.abdintl.com (28)

Cheung, Deborah, Institute For Natural Resources, Concord, CA. Tel: (925) 687-0860, FAX: (925) 609-2820, E-Mail: dcheung@biocorp.com (16)

Cheung, Deborah, United Systems c/o Biomed, Concord, CA. Tel: (925) 609-2820 (7)

Chevannes, Paul, Paul Chevannes, Brooklyn, NY. Tel: (718) 788-3550 (36)

Cheves, Angela, MD Anderson Cancer Center - Children's Art Project, Houston, TX. Tel: (713) 745-2575, (800) 231-1580, FAX: (713) 794-1950, E-Mail: krenner@mdanderson.org, Web Site: www.childrensart.org (1)

Chew, Susan, Nostrum Inc, Long Beach, CA. Tel: (562) 437-2200, Web Site: www.nostruminc.com (35)

Chewning Direct Marketing, Irvine, CA. Tel: (949) 854-5401, FAX: (949) 743-8395, E-Mail: hchewning@cdmdirect.com, Web Site: www.cdmdirect.com (21)

Chewning, Hugh, Chewning Direct Marketing, Irvine, CA. Tel: (949) 854-5401, FAX: (949) 743-8395, E-Mail: hchewning@cdmdirect.com, Web Site: www.cdmdirect.com (21)

Chhokar, Preet, NetSpend, San Mateo, CA. Tel: (866) 387-7363, Web Site: www.netspend.com (14)

Chiang, Emily, Advertising Age, New York, NY. Tel: (212) 210-0100, FAX: (212) 210-0111, Web Site: www.crain.com (43)

Chiang, Jim, Gero Vita, Costa Mesa, CA. Tel: (888) 382-9175, Web Site: www.gvi.com (16)

Chiarello, Guy, JP Morgan Chase & Co, New York, NY. Tel: (212) 270-6000, E-Mail: jpmcinvestorrelations@jpmchase.com, Web Site: www.jpmorgan.com (14)

Chiavelli, Jim, Evergreen Marketing, Shelton, CT. Tel: (203) 822-7782, E-Mail: jchiavelli@evergreenmarketing.com, Web Site: www.evergreenmarketing.com (23)

Chicago Association of Direct Marketing, Westmont, IL. Tel: (312) 849-2236, FAX: (312) 849-2239, E-Mail: info@cadm.org, Web Site: www.cadm.org (40)

Chicago Convention & Tourism Bureau, Chicago, IL. Tel: (312) 791-7000, FAX: (312) 567-8599, Web Site: www.choosechicago.com (1)

Chicago Magazine, Chicago, IL. Tel: (312) 222-8999, FAX: (312) 222-0287, Web Site: www.chicagomag.com (17)

Chicago Sun-Times, Chicago, IL. Tel: (312) 321-3000, FAX: (312) 321-9655, E-Mail: jmorawez@suntimes.com, Web Site: www.suntimes.com (31)

Chicago Tribune, Chicago, IL. Tel: (312) 222-3232, (800) 874-2863, FAX: (312) 222-2598, E-Mail: consumerservices@tribune.com, Web Site: www.chicagotribune.com (31)

Chick Harness & Supply Inc, Harrington, DE. Tel: (302) 398-4630, (800) 444-2441, FAX: (302) 398-3920, E-Mail: saddles@chicksaddlery.com, Web Site: www.chicksaddlery.com (11)

Chico's FAS Inc, Fort Myers, FL. Tel: (239) 277-6200, Web Site: www.chicos.com (2)

Chidambaram, Chidam, Johnny Appleseed's Inc, Middleton, MA. Tel: (978) 922-2040, (800) 546-4554, FAX: (978) 922-7001, Web Site: www.appleseeds.blair.com (2)

Chiddister, Bruce, MailGraphics Inc, Boulder, CO. Tel: (303) 449-4053, E-Mail: questions@mailgraphics.com, Web Site: www.mailgraphics.com (23)

Chidester, Becky, Wunderman Health, Saint Louis, MO. Tel: (314) 590-8300, FAX: (314) 590-8383, Web Site: www.wunderman.com/health (35)

Chief Executive Magazine, Greenwich, CT. Tel: (203) 930-2700, FAX: (203) 930-2701, Web Site: www.chiefexecutive.net (17)

Chief Marketer and Multichannel Merchant, New York, NY. Tel: (212) 204-4228 (17)

Chief Media LLC, New York, NY. Tel: (212) 300-8487, FAX: (212) 629-9505, E-Mail: info@chiefmedia.com, Web Site: www.chiefmedia.com (35)

Chilcott Direct Marketing, Edmond, OK. Tel: (405) 726-8780, FAX: (405) 726-8799, E-Mail: info@cdmlist.com, Web Site: www.cdmlist.com (24)

Chilcutt, Matt, Chilcutt Direct Marketing, Edmond, OK. Tel: (405) 726-8780, FAX: (405) 726-8799, E-Mail: info@cdmlist.com, Web Site: www.cdmlist.com (24)

Chilcutt, Scott R., Marketing Information Network, Edmond, OK. Tel: (405) 516-1215, FAX: (405) 516-1230, Web Site: www.minokc.com (22)

ChildFund International, Richmond, VA. Tel: (804) 756-2700, (800) 776-6767, FAX: (804) 756-2718, Web Site: www.christianchildrensfund.org (1)

ChildFund International, Richmond, VA. Tel: (804) 756-2700, Web Site: www.ChildFund.org (1)

Children International, Kansas City, MO. Tel: (816) 942-2000, (800) 888-3089, FAX: (816) 942-3714, E-Mail: RobS@cikc.org, Web Site: www.children.org (1)

Children of the Night, Van Nuys, CA. Tel: (818) 908-4474, (800) 551-1300, FAX: (818) 908-1468, E-Mail: llee@childrenofthenight.com, Web Site: www.childrenofthenight.org (1)

Children's Aid Society, New York, NY. Tel: (212) 949-4800, Web Site: www.childrensaidsociety.org (1)

Children's Better Health Institute, Indianapolis, IN. Tel: (317) 634-1100, FAX: (317) 684-8094, E-Mail: a.mcdowell@cbhi.org, Web Site: www.cbhi.org (1)

Children's Hospital Foundation, Silver Spring, MD. Tel: (202) 476-3000, (800) 884-LIFE, FAX: (202) 884-5999, Web Site: www.dcchildrens.com (1)

Children's Hospital of Pittsburgh, Pittsburgh, PA. Tel: (412) 692-5325, FAX: (412) 692-7140, Web Site: www.chp.edu (1)

Children's Miracle Network, Salt Lake City, UT. Tel: (801) 214-7400, Web Site: www.cmn.org (40)

Childs, Craig, Pinnacle Direct Marketing LLC, Columbus, OH. Tel: (800) 716-0173, FAX: (888) 754-4511, Web Site: www.pinnacledirectonline.com (35)

Childs, Ron, National Pen Corp, San Diego, CA. Tel: (858) 675-3000, FAX: (858) 675-3030, E-Mail: info@nationalpen.com, Web Site: www.pens.com (6)

Chiles, Dan, Watts Radiant, Springfield, MO. Tel: (417) 864-6108, (800) 276-2419, FAX: (417) 864-8161, Web Site: www.wattsheatway.com (9)

Chiles, Mike, Watts Radiant, Springfield, MO. Tel: (417) 864-6108, (800) 276-2419, FAX: (417) 864-8161, Web Site: www.wattsheatway.com (9)

Chin, Raymond T., GrayHair Software, Mount Laurel, NJ. Tel: (856) 727-9372, FAX: (856) 727-1315, Web Site: www.grayhairsoftware.com (22)

China Books & Periodicals Inc, South San Francisco, CA. Tel: (650) 872-7076, (800) 818-2017, FAX: (650) 872-7808, E-Mail: info@chinabooks.com, Web Site: www.chinabooks.com (17)

ChinaStock/WorldViews, Ann Arbor, MI. Tel: (734) 996-1440, (800) 315-4462, FAX: (734) 996-1481, E-Mail: decoxphoto@aol.com, Web Site: www.denniscox.com (38)

Chinn, Mike, SNL Financial, Charlottesville, VA. Tel: (434) 977-1600, FAX: (434) 977-4466, E-Mail: support@sni.com, Web Site: www.snl.com (17)

Chiorando, Rick, Austin & Williams, Hauppauge, NY. Tel: (631) 938-2279, FAX: (212) 434-7022, E-Mail: info@austin-williams.com, Web Site: www.austin-williams.com (35)

Chip Peterson Photos, Saint Paul, MN. Tel: (651) 699-4286, FAX: (651) 698-7667 (38)

Chipault, Raymond, Underwood Photo Archives Inc, Woodside, CA. Tel: (650) 851-5190, FAX: (650) 851-5193, E-Mail: ray@underwoodarchives.com, Web Site: www.underwoodarchives.com (38)

Chipman, Debra, Institute for International Research Inc, New York, NY. Tel: (212) 661-3500, (800) 345-8016, FAX: (212) 599-2192, E-Mail: register@iirusa.com, Web Site: www.iir-ny.com (16)

Chiquet, Maureen, Chanel Inc, New York, NY. Tel: (212) 688-5055, (800) 550-0005, FAX: (212) 752-1851, Web Site: www.chanel.com (16)

Chirico, Emanuel, Phillips-Van Heusen Corp, New York, NY. Tel: (212) 381-3500, (800) 388-9122, FAX: (212) 381-3950, Web Site: www.pvh.com (2)

Chittick, Denny, Insight Direct Inc, Tempe, AZ. Tel: (480) 333-3001, (800) 467-4448, FAX: (480) 902-1180, Web Site: www.insight.com (16)

Chiusano, Melissa, Challenge Industries Inc, Ithaca, NY. Tel: (607) 272-8990, FAX: (607) 277-7865, E-Mail: info@aboutchallenge.org, Web Site: www.aboutchallenge.org (28)

Chivari, Tony, Things Remembered, Highland Heights, OH. Tel: (440) 473-2000, (866) 902-4438, FAX: (440) 473-2018, E-Mail: customerservice@thingsremembered.com, Web Site: www.thingsremembered.com (6)

Choate, Timothy C., Aptimus, San Francisco, CA. Tel: (415) 896-2123, FAX: (415) 896-2561 (22)

Choice Courier Systems Inc, New York, NY. Tel: (212) 370-1999, FAX: (212) 370-0440, Web Site: www.choicecourier.com (16)

Choice Hotels International, Rockville, MD. Tel: (301) 592-5000, Web Site: www.choicehotels.com (16)

Choice Magazine, Middletown, CT. Tel: (860) 347-6933, (860) 347-1387, FAX: (860) 346-8586, E-Mail: adsales@ala-choice.org, Web Site: www.ala.org/ala/acrl/acrlpubs/choice/home.cfm (31)

Choice Media, Amherst, NH. Tel: (603) 672-3338, FAX: (603) 249-9732, E-Mail: choicemedia@ comcast.net (31)

Choice Point, Alpharetta, GA. Tel: (770) 752-6000, (800) 342-5339, FAX: (770) 752-6005, Web Site: www.choicepoint.com (16)

ChoiceConnex, Clearwater, FL. Tel: (727) 571-3302, Web Site: www.choiceconnex.com (29)

ChoicePoint Precision Marketing, Little Rock, AR. Tel: (978) 738-0544, (800) 937-4232, FAX: (978) 738-0582, Web Site: www.cp-pm.com (30)

Chong, Arthur, Safeco Insurance Co, Seattle, WA. Tel: (206) 545-5000, (800) 332-3226, FAX: (206) 545-5767/5651, Web Site: www.safeco.com (15)

Chopoorian, Donald, Supreme Specialty Advertising, Mount Arlington, NJ. Tel: (973) 770-8700, FAX: (973) 770-0808 (33)

Chopp, Steve, Pharmavite Corp LLC (HQ), Northridge, CA. Tel: (818) 221-6200, (800) 423-2405, FAX: (818) 221-6618, Web Site: www.pharmavite.com (16)

Chown, Amy, Atlanta Journal & Constitution, Atlanta, GA. Tel: (404) 526-5151, Web Site: www.ajc.com (17)

Christ, Peter, Crystal Records Inc, Camas, WA. Tel: (360) 834-7022, FAX: (360) 834-9680, E-Mail: info@crystalrecords.com, Web Site: www. crystalrecords.com (3)

Christensen, Apryl, Cooper Concepts Inc, Chicago, IL. Tel: (872) 206-8145, E-Mail: contact.hr@ cooperconcepts.com, Web Site: www. cooperconcepts-inc.com (35)

Christensen, Charles, Bedford/St Martin's, Boston, MA. Tel: (617) 426-7440, FAX: (617) 426-8582, Web Site: www.bedfordstmartins.com (17)

Christensen, Dickie, Leslie Jordan, Portland, OR. Tel: (503) 295-1987, (800) 935-3343, FAX: (503) 295-0939, E-Mail: ljsales@lesliejordan.com, Web Site: www.lesliejordan.com (2)

Christensen, Kristine S., Equitable Life & Casualty Insurance Co, Salt Lake City, UT. Tel: (801) 579-3400, FAX: (801) 579-3789, Web Site: www. equilife.com (15)

Christensen, Leif, Manistique Papers Inc, Manistique, MI. Tel: (906) 341-2175, FAX: (906) 341-5635 (25)

Christensen, Pixie, Wycliffe Bible Translators, Dallas, TX. Tel: (972) 708-7522, Web Site: www.wycliffe. org (17)

Christensen, Shirlee, Mostad & Christensen, Oak Harbor, WA. Tel: (360) 679-4164, (800) 654-1654, FAX: (360) 679-4167, E-Mail: marketing@mostad. com, Web Site: www.mostad.com (16)

Christian Appalachian Project, Paintsville, KY. Tel: (866) 270-4227, (866) 270-4CAP, FAX: (859) 792-6560, E-Mail: capinfo@chrisapp.org, Web Site: www.christianapp.org (1)

Christian Book Distributors Inc, Peabody, MA. Tel: (978) 532-5300, FAX: (978) 977-5010, E-Mail: javedisian@chrbook.com, Web Site: www.chrbook. com (17)

Christian Brands, Phoenix, AZ. Tel: (602) 243-5200, (800) 521-2914, FAX: (602) 232-1855, Web Site: www.christian-brands.com (16)

Christian Broadcasting Network Inc, Virginia Beach, VA. Tel: (757) 226-7000, FAX: (757) 226-2017, Web Site: www.cbn.com (1)

Christian Herald Association, New York, NY. Tel: (212) 684-2800, (800) BOWERY-1, FAX: (212) 684-3740, E-Mail: info@chaonline.org, Web Site: www.bowery.org (1)

Christian Relief Services Charities Inc, Alexandria, VA. Tel: (703) 317-9086, E-Mail: info@christianrelief. org, Web Site: www.christianrelief.org (1)

Christian Resource Management, Orange, CA. Tel: (714) 974-0754, FAX: (714) 974-7845, E-Mail: CRMOrange@aol.com, Web Site: www.crmorange. com (22)

The Christian Science Monitor, Boston, MA. Tel: (617) 450-2300, FAX: (617) 450-2031, Web Site: www. csmonitor.com (31)

The Christian Science Publishing Society, Boston, MA. Tel: (617) 450-2000, E-Mail: info@christianscience. com, Web Site: jsh.christianscience.com (17)

Christianity Today Inc, Carol Stream, IL. Tel: (630) 260-6200, FAX: (630) 260-0114, Web Site: www. christianitytoday.com (17)

Christiansen, Jaclyn, Einhorn Associates Inc, Milwaukee, WI. Tel: (414) 453-4488, FAX: (414) 453-4831, Web Site: www.einhornassociates.com (20)

Christianson, Camille, Timm Medical Technologies, Inc, Lake Forest, IL. Tel: (952) 947-9410, (800) 438-8592, FAX: (952) 947-9411, Web Site: www. timmmedical.com (16)

Christianson, Kory, St Joseph's Indian School, Chamberlain, SD. Tel: (605) 734-3300, Web Site: www. stjo.org (1)

Christides, Stephen, Nylon Net Co, Memphis, TN. Tel: (901) 526-6500, (800) 238-7529, (877) 893-6535, FAX: (901) 526-6538, E-Mail: nylonnet@nylonnet. com, Web Site: www.nylonnet.com (11)

Christy, Charles, Citizens Republic Bank, Flint, MI. Tel: (810) 766-7500, Web Site: www. citizensbanking.com (14)

Christy, Jr. Donald D., NADA Appraisal Guides, Costa Mesa, CA. Tel: (714) 556-8511, (800) 966-6232, FAX: (714) 957-0302, E-Mail: info@nadaguides. com, Web Site: www.nadaguides.com (17)

Christy, Julie, In-Sync Publications, Redondo Beach, CA. Tel: (310) 543-9045, FAX: (310) 543-9035, E-Mail: insyncpubs@aol.com, Web Site: www. insyncpubs.com (18)

Christy, Robert, In-Sync Publications, Redondo Beach, CA. Tel: (310) 543-9045, FAX: (310) 543-9035, E-Mail: insyncpubs@aol.com, Web Site: www. insyncpubs.com (18)

Chronister, Mark, MXT Card Services, LLC, New Castle, DE. Tel: (302) 323-6203, FAX: (302) 323-6219, Web Site: www.mxtcs.com (14)

Chrystie, Kim, EMC Corp, Hopkinton, MA. Tel: (888) 438-3622, Web Site: www.emc.com (16)

Chu, Cynthia, USA Network, New York, NY. Tel: (212) 664-4444, FAX: (212) 664-6365, Web Site: www.usanetwork.com (32)

Chu, Peter, BroadVision Inc, Redwood City, CA. Tel: (650) 295-0716, (866) 246-4887, FAX: (650) 364-3425, E-Mail: sales@broadvision.com, Web Site: www.broadvision.com (16)

Chu, Selena, Queens College/CUNY Professional and Continuing Studies (PCS), Flushing, NY. Tel: (718) 997-5700, FAX: (718) 997-5723, E-Mail: pcs@qc. cuny.edu, Web Site: www.qc.cuny.edu/pcs (41)

Chua, Mark, J&H Berge/The Lab Mart, South Plainfield, NJ. Tel: (908) 561-3002, (800) 684-1234, FAX: (908) 561-3002, E-Mail: info@jhberge.com, Web Site: www.jhberge.com (7)

The Chubb Corp, Warren, NJ. Tel: (908) 903-2000, FAX: (908) 903-2027, Web Site: www.chubb.com (20)

Chugh, Ash, Epic Marketing Solutions, Halifax, NS Canada. Tel: (902) 455-5100, (888) 323-6263, FAX: (902) 455-5103, E-Mail: info@epicmarketing.ca, Web Site: www.epicmarketing.ca (22)

Church Extension Plan, Salem, OR. Tel: (800) 821-1112, Web Site: www.cepnet.com (14)

Church Pension Fund, New York, NY. Tel: (866) 802-6333, (800) 223-6602, Web Site: www.cpg.org (1)

Church, Andrew G., Oneida Ltd, Oneida, NY. Tel: (315) 361-3000, (888) 263-7195, FAX: (315) 361-3700, Web Site: www.oneida.com (16)

Church, Dr. Nancy J., State University of New York-College of Plattsburgh, Plattsburgh, NY. Tel: (518) 564-2000, FAX: (518) 564-3183, E-Mail: nancy. church@plattsburgh.edu, Web Site: www. plattsburgh.edu (41)

Church, Ellen, CMS LLC, Reston, VA. Tel: (703) 258-0000, Web Site: www.craveronline.com (1)

Church, John, The Pillsbury Co, Minneapolis, MN. Tel: (763) 764-7600, (800) 248-7310, FAX: (763) 764-8330, Web Site: www.pillsbury.com (16)

Church, Mark, James Medical Rents & Sales Inc, Fort Wayne, IN. Tel: (260) 739-0874, E-Mail: sales@ jamesmedical.com, Web Site: www.jamesmedical. net (7)

Ann Chwatsky Photography, New York, NY. Tel: (212) 673-5689, FAX: (212) 673-5689, E-Mail: annphotog@aol.com, Web Site: www. annchwatskyphoto.com (37)

Chwatsky, Ann, Ann Chwatsky Photography, New York, NY. Tel: (212) 673-5689, FAX: (212) 673-5689, E-Mail: annphotog@aol.com, Web Site: www.annchwatskyphoto.com (37)

Ciaccia, Peter, New York Road Runners, New York, NY. Tel: (855) 5MY-NYRR, E-Mail: mynyrr@nyrr. org, Web Site: www.nyrr.org (13)

Ciarlo Consulting LLC, Waterbury, CT. Tel: (203) 232-6655 (20)

Cichanowski, Mike, We-No-Nah Canoe Inc, Winona, MN. Tel: (507) 454-5430, FAX: (507) 454-5448, E-Mail: info@wenonah.com, Web Site: www. wenonah.com (11)

Cigich, Erin, Clickbooth.com LLC, Sarasota, FL. Tel: (941) 483-4188, Web Site: www.clickbooth.com (35)

CIGNA International, Philadelphia, PA. Tel: (215) 761-1741, FAX: (215) 761-5515, Web Site: www.cigna. com (15)

Cilley, Charles, Cuddledown Inc, Yarmouth, ME. Tel: (800) 323-6793, FAX: (207) 761-1948, Web Site: www.cuddledown.com (8)

Cillo, Joanne, Tuttle Printing & Engraving, Rutland, VT. Tel: (802) 773-9171, (800) 776-7682, FAX: (802) 773-5785, E-Mail: info@tuttleprinting.com, Web Site: www.tuttleprinting.com (10)

Cincinnati Bell Inc, Cincinnati, OH. Tel: (888) CIN-BELL, Web Site: www.cincinnatibell.com (16)

Cinema World Studios, Greenpoint, NY. Tel: (718) 389-9800, FAX: (718) 389-9897, E-Mail: cinemaworldfd@verizon.net, Web Site: www. cinemaworldstudios.com (32)

Cinmar LP, West Chester, OH. Tel: (888) 263-9850, Web Site: www.frontgate.com (8)

Cinque. Adam, Allied Integrated Marketing, Boston, MA. Tel: (617) 859-4800, E-Mail: alliedimsocial@ alliedim.com, Web Site: alliedim.com (35)

Cintas, Cincinnati, OH. Tel: (513) 459-1200, Web Site: www.cintas.com (16)

Ciola, Kimberly, Berkshire Direct Inc, Williamstown, MA. Tel: (413) 458-1721, FAX: (413) 458-1727, E-Mail: info@berkshiredirect.com, Web Site: www. berkshiredirect.com (17)

Ciolli, Sue, Tower Hobbies/Hobbico, Champaign, IL. Tel: (217) 398-3636, (800) 637-6050, FAX: (217) 398-1104, Web Site: www.towerhobbies.com (11)

Cipolaro, Robert, Richard Bauer & Co Inc, Teaneck, NJ. Tel: (201) 692-1005, (800) 995-7881, FAX: (201) 692-8626, E-Mail: info@richardbauer.com, Web Site: www.richardbauer.com (25)

Cipolla, Jack, American Federation of Astrologers, Tempe, AZ. Tel: (480) 838-1751, (888) 301-7630, FAX: (480) 838-8293, E-Mail: afa@msn.com, Web Site: www.astrologers.com (1)

Circle K Stores Inc, Akron, OH. Tel: (330) 630-6300, Web Site: www.cirlcek.com (16)

Circulation Specialists Inc, Shelton, CT. Tel: (888) 315-2472, FAX: (888) 315-2507 (20)

Cirino, Paul, Foremost Industrial Exchange, Van Nuys, CA. Tel: (818) 988-6900, FAX: (818) 787-0293 (16)

Cisco Systems Inc, San Jose, CA. Tel: (408) 526-4000, (800) 553-NETS, FAX: (408) 526-4100, Web Site: www.cisco.com (22)

Cision US Inc, Chicago, IL. Tel: (312) 922-2400, (866) 639-5087, FAX: (312) 922-3126, E-Mail: info.us@cision.com, Web Site: us.cision.com (43)

Cissna, John L., Computermail South Inc. Saint Petersburg, FL. Tel: (727) 579-1000, FAX: (727) 823-5474, E-Mail: sales@computermailsouth.com, Web Site: www.computermailsouth.com (23)

Citi Cards / Citicorp Credit Services, Long Island City, NY. Tel: (718) 248-5400 (14)

Citibank, New York, NY. Tel: (212) 559-9425, (800) 285-3000, FAX: (212) 527-2318, Web Site: www.citibank.com (14)

CitiFinancial Credit Co, Baltimore, MD. Tel: (410) 332-3000, (800) 922-6235, (800) 995-2274, FAX: (410) 332-3489, Web Site: www.citifinancial.com (14)

Citigroup Inc, New York, NY. Tel: (212) 559-1000, (800) 285-3000, FAX: (212) 793-3946, Web Site: www.citigroup.com (14)

Citizens Against Government Waste, Washington, DC. Tel: (202) 467-5300, (800) USA-DEBT, FAX: (202) 467-4253, E-Mail: membership@cagw.org, Web Site: www.cagw.org (1)

Citizens Bank, Boston, MA. Tel: (617) 725-5900, FAX: (617) 725-5921, Web Site: www.citizensbank.com (14)

Citizens Republic Bank, Flint, MI. Tel: (810) 766-7500, Web Site: www.citizensbanking.com (14)

Citorino, Tom, PennWell Publishing, Tulsa, OK. Tel: (918) 835-3161, (800) 331-4463, E-Mail: headquarters@pennwell.com, Web Site: www.pennwell.com (17)

Citrix Systems, Inc, Fort Lauderdale, FL. Tel: (954) 267-3000, FAX: (954) 267-3101, Web Site: www.citrix.com (22)

City of Cerritos, Cerritos, CA. Tel: (562) 916-1319, Web Site: www.ci.cerritos.ca.us (1)

City of Hope National Medical Center, Duarte, CA. Tel: (626) 256-4673, FAX: (626) 301-8468, Web Site: www.cityofhope.org (1)

City of LaGrange, LaGrange, GA. Tel: (706) 883-2010, FAX: (706) 883-2020, Web Site: www.lagrange-ga.org (1)

CityTwist, Boca Raton, FL. Tel: (866) 798-2489, FAX: (561) 314-2692, Web Site: www.citytwist.com (32)

Civil Service Employees Insurance Group, Walnut Creek, CA. Tel: (415) 274-7803, (925) 817-6300, (800) 282-6848, Web Site: www.cseinsurance.com (15)

Civil War Preservation Trust, Washington, DC. Tel: (202) 367-1861, (800) 298-7878, E-Mail: info@civilwar.org, Web Site: www.civilwar.org (1)

CL&B Capital Management, Fayetteville, NY. Tel: (315) 637-0915, FAX: (815) 642-9396, E-Mail: webinquiry@clbcm.com, Web Site: www.clbcm.com (35)

Claiborne, Phil, Elks Magazine, Chicago, IL. Tel: (773) 755-4700, FAX: (773) 775-4792, E-Mail: elksmag@elks.org, Web Site: www.elks.org (17)

Clairol Inc, Stamford, CT. Tel: (203) 357-5000, (800) 252-4765, FAX: (203) 357-5003, Web Site: www.clairol.com (7)

Clampitt Paper Co, Dallas, TX. Tel: (214) 638-3300, FAX: (214) 634-7837, E-Mail: dcrew@clampitt.com, Web Site: www.clampitt.com (16)

Clampitt, Donald, Clampitt Paper Co, Dallas, TX. Tel: (214) 638-3300, FAX: (214) 634-7837, E-Mail: dcrew@clampitt.com, Web Site: www.clampitt.com (16)

Clapper, Darrell, Welch Allyn, Inc, Skaneateles Falls, NY. Tel: (315) 685-4100, Web Site: www.welchallyn.com (9)

Clapper, William M., MTI Information Technologies LLC, Langhorne, PA. Tel: (267) 569-2400, FAX: (215) 741-3898, Web Site: www.mtiadvantage.com (30)

Clare, Dan, Gulfstream Aerospace Corp, Savannah, GA. Tel: (912) 965-3000, E-Mail: info@gulfstream.com, Web Site: www.gulfstream.com (16)

Clarin by Hussey Seating, North Berwick, ME. Tel: (800) 341-0401, FAX: (207) 676-2222, Web Site: www.husseyseating.com (5)

Clario Analytics, Eden Prairie, MN. Tel: (952) 653-0980, (866) 849-3341, FAX: (952) 653-5900, E-Mail: sales@clarioanalytics.com, Web Site: www.clarioanalytics.com (20)

Claritas Express, Ithaca, NY. Tel: (607) 257-5757, (866) 737-7429, FAX: (607) 266-0425, E-Mail: info@claritas.com, Web Site: www.claritas.com/express (30)

Clarity Group LLC, Chapel Hill, NC. Tel: (919) 932-6036, Web Site: www.claritygroupinc.com (20)

Clark & Clark Inc, Saint Louis, MO. Tel: (314) 994-9155, FAX: (314) 994-0573, E-Mail: jim.clark@clark-clark.net, Web Site: clark-clark.net (33)

The Clark Grave Vault Co, Columbus, OH. Tel: (614) 294-3761, FAX: (614) 299-2324, Web Site: www.clarkvault.com (16)

Clark Johnson, Sue, Reno Gazette Journal, Reno, NV. Tel: (775) 788-6200, FAX: (775) 788-6563 (17)

Clark, Bart, Suez Energy North America, Houston, TX. Tel: (713) 636-0000, FAX: (713) 636-1364, Web Site: www.tractebelpowerinc.com (16)

Clark, Ben, LH Selman Ltd, Chicago, IL. Tel: (831) 427-1177, (800) 538-0766, FAX: (831) 427-0111 (6)

Clark, Darren, MacLaren McCann, Toronto, ON Canada. Tel: (416) 594-6000, FAX: (416) 643-7026, Web Site: www.maclaren.com (35)

Clark, David, The Weather Channel, Atlanta, GA. Tel: (770) 226-0000, FAX: (770) 226-2390, Web Site: www.weather.com (32)

Clark, Dennis, Fairfield Industries Inc, Sugar Land, TX. Tel: (281) 275-7500, (800) 231-9809, FAX: (281) 275-7550, E-Mail: jblattman@fairfield.com, Web Site: www.fairfield.com (16)

Clark, George L., Rose Resnick Lighthouse for the Blind & Visually Impaired, San Francisco, CA. Tel: (415) 431-1481, FAX: (415) 863-7568, E-Mail: executive@lighthouse-sf.org, Web Site: www.lighthouse-sf.org (1)

Clark, Gina, AmMed Direct, Parsons, TN. Tel: (615) 941-3900, (800) 282-3524, Web Site: www.arrivamedical.com (7)

Clark, James, JLS Mailing Services Inc, Brockton, MA. Tel: (508) 313-1050, (866) JLS-MAIL, FAX: (508) 313-1093, E-Mail: rparkinson@jlsms.com, Web Site: www.jlsms.com (28)

Clark, Jamie Rappaport, Defenders of Wildlife, Washington, DC. Tel: (202) 682-9400, (800) 385-9712, E-Mail: defenders@mail.defenders.org, Web Site: www.defenders.org (1)

Clark, Jim, Boys & Girls Clubs of America National Headquarters, Atlanta, GA. Tel: (404) 487-5700, FAX: (404) 815-5757, (404) 487-5757, E-Mail: info@bgca.org, Web Site: www.bgca.org (1)

Clark, Jim, Clark & Clark Inc, Saint Louis, MO. Tel: (314) 994-9155, FAX: (314) 994-0573, E-Mail: jim.clark@clark-clark.net, Web Site: clark-clark.net (33)

Clark, Jim, Penguin Group USA Inc, New York, NY. Tel: (212) 366-2000, Web Site: www.us.penguingroup.com (17)

Clark, Joan, Clark's Corvair Parts, Inc, Shelburne Falls, MA. Tel: (413) 625-9776, FAX: (413) 625-8498, E-Mail: clarks@corvair.com, Web Site: www.corvair.com (12)

Clark, Jr. Calvin, Clark's Corvair Parts, Inc, Shelburne Falls, MA. Tel: (413) 625-9776, FAX: (413) 625-8498, E-Mail: clarks@corvair.com, Web Site: www.corvair.com (12)

Clark, Juahn, American Baseball Coaches Association, Greensboro, NC. Tel: (336) 821-3140, FAX: (336) 886-0000, E-Mail: abca@abca.org, Web Site: www.abca.org (1)

Clark, Kenneth, YP Talk, Pittsburg, KS. Tel: (620) 308-6434, E-Mail: info@yptalk.com, Web Site: www.yptalk.com (31)

Clark, Kent A.D., AMVETS National Service Foundation, Lanham, MD. Tel: (301) 459-6181, (800) 810-7148, FAX: (301) 459-5578, Web Site: www.amvetsnsf.org (1)

Clark, Meg, Association for Audience Marketing Professionals (AAMP), North Hollywood, CA. Tel: (310) 323-7220, FAX: (310) 323-7231, E-Mail: mjordan@espcomp.com, Web Site: www.wfma.org (40)

Clark, Mike, Fitness Quest, Canton, OH. Tel: (330) 478-0755, (800) 321-9236, FAX: (330) 479-9213, E-Mail: customersupport@fitnessquest.com, Web Site: www.fitnessquest.com (16)

Clark, Mitch, LH Selman Ltd, Chicago, IL. Tel: (831) 427-1177, (800) 538-0766, FAX: (831) 427-0111 (6)

Clark, R. Kerry, Fluke Biomedical, Everett, WA. Tel: (425) 347-6100, (800) 850-4608, FAX: (425) 446-5116, Web Site: www.flukebiomedical.com (16)

Clark, Richard, Medco Health Solutions Inc, Franklin Lakes, NJ. Tel: (201) 269-3400, (800) 556-3326, FAX: (800) 222-1934, E-Mail: customersupport@medcosupply.com, Web Site: www.medco-athletics.com (7)

Clark, Richard T., Calbiochem-Novabiochem Corp, San Diego, CA. Tel: (858) 450-9600, (800) 854-3417, FAX: (858) 453-3552, E-Mail: customerservice@emdbioscience.com, Web Site: www.calbiochem.com (9)

Clark, Thomas W, Con-Way Freight, Ann Arbor, MI. Tel: (734) 994-6600, FAX: (734) 757-1153 (12)

Clarke, Chris, Habitat For Humanity International, Americus, GA. Tel: (229) 924-6935, (800) HABITAT, FAX: (229) 924-6541, Web Site: www.habitat.org (1)

Clarke, Chris, Miracle of Aloe, Dallas, TX. Tel: (800) 966-2563, FAX: (800) 859-9881, E-Mail: LJohnson@miracleofaloe.com, Web Site: www.miracleofaloe.com (7)

Clarke, Gwilym, Alfa Aesar-A Johnson Matthey Co, Ward Hill, MA. Tel: (800) 343-0660, FAX: (800) 322-4757, E-Mail: info@alfa.com, Web Site: www. alfa.com (9)

Clarke, III Jess F., Miracle of Aloe, Dallas, TX. Tel: (800) 966-2563, FAX: (800) 859-9881, E-Mail: LJohnson@miracleofaloe.com, Web Site: www. miracleofaloe.com (7)

Clarke, Jeffrey J., Eastman Kodak Co, Rochester, NY. Tel: (585) 724-4000, (800) 698-3324, FAX: (585) 724-1089, Web Site: www.kodak.com (27)

Clarke, Jr. Jess F., Miracle of Aloe, Dallas, TX. Tel: (800) 966-2563, FAX: (800) 859-9881, E-Mail: LJohnson@miracleofaloe.com, Web Site: www. miracleofaloe.com (7)

Clarke, Marcy, Service Mailers & Fulfillment Inc, Vernon, CA. Tel: (323) 292-0133, FAX: (323) 292-1038, E-Mail: dgsteinhart@gmail.com, Web Site: servicemailersandfulfillment.com (28)

Clarke, Marie, ActionAid, Washington, DC. Tel: (202) 835-1240, E-Mail: info@actionaid.org, Web Site: www.actionaidusa.org (1)

Clarke, Marla, Veer, Calgary, AB Canada. Tel: (403) 234-7901, Web Site: www.veer.com (16)

Clarke, Richard A., Fifteen Degrees, New York, NY. Tel: (212) 545-7400, FAX: (212) 545-7433, E-Mail: hello@fifteendegrees.com, Web Site: fifteendegrees. com (35)

Clarke, Shane, B-T-B Internet Marketing Solutions, Middle Island, NY. Tel: (631) 924-3888, E-Mail: linickgroup@gmail.com, Web Site: www.linick.net; 222.asklinick.com (39)

Clarke, Troy, Navistar, Lisle, IL. Tel: (331) 332-5000, Web Site: www.navistar.com (16)

Clarken, Tom, The Hyiad Group, Garden City, NY. Tel: (516) 433-3800, FAX: (516) 822-6670, Web Site: www.thehyaidgroup.com (22)

Clark's Corvair Parts, Inc, Shelburne Falls, MA. Tel: (413) 625-9776, FAX: (413) 625-8498, E-Mail: clarks@corvair.com, Web Site: www.corvair.com (12)

Clarkson Eyecare, Ellisville, MO. Tel: (636) 227-2600, (888) 393-2273, E-Mail: info@clarksoneyecare. com, Web Site: clarksoneyecare.com (5)

Classic Color, Broadview, IL. Tel: (708) 484-0000, FAX: (708) 344-2233, E-Mail: info@classic-color. com, Web Site: www.classic-color.com (27)

Classic Motorbooks Inc, Minneapolis, MN. Tel: (715) 294-3345, (800) 826-6600, FAX: (715) 294-4448, Web Site: www.motorbooks.com (17)

Classic Thermographers, North Mankato, MN. Tel: (623) 582-0002, (800) 727-4200, FAX: (800) 727-4202 (10)

Claudio, Solange, Moxie, Atlanta, GA. Tel: (678) 916-4500, E-Mail: info@moxieusa.com, Web Site: moxieusa.com (35)

Claudy, Guy, ColorEdge, Burbank, CA. Tel: (818) 842-1121, (800) 300-3686, FAX: (818) 842-0280, E-Mail: john.davies@crushcreative.com, Web Site: www.coloredge.com (27)

Claure, Marcelo, Sprint Corp, Overland Park, KS. Tel: (703) 433-4000, Web Site: www.sprint.com (3)

Clausen Enterprises, Hendersonville, NC. Tel: (828) 692-8535, E-Mail: jhclausen@mchsi.com, Web Site: www.copy-design.com (39)

Clausen, John, Clausen Enterprises, Hendersonville, NC. Tel: (828) 692-8535, E-Mail: jhclausen@mchsi. com, Web Site: www.copy-design.com (39)

Clavert, Pan, CRM Learning, Carlsbad, CA. Tel: (760) 431-9800, (800) 421-0833, FAX: (760) 931-5792, E-Mail: sales@crmlearning.com, Web Site: www. crmlearning.com (16)

Clawson, Angela, Texas Monthly, Austin, TX. Tel: (512) 320-6900, (800) 759-2000, FAX: (512) 476-9007, E-Mail: info@texasmonthly.com, Web Site: www.texasmonthly.com (17)

Clay Creative Group LLC, Lewis Center, OH. Tel: (740) 548-0307, FAX: (740) 548-0898, E-Mail: marketing@claycreativeresults.com, Web Site: www.claycreativeresults.com (35)

Clay, Franklin, Clay Creative Group LLC, Lewis Center, OH. Tel: (740) 548-0307, FAX: (740) 548-0898, E-Mail: marketing@claycreativeresults.com, Web Site: www.claycreativeresults.com (35)

Clay, Jessica, Clay Creative Group LLC, Lewis Center, OH. Tel: (740) 548-0307, FAX: (740) 548-0898, E-Mail: marketing@claycreativeresults.com, Web Site: www.claycreativeresults.com (35)

Clayman Promotional Group, Kansas City, KS. Tel: (913) 384-3600, FAX: (913) 384-1227, E-Mail: jloud@claymanpromo.com, Web Site: www. claymanpromo.com (33)

AT Clayton & Co Inc, Stamford, CT. Tel: (203) 658-1200, FAX: (203) 658-1201, E-Mail: webmaster@ atclayton.com, Web Site: www.atclayton.com (25)

Clayton, Jim, Scripps Networks Interactive Inc, Knoxville, TN. Tel: (865) 560-2700, Web Site: scrippsnetworksinteractive.com (17)

Clayton, Michelle, Lincoln Park Zoo, Chicago, IL. Tel: (312) 742-2000, FAX: (312) 742-2137, E-Mail: webmaster@lpzoo.com, Web Site: www.lpzoo.com (1)

Clean Lists Associates Inc, New York, NY. Tel: (212) 551-1013, FAX: (212) 551-1107, E-Mail: cleanlists@mindspring.com (27)

Clear Visions Inc, San Antonio, TX. Tel: (210) 496-6006, FAX: (210) 496-9225, E-Mail: bidrequest@ clearvisionsinc.com, Web Site: www. clearvisionsinc.com (27)

ClearOne Advantage, Baltimore, MD. Tel: (888) 785-5376, FAX: (888) 785-5365, Web Site: www. clearoneadvantage.com (14)

ClearSaleing Inc, Columbus, OH. Tel: (614) 448-2688, (800) 592-0463, Web Site: www.clearsaleing.com (16)

Cleary, Jeff, Catalyst, Rochester, NY. Tel: (585) 453-8300, (800) 836-7720, FAX: (585) 453-8360, E-Mail: info@catalystinc.com, Web Site: www. catalystinc.com (35)

Clegg Industries Inc, Gardena, CA. Tel: (310) 225-3800, FAX: (800) 250-9851, E-Mail: sales@clegg. xo.com, Web Site: www.cleggonline.com (16)

Clegg, Kevin, Clegg Industries Inc, Gardena, CA. Tel: (310) 225-3800, FAX: (800) 250-9851, E-Mail: sales@clegg.xo.com, Web Site: www.cleggonline. com (16)

Clemens, Annette, ListK, Atlanta, GA. Tel: (800) 600-3389, FAX: (770) 825-9188, E-Mail: questions@ listk.com, Web Site: www.listk.com (32)

Clemens, Micke, Veriad, Brea, CA. Tel: (714) 990-2700, (800) 962-0658, FAX: (800) 962-0658, E-Mail: info@veriad.com, Web Site: www.veriad. com (16)

Clement Communications, Buffalo, NY. Tel: (800) 253-6368, E-Mail: customerservice@clement.com, Web Site: www.clement.com (17)

Clement, Bob, The Allied Group, Cranston, RI. Tel: (401) 946-6100, Web Site: www.thealliedgrp.com (28)

Clement, Coy, ClementDIRECT, Chapel Hill, NC. Tel: (919) 338-2853, FAX: (206) 338-2511, Web Site: www.clementdirect.com (20)

Clement, George, Clement Communications, Buffalo, NY. Tel: (800) 253-6368, E-Mail: customerservice@clement.com, Web Site: www. clement.com (17)

Clement, Mark, Viahealth, Rochester, NY. Tel: (585) 922-4000, (585) 922-3677, FAX: (585) 922-3929, Web Site: www.viahealth.org (16)

Clement, Philip B., Aon Innovative Solutions, Chicago, IL. Tel: (312) 381-1000, Web Site: www.aon.com (16)

ClementDIRECT, Chapel Hill, NC. Tel: (919) 338-2853, FAX: (206) 338-2511, Web Site: www. clementdirect.com (20)

Clemente Novelties Inc, Utica, NY. Tel: (315) 732-4145, FAX: (315) 732-2251, E-Mail: clemente@ 6org.com (16)

Clemente, Anthony, Clemente Novelties Inc, Utica, NY. Tel: (315) 732-4145, FAX: (315) 732-2251, E-Mail: clemente@6org.com (16)

Mark Clements Research Inc, Mount Kisco, NY. Tel: (914) 241-1803, FAX: (914) 241-7763, E-Mail: mjfharvey@aol.com, Web Site: www. markclementsresearch.com (30)

Clements, Deborah Taylor, ColorTree of Virginia Inc, Richmond, VA. Tel: (804) 358-4245, FAX: (804) 358-0488, Web Site: www.colortree.com (26)

Clements, Louise, ICF Olson, Minneapolis, MN. Tel: (612) 215-9800, FAX: (612) 215-9801, E-Mail: info@olson.com, Web Site: www.olson.com (35)

Clements, Mark, Mark Clements Research Inc, Mount Kisco, NY. Tel: (914) 241-1803, FAX: (914) 241-7763, E-Mail: mjfharvey@aol.com, Web Site: www.markclementsresearch.com (30)

Clements, Rev. Patrick L., Church Extension Plan, Salem, OR. Tel: (800) 821-1112, Web Site: www. cepnet.com (14)

Clendenin, Thomas J., CNBC, Englewood Cliffs, NJ. Tel: (201) 735-2622, FAX: (201) 735-3200, Web Site: www.cnbc.com (32)

Clendenning, Rick, INX International Ink Co, Schaumburg, IL. Tel: (800) 631-7956, FAX: (847) 969-9758, E-Mail: info@inxink.com, Web Site: www. inxinternational.com (16)

Clenney, Laura, BenefitMall, Dallas, TX. Tel: (469) 791-3355, Web Site: www.benefitmall.com (15)

Cleveland Clinic Foundation, Cleveland, OH. Tel: (216) 444-2200, Web Site: www.clevelandclinic.org (1)

Cleveland Institute of Electronics, Cleveland, OH. Tel: (216) 781-9400, (800) 243-6446, FAX: (216) 781-0331, E-Mail: instruct@cie-wc.edu, Web Site: www.cie-wc.edu (13)

The Cleveland Orchestra, Cleveland, OH. Tel: (216) 231-7300, FAX: (216) 231-4038, Web Site: www. clevelandorchestra.com (1)

Clevenger, Gregg, GXS Corp, Gaithersburg, MD. Tel: (301) 340-4000, (800) 560-4347, FAX: (301) 340-5299, Web Site: www.gxs.com (30)

Clever, Al, Alpha Supply Inc, Bremerton, WA. Tel: (360) 373-3302, (800) 257-4211, FAX: (360) 377-9235 (16)

Click2Mail, Arlington, VA. Tel: (703) 521-9029, (866) 665-2787, FAX: (703) 358-8811, E-Mail: info@ click2mail.com, Web Site: www.click2mail.com (20)

Clickbooth.com LLC, Sarasota, FL. Tel: (941) 483-4188, Web Site: www.clickbooth.com (35)

ClickMail Marketing Inc, San Mateo, CA. Tel: (650) 653-8055, Web Site: clickmail.com (32)

ClickSpark LLC, Rochester, NY. Tel: (800) 878-5709, E-Mail: amy@clickspark.com, Web Site: www. clickspark.com (32)

ClickSquared, Boston, MA. Tel: (781) 622-1611, (866) 402-5425, FAX: (857) 246-7645, E-Mail: info@ clicksquared.com, Web Site: www.clicksquared.com (20)

Clients & Profits Worldwide, Oceanside, CA. Tel: (760) 945-4334, Web Site: www.clientsandprofits.com (14)

Clients First, Westfield, NJ. Tel: (908) 232-1200, (800) 634-0040, FAX: (908) 233-8833, E-Mail: info@ clientsfirst.com, Web Site: www.clientsfirst.com (27)

Clifford, Christina, Harlequin Enterprises Ltd, Don Mills, ON Canada. Tel: (416) 445-5860, FAX: (416) 445-8655, E-Mail: customer_ecare@harlequin.ca, Web Site: www.eharlequin.com (17)

Clifford, Patrick, StayWell/Krames, San Bruno, CA. Tel: (650) 742-0400, FAX: (650) 244-4568, Web Site: www.staywell.com (17)

Clifton, Diane, National Council on Compensation Insurance Inc, Boca Raton, FL. Tel: (561) 893-1000, (800) 622-4123, FAX: (561) 893-1191, Web Site: www.ncci.com (1)

Cline, Hollis, Society for Neuroscience, Washington, DC. Tel: (202) 962-4000, Web Site: www.sfn.org (1)

Cline, Thomas, Northwestern University, Evanston, IL. Tel: (847) 491-5665, FAX: (847) 491-5925, E-Mail: jimc@northwestern.edu, Web Site: www. northwestern.edu (41)

Clingman, Eugene, Nordskog Publishing Co, Ventura, CA. Tel: (805) 642-2070, FAX: (805) 642-1862, Web Site: www.nordskogpublishing.com (17)

Clingman, Sarah, DNP America Inc, New York, NY. Tel: (212) 503-1060, FAX: (212) 679-0613 (27)

ClingZ Inc, Rio Rancho, NM. Tel: (505) 892-2500, (800) 795-1415, FAX: (505) 892-2510, Web Site: www.clingz.com (9)

Clinton, Michael A., Hearst Magazines, New York, NY. Tel: (212) 649-2824, FAX: (212) 765-3528, Web Site: www.hearst.com/magazines (17)

Clipper Magazine, Mountville, PA. Tel: (888) 569-5100, FAX: (717) 569-5101, Web Site: www. clippermagazine.com (31)

Clippinger, Marni Z., Marketing Science Institute Review, Cambridge, MA. Tel: (617) 491-2060, FAX: (617) 491-2065, E-Mail: msi@msi.org, Web Site: www.msi.org (43)

Clobes, April, MSU Federal Credit Union, East Lansing, MI. Tel: (517) 333-2254, Web Site: www.msufcu. org (1)

Clock, Kirby, Mountain West Communications Inc, Hotchkiss, CO. Tel: (970) 872-2500, (800) 642-9378, FAX: (970) 872-3862, E-Mail: sales@ mountainwest.com, Web Site: www.mountainwest. com (29)

Cloninger, III Kriss, American Family Life Assurance Co of Columbus (AFLAC), Columbus, GA. Tel: (706) 323-3431, (800) 992-3522, FAX: (706) 660-7446, Web Site: www.aflac.com (15)

Cloonan, James B., American Association of Individual Investors, Chicago, IL. Tel: (312) 280-0170, FAX: (312) 280-9883, E-Mail: adam@aaii.com, Web Site: www.aaii.com (1)

The Clorox Co, Oakland, CA. Tel: (510) 271-7000, FAX: (510) 832-1463, Web Site: www. thecloroxcompany.com (16)

Close, Allyn D., Symetra Financial, Bellevue, WA. Tel: (425) 256-8000, (800) 426-7355, FAX: (425) 256-5737, Web Site: www.symetra.com (15)

Close, Carolyn, Integrated Merchandising Systems LLC, Morton Grove, IL. Tel: (877) 467-1200, E-Mail: doug.carlson@imsfastpak.com, Web Site: www.imsfastpak.com (21)

Closser, Ron, Balboa Life & Casualty, Irvine, CA. Tel: (949) 222-8000, (800) 854-6115, FAX: (949) 222-8777, Web Site: www.balboainsurance.com (15)

Clotworthy, Brian, The Information Refinery Inc, Mahwah, NJ. Tel: (201) 529-2600, (800) 529-9020, FAX: (201) 529-4030, E-Mail: info@inforefinery. com, Web Site: inforefinery.com (24)

Clotworthy, Gordon, The Information Refinery Inc, Mahwah, NJ. Tel: (201) 529-2600, (800) 529-9020, FAX: (201) 529-4030, E-Mail: info@inforefinery. com, Web Site: inforefinery.com (24)

Clotz, Kevin, Assurant Group, New York, NY. Tel: (305) 253-2244, FAX: (305) 252-6987, Web Site: www.assurant.com (15)

Clouse, Robert, Lead Me Media, Delray Beach, FL. Tel: (888) 445-3282, FAX: (561) 423-7890, E-Mail: info@leadmemedia.com, Web Site: www. leadmemedia.com (30)

Clubs of America, Lakemoor, IL. Tel: (815) 363-4000, (800) CLUB-USA, FAX: (815) 363-4677, E-Mail: info@greatclubs.com, Web Site: www. clubsofamerica.com (6)

Cluett Peabody, New York, NY. Tel: (212) 984-8900, FAX: (212) 984-8910, Web Site: www.arrowshirt. com (16)

Cluppert, Carol, Ripon Printers, Ripon, WI. Tel: (920) 748-3136, (800) 321-3136, FAX: (920) 748-3741, E-Mail: info@riponprinters.com, Web Site: www. riponprinters.com (27)

Clure, Lori, CertainSource Inc, Fairfield, CT. Tel: (203) 254-0404, (888) 655-0464, FAX: (203) 254-0411, E-Mail: neil@certainsource.com, Web Site: www. certainsource.com (32)

Clute, Harold, Air-Lec Industries Inc, Madison, WI. Tel: (608) 244-4754, FAX: (608) 246-7676, E-Mail: info@air-lec.com, Web Site: www.air-lec.com (16)

CO-OP Promotions, Hollywood, FL. Tel: (954) 922-2323, FAX: (954) 922-2071, E-Mail: art@co-oppromotions.com, Web Site: www.co-oppromotions.com (35)

Co-operations, Tualatin, OR. Tel: (503) 620-7977, (866) 228-6362, FAX: (503) 620-7917, E-Mail: info@ fsipdx.com, Web Site: www.fsipdx.com (28)

Coach, New York, NY. Tel: (212) 594-1850, (800) 444-3611, FAX: (212) 594-1682, Web Site: www.coach. com (2)

Coalter, Rick, JA Sexauer, Elmsford, NY. Tel: (914) 472-7501, (800) 431-1872, FAX: (914) 472-5834, Web Site: www.jasmro.com (16)

Coast Hotels Limited, Seattle, WA. Tel: (206) 826-2700, FAX: (206) 826-2701, Web Site: www. coasthotels.com (19)

Coast to Coast Inc, Englewood, CO. Tel: (303) 728-2267, Web Site: www.coastresorts.com (1)

Coastal Hotel Group, Bellevue, WA. Tel: (206) 388-0400, FAX: (206) 388-0401, E-Mail: info@ coastalhotel.com, Web Site: www.coastalhotels.com (1)

Coastal Living, Birmingham, AL. Tel: (205) 445-6000, FAX: (205) 445-7263, E-Mail: coastalliving@ customersvc.com, Web Site: www.coastalliving.com (43)

Coastal Tool & Supply, West Hartford, CT. Tel: (860) 233-8213, (877) 551-8665, FAX: (860) 233-6295, E-Mail: sales@coastaltool.com, Web Site: www. coastaltool.com (16)

Coastal Training Technologies Corp, Virginia Beach, VA. Tel: (877) 262-7825, FAX: (757) 498-3657, E-Mail: info@training.dupont.com, Web Site: www. coastalhealth.com (7)

Coates, Doreen, Accounting with Debits and Credits with Coates & Hutchinson PC, Odenton, MD. Tel: (410) 672-6339, (800) 833-5933, FAX: (301) 912-3364, E-Mail: info@awdc.org (14)

Coats, Janet, Posty Cards Inc, Kansas City, MO. Tel: (816) 231-2323, (800) 554-5018, FAX: (888) 577-3800, E-Mail: customerservice@postycards.com, Web Site: www.postycards.com (16)

Coats, Jeffrey, Autobytel Inc, Irvine, CA. Tel: (949) 225-4500, E-Mail: consumercareabtl@autobytel. com, Web Site: www.autobytel.com (12)

Cobalt, Seattle, WA. Tel: (206) 269-6363, (800) 909-8244, Web Site: www.cobalt.com (16)

Cobb, Ellen, Craver Mathews Smith & Co, Reston, VA. Tel: (703) 258-0000, FAX: (703) 258-0001, E-Mail: ellenc@cms1.com, Web Site: www.craveronline. com (1)

Cobb, Gregg, Ideas To Go Inc, Minneapolis, MN. Tel: (612) 331-1570, FAX: (612) 331-1602, E-Mail: cebert@ideastogo.com, Web Site: www.ideastogo. com (30)

Cobb, Jerry, Kolbe Corp, Phoenix, AZ. Tel: (602) 840-9770, (800) 642-2822, FAX: (602) 952-2706, E-Mail: info@kolbe.com, Web Site: www.kolbe. com (17)

Cobbey & Associates Marketing Research, Carson City, NV. Tel: (775) 847-0321, (877) 433-3242, E-Mail: cobbey@cobbey.com, Web Site: www.cobbey.com (30)

Cobbey, Robin, Cobbey & Associates Marketing Research, Carson City, NV. Tel: (775) 847-0321, (877) 433-3242, E-Mail: cobbey@cobbey.com, Web Site: www.cobbey.com (30)

Cobblestone Publishing, Peterborough, NH. Tel: (603) 924-7209, (800) 821-0115, FAX: (603) 924-7380, E-Mail: customerservice@caruspub.com, Web Site: www.cobblestonepub.com (17)

Coble, Scott, Time Logistics Inc, Columbia, TN. Tel: (866) 293-8463, FAX: (866) 591-5697, E-Mail: quote@timelogisticsinc.com, Web Site: www. timelogisticsinc.com (12)

The Coca-Cola Co, Atlanta, GA. Tel: (404) 676-2121, (800) 438-2653, FAX: (404) 676-6792, Web Site: www.cocacola.com (16)

Cocchia, Ann Marie, Aspen Publishers Inc, New York, NY. Tel: (212) 771-0600, (800) 638-8437, Web Site: www.aspenpublishers.com (17)

Cochran, Edmund, United Way Store, Alexandria, VA. Tel: (703) 212-6300, (800) 772-0008, FAX: (703) 212-6319, E-Mail: customerservice@ unitedwaystore.com, Web Site: www. unitedwaystore.com (34)

Cochran, Gerald D., Golden Gate Transportation District, San Rafael, CA. Tel: (415) 921-5858, FAX: (415) 923-2014, Web Site: www.goldengate.org (16)

Cochran, Steve, MXT Card Services, LLC, New Castle, DE. Tel: (302) 323-6203, FAX: (302) 323-6219, Web Site: www.mxtcs.com (14)

Cochran, Terry, Raven's Nest Herbals, LLC, Duluth, GA. Tel: (678) 642-6691, (678) 584-0830, E-Mail: info@ravensnestherbals.com, Web Site: www. ravensnestherbals.com (7)

Cochrane, Chuck, Blethen Maine Newspapers Inc, Portland, ME. Tel: (207) 791-6650, FAX: (207) 791-6925, Web Site: www.mainetoday.com (17)

Cochrane, Gregory J, Data Communications Management Corp, Brampton, ON Canada. Tel: (905) 791-3151, (800) 268-0128, FAX: (905) 791-3277, E-Mail: info@datacm.com, Web Site: www.datacm.com (21)

Coco, Andrew, Knoll Group, New York, NY. Tel: (212) 343-4000, FAX: (212) 343-4180 (16)

Coday, Dennis, National Catholic Reporter Publishing Co Inc, Kansas City, MO. Tel: (816) 531-0538, (800) 444-8910, FAX: (816) 968-2268, Web Site: www.ncronline.org (17)

Coe, Ben, Butler Schein Animal Health, Dublin, OH. Tel: (614) 761-9095, (888) 691-2724, FAX: (888) 329-3861, Web Site: www.butlerschein.com (16)

Coe, John M., B2BMarketing.com, Scottsdale, AZ. Tel: (602) 402-6588, Web Site: www.b2bmarketing.com (35)

Coerper, Phil, International Filing Corp LLC, Hattiesburg, MS. Tel: (601) 554-0521, FAX: (601) 554-0522, E-Mail: pcoerper@intfiling.com, Web Site: www.intfiling.com (26)

Coffeen, III William I., Nexxlinx (HQ), Atlanta, GA. Tel: (770) 250-0349, (877) 747-0658, Web Site: www.nexxlinx.com (22)

Coffeen, Steve, Las Vegas Review Journal, Las Vegas, NV. Tel: (702) 383-0211, FAX: (702) 383-4646, Web Site: www.lvrj.com (17)

Coffey, C. Edward, The Menninger Foundation, Houston, TX. Tel: (713) 275-5000, (800) 351-9058, FAX: (713) 275-5107, Web Site: www.menningerclinic.com (1)

Coffin, Lew C., Polyair Packaging, Chicago, IL. Tel: (773) 995-1818, (888) POLYAIR X444, FAX: (773) 995-7725, E-Mail: marketing@polyair.com, Web Site: www.polyair.com (9)

Coffman, Richard, Norman Control Co, Cary, IL. Tel: (847) 639-5721, FAX: (847) 639-5755, E-Mail: susan@coffmanmfg.com, Web Site: www.coffmanmfg.com (16)

Coffman, Susan, Norman Control Co, Cary, IL. Tel: (847) 639-5721, FAX: (847) 639-5755, E-Mail: susan@coffmanmfg.com, Web Site: www.coffmanmfg.com (16)

Cofield, Linda, Team Cheer, Geneseo, NY. Tel: (800) 350-1562, (877) 243-5268, E-Mail: custserv@teamcheer.com, Web Site: www.teamcheer.com (2)

Cofield, Randy, Team Cheer, Geneseo, NY. Tel: (800) 350-1562, (877) 243-5268, E-Mail: custserv@teamcheer.com, Web Site: www.teamcheer.com (2)

Cogensia, Schaumburg, IL. Tel: (847) 805-9800, FAX: (847) 805-9313, E-Mail: info@cac-group.com, Web Site: www.cogensia.com (22)

Coggin, Scott, DataDirect, Atlanta, GA. Tel: (678) 530-0034, FAX: (678) 530-9563, E-Mail: info@ddirect.com, Web Site: www.ddirect.com (40)

Coggin, Tom, DataDirect, Atlanta, GA. Tel: (678) 530-0034, FAX: (678) 530-9563, E-Mail: info@ddirect.com, Web Site: www.ddirect.com (40)

Cogland, Don, Ad-Lib Advertising Inc, Old Bridge, NJ. Tel: (732) 679-9226, (800) 622-3542, FAX: (732) 679-9511, E-Mail: info@adlibadvertising.com, Web Site: www.adlibadvertising.com (10)

Cogley, John, Daniel Smith Inc, Seattle, WA. Tel: (206) 223-9599, (800) 426-6740, FAX: (800) 238-4065, E-Mail: sales@danielsmith.com, Web Site: www.danielsmith.com (17)

CognitiveDATA Inc, Little Rock, AR. Tel: (501) 975-7580, (866) 243-7883, FAX: (501) 975-7681, E-Mail: info@cognitivedata.com, Web Site: www.cognitivedata.com (22)

Cognitronics Corp, Danbury, CT. Tel: (203) 830-3400, (888) 228-5061, FAX: (508) 624-0289, E-Mail: info@thinkengine.com, Web Site: www.cognitronics.com (34)

Cohasset Colonials, Ashburnham, MA. Tel: (978) 827-3001, (800) 288-2389, FAX: (978) 827-3227, E-Mail: cohassetcolonials.custservice@gmail.com, Web Site: www.cohassetcolonials.com (8)

Cohen & Co, Brooklyn, NY. Tel: (718) 875-5065, FAX: (718) 875-5065, E-Mail: herbertjcohen@aol.com (20)

Cohen, Andrew, Exposed Brick, New York, NY. Tel: (646) 454-0880, E-Mail: andrewc@exposedbrick.com, Web Site: www.exposedbrick.com (35)

Cohen, Arthur, Electric Media, New York, NY. Tel: (201) 461-5252 (30)

Cohen, Barbara, Kannon Consulting Inc, Chicago, IL. Tel: (312) 346-2244, FAX: (312) 346-3665, Web Site: www.kannon.com (20)

Cohen, Bob, Rio Brands, Philadelphia, PA. Tel: (215) 632-2800, FAX: (215) 824-1172 (16)

Cohen, David L., Databazaar.com, Miramar, FL. Tel: (954) 843-0483, (888) 335-3282, FAX: (954) 843-0429, E-Mail: rudy@databazaar.com, Web Site: www.databazaar.com (10)

Cohen, Dennis, Bauer Publishing Co, Englewood Cliffs, NJ. Tel: (201) 569-6699, FAX: (201) 569-5303, Web Site: www.bauerpublishing.com (17)

Cohen, Eitan, Monarch Direct Response, Sherman Oaks, CA. Tel: (818) 817-8000, Web Site: www.monarchdr.com (35)

Cohen, Elaine, Createch Marketing, Montvale, NJ. Tel: (201) 326-3000, (866) 808-1050, Web Site: www.createchmarketing.com (22)

Cohen, Eli, Polo Ralph Lauren, New York, NY. Tel: (212) 813-7868, (800) 377-7656, Web Site: www.ralphlauren.com (2)

Cohen, Gail, Power Seminars, Swampscott, MA. Tel: (781) 595-9990, FAX: (781) 595-0770, Web Site: www.gailcohen.com (29)

Cohen, Hal, KD Mailing & Fulfillment Service, Lincolnwood, IL. Tel: (847) 673-0186, (866) 330-6245, FAX: (874) 673-0188, E-Mail: dan@kdmailing.com, Web Site: www.kdmailing.com (28)

Cohen, Harvey, Graham Field Health Products Inc, Atlanta, GA. Tel: (770) 368-4700, (800) 347-5678, FAX: (800) 726-0601, E-Mail: cs@grahamfield.com, Web Site: www.grahamfield.com (7)

Cohen, Herbert J., Cohen & Co, Brooklyn, NY. Tel: (718) 875-5065, FAX: (718) 875-5065, E-Mail: herbertjcohen@aol.com (20)

Cohen, Herbert, Platinum Press, Killingworth, CT. Tel: (860) 663-3882, FAX: (718) 825-5065, E-Mail: herbertjcohen@aol.com (20)

Cohen, Jay, Oakton Community College, Des Plaines, IL. Tel: (847) 635-1600, FAX: (847) 635-1706, Web Site: www.oakton.edu (41)

Cohen, Jeff, Teleperformance Interactive, Miami Beach, FL. Tel: (786) 437-3300, FAX: (786) 276-8452, Web Site: www.teleperformance.com (29)

Cohen, Jeffrey, Sylvan Learning Inc, Baltimore, MD. Tel: (410) 843-8000, (800) 31-SUCCESS, FAX: (410) 843-8057, E-Mail: pr@sylvanlearning.com, Web Site: www.sylvanlearning.com (16)

Cohen, Jerry P., Ebbets Field Flannels Inc, Seattle, WA. Tel: (206) 382-7249, FAX: (206) 382-4411, E-Mail: clubhouse@ebbets.com, Web Site: www.ebbets.com (2)

Cohen, Jill, Prospect Direct Inc, Milwaukee, WI. Tel: (414) 271-3313, FAX: (414) 271-4244, E-Mail: info@prospect-direct.com, Web Site: www.prospect-direct.com (21)

Cohen, Lawrence H., Alliance Bernstein, New York, NY. Tel: (212) 969-1000, (800) 962-2134, FAX: (212) 969-2293, Web Site: www.alliancebernstein.com (14)

Cohen, Mark, Brooke Distributors Inc, Miami, FL. Tel: (305) 624-9752, (800) 275-8792, FAX: (305) 620-3988, E-Mail: sales@brookedms.com, Web Site: www.brookedist.com (3)

Cohen, Mark J., Rio Brands, Philadelphia, PA. Tel: (215) 632-2800, FAX: (215) 824-1172 (16)

Cohen, Ralph, New York Life Insurance Co/AARP, Tampa, FL. Tel: (813) 288-5500, FAX: (813) 288-5256, Web Site: www.nylaarp.com (15)

Cohen, Rita, Magazine Publishers of America, New York, NY. Tel: (212) 872-3700, FAX: (212) 888-4217, E-Mail: mpa@magazine.org, Web Site: www.magazine.org (12)

Cohen, Scott, Quattro Direct LLC, Berwyn, PA. Tel: (610) 993-0070, Web Site: www.quattrodirect.com (35)

Cohen, Sean, AWeber Communications, Chalfont, PA. Tel: (877) 293-2371, Web Site: www.aweber.com (24)

Cohen, Sharon, Aon's Affinity Insurance Services Inc, Hatboro, PA. Tel: (215) 773-4600, Web Site: www.aon.com (15)

Cohen, Stephen, Falcon Products Inc, Newport, TN. Tel: (314) 991-9200, (800) 873-3252, FAX: (314) 991-9227, E-Mail: info@falconproducts.com, Web Site: www.falconproducts.com (16)

Cohen, Steve, LMS Inc, Orlando, FL. Tel: (407) 876-5544, (800) 257-5902, Web Site: lmsonline.com (35)

Cohen, Warren, Rio Brands, Philadelphia, PA. Tel: (215) 632-2800, FAX: (215) 824-1172 (16)

Cohn, Alan J., Sage Financial Group, West Conshohocken, PA. Tel: (484) 342-4400, FAX: (484) 537-0550, E-Mail: sage@sagefinancial.com, Web Site: www.sagefinancial.com (14)

Cohn, David, Sage Financial Group, West Conshohocken, PA. Tel: (484) 342-4400, FAX: (484) 537-0550, E-Mail: sage@sagefinancial.com, Web Site: www.sagefinancial.com (14)

Cohn, John D., Rockwell Automation, Milwaukee, WI. Tel: (414) 382-2000, FAX: (414) 382-4444, Web Site: www.rockwellautomation.com (14)

Cohn, Stephen, Sage Financial Group, West Conshohocken, PA. Tel: (484) 342-4400, FAX: (484) 537-0550, E-Mail: sage@sagefinancial.com, Web Site: www.sagefinancial.com (14)

Coin Laundry Association, Oakbrook Terrace, IL. Tel: (630) 963-7920, (800) 570-5629, FAX: (630) 963-7925, Web Site: www.coinlaundry.org (1)

Coin World, Sidney, OH. Tel: (937) 498-0800, (800) 253-4555, FAX: (937) 498-0812, E-Mail: cwcustomerservice@coinworld.com, Web Site: www.coinworld.com (17)

Cok, Mike, Foremost Insurance Group, Grand Rapids, MI. Tel: (616) 956-8241, (800) 527-3905, FAX: (800) 325-1507, Web Site: www.foremost.com (15)

Coker, Joseph, Universal Vintage Tire Co, Hershey, PA. Tel: (717) 534-0175, (800) 233-3827, FAX: (717) 534-0719, E-Mail: sales@universaltire.com, Web Site: www.universaltire.com (11)

Col Voce Consulting, Exton, PA. Tel: (215) 266-2992, Web Site: www.colvoce.com (3)

Colantuono, Lori, Walter Karl Inc, Pearl River, NY. Tel: (845) 620-0700, FAX: (845) 620-1885, E-Mail: info@walterkarl.infousa.com, Web Site: www.walterkarl.com (22)

Colarelli Meyer & Associates Inc, Saint Louis, MO. Tel: (314) 721-1860, (800) 459-4548, FAX: (314) 721-1992, E-Mail: cmaconsult@cmaconsult.com, Web Site: www.cmaconsult.com (20)

Colby, Gordon, Voyageur Inc, Easley, SC. Tel: (802) 496-3127, (800) 311-7245, FAX: (802) 496-6247 (11)

Colca, Nick, EMED Co Inc, Buffalo, NY. Tel: (716) 626-1616, (800) 442-3633, FAX: (716) 626-1630, E-Mail: customerservice@emedco.com, Web Site: www.emedco.com (16)

Cold Spring Harbor Lab Press, Woodbury, NY. Tel: (516) 422-4100, (800) 843-4388, FAX: (516) 422-4097, E-Mail: cshpress@cshl.edu, Web Site: www.cshlpress.com (17)

Cold Stream Farm, Free Soil, MI. Tel: (231) 464-5809, E-Mail: info@coldstreamfarm.net, Web Site: www.coldstreamfarm.net (8)

Coldwater Creek, Cincinnati, OH. Tel: (800) 787-9196, FAX: (800) 262-0080, Web Site: www.coldwatercreek.com (2)

Cole & Weber United, Seattle, WA. Tel: (206) 447-9595, FAX: (206) 233-0178, E-Mail: info@cwunited.com, Web Site: www.cwunited.com (35)

Cole Information Services, Omaha, NE. Tel: (800) 403-5894, E-Mail: info@coleinformation.com, Web Site: www.coleinformation.com (23)

Cole-Parmer Instrument Co, Vernon Hills, IL. Tel: (847) 549-7600, (800) 323-4340, FAX: (847) 247-2929, E-Mail: info@coleparmer.com, Web Site: www.coleparmer.com (16)

Cole, Chris, Burden Sales Co, Lincoln, NE. Tel: (402) 474-4055, (800) 488-3407, FAX: (402) 474-5198, Web Site: www.burdensales.com (9)

Cole, Chris, Surplus Center, Lincoln, NE. Tel: (402) 474-4055, (800) 488-3407, FAX: (402) 474-5198, E-Mail: customerservice@surpluscenter.com, Web Site: www.surpluscenter.com (9)

Cole, Douglas D., TWL Knowledge Group, Carrollton, TX. Tel: (972) 309-4000, (800) 624-2272, FAX: (972) 309-5105, Web Site: www.twlk.com (3)

Cole, Kelly, Halls Kansas City, Kansas City, MO. Tel: (816) 274-3222, (800) 624-4034, FAX: (816) 274-3220, E-Mail: contact@halls.com, Web Site: www.halls.com (16)

Cole, Laura, The Berry Company, Dayton, OH. Tel: (937) 610-4100, (800) 877-0475, Web Site: www.theberrycompany.com (35)

Cole, Meghan, Laughlin Associates Inc, Carson City, NV. Tel: (775) 883-8484, (888) 273-8152, FAX: (775) 883-4874 (16)

Cole, Melissa, MWM Dexter Inc, Aurora, MO. Tel: (417) 841-1040, (888) 833-1242, FAX: (417) 841-1025, Web Site: www.mwmdexter.com (27)

Cole, Paulette, ABC Carpet & Home, New York, NY. Tel: (212) 473-3000, Web Site: www.abccarpet.com (8)

Cole, Timothy H., Belvoir Media Group LLC, Norwalk, CT. Tel: (203) 857-3100, FAX: (203) 857-3103, E-Mail: customer_service@belvoir.com, Web Site: www.belvoir.com (17)

Colella, Stephen, Calmark Inc, Chicago, IL. Tel: (773) 247-7200, FAX: (773) 247-3199, E-Mail: ljakobi@calmark-inc.com, Web Site: www.clamark-inc.com (28)

Coleman Frost LLP, Santa Monica, CA. Tel: (310) 576-7312, Web Site: www.colemanfrost.com (20)

Coleman Research Inc, Morrisville, NC. Tel: (919) 571-0000, FAX: (919) 571-9999, E-Mail: callcoleman@colemaninsights.com, Web Site: www.colemaninsights.com (30)

Coleman, Allen, Cross Country Stitching, Quakertown, PA. Tel: (215) 529-6430, (800) 231-8108, FAX: (215) 529-6434, E-Mail: www.crosscountrystitching.com (17)

Coleman, Dan, John Harland Co, Decatur, GA. Tel: (770) 981-5580, (800) 723-3690, FAX: (770) 593-5367, E-Mail: jhhwebmaster@harland.net, Web Site: www.harland.net (16)

Coleman, David, The College Board, New York, NY. Tel: (212) 713-8000, FAX: (212) 713-8143, Web Site: www.collegeboard.com (1)

Coleman, Derrick F, Coleman Frost LLP, Santa Monica, CA. Tel: (310) 576-7312, Web Site: www.colemanfrost.com (20)

Coleman, Frank, CBT Direct, Tarpon Springs, FL. Tel: (727) 724-8994, (877) 872-4646, FAX: (727) 797-9143, Web Site: www.cbtdirect.com (16)

Coleman, J. Edward, Unisys, Blue Bell, PA. Tel: (215) 986-4011, (800) 874-8647, FAX: (215) 986-2312, Web Site: www.unisys.com (16)

Coleman, J. Scott, Delaware Investments, Philadelphia, PA. Tel: (215) 255-1200, E-Mail: service@delinvest.com, Web Site: www.delawareinvestments.com (14)

Coleman, James E., Gateway Inc, Irvine, CA. Tel: (949) 471-7000, (800) 369-1409, FAX: (949) 471-7041, Web Site: www.gateway.com (16)

Coleman, Jean C., Integrity Music Inc, Mobile, AL. Tel: (251) 633-9000, FAX: (251) 633-5202, Web Site: www.integritymusic.com (16)

Coleman, Jon, Coleman Research Inc, Morrisville, NC. Tel: (919) 571-0000, FAX: (919) 571-9999, E-Mail: callcoleman@colemaninsights.com, Web Site: www.colemaninsights.com (30)

Coleman, Linda, Cross Country Stitching, Quakertown, PA. Tel: (215) 529-6430, (800) 231-8108, FAX: (215) 529-6434, Web Site: www.crosscountrystitching.com (17)

Coleman, Mike, Integrity Music Inc, Mobile, AL. Tel: (251) 633-9000, FAX: (251) 633-5202, Web Site: www.integritymusic.com (16)

Coleman, Milton, The Washington Post, Washington, DC. Tel: (202) 334-6000, (800) 627-1150, E-Mail: letters@washpost.com, Web Site: www.washingtonpost.com (17)

Cole's Appliance & Furniture Co, Chicago, IL. Tel: (773) 525-1797, Web Site: shopcoles.com (8)

Coles, Bob, Cornerstone Group of Companies, Toronto, ON Canada. Tel: (416) 932-9555, FAX: (416) 932-9566, E-Mail: info@cstonecanada.com, Web Site: www.cstonecanada.com (22)

Colgate-Palmolive Co, New York, NY. Tel: (212) 310-2000, (800) 468-6502, FAX: (212) 310-2475, Web Site: www.colgate.com (16)

Colinear Systems, Alpharetta, GA. Tel: (770) 643-0000, (800) COLINEAR, FAX: (770) 643-0265, E-Mail: sales@colinear.com, Web Site: www.colinear.com (22)

Collard, Elijah, Reading for Education, Murfreesboro, TN. Tel: (615) 896-3800 (16)

Colle+McVoy, Minneapolis, MN. Tel: (612) 305-6000, FAX: (612) 305-6500, E-Mail: info@collemcvoy.com, Web Site: www.collemcvoy.com (35)

Collectibles Today Network, Ltd, Niles, IL. Tel: (800) 323-5577 #6, Web Site: www.collectiblestoday.com (16)

Collective[i], New York, NY. Tel: (888) 890-0020, Web Site: www.collectivei.com (35)

Collective - The Audience Engine, New York, NY. Tel: (646) 722-8550, FAX: (646) 442-6529, Web Site: www.collective.com (22)

Collector Books & American Quilters Society, Paducah, KY. Tel: (270) 898-6211, (800) 626-5420, FAX: (270) 898-8890, E-Mail: info@collectorbooks.com, Web Site: www.collectorbooks.com (17)

Collector's Armoury Ltd, McDonough, GA. Tel: (678) 593-2660, (877) 276-6879, FAX: (678) 593-2660, E-Mail: sales@collectorsarmoury.com, Web Site: www.collectorsarmoury.com (6)

Collector's Teapot, Kingston, NY. Tel: (845) 339-1109, (800) 724-3306, FAX: (845) 339-5530, Web Site: www.collectorsteapot.com (6)

The College Board, New York, NY. Tel: (212) 713-8000, FAX: (212) 713-8143, Web Site: www.collegeboard.com (1)

College of Business, Cincinnati, OH. Tel: (513) 556-7002, FAX: (513) 556-4891, E-Mail: business@uc.edu, Web Site: www.business.uc.edu (41)

College of Business Administration, Philadelphia, PA. Tel: (215) 895-2145, Web Site: www.drexel.edu (41)

CollegeAmerica, Salt Lake City, UT. Tel: (801) 284-7553 (1)

The Collegebound Network, Staten Island, NY. Tel: (718) 761-4800, (888) 338-6960, FAX: (718) 761-3300, E-Mail: info@collegebound.net, Web Site: www.collegebound.net (32)

CollegeSource Inc, San Diego, CA. Tel: (858) 560-8051, (800) 854-2670, FAX: (858) 278-8960, Web Site: www.collegesource.com (17)

Collegiate Cap & Gown, Champaign, IL. Tel: (217) 351-9500, FAX: (217) 351-9214, Web Site: www.herff-jones.com (16)

Colleluori, John, AIN Plastics Inc, Yonkers, NY. Tel: (914) 668-6800, (800) 431-2451, FAX: (914) 668-8820, Web Site: www.ainplastics.com (16)

Colleton, Michael E., JR Cigar, Burlington, NC. Tel: (800) 572-4427, FAX: (800) 457-3299, E-Mail: manager@jrburlington.com, Web Site: www.jrcigars.com (5)

Collette Vacations, Pawtucket, RI. Tel: (401) 728-3805, FAX: (401) 727-9014, E-Mail: czesk@collettetours.com, Web Site: www.collettevacations.com (19)

Collida, Susan, Nostrum Inc, Long Beach, CA. Tel: (562) 437-2200, Web Site: www.nostruminc.com (35)

Collider Media, Austin, TX. Tel: (512) 745-8070, Web Site: collidermedia.com (9)

Collin Street Bakery, Corsicana, TX. Tel: (800) 292-7400, Web Site: www.collinstreetbakery.com (4)

Collinger & Associates, Saint Louis, MO. Tel: (314) 432-2058, FAX: (314) 991-9797, E-Mail: bcmktr@aol.com (20)

Collinger, Tom, Medill IMC/Northwestern University, Evanston, IL. Tel: (847) 467-3433 (1)

Collinger, William, Collinger & Associates, Saint Louis, MO. Tel: (314) 432-2058, FAX: (314) 991-9797, E-Mail: bcmktr@aol.com (20)

JJ Collins' Sons Inc, Woodridge, IL. Tel: (630) 960-2525, (800) 972-2296, FAX: (630) 960-7487, E-Mail: sales@jjcollins.com, Web Site: www.jjcollins.com (27)

Collins List Exchange Inc, Henderson, NV. Tel: (702) 369-6015, FAX: (702) 920-8115, E-Mail: listinfo@collinslist.com, Web Site: www.collinslist.com (23)

Collins, Artie, NPN360 Inc, Wheeling, IL. Tel: (847) 215-7300, FAX: (847) 215-7314, E-Mail: sales@npn360.com, Web Site: www.npn360.com (21)

Collins, Chad, Accellos Inc, Colorado Springs, CO. Tel: (719) 433-7000, Web Site: www.accellos.com (12)

Collins, Daniel, TMP Direct, Budd Lake, NJ. Tel: (973) 347-9400, (800) 328-2439, FAX: (973) 347-8773, E-Mail: ron.pearl@tmpwdirect.com, Web Site: www.tmpwdirect.com (29)

Collins, Douglas, Torqmaster International, Stamford, CT. Tel: (203) 326-5945, (888) 414-4643, FAX: (203) 326-5944, E-Mail: info@torqmaster.com, Web Site: www.torqmaster.com (9)

Collins, Emilio, National Basketball Association, New York, NY. Tel: (212) 407-8000, FAX: (212) 826-0579, Web Site: www.nba.com (1)

Collins, George J., T Rowe Price Associates Inc, Baltimore, MD. Tel: (410) 345-2000, (800) 638-7890, FAX: (410) 986-3618, E-Mail: info@troweprice.com, Web Site: www.troweprice.com (14)

Collins, George, Research & Response International Inc, New York, NY. Tel: (212) 489-8610, FAX: (212) 262-3474 (23)

Collins, Jana O., Jones & O'Malley, Toluca Lake, CA. Tel: (818) 762-8353, FAX: (818) 762-6736, Web Site: www.jonesomalley.com (35)

Collins, Jim, JJ Collins' Sons Inc, Woodridge, IL. Tel: (630) 960-2525, (800) 972-2296, FAX: (630) 960-7487, E-Mail: sales@jjcollins.com, Web Site: www.jjcollins.com (27)

Collins, John, Marquis Awards & Specialties Inc, Powell, WY. Tel: (307) 754-2272, (800) 327-2446, FAX: (307) 754-9577, E-Mail: marquisawards@bresnan.net, Web Site: www.rushawards.com (35)

Collins, John S., Bitstream Inc, Marlborough, MA. Tel: (617) 497-6222, FAX: (617) 868-0784, Web Site: www.bitstream.com (22)

Collins, Kevin, ModernAd Media LLC, Deerfield Beach, FL. Tel: (954) 312-4700, FAX: (954) 312-4853, Web Site: www.modernad.com (40)

Collins, Melody, Collins List Exchange Inc, Henderson, NV. Tel: (702) 369-6015, FAX: (702) 920-8115, E-Mail: listinfo@collinslist.com, Web Site: www.collinslist.com (23)

Collins, Mike, Skar Advertising, Omaha, NE. Tel: (402) 330-0110, (866) 330-0112, FAX: (402) 330-8791, E-Mail: skar@skar.com, Web Site: skar.com (35)

Collins, Peter, Nature Publishing Group, New York, NY. Tel: (212) 726-9200, FAX: (212) 696-9006, Web Site: www.nature.com (17)

Collins, Raymond A., Brown Brothers, Sterling, PA. Tel: (570) 689-9688, FAX: (570) 689-7873, E-Mail: info@brownbrothersusa.com, Web Site: www.brownbrothersusa.com (38)

Collins, Rob, Brentwood Benson Music Publishing, Brentwood, TN. Tel: (615) 261-3400, (800) 846-7664, FAX: (615) 261-3381, E-Mail: choral@brentwoodbensonmusic.com, Web Site: www.brentwoodbenson.com (17)

Collins, Steve, Altair Customer Intelligence, Franklin, TN. Tel: (615) 468-6800, (800) 241-6631, FAX: (615) 468-6878, E-Mail: asales@altairci.com, Web Site: www.altairci.com (23)

Collins, Steve, Cartouche Ltd, Alexandria, VA. Tel: (703) 823-7904, (800) AT-EGYPT, FAX: (888) 283-4978, E-Mail: sales@egyptianimports.com, Web Site: www.egyptianimports.com (6)

Collis Curve Catalog Sales, Brownsville, TX. Tel: (956) 546-4818, (800) 298-4818, FAX: (956) 546-4818, E-Mail: brushteeth@aol.com, Web Site: www.colliscurve.com (7)

Collis, David, Collis Curve Catalog Sales, Brownsville, TX. Tel: (956) 546-4818, (800) 298-4818, FAX: (956) 546-4818, E-Mail: brushteeth@aol.com, Web Site: www.colliscurve.com (7)

Collis, Steven H., AmerisourceBergen, Chesterbrook, PA. Tel: (610) 727-7000, (800) 829-3132, E-Mail: solutions@amerisourcebergan.com, Web Site: www.amerisourcebergan.com (7)

Collom, John, Morcon Industrial Specialty Inc, Mesquite, NV. Tel: (702) 346-3447, (888) 842-7953, Web Site: www.morcon-ind.com (9)

Colman, Richard, United Systems c/o Biomed, Concord, CA. Tel: (925) 609-2820 (7)

Colona, John G., AIG Marketing, New York, NY. Tel: (212) 770-7000, (212) 770-2237, Web Site: www.agac.com (15)

Colonial Life Insurance Co Texas, Fort Worth, TX. Tel: (817) 390-2350, (888) 227-5119, FAX: (817) 390-2209, E-Mail: insurance@colonialinsurance.com, Web Site: www.colonialinsurance.com (15)

Colonial Redi Record Co, Brooklyn, NY. Tel: (718) 972-7433, (800) 637-0040, FAX: (718) 972-7438, E-Mail: redirecord@aol.com, Web Site: www.colonialrediprecord.com (34)

Colonial Redi-Record Corp, Brooklyn, NY. Tel: (718) 972-7433, (800) 637-0040, FAX: (718) 972-7438, Web Site: www.asisupplier.com/81110 (10)

The Colonial Williamsburg Foundation, Williamsburg, VA. Tel: (757) 229-1000, (757) 220-7275, (800) 761-8331, Web Site: www.williamsburgmarketplace.com (1)

Colonna, Robert J., Innovative Systems Inc, Pittsburgh, PA. Tel: (412) 937-9300, (800) 622-6390, FAX: (412) 937-9309, E-Mail: info@innovativesystems.com, Web Site: www.innovativesystems.com (22)

Color Film Media Group LLC, Norwalk, CT. Tel: (203) 202-2930, E-Mail: info@itownstore.com, Web Site: www.itownstore.com (32)

ColorEdge, Burbank, CA. Tel: (818) 842-1121, (800) 300-3686, FAX: (818) 842-0280, E-Mail: john.davies@crushcreative.com, Web Site: www.coloredge.com (27)

Colorlith Corp, Providence, RI. Tel: (508) 837-6100, (800) 556-7171, FAX: (508) 677-4466, E-Mail: lep@colorlith.net, Web Site: www.colorlith.net (27)

ColorTree of Virginia Inc, Richmond, VA. Tel: (804) 358-4245, FAX: (804) 358-0488, Web Site: www.colortree.com (26)

Colorworks Graphics Inc, Chicago, IL. Tel: (312) 666-7642, FAX: (312) 666-0473, E-Mail: colorworks@ameritech.net, Web Site: www.colorworksgraphics.com (34)

Colton, Bob, Steppin' Out & See America, Las Vegas, NV. Tel: (702) 798-6522, FAX: 702 798-6562, E-Mail: sales@see-america.net, Web Site: steppinoutseeamerica.com (19)

Colturi, Tom, Lucky Heart Cosmetics Inc, Memphis, TN. Tel: (901) 526-7658, (800) 283-1014, FAX: (901) 526-7660, Web Site: www.luckyheart.com (7)

Colucci, Steve, Interact Medical, South Bend, IN. Tel: (415) 354-1777, Web Site: www.interactmedical.com (35)

Columbia Books & Information Services, Bethesda, MD. Tel: (202) 464-1662, (888) 265-0600, FAX: (202) 464-1775, E-Mail: info@columbiabooks.com, Web Site: www.columbiabooks.com (24)

Columbia College Chicago, Chicago, IL. Tel: (312) 663-1600, FAX: (312) 344-0869, Web Site: www.colum.edu (41)

Columbia Journalism Review, New York, NY. Tel: (212) 854-2718, (888) 625-7782, FAX: (212) 854-8367, Web Site: www.cjr.org (17)

Columbia Sportswear, Portland, OR. Tel: (503) 985-4203, (800) 622-6953, Web Site: www.columbia.com (2)

Columbia University, Annual Fund Programs, New York, NY. E-Mail: donorrelations@columbia.edu, Web Site: http://giving.columbia.edu (5)

The Columbian, Vancouver, WA. Tel: (360) 694-3391, FAX: (360) 735-4503, Web Site: www.columbian.com (17)

Columbian Mutual Life Insurance Co, Binghamton, NY. Tel: (607) 724-2472, (800) 423-9765 (15)

The Columbus Dispatch, Columbus, OH. Tel: (614) 461-5000, FAX: (614) 461-7551, E-Mail: csmith@the.dispatch.com, Web Site: www.dispatch.com (17)

Colvin, Donald, Caesars Entertainment Corp, Las Vegas, NV. Tel: (702) 407-6000, (800) 634-6001, FAX: (702) 407-6037, Web Site: www.caesars.com (16)

Colvin, Mary, Do-It Corp, South Haven, MI. Tel: (269) 637-1121, (800) 426-4822, FAX: (269) 637-7223, E-Mail: sales@do-it.com, Web Site: www.do-it.com (9)

Colwell & Salmon Communications Inc, Cresskill, NJ. Tel: (518) 482-1596, (800) 724-5318, FAX: (518) 482-1998, E-Mail: sales@colwell-salmon.com, Web Site: www.colwell-salmon.com (29)

Colwell, Scott, Carvel Corp, Atlanta, GA. Tel: (404) 255-3250, (800) 227-8353, FAX: (404) 255-4978, Web Site: www.carvel.com (4)

Colyer, Mike, Ward's Natural Science, Rochester, NY. Tel: (585) 359-2502, (800) 962-2660, FAX: (585) 334-6174, E-Mail: customer_service@wardsci.com, Web Site: www.wardsci.com (34)

Com-Pak. Berlin. CT. Tel: (856) 802-1900, (856) 802-3097, E-Mail: info@com-pak.com, Web Site: www.marketpointdirect.com (28)

Comazzi, Anthony J., The Newman Group Computer Services Corp, Ann Arbor, MI. Tel: (734) 426-3200, FAX: (734) 426-0777, E-Mail: anewman@newman.com (3)

Combe, Paul C., American Student Assistance, Boston, MA. Tel: (800) 999-9080, Web Site: www.asa.com (1)

Combined Insurance Co of America, Glenview, IL. Tel: (847) 953-8116, (800) 490-1322, FAX: (847) 953-8070, Web Site: www.combinedinsurance.com (15)

Combs, Diane, Donna Salyers' Fabulous-Bridal Inc, Covington, KY. Tel: (859) 291-3300, (800) 848-4650, E-Mail: abell@fabulousfurs.com, Web Site: fabulousfurs.com (2)

Combs, Dorothy, Project HOPE, Millwood, VA. Tel: (540) 837-2100, Web Site: www.projecthope.org (1)

Combs, Jason, Strategic Marketing & Mailing, Champaign, IL. Tel: (217) 355-2600, (800) 871-4524, Web Site: www.strategicmail.com (28)

Combs, Jeff, Strategic Marketing & Mailing, Champaign, IL. Tel: (217) 355-2600, (800) 871-4524, Web Site: www.strategicmail.com (28)

Combs, Karen, Daydots, Fort Worth, TX. Tel: (817) 590-4500, (800) 321-3687, FAX: (800) 438-7002, E-Mail: customercare@daydots.com, Web Site: www.daydots.com (16)

Combuchen, Andreas, Atmosphere Proximity, New York, NY. Tel: (212) 827-2500, FAX: (212) 827-2525, E-Mail: andreas.combuechen@atmospeherebbdo.com, Web Site: atmosphereproximity.com (35)

Comcast Corp, Philadelphia, PA. Tel: (215) 665-1700, Web Site: www.comcast.com (32)

Comcast Spectacor LP, Philadelphia, PA. Tel: (215) 336-3600, (800) 298-4200, FAX: (215) 389-9518, E-Mail: info@comcast-spectacor.com, Web Site: www.comcast-spectacor.com (16)

Comdata Corp, Brentwood, TN. Tel: (615) 370-7000, (800) 266-3282, FAX: (615) 370-7614, Web Site: www.comdata.com (14)

Comedy Central, New York, NY. Tel: (212) 767-8600, Web Site: www.cc.com (32)

Comer, Marjorie A., Axia Public Relations, Jacksonville, FL. Tel: (904) 425-1500, (866) 773-4768, Web Site: www.axiapr.com (35)

Comerica Inc, Dallas, TX. Tel: (800) 521-1190, FAX: (925) 941-1999, Web Site: www.comerica.com (14)

Wm F Comly & Son Inc, Philadelphia, PA. Tel: (215) 634-2500, Web Site: www.comly.com (9)

Comly, Daniel F, Wm F Comly & Son Inc, Philadelphia, PA. Tel: (215) 634-2500, Web Site: www.comly.com (9)

Command Financial, New York, NY. Tel: (212) 274-0070, FAX: (212) 274-8262, E-Mail: csd@commandfinancial.com, Web Site: www.commandfinancial.com (35)

Commemorative Brands Inc, Austin, TX. Tel: (512) 444-0571, FAX: (512) 444-0065 (16)

Commerce Bancshares Inc, Saint Louis, MO. Tel: (800) 453-2265, Web Site: www.commercebank.com (14)

Commerce Register Inc, Midland Park, NJ. Tel: (201) 445-3000, FAX: (201) 445-5806, E-Mail: cri@comreginc.com, Web Site: www.comreginc.com (22)

Commercial Atlas & Marketing Guide, Skokie, IL. Tel: (847) 329-8100, (800) 678-7263, FAX: (800) 934-3479, E-Mail: store@randmcnally.com, Web Site: www.randmcnally.com (43)

Commercial Data Processing Inc, Fairfield, NJ. Tel: (973) 882-1660, (800) 242-3731, FAX: (973) 882-0387, Web Site: www.dataprocess.com (22)

Commercial Envelope Manufacturing Co Inc, Deer Park, NY. Tel: (631) 242-2500, FAX: (631) 242-6935, Web Site: www.commercial-envelope.com (26)

Commercial Federal Bank, Omaha, NE. Tel: (402) 554-9200, FAX: (402) 390-3592 (14)

Commercial Lithographing Co Inc, Kansas City, MO. Tel: (816) 241-2218, FAX: (816) 241-6091, E-Mail: sjohnson@commercial-lithographing.com, Web Site: www.clitho.com (31)

Commercial Mailing Lists, Framingham, MA. Tel: (508) 879-2647, (800) 875-8345, FAX: (508) 879-2911 (23)

Commercial Travelers Mutual Insurance Co, Utica, NY. Tel: (315) 797-5200, (800) 422-6200, FAX: (315) 797-3198, E-Mail: comtravl@commercialtravelers.com, Web Site: www.commercialtravelers.com (15)

CommercialWare Inc, Natick, MA. Tel: (508) 655-7500, FAX: (508) 647-9495, Web Site: www.commercialware.com (22)

Commerford, Don, Consolidated Printing & Stationary Co Inc, Salina, KS. Tel: (785) 825-5426, (800) 432-0266, FAX: (785) 825-6536, Web Site: www.consolidatedprinting.com (35)

Commisso, Rocco B., Mediacom Communications Corp, Chester, NY. Tel: (855) 633-4226, FAX: (845) 698-4100, Web Site: www.mediacomcable.com (32)

Commonwealth Business Media Inc, Newark, NJ. Tel: (609) 371-7700, (800) 221-5488, FAX: (609) 371-7879, Web Site: www.cbizmedia.com (17)

Commonwealth Lists, Washington, DC. Tel: (202) 831-6202, FAX: (202) 831-6203, E-Mail: info@commonwealthlists.com, Web Site: www.commonwealthlists.com (23)

CommScope Inc, Hickory, NC. Tel: (828) 324-2200, (800) 982-1708, Web Site: www.commscope.com (16)

Communication Creativity, Buena Vista, CO. Tel: (720) 344-4388, (800) 331-8355, FAX: (866) 685-0307, E-Mail: steve@steveheimberg.com, Web Site: www.communicationcreativity.com (17)

Communication Industries Corp, Grafton, VT. Tel: (802) 869-6500, FAX: (802) 869-6565, E-Mail: info@cicmail.com, Web Site: www.careersatcic.com (10)

Communication Logistics, Inc, Plover, WI. Tel: (715) 341-6180, FAX: (715) 341-7971, Web Site: www.comloginc.com (22)

Communication Managers, LLC, Brookfield, CT. Tel: (203) 775-4213, FAX: (203) 775-6413, E-Mail: etalian@communicationmanagers.com, Web Site: www.communicationmanagers.com (20)

Communication Resources Inc, Beaufort, SC. Tel: (330) 266-1489, (800) 992-2144, FAX: (330) 493-3158, E-Mail: service@comresources.com, Web Site: www.comresources.com (18)

Communication Solutions LLC, Springfield, MO. Tel: (417) 862-4567, Web Site: www.comsolllc.com (29)

Communications Corp of America, Boston, VA. Tel: (540) 547-1700, FAX: (540) 302-8015, E-Mail: contact@cca.net, Web Site: www.cca.net (21)

Communications Unlimited Inc, Richmond, VA. Tel: (804) 754-7242, E-Mail: communicationsunlimited1@verizon.net (20)

Communicor, Milwaukee, WI. Tel: (414) 961-5999, FAX: (414) 961-5990, Web Site: www.communicor.com (36)

Communifx Corp, Cranberry, PA. Tel: (724) 935-8655, Web Site: www.communifax.com (27)

Communispond Inc, East Hampton, NY. Tel: (631) 907-8010, (800) 529-5925, FAX: (631) 907-8011, Web Site: www.communispond.com (20)

Community Coffee Co, Baton Rouge, LA. Tel: (225) 291-3900, (800) 884-5282, FAX: (800) 643-8199, E-Mail: customerservice@communitycoffee.com, Web Site: www.communitycoffee.com (4)

Community Food Bank, Tucson, AZ. Tel: (520) 622-0525, FAX: (520) 624-6349, Web Site: www.communityfoodbank.org (1)

Compact Information Systems, Redmond, WA. Tel: (425) 869-1379, (800) 632-1379, FAX: (425) 558-2638, E-Mail: pat@compactlists.com, Web Site: www.compactlists.com (23)

Companion Plants, Athens, OH. Tel: (740) 592-4643, FAX: (740) 593-3092, E-Mail: peter@companionplants.com, Web Site: www.companionplants.com (8)

The Company of Others, Houston, TX. Tel: (800) 994-1681, E-Mail: inquiry@thecompany.com, Web Site: www.thecompany.com (35)

The Company Store Inc, La Crosse, WI. Tel: (608) 785-1400, FAX: (608) 791-5790, Web Site: www.thecompanystore.com (16)

Compass Bank, Birmingham, AL. Tel: (205) 297-4900, (800) 239-4357, FAX: (205) 933-3702, Web Site: www.compassbank.com (14)

Compass Electronics, Forest Grove, OR. Tel: (503) 357-2111, FAX: (503) 357-2111 (9)

Compass Media, Gulf Shores, AL. Tel: (251) 968-4600, (800) 239-9880, E-Mail: info@compassmedia.com, Web Site: www.compassmedia.com (30)

Compass Ventures, Lincoln, NE. Tel: (402) 438-3222, FAX: (402) 438-3439, E-Mail: info@compassventures.com, Web Site: www.compassventures.com (23)

Compassion International, Colorado Springs, CO. Tel: (800) 336-7676, Web Site: www.compassion.com (1)

CompetiScan, Chicago, IL. Tel: (312) 546-3489, Web Site: www.competiscan.com (30)

Comphealth, Salt Lake City, UT. Tel: (801) 930-3000, (800) 453-3030, FAX: (801) 930-4517, E-Mail: info@comphealth.com, Web Site: www.comphealth.com (16)

COMPITSS Inc, Newbury Park, CA. Tel: (805) 823-2286, E-Mail: info@compitss.com, Web Site: www.compitss.com (22)

Complete Mailing Lists LLC, White Plains, NY. Tel: (914) 771-6640, (866) 314-5478, FAX: (914) 771-6645, E-Mail: info@completemailinglists.com, Web Site: completemailinglists.com (23)

Complete Mailing Service, Toronto, ON Canada. Tel: (416) 755-7761, (888) 683-2501, FAX: (416) 755-8231, E-Mail: sales@completemailing.com, Web Site: www.completemailing.com (22)

Complete Mailing Service Inc, Santa Cruz, CA. Tel: (831) 425-5556, FAX: (831) 425-0306, E-Mail: info@completemail.com, Web Site: www.completemail.com (28)

Complete Mailing Solutions, Inc, Englewood, CO. Tel: (303) 761-0681, (888) 843-9937, FAX: (303) 761-7837, Web Site: www.comp-mail.com (22)

Comppon, Bob, AGORA Inc, Baltimore, MD. Tel: (410) 783-8499, FAX: (410) 783-8414, E-Mail: csteam@agorapublishinggroup.com, Web Site: www.agora-inc.com (17)

Compton, Brett, Red Clay Interactive, Buford, GA. Tel: (770) 297-2430, (866) 251-2800, E-Mail: hello@redclayinteractive.com, Web Site: www.redclayinteractive.com (35)

Compton, Kathryn C., Mother Earth News Magazine, Topeka, KS. Tel: (785) 274-4300, (800) 678-5779, FAX: (785) 274-4305, E-Mail: bwelch@ogdenpubs.com, Web Site: www.cappers.com (17)

Compton, Kris Ellen, Alerus Financial National Assoc, Grand Forks, ND. Tel: (701) 795-3200, (800) 279-3200, Web Site: www2.alerusfinancial.com (14)

Compton, Lance, Red Clay Interactive, Buford, GA. Tel: (770) 297-2430, (866) 251-2800, E-Mail: hello@redclayinteractive.com, Web Site: www.redclayinteractive.com (35)

Compton, Larry, American Modern Insurance Group, Amelia, OH. Tel: (513) 943-7200, (800) 759-9008, FAX: (513) 947-4779, (800) 217-5150, E-Mail: customer_care@amig.com, Web Site: www.amig.com (15)

Compton, Paul H., JP Morgan Chase & Co, New York, NY. Tel: (212) 270-6000, E-Mail: jpmcinvestorrelations@jpmchase.com, Web Site: www.jpmorgan.com (14)

Compton, Tim, ActiveCampaign Inc, Chicago, IL. Tel: (800) 357-0402, E-Mail: help@activecampaign.com, Web Site: www.activecampaign.com (24)

Compu-Mail Direct Marketing, Grand Island, NY. Tel: (716) 775-8001, (800) 255-0607, FAX: (716) 775-5681, E-Mail: marketing@compu-mail.com, Web Site: compu-mail.com (21)

Computer Business Services Inc, Americus, GA. Tel: (229) 924-4408, (866) 924-4408, FAX: (229) 924-3644, E-Mail: nelson@combusser.com, Web Site: www.combusser.com (22)

Computer Dynamics Inc, Charlotte, NC. Tel: (866) 599-6512, FAX: (704) 586-9671, E-Mail: CDIsales@gefanuc.com, Web Site: www.cdynamics.com (3)

Computer Shopper, New York, NY. Tel: (646) 472-4000, FAX: (646) 472-3912, E-Mail: feedback@computershopper.com, Web Site: www.computershopper.com (31)

Computer Solutions Inc, Miami, FL. Tel: (305) 558-7000, FAX: (305) 557-0003, E-Mail: info@csiflorida.com, Web Site: www.csiflorida.com (22)

Computer Station Corp, Houston, TX. Tel: (713) 777-6860, FAX: (713) 777-3431, E-Mail: csc@computerstationcorp.com, Web Site: www.computerstationcorp.com (3)

The Computer Studio, Yonkers, NY. Tel: (914) 968-1212, FAX: (914) 968-1228, E-Mail: connect@webbusconnect.com, Web Site: www.webbusconnect.com (35)

The Computer Supply People, Menomonee Falls, WI. Tel: (262) 251-5511, (800) 242-2090, FAX: (262) 251-4737, E-Mail: medmgt@computersupplypeople.com, Web Site: www.computersupplypeople.com (3)

Computerized Research & Development Inc, Lincoln, CA. Tel: (916) 434-5690, E-Mail: info@computerizedresearch.com, Web Site: www.cradinc.com (23)

Computermail South Inc, Saint Petersburg, FL. Tel: (727) 579-1000, FAX: (727) 823-5474, E-Mail: sales@computermailsouth.com, Web Site: www.computermailsouth.com (23)

Computerworld DataBase Div, Framingham, MA. Tel: (508) 879-0700, (800) 343-6474, FAX: (508) 875-4394, Web Site: www.computerworld.com (22)

Comsearch, Ashburn, VA. Tel: (703) 726-5500, FAX: (703) 726-5600, Web Site: www.comsearch.com (30)

Comstock, Beth, General Electric Co, Fairfield, CT. Tel: (203) 373-2211, FAX: (203) 373-3131, Web Site: www.ge.com (16)

Con-Cor International, Tucson, AZ. Tel: (520) 721-8939, (888) 255-7688, FAX: (520) 721-8940, E-Mail: concor@con-cor.com, Web Site: www.con-cor.com (11)

Con-Way Freight, Ann Arbor, MI. Tel: (734) 994-6600, FAX: (734) 757-1153 (12)

Con-Way Truckload, Joplin, MO. Tel: (417) 623-5229, (800) CFI-DRIVE, FAX: (417) 623-8939, E-Mail: gnichols@cfi-us.com, Web Site: www.cfi-us.com (12)

Conant, Jeff, SDI Marketing, Toronto, ON Canada. Tel: (416) 674-9010, (877) SDI-TEAM, FAX: (416) 674-9011, E-Mail: info@sdicapital.com, Web Site: www.sdimarketing.com (14)

Conant, Vic, Nightingale-Conant Corp, Niles, IL. Tel: (847) 647-0300, (800) 557-1660, FAX: (847) 647-7145, Web Site: www.nightingale.com (17)

Concept Communications, Nashua, NH. Tel: (603) 577-9810, Web Site: www.conceptcommusa.com (20)

Concept Communications Co, Romeoville, IL. Tel: (630) 829-8450, (800) 323-3524, FAX: (630) 629-8415, E-Mail: info@cstore1.com, Web Site: www.cstore1.com (16)

Concept Media Partners Inc, Yorktown Heights, NY. Tel: (914) 767-0032, FAX: (914) 514-1711, E-Mail: karen@conceptmediapartners.com, Web Site: www.conceptmediapartners.com (35)

Concepts TV Productions Inc, Boonton, NJ. Tel: (973) 331-1500, FAX: (973) 331-1550, E-Mail: info@conceptstv.com, Web Site: www.conceptstv.com (32)

Concepts Unlimited, Frederick, CO. Tel: (303) 918-9416, E-Mail: conceptsunlimited@estreet.com, Web Site: www.conceptsunlimitedinc.com (35)

Concern Worldwide, New York, NY. Tel: (212) 557-8000, FAX: (212) 557-8004, Web Site: /www.concernusa.org (1)

Concinnity Marketing & Technology Inc, Winston-Salem, NC. Tel: (336) 245-4561, E-Mail: chris@concinnitymarketing.com, Web Site: www.concinnitymarketing.com (35)

Conclusive Analytics, Inc, Huntersville, NC. Tel: (704) 887-5600, FAX: (704) 887-5601, E-Mail: info@conclusivemarketing.com, Web Site: www.conclusiveanalytics.com (22)

Concord Litho, Concord, NH. Tel: (603) 225-3328, FAX: (603) 225-6120, E-Mail: print@concordlitho.com, Web Site: www.concordlitho.com (27)

Concordia Publishing House, Saint Louis, MO. Tel: (314) 268-1000, (800) 325-3040, FAX: (314) 268-1329, E-Mail: order@cph.org, Web Site: www.cph.org (17)

Concur, Bellevue, WA. Tel: (425) 702-590-5000, (800) 401-8412, FAX: (425) 590-5999, Web Site: www.concur.com (22)

Concurrent Computer Corp, Duluth, GA. Tel: (678) 228-4000, (877) 978-7363, FAX: (954) 977-5580, Web Site: www.ccur.com (3)

Conde Nast, New York, NY. Tel: (212) 286-2860, FAX: (212) 880-8289, Web Site: www.condenast.com (17)

Condolink, Omaha, NE. Tel: (402) 592-3525, (800) 877-9600, FAX: (402) 592-4122, E-Mail: info@condolink.com, Web Site: www.condolink.com (16)

John Condon & Associates, Greenwich, CT. Tel: (203) 869-7006, FAX: (203) 622-1488 (20)

Condon, Jr. John, John Condon & Associates, Greenwich, CT. Tel: (203) 869-7006, FAX: (203) 622-1488 (20)

Condrin, III J. Paul, Liberty Mutual Group, Inc, Boston, MA. Tel: (617) 357-9500, (800) 837-5274, Web Site: www.libertymutual.com (15)

Cone, Jason, Doctors Without Borders, New York, NY. Tel: (212) 679-6800, FAX: (212) 679-7016, Web Site: www.doctorswithoutborders.org (1)

Coneys, Brooke, Carl Bloom Associates Inc, White Plains, NY. Tel: (914) 761-2800, FAX: (914) 761-2744, E-Mail: info@carlbloom.com, Web Site: www.carlbloom.com (35)

The Conference Board Inc, New York, NY. Tel: (212) 759-0900, FAX: (212) 980-7014, Web Site: www.conference-board.org (16)

Conform Pacific, Lomita, CA. Tel: (800) CONFORM, FAX: (310) 496-2880, E-Mail: info@smartblock.com, Web Site: www.smartblock.com (16)

Conformer Expansion Products Inc, Great Neck, NY. Tel: (516) 504-6300, E-Mail: support@conformerinc.com, Web Site: www.conformerinc.com (26)

Conforti, Michele, Affinion Group, Stamford, CT. Tel: (203) 956-1000, (800) 282-3315, Web Site: www.affinion.com (35)

Conley, Helena, National Seminars Group, Shawnee Mission, KS. Tel: (913) 432-7755, (800) 258-7246, FAX: (913) 432-0824, E-Mail: cstserv@natsem.com, Web Site: www.natsem.com (16)

Conley, Vicki, Galveston Bay Foundation, Webster, TX. Tel: (281) 332-3381, Web Site: www.galvbay.org (1)

Conlon, Brian T., DL Blair Inc, Westbury, NY. Tel: (516) 746-3700, FAX: (516) 746-3889, Web Site: www.dlblair.com (35)

Conlon, E.T., Mountain Craft Shop Co, Proctor, WV. Tel: (877) 365-5869, FAX: (304) 455-1740, E-Mail: info@folktoys.com, Web Site: www.folktoys.com (11)

Conlon, Ginger, DM News, New York, NY. Tel: (646) 638-6000, (800) 558-1703, FAX: (212) 925-8752, E-Mail: dmnewssubs@haymarketmedia.com, Web Site: www.dmnews.com (43)

Conlon, Kathy, Kett Tool Co, Cincinnati, OH. Tel: (513) 271-0333, FAX: (513) 271-5318, E-Mail: info@kett-tool.com, Web Site: www.kett-tool.com (9)

Conlon, Mary, American Movie Classics Holding Corp, Jericho, NY. Tel: (516) 803-3000, FAX: (516) 803-3003, Web Site: www.amctv.com (16)

Conlon, Steve A., Mountain Craft Shop Co, Proctor, WV. Tel: (877) 365-5869, FAX: (304) 455-1740, E-Mail: info@folktoys.com, Web Site: www.folktoys.com (11)

Conlon, T.J., DL Blair Inc, Westbury, NY. Tel: (516) 746-3700, FAX: (516) 746-3889, Web Site: www.dlblair.com (35)

Conmio Inc, New York, NY. Tel: (917) 583-2651, Web Site: www.conmio.com (16)

Conn, Katrina, StrongView Systems Inc, Redwood City, CA. Tel: (650) 421-4200, (800) 971-0380, FAX: (650) 421-4201, E-Mail: info@strongview.com, Web Site: www.strongview.com (32)

Conn, William, Simpson Electric Co, Lac Du Flambeau, WI. Tel: (715) 588-3311, FAX: (715) 588-3327, E-Mail: cservice@simpsonelectric.com, Web Site: www.simpsonelectric.com (16)

Connecticut Color Inc, Meriden, CT. Tel: (203) 237-1400, FAX: (203) 440-3678, Web Site: www.connecticutcolor.com (27)

Connecticut Marketing Associates, Wilton, CT. Tel: (203) 761-9556, FAX: (203) 761-9763 (20)

The Connection Contact Center Services, Burnsville, MN. Tel: (952) 948-5335, (800) 883-5777, FAX: (952) 948-5498, E-Mail: sales@the-connection.com, Web Site: www.the-connection.com (29)

The Connection Outsourced Call Ctr, Burnsville, MN. Tel: (800) 883-5777, Web Site: www.the-connection.com (29)

Connel, Kelly, TALX Corp, Dallas, TX. Tel: (972) 755-2100, FAX: (972) 755-2080, E-Mail: consulting@managementinsights.com, Web Site: www.managementinsights.com (20)

Connell Communications Inc, Peterborough, NH. Tel: (603) 924-7271, (800) 677-8847, FAX: (603) 924-7013 (17)

Connell, Colleen, GaelSong, Seattle, WA. Tel: (206) 526-8350, Web Site: www.gaelsong.com (6)

S Connelly & Co Inc, Annandale, MN. Tel: (320) 274-7054, E-Mail: sconco@aol.com (39)

Connelly, Deirdre, GlaxoSmithKline USA, Philadelphia, PA. Tel: (888) 825-5249, Web Site: us.gsk.com (16)

Connelly, James A., xpedx, Loveland, OH. Tel: (513) 965-2900, FAX: (513) 965-2849, Web Site: www.xpedx.com (25)

Connelly, Jim, Creative Teaching Press, Cypress, CA. Tel: (714) 895-5047, (800) 287-8879 (17)

Connelly, Jr Thomas M., American Chemical Society, Washington, DC. Tel: (202) 872-4600, (800) 227-5558, FAX: (202) 452-8913, E-Mail: service@acs.org, Web Site: www.acs.org (1)

Connelly, Kevin M, SpencerStuart, Chicago, IL. Tel: (312) 822-0088, FAX: (312) 822-0116, Web Site: www.spencerstuart.com (20)

Connelly, Stephen P., S Connelly & Co Inc, Annandale, MN. Tel: (320) 274-7054, E-Mail: sconco@aol.com (39)

Conner, Jay Del, Pennsylvania Firebacks, Philadelphia, PA. Tel: (215) 722-1221, E-Mail: info@fireback.com, Web Site: www.fireback.com (8)

Connex International Inc, Danbury, CT. Tel: (203) 731-5400, (800) 426-6639, FAX: (203) 730-9060, E-Mail: marketing@connexintl.com, Web Site: www.connexintl.com (22)

Conney Safety Products LLC, Madison, WI. Tel: (888) 356-9100, FAX: (800) 845-9095, E-Mail: safety@conney.com, Web Site: www.conney.com (7)

CM Connolly, Sacramento, CA. Tel: (916) 897-8095, Web Site: www.cmconnolly.com (1)

Connolly, Catherine, CM Connolly, Sacramento, CA. Tel: (916) 897-8095, Web Site: www.cmconnolly.com (1)

Connolly, Eileen, BT Americas, Irving, TX. Tel: (972) 830-8169, FAX: (703) 755-6740, Web Site: www.btglobalservices.com (22)

Connolly, Evan, Creative Strategy Group Inc, Newtown, PA. Tel: (215) 860-3045, FAX: (215) 860-3129, E-Mail: csg@csgmarketing.com, Web Site: www.csg-design.com (35)

Connolly, Patrick J., Williams-Sonoma Inc, San Francisco, CA. Tel: (415) 421-7900, (800) 840-2591, Web Site: www.williams-sonomainc.com (8)

Connolly, Richard, OnTime Companies, Chelsea, MA. Tel: (617) 884-8488, Web Site: www.ontimecompanies.com (28)

Connor, Michael G, Continental Western Group, Des Moines, IA. Tel: (515) 473-3000, (800) 533-0303, FAX: (515) 473-3015, Web Site: www.cwgins.com (15)

Connor, Scott, Acurian, Horsham, PA. Tel: (215) 323-9000, (866) 566-5966, FAX: (215) 323-9001, Web Site: www.acurian.com (7)

Paul Connors Creative, Lake Forest, IL. Tel: (847) 295-8746 (39)

Connors, Martha, Technology Review, Cambridge, MA. Tel: (617) 475-8000, FAX: (617) 258-5850, Web Site: www.technologyreview.com (17)

Connors, Paul F., Paul Connors Creative, Lake Forest, IL. Tel: (847) 295-8746 (39)

Conrad Direct Inc, Cresskill, NJ. Tel: (201) 567-3200, FAX: (201) 567-1530, E-Mail: listinfo@conraddirect.com, Web Site: www.conraddirect.com (23)

Conrad, Deborah S., Intel Corp, Santa Clara, CA. Tel: (408) 765-8080, (800) 548-4725, FAX: (408) 765-6187, Web Site: www.intel.com (16)

Conradi, Tom, Chicago Magazine, Chicago, IL. Tel: (312) 222-8999, FAX: (312) 222-0287, Web Site: www.chicagomag.com (17)

Conroy, Jennifer, Canine Companions for Independence, Santa Rosa, CA. Tel: (707) 577-1700, (800) 572-2275, FAX: (707) 577-1711, E-Mail: info@cci.org, Web Site: www.caninecompanions.org (16)

Conseco Inc, Carmel, IN. Tel: (317) 817-6100, FAX: (317) 817-2847, Web Site: www.conseco.com (15)

Conseil, Dominique, Aveda Corp, Blaine, MN. Tel: (763) 951-4201, (800) 644-4831, Web Site: www.aveda.com (7)

Conservation International, Arlington, VA. Tel: (703) 341-2400, E-Mail: community@conservation.org (1)

Conslato, Laurie, Pioneer Hi-Bred International Inc, Johnston, IA. Tel: (515) 535-3200, FAX: (515) 535-4415, E-Mail: web.editor@pioneer.com, Web Site: www.pioneer.com (4)

Consolidated Electronics Inc, Dayton, OH. Tel: (937) 252-5662, (800) 543-3568, FAX: (937) 252-4066, E-Mail: scoy@ceitron.com, Web Site: www.ceitron.com (3)

Consolidated Mailing Corp, Shawnee Mission, KS. Tel: (913) 262-4400, (800) 706-6245, FAX: (913) 262-7801, E-Mail: cmcmail@swbell.net, Web Site: www.consolidatedmailing.com (28)

Consolidated Market Response, Charleston, IL. Tel: (217) 348-7050, FAX: (217) 348-7060 (29)

Consolidated Plastics Co Inc, Stow, OH. Tel: (330) 425-3900, (800) 362-1000, FAX: (330) 425-3333, Web Site: www.consolidatedplastics.com (9)

Consolidated Printing & Stationary Co Inc, Salina, KS. Tel: (785) 825-5426, (800) 432-0266, FAX: (785) 825-6536, Web Site: www.consolidatedprinting.com (35)

Consolidated Printing Inc, Philadelphia, PA. Tel: (215) 879-1400, (800) 347-0119, FAX: (215) 879-9130, Web Site: www.condrake.com (27)

Consolidated Technologies Group LLC, Cleveland, OH. Tel: (866) 742-0109, E-Mail: info@ctgconvergence.com, Web Site: www.ctgadvisor.com (28)

Constable, Bill, Armbrust Paper Tubes Inc, Chicago, IL. Tel: (773) 586-3232, FAX: (773) 586-8997, E-Mail: tubesrus@corecomm.net, Web Site: www.tubesrus.com (10)

Constable, Ken, Smith & Noble, Corona, CA. Tel: (888) 241-2134, E-Mail: contactus@smithnoble.com, Web Site: www.smithandnoble.com (8)

Constant Contact Inc, Waltham, MA. Tel: (781) 472-8100, FAX: (781) 472-8101, Web Site: www.constantcontact.com (32)

Constant, Pete, RBS Citizens Financial Group Inc, Dedham, MA. Tel: (781) 471-1565, Web Site: www.citizensbank.com (14)

Constantino, Tor, Bausch & Lomb Inc, Rochester, NY. Tel: (585) 338-6000, (800) 344-8815, FAX: (585) 338-6007, Web Site: www.bausch.com (16)

Constanza, Gloria, Dexposito & Partners, New York, NY. Tel: (646) 747-8800, Web Site: newamericanagency.com (35)

Consumer Benefit Services Inc, Naperville, IL. Tel: (630) 420-6200, (800) 657-8309, FAX: (630) 420-2294, E-Mail: dcarlson@consumerbenefit.com, Web Site: www.consumerbenefit.com (16)

Consumer Credit Advocates Inc, Salt Lake City, UT. Tel: (801) 265-9333, FAX: (801) 265-9595 (16)

Consumer Focus, Plano, TX. Tel: (972) 378-9697, (214) 542-8787, E-Mail: sstewart@consumerfocusco.com, Web Site: www.consumerfocusco.com (30)

Consumer Opinion Services Inc, Seattle, WA. Tel: (206) 241-6050, FAX: (206) 241-5213, E-Mail: info@cosvc.com, Web Site: www.cosvc.com (30)

Consumers Digest Inc, Deerfield, IL. Tel: (847) 607-3000, FAX: (847) 763-0200, E-Mail: postmaster@consumersdigest.com, Web Site: www.consumersdigest.com (17)

Consumer's Energy, Jackson, MI. Tel: (517) 788-0550, (800) 805-0490, FAX: (517) 788-1859, E-Mail: businesscenter@consumerenergy.com, Web Site: www.consumersenergy.com (16)

Consumers Union, Yonkers, NY. Tel: (914) 378-2000, FAX: (914) 378-2906, Web Site: www.consumersunion.org (17)

Contact Center Compliance, Santa Rosa, CA. Tel: (707) 303-4437, (800) 308-0258, Web Site: www.dnc.com (22)

Contact Marketing LLC, New York, NY. Tel: (201) 530-0200, E-Mail: info@contactmarketing.net, Web Site: www.contactmarketing.net (23)

The Container Store, Coppell, TX. Tel: (888) 266-8246, Web Site: www.containerstore.com (8)

Conte, Guy, Graphnet Inc, New York, NY. Tel: (212) 994-1100, (800) 327-1800, FAX: (212) 994-1188, E-Mail: custsvc@graphnet.com, Web Site: www.graphnet.com (28)

The Contest Center, Wappingers Falls, NY. Tel: (845) 297-4833, E-Mail: contestcen@aol.com, Web Site: www.contestcen.com (19)

Conti, Robert John, Neuberger & Berman Management, New York, NY. Tel: (212) 476-9000, (800) 877-9700, FAX: (212) 476-8937, Web Site: www.nb.com (14)

Continental Envelope Corp, Geneva, IL. Tel: (630) 262-8080, (800) 621-8155, FAX: (630) 262-1450, E-Mail: sales@continentalenvelope.com, Web Site: www.continentalenvelope.com (26)

Continental Plastic Card Co, Pompano Beach, FL. Tel: (954) 794-0040, (800) 543-0670, FAX: (954) 755-4493, E-Mail: info@continentalplasticcard.com, Web Site: www.continentalplasticcard.com (27)

Continental Supply Inc, Cleveland, OH. Tel: (440) 864-6231, (800) 672-0321, FAX: (888) 672-9808 (9)

Continental Web Press Inc, Itasca, IL. Tel: (630) 773-1903, FAX: (630) 773-1909, E-Mail: inquires@continentalweb.com, Web Site: www.continentalweb.com (27)

Continental Western Group, Des Moines, IA. Tel: (515) 473-3000, (800) 533-0303, FAX: (515) 473-3015, Web Site: www.cwgins.com (15)

Continenza, James, The Berry Company, Dayton, OH. Tel: (937) 610-4100, (800) 877-0475, Web Site: www.theberrycompany.com (35)

Continuing Education of the Bar (CEB), Oakland, CA. Tel: (510) 302-2000, (800) 232-3444, FAX: (510) 302-2001, Web Site: www.ceb.com (1)

Continuity Shippers Association, Woodstock, VT. Tel: (802) 672-3634 (20)

Continuum Global, San Francisco, CA. Tel: (415) 685-3301, Web Site: www.continuumglobal.com (30)

The Contrino Group, Lafayette, CO. Tel: (303) 664-1290, Web Site: www.thecontrinogroup.com (20)

Contrino, Kathleen, The Contrino Group, Lafayette, CO. Tel: (303) 664-1290, Web Site: www.thecontrinogroup.com (20)

ConvergeDirect, New York, NY. Tel: (212) 213-0111, E-Mail: info@convergedirect.com, Web Site: www.convergedirect.com (35)

Convergys Corp, Ogden, UT. Tel: (630) 668-6174, Web Site: www.convergys.com (29)

Conversant Inc, Chicago, IL. Tel: (312) 588-3671, Web Site: www.conversantmedia.com (32)

Conversational Voice Technologies Corp, Fox Lake, IL. Tel: (847) 265-4901, (800) 994-4400, FAX: (847) 265-4915, E-Mail: sales@conservit.com, Web Site: www.conservit.com (29)

ConversionVoodoo.com, San Diego, CA. Tel: (858) 625-4203, Web Site: www.conversionvoodoo.com (16)

Convertible Service, San Gabriel, CA. Tel: (626) 285-2255, (800) 333-1140, FAX: (626) 285-9004, Web Site: www.convertibleparts.com (16)

Convio Inc, Austin, TX. Tel: (512) 652-2600, (888) 528-9501, FAX: (512) 652-2699, Web Site: www.convio.com (22)

Conway, Anthony W., Alliance of Nonprofit Mailers, Washington, DC. Tel: (202) 462-5132, FAX: (202) 462-0423, E-Mail: alliance@nonprofitmailers.org, Web Site: www.nonprofitmailers.org (40)

Conway, Arthur, DialAmerica Marketing Inc, Mahwah, NJ. Tel: (201) 327-0200, (800) 531-3131, FAX: (201) 327-4875, Web Site: www.dialamerica.com (29)

Conway, David, Eadon Ventures, Alliance, OH. Tel: (330) 418-4298, Web Site: www.eadonventures.com (20)

Conway, Dawn ., Cision US Inc, Chicago, IL. Tel: (312) 922-2400, (866) 639-5087, FAX: (312) 922-3126, E-Mail: info.us@cision.com, Web Site: us.cision.com (43)

Conway, James, Con-Cor International, Tucson, AZ. Tel: (520) 721-8939, (888) 255-7688, FAX: (520) 721-8940, E-Mail: concor@con-cor.com, Web Site: www.con-cor.com (11)

Conway, Mike, Dow Corning Corp, Midland, MI. Tel: (989) 496-4400, (800) 248-2481, FAX: (989) 496-4572, Web Site: www.dowcorning.com (16)

Conway, William S., Mutual of America Life Insurance Co, New York, NY. Tel: (212) 224-1600, (800) 468-3785, FAX: (212) 207-3001, Web Site: www.mutualofamerica.com (14)

Conyer, Marilyn, The Flexi Group Inc, Bronx, NY. Tel: (718) 543-8699, (800) 665-8053, FAX: (718) 543-8609, E-Mail: info@flexigroup.com, Web Site: www.flexigroup.com (27)

Conzatti, Maria, Nassau Community College, Garden City, NY. Tel: (516) 572-7501, FAX: (516) 572-7497, E-Mail: marketing-communications@ncc.edu, Web Site: www.ncc.edu (41)

David C Cook, Colorado Springs, CO. Tel: (719) 536-0100, (800) 323-7543, FAX: (719) 536-3232, Web Site: www.davidccook.com (17)

T A Cook Consultants Inc, Raleigh, NC. Tel: (919) 510-8142, FAX: (919) 510-8143, E-Mail: info-us@tacook.com, Web Site: www.tacook.com (20)

Cook, Bill, Timm Medical Technologies, Inc, Lake Forest, IL. Tel: (952) 947-9410, (800) 438-8592, FAX: (952) 947-9411, Web Site: www.timmmedical.com (16)

Cook, Darel, PPAI Expo, Irving, TX. Tel: (972) 252-0404, (888) 426-7724, FAX: (972) 258-3004, E-Mail: expo@ppai.org, Web Site: expo.ppai.org (42)

Cook, David, Oliver Russell & Associates, Boise, ID. Tel: (208) 344-1734, E-Mail: info@oliverrussell.com, Web Site: www.oliverrussell.com (35)

Cook, David T., The Christian Science Publishing Society, Boston, MA. Tel: (617) 450-2000, E-Mail: info@christianscience.com, Web Site: jsh.christianscience.com (17)

Cook, Gerrard, Pearl River Graphics Printing, Choctaw, MS. Tel: (601) 656-3636, FAX: (601) 650-3961, E-Mail: prgp@pearlriverprinting.com, Web Site: pearlriverprinting.com (27)

Cook, Ian M., Colgate-Palmolive Co, New York, NY. Tel: (212) 310-2000, (800) 468-6502, FAX: (212) 310-2475, Web Site: www.colgate.com (16)

Cook, Jon, VML Inc, Kansas City, MO. Tel: (816) 283-0700, FAX: (816) 283-0954, E-Mail: dl-vmlcommarketing@vml.com, Web Site: www.vml.com (14)

Cook, Peter, Concord Litho, Concord, NH. Tel: (603) 225-3328, FAX: (603) 225-6120, E-Mail: print@concordlitho.com, Web Site: www.concordlitho.com (27)

Cook, Rina, BKV Inc, Atlanta, GA. Tel: (404) 233-0332, E-Mail: rina.cook@bkv.com, Web Site: www.bkv.com (35)

Cook, Tim, Apple Inc, Cupertino, CA. Tel: (408) 996-1010, FAX: (408) 996-0275, Web Site: www.apple.com (16)

Cook, Tom, Concord Litho, Concord, NH. Tel: (603) 225-3328, FAX: (603) 225-6120, E-Mail: print@concordlitho.com, Web Site: www.concordlitho.com (27)

Cook, Tracy, InterfaceFlor LLC, La Grange, GA. Tel: (706) 882-1891, (800) 336-0225, FAX: (706) 882-0500, Web Site: www.interfaceflor.com (16)

Cook, Vince, Grand Circle Travel, Boston, MA. Tel: (617) 350-7500, (800) 959-0405, FAX: (617) 346-6030, Web Site: www.gct.com (19)

Cookbook Publishers Inc, Lenexa, KS. Tel: (913) 492-5900, (800) 227-7282, FAX: (913) 492-5947, E-Mail: info@cookbookpublishers.com, Web Site: www.cookbookpublishers.com (17)

Cooke, Brent, Payless ShoeSource Inc, Topeka, KS. Tel: (785) 233-5171, (877) 474-6379, E-Mail: customerservice@csr.payless.com, Web Site: www.payless.com (2)

Cooke, Eugenia, Tuttle Printing & Engraving, Rutland, VT. Tel: (802) 773-9171, (800) 776-7682, FAX: (802) 773-5785, E-Mail: info@tuttleprinting.com, Web Site: www.tuttleprinting.com (10)

Cooley, Scott, Morningstar Inc, Chicago, IL. Tel: (312) 696-6000, Web Site: www.morningstar.com (14)

Cooney, Bob, NTN Buzztime Inc, Carlsbad, CA. Tel: (760) 438-7400, (877) 963-9200, FAX: (760) 438-3505, Web Site: www.buzztimebusiness.com (32)

Cooney, Ted, BMC Group, Peterborough, ON Canada. Tel: (705) 745-4766, (866) 311-7711, FAX: (705) 745-0177, E-Mail: hello@bmcgroup.ca, Web Site: bmcgroup.ca (35)

Cooper-Atkins Corp, Middlefield, CT. Tel: (860) 347-2256, (800) 835-5011, FAX: (860) 347-5135, E-Mail: info@cooper-atkins.com, Web Site: www.cooper-atkins.com (34)

Cooper Communities Inc, Rogers, AR. Tel: (479) 246-6500, (800) 648-6401, FAX: (479) 855-6256, E-Mail: coopernet@ccias.com, Web Site: www.cooper-communities.com (16)

Cooper Concepts Inc, Chicago, IL. Tel: (872) 206-8145, E-Mail: contact.hr@cooperconcepts.com, Web Site: www.cooperconcepts-inc.com (35)

The Cooper Group, New York, NY. Tel: (212) 696-2512, Web Site: www.thecoopergroup.com (35)

Cooper Surgical Inc, Trumbull, CT. Tel: (203) 601-5202, (800) 243-2974, FAX: (203) 601-1007, E-Mail: orders@coopersurgical.com, Web Site: www.coopersurgical.com (7)

Cooper Tire & Rubber Co Inc, Findlay, OH. Tel: (419) 423-1321, (800) 537-9523, FAX: (419) 424-4212, E-Mail: cooperinfo@coopertire.com, Web Site: www.coopertire.com (16)

Cooper Vision, Fairport, NY. Tel: (855) 526-6737, (800) 341-2020, Web Site: www.coopervision.com (7)

Cooper, Bob, PTI Pyramid Technologies LLC, Meriden, CT. Tel: (203) 238-0550, (888) 479-7264, FAX: (203) 634-1696, Web Site: www.pyramid-technologies.com (10)

Cooper, Bud, Fundamentals Co Inc, Bristol, VA. Tel: (800) 303-8861, (800) 303-8861 (Fax) (1)

Cooper, Daniel W., Cooper Communities Inc, Rogers, AR. Tel: (479) 246-6500, (800) 648-6401, FAX: (479) 855-6256, E-Mail: coopernet@ccias.com, Web Site: www.cooper-communities.com (16)

Cooper, George L., On-Hand Adhesives Inc, Lake Zurich, IL. Tel: (847) 437-7773, (800) 323-5158, FAX: (847) 437-8006, E-Mail: help@on-hand.com, Web Site: www.on-hand.com (16)

Cooper, Harold, The Cooper Group, New York, NY. Tel: (212) 696-2512, Web Site: www.thecoopergroup.com (35)

Cooper, Harry, CollegeSource Inc, San Diego, CA. Tel: (858) 560-8051, (800) 854-2670, FAX: (858) 278-8960, Web Site: www.collegesource.com (17)

Cooper, Jay, Archer Malmo Inc, Memphis, TN. Tel: (901) 523-2000, FAX: (901) 524-5578, Web Site: www.archermalmo.com (35)

Cooper, Joel, List Strategies Inc, New York, NY. Tel: (212) 767-1000, FAX: (212) 541-4408, E-Mail: info@liststrategies.com, Web Site: www.liststrategies.com (23)

Cooper, John, Lunar Cow, Akron, OH. Tel: (330) 253-9000, (800) 594-9620, FAX: (330) 253-9001, E-Mail: info@lunarcow.com, Web Site: www.lunarcow.com (35)

Cooper, Jonathan, Spectronics Corp, Westbury, NY. Tel: (516) 333-4840, (800) 274-8888, FAX: (800) 491-6868, E-Mail: vscherer@spectroline.com, Web Site: www.spectroline.com (9)

Cooper, Jr. John, Cooper Communities Inc, Rogers, AR. Tel: (479) 246-6500, (800) 648-6401, FAX: (479) 855-6256, E-Mail: coopernet@ccias.com, Web Site: www.cooper-communities.com (16)

Cooper, Karen, Betterway Books, Blue Ash, OH. Tel: (513) 531-2222, (800) 289-0963, FAX: (513) 531-4744, Web Site: www.fwpublications.com/books.asp (17)

Cooper, Kerry, CollegeSource Inc, San Diego, CA. Tel: (858) 560-8051, (800) 854-2670, FAX: (858) 278-8960, Web Site: www.collegesource.com (17)

Cooper, Leon, Home Safeguard Industries, Malibu, CA. Tel: (310) 457-5813, FAX: (310) 457-4862, E-Mail: expert@homesafeguard.com, Web Site: www.homesafeguard.com (9)

Cooper, Lisa, Ebbets Field Flannels Inc, Seattle, WA. Tel: (206) 382-7249, FAX: (206) 382-4411, E-Mail: clubhouse@ebbets.com, Web Site: www.ebbets.com (2)

Cooper, Louis, Calling Solutions, San Antonio, TX. Tel: (210) 801-9630, (800) 683-5500, FAX: (210) 491-1777, E-Mail: marketing@callingsolutions.com, Web Site: www.callingsolutions.com (29)

Cooper, Margaret, On-Hand Adhesives Inc, Lake Zurich, IL. Tel: (847) 437-7773, (800) 323-5158, FAX: (847) 437-8006, E-Mail: help@on-hand.com, Web Site: www.on-hand.com (16)

Cooper, Marshall, Chief Executive Magazine, Greenwich, CT. Tel: (203) 930-2700, FAX: (203) 930-2701, Web Site: www.chiefexecutive.net (17)

Cooper, Michael, On-Hand Adhesives Inc, Lake Zurich, IL. Tel: (847) 437-7773, (800) 323-5158, FAX: (847) 437-8006, E-Mail: help@on-hand.com, Web Site: www.on-hand.com (16)

Cooper, Perry, Customer Portfolios LLC, Boston, MA. Tel: (617) 224-9501, E-Mail: getstarted@customerportfolios.com, Web Site: www.customerportfolios.com (22)

Cooper, Tom, The Cooper Group, New York, NY. Tel: (212) 696-2512, Web Site: www.thecoopergroup.com (35)

Cooper, Wayne, Chief Executive Magazine, Greenwich, CT. Tel: (203) 930-2700, FAX: (203) 930-2701, Web Site: www.chiefexecutive.net (17)

Cooperman, Allen B., Transemantics Inc, Washington, DC. Tel: (202) 362-2505, FAX: (202) 686-5603, E-Mail: ili@transemantics.com, Web Site: www.transemantics.com (16)

Coors, Peter H., Molson Coors Brewing Co, Denver, CO. Tel: (303) 927-2337, (800) 665-7661, Web Site: www.molsoncoors.com (16)

Copeland, Chris, Outrider North America, Saint Louis, MO. Tel: (314) 209-1005, FAX: (314) 209-1126, Web Site: www.outrider.com (30)

Copilevitz & Canter, LLC, Kansas City, MO. Tel: (816) 472-9000, FAX: (816) 472-5000, Web Site: www.copilevitz-canter.com (14)

Copilevitz, Errol, Copilevitz & Canter, LLC, Kansas City, MO. Tel: (816) 472-9000, FAX: (816) 472-5000, Web Site: www.copilevitz-canter.com (14)

Coppa Woodworking, Inc, San Pedro, CA. Tel: (310) 548-4142, FAX: (310) 548-6740, E-Mail: info@coppawoodworking.com, Web Site: www.coppawoodworking.com (8)

Coppa, Ciro C., Coppa Woodworking, Inc, San Pedro, CA. Tel: (310) 548-4142, FAX: (310) 548-6740, E-Mail: info@coppawoodworking.com, Web Site: www.coppawoodworking.com (8)

Coppage, Michael, Mostad & Christensen, Oak Harbor, WA. Tel: (360) 679-4164, (800) 654-1654, FAX: (360) 679-4167, E-Mail: marketing@mostad.com, Web Site: www.mostad.com (16)

Copperman, Paul, Institute of Reading Development, Novato, CA. Tel: (415) 884-8100, (800) 964-2030, FAX: (415) 382-0760, E-Mail: contactus@readingprograms.org, Web Site: www.readingprograms.org (1)

Josiah R Coppersmythe, Harwich, MA. Tel: (508) 432-8590, (800) 426-8249, FAX: (508) 432-8587, E-Mail: kethompson@jrcoppersmythe.com, Web Site: www.jrcoppersmythe.com (8)

Coptech Inc, Saugus, MA. Tel: (781) 935-2679, (800) 934-1560, FAX: (781) 935-7673, Web Site: www.coptechinc.com (16)

The Copy Pro, Oradell, NJ. Tel: (201) 986-1080, FAX: (201) 986-1170, E-Mail: thecopypro@aol.com, Web Site: www.thecopypronj.com (39)

The Copy Shoppe, Mendham, NJ. Tel: (973) 543-2679, FAX: (973) 543-2679, E-Mail: catalogistics@juno.com, Web Site: www.catalogistics.com (39)

The Copy Works, San Diego, CA. Tel: (858) 676-6757, Web Site: www.thecopyworks.com (20)

CopyDirect, Plymouth, MA. Tel: (508) 732-9900, Web Site: www.belindabrewster.com (20)

Copywriter's Council of America - (Freelancers), Middle Island, NY. Tel: (631) 924-3888, FAX: (631) 924-8555, E-Mail: cca4dmcopy@gmail.com, Web Site: www.linick.net; www.andrewlinickdirectmarketing.com (39)

Corbat, Michael, Citigroup Inc, New York, NY. Tel: (212) 559-1000, (800) 285-3000, FAX: (212) 793-3946, Web Site: www.citigroup.com (14)

Corbeille, Michael, SMZ Advertising, Troy, MI. Tel: (248) 362-4242, FAX: (248) 362-2014, E-Mail: info@smz.com, Web Site: www.smz.com (35)

Corbeille-Lepel, Pamela, Lorton Data Inc, Arden Hills, MN. Tel: (651) 203-8200, FAX: (651) 203-8299, Web Site: www.lortondata.com (22)

Corbijn, Captain Nico, Windstar Cruises, Seattle, WA. Tel: (206) 292-9606, (800) 258-SAIL, FAX: (206) 340-0975, E-Mail: info@windstarcruises.com, Web Site: www.windstarcruises.com (19)

Corbin, Brad, Conseco Inc, Carmel, IN. Tel: (317) 817-6100, FAX: (317) 817-2847, Web Site: www.conseco.com (15)

Corbin, Frank, Gambro Inc, Lakewood, CO. Tel: (303) 232-6800, (800) 525-2623, FAX: (303) 222-6810, Web Site: www.gambro.com (16)

Corbis Images, New York, NY. Tel: (212) 777-6200, FAX: (212) 375-7700, Web Site: www.corbis.com (38)

Corcillo, Jane, Jane Corcillo, Norwalk, CT. Tel: (203) 866-2008, FAX: (203) 299-0844, E-Mail: queries@corcillodirect.com, Web Site: www.corcillodirect.com (39)

Corcorah, John, Star Sprinkler Inc, Lansdale, PA. Tel: (414) 570-5000, (800) 558-5236, FAX: (414) 570-5010, Web Site: www.starsprinkler.com (9)

Corcoran, Allison, Alfa Aesar-A Johnson Matthey Co, Ward Hill, MA. Tel: (800) 343-0660, FAX: (800) 322-4757, E-Mail: info@alfa.com, Web Site: www.alfa.com (9)

Corcoran, Dan, Sales & Marketing Management Magazine, New York, NY. Tel: (800) 821-6897, FAX: (905) 470-8561, E-Mail: joyce.cooney@nielsen.com, Web Site: www.salesandmarketing.com (16)

Corcoran, Peter N., Deloitte & Touche, Boston, MA. Tel: (617) 437-2000, FAX: (617) 437-2111, Web Site: www.deloitte.com (14)

CorCreative Group LLC, Boulder, CO. Tel: (917) 971-4847, E-Mail: ccginfo@corcreativegroup.com, Web Site: corcreativegroup.com (35)

Cordazzo, Christine, Esto Photographics Inc, Mamaroneck, NY. Tel: (914) 698-4060, FAX: (914) 698-1033, E-Mail: esto@esto.com, Web Site: www.esto.com (38)

Cordial, Melissa, Fallon Community Health Plan, Worcester, MA. Tel: (508) 799-2100, (800) 333-2535, Web Site: www.fchp.org (1)

Cordier, Steve, Sensient Technologies, Saint Louis, MO. Tel: (314) 889-7600, (800) 325-8110, FAX: (314) 658-7318, Web Site: www.sensient-tech.com (16)

Cordova, Sally, McKee Consulting LLC, Escondido, CA. Tel: (760) 738-8200, Web Site: www.trainyourcallcenter.com (20)

Core Technologies, Boulder, CO. Tel: (614) 231-3031, (866) 624-5927, FAX: (303) 395-1474, E-Mail: support@core-tech.com, Web Site: www.mailware.com (22)

CoreLogic Inc, Irvine, CA. Tel: (949) 214-1000, (800) 426-1466, Web Site: www.corelogic.com (22)

COREMedia Systems Inc, Fairfield, NJ. Tel: (973) 276-0882, FAX: (973) 276-0891, Web Site: www.coremedia-systems.com (22)

CoreMessagink, Lancaster, PA. Tel: (717) 207-0212, Web Site: www.cormessagink.com (39)

Coretto, Tony, PNT Marketing Services, Inc. Long Island City, NY. Tel: (718) 433-4063, (888) 768-2210, FAX: (914) 428-0504, E-Mail: tony@pntmarketingservices.com, Web Site: www.pntmarketingservices.com (22)

Corey, Michael P., Maine Potato Board, Presque Isle, ME. Tel: (207) 769-5061, FAX: (207) 764-4148, E-Mail: mainepotatoes@mainepotatoes.com, Web Site: www.mainepotatoes.com (1)

Corigliano, Mary, truTV, New York, NY. Tel: (212) 973-2800, (800) 268-7856, FAX: (212) 973-3210, Web Site: www.trutv.com (17)

Corinthian Media, New York, NY. Tel: (212) 279-5700, FAX: (212) 239-1772, E-Mail: info@mediabuying.com, Web Site: www.mediabuying.com (35)

Corkery, Tim, HubCast Inc, Wakefield, MA. Tel: (781) 221-7200, FAX: (781) 221-7223, Web Site: www.hubeast.com (27)

Corley, Christina, Zones Inc, Auburn, WA. Tel: (253) 205-3000, (800) 408-9663, FAX: (425) 430-3626, E-Mail: corpsales@zones.com, Web Site: www.zones.com (3)

Cormier, Casey, The Artists Co, New York, NY. Tel: (212) 679-7199, Web Site: blog.theartistscompany.com (32)

Cornell Lab of Ornithology, Ithaca, NY. Tel: (607) 254-2157, (800) 843-2473, FAX: (607) 254-2415, E-Mail: birdslides@cornell.edu, Web Site: www.birds.cornell.edu (1)

Cornell, Brian, Frito-Lay, Plano, TX. Tel: (972) 334-7000, (800) 352-4477, FAX: (972) 334-2019, Web Site: www.fritolay.com (16)

Cornell, Brian, The Quaker Oats Co, Chicago, IL. Tel: (312) 821-1000, (800) 367-6287, FAX: (312) 222-8323, Web Site: www.quakeroats.com (16)

Cornell, Helen W., Champion, Quincy, IL. Tel: (217) 222-5400, FAX: (217) 228-8260, Web Site: www.championpneumatic.com (16)

Cornell, Michael, Accellos Inc, Colorado Springs, CO. Tel: (719) 433-7000, Web Site: www.accellos.com (12)

Cornerstone Brands Inc, West Chester, OH. Tel: (513) 603-1400, Web Site: www.cornerstonebrands.com (5)

Cornerstone Business Services Inc, Green Bay, WI. Tel: (920) 436-9890, FAX: (920) 436-9894, E-Mail: sbushkie@cornerstone-business.com, Web Site: www.cornerstone-business.com (14)

Cornerstone Group of Companies, Toronto, ON Canada. Tel: (416) 932-9555, FAX: (416) 932-9566, E-Mail: info@cstonecanada.com, Web Site: www.cstonecanada.com (22)

Cornhusker Press, Hastings, NE. Tel: (402) 462-4141, FAX: (402) 460-4612, E-Mail: dlsales@dutton-lainson.com, Web Site: www.dutton-lainson.com (17)

Cornick, Jim, Successful Farming, Des Moines, IA. Tel: (515) 284-2143, (800) 678-2711, FAX: (515) 284-3127 (17)

Cornish, Edward, World Future Society, Chicago, IL. Tel: (301) 656-8274, (800) 989-8274, FAX: (301) 951-0394, E-Mail: info@wfs.org, Web Site: www.wfs.org (1)

Cornish, Jefferson, World Future Society, Chicago, IL. Tel: (301) 656-8274, (800) 989-8274, FAX: (301) 951-0394, E-Mail: info@wfs.org, Web Site: www.wfs.org (1)

Cornwall, Craig, KET, Lexington, KY. Tel: (859) 258-7000, (800) 432-0951, FAX: (606) 258-7396, E-Mail: rgriffin@ket.org, Web Site: www.ket.org (17)

Cornwell Data Services Inc, Paramus, NJ. Tel: (201) 261-1050, FAX: (201) 261-7569, E-Mail: info@cornwelldata.com, Web Site: www.cornwelldata.com (22)

Cornwell, Peter, Cornwell Data Services Inc, Paramus, NJ. Tel: (201) 261-1050, FAX: (201) 261-7569, E-Mail: info@cornwelldata.com, Web Site: www.cornwelldata.com (22)

Corona Cigar Co, Orlando, FL. Tel: (407) 248-1212, (888) 702-4427, FAX: (407) 248-1211, E-Mail: info@coronacigar.com, Web Site: www.coronacigar.com (5)

Corona-Lotus Inc, San Francisco, CA. Tel: (415) 956-8956, (800) 422-2924, FAX: (415) 956-4922, E-Mail: customerservice@biscoff.com, Web Site: www.biscoff.com (4)

Coronis Building Systems Inc, Columbus, NJ. Tel: (609) 723-2600, FAX: (609) 723-6700, E-Mail: coronis@trussframe.com, Web Site: www.trussframe.com (9)

Coronis Jr, Emanuel A., Coronis Building Systems Inc, Columbus, NJ. Tel: (609) 723-2600, FAX: (609) 723-6700, E-Mail: coronis@trussframe.com, Web Site: www.trussframe.com (9)

Corpora Consulting, Bethlehem, PA. Tel: (215) 313-9229 (20)

Corpora, Placido, Corpora Consulting, Bethlehem, PA. Tel: (215) 313-9229 (20)

Corporate Express US Inc, Broomfield, CO. Tel: (303) 664-2000, (888) 238-6329, FAX: (303) 664-3474, Web Site: www.cexp.com (22)

Corporate Graphics Direct Marketing Solutions, Arden Hills, MN. Tel: (651) 494-1740, (800) 728-2615, FAX: (651) 494-1750, E-Mail: contact@cgdms. com, Web Site: www.cgids.com (22)

CorporateRewards.com, New York, NY. Tel: (212) 689-1200, Web Site: www.corporaterewards.com (35)

Corpus Christi Museum of Science & History, Corpus Christi, TX. Tel: (361) 826-4667, FAX: (361) 884-7392, Web Site: www.ccmuseum.com (1)

Corr, William, CSPI/Nutrition Action Health Letter, Washington, DC. Tel: (202) 332-9110, FAX: (202) 265-4954, E-Mail: cspi@cspinet.org, Web Site: www.cspinet.org (17)

Corral, Rafael, Argent Trading LLC, New York, NY. Tel: (212) 697-8800, FAX: (212) 697-8606, Web Site: www.Argenttrading.com (16)

Corrente-Evans, Toni, Pacific Botanicals LLC, Grants Pass, OR. Tel: (541) 479-7777, FAX: (541) 479-7780, E-Mail: pacbot1@earthlink.net, Web Site: www.pacificbotanicals.com (7)

Corry Direct Marketing LLC, Ridgefield, CT. Tel: (203) 438-1478, FAX: (203) 431-0217, E-Mail: tom@ corrydirect.com, Web Site: www.corrydirect.com (20)

Corry, Thomas P., Corry Direct Marketing LLC, Ridgefield, CT. Tel: (203) 438-1478, FAX: (203) 431-0217, E-Mail: tom@corrydirect.com, Web Site: www.corrydirect.com (20)

CORS, Itasca, IL. Tel: (630) 250-8677, (800) 323-1352, FAX: (630) 250-7362, E-Mail: resume@cors.com, Web Site: www.cors.com (20)

Cortes, PhD Dario A., Berkeley College, West Paterson, NJ. Tel: (973) 278-5400, (800) 446-5400, FAX: (973) 278-6243, E-Mail: info@berkeleycollege.edu, Web Site: www.berkeleycollege.edu (13)

Cortez, Linus, Stuller Inc, Lafayette, LA. Tel: (800) 877-7777, FAX: (800) 444-4741, E-Mail: info@ stuller.com, Web Site: www.stuller.com (2)

Cortez, Steve, Arch Telecom Inc, Austin, TX. Tel: (512) 492-0735, (800) 890-7575, FAX: (512) 495-7101, Web Site: www.archtelecom.com (16)

Corty, Andrew P., Trend Magazines Inc, Saint Petersburg, FL. Tel: (727) 821-5800, (800) 821-5800, FAX: (727) 822-5083, E-Mail: feedback@fltrend. com, Web Site: www.floridatrend.com (17)

Cortz Inc, West Chicago, IL. Tel: (630) 876-1080, (800) 288-7946, Web Site: www.intheswim.com (5)

Corwin, MD Steven J., New York-Presbyterian/Columbia University Medical Center, New York, NY. Tel: (212) 305-2500, FAX: (212) 305-8023, Web Site: www.nyp.org (16)

Coryell, Gwen, Kroll Direct Marketing Inc, Wellington, FL. Tel: (609) 275-2900, E-Mail: lee@krolldirect. com, Web Site: www.krolldirect.com (23)

Cosco Industries Inc, Chicago, IL. Tel: (708) 867-5800, (800) 323-0253, FAX: (800) 323-0275 (16)

Cosgrove Associates, New York, NY. Tel: (212) 888-7202, FAX: (212) 888-7201, Web Site: www. cosgrovejuro.com (14)

Cosgrove, Brent, V12 Data, Wesley Chapel, FL. Tel: (813) 960-7800, FAX: (813) 960-7811, E-Mail: info@v12data.com, Web Site: www.v12data.com (22)

Cosgrove, Jerry, Cosgrove Associates, New York, NY. Tel: (212) 888-7202, FAX: (212) 888-7201, Web Site: www.cosgrovejuro.com (14)

Cosimini, Nancy, UndercoverWear Inc, Tewksbury, MA. Tel: (978) 851-8580, (800) 733-0007, FAX: (978) 640-2882, E-Mail: service@undercoverwear. com, Web Site: www.undercoverwear.com (2)

Cosmetique, Inc, Vernon Hills, IL. Tel: (847) 913-9099, (800) 621-8822, E-Mail: customerservice@ cosmetique.com, Web Site: www.cosmetique.com (13)

Cosmo International, Deerfield Beach, FL. Tel: (954) 798-4500, FAX: (954) 798-4514 (16)

Cosper, Amy, Entrepreneur Media Inc, Irvine, CA. Tel: (949) 261-2325, (800) 274-6229, FAX: (949) 261-0234, Web Site: www.entrepreneur.com (17)

Cossette, Quebec, QC Canada. Tel: (418) 647-2727, FAX: (418) 647-2564, E-Mail: info@cossette.com, Web Site: www.cossette.com (35)

Cost, Steven, Intergraph Corp, Madison, AL. Tel: (256) 730-2000, (800) 345-4856, FAX: (256) 730-2048, Web Site: www.intergraph.com (16)

Costa, Dan, Ziff Davis Media Inc, New York, NY. Tel: (212) 503-5100, FAX: (212) 503-5023, Web Site: www.ziffdavis.com (17)

Costa, Mark J., Eastman Chemical Co, Kingsport, TN. Tel: (423) 229-2000, (800) 325-4330, E-Mail: eastman1@eastman.com, Web Site: www.eastman. com (16)

Costco Wholesale, Issaquah, WA. Tel: (425) 313-8647, 800-774-2678, E-Mail: customerservice@ contactcostco.com, Web Site: www.costco.com (33)

Costello, John, First to the Finish Inc, Carlinville, IL. Tel: (800) 747-9013, FAX: (877) 631-9687, E-Mail: customer_service@fttf.com, Web Site: www. firsttothefinish.com (7)

Costello, Mark, Amcat TeleProfit Inc, Oklahoma City, OK. Tel: (405) 216-8080, (800) 364-5518, FAX: (405) 216-8063, E-Mail: smart@amcat.com, Web Site: www.amcat.com (16)

Costello, Peter D., Premier Farnell Corp, Richfield, OH. Tel: (216) 525-4300, (800) 458-3222, FAX: (216) 525-4509, E-Mail: information@premierfarnell. com, Web Site: www.premierfarnell.com (16)

Costello, Richard, Amcat TeleProfit Inc, Oklahoma City, OK. Tel: (405) 216-8080, (800) 364-5518, FAX: (405) 216-8063, E-Mail: smart@amcat.com, Web Site: www.amcat.com (16)

Costello, Stanley, Dalrada Financial Corp, San Diego, CA. Tel: (858) 791-6200, (877) 325-7232, FAX: (858) 277-3448, E-Mail: inquiries@dalrada.com, Web Site: www.dalrada.com (14)

Costopulos, Nancy, American Marketing Association, Chicago, IL. Tel: (312) 542-9000, (800) AMA-1150, FAX: (312) 542-9001, Web Site: www. marketingpower.com (40)

Cota, Tammy, The Internet Alliance, Washington, DC. Tel: (202) 861-2476, FAX: (202) 955-8081, E-Mail: info@internetalliance.org, Web Site: www. internetalliance.org (40)

Cote, David M., Honeywell, Morristown, NJ. Tel: (973) 455-2000, FAX: (973) 455-4807, Web Site: www. honeywell.com (16)

Cote, Ryan, The Ballantine Corp, Wayne, NJ. Tel: (973) 305-1500, E-Mail: connect@ballantine.com, Web Site: www.ballantine.com (27)

Cote, Victoria, Invacare Continuing Care Group, Saint Louis, MO. Tel: (519) 659-1395, (800) 347-5440, FAX: (636) 519-0044, Web Site: www.invacare-ccg.com (16)

Pamela Cotrupe, Las Vegas, NV. Tel: (818) 624-0087 (20)

Cotta Transmission Co, Beloit, WI. Tel: (608) 368-5600, FAX: (608) 368-5605, E-Mail: sales@cotta. com, Web Site: www.cotta.com (16)

Cotter, Mike, Ed Voyles Hyundai Inc, Smyrna, GA. Tel: (770) 952-8881, (877) 579-0642, FAX: (770) 612-9396, Web Site: www.edvoyleshyundai.com (16)

Cotter, Pete, Motor Coach Industries International Inc, Schaumburg, IL. Tel: (847) 285-2000, (800) 624-2622, Web Site: www.mcicoach.com (16)

Cottler, Dave, Coast Hotels Limited, Seattle, WA. Tel: (206) 826-2700, FAX: (206) 826-2701, Web Site: www.coasthotels.com (19)

Cottrell, Gregory B., Caraustar, Austell, GA. Tel: (770) 948-3101, E-Mail: info@caraustar.com, Web Site: www.caraustar.com (16)

Cottrell, Noel, Fitzgerald & CO, Atlanta, GA. Tel: (404) 504-6900, FAX: (404) 239-0548, E-Mail: dave. fitzgerald@fitzco.com, Web Site: www.fitzco.com (35)

Couch, Jeanelle, Harvest Communications, Redding, CA. Tel: (800) 303-6405, FAX: (800) 926-8038, Web Site: www.harvest-communications.com (20)

Cougar Mountain Software, Boise, ID. Tel: (208) 375-4455, (800) 388-3038, FAX: (208) 375-4460, E-Mail: sales@cougarmtn.com, Web Site: www. cougarmtn.com (14)

Coughlin, Cathy M., AT&T Inc, Dallas, TX. Tel: (210) 821-4105, Web Site: www.att.com (16)

Coughlin, Jack, Esrock Partners, Orland Park, IL. Tel: (708) 349-8400, (888) ESROCKS, FAX: (708) 349-8471, E-Mail: kwilson@esrock.com, Web Site: www.esrock.com (35)

Coultier, Theresa, New England Direct Marketing Association, Wellesley Hills, MA. Tel: (781) 237-1366, FAX: (781) 431-8118, E-Mail: info@nedma.com, Web Site: www.nedma.com (40)

Council for Advancement and Support of Education, Washington, DC. Tel: (202) 328-2273, Web Site: www.case.org (1)

Council of Better Business Bureaus - BBBOnline, Arlington, VA. Tel: (703) 276-0100, FAX: (703) 525-8277, Web Site: www.bbb.org (1)

Council on Foreign Relations Inc, New York, NY. Tel: (212) 434-9400, FAX: (212) 861-2759, E-Mail: editor@foreignaffairs.com, Web Site: www. foreignaffairs.org (17)

Counter, Nicholas, International Foundation of Employee Benefit Plans, Brookfield, WI. Tel: (262) 373-7758, FAX: (262) 786-8670, Web Site: www.ifebp. org (1)

The Country Bed Shop, Ashby, MA. Tel: (978) 386-7550, FAX: (978) 386-7263, E-Mail: alan@ countrybed.com, Web Site: www.countrybed.com (16)

Country Curtains Inc, Stockbridge, MA. Tel: (800) 937-1237, Web Site: www.countrycurtains.com (8)

Country Dance and Song Society, Easthampton, MA. Tel: (413) 203-5467, FAX: (413) 203-5471, E-Mail: office@cdss.org, Web Site: www.cdss.org (1)

Country Financial, Bloomington, IL. Tel: (309) 821-3000 (15)

The Country House Inc, Salisbury, MD. Tel: (410) 749-1959, (800) 331-3602, FAX: (410) 548-3224, E-Mail: web@thecountryhouse.com, Web Site: www.thecountryhouse.com (6)

Country Sampler Group, Saint Charles, IL. Tel: (630) 377-8000, FAX: (630) 377-8194, Web Site: www. sampler.com (17)

Countryman, Jim, Haines Direct, North Canton, OH. Tel: (866) 879-6379, E-Mail: sales@haines-direct. com, Web Site: www.haines-direct.com (21)

Countrywide Financial Corp, Calabasas, CA. Tel: (818) 225-3000, FAX: (818) 225-4051, Web Site: www. countrywide.com (14)

Counts, Jack, Glamour Shots Licensing, Oklahoma City, OK. Tel: (405) 947-8747, (888) GLAMOUR-SHOTS, FAX: (405) 951-7343, Web Site: www. glamourshots.com (16)

Courage Cards & Gifts, Golden Valley, MN. Tel: (800) 992-6872, Web Site: www.couragecards.org (1)

Courage, Catherine, Citrix Systems, Inc, Fort Lauderdale, FL. Tel: (954) 267-3000, FAX: (954) 267-3101, Web Site: www.citrix.com (22)

Course Technology, Cambridge, MA. Tel: (617) 225-2595, FAX: (617) 225-7976, E-Mail: ed.moura@cengage.com, Web Site: www.course.com (31)

Courtois, Patricia, C-Suite Communications, Sarasota, FL. Tel: (941) 365-2710, E-Mail: info@c-suitecomms.com, Web Site: www.c-suitecomms.com (35)

Coury, Robert J., Mylan NV, Canonsburg, PA. Tel: (724) 514-1800, (800) 231-3052, FAX: (281) 240-0002, E-Mail: communications@mylan.com, Web Site: www.mylan.com (7)

Cousineau, Mike, PMX Agency, New York, NY. Tel: (212) 387-0300, (888) 960-0177, FAX: (212) 387-7647, E-Mail: info@pmxagency.com, Web Site: www.pmxagency.com (23)

Couture, France, Voxdata Telecom, Montreal, QC Canada. Tel: (514) 871-1920, (800) 861-9599, FAX: (514) 871-0445, E-Mail: fcouture@voxdata.com, Web Site: www.voxdata.com (29)

Couture, Steven, Standard Publishing, Cincinnati, OH. Tel: (513) 931-4050, (800) 543-1301, FAX: (877) 867-5751, Web Site: www.standardpub.com (17)

Covalent Marketing, Denver, CO. Tel: (303) 588-7754, Web Site: www.covalentmarketing.com (22)

Covenant House International Headquarters, New York, NY. Tel: (212) 613-0300, (800) 388-3888, FAX: (212) 727-4992, Web Site: www.covenanthouse.org (1)

Coveo Solutions Inc, Quebec, QC Canada. Tel: (418) 263-1111, FAX: (418) 263-1221, Web Site: www.coveo.com (22)

CoverClicks Media Inc, New York, NY. Tel: (646) 434-1413, E-Mail: info@coverclicksmail.com, Web Site: www.coverclicks.com (23)

Coverdell & Co Inc, Chicago, IL. Tel: (404) 881-2227, (800) 992-2196, FAX: (404) 881-2222, Web Site: www.coverdell.com (15)

Coverdell Canada Corporation, Montreal, QC Canada. Tel: (514) 847-7800 (16)

Covert, David, Bank of the West, Los Angeles, CA. Tel: (509) 736-0131, Web Site: www.bankofthewest.com (14)

Covey, J. Kent, Plas-Tanks Industries Inc, Hamilton, OH. Tel: (513) 942-3800, FAX: (513) 942-3993, E-Mail: info@plastanks.com, Web Site: www.plastanks.com (9)

Covington, Denise, Infocore Inc, Carlsbad, CA. Tel: (760) 607-2500, FAX: (760) 607-2505, E-Mail: info@infocore.com, Web Site: www.infocore.com (23)

Cowan, Gregory L., VWR International, Radnor, PA. Tel: (610) 386-1700, (800) 932-5000, FAX: (610) 431-9174, Web Site: www.vwrsp.com (34)

Cowan, Mark, Elite Sportswear LP, Reading, PA. Tel: (610) 921-1469, (800) 345-4087, FAX: (610) 921-0208, E-Mail: gkelite@gkelite.com, Web Site: www.gk-elitesportswear.com (2)

Cowan, Rebecca, New Pig Corp, Tipton, PA. Tel: (814) 684-0101, (800) 468-4647, FAX: (814) 684-0961, E-Mail: hothogs@newpig.com, Web Site: www.newpig.com (9)

Cowdery, Clarisse, Potpourri Group Inc, North Billerica, MA. Tel: (978) 256-4100, FAX: (978) 256-1961/0344, Web Site: www.potpourrigroup.com (6)

Cowley, Anarew, Bureau Van Dijk, New York, NY. Tel: (212) 797-3550, FAX: (212) 797-3555, E-Mail: newyork@bvdinfo.com, Web Site: www.bvdinfo.com (22)

Cowley, Chuck, Mary Maxim Inc, Port Huron, MI. Tel: (810) 987-2000, (800) 962-9504, FAX: (810) 987-5056, E-Mail: info@marymaxim.com, Web Site: www.marymaxim.com (11)

Cox Communications Inc, Atlanta, GA. Tel: (404) 843-5000, (888) 566-7751, FAX: (404) 269-2243, Web Site: www.cox.com (16)

Cox Target Media Inc, St. Petersburg, FL. Tel: (727) 399-3000, (800) 678-2743, FAX: (727) 399-3061, E-Mail: info@coxtarget.com, Web Site: www.coxtarget.com (21)

Cox, Chris, National Rifle Association of America, Fairfax, VA. Tel: (703) 267-1000, (800) 672-3888, FAX: (703) 267-3957, E-Mail: nra.contact@nra.org, Web Site: www.nra.org (1)

Cox, Chris W., National Rifle Association of America, Fairfax, VA. Tel: (703) 267-1000, (800) 672-3888, FAX: (703) 267-3957, E-Mail: nra.contact@nra.org, Web Site: www.nra.org (1)

Cox, Dale, Good Advertising, Memphis, TN. Tel: (901) 761-0741, (800) 325-9857, FAX: (901) 682-2568, E-Mail: info@goodadvertising.com, Web Site: www.goodadvertising.com (35)

Cox, Dennis, ChinaStock/WorldViews, Ann Arbor, MI. Tel: (734) 996-1440, (800) 315-4462, FAX: (734) 996-1481, E-Mail: decoxphoto@aol.com, Web Site: www.denniscox.com (38)

Cox, Donna O, Mead Westvaco Consumer & Office Products, Richmond, VA. Tel: (937) 222-6323, (804) 444-1000, FAX: (937) 495-3192, Web Site: www.meadwestvaco.com (10)

Cox, Karen, The Bradford Group, Niles, IL. Tel: (847) 966-2770, FAX: (847) 581-8630, Web Site: www.collectiblestoday.com (16)

Cox, Lincoln, Edwin Watts Golf, Fort Walton Beach, FL. Tel: (850) 244-2066, (800) 874-0146, FAX: (850) 244-5217, Web Site: www.edwinwatts.com (11)

Cox, Sheryl, Farrington Transportation, Bolingbrook, IL. Tel: (630) 783-9200 (12)

Coxon, John, Northern Illinois Consulting Inc, Libertyville, IL. Tel: (847) 828-1999, Web Site: www.cmsbusiness.com (20)

Coy, Randall S., Communication Resources Inc, Beaufort, SC. Tel: (330) 266-1489, (800) 992-2144, FAX: (330) 493-3158, E-Mail: service@comresources.com, Web Site: www.comresources.com (18)

Coy, Steven S., Consolidated Electronics Inc, Dayton, OH. Tel: (937) 252-5662, (800) 543-3568, FAX: (937) 252-4066, E-Mail: scoy@ceitron.com, Web Site: www.ceitron.com (3)

Coyle, John D., Unitron Ltd, Commack, NY. Tel: (631) 589-6666, FAX: (631) 589-6795, E-Mail: johnc@unitronusa.com, Web Site: www.unitronusa.com (9)

Coyle, Walter, Luxe Collective Group, New York, NY. Tel: (212) 627-3300, FAX: (212) 627-3388, E-Mail: info@luxecg.com, Web Site: luxecg.com (35)

Coyne American Institute, Chicago, IL. Tel: (773) 935-2520, (800) 999-5220, FAX: (773) 935-2920, Web Site: www.coyneamerican.edu (16)

Coyne, Bill, Raley's Bel Air Markets, West Sacramento, CA. Tel: (916) 373-3333, FAX: (916) 373-6351, Web Site: www.raleys.com (16)

Coyne, Patrick, Delaware Investments, Philadelphia, PA. Tel: (215) 255-1200, E-Mail: service@delinvest.com, Web Site: www.delawareinvestments.com (14)

Crabtree & Evelyn Ltd, Westport, CT. Tel: (860) 928-2761, (800) CRABTREE, FAX: (860) 928-1296, Web Site: www.crabtree-evelyn.com (4)

Crabtree, Robert E., Crabtree & Evelyn Ltd, Westport, CT. Tel: (860) 928-2761, (800) CRABTREE, FAX: (860) 928-1296, Web Site: www.crabtree-evelyn.com (4)

The Cracker Box Inc, Blooming Glen, PA. Tel: (215) 443-7777, FAX: (215) 443-7777, E-Mail: walter@crackerboxkits.com, Web Site: www.crackerboxkits.com (16)

Craft-Diston Industries, Wichita, KS. Tel: (316) 838-4291, (800) 835-0028, FAX: (316) 838-8502, Web Site: www.craftdiston.com (16)

Cragun, Ken, Local Corp, Irvine, CA. Tel: (877) 784-0805, FAX: (949) 784-0880, Web Site: www.local.com (32)

The Ben Craig Center, Charlotte, NC. Tel: (704) 548-9113, Web Site: www.bencraigcenter.com (1)

Craig Envelope Corp, Long Island City, NY. Tel: (718) 786-4277, (888) 272-4436, FAX: (718) 937-8178, E-Mail: info@craigenvelope.com, Web Site: www.craigenvelope.com (26)

Craig/Vartorella International Marketing & Advertising Inc, Camden, SC. Tel: (803) 432-4353, FAX: (803) 432-4353, E-Mail: globebiz@juno.com, Web Site: www.colasc.com/Marketing_&_Fundraising (1)

Craig, Becky, National Research LLC, Washington, DC. Tel: (202) 686-9350, FAX: (202) 686-7163, E-Mail: survey@nationalres.com, Web Site: www.nationalres.com (30)

Craig, David, Lowrance Electronics, Tulsa, OK. Tel: (918) 437-6881, FAX: (918) 234-1707, Web Site: www.lowrance.com (11)

Craig, Irv, Townsend Communications LLC, Kansas City, MO. Tel: (816) 361-0616, (800) 274-8867, FAX: (816) 361-6164, Web Site: www.townsendprint.com (17)

Craig, J David, Centric Communications, Norfolk, VA. Tel: (757) 622-2724, E-Mail: info@centriccommunications.net, Web Site: centriccommunications.net (28)

Craig, Joanna B., Craig/Vartorella International Marketing & Advertising Inc, Camden, SC. Tel: (803) 432-4353, FAX: (803) 432-4353, E-Mail: globebiz@juno.com, Web Site: www.colasc.com/Marketing_&_Fundraising (1)

Craig, John, One Hanes Place Catalog, Winston Salem, NC. Tel: (336) 519-8080, (800) 300-2600, FAX: (336) 519-0655, Web Site: www.onehanesplace.com (2)

Craig, John, Sara Lee Direct Home Shopping, Winston-Salem, NC. Tel: (336) 519-4400, (800) 671-5056, E-Mail: ohp.manager@onehanesplace.com, Web Site: www.onehanesplace.com (2)

Craig, Julie, ESignal, Hayward, CA. Tel: (510) 266-6000, Web Site: www.esignal.com (14)

Craig, Marilyn, G-Plex Direct Mail, Holtsville, NY. Tel: (631) 447-9500, FAX: 631-447-9518, Web Site: www.g-plex.net (28)

Craig, Thomas W., LTD Supply Chain, Downingtown, PA. Tel: (610) 458-3636, FAX: (610) 458-8039, E-Mail: tomc@ltdsupplychain.com, Web Site: www.ltdsupplychain.com (20)

Craighead, Scott, IAEE Expo! Expo! Annual Meeting and Exhibition, Dallas, TX. Tel: (972) 458-8002, FAX: (972) 458-8119, E-Mail: info@iaee.com, Web Site: www.iaee.com (42)

Crail, Frank, Rocky Mountain Chocolate Factory, Durango, CO. Tel: (970) 259-0554, (888) 525-2462, FAX: (970) 259-5895, E-Mail: customerservice@rmcfusa.com, Web Site: www.rmcf.com (4)

Crain Communications Inc, Detroit, MI. Tel: (313) 446-6000, FAX: (313) 446-1616, Web Site: www.crain.com (17)

Crain, Andrew, Tully & Holland Inc, Wellesley, MA. Tel: (781) 239-2900, FAX: (781) 239-2901, E-Mail: info@tullyandholland.com, Web Site: www.tullyandholland.com (14)

Crain, Keith, Crain Communications Inc, Detroit, MI. Tel: (313) 446-6000, FAX: (313) 446-1616, Web Site: www.crain.com (17)

Crain, Rance, Crain Communications Inc, Detroit, MI. Tel: (313) 446-6000, FAX: (313) 446-1616, Web Site: www.crain.com (17)

Cram, William, Prism Data Services Ltd, Mississauga, ON Canada. Tel: (905) 278-5556, FAX: (905) 278-6603, E-Mail: sales@prism-data.com, Web Site: www.prism-data.com (21)

Cramb, Don, Fujitsu Transaction Solutions Inc, Richardson, TX. Tel: (972) 963-2300, (800) 340-4425, Web Site: www.fujitsu.com (16)

Cramer, Norwood, MA. Tel: (781) 278-2387, Web Site: www.crameronline.com (20)

Cramer-Krasselt, Chicago, IL. Tel: (312) 616-9600, FAX: (312) 616-3839, E-Mail: pkrivkov@c-k.com, Web Site: c-k.com (35)

Cramer, Martin A., RBC Funds, Milwaukee, WI. Tel: (800) 422-2766, Web Site: us.rbcgam.com (14)

Crampton, Kelly, Excelligence Learning Corp, Monterey, CA. Tel: (831) 333-2000, E-Mail: contactus@excelligence.com, Web Site: www.excelligencelearning.com (5)

Crandall Associates Inc, Port Washington, NY. Tel: (516) 767-6800, E-Mail: joyce@crandallassociates.com, Web Site: www.crandallassociates.com (20)

Crandall, Roderick, Select Press, Novato, CA. Tel: (415) 209-9838, E-Mail: selectpr@aol.com (17)

Crandall, Theodore D., Rockwell Automation, Milwaukee, WI. Tel: (414) 382-2000, FAX: (414) 382-4444, Web Site: www.rockwellautomation.com (16)

Crandell, Matt, Automation Control Products, Alpharetta, GA. Tel: (678) 990-0945, FAX: (678) 990-0951, E-Mail: info@thinmanager.com, Web Site: www.thinmanager.com (16)

Crane Duplicating Service Inc, Naples, FL. Tel: (305) 280-6742, FAX: (239) 732-8415, Web Site: www.craneduplicating.com (28)

Crane Pumps & Systems Inc, Piqua, OH. Tel: (937) 773-2442, FAX: (937) 773-2238, E-Mail: cranepumps@cranepumps.com, Web Site: www.cranepumps.com (16)

Crane, Andrea, Training Consultants Inc, Highland Park, IL. Tel: (847) 432-9428, FAX: (847) 432-9318, E-Mail: wetrain2@home.com (20)

Crane, Bob, Towers Watson, New York, NY. Tel: (212) 725-7550, FAX: (212) 644-7432, Web Site: www.towerswatson.com (20)

Crane, Valerie, Research Communications Ltd, Canton, MA. Tel: (781) 341-1190, FAX: (781) 341-1191, E-Mail: info@researchcommunications.com (30)

Crane, William, Myllykoski North America, Westmont, IL. Tel: (203) 229-7400, Web Site: www.myllykoski.com (25)

Cranley, Edward R., Willis Music Co, Florence, KY. Tel: (859) 283-2050, (800) 354-9799, FAX: (859) 283-1784, E-Mail: ordpt@willis-music.com, Web Site: www.willismusic.com (17)

Cranley, Kevin, Willis Music Co, Florence, KY. Tel: (859) 283-2050, (800) 354-9799, FAX: (859) 283-1784, E-Mail: ordpt@willis-music.com, Web Site: www.willismusic.com (17)

Crary, John, American Red Cross, Washington, DC. Tel: (202) 303-5214, (800) RED-CROSS, FAX: (202) 303-6604, Web Site: www.redcross.org (1)

Crate & Barrel, Northbrook, IL. Tel: (847) 272-2888, (800) 967-6696, FAX: (630) 369-4497, Web Site: www.crateandbarrell.com (8)

Cravener, Greg, Antique Electronic Supply, Tempe, AZ. Tel: (480) 820-5411, (800) 706-6789, FAX: (480) 820-4643, E-Mail: info@tubesandmore.com, Web Site: www.tubesandmore.com (3)

Cravener, Noreen, Antique Electronic Supply, Tempe, AZ. Tel: (480) 820-5411, (800) 706-6789, FAX: (480) 820-4643, E-Mail: info@tubesandmore.com, Web Site: www.tubesandmore.com (3)

Craver Mathews Smith & Co, Reston, VA. Tel: (703) 258-0000, FAX: (703) 258-0001, E-Mail: ellenc@cms1.com, Web Site: www.craveronline.com (1)

Crawford Advertising Associates Ltd, New City, NY. Tel: (914) 946-2444, FAX: (914) 946-9236, E-Mail: crawads@aol.com, Web Site: www.crawfordadv.com (35)

Crawford & Co, Atlanta, GA. Tel: (404) 300-1000, (800) 241-2541, FAX: (404) 300-1905, E-Mail: info@us.crawco.com, Web Site: us.crawfordandcompany.com (35)

Crawford Kerr, Karla, Hawthorne Direct Inc, Los Angeles, CA. Tel: (301) 248-3972, E-Mail: inquiries@hawthornedirect.com, Web Site: www.hawthornedirect.com (35)

Crawford, Janice, Inquiry Intelligence Systems, O'Fallon, MO. Tel: (636) 240-1800, (800) 467-2329, FAX: (636) 281-1517, E-Mail: sales@iqsalespro.com, Web Site: www.inquiry-tracking.com (22)

Crawford, Jesse C., Crawford & Co, Atlanta, GA. Tel: (404) 300-1000, (800) 241-2541, FAX: (404) 300-1905, E-Mail: info@us.crawco.com, Web Site: us.crawfordandcompany.com (35)

Crawford, Thomas J., Stewart Enterprises Inc, Jefferson, LA. Tel: (504) 729-1400, (800) 535-6017, FAX: (504) 729-1984, Web Site: www.stewartenterprises.com (16)

Crawshaw Design, San Rafael, CA. Tel: (415) 456-5544, FAX: (415) 456-4319, E-Mail: crawshawdesign@earthlink.net, Web Site: www.crawshawdesign.com (36)

Crawshaw, Todd, Crawshaw Design, San Rafael, CA. Tel: (415) 456-5544, FAX: (415) 456-4319, E-Mail: crawshawdesign@earthlink.net, Web Site: www.crawshawdesign.com (36)

Craycraft, Robert M., Ashland Inc, Covington, KY. Tel: (859) 815-3333, Web Site: www.ashland.com (16)

Crazy Crow Trading Post, Pottsboro, TX. Tel: (903) 786-2287, (800) 786-6210, FAX: (903) 786-9059, E-Mail: info@crazycrow.com, Web Site: www.crazycrow.com (11)

Creager, Mark A., American Heart Association, Dallas, TX. Tel: (214) 373-6300, (800) AHA-USA-1, FAX: (214) 373-3406, Web Site: www.americanheart.org (1)

Creasey, Jr. F. Clay, Toys "R" Us, Wayne, NJ. Tel: (973) 617-5879, FAX: (973) 617-4006, Web Site: www.toysrus.com (11)

Createch Marketing, Montvale, NJ. Tel: (201) 326-3000, (866) 808-1050, Web Site: www.createchmarketing.com (22)

Creating Results LLC, Woodbridge, VA. Tel: (703) 494-7888, (888) 205-8899, Web Site: www.creatingresults.com (35)

Creating Selling Opportunities, Houston, TX. Tel: (713) 622-6936, FAX: (713) 622-2924, E-Mail: annci@sbcglobal.net (20)

The Creative Alliance Inc, Lafayette, CO. Tel: (303) 665-8101, FAX: (303) 665-3136, E-Mail: info@thecreativealliance.com, Web Site: www.thecreativealliance.com (35)

Creative Awards by Lane, Elk Grove Village, IL. Tel: (847) 593-7700, FAX: (847) 593-1155, E-Mail: info@creativeawardsbylane.com, Web Site: www.creativeawardsbylane.com (33)

Creative Banner Assemblies, Minneapolis, MN. Tel: (763) 566-1118, Web Site: www.creativebanner.com (9)

Creative Catalogs Corp, Lemont, IL. Tel: (630) 783-2400, Web Site: www.personalcreations.com (6)

Creative Commerce LLC, West Chester, PA. Tel: (610) 918-8800, FAX: (610) 918-1349, E-Mail: info@creativecommerce.com, Web Site: creativecommerce.com (35)

Creative Compliance, Chicago, IL. Tel: (916) 216-3379, E-Mail: info@creativecompliance.com, Web Site: www.creativecompliance.com (29)

Creative Copywriting, Plainfield, IL. Tel: (815) 439-9160, FAX: (815) 439-9158 (39)

Creative Direct Marketing, Chapel Hill, NC. Tel: (919) 929-5757, E-Mail: jeffb.cdm@mindspring.com (39)

Creative Freelancers Inc, Sarasota, FL. Tel: (203) 532-2924, (800) 398-9544, E-Mail: cfonline@freelancers.com, Web Site: www.freelancers.com (39)

Creative Health Products, Plymouth, MI. Tel: (734) 996-5900, (800) 742-4478, FAX: (734) 996-4650, Web Site: www.chponline.com (16)

Creative Irish Gifts, Little Rock, AR. Tel: (330) 954-1200, FAX: (330) 650-8888, E-Mail: gifts@shopirish.com, Web Site: www.shopirish.com (6)

Creative Learning Systems Inc, Longmont, CO. Tel: (303) 772-6400, (800) 458-2880, FAX: (303) 772-6422, Web Site: www.clsinc.com (9)

Creative Lift Inc, San Francisco, CA. Tel: (415) 248-3170, E-Mail: hello@creativelift.net, Web Site: www.creativelift.net (35)

Creative Mailing & Marketing, Gardena, CA. Tel: (310) 637-7100, FAX: (714) 998-9001, Web Site: www.creativemandm.com (28)

Creative Marketing Alliance Inc, Princeton Junction, NJ. Tel: (609) 297-2235, FAX: (609) 799-7032, E-Mail: info@cmasolutions.com, Web Site: www.gotocma.com (35)

Creative Marketing Programs of Kansas City, Kansas City, MO. Tel: (816) 472-6843, (800) 373-6843, FAX: (816) 472-8184, E-Mail: getresults@cmpkc.com, Web Site: www.cmpkc.com (21)

Creative Media Inc, Nicholasville, KY. Tel: (859) 227-6513 (35)

Creative Packaging Solutions, Keyport, NJ. Tel: (732) 335-3700, (888) 826-1646, FAX: (732) 264-9313, E-Mail: info@packaging-usa.com, Web Site: www.packaging-usa.com (35)

Creative Printing Services Inc, Saint Louis, MO. Tel: (314) 863-4550, (800) 886-4551, FAX: (314) 863-6036, E-Mail: steve@cpsstl.com, Web Site: www.cpsstl.com (27)

Creative Publishing International, Minneapolis, MN. Tel: (612) 344-8100, FAX: (612) 344-8691, E-Mail: sales@creativepub.com, Web Site: www.creativepub.com (17)

Creative Strategy Group Inc, Newtown, PA. Tel: (215) 860-3045, FAX: (215) 860-3129, E-Mail: info@csgmarketing.com, Web Site: www.csg-design.com (35)

Creative Synergy Inc, Germantown, MD. Tel: (301) 515-9397, Web Site: kimschwalm.com (20)

Creative Teaching Associates, Clovis, CA. Tel: (559) 291-6626, (800) 767-4282, FAX: (559) 291-2953, Web Site: www.mastercta.com (16)

Creative Teaching Press, Cypress, CA. Tel: (714) 895-5047, (800) 287-8879 (17)

Creativity International, Ada, MI. Tel: (616) 956-0053, FAX: (616) 956-6957 (16)

Crecca, Diane, Arcade Marketing, Inc, Chattanooga, TN. Tel: (423) 624-3301, FAX: (423) 622-4635, E-Mail: resumes@arcadeinc.com (27)

Credit Union Executives Society, Fitchburg, WI. Tel: (608) 271-2664, FAX: (608) 271-2303, E-Mail: cues@cues.org, Web Site: www.cues.org (1)

Creditcards.com, Austin, TX. Tel: (512) 996-8663, Web Site: www.creditcards.com (20)

Creel Printing of California, Costa Mesa, CA. Tel: (714) 540-7005, FAX: (714) 979-1496, Web Site: www.creelprint.com (27)

Creel, Allan, Creel Printing of California, Costa Mesa, CA. Tel: (714) 540-7005, FAX: (714) 979-1496, Web Site: www.creelprint.com (27)

Creel, Jr. Alan, Creel Printing of California, Costa Mesa, CA. Tel: (714) 540-7005, FAX: (714) 979-1496, Web Site: www.creelprint.com (27)

Cregan, James C., Magazine Publishers of America, New York, NY. Tel: (212) 872-3700, FAX: (212) 888-4217, E-Mail: mpa@magazine.org, Web Site: www.magazine.org (17)

Cregg, Roger A., Del Webb, Bloomfield Hills, MI. Tel: (248) 644-7300, (888) 717-9777, FAX: (248) 433-4598, Web Site: www.delwebb.com (16)

Crescent Beach Productions, Bohemia, NY. Tel: (631) 588-6600, (888) 401-7700, FAX: (631) 918-5044, E-Mail: info@cbprod.com, Web Site: www.cbprod.com (32)

Crescenzo, Bob, Lancer Insurance Co, Long Beach, NY. Tel: (516) 431-4441, (800) 782-8902, FAX: (516) 889-5111, E-Mail: roneill@lancer-ins.com, Web Site: www.lancer-ins.com (15)

Cressley, William W., Leadership Directories Inc, New York, NY. Tel: (212) 627-4140, FAX: (212) 645-0931, E-Mail: info@leadershipdirectories.com, Web Site: www.leadershipdirectories.com (17)

Crest Healthcare Supply, Dassel, MN. Tel: (800) 328-8908, (800) 369-9207, Web Site: www.cresthealthcare.com (16)

Crestline Specialties, Inc, Lewiston, ME. Tel: (207) 777-7075, (866) 488-4975, FAX: (207) 784-5038, E-Mail: info@crestline.com, Web Site: www.crestline.com (16)

Crews, Diane L., Magna Visual Inc, Saint Louis, MO. Tel: (314) 843-9000, (800) 843-3399, FAX: (314) 843-0000, E-Mail: magna@magnavisual.com, Web Site: www.magnavisual.com (9)

Crews, Ted, Kansas City Chiefs, Kansas City, MO. Tel: (816) 920-9300, (888) 99-CHIEFS, FAX: (816) 923-4719, Web Site: www.kcchiefs.com (16)

Cribbs, Helen, Peerless Rattan, Plainwell, MI. Tel: (269) 685-1858, (877) 611-2263, E-Mail: sales@peerlessrattan.com, Web Site: www.peerlessrattan.com (14)

The Cricket Magazine Group, Chicago, IL. Tel: (603) 924-7209, (800) 821-0115, FAX: (815) 224-6615, Web Site: customerservice@caruspub.com, Web Site: www.cricketmag.com (17)

Crifasi, Camille, Greenbook Worldwide Directory of Marketing Research Companies & Services, Bradenton, FL. Tel: (212) 849-2752, (800) 792-9202, FAX: (212) 202-7920, E-Mail: info@greenbrook.org, Web Site: www.greenbook.org (43)

Crilly, John, Solarcom, Norcross, GA. Tel: (770) 449-6116, (888) SUN-DATA, FAX: (770) 448-7726, Web Site: www.solarcom.net (16)

Crisan, Jane, R2C Group, Portland, OR. Tel: (866) 402-1124, E-Mail: getintouch@r2cgroup.com, Web Site: www.r2cgroup.com (35)

Criscuoli, Joseph, EPI Colorspace, Gaithersburg, MD. Tel: (301) 230-2023, FAX: (301) 990-7890, E-Mail: jcriscuoli@epicolorspace.com, Web Site: www.epicolorspace.com (36)

Crisp, Adam, ClickSquared, Boston, MA. Tel: (781) 622-1611, (866) 402-5425, FAX: (857) 246-7645, E-Mail: info@clicksquared.com, Web Site: www.clicksquared.com (20)

Crispin Porter + Bogusky, Miami, FL. Tel: (305) 859-2070, FAX: (305) 854-3419, E-Mail: info@cpbgroup.com, Web Site: www.cpbgroup.com (35)

Critchely, Keith, PrintWest Communications Ltd, Regina, SK Canada. Tel: (306) 525-2304, (800) 236-6438, FAX: (306) 757-2439, E-Mail: general@printwest.com, Web Site: www.printwest.com (27)

Criteser, Patrick G., Tillamook County Creamery Association, Tillamook, OR. Tel: (503) 842-4481, Web Site: www.tillamook.com (4)

Croatti, Ronald, UniFirst Corp, Wilmington, MA. Tel: (270) 683-5250 X523, Web Site: www.unifirst.com (2)

Croft, Charles R., Kalmbach Publishing Co, Waukesha, WI. Tel: (262) 796-8776, (800) 558-1544, FAX: (262) 796-1143, Web Site: www.kalmbach.com (17)

Crofton, Jim, Penguin Group USA Inc, New York, NY. Tel: (212) 366-2000, Web Site: www.us.penguingroup.com (17)

Crohn's & Colitis Foundation of America, New York, NY. Tel: (212) 685-3440, (800) 932-2423, E-Mail: info@ccfa.org, Web Site: www.ccfa.org (1)

Cromheecke, Todd, Integrated Merchandising Systems LLC, Morton Grove, IL. Tel: (877) 467-1200, E-Mail: doug.carlson@imsfastpak.com, Web Site: www.imsfastpak.com (21)

Crone, Annette, CollegeSource Inc, San Diego, CA. Tel: (858) 560-8051, (800) 854-2670, FAX: (858) 278-8960, Web Site: www.collegesource.com (17)

Cronin & Co, Glastonbury, CT. Tel: (860) 659-0514, Web Site: www.cronin-co.com (11)

Cronin, Douglas, NFocus Consulting Inc, Lancaster, OH. Tel: (740) 654-5809, (800) 675-5809, FAX: 740 654-0934, Web Site: www.nfocusconsulting.com (22)

Cronin, W. Perry, Shelby Insurance Companies, Birmingham, AL. Tel: (800) 443-1573, FAX: (877) 837-8203, Web Site: www.vesta.com (15)

Crook & Grant Lithographers Ltd, North York, ON Canada. Tel: (416) 499-1011, FAX: (416) 499-1821 (27)

Crook, Carolyn, Chaffee & Communications, Barrington, RI. Tel: (401) 247-2300, FAX: (401) 247-2002, E-Mail: dchaffee@fullchannel.net, Web Site: www.chaffeecommunications.com (35)

Crook, David, Strategy Corps LLC, Brentwood, TN. Tel: (615) 221-8381, (888) 577-6933, FAX: (615) 221-8479, E-Mail: info@strategycorps.com, Web Site: www.strategycorps.com (16)

Crook, Steve, Crook & Grant Lithographers Ltd, North York, ON Canada. Tel: (416) 499-1011, FAX: (416) 499-1821 (27)

Crook, Tom, Reading for Education, Murfreesboro, TN. Tel: (615) 494-4000, FAX: (615) 895-9041, Web Site: www.readingforeducation.com (1)

Crooker, Cynthia, Choice Magazine, Middletown, CT. Tel: (860) 347-6933, (860) 347-1387, FAX: (860) 346-8586, E-Mail: adsales@ala-choice.org, Web Site: www.ala.org/ala/acrl/acrlpubs/choice/home.cfm (31)

Croom, Marshall A, Lowe's Companies Inc, Mooresville, NC. Tel: (704) 758-1000, (800) 445-6937, Web Site: www.lowes.com (8)

Crosby, Nancy C., Partners Village Store, Westport, MA. Tel: (508) 636-2572, FAX: (508) 636-2529, E-Mail: info@partnersvillagestore.com, Web Site: www.partnersvillagestore.com (11)

A T Cross Co, Lincoln, RI. Tel: (401) 333-1200, (800) 282-7677, FAX: (401) 334-2861, Web Site: www.cross.com (16)

Cross Country Automotive Services, Medford, MA. Tel: (781) 393-9300, Web Site: www.cchs.com (16)

Cross Country Computer Corp, Central Islip, NY. Tel: (631) 334-1810, E-Mail: inquiry@crosscountrycomputer.com, Web Site: www.crosscountrycomputer.com (22)

The Cross Country Group LLC, Medford, MA. Tel: (781) 396-3700, FAX: (781) 391-7504, E-Mail: info@crosscountrygroup.com, Web Site: www.ccgroup.com (13)

Cross Country Stitching, Quakertown, PA. Tel: (215) 529-6430, (800) 231-8108, FAX: (215) 529-6434, Web Site: www.crosscountrystitching.com (17)

Cross Country Travcorps, Boca Raton, FL. Tel: (800) 530-6125, FAX: (561) 998-8533, Web Site: www.crosscountrytravcorps.com (16)

Cross Marketing USA, Chicago, IL. Tel: (312) 440-3700, (866) 440-3700, FAX: (312) 943-5813, E-Mail: ronbernstein@crossmarketing.us, Web Site: www.crossmarketing.us (23)

Cross, John, BJU Press, Greenville, SC. Tel: (864) 242-5100, (800) 845-5731, FAX: (864) 271-8151, (800) 525-8398, E-Mail: bjupinfo@bjupress.com, Web Site: www.bjupress.com (17)

Cross, Thomas, Hearst Business Media, New York, NY. Tel: (212) 649-2000, Web Site: www.hearst.com/business-media (24)

Crossbow Group, Westport, CT. Tel: (203) 222-2244, FAX: (203) 226-7838, E-Mail: info@crossbowgroup.com, Web Site: www.crossbowgroup.com (40)

Crossley, Orin, Reserve National Insurance Co, Oklahoma City, OK. Tel: (405) 848-7931, Web Site: www.reservenational.com (15)

Crosslists Cross & Co, Lone Jack, MO. Tel: (816) 697-3306, FAX: (816) 697-3317, E-Mail: info@crosscompany.com, Web Site: www.crosscompany.com (23)

Crossman, Paul G., National Fire Protection Association, Quincy, MA. Tel: (617) 770-3000, FAX: (617) 770-0700, Web Site: www.nfpa.org (1)

Crossroads Films Inc, Los Angeles, CA. Tel: (310) 659-6220, FAX: (310) 659-3105, Web Site: www.crossroadfilms.com (32)

Crosstown Traders Inc, Tucson, AZ. Tel: (520) 745-4500 (2)

Crosthwaithe, K.C., Philip Morris USA Inc, Richmond, VA. Tel: (804) 274-2000, FAX: (804) 484-8231, Web Site: www.philipmorrisusa.com (16)

Croswhite, Brian, Nova Southeastern University Fischler College of Education, North Miami Beach, FL. Tel: (954) 262-8651, Web Site: www.schoolofed.nova.edu (1)

Crotchfelt, Karen, Indianapolis Newspapers Inc, Indianapolis, IN. Tel: (317) 444-4444, FAX: (317) 633-9414, Web Site: www.indystar.com (17)

Crouch, Gene, Tyco Valves & Controls, Houston, TX. Tel: (713) 986-4665, (800) 343-0990, FAX: (713) 937-5466, Web Site: www.tycovalves.com (16)

Crow, Jessica, Basic Research, Salt Lake City, UT. Tel: (801) 530-2911, (888) 865-5326, E-Mail: customerservice@basicresearch.com, Web Site: www.silversage.com (7)

Crow, Timothy M., The Home Depot Inc, Atlanta, GA. Tel: (770) 433-8211, (800) 466-3337, FAX: (770) 384-2356, Web Site: www.homedepot.com (16)

Crowder, Jerry, Bradford Health Services, Birmingham, AL. Tel: (205) 251-7753, (800) 217-2849, Web Site: www.bradfordhealth.com (16)

Crowe, Jesse, Voice Message Broadcasting Corp, Aliso Viejo, CA. Tel: (714) 437-0600, FAX: (714) 242-1989, Web Site: www.vmbc.com (32)

Crowe, John, Polyair Packaging, Chicago, IL. Tel: (773) 995-1818, (888) POLYAIR X444, FAX: (773) 995-7725, E-Mail: marketing@polyair.com, Web Site: www.polyair.com (9)

Crowley, Arthur M., Garon Products Inc, Wall, NJ. Tel: (732) 449-1776, (800) 631-5380, FAX: (732) 449-6937, Web Site: www.garonproducts.com (16)

Crowley, Joseph, American Telecast Products LLC, Exton, PA. Tel: (610) 430-7800, FAX: (484) 879-4046, E-Mail: info@americantelecast.com, Web Site: www.americantelecast.com (32)

Crowley, Tara, Garon Products Inc, Wall, NJ. Tel: (732) 449-1776, (800) 631-5380, FAX: (732) 449-6937, Web Site: www.garonproducts.com (16)

Crown, Eric, Insight Direct Inc, Tempe, AZ. Tel: (480) 333-3001, (800) 467-4448, FAX: (480) 902-1180, Web Site: www.insight.com (16)

Crown, Tim A., Insight Direct Inc, Tempe, AZ. Tel: (480) 333-3001, (800) 467-4448, FAX: (480) 902-1180, Web Site: www.insight.com (16)

CrownPeak Technology Inc, Los Angeles, CA. Tel: (310) 841-5920, FAX: (310) 841-5913, Web Site: www.crownpeak.com (22)

Crozier, Joan, Hooleon Corp, Melrose, NM. Tel: (575) 253-4503, (800) 937-1337, E-Mail: sales@hooleon.com, Web Site: www.hooleon.com (3)

Crozier, Robert F., Hooleon Corp, Melrose, NM. Tel: (575) 253-4503, (800) 937-1337, E-Mail: sales@hooleon.com, Web Site: www.hooleon.com (3)

Crozier, Sharon, Ruf Corp, Olathe, KS. Tel: (913) 782-8544, (800) 829-8544, FAX: (913) 782-0150, E-Mail: solutions@ruf.com, Web Site: www.ruf.com (30)

Crozzoli, Christina, Stagestep Inc, Philadelphia, PA. Tel: (215) 636-9000, (800) 523-0960, FAX: (267) 672-2912, E-Mail: stagestep@stagestep.com, Web Site: www.stagestep.com (5)

Crull, Michele, Rawle Murdy, Charleston, SC. Tel: (843) 577-7327, E-Mail: contact@rawlemurdy.com, Web Site: www.rawlemurdy.com (35)

Crumb, Dan, Kansas City Chiefs, Kansas City, MO. Tel: (816) 920-9300, (888) 99-CHIEFS, FAX: (816) 923-4719, Web Site: www.kcchiefs.com (16)

Crumpton, Jonathan, Brentwood Benson Music Publishing, Brentwood, TN. Tel: (615) 261-3400, (800) 846-7664, FAX: (615) 261-3381, E-Mail: choral@brentwoodbensonmusic.com, Web Site: www.brentwoodbenson.com (17)

Crutchfield Corp, Charlottesville, VA. Tel: (434) 817-1000, (800) 955-9091, FAX: (804) 817-1010, E-Mail: administration@crutchfield.com, Web Site: www.crutchfield.com (3)

Crutchfield, William G., Crutchfield Corp, Charlottesville, VA. Tel: (434) 817-1000, (800) 955-9091, FAX: (804) 817-1010, E-Mail: administration@crutchfield.com, Web Site: www.crutchfield.com (3)

Cruver, Cynthia, GCDirect, Seattle, WA. Tel: (206) 262-1999, E-Mail: info@gcdirect.com, Web Site: www.gcdirect.com (35)

Cruz, Joel, Interface Engineering, Portland, OR. Tel: (503) 382-2266, FAX: (503) 382-2262, E-Mail: solutions@interfaceengineering.com, Web Site: www.ieice.com (20)

Cruz, Rey, Shasho Jones Direct Inc, New York, NY. Tel: (212) 929-2300, E-Mail: glenda@sjdirect.com, Web Site: www.sjdirect.com (20)

Crystal Records Inc, Camas, WA. Tel: (360) 834-7022, FAX: (360) 834-9680, E-Mail: info@crystalrecords.com, Web Site: www.crystalrecords.com (3)

Crystek Corp, Fort Myers, FL. Tel: (239) 561-3311, (800) 237-3061, FAX: (239) 561-1025, E-Mail: sales@crystek.com, Web Site: www.crystek.com (9)

Csipak, Dr. James, State University of New York-College of Plattsburgh, Plattsburgh, NY. Tel: (518) 564-2000, FAX: (518) 564-3183, E-Mail: nancy.church@plattsburgh.edu, Web Site: www.plattsburgh.edu (41)

Cuba Cheese Shoppe, Cuba, NY. Tel: (585) 968-3949, FAX: (716) 968-1746, Web Site: www.cubacheese.com (4)

Cubine, Kim, Chapman Cubine Adams & Hussey, Arlington, VA. Tel: (703) 248-0025, Web Site: www.ahadirect.com (20)

Cucciniello, John, Direct Link Worldwide, Elizabeth, NJ. Tel: (908) 289-0703, (800) 223-7967, FAX: (908) 289-0705, E-Mail: infousa@directlink.com, Web Site: www.directlink.com (20)

Cucullu, Robert (Robby), Data Intelligence Group, Franklin, TN. Tel: (615) 861-3301, Web Site: www.wedigdata.com (22)

Cuddledown Inc, Yarmouth, ME. Tel: (800) 323-6793, FAX: (207) 761-1948, Web Site: www.cuddledown.com (8)

Cuffee, Michael, Eclipse Direct Marketing, Mineola, NY. Tel: (212) 931-8344, FAX: (516) 493-9122, E-Mail: jkaiser@eclipsedm.com, Web Site: www.eclipsedm.com (23)

Cuisinart, Stamford, CT. Tel: (203) 975-4600, FAX: (203) 975-4660, E-Mail: marketing@cuisinart.com, Web Site: www.cuisinart.com (16)

Culinary Parts Unlimited, San Francisco, CA. Tel: (800) 543-7549, FAX: (415) 495-5141, Web Site: www.culinaryparts.com (16)

Cullen, Carolyn, McGruff Specialty Products Office, Amsterdam, NY. Tel: (518) 842-4388, (888) 776-7763, FAX: (800) 995-5121, E-Mail: mcgruff@spocentral.com, Web Site: www.mcgruffspo.com (16)

Cullen, D. Timothy, DelStar Technologies Inc, Middletown, DE. Tel: (302) 378-8888, (800) 521-6713, FAX: (302) 378-4482, Web Site: www.delstarinc.com (16)

Culler, Lee, DSP Inc USA, Charlottesville, VA. Tel: (434) 202-7870, E-Mail: iorder@delfortgroup.com, Web Site: www.delfortgroup.com (10)

Cullinane, Sue, Direct Marketing Association of Saint Louis, Washington, MO. Tel: (866) 516-0121, FAX: (636) 239-2324, E-Mail: mparisien@mac.com, Web Site: www.dmastl.org (40)

Culman, Barry, Spectrum Systems Inc, Reston, VA. Tel: (703) 591-7400 X217, (800) 929-3781, FAX: (703) 591-9780, E-Mail: spectrum@spectrum-systems.com, Web Site: www.spectrum-systems.com (34)

Mary Culnan, Waltham, MA. Tel: (781) 891-2773, E-Mail: mculnan@bentley.edu (20)

Culver Pictures Inc, Long Island City, NY. Tel: (718) 752-9393, FAX: (718) 752-9394, Web Site: www.culverpictures.com (38)

Culver, Harriet L, Culver Pictures Inc, Long Island City, NY. Tel: (718) 752-9393, FAX: (718) 752-9394, Web Site: www.culverpictures.com (38)

Culver, J. Bart, Bart's Watersports, North Webster, IN. Tel: (574) 834-7666, (800) 348-5016, FAX: (574) 834-4246, E-Mail: info@barts.com, Web Site: www.bartswatersports.com (11)

Cumenal, Frederic, Tiffany & Co, New York, NY. Tel: (212) 755-8000, FAX: (212) 320-7550, Web Site: www.tiffany.com (6)

Cumings, Brad, DEFENDER Direct Inc, Indianapolis, IN. Tel: (317) 810-4720, (800) 860-0303, FAX: (317) 810-4723, Web Site: www.defenderdirect.com (32)

John Cummings & Partners LLC, Armonk, NY. Tel: (914) 273-4691, FAX: (914) 206-3007, E-Mail: john@dbmscan.com, Web Site: www.dbmscan.com (20)

Cummings, Jesse, The Burris Agency Inc, Greensboro, NC. Tel: (336) 378-1221, FAX: (336) 378-1221, E-Mail: info@burris.com, Web Site: www.burris.com (35)

Cummings, John J., John Cummings & Partners LLC, Armonk, NY. Tel: (914) 273-4691, FAX: (914) 206-3007, E-Mail: john@dbmscan.com, Web Site: www.dbmscan.com (20)

Cummings, Robert, John Cummings & Partners LLC, Armonk, NY. Tel: (914) 273-4691, FAX: (914) 206-3007, E-Mail: john@dbmscan.com, Web Site: www.dbmscan.com (20)

Cummings, Steven R., Oakstone Publishing LLC, Birmingham, AL. Tel: (205) 991-5188, (800) 952-0690, FAX: (205) 995-4656, E-Mail: info@oakstonepublishing.com, Web Site: www.oakstonepublishing.com (17)

Cummiskey, Susan, The Reader's Digest Association Inc, New York, NY. Tel: (800) 310-6261, Web Site: www.rda.com (17)

Cumpiano, Gerardo, Caribe Direct Inc, San Juan, PR. Tel: (787) 722-5188, FAX: (787) 723-6165, E-Mail: islaonline@prw.net, Web Site: www.islaonline.com (6)

CUNA Mutual Group, Madison, WI. Tel: (608) 238-5851, (800) 356-2644, FAX: (608) 231-8839, Web Site: www.cunamutual.com (15)

CUNA - Trade Association, Madison, WI. Tel: (608) 231-4215, (800) 356-9655, FAX: (608) 231-4333, Web Site: www.cuna.org (1)

Cuneo Advertising, Bloomington, MN. Tel: (952) 707-1212, FAX: (952) 707-1295, E-Mail: agency@cuneocom.com, Web Site: cuneocom.com (35)

Cuneo, Laurence A., Cuneo Advertising, Bloomington, MN. Tel: (952) 707-1212, FAX: (952) 707-1295, E-Mail: agency@cuneocom.com, Web Site: cuneocom.com (35)

Cunningham Group, Elmwood Park, IL. Tel: (708) 848-2300, (800) 962-1224, FAX: (708) 848-2174, E-Mail: cunngroup@cg-ins.com, Web Site: www.cg-ins.com (15)

Cunningham, Adam, Allied Integrated Marketing, Boston, MA. Tel: (617) 859-4800, E-Mail: alliedimsocial@alliedim.com, Web Site: alliedim.com (35)

Cunningham, Dr. Joseph, Blue Cross Blue Shield of Oklahoma, Tulsa, OK. Tel: (918) 560-3500, (800) 942-5837, E-Mail: info@bcbsok.com, Web Site: www.bcbsok.com (15)

Cunningham, Gerard, MGI Management Institute, Hawthorne, NY. Tel: (914) 428-6500, (800) 932-0191, FAX: (914) 428-0773, E-Mail: mgiusa@aol.com, Web Site: www.mgi.org (16)

Cunningham, Glenn, Thermal Product Solutions, White Deer, PA. Tel: (570) 538-7200, (800) 586-2473 (16)

Cunningham, Jack, American Period Lighting Inc, Lancaster, PA. Tel: (717) 392-5649, FAX: (717) 509-3127, E-Mail: info@americanperiodlighting.com, Web Site: www.americanperiodlighting.com (8)

Cunningham, James, Alternative Media Group, Naples, FL. Tel: (732) 741-0585, FAX: (732) 741-0489, Web Site: www.amg-global.com (31)

Cunningham, James H., Cunningham Group, Elmwood Park, IL. Tel: (708) 848-2300, (800) 962-1224, FAX: (708) 848-2174, E-Mail: cunngroup@cg-ins.com, Web Site: www.cg-ins.com (15)

Cunningham, Sheri, Skies America International Publishing & Communications, Beaverton, OR. Tel: (503) 520-1955, FAX: (503) 520-1275, E-Mail: skies@skies.com, Web Site: www.skies.com (36)

Cuno, Steve, Response Agency Inc, Sandy, UT. Tel: (801) 352-9100, E-Mail: info@responseagency.com, Web Site: www.responseagency.com (35)

Cuoto, Joe, Accellos Inc, Colorado Springs, CO. Tel: (719) 433-7000, Web Site: www.accellos.com (12)

Curcio, John, Professional Training Associates Inc, Duquesne, PA. Tel: (412) 460-0266, FAX: (412) 460-0269, E-Mail: info@ptainc.com, Web Site: www.ptainc.com (17)

Curcurito, David, Esquire Magazine, New York, NY. Tel: (212) 649-4020, FAX: (212) 649-4303, E-Mail: esquire@hearst.com, Web Site: www.esquire.com (17)

Curcuruto, Bob, NCC Media, New York, NY. Tel: (212) 548-3300, FAX: (212) 519-0099, Web Site: nccmedia.com (32)

Curling, Douglas C., Choice Point, Alpharetta, GA. Tel: (770) 752-6000, (800) 342-5339, FAX: (770) 752-6005, Web Site: www.choicepoint.com (16)

MJ Curran & Associates Inc, Boston, MA. Tel: (617) 247-7700, FAX: (617) 267-6429 (20)

Curran, Beth, A&P, Montvale, NJ. Tel: (201) 573-9700, (866) 44 FRESH, FAX: (201) 505-3054, E-Mail: apcustomerrel@aptea.com, Web Site: www.aptea.com (16)

Curran, Don, Virco Manufacturing Corp, Conway, AR. Tel: (501) 329-2901, (800) 448-4726, FAX: (800) 258-7367, E-Mail: info@virco.com, Web Site: www.virco.com (16)

Curran, Dorothy E., Mission: A Consulting Group, Westport, CT. Tel: (203) 227-9475, FAX: (203) 227-6512, E-Mail: info@mission-consulting.com, Web Site: www.mission-consulting.com (20)

Curran, Kevin, GCC Printers, Bedford, MA. Tel: (781) 275-5800, (800) 422-7777, FAX: (781) 275-1115, (800) 442-2329, E-Mail: sales@gccprinters.com, Web Site: www.gcctech.com (10)

Curran, Martin J., MJ Curran & Associates Inc, Boston, MA. Tel: (617) 247-7700, FAX: (617) 267-6429 (20)

Current USA Inc, Colorado Springs, CO. Tel: (719) 594-4100, (877) 665-4458, FAX: (719) 531-2283, Web Site: www.currentinc.com (6)

Curriculum Associates Inc, North Billerica, MA. Tel: (978) 667-8000, FAX: (978) 667-5706, E-Mail: cainfo@curriculumassociates.com, Web Site: www.curriculumassociates.com (35)

Currie, Dave, List Partners Inc, Atlanta, GA. Tel: (404) 350-0600, (800) 941-6562, E-Mail: contact@thelistinc.com, Web Site: listpartnersinc.com (24)

Currie, Peter, Daydots, Fort Worth, TX. Tel: (817) 590-4500, (800) 321-3687, FAX: (800) 438-7002, E-Mail: customercare@daydots.com, Web Site: www.daydots.com (16)

Curry, Claire L., The Nulman Group, Flemington, NJ. Tel: (908) 751-5299, (888) 440-3367, FAX: (908) 751-5621, E-Mail: info@nulmangroup.com, Web Site: www.nulmangroup.com (35)

Curry, Deborah L., Florida Institute of CPA's, Tallahassee, FL. Tel: (850) 224-2727, (800) 342-3197 (FL), FAX: (850) 222-8190, E-Mail: msc@ficpa.org, Web Site: www.ficpa.org (1)

Curry, Jeff, House of Onyx, Inc, Greenville, KY. Tel: (270) 338-2363, (800) 844-3100, FAX: (270) 338-9605, E-Mail: sales@houseofonyx.com, Web Site: www.houseofonyx.com (6)

Curry, Pam, United Air Specialists Inc, Cincinnati, OH. Tel: (513) 891-0400, (800) 992-4422, FAX: (513) 891-4882, E-Mail: uas@uasinc.com, Web Site: www.uasinc.com (16)

Curtain, Mike, SmartSource Corp, Bedford, MA. Tel: (781) 785-3375, (800) 239-0239, Web Site: www.smartsourceonline.com (32)

Curtin, Mary, 4Imprint Inc, Oshkosh, WI. Tel: (920) 236-7272, (877) 446-7746, (888) 298-8190, FAX: (800) 355-5043, E-Mail: administrator@4imprint.com, Web Site: www.4imprint.com (16)

Curtis 1000 Inc, Duluth, GA. Tel: (678) 380-9095, (877) 287-8715, FAX: (770) 717-1890, E-Mail: info@curtis1000.com, Web Site: www.curtis1000.com (27)

Curtis, Cybil, Great Chefs Television Publishing, New Orleans, LA. Tel: (504) 581-5000, (800) 321-1499, FAX: (504) 581-1188, E-Mail: info@greatchefs.com, Web Site: www.greatchefs.com (6)

Curtis, Glenn, Starz Entertainment LLC, Englewood, CO. Tel: (855) 807-2929, Web Site: www.starz.com (16)

Curtis, Mary E., Transaction Publishers, Piscataway, NJ. Tel: (732) 445-1245, FAX: (732) 748-9801, E-Mail: trans@transactionpub.com, Web Site: www.transactionpub.com (17)

Curtis, Steven, Toyota Motor Sales USA Inc, Torrance, CA. Tel: (310) 468-4000, (800) 331-4331, FAX: (310) 468-7841, Web Site: www.toyota.com (16)

Curtis, Susan, Santa Fe School of Cooking, Santa Fe, NM. Tel: (505) 983-4511, (800) 982-4688, FAX: (505) 983-7540, Web Site: www.santafeschoolofcooking.com (4)

Curtis, Tim, Mid America Motorworks, Effingham, IL. Tel: (217) 347-5591, (800) 500-1500, FAX: (217) 347-2952, E-Mail: mail@mamotorworks.com, Web Site: www.mamotorworks.com (12)

Cusack, Chris, Direct Logic Solutions, Peoria, IL. Tel: (309) 688-5500, FAX: (309) 688-5502, E-Mail: nedbarrett@direct-logic.com, Web Site: www.direct-logic.com (22)

Cusak, Tom, Enterprise Ireland, New York, NY. Tel: (212) 371-3600, FAX: (212) 371-6398, Web Site: www.enterprise-ireland.com (16)

Cushinsky, Steven, Act One Lists, Marblehead, MA. Tel: (781) 639-1919, (800) 228-5478, FAX: (781) 639-2733, E-Mail: info@act1lists.com, Web Site: www.actonelists.com (23)

Cushman Fruit Co Inc, West Palm Beach, FL. Tel: (561) 965-3535, (800) 776-2295, FAX: (800) 776-4329, E-Mail: info@honeybell.com, Web Site: www.honeybell.com (4)

Cushman, III John C., Boys' Life & Scouting Magazines, Irving, TX. Tel: (972) 580-2000, (866) 584-6589, FAX: (972) 580-2079, Web Site: www.boyslife.org (17)

Cushman, Michael, Cushman Fruit Co Inc, West Palm Beach, FL. Tel: (561) 965-3535, (800) 776-2295, FAX: (800) 776-4329, E-Mail: info@honeybell.com, Web Site: www.honeybell.com (4)

Cusick, Thomas B., Columbia Sportswear, Portland, OR. Tel: (503) 985-4203, (800) 622-6953, Web Site: www.columbia.com (2)

Cuss, Francis, Bristol-Myers Squibb Co, New York, NY. Tel: (212) 546-4000, FAX: (212) 546-9544, Web Site: www.bms.com (16)

Custom Accessories, Richmond, IL. Tel: (847) 966-6900, (800) 962-6676, FAX: (847) 966-9650, Web Site: www.causa.com (11)

Custom Direct, Colorado Springs, CO. Tel: (410) 679-3300 (16)

Custom Miniatures, Hudson, NH. Tel: (603) 882-6392 (6)

Custom Toll Free, Los Angeles, CA. Tel: (800) 933-3030, E-Mail: service@customtollfree.com, Web Site: www.customtollfree.com (5)

Customer Communications Group Inc, Lakewood, CO. Tel: (303) 525-0313, E-Mail: info@customer.com, Web Site: www.customer.com (35)

The Customer Connection Inc, Escondido, CA. Tel: (760) 489-8339, (800) 477-7166, FAX: (760) 489-1075, E-Mail: contact@custcon.com, Web Site: www.thecustomerconnection.com (22)

Customer Growth Inc, Fairfield, CT. Tel: (203) 226-8795, FAX: (203) 286-1049, E-Mail: info@customer-growth.com, Web Site: www.customer-growth.com (35)

Customer Marketing Group LLC, Weston, CT. Tel: (203) 226-9845, FAX: (203) 226-9837, E-Mail: bill@4cmg.com, Web Site: www.4cmg.com (35)

Customer Portfolios LLC, Boston, MA. Tel: (617) 224-9501, E-Mail: getstarted@customerportfolios.com, Web Site: www.customerportfolios.com (22)

Customer Retention Solutions, Portage, MI. Tel: (269) 324-7385 (20)

CustomerLink, Duluth, MN. Tel: (218) 722-2800, (866) 245-5569, FAX: (218) 722-3287, E-Mail: info@customerlinkone.com, Web Site: www.customerlinkone.com (29)

CustomerMining Inc, Soquel, CA. Tel: (831) 465-0898, FAX: (831) 465-1186, E-Mail: biz@customermining.com, Web Site: www.customermining.com (35)

Custometrics Inc, Richmond Hill, ON Canada. Tel: (905) 886-9020, E-Mail: info@custometrics.ca, Web Site: www.custometrics.com (30)

Customized Newspaper Advertising, Des Moines, IA. Tel: (515) 244-2145, (800) 227-7636, FAX: (515) 244-4855, Web Site: www.cnaads.com (18)

Custus, Laura R., World Press Review, New York, NY. Tel: (212) 982-8880, Web Site: www.worldpressreview.com (18)

Cutler, Alexander M., Eaton Corp, Raleigh, NC. Tel: (216) 523-4400, (800) 356-5794, FAX: (216) 523-4787, Web Site: www.eaton.com (16)

Cutler, Ken, Tower Hobbies/Hobbico, Champaign, IL. Tel: (217) 398-3636, (800) 637-6050, FAX: (217) 398-1104, Web Site: www.towerhobbies.com (11)

Cutting IV, Sam, Dakin Farm, Ferrisburgh, VT. Tel: (802) 425-3971, (800) 993-2546, FAX: (802) 425-2765, E-Mail: scutting@dakinfarm.com, Web Site: www.dakinfarm.com (4)

Cutting, Mary, Worcester Envelope, Auburn, MA. Tel: (508) 832-5394, (800) 343-1398, FAX: (508) 832-3796, E-Mail: sales@worcesterenvelope.com, Web Site: www.worcester-envelope.com (26)

Cuvaison Inc, Napa, CA. Tel: (707) 942-2455, E-Mail: info@cuvaison.com, Web Site: www.cuvaison.com (4)

Cyber City Teleservices Marketing Inc, Hackensack, NJ. Tel: (201) 487-1616, (800) 213-4144, E-Mail: info@cctll.com, Web Site: www.cctll.com (29)

CyberData, Hicksville, NY. Tel: (516) 942-8000, FAX: (516) 942-0800, E-Mail: info@cyberdata.com, Web Site: www.cyberdata.com (22)

Cygnus Business Media, Fort Atkinson, WI. Tel: (203) 227-4037, (800) 547-7377, FAX: (203) 227-4245, Web Site: www.cygnus.com (17)

Cymerys, Ed, Blue Shield Life, San Francisco, CA. Tel: (888) 800-2742, FAX: (800) 329-2742, Web Site: www.blueshieldca.com (15)

Cypress Media Group Inc, Atlanta, GA. Tel: (770) 640-9918, E-Mail: info@cypressmedia.net, Web Site: www.cypressmedia.net (1)

Cyr, Mr. Tom, Nowetah's American Indian Store & Museum, New Portland, ME. Tel: (207) 628-4981, Web Site: www.nowetahs.webs.com (6)

Cyr, Mrs. Nowetah, Nowetah's American Indian Store & Museum, New Portland, ME. Tel: (207) 628-4981, Web Site: www.nowetahs.webs.com (6)

Cyril-Scott Co, Lancaster, OH. Tel: (740) 654-2112, FAX: (740) 654-7712, E-Mail: mstephenson@cyrilscott.com, Web Site: www.cyrilscott.com (27)

Cystic Fibrosis Foundation, Bethesda, MD. Tel: (301) 951-4422, FAX: (301) 951-6378, E-Mail: info@cff.org, Web Site: www.cff.org (1)

Cytec Industries Inc, Olean, NY. Tel: (716) 372-9650, FAX: (716) 372-1594, Web Site: www.conap.com (16)

Czaplinski, Desiree, Aircraft Spruce & Specialty Co, Corona, CA. Tel: (909) 372-9555, (877) 4-Spruce, FAX: (909) 372-0555, E-Mail: info@aircraft-spruce.com, Web Site: www.aircraft-spruce.com (12)

Czubay, Kenneth, Southeast Toyota Distributors LLC, Deerfield Beach, FL. Tel: (954) 429-2000, Web Site: www.jmfamily.com (16)

Czyz, Cynthia, Champion America Inc, Branford, CT. Tel: (203) 315-1181, (877) 242-6709, FAX: (800) 336-3707, E-Mail: teamca@champion-america.com, Web Site: www.champion-america.com (10)

D

D&B, Parsippany, NJ. Tel: (973) 605-6000, FAX: (973) 605-6920, Web Site: www.dnb.com (22)

D&B Canada, Mississauga, ON Canada. Tel: (800) 463-6362, FAX: (800) 668-7800, Web Site: www.dnb.ca (30)

D&B Sales and Marketing Solutions, Waltham, MA. Tel: (781) 672-9200, (800) 590-0065, FAX: (781) 672-9290, Web Site: www.b2bsalesandmarketing.com (22)

D&D Associates Inc, Garden City, NY. Tel: (516) 326-8800, (800) 554-0347 (22)

D2: Direct, Denville, NJ. Tel: (973) 627-4410, FAX: (973) 627-3703, E-Mail: info@d2direct.com, Web Site: www.d2direct.com (35)

D'Agostino, Chicca, Focus USA Inc, Paramus, NJ. Tel: (201) 489-2525, FAX: (201) 489-4499, E-Mail: info@focus-usa-l.com, Web Site: www.focus-usa-l.com (23)

D'Agostino, Susan, Harris Connect LLC, Chesapeake, VA. Tel: (800) 877-6554, E-Mail: moreinfo@harrisconnect.com, Web Site: www.harrisconnect.com (35)

D'Alessandro, Dominic, John Hancock Financial Services Inc, Boston, MA. Tel: (617) 572-6000, (800) 732-5543, FAX: (617) 572-6451, Web Site: www.johnhancock.com (15)

D'Amelio, Frank, Pfizer Inc, New York, NY. Tel: (212) 733-2323, Web Site: www.pfizer.com (16)

D'Amelio, Mimi, Madison Executive Search, Ridgefield, CT. Tel: (203) 431-6565, FAX: (203) 431-6060, E-Mail: mimi@directexec.com, Web Site: www.directexec.com (20)

D'Angelo, Justin E., Arthur Blank & Co Inc, Boston, MA. Tel: (617) 325-9600, (800) 776-7333, FAX: (617) 327-1235, E-Mail: abco@abco.com, Web Site: www.arthurblank.com (27)

D'Antonio, Angela, Catholic Church Extension Society, Chicago, IL. Tel: (312) 795-5109, (800) 842-7804, FAX: (312) 236-5276, E-Mail: info@catholicextension.org, Web Site: www.catholicextension.org (16)

D'Antonio, Mila, 1to1 Media, Stamford, CT. Tel: (203) 989-2200, Web Site: www.1to1media.com (35)

D'April, Shane, Campaigns & Elections Magazine, Arlington, VA. Tel: (703) 778-4028, (800) 771-8252, FAX: (703) 778-4024, Web Site: www.campaignsandelections.com (17)

D'Auray, Terry, Orion Telescopes & Binoculars, Watsonville, CA. Tel: (831) 763-7000, (800) 447-1001, FAX: (408) 763-7017, E-Mail: sales@telescope.com, Web Site: www.telescope.com (11)

D'Aurizio, Kim, We Deliver America Inc, Englewood Cliffs, NJ. Tel: (201) 307-8888, FAX: (201) 307-1200, E-Mail: info@we-deliver-america.com, Web Site: www.we-deliver-america.com (31)

D'Lando, Matthew, Newsmax List Management, West Palm Beach, FL. Tel: (561) 674-0726, (800) 485-4350, FAX: (561) 494-0922, E-Mail: matthewd@newsmax.com, Web Site: www.newsmax.com/advertise/list-management (24)

D'Micco, Daniel, Nucor Corp, Charlotte, NC. Tel: (704) 366-7000, FAX: (704) 362-4208, E-Mail: info@nucor.com, Web Site: nucor.com (16)

D'Souza, Victor, Polyair Packaging, Chicago, IL. Tel: (773) 995-1818, (888) POLYAIR X444, FAX: (773) 995-7725, E-Mail: marketing@polyair.com, Web Site: www.polyair.com (9)

DAJ Direct Inc, Newport Beach, CA. Tel: (949) 722-0506, FAX: (949) 722-8026, E-Mail: orders@dajdirect.com, Web Site: www.dajdirect.com (24)

DB Alex Brown Inc, Baltimore, MD. Tel: (410) 727-1700, (800) 638-2956, Web Site: www.dbalexbrown.com (14)

DB Consulting, Harrison, NY. Tel: (914) 698-2008, E-Mail: darcybev@yahoo.com (20)

DBM Group Inc, Irvine, CA. Tel: (714) 727-0825, FAX: (714) 838-0327, E-Mail: sales@dbmgroup.com, Web Site: www.dbmgroup.com (35)

DBMCatalyst, Holliston, MA. Tel: (339) 227-7591 (20)

DCA, West Chester, PA. Tel: (610) 344-7488, (800) 638-6684, FAX: (610) 431-6500, E-Mail: ortho@dentalcorp.com, Web Site: www.dentalcorp.com (16)

DCI-Artform, Milwaukee, WI. Tel: (414) 228-7000, Web Site: www.dci-artform.com (35)

DCJ Consulting, Forest Hills, NY. Tel: (718) 575-8357 (20)

DDB Canada, Vancouver, BC Canada. Tel: (604) 687-7911, FAX: (604) 640-4343, E-Mail: vancouver.info@ddbcanada.com, Web Site: www.ddbcanada.com (35)

DDB North America, New York, NY. Tel: (212) 415-2000, FAX: (212) 415-3550, Web Site: ddbnorthamerica.com (35)

DDB Stock Photography LLC, Baton Rouge, LA. Tel: (225) 763-6235, FAX: (225) 763-6894, E-Mail: info@ddbstock.com, Web Site: www.ddbstock.com (38)

DFS Group Limited, San Francisco, CA. Tel: (415) 977-2700, FAX: (415) 977-2970, Web Site: www.dfsgalleria.com (5)

D/FW Grocers Association, Carrollton, TX. Tel: (972) 353-5885, FAX: (469) 574-5252, Web Site: www.dfwga.net (1)

dgs Marketing Engineers, Fishers, IN. Tel: (317) 813-2222, FAX: (317) 813-2233, E-Mail: info@dgsmarketingengineers.com, Web Site: www.dgsmarketingengineers.com (35)

DHL Express, Plantation, FL. Tel: (954) 888-7000, (800) 225-5345, FAX: (954) 888-7310, Web Site: www.dhl.com (28)

DHL Global Mail, Weston, FL. Tel: (954) 903-6300, (866) 616-MAIL, FAX: (954) 903-6310, E-Mail: contact@dhlglobalmail.com, Web Site: www.dhlglobalmail.com (28)

DIA - Nielsen USA Inc, Moorestown, NJ. Tel: (856) 642-9700, (800) 893-6361, FAX: (856) 642-9709, Web Site: www.dianielsen.com (16)

DKP & Associates, Inc, Skokie, IL. Tel: (847) 933-9808, FAX: (847) 933-9821, E-Mail: dpearlman@dkpassociates.com, Web Site: www.dkpassociates.com (22)

D'Lights, South El Monte, CA. Tel: (626) 246-1094, (800) 414-5109, FAX: (626) 433-0267, E-Mail: lizzy@spjlighting.com, Web Site: www.dlights.com (8)

DM Assistance Inc, Portsmouth, NH. Tel: (603) 964-6156 (20)

DM Data Solutions LLC, Alexandria, VA. Tel: (703) 415-6222, Web Site: www.dmdatasolutions.com (22)

DM Info, Naperville, IL. Tel: (630) 357-0732, FAX: (630) 527-8136, E-Mail: dminfo@dmcsweeney.com (20)

DM News, New York, NY. Tel: (646) 638-6000, (800) 558-1703, FAX: (212) 925-8752, E-Mail: dmnewssubs@haymarketmedia.com, Web Site: www.dmnews.com (43)

DMA Annual Marketing Conference, New York, NY. Tel: (212) 768-7277, Web Site: thedma.org (42)

DMA Events-Conference Programming/Exhibitors/Speakers, New York, NY. Tel: (212) 768-7277, E-Mail: info@thedma.org, Web Site: thedma.org (41)

DMA Statistical Fact Book, New York, NY. Tel: (212) 768-7277, Web Site: thedma.org (43)

DMB Financial, Beverly, MA. Tel: (866) 810-3210, FAX: (978) 338-2347, E-Mail: help@dmbfinancial.com, Web Site: www.dmbfinancial.com (14)

DMB Realty Network, Scottsdale, AZ. Tel: (480) 515-0148, Web Site: www.dmbrealty.com (16)

DMC Corp, Kearny, NJ. Tel: (973) 589-0606, (800) 275-4117, FAX: (973) 589-8931, Web Site: www.dmc-usa.com (16)

DMG Direct Inc, Tigard, OR. Tel: (503) 579-5609, (888) 282-2122, FAX: (503) 579-4919, E-Mail: dmg@dirmarketing.com, Web Site: www.dirmarketing.com/dmginc (40)

dmh Marketing Partners - Louisville, Louisville, KY. Tel: (502) 339-6442, E-Mail: data@dmhmarketingpartners.com, Web Site: www.dmhmarketingpartners.com (28)

DMN3, Houston, TX. Tel: (713) 893-4275, (888) 721-0377, E-Mail: sales@dmn3.com, Web Site: www.dmn3.com (35)

DMRA, Mountain View, CA. Tel: (650) 559-9988, FAX: (650) 559-0149, E-Mail: mikeg@dmrainc. com, Web Site: www.dmrainc.com (22)

DMRA & Matchkey Corp, Mountain View, CA. Tel: (650) 856-9988, FAX: (650) 856-9986 (30)

DMRS Group Inc, New York, NY. Tel: (212) 590-2340, FAX: (212) 590-2341, E-Mail: bgrossman@ dmrsgroup.com, Web Site: www.dmrsgroup.com (22)

DMS Insights, Dallas, TX. Tel: (800) 409-6262, FAX: (214) 222-6103, E-Mail: info@dmsinsights.com, Web Site: www.dmsdallas.com (30)

DMS Marketing Inc, Mission Viejo, CA. Tel: (888) 794-1777, E-Mail: inquiries@dms-marketing.com, Web Site: www.dms-marketing.com (35)

DMSA Inc, Newfoundland, PA. Tel: (570) 676-6000 (40)

DMW Worldwide LLC, Chesterbrook, PA. Tel: (610) 407-0407, (877) 744-3699, FAX: (610) 407-9201, E-Mail: info@dmwdirect.com, Web Site: www. dmwdirect.com (35)

DNI Corp, Nashville, TN. Tel: (615) 313-7000, Web Site: www.dnicorp.com (21)

DNP America Inc, New York, NY. Tel: (212) 503-1060, FAX: (212) 679-0613 (27)

DPC Computers, Monsey, NY. Tel: (845) 426-3790, (866) 513-CORP, FAX: (845) 426-6275, E-Mail: learnmore@salestax.com, Web Site: www.salestax. com (16)

Dr Ho's, Greensboro, GA. Tel: (905) 471-4735, (877) 374-6669, FAX: (877) 836-7466, Web Site: www. drhonow.com (7)

DRG, Berne, IN. Tel: (260) 589-4000, FAX: (260) 589-8093, Web Site: www.drgnetwork.com (17)

DS Graphics Inc, Lowell, MA. Tel: (978) 970-1359, E-Mail: sales@dsgraphics.com, Web Site: www. dsgraphics.com (21)

DS Services of North America LP, Lakeland, FL. Tel: (770) 933-1400, (800) 669-3402, FAX: (770) 956-9495, E-Mail: customerservice@water.com, Web Site: www.water.com (4)

DSP Inc USA, Charlottesville, VA. Tel: (434) 202-7870, E-Mail: iorder@delfortgroup.com, Web Site: www.delfortgroup.com (10)

DST Output, South Windsor, CT. Tel: (860) 290-7337, (800) 441-7587, Web Site: www.dstoutput.com (28)

DWS Associates, Saint Paul, MN. Tel: (602) 321-6512, Web Site: www.dwstevenson.com (20)

DWS Investments Service Co, Kansas City, MO. Tel: (800) 543-5776, Web Site: www.dws-investments. com (14)

DXP Postexperts, Saint-Laurent, QC Canada. Tel: (514) 934-4545, E-Mail: info@dxp-postexperts.com, Web Site: www.postdestination.com (28)

D, Elliot, Environmental Law Institute, Washington, DC. Tel: (202) 939-3800, FAX: (202) 939-3868, E-Mail: law@eli.org, Web Site: www.eli.org (17)

Da Costa, Debra, Direct Marketing Partners, Sacramento, CA. Tel: (916) 974-6969, (800) 909-2626, FAX: (916) 920-5156, E-Mail: info@dirmkt.com, Web Site: www.directmarketingpartners.com (29)

Da Costa, Debra I., United Nations Federal Credit Union, Long Island City, NY. Tel: (347) 686-6000, E-Mail: email@unfcu.org, Web Site: www.unfcu. org (1)

Da-Lite Screen Co Inc, Warsaw, IN. Tel: (574) 267-8101, (800) 622-3737, FAX: (574) 267-7804, E-Mail: info@da-lite.com, Web Site: www.da-lite. com (16)

Da Silva, Dilip, New Wave Media Inc, Emeryville, CA. Tel: (510) 250-5500, FAX: (510) 250-5700, Web Site: www.exponential.com (5)

Dabbs, Dale, Custom Direct, Colorado Springs, CO. Tel: (410) 679-3300 (16)

Dabbs, Karl, Tidbits Media, Montgomery, AL. Tel: (334) 290-0225, (800) 523-3096, FAX: (334) 386-0302, E-Mail: editors@tidbitsweekly.com, Web Site: www.tidbitsweekly.com (17)

Dabkowski, Laura, American Bible Society, New York, NY. Tel: (212) 408-1200, FAX: (212) 408-1264, Web Site: www.americanbible.org (1)

Dabrowski, Richard C., Shaker Workshops, Ashburnham, MA. Tel: (978) 827-9900, (800) 849-9121, FAX: (978) 827-6554, E-Mail: shakerworkshops. customerservice@gmail.com, Web Site: www. shakerworkshops.com (8)

Dabrowski, Richard, Cohasset Colonials, Ashburnham, MA. Tel: (978) 827-3001, (800) 288-2389, FAX: (978) 827-3227, E-Mail: cohassetcolonials. custservice@gmail.com, Web Site: www. cohassetcolonials.com (8)

Dachowski, Peter, CertainTeed Corp, Valley Forge, PA. Tel: (610) 341-7000/7739, (800) 233-8990, FAX: (610) 341-7777, Web Site: www.certainteed.com (16)

DaCruz, Leslie, USC Viterbi School of Engineering, Los Angeles, CA. Tel: (213) 740-7832, Web Site: viterbi.usc.edu (1)

Dada, Joe, Smarthome/INSTEON, Irvine, CA. Tel: (949) 221-0037, (800) 762-7846, FAX: (949) 221-9240, E-Mail: feedback@smarthome.com, Web Site: www.smarthome.com (32)

Dadarria, Robert, RAD Marketing, Mount Vernon, NY. Tel: (914) 668-3563, FAX: (914) 668-4247, E-Mail: cabletowns@verizon.net (24)

Daedalus Books Inc, Columbia, MD. Tel: (410) 309-2706, (800) 944-8879, E-Mail: custserv@ daedalusbooks.com, Web Site: www.salebooks.com (5)

Dael, Rima, Country Dance and Song Society, East-hampton, MA. Tel: (413) 203-5467, FAX: (413) 203-5471, E-Mail: office@cdss.org, Web Site: www.cdss.org (1)

Dagestad, Mark, Schnuck Markets Inc, Saint Louis, MO. Tel: (314) 994-9900, FAX: (314) 994-4465, Web Site: www.schnucks.com (16)

Dahart, Denise, Ariago Design and Communications, Campbell, CA. Tel: (408) 668-0400, FAX: (408) 688-0401, E-Mail: ddahart@ariago.com, Web Site: www.ariago.com (3)

Daher, Gerard, Speedeon Data Corp, Cleveland, OH. Tel: (866) 647-9219, Web Site: www.speedeondata. com (30)

Daher, Tonya, School Annual Publishing Co, State College, PA. Tel: (800) 436-6030, E-Mail: yearbook@ schoolannual.com, Web Site: www.schoolannual. com (17)

Dahl, Roy, Crescent Beach Productions, Bohemia, NY. Tel: (631) 588-6600, (888) 401-7700, FAX: (631) 918-5044, E-Mail: info@cbprod.com, Web Site: www.cbprod.com (32)

Dahlberg, Peter, American Health & Life Insurance Co, Fort Worth, TX. Tel: (817) 348-7500, (800) 995-2274, FAX: (817) 348-7553, Web Site: www. citifinancial.com (15)

Dahlgren, Kent, Victor Envelope Co, Bensenville, IL. Tel: (630) 616-2750, Web Site: www. victorenvelope.com (26)

Dahlquist, John, Aurora Marketing Inc, Princeton, NJ. Tel: (609) 520-8863, FAX: (908) 359-1108, E-Mail: aurora2@voicenet.com, Web Site: www. auroramarketing.net (30)

Dahltorp, Jeff, Fifth Gear LLC, Indianapolis, IN. Tel: (317) 631-0907, FAX: (317) 631-6585, Web Site: www.infifthgear.com (22)

Daigle, John, Overton's Inc, Greenville, NC. Tel: (252) 355-5783, (800) 334-6541, FAX: (252) 355-2923, E-Mail: service@overtons.com, Web Site: www. overtons.com (11)

Daigle, Luke, Underline Communications LLC, New York, NY. Tel: (212) 994-4340, FAX: (212) 686-8234, E-Mail: inquiries@underline.com, Web Site: www.underlinecom.com (35)

Dailey, Marc, The Columbian, Vancouver, WA. Tel: (360) 694-3391, FAX: (360) 735-4503, Web Site: www.columbian.com (17)

Daily Commercial News & Construction Record, Markham, ON Canada. Tel: (905) 752-5408, (800) 465-6475, FAX: (905) 752-5450, (888) 396-9413, E-Mail: dcnonl@reedbusiness.com, Web Site: www. dcnonl.com (17)

Daily Record & Dispatch Co, Dunn, NC. Tel: (910) 891-1234, FAX: (910) 891-5253, Web Site: www. mydailyrecord.com (17)

DaimlerChrysler Corp, Auburn Hills, MI. Tel: (248) 512-1879, Web Site: www.daimlerchrysler.com (12)

Daines, Gina, Basic Research, Salt Lake City, UT. Tel: (801) 530-2911, (888) 865-5326, E-Mail: customerservice@basicresearch.com, Web Site: www.silversage.com (7)

Dairy Council of California, Irvine, CA. Tel: (949) 756-7892, Web Site: www.dairycouncilofca.org (1)

Dairy Farmers of America Inc, Kansas City, MO. Tel: (816) 801-6455, (888) 332-6455, FAX: (816) 801-6456, E-Mail: webmail@dfamilk.com, Web Site: www.dfamilk.com (16)

Dairy Management Inc, Rosemont, IL. Tel: (847) 803-2000, FAX: (847) 803-2077, Web Site: www. nationaldairycouncil.org (1)

Dakin Farm, Ferrisburgh, VT. Tel: (802) 425-3971, (800) 993-2546, FAX: (802) 425-2765, E-Mail: scutting@dakinfarm.com, Web Site: www. dakinfarm.com (4)

Dakota Digital, Sioux Falls, SD. Tel: (605) 332-6513, (800) 593-4160, FAX: (605) 339-4106, E-Mail: sales@dakotadigital.com, Web Site: www. dakotadigital.com (12)

Dalco Electronics, Springboro, OH. Tel: (937) 743-8042, (800) 445-5342, FAX: (937) 743-9251, Web Site: www.dalco.com (3)

Dale, Chris, MWM Dexter Inc, Aurora, MO. Tel: (417) 841-1040, (888) 833-1242, FAX: (417) 841-1025, Web Site: www.mwmdexter.com (27)

Dale, Randy, Anderson Direct & Digital, Poway, CA. Tel: (888) 694-5094, Web Site: www.andersondd. com (35)

Daley, Anthony, Westcon, Tarrytown, NY. Tel: (914) 829-7000, FAX: (914) 829-7137, Web Site: www. westcon.com (16)

Daley, Dorian E., Eloqua Inc, Vienna, VA. Tel: (703) 584-2750, Web Site: www.eloqua.com (22)

Daley, Kevin, Communispond Inc, East Hampton, NY. Tel: (631) 907-8010, (800) 529-5925, FAX: (631) 907-8011, Web Site: www.communispond.com (20)

Daley, Mark, Dean & Deluca Brands Inc, Wichita, KS. Tel: (316) 683-1255, Web Site: www.deandeluca. com (4)

Dallas Midwest, Dallas, TX. Tel: (800) 527-2417, FAX: (800) 301-8314, Web Site: www.dallasmidwest.com (33)

Dalrada Financial Corp, San Diego, CA. Tel: (858) 791-6200, (877) 325-7232, FAX: (858) 277-3448, E-Mail: inquiries@dalrada.com, Web Site: www. dalrada.com (14)

Dalton, James F., Tektronix Inc, Beaverton, OR. Tel: (503) 627-7111, (800) 833-9200, FAX: (503) 627-3247, Web Site: www.tektronix.com (16)

Dalton, John, LeadFlash, Boca Raton, FL. Tel: (561) 997-5759, Web Site: www.leadflash.com (14)

Dalton, William, The Bender Group, Reno, NV. Tel: (775) 788-8800, (800) 621-9402, FAX: (775) 788-8811, E-Mail: salesinfo@benderwhs.com, Web Site: www.bendergroup.com (28)

Daly Communications, Chevy Chase, MD. Tel: (301) 951-9110, E-Mail: speaker@johnjaydaly.com, Web Site: www.johnjaydaly.com (20)

Daly Direct Marketing, Potomac, MD. Tel: (301) 365-3201, FAX: (301) 365-7514 (39)

Daly, Carl, Front Porch Inc, Sonora, CA. Tel: (209) 288-5500, (800) 728-1464, Web Site: www.frontporch.com (35)

Daly, Erin, New England Direct Marketing Association, Wellesley Hills, MA. Tel: (781) 237-1366, FAX: (781) 431-8118, E-Mail: info@nedma.com, Web Site: www.nedma.com (40)

Daly, James P., Celtic Life Insurance Co, Chicago, IL. Tel: (312) 332-5401, FAX: (312) 441-0341, E-Mail: info@celtic-net.com, Web Site: www.celtic-net.com (15)

Daly, John Jay, Daly Communications, Chevy Chase, MD. Tel: (301) 951-9110, E-Mail: speaker@johnjaydaly.com, Web Site: www.johnjaydaly.com (20)

Daly, Joseph P., Comdata Corp, Brentwood, TN. Tel: (615) 370-7000, (800) 266-3282, FAX: (615) 370-7614, Web Site: www.comdata.com (14)

Daly, M. Virginia, Daly Direct Marketing, Potomac, MD. Tel: (301) 365-3201, FAX: (301) 365-7514 (39)

Daly, Michael L., Carefirst Blue Cross Blue Shield, Washington, DC. Tel: (202) 479-8000, FAX: (301) 470-8049, Web Site: www.carefirst.com (15)

Daly, Peter, US Naval Institute, Annapolis, MD. Tel: (410) 268-6110, (800) 233-8764, FAX: (410) 571-1703, E-Mail: customer@usni.org, Web Site: www.usni.org (38)

Daly, Robert C., Toyota Motor Sales USA Inc, Torrance, CA. Tel: (310) 468-4000, (800) 331-4331, FAX: (310) 468-7841, Web Site: www.toyota.com (16)

Daly, Scott, Fisher Scientific, Pittsburgh, PA. Tel: (800) 766-7000, FAX: (800) 772-7702, Web Site: www.fishersci.com (16)

Daly, Tim, Texwipe Co, Kernersville, NC. Tel: (201) 684-1800, (800) TEXWIPE, FAX: (201) 684-1801, E-Mail: info@texwipe.com, Web Site: www.texwipe.com (16)

Chet Dalzell, New York, NY. Tel: (212) 725-2294 (20)

Damerow, Steve, Loyaltyworks Inc, Atlanta, GA. Tel: (678) 539-5000, (800) 844-5000, FAX: (678) 539-5173, Web Site: www.loyaltyworks.com (21)

Damiano, Paula, National Association for Female Executives, New York, NY. Tel: (800) 927-6233, E-Mail: info@nafe.com, Web Site: www.nafe.com (1)

Damilic Corp, Rockville, MD. Tel: (301) 251-2960, (800) 276-7749, FAX: (301) 251-8591, E-Mail: info@realsig.com, Web Site: www.realsig.com (16)

Daminato, Liliana, British Columbia Automobile Association, Burnaby, BC Canada. Tel: (604) 268-5000, (800) 564-6222, FAX: (604) 268-5585, Web Site: www.bcaa.com (15)

Damioli, Jack, Broadmoor Hotel Inc, Colorado Springs, CO. Tel: (719) 623-5112, (866) 837-9520, FAX: (719) 577-5738, Web Site: www.broadmoor.com (19)

Damman, Steve, QuantumDigital, Austin, TX. Tel: (800) 637-7373, Web Site: www.quantumdigital.com (28)

Dammann, Peter, 48HourPrint.com, Boston, MA. Tel: (800) 844-0599, Web Site: www.48hourprint.com (27)

Dan Smolen Direct Search LLC, Stafford, VA. Tel: (703) 835-9900, FAX: (703) 835-9966, E-Mail: dsmolen@dansmolen.com, Web Site: www.dansmolen.com (20)

Dana-Farber Cancer Institute, Boston, MA. Tel: (617) 632-3000, (866) 408-3324, FAX: (617) 632-4070, E-Mail: suzanne_fountain@dfci.harvard.edu, Web Site: www.dana-farber.org (1)

Dandrea, Michael, 1to1 Media, Stamford, CT. Tel: (203) 989-2200, Web Site: www.1to1media.com (35)

Danenhauer, Greg, Parker Boiler Co, Los Angeles, CA. Tel: (323) 727-9800, FAX: (323) 722-2848, E-Mail: mleeming@parkerboiler.com, Web Site: www.parkerboiler.com (34)

Danenhauer, Sid D., Parker Boiler Co, Los Angeles, CA. Tel: (323) 727-9800, FAX: (323) 722-2848, E-Mail: mleeming@parkerboiler.com, Web Site: www.parkerboiler.com (34)

Dang, Margaret, Bank of Hawaii, Honolulu, HI. Tel: (808) 537-8398, FAX: (808) 536-9433, Web Site: www.boh.com (14)

Daniel Gonzalez & Associates, New York, NY. Tel: (212) 682-0333 (20)

Daniel, Chris, Golden Trophy, Chicago, IL. Tel: (773) 282-2900, (800) 821-3882, FAX: (800) 835-6601, E-Mail: goldentrophy@bruss.com, Web Site: www.giftsteaksonline.com (4)

Daniel, David S, SpencerStuart, Chicago, IL. Tel: (312) 822-0088, FAX: (312) 822-0116, Web Site: www.spencerstuart.com (20)

Daniel, Sandra, Fire Light Group, Madison, WI. Tel: (608) 441-3473, E-Mail: info@firelightgroup.com, Web Site: firelightgroup.com (33)

Daniels, Dionne, Riverside Acquisition Group LLC, Moorestown, NJ. Tel: (856) 802-1900, Web Site: www.com-pak.com (28)

Daniels, Jeremy L., Cornhusker Press, Hastings, NE. Tel: (402) 462-4141, FAX: (402) 460-4612, E-Mail: dlsales@dutton-lainson.com, Web Site: www.dutton-lainson.com (17)

Daniels, Richard J., The Hartford Courant, Hartford, CT. Tel: (860) 241-6200, FAX: (860) 293-0178, Web Site: www.courant.com (31)

Daniels, Ronald J., University of Pennsylvania, Philadelphia, PA. Tel: (215) 898-5000, FAX: (215) 898-9659, Web Site: www.upenn.edu (1)

Daniels, Sharon, Achieve Global, Tampa, FL. Tel: (813) 631-5500, (800) 566-0630, FAX: (813) 631-5796, Web Site: www.achieveglobal.com (16)

Daniels, Terri, CCA Global Partners, Manchester, NH. Tel: (603) 626-0333, Web Site: www.ccaglobal.com (16)

Danielson, R., Amerikal Products, Waukegan, IL. Tel: (847) 244-3600, FAX: (847) 244-2860, E-Mail: info@amerikal.com, Web Site: www.amerikal.com (25)

Danker Laboratories Inc, Sarasota, FL. Tel: (800) 237-9641, FAX: (800) 665-5086, E-Mail: sales@dankerlabs.com, Web Site: www.dankerlabs.com (16)

Danker, Frederick, Danker Laboratories Inc, Sarasota, FL. Tel: (800) 237-9641, FAX: (800) 665-5086, E-Mail: sales@dankerlabs.com, Web Site: www.dankerlabs.com (16)

Dansk, Bristol, PA. Tel: (914) 697-6400, (800) 326-7528, FAX: (914) 697-6464, Web Site: www.dansk.com (16)

Dante University Press, Wellesley, MA. Tel: (781) 790-1059, FAX: (781) 790-1056, E-Mail: dante@danteuniversity.org, Web Site: www.danteuniversity.org (17)

Danziger, B., Brim Electronics Inc, Lodi, NJ. Tel: (201) 796-2886, FAX: (973) 778-2792, E-Mail: info@brimelectronics.com, Web Site: www.brimelectronics.com (3)

Danziger, Robin, Educational Coin Co, Highland, NY. Tel: (845) 691-6100, Web Site: www.educationalcoin.com (16)

Dapper, Steve, hawkeye, Dallas, TX. Tel: (214) 749-0080, E-Mail: sdapper@hawkeyeww.com, Web Site: www.hawkeyeww.com (35)

Daprile, Joseph, Premier Farnell Corp, Richfield, OH. Tel: (216) 525-4300, (800) 458-3222, FAX: (216) 525-4509, E-Mail: information@premierfarnell.com, Web Site: www.premierfarnell.com (16)

Darbelnet, Robert L., American Automobile Association, Heathrow, FL. Tel: (407) 444-8000, Web Site: www.aaa.com (16)

Darby, Christian, Ronco Corp, Austin, TX. Tel: (800) 486-1806, E-Mail: customerservice@ronco.com, Web Site: www.ronco.com (16)

Darby, Kristen, Marketing Research Association, Washington, DC. Tel: (860) 682-1000, (202) 800-2545, FAX: (860) 682-1010, (888) 512-1050, E-Mail: membership@marketingresearch.org, Web Site: www.mra-net.org (40)

Darby, Warren, Atlantic Publication Group LLC, Charleston, SC. Tel: (843) 747-0025, FAX: (843) 744-0816, E-Mail: info@atlanticpublicationgrp.com, Web Site: www.atlanticpublicationgrp.com (17)

Darco International Inc, Huntington, WV. Tel: (304) 522-4883, (800) 999-8866, FAX: (304) 522-0037, Web Site: www.darcointernational.com (9)

Darden School Foundation Executive Foundation, Charlottesville, VA. Tel: (434) 924-3900, Web Site: www.darden.virginia.edu/execed (1)

Dardes, Beth, MarketForce Corp, Havertown, PA. Tel: (610) 356-5220, FAX: (610) 356-5110, E-Mail: davethomas@marketforcecorp.com, Web Site: www.marketforcecorp.com (23)

Dargery, Joan S., The Conference Board Inc, New York, NY. Tel: (212) 759-0900, FAX: (212) 980-7014, Web Site: www.conference-board.org (16)

Darland, Terry, Christian Dior Perfumes, New York, NY. Tel: (877) 903-4671, (800) 929-3467, FAX: (212) 931-2954, Web Site: www.dior.com (7)

Darling, Stephen, Datamark Inc, El Paso, TX. Tel: (800) 477-1944, E-Mail: info@datamark.net, Web Site: www.datamark.net (35)

Darooge, Bill, Baudville Inc, Grand Rapids, MI. Tel: (616) 698-0889, (800) 728-0888, FAX: (616) 698-0554, E-Mail: service@baudville.com, Web Site: www.baudville.com (16)

Darr, Anne, DeHart & Darr Associates, McLean, VA. Tel: (703) 448-1000, FAX: (703) 790-3460 (20)

Darr, Lynette, Olan Mills Inc, Chattanooga, TN. Tel: (423) 622-5141, (800) 251-6320, FAX: (423) 629-8128, Web Site: www.olanmills.com (16)

Darrah, Jason, GuideOne Insurance, West Des Moines, IA. Tel: (877) 448-4331, Web Site: www.guideone.com (15)

Dartmouth-Hitchcock, Lebanon, NH. Tel: (603) 650-5000, Web Site: www.dmsnet.org (1)

The Dartnell Corp, Naples, FL. Tel: (585) 240-7301, (800) 447-4030, FAX: (585) 292-4392, E-Mail: customerservice@dartnellcorp.com, Web Site: www.dartnellcorp.com (17)

Darwill, Hillside, IL. Tel: (708) 236-4900, FAX: (708) 236-5820, Web Site: www.darwill.com (27)

Dassault Falcon Jet Corp, Little Ferry, NJ. Tel: (201) 440-6700, FAX: (201) 541-4515, Web Site: www.dassaultfalcon.com (16)

Data Analytics Corp, Plainsboro, NJ. Tel: (609) 936-8999, Web Site: www.dataanalyticscorp.com (30)

The Data Base Inc, Oakhurst, NJ. Tel: (732) 531-4600, FAX: (732) 531-4798, E-Mail: don.nissim@heritagedirectdm.com, Web Site: www.heritagedirectdm.com (22)

Data Communications Management Corp, Brampton, ON Canada. Tel: (905) 791-3151, (800) 268-0128, FAX: (905) 791-3277, E-Mail: info@datacm.com, Web Site: www.datacm.com (21)

Data Dallas Corp, Dallas, TX. Tel: (214) 638-2007, Web Site: www.datadallas.com (22)

Data Dash Inc, Saint Louis, MO. Tel: (314) 832-5788, (800) 211-5988, FAX: (314) 832-5775, E-Mail: info@datadash.com, Web Site: www.datadash.com (22)

Data Direct Group Inc, Mississauga, ON Canada. Tel: (905) 564-0150, FAX: (905) 564-7246, E-Mail: info@datadirect.ca, Web Site: datadirect.ca (21)

Data Direct Networks, Chatsworth, CA. Tel: (818) 700-7607, (800) 837-2298, FAX: (818) 700-7601, E-Mail: info@ddn.com, Web Site: www.datadirectnet.com (3)

Data.com, San Francisco, CA. Tel: (415) 901-7000, (800) 667-6389, Web Site: www.data.com (24)

Data-Dynamix Inc, Denver, CO. Tel: (720) 855-9282, (888) 314-0078, FAX: (720) 855-9099, E-Mail: sales@data-dynamix.com, Web Site: www.data-dynamix.com (23)

The Data Group, Orlando, FL. Tel: (800) 262-5609, E-Mail: questions@thedatagroup.com, Web Site: thedatagroup.com (23)

Data Intelligence Group, Franklin, TN. Tel: (615) 861-3301, Web Site: www.wedigdata.com (22)

Data-Mail Inc, Newington, CT. Tel: (860) 666-0399, FAX: (860) 665-1226, E-Mail: aliceh@data-mail.com, Web Site: www.data-mail.com (28)

Data Management & Marketing Services LLC, Broken Arrow, OK. Tel: (918) 994-7272, Web Site: www.dm-ms.net (22)

Data Management Inc, Mc Lean, VA. Tel: (703) 893-5627, (800) 334-8331, FAX: (703) 356-1698, E-Mail: info@data-management.com, Web Site: www.data-management.com (22)

Data Partners Inc, Fort Myers, FL. Tel: (239) 267-8762, (866) 423-1818, FAX: (239) 267-9043, E-Mail: info@data-partners.com, Web Site: datapartners.com (22)

Data Services Inc, Salisbury, MD. Tel: (410) 546-2206, (800) 432-4066, FAX: (410) 546-2274, Web Site: www.dataservicesinc.com (22)

Data Square LLC, Stamford, CT. Tel: (203) 964-9733, FAX: (203) 964-0783, E-Mail: info@datasquare.com, Web Site: www.datasquare.com (22)

Data Translation Inc, Marlborough, MA. Tel: (508) 481-3700, (800) 525-8528, FAX: (508) 481-8620, E-Mail: info@datatranslation.com, Web Site: www.datatranslation.com (34)

Data University, Lincoln, NE. Tel: (402) 742-2179, (866) 328-2848, E-Mail: info@datauniversity.com, Web Site: www.datauniversity.org (22)

Database Marketing Services, Guaynabo, PR. Tel: (787) 792-7005 (22)

Databazaar.com, Miramar, FL. Tel: (954) 843-0483, (888) 335-3282, FAX: (954) 843-0429, E-Mail: rudy@databazaar.com, Web Site: www.databazaar.com (10)

DataBridge Marketing Systems Corp, Montvale, NJ. Tel: (201) 690-6319, Web Site: www.databridgemarketing.com (22)

DataCal Enterprises, Gilbert, AZ. Tel: (480) 813-3100, (800) 223-0123, FAX: (480) 545-8090, E-Mail: info@datacal.com, Web Site: www.datacal.com (16)

Datacard Ga-Vehren Corp, Minnetonka, MN. Tel: (952) 933-1223, (800) 621-6972 x6930, FAX: (952) 931-0418, E-Mail: info@datacard.com, Web Site: www.gavehren.com (34)

DataCentral Inc, Kennesaw, GA. Tel: (770) 218-8200, (800) 411-5771, FAX: (770) 218-8211, E-Mail: info@datacentralinc.com, Web Site: www.datacentralinc.com (24)

DataCraft Inc, Kailua, HI. Tel: (808) 263-5583, FAX: (808) 262-4101, E-Mail: akamaidatasolutions@dcraftinc.com, Web Site: www.akamaidatasolutions.com (22)

DataDirect, Atlanta, GA. Tel: (678) 530-0034, FAX: (678) 530-9563, E-Mail: info@ddirect.com, Web Site: www.ddirect.com (40)

Datahouse Inc, Colorado Springs, CO. Tel: (866) 640-3282, E-Mail: data@datahouseinc.com, Web Site: www.datahouseinc.com (23)

DataLab USA, Germantown, MD. Tel: (301) 972-1430, (800) 972-1430, E-Mail: information@datalabusa.com, Web Site: datalabusa.com (21)

DataLever Corp, Boulder, CO. Tel: (303) 541-1515, Web Site: www.datalever.com (16)

Dataline Inc, Princeton, NJ. Tel: (609) 452-6014, FAX: (609) 951-0025, E-Mail: psobel@datalinedata.com, Web Site: datalinedata.com (23)

Datalogic Scanning, Eugene, OR. Tel: (800) 695-5700, FAX: (541) 345-7140, Web Site: www.scanning.datalogic.com (34)

Datamann Inc, Wilder, VT. Tel: (802) 295-6600, (800) 451-4263, FAX: (802) 296-3623, Web Site: www.datamann.com (22)

Datamark Inc, El Paso, TX. Tel: (800) 477-1944, E-Mail: info@datamark.net, Web Site: www.datamark.net (35)

Datamart Direct Inc, Bloomingdale, IL. Tel: (630) 307-7100, FAX: (630) 307-8059, E-Mail: info@datamartdirect.com, Web Site: www.datamartdirect.com (27)

Datamatics Technologies, Burlington, MA. Tel: (781) 425-5240, FAX: (781) 425-5232, Web Site: www.datamaticstech.com (22)

Datamatx Inc, Ashland, VA. Tel: (804) 365-1000, (800) 943-5240, FAX: (804) 550-2527, E-Mail: info@datamatx.com, Web Site: www.datamatx.com (27)

Datapoint USA Inc, San Antonio, TX. Tel: (210) 614-9977, FAX: (210) 614-2297, E-Mail: info@datapointusa.com, Web Site: www.datapointusa.com (16)

Dataprint Corp, San Mateo, CA. Tel: (650) 340-0550, (800) 227-6191, FAX: (650) 340-7028, Web Site: www.dataprint.com (34)

Datasystem Solutions Inc, Overland Park, KS. Tel: (913) 362-6969, FAX: (913) 362-6383, E-Mail: sales@mutipub.com, Web Site: www.datasystem.com (22)

Datavs, Sue, Prime Graphics Inc, Wood Dale, IL. Tel: (630) 227-1300, FAX: (630) 227-1823, E-Mail: moreinfo@primegraphicsinc.com, Web Site: primegraphicsinc.com (27)

Datillo, Michael, Water's Edge Resort & Spa, Westbrook, CT. Tel: (860) 399-5901, (800) 222-5901, FAX: (860) 399-8644, Web Site: www.watersedgeresort.com (19)

Datillo, Tina, Water's Edge Resort & Spa, Westbrook, CT. Tel: (860) 399-5901, (800) 222-5901, FAX: (860) 399-8644, Web Site: www.watersedgeresort.com (19)

Datran Media, New York, NY. Tel: (212) 706-9781, FAX: (212) 706-9758, Web Site: www.datranmedia.com (22)

Datt, Raj, Kennametal Inc, Latrobe, PA. Tel: (800) 222-9327, FAX: (800) 521-3319, E-Mail: mcs-na.service@kennmetal.com, Web Site: www.kennametal.com (16)

Datum Timing, Test & Measurement, Beverly, MA. Tel: (978) 927-8220, FAX: (978) 927-4099, E-Mail: wriley@datum.com, Web Site: www.datum.com (9)

David Dauber & Associates, New York, NY. Tel: (212) 564-1728, FAX: (212) 208-4524, E-Mail: advancedbc@aol.com (16)

Dauber, David, David Dauber & Associates, New York, NY. Tel: (212) 564-1728, FAX: (212) 208-4524, E-Mail: advancedbc@aol.com (16)

Daugherty, Carol, Our Designs Inc, Vancouver, WA. Tel: (859) 282-5500, (800) 382-5252, FAX: (859) 282-5508, E-Mail: sales@ourdesigns.com, Web Site: www.ourdesigns.com (16)

Daugherty, Mike, Our Designs Inc, Vancouver, WA. Tel: (859) 282-5500, (800) 382-5252, FAX: (859) 282-5508, E-Mail: sales@ourdesigns.com, Web Site: www.ourdesigns.com (16)

Dauman, Philippe, Viacom Inc, New York, NY. Tel: (212) 258-6000, FAX: (212) 258-6464, Web Site: www.viacom.com (16)

Dauman, Philippe, Viacom Media Networks, New York, NY. Tel: (212) 258-6000, Web Site: www.viacom.com (32)

Dave, Shaunak, WSI, Mississauga, ON Canada. Tel: (905) 678-7588, (888) 678-7588, FAX: (905) 678-7242, E-Mail: contact@wsiworld.com, Web Site: www.wsiworld.com (35)

Davenport Austin, Susan, BMI, Nashville, TN. Tel: (615) 401-2000, (800) 925-8451, FAX: (615) 401-2812, E-Mail: nashville@bmi.com, Web Site: www.bmi.com (1)

Davenport, Brandie, Fairytale Brownies, Phoenix, AZ. Tel: (800) 324-7982, FAX: (602) 489-5133, E-Mail: service@brownies.com, Web Site: www.brownies.com (4)

Davenport, Catherine M., BGE Home Products & Services Inc, Baltimore, MD. Tel: (888) 243-4663, Web Site: www.bgehome.com (16)

Dave's Soda & Pet City, Agawam, MA. Tel: (413) 786-3339, Web Site: www.daveratner.com (5)

Davey, Dena, Association of Bridal Consultants, New Milford, CT. Tel: (860) 355-0464, FAX: (860) 354-1404, E-Mail: office@bridalassn.com, Web Site: www.bridalassn.com (1)

David, Christine, LO-AD Communications, Pasadena, CA. Tel: (626) 304-7750, FAX: (626) 304-2716, Web Site: www.lo-ad.com (16)

David, Joe, The Midland Co, Amelia, OH. Tel: (513) 943-7200 (15)

David, Joleen, Skar Advertising, Omaha, NE. Tel: (402) 330-0110, (866) 330-0112, FAX: (402) 330-8791, E-Mail: skar@skar.com, Web Site: skar.com (35)

David, Leonard A., Henry Schein Inc, Melville, NY. Tel: (631) 843-5500, (800) 472-4346, FAX: (631) 843-5658, E-Mail: custserv@henryschein.com, Web Site: www.henryschein.com (16)

David, Mark, IEEE Media, New York, NY. Tel: (800) 261-2052, E-Mail: ieeemedia@ieeeglobalspec.com, Web Site: advertise.ieee.org (24)

Davidoff of Geneva Inc, Pinellas Park, FL. Tel: (727) 828-5400, (800) 328-4365, FAX: (203) 975-0090 (6)

Davidson, Brian, Association of National Advertisers Inc, New York, NY. Tel: (212) 697-5950, FAX: (212) 687-7310, Web Site: www.ana.net (40)

Davidson, Mark, Wrisco Industries Inc, Palm Beach Gardens, FL. Tel: (561) 626-5700, (800) 627-2646, FAX: (561) 627-3574, Web Site: www.wrisco.com (8)

Davidson, Michael C., State Farm Insurance Cos, Bloomington, IL. Tel: (309) 766-2311, FAX: (309) 766-3621, Web Site: www.statefarm.com (15)

Davidson, Shelley, Ten Speed Press, Emeryville, CA. Tel: (510) 559-1600, (800) 841-BOOK, FAX: (510) 559-1629, E-Mail: order@tenspeed.com, Web Site: www.tenspeed.com (17)

Davidson, Terry, International Foundation of Employee Benefit Plans, Brookfield, WI. Tel: (262) 373-7758, FAX: (262) 786-8670, Web Site: www.ifebp.org (1)

Davies, Bill, Jack Morton Worldwide, New York, NY. Tel: (212) 401-7000, (212) 401-7121, E-Mail: experience@jackmorton.com, Web Site: www.jackmorton.com (35)

Davies, Heath, Alterian, Chicago, IL. Tel: (312) 704-1700, FAX: (312) 704-1701, Web Site: www.alterian.com (22)

Davies, John, ColorEdge, Burbank, CA. Tel: (818) 842-1121, (800) 300-3686, FAX: (818) 842-0280, E-Mail: john.davies@crushcreative.com, Web Site: www.coloredge.com (27)

Davies, Mike, BI, Summit, NJ. Tel: (908) 516-1393, E-Mail: info@biworldwide.com, Web Site: www.biworldwide.com (33)

DaVinci Direct, Plymouth, MA. Tel: (508) 746-2555, FAX: (815) 301-9884, E-Mail: steve@davinci-direct.com, Web Site: www.davinci-direct.com (1)

Davis & Gilbert, New York, NY. Tel: (212) 468-4800, FAX: (212) 468-4888, Web Site: www.dglaw.com (20)

Davis Art Images, Worcester, MA. Tel: (508) 754-7201, (800) 533-2847, FAX: (508) 831-9260, (508) 753-3834, E-Mail: lkeenekendrick@davisart.com, Web Site: www.davisartimages.com (38)

Bert Davis Executive Search, New York, NY. Tel: (212) 838-4000, FAX: (212) 935-3291, E-Mail: info@bertdavis.com, Web Site: www.bertdavis.com (20)

The Davis Center, Succasunna, NJ. Tel: (862) 251-4637, FAX: (862) 251-4642, E-Mail: info@thedaviscenter.com, Web Site: www.thedaviscenter.com (16)

Dick Davis Digest, Salem, MA. Tel: (978) 745-5532, FAX: (978) 745-1283, E-Mail: marketing@dickdavis.com, Web Site: www.dickdavis.com (17)

Davis Instruments Corp, Hayward, CA. Tel: (510) 732-9229, (510) 670-0589, (800) 678-3669, FAX: (510) 732-9188, E-Mail: info@davisnet.com, Web Site: www.davisnet.com (8)

Davis Publications Inc, Worcester, MA. Tel: (508) 754-7201, (800) 533-2847, FAX: (508) 753-3834, Web Site: www.davisart.com (17)

Davis, Amy, Mayo Clinic, Rochester, MN. Tel: (507) 284-2511, Web Site: www.mayoclinic.org (17)

Davis, Bert, Bert Davis Executive Search, New York, NY. Tel: (212) 838-4000, FAX: (212) 935-3291, E-Mail: info@bertdavis.com, Web Site: www.bertdavis.com (20)

Davis, Betsy, Quantum Group, Morton Grove, IL. Tel: (847) 967-3600, FAX: (847) 967-3610, Web Site: www.quantumgroup.com (35)

Davis, Bob, Northern Greenhouse Sales, Neche, ND. Tel: (204) 327-5540, FAX: (204) 327-5527, E-Mail: info@northerngreenhouse.com, Web Site: www.northerngreenhouse.com (8)

Davis, Brad, NRS, Decatur, TX. Tel: (940) 627-3949, Web Site: www.nrsworld.com (11)

Davis, Brandon, MAX Federal Credit Union, Montgomery, AL. Tel: (334) 260-2600, (800) 776-6776, FAX: (334) 270-0921, Web Site: www.mymax.com (14)

Davis, Bryan, Brookfield Office Properties, New York, NY. Tel: (212) 417-7000, FAX: (212) 417-7214, Web Site: brookfieldofficeproperties.com (16)

Davis, Carol, One Hanes Place Catalog, Winston Salem, NC. Tel: (336) 519-8080, (800) 300-2600, FAX: (336) 519-0655, Web Site: www.onehanesplace.com (2)

Davis, Catherine, The Container Store, Coppell, TX. Tel: (888) 266-8246, Web Site: www.containerstore.com (8)

Davis, Chad, Curtis 1000 Inc, Duluth, GA. Tel: (678) 380-9095, (877) 287-8715, FAX: (770) 717-1890, E-Mail: info@curtis1000.com, Web Site: www.curtis1000.com (27)

Davis, D. Scott, United Parcel Service, Atlanta, GA. Tel: (404) 828-6000, (800) 874-5877, FAX: (404) 828-6562, Web Site: www.ups.com (28)

Davis, David H., Aptimus, San Francisco, CA. Tel: (415) 896-2123, FAX: (415) 896-2561 (22)

Davis, Dee, Pittman & Davis Inc, Harlingen, TX. Tel: (956) 423-2154, (800) 289-7829, FAX: (866) 329-7829, E-Mail: fruit@pittmandavis.com, Web Site: www.pittmandavis.com (4)

Davis, Don, Dexposito & Partners, New York, NY. Tel: (646) 747-8800, Web Site: newamericanagency.com (35)

Davis, Don, StayWell/Krames, San Bruno, CA. Tel: (650) 742-0400, FAX: (650) 244-4568, Web Site: www.staywell.com (17)

Davis, Dorinne S., The Davis Center, Succasunna, NJ. Tel: (862) 251-4637, FAX: (862) 251-4642, E-Mail: info@thedaviscenter.com, Web Site: www.thedaviscenter.com (16)

Davis, Dr. Jacob A., Solitron Devices Inc, West Palm Beach, FL. Tel: (561) 848-4311, FAX: (561) 863-5946, E-Mail: sales@solitrondevices.com, Web Site: www.solitrondevices.com (16)

Davis, Fred, Price Weber Marketing Communications Inc, Louisville, KY. Tel: (502) 499-9220, FAX: (502) 491-5593, E-Mail: info@priceweber.com, Web Site: www.priceweber.com (35)

Davis, George, The Hershey Co, Hershey, PA. Tel: (717) 534-4200, (800) 454-7737, FAX: (717) 534-5204, Web Site: www.hersheygifts.com (4)

Davis, James, PMIC, Los Angeles, CA. Tel: (323) 954-0224, (800) 633-4215, FAX: (323) 954-0253, Web Site: pmiconline.stores.yahoo.net (17)

Davis, Jim, BJU Press, Greenville, SC. Tel: (864) 242-5100, (800) 845-5731, FAX: (864) 271-8151, (800) 525-8398, E-Mail: bjupinfo@bjupress.com, Web Site: www.bjupress.com (17)

Davis, Jim, Thomson Reuters LPC, New York, NY. Tel: (646) 223-6890, E-Mail: lpc.americas@reuters.com, Web Site: www.loanpricing.com (14)

Davis, Jocelyn, AARP, Washington, DC. Tel: (202) 434-2277, FAX: (202) 434-2525, Web Site: www.aarp.org (1)

Davis, John, Photographic Society of America Inc (PSA), Oklahoma City, OK. Tel: (405) 843-1437, (855) 772-4636, FAX: (405) 843-1438, E-Mail: HQ@psa-photo.org, Web Site: www.psa-photo.org (40)

Davis, Ken, Christian Book Distributors Inc, Peabody, MA. Tel: (978) 532-5300, FAX: (978) 977-5010, E-Mail: javedisian@chrbook.com, Web Site: www.chrbook.com (17)

Davis, Larry, Ross-Simons, Cranston, RI. Tel: (401) 463-3100, (800) 835-0919, FAX: (401) 463-8599, Web Site: www.ross-simons.com (6)

Davis, Margaret, Northern Greenhouse Sales, Neche, ND. Tel: (204) 327-5540, FAX: (204) 327-5527, E-Mail: info@northerngreenhouse.com, Web Site: www.northerngreenhouse.com (8)

Davis, Mark, Davis Publications Inc, Worcester, MA. Tel: (508) 754-7201, (800) 533-2847, FAX: (508) 753-3834, Web Site: www.davisart.com (17)

Davis, Martin D., Catalog Music Corp, Nashville, TN. Tel: (615) 298-4338, (800) 744-8204, FAX: (615) 298-4628, Web Site: www.catalogmusic.com (3)

Davis, Marvin, ServiceMaster Co, Memphis, TN. Tel: (901) 766-1400, (866) 782-6787, Web Site: www.servicemaster.com (8)

Davis, Mary, Special Olympics International, Washington, DC. Tel: (202) 628-3630, (800) 700-8585, FAX: (202) 824-0200, E-Mail: info@specialolympics.org, Web Site: www.specialolympics.org (1)

Davis, Michael L., The Pillsbury Co, Minneapolis, MN. Tel: (763) 764-7600, (800) 248-7310, FAX: (763) 764-8330, Web Site: www.pillsbury.com (16)

Davis, Michael, Manchester Farms Inc, Columbia, SC. Tel: (803) 845-0421, FAX: (803) 227-3103, E-Mail: customerservice@manchesterfarms.com, Web Site: www.manchesterfarms.com (4)

Davis, Ned, Pittman & Davis Inc, Harlingen, TX. Tel: (956) 423-2154, (800) 289-7829, FAX: (866) 329-7829, E-Mail: fruit@pittmandavis.com, Web Site: www.pittmandavis.com (4)

Davis, Pam, Homesteaders Life Co, West Des Moines, IA. Tel: (515) 440-7777, (800) 477-3633, E-Mail: service@homesteaderslife.com, Web Site: www.homesteaderslife.com (15)

Davis, Peter, Gaco Western Inc, Seattle, WA. Tel: (206) 575-0450, (800) 456-4226, FAX: (206) 575-0587, E-Mail: info@gaco.com, Web Site: www.gaco.com (16)

Davis, Rich, WPG Americas Inc, San Jose, CA. Tel: (408) 392-8100, FAX: (408) 436-9551, E-Mail: northerncalifornia.sales@wpgamericas.com, Web Site: www.wpgamericas.com (20)

Davis, Richard K., US Bancorp, Minneapolis, MN. Tel: (651) 466-3000, (800) 872-2657, FAX: (612) 303-0782, Web Site: www.usbank.com (14)

Davis, Robert D., Rent-A-Center Inc, Plano, TX. Tel: (972) 801-1100, (800) 275-2996, FAX: (972) 943-0113, Web Site: www.rentacenter.com (16)

Davis, Robert, Mazda Motor of America Inc, Irvine, CA. Tel: (949) 727-1990, (800) 222-6500, FAX: (949) 727-6101, Web Site: www.mazdausa.com (16)

Davis, Ron, Milwaukee Direct Marketing Inc, Brookfield, WI. Tel: (262) 789-2240, FAX: (262) 789-2250, E-Mail: info@milwaukeedirect.com, Web Site: milwaukeedirect.com (35)

Davis, Sally Ann, Baltimore Magazine, Baltimore, MD. Tel: (410) 752-4200, (800) 935-0838, FAX: (410) 625-0280, E-Mail: blori@baltimoremagazine.net, Web Site: www.baltimoremagazine.net (17)

Davis, Sara, Sunrise Greetings, Kansas City, MO. Tel: (812) 336-4045, (800) 457-4045, FAX: (812) 336-8712, E-Mail: info@interart.com, Web Site: www.interartdistribution.com (17)

Davis, Steve, Booth Michigan, Grand Rapids, MI. Tel: (616) 222-5824, FAX: (616) 222-5318, Web Site: www.boothnewspapers.com (17)

Davis, Tom, Lexinet Corp, Council Grove, KS. Tel: (620) 767-7000, FAX: (620) 767-7100, E-Mail: tlc@lexinetcorporation.com (22)

Davis, Tom, USA 800 Inc, Raytown, MO. Tel: (816) 358-1303, (800) 821-7539, FAX: (816) 358-8845, E-Mail: dlabatt@usa-800.com, Web Site: www.usa-800.com (29)

Davis, Wade, Viacom Inc, New York, NY. Tel: (212) 258-6000, FAX: (212) 258-6464, Web Site: www.viacom.com (16)

Davis-Trier, Lynn, Winterthur Museum & Country Estate, Wilmington, DE. Tel: (302) 888-4600, (800) 448-3883, FAX: (302) 888-4730, E-Mail: tourinfo@winterthur.org, Web Site: www.winterthur.org (6)

Davison, Hamilton, American Catalog Mailers Association, Providence, RI. Tel: (800) 509-9514, E-Mail: info@catalogmailers.org, Web Site: www.catalogmailers.org (1)

Davison, John M., Four Seasons Hotels & Resorts, Toronto, ON Canada. Tel: (416) 449-1750, (800) 819-5053, FAX: (416) 441-4437, Web Site: www.fourseasons.com (19)

Dawe, Barnaby, HarperCollins, New York, NY. Tel: (212) 207-7000, (800) 242-7737, FAX: (212) 207-7145, Web Site: www.harpercollins.com (17)

Dawley, Matthew, Graphic Communications Holdings Inc, Hudson, OH. Tel: (330) 650-5522, FAX: (330) 650-8998, E-Mail: info@graphiccommunications.com, Web Site: www.graphiccommunications.com (25)

Thomas Dawson, Palm Coast, FL. Tel: (303) 250-9000 (20)

Dawson, Beccie C., Sage Software Inc, Irvine, CA. Tel: (949) 753-1222, (800) 854-3415, FAX: (949) 753-0374, Web Site: www.sagesoftware.com (16)

Dawson, Charles T., Harland Clarke Marketing Services, San Antonio, TX. Tel: (210) 697-8888, Web Site: www.harlandclarke.com (31)

Dawson, David, The Herald & Review, Decatur, IL. Tel: (217) 429-5151, FAX: (217) 421-6913, E-Mail: hrdirect@herald-review.com, Web Site: www.herald-review.com (17)

Dawson, Jackie, Curriculum Associates Inc, North Billerica, MA. Tel: (978) 667-8000, FAX: (978) 667-5706, E-Mail: cainfo@curriculumassociates.com, Web Site: www.curriculumassociates.com (17)

Dawson, Ken, Integretel Inc, San Jose, CA. Tel: (408) 362-4000, FAX: (408) 362-2795, Web Site: www.integretel.com (16)

Dawson, Michelle S., Ad Facts Inc, Cary, NC. Tel: (919) 388-3015, (800) 923-3228, E-Mail: adfacts@adfacts.com, Web Site: www.adfacts.com (30)

Dawson, Scott, School of Business Administration, Portland, OR. Tel: (503) 725-3712, FAX: (503) 725-5850, E-Mail: info@sba.pdx.edu, Web Site: www.sba.pdx.edu (41)

Dawson, Shaun, BellTower Technologies LLC, Richardson, TX. Tel: (214) 220-8000, Web Site: www.belltowertech.com (18)

Dawson, Steve, Tektronix Inc, Beaverton, OR. Tel: (503) 627-7111, (800) 833-9200, FAX: (503) 627-3247, Web Site: www.tektronix.com (16)

Day Runner Direct, Sidney, NY. Tel: (800) 643-9923, FAX: (800) 643-9927, Web Site: www.dayrunner.com (10)

Day-Timer, East Texas, PA. Tel: (610) 398-1151, (800) 457-5702, (800) 225-5005, FAX: (800) 452-7398, E-Mail: connie@lomottastrategic.com, Web Site: www.daytimer.com (13)

Day, Beth, DHL Global Mail, Weston, FL. Tel: (954) 903-6300, (866) 616-MAIL, FAX: (954) 903-6310, E-Mail: contact@dhlglobalmail.com, Web Site: www.dhlglobalmail.com (28)

Day, Jack, John Wiley & Sons Inc, Hoboken, NJ. Tel: (201) 748-6000, FAX: (201) 748-6088, E-Mail: info@wiley.com, Web Site: www.wiley.com (17)

Day, Rosanne, PacNet Services Ltd, Vancouver, BC Canada. Tel: (604) 689-0399, FAX: (604) 689-0313, E-Mail: info@pacnetservices.com, Web Site: www.pacnetservices.com (14)

Daya, Moaiz F., Numark Brands. Edison, NJ. Tel: (732) 417-1870, (800) 338-8079, FAX: (732) 225-0066, E-Mail: newmark@injersey.com (7)

Dayan, Bonnie, Triangle Printers Inc, Skokie, IL. Tel: (847) 675-3700, FAX: (847) 674-1230, E-Mail: blevin@triangleprinters.com, Web Site: www.triangleprinters.com (27)

Daydots, Fort Worth, TX. Tel: (817) 590-4500, (800) 321-3687, FAX: (800) 438-7002, E-Mail: customercare@daydots.com, Web Site: www.daydots.com (16)

Dayoob, Ed, Fred Meyer Jewelers Inc. Portland, OR. Tel: (503) 232-8844, (800) 457-5977, FAX: (503) 797-7616, Web Site: www.fredmeyerjewelers.com (16)

Days Inns Worldwide Inc, Parsippany, NJ. Tel: (973) 753-6000, (800) 441-1618, Web Site: www.daysinn.com (16)

Daystar Data Group Inc, Schaumburg, IL. Tel: (847) 202-0100, FAX: (847) 202-0107, E-Mail: sales@daystardg.com, Web Site: www.daystardg.com (22)

Dayton Daily News, Dayton, OH. Tel: (937) 222-5700, (888) 397-6397, FAX: (937) 225-2153, E-Mail: daytondaily@coxohio.com, Web Site: www.daytondailynews.com (18)

de Emley & Associates Inc, San Juan Capistrano, CA. Tel: (949) 493-5117, FAX: (949) 493-6382 (33)

de Jong, Rienk, Premier World Marketing LLC, Miami, FL. Tel: (305) 445-1077, FAX: (305) 445-1075, Web Site: pwmktg.com (35)

De Korne, Steven, Vertical Communications Inc, Santa Clara, CA. Tel: (408) 404-1600, (800) COMDIAL, FAX: (408) 969-9601, Web Site: www.comdial.com (34)

De La Cruz, John P, Sweetgrass Marketing LLC. Charleston, SC. Tel: (843) 834-1884, Web Site: sweetgrassmarketing.net (35)

de la Cueva-Peterson, Rosa Maria, Chip Peterson Photos, Saint Paul, MN. Tel: (651) 699-4286, FAX: (651) 698-7667 (38)

de la Uz, Michelle, Fifth Avenue Committee, Brooklyn, NY. Tel: (718) 237-2017, FAX: (718) 237-5366, Web Site: www.fifthave.org (1)

De Lacluyse, Mike, Lesman Instrument Co, Bensenville, IL. Tel: (630) 595-8400, (800) 953-7626, FAX: (630) 595-2386, E-Mail: sales@lesman.com, Web Site: www.lesman.com (9)

de Lacoste, Arnaud, Sitel, Nashville, TN. Tel: (615) 301-7100, (866) 95-SITEL, Web Site: www.sitel.com (29)

De Meo, Rosalba, Dentino Marketing, Princeton, NJ. Tel: (609) 454-3202, FAX: (609) 454-3239, E-Mail: karl@dentinomarketing.com, Web Site: www.dentinomarketing.com (35)

De Paul, Paulette, Christianity Today Inc, Carol Stream, IL. Tel: (630) 260-6200, FAX: (630) 260-0114, Web Site: www.christianitytoday.com (17)

de Rham & Co Inc, Dorset, VT. Tel: (802) 867-0155, (888) 867-0155, FAX: (802) 867-0361, Web Site: www.derham.com (20)

de Rham, Abbott, de Rham & Co Inc, Dorset, VT. Tel: (802) 867-0155, (888) 867-0155, FAX: (802) 867-0361, Web Site: www.derham.com (20)

De Saint-Affrique, Antoine, Unilever Best Foods, Englewood Cliffs, NJ. Tel: (201) 567-8000, FAX: (201) 871-8257, E-Mail: comments@unilever.com, Web Site: www.unilever.com (16)

De Shon, Larry, Avis World Headquarters, Parsippany, NJ. Tel: (973) 496-3500, Web Site: www.avis.com (19)

De Turk, Nanette P., Highmark Blue Cross Blue Shield, Pittsburgh, PA. Tel: (412) 544-7000, FAX: (412) 544-5350, Web Site: www.highmark.com (15)

De Yager, Peter W., Profit Potentials Inc, Hull, IA. Tel: (712) 439-1496, (800) 543-5480, FAX: (712) 439-1434, Web Site: www.profitpotentials.com (1)

de Young, Gary, 1000 Islands International Tourism Council, Alexandria Bay, NY. Tel: (315) 482-2520, (800) 847-5263, (800) 456-2267, FAX: (315) 482-5906, E-Mail: info@visit1000islands.com, Web Site: www.visit1000islands.com/visitorinfo/ (19)

DealerTrack, New Hyde Park, NY. Tel: (516) 734-3600, Web Site: www.dealertract.com (14)

Dean & Deluca Brands Inc, Wichita, KS. Tel: (316) 683-1255, Web Site: www.deandeluca.com (4)

Dean, Harvey, Hearlihy & Co, Pittsburg, KS. Tel: (800) 622-1000, (866) 622-1003, FAX: (800) 443-2260, Web Site: www.hearlihy.com (17)

Dean, Jay, AcquireWEB Inc, Foster City, CA. Tel: (650) 212-2233, FAX: (650) 212-2234, E-Mail: sales@aquireweb.com, Web Site: www.acquireWEB.com (22)

Dean, Jill Brown, Coldwater Creek, Cincinnati, OH. Tel: (800) 787-9196, FAX: (800) 262-0080, Web Site: www.coldwatercreek.com (2)

Dean, John C., Central Pacific Bank, Honolulu, HI. Tel: (808) 544-0500, (800) 544-0500, (800) 342-8422, FAX: (808) 531-2875, Web Site: www.centralpacificbank.com (14)

Dean, John S., Steelcase Inc, Grand Rapids, MI. Tel: (616) 247-2710, FAX: (616) 475-2270, Web Site: www.steelcase.com (16)

Dean, L. Marcus, Graphics International Inc, Dallas, TX. Tel: (214) 352-7565, FAX: (214) 528-0114 (27)

DeAngelis, Dawn, New Hampshire Public Television, Durham, NH. Tel: (603) 868-1100, E-Mail: themailbox@nhptv.org, Web Site: www.nhptv.org (32)

DeAngelo, Joseph J., HD Supply, San Diego, CA. Tel: (877) 610-6912, FAX: (877) 219-8526, Web Site: www.hdsupplysolutions.com (34)

Dearing, Kristen, Brierley & Partners, Dallas, TX. Tel: (214) 760-8700, FAX: (214) 743-5511, E-Mail: bpayton@brierley.com, Web Site: www.brierley.com (24)

Dearn, Stephen F, Con-Way Freight, Ann Arbor, MI. Tel: (734) 994-6600, FAX: (734) 757-1153 (12)

Deas, Jr. Thomas C., FMC Corp, Philadelphia, PA. Tel: (215) 299-6000, FAX: (215) 299-5998, Web Site: www.fmc.com (16)

Deasy, Dave, TRUSTe, San Francisco, CA. Tel: (415) 520-3490, FAX: (415) 520-3420, Web Site: www.truste.org (22)

Deaton, Luther, Kentucky Bankers Association, Louisville, KY. Tel: (502) 582-2453, FAX: (502) 584-6390, Web Site: www.kybanks.com (1)

Deaton, Nancy, eBureau LLC, Saint Cloud, MN. Tel: (320) 534-5000, FAX: (320) 534-5020, Web Site: www.ebureau.com (22)

Debacker, Travis, NuNaturals, Eugene, OR. Tel: (541) 344-9785, (800) 753-4372, FAX: (541) 343-0915, E-Mail: info@nunaturals.com, Web Site: www.nunaturals.com (16)

DeBellis & Ferrara, Vienna, VA. Tel: (888) 748-2133, FAX: (888) 979-6345, E-Mail: info@debellis-ferrara.com, Web Site: www.debellis-ferrara.com (35)

DeBiasi, Gerard A., IPacesetters, Montvale, NJ. Tel: (201) 391-1500, FAX: (201) 391-8357, Web Site: www.ipacesetters.com (22)

DeBlasio Jr, James, JD Graphic Co, Elk Grove Village, IL. Tel: (847) 364-4000, (888) 364-6216, FAX: (847) 364-4024, E-Mail: sakes@jdgraphic.com, Web Site: www.jdgraphic.com (27)

DeBoer, Bryan B, Lithia Motors Inc, Medford, OR. Tel: (541) 774-7602 (12)

DeBow Communications Ltd, New York, NY. Tel: (212) 977-8815, FAX: (212) 977-8376, E-Mail: info@debow.com, Web Site: www.debow.com (35)

DeBow, Suzanne Hayat, DeBow Communications Ltd, New York, NY. Tel: (212) 977-8815, FAX: (212) 977-8376, E-Mail: info@debow.com, Web Site: www.debow.com (35)

DeBow, Tom, DeBow Communications Ltd, New York, NY. Tel: (212) 977-8815, FAX: (212) 977-8376, E-Mail: info@debow.com, Web Site: www.debow.com (35)

DeBrosse, Nancy, Projection Video Services, Springfield, VA. Tel: (703) 912-1334, (800) 377-7650, FAX: (703) 912-1350, Web Site: www.projection.com (16)

Debuque, Kenneth, Guaranty Bank, Brown Deer, WI. Tel: (414) 362-4000, (800) 235-4636, Web Site: www.guarantybank.com (14)

Debus, Liza, Tom Snyder Productions, Watertown, MA. Tel: (617) 926-6000, (800) 342-0236, FAX: (800) 304-1254, E-Mail: ask@tomsnyder.com, Web Site: www.tomsnyder.com (16)

deButts, Read, OTM Partners, Arlington, VA. Tel: (800) 759-2244, Web Site: otmpartners.com (35)

Decal Shop, Jacksonville, FL. Tel: (800) 634-1889, FAX: (253) 276-3467, E-Mail: decalshop@decalshop.com (10)

DeCarlo, Sara, FW Media, Cincinnati, OH. Tel: (513) 531-2690, Web Site: www.fwpublications.com (17)

DeCarlucci, Karen, The Wig Co, Pittsburgh, PA. Tel: (800) 568-3499, E-Mail: custserv@twcwigs.com, Web Site: www.thewigcompany.com (2)

DeCarlucci, Vincent James, The Wig Co, Pittsburgh, PA. Tel: (800) 568-3499, E-Mail: custserv@twcwigs.com, Web Site: www.thewigcompany.com (2)

DeCaspers, Carl, New Pig Corp, Tipton, PA. Tel: (814) 684-0101, (800) 468-4647, FAX: (814) 684-0961, E-Mail: hothogs@newpig.com, Web Site: www.newpig.com (9)

Decenzo, Georgiann, Advanstar Communications Inc, North Olmstead, OH. Tel: (440) 243-8100, (800) 225-4569, FAX: (440) 891-2651, E-Mail: info@advanstar.com, Web Site: www.advanstarlists.com (17)

Decision Analyst Inc, Arlington, TX. Tel: (817) 640-6166, (800) 262-5974, FAX: (817) 640-6567, E-Mail: jthomas@decisionanalyst.com, Web Site: www.decisionanalyst.com (30)

Decision Demographics, Arlington, VA. Tel: (703) 931-9200, FAX: (703) 527-1448, E-Mail: tordella@decision-demographics.com, Web Site: www.decision-demographics.com (30)

Decision One, Devon, PA. Tel: (610) 296-6000, (800) 767-2876, FAX: (610) 296-2910, Web Site: www.decisionone.com (34)

Decision Software Inc, Hyattsville, MD. Tel: (301) 459-9000, FAX: (301) 459-3072, E-Mail: info@dsoftware.biz, Web Site: www.dsimarketingservices.com (22)

Deck the Walls Inc, Saint Peters, MO. Tel: (314) 719-8200, (866) 719-8200, FAX: (314) 719-8290, E-Mail: dtwcontact@fcibiz.com, Web Site: www.deckthewalls.com (5)

Decker Communications Inc, San Francisco, CA. Tel: (415) 543-8100, (877) 485-0700, FAX: (415) 543-8103, E-Mail: info@deckercommunications.com, Web Site: www.deckercommunications.com (20)

Decker, Ben, Decker Communications Inc, San Francisco, CA. Tel: (415) 543-8100, (877) 485-0700, FAX: (415) 543-8103, E-Mail: info@deckercommunications.com, Web Site: www.deckercommunications.com (20)

Decker, Bert, Decker Communications Inc, San Francisco, CA. Tel: (415) 543-8100, (877) 485-0700, FAX: (415) 543-8103, E-Mail: info@deckercommunications.com, Web Site: www.deckercommunications.com (20)

Decker, Jack, American Printing House for the Blind, Louisville, KY. Tel: (502) 895-2405, (800) 223-1839, FAX: (502) 899-2274, E-Mail: info@aph.org, Web Site: www.aph.org (7)

Decker, Kelly, Decker Communications Inc, San Francisco, CA. Tel: (415) 543-8100, (877) 485-0700, FAX: (415) 543-8103, E-Mail: info@deckercommunications.com, Web Site: www.deckercommunications.com (20)

Decker, Matthew, Wholesale Tool Co, Warren, MI. Tel: (800) 521-3420, FAX: (800) 521-3661, E-Mail: wtmich@aol.com, Web Site: www.wttool.com (9)

Decko Products Inc, Sandusky, OH. Tel: (419) 626-5757, FAX: (419) 626-3135, Web Site: www.decko.com (4)

DeCorso, Bill, Block & DeCorso, Verona, NJ. Tel: (973) 857-3900, FAX: (973) 857-4041, E-Mail: bdecorso@blockdecorso.com, Web Site: www.blockdecorso.com (35)

DeCosmo, Joe, Chicago Association of Direct Marketing, Westmont, IL. Tel: (312) 849-2236, FAX: (312) 849-2239, E-Mail: info@cadm.org, Web Site: www.cadm.org (40)

DeCross, Derek, American Airlines Inc, Fort Worth, TX. Tel: (817) 963-1234, FAX: (817) 967-2841, Web Site: www.aa.com (19)

Dee, David, The Dartnell Corp, Naples, FL. Tel: (585) 240-7301, (800) 447-4030, FAX: (585) 292-4392, E-Mail: customerservice@dartnellcorp.com, Web Site: www.dartnellcorp.com (17)

Deeds, Stephen, Bowers & Merena Auctions, Irvine, CA. Tel: (949) 253-0916, (800) 458-4646, FAX: (949) 253-4091, E-Mail: auction@bowersandmerena.com, Web Site: www.bowersandmerena.com (16)

Deely, Brendan J., USG Corp, Chicago, IL. Tel: (312) 436-4000, (800) 621-9622, FAX: (312) 672-4093, Web Site: www.usg.com (34)

Deere & Co, Moline, IL. Tel: (309) 765-8000, FAX: (309) 748-0114, Web Site: www.deere.com (16)

Deering, Suzy, Moxie, Atlanta, GA. Tel: (678) 916-4500, E-Mail: info@moxieusa.com, Web Site: moxieusa.com (17)

Dees, Jr John Allen, Sales by Dees, Montgomery, AL. Tel: (334) 333-1567, E-Mail: dees@sbdees.com, Web Site: www.sbdees.com (35)

Dees, Lee, Kendall Products/Dri-Dek, Naples, FL. Tel: (239) 643-2244, (800) 348-2398, FAX: (800) 828-4248, E-Mail: info@dri-dek.com, Web Site: www.dri-dek.com (16)

Deese, Willie A., Calbiochem-Novabiochem Corp, San Diego, CA. Tel: (858) 450-9600, (800) 854-3417, FAX: (858) 453-3552, E-Mail: customerservice@emdbioscience.com, Web Site: www.calbiochem.com (9)

Deese, Willie A., Merck & Co Inc, Whitehouse Station, NJ. Tel: (908) 423-1000, Web Site: www.merck.com (16)

Deeter. Tom, American Teleservices Association, Indianapolis, IN. Tel: (317) 816-9336, (877) 779-3974, FAX: (317) 218-0323, Web Site: www.ataconnect.org (14)

DEFENDER Direct Inc, Indianapolis, IN. Tel: (317) 810-4720, (800) 860-0303, FAX: (317) 810-4723, Web Site: www.defenderdirect.com (32)

Defenders of Wildlife, Washington, DC. Tel: (202) 682-9400, (800) 385-9712, E-Mail: defenders@mail.defenders.org, Web Site: www.defenders.org (1)

Defense News Media Group, Springfield, VA. Tel: (703) 848-0490, FAX: (703) 848-0480, E-Mail: mgrant@atpco.com, Web Site: www.defensenews.com (17)

DeFrancesco, Therese, CORS, Itasca, IL. Tel: (630) 250-8677, (800) 323-1352, FAX: (630) 250-7362, E-Mail: resume@cors.com, Web Site: www.cors.com (20)

DeFranco, Bobbi, Huck Spaulding Enterprises, Voorheesville, NY. Tel: (518) 768-2070, (888) 982-8866, FAX: (518) 768-2240, E-Mail: orders@spaulding-rogers.com, Web Site: www.spaulding-rogers.com (16)

Defy Media Inc, New York, NY. E-Mail: info@defymedia.com, Web Site: www.defymedia.com (35)

Degennaro, Louis J., The Leukemia & Lymphoma Society, Rye Brook, NY. Tel: (914) 949-5213, FAX: (914) 949-6691, Web Site: www.lls.org (1)

Degnan, Thomas James, Pactiv Corp, Lake Forest, IL. Tel: (847) 482-2000, (800) 828-2850, FAX: (847) 482-4738, Web Site: www.pactiv.com (26)

Degorter, Jennifer, Jenco Productions Inc, San Bernardino, CA. Tel: (909) 381-9453, FAX: (909) 383-1106, Web Site: www.jencoproductions.com (28)

DeHart & Darr Associates, McLean, VA. Tel: (703) 448-1000, FAX: (703) 790-3460 (20)

Dehoche, Stephane, Neolane, Newton, MA. Tel: (617) 467-6760, FAX: (617) 467-6701, Web Site: www.neolane.com (22)

Deighan, Janine, Troy Biologicals Inc, Troy, MI. Tel: (248) 585-9720, (800) 521-0445, FAX: (248) 585-2490, E-Mail: info@troybio.com, Web Site: www.troybio.com (7)

Deisher, Beth, Coin World, Sidney, OH. Tel: (937) 498-0800, (800) 253-4555, FAX: (937) 498-0812, E-Mail: cwcustomerservice@coinworld.com, Web Site: www.coinworld.com (17)

Deisinger, Robert, American Technical Publishers Inc, Orland Park, IL. Tel: (708) 957-1100, (800) 323-3471, FAX: (708) 957-1101, E-Mail: service@americantech.net, Web Site: www.atplearning.com (17)

Dejanovic, Darko, ACTIVE Network LLC, Dallas, TX. Tel: (858) 964-6064, (877) 228-4808, Web Site: www.activenetwork.com (22)

DeKraker, Glenn, COREMedia Systems Inc, Fairfield, NJ. Tel: (973) 276-0882, FAX: (973) 276-0891, Web Site: www.coremedia-systems.com (22)

Del Cielo, Robert, The Bradford Group, Niles, IL. Tel: (847) 966-2770, FAX: (847) 581-8630, Web Site: www.collectiblestoday.com (16)

Del Monte, Ray, Wolff/SMG, Macedon, NY. Tel: (315) 986-1155, FAX: (315) 986-1161, E-Mail: rdelmonte@wolff-smg.com, Web Site: www.wolff-smg.com (28)

Del Polito, Gene A., Association for Postal Commerce, Alexandria, VA. Tel: (703) 524-0096, FAX: (703) 524-1871, Web Site: www.postcom.org (40)

Del Vecchio, Claudio, Brooks Brothers, New York, NY. Tel: (212) 682-8800, (800) 274-1815, FAX: (212) 309-7273, Web Site: www.brooksbrothers.com (2)

Del Vecchio, Debra, Brooks Brothers, New York, NY. Tel: (212) 682-8800, (800) 274-1815, FAX: (212) 309-7273, Web Site: www.brooksbrothers.com (2)

Del Vecchio, Leonardo, Luxottica Retail, Mason, OH. Tel: (513) 765-6956, Web Site: www.luxottica.com (2)

Del Webb, Bloomfield Hills, MI. Tel: (248) 644-7300, (888) 717-9777, FAX: (248) 433-4598, Web Site: www.delwebb.com (16)

Delahaye, Bruno, KXEN Inc, San Francisco, CA. Tel: (415) 904-4160, FAX: (415) 904-9041, Web Site: www.kxen.com (22)

DeLaney, Doreen, Balboa Life & Casualty, Irvine, CA. Tel: (949) 222-8000, (800) 854-6115, FAX: (949) 222-8777, Web Site: www.balboainsurance.com (15)

Delaney, Jay, McMaster-Carr Supply Co (HQ), Elmhurst, IL. Tel: (630) 834-9600, FAX: (630) 834-9427, E-Mail: chi.sales@mcmaster.com, Web Site: www.mcmaster.com (9)

Delaney, John E, Strongwell, Bristol, VA. Tel: (276) 645-8000, FAX: (276) 645-8132, E-Mail: gbarefoot@strongwell.com, Web Site: www.strongwell.com (9)

Delaney, Jr. David P., Lancer Insurance Co, Long Beach, NY. Tel: (516) 431-4441, (800) 782-8902, FAX: (516) 889-5111, E-Mail: roneill@lancer-ins.com, Web Site: www.lancer-ins.com (15)

Delaney, Karin, Birthday Keepsakes, Loveland, CO. Tel: (970) 669-5506, Web Site: www.bkeepsakes.com (4)

Delaney, Kris, Professional Photographer Magazine, Atlanta, GA. Tel: (404) 522-8600, (800) 786-6277, FAX: (404) 614-6405, E-Mail: csc@ppa.com, Web Site: www.ppa.com (17)

Delaney, Mike, National Pen Corp, San Diego, CA. Tel: (858) 675-3000, FAX: (858) 675-3030, E-Mail: info@nationalpen.com, Web Site: www.pens.com (6)

Delaney, Timothy D., Lancer Insurance Co, Long Beach, NY. Tel: (516) 431-4441, (800) 782-8902, FAX: (516) 889-5111, E-Mail: roneill@lancer-ins.com, Web Site: www.lancer-ins.com (15)

Delano, Michael, The Country House Inc, Salisbury, MD. Tel: (410) 749-1959, (800) 331-3602, FAX: (410) 548-3224, E-Mail: web@thecountryhouse.com, Web Site: www.thecountryhouse.com (6)

Delauner, Trish, SRDS, Des Plaines, IL. Tel: (800) 851-7737, FAX: (847) 375-5001, Web Site: www.srds.com (17)

DeLaVergne, Ann, Ecoenvelopes, Eden Prairie, MN. Tel: (612) 605-4885, (888) 428-4364, FAX: (651) 392-8924, E-Mail: info@ecoenvelopes.com, Web Site: www.ecoenvelopes.com (20)

Delaware Investments, Philadelphia, PA. Tel: (215) 255-1200, E-Mail: service@delinvest.com, Web Site: www.delawareinvestments.com (14)

Robert DeLay, Tucson, AZ. Tel: (520) 615-8235 (20)

DeLee, Debra, Americans for Peace Now, Washington, DC. Tel: (202) 408-9898, FAX: (202) 408-9899, E-Mail: apndc@peacenow.org, Web Site: www.peacenow.org (1)

Delettre, Cecile, French Trade Office Embassy of France, New York, NY. Tel: (212) 400-2167, Web Site: www.missioneco.org (1)

Delia, Gina Marie, Direct Marketing Market Place, New Providence, NJ. Tel: (908) 517-0780, (844) 592-4197, FAX: (908) 608-3012, Web Site: www.dirmktgplace.com (43)

Delicious Orchards, Colts Neck, NJ. Tel: (732) 462-1989, FAX: (732) 409-4993, E-Mail: info@deliciousorchardsnj.com, Web Site: www.deliciousorchardsnjonline.com (4)

Delivra, Indianapolis, IN. Tel: (317) 915-9400, (866) 915-9465, Web Site: www.delivra.com (32)

Dell Computer Corp, Round Rock, TX. Tel: (512) 338-4400, FAX: (512) 283-6161, Web Site: www.dell.com (16)

Dell, Michael S., Dell Computer Corp, Round Rock, TX. Tel: (512) 338-4400, FAX: (512) 283-6161, Web Site: www.dell.com (16)

Della Rossa, James, Array Marketing Group Inc, Toronto, ON Canada. Tel: (416) 299-4865, FAX: (416) 292-9759, E-Mail: inquiry@arraymarketing.com, Web Site: arraymarketing.com (35)

Della Torre, Alex, Direct Marketing Association of Detroit, Royal Oak, MI. Tel: (248) 478-4888, FAX: (248) 478-6437, E-Mail: dmad@ameritech.net, Web Site: www.dmad.org (40)

Della Torre, Stefano, SipcamAdvan, Durham, NC. Tel: (800) 295-0733, FAX: (919) 226-1196, Web Site: www.sipcamadvan.com (5)

Dellavilla, Jim, SIGMA Marketing Group LLC, Rochester, NY. Tel: (585) 473-7300, (888) 277-9837, FAX: (585) 473-0332, E-Mail: mbush@sigmamarketing.com, Web Site: www.sigmamarketing.com; www.jthgearanalytics.com (Blog) (20)

Delmmar Communications, Cameron, MO. Tel: (816) 632-1583, (800) 872-2627, FAX: (816) 632-5107, E-Mail: sales@eradiostore.com, Web Site: www.delmmar.com (16)

Deloitte & Touche, Boston, MA. Tel: (617) 437-2000, FAX: (617) 437-2111, Web Site: www.deloitte.com (14)

DeLong, James, ANCOR, Troy, MI. Tel: (248) 740-8866, (800) 229-3860, FAX: (248) 740-9025, Web Site: www.anchorinfo.com (22)

Delong, Joe, Raritan Inc, Somerset, NJ. Tel: (732) 764-8886, FAX: (732) 764-8887, Web Site: raritan.com (22)

DeLorenzo, Dennis, Hilton Grand Vacations Co, Orlando, FL. Tel: (407) 722-3100, FAX: (407) 521-3112, Web Site: www.hiltongrandvacations.com (19)

DeLorme Mapping, Yarmouth, ME. Tel: (207) 846-7100, (800) 642-0970, FAX: (207) 846-7051, E-Mail: caleb.mason@delorme.com, Web Site: www.delorme.com (3)

Delorme, David, DeLorme Mapping, Yarmouth, ME. Tel: (207) 846-7100, (800) 642-0970, FAX: (207) 846-7051, E-Mail: caleb.mason@delorme.com, Web Site: www.delorme.com (3)

DelStar Technologies Inc, Middletown, DE. Tel: (302) 378-8888, (800) 521-6713, FAX: (302) 378-4482, Web Site: www.delstarinc.com (16)

Delta Market Research Inc, Hatboro, PA. Tel: (215) 674-1180, (267) 960-1033, FAX: (215) 674-1271, E-Mail: information@deltamarketresearch.com, Web Site: www.deltamarketresearch.com (30)

Delta Tech Industries, Ontario, CA. Tel: (714) 577-8028, FAX: (714) 577-0140, E-Mail: sales@deltatechindustries.com, Web Site: www.deltatechindustries.com (12)

Delta Upsilon International Fraternity, Indianapolis, IN. Tel: (317) 875-8900, FAX: (317) 876-1629, E-Mail: ihq@deltau.org, Web Site: www.deltau.org (16)

Delta Vacations, Atlanta, GA. Tel: (404) 559-2270, (800) 800-1504, Web Site: www.deltavacations.com (19)

DeLuca, Jim, Western-Southern Life, Cincinnati, OH. Tel: (513) 629-1800, Web Site: www.westernsouthernlife.com (15)

DeLuca, Michael, Meister Media Worldwide, Willoughby, OH. Tel: (440) 942-2000, (800) 572-7740, FAX: (440) 975-3447, E-Mail: info@meistermedia.com, Web Site: www.meistermedia.com (17)

DeLuca, Victoria, Ad-Lib Advertising Inc, Old Bridge, NJ. Tel: (732) 679-9226, (800) 622-3542, FAX: (732) 679-9511, E-Mail: info@adlibadvertising.com, Web Site: www.adlibadvertising.com (10)

Deluxe Corp, Shoreview, MN. Tel: (651) 483-7111, FAX: (651) 481-4477, Web Site: www.deluxe.com (27)

DeLuxe Laboratories Inc, Hollywood, CA. Tel: (323) 462-6171, FAX: (323) 960-7016, E-Mail: steven.vananda@bydeluxe.com, Web Site: www.bydeluxe.com (16)

Demand Telemarketing Inc, Grosse Pointe, MI. Tel: (313) 823-8598, (888) 977-2256, FAX: (313) 823-8598, E-Mail: info@create-demand.com, Web Site: www.create-demand.com (29)

Demandbase Inc, San Francisco, CA. Tel: (415) 683-2660, E-Mail: info@demandbase.com, Web Site: www.demandbase.com (22)

DeMarco, Michelle, Pensions & Investments, New York, NY. Tel: (212) 210-0100, FAX: (212) 210-0117, Web Site: www.pionline.com (17)

DeMarco, Tony, Signature Communications Inc, Philadelphia, PA. Tel: (215) 922-3022, FAX: (215) 922-3033, Web Site: www.signatureteam.com (21)

DeMarie, Jr. Donald J., Masco Corp, Taylor, MI. Tel: (313) 274-7400, FAX: (313) 792-6135, E-Mail: webmaster@mascohq.com, Web Site: www.masco.com (16)

DeMarsh, Dave, I-Behavior Inc, Louisville, CO. Tel: (303) 228-5000, E-Mail: ib-sales@i-behavior.com, Web Site: www.i-behavior.com (23)

DeMarsh, Dave, KBM Group, Louisville, CO. Tel: (800) 579-1950, E-Mail: sales@kbmg.com, Web Site: www.kbmg.com (22)

DeMartine, Chris, Statlistics, Danbury, CT. Tel: (203) 778-8700, FAX: (203) 778-4839, E-Mail: info@statlistics.com, Web Site: www.statlistics.com (23)

DeMartine, Chris, Vermont/New Hampshire Direct Marketing Group, Woodstock, VT. Tel: (802) 457-2807, FAX: (802) 457-2807, E-Mail: vtnhmg@vtnhmg, Web Site: www.vtnhmg.org (40)

DeMartino, Angelo, ADM Productions Inc, Port Washington, NY. Tel: (516) 484-6900, (800) ADM-DIAL, FAX: (516) 621-2531, Web Site: www.admpro.com (16)

DeMartino, Anthony, ADM Productions Inc, Port Washington, NY. Tel: (516) 484-6900, (800) ADM-DIAL, FAX: (516) 621-2531, Web Site: www.admpro.com (16)

DeMartins, Paul, Medco Supply Co Inc, Tonawanda, NY. Tel: (716) 743-8400, (800) 556-3326, FAX: (800) 222-1934, E-Mail: sales@medcosupply.com, Web Site: www.medcosupply.com (7)

Dembicki, Dan, Direct Marketing Association of Detroit, Royal Oak, MI. Tel: (248) 478-4888, FAX: (248) 478-6437, E-Mail: dmad@ameritech.net, Web Site: www.dmad.org (40)

Demco Inc, Madison, WI. Tel: (608) 241-1201, (800) 356-1200, FAX: (608) 241-1799, E-Mail: custserv@demco.com, Web Site: www.demco.com (10)

Demi, Mike, Direct Marketing News, Markham, ON Canada. Tel: (905) 201-6600, (800) 668-1838, FAX: (905) 201-6601, E-Mail: home@dmn.ca, Web Site: www.dmn.ca (43)

DeMichael, Cheryl, Tauck World Discovery, Norwalk, CT. Tel: (203) 899-6760, Web Site: www.tauck.com (19)

Demme, Robert, Micro Center, Hilliard, OH. Tel: (614) 850-3675, (800) 634-3478, FAX: (614) 777-2620, E-Mail: csrs@microcenterorder.com, Web Site: www.microcenter.com (3)

Democratic Congressional Campaign Committee, Washington, DC. Tel: (202) 863-1500, FAX: (202) 485-3436, Web Site: www.dccc.org (1)

Demographic Research Co, Denver, CO. Tel: (310) 766-5590, FAX: (303) 831-9181, Web Site: www.drcmodel.com (22)

DeMontmollin, Steve, AvMed Health Plan Inc, Miami, FL. Tel: (305) 671-5437, FAX: (305) 671-4782, Web Site: www.avmed.org (1)

DeMoss, Michelle, Stetson University, Deland, FL. Tel: (904) 822-7405/7406, FAX: (904) 822-7430, Web Site: www.stetson.edu (41)

Demoulin, Chris, Advanstar Communications Inc, North Olmstead, OH. Tel: (440) 243-8100, (800) 225-4569, FAX: (440) 891-2651, E-Mail: info@advanstar.com, Web Site: www.advanstarlists.com (17)

Dempsey, James J., Neuberger & Berman Management, New York, NY. Tel: (212) 476-9000, (800) 877-9700, FAX: (212) 476-8937, Web Site: www.nb.com (14)

Demsey, John, Estee Lauder Inc, New York, NY. Tel: (212) 572-4200, FAX: (212) 893-7782, Web Site: www.esteelauder.com (16)

DeMuth, David, Doner, Baltimore, MDSouthfield, MI. Tel: (248) 354-9700, FAX: (248) 827-0880, Web Site: www.doner.com (35)

Denaci, David, RPM Direct LLC, Lambertville, NJ. Tel: (609) 566-7150, FAX: (609) 566-7155, E-Mail: jimarslan@rpmdirectllc.com, Web Site: www.rpmdirectllc.com (35)

Denault, Leo, Entergy, New Orleans, LA. Tel: (504) 576-4000, (800) ENTERGY, FAX: (504) 576-4428, Web Site: www.entergy.com (16)

DenBoer, Dennis, Advanced Direct Marketing Inc, Loveland, CO. Tel: (970) 669-9800, FAX: (970) 669-1920, E-Mail: sales@admimail.com, Web Site: www.admimail.com (21)

Denenberg, Marc, Madison Sales Group, Northbrook, IL. Tel: (847) 480-2370, FAX: (847) 480-7437, E-Mail: sales@madisonsalesgroup.com, Web Site: madisonsalesgroup.com (33)

Denham, Charles R., Health Care Concepts Inc, Austin, TX. Tel: (512) 479-8508, (800) 628-4201, FAX: (512) 479-8741 (16)

Denham, Jerry, Bear Computer Systems Inc, Dallas, TX. Tel: (818) 509-0459, (800) 252-1691, FAX: (818) 769-3055, E-Mail: info@bearcom.com, Web Site: www.bearcom.com (16)

Denhof, Dave, National Bulk Equipment Inc, Holland, MI. Tel: (616) 399-2220, FAX: (616) 399-7365, E-Mail: sales@nbe-inc.com, Web Site: www.nbe-inc.com (16)

Denis, Alison, TPG Direct Inc, Philadelphia, PA. Tel: (215) 592-8381, FAX: (215) 574-8316, E-Mail: slongley@tpgdirect.com, Web Site: www.tpgdirect.com (35)

Denison, Jay, THD Inc, Lexington, MA. Tel: (781) 859-1400, FAX: (781) 859-1500, E-Mail: info@thdinc.com, Web Site: www.thdinc.com (1)

Denka, Andrew, Accountemps, Menlo Park, CA. Tel: (650) 234-6000, (800) 803-8367, FAX: (650) 234-6998, Web Site: www.accountemps.com (16)

Denley, Bryan, Memphis Net & Twine Co Inc, Memphis, TN. Tel: (901) 458-2656, (888) 674-7638, FAX: (901) 458-1601, E-Mail: fishinfo@memphisnet.net, Web Site: www.memphisnet.net (11)

Denmark Francisco, New York, NY. Tel: (212) 444-8157, Web Site: www.dsfnyc.com (20)

Denn, David, Premier Packaging Corp, Victor, NY. Tel: (877) 924-8460, FAX: (585) 924-8753, E-Mail: info@premiercustompkg.com, Web Site: www.premiercustompkg.com (16)

Denning, Laura, Selman & Co, Cleveland, OH. Tel: (440) 646-9336, (800) 735-6262, FAX: (440) 646-9339, E-Mail: ldenning@selmaninsurance.com, Web Site: www.sel-co.com (15)

Dennis Jourdan Photography Inc, Buffalo Grove, IL. Tel: (847) 564-2570, FAX: (847) 255-5976, E-Mail: info@djphoto.com, Web Site: www.djphoto.com (37)

Dennis, Barry, Netweb/Omni LLC, Ellicott City, MD. Tel: (410) 591-1900, E-Mail: barry@netwebomni.com, Web Site: www.netwebomni.com (40)

Dennis, Daniel, Netweb/Omni LLC, Ellicott City, MD. Tel: (410) 591-1900, E-Mail: barry@netwebomni.com, Web Site: www.netwebomni.com (40)

Dennis, Robert J., Genesco Inc, Nashville, TN. Tel: (615) 367-7000, (888) 324-6189, FAX: (615) 367-8278, Web Site: www.genesco.com (2)

Dennis, Sharon, JHL Mail Marketing Inc, Stevens Point, WI. Tel: (715) 341-0581, (800) 236-0581, FAX: (715) 341-9645, E-Mail: ren@jhl.com, Web Site: www.jhl.com (28)

Dennison-Bauer, Jane, Knowledge Networks/SRI, Cranford, NJ. Tel: (908) 497-8000, FAX: (908) 497-8001, E-Mail: mclancey@knowledgenetworks.com, Web Site: www.knowledgenetworks.com (30)

Dennon, G.B., Jerden Records/SpeechWorks, Redmond, WA. Tel: (425) 882-3344, (888) 401-4487, FAX: (425) 882-3494, E-Mail: jerden@aol.com, Web Site: www.soundworks.net (16)

Denny, Mike, Cenveo Color Art Inc, Saint Louis, MO. Tel: (314) 966-2000, FAX: (314) 966-4725, E-Mail: mikedenny@cenveo.com, Web Site: www.colorart.com (27)

Denson, Charles D., Nike Inc, Beaverton, OR. Tel: (503) 671-4565, (800) 344-6543, FAX: (503) 671-6300, Web Site: www.nike.com (2)

Denson, Russel, Reiman Publications, Greendale, WI. Tel: (414) 423-0100, (800) 344-6913, FAX: (414) 423-3840, Web Site: www.reimanpub.com (17)

Dent, Beth, AGORA Inc, Baltimore, MD. Tel: (410) 783-8499, FAX: (410) 783-8414, E-Mail: csteam@agorapublishinggroup.com, Web Site: www.agora-inc.com (17)

Dental Economics, Tulsa, OK. Tel: (800) 331-4633, E-Mail: christopherp@pennwell.com, Web Site: www.dentaleconomics.com (17)

Dental Products Report, New York, NY. Tel: (847) 441-3700, FAX: (847) 441-3702, Web Site: www.dentalproducts.net (17)

Dentino Marketing, Princeton, NJ. Tel: (609) 454-3202, FAX: (609) 454-3239, E-Mail: karl@dentinomarketing.com, Web Site: www.dentinomarketing.com (35)

Dentino, Karl, Dentino Marketing, Princeton, NJ. Tel: (609) 454-3202, FAX: (609) 454-3239, E-Mail: karl@dentinomarketing.com, Web Site: www.dentinomarketing.com (35)

Denton, Mike, Formal Approach, Jefferson City, TN. Tel: (865) 475-8641, Web Site: www.formalapproach.com (2)

Denton, Neal, Alliance of Nonprofit Mailers, Washington, DC. Tel: (202) 462-5132, FAX: (202) 462-0423, E-Mail: alliance@nonprofitmailers.org, Web Site: www.nonprofitmailers.org (40)

Dentsply International, York, PA. Tel: (844) 848-0137, (800) 877-0020, E-Mail: contact@dentsplysirona.com, Web Site: www.dentsply.com (7)

Denver Metro Convention & Visitors Bureau, Denver, CO. Tel: (303) 892-1112, (800) 233-6837, FAX: (303) 892-1636, Web Site: www.denver.org (1)

Denver Tax Software Inc, Littleton, CO. Tel: (303) 796-7780, (800) 326-6686, FAX: (888) 326-6686, Web Site: www.denvertax.com (16)

DePaul University, Chicago, IL. Tel: (312) 362-8000, (800) 4-DEPAUL, FAX: (312) 362-6639, E-Mail: skelly@wppost.depaul.edu, Web Site: www.depaul.edu (41)

DePaulo, Joseph, SLM Corp, Newark, DE. Web Site: www.salliemae.com (16)

Depeau, Jamie, TIAA-CREF, New York, NY. Tel: (212) 490-9000, FAX: (212) 916-6505, Web Site: www.tiaa-cref.org (15)

Dependable Business Forms, Villa Park, IL. Tel: (630) 530-1734, FAX: (630) 530-1789, E-Mail: j.zawaski@comcast.net, Web Site: www.dependablebusinessforms.com (27)

Depue, Robert, The Bowery Mission, New York, NY. Tel: (212) 684-2800, Web Site: www.bowery.org (1)

Derakhshan, Behrange, DataDirect, Atlanta, GA. Tel: (678) 530-0034, FAX: (678) 530-9563, E-Mail: info@ddirect.com, Web Site: www.ddirect.com (40)

Derke, Hanns, Advanced Machinery, New Castle, DE. Tel: (302) 322-2226, (800) 727-6553, FAX: (866) 686-1615, E-Mail: jean@advmachinery.com, Web Site: www.advmachinery.com (9)

Derke, Wolfgang, Advanced Machinery, New Castle, DE. Tel: (302) 322-2226, (800) 727-6553, FAX: (866) 686-1615, E-Mail: jean@advmachinery.com, Web Site: www.advmachinery.com (9)

Derks, Steven M., Muscular Dystrophy Association, Chicago, IL. Tel: (800) 572-1717, Web Site: www.mda.org (1)

Dermac Labs Inc, Salem, OR. Tel: (503) 399-8181, (800) 547-9164, FAX: (503) 581-7439, Web Site: www.touchofmink.com (16)

Dernburg, Michael, MPBS Industries, Los Angeles, CA. Tel: (323) 268-8514, (800) 421-6265, FAX: (323) 268-6305, Web Site: www.mpbs.com (16)

DeRodes, Robert, Target Corp, Minneapolis, MN. Tel: (612) 304-6073, Web Site: www.target.com (16)

Derr, Catherine, 3Com Corp, Marlborough, MA. Tel: (508) 323-5000, FAX: (508) 323-1111 (22)

Derry, Kevin, Cookbook Publishers Inc, Lenexa, KS. Tel: (913) 492-5900, (800) 227-7282, FAX: (913) 492-5947, E-Mail: info@cookbookpublishers.com, Web Site: www.cookbookpublishers.com (17)

DeRuggiero, Erin, Social Reality Inc, Los Angeles, CA. Tel: (323) 694-9800, Web Site: www.socialreality.com (35)

Des Plaines Printing Co, Des Plaines, IL. Tel: (847) 824-1111, (800) 283-1776, FAX: (847) 824-1112, E-Mail: custserv@dppc.com (27)

Des Prez, III John D., John Hancock Financial Services Inc, Boston, MA. Tel: (617) 572-6000, (800) 732-5543, FAX: (617) 572-6451, Web Site: www.johnhancock.com (15)

Des Rosiers, Bert, GlaserDirect Inc, Glen Ellyn, IL. Tel: (630) 469-2075, (888) 380-1356, FAX: (630) 790-5244, E-Mail: info@glaserdirect.com, Web Site: www.glaserdirect.com (23)

Desai, Alka, FDAnews, Falls Church, VA. Tel: (703) 538-7600, (888) 838-5578, FAX: (703) 538-7676, E-Mail: customerservice@fdanews.com, Web Site: www.fdanews.com (17)

Desai, Sandip, Amanet, Canoga Park, CA. Tel: (818) 786-1113, FAX: (818) 786-5736, E-Mail: info@amanet-usa.com, Web Site: www.amanet.com (16)

DeSalva, AnnaMaria, E I DuPont De Nemours & Co, Wilmington, DE. Tel: (302) 774-1000, (800) 441-7515, FAX: (302) 774-7321, Web Site: www.dupont.com (16)

DeSantis Holster & Leather Goods Co, Amityville, NY. Tel: (631) 841-6300, (800) GUNHIDE, FAX: (631) 841-6320, E-Mail: contact@desantisholster.com, Web Site: www.desantisholster.com (34)

DeSantis, Gene, DeSantis Holster & Leather Goods Co, Amityville, NY. Tel: (631) 841-6300, (800) GUN-HIDE, FAX: (631) 841-6320, E-Mail: contact@desantisholster.com, Web Site: www.desantisholster.com (34)

DeSantis, Helen, DeSantis Holster & Leather Goods Co, Amityville, NY. Tel: (631) 841-6300, (800) GUN-HIDE, FAX: (631) 841-6320, E-Mail: contact@desantisholster.com, Web Site: www.desantisholster.com (34)

DeSantis, Susan, Who's Calling, College Station, TX. Tel: (866) 688-9300, FAX: (888) 821-4260, E-Mail: contact@whoscalling.com, Web Site: www.whoscalling.com (30)

DeSantis, Vincent, Payless ShoeSource Inc, Topeka, KS. Tel: (785) 233-5171, (877) 474-6379, E-Mail: customerservice@csr.payless.com, Web Site: www.payless.com (2)

Desborough, Jim, Directory of Premium, Incentive & Travel Buyers, Richmond, VA. Tel: (804) 762-4455, (800) 223-1797, FAX: (804) 935-0271, E-Mail: amdouglas4@aol.com, Web Site: www.douglaspublications.com (43)

Deseret Book, Salt Lake City, UT. Tel: (801) 534-1515, (800) 453-4532, FAX: (801) 517-3392, Web Site: www.deseretbook.com (16)

Desert Rat Truck Centers, Tucson, AZ. Tel: (520) 790-8502, (866) 444-5337, FAX: (520) 750-1918, Web Site: www.desertrat.com (12)

Design Distributors, Inc, Deer Park, NY. Tel: (631) 242-2000, FAX: (631) 242-7367, E-Mail: info@designdistributors.com, Web Site: www.designdistributors.com (21)

Design Matters Inc!, New York, NY. Tel: (212) 560-0681, FAX: (646) 478-9149, E-Mail: stephen@designmattersinc.com, Web Site: www.designmattersinc.com (35)

Design Toscano, Inc, Elk Grove Village, IL. Tel: (847) 952-0100, (800) 525-5141, FAX: (847) 952-8992, Web Site: www.designtoscano.com (6)

DeSimone, Linda S., Amerisure Insurance Cos, Farmington Hills, MI. Tel: (248) 615-9000, (800) 257-1900, FAX: (248) 615-8224, Web Site: www.amerisure.com (15)

DeSimone, Rich, The EGC Group, Melville, NY. Tel: (516) 935-4944, FAX: (516) 935-7030, E-Mail: contact@egcgroup.com, Web Site: www.egcgroup.com (35)

DesJardin, Bonny, Jesco Industries Inc, Litchfield, MI. Tel: (517) 542-2903, (866) 638-8577, FAX: (517) 542-2501, E-Mail: jesco@jescoonline.com, Web Site: www.jescoonline.com (34)

Desjardins Financial Securities, Levis, QC Canada. Tel: (418) 838-7870, FAX: (418) 833-5985, Web Site: www.desjardinsfinancialsecurity.com (15)

Desjardins, Luc, Telemedia Communications US, North York, ON Canada. Tel: (416) 733-7600, (800) 461-3773 U.S., (888) 290-1466 Can., FAX: (416) 733-3563, E-Mail: info@transcontinental.ca, Web Site: www.transcontinental.com (17)

Desmond, Bevin, Morningstar Inc, Chicago, IL. Tel: (312) 696-6000, Web Site: www.morningstar.com (14)

Desmond, Kevin, Star Tribune Media Co, Minneapolis, MN. Tel: (612) 673-4000, FAX: (612) 673-4359, Web Site: www.startribunecompany.com (17)

Desmond, Laura, Starcom MediaVest Group, Chicago, IL. Tel: (312) 220-3535, Web Site: smvgroup.com (35)

Desrochers, Darrel, Tyco Valves & Controls, Houston, TX. Tel: (713) 986-4665, (800) 343-0990, FAX: (713) 937-5466, Web Site: www.tycovalves.com (16)

Desroches, Andre, CFA Communications, Toronto, ON Canada. Tel: (416) 504-5071, FAX: (416) 504-7390, Web Site: www.cfacommunications.com (32)

Destailleur, Elisabeth, Sitel, Nashville, TN. Tel: (615) 301-7100, (866) 95-SITEL, Web Site: www.sitel.com (29)

DeStefano, Gary M., Nike Inc, Beaverton, OR. Tel: (503) 671-4565, (800) 344-6543, FAX: (503) 671-6300, Web Site: www.nike.com (2)

DeStefano, Robert, Echomax, Teaneck, NJ. Tel: (201) 837-1371, FAX: (201) 837-6142 (35)

Destination Maternity Corp, Philadelphia, PA. Tel: (215) 873-2200, Web Site: www.motherswork.com (2)

Destinations Ireland & Beyond, Kingston, NY. Tel: (800) 832-1848, FAX: (845) 810-7678, E-Mail: info@digbtravel.com, Web Site: www.allgolftravel.com/tours (19)

Details Interactive LLC, Westfield, NJ. Tel: (917) 331-0685, E-Mail: mark@detailsinteractive.com, Web Site: www.detailsinteractive.com (16)

DeThorne, Raymond, The Field Museum, Chicago, IL. Tel: (312) 665-7600, FAX: (312) 665-7601, E-Mail: events@fieldmuseum.org, Web Site: www.fieldmuseum.org (1)

The Detroit Institute of Arts, Detroit, MI. Tel: (313) 833-7900, FAX: (313) 833-1390, Web Site: www.dia.org (14)

Detroit Newspapers, Detroit, MI. Tel: (313) 222-2300, FAX: (313) 496-5400, E-Mail: newsroom@detnews.com, Web Site: www.freep.com (18)

Deuschle, James, Rich Products Corp, Buffalo, NY. Tel: (716) 878-8000, (800) 828-2021, FAX: (716) 878-8765, Web Site: www.richs.com (16)

Deutsch, Maury, Mercury Envelope Co Inc, Rockville Centre, NY. Tel: (516) 678-6744, FAX: (516) 678-6764, E-Mail: mercuryenvelope@aol.com (26)

Deutsch, Scott, Mercury Envelope Co Inc, Rockville Centre, NY. Tel: (516) 678-6744, FAX: (516) 678-6764, E-Mail: mercuryenvelope@aol.com (26)

Deutsche Bank Alex Brown Inc, New York, NY. Tel: (212) 250-2500, FAX: (212) 797-4664, Web Site: www.db.com (14)

Devanna, Len, Trepoint, New York, NY. Tel: (646) 867-2252, E-Mail: challengeus@trepoint.com, Web Site: www.trepoint.com (35)

DeVard, Jerri, ADT LLC, Boca Raton, FL. Tel: (561) 988-3600, FAX: (561) 988-3673, Web Site: www.adt.com (16)

Development Dimensions International, Bridgeville, PA. Tel: (412) 257-0600, (800) 933-4463, FAX: (412) 220-2942, E-Mail: info@ddiworld.com, Web Site: www.ddiworld.com (16)

The Devereux Group, Marblehead, MA. Tel: (781) 631-9213, FAX: (781) 639-3044, E-Mail: roeser@devereuxgroup.com, Web Site: www.devereuxgroup.com (20)

Devessa, David, Music Choice, Horsham, PA. Tel: (215) 784-5840, Web Site: www.musicchoice.com (16)

Devin, Jeff, Postal En Espanol Inc, Tampa, FL. Tel: (813) 885-8888, Web Site: www.postalenespanol.com (20)

Devincenzi, Kevin, Rapid Response Marketing, Las Vegas, NV. Tel: (702) 475-5235, Web Site: www.rapidresponseonline.com (32)

Devine, Megan, d.trio marketing group, Minneapolis, MN. Tel: (612) 787-3333, FAX: (612) 436-0324, E-Mail: greatideas@dtrio.com, Web Site: www.dtrio.com (35)

Devine, Robert, Chem-Tainer Industries Inc, North Babylon, NY. Tel: (631) 661-8300, (800) 275-2436, (800) ASK-CHEM, FAX: (631) 661-8209, E-Mail: sales@chemtainer.com, Web Site: www.chemtainer.com (9)

Devitt, John, International Coins & Currency Inc, Montpelier, VT. Tel: (802) 223-6331, (800) 451-4463, FAX: (800) 229-3239, E-Mail: info@iccoin.org, Web Site: www.iccoin.com (6)

DeVitto, Ralph, American Cancer Society, Atlanta, GA. Tel: (404) 320-3333, (800) ACS-2345, FAX: (404) 329-5787, Web Site: www.cancer.org (1)

Devlin, Edward, PlusNetMarketing Inc, Exton, PA. Tel: (610) 458-0707, E-Mail: info@pnmarketing.com, Web Site: www.plusnetmarketing.com (21)

Devlin, Sherry, The Missoulian, Missoula, MT. Tel: (406) 523-5200, (800) 366-7102, FAX: (406) 523-5221, Web Site: www.missoulian.com (31)

DeVoldre, John A., Transcat, Rochester, NY. Tel: (585) 352-9460, (800) 800-5001, FAX: (585) 352-1486, Web Site: www.transcat.com (17)

DeVore, Irven, Anthro Photo File, Cambridge, MA. Tel: (617) 497-7227, FAX: (617) 484-6428, Web Site: www.anthrophoto.com (38)

DeVries, Wes, DM Assistance Inc, Portsmouth, NH. Tel: (603) 964-6156 (20)

DeVry Education Group, Downers Grove, IL. Tel: (630) 515-7700, (800) 73-DEVRY, E-Mail: inquiries@devrygroup.com, Web Site: www.devryeducationgroup.com (16)

Dew, III Matthew J., NGL Insurance Group, Madison, WI. Tel: (608) 257-5611, (800) 548-2962, FAX: (608) 257-9340, Web Site: www.nglic.com (15)

DeWalt, Stacy, Learning Care Group, Novi, MI. Tel: (248) 697-9115, Web Site: www.learningcaregroup.com (16)

Dewhurst, Moray P., Florida Power & Light Co, Juno Beach, FL. Tel: (305) 552-3552, (800) 468-8243, FAX: (305) 552-2487, Web Site: www.fpl.com (16)

DeWitt, Eric, 5MetaCom, Carmel, IN. Tel: (317) 580-7540, FAX: (317) 580-7550, E-Mail: mail@5metacom.com, Web Site: www.5metacom.com (35)

DeWitz, Jerry, ITW Bee Leitzke, Iron Ridge, WI. Tel: (920) 625-2342, FAX: (920) 625-2643, Web Site: www.itwbeeleitzke.com (16)

Dex Direct Marketing, Lone Tree, CO. Tel: (800) 999-4630, Web Site: www.dexlist.com (31)

Dex Media, Dallas-Fort Worth Airport, TX. Tel: (972) 453-7000, Web Site: www.dexmedia.com (31)

Dexposito & Partners, New York, NY. Tel: (646) 747-8800, Web Site: newamericanagency.com (35)

Dexta Corp, Napa, CA. Tel: (707) 255-2454, (800) 733-3982, FAX: (707) 255-8520, Web Site: www.dexta.com (16)

Dexter, Roger, B-T-B Internet Marketing Solutions, Middle Island, NY. Tel: (631) 924-3888, E-Mail: linickgroup@gmail.com, Web Site: www.linick.net; 222.asklinick.com (39)

Dexter, Roger, Copywriter's Council of America - (Freelancers), Middle Island, NY. Tel: (631) 924-3888, FAX: (631) 924-8555, E-Mail: cca4dmcopy@gmail.com, Web Site: www.linick.net; www.andrewlinickdirectmarketing.com (39)

Deyling, Jim, Blue Cross Blue Shield of South Carolina, Columbia, SC. Tel: (803) 788-0222, (800) 288-2227, FAX: (803) 736-4516, Web Site: www.bcbssc.com (15)

Deyo, Charles, Cendyn, Boca Raton, FL. Tel: (800) 760-8152, FAX: (561) 750-6795, E-Mail: info@cendyn.com, Web Site: www.cendyn.com (32)

DeYulis, Mark, New Pig Corp, Tipton, PA. Tel: (814) 684-0101, (800) 468-4647, FAX: (814) 684-0961, E-Mail: hothogs@newpig.com, Web Site: www.newpig.com (9)

Dhanuka, Pankaj, O'Currance Inc, Draper, UT. Tel: (801) 736-0500, (888) 628-7726, FAX: (801) 736-0510, E-Mail: sales@ocurrance.com, Web Site: www.ocurance.com (18)

Dharma Trading Co, Petaluma, CA. Tel: (415) 456-1211, (800) 542-5227, FAX: (415) 456-8747, E-Mail: service@dharmatrading.com, Web Site: www.dharmatrading.com (2)

Di Biase, David, Pilot Interactive Inc, Toronto, ON Canada. Tel: (416) 840-6438, E-Mail: hello@pilotinteractive.ca, Web Site: pilotinteractive.ca (35)

Di Giovanni, Rico, Marketing Agencies Association Worldwide, Edina, MN. Tel: (952) 922-0130, FAX: (203) 969-1499, E-Mail: keith.mccracker@maaw.org, Web Site: www.maaw.org (40)

Di Leo, Bruno V., IBM Corp, Armonk, NY. Tel: (914) 765-1900, FAX: (914) 765-6633, Web Site: www.ibm.com (16)

Diagraph Corp, Saint Charles, MO. Tel: (636) 300-2000, (800) 722-1125, FAX: (636) 300-2004, E-Mail: info@diagraph.com, Web Site: www.diagraph.com (16)

Diakon Lutheran Social Ministries, Allentown, PA. Tel: (877) 342-5667, FAX: (610) 682-1559, E-Mail: swangerb@diakon.org, Web Site: www.diakon.org (1)

Dial 800 LLC, Los Angeles, CA. Tel: (310) 273-9023, (800) 700-1987, E-Mail: sales@dial800.com, Web Site: www.dial800.com (32)

DialAmerica Marketing Inc, Mahwah, NJ. Tel: (201) 327-0200, (800) 531-3131, FAX: (201) 327-4875, Web Site: www.dialamerica.com (29)

The Dialog Corp, Morrisville, NC. Tel: (919) 804-6400, (800) 3 DIALOG, FAX: (919) 804-6410, E-Mail: customer@dialog.com, Web Site: www.dialog.com (30)

Dialog Direct, Highland Park, MI. Tel: (800) 523-5867, E-Mail: sales@dialog-direct.com, Web Site: www.dialog-direct.com (35)

DialogDirect, Troy, MI. Tel: (734) 374-8400, (800) 523-5867, FAX: (248) 836-2601, Web Site: www.dialogue-marketing.com (29)

Diamond Envelope Corp, Aurora, IL. Tel: (630) 499-2800, FAX: (630) 499-2801 (26)

Diamond Essence, Edison, NJ. Tel: (800) 909-2525, E-Mail: info@diamondessence.com, Web Site: www.diamond-essence.com (2)

Diamond Machining Technology, Marlborough, MA. Tel: (508) 481-5944, (800) 666-4368, FAX: (508) 485-3924, Web Site: www.dmtsharp.com (9)

Diamond Marketing Solutions, Carol Stream, IL. Tel: (630) 597-9100, E-Mail: info@dmsolutions.com, Web Site: www.dmsolutions.com (35)

Diamond, David A., Mutual of Omaha, Omaha, NE. Tel: (402) 342-7600, (800) 775-6000, FAX: (402) 351-2775, Web Site: www.mutualofomaha.com (15)

Diamond, Matthew C, Defy Media Inc, New York, NY. E-Mail: info@defymedia.com, Web Site: www.defymedia.com (33)

Diamonds By Rennie Ellen, New York, NY. Tel: (212) 869-5525, FAX: (212) 869-5526, Web Site: www.rennieellen.com (6)

Diane Publishing Co, Darby, PA. Tel: (610) 461-6200, E-Mail: hbaron@dianepublishing.net, Web Site: www.dianepublishing.net (43)

Diapers.com, Jersey City, NJ. Tel: (800) 342-7377, E-Mail: customercare@diapers.com, Web Site: www.diapers.com (5)

Diaz, Paula, Special Libraries Association (SLA), Alexandria, VA. Tel: (703) 647-4900, FAX: (703) 647-4901, E-Mail: sla@sla.org, Web Site: www.sla.org (40)

Dibben, David W., Central States Health & Life Co of Omaha, Omaha, NE. Tel: (402) 397-1111, (800) 826-6587, FAX: (402) 391-3772, Web Site: www.cso.com (15)

DiBlasi, Barbara, Marshall Fields Dept Stores, Minneapolis, MN. Tel: (612) 375-3004, Web Site: www.fields.com (5)

Diboll, Neil, Prairie Nursery, Westfield, WI. Tel: (800) 476-9453, FAX: (608) 296-2741, Web Site: www.prairienursery.com (8)

Dickenson, Sicily, Reliant Energy, Houston, TX. Tel: (713) 497-7794, (866) 222-7100, Web Site: www.reliant.com (16)

Dickerson, David, Globe Specialty Products Inc, Millbury, MA. Tel: (508) 871-1900 (17)

Dickerson, Jeff, Neat Co, Philadelphia, PA. Tel: (215) 382-3300, (866) 632-8732, FAX: (215) 386-2536, Web Site: neatco.com (22)

Dickinson, Marke, AAA Mid-Atlantic Insurance Groups, Wilmington, DE. Tel: (302) 299-4700, (800) 451-5921, FAX: (215) 864-5486, Web Site: www.aaamidatlantic.com (15)

Dickinson, Martin, Environmental Law Institute, Washington, DC. Tel: (202) 939-3800, FAX: (202) 939-3868, E-Mail: law@eli.org, Web Site: www.eli.org (17)

Dickman, James G., Lewis Direct, Baltimore, MD. Tel: (410) 539-5100, FAX: (410) 539-4700 (22)

Dickson, Sally, Marketing & Media Services LLC, Warwick, RI. Tel: (401) 737-7730, FAX: (401) 737-6465, Web Site: www.mmsipitv.com (30)

DiCola, James, Urban Response LLC, Hartville, OH. Tel: (330) 877-0800, (866) 550-3501, FAX: (330) 877-0802 (17)

Dicosmo, Nino A, Tridium Inc, Richmond, VA. Tel: (804) 525-1648, Web Site: www.tridium.com (9)

Dictionary of Marketing Terms, Hauppauge, NY. Tel: (631) 434-3311, (800) 645-3476, FAX: (631) 434-3723, E-Mail: barrons@barronseduc.com, Web Site: www.barronseduc.com (43)

Didactic Systems, Cranford, NJ. Tel: (908) 276-5413, FAX: (908) 276-7174, E-Mail: didacticra@aol.com (20)

Didit, Mineola, NY. Tel: (212) 631-0157, Web Site: www.did-it.com (16)

Diebel, Don, Gemini Publishing Co, Webster, TX. Tel: (281) 316-4276, E-Mail: getgirls@getgirls.com, Web Site: www.getgirls.com (17)

Diebel, Michele, Gemini Publishing Co, Webster, TX. Tel: (281) 316-4276, E-Mail: getgirls@getgirls.com, Web Site: www.getgirls.com (17)

Diebold Inc, North Canton, OH. Tel: (330) 490-4000, (800) DIEBOLD, Web Site: www.diebold.com (16)

Diebold, Marc, dgs Marketing Engineers, Fishers, IN. Tel: (317) 813-2222, FAX: (317) 813-2233, E-Mail: info@dgsmarketingengineers.com, Web Site: www.dgsmarketingengineers.com (35)

Diehl, Donna, Plymouth Rock Assurance, Lincroft, NJ. Tel: (732) 978-6255, Web Site: www.highpointins.com (15)

Diehl, Frederick, 2-10 Home Buyers Warranty, Denver, CO. Tel: (720) 747-6000, Web Site: www.2-10.com (15)

Diehl, Irene, Strategic Data Intelligence LLC, Northbrook, IL. Tel: (847) 897-5707, FAX: (847) 897-5715, E-Mail: info@sdintelligence.com, Web Site: www.sdintelligence.com (22)

Dieleman, Ann, ARAG, Des Moines, IA. Tel: (800) 247-4184, FAX: (515) 246-8710, E-Mail: service@ARAGgroup.com, Web Site: www.araggroup.com (15)

Dieme, Verena, Thieme Medical Publishers Inc, New York, NY. Tel: (212) 760-0888, (800) 782-3488, FAX: (212) 947-1112, E-Mail: info@thieme.com, Web Site: www.thieme.com (17)

Diemoz, Doug, Crate & Barrel, Northbrook, IL. Tel: (847) 272-2888, (800) 967-6696, FAX: (630) 369-4497, Web Site: www.crateandbarrell.com (8)

Dier, Kelly E., The Marmon Group LLC, Chicago, IL. Tel: (312) 372-9500, FAX: (312) 845-5305, Web Site: www.marmon.com (16)

Dierke, David, AccountMate Software Corp, Petaluma, CA. Tel: (707) 774-7500, FAX: (707) 774-7590, E-Mail: information@accountmate.com, Web Site: www.accountmate.com (22)

Diers, Michael, Old World Mouldings Inc, Bohemia, NY. Tel: (631) 563-8660, FAX: (631) 563-8815, E-Mail: mouldings@optonline.com, Web Site: www.oldworldmouldings.com (9)

Dieschbourg, Ed, Replogle Globes Inc, Broadview, IL. Tel: (708) 343-0900, FAX: (708) 343-0923, E-Mail: info@replogleglobes.com, Web Site: www.replogleglobes.com (16)

Dieste, Dallas, TX. Tel: (214) 259-8000, FAX: (214) 259-8040, E-Mail: contact@dieste.com, Web Site: www.dieste.com (35)

Dieste, Tony, Dieste, Dallas, TX. Tel: (214) 259-8000, FAX: (214) 259-8040, E-Mail: contact@dieste.com, Web Site: www.dieste.com (35)

Dietrich, Brian, Gaw-O'Hara Envelope Co, Chicago, IL. Tel: (773) 638-1200 (26)

Dietrich, Liane, LinkShare Corp, New York, NY. Tel: (646) 943-8200, FAX: (646) 943-8204, Web Site: www.linkshare.com (32)

Dietrich, Robert, Dalrada Financial Corp, San Diego, CA. Tel: (858) 791-6200, (877) 325-7232, FAX: (858) 277-3448, E-Mail: inquiries@dalrada.com, Web Site: www.dalrada.com (14)

Dietz, Brian, INTX - The Internet & Televison Expo, Washington, DC. Tel: (202) 222-2430, FAX: (202) 222-2431, E-Mail: infointx@ncta.com, Web Site: www.intxshow.com (42)

DiFato, Roger, Healthy Directions LLC, Bethesda, MD. Tel: (301) 340-2100, FAX: (301) 309-8516, Web Site: www.healthydirections.com (34)

DiFoglio, Kristin, JDRF, New York, NY. Tel: (212) 689-2860, (800) 533-CURE, FAX: (212) 785-9595, E-Mail: newyorkchapter@jdrf.org, Web Site: www.jdrf.org (1)

DigDev Direct, Deerfield Beach, FL. Tel: (954) 949-9500, (800) 873-5137, FAX: (954) 337-0251, E-Mail: info@digdev.com, Web Site: www.digdevdirect.com (35)

DigDev Direct, Deerfield Beach, FL. Tel: (954) 949-9500, Web Site: www.foundationmediagroup.com (16)

Digi International, Minnetonka, MN. Tel: (952) 912-3444, (877) 912-3444, FAX: (952) 912-4952, Web Site: www.digi.com (3)

Digi-Key Corp, Thief River Falls, MN. Tel: (218) 681-6674, (800) 344-4539, FAX: (218) 681-3380, E-Mail: sales@digikey.com, Web Site: www.digikey.com (3)

Digioia, Frank, The Fort Group, Ridgefield Park, NJ. Tel: (201) 445-0202, FAX: (201) 445-0626, E-Mail: info@fortgroupinc.com, Web Site: www.fortgroupinc.com (35)

DiGiovanni, Paul, Christian Brands, Phoenix, AZ. Tel: (602) 243-5200, (800) 521-2914, FAX: (602) 232-1855, Web Site: www.christian-brands.com (16)

DiGiovanni, Tom, Christian Brands, Phoenix, AZ. Tel: (602) 243-5200, (800) 521-2914, FAX: (602) 232-1855, Web Site: www.christian-brands.com (16)

Digital Speech Systems, Richardson, TX. Tel: (972) 235-2999, FAX: (972) 235-3036, E-Mail: sales@digitalspeech.com, Web Site: www.digitalspeech.com (3)

Digital Vision Resources Group - DVRG, Lenexa, KS. Tel: (913) 402-5900, E-Mail: info@dvrg.com, Web Site: www.dvrg.com (27)

DigitasLBi, Boston, MA. Tel: (617) 867-1000, E-Mail: newbusiness@digitas.com, Web Site: www.digitaslbi.com (35)

Dignan, Tom, Reputation.com, Redwood City, CA. Tel: (877) 425-5792, E-Mail: info@reputation.com, Web Site: www.reputation.com (32)

Dik & Associates Direct Marketing, Honolulu, HI. Tel: (808) 734-8868, FAX: (808) 734-8868, E-Mail: susandik@gmail.com (35)

Dik, Susan, Dik & Associates Direct Marketing, Honolulu, HI. Tel: (808) 734-8868, FAX: (808) 734-8868, E-Mail: susandik@gmail.com (35)

Dilenschneider, Robert L., The Dartnell Corp, Naples, FL. Tel: (585) 240-7301, (800) 447-4030, FAX: (585) 292-4392, E-Mail: customerservice@dartnellcorp.com, Web Site: www.dartnellcorp.com (17)

DiLeonardo, Albert, Vector Marketing Corp, Olean, NY. Tel: (716) 373-6141, (267) 880-1750, FAX: (716) 373-6145, Web Site: www.cutco.com (5)

Dill, Chris, Computer Business Services Inc, Americus, GA. Tel: (229) 924-4408, (866) 924-4408, FAX: (229) 924-3644, E-Mail: nelson@combusser.com, Web Site: www.combusser.com (3)

Dill, Marcy, Technology Review, Cambridge, MA. Tel: (617) 475-8000, FAX: (617) 258-5850, Web Site: www.technologyreview.com (17)

Dillard, Felicia, AIIM International, Silver Spring, MD. Tel: (301) 587-8202, (800) 477-2446, FAX: (301) 587-2711, E-Mail: aiim@aiim.org, Web Site: www.aiim.org (1)

Dille, Steve, Message Systems, Columbia, MD. Tel: (410) 872-4910, (877) 887-3031, FAX: (410) 872-4912, E-Mail: information@messagesystems.com, Web Site: www.messagesystems.com (32)

Diller, Barry, HSN Inc, Saint Petersburg, FL. Tel: (727) 872-1000, (800) 284-5757, Web Site: www.hsn.com (5)

Dillmann, Thomas, IJHANA, Los Angeles, CA. Tel: (213) 268-4283, (888) 421-9222, E-Mail: info@ijhana.com, Web Site: www.ijhana.com (20)

Dillon, Dan, Replogle Globes Inc, Broadview, IL. Tel: (708) 343-0900, FAX: (708) 343-0923, E-Mail: info@replogleglobes.com, Web Site: www.replogleglobes.com (16)

Dillon, G. Scott, Whitaker National, Huntington, WV. Tel: (304) 525-0852, (800) 377-8721, FAX: (304) 525-0874, Web Site: www.neshold.com (16)

Dillon, Mary, ULTA Salon Cosmetics Fragrance, Bolingbrook, IL. Tel: (630) 410-4800, (866) 983-8582 (7)

DiLucente, Anthony, ServiceMaster Co, Memphis, TN. Tel: (901) 766-1400, (866) 782-6787, Web Site: www.servicemaster.com (8)

Dimaio, Alicia, Special Libraries Association (SLA), Alexandria, VA. Tel: (703) 647-4900, FAX: (703) 647-4901, E-Mail: sla@sla.org, Web Site: www.sla.org (40)

Dimas, Constantine S., Loews Hotels, Inc, New York, NY. Tel: (212) 521-2000, (866) 563-9792, FAX: (212) 521-2379, Web Site: www.loewshotels.com (19)

The Dime Savings Bank of New York FSB, New York, NY. Tel: (212) 326-6170, FAX: (212) 326-6194, Web Site: www.dimewill.com (14)

DiMemmo, Vincent, Savvis Inc, Town and Country, MO. Tel: (314) 628-7000, (800) 728-8471, FAX: (703) 667-6298 (22)

Dimmock Hill Golf Course Pro Shop, Binghamton, NY. Tel: (607) 729-5511, (800) 727-5511, FAX: (607) 797-7434, Web Site: www.dimmockhill.com (11)

Dimon, James, JP Morgan Chase & Co, New York, NY. Tel: (212) 270-6000, E-Mail: jpmcinvestorrelations@jpmchase.com, Web Site: www.jpmorgan.com (14)

DiMuccio, Robert A., Amica Insurance, Lincoln, RI. Tel: (401) 334-6000, (800) 652-6422, FAX: (401) 334-4241, Web Site: www.amica.com (15)

DineEquity Inc, Glendale, CA. Tel: (866) 995-DINE, Web Site: dineequity.com (16)

DineWise, Farmingdale, NY. Tel: (631) 694-1111, (800) 749-1170, FAX: (631) 694-4064, E-Mail: info@dinewise.com, Web Site: www.dinewise.com (4)

The Dingley Press, Lisbon, ME. Tel: (207) 353-4151, (800) 317-4574, FAX: (207) 353-9886, E-Mail: webrequest@dingley.com, Web Site: www.dingley.com (27)

Dingus, Teresa, CPM Delta 1, Inc, Dallas, TX. Tel: (214) 349-6886, (800) 627-0252, FAX: (214) 503-1557, Web Site: www.cpmdelta1.com (11)

Dingwerth, Jared, VastCast Media Inc, Las Vegas, NV. Tel: (702) 221-8261, (800) 946-7112, FAX: (702) 666-8553, E-Mail: support@vastcast.com, Web Site: www.vastcastmedia.com (35)

Dinn Brothers Inc, West Springfield, MA. Tel: (413) 750-3466, (800) 628-9657, FAX: (800) 876-7497, E-Mail: sales@dinntrophy.com, Web Site: www.dinntrophy.com (16)

Dinn, Bill, Dinn Brothers Inc, West Springfield, MA. Tel: (413) 750-3466, (800) 628-9657, FAX: (800) 876-7497, E-Mail: sales@dinntrophy.com, Web Site: www.dinntrophy.com (16)

Dinn, Michael, Dinn Brothers Inc, West Springfield, MA. Tel: (413) 750-3466, (800) 628-9657, FAX: (800) 876-7497, E-Mail: sales@dinntrophy.com, Web Site: www.dinntrophy.com (16)

Dinozzi, John, Access Direct Systems Inc, Farmingdale, NY. Tel: (631) 420-0700, Web Site: www.accessdirect.com (28)

Dinozzi, John V., Access Direct Systems Inc, Farmingdale, NY. Tel: (631) 420-0700, Web Site: www.accessdirect.com (28)

Dinsmoor, Alex, Script to Screen Inc, Santa Ana, CA. Tel: (714) 558-3971, (800) 453-0003, FAX: (714) 558-1759, E-Mail: newbusiness@scripttoscreen.com, Web Site: www.scripttoscreen.com (32)

Dinyari Inc, San Jose, CA. Tel: (408) 289-5400, (888) 997-0400, Web Site: www.dinyari.com (9)

Dinyari, Farbod, Dinyari Inc, San Jose, CA. Tel: (408) 289-5400, (888) 997-0400, Web Site: www.dinyari.com (9)

Dionisio, Michelle, Benevilla, Surprise, AZ. Tel: (623) 584-4999, FAX: (623) 546-1589, Web Site: www.interfaithcommunitycare.org (1)

Christian Dior Perfumes, New York, NY. Tel: (877) 903-4671, (800) 929-3467, FAX: (212) 931-2954, Web Site: www.dior.com (7)

Diorio, James, Dial 800 LLC, Los Angeles, CA. Tel: (310) 273-9023, (800) 700-1987, E-Mail: sales@dial800.com, Web Site: www.dial800.com (32)

DiOrio, Steven, Handy Store Fixtures Inc, Newark, NJ. Tel: (973) 242-1600, (800) 631-4280, FAX: (973) 642-6222, Web Site: www.handystorefixtures.com (8)

Dipert Brown, Autumn, Dan Dipert Travel Service Inc, Arlington, TX. Tel: (817) 543-3700, (800) 433-5335, FAX: (817) 543-3728, Web Site: www.dandipert.com (19)

Dan Dipert Travel Service Inc, Arlington, TX. Tel: (817) 543-3700, (800) 433-5335, FAX: (817) 543-3728, Web Site: www.dandipert.com (19)

Dipert, Dan W., Dan Dipert Travel Service Inc, Arlington, TX. Tel: (817) 543-3700, (800) 433-5335, FAX: (817) 543-3728, Web Site: www.dandipert.com (19)

Dipert, Linda, Dan Dipert Travel Service Inc, Arlington, TX. Tel: (817) 543-3700, (800) 433-5335, FAX: (817) 543-3728, Web Site: www.dandipert.com (19)

DiPietro, Dave, Atlanta Cutlery Corp, Conyers, GA. Tel: (770) 922-3700, (800) 833-8838, FAX: (770) 760-8993, E-Mail: webmaster@atlantacutlery.com, Web Site: www.atlantacutlery.com (11)

Direct Access Marketing Services Inc, Syosset, NY. Tel: (516) 364-2777, FAX: (516) 364-0644, E-Mail: info@daxcess.com, Web Site: www.daxcess.com (22)

Direct Advantage Marketing, Pittsburgh, PA. Tel: (412) 381-2300, E-Mail: information@dam.com, Web Site: www.dam.com (29)

Direct Advantage Partners, Rowayton, CT. Tel: (203) 286-7100 (20)

Direct Auto Insurance, Nashville, TN. Tel: (615) 399-4859, Web Site: www.directgeneral.com (15)

Direct Brands Inc, New York, NY. Tel: (212) 930-4949, Web Site: www.columbiahouse.com (13)

Direct Channel Inc, West Bridgewater, MA. Tel: (508) 588-4448, FAX: (508) 588-4644, E-Mail: sales@directchannel.com, Web Site: www.directchannel.com (23)

The Direct Channels Group, New York, NY. Tel: (212) 208-1479, FAX: (631) 514-8716, E-Mail: info@ directchannelsgroup.com, Web Site: www. directchannelsgroup.com (35)

Direct Choice Inc, Wayne, PA. Tel: (610) 995-8201, (866) 995-2111, E-Mail: hello@directchoice.com, Web Site: www.directchoiceinc.com (35)

Direct Cinema Ltd Inc, Santa Monica, CA. Tel: (310) 636-8200, FAX: (310) 636-8228, E-Mail: dclvideo@aol.com, Web Site: www.directcinema. com (35)

Direct Connect Group, Cleveland, OH. Tel: (216) 651-9500, Web Site: www.directconnectgroup.com (35)

Direct Creative, Westerville, OH. Tel: (614) 882-8823, E-Mail: dean@directcreative.com, Web Site: www. directcreative.com (39)

Direct Data Capture Ltd, Evergreen, CO. Tel: (631) 547-5500, FAX: (631) 547-6800, E-Mail: jan@ datacapture.com, Web Site: www.datacapture.com (22)

Direct Dynamics LLC, Killingworth, CT. Tel: (860) 614-4816, E-Mail: info@direct-dynamics.com, Web Site: direct-dynamics.com (20)

Direct Energy, Toronto, ON Canada. Tel: (416) 758-8700, (800) 348-2999 (16)

Direct Gardening Association, La Grange, GA. Tel: (706) 298-0022, FAX: (706) 883-8215, Web Site: www.directgardeningassociation.com (1)

Direct Impact Group, Needham, MA. Tel: (781) 453-2200, FAX: (781) 453-1200, E-Mail: info@ directimpactgroup.com, Web Site: www. directimpactgroup.com (35)

Direct Impact Inc, Saint Louis, MO. Tel: (314) 336-1300, FAX: (314) 336-0013, E-Mail: info@ directimpactinc.com, Web Site: www. directimpactinc.com (35)

Direct Link Worldwide, Elizabeth, NJ. Tel: (908) 289-0703, (800) 223-7967, FAX: (908) 289-0705, E-Mail: infousa@directlink.com, Web Site: www. directlink.com (28)

Direct List Technology Inc, Orange, CA. Tel: (714) 772-3282, (888) 341-1117, FAX: (714) 772-6947, E-Mail: info@directlist.com, Web Site: www. directlist.com (23)

Direct Logic Solutions, Peoria, IL. Tel: (309) 688-5500, FAX: (309) 688-5502, E-Mail: nedbarrett@direct-logic.com, Web Site: www.direct-logic.com (22)

Direct Mail Center, San Francisco, CA. Tel: (415) 252-1600, FAX: (415) 252-9100, E-Mail: dmc@ directmailctr.com, Web Site: www.directmailctr. com (21)

Direct Mail Depot Inc, Piscataway, NJ. Tel: (732) 469-5900, FAX: (732) 469-8414, E-Mail: sales@ directmaildepot.com, Web Site: www. directmaildepot.com (28)

Direct Mail of NY-PostHaste, Buchanan, NY. Tel: (914) 736-2239 (28)

Direct Mail Service Inc, Pittsburgh, PA. Tel: (412) 471-6300, FAX: (412) 321-6061, E-Mail: info@ dirmailserv.com, Web Site: www.dirmailserv.com (21)

Direct Mail Solutions, Richmond, VA. Tel: (804) 254-8300, (877) 367-0800, Web Site: www. directmailsolutions.com (28)

Direct Mail Solutions LLC, Carol Stream, IL. Tel: (630) 653-6863, FAX: (630) 653-7144, E-Mail: support@ dmspostal.com, Web Site: www.dmspostal.com (28)

Direct Mail Source, Wilmette, IL. Tel: (847) 676-3744, E-Mail: dms@directmailsource.net (28)

Direct Mail Strategy Group (DMSG), Cresskill, NJ. Tel: (201) 567-3200, FAX: (201) 567-1530, E-Mail: listinfo@conraddirect.com, Web Site: www. conraddirect.com (31)

Direct Mail Systems, Clearwater, FL. Tel: (727) 573-1985, (800) 683-6245, FAX: (727) 573-1747, E-Mail: info@direct-mail-systems.com, Web Site: www.direct-mail-systems.com (20)

Direct Mail Trackers, Medford, NY. Tel: (631) 758-0984, E-Mail: info@dmtrackers.com, Web Site: www.dmtrackers.com (28)

Direct Market Designs Inc, Paterson, NJ. Tel: (973) 925-9600, Web Site: www.dmd-liberty.com (28)

Direct Marketers On Call Inc (DMOC), New York, NY. Tel: (212) 691-1942, FAX: (212) 924-1331, E-Mail: info@dmoc-inc.com, Web Site: www.dmoc-inc.com (20)

The Direct Marketing Association, New York, NY. Tel: (212) 768-7277, E-Mail: info@the-dma.org, Web Site: thedma.org (1)

Direct Marketing Association of Detroit, Royal Oak, MI. Tel: (248) 478-4888, FAX: (248) 478-6437, E-Mail: dmad@ameritech.net, Web Site: www. dmad.org (40)

Direct Marketing Association of Northern California, Morgan Hill, CA. Tel: (800) 613-9266, FAX: (800) 613-8819, E-Mail: lbeasley@beasleydirect.com, Web Site: www.dmanc.org (40)

Direct Marketing Association of Saint Louis, Washington. MO. Tel: (866) 516-0121, FAX: (636) 239-2324, E-Mail: mparisien@mac.com, Web Site: www.dmastl.org (40)

Direct Marketing Association of Southern California, Newbury Park, CA. Tel: (818) 541-1152, FAX: (818) 541-1959, Web Site: www.ladma.org (40)

Direct Marketing Association of Toronto, Toronto, ON Canada. Tel: (905) 564-0150 X108, FAX: (905) 564-6621, E-Mail: pete@themose.ca, Web Site: www.dmatoronto.org (40)

Direct Marketing Association of Washington, Reston, VA. Tel: (703) 689-DMAW, FAX: (703) 481-DMAW, E-Mail: info@dmaw.org, Web Site: www. dmaw.org (40)

Direct Marketing Audit Systems, Bridgeton, MO. Tel: (314) 739-7480, FAX: (314) 739-7284, Web Site: www.dmasinc.com (22)

The Direct Marketing Club of New York Inc, Garden City, NY. Tel: (516) 746-6700, FAX: (516) 294-8141, E-Mail: info@dmcny.org, Web Site: www. dmcny.org (1)

Direct Marketing Consultant, Sharon, PA. Tel: (724) 699-0230 (20)

Direct Marketing Designs Inc, Greenwood Village, CO. Tel: (303) 649-9888, FAX: (303) 649-1917, E-Mail: info@directmarketingdesigns.com, Web Site: www. directmarketingdesigns.com (35)

Direct Marketing Digest, Minneapolis, MN. Tel: (612) 788-1673, E-Mail: info@nmoa.org, Web Site: www. nmoa.org (43)

Direct Marketing Dynamics Inc, Germantown, MD. Tel: (301) 916-3900, FAX: (301) 515-0404, E-Mail: jim@directmarketingdynamics.com, Web Site: www.directmarketingdynamics.com (35)

Direct Marketing Group, Eden Prairie, MN. Tel: (952) 975-5060, (888) 397-5060, FAX: (952) 906-0608, Web Site: www.directmg.com (35)

Direct Marketing Insights Inc, Goodyear, AZ. Tel: (843) 817-7488, E-Mail: jimp@dminsights.com, Web Site: www.dminsights.com (20)

Direct Marketing Market Place, New Providence, NJ. Tel: (908) 517-0780, (844) 592-4197, FAX: (908) 608-3012, Web Site: www.dirmktgplace.com (43)

Direct Marketing News, Markham, ON Canada. Tel: (905) 201-6600, (800) 668-1838, FAX: (905) 201-6601, E-Mail: home@dmn.ca, Web Site: www.dmn. ca (43)

Direct Marketing Partners, Sacramento, CA. Tel: (916) 974-6969, (800) 909-2626, FAX: (916) 920-5156, E-Mail: info@dirmkt.com, Web Site: www. directmarketingpartners.com (29)

Direct Marketing Resources, Charlotte, NC. Tel: (704) 845-5890, (888) 644-4DMR, E-Mail: dan@ dmresources.com, Web Site: www.dmresources.com (20)

Direct Marketing Resources Group Inc, Raleigh, NC. Tel: (919) 231-2728, (800) 517-5253, Web Site: www.improvedmarketingresults.com (20)

Direct Marketing Solutions Inc, Portland, OR. Tel: (503) 281-1400, FAX: (503) 249-5120, Web Site: www.teamdms.com (35)

The Direct Marketing Specialists Inc, Chicago, IL. Tel: (312) 266-7906, FAX: (312) 266-9230, E-Mail: rwinedms@networkgci.com, Web Site: thedirectmarketingspecialists.com (35)

Direct Marketing Strategy, Planning & Execution, Blacklick, OH. Tel: (614) 755-4152, (800) 722-4726, Web Site: www.mcgraw-hill.com (43)

Direct Marketing Tool Kit for Small Business, Minneapolis, MN. Tel: (612) 788-1673, E-Mail: info@ nmoa.org, Web Site: www.nmoa.org/ directmarketingtoolkit (43)

Direct One Inc, Winter Park, FL. Tel: (407) 673-4500, FAX: (407) 673-4501, E-Mail: wariagno@ directoneinc.com, Web Site: www.directoneinc.com (28)

Direct Options, West Chester, OH. Tel: (513) 779-4416, (800) 749-3678, FAX: (513) 779-4426, E-Mail: info@directoptions.com, Web Site: www. directoptions.com (35)

Direct Partners, Marina Del Rey, CA. Tel: (310) 482-4200, FAX: (310) 482-4201, Web Site: www. directpartners.com (35)

Direct Resources Group Inc, Seattle, WA. Tel: (206) 455-6157, FAX: (206) 749-0005, E-Mail: results@ drg.com, Web Site: www.drg.com (35)

Direct Response Academy, Austin, TX. Tel: (512) 301-5900, FAX: (512) 301-7900, Web Site: www. directresponseacademy.com (41)

Direct Response Consulting, McLean, VA. Tel: (703) 749-3100, FAX: (703) 749-0962, E-Mail: info@ drcs.com, Web Site: www.drcs.com (17)

Direct Response Enhancements LLC, Scottsdale, AZ. Tel: (480) 451-7384, FAX: (480) 661-8460, Web Site: www.dreteleconsultants.com (29)

Direct Response Marketing, Clearwater, FL. Tel: (727) 573-1985, (800) 683-6245, FAX: (727) 573-1747, E-Mail: drmclwr@tampabay.rr.com, Web Site: www.dmsmails.com (28)

Direct Response Media Group, Oakville, ON Canada. Tel: (905) 465-1233, (866) 993-0600, FAX: (905) 465-1228, E-Mail: info@drmg.ca, Web Site: www. drmg.com (21)

Direct Response Services, Glen Carbon, IL. Tel: (618) 288-8811, (800) 795-5478, FAX: (618) 288-3005, E-Mail: drs@drslist.com, Web Site: www.drslist. com (23)

Direct Results, West Springfield, MA. Tel: (413) 732-8310, FAX: (413) 732-8361 (21)

Direct SAT TV LLC, Southern Pines, NC. Tel: (910) 693-3042, (800) 595-4101, FAX: (866) 935-4097, Web Site: www.directsattv.com (3)

Direct Selling Association, Washington, DC. Tel: (202) 452-8866, FAX: (202) 452-9010, E-Mail: info@dsa. org, Web Site: www.dsa.org (40)

Direct Selling Education Foundation, Washington, DC. Tel: (202) 452-8866, FAX: (202) 452-9015, E-Mail: info@dsef.org, Web Site: www.dsef.org (40)

Direct Sports Supply, Pearisburg, VA. Tel: (540) 921-1243, (800) 456-0072, FAX: (540) 921-1475, Web Site: www.directsports.com (11)

Direct Success Communications Inc, Chester Springs, PA. Tel: (610) 321-0321, FAX: (610) 321-0322 (35)

Direct Supply Inc, Milwaukee, WI. Tel: (414) 358-2805, (800) 634-7328, FAX: (414) 358-2397, E-Mail: deardirect@directs.com, Web Site: www.directsupply.net (16)

Direct Tech Inc, Omaha, NE. Tel: (402) 895-2100, Web Site: www.direct-tech.com (34)

Direct Ventures Inc, Rye, NY. Tel: (914) 833-9842, FAX: (914) 834-3883, E-Mail: bsideroff@directventuresmcinc.wm (20)

DirectBuy Inc, Merrillville, IN. Tel: (219) 736-1100, FAX: (219) 755-6279, Web Site: www.ucctotalhome.com (1)

DirecTech Holding Company Inc, Maysville, KY. Tel: (866) 550-5030, E-Mail: ceo@directech.com, Web Site: www.directech.com (22)

DirectInnovations Inc, Suwanee, GA. Tel: (404) 402-2825, E-Mail: htorgersen@directinnovations.biz, Web Site: www.directinnovations.biz (24)

Directions Marketing, Ann Arbor, MI. Tel: (734) 930-2820, FAX: (734) 930-9189, E-Mail: directions@directions.com.eg, Web Site: www.directions.com. eg (20)

Directives/Targeted Marketing and Communications, Plymouth, MA. Tel: (215) 546-7817, Web Site: www.directivesmarketing.com (20)

DirectMail.com, Prince Frederick, MD. Tel: (888) 690-2252, FAX: (301) 855-9810, Web Site: www.directmail.com (28)

The Directors Network, Encino, CA. Tel: (818) 906-0006, E-Mail: info@tdnartists.com, Web Site: www.tdnartists.com (35)

Directory of American Business & Insurance Attorneys, New York, NY. Tel: (732) 458-7788, (800) 445-7995, FAX: (732) 458-7710. E-Mail: staff@abialaw.com, Web Site: www.abialaw.com (15)

The Directory of Business Information Resources, Amenia, NY. Tel: (845) 373-8263, E-Mail: cstupak@greyhouse.com, Web Site: www.greyhouse.com (43)

Directory of Mail Order Catalogs, Minneapolis, MN. Tel: (612) 788-1673, E-Mail: info@nmoa.org, Web Site: www.nmoa.org (43)

Directory of Mail Order Catalogs, Amenia, NY. Tel: (518) 789-8700, (800) 562-2139, FAX: (518) 789-0556, E-Mail: cstupak@greyhouse.com, Web Site: www.greyhouse.com (43)

Directory of Major Mailers & What They Mail, Philadelphia, PA. Tel: (215) 238-5300, (800) 777-8074, FAX: (215) 238-5412, E-Mail: customerservice@napco.com, Web Site: www.majormailers.com (43)

Directory of Major Malls Inc, Nyack, NY. Tel: (845) 348-7000, (800) 898-6255, Web Site: shoppingcenters.com (23)

Directory of Premium, Incentive & Travel Buyers, Richmond, VA. Tel: (804) 762-4455, (800) 223-1797, FAX: (804) 935-0271, E-Mail: amdouglas4@aol.com, Web Site: www.douglaspublications.com (43)

DirectSmile LLC, Bloomfield, NJ. Tel: (973) 338-9368, Web Site: www.directsmile.com (22)

DIRECTV LLC, El Segundo, CA. Tel: (310) 535-5000, FAX: (310) 535-5225, Web Site: www.directv.com (16)

Direxxis Inc, Needham, MA. Tel: (781) 444-7900, FAX: (781) 444-7909, Web Site: www.direxxismarketing.com (22)

Dirmark Group Inc, Roswell, GA. Tel: (678) 245-1831, (888) 221-4968, E-Mail: dirmarkonline@dirmark.com, Web Site: dirmark.com (23)

DiRosa, James R., Quartermaster Uniform & Equipment Co, Cerritos, CA. Tel: (866) 673-7645, FAX: (562) 304-7335, E-Mail: help@qmuniforms.com, Web Site: www.qmuniforms.com (2)

Diruzza, Joe, MFE Instruments, Salem, NH. Tel: (603) 893-8778, (800) 843-8011, FAX: (603) 893-8851, Web Site: www.stockeryale.com (9)

Dirxion, Saint Louis, MO. Tel: (636) 717-2300, Web Site: www.dirxion.com (16)

Disabled American Veterans, Cincinnati, OH. Tel: (859) 441-7300, FAX: (859) 442-2084, E-Mail: feedback@davmail.org, Web Site: www.dav.org (1)

DiSalle, Tony, Buick, Detroit, MI. Tel: (313) 556-5000, (800) 521-7300, FAX: (313) 556-5108, Web Site: www.buick.com (16)

Disc Graphics Inc, Hauppauge, NY. Tel: (631) 234-1400, FAX: (631) 234-1460, E-Mail: info@discgraphics.com, Web Site: www.discgraphics.com (27)

Disc Makers, New York, NY. Tel: (800) 468-9353, Web Site: www.discmakers.com (3)

Disch, Thomas R., Handi-Ramp Inc, Libertyville, IL. Tel: (847) 680-7700, (800) 876-RAMP, FAX: (847) 816-7689, E-Mail: info@handiramp.com, Web Site: www.handiramp.com (7)

DiscMail Direct Coalition, Port Washington, NY. Tel: (516) 757-6720, Web Site: http://mesalliance.org/ (40)

Discover Financial Services, Riverwoods, IL. Tel: (224) 405-0900 (14)

Discover Publications, Worthington, OH. Tel: (877) 872-3080, FAX: (614) 431-3324, E-Mail: info@discoverpubs.com, Web Site: www.discoverpubs.com (17)

Discovery, Eatontown, NJ. Tel: (732) 933-1899, Web Site: www.discoveryco.com (9)

Discovery Communications Inc, Silver Spring, MD. Tel: (240) 662-2000, FAX: (240) 662-1868, Web Site: corporate.discovery.com (16)

Discovery Toys, Livermore, CA. Tel: (925) 606-2600, (800) 426-4777, FAX: (925) 370-0289, Web Site: www.discoverytoysinc.net (16)

Disieno, Denise, PPS - Packaging Printing Specialists, Saint Charles, IL. Tel: (630) 513-8060, (877) 573-8060, FAX: (630) 513-8062, E-Mail: pps@ppsofil.com, Web Site: www.PPSofIL.com (27)

Diskin, Jeff, Hilton HHonors, McLean, VA. Tel: (703) 883-1000, Web Site: hhonors.hilton.com (16)

Dismukes, Phil, GreatLists.com, Herndon, VA. Tel: (703) 821-8130, FAX: (703) 821-8243. E-Mail: info@greatlists.com, Web Site: greatlists.com (23)

Disney/ABC Television Group, Burbank, CA. Tel: (818) 460-7477, Web Site: www.disneyabctv.com (32)

Disney Vacation Club, Kissimmee, FL. Tel: (407) 566-3000, (800) 500-3990, FAX: (407) 566-3393 (19)

Walt Disney Parks & Resorts, Lake Buena Vista, FL. Tel: (407) 824-2222, FAX: (407) 566-5700, Web Site: www.disneyworld.com (19)

Dispatch Letter Service, New York, NY. Tel: (212) 307-5943, FAX: (212) 307-6103, Web Site: www.dispatchletterservice.com (28)

Dispensa-Matic Label Dispensers, Saint Louis, MO. Tel: (314) 231-6006, (800) 325-7303, FAX: (314) 621-1602, E-Mail: info@dispensamatic.com, Web Site: www.dispensa-matic.com (34)

Disser, David, Customer Retention Solutions, Portage, MI. Tel: (269) 324-7385 (20)

Dissette, Mark R., Holy Cross Hospital, Fort Lauderdale, FL. Tel: (954) 771-8000, FAX: (954) 229-8597, Web Site: www.holy-cross.com (16)

Distribution Postal Co Inc, Baltimore, MD. Tel: (410) 488-1002, (800) 992-4525, FAX: (410) 488-2344, E-Mail: louishaber@distpost.com, Web Site: www.distpost.com (28)

Ditmer, Dale, Dalco Electronics, Springboro, OH. Tel: (937) 743-8042, (800) 445-5342, FAX: (937) 743-9251, Web Site: www.dalco.com (3)

Dittman, Terrie, Harcourt Educational Measurement, San Antonio, TX. Tel: (210) 299-1061, (800) 211-8378, FAX: (800) 232-1223, Web Site: www.harcourtassessment.com (17)

Diversified Healthcare Services, Richardson, TX. Tel: (972) 238-1492, FAX: (972) 907-8283, Web Site: www.dhscorp.com (15)

Diversified Investment Advisors, Harrison, NY. Tel: (914) 627-3000, FAX: (914) 627-3280, Web Site: www.divinvest.com (14)

Diversified Photo Supply Corp, Gardena, CA. Tel: (310) 328-8577, (800) 544-1609, FAX: (310) 328-8518, Web Site: www.diversifiedphoto.com (10)

The Diversified Services Group Inc, Wayne, PA. Tel: (610) 989-1710, FAX: (610) 989-1730, E-Mail: rfgrieb@dsg-network.com, Web Site: www.dsg-network.com (20)

Divine Word Missionaries, Techny, IL. Tel: (847) 412-7233, (800) 275-0626, Web Site: www.svdmissions.org (1)

Dixit, Jay, Sussex Publishers Inc, New York, NY. Tel: (212) 260-7210, FAX: (212) 260-7445, Web Site: www.blues-buster.com (17)

Dixon Direct, Dixon, IL. Tel: (815) 284-2211, FAX: (630) 810-1934, E-Mail: info@dixondirect.com, Web Site: dixondirect.com (35)

Dixon, Diane B., Avery Dennison Corp, Brea, CA. Tel: (714) 674-8500, (800) 462-8379, FAX: (714) 674-6929, Web Site: www.avery.com (10)

Dixon, Drew, Inmar, Winston-Salem, NC. Tel: (336) 631-2500, FAX: (336) 631-2888, E-Mail: ibizdev@inmar.com, Web Site: www.promotionslogistics.com (14)

Dixon, J. Gordon, ARI, Orchard Hill, GA. Tel: (770) 227-8222, (800) 241-5064, FAX: (770) 227-9190, Web Site: www.halt.com (16)

Dizon, Marc A., Georgetown University Law Center, Washington, DC. Tel: (202) 662-9890, FAX: (202) 662-9891, E-Mail: cle@law.georgetown.edu, Web Site: www.law.georgetown.edu (13)

Dlaboha, Lila, The Granger Collection, New York, NY. Tel: (212) 447-1789, FAX: (212) 447-1492, Web Site: www.granger.com (38)

Dlesk, Sr. Richard, Mail America Inc, Wheeling, WV. Tel: (304) 242-8081, (800) 421-2150, FAX: (304) 242-8082, E-Mail: sales@mailamerica.com, Web Site: www.mailamerica.com (35)

DM Communications Inc, Sarasota, FL. Tel: (617) 482-5900, E-Mail: cmay@dmcommunications.com, Web Site: www.dmcommunications.com (35)

DME Holdings, Daytona Beach, FL. Tel: (877) 720-0082, E-Mail: info@dmedelivers.com, Web Site: dmedelivers.com (21)

DMXENGAGE, Centennial, CO. Tel: (303) 339-9300, FAX: (303) 388-6363, E-Mail: workwithus@dmxengage.com, Web Site: dmxengage.com (21)

DNE Nutraceuticals Inc, Farmingdale, NJ. Tel: (212) 235-5200, (800) 221-1833, FAX: (212) 235-5243, E-Mail: info@dnenutra.com, Web Site: www.dnenutra.com (7)

Do-It Corp, South Haven, MI. Tel: (269) 637-1121, (800) 426-4822, FAX: (269) 637-7223, E-Mail: sales@do-it.com, Web Site: www.do-it.com (9)

Do It Yourself Direct Marketing, Hoboken, NJ. Tel: (201) 748-6000, FAX: (201) 748-6088, E-Mail: info@wiley.com, Web Site: www.wiley.com (43)

DoAll Co, Wheeling, IL. Tel: (847) 824-1122, (800) 92-DOALL, FAX: (847) 699-7524, E-Mail: info@doall.com, Web Site: www.doall.com (16)

Doane, Saint Louis, MO. Tel: (314) 569-2700, (866) 647-0918, FAX: (314) 569-1083, Web Site: www.doane.com (17)

Dobbin, Daniel, Action Mailers Inc, Aston, PA. Tel: (610) 859-0500, (800) 258-5992, FAX: (610) 859-0505, Web Site: www.actionmailer.com (27)

Dobbin, Kathy, Action Mailers Inc, Aston, PA. Tel: (610) 859-0500, (800) 258-5992, FAX: (610) 859-0505, Web Site: www.actionmailer.com (27)

Dobbins, Mike, Perimeter Technology Inc, Manchester, NH. Tel: (603) 645-1616, (800) 645-1650, FAX: (603) 645-1424, Web Site: www.perimetertechnology.com (34)

Dobin, Bruce, Reliable Mail Service Inc, Edison, NJ. Tel: (732) 346-9779, (800) 773-6338, FAX: (732) 346-9799, E-Mail: bdobin@reliablemailservice.com, Web Site: www.reliablemailservice.com (28)

Dobina, Don, MPC Louisville Promotions, Louisville, KY. Tel: (800) 331-0989, FAX: (888) 451-8475, E-Mail: sales@mpcpromotions.com, Web Site: www.mpcpromotions.com (33)

Dobkin, Jeffrey, Danielle Adams Publishing Co, Merion Station, PA. Tel: (610) 642-1000, E-Mail: jeff@dobkin.com, Web Site: www.danielleadams.com (35)

Dobos, Greg, Catalyst Inc, Providence, RI. Tel: (401) 732-1886, FAX: (401) 732-5528, Web Site: www.catalystb2b.com (35)

Dobrin, Ellen, USA TODAY, Mc Lean, VA. Tel: (703) 854-3400, (800) 872-0001, E-Mail: accuracy@usatoday.com, Web Site: www.usatoday.com (17)

Dobrus, Stefan, Civil Service Employees Insurance Group, Walnut Creek, CA. Tel: (415) 274-7803, (925) 817-6300, (800) 282-6848, Web Site: www.cseinsurance.com (15)

Dobson, Mark, WSI, Mississauga, ON Canada. Tel: (905) 678-7588, (888) 678-7588, FAX: (905) 678-7242, E-Mail: contact@wsiworld.com, Web Site: www.wsiworld.com (35)

Docherty, Robert, Direct Marketing Market Place, New Providence, NJ. Tel: (908) 517-0780, (844) 592-4197, FAX: (908) 608-3012, Web Site: www.dirmktgplace.com (43)

Dochtermann, Erik, MODCo Media, New York, NY. Tel: (212) 686-0006, FAX: (212) 686-6991, Web Site: modcomedia.com (35)

Dockeray, Tara, Fixed Address Marketing Inc, Aurora, ON Canada. Tel: (905) 750-0029, E-Mail: dockeray@fixedaddressmarketing.com, Web Site: www.fixedaddressmarketing.com (23)

Dockerman, David, Tom Snyder Productions, Watertown, MA. Tel: (617) 926-6000, (800) 342-0236, FAX: (800) 304-1254, E-Mail: ask@tomsnyder.com, Web Site: www.tomsnyder.com (16)

Dockery House Publishing Inc, Lindale, TX. Tel: (903) 882-6900, FAX: (903) 882-6902, E-Mail: questions@dockerypublishing.com, Web Site: www.dockerypublishing.com (27)

Dockery, Rod, Dockery House Publishing Inc, Lindale, TX. Tel: (903) 882-6900, FAX: (903) 882-6902, E-Mail: questions@dockerypublishing.com, Web Site: www.dockerypublishing.com (27)

Dockter, James E., PBD Worldwide Fulfillment Services, Alpharetta, GA. Tel: (770) 442-8633, FAX: (770) 442-9742, E-Mail: sales.marketing@pbd.com, Web Site: www.pbd.com (28)

Doctor's Best Inc, San Clemente, CA. Tel: (949) 498-3628, (800) 333-6977, FAX: (800) 754-2036, (949) 498-3952, E-Mail: info@drbvitamins.com, Web Site: www.drbvitamins.com (16)

The Doctor's Inc, Napa, CA. Tel: (707) 226-0176, E-Mail: info@thedoctors.com, Web Site: www.thedoctors.com (15)

Drs Foster & Smith Inc, Rhinelander, WI. Tel: (715) 369-3305, Web Site: www.drsfostersmith.com (2)

Doctors Without Borders, New York, NY. Tel: (212) 679-6800, FAX: (212) 679-7016, Web Site: www.doctorswithoutborders.org (1)

Dodd, Jason, Tiziani Whitmyre Inc, Sharon, MA. Tel: (781) 793-9380, FAX: (781) 793-9395, E-Mail: info@tizinc.com, Web Site: www.tizinc.com (21)

Dodds, Diane, Rapids Wholesale Equipment, Marion, IA. Tel: (319) 447-1670, (800) 472-7431, FAX: (319) 447-1680, (800) 858-0327, E-Mail: judys@rapidswholesale.com, Web Site: www.rapidswholesale.com (16)

Dodds, Joe, Rapids Wholesale Equipment, Marion, IA. Tel: (319) 447-1670, (800) 472-7431, FAX: (319) 447-1680, (800) 858-0327, E-Mail: judys@rapidswholesale.com, Web Site: www.rapidswholesale.com (16)

Doddy, Aine, Concern Worldwide, New York, NY. Tel: (212) 557-8000, FAX: (212) 557-8004, Web Site: /www.concernusa.org (1)

Dodenhoff, Steve, Syntellect, Phoenix, AZ. Tel: (602) 789-2800, (800) 788-9733, FAX: (602) 789-2899, Web Site: www.syntellect.com (16)

Dodge, Jason, I-Behavior Inc, Louisville, CO. Tel: (303) 228-5000, E-Mail: ib-sales@i-behavior.com, Web Site: www.i-behavior.com (23)

Dodge, Jason, KBM Group, Louisville, CO. Tel: (800) 579-1950, E-Mail: sales@kbmg.com, Web Site: www.kbmg.com (22)

Dodge, Larry, Booth Michigan, Grand Rapids, MI. Tel: (616) 222-5824, FAX: (616) 222-5318, Web Site: www.boothnewspapers.com (17)

Dodson & Associates, Dallas, TX. Tel: (972) 931-9200 (20)

Dodson, David, Chattanooga Shooting Supplies Inc, Chattanooga, TN. Tel: (423) 894-3007, (800) 251-4808, FAX: (423) 855-5513, Web Site: www.chattanoogashooting.com (16)

Dodson, Denise, Issues & Answers Network Inc, Virginia Beach, VA. Tel: (757) 456-1100, FAX: (757) 456-0377, E-Mail: info@issans.com, Web Site: www.issans.com (30)

Dodson, Gordon O., Dodson & Associates, Dallas, TX. Tel: (972) 931-9200 (20)

Dodson, Larry, Dorothy Biddle Service, Greeley, PA. Tel: (570) 226-3239, FAX: (570) 226-0349, E-Mail: info@dorothybiddle.com, Web Site: www.dorothybiddle.com (8)

Dodson, Lynne, Dorothy Biddle Service, Greeley, PA. Tel: (570) 226-3239, FAX: (570) 226-0349, E-Mail: info@dorothybiddle.com, Web Site: www.dorothybiddle.com (8)

Doehner, George J., Bulkley Dunton Publishing Group, New York, NY. Tel: (212) 863-1800, FAX: (212) 863-1870, Web Site: www.internationalpaper.com (25)

Doerfler, Ronald J., The Hearst Corp, New York, NY. Tel: (212) 649-2000, FAX: (212) 649-2108, Web Site: www.hearst.com/magazines/ (17)

Doering, Tim, PNC Bank Corp, Pittsburgh, PA. Tel: (412) 762-2000/3514, (800) 422-6537, FAX: (412) 762-4482 (14)

Doerr, R. Chris, Blue Cross Blue Shield of Florida, Jacksonville, FL. Tel: (904) 791-6111, (800) 477-3736, FAX: (904) 905-6638, E-Mail: katie.magee@bcbsfl.com, Web Site: www.bcbsfl.com (15)

Doerr, Rick, Rapp, New York, NY. Tel: (212) 817-6800, FAX: (212) 686-7047, E-Mail: rick.doerr@rapp.com, Web Site: www.rapp.com (15)

Doheny, II Edward L., P & H Mining Equipment, Milwaukee, WI. Tel: (414) 671-4400, FAX: (414) 671-7618, Web Site: www.phmining.com (16)

Doherty, Dave, Digi-Key Corp, Thief River Falls, MN. Tel: (218) 681-6674, (800) 344-4539, FAX: (218) 681-3380, E-Mail: sales@digikey.com, Web Site: www.digikey.com (3)

Doherty, Mike, Cole & Weber United, Seattle, WA. Tel: (206) 447-9595, FAX: (206) 233-0178, E-Mail: info@cwunited.com, Web Site: www.cwunited.com (35)

Doherty, Robert B, American College of Physicians, Philadelphia, PA. Tel: (215) 351-2600, (800) 523-1546, FAX: (215) 351-2686, Web Site: www.acponline.org (17)

Doi, Tracey C., Toyota Motor Sales USA Inc, Torrance, CA. Tel: (310) 468-4000, (800) 331-4331, FAX: (310) 468-7841, Web Site: www.toyota.com (16)

Doiel, Ron, EMED Co Inc, Buffalo, NY. Tel: (716) 626-1616, (800) 442-3633, FAX: (716) 626-1630, E-Mail: customerservice@emedco.com, Web Site: www.emedco.com (16)

Dolaher, Mary, IDG World Expo, Framingham, MA. Tel: (508) 879-0700, E-Mail: info@idgworldexpo.com, Web Site: www.idgworldexpo.com (42)

Dolak, John, Sony Electronics Inc, San Diego, CA. Tel: (858) 942-2400, Web Site: www.sony.com (16)

Dolan, Charles F., Cablevision Systems Corp, Bethpage, NY. Tel: (516) 803-2300, FAX: (516) 803-3134, Web Site: www.cablevision.com (16)

Dolan, James L., Cablevision Systems Corp, Bethpage, NY. Tel: (516) 803-2300, FAX: (516) 803-3134, Web Site: www.cablevision.com (16)

Dolan, John P., Union Switch & Signal Inc, Pittsburgh, PA. Tel: (412) 688-2400, (800) 351-1520, FAX: (412) 688-2399, Web Site: www.switch.com (16)

Dolan, Kristin A., Cablevision Systems Corp, Bethpage, NY. Tel: (516) 803-2300, FAX: (516) 803-3134, Web Site: www.cablevision.com (16)

Dolan, Michael, Data Square LLC, Stamford, CT. Tel: (203) 964-9733, FAX: (203) 964-0783, E-Mail: info@datasquare.com, Web Site: www.datasquare.com (22)

Dolan, Tom, Westcon, Tarrytown, NY. Tel: (914) 829-7000, FAX: (914) 829-7137, Web Site: www.westcon.com (16)

Dole, Paul, KCEOC Community Action Partnership Inc, Barbourville, KY. Tel: (606) 546-3152, Web Site: kceoc.com (1)

Dolling, Jill, Felco Printing & Mailing, Kansas City, MO. Tel: (816) 421-5164, (800) 467-0805, FAX: (816) 421-1607, E-Mail: jill@felco.net, Web Site: www.felco.net (27)

Dollison, Mary, Service Mailers & Fulfillment Inc, Vernon, CA. Tel: (323) 292-0133, FAX: (323) 292-1038, E-Mail: dgsteinhart@gmail.com, Web Site: servicemailersandfulfillment.com (28)

Dolney, Chris, The Marek Group, Waukesha, WI. Tel: (262) 549-8900, FAX: (262) 49-8910, E-Mail: info@marekgroup.com, Web Site: www.marekgroup.com (21)

Doman, Mark, eBureau LLC, Saint Cloud, MN. Tel: (320) 534-5000, FAX: (320) 534-5020, Web Site: www.ebureau.com (22)

Domanico, Ronald J., Caraustar, Austell, GA. Tel: (770) 948-3101, E-Mail: info@caraustar, Web Site: www.caraustar.com (16)

Domaschko, John, PBS Distribution, Arlington, VA. Tel: (617) 208-0720, Web Site: shoppbs.org (3)

Dome Printing, Sacramento, CA. Tel: (800) 343-3139 (27)

Domeck, Brian C., The Progressive Corp, Mayfield Village, OH. Tel: (440) 461-5000, (800) PROGRESSIVE, (800) 776-4737, FAX: (800) 456-6590, Web Site: www.progressive.com (15)

Domestic Bank, Providence, RI. Tel: (401) 943-1600, (800) 566-6600, FAX: (401) 943-6708, Web Site: www.domesticbank.com (14)

Dominick, Don, George Sterne Agency Inc, Fallbrook, CA. Tel: (760) 432-6913, (800) 772-8174, FAX: (760) 432-9570, E-Mail: info@georgesterneagency.net, Web Site: georgesterneagency.net (23)

Dominick, Lynne, Woman's Day Special Interest Publications, New York, NY. Tel: (212) 767-6000, FAX: (212) 767-5612, Web Site: www.womensday.com (17)

Dominion Enterprises, Norfolk, VA. Tel: (757) 351-7000, Web Site: www.dominionenterprises.com (32)

Dominion Retail Inc, Richmond, VA. Tel: (804) 819-2268, Web Site: www.dom.com (16)

Domino Amjet Inc, Gurnee, IL. Tel: (847) 244-2501, FAX: (847) 244-1421, Web Site: www.dominoamjet.com (27)

Domme, Jack, Hitachi Data Systems, Santa Clara, CA. Tel: (408) 970-1000, FAX: (408) 727-8036, Web Site: www.hds.com (22)

Domorski, Paul, EMS Technologies, Norcross, GA. Tel: (770) 263-9200, FAX: (770) 447-4405, Web Site: www.ems-t.com (16)

Domtar Inc, Fort Mill, SC. Tel: (270) 927-7204, (803) 802-7500, FAX: (270) 927-8714, Web Site: www.domtar.com (25)

Domville, Sara, Betterway Books, Blue Ash, OH. Tel: (513) 531-2222, (800) 289-0963, FAX: (513) 531-4744, Web Site: www.fwpublications.com/books.asp (17)

Domville, Sara, F&W Media Inc, Blue Ash, OH. Tel: (513) 531-2690, FAX: (513) 531-0293, Web Site: www.fwmedia.com (17)

Edward Don & Co, Woodridge, IL. Tel: (708) 442-9400, (800) 777-4366, FAX: (708) 442-0436, Web Site: www.don.com (16)

Don, Robert E., Edward Don & Co, Woodridge, IL. Tel: (708) 442-9400, (800) 777-4366, FAX: (708) 442-0436, Web Site: www.don.com (16)

Don, Steven R., Edward Don & Co, Woodridge, IL. Tel: (708) 442-9400, (800) 777-4366, FAX: (708) 442-0436, Web Site: www.don.com (16)

Dona, Salvatore, Check Point Systems, Thorofare, NJ. Tel: (856) 848-1800, (800) 257-5540, FAX: (856) 848-0937, Web Site: www.checkpointsystems.com (34)

Donahue, Caroline, Intuit, Mountain View, CA. Tel: (650) 944-6000, Web Site: www.inuit.com (10)

Donahue, Christopher, Rapid City Journal, Rapid City, SD. Tel: (605) 394-8300, FAX: (605) 394-8462, E-Mail: classifieds@rapidcityjournal.com, Web Site: www.rapidcityjournal.com (18)

Donahue, J. Christopher, Federated Investors Co, Pittsburgh, PA. Tel: (412) 288-1900, (800) 341-7400, FAX: (412) 288-1171, Web Site: www.federatedinvestors.com (14)

Donahue, Michael D., American Association of Advertising Agencies, New York, NY. Tel: (212) 682-2500, FAX: (212) 682-8391, Web Site: www.aaaa.org (40)

Donaldson, Jerry L., Fostoria Industries Inc, Johnson City, TN. Tel: (419) 435-9201, (800) 495-4525, FAX: (419) 435-0842, E-Mail: email@fostoriaindustries.com, Web Site: www.fostoriaindustries.com (9)

Donaldson, Samantha, Federal Citizen Information Center, Pueblo, CO. Tel: (719) 295-2675, (888) 8-PUEBLO, FAX: (719) 948-9724, E-Mail: pueblo@gpo.gov, Web Site: www.pueblo.gsa.gov (5)

Donatelli, David A., EMC Corp, Hopkinton, MA. Tel: (888) 438-3622, Web Site: www.emc.com (16)

Donato, Thomas, Nielsen Trade Dimensions, Wilton, CT. Tel: (203) 222-5750, (800) 291-0410, FAX: (203) 222-5701, E-Mail: tradedimensions.info@nielsen.com, Web Site: www.tradedimensions.com (17)

Doner, Southfield, MI. Tel: (248) 354-9700, FAX: (248) 827-0880, Web Site: www.doner.com (35)

Doney, Marshall L., American Automobile Association, Heathrow, FL. Tel: (407) 444-8000, Web Site: www.aaa.com (16)

Donihe Graphics Inc, Kingsport, TN. Tel: (423) 246-2800, (800) 251-0337, FAX: (423) 246-7297, Web Site: www.donihe.com (27)

Donikian, Claudine, Pentera Inc, Indianapolis, IN. Tel: (617) 277-5033, Web Site: www.pentera.com (28)

Donio, Elena, Concur, Bellevue, WA. Tel: (425) 702-590-5000, (800) 401-8412, FAX: (425) 590-5999, Web Site: www.concur.com (22)

Donio, Father Frank, Pallottine Center for Apostolic Causes Inc/St Jude Shrine, Baltimore, MD. Tel: (410) 685-6026, (877) 278-5833, FAX: (410) 234-1459, E-Mail: info@stjudeshrine.org, Web Site: www.stjudeshrine.org (1)

Donlon, J.P., Chief Executive Magazine, Greenwich, CT. Tel: (203) 930-2700, FAX: (203) 930-2701, Web Site: www.chiefexecutive.net (17)

Donna Salyers' Fabulous-Bridal Inc, Covington, KY. Tel: (859) 291-3300, (800) 848-4650, E-Mail: abell@fabulousfurs.com, Web Site: fabulousfurs.com (2)

Donnelley Marketing, Pearl River, NY. Tel: (201) 476-2300, FAX: (201) 476-2151, Web Site: www.infousa.com (3)

RR Donnelley & Sons Co, Chicago, IL. Tel: (312) 326-8000, (800) 742-4455, FAX: (312) 326-7156, Web Site: www.rrdonnelly.com (31)

Donnelly, Louise, Marketrac Inc, Westbury, NY. Tel: (516) 365-4330, FAX: (516) 365-5789 (20)

Donnelly, Michael, Hinda Incentives, Chicago, IL. Tel: (773) 890-5900, FAX: (773) 890-4606, E-Mail: contact@hinda.com, Web Site: www.hinda.com (33)

Donnelly, Michael, Life-Study Fellowship Foundation Inc, Darien, CT. Tel: (203) 655-1436, FAX: (203) 655-1392, Web Site: www.lifestudyfellowship.com (17)

Donnelly, Michael, Starcrest Products of California Inc, Perris, CA. Tel: (909) 943-2011, FAX: (909) 943-2971, E-Mail: tmc@tstonramp.com (16)

Donnelly, Patrick L., SiriusXM Radio Inc, New York, NY. Tel: (212) 584-5100, Web Site: www.siriusxm.com (16)

Donnelly, Timothy J., Amvac Chemical Corp, Los Angeles, CA. Tel: (323) 264-3910, (888) 462-6822, Web Site: www.amvac-chemical.com (8)

Donoghue, Jerry, Asheville Compassionate Communication Center, Asheville, NC. Tel: (828) 252-0538, E-Mail: jerry@ashevilleccc.com, Web Site: ashevilleccc.com (13)

Donoghue, Marlene, Creative Health Products, Plymouth, MI. Tel: (734) 996-5900, (800) 742-4478, FAX: (734) 996-4650, Web Site: www.chponline.com (16)

Donoghue, W.C., Creative Health Products, Plymouth, MI. Tel: (734) 996-5900, (800) 742-4478, FAX: (734) 996-4650, Web Site: www.chponline.com (16)

Donohoe, Marina, Enterprise Ireland, New York, NY. Tel: (212) 371-3600, FAX: (212) 371-6398, Web Site: www.enterprise-ireland.com (16)

Donohue, Brendan, National Basketball Association, New York, NY. Tel: (212) 407-8000, FAX: (212) 826-0579, Web Site: www.nba.com (1)

Donohue, Gail E., DeBellis & Ferrara, Vienna, VA. Tel: (888) 748-2133, FAX: (888) 979-6345, E-Mail: info@debellis-ferrara.com, Web Site: www.debellis-ferrara.com (16)

Donohue, Margaret, The Tog Shop Inc, Beverly, MA. Tel: (800) 262-8888, FAX: (800) 755-7557, Web Site: www.togshop.com (2)

Donohue, Thomas J., US Chamber of Commerce, Washington, DC. Tel: (202) 659-6000, (800) 638-6582, FAX: (202) 887-3430, Web Site: www.uschamber.com (1)

Donor Services Group, Los Angeles, CA. Tel: (310) 788-9000, (888) 474-1900, Web Site: www.donorservicesgroup.com (1)

Donovan Advertising, Lititz, PA. Tel: (717) 560-1333, FAX: (717) 560-2034, Web Site: www.donovanadv.com (35)

Donovan, Jr. William, Donovan Advertising, Lititz, PA. Tel: (717) 560-1333, FAX: (717) 560-2034, Web Site: www.donovanadv.com (35)

Donovan, Randi, The Law Offices of James Sokolove, Wellesley Hills, MA. Tel: (617) 742-0696, Web Site: www.jimsokolove.com (14)

Donovan, Sheila, Global DM Solutions Inc, Boonton, NJ. Tel: (973) 402-2205, (866) 402-2205, FAX: (973) 402-2305, E-Mail: contact@globaldmsolutions.com, Web Site: www.globaldmsolutions.com (23)

Dontas, Peter, Bank of America, Charlotte, NC. Tel: (704) 386-5681, (800) 841-4000, FAX: (704) 386-6699, Web Site: www.bankofamerica.com (14)

Doody, Joseph G, Staples Inc, Framingham, MA. Tel: (508) 253-5000, FAX: (508) 253-7803, Web Site: www.staples.com (10)

Doody, Mike, DCI-Artform, Milwaukee, WI. Tel: (414) 228-7000, Web Site: www.dci-artform.com (35)

Dooley, Thomas E., Viacom Inc, New York, NY. Tel: (212) 258-6000, FAX: (212) 258-6464, Web Site: www.viacom.com (16)

Doombos, Chris, David C Cook, Colorado Springs, CO. Tel: (719) 536-0100, (800) 323-7543, FAX: (719) 536-3232, Web Site: www.davidccook.com (17)

Doon, Loretta, California Society of CPA's, San Mateo, CA. Tel: (800) 922-5272, FAX: (650) 522-3009, E-Mail: info@culcpa.org, Web Site: www.calcpa.org (1)

Doonan, Judith, A & A Research, Kalispell, MT. Tel: (406) 752-7857 (30)

Dopp, Liz, Rochester Institute of Technology, Rochester, NY. Tel: (585) 475-7436, Web Site: www.rit.edu (1)

Doran & Forgacs Inc, West Chester, PA. Tel: (610) 344-0570, FAX: (610) 344-7203, E-Mail: bdoran@doranforgacs.com, Web Site: www.doranforgacs.com (35)

Doran, Barbara H., Doran & Forgacs Inc, West Chester, PA. Tel: (610) 344-0570, FAX: (610) 344-7203, E-Mail: bdoran@doranforgacs.com, Web Site: www.doranforgacs.com (35)

Dore, James P., Bitstream Inc, Marlborough, MA. Tel: (617) 497-6222, FAX: (617) 868-0784, Web Site: www.bitstream.com (22)

Doremus & Co, New York, NY. Tel: (212) 366-3000, FAX: (212) 366-3060, E-Mail: mbroom@doremus. com, Web Site: www.doremus.com (35)

Doren, Andre, AVD Marketing, Hollywood, FL. Tel: (954) 410-9000, Web Site: www.avdmarketing.com (20)

Dorer, Benno, The Clorox Co, Oakland, CA. Tel: (510) 271-7000, FAX: (510) 832-1463, Web Site: www. thecloroxcompany.com (16)

Doretti, Dirk J., Clubs of America, Lakemoor, IL. Tel: (815) 363-4000, (800) CLUB-USA, FAX: (815) 363-4677, E-Mail: info@greatclubs.com, Web Site: www.clubsofamerica.com (6)

Doretti, Douglas M., Clubs of America, Lakemoor, IL. Tel: (815) 363-4000, (800) CLUB-USA, FAX: (815) 363-4677, E-Mail: info@greatclubs.com, Web Site: www.clubsofamerica.com (6)

Dorman, Robin Boss, A T Cross Co, Lincoln, RI. Tel: (401) 333-1200, (800) 282-7677, FAX: (401) 334-2861, Web Site: www.cross.com (16)

Dorn Marketing, Geneva, IL. Tel: (630) 232-2010, FAX: (630) 232-2033, E-Mail: info@ dornmarketing.com, Web Site: www.dornmarketing. com (35)

Dorn, Brian, Dorn Marketing, Geneva, IL. Tel: (630) 232-2010, FAX: (630) 232-2033, E-Mail: info@ dornmarketing.com, Web Site: www.dornmarketing. com (35)

Dorn, Elizabeth, Dorn Marketing, Geneva, IL. Tel: (630) 232-2010, FAX: (630) 232-2033, E-Mail: info@dornmarketing.com, Web Site: www. dornmarketing.com (35)

Dorn, Gregory, Hearst Business Media, New York, NY. Tel: (212) 649-2000, Web Site: www.hearst.com/ business-media (24)

Dorogoff, John Alexander, Neuberger & Berman Management, New York, NY. Tel: (212) 476-9000, (800) 877-9700, FAX: (212) 476-8937, Web Site: www.nb.com (14)

Dorothy Biddle Service, Greeley, PA. Tel: (570) 226-3239, FAX: (570) 226-0349, E-Mail: info@ dorothybiddle.com, Web Site: www.dorothybiddle. com (8)

Dorothy's Ruffled Originals Inc, Wilmington, NC. Tel: (800) 367-6849, FAX: (910) 791-0729, E-Mail: curtains@dorothysoriginals.com, Web Site: www. dorothysoriginals.com (8)

Dorr, Marjorie, Anthem Blue Cross Blue Shield, North Haven, CT. Tel: (203) 239-8381, (800) 545-0948, FAX: (203) 985-7918, Web Site: www.anthem.com (15)

Dorsey, Scott, ExactTarget, Indianapolis, IN. Tel: (317) 423-3928, FAX: (317) 396-1592, Web Site: www. exacttarget.com (32)

Dorsman, Peter, NCR Corp, Duluth, GA. Tel: (937) 445-1936, (800) CALL-NCR, FAX: (937) 445-1682, Web Site: www.ncr.com (16)

Doster, Steven, American General Life & Accident Insurance, Nashville, TN. Tel: (615) 749-1000, (800) 888-2452, Web Site: www.agla.com (15)

Double Envelope, Gainesville, FL. Tel: (800) 543-5275, Web Site: www.double-envelope.com (26)

Doubletree Suites by Hilton, Boston, MA. Tel: (617) 783-0090, (800) 222-TREE, FAX: (617) 783-0897, E-Mail: doubletree1@hilton.com (19)

DoubleVerify, New York, NY. Tel: (212) 631-2111, Web Site: www.doubleverify.com (9)

Dougan, Sally, Bert Davis Executive Search, New York, NY. Tel: (212) 838-4000, FAX: (212) 935-3291, E-Mail: info@bertdavis.com, Web Site: www. bertdavis.com (20)

Dougherty, Joe, Course Technology, Cambridge, MA. Tel: (617) 225-2595, FAX: (617) 225-7976, E-Mail: ed.moura@cengage.com, Web Site: www.course. com (31)

Dougherty, Kris, Delivra, Indianapolis, IN. Tel: (317) 915-9400, (866) 915-9465, Web Site: www.delivra. com (32)

Dougherty, Paul, Premier Packaging Corp, Victor, NY. Tel: (877) 924-8460, FAX: (585) 924-8753, E-Mail: info@premiercustompkg.com, Web Site: www. premiercustompkg.com (16)

Douglas Press Inc, Bellwood, IL. Tel: (708) 547-8400, (800) 323-0705, FAX: (708) 547-0296, Web Site: www.douglaspress.com (16)

Douglas Shaw & Associates, Naperville, IL. Tel: (630) 562-1321, Web Site: www.douglasshaw.com (1)

Douglas, Brad, Direct Resources Group Inc, Seattle, WA. Tel: (206) 455-6157, FAX: (206) 749-0005, E-Mail: results@drg.com, Web Site: www.drg.com (35)

Douglas, Brian, Association of Energy Engineers, Atlanta, GA. Tel: (770) 447-5083 x210, FAX: (770) 446-3969, E-Mail: info@aeecenter.org, Web Site: www.aeecenter.org (40)

Douglas, Bruce, Education Dynamics LLC, Hoboken, NJ. Tel: (201) 377-3000, FAX: (201) 377-3081, Web Site: www.educationdynamics.com (30)

Douglas, Dean, Sterling Fluid Systems, Indianapolis, IN. Tel: (317) 925-9661, (800) 879-0182, FAX: (317) 924-7388, Web Site: www.peerlesspump.com (16)

Douglas, Dwight, Media Monitors Inc, White Plains, NY. Tel: (914) 428-5971, FAX: (914) 428-4541, E-Mail: jselig@mediamonitors.com, Web Site: www.mediamonitors.com (30)

Douglas, Jaime, The Black Dog Tavern Co Inc, Vineyard Haven, MA. Tel: (800) 626-1991, E-Mail: contactus@theblackdog.com, Web Site: www. theblackdog.com; www.theblackdogtshirt.com (2)

Douglas, Peter, Lake County Press Inc, Waukegan, IL. Tel: (847) 336-4333, FAX: (847) 336-5846, Web Site: www.lakecountypress.com (27)

Douglas, Robert S., The Black Dog Tavern Co Inc, Vineyard Haven, MA. Tel: (800) 626-1991, E-Mail: contactus@theblackdog.com, Web Site: www. theblackdog.com; www.theblackdogtshirt.com (2)

Douglass, David M., Photoworks, Cleveland, OH. Tel: (206) 281-1390, (800) PHOTOWORKS, FAX: (206) 284-5357, E-Mail: info@photoworks.com, Web Site: www.photoworks.com (16)

Douthat, Annette, AllBrands.com Sewing Machine Superstore, Baton Rouge, LA. Tel: (225) 923-1285, (866) 255-2726, FAX: (225) 923-1261, E-Mail: info@allbrands.com, Web Site: www.allbrands.com (11)

Douthat, John M., AllBrands.com Sewing Machine Superstore, Baton Rouge, LA. Tel: (225) 923-1285, (866) 255-2726, FAX: (225) 923-1261, E-Mail: info@allbrands.com, Web Site: www.allbrands.com (11)

Dove, Peter, ColorTree of Virginia Inc, Richmond, VA. Tel: (804) 358-4245, FAX: (804) 358-0488, Web Site: www.colortree.com (16)

Dover Publications Inc, Mineola, NY. Tel: (516) 294-7000, FAX: (516) 742-6953, Web Site: www. doverpublications.com (17)

Dover Saddlery, Littleton, MA. Tel: (978) 952-8062, (800) 406-8204, Web Site: www.doversaddlery.com (11)

Dovetail, Littleton, CO. Tel: (303) 904-4771, FAX: (303) 904-4776, E-Mail: welcome@dovetailnet. com, Web Site: www.dovetailnet.com (22)

Dovetail Art & Design Inc, Dover, OH. Tel: (330) 343-3764, Web Site: www.dovetailart.com (20)

The Dow Chemical Co, Midland, MI. Tel: (989) 636-1000, (800) 258-2436, FAX: (989) 832-1556, Web Site: www.dow.com (16)

Dow Corning Corp, Midland, MI. Tel: (989) 496-4400, (800) 248-2481, FAX: (989) 496-4572, Web Site: www.dowcorning.com (16)

Dow Jones & Co, Princeton, NJ. Tel: (609) 520-4000, FAX: (212) 416-4348, Web Site: www.dowjones. com/corp/index.html (17)

Dow Theory Forecasts, Hammond, IN. Tel: (219) 931-6480, (800) 233-5922, FAX: (219) 931-6487, E-Mail: custserv@horizonpublishing.com, Web Site: www.dowtheory.com (17)

Dow, Michael P., Society of Financial Service Professionals, Newtown Square, PA. Tel: (610) 526-2500, FAX: (610) 359-8115, E-Mail: info@financialpro. org, Web Site: www.financialpro.org (1)

Dow, Roger, US Travel Association, Washington, DC. Tel: (202) 408-8422, FAX: (202) 408-1255, E-Mail: feedback@ustravel.org, Web Site: www.ustravel.org (1)

Patricia Dowd Inc, Atascadero, CA. Tel: (805) 985-8243, E-Mail: pdowd@pdisearch.com, Web Site: www.pdisearch.com (20)

Dowd, Patricia, Patricia Dowd Inc, Atascadero, CA. Tel: (805) 985-8243, E-Mail: pdowd@pdisearch. com, Web Site: www.pdisearch.com (20)

Dowden, C. James, Alliance of Area Business Publications, Redondo Beach, CA. Tel: (310) 379-8261, FAX: (310) 379-8283, E-Mail: info@bizpubs.org, Web Site: www.bizpubs.org (1)

Dowdle, Don, Mastergrip Inc, Irving, TX. Tel: (972) 554-4450, (800) 275-1100, FAX: (972) 554-1109, Web Site: www.mastergrip.com (11)

Dowdle, Mike, Bonneville International, Salt Lake City, UT. Tel: (801) 575-7500, FAX: (801) 575-5820, E-Mail: bonneville@bonneville.com, Web Site: www.bonneville.com (35)

Dowdy, Mark, Wholesale Tool Co, Warren, MI. Tel: (800) 521-3420, FAX: (800) 521-3661, E-Mail: wtmich@aol.com, Web Site: www.wttool.com (9)

Dowe, Tilema, Eastbay Running Store Inc, Wausau, WI. Tel: (715) 845-5538, (800) 826-2205, FAX: (715) 261-9500, Web Site: www.eastbay.com (2)

Dowhan, David, eBureau LLC, Saint Cloud, MN. Tel: (320) 534-5000, FAX: (320) 534-5020, Web Site: www.ebureau.com (22)

Dowling, Alan F., American Health Information Management Association, Chicago, IL. Tel: (312) 233-1100, (800) 335-5535, FAX: (312) 233-1090, E-Mail: info@ahima.org, Web Site: www.ahima.org (1)

Dowling, Bernadette M., Data Services Inc, Salisbury, MD. Tel: (410) 546-2206, (800) 432-4066, FAX: (410) 546-2274, Web Site: www.dataservicesinc. com (22)

Dowling, Jack, Westbeth Gallery, New York, NY. Tel: (212) 989-4650 (36)

Dowling, Stephen, Sani Serv, Mooresville, IN. Tel: (317) 831-7030, FAX: (317) 381-7036, Web Site: www.saniserv.com (16)

Down Home Comforts, Putnam Station, NY. Tel: (518) 547-8966, (518) 223-2193, Web Site: downhomecomforts.com (8)

Downey, Janie, New England Mail Order Association, Scarborough, ME. Tel: (207) 885-0090, (860) 691-1260, FAX: (207) 885-0097, Web Site: www. nemoa.org (40)

Downie, Jr. Leonard, The Washington Post, Washington, DC. Tel: (202) 334-6000, (800) 627-1150, E-Mail: letters@washpost.com, Web Site: www. washingtonpost.com (17)

Downing, Jonathan, The Ad Farm, Ottawa Hills, OH. Tel: (419) 720-5676, Web Site: www.theadfarm. com (20)

Downing, Sue, Dakin Farm, Ferrisburgh, VT. Tel: (802) 425-3971, (800) 993-2546, FAX: (802) 425-2765, E-Mail: scutting@dakinfarm.com, Web Site: www. dakinfarm.com (4)

Downing, Tom, Random House Direct Marketing, New York, NY. Tel: (212) 572-4985, (800) 678-5681, FAX: (212) 572-6018, Web Site: www. randomhousedirect.com (17)

Doyal, Clark R., ADS Media Group Inc, San Antonio, TX. Tel: (210) 655-6613, FAX: (210) 655-6269, Web Site: www.adsmediagroup.com (27)

Doyle, Corbette, AON Center, Chicago, IL. Tel: (312) 381-1000, FAX: (312) 381-6032, Web Site: www. aon.com (15)

Doyle, Courtney, CP Travel, Boston, MA. Tel: (617) 521-5400, Web Site: travel.connellypartners.com (35)

Doyle, Dan, Neat Co, Philadelphia, PA. Tel: (215) 382-3300, (866) 632-8732, FAX: (215) 386-2536, Web Site: neatco.com (22)

Doyle, Daniel S., Mal Warwick Associates, Berkeley, CA. Tel: (510) 843-8888, FAX: (510) 843-0142, E-Mail: info@malwarwick.com, Web Site: www. malwarwick.com (1)

Doyle, Gene, Creative Media Inc, Nicholasville, KY. Tel: (859) 227-6513 (35)

Doyle, Hilary, Byrum & Fleming, San Anselmo, CA. Tel: (415) 457-1700, (800) 850-1711, E-Mail: hilary@byrumfleming.com, Web Site: www. byrumfleming.com (23)

Doyle, Hugh, The Services Group (TSG), Arlington, VA. Tel: (703) 528-7444, FAX: (703) 522-2329, E-Mail: tsq@tsginc.com, Web Site: www.tsginc. com (20)

Doyle, III William, Callaway Gardens, Pine Mountain, GA. Tel: (706) 663-2281, (800) CALLAWAY, FAX: (706) 663-6812, E-Mail: info@ callawaygardens.com, Web Site: www. callawaygardens.com/where-to-stay (19)

Doyle, Jack, Amergent, Peabody, MA. Tel: (800) 370-7500, FAX: (978) 531-0400, Web Site: www. amergent.com (1)

Doyle, John, Universal Training, Lake Forest, IL. Tel: (847) 235-2170, E-Mail: information@ universaltraining.com, Web Site: www. universaltraining.com (16)

Doyle, Jr. Donald W., Blanchard & Co Inc, New Orleans, LA. Tel: (504) 837-3010, (800) 880-4653, FAX: (504) 837-4884, Web Site: www. blanchardonline.com (22)

Doyle, Patrick, Barton & Cooney, Burlington, NJ. Tel: (609) 747-9300, FAX: (609) 747-9700, E-Mail: pmdoyle@bartoncooney.com, Web Site: www. bartoncooney.com (28)

Doyle, Patrick T., DIRECTV LLC, El Segundo, CA. Tel: (310) 535-5000, FAX: (310) 535-5225, Web Site: www.directv.com (16)

Dozier Equipment International, Milwaukee, WI. Tel: (800) 251-1234, FAX: (800) 336-6608, Web Site: www.dozierequip.com (9)

Dr Jays, San Diego, CA. Tel: (212) 334-7999, Web Site: drjays.com (2)

Dr Leonard's Healthcare Corp, Edison, NJ. Tel: (732) 225-0100, (800) 455-1918, FAX: (732) 225-0302, Web Site: www.doctorleonard.com (7)

Draeger, Paul, Center for Creative Leadership, Greensboro, NC. Tel: (336) 545-2810, FAX: (336) 282-3284, E-Mail: info@ccl.org, Web Site: www.ccl.org (16)

Dragich Auto Literature, Princeton, MN. Tel: (763) 389-8600, FAX: (763) 389-8222, E-Mail: mail@ dragich.com, Web Site: www.dragich.com (16)

Dragich, John, Dragich Auto Literature, Princeton, MN. Tel: (763) 389-8600, FAX: (763) 389-8222, E-Mail: mail@dragich.com, Web Site: www.dragich.com (16)

Dragin, Stephen, Allyn & Bacon, Upper Saddle River, NJ. Tel: (617) 848-7216, FAX: (781) 455-1220 (17)

Dragisic, John, Charlton, Madison, WI. Tel: (608) 259-8004, FAX: (608) 259-8061, E-Mail: jdragisic@ tcgcorp.net, Web Site: www.tcgcorp.net (29)

Dragone, Allan, Graphic Communications Holdings Inc, Hudson, OH. Tel: (330) 650-5522, FAX: (330) 650-8998, E-Mail: info@graphiccommunications.com, Web Site: www.graphiccommunications.com (25)

Dragonette, Rob, Barton-Cotton, Baltimore, MD. Tel: (410) 247-4800, (800) 348-1102, FAX: (410) 536-0491, E-Mail: info@bartoncotton.com, Web Site: www.bartoncotton.com (16)

Drake Direct, New York, NY. Tel: (212) 759-1225, (914) 299-4956, FAX: (212) 759-9756, E-Mail: Rhonda@DrakeDirect.com, Web Site: www. drakedirect.com (22)

Drake, Chuck, Crane Pumps & Systems Inc, Piqua, OH. Tel: (937) 773-2442, FAX: (937) 773-2238, E-Mail: cranepumps@cranepumps.com, Web Site: www. cranepumps.com (16)

Drake, O. Burtch, American Association of Advertising Agencies, New York, NY. Tel: (212) 682-2500, FAX: (212) 682-8391, Web Site: www.aaaa.org (40)

Drake, Perry, Drake Direct, New York, NY. Tel: (212) 759-1225, (914) 299-4956, FAX: (212) 759-9756, E-Mail: Rhonda@DrakeDirect.com, Web Site: www.drakedirect.com (22)

Drake, R. Glenn, Tupperware Brands Corp, Orlando, FL. Tel: (407) 826-5050, (800) 366-3800, FAX: (407) 826-8874, Web Site: www.tupperwarebrands. com (16)

Drake, Rhonda Knehans, Drake Direct, New York, NY. Tel: (212) 759-1225, (914) 299-4956, FAX: (212) 759-9756, E-Mail: Rhonda@DrakeDirect.com, Web Site: www.drakedirect.com (22)

Dranikoff, Lee, American Securities Capital Partners, New York, NY. Tel: (212) 476-8000, Web Site: www.american-securities.com (15)

Drapeau, Anne, VistaPrint USA Inc, Lexington, MA. Tel: (800) 961-2075, Web Site: www.vistaprint.com (27)

Draper, Mike, Pastime Publications Inc, Denver, CO. Tel: (303) 534-7867, (888) 650-8665, FAX: (630) 214-7600, E-Mail: post@pastimecompany.com, Web Site: www.pastimecompany.com (17)

Draper's & Damon's, Irvine, CA. Tel: (949) 784-3000, (800) 843-1174, FAX: (949) 784-3400, E-Mail: jilld@drapers.com, Web Site: www.drapers.com (2)

Drapkin, Lisa, American Express Co, New York, NY. Tel: (212) 640-2000, FAX: (212) 619-9802, Web Site: www.americanexpress.com (14)

Draught, Eric J., Kemper Corp, Chicago, IL. Tel: (312) 661-4600, (800) 733-7366, FAX: (312) 494-6995, Web Site: www.kemper.com (15)

Drawing Board Inc, Waynesboro, PA. Tel: (301) 739-4487, (800) 527-9530, FAX: (800) 253-1838, E-Mail: customerservice@drawingboard.com, Web Site: www.drawingboard.com (16)

Drayton, John, University of Oklahoma Press, Norman, OK. Tel: (800) 627-7377, FAX: (405) 364-5798, Web Site: www.oupress.com (17)

Dream Products Inc, Van Nuys, CA. Tel: (818) 773-4233, (800) 410-2153, FAX: (816) 206-8061, Web Site: www.dreamproducts.net (5)

Dreher, Gary, Advanced Mail Inc, Eau Claire, WI. Tel: (715) 839-8801, 888-624-5255, FAX: (715) 839-8906, Web Site: www.amailinc.com (28)

Dreher, Lincoln, Hansen Corp, Princeton, IN. Tel: (812) 385-3415, FAX: (812) 385-3013, E-Mail: sales@ hansen-motor.com, Web Site: www.hansen-motor. com (16)

Dreis & Krump Manufacturing Co, Peotone, IL. Tel: (708) 258-1200, FAX: (708) 258-9682, E-Mail: chicago@dreis-krump.com, Web Site: www.dreis-krump.com (16)

Dreishpoon, Ph.D. Douglas, The Gallery Shop, Buffalo, NY. Tel: (716) 882-8700 X258, FAX: (716) 882-1958, E-Mail: gallshop@albrightknox.org, Web Site: www.albrightknox.org (6)

Dreller, Mike, Falcon Products Inc, Newport, TN. Tel: (314) 991-9200, (800) 873-3252, FAX: (314) 991-9227, E-Mail: info@falconproducts.com, Web Site: www.falconproducts.com (16)

Dremann, Craig C., Redwood City Seed Co, Redwood City, CA. Tel: (650) 325-7333, FAX: (650) 325-4056, Web Site: www.ecoseeds.com (8)

Dremann, Sue, Redwood City Seed Co, Redwood City, CA. Tel: (650) 325-7333, FAX: (650) 325-4056, Web Site: www.ecoseeds.com (8)

Drenning, Ron, pii, Bloomington, IL. Tel: (800) 664-0444, FAX: (309) 662-2055, E-Mail: sales@ whateverittakes.com, Web Site: www. whateverittakes.com (35)

Drenning, Ronald, First Marketing Co, Pompano Beach, FL. Tel: (954) 979-0700, FAX: (954) 971-4707, Web Site: www.first-marketing.com (31)

Dresden Direct Inc, Palm Beach Gardens, FL. Tel: (561) 622-3400 (23)

Dresden, Phillip, Dresden Direct Inc, Palm Beach Gardens, FL. Tel: (561) 622-3400 (23)

Dresdow, Mary A., ACNielsen Corp, New York, NY. Tel: (646) 654-5000, FAX: (646) 654-5002, E-Mail: globalc@nielsen.com, Web Site: www.acnielsen. com/us (30)

Dresser, Mark, American 3B Scientific, Tucker, GA. Tel: (770) 492-9111, Web Site: www.a3bs.com (16)

Dresser, Mark, Sportime International, Norcross, GA. Tel: (770) 449-5700, (800) 283-5700, FAX: (770) 510-7290, E-Mail: orders@sportime.com, Web Site: www.sportime.com (11)

Drevlow, Lauren, American Spirit Graphics Corp, Minneapolis, MN. Tel: (612) 623-3333, FAX: (612) 623-9314, E-Mail: asgc@asgc.com, Web Site: www.asgc.com (27)

Drew, Michael, Professional Binding Products Inc, Thousand Oaks, CA. Tel: (800) 443-7557, (800) 545-9413, E-Mail: sales@probinding.com, Web Site: www.probinding.com (16)

Drew, Mike, Telect Inc, Liberty Lake, WA. Tel: (509) 926-6000, FAX: (509) 926-8915, E-Mail: getinfo@ telect.com, Web Site: www.telect.com (16)

Drexel University Goodwin College of Professional Studies, Philadelphia, PA. Tel: (215) 895-2159, E-Mail: goodwin@drexel.edu, Web Site: goodwin. drexel.edu (16)

Drexel, George, Industrial Arts & Graphics, Middleburg, VA. Tel: (540) 687-6770, (866) 324-7746, FAX: (540) 687-4678, E-Mail: gdrex@ industrialarts.us (27)

The Dreyfus Corp, New York, NY. Tel: (212) 922-6000, FAX: (212) 922-6880, Web Site: www. dreyfus.com (14)

Driasi, Chanhassen, MN. Tel: (952) 556-5600, (800) 688-0760, FAX: (952) 556-8200, E-Mail: tpa@ driasi.com, Web Site: www.driasi.com (21)

Drinan, Helen G., Simmons College, Boston, MA. Tel: (617) 521-2000, Web Site: www.simmons.edu (1)

Drinko, J. Randall, Cleveland Institute of Electronics, Cleveland, OH. Tel: (216) 781-9400, (800) 243-6446, FAX: (216) 781-0331, E-Mail: instruct@cie-wc.edu, Web Site: www.cie-wc.edu (13)

Drinnan, Faith, The Oyster Group, Dartmouth, NS Canada. Tel: (877) 405-4858, E-Mail: fdrinnan@ theoystergroup.ca, Web Site: www.theoystergroup. ca (22)

Driscoll Label Co Inc, East Hanover, NJ. Tel: (973) 585-7291, FAX: (800) 342-1195, (973) 585-7295, E-Mail: info@driscolllabel.com, Web Site: www. driscolllabel.com (27)

Driscoll, Dan, September Productions, Nantucket, MA. Tel: (508) 332-3577, FAX: (508) 228-3853, E-Mail: info@september.com, Web Site: www.september. com (32)

Driver, Carrie, Foundation of FirstHealth, Pinehurst, NC. Tel: (910) 695-7500, Web Site: www. firsthealth.org/foundation (1)

Driver, Fred, d.trio marketing group, Minneapolis, MN. Tel: (612) 787-3333, FAX: (612) 436-0324, E-Mail: greatideas@dtrio.com, Web Site: www.dtrio.com (35)

Driver, Louann, Global Demand Publishing Inc, Jacksonville, NC. Tel: (910) 937-0562, FAX: (910) 455-1937, E-Mail: globaldemandpublishing@yahoo.com (17)

Drobenko, Walter, Beluga Bar by Caviarteria, New York, NY. Tel: (212) 759-7410, (800) 422-8427, FAX: (212) 750-0358, E-Mail: info@caviarteria. com, Web Site: www.caviarteria.com (4)

Drolet, Patricia, Corpus Christi Museum of Science & History, Corpus Christi, TX. Tel: (361) 826-4667, FAX: (361) 884-7392, Web Site: www.ccmuseum. com (1)

Droll Yankees Inc, Plainfield, CT. Tel: (860) 799-8980, (800) 352-9164, FAX: (860) 564-8031, E-Mail: drollbird@drollyankees.com, Web Site: www. drollyankees.com (8)

Drozd, Ann Marie, Beber Silverstein Group, Miami, FL. Tel: (305) 856-9800, FAX: (305) 854-7686, E-Mail: jennifer@thinkbsg.com, Web Site: www.thinkbsg. com (35)

Drozdenko, Ronald, Western Connecticut State University, Danbury, CT. Tel: (203) 837-8200, FAX: (203) 837-8527, E-Mail: hills@wcsu.edu, Web Site: www. wcsu.edu (41)

Drucker, Charles, Fifth Third Bank, Cincinnati, OH. Tel: (800) 972-3030, FAX: (231) 922-4060, Web Site: www.53.com (14)

Drug Information Association, Horsham, PA. Tel: (215) 442-6100, FAX: (215) 442-6199, Web Site: www. diahome.org (1)

Drug Policy Alliance, New York, NY. Tel: (212) 613-8020, FAX: (212) 613-8021, E-Mail: nyc@ drugpolicy.org, Web Site: www.drugpolicy.org (1)

Drum, Jason, Voxdata Telecom, Montreal, QC Canada. Tel: (514) 871-1920, (800) 861-9599, FAX: (514) 871-0445, E-Mail: fcouture@voxdata.com, Web Site: www.voxdata.com (29)

Drumbeat Indian Arts Inc, Phoenix, AZ. Tel: (602) 266-4823, (800) 895-4859, FAX: (602) 265-2402, E-Mail: info@drumbeatindianarts.com, Web Site: www.drumbeatindianarts.com (6)

Drumm, Robert, Alexander + Roberts, Keene, NH. Tel: (603) 357-5033, (800) 221-2216, FAX: (603) 357-4548, E-Mail: info@generaltours.com, Web Site: www.generaltours.com (19)

Drumm, Wesley, The Metal Ware Corp, Two Rivers, WI. Tel: (920) 793-1368, (800) 288-4545, FAX: (920) 794-3161, Web Site: www.nesco.com (32)

Drummond, David C., Google Inc, Mountain View, CA. Tel: (650) 253-0000, FAX: (650) 253-0001, Web Site: www.google.com (31)

Drury, Tom, Lab Safety Supply Inc, Janesville, WI. Tel: (608) 754-2345, (800) 356-2855, FAX: (800) 543-9910, Web Site: www.labsafety.com (5)

Dryden, Ed, Power Direct, Mission Viejo, CA. Tel: (877) 737-8977, FAX: (949) 253-3458, E-Mail: info@powerdirect.net, Web Site: www.powerdirect. net (35)

Drysdale, Ross, Arrowhead Mountain Spring Water, Wilkes Barre, PA. Tel: (800) 873-7775, Web Site: www.arrowheadwater.com (16)

Drzik, John, Oliver Wyman, New York, NY. Tel: (212) 345-8000, (212) 541-8100, Web Site: www. oliverwyman.com (14)

DS Direct Response, Torrance, CA. Tel: (310) 251-1830, E-Mail: info@dsdirectresponse.com, Web Site: dsdirectresponse.com (23)

d.trio marketing group, Minneapolis, MN. Tel: (612) 787-3333, FAX: (612) 436-0324, E-Mail: greatideas@dtrio.com, Web Site: www.dtrio.com (35)

The Du-Rite Group Inc, Englewood, NJ. Tel: (201) 387-7000, FAX: (201) 385-8513, E-Mail: information@ duriteconstruction.com, Web Site: www. duriteconstruction.com (16)

Duarte, Bernarda, MundoFOX22, Los Angeles, CA. Tel: (213) 344-3700, E-Mail: info@canal22.tv, Web Site: www.mundofox22.com (32)

Dubasek, J., Adams Manufacturing Co, Cleveland, OH. Tel: (216) 587-6801, FAX: (216) 587-6807, E-Mail: adamsx@att.net, Web Site: www. adamsmanufacturing.com (9)

Dubin, Burt, Personal Achievement Institute, Kingman, AZ. Tel: (928) 753-7546, (800) 321-1225, FAX: (928) 753-7554, E-Mail: burt@burtdubin.com, Web Site: www.speakingbizsuccess.com (17)

Dubin, Thomas, MNI, Evanston, IL. Tel: (847) 864-7000, (888) 752-5200, FAX: (847) 332-1100, Web Site: mni.net (23)

DuBois, David, IAEE Expo! Expo! Annual Meeting and Exhibition, Dallas, TX. Tel: (972) 458-8002, FAX: (972) 458-8119, E-Mail: info@iaee.com, Web Site: www.iaee.com (42)

DuBois, Molly M., C H Robinson Worldwide Inc, Eden Prairie, MN. Tel: (952) 937-8500, FAX: (952) 937-6740, E-Mail: info@chrobinson.com, Web Site: www.chrobinson.com (16)

Dubos, Jean-Francois, Vivendi SA, New York, NY. Tel: (212) 572-7000, FAX: (212) 572-1080, Web Site: www.vivendi.com (16)

Dubrow, Lee, Straw Hat Cooperative Corp, San Ramon, CA. Tel: (925) 837-3400, FAX: (925) 820-1080, E-Mail: info@strawhatpizza.com, Web Site: www. strawhatpizza.com (16)

Dubuc, Nancy, A+E Television Networks LLC, New York, NY. Tel: (212) 210-1400, FAX: (212) 210-1326, E-Mail: aefeedback@aenetworks.com, Web Site: www.aenetworks.com (16)

Ducatelli, Tom, Zones Inc, Auburn, WA. Tel: (253) 205-3000, (800) 408-9663, FAX: (425) 430-3626, E-Mail: corpsales@zones.com, Web Site: www. zones.com (3)

Duccilli, Steve, ST Media Group International, Cincinnati, OH. Tel: (513) 421-2050, (800) 925-1110, FAX: (513) 421-5144, E-Mail: customer@ stmediagroup.com, Web Site: www.signweb.com (17)

Duchene, Mark, AIG Marketing, New York, NY. Tel: (212) 770-7000, (212) 770-2237, Web Site: www. agac.com (15)

Duchesne, Rupert, Aimia Inc, Montreal, QC Canada. Web Site: www.aimia.com (35)

Duchin, Susan, Data-Dynamix Inc, Denver, CO. Tel: (720) 855-9282, (888) 314-0078, FAX: (720) 855-9099, E-Mail: sales@data-dynamix.com, Web Site: www.data-dynamix.com (23)

Ducks Unlimited, Memphis, TN. Tel: (901) 758-3825, (800) 45DUCKS, FAX: (901) 758-3850, Web Site: www.ducks.org (1)

Ducktrap River Fish Farm, Belfast, ME. Tel: (207) 338-6280, (800) 828-3825, FAX: (207) 338-6288, E-Mail: smoked@ducktrap.com, Web Site: www. ducktrap.com (4)

Duclos, Lorraine, PDQ Post Group, Surrey, BC Canada. Tel: (604) 888-0676, (888) 998-9878, FAX: (604) 888-4467, E-Mail: sales@pdqpostgroup.com, Web Site: www.pdqpostgroup.com (21)

Duda, Donald, Methode Electronics Inc, Chicago, IL. Tel: (708) 867-6777, FAX: (708) 867-6999, E-Mail: info@methode.com, Web Site: www.methode.com (9)

Duda, Teri, Berkeley College, West Paterson, NJ. Tel: (973) 278-5400, (800) 446-5400, FAX: (973) 278-6243, E-Mail: info@berkeleycollege.edu, Web Site: www.berkeleycollege.edu (13)

Dudek, Andrew, Telcordia Technologies, Piscataway, NJ. Tel: (732) 699-2000, FAX: (973) 829-2458, Web Site: www.telcordia.com (16)

Dudek, Sue, Sculptz, Feasterville Trevose, PA. Tel: (215) 494-2900, E-Mail: sdudek@sculptz.com, Web Site: www.silkies.com (2)

Dudka, Nicole, Chicago Magazine, Chicago, IL. Tel: (312) 222-8999, FAX: (312) 222-0287, Web Site: www.chicagomag.com (17)

Dudley, Frank, Guideline Washington DC, Washington, DC. Tel: (703) 312-6004, (866) GUIDELINE, E-Mail: fdudley@guideline.com, Web Site: www. guideline.com (30)

Dudley, Tom, ASM International, Materials Park, OH. Tel: (440) 338-5151, (800) 336-5152, FAX: (440) 338-4634, E-Mail: customerservice@ asminternational.org, Web Site: www. asminternational.org (1)

Dudnyk, Horsham, PA. Tel: (215) 443-9406, (800) 438-3695, E-Mail: fpowers@dudnyk.com, Web Site: dudnyk.com (35)

Duerr, Charlie, Hatteras Press Inc, Tinton Falls, NJ. Tel: (732) 223-9888, (800) 695-0719, FAX: (732) 223-1232, E-Mail: connect@hatteras.us, Web Site: www.hatterascpc.com (27)

Duerr, John, Spectronics Corp, Westbury, NY. Tel: (516) 333-4840, (800) 274-8888, FAX: (800) 491-6868, E-Mail: vscherer@spectroline.com, Web Site: www.spectroline.com (9)

Duff, Stephen D., FM Howell & Co, Elmira, NY. Tel: (607) 734-6291, FAX: (607) 735-0464, E-Mail: best@howellpkg.com, Web Site: www.howellpkg. com (16)

Duffey Petrosky, Farmington Hills, MI. Tel: (248) 489-8300, FAX: (248) 994-1600, Web Site: www.duffeypetrosky.com (35)

Dufford Marketing, Pasadena, CA. Tel: (626) 665-2268, E-Mail: donnduff@aol.com (21)

Dufford, Donn, Dufford Marketing, Pasadena, CA. Tel: (626) 665-2268, E-Mail: donnduff@aol.com (21)

Duffy, Brian, Lea & Perrins Inc, Fair Lawn, NJ. Tel: (201) 791-1600, FAX: (201) 791-8945, Web Site: www.leaperrins.com (16)

Duffy, Dennis, Loyalogy, Asheville, NC. Tel: (828) 333-5860, Web Site: loyalogy.com (35)

Duffy, Michael, Paymentech, Salem, NH. Tel: (603) 896-6000, FAX: (603) 896-8717, Web Site: www.paymentech.com (14)

Duffy, Mike, Norman Rockwell Museum, Stockbridge, MA. Tel: (413) 298-4100, (800) 742-9450, FAX: (413) 298-4144, E-Mail: emazzer@nrm.org, Web Site: www.nrm.org (16)

Duffy, William, iKnowtion LLC, Burlington, MA. Tel: (781) 494-9989, Web Site: www.iknowtion.com (20)

Dugan, William, Publishing Fulfillment Consulting LLC, Brewster, NY. Tel: (845) 278-2800, Web Site: www.fulfillmentconsulting.com (20)

Dugas, Jr. Richard J., Del Webb, Bloomfield Hills, MI. Tel: (248) 644-7300, (888) 717-9777, FAX: (248) 433-4598, Web Site: www.delwebb.com (16)

Duggan & Brown Inc, Barrington, IL. Tel: (847) 381-8484, FAX: (847) 381-8499, E-Mail: evan@dugganandbrown.com, Web Site: www.dugganandbrown.com (20)

Duggan & Brown Inc, Abington, PA. Tel: (215) 657-3400, FAX: (215) 657-6119, E-Mail: john@dugganandbrown.com, Web Site: www.dugganandbrown.com (16)

Duggan, John, Duggan & Brown Inc, Abington, PA. Tel: (215) 657-3400, FAX: (215) 657-6119, E-Mail: john@dugganandbrown.com, Web Site: www.dugganandbrown.com (16)

Dukart, Eric, Sundog, Fargo, ND. Tel: (701) 235-5525, (888) 9-SUNDOG, FAX: (701) 235-8941, E-Mail: info@sundoginteractive.com, Web Site: www.sundoginteractive.com (35)

Dukat, Gregory, Ventyx, Atlanta, GA. Tel: (770) 952-8444, (800) 868-0497, FAX: (770) 955-2977, E-Mail: support@ventyx.com, Web Site: www.ventyx.com (16)

Duke, Marlies, New England Mail Order Association, Scarborough, ME. Tel: (207) 885-0090, (860) 691-1260, FAX: (207) 885-0097, Web Site: www.nemoa.org (40)

Dukky Inc, Mandeville, LA. Tel: (888) 662-9096, E-Mail: info@dukky.com, Web Site: www.dukky.com (32)

Dulckeit, Selinde, Geometry Global, New York, NY. Tel: (212) 537-3700, E-Mail: press@geometry.com, Web Site: www.geometry.com (35)

Dullea, John, As We Change, Oshkosh, WI. Tel: (619) 213-2200, (855) 202-7392, (800) 699-6993, FAX: (888) 534-8469, E-Mail: help@aswechange.com, Web Site: www.aswechange.com (7)

Duloc, Michael P., Kable Fulfillment Services, Mount Morris, IL. Tel: (815) 734-4151, FAX: (815) 734-5228 (22)

Duluth Trading Co Inc, Belleville, WI. Tel: (800) 300-9719, FAX: (888) 950-3199, E-Mail: customerservice@duluthtrading.com, Web Site: www.duluthtrading.com (8)

Duman, Mike, Skar Advertising, Omaha, NE. Tel: (402) 330-0110, (866) 330-0112, FAX: (402) 330-8791, E-Mail: skar@skar.com, Web Site: skar.com (35)

Dumas, Axel, Hermes of Paris, New York, NY. Tel: (212) 759-7585, (800) 441-4488, FAX: (212) 644-2132 (2)

Dumas, Heather, Gates Corp, Denver, CO. Tel: (303) 744-1911, FAX: (303) 744-4000, Web Site: www.gates.com (9)

Dunay, Brian, Meister Media Worldwide, Willoughby, OH. Tel: (440) 942-2000, (800) 572-7740, FAX: (440) 975-3447, E-Mail: info@meistermedia.com, Web Site: www.meistermedia.com (17)

Dunay, Darren, National Association of Publishers Representatives, Hoffman Estates, IL. Tel: (877) 263-9640, FAX: (847) 885-8393, E-Mail: info@napronline.com, Web Site: www.napronline.com (1)

Dunbar, Yolanda, Frederick's of Hollywood Group Inc, Los Angeles, CA. Tel: (323) 466-5151, (855) 655-2514, FAX: (323) 464-5149, E-Mail: support@fredericks.com, Web Site: www.fredericks.com (2)

Duncan Aviation, Lincoln, NE. Tel: (402) 475-2611, (800) 228-4277, FAX: (402) 475-5541, Web Site: www.duncanaviation.com (16)

Duncan Direct Associates, Peterborough, NH. Tel: (603) 924-3121, FAX: (603) 924-8511, E-Mail: duncandirect@pobox.com, Web Site: www.duncandirect.com (39)

Duncan Thompson, John, Cotta Transmission Co, Beloit, WI. Tel: (608) 368-5600, FAX: (608) 368-5605, E-Mail: sales@cotta.com, Web Site: www.cotta.com (16)

Duncan, Bill, Maxon Furniture Inc, Muscatine, IA. Tel: (253) 395-4139, (800) 876-4274, FAX: (800) 257-2635, Web Site: www.maxonfurniture.com (10)

Duncan, Candace, Alliance Defense Fund, Scottsdale, AZ. Tel: (480) 444-0020, Web Site: www.telladf.org (1)

Duncan, George, Duncan Direct Associates, Peterborough, NH. Tel: (603) 924-3121, FAX: (603) 924-8511, E-Mail: duncandirect@pobox.com, Web Site: www.duncandirect.com (39)

Duncan, J. Robert, Duncan Aviation, Lincoln, NE. Tel: (402) 475-2611, (800) 228-4277, FAX: (402) 475-5541, Web Site: www.duncanaviation.com (16)

Duncan, Pat, Helzberg Diamonds, North Kansas City, MO. Tel: (816) 842-7780, (800) HELZBERG, FAX: (816) 480-0294, Web Site: www.helzberg.com (16)

Duncanson, Donald M., Dynacolor Graphics Inc, Hialeah, FL. Tel: (305) 625-5388, (800) 624-8840, FAX: (305) 888-9903, E-Mail: dmail@dynacolor.com, Web Site: www.dynacolor.com (27)

Duncomb, Andrew, Tony Stone Images, Chicago, IL. Tel: (800) 234-7880, FAX: (312) 922-9075, Web Site: www.getty-images.com (38)

Duncraft Inc, Concord, NH. Tel: (603) 224-0200, (800) 593-5656, FAX: (603) 226-3735, E-Mail: info@duncraft.com, Web Site: www.duncraft.com (16)

Dundee Internet Services Inc, Dundee, MI. Tel: (734) 529-5331, FAX: (734) 529-5085, E-Mail: pat@dundee.net, Web Site: mailing-list-services.com/dundee.net (22)

Dungan, David N., Answerthink, Miami, FL. Tel: (305) 375-8005, (866) 844-6514, FAX: (305) 379-8810, Web Site: www.answerthink.com (35)

Dungan, Virginia B, National Humane Education Society, Charles Town, WV. Tel: (304) 725-0506, FAX: (304) 725-1523, E-Mail: information@nhes.org, Web Site: www.nhes.org (1)

Dunham & Co. Plano, TX. Tel: (469) 454-0100 (1)

Dunham, Lisa, Smithsonian Enterprises, New York, NY. Tel: (212) 916-1300, (800) 766-2149, FAX: (212) 490-0058, Web Site: www.smithsonianmag.com (17)

Dunham, Paul, Pace Inc, Southern Pines, NC. Tel: (910) 695-7223, FAX: (910) 695-1594, E-Mail: support@paceworldwide.com, Web Site: www.paceworldwide.com/index.asp (16)

Dunham, Rick, Dunham & Co, Plano, TX. Tel: (469) 454-0100 (1)

Dunham, Sandra, Pace Inc, Southern Pines, NC. Tel: (910) 695-7223, FAX: (910) 695-1594, E-Mail: support@paceworldwide.com, Web Site: www.paceworldwide.com/index.asp (16)

Hugo Dunhill Mailing Lists Inc, Omaha, NE. Tel: (800) 223-6454, FAX: (402) 255-9099, E-Mail: sales@hdml.com, Web Site: www.hdml.com (23)

Dunhill International List Co Inc, Boca Raton, FL. Tel: (561) 998-7800, (800) 386-4455, FAX: (561) 998-7880, E-Mail: dunhill@dunhills.com, Web Site: www.dunhills.com (23)

Dunhill, Cindy, Dunhill International List Co Inc, Boca Raton, FL. Tel: (561) 998-7800, (800) 386-4455, FAX: (561) 998-7880, E-Mail: dunhill@dunhills.com, Web Site: www.dunhills.com (23)

Dunhill, Robert, Dunhill International List Co Inc, Boca Raton, FL. Tel: (561) 998-7800, (800) 386-4455, FAX: (561) 998-7880, E-Mail: dunhill@dunhills.com, Web Site: www.dunhills.com (23)

Dunlap, Dennis, American Marketing Association, Chicago, IL. Tel: (312) 542-9000, (800) AMA-1150, FAX: (312) 542-9001, Web Site: www.marketingpower.com (40)

Dunlap, Larry E., Fostoria Industries Inc, Johnson City, TN. Tel: (419) 435-9201, (800) 495-4525, FAX: (419) 435-0842, E-Mail: email@fostoriaindustries.com, Web Site: www.fostoriaindustries.com (9)

Dunleavey, Jennifer, Direct Selling Association, Washington, DC. Tel: (202) 452-8866, FAX: (202) 452-9010, E-Mail: info@dsa.org, Web Site: www.dsa.org (40)

Dunn, Anna Marie, AMD Research & Marketing LLC, Safety Harbor, FL. Tel: (727) 409-1087, Web Site: www.amdresearch-marketing.com (30)

Dunn, Dennis, Growing Child, Inc, West Lafayette, IN. Tel: (765) 464-0920, (800) 927-7289, FAX: (765) 423-4495, E-Mail: service@growingchild.com, Web Site: www.growingchild.com (17)

Dunn, Gregory, Alliant, Brewster, NY. Tel: (845) 276-2600, FAX: (845) 276-2605, Web Site: www.alliantdata.com (22)

Dunn, Gregory W., Gifts Corp, Barrie, ON Canada. Tel: (905) 670-1126, (800) 565-3130, FAX: (905) 670-1127, E-Mail: customerservice@regal.ca, Web Site: www.regalgreetings.com (35)

Dunn, James, The New York Times Co, New York, NY. Tel: (212) 556-1234, Web Site: www.nytimes.com (17)

Dunn, Jeffrey D., Sesame Workshop, New York, NY. Tel: (212) 875-6677, Web Site: www.sesameworkshop.org (1)

Dunn, John, ADM Productions Inc, Port Washington, NY. Tel: (516) 484-6900, (800) ADM-DIAL, FAX: (516) 621-2531, Web Site: www.admpro.com (16)

Dunn, John, PRIORITY Data Systems Inc, Omaha, NE. Tel: (402) 592-2550, (877) 273-7774, FAX: (402) 592-5052, E-Mail: sales@pdomaha.com, Web Site: www.priority-data.com (22)

Dunn, Kevin, World Wrestling Entertainment Inc, Stamford, CT. Tel: (203) 352-8600, FAX: (203) 359-5180, Web Site: www.wwe.com (16)

Dunn, Melanie, Cossette, Quebec, QC Canada. Tel: (418) 647-2727, FAX: (418) 647-2564, E-Mail: info@cossette.com, Web Site: www.cossette.com (35)

Dunn, Michael M., Duncraft Inc, Concord, NH. Tel: (603) 224-0200, (800) 593-5656, FAX: (603) 226-3735, E-Mail: info@duncraft.com, Web Site: www.duncraft.com (16)

Dunn, Mike, DME Holdings, Daytona Beach, FL. Tel: (877) 720-0082, E-Mail: info@dmedelivers.com, Web Site: dmedelivers.com (21)

Dunn, Sharon, Duncraft Inc, Concord, NH. Tel: (603) 224-0200, (800) 593-5656, FAX: (603) 226-3735, E-Mail: info@duncraft.com, Web Site: www.duncraft.com (16)

Dunn, Stephen, DunnData Co, Brewster, NY. Tel: (845) 278-1200, Web Site: www.dunndataco.com (23)

DunnData Co, Brewster, NY. Tel: (845) 278-1200, Web Site: www.dunndataco.com (23)

Dunning, Patty, Horticulture Magazine, Cincinnati, OH. Tel: (513) 531-2690, FAX: (513) 891-7153, Web Site: www.hortmag.com (17)

Dunphy, Peter, Doctor's Best Inc, San Clemente, CA. Tel: (949) 498-3628, (800) 333-6977, FAX: (800) 754-2036, (949) 498-3952, E-Mail: info@drbvitamins.com, Web Site: www.drbvitamins.com (16)

Duplication Factory Inc, Chaska, MN. Tel: (952) 448-9912, (800) 279-2009, FAX: (952) 448-3983, E-Mail: info@duplicationfactory.com, Web Site: www.duplicationfactory.com (31)

Dupont Color Proofing, Wilmington, DE. Tel: (800) 441-7515, FAX: (302) 892-8030, Web Site: www.dupont.com/proofing (27)

E I DuPont De Nemours & Co, Wilmington, DE. Tel: (302) 774-1000, (800) 441-7515, FAX: (302) 774-7321, Web Site: www.dupont.com (16)

Dupuis, Sharon, Photri Images LLC, Fairfax, VA. Tel: (703) 978-0129, E-Mail: info@photriimages.com, Web Site: www.photriimages.com (38)

Duque, Milette, Peet's Coffee & Tea Inc, Berkeley, CA. Tel: (510) 525-3207, (800) 999-2132, FAX: (510) 594-2180, E-Mail: mailorder@peets.com, Web Site: www.peets.com (4)

Duracell, Bethel, CT. Tel: (800) 551-2355, Web Site: www.duracell.com (16)

Durand, Bob, Atlantic Publication Group LLC, Charleston, SC. Tel: (843) 747-0025, FAX: (843) 744-0816, E-Mail: info@atlanticpublicationgrp.com, Web Site: www.atlanticpublicationgrp.com (17)

Durasol Corp, Amesbury, MA. Tel: (978) 388-2020, (800) 370-0683, FAX: (978) 388-9762, Web Site: www.durasolcorp.com (34)

Durate, Bernarda, 21st Century Insurance, Woodland Hills, CA. Tel: (818) 704-3700, FAX: (818) 226-1198, E-Mail: executiveoffice@21st.com, Web Site: www.21st.com (15)

The Durham Manufacturing Co, Durham, CT. Tel: (860) 349-3427, (800) 243-3774, FAX: (860) 349-8572, (800) 782-5499, E-Mail: info@durhammfg.com, Web Site: www.durhammfg.com (16)

Durian, Bogdan, Delta Tech Industries, Ontario, CA. Tel: (714) 577-8028, FAX: (714) 577-0140, E-Mail: sales@deltatechindustries.com, Web Site: www.deltatechindustries.com (12)

During, Kimberly, WinterSilks LLC, Warren, PA. Tel: (904) 645-6000, Web Site: www.wintersilks.com (2)

Durio Nursery, Opelousas, LA. Tel: (337) 948-3696, FAX: (337) 942-6404, E-Mail: dalton@durionursery.biz, Web Site: www.durionursery.com (8)

Durio, Belle, Durio Nursery, Opelousas, LA. Tel: (337) 948-3696, FAX: (337) 942-6404, E-Mail: dalton@durionursery.biz, Web Site: www.durionursery.com (8)

Durio, Dalton, Durio Nursery, Opelousas, LA. Tel: (337) 948-3696, FAX: (337) 942-6404, E-Mail: dalton@durionursery.biz, Web Site: www.durionursery.com (8)

Durley, Dale H., American Tax Associates Inc, Columbus, OH. Tel: (614) 443-5343, FAX: (614) 443-0279 (20)

Durning, Andrea, Bellomy Research Inc, Winston Salem, NC. Tel: (336) 721-1140, (800) 443-7344, FAX: (336) 721-1597, E-Mail: bellomy@interpath.com, Web Site: www.bellomyresearch.com (30)

Durrah, Elaine, Reliance Electric, Fort Smith, AR. Tel: (479) 646-4711, FAX: (479) 648-5792, E-Mail: smtraylor@powersystems.rockwell.com, Web Site: www.reliance.com (9)

Durrett, Jason, B Shackman & Co Inc, Galesburg, MI. Tel: (269) 484-1000, (800) 221-7656, FAX: (269) 484-1010, Web Site: www.shackman.com (6)

Durrett, Johanna, B Shackman & Co Inc, Galesburg, MI. Tel: (269) 484-1000, (800) 221-7656, FAX: (269) 484-1010, Web Site: www.shackman.com (6)

Durs, Don, Stile-Tile Like Metal Roofing, Sellersburg, IN. Tel: (812) 246-1866, (800) 999-7777, FAX: (800) 477-9318, (800) 944-6884, Web Site: www.mtsales.com (9)

Dursi, Bonnie, Hotline List Corp, New York, NY. Tel: (212) 840-8135, FAX: (212) 840-8139 (23)

Dustman, Wesley, Selkirk Press, Sandpoint, ID. Tel: (208) 263-7523, FAX: (208) 263-2229, E-Mail: weprint@selkirkpress.com (27)

Dutch Gardens USA Inc, Bloomington, IL. Tel: (800) 944-2250, E-Mail: customerservice@dutchgardens.com, Web Site: www.dutchgardens.com (8)

Dutcher, John, Isuzu Motors America LLC, Anaheim, CA. Tel: (562) 229-5000, (800) 255-6727, FAX: (562) 229-5463, Web Site: www.isuzu.com (16)

Duval, Christopher, McCabe Duval + Associates, Portland, ME. Tel: (207) 347-8614, FAX: (207) 773-7245, E-Mail: cduval@mccabe-duval.com, Web Site: www.mccabe-duval.com (35)

Dvorak, Kathleen, Richardson Electronics Ltd, Lafox, IL. Tel: (630) 208-2200, FAX: (630) 208-2550, E-Mail: edg@rell.com, Web Site: www.rell.com (16)

Dvorak, Kathleen S., United Stationers, Deerfield, IL. Tel: (847) 627-7000, FAX: (847) 647-7001, Web Site: www.unitedstationers.com (25)

Dworman, Steven, It Really Works Inc, Beverly Hills, CA. Tel: (310) 888-4009, FAX: (310) 888-4025, E-Mail: steve@itreallyworks.tv, Web Site: www.itreallyworks.tv (32)

Dworsky, Bruce, Jordan Direct LLC, Saint Petersburg, FL. Tel: (727) 452-7718, E-Mail: bruce@jordandirecttv.com, Web Site: www.jordandirecttv.com (32)

Dworsky, Shannon, Jordan Direct LLC, Saint Petersburg, FL. Tel: (727) 452-7718, E-Mail: bruce@jordandirecttv.com, Web Site: www.jordandirecttv.com (32)

The Dwyer Group, Waco, TX. Tel: (254) 759-5850, Web Site: www.dwyergroup.com (16)

Dwyer Instruments Inc, Michigan City, IN. Tel: (219) 879-8868, Web Site: www.dwyer-inst.com (16)

Dwyer, Kerry Ann, FCB Health, New York, NY. Tel: (212) 672-2300, FAX: (212) 672-2301, E-Mail: hello@fcbhealthcare.com, Web Site: fcbhealthcare.com (35)

Dwyer, Paul, Plan International USA, Warwick, RI. Tel: (401) 562-8400, (800) 556-7918, FAX: (401) 738-5608, Web Site: www.planusa.org (1)

Dwyre, Loretta, Luster Care Products, Saint Louis, MO. Tel: (636) 272-1885, (800) 291-5223, FAX: (636) 272-1869, Web Site: www.lusterlace.com (16)

DX Engineering, Akron, OH. Tel: (800) 777-0703, FAX: (330) 572-3279, E-Mail: info@comteksystems.com, Web Site: www.comteksystems.com (16)

Dyck, A.R., Poker Player, Sherman Oaks, CA. Tel: (310) 674-3365, FAX: (310) 674-3205, E-Mail: ard@gamblingtimes.com, Web Site: www.gamblingtimes.com (17)

Dye, Kim, Nu-Parr Swimwear, Phoenix, AZ. Tel: (602) 279-4044, (800) 230-7277, FAX: (602) 212-2636, E-Mail: info@nu-parr.com, Web Site: www.nu-parr.com (2)

Dyer, Christopher, ListAbility Inc, Venice, FL. Tel: (866) 446-2055, E-Mail: info@listability.com, Web Site: www.listability.com (23)

Dyer, Dr. Esther R., National Medical Fellowships, New York, NY. Tel: (212) 483-8880, FAX: (212) 483-8897, E-Mail: info@nmf-online.org, Web Site: www.nmf-online.org (1)

Dyer, Kerry, US News & World Report, Washington, DC. Tel: (202) 955-2000, Web Site: www.usnews.com (17)

Dyer, Peggy, American Red Cross, Washington, DC. Tel: (202) 303-5214, (800) RED-CROSS, FAX: (202) 303-6604, Web Site: www.redcross.org (1)

Dyer, Shelli, ListAbility Inc, Venice, FL. Tel: (866) 446-2055, E-Mail: info@listability.com. Web Site: www.listability.com (23)

Dyess, Carl D., International Specialized Book Services Inc, Portland, OR. Tel: (503) 287-3093, (800) 944-6190, FAX: (503) 280-8832, E-Mail: isbs_sales@isbs.com, Web Site: www.isbscatalog.com (16)

Dykstra, Karen, AOL Corp, New York, NY. Tel: (212) 206-4400, Web Site: www.aol.com (32)

Dykun, L, Ventriloquist Voice Solutions International Inc, Mississauga, ON Canada. Tel: (866) 446-0860, E-Mail: info@ventriloquistsolutions.com, Web Site: www.ventriloquistsolutions.com (29)

Dylla, H. Frederick, American Institute of Physics, Melville, NY. Tel: (516) 576-2200, (800) 892-8259, FAX: (516) 576-2374, E-Mail: aipinfo@aip.org, Web Site: www.aip.org (17)

Dynacolor Graphics Inc, Hialeah, FL. Tel: (305) 625-5388, (800) 624-8840, FAX: (305) 888-9903, E-Mail: dmail@dynacolor.com, Web Site: www.dynacolor.com (27)

Dynamic Development Co, Mission Viejo, CA. Tel: (949) 768-5798, E-Mail: antiwear@dynamicdevelopment.com, Web Site: www.dynamicdevelopment.com (12)

Dynamic Engineering, Santa Cruz, CA. Tel: (831) 457-8891, FAX: (831) 457-4793, E-Mail: sales@dyneng.com, Web Site: www.dyneng.com (3)

Dynamics Research Corp, Andover, MA. Tel: (978) 475-9090, (800) 522-4321, FAX: (978) 475-8205, Web Site: www.drc.com (16)

Dysert, Scott, Liebert Corp, Columbus, OH. Tel: (614) 841-6700, (800) LIEBERT, FAX: (614) 841-6022, Web Site: www.liebert.com (16)

Dyson, Peter, American Society of Media Photographers (ASMP), Philadelphia, PA. Tel: (215) 451-ASMP, FAX: (215) 451-0880, Web Site: www.asmp.org (40)

Dyvig, Maureen, d.trio marketing group, Minneapolis, MN. Tel: (612) 787-3333, FAX: (612) 436-0324, E-Mail: greatideas@dtrio.com, Web Site: www.dtrio.com (35)

Dziurman Dzign Inc, Clawson, MI. Tel: (248) 288-8800, FAX: (248) 288-8804, E-Mail: dziurman@dzdzign.com, Web Site: www.dzdzign.com (35)

Dziurman, Mark, Dziurman Dzign Inc, Clawson, MI. Tel: (248) 288-8800, FAX: (248) 288-8804, E-Mail: dziurman@dzdzign.com, Web Site: www.dzdzign.com (35)

E

E&D Web Printing Inc, Rochelle, IL. Tel: (708) 656-6600, (815) 562-5800, FAX: (708) 656-4154, E-Mail: info@eanddweb.com, Web Site: www.eanddweb.com (27)

E+M Advertising Inc, New York, NY. Tel: (212) 981-5900, E-Mail: jtarsitano@emadv.com, Web Site: www.emadv.com (35)

E&M Media Group Inc, New York, NY. Tel: (212) 455-0177, FAX: (212) 455-0176, Web Site: www.emtvsales.com (35)

E! Entertainment Television, Los Angeles, CA. Tel: (323) 954-2400, FAX: (323) 954-2665, Web Site: www.eonline.com (32)

E Media Advantage, Livingston, NJ. Tel: (917) 994-3685, FAX: (973) 455-1312, E-Mail: tnevitt@emediaadvantage.com, Web Site: emediaadvantage.com (20)

E-Miles.com, Plano, TX. Tel: (214) 743-5555, Web Site: www.e-miles.com (19)

e-Pipeconnection, Evansville, IN. Tel: (812) 474-4529, (800) 262-4300, FAX: (812) 474-4531, E-Mail: sales@e-pipeconnection.com, Web Site: www.e-pipeconnection.com (9)

E3 Local Marketing Solutions, Cincinnati, OH. Tel: (513) 699-3300, (888) 878-2768, FAX: (513) 699-3310, Web Site: e3local.com (35)

EU Services, Stevensville, MD. Tel: (410) 643-7900, FAX: (410) 643-7933, E-Mail: clyde_sisk@siskmail.com, Web Site: www.siskmail.com (28)

E-Z-EM Inc, Lake Success, NY. Tel: (516) 333-8230, (800) 544-4624, FAX: (516) 333-8278, E-Mail: webmaster@ezem.com, Web Site: www.ezem.com (7)

EBM Direct Marketing Services LLC, Port Washington, NY. Tel: (516) 874-7839, Web Site: www.ebmdirectmarketing.com (20)

EBSCO Reception Room Subscription Services, Birmingham, AL. Tel: (205) 991-1409, (800) 527-5901, FAX: (205) 995-1621, Web Site: www.ebsco.com/errss (18)

EDC Publishing, Tulsa, OK. Tel: (918) 622-4522, (800) 475-4522, FAX: (800) 747-4509, Web Site: www.edcpub.com (17)

eFootage, Pasadena, CA. Tel: (626) 395-9593, FAX: (626) 395-5394, E-Mail: info@efootage.com, Web Site: www.efootage.com (38)

The EGC Group, Melville, NY. Tel: (516) 935-4944, FAX: (516) 935-7030, E-Mail: contact@egcgroup.com, Web Site: www.egcgroup.com (35)

EMC Corp, Hopkinton, MA. Tel: (888) 438-3622, Web Site: www.emc.com (16)

EMED Co Inc, Buffalo, NY. Tel: (716) 626-1616, (800) 442-3633, FAX: (716) 626-1630, E-Mail: customerservice@emedco.com, Web Site: www.emedco.com (16)

EMI Strategic Marketing Inc, Boston, MA. Tel: (617) 224-1101, E-Mail: info@emiboston.com, Web Site: emiboston.com (35)

EMS Technologies, Norcross, GA. Tel: (770) 263-9200, FAX: (770) 447-4405, Web Site: www.ems-t.com (16)

EOS International Inc, Carlsbad, CA. Tel: (760) 431-8400, (800) 876-5484, FAX: (760) 431-8448, Web Site: www.eosintl.com (5)

EPI Colorspace, Gaithersburg, MD. Tel: (301) 230-2023, FAX: (301) 990-7890, E-Mail: jcriscuoli@epicolorspace.com, Web Site: www.epicolorspace.com (36)

ERA D2C Convention, Washington, DC. Tel: (703) 841-1751, (800) 987-6462, FAX: (425) 977-1036, E-Mail: webadmin@retailing.org, Web Site: retailing.org/d2c (42)

ESL Federal Credit Union, Rochester, NY. Tel: (585) 336-1000, (800) 848-2265, FAX: (585) 336-1138, Web Site: www.esl.org (14)

ESP Printing & Mailing Inc, Boise, ID. Tel: (208) 345-4644, (888) 845-7665, FAX: (208) 345-4765, E-Mail: info@espdirectmail.com (28)

ESPN, Bristol, CT. Tel: (212) 456-4995 (5)

ETI Sales Support, Valhalla, NY. Tel: (914) 747-3030, (800) 466-4384, FAX: (914) 747-3466, E-Mail: info@etisales.com, Web Site: www.etisales.com (29)

ETR Associates, Scotts Valley, CA. Tel: (800) 321-4407, E-Mail: customerservice@etr.org, Web Site: www.etr.org (7)

ETTSI Premiums & Incentives, Daytona Beach, FL. Tel: (386) 271-0204, Web Site: www.ettsi.com (16)

EU Services, Rockville, MD. Tel: (301) 424-3300, (800) 230-3362, FAX: (301) 424-3696, E-Mail: marketing@euservices.com, Web Site: www.euservices.com (21)

EWA & Miniature Cars USA Inc, Berkeley Heights, NJ. Tel: (732) 424-7811, (800) 392-4454, FAX: (732) 424-7814, E-Mail: ewa@ewacars.com (11)

EXL, Jersey City, NJ. Tel: (201) 748-4729 (16)

The EZ-Forms Co, Kerrville, TX. Tel: (281) 667-4414, FAX: (281) 667-4415, E-Mail: ezformscontactus@gmail.com, Web Site: www.ez-forms.com (21)

Eadon Ventures, Alliance, OH. Tel: (330) 418-4298, Web Site: www.eadonventures.com (20)

Eager, Bill, CARFAX Inc, Centreville, VA. Tel: (703) 934-2664, Web Site: www.carfax.com (12)

Eagle Asset Management Inc, Saint Petersburg, FL. Tel: (727) 573-2453, FAX: (727) 573-8655, Web Site: www.eagleasset.com (14)

Eagle Claw Fishing Tackle, Denver, CO. Tel: (720) 941-8700, FAX: (303) 321-4750, E-Mail: info@eagleclaw.com, Web Site: www.eagleclaw.com (11)

Eagle Marketing Services Inc, San Diego, CA. Tel: (619) 223-1273, E-Mail: info@eaglemarketing.com, Web Site: www.eaglemarketing.com (35)

Eagle Publishing, Washington, DC. Tel: (202) 216-0600, FAX: (202) 216-0612, Web Site: www.eaglepub.com (17)

Eagle, Denise, ZCard North America, New York, NY. Tel: (212) 797-3450, Web Site: www.zcard.com (31)

Eagle:xm, Denver, CO. Tel: (303) 320-5411, (800) 426-5376, FAX: (303) 393-6584, E-Mail: extendedmedia@eaglexm.com, Web Site: www.eaglexm.com (21)

Eaker, Dean, Wired Assets Data Corp, Greenwich, CT. Tel: (203) 340-2316, Web Site: www.wiredassets.com (22)

Ealy, C. Cato, International Paper, Memphis, TN. Tel: (901) 419-9000, (800) 207-4003, E-Mail: internationalpaper.comm@ipaper.com, Web Site: www.internationalpaper.com (16)

Earl, Rachel, St Labre Indian School, Ashland, MT. Tel: (406) 784-4500, Web Site: www.stlabre.org (1)

Earlywine, Lisa, World Publications Inc, Winter Park, FL. Tel: (407) 628-4802, FAX: (407) 628-7061, Web Site: www.worldpub.net (17)

Earthrise, Irvine, CA. Tel: (949) 623-0980, FAX: (949) 623-0990, E-Mail: info@earthrise.com, Web Site: www.earthrise.com (16)

East Coast Industrial Equipment & Tire, Jacksonville, FL. Tel: (904) 358-5681, (800) 874-1942, FAX: (904) 354-0888 (34)

Eastabrook, Lucy, National Business Furniture Inc, Milwaukee, WI. Tel: (414) 276-8511, (800) 558-1010, FAX: (414) 276-8371, Web Site: www.nationalbusinessfurniture.com (10)

Eastbay Running Store Inc, Wausau, WI. Tel: (715) 845-5538, (800) 826-2205, FAX: (715) 261-9500, Web Site: www.eastbay.com (2)

Easter Seals, Chicago, IL. Tel: (312) 726-6200, (800) 221-6827, FAX: (312) 726-1494, Web Site: www.easter-seals.org (1)

Easterday, Vickie, Burkholder Flint Associates, Columbus, OH. Tel: (614) 228-2425, FAX: (614) 228-0631, E-Mail: easterday@burkholderflint.com, Web Site: www.burkholderflint.com (23)

Easterly, David G., American Appraisal Associates, Milwaukee, WI. Tel: (414) 271-7240, (800) 558-8650, FAX: (414) 221-7065, Web Site: www.american-appraisal.com (14)

Eastern Bank, Boston, MA. Tel: (617) 897-1008, (800) EASTERN, FAX: (617) 897-1105, Web Site: www.easternbank.com (14)

Eastern Collection Corp, Sag Harbor, NY. Tel: (631) 563-2112, (800) 243-1204, FAX: (631) 563-2471, E-Mail: ecc1626@aol.com (20)

Eastern Michigan University, Ypsilanti, MI. Tel: (734) 487-1849, FAX: (734) 484-1151, Web Site: www.emich.edu (16)

Eastern Mountain Sports, Peterborough, NH. Tel: (603) 924-9571, (888) 463-6367, FAX: (603) 924-4320, Web Site: www.ems.com (16)

Easthill Group Inc, Pottstown, PA. Tel: (610) 323-9063, (610) 323-9099, (610) 323-2200, (800) 345-1178, (888) 869-4433, FAX: (610) 323-6268, Web Site: www.eastwoodcompany.com (12)

Eastman Chemical Co, Kingsport, TN. Tel: (423) 229-2000, (800) 325-4330, E-Mail: eastman1@eastman.com, Web Site: www.eastman.com (16)

Eastman Kodak Co, Rochester, NY. Tel: (585) 724-4000, (800) 698-3324, FAX: (585) 724-1089, Web Site: www.kodak.com (27)

Eastman Vidal, Jill, 1-800-Flowers.com, Carle Place, NY. Tel: (516) 237-6000, Web Site: www.1800flowers.com (16)

Eastman, David, Agency.com, New York, NY. Tel: (212) 358-2600, FAX: (212) 358-2604, Web Site: www.agency.com (20)

Eastman, Deanna, Musician's Friend, Westlake Village, CA. Tel: (541) 772-5173, (800) 449-9128, Web Site: www.musiciansfriend.com (5)

Eastman, Rob, Musician's Friend, Westlake Village, CA. Tel: (541) 772-5173, (800) 449-9128, Web Site: www.musiciansfriend.com (5)

David Easton Inc, New York, NY. Tel: (212) 334-3820, FAX: (212) 334-3821, Web Site: www.davideastoninc.com (16)

Easton, David, David Easton Inc, New York, NY. Tel: (212) 334-3820, FAX: (212) 334-3821, Web Site: www.davideastoninc.com (16)

Eastwood, Michael, Time Communications, Saint Paul, MN. Tel: (800) 486-8581, FAX: (612) 298-1945, E-Mail: info@timecommunications.biz, Web Site: www.timecommunications.biz (29)

Easy Analytic Software Inc, Bellmawr, NJ. Tel: (856) 931-5780, FAX: (856) 931-4115, Web Site: www. easidemographics.com (22)

EasyLink Services International Corp, Piscataway, NJ. Tel: (800) 828-7115, FAX: (732) 652-3810, E-Mail: sales@easylink.com, Web Site: www.easylink.com (16)

Eaton Corp, Raleigh, NC. Tel: (216) 523-4400, (800) 356-5794, FAX: (216) 523-4787, Web Site: www. eaton.com (16)

Eaton, Jon, International Marine, Camden, ME. Tel: (207) 236-4837, FAX: (207) 236-6314, Web Site: www.internationalmarine.com (17)

Eaton, Robert J, DaimlerChrysler Corp, Auburn Hills, MI. Tel: (248) 512-1879, Web Site: www. daimlerchrysler.com (12)

Eaton-Pregler, Kimberly, Greater Fort Worth Builders Association, Fort Worth, TX. Tel: (817) 284-3566, FAX: (817) 284-6465, E-Mail: info@ fortworthbuilders.org, Web Site: www. forthworthbuilders.org (1)

Ebanks, Michele, Essence Communications Inc, New York, NY. Tel: (212) 522-1212, FAX: (212) 921-5173, Web Site: www.essence.com (17)

eBay Inc, San Jose, CA. Tel: (408) 376-7400, (800) 322-7400, Web Site: www.ebayinc.com (16)

Ebbets Field Flannels Inc, Seattle, WA. Tel: (206) 382-7249, FAX: (206) 382-4411, E-Mail: clubhouse@ ebbets.com, Web Site: www.ebbets.com (2)

Ebel, Greg, 4Imprint Inc, Oshkosh, WI. Tel: (920) 236-7272, (877) 446-7746, (888) 298-8190, FAX: (800) 355-5043, E-Mail: administrator@4imprint.com, Web Site: www.4imprint.com (16)

Eberle & Associates Inc, McLean, VA. Tel: (703) 821-1550, FAX: (703) 821-0920, E-Mail: info@eberle1. com, Web Site: www.eberleassociates.com (1)

Eberle Associates Inc, McLean, VA. Tel: (703) 821-1550, FAX: (703) 821-0920, Web Site: www. eberleassociates.com (35)

Eberle Walker, Kate, The Princeton Review, Natick, MA. Tel: (800) 273-8439, E-Mail: prep@review. com, Web Site: www.princetonreview.com (16)

Eberle, Bruce, Eberle Associates Inc, McLean, VA. Tel: (703) 821-1550, FAX: (703) 821-0920, Web Site: www.eberleassociates.com (35)

Eberle, Bruce W., Eberle & Associates Inc, McLean, VA. Tel: (703) 821-1550, FAX: (703) 821-0920, E-Mail: info@eberle1.com, Web Site: www. eberleassociates.com (1)

Eberle, Karl M, Harley-Davidson Inc, Milwaukee, WI. Tel: (414) 343-7286, FAX: (414) 343-4806, Web Site: www.harley-davidson.com (12)

Eberle, Terry, Florida Today, Melbourne, FL. Tel: (321) 242-3500, (877) 424-0156, FAX: (321) 242-3729, Web Site: www.floridatoday.com (17)

Eberlein, Gail K., Direct Response Enhancements LLC, Scottsdale, AZ. Tel: (480) 451-7384, FAX: (480) 661-8460, Web Site: www.dreteleconsultants.com (29)

Ebersole Lapidary Supply Inc, Wichita, KS. Tel: (316) 945-4771, (877) EBERSOLE, FAX: (316) 945-4773, E-Mail: ebersolerocks@sbcglobal.net, Web Site: www.ebersolelapidary.com (11)

Ebersole, Del, Ebersole Lapidary Supply Inc, Wichita, KS. Tel: (316) 945-4771, (877) EBERSOLE, FAX: (316) 945-4773, E-Mail: ebersolerocks@sbcglobal. net, Web Site: www.ebersolelapidary.com (11)

Ebersole, Len, Ebersole Lapidary Supply Inc, Wichita, KS. Tel: (316) 945-4771, (877) EBERSOLE, FAX: (316) 945-4773, E-Mail: ebersolerocks@sbcglobal. net, Web Site: www.ebersolelapidary.com (11)

Eberwein, Elise R, American Airlines, Fort Worth, TX. Tel: (817) 963-1234 (12)

Ebling, Ken, MDE Marketing, Mahwah, NJ. Tel: (201) 891-7010, Web Site: www.wdemarketing.com (16)

Eboli, Carla, Dieste, Dallas, TX. Tel: (214) 259-8000, FAX: (214) 259-8040, E-Mail: contact@dieste.com, Web Site: www.dieste.com (35)

eBureau LLC, Saint Cloud, MN. Tel: (320) 534-5000, FAX: (320) 534-5020, Web Site: www.ebureau.com (22)

Echenberg, Michael, Weight Watchers International, New York, NY. Tel: (516) 390-1400, FAX: (516) 390-1302, Web Site: www.weight-watchers.com (16)

Echnologist Scrub Tech, Mesquite, TX. Tel: (520) 208-6314 (34)

Echo Data Group, New Holland, PA. Tel: (800) 511-3870, E-Mail: sroberts@echodata.com, Web Site: www.echodata.com (22)

Echohawk, John E., Native American Rights Fund, Boulder, CO. Tel: (303) 447-8760, FAX: (303) 443-7776, Web Site: www.narf.org (1)

Echols, Terumi, Christianity Today Inc, Carol Stream, IL. Tel: (630) 260-6200, FAX: (630) 260-0114, Web Site: www.christianitytoday.com (17)

Echols, Tracy, MISSCO Corp, Flowood, MS. Tel: (601) 948-8600, (800) 647-5333, FAX: (601) 987-3038 (16)

Echomax, Teaneck, NJ. Tel: (201) 837-1371, FAX: (201) 837-6142 (35)

Echotouch Corp, Austin, TX. Tel: (512) 327-5638, Web Site: www.echotouch.com (20)

Eck, Robert, Beeman Precision Airguns, Santa Fe Springs, CA. Tel: (562) 968-5891, (800) 227-2744, FAX: (562) 968-5823, E-Mail: sales@beeman.com, Web Site: www.beeman.com (11)

Eckankar, Minneapolis, MN. Tel: (612) 544-3001, (800) 327-5113, FAX: (612) 474-1127, Web Site: www. eckankar.org (17)

Eckels, Jeff, e-Pipeconnection, Evansville, IN. Tel: (812) 474-4529, (800) 262-4300, FAX: (812) 474-4531, E-Mail: sales@e-pipeconnection.com, Web Site: www.e-pipeconnection.com (9)

Eckert, Mark, JLG Industries Inc, McConnellsburg, PA. Tel: (717) 485-5161, (877) JLG-SELL, FAX: (717) 485-6417, E-Mail: comments@jlg.com, Web Site: www.jlg.com (16)

Ecklers, Titusville, FL. Tel: (888) 787-3626, (800) 284-3906, E-Mail: custsvc@ecklers.net, Web Site: www. ecklers.com (1)

Eckman, Jamie, Brookhollow Cards, Rexburg, ID. Tel: (800) 822-0256, FAX: (800) 443-8847, E-Mail: service@brookhollowcards.com, Web Site: www. brookhollowcards.com (10)

Eckmann, Juergen, Nautilus Inc, Vancouver, WA. Tel: (360) 859-2900, (800) 675-0171, FAX: (360) 694-2755, Web Site: www.nautilus.com (11)

Eckstein, Joseph, Berkshire Record Outlet Inc, Lee, MA. Tel: (413) 243-4080, FAX: (413) 243-4340, E-Mail: broinc@berkshirerecordoutlet.com, Web Site: www2.broinc.com (3)

Eckstein, Stacy, Gun Video Catalog/LMP, San Diego, CA. Tel: (858) 569-4000, (800) 942-8273, FAX: (858) 569-0505, Web Site: www.gunvideo.com; www.glockstore.com (11)

Eckstein, Yechiel, International Fellowship of Christians and Jews, Washington, DC. Tel: (312) 641-7200, (800) 486-8844, Web Site: www.ifcj.org (1)

Eckweiler, Tania, SmartReply Inc, Irvine, CA. Tel: (949) 340-0700, Web Site: www.smartreply.com (29)

Eclipse Direct Marketing, Mineola, NY. Tel: (212) 931-8344, FAX: (516) 493-9122, E-Mail: jkaiser@ eclipsedm.com, Web Site: www.eclipsedm.com (23)

Eclipse Marketing Services Inc, Cedar Knolls, NJ. Tel: (800) 837-4648, E-Mail: hello@eclipse2.com, Web Site: www.eclipsemarketingservices.com (35)

Ecoenvelopes, Eden Prairie, MN. Tel: (612) 605-4885, (888) 428-4364, FAX: (651) 392-8924, E-Mail: info@ecoenvelopes.com, Web Site: www. ecoenvelopes.com (20)

Ecolab Professional Products, Saint Paul, MN. Tel: (651) 293-4248, FAX: (651) 225-3025, E-Mail: ecolabs@ecolabs.com, Web Site: www.ecolab.com (16)

Ecological Fibers Inc, Lunenburg, MA. Tel: (978) 537-0003, FAX: (978) 537-2238, E-Mail: jquill@ ecofibers.com (25)

Economaki, John, Bridge City Tool Works Inc, Portland, OR. Tel: (503) 282-6997, (800) 253-3332, FAX: (503) 287-1085, E-Mail: jjeconomaki@ comcast.net, Web Site: www.bridgecitytools.com (9)

The Economist Newspaper NA Inc, New York, NY. Tel: (212) 554-0600, FAX: (212) 586-1191, Web Site: www.economist.com (1)

Economy Handicrafts, Brooklyn, NY. Tel: (718) 431-9300, (800) 216-1601, FAX: (718) 431-9309, Web Site: www.vanguardcrafts.com (16)

Ecton, Virgil, NAACP, Baltimore, MD. Tel: (410) 580-5777, Web Site: www.naacp.org (1)

The Edbraham Group, Westbrook, CT. Tel: (860) 664-4120, Web Site: www.theedbrahamgroup.com (20)

Edbrooke, Shirley, The Edbraham Group, Westbrook, CT. Tel: (860) 664-4120, Web Site: www. theedbrahamgroup.com (20)

Eddy, Bob, BJ's Wholesale Club Inc, Westborough, MA. Tel: (508) 651-7400, FAX: (508) 651-6167, Web Site: www.bjs.com (13)

Eddy, George, Heinrich, Denver, CO. Tel: (303) 233-8660, (800) 356-5036, FAX: (303) 239-5352, E-Mail: info@heinrich.com, Web Site: www. heinrich.com (35)

Edelman Direct Marketing Inc, Great Neck, NY. Tel: (516) 829-9398 (20)

Edelman, Barbara A., Gebbie Press Inc, New Paltz, NY. Tel: (845) 255-7560, FAX: (888) 345-2790, E-Mail: gebbiepress@pipeline.com, Web Site: www. gebbieinc.com (17)

Edelman, Barbara, All-In-One Directory, New Paltz, NY. Tel: (845) 255-7560, FAX: (888) 345-2790, E-Mail: gebbiepress@pipeline.com, Web Site: www.gebbieinc.com (43)

Edelman, Michelle, Peter A Mayer Advertising Inc, New Orleans, LA. Tel: (504) 581-7191, FAX: (504) 581-3009, E-Mail: contact@petermayer.com, Web Site: www.peteramayer.com (35)

Edelman, Robert, Edelman Direct Marketing Inc, Great Neck, NY. Tel: (516) 829-9398 (20)

Edelman, Scott A., KCET, Burbank, CA. Tel: (747) 201-5000, FAX: (747) 201-5877, E-Mail: contact@ kcet.org, Web Site: www.kcet.org (1)

Edelman, Vladimir, NTN Buzztime Inc, Carlsbad, CA. Tel: (760) 438-7400, (877) 963-9200, FAX: (760) 438-3505, Web Site: www.buzztimebusiness.com (32)

Edelmann Scott Inc, Richmond, VA. Tel: (804) 643-1931, FAX: (804) 643-1934 (35)

Edelson, Maurice, Time Inc, New York, NY. Tel: (212) 522-1212, Web Site: www.timeinc.com (17)

Edelston, Marty, Boardroom Inc, Stamford, CT. Tel: (203) 973-5900, FAX: (203) 967-3086, Web Site: www.bottomlinepublications.com (17)

Edelstone, Charles, Dassault Falcon Jet Corp, Little Ferry, NJ. Tel: (201) 440-6700, FAX: (201) 541-4515, Web Site: www.dassaultfalcon.com (16)

Eden, Maria, Mercury Media, Santa Monica, CA. Tel: (310) 451-2900, FAX: (310) 451-0180, Web Site: www.mercurymedia.com (32)

Edgar, Howard, Practice Builders, Irvine, CA. Tel: (800) 679-1262, FAX: (714) 751-7801, E-Mail: info@practicebuilders.com, Web Site: www.practicebuilders.com (35)

Edge Teleservices, Inc, Oak Lawn, IL. Tel: (708) 857-5000, (800) 394-2323, FAX: (708) 857-5029, E-Mail: contactme@edgeteleservices.com, Web Site: www.edgeteleservices.com (29)

Edgecliffe-Johnson, Paul, InterContinental Hotels Group, Atlanta, GA. Tel: (800) 621-0555, FAX: (801) 975-1846, Web Site: www.ichotelsgroup.com (19)

EdgeMark Partners Inc, Glen Allen, VA. Tel: (804) 967-2000, (800) 488-0289, FAX: (804) 967-2111, E-Mail: info@edgemarkpartners.com, Web Site: www.edgemarkpartners.com (35)

Edgerton, Brendan, Crutchfield Corp, Charlottesville, VA. Tel: (434) 817-1000, (800) 955-9091, FAX: (804) 817-1010, E-Mail: administration@crutchfield.com, Web Site: www.crutchfield.com (3)

Edible Landscaping, Afton, VA. Tel: (434) 361-9134, (800) 524-4156, FAX: (434) 361-1916, E-Mail: info@ediblelandscaping.com, Web Site: www.eat-it.com (8)

Edison Electric Institute, Washington, DC. Tel: (202) 508-5000, FAX: (202) 508-5096, Web Site: www.eei.org (1)

Editorial Code & Data Inc, Walled Lake, MI. Tel: (248) 926-5187, FAX: (248) 926-6047, E-Mail: Monique@marketsize.com, Web Site: www.marketsize.com (30)

Editorial Freelance Association, New York, NY. Tel: (212) 929-5400, (866) 929-5425, FAX: (212) 929-5439, E-Mail: office@the-efa.org, Web Site: www.the-efa.org (31)

Editorial Projects in Education Inc, Bethesda, MD. Tel: (301) 280-3100, (800) 346-1834, FAX: (301) 280-3250, Web Site: www.edweek.org (17)

Editors Press Inc, Hyattsville, MD. Tel: (301) 853-4900, (888) 853-4900, FAX: (301) 853-4961, Web Site: www.edpress.com (27)

Edlund, Campbell, EMI Strategic Marketing Inc, Boston, MA. Tel: (617) 224-1101, E-Mail: info@emiboston.com, Web Site: emiboston.com (35)

Edman, Jeff, PC World, San Francisco, CA. Tel: (415) 243-0500, FAX: (415) 442-1891, Web Site: www.pcworld.com (17)

Edmonds Associates Inc, Vienna, VA. Tel: (703) 448-8000, E-Mail: tedmonds@edmondsassociates.com, Web Site: www.edmondsassociates.com (35)

Edmonds, Gary, Food for the Hungry Inc, Phoenix, AZ. Tel: (480) 998-3100, (800) 248-6437, FAX: (480) 998-4806, E-Mail: hunger@fh.org, Web Site: www.fh.org (1)

Edmonds, Lynn S., LW Robbins Associates, Holliston, MA. Tel: (508) 893-0210, (800) 229-5972, FAX: (508) 893-0212, E-Mail: ppapsador@lwra.com, Web Site: www.lwra.com (1)

Edmonds, Mel, MISSCO Corp, Flowood, MS. Tel: (601) 948-8600, (800) 647-5333, FAX: (601) 987-3038 (16)

Edmonds, Thomas, Edmonds Associates Inc, Vienna, VA. Tel: (703) 448-8000, E-Mail: tedmonds@edmondsassociates.com, Web Site: www.edmondsassociates.com (35)

Edmund Optics Inc, Barrington, NJ. Tel: (856) 573-6250, (800) 363-1992, FAX: (856) 573-6295, E-Mail: sales@edmundoptic.com, Web Site: www.edmundoptics.com (9)

Edmund, Marisa, Edmund Optics Inc, Barrington, NJ. Tel: (856) 573-6250, (800) 363-1992, FAX: (856) 573-6295, E-Mail: sales@edmundoptic.com, Web Site: www.edmundoptics.com (9)

Edmund, Robert M., Edmund Optics Inc, Barrington, NJ. Tel: (856) 573-6250, (800) 363-1992, FAX: (856) 573-6295, E-Mail: sales@edmundoptic.com, Web Site: www.edmundoptics.com (9)

Edo Interactive, Nashville, TN. Tel: (615) 297-6080, Web Site: www.edointeractive.com (16)

Edroy Products Co Inc, Nyack, NY. Tel: (845) 358-6600, (800) 233-8803, FAX: (845) 358-4098, E-Mail: sales@edroyproducts.com, Web Site: www.edroyproducts.com (16)

Edsall, Jr. Robert, Sun Harvest Citrus, Fort Myers, FL. Tel: (239) 768-2686, (800) 743-1480, FAX: (239) 768-9255, E-Mail: info@sunharvestcitrus.com, Web Site: www.SunHarvestCitrus.com (6)

Edson, B. Montgomery, Guarantee Trust Life Insurance Co, Glenview, IL. Tel: (847) 298-0670, FAX: (847) 298-1215, E-Mail: pr@gtlic.com, Web Site: www.gtlic.com (15)

Education Direct, Scranton, PA. Tel: (570) 342-7701, FAX: (570) 961-4851, Web Site: www.educationdirect.com (16)

Education Dynamics LLC, Hoboken, NJ. Tel: (201) 377-3000, FAX: (201) 377-3081, Web Site: www.educationdynamics.com (30)

Education Management Corp, Pittsburgh, PA. Tel: (412) 562-0900, FAX: (412) 562-0598, Web Site: www.edmc.edu (1)

Educational Coin Co, Highland, NY. Tel: (845) 691-6100, Web Site: www.educationalcoin.com (16)

Educational First Steps, Dallas, TX. Tel: (214) 824-7940), FAX: (214) 824-7428, Web Site: educationalfirststeps.org (1)

Educational Insights, Inc, Gardena, CA. Tel: (310) 884-2000, (888) 591-9334, FAX: (310) 886-8850, E-Mail: service@edin.com, Web Site: www.educationalinsights.com (16)

Educational Testing Service, Princeton, NJ. Tel: (609) 921-9000, FAX: (609) 734-5410, Web Site: www.ets.org (16)

Educators Progress Service Inc, Randolph, WI. Tel: (920) 326-3126, (888) 951-4469, Web Site: www.freeteachingaids.com (17)

EduTrek, Salt Lake City, UT. Tel: (801) 716-3924, Web Site: edutrek.com (16)

S Wallace Edwards & Sons Inc, Surry, VA. Tel: (757) 294-3121, (800) 290-9213, FAX: (757) 294-5378, E-Mail: info@virginiatraditions.com, Web Site: www.virginiatraditions.com (4)

Edwards Sakach, Deborah, American Historic Inns Inc, Dana Point, CA. Tel: (949) 497-2232, (800) 397-4667, FAX: (949) 497-9228, E-Mail: comments@iloveinns.com, Web Site: www.iloveinns.com (17)

Edwards, Ashley, IZEA, Orlando, FL. Tel: (321) 332-6830, Web Site: www.izea.com (20)

Edwards, Barrie, Music Sales Corp, New York, NY. Tel: (212) 254-2100, FAX: (212) 254-2013, E-Mail: info@musicsales.com, Web Site: www.musicsales.com (17)

Edwards, Brenda, TNS Intersearch, White Plains, NY. Tel: (914) 684-6100, FAX: (914) 684-6078, Web Site: www.tns-global.com (30)

Edwards, Carrie, White64, Vienna, VA. Tel: (703) 793-3000, E-Mail: info@white64.com, Web Site: white64.com (35)

Edwards, Chris, Winetasting.com, Napa, CA. Tel: (800) 435-2225, FAX: (707) 257-7470, Web Site: www.winetasting.com (4)

Edwards, Darrell, HCI Direct, Bensalem, PA. Tel: (215) 244-9600, (888) 765-0062, FAX: (215) 244-0328, Web Site: www.silkies.com (16)

Edwards, III Samuel W., S Wallace Edwards & Sons Inc, Surry, VA. Tel: (757) 294-3121, (800) 290-9213, FAX: (757) 294-5378, E-Mail: info@virginiatraditions.com, Web Site: www.virginiatraditions.com (4)

Edwards, Jeff, Nissan Motor Acceptance Corp, Irving, TX. Tel: (972) 929-7214, (800) 647-7261, Web Site: www.nissanusa.com (14)

Edwards, Jeffrey L., Allergan Inc, Irvine, CA. Tel: (714) 246-4500, (800) 347-4500, FAX: (714) 246-6987, Web Site: www.allergan.com (16)

Edwards, Jess, Nissan Motor Acceptance Corp, Irving, TX. Tel: (972) 929-7214, (800) 647-7261, Web Site: www.nissanusa.com (14)

Edwards, Jr. Marvin S., CommScope Inc, Hickory, NC. Tel: (828) 324-2200, (800) 982-1708, Web Site: www.commscope.com (16)

Edwards, Valerie Grudier, Gard Communications, Portland, OR. Tel: (503) 221-0100, (800) 800-7132, E-Mail: lfuller@gardcommunications.com, Web Site: gardcommunications.com (35)

Edwards, Virginia B., Editorial Projects in Education Inc, Bethesda, MD. Tel: (301) 280-3100, (800) 346-1834, FAX: (301) 280-3250, Web Site: www.edweek.org (17)

Edwards-Pullin, Jan, Publication Fulfillment Svcs, Cypress, CA. Tel: (714) 226-9785, FAX: (714) 226-9733, E-Mail: janpullin@pfsmag.com, Web Site: www.pfsmag.com (20)

Edwin Watts Golf, Fort Walton Beach, FL. Tel: (850) 244-2066, (800) 874-0146, FAX: (850) 244-5217, Web Site: www.edwinwatts.com (11)

Eechambadi, Naras, Quaero Corp, Charlotte, NC. Tel: (704) 414-0200, FAX: (704) 414-2195, Web Site: www.quaero.com (22)

Eenigenburg & Co, Bellevue, WA. Tel: (425) 649-0777, FAX: (425) 649-0719 (35)

Eenigenburg, Jill, Eenigenburg & Co, Bellevue, WA. Tel: (425) 649-0777, FAX: (425) 649-0719 (35)

Effective Marketing Associates, Inc, West Linn, OR. Tel: (503) 657-5859, FAX: (503) 657-5886, Web Site: www.e-m-a.com (20)

Effective Promotions Inc, Fort Johnson, NY. Tel: (518) 274-0291, (888) 467-3514, FAX: (518) 274-0290, Web Site: www.efpromotions.com (16)

Effrem, Deborah, Wood Carvers Supply Inc, Englewood, FL. Tel: (941) 698-0123, (800) 284-6229, FAX: (941) 698-0329, E-Mail: info@woodcarverssupply.com, Web Site: www.woodcarverssupply.com (9)

Effrem, Timothy, Wood Carvers Supply Inc, Englewood, FL. Tel: (941) 698-0123, (800) 284-6229, FAX: (941) 698-0329, E-Mail: info@woodcarverssupply.com, Web Site: www.woodcarverssupply.com (9)

Effron, Mark, TitanTV Media, Cedar Rapids, IA. Tel: (319) 365-5597, (800) 365-7629, FAX: (319) 365-5694, E-Mail: mktg@titantv.com, Web Site: www.titantv.com (20)

Efston, Irene, Efstonscience Inc, Toronto, ON Canada. Tel: (416) 787-4581, (888) 777-5255, FAX: (416) 787-5140, E-Mail: info@escience.ca, Web Site: www.e-sci.com (3)

Efston, Nick, Efstonscience Inc, Toronto, ON Canada. Tel: (416) 787-4581, (888) 777-5255, FAX: (416) 787-5140, E-Mail: info@escience.ca, Web Site: www.e-sci.com (3)

Efstonscience Inc, Toronto, ON Canada. Tel: (416) 787-4581, (888) 777-5255, FAX: (416) 787-5140, E-Mail: info@escience.ca, Web Site: www.e-sci.com (3)

Egan, Dean, Roosevelt Paper Co, Mount Laurel, NJ. Tel: (856) 303-4100, (856) 303-4200, (800) 523-3470, FAX: (856) 642-1950, (856) 642-1949, Web Site: www.rooseveltpaper.com (25)

Egan, Shane, Phoenix Learning Group Inc, Maryland Heights, MO. Tel: (314) 569-0211, (800) 221-1274, FAX: (314) 569-2834, E-Mail: dealersales@phoenixlearninggroup.com, Web Site: www.phoenixlearninggroup.com (16)

Egasti, Jaime, Catalina Marketing Corp, Saint Petersburg, FL. Tel: (727) 579-5000, FAX: (727) 556-2700, Web Site: www.catalinamarketing.com (31)

Egger, Terrence C.Z., The Plain Dealer, Cleveland, OH. Tel: (216) 999-5000, (800) 362-0727, FAX: (216) 999-6356, Web Site: www.plaindealer.com (18)

Egger, Terry, St Louis Post-Dispatch, Saint Louis, MO. Tel: (314) 340-8000, (800) 365-0820, FAX: (314) 340-3140, Web Site: www.stltoday.com (17)

Eggers, Tony, Bellomy Research Inc, Winston Salem, NC. Tel: (336) 721-1140, (800) 443-7344, FAX: (336) 721-1597, E-Mail: bellomy@interpath.com, Web Site: www.bellomyresearch.com (30)

Eggs by Byrd, Wappapello, MO. Tel: (573) 222-7999, (800) 235-EGGS, FAX: (573) 222-8009, E-Mail: eggsbybyrd@dishmail.net (10)

Ehardt, Thomas, Advanstar Communications Inc, North Olmstead, OH. Tel: (440) 243-8100, (800) 225-4569, FAX: (440) 891-2651, E-Mail: info@advanstar.com, Web Site: www.advanstarlists.com (17)

Ehmann, Elizabeth, Petsky Prunier LLC, New York, NY. Tel: (212) 842-6001, FAX: (212) 842-6039, Web Site: www.petskyprunier.com (14)

Ehmke, L.A., BFS Credit Services Co, Brook Park, OH. Tel: (216) 362-5094, FAX: (216) 362-5236, E-Mail: lupinettijim@bfsusa.com (16)

Ehringer, Ann, KCET, Burbank, CA. Tel: (747) 201-5000, FAX: (747) 201-5877, E-Mail: contact@kcet.org, Web Site: www.kcet.org (1)

Ehrlich, Jeffrey, Fulfillment Plus Inc, Holtsville, NY. Tel: (631) 758-8300, FAX: (631) 758-8360, E-Mail: jeff.ehrlich@fulfillmentplusny.com, Web Site: www.fulfillmentplusny.com (28)

Ehrlich, Matthew, Profit Center Software Inc, Uniondale, NY. Tel: (516) 414-6300, (888) 446-6240, FAX: (516) 414-6304, E-Mail: jmarrah@profitcenter.com, Web Site: www.profitcenter.com (22)

Eichinger, Marilynne, Informal Education Products, Milwaukie, OR. Tel: (503) 794-7045, (888) 444-5500, FAX: (503) 794-7111, E-Mail: sales@museumtour.com, Web Site: www.museumtour.com (11)

Eichler, Aaron, Bank of America, Charlotte, NC. Tel: (704) 386-5681, (800) 841-4000, FAX: (704) 386-6699, Web Site: www.bankofamerica.com (14)

Eichman, Donald, Alcom, Harleysville, PA. Tel: (215) 513-1600, E-Mail: stucker@alcomprinting.com, Web Site: www.alcomprinting.com (21)

Eichten, Doug, Greater Public, Minneapolis, MN. Tel: (612) 677-1505, (888) 454-2314, Web Site: www.deiworksite.org (1)

Eichten's Hidden Acres, Center City, MN. Tel: (651) 257-4752, FAX: (651) 257-6286, E-Mail: eichtens@frontiernet.net, Web Site: www.specialtycheese.com (4)

A Eicoff & Co, Chicago, IL. Tel: (312) 527-7183, (800) 333-6605, FAX: (312) 527-7192, E-Mail: bill.mccabe@eicoff.com, Web Site: www.eicoff.com (35)

800 Call KC, Kansas City, MO. Tel: (816) 231-4321, (800) 722-5554, FAX: (816) 241-2743, E-Mail: sales@call-kc.com, Web Site: www.call-kc.com (29)

800 Response, Burlington, VT. Tel: (802) 860-0378, (800) 639-7253, FAX: (800) 639-6733, E-Mail: sales@800response.com, Web Site: www.800response.com (32)

802 Creative Partners Inc, Montpelier, VT. Tel: (802) 234-9755, FAX: (802) 732-9056, E-Mail: info@802creative.com, Web Site: www.802creative.com (35)

89 Degrees, Burlington, MA. Tel: (781) 221-5400, Web Site: www.89degrees.com (9)

Eilenberger's Bakery Inc, Palestine, TX. Tel: (903) 729-2176, (800) 831-2544, FAX: (903) 723-2915, Web Site: www.eilenbergerbakery.com (4)

Einhaus, Brian, ClickSpark LLC, Rochester, NY. Tel: (800) 878-5709, E-Mail: amy@clickspark.com, Web Site: www.clickspark.com (32)

Einhorn Associates Inc, Milwaukee, WI. Tel: (414) 453-4488, FAX: (414) 453-4831, Web Site: www.einhornassociates.com (20)

Einhorn, Nancy, Einhorn Associates Inc, Milwaukee, WI. Tel: (414) 453-4488, FAX: (414) 453-4831, Web Site: www.einhornassociates.com (20)

Einhorn, Stephen, Einhorn Associates Inc, Milwaukee, WI. Tel: (414) 453-4488, FAX: (414) 453-4831, Web Site: www.einhornassociates.com (20)

Eire Direct, Chicago, IL. Tel: (312) 640-4000, FAX: (312) 640-0324, E-Mail: info@eiredirect.com, Web Site: www.eiredirect.com (16)

Eisel, John, InnerWorkings Inc, Chicago, IL. Tel: (317) 642-3700, (866) 766-5176, E-Mail: info@inwk.com, Web Site: www.inwk.com (35)

Eiseman, Jim, US Tape & Label Corp, Saint Louis, MO. Tel: (314) 824-4444, (800) 569-1906, FAX: (314) 824-4400, E-Mail: harrisonc@ustl.com, Web Site: www.ustl.com (27)

Eisen, James, Visionworks of America Inc, San Antonio, TX. Tel: (210) 340-3531, (800) 669-1183, FAX: (210) 201-8445, E-Mail: websupport@visionworks.com, Web Site: www.visionworks.com (7)

Eisenberg, Geoff, Tidewater Direct LLC, Centreville, MD. Tel: (410) 758-1500, FAX: (410) 758-2478, Web Site: www.tidewaterdirect.com (27)

Eisenberg, Geoffrey A., West Marine Inc, Watsonville, CA. Tel: (831) 728-2700, (800) 262-8464, (800) BOATING, FAX: (831) 768-5000, E-Mail: customercare@westmarine.com, Web Site: www.westmarine.com (11)

Eisenberg, Jeff, Mercury Commerce Inc, Westbury, NY. Tel: (212) 307-7001, FAX: (646) 219-3982, E-Mail: info@mercury-commerce.com, Web Site: www.mercury-commerce.com (22)

Eisenberg, Ken S., Industrial Marketing Associates, Cranford, NJ. Tel: (908) 276-4256, E-Mail: ken@industrialmarketingassociates.com, Web Site: www.industrialmarketingassociates.com (30)

Eisenberg, Michael, Birthday Express Inc, Kirkland, WA. Tel: (425) 250-1064, (800) 247-8432, FAX: (425) 641-2028, Web Site: www.birthdayexpress.com (5)

Eisenbrown, Steven A., Rockwell Automation, Milwaukee, WI. Tel: (414) 382-2000, FAX: (414) 382-4444, Web Site: www.rockwellautomation.com (16)

Eisenhauer, Elizabeth, Down Home Comforts, Putnam Station, NY. Tel: (518) 547-8966, (518) 223-2193, Web Site: downhomecomforts.com (8)

Ekberg, Daniel, Diamond Machining Technology, Marlborough, MA. Tel: (508) 481-5944, (800) 666-4368, FAX: (508) 485-3924, Web Site: www.dmtsharp.com (9)

Ekman, Anders, V12 Data, Wesley Chapel, FL. Tel: (813) 960-7800, FAX: (813) 960-7811, E-Mail: info@v12data.com, Web Site: www.v12data.com (22)

Ekroth, Chad, Bull Dog Media Group Inc, Madison, SD. Tel: (605) 256-9103, Web Site: www.commissionsoup.com (20)

Ekroth, Chad, Bulldog Media Group Inc, Madison, SD. Tel: (866) 309-7687, E-Mail: info@bulldogmediagroup.com, Web Site: www.bulldogmediagroup.com (32)

Elam, Mike, Continental Western Group, Des Moines, IA. Tel: (515) 473-3000, (800) 533-0303, FAX: (515) 473-3015, Web Site: www.cwgins.com (15)

Elbel, Tim, Esco Corp, Portland, OR. Tel: (503) 228-2141, FAX: (503) 778-6682, Web Site: www.escocorp.com (16)

Elbing, Steve, Service Litho Print Inc, Oshkosh, WI. Tel: (920) 231-3060, (800) 544-1493, FAX: (920) 231-1272, E-Mail: slp@service-litho.com (27)

Elcom International Inc, Norwood, MA. Tel: (781) 501-4000, FAX: (781) 762-1540, Web Site: www.elcominternational.com (22)

Elder, Bonny, Gift Services Inc, Vancouver, WA. Tel: (800) 379-4065, FAX: (360) 699-0597, E-Mail: corpsales@gifttree.com, Web Site: www.gifttree.com (6)

Elder, Derek, Concurrent Computer Corp, Duluth, GA. Tel: (678) 228-4000, (877) 978-7363, FAX: (954) 977-5580, Web Site: www.ccur.com (3)

Elder, James, Message Systems, Columbia, MD. Tel: (410) 872-4910, (877) 887-3031, FAX: (410) 872-4912, E-Mail: information@messagesystems.com, Web Site: www.messagesystems.com (32)

Elderhostel Inc, Lowell, MA. Tel: (978) 323-4291, (800) 454-5678, FAX: (617) 426-2166, Web Site: www.elderhostel.org (1)

Elderly Instruments, Lansing, MI. Tel: (517) 372-7890, (888) 473-5810, FAX: (517) 372-5155, E-Mail: web@elderly.com, Web Site: www.elderly.com (5)

Electric Insurance Co, Beverly, MA. Tel: (978) 921-2080, (800) 227-2757, FAX: (978) 524-5583, E-Mail: sales@electricinsurance.com, Web Site: www.electricinsurance.com (15)

Electric Media, New York, NY. Tel: (201) 461-5252 (30)

Electronic Arts Inc, Redwood City, CA. Tel: (650) 628-1500, Web Site: www.ea.com (3)

Electrosonic Group, Burbank, CA. Tel: (818) 333-3600, FAX: (818) 641-6384, E-Mail: info@electrosonic.com, Web Site: www.electrosonic.com (32)

ElectroWarmth Products LLC, Danville, OH. Tel: (800) 990-4622, E-Mail: sales@electrowarmth.com, Web Site: www.electrowarmth.com (8)

Elemental Scientific LLC, Appleton, WI. Tel: (920) 882-1277, E-Mail: info@elementalscientific.net, Web Site: www.elementalscientific.net (9)

Elephant Group Inc, Fort Lauderdale, FL. Tel: (954) 657-9611, FAX: (866) 699-5786, Web Site: www.elephantgroup.com (30)

Eleven Inc, San Francisco, CA. Tel: (415) 707-1111, Web Site: www.eleveninc.com (35)

Edward Elgar Publishing Inc, Northampton, MA. Tel: (413) 584-5551, FAX: (413) 584-9933, E-Mail: sales@e-elgar.com, Web Site: www.e-elgar.com (17)

Eli Journals, Durham, NC. Tel: (585) 203-5248, (800) 223-8720, FAX: (585) 292-4392, Web Site: www.elijournals.com (16)

Eli, Rafael, Schramm Marketing Group, New York, NY. Tel: (212) 983-0219, E-Mail: info@schrammnyc.com, Web Site: www.schrammnyc.com (35)

Elia, Michael, Gerber Garment Technology Inc, Toll-and, CT. Tel: (800) 826-3243, FAX: (860) 871-6007, E-Mail: info@gerbertechnology.com, Web Site: www.gerbertechnology.com (34)

JS Eliezer Associates Inc, Stamford, CT. Tel: (203) 658-1300 (20)

Elinsky, Sherry, United States Tennis Association, White Plains, NY. Tel: (914) 696-7000, (800) 990-8782, E-Mail: memberservices@usta.com, Web Site: www.usta.com (1)

Elisman, Boris, ACCO Brands Corp, Lake Zurich, IL. Tel: (800) 222-6462, FAX: (800) 247-1317, Web Site: www.accobrands.com (16)

Elite Debit, Sun Valley, CA. Tel: (435) 688-0634 X302, Web Site: www.elitedebit.com (14)

Elite Sportswear LP, Reading, PA. Tel: (610) 921-1469, (800) 345-4087, FAX: (610) 921-0208, E-Mail: gkelite@gkelite.com, Web Site: www.gk-elitesportswear.com (2)

Elkhart Cases, Elkhart, IN. Tel: (574) 295-7700, (800) 582-0319, FAX: (574) 295-7761, E-Mail: elkcases@aol.com (2)

Elkins, James, The Legal Studies Forum, Morgantown, WV. Tel: (304) 293-5301, FAX: (304) 293-6891, E-Mail: wvulaw@mail.wvu.edu (1)

Elkon, Idan, Graphnet Inc, New York, NY. Tel: (212) 994-1100, (800) 327-1800, FAX: (212) 994-1188, E-Mail: custsvc@graphnet.com, Web Site: www.graphnet.com (28)

Elkon, Yaakov, Graphnet Inc, New York, NY. Tel: (212) 994-1100, (800) 327-1800, FAX: (212) 994-1188, E-Mail: custsvc@graphnet.com, Web Site: www.graphnet.com (28)

Elkow, Mike, Crohn's & Colitis Foundation of America, New York, NY. Tel: (212) 685-3440, (800) 932-2423, E-Mail: info@ccfa.org, Web Site: www.ccfa.org (1)

Elks Magazine, Chicago, IL. Tel: (773) 755-4700, FAX: (773) 775-4792, E-Mail: elksmag@elks.org, Web Site: www.elks.org (17)

Ellen, Rennie, Diamonds By Rennie Ellen, New York, NY. Tel: (212) 869-5525, FAX: (212) 869-5526, Web Site: www.rennieellen.com (6)

Ellen, Shawn, Ability Commerce, Delray Beach, FL. Tel: (561) 330-3151, Web Site: www.abilitycommerce.com (20)

Ellerbusch Instrument Co, Cincinnati, OH. Tel: (513) 641-1800, (800) 582-2644, FAX: (513) 641-4360, E-Mail: info@ellerbusch.com, Web Site: www.ellerbusch.com (9)

Ellerbusch, Michael, Ellerbusch Instrument Co, Cincinnati, OH. Tel: (513) 641-1800, (800) 582-2644, FAX: (513) 641-4360, E-Mail: info@ellerbusch.com, Web Site: www.ellerbusch.com (9)

Ellett, Bob, The RYTEX Co, Peru, IN. Tel: (317) 872-8553, (800) 277-5458, FAX: (317) 872-8535, (800) 329-1669, Web Site: www.rytex.com (17)

Ellett, John, nFusion Group LLC, Austin, TX. Tel: (512) 716-7000, FAX: (512) 716-7001, E-Mail: info@nfusion.com, Web Site: www.nfusion.com (35)

Elliot, Kristina, The Copy Pro, Oradell, NJ. Tel: (201) 986-1080, FAX: (201) 986-1170, E-Mail: thecopypro@aol.com, Web Site: www.thecopypronj.com (39)

Elliot, Robin, Parkinson's Disease Foundation, New York, NY. Tel: (212) 923-4700, (800) 457-6676, FAX: (212) 923-4778, E-Mail: info@pdf.org, Web Site: www.pdf.org (1)

Elliott Marketing Group Inc, Pittsburgh, PA. Tel: (412) 831-1183 (22)

Elliott, Bob, Aerovox Inc, New Bedford, MA. Tel: (508) 994-9661, (888) AEROVOX, FAX: (508) 995-3000, E-Mail: sales1@aerovox.com, Web Site: www.aerovox.com (16)

Elliott, David, Elcom International Inc, Norwood, MA. Tel: (781) 501-4000, FAX: (781) 762-1540, Web Site: www.elcominternational.com (22)

Elliott, Garth, Medical Marketing Service Inc, Schaumburg, IL. Tel: (630) 350-1717, (800) 633-5478, E-Mail: sales@mmslists.com, Web Site: www.mmslists.com (24)

Elliott, Jamie, Coastal Living, Birmingham, AL. Tel: (205) 445-6000, FAX: (205) 445-7263, E-Mail: coastalliving@customersvc.com, Web Site: www.coastalliving.com (43)

Elliott, John, Elliott Marketing Group Inc, Pittsburgh, PA. Tel: (412) 831-1183 (22)

Elliott, Kirk, Medical Marketing Service Inc, Schaumburg, IL. Tel: (630) 350-1717, (800) 633-5478, E-Mail: sales@mmslists.com, Web Site: www.mmslists.com (24)

Elliott, Richard M., Medical Marketing Service Inc, Schaumburg, IL. Tel: (630) 350-1717, (800) 633-5478, E-Mail: sales@mmslists.com, Web Site: www.mmslists.com (24)

Elliott, Ross, Accellos Inc, Colorado Springs, CO. Tel: (719) 433-7000, Web Site: www.accellos.com (12)

Elliott, Stacy Weiss, Your Choice Or Mine, San Mateo, CA. Tel: (650) 340-7959, FAX: (650) 340-0449 (16)

Elliott, Thomas, Your Choice Or Mine, San Mateo, CA. Tel: (650) 340-7959, FAX: (650) 340-0449 (16)

Ellis Systems Corp, Lake Forest, IL. Tel: (847) 371-0200, (800) 253-5547, FAX: (847) 371-0202, E-Mail: tom@ellisfiling.com, Web Site: www.ellismh.com (9)

Ellis, Arthur, Spadet, New York, NY. Tel: (781) 275-8363, E-Mail: soapfac@verizon.net, Web Site: www.alcasoft.com/soapfact/ (7)

Ellis, Gary, Medtronic Inc, Minneapolis, MN. Tel: (763) 514-4000, (800) 328-2518, FAX: (763) 514-4879, Web Site: www.medtronic.com (16)

Ellis, Jim, The Adcentive Group Inc, San Diego, CA. Tel: (858) 278-9200, FAX: (858) 571-2832, Web Site: www.brownandbigelow.com (35)

Ellis, Lynda, Capitol Concierge Inc, Washington, DC. Tel: (202) 223-4765, FAX: (202) 833-2287, E-Mail: onlineconcierge@capitolconcierge.com, Web Site: www.capitolconcierge.com (16)

Ellis, Marietta, Spadet, New York, NY. Tel: (781) 275-8363, E-Mail: soapfac@verizon.net, Web Site: www.alcasoft.com/soapfact/ (7)

Ellis, Pete, Spa-Finder Inc, New York, NY. Tel: (305) 307-5852, (800) ALL-SPAS, Web Site: www.spafinder.com (7)

Ellis, Susie, Spa-Finder Inc, New York, NY. Tel: (305) 307-5852, (800) ALL-SPAS, Web Site: www.spafinder.com (7)

Ellis, Thomas, Priester Pecan Co Inc, Fort Deposit, AL. Tel: (334) 227-4301, (800) 277-3226, FAX: (334) 227-4294, E-Mail: customerservice@priester.com, Web Site: www.priesters.com (4)

Ellison, Denise, Baber Direct Marketing, Memphis, TN. Tel: (901) 332-6300, (800) 847-7040, FAX: (901) 332-6441, E-Mail: info@baberweb.com, Web Site: www.baberweb.com (21)

Ellison, Jay, US Cellular, Chicago, IL. Tel: (888) 944-9400, Web Site: www.uscellular.com (32)

Ellison, Larry, Oracle Corp, Redwood Shores, CA. Tel: (650) 506-7000, (800) 633-0738, FAX: (650) 506-7200, Web Site: www.oracle.com (16)

Ellison, Marvin R., JC Penney Inc, Plano, TX. Tel: (972) 431-1000, FAX: (972) 431-1977, Web Site: www.jcpenney.com (5)

Ellsworth, Robert K., Hook & Hackle Co Inc, Homestead, PA. Tel: (412) 476-8620, (800) 652-8342, FAX: (412) 476-8639, E-Mail: ron@hookhack.com, Web Site: www.hookhack.com (11)

Elmers Products Inc, Westerville, OH. Tel: (614) 985-2600, (800) 848-9400, FAX: (614) 985-2605, E-Mail: comments@elmers.com, Web Site: www.elmers.com (25)

Elmore, Shelly, Alliance of Area Business Publications, Redondo Beach, CA. Tel: (310) 379-8261, FAX: (310) 379-8283, E-Mail: info@bizpubs.org, Web Site: www.bizpubs.org (1)

Elms, Jim, Initiative, New York, NY. Tel: (212) 605-7000, FAX: (212) 605-7200, Web Site: www.initiative.com (32)

Elmwood Spa, Toronto, ON Canada. Tel: (416) 964-4515, (877) 284-6348, E-Mail: spa@elmwoodspa.com, Web Site: www.elmwoodspa.com (19)

Eloqua Inc, Vienna, VA. Tel: (703) 584-2750, Web Site: www.eloqua.com (22)

Elouazzani, Kenza, Ken Elo, Montreal, QC Canada. Tel: (514) 926-6945 (20)

Elrod, Bill, University of Alabama, Tuscaloosa, AL. Tel: (205) 348-6330, (866) 307-3917, FAX: (205) 348-9246, Web Site: continuingstudies.ua.edu (13)

Elsarky, Mohamed, Godiva Chocolatier, New York, NY. Tel: (212) 984-5900, (800) 946-3482, Web Site: www.godiva.com (4)

Elsberry, Greg, Cole Information Services, Omaha, NE. Tel: (800) 403-5894, E-Mail: info@coleinformation.com, Web Site: www.coleinformation.com (23)

Elseth, Chad, Alamo Mailing, San Antonio, TX. Tel: (210) 637-0404, FAX: (210) 637-0081 (28)

Elsevier, New York, NY. Tel: (212) 633-3805, FAX: (212) 633-3880, Web Site: www.elsevier.com (17)

Elston, Jason, CityTwist, Boca Raton, FL. Tel: (866) 798-2489, FAX: (561) 314-2692, Web Site: www.citytwist.com (32)

Elter, Kathy, Walter Karl Inc, Pearl River, NY. Tel: (845) 620-0700, FAX: (845) 620-1885, E-Mail: info@walterkarl.infousa.com, Web Site: www.walterkarl.com (22)

Elverding, Peter, ING, Minneapolis, MN. Tel: (612) 342-7061, (800) 333-6965, FAX: (612) 372-5339, Web Site: www.ing.com (15)

Ely, Ross, ProLogic Retail Services, Delray Beach, FL. E-Mail: info@prologicretail.com, Web Site: www.prologicretail.com (35)

ElZayn, Haytehm, National Administrative Service Co LLC, Dublin, OH. Tel: (614) 358-1500 (29)

Emailogics Inc/Emailbrain, Vancouver, WA. Tel: (866) 873-3019, Web Site: www.emailbrain.com (20)

eMarketing Strategy Group, New York, NY. Tel: (212) 679-6486, Web Site: www.ruthstevens.com (20)

Embassy Digital, Oakville, ON Canada. Tel: (905) 829-9969, (888) 477-8629, FAX: (905) 829-9429, E-Mail: info@embassydigital.com, Web Site: www.embassydigital.com (27)

Emberson, Dick, America's Call Center, Jacksonville, FL. Tel: (904) 224-2000, (800) 598-2580, FAX: (904) 737-1107, E-Mail: info@webcallusa.com, Web Site: www.webcallusa.com (29)

Embke, Tia, NBI Inc, Eau Claire, WI. Tel: (715) 835-8525, Web Site: www.nbi-sems.com (1)

Emblem & Badge Inc, Johnston, RI. Tel: (401) 365-1265, (800) 875-5444, FAX: (401) 365-1263, E-Mail: sales@recognition.com, Web Site: www.recognition.com (6)

Embrace Home Loans, Middletown, RI. Tel: (401) 846-3100, Web Site: www.afsfitfinance.com (14)

Embrey, Michael T., FunME Events, Dekalb, IL. Tel: (800) 386-6321, FAX: (815) 787-3100, E-Mail: funMEevents@aol.com, Web Site: www.funMEevents.com (20)

Emergency Essentials Inc, Orem, UT. Tel: (801) 222-9596, FAX: (801) 222-9598, E-Mail: webmaster@beprepared.com, Web Site: www.beprepared.com (16)

Emerging Marketing, Columbus, OH. Tel: (614) 923-6000, FAX: (614) 424-6200, E-Mail: info@emergingmarketing.com, Web Site: www.emergingmarketing.com (35)

Emerson Ecologics, Manchester, NH. Tel: (603) 656-9778, (800) 654-4432, FAX: (603) 656-9797, (800) 718-7238, E-Mail: cs@emersonecologics.com (7)

Emerson, Francis B., Deere & Co, Moline, IL. Tel: (309) 765-8000, FAX: (309) 748-0114, Web Site: www.deere.com (16)

Emerson, Jeff, McArdle Printing Co Inc, Upper Marlboro, MD. Tel: (301) 390-8500, FAX: (301) 390-8052, Web Site: www.mcardleprinting.com (27)

Emerson, Stewart, Supremex Inc, La Salle, QC Canada. Tel: (514) 595-0555, FAX: (514) 595-1112, E-Mail: vente@supremex.com, Web Site: www.supremex.com (26)

Emerson, Stewart, Supremex Inc, Etobicoke, ON Canada. Tel: (416) 675-9370, (800) 465-7603, FAX: (416) 675-1952, (416) 848-8388, E-Mail: sales.central@supremex.com, Web Site: www.supremex.com (26)

Emery, Jr. Sidney W., MTS Systems Corp, Eden Prairie, MN. Tel: (952) 937-4000, (800) 328-2255, FAX: (952) 937-4515, E-Mail: info@mts.com, Web Site: www.mts.com (16)

Emfluence, Kansas City, MO. Tel: (816) 472-4455, (877) 81-EMAIL, FAX: (816) 472-8855, E-Mail: expert@emfluence.com, Web Site: www.emfluence.com (21)

Emigrant Savings Bank, New York, NY. Tel: (212) 850-4521, (800) EMIGRANT, FAX: (212) 850-4372, Web Site: www.emigrant.com (14)

Emisare Inc, Greensboro, NC. Tel: (336) 378-0510, E-Mail: info@emisare.com, Web Site: www.emisare.com (32)

Emitte, Douglas, Ameriprise Financial Services Inc, Minneapolis, MN. Tel: (612) 671-3131, (651) 671-3434, (800) 386-2042, FAX: (612) 547-2736, Web Site: www.ameriprise.com (14)

Emley, Fredi Thorndike, de Emley & Associates Inc, San Juan Capistrano, CA. Tel: (949) 493-5117, FAX: (949) 493-6382 (33)

Emma, Nashville, TN. Tel: (800) 595-4401, E-Mail: hi@myemma.com, Web Site: myemma.com (24)

Emma, James P., Nova Communications Inc, Geneva, IL. Tel: (630) 377-1889, (800) 816-6682, FAX: (630) 377-1899, E-Mail: jim@novacominc.com, Web Site: www.novacominc.com (35)

Emond, Gary, GRP Funding LLC, Springfield, MA. Tel: (877) 571-7999, E-Mail: info@grpfunding.com, Web Site: www.grpfunding.com (14)

Emonds, Lisa, Fire Mountain Gems, Grants Pass, OR. Tel: (541) 956-7890, (800) 355-2137, (800) 423-2319, FAX: (541) 470-GEMS, E-Mail: questions@firemtn.com, Web Site: www.firemtn.com (16)

Emperor Clock LLC, Amherst, VA. Tel: (800) 642-0011, FAX: (434) 946-1420, E-Mail: emperor@emperorclock.com, Web Site: www.emperorclock.com (16)

Empire Blue Cross & Blue Shield, New York, NY. Tel: (212) 476-1000, (877) 476-7111, FAX: (212) 476-1281, Web Site: www.empireblue.com (15)

Empire City Casino at Yonkers Raceway, Yonkers, NY. Tel: (914) 968-4200, Web Site: www.empirecitygaming.com (19)

Empire Coffee & Tea Co, New York, NY. Tel: (212) 268-1220, (800) 262-5908, E-Mail: owners@empirecoffeetea.com, Web Site: www.empirecoffeetea.com (4)

Empire Imports Inc, Amherst, MA. Tel: (413) 256-4917, (800) 544-4744, FAX: (413) 256-4645, E-Mail: custsvc@empireimports.com, Web Site: www.empireimports.com (34)

Empire Scientific, Deer Park, NY. Tel: (631) 595-9206, (800) 645-7220, FAX: (631) 595-9384, (800) 343-5733, E-Mail: sales@empirescientific.com, Web Site: www.empirescientific.com (16)

Employers Group, El Segundo, CA. Tel: (800) 748-8484, Web Site: www.employersgroup.com (20)

EMPLOYERS Insurance, Reno, NV. Tel: (775) 327-2677, Web Site: www.employers.com (15)

Employment Publishing Inc, Wayne, PA. Tel: (610) 975-4539, FAX: (610) 687-7860, E-Mail: jfannin@employment911.com (17)

Emrey, Tom W., DineEquity Inc, Glendale, CA. Tel: (866) 995-DINE, Web Site: dineequity.com (16)

Emrich, Bryan, Old World Ind, Northbrook, IL. Tel: (847) 559-2000, FAX: (847) 559-2266, Web Site: www.oldworldind.com (34)

Emslie, Scott G., Sunshine Glassworks Ltd, Buffalo, NY. Tel: (716) 668-2918, (800) 828-7159, FAX: (716) 668-2932, E-Mail: info23@sunshineglass.com, Web Site: www.sunshineglass.com (11)

En ESPANOL Publishing Group LLC, Beverly Hills, CA. Tel: (310) 248-2680 (17)

Encircle, Miami, FL. Tel: (305) 592-7800, FAX: (305) 470-2662, E-Mail: merchantservices@encirclepayments.com, Web Site: www.insta-check.com (14)

Enco Manufacturing Co, Fernley, NV. Tel: (775) 788-7175, (800) 873-3626, FAX: (800) 965-5857, E-Mail: milanesp@use-enco.com, Web Site: www.use-enco.com (9)

Encore Marketing International, Lanham, MD. Tel: (301) 459-8020, (800) 846-9398, FAX: (301) 731-0525, E-Mail: customerservice@encoremarketing.com, Web Site: www.encoremarketing.com (16)

Encyclopaedia Britannica Inc, Chicago, IL. Tel: (312) 347-7159, (800) 323-1229, FAX: (312) 294-2104, Web Site: www.britannica.com (17)

Ende, John, Argent Trading LLC, New York, NY. Tel: (212) 697-8800, FAX: (212) 697-8606, Web Site: www.Argenttrading.com (16)

Ender, Ph.D. Kenneth L., Harper College, Palatine, IL. Tel: (847) 925-6000, Web Site: www.harpercollege.com (1)

Enderle, Robert, Advanced Marketing Direct, Buffalo, NY. Tel: (800) 696-7567, FAX: 716-821-5300, Web Site: www.amdirect.com (28)

Energizer Holdings Inc, Saint Louis, MO. Tel: (314) 985-2000, (800) 383-7323, FAX: (636) 733-4001, Web Site: www.energizer.com (16)

Enerpac, Menomonee Falls, WI. Tel: (262) 781-6600, (800) 433-2766, FAX: (262) 781-1028, Web Site: www.enerpac.com (16)

Enertex Marketing, New York, NY. Tel: (212) 532-3115, FAX: (212) 532-1878, E-Mail: info@enertexmarketing.com, Web Site: www.enertexmarketing.com (22)

Engagenextgen LLC, Mound, MN. Tel: (952) 905-4474 (20)

Engel, Dorothy, Seybold Publications, Gilbertsville, PA. Tel: (610) 327-3958, (888) 544-7104, FAX: (888) 463-4814, E-Mail: molly@thejossgroup, Web Site: www.seyboldreports.com (17)

Engel, Fred, KET, Lexington, KY. Tel: (859) 258-7000, (800) 432-0951, FAX: (606) 258-7396, E-Mail: rgriffin@ket.org, Web Site: www.ket.org (17)

Engel, John D., Donna Salyers' Fabulous-Bridal Inc, Covington, KY. Tel: (859) 291-3300, (800) 848-4650, E-Mail: abell@fabulousfurs.com, Web Site: fabulousfurs.com (2)

Engel, John J., WESCO, Pittsburgh, PA. Tel: (412) 454-2200, (800) 343-1201, E-Mail: info@wesco.com, Web Site: www.wescodist.com (16)

Engel, Laura, Angel Sales Inc, Chicago, IL. Tel: (773) 883-8858, FAX: (773) 883-8889, E-Mail: info@angelsales.com, Web Site: www.angelsales.com (31)

Engel, Paul, AIIM International, Silver Spring, MD. Tel: (301) 587-8202, (800) 477-2446, FAX: (301) 587-2711, E-Mail: aiim@aiim.org, Web Site: www.aiim.org (1)

Engel, Robert, Angel Sales Inc, Chicago, IL. Tel: (773) 883-8858, FAX: (773) 883-8889, E-Mail: info@angelsales.com, Web Site: www.angelsales.com (31)

Engelhorn, Lorinda, American Horse Products, San Juan Capistrano, CA. Tel: (949) 248-5300, (800) 500-0799, FAX: (949) 248-5305, E-Mail: zjim@sbcglobal.net, Web Site: www.americanhorseproducts.com (11)

Engineering Services & Products Co, South Windsor, CT. Tel: (860) 528-1119, (800) 835-7877, FAX: (800) 457-8887, Web Site: www.teksupply.com (9)

England, Andrew J., MillerCoors LLC, Chicago, IL. Tel: (312) 496-2700, (800) 645-5376, Web Site: www.millercoors.com (4)

Englander, Robert, Belvoir Media Group LLC, Norwalk, CT. Tel: (203) 857-3100, FAX: (203) 857-3103, E-Mail: customer_service@belvoir.com, Web Site: www.belvoir.com (17)

Engle, Barry, Ambassador Press, Minneapolis, MN. Tel: (612) 521-0123, (800) 544-9112, FAX: (612) 521-4587, E-Mail: info@ambpress.com, Web Site: www.ambpress.com (27)

Engle, Bernard, Ambassador Press, Minneapolis, MN. Tel: (612) 521-0123, (800) 544-9112, FAX: (612) 521-4587, E-Mail: info@ambpress.com, Web Site: www.ambpress.com (27)

Engleman, Michael, Syfy, New York, NY. Tel: (212) 664-4444, Web Site: www.syfy.com (32)

English, Flaurel, Toyota Motor Sales USA Inc, Torrance, CA. Tel: (310) 468-4000, (800) 331-4331, FAX: (310) 468-7841, Web Site: www.toyota.com (16)

English, Glenn, National Rural Electric Cooperative Association, Arlington, VA. Tel: (703) 907-5500, FAX: (703) 907-5528, Web Site: www.nreca.org (1)

English, Jeannine, AARP, Washington, DC. Tel: (202) 434-2277, FAX: (202) 434-2525, Web Site: www.aarp.org (1)

English, Jeffrey, Empire Scientific, Deer Park, NY. Tel: (631) 595-9206, (800) 645-7220, FAX: (631) 595-9384, (800) 343-5733, E-Mail: sales@empirescientific.com, Web Site: www.empirescientific.com (16)

English, William, Scope 1, Kalamazoo, MI. Tel: (269) 323-1333, (877) 7SCOPE1, Web Site: www.scope1.com (16)

Engstrom, Erik, Reed Elsevier, New York, NY. Tel: (212) 309-8100, FAX: (212) 309-8187, Web Site: www.reedelsevier.com (17)

Engstrom, John, DBM Group Inc, Irvine, CA. Tel: (714) 727-0825, FAX: (714) 838-0327, E-Mail: sales@dbmgroup.com, Web Site: www.dbmgroup.com (35)

Enke, Roger, Action-AD, Bettendorf, IA. Tel: (563) 355-9581, FAX: (563) 355-9586 (35)

ENMAX Corp, Calgary, AB Canada. Tel: (403) 514-3122, Web Site: www.enmax.com (9)

Ennis Inc, Midlothian, TX. Tel: (972) 775-9801, (800) 962-0944, FAX: (800) 645-8339, Web Site: www.ennis.com (16)

Enos, Jim, PennWell Publishing, Tulsa, OK. Tel: (918) 835-3161, (800) 331-4463, E-Mail: headquarters@pennwell.com, Web Site: www.pennwell.com (17)

Enright, Patty, Publicis Worldwide North America, New York, NY. Tel: (212) 279-5550, E-Mail: andrew.bruce@publicisna.com, Web Site: publicisna.com (35)

Entergy, New Orleans, LA. Tel: (504) 576-4000, (800) ENTERGY, FAX: (504) 576-4428, Web Site: www.entergy.com (16)

Enterprex International Corp, Arcadia, CA. Tel: (626) 256-1444, FAX: (626) 256-1404, E-Mail: premium@enterprex.com, Web Site: www.enterprex.com (16)

Enterprise Ireland, New York, NY. Tel: (212) 371-3600, FAX: (212) 371-6398, Web Site: www.enterprise-ireland.com (16)

Enterprise Rent-A-Car, Saint Louis, MO. Tel: (314) 512-5000, FAX: (314) 512-4706, Web Site: www.enterprise.com (19)

Carol Enters List Co Inc, Fairfax, VA. Tel: (703) 425-0052, FAX: (703) 425-0056, E-Mail: listmanagement@carolenters.com, Web Site: www.carolenters.com (23)

Entertainment Music Marketing Corp, Baldwin, NY. Tel: (631) 243-0600, FAX: (631) 243-0605, E-Mail: emmcmusic@aol.com, Web Site: www.emmcmusic.com (16)

Entertainment Publications Inc, Troy, MI. Tel: (248) 404-1000, (888) 231-SAVE, FAX: (248) 404-1915, Web Site: www.entertainment.com (31)

Entrepreneur Media Inc, Irvine, CA. Tel: (949) 261-2325, (800) 274-6229, FAX: (949) 261-0234, Web Site: www.entrepreneur.com (17)

Entrepreneur Partners, Philadelphia, PA. Tel: (267) 322-7000, FAX: (267) 322-7001, E-Mail: info@epfunds.com, Web Site: www.epfunds.com (14)

The Envelope Connection Inc, Chicago, IL. Tel: (773) 774-4600, FAX: (773) 774-4601, E-Mail: sales@envelopeconnection.com, Web Site: envelopeconnection.com (28)

Envelope Manufacturers Association, Alexandria, VA. Tel: (703) 739-2200, FAX: (703) 739-2209, Web Site: www.envelope.org (1)

Environmental Defense Fund, Washington, DC. Tel: (202) 387-3500, (800) 684- (1)

Environmental Law Institute, Washington, DC. Tel: (202) 939-3800, FAX: (202) 939-3868, E-Mail: law@eli.org, Web Site: www.eli.org (17)

Environmental Research Associates, Havertown, PA. Tel: (610) 449-7400 (30)

Envision, Newport, RI. Tel: (401) 619-1500, (800) 524-8238, FAX: (401) 619-0130, E-Mail: envision@att.net, Web Site: www.envision-stock.com (38)

Eperformax Inc, Thompsons Station, TN. Tel: (901) 751-4800, (888) 384-7004, FAX: (901) 751-4805, E-Mail: info0609@eperformax.com, Web Site: www.eperformax.com (29)

Epic Marketing Solutions, Halifax, NS Canada. Tel: (902) 455-5100, (888) 323-6263, FAX: (902) 455-5103, E-Mail: info@epicmarketing.ca, Web Site: www.epicmarketing.ca (22)

Epic Research LLC, Greenville, DE. Tel: (302) 467-5445, Web Site: www.epicresearch.net (20)

Epilepsy Foundation, Landover, MD. Tel: (800) 332-1000, E-Mail: contactus@efa.org, Web Site: www.efa.org (1)

Episcopal Relief & Development, New York, NY. Tel: (855) 312-4325, FAX: (212) 687-5302, Web Site: www.er-d.org (1)

Epler, Barbara, New Directions Publishing Corp, New York, NY. Tel: (212) 255-0230, FAX: (212) 255-0231, E-Mail: editorial@ndbooks.com, Web Site: www.ndbooks.com (17)

Epling, Bill, FileMaker Inc, Santa Clara, CA. Tel: (408) 987-7000, FAX: (408) 987-3823, Web Site: www.filemaker.com (22)

Epp, Tyler, Kansas City Chiefs, Kansas City, MO. Tel: (816) 920-9300, (888) 99-CHIEFS, FAX: (816) 923-4719, Web Site: www.kcchiefs.com (16)

Epperson, Christine, The Virginia Diner Inc, Wakefield, VA. Tel: (888) 823-4637, E-Mail: vadiner@vadiner.com, Web Site: www.vadiner.com (4)

Eppinger, Nick, AAA Mid-Atlantic Insurance Groups, Wilmington, DE. Tel: (302) 299-4700, (800) 451-5921, FAX: (215) 864-5486, Web Site: www.aaamidatlantic.com (15)

Eppley, Mark, Laplink Software Inc, Bellevue, WA. Tel: (425) 952-6000, (800) 527-5465, FAX: (425) 952-6002, E-Mail: marketing@laplink.com, Web Site: www.laplink.com (3)

Epps, Monique Van, Booth Michigan, Grand Rapids, MI. Tel: (616) 222-5824, FAX: (616) 222-5318, Web Site: www.boothnewspapers.com (17)

Epsilon, Irving, TX. Tel: (469) 262-0600, Web Site: www.epsilon.com (35)

Epskamp, Scott, Leapfrog Online, Evanston, IL. Tel: (847) 492-1968, Web Site: www.leapfrogonline.com (35)

Epson America, Long Beach, CA. Tel: (562) 981-3840, (800) 873-7766, FAX: (562) 290-5220, Web Site: www.epson.com (10)

Epstein, Ann, HighScope Educational Research Foundation, Ypsilanti, MI. Tel: (800) 587-5639, FAX: (734) 485-0704, E-Mail: info@highscope.org, Web Site: www.highscope.org (17)

Epstein, Barbara, Nyrev Inc, New York, NY. Tel: (212) 757-8070, FAX: (212) 333-5374, E-Mail: mail@nybooks.com, Web Site: www.nybooks.com (17)

Epstein, David, Novartis Pharmaceuticals Corp, East Hanover, NJ. Tel: (862) 778-2100, (800) 669-6682, FAX: (973) 781-8119, Web Site: www.novartis.com (7)

Epstein, Jay A., NewPage Corp, Miamisburg, OH. Tel: (937) 242-9345, (877) 855-7243, FAX: (937) 242-9327, Web Site: www.newpagecorp.com (25)

Epstein, John, Direct Results, West Springfield, MA. Tel: (413) 732-8310, FAX: (413) 732-8361 (21)

Epton, Terrence J., USA Hosts Ltd, New Orleans, LA. Tel: (504) 524-8687, FAX: (504) 524-8842, Web Site: www.usahosts.com (19)

Equifax Credit Information Services Inc, Atlanta, GA. Tel: (404) 885-8000, (800) 685-5000, FAX: (404) 885-8988, Web Site: www.equifax.com (20)

Equifax Database Marketing, Wakefield, MA. Tel: (781) 876-2000, (800) 660-5125, FAX: (781) 246-3720, E-Mail: monica.baker@equifax.com, Web Site: www.equifax.com/databaseservices (22)

Equifax Online Marketing, Atlanta, GA. Tel: (404) 885-8000, Web Site: www.equifax.com/business/online-marketing (23)

Equitable Life & Casualty Insurance Co, Salt Lake City, UT. Tel: (801) 579-3400, FAX: (801) 579-3789, Web Site: www.equilife.com (15)

Equity Management Inc, San Diego, CA. Tel: (858) 558-2500, FAX: (858) 558-2547, Web Site: www.equitymanagementinc.com (20)

Equity Residential Properties, Chicago, IL. Tel: (312) 474-1300, FAX: (312) 474-8703, E-Mail: mgraycraddock@eqr.com, Web Site: www.eqr.com (20)

Erdahl, Randy, Clario Analytics, Eden Prairie, MN. Tel: (952) 653-0900, (866) 849-3341, FAX: (952) 653-5900, E-Mail: sales@clarioanalytics.com, Web Site: www.clarioanalytics.com (20)

Erdo, Peter, Graves Lapidary Co, Pompano Beach, FL. Tel: (954) 960-0300, (800) 327-9103, FAX: (954) 960-0301, E-Mail: sales@gravescompany.com, Web Site: www.gravescompany.com (9)

Erdo, Victoria, Graves Lapidary Co, Pompano Beach, FL. Tel: (954) 960-0300, (800) 327-9103, FAX: (954) 960-0301, E-Mail: sales@gravescompany.com, Web Site: www.gravescompany.com (9)

Erdos & Morgan Inc, Syosset, NY. Tel: (516) 935-6959, FAX: (516) 935-4040, E-Mail: info@erdosmorgan.com, Web Site: www.erdosmorgan.com (30)

Eric Mower + Associates, Syracuse, NY. Tel: (315) 466-1000, Web Site: www.mower.com (35)

Erickson, Annmarie, The Detroit Institute of Arts, Detroit, MI. Tel: (313) 833-7900, FAX: (313) 833-1390, Web Site: www.dia.org (16)

Erickson, Jeff, DKP & Associates, Inc, Skokie, IL. Tel: (847) 933-9808, FAX: (847) 933-9821, E-Mail: dpearlman@dkpassociates.com, Web Site: www.dkpassociates.com (22)

Erickson, Jodie, Power Music, Salt Lake City, UT. Tel: (801) 292-2418, (800) 777-BEAT, FAX: (801) 292-2462, Web Site: www.powermusic.com (16)

Erickson, John, IC System Inc, Saint Paul, MN. Tel: (800) 443-4123, Web Site: www.icsystem.com (20)

Erickson, Peter C., The Pillsbury Co, Minneapolis, MN. Tel: (763) 764-7600, (800) 248-7310, FAX: (763) 764-8330, Web Site: www.pillsbury.com (16)

Erickson, Peter H., Hall-Erickson Inc, Westmont, IL. Tel: (630) 434-7779, FAX: (630) 434-1216 (16)

Erickson, Terri L., J Peterman Co, Lexington, KY. Tel: (888) 647-2555, FAX: (859) 254-0869, Web Site: www.jpeterman.com (5)

Erickson, Tom, Northern Tool & Equipment Inc, Burnsville, MN. Tel: (952) 894-9510, (800) 221-0516, FAX: (952) 894-1020, Web Site: www.northerntool.com (16)

Erikson, John R., American Capital, Bethesda, MD. Tel: (301) 951-6122, FAX: (301) 654-6714, E-Mail: info@americancapital.com, Web Site: www.americancapital.com (15)

Erikson, Pam, PDQ Post Group, Surrey, BC Canada. Tel: (604) 888-0676, (888) 998-9878, FAX: (604) 888-4467, E-Mail: sales@pdqpostgroup.com, Web Site: www.pdqpostgroup.com (21)

Erkes, Ronald D., Ronald Erkes & Associates Inc, Palm Harbor, FL (35)

Erlandson Associates, Leesburg, VA. Tel: (703) 669-0889, E-Mail: bgerlandso@aol.com (20)

Erlandson, Barbara, Erlandson Associates, Leesburg, VA. Tel: (703) 669-0889, E-Mail: bgerlandso@aol.com (20)

Erlandson, Greg, Our Sunday Visitor Publishing, Huntington, IN. Tel: (260) 356-8400, (800) 348-2440, FAX: (260) 356-8472, E-Mail: athomas@osv.com, Web Site: www.osv.com (17)

Erlewine, Dan, Stewart-MacDonald, Athens, OH. Tel: (740) 592-3021, (800) 848-2273, FAX: (740) 593-7922, E-Mail: hostetler@stewmac.com, Web Site: www.stewmac.com (16)

Erna, Christine J., New England Direct Marketing Association, Wellesley Hills, MA. Tel: (781) 237-1366, FAX: (781) 431-8118, E-Mail: info@nedma.com, Web Site: www.nedma.com (40)

Ernan Roman Direct Marketing Corp, Little Neck, NY. Tel: (718) 225-4151, FAX: (718) 225-4889, E-Mail: ernan@erdm.com, Web Site: www.erdm.com (20)

Ernest, Scott, Cessna Aircraft Co, Wichita, KS. Tel: (316) 517-6000, (800) 4-CESSNA, FAX: (316) 517-6640, Web Site: www.cessna.com (16)

Ernst & Young LLP, New York, NY. Tel: (212) 773-6146, FAX: (312) 879-4000, Web Site: www.ey.com (20)

Ernst, Connie P., Stewart Enterprises Inc, Jefferson, LA. Tel: (504) 729-1400, (800) 535-6017, FAX: (504) 729-1984, Web Site: www.stewartenterprises.com (16)

Ernst, Roger, Case Design Corp, Telford, PA. Tel: (215) 703-0130, (800) 847-4176, FAX: (215) 703-0139, E-Mail: sales@casedesigncorp.com, Web Site: www.casedesigncorp.com (34)

Ertel, Louis, Foote-Jones/Illinois Gear, Aberdeen, SD. Tel: (605) 225-0360, FAX: (605) 225-0567, Web Site: www.footejones.com (16)

Ertel, Mike, IWCO Direct, Chanhassen, MN. Tel: (952) 474-0961, FAX: (952) 474-6467, Web Site: www.iwco.com (21)

Ervey, Al, Mercury Print & Mail Co Inc, Pawtucket, RI. Tel: (401) 724-7600, FAX: (401) 724-9920, Web Site: www.mpmri.com (28)

Escalante, David, SK&A, Irvine, CA. Tel: (800) 752-5478, FAX: (949) 476-9131, E-Mail: skasales@skainfo.com, Web Site: www.skainfo.com (23)

Esco Corp, Portland, OR. Tel: (503) 228-2141, FAX: (503) 778-6682, Web Site: www.escocorp.com (16)

Escoe, Steven, Facts 'n Figures, Sherman Oaks, CA. Tel: (661) 222-2278, (818) 986-6600, FAX: (661) 222-2287, Web Site: www.factsnfiguresinc.com (30)

Escort Inc, West Chester, OH. Tel: (513) 870-8500, (800) 964-3138, FAX: (513) 870-8509, E-Mail: sales@escortradar.com, Web Site: www.escortradar.com (16)

Eshelman, David, DeLorme Mapping, Yarmouth, ME. Tel: (207) 846-7100, (800) 642-0970, FAX: (207) 846-7051, E-Mail: caleb.mason@delorme.com, Web Site: www.delorme.com (3)

ESignal, Hayward, CA. Tel: (510) 266-6000, Web Site: www.esignal.com (14)

Esler, Susan B., Ashland Inc, Covington, KY. Tel: (859) 815-3333, Web Site: www.ashland.com (16)

Espeland, Curt E., Eastman Chemical Co, Kingsport, TN. Tel: (423) 229-2000, (800) 325-4330, E-Mail: eastman1@eastman.com, Web Site: www.eastman.com (16)

Espinola, Jill, Morgan Kaufmann Publishers Inc, Burlington, MA. Tel: (781) 313-4700, E-Mail: order@mkp.com, Web Site: www.mkp.com (17)

Esprit Line Co Ltd USA, Greenwich, CT. Tel: (203) 629-5124 (16)

Esquire Magazine, New York, NY. Tel: (212) 649-4020, FAX: (212) 649-4303, E-Mail: esquire@hearst.com, Web Site: www.esquire.com (17)

Esquivel, Claudia, GS Marketing, Houston, TX. Tel: (713) 580-3900, FAX: (713) 580-5935, E-Mail: contactus@gsmarketing.com, Web Site: www.gsmarketing.com (21)

ESRI, Redlands, CA. Tel: (909) 793-2853, Web Site: www.esri.com (22)

Esrock Partners, Orland Park, IL. Tel: (708) 349-8400, (888) ESROCKS, FAX: (708) 349-8471, E-Mail: kwilson@esrock.com, Web Site: www.esrock.com (35)

Esselte Americas, Melville, NY. Tel: (631) 675-5700, (800) 645-6051, FAX: (631) 622-1970, Web Site: www.curtis.com (16)

Essence Communications Inc, New York, NY. Tel: (212) 522-1212, FAX: (212) 921-5173, Web Site: www.essence.com (17)

Essential Products Co Inc, New York, NY. Tel: (212) 344-4288 (7)

Esser, Patrick J., Cox Communications Inc, Atlanta, GA. Tel: (404) 843-5000, (888) 566-7751, FAX: (404) 269-2243, Web Site: www.cox.com (16)

Essex Printing Co Inc, Croton On Hudson, NY. Tel: (212) 688-4720, (800) 443-9113, FAX: (212) 308-2764, E-Mail: essexptg@aol.com, Web Site: www.essex-printing.com (27)

Estee Lauder Inc, New York, NY. Tel: (212) 572-4200, FAX: (212) 893-7782, Web Site: www.esteelauder.com (14)

Estee Marketing Group Inc, Rye Brook, NY. Tel: (914) 235-7080, FAX: (914) 235-6518, E-Mail: info@esteemarketing.com, Web Site: www.esteemarketing.com (24)

Estepa, Jim, Journeys, Nashville, TN. Tel: (615) 367-7000, (888) 324-6356, FAX: (615) 367-8123, Web Site: www.journeys.com (2)

Esterly, Diana E., Speed-Mat, Biddeford, ME. Tel: (207) 294-4358, (800) 882-7017, FAX: (207) 882-9279, E-Mail: info@speed-mat.com, Web Site: www.speed-mat.com (16)

Esterly, Harry F., Speed-Mat, Biddeford, ME. Tel: (207) 294-4358, (800) 882-7017, FAX: (207) 882-9279, E-Mail: info@speed-mat.com, Web Site: www.speed-mat.com (16)

Esterow, Milton, Art News Magazine, New York, NY. Tel: (212) 398-1690, FAX: (212) 819-0394, E-Mail: info@artnews.com, Web Site: www.artnews.com (17)

Estes Industries, Penrose, CO. Tel: (719) 372-6565, FAX: (719) 372-3419, Web Site: www.estesrockets.com (11)

Estes, Ph.D. Carroll L., National Committee to Preserve Social Security & Medicare, Washington, DC. Tel: (202) 216-0420, (800) 966-1935, FAX: (202) 216-0446, E-Mail: kreard@ncpssm.org, Web Site: www.ncpssm.org (1)

Estka, Robert J., Special Markets Sales Co, Indianapolis, IN. Tel: (317) 595-6587, FAX: (317) 595-9853, E-Mail: info@specialmkts.com, Web Site: www.specialmkts.com (33)

Esto Photographics Inc, Mamaroneck, NY. Tel: (914) 698-4060, FAX: (914) 698-1033, E-Mail: esto@esto.com, Web Site: www.esto.com (38)

eStock Photo, Long Island City, NY. Tel: (718) 433-4295, (800) 284-3399, E-Mail: sales@estockphoto.com, Web Site: www.estockphoto.com (38)

Estok, Marcy, SAE International, Warrendale, PA. Tel: (724) 776-4841, Web Site: www.sae.org (6)

eTargetMedia.com Inc, Coconut Creek, FL. Tel: (954) 480-8470, (888) 805-3282, FAX: (954) 480-8489, E-Mail: info@etargetmedia.com, Web Site: www.etargetmedia.com (32)

Etchworld, Hawthorne, NJ. Tel: (973) 423-4002, (800) 872-3458, FAX: (973) 427-8823, Web Site: www.etchworld.com (11)

Etech Inc, Lufkin, TX. Tel: (936) 633-9333, Web Site: www.effectiveteleservices.com (29)

Ethel M Chocolates Inc, Henderson, NV. Tel: (702) 435-2655, (800) 471-0352, FAX: (702) 451-8379, E-Mail: chocolatier@ethelm.com, Web Site: www.ethelm.com (4)

Ethen, Troy, Taymark Inc, White Bear Lake, MN. Tel: (651) 426-1667, (800) 479-2043, FAX: (651) 426-0275, Web Site: www.taymarkinc.com (1)

Etheridge, Chris, The Lead Connection Inc, Denison, TX. Tel: (903) 337-1636, (888) 267-3165, FAX: (903) 337-1640, E-Mail: chriswithtlc@gmail.com, Web Site: www.leadconnections.com (28)

Ethnic Technologies LLC, South Hackensack, NJ. Tel: (201) 440-8923, (866) 333-8324, FAX: (201) 440-2168, E-Mail: karens@ethnictechnologies.com, Web Site: www.ethnictechnologies.com (23)

Ethridge, Will, Pearson Education, Upper Saddle River, NJ. Tel: (201) 236-7000, FAX: (201) 236-3290, Web Site: www.pearsoned.com (17)

Ethyl Corp, Richmond, VA. Tel: (804) 788-5000, FAX: (804) 788-5688, Web Site: www.ethyl.com (16)

Ettelson, John R., William Blair & Co LLC, Chicago, IL. Tel: (312) 236-1600, (800) 621-0687, FAX: (312) 368-9418, E-Mail: info@williamblair.com, Web Site: www.williamblair.com (14)

Ettinger, Jeffrey M., Hormel Foods Corp, Austin, MN. Tel: (507) 437-5611, (800) 523-4635, FAX: (507) 437-5158, Web Site: www.hormelfoods.com (16)

Ettinger, Mark, Linguistic Systems Inc, Cambridge, MA. Tel: (877) 654-5006, FAX: (617) 528-7491, E-Mail: info@linguist.com, Web Site: www.linguist.com (27)

Etzcorn, Janis L., Landscape Forms Inc, Kalamazoo, MI. Tel: (616) 381-0490, (800) 430-6209, FAX: (616) 381-3455, E-Mail: specify@landscapeforms.com, Web Site: www.landscapeforms.com (16)

Etzel, Tom, National Graphics Inc, North Branford, CT. Tel: (203) 481-2351, FAX: (203) 483-0256, E-Mail: inquiries@natgraphics.com, Web Site: www.natgraphics.com (27)

Euclide, Brian, TEC Mailing Solutions, LLC, Sun Prairie, WI. Tel: (608) 825-8525, (866) 379-9437, FAX: (608) 825-8526, E-Mail: info@tecmailing.com (22)

Eudaley, Deborah, Lyris Inc, Emeryville, CA. Tel: (510) 844-1551, (800) 768-2929, FAX: (510) 844-1598, E-Mail: sales@lyris.com, Web Site: www.lyris.com (32)

Evans, Brad, CPM Delta 1, Inc, Dallas, TX. Tel: (214) 349-6886, (800) 627-0252, FAX: (214) 503-1557, Web Site: www.cpmdelta1.com (11)

Evans, Carol, Working Mother, New York, NY. Tel: (212) 221-9595, FAX: (212) 219-7448, Web Site: www.workingmother.com (31)

Evans, Dennis, Cookbook Publishers Inc, Lenexa, KS. Tel: (913) 492-5900, (800) 227-7282, FAX: (913) 492-5947, E-Mail: info@cookbookpublishers.com, Web Site: www.cookbookpublishers.com (17)

Evans, Glenn, RG Barry Corp, Pickerington, OH. Tel: (614) 864-6400, (800) 848-7560, FAX: (614) 866-9787, E-Mail: sales@rgbarry.com, Web Site: www.rgbarry.com (2)

Evans, Gregory P., Indium Corp of America, Clinton, NY. Tel: (315) 853-4900, (800) 446-3486, FAX: (800) 221-5759, E-Mail: askus@indium.com, Web Site: www.indium.com (16)

Evans, Janet, American Biographical Institute Inc, Raleigh, NC. Tel: (919) 781-8710, FAX: (919) 781-8712 (17)

Evans, John, British Columbia Automobile Association, Burnaby, BC Canada. Tel: (604) 268-5000, (800) 564-6222, FAX: (604) 268-5585, Web Site: www.bcaa.com (15)

Evans, John, SilverState Marketing Solutions, Las Vegas, NV. Tel: (702) 489-2124, Web Site: www.silverstateprintmail.com (28)

Evans, Kenneth, Summit Industries Inc, Marietta, GA. Tel: (770) 590-0600, (800) 241-6996, FAX: (770) 590-0714, E-Mail: info@summitinds.com, Web Site: www.summitinds.com (5)

Evans, Marge, Annie's Attic LLC, Big Sandy, TX. Tel: (903) 636-4303, (800) 282-6643, FAX: (903) 636-4088, Web Site: www.anniesattic.com (11)

Evans, Michael, BowTie Inc, Irvine, CA. Tel: (949) 855-8822, FAX: (949) 855-1850, E-Mail: mevans@bowtieinc.com, Web Site: www.animalnetwork.com (17)

Evans, N., Sedlak, Highland Hills, OH. Tel: (216) 206-4700, FAX: (216) 206-4840, E-Mail: info@jasedlak.com, Web Site: www.jasedlak.com (20)

Evans, Peter, ActiveCampaign Inc, Chicago, IL. Tel: (800) 357-0402, E-Mail: help@activecampaign.com, Web Site: www.activecampaign.com (24)

Evans, Robert, Liberty Life Insurance Co, Greenville, SC. Tel: (864) 609-8111, (800) 344-5834 (Mktg), FAX: (864) 609-4411, Web Site: www.libertycorp.com (15)

Evans, Ronald W., Interex, Amesbury, MA. Tel: (978) 388-8755, (800) INTEREX, FAX: (978) 388-8747, Web Site: www.interexhibits.com (17)

Evans, Steve, Scott Sign Systems Inc, Sarasota, FL. Tel: (941) 355-5171, (800) 237-9447, FAX: (941) 351-1787, E-Mail: mail@scottsigns.com, Web Site: www.scottsigns.com (16)

Evans, Tony, Lorton Data Inc, Arden Hills, MN. Tel: (651) 203-8200, FAX: (651) 203-8299, Web Site: www.lortondata.com (22)

Evenson, Jennifer, Lehigh Direct, Broadview, IL. Tel: (708) 681-3612, FAX: (708) 681-4694, Web Site: www.lehighdirect.com (27)

Event 360 Inc, Chicago, IL. Tel: (773) 247-5360, Web Site: www.event360.com (1)

Eventful Inc, San Diego, CA. Tel: (858) 882-0360, FAX: (858) 964-4640, Web Site: www.eventful.com (19)

Everest Direct Mail & Marketing, Asheville, NC. Tel: (866) 811-1553, E-Mail: info@everestdmm.com, Web Site: www.everestdmm.com (21)

Everett, John, Utilities Supply Corp, Woburn, MA. Tel: (781) 395-9023, (800) 343-7555, FAX: (800) 232-8726, (781) 395-2329, E-Mail: jge@fwwebb.com, Web Site: www.uscosupply.com (16)

Everett, Teri, Time Inc, New York, NY. Tel: (212) 522-1212, Web Site: www.timeinc.com (17)

Everex Computer Systems Inc, Fremont, CA. Tel: (800) 383-7391, (866) 850-8835, FAX: (510) 683-2186, E-Mail: customerservice@everex.com, Web Site: www.everex.com (16)

Everfast Inc, Kennett Square, PA. Tel: (800) 213-6366, Web Site: www.calicocorners.com (8)

Evergreen Enterprises Inc, Richmond, VA. Tel: (800) 774-3837, E-Mail: customerservice@myevergreen.com, Web Site: www.myevergreen.com (8)

Evergreen Marketing, Shelton, CT. Tel: (203) 822-7782, E-Mail: jchiavelli@evergreenmarketing.com, Web Site: www.evergreenmarketing.com (23)

Everly, Joseph W., Amtelco, McFarland, WI. Tel: (608) 838-4194, (800) 356-9148, FAX: (608) 838-8998, E-Mail: info@amtelco.com, Web Site: www.amtelco.com (16)

Evert, Cary, Hilti North America, Tulsa, OK. Tel: (866) 445-8827, FAX: (800) 879-7000, Web Site: www.hilti.com (34)

Everyday Media, Garrison, NY. Tel: (845) 788-3900, FAX: (212) 481-7800, Web Site: www.everydaymedia.com (31)

Ewald, Robert, Silicon Graphics Inc, Fremont, CA. Tel: (510) 933-8300, Web Site: www.sgi.com (16)

Ewen, David, EMED Co Inc, Buffalo, NY. Tel: (716) 626-1616, (800) 442-3633, FAX: (716) 626-1630, E-Mail: customerservice@emedco.com, Web Site: www.emedco.com (16)

Ewer, Marilyn, MKE Enterprises, North Reading, MA. Tel: (978) 664-3877, FAX: (978) 664-2835, E-Mail: e.marilyn@mke-enterprises.com, Web Site: www.mke-enterprises.com (35)

Ewert, Doug, Joseph A Bank Clothiers Inc, Hampstead, MD. Tel: (410) 239-2700, (800) 285-2265, FAX: (410) 239-5911, E-Mail: service@jos-a-bank.com, Web Site: www.josbank.com (2)

Ewing, William D., The Foxon Co, Providence, RI. Tel: (401) 421-2386, (800) 556-6943, FAX: (401) 421-8996 (27)

Ewoldt, Kriston, Business Marketing Association, Naperville, IL. Tel: (630) 544-5054, FAX: (630) 544-5055, E-Mail: info@marketing.org, Web Site: www.marketing.org (40)

ExactTarget, Indianapolis, IN. Tel: (317) 423-3928, FAX: (317) 396-1592, Web Site: www.exacttarget.com (32)

Excalibur Enterprises Inc, Winston Salem, NC. Tel: (336) 744-5000, (800) 441-4193, FAX: (336) 767-8257, E-Mail: info@excaliburmail.com, Web Site: www.excaliburmail.com (28)

Excelligence Learning Corp, Monterey, CA. Tel: (831) 333-2000, E-Mail: contactus@excelligence.com, Web Site: www.excelligencelearning.com (5)

Executive Connections LLC, Sarasota, FL. Tel: (941) 323-8300, Web Site: www.executiveconnectionsllc.com (20)

Executive Enterprises Inc, Hawthorne, NY. Tel: (860) 701-5900, (800) 831-8333, FAX: (860) 701-5909, (800) 250-3861, E-Mail: info@eeiconferences.com, Web Site: www.eeiconferences.com (16)

Executive Protection Products Inc, Napa, CA. Tel: (707) 253-7142, FAX: (707) 253-7149, E-Mail: services@epsecuritysolutions.com, Web Site: epsecuritysolutions.com (16)

Executive Search International, Newton, MA. Tel: (617) 527-8787, E-Mail: info@execsearchintl.com, Web Site: www.execsearchintl.com (20)

Exhibitgroup/Giltspur, Roselle, IL. Tel: (972) 538-3031, (800) 843-3944, Web Site: www.e-g.com (30)

Exhibitrac Direct Marketing, Las Vegas, NV. Tel: (702) 824-9651, (866) 988-6601, FAX: (702) 824-9376, E-Mail: sales@exhibitrac.com, Web Site: www.exhibitrac.com (23)

Expedia Inc, Bellevue, WA. Tel: (425) 679-7200, Web Site: www.expedia.com (19)

Experian, Costa Mesa, CA. Tel: (714) 830-7000, (888) EXPERIAN, FAX: (949) 242-2938, Web Site: www.experian.com (30)

Experian Simmons, New York, NY. Tel: (212) 749-3162, FAX: (212) 471-2940, E-Mail: ellenr@smrb.com, Web Site: www.smrb.com (30)

Experience In Software Inc, Berkeley, CA. Tel: (510) 644-0694, (800) 678-7008, FAX: (510) 644-3823, Web Site: www.projectkickstart.com (16)

Exposed Brick, New York, NY. Tel: (646) 454-0880, E-Mail: andrewc@exposedbrick.com, Web Site: www.exposedbrick.com (35)

Exposito-Ulla, Daisy, Dexposito & Partners, New York, NY. Tel: (646) 747-8800, Web Site: newamericanagency.com (35)

Express LLC, Columbus, OH. Tel: (614) 474-7000, Web Site: www.expressfashion.com (2)

Expressions Custom Furniture, Hickory, NC. Tel: (828) 328-1851, FAX: (828) 328-2176, Web Site: www.expressionsfurniture.com (16)

Exum, Ashe B., Happy Jack Inc, Snow Hill, NC. Tel: (252) 747-2911, (800) 326-5225, FAX: (252) 747-4111, E-Mail: happyjack@happyjackinc.com, Web Site: www.happyjackinc.com (11)

Exum, Joe, Happy Jack Inc, Snow Hill, NC. Tel: (252) 747-2911, (800) 326-5225, FAX: (252) 747-4111, E-Mail: happyjack@happyjackinc.com, Web Site: www.happyjackinc.com (11)

Ey, Fred, FocalPoint Marketing LLC, Metuchen, NJ. Tel: (877) 252-4305, Web Site: www.focalpoint-emarketing.com (35)

Eyeglass Service Industries, Lynbrook, NY. Tel: (516) 599-1135, FAX: (516) 599-4825 (2)

F

F&W Media Inc, Blue Ash, OH. Tel: (513) 531-2690, FAX: (513) 531-0293, Web Site: www.fwmedia.com (17)

F P International, Fremont, CA. Tel: (650) 261-5300, (800) 866-9946, FAX: (650) 361-1713, Web Site: www.fpintl.com (16)

The FX Matt Brewing Co, Utica, NY. Tel: (315) 624-2400, (800) 765-6288, FAX: (315) 624-2401, E-Mail: info@saranac.com, Web Site: www.saranac.com (4)

FAFCO Inc, Chico, CA. Tel: (530) 332-2100, (800) 994-7652, FAX: (530) 332-2109, Web Site: www.fafco.com (16)

FCB Health, New York, NY. Tel: (212) 672-2300, FAX: (212) 672-2301, E-Mail: hello@fcbhealthcare.com, Web Site: fcbhealthcare.com (35)

FCIA Management Co Inc, New York, NY. Tel: (212) 885-1500, FAX: (212) 885-1535, E-Mail: service@fcia.com, Web Site: www.fcia.com (15)

FCL Graphics Inc, Harwood Heights, IL. Tel: (708) 867-5500, (800) 274-3380, FAX: (708) 867-7768, Web Site: www.fclgraphics.com (27)

FDAnews, Falls Church, VA. Tel: (703) 538-7600, (888) 838-5578, FAX: (703) 538-7676, E-Mail: customerservice@fdanews.com, Web Site: www.fdanews.com (17)

FG Companies, Wayzata, MN. Tel: (952) 476-8900, E-Mail: mmelius@fgcompanies.com, Web Site: www.fgcompanies.com (22)

FGI Research Inc, Chapel Hill, NC. Tel: (919) 929-7759, FAX: (919) 932-8829, E-Mail: info@fgiresearch.com, Web Site: www.fgiresearch.com (35)

FIU Online, Miami, FL. Tel: (305) 348-2000 (1)

FJ Associates LLC, Wilmington, NC. Tel: (910) 452-2643, FAX: (630) 982-1056 (23)

FLM Graphics Corp, Fairfield, NJ. Tel: (973) 575-9450, E-Mail: info@flmgraphics.com, Web Site: www.flmgraphics.com (16)

FMC Corp, Philadelphia, PA. Tel: (215) 299-6000, FAX: (215) 299-5998, Web Site: www.fmc.com (16)

FMP Direct Inc, Libertyville, IL. Tel: (847) 816-1919, (800) 995-3343, FAX: (847) 816-1969, E-Mail: info@fmpdirect.com, Web Site: www.fmpdirect.com (21)

FMS Direct, Tarzana, CA. Tel: (818) 708-7814, FAX: (818) 708-7842, E-Mail: info@fmsdirect.com, Web Site: www.fmsdirect.com (35)

FNC INC, Oxford, MS. Tel: (662) 236-8254, Web Site: www.fncinc.com (14)

FP Mailing Solutions, Addison, IL. Tel: (630) 827-5500, (800) 341-6052, FAX: (630) 693-0626, E-Mail: custserv@fp-usa.com, Web Site: www.fp-usa.com (34)

FPS Marketing Communications, Milford, CT. Tel: (203) 783-1940, FAX: (203) 685-1940, E-Mail: info@fpsmarketing.com, Web Site: www.fpsmarketing.com (35)

FTD Companies Inc, Downers Grove, IL. Tel: (630) 719-7800, Web Site: www.ftdcompanies.com (16)

FTD Group Inc, Downers Grove, IL. Tel: (630) 719-7800, (800) 788-9000, FAX: (630) 719-6170, E-Mail: ftdmemberservices@ftdi.com, Web Site: www.ftdi.com (29)

FW Media, Cincinnati, OH. Tel: (513) 531-2690, Web Site: www.fwpublications.com (17)

Faberman, APR Rhea K., Foundation Fighting Blindness, Columbia, MD. Tel: (410) 423-0600, (800) 683-5555, Web Site: www.fightblindness.org (1)

Fabrizi, Michele, Marc USA, Pittsburgh, PA. Tel: (412) 562-2000, FAX: (412) 562-2022, E-Mail: pittsburgh@marcusa.com, Web Site: www.marcusa.com (35)

Faccomonto, Donald, Innovative Plastic Printing Corp, Roselle, IL. Tel: (630) 539-4400, (800) 238-7686, FAX: (630) 529-2109, E-Mail: dan@innov8cards.com, Web Site: www.innov8cards.com (27)

Facebook Inc, Menlo Park, CA. Tel: (650) 543-4800, Web Site: www.facebook.com (31)

Facts 'n Figures, Sherman Oaks, CA. Tel: (661) 222-2278, (818) 986-6600, FAX: (661) 222-2287, Web Site: www.factsnfiguresinc.com (30)

Facts On File Inc, New York, NY. Tel: (212) 967-8800, (800) 322-8755, FAX: (212) 678-3633, Web Site: www.infobasepublishing.com (17)

Fadel, Mitchell, Rent-A-Center Inc, Plano, TX. Tel: (972) 801-1100, (800) 275-2996, FAX: (972) 943-0113, Web Site: www.rentacenter.com (16)

Fagan, III Charles E., Credit Union Executives Society, Fitchburg, WI. Tel: (608) 271-2664, FAX: (608) 271-2303, E-Mail: cues@cues.org, Web Site: www.cues.org (1)

Fagan, Ray, HF Direct, Birmingham, AL. Tel: (205) 458-8200, FAX: (205) 458-8206, E-Mail: info@hfdirect.com, Web Site: www.hfdirect.com (35)

Fagnan, Nathalie, Publicis Worldwide North America, New York, NY. Tel: (212) 279-5550, E-Mail: andrew.bruce@publicisna.com, Web Site: publicisna.com (35)

Fahey, John, National Geographic Society, Washington, DC. Tel: (202) 862-8638, (800) 373-1717, Web Site: www.nationalgeographic.com (17)

Fahlbeck, Dale D., Elkhart Cases, Elkhart, IN. Tel: (574) 295-7700, (800) 582-0319, FAX: (574) 295-7761, E-Mail: elkcases@aol.com (2)

Fahlgren Mortine, Columbus, OH. Tel: (800) 731-8927, E-Mail: info@fahlgren.com, Web Site: www.fahlgrenmortine.com (35)

Fahmie, Tom, Commercial Data Processing Inc, Fairfield, NJ. Tel: (973) 882-1660, (800) 242-3731, FAX: (973) 882-0387, Web Site: www.dataprocess.com (22)

Faidley, David, Ability Commerce, Delray Beach, FL. Tel: (561) 330-3151, Web Site: www.abilitycommerce.com (20)

Fain, Bruce, Pacific Botanicals LLC, Grants Pass, OR. Tel: (541) 479-7777, FAX: (541) 479-7780, E-Mail: pacbot1@earthlink.net, Web Site: www.pacificbotanicals.com (7)

Fain, Deborah, Infomorphosis/Marketing Solutions, New York, NY. Tel: (212) 366-6216, FAX: (212) 255-4784, E-Mail: dfain@nyc.rr.com (20)

Fainman, Burt, Butler Specialty Co, Chicago, IL. Tel: (773) 221-1200, (800) 799-2857, FAX: (773) 221-5892, Web Site: www.butlerspecialty.net (16)

Fainstein, Boris, Medco Health Solutions Inc, Franklin Lakes, NJ. Tel: (201) 269-3400, (800) 556-3326, FAX: (800) 222-1934, E-Mail: customersupport@medcosupply.com, Web Site: www.medco-athletics.com (7)

Fair Indigo, Madison, WI. Tel: (608) 824-8974, (800) 520-1806, E-Mail: service@fairindigo.com, Web Site: www.fairindigo.com (2)

Fair Isaac Corp, Saint Paul, MN. Tel: (651) 636-4509, E-Mail: info@fairisaac.com, Web Site: www.fairisaac.com (22)

Fairbanks, John, Accountants' Supply House, Lancaster, CA. Tel: (856) 384-1144, (800) 342-5274, FAX: (800) 468-4446, Web Site: www.rapidforms.com (10)

Fairbanks, John F., NEBS, Groton, MA. Tel: (978) 448-6111, (800) 225-6380, (888) 823-6327, FAX: (978) 448-3653, (800) 234-4324, E-Mail: customerservice@nebs.com, Web Site: www.nebs.com (10)

Fairbrother, Jay P., Direct Advantage Marketing, Pittsburgh, PA. Tel: (412) 381-2300, E-Mail: information@dam.com, Web Site: www.dam.com (29)

Fairchild Books, New York, NY. Tel: (212) 419-5292, Web Site: www.fairchildbooks.com (17)

Fairchild Fashion Media, New York, NY. Tel: (212) 286-2860, Web Site: www.condenast.com/fairchild (17)

Fairchild, Nancy, Air Chek Inc, Naples, NC. Tel: (828) 684-0893, (800) AIR-CHEK, FAX: (828) 684-8498, Web Site: www.radon.com (9)

Faircloth, James B., Alerus Financial National Assoc, Grand Forks, ND. Tel: (701) 795-3200, (800) 279-3200, Web Site: www2.alerusfinancial.com (14)

Faire Harbour Limited, Scituate, MA. Tel: (781) 545-2465, FAX: (781) 545-2465 (5)

Fairey, David, Clickbooth.com LLC, Sarasota, FL. Tel: (941) 483-4188, Web Site: www.clickbooth.com (35)

Fairfield Industries Inc, Sugar Land, TX. Tel: (281) 275-7500, (800) 231-9809, FAX: (281) 275-7550, E-Mail: jblattman@fairfield.com, Web Site: www.fairfield.com (16)

Fairfield Marketing Group Inc, Easton, CT. Tel: (203) 261-5585 X202, (203) 261-5568, FAX: (203) 261-0884, E-Mail: info@fairfieldmarketing.com, Web Site: www.fairfieldmarketing.com (22)

Fairise, Alain, Neopost USA, Milford, CT. Tel: (203) 301-3400, Web Site: www.neopostusa.com (16)

Fairman, Mark, Potpourri Group Inc, North Billerica, MA. Tel: (978) 256-4100, FAX: (978) 256-1961/0344, Web Site: www.potpourrigroup.com (6)

Fairytale Brownies, Phoenix, AZ. Tel: (800) 324-7982, FAX: (602) 489-5133, E-Mail: service@brownies.com, Web Site: www.brownies.com (4)

Fakiri, Sha, MyPoints.com Inc, San Francisco, CA. Tel: (415) 856-0877, FAX: (415) 615-1122, E-Mail: memberservices@mypoints.com, Web Site: www.mypoints.com (35)

Falato, Rory, Chase Industries, Inc, Cincinnati, OH. Tel: (513) 860-5565, (800) 543-4455, FAX: (800) 245-7045, Web Site: www.chasedoors.com (16)

Falchuk, Evan, Doctor's Best Inc, San Clemente, CA. Tel: (949) 498-3628, (800) 333-6977, FAX: (800) 754-2036, (949) 498-3952, E-Mail: info@drbvitamins.com, Web Site: www.drbvitamins.com (16)

Falco, Jason, TMone LLC, Iowa City, IA. Tel: (868) 577-2461, E-Mail: info@massmarkets.com, Web Site: www.massmarkets.com (29)

Falcon Products Inc, Newport, TN. Tel: (314) 991-9200, (800) 873-3252, FAX: (314) 991-9227, E-Mail: info@falconproducts.com, Web Site: www.falconproducts.com (16)

Falcon Safety Products, Branchburg, NJ. Tel: (908) 707-4900, FAX: (908) 707-8855, Web Site: www.falconsafety.com (16)

Falcone, Marcello, Fujii Communications Inc, Lincolnwood, IL. Tel: (847) 677-0542, FAX: (847) 677-0523, E-Mail: fci@fujiicommunications.com, Web Site: www.fujiicommunications.com (35)

Falcone, Robert S., Nautilus Inc, Vancouver, WA. Tel: (360) 859-2900, (800) 675-0171, FAX: (360) 694-2755, Web Site: www.nautilus.com (11)

Falk, Lisa, American Hotel Register Co, Vernon Hills, IL. Tel: (708) 743-4163, FAX: (708) 564-5797, Web Site: www.americanhotel.com (23)

Falk, Thomas J., Kimberly-Clark Corp, Neenah, WI. Tel: (920) 721-2000, (888) 525-8388, FAX: (920) 721-7722, Web Site: www.kimberly-clark.com (16)

Falkson, Michael, ETI Sales Support, Valhalla, NY. Tel: (914) 747-3030, (800) 466-4384, FAX: (914) 747-3466, E-Mail: info@etisales.com, Web Site: www.etisales.com (29)

Fallon, Minneapolis, MN. Tel: (612) 758-2345, FAX: (612) 758-2346, E-Mail: info@fallon.com, Web Site: www.fallon.com (35)

Fallon Community Health Plan, Worcester, MA. Tel: (508) 799-2100, (800) 333-2535, Web Site: www.fchp.org (1)

Fallon, Art, Houston Direct Marketing Association, Houston, TX. Tel: (281) 931-8883, FAX: (281) 820-4023, Web Site: www.houstondma.org (40)

Fallon, Dave, Atomic Direct LLC, Portland, OR. Tel: (503) 296-6131, FAX: (503) 296-9890, Web Site: www.atomicdirect.com (35)

Fallon, John, Pearson Education, Upper Saddle River, NJ. Tel: (201) 236-7000, FAX: (201) 236-3290, Web Site: www.pearsoned.com (17)

R Falls Agency, Minneapolis, MN. Tel: (612) 872-6372, (800) 339-1119, FAX: (612) 872-1018, E-Mail: info@fallsagency.com, Web Site: fallsagency.com (35)

Falor, John, American Bronzing Co, Columbus, OH. Tel: (614) 252-7388, (800) 423-5678, FAX: (614) 252-4602, E-Mail: bronzeinfo@bronshoe.com, Web Site: www.abcbronze.com (16)

Faltischek, Michael, Ruskin, Moscou, Faltischek, PC, Uniondale, NY. Tel: (516) 663-6600, FAX: (516) 663-6601, E-Mail: info@rmfpc.com, Web Site: www.rmfpc.com (14)

Falzone & Associates LLC, Sellersville, PA. Tel: (215) 822-8941 (29)

Falzone, Mary Ann, Falzone & Associates LLC, Sellersville, PA. Tel: (215) 822-8941 (29)

Family Album, Kinzers, PA. Tel: (717) 442-0220, FAX:
(717) 442-7904, E-Mail: rarebooks@pobox.com (6)

Family Christian Stores, Grand Rapids, MI. Tel: (888)
887-6555, E-Mail: customerservice@
familychristian.com, Web Site: www.
familychristian.com (5)

Family Circle Magazine Inc, New York, NY. Tel: (212)
557-6600, Web Site: www.familycircle.com (31)

The Family Handyman, Eagan, MN. Tel: (651) 454-
9200, FAX: (651) 994-2250 (17)

Famous Smoke Shop Inc, Easton, PA. Tel: (610) 559-
7000, (800) 672-5544, FAX: (610) 559-7170,
E-Mail: info@famous-smoke.com, Web Site: www.
famous-smoke.com (16)

Fanandakis, Nicholas C., E I DuPont De Nemours &
Co, Wilmington, DE. Tel: (302) 774-1000, (800)
441-7515, FAX: (302) 774-7321, Web Site: www.
dupont.com (16)

Fancy Fronds, Gold Bar, WA. Tel: (360) 793-1472,
E-Mail: fancyfronts@gmail.com, Web Site: www.
fancyfronds.com (8)

Faneuil ISG, Hampton, VA. Tel: (757) 722-3235, FAX:
757-722-5293, Web Site: www.faneuil.com (30)

Fankhauser, Brent, Data-Dynamix Inc, Denver, CO.
Tel: (720) 855-9282, (888) 314-0078, FAX: (720)
855-9099, E-Mail: sales@data-dynamix.com, Web
Site: www.data-dynamix.com (23)

Fannin, Jake, Employment Publishing Inc, Wayne, PA.
Tel: (610) 975-4539, FAX: (610) 687-7860, E-Mail:
jfannin@employment911.com (17)

Fanolis, George C., Fosdick Fulfillment Corp, Wallingford, CT. Tel: (203) 269-0211, (800) 759-5588,
FAX: (203) 679-3290, E-Mail: sales@fosdickcorp.
com, Web Site: www.fosdickfulfillment.com (28)

Fansworth, Bob, GameTime Inc, Fort Payne, AL. Tel:
(256) 845-5610, (800) 235-2440, FAX: (256) 845-
9361/2649, Web Site: www.gametime.com (11)

Fanter, Jeff, Ivy Tech Community College of Indiana,
Indianapolis, IN. Tel: (317) 921-4800, (888) IVY-
LINE, FAX: (317) 921-4753, Web Site: www.
ivytech.edu (13)

Fantle, Susan, The Copy Works, San Diego, CA. Tel:
(858) 676-6757, Web Site: www.thecopyworks.com
(20)

Fanton, Ian, Harvard Business School Publishing, Boston, MA. Tel: (617) 783-7400, Web Site: www.
harvardbusiness.org (17)

Far West Media Services, Long Beach, CA. Tel: (562)
496-3342, FAX: (562) 496-4329, E-Mail: info@
farwestmedia.com, Web Site: www.farwestmedia.
com (32)

Faraci, John V., International Paper, Memphis, TN. Tel:
(901) 419-9000, (800) 207-4003, E-Mail:
internationalpaper.comm@ipaper.com, Web Site:
www.internationalpaper.com (16)

Faragi, Francine, The First Occupational Center of New
Jersey, Orange, NJ. Tel: (973) 672-5800, FAX:
(973) 672-0065, E-Mail: ocnj@ocnj.org, Web Site:
www.ocnj.org (28)

Farber, Ben, Bristol Associates Inc, Los Angeles, CA.
Tel: (310) 670-0525, FAX: (310) 670-4075, E-Mail:
lfarber@bristolassoc.com, Web Site: www.
bristolassoc.com (20)

Farber, Naomi, Conde Nast, New York, NY. Tel: (212)
286-2860, FAX: (212) 880-8289, Web Site: www.
condenast.com (17)

Farber, Steve, Triangle Printers Inc, Skokie, IL. Tel:
(847) 675-3700, FAX: (847) 674-1230, E-Mail:
blevin@triangleprinters.com, Web Site: www.
triangleprinters.com (27)

Faria, Thom, Cramer, Norwood, MA. Tel: (781) 278-
2387, Web Site: www.crameronline.com (20)

Faris Mailing Inc, Indianapolis, IN. Tel: (317) 246-
3315, FAX: (317) 246-3330, E-Mail: info@
farismailing.net, Web Site: farismailing.com (28)

Faris, Bill, Avatar Studios, Saint Louis, MO. Tel: (314)
533-2242, FAX: (314) 533-3349, Web Site: www.
avatar-studios.com (32)

Faris, Jr Robert L., Faris Mailing Inc, Indianapolis, IN.
Tel: (317) 246-3315, FAX: (317) 246-3330, E-Mail:
info@farismailing.net, Web Site: farismailing.com
(28)

Farley, Ed, Ashrae Learning Institute, Atlanta, GA. Tel:
(404) 636-8400, (800) 527-4723, FAX: (404) 321-
5478, E-Mail: ashrae@ashrae.org, Web Site: www.
ashrae.org (31)

Farley, James D., Ford Motor Co, Dearborn, MI. Tel:
(313) 845-8540, (800) 555-5259, FAX: (313) 845-
6073, Web Site: www.ford.com (16)

Farley, Richard, Marshall Cavendish Corp, Tarrytown,
NY. Tel: (914) 332-8888, (800) 821-9881, FAX:
(914) 332-1888, Web Site: www.marshallcavendish.
com (17)

Farley, Tom, Brookfield Office Properties, New York,
NY. Tel: (212) 417-7000, FAX: (212) 417-7214,
Web Site: brookfieldofficeproperties.com (16)

FARM, Depew, NY. Tel: (716) 989-3200, FAX: (716)
989-3220, E-Mail: bizdev@farmbuffalo.com, Web
Site: www.growwiththefarm.com (35)

Farm Bureau Insurance, Lansing, MI. Tel: (517) 323-
7000, (800) 292-2680, FAX: (517) 327-0208, Web
Site: www.farmbureauinsurance-mi.com (15)

Farm Home Offices, Richfield, MN. Tel: (612) 920-
0907, (800) 788-7218, FAX: (866) 404-0257, Web
Site: www.sylvette.com (10)

Farm Journal Inc, Philadelphia, PA. Tel: (215) 557-
8937, FAX: (215) 568-4238 (17)

Farm Market iD, Westmont, IL. Tel: (844) 487-6322,
E-Mail: sales@farmmarketid.com, Web Site: www.
farmmarketid.com (23)

Farm Progress Co, Saint Charles, IL. Tel: (630) 690-
5600, FAX: (630) 462-2202, E-Mail: dwilson@
farmprogress.com, Web Site: www.farmprogress.
com (17)

Farmer, Brad, Draper's & Damon's, Irvine, CA. Tel:
(949) 784-3000, (800) 843-1174, FAX: (949) 784-
3400, E-Mail: jilld@drapers.com, Web Site: www.
drapers.com (2)

Farmer, Bradley D., Boy Scouts of America/National
Supply Group, Charlotte, NC. Tel: (800) 323-0736,
FAX: (704) 588-5822, E-Mail: customerservice@
scoutstuff.org, Web Site: www.scoutstuff.org (1)

Farmer, Gary, AAVIM, Winterville, GA. Tel: (706)
742-5355, (800) 228-4689, FAX: (706) 742-7005,
E-Mail: gary@aavim.com, Web Site: www.aavim.
com (31)

Farmer, Jody, Creditcards.com, Austin, TX. Tel: (512)
996-8663, Web Site: www.creditcards.com (20)

Farmer, Lisa, Daily Record & Dispatch Co, Dunn, NC.
Tel: (910) 891-1234, FAX: (910) 891-5253, Web
Site: www.mydailyrecord.com (17)

Farmer, Scott D., Cintas, Cincinnati, OH. Tel: (513)
459-1200, Web Site: www.cintas.com (16)

Farmers Insurance, Los Angeles, CA. Tel: (410) 338-
1633, (410) 366-1000, (800) 327-6377, FAX: (410)
554-1926, Web Site: www.farmers.com (15)

Farnsworth, Peter W., American Kennel Club, New
York, NY. Tel: (212) 696-8200, FAX: (212) 696-
8217, (212) 696-8299, Web Site: www.akc.org (17)

Farooq, Omar, CIT, Livingston, NJ. Tel: (973) 740-
5000, FAX: (973) 740-5383, Web Site: www.cit.
com (14)

Farr, Kevin M., Fisher-Price, East Aurora, NY. Tel:
(716) 687-3000, FAX: (716) 687-3636, Web Site:
www.fisherprice.com (16)

Farr, Kevin, Mattel Inc, El Segundo, CA. Tel: (310)
252-2000, FAX: (310) 252-2180, Web Site: www.
mattel.com (16)

Farr-Jones, Stephen, ADM Marketing, Burbank, CA.
Tel: (888) 800-1001 (20)

Farrar Straus & Giroux Inc, New York, NY. Tel: (212)
741-6900, Web Site: us.macmillan.com/fsg.aspx
(17)

Farrell, Caryn, American Preferred Reader's Service Inc,
Fort Lauderdale, FL. Tel: (954) 767-6022, (888)
482-2443, FAX: (954) 767-6065, E-Mail: jfarrell@
amerpref.com, Web Site: www.amerpref.com (18)

Farrell, Christine, Suntrust Banks Inc, Atlanta, GA. Tel:
(404) 588-7914, (800) 786-8787, FAX: (404) 532-
0550, E-Mail: emmett.harmon@suntrust.com, Web
Site: www.suntrust.com (14)

Farrell, Hilery, McCourt Label Co, Lewis Run, PA. Tel:
(800) 458-2390, FAX: (814) 362-4156, Web Site:
www.mccourtlabel.com (27)

Farrell, Lawrence, Sunstar, Chicago, IL. Tel: (773) 777-
4000, FAX: (773) 777-1417, E-Mail: dominico@
sunstar.com, Web Site: www.sunstar.com (16)

Farrell, Patrick T., Alamo Rent A Car, Saint Louis, MO.
Tel: (314) 512-2880, Web Site: www.alamo.com
(16)

Farrell, Sr James H., American Preferred Reader's Service Inc, Fort Lauderdale, FL. Tel: (954) 767-6022,
(888) 482-2443, FAX: (954) 767-6065, E-Mail:
jfarrell@amerpref.com, Web Site: www.amerpref.
com (18)

Farrey, James, Jameco Electronics, Belmont, CA. Tel:
(650) 592-8097, (800) 831-4242, FAX: (650) 592-
2503, (800) 237-6948, E-Mail: domestic@jameco.
com, Web Site: www.jameco.com (16)

Farrington Transportation, Bolingbrook, IL. Tel: (630)
783-9200 (12)

Farros, Royal P., IMSI/Design LLC, Novato, CA. Tel:
(415) 483-8000, (800) 833-4674, FAX: (415) 884-
9023, Web Site: www.imsidesign.com (34)

Farrow Group, Windsor, ON Canada. Tel: (519) 966-
3003, E-Mail: info@farrow.com, Web Site: www.
farrow.com (16)

Farrow Logistics, Windsor, ON Canada. Tel: (844) 532-
7769, E-Mail: info@farrowlogistics.com, Web Site:
www.farrowlogistics.com (28)

Farrow, John, Farrow Group, Windsor, ON Canada.
Tel: (519) 966-3003, E-Mail: info@farrow.com,
Web Site: www.farrow.com (16)

Farrow, Rick, Farrow Group, Windsor, ON Canada.
Tel: (519) 966-3003, E-Mail: info@farrow.com,
Web Site: www.farrow.com (16)

Farstar Inc, Frisco, TX. Tel: (214) 649-0422, E-Mail:
realhuman@wedontplay.com, Web Site: blog.
wedontplayfair.com (35)

Fashion Institute of Technology Library, New York,
NY. Tel: (212) 217-7999, FAX: (212) 217-4371,
Web Site: www.fitnyc.edu (1)

Fasking, Greg, Infinity Insurance Co, Birmingham, AL.
Tel: (800) 527-5412, Web Site: www.infinityauto.
com (15)

Fasnacht, Jill Howell, American College of Physician
Executives, Tampa, FL. Tel: (813) 287-2000, (800)
562-8088, FAX: (813) 287-8993, E-Mail: acpe@
acpe.org, Web Site: www.acpe.org (1)

Faso, Lawrence, eFootage, Pasadena, CA. Tel: (626)
395-9593, FAX: (626) 395-5394, E-Mail: info@
efootage.com, Web Site: www.efootage.com (38)

Faso, Steven, Brand New Products LLC, Chicago, IL. Tel: (773) 486-8813, Web Site: www.brandnewllc.com (4)

Fasolo, PhD Peter M., Johnson & Johnson, New Brunswick, NJ. Tel: (732) 524-0400, FAX: (732) 214-0332, Web Site: www.jnj.com (16)

Fasseel, Jeff, Advertising Network Solutions, Oxford, MI. Tel: (248) 475-7845, Web Site: www.adnetworksolutions.com (20)

Fassett, Sean, American Movie Classics Holding Corp, Jericho, NY. Tel: (516) 803-3000, FAX: (516) 803-3003, Web Site: www.amctv.com (16)

Fassnacht, Michael, Foote, Cone & Belding, Chicago, IL. Tel: (312) 425-5000, FAX: (312) 425-5010, E-Mail: chicago@fcb.com, Web Site: www.fcb.com (35)

Fasson Roll Div, Mentor, OH. Tel: (440) 354-7900, FAX: (440) 358-4712, (440) 358-6025, Web Site: www.fasson.com (16)

Fastlicht, Michaelle, En ESPANOL Publishing Group LLC, Beverly Hills, CA. Tel: (310) 248-2680 (17)

Fasulo, Mike, Sony Electronics Inc, San Diego, CA. Tel: (858) 942-2400, Web Site: www.sony.com (16)

Father Flanagan's Boy's Home, Boys Town, NE. Tel: (402) 498-1111, FAX: (402) 498-1969, Web Site: www.boystown.org (1)

Fathers of St Edmund Southern Missions Inc, Selma, AL. Tel: (334) 872-2359, FAX: (334) 875-8189, E-Mail: jm1428@aol.com, Web Site: www.edmunditemissions.org (1)

FATHOM Works, Saint Joseph, MI. Tel: (269) 932-3623, (800) 800-9547, Web Site: fathom-works.com (35)

Fatt, Rory, Firepower Marketing Inc, Blaine, WA. Tel: (888) 353-5012, FAX: (800) 253-1633, Web Site: www.firepowermarketing.com (35)

FatWallet, Beloit, WI. Tel: (888) 634-0098, Web Site: www.fatwallet.com (14)

Faulhaber, Glen, G-Plex Direct Mail, Holtsville, NY. Tel: (631) 447-9500, FAX: 631-447-9518, Web Site: www.g-plex.net (28)

Faultless Starch/Bon Ami Co, Kansas City, MO. Tel: (816) 842-1230, FAX: (816) 842-3417, E-Mail: info@faultless.com, Web Site: www.faultless.com (16)

Fauntleroy Supply Co/Wing Supply, Greenville, KY. Tel: (270) 338-5866, (800) 388-9464, FAX: (270) 338-0057, Web Site: www.wingsupply.com (11)

Fauntleroy, Walter, Fauntleroy Supply Co/Wing Supply, Greenville, KY. Tel: (270) 338-5866, (800) 388-9464, FAX: (270) 338-0057, Web Site: www.wingsupply.com (11)

Faust, Doug, Masterpiece Studios Inc, Mankato, MN. Tel: (507) 388-8788, (800) 447-0219, FAX: (507) 344-4606, E-Mail: masterpiecestudios@masterpiecestudios.com, Web Site: www.masterpiecestudios.com (16)

Faust, Richard, Membership Cards Only LLC, Vienna, VA. Tel: (800) 772-2737, E-Mail: rfaust@membershipcards.com, Web Site: wwww.membershipcards.com (27)

Faver, Rosy, DunnData Co, Brewster, NY. Tel: (845) 278-1200, Web Site: www.dunndataco.com (23)

Fay, Bill, Amos Press, Inc, Sidney, OH. Tel: (937) 498-2111, FAX: (937) 498-0876, Web Site: www.amospress.com (17)

Fay, Sharon E., Alliance Bernstein, New York, NY. Tel: (212) 969-1000, (800) 962-2134, FAX: (212) 969-2293, Web Site: www.alliancebernstein.com (14)

Fayad, John, Concept Communications, Nashua, NH. Tel: (603) 577-9810, Web Site: www.conceptcommusa.com (20)

Fayard, Gary P., The Coca-Cola Co, Atlanta, GA. Tel: (404) 676-2121, (800) 438-2653, FAX: (404) 676-6792, Web Site: www.cocacola.com (16)

Fayenweather, William, Direxxis Inc, Needham, MA. Tel: (781) 444-7900, FAX: (781) 444-7909, Web Site: www.direxxismarketing.com (22)

Fazer, Bernard, The Hamilton Group Ltd Inc, Jacksonville, FL. Tel: (904) 279-1300, FAX: (904) 279-1414, Web Site: www.collectibletoday.com (16)

Fazzio, James, Boston Research Group, Hopkinton, MA. Tel: (508) 497-2555, FAX: (508) 497-2592, E-Mail: BRGrep@BostonResearchGroup.com, Web Site: www.bostonresearchgroup.com (30)

Fearon, Richard H., Eaton Corp, Raleigh, NC. Tel: (216) 523-4400, (800) 356-5794, FAX: (216) 523-4787, Web Site: www.eaton.com (16)

Fears, Linda, Family Circle Magazine Inc, New York, NY. Tel: (212) 557-6600, Web Site: www.familycircle.com (31)

Feasel, Joanne, Airomat Corp, Fort Wayne, IN. Tel: (260) 747-7408, (800) 348-4905, FAX: (260) 747-7409, E-Mail: airomat@airomat.com, Web Site: www.mymatting.com (16)

Feder, Teodore, Art Resource Inc, New York, NY. Tel: (212) 505-8700, FAX: (212) 505-2053, E-Mail: requests@artres.com, Web Site: www.artres.com (38)

Federal Citizen Information Center, Pueblo, CO. Tel: (719) 295-2675, (888) 8-PUEBLO, FAX: (719) 948-9724, E-Mail: pueblo@gpo.gov, Web Site: www.pueblo.gsa.gov (5)

Federal Direct, Clifton, NJ. Tel: (973) 667-9800, (800) 927-5123, Web Site: www.feddirect.com (27)

Federal Envelope Co, Bensenville, IL. Tel: (630) 595-2000, FAX: (630) 595-1212, E-Mail: postmaster@federalenvelope.com, Web Site: www.federalenvelope.com (26)

Federated Investors Co, Pittsburgh, PA. Tel: (412) 288-1900, (800) 341-7400, FAX: (412) 288-1171, Web Site: www.federatedinvestors.com (14)

Federico, Paul, Princeton Partners Inc, Princeton, NJ. Tel: (609) 452-8500, FAX: (609) 452-7212, E-Mail: moreinfo@princetonpartners.com, Web Site: www.princetonpartners.com (35)

FedEx Corp, Memphis, TN. Tel: (901) 369-3600, FAX: (901) 395-5082, Web Site: www.fedex.com (16)

FedEx Ground, Coraopolis, PA. Tel: (412) 269-1000, (800) 762-3725, FAX: (412) 747-4295, Web Site: www.fedex.com/us/ground/main (16)

Fedus, Gary, Mitchell Graphics Inc, Petoskey, MI. Tel: (231) 347-5650, (800) 583-9401, FAX: (231) 347-9255, E-Mail: mgi@mitchellgraphics.com, Web Site: www.mitchellgraphics.com (27)

Feece, Julie, Royal Performance Group, Lisle, IL. Tel: (630) 353-7900, (888) 774-0125, FAX: (630) 353-7902, E-Mail: info@rpgglobal.com, Web Site: www.rpggiftcards.com (34)

Feed the Children, Oklahoma City, OK. Tel: (800) 627-4556, Web Site: www.feedthechildren.org (1)

FEEDING AMERICA, Chicago, IL. Tel: (312) 263-2303, FAX: (312) 263-5626, Web Site: www.secondharvest.org (1)

Feeser, Robert A, Mead Westvaco Consumer & Office Products, Richmond, VA. Tel: (937) 222-6323, (804) 444-1000, FAX: (937) 495-3192, Web Site: www.meadwestvaco.com (10)

Fegley, Kent, Accountants' Supply House, Lancaster, CA. Tel: (856) 384-1144, (800) 342-5274, FAX: (800) 468-4446, Web Site: www.rapidforms.com (10)

Feierbend, Janel, Book Passage Cafe, Corte Madera, CA. Tel: (415) 927-0960, (800) 999-7909, FAX: (415) 924-3838, Web Site: www.BookPassage.com (17)

Feinberg, Bob, Stephan Partners Inc, New York, NY. Tel: (212) 524-8583, E-Mail: george@stephenpartners.com, Web Site: www.stephanpartners.com (35)

Feinberg, David A., New York-Presbyterian/Columbia University Medical Center, New York, NY. Tel: (212) 305-2500, FAX: (212) 305-8023, Web Site: www.nyp.org (16)

Feinberg, Stan, SF Global Sourcing Inc, San Francisco, CA. Tel: (415) 288-9400, (800) 545-5865, FAX: (415) 288-9410, E-Mail: selfservice@sfvideo.com, Web Site: www.sfvideo.com (16)

Feinberg, Steven, SF Global Sourcing Inc, San Francisco, CA. Tel: (415) 288-9400, (800) 545-5865, FAX: (415) 288-9410, E-Mail: selfservice@sfvideo.com, Web Site: www.sfvideo.com (3)

Feingold, David, Emigrant Savings Bank, New York, NY. Tel: (212) 850-4521, (800) EMIGRANT, FAX: (212) 850-4372, Web Site: www.emigrant.com (14)

Feingold, Reenie, Visual Horizons, Rochester, NY. Tel: (585) 424-5300, (800) 424-1011, FAX: (800) 424-5411, E-Mail: cs@visualhorizons.com, Web Site: www.visualhorizons.com (16)

Feingold, Stanley Z., Visual Horizons, Rochester, NY. Tel: (585) 424-5300, (800) 424-1011, FAX: (800) 424-5411, E-Mail: cs@visualhorizons.com, Web Site: www.visualhorizons.com (16)

Feinsod, Joan, Graphik Dimensions Ltd, High Point, NC. Tel: (336) 887-3500, (800) 221-0262, FAX: (336) 887-3773, E-Mail: customercare@pictureframes.com, Web Site: www.pictureframes.com (16)

Feinson, Jim, Gardener's Supply Co, Burlington, VT. Tel: (888) 833-1412, FAX: (800) 551-6712, E-Mail: info@gardeners.com, Web Site: www.gardeners.com (8)

Feinstein, Peter, Higher Power Marketing, Phoenix, AZ. Tel: (480) 837-3580, (888) 501-5544, FAX: (480) 837-3589, E-Mail: info@hpowermarketing.com, Web Site: www.hpowermarketing.com (30)

Felco Printing & Mailing, Kansas City, MO. Tel: (816) 421-5164, (800) 467-0805, FAX: (816) 421-1607, E-Mail: jill@felco.net, Web Site: www.felco.net (27)

Feld, Lori, MRM//McCann, New York, NY. Tel: (646) 865-6230, E-Mail: gbc@mrm-mccann.com, Web Site: mrm-mccann.com (35)

Feldman & Associates Inc, Glenview, IL. Tel: (630) 684-0404, FAX: (847) 272-0664, E-Mail: rfeldman@feldmans.net, Web Site: www.feldmans.net (35)

Samuel Feldman, New York, NY. Tel: (212) 362-9517, E-Mail: samuelfeldman@verizon.net (39)

Feldman, Harvey A., Harvey Associates, Cresskill, NJ. Tel: (201) 962-8463, E-Mail: harveyfnj@optonline.net, Web Site: harveyfeldmanassociates.com (35)

Feldman, Jerome I., General Physics Corp, Elkridge, MD. Tel: (410) 379-3600, (800) 727-6677, FAX: (410) 540-5302, E-Mail: info@gpworldwide.com, Web Site: www.gpworldwide.com (16)

Feldman, Martin J, Mark Clements Research Inc, Mount Kisco, NY. Tel: (914) 241-1803, FAX: (914) 241-7763, E-Mail: mjfharvey@aol.com, Web Site: www.markclementsresearch.com (30)

Feldman, Rich, Source, Norwalk, CT. Tel: (203) 291-4000, FAX: (203) 291-4010, E-Mail: info@sourcecxm.com, Web Site: www.sourcecxm.com (35)

Feldman, Roger S., Feldman & Associates Inc, Glenview, IL. Tel: (630) 684-0404, FAX: (847) 272-0664, E-Mail: rfeldman@feldmans.net, Web Site: www.feldmans.net (35)

Feldman, Samuel, Samuel Feldman, New York, NY. Tel: (212) 362-9517, E-Mail: samuelfeldman@verizon.net (39)

Feldner, Scott, DCI-Artform, Milwaukee, WI. Tel: (414) 228-7000, Web Site: www.dci-artform.com (35)

Felhorfer, Jim, JHL Mail Marketing Inc, Stevens Point, WI. Tel: (715) 341-0581, (800) 236-0581, FAX: (715) 341-9645, E-Mail: ren@jhl.com, Web Site: www.jhl.com (28)

Feliz, Freddy, Marketing 1by1 Inc, Fairfax, VA. Tel: (703) 934-6020, FAX: (703) 591-3049, Web Site: marketing1by1.com (22)

Felke, Kathryn, IMPACT International Marketing, Lake Havasu City, AZ. Tel: (866) 389-9798, E-Mail: sales@iimgroup.com, Web Site: iimgroup.com (35)

Fellin, Paolo, Caterpillar Inc, Peoria, IL. Tel: (309) 675-0545, Web Site: www.cat.com (16)

Felmer, Tom, Brady Corp, Milwaukee, WI. Tel: (414) 358-6600, (800) 541-1686, FAX: (800) 292-2289, Web Site: www.bradycorp.com (16)

Feltheimer, John, Lionsgate Entertainment Inc, New York, NY. Tel: (212) 577-2400, FAX: (212) 962-2872, Web Site: www.lionsgate.com (32)

Feltheimer, Jon, Lionsgate Television Corp, Santa Monica, CA. Tel: (310) 449-9200, FAX: (310) 255-3870, Web Site: www.lionsgate.com (16)

George Fencik Associates, Point Pleasant, NJ. Tel: (732) 295-8092, (800) 443-6743, FAX: (732) 295-1729, E-Mail: gfencik@aol.com (16)

Fencik, George, George Fencik Associates, Point Pleasant, NJ. Tel: (732) 295-8092, (800) 443-6743, FAX: (732) 295-1729, E-Mail: gfencik@aol.com (16)

Fendler, Stephen, CM Almy & Son Inc, Armonk, NY. Tel: (800) 225-2569, FAX: (800) 426-2569, E-Mail: almyaccess@almy.com, Web Site: www.almy.com (5)

Fenimore, Lorna, Datasystem Solutions Inc, Overland Park, KS. Tel: (913) 362-6969, FAX: (913) 362-6383, E-Mail: sales@mutipub.com, Web Site: www.datasystem.com (22)

Fenkel, William R., Styled Packaging LLC, Philadelphia, PA. Tel: (610) 529-4122, FAX: (610) 520-9662, E-Mail: bill@styledpackaging.com, Web Site: www.styledpackaging.com (34)

Fenner, Elizabeth, Chicago Magazine, Chicago, IL. Tel: (312) 222-8999, FAX: (312) 222-0287, Web Site: www.chicagomag.com (17)

Fennessey, Kevin, Pernod Ricard USA, Purchase, NY. Tel: (914) 848-4800, Web Site: www.pernod-ricard-usa.com (16)

Fenske Media Corp, Rapid City, SD. Tel: (605) 343-6070, (800) 821-6343, FAX: (605) 348-2108, E-Mail: tomf@fenskemedia.com, Web Site: www.fenskemedia.com (34)

Fenske, Tom, Fenske Media Corp, Rapid City, SD. Tel: (605) 343-6070, (800) 821-6343, FAX: (605) 348-2108, E-Mail: tomf@fenskemedia.com, Web Site: www.fenskemedia.com (34)

Fenton, John, Affinity Federal Credit Union, Basking Ridge, NJ. Tel: (908) 860-7300, FAX: (908) 860-3883, Web Site: www.affinityfcu.org (1)

Fenton, Tracy Redmond, Institutional Investor Inc, New York, NY. Tel: (212) 224-3300, FAX: (212) 224-3592, Web Site: www.institutionalinvestor.com (17)

Fenwick, Katherine, CNA, Chicago, IL. Tel: (312) 822-5000, (800) 262-2000, E-Mail: cna_help@cna.com, Web Site: www.cna.com (15)

Feragen, Jody H., Hormel Foods Corp, Austin, MN. Tel: (507) 437-5611, (800) 523-4635, FAX: (507) 437-5158, Web Site: www.hormelfoods.com (16)

Ferari, William, Forecast Direct Marketing Group, Pittsburgh, PA. Tel: (412) 481-4977, FAX: (412) 481-0872, Web Site: forecastdirect.com (21)

Ferguson Publishing Co, New York, NY. Tel: (800) 322-8755, FAX: (800) 678-3633, Web Site: www.infobasepublishing.com (17)

Ferguson, Catherine, San Antonio Express-News, San Antonio, TX. Tel: (210) 250-2000, E-Mail: feedabck@express-news.net, Web Site: www.expressnews.com (17)

Ferguson, Daniel, Universal Engineering Corp, Cedar Rapids, IA. Tel: (319) 365-0441, (800) 366-2051, FAX: (319) 369-5440, E-Mail: info@universalcrusher.com, Web Site: www.universalcrusher.com (16)

Ferguson, Dave, McCourt Label Co, Lewis Run, PA. Tel: (800) 458-2390, FAX: (814) 362-4156, Web Site: www.mccourtlabel.com (27)

Ferguson, Frank E., Curriculum Associates Inc, North Billerica, MA. Tel: (978) 667-8000, FAX: (978) 667-5706, E-Mail: cainfo@curriculumassociates.com, Web Site: www.curriculumassociates.com (17)

Ferguson, Jack, PC Connection, Merrimack, NH. Tel: (603) 683-2167, (800) 800-0014, FAX: (603) 683-5773, E-Mail: pr@pcconnection.com, Web Site: www.pcconnection.com, macconnection.com (22)

Ferguson, Rodney, Potawatomi Bingo Casino, Milwaukee, WI. Tel: (414) 645-6888, (800) PAYS-BIG, FAX: (414) 847-7727, Web Site: www.paysbig.com (19)

Ferguson, Stanley L., USG Corp, Chicago, IL. Tel: (312) 436-4000, (800) 621-9622, FAX: (312) 672-4093, Web Site: www.usg.com (34)

Ferillo & Associates Inc, Columbia, SC. Tel: (803) 771-6106, FAX: (803) 799-8019 (35)

Ferillo, Charles, Ferillo & Associates Inc, Columbia, SC. Tel: (803) 771-6106, FAX: (803) 799-8019 (35)

Fernandez, Christina B., National Humane Education Society, Charles Town, WV. Tel: (304) 725-0506, FAX: (304) 725-1523, E-Mail: information@nhes.org, Web Site: www.nhes.org (1)

Fernandez, Fernando, Dexposito & Partners, New York, NY. Tel: (646) 747-8800, Web Site: newamericanagency.com (35)

Fernandez, James N, Tiffany & Co, New York, NY. Tel: (212) 755-8000, FAX: (212) 320-7550, Web Site: www.tiffany.com (6)

Fernandez, Luis, Carson's, Milwaukee, WI. Tel: (414) 347-1152, FAX: (414) 278-5748, Web Site: www.carsons.com (16)

Fernandez, Manuel, Bellak Color Corp, Miami, FL. Tel: (305) 854-8525, FAX: (305) 858-8783, Web Site: www.foilmania.com (27)

Fernandez, Ted A., Answerthink, Miami, FL. Tel: (305) 375-8005, (866) 844-6514, FAX: (305) 379-8810, Web Site: www.answerthink.com (35)

Ferranti, Tony, Marketing & Media Services LLC, Warwick, RI. Tel: (401) 737-7730, FAX: (401) 737-6465, Web Site: www.mmsipitv.com (30)

Ferrara Bakery & Cafe Inc, New York, NY. Tel: (212) 226-6150, FAX: (212) 226-0667, E-Mail: information@ferraracafe.com, Web Site: www.ferraracafe.com (4)

Ferrara, Kellie, Stewart Enterprises Inc, Jefferson, LA. Tel: (504) 729-1400, (800) 535-6017, FAX: (504) 729-1984, Web Site: www.stewartenterprises.com (16)

Ferrara, Michael C., Microfluidics Corp, Westwood, MA. Tel: (617) 969-5452, (800) 370-5452, FAX: (617) 965-1213, E-Mail: info@mfics.com, Web Site: www.microfluidicscorp.com (16)

Ferree, Thomas J., Paperweight Development Corp, Appleton, WI. Tel: (920) 734-9841, FAX: (920) 991-8796, Web Site: www.appletonideas.com (25)

Ferretti, John, Foxfire Printing & Packaging Inc, Newark, DE. Tel: (302) 368-9466, (800) 497-0516, FAX: (302) 368-5164, E-Mail: info@foxfiresigns.com, Web Site: www.foxfiresigns.com (27)

Ferriero, David S., National Archives & Records Administration, Washington, DC. Tel: (202) 357-5000, (866) 325-7208, Web Site: www.archives.gov (17)

Ferrigno, Samantha, International Fund for Animal Welfare, Yarmouth Port, MA. Tel: (508) 744-2000, (800) 932-4329, FAX: (508) 744-2099, E-Mail: info-int@ifaw.org, Web Site: www.ifaw.org (1)

Ferrin, Lynn, Select Comfort Corp, Minneapolis, MN. Tel: (763) 551-7000, (888) 411-2188, FAX: (763) 551-7826, Web Site: www.selectcomfort.com (16)

Ferrini, John, JF Direct Marketing Inc, Ossining, NY. Tel: (914) 762-1975, FAX: (914) 762-9247, E-Mail: jfdirect@bestweb.net, Web Site: www.jfdirectmarketing.com (23)

Ferriolo, William, Autobytel Inc, Irvine, CA. Tel: (949) 225-4500, E-Mail: consumercareabtl@autobytel.com, Web Site: www.autobytel.com (12)

Ferrise, Sam, Baldwin Filters, Kearney, NE. Tel: (308) 234-1951, (800) 822-5394, FAX: (800) 828-4453, E-Mail: info@baldwinfilter.com, Web Site: www.baldwinfilter.com (16)

Ferruzza, Gene, Communifx Corp, Cranberry, PA. Tel: (724) 935-8655, Web Site: www.communifax.com (27)

Ferry, Miguel, TPG Direct Inc, Philadelphia, PA. Tel: (215) 592-8381, FAX: (215) 574-8316, E-Mail: slongley@tpgdirect.com, Web Site: www.tpgdirect.com (35)

Fertik, Michael, Reputation.com, Redwood City, CA. Tel: (877) 425-5792, E-Mail: info@reputation.com, Web Site: www.reputation.com (32)

Festa, Fred, W R Grace & Co, Columbia, MD. Tel: (410) 531-4000, FAX: (410) 531-4367, Web Site: www.grace.com (16)

Fetherstonhaugh, Brian, OgilvyOne Worldwide, New York, NY. Tel: (212) 237-4000, Web Site: www.ogilvy.com (35)

Fetner, John, Kellyco Metal Detector Distributors, Winter Springs, FL. Tel: (407) 699-8700, (800) 327-9697, FAX: (407) 695-6671, E-Mail: customerservice@kellycodetectors.com, Web Site: www.kellycodetectors.com (11)

Fetter Printing Company Inc, Louisville, KY. Tel: (502) 634-4771, (800) 234-4771, FAX: (502) 634-3587, E-Mail: info@fettergroup.com (27)

Fettig, Jeff, Whirlpool Corp, Benton Harbor, MI. Tel: (269) 923-5000, E-Mail: info@whirlpool.com, Web Site: www.whirlpoolcorp.com (16)

Feuss, Linda, C H Robinson Worldwide Inc, Eden Prairie, MN. Tel: (952) 937-8500, FAX: (952) 937-6740, E-Mail: info@chrobinson.com, Web Site: www.chrobinson.com (16)

Fey, Robert A., BeaconFey LLC, Baltimore, MD. Tel: (410) 583-1203, FAX: (410) 583-1506, E-Mail: info@beaconfey.com, Web Site: www.beaconfey.com (35)

Ficke, Randy, Associated Premium Corp, Cincinnati, OH. Tel: (513) 679-4444, FAX: (513) 679-4447, E-Mail: inof@associatedpremium.com, Web Site: www.associatedpremium.com (33)

Fiddler's Rock Communications Inc, McLean, VA. Tel: (703) 406-1500, E-Mail: customerservice@frcmktg. com, Web Site: www.frcmarketing.com (33)

The Fidelis Group Inc, Little Ferry, NJ. Tel: (410) 721-3450, Web Site: www.thefidelisgroup.net (22)

Fidelity Investments, Boston, MA. Tel: (617) 563-7000, (800) 343-3548, FAX: (617) 476-6150, Web Site: www.fidelity.com (14)

Fidelity Security Life Insurance Co, Kansas City, MO. Tel: (816) 756-1060, (800) 648-8624, FAX: (816) 968-0580, E-Mail: info@fslins.com, Web Site: www.fslins.com (15)

Fiedler, Maryanne, Voice Systems Engineering Inc, Langhorne, PA. Tel: (215) 953-8568, E-Mail: info@vseinc.com, Web Site: www.vseinc.com (32)

The Field Companies Fulfillment Center Inc, Watertown, MA. Tel: (617) 926-5550, (800) 346-6552, FAX: (617) 924-9011, E-Mail: info@fieldcompanies.com, Web Site: www.fieldcompanies.com (21)

The Field Museum, Chicago, IL. Tel: (312) 665-7600, FAX: (312) 665-7601, E-Mail: events@fieldmuseum.org, Web Site: www.fieldmuseum.org (1)

Field, Diane, Continental Web Press Inc, Itasca, IL. Tel: (630) 773-1903, FAX: (630) 773-1909, E-Mail: inquires@continentalweb.com, Web Site: www.continentalweb.com (27)

Field, Kenneth, Continental Web Press Inc, Itasca, IL. Tel: (630) 773-1903, FAX: (630) 773-1909, E-Mail: inquires@continentalweb.com, Web Site: www.continentalweb.com (27)

Fielder, Lynn, Planned Parenthood Mar Monte, San Jose, CA. Tel: (408) 287-7532, FAX: (408) 971-6935, Web Site: www.plannedparenthood.org (1)

Fielder's Choice Direct, Monticello, IN. Tel: (812) 492-1700, FAX: (812) 492-1799, Web Site: monsanto. com (8)

Fielding, Jennifer, Electric Insurance Co, Beverly, MA. Tel: (978) 921-2080, (800) 227-2757, FAX: (978) 524-5583, E-Mail: sales@electricinsurance.com, Web Site: www.electricinsurance.com (15)

Fielding, Richard, Kantar Media, New York, NY. Tel: (212) 991-6000, (800) 497-8450, FAX: (212) 991-6100, Web Site: kantarmedia.us (32)

Fieldler, David L., ESL Federal Credit Union, Rochester, NY. Tel: (585) 336-1000, (800) 848-2265, FAX: (585) 336-1138, Web Site: www.esl.org (14)

Fieldman, Josh, Ambassador Press, Minneapolis, MN. Tel: (612) 521-0123, (800) 544-9112, FAX: (612) 521-4587, E-Mail: info@ambpress.com, Web Site: www.ambpress.com (27)

Cynthia Fields & Co (CFC), New York, NY. Tel: (212) 242-6063 (20)

Fields, Cynthia, Cynthia Fields & Co (CFC), New York, NY. Tel: (212) 242-6063 (20)

Fields, Mark, Ford Motor Co, Dearborn, MI. Tel: (313) 845-8540, (800) 555-5259, FAX: (313) 845-6073, Web Site: www.ford.com (16)

Fields, Valerie, North Shore Animal League America Inc, Port Washington, NY. Tel: (516) 883-7575, Web Site: www.animalleague.org (1)

Fieldstone Gardens Inc, Vassalboro, ME. Tel: (207) 923-3836, FAX: (207) 923-3836, Web Site: www.fieldstonegardens.com (8)

Fienberg, Debra, Douglas Press Inc, Bellwood, IL. Tel: (708) 547-8400, (800) 323-0705, FAX: (708) 547-0296, Web Site: www.douglaspress.com (16)

Fienberg, Frank, Douglas Press Inc, Bellwood, IL. Tel: (708) 547-8400, (800) 323-0705, FAX: (708) 547-0296, Web Site: www.douglaspress.com (16)

Fiengold, Reenie, Store Smart Express/Visual Horizons, Rochester, NY. Tel: (585) 424-5300, (800) 424-1011, FAX: (585) 424-1064, E-Mail: cs@storesmart.com, Web Site: www.storesmart.com (16)

Fiengold, Stan, Store Smart Express/Visual Horizons, Rochester, NY. Tel: (585) 424-5300, (800) 424-1011, FAX: (585) 424-1064, E-Mail: cs@storesmart.com, Web Site: www.storesmart.com (16)

Fierko, Ed, Osmonics Inc, Minnetonka, MN. Tel: (952) 264-3937, (800) 605-6698, FAX: (952) 536-3301, Web Site: www.osmonics.com (16)

Fifteen Degrees, New York, NY. Tel: (212) 545-7400, FAX: (212) 545-7433, E-Mail: hello@fifteendegrees.com, Web Site: fifteendegrees.com (35)

Fifth Avenue Committee, Brooklyn, NY. Tel: (718) 237-2017, FAX: (718) 237-5366, Web Site: www.fifthave.org (1)

Fifth Gear LLC, Indianapolis, IN. Tel: (317) 631-0907, FAX: (317) 631-6585, Web Site: www.infifthgear.com (22)

Fifth Third Bank, Cincinnati, OH. Tel: (800) 972-3030, FAX: (231) 922-4060, Web Site: www.53.com (14)

Figi's Inc, Marshfield, WI. Tel: (715) 387-1771, (800) 422-3444, FAX: (715) 384-1129, Web Site: www.figis.com (4)

Figone, Joe, Coast Hotels Limited, Seattle, WA. Tel: (206) 826-2700, FAX: (206) 826-2701, Web Site: www.coasthotels.com (19)

Figurs*, Toronto, ON Canada. Tel: (416) 826-9083 (20)

Figurski, Dan, Sunburst Digital Inc, Hoffman Estates, IL. Tel: (800) 321-7511, E-Mail: sales@sunburst. com, Web Site: www.sunburst.com (17)

Filek, Judith, Impact Communications Inc, Long Grove, IL. Tel: (847) 438-4480, E-Mail: info@impactcommunicationsinc.com, Web Site: www.impactcommunicationsinc.com (32)

FileMaker Inc, Santa Clara, CA. Tel: (408) 987-7000, FAX: (408) 987-3823, Web Site: www.filemaker. com (22)

Filios, Matt, Net-Results, Golden, CO. Tel: (303) 771-2552, E-Mail: info@net-results.com, Web Site: www.net-results.com (32)

Filipopoulas, Anna, Direct Energy, Toronto, ON Canada. Tel: (416) 758-8700, (800) 348-2999 (16)

Filkins, Dan, Aerovox Inc, New Bedford, MA. Tel: (508) 994-9661, (888) AEROVOX, FAX: (508) 995-3000, E-Mail: sales1@aerovox.com, Web Site: www.aerovox.com (16)

Filla, Tom, Houston Direct Marketing Association, Houston, TX. Tel: (281) 931-8883, FAX: (281) 820-4023, Web Site: www.houstondma.org (40)

Filmore, Charles Rickert, Unity School of Christianity, Unity Village, MO. Tel: (816) 254-3550, FAX: (816) 251-3554, E-Mail: unity@unityonline.org, Web Site: www.unityonline.org (17)

Films Media Group, New York, NY. Tel: (800) 322-8755, FAX: (800) 678- 3633, E-Mail: custserv@films.com, Web Site: www.films.com (3)

Fimmano, Frank J., Aon Consulting New York, New York, NY. Tel: (212) 792-9700, (212) 792-9759, (212) 441-2000, FAX: (212) 792-9720, E-Mail: garry_sullivan@aoncons.com (15)

Fimpler, Jr. William, Cane & Basket Supply Co, Los Angeles, CA. Tel: (323) 939-9644, FAX: (323) 939-7237, E-Mail: info@caneandbasket.com, Web Site: www.caneandbasket.com (8)

Fimpler, William L., Cane & Basket Supply Co, Los Angeles, CA. Tel: (323) 939-9644, FAX: (323) 939-7237, E-Mail: info@caneandbasket.com, Web Site: www.caneandbasket.com (8)

Michael C Fina, New York, NY. Tel: (212) 557-2500, Web Site: www.michaelcfina.com (6)

Fina, George, Michael C Fina, New York, NY. Tel: (212) 557-2500, Web Site: www.michaelcfina.com (6)

Financial Executives International, Morristown, NJ. Tel: (973) 765-1000, FAX: (973) 765-1018, Web Site: www.financialexecutives.com (1)

Financial Publishing Co, South Bend, IN. Tel: (800) 247-3214, FAX: (574) 243-6060, Web Site: www.financial-publishing.com (17)

Financial Services International Corp, Seattle, WA. Tel: (206) 386-5475, FAX: (206) 654-0499 (14)

The Financial Times Group, New York, NY. Tel: (212) 641-6500, Web Site: www.ft.com (17)

Finch Paper, Glens Falls, NY. Tel: (518) 793-2541, (800) 833-9983, FAX: (518) 793-7364, E-Mail: info@finchpaper.com, Web Site: www.finchpaper.com (25)

Finck Cigar Co, San Antonio, TX. Tel: (210) 341-8888, (800) 221-0638, FAX: (210) 341-8890, E-Mail: custser@finckcigarcompany.com, Web Site: www.finckcigar.com (5)

Finck Jr, Bill, Finck Cigar Co, San Antonio, TX. Tel: (210) 341-8888, (800) 221-0638, FAX: (210) 341-8890, E-Mail: custser@finckcigarcompany.com, Web Site: www.finckcigar.com (5)

Findley, Jean. University of Pennsylvania, Philadelphia, PA. Tel: (215) 898-5000, FAX: (215) 898-9659, Web Site: www.upenn.edu (1)

Fine Architectural Metalsmiths, Chester, NY. Tel: (845) 651-7550, FAX: (845) 651-7857, Web Site: www.iceforge.com (16)

Fine, Deborah, Bookspan, New York, NY. Tel: (516) 490-4561, FAX: (516) 490-4856, E-Mail: info@directbrands.com, Web Site: bookspan.com (13)

Fine, Deborah, Direct Brands Inc, New York, NY. Tel: (212) 930-4949, Web Site: www.columbiahouse. com (13)

Fine, Deborah, The History Book Club Inc, Mechanicsburg, PA. Tel: (718) 918-2665, E-Mail: paula.batson@dgna.com, Web Site: www.historybookclub.com (13)

Finerty & Wolfe Advertising Inc, Chicago, IL. Tel: (773) 348-3918, FAX: (773) 348-5873 (35)

Finerty, Judith E., Finerty & Wolfe Advertising Inc, Chicago, IL. Tel: (773) 348-3918, FAX: (773) 348-5873 (35)

Finest LED Signs, Fort Lauderdale, FL. Tel: (954) 771-5488, E-Mail: finestservices@bellsouth.net, Web Site: www.finestledsigns.com (31)

Finishing Plus, Inc, Chicago, IL. Tel: (773) 523-5510, FAX: (773) 523-9155, E-Mail: info@finishingplus. com, Web Site: www.finishingplus.com (28)

Fink, Elissa, Tableau Software, Seattle, WA. Tel: (206) 633-3400, FAX: (206) 633-3004, Web Site: www.tableausoftware.com (22)

Fink, Gregg, PNC Bank Corp, Pittsburgh, PA. Tel: (412) 762-2000/3514, (800) 422-6537, FAX: (412) 762-4482 (14)

Fink, Martin, Hewlett-Packard Co, Palo Alto, CA. Tel: (650) 857-1501, (800) 752-0900, FAX: (650) 857-5518, Web Site: www.hp.com (16)

Finke, Evan, Specialty Store Services Inc, Des Plaines, IL. Tel: (847) 470-7000, (888) 441-4440, FAX: (847) 470-5355, Web Site: www.specialtystoreservices.com (16)

Finke, Malcom, Specialty Store Services Inc, Des Plaines, IL. Tel: (847) 470-7000, (888) 441-4440, FAX: (847) 470-5355. Web Site: www. specialtystoreservices.com (16)

Finkelstein, Steven, Carnival Creations, Irvine, CA. Tel: (949) 833-9370, FAX: (949) 955-2078 (39)

Finlaysonitsj, Richard, Overton's Inc, Greenville, NC. Tel: (252) 355-5783, (800) 334-6541, FAX: (252) 355-2923, E-Mail: service@overtons.com, Web Site: www.overtons.com (11)

Finley Products Inc, Lancaster, PA. Tel: (717) 735-8200, (888) 626-5301, FAX: (717) 735-8210, E-Mail: fininfo@finleyproducts.com, Web Site: www.2X4basics.com (16)

Finley, Guy, MESA Media & Entertainment Services Alliancce, Port Washington, NY. Tel: (516) 767-6720, Web Site: www.mesalliance.org/ (22)

Finn, Patrick, Results Producers, Los Angeles, CA. Tel: (818) 985-9200, E-Mail: info@resultsproducers. com, Web Site: resultsproducers.com (32)

Finnegan, Jr, John H., The Hope Co Inc, Bridgeton, MO. Tel: (314) 739-7254, (800) 325-4026, FAX: (314) 739-7786, E-Mail: info@hopecompany.com (16)

Finnegan, Raymond, A+ Letter Service, Lakewood, NJ. Tel: (732) 905-2010, FAX: (732) 905-4662, E-Mail: aplus@aplusletter.com, Web Site: www.aplusletters. com (28)

Finnegan, Sr, John H., The Hope Co Inc, Bridgeton, MO. Tel: (314) 739-7254, (800) 325-4026, FAX: (314) 739-7786, E-Mail: info@hopecompany.com (16)

Finney, Elisha W, Varian Medical Systems, Palo Alto, CA. Tel: (650) 493-4000, FAX: (650) 842-5196, Web Site: www.varian.com (9)

Finney, Gary, Virido LLC, Scottsdale, AZ. Tel: (480) 419-9063, Web Site: www.virido.com (29)

Finocchiaro, Kevin, Whitehat Inc, Tempe, AZ. Tel: (480) 858-9000, FAX: (480) 858-9001, E-Mail: sales@whitehat.com, Web Site: www.whitehat.com (32)

Fiore, Dave, Balfour, Austin, TX. Tel: (512) 444-0571, FAX: (512) 440-1138, Web Site: www.artcarved. com (16)

Fiorella's Jack Stack Barbecue, Kansas City, MO. Tel: (816) 942-9141, Web Site: www.jackstackbbq.com (4)

Fiorello, Vince, FLM Graphics Corp, Fairfield, NJ. Tel: (973) 575-9450, E-Mail: info@flmgraphics.com, Web Site: www.flmgraphics.com (16)

Fiorentino, Lisa, University of Pittsburgh at Bradford, Bradford, PA. Tel: (814) 362-7500, FAX: (814) 362-5150, E-Mail: admissions@upb.pitt.edu, Web Site: www.upd.pitt.edu (41)

Fiorile, Michael J., The Columbus Dispatch, Columbus, OH. Tel: (614) 461-5000, FAX: (614) 461-7551, E-Mail: csmith@the.dispatch.com, Web Site: www. dispatch.com (17)

Fire Light Group, Madison, WI. Tel: (608) 441-3473, E-Mail: info@firelightgroup.com, Web Site: firelightgroup.com (33)

Fire Mountain Gems, Grants Pass, OR. Tel: (541) 956-7890, (800) 355-2137, (800) 423-2319, FAX: (541) 470-GEMS, E-Mail: questions@firemtn.com, Web Site: www.firemtn.com (16)

Fire, Dino, FGI Research Inc, Chapel Hill, NC. Tel: (919) 929-7759, FAX: (919) 932-8829, E-Mail: info@fgiresearch.com, Web Site: www.fgiresearch. com (35)

Firebrand Group, New York, NY. Tel: (866) 757-3362, E-Mail: info@firebrandgroup.com, Web Site: www. firebrandgroup.com (32)

Fireman's Fund Insurance Co, Novato, CA. Tel: (415) 899-2000, FAX: (415) 899-3600, Web Site: www. firemansfund.com (14)

Fireng, Steve, KeyPath Education, Lenexa, KS. Tel: (913) 254-6000, Web Site: keypathedu.com (35)

Firepower Marketing Inc, Blaine, WA. Tel: (888) 353-5012, FAX: (800) 253-1633, Web Site: www. firepowermarketing.com (35)

Firestone, James A., Xerox Corp. Norwalk, CT. Tel: (800) 275-9376, Web Site: www.xerox.com (14)

First Advantage Membership Services, Poway, CA. Tel: (866) 424-3223, FAX: (619) 938-7017, Web Site: www.fmembershipservices.com (14)

First Banks Inc, Clayton, MO. Tel: (314) 854-4600, FAX: (314) 592-6840, Web Site: www.firstbanks. com (14)

First Class Inc, Chicago, IL. Tel: (773) 378-1009, FAX: (773) 378-1018, Web Site: www.firstclassinc.com (21)

First Cyber Services, Omaha, NE. Tel: (402) 330-3222, (888) 977-3222, FAX: (402) 330-3444, E-Mail: cat@lcsinc.com, Web Site: www.firstcyberserv.com (31)

First Data Corp, Greenwood Village, CO. Tel: (303) 488-8000, (800) 735-3362, Web Site: www.firstdata. com (28)

First Data Merchant Services, Atlanta, GA. Tel: (404) 890-2000, FAX: (303) 967-5188, Web Site: www. firstdata.com (14)

First Direct Corp, Hopewell Junction, NY. Tel: (845) 221-3800, (800) 935-4386, E-Mail: info@1stdirect. com, Web Site: www.1stdirect.com (35)

First Direct Inc, Bellevue, NE. Tel: (402) 403-0000, (866) 363-9575, FAX: (402) 403-0001, E-Mail: sales@firstdirectmarketing.com, Web Site: www. firstdirectmarketing.com (23)

First Hawaiian Bank, Honolulu, HI. Tel: (808) 525-6273, (888) 844-4444, FAX: (808) 525-5798, E-Mail: bfarias@fhb.com, Web Site: www.fhb.com (14)

First Marketing Co, Pompano Beach, FL. Tel: (954) 979-0700, FAX: (954) 971-4707, Web Site: www. first-marketing.com (31)

First Media Communications Inc, Brentwood, TN. Tel: (615) 661-0826, FAX: (615) 661-4084, Web Site: www.first-media.com (16)

First Merit Bank (HQ), Akron, OH. Tel: (330) 996-6300, (888) 554-4362, Web Site: www.firstmerit. com (14)

First National Information Network, Burbank, CA. Tel: (855) 909-6800, (800) 562-1999, FAX: (818) 558-6663, E-Mail: info@fnin.com, Web Site: www.fnin. com (30)

The First Occupational Center of New Jersey, Orange, NJ. Tel: (973) 672-5800, FAX: (973) 672-0065, E-Mail: ocnj@ocnj.org, Web Site: www.ocnj.org (28)

First of Omaha Merchant Processing, Omaha, NE. Tel: (402) 341-0500, (800) 228-2443 (20)

First Tennessee Bank, Memphis, TN. Tel: (901) 523-4883, FAX: (901) 523-4030, Web Site: www. firsttennessee.com (14)

First to the Finish Inc, Carlinville, IL. Tel: (800) 747-9013, FAX: (877) 631-9687, E-Mail: customer_service@fttf.com, Web Site: www. firsttothefinish.com (7)

First Wave Technologies Inc, Atlanta, GA. Tel: (678) 672-3100, Web Site: www.firstwave.com (22)

Firstenberg, Jean, The American Film Institute, Los Angeles, CA. Tel: (323) 856-7600, FAX: (323) 467-4578, Web Site: www.afi.com (1)

FirstGroup America, Cincinnati, OH. Tel: (513) 241-2200, FAX: (513) 419-3242, Web Site: www. firstgroup.com/north_america (12)

FIrstMark Inc, Campton, NH. Tel: (603) 726-4800, (800) 729-2600, FAX: (603) 726-4840, E-Mail: sales@firstmark.com, Web Site: www.firstmark. com (23)

Fischbein, Stephen, Just Packaging Inc, South Plainfield, NJ. Tel: (908) 753-6700, FAX: (908) 753-6709, E-Mail: sfischbein@justpackaging.com, Web Site: www.justpackaging.com (28)

Carl Fischer Music, New York, NY. Tel: (212) 777-0900, (800) 762-2328, FAX: (212) 477-6996, E-Mail: cf-info@carlfischer.com, Web Site: www. carlfischer.com (17)

Fischer, Debbie, Mithun Agency, Minneapolis, MN. Tel: (612) 347-1000, FAX: (612) 347-1515, Web Site: www.everythingtalks.com (35)

Fischer, Diane, L & D Mail Masters, New Albany, IN. Tel: (812) 981-7161, FAX: (812) 981-7169, E-Mail: info@ldmailmasters.com, Web Site: www. ldmailmasters.com (21)

Fischer, George, CA Inc, Islandia, NY. Tel: (800) 225-5224, FAX: (631) 342-3300, E-Mail: info@ca.com, Web Site: www.ca.com (16)

Fischer, John, SalesLeads.tv Inc, Boca Raton, FL. Tel: (561) 239-0364, (800) 590-5323, FAX: (561) 981-8786, E-Mail: bear@salesleads.tv, Web Site: www. salesleads.tv (23)

Fischer, Marcus, Carmichael Lynch Inc, Minneapolis, MN. Tel: (612) 334-6000, FAX: (612) 334-6101, E-Mail: inquiry@clynch.com, Web Site: www. carmichaellynch.com (35)

Fischetti, Michael, National Contract Management Association, Ashburn, VA. Tel: (571) 382-0082, (800) 344-8096, FAX: (703) 448-0939, E-Mail: memberservices@ncmghq.org, Web Site: www. ncmahq.org (1)

Fiser, Randy W., American Society of Interior Designers, Washington, DC. Tel: (202) 546-3480, FAX: (202) 546-3240, E-Mail: membership@asid.org, Web Site: www.asid.org (1)

Fiserv, Norcross, GA. Tel: (678) 375-3000, Web Site: www.checkfreecorp.com (14)

Fish, Jon, The Advertising Council Inc, New York, NY. Tel: (212) 922-1500, FAX: (212) 922-1676, E-Mail: info@adcouncil.org, Web Site: www.adcouncil.org (1)

Fish, Laura, Universal Media Syndicate Inc, Canton, OH. Tel: (330) 966-9000, E-Mail: lfish@uni-syn. com, Web Site: www.universalmediasyndicate.com (35)

Fishbein, Larry, The Kiplinger Washington Editors Inc, Washington, DC. Tel: (202) 887-6400, (800) 544-0155, FAX: (202) 496-1817, Web Site: www. kiplinger.com (17)

Fisher Group Inc, Hiawatha, IA. Tel: (319) 393-5405, FAX: (319) 393-2738, E-Mail: info@fishergroup. com, Web Site: www.fishergroup.com (27)

Fisher Investments, Woodside, CA. Tel: (650) 851-3334, (800) 587-5512, FAX: (650) 350-1436, E-Mail: info@fi.com, Web Site: www.fi.com (14)

Fisher-Price, East Aurora, NY. Tel: (716) 687-3000, FAX: (716) 687-3636, Web Site: www.fisherprice. com (16)

Fisher Scientific, Pittsburgh, PA. Tel: (800) 766-7000, FAX: (800) 772-7702, Web Site: www.fishersci. com (16)

Fisher, Dave, Bunzl Distribution USA, Inc, Saint Louis, MO. Tel: (314) 997-5959, (888) 997-5959, FAX: (314) 997-1405, Web Site: www.bunzldistribution. com (16)

Fisher, George, Oral Roberts University, Tulsa, OK. Tel: (918) 495-6161, FAX: (918) 495-6222, E-Mail: admissions@oru.edu, Web Site: www.oru.edu (1)

Fisher, Greg, PayPal Inc, San Jose, CA. Tel: (402) 935-2050, Web Site: www.paypal.com (14)

Fisher, James B., Innovative Marketing Services Inc, Houston, TX. Tel: (281) 398-0321, (800) 231-4678, FAX: (281) 398-0679, E-Mail: mfisher@imstcorp. com, Web Site: www.imstcorp.com (30)

Fisher, Jay, Island Pacific Inc, Irvine, CA. Tel: (949) 476-2212, (800) 569-1122, FAX: (949) 476-0177, Web Site: www.islandpacific.com (22)

Fisher, Joseph C., Interdata Inc, Sanibel, FL. Tel: (239) 472-2700, FAX: (941) 472-4272, E-Mail: jfisher435@aol.com, Web Site: www.interdata.org (30)

Fisher, Keith, Bartash Media Group, Philadelphia, PA. Tel: (215) 724-1700, (800) 599-9792, FAX: (215) 724-3313, Web Site: www.bartash.com (27)

Fisher, Ken, Fisher Investments, Woodside, CA. Tel: (650) 851-3334, (800) 587-5512, FAX: (650) 350-1436, E-Mail: info@fi.com, Web Site: www.fi.com (14)

Fisher, Mark, NextScreen LLC, Austin, TX. Tel: (512) 892-8682, Web Site: www.avguide.com (17)

Fisher, Matthew, Local Search Association, Troy, MI. Tel: (248) 244-6200, FAX: (248) 244-0700, Web Site: www.localsearchassociation.org (1)

Fisher, MD Richard I., Fox Chase Cancer Center, Philadelphia, PA. Tel: (215) 728-6900, (888) 369-2427, FAX: (215) 728-2594, Web Site: www.fccc.edu (1)

Fisher, Patricia, Johnson & Wales University, Providence, RI. Tel: (401) 598-1000, (800) DIAL-JWU, FAX: (401) 598-1833, Web Site: www.jwu.edu (41)

Fisher, Patti, Sea Bear, Anacortes, WA. Tel: (360) 293-4661, (800) 645-3474, FAX: (888) 487-6427, Web Site: www.seabear.com (16)

Fisher, Robin, Telesystems Marketing Inc, Houston, TX. Tel: (713) 784-3439, (800) 622-0190, FAX: (713) 780-5974, E-Mail: kimberly@nwpros.com, Web Site: www.telesystemsmarketing.com (29)

Fisher, Stefani, Van Groesbeck & Co, Richmond, VA. Tel: (804) 285-3176, FAX: (804) 359-7271, E-Mail: info@vangroesbeckco.com, Web Site: www. vangroesbeckco.com (1)

Fisher, Steve, eBay Inc, San Jose, CA. Tel: (408) 376-7400, (800) 322-7400, Web Site: www.ebayinc.com (16)

Fisher, Steven R., Communications Corp of America, Boston, VA. Tel: (540) 547-1700, FAX: (540) 302-8015, E-Mail: contact@cca.net, Web Site: www.cca. net (21)

Fishman, Bob, NCR Corp, Duluth, GA. Tel: (937) 445-1936, (800) CALL-NCR, FAX: (937) 445-1682, Web Site: www.ncr.com (16)

Fiske, David, Massachusetts Horticultural Society, Wellesley, MA. Tel: (617) 933-4900, (617) 933-4929, FAX: (617) 933-4901, E-Mail: hort_line@ masshort.org, Web Site: www.masshort.org (1)

Fissinger, Tim, Volvo Cars of North America LLC, Northvale, NJ. Tel: (201) 768-7300, (800) 458-1552, E-Mail: customercare@volvocars.com, Web Site: www.volvocars.com (16)

Fite, Stephanie, Henry Wurst Inc, North Kansas City, MO. Tel: (816) 842-3113, FAX: (816) 472-6221, E-Mail: info@henrywurst.com, Web Site: www. henrywurst.com (27)

Fiterman, Mike, Presentation Packaging, Minneapolis, MN. Tel: (763) 540-9544, (800) 818-2698, FAX: (763) 540-9522, E-Mail: customerservice@ presentationpackaging.com, Web Site: www. presentationpackaging.com (35)

Fitness Quest, Canton, OH. Tel: (330) 478-0755, (800) 321-9236, FAX: (330) 479-9213, E-Mail: customersupport@fitnessquest.com, Web Site: www.fitnessquest.com (16)

Fitness Systems Manufacturing Corp, Wyomissing, PA. Tel: (800) 822-9995, FAX: (610) 670-0135, E-Mail: vitaminout@aol.com, Web Site: www.fitness-systems.net (7)

Fitness USA Super Centers, West Bloomfield, MI. Tel: (248) 737-7200, (800) GET-FIT-1, FAX: (248) 932-3300, Web Site: www.fitnessusa.com (16)

Fitter International Inc, Calgary, AB Canada. Tel: (403) 243-6830, (800) 348-8371, FAX: (403) 229-1230, E-Mail: sales2@fiiler1.com, Web Site: www.fitter1. com (1)

Fitzgerald & CO, Atlanta, GA. Tel: (404) 504-6900, FAX: (404) 239-0548, E-Mail: dave.fitzgerald@ fitzco.com, Web Site: www.fitzco.com (35)

Fitzgerald, David. Fitzgerald & CO, Atlanta, GA. Tel: (404) 504-6900, FAX: (404) 239-0548, E-Mail: dave.fitzgerald@fitzco.com, Web Site: www.fitzco. com (35)

Fitzgerald, Gary T., Meister Media Worldwide, Willoughby, OH. Tel: (440) 942-2000, (800) 572-7740, FAX: (440) 975-3447, E-Mail: info@meistermedia. com, Web Site: www.meistermedia.com (17)

Fitzgerald, James, Calmark Inc, Chicago, IL. Tel: (773) 247-7200, FAX: (773) 247-3199, E-Mail: ljakobi@ calmark-inc.com, Web Site: www.clamark-inc.com (28)

Fitzgerald, James, Taradel LLC, Glen Allen, VA. Tel: (804) 364-8444, (800) 481-1656, FAX: (888) 241-3023, E-Mail: info@taradel.com, Web Site: www. taradel.com (21)

Fitzgerald, Julia, Sylvan Learning Inc, Baltimore, MD. Tel: (410) 843-8000, (800) 31-SUCCESS, FAX: (410) 843-8057, E-Mail: pr@sylvanlearning.com, Web Site: www.sylvanlearning.com (16)

Fitzgerald, Ken, Catalyst, Rochester, NY. Tel: (585) 453-8300, (800) 836-7720, FAX: (585) 453-8360, E-Mail: info@catalystinc.com, Web Site: www. catalystinc.com (35)

Fitzgerald, Sr James, Rand Material Handling Equipment Co Inc, Janesville, WI. Tel: (401) 751-7657, (800) 366-2300, FAX: (800) 755-7263, E-Mail: cs@ randmh.com, Web Site: www.randmh.com (16)

FitzGerald, Tamara, Statlistics, Danbury, CT. Tel: (203) 778-8700, FAX: (203) 778-4839, E-Mail: info@ statlistics.com, Web Site: www.statlistics.com (23)

Fitzgerald, Timothy J., The Middleby Corp, Elgin, IL. Tel: (847) 741-3300, FAX: (847) 741-0015, E-Mail: sales@middleby.com, Web Site: www.middleby. com (18)

Fitzgibbon, Mo, Walker/Fitzgibbon TV & Film Productions, Los Angeles, CA. Tel: (323) 469-6800, FAX: (323) 878-0600, E-Mail: mo@walkerfitzgibbon. com, Web Site: www.walkerfitzgibbon.com (32)

Fitzgibbons, Ruth, Richards Partners, Dallas, TX. Tel: (214) 891-5700, FAX: (214) 891-3515, E-Mail: ruth_fitzgibbons@richards.com, Web Site: richardspartners.com (35)

Fitzhenry, Paul, Goodyear Tire & Rubber Co, Akron, OH. Tel: (330) 796-2121, (800) 321-2136, FAX: (330) 796-2222, Web Site: www.goodyear.com (16)

Fitzmorris, Andy, First Cyber Services, Omaha, NE. Tel: (402) 330-3222, (888) 977-3222, FAX: (402) 330-3444, E-Mail: cat@1csinc.com, Web Site: www.firstcyberserv.com (31)

Fitzpatrick, Bee, Orient Expressed Imports Inc, New Orleans, LA. Tel: (888) 856-3948, FAX: (504) 899-5566, E-Mail: orient@orientexpressed.com, Web Site: www.orientexpressed.com (2)

Fitzpatrick, Daniel M., ITT Educational Services Inc, Carmel, IN. Tel: (317) 706-9200, Web Site: www. ittesi.com (16)

Fitzpatrick, J. Michael, Rohm & Haas Co, Philadelphia, PA. Tel: (215) 592-3000, (877) 288-5881, FAX: (215) 592-3377, Web Site: www.rohmhaas.com (16)

Fitzpatrick, John W., Cornell Lab of Ornithology, Ithaca, NY. Tel: (607) 254-2157, (800) 843-2473, FAX: (607) 254-2415, E-Mail: birdslides@cornell.edu, Web Site: www.birds.cornell.edu (1)

Fitzpatrick, Lisa A., The Bureau of National Affairs, Inc, Arlington, VA. Tel: (703) 341-3000, (800) 372-1033, FAX: (703) 341-1688, Web Site: www.bna. com (17)

5MetaCom, Carmel, IN. Tel: (317) 580-7540, FAX: (317) 580-7550, E-Mail: mail@5metacom.com, Web Site: www.5metacom.com (35)

Fixed Address Marketing Inc, Aurora, ON Canada. Tel: (905) 750-0029, E-Mail: dockeray@ fixedaddressmarketing.com, Web Site: www. fixedaddressmarketing.com (23)

Fixel, Gary, Spectronics Corp, Westbury, NY. Tel: (516) 333-4840, (800) 274-8888, FAX: (800) 491-6868, E-Mail: vscherer@spectroline.com, Web Site: www.spectroline.com (9)

Flach, Bill, Clario Analytics, Eden Prairie, MN. Tel: (952) 653-0980, (866) 849-3341, FAX: (952) 653-5900, E-Mail: sales@clarioanalytics.com, Web Site: www.clarioanalytics.com (20)

Fladung, Thomas, The Plain Dealer, Cleveland, OH. Tel: (216) 999-5000, (800) 362-0727, FAX: (216) 999-6356, Web Site: www.plaindealer.com (18)

Flagg Management Inc, New York, NY. Tel: (212) 286-0333, FAX: (212) 286-0086, E-Mail: flaggmgmt@ msn.com, Web Site: www.flaggmgmt.com (41)

Flagg, Russell E., Flagg Management Inc, New York, NY. Tel: (212) 286-0333, FAX: (212) 286-0086, E-Mail: flaggmgmt@msn.com, Web Site: www. flaggmgmt.com (41)

Flaghouse Inc, Hasbrouck Heights, NJ. Tel: (201) 288-7600, (800) 793-7900, FAX: (800) 793-7922, E-Mail: sales@flaghouse.com, Web Site: www. flaghouse.com (5)

Flaherty, Brendan, Warrior Custom Golf Inc, Irvine, CA. Tel: (949) 699-2499, (800) 600-5113, Web Site: www.warriorcustomgolf.com (11)

Flaherty, Dennis, Victory Corps, New Hope, MN. Tel: (763) 561-5600, (800) 328-6120, FAX: (763) 561-8523, E-Mail: cs@victorycorps.com, Web Site: www.victorycorps.com (16)

Flaherty, Lee F., Flair Communications Agency Inc, Chicago, IL. Tel: (312) 943-5959, (800) 621-8317, FAX: (312) 943-0881, E-Mail: lflaherty@ flairagency.com, Web Site: www.flairpromo.com (35)

Flaherty, Pamela M., American Health & Life Insurance Co, Fort Worth, TX. Tel: (817) 348-7500, (800) 995-2274, FAX: (817) 348-7553, Web Site: www. citifinancial.com (15)

Flaherty, Patricia C., Putnam Investments, Boston, MA. Tel: (617) 292-1400, (800) 225-1581, FAX: (617) 292-1683, Web Site: www.putnam.com (14)

Flaherty, Rob, Ketchum, New York, NY. Tel: (646) 935-3900, Web Site: www.ketchum.com (35)

Flair Communications Agency Inc, Chicago, IL. Tel: (312) 943-5959, (800) 621-8317, FAX: (312) 943-0881, E-Mail: lflaherty@flairagency.com, Web Site: www.flairpromo.com (35)

Flajs, Ken, Graphic Communications Holdings Inc, Hudson, OH. Tel: (330) 650-5522, FAX: (330) 650-8998, E-Mail: info@graphiccommunications.com, Web Site: www.graphiccommunications.com (25)

Flanagan, Bryan, Zig Ziglar Corp, Plano, TX. Tel: (972) 233-9191, (800) 527-0306, FAX: (469) 321-7556, E-Mail: info@ziglar.com, Web Site: www.zigziglar.com (16)

Flanagan, John F., Goodheart-Willcox Publisher, Tinley Park, IL. Tel: (708) 687-5000, (800) 323-0440, FAX: (708) 687-0315, E-Mail: custserv@g-w.com, Web Site: www.g-w.com (17)

Flanagan, Sandy, APW-Wright Line, Worcester, MA. Tel: (508) 852-4300, (800) 225-7348, FAX: (508) 852-3060, Web Site: www.wrightline.com (16)

Flanders, Scott N., Playboy Enterprises Inc, Beverly Hills, CA. Tel: (310) 860-1215, Web Site: www.playboyenterprises.com (17)

Caimin Flannery & Associates, Naperville, IL. Tel: (630) 236-1955 (14)

Flannery, Caimin, Caimin Flannery & Associates, Naperville, IL. Tel: (630) 236-1955 (14)

Flannery, Donald, Maine Potato Board, Presque Isle, ME. Tel: (207) 769-5061, FAX: (207) 764-4148, E-Mail: mainepotatoes@mainepotatoes.com, Web Site: www.mainepotatoes.com (1)

Flannery, Marlene, Caimin Flannery & Associates, Naperville, IL. Tel: (630) 236-1955 (14)

Flannery, Michael D., Redwood Partners Ltd, New York, NY. Tel: (212) 843-8585, FAX: (212) 843-9093, E-Mail: info@redwoodpartners.com, Web Site: www.redwoodpartners.com (20)

FlarePath LLC, Canaan, NY. Tel: (212) 927-1296 (20)

Flaten, Don D., International Direct Media Co & Information Publishing Co, San Francisco, CA. Tel: (415) 661-4730, E-Mail: infopubsf@aol.com, Web Site: www.bookwormproductions.com (17)

Flater, Kerry, Nutritional Research Associates Inc, South Whitley, IN. Tel: (260) 723-4931, (800) 456-4931, FAX: (260) 723-6297, E-Mail: info@nrfeeds.com, Web Site: www.nrfeeds.com (16)

Flatow, Kelly, National Basketball Association, New York, NY. Tel: (212) 407-8000, FAX: (212) 826-0579, Web Site: www.nba.com (1)

Flatt, J. Bruce, General Growth Properties, Chicago, IL. Tel: (312) 960-5000, Web Site: www.generalgrowth.com (5)

Flatz, Sheila, University of Minnesota, Minneapolis, MN. Tel: (612) 625-0256, Web Site: www.twin-cities.umn.edu (1)

Flaxenburg, Eric, French Creek Sheep & Wool Co Inc, Elverson, PA. Tel: (610) 286-5700, (800) 977-4337, FAX: (610) 286-0324, E-Mail: info@frenchcreeksw.com, Web Site: www.frenchcreeksw.com (2)

Flaxenburg, Jean, French Creek Sheep & Wool Co Inc, Elverson, PA. Tel: (610) 286-5700, (800) 977-4337, FAX: (610) 286-0324, E-Mail: info@frenchcreeksw.com, Web Site: www.frenchcreeksw.com (2)

Fleck, Steve, Jofco Inc, Jasper, IN. Tel: (812) 482-5154, (800) 23-JOFCO, FAX: (812) 634-2392, E-Mail: furniture@jofco.com, Web Site: www.jofco.com (16)

Fleet One LLC, Antioch, TN. Tel: (615) 523-6465, Web Site: www.fleetone.com (14)

Fleet, Cliff B., Philip Morris USA Inc, Richmond, VA. Tel: (804) 274-2000, FAX: (804) 484-8231, Web Site: www.philipmorrisusa.com (16)

Fleischer, Lee A., University of Pennsylvania, Philadelphia, PA. Tel: (215) 898-5000, FAX: (215) 898-9659, Web Site: www.upenn.edu (1)

Fleischman, Matt, Moxie, Atlanta, GA. Tel: (678) 916-4500, E-Mail: info@moxieusa.com, Web Site: moxieusa.com (35)

Fleischman, Virginia, VMF Inc, Washington, DC. Tel: (202) 966-3361, FAX: (202) 362-8409, E-Mail: veflei@aol.com (20)

Fleischmann, John, Potpourri Group Inc, North Billerica, MA. Tel: (978) 256-4100, FAX: (978) 256-1961/0344, Web Site: www.potpourrigroup.com (6)

Fleischner, Michael H., Peterson's, Lawrenceville, NJ. Tel: (609) 896-1800, FAX: (609) 896-1811, E-Mail: custsvc@petersons.com, Web Site: www.petersons.com (17)

Fleming, Alan B., Las Vegas Review Journal, Las Vegas, NV. Tel: (702) 383-0211, FAX: (702) 383-4646, Web Site: www.lvrj.com (17)

Fleming, Connie, Oakstone Publishing LLC, Birmingham, AL. Tel: (205) 991-5188, (800) 952-0690, FAX: (205) 995-4656, E-Mail: info@oakstonepublishing.com, Web Site: www.oakstonepublishing.com (17)

Fleming, Kim, AIFS, Stamford, CT. Tel: (203) 399-5000, (866) 906-2437, FAX: (203) 599-5590, E-Mail: info@aifs.com, Web Site: www.aifs.com (19)

Fleming, Mark, School Specialty Inc, Greenville, WI. Tel: (920) 734-5712, (888) 388-3224, FAX: (920) 734-5112, E-Mail: info@schoolspecialty.com, Web Site: www.schoolspecialty.com (16)

Fleming, Richard, Harbour Bay Inc, Oakland, NJ. Tel: (845) 368-2857, FAX: (845) 368-2349 (16)

Fleming, Robert, Byrum & Fleming, San Anselmo, CA. Tel: (415) 457-1700, (800) 850-1711, E-Mail: hilary@byrumfleming.com, Web Site: www.byrumfleming.com (23)

Fleming, Robert L., Chick Harness & Supply Inc, Harrington, DE. Tel: (302) 398-4630, (800) 444-2441, FAX: (302) 398-3920, E-Mail: saddles@chicksaddlery.com, Web Site: www.chicksaddlery.com (11)

Fleming, Steve, RedEnvelope Inc, San Diego, CA. Tel: (619) 528-4888, (877) 733-3683, Web Site: www.redenvelope.com (6)

Fletcher Direct, Cary, NC. Tel: (919) 880-5301, FAX: (919) 459-6816, E-Mail: billf@fletcherdirect.com, Web Site: www.fletcherdirect.com (35)

Fletcher, Alan, Demandbase Inc, San Francisco, CA. Tel: (415) 683-2660, E-Mail: info@demandbase.com, Web Site: www.demandbase.com (22)

Fletcher, Bill, The Right Lists Ltd, Gaithersburg, MD. Tel: (301) 869-2020, FAX: bfletch@rightlists.com, Web Site: www.rightlists.com (23)

Fletcher, Jay, Food Chemical News, Arlington, VA. Tel: (202) 887-6320, (888) 732-7070, FAX: (202) 887-6335, E-Mail: cs@foodregulation.com, Web Site: www.foodchemicalnews.com (17)

Fletcher, Keith, Florida Direct Marketing Association, Tamarac, FL. Tel: (786) 357-3275, E-Mail: president@fdma.org, Web Site: www.fdma.org (40)

Fletcher, Robyn P., Gardens Of The Blue Ridge Inc, Pineola, NC. Tel: (828) 733-2417, FAX: (828) 733-8894, E-Mail: contact@gardensoftheblueridge.com, Web Site: www.gardensoftheblueridge.com (8)

Fletcher, Sarah, Catalog Design Studios, Providence, RI. Tel: (866) 849-4264, E-Mail: sfletcher@catalogdesignstudios.com, Web Site: www.catalogdesignstudios.com (21)

Fletcher, William E., Diamond Machining Technology, Marlborough, MA. Tel: (508) 481-5944, (800) 666-4368, FAX: (508) 485-3924, Web Site: www.dmtsharp.com (9)

Fletcher, William U., Fletcher Direct, Cary, NC. Tel: (919) 880-5301, FAX: (919) 459-6816, E-Mail: billf@fletcherdirect.com, Web Site: www.fletcherdirect.com (35)

Flex Products, Carlstadt, NJ. Tel: (636) 282-6800, (800) 526-6273, FAX: (6361) 282-6888, E-Mail: info@flex-products.com, Web Site: www.flex-products.com (34)

FLEXcon, Spencer, MA. Tel: (508) 885-8200, Web Site: www.flexcon.com (16)

The Flexi Group Inc, Bronx, NY. Tel: (718) 543-8699, (800) 665-8053, FAX: (718) 543-8609, E-Mail: info@flexigroup.com, Web Site: www.flexigroup.com (27)

Flick, Kenneth E., Omega Research & Development, Douglasville, GA. Tel: (770) 942-9876, (800) 554-4053, Web Site: www.caralarm.com (12)

Flickinger, Richard, Flickinger's Nursery, Beyer, PA. Tel: (800) 368-7381, FAX: (724) 783-6528, Web Site: www.flicknursery.com (8)

Flickinger's Nursery, Beyer, PA. Tel: (800) 368-7381, FAX: (724) 783-6528, Web Site: www.flicknursery.com (8)

Flight Form Cases Inc, Bedford Park, IL. Tel: (708) 458-8989, (800) 657-1199, FAX: (708) 458-9023, E-Mail: info@caseguys.net, Web Site: www.flightform.com (9)

The Flinchbaugh Co Inc, Manchester, PA. Tel: (717) 266-2202, FAX: (717) 266-7055, E-Mail: flinchbaugh@blazenet.net, Web Site: www.flinchbaugh.com (16)

Flint Communications, Fargo, ND. Tel: (701) 237-4850, FAX: (701) 234-9680, Web Site: www.flintcom.com (35)

Flint, Alan, Automated Graphic Systems LLC, White Plains, MD. Tel: (800) 678-8760, FAX: (240) 222-3419, E-Mail: info@ags.com, Web Site: www.ags.com (31)

Flom, Robert, Win Craft Inc, Winona, MN. Tel: (507) 454-5510, (800) 533-8100, FAX: (507) 454-6403, E-Mail: inquiries@wincraftschool.com, Web Site: www.wincraftschool.com (5)

Flood, Bill, Upstart, Madison, WI. Tel: (920) 563-9571, FAX: (800) 448-5828, Web Site: www.highsmith.com (16)

Flood, Stephen, FCL Graphics Inc, Harwood Heights, IL. Tel: (708) 867-5500, (800) 274-3380, FAX: (708) 867-7768, Web Site: www.fclgraphics.com (27)

Flood, Stephen J, Universal Wilde, Westwood, MA. Tel: (781) 251-2700, FAX: (781) 251-2613, E-Mail: marketing@universalwilde.com, Web Site: www.universalwilde.com (21)

Flor, Kristin, HackerAgency Inc, Seattle, WA. Tel: (206) 805-1500, Web Site: www.hal2l.com (35)

Flora, Carlin, Sussex Publishers Inc, New York, NY. Tel: (212) 260-7210, FAX: (212) 260-7445, Web Site: www.blues-buster.com (17)

Flores, Eliezer, Action Direct Inc, Miami, FL. Tel: (305) 969-0056, E-Mail: info@action-direct.com, Web Site: www.action-direct.com (11)

Flores, J.O., Action Direct Inc, Miami, FL. Tel: (305) 969-0056, E-Mail: info@action-direct.com, Web Site: www.action-direct.com (11)

Flores, Omar, Action Direct Inc, Miami, FL. Tel: (305) 969-0056, E-Mail: info@action-direct.com, Web Site: www.action-direct.com (11)

Flores, Peter P., Texas Parks & Wildlife Dept, Austin, TX. Tel: (512) 389-4800, (800) 792-1112, FAX: (512) 389-8029, Web Site: www.tpwd.state.tx.us (1)

Flores, Robert, Luster Care Products, Saint Louis, MO. Tel: (636) 272-1885, (800) 291-5223, FAX: (636) 272-1869, Web Site: www.lusterlace.com (16)

Florian Tools, Southington, CT. Tel: (860) 628-9643, (800) 275-3618, E-Mail: info@floriantools.com, Web Site: www.floriantools.com (8)

Florian, Jared, What on Earth, Hudson, OH. Tel: (330) 963-6554, (800) 945-2552, FAX: (800) 950-9569, Web Site: www.whatonearthcatalog.com (5)

Florida A&M University, Tallahassee, FL. Tel: (850) 599-3379, E-Mail: sjgc@famu.edu, Web Site: sjgc.famu.edu (16)

Florida Credit Union, Gainesville, FL. Tel: (352) 377-4141, Web Site: www.flcu.org (14)

Florida Direct Marketing Association, Tamarac, FL. Tel: (786) 357-3275, E-Mail: president@fdma.org, Web Site: www.fdma.org (40)

Florida Gift Fruit Shippers Association, Orlando, FL. Tel: (407) 295-1491, FAX: (407) 290-0918, E-Mail: info@fgfsa.com, Web Site: www.fgfsa.com (1)

Florida Institute of CPA's, Tallahassee, FL. Tel: (850) 224-2727, (800) 342-3197 (FL), FAX: (850) 222-8190, E-Mail: msc@ficpa.org, Web Site: www.ficpa.org (1)

Florida Power & Light Co, Juno Beach, FL. Tel: (305) 552-3552, (800) 468-8243, FAX: (305) 552-2487, Web Site: www.fpl.com (16)

Florida Today, Melbourne, FL. Tel: (321) 242-3500, (877) 424-0156, FAX: (321) 242-3729, Web Site: www.floridatoday.com (17)

Florin, Dave, The Hiebing Group, Madison, WI. Tel: (608) 256-6357, FAX: (608) 256-0693, E-Mail: ideas@hiebing.com, Web Site: www.hiebing.com (35)

Flory III, Curtis B., Zircon Co Inc, Salem, MA. Tel: (978) 741-7000, FAX: (978) 532-0012 (22)

Floyd, Craig, National Law Enforcement Officers Memorial Fund, Washington, DC. Tel: (202) 737-3400, Web Site: www.nleomf.com (1)

Floyd, Elson S., University of Missouri, Columbia, MO. Tel: (573) 882-6333, (800) 856-2181, FAX: (573) 882-2721, E-Mail: visitus@missouri.edu, Web Site: www.missouri.edu (41)

Fluid Metering Inc, Syosset, NY. Tel: (516) 922-6050, (800) 223-3388, FAX: (516) 624-8261, E-Mail: pumps@fmipump.com, Web Site: www.fmipump.com (16)

Fluke Biomedical, Everett, WA. Tel: (425) 347-6100, (800) 850-4608, FAX: (425) 446-5116, Web Site: www.flukebiomedical.com (16)

Fluke, John M., PACCAR Inc, Bellevue, WA. Tel: (425) 468-7400, FAX: (425) 468-8216, Web Site: www.paccar.com (16)

Flynn, III Edward B., ADP Inc, Roseland, NJ. Tel: (973) 974-5000, (800) 225-5237, FAX: (973) 974-3334, Web Site: www.adp.com (16)

Flynn, Jim, Hult Marketing, Peoria, IL. Tel: (309) 673-8191, FAX: (309) 674-5530, E-Mail: jflynn@hultmarketing.com, Web Site: www.hultmarketing.com (35)

Flynn, Kris, LO-AD Communications, Pasadena, CA. Tel: (626) 304-7750, FAX: (626) 304-2716, Web Site: www.lo-ad.com (16)

Flynn, Larry, Gulfstream Aerospace Corp, Savannah, GA. Tel: (912) 965-3000, E-Mail: info@gulfstream.com, Web Site: www.gulfstream.com (16)

Flynn, Liz, Marsh US Consumer, Urbandale, IA. Tel: (515) 365-6102 (15)

Flynn, Richard, Wolters Kluwer Financial Services, Minneapolis, MN. Tel: (612) 656-7700, (800) 552-9408, Web Site: www.wolterskluwerfs.com (14)

Flynn, Terry, Hello Direct, Nashua, NH. Tel: (408) 972-1990, (800) 435-5634, FAX: (408) 972-8155, Web Site: www.hello-direct.com (16)

Flynn, Timothy Patrick, BT Americas, Irving, TX. Tel: (972) 830-8169, FAX: (703) 755-6740, Web Site: www.btglobalservices.com (22)

Flynn, William J., Mutual of America Life Insurance Co, New York, NY. Tel: (212) 224-1600, (800) 468-3785, FAX: (212) 207-3001, Web Site: www.mutualofamerica.com (14)

FM Howell & Co, Elmira, NY. Tel: (607) 734-6291, FAX: (607) 735-0464, E-Mail: best@howellpkg.com, Web Site: www.howellpkg.com (16)

FocalPoint Marketing LLC, Metuchen, NJ. Tel: (877) 252-4305, Web Site: www.focalpoint-emarketing.com (35)

Focus on the ROI, Massapequa Park, NY. Tel: (917) 620-1838 (20)

Focus Plus Inc, New York, NY. Tel: (212) 675-0142, (800) 340-8846, FAX: (212) 645-3171, E-Mail: info@focusplusny.com, Web Site: www.focusplusny.com (30)

Focus USA Inc, Paramus, NJ. Tel: (201) 489-2525, FAX: (201) 489-4499, E-Mail: info@focus-usa-l.com, Web Site: www.focus-usa-l.com (23)

Fogel, Bob, Uniforms & Scrubs.com, Ballwin, MO. Tel: (636) 391-9200, (855) 391-9200, FAX: (636) 391-9205, E-Mail: questions@uniformsandscrubs.com, Web Site: www.uniformsandscrubs.com (7)

Fogel, Suzanne L., DePaul University, Chicago, IL. Tel: (312) 362-8000, (800) 4-DEPAUL, FAX: (312) 362-6639, E-Mail: skelly@wppost.depaul.edu, Web Site: www.depaul.edu (41)

Fogerty, Tim, Bissinger French Confections, Saint Louis, MO. Tel: (314) 615-2436, (800) 325-8881, Web Site: www.bissingers.com (4)

Foggle, Glen, American Century Investments, Kansas City, MO. Tel: (816) 531-5575, (800) 345-2021, FAX: (816) 340-4964, Web Site: www.americancentury.com (14)

Fogle, Bob, Rhythm Band Inc, Fort Worth, TX. Tel: (817) 335-2561, (800) 424-4724, FAX: (800) 784-9401, E-Mail: sales@rhythmband.com, Web Site: www.rhythmband.com (11)

Fohl, Blake, True Value Co, Chicago, IL. Tel: (773) 695-5000, Web Site: www.truevaluecompany.com (16)

Folder Factory Inc, Mount Jackson, VA. Tel: (540) 984-8852, (800) 296-4321, FAX: (540) 477-9677, E-Mail: webmaster@folders.com, Web Site: www.folders.com (27)

Foley, Kevin, ACCENT Marketing Services LLC, Jeffersonville, IN. Tel: (812) 206-6200, Web Site: www.accentonline.com (20)

Foley, Kevin S., Business Planners & Consultants Inc, New York, NY. Tel: (212) 972-1970, FAX: (212) 972-1126 (15)

Foley, Nick, Home Planners, Tucson, AZ. Tel: (520) 297-8200, FAX: (520) 297-6219, E-Mail: sales@homeplanners.com, Web Site: www.homeplanners.com (17)

Foley, Nick, The Media Crew, Largo, FL. Tel: (813) 551-0902, E-Mail: marketing@themediacrew.com, Web Site: www.themediacrew.com (35)

Foley, Rich, Cengage Learning, Independence, KY. Tel: (800) 354-9706, FAX: (800) 487-8488, Web Site: www.delmar.com (17)

Foliano, Jay, Beechtree Assoc Inc, Cary, NC. Tel: (919) 852-1800, FAX: (919) 852-4400, E-Mail: jfoliano@aol.com (20)

Folkerth, John R., Shopsmith Inc, Dayton, OH. Tel: (937) 898-6070, (800) 543-7586, FAX: (937) 890-5197, Web Site: www.shopsmith.com (16)

Folkerth, Robert, Shopsmith Inc, Dayton, OH. Tel: (937) 898-6070, (800) 543-7586, FAX: (937) 890-5197, Web Site: www.shopsmith.com (16)

Folks, Valerie, USC Marshall School of Business Dept of Marketing, Los Angeles, CA. Tel: (213) 740-5033, FAX: (213) 740-7828, E-Mail: dennis.rook@marshall.usc.edu (41)

Folkwein, Kristy, Dow Corning Corp, Midland, MI. Tel: (989) 496-4400, (800) 248-2481, FAX: (989) 496-4572, Web Site: www.dowcorning.com (16)

Follett School Solutions Inc, McHenry, IL. Tel: (815) 759-1700, (888) 511-5114, FAX: (800) 852-5458, E-Mail: customerservice@follett.com, Web Site: www.flr.follett.com (16)

Follett, Charles, Dow Theory Forecasts, Hammond, IN. Tel: (219) 931-6480, (800) 233-5922, FAX: (219) 931-6487, E-Mail: custserv@horizonpublishing.com, Web Site: www.dowtheory.com (17)

Follo, James M., The New York Times Co, New York, NY. Tel: (212) 556-1234, Web Site: www.nytimes.com (17)

Folta, Carl D., Viacom Inc, New York, NY. Tel: (212) 258-6000, FAX: (212) 258-6464, Web Site: www.viacom.com (16)

Fonk, Catherine, Direct Connect Group, Cleveland, OH. Tel: (216) 651-9500, Web Site: www.directconnectgroup.com (35)

Fonner, Pat, Esco Corp, Portland, OR. Tel: (503) 228-2141, FAX: (503) 778-6682, Web Site: www.escocorp.com (16)

Fontaine, Chantal, Promotional Product Professionals of Canada, Dorval, QC Canada. Tel: (514) 489-5359, FAX: (800) 489-8741, (514) 489-7760, E-Mail: gladys@pppc.ca, Web Site: www.pppc.ca (1)

Fontaine, Richard, Martha Stewart Living Omnimedia, New York, NY. Tel: (212) 827-8000, Web Site: www.marthastewart.com (17)

Fontana, Christine, BannerDirect, Westhampton Beach, NY. Tel: (212) 858-9883, E-Mail: info@bannerdirect.com, Web Site: www.bannerdirect.com (35)

Fontana, Frank, Dover Publications Inc, Mineola, NY. Tel: (516) 294-7000, FAX: (516) 742-6953, Web Site: www.doverpublications.com (17)

Fontana, Paula, Executive Connections LLC, Sarasota, FL. Tel: (941) 323-8300, Web Site: www.executiveconnectionsllc.com (20)

Fontana, PhD Lynn A., Sylvan Learning Inc, Baltimore, MD. Tel: (410) 843-8000, (800) 31-SUCCESS, FAX: (410) 843-8057, E-Mail: pr@sylvanlearning.com, Web Site: www.sylvanlearning.com (16)

Fontanes, A. Alexander, Liberty Mutual Group, Inc, Boston, MA. Tel: (617) 357-9500, (800) 837-5274, Web Site: www.libertymutual.com (15)

Fontes, Chris, Clement Communications, Buffalo, NY. Tel: (800) 253-6368, E-Mail: customerservice@clement.com, Web Site: www.clement.com (16)

Fontes, Kimberly A., National Fire Protection Association, Quincy, MA. Tel: (617) 770-3000, FAX: (617) 770-0700, Web Site: www.nfpa.org (1)

Food & Water Watch, Washington, DC. Tel: (202) 683-2500, E-Mail: info@fwwatch.org, Web Site: www.foodandwaterwatch.org (1)

Food Chemical News, Arlington, VA. Tel: (202) 887-6320, (888) 732-7070, FAX: (202) 887-6335, E-Mail: cs@foodregulation.com, Web Site: www.foodchemicalnews.com (17)

Food for the Hungry Inc, Phoenix, AZ. Tel: (480) 998-3100, (800) 248-6437, FAX: (480) 998-4806, E-Mail: hunger@fh.org, Web Site: www.fh.org (1)

Food for the Poor Inc, Coconut Creek, FL. Tel: (954) 427-2222, Web Site: www.foodforthepoor.com (1)

Food Marketing Institute (FMI), Arlington, VA. Tel: (202) 452-8444, FAX: (202) 429-4519, E-Mail: fmi@fmi.org, Web Site: www.fmi.org (40)

Foos, Brian, ST Media Group International, Cincinnati, OH. Tel: (513) 421-2050, (800) 925-1110, FAX: (513) 421-5144, E-Mail: customer@stmediagroup. com, Web Site: www.signweb.com (17)

Foote, Cone & Belding, Chicago, IL. Tel: (312) 425-5000, FAX: (312) 425-5010, E-Mail: chicago@fcb. com, Web Site: www.fcb.com (35)

Foote, Francisco & Co, West Caldwell, NJ. Tel: (973) 226-1212, FAX: (973) 226-3409 (1)

Foote-Jones/Illinois Gear, Aberdeen, SD. Tel: (605) 225-0360, FAX: (605) 225-0567, Web Site: www. footejones.com (16)

Foote, Willy, Foote, Francisco & Co, West Caldwell, NJ. Tel: (973) 226-1212, FAX: (973) 226-3409 (1)

Forbes Inc, New York, NY. Tel: (212) 620-1887, (800) 295-0893, Web Site: www.forbes.com (17)

Forbes, Elroy, Houston Direct Marketing Association, Houston, TX. Tel: (281) 931-8883, FAX: (281) 820-4023, Web Site: www.houstondma.org (40)

Forchon, Stephen, RI Direct + Digital, Toronto, ON Canada. Tel: (416) 368-6211, E-Mail: info@ responseinnovations.com, Web Site: www. responseinnovations.com (35)

Ford Foundation Office of Communications, New York, NY. Tel: (212) 573-5000, E-Mail: office-of-communications@fordfound.org, Web Site: www. fordfound.org (5)

Ford Motor Co, Dearborn, MI. Tel: (313) 845-8540, (800) 555-5259, FAX: (313) 845-6073, Web Site: www.ford.com (16)

Ford, Charlotte, Drexel University Goodwin College of Professional Studies, Philadelphia, PA. Tel: (215) 895-2159, E-Mail: goodwin@drexel.edu, Web Site: goodwin.drexel.edu (16)

Ford, Charlotte, Charlotte Ford Trunks, Dumas, TX. Tel: (806) 934-8477, (800) 659-5614, FAX: (806) 372-3061, E-Mail: charolette@charolettefordtrunks. com, Web Site: www.charolettefordtrunks.com (11)

Ford, Freeman A., FAFCO Inc, Chico, CA. Tel: (530) 332-2100, (800) 994-7652, FAX: (530) 332-2109, Web Site: www.fafco.com (16)

Ford, Jon, Paladin Press, Boulder, CO. Tel: (303) 443-7250, (800) 392-2400, FAX: (303) 442-8741, E-Mail: service@paladin-press.com, Web Site: www.paladin-press.com (17)

Ford, Linda, Virginia Port Authority, Norfolk, VA. Tel: (757) 683-8000, (800) 446-8098, FAX: (757) 683-2897, Web Site: www.portofvirginia.com (16)

Ford, Marshall, Sage Software Inc, Irvine, CA. Tel: (949) 753-1222, (800) 854-3415, FAX: (949) 753-0374, Web Site: www.sagesoftware.com (16)

Ford, Michael H., Des Plaines Printing Co, Des Plaines, IL. Tel: (847) 824-1111, (800) 283-1776, FAX: (847) 824-1112, E-Mail: custserv@dppc.com (27)

Ford, Mike, Simplex Grinnell, Westminster, MA. Tel: (978) 731-2500, (800) SIMPLEX, FAX: (978) 731-7856, Web Site: www.simplexgrinnel.com (16)

Ford, Rod, CognitiveDATA Inc, Little Rock, AR. Tel: (501) 975-7580, (866) 243-7883, FAX: (501) 975-7681, E-Mail: info@cognitivedata.com, Web Site: www.cognitivedata.com (22)

Ford, Steven G., Muscular Dystrophy Association, Chicago, IL. Tel: (800) 572-1717, Web Site: www.mda. org (1)

Ford, Tony, Alfa CTP Systems, Tewksbury, MA. Tel: (603) 689-1101, FAX: (603) 689-1197, Web Site: www.alfactp.com (10)

Ford, William Clay, Ford Motor Co, Dearborn, MI. Tel: (313) 845-8540, (800) 555-5259, FAX: (313) 845-6073, Web Site: www.ford.com (16)

Forde, Joan, Midwest Direct Marketing Association Inc, Saint Paul, MN. Tel: (651) 999-5351, FAX: (651) 917-1835, E-Mail: mdma@mdma.org, Web Site: www.mdma.org (40)

Forde, Joan, US Bank, Minneapolis, MN. Tel: (612) 973-1111, Web Site: www.usbank.com (14)

Fordham University Graduate School of Business Administration, New York, NY. Tel: (212) 636-6200, (800) 825-4422, FAX: (212) 636-7076, Web Site: www.fordham.edu (41)

Forecast Direct Marketing Group, Pittsburgh, PA. Tel: (412) 481-4977, FAX: (412) 481-0872, Web Site: forecastdirect.com (21)

Forecaster Publishing Co Inc, Tarzana, CA. Tel: (818) 345-4421 (14)

Foreman, Bart, Group 3 Marketing, Wayzata, MN. Tel: (952) 475-3269, (888) 571-6554, FAX: (952) 449-0403, E-Mail: info@group3marketing.com, Web Site: www.group3marketing.com (20)

Foreman, Jay, Sybase Inc, Dublin, CA. Tel: (925) 236-5000, FAX: (925) 236-4321, Web Site: www. sybase.com/product/datawarehousing (22)

Foremaster, Cindy, Laitram Machinery, Harahan, LA. Tel: (504) 733-6000, FAX: (504) 733-6111 (16)

Foremost Industrial Exchange, Van Nuys, CA. Tel: (818) 988-6900, FAX: (818) 787-0293 (16)

Foremost Insurance Group, Grand Rapids, MI. Tel: (616) 956-8241, (800) 527-3905, FAX: (800) 325-1507, Web Site: www.foremost.com (15)

ForeSee Results Inc, Ann Arbor, MI. Tel: (734) 205-2600, (800) 621-2850, FAX: (734) 205-2601, Web Site: www.foreseeresults.com (30)

Forest Envelope Co, Lisle, IL. Tel: (630) 515-1200, FAX: (630) 515-1212, Web Site: forestenvelope. com (26)

Foresters, Toronto, ON Canada. Tel: (416) 467-2544, Web Site: www.foresters.com (15)

Forestry Suppliers Inc, Jackson, MS. Tel: (601) 354-3565, (800) 647-5368, FAX: (601) 292-0165, E-Mail: fsi@forestry-suppliers.com, Web Site: www.forestry-suppliers.com (9)

Forethought Financial Services Inc, Batesville, IN. Tel: (812) 934-7139, (800) 331-8853, FAX: (812) 934-8564, Web Site: www.forethought.com (15)

Forgacs, Frank, Doran & Forgacs Inc, West Chester, PA. Tel: (610) 344-0570, FAX: (610) 344-7203, E-Mail: bdoran@doranforgacs.com, Web Site: www.doranforgacs.com (35)

Form House Inc, Chicago, IL. Tel: (773) 577-8500, E-Mail: ktalbot@theformhouse.com, Web Site: www.theformhouse.com (28)

Formal Approach, Jefferson City, TN. Tel: (865) 475-8641, Web Site: www.formalapproach.com (2)

Forman, Bruce, Commercial Mailing Lists, Framingham, MA. Tel: (508) 879-2647, (800) 875-8345, FAX: (508) 879-2911 (23)

Forman, Charles, M2Media 360, Park Ridge, IL. Tel: (760) 318-7000, E-Mail: cnaughton@m2media360. com, Web Site: www.m2media360.com (17)

Forman, Nancy, Media People Inc, New York, NY. Tel: (212) 779-7172, FAX: (212) 779-7248, E-Mail: info@mediapeople.com, Web Site: www. mediapeople.com (31)

Formant, Christopher, MCI Communications Services Inc, Basking Ridge, NJ. Tel: (877) 297-7816, Web Site: www.mci.com (16)

Formica, Bob, Fosdick Fulfillment Corp, Wallingford, CT. Tel: (203) 269-0211, (800) 759-5588, FAX: (203) 679-3290, E-Mail: sales@fosdickcorp.com, Web Site: www.fosdickfulfillment.com (28)

Formica, Pat, Apollo Technologies Inc, Smyrna, GA. Tel: (770) 433-0210, (800) 533-3548, FAX: (770) 433-0132, E-Mail: customerservice@apolloind.com, Web Site: www.apolloind.com (34)

Formsource, Lewiston, ME. Tel: (207) 782-3311, (877) 782-3311, FAX: (207) 783-0157, E-Mail: service@ formsource1.com, Web Site: www.formsource1.com (27)

Forquer, M. William, Open Text Inc, Waterloo, ON Canada. Tel: (519) 888-9933, (800) 499-6544, FAX: (519) 888-0677, E-Mail: support@opentext.com, Web Site: www.opentext.com (16)

Forrest, Jack W., Remington College, Heathrow, FL. Tel: (407) 562-5691, (800) 560-6192, Web Site: www.remingtoncollege.edu (13)

Forrester, Jalayne, Sunset Magazine, Menlo Park, CA. Tel: (650) 321-3600, FAX: (650) 328-6215 (17)

Forsyth, John, Wellmark Blue Cross & Blue Shield of Iowa, Des Moines, IA. Tel: (515) 376-4500, (800) 524-9242, FAX: (515) 323-7722, Web Site: www. wellmark.com (15)

Forsythe, Michael, CNY Awards & Apparel Inc, New Hartford, NY. Tel: (315) 733-0931, FAX: (800) 732-3617, Web Site: www.cnyapprel.com (5)

The Fort Group, Ridgefield Park, NJ. Tel: (201) 445-0202, FAX: (201) 445-0626, E-Mail: info@ fortgroupinc.com, Web Site: www.fortgroupinc.com (35)

Fort Hays State University, Hays, KS. Tel: (785) 628-FHSU, FAX: (785) 628-4046, Web Site: www.fhsu. edu (41)

Forte, Deborah A, Scholastic Inc, New York, NY. Tel: (212) 343-6100, (800) SCHOLASTIC, FAX: (212) 343-6484, Web Site: www.scholastic.com (17)

Fortier, Richard, Desjardins Financial Securities, Levis, QC Canada. Tel: (418) 838-7870, FAX: (418) 833-5985, Web Site: www.desjardinsfinancialsecurity. com (15)

Fortin, Dana, Embrace Home Loans, Middletown, RI. Tel: (401) 846-3100, Web Site: www.afsfitfinance. com (14)

Fortson, Nicholas, University Bank, Ann Arbor, MI. Tel: (734) 741-5858, FAX: (734) 741-5859, E-Mail: ranzini@university-bank.com, Web Site: www. university-bank.com (14)

Fortunato, Joseph, General Nutrition Corp, Pittsburgh, PA. Tel: (412) 288-4600, (877) 462-4700, FAX: (412) 402-7218, Web Site: www.gnc.com (7)

48HourPrint.com, Boston, MA. Tel: (800) 844-0599, Web Site: www.48hourprint.com (27)

The Forum Corp, Boston, MA. Tel: (617) 523-7300, (800) 367-8611, FAX: (617) 371-3300, E-Mail: forum@forum.com, Web Site: www.forum.com (20)

Forum Publishing Co, Centerport, NY. Tel: (631) 754-5000, (800) 635-7654, FAX: (631) 754-0630, E-Mail: forumpublishing@aol.com, Web Site: www.forum123.com (17)

Fosdick Fulfillment Corp, Wallingford, CT. Tel: (203) 269-0211, (800) 759-5588, FAX: (203) 679-3290, E-Mail: sales@fosdickcorp.com, Web Site: www. fosdickfulfillment.com (28)

Fosdyck, Vicki, Direct One Inc, Winter Park, FL. Tel: (407) 673-4500, FAX: (407) 673-4501, E-Mail: wariagno@directoneinc.com, Web Site: www. directoneinc.com (14)

Fosina Marketing Group Inc, Danbury, CT. Tel: (203) 790-0013, E-Mail: info@fosinamarketing.com, Web Site: fosinamarketinggroup.com (35)

Fosina, Jim, Fosina Marketing Group Inc, Danbury, CT. Tel: (203) 790-0013, E-Mail: info@ fosinamarketing.com, Web Site: fosinamarketinggroup.com (35)

Foss, Eric, Aramark Uniform Services, Burbank, CA. Tel: (800) 272-6275, Web Site: www.aramark-uniform.com (2)

Fossil, Richardson, TX. Tel: (469) 587-2628, Web Site: www.fossil.com (2)

Stephen Fossler Co Inc, Des Plaines, IL. Tel: (847) 635-7200, (800) 762-0030, FAX: (800) 424-9292, E-Mail: customerservice@fossler.com, Web Site: sfc.stephen-fossler.com (27)

Fossum, Polly, Victory Corps, New Hope, MN. Tel: (763) 561-5600, (800) 328-6120, FAX: (763) 561-8523, E-Mail: cs@victorycorps.com, Web Site: www.victorycorps.com (16)

Foster Keencut, Montgomeryville, PA. Tel: (267) 413-6220, (800) 523-4855, FAX: (267) 413-6227, E-Mail: information@fostermfg.com, Web Site: www.fostermfg.com (34)

Foster Marketing LLC, Lafayette, LA. Tel: (337) 235-1848, FAX: (337) 237-7246, E-Mail: gfoster@ fostermarketing.com, Web Site: fostermarketing.com (35)

Foster Travel Publishing, Berkeley, CA. Tel: (510) 549-2202, FAX: (510) 549-1131, E-Mail: lee@ fostertravel.com, Web Site: www.fostertravel.com (38)

Foster, Careen, Fractal Analytics, Jersey City, NJ. Tel: (201) 469-0600, Web Site: www.fractalanalytics.com (35)

Foster, Craig, Amobee, Foster City, CA. Tel: (650) 802-8871, Web Site: www.amobee.com (32)

Foster, Frank, Medals of America, Fountain Inn, SC. Tel: (864) 862-0635, (800) 308-0849, FAX: (800) 407-8640, E-Mail: medals@usmedals.com, Web Site: www.usmedals.com (6)

Foster, George, Foster Marketing LLC, Lafayette, LA. Tel: (337) 235-1848, FAX: (337) 237-7246, E-Mail: gfoster@fostermarketing.com, Web Site: fostermarketing.com (35)

Foster, Kim, Reno Gazette Journal, Reno, NV. Tel: (775) 788-6200, FAX: (775) 788-6563 (17)

Foster, Lee, Foster Travel Publishing, Berkeley, CA. Tel: (510) 549-2202, FAX: (510) 549-1131, E-Mail: lee@fostertravel.com, Web Site: www.fostertravel.com (38)

Foster, Leo, Campbell Tools Co, Springfield, OH. Tel: (937) 882-6716, FAX: (937) 882-6648, E-Mail: campbell@campbelltools.com, Web Site: www.campbelltools.com (9)

Foster, Linda, Medals of America, Fountain Inn, SC. Tel: (864) 862-0635, (800) 308-0849, FAX: (800) 407-8640, E-Mail: medals@usmedals.com, Web Site: www.usmedals.com (6)

Foster, Ryan, Business Marketing Association, Naperville, IL. Tel: (630) 544-5054, FAX: (630) 544-5055, E-Mail: info@marketing.org, Web Site: www.marketing.org (40)

Foster, Todd, Intelligencer Printing Co, Lancaster, PA. Tel: (717) 291-3100, (800) 233-0107, FAX: (717) 569-2643, Web Site: www.intellprinting.com (27)

Foster, William K., FMC Corp, Philadelphia, PA. Tel: (215) 299-6000, FAX: (215) 299-5998, Web Site: www.fmc.com (16)

Fostoria Industries Inc, Johnson City, TN. Tel: (419) 435-9201, (800) 495-4525, FAX: (419) 435-0842, E-Mail: email@fostoriaindustries.com, Web Site: www.fostoriaindustries.com (9)

Fotch, Katherine, System Pavers, Newport Beach, CA. Tel: (949) 263-8300, Web Site: www.systempavers.com (16)

Fote, Charlie T., First Data Merchant Services, Atlanta, GA. Tel: (404) 890-2000, FAX: (303) 967-5188, Web Site: www.firstdata.com (14)

FotoBed.com, Birmingham, AL. Tel: (888) 368-6233, E-Mail: service@fotobed.com, Web Site: www.fotobed.com (20)

Foulkes, Helena B, CVS Caremark, Woonsocket, RI. Tel: (401) 765-1500, FAX: (401) 769-4488, Web Site: www.cvs.com (7)

Foundation Fighting Blindness, Columbia, MD. Tel: (410) 423-0600, (800) 683-5555, Web Site: www.fightblindness.org (1)

Foundation for Chiropractic Education & Research, Norwalk, IA. Tel: (515) 981-9888 (1)

Foundation of FirstHealth, Pinehurst, NC. Tel: (910) 695-7500, Web Site: www.firsthealth.org/foundation (1)

Founder, Jeanniey Mullen, Zinio Systems Inc, San Francisco, CA. Tel: (415) 494-2700, FAX: (415) 494-2701, Web Site: www.zinio.com (31)

Four Corners Direct Inc, Sarasota, FL. Tel: (941) 364-8585 (16)

4Imprint Inc, Oshkosh, WI. Tel: (920) 236-7272, (877) 446-7746, (888) 298-8190, FAX: (800) 355-5043, E-Mail: administrator@4imprint.com, Web Site: www.4imprint.com (16)

Four Seasons Hotels & Resorts, Toronto, ON Canada. Tel: (416) 449-1750, (800) 819-5053, FAX: (416) 441-4437, Web Site: www.fourseasons.com (19)

Four Seasons Solar Products LLC, Holbrook, NY. Tel: (631) 563-4000, (800) 368-7732, FAX: (631) 563-4010, E-Mail: info@fourseasonssunrooms.com, Web Site: www.fourseasonssunrooms.com (8)

Four Star Marketing Inc, Lincolnwood, IL. Tel: (800) 888-2991, FAX: (847) 679-6449, E-Mail: cari@ fourstarmarketing.com, Web Site: www.conventionbags.com (33)

Four Wheel Drive Hardware LLC, Columbiana, OH. Tel: (330) 482-4924, FAX: (330) 482-5035, E-Mail: info@4wd.com, Web Site: www.4wd.com (12)

Fournier, Dab, Arthur Blank & Co Inc, Boston, MA. Tel: (617) 325-9600, (800) 776-7333, FAX: (617) 327-1235, E-Mail: abco@abco.com, Web Site: www.arthurblank.com (27)

Fourshee, Coleman, Klingspor's Woodworking Shop, Hickory, NC. Tel: (828) 326-WOOD, (800) 228-0000, FAX: (828) 327-4634, E-Mail: sales@ woodworkingshop.com, Web Site: www.woodworkingshop.com (9)

Fouse, Mel, Mustek Inc, Tustin, CA. Tel: (949) 790-3800, FAX: (949) 788-3670, Web Site: www.mustek.com (3)

Fowden, Jerry, DS Services of North America LP, Lakeland, FL. Tel: (770) 933-1400, (800) 669-3402, FAX: (770) 956-9495, E-Mail: customerservice@water.com, Web Site: www.water.com (4)

Fowke, Ben, Xcel Energy, Minneapolis, MN. Tel: (612) 330-6783, Web Site: xcelenergy.com (5)

Fowkes, Rick, Kett Tool Co, Cincinnati, OH. Tel: (513) 271-0333, FAX: (513) 271-5318, E-Mail: info@ kett-tool.com, Web Site: www.kett-tool.com (9)

Fowler, Alison Mori, Eleven Inc, San Francisco, CA. Tel: (415) 707-1111, Web Site: www.eleveninc.com (35)

Fowler, Jeff, Decision Software Inc, Hyattsville, MD. Tel: (301) 459-9000, FAX: (301) 459-3072, E-Mail: info@dsoftware.biz, Web Site: www.dsimarketingservices.com (22)

Fowler, Jim, National Review, New York, NY. Tel: (212) 679-7330, FAX: (212) 849-2852, Web Site: www.nationalreview.com (17)

Fowler, Richard C., Market Focus Inc, Evanston, IL. Tel: (847) 328-2900, FAX: (847) 328-8121 (30)

Fowler, Richard M., Texas Industries Inc, Dallas, TX. Tel: (972) 647-6700, FAX: (972) 647-3878, Web Site: www.txi.com (16)

Fowler, Steve, Houston Direct Marketing Association, Houston, TX. Tel: (281) 931-8883, FAX: (281) 820-4023, Web Site: www.houstondma.org (40)

Fowler's Chocolates Inc, Buffalo, NY. Tel: (716) 877-9983, (800) 824-2263, FAX: (716) 877-9959, E-Mail: customerservice@fowlerschocolates.com, Web Site: www.fowlerschocolates.com (4)

Fox Associates Inc, Chicago, IL. Tel: (312) 644-3888, FAX: (312) 644-8718, E-Mail: sales@foxrep.com, Web Site: www.foxrep.com (31)

Fox Chase Cancer Center, Philadelphia, PA. Tel: (215) 728-6900, (888) 369-2427, FAX: (215) 728-2594, Web Site: www.fccc.edu (1)

Larry Fox & Co Ltd, Valley Stream, NY. Tel: (516) 791-7929, (800) 397-7923, FAX: (516) 791-1022, E-Mail: larry@larryfox.com, Web Site: www.larryfox.com (16)

Fox Lite, Inc, Fairborn, OH. Tel: (937) 864-1966, FAX: (937) 864-7010, E-Mail: doug@foxlite.com, Web Site: www.foxlite.com (9)

Fox Media Lab, Natick, MA. Tel: (508) 655-5665, FAX: (508) 655-2051, E-Mail: foxmedialabs@gmail.com (32)

Rich Fox & Associates Inc, Carmel Valley, CA. Tel: (831) 659-1123 (1)

Fox Valley Systems Inc, Brookfield, CT. Tel: (844) 627-5255, E-Mail: info@foxvalleypaint.com, Web Site: www.foxvalleypaint.com (9)

Fox, Allison, The Bradford Group, Niles, IL. Tel: (847) 966-2770, FAX: (847) 581-8630, Web Site: www.collectiblestoday.com (16)

Fox, Anthony, Uncle Ben's Inc, Greenville, MS. Tel: (601) 335-8000, (800) 54-UNCLE, (800) 548-6253, FAX: (601) 378-4370, E-Mail: info@unclebens.com, Web Site: www.unclebens.com (4)

Fox, Graham, IRPP, Montreal, QC Canada. Tel: (514) 985-2461, FAX: (514) 985-2559, E-Mail: irpp@irpp.org, Web Site: www.irpp.org (30)

Fox, Gregory C., Burlington Northern & Santa Fe LLC, Fort Worth, TX. Tel: (817) 878-2000, (800) 795-2673, FAX: (817) 333-7593, Web Site: www.bnsf.com (16)

Fox, Joseph M., Fox Media Lab, Natick, MA. Tel: (508) 655-5665, FAX: (508) 655-2051, E-Mail: foxmedialabs@gmail.com (32)

Fox, Kelly, American Institute for Economic Research, Great Barrington, MA. Tel: (413) 528-1216, (888) 528-1216, FAX: (413) 528-0103, E-Mail: info@aier.org, Web Site: www.aier.org (1)

Fox, Ken, Berry Hill Ltd, Saint Thomas, ON Canada. Tel: (519) 631-0480, (800) 668-3072, FAX: (519) 631-8935, E-Mail: customerservice@berryhill.ca, Web Site: www.berryhilllimited.com (8)

Fox, Larry, Larry Fox & Co Ltd, Valley Stream, NY. Tel: (516) 791-7929, (800) 397-7923, FAX: (516) 791-1022, E-Mail: larry@larryfox.com, Web Site: www.larryfox.com (16)

Fox, Leigh, Cincinnati Bell Inc, Cincinnati, OH. Tel: (888) CIN-BELL, Web Site: www.cincinnatibell.com (16)

Fox, Marlys, Fox Associates Inc, Chicago, IL. Tel: (312) 644-3888, FAX: (312) 644-8718, E-Mail: sales@foxrep.com, Web Site: www.foxrep.com (31)

Fox, Michael J., Rogers Publishing Ltd, Toronto, ON Canada. Tel: (416) 935-7777, FAX: (416) 935-3597, Web Site: www.rogerspublishing.ca (17)

Fox, Randy, Jet LithoColor Inc, Downers Grove, IL. Tel: (630) 932-9000, (800) 932-1538, (800) 932-1JET, FAX: (630) 932-9101, E-Mail: sales@jetlitho. com, Web Site: www.jetlitho.com (27)

Fox, Rich, Rich Fox & Associates Inc, Carmel Valley, CA. Tel: (831) 659-1123 (1)

Fox, Steve, PC World, San Francisco, CA. Tel: (415) 243-0500, FAX: (415) 442-1891, Web Site: www. pcworld.com (17)

Fox, Thomas, National Catholic Reporter Publishing Co Inc, Kansas City, MO. Tel: (816) 531-0538, (800) 444-8910, FAX: (816) 968-2268, Web Site: www. ncronline.org (17)

Foxfire Printing & Packaging Inc, Newark, DE. Tel: (302) 368-9466, (800) 497-0516, FAX: (302) 368-5164, E-Mail: info@foxfiresigns.com, Web Site: www.foxfiresigns.com (27)

Foxhall Corporation, McLean, VA. Tel: (703) 749-3126 (20)

The Foxon Co, Providence, RI. Tel: (401) 421-2386, (800) 556-6943, FAX: (401) 421-8996 (27)

Foxx, Lucia M., Ronell Clock Co, Grants Pass, OR. Tel: (800) 334-0135, FAX: (541) 471-0099, E-Mail: info@ronellclock.com, Web Site: www. ronellclock.com (5)

Fractal Analytics, Jersey City, NJ. Tel: (201) 469-0600, Web Site: www.fractalanalytics.com (35)

Fradin, Russell, Sungard Computer Services, Wayne, PA. Tel: (484) 582-5673, E-Mail: GetInfo@ SunGard.com, Web Site: www.sungard.com (22)

Fraenkel, Sallie, Spa-Finder Inc, New York, NY. Tel: (305) 307-5852, (800) ALL-SPAS, Web Site: www. spafinder.com (7)

Fragrance International Inc, Youngstown, OH. Tel: (330) 747-3341, (888) 547-8355, FAX: (330) 747-3343, E-Mail: comments@kisstell.com, Web Site: www.kisstell.com (16)

Frahman, Dennis, Sage Software Inc, Irvine, CA. Tel: (949) 753-1222, (800) 854-3415, FAX: (949) 753-0374, Web Site: www.sagesoftware.com (16)

Fraim, William L., AcuSport Corp, Bellefontaine, OH. Tel: (937) 593-7010, FAX: (937) 592-5625, E-Mail: mwsales@acusport.com, Web Site: www.acusport. com (11)

Fraizer, Michael D., Genworth Financial Inc, Richmond, VA. Tel: (804) 281-6000, (888) 436-9678, FAX: (804) 662-2414, Web Site: www.genworth.com (14)

Frakenfield, Jack, Bob Barker Co Inc, Fuquay Varina, NC. Tel: (800) 334-9880, FAX: (800) 322-7537, Web Site: www.bobbarker.com (5)

Francesco, John Di, Gump's By Mail Inc, San Francisco, CA. Tel: (415) 982-1616, (800) 882-8055, FAX: (800) 984-9361, Web Site: www.gumpsbymail.com (6)

Franchino, Michael, Peppermill Marketing Inc, Los Angeles, CA. Tel: (866) 737-5478, E-Mail: inquiry@ peppermillmarketing.com, Web Site: peppermillmarketing.com (23)

Francis, Jennifer, Philadelphia Museum of Art, Philadelphia, PA. Tel: (215) 684-7840, FAX: (215) 235-0042, E-Mail: memberservices@philamuseum.org, Web Site: www.philamuseum.org (1)

Francis, Merle, Blue Cross Blue Shield of Louisiana, Baton Rouge, LA. Tel: (225) 295-3307, (800) 599-2583, FAX: (225) 295-2054, E-Mail: help@bcbsla. com, Web Site: www.bcbsla.com (15)

Francis, Ron, Wire Works, Chester, PA. Tel: (610) 485-1981, (800) 292-1940, Web Site: www.wire-works. com (9)

Francis, Scott, Photographer's Market, Blue Ash, OH. Tel: (513) 531-2690, FAX: (513) 531-2686, E-Mail: photomarket@fwpubs.com, Web Site: www. photographersmarket.com (43)

Francis, Steve, GMC Software Technology Inc, Charlestown, MA. Tel: (800) 250-1850, FAX: (617) 241-5665, Web Site: www.gmc.net (22)

Francis, Susanne, Spinneybeck Enterprises, Getzville, NY. Tel: (716) 446-2380, (800) 482-7777, FAX: (716) 446-2396, E-Mail: sales@spinneybeck.com, Web Site: www.spinneybeck.com (16)

Franciscan Friars of the Atonement - Graymoor, Garrison, NY. Tel: (845) 424-3671, (800) 338-2620, FAX: (845) 424-2168, E-Mail: info@ atonementfriars.org, Web Site: www. atonementfriars.org (1)

Franciscan Mission Associates, Mount Vernon, NY. Tel: (914) 664-5604, FAX: (914) 664-3017, E-Mail: admin@franciscanmissionassoc.org, Web Site: www.franciscanmissionassoc.org (1)

Francke, Filip, Helly-Hansen, Auburn, WA. Tel: (800) 435-5901, FAX: (425) 649-3740, Web Site: www. hellyhansen.com (16)

Franco, Adolfo, Direct Selling Association, Washington, DC. Tel: (202) 452-8866, FAX: (202) 452-9010, E-Mail: info@dsa.org, Web Site: www.dsa.org (40)

Franco, Lawrence, D&B Canada, Mississauga, ON Canada. Tel: (800) 463-6362, FAX: (800) 668-7800, Web Site: www.dnb.ca (30)

Franco, Lynn, The Conference Board Inc, New York, NY. Tel: (212) 759-0900, FAX: (212) 980-7014, Web Site: www.conference-board.org (16)

Frandsen, Laura, Cade & Associates Advertising Inc, Tallahassee, FL. Tel: (850) 385-0300, (800) 715-CADE, FAX: (850) 385-1165, E-Mail: webmaster@ cade1.com, Web Site: www.cade1.com (35)

Franey, Christopher, Kensington Computer Products Group, Redwood Shores, CA. Tel: (650) 572-2700, FAX: (650) 267-2800, Web Site: www.kensington. com (16)

Frank Joseph, Chevy Chase, MD. Tel: (301) 656-8753, E-Mail: mr.dm@verizon.net (39)

Frank Mobility Systems Inc, Oakdale, PA. Tel: (888) 426-8581, FAX: (724) 695-3710, E-Mail: info@ lfrankmobility.com, Web Site: www.lifestandusa. com (13)

Frank Siteman Photography, Winchester, MA. Tel: (781) 729-3747, E-Mail: frank@franksiteman.com, Web Site: www.franksiteman.com (37)

Frank, Gerald, Tridium Inc, Richmond, VA. Tel: (804) 525-1648, Web Site: www.tridium.com (9)

Frank, Harley, Admiral Packaging Inc, Providence, RI. Tel: (401) 274-7000, (800) 262-0027, FAX: (401) 331-1910, Web Site: www.admiralpkg.com (26)

Frank, Robert L., Air Force Sergeants Association, Suitland, MD. Tel: (301) 899-3500, (800) 638-0594, FAX: (301) 899-8136, E-Mail: staff@hqafsa.org, Web Site: www.hqafsa.org (1)

Frank, Terry, Bunzl Distribution USA, Inc, Saint Louis, MO. Tel: (314) 997-5959, (888) 997-5959, FAX: (314) 997-1405, Web Site: www.bunzldistribution. com (16)

Franke, Jim, Cision US Inc, Chicago, IL. Tel: (312) 922-2400, (866) 639-5087, FAX: (312) 922-3126, E-Mail: info.us@cision.com, Web Site: us.cision. com (43)

Frankel, Rich, CMEinfo.com, Birmingham, AL. Tel: (205) 991-9188, (800) 284-8433, FAX: (800) 284-5964, Web Site: www.cmeinfo.com (16)

Franken, Linda A., New York Road Runners, New York, NY. Tel: (855) 5MY-NYRR, E-Mail: mynyrr@nyrr.org, Web Site: www.nyrr.org (13)

Frankhouse, Dale, Adventure Creations Inc, Costa Mesa, CA. Tel: (949) 515-3600, FAX: (949) 515-3933, E-Mail: sales@adv-creations.com, Web Site: www.adv-creations.com (16)

Frankio, Phil, Speakers Guild Inc, Sandwich, MA. Tel: (508) 888-6702, (800) 343-4530, FAX: (508) 888-6771, E-Mail: info@speakersguild.com, Web Site: www.speakersguild.com (16)

Franklin & Welker Direct Marketing Services, Miami, FL. Tel: (305) 758-6690, FAX: (305) 758-9399 (30)

Franklin Estimating Systems, Woods Cross, UT. Tel: (801) 303-6083, (800) 346-7363, FAX: (801) 303-4540, E-Mail: management@franklinestimating. com, Web Site: www.fesys.com (17)

The Franklin Mint, Exton, PA. Tel: (610) 497-4800, (800) THE-MINT, FAX: (610) 497-4956, E-Mail: support@franklinmint.com, Web Site: www. franklinmint.com (16)

Franklin, Bob, San Francisco Bay Area Rapid Transit District (BART), Oakland, CA. Tel: (510) 464-6000, FAX: (510) 464-7103, Web Site: www.bart.gov (16)

Franklin, Cal, TN Marketing, Wayzata, MN. Tel: (763) 577-1200, Web Site: www.tnmarketing.com (35)

Franklin, Erin, PNT Marketing Services, Inc, Long Island City, NY. Tel: (718) 433-4063, (888) 768-2210, FAX: (914) 428-0504, E-Mail: tony@ pntmarketingservices.com, Web Site: www. pntmarketingservices.com (22)

Franklin, Garrett, Atmosphere Proximity, New York, NY. Tel: (212) 827-2500, FAX: (212) 827-2525, E-Mail: andreas.combuechen@atmospeherebbdo. com, Web Site: www.atmosphereproximity.com (35)

Franklin, Leonard G., Franklin & Welker Direct Marketing Services, Miami, FL. Tel: (305) 758-6690, FAX: (305) 758-9399 (30)

Franklin, Lindley, FCIA Management Co Inc, New York, NY. Tel: (212) 885-1500, FAX: (212) 885-1535, E-Mail: service@fcia.com, Web Site: www. fcia.com (15)

Franklin, Martin E., Jarden Corp, Boca Raton, FL. Tel: (561) 912-4395, Web Site: www.jarden.com (16)

Franklin, Rebecca, Gibson Auer LLC, Victor, ID. Tel: (208) 201-3143, (888) 425-2250, E-Mail: helpdesk@galabs.com, Web Site: www. spiralenergetics.com (7)

Franklin, Robert, McFarland & Co Inc Publishers, Jefferson, NC. Tel: (336) 246-4460, (800) 253-2187, FAX: (336) 246-5018, E-Mail: info@mcfarlandpub. com, Web Site: www.mcfarlandpub.com (17)

Franklin, Rusty, Sellstrom Manufacturing Co, Schaumburg, IL. Tel: (847) 358-2000, (800) 323-7402, FAX: (847) 358-8564, E-Mail: sellstrom@sellstrom. com, Web Site: www.sellstrom.com (16)

Franks, Carli, Print Services Distribution Association, Chicago, IL. Tel: (800) 230-0175, FAX: (312) 673-6880, Web Site: www.psda.org (1)

Fran's Basket House, Inc, Succasunna, NJ. Tel: (973) 584-2230, (800) 372-6799, E-Mail: sales@ franswicker.com, Web Site: www.franswicker.com (8)

Franzblau, R.M., Thompson Cigar Co, Tampa, FL. Tel: (813) 884-6344, (800) 216-7107, FAX: (813) 882-4605, Web Site: www.thompsoncigar.com (6)

Franzen, Tim, American Spirit Graphics Corp, Minneapolis, MN. Tel: (612) 623-3333, FAX: (612) 623-9314, E-Mail: asgc@asgc.com, Web Site: www. asgc.com (27)

Frappier, Renee, PacNet Services Ltd, Vancouver, BC Canada. Tel: (604) 689-0399, FAX: (604) 689-0313, E-Mail: info@pacnetservices.com, Web Site: www. pacnetservices.com (14)

Fratoni, Doreen, Jaypro Sports, Waterford, CT. Tel: (860) 447-3001, (800) 243-0533, FAX: (800) 988-3363, E-Mail: info@jaypro.com, Web Site: www.jaypro.com (11)

Frattarda, Robert, Herbert L Jamison & Co LLC, West Orange, NJ. Tel: (973) 731-0806, (800) 526-4766, (800) JAMISON, FAX: (973) 731-3035, Web Site: www.jamisongroup.com (15)

Frattaroli, Brian, Intromark Inc, Pittsburgh, PA. Tel: (412) 288-1300, (800) 851-6030 X1368, FAX: (412) 338-0497, E-Mail: licensing@intromark.com (16)

Fraud & Theft Information Bureau, Boynton Beach, FL. Tel: (561) 737-8700, FAX: (561) 737-5800, E-Mail: sales@fraudandtheft.com, Web Site: www.fraudandtheftinfo.com (43)

Frausto, Ernie, NestFamily.com, Lewisville, TX. Tel: (800) 596-7386, FAX: (972) 629-7181, Web Site: www.nestfamily.com (3)

Frawley, Andy, Epsilon, Irving, TX. Tel: (469) 262-0600, Web Site: www.epsilon.com (35)

Frayne, Heather, Direct Marketers On Call Inc (DMOC), New York, NY. Tel: (212) 691-1942, FAX: (212) 924-1331, E-Mail: info@dmoc-inc.com, Web Site: www.dmoc-inc.com (20)

David R Frazier Photolibrary Inc, Boise, ID. Tel: (208) 342-9250, (800) 342-3283, FAX: (208) 342-2307, E-Mail: dave@drfphoto.com, Web Site: www.drfphoto.com (38)

Frazier, David R., David R Frazier Photolibrary Inc, Boise, ID. Tel: (208) 342-9250, (800) 342-3283, FAX: (208) 342-2307, E-Mail: dave@drfphoto.com, Web Site: www.drfphoto.com (38)

Frazier, Gary, USC Marshall School of Business Dept of Marketing, Los Angeles, CA. Tel: (213) 740-5033, FAX: (213) 740-7828, E-Mail: dennis.rook@marshall.usc.edu (41)

Frazier, Kenneth C., Merck & Co Inc, Whitehouse Station, NJ. Tel: (908) 423-1000, Web Site: www.merck.com (16)

Frazzini, Maria, Washington Gas Energy Services, Herndon, VA. Tel: (703) 793-7500, Web Site: www.wges.com (16)

Frear, David J., SiriusXM Radio Inc, New York, NY. Tel: (212) 584-5100, Web Site: www.siriusxm.com (16)

Freda, Fabrizio, Estee Lauder Inc, New York, NY. Tel: (212) 572-4200, FAX: (212) 893-7782, Web Site: www.esteelauder.com (16)

Freddie Mac, McLean, VA. Tel: (703) 903-2000, (800) 424-5401, Web Site: www.freddiemac.com (14)

Fredel, Alfred, Carl Fischer Music, New York, NY. Tel: (212) 777-0900, (800) 762-2328, FAX: (212) 477-6996, E-Mail: cf-info@carlfischer.com, Web Site: www.carlfischer.com (17)

Frederick, Aaron, Alfa Aesar-A Johnson Matthey Co, Ward Hill, MA. Tel: (800) 343-0660, FAX: (800) 322-4757, E-Mail: info@alfa.com, Web Site: www.alfa.com (16)

Frederick, Sherman R., Las Vegas Review Journal, Las Vegas, NV. Tel: (702) 383-0211, FAX: (702) 383-4646, Web Site: www.lvrj.com (17)

Frederick's of Hollywood Group Inc, Los Angeles, CA. Tel: (323) 466-5151, (855) 655-2514, FAX: (323) 464-5149, E-Mail: support@fredericks.com, Web Site: www.fredericks.com (2)

Frederickson, Flemming, Laitram Machinery, Harahan, LA. Tel: (504) 733-6000, FAX: (504) 733-6111 (16)

Paul Fredrick Menstyle, Fleetwood, PA. Tel: (610) 944-0909, (800) 247-1417, FAX: (610) 944-6452, E-Mail: custserv@menstyle.com, Web Site: www.paulfredricks.com (2)

Free, Vicky, Black Entertainment Television Inc, Washington, DC. Tel: (202) 608-2000, Web Site: www.bet.com (16)

Freed, Bernie, 925 Business Furniture, Kensington, MD. Tel: (301) 946-7288, (800) 525-0302, FAX: (302) 349-4587, E-Mail: bjfreed@erols.com, Web Site: www.natcofurniture.com (34)

Freedman, Christlin, Fire Mountain Gems, Grants Pass, OR. Tel: (541) 956-7890, (800) 355-2137, (800) 423-2319, FAX: (541) 470-GEMS, E-Mail: questions@firemtn.com, Web Site: www.firemtn.com (16)

Freedman, Mark, The Company Store Inc, La Crosse, WI. Tel: (608) 785-1400, FAX: (608) 791-5790, Web Site: www.thecompanystore.com (16)

Freedman, Stuart, Fire Mountain Gems, Grants Pass, OR. Tel: (541) 956-7890, (800) 355-2137, (800) 423-2319, FAX: (541) 470-GEMS, E-Mail: questions@firemtn.com, Web Site: www.firemtn.com (16)

Freedom Graphic Systems Inc, Milton, WI. Tel: (608) 868-7007, (800) 334-3540, FAX: (608) 868-7006, E-Mail: information@fgs.com, Web Site: www.freedomgraphicsystems.com (28)

Freel, Michael, Polyair Packaging, Chicago, IL. Tel: (773) 995-1818, (888) POLYAIR X444, FAX: (773) 995-7725, E-Mail: marketing@polyair.com, Web Site: www.polyair.com (9)

Freeman Decorating Co, Kearny, NJ. Tel: (201) 998-6006 (16)

Freeman, Jack, The Keystone Equities Group, Oaks, PA. Tel: (610) 415-6300, (800) 715-9905, FAX: (610) 415-6328, Web Site: www.keystoneequities.com (20)

Freeman, Lawrence, Value Line Publishing Inc, New York, NY. Tel: (212) 907-1500, FAX: (212) 818-9747, Web Site: www.valueline.com (17)

Freeman, Russell, Coyne American Institute, Chicago, IL. Tel: (773) 935-2520, (800) 999-5220, FAX: (773) 935-2920, Web Site: www.coyneamerican.edu (16)

Freeport Music Inc, Farmingville, NY. Tel: (631) 549-4108, (888) 549-4108, E-Mail: sales@musicalinstruments.com; sales@freeportmusic.com, Web Site: www.musicalinstruments.com (11)

Freestate, Donna, REGIT Inc, Glen Ellyn, IL. Tel: (630) 495-1500, (800) 537-9786, FAX: (630) 495-1611, E-Mail: regit@regitinc.com, Web Site: www.regitinc.com (15)

Freestone, Robin, Pearson Education, Upper Saddle River, NJ. Tel: (201) 236-7000, FAX: (201) 236-3290, Web Site: www.pearsoned.com (17)

Freestyle Photographic Supplies, Los Angeles, CA. Tel: (323) 660-3640, (800) 292-6137, FAX: (323) 284-0050, Web Site: www.freestylephoto.biz (5)

Freestyle Solutions, Parsippany, NJ. Tel: (973) 237-9415, (800) 858-3666, FAX: (973) 237-9043, E-Mail: sales@dydacomp.com, Web Site: www.dydacomp.com (22)

Frehner, Jeff, Pacific Cycle Inc, Madison, WI. Tel: (608) 268-2468, (800) 724-9466, FAX: (847) 236-3692, (847) 573-0602, E-Mail: info@pacificcycle.com, Web Site: www.pacificcycle.com (16)

Freidus, Marc, Victor Machinery Exchange, Brooklyn, NY. Tel: (800) 723-5359, FAX: (718) 366-7026, E-Mail: sales@victornet.com, Web Site: www.victornet.com (9)

Freifeld, Lorrie, Sales & Marketing Management Magazine, New York, NY. Tel: (800) 821-6897, FAX: (905) 470-8561, E-Mail: joyce.cooney@nielsen.com, Web Site: www.salesandmarketing.com (16)

Freitag, Randal J., Lincoln Financial Group, Radnor, PA. Tel: (215) 448-1400, (877) 275-5462, FAX: (215) 448-3962, Web Site: www.lfg.com (15)

French Creek Sheep & Wool Co Inc, Elverson, PA. Tel: (610) 286-5700, (800) 977-4337, FAX: (610) 286-0324, E-Mail: info@frenchcreeksw.com, Web Site: www.frenchcreeksw.com (16)

French Trade Office Embassy of France, New York, NY. Tel: (212) 400-2167, Web Site: www.missioneco.org (1)

French, Don, The Source Stock Footage Library Inc, Tucson, AZ. Tel: (520) 298-4810, FAX: (520) 290-8831, E-Mail: requests@sourcefootage.com, Web Site: www.sourcefootage.com (38)

French, Ian, Northern Lights Direct, Chicago, IL. Tel: (312) 263-8686, FAX: (312) 600-9050, E-Mail: contact@northernlightsdirect.com, Web Site: www.northernlightsdirect.com (32)

French, John, Cygnus Business Media, Fort Atkinson, WI. Tel: (203) 227-4037, (800) 547-7377, FAX: (203) 227-4245, Web Site: www.cygnus.com (17)

French, Jr R. Reid, Intergraph Corp, Madison, AL. Tel: (256) 730-2000, (800) 345-4856, FAX: (256) 730-2048, Web Site: www.intergraph.com (16)

French, Sandy, Northern Lights Direct, Chicago, IL. Tel: (312) 263-8686, FAX: (312) 600-9050, E-Mail: contact@northernlightsdirect.com, Web Site: www.northernlightsdirect.com (32)

Frenkel, Lev, Digital Speech Systems, Richardson, TX. Tel: (972) 235-2999, FAX: (972) 235-3036, E-Mail: sales@digitalspeech.com, Web Site: www.digitalspeech.com (3)

Frenz, Thomas R., List Advisor Inc, Farmingdale, NY. Tel: (631) 777-2900, FAX: (631) 777-3050 (23)

FreshAddress Inc, Newton, MA. Tel: (617) 965-4500, (800) 321-3009, FAX: (617) 965-4551, Web Site: www.freshaddress.com (22)

FreshDirect, Long Island City, NY. Tel: (212) 796-8002 (5)

Fresno Oxygen, Fresno, CA. Tel: (559) 233-6684, (800) 404-9353, FAX: (559) 233-4206, E-Mail: info@fresnooxygen.com, Web Site: www.fresnooxygen.com (9)

Fretz, Jr. William B., The Keystone Equities Group, Oaks, PA. Tel: (610) 415-6300, (800) 715-9905, FAX: (610) 415-6328, Web Site: www.keystoneequities.com (20)

Fretz, L. Keith, The Keystone Equities Group, Oaks, PA. Tel: (610) 415-6300, (800) 715-9905, FAX: (610) 415-6328, Web Site: www.keystoneequities.com (20)

Freund, Ronald, Midpoint National Inc, Kansas City, KS. Tel: (913) 362-7400, (800) 228-4321, FAX: (913) 362-7401, E-Mail: info@midpt.com, Web Site: www.midpointorderfulfillment.com (28)

Frevert, Mark C., Grand Circle Travel, Boston, MA. Tel: (617) 350-7500, (800) 959-0405, FAX: (617) 346-6030, Web Site: www.gct.com (19)

Frey, Edward, ArcelorMittal, Coatesville, PA. Tel: (610) 383-2000, FAX: (610) 383-5036, Web Site: www.arcelormittal.com (16)

Frey, Gerry, Avnet Inc, Phoenix, AZ. Tel: (480) 643-2000, FAX: (480) 643-7240, Web Site: www.avnet.com (16)

Frey, Robyn, BolchalkFReY Marketing, Tucson, AZ. Tel: (520) 745-8221, FAX: (520) 745-5540, E-Mail: info-mb@adwiz.com, Web Site: www.adwiz.com (35)

Frey, Scott, PossibleNOW Inc, Duluth, GA. Tel: (770) 255-1020, FAX: (770) 255-1025, Web Site: www.dncsolution.com (22)

Frey, Stephen, Disc Graphics Inc, Hauppauge, NY. Tel: (631) 234-1400, FAX: (631) 234-1460, E-Mail: info@discgraphics.com, Web Site: www. discgraphics.com (27)

Frid, Peter A., New Hampshire Public Television, Durham, NH. Tel: (603) 868-1100, E-Mail: themailbox@nhptv.org, Web Site: www.nhptv.org (32)

Friday Report, Garden City, NY. Tel: (516) 746-6700, FAX: (516) 294-8141 (43)

Friday, Denise S., AMA Insurance Agency Inc, Chicago, IL. Tel: (312) 464-2425, (800) 458-5736, FAX: (312) 419-5096, Web Site: www.amainsure.com (15)

Fried-Cassorla Communications Inc, Melrose Park, PA. Tel: (215) 635-5189, FAX: (215) 635-0461, E-Mail: albert@fried-cas.com, Web Site: www.fried-cas. com (35)

Fried-Cassorla, Albert, Fried-Cassorla Communications Inc, Melrose Park, PA. Tel: (215) 635-5189, FAX: (215) 635-0461, E-Mail: albert@fried-cas.com, Web Site: www.fried-cas.com (35)

Friedenberg, Michael, IDG Enterprise, Framingham, MA. Tel: (508) 872-0080, Web Site: www. idgenterprise.com (17)

Friedhoff, Ed, Flex Products, Carlstadt, NJ. Tel: (636) 282-6800, (800) 526-6273, FAX: (6361) 282-6888, E-Mail: info@flex-products.com, Web Site: www. flex-products.com (34)

Friedland, Jim, McMaster-Carr Supply Co (HQ), Elmhurst, IL. Tel: (630) 834-9600, FAX: (630) 834-9427, E-Mail: chi.sales@mcmaster.com, Web Site: www.mcmaster.com (9)

Friedlander, David H., Vitamin Power Inc, Hauppauge, NY. Tel: (516) 378-0900, (800) 645-6567, FAX: (631) 273-4394, E-Mail: contactus@vitaminpower. com, Web Site: www.vitaminpower.com (7)

Friedlander, Edward, Vitamin Power Inc, Hauppauge, NY. Tel: (516) 378-0900, (800) 645-6567, FAX: (631) 273-4394, E-Mail: contactus@vitaminpower. com, Web Site: www.vitaminpower.com (7)

A I Friedman Inc, New York, NY. Tel: (212) 243-9000, (800) 204-6352, FAX: (212) 929-7320, Web Site: www.aifriedman.com (10)

Jonathan Friedman, Hollywood, FL. Tel: (954) 416-3419 (20)

Friedman Marketing Svcs, Harrison, NY. Tel: (914) 698-0800, FAX: (914) 698-0485, E-Mail: paula. wynne@gfk.com, Web Site: www.friedmanmktg. com (30)

Friedman Rafferty, Barri, Ketchum, New York, NY. Tel: (646) 935-3900, Web Site: www.ketchum.com (35)

Friedman, Donald R., CA Inc, Islandia, NY. Tel: (800) 225-5224, FAX: (631) 342-3300, E-Mail: info@ca. com, Web Site: www.ca.com (16)

Friedman, Jacki, Furman Roth Advertising, New York, NY. Tel: (212) 687-2300, FAX: (212) 687-0858, E-Mail: eroth@furmanroth.com, Web Site: www. furmanroth.com (35)

Friedman, Jay, Goodway Group, Jenkintown, PA. Tel: (626) 355-7800, E-Mail: info@goodwaygroup.com, Web Site: goodwaygroup.com (35)

Friedman, Ken, Gates Corp, Denver, CO. Tel: (303) 744-1911, FAX: (303) 744-4000, Web Site: www. gates.com (9)

Friedman, Laura, Homeowners Marketing Services Inc, North Hollywood, CA. Tel: (888) 743-3037, E-Mail: inquiry@homeownersmarketingservices.com, Web Site: www.homeownersmarketingservices.com (23)

Friedman, Mark, SoundBite Communications, Bedford, MA. Tel: (877) SOUNDBITE, Web Site: www. soundbite.com (32)

Friedman, Marvin, Better Health Fitness, Brooklyn, NY. Tel: (718) 436-4693, FAX: (718) 854-3381, Web Site: www.betterhealthfitness.com (11)

Friedman, Scott, SWB&R Inc, Bethlehem, PA. Tel: (610) 866-0611, (877) 377-9286, FAX: (610) 866-8650, E-Mail: swbr@swbrinc.com, Web Site: www. swbrinc.com (35)

Friedman, Stephen, Pace University, New York, NY. Tel: (212) 346-1781, (866) 722-3338, FAX: (212) 346-1821, Web Site: www.pace.edu (16)

Friedman-Steele, Julie, World Future Society, Chicago, IL. Tel: (301) 656-8274, (800) 989-8274, FAX: (301) 951-0394, E-Mail: info@wfs.org, Web Site: www.wfs.org (1)

Friedrich, Dennis, Brookfield Office Properties, New York, NY. Tel: (212) 417-7000, FAX: (212) 417-7214, Web Site: brookfieldofficeproperties.com (16)

Friend, David, WLNY-TV 10/55, Melville, NY. Tel: (631) 777-8855, Web Site: newyork.cbslocal.com/ station/wlny (32)

Friend, Michael, Catalyst Inc, Providence, RI. Tel: (401) 732-1886, FAX: (401) 732-5528, Web Site: www.catalystb2b.com (35)

Friendly, Ian R., The Pillsbury Co, Minneapolis, MN. Tel: (763) 764-7600, (800) 248-7310, FAX: (763) 764-8330, Web Site: www.pillsbury.com (16)

Pat Friesen & Co LLC, Leawood, KS. Tel: (913) 341-1211, FAX: (913) 341-4343, Web Site: www. patfriesen.com (36)

Friesen, Patricia, Pat Friesen & Co LLC, Leawood, KS. Tel: (913) 341-1211, FAX: (913) 341-4343, Web Site: www.patfriesen.com (36)

Friesen, Rod, Truitt Brothers Inc, Salem, OR. Tel: (503) 362-3674, (800) 547-8712, FAX: (503) 588-2868, E-Mail: truittbrothers@truittbros.com, Web Site: www.truittbros.com (16)

Frigon, Lloyd, Stonwurks, Eden Prairie, MN. Tel: (785) 526-7847, (888) 884-7881, FAX: (785) 526-7841, E-Mail: stonwurks@stonwurks.com, Web Site: www.stonwurks.com (16)

Frigstad, David, Frost & Sullivan Inc, Mountain View, CA. Tel: (877) 463-7678, (877) 690-3329, FAX: (877) 690-3329, E-Mail: myfrost@frost.com, Web Site: www.frost.com (30)

Frisen, Lisa, Winnipeg Art Gallery, Winnipeg, MB Canada. Tel: (204) 786-6641, FAX: (204) 788-4998, E-Mail: inquiries@wag.mb.ca, Web Site: www.wag. ca (1)

Frishman, P.J., RocketWear, New York, NY. Tel: (212) 977-9227, E-Mail: info@rocketwear.com, Web Site: www.rocketwear.net (2)

Frisk, Patrik, Timberland LLC, Stratham, NH. Tel: (603) 772-9500, (888) 802-9947, Web Site: www. timberland.com (16)

Frith, Scott, Lawn Doctor Inc, Holmdel, NJ. Tel: (732) 946-0029, (800) 631-5660, FAX: (732) 946-9089, Web Site: www.lawndoctor.com (16)

Frito-Lay, Plano, TX. Tel: (972) 334-7000, (800) 352-4477, FAX: (972) 334-2019, Web Site: www. fritolay.com (16)

Fritz, Mike, Estes Industries, Penrose, CO. Tel: (719) 372-6565, FAX: (719) 372-3419, Web Site: www. estesrockets.com (11)

FRM Inc, Garden City, NY. Tel: (516) 746-6700, FAX: (516) 294-8141 (43)

Froese, Garth, PacificEast, Beaverton, OR. Tel: (800) 665-8400, Web Site: www.pacificeast.com (22)

Frog Tool Co Ltd, Dixon, IL. Tel: (815) 288-3811, E-Mail: info@frogwoodtools.com, Web Site: www. frogwoodtools.com (11)

Frohlich, Kate, Trumble Greetings, Boulder, CO. Tel: (800) 525-0656, FAX: (303) 530-5124, E-Mail: info@leanintree.com, Web Site: www.leanintree. com (6)

Frojd, Tim, Martin Williams Advertising, Minneapolis, MN. Tel: (612) 342-9739, FAX: (612) 342-9700, Web Site: www.martinwilliams.com (35)

Fromm, Allan, AnSer Services, Green Bay, WI. Tel: (920) 490-7000, (800) 723-0000, E-Mail: allanf@ anser.com, Web Site: www.anser.com (29)

Fromm, Dave, Barkley, Kansas City, MO. Tel: (816) 842-1500, E-Mail: 411@barkleyus.com, Web Site: www.barkleyus.com (35)

Fromm, Nicole, Association for Audience Marketing Professionals (AAMP), North Hollywood, CA. Tel: (310) 323-7220, FAX: (310) 323-7231, E-Mail: mjordan@espcomp.com, Web Site: www.wfma.org (40)

Fromm, Ronald, Brown Shoe Co, Saint Louis, MO. Tel: (314) 854-4000, FAX: (314) 854-4274, Web Site: www.brownshoe.com (16)

Front Porch Inc, Sonora, CA. Tel: (209) 288-5500, (800) 728-1464, Web Site: www.frontporch.com (35)

Frontier Communications Corp, Stamford, CT. Tel: (203) 614-5600, Web Site: www.frontier.com (29)

Frontier Natural Products Co-op, Norway, IA. Tel: (800) 669-3275, FAX: (800) 717-4372, E-Mail: info@frontiercoop.com, Web Site: www. frontiercoop.com (7)

Frost & Sullivan Inc, Mountain View, CA. Tel: (877) 463-7678, (877) 690-3329, FAX: (877) 690-3329, E-Mail: myfrost@frost.com, Web Site: www.frost. com (30)

Frost Bank, San Antonio, TX. Tel: (210) 220-4011, Web Site: www.frostbank.com (14)

Frost, JB, Coleman Frost LLP, Santa Monica, CA. Tel: (310) 576-7312, Web Site: www.colemanfrost.com (20)

Frost, Tony, National Enquirer, New York, NY. Tel: (212) 545-4800, Web Site: www.nationalenquirer. com (17)

Fruechte, Christine, Colle+McVoy, Minneapolis, MN. Tel: (612) 305-6000, FAX: (612) 305-6500, E-Mail: info@collemcvoy.com, Web Site: www. collemcvoy.com (35)

Frustieri, Jim, DataBridge Marketing Systems Corp, Montvale, NJ. Tel: (201) 690-6319, Web Site: www. databridgemarketing .com (22)

Fruth, Steve, Fostoria Industries Inc, Johnson City, TN. Tel: (419) 435-9201, (800) 495-4525, FAX: (419) 435-0842, E-Mail: email@fostoriaindustries.com, Web Site: www.fostoriaindustries.com (9)

Fry Communications Inc, Mechanicsburg, PA. Tel: (717) 766-0211, (800) 334-1429, FAX: (717) 691-0341, Web Site: www.frycomm.com (27)

Fry Consultants Inc, Atlanta, GA. Tel: (770) 226-8888, FAX: (770) 226-8899, E-Mail: lynesmith@ fryconsultants.com, Web Site: www.fryconsultants. com (30)

Fry, Carl, Craft-Diston Industries, Wichita, KS. Tel: (316) 838-4291, (800) 835-0028, FAX: (316) 838-8502, Web Site: www.craftdiston.com (16)

Fry, Jacki, Jon-Don, Roselle, IL. Tel: (630) 893-4747, (800) 556-6366, FAX: (888) 344-6878, Web Site: www.jondon.com (34)

Fryer, William R., SBDP Corp, Cincinnati, OH. Tel: (513) 871-7019, FAX: (513) 871-0134, E-Mail: info@sbdp.com, Web Site: www.sbdp.com (22)

Fucci, Ralph, Vanguard Direct, New York, NY. Tel: (212) 736-0770, FAX: (212) 736-8305, Web Site: www.vanguarddirect.com (35)

Fuchs, Brooke, Greater Public, Minneapolis, MN. Tel: (612) 677-1505, (888) 454-2314, Web Site: www.deiworksite.org (1)

Fuchs, Steve, True North Inc, New York, NY. Tel: (212) 557-4202, Web Site: truenorthinc.com (35)

Fucich, Mark, Tyco Valves & Controls, Houston, TX. Tel: (713) 986-4665, (800) 343-0990, FAX: (713) 937-5466, Web Site: www.tycovalves.com (16)

Fuersich, Lawrence, Visual Reference Publications, New York, NY. Tel: (212) 279-7000, (800) 251-4545, FAX: (212) 279-7014 (17)

Fugate, Lisa, First Data Corp, Greenwood Village, CO. Tel: (303) 488-8000, (800) 735-3362, Web Site: www.firstdata.com (28)

Fugiel, Dave, Nimlok, Niles, IL. Tel: (847) 647-1012, (800) 233-8870, FAX: (847) 647-2044, E-Mail: info@nimlok.com, Web Site: www.nimlok.com (16)

Fuguitt, Gayle, Advertising Research Foundation, New York, NY. Tel: (212) 751-5656, FAX: (212) 319-5265, E-Mail: info@thearf.org, Web Site: www.thearf.org (40)

Fuguitt, Gayle, ARF Events, New York, NY. Tel: (212) 751-5656, FAX: (212) 319-5265, E-Mail: info@theARF.org, Web Site: theARF.org (42)

Fujifilm Holdings America Corp, Valhalla, NY. Tel: (914) 789-8100, (800) 755-3854, FAX: (914) 789-8295, Web Site: www.fujifilmusa.com (16)

Fujii Communications Inc, Lincolnwood, IL. Tel: (847) 677-0542, FAX: (847) 677-0523, E-Mail: fci@fujiicommunications.com, Web Site: www.fujiicommunications.com (35)

Fujii Falcone, Laurie, Fujii Communications Inc, Lincolnwood, IL. Tel: (847) 677-0542, FAX: (847) 677-0523, E-Mail: fci@fujiicommunications.com, Web Site: www.fujiicommunications.com (35)

Fujii, Ted, Mark James & Associates Inc, Oswego, IL. Tel: (630) 548-8100, FAX: (630) 548-6107, E-Mail: info@markjamesassociates.com, Web Site: www.markjamesassociates.com/contact.html (16)

Fujisankei Communications International Inc, New York, NY. Tel: (212) 753-8100, FAX: (212) 702-0420, Web Site: www.fujisankei.com (32)

Fujita, Victor, IMC Direct, Honolulu, HI. Tel: (808) 545-1680, FAX: (808) 528-4293, E-Mail: vfujita@imcdm.com (35)

Fujitsu America Inc, Sunnyvale, CA. Tel: (408) 746-6000, (800) 831-3183, FAX: (408) 992-2674, E-Mail: solutions@us.fujitsu.com, Web Site: www.fujitsu.com (22)

Fujitsu Transaction Solutions Inc, Richardson, TX. Tel: (972) 963-2300, (800) 340-4425, Web Site: www.fujitsu.com (16)

Fukagawa, Mikako, Potpourri Group Inc, North Billerica, MA. Tel: (978) 256-4100, FAX: (978) 256-1961/0344, Web Site: www.potpourrigroup.com (6)

Fukasawa, Kenji, Nihon Keizai Shimbun America Inc, New York, NY. Tel: (212) 261-6230, FAX: (212) 261-6239, Web Site: www.nikkeius.com (17)

Fulcrum, New York, NY. Tel: (212) 651-7000, (888) 245-9450 (22)

Fulcrum Publishing, Golden, CO. Tel: (303) 277-1623, (800) 992-2908, FAX: (303) 279-7111, Web Site: www.fulcrum-books.com (17)

Fulfillment Express Inc, Pico Rivera, CA. Tel: (562) 948-4400, (800) 700-9295, FAX: (562) 948-4459, E-Mail: information@fex.com, Web Site: www.fex.com (28)

Fulfillment Plus Inc, Holtsville, NY. Tel: (631) 758-8300, FAX: (631) 758-8360, E-Mail: jeff.ehrlich@fulfillmentplusny.com, Web Site: www.fulfillmentplusny.com (28)

The Fuller Brush Co, Great Bend, KS. Tel: (800) 522-0499, FAX: (620) 792-1906, E-Mail: custom@fuller.com, Web Site: www.fuller.com (5)

The Fuller Theological Seminary, Pasadena, CA. Tel: (626) 584-5200, (800) 235-2222, FAX: (626) 584-5449, Web Site: www.fuller.edu (16)

Fuller, Craig, Aircraft Owners & Pilots Association, Frederick, MD. Tel: (301) 695-2000, (800) 872-2672, FAX: (301) 695-2375, E-Mail: aopahq@aopa.org, Web Site: www.aopa.org (1)

Fuller, Liz, Gard Communications, Portland, OR. Tel: (503) 221-0100, (800) 800-7132, E-Mail: lfuller@gardcommunications.com, Web Site: gardcommunications.com (35)

Fuller, Shawna, Gift Services Inc, Vancouver, WA. Tel: (800) 379-4065, FAX: (360) 699-0597, E-Mail: corpsales@gifttree.com, Web Site: www.gifttree.com (6)

Fullington, Robert, LOTSolutions, Jacksonville, FL. Tel: (888) 784-3539, Web Site: www.lotsolutions.com (14)

Fulton, Sharon, Travelclick, Schaumburg, IL. Tel: (847) 585-5016 (19)

Funasaki, Mark, Fred Meyer Jewelers Inc, Portland, OR. Tel: (503) 232-8844, (800) 457-5977, FAX: (503) 797-7616, Web Site: www.fredmeyerjewelers.com (16)

Funches, Venessa, Auburn University at Montgomery, Montgomery, AL. Tel: (334) 244-3621, (800) 227-2649, FAX: (334) 244-3826, Web Site: www.aum.edu (41)

Fund for Public Interest Research, Washington, DC. Tel: (202) 546-3965, Web Site: www.ffpir.org (1)

Fund, Ken, Creative Publishing International, Minneapolis, MN. Tel: (612) 344-8100, FAX: (612) 344-8691, E-Mail: sales@creativepub.com, Web Site: www.creativepub.com (17)

Fund, Ken, Quayside Publishing Group, Minneapolis, MN. Tel: (612) 344-8100, FAX: (612) 344-8691, Web Site: www.quaysidepub.com (17)

Fundamental Photographs, New York, NY. Tel: (212) 473-5770, FAX: (212) 228-5059, E-Mail: mail@fphoto.com, Web Site: www.fphoto.com (38)

Fundamentals Co Inc, Bristol, VA. Tel: (800) 303-8861, (800) 303-8861 (Fax) (1)

FunME Events, Dekalb, IL. Tel: (800) 386-6321, FAX: (815) 787-3100, E-Mail: funMEevents@aol.com, Web Site: www.funMEevents.com (20)

Fuqua, Mike, SIGMA Marketing Group LLC, Rochester, NY. Tel: (585) 473-7300, (888) 277-9837, FAX: (585) 473-0332, E-Mail: mbush@sigmamarketing.com, Web Site: www.sigmamarketing.com; www.jthgearanalytics.com (Blog) (20)

Furbush, III Douglas D., Gallagher Affinity, Lakewood Ranch, FL. Tel: (941) 757-1445, (888) 437-6611, Web Site: www.gallagher-affinity.com (15)

Fureman, Brandy, Epilepsy Foundation, Landover, MD. Tel: (800) 332-1000, E-Mail: contactus@efa.org, Web Site: www.efa.org (1)

Furgiuele & Co Inc, Crestwood, NY. Tel: (914) 793-0045, FAX: (914) 779-6447, E-Mail: fci@fcidms.com, Web Site: www.fcidms.com (20)

Furgiuele, Joseph, Furgiuele & Co Inc, Crestwood, NY. Tel: (914) 793-0045, FAX: (914) 779-6447, E-Mail: fci@fcidms.com, Web Site: www.fcidms.com (20)

Furlo, Paul, Morley Companies, Saginaw, MI. Tel: (989) 791-2550, (800) 336-5554, FAX: (800) 426-6753, Web Site: www.morleynet.com (33)

Furlong-Weber, Maureen, The Peter A Tobin College of Business, Jamaica, NY. Tel: (718) 990-2600, FAX: (718) 990-1868, Web Site: www.stjohns.edu (41)

Alan Furman & Co, Rockville, MD. Tel: (202) 397-8463, (800) 654-7184, FAX: (301) 881-0810, E-Mail: watches@alanfurman.com, Web Site: www.alanfurman.com (2)

Furman Roth Advertising, New York, NY. Tel: (212) 687-2300, FAX: (212) 687-0858, E-Mail: eroth@furmanroth.com, Web Site: www.furmanroth.com (35)

Furman, Alan, Alan Furman & Co, Rockville, MD. Tel: (202) 397-8463, (800) 654-7184, FAX: (301) 881-0810, E-Mail: watches@alanfurman.com, Web Site: www.alanfurman.com (2)

Furnia, Joseph, Intelitec, Granby, MA. Tel: (413) 467-9476, E-Mail: info@intelitec.com, Web Site: intelitec.com (23)

Furrier, Jack, Desert Rat Truck Centers, Tucson, AZ. Tel: (520) 790-8502, (866) 444-5337, FAX: (520) 750-1918, Web Site: www.desertrat.com (12)

Furrier, Mike, Desert Rat Truck Centers, Tucson, AZ. Tel: (520) 790-8502, (866) 444-5337, FAX: (520) 750-1918, Web Site: www.desertrat.com (12)

Eduardo Fuss, Santa Fe, NM. Tel: (505) 424-0304, FAX: (505) 424-0602 (37)

Fuss, Eduardo, Eduardo Fuss, Santa Fe, NM. Tel: (505) 424-0304, FAX: (505) 424-0602 (37)

G

G&A Marketing, Cincinnati, OH. Tel: (800) 688-1370, FAX: (513) 688-1570, E-Mail: info@gamarketing.com, Web Site: www.gamarketing.com (35)

G&S Fruit Packers LLC, Weirsdale, FL. Tel: (352) 821-2251, (800) 949-9074, FAX: (352) 821-0278, E-Mail: info@gsfruitpackers.com, Web Site: www.gsfruitpackers.com (16)

G H Bass & Co, New York, NY. Tel: (212) 381-3900, FAX: (212) 381-3950, E-Mail: help@ghbass.com, Web Site: www.ghbass.com (16)

G-Neil Direct Mail, Sunrise, FL. Tel: (800) 999-9111, FAX: (954) 851-1264, E-Mail: tcs@gneil.com, Web Site: www.gneil.com (10)

G-Plex Direct Mail, Holtsville, NY. Tel: (631) 447-9500, FAX: 631-447-9518, Web Site: www.g-plex.net (28)

GBE Plus, Hartford, CT. Tel: (860) 727-9100, (800) 842-0139, FAX: (860) 527-6041, Web Site: www.gbeplus.com (26)

GBH Communications, Monrovia, CA. Tel: (818) 246-9900, (800) 222-5424, FAX: (818) 246-5850, E-Mail: customerservice@gbh.com, Web Site: www.gbh.com (3)

GC Services, Houston, TX. Tel: (713) 777-4441, FAX: (713) 776-6535, E-Mail: marketing.communications@gcserv.com, Web Site: www.gcserv.com (20)

GCC Printers, Bedford, MA. Tel: (781) 275-5800, (800) 422-7777, FAX: (781) 275-1115, (800) 442-2329, E-Mail: sales@gccprinters.com, Web Site: www.gcctech.com (10)

GE Canada, Mississauga, ON Canada. Tel: (905) 858-5100, Web Site: www.ge.com/canada (9)

GE Lighting North America, Cleveland, OH. Tel: (216) 266-2121, FAX: (216) 266-2930, Web Site: www.gelighting.com/na (16)

GE Money, Alpharetta, GA. Tel: (678) 518-2403 (14)

GE Partnership Marketing Group, Schaumburg, IL. Tel: (847) 605-3000, FAX: (847) 605-3044, Web Site: www.gepmg.com (14)

GEICO Direct, Washington, DC. Tel: (301) 986-2842, (800) 841-3000, FAX: (301) 986-2068, Web Site: www.geico.com (15)

GG Direct, Portland, ME. Tel: (207) 772-0414, FAX: (207) 871-1444, E-Mail: data@ggdirect.com, Web Site: www.ggdirect.com (21)

GHW Associates, Lake Suzy, FL. Tel: (941) 625-4293, E-Mail: info@ghw-associates.com, Web Site: www.ghw-associates.com (35)

GIE Corporation, Columbus, OH. Tel: (614) 888-5850, Web Site: www.giecorporation.net (33)

GKV, Baltimore, MD. Tel: (410) 539-5400, FAX: (410) 234-2441, E-Mail: newbusiness@gkv.com, Web Site: gvk.com (35)

GLM Communications, New York, NY. Tel: (212) 929-1300, FAX: (212) 929-9574, E-Mail: info@glmcommunications.com, Web Site: www.glmcommunications.com (31)

GM Customer Relationship Management, Detroit, MI. Tel: (313) 665-6605, Web Site: www.gm.com (35)

GMC Software Technology Inc, Charlestown, MA. Tel: (800) 250-1850, FAX: (617) 241-5665, Web Site: www.gmc.net (22)

GMG Productions Inc, Roslyn, NY. Tel: (516) 482-0093, FAX: (516) 482-0097, Web Site: www.gmgproductions.com (3)

GMI Distribution, Somerset, NJ. Tel: (732) 846-4800, FAX: (732) 846-4709, E-Mail: keith@gmidistribution.com, Web Site: www.gmidistribution.com (28)

GN Netcom, Nashua, NH. Tel: (603) 598-1100, (800) 345-8639, FAX: (603) 598-1122, Web Site: www.jabra.com (16)

The GRI Marketing Group Inc, Trumbull, CT. Tel: (203) 261-3337, FAX: (203) 261-1113, E-Mail: bsnider@gridirect.com, Web Site: www.gridirect.com (35)

GRP Funding LLC, Springfield, MA. Tel: (877) 571-7999, E-Mail: info@grpfunding.com, Web Site: www.grpfunding.com (14)

GS&F, Nashville, TN. Tel: (615) 385-1100, (800) 241-3325, FAX: (615) 783-0500, E-Mail: biz@gsandf.com, Web Site: www.gsandf.com (35)

GS Direct Inc, Eden Prairie, MN. Tel: (952) 942-6115, (800) 234-3729, FAX: (952) 942-0216, Web Site: www.gsdirect.net (34)

GS Marketing, Houston, TX. Tel: (713) 580-3900, FAX: (713) 580-5935, E-Mail: contactus@gsmarketing.com, Web Site: www.gsmarketing.com (21)

GSD&M, Austin, TX. Tel: (512) 242-4736, Web Site: www.gsdm.com (35)

GTM Sportswear, Manhattan, KS. Tel: (877) 569-3095, Web Site: www.gtmsportswear.com (2)

GWR Wealth Management, Omaha, NE. Tel: (402) 452-3737, FAX: (402) 452-3676, Web Site: www.gwrwealth.com (14)

GXS Corp, Gaithersburg, MD. Tel: (301) 340-4000, (800) 560-4347, FAX: (301) 340-5299, Web Site: www.gxs.com (30)

GA Wright Sales Inc, Denver, CO. Tel: (303) 333-4453, FAX: (303) 393-5320, E-Mail: info@gawright.com, Web Site: www.gawrightsales.com (35)

Gabler, Joe, Major Brands Group, Minneapolis, MN. Tel: (763) 767-6800, FAX: (763) 767-1264, E-Mail: mbgcustomerservice@mrgmn.com, Web Site: www.mrgrp.com (31)

Gabor, Lisa, American Express Publishing Corp, New York, NY. Tel: (212) 382-5600, (888) 461-6180, FAX: (212) 827-6496, E-Mail: aepc@custmersvc.com, Web Site: www.amexpub.com (17)

Gabriel Group, Earth City, MO. Tel: (314) 743-5700, FAX: (314) 743-5800, E-Mail: sales@gabrielgr.com, Web Site: gabrielgr.com (21)

Gabrielson, Charles, USA Weekend, New York, NY. Tel: (800) 487-4956, FAX: (703) 854-2122, Web Site: www.usaweekend.com (31)

Gaches, Greg, Cable Connection, Fremont, CA. Tel: (510) 249-9000, E-Mail: cables4u@cable-connection.com, Web Site: www.cable-connection.com (3)

Gaco Western Inc, Seattle, WA. Tel: (206) 575-0450, (800) 456-4226, FAX: (206) 575-0587, E-Mail: info@gaco.com, Web Site: www.gaco.com (16)

Gadbois, Greg, Service Net Warranty LLC, Jeffersonville, IN. Tel: (812) 258-4700, (812) 258-4722, FAX: (812) 258-4693, Web Site: www.servicenet.com (22)

Gadbut, Albert, AcquireWEB Inc, Foster City, CA. Tel: (650) 212-2233, FAX: (650) 212-2234, E-Mail: sales@aquireweb.com, Web Site: www.acquireWEB.com (22)

Gaddis, Evan R., National Electrical Manufacturers Association (NEMA), Rosslyn, VA. Tel: (703) 841-3200, FAX: (703) 841-5900, E-Mail: communications@nema.org, Web Site: www.nema.org (34)

Gade, Chris, Mayo Clinic, Rochester, MN. Tel: (507) 284-2511, Web Site: www.mayoclinic.org (17)

Gady, Wendy, Pohaku Inc, Kaneohe, HI. Tel: (319) 653-2569, Web Site: www.gopohaku.com (20)

GaelSong, Seattle, WA. Tel: (206) 526-8350, Web Site: www.gaelsong.com (6)

Gaffer, Kevin, Renkim Corp, Southgate, MI. Tel: (734) 374-8300, FAX: (734) 374-9165, E-Mail: info@renkim.com, Web Site: www.renkim.com (22)

Gaffney, Julie, The Arizona Direct Marketing Association, Scottsdale, AZ. Tel: (480) 970-8643, FAX: (480) 893-1157, E-Mail: julie@brownies.com, Web Site: www.azdma.org (40)

Gaffney, Michael, Wiland Direct, Longmont, CO. Tel: (303) 485-8686, Web Site: www.wilanddirect.com (22)

Gage, Minneapolis, MN. Tel: (763) 595-3800, FAX: (763) 595-5845, Web Site: www.gage.com (35)

Gagliano, Anthony, St Joseph Communications, Concord, ON Canada. Tel: (905) 660-3111, FAX: (905) 669-1972, Web Site: www.stjoseph.com (27)

Gagliardi, Leo, A&R Mailing Machine Inc, East Hartford, CT. Tel: (860) 290-6640, FAX: (860) 290-6644, E-Mail: info@a-r-machine.com, Web Site: a-r-machine.com (34)

Gagliardo, Coleen, Gaylord Brothers, Syracuse, NY. Tel: (315) 634-8440, Web Site: www.gaylord.com (16)

Gagne, Gaetan, L'Entraide Assurance, Quebec, QC Canada. Tel: (418) 658-0663, FAX: (418) 658-5065, E-Mail: service@lentraide.com, Web Site: www.lentraide.com (15)

Gagne, Patrick, Komunik, Montreal, QC Canada. Tel: (514) 904-0710, Web Site: www.komunik.com (20)

Gagnon, Bodie, LinkShare Corp, New York, NY. Tel: (646) 943-8200, FAX: (646) 943-8204, Web Site: www.linkshare.com (32)

Gagnon, Donald, AAA Mid-Atlantic Insurance Groups, Wilmington, DE. Tel: (302) 299-4700, (800) 451-5921, FAX: (215) 864-5486, Web Site: www.aaamidatlantic.com (15)

Gagnon, Rik, White Cap Wholesale Contractors Supplies, Costa Mesa, CA. Tel: (800) 944-8322, FAX: (866) 791-8396, E-Mail: customerservice@whitecap.com, Web Site: www.whitecapdirect.com (16)

Gahleiter, Michael, Hilti North America, Tulsa, OK. Tel: (866) 445-8827, FAX: (800) 879-7000, Web Site: www.hilti.com (34)

Gaiam Inc, Boulder, CO. Tel: (877) 989-6321, Web Site: life.gaiam.com (9)

Gaier, Mark, RR Donnelley Response Marketing Services, Warrenville, IL. Tel: (630) 963-9494, (800) 722-9001, FAX: (630) 322-6270, Web Site: www.rms.rrd.com (31)

Gaige, Marianne W., Cathedral Corp, Rome, NY. Tel: (315) 338-0021, (800) 698-0299, FAX: (315) 338-5874, E-Mail: sales@cathedralstewardship.com, Web Site: www.cathedralcorporation.com (21)

Gail, Shelley, Safian Communications Inc, Maplewood, NJ. Tel: (973) 378-3672, FAX: (973) 378-2456, E-Mail: gail.safian@safianhealth.com, Web Site: safianhealth.com (35)

Gaines, Tammy, The United Methodist Publishing House, Nashville, TN. Tel: (615) 749-6000, (800) 672-1789, FAX: (615) 749-6417, E-Mail: productsandservices@umpublishing.com, Web Site: www.umpublishing.com (17)

Gaiter, Jatrice Martel, Volunteers of America, Alexandria, VA. Tel: (703) 341-5000, (800) 899-0089, FAX: (703) 341-7000, E-Mail: info@voa.org, Web Site: www.voa.org (1)

Galanti, Lisa, Fitzgerald & CO, Atlanta, GA. Tel: (404) 504-6900, FAX: (404) 239-0548, E-Mail: dave.fitzgerald@fitzco.com, Web Site: www.fitzco.com (35)

Galantic, John, Chanel Inc, New York, NY. Tel: (212) 688-5055, (800) 550-0005, FAX: (212) 752-1851, Web Site: www.chanel.com (16)

Galanty & Co Inc, Santa Monica, CA. Tel: (310) 451-2525, FAX: (310) 451-5020, Web Site: www.galanty.com (35)

Galanty, Mark, Galanty & Co Inc, Santa Monica, CA. Tel: (310) 451-2525, FAX: (310) 451-5020, Web Site: www.galanty.com (35)

Galassi, Daniel, SP Express, Tempe, AZ. Tel: (866) 773-7363, E-Mail: info@spexpress.com, Web Site: www.spexpress.com (28)

Galassi, Jonathan, Farrar Straus & Giroux Inc, New York, NY. Tel: (212) 741-6900, Web Site: us.macmillan.com/fsg.aspx (17)

Galbraith, Robert, Union Switch & Signal Inc, Pittsburgh, PA. Tel: (412) 688-2400, (800) 351-1520, FAX: (412) 688-2399, Web Site: www.switch.com (16)

Galbreath, Diane, White Cap Wholesale Contractors Supplies, Costa Mesa, CA. Tel: (800) 944-8322, FAX: (866) 791-8396, E-Mail: customerservice@whitecap.com, Web Site: www.whitecapdirect.com (16)

Galbreath, Leslie, dgs Marketing Engineers, Fishers, IN. Tel: (317) 813-2222, FAX: (317) 813-2233, E-Mail: info@dgsmarketingengineers.com, Web Site: www.dgsmarketingengineers.com (35)

Gale, Farmington Hills, MI. Tel: (248) 699-4253, Web Site: www.gale.cengage.com (17)

Gale, Wayne, Stokes Seeds Inc, Buffalo, NY. Tel: (800) 396-9238, FAX: (800) 272-5560, E-Mail: stokes@stokeseeds.com, Web Site: www.stokeseeds.com (8)

Gale, William C., Cintas, Cincinnati, OH. Tel: (513) 459-1200, Web Site: www.cintas.com (16)

Galea, John A., Interval International, South Miami, FL. Tel: (305) 666-1884, (800) 468-3782, FAX: (305) 667-5321, Web Site: www.intervalworld.com (16)

Galen Williams Landscaping & Garden Design, East Hampton, NY. Tel: (631) 324-6220, FAX: (631) 329-3684 (16)

Galer, Mike, Amigo Mobility International Inc, Bridgeport, MI. Tel: (989) 777-0910, (800) 692-6446, FAX: (989) 777-8184, E-Mail: info@myamigo.com, Web Site: www.myamigo.com (16)

Galka, Chet, Datalogic Scanning, Eugene, OR. Tel: (800) 695-5700, FAX: (541) 345-7140, Web Site: www.scanning.datalogic.com (34)

Gallagher Affinity, Lakewood Ranch, FL. Tel: (941) 757-1445, (888) 437-6611, Web Site: www.gallagher-affinity.com (15)

Gallagher, Brian, United Way Worldwide, Alexandria, VA. Tel: (703) 836-7112, Web Site: www.unitedway.org (1)

Gallagher, Dan, Booyah! Online Advertising, Denver, CO. Tel: (303) 345-6100, (303) 345-6700, E-Mail: info@booyahadvertising.ocm, Web Site: www.booyahadvertising.com (35)

Gallagher, Dan, Comcast Spectacor LP, Philadelphia, PA. Tel: (215) 336-3600, (800) 298-4200, FAX: (215) 389-9518, E-Mail: info@comcast-spectacor.com, Web Site: www.comcast-spectacor.com (16)

Gallagher, Kevin, Body by Jake Global LLC, Los Angeles, CA. Tel: (310) 571-7101, FAX: (310) 571-7107, E-Mail: info@bodybyjake.com, Web Site: www.bodybyjake.com (16)

Gallagher, Patricia, Liberty Fund Inc, Indianapolis, IN. Tel: (317) 842-0880, Web Site: www.libertyfund.org (1)

Gallagher, R.F., Hampton Marketing Corp, Medford, NY. Tel: (516) 924-1335, (800) 229-1019, FAX: (516) 924-1669, Web Site: www.hamptonstamp.com (16)

Gallagher, Ronald T., Hampton Marketing Corp, Medford, NY. Tel: (516) 924-1335, (800) 229-1019, FAX: (516) 924-1669, Web Site: www.hamptonstamp.com (16)

Gallagher, Shay, The Bradford Group, Niles, IL. Tel: (847) 966-2770, FAX: (847) 581-8630, Web Site: www.collectiblestoday.com (16)

Gallagher, Steven, Hampton Marketing Corp, Medford, NY. Tel: (516) 924-1335, (800) 229-1019, FAX: (516) 924-1669, Web Site: www.hamptonstamp.com (16)

Gallagher, Thomas "Tom" J., American Radio Relay League, Newington, CT. Tel: (860) 594-0200, FAX: (860) 594-0259, Web Site: www.arrl.org (1)

Gallagher, Thomas P., Dairy Management Inc, Rosemont, IL. Tel: (847) 803-2000, FAX: (847) 803-2077, Web Site: www.nationaldairycouncil.org (1)

Gallaher, John, American Mailing Service Inc, Ashland, KY. Tel: (606) 329-2741, (800) 678-8384, FAX: (606) 325-8558, Web Site: www.thegallahergroup.com (28)

Gallaher, Stephanie, American Mailing Service Inc, Ashland, KY. Tel: (606) 329-2741, (800) 678-8384, FAX: (606) 325-8558, Web Site: www.thegallahergroup.com (28)

Gallaiford, Neal, Stephen Thomas, Toronto, ON Canada. Tel: (416) 690-8801, FAX: (416) 690-7256, E-Mail: mail@stephenthomas.ca, Web Site: www.stephenthomas.ca (1)

Gallarneau, Cliff, Lion Apparel, Dayton, OH. Tel: (937) 898-1949, (800) 548-6614, FAX: (937) 913-5667, Web Site: www.lionprotects.com (2)

Gallatin, David, Mailing Specialists Inc, Greensburg, PA. Tel: (724) 832-3840, (888) 216-1056, FAX: (724) 832-8419, E-Mail: sales@mailmsi.com, Web Site: www.mailmsi.com (28)

Gallego, Fernando, Lladro USA Inc, Moonachie, NJ. Tel: (201) 807-1177, (800) 634-9088, FAX: (201) 807-1293, E-Mail: customer-services@us.lladro.com, Web Site: www.lladro.com (16)

Galler, Rosie, Rock-Tred Corp, Waukegan, IL. Tel: (847) 673-8200, (800) 762-8733, FAX: (847) 679-6665, Web Site: www.rocktred.com (9)

Gallery of Cats, Valencia, CA. Tel: (818) 782-6264, E-Mail: helpdesk@galleryofcats.com, Web Site: www.galleryofcats.com (6)

The Gallery Shop, Buffalo, NY. Tel: (716) 882-8700 X258, FAX: (716) 882-1958, E-Mail: gallshop@albrightknox.org, Web Site: www.albrightknox.org (6)

Gallimore, Dave, Encore Marketing International, Lanham, MD. Tel: (301) 459-8020, (800) 846-9398, FAX: (301) 731-0525, E-Mail: customerservice@encoremarketing.com, Web Site: www.encoremarketing.com (16)

Galling, Debbie, SA-SO/Time Wise, Arlington, TX. Tel: (972) 641-4911, (800) 523-8060, FAX: (972) 660-5684, E-Mail: info@sa-so.com, Web Site: www.sa-so.com (33)

Gallion, Karen, Sunset Magazine, Menlo Park, CA. Tel: (650) 321-3600, FAX: (650) 328-6215 (17)

Diane Gallo Associates, Gilbertsville, NY. Tel: (607) 783-2386, E-Mail: dgallo@stny.rr.com, Web Site: www.dianegallo.com (39)

Gallo, Anthony, Association for Postal Commerce, Alexandria, VA. Tel: (703) 524-0096, FAX: (703) 524-1871, Web Site: www.postcom.org (40)

Gallo, Diane, Diane Gallo Associates, Gilbertsville, NY. Tel: (607) 783-2386, E-Mail: dgallo@stny.rr.com, Web Site: www.dianegallo.com (39)

Gallo, Mark, Magellan's Catalog, Chelmsford, MA. Tel: (800) 450-7715, FAX: (800) 866-3235, E-Mail: sales@magellans.com, Web Site: www.magellans.com (5)

Galloway Farms, Miami, FL. Tel: (305) 274-7472, FAX: (305) 274-3233, E-Mail: galloway_inc@bellsouth.net, Web Site: www.gallowayfarm.com (8)

Galloway Research Service, San Antonio, TX. Tel: (210) 734-4346, FAX: (210) 732-4500, E-Mail: info@gallowayresearch.com, Web Site: www.gallowayresearch.com (30)

Galloway, Maryann, The Virginia Diner Inc, Wakefield, VA. Tel: (888) 823-4637, E-Mail: vadiner@vadiner.com, Web Site: www.vadiner.com (4)

Gall's Inc, Lexington, KY. Tel: (859) 266-7227, (800) 477-7766, FAX: (859) 268-5954, E-Mail: helpdesk@galls.com, Web Site: www.galls.com (16)

Gallup Inter-Tribal Indian Ceremonial, Gallup, NM. Tel: (505) 863-3896, E-Mail: cermonial@qwestoffice.net, Web Site: www.theceremonial.com (1)

Galonek, Brian A., All Star Premium Products Inc, Fiskdale, MA. Tel: (800) 526-8629, E-Mail: info@incentiveusa.com, Web Site: www.incentiveusa.com (33)

Galonek, Sr Ed, All Star Premium Products Inc, Fiskdale, MA. Tel: (800) 526-8629, E-Mail: info@incentiveusa.com, Web Site: www.incentiveusa.com (33)

Galterio, Clare, Empire City Casino at Yonkers Raceway, Yonkers, NY. Tel: (914) 968-4200, Web Site: www.empirecitygaming.com (19)

Jack Galub, New York, NY. Tel: (212) 737-9013 (39)

Galub, Jack, Jack Galub, New York, NY. Tel: (212) 737-9013 (39)

Galvan, Mauricio, Dexposito & Partners, New York, NY. Tel: (646) 747-8800, Web Site: newamericanagency.com (35)

Galveston Bay Foundation, Webster, TX. Tel: (281) 332-3381, Web Site: www.galvbay.org (1)

Galvin, John, Collette Vacations, Pawtucket, RI. Tel: (401) 728-3805, FAX: (401) 727-9014, E-Mail: czesk@collettetours.com, Web Site: www.collettevacations.com (19)

Gamache, Larry, CARFAX Inc, Centreville, VA. Tel: (703) 934-2664, Web Site: www.carfax.com (12)

Gambill, Brad, Tyco Electronics Corp, Berwyn, PA. Tel: (610) 893-9800, Web Site: www.te.com (16)

Gamble, Richard G., Brookfield Zoo, Brookfield, IL. Tel: (708) 485-0263, (800) 201-0784, FAX: (708) 485-3532, Web Site: www.brookfieldzoo.org (1)

Gambro Inc, Lakewood, CO. Tel: (303) 232-6800, (800) 525-2623, FAX: (303) 222-6810, Web Site: www.gambro.com (16)

Game Show Placements Ltd, Hollywood, CA. Tel: (323) 874-7818, E-Mail: gsp@ix.netcom.com, Web Site: www.gameshowplacements.com (35)

Gamer, Richard, Mason Inc, Bethany, CT. Tel: (203) 393-1101, Web Site: mason23.com (35)

GameTime Inc, Fort Payne, AL. Tel: (256) 845-5610, (800) 235-2440, FAX: (256) 845-9361/2649, Web Site: www.gametime.com (11)

Gamino, Linda, UGL Equis Corp, Chicago, IL. Tel: (312) 424-8000, FAX: (312) 424-8080, Web Site: www.equiscorp.com (16)

Gamma Photo Labs LLC, Chicago, IL. Tel: (312) 337-0022, FAX: (312) 337-3753, Web Site: www.photobition.com (16)

Gandotra, Akshay, Infogroup Media Solutions, Papillion, NE. Tel: (800) 223-2194, E-Mail: infogroupmediasolutions@infogroup.com, Web Site: www.infogroupmediasolutions.com (23)

Ganeless, Michele, Comedy Central, New York, NY. Tel: (212) 767-8600, Web Site: www.cc.com (32)

Gangemi, Dr. Richard, Viahealth, Rochester, NY. Tel: (585) 922-4000, (585) 922-3677, FAX: (585) 922-3929, Web Site: www.viahealth.org (16)

Gannett Co Inc, Mc Lean, VA. Tel: (703) 854-6000, FAX: (703) 854-2046, Web Site: www.gannett.com (16)

Gannon, Kevin T., Robert A Stanger & Co Inc, Shrewsbury, NJ. Tel: (732) 389-3600, FAX: (732) 389-1751, E-Mail: info@rastanger.com, Web Site: www.rastranger.com (14)

Gant, Russell, Supelco Inc, Bellefonte, PA. Tel: (814) 359-3441, (800) 359-3041, FAX: (814) 359-3044, E-Mail: supelco@sial.com, Web Site: www.sigma-aldrich.com (16)

Ganz, David L., Relationship1, Pearl River, NY. Tel: (845) 732-8300, E-Mail: inforequest@relationship1.com, Web Site: www.relationship1.com (21)

Ganzert, Robin R., American Humane Association, Washington, DC. Tel: (303) 925-9497, Web Site: www.americanhumane.org (1)

Garber, Ann, Market Square Communications Inc, Stevens Point, WI. Tel: (715) 344-4609, FAX: (715) 344-6885 (20)

Garbutt, Chris, TBWA/Chiat/Day Inc, New York, NY. Tel: (212) 804-1000, FAX: (212) 804-1200, Web Site: www.tbwachiatdayny.com (35)

Garcia, Abel, Apperson Inc, Cerritos, CA. Tel: (562) 356-3333, (800) 877-2341, FAX: (562) 356-3310, E-Mail: sales@appersonprint.com, Web Site: www.appersonprint.com (27)

Garcia, Candie, Clampitt Paper Co, Dallas, TX. Tel: (214) 638-3300, FAX: (214) 634-7837, E-Mail: dcrew@clampitt.com, Web Site: www.clampitt.com (16)

Garcia, Erika, Blue Strawberry Resorts LLC, Miami, FL. Tel: (756) 513-1456, (800) 873-1440, Web Site: www.bluestrawberry-resorts.com (19)

Garcia, Gerald, Data Dallas Corp, Dallas, TX. Tel: (214) 638-2007, Web Site: www.datadallas.com (22)

Garcia, Joanne. John Sutherland & Associates, San Diego, CA. Tel: (858) 535-1139, (800) 545-9591, FAX: (858) 535-9124 (15)

Garcia, Jonathan, PFE Inc, Irvine, CA. Tel: (949) 417-0330, FAX: (949) 417-0331, Web Site: www.pfeinc.com (34)

Garcia, Patrick, Biomerica Inc. Irvine, CA. Tel: (949) 645-2111, (800) 854-3002, FAX: (949) 553-1231, E-Mail: info@biomerica.com, Web Site: www.biomerica.com (7)

Garcia-Ruiz, Emilio, Washington Post Digital, Washington, DC. Tel: (202) 334-9900 (17)

Gard Communications, Portland, OR. Tel: (503) 221-0100, (800) 800-7132, E-Mail: lfuller@gardcommunications.com, Web Site: gardcommunications.com (35)

Gard, Brian, Gard Communications, Portland, OR. Tel: (503) 221-0100, (800) 800-7132, E-Mail: lfuller@gardcommunications.com, Web Site: gardcommunications.com (35)

Garda, Donna, Lazarus Direct Inc, Uniondale, NY. Tel: (516) 880-7000, E-Mail: inquiries@lazarusdirect.com, Web Site: www.lazarusmarketing.com (21)

Garden Botanika Inc, Saint Louis, MO. Tel: (425) 881-9603, (800) 724-7227, FAX: (314) 633-4804, E-Mail: customercare@zidle.com, Web Site: www.zidle.com (7)

Garden Perennials, Wayne, NE. Tel: (402) 375-3615, (888) 375-3615, Web Site: www.gardenperennials.net (8)

Gardener's Supply Co, Burlington, VT. Tel: (888) 833-1412, FAX: (800) 551-6712, E-Mail: info@gardeners.com, Web Site: www.gardeners.com (8)

Gardens Alive! Inc, Lawrenceburg, IN. Tel: (513) 354-1483, FAX: (513) 354-1484, E-Mail: service@gardensalive.com, Web Site: www.gardensalive.com (8)

Gardens Of The Blue Ridge Inc, Pineola, NC. Tel: (828) 733-2417, FAX: (828) 733-8894, E-Mail: contact@gardensoftheblueridge.com, Web Site: www.gardensoftheblueridge.com (8)

Garder, Dimitri, Global-Z International Inc, Bennington, VT. Tel: (802) 445-1011, FAX: (802) 445-1016, E-Mail: info@globalz.com, Web Site: www.globalz.com (22)

Garder, Sasha, Global-Z International Inc, Bennington, VT. Tel: (802) 445-1011, FAX: (802) 445-1016, E-Mail: info@globalz.com, Web Site: www.globalz.com (22)

Gardner, Barry, Food for the Hungry Inc, Phoenix, AZ. Tel: (480) 998-3100, (800) 248-6437, FAX: (480) 998-4806, E-Mail: hunger@fh.org, Web Site: www.fh.org (1)

Gardner, David, The Motley Fool, Alexandria, VA. Tel: (703) 838-3665, FAX: (703) 254-1999, E-Mail: cs@fool.com, Web Site: www.Fool.com (14)

Gardner, Gary, SG360, Wheeling, IL. Tel: (847) 541-1080, FAX: (847) 541-5237, Web Site: www.sg360.com, (27)

Gardner, Jeff, Windstream Communications Inc, Little Rock, AR. Tel: (501) 748-7000, Web Site: www.windstream.com (32)

Gardner, John. Integrative Logic LLC, Lawrenceville, GA. Tel: (678) 638-2600, FAX: (678) 638-2601, Web Site: www.integrativelogic.com (30)

Gardner, Mark, Sappi Fine Paper North America, Boston, MA. Tel: (617) 423-7300, FAX: (617) 423-5494, Web Site: www.sappi.com (25)

Gardner, Melanie, University of Southern Mississippi, Hattiesburg, MS. Tel: (601) 266-1000, Web Site: www.usm.edu (1)

Gardner, Mickey, Current USA Inc, Colorado Springs, CO. Tel: (719) 594-4100, (877) 665-4458, FAX: (719) 531-2283, Web Site: www.currentinc.com (6)

Gardner, Nancy, TechniServe Inc, Troy, MI. Tel: (248) 989-0100, FAX: (248) 989-0111, E-Mail: info@techni-serve.com, Web Site: www.techni-serve.com (22)

Gardner, Robert, J&H Berge/The Lab Mart, South Plainfield, NJ. Tel: (908) 561-3002, (800) 684-1234, FAX: (908) 561-3002, E-Mail: info@jhberge.com, Web Site: www.jhberge.com (7)

Gardner, Tom, The Motley Fool, Alexandria, VA. Tel: (703) 838-3665, FAX: (703) 254-1999, E-Mail: cs@fool.com, Web Site: www.Fool.com (14)

Gardner, Tony, Continental Plastic Card Co, Pompano Beach, FL. Tel: (954) 794-0040, (800) 543-0670, FAX: (954) 755-4493, E-Mail: info@continentalplasticcard.com, Web Site: www.continentalplasticcard.com (27)

Garduno, Christena, Koeppel Direct, Dallas, TX. Tel: (972) 732-6110, FAX: (972) 248-2759, E-Mail: pkoeppel@koeppelinc.com, Web Site: www.koeppeldirect.com (32)

Garfield, Gary, Bridgestone Americas Inc, Nashville, TN. Tel: (615) 937-1000, (800) 543-7522, FAX: (615) 937-3721, Web Site: www.bridgestonetire.com (16)

Garfinkel Andrews, Alison, Call Compliance Inc, Glen Cove, NY. Tel: (516) 674-4545, FAX: (516) 676-2420, E-Mail: sales@callcompliance.com, Web Site: www.callcompliance.com (29)

Garfinkel, Dean, Quality Contact Solutions Inc, Aurora, NE. Tel: (402) 210-2692, (866) 963-2889, FAX: (402) 210-2692, E-Mail: info@qualitycontactsolutions.com, Web Site: www.qualitycontactsolutions.com (29)

Garfinkle, Phil, Planet Cotton, Gaithersburg, MD. Tel: (301) 948-0400, FAX: (301) 948-9031, Web Site: www.planetcotton.com (2)

Gargiulo, PhD Leslie, Ashworth College, Norcross, GA. Tel: (770) 729-8400, (800) 957-5412, FAX: (770) 729-9294, Web Site: www.ashworthcollege.edu (13)

Garland, Amy, Blue Sky Factory, Baltimore, MD. Tel: (410) 230-0061, Web Site: www.blueskyfactory.com (32)

Garland, Donna, National Archives & Records Administration, Washington, DC. Tel: (202) 357-5000, (866) 325-7208, Web Site: www.archives.gov (17)

Garling, Mary Ellen, Oakstone Publishing LLC, Birmingham, AL. Tel: (205) 991-5188, (800) 952-0690, FAX: (205) 995-4656, E-Mail: info@oakstonepublishing.com, Web Site: www.oakstonepublishing.com (17)

Garlinghouse Co, Beaufort, SC. Tel: (703) 547-4115, (800) 235-5700, FAX: (703) 222-9705, Web Site: www.familyhomeplans.com (17)

Garn, Randy, Prosper Inc, Provo, UT. Tel: (801) 371-0755, (800) 748-5799, FAX: (801) 374-2358, E-Mail: support@prospering.com, Web Site: www.prospering.com (32)

Garner, J Kenneth, Who's Who - The MFSA Buyers' Guide to Blue Ribbon Mailing Services, Alexandria, VA. Tel: (703) 836-9200, FAX: (703) 548-8204, E-Mail: masa-mail@masa.org, Web Site: www.mfsanet.org (43)

Garner, Kenneth, Association of Marketing Service Providers, Alexandria, VA. Tel: (703) 836-9200, (800) 333-6272, FAX: (703) 548-8204, E-Mail: mfsa-mail@mfsanet.org, Web Site: www.mfsanet.org (40)

Garner, Stephen B., Effective Marketing Associates, Inc, West Linn, OR. Tel: (503) 657-5859, FAX: (503) 657-5886, Web Site: www.e-m-a.com (20)

Garnet Hill Inc, Franconia, NH. Tel: (603) 823-5545, (800) 870-3513, FAX: (888) 842-9696, Web Site: www.garnethill.com (2)

Garnett, Doug, Atomic Direct LLC, Portland, OR. Tel: (503) 296-6131, FAX: (503) 296-9890, Web Site: www.atomicdirect.com (35)

Garnys, Greg, ClickSquared, Boston, MA. Tel: (781) 622-1611, (866) 402-5425, FAX: (857) 246-7645, E-Mail: info@clicksquared.com, Web Site: www.clicksquared.com (20)

Garofalo, Regina, Anheuser-Busch Inc Promotional Products Group, Shelton, CT. Tel: (800) 742-5283, Web Site: www.budshop.com (6)

Garon Products Inc, Wall, NJ. Tel: (732) 449-1776, (800) 631-5380, FAX: (732) 449-6937, Web Site: www.garonproducts.com (16)

Garrard, Ted, SickKids Foundation, Toronto, ON Canada. Tel: (800) 661-1083, FAX: (416) 813-5024, Web Site: www.sickkidsfoundation.com (1)

Garren, Donna, Florida Gift Fruit Shippers Association, Orlando, FL. Tel: (407) 295-1491, FAX: (407) 290-0918, E-Mail: info@fgfsa.com, Web Site: www.fgfsa.com (1)

Garret, Desta, Nordskog Publishing Co, Ventura, CA. Tel: (805) 642-2070, FAX: (805) 642-1862, Web Site: www.nordskogpublishing.com (17)

Garreton, Catalina, Nimblefish Technologies, San Francisco, CA. Tel: (415) 247-7000, Web Site: www.nimblefish.com (30)

Garrett, Audrey, Winfield Marketing Corp, Chicago, IL. Tel: (773) 743-8784, FAX: (440) 764-4871 (31)

Garrett, Jody, Woodcraft Supply Corp LLC, Parkersburg, WV. Tel: (304) 422-5412, (800) 344-3348, FAX: (304) 422-5417, Web Site: www.woodcraft.com (9)

Garrett, Karen, Anheuser-Busch Inc Promotional Products Group, Shelton, CT. Tel: (800) 742-5283, Web Site: www.budshop.com (6)

Garrett, Karen, Direct Selling Association, Washington, DC. Tel: (202) 452-8866, FAX: (202) 452-9010, E-Mail: info@dsa.org, Web Site: www.dsa.org (40)

Garrett, Mark, Adobe Systems Inc, San Jose, CA. Tel: (408) 536-6000, (800) 833-6687, FAX: (408) 537-6000, Web Site: www.adobe.com (22)

Garrett, Patrick, Sickafus Sheepskins, Strausstown, PA. Tel: (610) 488-1782, (888) 751-1300, FAX: (610) 488-1576, E-Mail: pat@patgarrett.com, Web Site: www.sheepcoat.com (2)

Garrett, Scott, Beckman Coulter Inc, Brea, CA. Tel: (714) 993-5321, (800) 526-3821, FAX: (800) 232-3828, Web Site: www.beckmancoulter.com (16)

Garris, Bert, DataDirect, Atlanta, GA. Tel: (678) 530-0034, FAX: (678) 530-9563, E-Mail: info@ddirect.com, Web Site: www.ddirect.com (40)

Garrison, Beth, Hearlihy & Co, Pittsburg, KS. Tel: (800) 622-1000, (866) 622-1003, FAX: (800) 443-2260, Web Site: www.hearlihy.com (17)

Garrison, Glenn, Mr G's Enterprises, Fort Worth, TX. Tel: (817) 831-3501, FAX: (817) 831-0638, E-Mail: mrgs@mrgusa.com, Web Site: www.mrgusa.com (16)

Garrison, Neal, Oliver of Adrian Inc, Adrian, MI. Tel: (517) 263-2132, (877) 668-0885, FAX: (517) 265-8698, E-Mail: info@oliverinstrument.com, Web Site: www.oliverofadrian.com (16)

Garrison, Stanley M., Choice Point, Alpharetta, GA. Tel: (770) 752-6000, (800) 342-5339, FAX: (770) 752-6005, Web Site: www.choicepoint.com (16)

Garriss, Steve, Compass Electronics, Forest Grove, OR. Tel: (503) 357-2111, FAX: (503) 357-2111 (9)

Garritano Group, Wayzata, MN. Tel: (612) 333-3775, FAX: (612) 333-3778, Web Site: garritano-group. com (35)

Garritano, Joe, Garritano Group, Wayzata, MN. Tel: (612) 333-3775, FAX: (612) 333-3778, Web Site: garritano-group.com (35)

Garrity, William E., Consumer's Energy, Jackson, MI. Tel: (517) 788-0550, (800) 805-0490, FAX: (517) 788-1859, E-Mail: businesscenter@ consumerenergy.com, Web Site: www. consumersenergy.com (16)

Garrubbo, Edwin, Creative Commerce LLC, West Chester, PA. Tel: (610) 918-8800, FAX: (610) 918-1349, E-Mail: info@creativecommerce.com, Web Site: creativecommerce.com (35)

Walter Garson Jr & Associates Inc, Bensalem, PA. Tel: (215) 245-6610, FAX: (215) 245-0281, E-Mail: walt@garsonmail.com (28)

Garson, Jr. Walter, Walter Garson Jr & Associates Inc, Bensalem, PA. Tel: (215) 245-6610, FAX: (215) 245-0281, E-Mail: walt@garsonmail.com (28)

Gartenberg, David, Selltel Inc, Brick, NJ. Tel: (732) 920-8700, (888) 840-9481, FAX: (732) 903-0836, E-Mail: info@nationalprotection.com (29)

Gartner Inc, San Jose, CA. Tel: (408) 468-8000, (800) 419-3282, FAX: (408) 954-1780, E-Mail: tom. mccall@gartner.com, Web Site: www.gartner.com (20)

Garver Advertising Service Inc, New York, NY. Tel: (212) 371-3325, E-Mail: garverads@aol.com (35)

The Garvey Group, Niles, IL. Tel: (847) 647-1900, FAX: (847) 647-6550, E-Mail: info@ thegarveygroup.com, Web Site: www. thegarveygroup.com (27)

Garvey, Gary, National Mail-It Inc, Shreveport, LA. Tel: (318) 683-0093, Web Site: www.nationalmailit. com (27)

Garvey, Jr. Ed J., The Garvey Group, Niles, IL. Tel: (847) 647-1900, FAX: (847) 647-6550, E-Mail: info@thegarveygroup.com, Web Site: www. thegarveygroup.com (27)

Garvey, Lee, Click2Mail, Arlington, VA. Tel: (703) 521-9029, (866) 665-2787, FAX: (703) 358-8811, E-Mail: info@click2mail.com, Web Site: www. click2mail.com (20)

Gary, Ken, O'Halloran Advertising, Westport, CT. Tel: (203) 341-9400 (39)

Gary's Perennials, LLC, Maple Glen, PA. Tel: (215) 628-4070, (800) 898-6653, FAX: (215) 628-0216, E-Mail: roots@garysperennials.com, Web Site: www.garysperennials.com; www.perennialmarket. com (8)

Garza, Laura, Workforce Advantage USA, Elizabeth, NJ. Tel: (908) 355-2299, FAX: (908) 352-2931, Web Site: www.workforceadvantageusa.com (13)

Garza, Linda, Pecan Producers International, Corsicana, TX. Tel: (903) 872-1337, (800) 732-2648, FAX: (903) 874-7143 (4)

Gaskins, Matthew, Kenney Marketing & Advertising Inc, King of Prussia, PA. Tel: (610) 341-0430, FAX: (610) 341-0480, E-Mail: info@kenneymarketing. com, Web Site: www.kmaphl.com (35)

Gaspari, John, Specialty Print Communications Inc, Niles, IL. Tel: (847) 588-2580, FAX: (847) 588-2146, Web Site: www.specialtyprintcomm.com (27)

GasPedal, Chicago, IL. Tel: (312) 932-9000, Web Site: www.gaspedal.net (20)

Gast, Ann, Anheuser-Busch Inc Promotional Products Group, Shelton, CT. Tel: (800) 742-5283, Web Site: www.budshop.com (6)

Gaston, Dave, MSI, Chicago, IL. Tel: (312) 565-0044, FAX: (312) 946-6100, E-Mail: info@agencymsi. com, Web Site: agencymsi.com (35)

Gately, Jerry, Direct Mail Solutions LLC, Carol Stream, IL. Tel: (630) 653-6863, FAX: (630) 653-7144, E-Mail: support@dmspostal.com, Web Site: www. dmspostal.com (28)

Gates Corp, Denver, CO. Tel: (303) 744-1911, FAX: (303) 744-4000, Web Site: www.gates.com (9)

Gates Marketing, Atlanta, GA. Tel: (770) 455-9662, FAX: (770) 455-8785 (22)

Gates, Greg, Manning Materials, Birdsboro, PA. Tel: (610) 385-6797, (800) 445-1719, FAX: (610) 385-7524, E-Mail: mmsupport@manningmaterials.com, Web Site: www.manningmaterials.com (16)

Gates, Jim, BuyFilters.com LLC, Silverhill, AL. Tel: (866) 863-1262, E-Mail: customerservice@ buyfilters.com, Web Site: www.buyfilters.com (5)

Gates, Robert, Gates Marketing, Atlanta, GA. Tel: (770) 455-9662, FAX: (770) 455-8785 (22)

Gates, Robert, VF Imagewear, Greensboro, NC. Tel: (336) 424-6000, (800) 733-5271, FAX: www. vfimagewear.com (2)

Gateway Bank and Trust, Raleigh, NC. Tel: (919) 789-2799, Web Site: www.gatewaybankandtrust.com (14)

Gateway Inc, Irvine, CA. Tel: (949) 471-7000, (800) 369-1409, FAX: (949) 471-7041, Web Site: www. gateway.com (3)

Gatsch, Mary E., Peterson's, Lawrenceville, NJ. Tel: (609) 896-1800, FAX: (609) 896-1811, E-Mail: custsvc@petersons.com, Web Site: www.petersons. com (17)

Gattinella, Wayne, DoubleVerify, New York, NY. Tel: (212) 631-2111, Web Site: www.doubleverify.com (9)

Gattone, Phil, Epilepsy Foundation, Landover, MD. Tel: (800) 332-1000, E-Mail: contactus@efa.org, Web Site: www.efa.org (1)

Gauger, Jeff, News & Record, Greensboro, NC. Tel: (336) 373-7000, (800) 553-6880 (31)

Gault, Marc G., Marc G Gault Consulting, Stone Mountain, GA. Tel: (770) 938-0781 (35)

Gauri, Rajinder, Data Square LLC, Stamford, CT. Tel: (203) 964-9733, FAX: (203) 964-0783, E-Mail: info@datasquare.com, Web Site: www.datasquare. com (22)

Gautschi, David A., Fordham University Graduate School of Business Administration, New York, NY. Tel: (212) 636-6200, (800) 825-4422, FAX: (212) 636-7076, Web Site: www.fordham.edu (41)

Gauvin, Guy, Coveo Solutions Inc, Quebec, QC Canada. Tel: (418) 263-1111, FAX: (418) 263-1221, Web Site: www.coveo.com (22)

Gaw-O'Hara Envelope Co, Chicago, IL. Tel: (773) 638-1200 (26)

Gay Men's Health Crisis, New York, NY. Tel: (212) 367-1000, FAX: (212) 367-1220, E-Mail: webmaster@gmhc.org, Web Site: www.gmhc.org (1)

Gay, Brian, Champs Software Inc, Crystal River, FL. Tel: (352) 795-2362, FAX: (352) 795-9100, E-Mail: champs@champsinc.com, Web Site: www. champsinc.com (3)

Gaylord Brothers, Syracuse, NY. Tel: (315) 634-8440, Web Site: www.gaylord.com (16)

Gaylord Communications Unlimited, Bridgewater, VT. Tel: (802) 672-6200, FAX: (802) 672-6226 (35)

Gaylord, Amy, Westlake Plastics Co, Lenni, PA. Tel: (610) 459-1000, (800) 999-1700, FAX: (610) 459-1084, Web Site: www.westlakeplastics.com (16)

Gaylord, Jeremy P., Gaylord Communications Unlimited, Bridgewater, VT. Tel: (802) 672-6200, FAX: (802) 672-6226 (35)

Gaynor, Paul, Market Focus Direct, Markham, ON Canada. Tel: (905) 477-0801, FAX: (905) 477-4473, E-Mail: info@market-focus.com, Web Site: www. market-focus.com (28)

Gazette Communications Inc, Cedar Rapids, IA. Tel: (319) 398-8211, (800) 397-8211, FAX: (319) 368-8834, Web Site: www.gazettecommunications.com (17)

Gazette Direct Marketing Co, Cedar Rapids, IA. Tel: (319) 399-5997, FAX: (319) 399-5998, Web Site: www.gazette.com (20)

GCDirect, Seattle, WA. Tel: (206) 262-1999, E-Mail: info@gcdirect.com, Web Site: www.gcdirect.com (35)

Gearen, Mark D.. Hobart & William Smith Colleges, Geneva, NY. Tel: (315) 781-3540, (800) 852-2256, FAX: (315) 781-3400, Web Site: www.hws.edu (19)

Geary's of Beverly Hills, Beverly Hills, CA. Tel: (310) 273-4741, (800) 793-6670, FAX: (310) 858-7555, Web Site: www.gearys.com (6)

Gebbie Press Inc, New Paltz, NY. Tel: (845) 255-7560, FAX: (888) 345-2790, E-Mail: gebbiepress@ pipeline.com, Web Site: www.gebbieinc.com (17)

Gebbie, Mark, All-In-One Directory, New Paltz, NY. Tel: (845) 255-7560, FAX: (888) 345-2790, E-Mail: gebbiepress@pipeline.com, Web Site: www. gebbieinc.com (43)

Gebbie, Mark, Gebbie Press Inc, New Paltz, NY. Tel: (845) 255-7560, FAX: (888) 345-2790, E-Mail: gebbiepress@pipeline.com, Web Site: www. gebbieinc.com (17)

Gebert, Richard, Grant Thornton LLP, Philadelphia, PA. Tel: (215) 561-4200, FAX: (215) 561-1066, Web Site: www.grantthornton.com (20)

Gebhart, Walter M., Phillips Kiln Service LTD, South Sioux City, NE. Tel: (402) 494-6837, (800) 831-0876, FAX: (402) 494-6858, E-Mail: info@kiln. com, Web Site: www.kiln.com (16)

Gebre, Tefere, AFL-CIO, Washington, DC. Tel: (202) 637-5000, FAX: (202) 637-5323, (202) 637-5058, Web Site: www.aflcio.org (1)

Karen Gedney Communications, Brooklyn, NY. Tel: (718) 680-1627, FAX: (917) 591-5547 (35)

Gedney, Karen, Karen Gedney Communications, Brooklyn, NY. Tel: (718) 680-1627, FAX: (917) 591-5547 (35)

Gee, Jim, Leadership Directories Inc, New York, NY. Tel: (212) 627-4140, FAX: (212) 645-0931, E-Mail: info@leadershipdirectories.com, Web Site: www. leadershipdirectories.com (17)

Geer, David, Listmasters Direct Mail Services, Philadelphia, PA. Tel: (215) 633-8200, E-Mail: sales@ listmastersdirect.com, Web Site: www. listmastersdirect.com (23)

Gegax, Tom, CSPI/Nutrition Action Health Letter, Washington, DC. Tel: (202) 332-9110, FAX: (202) 265-4954, E-Mail: cspi@cspinet.org, Web Site: www.cspinet.org (17)

Gehner, Scott, Parcel Insurance Plan Inc, Saint Louis, MO. Tel: (314) 692-0300, (800) 325-7390, FAX: (314) 692-7598, E-Mail: office@pipinsure.com, Web Site: www.pipinsure.com (15)

Geiger Brothers, Lewiston, ME. Tel: (207) 755-2000, (888) 953-9340, E-Mail: geigerorders@geiger.com, Web Site: www.geiger.com (33)

Geiger, Eugene, Geiger Brothers, Lewiston, ME. Tel: (207) 755-2000, (888) 953-9340, E-Mail: geigerorders@geiger.com, Web Site: www.geiger. com (33)

Geiger, Kevin, Standard Buying Service Ltd, New York, NY. Tel: (212) 686-6800, FAX: (212) 532-4102, E-Mail: info@sbspromo.com, Web Site: www.standardbuying.com (33)

Geiger, Peter, Geiger Brothers, Lewiston, ME. Tel: (207) 755-2000, (888) 953-9340, E-Mail: geigerorders@geiger.com, Web Site: www.geiger.com (33)

Geiger, Steve, Curtis 1000 Inc, Duluth, GA. Tel: (678) 380-9095, (877) 287-8715, FAX: (770) 717-1890, E-Mail: info@curtis1000.com, Web Site: www.curtis1000.com (27)

Geilenkrichen, Katie, Vente Inc, Omaha, NE. Tel: (402) 898-6800, (877) 899-9691, FAX: (402) 334-4829, Web Site: www.venteinc.com (30)

Geissler, Werner, The Procter & Gamble Co, Cincinnati, OH. Tel: (513) 983-1100, Web Site: www.pg.com (16)

Geist, Marjorie, American College of Emergency Physicians, Irving, TX. Tel: (972) 550-0911, (800) 798-1822, FAX: (972) 580-2816, Web Site: www.acep.org (1)

Gelb, Peter, The Metropolitan Opera, New York, NY. Tel: (212) 362-6000, (212) 799-3100, FAX: (212) 870-7695, Web Site: www.metoperafamily.org (1)

Gelco Information Network, Eden Prairie, MN. Tel: (952) 947-1500, (800) 444-6588, FAX: (952) 947-1525, Web Site: www.gelco.com (16)

Gelderman Group Inc, Brookfield, CT. Tel: (203) 740-9000, FAX: (203) 702-7096, E-Mail: geldermangroup@earthlink.net (23)

Gelfand, Sergei, American Mathematical Society, Providence, RI. Tel: (401) 455-4000, (800) 321-4267, FAX: (401) 331-3842, E-Mail: ams@ams.org, Web Site: www.ams.org (17)

Gelinas, R. Gerald, Thousand Trails LP, Chicago, IL. Tel: (214) 618-7200, (800) 205-0606, FAX: (214) 618-7324, Web Site: www.1000trails.com (16)

David Geller Associates, New York, NY. Tel: (212) 455-0100, FAX: (212) 455-0164 (31)

Lois Geller Marketing Group, Aventura, FL. Tel: (646) 723-3231, E-Mail: info2@loisgellermarketinggroup.com, Web Site: www.loisgellermarketinggroup.com (35)

Geller, Allan, Visions Marketing Services, Lancaster, PA. Tel: (717) 381-2100, (800) 222-1577, FAX: (717) 295-8020, Web Site: www.wecloseloans.com (29)

Geller, Lois, Lois Geller Marketing Group, Aventura, FL. Tel: (646) 723-3231, E-Mail: info2@loisgellermarketinggroup.com, Web Site: www.loisgellermarketinggroup.com (35)

Geltner, Sharon, Mark James & Associates Inc, Oswego, IL. Tel: (630) 548-8100, FAX: (630) 548-6107, E-Mail: info@markjamesassociates.com, Web Site: www.markjamesassociates.com/contact.html (16)

Gemalto Inc, Montgomeryville, PA. Tel: (215) 390-2000, E-Mail: us.sales@gemalto.com, Web Site: www.gemalto.com (16)

Gemini Publishing Co, Webster, TX. Tel: (281) 316-4276, E-Mail: getgirls@getgirls.com, Web Site: www.getgirls.com (17)

Gems Sensors & Controls, Plainville, CT. Tel: (860) 747-3000, (800) 378-1600, FAX: (860) 747-4244, E-Mail: info@gemssensors.com, Web Site: www.gemssensors.com (9)

Gendelev, Boris, B2BMarketing.com, Scottsdale, AZ. Tel: (602) 402-6588, Web Site: www.b2bmarketing.com (35)

Gendelev, Boris, Wheaton Group, Chapel Hill, NC. Tel: (919) 969-8859, FAX: (425) 675-6014, E-Mail: jim.wheaton@wheatongroup.com, Web Site: www.wheatongroup.com (22)

Gendreau, Kyle Francis, Samsonite International SA, Mansfield, MA. Tel: (508) 851-1400, (800) 547-BAGS, FAX: (303) 373-8715, Web Site: www.samsonite.com (16)

Gendreau, Ronald R., The Hartford Financial Services Inc, Southington, CT. Tel: (860) 547-5000, (860) 843-8070, FAX: (860) 547-2680, Web Site: www.thehartford.com (15)

General Binding Corp, Northbrook, IL. Tel: (800) 723-4000, (847) 272-1389, (800) 952-1166, Web Site: www.gbc.com (10)

General Electric Co, Fairfield, CT. Tel: (203) 373-2211, FAX: (203) 373-3131, Web Site: www.ge.com (16)

General Growth Properties, Chicago, IL. Tel: (312) 960-5000, Web Site: www.generalgrowth.com (5)

General Mills Inc, Minneapolis, MN. Tel: (800) 248-7310, FAX: (763) 764-8330, Web Site: www.generalmills.com (8)

General Motivation Co, Grand Rapids, MI. Tel: (616) 647-3085, (888) 664-6449, FAX: (616) 647-5909, E-Mail: i2k@generalmotivation.com, Web Site: www.generalmotivation.com (33)

General Nutrition Corp, Pittsburgh, PA. Tel: (412) 288-4600, (877) 462-4700, FAX: (412) 402-7218, Web Site: www.gnc.com (7)

General Pencil Co Inc, Jersey City, NJ. Tel: (201) 653-5351, FAX: (201) 653-2298, E-Mail: info@generalpencil.com, Web Site: www.generalpencil.com (16)

General Physics Corp, Elkridge, MD. Tel: (410) 379-3600, (800) 727-6677, FAX: (410) 540-5302, E-Mail: info@gpworldwide.com, Web Site: www.gpworldwide.com (16)

General Vitamin Corp, Raleigh, NC. Tel: (919) 929-5785, (800) 323-8432, FAX: (919) 929-2458, E-Mail: support@generalvitamin.com, Web Site: www.generalvitamin.com (16)

Generali, Philippe, Media Monitors Inc, White Plains, NY. Tel: (914) 428-5971, FAX: (914) 428-4541, E-Mail: jselig@mediamonitors.com, Web Site: www.mediamonitors.com (30)

Genereaux, Scott, Data Direct Networks, Chatsworth, CA. Tel: (818) 700-7607, (800) 837-2298, FAX: (818) 700-7601, E-Mail: info@ddn.com, Web Site: www.datadirectnet.com (3)

Genesco Inc, Nashville, TN. Tel: (615) 367-7000, (888) 324-6189, FAX: (615) 367-8278, Web Site: www.genesco.com (2)

GENESYS Sampling Systems, Horsham, PA. Tel: (215) 653-7100, (800) 336-7674, FAX: (215) 653-7115, E-Mail: alambert@m-s-g.com, Web Site: www.m-s-g.com (30)

Genetica DNA Laboratories Inc, Cincinnati, OH. Tel: (513) 985-9777, (800) 433-6848, FAX: (513) 985-9983, Web Site: www.genetica.com (16)

Gengler, Charles, Baruch College - Dept of Mktg & International Bus, New York, NY. Tel: (646) 312-3270, FAX: (646) 312-3271, E-Mail: mktlB@baruch.cuny.edu, Web Site: www.baruch.cuny.edu (41)

Genium Publishing, Amsterdam, NY. Tel: (518) 842-4111, FAX: (518) 842-1843, E-Mail: sales@genium.com, Web Site: www.genium.com (17)

Gennaco, Joseph P., The Boston Co Asset Management LLC, Boston, MA. Tel: (617) 722-7029, FAX: (617) 722-3928, Web Site: www.thebostoncompany.com (14)

Gennera Knab & Co, Studio City, CA(35)

Gennett, Sara, Crispin Porter + Bogusky, Miami, FL. Tel: (305) 859-2070, FAX: (305) 854-3419, E-Mail: info@cpbgroup.com, Web Site: www.cpbgroup.com (35)

Genovese, Ralph, Paramount Lists Inc, Erie, PA. Tel: (814) 459-8787, (800) 723-5478, FAX: (814) 459-1398, E-Mail: info@paramountlists.com, Web Site: www.paramountdirectmarketing.com (23)

Genovese, Tina, Gulf Coast List Service, Tampa, FL. Tel: (813) 962-3594, FAX: (813) 907-8463, E-Mail: tg@gulfcoastlist.com (23)

Gentile, Dave, Folder Factory Inc, Mount Jackson, VA. Tel: (540) 984-8852, (800) 296-4321, FAX: (540) 477-9677, E-Mail: webmaster@folders.com, Web Site: www.folders.com (27)

Gentile, Pam, RG Barry Corp, Pickerington, OH. Tel: (614) 864-6400, (800) 848-7560, FAX: (614) 866-9787, E-Mail: sales@rgbarry.com, Web Site: www.rgbarry.com (2)

Gentry, Bern L., The Pin Man, Tulsa, OK. Tel: (918) 587-2405, (918) 745-2162, Web Site: www.positivepin.com (16)

Gentry, Julie, Richardson Electronics Ltd, Lafox, IL. Tel: (630) 208-2200, FAX: (630) 208-2550, E-Mail: edg@rell.com, Web Site: www.rell.com (16)

Gentry, Marilyn, American Institute for Cancer Research, Washington, DC. Tel: (202) 328-7744, (800) 843-8114, FAX: (202) 328-7226, E-Mail: aicrweb@aicr.org, Web Site: www.aicr.org (1)

Gentry, Michelle, The Pin Man, Tulsa, OK. Tel: (918) 587-2405, FAX: (918) 745-2162, Web Site: www.positivepin.com (16)

Gentzel, Thomas J., National School Boards Association Inc, Alexandria, VA. Tel: (703) 838-6722, FAX: (703) 683-7590, E-Mail: info@nsba.org, Web Site: www.nsba.org (1)

Genworth Financial Inc, Richmond, VA. Tel: (804) 281-6000, (888) 436-9678, FAX: (804) 662-2414, Web Site: www.genworth.com (14)

Geometry Global, New York, NY. Tel: (212) 537-3700, E-Mail: press@geometry.com, Web Site: www.geometry.com (35)

George, Bill, Synergy Arts Interactive, White Plains, NY. Tel: (914) 997-7222, FAX: (914) 997-9893, E-Mail: bgeorge@synergyarts.com, Web Site: www.synergyarts.com (36)

George, Julie, Emperor Clock LLC, Amherst, VA. Tel: (800) 642-0011, FAX: (434) 946-1420, E-Mail: emperor@emperorclock.com, Web Site: www.emperorclock.com (16)

George, Larry, Univenture Inc, Marysville, OH. Tel: (937) 645-4600, FAX: (937) 645-4700, Web Site: www.univenture.com (27)

George, Michael, Consolidated Printing Inc, Philadelphia, PA. Tel: (215) 879-1400, (800) 347-0119, FAX: (215) 879-9130, Web Site: www.condrake.com (27)

George, Mike, QVC Inc, West Chester, PA. Tel: (484) 701-1000, FAX: (484) 701-8500, Web Site: www.qvc.com (32)

George, William, Partners Health, Philadelphia, PA. Tel: (215) 849-9600, (800) 553-0784, E-Mail: sroberts@healthpart.com, Web Site: www.healthpart.com (15)

Georgetown University Law Center, Washington, DC. Tel: (202) 662-9890, FAX: (202) 662-9891, E-Mail: cle@law.georgetown.edu, Web Site: www.law.georgetown.edu (13)

Georgetown University McDonough School of Business, Washington, DC. Tel: (202) 687-3883, Web Site: www.msb.edu (1)

Georgia Institute of Technology, Atlanta, GA. Tel: (404) 894-2000, Web Site: www.dlpe.gatech.edu (1)

Georgia-Pacific Corp LLC, Atlanta, GA. Tel: (404) 652-4000, FAX: (404) 230-7052, Web Site: www.gp.com (25)

Georgia Power, Atlanta, GA. Tel: (404) 506-3440 (16)

Geoscape, Miami, FL. Tel: (305) 860-1460, FAX: (305) 860-6161, Web Site: www.geoscape.com (22)

Geraghty, Patrick, Blue Cross Blue Shield of Florida, Jacksonville, FL. Tel: (904) 791-6111, (800) 477-3736, FAX: (904) 905-6638, E-Mail: katie.magee@bcbsfl.com, Web Site: www.bcbsfl.com (15)

Gerald, Bernadette, Berway Visual Products Inc, Wilmington, MA. Tel: (978) 694-9195, (800) 452-0410, FAX: (978) 694-9212, E-Mail: sales@berway.com, Web Site: www.berway.com (3)

Gerald, Wayne E., Berway Visual Products Inc, Wilmington, MA. Tel: (978) 694-9195, (800) 452-0410, FAX: (978) 694-9212, E-Mail: sales@berway.com, Web Site: www.berway.com (3)

Gerber Garment Technology Inc, Tolland, CT. Tel: (800) 826-3243, FAX: (860) 871-6007, E-Mail: info@gerbertechnology.com, Web Site: www.gerbertechnology.com (34)

Gerber Life Insurance Co, White Plains, NY. Tel: (914) 272-4000, (800) 704-2180, FAX: (914) 272-4099, Web Site: www.gerberlife.com (15)

Gerber Products Co, Florham Park, NJ. Tel: (973) 593-7500, (800) 284-9488, Web Site: www.gerber.com (16)

Gerber, Larry, American Student Marketing LLC, Highland Park, IL. Tel: (847) 432-4329, FAX: (847) 432-4811, E-Mail: admin@asmdm.com, Web Site: www.asmdm.com (23)

Gerber, Steven, Zeta Interactive, New York, NY. Tel: (212) 660-2500, FAX: (212) 967-1028, E-Mail: info@zetainteractive.com, Web Site: www.zetainteractive.com (32)

Gerber, William J., TD Ameritrade Holding Corp, Omaha, NE. Tel: (800) 237-8692, Web Site: www.amtd.com (16)

Gerchen, Gary, Midland Marketing Group, Saint Joseph, MO. Tel: (816) 261-9007, FAX: (816) 233-0859, E-Mail: info@midlandmarketinggroup.com, Web Site: www.midlandmarketinggroup.com (16)

Gerhardt, Mike, Impact Ratings Inc, Newtown, PA. Tel: (610) 353-8311, FAX: (610) 353-8311 (30)

Gerhold, John, Yenkin-Majestic, Columbus, OH. Tel: (614) 253-8511, FAX: (614) 253-6327 (16)

Gerlach, John B., T Marzetti Co Inc, Columbus, OH. Tel: (614) 846-2232, FAX: (614) 848-8330, Web Site: www.marzetti.com (4)

Germain, Steven, BJ's Wholesale Club Inc, Westborough, MA. Tel: (508) 651-7400, FAX: (508) 651-6167, Web Site: www.bjs.com (13)

German, Sarah, XL Environmental, Exton, PA. Tel: (610) 968-9500, (800) 327-1414, FAX: (610) 458-9109, E-Mail: webinfo.xli@xlgroup.com, Web Site: www.xlenvironmental.com (15)

Germany, Rhonda, Honeywell, Morristown, NJ. Tel: (973) 455-2000, FAX: (973) 455-4807, Web Site: www.honeywell.com (16)

Gero Vita, Costa Mesa, CA. Tel: (888) 382-9175, Web Site: www.gvi.com (16)

Gerrity, Tim, InterMedia Advertising, Woodland Hills, CA. Tel: (818) 995-1455, (800) 846-3289, FAX: (818) 719-9977, E-Mail: sales@intermedia-advertising.com, Web Site: www.intermedia-advertising.com (35)

Bill Gershon Marketing Communications, Skokie, IL. Tel: (847) 676-9452, FAX: (847) 674-7205, E-Mail: gershcom@yahoo.com (39)

Gershon, Bill, Bill Gershon Marketing Communications, Skokie, IL. Tel: (847) 676-9452, FAX: (847) 674-7205, E-Mail: gershcom@yahoo.com (39)

Gershon, Edwin M., National 4-H Supply Service, Chevy Chase, MD. Tel: (301) 961-2959, FAX: (301) 961-2937, E-Mail: 4hsupply@fourhcouncil.edu, Web Site: www.fourhcouncil.edu (16)

Gersie, Michael H., The Principal Financial Group, Des Moines, IA. Tel: (515) 247-5111, (800) 986-3343, FAX: (515) 246-5475, Web Site: www.principal.com (15)

Gerspach, John C., Citigroup Inc, New York, NY. Tel: (212) 559-1000, (800) 285-3000, FAX: (212) 793-3946, Web Site: www.citigroup.com (14)

Gerstner Woodworks, Dayton, OH. Tel: (937) 228-1662, FAX: (937) 228-8557, E-Mail: info@gerstnerusa.com, Web Site: www.gerstnerusa.com (6)

Gerten, Nick, Meyer Associates Teleservices, Saint Cloud, MN. Tel: (320) 259-4000, (800) 676-9233, FAX: (320) 259-4044, E-Mail: info@callmeyer.com, Web Site: www.callmeyer.com (29)

Gertler, Todd, Gilson Co Inc, Lewis Center, OH. Tel: (740) 548-7298, (800) 444-1508, FAX: (740) 548-5314, E-Mail: sales@gilsonco.com, Web Site: www.globalgilson.com (9)

Gertz, William, AIFS, Stamford, CT. Tel: (203) 399-5000, (866) 906-2437, FAX: (203) 599-5590, E-Mail: info@aifs.com, Web Site: www.aifs.com (19)

Geruson, Richard J., Phoenix Technologies Ltd, Campbell, CA. Tel: (408) 570-1000, (800) 677-7305, FAX: (408) 570-1001, Web Site: www.phoenix.com (22)

Get Seen Media Group, Los Angeles, CA. Tel: (323) 424-4669, Web Site: www.getseenmedia.com (16)

GetResponse Services Inc, Wilmington, DE. Tel: (877) 362-4547, Web Site: www.getresponse.com (24)

Getronics, Tewksbury, MA. Tel: (978) 625-5000, Web Site: www.getronics.com (16)

Gettman, Ken D., Longview Fibre Co, Longview, WA. Tel: (360) 425-1550, FAX: (360) 230-5135, E-Mail: info@longviewfibre.com, Web Site: www.longfibre.com (25)

Getty Images, Seattle, WA. Tel: (206) 925-5000, (888) 888-5889, Web Site: www.gettyimages.com (38)

Getty, Mark, Getty Images, Seattle, WA. Tel: (206) 925-5000, (888) 888-5889, Web Site: www.gettyimages.com (38)

Getty, Mark, The Image Bank, New York, NY. Tel: (646) 613-4000, FAX: (646) 613-4601, Web Site: www.gettyimages.com (38)

Gevicchi, Paul, Suez Energy North America, Houston, TX. Tel: (713) 636-0000, FAX: (713) 636-1364, Web Site: www.tractebelpowerinc.com (16)

Geyer, Jeff, American Color, Irving, TX. Tel: (602) 333-1000, FAX: (602) 333-1099, Web Site: www.amcolor.com (27)

Geyer, Jeff, Truitt Brothers Inc, Salem, OR. Tel: (503) 362-3674, (800) 547-8712, FAX: (503) 588-2868, E-Mail: truittbrothers@truittbros.com, Web Site: www.truittbros.com (16)

GfK Custom Research LLC, New York, NY. Tel: (212) 240-5300, (800) 274-3577, FAX: (212) 240-5353, E-Mail: info@gfkamerica.com, Web Site: www.gfkamerica.com (30)

Ghent Manufacturing Inc, Lebanon, OH. Tel: (513) 932-3445, (800) 543-0550, FAX: (513) 932-9252, E-Mail: customer_service@ghent.com, Web Site: www.ghent.com (10)

Ghirardelli Chocolate Co, San Leandro, CA. Tel: (510) 483-6970, (800) 877-9338, FAX: (510) 297-2649, Web Site: www.ghirardelli.com (16)

Ghort, Michael, Retrieval Masters Creditors Bureau Inc, Elmsford, NY. Tel: (914) 592-0055, (800) 666-8097, FAX: (914) 345-5023, E-Mail: info@retrievalmasters.com, Web Site: www.retrievalmasters.com (20)

Ghosn, Carlos, Nissan North America Inc, Franklin, TN. Tel: (615) 725-1000, Web Site: www.nissanusa.com (16)

Ghuman, Donna, Marketlinc, Saskatoon, SK Canada. Tel: (306) 956-7000, FAX: (306) 668-5812, E-Mail: info@marketlinc.com, Web Site: www.marketlinc.com (29)

Giagkou, Anna, BBM Canada Inc, Don Mills, ON Canada. Tel: (416) 445-9800, FAX: (416) 445-8644, E-Mail: info@bbm.ca, Web Site: www.bbm.ca (30)

Giamalva, Peter, RCI LLC, Carmel, IN. Tel: (317) 805-9000, FAX: (317) 805-9335, Web Site: www.rci.com (19)

Giambruno, John, Planned Parenthood Mar Monte, San Jose, CA. Tel: (408) 287-7532, FAX: (408) 971-6935, Web Site: www.plannedparenthood.org (1)

Giampietro, Susan, Specialists Marketing Services Inc, Hasbrouck Heights, NJ. Tel: (201) 865-5800, FAX: (201) 288-4295, E-Mail: info@sms-inc.com, Web Site: www.sms-inc.com (23)

Gianfagna Strategic Marketing Inc, Westlake, OH. Tel: (440) 808-4700, FAX: (440) 808-4707, E-Mail: tellmemore@gianfagnamarketing.com, Web Site: www.gianfagnamarketing.com (35)

Gianfagna, Jean M., Gianfagna Strategic Marketing Inc, Westlake, OH. Tel: (440) 808-4700, FAX: (440) 808-4707, E-Mail: tellmemore@gianfagnamarketing.com, Web Site: www.gianfagnamarketing.com (35)

Gianfagna, Jim, Gianfagna Strategic Marketing Inc, Westlake, OH. Tel: (440) 808-4700, FAX: (440) 808-4707, E-Mail: tellmemore@gianfagnamarketing.com, Web Site: www.gianfagnamarketing.com (35)

Gianinno, Susan, Publicis Worldwide North America, New York, NY. Tel: (212) 279-5550, E-Mail: andrew.bruce@publicisna.com, Web Site: publicisna.com (35)

Giannetti, Stephen P., Smithsonian Enterprises, New York, NY. Tel: (212) 916-1300, (800) 766-2149, FAX: (212) 490-0058, Web Site: www.smithsonianmag.com (17)

Gianni, Patrice, Marketing Results Inc, Sicklerville, NJ. Tel: (856) 740-3334, FAX: (856) 740-3335, Web Site: www.marketingresults.net (16)

Gianoni, Michael "Mike", Blackbaud Inc, Charleston, SC. Tel: (843) 216-6200, (800) 443-9441, FAX: (843) 216-6100, Web Site: www.blackbaud.com (22)

Giardini, Anne, Weyerhaeuser Co, Federal Way, WA. Tel: (253) 924-2345, (800) 525-5440, FAX: (253) 924-2685, Web Site: www.wy.com (25)

Gibb, Tara, United Business Media, Manhasset, NY. Tel: (516) 562-5000, Web Site: www.ubmtechnology.com (17)

Gibbins, Deborah, Mary Kay Cosmetics Inc, Addison, TX. Tel: (972) 687-6300, (800) MARY KAY, FAX: (972) 687-1611, Web Site: www.marykay.com (16)

Gibble, Ernie, DeVry Education Group, Downers Grove, IL. Tel: (630) 515-7700, (800) 73-DEVRY, E-Mail: inquiries@devrygroup.com, Web Site: www.devryeducationgroup.com (16)

Gibbons, Denise, CommercialWare Inc, Natick, MA. Tel: (508) 655-7500, FAX: (508) 647-9495, Web Site: www.commercialware.com (22)

Gibbons, Roland, GS&F, Nashville, TN. Tel: (615) 385-1100, (800) 241-3325, FAX: (615) 783-0500, E-Mail: biz@gsandf.com, Web Site: www.gsandf.com (35)

Gibbons, Thomas P., BNY Mellon, New York, NY. Tel: (412) 234-5000, (212) 495-1784, FAX: (412) 635-1799, Web Site: www.bnymellon.com (14)

Gibbs, David, Pizza Hut Inc, Plano, TX. Tel: (972) 338-7700, (866) 298-6986, FAX: (972) 338-6869, Web Site: www.pizzahut.com (16)

Gibbs, David, Strongwell, Bristol, VA. Tel: (276) 645-8000, FAX: (276) 645-8132, E-Mail: gbarefoot@strongwell.com, Web Site: www.strongwell.com (9)

Gibson Auer LLC, Victor, ID. Tel: (208) 201-3143, (888) 425-2250, E-Mail: helpdesk@galabs.com, Web Site: www.spiralenergetics.com (7)

Gibson Direct Inc, Coppell, TX. Tel: (972) 462-7580, FAX: (972) 304-9202 (20)

Gibson, Beth, New York Blood Center Inc, New York, NY. Tel: (212) 570-3000, (800) 933-2566, FAX: (212) 570-3195, Web Site: www.nybloodcenter.org (1)

Gibson, Frank A., Memphis Net & Twine Co Inc, Memphis, TN. Tel: (901) 458-2656, (888) 674-7638, FAX: (901) 458-1601, E-Mail: fishinfo@memphisnet.net, Web Site: www.memphisnet.net (11)

Gibson, George, Walker Publishing Co Inc, New York, NY. Tel: (212) 727-8300, (800) 289-2553, FAX: (212) 727-0984 (17)

Gibson, Mark, AccuTrade Inc, Bellevue, NE. Tel: (402) 970-7400, (800) 882-4887, FAX: (816) 243-3762, E-Mail: info@accutrade.com (14)

Gibson, Steve E., Gibson Direct Inc, Coppell, TX. Tel: (972) 462-7580, FAX: (972) 304-9202 (20)

Gibson, Tom, Ross-Simons, Cranston, RI. Tel: (401) 463-3100, (800) 835-0919, FAX: (401) 463-8599, Web Site: www.ross-simons.com (6)

Giera, Christie, DDB North America, New York, NY. Tel: (212) 415-2000, FAX: (212) 415-3550, Web Site: ddbnorthamerica.com (35)

Gieseler, Tim J., Orion Telescopes & Binoculars, Watsonville, CA. Tel: (831) 763-7000, (800) 447-1001, FAX: (408) 763-7017, E-Mail: sales@telescope.com, Web Site: www.telescope.com (11)

Gieselman, Dave, Blue Cross Blue Shield of Illinois, Chicago, IL. Tel: (312) 938-6000, FAX: (312) 938-5722, Web Site: www.bcbsil.com (15)

Giesler, Louis, AmeriMark Direct LLC, Middleburg Heights, OH. Tel: (440) 325-2000, FAX: (440) 234-8925, E-Mail: affiliate@amerimark.com, Web Site: www.amerimark.com (2)

Giesler, Michael F., FMC Corp, Philadelphia, PA. Tel: (215) 299-6000, FAX: (215) 299-5998, Web Site: www.fmc.com (16)

Giesmann, Jean, New England Mail Order Association, Scarborough, ME. Tel: (207) 885-0090, (860) 691-1260, FAX: (207) 885-0097, Web Site: www.nemoa.org (40)

Gifford, Roy, US Playing Card Co, Erlanger, KY. Tel: (800) 543-2273, FAX: (859) 815-7566, E-Mail: sales@usplayingcard.com, Web Site: www.usplayingcard.com (16)

Gift Services Inc, Vancouver, WA. Tel: (800) 379-4065, FAX: (360) 699-0597, E-Mail: corpsales@gifttree.com, Web Site: www.gifttree.com (6)

Gifts Corp, Barrie, ON Canada. Tel: (905) 670-1126, (800) 565-3130, FAX: (905) 670-1127, E-Mail: customerservice@regal.ca, Web Site: www.regalgreetings.com (6)

Gigante, Alex, Penguin Group USA Inc, New York, NY. Tel: (212) 366-2000, Web Site: www.us.penguingroup.com (17)

Giger, Sherri, National Multiple Sclerosis Society, Denver, CO. Tel: (303) 813-1052, Web Site: www.nmss.org (1)

Gigliotti, Steven, Scripps Networks Interactive Inc, Knoxville, TN. Tel: (865) 560-2700, Web Site: scrippsnetworksinteractive.com (17)

Gil, Frank, New Win Publishing Inc, El Monte, CA. Tel: (626) 448-3448, FAX: (626) 602-3817, E-Mail: info@AcademicLearningCompany.com, Web Site: www.newwinpublishing.com (17)

Gilbert, Christian, The Jackson Laboratory JAX Research Systems, Bar Harbor, ME. Tel: (800) 422-6423, Web Site: www.jax.org/jaxmice (1)

Gilbert, Eric, Upbeat Inc, Saint Louis, MO. Tel: (314) 535-5005, (800) 325-3047, FAX: (314) 535-4419, E-Mail: custservice@upbeat.com, Web Site: www.upbeat.com (9)

Gilbert, Ernest, Video Artists International, Pleasantville, NY. Tel: (914) 769-3691, (800) 477-7146, FAX: (914) 769-5407, E-Mail: orders@vaimusic.com, Web Site: www.vaimusic.com (3)

Gilbert, Gerry, Paymentech, Salem, NH. Tel: (603) 896-6000, FAX: (603) 896-8717, Web Site: www.paymentech.com (14)

Gilbert, Mike, GCDirect, Seattle, WA. Tel: (206) 262-1999, E-Mail: info@gcdirect.com, Web Site: www.gcdirect.com (35)

Gilbert, Steven, Affinitas Corp, Boys Town, NE. Tel: (402) 397-7077, (800) 369-6495, FAX: (402) 397-7576, Web Site: www.affinitas.net (29)

Gilboyne, Mark T., Westwood Publishing Co, Glendale, CA. Tel: (818) 242-1159, FAX: (818) 247-9379 (17)

Gilchrist & Partners, Boston, MA. Tel: (617) 314-4096, (866) 617-5070 (20)

Gilchrist, Andrew D., RJ Reynolds Tobacco Co, Winston Salem, NC. Tel: (336) 741-5111, (800) 341-5211, Web Site: www.rjrt.com (16)

Giles, Jane, Cambey & West Inc, Congers, NY. Tel: (845) 267-3006, FAX: (845) 267-3503, E-Mail: info@cambeywest.com, Web Site: www.cambeywest.com (22)

Gilkey, Gregg, Consolidated Plastics Co Inc, Stow, OH. Tel: (330) 425-3900, (800) 362-1000, FAX: (330) 425-3333, Web Site: www.consolidatedplastics.com (9)

Gill, Terry, Fetter Printing Company Inc, Louisville, KY. Tel: (502) 634-4771, (800) 234-4771, FAX: (502) 634-3587, E-Mail: info@fettergroup.com (27)

Gillan, Eugenia, Zoom Information Inc, Waltham, MA. Tel: (781) 693-7500, FAX: (781) 693-7510, Web Site: www.zoominfo.com (22)

Gillespie Magazine Marketing & Publishing, Lawrenceville, NJ. Tel: (609) 895-0200, FAX: (609) 895-0222, Web Site: www.gillespie.com (20)

Gillett, Stephen, Symantec, Mountain View, CA. Tel: (408) 517-8000, FAX: (408) 517-8186, Web Site: www.symantec.com (16)

Gillette Children's Specialty Healthcare, Saint Paul, MN. Tel: (651) 291-2848, Web Site: www.gillettechildrens.org (1)

Gillette, Robert J, ServiceMaster Co, Memphis, TN. Tel: (901) 766-1400, (866) 782-6787, Web Site: www.servicemaster.com (8)

Gillham, Simon, Vivendi SA, New York, NY. Tel: (212) 572-7000, FAX: (212) 572-1080, Web Site: www.vivendi.com (16)

Gilliam, Jeff, Toter Inc, Statesville, NC. Tel: (704) 872-8171, (800) 424-0422, FAX: (704) 878-0734, E-Mail: info@toter.com, Web Site: www.toter.com (16)

Gillien, Wayne, Ruud Lighting Inc, Racine, WI. Tel: (262) 886-1900, (800) 236-7000, FAX: (800) 236-7500, E-Mail: sales@ruudlighting.com, Web Site: www.ruudlighting.com (9)

Gilligan, Edward, American Express Co, New York, NY. Tel: (212) 640-2000, FAX: (212) 619-9802, Web Site: www.americanexpress.com (14)

Gilliland, Mike, Airlines Reporting Corp, Arlington, VA. Tel: (703) 816-8135, FAX: (703) 816-8104, E-Mail: corpcom@arccorp.com, Web Site: www.arccorp.com (16)

Gillis Odelbo, Catherine, Morningstar Inc, Chicago, IL. Tel: (312) 696-6000, Web Site: www.morningstar.com (14)

Gillogly, Bridget, Robert J Matthews Co, Massillon, OH. Tel: (330) 834-3000, (800) 578-9234, FAX: (330) 830-2762, E-Mail: email@rjmatthews.com, Web Site: www.pbsanimalhealth.com (7)

Gillund, Laura, C H Robinson Worldwide Inc, Eden Prairie, MN. Tel: (952) 937-8500, FAX: (952) 937-6740, E-Mail: info@chrobinson.com, Web Site: www.chrobinson.com (16)

Gilman, Robert, Gilman's Lapidary Supply, Hellertown, PA. Tel: (610) 838-8767, FAX: (610) 838-2961, E-Mail: info@lostcave.com, Web Site: www.lostcave.com (11)

Gilman's Lapidary Supply, Hellertown, PA. Tel: (610) 838-8767, FAX: (610) 838-2961, E-Mail: info@lostcave.com, Web Site: www.lostcave.com (11)

Gilner, Paul, Life Extension Foundation, Fort Lauderdale, FL. Tel: (954) 766-8144, (800) 678-8989, FAX: (954) 771-2827, E-Mail: info@lef.org, Web Site: www.lef.org (7)

Gilroy, Maureen E, OfficeMax Inc, Boca Raton, FL. Tel: (877) 633-4236, Web Site: www.officemax.com (10)

Gilson Co Inc, Lewis Center, OH. Tel: (740) 548-7298, (800) 444-1508, FAX: (740) 548-5314, E-Mail: sales@gilsonco.com, Web Site: www.globalgilson.com (9)

Gilson, Rob, Imperial Supplies, Green Bay, WI. Tel: (920) 494-5403, (800) 558-2808, FAX: (800) 553-8769, Web Site: www.imperialsupplies.com (16)

Gimbel, Diane, Gimbels of Maine Inc, Boothbay Harbor, ME. Tel: (207) 633-5088, FAX: (207) 633-5128, Web Site: www.gimbelscollectibles.com (6)

Gimbel, Mark S., Gimbels of Maine Inc, Boothbay Harbor, ME. Tel: (207) 633-5088, FAX: (207) 633-5128, Web Site: www.gimbelscollectibles.com (6)

Gimbels of Maine Inc, Boothbay Harbor, ME. Tel: (207) 633-5088, FAX: (207) 633-5128, Web Site: www.gimbelscollectibles.com (6)

Gimlin, Hal F., Omni Farm, West Jefferson, NC. Tel: (336) 982-3475, (800) TREE-FARM, FAX: (336) 982-4163, E-Mail: omnifarm@omnifarm.com, Web Site: www.omnifarm.com (16)

Gincel, Sherry, Air Ambulance Network Inc, Palm Harbor, FL. Tel: (727) 934-3999, (800) 327-1966, FAX: (727) 937-0276, Web Site: www.airambulancenetwork.com (16)

Ginger, Andrew R., Snap-on Inc, Kenosha, WI. Tel: (262) 656-5200, (800) 866-5748, (800) 786-6600, FAX: (262) 656-5577, Web Site: www.snapon.com (9)

Gingrich, James A., Alliance Bernstein, New York, NY. Tel: (212) 969-1000, (800) 962-2134, FAX: (212) 969-2293, Web Site: www.alliancebernstein.com (14)

Ginsberg O'Sullivan, Susan, TransitCenter Inc, New York, NY. Tel: (646) 395-9555, E-Mail: info@transitcenter.org, Web Site: www.transitcenter.org (1)

Ginsberg, Ari, Contact Marketing LLC, New York, NY. Tel: (201) 530-0200, E-Mail: info@contactmarketing.net, Web Site: www.contactmarketing.net (23)

Ginsberg, Frank, CWC Inventories Inc, Saint Louis, MO. Tel: (314) 739-1311 (33)

Ginsberg, Gary L., Time Warner Inc, New York, NY. Tel: (212) 484-8000, Web Site: www.timewarner.com (16)

Ginsburg Global LLC, Stamford, CT. Tel: (203) 359-2420, FAX: (203) 325-4443, E-Mail: gerry@ginsburgglobal.com, Web Site: www.ginsburgglobal.com (24)

Ginsburg, Gerry, Ginsburg Global LLC, Stamford, CT. Tel: (203) 359-2420, FAX: (203) 325-4443, E-Mail: gerry@ginsburgglobal.com, Web Site: www.ginsburgglobal.com (24)

Ginsburg, Richard, Protection One Inc, Lawrence, KS. Tel: (785) 856-5500, (800) GET-HELP, Web Site: www.protectionone.com (16)

Ginzburg, Mitchell, TRANZACT, Fort Lee, NJ. Tel: (201) 461-5665, E-Mail: info@tranzact.net, Web Site: www.tranzact.net (35)

Gioia, Joyce L., The Herman Group, Austin, TX. Tel: (336) 210-3547, E-Mail: info@hermangroup.com, Web Site: www.hermangroup.com (20)

Giokas, Lisa, H Armstrong Roberts Inc, Philadelphia, PA. Tel: (212) 685-3870, (800) 786-6300, FAX: (800) 786-1920, E-Mail: info@robertstock.com, Web Site: www.robertstock.com (38)

Gion, Ron, Impressions Unlimited Inc, Deerfield, IL. Tel: (630) 705-6464, FAX: (630) 705-1598, E-Mail: info@impressionsunltd.com, Web Site: www.impressionsunltd.com (27)

Giordana, Jerry, Publishers Circulation Fulfillment Inc, Towson, MD. Tel: (410) 821-8614, E-Mail: sales@pcfcorp.com, Web Site: www.pcfcorp.com (32)

Giordano, Andrea, Riverside Acquisition Group LLC, Moorestown, NJ. Tel: (856) 802-1900, Web Site: www.com-pak.com (28)

Giordano, Pat, Hampshire Agency, Great Neck, NY. Tel: (516) 466-3814, FAX: (516) 466-0910 (14)

Giordano, Vittorio, Urbani Truffles USA Corp, New York, NY. Tel: (212) 247-8800, FAX: (212) 247-8900, E-Mail: info@urbani.com, Web Site: www.urbani.com (4)

Girardi, Bob, SofTrek Corp, Amherst, NY. Tel: (716) 691-2800, (800) 442-9211, FAX: (716) 691-2828, Web Site: www.softrek.com (22)

Girardi, Theresa, Magna Publications Inc, Madison, WI. Tel: (608) 246-3590, FAX: (608) 246-3597, Web Site: www.magnapubs.com (17)

Girl Scouts of the USA, New York, NY. Tel: (212) 852-8000, (800) 478-7248, Web Site: www.girlscouts.org (1)

Giroux, Nathalie, Cancer Research Society, Montreal, QC Canada. Tel: (514) 861-9227, (888) 766-2262, FAX: (514) 861-9220, E-Mail: info@crs-src.ca, Web Site: www.cancerresearchsociety.ca (1)

Gisel, Jr. William G., Rich Products Corp, Buffalo, NY. Tel: (716) 878-8000, (800) 828-2021, FAX: (716) 878-8765, Web Site: www.richs.com (16)

Githens, William F., RMA-The Risk Management Association, Philadelphia, PA. Tel: (215) 446-4000, FAX: (215) 446-4101, E-Mail: customers@rmahq.org, Web Site: www.rmahq.org (1)

Gitow, David, Direct Brands Inc, New York, NY. Tel: (212) 930-4949, Web Site: www.columbiahouse.com (13)

Gittus, Kathleen, Nancy's Notions LLC, Beaver Dam, WI. Tel: (920) 887-0321, (800) 833-0690, FAX: (800) 255-8119, E-Mail: comments@nancysnotions.com, Web Site: www.nancysnotions.com (11)

Giufre, Tina, Sun Harvest Citrus, Fort Myers, FL. Tel: (239) 768-2686, (800) 743-1480, FAX: (239) 768-9255, E-Mail: info@sunharvestcitrus.com, Web Site: www.SunHarvestCitrus.com (6)

Giugni, June, Cosmetique, Inc, Vernon Hills, IL. Tel: (847) 913-9099, (800) 621-8822, E-Mail: customerservice@cosmetique.com, Web Site: www.cosmetique.com (13)

Giuliani, Tony, 21st Century Marketing, Altamonte Springs, FL. Tel: (321) 663-4640, E-Mail: tony@21stcenturymarketingonline.com, Web Site: 21stcenturymarketingonline.com (24)

Giurleo, Rich, SmartSource Corp, Bedford, MA. Tel: (781) 785-3375, (800) 239-0239, Web Site: www.smartsourceonline.com (32)

Givens, Michele, Editorial Projects in Education Inc, Bethesda, MD. Tel: (301) 280-3100, (800) 346-1834, FAX: (301) 280-3250, Web Site: www.edweek.org (17)

Giza, Dennis F., Columbia Journalism Review, New York, NY. Tel: (212) 854-2718, (888) 625-7782, FAX: (212) 854-8367, Web Site: www.cjr.org (17)

Gladden, Ray, Carolina Biological Supply Co, Burlington, NC. Tel: (800) 334-5551, (800) 222-7112, E-Mail: carolina@carolina.com, Web Site: www.carolina.com (9)

Glader, Bonita, OAG Worldwide, Downers Grove, IL. Tel: (630) 515-5300, FAX: (630) 515-5301, E-Mail: custsvc@oag.com, Web Site: www.oag.com (17)

Glahn, Ted, Solarcom, Norcross, GA. Tel: (770) 449-6116, (888) SUN-DATA, FAX: (770) 448-7726, Web Site: www.solarcom.net (16)

Glamour Shots Licensing, Oklahoma City, OK. Tel: (405) 947-8747, (888) GLAMOUR-SHOTS, FAX: (405) 951-7343, Web Site: www.glamourshots.com (16)

Glancy, Paul, JetSpring, Richmond, VA. Tel: (804) 359-8295, FAX: (804) 359-1686, Web Site: www.jetspring.com (30)

Glas-Col, Terre Haute, IN. Tel: (812) 235-6167, FAX: (812) 234-6975, Web Site: www.i-2-r.com (16)

Glasco, Doug, EdgeMark Partners Inc, Glen Allen, VA. Tel: (804) 967-2000, (800) 488-0289, FAX: (804) 967-2111, E-Mail: info@edgemarkpartners.com, Web Site: www.edgemarkpartners.com (35)

Glasco, Rick, EdgeMark Partners Inc, Glen Allen, VA. Tel: (804) 967-2000, (800) 488-0289, FAX: (804) 967-2111, E-Mail: info@edgemarkpartners.com, Web Site: www.edgemarkpartners.com (35)

Steve A Glaser Communications Services, Champaign, IL. Tel: (217) 351-0981, FAX: (217) 351-0981, E-Mail: steve@sagcs.net, Web Site: www.sags.net (39)

Glaser, Alvin B., Essex Printing Co Inc, Croton On Hudson, NY. Tel: (212) 688-4720, (800) 443-9113, FAX: (212) 308-2764, E-Mail: essexptg@aol.com, Web Site: www.essex-printing.com (27)

Glaser, Joseph, GlaserDirect Inc, Glen Ellyn, IL. Tel: (630) 469-2075, (888) 380-1356, FAX: (630) 790-5244, E-Mail: info@glaserdirect.com, Web Site: www.glaserdirect.com (23)

Glaser, Steve A., Steve A Glaser Communications Services, Champaign, IL. Tel: (217) 351-0981, FAX: (217) 351-0981, E-Mail: steve@sagcs.net, Web Site: www.sags.net (39)

GlaserDirect Inc, Glen Ellyn, IL. Tel: (630) 469-2075, (888) 380-1356, FAX: (630) 790-5244, E-Mail: info@glaserdirect.com, Web Site: www.glaserdirect.com (23)

Peter Glass Photography, East Hartford, CT. Tel: (860) 528-8559, E-Mail: peter@peterglass.com, Web Site: www.peterglass.com (37)

Glass, Dennis R., Lincoln Financial Group, Radnor, PA. Tel: (215) 448-1400, (877) 275-5462, FAX: (215) 448-3962, Web Site: www.lfg.com (15)

Glass, Dennis, Scorecards USA, North Kingstown, RI. Tel: (401) 294-4049, (800) 553-4154, FAX: (401) 294-4076, E-Mail: sales@scorecardsusa.com, Web Site: www.scorecardsusa.com (16)

Glass, Kelly, Affinity Express, Elgin, IL. Tel: (847) 930-3200, FAX: (847) 930-3299, E-Mail: kellyg@affinityexpress.com, Web Site: www.affinityexpress.com (16)

Glass, Peter, Peter Glass Photography, East Hartford, CT. Tel: (860) 528-8559, E-Mail: peter@peterglass.com, Web Site: www.peterglass.com (37)

Glasser, Dr. Gerald J., Knowledge Networks/SRI, Cranford, NJ. Tel: (908) 497-8000, FAX: (908) 497-8001, E-Mail: mclancey@knowledgenetworks.com, Web Site: www.knowledgenetworks.com (30)

Glassman, Judy, Smithsonian Enterprises, New York, NY. Tel: (212) 916-1300, (800) 766-2149, FAX: (212) 490-0058, Web Site: www.smithsonianmag.com (17)

Glastris, Paul, The Washington Monthly Co, Washington, DC. Tel: (202) 955-9010, FAX: (202) 955-9011, E-Mail: editors@washingtonmonthly.com, Web Site: www.washingtonmonthly.com (17)

Glatfelter, York, PA. Tel: (717) 225-4711, (866) 744-7380, FAX: (717) 225-6834, E-Mail: info@glatfelter.com, Web Site: www.glatfelter.com (25)

Glauberman, Jay, Malco Products Inc, Barberton, OH. Tel: (330) 753-0361, (800) 253-2526, FAX: (330) 753-2025, Web Site: www.malcopro.com (16)

Glauberman, Stuart, Malco Products Inc, Barberton, OH. Tel: (330) 753-0361, (800) 253-2526, FAX: (330) 753-2025, Web Site: www.malcopro.com (16)

GlaxoSmithKline USA, Philadelphia, PA. Tel: (888) 825-5249, Web Site: us.gsk.com (16)

Glazer-Kennedy Insider Circle, Chicago, IL. Tel: (410) 825-8600, Web Site: www.dankennedy.com (20)

Glazer, William, Glazer-Kennedy Insider Circle, Chicago, IL. Tel: (410) 825-8600, Web Site: www.dankennedy.com (20)

Glazier, Jordan, Eventful Inc, San Diego, CA. Tel: (858) 882-0360, FAX: (858) 964-4640, Web Site: www.eventful.com (19)

Gleeson, Kathleen A., Response Insurance, Scranton, PA. Tel: (203) 634-7255, (800) 518-2984, FAX: (203) 634-7319, E-Mail: webcs@response.com, Web Site: www.response.com (15)

Glendinning, Stewart, Molson Coors Brewing Co, Denver, CO. Tel: (303) 927-2337, (800) 665-7661, Web Site: www.molsoncoors.com (16)

Glengarry Marketing, Austin, TX. Tel: (800) 883-1924 (20)

Peter Glenn Publications, Delray Beach, FL. Tel: (561) 404-4290, (888) 332-6700, FAX: (561) 892-5786, E-Mail: gregjames@pgdirect.com, Web Site: www.pgdirect.com (17)

Glenn, Don, The Vane Brothers Co, Baltimore, MD. Tel: (410) 631-5096, FAX: (410) 631-7781, E-Mail: webmaster@vanebros.com, Web Site: www. vanebros.com (16)

Glenn, T Michael, FedEx Corp, Memphis, TN. Tel: (901) 369-3600, FAX: (901) 395-5082, Web Site: www.fedex.com (16)

Glennon, Amy, Atlanta Journal & Constitution, Atlanta, GA. Tel: (404) 526-5151, Web Site: www.ajc.com (17)

Glens Falls Hospital Foundation, Glens Falls, NY. Tel: (518) 926-5960, FAX: (518) 926-7012, Web Site: www.glensfallshospital.org (1)

Glenview Capital Management, New York, NY. Tel: (212) 812-4700 (14)

Glenview State Bank, Glenview, IL. Tel: (847) 729-1900, FAX: (847) 729-5847, E-Mail: info@gsb.com, Web Site: www.glenviewstatebank.com (14)

Glerum, Matt, Sportif Mail Order Inc, Sparks, NV. Tel: (888) 260-7676, FAX: (775) 356-3567, Web Site: www.sportif.com (2)

Glick, Angie, Sunshine Farm & Gardens, Renick, WV. Tel: (304) 497-2208, E-Mail: barry@sunfarm.com, Web Site: www.sunfarm.com (8)

Glick, Art, Almost Heaven Group, Renick, WV. Tel: (304) 645-2310, FAX: (304) 497-2698, E-Mail: art@almostheaven.net, Web Site: www. almostheaven.net (16)

Glick, Barry, Sunshine Farm & Gardens, Renick, WV. Tel: (304) 497-2208, E-Mail: barry@sunfarm.com, Web Site: www.sunfarm.com (8)

Glick, Charles, Unum Corp, Portland, ME. Tel: (207) 770-2211, (800) 421-0344, FAX: (207) 770-4510, Web Site: www.unum.com (15)

Glick, Zak, Sunshine Farm & Gardens, Renick, WV. Tel: (304) 497-2208, E-Mail: barry@sunfarm.com, Web Site: www.sunfarm.com (8)

Glickman Research Associates/GRA Focus Center, Northvale, NJ. Tel: (201) 767-8888, (800) 334-3978, FAX: (201) 767-6933, E-Mail: j.glickman@ glickmanresearch.com, Web Site: www. glickmanresearch.com (30)

Glickman, Bob, Harbor Freight Tools, Camarillo, CA. Tel: (805) 445-4791, (800) 423-2567, FAX: (800) 445-4925, Web Site: www.harborfreight.com (9)

Glickman, James, Glickman Research Associates/GRA Focus Center, Northvale, NJ. Tel: (201) 767-8888, (800) 334-3978, FAX: (201) 767-6933, E-Mail: j. glickman@glickmanresearch.com, Web Site: www. glickmanresearch.com (30)

Glicksman, Russell, The Beam Group, Gladwyne, PA. Tel: (215) 988-2100, FAX: (215) 988-1558, Web Site: www.beamgroup.com (20)

Glisan, George, The Hickory Printing Solutions LLC, Conover, NC. Tel: (828) 465-3431, (800) 442-5679, FAX: (828) 465-2517, E-Mail: gglisan@ hickoryprinting.com, Web Site: www. hickoryprinting.com (27)

Glista, Elizabeth Stephenson, ICMA Retirement Corp, Washington, DC. Tel: (202) 962-4600, (800) 669-7400, FAX: (202) 962-4601, E-Mail: investorservices@icmarc.org, Web Site: www. icmarc.org (14)

Global Business Information Services Inc (GLoBIS), Chicago, IL. Tel: (877) 456-2478, FAX: (877) 456-2478, E-Mail: info@glo-bis.com, Web Site: www. glo-bis.com (30)

Global Computer Corp, Port Jefferson, NY. Tel: (516) 625-4300, (888) 845-6225, FAX: (516) 625-4072, Web Site: www.globalcomputer.com (3)

Global Computer Supplies, Port Washington, NY. Tel: (516) 403-2800, (800) 446-9662, FAX: (516) 625-6683, Web Site: www.globalcomputer.com (34)

Global Demand Publishing Inc, Jacksonville, NC. Tel: (910) 937-0562, FAX: (910) 455-1937, E-Mail: globaldemandpublishing@yahoo.com (17)

Global DM Solutions Inc, Boonton, NJ. Tel: (973) 402-2205, (866) 402-2205, FAX: (973) 402-2305, E-Mail: contact@globaldmsolutions.com, Web Site: www.globaldmsolutions.com (23)

Global Equipment Co Inc, Port Washington, NY. Tel: (516) 484-3100, (888) 381-2861, FAX: (516) 608-7111, E-Mail: sales@globalindustrial.com, Web Site: www.globalindustrial.com (9)

Global Infomercial Services Inc, Burr Ridge, IL. Tel: (708) 229-2424, FAX: (708) 229-2407, E-Mail: info@giservices.tv, Web Site: www.giservices.tv (34)

Global IntelliSystems, Evergreen, CO. Tel: (970) 315-3637, (800) 707-7074, FAX: (970) 432-7190, Web Site: www.globalintellisystems.com (22)

Global Marketing Group Ltd, New York, NY. Tel: (212) 247-6060, FAX: (212) 586-5446, E-Mail: kimglobal@aol.com, Web Site: www.gmgsolution.com (20)

Global Response Corp, Margate, FL. Tel: (954) 973-7300, (800) 537-8000, FAX: (954) 968-9862, E-Mail: wendys@globalresponse.com, Web Site: www.globalresponse.com (29)

Global Specialties, Wallingford, CT. Tel: (203) 272-3285, FAX: (203) 272-4330, Web Site: www. globalspecialties.com (16)

Global Turnkey Systems Inc, Parsippany, NJ. Tel: (973) 331-1010, FAX: (973) 331-0042, E-Mail: sales@ gtsystems.com, Web Site: www.gtsystems.com (22)

Global Village Marketing & Data Services Inc, Cheyenne, WY. Tel: (307) 222-4135, E-Mail: sales@ globalvillagemktg.com, Web Site: www. globalvillagemktg.com (41)

Global Ware Solutions, Haverhill, MA. Tel: (800) 469-7500, FAX: (978) 469-7373, E-Mail: sales@ gwsmail.com, Web Site: www.globalwaresolutions. com (22)

Global-Z International Inc, Bennington, VT. Tel: (802) 445-1011, FAX: (802) 445-1016, E-Mail: info@ globalz.com, Web Site: www.globalz.com (22)

Globalization Partners International, Mc Lean, VA. Tel: (703) 268-2193, (866) 272-5874, FAX: (202) 478-0956, E-Mail: info@globalizationpartners.com, Web Site: www.globalizationpartners.com (35)

Globe Marketing Systems Inc, Coral Springs, FL. Tel: (954) 753-7173, (800) 382-9013, FAX: (954) 337-0650, Web Site: www.internetprintcenter.com (27)

Globe Photos Inc, West Islip, NY. Tel: (631) 661-3131 (38)

Globe Specialty Products Inc, Millbury, MA. Tel: (508) 871-1900 (17)

Globe Ticket & Label Co, Carol Stream, IL. Tel: (404) 762-9711, (800) 523-5968, FAX: (404) 762-7019, Web Site: www.globeticket.com (16)

Glosser, Roy J., American Locker Security Systems Inc, Coppell, TX. Tel: (817) 329-1600, (800) 828-9118, E-Mail: info@americanlocker.com, Web Site: www. americanlocker.com (16)

Glouatts, John, Tristar Products, Fairfield, NJ. Tel: (973) 575-5400, FAX: (973) 683-6708, E-Mail: infotp@tristarproductsinc.com, Web Site: www. tristarproductsinc.com (16)

Glover, David, cbsi, Fort Worth, TX. Tel: (817) 332-3681, FAX: (817) 332-3686, Web Site: www. buxtonco.com (30)

Glover, Jerry, EdgeMark Partners Inc, Glen Allen, VA. Tel: (804) 967-2000, (800) 488-0289, FAX: (804) 967-2111, E-Mail: info@edgemarkpartners.com, Web Site: www.edgemarkpartners.com (35)

Glover, William, The Granger Collection, New York, NY. Tel: (212) 447-1789, FAX: (212) 447-1492, Web Site: www.granger.com (38)

Glovin, Martin, Marden-Kane Inc, Woodbury, NY. Tel: (516) 365-3999, FAX: (516) 365-5250, E-Mail: expert@mardenkane.com, Web Site: www. mardenkane.com (35)

Glovsky, Staci, Vitamin Research Products, Cottonwood, AZ. Tel: (888) 362-1699, FAX: (775) 884-1331, E-Mail: customerservice@vrp.com, Web Site: www.vrp.com (7)

Gluck, Brian, Vcom International Multi-Media Corp, South Hackensack, NJ. Tel: (201) 229-9800, (800) 572-6373, FAX: (973) 439-1522, E-Mail: info@ vcomimc.com, Web Site: www.vcomimc.com (3)

Gluck, Robert, Harris Connect LLC, Chesapeake, VA. Tel: (800) 877-6554, Web Site: www.harrisconnect. com (1)

Glynn Denney, Barbara, Arizona Highways Magazine, Phoenix, AZ. Tel: (602) 712-2200, FAX: (602) 254-4505, E-Mail: editor@arizonahighways.com, Web Site: www.arizonahighways.com (17)

Go Ahead Vacations, Cambridge, MA. Tel: (617) 619-1000, (800) 242-4686, FAX: (617) 619-1001, E-Mail: goahead@et.com, Web Site: www. goaheadvacations.com (16)

Go Promos, Amsterdam, NY. Tel: (800) 523-9909, FAX: (800) 523-3292, E-Mail: customerservice@ gopromos.com, Web Site: www.gopromos.com (5)

Go, Robert, Air Power USA, Los Angeles, CA. Tel: (310) 641-0830, (888) 888-8231, FAX: (310) 641-8515, Web Site: www.airpowerusa.com (12)

Goddard Manufacturing Co, Logan, KS. Tel: (785) 689-4341, (800) 536-4341, Web Site: www.spiral-staircases.com (8)

Goddard, Anne Lynam, ChildFund International, Richmond, VA. Tel: (804) 756-2700, (800) 776-6767, FAX: (804) 756-2718, Web Site: www. christianchildrensfund.org (1)

Goddard, Doug, Gamma Photo Labs LLC, Chicago, IL. Tel: (312) 337-0022, FAX: (312) 337-3753, Web Site: www.photobition.com (16)

Goddard, Jeffrey, TVA Media Group, Studio City, CA. Tel: (818) 505-8300, (888) 322-4296, FAX: (818) 505-8370, E-Mail: info@tvamediagroup.com, Web Site: www.tvamediagroup.com (35)

Goddard, Jerry, Goddard Manufacturing Co, Logan, KS. Tel: (785) 689-4341, (800) 536-4341, Web Site: www.spiral-staircases.com (8)

Godfrey, Lynn, Girl Scouts of the USA, New York, NY. Tel: (212) 852-8000, (800) 478-7248, Web Site: www.girlscouts.org (1)

Godfrey, Nick, Customer Portfolios LLC, Boston, MA. Tel: (617) 224-9501, E-Mail: getstarted@ customerportfolios.com, Web Site: www. customerportfolios.com (22)

Godfrey, Patty L., Insurance Publications Inc, Overland Park, KS. Tel: (913) 383-9191, (800) 762-3387, FAX: (913) 383-1247, E-Mail: brokerwrld@ primary.net, Web Site: www.brokerworldmag.com (17)

Godin, Gary, MFE Instruments, Salem, NH. Tel: (603) 893-8778, (800) 843-8011, FAX: (603) 893-8851, Web Site: www.stockeryale.com (9)

Godiva Chocolatier, New York, NY. Tel: (212) 984-5900, (800) 946-3482, Web Site: www.godiva.com (4)

Godlasky, Thomas C., Aviva USA Corp, Des Moines, IA. Tel: (515) 362-3600, FAX: (800) 531-0038, Web Site: www.avivausa.com (14)

Godlewski, Rob, Powr-Flite, a Tacony Co, Fort Worth, TX. Tel: (800) 880-2913, FAX: (817) 551-0719, Web Site: www.powrflite.com (9)

Godley, Benjamin, WGBH Educational Foundation, Brighton, MA. Tel: (617) 300-2000, FAX: (617) 300-1026, Web Site: www.wgbh.org (1)

Goergens, Doug, West End Diving Centers Inc, Bridgeton, MO. Tel: (314) 209-7200, (888) 843-3483, E-Mail: info@2dive.com, Web Site: www.westenddiving.com (19)

Goertz, Elena, American Society of Media Photographers (ASMP), Philadelphia, PA. Tel: (215) 451-ASMP, FAX: (215) 451-0880, Web Site: www.asmp.org (40)

Goethel, Mike, Demco Inc, Madison, WI. Tel: (608) 241-1201, (800) 356-1200, FAX: (608) 241-1799, E-Mail: custserv@demco.com, Web Site: www.demco.com (16)

Goff, Isaac, Dharma Trading Co, Petaluma, CA. Tel: (415) 456-1211, (800) 542-5227, FAX: (415) 456-8747, E-Mail: service@dharmatrading.com, Web Site: www.dharmatrading.com (2)

Goggin, Mark W., Golden State Envelopes, Thousand Oaks, CA. Tel: (818) 865-7940, (800) 252-7600, FAX: (818) 865-0012, E-Mail: answers@golden-state-env.com, Web Site: www.golden-state-env.com (26)

Gogoel, Michael, BYK-Gardner USA, Columbia, MD. Tel: (310) 483-6500, Web Site: www.byk.com (16)

Gogue, Jay, Auburn University at Montgomery, Montgomery, AL. Tel: (334) 244-3621, (800) 227-2649, FAX: (334) 244-3826, Web Site: www.aum.edu (41)

Gohn Brothers, Middlebury, IN. Tel: (574) 825-2400, (800) 595-0031, E-Mail: gohnbrothers@gmail.com, Web Site: www.gohnbrothers.com (5)

Goings, Rick, Tupperware Brands Corp, Orlando, FL. Tel: (407) 826-5050, (800) 366-3800, FAX: (407) 826-8874, Web Site: www.tupperwarebrands.com (16)

Barbara Gold, New York, NY. Tel: (917) 750-4038 (20)

Gold Medal Hair Products Inc, Farmingdale, NY. Tel: (631) 465-0202, FAX: (631) 465-0207, E-Mail: customerservice@goldmedalhair.com, Web Site: www.goldmedalhair.com (7)

Gold Medal Products Co, Cincinnati, OH. Tel: (513) 769-7676, (800) 543-0862, FAX: (800) 542-1496, E-Mail: info@gmpopcorn.com, Web Site: www.gmpopcorn.com (16)

Gold, James J, Neiman-Marcus Group, Dallas, TX. Tel: (214) 339-0396, (888) 888-4757, Web Site: www.neimanmarcus.com (8)

Gold, Keith, Flaghouse Inc, Hasbrouck Heights, NJ. Tel: (201) 288-7600, (800) 793-7900, FAX: (800) 793-7922, E-Mail: sales@flaghouse.com, Web Site: www.flaghouse.com (5)

Gold, Lila Teich, Nightingale Resources, Cold Spring, NY. Tel: (718) 338-3976, (212) 753-5383, (800) 953-9929 (17)

Goldberg, Andrew, Publishers Clearing House, Port Washington, NY. Tel: (516) 883-5432, FAX: (516) 767-4567, E-Mail: cirving@pch.com, Web Site: www.pch.com (18)

Goldberg, Bill, The StayWell Co, Yardley, PA. Tel: (267) 685-2800, Web Site: www.staywell.com (7)

Goldberg, Dan, KD Mailing & Fulfillment Service, Lincolnwood, IL. Tel: (847) 673-0186, (866) 330-6245, FAX: (874) 673-0188, E-Mail: dan@kdmailing.com, Web Site: www.kdmailing.com (28)

Goldberg, Howard, AP Images, New York, NY. FAX: (212) 621-1679, E-Mail: apimages_us@ap.org, Web Site: www.apimages.com (38)

Goldberg, Marc S., Advertising Idea Stores, Ardmore, PA. Tel: (484) 416-0004, E-Mail: marc@uniongoods.com, Web Site: www.uniongoods.com (35)

Goldberg, Marilyn, Museum Masters Inc, New York, NY. Tel: (212) 360-7100, (917) 273-8710, FAX: (212) 360-7102, E-Mail: MMIMarilyn@aol.com, Web Site: www.museummasters.com (16)

Goldberg, Michael, Zimmerman Advertising, Fort Lauderdale, FL. Tel: (954) 644-4000, E-Mail: contact@zadv.com, Web Site: www.zadv.com (35)

Goldberg, Richard, AsiaEXP, Miami, FL. Tel: (305) 675-5969, Web Site: www.asiaexp.com (16)

Goldberg, Scott L., Bankers Life & Casualty Co, Chicago, IL. Tel: (312) 396-6000, (800) 231-9150, Web Site: www.bankerslife.com (15)

Goldberg, Stanley R., Hampshire Agency, Great Neck, NY. Tel: (516) 466-3814, FAX: (516) 466-0910 (14)

Goldberg, Steve, Media Recruiting Group Inc, Irvington, NY. Tel: (914) 591-5511, FAX: (914) 591-8911, E-Mail: resume@mediarecruiting.com, Web Site: www.mediarecruiting.com (20)

Goldberg, Stuart, Informed Sources Inc, Plainview, NY. Tel: (800) 201-6060, FAX: (516) 576-0249, E-Mail: info@informed-sources.com, Web Site: www.informed-sources.com (30)

Goldbrenner, Joseph, The Goldmark Group Inc, Clifton, NJ. Tel: (973) 777-5720, (800) 632-9632, FAX: (973) 777-2390, E-Mail: info@goldmarkgroup.com, Web Site: www.goldmarkgroup.com (35)

Golden Bison LLC, Denver, CO. Tel: (303) 962-0018, Web Site: www.highplainsbison.com (4)

Ed Golden & Associates, Austin, TX. Tel: (512) 458-8222, FAX: (512) 454-3536 (20)

Golden Fleece Designs Inc, Burbank, CA. Tel: (818) 848-7724, FAX: (818) 566-7100, Web Site: www.mandonia.com (16)

Golden Gate Transportation District, San Rafael, CA. Tel: (415) 921-5858, FAX: (415) 923-2014, Web Site: www.goldengate.org (16)

Golden Key International Honour Society, Atlanta, GA. Tel: (678) 689-2200, (800) 377-2401, FAX: (678) 689-2297, E-Mail: memberservices@goldenkey.org, Web Site: www.goldenkey.org (1)

Golden Millennium Productions Inc, Pasadena, CA. Tel: (818) 500-1099, FAX: (866) 886-5802, E-Mail: info@goldenproductions.com, Web Site: www.goldenproductions.com (32)

Golden Rule Insurance Co, Indianapolis, IN. Tel: (317) 297-4123, FAX: (317) 297-0908, Web Site: www.goldenrule.com (15)

Golden State Envelopes, Thousand Oaks, CA. Tel: (818) 865-7940, (800) 252-7600, FAX: (818) 865-0012, E-Mail: answers@golden-state-env.com, Web Site: www.golden-state-env.com (26)

Golden Trophy, Chicago, IL. Tel: (773) 282-2900, (800) 821-3882, FAX: (800) 835-6601, E-Mail: goldentrophy@bruss.com, Web Site: www.giftsteaksonline.com (4)

Golden, Ed, Ed Golden & Associates, Austin, TX. Tel: (512) 458-8222, FAX: (512) 454-3536 (20)

Golden, Lawrence, RSVP Publications, Tampa, FL. Tel: (813) 960-7787, FAX: (866) 554-3003, Web Site: www.MailToTheAffluent.com (31)

Golden, Michael, Stephen Gould Paper Co Inc, Whippany, NJ. Tel: (973) 428-1500, FAX: (973) 428-5274, Web Site: www.stephengould.com (27)

Golden, Michael, The New York Times Co, New York, NY. Tel: (212) 556-1234, Web Site: www.nytimes.com (17)

Goldenberg, Norman, Terminix International, The Trugreen Companies, Memphis, TN. Tel: (901) 766-1105, Web Site: www.trugreenchemlawn.com (16)

Goldfarb, Debra, Institute Lists, Portland, OR. Tel: (917) 751-8439, E-Mail: info@institutelists.com, Web Site: institutelists.com (24)

Goldfarb, Eric, Bearingpoint Inc, Dallas, TX. Tel: (703) 747-3000, FAX: (703) 747-3215, Web Site: www.bearingpoint.com (14)

Goldfarb, Jeff, A I Friedman Inc, New York, NY. Tel: (212) 243-9000, (800) 204-6352, FAX: (212) 929-7320, Web Site: www.aifriedman.com (10)

Goldfedder, Judd, The Customer Connection Inc, Escondido, CA. Tel: (760) 489-8339, (800) 477-7166, FAX: (760) 489-1075, E-Mail: contact@custcon.com, Web Site: www.thecustomerconnection.com (22)

Goldie, Melissa, Phillips-Van Heusen Corp, New York, NY. Tel: (212) 381-3500, (800) 388-9122, FAX: (212) 381-3950, Web Site: www.pvh.com (2)

Goldinger, Ferko, Appleton Coated LLC, Combined Locks, WI. Tel: (920) 788-3550, FAX: (920) 687-3420, Web Site: www.appletoncoated.com (25)

Goldklank, Mitchell, Direct Mail Depot Inc, Piscataway, NJ. Tel: (732) 469-5900, FAX: (732) 469-8414, E-Mail: sales@directmaildepot.com, Web Site: www.directmaildepot.com (28)

Goldleaf Data Inc, Suwanee, GA. Tel: (888) 936-3282, E-Mail: info@goldleafdata.com, Web Site: goldleafdata.com (23)

Goldman, Jeremy, Firebrand Group, New York, NY. Tel: (866) 757-3362, E-Mail: info@firebrandgroup.com, Web Site: www.firebrandgroup.com (32)

Goldman, Ken, Yahoo! Inc, Sunnyvale, CA. Tel: (408) 349-3300, Web Site: www.yahoo.com (32)

Goldman, Matthew, Fujitsu America Inc, Sunnyvale, CA. Tel: (408) 746-6000, (800) 831-3183, FAX: (408) 992-2674, E-Mail: solutions@us.fujitsu.com, Web Site: www.fujitsu.com (22)

Goldman, Michael, Boys' Life & Scouting Magazines, Irving, TX. Tel: (972) 580-2000, (866) 584-6589, FAX: (972) 580-2079, Web Site: www.boyslife.org (17)

Goldman, Phyllis B., Monkeyshines Publishers, Greensboro, NC. Tel: (336) 292-6999, FAX: (336) 292-6999, E-Mail: mkshines@nr.infi.net, Web Site: www.monkeyshinespublishers.com (17)

Goldman, Richard, CompetiScan, Chicago, IL. Tel: (312) 546-3489, Web Site: www.competiscan.com (30)

Goldman, Rick, Dream Products Inc, Van Nuys, CA. Tel: (818) 773-4233, (800) 410-2153, FAX: (816) 206-8061, Web Site: www.dreamproducts.net (5)

The Goldmark Group Inc, Clifton, NJ. Tel: (973) 777-5720, (800) 632-9632, FAX: (973) 777-2390, E-Mail: info@goldmarkgroup.com, Web Site: www.goldmarkgroup.com (35)

Goldner, Brian D, Hasbro Inc, Pawtucket, RI. Tel: (401) 431-8697, (800) 242-7276, FAX: (401) 727-5121, Web Site: www.hasbro.com (11)

Goldner, Mark, Parker Steel Co, Toledo, OH. Tel: (419) 473-2481, (800) 333-4140, FAX: (419) 471-2655, Web Site: www.metricmetal.com (16)

Goldner, Paul, Parker Steel Co, Toledo, OH. Tel: (419) 473-2481, (800) 333-4140, FAX: (419) 471-2655, Web Site: www.metricmetal.com (16)

Goldner, Sharon, Parker Steel Co, Toledo, OH. Tel: (419) 473-2481, (800) 333-4140, FAX: (419) 471-2655, Web Site: www.metricmetal.com (16)

Goldrich, Kathy, LS Direct Marketing, Suffern, NY. Tel: (845) 357-1238, E-Mail: info@lsdirect.com, Web Site: www.lsdirect.com (23)

Goldring, Norm, CPO Direct Inc, Lake Forest, IL. Tel: (847) 735-7365, FAX: (847) 735-9825, E-Mail: ngoldring@cpodirect.com, Web Site: www.cpodirect.com (35)

Goldsberry, John P., Gateway Inc, Irvine, CA. Tel: (949) 471-7000, (800) 369-1409, FAX: (949) 471-7041, Web Site: www.gateway.com (3)

Goldsbury, Rich, Bobcat Co, West Fargo, ND. Tel: (701) 241-8700, FAX: (701) 241-8704, Web Site: www.bobcat.com (16)

Goldschein, Perry, SRB Marketing Inc, New Paltz, NY. Tel: (866) 210-1183, Web Site: www.srbmarketing.com (30)

Goldschmidt, Robert, Roto-Rooter Services Co, Cincinnati, OH. Tel: (513) 762-6690, FAX: (513) 762-6590, Web Site: www.rotorooter.com (16)

Goldshein, Sandy, Sandy Goldshein Associates Inc, New York, NY. Tel: (212) 366-5105, E-Mail: info@sgany.com, Web Site: www.sgany.com (35)

Goldsher, Barry, Engineering Services & Products Co, South Windsor, CT. Tel: (860) 528-1119, (800) 835-7877, FAX: (800) 457-8887, Web Site: www.teksupply.com (9)

Goldsmith, Brian, Lionsgate Entertainment Inc, New York, NY. Tel: (212) 577-2400, FAX: (212) 962-2872, Web Site: www.lionsgate.com (32)

Goldsmith, Brian, Lionsgate Television Corp, Santa Monica, CA. Tel: (310) 449-9200, FAX: (310) 255-3870, Web Site: www.lionsgate.com (16)

Goldsmith, Richard, The Horah Group, Pleasantville, NY. Tel: (914) 495-3200, E-Mail: dgoldsmith@horah.com, Web Site: www.horah.com (21)

Goldstein, Alan J., The Computer Studio, Yonkers, NY. Tel: (914) 968-1212, FAX: (914) 968-1228, E-Mail: connect@webbusconnect.com, Web Site: www.webbusconnect.com (35)

Goldstein, Ben, Ben Loeb Inc, Fairfield, NJ. Tel: (908) 788-0542, FAX: (908) 788-6861, E-Mail: tbecker@bsloeb.com, Web Site: www.bsloeb.com (33)

Goldstein, Cary, Blue Cross Blue Shield of Illinois, Chicago, IL. Tel: (312) 938-6000, FAX: (312) 938-5722, Web Site: www.bcbsil.com (15)

Goldstein, David, Jerry's Artarama, Raleigh, NC. Tel: (919) 878-8478, (800) U-ARTIST, FAX: (919) 873-9565, E-Mail: micah@jerrysartarama.com, Web Site: www.jerrysartarama.com (10)

Goldstein, Ira, Jerry's Artarama, Raleigh, NC. Tel: (919) 878-8478, (800) U-ARTIST, FAX: (919) 873-9565, E-Mail: micah@jerrysartarama.com, Web Site: www.jerrysartarama.com (10)

Goldstein, Jeff, IDMS Inc, Melville, NY. Tel: (631) 249-7744, (800) 582-5831, FAX: (631) 249-4425, E-Mail: sales@idmsinc.com, Web Site: www.idmsinc.com (16)

Goldstein, Jennifer, Publications International Ltd, Lincolnwood, IL. Tel: (847) 676-3470, (800) 595-8484, FAX: (847) 676-3671, Web Site: www.pubint.com (17)

Goldstein, Jeremy, Navitar Inc, Rochester, NY. Tel: (585) 359-4000, (800) 828-6778, FAX: (585) 359-4999, E-Mail: info@navitar.com, Web Site: www.navitar.com (16)

Goldstein, Josh, Data Direct Networks, Chatsworth, CA. Tel: (818) 700-7607, (800) 837-2298, FAX: (818) 700-7601, E-Mail: info@ddn.com, Web Site: www.datadirectnet.com (3)

Goldstein, Julian, Navitar Inc, Rochester, NY. Tel: (585) 359-4000, (800) 828-6778, FAX: (585) 359-4999, E-Mail: info@navitar.com, Web Site: www.navitar.com (16)

Goldstein, Kymn, Allied Integrated Marketing, Boston, MA. Tel: (617) 859-4800, E-Mail: alliedimsocial@alliedim.com, Web Site: alliedim.com (35)

Goldstein, Lauren, Babcock & Jenkins, Portland, OR. Tel: (503) 382-8500, E-Mail: laureng@bnj.com, Web Site: www.bnj.com (35)

Goldstein, Leslie, IDMS Inc, Melville, NY. Tel: (631) 249-7744, (800) 582-5831, FAX: (631) 249-4425, E-Mail: sales@idmsinc.com, Web Site: www.idmsinc.com (16)

Goldstein, Marc, Profile Mailing Service Inc, Syosset, NY. Tel: (516) 802-3974 (16)

Goldstein, Michael, Islands Tropicals, Keaau, HI. Tel: (808) 961-0606, (800) 367-5155, FAX: (808) 966-7684, Web Site: www.islandtropicals.com (6)

Goldstein, Patricia, Emigrant Savings Bank, New York, NY. Tel: (212) 850-4521, (800) EMIGRANT, FAX: (212) 850-4372, Web Site: www.emigrant.com (14)

Goldstein, Sheldon, Vcom International Multi-Media Corp, South Hackensack, NJ. Tel: (201) 229-9800, (800) 572-6373, FAX: (973) 439-1522, E-Mail: info@vcomimc.com, Web Site: www.vcomimc.com (3)

Goldston, Georgie, Health Affairs, Bethesda, MD. Tel: (301) 656-7401, FAX: (301) 654-2845, Web Site: www.healthaffairs.org (17)

Goldstone, Jerry A., BCR Enterprises Inc, Downers Grove, IL. Tel: (630) 986-1432, (800) 227-1234, FAX: (630) 323-5324, Web Site: www.bcr.com (17)

Goldwasser, Dawn, Renton's Inc, Parker, CO. Tel: (303) 865-7025, (800) 365-6644, E-Mail: info@rentons.com, Web Site: www.rentons.com (10)

Golec, Chris, Demandbase Inc, San Francisco, CA. Tel: (415) 683-2660, E-Mail: info@demandbase.com, Web Site: www.demandbase.com (22)

Golestani, Clark, Merck & Co Inc, Whitehouse Station, NJ. Tel: (908) 423-1000, Web Site: www.merck.com (16)

Golf Card International, Englewood, CO. Tel: (303) 792-7284, (800) 321-8269, Web Site: www.golfcard.com (1)

Golf Digest Co, Wilton, CT. Tel: (203) 761-5100, FAX: (203) 371-2572, Web Site: www.golfdigest.com (17)

Golf Haus, Lansing, MI. Tel: (517) 482-8842, FAX: (517) 482-8843 (11)

Golfsmith International Inc, Austin, TX. Tel: (512) 821-4050, (800) 813-6897, FAX: (512) 837-9347, E-Mail: comments@golfsmith.com, Web Site: www.golfsmith.com (11)

Golio, Vic, Chief Media LLC, New York, NY. Tel: (212) 300-8487, FAX: (212) 629-9505, E-Mail: info@chiefmedia.com, Web Site: www.chiefmedia.com (35)

Gollaher, Greg, Polynesian Cultural Center, Honolulu, HI. Tel: (808) 293-3333, (800) 367-7060, FAX: (888) 722-7339, E-Mail: internetrez@polynesia.com, Web Site: www.polynesia.com (16)

Gomez, Cynthia, The Dartnell Corp, Naples, FL. Tel: (585) 240-7301, (800) 447-4030, FAX: (585) 292-4392, E-Mail: customerservice@dartnellcorp.com, Web Site: www.dartnellcorp.com (17)

Gomez, Henry, Hewlett-Packard Co, Palo Alto, CA. Tel: (650) 857-1501, (800) 752-0900, FAX: (650) 857-5518, Web Site: www.hp.com (16)

Gonier, Dennis E., DMS Insights, Dallas, TX. Tel: (800) 409-6262, FAX: (214) 222-6103, E-Mail: info@dmsinsights.com, Web Site: www.dmsdallas.com (30)

Gonzales, Scott, Three Georges and the Nuthouse, Mobile, AL. Tel: (334) 433-1689, FAX: (334) 433-3364, E-Mail: sales@threegeorges.com, Web Site: www.threegeorges.com (16)

Gonzales, Siobhan, Three Georges and the Nuthouse, Mobile, AL. Tel: (334) 433-1689, FAX: (334) 433-3364, E-Mail: sales@threegeorges.com, Web Site: www.threegeorges.com (16)

Gonzalez, Cesar A, Creditcards.com, Austin, TX. Tel: (512) 996-8663, Web Site: www.creditcards.com (20)

Gonzalez, Daniel, Daniel Gonzalez & Associates, New York, NY. Tel: (212) 682-0333 (20)

Gonzalez, Jackie, Mailmen Inc, Hauppauge, NY. Tel: (631) 582-6900, FAX: (631) 582-6948, E-Mail: getresults@mailmeninc.com, Web Site: www.mailmeninc.com (28)

Gonzalez, Jaime, Cardflex Financial Services, Costa Mesa, CA. Tel: (714) 361-1900, E-Mail: aphillips@cliq.com, Web Site: www.flex1.com (14)

Gonzalez, Jane, Collis Curve Catalog Sales, Brownsville, TX. Tel: (956) 546-4818, (800) 298-4818, FAX: (956) 546-4818, E-Mail: brushteeth@aol.com, Web Site: www.colliscurve.com (7)

Gonzalez, Jose, Severini Communications LLC, New York, NY. Tel: (917) 734-3991, E-Mail: mark@severinicommunications.com, Web Site: www.severinicommunications.com (20)

Gonzalez, Saul, Con-Way Truckload, Joplin, MO. Tel: (417) 623-5229, (800) CFI-DRIVE, FAX: (417) 623-8939, E-Mail: gnichols@cfi-us.com, Web Site: www.cfi-us.com (12)

Gooch, Jaime, Level 5 Communications Inc, Dublin, NH. Tel: (603) 563-1631, FAX: (603) 563-8912, E-Mail: de-news@deskeng.com, Web Site: www.deskeng.com (16)

Good Advertising, Memphis, TN. Tel: (901) 761-0741, (800) 325-9857, FAX: (901) 682-2568, E-Mail: info@goodadvertising.com, Web Site: www.goodadvertising.com (35)

Good Directions Co Inc, Danbury, CT. Tel: (203) 743-3775, FAX: (203) 743-5226, E-Mail: contact@gooddirections.com, Web Site: www.gooddirections.com (8)

Good, Kyle, Scholastic Inc, New York, NY. Tel: (212) 343-6100, (800) SCHOLASTIC, FAX: (212) 343-6484, Web Site: www.scholastic.com (17)

Good, Vicki, Harvard Business School - Executive Education, Boston, MA. Tel: (617) 496-2193, (800) 427-5577, E-Mail: executive_education@hbs.edu, Web Site: www.exed.hbs.edu (1)

The Jane Goodall Institute, Vienna, VA. Tel: (703) 682-9220, Web Site: www.janegoodall.org (1)

Goodall, Dr. Jane, The Jane Goodall Institute, Vienna, VA. Tel: (703) 682-9220, Web Site: www.janegoodall.org (1)

Goodell, Jackie, Diagraph Corp, Saint Charles, MO. Tel: (636) 300-2000, (800) 722-1125, FAX: (636) 300-2004, E-Mail: info@diagraph.com, Web Site: www.diagraph.com (16)

Goodfader, Joel, AMI Instore, Framingham, MA. Tel: (508) 652-0200, (877) 652-0200, FAX: (508) 652-0101, E-Mail: info@advancemarketing.com, Web Site: www.advancemarketing.com (31)

Goodgame, Ken, True Value Co, Chicago, IL. Tel: (773) 695-5000, Web Site: www.truevaluecompany.com (16)

Goodheart-Willcox Publisher, Tinley Park, IL. Tel: (708) 687-5000, (800) 323-0440, FAX: (708) 687-0315, E-Mail: custserv@g-w.com, Web Site: www.g-w.com (17)

Goodin, Stephanie, Gold Medal Products Co, Cincinnati, OH. Tel: (513) 769-7676, (800) 543-0862, FAX: (800) 542-1496, E-Mail: info@gmpopcorn.com, Web Site: www.gmpopcorn.com (16)

Goodkind & Goodkind Direct Inc, Arcata, CA. Tel: (712) 347-6114, (800) 690-9342, FAX: (712) 347-5754, E-Mail: mail@goodkind.com, Web Site: www.goodkind.com (28)

Goodkind, Dan, Goodkind & Goodkind Direct Inc, Arcata, CA. Tel: (712) 347-6114, (800) 690-9342, FAX: (712) 347-5754, E-Mail: mail@goodkind.com, Web Site: www.goodkind.com (28)

Goodkind, Kathi, Goodkind & Goodkind Direct Inc, Arcata, CA. Tel: (712) 347-6114, (800) 690-9342, FAX: (712) 347-5754, E-Mail: mail@goodkind.com, Web Site: www.goodkind.com (28)

Goodloe, Shantae, Federal Citizen Information Center, Pueblo, CO. Tel: (719) 295-2675, (888) 8-PUEBLO, FAX: (719) 948-9724, E-Mail: pueblo@gpo.gov, Web Site: www.pueblo.gsa.gov (5)

Goodman & Co, New York, NY. Tel: (212) 579-0020, Web Site: www.goodmancompany.com (20)

Goodman Marketing Partners Inc, San Rafael, CA. Tel: (415) 507-9060, FAX: (415) 507-9067, E-Mail: info@goodmanmarketing.com, Web Site: www.goodmanmarketing.com (35)

Goodman Media Group Inc, New York, NY. Tel: (212) 262-2247, FAX: (212) 262-2278, E-Mail: jgoodman@gmgpub.com, Web Site: www.goodmanmediagroup.dev.hotresponse.com (17)

Goodman, Adam, St Louis Post-Dispatch, Saint Louis, MO. Tel: (314) 340-8000, (800) 365-0820, FAX: (314) 340-3140, Web Site: www.stltoday.com (17)

Goodman, Alyce, Lillian Vernon Corp, Colorado Springs, CO. Tel: (757) 427-7923, (800) 545-5426, FAX: (757) 427-7819, E-Mail: publicrelations@lillianvernon.com, Web Site: www.lillianvernon.com (6)

Goodman, Bruce, Vector Marketing Corp, Olean, NY. Tel: (716) 373-6141, (267) 880-1750, FAX: (716) 373-6145, Web Site: www.cutco.com (5)

Goodman, Carolyn, Goodman Marketing Partners Inc, San Rafael, CA. Tel: (415) 507-9060, FAX: (415) 507-9067, E-Mail: info@goodmanmarketing.com, Web Site: www.goodmanmarketing.com (35)

Goodman, Don, Tuttle Printing & Engraving, Rutland, VT. Tel: (802) 773-9171, (800) 776-7682, FAX: (802) 773-5785, E-Mail: info@tuttleprinting.com, Web Site: www.tuttleprinting.com (10)

Goodman, Eleanor, Pennsylvania State University Press, University Park, PA. Tel: (814) 865-1327, (800) 326-9180, FAX: (814) 863-1408, Web Site: www.psupress.org (17)

Goodman, Eric, Transamerica Occidental Life Co, Los Angeles, CA. Tel: (213) 742-3111, FAX: (213) 741-6623, Web Site: www.transamerica.com (15)

Goodman, Jason, Goodman Media Group Inc, New York, NY. Tel: (212) 262-2247, FAX: (212) 262-2278, E-Mail: jgoodman@gmgpub.com, Web Site: www.goodmanmediagroup.dev.hotresponse.com (17)

Goodman, John, Technical Assistance Research Programs (TARP), Arlington, VA. Tel: (703) 524-1456, FAX: (703) 524-6374, Web Site: www.tarp.com (20)

Goodman, Keith, Modern Postcard, Carlsbad, CA. Tel: (800) 959-8365, Web Site: www.modernpostcard.com (10)

Goodman, Kim, Tom Snyder Productions, Watertown, MA. Tel: (617) 926-6000, (800) 342-0236, FAX: (800) 304-1254, E-Mail: ask@tomsnyder.com, Web Site: www.tomsnyder.com (16)

Goodman, Meg, PCG, Inc, Batavia, IL. Tel: (630) 482-9300, FAX: (630) 454-3750, E-Mail: sasmith@pcgnow.com, Web Site: www.pcgnow.com (20)

Goodman, Michael, Shepard's Inc, Bethel, CT. Tel: (203) 830-8300, (800) 243-0993, FAX: (203) 794-1296, E-Mail: mleahy@shepardsinc.com, Web Site: www.shepardsinc.com (22)

Goodman, Susan, Goodman & Co, New York, NY. Tel: (212) 579-0020, Web Site: www.goodmancompany.com (20)

Goodman, Will, Guidance Associates, Mount Kisco, NY. Tel: (914) 666-4100, (800) 431-1242, FAX: (914) 666-5319, E-Mail: willg1961@gmail.com, Web Site: www.guidanceassociates.com (31)

Goodnight, Dr. James H., SAS Institute, Cary, NC. Tel: (919) 677-8000, FAX: (919) 677-4444, Web Site: www.sas.com (22)

Goodnight, Keith, Infolure, Phoenix, AZ. Tel: (602) 308-6700, FAX: (602) 308-6801, E-Mail: glenn.gottfried@infolure.com, Web Site: www.infolure.com (22)

Goodreds, Steve, Mediamark Research Inc, New York, NY. Tel: (212) 884-9200, (800) 310-3305, FAX: (212) 884-9339, Web Site: www.mediamark.com (30)

Goodrich, Donna C., Branch Banking & Trust Co, Winston-Salem, NC. Tel: (336) 733-2000, FAX: (336) 733-2189, Web Site: www.bbt.com (14)

Goodrich, Garry, Propay USA Inc, Lehi, UT. Tel: (801) 766-3758, Web Site: www.propay.com (14)

Goodrich, Mike, Potawatomi Bingo Casino, Milwaukee, WI. Tel: (414) 645-6888, (800) PAYS-BIG, FAX: (414) 847-7727, Web Site: www.paysbig.com (19)

Goodrich, Stephen, PowerPay, Portland, ME. Tel: (207) 775-6900, (877) 877-3737, FAX: (888) 204-4040, Web Site: www.powerpay.biz (14)

Goodroe, J. Glenn, White Point Leads Group LLC, Gulf Breeze, FL. Tel: (850) 934-5577, Web Site: www.whitepointleads.com (29)

Goodson, Maureen, National Postal Forum, Fairfax, VA. Tel: (703) 218-5015, FAX: (703) 218-5020, E-Mail: info@npf.org, Web Site: www.npf.org (42)

Goodstein, Barbara, Vonage, Holmdel, NJ. Tel: (732) 528-2600, Web Site: www.vonage.com (32)

Goodvin, Grant, Heart Thoughts Inc, Wichita, KS. Tel: (316) 688-5781, (800) 524-2229, FAX: (316) 687-2846, Web Site: www.heart-thoughts.com (27)

Goodway Group, Jenkintown, PA. Tel: (626) 355-7800, E-Mail: info@goodwaygroup.com, Web Site: goodwaygroup.com (35)

Goodwill Industries of San Francisco, San Francisco, CA. Tel: (415) 575-2240, FAX: (415) 575-2170, Web Site: www.sfgoodwill.org (1)

Goodwin, Elinor, Berkshire Direct Inc, Williamstown, MA. Tel: (413) 458-1721, FAX: (413) 458-1727, E-Mail: info@berkshiredirect.com, Web Site: www.berkshiredirect.com (17)

Goodwin, Greg, Maus & Hoffman Inc, Fort Lauderdale, FL. Tel: (800) 628-6287, FAX: (954) 463-8735, E-Mail: info@mausandhoffman.com, Web Site: www.mausandhoffman.com (2)

Goodwin, Jeff, EOS International Inc, Carlsbad, CA. Tel: (760) 431-8400, (800) 876-5484, FAX: (760) 431-8448, Web Site: www.eosintl.com (5)

Goodwin, Jodee, The Creative Alliance Inc, Lafayette, CO. Tel: (303) 665-8101, FAX: (303) 665-3136, E-Mail: info@thecreativealliance.com, Web Site: www.thecreativealliance.com (35)

Goodwin, Scott, Cenveo Inc, Stamford, CT. Tel: (410) 633-4200, (800) 638-2850, FAX: (410) 633-1202, Web Site: www.cenveo.com (27)

Goodwin, William M., WESCO, Pittsburgh, PA. Tel: (412) 454-2200, (800) 343-1201, E-Mail: info@wesco.com, Web Site: www.wescodist.com (16)

Goodyear Tire & Rubber Co, Akron, OH. Tel: (330) 796-2121, (800) 321-2136, FAX: (330) 796-2222, Web Site: www.goodyear.com (16)

Goodyear, Steve, Nestle HealthCare Nutrition, Florham Park, NJ. Tel: (800) 422-2752, Web Site: www.nestle-nutrition.com (16)

Google Inc, Mountain View, CA. Tel: (650) 253-0000, FAX: (650) 253-0001, Web Site: www.google.com (31)

Goolara LLC, Alameda, CA. Tel: (510) 522-8000, (888) 362-4575, FAX: (510) 522-2457, E-Mail: info@goolara.com, Web Site: www.goolara.com (32)

Goosman, Tom, True North Inc, New York, NY. Tel: (212) 557-4202, Web Site: truenorthinc.com (35)

Gorchels, Linda, University of Wisconsin-Madison School of Business, Madison, WI. Tel: (608) 262-1550, E-Mail: info@bus.wisc.edu, Web Site: bus.wisc.edu (1)

Joel Gordon Photography, New York, NY. Tel: (212) 254-1688, E-Mail: joel.gordon@verizon.net, Web Site: www.joelgordonphotography.com (38)

Gordon Management Inc, Somerset, NJ. Tel: (732) 846-4800, FAX: (732) 846-4709, E-Mail: keith@gmidistribution.com, Web Site: www.gmidistribution.com (28)

Gordon, Alan R., Iroquois Products, Chicago, IL. Tel: (773) 436-3900, (800) 453-3355, FAX: (773) 436-4908, E-Mail: sales@iroquoisproducts.com, Web Site: www.iroquoisproducts.com (10)

Gordon, Andrew, Direct Impact Group, Needham, MA. Tel: (781) 453-2200, FAX: (781) 453-1200, E-Mail: info@directimpactgroup.com, Web Site: www.directimpactgroup.com (35)

Gordon, Anne, The Philadelphia Inquirer & Daily News, Philadelphia, PA. Tel: (215) 854-2000, FAX: (215) 854-4788, Web Site: www.phil.com/inquirer (31)

Gordon, Christopher, Accountants' Supply House, Lancaster, CA. Tel: (856) 384-1144, (800) 342-5274, FAX: (800) 468-4446, Web Site: www.rapidforms.com (10)

Gordon, Clifford, DoAll Co, Wheeling, IL. Tel: (847) 824-1122, (800) 92-DOALL, FAX: (847) 699-7524, E-Mail: info@doall.com, Web Site: www.doall.com (16)

Gordon, Joel, Joel Gordon Photography, New York, NY. Tel: (212) 254-1688, E-Mail: joel.gordon@verizon.net, Web Site: www.joelgordonphotography.com (38)

Gordon, Keith, GMI Distribution, Somerset, NJ. Tel: (732) 846-4800, FAX: (732) 846-4709, E-Mail: keith@gmidistribution.com, Web Site: www.gmidistribution.com (28)

Gordon, Keith, Gordon Management Inc, Somerset, NJ. Tel: (732) 846-4800, FAX: (732) 846-4709, E-Mail: keith@gmidistribution.com, Web Site: www.gmidistribution.com (28)

Gordon, Kenneth, Gordon Management Inc, Somerset, NJ. Tel: (732) 846-4800, FAX: (732) 846-4709, E-Mail: keith@gmidistribution.com, Web Site: www.gmidistribution.com (28)

Gordon, Megan, American Diabetes Association, Alexandria, VA. Tel: (703) 549-1500, (800) 342-2383, Web Site: www.diabetes.org (1)

Gordon, Nancy, HAVE Inc, Hudson, NY. Tel: (518) 828-2000, (800) 999-HAVE (4283), FAX: (518) 828-2008, E-Mail: kstein@haveinc.com, Web Site: www.haveinc.com (3)

Gordon, Rafi, Baseline FT, Los Angeles, CA. Tel: (212) 254-8235, (310) 393-9999, (800) 242-7546, FAX: (212) 529-3330, E-Mail: info@baseline.hollywood. com, Web Site: www.baseline.hollywood.com (17)

Gordon, Tomas, ClearOne Advantage, Baltimore, MD. Tel: (888) 785-5376, FAX: (888) 785-5365, Web Site: www.clearoneadvantage.com (14)

Gordon, Trina, Boyden Global Executive Search, Purchase, NY. Tel: (914) 747-0093, E-Mail: inquiry@boyden.com, Web Site: www.boyden.com (20)

WL Gore & Associates Inc, Newark, DE. Tel: (410) 506-7787, (888) 914-4673, E-Mail: info@wlgore. com, Web Site: www.wlgore.com (2)

Gore, Les, Executive Search International, Newton, MA. Tel: (617) 527-8787, E-Mail: info@execsearchintl.com, Web Site: www.execsearchintl.com (20)

Gorelkin, Amy, Beta Research Corp, Syosset, NY. Tel: (516) 935-3800, FAX: (516) 935-4092, E-Mail: beta@nybeta.com, Web Site: www.nybeta.com (30)

Gorelkin, Jason, Beta Research Corp, Syosset, NY. Tel: (516) 935-3800, FAX: (516) 935-4092, E-Mail: beta@nybeta.com, Web Site: www.nybeta.com (30)

Gorges, Lynn, Battleground Antiques Inc, New Bern, NC. Tel: (252) 636-3039, FAX: (252) 637-1862, E-Mail: tarheelrebel2000@aol.com, Web Site: www.civilwarantiques.com (6)

Gorges, William D., Battleground Antiques Inc, New Bern, NC. Tel: (252) 636-3039, FAX: (252) 637-1862, E-Mail: tarheelrebel2000@aol.com, Web Site: www.civilwarantiques.com (6)

Gorgonne, Tom, Magnet LLC, Washington, MO. Tel: (636) 239-5661, (800) 458-9457, FAX: (636) 239-4490, E-Mail: contactus@themagnetgroup.com, Web Site: www.magnetllc.com (16)

Gorham, Phyllis, Call Compliance Inc, Glen Cove, NY. Tel: (516) 674-4545, FAX: (516) 676-2420, E-Mail: sales@callcompliance.com, Web Site: www.callcompliance.com (29)

Gorham's Inc, Springfield, IL. Tel: (217) 544-1727, FAX: (217) 544-1623, E-Mail: gorhams@gorhams.com, Web Site: www.gorhams.com (33)

Gorman, Kathleen A., RBC Funds, Milwaukee, WI. Tel: (800) 422-2766, Web Site: us.rbcgam.com (14)

Gornitsky, Rhonda, International Masters Publishers Inc, Montoursville, PA. Tel: (800) 570-5718, E-Mail: customerservice@imp-usa.com, Web Site: www.imponline.com (17)

Gornnert, Margie, Concept Media Partners Inc, Yorktown Heights, NY. Tel: (914) 767-0032, FAX: (914) 514-1711, E-Mail: karen@conceptmediapartners.com, Web Site: www.conceptmediapartners.com (35)

Gorsky, Alex, Johnson & Johnson, New Brunswick, NJ. Tel: (732) 524-0400, FAX: (732) 214-0332, Web Site: www.jnj.com (16)

Gorsuch Ltd, Vail, CO. Tel: (970) 476-2294, (800) 525-9808, FAX: (970) 476-4323, Web Site: www.gorsuchltd.com (2)

Gorsuch, David, Gorsuch Ltd, Vail, CO. Tel: (970) 476-2294, (800) 525-9808, FAX: (970) 476-4323, Web Site: www.gorsuchltd.com (2)

Gorsuch, Gary, Mercury International Trading, North Attleboro, MA. Tel: (508) 699-9000, FAX: (508) 699-9088, Web Site: www.mercuryfootwear.com (2)

Gorsuch, Renie, Gorsuch Ltd, Vail, CO. Tel: (970) 476-2294, (800) 525-9808, FAX: (970) 476-4323, Web Site: www.gorsuchltd.com (2)

Gorvine, Tara, Edward Elgar Publishing Inc, Northampton, MA. Tel: (413) 584-5551, FAX: (413) 584-9933, E-Mail: sales@e-elgar.com, Web Site: www.e-elgar.com (17)

Goss International, Durham, NH. Tel: (603) 749-6600, FAX: (603) 750-6860, Web Site: www.gossinternational.com (27)

Gosse, Jonathan, American Technical Publishers Inc, Orland Park, IL. Tel: (708) 957-1100, (800) 323-3471, FAX: (708) 957-1101, E-Mail: service@americantech.net, Web Site: www.atplearning.com (17)

Gosselin, Nick, VistaPrint USA Inc, Lexington, MA. Tel: (800) 961-2075, Web Site: www.vistaprint.com (27)

Gossett, Chuck, Cougar Mountain Software, Boise, ID. Tel: (208) 375-4455, (800) 388-3038, FAX: (208) 375-4460, E-Mail: sales@cougarmtn.com, Web Site: www.cougarmtn.com (14)

Gossett, Elaine, Image Makers Marketing Inc, Marietta, GA. Tel: (770) 926-9552, FAX: (770) 926-9558, E-Mail: elaine.gossett@immmail.com, Web Site: www.imagemakersmarketing.com (21)

Gossett, Jon, Minnesota Public Radio, Saint Paul, MN. Tel: (651) 290-1500, (800) 228-7123, FAX: (651) 290-1260, E-Mail: mail@mpr.org, Web Site: www.mpr.org (1)

Gossett, Natalie, Hunt Marketing Group, Seattle, WA. Tel: (206) 447-5665, FAX: (206) 447-5789, E-Mail: info@hmgseattle.com, Web Site: www.hmgseattle.com (35)

Gossett, Steve, Image Makers Marketing Inc, Marietta, GA. Tel: (770) 926-9552, FAX: (770) 926-9558, E-Mail: elaine.gossett@immmail.com, Web Site: www.imagemakersmarketing.com (21)

Gossler Farms Nursery, Springfield, OR. Tel: (541) 746-3922, FAX: (541) 744-7924, Web Site: www.gosslerfarms.com (8)

Gossler, Marjory, Gossler Farms Nursery, Springfield, OR. Tel: (541) 746-3922, FAX: (541) 744-7924, Web Site: www.gosslerfarms.com (8)

Gossler, Roger, Gossler Farms Nursery, Springfield, OR. Tel: (541) 746-3922, FAX: (541) 744-7924, Web Site: www.gosslerfarms.com (8)

Gossman, Bill, Advanced Software Applications Corp, Morgan, PA. Tel: (412) 220-9300, FAX: (412) 220-3878, E-Mail: asa@asacorp.com, Web Site: www.asacorp.com (22)

Gostic, Julia, Sweepstakes Clearinghouse, Dallas, TX. Tel: (214) 915-7100, (800) 481-2631, FAX: (214) 915-7458, E-Mail: customersupport@sweepstakesclearinghouse.com, Web Site: www.schstore.com (16)

Gotbetter, Amy, Direct Marketers On Call Inc (DMOC), New York, NY. Tel: (212) 691-1942, FAX: (212) 924-1331, E-Mail: info@dmoc-inc.com, Web Site: www.dmoc-inc.com (20)

Gotfredson, Mike, Road Runner Sports Inc, San Diego, CA. Tel: (858) 974-4455, (800) 636-3560, FAX: (800) 453-5443, Web Site: www.roadrunnersports.com (11)

Gothic Arch Greenhouses Inc, Mobile, AL. Tel: (251) 471-5238, (800) 531-4769, FAX: (251) 471-5465, E-Mail: info@gothicarchgreenhouses.net, Web Site: www.GothicArchGreenhouses.com (8)

Gotsch, Kenneth C., Columbia College Chicago, Chicago, IL. Tel: (312) 663-1600, FAX: (312) 344-0869, Web Site: www.colum.edu (41)

Gottehrer, Rita, Better Health Fitness, Brooklyn, NY. Tel: (718) 436-4693, FAX: (718) 854-3381, Web Site: www.betterhealthfitness.com (11)

Gottlieb, Bruce, National Journal Group, Washington, DC. Tel: (202) 739-8400, (800) 613-6701, FAX: (202) 833-8069, Web Site: www.nationaljournal.com (17)

Gottlieb, Richard, Directory of Mail Order Catalogs, Amenia, NY. Tel: (518) 789-8700, (800) 562-2139, FAX: (518) 789-0556, E-Mail: cstupak@greyhouse.com, Web Site: www.greyhouse.com (43)

Gottlieb, Richard, Grey House Publishing, Amenia, NY. Tel: (518) 789-8700, (800) 562-2139, FAX: (518) 789-0556, E-Mail: books@greyhouse.com, Web Site: www.greyhouse.com (43)

Gottlieb, Richard, The Directory of Business Information Resources, Amenia, NY. Tel: (845) 373-8263, E-Mail: cstupak@greyhouse.com, Web Site: www.greyhouse.com (43)

Gottung, Lizanne C., Kimberly-Clark Corp, Neenah, WI. Tel: (920) 721-2000, (888) 525-8388, FAX: (920) 721-7722, Web Site: www.kimberly-clark.com (16)

Gotwald, Bruce C., Ethyl Corp, Richmond, VA. Tel: (804) 788-5000, FAX: (804) 788-5688, Web Site: www.ethyl.com (16)

Gotwald, Thomas E., Ethyl Corp, Richmond, VA. Tel: (804) 788-5000, FAX: (804) 788-5688, Web Site: www.ethyl.com (16)

Goudeseune, Scott, American Council on Exercise, San Diego, CA. Tel: (858) 576-6500, (888) 825-3636, FAX: (858) 576-6564, Web Site: www.acefitness.org (1)

Goudis, Richard, Herbalife International of America Inc, Los Angeles, CA. Tel: (310) 216-9661, (866) 866-4744, FAX: (310) 258-7019, Web Site: www.herbalife.com (7)

Gough, Al, Cablexpress Technologies, Syracuse, NY. Tel: (315) 476-3000, (800) 913-9467, FAX: (315) 455-1800, E-Mail: info@cablexpress.com, Web Site: www.CXTec.com (10)

Gould & Goodrich, Lillington, NC. Tel: (910) 893-2071, (800) 277-0732, FAX: (910) 893-4742, E-Mail: service@gouldusa.com, Web Site: www.gouldusa.com (2)

Gould Paper Corp, New York, NY. Tel: (212) 301-0001, (800) 221-3043, FAX: (212) 481-0392, Web Site: www.gouldpaper.com (25)

Stephen Gould Paper Co Inc, Whippany, NJ. Tel: (973) 428-1500, FAX: (973) 428-5274, Web Site: www.stephengould.com (27)

Gould, C.W.D., Broadway Play Publishing Inc, New York, NY. Tel: (212) 772-8334, FAX: (212) 772-8358, E-Mail: sara@broadwayplaypubl.com, Web Site: www.broadwayplaypubl.com (17)

Gould, Carolyn, Directives/Targeted Marketing and Communications, Plymouth, MA. Tel: (215) 546-7817, Web Site: www.directivesmarketing.com (20)

Gould, David, Thermo Pro, Duluth, GA. Tel: (678) 475-1647, (800) 523-5542, FAX: (678) 475-1747, Web Site: www.thermopro.com (16)

Gould, Donald, Medifast Inc, Owings Mills, MD. Tel: (410) 581-8042, (800) 209-0878, FAX: 410 581-8070, Web Site: www.medifastdiet.com (4)

Gould, Harry E., Gould Paper Corp, New York, NY. Tel: (212) 301-0001, (800) 221-3043, FAX: (212) 481-0392, Web Site: www.gouldpaper.com (25)

Gould, Jerry, Conrad Direct Inc, Cresskill, NJ. Tel: (201) 567-3200, FAX: (201) 567-1530, E-Mail: listinfo@conraddirect.com, Web Site: www.conraddirect.com (23)

Gould, Michael L., Thermo Pro, Duluth, GA. Tel: (678) 475-1647, (800) 523-5542, FAX: (678) 475-1747, Web Site: www.thermopro.com (16)

Gould, Rick, Ohio Envelope Manufacturing Co, Cleveland, OH. Tel: (216) 267-2920, (800) 989-0336, FAX: (216) 267-1765, E-Mail: mgmt@ohioenvelope.com, Web Site: www.ohioenvelope.com (26)

Goupil, Dominique Philippe, FileMaker Inc, Santa Clara, CA. Tel: (408) 987-7000, FAX: (408) 987-3823, Web Site: www.filemaker.com (22)

Gourlay, Alex, Walgreens Co, Deerfield, IL. Tel: (800) 925-4733, Web Site: www.walgreens.com (7)

Gourlay, John, American Craft Council, Minneapolis, MN. Tel: (212) 274-0630, FAX: (212) 274-0650, E-Mail: council@craftcouncil.org, Web Site: www.craftcouncil.org (17)

The Gourley Group, Henderson, NV. Tel: (888) 656-1324, E-Mail: issuestoday@yahoo.com, Web Site: www.issuestodayradio.com (32)

Gourley, Bob, The Gourley Group, Henderson, NV. Tel: (888) 656-1324, E-Mail: issuestoday@yahoo.com, Web Site: www.issuestodayradio.com (32)

Governing Magazine, Washington, DC. Tel: (202) 862-8802, Web Site: www.governing.com (17)

Government of India Tourist Office, New York, NY. Tel: (212) 586-4901, (800) 953-9399, FAX: (212) 582-3274, Web Site: www.incredibleindia.org (1)

Gow, Frank, Audio Classics Ltd, Vestal, NY. Tel: (607) 766-3501, FAX: (607) 766-3502, E-Mail: steve@audioclassics.com, Web Site: www.audioclassics.com (3)

Grabin, Bill, Renaissance Greeting Cards Inc, Downers Grove, IL. Tel: (800) 736-3383, Web Site: www.ftd.com (5)

Grabowski, Jim, Hasco First Photo, Saint Charles, MO. Tel: (636) 946-5115, FAX: (636) 946-7148, Web Site: www.growingfamily.com (16)

Grabowski, Simon, GetResponse Services Inc, Wilmington, DE. Tel: (877) 362-4547, Web Site: www.getresponse.com (24)

W R Grace & Co, Columbia, MD. Tel: (410) 531-4000, FAX: (410) 531-4367, Web Site: www.grace.com (16)

Grace, Alfred, Polynesian Cultural Center, Honolulu, HI. Tel: (808) 293-3333, (800) 367-7060, FAX: (888) 722-7339, E-Mail: internetrez@polynesia.com, Web Site: www.polynesia.com (16)

Graceland, Memphis, TN. Tel: (901) 332-3322, (800) 238-2010, FAX: (901) 344-3120, Web Site: www.elvis.com (6)

Graci, Joseph, Sleepy's Inc, Hicksville, NY. Tel: (516) 844-8800, (800) sleepys, FAX: (516) 844-8847, Web Site: www.sleepys.com (16)

Graddick Weir, Mirian, Calbiochem-Novabiochem Corp, San Diego, CA. Tel: (858) 450-9600, (800) 854-3417, FAX: (858) 453-3552, E-Mail: customerservice@emdbioscience.com, Web Site: www.calbiochem.com (9)

Grade Finders Inc, Philadelphia, PA. Tel: (800) 777-8074, E-Mail: info@gradefinders.com, Web Site: www.gradefinders.com (17)

Graduate Management Admission Council, Reston, VA. Tel: (703) 668-9813, Web Site: www.mba.com (20)

Graduate School USA, Washington, DC. Tel: (202) 314-3300, FAX: (202) 690-6577, E-Mail: pubaffairs@grad.usda.gov, Web Site: www.grad.usda.gov (1)

Grady, Jarell D, Special Libraries Association (SLA), Alexandria, VA. Tel: (703) 647-4900, FAX: (703) 647-4901, E-Mail: sla@sla.org, Web Site: www.sla.org (40)

Graf, David, TRANZACT, Fort Lee, NJ. Tel: (201) 461-5665, E-Mail: info@tranzact.net, Web Site: www.tranzact.net (35)

Graf, Dennis, Form House Inc, Chicago, IL. Tel: (773) 577-8500, E-Mail: ktalbot@theformhouse.com, Web Site: www.theformhouse.com (28)

Graf, John, Forethought Financial Services Inc, Batesville, IN. Tel: (812) 934-7139, (800) 331-8853, FAX: (812) 934-8564, Web Site: www.forethought.com (15)

Graff, Brian, The Jane Goodall Institute, Vienna, VA. Tel: (703) 682-9220, Web Site: www.janegoodall.org (1)

Graff, Michael, Sandy Alexander Inc, Clifton, NJ. Tel: (973) 470-8100, FAX: (973) 470-9269, E-Mail: sandy@sandyinc.com, Web Site: www.sandyinc.com (32)

Grafica Group, Morristown, NJ. Tel: (973) 309-7500, FAX: (973) 309-7501, E-Mail: information@grafica.com, Web Site: www.grafica.com (35)

Gragg Advertising, Kansas City, MO. Tel: (877) GRAGGADV, FAX: (816) 931-2227, E-Mail: contact@graggadv.com, Web Site: www.graggadv.com (35)

Gragg, Greg, Gragg Advertising, Kansas City, MO. Tel: (877) GRAGGADV, FAX: (816) 931-2227, E-Mail: contact@graggadv.com, Web Site: www.graggadv.com (35)

Gragg, Sam, Teradata Corp. Miamisburg, OH. Tel: (937) 242-4800, Web Site: www.teradata.com (22)

Billy Graham Evangelistic Association, Charlotte, NC. Tel: (704) 401-2432, (877) 247-2426, Web Site: www.billygraham.org (1)

Graham Field Health Products Inc, Atlanta, GA. Tel: (770) 368-4700, (800) 347-5678, FAX: (800) 726-0601, E-Mail: cs@grahamfield.com, Web Site: www.grahamfield.com (7)

Graham, Arnold, NYK Rapp Enterprises LLC, Hallandale, FL. Tel: (954) 457-9100, FAX: (954) 457-9015, Web Site: www.nykrapp.com (35)

Graham, Bill, CAA Auto Club & Travel Agency Inc, Thornhill, ON Canada. Tel: (905) 371-3000, (866) 988-, FAX: (905) 371-3101, E-Mail: membership@caasco.ca, Web Site: www.central.on.caa.ca (1)

Graham, Billy, Billy Graham Evangelistic Association, Charlotte, NC. Tel: (704) 401-2432, (877) 247-2426, Web Site: www.billygraham.org (1)

Graham, Donald E., The Washington Post, Washington, DC. Tel: (202) 334-6000, (800) 627-1150, E-Mail: letters@washpost.com, Web Site: www.washingtonpost.com (17)

Graham, Franklin, Billy Graham Evangelistic Association, Charlotte, NC. Tel: (704) 401-2432, (877) 247-2426, Web Site: www.billygraham.org (1)

Graham, Jennifer, Dirxion, Saint Louis, MO. Tel: (636) 717-2300, Web Site: www.dirxion.com (16)

Graham, Judge, Ansira, Saint Louis, MO. Tel: (314) 783-2300, FAX: (314) 783-2301, E-Mail: dl-newbusiness@ansira.com, Web Site: ansira.com (35)

Graham, Marianne, The Hamilton Collection, Jacksonville, FL. Tel: (904) 279-1300, (866) 323-5577, FAX: (904) 279-1495, Web Site: www.hamiltoncollection.com (6)

Graham, Mark, Data University, Lincoln, NE. Tel: (402) 742-2179, (866) 328-2848, E-Mail: info@datauniversity.com, Web Site: www.datauniversity.org (22)

Graham, Richie, Impressions Direct, Saint Louis, MO. Tel: (314) 951-2100, Web Site: www.impressionsdirect.com (28)

Graham, Ronald M., Ennis Inc, Midlothian, TX. Tel: (972) 775-9801, (800) 962-0944, FAX: (800) 645-8339, Web Site: www.ennis.com (16)

Graham, Thomas P., The Cross Country Group LLC, Medford, MA. Tel: (781) 396-3700, FAX: (781) 391-7504, E-Mail: info@crosscountrygroup.com, Web Site: www.ccgroup.com (13)

Graham, Tom, Mutual of Omaha, Omaha, NE. Tel: (402) 342-7600, (800) 775-6000, FAX: (402) 351-2775, Web Site: www.mutualofomaha.com (15)

Grahek, Greg, The American Phytopathological Society, Saint Paul, MN. Tel: (651) 454-7250, FAX: (651) 454-0766, E-Mail: apsheadquarters@scisoc.org, Web Site: www.apsnet.org (1)

Grainger Industrial Supply, North Brook, IL. Tel: (847) 498-5900, FAX: (847) 498-3402, Web Site: www.grainger.com (16)

W W Grainger Inc, Bradenton, FL. Tel: (941) 747-5566, (800) 472-4643, E-Mail: info@grainger.com, Web Site: www.grainger.com (5)

WW Grainger Inc, Lake Forest, IL. Tel: (847) 535-1000, (800) 472-4643, FAX: (847) 535-9122, Web Site: www.grainger.com (9)

Gramkow, Ted, InterMedia Outdoors Inc, New York, NY. Tel: (212) 852-6641, FAX: (212) 302-4472, Web Site: imomages.com (31)

Gramma's Graphics Inc, Lancaster, VA. Tel: (804) 462-0884, FAX: (804) 462-0884, E-Mail: sunprints@grandloving.com, Web Site: www.bubblink.com/donnelly (36)

Grammer-Williams, Jill, American Name Services Inc, Orem, UT. Tel: (801) 235-8061, (800) 434-1851, FAX: (801) 764-0613, E-Mail: sales@americannameservices.com, Web Site: www.americannameservices.com (23)

Granados, Patricia, Triton College, River Grove, IL. Tel: (708) 456-0300, FAX: (708) 583-3121, Web Site: www.triton.edu (16)

Granat, Bob, Johnson & Quin Inc, Niles, IL. Tel: (847) 588-4800, FAX: (847) 647-6949, E-Mail: jqinfo@j-quin.com, Web Site: www.j-quin.com (28)

Granat, Peter, Cision US Inc, Chicago, IL. Tel: (312) 922-2400, (866) 639-5087, FAX: (312) 922-3126, E-Mail: info.us@cision.com, Web Site: us.cision.com (43)

Granchos, Louis, The Gallery Shop, Buffalo, NY. Tel: (716) 882-8700 X258, FAX: (716) 882-1958, E-Mail: gallshop@albrightknox.org, Web Site: www.albrightknox.org (6)

Grand Canyon Association, Grand Canyon, AZ. Tel: (928) 638-2481, (800) 858-2808, FAX: (928-638-2484, E-Mail: gcassociation@grandcanyon.org, Web Site: www.grandcanyon.org (1)

Grand Canyon University, Phoenix, AZ. Tel: (602) 639-7500, (877) 860-3951, Web Site: www.gcu.edu (13)

Grand Circle Travel, Boston, MA. Tel: (617) 350-7500, (800) 959-0405, FAX: (617) 346-6030. Web Site: www.gct.com (19)

Grand Pacific Resorts, Carlsbad, CA. Tel: (760) 827-4100, (800) 374-7779, Web Site: www.grandpacificresorts.com (19)

Grandma Brown's Beans Inc, Mexico, NY. Tel: (315) 963-7221, FAX: (315) 963-4072 (4)

Grandos, Jim, Print Management Partners, Des Plaines, IL. Tel: (847) 699-2999, FAX: (847) 699-2935, Web Site: www.ourpartners.com (27)

Grange, Carey, Murad Inc, El Segundo, CA. Tel: (310) 726-0600, (888) 996-8723, Web Site: www.murad.com (7)

The Granger Collection, New York, NY. Tel: (212) 447-1789, FAX: (212) 447-1492, Web Site: www.granger.com (38)

Mary Elizabeth Granger & Associates Inc, Baltimore, MD. Tel: (410) 842-1170, FAX: (410) 842-1185, E-Mail: info@maryegranger.com, Web Site: www.maryegranger.com (23)

Granger, Bonnie, Mary Elizabeth Granger & Associates Inc, Baltimore, MD. Tel: (410) 842-1170, FAX: (410) 842-1185, E-Mail: info@maryegranger.com, Web Site: www.maryegranger.com (23)

Granger, David, Esquire Magazine, New York, NY. Tel: (212) 649-4020, FAX: (212) 649-4303, E-Mail: esquire@hearst.com, Web Site: www.esquire.com (17)

Grano, Joseph, UBS Wealth Management US, Weehawken, NJ. Tel: (201) 352-3000, (888) 279-3343, FAX: (201) 617-8589, Web Site: www.ubs.com/financialservicesinc (14)

Grant, Gerald, SMY Media Inc, Chicago, IL. Tel: (312) 621-9600, FAX: (312) 621-0924, E-Mail: info@smymedia.com, Web Site: www.smymedia.com (32)

Grant, Hallie, Sailrite Enterprises, Inc, Columbia City, IN. Tel: (260) 693-2242, (800) 348-2769, FAX: (260) 693-2246, E-Mail: sailrite@sailrite.com, Web Site: www.sailrite.com (11)

Grant, Hugh, Fielder's Choice Direct, Monticello, IN. Tel: (812) 492-1700, FAX: (812) 492-1799, Web Site: monsanto.com (8)

Grant, Jr. W. King, KEH.com, Smyrna, GA. Tel: (770) 333-4200, (800) 342-5534, FAX: (770) 333-4242, E-Mail: sales@keh.com, Web Site: www.keh.com (16)

Grant, Matthew, Sailrite Enterprises, Inc, Columbia City, IN. Tel: (260) 693-2242, (800) 348-2769, FAX: (260) 693-2246, E-Mail: sailrite@sailrite.com, Web Site: www.sailrite.com (11)

Grant, Maurice, Defense News Media Group, Springfield, VA. Tel: (703) 848-0490, FAX: (703) 848-0480, E-Mail: mgrant@atpco.com, Web Site: www.defensenews.com (17)

Grant, Nina, Practice Builders, Irvine, CA. Tel: (800) 679-1262, FAX: (714) 751-7801, E-Mail: info@practicebuilders.com, Web Site: www.practicebuilders.com (35)

Grant's Mailing Services Inc, Mississauga, ON Canada. Tel: (905) 826-1411, FAX: (905) 826-1450, E-Mail: mstephens@innovativeresponse.ca, Web Site: www.grants-mailing.ca (27)

Granum, Patricia, Co-operations, Tualatin, OR. Tel: (503) 620-7977, (866) 228-6362, FAX: (503) 620-7917, E-Mail: info@fsipdx.com, Web Site: www.fsipdx.com (28)

The Graph Co, Vineland, NJ. Tel: (856) 825-9199, FAX: (856) 825-5573, E-Mail: graphco2@verizon.net (14)

Graphic Arts Center, Garland, TX. Tel: (972) 543-1250, (800) 865-7086, FAX: (972) 271-8392 (27)

Graphic Arts Information Network (GAIN), Sewickley, PA. Tel: (412) 741-6860, (800) 910-4283, FAX: (412) 741-2311, E-Mail: printing@printing.org, Web Site: www.gain.net (27)

Graphic Communications Center, Appleton, WI. Tel: (920) 733-4483, (800) 422-3696, FAX: (920) 733-1700 (27)

Graphic Communications Holdings Inc, Hudson, OH. Tel: (330) 650-5522, FAX: (330) 650-8998, E-Mail: info@graphiccommunications.com, Web Site: www.graphiccommunications.com (25)

Graphic Converting Inc, Elmhurst, IL. Tel: (630) 758-4100, (800) 447-1935, FAX: (630) 833-1058, E-Mail: sales@graphicconverting.com, Web Site: www.graphicconverting.com (36)

Graphics International Inc, Dallas, TX. Tel: (214) 352-7565, FAX: (214) 528-0114 (27)

Graphik Dimensions Ltd, High Point, NC. Tel: (336) 887-3500, (800) 221-0262, FAX: (336) 887-3773, E-Mail: customercare@pictureframes.com, Web Site: www.pictureframes.com (16)

Graphnet Inc, New York, NY. Tel: (212) 994-1100, (800) 327-1800, FAX: (212) 994-1188, E-Mail: custsvc@graphnet.com, Web Site: www.graphnet.com (28)

Grasee, Mike, Demco Inc, Madison, WI. Tel: (608) 241-1201, (800) 356-1200, FAX: (608) 241-1799, E-Mail: custserv@demco.com, Web Site: www.demco.com (10)

Grassi, Judith, Academic Management Services, Swansea, MA. Tel: (508) 235-2870, (800) 891-4203, FAX: (508) 235-2991, E-Mail: info@amsweb.com, Web Site: www.amsweb.com (14)

Grassmyer, Bill, MediaTree, Parsippany, NJ. Tel: (973) 781-1070, (800) 475-8703, FAX: (973) 781-1071, E-Mail: sales@mediatreegroup.com, Web Site: www.mediatreegroup.com (27)

Grasso, Ethel, Ulano Corp, Brooklyn, NY. Tel: (718) 237-4700, (800) 221-0616, FAX: (718) 802-1119, E-Mail: ulano@ulano.com, Web Site: www.ulano.com (34)

Grausam, Michael, Thermal Product Solutions, White Deer, PA. Tel: (570) 538-7200, (800) 586-2473 (16)

Graves Lapidary Co, Pompano Beach, FL. Tel: (954) 960-0300, (800) 327-9103, FAX: (954) 960-0301, E-Mail: sales@gravescompany.com, Web Site: www.gravescompany.com (9)

Graves, Bill, American Trucking Association, Arlington, VA. Tel: (703) 838-1700, FAX: (800) 254-2571, E-Mail: atamembership@trucking.org, Web Site: www.trucking.org (1)

Graves, Chris, Team One Advertising, Los Angeles, CA. Tel: (310) 437-2500, Web Site: www.teamone-usa.com (35)

Graves, Earl Butch, Black Enterprise Magazine, New York, NY. Tel: (212) 242-8000, FAX: (212) 886-9618, Web Site: www.blackenterprise.com (17)

Graves, Jeffrey B., Sedlak, Highland Hills, OH. Tel: (216) 206-4700, FAX: (216) 206-4840, E-Mail: info@jasedlak.com, Web Site: www.jasedlak.com (20)

Graves, John, Herrmann Global LLC, Lake Lure, NC. Tel: (828) 625-9153, (800) 432-4234, E-Mail: info@hbdi.com, Web Site: www.herrmannsolutions.com (35)

Graves, Mark, Cole-Parmer Instrument Co, Vernon Hills, IL. Tel: (847) 549-7600, (800) 323-4340, FAX: (847) 247-2929, E-Mail: info@coleparmer.com, Web Site: www.coleparmer.com (16)

Graves, Matt, Infogroup, Papillion, NE. Tel: (402) 836-5290, E-Mail: contentfeedback@infogroup.com, Web Site: www.infogroup.com (32)

Graves, Michael, Black Enterprise Magazine, New York, NY. Tel: (212) 242-8000, FAX: (212) 886-9618, Web Site: www.blackenterprise.com (17)

Graves, Michael, Midland Paper, Wheeling, IL. Tel: (847) 777-2700, (800) 323-8522, FAX: (847) 777-2552, E-Mail: whl@midlandpaper.com, Web Site: www.midlandpaper.com (25)

Graves, Sr. Earl G., Black Enterprise Magazine, New York, NY. Tel: (212) 242-8000, FAX: (212) 886-9618, Web Site: www.blackenterprise.com (17)

Gravitt, Mark, Raven's Nest Herbals, LLC, Duluth, GA. Tel: (678) 642-6691, (678) 584-0830, E-Mail: info@ravensnestherbals.com, Web Site: www.ravensnestherbals.com (7)

Gray & Graham Inc, Westport, CT. Tel: (203) 227-3900, FAX: (203) 227-3593, E-Mail: info@graygraham.com, Web Site: www.graygraham.com (35)

Gray Craddock, Mary, Equity Residential Properties, Chicago, IL. Tel: (312) 474-1300, FAX: (312) 474-8703, E-Mail: mgraycraddock@eqr.com, Web Site: www.eqr.com (20)

The Gray Printing Co, Fostoria, OH. Tel: (419) 435-6638 (27)

Gray, Bill, Innovation Printing Inc, Philadelphia, PA. Tel: (215) 969-4600, FAX: (215) 464-7664, Web Site: www.innovationprinting.com (27)

Gray, Donna, Melitta USA, Clearwater, FL. Tel: (727) 535-2111, Web Site: www.melitta.com (4)

Gray, Jeff R., Gray & Graham Inc, Westport, CT. Tel: (203) 227-3900, FAX: (203) 227-3593, E-Mail: info@graygraham.com, Web Site: www.graygraham.com (35)

Gray, Jonathan, Revana Digital, San Dimas, CA. Tel: (909) 599-8885, (866) 922-4632, Web Site: www.revanadigital.com (35)

Gray, Jonathon, Revana Inc, Tempe, AZ. Tel: (408) 902-5900, (800) 535-0343, Web Site: www.revana.com (35)

Gray, Mark, Katz Media Group, New York, NY. Tel: (212) 424-6000, Web Site: www.katz-media.com (32)

Gray, Michael W., Marketing & Promotions Group, Ridgewood, NJ. Tel: (201) 251-8339, FAX: (201) 251-8340, E-Mail: michael@promowaves.com, Web Site: www.promowaves.com (35)

Gray, Richard F., Arich Corp, New York, NY. Tel: (212) 247-1800, FAX: (212) 247-2231, Web Site: www.arichinc.com (20)

Gray, Robert A., The Gray Printing Co, Fostoria, OH. Tel: (419) 435-6638 (27)

Gray, Roger, GKV, Baltimore, MD. Tel: (410) 539-5400, FAX: (410) 234-2441, E-Mail: newbusiness@gkv.com, Web Site: gvk.com (35)

Gray, Stacie, iN DEMAND LLC, New York, NY. Tel: (646) 638-8200, FAX: (646) 486-0855, Web Site: www.indemand.com (32)

Graycar, Edward W., Physicians Mutual Insurance Co, Omaha, NE. Tel: (402) 633-1604, (888) 932-7642, FAX: (402) 633-1604, Web Site: www.physiciansmutual.com (15)

Graye, Mitchell T.G., Great-West Life, Greenwood Village, CO. Tel: (800) 537-2033, Web Site: www.greatwest.com (15)

GrayHair Software, Mount Laurel, NJ. Tel: (856) 727-9372, FAX: (856) 727-1315, Web Site: www.grayhairsoftware.com (22)

Grayson, David, American Fine Paper Co, Appleton, WI. Tel: (920) 733-6100, (800) 458-5446, FAX: (920) 380-8711, E-Mail: found@americanfinepaper.com, Web Site: www.americanfinepaper.com (25)

Graziani, Cheryl, Bay Manufacturing, Milan, OH. Tel: (419) 499-4602, FAX: (419) 499-4603, Web Site: www.baymfg.com (16)

The Great Amarillo Directory, Amarillo, TX. Tel: (806) 353-5155, FAX: (806) 359-2974, Web Site: www.worldpages.com (17)

The Great Books Foundation, Chicago, IL. Tel: (312) 332-5870, (800) 222-5870, FAX: (312) 407-0224, Web Site: www.greatbooks.org (1)

Great Chefs Television Publishing, New Orleans, LA. Tel: (504) 581-5000, (800) 321-1499, FAX: (504) 581-1188, E-Mail: info@greatchefs.com, Web Site: www.greatchefs.com (6)

Great Ideas Inc/CSP, Highland Park, IL. Tel: (800) 611-5515, FAX: (847) 432-8557, E-Mail: art@greatideasinc.com, Web Site: www.greatideasinc.com (33)

Great Lakes Integrated, Cleveland, OH. Tel: (216) 651-1500, (800) 745-4846, FAX: (216) 651-8311, E-Mail: bbemer@glintergrated.com, Web Site: www.gll.com (27)

Great Lakes List Management, Erie, PA. Tel: (814) 456-2175, (800) 964-5478, FAX: (814) 455-1942, E-Mail: info@greatlakeslists.com, Web Site: www.greatlakeslists.com (24)

Great-West Life, Greenwood Village, CO. Tel: (800) 537-2033, Web Site: www.greatwest.com (15)

Great Western Bank, Sioux Falls, SD. Tel: (605) 334-2545, Web Site: greatwesternbank.com (14)

Great Western Supply, Dallas, TX. Tel: (972) 481-6100, (800) 527-2782, FAX: (972) 481-6215, Web Site: www.proforma.com/greatwesternsupply (16)

Greater Fort Worth Builders Association, Fort Worth, TX. Tel: (817) 284-3566, FAX: (817) 284-6465, E-Mail: info@fortworthbuilders.org, Web Site: www.forthworthbuilders.org (1)

Greater Public, Minneapolis, MN. Tel: (612) 677-1505, (888) 454-2314, Web Site: www.deiworksite.org (1)

GreatLists.com, Herndon, VA. Tel: (703) 821-8130, FAX: (703) 821-8243, E-Mail: info@greatlists.com, Web Site: greatlists.com (23)

Greatrex, Mark, Cox Communications Inc, Atlanta, GA. Tel: (404) 843-5000, (888) 566-7751, FAX: (404) 269-2243, Web Site: www.cox.com (16)

Grebow, Ed, Union Privilege, AFL-CIO, Washington, DC. Tel: (202) 293-5311, (800) 472-2005, FAX: (202) 293-5311, E-Mail: info@unionprivilege.org, Web Site: www.unionplus.org (1)

Grech, Paul A., Dispatch Letter Service, New York, NY. Tel: (212) 307-5943, FAX: (212) 307-6103, Web Site: www.dispatchletterservice.com (28)

Greco, Tom, Frito-Lay, Plano, TX. Tel: (972) 334-7000, (800) 352-4477, FAX: (972) 334-2019, Web Site: www.fritolay.com (16)

Green Mountain Coffee Roasters, Inc, Waterbury, VT. Tel: (802) 244-5621, (800) 545-2326, FAX: (802) 244-5436, Web Site: www.gmcr.com (4)

Green, Barry, Hooleon Corp, Melrose, NM. Tel: (575) 253-4503, (800) 937-1337, E-Mail: sales@hooleon.com, Web Site: www.hooleon.com (3)

Green, Charles, National Journal Group, Washington, DC. Tel: (202) 739-8400, (800) 613-6701, FAX: (202) 833-8069, Web Site: www.nationaljournal.com (17)

Green, Charles, Thomas Computer Corp, Orlando, FL. Tel: (407) 855-2020, (800) 621-3906, FAX: (407) 426-2805, E-Mail: hildap@thomascompute.com, Web Site: www.thomascomputer.com (16)

Green, David I., Results Advertising Inc, Hasbrouck Heights, NJ. Tel: (201) 288-7888, FAX: (201) 288-5112, E-Mail: info@resultsinc.com, Web Site: www.resultsinc.com (35)

Green, Jessica A., Keeneland Association Inc, Lexington, KY. Tel: (859) 254-3412, (800) 456-3412, FAX: (859) 255-2484, Web Site: www.keeneland.com (16)

Green, Jr. Robert A., The Verdi Group Inc, Pittsford, NY. Tel: (585) 381-4275, FAX: (585) 381-4293, E-Mail: info@theverdigroup.com, Web Site: www.theverdigroup.com (35)

Green, Kevin, Lillian Vernon Corp, Colorado Springs, CO. Tel: (757) 427-7923, (800) 545-5426, FAX: (757) 427-7819, E-Mail: publicrelations@lillianvernon.com, Web Site: www.lillianvernon.com (6)

Green, Kevin, Vanguard Direct, New York, NY. Tel: (212) 736-0770, FAX: (212) 736-8305, Web Site: www.vanguarddirect.com (35)

Green, Lori, Peruvian Connection Ltd, Tonganoxie, KS. Tel: (913) 845-2450, (800) 221-8520, E-Mail: sales@peruvianconnection.com, Web Site: www.peruvianconnection.com (2)

Green, Michael E., DMRA, Mountain View, CA. Tel: (650) 559-9988, FAX: (650) 559-0149, E-Mail: mikeg@dmrainc.com, Web Site: www.dmrainc.com (22)

Green, Michael E., DMRA & Matchkey Corp, Mountain View, CA. Tel: (650) 856-9988, FAX: (650) 856-9986 (30)

Green, Stanley, Thomas Computer Corp, Orlando, FL. Tel: (407) 855-2020, (800) 621-3906, FAX: (407) 426-2805, E-Mail: hildap@thomascompute.com, Web Site: www.thomascomputer.com (16)

Green, Todd, Kipp Brothers Inc, Greenfield, IN. Tel: (800) 428-1153, E-Mail: support@kippbrothers.com, Web Site: kippbrothers.com (33)

Greenawalt, Andy, Cole-Parmer Instrument Co, Vernon Hills, IL. Tel: (847) 549-7600, (800) 323-4340, FAX: (847) 247-2929, E-Mail: info@coleparmer.com, Web Site: www.coleparmer.com (16)

Greenberg, Daniel, Norman Hecht Research Inc, Syosset, NY. Tel: (516) 496-8866, FAX: (516) 496-8165, E-Mail: nhr@normanhechtresearch.com, Web Site: www.normanhechtresearch.com (30)

Greenberg, Laura, Norman Hecht Research Inc, Syosset, NY. Tel: (516) 496-8866, FAX: (516) 496-8165, E-Mail: nhr@normanhechtresearch.com, Web Site: www.normanhechtresearch.com (30)

Greenberg, Mort, Katz Media Group, New York, NY. Tel: (212) 424-6000, Web Site: www.katz-media.com (32)

Greenblatt, Jonathan, Anti-Defamation League, New York, NY. Tel: (212) 885-7700, Web Site: www.adl.org (1)

Greenbook Worldwide Directory of Marketing Research Companies & Services, Bradenton, FL. Tel: (212) 849-2752, (800) 792-9202, FAX: (212) 202-7920, E-Mail: info@greenbrook.org, Web Site: www.greenbook.org (43)

Greenburg, Eric, Life Line Screening, Austin, TX. Tel: (216) 581-6556, (800) 449-2350, Web Site: www.lifelinescreening.com (7)

Greenbury, Jeff, NPN360 Inc, Wheeling, IL. Tel: (847) 215-7300, FAX: (847) 215-7314, E-Mail: sales@npn360.com, Web Site: www.npn360.com (21)

Greene, Chuck, Enertex Marketing, New York, NY. Tel: (212) 532-3115, FAX: (212) 532-1878, E-Mail: info@enertexmarketing.com, Web Site: www.enertexmarketing.com (22)

Greene, Mark, Data Square LLC, Stamford, CT. Tel: (203) 964-9733, FAX: (203) 964-0783, E-Mail: info@datasquare.com, Web Site: www.datasquare.com (22)

Greene, Mark N., Fair Isaac Corp, Saint Paul, MN. Tel: (651) 636-4509, E-Mail: info@fairisaac.com, Web Site: www.fairisaac.com (22)

Greene, Robert E., Branch Banking & Trust Co, Winston-Salem, NC. Tel: (336) 733-2000, FAX: (336) 733-2189, Web Site: www.bbt.com (14)

Greene, Roger, Ipswitch Inc, Lexington, MA. Tel: (781) 676-5700, FAX: (781) 676-5710, Web Site: www.whatsupgold.com (22)

Greene, Ted, United Security Products Inc, Poway, CA. Tel: (858) 413-0149, (800) 227-1592, FAX: (858) 413-0124, E-Mail: usp@unitedsecurity.com, Web Site: www.unitedsecurity.com (16)

Greenfield, David W., Kennametal Inc, Latrobe, PA. Tel: (800) 222-9327, FAX: (800) 521-3319, E-Mail: mcs-na.service@kennmetal.com, Web Site: www.kennametal.com (16)

Greenfield, Tamra, International Specialized Book Services Inc, Portland, OR. Tel: (503) 287-3093, (800) 944-6190, FAX: (503) 280-8832, E-Mail: isbs_sales@isbs.com, Web Site: www.isbscatalog.com (16)

Greenglass, Cyndi, Diamond Marketing Solutions, Carol Stream, IL. Tel: (630) 597-9100, E-Mail: info@dmsolutions.com, Web Site: www.dmsolutions.com (35)

Greenhut, Jonathan, Canyon Marketing, Hicksville, NY (7)

GreenPath Sustainability Consultants, New City, NY. Tel: (914) 980-8346 (20)

Greenpeace USA, Washington, DC. Tel: (202) 462-1177, Web Site: www.greenpeace.org (40)

Greenstein, Scott, SiriusXM Radio Inc, New York, NY. Tel: (212) 584-5100, Web Site: www.siriusxm.com (16)

Greenwood Publishing Group Inc, Portsmouth, NH. Tel: (203) 226-3571, FAX: (203) 222-1502, E-Mail: sales@greenwood.com, Web Site: www.greenwood.com (17)

Greenwood, Alex, Spectra Merchandising International Inc, Chicago, IL. Tel: (773) 202-8408, FAX: (773) 202-8409 (16)

Greenwood, Sara, Spa-Finder Inc, New York, NY. Tel: (305) 307-5852, (800) ALL-SPAS, Web Site: www.spafinder.com (7)

Greer, Charles, Commerce Register Inc, Midland Park, NJ. Tel: (201) 445-3000, FAX: (201) 445-5806, E-Mail: cri@comreginc.com, Web Site: www.comreginc.com (22)

Greer, Emily S., ALSAC - St Jude, Memphis, TN. Tel: (901) 495-3300, (800) 278-5833, FAX: (901) 495-3966, Web Site: www.stjude.org (1)

Greer, Shane, Campaigns & Elections Magazine, Arlington, VA. Tel: (703) 778-4028, (800) 771-8252, FAX: (703) 778-4024, Web Site: www.campaignsandelections.com (17)

Grefe, Richard, American Institute of Graphic Arts (AIGA), New York, NY. Tel: (212) 807-1990, FAX: (212) 807-1799, E-Mail: grefe@aiga.org, Web Site: www.aiga.org (40)

Gregerson, Bob, Yellow Book USA, Uniondale, NY. Tel: (516) 730-1900, (800) 666-8230, FAX: (845) 278-3299, Web Site: www.yellowbook.com (17)

Gregitis, David, Patriot Communications LLC, West Hollywood, CA. Tel: (888) 833-4711, FAX: (310) 482-6701, E-Mail: dlivingston@patriotllc.com, Web Site: www.patriotllc.com (17)

Gregor, Jeff, Turner Network Television (TNT), Atlanta, GA. Tel: (404) 827-1700, E-Mail: tnt@turner.com, Web Site: www.turner.com (32)

Gregory, James, Tenet Partners, New York, NY. Tel: (212) 329-3030, FAX: (212) 329-3031, Web Site: tenetpartners.com (35)

Gregory, Roy, NextScreen LLC, Austin, TX. Tel: (512) 892-8682, Web Site: www.avguide.com (17)

Gregory, Scott, Triggerfish Marketing, San Francisco, CA. Tel: (415) 671-4699, Web Site: www.triggerfish.com (30)

Greig, Paul G., First Merit Bank (HQ), Akron, OH. Tel: (330) 996-6300, (888) 554-4362, Web Site: www.firstmerit.com (14)

Greis, Jan, US Tape & Label Corp, Saint Louis, MO. Tel: (314) 824-4444, (800) 569-1906, FAX: (314) 824-4400, E-Mail: harrisonc@ustl.com, Web Site: www.ustl.com (27)

Gremillet, Andre, The Cleveland Orchestra, Cleveland, OH. Tel: (216) 231-7300, FAX: (216) 231-4038, Web Site: www.clevelandorchestra.com (1)

Grenier, Bart A., The Boston Co Asset Management LLC, Boston, MA. Tel: (617) 722-7029, FAX: (617) 722-3928, Web Site: www.thebostoncompany.com (14)

Greskiewicz, Michael, Business Marketing Association, Naperville, IL. Tel: (630) 544-5054, FAX: (630) 544-5055, E-Mail: info@marketing.org, Web Site: www.marketing.org (40)

Gressett, Wayne, Harcourt Educational Measurement, San Antonio, TX. Tel: (210) 299-1061, (800) 211-8378, FAX: (800) 232-1223, Web Site: www.harcourtassessment.com (17)

Gretschel, Gerry, List America, Washington, DC. Tel: (202) 298-9206, FAX: (202) 244-7294, Web Site: mdginc.org (23)

Gretschel, W. Michael, Market Development Group Inc, Washington, DC. Tel: (202) 298-8030, FAX: (202) 244-4999, Web Site: www.mdginc.org (1)

Greve, Ryann, Bader Rutter, Brookfield, WI. Tel: (262) 784-7200, FAX: (262) 938-5595, Web Site: www.baderrutter.com (35)

Greving, Robert C., Unum Corp, Portland, ME. Tel: (207) 770-2211, (800) 421-0344, FAX: (207) 770-4510, Web Site: www.unum.com (15)

Grewal, Harpreet, Constant Contact Inc, Waltham, MA. Tel: (781) 472-8100, FAX: (781) 472-8101, Web Site: www.constantcontact.com (32)

Grey Birch Group LLC, Irvington, NY. Tel: (914) 479-5088, Web Site: www.greybirch.com (20)

Grey Healthcare Group, New York, NY. Tel: (212) 886-3000, FAX: (212) 886-3297, E-Mail: info@ghgroup.com, Web Site: www.ghgroup.com (35)

Grey House Publishing, Amenia, NY. Tel: (518) 789-8700, (800) 562-2139, FAX: (518) 789-0556, E-Mail: books@greyhouse.com, Web Site: www.greyhouse.com (43)

Grey, Chris, Emigrant Savings Bank, New York, NY. Tel: (212) 850-4521, (800) EMIGRANT, FAX: (212) 850-4372, Web Site: www.emigrant.com (14)

Grey, Ethan, Magazine Publishers of America, New York, NY. Tel: (212) 872-3700, FAX: (212) 888-4217, E-Mail: mpa@magazine.org, Web Site: www.magazine.org (17)

Greystone Graphics, Kansas City, MO. Tel: (913) 342-1393, (800) 458-7407, FAX: (913) 621-4856, E-Mail: info@greystonegraphics.com, Web Site: www.greystonegraphics.com (27)

Greystone Services Inc, Beverly, MA. Tel: (978) 535-9185, FAX: (978) 535-7826, E-Mail: lee@gstone.biz, Web Site: www.gstone.biz (35)

Gribble, George, IPD Printing & Distributing Inc, Atlanta, GA. Tel: (770) 458-6351, FAX: (770) 454-6236, Web Site: www.rrdonnelley.com (27)

Gribble, James, Direct Marketing Dynamics Inc, Germantown, MD. Tel: (301) 916-3900, FAX: (301) 515-0404, E-Mail: jim@directmarketingdynamics.com, Web Site: www.directmarketingdynamics.com (35)

Gridley & Co LLC, New York, NY. Tel: (212) 400-9720, Web Site: www.gridleyco.com (14)

Gridley, Linda, Gridley & Co LLC, New York, NY. Tel: (212) 400-9720, Web Site: www.gridleyco.com (14)

Grieb, Deborah L., AutoPacific Inc, Tustin, CA. Tel: (714) 838-4234, FAX: (714) 838-4260, Web Site: www.autopacific.com (30)

Grieb, Robert F., The Diversified Services Group Inc, Wayne, PA. Tel: (610) 989-1710, FAX: (610) 989-1730, E-Mail: rfgrieb@dsg-network.com, Web Site: www.dsg-network.com (20)

Grieder, Daniel, Tommy Hilfiger, New York, NY. Tel: (212) 548-1368, Web Site: www.tommy.com (2)

Grier, Scott, Power Direct, Mission Viejo, CA. Tel: (877) 737-8977, FAX: (949) 253-3458, E-Mail: info@powerdirect.net, Web Site: www.powerdirect.net (35)

Griesemer, Ken, American General Co, Neptune, NJ. Tel: (732) 922-7000, FAX: (732) 922-7595 (15)

Griesen, Thomas, Rohlik Specialties Co, Bloomfield Hills, MI. Tel: (248) 858-8880, FAX: (248) 858-7323 (33)

Griffin, Bill, StrongView Systems Inc, Redwood City, CA. Tel: (650) 421-4200, (800) 971-0380, FAX: (650) 421-4201, E-Mail: info@strongview.com, Web Site: www.strongview.com (32)

Griffin, Brian, Empire Blue Cross & Blue Shield, New York, NY. Tel: (212) 476-1000, (877) 476-7111, FAX: (212) 476-1281, Web Site: www.empireblue.com (14)

Griffin, Chad, Human Rights Campaign, Washington, DC. Tel: (202) 216-1500, (800) 777-4723, Web Site: www.hrc.org (40)

Griffin, Christopher R., USG Corp, Chicago, IL. Tel: (312) 436-4000, (800) 621-9622, FAX: (312) 672-4093, Web Site: www.usg.com (34)

Griffin, Linda, SHSMD Annual Conference, Chicago, IL. Tel: (312) 422-3888, FAX: (312) 278-0883, E-Mail: shsmd@aha.org, Web Site: www.shsmd.org (42)

Griffin, Lyndon, CityTwist, Boca Raton, FL. Tel: (866) 798-2489, FAX: (561) 314-2692, Web Site: www.citytwist.com (32)

Griffin, Mary Ellen, Pernod Ricard USA, Purchase, NY. Tel: (914) 848-4800, Web Site: www.pernod-ricard-usa.com (16)

Griffin, Neil, JAM Communications Inc, Washington, DC. Tel: (202) 986-4750, FAX: (202) 232-9146, E-Mail: neil@jamagency.com, Web Site: www.jamagency.com (35)

Griffin, Raymond, Scan Optics Inc, Manchester, CT. Tel: (860) 645-7878, (800) 745-6001, FAX: (860) 645-7995, E-Mail: info@scanoptics.com, Web Site: www.scanoptics.com (16)

Griffing, Jeff, Star Tribune Media Co, Minneapolis, MN. Tel: (612) 673-4000, FAX: (612) 673-4359, Web Site: www.startribunecompany.com (17)

Griffis, Terry, DSP Inc USA, Charlottesville, VA. Tel: (434) 202-7870, E-Mail: iorder@delfortgroup.com, Web Site: www.delfortgroup.com (10)

Griffith, Andrew, Sage Software Inc, Irvine, CA. Tel: (949) 753-1222, (800) 854-3415, FAX: (949) 753-0374, Web Site: www.sagesoftware.com (16)

Griffith, Ann Marie, Power Direct, Mission Viejo, CA. Tel: (877) 737-8977, FAX: (949) 253-3458, E-Mail: info@powerdirect.net, Web Site: www.powerdirect.net (35)

Griffith, Bill, Nationwide Displays Inc, Ronkonkoma, NY. Tel: (631) 467-2034, FAX: (631) 467-2079, E-Mail: info@nationwidedisplays.com, Web Site: www.nationwidedisplays.com (16)

Griffith, Deborah, Towne AllPoints, Santa Ana, CA. Tel: (714) 540-3095, (800) 243-8099, FAX: (714) 540-4192, E-Mail: info@towne.com, Web Site: www.towne.com (21)

Griffith, John, Target Corp, Minneapolis, MN. Tel: (612) 304-6073, Web Site: www.target.com (16)

Griffith, Nancy, Aviation Book Co, Seattle, WA. Tel: (206) 767-5232, FAX: (206) 763-3428, E-Mail: sales@aviationbook.com, Web Site: www.aviationbook.com (17)

Griffith, Richard, Commercial Travelers Mutual Insurance Co, Utica, NY. Tel: (315) 797-5200, (800) 422-6200, FAX: (315) 797-3198, E-Mail: comtravl@commercialtravelers.com, Web Site: www.commercialtravelers.com (15)

Griffith, Scott, Voyageur Inc, Easley, SC. Tel: (802) 496-3127, (800) 311-7245, FAX: (802) 496-6247 (11)

Griffith, Steve, Nationwide Displays Inc, Ronkonkoma, NY. Tel: (631) 467-2034, FAX: (631) 467-2079, E-Mail: info@nationwidedisplays.com, Web Site: www.nationwidedisplays.com (16)

Griffiths, William D., Eberle & Associates Inc, McLean, VA. Tel: (703) 821-1550, FAX: (703) 821-0920, E-Mail: info@eberle1.com, Web Site: www.eberleassociates.com (1)

Griggs, Brent, Protective Life Corp, Deerfield, IL. Tel: (847) 948-8988, (800) 323-5771, FAX: (847) 948-1156, Web Site: www.protective.com (15)

Grijalva, Frank, Adwest Mailers Inc, Northridge, CA. Tel: (818) 982-3720, FAX: (818) 982-3786, E-Mail: sales@adwest.com, Web Site: www.adwest.com (28)

Grill, Glenn R., NewPage Corp, Miamisburg, OH. Tel: (937) 242-9345, (877) 855-7243, FAX: (937) 242-9327, Web Site: www.newpagecorp.com (25)

Grill, John, WorleyParsons, Reading, PA. Tel: (610) 855-2000, FAX: (610) 885-2001, Web Site: www.worleyparsons.com (16)

Grimes Horticulture Inc, Concord, OH. Tel: (800) 241-7333, FAX: (440) 352-1800, E-Mail: sales@grimes-hort.com, Web Site: www.grimesseeds.com (8)

Grimes, Angela, Born Free USA, Washington, DC. Tel: (202) 450-3168, (800) 348-7387, FAX: (202) 450-3581, E-Mail: info@bornfreeusa.org, Web Site: www.bornfreeusa.org (1)

Grimes, Brian, Plastic Graphic, Wauconda, IL. Tel: (847) 487-2030, FAX: (847) 487-2050, E-Mail: bgrimespgc@sbcglobal.net, Web Site: www.plasticgraphic.com (27)

Grimm, Foster, Video Artists International, Pleasantville, NY. Tel: (914) 769-3691, (800) 477-7146, FAX: (914) 769-5407, E-Mail: orders@vaimusic.com, Web Site: www.vaimusic.com (3)

Grimwood, Paul, Nestle USA, Glendale, CA. Tel: (818) 549-6000, (800) 225-2270, FAX: (818) 553-3547, Web Site: www.nestleusa.com (4)

Grindel, Karl, Delta Upsilon International Fraternity, Indianapolis, IN. Tel: (317) 875-8900, FAX: (317) 876-1629, E-Mail: ihq@deltau.org, Web Site: www.deltau.org (16)

Grindle, Dan, ElectroWarmth Products LLC, Danville, OH. Tel: (800) 990-4622, E-Mail: sales@electrowarmth.com, Web Site: www.electrowarmth.com (8)

Grindrod, Jeff, Nova Marketing Services, Avon, CT. Tel: (800) 879-0288, Web Site: www.nova-marketing.com (35)

Grinnell, Dave C., Beyond Quota LLC, Lake Forest, IL. Tel: (847) 234-9475, FAX: (847) 234-5260, E-Mail: megrinnell@beyondquota.com, Web Site: www.beyondquota.com (35)

Grinnell, Maureen Eddy, Beyond Quota LLC, Lake Forest, IL. Tel: (847) 234-9475, FAX: (847) 234-5260, E-Mail: megrinnell@beyondquota.com, Web Site: www.beyondquota.com (35)

Grissom, Kathleen, Luzier Personalized Cosmetics, Grandview, MO. Tel: (816) 531-8338, (800) 821-6632, FAX: (816) 531-6979, E-Mail: customerservice@luzier.com, Web Site: www.luzier.com (7)

Griswald, Marlee, Patagonia Mail Order Inc, Reno, NV. Tel: (775) 747-1992, (800) 638-6464, FAX: (775) 747-6159, Web Site: www.patagonia.com (2)

Gritzmacher, John, Herrschners Inc, Stevens Point, WI. Tel: (715) 341-8686, (800) 441-0838, FAX: (715) 341-2250, E-Mail: customerservice@herrschners.com, Web Site: www.herrschners.com (11)

Grizzard Communications Group Inc, Atlanta, GA. Tel: (404) 522-8330, (800) 241-9351, Web Site: www.grizzard.com (35)

Grizzard, Chip, Grizzard Communications Group Inc, Atlanta, GA. Tel: (404) 522-8330, (800) 241-9351, Web Site: www.grizzard.com (35)

Grizzly Industrial Inc, Bellingham, WA. Tel: (360) 647-0801, (800) 523-4777, FAX: (360) 671-8375, E-Mail: csr@grizzly.com, Web Site: www.grizzly.com (9)

Grodsky, Mark, Rich Brands, Phoenix, AZ. Tel: (602) 889-4800, (877) 856-1753, FAX: (602) 889-4830, E-Mail: sales@esscentualbrands.com, Web Site: esscentualbrands.com (16)

Groeninger, Steve, Magnaflux, Glenview, IL. Tel: (847) 657-5300, FAX: (847) 657-5388, Web Site: www.magnaflux.com (16)

Groese, Jennifer, List Partners Inc, Atlanta, GA. Tel: (404) 350-0600, (800) 941-6562, E-Mail: contact@thelistinc.com, Web Site: listpartnersinc.com (24)

Groff DRTV LLC, Portland, ME. Tel: (207) 415-1374, FAX: (207) 771-5320, E-Mail: regfilm@gmail.com, Web Site: www.groffdrtv.com (32)

Groff, Reginald, Groff DRTV LLC, Portland, ME. Tel: (207) 415-1374, FAX: (207) 771-5320, E-Mail: regfilm@gmail.com, Web Site: www.groffdrtv.com (32)

Grogan, Jim, MBI Direct Mail, Deland, FL. Tel: (386) 736-9998, (800) 359-4780, FAX: (386) 736-1100, E-Mail: sales@mbidirectmail.com, Web Site: www.directmail-mbi.com (28)

Grogan, Mike, MBI Direct Mail, Deland, FL. Tel: (386) 736-9998, (800) 359-4780, FAX: (386) 736-1100, E-Mail: sales@mbidirectmail.com, Web Site: www.directmail-mbi.com (28)

Grohs, Aaron T., AlphaGraphics World Headquarters, Salt Lake City, UT. Tel: (801) 595-7270, (800) 955-6246, FAX: (801) 595-7271, E-Mail: contactus@alphagraphics.com, Web Site: www.alphagraphics.com (27)

Groobey, Carolyn, Bill Me Later Inc, Timonium, MD. Tel: (443) 921-1900, FAX: (443) 921-1985, Web Site: www.billmelater.com (14)

Groom, Judy, Computerized Research & Development Inc, Lincoln, CA. Tel: (916) 434-5690, E-Mail: info@computerizedresearch.com, Web Site: www.cradinc.com (23)

Grosch, Greg, White Cap Wholesale Contractors Supplies, Costa Mesa, CA. Tel: (800) 944-8322, FAX: (866) 791-8396, E-Mail: customerservice@whitecap.com, Web Site: www.whitecapdirect.com (16)

Groser, Fred, Newsday, Melville, NY. Tel: (800) 639-7329, Web Site: www.newsday.com (17)

Gross, Adam, The Jordan Edmiston Group Inc, New York, NY. Tel: (212) 754-0710, FAX: (212) 754-0337, Web Site: www.jegi.com (14)

Gross, Brent, Ignition Network, Chicago, IL. Tel: (312) 893-5000, E-Mail: inquiries@ignitionnetwork.com, Web Site: www.ignitionnetwork.com (35)

Gross, Karen, DoubleVerify, New York, NY. Tel: (212) 631-2111, Web Site: www.doubleverify.com (9)

Gross, Martin, Martin Gross & Friends, New York, NY. Tel: (212) 689-0772, FAX: (212) 481-0552, E-Mail: grossdirect@aol.com (39)

Gross, Ron, Wimmer's Meat Products Inc, West Point, NE. Tel: (800) 762-9865, E-Mail: consumer.affairs@landofrost.com, Web Site: www.wimmersmeats.com (4)

Grossano, Gerard, Neopost USA, Milford, CT. Tel: (203) 301-3400, Web Site: www.neopostusa.com (34)

Grossblatt, Harvey B., Universal Security Instruments Inc, Owings Mills, MD. Tel: (410) 363-3000, FAX: (410) 363-3218, E-Mail: sales@universalsecurity.com, Web Site: www.universalsecurity.com (16)

Gordon W Grossman Inc, Pound Ridge, NY. Tel: (914) 238-9387, FAX: (914) 238-1635 (20)

Henry Grossman, New York, NY. Tel: (212) 580-7751, E-Mail: info.grossmanenterprises@gmail.com (37)

Grossman, Bernice, DMRS Group Inc, New York, NY. Tel: (212) 590-2340, FAX: (212) 590-2341, E-Mail: bgrossman@dmrsgroup.com, Web Site: www.dmrsgroup.com (22)

Grossman, Gordon W., Gordon W Grossman Inc, Pound Ridge, NY. Tel: (914) 238-9387, FAX: (914) 238-1635 (20)

Grossman, Henry, Henry Grossman, New York, NY. Tel: (212) 580-7751, E-Mail: info.grossmanenterprises@gmail.com (37)

Grossman, M.D. Robert I., New York University Medical Center, New York, NY. Tel: (212) 263-7800, FAX: (212) 263-8426, Web Site: www.med.nyu.edu (1)

Grossman, Mindy F., Improvements, West Chester, OH. Tel: (800) 634-9484, Web Site: www.improvementscatalog.com (8)

Grossman, Mindy, HSN Inc, Saint Petersburg, FL. Tel: (727) 872-1000, (800) 284-5757, Web Site: www.hsn.com (5)

Grosvenor, Gilbert, National Geographic Society, Washington, DC. Tel: (202) 862-8638, (800) 373-1717, Web Site: www.nationalgeographic.com (17)

Grosz, Geoff, Cooper-Atkins Corp, Middlefield, CT. Tel: (860) 347-2256, (800) 835-5011, FAX: (860) 347-5135, E-Mail: info@cooper-atkins.com, Web Site: www.cooper-atkins.com (34)

Al Grotell, Underwater Photography, New York, NY. Tel: (212) 349-3165, FAX: (212) 349-4363 (38)

Grotell, Al, Al Grotell, Underwater Photography, New York, NY. Tel: (212) 349-3165, FAX: (212) 349-4363 (38)

Grothe, Chris, Prism Marketing Group, Schaller, IA. Tel: (800) 862-4827, FAX: (712) 275-4855, E-Mail: cjgrothe@schallertel.net, Web Site: www.prismktg.com (29)

Grounds, Deborah, Financial Publishing Co, South Bend, IN. Tel: (800) 247-3214, FAX: (574) 243-6060, Web Site: www.financial-publishing.com (17)

Group f/64, Winston-Salem, NC. Tel: (336) 748-8272, FAX: (336) 748-8780 (20)

Group M Inc, Nyack, NY. Tel: (845) 535-3453, E-Mail: gmi.prm@gmail.com, Web Site: www.groupm.org (35)

Group Mojo, Portland, OR. Tel: (503) 493-2242, FAX: (503) 493-2246, E-Mail: sam@groupmojo.com, Web Site: www.groupmojo.com (32)

Group O Inc, Milan, IL. Tel: (309) 736-8300, FAX: (309) 736-8301, Web Site: www.groupo.com (30)

Group 1 Software Inc, Lanham, MD. Tel: (301) 731-2300, (888) 413-6763, FAX: (301) 731-0360, E-Mail: info@g1.com, Web Site: www.g1.com (22)

Group 3 Marketing, Wayzata, MN. Tel: (952) 475-3269, (888) 571-6554, FAX: (952) 449-0403, E-Mail: info@group3marketing.com, Web Site: www.group3marketing.com (20)

Group 236, Oakland, CA. Tel: (510) 874-0141, Web Site: group236.com (32)

GroupLevinson, Philadelphia, PA. Tel: (215) 627-3030, Web Site: grouplevinson.com (35)

GroupM Direct, New York, NY. Tel: (212) 474-0830, Web Site: www.groupm.com (35)

Grove Communications, Crystal Lake, IL. Tel: (815) 459-4552, FAX: (815) 459-4553, E-Mail: bobg@grovecommunications.com, Web Site: www.grovecommunications.com (35)

Grove Enterprises Inc, Brasstown, NC. Tel: (828) 837-9200, (800) 438-8155, FAX: (828) 837-2216, E-Mail: judy@grove-ent.com, Web Site: www.grove-ent.com (16)

Grove, Judy A., Grove Enterprises Inc, Brasstown, NC. Tel: (828) 837-9200, (800) 438-8155, FAX: (828) 837-2216, E-Mail: judy@grove-ent.com, Web Site: www.grove-ent.com (16)

Grove, Laurel, Rapid City Journal, Rapid City, SD. Tel: (605) 394-8300, FAX: (605) 394-8462, E-Mail: classifieds@rapidcityjournal.com, Web Site: www.rapidcityjournal.com (18)

Grove, Robert, Grove Enterprises Inc, Brasstown, NC. Tel: (828) 837-9200, (800) 438-8155, FAX: (828) 837-2216, E-Mail: judy@grove-ent.com, Web Site: www.grove-ent.com (16)

Groveman, George, Audio-Digest Foundation, Glendale, CA. Tel: (818) 240-7500, (800) 423-2308, FAX: (818) 240-7379, Web Site: www.audio-digest.org (1)

Grover Co, Mesa, AZ. Tel: (480) 827-8011, FAX: (480) 827-8014 (16)

Grover, John, Grover Co, Mesa, AZ. Tel: (480) 827-8011, FAX: (480) 827-8014 (16)

Grover, Rande, Grover Co, Mesa, AZ. Tel: (480) 827-8011, FAX: (480) 827-8014 (16)

Groves, David, PHE Inc, Hillsborough, NC. Tel: (919) 644-8100, (800) 293-4654, FAX: (919) 644-8150, E-Mail: custserv@adameve.com (5)

Grower's Supply Co, Dexter, MI. Tel: (734) 426-5852, FAX: (734) 426-5750, E-Mail: growers@grower-supply.com, Web Site: www.growerssupplycompany.com (8)

Growing Child, Inc, West Lafayette, IN. Tel: (765) 464-0920, (800) 927-7289, FAX: (765) 423-4495, E-Mail: service@growingchild.com, Web Site: www.growingchild.com (17)

Growing Family Portraits, Seattle, WA. Tel: (206) 587-0333, Web Site: www.silversand.com (16)

Growth Platforms Institute, Wilton, CT. Tel: (203) 529-0500, E-Mail: info@growthplatforms.org, Web Site: www.growthplatforms.org (20)

Gruaz, Bruno, DoAll Co, Wheeling, IL. Tel: (847) 824-1122, (800) 92-DOALL, FAX: (847) 699-7524, E-Mail: info@doall.com, Web Site: www.doall.com (16)

Gruber & Allison Inc, Boynton Beach, FL. Tel: (561) 752-9960, FAX: (561) 752-0085 (17)

Gruber, Andrew, JS Eliezer Associates Inc, Stamford, CT. Tel: (203) 658-1300 (20)

Gruber, J.H., Gruber & Allison Inc, Boynton Beach, FL. Tel: (561) 752-9960, FAX: (561) 752-0085 (17)

Gruber, Jeff, Fran's Basket House, Inc, Succasunna, NJ. Tel: (973) 584-2230, (800) 372-6799, E-Mail: sales@franswicker.com, Web Site: www.franswicker.com (8)

Gruber, John, Wenner Media LLC, New York, NY. Tel: (212) 484-1616, FAX: (212) 484-1713 (17)

Gruber, Philip, Inkwell Inc, Cresco, PA. Tel: (570) 595-3344, E-Mail: philip@inkwellinc.com (36)

Grubman, James, Media Printing Corp, Pompano Beach, FL. Tel: (954) 984-7300, FAX: (954) 984-7303 (27)

Grucci, Vince, CGT Marketing LLC, Amityville, NY. Tel: (631) 842-4600, E-Mail: info@cgtmarketing.com, Web Site: www.cgtmarketing.com (35)

Grudy, J. Lee, Strang Communications Co, Lake Mary, FL. Tel: (407) 333-0600, FAX: (407) 333-7100, E-Mail: magcustsvc@strang.com, Web Site: www.strang.com (17)

Grudzinski, Phil, American Teleservices Association, Indianapolis, IN. Tel: (317) 816-9336, (877) 779-3974, FAX: (317) 218-0323, Web Site: www.ataconnect.org (40)

Grunow, Randy, Mediaspace Solutions, Hopkins, MN. Tel: (612) 253-3900, (888) 672-2100, FAX: (612) 454-2848, E-Mail: bstcy@mediaspace.com, Web Site: www.mediaspacesolutions.com (31)

Gruppo Levey & Co, New York, NY. Tel: (212) 867-, FAX: (212) 949-7294, E-Mail: info@glconline.com, Web Site: www.glconline.com (14)

Gruppo, Claire, Gruppo Levey & Co, New York, NY. Tel: (212) 867-, FAX: (212) 949-7294, E-Mail: info@glconline.com, Web Site: www.glconline.com (14)

Grzelewski, Robert, Grove Communications, Crystal Lake, IL. Tel: (815) 459-4552, FAX: (815) 459-4553, E-Mail: bobg@grovecommunications.com, Web Site: www.grovecommunications.com (35)

Grzywa, Tom, The Miller Group, Dupo, IL. Tel: (800) 325-3350, FAX: (618) 286-6202, E-Mail: info@miller-group.com, Web Site: www.multiplexdisplays.com (5)

Guarantee Trust Life Insurance Co, Glenview, IL. Tel: (847) 298-0670, FAX: (847) 298-1215, E-Mail: pr@gtlic.com, Web Site: www.gtlic.com (15)

Guaranty Bank, Brown Deer, WI. Tel: (414) 362-4000, (800) 235-4636, Web Site: www.guarantybank.com (14)

Guarderas, Darwin, Direct Market Designs Inc, Paterson, NJ. Tel: (973) 925-9600, Web Site: www.dmd-liberty.com (28)

The Guardian Life Insurance Co, New York, NY. Tel: (212) 598-8000, Web Site: www.guardianlife.com (15)

Guay, Charles, Standard Life, Montreal, QC Canada. Tel: (514) 499-8855, (877) 499-9555, FAX: (514) 499-4908, Web Site: www.standardlife.ca (15)

Gudat, Sandra, Customer Communications Group Inc, Lakewood, CO. Tel: (303) 525-0313, E-Mail: info@customer.com, Web Site: www.customer.com (35)

Guercio, Alfred, Ulano Corp, Brooklyn, NY. Tel: (718) 237-4700, (800) 221-0616, FAX: (718) 802-1119, E-Mail: ulano@ulano.com, Web Site: www.ulano.com (34)

Guerra, Jr. Michael J., Benton Announcements Inc, Buffalo, NY. Tel: (716) 836-4100, FAX: (716) 836-4161 (27)

Guerra, Maria, Crystek Corp, Fort Myers, FL. Tel: (239) 561-3311, (800) 237-3061, FAX: (239) 561-1025, E-Mail: sales@crystek.com, Web Site: www.crystek.com (9)

Guerra, Philip J., Benton Announcements Inc, Buffalo, NY. Tel: (716) 836-4100, FAX: (716) 836-4161 (27)

Guerra, Sr. Michael J., Benton Announcements Inc, Buffalo, NY. Tel: (716) 836-4100, FAX: (716) 836-4161 (27)

Guerrero, Penny, Greenbook Worldwide Directory of Marketing Research Companies & Services, Bradenton, FL. Tel: (212) 849-2752, (800) 792-9202, FAX: (212) 202-7920, E-Mail: info@greenbrook.org, Web Site: www.greenbook.org (43)

Guerrero, Susan, Stein IAS, New York, NY. Tel: (212) 213-1112, Web Site: www.steinias.com (35)

Guerriero, Tracy, Thurston Moore Country Ltd, Madison, TN. Tel: (615) 868-7448, FAX: (615) 868-3738 (16)

Guertin, M. K., Best Western International, Phoenix, AZ. Tel: (602) 957-4200, FAX: (623) 780-6199, Web Site: www.bestwestern.com (19)

Guevara, Mario, BIC Corp, Shelton, CT. Tel: (203) 783-2000, FAX: (203) 783-2081, Web Site: www.bicworld.com (16)

Gugalal, Dave, Sandy Corp, Troy, MI. Tel: (800) 733-4739, FAX: (248) 729-4701, E-Mail: info@sandycorp.com, Web Site: www.sandycorp.com (16)

Gugino, Ann, Patterson Dental, Saint Paul, MN. Tel: (651) 686-1600, (800) 328-5536, FAX: (651) 686-9331, Web Site: www.pattersondental.com (10)

Guice, Rev. Gregory, Unity School of Christianity, Unity Village, MO. Tel: (816) 254-3550, FAX: (816) 251-3554, E-Mail: unity@unityonline.org, Web Site: www.unityonline.org (17)

Guida, Kent, Houston Direct Marketing Association, Houston, TX. Tel: (281) 931-8883, FAX: (281) 820-4023, Web Site: www.houstondma.org (40)

Guidance Associates, Mount Kisco, NY. Tel: (914) 666-4100, (800) 431-1242, FAX: (914) 666-5319, E-Mail: willg1961@gmail.com, Web Site: www.guidanceassociates.com (31)

Guide to American & International Directories, Delray Beach, FL. Tel: (561) 496-3316, FAX: (561) 451-0803, E-Mail: bkleinpub@aol.com (43)

Guideline, New York, NY. Tel: (212) 463-6232, (866) GUIDELINE, FAX: (212) 645-7681, Web Site: www.findsvp.com (30)

Guideline Research Corp, New York, NY. Tel: (212) 947-5140, FAX: (212) 629-0061, Web Site: www.guidelineresearch.com (30)

Guideline Washington DC, Washington, DC. Tel: (703) 312-6004, (866) GUIDELINE, E-Mail: fdudley@guideline.com, Web Site: www.guideline.com (30)

GuideOne Insurance, West Des Moines, IA. Tel: (877) 448-4331, Web Site: www.guideone.com (15)

Guideposts, Danbury, CT. Tel: (800) 932-2154, Web Site: www.guideposts.org (1)

Guiding Eyes for the Blind, Yorktown Heights, NY. Tel: (914) 245-4042, (800) 942-0149, FAX: (914) 245-1609, Web Site: www.guidingeyes.org (16)

Guido, III Umberto, Peter Glenn Publications, Delray Beach, FL. Tel: (561) 404-4290, (888) 332-6700, FAX: (561) 892-5786, E-Mail: gregjames@pgdirect.com, Web Site: www.pgdirect.com (17)

Guilford Publications Inc, New York, NY. Tel: (212) 431-9800, (800) 365-7006, FAX: (212) 966-6708, E-Mail: info@guilford.com, Web Site: www.guilford.com (17)

Guilford, Ryan, Location3 Media, Denver, CO. Tel: (720) 881-8510, FAX: (303) 298-1986, E-Mail: info@location3.com, Web Site: www.location3.com (32)

Guiliano, Edward, School of Management, Old Westbury, NY. Tel: (516) 686-1000, (800) 345-NYIT, (800) 345-6948, E-Mail: asknyit@nyit.edu, Web Site: www.nyit.edu (41)

Guiney, Alice, Things Remembered, Highland Heights, OH. Tel: (440) 473-2000, (866) 902-4438, FAX: (440) 473-2018, E-Mail: customerservice@thingsremembered.com, Web Site: www.thingsremembered.com (6)

Guinn, Clyde, Days Inns Worldwide Inc, Parsippany, NJ. Tel: (973) 753-6000, (800) 441-1618, Web Site: www.daysinn.com (16)

Guinness, Peter, Issues & Answers Network Inc, Virginia Beach, VA. Tel: (757) 456-1100, FAX: (757) 456-0377, E-Mail: info@issans.com, Web Site: www.issans.com (30)

Guionnet, Philippe, RCI LLC, Carmel, IN. Tel: (317) 805-9000, FAX: (317) 805-9335, Web Site: www.rci.com (19)

Gulam, Ray, MARKOTS, Brentwood, CA. Tel: (925) 240-0093, (877) 946-7253, FAX: (925) 240-0097, E-Mail: info@markots.com, Web Site: www.markots.com (35)

Gulbenkian Swim Inc, Danbury, CT. Tel: (203) 790-0800, (800) 431-2586, Web Site: www.gulbenkianswim.com (33)

Gulbenkian, Jr. Ed, Gulbenkian Swim Inc, Danbury, CT. Tel: (203) 790-0800, (800) 431-2586, Web Site: www.gulbenkianswim.com (33)

Gulden, Dan, Outdoor Research, Seattle, WA. Tel: (206) 467-1496, (888) 467-4327, FAX: (206) 467-0374, Web Site: www.outdoorresearch.com (11)

Gulf Coast Data Supply Inc, Milton, FL. Tel: (850) 994-7042, (800) 226-DISK, FAX: (850) 479-4441, Web Site: www.gulfdata.com (3)

Gulf Coast List Service, Tampa, FL. Tel: (813) 962-3594, FAX: (813) 907-8463, E-Mail: tg@gulfcoastlist.com (3)

Gulf Publishing Co, Houston, TX. Tel: (713) 529-4301, FAX: (713) 520-4433, E-Mail: publications@gulfpub.com, Web Site: www.gulfpub.com (17)

Gulfstream Aerospace Corp, Savannah, GA. Tel: (912) 965-3000, E-Mail: info@gulfstream.com, Web Site: www.gulfstream.com (16)

Gullette, Fred, Book News Inc, Portland, OR. Tel: (503) 281-9230, FAX: (503) 287-4485, E-Mail: info@booknews.com (43)

Gullickson, Michael, Jaypro Sports, Waterford, CT. Tel: (860) 447-3001, (800) 243-0533, FAX: (800) 988-3363, E-Mail: info@jaypro.com, Web Site: www.jaypro.com (11)

Gulmi, James S., Genesco Inc, Nashville, TN. Tel: (615) 367-7000, (888) 324-6189, FAX: (615) 367-8278, Web Site: www.genesco.com (2)

Guloien, Donald A., Manulife Financial Inc, Toronto, ON Canada. Tel: (416) 229-4515, (800) 387-0990, FAX: (416) 229-3028, Web Site: www.manulife.com (15)

Gumas Advertising, San Francisco, CA. Tel: (415) 621-7575, FAX: (415) 255-8804, E-Mail: jgumas@gumas.com, Web Site: www.gumas.com (35)

Gumas, John, Gumas Advertising, San Francisco, CA. Tel: (415) 621-7575, FAX: (415) 255-8804, E-Mail: jgumas@gumas.com, Web Site: www.gumas.com (35)

Gumbert, Jerry, Audience Research & Development, Fort Worth, TX. Tel: (817) 924-6922, FAX: (817) 924-7539, E-Mail: jgumbert@ar-d.com, Web Site: www.ar-d.com (20)

Gummed Papers of America, Mc Cook, IL. Tel: (773) 650-2020, (800) 395-9000, FAX: (708) 485-8603, (800) 395-3581, E-Mail: info@labelexperts.com, Web Site: www.labelexperts.com (34)

Gump's By Mail Inc, San Francisco, CA. Tel: (415) 982-1616, (800) 882-8055, FAX: (800) 984-9361, Web Site: www.gumpsbymail.com (6)

Gun Video Catalog/LMP, San Diego, CA. Tel: (858) 569-4000, (800) 942-8273, FAX: (858) 569-0505, Web Site: www.gunvideo.com; www.glockstore. com (11)

Gunasekaram, Kishan, The Helicopter Group, Richmond Hill, ON Canada. Tel: (416) 222-3835, Web Site: www.thehelicoptergroup.com (28)

Gundersen Partners LLC, New York, NY. Tel: (212) 677-7660, FAX: (212) 358-0275, Web Site: www. gundersenpartners.com (20)

Gundersen, Jeff, Executive Connections LLC, Sarasota, FL. Tel: (941) 323-8300, Web Site: www. executiveconnectionsllc.com (20)

Gundersen, Steven, Gundersen Partners LLC, New York, NY. Tel: (212) 677-7660, FAX: (212) 358-0275, Web Site: www.gundersenpartners.com (20)

Gunning, Pat, G&A Marketing, Cincinnati, OH. Tel: (800) 688-1370, FAX: (513) 688-1570, E-Mail: info@gamarketing.com, Web Site: www. gamarketing.com (35)

Gunzenhauser, Chris, Concinnity Marketing & Technology Inc, Winston-Salem, NC. Tel: (336) 245-4561, E-Mail: chris@concinnitymarketing.com, Web Site: www.concinnitymarketing.com (35)

Gupa, Vanita Vanita Gupta, Ashrae Learning Institute, Atlanta, GA. Tel: (404) 636-8400, (800) 527-4723, FAX: (404) 321-5478, E-Mail: ashrae@ashrae.org, Web Site: www.ashrae.org (31)

Gupta, Raj L., Rohm & Haas Co, Philadelphia, PA. Tel: (215) 592-3000, (877) 288-5881, FAX: (215) 592-3377, Web Site: www.rohmhaas.com (16)

Gupta, Vin, American Business Directories, Omaha, NE. Tel: (402) 593-4600, (800) 555-6124, FAX: (402) 596-0475, Web Site: www.infousa.com (43)

Gureck, W. Scott, US Naval Institute, Annapolis, MD. Tel: (410) 268-6110, (800) 233-8764, FAX: (410) 571-1703, E-Mail: customer@usni.org, Web Site: www.usni.org (38)

Gurley, Wayne, Allegiant Direct Inc, Brentwood, TN. Tel: (615) 373-2042, FAX: (615) 373-2099, E-Mail: welcome@allegiantdirect.com, Web Site: www. allegiantdirect.com (35)

Gurn, Jim, MRI Norwalk, Pompano Beach, FL. Tel: (203) 926-1200, FAX: (203) 926-1211, E-Mail: jbgurn@mricoastalgroup.com, Web Site: www. mricoastalgroup.com (20)

Gurney, John, Atomic Direct LLC, Portland, OR. Tel: (503) 296-6131, FAX: (503) 296-9890, Web Site: www.atomicdirect.com (35)

Gurney, Larry, Fitness USA Super Centers, West Bloomfield, MI. Tel: (248) 737-7200, (800) GET-FIT-1, (248) 932-3300, Web Site: www. fitnessusa.com (16)

Gurshaney, Naren K., ADT LLC, Boca Raton, FL. Tel: (561) 988-3600, FAX: (561) 988-3673, Web Site: www.adt.com (16)

Gurtman, Arthur, GMG Productions Inc, Roslyn, NY. Tel: (516) 482-0093, FAX: (516) 482-0097, Web Site: www.gmgproductions.com (3)

Gurtman, Bernard, GMG Productions Inc, Roslyn, NY. Tel: (516) 482-0093, FAX: (516) 482-0097, Web Site: www.gmgproductions.com (3)

Gusfeld, Edward, Time Products International, Del Rio, TX. Tel: (847) 459-8885, FAX: (847) 459-8111, E-Mail: cttpi@aol.com, Web Site: www.tpi2000. com (16)

Gust, David, American Health & Safety Inc, Stoughton, WI. Tel: (630) 413-5662, (800) 522-7554, FAX: (800) 326-3245, Web Site: www.ahsafety.com (16)

Gutfreud, Jaime, Wunderman, New York, NY. Tel: (212) 941-3000, Web Site: www.wunderman.com (35)

Guth, Robert E., The Reader's Digest Association Inc, New York, NY. Tel: (800) 310-6261, Web Site: www.rda.com (17)

Guthrie, David M., Premiere Global Services Inc, Atlanta, GA. Tel: (404) 262-8400, (800) 546-1541, FAX: (404) 262-8540, Web Site: www.pgi.com (22)

Guthrie, Mary, National Postal Forum, Fairfax, VA. Tel: (703) 218-5015, FAX: (703) 218-5020, E-Mail: info@npf.org, Web Site: www.npf.org (42)

Guthrie, Matthew, DMB Financial, Beverly, MA. Tel: (866) 810-3210, FAX: (978) 338-2347, E-Mail: help@dmbfinancial.com, Web Site: www. dmbfinancial.com (14)

Guthy-Renker Corp, Santa Monica, CA. Tel: (310) 581-6250, FAX: (310) 581-3232, Web Site: www.guthy-renker.com (32)

Guthy, Bill, Guthy-Renker Corp, Santa Monica, CA. Tel: (310) 581-6250, FAX: (310) 581-3232, Web Site: www.guthy-renker.com (32)

Gutman, Amy, University of Pennsylvania, Philadelphia, PA. Tel: (215) 898-5000, FAX: (215) 898-9659, Web Site: www.upenn.edu (1)

Gutman, Luisa, Holy Cross Hospital, Fort Lauderdale, FL. Tel: (954) 771-8000, FAX: (954) 229-8597, Web Site: www.holy-cross.com (16)

Gutnick, Todd M., Anti-Defamation League, New York, NY. Tel: (212) 885-7700, Web Site: www.adl. org (1)

Guttenberg, Edward, Foremost Industrial Exchange, Van Nuys, CA. Tel: (818) 988-6900, FAX: (818) 787-0293 (16)

Guttosch, Bob, Cole-Parmer Instrument Co, Vernon Hills, IL. Tel: (847) 549-7600, (800) 323-4340, FAX: (847) 247-2929, E-Mail: info@coleparmer. com, Web Site: www.coleparmer.com (16)

Guy, Dana, International Crystal Manufacturing Co, Oklahoma City, OK. Tel: (405) 236-3741, (800) 252-6780, FAX: (405) 235-1904, E-Mail: info@ icmfg.com, Web Site: www.icmfg.com (16)

Guyer, Douglas, IDR Marketing Partners LLC, Berwyn, PA. Tel: (610) 993-0500, FAX: (610) 993-9938, E-Mail: idr@idronline.com, Web Site: www. idronline.com (23)

Guzman, Emanuel, Cengage Learning, Independence, KY. Tel: (800) 354-9706, FAX: (800) 487-8488, Web Site: www.delmar.com (1)

Guzman, Sergio, United Farm Workers of America, AFL-CIO, Keene, CA. Tel: (661) 823-6151, FAX: (661) 823-6177, E-Mail: execoffice@ufw.org, Web Site: www.ufw.org (1)

Guzzo, Paulo, Merchant E-Solutions, Redwood City, CA. Tel: (509) 232-5639, (866) 663-6132, FAX: (509) 232-5625, E-Mail: help@merchante-solutions. com, Web Site: www.merchante-solutions.com (14)

Gwaltney, Jill, Rauxa, Costa Mesa, CA. Tel: (714) 427-1271, E-Mail: newbiz@rauxa.com, Web Site: www. rauxa.com (35)

Gwaltney, John, Forestry Suppliers Inc, Jackson, MS. Tel: (601) 354-3565, (800) 647-5368, FAX: (601) 292-0165, E-Mail: fsi@forestry-suppliers.com, Web Site: www.forestry-suppliers.com (9)

Gyllenhaal, Anders, McClatchy Co, Sacramento, CA. Tel: (916) 321-1855, FAX: (916) 321-1869, Web Site: www.mcclatchy.com (17)

The Gymboree Corp, San Francisco, CA. Tel: (877) 449-6932, Web Site: www.gymboree.com (2)

H

H & H Graphics, Lancaster, PA. Tel: (717) 393-3941, (866) 338-7569, E-Mail: info@thehandhgroup.com, Web Site: www.hhgraphicsgroup.com (31)

H&R Block Inc, Kansas City, MO. Tel: (816) 854-3000, (800) 472-5625, FAX: (816) 854-8500, Web Site: www.hrblock.com (14)

HR Direct Inc, Fairfield, IA. Tel: (641) 472-7188, FAX: (641) 472-5729, E-Mail: info@hrdirect.net, Web Site: www.hrdirect.net (23)

HB Communications, North Haven, CT. Tel: (203) 234-9246, (800) 243-4414, FAX: (203) 234-2013, E-Mail: info@hbcommunications.com, Web Site: www.hbcommunications.com (34)

HB Distributors, Chatsworth, CA. Tel: (818) 882-0000, (800) 266-3478, FAX: (818) 700-1808, E-Mail: info@hbdistributors.com, Web Site: www. hddistributors.com (34)

HBP, Falls Church, VA. Tel: (703) 289-9000, FAX: (703) 289-9143, E-Mail: info@hbp.com, Web Site: www.hbp.com (27)

HCI Direct, Bensalem, PA. Tel: (215) 244-9600, (888) 765-0062, FAX: (215) 244-0328, Web Site: www. silkies.com (16)

HD Supply, San Diego, CA. Tel: (877) 610-6912, FAX: (877) 219-8526, Web Site: www.hdsupplysolutions. com (34)

HDA Inc, Saint Louis, MO. Tel: (314) 770-2222, (800) 533-4350, FAX: (314) 770-1454, E-Mail: plans@ hdainc.com, Web Site: www.designamerica.com (17)

HDI Group, San Francisco, CA. Tel: (415) 794-3320, Web Site: www.hobbsdirect.com (20)

HF Direct, Birmingham, AL. Tel: (205) 458-8200, FAX: (205) 458-8206, E-Mail: info@hfdirect.com, Web Site: www.hfdirect.com (35)

HIMSS, Chicago, IL. Tel: (312) 664-4467, FAX: (312) 664-6143, Web Site: www.himss.org (1)

HK Systems Inc, New Berlin, WI. Tel: (262) 860-7000, (800) HK SYSTEMS, FAX: (262) 860-7010, E-Mail: hkinfo@hksystems.com, Web Site: www. hksystems.com (34)

HP Indigo & Inkjet Press Solutions, Vancouver, WA. Tel: (360) 795-5000, Web Site: www.hp.com (16)

HR Direct, Sunrise, FL. Tel: (800) 346-1231, FAX: (800) 350-7760, Web Site: www.hrdirect.com (10)

HSBC Bank USA, NA, New York, NY. Tel: (716) 841-2424, FAX: (716) 841-5391, Web Site: www. banking.us.hsbc.com (14)

HSN Inc, Saint Petersburg, FL. Tel: (727) 872-1000, (800) 284-5757, Web Site: www.hsn.com (5)

HSP Direct, Ashburn, VA. Tel: (703) 793-3220, FAX: (703) 723-5405, E-Mail: info@hspdirect.com, Web Site: www.hspdirect.com (1)

Haaland, Mark, Telpro Inc, Grand Forks, ND. Tel: (701) 775-0551, FAX: (701) 775-0629 (9)

Haank, Derk, Springer Science & Business Media LLC, New York, NY. Tel: (212) 460-1500, FAX: (212) 460-1575, Web Site: www.springer.com (17)

Haas, Hugh, Sandy Alexander Inc, Clifton, NJ. Tel: (973) 470-8100, FAX: (973) 470-9269, E-Mail: sandy@sandyinc.com, Web Site: www.sandyinc. com (32)

Haas, Mike, Guarantee Trust Life Insurance Co, Glenview, IL. Tel: (847) 298-0670, FAX: (847) 298-1215, E-Mail: pr@gtlic.com, Web Site: www.gtlic. com (1)

Haas, Pam, The Direct Marketing Club of New York Inc, Garden City, NY. Tel: (516) 746-6700, FAX: (516) 294-8141, E-Mail: info@dmcny.org, Web Site: www.dmcny.org (1)

Haas, Ted, Global-Z International Inc, Bennington, VT. Tel: (802) 445-1011, FAX: (802) 445-1016, E-Mail: info@globalz.com, Web Site: www.globalz.com (22)

Haband Co Inc, Oakland, NJ. Tel: (201) 651-1000, FAX: (201) 405-7777, Web Site: www.haband.blair. com (2)

Habbee, John, The NH Broadcaster, Lowell, MA. Tel: (978) 458-7100, Web Site: www.nhbroadcaster.com (31)

Haber, Louis, Distribution Postal Co Inc, Baltimore, MD. Tel: (410) 488-1002, (800) 992-4525, FAX: (410) 488-2344, E-Mail: louishaber@distpost.com, Web Site: www.distpost.com (28)

Habing, Cheryl, Mid America Designs Inc, Effingham, IL. Tel: (217) 540-4200, (800) 350-4543, FAX: (217) 540-4800, E-Mail: mail@mamotorworks.com, Web Site: www.mamotorworks.com (12)

Habitat For Humanity International, Americus, GA. Tel: (229) 924-6935, (800) HABITAT, FAX: (229) 924-6541, Web Site: www.habitat.org (1)

Habyan, Bonnie, Arbor Commercial Mortgage, Uniondale, NY. Tel: (516) 229-6615, Web Site: www. thearbornet.com (14)

Hack, Brian, Stephan Partners Inc, New York, NY. Tel: (212) 524-8583, E-Mail: george@stephenpartners. com, Web Site: www.stephanpartners.com (35)

Hack, Rob, Oneida Ltd, Oneida, NY. Tel: (315) 361-3000, (888) 263-7195, FAX: (315) 361-3700, Web Site: www.oneida.com (16)

HackerAgency Inc, Seattle, WA. Tel: (206) 805-1500, Web Site: www.hal21.com (35)

Hackett, James P., Steelcase Inc, Grand Rapids, MI. Tel: (616) 247-2710, FAX: (616) 475-2270, Web Site: www.steelcase.com (16)

Haddox, Darryl, Magnet LLC, Washington, MO. Tel: (636) 239-5661, (800) 458-9457, FAX: (636) 239-4490, E-Mail: contactus@themagnetgroup.com, Web Site: www.magnetllc.com (16)

Hadeed, Charles P., Transcat, Rochester, NY. Tel: (585) 352-9460, (800) 800-5001, FAX: (585) 352-1486, Web Site: www.transcat.com (16)

Hadley Fruit Orchards Inc, Cabazon, CA. Tel: (951) 849-5255, FAX: (951) 849-5255, Web Site: www. hadleys.com (4)

Haefner, Bob, Stellar Technology Inc, Amherst, NY. Tel: (716) 250-1900, (800) 274-1846, FAX: (716) 250-1909, E-Mail: info@stellartech.com, Web Site: www.stellartech.com (9)

Hafford, Patrick, The Christian Science Publishing Society, Boston, MA. Tel: (617) 450-2000, E-Mail: info@christianscience.com, Web Site: jsh. christianscience.com (17)

Haffreingue, Xavier, KXEN Inc, San Francisco, CA. Tel: (415) 904-4160, FAX: (415) 904-9041, Web Site: www.kxen.com (22)

Hafkin, Matt, Rapp, New York, NY. Tel: (212) 817-6800, FAX: (212) 686-7047, E-Mail: rick.doerr@ rapp.com, Web Site: www.rapp.com (35)

Hagadone Printing Co, Honolulu, HI. Tel: (808) 847-5310, (800) 491-4888, FAX: (808) 841-0094, E-Mail: sales@hagadoneprinting.com, Web Site: www.hagadoneprinting.com (27)

Hagale, Jim, Bass Pro Shops, Springfield, MO. Tel: (417) 887-7334, FAX: (417) 873-5882, Web Site: www.basspro.com (11)

Hagata, Tadaaki, Epson America, Long Beach, CA. Tel: (562) 981-3840, (800) 873-7766, FAX: (562) 290-5220, Web Site: www.epson.com (10)

Hagedorn, James, The Scotts Co LLC, Marysville, OH. Tel: (888) 270-3714, Web Site: www.scotts.com (8)

Hagedorn, Jim, Scotts-Sierra Horticultural, Marysville, OH. Tel: (888) 270-3714, Web Site: www. scottscompany.com (16)

Hagee, Lisa, NCO Financial Systems, Horsham, PA. Tel: (215) 441-3000, (800) 220-2274, FAX: (215) 441-3923, E-Mail: marketing@ncogroup.com, Web Site: www.ncogroup.com (29)

Hagemeyer - North America, Charleston, SC. Tel: (843) 745-2400, FAX: (843) 745-6942, E-Mail: info@ hagemeyerna.com, Web Site: www.hagemeyerna. com (16)

Hagen, Jarom, Relevate Group Inc, Springfield, VA. Tel: (703) 658-8300, (800) 523-7346, FAX: (703) 658-8301, E-Mail: sales@relevategroup.com, Web Site: www.relevategroup.com (22)

Hagen, Larry, Miller Stockman, Denver, CO. Tel: (303) 428-5696, FAX: (303) 430-1130 (2)

Hagen, Lisa, Elizabeth Arden Spas LLC, Stamford, CT. Tel: (203) 905-1700, FAX: (203) 905-1716, Web Site: www.reddoorspas.com (19)

Hagen, Paulette, Agco Spra-Coup, Duluth, GA. Tel: (320) 231-9400, FAX: (320) 231-9413, Web Site: www.agcocorp.com (16)

Hagen, Vickie, Omaha Creative Group Inc, Omaha, NE. Tel: (402) 597-3000, (800) 228-9872, FAX: (800) 428-1593, Web Site: www.omahasteaks.com (4)

Hagerman, Douglas M., Rockwell Automation, Milwaukee, WI. Tel: (414) 382-2000, FAX: (414) 382-4444, Web Site: www.rockwellautomation.com (16)

Hagey, Alec, Toyota Motor Sales USA Inc, Torrance, CA. Tel: (310) 468-4000, (800) 331-4331, FAX: (310) 468-7841, Web Site: www.toyota.com (16)

Haggerty, Diane, Tuttle Printing & Engraving, Rutland, VT. Tel: (802) 773-9171, (800) 776-7682, FAX: (802) 773-5785, E-Mail: info@tuttleprinting.com, Web Site: www.tuttleprinting.com (10)

Haggerty, Greg, Telecom Inc, Oakland, CA. Tel: (510) 873-8283, (800) 243-3101, FAX: (510) 873-8293, Web Site: www.telecominc.com (29)

Haggerty, Michael, Physicians Planning Association Services, Deerfield Beach, FL. Tel: (954) 571-1877, (800) 221-2168, FAX: (954) 571-8582, E-Mail: insurance@assnservices.com, Web Site: www. physiciansplanning.com (16)

Haggstrom, Don, Russ Reid Co, Pasadena, CA. Tel: (626) 449-6100, FAX: (626) 449-6190, E-Mail: info@russreid.com, Web Site: www.russreid.com (35)

Hagie Manufacturing Co, Clarion, IA. Tel: (515) 532-2861, (800) 247-4885, FAX: (515) 532-3553, E-Mail: info@hagie.com, Web Site: www.hagie. com (9)

Hagie, Alan, Hagie Manufacturing Co, Clarion, IA. Tel: (515) 532-2861, (800) 247-4885, FAX: (515) 532-3553, E-Mail: info@hagie.com, Web Site: www. hagie.com (9)

Hagie, John, Hagie Manufacturing Co, Clarion, IA. Tel: (515) 532-2861, (800) 247-4885, FAX: (515) 532-3553, E-Mail: info@hagie.com, Web Site: www. hagie.com (9)

Hagood, Louis, Oxbridge Communications Inc, New York, NY. Tel: (212) 741-0231, (800) 955-0231, FAX: (212) 633-2938, E-Mail: custserv@oxbridge. com, Web Site: www.mediafinder.com; www. oxbridge.com (30)

Hagood, Patricia, Oxbridge Communications Inc, New York, NY. Tel: (212) 741-0231, (800) 955-0231, FAX: (212) 633-2938, E-Mail: custserv@oxbridge. com, Web Site: www.mediafinder.com; www. oxbridge.com (30)

Hahn, Lisa C., Caugherty Hahn Communications, Glen Rock, NJ. Tel: (201) 251-7778, FAX: (201) 251-7779, Web Site: www.chcomm.com (20)

Hahn, Mark, FLM Graphics Corp, Fairfield, NJ. Tel: (973) 575-9450, E-Mail: info@flmgraphics.com, Web Site: www.flmgraphics.com (16)

Hahs, Jennifer, Martin Williams Advertising, Minneapolis, MN. Tel: (612) 342-9739, FAX: (612) 342-9700, Web Site: www.martinwilliams.com (35)

Haight, Bill, Magna Publications Inc, Madison, WI. Tel: (608) 246-3590, FAX: (608) 246-3597, Web Site: www.magnapubs.com (17)

Haile, Zack, American Baseball Coaches Association, Greensboro, NC. Tel: (336) 821-3140, FAX: (336) 886-0000, E-Mail: abca@abca.org, Web Site: www. abca.org (1)

Hain Celestial Group Inc, Boulder, CO. Tel: (800) 434-4246, Web Site: www.hain-celestial.com (16)

Haines Direct, North Canton, OH. Tel: (866) 879-6379, E-Mail: sales@haines-direct.com, Web Site: www. haines-direct.com (21)

Haines, Anthony, Toronto Hydro-Electric System, Toronto, ON Canada. Tel: (416) 542-8000, Web Site: www.torontohydro.com (1)

Haines, Ken, Raycom Sports, Charlotte, NC. Tel: (704) 378-4456/4400, FAX: (704) 378-4465, E-Mail: whicks@raycomsports.com, Web Site: raycomsports.com (16)

Haining, Kevin, Direct Mail Trackers, Medford, NY. Tel: (631) 758-0984, E-Mail: info@dmtrackers.com, Web Site: www.dmtrackers.com (28)

Haire, John E., Parade Publications, New York, NY. Tel: (212) 450-7000, FAX: (212) 450-7287, Web Site: www.parade.com (31)

Hal Levy & Associates, High Falls, NY. Tel: (845) 687-4400 (20)

Halbritter, Ray, Indian Country Today Media Network, New York, NY. Tel: (212) 600-2086, Web Site: www.indiancountrytodaymedianetwork.com (17)

Halbur, Jim, Farm Home Offices, Richfield, MN. Tel: (612) 920-0907, (800) 788-7218, FAX: (866) 404-0257, Web Site: www.sylvette.com (10)

Haldy, Joe, Gazette Direct Marketing Co, Cedar Rapids, IA. Tel: (319) 399-5997, FAX: (319) 399-5998, Web Site: www.gazette.com (20)

Hale Indian River Groves Inc, Vero Beach, FL. Tel: (800) 356-7264, FAX: (877) 329-4253, E-Mail: marketing@halegroves.com, Web Site: www.hales. com (16)

Hale, Beth, Indian Arts & Crafts Association, Albuquerque, NM. Tel: (505) 265-9149, FAX: (505) 265-8251, E-Mail: info@iaca.com, Web Site: www.iaca. com (1)

Hale, Houston, Zouire, Leawood, KS. Tel: (913) 384-6888, (800) 346-8991, FAX: (913) 384-5757, E-Mail: info@zouire.com, Web Site: www.zouire. com (33)

Hale, III Stephen, Hale Indian River Groves Inc, Vero Beach, FL. Tel: (800) 356-7264, FAX: (877) 329-4253, E-Mail: marketing@halegroves.com, Web Site: www.hales.com (16)

Hale, Kyler, JDRF, New York, NY. Tel: (212) 689-2860, (800) 533-CURE, FAX: (212) 785-9595, E-Mail: newyorkchapter@jdrf.org, Web Site: www. jdrf.org (1)

Hale, Maria, Movie Central, Toronto, ON Canada. Tel: (416) 479-6784, E-Mail: info@moviecentral.ca, Web Site: www.moviecentral.ca (32)

Hale, Mark, Scripps Networks Interactive Inc, Knoxville, TN. Tel: (865) 560-2700, Web Site: scrippsnetworksinteractive.com (17)

Hale, Robert, Shipping Solutions, Eagan, MN. Tel: (651) 905-1727, (888) 890-7447, FAX: (651) 905-1827, E-Mail: info@shipsolutions.com, Web Site: www.shipsolutions.com (16)

Haley, Ellen, CTB/McGraw-Hill LLC, Monterey, CA. Tel: (800) 538-9547, FAX: (800) 282-0266, E-Mail: customer_service_ind@ctb.com, Web Site: www.ctb.com (16)

Haley, Roy W., WESCO, Pittsburgh, PA. Tel: (412) 454-2200, (800) 343-1201, E-Mail: info@wesco.com, Web Site: www.wescodist.com (16)

Robert Half International Inc, Menlo Park, CA. Tel: (650) 234-6000, FAX: (650) 234-6930, E-Mail: webmaster@rhi.com, Web Site: www.rhii.com (20)

Hall-Erickson Inc, Westmont, IL. Tel: (630) 434-7779, FAX: (630) 434-1216 (16)

Hall, Alan, Russ Reid Co, Pasadena, CA. Tel: (626) 449-6100, FAX: (626) 449-6190, E-Mail: info@russreid.com, Web Site: www.russreid.com (35)

Hall, Anthony, ASH Recruitment Solutions, Exeter, NH. Tel: (603) 778-8888, E-Mail: t.hall@ashrecruit.com, Web Site: www.ashrecruit.com (20)

Hall, Brian, Westgroup, Eagan, MN. Tel: (800) 344-5008, Web Site: www.westgroup.com (17)

Hall, Carolyn, AARP, Washington, DC. Tel: (202) 434-2277, FAX: (202) 434-2525, Web Site: www.aarp.org (1)

Hall, David E., Hallmark Cards Inc, Kansas City, MO. Tel: (816) 274-5111, (800) 425-5627, FAX: (816) 274-7276, Web Site: www.hallmark.com (16)

Hall, Douglas B., Richard Saunders International, Cincinnati, OH. Tel: (513) 271-9911, FAX: (513) 271-9966, E-Mail: doug@eurekaranch.com, Web Site: www.eurekaranch.com (20)

Hall, Elizabeth, Haymarket Group Ltd, New York, NY. Tel: (212) 239-0855, FAX: (212) 967-4184, Web Site: www.chocalatiermagazine.com (17)

Hall, Erin, Thermal Product Solutions, White Deer, PA. Tel: (570) 538-7200, (800) 586-2473 (16)

Hall, James Spencer, Script to Screen Inc, Santa Ana, CA. Tel: (714) 558-3971, (800) 453-0003, FAX: (714) 558-1759, E-Mail: newbusiness@scripttoscreen.com, Web Site: www.scripttoscreen.com (32)

Hall, Jan, Partners Village Store, Westport, MA. Tel: (508) 636-2572, FAX: (508) 636-2529, E-Mail: info@partnersvillagestore.com, Web Site: www.partnersvillagestore.com (11)

Hall, Jr O. B. Grayson, Regions, Birmingham, AL. Tel: (205) 944-1300, FAX: (205) 326-4072, Web Site: www.regions.com (14)

Hall, Jr. Donald J., Hallmark Cards Inc, Kansas City, MO. Tel: (816) 274-5111, (800) 425-5627, FAX: (816) 274-7276, Web Site: www.hallmark.com (16)

Hall, Lisa, Maxwell + Miller, Kalamazoo, MI. Tel: (269) 382-4060, FAX: (269) 382-0504, E-Mail: info@maxwellandmiller.com, Web Site: www.maxwellandmiller.com (35)

Hall, Mary, Physical Therapy Institute Inc, Poway, CA. Tel: (858) 485-7103 (16)

Hall, Michael E., Fidelity Security Life Insurance Co, Kansas City, MO. Tel: (816) 756-1060, (800) 648-8624, FAX: (816) 968-0580, E-Mail: info@fslins.com, Web Site: www.fslins.com (15)

Hall, Paul, Mastery Marketing Group, Columbus, OH. Tel: (203) 544-8997, (703) 938-0101, (800) MKT-0121, FAX: (203) 544-8397, (703) 938-0144, E-Mail: info@masterymg.com, Web Site: www.masterymktgrp.com (20)

Hall, Rick, Fifth Gear LLC, Indianapolis, IN. Tel: (317) 631-0907, FAX: (317) 631-6585, Web Site: www.infifthgear.com (22)

Hall, Robert J., The Philadelphia Inquirer & Daily News, Philadelphia, PA. Tel: (215) 854-2000, FAX: (215) 854-4788, Web Site: www.phil.com/inquirer (31)

Hallelujah Acres, Gastonia, NC. Tel: (704) 481-1700, (800) 915-9355, Web Site: www.myhdiet.com (5)

Haller, Lou, Ampersand Press, Port Townsend, WA. Tel: (360) 379-5187, (800) 624-4263, FAX: (360) 379-0324, E-Mail: info@ampersandpress.com, Web Site: www.ampersandpress.com (11)

Haller, Maureen, Easter Seals, Chicago, IL. Tel: (312) 726-6200, (800) 221-6827, FAX: (312) 726-1494, Web Site: www.easter-seals.org (1)

Halliday, Stephen, Affinity4, Norfolk, VA. Tel: (757) 465-4602, Web Site: www.affinity4.com (16)

Halligan, Katy, Potpourri Group Inc, North Billerica, MA. Tel: (978) 256-4100, FAX: (978) 256-1961/0344, Web Site: www.potpourrigroup.com (6)

Hallinan, Patrick, Moen Inc, North Olmsted, OH. Tel: (440) 962-2000, Web Site: www.moen.com (16)

Halliwell, Gary, NetProspex Inc, Waltham, MA. Tel: (888) 826-4877, E-Mail: sales@netprospex.com, Web Site: www.netprospex.com (22)

Hallmark Cards Inc, Kansas City, MO. Tel: (816) 274-5111, (800) 425-5627, FAX: (816) 274-7276, Web Site: www.hallmark.com (16)

Hallock, Andy, Hubert Co, Harrison, OH. Tel: (513) 367-8767, (800) 543-7374, FAX: (513) 367-8823, Web Site: www.hubert.com (16)

Hallquist, Connie, Healthy Directions LLC, Bethesda, MD. Tel: (301) 340-2100, FAX: (301) 309-8516, Web Site: www.healthydirections.com (34)

Halls Kansas City, Kansas City, MO. Tel: (816) 274-3222, (800) 624-4034, FAX: (816) 274-3220, E-Mail: contact@halls.com, Web Site: www.halls.com (16)

Halo Branded Solutions, Sterling, IL. Tel: (815) 625-0980, (866) 840-6401, Web Site: www.halo.com (33)

Halogen Response Media, New York, NY. Tel: (212) 468-4000, Web Site: www.halogenresponse.com (31)

Halsom Home Care Inc, Centerville, OH. Tel: (937) 438-6600, (800) 345-5438, FAX: (937) 438-6620, E-Mail: main@halsom.com, Web Site: www.halsom.com (16)

Halverson, Bradley M., Caterpillar Inc, Peoria, IL. Tel: (309) 675-0545, Web Site: www.cat.com (16)

Halverson, Glen, Vemma Nutrition Co, Tempe, AZ. Tel: (480) 927-8999, (800) 577-0777, FAX: (888) 314-9827, E-Mail: ms@vemma.com, Web Site: www.vemma.com (7)

Halvorsrude, Ken, Doctor's Best Inc, San Clemente, CA. Tel: (949) 498-3628, (800) 333-6977, FAX: (800) 754-2036, (949) 498-3952, E-Mail: info@drbvitamins.com, Web Site: www.drbvitamins.com (16)

Hamada, Rick, Avnet Inc, Phoenix, AZ. Tel: (480) 643-2000, FAX: (480) 643-7240, Web Site: www.avnet.com (16)

Hamakor Judaica Inc, Skokie, IL. Tel: (847) 966-4040, (800) 677-4150, FAX: (847) 966-4033, E-Mail: service@ewishource.com, Web Site: www.jewishsource.com (5)

Hamann, Beth, Smart Practice, Phoenix, AZ. Tel: (800) 522-0800, FAX: (800) 522-8329, E-Mail: info@smartpractice.com, Web Site: www.smartpractice.com (17)

Hamann, Dr. Curt, Smart Practice, Phoenix, AZ. Tel: (800) 522-0800, FAX: (800) 522-8329, E-Mail: info@smartpractice.com, Web Site: www.smartpractice.com (17)

Hamburger, Daniel, DeVry Education Group, Downers Grove, IL. Tel: (630) 515-7700, (800) 73-DEVRY, E-Mail: inquiries@devrygroup.com, Web Site: www.devryeducationgroup.com (16)

Hamburger, Kathleen, Affina, Peoria, IL. Tel: (309) 685-5901, (877) 4 AFFINA, FAX: (309) 679-4199, Web Site: www.affina.com (30)

Hamerman, Felicia, United Business Media, Manhasset, NY. Tel: (516) 562-5000, Web Site: www.ubmtechnology.com (17)

Hamill, Jeff, Hearst Direct Response Advertising Sales, New York, NY. Tel: (212) 649-2000, Web Site: www.hearst.com (31)

Hamilton Beach Brands Inc, Glen Allen, VA. Tel: (804) 273-9777, FAX: (804) 527-7142, Web Site: www.hamiltonbeach.com (16)

Hamilton Campaigns, Washington, DC. Tel: (202) 686-5900, FAX: (202) 686-7080, E-Mail: info@hamiltoncampaigns.com, Web Site: www.hamiltoncampaigns.com (30)

The Hamilton Collection, Jacksonville, FL. Tel: (904) 279-1300, (866) 323-5577, FAX: (904) 279-1495, Web Site: www.hamiltoncollection.com (6)

The Hamilton Group Ltd Inc, Jacksonville, FL. Tel: (904) 279-1300, FAX: (904) 279-1414, Web Site: www.collectibletoday.com (16)

Hamilton Sorter Co, Fairfield, OH. Tel: (513) 870-4400, (800) 503-9966, FAX: (800) 503-9963, E-Mail: sstreight@hamiltonsorter.com, Web Site: www.hamiltonsorter.com (34)

Hamilton Watch, Weehawken, NJ. Tel: (201) 271-1400, (800) 243-8463, Web Site: www.hamiltonwatches.com (16)

Hamilton, Dana L., Fidelity Security Life Insurance Co, Kansas City, MO. Tel: (816) 756-1060, (800) 648-8624, FAX: (816) 968-0580, E-Mail: info@fslins.com, Web Site: www.fslins.com (15)

Hamilton, Dave, ListSource, Irvine, CA. Tel: (866) 774-3282, E-Mail: sales@corelogic.com, Web Site: www.listsource.com (23)

Hamilton, David, Brant Publications Inc, New York, NY. Tel: (212) 941-2800, FAX: (212) 941-2885, Web Site: www.interviewmagazine.com (17)

Hamilton, Donna, Alliant, Brewster, NY. Tel: (845) 276-2600, FAX: (845) 276-2605, Web Site: www.alliantdata.com (22)

Hamilton, Kyle, American Church Inc, Youngstown, OH. Tel: (330) 758-4545, (800) 250-7112, FAX: (800) 763-8772, E-Mail: sales@americanchurch.com, Web Site: www.americanchurch.com (26)

Hamilton, Laura B., MTS Systems Corp, Eden Prairie, MN. Tel: (952) 937-4000, (800) 328-2255, FAX: (952) 937-4515, E-Mail: info@mts.com, Web Site: www.mts.com (16)

Hamilton, Richard, University of Missouri/Kansas City, Kansas City, MO. Tel: (816) 235-2215, FAX: (816) 235-2312, Web Site: www.umkc.edu (41)

Hamlin, Pam, Arnold Worldwide Boston, Boston, MA. Tel: (617) 587-8000, FAX: (617) 587-8004, Web Site: www.arn.com (35)

Hamlin, Tom, Catalyst Inc, Providence, RI. Tel: (401) 732-1886, FAX: (401) 732-5528, Web Site: www.catalystb2b.com (35)

Hamm, Don, Assurant Health, Milwaukee, WI. Tel: (414) 244-0658, (800) 800-1212, FAX: (414) 224-0472, Web Site: www.assuranthealth.com (15)

Hamm, Jon, Geometry Global, New York, NY. Tel: (212) 537-3700, E-Mail: press@geometry.com, Web Site: www.geometry.com (35)

Hammacher Schlemmer & Co Inc, Niles, IL. Tel: (847) 581-8600, (800) 233-4800, FAX: (847) 581-8616, Web Site: www.hammacher.com (16)

Hamman, Robert, SCA Promotions Inc, Dallas, TX. Tel: (214) 860-3700, (888) 860-3700, FAX: (214) 860-3723, E-Mail: scainfo@scapromo.com, Web Site: www.scapromo.com (15)

Hammelman, David H., GameTime Inc, Fort Payne, AL. Tel: (256) 845-5610, (800) 235-2440, FAX: (256) 845-9361/2649, Web Site: www.gametime. com (11)

Hammer, Bonnie, Syfy, New York, NY. Tel: (212) 664-4444, Web Site: www.syfy.com (32)

Hammer, Bonnie, USA Network, New York, NY. Tel: (212) 664-4444, FAX: (212) 664-6365, Web Site: www.usanetwork.com (32)

Hammergren, John H., McKesson Corp, San Francisco, CA. Tel: (415) 983-8300, FAX: (415) 983-7160, Web Site: www.mckesson.com (7)

Hammersley, John, Eclipse Direct Marketing, Mineola, NY. Tel: (212) 931-8344, FAX: (516) 493-9122, E-Mail: jkaiser@eclipsedm.com, Web Site: www. eclipsedm.com (23)

Hammes, Lynda, Council on Foreign Relations Inc, New York, NY. Tel: (212) 434-9400, FAX: (212) 861-2759, E-Mail: editor@foreignaffairs.com, Web Site: www.foreignaffairs.org (17)

Hammilton, Dennis, LO-AD Communications, Pasadena, CA. Tel: (626) 304-7750, FAX: (626) 304-2716, Web Site: www.lo-ad.com (16)

Hammock Publishing Inc, Nashville, TN. Tel: (615) 690-3400, FAX: (615) 690-3401, E-Mail: info@ hammock.com, Web Site: www.hammock.com (17)

Hammond Communications Group Inc, Lexington, KY. Tel: (859) 254-1878, (888) 424-1878, FAX: (859) 254-4290, E-Mail: info@hammondcg.com, Web Site: www.hammondcg.com (35)

Hammond, Brian, Telecommunications Reports International Inc, Washington, DC. Tel: (202) 312-6060, (800) 234-1660, FAX: (202) 312-6111, E-Mail: bhammond@tr.com, Web Site: www.tr.com (17)

Hammond, Edward H., Fort Hays State University, Hays, KS. Tel: (785) 628-FHSU, FAX: (785) 628-4046, Web Site: www.fhsu.edu (41)

Hammond, Steven, Sweepstakes Clearinghouse, Dallas, TX. Tel: (214) 915-7100, (800) 481-2631, FAX: (214) 915-7458, E-Mail: customersupport@ sweepstakesclearinghouse.com, Web Site: www. schstore.com (16)

Hammond, Tom, Hammond Communications Group Inc, Lexington, KY. Tel: (859) 254-1878, (888) 424-1878, FAX: (859) 254-4290, E-Mail: info@ hammondcg.com, Web Site: www.hammondcg.com (35)

Hammonds, Lisa, Medcom Inc, Cypress, CA. Tel: (800) 877-1443, FAX: (714) 891-3140, E-Mail: lhammonds@medcominc.com, Web Site: www. medcominc.com (17)

Hammonds, Tim, Food Marketing Institute (FMI), Arlington, VA. Tel: (202) 452-8444, FAX: (202) 429-4519, E-Mail: fmi@fmi.org, Web Site: www.fmi. org (40)

Hamood, Samuel Allen, Trans Union Corp, Chicago, IL. Tel: (312) 985-2000, Web Site: www.transunion. com (14)

Hampden Papers Inc, Holyoke, MA. Tel: (413) 536-1000, FAX: (413) 532-9161, Web Site: www. hampdenpapers.com (25)

Hampshire Agency, Great Neck, NY. Tel: (516) 466-3814, FAX: (516) 466-0910 (14)

Hampshire Pewter Co, Somersworth, NH. Tel: (603) 569-4944, (800) 639-7704, FAX: (603) 569-4524, E-Mail: gifts@hampshirepewter.com, Web Site: www.hampshirepewter.com (6)

Hampton Marketing Corp, Medford, NY. Tel: (516) 924-1335, (800) 229-1019, FAX: (516) 924-1669, Web Site: www.hamptonstamp.com (16)

Hampton, Renee, Booth Michigan, Grand Rapids, MI. Tel: (616) 222-5824, FAX: (616) 222-5318, Web Site: www.boothnewspapers.com (17)

Hampton, William B., Colonial Life Insurance Co Texas, Fort Worth, TX. Tel: (817) 390-2350, (888) 227-5119, FAX: (817) 390-2209, E-Mail: insurance@colonialinsurance.com, Web Site: www. colonialinsurance.com (15)

Hamsa, William R., Physicians Mutual Insurance Co, Omaha, NE. Tel: (402) 633-1604, (888) 932-7642, FAX: (402) 633-1604, Web Site: www. physiciansmutual.com (15)

Hana, Sandy, Wag/Aero Group, Lyons, WI. Tel: (262) 763-9586, (800) 558-6868, FAX: (262) 763-7595, E-Mail: wagaero-sales@wagaero.com, Web Site: www.wagaero.com (16)

Hanapole, Edward, Kaplan Inc, Fort Lauderdale, FL. Tel: (954) 515-3993, Web Site: www.kaplan.com (16)

Hancock, Harley D., Input Systems Inc, Paramount, CA. Tel: (562) 634-1170, (800) 327-9337, FAX: (562) 634-0993, E-Mail: info@sweepssoftware.com, Web Site: www.sweepssoftware.com (22)

Hancock, Peter D., Chartis, New York, NY. Tel: (212) 770-8013, Web Site: www.chartisinsurance.com/pcg (15)

Hand Assembly & Packaging Inc (HAPI), Plainview, NY. Tel: (718) 699-3400, FAX: (718) 699-3409 (28)

Hand, Judi, Revana Digital, San Dimas, CA. Tel: (909) 599-8885, (866) 922-4632, Web Site: www. revanadigital.com (35)

Hand, Judi, Revana Inc, Tempe, AZ. Tel: (408) 902-5900, (800) 535-0343, Web Site: www.revana.com (35)

Handeland, Stacy, Victory Corps, New Hope, MN. Tel: (763) 561-5600, (800) 328-6120, FAX: (763) 561-8523, E-Mail: cs@victorycorps.com, Web Site: www.victorycorps.com (16)

Handi-Ramp Inc, Libertyville, IL. Tel: (847) 680-7700, (800) 876-RAMP, FAX: (847) 816-7689, E-Mail: info@handiramp.com, Web Site: www.handiramp. com (7)

Handley, Mark, International Crystal Manufacturing Co, Oklahoma City, OK. Tel: (405) 236-3741, (800) 252-6780, FAX: (405) 235-1904, E-Mail: info@ icmfg.com, Web Site: www.icmfg.com (16)

Handy Store Fixtures Inc, Newark, NJ. Tel: (973) 242-1600, (800) 631-4280, FAX: (973) 642-6222, Web Site: www.handystorefixtures.com (8)

Hanesbrands Inc, Winston Salem, NC. Tel: (336) 519-8080, Web Site: www.hanesbrands.com (2)

Haney, Carl, Estee Lauder Inc, New York, NY. Tel: (212) 572-4200, FAX: (212) 893-7782, Web Site: www.esteelauder.com (16)

Hanfling, Renita, Amacom Books, New York, NY. Tel: (212) 903-8376, FAX: (212) 903-8083, E-Mail: customerservice@amanet.org, Web Site: www. amacombooks.org (17)

Hang, Sherry, Yeck Brothers Co, Dayton, OH. Tel: (937) 294-4000, (800) 417-2767, FAX: (937) 294-6985, E-Mail: byeck@yeck.com, Web Site: www. yeck.com (35)

Hanika, Mike, Culinary Parts Unlimited, San Francisco, CA. Tel: (800) 543-7549, FAX: (415) 495-5141, Web Site: www.culinaryparts.com (16)

Hanisko, Gayle, Charter One Bank, Cleveland, OH. Tel: (216) 566-5300, (877) CHARTER, (877) 242-7837, FAX: (216) 664-1481, Web Site: www.charterone. com (14)

Hanley Wood LLC, Washington, DC. Tel: (202) 452-0800, FAX: (202) 785-1974, Web Site: www. hanleywood.com (16)

Hanley, Brian F., Leadership Directories Inc, New York, NY. Tel: (212) 627-4140, FAX: (212) 645-0931, E-Mail: info@leadershipdirectories.com, Web Site: www.leadershipdirectories.com (17)

Hanley, Tom, Smith Hanley Associates, Southport, CT. Tel: (203) 319-4300, (888) 221-2900, FAX: (203) 319-4320, Web Site: www.smithhanley.com (20)

Hanlon, Mark, Compassion International, Colorado Springs, CO. Tel: (800) 336-7676, Web Site: www. compassion.com (1)

Hanna Instruments Inc, Woonsocket, RI. Tel: (401) 765-7500, (800) 426-6287, FAX: (401) 765-7575, E-Mail: custsvc@hannainst.com, Web Site: www. hannainst.com (16)

Hannah, Jerome, Penn Herb Co Ltd, Philadelphia, PA. Tel: (215) 632-6100, (800) 523-9971, FAX: (215) 632-7945, E-Mail: information@pennherb.com, Web Site: www.pennherb.com (7)

Hannah, Marcia, CertainTeed Corp, Valley Forge, PA. Tel: (610) 341-7000/7739, (800) 233-8990, FAX: (610) 341-7777, Web Site: www.certainteed.com (16)

Hannan, James B., Georgia-Pacific Corp LLC, Atlanta, GA. Tel: (404) 652-4000, FAX: (404) 230-7052, Web Site: www.gp.com (25)

Hannasch, Brian, Circle K Stores Inc, Akron, OH. Tel: (330) 630-6300, Web Site: www.cirlcek.com (16)

Hannecke Display Systems Inc, Boonton, NJ. Tel: (973) 335-0434, FAX: (973) 335-1274, E-Mail: info.usa@ hannecke.com, Web Site: www.hannecke.com (27)

Hanobik Communications, Coraopolis, PA. Tel: (412) 264-3077, FAX: (412) 264-0321 (35)

Hanobik, Raymond G., Hanobik Communications, Coraopolis, PA. Tel: (412) 264-3077, FAX: (412) 264-0321 (35)

Hanorof, Debbi, Hofstra University, Hempstead, NY. Tel: (516) 463-7200, FAX: (516) 463-4833, E-Mail: ce@hofstra.edu, Web Site: www.hofstra.edu/ Academics/CE (41)

Hanover Direct Inc, Weehawken, NJ. Tel: (201) 863-7300, FAX: (201) 272-3465, Web Site: www. hanoverdirect.com (5)

The Hanover Shoe Co, Newton, MA. Tel: (617) 964-1222, FAX: (617) 243-4210, Web Site: www.clarks. com (16)

Hanrahan, Don, Dick Davis Digest, Salem, MA. Tel: (978) 745-5532, FAX: (978) 745-1283, E-Mail: marketing@dickdavis.com, Web Site: www. dickdavis.com (17)

Hans, Paul, Genium Publishing, Amsterdam, NY. Tel: (518) 842-4111, FAX: (518) 842-1843, E-Mail: sales@genium.com, Web Site: www.genium.com (17)

Hanscomb, Neil, San Francisco Herb & Natural Food Co, San Francisco, CA. Tel: (510) 770-1215, (800) 227-2830, FAX: (510) 770-9021, E-Mail: customerservice@herbspicetea.com, Web Site: www.herbspicetea.com (4)

Hansee, Donna, WILD Flavors Inc, Erlanger, KY. Tel: (859) 342-3600, FAX: (859) 342-3610, Web Site: www.wildflavors.com (4)

Hansell, Raymond, ToonUp Coach, Wayne, PA. Tel: (610) 902-0430, (866) 866-6877, E-Mail: info@ toonupcoach.com, Web Site: www.toonupcoach. com (13)

Chris Hansen, New Berlin, WI. Tel: (414) 607-5700, FAX: (414) 607-5704, Web Site: www.chr-hansen. com (16)

Hansen Corp, Princeton, IN. Tel: (812) 385-3415, FAX: (812) 385-3013, E-Mail: sales@hansen-motor.com, Web Site: www.hansen-motor.com (16)

Hansen, Jes Munk, OSRAM Sylvania, Danvers, MA. Tel: (978) 777-1900, (800) LIGHTBULB, FAX: (978) 750-2152, Web Site: www.sylvania.com (16)

Hansen, Mark, Horace Mann Educators Corp, Springfield, IL. Tel: (217) 789-2500, FAX: (217) 788-5161, Web Site: www.horacemann.com (15)

Hansen, Michael, Calendar Marketing Association, Wheaton, IL. Tel: (630) 510-4564, FAX: (630) 510-4501, E-Mail: info@calendarassociation.org, Web Site: www.calendarassociation.org (1)

Hansen, Michael R., Lone Star Web Inc, Dallas, TX. Tel: (214) 638-4946, FAX: (214) 630-4364, E-Mail: jerry@lonestarweb.com, Web Site: www.lonestarweb.com (27)

Hansen, Michael, The Psychological Corp, San Antonio, TX. Tel: (800) 211-8378, FAX: (800) 232-1223, Web Site: www.psychcorp.com (17)

Hansen, Mike, Amateur Electronic Supply LLC, Milwaukee, WI. Tel: (414) 558-0333, (800) 558-0411, FAX: (414) 358-3337, Web Site: www.aesham.com (16)

Hansen, Ray, Forestry Suppliers Inc, Jackson, MS. Tel: (601) 354-3565, (800) 647-5368, FAX: (601) 292-0165, E-Mail: fsi@forestry-suppliers.com, Web Site: www.forestry-suppliers.com (9)

Hansen, Richard A., The Keystone Equities Group, Oaks, PA. Tel: (610) 415-6300, (800) 715-9905, FAX: (610) 415-6328, Web Site: www.keystoneequities.com (20)

Hansen, Rick, Visions Inc, Brooklyn Park, MN. Tel: (763) 425-4251, FAX: (763) 425-4614, E-Mail: general@visionsfirst.com, Web Site: www.visionsfirst.com (35)

Hansen, Robert D., Dow Corning Corp, Midland, MI. Tel: (989) 496-4400, (800) 248-2481, FAX: (989) 496-4572, Web Site: www.dowcorning.com (16)

Hansen, Scott, Harland Financial Solutions Inc, Lake Mary, FL. Tel: (407) 804-6600, (800) 815-5592, FAX: (407) 829-6702, Web Site: www.harlandfinancialsolutions.com (16)

Hansen, Steven, Levenger, Delray Beach, FL. Tel: (561) 276-2436, (800) 544-0880, FAX: (800) 544-6910, E-Mail: corpsales@levenger.com, Web Site: www.levenger.com (5)

Hansen, Tracy, Renaissance Learning, Wisconsin Rapids, WI. Tel: (715) 424-3636, (800) 338-4204, FAX: (877) 280-7642, E-Mail: electronicorders@renaissance.com, Web Site: www.renlearn.com (5)

Hansen, Trevor, Senior Publishers Media Group, San Diego, CA. Tel: (858) 272-9023, (800) 727-3646, FAX: (858) 272-7275, E-Mail: info@spmg.com, Web Site: www.spmg.com (31)

Hanson Inc, Maumee, OH. Tel: (419) 327-6100, FAX: (419) 327-6101, Web Site: www.hansoninc.com (30)

Hanson, Daniel G., Columbia Sportswear, Portland, OR. Tel: (503) 985-4203, (800) 622-6953, Web Site: www.columbia.com (2)

Hanson, Gene, Infolure, Phoenix, AZ. Tel: (602) 308-6700, FAX: (602) 308-6801, E-Mail: glenn.gottfried@infolure.com, Web Site: www.infolure.com (22)

Hanson, James L., Mutual of Omaha, Omaha, NE. Tel: (402) 342-7600, (800) 775-6000, FAX: (402) 351-2775, Web Site: www.mutualofomaha.com (15)

Hanson, John, P & H Mining Equipment, Milwaukee, WI. Tel: (414) 671-4400, FAX: (414) 671-7618, Web Site: www.phmining.com (16)

Hanson, Nathan, Apothecary Products Inc, Burnsville, MN. Tel: (952) 890-1940, (800) 328-2742, FAX: (800) 328-1584, E-Mail: info@apothecaryproducts.com, Web Site: www.apothecaryproducts.com (7)

Hanson, Steve, Hanson Inc, Maumee, OH. Tel: (419) 327-6100, FAX: (419) 327-6101, Web Site: www.hansoninc.com (30)

Hansraj, Bharat, Omega Direct Response Inc, Richmond Hill, ON Canada. Tel: (905) 482-2340, FAX: (905) 482-9721, E-Mail: odrsales@omegadirect.com, Web Site: www.omegadirect.com (29)

Hanton, Carl, The World Bank, Washington, DC. Tel: (202) 473-1000, FAX: (202) 477-6391, Web Site: www.worldbank.org (17)

Hanway, H. Edward, CIGNA International, Philadelphia, PA. Tel: (215) 761-1741, FAX: (215) 761-5515, Web Site: www.cigna.com (15)

Hapoienu, Spencer, Insight Out of Chaos, New York, NY. Tel: (212) 935-0044, FAX: (212) 742-0469, E-Mail: info@iooc.com, Web Site: www.iooc.com (22)

Happy Jack Inc, Snow Hill, NC. Tel: (252) 747-2911, (800) 326-5225, FAX: (252) 747-4111, E-Mail: happyjack@happyjackinc.com, Web Site: www.happyjackinc.com (11)

Happy Trails Resort, Surprise, AZ. Tel: (623) 584-0066, (800) 872-4579, FAX: (623) 546-6293, E-Mail: happytrails@uccinc.net, Web Site: www.htresort.com (19)

Haque, Gavin, HighScope Educational Research Foundation, Ypsilanti, MI. Tel: (800) 587-5639, FAX: (734) 485-0704, E-Mail: info@highscope.org, Web Site: www.highscope.org (17)

Har Court Inc, Orlando, FL. Tel: (407) 345-2000, FAX: (407) 345-1052 (17)

Hara, Carolyn, Hawaiian Host Inc, Honolulu, HI. Tel: (808) 848-0500, (866) 972-6879, E-Mail: info@hawaiianhost.com, Web Site: www.hawaiianhost.com (4)

Harada, Yasuyuki, ITOCHU International Inc, New York, NY. Tel: (212) 818-8000, FAX: (212) 818-8282, Web Site: www.adpackusa.com (25)

Haran, Edward J., Standard & Poor's Corp, New York, NY. Tel: (212) 438-2000, FAX: (212) 438-7375, Web Site: www.standardandpoors.com (17)

Harbin, Ben, LifeWay Christian Resources, Nashville, TN. Tel: (615) 251-5822, Web Site: www.lifeway.com (1)

Harbin, Roger F., Symetra Financial, Bellevue, WA. Tel: (425) 256-8000, (800) 426-7355, FAX: (425) 256-5737, Web Site: www.symetra.com (15)

Harbison, Erik, AWeber Communications, Chalfont, PA. Tel: (877) 293-2371, Web Site: www.aweber.com (24)

Harbor Freight Tools, Camarillo, CA. Tel: (805) 445-4791, (800) 423-2567, FAX: (800) 445-4925, Web Site: www.harborfreight.com (9)

Harbour Bay Inc, Oakland, NJ. Tel: (845) 368-2857, FAX: (845) 368-2349 (16)

Harcourt Educational Measurement, San Antonio, TX. Tel: (210) 299-1061, (800) 211-8378, FAX: (800) 232-1223, Web Site: www.harcourtassessment.com (17)

Hardam, Gary, International Mailing Solutions LLC, Burlington, MA. Tel: (718) 376-5000, Web Site: www.mailims.com (28)

Hardenbergh, David, Rural Alaska Community Action Program Inc, Anchorage, AK. Tel: (907) 279-2511, FAX: (907) 278-2309, Web Site: www.ruralcap.com (1)

Hardiman, Dennis, Advanced Financial Services, Middletown, RI. Tel: (401) 849-0892, (800) 620-6292, FAX: (401) 851-5621, Web Site: www.embracehomeloans.com (14)

Hardin, Joe, SRDS, Des Plaines, IL. Tel: (800) 851-7737, FAX: (847) 375-5001, Web Site: www.srds.com (17)

Harding, Carol, Kozak Auto Drywash Inc, Batavia, NY. Tel: (716) 343-8111, (800) 237-9927, FAX: (585) 343-3732, E-Mail: info@kozak.com, Web Site: www.dryautowash.com (16)

Harding, Craig, Direct Tech Inc, Omaha, NE. Tel: (402) 895-2100, Web Site: www.direct-tech.com (34)

Harding, Derek, Innovyx Inc, Seattle, WA. Tel: (206) 674-8720, Web Site: www.innovyx.com (32)

Harding, Edward R., Kozak Auto Drywash Inc, Batavia, NY. Tel: (716) 343-8111, (800) 237-9927, FAX: (585) 343-3732, E-Mail: info@kozak.com, Web Site: www.dryautowash.com (16)

Harding, Jonathan, Golden Bison LLC, Denver, CO. Tel: (303) 962-0018, Web Site: www.highplainsbison.com (4)

Harding, Peter, AT Clayton & Co Inc, Stamford, CT. Tel: (203) 658-1200, FAX: (203) 658-1201, E-Mail: webmaster@atclayton.com, Web Site: www.atclayton.com (25)

Harding, Shawn, Infinity Direct Inc, Plymouth, MN. Tel: (763) 559-1111, Web Site: www.infinitydirect.com (35)

Harding, Steve, Geometry Global, New York, NY. Tel: (212) 537-3700, E-Mail: press@geometry.com, Web Site: www.geometry.com (35)

Harding, Susan, Prime Media Equine Group, Gaithersburg, MD. Tel: (301) 977-3900, FAX: (301) 990-9015, Web Site: www.equisearch.com (17)

Harding, Tom, Infinity Direct Inc, Plymouth, MN. Tel: (763) 559-1111, Web Site: www.infinitydirect.com (35)

Hardison, Matt, National Railroad Passenger Corp, Washington, DC. Tel: (202) 906-3000, (800) USA-RAIL, FAX: (202) 906-3306, Web Site: www.amtrak.com (16)

Hardy, Darren, Success Magazine, Lake Dallas, TX. Tel: (877) 243-8383, E-Mail: editor@success.com, Web Site: www.successmagazine.com (17)

Hardy, Diane, National Fundraising Lists, Bowie, MD. Tel: (410) 721-5700, FAX: (410) 721-5795, E-Mail: info@nflists.com, Web Site: www.nflists.com (23)

Hardy, Patrick, Tierney Communications, Philadelphia, PA. Tel: (215) 790-4100, FAX: (215) 790-4363, Web Site: www.tierneyagency.com (35)

Hardy, Robert C., Uniway Management Corp, Forest Park, GA. Tel: (404) 363-6200, (888) 386-4929, FAX: (404) 363-8848, E-Mail: uniway@bellsouth.net, Web Site: www.uniway.com (16)

Hardy, Scott W., Polaroid Corp, Minnetonka, MN. Tel: (781) 386-2000, (800) 765-2764, FAX: (781) 386-3263, E-Mail: marketing@polaroid.com, Web Site: www.polaroid.com (16)

Hare, David, New England List Services Inc, Danville, VT. Tel: (802) 684-1179, (877) 252-2100, FAX: (802) 684-2113, E-Mail: dave@nelists.com, Web Site: www.nelists.com (23)

Hare, Loralee, Telerx, Horsham, PA. Tel: (800) 2TELERX, Web Site: www.telerx.com (29)

Hare, Stephen E., Office Depot, Boca Raton, FL. Tel: (561) 438-4800, (800) 463-3768, FAX: (561) 438-4001, Web Site: www.officedepot.com (16)

Hare, Stephen E., OfficeMax Inc, Boca Raton, FL. Tel: (877) 633-4236, Web Site: www.officemax.com (10)

Hare, Susan, Sunrise Greetings, Kansas City, MO. Tel: (812) 336-4045, (800) 457-4045, FAX: (812) 336-8712, E-Mail: info@interart.com, Web Site: www.interartdistribution.com (17)

Haren, Jack, Mohawk Fine Papers Inc, Cohoes, NY. Tel: (518) 237-1740, (800) 843-6455, FAX: (518) 237-7394, E-Mail: info@mohawkpaper.com, Web Site: www.mohawkconnects.com (25)

Harenchar, Jim, Response Marketing Group, Richmond, VA. Tel: (866) 574-7665, E-Mail: info@rmg-info.com, Web Site: rmg-usa.com (35)

Harenski, Hallie, MetLife International, Long Island City, NY. Tel: (212) 578-3128 (15)

Harff, Judy, Creating Results LLC, Woodbridge, VA. Tel: (703) 494-7888, (888) 205-8899, Web Site: www.creatingresults.com (35)

Harff, Todd, Creating Results LLC, Woodbridge, VA. Tel: (703) 494-7888, (888) 205-8899, Web Site: www.creatingresults.com (35)

Hargis, Jonathan, Charter Communications, Stamford, CT. Tel: (203) 905-7801, Web Site: www.charter.com (16)

Hargis, Kenny, Venture Encoding Service Inc, Fort Worth, TX. Tel: (817) 283-9500, FAX: (817) 540-6966, E-Mail: sales@venture-encoding.com, Web Site: www.venture-encoding.com (27)

Hargreaves, Linda, Lotions & Lace, Riverside, CA. Tel: (951) 686-5223, FAX: (951) 686-5765, E-Mail: linda@ez-access.com, Web Site: www.sexyvideos.com (2)

Hargreaves, Ray, Lotions & Lace, Riverside, CA. Tel: (951) 686-5223, FAX: (951) 686-5765, E-Mail: linda@ez-access.com, Web Site: www.sexyvideos.com (2)

Harington, Robert M., American Mathematical Society, Providence, RI. Tel: (401) 455-4000, (800) 321-4267, FAX: (401) 331-3842, E-Mail: ams@ams.org, Web Site: www.ams.org (17)

Harkin, Emilie, Council on Foreign Relations Inc, New York, NY. Tel: (212) 434-9400, FAX: (212) 861-2759, E-Mail: editor@foreignaffairs.com, Web Site: www.foreignaffairs.org (17)

Harkness, Andy, SDI Marketing, Toronto, ON Canada. Tel: (416) 674-9010, (877) SDI-TEAM, FAX: (416) 674-9011, E-Mail: info@sdicapital.com, Web Site: www.sdimarketing.com (14)

Harland Clarke Marketing Services, San Antonio, TX. Tel: (210) 697-8888, Web Site: www.harlandclarke.com (31)

Harland Financial Solutions Inc, Lake Mary, FL. Tel: (407) 804-6600, (800) 815-5592, FAX: (407) 829-6702, Web Site: www.harlandfinancialsolutions.com (16)

John Harland Co, Decatur, GA. Tel: (770) 981-5580, (800) 723-3690, FAX: (770) 593-5367, E-Mail: jhhwebmaster@harland.net, Web Site: www.harland.net (16)

Harland, Brent, Consolidated Plastics Co Inc, Stow, OH. Tel: (330) 425-3900, (800) 362-1000, FAX: (330) 425-3333, Web Site: www.consolidatedplastics.com (9)

Harlequin Enterprises Ltd, Don Mills, ON Canada. Tel: (416) 445-5860, FAX: (416) 445-8655, E-Mail: customer_ecare@harlequin.ca, Web Site: www.eharlequin.com (17)

Harley-Davidson Inc, Milwaukee, WI. Tel: (414) 343-7286, FAX: (414) 343-4806, Web Site: www.harley-davidson.com (12)

Harling Marketing Inc, Kirkland, QC Canada. Tel: (514) 695-1430, FAX: (514) 695-0530, E-Mail: info@harlingdirect.com, Web Site: www.harlingdirect.com (21)

Harlow, Kevin, ICS Marketing Services, Lansing, MI. Tel: (517) 394-1890, (888) 394-1890, FAX: (517) 394-7408, E-Mail: sales@icshq.com, Web Site: icshq.com (21)

Harman's Cheese & Country Store Inc, Sugar Hill, NH. Tel: (603) 823-8000, E-Mail: cheese@harmanscheese.com, Web Site: www.HarmansCheese.com (4)

Harmelin Media, Bala Cynwyd, PA. Tel: (610) 668-7900, FAX: (610) 668-9257, E-Mail: info@harmelin.com, Web Site: www.harmelin.com (32)

Harmelin, Joanne, Harmelin Media, Bala Cynwyd, PA. Tel: (610) 668-7900, FAX: (610) 668-9257, E-Mail: info@harmelin.com, Web Site: www.harmelin.com (32)

Harmening, Jeffrey L., General Mills Inc, Minneapolis, MN. Tel: (800) 248-7310, FAX: (763) 764-8330, Web Site: www.generalmills.com (8)

Harmon, Andy, The Levenson Group, Dallas, TX. Tel: (214) 932-6000, E-Mail: hello@levensongroup.com, Web Site: levensongroup.com (35)

Harmon, Brenda, Cooper Tire & Rubber Co Inc, Findlay, OH. Tel: (419) 423-1321, (800) 537-9523, FAX: (419) 424-4212, E-Mail: cooperinfo@coopertire.com, Web Site: www.coopertire.com (16)

Harmon, Emmett, Suntrust Banks Inc, Atlanta, GA. Tel: (404) 588-7914, (800) 786-8787, FAX: (404) 532-0550, E-Mail: emmett.harmon@suntrust.com, Web Site: www.suntrust.com (14)

Harmon, Raymond W., Hasco First Photo, Saint Charles, MO. Tel: (636) 946-5115, FAX: (636) 946-7148, Web Site: www.growingfamily.com (16)

Harnetiaux, Tom, Nevco Scoreboard Co, Greenville, IL. Tel: (618) 664-0360, (800) 851-4040, FAX: (618) 664-0398, E-Mail: sales@nevcoscoreboards.com, Web Site: www.nevcoscoreboards.com (16)

Haro, Tari, iCrossing, New York, NY. Tel: (212) 649-3900, FAX: (646) 280-1091, Web Site: www.icrossing.com (32)

Harold Walter Siebens School of Business, Storm Lake, IA. Tel: (712) 749-2410, (800) 383-2821, FAX: (712) 749-2037, Web Site: www2.bvu.edu/academics/business (41)

Harper College, Palatine, IL. Tel: (847) 925-6000, Web Site: www.harpercollege.com (1)

Harper, Bill, Vegetarian Times, El Segundo, CA. Tel: (310) 356-4100, FAX: (310) 356-4110, Web Site: www.vegetariantimes.com (31)

Harper, Bret, KBM Group, Louisville, CO. Tel: (800) 579-1950, E-Mail: sales@kbmg.com, Web Site: www.kbmg.com (22)

Harper, Kellie, Merrick Bank, South Jordan, UT. Tel: (801) 545-6647, Web Site: www.merrickbank.com (14)

Harper, Lisa M., Hot Topic Inc, City of Industry, CA. Tel: (626) 839-4681, (800) 275-9169, FAX: (626) 839-4686, Web Site: www.hottopic.com (2)

Harper, Susan, Caudill & Associates Inc, Orange, CA. Tel: (714) 210-2585, FAX: (714) 210-2595, E-Mail: bobc@caudill4production.com, Web Site: www.caudill4production.com (32)

HarperCollins, New York, NY. Tel: (212) 207-7000, (800) 242-7737, FAX: (212) 207-7145, Web Site: www.harpercollins.com (17)

Harper's Magazine, New York, NY. Tel: (212) 420-5720, FAX: (212) 228-5889, Web Site: www.harpers.org (17)

Harraman, Brad, E-Miles.com, Dallas, TXPlano, TX. Tel: (214) 743-5555, Web Site: www.e-miles.com (19)

Harransky, Charles, Squadron Mail Order, Carrollton, TX. Tel: (972) 242-8663, (877) 414-0434, FAX: (972) 242-3775, E-Mail: mailorder@squadron.com, Web Site: www.squadron.com (16)

Harrell, Henry H., Universal Corp, Richmond, VA. Tel: (804) 359-9311, FAX: (804) 254-3582, Web Site: www.universalcorp.com (16)

Harrell, Suzanne, Center for Professional Development, Tallahassee, FL. Tel: (850) 487-1691, (850) 644-8004, FAX: (850) 644-2589, Web Site: www.Learningforlife.fsu.com (16)

Harriet Carter Gifts, Inc, Montgomeryville, PA (6)

Harriman, Dann, Saunders Manufacturing Co Inc, Readfield, ME. Tel: (207) 685-3385, (800) 341-4674, FAX: (207) 685-9918, E-Mail: jsherwood@saunders-usa.com, Web Site: www.saunders-usa.com (16)

Harrington, Jessica, Schultz & Williams Inc, Philadelphia, PA. Tel: (215) 625-9955, FAX: (215) 625-2701, E-Mail: mail@schultzwilliams.com, Web Site: www.sw-inc.com (1)

Harrington, Judy B., Partners Health, Philadelphia, PA. Tel: (215) 849-9600, (800) 553-0784, E-Mail: sroberts@healthpart.com, Web Site: www.healthpart.com (15)

Harrington, Tara, Direct Auto Insurance, Nashville, TN. Tel: (615) 399-4859, Web Site: www.directgeneral.com (15)

Harrington's of Vermont Inc, Richmond, VT. Tel: (802) 434-4444, E-Mail: info@harringtonham.com, Web Site: www.harringtonham.com (4)

Harris Bancorp Inc, Chicago, IL. Tel: (312) 461-2121, (888) 340-BANK, FAX: (312) 461-7869, E-Mail: onlineservices@harrisbank.com, Web Site: www.harrisbank.com (14)

Harris Connect LLC, Chesapeake, VA. Tel: (800) 877-6554, E-Mail: moreinfo@harrisconnect.com, Web Site: www.harrisconnect.com (35)

Harris Connect LLC, Chesapeake, VA. Tel: (800) 877-6554, Web Site: www.harrisconnect.com (1)

Harris Corp, Melbourne, FL. Tel: (321) 727-9100, (800) 442-7747, E-Mail: webmaster@harris.com, Web Site: harris.com (16)

Harris Direct, Woodland Hills, CA. Tel: (818) 222-3470 x102, Web Site: www.harris-direct.com (1)

Harris Interactive, Rochester, NY. Tel: (585) 272-8400, (800) 866-7655, FAX: (585) 272-8680, E-Mail: info@harrisinteractive.com, Web Site: www.harrisinteractive.com (30)

Harris Marketing Group, Birmingham, MI. Tel: (248) 723-6300, FAX: (248) 723-6301, E-Mail: info@harris-hmg.com, Web Site: www.harris-hmg.com (35)

Harris Marketing Inc, Indianapolis, IN. Tel: (317) 251-9729, FAX: (317) 251-9733, E-Mail: hmdataindy@msn.com, Web Site: www.listsandmail.com (23)

Harris, Amina, Moon Shine Trading Co, Woodland, CA. Tel: (530) 668-0660, (800) 678-1226, FAX: (530) 668-6061, E-Mail: store@moonshinetrading.com, Web Site: www.moonshinetrading.com (4)

Harris, Benjamin C., Unicall International Inc, Fairlawn, OH. Tel: (330) 864-9364, FAX: (330) 864-9367, E-Mail: harrisb@unicallinc.com, Web Site: www.unicallinc.com (29)

Harris, Benjamin, Lunar Cow, Akron, OH. Tel: (330) 253-9000, (800) 594-9620, FAX: (330) 253-9001, E-Mail: info@lunarcow.com, Web Site: www.lunarcow.com (35)

Harris, Bob, Hot Sauce Harry's, North Port, FL. Tel: (214) 902-8552, (800) 588-8979, FAX: (214) 956-9885, E-Mail: info@hotsauceharrys.com, Web Site: www.hotsauceharrys.com (4)

Harris, Brett C, Speedway, Lincoln, NE. Tel: (402) 323-3100, FAX: (402) 477-7476 (12)

Harris, Brian, Mary Maxim Inc, Port Huron, MI. Tel: (810) 987-2000, (800) 962-9504, FAX: (810) 987-5056, E-Mail: info@marymaxim.com, Web Site: www.marymaxim.com (11)

Harris, Brian, Paradigm Promotions LLC, San Francisco, CA. Tel: (415) 387-2158, FAX: (415) 387-2185, E-Mail: brian@brianharris.com, Web Site: www.paradigmpromotions.com (35)

Harris, Charles, Natural History Magazine, Durham, NC. Tel: (646) 356-6500, FAX: (646) 356-6511, E-Mail: nhmag@naturalhistorymag.com, Web Site: www.naturalhistorymag.com (17)

Harris, Chris, Creative Commerce LLC, West Chester, PA. Tel: (610) 918-8800, FAX: (610) 918-1349, E-Mail: info@creativecommerce.com, Web Site: creativecommerce.com (35)

Harris, Cy, Prime Graphics Inc, Wood Dale, IL. Tel: (630) 227-1300, FAX: (630) 227-1823, E-Mail: moreinfo@primegraphicsinc.com, Web Site: www.primegraphicsinc.com (27)

Harris, Greg, Jameco Electronics, Belmont, CA. Tel: (650) 592-8097, (800) 831-4242, FAX: (650) 592-2503, (800) 237-6948, E-Mail: domestic@jameco.com, Web Site: www.jameco.com (3)

Harris, Helaine, Daedalus Books Inc, Columbia, MD. Tel: (410) 309-2706, (800) 944-8879, E-Mail: custserv@daedalusbooks.com, Web Site: www.salebooks.com (5)

Harris, II J. Robert, JRH Marketing Services Inc, Jamaica, NY. Tel: (718) 805-7300, FAX: (718) 805-7303, E-Mail: office@jrhmarketingservices.com, Web Site: www.jrhmarketingservices.com (30)

Harris, Janet, Harris Marketing Inc, Indianapolis, IN. Tel: (317) 251-9729, FAX: (317) 251-9733, E-Mail: hmdataindy@msn.com, Web Site: www.listsandmail.com (23)

Harris, Jeffrey, Inte Q, Oakbrook Terrace, IL. Tel: (630) 874-2424, Web Site: www.inteqinsights.com (21)

Harris, Jr. Henry E., Kenmore Stamp Co, Milford, NH. Tel: (603) 673-1745, (800) 225-5059, FAX: (603) 673-3222, Web Site: www.kenmorestamp.com (6)

Harris, Keith, The Los Angeles Lakers Inc, El Segundo, CA. Tel: (310) 426-6000, FAX: (310) 426-6110, E-Mail: vlawlor@la-lakers.com, Web Site: www.nba.com/lakers (11)

Harris, Kenneth, Swanson Health Products, Fargo, ND. Tel: (701) 356-2700, (800) 824-4491, FAX: (701) 356-2708, E-Mail: customercare@swansonvitamins.com, Web Site: www.swansonvitamins.com (4)

Harris, Kevin, Hot Sauce Harry's, North Port, FL. Tel: (214) 902-8552, (800) 588-8979, FAX: (214) 956-9885, E-Mail: info@hotsauceharrys.com, Web Site: www.hotsauceharrys.com (4)

Harris, Mark, NCP Solutions, Birmingham, AL. Tel: (250) 849-5200, Web Site: www.ncprint.com (21)

Harris, Mark, Wolfe Publishing Co Inc, Prescott, AZ. Tel: (928) 445-7810, (800) 899-7810, FAX: (928) 778-5124, E-Mail: wolfepub@riflemag.com, Web Site: www.riflemagazine.com (17)

Harris, Matt, Arbor Day Foundation, Nebraska City, NE. Tel: (402) 474-5655, (888) 448-7337, Web Site: www.arborday.org (1)

Harris, Michelle, Our Data Works Inc, Lewisville, TX. Tel: (469) 546-3000, (800) 268-2505, FAX: (469) 546-3013, E-Mail: info@ourdataworks.com, Web Site: www.ourdataworks.com (29)

Harris, Steve, Concordia Publishing House, Saint Louis, MO. Tel: (314) 268-1000, (800) 325-3040, FAX: (314) 268-1329, E-Mail: order@cph.org, Web Site: www.cph.org (17)

Harris, Steven, Cable Shopping Network, Scottsdale, AZ. Tel: (480) 624-4446, Web Site: www.shopcsntv.com (16)

Harris, Tiffany, Foster Marketing LLC, Lafayette, LA. Tel: (337) 235-1848, FAX: (337) 237-7246, E-Mail: gfoster@fostermarketing.com, Web Site: fostermarketing.com (35)

Harris, Tim, Ivy Tech Community College of Indiana, Indianapolis, IN. Tel: (317) 921-4800, (888) IVY-LINE, FAX: (317) 921-4753, Web Site: www.ivytech.edu (13)

Harrison, Ashton, Shades of Light, Richmond, VA. Tel: (804) 288-6515, (877) 288-5029, E-Mail: customercare@shadesoflight.com, Web Site: www.shadesoflight.com (8)

Harrison, Gregory, Franklin Estimating Systems, Woods Cross, UT. Tel: (801) 303-6083, (800) 346-7363, FAX: (801) 303-4540, E-Mail: management@franklinestimating.com, Web Site: www.fesys.com (17)

Harrison, John J., The Keystone Equities Group, Oaks, PA. Tel: (610) 415-6300, (800) 715-9905, FAX: (610) 415-6328, Web Site: www.keystoneequities.com (20)

Harrison, Mary E., Mary's Plant Farm & Landscaping, Hamilton, OH. Tel: (513) 894-0022, FAX: (513) 892-2053, E-Mail: marysplantfarm@zoomtown.com, Web Site: www.marysplantfarm.com (8)

Harrison, Sam, Linett & Harrison, Montville, NJ. Tel: (908) 686-0606, FAX: (908) 686-0623, E-Mail: sharrison@linettandharrison.com, Web Site: www.linettandharrison.com (35)

Harrison, Steve, Russ Reid Co, Pasadena, CA. Tel: (626) 449-6100, FAX: (626) 449-6190. E-Mail: info@russreid.com, Web Site: www.russreid.com (35)

Harrobin, John, MCI Communications Services Inc, Basking Ridge, NJ. Tel: (877) 297-7816, Web Site: www.mci.com (16)

Harrold, Jim, Woodcraft Supply Corp LLC, Parkersburg, WV. Tel: (304) 422-5412, (800) 344-3348, FAX: (304) 422-5417, Web Site: www.woodcraft.com (9)

Harry & David Holdings Inc, Medford, OR. Tel: (541) 864-2362, (877) 322-1200, FAX: (800) 648-6640, Web Site: www.hndcorp.com (4)

Hart, Ann Weaver, Temple University, Philadelphia, PA. Tel: (215) 204-7282, FAX: (215) 204-4554, Web Site: www.sbm.temple.edu (41)

Hart, David G., Convio Inc, Austin, TX. Tel: (512) 652-2600, (888) 528-9501, FAX: (512) 652-2699, Web Site: www.convio.com (22)

Hart, Devin, The Marx Group, San Rafael, CA. Tel: (415) 453-0844, FAX: (415) 451-0166, E-Mail: info@themarxgrp.com, Web Site: www.themarxgrp.com (35)

Hart, Julie, Teachers' Discovery, Auburn Hills, MI. Tel: (800) 832-2437, FAX: (800) 287-4509, E-Mail: orders@teachersdiscovery.com, Web Site: teachersdiscovery.com (5)

Hart, Karl, Wendell August Forge Inc, Grove City, PA. Tel: (724) 458-8360, (800) 923-1390, FAX: (724) 458-0906, E-Mail: info@wendell.com, Web Site: www.wendellaugust.com (6)

Hart, Lora Lee, Trigon Blue Cross/Blue Shield, Roanoke, VA. Tel: (540) 853-5000, (800) 553-3164, FAX: (540) 853-3053, Web Site: www.trigon.com (15)

Hart, Michael, Web Graphics, Glens Falls, NY. Tel: (518) 792-6501, (800) 833-8863, FAX: (518) 792-9353, (800) 833-8861, E-Mail: proofs&pos@printatweb.com, Web Site: www.printatweb.com (27)

Hart, Patti, Times Union, Albany, NY. Tel: (518) 454-5694, FAX: (518) 454-5628, Web Site: www.timesunion.com (18)

Hart, Rachel, Seattle Magazine, Seattle, WA. Tel: (206) 284-1750, (800) 637-0334, FAX: (206) 284-2550, E-Mail: customerservice@seattlemag.com, Web Site: www.seattlemag.com (17)

Hart, Sue, IPD Co Inc, Portland, OR. Tel: (503) 257-7500, (800) 444-6473, FAX: (503) 257-7596, E-Mail: info@ipdusa.com, Web Site: www.ipdusa.com (12)

Hart, Tracy, American Kidney Fund, Rockville, MD. Tel: (301) 881-3052, (800) 638-8299, FAX: (301) 881-0898, Web Site: www.kidneyfund.org (1)

Harte-Hanks, San Antonio, TX. Tel: (210) 829-9000, FAX: (210) 829-9403, Web Site: www.hartehanks.com (22)

The Hartford Courant, Hartford, CT. Tel: (860) 241-6200, FAX: (860) 293-0178, Web Site: www.courant.com (31)

The Hartford Financial Services Inc, Southington, CT. Tel: (860) 547-5000, (860) 843-8070, FAX: (860) 547-2680, Web Site: www.thehartford.com (15)

Hartford, Jeff. Audience Development, Norwalk, CT. Tel: (203) 854-6730, FAX: (203) 854-6735, E-Mail: inolan@red7media.com, Web Site: www.audiencedevelopment.com (43)

Hartle, Charles, Rod's Western Palace, Columbus, OH. Tel: (614) 268-8200, (800) 325-8508, FAX: (800) 330-7637, E-Mail: rods@rods.com, Web Site: www.rods.com (2)

Hartle, Scott, Rod's Western Palace, Columbus, OH. Tel: (614) 268-8200, (800) 325-8508, FAX: (800) 330-7637, E-Mail: rods@rods.com, Web Site: www.rods.com (2)

Hartless, Frank, Starcrest Products of California Inc, Perris, CA. Tel: (909) 943-2011, FAX: (909) 943-2971, E-Mail: tmc@tstonramp.com (16)

Elizabeth Hartman, Syosset, NY. Tel: (516) 650-8862 (20)

Hartman, Bobbie, FirstGroup America, Cincinnati, OH. Tel: (513) 241-2200, FAX: (513) 419-3242, Web Site: www.firstgroup.com/north_america (12)

Hartman, Carl, Geometry Global, New York, NY. Tel: (212) 537-3700, E-Mail: press@geometry.com, Web Site: www.geometry.com (35)

Hartman, Carolyn, Kraftbilt, Tulsa, OK. Tel: (918) 628-1260, (800) 331-7290, FAX: (918) 632-7371, Web Site: www.kraftbilt.com (10)

Hartman, Elizabeth, Elizabeth Hartman, Syosset, NY. Tel: (516) 650-8862 (20)

Hartman, John, True Value Co, Chicago, IL. Tel: (773) 695-5000, Web Site: www.truevaluecompany.com (16)

Hartman, Nicole. J&H Berge/The Lab Mart, South Plainfield, NJ. Tel: (908) 561-3002, (800) 684-1234, FAX: (908) 561-3002, E-Mail: info@jhberge.com, Web Site: www.jhberge.com (27)

Hartman, Robert, ACBL, Horn Lake, MS. Tel: (662) 253-3100, FAX: (662) 253-3187, E-Mail: service@acbl.org, Web Site: www.acbl.org (1)

Hartmann, John, Compass Ventures, Lincoln, NE. Tel: (402) 438-3222, FAX: (402) 438-3439, E-Mail: info@compassventures.com, Web Site: www.compassventures.com (23)

Hartmann, Matthias, GfK Custom Research LLC, New York, NY. Tel: (212) 240-5300, (800) 274-3577, FAX: (212) 240-5353, E-Mail: info@gfkamerica.com, Web Site: www.gfkamerica.com (30)

Hartmann, Tobias, Radial Inc, King of Prussia, PA. Tel: (610) 491-7000, Web Site: www.radial.com (28)

Hartnack, Richard C., US Bancorp, Minneapolis, MN. Tel: (651) 466-3000, (800) 872-2657, FAX: (612) 303-0782, Web Site: www.usbank.com (14)

Hartnett, John, Thomson Reuters, New York, NY. Tel: (212) 367-6300, (800) 950-1216, FAX: (212) 367-6301, Web Site: www.riahome.com (17)

Hartnett, Mark, Formsource, Lewiston, ME. Tel: (207) 782-3311, (877) 782-3311, FAX: (207) 783-0157, E-Mail: service@formsource1.com, Web Site: www.formsource1.com (27)

Hartrick, Gretchen, Advanced Business Teleservices, Inc, Talent, OR. Tel: (541) 535-7878, (800) 866-9225, FAX: (541) 535-6942, Web Site: www.abtc.com (29)

Hartsaw, Teresa, Eperformax Inc, Thompsons Station, TN. Tel: (901) 751-4800, (888) 384-7004, FAX: (901) 751-4805, E-Mail: info0609@eperformax.com, Web Site: www.eperformax.com (29)

Hartwell, John, Innovairre Communications LLC, Cherry Hill, NJ. Tel: (856) 663-2500, E-Mail: info@innovairre.com, Web Site: www.innovairre.com (35)

Hartwig, Vicky, Leslie Jordan, Portland, OR. Tel: (503) 295-1987, (800) 935-3343, FAX: (503) 295-0939, E-Mail: ljsales@lesliejordan.com, Web Site: www.lesliejordan.com (2)

Harty Integrated Solutions, New Haven, CT. Tel: (203) 562-5112, (800) 654-0562, FAX: (203) 782-9168, E-Mail: gplatt@hartynet.com, Web Site: www.hartynet.com (21)

Harty, Tom, Meredith Corp, Des Moines, IA. Tel: (515) 284-3000, FAX: (515) 284-2700, Web Site: www.meredith.com (17)

The Hartz Mountain Corp, Secaucus, NJ. Tel: (201) 271-4800, (800) 275-1414, FAX: (201) 271-0068, Web Site: www.hartz.com (16)

Harvard Business Review, Boston, MA. Tel: (617) 783-7410, FAX: (617) 783-7493, Web Site: hbr.org (17)

Harvard Business School - Executive Education, Boston, MA. Tel: (617) 496-2193, (800) 427-5577, E-Mail: executive_education@hbs.edu, Web Site: www.exed.hbs.edu (1)

Harvard Business School Publishing, Boston, MA. Tel: (617) 783-7400, Web Site: www.harvardbusiness.org (17)

Harvard Pilgrim Health Care, Wellesley, MA. Tel: (617) 509-1000, (888) 888-4742, FAX: (617) 509-7590, Web Site: www.harvardpilgrim.org (17)

Harvard Square Records, Austin, TX. Tel: (877) 465-7669, E-Mail: LPnow@yahoo.com, Web Site: www.lpnow.com (3)

Harvest Communications, Redding, CA. Tel: (800) 303-6405, FAX: (800) 926-8038, Web Site: www.harvest-communications.com (20)

Harvey Associates, Cresskill, NJ. Tel: (201) 962-8463, E-Mail: harveyfnj@optonline.net, Web Site: harveyfeldmanassociates.com (35)

Harvey, Duanne, Tucker Electronics Co, Garland, TX. Tel: (214) 348-8800, (887) 667-6044, FAX: (214) 348-0367, E-Mail: sales@tucker.com, Web Site: www.tucker.com (2)

Harvey, Katherine, Curriculum Associates Inc, North Billerica, MA. Tel: (978) 667-8000, FAX: (978) 667-5706, E-Mail: cainfo@curriculumassociates.com, Web Site: www.curriculumassociates.com (17)

Harvey, Kathy, Potpourri Group Inc, North Billerica, MA. Tel: (978) 256-4100, FAX: (978) 256-1961/0344, Web Site: www.potpourrigroup.com (6)

Harvey, Kay, Bethesda Hospital Foundation, Boynton Beach, FL. Tel: (561) 737-7733, FAX: (561) 735-7942 (1)

Harvey, Peter E., Intellidyn Corp, Hingham, MA. Tel: (781) 741-5503, (866) 773-5756, FAX: (781) 741-5545, E-Mail: kmf@intellidyn.com, Web Site: www.intellidyn.com (22)

Harvey, William L., Interval International, South Miami, FL. Tel: (305) 666-1884, (800) 468-3782, FAX: (305) 667-5321, Web Site: www.intervalworld.com (35)

Harwil Corp, Oxnard, CA. Tel: (805) 988-6800, (800) 562-2447, FAX: (805) 988-6804, E-Mail: harwil@harwil.com, Web Site: www.harwil.com (9)

Harwood, Brent A, Mead Westvaco Consumer & Office Products, Richmond, VA. Tel: (937) 222-6323, (804) 444-1000, FAX: (937) 495-3192, Web Site: www.meadwestvaco.com (10)

Harwood, Chip, ValCom Inc, Boonton, NJ. Tel: (973) 588-7084, FAX: (973) 257-7216, E-Mail: info@valcom.tv, Web Site: www.valcom.tv (32)

Harwood, Thomas A., Mutual of America Life Insurance Co, New York, NY. Tel: (212) 224-1600, (800) 468-3785, FAX: (212) 207-3001, Web Site: www.mutualofamerica.com (14)

Hasbro Inc, Pawtucket, RI. Tel: (401) 431-8697, (800) 242-7276, FAX: (401) 727-5121, Web Site: www.hasbro.com (11)

Hasco First Photo, Saint Charles, MO. Tel: (636) 946-5115, FAX: (636) 946-7148, Web Site: www.growingfamily.com (16)

Hasen, Jeff, HipCricket Inc, Kirkland, WA. Tel: (425) 452-1111, Web Site: www.hipcricket.com (16)

Hasler Inc, Milford, CT. Tel: (203) 301-3400, (800) 995-2035, FAX: (203) 301-2600, E-Mail: info@haslerinc.com, Web Site: www.haslerinc.com (34)

Hassan, John, Champion Printing Inc, Cincinnati, OH. Tel: (513) 541-1100, (800) 543-1957, FAX: (513) 541-9398, E-Mail: cpi@championprintinginc.com, Web Site: www.championprintinginc.com (27)

Hasselbaum, Richard, Periodical Publisher's Service Bureau Inc, Fresno, CA. Tel: (419) 626-0623, (888) 206-0350, FAX: (419) 626-4576, Web Site: www.ppsb.com (18)

Hassell, Gerald L., BNY Mellon, New York, NY. Tel: (412) 234-5000, (212) 495-1784, FAX: (412) 635-1799, Web Site: www.bnymellon.com (14)

Hassell, Joel, Canoe Ventures LLC, Englewood, CO. Tel: (212) 364-3600, FAX: (212) 364 3601, Web Site: www.canoe-ventures.com (32)

Hasson, Janet, The Journal News, White Plains, NY. Tel: (914) 694-9300, FAX: (914) 696-8152, Web Site: www.nyjournalnews.com (17)

Hastings, Barry G., The Northern Trust Co, Chicago, IL. Tel: (312) 630-6000, (888) 289-6542, FAX: (312) 444-5244, Web Site: www.ntrs.com (14)

Hastings, Chuck, Almore International Inc, Beaverton, OR. Tel: (503) 643-6633, (800) 547-1511, FAX: (503) 643-9748, E-Mail: info@almore.com, Web Site: www.almore.com (7)

Hastings, Lionel K., Magna-Tel Inc, Cape Girardeau, MO. Tel: (573) 334-3096, (800) 467-2537, FAX: (573) 335-1715, Web Site: www.magna.tel.com (5)

Hastings, Lyn, Random House Direct Marketing, New York, NY. Tel: (212) 572-4985, (800) 678-5681, FAX: (212) 572-6018, Web Site: www.randomhousedirect.com (17)

Hatami, Derrick, Nissan North America Inc, Franklin, TN. Tel: (615) 725-1000, Web Site: www.nissanusa.com (16)

Denny Hatch Associates Inc, Philadelphia, PA. Tel: (215) 627-9103, FAX: (215) 627-6610, E-Mail: dennyhatch@yahoo.com, Web Site: dennyhatch.com (20)

Hatch, Denny, Denny Hatch Associates Inc, Philadelphia, PA. Tel: (215) 627-9103, FAX: (215) 627-6610, E-Mail: dennyhatch@yahoo.com, Web Site: www.dennyhatch.com (20)

Hatch, Peggy, Target Marketing Group, Philadelphia, PA. Tel: (215) 238-5300, Web Site: www.targetonline.com (31)

Hatch, Peggy, Target Marketing Magazine, Philadelphia, PA. Tel: (215) 238-5300, (800) 777-8074, FAX: (215) 238-5270, Web Site: www.targetmarketingmag.com (43)

Hatchell, David, David C Cook, Colorado Springs, CO. Tel: (719) 536-0100, (800) 323-7543, FAX: (719) 536-3232, Web Site: www.davidccook.com (17)

Hatchholdings LLC, Plano, TX. Tel: (214) 505-4697 (20)

Hatfield, David, Energizer Holdings Inc, Saint Louis, MO. Tel: (314) 985-2000, (800) 383-7323, FAX: (636) 733-4001, Web Site: www.energizer.com (16)

Hathaway, Diane M., Recycled Software Inc, Palm Springs, CA. Tel: (760) 655-5666, (760) 534-5338, FAX: (702) 323-5333, E-Mail: support@recycledsoftware.com, Web Site: www.recycledsoftware.com (3)

Hathaway, Misty, Mayo Clinic, Rochester, MN. Tel: (507) 284-2511, Web Site: www.mayoclinic.org (17)

Hatlestad, Tim, CCIM Institute, Chicago, IL. Tel: (312) 321-4460, (800) 621-7027, FAX: (312) 321-4530, Web Site: www.ccim.com (1)

Hattaway, Ann, Target MarkeTeam, Atlanta, GA. Tel: (770) 274-3700, FAX: (770) 274-3730, E-Mail: inquiries@tmtinc.com, Web Site: www.tmtinc.com (35)

Hatteras Press Inc, Tinton Falls, NJ. Tel: (732) 223-9888, (800) 695-0719, FAX: (732) 223-1232, E-Mail: connect@hatteras.us, Web Site: www.hatterascpc.com (27)

Hattersley, Gavin, Molson Coors Brewing Co, Denver, CO. Tel: (303) 927-2337, (800) 665-7661, Web Site: www.molsoncoors.com (16)

Hatton-Brown Publishers Inc, Montgomery, AL. Tel: (334) 834-1170, FAX: (334) 834-4525, E-Mail: webman@hattonbrown.com, Web Site: www.hattonbrown.com (17)

Hau, Robert, Tyco Electronics Corp, Berwyn, PA. Tel: (610) 893-9800, Web Site: www.te.com (16)

Hauber, Steve, Clipper Magazine, Mountville, PA. Tel: (888) 569-5100, FAX: (717) 569-5101, Web Site: www.clippermagazine.com (31)

Haublein, James, Stezzi Direct Inc, Atlanta, GA. Tel: (770) 448-9900, (800) 954-5100, FAX: (770) 448-9480, E-Mail: info@stezzi.com, Web Site: www.stezzi.com (21)

Hauf, Brian, Convio Inc, Austin, TX. Tel: (512) 652-2600, (888) 528-9501, FAX: (512) 652-2699, Web Site: www.convio.com (22)

Haugen, Janet B., Unisys, Blue Bell, PA. Tel: (215) 986-4011, (800) 874-8647, FAX: (215) 986-2312, Web Site: www.unisys.com (16)

Haugland, Henry, WebReply Inc, Natick, MA. Tel: (508) 318-4600, E-Mail: info@webreply.com, Web Site: www.webreply.com (35)

Haun, James, Oleda & Co Inc, Fort Worth, TX. Tel: (817) 731-1147, (800) 731-4247, FAX: (817) 731-1149, E-Mail: oleda@oleda.com, Web Site: www.oleda.com (16)

Haus, Jennifer, Songbird Hearing Inc, North Brunswick, NJ. Tel: (732) 422-7203, (800) 647-5560, Web Site: www.songbirdhearing.com (7)

Hausbeck, Janet, Amigo Mobility International Inc, Bridgeport, MI. Tel: (989) 777-0910, (800) 692-6446, FAX: (989) 777-8184, E-Mail: info@myamigo.com, Web Site: www.myamigo.com (16)

Hauser List Services, NMIS, East Meadow, NY. Tel: (516) 935-8603, FAX: (516) 935-8626, E-Mail: david@hausernet.com, Web Site: www.hausertrack.com (20)

Hauser, Barry, Hauser List Services, NMIS, East Meadow, NY. Tel: (516) 935-8603, FAX: (516) 935-8626, E-Mail: david@hausernet.com, Web Site: www.hausertrack.com (20)

Hauser, David, Hauser List Services, NMIS, East Meadow, NY. Tel: (516) 935-8603, FAX: (516) 935-8626, E-Mail: david@hausernet.com, Web Site: www.hausertrack.com (20)

Hauser, Laura, Moritt, Hock, Hamroff & Horowitz, Garden City, NY. Tel: (516) 873-2000, FAX: (516) 873-2010, E-Mail: lhauser@morritthock.com, Web Site: www.morritthock.com (16)

Hauser, Leela, Bureau Van Dijk, New York, NY. Tel: (212) 797-3550, FAX: (212) 797-3555, E-Mail: newyork@bvdinfo.com, Web Site: www.bvdinfo.com (22)

Hausner, Larry, American Diabetes Association, Alexandria, VA. Tel: (703) 549-1500, (800) 342-2383, Web Site: www.diabetes.org (1)

Hausrath, David L., Ashland Inc, Covington, KY. Tel: (859) 815-3333, Web Site: www.ashland.com (16)

Hausske, Jarett, Eleven Inc, San Francisco, CA. Tel: (415) 707-1111, Web Site: www.eleveninc.com (35)

Haut, Judith, Random House Children's Books, New York, NY. Tel: (212) 782-9000, (800) 726-0600, E-Mail: rhkidspublicity@randomhouse.com, Web Site: www.randomhousekids.com (13)

Havas Worldwide LLC, New York, NY. Tel: (212) 886-2000, FAX: (212) 886-5013, Web Site: www.havasworldwide.com (35)

HAVE Inc, Hudson, NY. Tel: (518) 828-2000, (800) 999-HAVE (4283), FAX: (518) 828-2008, E-Mail: kstein@haveinc.com, Web Site: www.haveinc.com (3)

Havel's Inc, Cincinnati, OH. Tel: (513) 271-2117, (800) 638-4770, FAX: (800) 628-3458, E-Mail: customercare@havels.com, Web Site: www.havels.com (17)

Havens, Gary, The Family Handyman, Eagan, MN. Tel: (651) 454-9200, FAX: (651) 994-2250 (17)

Havens, M. Scott, The Atlantic Monthly, Washington, DC. Tel: (202) 266-6000, (800) 234-2411, FAX: (202) 266-6001, Web Site: www.theatlantic.com (17)

Havens, Rob, The Newman Group Computer Services Corp, Ann Arbor, MI. Tel: (734) 426-3200, FAX: (734) 426-0777, E-Mail: anewman@newman.com (3)

Havranek, Alan D., Old World Mouldings Inc, Bohemia, NY. Tel: (631) 563-8660, FAX: (631) 563-8815, E-Mail: mouldings@optonline.com, Web Site: www.oldworldmouldings.com (9)

Havro, Tina, Indoor Gardening Supplies, Dexter, MI. Tel: (800) 823-5740, Web Site: www.indoorgardensupplies.com (8)

Hawaiian Host Inc, Honolulu, HI. Tel: (808) 848-0500, (866) 972-6879, E-Mail: info@hawaiianhost.com, Web Site: www.hawaiianhost.com (4)

Hawco, Steven, Lego Direct Marketing, Enfield, CT. Tel: (860) 749-2291, (800) 838-4386, FAX: (860) FAX-LEGO, Web Site: www.lego.com (11)

Hawk, Jeffrey A., American Trim, Lima, OH. Tel: (419) 228-1145, FAX: (419) 996-4850, E-Mail: sales@amtrim.com, Web Site: www.amtrim.com (9)

hawkeye, Dallas, TX. Tel: (214) 749-0080, E-Mail: sdapper@hawkeyeww.com, Web Site: www.hawkeyeww.com (35)

Hawkins, Arlene, Tom Snyder Productions, Watertown, MA. Tel: (617) 926-6000, (800) 342-0236, FAX: (800) 304-1254, E-Mail: ask@tomsnyder.com, Web Site: www.tomsnyder.com (16)

Hawkins, David, Gabriel Group, Earth City, MO. Tel: (314) 743-5700, FAX: (314) 743-5800, E-Mail: sales@gabrielgr.com, Web Site: www.gabrielgr.com (21)

Hawkins, John, ab + c Creative Intelligence, Wilmington, DE. Tel: (302) 655-1552, (800) 848-1552, FAX: (302) 655-3105, Web Site: www.a-b-c.com (35)

Hawkins, Terri, Suntrust Banks Inc, Atlanta, GA. Tel: (404) 588-7914, (800) 786-8787, FAX: (404) 532-0550, E-Mail: emmett.harmon@suntrust.com, Web Site: www.suntrust.com (14)

Haworth College of Business, Kalamazoo, MI. Tel: (616) 387-5050, FAX: (616) 387-5710, E-Mail: jessica.pelkey@wmich.edu, Web Site: www.wmich.edu/business (41)

Haworth Inc, Holland, MI. Tel: (616) 393-3000, (800) 344-2600, FAX: (616) 393-1570, Web Site: www.haworth.com (34)

Haworth, Dave, Cougar Mountain Software, Boise, ID. Tel: (208) 375-4455, (800) 388-3038, FAX: (208) 375-4460, E-Mail: sales@cougarmtn.com, Web Site: www.cougarmtn.com (14)

Haworth, G. W., Haworth Inc, Holland, MI. Tel: (616) 393-3000, (800) 344-2600, FAX: (616) 393-1570, Web Site: www.haworth.com (34)

Hawthorne Direct Inc, Los Angeles, CA. Tel: (301) 248-3972, E-Mail: inquiries@hawthornedirect.com, Web Site: www.hawthornedirect.com (35)

Hawthorne, David, HR Direct Inc, Fairfield, IA. Tel: (641) 472-7188, FAX: (641) 472-5729, E-Mail: info@hrdirect.net, Web Site: www.hrdirect.net (23)

Hawthorne, Timothy R., Hawthorne Direct Inc, Los Angeles, CA. Tel: (301) 248-3972, E-Mail: inquiries@hawthornedirect.com, Web Site: www.hawthornedirect.com (35)

Hayden, Deborah, Houston Direct Marketing Association, Houston, TX. Tel: (281) 931-8883, FAX: (281) 820-4023, Web Site: www.houstondma.org (40)

Hayden, Robin, Country Dance and Song Society, Easthampton, MA. Tel: (413) 203-5467, FAX: (413) 203-5471, E-Mail: office@cdss.org, Web Site: www.cdss.org (1)

Haydock, John, Crutchfield Corp, Charlottesville, VA. Tel: (434) 817-1000, (800) 955-9091, FAX: (804) 817-1010, E-Mail: administration@crutchfield.com, Web Site: www.crutchfield.com (3)

Haydock, John, The Plow & Hearth Inc, Madison, VA. Tel: (800) 494-7544, Web Site: www.plowhearth.com (8)

Haydu, Lucy, Marketing Research Association, Washington, DC. Tel: (860) 682-1000, (202) 800-2545, FAX: (860) 682-1010, (888) 512-1050, E-Mail: membership@marketingresearch.org, Web Site: www.mra-net.org (40)

Hayes, Dana, Harlequin Enterprises Ltd, Don Mills, ON Canada. Tel: (416) 445-5860, FAX: (416) 445-8655, E-Mail: customer_ecare@harlequin.ca, Web Site: www.eharlequin.com (17)

Hayes, Gwen, Elmwood Spa, Toronto, ON Canada. Tel: (416) 964-4515, (877) 284-6348, E-Mail: spa@elmwoodspa.com, Web Site: www.elmwoodspa.com (19)

Hayes, Jeremy, Active Graphics Inc, Cicero, IL. Tel: (708) 656-8900, FAX: (708) 656-2176, E-Mail: support@active-us.com, Web Site: www.active-us.com (21)

Hayes, Joseph, SRDS, Des Plaines, IL. Tel: (800) 851-7737, FAX: (847) 375-5001, Web Site: www.srds.com (17)

Hayes, Kevin, Methode Electronics Inc, Chicago, IL. Tel: (708) 867-6777, FAX: (708) 867-6999, E-Mail: info@methode.com, Web Site: www.methode.com (9)

Hayes, Lisa, Menardi Mikropul LLC, Trenton, SC. Tel: (803) 663-6551, (800) 321-3218, FAX: (803) 663-4029, E-Mail: info@menardifilters.com, Web Site: www.menardifilters.com (16)

Hayes, M.C., DX Engineering, Akron, OH. Tel: (800) 777-0703, FAX: (330) 572-3279, E-Mail: info@comteksystems.com, Web Site: www.comteksystems.com (16)

Hayes, Ron, Convertible Service, San Gabriel, CA. Tel: (626) 285-2255, (800) 333-1140, FAX: (626) 285-9004, Web Site: www.convertibleparts.com (16)

Hayes, Steve, Aradius Group, Omaha, NE. Tel: (402) 734-4400, (800) 369-0033, FAX: (402) 734-7492, E-Mail: info@aradiusgroup.com, Web Site: www.aradiusgroup.com (21)

Hayes, Thomas J., DX Engineering, Akron, OH. Tel: (800) 777-0703, FAX: (330) 572-3279, E-Mail: info@comteksystems.com, Web Site: www.comteksystems.com (16)

Haymarket Group Ltd, New York, NY. Tel: (212) 239-0855, FAX: (212) 967-4184, Web Site: www.chocalatiermagazine.com (17)

Haynes Marketing Network Inc, Macon, GA. Tel: (912) 742-5266, Web Site: www.haynesmarketing.com (35)

Haynes, Amelia, Haynes Marketing Network Inc, Macon, GA. Tel: (912) 742-5266, Web Site: www.haynesmarketing.com (35)

Haynes, Janel Bell, Alabama State University/College of Business Administration, Montgomery, AL. Tel: (334) 229-4124, FAX: (334) 229-4870, Web Site: coba.alasu.edu (41)

Haynes, John, American Institute of Physics, Melville, NY. Tel: (516) 576-2200, (800) 892-8259, FAX: (516) 576-2374, E-Mail: aipinfo@aip.org, Web Site: www.aip.org (17)

Haynes, John, Pete Rickard Inc, Cobleskill, NY. Tel: (518) 234-2731, (800) 282-5663, FAX: (518) 234-2454, E-Mail: info@peterickard.com, Web Site: www.peterickard.com (11)

Haynes, Phil, Haynes Marketing Network Inc, Macon, GA. Tel: (912) 742-5266, Web Site: www.haynesmarketing.com (35)

Haynes, Shawn, Markwins International Corp, City of Industry, CA. Tel: (909) 595-8898, FAX: (909) 595-8820, Web Site: www.markwins.com (16)

Hayward, Al, Pacific Propeller Inc, Kent, WA. Tel: (253) 872-7767, (800) 722-7767, FAX: (253) 872-7221, E-Mail: jheikke@pacprop.com, Web Site: www.pacificpropeller.com (16)

Hayward, Jon, PlusNetMarketing Inc, Exton, PA. Tel: (610) 458-0707, E-Mail: info@pnmarketing.com, Web Site: www.plusnetmarketing.com (21)

Hayward, Lisa, The Metropolitan Opera, New York, NY. Tel: (212) 362-6000, (212) 799-3100, FAX: (212) 870-7695, Web Site: www.metoperafamily.org (1)

Haywood, Jerry, Hess Print Solutions, Kent, OH. Tel: (800) 678-1222, E-Mail: info@hessprintsolutions.com, Web Site: www.thepressofohio.com (27)

Hazelden, Center City, MN. Tel: (651) 213-4200, (800) 257-7810, FAX: (651) 213-4411, E-Mail: info@hazeldenbettyford.org, Web Site: www.hazelden.org (7)

Head, Don, BBM Canada Inc, Don Mills, ON Canada. Tel: (416) 445-9800, FAX: (416) 445-8644, E-Mail: info@bbm.ca, Web Site: www.bbm.ca (30)

Healey, Chris, Source, Norwalk, CT. Tel: (203) 291-4000, FAX: (203) 291-4010, E-Mail: info@sourcecxm.com, Web Site: www.sourcecxm.com (35)

Health Affairs, Bethesda, MD. Tel: (301) 656-7401, FAX: (301) 654-2845, Web Site: www.healthaffairs.org (17)

Health Alliance Plan, Detroit, MI. Tel: (248) 443-1075, FAX: (248) 443-8851, E-Mail: alandin1@hapcorp.org, Web Site: www.hapcorp.org (15)

Health Care Concepts Inc, Austin, TX. Tel: (512) 479-8508, (800) 628-4201, FAX: (512) 479-8741 (16)

Health Care Logistics, Circleville, OH. Tel: (800) 848-1633, Web Site: www.healthcarelogistics.com (16)

Health International Corp, Tampa, FL. Tel: (800) 780-6744, FAX: (727) 595-6456, E-Mail: info@tonylittle.com, Web Site: www.tonylittle.com (32)

Health O Meter, Countryside, IL. Tel: (708) 377-0600, (800) 815-6615, FAX: (708) 377-0601, E-Mail: HomProCS@homscales.com, Web Site: www.homscales.com (16)

HealthPlan Services, Tampa, FL. Tel: (813) 289-1000, (800) 545-6441, Web Site: www.healthplan.com (15)

Health Sciences Consortium, Chapel Hill, NC. Tel: (919) 942-8731, FAX: (919) 942-3689, E-Mail: tony.penta@edtsi.com, Web Site: www.healthsciencesconsortium.org (17)

HealthInfo Direct, Schaumburg, IL. Tel: (630) 936-9465 (20)

HealthRight International, New York, NY. Tel: (212) 226-9890, Web Site: www.healthright.org (1)

The Healthy Back Store, Beltsville, MD. Tel: (703) 339-1700, (800) 4 MY BACK, FAX: (703) 339-0671, E-Mail: service@healthyback.com, Web Site: www.healthyback.com (16)

Healthy Directions LLC, Bethesda, MD. Tel: (301) 340-2100, FAX: (301) 309-8516, Web Site: www.healthydirections.com (34)

Healthy Offers Inc, Scottsdale, AZ. Tel: (480) 614-0060, FAX: (480) 614-0160, E-Mail: info@medicxmedia.com, Web Site: www.medicxmedia.com (23)

Healy List Marketing, Danvers, MA. Tel: (800) 281-8956, FAX: (978) 336-0463, E-Mail: info@healylistmarketing.com, Web Site: www.healylistmarketing.com (23)

Healy, Gigi, The Right Start Inc, Denver, CO. Tel: (303) 320-8312, (888) 856-8004, E-Mail: customerservice@rightstart.org, Web Site: www.rightstart.com (5)

Healy, Jim, Healy List Marketing, Danvers, MA. Tel: (800) 281-8956, FAX: (978) 336-0463, E-Mail: info@healylistmarketing.com, Web Site: www.healylistmarketing.com (23)

Healy, John, MBS, Central Islip, NY. Tel: (631) 851-5000, Web Site: www.mbsinsight.com (22)

Healy, Michael, Gillette Children's Specialty Healthcare, Saint Paul, MN. Tel: (651) 291-2848, Web Site: www.gillettechildrens.org (1)

Healy, Patrick, Quinnipiac College, Hamden, CT. Tel: (203) 582-8200, (203) 582-8600, (800) 462-1944, FAX: (203) 281-8664, Web Site: www.quinnipiac.edu (41)

Healy, Sue, Leadership Directories Inc, New York, NY. Tel: (212) 627-4140, FAX: (212) 645-0931, E-Mail: info@leadershipdirectories.com, Web Site: www.leadershipdirectories.com (17)

Hear Music, Beverly Hills, CA. Tel: (425) 452-5534, E-Mail: gail@hearmusic.com, Web Site: www.hearmusic.com (3)

Heard, Melissa, Sellstrom Manufacturing Co, Schaumburg, IL. Tel: (847) 358-2000, (800) 323-7402, FAX: (847) 358-8564, E-Mail: sellstrom@sellstrom.com, Web Site: www.sellstrom.com (16)

Hearlihy & Co, Pittsburg, KS. Tel: (800) 622-1000, (866) 622-1003, FAX: (800) 443-2260, Web Site: www.hearlihy.com (17)

Hearlihy, Sandra, Hearlihy & Co, Pittsburg, KS. Tel: (800) 622-1000, (866) 622-1003, FAX: (800) 443-2260, Web Site: www.hearlihy.com (17)

Hearn, Daniel, Stephan & Brady Inc, Madison, WI. Tel: (608) 241-4141, FAX: (608) 241-4246, E-Mail: gwhitely@stephanbrady.com, Web Site: www.stephanbrady.com (35)

Hearst Business Media, New York, NY. Tel: (212) 649-2000, Web Site: www.hearst.com/business-media (24)

The Hearst Corp, New York, NY. Tel: (212) 649-2000, FAX: (212) 649-2108, Web Site: www.hearst.com/magazines/ (17)

Hearst Direct Response Advertising Sales, New York, NY. Tel: (212) 649-2000, Web Site: www.hearst.com (31)

Hearst Magazines, New York, NY. Tel: (212) 649-2824, FAX: (212) 765-3528, Web Site: www.hearst.com/magazines (17)

Hearst, III William R., The Hearst Corp, New York, NY. Tel: (212) 649-2000, FAX: (212) 649-2108, Web Site: www.hearst.com/magazines/ (17)

Heart Thoughts Inc, Wichita, KS. Tel: (316) 688-5781, (800) 524-2229, FAX: (316) 687-2846, Web Site: www.heart-thoughts.com (27)

Hearthside Quilts & Supplies, Hinesburg, VT. Tel: (802) 482-7800, (800) 451-3533, FAX: (802) 482-7803, E-Mail: hearthsidequilts@att.net, Web Site: www.hearthsidequilts.com (11)

Heartland America, Chaska, MN. Tel: (952) 361-3640, (800) 229-2901, FAX: (952) 368-3452, E-Mail: info@heartlandamerica.com, Web Site: www.heartlandamerica.com (3)

Heartland Boating Magazine, Saint Louis, MO. Tel: (314) 241-4310, (800) 366-9630, FAX: (314) 241-4207, E-Mail: info@heartlandboating.com, Web Site: www.heartlandboating.com (17)

Heartstrings Press, Lancaster, VA. Tel: (804) 462-0884, (800) 462-0884, FAX: (716) 462-0884, E-Mail: sue@grandloving.com, Web Site: www.grandloving.com (17)

Heath, Barb, Klockit, Lake Geneva, WI. Tel: (262) 248-7000, (800) 556-2548, FAX: (262) 248-9899, E-Mail: klockit@klockit.com, Web Site: www.klockit.com (6)

Heath, David, Redleaf Press, Saint Paul, MN. Tel: (651) 641-6621, (800) 423-8309, FAX: (800) 641-0115, E-Mail: jvoltz@redleafpress.org, Web Site: www.redleafpress.org (17)

Heath, Gary, Gambro Inc, Lakewood, CO. Tel: (303) 232-6800, (800) 525-2623, FAX: (303) 222-6810, Web Site: www.gambro.com (16)

Heath, Jinger L., Beauticontrol Cosmetics Inc, Carrollton, TX. Tel: (972) 458-0601, (800) BEAUTI-1, FAX: (972) 458-6904, E-Mail: clientservices@beauticontrol.com, Web Site: www.beauticontrol.com (7)

Heathman, James, O2 Agency Inc, New York, NY. Tel: (212) 675-7334, E-Mail: newbiz@o2agency.com, Web Site: o2agency.strikingly.com (35)

Heaton, Amy, Pfaelzer Brothers, Maumee, OH. Tel: (419) 893-7611, (800) 345-9290, FAX: (419) 893-0164, Web Site: www.phaelzerbrothers.com (16)

Heator, Marty, Schoolcraft College, Livonia, MI. Tel: (734) 462-4400, Web Site: www.schoolcraft.edu (1)

Heaven & Earth, Virginia Beach, VA. Tel: (757) 420-3576, E-Mail: heavenandearthkr8@gmail.com, Web Site: www.heavenandearth.com (5)

Heavy Rotation, Milwaukee, WI. Tel: (414) 384-5200, (800) 886-4759, FAX: (414) 434-9318, E-Mail: info@holoubekstudios.com, Web Site: heavytees.com (27)

Hebden Direct, Philadelphia, PA. Tel: (215) 923-3891, E-Mail: hebdendirect@comcast.net (39)

Hebden, William, Hebden Direct, Philadelphia, PA. Tel: (215) 923-3891, E-Mail: hebdendirect@comcast.net (39)

Hebeler, Rose, O'Halloran Advertising, Westport, CT. Tel: (203) 341-9400 (39)

Hebert, Jr. Curt L., Entergy, New Orleans, LA. Tel: (504) 576-4000, (800) ENTERGY, FAX: (504) 576-4428, Web Site: www.entergy.com (16)

Hebron Academy, Hebron, ME. Tel: (207) 966-2100, (888) 432-7664, Web Site: www.habronacademy.org (1)

Norman Hecht Research Inc, Syosset, NY. Tel: (516) 496-8866, FAX: (516) 496-8165, E-Mail: nhr@normanhechtresearch.com, Web Site: www.normanhechtresearch.com (30)

Hecht Rubber Corp, Jacksonville, FL. Tel: (904) 731-3401, (800) 872-3401, FAX: (904) 730-0066, Web Site: www.hechtrubber.com (16)

Hecht, Larry M., Hecht Rubber Corp, Jacksonville, FL. Tel: (904) 731-3401, (800) 872-3401, FAX: (904) 730-0066, Web Site: www.hechtrubber.com (16)

Hecht, Stuart, Hecht Rubber Corp, Jacksonville, FL. Tel: (904) 731-3401, (800) 872-3401, FAX: (904) 730-0066, Web Site: www.hechtrubber.com (16)

Hechtkopf, Bram, Kobie Marketing Inc, Saint Petersburg, FL. Tel: (727) 822-5353, (800) 821-7892, FAX: (727) 822-5265, E-Mail: info@kobie.com, Web Site: www.kobie.com (35)

Heck, Kirby, Current USA Inc, Colorado Springs, CO. Tel: (719) 594-4100, (877) 665-4458, FAX: (719) 531-2283, Web Site: www.currentinc.com (6)

Heckert, Christine, Brocade Communications Systems Inc, San Jose, CA. Tel: (408) 333-8000, FAX: (408) 333-8101, E-Mail: info@brocade.com, Web Site: www.brocade.com (16)

Heckman, Peter H., Horace Mann Educators Corp, Springfield, IL. Tel: (217) 789-2500, FAX: (217) 788-5161, Web Site: www.horacemann.com (15)

Hedden, Andrew S, Scholastic Inc, New York, NY. Tel: (212) 343-6100, (800) SCHOLASTIC, FAX: (212) 343-6484, Web Site: www.scholastic.com (17)

Hederman, Rea, Nyrev Inc, New York, NY. Tel: (212) 757-8070, FAX: (212) 333-5374, E-Mail: mail@nybooks.com, Web Site: www.nybooks.com (17)

Hedlund, Greg, Charnstrom, Shakopee, MN. Tel: (952) 403-0303, (800) 328-2962, FAX: (800) 916-3215, E-Mail: customerservice@charnstrom.com, Web Site: www.charnstrom.com (28)

Heffernan, Ed, Alliance Data, Plano, TX. Tel: (972) 348-5100, E-Mail: info@thealliedgrp.com, Web Site: www.alliancedata.com (22)

Heffernan, Jim, Imagine Fulfillment Services, La Mirada, CA. Tel: (310) 217-4610, FAX: (310) 217-9632, E-Mail: andya@imaginefulfillment.com, Web Site: www.imaginefulfillment.com (28)

Heggen, Arthur, Safeware, The Insurance Agency Inc, Columbus, OH. Tel: (614) 781-1492, (800) 800-1492, FAX: (614) 781-0559, E-Mail: service@safeware.com Web Site: www.safeware.com (15)

Hegner, Mike, Chase Industries, Inc, Cincinnati, OH. Tel: (513) 860-5565, (800) 543-4455, FAX: (800) 245-7045, Web Site: www.chasedoors.com (16)

Heh, Greg, Jersey Printing Associates Inc, Atlantic Highlands, NJ. Tel: (732) 872-9654, FAX: (732) 872-9309, E-Mail: sales@jerseyprinting.com, Web Site: www.jerseyprinting.com (27)

Heid, Francis, Advanstar Communications Inc, North Olmstead, OH. Tel: (440) 243-8100, (800) 225-4569, FAX: (440) 891-2651, E-Mail: info@advanstar.com, Web Site: www.advanstarlists.com (17)

Heidemann, Rob, Daydots, Fort Worth, TX. Tel: (817) 590-4500, (800) 321-3687, FAX: (800) 438-7002, E-Mail: customercare@daydots.com, Web Site: www.daydots.com (16)

Heiden, Mark, Point To Point Marketing Inc, Fort Collins, CO. Tel: (513) 231-0344, E-Mail: info@ptpmarketing.com, Web Site: ptpmarketing.com (35)

Heiderer, Cody, Marketing Economics Inc, Chicago, IL. Tel: (312) 642-2188, FAX: (312) 642-3091, E-Mail: codyh@meimedia.com, Web Site: www.meimedia.com (23)

Heikke, Jeff, Pacific Propeller Inc, Kent, WA. Tel: (253) 872-7767, (800) 722-7767, FAX: (253) 872-7221, E-Mail: jheikke@pacprop.com, Web Site: www.pacificpropeller.com (16)

Heil, Sonya Kim, Theodore Presser Co, King Of Prussia, PA. Tel: (610) 592-1222, FAX: (610) 592-1229, E-Mail: webmaster@presser.com, Web Site: www.presser.com (17)

Heiland, Chris, Sierra Scientific Inc, Phoenix, AZ. Tel: (602) 256-0540, FAX: (602) 252-1972, Web Site: www.value-tek.com (9)

Heiland, George, Sierra Scientific Inc, Phoenix, AZ. Tel: (602) 256-0540, FAX: (602) 252-1972, Web Site: www.value-tek.com (9)

Grant Heilman Photography Inc, Lititz, PA. Tel: (717) 626-0296, (800) 622-2046, FAX: (717) 626-0971, E-Mail: info@heilmanphoto.com, Web Site: www.heilmanphoto.com (38)

Heilmann, Michael, StrongView Systems Inc, Redwood City, CA. Tel: (650) 421-4200, (800) 971-0380, FAX: (650) 421-4201, E-Mail: info@strongview.com, Web Site: www.strongview.com (32)

Heim, Tom, Infocus Marketing Inc, Warrenton, VA. Tel: (800) 708-5478, FAX: (866) 708-5478, E-Mail: sales@infocusmarketing.com, Web Site: www.infocusmarketing.com (23)

Heim, Wolf, Zotos International, Darien, CT. Tel: (203) 655-8911, (800) 242-9283, (800) 242-WAVE, FAX: (203) 656-7890, E-Mail: HumanResources@zotosintl.com, Web Site: www.zotos.com (16)

Heimberg, Steve, Communication Creativity, Buena Vista, CO. Tel: (720) 344-4388, (800) 331-8355, FAX: (866) 685-0307, E-Mail: steve@steveheimberg.com, Web Site: www.communicationcreativity.com (17)

Heimerman, Jon, Eagle Publishing, Washington, DC. Tel: (202) 216-0600, FAX: (202) 216-0612, Web Site: www.eaglepub.com (17)

Hein, Linda, JIST Publishing, Saint Paul, MN. Tel: (800) 328-4564, FAX: (800) 328-1452, E-Mail: educate@emcp.com, Web Site: jist.emcp.com (17)

Hein, Linda, Redleaf Press, Saint Paul, MN. Tel: (651) 641-6621, (800) 423-8309, FAX: (800) 641-0115, E-Mail: jvoltz@redleafpress.org, Web Site: www.redleafpress.org (17)

Hein, Meredith, Advanta Corp, Conshohocken, PA. Tel: (215) 657-4000, (800) 255-0022, Web Site: www.advanta.com (14)

Heinbuch, Kirk, Summit Racing Equipment, Tallmadge, OH. Tel: (330) 630-0250, (800) 230-3030, FAX: (330) 630-5571, Web Site: www.summitracing.com (12)

Heinlein, James, ALSTOM Signaling Inc, West Henrietta, NY. Tel: (585) 279-2228, Web Site: www.alstomsignalingsolutions.com (16)

Heinlen, Chuck, Paslode, Vernon Hills, IL. Tel: (847) 634-1900, (800) 222-6990, FAX: (847) 634-6602, E-Mail: tech@paslode.com, Web Site: www.paslode.com (16)

Heinrich, Denver, CO. Tel: (303) 233-8660, (800) 356-5036, FAX: (303) 239-5352, E-Mail: info@heinrich.com, Web Site: www.heinrich.com (35)

Heintzelman, Mark, The Missoulian, Missoula, MT. Tel: (406) 523-5200, (800) 366-7102, FAX: (406) 523-5221, Web Site: www.missoulian.com (31)

Heist, Richard L., Our Lady of Victory Homes of Charity, Lackawanna, NY. Tel: (716) 828-9648, FAX: (716) 828-9643, E-Mail: rheist@olv-bvs.org, Web Site: www.ourladyofvictory.org (1)

Heisz, Deborah, Success Magazine, Lake Dallas, TX. Tel: (877) 243-8383, E-Mail: editor@success.com, Web Site: www.successmagazine.com (43)

Heitman, Christopher J., Pegasus Auto Racing Supplies Inc, New Berlin, WI. Tel: (262) 317-1234, (800) 688-6946, FAX: (262) 317-1201, E-Mail: info@pegasusautoracing.com, Web Site: www.pegasusautoracing.com (12)

Heitman, David, The Creative Alliance Inc, Lafayette, CO. Tel: (303) 665-8101, FAX: (303) 665-3136, E-Mail: info@thecreativealliance.com, Web Site: www.thecreativealliance.com (35)

Held, Joe, The Reader's Digest Association Inc, New York, NY. Tel: (800) 310-6261, Web Site: www.rda.com (17)

Held, Lori, Trout Unlimited, Arlington, VA. Tel: (703) 522-0200, (800) 834-2419, FAX: (703) 284-9400, E-Mail: trout@tu.org, Web Site: www.tu.org (1)

Heldref Publications, Washington, DC. Tel: (202) 296-6267, (215) 625-8900, FAX: (202) 296-5149, Web Site: www.heldref.org (17)

The Helicopter Group, Richmond Hill, ON Canada. Tel: (416) 222-3835, Web Site: www.thehelicoptergroup.com (28)

Heller Financial, Chicago, IL. Tel: (312) 441-7000, FAX: (312) 441-7499, Web Site: www.hellerfin.com (14)

W C Heller & Co, Montpelier, OH. Tel: (419) 485-3176, FAX: (419) 485-8694 (16)

Walter E Heller College of Business Administration, Chicago, IL. Tel: (312) 281-3293, FAX: (312) 281-3290, Web Site: www.roosevelt.edu (41)

Heller, Andrew M., W C Heller & Co, Montpelier, OH. Tel: (419) 485-3176, FAX: (419) 485-8694 (16)

Heller, Caren, Crohn's & Colitis Foundation of America, New York, NY. Tel: (212) 685-3440, (800) 932-2423, E-Mail: info@ccfa.org, Web Site: www.ccfa.org (1)

Heller, R.L., W C Heller & Co, Montpelier, OH. Tel: (419) 485-3176, FAX: (419) 485-8694 (16)

Heller, Scott, Communication Industries Corp, Grafton, VT. Tel: (802) 869-6500, FAX: (802) 869-6565, E-Mail: info@cicmail.com, Web Site: www.careersatcic.com (10)

Hellhake, Paul, Rajant Corp, Malvern, PA. Tel: (484) 595-0233, FAX: (484) 595-0244, E-Mail: support@rajant.com, Web Site: www.rajant.com (32)

Hello Direct, Nashua, NH. Tel: (408) 972-1990, (800) 435-5634, FAX: (408) 972-8155, Web Site: www.hello-direct.com (16)

Helly-Hansen, Auburn, WA. Tel: (800) 435-5901, FAX: (425) 649-3740, Web Site: www.hellyhansen.com (16)

Helm, Peyton Randolph, UMass Dartmouth, North Dartmouth, MA. Tel: (508) 999-8000, (508) 999-9250, Web Site: www.umassd.edu (1)

Helm, Sally, The Sailing Co, Palm Coast, FL. Tel: (866) 436-2460, FAX: (401) 848-5048, Web Site: www.sailingworld.com (17)

Helman Group Ltd, Oxnard, CA. Tel: (805) 487-7772, FAX: (805) 487-9975, E-Mail: barryh@helmangroup.com, Web Site: www.helmangroup.com (16)

Helman, Andy, Helman Group Ltd, Oxnard, CA. Tel: (805) 487-7772, FAX: (805) 487-9975, E-Mail: barryh@helmangroup.com, Web Site: www.helmangroup.com (16)

Helman, Barry, Helman Group Ltd, Oxnard, CA. Tel: (805) 487-7772, FAX: (805) 487-9975, E-Mail: barryh@helmangroup.com, Web Site: www.helmangroup.com (16)

Helmer, Dan, Wilton Armetale, Mount Joy, PA. Tel: (717) 653-4444, (800) 553-2048, FAX: (717) 653-6573, E-Mail: cservice@armetale.com, Web Site: www.armetale.com (16)

Helmers, Cathy, Peter Li Education Group, Dayton, OH. Tel: (937) 293-1415, (800) 523-4625, FAX: (937) 293-1310, Web Site: www.peterli.com (17)

Helms, Jack P., Lazard Middle Market LLC, Minneapolis, MN. Tel: (612) 339-0500, FAX: (612) 339-0507, Web Site: www.lazardmm.com (23)

Helsley, James, Houston Direct Marketing Association, Houston, TX. Tel: (281) 931-8883, FAX: (281) 820-4023, Web Site: www.houstondma.org (40)

Helsley, Tom, Automated Mailing Systems Corp, Dallas, TX. Tel: (972) 869-2844, (800) 527-1668, FAX: (972) 869-2735, E-Mail: amsco@amscodallas.com (34)

Helzberg Diamonds, North Kansas City, MO. Tel: (816) 842-7780, (800) HELZBERG, FAX: (816) 480-0294, Web Site: www.helzberg.com (16)

Hemisphere Marketing, Kansas City, MO. Tel: (816) 444-5439, Web Site: www.hemispheremarketing.com (20)

Hemmer, Jim, CorporateRewards.com, New York, NY. Tel: (212) 689-1200, Web Site: www.corporaterewards.com (35)

Hemmings Motor News, Bennington, VT. Tel: (800) 227-4373, FAX: (802) 447-9631, Web Site: www.hmn.com (17)

Hemmingson, John, Esco Corp, Portland, OR. Tel: (503) 228-2141, FAX: (503) 778-6682, Web Site: www.escocorp.com (16)

Hemus, Simon, Tupperware Brands Corp, Orlando, FL. Tel: (407) 826-5050, (800) 366-3800, FAX: (407) 826-8874, Web Site: www.tupperwarebrands.com (16)

Hen, Sam, Unicom Electric Inc, Walnut, CA. Tel: (626) 964-7873, (800) 346-6668, FAX: (626) 964-7880, E-Mail: info@unicomlink.com, Web Site: www.unicomlink.com (16)

Henderson, Ann, Nevada Magazine, Carson City, NV. Tel: (775) 687-5416, FAX: (775) 687-6159, E-Mail: editor@nevadamagazine.com, Web Site: www.nevadamagazine.com (17)

Henderson, Bruce, Jack Morton Worldwide, New York, NY. Tel: (212) 401-7000, (212) 401-7121, E-Mail: experience@jackmorton.com, Web Site: www.jackmorton.com (35)

Henderson, David L., American Locker Security Systems Inc, Coppell, TX. Tel: (817) 329-1600, (800) 828-9118, E-Mail: info@americanlocker.com, Web Site: www.americanlocker.com (16)

Henderson, George, Burlington Industries Inc, Greensboro, NC. Tel: (336) 379-2000, FAX: (336) 379-2498, Web Site: www.burlington.com (16)

Henderson, Lynn O., Doane, Saint Louis, MO. Tel: (314) 569-2700, (866) 647-0918, FAX: (314) 569-1083, Web Site: www.doane.com (17)

Henderson, Rick, American Speech-Language-Hearing Association, Rockville, MD. Tel: (301) 897-5700, (800) 638-8255, FAX: (301) 296-8580, E-Mail: productsales@asha.org, Web Site: www.asha.org (1)

Hendley, Audrey, American Express Co, New York, NY. Tel: (212) 640-2000, FAX: (212) 619-9802, Web Site: www.americanexpress.com (14)

Hendren, Tom, Array Marketing Group Inc, Toronto, ON Canada. Tel: (416) 299-4865, FAX: (416) 292-9759, E-Mail: inquiry@arraymarketing.com, Web Site: arraymarketing.com (35)

Hendrick, Jacqueline, LearnCom HR Consulting & Training, Irvine, CA. Tel: (515) 440-0890, (800) 698-8263, FAX: (515) 221-3149, E-Mail: nhartline@learncom.com, Web Site: www.learncomhr.com (16)

Hendricks, Daryl, American Kennel Club, New York, NY. Tel: (212) 696-8200, FAX: (212) 696-8217, (212) 696-8299, Web Site: www.akc.org (17)

Hendricks, John, Discovery Communications Inc, Silver Spring, MD. Tel: (240) 662-2000, FAX: (240) 662-1868, Web Site: corporate.discovery.com (16)

Hendricks, Todd, ASPCA, New York, NY. Tel: (212) 876-7700, Web Site: www.aspca.org (1)

Hendricks, Virgil, Mid West Floor Co Inc, Saint Louis, MO. Tel: (314) 647-6060, FAX: (314) 647-9189, E-Mail: sales@mid-westfloor.com, Web Site: www.mid-westfloor.com (16)

Hendrickson, Ray, Christian Book Distributors Inc, Peabody, MA. Tel: (978) 532-5300, FAX: (978) 977-5010, E-Mail: javedisian@chrbook.com, Web Site: www.chrbook.com (16)

Hendrix, Darrell, Milwaukee Electric Tool Corp, Brookfield, WI. Tel: (262) 781-3600, (800) 729-3878, FAX: (800) 638-9582, Web Site: www.milwaukeetool.com (16)

Hendrix, Dave, Convio Inc, Austin, TX. Tel: (512) 652-2600, (888) 528-9501, FAX: (512) 652-2699, Web Site: www.convio.com (22)

Hendry, Jon H., Alerus Financial National Assoc, Grand Forks, ND. Tel: (701) 795-3200, (800) 279-3200, Web Site: www2.alerusfinancial.com (14)

Hendryx, Carolyn, Ebersole Lapidary Supply Inc, Wichita, KS. Tel: (316) 945-4771, (877) EBERSOLE, FAX: (316) 945-4773, E-Mail: ebersolerocks@sbcglobal.net, Web Site: www.ebersolelapidary.com (11)

David Heneberry Associates, West Grove, PA. Tel: (203) 778-0692, FAX: (203) 778-0699 (20)

Heneberry, David, David Heneberry Associates, West Grove, PA. Tel: (203) 778-0692, FAX: (203) 778-0699 (20)

Henerson, Paula, Bethesda Hospital Foundation, Boynton Beach, FL. Tel: (561) 737-7733, FAX: (561) 735-7942 (1)

Hengesbaugh, Bernard L., American Medical Association, Chicago, IL. Tel: (312) 464-5000, (800) 621-8335, FAX: (312) 464-4184, Web Site: www.ama-assn.org (1)

Henke & Associates Inc, Cedarburg, WI. Tel: (262) 375-9090, FAX: (262) 375-2262, E-Mail: info@henkeinc.com, Web Site: www.henkeinc.com (35)

Henke, Bill, Henke & Associates Inc, Cedarburg. WI. Tel: (262) 375-9090, FAX: (262) 375-2262, E-Mail: info@henkeinc.com, Web Site: www.henkeinc.com (35)

Henke, Jack, Henke & Associates Inc, Cedarburg, WI. Tel: (262) 375-9090, FAX: (262) 375-2262, E-Mail: info@henkeinc.com, Web Site: www.henkeinc.com (35)

Henkel, Andrew, Johnson & Quin Inc, Niles, IL. Tel: (847) 588-4800, FAX: (847) 647-6949, E-Mail: jqinfo@j-quin.com, Web Site: www.j-quin.com (28)

Henkel, Dave, Johnson & Quin Inc, Niles, IL. Tel: (847) 588-4800, FAX: (847) 647-6949, E-Mail: jqinfo@j-quin.com, Web Site: www.j-quin.com (28)

Henley, Deborah, Newsday, Melville, NY. Tel: (800) 639-7329, Web Site: www.newsday.com (17)

Henley, Jeffrey O., Oracle Corp, Redwood Shores, CA. Tel: (650) 506-7000, (800) 633-0738, FAX: (650) 506-7200, Web Site: www.oracle.com (16)

Hennelly, Fran, Independent Living Aids, Buffalo, NY. Tel: (516) 450-3829, (800) 537-2118, FAX: (516) 937-3906, E-Mail: techsupport@independentliving.com, Web Site: www.independentliving.com (7)

Hennen, Mike, Cannella Response Television Inc, Burlington, WI. Tel: (262) 763-4810, FAX: (262) 763-2875, Web Site: www.drtv.com (32)

Hennenfent, Ken, American Teleservices Association, Indianapolis, IN. Tel: (317) 816-9336, (877) 779-3974, FAX: (317) 218-0323, Web Site: www.ataconnect.org (40)

Hennerberg Group Inc, Colleyville, TX. Tel: (817) 318-8100, E-Mail: gary@hennerberg.com, Web Site: hennerberg.com (35)

Hennerberg, Gary, Hennerberg Group Inc, Colleyville, TX. Tel: (817) 318-8100, E-Mail: gary@hennerberg.com, Web Site: hennerberg.com (35)

Hennessey, Edward, Littleton Coin Co Inc, Littleton, NH. Tel: (603) 444-5386, (800) 645-3122, FAX: (603) 444-0121, E-Mail: jhennessey@littletoncoin.com, Web Site: www.littletoncoin.com (6)

Hennessey, Theresa, Playboy Enterprises Inc, Beverly Hills, CA. Tel: (310) 860-1215, Web Site: www.playboyenterprises.com (17)

Hennigan, Joseph, Welch Allyn, Inc, Skaneateles Falls, NY. Tel: (315) 685-4100, Web Site: www.welchallyn.com (3)

Hennighausen, Charles E., Lorillard Tobacco Co, Greensboro, NC. Tel: (336) 335-7000, (877) 703-0386, FAX: (336) 373-6917, E-Mail: externalaffairs@lortobco.com, Web Site: www.lorillard.com (17)

Henning. Richard, Edward Elgar Publishing Inc, Northampton, MA. Tel: (413) 584-5551, FAX: (413) 584-9933, E-Mail: sales@e-elgar.com, Web Site: www.e-elgar.com (17)

Henningfield, Mary Pat, Wag/Aero Group, Lyons, WI. Tel: (262) 763-9586, (800) 558-6868, FAX: (262) 763-7595, E-Mail: wagaero-sales@wagaero.com, Web Site: www.wagaero.com (16)

Henricks, Susan, Arbor Capital 1, Omaha, NE. Tel: (402) 991-4962 (14)

Henricson, C. Robert, New England Life Insurance Co, Boston, MA. Tel: (617) 578-2000, FAX: (617) 536-2393, Web Site: www.nefn.metlife.com (15)

Leon Henry Inc, Hartsdale, NY. Tel: (914) 285-3456, FAX: (914) 285-3450, E-Mail: lh@leonhenryinc.com, Web Site: www.leonhenryinc.com (23)

Henry, Gail, Leon Henry Inc, Hartsdale, NY. Tel: (914) 285-3456, FAX: (914) 285-3450, E-Mail: lh@leonhenryinc.com, Web Site: www.leonhenryinc.com (23)

Henry, Gordon, Dex Media, Dallas-Fort Worth Airport, TX. Tel: (972) 453-7000, Web Site: www.dexmedia.com (31)

Henry, James L., United Church Homes, Marion, OH. Tel: (740) 382-4885, (800) 837-2211, FAX: (740) 382-4884, Web Site: www.unitedchurchhomes.org (1)

Henry, Mark, TEC Mailing Solutions, LLC, Sun Prairie, WI. Tel: (608) 825-8525, (866) 379-9437, FAX: (608) 825-8526, E-Mail: info@tecmailing.com (22)

Henry, Peter, O'Keefe Henry Direct Inc, Deerfield, IL. Tel: (847) 681-9200, FAX: (847) 681-9299, Web Site: www.okeefehenrydirect.com (20)

Hensel, Nancy P., The Popcorn Factory, Lake Forest, IL. Tel: (847) 247-3342, (888) 238-8107, FAX: (888) 333-4595, E-Mail: service@thepopcornfactory.com, Web Site: www.thepopcornfactory.com (4)

Henshall, David J., Citrix Systems, Inc, Fort Lauderdale, FL. Tel: (954) 267-3000, FAX: (954) 267-3101, Web Site: www.citrix.com (22)

Henson, Mary Beth, National Audubon Society, New York, NY. Tel: (212) 979-3000, FAX: (212) 979-3188, Web Site: www.audubon.org (17)

Henthorn, Lisa, PartnerData LLC, Evanston, IL. Tel: (847) 733-0819 (30)

Heppelman, James E., PTC, Needham, MA. Tel: (781) 370-5000, (877) 275-4782, Web Site: www.ptc.com (22)

The Herald & Review, Decatur, IL. Tel: (217) 429-5151, FAX: (217) 421-6913, E-Mail: hrdirect@herald-review.com, Web Site: www.herald-review.com (17)

Herb, Ike, Pfaelzer Brothers, Maumee, OH. Tel: (419) 893-7611, (800) 345-9290, FAX: (419) 893-0164, Web Site: www.phaelzerbrothers.com (16)

Herbach & Rademan Co, Moorestown, NJ. Tel: (856) 802-0422, (800) 848-8001, FAX: (856) 802-0465, E-Mail: sales@herbach.com, Web Site: www.herbach.com (9)

Herbalife International of America Inc, Los Angeles, CA. Tel: (310) 216-9661, (866) 866-4744, FAX: (310) 258-7019, Web Site: www.herbalife.com (7)

Herbert, Mark, Loyaltyworks Inc, Atlanta, GA. Tel: (678) 539-5000, (800) 844-5000, FAX: (678) 539-5173, Web Site: www.loyaltyworks.com (21)

Herbert, Pat, Omni Farm, West Jefferson, NC. Tel: (336) 982-3475, (800) TREE-FARM, FAX: (336) 982-4163, E-Mail: omnifarm@omnifarm.com, Web Site: www.omnifarm.com (16)

Herbst, James E., Henry Wurst Inc, North Kansas City, MO. Tel: (816) 842-3113, FAX: (816) 472-6221, E-Mail: info@henrywurst.com, Web Site: www.henrywurst.com (27)

Herceg, Lisa, National Association of Realtors, Chicago, IL. Tel: (312) 329-8526, (800) 874-6500, Web Site: www.realtors.org (1)

Hercky-Pasqua-Herman, Roselle Park, NJ. Tel: (908) 241-9474, FAX: (908) 241-8961, E-Mail: hercky@hph-comm.com, Web Site: www.hph-comm.com (35)

Hercky, Peter, Hercky-Pasqua-Herman, Roselle Park, NJ. Tel: (908) 241-9474, FAX: (908) 241-8961, E-Mail: hercky@hph-comm.com, Web Site: www.hph-comm.com (35)

Herd, Ronald, Orbit Manufacturing Co, Perkasie, PA. Tel: (215) 257-0727, (888) 895-0958, FAX: (215) 257-7399, Web Site: www.orbitmfg.com (9)

Herdzina, Jeff, US Data Corp, Omaha, NE. Tel: (402) 502-5623, (888) 578-3282, FAX: (402) 502-5623, E-Mail: info@usdatacorporation.com, Web Site: www.usdatacorporation.com (29)

Hergesell, Janine, Specialized Information Publishers Association, Vienna, VA. Tel: (781) 754-4771, FAX: (703) 992-7512, E-Mail: nbrand@sia.net, Web Site: www.siia.net (1)

The Heritage Co, North Little Rock, AR. Tel: (501) 835-5000 x1142, FAX: (501) 835-5834, Web Site: www.theheritagecompany.com (29)

Heritage Direct, Oakhurst, NJ. Tel: (732) 531-2212, FAX: (732) 531-4798, Web Site: www.actionmarkets.com (22)

Herklots, Michael, Davidoff of Geneva Inc, Pinellas Park, FL. Tel: (727) 828-5400, (800) 328-4365, FAX: (203) 975-0090 (6)

The Herman Group, Austin, TX. Tel: (336) 210-3547, E-Mail: info@hermangroup.com, Web Site: www.hermangroup.com (20)

Herman Miller Inc, Zeeland, MI. Tel: (616) 654-3000, FAX: (616) 654-5234, E-Mail: investor@hermanmiller.com, Web Site: www.hermanmiller.com (16)

Herman, Aaron M., Latest Products Corp, Woodbury, NY. Tel: (516) 367-4700, (800) 288-3547, FAX: (516) 367-4714, E-Mail: lpcorp@aol.com, Web Site: www.latestproducts.net (7)

Herman, Edie, Warren Communications News, Washington, DC. Tel: (202) 872-9200, (800) 771-9202, FAX: (202) 318-8350, E-Mail: info@warren-news.com, Web Site: www.warren-news.com (17)

Herman, Rhonda, McFarland & Co Inc Publishers, Jefferson, NC. Tel: (336) 246-4460, (800) 253-2187, FAX: (336) 246-5018, E-Mail: info@mcfarlandpub.com, Web Site: www.mcfarlandpub.com (17)

Herman, Rob, North American Communications Inc, Katonah, NY. Tel: (914) 273-8620, E-Mail: info@nacmail.com, Web Site: www.nacmail.com (21)

Herman, Robert, North American Communications Inc (East), Duncansville, PA. Tel: (814) 696-3553, (800) 624-1533, FAX: (814) 696-1180, E-Mail: marketing@nacmail.com, Web Site: www.nacmail.com (26)

Herman, Susan N., American Civil Liberties Union Foundation, New York, NY. Tel: (212) 549-2500, Web Site: www.aclu.org (1)

Hermann, Scott, First Advantage Membership Services, Poway, CA. Tel: (866) 424-3223, FAX: (619) 938-7017, Web Site: www.fmembershipservices.com (14)

Hermes of Paris, New York, NY. Tel: (212) 759-7585, (800) 441-4488, FAX: (212) 644-2132 (2)

Hermes, Charles R., Cornhusker Press, Hastings, NE. Tel: (402) 462-4141, FAX: (402) 460-4612, E-Mail: dlsales@dutton-lainson.com, Web Site: www.dutton-lainson.com (17)

Hernandez, Briseida, Elks Magazine, Chicago, IL. Tel: (773) 755-4700, FAX: (773) 775-4792, E-Mail: elksmag@elks.org, Web Site: www.elks.org (17)

Hernandez, Carrie, HighScope Educational Research Foundation, Ypsilanti, MI. Tel: (800) 587-5639, FAX: (734) 485-0704, E-Mail: info@highscope.org, Web Site: www.highscope.org (17)

Hernandez, Jorge, Solo Printing, Miami, FL. Tel: (305) 594-8699, FAX: (305) 599-5245, Web Site: www.soloprinting.com (17)

Hernandez, Robert, Golden Millennium Productions Inc, Pasadena, CA. Tel: (818) 500-1099, FAX: (866) 886-5802, E-Mail: info@goldenproductions.com, Web Site: www.goldenproductions.com (32)

Hernandez, Robert M., USX, Pittsburgh, PA. Tel: (412) 433-1121, E-Mail: webmaster@usx.com, Web Site: www.usx.com (16)

Hernandez, Ruben, Mercury Media, Santa Monica, CA. Tel: (310) 451-2900, FAX: (310) 451-0180, Web Site: www.mercurymedia.com (32)

Hernandez, William H., Safti First, Brisbane, CA. Tel: (415) 824-4900, (888) 653-3333, FAX: (415) 824-5900, (888) 653-4444, E-Mail: info@safti.com, Web Site: www.safti.com (16)

Herndon, Lisa M., Catch The Wind Kite Shop, Lincoln City, OR. Tel: (541) 994-9500, (800) 227-7878, FAX: (541) 994-4766, E-Mail: catchthewindkites@yahoo.com, Web Site: www.catchthewind.com (11)

Herntier, John, Charnstrom, Shakopee, MN. Tel: (952) 403-0303, (800) 328-2962, FAX: (800) 916-3215, E-Mail: customerservice@charnstrom.com, Web Site: www.charnstrom.com (28)

Herold-Martinez, Kelly, XPO, Torrance, CA. Tel: (310) 784-8485, Web Site: www.xpomail.com (28)

Heroux, Dr. Lise, State University of New York-College of Plattsburgh, Plattsburgh, NY. Tel: (518) 564-2000, FAX: (518) 564-3183, E-Mail: nancy.church@plattsburgh.edu, Web Site: www.plattsburgh.edu (41)

Herr Foods Inc, Nottingham, PA. Tel: (610) 932-9330, (800) 344-3777, FAX: (610) 932-2137, E-Mail: info@herrs.com, Web Site: www.herrs.com (16)

Herr, Edwin, Herr Foods Inc, Nottingham, PA. Tel: (610) 932-9330, (800) 344-3777, FAX: (610) 932-2137, E-Mail: info@herrs.com, Web Site: www.herrs.com (16)

Herr, J.M., Herr Foods Inc, Nottingham, PA. Tel: (610) 932-9330, (800) 344-3777, FAX: (610) 932-2137, E-Mail: info@herrs.com, Web Site: www.herrs.com (16)

Herr, Rick, Connecticut Color Inc, Meriden, CT. Tel: (203) 237-1400, FAX: (203) 440-3678, Web Site: www.connecticutcolor.com (27)

Herre, Tom, Referee Enterprises, Racine, WI. Tel: (800) 733-6100, FAX: (262) 632-5460, E-Mail: questions@referee.com, Web Site: www.referee.com (1)

Herres, Gen, USAA, San Antonio, TX. Tel: (512) 498-6524, FAX: (512) 498-8000 (15)

Herrick, David, Names in the News, Oakland, CA. Tel: (415) 989-3350, FAX: (415) 433-7796, E-Mail: susananstrand@nincal.com, Web Site: www.nincal.com (23)

Herrick, Gregory, Historic Aviation, Minneapolis, MN. Tel: (651) 635-0100, (800) 225-5575, FAX: (651) 635-0700, E-Mail: info@historicaviation.com, Web Site: www.historicaviation.com (12)

Herrington, Londonderry, NH. Tel: (603) 437-1600, (800) 903-2878, FAX: (603) 437-1340, (603) 437-3492, E-Mail: customerservice@herringtoncatalog.com, Web Site: www.herringtoncatalog.com (16)

Herrington, Lee R., Herrington, Londonderry, NH. Tel: (603) 437-1600, (800) 903-2878, FAX: (603) 437-1340, (603) 437-3492, E-Mail: customerservice@herringtoncatalog.com, Web Site: www.herringtoncatalog.com (16)

Herrmann Global LLC, Lake Lure, NC. Tel: (828) 625-9153, (800) 432-4234, E-Mail: info@hbdi.com, Web Site: www.herrmannsolutions.com (35)

Herrmann-Nehdi, Ann, Herrmann Global LLC, Lake Lure, NC. Tel: (828) 625-9153, (800) 432-4234, E-Mail: info@hbdi.com, Web Site: www.herrmannsolutions.com (35)

Herrschners Inc, Stevens Point, WI. Tel: (715) 341-8686, (800) 441-0838, FAX: (715) 341-2250, E-Mail: customerservice@herrschners.com, Web Site: www.herrschners.com (11)

Herschend Family Entertainment, Norcross, GA. Tel: (417) 338-3810, FAX: (417) 338-8144, Web Site: www.hfecorp.com (5)

Hersh, Anita K., Lister Butler Inc, New York, NY. Tel: (212) 951-6100, FAX: (212) 481-0230, Web Site: www.listerbutler.com (20)

Hersh, Bob, Lefty's Corner, Clarks Summit, PA. Tel: (570) 586-5338, (570) 586-LEFT, FAX: (570) 585-2906, E-Mail: info@leftyscorner.com, Web Site: www.leftyscorner.com (6)

Hersh, Dale, Lefty's Corner, Clarks Summit, PA. Tel: (570) 586-5338, (570) 586-LEFT, FAX: (570) 585-2906, E-Mail: info@leftyscorner.com, Web Site: www.leftyscorner.com (6)

Hersh, Randi, Ultra Direct Marketing Inc, Jackson, NJ. Tel: (732) 364-8337, (800) 365-8587, FAX: (732) 364-9598, E-Mail: contact@ultradirect.com, Web Site: www.ultradirect.com (16)

Hershberger, Julia, Sustainable Forestry Initiative Inc, Washington, DC. Tel: (202) 596-3450, FAX: (202) 596-3451, E-Mail: info@sfiprogram.org, Web Site: www.sfiprogram.org (1)

Hersheiser, Dave, Omaha Steaks Inc, Omaha, NE. Tel: (402) 597-8370, FAX: (402) 597-8125, E-Mail: info@omahasteaks.com, Web Site: www.omahasteaks.com (4)

The Hershey Co, Hershey, PA. Tel: (717) 534-4200, (800) 454-7737, FAX: (717) 534-5204, Web Site: www.hersheygifts.com (4)

Hershey Park, Hershey, PA. Tel: (717) 534-3149, (800) HERSHEY, E-Mail: info@hersheypa.com, Web Site: www.hersheypark.com (19)

Hershey, Douglas, New Pig Corp, Tipton, PA. Tel: (814) 684-0101, (800) 468-4647, FAX: (814) 684-0961, E-Mail: hothogs@newpig.com, Web Site: www.newpig.com (9)

Hersum, Mark, AAI, Boston, MA. Tel: (508) 544-1250, (877) 866-8500, FAX: (508) 544-1253, E-Mail: info@aai-agency.com, Web Site: www.aai-agency.com (35)

Hertz Corp, Park Ridge, NJ. Tel: (201) 307-2000, FAX: (201) 307-2644, Web Site: www.hertz.com (19)

Hertz, Paul, A&P, Montvale, NJ. Tel: (201) 573-9700, (866) 44 FRESH, FAX: (201) 505-3054, E-Mail: apcustomerrel@aptea.com, Web Site: www.aptea.com (16)

Hervieu, Philippe, Yves Rocher North America Inc, Exton, PA. Tel: (450) 442-9555, (888) 909-0771, E-Mail: customer_services@yrnet.com, Web Site: www.yvesrocherusa.com (7)

Herweh, Bill, Specialty Envelope Inc, Cincinnati, OH. Tel: (513) 542-4700, (800) 288-8884, FAX: (513) 542-5260, E-Mail: info@specialtyenvelope.com, Web Site: www.specialtyenvelope.com (26)

Herzig, Jill, Redbook Magazine, New York, NY. Tel: (212) 649-2000, (800) 888-0008, FAX: (212) 581-7605, Web Site: www.redbookmag.com (17)

Herzog, Doug, Viacom Media Networks, New York, NY. Tel: (212) 258-6000, Web Site: www.viacom.com (32)

Herzog, Robert F., Berkeley College, West Paterson, NJ. Tel: (973) 278-5400, (800) 446-5400, FAX: (973) 278-6243, E-Mail: info@berkeleycollege.edu, Web Site: www.berkeleycollege.edu (13)

Herzog, Sylviane, Answering 365, Los Angeles, CA. Tel: (310) 854-4411, (800) 800-4411, FAX: (310) 854-0551, Web Site: www.concordecommunications.com (29)

Hesemann, Ted, Herrschners Inc, Stevens Point, WI. Tel: (715) 341-8686, (800) 441-0838, FAX: (715) 341-2250, E-Mail: customerservice@herrschners.com, Web Site: www.herrschners.com (11)

Hess Print Solutions, Kent, OH. Tel: (800) 678-1222, E-Mail: info@hessprintsolutions.com, Web Site: www.thepressofohio.com (27)

Hess, Carol, Political Resources Inc, Lake Worth, FL. Tel: (800) 423-2677, FAX: (561) 533-0104, E-Mail: chess@politicalresources.com, Web Site: www.politicalresources.com (23)

Hess, Sara, Farm Progress Co, Saint Charles, IL. Tel: (630) 690-5600, FAX: (630) 462-2202, E-Mail: dwilson@farmprogress.com, Web Site: www.farmprogress.com (17)

Hester, Walter, Maui Jim Inc, Peoria, IL. Tel: (309) 691-3700, FAX: (309) 683-2202, Web Site: www.mauijim.com (16)

Heth, Todd, Cuvaison Inc, Napa, CA. Tel: (707) 942-2455, E-Mail: info@cuvaison.com, Web Site: www.cuvaison.com (4)

Hetzuer, Frances E., Amigo Mobility International Inc, Bridgeport, MI. Tel: (989) 777-0910, (800) 692-6446, FAX: (989) 777-8184, E-Mail: info@myamigo.com, Web Site: www.myamigo.com (16)

Hewlett-Packard Co, Palo Alto, CA. Tel: (650) 857-1501, (800) 752-0900, FAX: (650) 857-5518, Web Site: www.hp.com (16)

Hewson, Marilyn A., Lockheed Martin Corp, Bethesda, MD. Tel: (301) 897-6000, Web Site: www.lockheedmartin.com (16)

Heydendael, Arthur G., America Direct Book Service Custom Publishing, Ossining, NY. Tel: (914) 271-3640, FAX: (914) 271-3641, E-Mail: info@americadirectbook.com, Web Site: www.americadirectbook.com (17)

Heyder, Markus B, Center For Information Policy Leadership, Washington, DC. Tel: (202) 778-2264, FAX: (202) 778-2201, Web Site: www.policyleaders.com (20)

Heyer Corp, Roselle, IL. Tel: (773) 884-0815, FAX: (708) 952-4491. E-Mail: info@heyerco.com, Web Site: www.heyerco.com (34)

Heyman, Bruce, Metropolitan Window Fashions at Fabricland, North Plainfield, NJ. Tel: (908) 755-4700, (877) 722-1100, FAX: (908) 755-6368 (8)

Heynes, Bill, KD Mailing & Fulfillment Service, Lincolnwood, IL. Tel: (847) 673-0186, (866) 330-6245, FAX: (874) 673-0188, E-Mail: dan@kdmailing.com, Web Site: www.kdmailing.com (28)

Hi-C Production, New Hyde Park, NY. Tel: (516) 746-2142, FAX: (516) 294-1964, E-Mail: haponte435@aol.com (27)

Hiban, Michael, Omega List Co, McLean, VA. Tel: (703) 821-1890, FAX: (703) 821-8794, E-Mail: listmanager@omegalist.com, Web Site: omegalist.com (23)

Hibbard, Jay, Bluespire Senior Living, West Hartford, CT. Tel: (888) 818-4715, Web Site: www.bluespireseniorliving.com (35)

Hibbard, Timothy A., WESCO, Pittsburgh, PA. Tel: (412) 454-2200, (800) 343-1201, E-Mail: info@wesco.com, Web Site: www.wescodist.com (16)

The Hibbert Group, Trenton, NJ. Tel: (609) 394-7500, (800) 545-4747, FAX: (609) 695-6553, Web Site: www.hibbertco.com (28)

Hibbert, J Andrew, The Aldrich Group, Woodbury, CT. Tel: (860) 274-7693, (203) 263-5505, FAX: (203) 263-5572, E-Mail: jeff.aldrich@aldrichsearch.com, Web Site: www.aldrichsearch.com (20)

Hibbs, Erin, Native American Heritage Association, Black Hawk, SD. Tel: (605) 341-9110, FAX: (605) 341-91413, E-Mail: info@naha-inc.org, Web Site: www.naha-inc.org (1)

Hibbs, Jr Ralph L, American College of Physicians, Philadelphia, PA. Tel: (215) 351-2600, (800) 523-1546, FAX: (215) 351-2686, Web Site: www.acponline.org (17)

Hickey, Mark, Telephony, Chicago, IL. Tel: (312) 595-1080, (800) 458-0479, FAX: (312) 595-0295, Web Site: www.internettelephony.com (17)

Hickey, Michael, 802 Creative Partners Inc, Montpelier, VT. Tel: (802) 234-9755, FAX: (802) 732-9056, E-Mail: info@802creative.com, Web Site: www.802creative.com (35)

Hickey, Michael, Group 1 Software Inc, Lanham, MD. Tel: (301) 731-2300, (888) 413-6763, FAX: (301) 731-0360, E-Mail: info@g1.com, Web Site: www.g1.com (22)

Hickle, Kevin, Amazon Drygoods, Osgood, IN. FAX: (812)852-1780, Web Site: www.amazondrygoods.com (2)

Hickle, Samantha, Amazon Drygoods, Osgood, IN. FAX: (812)852-1780, Web Site: www.amazondrygoods.com (2)

Hickner, Joe, Woodwind & Brasswind Inc, Westlake Village, CA. Tel: (574) 251-3500, (800) 348-5003, FAX: (800) 266-5962, Web Site: www.wwbw.com (5)

Hickok, Chris, Academy of Marketing Science Journal, Thousand Oaks, CA. Tel: (800) 818-7243, FAX: (800) 583-2665, E-Mail: journals@sagepub.com, Web Site: www.sagepub.com (43)

Hickok, Lori, Scripps Networks Interactive Inc, Knoxville, TN. Tel: (865) 560-2700, Web Site: scrippsnetworksinteractive.com (17)

Hickory Farms, Maumee, OH. Tel: (419) 893-7611, (800) 776-4111, (800) 442-5671, FAX: (419) 893-0164, Web Site: www.hickoryfarms.com (4)

The Hickory Printing Solutions LLC, Conover, NC. Tel: (828) 465-3431, (800) 442-5679, FAX: (828) 465-2517, E-Mail: gglisan@hickoryprinting.com, Web Site: www.hickoryprinting.com (27)

Hicks, Barbara, Houston Direct Marketing Association, Houston, TX. Tel: (281) 931-8883, FAX: (281) 820-4023, Web Site: www.houstondma.org (40)

Hicks, Deborah A., Harvard Pilgrim Health Care, Wellesley, MA. Tel: (617) 509-1000, (888) 888-4742, FAX: (617) 509-7590, Web Site: www.harvardpilgrim.org (7)

Hicks, Frank, Healthy Offers Inc, Scottsdale, AZ. Tel: (480) 614-0060, FAX: (480) 614-0160, E-Mail: info@medicxmedia.com, Web Site: www.medicxmedia.com (23)

Hicks, Gunner, Allied Printing Services Inc, Manchester, CT. Tel: (860) 643-1101, (800) 225-8777, (800) 224-8894, FAX: (860) 646-7954, E-Mail: allied@alliedprinting.com, Web Site: www.alliedprinting.com (27)

Hicks, James, Trigon Blue Cross/Blue Shield, Roanoke, VA. Tel: (540) 853-5000, (800) 553-3164, FAX: (540) 853-3053, Web Site: www.trigon.com (15)

Hicks, Randy, Solarcom, Norcross, GA. Tel: (770) 449-6116, (888) SUN-DATA, FAX: (770) 448-7726, Web Site: www.solarcom.net (16)

Hicks, Robert, List Media Inc, Aurora, OH. Tel: (330) 995-0864, FAX: (330) 995-0873, E-Mail: sales@admail.net, Web Site: www.admail.net (32)

Hicks, Tyler G., How I Grossed More Than $1 Million in Direct Mail Order Starting with Little Cash & Less Know How, Rockville Centre, NY. Tel: (516) 766-5850, (800) 323-0548, FAX: (516) 766-5919, E-Mail: admin@iwsmony.com, Web Site: www.iwsmoney.com (43)

Hickson, Mark E., Florida Power & Light Co, Juno Beach, FL. Tel: (305) 552-3552, (800) 468-8243, FAX: (305) 552-2487, Web Site: www.fpl.com (16)

Hidalgo, Jerry, Parker Steel Co, Toledo, OH. Tel: (419) 473-2481, (800) 333-4140, FAX: (419) 471-2655, Web Site: www.metricmetal.com (16)

Hiebert, Crystal, Winnipeg Art Gallery, Winnipeg, MB Canada. Tel: (204) 786-6641, FAX: (204) 788-4998, E-Mail: inquiries@wag.mb.ca, Web Site: www.wag.ca (1)

The Hiebing Group, Madison, WI. Tel: (608) 256-6357, FAX: (608) 256-0693, E-Mail: ideas@hiebing.com, Web Site: www.hiebing.com (35)

Hiendarto, Joyce V., The Fuller Theological Seminary, Pasadena, CA. Tel: (626) 584-5200, (800) 235-2222, FAX: (626) 584-5449, Web Site: www.fuller.edu (16)

Hier, Rabbi Marvin, Simon Wiesenthal Center, Los Angeles, CA. Tel: (310) 553-9036, (800) 900-9036, FAX: (310) 553-4521, E-Mail: information@wiesenthal.com, Web Site: wiesenthal.com (1)

Hietikko, Donna, Mary Maxim Inc, Port Huron, MI. Tel: (810) 987-2000, (800) 962-9504, FAX: (810) 987-5056, E-Mail: info@marymaxim.com, Web Site: www.marymaxim.com (11)

Higgins, Becky, Helzberg Diamonds, North Kansas City, MO. Tel: (816) 842-7780, (800) HELZBERG, FAX: (816) 480-0294, Web Site: www.helzberg.com (18)

Higgins, Ron, Gulf Publishing Co, Houston, TX. Tel: (713) 529-4301, FAX: (713) 520-4433, E-Mail: publications@gulfpub.com, Web Site: www.gulfpub.com (17)

Higgins, Shaun, The Spokesman-Review, Spokane, WA. Tel: (509) 459-5060, FAX: (509) 459-5083, E-Mail: shaunh@spokesman.com, Web Site: www.spokane.net (17)

High Cotton, Birmingham, AL. Tel: (877) 838-2345, FAX: (205) 836-5587, E-Mail: sales@highscottonusa.com, Web Site: www.highcottonusa.com (28)

High Note Media Inc, Chicago, IL. Tel: (773) 980-6873, Web Site: www.highnotemedia.com (20)

Higher Power Marketing, Phoenix, AZ. Tel: (480) 837-3580, (888) 501-5544, FAX: (480) 837-3589, E-Mail: info@hpowermarketing.com, Web Site: www.hpowermarketing.com (30)

Highfill, Scott, Response Marketing Group, Richmond, VA. Tel: (866) 574-7665, E-Mail: info@rmg-info.com, Web Site: rmg-usa.com (35)

Highley, Jay, ChaCha Mobile Answers, Carmel, IN. Tel: (317) 660-6680, Web Site: partners.chacha.com (20)

Highlights For Children, Columbus, OH. Tel: (614) 487-2601, (800) 848-8922, FAX: (614) 487-2700, Web Site: www.highlights.com (17)

Highmark Blue Cross Blue Shield, Pittsburgh, PA. Tel: (412) 544-7000, FAX: (412) 544-5350, Web Site: www.highmark.com (15)

HighScope Educational Research Foundation, Ypsilanti, MI. Tel: (800) 587-5639, FAX: (734) 485-0704, E-Mail: info@highscope.org, Web Site: www.highscope.org (17)

Higley, Karen, Fluke Biomedical, Everett, WA. Tel: (425) 347-6100, (800) 850-4608, FAX: (425) 446-5116, Web Site: www.flukebiomedical.com (16)

Higman, Rebecca, Network for Good, Washington, DC. Tel: (240) 482-3211, Web Site: www.networkforgood.org (1)

Hiland, Mark, The Arizona Republic, Phoenix, AZ. Tel: (602) 444-8000, Web Site: www.azcentral.com (17)

Hilbert, Greg, S&S Worldwide, Colchester, CT. Tel: (860) 537-3451, (800) 288-9941, FAX: (860) 537-2866, E-Mail: cservice@ssww.com, Web Site: www.ssww.com (11)

Hilbert, Stan, Telect Inc, Liberty Lake, WA. Tel: (509) 926-6000, FAX: (509) 926-8915, E-Mail: getinfo@ telect.com, Web Site: www.telect.com (16)

Tommy Hilfiger, New York, NY. Tel: (212) 548-1368, Web Site: www.tommy.com (2)

Hilger, Joe, G-Neil Direct Mail, Sunrise, FL. Tel: (800) 999-9111, FAX: (954) 851-1264, E-Mail: tcs@gneil. com, Web Site: www.gneil.com (10)

Hilkemann, Aaron C., Duncan Aviation, Lincoln, NE. Tel: (402) 475-2611, (800) 228-4277, FAX: (402) 475-5541, Web Site: www.duncanaviation.com (16)

Hilkert, Tom, Merchandising Equipment Group (MEG), Cambridge City, IN. Tel: (765) 478-3141, (800) 645-3315, FAX: (765) 478-4439, E-Mail: meginfo@ megfixtures.com, Web Site: www.megfixtures.com (34)

BW Hill & Associates LLC, Oak Park, IL. Tel: (312) 268-6361, (800) 431-3183, Web Site: www. bwhillassociates.com (30)

Hill Holliday, Boston, MA. Tel: (617) 366-4000, Web Site: www.hhcc.com (35)

James J Hill Reference Library, Saint Paul, MN. Tel: (651) 265-5500, Web Site: www.jjhill.org (1)

Hill Mailing & Printing of Florida Inc, Brandon, FL. Tel: (813) 258-5220, (888) 662-6951, FAX: (813) 944-2882, E-Mail: mail@hillmailing.com, Web Site: hillmailing.com (21)

Hill, Andrea, Rio Grande, Albuquerque, NM. Tel: (505) 839-3000, (800) 545-6566, FAX: (800) 965-2329, E-Mail: info@riogrande.com, Web Site: www. riogrande.com (16)

Hill, Barb, Townsend Communications LLC, Kansas City, MO. Tel: (816) 361-0616, (800) 274-8867, FAX: (816) 361-6164, Web Site: www. townsendprint.com (17)

Hill, Benjamin, BW Hill & Associates LLC, Oak Park, IL. Tel: (312) 268-6361, (800) 431-3183, Web Site: www.bwhillassociates.com (30)

Hill, Constance, TFC Inc, Napa, CA. Tel: (707) 224-6161, Web Site: www.tfcinc.com (27)

Hill, David, Perfection Tip Co/Camping Products Co, Long Beach, CA. Tel: (562) 491-0076, (800) 525-4835, FAX: (562) 435-7599 (16)

Hill, Derryl, MarketAide Services Inc, Hutchinson, KS. Tel: (785) 825-7161, (800) 204-2433, FAX: (785) 825-4697, E-Mail: creative@marketaide.com, Web Site: www.marketaide.com (21)

Hill, Gregory, Titan Manufacturing, Holbrook, MA. Tel: (781) 767-1963, Web Site: www.americantitan. com (34)

Hill, Jim, The Psychological Corp, San Antonio, TX. Tel: (800) 211-8378, FAX: (800) 232-1223, Web Site: www.psychcorp.com (17)

Hill, Marc, US Playing Card Co, Erlanger, KY. Tel: (800) 543-2273, FAX: (859) 815-7566, E-Mail: sales@usplayingcard.com, Web Site: www. usplayingcard.com (16)

Hill, Richard, Rent Mother Nature, Cambridge, MA. Tel: (617) 868-5059, (800) 232-4048, FAX: (617) 868-5861, Web Site: www.rentmothernature.com (4)

Hill, Steven D., Zoom Information Inc, Waltham, MA. Tel: (781) 693-7500, FAX: (781) 693-7510, Web Site: www.zoominfo.com (22)

Hill, Tom, Micro Plastics Inc, Flippin, AR. Tel: (870) 453-2261, (800) 466-1467, FAX: (870) 453-8676, E-Mail: mpsales@microplastics.com, Web Site: www.microplastics.com (16)

Hilleary, Rick, RealData Services Inc, Glenwood Springs, CO. Tel: (970) 945-2456, FAX: (970) 945-5356, E-Mail: rick@realdataservices.com, Web Site: www.realdataservices.com (22)

Hilliard, Curt, DirectBuy Inc, Merrillville, IN. Tel: (219) 736-1100. FAX: (219) 755-6279, Web Site: www.ucctotalhome.com (1)

Hillin, Andrew, Carhill Enterprises Inc, Saint Louis, MO. Tel: (314) 621-7646, Web Site: www. cahillinsight.com (15)

Hillis, Jay, Wildlife Education Ltd, Park Hills, KY. Tel: (858) 513-7600, FAX: (858) 513-7660, E-Mail: animals@zoobooks.com, Web Site: www.zoobooks. com (17)

Hillis, John, StatSoft Inc, Tulsa, OK. Tel: (918) 749-1119, FAX: (918) 749-2217, E-Mail: info@statsoft. com, Web Site: www.statsoft.com (9)

Hillis, Robert J., Direct Supply Inc, Milwaukee, WI. Tel: (414) 358-2805, (800) 634-7328, FAX: (414) 358-2397, E-Mail: deardirect@directs.com, Web Site: www.directsupply.net (9)

Hills, Laura, Freestyle Solutions, Parsippany, NJ. Tel: (973) 237-9415, (800) 858-3666, FAX: (973) 237-9043, E-Mail: sales@dydacomp.com, Web Site: www.dydacomp.com (22)

Hillside Wire Cloth Co, Belleville, NJ. Tel: (973) 751-3131, (800) 826-7395, FAX: (973) 470-8183, E-Mail: info@hillsidewirecloth.com, Web Site: www.hillsidewirecloth.com (9)

Hillyer, MD Christopher D., New York Blood Center Inc, New York, NY. Tel: (212) 570-3000, (800) 933-2566, FAX: (212) 570-3195, Web Site: www. nybloodcenter.org (1)

Hilsheimer, Lawrence A., Nationwide Mutual Insurance Co, Columbus, OH. Tel: (614) 249-7111, (800) 882-2822, FAX: (614) 854-3676, Web Site: www. nationwide.com (15)

Hiltenbrand, Danny, Graceland, Memphis, TN. Tel: (901) 332-3322, (800) 238-2010, FAX: (901) 344-3120, Web Site: www.elvis.com (6)

Hilti North America, Tulsa, OK. Tel: (866) 445-8827, FAX: (800) 879-7000, Web Site: www.hilti.com (34)

Conrad N Hilton College of Hotel & Restaurant Management University of Houston, Houston, TX. Tel: (713) 743-2255 (1)

Hilton Grand Vacations Co, Orlando, FL. Tel: (407) 722-3100, FAX: (407) 521-3112, Web Site: www. hiltongrandvacations.com (16)

Hilton HHonors, McLean, VA. Tel: (703) 883-1000, Web Site: hhonors.hilton.com (16)

Hilton Hotels Corp, Mc Lean, VA. Tel: (703) 883-1000, (800) HILTONS, FAX: (310) 205-3670, Web Site: www.hilton.com (19)

Hilton, Larry, Spectrum Chemicals & Laboratory Products, Gardena, CA. Tel: (310) 516-8000, Web Site: www.spectrumchemical.com (16)

Hilton, Scott, Diapers.com, Jersey City, NJ. Tel: (800) 342-7377, E-Mail: customercare@diapers.com, Web Site: www.diapers.com (5)

Hilzinger, Kurt, Hopkins Medical Products, Baltimore, MD. Tel: (410) 484-2036, (800) 835-1995, FAX: (410) 484-4036, E-Mail: customerservice@ hopkinsmedical.net, Web Site: www. hopkinsmedicalproducts.com (7)

Hilzinger, Matthew F., USG Corp, Chicago, IL. Tel: (312) 436-4000, (800) 621-9622, FAX: (312) 672-4093, Web Site: www.usg.com (34)

Himmel, Jr. Keith L., J Peterman Co, Lexington, KY. Tel: (888) 647-2555, FAX: (859) 254-0869, Web Site: www.jpeterman.com (5)

Hinaga, Steven, DataCraft Inc, Kailua, HI. Tel: (808) 263-5583, FAX: (808) 262-4101, E-Mail: akamaidatasolutions@dcraftinc.com, Web Site: www.akamaidatasolutions.com (22)

Hinda Incentives, Chicago, IL. Tel: (773) 890-5900, FAX: (773) 890-4606, E-Mail: contact@hinda.com, Web Site: www.hinda.com (33)

Hinds, Ossie, Cornerstone Group of Companies, Toronto, ON Canada. Tel: (416) 932-9555, FAX: (416) 932-9566, E-Mail: info@cstonecanada.com, Web Site: www.cstonecanada.com (22)

Hinds, Tim, American Recreation Products Inc, Saint Louis, MO. Tel: (314) 576-8000, FAX: (314) 576-8072 (11)

Hiner, Sarah, Boardroom Inc, Stamford, CT. Tel: (203) 973-5900, FAX: (203) 967-3086, Web Site: www. bottomlinepublications.com (17)

Hines, Thomas A., JJ Keller & Associates Inc, Neenah, WI. Tel: (920) 722-2848, (800) 327-6868, FAX: (800) 727-7516, E-Mail: thines@jjkeller.com, Web Site: www.jjkeller.com/jjk (33)

Hines, Vivian, Baber Direct Marketing, Memphis, TN. Tel: (901) 332-6300, (800) 847-7040, FAX: (901) 332-6441, E-Mail: info@baberweb.com, Web Site: www.baberweb.com (21)

Hing, Kevin, Danker Laboratories Inc, Sarasota, FL. Tel: (800) 237-9641, FAX: (800) 665-5086, E-Mail: sales@dankerlabs.com, Web Site: www.dankerlabs. com (16)

Hinkle, April Brumley, Texas Monthly, Austin, TX. Tel: (512) 320-6900, (800) 759-2000, FAX: (512) 476-9007, E-Mail: info@texasmonthly.com, Web Site: www.texasmonthly.com (17)

Hinnant, Keith, Cystic Fibrosis Foundation, Bethesda, MD. Tel: (301) 951-4422, FAX: (301) 951-6378, E-Mail: info@cff.org, Web Site: www.cff.org (1)

Hinrichs, Joseph R., Ford Motor Co, Dearborn, MI. Tel: (313) 845-8540, (800) 555-5259, FAX: (313) 845-6073, Web Site: www.ford.com (16)

Hinrichs, Melissa, Quality Contact Solutions Inc, Aurora, NE. Tel: (402) 210-2692, (866) 963-2889, FAX: (402) 210-2692, E-Mail: info@ qualitycontactsolutions.com, Web Site: www. qualitycontactsolutions.com (29)

Hinson, Ron, Georgia Power, Atlanta, GA. Tel: (404) 506-3440 (16)

Hinton, Patricia, Ansar Inc, Thompsons Station, TN. Tel: (615) 368-2025, Web Site: www.ansarinc.com (1)

HipCricket Inc, Kirkland, WA. Tel: (425) 452-1111, Web Site: www.hipcricket.com (16)

Hipelius, Angela, Liberty Creative Solutions, Tinley Park, IL. Tel: (708) 633-7450, FAX: (708) 633-7449, E-Mail: info@libertycreativesolutions.com, Web Site: www.libertycreativesolutions.com (21)

Hipp, Charlie, Taylor Communications, North Mankato, MN. Tel: (800) 755-6405, Web Site: www. taylorcommunications.com (21)

Hippo Direct, Solon, OH. Tel: (440) 519-0730, FAX: (440) 519-0727, E-Mail: rapidresponse@ hippodirect.com, Web Site: www.hippodirect.com (23)

Hireko Golf, City of Industry, CA. Tel: (626) 330-5525, (800) 367-8912, FAX: (888) 367-8912, E-Mail: support@hirekogolf.com, Web Site: www.hireko. com (11)

Hirsch, Harvey, Media Consultants, Lyndhurst, NJ. Tel: (201) 933-2015, FAX: (201) 933-6314, E-Mail: info@mediaconsultants.net, Web Site: mediaconsultants.net (35)

Hirson, Mona, Weingeroff Enterprises Inc, Cranston, RI. Tel: (401) 467-2200, FAX: (401) 785-1320, Web Site: www.weingeroff.com (16)

Hirst, Steve, Calibre Press Inc, San Francisco, CA. Tel: (214) 545-3060, (800) 323-0037, FAX: (866) 225-4273, Web Site: www.calibrepress.com (17)

Hiskett, Mike, Money Mailer LLC, Garden Grove, CA. Tel: (800) 624-5371, Web Site: www.moneymailer.net (31)

Historic Aviation, Minneapolis, MN. Tel: (651) 635-0100, (800) 225-5575, FAX: (651) 635-0700, E-Mail: info@historicaviation.com, Web Site: www.historicaviation.com (12)

Historical Replications Inc, Jackson, MS. Tel: (800) 426-5628, FAX: (601) 981-8185, E-Mail: info@historicaldesigns.com, Web Site: www.historicaldesigns.com (8)

The Historical Research Center International Inc, Boynton Beach, FL. Tel: (561) 732-5263, (800) 985-9956, FAX: (561) 940-7991, E-Mail: custsvc@names.com, Web Site: www.historicalresearchcenter.net (16)

The History Book Club Inc, Mechanicsburg, PA. Tel: (718) 918-2665, E-Mail: paula.batson@dgna.com, Web Site: www.historybookclub.com (13)

Hitachi Data Systems, Santa Clara, CA. Tel: (408) 970-1000, FAX: (408) 727-8036, Web Site: www.hds.com (22)

Hitchcock Shoes Inc, Hingham, MA. Tel: (781) 749-3571, (888) 599-9433, FAX: (781) 749-3576, E-Mail: hitchcock@wideshoes.com, Web Site: www.wideshoes.com (2)

Hively, Michael, Bland Farms, Glennville, GA. Tel: (912) 654-1300, Web Site: www.blandfarms.com (4)

Hladky, Joe F., Gazette Communications Inc, Cedar Rapids, IA. Tel: (319) 398-8211, (800) 397-8211, FAX: (319) 368-8834, Web Site: www.gazettecommunications.com (17)

Hlavac, Randy, Marketing Synergy Inc, Naperville, IL. Tel: (630) 328-9550, FAX: (630) 328-9552, E-Mail: info@MSINetwork.com, Web Site: www.msinetwork.com (30)

Hnatek, Richard, Falcon Products Inc, Newport, TN. Tel: (314) 991-9200, (800) 873-3252, FAX: (314) 991-9227, E-Mail: info@falconproducts.com, Web Site: www.falconproducts.com (16)

Ho, Florence, Wyndham Hotel Group, Parsippany, NJ. Tel: (973) 753-8925, Web Site: www.cendant.com (19)

Ho, Monica, TMP Directional Marketing, Boston, MA. Tel: (212) 351-7595, Web Site: www.tmpdm.com (30)

Ho, Vincent, Dr Ho's, Greensboro, GA. Tel: (905) 471-4735, (877) 374-6669, FAX: (877) 836-7466, Web Site: www.drhonow.com (7)

Hoare, Toby, Geometry Global, New York, NY. Tel: (212) 537-3700, E-Mail: press@geometry.com, Web Site: www.geometry.com (35)

Hoarty, Thomas, Microfluidics Corp, Westwood, MA. Tel: (617) 969-5452, (800) 370-5452, FAX: (617) 965-1213, E-Mail: info@mfics.com, Web Site: www.microfluidicscorp.com (16)

Hobart & William Smith Colleges, Geneva, NY. Tel: (315) 781-3540, (800) 852-2256, FAX: (315) 781-3400, Web Site: www.hws.edu (19)

Hobbs, David, InterfaceFlor LLC, La Grange, GA. Tel: (706) 882-1891, (800) 336-0225, FAX: (706) 882-0500, Web Site: www.interfaceflor.com (16)

Hobbs, Michele, HDI Group, San Francisco, CA. Tel: (415) 794-3320, Web Site: www.hobbsdirect.com (20)

Hobbs, Steven, Hearst Business Media, New York, NY. Tel: (212) 649-2000, Web Site: www.hearst.com/business-media (24)

Hobby Builders Supply, Atlanta, GA. Tel: (770) 242-1498, (800) 223-7171, FAX: (770) 242-1497, (800) 926-6464, E-Mail: hbs@miniatures.com, Web Site: www.miniatures.com (11)

Hobby Surplus Sales, New Britain, CT. Tel: (860) 223-0600, (800) 233-0872, FAX: (860) 225-5316, E-Mail: amatohobby@sbcglobal.net, Web Site: www.hobbysurplus.com (11)

Hobday, Sean, Zones Inc, Auburn, WA. Tel: (253) 205-3000, (800) 408-9663, FAX: (425) 430-3626, E-Mail: corpsales@zones.com, Web Site: www.zones.com (3)

Hober, Rosemary M, The Hibbert Group, Trenton, NJ. Tel: (609) 394-7500, (800) 545-4747, FAX: (609) 695-6553, Web Site: www.hibbertco.com (28)

Hobert, Kevin J, Carestream Health Inc, Rochester, NY. Tel: (585) 627-1800, (888) 777-2072, E-Mail: corporatesecurity@carestream.com, Web Site: www.carestreamhealth.com (7)

Hobson, Paul, The Stratosphere Las Vegas, Las Vegas, NV. Tel: (702) 380-7777, (800) 998-6937, FAX: (702) 383-4755, Web Site: www.stratospherehotel.com (19)

Hobsons, Cincinnati, OH. Tel: (513) 985-4186, Web Site: www.hobsons.com (16)

Hochhauser, Hal, Shakespeare Mailing Service, Union City, NJ. Tel: (212) 560-8958, E-Mail: support@shakespearemailing.com, Web Site: www.shakespearemailing.com (28)

Hochman, Karen, Ad Hoc Marketing Resources Inc, New York, NY. Tel: (212) 595-1800, FAX: (212) 656-1860, E-Mail: adhocmrktg@aol.com, Web Site: www.members.aol.com/adhocmrktg (20)

Hock, Alan, Moritt, Hock, Hamroff & Horowitz, Garden City, NY. Tel: (516) 873-2000, FAX: (516) 873-2010, E-Mail: lhauser@morritthock.com, Web Site: www.morritthock.com (16)

Hock, Jackie, Eagle Claw Fishing Tackle, Denver, CO. Tel: (720) 941-8700, FAX: (303) 321-4750, E-Mail: info@eagleclaw.com, Web Site: www.eagleclaw.com (11)

Hocking, Alice, Diversified Investment Advisors, Harrison, NY. Tel: (914) 627-3000, FAX: (914) 627-3280, Web Site: www.divinvest.com (14)

Hodel, Eugene, Hilti North America, Tulsa, OK. Tel: (866) 445-8827, FAX: (800) 879-7000, Web Site: www.hilti.com (34)

Hodes Photography, Buffalo Grove, IL. Tel: (847) 215-3939, E-Mail: hodesphotography@comcast.net, Web Site: www.hodesphotography.com (37)

Hodes, Chuck, Hodes Photography, Buffalo Grove, IL. Tel: (847) 215-3939, E-Mail: hodesphotography@comcast.net, Web Site: www.hodesphotography.com (37)

Hodges, Lawrence A., Ameristar Casinos Inc, Las Vegas, NV. Tel: (702) 567-7000, FAX: (702) 369-8860, Web Site: www.ameristarcasinos.com (19)

Hodgkins, Phillip, Creative Mailing & Marketing, Gardena, CA. Tel: (310) 637-7100, FAX: (714) 998-9001, Web Site: www.creativemandm.com (28)

Hodgkins, Rebecca, Cramer, Norwood, MA. Tel: (781) 278-2387, Web Site: www.crameronline.com (20)

Hodgson, Daniel, Crutchfield Corp, Charlottesville, VA. Tel: (434) 817-1000, (800) 955-9091, FAX: (804) 817-1010, E-Mail: administration@crutchfield.com, Web Site: www.crutchfield.com (3)

Hodson, Nancy, Cold Spring Harbor Lab Press, Woodbury, NY. Tel: (516) 422-4100, (800) 843-4388, FAX: (516) 422-4097, E-Mail: cshpress@cshl.edu, Web Site: www.cshlpress.com (17)

Hoeg, Krystyna T., Sunlife of Canada, Wellesley Hills, MA. Tel: (781) 237-6030, (800) SUNLIFE, FAX: (781) 446-1779, Web Site: www.sunlife-usa.com (15)

Hoelscher Marketing Group, El Cajon, CA. Tel: (619) 588-2155, FAX: (619) 588-9103, E-Mail: rvhmedia@aol.com (31)

Hoelscher, Russ, Hoelscher Marketing Group, El Cajon, CA. Tel: (619) 588-2155, FAX: (619) 588-9103, E-Mail: rvhmedia@aol.com (31)

Hoerres, Peg, Smith Hanley Associates, Southport, CT. Tel: (203) 319-4300, (888) 221-2900, FAX: (203) 319-4320, Web Site: www.smithhanley.com (20)

Hoesly, Michael, Rainbow Group LLC, Middleton, WI. Tel: (608) 824-0068, Web Site: www.beaconathletics.com (11)

Hoetger, William, Mott Media LLC, Fenton, MI. Tel: (810) 714-4280, FAX: (810) 714-2077, E-Mail: info@mottmedia.com, Web Site: www.mottmedia.com (17)

Hoey, B. Douglas, National Community Pharmacists Association, Alexandria, VA. Tel: (703) 683-8200, (800) 544-7447, FAX: (703) 683-3619, E-Mail: info@ncpanet.org, Web Site: www.ncpanet.org (1)

Hofer, Jeff, Liberty Creative Solutions, Tinley Park, IL. Tel: (708) 633-7450, FAX: (708) 633-7449, E-Mail: info@libertycreativesolutions.com, Web Site: www.libertycreativesolutions.com (21)

Hofer, Thomas W., Spring-Green Lawn Care Corp, Plainfield, IL. Tel: (815) 436-8777, FAX: (815) 436-9056, Web Site: www.spring-green.com (16)

Hoff Communications Inc, Lansdowne, PA. Tel: (610) 623-2091, FAX: (610) 623-2041, E-Mail: service@hoffcomm.com, Web Site: hoffcomm.com (35)

Hoff, Clay, House of Eyes, Greensboro, NC. Tel: (336) 852-7107, FAX: (336) 854-0311 (2)

Hoff, Don, American Slide-Chart Corp, Carol Stream, IL. Tel: (630) 665-3333, (800) 323-4433, FAX: (630) 665-3491, E-Mail: info2@americanslidechart.com, Web Site: www.americanslidechart.com (27)

Hoff, Don, Perrygraf, Carol Stream, IL. Tel: (630) 665-3333, (800) 323-4433, FAX: (630) 665-3491, E-Mail: info2@americanperrygraf.com, Web Site: www.perrygraf.com (16)

Hoff, Jeff, House of Eyes, Greensboro, NC. Tel: (336) 852-7107, FAX: (336) 854-0311 (2)

Hoff, Jennifer, Hoff Communications Inc, Lansdowne, PA. Tel: (610) 623-2091, FAX: (610) 623-2041, E-Mail: service@hoffcomm.com, Web Site: hoffcomm.com (35)

Hoff, Jennifer, Houston Direct Marketing Association, Houston, TX. Tel: (281) 931-8883, FAX: (281) 820-4023, Web Site: www.houstondma.org (40)

Hoff, Joseph W., HSBC Bank USA, NA, New York, NY. Tel: (716) 841-2424, FAX: (716) 841-5391, Web Site: www.banking.us.hsbc.com (14)

Hoff, Tammy, House of Eyes, Greensboro, NC. Tel: (336) 852-7107, FAX: (336) 854-0311 (2)

Deborah Hoffman Copywriting, Corrales, NM. Tel: (505) 440-8725 (20)

Hoffman Mint, Fort Lauderdale, FL. Tel: (954) 971-5451, (800) 227-5813, (800) 441-0292, FAX: (954) 917-3079, E-Mail: sales@hoffmanmint.com, Web Site: www.hoffmanmint.com (6)

Hoffman, Bradley J., Arandell Corp, Menomonee Falls, WI. Tel: (262) 255-4400, (800) 558-8724, FAX: (262) 253-3162, E-Mail: jft@arandell.com, Web Site: www.arandell.com (27)

Hoffman, Brendan L., Carson's, Milwaukee, WI. Tel: (414) 347-1152, FAX: (414) 278-5748, Web Site: www.carsons.com (16)

Hoffman, Carrie, TVGuide.com, New York, NY. Tel: (212) 626-2500, Web Site: www.tvguide.com (31)

Hoffman, Cindy, Defenders of Wildlife, Washington, DC. Tel: (202) 682-9400, (800) 385-9712, E-Mail: defenders@mail.defenders.org, Web Site: www. defenders.org (1)

Hoffman, David, Fitness Systems Manufacturing Corp, Wyomissing, PA. Tel: (800) 822-9995, FAX: (610) 670-0135, E-Mail: vitaminout@aol.com, Web Site: www.fitness-systems.net (7)

Hoffman, Desiree, YWCA of the USA, Washington, DC. Tel: (202) 467-0801, FAX: (202) 467-0802, E-Mail: info@ywca.org, Web Site: www.ywca.org (1)

Hoffman, Donna, Association for Postal Commerce, Alexandria, VA. Tel: (703) 524-0096, FAX: (703) 524-1871, Web Site: www.postcom.org (40)

Hoffman, Howard, Dow Jones & Co, Princeton, NJ. Tel: (609) 520-4000, FAX: (212) 416-4348, Web Site: www.dowjones.com/corp/index.html (17)

Hoffman, Jeff, The Chubb Corp, Warren, NJ. Tel: (908) 903-2000, FAX: (908) 903-2027, Web Site: www. chubb.com (20)

Hoffman, Joseph, Colarelli Meyer & Associates Inc, Saint Louis, MO. Tel: (314) 721-1860, (800) 459-4548, FAX: (314) 721-1992, E-Mail: cmaconsult@ cmaconsult.com, Web Site: www.cmaconsult.com (20)

Hoffman, Lance, CRC Data Systems, Long Island City, NY. Tel: (718) 729-2622, E-Mail: jrafael@ opinionaccess.com, Web Site: www.opinionaccess. com (22)

Hoffman, Mark, CNBC, Englewood Cliffs, NJ. Tel: (201) 735-2622, FAX: (201) 735-3200, Web Site: www.cnbc.com (32)

Hoffman, Michael, Hoffman Mint, Fort Lauderdale, FL. Tel: (954) 971-5451, (800) 227-5813, (800) 441-0292, FAX: (954) 917-3079, E-Mail: sales@ hoffmanmint.com, Web Site: www.hoffmanmint. com (6)

Hoffman, Mike, The Toro Co, Bloomington, MN. Tel: (952) 888-8801, (800) 348-2424, FAX: (952) 887-8258, E-Mail: companyinfo@thetorocompany.com, Web Site: www.thetorocompany.com (16)

Hoffman, Robin, Audience Research & Development, Fort Worth, TX. Tel: (817) 924-6922, FAX: (817) 924-7539, E-Mail: jgumbert@ar-d.com, Web Site: www.ar-d.com (20)

Hoffman, Rowe, Kett Tool Co, Cincinnati, OH. Tel: (513) 271-0333, FAX: (513) 271-5318, E-Mail: info@kett-tool.com, Web Site: www.kett-tool.com (9)

Hoffman, Steve, Modern Postcard, Carlsbad, CA. Tel: (800) 959-8365, Web Site: www.modernpostcard. com (10)

Hoffmann, John, Infogroup, Papillion, NE. Tel: (402) 836-5290, E-Mail: contentfeedback@infogroup. com, Web Site: www.infogroup.com (32)

Hofland, Brian, Research To Prevent Blindness Inc, New York, NY. Tel: (212) 752-4333, (800) 621-0026, FAX: (212) 688-6231, E-Mail: inforequest@ rpbusa.org, Web Site: www.rpbusa.org (1)

Hofmann, Sheryl, Time/System, Chicopee, MA. Tel: (800) 637-9942, FAX: (800) 269-3075, E-Mail: customerservice@timesystem.us, Web Site: www. timesystem.us (16)

Hofstra University, Hempstead, NY. Tel: (516) 463-7200, FAX: (516) 463-4833, E-Mail: ce@hofstra. edu, Web Site: www.hofstra.edu/Academics/CE (41)

Hoga, Takashi, Fujisankei Communications International Inc, New York, NY. Tel: (212) 753-8100, FAX: (212) 702-0420, Web Site: www.fujisankei.com (32)

The Hogan Co, Knoxville, TN. Tel: (865) 546-7661, FAX: (865) 523-7300 (35)

Hogan, Douglas W., The Hogan Co, Knoxville, TN. Tel: (865) 546-7661, FAX: (865) 523-7300 (35)

Hogan, Jack, LifeScript, Newport Beach, CA. Tel: (949) 454-0422, (800) 637-9382, Web Site: www. lifescript.com (7)

Hogan, Jamie, HSP Direct, Ashburn, VA. Tel: (703) 793-3220, FAX: (703) 723-5405, E-Mail: info@ hspdirect.com, Web Site: www.hspdirect.com (1)

Hogan, Joe, Biosciences-Amersham, Piscataway, NJ. Tel: (732) 457-8000, FAX: (732) 457-0557, Web Site: www.amersham.com (16)

Hogan, Michael, Delaware Investments, Philadelphia, PA. Tel: (215) 255-1200, E-Mail: service@ delinvest.com, Web Site: www. delawareinvestments.com (14)

Hogan, Thomas H., Literary Market Place, Medford, NJ. Tel: (609) 654-6266. FAX: (609) 654-4309, E-Mail: custserv@infotoday.com, Web Site: www. literarymarketplace.com (43)

Hogard Business Services Inc, Kankakee, IL. Tel: (815) 932-1835, FAX: (815) 932-4793, E-Mail: hogards@ att.net, Web Site: www.hogardbusinessservices.com (28)

Hogben, Andrea, The Plain Dealer, Cleveland, OH. Tel: (216) 999-5000, (800) 362-0727, FAX: (216) 999-6356, Web Site: www.plaindealer.com (18)

Hogsett, Scott, Shakespeare Co, Columbia, SC. Tel: (803) 754-7000, (800) 347-3759, FAX: (803) 754-7342, Web Site: www.shakespeare-fishing.com (11)

Hogue, Ilyse, NARAL Pro-Choice America, Washington, DC. Tel: (202) 973-3000, FAX: (202) 973-3096, Web Site: www.naral.com (1)

Hohener, John W., White Electronic Designs, Phoenix, AZ. Tel: (614) (602) 437-1520, FAX: (602) 437-9120, Web Site: www.whiteedc.com (27)

Hohman, Jennifer, Kirshenbaum Bond Senecal & Partners, New York, NY. Tel: (212) 633-0080, FAX: (212) 463-8643, E-Mail: press@kbsp.com, Web Site: www.kbsp.com (35)

Hohne, Bob, Front Porch Inc, Sonora, CA. Tel: (209) 288-5500, (800) 728-1464, Web Site: www. frontporch.com (35)

Hoiberg, Dale, Encyclopaedia Britannica Inc, Chicago, IL. Tel: (312) 347-7159, (800) 323-1229, FAX: (312) 294-2104, Web Site: www.britannica.com (17)

Hoing, Jim, Omaha Vaccine Co, Omaha, NE. Tel: (402) 731-9600, (800) 367-4444, FAX: (800) 242-9447, E-Mail: customerservice@OmahaVaccine.com, Web Site: www.omahavaccine.com (35)

Hoke Communications Inc, Garden City, NY. Tel: (516) 746-6700, FAX: (516) 294-8141 (17)

Hoke, Henry, FRM Weekly, Garden City, NY. Tel: (516) 746-6700, FAX: (516) 294-8141 (43)

Hoke, III Henry Reed, Hoke Communications Inc, Garden City, NY. Tel: (516) 746-6700, FAX: (516) 294-8141 (17)

Holbrook, Kevin, Boca Java, Miami, FL. Tel: (954) 949-2010, (888) 262-2528, Web Site: www. bocajava.com (4)

Holden Copywriting, Deerfield, IL. Tel: (847) 236-0669, E-Mail: holdendm@aol.com (39)

Holden, Eric, Association for Audience Marketing Professionals (AAMP), North Hollywood, CA. Tel: (310) 323-7220, FAX: (310) 323-7231, E-Mail: mjordan@espcomp.com, Web Site: www.wfma.org (40)

Holden, Stan, Holden Copywriting, Deerfield, IL. Tel: (847) 236-0669, E-Mail: holdendm@aol.com (39)

Holden, Win, Arizona Highways Magazine, Phoenix, AZ. Tel: (602) 712-2200, FAX: (602) 254-4505, E-Mail: editor@arizonahighways.com, Web Site: www.arizonahighways.com (17)

Holden-Bache, Adam, Mass Transmit, New York, NY. Tel: (646) 797-4349, E-Mail: info@masstransmit. com, Web Site: www.masstransmit.com (32)

Holder, Diane, UPMC Health Plan, Pittsburgh, PA. Tel: (888) 876-2756, (800) 361-2629, Web Site: www. upmchealthplan.com (1)

Holder, Jean, Merkle Inc, Columbia, MD. Tel: (443) 542-4000, (877) 9MERKLE, FAX: (443) 542-4758, Web Site: www.merkleinc.com (22)

Holian, Janet, VistaPrint USA Inc, Lexington, MA. Tel: (800) 961-2075, Web Site: www.vistaprint.com (27)

Holiber, William D., US News & World Report, Washington, DC. Tel: (202) 955-2000, Web Site: www. usnews.com (17)

Holiday Travel of America, Carlsbad, CA. Tel: (760) 431-8600, (888) 732-2479, FAX: (760) 431-3131, E-Mail: sales@htoa.com, Web Site: www.htoa.com (19)

Holiday Vacations, Eau Claire, WI. Tel: (715) 834-5555, (800) 826-2266, FAX: (715) 834-8554, E-Mail: info@holidayvacations.net, Web Site: www.holidayvacations.net (19)

Holl, David B., Mary Kay Cosmetics Inc, Addison, TX. Tel: (972) 687-6300, (800) MARY KAY, FAX: (972) 687-1611, Web Site: www.marykay.com (16)

Holland Wildflower Farm, Elkins, AR. Tel: (479) 643-2622, (800) 684-3734, E-Mail: info@ hollandwildflowerfarm.com, Web Site: www. hollandwildflowerfarm.com (8)

Holland, Angela, Suntrust Banks Inc, Atlanta, GA. Tel: (404) 588-7914, (800) 786-8787, FAX: (404) 532-0550, E-Mail: emmett.harmon@suntrust.com, Web Site: www.suntrust.com (14)

Holland, Deborah, St Petersburg/Clearwater Area CVB, Clearwater, FL. Tel: (727) 464-7200, Web Site: www.floridasbeach.com (1)

Holland, Hillary K., Winterthur Museum & Country Estate, Wilmington, DE. Tel: (302) 888-4600, (800) 448-3883, FAX: (302) 888-4730, E-Mail: tourinfo@ winterthur.org, Web Site: www.winterthur.org (6)

Holland, Jeff, Vertical Media Group, Fort Lee, NJ. Tel: (201) 245-7935 (20)

Holland, Julie, Holland Wildflower Farm, Elkins, AR. Tel: (479) 643-2622, (800) 684-3734, E-Mail: info@hollandwildflowerfarm.com, Web Site: www. hollandwildflowerfarm.com (8)

Holland, Mike, Byron Plantation, Vidalia, GA. Tel: (800) 356-0171, FAX: (912) 538-8043, E-Mail: greenlinebyron@bellsouth.net, Web Site: www. byronplantation.com (4)

Holland, Timothy, Saint Gregory Group, Cincinnati, OH. Tel: (513) 769-8440, FAX: (513) 769-1640, E-Mail: info@stgregory.com, Web Site: www. stgregory.com (35)

Kenneth Hollander Associates Inc, Mendocino, CA. Tel: (707) 962-1648, FAX: (707) 962-1635, Web Site: www.kharesearch.com (30)

Hollander, Bruce, Don Jagoda Associates Inc, Melville, NY. Tel: (631) 454-1800, FAX: (631) 454-1834, E-Mail: information@dja.com, Web Site: www.dja. com (35)

Hollander, Bruce, Innovative Packaging of Westchester, Spring Valley, NY. Tel: (845) 364-9500 (26)

Hollander, Ken, Kenneth Hollander Associates Inc, Mendocino, CA. Tel: (707) 962-1648, FAX: (707) 962-1635, Web Site: www.kharesearch.com (30)

Hollander, Marc, CorporateRewards.com, New York, NY. Tel: (212) 689-1200, Web Site: www. corporaterewards.com (35)

Hollars, W. Michael, Hansen Corp, Princeton, IN. Tel: (812) 385-3415, FAX: (812) 385-3013, E-Mail: sales@hansen-motor.com, Web Site: www.hansen-motor.com (16)

Holleman, Shannon, Huntsinger & Jeffer, Richmond, VA. Tel: (804) 266-2499, FAX: (804) 266-8563, E-Mail: info@huntsinger-jeffer.com, Web Site: www.huntsinger-jeffer.com (21)

Holley, Jeffrey D., CUNA Mutual Group, Madison, WI. Tel: (608) 238-5851, (800) 356-2644, FAX: (608) 231-8839, Web Site: www.cunamutual.com (15)

Holley, Jr. Charles M., WalMart Stores Inc, Bentonville, AR. Tel: (479) 273-4000, (800) 925-6278, FAX: (479) 277-1830, Web Site: www.walmart.com (16)

Hollfelder, Jack, Marketing News, Chicago, IL. Tel: (312) 542-9000, (800) 262-1150, FAX: (312) 542-9001, E-Mail: news@ama.org, Web Site: www.ama.org (43)

Hollis, Jack, Toyota Motor Sales USA Inc, Torrance, CA. Tel: (310) 468-4000, (800) 331-4331, FAX: (310) 468-7841, Web Site: www.toyota.com (16)

Hollister Inc, Libertyville, IL. Tel: (847) 680-1000, (888) 740-8999, FAX: (847) 680-2123, Web Site: www.hollister.com (16)

Hollister, Dean, Martindale-Hubbell, New Providence, NJ. Tel: (908) 771-7777, (800) 526-4902, FAX: (908) 771-8704, Web Site: www.martindale.com (17)

Hollister, Glenn, Ideal Industries Inc, Sycamore, IL. Tel: (815) 895-5181, (800) 435-0705, FAX: (815) 895-4800, E-Mail: ideal_industries@idealindustries.com, Web Site: www.idealindustries.com (16)

Hollister, Joyce, Nevada Magazine, Carson City, NV. Tel: (775) 687-5416, FAX: (775) 687-6159, E-Mail: editor@nevadamagazine.com, Web Site: www.nevadamagazine.com (17)

Holloman, J. Philip, Cintas, Cincinnati, OH. Tel: (513) 459-1200, Web Site: www.cintas.com (16)

Holloway, J. David, American Technical Publishers Inc, Orland Park, IL. Tel: (708) 957-1100, (800) 323-3471, FAX: (708) 957-1101, E-Mail: service@americantech.net, Web Site: www.atplearning.com (17)

Hollywood Film Archive, Los Angeles, CA. Tel: (323) 655-4968, Web Site: www.hfarchive.com (17)

Holm, Jan, Laerdal Medical, Wappingers Falls, NY. Tel: (845) 297-7770, FAX: (800) 227-1143, Web Site: www.laerdal.com (34)

Holm, Tom, Enertex Marketing, New York, NY. Tel: (212) 532-3115, FAX: (212) 532-1878, E-Mail: info@enertexmarketing.com, Web Site: www.enertexmarketing.com (22)

Holmberg, Laura, US Travel Association, Washington, DC. Tel: (202) 408-8422, FAX: (202) 408-1255, E-Mail: feedback@ustravel.org, Web Site: www.ustravel.org (1)

Holmes, Barry, Accurate Marketing Systems, River Edge, NJ. Tel: (201) 265-5198 (22)

Holmes, Heather, Technology Review, Cambridge, MA. Tel: (617) 475-8000, FAX: (617) 258-5850, Web Site: www.technologyreview.com (17)

Holmes, John, Datamark Inc, El Paso, TX. Tel: (800) 477-1944, E-Mail: info@datamark.net, Web Site: www.datamark.net (35)

Holmes, Mac, Carter & Holmes Inc, Newberry, SC. Tel: (803) 276-0579, FAX: (803) 276-0588, E-Mail: orchids@carterandholmes.com, Web Site: www.carterandholmes.com (8)

Holmes, Mary, Garden Botanika Inc, Saint Louis, MO. Tel: (425) 881-9603, (800) 724-7227, FAX: (314) 633-4804, E-Mail: customercare@zidle.com, Web Site: www.zidle.com (7)

Holmes, Nancy, Westminster International Inc, Markham, ON Canada. Tel: (416) 494-6245, (866) 635-8050, FAX: (905) 771-9349, E-Mail: info@westminster.ca, Web Site: www.westminster.ca (21)

Holmes, Tony, Bronx Council on the Arts, Bronx, NY. Tel: (718) 931-9500, FAX: (718) 409-6445, E-Mail: info@bronxarts.org, Web Site: www.bronxarts.org (1)

Holmgren, Dale, Oakwood Homes Corp, Greensboro, NC. Tel: (336) 664-2400, (800) 822-0633, FAX: (336) 315-3249, Web Site: www.oakwoodhomes.com (16)

Holoubek, Brian, Heavy Rotation, Milwaukee, WI. Tel: (414) 384-5200, (800) 886-4759, FAX: (414) 434-9318, E-Mail: info@holoubekstudios.com, Web Site: heavytees.com (27)

Holowacz, Phillip, Unadilla Laminated Products, Unadilla, NY. Tel: (607) 369-9341, FAX: (607) 369-3608, E-Mail: info@unalam.com, Web Site: www.unalam.com (16)

Holpp, Abby, Nostrum Inc, Long Beach, CA. Tel: (562) 437-2200, Web Site: www.nostruminc.com (35)

Holsinger, Chad, Steel Media Inc, New York, NY. Tel: (212) 601-2840, E-Mail: info@steelmediainc.com, Web Site: www.steelmediainc.com (35)

Holson, III Richard S., Guarantee Trust Life Insurance Co, Glenview, IL. Tel: (847) 298-0670, FAX: (847) 298-1215, E-Mail: pr@gtlic.com, Web Site: www.gtlic.com (15)

Holsted Marketing Inc, New York, NY. Tel: (212) 686-8537, FAX: (212) 481-0415, E-Mail: preulbach@holstedmarketing.com, Web Site: www.holstedmarketing.com (35)

Holt, Dennis, Patriot Communications LLC, West Hollywood, CA. Tel: (888) 833-4711, FAX: (310) 482-6701, E-Mail: dlivingston@patriotllc.com, Web Site: www.patriotllc.com (32)

Holt, Jo, Louisville Direct Marketing Association, Louisville, KY. Tel: (888) 392-1941, E-Mail: ldmacontact@ldma.org, Web Site: www.ldma.org (40)

Holt, John W., Cobalt, Seattle, WA. Tel: (206) 269-6363, (800) 909-8244, Web Site: www.cobalt.com (16)

Holt, Sara, Commonwealth Lists, Washington, DC. Tel: (202) 831-6202, FAX: (202) 831-6203, E-Mail: info@commonwealthlists.com, Web Site: www.commonwealthlists.com (23)

Holt, Stuart, Response Marketing Group, Richmond, VA. Tel: (866) 574-7665, E-Mail: info@rmg-info.com, Web Site: rmg-usa.com (35)

Holt, William M., Intel Corp, Santa Clara, CA. Tel: (408) 765-8080, (800) 548-4725, FAX: (408) 765-6187, Web Site: www.intel.com (16)

Holton, Michael, Hickory Farms, Maumee, OH. Tel: (419) 893-7611, (800) 776-4111, (800) 442-5671, FAX: (419) 893-0164, Web Site: www.hickoryfarms.com (4)

Holtscheider, Rev. Dennis H., DePaul University, Chicago, IL. Tel: (312) 362-8000, (800) 4-DEPAUL, FAX: (312) 362-6639, E-Mail: skelly@wppost.depaul.edu, Web Site: www.depaul.edu (41)

Holy Cross Hospital, Fort Lauderdale, FL. Tel: (954) 771-8000, FAX: (954) 229-8597, Web Site: www.holy-cross.com (16)

Homar, Barb, Four Seasons Solar Products LLC, Holbrook, NY. Tel: (631) 563-4000, (800) 368-7732, FAX: (631) 563-4010, E-Mail: info@fourseasonssunrooms.com, Web Site: www.fourseasonssunrooms.com (8)

Home Decorators Collection Inc, Marietta, GA. Tel: (800) 245-2217, Web Site: www.homedecoratorscom (8)

The Home Depot Inc, Atlanta, GA. Tel: (770) 433-8211, (800) 466-3337, FAX: (770) 384-2356, Web Site: www.homedepot.com (16)

Home Interiors & Gifts Inc, Carrollton, TX. Tel: (972) 695-1000, FAX: (972) 695-1112 (16)

Home Loan Investment Bank, Warwick, RI. Tel: (401) 739-8800, (800) 223-1700 X278, FAX: (401) 739-9675, E-Mail: contactus@homeloanbank.com, Web Site: www.homeloanbankfsb.com (14)

Home 123 Mortgage, Riverwoods, IL. Tel: (888) 215-0080, E-Mail: info@home123.com, Web Site: www.home123.com (14)

Home Planners, Tucson, AZ. Tel: (520) 297-8200, FAX: (520) 297-6219, E-Mail: sales@homeplanners.com, Web Site: www.homeplanners.com (17)

Home Safeguard Industries, Malibu, CA. Tel: (310) 457-5813, FAX: (310) 457-4862, E-Mail: expert@homesafeguard.com, Web Site: www.homesafeguard.com (9)

Home-Sew Inc, Bethlehem, PA. Tel: (610) 867-3833, (800) 344-4739, FAX: (610) 867-9717, E-Mail: customerservice@homesew.com, Web Site: www.homesew.com (11)

Home Shopping Network, Saint Petersburg, FL. Tel: (727) 872-1000, FAX: (727) 872-7292, Web Site: www.hsn.com (32)

HomeAway.com Inc, Austin, TX. Tel: (512) 684-1100, (877) 228-3145, Web Site: www.homeaway.com (19)

Homecraft Veneer & Woodworker Supply, Latrobe, PA. Tel: (724) 537-8435, (800) 796-6348, FAX: (724) 537-0543, E-Mail: woodman@homecraftveneer.com, Web Site: www.homecraftveneer.com (8)

HomeData, Goleta, CA. Tel: (805) 683-6551, FAX: (805) 683-6553, E-Mail: doreen@avrick.com, Web Site: avrickdirect.com/homedata (24)

Homeowner Data Services Inc, Lawrenceville, GA. Tel: (770) 925-9000, FAX: (770) 925-8977, E-Mail: hdsi@newhomedata.net, Web Site: www.newhomedata.net (23)

Homeowners Marketing Services Inc, North Hollywood, CA. Tel: (888) 743-3037, E-Mail: inquiry@homeownersmarketingservices.com, Web Site: www.homeownersmarketingservices.com (23)

Homer, MD Kenneth, Holy Cross Hospital, Fort Lauderdale, FL. Tel: (954) 771-8000, FAX: (954) 229-8597, Web Site: www.holy-cross.com (16)

Homer, Michael, Psion Teklogix Inc, Mississauga, ON Canada. Tel: (905) 813-9900, (800) 322-3437, E-Mail: ptinfo@psion.com, Web Site: www.psionteklogix.com (17)

Homes, Suzanne, Networking Alternatives for Publishers, Retailers & Artists, Inc, Eastsound, WA. Tel: (360) 376-2702, (800) 367-1907, FAX: (360) 376-2704, E-Mail: futureweb@rockisland.com (40)

Homespun Tapes Music Instruction, Woodstock, NY. Tel: (845) 246-2550, (800) 338-2737, FAX: (845) 246-5282, E-Mail: info@homespuntapes.com, Web Site: www.homespuntapes.com (3)

Homesteaders Life Co, West Des Moines, IA. Tel: (515) 440-7777, (800) 477-3633, E-Mail: service@homesteaderslife.com, Web Site: www.homesteaderslife.com (15)

Hometown Mailing Lists & Direct Mail, Dallas, TX. Tel: (800) 798-4811, E-Mail: tinkham@hometownlists.com, Web Site: www.hometownlists.com (23)

The Honey Agency, Sacramento, CA. Tel: (916) 444-0203, E-Mail: buzz@honeyagency.com, Web Site: honeyagency.com (35)

The HoneyBaked Ham Co, Holland, OH. Tel: (419) 724-4267, (866) 492-4267, E-Mail: info@honeybaked.com, Web Site: www.honeybaked.com (4)

Honeywell, Morristown, NJ. Tel: (973) 455-2000, FAX: (973) 455-4807, Web Site: www.honeywell.com (16)

Hong, Corry S., UNICOM Government Inc, Herndon, VA. Tel: (703) 502-2000, FAX: (703) 463-5011, Web Site: unicomgov.com (16)

Honnold, Scott, Goodyear Tire & Rubber Co, Akron, OH. Tel: (330) 796-2121, (800) 321-2136, FAX: (330) 796-2222, Web Site: www.goodyear.com (16)

Hood, Andy, The Newman Group Computer Services Corp, Ann Arbor, MI. Tel: (734) 426-3200, FAX: (734) 426-0777, E-Mail: anewman@newman.com (3)

Hood, George, The Salvation Army National Headquarters, Alexandria, VA. Tel: (703) 684-5500, Web Site: www.salvationarmyusa.org (1)

Hood, Julia, DM News, New York, NY. Tel: (646) 638-6000, (800) 558-1703, FAX: (212) 925-8752, E-Mail: dmnewssubs@haymarketmedia.com, Web Site: www.dmnews.com (43)

Hood, Kim, American Fidelity Assurance Co, Oklahoma City, OK. Tel: (405) 525-6900, FAX: (405) 523-5215, Web Site: www.afadvantage.com (15)

Hood, Mark E., Brown Shoe Co, Saint Louis, MO. Tel: (314) 854-4000, FAX: (314) 854-4274, Web Site: www.brownshoe.com (16)

Hood, Shawn, Sherman Specialty Toy Co Inc, Jericho, NY. Tel: (516) 861-6420, (516) 546-7400, (800) 645-6513, FAX: (516) 861-1033, (800) 853-8697, E-Mail: orders@shermanspecialty.com, Web Site: www.shermanspecialty.com (16)

Hoody, Mike, Central States Indemnity, Omaha, NE. Tel: (402) 997-8000, (402) 397-1111, (800) 445-6500, Web Site: www.csi-omaha.com (15)

Hook & Hackle Co Inc, Homestead, PA. Tel: (412) 476-8620, (800) 652-8342, FAX: (412) 476-8639, E-Mail: ron@hookhack.com, Web Site: www.hookhack.com (11)

Hook, Lisa, Neustar Inc, Sterling, VA. Tel: (571) 434-5400, (877) 245-5277, E-Mail: billingsupport@neustar.biz, Web Site: www.neustar.biz (29)

Hooker, Betty, Wendover Associates Inc, Greensboro, NC. Tel: (336) 299-6611, FAX: (336) 292-4261, E-Mail: wendover@wendoverassociates.com, Web Site: www.wendoverassociates.com (35)

Hooker, E. Stanton, Midland Paper, Wheeling, IL. Tel: (847) 777-2700, (800) 323-8522, FAX: (847) 777-2552, E-Mail: whl@midlandpaper.com, Web Site: www.midlandpaper.com (25)

Hooks, Simon, CCG Marketing Solutions, West Caldwell, NJ. Tel: (973) 808-0009, (866) 902-2807, FAX: (973) 808-9740, E-Mail: info@corpcomm.com, Web Site: home.corpcomm.com (21)

Hoole, David, Nature Publishing Group, New York, NY. Tel: (212) 726-9200, FAX: (212) 696-9006, Web Site: www.nature.com (17)

Hooleon Corp, Melrose, NM. Tel: (575) 253-4503, (800) 937-1337, E-Mail: sales@hooleon.com, Web Site: www.hooleon.com (3)

Hooper, Ann, Lathem Time Corp, Atlanta, GA. Tel: (404) 691-0400, (800) 241-4990, FAX: (404) 696-6048, Web Site: www.lathem.com (16)

Hoover, David R., Hoover's Mfg Co, Peru, IL. Tel: (815) 223-1159, FAX: (815) 333-1499, Web Site: www.hmchonors.com (2)

Hoover's Inc, Austin, TX. Tel: (512) 374-4500, FAX: (512) 374-4051, Web Site: www.hoovers.com (22)

Hoover's Mfg Co, Peru, IL. Tel: (815) 223-1159, FAX: (815) 333-1499, Web Site: www.hmchonors.com (2)

The Hope Co Inc, Bridgeton, MO. Tel: (314) 739-7254, (800) 325-4026, FAX: (314) 739-7786, E-Mail: info@hopecompany.com (16)

Hope Counts, Rita, BrightKey, Annapolis Junction, MD. Tel: (301) 604-3305 (28)

Hope, Amy, The American Phytopathological Society, Saint Paul, MN. Tel: (651) 454-7250, FAX: (651) 454-0766, E-Mail: apsheadquarters@scisoc.org, Web Site: www.apsnet.org (1)

Hope, Dave, American Crane & Equipment Corp, Douglassville, PA. Tel: (610) 385-4876, (877) 877-6778, FAX: (610) 385-3191, E-Mail: info@americancrane.com, Web Site: www.americancrane.com (16)

Hopkins Medical Products, Baltimore, MD. Tel: (410) 484-2036, (800) 835-1995, FAX: (410) 484-4036, E-Mail: customerservice@hopkinsmedical.net, Web Site: www.hopkinsmedicalproducts.com (7)

Hopkins, Jr. George E., The Maine Connection, Portland, ME. Tel: (207) 780-4355, FAX: (207) 780-4239, E-Mail: mainelaw@maine.edu (27)

Hopkins, Mark, Fox Lite, Inc, Fairborn, OH. Tel: (937) 864-1966, FAX: (937) 864-7010, E-Mail: doug@foxlite.com, Web Site: www.foxlite.com (9)

Hopkins, Rick, Love To Learn Inc, Salem, UT. Tel: (801) 423-2009, (888) 771-1034, FAX: (801) 423-9188, E-Mail: customerservice@lovetolearn.net, Web Site: www.lovetolearn.net (5)

Hopkins, Robert, Direct Mail Solutions LLC, Carol Stream, IL. Tel: (630) 653-6863, FAX: (630) 653-7144, E-Mail: support@dmspostal.com, Web Site: www.dmspostal.com (28)

Hopkins, Rusty, Directory of Premium, Incentive & Travel Buyers, Richmond, VA. Tel: (804) 762-4455, (800) 223-1797, FAX: (804) 935-0271, E-Mail: amdouglas4@aol.com, Web Site: www.douglaspublications.com (43)

Hopkins, Scott, Anderson Direct & Digital, Poway, CA. Tel: (888) 694-5094, Web Site: www.andersondd.com (35)

Hopkins, Shae, KET, Lexington, KY. Tel: (859) 258-7000, (800) 432-0951, FAX: (606) 258-7396, E-Mail: rgriffin@ket.org, Web Site: www.ket.org (17)

Hopkins, Suzanne, The Economist Newspaper NA Inc, New York, NY. Tel: (212) 554-0600, FAX: (212) 586-1191, Web Site: www.economist.com (17)

Hoplamazian, Mark, Hyatt Hotels Corp, Chicago, IL. Tel: (312) 750-1234, FAX: (312) 780-5289, Web Site: www.hyatt.com (16)

Hopp, Jeffrey, Leslie Shoe Co Inc, Rogers City, MI. Tel: (989) 734-4030, (800) 716-8617, E-Mail: info@sexyshoes.com, Web Site: www.sexyshoes.com (2)

Hopple, Richard V., Guideposts, Danbury, CT. Tel: (800) 932-2154, Web Site: www.guideposts.org (1)

Hoquet, Karen M., Macy's Marketing, New York, NY. Tel: (212) 695-4400, FAX: (212) 494-1517, Web Site: www.macys.com (16)

Horace Mann Educators Corp, Springfield, IL. Tel: (217) 789-2500, FAX: (217) 788-5161, Web Site: www.horacemann.com (15)

The Horah Group, Pleasantville, NY. Tel: (914) 495-3200, E-Mail: dgoldsmith@horah.com, Web Site: www.horah.com (21)

Horizon Lists, Congers, NY. Tel: (845) 300-4932, E-Mail: sales@horizonlists.com, Web Site: www.horizonlists.com (23)

Horizon Paper Co Inc, Stamford, CT. Tel: (203) 358-0855, (866) 358-0855, FAX: (203) 358-0828, Web Site: www.horizonpaper.com (25)

Hormel Foods Corp, Austin, MN. Tel: (507) 437-5611, (800) 523-4635, FAX: (507) 437-5158, Web Site: www.hormelfoods.com (16)

Horn, Michael, Volkswagen Group of America Inc, Herndon, VA. Tel: (248) 754-5000, Web Site: www.volkswagengroupamerica.com (16)

Hornbaker, Ron, Rockler Woodworking & Hardware, Medina, MN. Tel: (763) 478-8200, (800) 279-4441, FAX: (800) 865-1229, E-Mail: info@rockler.com, Web Site: www.rockler.com (8)

Hornberger, Jim, Golf Haus, Lansing, MI. Tel: (517) 482-8842, FAX: (517) 482-8843 (11)

Hornbuster, Louis, Mel Bay Publications Inc, Pacific, MO. Tel: (800) 8-MELBAY, FAX: (636) 257-5062, E-Mail: email@melbay.com, Web Site: www.melbay.com (17)

Hornstein, Lee, (C) Systems LLC, Edison, NJ. Tel: (732) 548-6100, FAX: (732) 548-3883, Web Site: www.csystemsllc.net (27)

Hornstein, Scott, Erman Roman Direct Marketing Corp, Little Neck, NY. Tel: (718) 225-4151, FAX: (718) 225-4889, E-Mail: ernan@erdm.com, Web Site: www.erdm.com (20)

David K Horowitz Studio Inc, Philadelphia, PA. Tel: (215) 765-3600, FAX: (215) 763-1056 (37)

Horowitz, Jeff, LS Direct Marketing, Suffern, NY. Tel: (845) 357-1238, E-Mail: info@lsdirect.com, Web Site: www.lsdirect.com (23)

Horowitz, Steve, Ziff Davis Media Inc, New York, NY. Tel: (212) 503-5100, FAX: (212) 503-5023, Web Site: www.ziffdavis.com (17)

Horstmann, Stephen F., BullsEye Marketing Systems LLC, West Chester, PA. Tel: (484) 356-2240, E-Mail: info@bullseyemarketingsystems.com, Web Site: bullseyemarketingsystems.com (35)

Horticulture Magazine, Cincinnati, OH. Tel: (513) 531-2690, FAX: (513) 891-7153, Web Site: www.hortmag.com (17)

Horton Interpreting Inc, Providence, RI. Tel: (401) 331-4798, (800) 345-2135, FAX: (401) 331-2822, Web Site: www.language-link.com (30)

Horton, Juana I, Horton Interpreting Inc, Providence, RI. Tel: (401) 331-4798, (800) 345-2135, FAX: (401) 331-2822, Web Site: www.language-link.com (30)

Horwitz, Allen, IClimber Inc, Burbank, CA. Tel: (818) 567-3030, Web Site: www.iclimber.com (16)

Hoskins, Marla, The Response Shop Inc, Palm Desert, CA. Tel: (858) 735-7646, FAX: (858) 777-5418, E-Mail: marla@responseshop.com, Web Site: www.responseshop.com (35)

Hoslins, Marla, The Testimonial Wrangler, La Jolla, CA. Tel: (858) 735-7646, FAX: (858) 777-5418 (35)

Hostetler, Jay, Stewart-MacDonald, Athens, OH. Tel: (740) 592-3021, (800) 848-2273, FAX: (740) 593-7922, E-Mail: hostetler@stewmac.com, Web Site: www.stewmac.com (16)

Hot Sauce Harry's, North Port, FL. Tel: (214) 902-8552, (800) 588-8979, FAX: (214) 956-9885, E-Mail: info@hotsauceharrys.com, Web Site: www. hotsauceharrys.com (4)

Hot Topic Inc, City of Industry, CA. Tel: (626) 839-4681, (800) 275-9169, FAX: (626) 839-4686, Web Site: www.hottopic.com (2)

Hotaling, Veronica, Syracuse University, Syracuse, NY. Tel: (315) 443-1870, (315) 443-4226, E-Mail: orange@syr.edu, Web Site: syr.edu (1)

Hotline List Corp, New York, NY. Tel: (212) 840-8135, FAX: (212) 840-8139 (23)

Houlihan Lokey Howard & Zukin, Los Angeles, CA. Tel: (310) 553-8871, (800) 788-5300, FAX: (310) 553-2173, Web Site: www.hlhz.com (14)

Houlihan, Mary, Anheuser-Busch Inc Promotional Products Group, Shelton, CT. Tel: (800) 742-5283, Web Site: www.budshop.com (6)

Houlne, Tim, WS Live LLC, Dubuque, IA. Tel: (563) 582-9501, (800) 582-9501, FAX: (563) 582-2003, Web Site: www.wslive.com (29)

House of Eyes, Greensboro, NC. Tel: (336) 852-7107, FAX: (336) 854-0311 (2)

House of Marketing Research, Pasadena, CA. Tel: (626) 486-1400, FAX: (626) 486-1404, Web Site: www. hmr-research.com (30)

House of Oldies, New York, NY. Tel: (212) 243-0500, FAX: (212) 989-1697, E-Mail: rabramson@ houseofoldies.com, Web Site: www.houseofoldies. com (6)

House of Onyx, Inc, Greenville, KY. Tel: (270) 338-2363, (800) 844-3100, FAX: (270) 338-9605, E-Mail: sales@houseofonyx.com, Web Site: www. houseofonyx.com (6)

House of Orange, Brentwood Bay, BC Canada. Tel: (866) 401-9174, FAX: (250) 652-8673, E-Mail: houseoforange@shaw.ca, Web Site: www. houseoforangeltd.com (2)

House of Wesley Inc, Bloomington, IL. Tel: (309) 664-7334, E-Mail: customercare@houseofwesley.com, Web Site: www.houseofwesley.com (8)

House Party Inc, Irvington, NY. Tel: (720) 496-2503, (888) 591-1678, FAX: (914) 591-4561, E-Mail: help@houseparty.com, Web Site: www.houseparty. com (30)

House, Dave, Brocade Communications Systems Inc, San Jose, CA. Tel: (408) 333-8000, FAX: (408) 333-8101, E-Mail: info@brocade.com, Web Site: www. brocade.com (16)

House, Gerry, Institute for Student Achievement, Carle Place, NY. Tel: (516) 812-6700, Web Site: www. studentachievement.org (1)

House, Gwen, Potpourri Group Inc, North Billerica, MA. Tel: (978) 256-4100, FAX: (978) 256-1961/0344, Web Site: www.potpourrigroup.com (6)

House, Maria, Daily Record & Dispatch Co, Dunn, NC. Tel: (910) 891-1234, FAX: (910) 891-5253, Web Site: www.mydailyrecord.com (17)

Housely, James, Facts On File Inc, New York, NY. Tel: (212) 967-8800, (800) 322-8755, FAX: (212) 678-3633, Web Site: www.infobasepublishing.com (17)

Housley, James, Cambridge Educational, New York, NY. Tel: (800) 257-5126, FAX: (917) 339-0325, Web Site: www.filmsmediagroup.com (12)

Houss, Max, Interstate EDP & Direct Mail Center Inc, Brooklyn, NY. Tel: (718) 965-2500, FAX: (718) 965-2504, E-Mail: info@interstateedp.com, Web Site: www.interstateedp.com (28)

The Houston Chronicle, Houston, TX. Tel: (713) 362-7171, FAX: (713) 362-3575, Web Site: www. houstonchronicle.com (31)

Houston Direct Marketing Association, Houston, TX. Tel: (281) 931-8883, FAX: (281) 820-4023, Web Site: www.houstondma.org (40)

Houston, H. Rika, School of Business & Economics, Los Angeles, CA. Tel: (323) 343-2800, FAX: (323) 343-2813, Web Site: cbe.calstatela.edu (41)

Hovan, Nadine, Practicing Law Institute, New York, NY. Tel: (212) 824-5700, (800) 260 4PLI, FAX: (800) 321-0093, E-Mail: info@pli.edu, Web Site: www.pli.edu (16)

How I Grossed More Than $1 Million in Direct Mail Order Starting with Little Cash & Less Know How, Rockville Centre, NY. Tel: (516) 766-5850, (800) 323-0548, FAX: (516) 766-5919, E-Mail: admin@ iwsmoney.com, Web Site: www.iwsmoney.com (43)

Howard Rice Nemerovski Canady Falk & Rabkin, San Francisco, CA. Tel: (415) 464-1600, FAX: (415) 217-5910, Web Site: www.howardrice.com (14)

Howard-Sloan-Koller Group, New York, NY. Tel: (212) 661-5250, FAX: (212) 557-9178, E-Mail: ekoller@ hsksearch.com, Web Site: www.hsksearch.com (20)

Howard, A., Air-Scent International, Pittsburgh, PA. Tel: (800) 247-0770, FAX: (412) 252-2000, E-Mail: laura@aromaresource.com, Web Site: www. airscent.com (16)

Howard, Alan B., Southern Poverty Law Center, Montgomery, AL. Tel: (334) 956-8200, (888) 414-7752, FAX: (334) 956-8483, Web Site: www.splcenter.org (1)

Howard, Cherene, Pennsylvania State University Press, University Park, PA. Tel: (814) 865-1327, (800) 326-9180, FAX: (814) 863-1408, Web Site: www. psupress.org (17)

Howard, Elaine, Army Times Publishing Co, Springfield, VA. Tel: (703) 750-9000, (800) 336-4590, FAX: (703) 750-8129, E-Mail: cust-svc@atpco.com, Web Site: www.armytimes.com (17)

Howard, Hope E., Insurance Publications Inc, Overland Park, KS. Tel: (913) 383-9191, (800) 762-3387, FAX: (913) 383-1247, E-Mail: brokerwrld@ primary.net, Web Site: www.brokerworldmag.com (17)

Howard, Jerry, National Association of Home Builders, Washington, DC. Tel: (202) 266-8200, (800) 368-5242, FAX: (202) 266-8400, Web Site: www.nahb. org (1)

Howard, Jim, CrownPeak Technology Inc, Los Angeles, CA. Tel: (310) 841-5920, FAX: (310) 841-5913, Web Site: www.crownpeak.com (22)

Howard, Marilyn, Creative Freelancers Inc, Sarasota, FL. Tel: (203) 532-2924, (800) 398-9544, E-Mail: cfonline@freelancers.com, Web Site: www. freelancers.com (39)

Howard, Peter, Staples Inc, Framingham, MA. Tel: (508) 253-5000, FAX: (508) 253-7803, Web Site: www.staples.com (10)

Howard, Stephen P., Insurance Publications Inc, Overland Park, KS. Tel: (913) 383-9191, (800) 762-3387, FAX: (913) 383-1247, E-Mail: brokerwrld@ primary.net, Web Site: www.brokerworldmag.com (17)

Howard, Susan, American General Life Insurance Co, Houston, TX. Tel: (713) 522-1111, FAX: (713) 522-8531, Web Site: www.aglife.com (15)

Howard, Vicki, Christianity Today Inc, Carol Stream, IL. Tel: (630) 260-6200, FAX: (630) 260-0114, Web Site: www.christianitytoday.com (17)

Howe, Dave, Syfy, New York, NY. Tel: (212) 664-4444, Web Site: www.syfy.com (32)

Howe, III Rick, Saint Mary's Paper Corp, Wheaton, IL. Tel: (630) 668-6279, FAX: (630) 668-6292, Web Site: www.stmarys-paper.com (25)

Howe, Keith, Echnologist Scrub Tech, Mesquite, TX. Tel: (520) 208-6314 (34)

Howe, Scott E., Acxiom Corp, Little Rock, AR. Tel: (501) 342-1000, FAX: (501) 342-3913, Web Site: www.acxiom.com (22)

Howell Marketing Services, Elmira, NY. Tel: (607) 734-6291, FAX: (607) 734-6759, E-Mail: jjs@ howellmarketingservices.com, Web Site: www. howellmarketingservices.com (28)

Howell, George, FM Howell & Co, Elmira, NY. Tel: (607) 734-6291, FAX: (607) 735-0464, E-Mail: best@howellpkg.com, Web Site: www.howellpkg. com (16)

Howell, Stephen, The Nature Conservancy, Arlington, VA. Tel: (703) 841-5300, (800) 628-6860, FAX: (703) 841-1283, Web Site: www.nature.org (1)

Howland, MaryAnne, Ibis Communications Inc, Nashville, TN. Tel: (615) 777-1900, FAX: (615) 777-1906, E-Mail: mhowland@ibiscommunications. com, Web Site: www.ibiscommunications.com (35)

Howley, Nicolas, Marathon Norco Aerospace Inc, Waco, TX. Tel: (254) 776-0650, FAX: (254) 776-6558, Web Site: www.mptc.com (16)

Howse, Jennifer, March of Dimes Foundation, White Plains, NY. Tel: (914) 997-4488, Web Site: www. marchofdimes.org (1)

Hoy, Douglas, Fox Lite, Inc, Fairborn, OH. Tel: (937) 864-1966, FAX: (937) 864-7010, E-Mail: doug@ foxlite.com, Web Site: www.foxlite.com (9)

Hoy, Stephanie, Direct Mail Solutions, Richmond, VA. Tel: (804) 254-8300, (877) 367-0800, Web Site: www.directmailsolutions.com (28)

Hoy, Walt, Fox Lite, Inc, Fairborn, OH. Tel: (937) 864-1966, FAX: (937) 864-7010, E-Mail: doug@foxlite. com, Web Site: www.foxlite.com (9)

Hoyle, Mark, Mountain Media Enterprises, Fort Collins, CO. Tel: (970) 493-2499, FAX: (970) 493-3598, E-Mail: info@mountain-media.com, Web Site: fortcollinsdigitalprinting.com (21)

Coleman W Hoyt Consultant, Woodstock, VT. Tel: (802) 672-3634, FAX: (802) 672-5116, E-Mail: cwhoyt@vermontel.net (20)

Hoyt, Coleman, Continuity Shippers Association, Woodstock, VT. Tel: (802) 672-3634 (20)

Hoyt, Coleman W., Coleman W Hoyt Consultant, Woodstock, VT. Tel: (802) 672-3634, FAX: (802) 672-5116, E-Mail: cwhoyt@vermontel.net (20)

Hrabak, DeAnne, Vita-Mix Corp, Cleveland, OH. Tel: (440) 235-4840, (800) VITA-MIX, FAX: (440) 235-3726, E-Mail: service@vitamix.com, Web Site: www.vitamix.com (16)

Hradel, Craig, Cold Stream Farm, Free Soil, MI. Tel: (231) 464-5809, E-Mail: info@coldstreamfarm.net, Web Site: www.coldstreamfarm.net (8)

Hren, Eddie, Martin Worldwide Inc, Oak Park, CA. Tel: (888) 694-5478, Web Site: www.martinworldwide. net (23)

Hritzak, Adam, ClearSaleing Inc, Columbus, OH. Tel: (614) 448-2688, (800) 592-0463, Web Site: www. clearsaleing.com (16)

Hron, Ihor, North American Co for Life & Health Insurance, Chicago, IL. Tel: (312) 648-7600, (800) 800-3656, FAX: (312) 648-7796, Web Site: www. nacolah.com (15)

Hsu, Charles J., Retawmatic Corp, Flushing, NY. Tel: (718) 886-0502 (9)

Hsu, Ching-I, Raritan Inc, Somerset, NJ. Tel: (732) 764-8886, FAX: (732) 764-8887, Web Site: www. raritan.com (22)

Huisingh, Rosemary, LinguiSystems, East Moline, IL. Tel: (309) 755-2300, (800) 776-4332, FAX: (800) 577-4555, E-Mail: service@linguisystems.com, Web Site: www.linguisystems.com (17)

Hull, Lucy M., Selltel Inc, Brick, NJ. Tel: (732) 920-8700, (888) 840-9481, FAX: (732) 903-0836, E-Mail: info@nationalprotection.com (29)

Hullinger, Margret S., The Bureau of National Affairs, Inc, Arlington, VA. Tel: (703) 341-3000, (800) 372-1033, FAX: (703) 341-1688, Web Site: www.bna.com (17)

Hulon, Wade, Anritsu Co, Morgan Hill, CA. Tel: (408) 778-2000, (800) 267-4878, FAX: (408) 776-1744, Web Site: www.us.anritsu.com (16)

Hulse, Chris, Madison Direct Marketing Ltd, Stamford, CT. Tel: (203) 653-3200, FAX: (203) 316-0518, Web Site: www.madisondm.com (31)

Hult Marketing, Peoria, IL. Tel: (309) 673-8191, FAX: (309) 674-5530, E-Mail: jflynn@hultmarketing.com, Web Site: www.hultmarketing.com (35)

Hulton, Dennis, Valley Forge Tape & Label Co Inc, Exton, PA. Tel: (610) 524-8900, (800) 345-1323, FAX: (610) 524-8906, E-Mail: vfsales@vftl.com, Web Site: www.vftl.com (27)

Hultquist, Timothy A., Morgan Stanley, New York, NY. Tel: (212) 761-4000, FAX: (212) 761-0096 (14)

Human Resource Development Press, Amherst, MA. Tel: (413) 253-3488, (800) 822-2801, FAX: (413) 253-3490, E-Mail: info@hrdpress.com, Web Site: www.hrdpress.com (17)

Human Rights Campaign, Washington, DC. Tel: (202) 216-1500, (800) 777-4723, Web Site: www.hrc.org (40)

Humana Inc, Louisville, KY. Tel: (502) 580-5005, (800) 486-2620, FAX: (502) 580-3141, Web Site: www.humana.com (7)

The Humane Society of the US, Washington, DC. Tel: (202) 452-1100, (866) 720-2676, Web Site: www.hsus.org (1)

Hume, Linda, KET, Lexington, KY. Tel: (859) 258-7000, (800) 432-0951, FAX: (606) 258-7396, E-Mail: rgriffin@ket.org, Web Site: www.ket.org (17)

Hummel Integrated Marketing Solutions, Union, NJ. Tel: (908) 688-5300, FAX: (908) 688-6020, E-Mail: info@hummelsolutions.com, Web Site: www.hummelsolutions.com (21)

Hummel, Dennis, Maritz, Fenton, MO. Tel: (636) 827-4000, Web Site: www.maritz.com (35)

Hummel, John, Hummel Integrated Marketing Solutions, Union, NJ. Tel: (908) 688-5300, FAX: (908) 688-6020, E-Mail: info@hummelsolutions.com, Web Site: www.hummelsolutions.com (21)

Humphrey, Karla, Click2Mail, Arlington, VA. Tel: (703) 521-9029, (866) 665-2787, FAX: (703) 358-8811, E-Mail: info@click2mail.com, Web Site: www.click2mail.com (20)

Humphrey, Sam, Mi-T-M Corp, Peosta, IA. Tel: (563) 556-7484, Web Site: www.mitm.com (9)

Humphries, Melita, Schermer Pecans, Glennville, GA. Tel: (912) 654-2230, (800) 841-3403, E-Mail: information@schermerpecans.com, Web Site: www.pecantreats.com (4)

Hungerford, William, Strategic Software Systems LLC, Richmond, VA. Tel: (804) 288-8827x110, Web Site: www.sss1.com (22)

Hungsberg, Jill, Marshall Fields Dept Stores, Minneapolis, MN. Tel: (612) 375-3004, Web Site: www.fields.com (5)

Hunsinger, Peter King, Golf Digest Co, Wilton, CT. Tel: (203) 761-5100, FAX: (203) 371-2572, Web Site: www.golfdigest.com (17)

Hunt Marketing Group, Seattle, WA. Tel: (206) 447-5665, FAX: (206) 447-5789, E-Mail: info@hmgseattle.com, Web Site: www.hmgseattle.com (35)

Hunt, Brian, Hunt Marketing Group, Seattle, WA. Tel: (206) 447-5665, FAX: (206) 447-5789, E-Mail: info@hmgseattle.com, Web Site: www.hmgseattle.com (35)

Hunt, C, Ventriloquist Voice Solutions International Inc, Mississauga, ON Canada. Tel: (866) 446-0860, E-Mail: info@ventriloquistsolutions.com, Web Site: www.ventriloquistsolutions.com (29)

Hunt, Clark, Kansas City Chiefs, Kansas City, MO. Tel: (816) 920-9300, (888) 99-CHIEFS, FAX: (816) 923-4719, Web Site: www.kcchiefs.com (16)

Hunt, Courtney, Baton Rouge Conventions & Visitors Bureau, Baton Rouge, LA. Tel: (225) 383-1825, (800) LA-ROUGE, FAX: (225) 346-1253, E-Mail: karron@visitbatonrouge.com, Web Site: www.bracvb.com (1)

Hunt, Dan, Mason Companies Inc, Chippewa Falls, WI. Tel: (715) 723-1871, (800) 826-7030, FAX: (715) 720-4247, Web Site: www.masoncompaniesinc.com (2)

Hunt, Eric, Welch Allyn, Inc, Skaneateles Falls, NY. Tel: (315) 685-4100, Web Site: www.welchallyn.com (9)

Hunt, F. Randal, Aerovox Inc, New Bedford, MA. Tel: (508) 994-9661, (888) AEROVOX, FAX: (508) 995-3000, E-Mail: sales1@aerovox.com, Web Site: www.aerovox.com (16)

Hunt, J., Ventriloquist Voice Solutions International Inc, Mississauga, ON Canada. Tel: (866) 446-0860, E-Mail: info@ventriloquistsolutions.com, Web Site: www.ventriloquistsolutions.com (29)

Hunt, Kia, Lundmark Advertising + Design Inc, Kansas City, MO. Tel: (816) 842-5236, Web Site: lundmarkadvertising.com (35)

Hunt, Lorraine, Nevada Commission on Tourism, Carson City, NV. Tel: (775) 687-4322, (800) NEVADA 8, FAX: (775) 687-6779, Web Site: www.travelnevada.com (1)

Hunt, Mariah, New England Direct Marketing Association, Wellesley Hills, MA. Tel: (781) 237-1366, FAX: (781) 431-8118, E-Mail: info@nedma.com, Web Site: www.nedma.com (40)

Hunt, Matt, Hunt Marketing Group, Seattle, WA. Tel: (206) 447-5665, FAX: (206) 447-5789, E-Mail: info@hmgseattle.com, Web Site: www.hmgseattle.com (35)

Hunt, Robert, New Day Marketing Ltd, Santa Barbara, CA. Tel: (805) 965-7833, FAX: (805) 965-1284, E-Mail: robert@ndm.tv, Web Site: www.newdaymarketing.com (35)

Hunt, Vince, Shop.com, Miami, FL. Tel: (866) 420-1709, E-Mail: customerservice@shop.com, Web Site: www.shop.com (16)

Hunter Business Group LLC, Milwaukee, WI. Tel: (414) 203-8060, (800) 423-4010, FAX: (414) 203-8225, E-Mail: hunter@hunterbusiness.com, Web Site: www.hunterbusiness.com (20)

Hunter, Barbara, Air Ambulance Network Inc, Palm Harbor, FL. Tel: (727) 934-3999, (800) 327-1966, FAX: (727) 937-0276, Web Site: www.airambulancenetwork.com (16)

Hunter, Clifford M., Broadcast Media Associates, Santa Maria, CA. Tel: (805) 937-1553, E-Mail: cliffhunter@cliffhunter.com, Web Site: www.broadcastmediabroker.com (30)

Hunter, Jennifer, Scott's Directories, Toronto, ON Canada. Tel: (416) 510-5131, FAX: (416) 510-5129, E-Mail: info@scottsinfo.com, Web Site: scottsinfo.com (31)

Hunter, Joyce, Miller Stockman, Denver, CO. Tel: (303) 428-5696, FAX: (303) 430-1130 (2)

Hunter, Kathleen, Association of National Advertisers Inc, New York, NY. Tel: (212) 697-5950, FAX: (212) 687-7310, Web Site: www.ana.net (40)

Hunter, Lindsay, The Direct Marketing Association, New York, NY. Tel: (212) 768-7277, E-Mail: info@the-dma.org, Web Site: thedma.org (1)

Hunter, Mark, Molson Coors Brewing Co, Denver, CO. Tel: (303) 927-2337, (800) 665-7661, Web Site: www.molsoncoors.com (16)

Hunter, Mason, BMI, Nashville, TN. Tel: (615) 401-2000, (800) 925-8451, FAX: (615) 401-2812, E-Mail: nashville@bmi.com, Web Site: www.bmi.com (1)

Hunter, Richard, Air Ambulance Network Inc, Palm Harbor, FL. Tel: (727) 934-3999, (800) 327-1966, FAX: (727) 937-0276, Web Site: www.airambulancenetwork.com (16)

Hunter, Tony W., Chicago Tribune, Chicago, IL. Tel: (312) 222-3232, (800) 874-2863, FAX: (312) 222-2598, E-Mail: consumerservices@tribune.com, Web Site: www.chicagotribune.com (17)

Hunter, Victor, Hunter Business Group LLC, Milwaukee, WI. Tel: (414) 203-8060, (800) 423-4010, FAX: (414) 203-8225, E-Mail: hunter@hunterbusiness.com, Web Site: www.hunterbusiness.com (20)

Hunter, Warren, DMW Worldwide LLC, Chesterbrook, PA. Tel: (610) 407-0407, (877) 744-3699, FAX: (610) 407-9201, E-Mail: info@dmwdirect.com, Web Site: www.dmwdirect.com (35)

Huntington Bancshares, Columbus, OH. Tel: (614) 480-5160, (800) 480-BANK, FAX: (614) 480-5284, Web Site: www.huntington.com (14)

Huntoon, Keith, Blue Hill Marketing Solutions Inc, Pearl River, NY. Tel: (845) 627-6600, FAX: (845) 735-3985, E-Mail: sales@liftengine.com, Web Site: www.liftengine.com (22)

Huntsinger & Jeffer, Richmond, VA. Tel: (804) 266-2499, FAX: (804) 266-8563, E-Mail: info@huntsinger-jeffer.com, Web Site: www.huntsinger-jeffer.com (21)

Hupp, Dennis, Direct Marketing Audit Systems, Bridgeton, MO. Tel: (314) 739-7460, FAX: (314) 739-7284, Web Site: www.dmasinc.com (22)

Hupping, Carol, The Jewish Publication Society, Philadelphia, PA. Tel: (215) 832-0600, (800) 234-3151, FAX: (215) 568-2017, Web Site: www.jewishpub.org (17)

Hurd, Mark, Oracle Corp, Redwood Shores, CA. Tel: (650) 506-7000, (800) 633-0738, FAX: (650) 506-7200, Web Site: www.oracle.com (16)

Hurlbut, Annie, Peruvian Connection Ltd, Tonganoxie, KS. Tel: (913) 845-2450, (800) 221-8520, E-Mail: sales@peruvianconnection.com, Web Site: www.peruvianconnection.com (2)

Hurletron Inc, Libertyville, IL. Tel: (847) 680-7022, FAX: (847) 680-7338, E-Mail: sales@hurletron.com, Web Site: www.hurletron.com (34)

Hurley, Cheryl, The Library of America, New York, NY. Tel: (212) 308-3360, (800) 964-5778, FAX: (212) 750-8352, E-Mail: info@loa.org, Web Site: www.loa.org (13)

Hurley, Gerry, Vertex Inc, Berwyn, PA. Tel: (610) 640-4200, (800) 355-3500, FAX: (610) 640-5892, Web Site: www.vertexinc.com (16)

Hurt, Dwayne, Bacompt Systems Inc, Carmel, IN. Tel: (317) 574-7474, (800) 533-7109, FAX: (317) 574-7475, E-Mail: customer.service@bacompt.com, Web Site: www.bacompt.com (21)

Hurteau, Claudia, Roseberry Direct List Management & Brokerage, Elon, NC. Tel: (336) 532-1000, FAX: (336) 532-1003, E-Mail: churteau@roseberrydirect. com, Web Site: roseberrydirect.com (23)

Hurvis, John Thomas, Old World Ind, Northbrook, IL. Tel: (847) 559-2000, FAX: (847) 559-2266, Web Site: www.oldworldind.com (34)

Hurwitz, Marty, MVI Marketing Ltd, San Luis Obispo, CA. Tel: (805) 239-2994, (805) 459-4455, FAX: (805) 239-2947, E-Mail: info@mvimarketing.com, Web Site: www.mvimarketing.com (20)

Husain, Dave, Leapfrog Online, Evanston, IL. Tel: (847) 492-1968, Web Site: www.leapfrogonline.com (35)

Huse, Paul, Joyce Meyer Ministries, Fenton, MO. Tel: (636) 349-0303, Web Site: www.joycemeyer.org (1)

Huseby, Michael P., BarnesandNoble.com, New York, NY. Tel: (212) 414-6000, (800) THE-BOOK, FAX: (212) 414-6140, E-Mail: service@barnesandnoble. com, Web Site: www.barnesandnoble.com (16)

Huser, Matt, nFusion Group LLC, Austin, TX. Tel: (512) 716-7000, FAX: (512) 716-7001, E-Mail: info@nfusion.com, Web Site: nfusion.com (35)

Husky Envelope Products, Walled Lake, MI. Tel: (248) 624-7070, FAX: (248) 624-5990, E-Mail: bmuehl@ huskyenvelope.com, Web Site: www. huskyenvelope.com (26)

Hussey, James, Chapman Cubine Adams & Hussey, Arlington, VA. Tel: (703) 248-0025, Web Site: www. ahadirect.com (20)

Hussey, Jay, Baldwin Filters, Kearney, NE. Tel: (308) 234-1951, (800) 822-5394, FAX: (800) 828-4453, E-Mail: info@baldwinfilter.com, Web Site: www. baldwinfilter.com (16)

Hussey, Michael E., Professional Education Institute, Chicago, IL. Tel: (312) 521-8002, (800) 320-7517, Web Site: www.thepei.com (13)

Hussey, Phil, 89 Degrees, Burlington, MA. Tel: (781) 221-5400, Web Site: www.89degrees.com (9)

Hussey, Tim, Clarin by Hussey Seating, North Berwick, ME. Tel: (800) 341-0401, FAX: (207) 676-2222, Web Site: www.husseyseating.com (5)

Hutchins, Peter, American Forests, Washington, DC. Tel: (202) 737-1944, FAX: (202) 737-2457, E-Mail: info@amfor.org, Web Site: www.americanforests. org (1)

Hutchins, Traver, Remedy Magazine, New York, NY. Tel: (212) 695-2223, FAX: (212) 695-2936, E-Mail: info@rmedizine.com, Web Site: www.medizine. com (17)

Hutchinson, Imogene Akins, Leadership Directories Inc, New York, NY. Tel: (212) 627-4140, FAX: (212) 645-0931, E-Mail: info@leadershipdirectories.com, Web Site: www.leadershipdirectories.com (17)

Hutchinson, R. Kenneth, University of Missouri, Columbia, MO. Tel: (573) 882-6333, (800) 856-2181, FAX: (573) 882-2721, E-Mail: visitus@missouri. edu, Web Site: www.missouri.edu (41)

Hutchinson, Theresa, Accounting with Debits and Credits with Coates & Hutchinson PC, Odenton, MD. Tel: (410) 672-6339, (800) 833-5933, FAX: (301) 912-3364, E-Mail: info@awdc.org (14)

Hutchison, Kristi, Big Brothers Big Sisters of Greater Kansas City, Kansas City, MO. Tel: (816) 561-5269, FAX: (816) 561-5273, Web Site: www. bigbrothersbigsisterskc.org (1)

Hutney, Beverly, The Stelter Co, Des Moines, IA. Tel: (800) 331-6881 (20)

Hutsen, Yogi, Coastal Hotel Group, Bellevue, WA. Tel: (206) 388-0400, FAX: (206) 388-0401, E-Mail: info@coastalhotel.com, Web Site: www. coastalhotels.com (1)

Hutson, Daryl, InteliSpend Prepaid Solutions, Fenton, MO. Tel: (888) 234-7725, E-Mail: saleads@ intelispend.com, Web Site: www.my.intelispend. com (5)

Hutton, Scotti, ActionAid, Washington, DC. Tel: (202) 835-1240, E-Mail: info@actionaid.org, Web Site: www.actionaidusa.org (1)

Huvar, Jeff, The Print Box Inc, Brooklyn, NY. Tel: (212) 741-1381, (800) 546-4011, FAX: (212) 463-9071, E-Mail: info@promobrands.com, Web Site: www.promobrands.com (33)

Huxta, Wendy, Current USA Inc, Colorado Springs, CO. Tel: (719) 594-4100, (877) 665-4458, FAX: (719) 531-2283, Web Site: www.currentinc.com (6)

Huyser, Karen, Thorndike Press, Waterville, ME. Tel: (207) 859-1000, (800) 223-1244, E-Mail: gale. salesassistance@cengage.com, Web Site: www. galegroup.com (17)

Hwang, Lawrence, SECO-LARM USA Inc, Irvine, CA. Tel: (949) 261-2999, (800) 662-0800, FAX: (949) 261-7326, E-Mail: info@seco-larm.com, Web Site: www.seco-larm.com (16)

Hy Cite Corp, Madison, WI. Tel: (608) 273-3373, (877) 494-2289, FAX: (608) 273-0936, Web Site: www. hycite.com (16)

HY-KO Products Co, Northfield, OH. Tel: (330) 467-7446, Web Site: www.hy-ko.com (16)

Hyatt Fruit Co, Vero Beach, FL. Tel: (772) 567-3766, (866) 991-8889, FAX: (772) 567-0973, Web Site: www.hyattfruitco.com (4)

Hyatt Hotels Corp, Chicago, IL. Tel: (312) 750-1234, FAX: (312) 780-5289, Web Site: www.hyatt.com (16)

Hyatt Legal Plans Inc, Cleveland, OH. Tel: (216) 241-0022, FAX: (216) 694-4305, Web Site: www. legalplans.com (16)

Hyatt, Caitlin, Direct Gardening Association, La Grange, GA. Tel: (706) 298-0022, FAX: (706) 883-8215, Web Site: www.directgardeningassociation. com (1)

Hyde, Bill, Duffey Petrosky, Farmington Hills, MI. Tel: (248) 489-8300, FAX: (248) 994-1600, Web Site: www.duffeypetrosky.com (35)

Hydra Group LLC, Los Angeles, CA. Tel: (310) 526-6680, FAX: (310) 526-6682, Web Site: www. hydragroup.com (9)

Hygienic Fabrics & Filters Inc, Sheboygan, WI. Tel: (920) 457-7383, (800) 876-2009, FAX: (920) 457-2558, Web Site: www.hyfab.com (16)

The Hyiad Group, Garden City, NY. Tel: (516) 433-3800, FAX: (516) 822-6670, Web Site: www. thehyiadgroup.com (22)

Hylton, Annie, City of Cerritos, Cerritos, CA. Tel: (562) 916-1319, Web Site: www.ci.cerritos.ca.us (1)

Hylton, Christa, USA Weekend, New York, NY. Tel: (800) 487-4956, FAX: (703) 854-2122, Web Site: www.usaweekend.com (31)

Hyman's, Hanahan, SC. Tel: (843) 571-7870, (800) 354-9626, FAX: (843) 571-7575, E-Mail: support@ hymans.com, Web Site: www.hymans.com (2)

Hyme, Mier, Hyman's, Hanahan, SC. Tel: (843) 571-7870, (800) 354-9626, FAX: (843) 571-7575, E-Mail: support@hymans.com, Web Site: www. hymans.com (2)

Hynes, Bryan, Austin & Williams, Hauppauge, NY. Tel: (631) 938-2279, FAX: (212) 434-7022, E-Mail: info@austin-williams.com, Web Site: www.austin-williams.com (2)

Hynes, Tom, Ellis Systems Corp, Lake Forest, IL. Tel: (847) 371-0200, (800) 253-5547, FAX: (847) 371-0202, E-Mail: tom@ellisfiling.com, Web Site: www.ellismh.com (9)

Hyson, Kevin, National Enquirer, New York, NY. Tel: (212) 545-4800, Web Site: www.nationalenquirer. com (17)

Hyzy, Brian, Personal Creations, Lemont, IL. Tel: (630) 783-2400, (866) 834-7695, Web Site: www. personalcreations.com (6)

I

I-Behavior Inc, Louisville, CO. Tel: (303) 228-5000, E-Mail: ib-sales@i-behavior.com, Web Site: www.i-behavior.com (23)

IAEE Expo! Expo! Annual Meeting and Exhibition, Dallas, TX. Tel: (972) 458-8002, FAX: (972) 458-8119, E-Mail: info@iaee.com, Web Site: www.iaee. com (42)

IBM Corp, Armonk, NY. Tel: (914) 765-1900, FAX: (914) 765-6633, Web Site: www.ibm.com (16)

IC International, Hicksville, NY. Tel: (516) 479-2200, (800) 631-0209, FAX: (516) 479-2215, E-Mail: info@ic-mr.com, Web Site: www.ic-mr.com (30)

IC System Inc, Saint Paul, MN. Tel: (800) 443-4123, Web Site: www.icsystem.com (20)

ICF Olson, Minneapolis, MN. Tel: (612) 215-9800, FAX: (612) 215-9801, E-Mail: info@olson.com, Web Site: www.olson.com (35)

ICIS Inc, Upper Black Eddy, PA. Tel: (610) 982-0429, E-Mail: icis@ptdprolog.net, Web Site: www. icisjewelry.com (2)

ICMA Retirement Corp, Washington, DC. Tel: (202) 962-4600, (800) 669-7400, FAX: (202) 962-4601, E-Mail: investorservices@icmarc.org, Web Site: www.icmarc.org (14)

ICS Corp, West Deptford, NJ. Tel: (215) 427-3355, E-Mail: mefstathios@ics-corporation.com, Web Site: www.ics-corporation.com (21)

ICS Marketing Services, Lansing, MI. Tel: (517) 394-1890, (888) 394-1890, FAX: (517) 394-7408, E-Mail: sales@icshq.com, Web Site: icshq.com (21)

IDC, Ltd, Henderson, NV. Tel: (702) 450-1000, FAX: (702) 450-1020, E-Mail: info@goidc.com, Web Site: www.goidc.com (1)

IDG Enterprise, Framingham, MA. Tel: (508) 872-0080, Web Site: www.idgenterprise.com (17)

IDG List Services, Framingham, MA. Tel: (508) 766-5633, E-Mail: stozeski@idglist.com, Web Site: www.idglist.com (24)

IDG World Expo, Framingham, MA. Tel: (508) 879-0700, E-Mail: info@idgworldexpo.com, Web Site: www.idgworldexpo.com (42)

IDM Inc, Reston, VA. Tel: (703) 547-4961, E-Mail: info@integrated-dm.com, Web Site: www.idm.us. com (23)

IDMS Inc, Melville, NY. Tel: (631) 249-7744, (800) 582-5831, FAX: (631) 249-4425, E-Mail: sales@ idmsinc.com, Web Site: www.idmsinc.com (16)

IDR Marketing Partners LLC, Berwyn, PA. Tel: (610) 993-0500, FAX: (610) 993-9938, E-Mail: idr@ idronline.com, Web Site: www.idronline.com (23)

The IDT Group, Philadelphia, PA. Tel: (215) 487-4420, FAX: (215) 487-3110, Web Site: www. idthospitality.com (22)

IEEE Media, New York, NY. Tel: (800) 261-2052, E-Mail: ieeemedia@ieeeglobalspec.com, Web Site: advertise.ieee.org (24)

The IEI Corp, Princeton, NJ. Tel: (609) 987-2700, FAX: (609) 987-2703 (6)

Ifbyphone, Chicago, IL. Tel: (877) 295-5100, (877) 387-7192, Web Site: www.ifbyphone.com (30)

IHFRA, High Point, NC. Tel: (336) 889-3920, FAX: (336) 464-2125, E-Mail: ihfra@ihfra.org, Web Site: www.ihfra.org (1)

IHS Markit, Englewood, CO. Tel: (303) 858-6187, (800) 447-2273, Web Site: www.ihs.com (17)

IJHANA, Los Angeles, CA. Tel: (213) 268-4283, (888) 421-9222, E-Mail: info@ijhana.com, Web Site: www.ijhana.com (20)

IMA Executive Summit, Minneapolis, MN. Tel: (952) 928-4649, E-Mail: info@incentivemarketing.com, Web Site: www.incentivemarketing.com (42)

IMC Direct, Honolulu, HI. Tel: (808) 545-1680, FAX: (808) 528-4293, E-Mail: vfujita@imcdm.com (35)

IMC - Multi Media Marketing, Jenkintown, PA. Tel: (215) 887-5700 X107, FAX: (215) 887-7076, E-Mail: berylwolk@aol.com, Web Site: berylsworld.com (31)

IMN, Waltham, MA. Tel: (781) 672-7000, (866) 964-6397, FAX: (781) 890-4701, E-Mail: support@imninc.com, Web Site: www.imninc.com (32)

IMSI/Design LLC, Novato, CA. Tel: (415) 483-8000, (800) 833-4674, FAX: (415) 884-9023, Web Site: www.imsidesign.com (34)

IMV, Des Plaines, IL. Tel: (847) 297-1404, FAX: (847) 297-5010, E-Mail: sales@imvinfo.com, Web Site: www.imvlimited.com (20)

INC Magazine, New York, NY. Tel: (212) 389-5377, FAX: (617) 248-8090, E-Mail: mail@inc.com, Web Site: www.inc.com (17)

ING, Minneapolis, MN. Tel: (612) 342-7061, (800) 333-6965, FAX: (612) 372-5339, Web Site: www.ing.com (15)

ING USA Annuity & Life Ins Co, Des Moines, IA. Tel: (515) 698-7100, FAX: (515) 698-2001, Web Site: www.ing-usa.com (15)

INSP LLC, Charlotte, NC. Tel: (803) 578-1000, FAX: (803) 578-1725, E-Mail: info@insp.com, Web Site: www.insp.com (32)

INTX - The Internet & Televison Expo, Washington, DC. Tel: (202) 222-2430, FAX: (202) 222-2431, E-Mail: infointx@ncta.com, Web Site: www.intxshow.com (42)

INX International Ink Co, Schaumburg, IL. Tel: (800) 631-7956, FAX: (847) 969-9758, E-Mail: info@inxink.com, Web Site: www.inxinternational.com (16)

IPD Co Inc, Portland, OR. Tel: (503) 257-7500, (800) 444-6473, FAX: (503) 257-7596, E-Mail: info@ipdusa.com, Web Site: www.ipdusa.com (12)

IPD Printing & Distributing Inc, Atlanta, GA. Tel: (770) 458-6351, FAX: (770) 454-6236, Web Site: www.rrdonnelley.com (27)

IPG, New York, NY. Tel: (646) 229-2255 (20)

IPS - Sendero Corp, Norcross, GA. Tel: (480) 941-8112, (800) 879-1996, FAX: (770) 409-1735, E-Mail: sales@ips-sendero.com, Web Site: www.ips-sendero.com (14)

IQ Agency, Atlanta, GA. Tel: (404) 255-3550, E-Mail: newbiz@iqagency.com, Web Site: iqagency.com (35)

IRPP, Montreal, QC Canada. Tel: (514) 985-2461, FAX: (514) 985-2559, E-Mail: irpp@irpp.org, Web Site: www.irpp.org (30)

ISA International Sign Expo, Alexandria, VA. Tel: (703) 836-4012, FAX: (703) 836-8353, Web Site: signexpo.org (42)

ISA-The International Society of Automation, Research Triangle Park, NC. Tel: (919) 549-8411, FAX: (919) 549-8288, E-Mail: info@isa.org, Web Site: www.isa.org (1)

ITAGroup, West Des Moines, IA. Tel: (800) 257-1985, E-Mail: drivenbyloyalty@itagroup.com, Web Site: www.itagroup.com (33)

ITT Educational Services Inc, Carmel, IN. Tel: (317) 706-9200, Web Site: www.ittesi.com (16)

ITW Bee Leitzke, Iron Ridge, WI. Tel: (920) 625-2342, FAX: (920) 625-2643, Web Site: www.itwbeeleitzke.com (16)

ITW Vortec, Cincinnati, OH. Tel: (513) 891-7474, (800) 441-7475, FAX: (513) 891-4092, E-Mail: techsupport@vortec.com, Web Site: www.vortec.com (16)

IWCO Direct, Chanhassen, MN. Tel: (952) 474-0961, FAX: (952) 474-6467, Web Site: www.iwco.com (21)

IZEA, Orlando, FL. Tel: (321) 332-6830, Web Site: www.izea.com (20)

Iaccarino, Michael, Infogroup, Papillion, NE. Tel: (402) 836-5290, E-Mail: contentfeedback@infogroup.com, Web Site: www.infogroup.com (32)

Iacobacci, Charlene, Jaz Holdings LLC, Liberty Corner, NJ. Tel: (973) 574-7600, (800) 999-9554, FAX: (973) 944-5073, E-Mail: webmaster@regentbook.com, Web Site: www.regentbook.com (16)

The Iams Co, Mason, OH. Tel: (800) 675-3849, Web Site: www.iams.com (16)

Iannaccone, Dominick, Advertising Distributors of America Inc, Ronkonkoma, NY. Tel: (631) 231-5700, FAX: (631) 434-1063 (21)

Iannini, Robert E., Information Unlimited Inc, Mont Vernon, NH. Tel: (603) 673-4730, (800) 221-1705, FAX: (603) 672-5406, E-Mail: wako2@xtdl.com, Web Site: www.amazing1.com (11)

Iaquinto, Kevin, JDA Software Group Inc, Scottsdale, AZ. Tel: (480) 308-3000, (800) 479-7382, FAX: (480) 308-3001, E-Mail: info@jda.com, Web Site: www.jda.com (22)

Iazzetto, Joe, Unicom Marketing Group Inc, Broadview, IL. Tel: (312) 738-1404, FAX: (312) 738-1405 (35)

Ibarra, Jose, RG Barry Corp, Pickerington, OH. Tel: (614) 864-6400, (800) 848-7560, FAX: (614) 866-9787, E-Mail: sales@rgbarry.com, Web Site: www.rgbarry.com (2)

Ibis Communications Inc, Nashville, TN. Tel: (615) 777-1900, FAX: (615) 777-1906, E-Mail: mhowland@ibiscommunications.com, Web Site: www.ibiscommunications.com (35)

IBSDirect, King of Prussia, PA. Tel: (610) 265-8210, FAX: (610) 265-7997, Web Site: www.ibsdm.com (27)

Ice, Carl R., Burlington Northern & Santa Fe LLC, Fort Worth, TX. Tel: (817) 878-2000, (800) 795-2673, FAX: (817) 333-7593, Web Site: www.bnsf.com (16)

IClimber Inc, Burbank, CA. Tel: (818) 567-3030, Web Site: www.iclimber.com (16)

The Icon, Los Angeles, CA. Tel: (323) 933-1666, E-Mail: icon@iconia.com, Web Site: www.iconia.com (37)

Icon Marketing Communications, Fort Mitchell, KY. Tel: (859) 647-7271, FAX: (859) 647-0615, E-Mail: shawn@iconmc.com, Web Site: iconmc.com (21)

Icon Media Direct Inc, Sherman Oaks, CA. Tel: (818) 995-6400, FAX: (818) 995-6405, E-Mail: info@iconmediadirect.com, Web Site: www.iconmediadirect.com (35)

iContact LLC, Morrisville, NC. Tel: (919) 820-7837, (877) 820-7837, E-Mail: sales@icontact.com, Web Site: www.icontact.com (32)

iCrossing, New York, NY. Tel: (212) 649-3900, FAX: (646) 280-1091, Web Site: www.icrossing.com (32)

Idea Art Inc, Colorado Springs, CO. Tel: (719) 594-4100, (800) 433-2278, FAX: (719) 534-6313, E-Mail: customerservice@ideaart.com, Web Site: www.ideaart.com (25)

I/D/E/A Inc, Caldwell, ID. Tel: (208) 459-6357, (800) 635-9261, FAX: (208) 459-6484, Web Site: www.relyonidea.com (16)

Ideagroup Mail Service, Saint Paul, MN. Tel: (651) 490-2903, FAX: (651) 490-0728, E-Mail: ideagroup@visi.com (28)

Ideal Industries (Canada) Corp, Ajax, ON Canada. Tel: (905) 683-3400, (800) 824-3325, FAX: (905) 683-0209, E-Mail: nick.shkordoff@idealindustries.com, Web Site: www.idealindustries.com (9)

Ideal Industries Inc, Sycamore, IL. Tel: (815) 895-5181, (800) 435-0705, FAX: (815) 895-4800, E-Mail: ideal_industries@idealindustries.com, Web Site: www.idealindustries.com (16)

Idealliance, Alexandria, VA. Tel: (703) 837-1070, FAX: (703) 837-1072 (40)

Ideals Publications Inc, Nashville, TN. Tel: (615) 333-0478, FAX: (615) 781-1447, Web Site: www.idealspublications.com (17)

Idearc Media Corp, Dallas, TX. Tel: (972) 453-7797 (16)

Ideas in SEO, Miami, FL. Tel: (786) 280-6051 (20)

Ideas To Go Inc, Minneapolis, MN. Tel: (612) 331-1570, FAX: (612) 331-1602, E-Mail: cebert@ideastogo.com, Web Site: www.ideastogo.com (30)

iDfour, Houston, TX. Tel: (281) 497-7606, FAX: (281) 497-7616, E-Mail: scotthaney@interdirectusa.com, Web Site: www.idfour.com (21)

Idowu, Olajire, Narrow Way, Lafayette, CA. Tel: (925) 283-4074 (6)

Iglehart, John, Health Affairs, Bethesda, MD. Tel: (301) 656-7401, FAX: (301) 654-2845, Web Site: www.healthaffairs.org (17)

Ignatius, Adi, Harvard Business Review, Boston, MA. Tel: (617) 783-7410, FAX: (617) 783-7493, Web Site: hbr.org (17)

Ignition Network, Chicago, IL. Tel: (312) 893-5000, E-Mail: inquiries@ignitionnetwork.com, Web Site: www.ignitionnetwork.com (35)

Iida, Yaz, LinkShare Corp, New York, NY. Tel: (646) 943-8200, FAX: (646) 943-8204, Web Site: www.linkshare.com (32)

iKnowtion LLC, Burlington, MA. Tel: (781) 494-9989, Web Site: www.iknowtion.com (20)

Ikon Communications Consultants Inc, Wellesley, MA. Tel: (781) 237-6060, FAX: (781) 235-3504, E-Mail: info@ikoncommunications.com, Web Site: www.ikoncommunications.com (35)

Ilardi, Marco, Adknowledge, Kansas City, MO. Tel: (816) 931-1771, (866) 730-2109, Web Site: www.adknowledge.com (32)

Illy Caffe North America, Rye Brook, NY. Tel: (914) 253-4500, (877) 469-4559, E-Mail: info@illyusa.com, Web Site: www.illyusa.com (4)

Illy, Andrea, Illy Caffe North America, Rye Brook, NY. Tel: (914) 253-4500, (877) 469-4559, E-Mail: info@illyusa.com, Web Site: www.illyusa.com (4)

iLoop Mobile Inc, San Jose, CA. Tel: (408) 907-3360, Web Site: www.iloopmobile.com (16)

Iltis, Carolee E., Ford Foundation Office of Communications, New York, NY. Tel: (212) 573-5000, E-Mail: office-of-communications@fordfound.org, Web Site: www.fordfound.org (5)

The Image Bank, New York, NY. Tel: (646) 613-4000, FAX: (646) 613-4601, Web Site: www.gettyimages.com (38)

Image Checks, Bel Air, MD. Tel: (800) 562-8768, FAX: (410) 676-8269, Web Site: www.imagechecks.com (27)

Image Makers Marketing Inc, Marietta, GA. Tel: (770) 926-9552, FAX: (770) 926-9558, E-Mail: elaine. gossett@immmail.com, Web Site: www. imagemakersmarketing.com (21)

Image Photos/Clemens Kalischer, Stockbridge, MA. Tel: (413) 298-5500, FAX: (413) 298-5500, E-Mail: inform@bcn.net (38)

The Image Works Inc, Woodstock, NY. Tel: (845) 679-8500, (800) 475-8801, FAX: (845) 679-0606, E-Mail: info@theimageworks.com, Web Site: www. theimageworks.com (38)

Imagination Works, Trumbull, CT. Tel: (203) 377-1747, FAX: (203) 377-7401, E-Mail: jim@ imaginationworks.net, Web Site: www. imaginationworks.net (20)

Imagine Fulfillment Services, La Mirada, CA. Tel: (310) 217-4610, FAX: (310) 217-9632, E-Mail: andya@imaginefulfillment.com, Web Site: www. imaginefulfillment.com (28)

Imagine 360 Marketing, New York, NY. Tel: (212) 313-9616, Web Site: www.i360m.com (20)

iMarketing Solutions Group Inc, Milwaukee, WI. Tel: (414) 224-0701, (800) 879-0076, FAX: (414) 224-0943, Web Site: imarketingsolutionsgroup.com (29)

Imber, Jane, Gorsuch Ltd, Vail, CO. Tel: (970) 476-2294, (800) 525-9808, FAX: (970) 476-4323, Web Site: www.gorsuchltd.com (2)

Imbriani, Jennifer, Jenco Productions Inc, San Bernardino, CA. Tel: (909) 381-9453, FAX: (909) 383-1106, Web Site: www.jencoproductions.com (28)

Imbriani, Roger, Jenco Productions Inc, San Bernardino, CA. Tel: (909) 381-9453, FAX: (909) 383-1106, Web Site: www.jencoproductions.com (28)

Imbrogno, Karen, Insurance.com, Solon, OH. Tel: (440) 715-0075, Web Site: www.insurance.com (15)

Imig, Gary, Sierra Trading Post, Cheyenne, WY. Tel: (800) 713-4534, FAX: (800) 378-8946, E-Mail: customerservice@sierratradingpost.com, Web Site: www.sierratradingpost.com (2)

Immelt, Jeffrey R., GE Partnership Marketing Group, Schaumburg, IL. Tel: (847) 605-3000, FAX: (847) 605-3044, Web Site: www.gepmg.com (14)

Immelt, Jeffrey R., General Electric Co, Fairfield, CT. Tel: (203) 373-2211, FAX: (203) 373-3131, Web Site: www.ge.com (16)

Immergluck, Phillip S., PSI Marketing Consultants Inc, Rolling Meadows, IL. Tel: (773) 878-0800, (800) 933-4774, FAX: (773) 878-4219 (29)

Impact Communications Inc, Long Grove, IL. Tel: (847) 438-4480, E-Mail: info@ impactcommunicationsinc.com, Web Site: www. impactcommunicationsinc.com (32)

IMPACT International Marketing, Lake Havasu City, AZ. Tel: (866) 389-9798, E-Mail: sales@iimgroup. com, Web Site: iimgroup.com (35)

Impact Mailing, Minneapolis, MN. Tel: (612) 521-6245, FAX: (612) 521-1349, E-Mail: sales@ impactmailing.com, Web Site: www.impactmailing. com (28)

IMPACT Publishing Inc, Bradenton, FL. Tel: (941) 739-2611, (800) 4-A-NEW-ME, FAX: (941) 756-0315, Web Site: www.potentialsunlimited.com (17)

Impact Ratings Inc, Newtown, PA. Tel: (610) 353-8311, FAX: (610) 353-8311 (30)

Imperial Supplies, Green Bay, WI. Tel: (920) 494-5403, (800) 558-2808, FAX: (800) 553-8769, Web Site: www.imperialsupplies.com (16)

Impressions Direct, Saint Louis, MO. Tel: (314) 951-2100, Web Site: www.impressions-direct.com (28)

Impressions Unlimited Inc, Deerfield, IL. Tel: (630) 705-6464, FAX: (630) 705-1598, E-Mail: info@ impressionsunltd.com, Web Site: www. impressionsunltd.com (27)

Improvements, West Chester, OH. Tel: (800) 634-9484, Web Site: www.improvementscatalog.com (8)

iN DEMAND LLC, New York, NY. Tel: (646) 638-8200, FAX: (646) 486-0855, Web Site: www. indemand.com (32)

In-Sync Publications, Redondo Beach, CA. Tel: (310) 543-9045, FAX: (310) 543-9035, E-Mail: insyncpubs@aol.com, Web Site: www.insyncpubs. com (18)

In Touch Ministries, Atlanta, GA. Tel: (800) 789-1473, Web Site: www.intouch.org (1)

Inaba, Yoshima, Toyota Motor Sales USA Inc, Torrance, CA. Tel: (310) 468-4000, (800) 331-4331, FAX: (310) 468-7841, Web Site: www.toyota.com (16)

Incentive Associates Inc, Overland Park, KS. Tel: (913) 722-2848, E-Mail: incentiveassociate@sbcglobal.net (33)

Incentive Manufacturers Representatives Association (IMRA), Naperville, IL. Tel: (630) 369-7786, FAX: (630) 369-3773, E-Mail: nicole@ incentivemarketing.org, Web Site: www.imraonline. org (40)

Incept Corp, Canton, OH. Tel: (330) 649-8000, Web Site: www.inceptcorp.com (29)

Inchcoombe, Steven, Nature Publishing Group, New York, NY. Tel: (212) 726-9200, FAX: (212) 696-9006, Web Site: www.nature.com (17)

INCOMPAS Show, Washington, DC. Tel: (202) 296-6650, FAX: (202) 296-7585, Web Site: show. incompas.org (42)

Indenbaum, Laurie, Rubber Stamps of America, Dublin, NH. Tel: (800) 553-5031, FAX: (603) 563-8102, E-Mail: stampusa@verizon.net, Web Site: www. stampusa.com (6)

Independent Consultant, Saint Paul, MN. Tel: (612) 239-6572 (20)

Independent Insurance Agents & Brokers of America, Alexandria, VA. Tel: (703) 683-4422, (800) 221-7917, FAX: (703) 683-7556, E-Mail: info@iiaba. org, Web Site: www.iiaba.org (1)

Independent Living Aids, Buffalo, NY. Tel: (516) 450-3829, (800) 537-2118, FAX: (516) 937-3906, E-Mail: techsupport@independentliving.com, Web Site: www.independentliving.com (7)

Indian Arts & Crafts Association, Albuquerque, NM. Tel: (505) 265-9149, FAX: (505) 265-8251, E-Mail: info@iaca.com, Web Site: www.iaca.com (1)

Indian Country Today Media Network, New York, NY. Tel: (212) 600-2086, Web Site: www. indiancountrytodaymedianetwork.com (17)

Indian House Records & Tapes, Taos, NM. Tel: (575) 776-2953, (800) 748-0522, FAX: (575) 776-2804, E-Mail: music@indianhouse.com, Web Site: www. indianhouse.com (3)

Indianapolis Motor Speedway, Indianapolis, IN. Tel: (317) 492-8500, FAX: (317) 492-6571, Web Site: www.indianapolismotorspeedway.com (19)

Indianapolis Newspapers Inc, Indianapolis, IN. Tel: (317) 444-4444, FAX: (317) 633-9414, Web Site: www.indystar.com (17)

Indium Corp of America, Clinton, NY. Tel: (315) 853-4900, (800) 446-3486, FAX: (800) 221-5759, E-Mail: askus@indium.com, Web Site: www. indium.com (16)

Indoor Gardening Supplies, Dexter, MI. Tel: (800) 823-5740, Web Site: www.indoorgardensupplies.com (8)

Indrigo, Peter I., Unitron Ltd, Commack, NY. Tel: (631) 589-6666, FAX: (631) 589-6795, E-Mail: johnc@ unitronusa.com, Web Site: www.unitronusa.com (9)

Indros Group, Brooklyn, NY. Tel: (866) 463-7671, E-Mail: info@indrosgroup.com, Web Site: www. indrosgroup.com (35)

Indus-Tool, Chicago, IL. Tel: (312) 226-2473, (800) 662-5021, FAX: (312) 226-2480, E-Mail: sales@ indus-tool.com, Web Site: www.indus-tool.com (12)

Industrial Arts & Graphics, Middleburg, VA. Tel: (540) 687-6770, (866) 324-7746, FAX: (540) 687-4678, E-Mail: gdrex@industrialarts.us (27)

Industrial Instruments & Supplies Inc, Southampton, PA. Tel: (215) 396-0822, (800) 523-6079, FAX: (215) 396-0833, E-Mail: customerservice@iisusa. com, Web Site: www.iisusa.com (9)

Industrial Marketing Associates, Cranford, NJ. Tel: (908) 276-4256, E-Mail: ken@ industrialmarketingassociates.com, Web Site: www. industrialmarketingassociates.com (30)

Industrial Uniform Co Inc, Wichita, KS. Tel: (316) 264-2871, (800) 333-3666, FAX: (316) 264-2708, E-Mail: info@logodepotweb.com, Web Site: www. industrialuniform.com (2)

Infante, Peter, Butler Till Media Services, Rochester, NY. Tel: (855) 472-5100, FAX: (855) 274-5199, Web Site: www.butlertill.com (31)

Infantino, Bob, The Hanover Shoe Co, Newton, MA. Tel: (617) 964-1222, FAX: (617) 243-4210, Web Site: www.clarks.com (16)

Infantino, Robert, C & J Clark America Inc, Newton Upper Falls, MA. Tel: (617) 964-1222, (800) 925-4315, FAX: (617) 243-4213, Web Site: www.clarks. com (16)

Infinite Media Concepts Inc, White Plains, NY. Tel: (914) 948-8300, FAX: (914) 949-1605, Web Site: mailinglists.com (23)

Infinity Direct Inc, Plymouth, MN. Tel: (763) 559-1111, Web Site: www.infinitydirect.com (35)

Infinity Insurance Co, Birmingham, AL. Tel: (800) 527-5412, Web Site: www.infinityauto.com (15)

Infinity Trading Co Inc, Spring, TX. Tel: (281) 292-8509, FAX: (281) 931-8139, E-Mail: sales@ infinitytradingcompany.com, Web Site: www. infinitytradingcompany.com (34)

Influent Inc, Dublin, OH. Tel: (614) 280-1600, (800) 856-6768, FAX: (614) 280-1610, E-Mail: info@ influentinc.com, Web Site: www.influentinc.com (29)

InfoUSA, Papillion, NE. Tel: (800) 835-5856, Web Site: www.infousa.com (23)

InfoCanada, Mississauga, ON Canada. Tel: (800) 565-7224, FAX: (905) 803-7195, E-Mail: info@ infocanada.ca, Web Site: infogroup.infocanada.ca (23)

InfoCision Management Corp, Akron, OH. Tel: (330) 668-1400, FAX: (330) 668-1401, E-Mail: infocision@infocision.com, Web Site: www. infocision.com (29)

Infocore Inc, Carlsbad, CA. Tel: (760) 607-2500, FAX: (760) 607-2505, E-Mail: info@infocore.com, Web Site: www.infocore.com (23)

Infocus Marketing Inc, Warrenton, VA. Tel: (800) 708-5478, FAX: (866) 708-5478, E-Mail: sales@ infocusmarketing.com, Web Site: www. infocusmarketing.com (23)

Infogroup, Papillion, NE. Tel: (402) 836-5290, E-Mail: contentfeedback@infogroup.com, Web Site: www. infogroup.com (32)

Infogroup Media Solutions, Papillion, NE. Tel: (800) 223-2194, E-Mail: infogroupmediasolutions@ infogroup.com, Web Site: www. infogroupmediasolutions.com (23)

Infolure, Phoenix, AZ. Tel: (602) 308-6700, FAX: (602) 308-6801, E-Mail: glenn.gottfried@infolure.com, Web Site: www.infolure.com (22)

Infomart, Dallas, TX. Tel: (214) 800-8000, FAX: (214) 800-8100, Web Site: www.infomartusa.com (16)

InfoMat Inc, Torrance, CA. Tel: (310) 212-5944, FAX: (310) 212-3026, E-Mail: listmgr@infomatbiz.com, Web Site: www.infomatbiz.com (23)

Infomercial Monitoring Service Inc, West Chester, PA. Tel: (610) 328-6902, FAX: (610) 328-6791, E-Mail: catanese@imstv.com, Web Site: www.imstv.com (20)

Infomercial Sales Inc, Las Vegas, NV. Tel: (702) 253-0433, FAX: (702) 871-0759, Web Site: www. infomercialsalesinc.com (32)

Infomercial Solutions Inc, Agoura Hills, CA. Tel: (818) 879-1140, FAX: (818) 879-1148, E-Mail: david@ infomercialsolutions.com, Web Site: www. infomercialsolutions.com (32)

Infomorphosis/Marketing Solutions, New York, NY. Tel: (212) 366-6216, FAX: (212) 255-4784, E-Mail: dfain@nyc.rr.com (20)

Infor, Alpharetta, GA. Tel: (678) 319-8000, Web Site: www.infor.com (22)

Informal Education Products, Milwaukie, OR. Tel: (503) 794-7045, (888) 444-5500, FAX: (503) 794-7111, E-Mail: sales@museumtour.com, Web Site: www.museumtour.com (11)

Information Command Inc, Chicago, IL. Tel: (312) 245-1111, (800) 376-6654, FAX: (312) 245-1128, E-Mail: gon@phonebiz2000.com, Web Site: www. info2u.com (22)

The Information Engine, Bradenton, FL. Tel: (904) 645-6000, Web Site: www.informationeng.com (22)

Information for Public Affairs, Inc, Sacramento, CA. Tel: (916) 444-0840, (800) 726-4566, FAX: (916) 446-5369, E-Mail: info@statenet.com, Web Site: www.statenet.com (17)

The Information Refinery Inc, Mahwah, NJ. Tel: (201) 529-2600, (800) 529-9020, FAX: (201) 529-4030, E-Mail: info@inforefinery.com, Web Site: inforefinery.com (24)

Information Resources Inc, Chicago, IL. Tel: (312) 726-1221, FAX: (312(726-8214, Web Site: www. infores.com (30)

Information Sources Inc, Walnut Creek, CA. Tel: (510) 525-6220, FAX: (510) 525-1568, Web Site: www. tectrends.com (22)

Information Unlimited Inc, Mont Vernon, NH. Tel: (603) 673-4730, (800) 221-1705, FAX: (603) 672-5406, E-Mail: wako2@xtdl.com, Web Site: www. amazing1.com (11)

Informed Sources Inc, Plainview, NY. Tel: (800) 201-6060, FAX: (516) 576-0249, E-Mail: info@ informed-sources.com, Web Site: www.informed-sources.com (30)

Inforonics Global Services LLC, Littleton, MA. Tel: (315) 261-7525, FAX: (978) 698-7500, E-Mail: info@inforonics.com, Web Site: www.inforonics. com (22)

InfoSource Inc, Oviedo, FL. Tel: (407) 796-5200, (800) 393-4636, FAX: (407) 796-5190, E-Mail: isisale@ howtomaster.com, Web Site: www. infosourcelearning.com (3)

Infotrends Inc, Weymouth, MA. Tel: (781) 616-2100, FAX: (781) 616-2121, E-Mail: info@infotrends. com, Web Site: www.infotrends.com (35)

Infutor Data Solutions, Oakbrook Terrace, IL. Tel: (312) 348-7900, E-Mail: sales@infutor.com, Web Site: www.infutor.com (23)

Ingber, Ellen, Larry Fox & Co Ltd, Valley Stream, NY. Tel: (516) 791-7929, (800) 397-7923, FAX: (516) 791-1022, E-Mail: larry@larryfox.com, Web Site: www.larryfox.com (16)

Ingebritson, Britt, Williamson-Dickie Manufacturing Co, Fort Worth, TX. Tel: (800) 336-7201, FAX: (817) 877-5027, E-Mail: customerservice@dickies. com, Web Site: www.dickies.com (2)

Ingenio LLC, San Francisco, CA. Tel: (877) 529-1193, Web Site: www.ingenio.com (32)

Ingenito, Alphonse, Enertex Marketing, New York, NY. Tel: (212) 532-3115, FAX: (212) 532-1878, E-Mail: info@enertexmarketing.com, Web Site: www. enertexmarketing.com (22)

Ingersoll, John, Farmers Insurance, Los Angeles, CA. Tel: (410) 338-1613, (410) 366-1000, (800) 327-6377, FAX: (410) 554-1926, Web Site: www. farmers.com (15)

Inglis, John, Cold Spring Harbor Lab Press, Woodbury, NY. Tel: (516) 422-4100, (800) 843-4388, FAX: (516) 422-4097, E-Mail: cshpress@cshl.edu, Web Site: www.cshlpress.com (17)

Ingram Book Group, La Vergne, TN. Tel: (615) 793-5000, (800) 937-8000, FAX: (800) 876-0186, Web Site: www.ipage.ingrambook.com (16)

Ingram, Ardith, Business Automation Systems Inc, Nashville, TN. Tel: (615) 329-4585, FAX: (615) 320-0206, Web Site: www.bas-solutions.com (16)

Ingram, Barbara, Solarcom, Norcross, GA. Tel: (770) 449-6116, (888) SUN-DATA, FAX: (770) 448-7726, Web Site: www.solarcom.net (16)

Ingram, Chip, Walk Thru The Bible Ministries Inc, Nor-cross, GA. Tel: (770) 458-9300, (800) 361-6131, Web Site: www.walkthru.org (1)

Ingram, Mark A., CSPI/Nutrition Action Health Letter, Washington, DC. Tel: (202) 332-9110, FAX: (202) 265-4954, E-Mail: cspi@cspinet.org, Web Site: www.cspinet.org (17)

Ingram, Raymond E., Business Automation Systems Inc, Nashville, TN. Tel: (615) 329-4585, FAX: (615) 320-0206, Web Site: www.bas-solutions.com (16)

Initiative, New York, NY. Tel: (212) 605-7000, FAX: (212) 605-7200, Web Site: www.initiative.com (32)

Inkwell Inc, Cresco, PA. Tel: (570) 595-5344, E-Mail: philip@inkwellinc.com (36)

Inland Press, Detroit, MI. Tel: (313) 961-6000, FAX: (313) 961-7817, Web Site: www.inlandpress.com (27)

Inmar, Winston-Salem, NC. Tel: (336) 631-2500, FAX: (336) 631-2888, E-Mail: ibizdev@inmar.com, Web Site: www.promotionslogistics.com (14)

InnerWorkings Inc, Chicago, IL. Tel: (317) 642-3700, (866) 766-5176, E-Mail: info@inwk.com, Web Site: www.inwk.com (35)

Innis Maggiore Group Inc, Canton, OH. Tel: (330) 492-5500, (800) 460-4111, FAX: (330) 492-5568, E-Mail: dick@innismaggiore.com, Web Site: www. innismaggiore.com (35)

Innotrac Corp, Duluth, GA. Tel: (678) 584-4000, FAX: (678) 475-5840, Web Site: www.innotrac.com (23)

Innovaire Communications LLC, Cherry Hill, NJ. Tel: (856) 663-2500, E-Mail: info@innovairre.com, Web Site: www.innovairre.com (35)

The Innovation Machine, Chicago, IL. Tel: (312) 238-9362, E-Mail: contact@theinnovationmachine.com, Web Site: www.theinnovationmachine.com (1)

Innovation Printing Inc, Philadelphia, PA. Tel: (215) 969-4600, FAX: (215) 464-7664, Web Site: www. innovationprinting.com (27)

Innovative Industries Inc, Carthage, MO. Tel: (417) 358-6891, (800) 344-7467, FAX: (417) 358-1849, E-Mail: info@innovativeindustries.com, Web Site: www.innovativeindustries.com (28)

Innovative Marketing Direct Inc, Tampa, FL. Tel: (813) 873-7909, FAX: (813) 873-7918, E-Mail: mail@ innovativedirectmail.com, Web Site: www. innovativedirectmail.com (21)

Innovative Marketing Services Inc, Houston, TX. Tel: (281) 398-0321, (800) 231-4678, FAX: (281) 398-0679, E-Mail: mfisher@imstcorp.com, Web Site: www.imstcorp.com (30)

Innovative Marketing Solutions LLC, Bangor, ME. Tel: (207) 262-6233, Web Site: www.imsmaine.net (29)

Innovative Packaging of Westchester, Spring Valley, NY. Tel: (845) 364-9500 (26)

Innovative Plastic Printing Corp, Roselle, IL. Tel: (630) 539-4400, (800) 238-7686, FAX: (630) 529-2109, E-Mail: dan@innov8cards.com, Web Site: www. innov8cards.com (27)

Innovative Systems Inc, Pittsburgh, PA. Tel: (412) 937-9300, (800) 622-6390, FAX: (412) 937-9309, E-Mail: info@innovativesystems.com, Web Site: www.innovativesystems.com (22)

Innovyx Inc, Seattle, WA. Tel: (206) 674-8720, Web Site: www.innovyx.com (32)

Input Systems Inc, Paramount, CA. Tel: (562) 634-1170, (800) 327-9337, FAX: (562) 634-0993, E-Mail: info@sweepssoftware.com, Web Site: www.sweepssoftware.com (22)

Inquiry Intelligence Systems, O'Fallon, MO. Tel: (636) 240-1800, (800) 467-2329, FAX: (636) 281-1517, E-Mail: sales@iqsalespro.com, Web Site: www. inquiry-tracking.com (22)

Insetta, Bob, ArcelorMittal, Coatesville, PA. Tel: (610) 383-2000, FAX: (610) 383-5036, Web Site: www. arcelormittal.com (1)

Inside Direct Mail, Philadelphia, PA. Tel: (215) 238-5300, (800) 777-8074, FAX: (215) 238-5412, E-Mail: customservice@napco.com, Web Site: www.insidedirectmail.com (43)

Insight Direct Inc, Tempe, AZ. Tel: (480) 333-3001, (800) 467-4448, FAX: (480) 902-1180, Web Site: www.insight.com (16)

Insight Out of Chaos, New York, NY. Tel: (212) 935-0044, FAX: (212) 742-0469, E-Mail: info@iooc. com, Web Site: www.iooc.com (22)

Insolia, Spencer, Drs Foster & Smith Inc, Rhinelander, WI. Tel: (715) 369-3305, Web Site: www. drsfostersmith.com (2)

The Inspiration Networks, Charlotte, NC. Tel: (704) 561-7872, (803) 578-1000, FAX: (803) 578-1735, Web Site: www.insptoday.com (1)

Institute for International Research Inc, New York, NY. Tel: (212) 661-3500, (800) 345-8016, FAX: (212) 599-2192, E-Mail: register@iirusa.com, Web Site: www.iir-ny.com (16)

Institute For Natural Resources, Concord, CA. Tel: (925) 687-0860, FAX: (925) 609-2820, E-Mail: dcheung@biocorp.com (16)

Institute for Student Achievement, Carle Place, NY. Tel: (516) 812-6700, Web Site: www. studentachievement.org (1)

Institute Lists, Portland, OR. Tel: (917) 751-8439, E-Mail: info@institutelists.com, Web Site: institutelists.com (24)

Institute of Business Forecasting, Great Neck, NY. Tel: (516) 504-7576, E-Mail: info@ibf.org, Web Site: www.ibf.org (1)

Institute of Management Accountants Inc, Montvale, NJ. Tel: (201) 573-9000, (800) 638-4427, FAX: (201) 474-1600, E-Mail: ima@imanet.org, Web Site: www.imanet.org (1)

Institute of Management & Administration (IOMA), Bethesda, MD. Tel: (703) 341-3500, (800) 372-1033, FAX: (800) 253-0332, Web Site: www.ioma.com (17)

Institute of Reading Development, Novato, CA. Tel: (415) 884-8100, (800) 964-2030, FAX: (415) 382-0760, E-Mail: contactus@readingprograms.org, Web Site: www.readingprograms.org (1)

Institute of Real Estate Management, Chicago, IL. Tel: (312) 329-6000, (800) 837-0706, FAX: (800) 338-4736, E-Mail: custserv@irem.org, Web Site: www.irem.org (1)

Institutional Advancement Programs Inc, Tuckahoe, NY. Tel: (914) 779-4092, FAX: (914) 961-4202 (1)

Institutional Investor Inc, New York, NY. Tel: (212) 224-3300, FAX: (212) 224-3592, Web Site: www.institutionalinvestor.com (17)

Institutional Real Estate Inc, San Ramon, CA. Tel: (925) 244-0500, FAX: (925) 244-0520, Web Site: www.irei.com (17)

Instructor's Choice Dancewear, Massapequa Park, NY. Tel: (516) 799-6000, FAX: (516) 799-7993, E-Mail: customerservice@instructorschoice.com, Web Site: www.instructorschoice.net (2)

The Instrument Workshop, Ashland, OR. Tel: (541) 552-0989, (800) 442-6038, FAX: (541) 488-5846, E-Mail: shop77@fortepiano.com, Web Site: www.fortepiano.com (16)

Insurance.com, Solon, OH. Tel: (440) 715-0075, Web Site: www.insurance.com (15)

Insurance Publications Inc, Overland Park, KS. Tel: (913) 383-9191, (800) 762-3387, FAX: (913) 383-1247, E-Mail: brokerwrld@primary.net, Web Site: www.brokerworldmag.com (17)

Inte Q, Oakbrook Terrace, IL. Tel: (630) 874-2424, Web Site: www.inteqinsights.com (21)

Integer Group, Des Moines, IA. Tel: (515) 288-7910, FAX: (515) 288-8439, E-Mail: fmaher@integermidwest.com, Web Site: www.integer.com (35)

Integrated Advertising Inc, Jacksonville, FL. Tel: (904) 296-2585, FAX: (904) 296-2586, E-Mail: mary@intadvertising.com, Web Site: www.intadvertising.com (35)

Integrated Alliance Limited Partnership, Denton, TX. Tel: (940) 565-9415, FAX: (940) 383-1876, E-Mail: ryoung@integratedalliance.com, Web Site: www.integratedalliance.com (29)

Integrated Business Services Inc, Lake Forest, IL. Tel: (847) 735-1690, (800) 451-5478, Web Site: www.medbase200.com (22)

Integrated Mail Industries Ltd, Milwaukee, WI. Tel: (414) 908-3500, FAX: (414) 449-2906, E-Mail: sales@integratedmail.com, Web Site: www.integratedmail.com (28)

Integrated Marketing Solutions (IMS), Ashland, NE. Tel: (402) 486-3151, FAX: (402) 486-3161 (20)

Integrated Marketing Technology Inc, San Francisco, CA. Tel: (415) 699-2280, FAX: (917) 591-5333, E-Mail: information@imtnetwork.com, Web Site: www.imtnetwork.com (22)

Integrated Merchandising Systems LLC, Morton Grove, IL. Tel: (877) 467-1200, E-Mail: doug.carlson@imsfastpak.com, Web Site: www.imsfastpak.com (21)

Integrated Messaging Inc, Winnipeg, MB Canada. Tel: (204) 786-7630, (800) 561-3734, FAX: (204) 786-7718, E-Mail: sales@imi.mb.ca, Web Site: www.imi.mb.ca (29)

Integrated Print & Graphics, South Elgin, IL. Tel: (847) 695-6777, FAX: (847) 741-4090, E-Mail: info@ipandginc.com, Web Site: www.ipandginc.com (27)

Integrative Logic LLC, Lawrenceville, GA. Tel: (678) 638-2600, FAX: (678) 638-2601, Web Site: www.integrativelogic.com (30)

Integretel Inc, San Jose, CA. Tel: (408) 362-4000, FAX: (408) 362-2795, Web Site: www.integretel.com (16)

Integrity Music Inc, Mobile, AL. Tel: (251) 633-9000, FAX: (251) 633-5202, Web Site: www.integritymusic.com (16)

Intel Corp, Santa Clara, CA. Tel: (408) 765-8080, (800) 548-4725, FAX: (408) 765-6187, Web Site: www.intel.com (16)

Intelesure LLC, Meridian, ID. Tel: (866) 808-7366, Web Site: www.intelesure.com (29)

InteliSpend Prepaid Solutions, Fenton, MO. Tel: (888) 234-7725, E-Mail: saleads@intellispend.com, Web Site: www.my.intelispend.com (5)

Intelitec, Granby, MA. Tel: (413) 467-9476, E-Mail: info@intelitec.com, Web Site: intelitec.com (23)

Intelius Inc, Bellevue, WA. Tel: (425) 974-6100, Web Site: www.intelius.com (22)

Intellidyn Corp, Hingham, MA. Tel: (781) 741-5503, (866) 773-5756, FAX: (781) 741-5545, E-Mail: kmf@intellidyn.com, Web Site: www.intellidyn.com (22)

Intelligencer Printing Co, Lancaster, PA. Tel: (717) 291-3100, (800) 233-0107, FAX: (717) 569-2643, Web Site: www.intellprinting.com (27)

Intelligent Direct, Wellsboro, PA. Tel: (570) 724-7355, Web Site: www.marketmaps.com (9)

IntelliQuote Insurance Services, El Dorado Hills, CA. Tel: (800) 543-3467, Web Site: www.intelliquote.com (15)

Inter7 Internet Technologies Inc, Galena, IL. Tel: (815) 776-9465, Web Site: www.inter7.com (3)

Interact Direct Marketing Inc, London, ON Canada. Tel: (519) 439-6245, Web Site: www.interactdirect.com (28)

Interact Medical, South Bend, IN. Tel: (415) 354-1777, Web Site: www.interactmedical.com (35)

Interactive Marketing Group LLC, Brownsburg, IN. Tel: (317) 965-9215, Web Site: www.immarkgrp.com (32)

Interactive Marketing Institute, Richmond, VA. Tel: (800) 925-5308, Web Site: www.imi.vcu.edu (41)

Interactive Marketing Solutions, Stamford, CT. Tel: (203) 653-2762, FAX: (203) 653-2767, E-Mail: solutions@ims-dm.com (22)

Interactive Response Technologies Inc, Fort Lauderdale, FL. Tel: (954) 484-4973, (800) 700-3033, FAX: (954) 484-0818, E-Mail: hglass@callcenter.com, Web Site: www.callcenter.com (29)

Interactive Search Group, Cleveland, OH. Tel: (216) 255-3388, Web Site: www.isgstaffingnow.com (20)

InterContinental Hotels Group, Atlanta, GA. Tel: (800) 621-0555, FAX: (801) 975-1846, Web Site: www.ichotelsgroup.com (19)

Interdata Inc, Sanibel, FL. Tel: (239) 472-2700, FAX: (941) 472-4272, E-Mail: jfisher435@aol.com, Web Site: www.interdata.org (30)

Interdisciplinary Design Team, Southhampton, PA. Tel: (215) 364-5608, FAX: (215) 364-6509, E-Mail: rich.bomze@gmail.com (36)

Interex, Amesbury, MA. Tel: (978) 388-8755, (800) IN-TEREX, FAX: (978) 388-8747, Web Site: www.interexexhibits.com (17)

Interface Engineering, Portland, OR. Tel: (503) 382-2266, FAX: (503) 382-2262, E-Mail: solutions@interfaceengineering.com, Web Site: www.ieice.com (20)

InterfaceFlor LLC, La Grange, GA. Tel: (706) 882-1891, (800) 336-0225, FAX: (706) 882-0500, Web Site: www.interfaceflor.com (16)

The Interfaith Alliance, Washington, DC. Tel: (202) 466-0567, Web Site: www.interfaithalliance.org (1)

Intergraph Corp, Madison, AL. Tel: (256) 730-2000, (800) 345-4856, FAX: (256) 730-2048, Web Site: www.intergraph.com (16)

Interior Concepts Corp, Spring Lake, MI. Tel: (616) 842-5550, (800) 678-5550, FAX: (616) 846-3925, Web Site: www.interiorconcepts.com (34)

Interline Creative Group Inc, Palatine, IL. Tel: (847) 358-4848, FAX: (847) 358-8089, E-Mail: info@interlinegroup.com, Web Site: www.interlinegroup.com (35)

Intermap Technologies, Englewood, CO. Tel: (303) 708-0955, FAX: (303) 708-0952, E-Mail: info@intermap.com, Web Site: www.intermap.com (32)

InterMedia Advertising, Woodland Hills, CA. Tel: (818) 995-1455, (800) 846-3289, FAX: (818) 719-9977, E-Mail: sales@intermedia-advertising.com, Web Site: www.intermedia-advertising.com (35)

Intermedia Consultants Inc, Princeton, NJ. Tel: (609) 430-8460, Web Site: www.interprintmedia.com (35)

InterMedia Outdoors Inc, New York, NY. Tel: (212) 852-6641, FAX: (212) 302-4472, Web Site: imomages.com (31)

International Academy - Compounding Pharmacists, Missouri City, TX. Tel: (281) 933-8400, Web Site: www.iacprx.org (1)

International Advertising Association, New York, NY. Tel: (646) 722-2612, FAX: (646) 722-2501, E-Mail: iaa@iaaglobal.com, Web Site: www.iaaglobal.org (1)

International Auto Parts, Charlottesville, VA. Tel: (434) 973-0550, (800) 953-0813, FAX: (434) 973-2368, E-Mail: iap1@international-auto.com, Web Site: www.international-auto.com (12)

International City/County Management Association, Washington, DC. Tel: (202) 289-4262, FAX: (202) 962-3500, E-Mail: customerservice@icma.org, Web Site: www.icma.org (1)

International Coins & Currency Inc, Montpelier, VT. Tel: (802) 223-6331, (800) 451-4463, FAX: (800) 229-3239, E-Mail: info@iccoin.org, Web Site: www.iccoin.com (6)

International Corp, Hasbrouck Heights, NJ. Tel: (201) 203-3083, Web Site: www.datadirectsolutions.com (20)

International Crystal Manufacturing Co, Oklahoma City, OK. Tel: (405) 236-3741, (800) 252-6780, FAX: (405) 235-1904, E-Mail: info@icmfg.com, Web Site: www.icmfg.com (16)

International Currency LLC, Beaumont, TX. Tel: (409) 866-0588 (11)

International Data Management - a Dmh Marketing Partners Co, Akron, OH. Tel: (330) 869-8500, FAX: (330) 869-4027, Web Site: www.idmi.com (22)

International Direct Marketing Consultants Inc, Dallas, TX. Tel: (214) 443-9494, FAX: (214) 443-9512, E-Mail: billmcnutt@charter.net, Web Site: www.dmtrademissions.com (20)

International Direct Media Co & Information Publishing Co, San Francisco, CA. Tel: (415) 661-4730, E-Mail: infopubsf@aol.com, Web Site: www.bookwormproductions.com (17)

International Direct Response Services Ltd, Delta, BC Canada. Tel: (604) 951-6855, Web Site: www.idrs. ca (28)

International Fellowship of Christians and Jews, Washington, DC. Tel: (312) 641-7200, (800) 486-8844, Web Site: www.ifcj.org (1)

International Filing Corp LLC, Hattiesburg, MS. Tel: (601) 554-0521, FAX: (601) 554-0522, E-Mail: pcoerper@intfiling.com, Web Site: www.intfiling. com (26)

International Foundation of Employee Benefit Plans, Brookfield, WI. Tel: (262) 373-7758, FAX: (262) 786-8670, Web Site: www.ifebp.org (1)

International Fulfillment Inc, Philadelphia, PA. Tel: (215) 638-8060, (800) 962-8080, FAX: (215) 638-8091, Web Site: www.ifionline.net (27)

International Fund for Animal Welfare, Yarmouth Port, MA. Tel: (508) 744-2000, (800) 932-4329, FAX: (508) 744-2099, E-Mail: info-int@ifaw.org, Web Site: www.ifaw.org (1)

International Gamco Inc, Omaha, NE. Tel: (402) 571-2449, (800) 524-2626, FAX: (402) 571-7941, E-Mail: mark.stevens@intlgamco.com, Web Site: www.intlgamco.com (31)

International Irrigation Systems, St. Catherines, ON Canada. Tel: (905) 688-4090, (877) 477-4476, FAX: (905) 688-4093, Web Site: www.irrigro.com (8)

International Mailing Solutions LLC, Burlington, MA. Tel: (718) 376-5000, Web Site: www.mailims.com (28)

International Manufacturing Co, Whitesburg, GA. Tel: (770) 834-2094, FAX: (770) 834-2096, E-Mail: textilenterprise@aol.net (8)

International Marine, Camden, ME. Tel: (207) 236-4837, FAX: (207) 236-6314, Web Site: www. internationalmarine.com (17)

International Marketing Partners Ltd, Los Angeles, CA. Tel: (310) 665-1155, FAX: (310) 665-1155, E-Mail: info@intermarketingonline.com, Web Site: www. intermarketingonline.com (35)

International Masters Publishers Inc, Montoursville, PA. Tel: (800) 570-5718, E-Mail: customerservice@ imp-usa.com, Web Site: www.imponline.com (17)

International Paper, Memphis, TN. Tel: (901) 419-9000, (800) 207-4003, E-Mail: internationalpaper.comm@ ipaper.com, Web Site: www.internationalpaper.com (16)

International Planned Parenthood Federation Western Hemisphere Region Inc, New York, NY. Tel: (212) 248-6400, (866) IPPFWHR, FAX: (212) 248-4221, E-Mail: info@ippfwhr.org, Web Site: www.ippfwhr. org (1)

International Prepaid Communications Association, Washington, DC. Tel: (202) 544-4448, (800) 333-3513, FAX: (202) 547-7417 (40)

International Resource Management Co, Bedford, TX. Tel: (817) 861-9191, FAX: (817) 277-0868, E-Mail: james@irmco.net, Web Site: www.irmco.net (20)

International Sign Association, Alexandria, VA. Tel: (703) 836-4012, FAX: (703) 836-8353, E-Mail: info@signs.org, Web Site: www.signs.org (1)

International Society for Technology in Education, Eugene, OR. Tel: (800) 336-5191, FAX: (541) 302-3778, Web Site: www.iste.org (1)

International Specialized Book Services Inc, Portland, OR. Tel: (503) 287-3093, (800) 944-6190, FAX: (503) 280-8832, E-Mail: isbs_sales@isbs.com, Web Site: www.isbscatalog.com (16)

International Wine Accessories Inc, Petaluma, CA. Tel: (214) 349-6097, (800) 527-4072, FAX: (214) 349-8712, E-Mail: customerservice@iwawine.com, Web Site: www.iwawine.com (4)

The Internet Alliance, Washington, DC. Tel: (202) 861-2476, FAX: (202) 955-8081, E-Mail: info@ internetalliance.org, Web Site: www. internetalliance.org (40)

Internet Direct Response, Inc, Austin, TX. Tel: (512) 551-8417, FAX: (888) 763-5177, E-Mail: tbroderick@internet-direct-response.com, Web Site: www.internet-direct-response.com (35)

Interprint Web & Sheetfed, Clearwater, FL. Tel: (727) 531-8957, (800) 749-5152, FAX: (727) 536-0647, E-Mail: customerservice@printerusa.com, Web Site: www.printerusa.com (27)

The Interprovincial Group, Scarborough, ON Canada. Tel: (416) 283-5555, FAX: (416) 283-6643, E-Mail: info@interprovincialgroup.com, Web Site: www. interprovincialgroup.com (21)

Interrante, Steve, Freeport Music Inc, Farmingville, NY. Tel: (631) 549-4108, (888) 549-4108, E-Mail: sales@musicalinstruments.com; sales@ freeportmusic.com, Web Site: www. musicalinstruments.com (11)

Intersections, Chantilly, VA. Tel: (703) 488-6100, Web Site: www.charteredmarketing.com (14)

Interstate EDP & Direct Mail Center Inc, Brooklyn, NY. Tel: (718) 965-2500, FAX: (718) 965-2504, E-Mail: info@interstateedp.com, Web Site: www. interstateedp.com (28)

Interstate Printing Co, Omaha, NE. Tel: (402) 341-8028, (800) 788-4177, FAX: (402) 341-6168, E-Mail: printer@interstateprinting.com, Web Site: www. interstateprinting.com (27)

interTrend Communications Inc, Long Beach, CA. Tel: (562) 733-1888, E-Mail: info@intertrend.com, Web Site: www.intertrend.com (35)

Interval International, South Miami, FL. Tel: (305) 666-1884, (800) 468-3782, FAX: (305) 667-5321, Web Site: www.intervalworld.com (35)

Intra Business Systems Inc, South Bend, IN. Tel: (574) 257-7940, FAX: (574) 257-7944, E-Mail: info@ intrabusinesssystems.com, Web Site: www. intrabusinesssystems.com (16)

Intromark Inc, Pittsburgh, PA. Tel: (412) 288-1300, (800) 851-6030 X1368, FAX: (412) 338-0497, E-Mail: licensing@intromark.com (16)

Intuit, Mountain View, CA. Tel: (650) 944-6000, Web Site: www.inuit.com (10)

Invacare Continuing Care Group, Saint Louis, MO. Tel: (519) 659-1395, (800) 347-5440, FAX: (636) 519-0044, Web Site: www.invacare-ccg.com (16)

Invacare Supply Group, Milford, MA. Tel: (508) 429-1000, (800) 225-4792, FAX: (508) 429-1581, E-Mail: service.isg@invacare.com, Web Site: www. invacaresupplygroup.com (16)

Invenda Corp, Bethesda, MD. Tel: (240) 333-6111, E-Mail: sales@invenda.com, Web Site: www. invenda.com (32)

InventHelp's INPEX, Pittsburgh, PA. Tel: (412) 288-1343, (888) 544-6739, FAX: (412) 288-4546, E-Mail: info@inpex.com, Web Site: www.inpex. com (42)

InvestorPlace Lists, Rockville, MD. Tel: (601) 620-4135, FAX: (703) 940-7749, E-Mail: dferry@ investormedia.com, Web Site: www. investorplacelists.com (24)

Investors Alliance Inc, Austin, TX. Tel: (512) 480-8100, FAX: (512) 480-9100, E-Mail: info@powerinvestor. com, Web Site: www.powerinvestor.com (1)

Investors Marketing Services, Danvers, MA. Tel: (978) 774-2990, (800) 462-2551, FAX: (978) 774-4249, Web Site: www.investorsmarketing.com (14)

Invitation Hotline, Manalapan, NJ. Tel: (732) 536-9115, (800) 800-4355, FAX: (732) 972-4875, E-Mail: info@invitationhotline.com, Web Site: www. invitationhotline.com (27)

Involve Social, Fremont, CA. Tel: (510) 396-3941, Web Site: www.involvesocial.com (1)

INWAVE Internet, Janesville, WI. Tel: (888) 469-2831, FAX: (608) 752-8981, Web Site: www.inwave.com (16)

Iomega Corp, Roy, UT. Tel: (801) 332-1000, (888) 446-6342, FAX: (801) 332-3158, Web Site: www. iomega.com (16)

Ion Exhibits, Itasca, IL. Tel: (877) 499-6197, FAX: (630) 235-9501, E-Mail: info@ionexhibits.com, Web Site: www.ionexhibits.com (36)

Ion Media Networks Inc, West Palm Beach, FL. Tel: (561) 659-4122, (800) 646-7296, FAX: (561) 659-4252, Web Site: www.ionmedia.tv (32)

Iowa Medical Society, Des Moines, IA. Tel: (515) 223-1401, (800) 747-3070, FAX: (515) 223-0590, Web Site: www.iowamedical.org (1)

Iowa Student Loan Liquidity Corp, West Des Moines, IA. Tel: (515) 243-5626, Web Site: www. studentloan.org (1)

IPacesetters, Montvale, NJ. Tel: (201) 391-1500, FAX: (201) 391-8357, Web Site: www.ipacesetters.com (22)

Ipema, Tim, Unity School of Christianity, Unity Village, MO. Tel: (816) 254-3550, FAX: (816) 251-3554, E-Mail: unity@unityonline.org, Web Site: www. unityonline.org (17)

Ippolito, Michael, SC Direct, West Bridgewater, MA. Tel: (800) 343-9695, Web Site: www.scdirect.com (2)

Ipsos America Inc, New York, NY. Tel: (212) 265-3200, FAX: (212) 265-3790, E-Mail: info@ipsos-asi.com, Web Site: www.ipsos-asi.com (30)

Ipswitch Inc, Lexington, MA. Tel: (781) 676-5700, FAX: (781) 676-5710, Web Site: www. whatsupgold.com (22)

Irani, Zackary, Biomerica Inc, Irvine, CA. Tel: (949) 645-2111, (800) 854-3002, FAX: (949) 553-1231, E-Mail: info@biomerica.com, Web Site: www. biomerica.com (7)

Iris Marketing, Bel Air, MD. Tel: (443) 742-1232 (20)

Irizarry, Michael S., US Cellular, Chicago, IL. Tel: (888) 944-9400, Web Site: www.uscellular.com (32)

Iron Mountain Fulfillment Services, Milpitas, CA. Tel: (408) 945-1600, FAX: (408) 946-1135, E-Mail: info@comac.com, Web Site: www.ironmountain. com (28)

Iroquois Products, Chicago, IL. Tel: (773) 436-3900, (800) 453-3355, FAX: (773) 436-4908, E-Mail: sales@iroquoisproducts.com, Web Site: www. iroquoisproducts.com (10)

Irresistible Ink Inc, Duluth, MN. Tel: (218) 336-4200, (800) 543-8396, Web Site: www.irresistibleink.com (28)

Irvine, Donald, Accuracy in Media Inc, Bethesda, MD. Tel: (202) 364-4401, FAX: (202) 364-4098, E-Mail: info@aim.org, Web Site: www.aim.org (1)

Irving, Blake, Mad Mimi, Scottsdale, AZ. Tel: (480) 505-8800, FAX: (480) 505-8844, E-Mail: support@ madmimi.com, Web Site: madmimi.com (24)

Irving, Mark, Atlantic Spice Co, North Truro, MA. Tel: (508) 487-6100, (800) 316-7965, FAX: (508) 487-2550, E-Mail: weborders@atlanticspice.com, Web Site: www.atlanticspice.com (4)

Irwin, Dave, The Allant Group, Naperville, IL. Tel: (800) 367-7311, FAX: (630) 355-3090, E-Mail: dirwin@allantgroup.com, Web Site: www. allantgroup.com (22)

Irwin, Jim, Aircraft Spruce & Specialty Co, Corona, CA. Tel: (909) 372-9555, (877) 4-Spruce, FAX: (909) 372-0555, E-Mail: info@aircraft-spruce.com, Web Site: www.aircraft-spruce.com (12)

Irwin, Nanci, Aircraft Spruce & Specialty Co, Corona, CA. Tel: (909) 372-9555, (877) 4-Spruce, FAX: (909) 372-0555, E-Mail: info@aircraft-spruce.com, Web Site: www.aircraft-spruce.com (12)

Isaacman, Ellen, Good Advertising, Memphis, TN. Tel: (901) 761-0741, (800) 325-9857, FAX: (901) 682-2568, E-Mail: info@goodadvertising.com, Web Site: www.goodadvertising.com (35)

Isaacs, Tony, Indian House Records & Tapes, Taos, NM. Tel: (575) 776-2953, (800) 748-0522, FAX: (575) 776-2804, E-Mail: music@indianhouse.com, Web Site: www.indianhouse.com (35)

Isaacson, Peter, Demandbase Inc, San Francisco, CA. Tel: (415) 683-2660, E-Mail: info@demandbase.com, Web Site: www.demandbase.com (22)

Isacson, Alan, ABI Inc, New York, NY. Tel: (212) 529-4500, FAX: (212) 529-4442, E-Mail: info@abipr.com, Web Site: www.abipr.com (35)

Iseli, Carl, The Washington Monthly Co, Washington, DC. Tel: (202) 955-9010, FAX: (202) 955-9011, E-Mail: editors@washingtonmonthly.com, Web Site: www.washingtonmonthly.com (17)

Iseli, Claire, The Washington Monthly Co, Washington, DC. Tel: (202) 955-9010, FAX: (202) 955-9011, E-Mail: editors@washingtonmonthly.com, Web Site: www.washingtonmonthly.com (17)

Isham, David, NRS, Decatur, TX. Tel: (940) 627-3949, Web Site: www.nrsworld.com (11)

Ishaug, Kurt, Datacard Ga-Vehren Corp, Minnetonka, MN. Tel: (952) 933-1223, (800) 621-6972 x6930, FAX: (952) 931-0418, E-Mail: info@datacard.com, Web Site: www.gavehren.com (34)

Ishii, Shin, Itochu Chemicals America Inc, White Plains, NY. Tel: (914) 333-7800, (800) 423-6870, FAX: (914) 333-7848, Web Site: www.itochu-sc.com (16)

Ishrak, Omar, Medtronic, Minneapolis, MN. Tel: (763) 514-4000, (800) 633-8766, Web Site: www.covidien.com (7)

Ishrak, Omar, Medtronic Inc, Minneapolis, MN. Tel: (763) 514-4000, (800) 328-2518, FAX: (763) 514-4879, Web Site: www.medtronic.com (16)

Isip, Vicki, Ghirardelli Chocolate Co, San Leandro, CA. Tel: (510) 483-6970, (800) 877-9338, FAX: (510) 297-2649, Web Site: www.ghirardelli.com (16)

Island Pacific Inc, Irvine, CA. Tel: (949) 476-2212, (800) 569-1122, FAX: (949) 476-0177, Web Site: www.islandpacific.com (22)

Islands Tropicals, Keaau, HI. Tel: (808) 961-0606, (800) 367-5155, FAX: (808) 966-7684, Web Site: www.islandtropicals.com (6)

Isler, Adam, PNT Marketing Services, Inc, Long Island City, NY. Tel: (718) 433-4063, (888) 768-2210, FAX: (914) 428-0504, E-Mail: tony@pntmarketingservices.com, Web Site: www.pntmarketingservices.com (22)

Israel, David, Playboy Enterprises Inc, Beverly Hills, CA. Tel: (310) 860-1215, Web Site: www.playboyenterprises.com (17)

Israel, James A., John Deere Financial, Johnston, IA. Tel: (515) 267-3000, (800) 275-5322, FAX: (515) 267-3292, Web Site: www.deere.com (14)

Israel, Lisa J., Durasol Corp, Amesbury, MA. Tel: (978) 388-2020, (800) 370-0683, FAX: (978) 388-9762, Web Site: www.durasolcorp.com (34)

Israel, Walter, Durasol Corp, Amesbury, MA. Tel: (978) 388-2020, (800) 370-0683, FAX: (978) 388-9762, Web Site: www.durasolcorp.com (34)

Issues & Answers Network Inc, Virginia Beach, VA. Tel: (757) 456-1100, FAX: (757) 456-0377, E-Mail: info@issans.com, Web Site: www.issans.com (30)

Isuzu Motors America LLC, Anaheim, CA. Tel: (562) 229-5000, (800) 255-6727, FAX: (562) 229-5463, Web Site: www.isuzu.com (16)

It Really Works Inc, Beverly Hills, CA. Tel: (310) 888-4009, FAX: (310) 888-4025, E-Mail: steve@itreallyworks.tv, Web Site: www.itreallyworks.tv (32)

iThink Direct LLC, West Harrison, NY. Tel: (914) 984-2109, E-Mail: info@ithinkdirect.com, Web Site: www.ithinkdirect.com (31)

Itochu Chemicals America Inc, White Plains, NY. Tel: (914) 333-7800, (800) 423-6870, FAX: (914) 333-7848, Web Site: www.itochu-sc.com (16)

ITOCHU International Inc, New York, NY. Tel: (212) 818-8000, FAX: (212) 818-8282, Web Site: www.adpackusa.com (25)

Ivanov, Sergey, Heldref Publications, Washington, DC. Tel: (202) 296-6267, (215) 625-8900, FAX: (202) 296-5149, Web Site: www.heldref.org (17)

Iverson, Ann C., Creating Selling Opportunities, Houston, TX. Tel: (713) 622-6936, FAX: (713) 622-2924, E-Mail: annci@sbcglobal.net (20)

Ives, Debi S., Wildlife Education Ltd, Park Hills, KY. Tel: (858) 513-7600, FAX: (858) 513-7660, E-Mail: animals@zoobooks.com, Web Site: www.zoobooks.com (17)

Ivie & Associates Inc, Flower Mound, TX. Tel: (972) 899-5000, FAX: (972) 899-5050, Web Site: www.ivieinc.com (35)

Ivie, Brandon, Ivie & Associates Inc, Flower Mound, TX. Tel: (972) 899-5000, FAX: (972) 899-5050, Web Site: www.ivieinc.com (35)

Ivie, Kay, Ivie & Associates Inc, Flower Mound, TX. Tel: (972) 899-5000, FAX: (972) 899-5050, Web Site: www.ivieinc.com (35)

Ivie, Warren, Ivie & Associates Inc, Flower Mound, TX. Tel: (972) 899-5000, FAX: (972) 899-5050, Web Site: www.ivieinc.com (35)

iVisionMobile Inc, Chatsworth, CA. Tel: (866) 655-5302, FAX: (818) 812-6126, E-Mail: sales@ivisionmobile.com, Web Site: www.ivisionmobile.com (35)

Ivy Tech Community College of Indiana, Indianapolis, IN. Tel: (317) 921-4800, (888) IVY-LINE, FAX: (317) 921-4753, Web Site: www.ivytech.edu (13)

Iwata, Erin, Heinrich, Denver, CO. Tel: (303) 233-8660, (800) 356-5036, FAX: (303) 239-5352, E-Mail: info@heinrich.com, Web Site: www.heinrich.com (35)

Iwata, Jon C., IBM Corp, Armonk, NY. Tel: (914) 765-1900, FAX: (914) 765-6633, Web Site: www.ibm.com (16)

IXI Services, McLean, VA. Tel: (703) 848-3800, FAX: (703) 848-3868, E-Mail: info.ixiservices@equifax.com, Web Site: www.ixicorp.com (35)

Iyer, Bala, Telebrands Corp, Fairfield, NJ. Tel: (973) 247-8777, Web Site: www.telebrands.com (21)

Izenstark, Gail S., Direct Mail Source, Wilmette, IL. Tel: (847) 676-3744, E-Mail: dms@directmailsource.net (28)

J

J&L Concepts Inc, Valdosta, GA. Tel: (229) 247-5731, E-Mail: promo@jlconcepts.com, Web Site: www.jlconcepts.com (33)

J&L Industrial Supply, Southfield, MI. Tel: (734) 458-7000, (800) 521-9520, FAX: (734) 261-0352, Web Site: www.jlindustrial.com (9)

J&P Cycles, Anamosa, IA. Tel: (319) 462-4819, (800) 318-4817, Web Site: www.j-pcycles.com (12)

JB Dollar Stretcher Magazine, Richfield, OH. Tel: (330) 659-3590, (800) 673-2531, FAX: (330) 659-6741, Web Site: www.jbdollar.com (31)

JC Direct Mail Inc, Groveport, OH. Tel: (614) 836-4848, FAX: (614) 836-4847 (28)

JC Penney Inc, Plano, TX. Tel: (972) 431-1000, FAX: (972) 431-1977, Web Site: www.jcpenney.com (5)

JC Whitney, Chicago, IL. Tel: (312) 431-6000, FAX: (312) 431-5650, (800) 537-2700, Web Site: www.jcwhitney.com (12)

JD Graphic Co, Elk Grove Village, IL. Tel: (847) 364-4000, (888) 364-6216, FAX: (847) 364-4024, E-Mail: sakes@jdgraphic.com, Web Site: www.jdgraphic.com (27)

JDR Microdevices, Dublin, CA. Tel: (650) 625-1400, (800) 538-5000, FAX: (800) 538-5005, E-Mail: sales@jdr.com, Web Site: www.jdr.com (3)

JDRF, New York, NY. Tel: (212) 689-2860, (800) 533-CURE, FAX: (212) 785-9595, E-Mail: newyorkchapter@jdrf.org, Web Site: www.jdrf.org (1)

JDS Uniphase Corp, Milpitas, CA. Tel: (408) 546-5000, FAX: (408) 546-4300, Web Site: www.jdsu.com (32)

JF Direct Marketing Inc, Ossining, NY. Tel: (914) 762-1975, FAX: (914) 762-9247, E-Mail: jfdirect@bestweb.net, Web Site: www.jfdirectmarketing.com (23)

JHL Mail Marketing Inc, Stevens Point, WI. Tel: (715) 341-0581, (800) 236-0581, FAX: (715) 341-9645, E-Mail: ren@jhl.com, Web Site: www.jhl.com (28)

JIST Publishing, Saint Paul, MN. Tel: (800) 328-4564, FAX: (800) 328-1452, E-Mail: educate@emcp.com, Web Site: jist.emcp.com (17)

JJI International Inc, Cranston, RI. Tel: (401) 780-8668 (35)

JK Associates LLC, Palo Alto, CA. Tel: (650) 838-9816, FAX: (650) 838-9867, Web Site: www.jk-associates.com (20)

JLG Industries Inc, McConnellsburg, PA. Tel: (717) 485-5161, (877) JLG-SELL, FAX: (717) 485-6417, E-Mail: comments@jlg.com, Web Site: www.jlg.com (16)

JLMC, New York, NY. Tel: (917) 476-3072 (20)

JLS Mailing Services Inc, Brockton, MA. Tel: (508) 313-1050, (866) JLS-MAIL, FAX: (508) 313-1093, E-Mail: rparkinson@jlsms.com, Web Site: www.jlsms.com (28)

Jos A Bank Clothiers Inc, Hampstead, MD. Tel: (410) 239-2700, Web Site: www.josbank.com (2)

JP Morgan Chase & Co, New York, NY. Tel: (212) 270-6000, E-Mail: jpmcinvestorrelations@jpmchase.com, Web Site: www.jpmorgan.com (14)

JPL Integrated Communications Inc, Harrisburg, PA. Tel: (717) 558-8048, E-Mail: jpl@jplcreative.com, Web Site: www.jplcreative.com (35)

JR Cigar, Burlington, NC. Tel: (800) 572-4427, FAX: (800) 457-3299, E-Mail: manager@jrburlington.com, Web Site: www.jrcigars.com (5)

JR Direct Response International Inc, Delta, BC Canada. Tel: (604) 940-0277, (877) 940-0277, FAX: (604) 946-1419, E-Mail: contactus@jrdirect.com, Web Site: www.jrdirect.com (23)

JRB Marketing Group, East Windsor, NJ. Tel: (301) 758-2334, FAX: (302) 348-2490, E-Mail: jrblitman@gmail.com (20)

JRH Marketing Services Inc, Jamaica, NY. Tel: (718) 805-7300, FAX: (718) 805-7303, E-Mail: office@jrhmarketingservices.com, Web Site: www.jrhmarketingservices.com (30)

JS Direct Address Ltd, North Vancouver, BC Canada. Tel: (604) 987-1282, FAX: (604) 987-1283, E-Mail: jim.slight@jsdirect.com, Web Site: www.jsdirect. com (23)

JSA Creative Services LLC, Chicago, IL. Tel: (773) 772-3445, FAX: (773) 772-3446, E-Mail: jsacreative@comcast.net, Web Site: www. jsacreative.com (39)

JSR Advertising Corp, New York, NY. Tel: (212) 995-1661, E-Mail: jay@tqm1.com, Web Site: www. quantmethod.com (18)

JT International, Teaneck, NJ. Tel: (201) 871-1210, Web Site: www.jti.com (16)

JVW Direct, Pittsburgh, PA. Tel: (412) 241-5920, FAX: (412) 241-5850, E-Mail: john@jvwdirect.com (35)

JWT Inside, Los Angeles, CA. Tel: (310) 309-8282, (877) 665-8768, FAX: (310) 309-8283, E-Mail: conversations@jwtinside.com, Web Site: www. jwtinside.com (35)

JZ Marketing, Lehigh Acres, FL. Tel: (239) 693-7567, Web Site: www.jzmktg.com (20)

Jabin, Chris, Brookfield Zoo, Brookfield, IL. Tel: (708) 485-0263, (800) 201-0784, FAX: (708) 485-3532, Web Site: www.brookfieldzoo.org (1)

Jaccard, Walter B., Thousand Trails LP, Chicago, IL. Tel: (214) 618-7200, (800) 205-0606, FAX: (214) 618-7324, Web Site: www.1000trails.com (16)

Jack Morton Worldwide, New York, NY. Tel: (212) 401-7000, (212) 401-7121, E-Mail: experience@ jackmorton.com, Web Site: www.jackmorton.com (35)

Jack Schecterson visualmarketing Consultants, Little Neck, NY. Tel: (718) 225-3536 (20)

Jackman, Michael, DeLuxe Laboratories Inc, Hollywood, CA. Tel: (323) 462-6171, FAX: (323) 960-7016, E-Mail: steven.vananda@bydeluxe.com, Web Site: www.bydeluxe.com (16)

The Jackson Consulting Group Ltd, Middletown, DE. Tel: (302) 378-0218, (866) 450-7005, FAX: (302) 378-0219, E-Mail: djack98489@aol.com, Web Site: www.jcg-ltd.com (20)

The Jackson Group, Indianapolis, IN. Tel: (317) 791-9000, (888) 522-5766, FAX: (317) 791-9800, Web Site: www.jacksongroup.com (35)

The Jackson Laboratory JAX Research Systems, Bar Harbor, ME. Tel: (800) 422-6423, Web Site: www. jax.org/jaxmice (1)

Jackson, Ann Rockler, Rockler Woodworking & Hardware, Medina, MN. Tel: (763) 478-8200, (800) 279-4441, FAX: (800) 865-1229, E-Mail: info@rockler. com, Web Site: www.rockler.com (8)

Jackson, Barbara, Animal Health Express, Inc, Tucson, AZ. Tel: (520) 888-0294, (800) 533-8115, FAX: (520) 888-0297, (800) 437-9898, E-Mail: info@ animalhealthexpress.com, Web Site: www. animalhealthexpress.com (5)

Jackson, Carolyn, UCEA, New York, NY. FAX: (212) 781-6500, Web Site: www.revike.org (1)

Jackson, Dolores, Woman's Missionary Union, Birmingham, AL. Tel: (205) 991-8100, FAX: (205) 991-4990, E-Mail: email@wmu.org, Web Site: www. wmu.org (17)

Jackson, Donald R., The Jackson Consulting Group Ltd, Middletown, DE. Tel: (302) 378-0218, (866) 450-7005, FAX: (302) 378-0219, E-Mail: djack98489@ aol.com, Web Site: www.jcg-ltd.com (20)

Jackson, Henry G., Society for Human Resource Management, Alexandria, VA. Tel: (703) 548-3440, (800) 283-7476, FAX: (703) 535-6490, E-Mail: shrmstore@shrm.org, Web Site: www.shrm.org (1)

Jackson, Kathryn E., Response Design Corp, Ocean City, NJ. Tel: (609) 601-5866, (800) 366-4732, FAX: (609) 788-3619, E-Mail: rdc@responsedesign. com, Web Site: www.responsedesign.com (20)

Jackson, Marianne, Blue Shield Life, San Francisco, CA. Tel: (888) 800-2742, FAX: (800) 329-2742, Web Site: www.blueshieldca.com (15)

Jackson, Michael J., iCrossing, New York, NY. Tel: (212) 649-3900, FAX: (646) 280-1091, Web Site: www.icrossing.com (32)

Jackson, Nigel D., Intermap Technologies, Englewood, CO. Tel: (303) 708-0955, FAX: (303) 708-0952, E-Mail: info@intermap.com, Web Site: www. intermap.com (32)

Jackson, Patricia, Regnery Publishing, Washington, DC. Tel: (202) 216-0600, FAX: (202) 216-0612, Web Site: www.regnery.com (17)

Jackson, Regina, Warner Press, Anderson, IN. Tel: (765) 644-7721, (800) 741-7721, FAX: (765) 640-8005, E-Mail: wporders@warnerpress.org, Web Site: www.warnerpress.com (17)

Jackson, Rex, JDS Uniphase Corp, Milpitas, CA. Tel: (408) 546-5000, FAX: (408) 546-4300, Web Site: www.jdsu.com (32)

Jackson, Tasha, Marketing Research Association, Washington, DC. Tel: (860) 682-1000, (202) 800-2545, FAX: (860) 682-1010, (888) 512-1050, E-Mail: membership@marketingresearch.org, Web Site: www.mra-net.org (40)

Jackson, Tim, Animal Health Express, Inc, Tucson, AZ. Tel: (520) 888-0294, (800) 533-8115, FAX: (520) 888-0297, (800) 437-9898, E-Mail: info@ animalhealthexpress.com, Web Site: www. animalhealthexpress.com (5)

Jackson, Tyrone W., School of Business & Economics, Los Angeles, CA. Tel: (323) 343-2800, FAX: (323) 343-2813, Web Site: cbe.calstatela.edu (41)

Jackson, Vincent, Plan International USA, Warwick, RI. Tel: (401) 562-8400, (800) 556-7918, FAX: (401) 738-5608, Web Site: www.planusa.org (1)

Jackson, Wendy, Redirect, Salt Lake City, UT. Tel: (801) 453-0100, E-Mail: hello@redirectdigital.com, Web Site: redirectdigital.com (35)

Jacob, Dabney, Orient Expressed Imports Inc, New Orleans, LA. Tel: (888) 856-3948, FAX: (504) 899-5566, E-Mail: orient@orientexpressed.com, Web Site: www.orientexpressed.com (2)

Jacob, Jeffrey, New York Blood Center Inc, New York, NY. Tel: (212) 570-3000, (800) 933-2566, FAX: (212) 570-3195, Web Site: www.nybloodcenter.org (1)

Jacob, Jenny, Hanson Inc, Maumee, OH. Tel: (419) 327-6100, FAX: (419) 327-6101, Web Site: www. hansoninc.com (30)

Jacobovitz, Shalom, American College of Cardiology, Washington, DC. Tel: (202) 375-6000, FAX: (202) 375-7000, E-Mail: resource@acc.org, Web Site: www.acc.org (1)

Jacobs & Clevenger Inc, Chicago, IL. Tel: (312) 894-3000, FAX: (312) 645-9825, E-Mail: mail2350@ jacobsclevenger.com, Web Site: www. jacobsclevenger.com (35)

Jacobs, Andrew, Influent Inc, Dublin, OH. Tel: (614) 280-1600, (800) 856-6768, FAX: (614) 280-1610, E-Mail: info@influentinc.com, Web Site: www. influentinc.com (29)

Jacobs, Daniel, DAJ Direct Inc, Newport Beach, CA. Tel: (949) 722-0506, FAX: (949) 722-8026, E-Mail: orders@dajdirect.com, Web Site: www.dajdirect. com (24)

Jacobs, Daniel, MSI Direct Response Inc, Newport Beach, CA. Tel: (949) 722-2524, FAX: (949) 650-0989, E-Mail: sales@mailingteam.com, Web Site: mailingteam.com (24)

Jacobs, Ed, Wind River Group, Akron, OH. Tel: (330) 644-7774, FAX: (330) 645-2045 (20)

Jacobs, Frank, Falcon Products Inc, Newport, TN. Tel: (314) 991-9200, (800) 873-3252, FAX: (314) 991-9227, E-Mail: info@falconproducts.com, Web Site: www.falconproducts.com (16)

Jacobs, Kevin J., Hilton Hotels Corp, Mc Lean, VA. Tel: (703) 883-1000, (800) HILTONS, FAX: (310) 205-3670, Web Site: www.hilton.com (19)

Jacobs, Kyla, TBWA/Chiat/Day Inc, New York, NY. Tel: (212) 804-1000, FAX: (212) 804-1200, Web Site: www.tbwachiatdayny.com (35)

Jacobs, Leonard, Kalmed Dental Products Inc, Marietta, GA. Tel: (770) 971-8815, (800) 322-8815, FAX: (770) 509-8823, E-Mail: sales@kalmed.com, Web Site: www.kalmed.com (7)

Jacobs, Michael, Harry N Abrams Inc, New York, NY. Tel: (212) 206-7715, FAX: (212) 645-8437, Web Site: www.hnabooks.com (17)

Jacobs, Norman, Lakeside Publishing Co LLC, Evanston, IL. Tel: (847) 491-6440, FAX: (847) 491-0459, E-Mail: cs@centurysports.net, Web Site: www. centurysports.net (17)

Jacobs, Randall, Artemis International Solutions Corp, Austin, TX. Tel: (512) 201-8222, FAX: (512) 874-8900, Web Site: www.aisc.com (32)

Jacobs, Richard P., Eaton Corp, Raleigh, NC. Tel: (216) 523-4400, (800) 356-5794, FAX: (216) 523-4787, Web Site: www.eaton.com (16)

Jacobs, Robert, DAJ Direct Inc, Newport Beach, CA. Tel: (949) 722-0506, FAX: (949) 722-8026, E-Mail: orders@dajdirect.com, Web Site: www.dajdirect. com (24)

Jacobs, Ron, Jacobs & Clevenger Inc, Chicago, IL. Tel: (312) 894-3000, FAX: (312) 645-9825, E-Mail: mail2350@jacobsclevenger.com, Web Site: www. jacobsclevenger.com (35)

Jacobs, Sheldon, No Load Fund Investor, Brentwood, TN. Tel: (800) 706-6364, FAX: (800) 785-9212, E-Mail: NoLoad@mleesmith.com, Web Site: www. noloadfundinvestor.com (14)

Jacobs, Tom, Reliable Racing Supply, Queensbury, NY. Tel: (518) 793-5677, FAX: (518) 793-6491, Web Site: www.reliableracing.com (11)

Jacobsen Lenticular Tool & Cylinder Engraving Technologies Co (Jacotech), Itasca, IL. Tel: (630) 467-0900, FAX: (630) 467-0900, E-Mail: sales@ lenticlearlens.com, Web Site: www.jacotech.ww. lenticlearlens.com (34)

Jacobsen, Harlan, Single Scene News, Tempe, AZ. Tel: (480) 945-6746, FAX: (480) 945-6746, E-Mail: publisher@azsinglescene.com, Web Site: www. azsinglescene.com (17)

Jacobsen, Janet, Single Scene News, Tempe, AZ. Tel: (480) 945-6746, FAX: (480) 945-6746, E-Mail: publisher@azsinglescene.com, Web Site: www. azsinglescene.com (17)

Jacobsen, Jeff, Single Scene News, Tempe, AZ. Tel: (480) 945-6746, FAX: (480) 945-6746, E-Mail: publisher@azsinglescene.com, Web Site: www. azsinglescene.com (17)

Jacobsen, Ph.D. Gary A., Jacobsen Lenticular Tool & Cylinder Engraving Technologies Co (Jacotech), Itasca, IL. Tel: (630) 467-0900, FAX: (630) 467-0900, E-Mail: sales@lenticlearlens.com, Web Site: www.jacotech.ww.lenticlearlens.com (34)

Jacobsohn Consulting Associates, Highland Park, IL. Tel: (312) 543-3330, E-Mail: jacobsohnr@aol.com (20)

Jacobsohn, Richard H., Jacobsohn Consulting Associates, Highland Park, IL. Tel: (312) 543-3330, E-Mail: jacobsohnr@aol.com (20)

Jacobson, Kenneth, Anti-Defamation League, New York, NY. Tel: (212) 885-7700, Web Site: www.adl. org (1)

Jacobson, Mitchell, MSC Industrial Supply Co, Melville, NY. Tel: (516) 812-2000, (800) 645-7270, FAX: (800) 255-5067, E-Mail: executive@ mscdirect.com, Web Site: www.mscdirect.com (9)

Jacobson, Ph.D. Michael F., CSPI/Nutrition Action Health Letter, Washington, DC. Tel: (202) 332-9110, FAX: (202) 265-4954, E-Mail: cspi@cspinet. org, Web Site: www.cspinet.org (17)

Jacobson, Ted, Polynesian Cultural Center, Honolulu, HI. Tel: (808) 293-3333, (800) 367-7060, FAX: (888) 722-7339, E-Mail: internetrez@polynesia. com, Web Site: www.polynesia.com (16)

Jadin, Ronald L., Grainger Industrial Supply, North Brook, IL. Tel: (847) 498-5900, FAX: (847) 498-3402, Web Site: www.grainger.com (16)

Jadin, Ronald L., WW Grainger Inc, Lake Forest, IL. Tel: (847) 535-1000, (800) 472-4643, FAX: (847) 535-9122, Web Site: www.grainger.com (9)

Jaeck, Glenn, Ty Pac, Baldwinsville, NY. Tel: (315) 638-9431, (800) 356-8964, FAX: (315) 638-9433, E-Mail: info@typac.com, Web Site: www.typack. com (34)

Jaeger, Jo-Anne C., Beauticontrol Cosmetics Inc, Carrollton, TX. Tel: (972) 458-0601, (800) BEAUTI-1, FAX: (972) 458-6904, E-Mail: clientservices@ beauticontrol.com, Web Site: www.beauticontrol. com (7)

Jaehnert, Frank M., Brady Corp, Milwaukee, WI. Tel: (414) 358-6600, (800) 541-1686, FAX: (800) 292-2289, Web Site: www.bradycorp.com (16)

Jafarey, Azmi, Ipswitch Inc, Lexington, MA. Tel: (781) 676-5700, FAX: (781) 676-5710, Web Site: www. whatsupgold.com (22)

Jaff Marketing Group Inc, Spring, TX. Tel: (281) 353-0004, FAX: (281) 288-0970 (16)

Jaffe Brothers Natural Foods, Valley Center, CA. Tel: (760) 749-1133, (877) 975-2333, FAX: (760) 749-1282, E-Mail: jaffebros@att.net, Web Site: www. organicfruitsandnuts.com (4)

Michael Jaffe Stamps Inc/Brookman Stamp Co, Vancouver, WA. Tel: (360) 695-6161, (800) 782-6770, FAX: (360) 695-1616, E-Mail: mjaffe@ brookmanstamps.com, Web Site: www. brookmanstamps.com (6)

Jaffe, David, Charming Shoppes Inc., Bensalem, PA. Tel: (215) 245-9100, Web Site: www. charmingshoppers.com (2)

Jaffe, Jay M., Actuarial Enterprises Ltd, Chicago, IL. Tel: (312) 397-0099, E-Mail: jay@actentltd.com (20)

Jaffe, Lawrence, Jaffe Brothers Natural Foods, Valley Center, CA. Tel: (760) 749-1133, (877) 975-2333, FAX: (760) 749-1282, E-Mail: jaffebros@att.net, Web Site: www.organicfruitsandnuts.com (4)

Jaffe, Michael, Michael Jaffe Stamps Inc/Brookman Stamp Co, Vancouver, WA. Tel: (360) 695-6161, (800) 782-6770, FAX: (360) 695-1616, E-Mail: mjaffe@brookmanstamps.com, Web Site: www. brookmanstamps.com (6)

Jaffee, Larry, Promo Magazine, New York, NY. Tel: (203) 358-9900, (800) 927-5007, FAX: (203) 358-5816, E-Mail: larry.jaffee@penton.com, Web Site: www.promomagazine.com (17)

Jafra Cosmetics International Inc, Westlake Village, CA. Tel: (260) 423-9571, (888) 848-4077, FAX: (960) 423-6742, Web Site: www.jafra.com (7)

Don Jagoda Associates Inc, Melville, NY. Tel: (631) 454-1800, FAX: (631) 454-1834, E-Mail: information@dja.com, Web Site: www.dja.com (35)

Jagoda, Don, Don Jagoda Associates Inc, Melville, NY. Tel: (631) 454-1800, FAX: (631) 454-1834, E-Mail: information@dja.com, Web Site: www.dja.com (35)

Jahn, Calvin, Graphic Arts Center, Garland, TX. Tel: (972) 543-1250, (800) 865-7086, FAX: (972) 271-8392 (27)

Jahn, Martin, Paslode, Vernon Hills, IL. Tel: (847) 634-1900, (800) 222-6990, FAX: (847) 634-6602, E-Mail: tech@paslode.com, Web Site: www. paslode.com (16)

Jain, Naveen, Intelius Inc, Bellevue, WA. Tel: (425) 974-6100, Web Site: www.intelius.com (22)

Jain, Vivek, Fluke Biomedical, Everett, WA. Tel: (425) 347-6100, (800) 850-4608, FAX: (425) 446-5116, Web Site: www.flukebiomedical.com (16)

Jaitlin, Geraldine, Cold Spring Harbor Lab Press, Woodbury, NY. Tel: (516) 422-4100, (800) 843-4388, FAX: (516) 422-4097, E-Mail: cshpress@cshl.edu, Web Site: www.cshlpress.com (17)

JAK Productions, Atlanta, GA. Tel: (404) 883-2450, FAX: (404) 883-2672, E-Mail: info@jak-productions.com (29)

Jakobsen, Kasper, Mead Johnson Co, Evansville, IN. Tel: (812) 429-5204, Web Site: www.MeadJohnson. com (7)

Jalili, Houshang, Carabella Collection, Irvine, CA. Tel: (949) 263-2300, (800) 227-2235, FAX: (949) 263-2323, Web Site: www.carabella.com (2)

Jalili, Monir, Carabella Collection, Irvine, CA. Tel: (949) 263-2300, (800) 227-2235, FAX: (949) 263-2323, Web Site: www.carabella.com (2)

Jalufka, Frank, Education Management Corp, Pittsburgh, PA. Tel: (412) 562-0900, FAX: (412) 562-0598, Web Site: www.edmc.edu (1)

JAM Communications Inc, Washington, DC. Tel: (202) 986-4750, FAX: (202) 232-9146, E-Mail: neil@ jamagency.com, Web Site: www.jamagency.com (35)

Jamax Direct LLC, Englewood Cliffs, NJ. Tel: (201) 569-4540 (23)

Jameco Electronics, Belmont, CA. Tel: (650) 592-8097, (800) 831-4242, FAX: (650) 592-2503, (800) 237-6948, E-Mail: domestic@jameco.com, Web Site: www.jameco.com (3)

James M Sears Associates, Bergenfield, NJ. Tel: (201) 501-9977, FAX: (201) 453-0833 (30)

James Medical Rents & Sales Inc, Fort Wayne, IN. Tel: (260) 739-0874, E-Mail: sales@jamesmedical.com, Web Site: www.jamesmedical.net (7)

Robert James Co Inc, Moody, AL. Tel: (205) 640-7081, (800) 633-8296, FAX: (205) 640-7087 (10)

Victoria James Executive Search Inc, South Kent, CT. Tel: (203) 750-8838 X101, FAX: (203) 547-6284, E-Mail: vjames@victoriajames.com, Web Site: www.victoriajames.com (20)

James, Ashton, Kelly's Kids, Natchez, MS. Tel: (601) 442-5332, (800) 837-2066, FAX: (601) 442-4399, E-Mail: hello@kellyskids.com, Web Site: www. kellyskids.com (2)

James, Daniel E., Carolina Biological Supply Co, Burlington, NC. Tel: (800) 334-5551, (800) 222-7112, E-Mail: carolina@carolina.com, Web Site: www. carolina.com (9)

James, David, Bethesda List Center Inc, Bethesda, MD. Tel: (301) 986-1455, FAX: (301) 907-4870, E-Mail: info@bethesda-list.com, Web Site: www.bethesda-list.com (24)

James, Diane, CAIG Laboratories Inc, Poway, CA. Tel: (858) 486-8388, FAX: (858) 486-8398, E-Mail: caig123@caig.com, Web Site: www.caig.com (9)

James, Donald M., Vulcan Materials Co, Birmingham, AL. Tel: (205) 298-3000, FAX: (205) 298-2960, Web Site: www.vulcanmaterials.com (16)

James, Doug, James Medical Rents & Sales Inc, Fort Wayne, IN. Tel: (260) 739-0874, E-Mail: sales@ jamesmedical.com, Web Site: www.jamesmedical. net (7)

James, Drew, Target Marketing Magazine, Philadelphia, PA. Tel: (215) 238-5300, (800) 777-8074, FAX: (215) 238-5270, Web Site: www. targetmarketingmag.com (43)

James, Gregory, Peter Glenn Publications, Delray Beach, FL. Tel: (561) 404-4290, (888) 332-6700, FAX: (561) 892-5786, E-Mail: gregjames@pgdirect. com, Web Site: www.pgdirect.com (17)

James, Lynn, Kelly's Kids, Natchez, MS. Tel: (601) 442-5332, (800) 837-2066, FAX: (601) 442-4399, E-Mail: hello@kellyskids.com, Web Site: www. kellyskids.com (2)

James, Renee J. Intel Corp. Santa Clara, CA. Tel: (408) 765-8080, (800) 548-4725, FAX: (408) 765-6187, Web Site: www.intel.com (16)

James, Rich, New England Stock Photo, Glastonbury, CT. Tel: (860) 659-4949, FAX: (860) 659-3235 (38)

James, Robert, Balboa Life & Casualty, Irvine, CA. Tel: (949) 222-8000, (800) 854-6115, FAX: (949) 222-8777, Web Site: www.balboainsurance.com (15)

James, Robert M., Kross Inc, Santa Clarita, CA. Tel: (661) 284-3557, (800) 456-3699, FAX: (661) 257-1914, Web Site: www.krosskits.com (16)

James, Tiffany, UndercoverWear Inc, Tewksbury, MA. Tel: (978) 851-8580, (800) 733-0007, FAX: (978) 640-2882, E-Mail: service@undercoverwear.com, Web Site: www.undercoverwear.com (2)

James, Victoria, Victoria James Executive Search Inc, South Kent, CT. Tel: (203) 750-8838 X101, FAX: (203) 547-6284, E-Mail: vjames@victoriajames. com, Web Site: www.victoriajames.com (20)

James, Victoria, Women in Direct Marketing International, New York, NY. Tel: (516) 746-6700, FAX: (516) 294-8141, Web Site: www.wdmi.org (40)

James, Walter, UndercoverWear Inc, Tewksbury, MA. Tel: (978) 851-8580, (800) 733-0007, FAX: (978) 640-2882, E-Mail: service@undercoverwear.com, Web Site: www.undercoverwear.com (2)

Jameson, Piper, Lincoln Educational Services Corp, West Orange, NJ. Tel: (973) 736-9340, Web Site: www.lincolnedu.com (13)

Herbert L Jamison & Co LLC, West Orange, NJ. Tel: (973) 731-0806, (800) 526-4766, (800) JAMISON, FAX: (973) 731-3035, Web Site: www. jamisongroup.com (15)

Jamitkowski, Jamie, UndercoverWear Inc, Tewksbury, MA. Tel: (978) 851-8580, (800) 733-0007, FAX: (978) 640-2882, E-Mail: service@undercoverwear. com, Web Site: www.undercoverwear.com (2)

Janacek, Ike, Chateau Le Combe, Edmonton, AB Canada. Tel: (780) 428-6611, (800) 661-8801, FAX: (780) 425-6564, E-Mail: info@chateaulecombe. com, Web Site: www.chateaulecombe.com (19)

Janc, Ken, Lorex Inc, Elk River, MN. Tel: (763) 441-0055, (800) 792-8812, E-Mail: customerservice@ lorexinc.com, Web Site: www.lorexinc.com (35)

Jandron, Paul, Invacare Supply Group, Milford, MA. Tel: (508) 429-1000, (800) 225-4792, FAX: (508) 429-1581, E-Mail: service.isg@invacare.com, Web Site: www.invacaresupplygroup.com (16)

Jane Corcillo, Norwalk, CT. Tel: (203) 866-2008, FAX: (203) 299-0844, E-Mail: queries@corcillodirect. com, Web Site: www.corcillodirect.com (39)

Janes, Gabriele, CMA Awards, Don Mills, ON Canada. Tel: (416) 391-2362, FAX: (416) 441-4062, E-Mail: info@the-cma.org, Web Site: www.the-cma.org/ awards (42)

Janes, Gabriele, CMA Events & Education, Don Mills, ON Canada. Tel: (416) 391-2362, FAX: (416) 441-4062, E-Mail: info@the-cma.org, Web Site: www. the-cma.org (42)

Jania, AJ, Diamond Envelope Corp, Aurora, IL. Tel: (630) 499-2800, FAX: (630) 499-2801 (26)

Jania, Alan, Diamond Envelope Corp, Aurora, IL. Tel: (630) 499-2800, FAX: (630) 499-2801 (26)

Jania, Michael, Diamond Envelope Corp, Aurora, IL. Tel: (630) 499-2800, FAX: (630) 499-2801 (26)

Jania, Susan, Diamond Envelope Corp, Aurora, IL. Tel: (630) 499-2800, FAX: (630) 499-2801 (26)

Janice's LLC, Hartford, CT. Tel: (860) 523-4479, (800) 526-4237, FAX: (860) 523-4178, E-Mail: dlerner@ janices.com, Web Site: www.janices.com (8)

Janicki, Harry, Nomadics Tipi Makers, Bend, OR. Tel: (541) 389-3980, FAX: (541) 389-3980, Web Site: www.tipi.com (11)

Jankey, Molly, Andrea Electronics Corp, Bohemia, NY. Tel: (631) 719-1800, (800) 442-7787, FAX: (631) 719-1950, Web Site: www.andreaelectronics.com (16)

Jankowski, Ed, Godiva Chocolatier, New York, NY. Tel: (212) 984-5900, (800) 946-3482, Web Site: www.godiva.com (4)

Jankowski, Kim, Automotive Headphones, Sterling Heights, MI. Tel: (586) 292-6166 (16)

Jann, Bill, Media Dynamics LLC, Greenwich, CT. Tel: (203) 531-6600, FAX: (203) 531-6661, E-Mail: bjann@mediadynamx.com, Web Site: www.Media-Dynamics.com (31)

Janos, Edward H., Support Plus, Hudson, OH. Tel: (866) 553-8875, (800) 229-2910, FAX: (800) 950-9569, E-Mail: cs@supportplus.com, Web Site: www.supportplus.com (7)

Janos, Eloise, Support Plus, Hudson, OH. Tel: (866) 553-8875, (800) 229-2910, FAX: (800) 950-9569, E-Mail: cs@supportplus.com, Web Site: www. supportplus.com (7)

Janssen, Debra A., CDS Global, Des Moines, IA. Tel: (515) 246-6837, FAX: (515) 246-6687, E-Mail: dluther@cdsfulfillment.com, Web Site: www. cdsglobal.com (22)

Jantz Supply Koval Knives, Davis, OK. Tel: (580) 369-2316, (800) 351-8900, FAX: (580) 369-3082, Web Site: www.knifemaking.com (9)

Janulewicz, Tony, Roosevelt Paper Co, Mount Laurel, NJ. Tel: (856) 303-4100, (856) 303-4200, (800) 523-3470, FAX: (856) 642-1950, (856) 642-1949, Web Site: www.rooseveltpaper.com (25)

Japinga, Ronald, West Marine Inc, Watsonville, CA. Tel: (831) 728-2700, (800) 262-8464, (800) BOAT-ING, FAX: (831) 768-5000, E-Mail: customercare@ westmarine.com, Web Site: www.westmarine.com (11)

Japs-Olson Co, Saint Louis Park, MN. Tel: (952) 932-9393, (800) 548-2897, FAX: (612) 912-1900, Web Site: www.japsolson.com (27)

Jarashow, Daniel, Campmor Inc, Mahwah, NJ. Tel: (201) 335-9064, (800) 525-4784, FAX: (201) 236-3601, Web Site: www.campmor.com (17)

Jarashow, Morton, Campmor Inc, Mahwah, NJ. Tel: (201) 335-9064, (800) 525-4784, FAX: (201) 236-3601, Web Site: www.campmor.com (17)

Jarden Corp, Boca Raton, FL. Tel: (561) 912-4395, Web Site: www.jarden.com (16)

Jaritz, Alexandra, Choice Hotels International, Rockville, MD. Tel: (301) 592-5000, Web Site: www.choicehotels.com (16)

Jaros, Karin, The Morton Arboretum, Lisle, IL. Tel: (630) 968-0074, Web Site: www.mortonarb.org (1)

Jarr, Robert, Communicor, Milwaukee, WI. Tel: (414) 961-5999, FAX: (414) 961-5990, Web Site: www. communicor.com (36)

Jarvis, John, The Lacek Group, Minneapolis, MN. Tel: (612) 359-3700, FAX: (612) 359-9395, E-Mail: info@lacek.com, Web Site: www.lacek.com (35)

Jarvis, Mike, Chain Store Guide, Tampa, FL. Tel: (800) 927-9292, FAX: (813) 627-6882, E-Mail: info@ csgis.com, Web Site: www.csgis.com (17)

Jarymiszyn, Phil, PNT Marketing Services, Inc, Long Island City, NY. Tel: (718) 433-4063, (888) 768-2210, FAX: (914) 428-0504, E-Mail: tony@ pntmarketingservices.com, Web Site: www. pntmarketingservices.com (22)

Jasek Enterprises, Westlake Village, CA. Tel: (805) 379-2871, FAX: (805) 379-9839 (20)

Jason Natural Personal Care Products, Boulder, CO. Tel: (88) 659-7730, Web Site: www.jason-natural. com (7)

Jason, Debra, The Write Direction, Boulder, CO. Tel: (808) 635-8031, E-Mail: debra@writedirection.com, Web Site: www.writedirection.com (39)

Jason, Tracey, Nielsen Trade Dimensions, Wilton, CT. Tel: (203) 222-5750, (800) 291-0410, FAX: (203) 222-5701, E-Mail: tradedimensions.info@nielsen. com, Web Site: www.tradedimensions.com (17)

Jasper, Robert G., Marketing Horizons Inc, Saint Louis, MO. Tel: (314) 432-1957, (800) 669-0839, FAX: (314) 432-7014, E-Mail: jkramer@mhorizons.com (30)

Jastrem, John, Exhibitgroup/Giltspur, Roselle, IL. Tel: (972) 538-3031, (800) 843-3944, Web Site: www.e-g.com (30)

Jauzapaitis, Stephen, Arbus Capital Ltd, Schaumburg, IL. Tel: (847) 290-9600, FAX: (847) 290-9601 (16)

Javaherian, Parham, Practice Builders, Irvine, CA. Tel: (800) 679-1262, FAX: (714) 751-7801, E-Mail: info@practicebuilders.com, Web Site: www. practicebuilders.com (35)

Javelin Marketing Group, Irving, TX. Tel: (972) 443-7000, FAX: (972) 443-7194, E-Mail: info@javelin. mg, Web Site: www.javelin.mg (30)

Jay, Al, Colorworks Graphics Inc, Chicago, IL. Tel: (312) 666-7642, FAX: (312) 666-0473, E-Mail: colorworks@ameritech.net, Web Site: www. colorworksgraphics.com (34)

Jayne, Fairman, Sandy Mush Herb Nursery, Leicester, NC. Tel: (828) 683-2014, E-Mail: info@ sandymushherbs.com, Web Site: www. sandymushherbs.com (8)

Jayne, Kate, Sandy Mush Herb Nursery, Leicester, NC. Tel: (828) 683-2014, E-Mail: info@ sandymushherbs.com, Web Site: www. sandymushherbs.com (8)

Jaypro Sports, Waterford, CT. Tel: (860) 447-3001, (800) 243-0533, FAX: (800) 988-3363, E-Mail: info@jaypro.com, Web Site: www.jaypro.com (11)

Jaz Holdings LLC, Liberty Corner, NJ. Tel: (973) 574-7600, (800) 999-9554, FAX: (973) 944-5073, E-Mail: webmaster@regentbook.com, Web Site: www.regentbook.com (16)

Jazwiec, John G., WennSoft, New Berlin, WI. Tel: (262) 821-4100, FAX: (262) 821-3838, Web Site: www.wennsoft.com (22)

Jazzercise Inc, Carlsbad, CA. Tel: (760) 476-1750, FAX: (760) 602-7180, E-Mail: customercare@ jazzercise.com, Web Site: www.jazzercise.com (2)

JazzTimes Magazine Inc, Quincy, MA. Tel: (617) 706-9110, FAX: (617) 536-0102, E-Mail: info@ jazztimes.com, Web Site: www.jazztimes.com (17)

JDA Software Group Inc, Scottsdale, AZ. Tel: (480) 308-3000, (800) 479-7382, FAX: (480) 308-3001, E-Mail: info@jda.com, Web Site: www.jda.com (22)

Jean, Phil, Trends International LLC, Indianapolis, IN. Tel: (317) 388-1212, (800) 354-4639, FAX: (317) 388-1414, E-Mail: info@trendsinternational.com, Web Site: www.trendsinternational.com (38)

Jedele, Mary Sue, Marketing/Media Dynamics Inc, Harpers Ferry, WV. Tel: (304) 725-1119 (20)

Jeffers & Co, Dothan, AL. Tel: (334) 793-6257, (800) 533-3377, FAX: (334) 793-5179, E-Mail: customerservice@jefferspet.com, Web Site: www. jefferspet.com (5)

Jeffers, Dorothy, Jeffers & Co, Dothan, AL. Tel: (334) 793-6257, (800) 533-3377, FAX: (334) 793-5179, E-Mail: customerservice@jefferspet.com, Web Site: www.jefferspet.com (5)

Jeffers, Ruth, Jeffers & Co, Dothan, AL. Tel: (334) 793-6257, (800) 533-3377, FAX: (334) 793-5179, E-Mail: customerservice@jefferspet.com, Web Site: www.jefferspet.com (5)

Jefferson National, Louisville, KY. Tel: (502) 587-3853, Web Site: www.jeffnat.com (14)

Jeffery, Jeannie, Butler Schein Animal Health, Dublin, OH. Tel: (614) 761-9095, (888) 691-2724, FAX: (888) 329-3861, Web Site: www.butlerschein.com (16)

Jeffress, Dr. Conway A., Schoolcraft College, Livonia, MI. Tel: (734) 462-4400, Web Site: www. schoolcraft.edu (1)

Jeffrey Lant Associates Inc, Cambridge, MA. Tel: (617) 547-6372, FAX: (617) 547-0061, E-Mail: drjlant@ worldprofit.com, Web Site: www.thejeffreylanttrust. org (5)

Jeffrey, Scott, ABCO Inc, Dallas, TX. Tel: (214) 565-1191, Web Site: www.abcoinc.com (20)

Jeffs, Dirk, Ultradent Products Inc, South Jordan, UT. Tel: (801) 572-4200, FAX: (801) 553-4600, E-Mail: onlineordersupport@ultradent.com, Web Site: www. ultradent.com (7)

Jelinek, Craig, Costco Wholesale, Issaquah, WA. Tel: (425) 313-8647, 800-774-2678, E-Mail: customerservice@contactcostco.com, Web Site: www.costco.com (33)

Jellinek, Jimmy, Playboy Enterprises Inc, Beverly Hills, CA. Tel: (310) 860-1215, Web Site: www. playboyenterprises.com (17)

Jellison, Bob, PAPYRUS, Fairfield, CA. Tel: (707) 428-0200, Web Site: www.papyrusonline.com (5)

Jencks, John, Applications Development Corp, Dekalb, IL. Tel: (815) 754-7432, Web Site: www. appdevcorp.com (20)

Jenco Productions Inc, San Bernardino, CA. Tel: (909) 381-9453, FAX: (909) 383-1106, Web Site: www. jencoproductions.com (28)

Jendra, Bryan, Royal Performance Group, Lisle, IL. Tel: (630) 353-7900, (888) 774-0125, FAX: (630) 353-7902, E-Mail: info@rpgglobal.com, Web Site: www.rpggiftcards.com (34)

Jenkin, Tom, Caesars Entertainment Corp, Las Vegas, NV. Tel: (702) 407-6000, (800) 634-6001, FAX: (702) 407-6037, Web Site: www.caesars.com (16)

Jenkins, Dave, Traction On Demand, Burnaby, BC Canada. Tel: (604) 620-6040, Web Site: www.tractionondemand.com (35)

Jenkins, Gregory, The Flinchbaugh Co Inc, Manchester, PA. Tel: (717) 266-2202, FAX: (717) 266-7055, E-Mail: flinchbaugh@blazenet.net, Web Site: www.flinchbaugh.com (16)

Jenkins, Jo Ann, AARP, Washington, DC. Tel: (202) 434-2277, FAX: (202) 434-2525, Web Site: www.aarp.org (1)

Jenkins, Michael, MarketLeverage, Lake Mary, FL. Tel: (407) 268-7700, FAX: (407) 268-7654, Web Site: www.precisionplaymedia.com (22)

Jenkins, Michael, Precision Play Media / MarketLeverage, Lake Mary, FL. Tel: (407) 805-8800, Web Site: www.precisionplaymedia.com (22)

Jenkins, P. Thomas, Open Text Inc, Waterloo, ON Canada. Tel: (519) 888-9933, (800) 499-6544, FAX: (519) 888-0677, E-Mail: support@opentext.com, Web Site: www.opentext.com (16)

Jenkins, Tracy, Lending Tree/Home Loan Center, Charlotte, NC. Tel: (704) 541-5351, (800) 555-8733, FAX: (704) 541-1824, Web Site: www.lendingtree.com (14)

Jenks, Tom, BBM Canada Inc, Don Mills, ON Canada. Tel: (416) 445-9800, FAX: (416) 445-8644, E-Mail: info@bbm.ca, Web Site: www.bbm.ca (30)

Jenks, William, Safeco Insurance Co, Seattle, WA. Tel: (206) 545-5000, (800) 332-3226, FAX: (206) 545-5767/5651, Web Site: www.safeco.com (15)

Jenloz, Claude, The Renovator's Supply Inc, Millers Falls, MA. Tel: (413) 423-3300, (800) 659-2211, FAX: (413) 423-3800, E-Mail: customercare@rensup.com, Web Site: www.rensup.com (9)

Jennemann, Mark, Bullseye Database Marketing LLC, Tulsa, OK. Tel: (918) 587-1731, FAX: (918) 587-0450, E-Mail: inquiries@bullseyedm.com, Web Site: www.bullseyedm.com (35)

Brian Jenner Inc, Pasco, WA. Tel: (509) 735-2172, FAX: (509) 783-8042 (6)

Jenner, Brian, Brian Jenner Inc, Pasco, WA. Tel: (509) 735-2172, FAX: (509) 783-8042 (6)

Jenney Laffey, Noreen S., Celebrity Endorsement Network (CEN), Calabasas, CA. Tel: (818) 225-7090, FAX: (818) 880-0898, E-Mail: info@celebrityendorsement.com, Web Site: www.celebrityendorsement.com (35)

Jennings, Vince, National Mail/Marketing Corp, Broomall, PA. Tel: (610) 544-8200, FAX: (610) 544-1819, Web Site: www.natlmail.com (20)

Jenny Products Inc, Somerset, PA. Tel: (814) 445-3400, FAX: (814) 445-2280, Web Site: www.jennyproducts.com (16)

Jensen, Jeff, Specialized Association Services, Irving, TX. Tel: (469) 524-5000, E-Mail: hvincent@1sas.com, Web Site: www.1sas.com (1)

Jensen, Jeffrey J., National Motor Club of America Inc, Irving, TX. Tel: (972) 999-4400, (800) 523-4582, FAX: (972) 999-4405, Web Site: www.nmca.com (1)

Jensen, Jim, F P International, Fremont, CA. Tel: (650) 261-5300, (800) 866-9946, FAX: (650) 361-1713, Web Site: www.fpintl.com (16)

Jensen, Jon A., L-Com Inc, North Andover, MA. Tel: (978) 682-6936, FAX: (978) 689-9484, Web Site: www.L-com.com (22)

Jensen, Joseph, Astronomical Society of the Pacific, San Francisco, CA. Tel: (415) 337-1100, (800) 335-2624, FAX: (415) 337-5205, E-Mail: service@astrosociety.org, Web Site: www.astrosociety.org (1)

Jensen, Kenneth R., Coast to Coast Inc, Englewood, CO. Tel: (303) 728-2267, Web Site: www.coastresorts.com (1)

Jensen, Lance, Hill Holliday, Boston, MA. Tel: (617) 366-4000, Web Site: www.hhcc.com (35)

Jensen, Stephan, Direct Resources Group Inc, Seattle, WA. Tel: (206) 455-6157, FAX: (206) 749-0005, E-Mail: results@drg.com, Web Site: www.drg.com (35)

Jensen, William T., Methode Electronics Inc, Chicago, IL. Tel: (708) 867-6777, FAX: (708) 867-6999, E-Mail: info@methode.com, Web Site: www.methode.com (9)

Jenson, Mark, NTP Distribution, Wilsonville, OR. Tel: (503) 570-0171, FAX: (888) 570-0342, Web Site: www.ntpdistribution.com (34)

Jenson, Warren C., Acxiom Corp, Little Rock, AR. Tel: (501) 342-1000, FAX: (501) 342-3913, Web Site: www.acxiom.com (22)

Jeppesen, Englewood, CO. Tel: (303) 799-9090, (800) 353-2107, Web Site: www.jeppesen.com (22)

Jerauld, Marc, Speedeon Data Corp, Cleveland, OH. Tel: (866) 647-9219, Web Site: www.speedeondata.com (30)

Jerchower, Barbara, Williams, Caliri, Miller & Otley, Wayne, NJ. Tel: (973) 694-0800, FAX: (973) 694-0302, Web Site: www.wcmolaw.com (20)

Jerden Records/SpeechWorks, Redmond, WA. Tel: (425) 882-3344, (888) 401-4487, FAX: (425) 882-3494, E-Mail: jerden@aol.com, Web Site: www.soundworks.net (16)

Jerden, Cris, Direct Marketing Group, Eden Prairie, MN. Tel: (952) 975-5060, (888) 397-5060, FAX: (952) 906-0608, Web Site: www.directmg.com (35)

Jerick, Marty, ICS Marketing Services, Lansing, MI. Tel: (517) 394-1890, (888) 394-1890, FAX: (517) 394-7408, E-Mail: sales@icshq.com, Web Site: icshq.com (21)

Jeroboam, San Francisco, CA. Tel: (415) 824-8085 cell, E-Mail: jeroboamster@gmail.com (38)

Jerry's Artarama, Raleigh, NC. Tel: (919) 878-8478, (800) U-ARTIST, FAX: (919) 873-9565, E-Mail: micah@jerrysartarama.com, Web Site: www.jerrysartarama.com (10)

Jersey Printing Associates Inc, Atlantic Highlands, NJ. Tel: (732) 872-9654, FAX: (732) 872-9309, E-Mail: sales@jerseyprinting.com, Web Site: www.jerseyprinting.com (27)

Jesco Industries Inc, Litchfield, MI. Tel: (517) 542-2903, (866) 638-8577, FAX: (517) 542-2501, E-Mail: jesco@jescoonline.com, Web Site: www.jescoonline.com (34)

Jesinoski, Barry A., Disabled American Veterans, Cincinnati, OH. Tel: (859) 441-7300, FAX: (859) 442-2084, E-Mail: feedback@davmail.org, Web Site: www.dav.org (1)

Jeske, Doug, Meyocks, West Des Moines, IA. Tel: (515) 225-1200, FAX: (515) 225-6400, E-Mail: meanmore@meyocks.com, Web Site: www.meyocks.com (35)

Jessee, Lance H., Posty Cards Inc, Kansas City, MO. Tel: (816) 231-2323, (800) 554-5018, FAX: (888) 577-3800, E-Mail: customerservice@postycards.com, Web Site: www.postycards.com (16)

Jessup, Bill, Psion Teklogix Inc, Mississauga, ON Canada. Tel: (905) 813-9900, (800) 322-3437, E-Mail: ptinfo@psion.com, Web Site: www.psionteklogix.com (3)

Jet LithoColor Inc, Downers Grove, IL. Tel: (630) 932-9000, (800) 932-1538, (800) 932-1JET, FAX: (630) 932-9101, E-Mail: sales@jetlitho.com, Web Site: www.jetlitho.com (27)

JetSpring, Richmond, VA. Tel: (804) 359-8295, FAX: (804) 359-1686, Web Site: www.jetspring.com (30)

Jewell, Jan, Birthday Express Inc, Kirkland, WA. Tel: (425) 250-1064, (800) 247-8432, FAX: (425) 641-2028, Web Site: www.birthdayexpress.com (5)

Jewell, Michael, Birthday Express Inc, Kirkland, WA. Tel: (425) 250-1064, (800) 247-8432, FAX: (425) 641-2028, Web Site: www.birthdayexpress.com (5)

Jewett, Dwight, Globe Marketing Systems Inc, Coral Springs, FL. Tel: (954) 753-7173, (800) 382-9013, FAX: (954) 337-0650, Web Site: www.internetprintcenter.com (27)

Jewett, Rebecca, Windward Group, Shelburne, VT. Tel: (802) 985-3631, Web Site: www.windwardgroup.us (20)

The Jewish Federation of Greater Washington, North Bethesda, MD. Tel: (301) 230-7200, Web Site: www.shalomdc.org (1)

The Jewish Publication Society, Philadelphia, PA. Tel: (215) 832-0600, (800) 234-3151, FAX: (215) 568-2017, Web Site: www.jewishpub.org (17)

Jezouit, Allen, Berkshire Direct Inc, Williamstown, MA. Tel: (413) 458-1721, FAX: (413) 458-1727, E-Mail: info@berkshiredirect.com, Web Site: www.berkshiredirect.com (17)

J Jill Group, Inc, Quincy, MA. Tel: (617) 376-4300, (800) 642-9989, FAX: (617) 769-0177, Web Site: www.jjillgroup.com (2)

Jillian, Louise, Go Ahead Vacations, Cambridge, MA. Tel: (617) 619-1000, (800) 242-4686, FAX: (617) 619-1001, E-Mail: goahead@et.com, Web Site: www.goaheadvacations.com (16)

Jilling, John, Eagle Claw Fishing Tackle, Denver, CO. Tel: (720) 941-8700, FAX: (303) 321-4750, E-Mail: info@eagleclaw.com, Web Site: www.eagleclaw.com (11)

Jimenez, Charisse, American College of Physician Executives, Tampa, FL. Tel: (813) 287-2000, (800) 562-8088, FAX: (813) 287-8993, E-Mail: acpe@acpe.org, Web Site: www.acpe.org (1)

Jimenez, Joseph, Novartis Pharmaceuticals Corp, East Hanover, NJ. Tel: (862) 778-2100, (800) 669-6682, FAX: (973) 781-8119, Web Site: www.novartis.com (7)

Jimenez, Selena, KHL Engineered Packaging Solutions, Buena Park, CA. Tel: (714) 690-6361 (16)

Jin, Yuangie, Boundless Corp, Phelps, NY. Tel: (631) 962-1500, (800) 231-5445, FAX: (631) 962-1505, E-Mail: sales@boundless.com, Web Site: www.boundless.com (16)

Jobscope Corp, Greenville, SC. Tel: (864) 458-3143, (800) 443-5794, FAX: (864) 234-4852, E-Mail: marketing@jobscope.com, Web Site: www.jobscope.com (16)

Jobse, Tracey, Progressive Distribution Services Inc, Grand Rapids, MI. Tel: (616) 957-5900, (800) 304-3699, FAX: (616) 957-2990, E-Mail: sales@progressive-commerce.com, Web Site: www.prodist.com (28)

Jobson, James, Rigden Inc, Boulder, CO. Tel: (303) 442-8190, FAX: (303) 442-8686, E-Mail: rigden@rigden.com, Web Site: www.rigden.com (22)

Jockey International Global Inc, Kenosha, WI. Tel: (262) 658-8111 (2)

Jodie, Kregg, Mary Kay Cosmetics Inc, Addison, TX. Tel: (972) 687-6300, (800) MARY KAY, FAX: (972) 687-1611, Web Site: www.marykay.com (16)

Joers, Barbara, Gillette Children's Specialty Healthcare, Saint Paul, MN. Tel: (651) 291-2848, Web Site: www.gillettechildrens.org (1)

Jofco Inc, Jasper, IN. Tel: (812) 482-5154, (800) 23-JOFCO, FAX: (812) 634-2392, E-Mail: furniture@jofco.com, Web Site: www.jofco.com (16)

Joffe, Karen, Public Issues Management, Piedmont, CA. Tel: (510) 654-9114, FAX: (510) 654-0196 (20)

Joffe, Rodney, Whitehat Inc, Tempe, AZ. Tel: (480) 858-9000, FAX: (480) 858-9001, E-Mail: sales@whitehat.com, Web Site: www.whitehat.com (32)

Joffrey Long Consultants, Granada Hills, CA. Tel: (818) 635-1777, Web Site: www.southwestbancorp.com (20)

Joggerst, Patrick, Telcordia Technologies, Piscataway, NJ. Tel: (732) 699-2000, FAX: (973) 829-2458, Web Site: www.telcordia.com (16)

Johannes, Dave, IWCO Direct, Chanhassen, MN. Tel: (952) 474-0961, FAX: (952) 474-6467, Web Site: www.iwco.com (21)

Johannes, Eric, IC System Inc, Saint Paul, MN. Tel: (800) 443-4123, Web Site: www.icsystem.com (20)

John Deere Financial, Johnston, IA. Tel: (515) 267-3000, (800) 275-5322, FAX: (515) 267-3292, Web Site: www.deere.com (14)

John Hancock Financial Services Inc, Boston, MA. Tel: (617) 572-6000, (800) 732-5543, FAX: (617) 572-6451, Web Site: www.johnhancock.com (15)

John Hancock Retirement Plan Services, Toronto, ON Canada. Tel: (416) 852-1035, Web Site: www.jhancock.com (14)

John Henry Packaging, Lansing, MI. Tel: (707) 778-1250, (800) 327-5997, FAX: (707) 762-1253, Web Site: www.jhpackaging.com (27)

John, Roxanne, Institute for International Research Inc, New York, NY. Tel: (212) 661-3500, (800) 345-8016, FAX: (212) 599-2192, E-Mail: register@iirusa.com, Web Site: www.iir-ny.com (16)

Johnny Appleseed's Inc, Middleton, MA. Tel: (978) 922-2040, (800) 546-4554, FAX: (978) 922-7001, Web Site: www.appleseeds.blair.com (2)

Johns, Andy, Ziff Davis Media Inc, New York, NY. Tel: (212) 503-5100, FAX: (212) 503-5023, Web Site: www.ziffdavis.com (17)

Johns, Chris, National Geographic Society, Washington, DC. Tel: (202) 862-8638, (800) 373-1717, Web Site: www.nationalgeographic.com (17)

Johns, Donna, PromarkDirect Inc, Ramsey, NJ. Tel: (201) 489-0532, (800) 776-6275, FAX: (201) 489-2680, E-Mail: solutions@promarkdirect.com, Web Site: www.promarkdirect.com (21)

Johns, John D., Protective Life Corp, Deerfield, IL. Tel: (847) 948-8988, (800) 323-5771, FAX: (847) 948-1156, Web Site: www.protective.com (15)

Johns, John E., Protective Life Insurance Co, Birmingham, AL. Tel: (205) 268-1000, (800) 866-3555, FAX: (205) 868-3086, Web Site: www.protective.com (15)

Johns, Mickey, Wyandotte West Communications Inc, Kansas City, KS. Tel: (913) 788-5565, FAX: (913) 788-9812, E-Mail: news@wyandottewest.com, Web Site: www.wyandottewest.com (17)

Johnson & Johnson, New Brunswick, NJ. Tel: (732) 524-0400, FAX: (732) 214-0332, Web Site: www.jnj.com (16)

Johnson & Quin Inc, Niles, IL. Tel: (847) 588-4800, FAX: (847) 647-6949, E-Mail: jqinfo@j-quin.com, Web Site: www.j-quin.com (28)

Johnson & Wales University, Providence, RI. Tel: (401) 598-1000, (800) DIAL-JWU, FAX: (401) 598-1833, Web Site: www.jwu.edu (41)

Johnson Direct LLC, Brookfield, WI. Tel: (262) 782-2750, (800) 710-2750, FAX: (262) 782-2751, E-Mail: info@responsory.com, Web Site: www.johnsondirect.com (35)

Johnson Wilshire Distributors Service Corp, Santa Fe Springs, CA. Tel: (562) 777-0088, (800) 922-2456, FAX: (562) 777-0099, (800) 993-9699, E-Mail: jwigloves@aol.com, Web Site: www.johnsonwilshire.com (34)

Johnson, Alan, Gulf Coast Data Supply Inc, Milton, FL. Tel: (850) 994-7042, (800) 226-DISK, FAX: (850) 479-4441, Web Site: www.gulfdata.com (3)

Johnson, Allen, Westhoff Machine Co, Saint Louis, MO. Tel: (314) 963-7130, (800) 364-0280, FAX: (800) 324-1942, E-Mail: mail@westhoffinc.com, Web Site: www.westhoffinc.com (9)

Johnson, Alyson, Days Inns Worldwide Inc, Parsippany, NJ. Tel: (973) 753-6000, (800) 441-1618, Web Site: www.daysinn.com (16)

Johnson, Andy, Cadmus Communications, Richmond, VA. Tel: (804) 261-3000, (800) 888-2973, Web Site: www.cenveo.com (35)

Johnson, Bill, Tennessee Valley Authority, Knoxville, TN. Tel: (865) 632-2101, Web Site: www.tva.gov (16)

Johnson, Billy R., The American Legion National Headquarters, Indianapolis, IN. Tel: (317) 860-3100, (800) 433-2700, FAX: (317) 860-3001, Web Site: www.legion.org (1)

Johnson, Bob, Facts 'n Figures, Sherman Oaks, CA. Tel: (661) 222-2278, (818) 986-6600, FAX: (661) 222-2287, Web Site: www.factsnfiguresinc.com (30)

Johnson, Brenda, Mays Mission for the Handicapped Inc, Heber Springs, AR. Tel: (501) 362-7526, (888) 503-7955, FAX: (501) 362-7529, E-Mail: info@maysmission.org, Web Site: www.maysmission.org (27)

Johnson, Brett, Optronics Inc, Muskogee, OK. Tel: (918) 683-9514, (800) 364-5483, FAX: (918) 683-9517, E-Mail: sales@optronicsinc.com, Web Site: www.optronicsinc.com (11)

Johnson, Bruce W., Strata Marketing Inc, Chicago, IL. Tel: (312) 222-1555, FAX: (312) 222-2510, Web Site: www.stratag.com (30)

Johnson, Carolyn M., Protective Life Corp, Deerfield, IL. Tel: (847) 948-8988, (800) 323-5771, FAX: (847) 948-1156, Web Site: www.protective.com (15)

Johnson, Chris, Jostens, Inc, Minneapolis, MN. Tel: (952) 830-3300, FAX: (952) 830-3293, Web Site: www.jostens.com (16)

Johnson, Christopher C., Roberts Stock/Classic Stock, Philadelphia, PA. Tel: (213) 386-4600, (800) 786-6300. FAX: (213) 365-7171, E-Mail: aspstockpix@earthlink.net, Web Site: www.americanstockphotos.com (38)

Johnson, Colin, Symetra Financial, Bellevue, WA. Tel: (425) 256-8000, (800) 426-7355, FAX: (425) 256-5737, Web Site: www.symetra.com (15)

Johnson, Dan, Team Cheer, Geneseo, NY. Tel: (800) 350-1562, (877) 243-5268, E-Mail: custserv@teamcheer.com, Web Site: www.teamcheer.com (2)

Johnson, Dave, iCrossing, New York, NY. Tel: (212) 649-3900, FAX: (646) 280-1091, Web Site: www.icrossing.com (32)

Johnson, David, HF Direct, Birmingham, AL. Tel: (205) 458-8200, FAX: (205) 458-8206, E-Mail: info@hfdirect.com, Web Site: www.hfdirect.com (35)

Johnson, David, Live Design, New York, NY. Tel: (212) 204-4268, FAX: (212) 204-4291, Web Site: livedesignonline.com (17)

Johnson, David M., The Hartford Financial Services Inc, Southington, CT. Tel: (860) 547-5000, (860) 843-8070, FAX: (860) 547-2680, Web Site: www.thehartford.com (15)

Johnson, David, School Specialty Inc, Greenville, WI. Tel: (920) 734-5712, (888) 388-3224, FAX: (920) 734-5112, E-Mail: info@schoolspecialty.com, Web Site: www.schoolspecialty.com (16)

Johnson, David T., Amvac Chemical Corp, Los Angeles, CA. Tel: (323) 264-3910, (888) 462-6822, Web Site: www.amvac-chemical.com (8)

Johnson, David, Tova Corp, West Chester, PA. Tel: (800) 852-9999, Web Site: www.beautybytova.com (7)

Johnson, Debbie, American Diabetes Association, Alexandria, VA. Tel: (703) 549-1500, (800) 342-2383, Web Site: www.diabetes.org (1)

Johnson, Don, JohnsonRauhoff Inc, Saint Joseph, MI. Tel: (269) 428-3377, (800) 572-3996, FAX: (269) 428-3312, E-Mail: questions@johnson-rauhoff.com, Web Site: www.johnsonrauhoff.com (35)

Johnson, Ed, House of Orange, Brentwood Bay, BC Canada. Tel: (866) 401-9174, FAX: (250) 652-8673, E-Mail: houseoforange@shaw.ca, Web Site: www.houseoforangeltd.com (2)

Johnson, Edward C., Fidelity Investments, Boston, MA. Tel: (617) 563-7000, (800) 343-3548, FAX: (617) 476-6150, Web Site: www.fidelity.com (14)

Johnson, Edward, Dynamics Research Corp, Andover, MA. Tel: (978) 475-9090, (800) 522-4321, FAX: (978) 475-8205, Web Site: www.drc.com (16)

Johnson, Eric, The Orvis Co Inc, Manchester, VT. Tel: (802) 362-3622, FAX: (802) 362-3525, Web Site: www.orvis.com (11)

Johnson, Eric, Win Craft Inc, Winona, MN. Tel: (507) 454-5510, (800) 533-8100, FAX: (507) 454-6403, E-Mail: inquiries@wincraftschool.com, Web Site: www.wincraftschool.com (5)

Johnson, Erik S., Hy Cite Corp, Madison, WI. Tel: (608) 273-3373, (877) 494-2289, FAX: (608) 273-0936, Web Site: www.hycite.com (16)

Johnson, F.B., Gramma's Graphics Inc, Lancaster, VA. Tel: (804) 462-0884, FAX: (804) 462-0884, E-Mail: sunprints@grandloving.com, Web Site: www.bubblink.com/donnelly (36)

Johnson, F.B., Heartstrings Press, Lancaster, VA. Tel: (804) 462-0884, (800) 462-0884, FAX: (716) 462-0884, E-Mail: sue@grandloving.com, Web Site: www.grandloving.com (17)

Johnson, Grant A., Johnson Direct LLC, Brookfield, WI. Tel: (262) 782-2750, (800) 710-2750, FAX: (262) 782-2751, E-Mail: info@responsory.com, Web Site: www.johnsondirect.com (35)

Johnson, Grant, ClickMail Marketing Inc, San Mateo, CA. Tel: (650) 653-8055, Web Site: clickmail.com (32)

Johnson, James E., International Resource Management Co, Bedford, TX. Tel: (817) 861-9191, FAX: (817) 277-0868, E-Mail: james@irmco.net, Web Site: www.irmco.net (20)

Johnson, James, Safeware, The Insurance Agency Inc, Columbus, OH. Tel: (614) 781-1492, (800) 800-1492, FAX: (614) 781-0559, E-Mail: service@safeware.com, Web Site: www.safeware.com (15)

Johnson, James W., Automation Mailing & Shipping Solutions Inc, Cleveland, OH. Tel: (216) 241-4487, (800) 883-7935, FAX: (216) 241-5918, E-Mail: service@mailshipsolutions.com, Web Site: www.mailshipsolutions.com (16)

Johnson, Janice Westhoff, Westhoff Machine Co, Saint Louis, MO. Tel: (314) 963-7130, (800) 364-0280, FAX: (800) 324-1942, E-Mail: mail@westhoffinc.com, Web Site: www.westhoffinc.com (9)

Johnson, Jim, Cable Connection, Fremont, CA. Tel: (510) 249-9000, E-Mail: cables4u@cable-connection.com, Web Site: www.cable-connection.com (3)

Johnson, Jim, Liberty Orchards Co Inc, Cashmere, WA. Tel: (509) 782-2191, (800) 888-5696, FAX: (509) 782-1487, E-Mail: service@libertyorchards.com, Web Site: www.libertyorchards.com (16)

Johnson, Jim, Solarcom, Norcross, GA. Tel: (770) 449-6116, (888) SUN-DATA, FAX: (770) 448-7726, Web Site: www.solarcom.net (16)

Johnson, Kari, Luzier Personalized Cosmetics, Grandview, MO. Tel: (816) 531-8338, (800) 821-6632, FAX: (816) 531-6979, E-Mail: customerservice@luzier.com, Web Site: www.luzier.com (7)

Johnson, Ken, Position Technologies Inc, Geneva, IL. Tel: (630) 262-5300, FAX: (630) 232-2998, Web Site: www.positiontech.com (16)

Johnson, Kent S., Highlights For Children, Columbus, OH. Tel: (614) 487-2601, (800) 848-8922, FAX: (614) 487-2700, Web Site: www.highlights.com (17)

Johnson, Kevin, Starbucks Corp, Seattle, WA. Tel: (206) 447-1575, (800) 344-1575, FAX: (206) 447-0828, Web Site: www.starbucks.com (4)

Johnson, Kevin, Straw Hat Cooperative Corp, San Ramon, CA. Tel: (925) 837-3400, FAX: (925) 820-1080, E-Mail: info@strawhatpizza.com, Web Site: www.strawhatpizza.com (16)

Johnson, Lain Barrie, Alterian, Chicago, IL. Tel: (312) 704-1700, FAX: (312) 704-1701, Web Site: www.alterian.com (22)

Johnson, Michael O., Herbalife International of America Inc, Los Angeles, CA. Tel: (310) 216-9661, (866) 866-4744, FAX: (310) 258-7019, Web Site: www.herbalife.com (7)

Johnson, Michael, The Washingtonian, Washington, DC. Tel: (202) 296-3600, E-Mail: editorial@washingtonian.com, Web Site: www.washingtonian.com (17)

Johnson, Michelle, Howard Rice Nemerovski Canady Falk & Rabkin, San Francisco, CA. Tel: (415) 464-1600, FAX: (415) 217-5910, Web Site: www.howardrice.com (14)

Johnson, Nick, Thomson Reuters, New York, NY. Tel: (646) 223-4000, Web Site: www.thomsonreuters.com (34)

Johnson, Nora, Alexian Brothers Bonaventure House, Chicago, IL. Tel: (773) 327-9921, FAX: (773) 327-9113, E-Mail: info@abam.org, Web Site: www.bonaventurehouse.org (1)

Johnson, Paul, LinguiSystems, East Moline, IL. Tel: (309) 755-2300, (800) 776-4332, FAX: (800) 577-4555, E-Mail: service@linguisystems.com, Web Site: www.linguisystems.com (17)

Johnson, Phil, Colle+McVoy, Minneapolis, MN. Tel: (612) 305-6000, FAX: (612) 305-6500, E-Mail: info@collemcvoy.com, Web Site: www.collemcvoy.com (35)

Johnson, Rachel, American Library Association-Publishing Services, Chicago, IL. Tel: (312) 944-6780, (800) 545-2433, FAX: (312) 440-9374, Web Site: www.ala.org (1)

Johnson, Ralph, Lake County Press Inc, Waukegan, IL. Tel: (847) 336-4333, FAX: (847) 336-5846, Web Site: www.lakecountypress.com (27)

Johnson, Robert, US Naval Institute, Annapolis, MD. Tel: (410) 268-6110, (800) 233-8764, FAX: (410) 571-1703, E-Mail: customer@usni.org, Web Site: www.usni.org (38)

Johnson, Scott, Dakota Digital, Sioux Falls, SD. Tel: (605) 332-6513, (800) 593-4160, FAX: (605) 339-4106, E-Mail: sales@dakotadigital.com, Web Site: www.dakotadigital.com (12)

Johnson, Scott, Phoenix Data Processing LLC, Westmont, IL. Tel: (630) 654-4400, FAX: (630) 654-4470, E-Mail: sales@phoenixdataprocessing.com, Web Site: www.phoenixdataprocessing.com (22)

Johnson, Sonia, Waytek, Chanhassen, MN. Tel: (952) 465-0431, Web Site: www.waytekwire.com (16)

Johnson, Stuart, SUCCESS Partners Co, Lake Dallas, TX. Tel: (940) 497-9700, (800) 752-2030, FAX: (940) 497-9987, Web Site: successpartners.com (32)

Johnson, Sue, Heartstrings Press, Lancaster, VA. Tel: (804) 462-0884, (800) 462-0884, FAX: (716) 462-0884, E-Mail: sue@grandloving.com, Web Site: www.grandloving.com (17)

Johnson, Sue, Hobby Builders Supply, Atlanta, GA. Tel: (770) 242-1498, (800) 223-7171, FAX: (770) 242-1497, (800) 926-6464, E-Mail: hbs@miniatures.com, Web Site: www.miniatures.com (11)

Johnson, Susan, Gramma's Graphics Inc, Lancaster, VA. Tel: (804) 462-0884, FAX: (804) 462-0884, E-Mail: sunprints@grandloving.com, Web Site: www.bubblink.com/donnelly (36)

Johnson, T.J., The Direct Channels Group, New York, NY. Tel: (212) 208-1479, FAX: (631) 514-8716, E-Mail: info@directchannelsgroup.com, Web Site: www.directchannelsgroup.com (35)

Johnson, Thomas A., Spokane Teachers Credit Union, Liberty Lake, WA. Tel: (509) 326-1954, Web Site: www.stcu.org (14)

Johnson, Tom, E-Z-EM Inc, Lake Success, NY. Tel: (516) 333-8230, (800) 544-4624, FAX: (516) 333-8278, E-Mail: webmaster@ezem.com, Web Site: www.ezem.com (7)

Johnson, Zelma, Uncle Ben's Inc, Greenville, MS. Tel: (601) 335-8000, (800) 54-UNCLE, (800) 548-6253, FAX: (601) 378-4370, E-Mail: info@unclebens.com, Web Site: www.unclebens.com (4)

Johnsong, Kirk, Longevity Network Ltd, Henderson, NV. Tel: (702) 454-7000, (800) 242-1000, FAX: (702) 434-8259, E-Mail: info@longevity.com, Web Site: www.longevity.com (7)

JohnsonRauhoff Inc, Saint Joseph, MI. Tel: (269) 428-3377, (800) 572-3996, FAX: (269) 428-3312, E-Mail: questions@johnson-rauhoff.com, Web Site: www.johnsonrauhoff.com (35)

Johnsos, Judith, Business Graphics Inc, Elmhurst, IL. Tel: (815) 338-8222, (800) 435-4874, FAX: (815) 338-2652, E-Mail: busgraph@mc.net, Web Site: www.businessgraphics.com (16)

Johnsos, Luke, Business Graphics Inc, Elmhurst, IL. Tel: (815) 338-8222, (800) 435-4874, FAX: (815) 338-2652, E-Mail: busgraph@mc.net, Web Site: www.businessgraphics.com (16)

Johnsten, Christine, Wysong Corp, Midland, MI. Tel: (989) 631-0009, (800) 748-0188, FAX: (989) 631-9280, E-Mail: wysong@wysong.net, Web Site: www.wysong.net (7)

Johnston, Andrew, Publishers Computer Corp, New Milford, NJ. Tel: (201) 261-3700, FAX: (201) 261-9110, E-Mail: mail@publisherscomputer.com, Web Site: www.publisherscomputer.com (22)

Johnston, Charlie, Nevada Magazine, Carson City, NV. Tel: (775) 687-5416, FAX: (775) 687-6159, E-Mail: editor@nevadamagazine.com, Web Site: www.nevadamagazine.com (17)

Johnston, Howard, American Megatrends Inc, Norcross, GA. Tel: (770) 246-8600, (800) 828-9264, FAX: (770) 246-8790, Web Site: www.ami.com (3)

Johnston, Jr. John, Pete Rickard Inc, Cobleskill, NY. Tel: (518) 234-2731, (800) 282-5663, FAX: (518) 234-2454, E-Mail: info@peterickard.com, Web Site: www.peterickard.com (11)

Johnston, Kristi, Bert Davis Executive Search, New York, NY. Tel: (212) 838-4000, FAX: (212) 935-3291, E-Mail: info@bertdavis.com, Web Site: www.bertdavis.com (20)

Johnston, Reginald, The Graph Co, Vineland, NJ. Tel: (856) 825-9199, FAX: (856) 825-5573, E-Mail: graphco2@verizon.net (14)

Johnston, Robert, Supremex Inc, Etobicoke, ON Canada. Tel: (416) 675-9370, (800) 465-7603, FAX: (416) 675-1952, (416) 848-8388, E-Mail: sales.central@supremex.com, Web Site: www.supremex.com (26)

Johnston, Steve, The National Underwriter Co, Erlanger, KY. Tel: (800) 543-0874, FAX: (856) 692-2246, E-Mail: customerservice@nuco.com, Web Site: www.nuco.com (17)

Johnston, Thomas, AG Interactive, Cleveland, OH. Tel: (216) 252-7300, (800) 711-4474, FAX: (216) 252-6778, Web Site: www.americangreetings.com (32)

Joint Commission, Oakbrook Terrace, IL. Tel: (630) 792-5000, Web Site: www.jcaho.org (1)

Joly, Hubert, Best Buy, Richfield, MN. Tel: (612) 291-1000, Web Site: www.bestbuy.com (3)

Jon-Don, Roselle, IL. Tel: (630) 893-4747, (800) 556-6366, FAX: (888) 344-6878, Web Site: www.jondon.com (34)

Jondal, Dan, Sea Bear, Anacortes, WA. Tel: (360) 293-4661, (800) 645-3474, FAX: (888) 487-6427, Web Site: www.seabear.com (16)

Jones & O'Malley, Toluca Lake, CA. Tel: (818) 762-8353, FAX: (818) 762-6736, Web Site: www.jonesomalley.com (35)

Jones & Thomas Inc, Decatur, IL. Tel: (217) 423-1889, FAX: (217) 425-0680, E-Mail: corp@jonesthomas.com, Web Site: www.jonesthomas.com (35)

Edward Jones, Des Peres, MO. Tel: (314) 515-2000, FAX: (314) 515-3269, Web Site: www.edwardjones.com (14)

Jones International Ltd, Centennial, CO. Tel: (303) 792-3111, (800) 525-7002, FAX: (303) 784-8508, E-Mail: publicrelations@jones.com, Web Site: www.jones.com (16)

Marlin P Jones & Associates Inc, West Palm Beach, FL. Tel: (561) 848-1414, (800) 652-6733, FAX: (561) 844-8764, E-Mail: mpja@mpja.com, Web Site: www.mpja.com (3)

Jones Publishing Inc, Iola, WI. Tel: (715) 445-5000, (800) 331-0038, FAX: (715) 445-4053, E-Mail: jonespub@jonespublishing.com, Web Site: www.jonespublishing.com (16)

Jones School Supply Co Inc, Irmo, SC. Tel: (803) 772-3796, FAX: (800) 942-5921, Web Site: www.jonesawards.com (6)

Susan K Jones & Associates, Grand Rapids, MI. Tel: (616) 458-0305, E-Mail: sjones9200@aol.com (39)

Tylie Jones & Associates, Burbank, CA. Tel: (855) 955-7600, E-Mail: email@tylie.com, Web Site: www.tylie.com (32)

Jones, Amy, Zig Ziglar Corp, Plano, TX. Tel: (972) 233-9191, (800) 527-0306, FAX: (469) 321-7556, E-Mail: info@ziglar.com, Web Site: www.zigziglar.com (16)

Jones, Becca, Lutheran Church Extension Fund - Missouri Synod, Saint Louis, MO. Tel: (800) 843-5233, FAX: (314) 996-1131, Web Site: www.lcef.org (1)

Jones, Bethea, Quality Products Inc, Columbus, MS. Tel: (662) 328-1477, (800) 647-1057, FAX: (800) 824-8510, E-Mail: kshep@classroomsupply.com, Web Site: www.classroomsupply.com (10)

Jones, Boland, Premiere Global Services Inc, Atlanta, GA. Tel: (404) 262-8400, (800) 546-1541, FAX: (404) 262-8540, Web Site: www.pgi.com (22)

Jones, Brad, Jazzercise Inc, Carlsbad, CA. Tel: (760) 476-1750, FAX: (760) 602-7180, E-Mail: customercare@jazzercise.com, Web Site: www.jazzercise.com (2)

Jones, Brian, AWeber Communications, Chalfont, PA. Tel: (877) 293-2371, Web Site: www.aweber.com (24)

Jones, Christopher, Initiative, New York, NY. Tel: (212) 605-7000, FAX: (212) 605-7200, Web Site: www.initiative.com (32)

Jones, Christy, American Association of University Women, Washington, DC. Tel: (202) 785-7700, FAX: (202) 872-1425, E-Mail: connect@aauw.org, Web Site: www.aauw.org (1)

Jones, Dale, Agco Spra-Coup, Duluth, GA. Tel: (320) 231-9400, FAX: (320) 231-9413, Web Site: www.agcocorp.com (16)

Jones, Dana, Tandy Leather Co, Fort Worth, TX. Tel: (817) 872-3200, FAX: (817) 496-7859, E-Mail: tlfhelp@tandyleather.com, Web Site: www.tandyleatherfactory.com (11)

Jones, David A., Marlin P Jones & Associates Inc, West Palm Beach, FL. Tel: (561) 848-1414, (800) 652-6733, FAX: (561) 844-8764, E-Mail: mpja@mpja.com, Web Site: www.mpja.com (3)

Jones, David P., The Bowery Mission, New York, NY. Tel: (212) 684-2800, Web Site: www.bowery.org (1)

Jones, Doug, Stretch Multimedia LLC, Dublin, OH. Tel: (614) 363-4444, FAX: (614) 363-3772, E-Mail: dougj@stretch-multimedia.com, Web Site: www.stretch-multimedia.com (35)

Jones, Elizabeth, Safeguard Business Systems Inc, Dallas, TX. Tel: (214) 905-3935, (800) 523-2422, FAX: (800) 439-8423, Web Site: www.gosafeguard.com (16)

Jones, Fred, Quality Products Inc, Columbus, MS. Tel: (662) 328-1477, (800) 647-1057, FAX: (800) 824-8510, E-Mail: kshep@classroomsupply.com, Web Site: www.classroomsupply.com (10)

Jones, Glen, Jones International Ltd, Centennial, CO. Tel: (303) 792-3111, (800) 525-7002, FAX: (303) 784-8508, E-Mail: publicrelations@jones.com, Web Site: www.jones.com (16)

Jones, Glen, Vulcan Information Packaging, Vincent, AL. Tel: (205) 672-2241, (800) 633-4526, FAX: (205) 672-1276, Web Site: www.vulcan-online.com (16)

Jones, Greg, China Books & Periodicals Inc, South San Francisco, CA. Tel: (650) 872-7076, (800) 818-2017, FAX: (650) 872-7808, E-Mail: info@chinabooks.com, Web Site: www.chinabooks.com (17)

Jones, Gregory P., Gilbert H Wild & Son Inc, Reeds, MO. Tel: (417) 548-3514, (888) 449-4537, FAX: (417) 548-6831, E-Mail: gregj@gilberthwild.com, Web Site: www.gilberthwild.com (8)

Jones, II Jeffrey J., Target Corp, Minneapolis, MN. Tel: (612) 304-6073, Web Site: www.target.com (16)

Jones, Jeff, Innovation Printing Inc, Philadelphia, PA. Tel: (215) 969-4600, FAX: (215) 464-7664, Web Site: www.innovationprinting.com (27)

Jones, Jeff, Innovative Industries Inc, Carthage, MO. Tel: (417) 358-6891, (800) 344-7467, FAX: (417) 358-1849, E-Mail: info@innovativeindustries.com, Web Site: www.innovativeindustries.com (28)

Jones, Jennifer, Hyatt Fruit Co, Vero Beach, FL. Tel: (772) 567-3766, (866) 991-8889, FAX: (772) 567-0973, Web Site: www.hyattfruitco.com (4)

Jones, Jerry, Kappler Protective Apparel & Fabrics, Guntersville, AL. Tel: (256) 505-4005, (800) 600-4019, FAX: (256) 505-4151, E-Mail: customerservice@kappler.com, Web Site: www.kappler.com (2)

Jones, Jerry, Partners Marketing Inc, Saint Charles, IL. Tel: (630) 524-9901, FAX: (630) 524-9909, E-Mail: georgeb@partnersmarketing.com, Web Site: www.partnersmarketing.com (22)

Jones, Jerry, Twin City Engraving/Premier Promotions, Saint Joseph, MI. Tel: (616) 983-0601, (800) 222-7752, FAX: (616) 983-3571, Web Site: www.premierpromos.com (33)

Jones, Jim, Edward Don & Co, Woodridge, IL. Tel: (708) 442-9400, (800) 777-4366, FAX: (708) 442-0436, Web Site: www.don.com (16)

Jones, Joe, ACBL, Horn Lake, MS. Tel: (662) 253-3100, FAX: (662) 253-3187, E-Mail: service@acbl.org, Web Site: www.acbl.org (1)

Jones, Joe, Jones Publishing Inc, Iola, WI. Tel: (715) 445-5000, (800) 331-0038, FAX: (715) 445-4053, E-Mail: jonespub@jonespublishing.com, Web Site: www.jonespublishing.com (17)

Jones, John W., Deck the Walls Inc, Saint Peters, MO. Tel: (314) 719-8200, (866) 719-8200, FAX: (314) 719-8290, E-Mail: dtwcontact@fcibiz.com, Web Site: www.deckthewalls.com (5)

Jones, Judith, Fancy Fronds, Gold Bar, WA. Tel: (360) 793-1472, E-Mail: fancyfronts@gmail.com, Web Site: www.fancyfronds.com (8)

Jones, Justin, WSI, Mississauga, ON Canada. Tel: (905) 678-7588, (888) 678-7588, FAX: (905) 678-7242, E-Mail: contact@wsiworld.com, Web Site: www.wsiworld.com (35)

Jones, Kelly, Premera Blue Cross, Spokane, WA. Tel: (425) 670-4000, (800) 422-0032, FAX: (425) 670-5853, Web Site: www.premera.com (15)

Jones, Kelly, Telect Inc, Liberty Lake, WA. Tel: (509) 926-6000, FAX: (509) 926-8915, E-Mail: getinfo@telect.com, Web Site: www.telect.com (16)

Jones, Ken, Inter7 Internet Technologies Inc, Galena, IL. Tel: (815) 776-9465, Web Site: www.inter7.com (3)

Jones, Kenneth, Bunchball, Redwood City, CA. Tel: (408) 985-2034, Web Site: www.bunchball.com (32)

Jones, Kimberely, Butler Till Media Services, Rochester, NY. Tel: (855) 472-5100, FAX: (855) 274-5199, Web Site: www.butlertill.com (31)

Jones, Lee, USA TODAY, Mc Lean, VA. Tel: (703) 854-3400, (800) 872-0001, E-Mail: accuracy@usatoday.com, Web Site: www.usatoday.com (17)

Jones, Linda, American Society on Aging, San Francisco, CA. Tel: (415) 974-9600, (800) 537-9728, FAX: (415) 974-0300, E-Mail: info@asaging.org, Web Site: www.asaging.org (1)

Jones, Lisa, Alliance of Area Business Publications, Redondo Beach, CA. Tel: (310) 379-8261, FAX: (310) 379-8283, E-Mail: info@bizpubs.org. Web Site: www.bizpubs.org (1)

Jones, Marlin L., Marlin P Jones & Associates Inc, West Palm Beach, FL. Tel: (561) 848-1414, (800) 652-6733, FAX: (561) 844-8764, E-Mail: mpja@mpja.com, Web Site: www.mpja.com (3)

Jones, Marlin P., Marlin P Jones & Associates Inc, West Palm Beach, FL. Tel: (561) 848-1414, (800) 652-6733, FAX: (561) 844-8764, E-Mail: mpja@mpja.com, Web Site: www.mpja.com (3)

Jones, Melanie, DataDirect, Atlanta, GA. Tel: (678) 530-0034, FAX: (678) 530-9563, E-Mail: info@ddirect.com, Web Site: www.ddirect.com (40)

Jones, Michael, Landmark Graphics Corp, Houston, TX. Tel: (713) 839-2000, FAX: (713) 839-2015, Web Site: www.landmarksoftware.com (16)

Jones, Patty, DDB Canada, Vancouver, BC Canada. Tel: (604) 687-7911, FAX: (604) 640-4343, E-Mail: vancouver.info@ddbcanada.com, Web Site: www.ddbcanada.com (35)

Jones, Paul W., AO Smith Corp, Milwaukee, WI. Tel: (414) 359-4000, FAX: (414) 359-4064, Web Site: www.aosmith.com (16)

Jones, Renee, American Clearinghouse Inc, Louisville, KY. Tel: (502) 499-4185, (800) 944-6361 (23)

Jones, Richard F., Fidelity Security Life Insurance Co, Kansas City, MO. Tel: (816) 750-1160, (800) 648-8624, FAX: (816) 968-0580, E-Mail: info@fslins.com, Web Site: www.fslins.com (15)

Jones, Rick, HBP, Falls Church, VA. Tel: (703) 289-9000, FAX: (703) 289-9143, E-Mail: info@hbp.com, Web Site: www.hbp.com (27)

Jones, Ryan, Jones Publishing Inc, Iola, WI. Tel: (715) 445-5000, (800) 331-0038, FAX: (715) 445-4053, E-Mail: jonespub@jonespublishing.com, Web Site: www.jonespublishing.com (17)

Jones, Sarah, Jones School Supply Co Inc, Irmo, SC. Tel: (803) 772-3796, FAX: (800) 942-5921, Web Site: www.jonesawards.com (6)

Jones, Steve, Golfsmith International Inc, Austin, TX. Tel: (512) 821-4050, (800) 813-6897, FAX: (512) 837-9347, E-Mail: comments@golfsmith.com, Web Site: www.golfsmith.com (11)

Jones, Steven D., Fieldstone Gardens Inc, Vassalboro, ME. Tel: (207) 923-3836, FAX: (207) 923-3836, Web Site: www.fieldstonegardens.com (8)

Jones, Susan K., Susan K Jones & Associates, Grand Rapids, MI. Tel: (616) 458-0305, E-Mail: sjones9200@aol.com (39)

Jones, Terri L., BC Incentives, Fate, TX. Tel: (800) 275-1298, E-Mail: terri@bcincentives.com, Web Site: www.bcincentives.com (33)

Jones, Tim, ZenithOptimedia Direct, New York, NY. Tel: (212) 859-5100, FAX: (212) 757-9495, Web Site: www.zenithoptimedia.com (35)

Jones, Tom, Infomart, Dallas, TX. Tel: (214) 800-8000, FAX: (214) 800-8100, Web Site: www.infomartusa.com (16)

Jones, Tom, Ingram Book Group, La Vergne, TN. Tel: (615) 793-5000, (800) 937-8000, FAX: (800) 876-0186, Web Site: www.ipage.ingrambook.com (16)

Jones, Tom R., Hyatt Fruit Co, Vero Beach, FL. Tel: (772) 567-3766, (866) 991-8889, FAX: (772) 567-0973, Web Site: www.hyattfruitco.com (4)

Jones, Tom, Sportime International, Norcross, GA. Tel: (770) 449-5700, (800) 283-5700, FAX: (770) 510-7290, E-Mail: orders@sportime.com, Web Site: www.sportime.com (11)

Jones, Tylie, Tylie Jones & Associates, Burbank, CA. Tel: (855) 955-7600, E-Mail: email@tylie.com, Web Site: www.tylie.com (32)

Jones, W. Paul, Payless ShoeSource Inc, Topeka, KS. Tel: (785) 233-5171, (877) 474-6379, E-Mail: customerservice@csr.payless.com, Web Site: www.payless.com (2)

Jones, William B., The Virginia Diner Inc, Wakefield, VA. Tel: (888) 823-4637, E-Mail: vadiner@vadiner.com, Web Site: www.vadiner.com (4)

Jonesi, David, C&S Sales Inc, Wheeling, IL. Tel: (847) 541-0710, (800) 292-7711, FAX: (847) 541-9904, E-Mail: sales@cs-sales.com, Web Site: www.cs_sales.com (9)

Joos, Chris, Grizzard Communications Group Inc, Atlanta, GA. Tel: (404) 522-8330, (800) 241-9351, Web Site: www.grizzard.com (35)

Joos, David W., Consumer's Energy, Jackson, MI. Tel: (517) 788-0550, (800) 805-0490, FAX: (517) 788-1859, E-Mail: businesscenter@consumerenergy.com, Web Site: www.consumersenergy.com (16)

Jordan Direct LLC, Saint Petersburg, FL. Tel: (727) 452-7718, E-Mail: bruce@jordandirecttv.com, Web Site: www.jordandirecttv.com (32)

The Jordan Edmiston Group Inc, New York, NY. Tel: (212) 754-0710, FAX: (212) 754-0337, Web Site: www.jegi.com (14)

Jordan, Austin, FreshAddress Inc, Newton, MA. Tel: (617) 965-4500, (800) 321-3009, FAX: (617) 965-4551, Web Site: www.freshaddress.com (22)

Jordan, Greg, Centric Communications, Norfolk, VA. Tel: (757) 622-2724, E-Mail: info@centriccommunications.net, Web Site: centriccommunications.net (28)

Jordan, Jack, Engineering Services & Products Co, South Windsor, CT. Tel: (860) 528-1119, (800) 835-7877, FAX: (800) 457-8887, Web Site: www.teksupply.com (9)

Jordan, Jacqueline E., Envelope Manufacturers Association, Alexandria, VA. Tel: (703) 739-2200, FAX: (703) 739-2209, Web Site: www.envelope.org (1)

Jordan, Leslie, Leslie Jordan, Portland, OR. Tel: (503) 295-1987, (800) 935-3343, FAX: (503) 295-0939, E-Mail: ljsales@lesliejordan.com, Web Site: www.lesliejordan.com (2)

Jordan, Matt, Ecklers, Titusville, FL. Tel: (888) 787-3626, (800) 284-3906, E-Mail: custsvc@ecklers.net, Web Site: www.ecklers.com (12)

Jordan, Peter, CRM Learning, Carlsbad, CA. Tel: (760) 431-9800, (800) 421-0833, FAX: (760) 931-5792, E-Mail: sales@crmlearning.com, Web Site: www.crmlearning.com (16)

Jordan, Philip, CTC Corp, Bennington, VT. Tel: (802) 442-6371, FAX: (802) 442-8526 (16)

Jordan, Todd, Rappahannock Electric Cooperative, Fredericksburg, VA. Tel: (540) 898-8500, (800) 552-3904, E-Mail: office@myrec.coop, Web Site: www.myrec.coop (1)

Jordan, Tom, Automation Control Products, Alpharetta, GA. Tel: (678) 990-0945, FAX: (678) 990-0951, E-Mail: info@thinmanager.com, Web Site: www.thinmanager.com (16)

Josen, Bob, Things Deco, New York, NY. Tel: (212) 362-8961, E-Mail: thingsdeco@hotmail.com, Web Site: www.thingsdeco.com (6)

Joseph, Brian, National Motor Club of America Inc, Irving, TX. Tel: (972) 999-4400, (800) 523-4582, FAX: (972) 999-4405, Web Site: www.nmca.com (1)

Joseph, Frank, Frank Joseph, Chevy Chase, MD. Tel: (301) 656-8753, E-Mail: mr.dm@verizon.net (39)

Joseph, James E., Oneida Ltd, Oneida, NY. Tel: (315) 361-3000, (888) 263-7195, FAX: (315) 361-3700, Web Site: www.oneida.com (16)

Joseph, Jr. Robert H., Alliance Bernstein, New York, NY. Tel: (212) 969-1000, (800) 962-2134, FAX: (212) 969-2293, Web Site: www.alliancebernstein.com (14)

Josephson, Joseph P., Magnaplan Corp, Champlain, NY. Tel: (518) 298-8404, (800) 361-1192, FAX: (518) 298-2368, E-Mail: info@visualplanning.com, Web Site: www.visualplanning.com (10)

Joslin Photo Puzzle Co, Southampton, PA. Tel: (215) 357-8346, FAX: (215) 357-0307, E-Mail: 2832@comcast.net, Web Site: www.jigsawpuzzle.com (16)

Joslin, Jeffrey L., Joslin Photo Puzzle Co, Southampton, PA. Tel: (215) 357-8346, FAX: (215) 357-0307, E-Mail: 2832@comcast.net, Web Site: www.jigsawpuzzle.com (16)

Joslin, Marcia S., Joslin Photo Puzzle Co, Southampton, PA. Tel: (215) 357-8346, FAX: (215) 357-0307, E-Mail: 2832@comcast.net, Web Site: www.jigsawpuzzle.com (16)

Jossey-Bass Inc Publishers, San Francisco, CA. Tel: (415) 433-1740, FAX: (415) 433-0499, Web Site: www.josseybass.com (17)

Jost, Kenneth, Redstone Federal Credit Union, Huntsville, AL. Tel: (256) 837-6110, Web Site: www.redfcu.org (1)

Jostens, Inc, Minneapolis, MN. Tel: (952) 830-3300, FAX: (952) 830-3293, Web Site: www.jostens.com (16)

Jourdan, Dennis, Dennis Jourdan Photography Inc, Buffalo Grove, IL. Tel: (847) 564-2570, FAX: (847) 255-5976, E-Mail: info@djphoto.com, Web Site: www.djphoto.com (37)

The Journal News, White Plains, NY. Tel: (914) 694-9300, FAX: (914) 696-8152, Web Site: www.nyjournalnews.com (17)

Journal of Commerce Group, Newark, NJ. Tel: (973) 848-7000, FAX: (973) 848-7004, Web Site: www.joc.com (17)

Journal of Marketing Research, Chicago, IL. Tel: (312) 542-9000, (800) AMA-1150, FAX: (312) 542-9001, E-Mail: info@ama.org, Web Site: www.marketingpower.org (43)

Journal Star, Peoria, IL. Tel: (309) 686-3026, FAX: (309) 686-3265, Web Site: www.pjstar.com (17)

Journey, R. Bruce, Technology Review, Cambridge, MA. Tel: (617) 475-8000, FAX: (617) 258-5850, Web Site: www.technologyreview.com (17)

Journeys, Nashville, TN. Tel: (615) 367-7000, (888) 324-6356, FAX: (615) 367-8123, Web Site: www.journeys.com (2)

Joutras, Richard, Segerdahl Graphics Inc, Wheeling, IL. Tel: (847) 850-8800, FAX: (847) 850-8801, Web Site: www.segerdahlgraphics.com (27)

Joutras, Rick, SG360, Wheeling, IL. Tel: (847) 541-1080, FAX: (847) 541-5237, Web Site: www.sg360.com, (27)

Jovanelly, Linda, Marshall & Swift, Los Angeles, CA. Tel: (213) 683-9000, FAX: (213) 683-9010, Web Site: www.marshallswift.com (17)

Jow, Annie, Computer Station Corp, Houston, TX. Tel: (713) 777-6860, FAX: (713) 777-3431, E-Mail: csc@computerstationcorp.com, Web Site: www.computerstationcorp.com (3)

Jow, Jeff T., Computer Station Corp, Houston, TX. Tel: (713) 777-6860, FAX: (713) 777-3431, E-Mail: csc@computerstationcorp.com, Web Site: www.computerstationcorp.com (3)

Joyce, Leon, Carolina Biological Supply Co, Burlington, NC. Tel: (800) 334-5551, (800) 222-7112, E-Mail: carolina@carolina.com, Web Site: www.carolina.com (9)

Joyce, Stephen, Choice Hotels International, Rockville, MD. Tel: (301) 592-5000, Web Site: www.choicehotels.com (17)

Joyce, Tom, Beckman Coulter Inc, Brea, CA. Tel: (714) 993-5321, (800) 526-3821, FAX: (800) 232-3828, Web Site: www.beckmancoulter.com (16)

Joyner, Robert B., Horace Mann Educators Corp, Springfield, IL. Tel: (217) 789-2500, FAX: (217) 788-5161, Web Site: www.horacemann.com (15)

Juba, Mark, Best Buy, Richfield, MN. Tel: (612) 291-1000, Web Site: www.bestbuy.com (3)

Judge, Bob, Edelmann Scott Inc, Richmond, VA. Tel: (804) 643-1931, FAX: (804) 643-1934 (35)

Judge, Tom, Direct Marketing Partners, Sacramento, CA. Tel: (916) 974-6969, (800) 909-2626, FAX: (916) 920-5156, E-Mail: info@dirmkt.com, Web Site: www.directmarketingpartners.com (29)

Jue, Susanna, interTrend Communications Inc, Long Beach, CA. Tel: (562) 733-1888, E-Mail: info@intertrend.com, Web Site: www.intertrend.com (35)

Juenger, Lisa, American Ostomy Supply, Earth City, MO. Tel: (314) 291-2900, (800) 858-5858, FAX: (800) 545-0065 (16)

Juergens, Jennifer, Sales & Marketing Management Magazine, New York, NY. Tel: (800) 821-6897, FAX: (905) 470-8561, E-Mail: joyce.cooney@nielsen.com, Web Site: www.salesandmarketing.com (16)

Juge, Richard E., CCIM Institute, Chicago, IL. Tel: (312) 321-4460, (800) 621-7027, FAX: (312) 321-4530, Web Site: www.ccim.com (1)

Jukes, Terence, Ability Commerce, Delray Beach, FL. Tel: (561) 330-3151, Web Site: www.abilitycommerce.com (20)

Jukes, Terry, Logicnology Inc, Sunrise, FL. Tel: (954) 851-1200, FAX: (954) 846-8552 (22)

Jule, Tom, Accountants' Supply House, Lancaster, CA. Tel: (856) 384-1144, (800) 342-5274, FAX: (800) 468-4446, Web Site: www.rapidforms.com (10)

Julian, Paul C., McKesson Corp, San Francisco, CA. Tel: (415) 983-8300, FAX: (415) 983-7160, Web Site: www.mckesson.com (7)

Juliano, Donna, Vision Media Inc, Sunrise, FL. Tel: (877) 877-2047, Web Site: www.visionmediainc.com (35)

Juliano, Jay, Vision Media Inc, Sunrise, FL. Tel: (877) 877-2047, Web Site: www.visionmediainc.com (35)

Jump Technologies Inc, Eagan, MN. Tel: (651) 287-6000, FAX: (651) 287-6020, E-Mail: info@jumptech.com, Web Site: www.jumptech.com (32)

Jun, Ted, The Hiebing Group, Madison, WI. Tel: (608) 256-6357, FAX: (608) 256-0693, E-Mail: ideas@hiebing.com, Web Site: www.hiebing.com (35)

JW Jung Seed Co, Randolph, WI. Tel: (800) 297-3123, Web Site: www.jungseed.com (1)

Jung, Aaron, Missouri Landscape & Nursery Association, Bowling Green, MO. Tel: (636) 542-1234, E-Mail: admin@mlng.org, Web Site: www.mlna.org (1)

Jung, Pat, Surdell & Partners, Omaha, NE. Tel: (402) 501-7400, (800) 733-7765, FAX: (402) 733-2083, E-Mail: info@surdellpartners.com, Web Site: www.surdellpartners.com (27)

Jungle Consulting, Colorado Springs, CO. Tel: (702) 596-4366 (20)

Junior's Cheesecake, Brooklyn, NY. Tel: (718) 852-5257, (800) 458-6467, FAX: (718) 260-9849, E-Mail: info@juniorscheesecake.com, Web Site: www.juniorscheesecake.com (16)

Juredini, Serge, Arcade Marketing, Inc, Chattanooga, TN. Tel: (423) 624-3301, FAX: (423) 622-4635, E-Mail: resumes@arcadeinc.com (27)

Jurgena, Richard, Mail Advertising Services Inc, Darnestown, MD. Tel: (301) 762-9015 (28)

Just Packaging Inc, South Plainfield, NJ. Tel: (908) 753-6700, FAX: (908) 753-6709, E-Mail: sfischbein@justpackaging.com, Web Site: www.justpackaging.com (28)

JustThink Inc, Sherwood Park, AB Canada. Tel: (780) 416-0244 (16)

K

K-D Lamp Co, Andover, OH. Tel: (440) 293-4064, FAX: (440) 293-4591, E-Mail: admin@atc-lighting-plastics.com, Web Site: www.k-dlamp.com (12)

K-Log, Zion, IL. Tel: (800) 872-6611, FAX: (847) 872-3728, E-Mail: info@k-log.com, Web Site: www.k-log.com (8)

K Public Relations LLC, New York, NY. Tel: (646) 756-4217, FAX: (646) 688-3017, Web Site: www.kpr-nyc.com (35)

K-tel International, Golden Valley, MN. Tel: (204) 889-5430, (800) 665-5021, FAX: (612) 559-6803, Web Site: www.ktel.com (16)

Kantar Media, New York, NY. Tel: (212) 991-6000, (800) 497-8450, FAX: (212) 991-6100, Web Site: kantarmedia.us (32)

KAR Graphics, Mashpee, MA. Tel: (800) 760-5192, FAX: (508) 539-1108, E-Mail: hoop@cape.com, Web Site: www.hoophouse.com (8)

KBM Group, Louisville, CO. Tel: (800) 579-1950, E-Mail: sales@kbmg.com, Web Site: www.kbmg.com (22)

KCEOC Community Action Partnership Inc, Barbourville, KY. Tel: (606) 546-3152, Web Site: kceoc.com (1)

KCET, Burbank, CA. Tel: (747) 201-5000, FAX: (747) 201-5877, E-Mail: contact@kcet.org, Web Site: www.kcet.org (1)

KCI Communications Inc, Falls Church, VA. Tel: (703) 394-4931, FAX: (703) 905-8100, Web Site: www.kci-com.com (17)

KEH.com, Smyrna, GA. Tel: (770) 333-4200, (800) 342-5534, FAX: (770) 333-4242, E-Mail: sales@keh.com, Web Site: www.keh.com (16)

KET, Lexington, KY. Tel: (859) 258-7000, (800) 432-0951, FAX: (606) 258-7396, E-Mail: rgriffin@ket.org, Web Site: www.ket.org (17)

KHL Engineered Packaging Solutions, Buena Park, CA. Tel: (714) 690-6361 (16)

KICU-TV36, Oakland, CA. Tel: (510) 834-1212, E-Mail: kicu.public@coxmg.com, Web Site: www.ktvu.com/kicu/index (32)

KMA Direct Communications, Dallas, TX. Tel: (214) 866-7700, E-Mail: info@pursuant.com, Web Site: www.pursuant.com/kma (1)

KNG Inc, Nampa, ID. Tel: (208) 318-0188, Web Site: www.kng.com (34)

KPBS FM/TV, San Diego, CA. Tel: (619) 594-1515, Web Site: www.kpbs.org (1)

KTM Sportmotorcycle USA Inc, Amherst, OH. Tel: (440) 985-3553, FAX: (440) 985-3060, Web Site: www.ktmusa.com (16)

KV Vet Supply Co, Inc, David City, NE. Tel: (402) 367-6047, Web Site: www.kvvet.com (5)

KXEN Inc, San Francisco, CA. Tel: (415) 904-4160, FAX: (415) 904-9041, Web Site: www.kxen.com (22)

KZSW Advertising Inc, East Setauket, NY. Tel: (631) 348-1440, FAX: (631) 348-1449, E-Mail: contact@kzswadvertising.com, Web Site: kzsadvertising.com (35)

Kaasila, Sampo, Bitstream Inc, Marlborough, MA. Tel: (617) 497-6222, FAX: (617) 868-0784, Web Site: www.bitstream.com (22)

Kabakow, James, Media Horizons Inc, Norwalk, CT. Tel: (203) 857-0770, FAX: (203) 857-0296, E-Mail: info@mediahorizons.com, Web Site: www.mediahorizons.com (21)

Kabat, Kevin T., Fifth Third Bank, Cincinnati, OH. Tel: (800) 972-3030, FAX: (231) 922-4060, Web Site: www.53.com (14)

Kable Fulfillment Services, Mount Morris, IL. Tel: (815) 734-4151, FAX: (815) 734-5228 (22)

Kachain, Harry, Graphic Communications Center, Appleton, WI. Tel: (920) 733-4483, (800) 422-3696, FAX: (920) 733-1700 (27)

Kadant Johnson Inc, Three Rivers, MI. Tel: (269) 278-1715, FAX: (269) 279-5980, Web Site: www.kadantjohnson.com (16)

Kadlic, John, Resource/Ammirati, Columbus, OH. Tel: (614) 621-2888, FAX: (614) 621-2873, E-Mail: businessdevelopment@resourceammirati.com, Web Site: www.resourceammirati.com (35)

Kaduri, Arie, NYK Rapp Enterprises LLC, Hallandale, FL. Tel: (954) 457-9100, FAX: (954) 457-9015, Web Site: nykrapp.com (35)

Kaenel, Bob, Sunrise Medical Inc, Boulder, CO. Tel: (303) 218-4500, (800) 333-4000, FAX: (303) 218-4949, Web Site: www.sunrisemedical.com (16)

Kagel, David, Magnet LLC, Washington, MO. Tel: (636) 239-5661, (800) 458-9457, FAX: (636) 239-4490, E-Mail: contactus@themagnetgroup.com, Web Site: www.magnetllc.com (16)

Kahana, Yoram, Shooting Star International, Hollywood, CA. Tel: (323) 469-2020, FAX: (323) 464-0880, Web Site: www.shootingstaragency.com (38)

Kahler, Michael E., Poly One Corp, Avon Lake, OH. Tel: (440) 930-1000, (866) POLY-ONE, FAX: (440) 930-1428, Web Site: www.polyone.com (16)

Kahlow, Thad, BusinessOnline, San Diego, CA. Tel: (619) 699-0767, Web Site: www.businessol.com (16)

Kahn, Ellis, Media Response Inc, Hollywood, FL. Tel: (954) 967-9899, E-Mail: info@media-response.com, Web Site: www.media-response.com (35)

Kahn, Kenneth, The Dartnell Corp, Naples, FL. Tel: (585) 240-7301, (800) 447-4030, FAX: (585) 292-4392, E-Mail: customerservice@dartnellcorp.com, Web Site: www.dartnellcorp.com (17)

Kahn, Linda, The Ohlmann Group, Dayton, OH. Tel: (937) 278-0681, FAX: (937) 277-1723, E-Mail: info@ohlmanngroup.com, Web Site: ohlmanngroup.com (35)

Kahn, Perry, Infolure, Phoenix, AZ. Tel: (602) 308-6700, FAX: (602) 308-6801, E-Mail: glenn.gottfried@infolure.com, Web Site: www.infolure.com (22)

Kahren, John, Sterling Fluid Systems, Indianapolis, IN. Tel: (317) 925-9661, (800) 879-0182, FAX: (317) 924-7388, Web Site: www.peerlesspump.com (16)

Kahwaty, Patti, Penton Learning Systems Inc, New York, NY. Tel: (212) 885-2700, FAX: (212) 885-2703, E-Mail: info@iqpc.com, Web Site: www.iqpc.com (16)

Kaill, David, Photoworks, Cleveland, OH. Tel: (206) 281-1390, (800) PHOTOWORKS, FAX: (206) 284-5357, E-Mail: info@photoworks.com, Web Site: www.photoworks.com (16)

Kaines, Ellen, National Bulk Equipment Inc, Holland, MI. Tel: (616) 399-2220, FAX: (616) 399-7365, E-Mail: sales@nbe-inc.com, Web Site: www.nbe-inc.com (16)

Kaiser Foundation Health Plan of the Mid-Atlantic States Inc, Rockville, MD. Tel: (301) 816-5641, Web Site: kp.org (1)

The Kaiser Group Inc, Waukesha, WI. Tel: (262) 544-4971, FAX: (262) 544-6271, Web Site: www.kaisergrp.com (20)

Kaiser, Bonnie, Printing + Quick Copy, Philadelphia, PA. Tel: (215) 331-5999, FAX: (215) 333-2577, E-Mail: copyman@aol.com (27)

Kaiser, Ed, Polyline LLC, Elmhurst, IL. Tel: (800) 701-7689, FAX: (630) 834-6800, E-Mail: customerservice@polylinecorp.com, Web Site: www.polylinecorp.com (3)

Kaiser, Gina, Florida Today, Melbourne, FL. Tel: (321) 242-3500, (877) 424-0156, FAX: (321) 242-3729, Web Site: www.floridatoday.com (17)

Kaiser, Jane, Eclipse Direct Marketing, Mineola, NY. Tel: (212) 931-8344, FAX: (516) 493-9122, E-Mail: jkaiser@eclipsedm.com, Web Site: www.eclipsedm.com (23)

Kaiser, Joseph B., USI Affinity, Philadelphia, PA. Tel: (610) 833-2876, (800) 625-2876, FAX: (610) 265-2876, E-Mail: info@usiaffinity.com, Web Site: www.brcorp.com (15)

Kaiser, Peter, The Kaiser Group Inc, Waukesha, WI. Tel: (262) 544-4971, FAX: (262) 544-6271, Web Site: www.kaisergrp.com (20)

Kaiser, Ray, Polyline LLC, Elmhurst, IL. Tel: (800) 701-7689, FAX: (630) 834-6800, E-Mail: customerservice@polylinecorp.com, Web Site: www.polylinecorp.com (3)

Kaiser, Winfried, Champion, Quincy, IL. Tel: (217) 222-5400, FAX: (217) 228-8260, Web Site: www.championpneumatic.com (16)

Kaitz, James A., Association for Financial Professionals, Bethesda, MD. Tel: (301) 907-2862, FAX: (301) 907-2864, Web Site: www.afponline.org (14)

Kakalik, John, Western Connecticut State University, Danbury, CT. Tel: (203) 837-8200, FAX: (203) 837-8527, E-Mail: hills@wcsu.edu, Web Site: www.wcsu.edu (41)

Kalafa, Victor, Cross Country Travcorps, Boca Raton, FL. Tel: (800) 530-6125, FAX: (561) 998-8533, Web Site: www.crosscountrytravcorps.com (16)

Kalathur, Rajesh, Deere & Co, Moline, IL. Tel: (309) 765-8000, FAX: (309) 748-0114, Web Site: www.deere.com (16)

Ben Kalb Productions, Las Vegas, NV. Tel: (702) 871-8787, FAX: (702) 597-0741, E-Mail: benkalb@benkalbproductions.com, Web Site: www.benkalbproductions.com (32)

Kalb, Ben, Ben Kalb Productions, Las Vegas, NV. Tel: (702) 871-8787, FAX: (702) 597-0741, E-Mail: benkalb@benkalbproductions.com, Web Site: www.benkalbproductions.com (32)

Kalb, Donald R., American Telecast Products LLC, Exton, PA. Tel: (610) 430-7800, FAX: (484) 879-4046, E-Mail: info@americantelecast.com, Web Site: www.americantelecast.com (32)

Kaldor, Dave, Driasi, Chanhassen, MN. Tel: (952) 556-5600, (800) 688-0760, FAX: (952) 556-8200, E-Mail: tpa@driasi.com, Web Site: www.driasi.com (21)

Kaler, Eric W., University of Minnesota, Minneapolis, MN. Tel: (612) 625-0256, Web Site: www.twin-cities.umn.edu (1)

Kalian, Dennis, The Roblin Group Inc, White Plains, NY. Tel: (914) 686-7221, FAX: (914) 372-1028, E-Mail: freethingsusa@yahoo.com, Web Site: www.freethingsusa.com (17)

Kalian, Linda, The Roblin Group Inc, White Plains, NY. Tel: (914) 686-7221, FAX: (914) 372-1028, E-Mail: freethingsusa@yahoo.com, Web Site: www.freethingsusa.com (17)

Kalian, Robert, The Roblin Group Inc, White Plains, NY. Tel: (914) 686-7221, FAX: (914) 372-1028, E-Mail: freethingsusa@yahoo.com, Web Site: www.freethingsusa.com (17)

Kalinka, John, Foremost Insurance Group, Grand Rapids, MI. Tel: (616) 956-8241, (800) 527-3905, FAX: (800) 325-1507, Web Site: www.foremost.com (15)

Kalischer, Clemens, Image Photos/Clemens Kalischer, Stockbridge, MA. Tel: (413) 298-5500, FAX: (413) 298-5500, E-Mail: inform@bcn.net (38)

Kallenberg, Jim, MPBS Industries, Los Angeles, CA. Tel: (323) 268-8514, (800) 421-6265, FAX: (323) 268-6305, Web Site: www.mpbs.com (16)

Kalmbach Publishing Co, Waukesha, WI. Tel: (262) 796-8776, (800) 558-1544, FAX: (262) 796-1143, Web Site: www.kalmbach.com (17)

Kalmed Dental Products Inc, Marietta, GA. Tel: (770) 971-8815, (800) 322-8815, FAX: (770) 509-8823, E-Mail: sales@kalmed.com, Web Site: www.kalmed.com (7)

Kalogridis, George A., Walt Disney Parks & Resorts, Lake Buena Vista, FL. Tel: (407) 824-2222, FAX: (407) 566-5700, Web Site: www.disneyworld.com (19)

Kalra-ali, Sonia, Daily Commercial News & Construction Record, Markham, ON Canada. Tel: (905) 752-5408, (800) 465-6475, FAX: (905) 752-5450, (888) 396-9413, E-Mail: dcnonl@reedbusiness.com, Web Site: www.dcnonl.com (17)

Kalt, Bernard, School Annual Publishing Co, State College, PA. Tel: (800) 436-6030, E-Mail: yearbook@schoolannual.com, Web Site: www.schoolannual.com (17)

Kalter, Dr. Marjorie, New York University, New York, NY. Tel: (212) 992-3221, Web Site: www.scps.nyu.edu (1)

Kamin, John V., Forecaster Publishing Co Inc, Tarzana, CA. Tel: (818) 345-4421 (14)

Kaminski, Amos, Bitstream Inc, Marlborough, MA. Tel: (617) 497-6222, FAX: (617) 868-0784, Web Site: www.bitstream.com (22)

Kaminsky, Erich, US Data Corp, Omaha, NE. Tel: (402) 758-0290, (888) 578-3282, FAX: (402) 934-3885, E-Mail: info@usdatacorporation.com, Web Site: www.usdatacorp.net (23)

Kampars, John, Intra Business Systems Inc, South Bend, IN. Tel: (574) 257-7940, FAX: (574) 257-7944, E-Mail: info@intrabusinesssystems.com, Web Site: www.intrabusinesssystems.com (16)

Kampfe, John E., Turner Broadcasting System Inc, Atlanta, GA. Tel: (404) 827-1700, Web Site: www.turner.com (32)

Kampfer, Thomas, Iomega Corp, Roy, UT. Tel: (801) 332-1000, (888) 446-6342, FAX: (801) 332-3158, Web Site: www.iomega.com (16)

Kan, David, Mustek Inc, Tustin, CA. Tel: (949) 790-3800, FAX: (949) 788-3670, Web Site: www.mustek.com (3)

Kananowicz, Cheryl, DST Output, South Windsor, CT. Tel: (860) 290-7337, (800) 441-7587, Web Site: www.dstoutput.com (28)

Kane, Cameron, ClickMail Marketing Inc, San Mateo, CA. Tel: (650) 653-8055, Web Site: clickmail.com (32)

Kane, Rachel, Perennial Pleasures Nursery, East Hardwick, VT. Tel: (802) 472-5104, FAX: (802) 472-6572, E-Mail: annex@perennialpleasures.net, Web Site: www.perennialpleasures.net (8)

Kaneda, Hiroo, Sunstar, Chicago, IL. Tel: (773) 777-4000, FAX: (773) 777-1417, E-Mail: dominico@sunstar.com, Web Site: www.sunstar.com (16)

Kaneshiro, June, Bank of Hawaii, Honolulu, HI. Tel: (808) 537-8398, FAX: (808) 536-9433, Web Site: www.boh.com (14)

Kaney, Howard, West Bend, West Bend, WI. Tel: (262) 334-5107, (866) 290-1851, FAX: (262) 334-6800, Web Site: www.focuselectrics.com (16)

Kanfer, Ronald, Response Dynamics Inc, Vienna, VA. Tel: (703) 442-7595, FAX: (703) 442-4565, E-Mail: info@responsedynamicsinc.com, Web Site: www.responsedynamicsinc.com (35)

Kangaju, Eustace, Temple University, Philadelphia, PA. Tel: (215) 204-7282, FAX: (215) 204-4554, Web Site: www.sbm.temple.edu (41)

Kani, Brick, Creative Learning Systems Inc, Longmont, CO. Tel: (303) 772-6400, (800) 458-2880, FAX: (303) 772-6422, Web Site: www.clsinc.com (9)

Kannan, Victor, American Megatrends Inc, Norcross, GA. Tel: (770) 246-8600, (800) 828-9264, FAX: (770) 246-8790, Web Site: www.ami.com (3)

Kanner, Robert H., Aspen Imaging International Inc, Cleveland, OH. Tel: (216) 881-5300, (800) 955-5555, FAX: (216) 881-8380, (800) 756-0990 (34)

Kannon Consulting Inc, Chicago, IL. Tel: (312) 346-2244, FAX: (312) 346-3665, Web Site: www.kannon.com (20)

Kano Laboratories, Nashville, TN. Tel: (615) 833-4101, (800) 311-3374, FAX: (615) 833-5790, Web Site: www.kanolabs.com (16)

Kanodia, Rahul L., Datamatics Technologies, Burlington, MA. Tel: (781) 425-5240, FAX: (781) 425-5232, Web Site: www.datamaticstech.com (22)

Kanofsky, Gordon R., Ameristar Casinos Inc, Las Vegas, NV. Tel: (702) 567-7000, FAX: (702) 369-8860, Web Site: www.ameristarcasinos.com (19)

Kansas City Chiefs, Kansas City, MO. Tel: (816) 920-9300, (888) 99-CHIEFS, FAX: (816) 923-4719, Web Site: www.kcchiefs.com (16)

Kansas City Direct Marketing Association, Kansas City, MO. Tel: (816) 561-5323, FAX: (816) 561-1991, E-Mail: info@kcdma.org, Web Site: www.kcdma.org (40)

Kansas State University Division of Continuing Education, Manhattan, KS. Tel: (785) 532-5888, Web Site: www.dce.ksu.edu (1)

Kanter, David, AccuList Inc, San Antonio, TX. Tel: (210) 807-9940, (877) 505-8747, FAX: (210) 494-5478, E-Mail: sales@acculistusa.com, Web Site: www.acculistusa.com (23)

Kantrowitz, Jonathan, Queue Inc, Stratford, CT. Tel: (203) 335-0906, (800) 232-2224, FAX: (800) 775-2729, E-Mail: jdk@queueinc.com, Web Site: www.qworkbooks.com (17)

Kao Brands, Cincinnati, OH. Tel: (512) 421-1400, Web Site: www.kaobrands.com (17)

Kao, Richard H., School of Business & Economics, Los Angeles, CA. Tel: (323) 343-2800, FAX: (323) 343-2813, Web Site: cbe.calstatela.edu (41)

Kaplan Inc, Fort Lauderdale, FL. Tel: (954) 515-3993, Web Site: www.kaplan.com (16)

Kaplan Publishing, Chicago, IL. Tel: (312) 606-8905, (800) 245-2665, FAX: (312) 606-8985, Web Site: www.kaplanpublishing.com (17)

Kaplan Test Prep, New York, NY. Tel: (212) 997-5800, Web Site: www.kaptest.com (1)

Kaplan, Anita, Siquis Ltd, Baltimore, MD. Tel: (410) 323-4800, FAX: (410) 323-4113, Web Site: www.siquis.com (35)

Kaplan, Bill, FreshAddress Inc, Newton, MA. Tel: (617) 965-4500, (800) 321-3009, FAX: (617) 965-4551, Web Site: www.freshaddress.com (22)

Kaplan, Bo, Toys To Grow On, Carson, CA. Tel: (310) 537-8600, (800) 874-4242, FAX: (800) 537-5403, E-Mail: toyinfo@toystogrowon.com, Web Site: www.ttgo.com (11)

Kaplan, Charles, Toys To Grow On, Carson, CA. Tel: (310) 537-8600, (800) 874-4242, FAX: (800) 537-5403, E-Mail: toyinfo@toystogrowon.com, Web Site: www.ttgo.com (11)

Kaplan, David, Tafford Uniforms, Charlotte, NC. Tel: (215) 643-9666, E-Mail: customerservice@tafford.com, Web Site: www.tafford.com (2)

Kaplan, Jon E., TeleDevelopment Services Inc, Richfield, OH. Tel: (330) 659-4441, FAX: (330) 659-4442, E-Mail: jkaplan@teledevelopment.com, Web Site: www.teledevelopment.com (20)

Kaplan, Karen, Hill Holliday, Boston, MA. Tel: (617) 366-4000, Web Site: www.hhcc.com (35)

Kaplan. Larry, Tele Business USA, Northbrook, IL. Tel: (847) 480-1560, FAX: (847) 897-4120, Web Site: www.tbiz.com (29)

Kaplan, Leon, ABCO Inc, Dallas, TX. Tel: (214) 565-1191, Web Site: www.abcoinc.com (20)

Kaplan, Marjorie, TLC, Silver Spring, MD. Tel: (240) 662-2000, Web Site: www.tlc.com (32)

Kaplan, Michael, Toys To Grow On, Carson, CA. Tel: (310) 537-8600, (800) 874-4242, FAX: (800) 537-5403, E-Mail: toyinfo@toystogrowon.com, Web Site: www.ttgo.com (11)

Kaplan, Peter W., Fairchild Fashion Media, New York, NY. Tel: (212) 286-2860, Web Site: www.condenast.com/fairchild (1)

Kaplan, Stuart R., US Games Systems Inc, Stamford, CT. Tel: (203) 353-8400, (800) 544-2637, FAX: (203) 353-8431, Web Site: www.usgamesinc.com (11)

Kaporis, Kathy, Taylor Capital Group, Inc, Rosemont, IL. Tel: (847) 653-7978, FAX: (847) 653-7890, E-Mail: investor.relations@coletaylor.com, Web Site: www.taylorcapitalgroup.com (14)

Kapotes, Jim, The Lifestyle Marketing Corp, Glen Rock, NJ. Tel: (201) 670-7985, FAX: (201) 251-2443 (35)

Kappa Publishing Group, Blue Bell, PA. Tel: (215) 643-6385, FAX: (215) 628-3571, Web Site: www.kappapublishing.com (17)

Kappa Studios, Burbank, CA. Tel: (818) 843-3400, FAX: (818) 559-5684, E-Mail: info@kappastudios.com, Web Site: www.kappastudios.com (32)

Kappler Protective Apparel & Fabrics, Guntersville, AL. Tel: (256) 505-4005, (800) 600-4019, FAX: (256) 505-4151, E-Mail: customerservice@kappler.com, Web Site: www.kappler.com (2)

Kappler, George, Kappler Protective Apparel & Fabrics, Guntersville, AL. Tel: (256) 505-4005, (800) 600-4019, FAX: (256) 505-4151, E-Mail: customerservice@kappler.com, Web Site: www.kappler.com (2)

Kaprelyan, Raffi, Knott's Berry Farm Foods, Orrville, OH. Tel: (714) 220-5200, (866) 828-5502, FAX: (714) 220-5148, Web Site: www.knottsberryfarmfoods.com (4)

Kapur, Sundeep, Vermont/New Hampshire Direct Marketing Group, Woodstock, VT. Tel: (802) 457-2807, FAX: (802) 457-2807, E-Mail: vtnhmg@vtnhmg.org, Web Site: www.vtnhmg.org (40)

Karaban Media Services Inc, Westfield, NJ. Tel: (212) 840-0660, E-Mail: gkaraban@karabanmediaservices.com, Web Site: www.klapublishing.com (31)

Karaban, Glenn, Karaban Media Services Inc, Westfield, NJ. Tel: (212) 840-0660, E-Mail: gkaraban@karabanmediaservices.com, Web Site: www.klapublishing.com (31)

Karaoke USA, Largo, FL. Tel: (727) 209-1313, (800) 776-7464, FAX: (702) 209-1312, Web Site: www.karaokeusa.com (5)

Karbowiak, Christine, Bridgestone Americas Inc, Nashville, TN. Tel: (615) 937-1000, (800) 543-7522, FAX: (615) 937-3721, Web Site: www.bridgestonetire.com (16)

Karcy, Bob, VIEW Video Inc/Arcadia Entertainment Corp, Saugerties, NY. Tel: (845) 246-9955, FAX: (845) 246-9966, E-Mail: sales@view.com, Web Site: www.view.com (16)

Karfunkel, Barry, National General Insurance, Winston-Salem, NC. Tel: (888) 293-5108, Web Site: www.nationalgeneral.com (15)

Karfunkel, Michael, National General Insurance, Winston-Salem, NC. Tel: (888) 293-5108, Web Site: www.nationalgeneral.com (15)

Kari, Ross, Safeco Insurance Co, Seattle, WA. Tel: (206) 545-5000, (800) 332-3226, FAX: (206) 545-5767/5651, Web Site: www.safeco.com (15)

Walter Karl Inc, Pearl River, NY. Tel: (845) 620-0700, FAX: (845) 620-1885, E-Mail: info@walterkarl.infousa.com, Web Site: www.walterkarl.com (22)

Karl, Bob, New Customer Acquisition, Medford, OR. Tel: (541) 779-9999, FAX: (541) 779-1935, E-Mail: bobk@postage-exempt.com (31)

Karlicek, Beth, Alexander + Roberts, Keene, NH. Tel: (603) 357-5033, (800) 221-2216, FAX: (603) 357-4548, E-Mail: info@generaltours.com, Web Site: www.generaltours.com (19)

Karlovic, Eric, HughesLeahyKarlovic, Saint Louis, MO. Tel: (314) 571-6300, FAX: (314) 862-1616, E-Mail: hello@hlkagency.com, Web Site: hlkagency.com (35)

Karlstad Flom, Linda, Midwest Technology Products & Services, Sioux City, IA. Tel: (712) 252-3601, (800) 831-5904, FAX: (800) 258-7054, E-Mail: web@midwesttechnology.com, Web Site: www.midwesttechnology.com (9)

Karmele, Gerald, Freestyle Photographic Supplies, Los Angeles, CA. Tel: (323) 660-3640, (800) 292-6137, FAX: (323) 284-0050, Web Site: www.freestylephoto.biz (5)

Karol Media, Wilkes-Barre, PA. Tel: (570) 822-8899, (800) 526-4773, FAX: (570) 822-8226, Web Site: www.karolmedia.com (28)

Karow, Al, TruGreen/ChemLawn, Lewis Center, OH. Tel: (614) 846-1800, (800) TRUE-GREEN, FAX: (614) 431-0155, Web Site: www.trugreen.com (16)

Karp, Jonathan, Simon & Schuster Inc, New York, NY. Tel: (212) 698-7000, (800) 223-2348, Web Site: www.simonandschuster.com (17)

Karpowicz, Paul, Meredith Corp, Des Moines, IA. Tel: (515) 284-3000, FAX: (515) 284-2700, Web Site: www.meredith.com (17)

Karsh, Bruce A., Tribune Co, Chicago, IL. Tel: (312) 222-9100, FAX: (312) 222-1573, Web Site: www.tribune.com (17)

Karstedt, Chris, Bowers & Merena Auctions, Irvine, CA. Tel: (949) 253-0916, (800) 458-4646, FAX: (949) 253-4091, E-Mail: auction@bowersandmerena.com, Web Site: www.bowersandmerena.com (16)

Karten, Stuart, Stuart Karten Design, Marina Del Rey, CA. Tel: (310) 827-8722, FAX: (310) 821-4492, Web Site: www.kartendesign.com (16)

Kartsotis, Kosta N., Fossil, Richardson, TX. Tel: (469) 587-2628, Web Site: www.fossil.com (2)

Kartsounes, Scott, MNI, Evanston, IL. Tel: (847) 864-7000, (888) 752-5200, FAX: (847) 332-1100, Web Site: mni.net (23)

Kartychak, Darr, Intermedia Consultants Inc, Princeton, NJ. Tel: (609) 430-8460, Web Site: www.interprintmedia.com (35)

Kasander, Bonnie, Encore Marketing International, Lanham, MD. Tel: (301) 459-8020, (800) 846-9398, FAX: (301) 731-0525, E-Mail: customerservice@encoremarketing.com, Web Site: www.encoremarketing.com (16)

Kasanders, Paul, Visible Computer Supply Corp, Saint Charles, IL. Tel: (630) 377-2586, (800) 323-0628, FAX: (800) 233-2016, Web Site: www.wallace.com (16)

Kash, Rick, The Nielsen Co, New York, NY. Tel: (800) 864-1224, Web Site: www.nielsen.com (17)

Kashan, Robert, LP Thebault Co, Parsippany, NJ. Tel: (973) 884-1300, FAX: (973) 952-8282, E-Mail: info@earthcolor.com, Web Site: www.earthcolor.com (27)

Kashgegian, Glen A., Blue Raven Technology, Wilmington, MA. Tel: ((978) 658-4676, (800) 274-5343, (800) 20RAVEN, FAX: (781) 778-4848, E-Mail: sales@blueraven.com, Web Site: www.blueraven.com (3)

Kasp, Gladys, Promotional Product Professionals of Canada, Dorval, QC Canada. Tel: (514) 489-5359, FAX: (800) 489-8741, (514) 489-7760, E-Mail: gladys@pppc.ca, Web Site: www.pppc.ca (1)

Kasper, Robert, Informed Sources Inc, Plainview, NY. Tel: (800) 201-6060, FAX: (516) 576-0249, E-Mail: info@informed-sources.com, Web Site: www.informed-sources.com (30)

Kass, Jonathan, Innovative Marketing Direct Inc, Tampa, FL. Tel: (813) 873-7909, FAX: (813) 873-7918, E-Mail: mail@innovativedirectmail.com, Web Site: www.innovativedirectmail.com (21)

Kassel, Norman, Nationwide Beauty & Barber Supply, Syracuse, NY. Tel: (315) 446-9026, FAX: (315) 446-8943, E-Mail: sales@nationwidebeauty.com, Web Site: www.nationwidebeauty.com (16)

Kassel, Richard, Nationwide Beauty & Barber Supply, Syracuse, NY. Tel: (315) 446-9026, FAX: (315) 446-8943, E-Mail: sales@nationwidebeauty.com, Web Site: www.nationwidebeauty.com (16)

Kasten, Alan, United States Bronze Sign Co Inc, New Hyde Park, NY. Tel: (516) 352-5155, (800) 872-5155, FAX: (516) 253-2328, E-Mail: peter@usbronze.com, Web Site: www.usbronze.com (1)

Kasten, Peter, United States Bronze Sign Co Inc, New Hyde Park, NY. Tel: (516) 352-5155, (800) 872-5155, FAX: (516) 253-2328, E-Mail: peter@usbronze.com, Web Site: www.usbronze.com (1)

Kastning, Tracy, Saunders Manufacturing Co Inc, Readfield, ME. Tel: (207) 685-3385, (800) 341-4674, FAX: (207) 685-9918, E-Mail: jsherwood@saunders-usa.com, Web Site: www.saunders-usa.com (16)

Katalin, Spencer, Spear Engineering Co, Colorado Springs, CO. Tel: (719) 471-9850 (16)

Katalyst Partners Inc, New York, NY. Tel: (203) 257-4277, E-Mail: bpetisi@katalystresponse.com, Web Site: www.katalystresponse.com (21)

Katchian, Sonia, Photo Shuttle Japan, Chapel Hill, NC. Tel: (919) 967-1585, E-Mail: sonia@photoshuttle.com, Web Site: www.photoshuttle.com (37)

Kathan, Ken, BCC Software Inc, Rochester, NY. Tel: (585) 272-9130, (800) 453-3130, FAX: (585) 272-9141, Web Site: www.bccsoftware.com (22)

Katz Media Group, New York, NY. Tel: (212) 424-6000, Web Site: www.katz-media.com (32)

Katz, Andrew, PetEdge, Beverly, MA. Tel: (978) 998-8100, (800) 738-3343, FAX: (978) 887-8499, E-Mail: support@petedge.com, Web Site: www.petedge.com (16)

Katz, Ed, Choice Courier Systems Inc, New York, NY. Tel: (212) 370-1999, FAX: (212) 370-0440, Web Site: www.choicecourier.com (16)

Katz, Karen, Neiman-Marcus Group, Dallas, TX. Tel: (214) 339-0396, (888) 888-4757, Web Site: www.neimanmarcus.com (8)

Katz, Leslie, American Speech-Language-Hearing Association, Rockville, MD. Tel: (301) 897-5700, (800) 638-8255, FAX: (301) 296-8580, E-Mail: productsales@asha.org, Web Site: www.asha.org (1)

Katz, Michael, Choice Courier Systems Inc, New York, NY. Tel: (212) 370-1999, FAX: (212) 370-0440, Web Site: www.choicecourier.com (16)

Katz, Paul, PartyLite Gifts Inc, Norwell, MA. Tel: (508) 830-3100, (888)999-5706, FAX: (508) 830-0026, E-Mail: infona@partylite.com, Web Site: www.partylite.com (8)

Katz, Robert A., Vail Resorts Inc, Broomfield, CO. Tel: (303) 404-1800, FAX: (303) 404-6415, Web Site: www.vailresorts.com (19)

Katz, Robert M., Easy Analytic Software Inc, Bellmawr, NJ. Tel: (856) 931-5780, FAX: (856) 931-4115, Web Site: www.easidemographics.com (22)

Katz, Stan, ACBL, Horn Lake, MS. Tel: (662) 253-3100, FAX: (662) 253-3187, E-Mail: service@acbl.org, Web Site: www.acbl.org (1)

Katz, Steven, Mother Jones Magazine, San Francisco, CA. Tel: (415) 321-1700, Web Site: www.motherjones.com (17)

Katzman, Ken, Dover Publications Inc, Mineola, NY. Tel: (516) 294-7000, FAX: (516) 742-6953, Web Site: www.doverpublications.com (17)

Kauffman, Kerri, Lamkin Corp, San Diego, CA. Tel: (619) 661-7090, (800) 642-7755, FAX: (619) 661-0014, E-Mail: info@lamkingrips.com, Web Site: www.lamkingrips.com (11)

Kaufman, Jay, Paragon Laboratories, Torrance, CA. Tel: (310) 370-1563, (800) 231-3670, FAX: (310) 370-7354, E-Mail: sales@paragonlabsusa.com, Web Site: www.paragonlabsusa.com (16)

Kaufman, Kenneth A., Omni Print Inc, Lanham, MD. Tel: (301) 731-7000, FAX: (301) 731-7001, E-Mail: info@omniprint.net, Web Site: www.omniprint.net (27)

Kaufman, Lauren, Spring O'Brien & Co, New York, NY. Tel: (212) 620-7100, FAX: (212) 620-7166, E-Mail: info@spring-obrien.com, Web Site: www.spring-obrien.com (35)

Kaufman, Lois, Environmental Research Associates, Havertown, PA. Tel: (610) 449-7400 (30)

Kaufman, Marlin, Concord Litho, Concord, NH. Tel: (603) 225-3328, FAX: (603) 225-6120, E-Mail: print@concordlitho.com, Web Site: www.concordlitho.com (27)

Kaufman, Mike, Promotion Marketing Association (PMA) Inc, New York, NY. Tel: (212) 420-1100, FAX: (212) 533-7622, E-Mail: pma@pmalink.org, Web Site: www.pmalink.org (1)

Kaufman, Pete, Valentine Research Inc, Cincinnati, OH. Tel: (513) 984-8900, (800) 331-3030, FAX: (513) 984-8976, E-Mail: sales@valentine1.com, Web Site: www.valentine1.com (16)

Kaufman, Richard, Paragon Laboratories, Torrance, CA. Tel: (310) 370-1563, (800) 231-3670, FAX: (310) 370-7354, E-Mail: sales@paragonlabsusa.com, Web Site: www.paragonlabsusa.com (16)

Kaufmann, Anne, Frank W Cawood & Associates, Peachtree City, GA. Tel: (770) 487-6307, Web Site: www.fca.com (35)

Kaufmann, Dave, Denver Tax Software Inc, Littleton, CO. Tel: (303) 796-7780, (800) 326-6686, FAX: (888) 326-6686, Web Site: www.denvertax.com (16)

Kaul, Ajay, Lenovo, Morrisville, NC. Tel: (919) 257-6315, (855) 253-6686, Web Site: www.uslenovo.com (3)

Kaupe, Chris, Tully & Holland Inc, Wellesley, MA. Tel: (781) 239-2900, FAX: (781) 239-2901, E-Mail: info@tullyandholland.com, Web Site: www.tullyandholland.com (14)

Kauppila, John, Duncan Aviation, Lincoln, NE. Tel: (402) 475-2611, (800) 228-4277, FAX: (402) 475-5541, Web Site: www.duncanaviation.com (16)

Kautz, John, Rawle Murdy, Charleston, SC. Tel: (843) 577-7327, E-Mail: contact@rawlemurdy.com, Web Site: www.rawlemurdy.com (35)

Kavanagh, Kim, Potpourri Group Inc, North Billerica, MA. Tel: (978) 256-4100, FAX: (978) 256-1961/0344, Web Site: www.potpourrigroup.com (6)

Kawada, Yoshikatsu, Seiko Corp of America, Mahwah, NJ. Tel: (201) 529-3316, E-Mail: custserv@seikousa.com, Web Site: www.seikousa.com (16)

Kaye-Smith, Renton, WA. Tel: (425) 228-8600, (800) 822-9987, FAX: (425) 291-3167, E-Mail: info@kayesmith.com, Web Site: www.kayesmith.com (21)

Kaye, Candy, Lazarus Direct Inc, Uniondale, NY. Tel: (516) 880-7000, E-Mail: inquiries@lazarusdirect.com, Web Site: www.lazarusmarketing.com (21)

Kaye, David, The Economist Newspaper NA Inc, New York, NY. Tel: (212) 554-0600, FAX: (212) 586-1191, Web Site: www.economist.com (17)

Kaye, Paul, I/D/E/A Inc, Caldwell, ID. Tel: (208) 459-6357, (800) 635-9261, FAX: (208) 459-6484, Web Site: www.relyonidea.com (16)

Kaye, Sandy, Porta-Bote International, Mountain View, CA. Tel: (650) 961-5334, (800) 227-8882, Web Site: www.porta-bote.com (11)

Kaylor, Dan, Kaylor's School Supply, Albertville, AL. Tel: (256) 878-1200, (800) 239-9999, FAX: (800) 239-9998, E-Mail: sales@kaylorsinc.com, Web Site: www.kaylorsinc.com (16)

Kaylor, Jesse, Kaylor's School Supply, Albertville, AL. Tel: (256) 878-1200, (800) 239-9999, FAX: (800) 239-9998, E-Mail: sales@kaylorsinc.com, Web Site: www.kaylorsinc.com (16)

Kaylor's School Supply, Albertville, AL. Tel: (256) 878-1200, (800) 239-9999, FAX: (800) 239-9998, E-Mail: sales@kaylorsinc.com, Web Site: www.kaylorsinc.com (16)

Kayne & Son Custom Hardware Inc, Candler, NC. Tel: (828) 667-8868, FAX: (828) 665-8303, Web Site: www.customforgedhardware.com (8)

Kayne, David, Kayne & Son Custom Hardware Inc, Candler, NC. Tel: (828) 667-8868, FAX: (828) 665-8303, Web Site: www.customforgedhardware.com (8)

Kaynes, Jr. Robert, American Bronzing Co, Columbus, OH. Tel: (614) 252-7388, (800) 423-5678, FAX: (614) 252-4602, E-Mail: bronzeinfo@bronshoe.com, Web Site: www.abcbronze.com (16)

Kayser-Roth Corp Inc, Greensboro, NC. Tel: (800) 575-3497, Web Site: www.nononsense.com (16)

KD Mailing & Fulfillment Service, Lincolnwood, IL. Tel: (847) 673-0186, (866) 330-6245, FAX: (874) 673-0188, E-Mail: dan@kdmailing.com, Web Site: www.kdmailing.com (28)

Keane, Jr. John, Life-Study Fellowship Foundation Inc, Darien, CT. Tel: (203) 655-1436, FAX: (203) 655-1392, Web Site: www.lifestudyfellowship.com (17)

Keane, Marylee, American Marketing Association/New York Chapter, New York, NY. Tel: (212) 687-3280, FAX: (212) 557-9242, E-Mail: mlkeane@nyama.org, Web Site: www.nyama.org (40)

Keane, Michael, Life-Study Fellowship Foundation Inc, Darien, CT. Tel: (203) 655-1436, FAX: (203) 655-1392, Web Site: www.lifestudyfellowship.com (17)

Keane, Robert, VistaPrint USA Inc, Lexington, MA. Tel: (800) 961-2075, Web Site: www.vistaprint.com (27)

Kearney, Doug, Dialog Direct, Highland Park, MI. Tel: (800) 523-5867, E-Mail: sales@dialog-direct.com, Web Site: www.dialog-direct.com (35)

Kearney, Jim, Eire Direct, Chicago, IL. Tel: (312) 640-4000, FAX: (312) 640-0324, E-Mail: info@eiredirect.com, Web Site: www.eiredirect.com (16)

Kearney, Louisa D., World Press Review, New York, NY. Tel: (212) 982-8880, Web Site: www.worldpressreview.com (18)

Kearns, Bill, Clement Communications, Buffalo, NY. Tel: (800) 253-6368, E-Mail: customerservice@clement.com, Web Site: www.clement.com (17)

Keating Magee, Metairie, LA. Tel: (504) 299-8000, FAX: (504) 525-6647, E-Mail: info@keatingmagee.com, Web Site: www.keatingmagee.com (35)

Keating, Cheryl, Mailing Source, Costa Mesa, CA. Tel: (949) 722-9391 (28)

Keaton, Earl, Saunders Military Insignia, Naples, FL. Tel: (239) 298-8228, (800) 442-3133, FAX: (239) 774-3323, E-Mail: info@saundersinsignia.com, Web Site: www.saundersinsignia.com (6)

Keaveney, James, ISA-The International Society of Automation, Research Triangle Park, NC. Tel: (919) 549-8411, FAX: (919) 549-8288, E-Mail: info@isa.org, Web Site: www.isa.org (1)

Kee, Gilbert, Promotional Products Fulfillment & Distribution Ltd, Whitby, ON Canada. Tel: (905) 668-5060, (800) 263-4678, FAX: (905) 668-1195, E-Mail: sales@ppfd.com, Web Site: www.ppfd.com (22)

Keefe, Donald J., American Printing House for the Blind, Louisville, KY. Tel: (502) 895-2405, (800) 223-1839, FAX: (502) 899-2274, E-Mail: info@aph.org, Web Site: www.aph.org (7)

Keefe, Mark, PrimeNet, Clearwater, FL. Tel: (651) 405-4000, FAX: (651) 405-4100, Web Site: www.pnms.com (22)

Keefhaver, Joe, Wyandotte West Communications Inc, Kansas City, KS. Tel: (913) 788-5565, FAX: (913) 788-9812, E-Mail: news@wyandottewest.com, Web Site: www.wyandottewest.com (17)

The Keehn Co, Pound Ridge, NY. Tel: (914) 764-8591, FAX: (914) 764-5388, E-Mail: dkeehnco@optonline.net (35)

Keehn, Dennis, The Keehn Co, Pound Ridge, NY. Tel: (914) 764-8591, FAX: (914) 764-5388, E-Mail: dkeehnco@optonline.net (35)

Keelty, Mary Beth, PMX Agency, New York, NY. Tel: (212) 387-0300, (888) 960-0177, FAX: (212) 387-7647, E-Mail: info@pmxagency.com, Web Site: www.pmxagency.com (23)

Keely, William G., Whitaker National, Huntington, WV. Tel: (304) 525-0852, (800) 377-8721, FAX: (304) 525-0874, Web Site: www.neshold.com (16)

Keeman, Deb, Stream International, Wellesley, MA. Tel: (781) 304-1800, (888) 264-5834, FAX: (781) 575-6999, Web Site: www.stream.com (16)

Keenan, Anne, USI Affinity, Philadelphia, PA. Tel: (610) 833-2876, (800) 625-2876, FAX: (610) 265-2876, E-Mail: info@usiaffinity.com, Web Site: www.brcorp.com (17)

Keenan, Jack L., Tele Resources Inc, Duluth, MN. Tel: (888) 698-8787 X114, FAX: (218) 724-2466, E-Mail: mark.swanson@teleresources.net, Web Site: www.teleresources.net (29)

Keenan, John, Anthem Marketing, Chicago, IL. Tel: (312) 441-0382 (22)

Keene, Michael, The John Roberts Co, Minneapolis, MN. Tel: (763) 755-5500, (800) 551-1534, FAX: (763) 755-0394, E-Mail: jfoster@johnroberts.com, Web Site: www.johnroberts.com (28)

Keene-Kendrick, Lydia, Davis Art Images, Worcester, MA. Tel: (508) 754-7201, (800) 533-2847, FAX: (508) 831-9260, (508) 753-3834, E-Mail: lkeenekendrick@davisart.com, Web Site: www.davisartimages.com (38)

Keeneland Association Inc, Lexington, KY. Tel: (859) 254-3412, (800) 456-3412, FAX: (859) 255-2484, Web Site: www.keeneland.com (16)

Keeney, Tyler, Who's Who - The MFSA Buyers' Guide to Blue Ribbon Mailing Services, Alexandria, VA. Tel: (703) 836-9200, FAX: (703) 548-8204, E-Mail: masa-mail@masa.org, Web Site: www.mfsanet.org (43)

Keessen. Robert H., Scott Publications, Inc, Muskegon, MI. Tel: (231) 755-2200, (866) 733-9382, FAX: (231) 755-1003, Web Site: www.scottpublications.com (17)

Kehoe, Debra, Daniel Smith Inc, Seattle, WA. Tel: (206) 223-9599, (800) 426-6740, FAX: (800) 238-4065, E-Mail: sales@danielsmith.com, Web Site: www.danielsmith.com (10)

Kehoe, John, Trinity Direct LLC, Butler, NJ. Tel: (973) 283-3600, FAX: (973) 283-3606, E-Mail: trinity.info@trinitydirect.net, Web Site: www.trinitydirect.net (23)

Kehoe, Sean, Trinity Direct LLC, Butler, NJ. Tel: (973) 283-3600, FAX: (973) 283-3606, E-Mail: trinity.info@trinitydirect.net, Web Site: www.trinitydirect.net (23)

Keifer, Joy, Babyshoe.com, Hendersonville, NC. Tel: (828) 697-5811, (800) 543-8566, FAX: (828) 697-5815, E-Mail: info@babyshoe.com, Web Site: www.babyshoe.com (6)

Keilitz, Craig, American Baseball Coaches Association, Greensboro, NC. Tel: (336) 821-3140, FAX: (336) 886-0000, E-Mail: abca@abca.org, Web Site: www.abca.org (1)

Keir, Gerald J., First Hawaiian Bank, Honolulu, HI. Tel: (808) 525-6273, (888) 844-4444, FAX: (808) 525-5798, E-Mail: bfarias@fhb.com, Web Site: www.fhb.com (14)

Keiser, Lauren, Carl Fischer Music, New York, NY. Tel: (212) 777-0900, (800) 762-2328, FAX: (212) 477-6996, E-Mail: cf-info@carlfischer.com, Web Site: www.carlfischer.com (17)

Keith, Jason, VistaPrint USA Inc, Lexington, MA. Tel: (800) 961-2075, Web Site: www.vistaprint.com (27)

Keith, MD Stephen N., National Medical Fellowships, New York, NY. Tel: (212) 483-8880, FAX: (212) 483-8897, E-Mail: info@nmf-online.org, Web Site: www.nmf-online.org (1)

Kelco Supply Co, Big Lake, MN. Tel: (763) 493-1260, (800) 328-7720, FAX: (763) 493-1261, E-Mail: info@kelcosupply.com, Web Site: www.kelcosupply.com (16)

Keleher, David, Dynamics Research Corp, Andover, MA. Tel: (978) 475-9090, (800) 522-4321, FAX: (978) 475-8205, Web Site: www.drc.com (16)

Kelleher, Patrick, Genworth Financial Inc, Richmond, VA. Tel: (804) 281-6000, (888) 436-9678, FAX: (804) 662-2414, Web Site: www.genworth.com (14)

Kellen, Mike, Assurant Health, Milwaukee, WI. Tel: (414) 244-0658, (800) 800-1212, FAX: (414) 224-0472, Web Site: www.assuranthealth.com (15)

Kellenberger, Dan, Cadie Products Corp, Paterson, NJ. Tel: (973) 278-8300, FAX: (973) 278-0303, E-Mail: emeyers@cadie.com, Web Site: www. cadieproducts.com (16)

JJ Keller & Associates Inc, Neenah, WI. Tel: (920) 722-2848, (800) 327-6868, FAX: (800) 727-7516, E-Mail: thines@jjkeller.com, Web Site: www. jjkeller.com/jjk (16)

Keller, Barb, We Deliver America Inc, Englewood Cliffs, NJ. Tel: (201) 307-8888, FAX: (201) 307-1200, E-Mail: info@we-deliver-america.com, Web Site: www.we-deliver-america.com (31)

Keller, Don, World Book Inc, Chicago, IL. Tel: (312) 729-5800, (800) 255-1750, FAX: (312) 729-5600, Web Site: www.worldbook.com (17)

Keller, Guy, ProLogic Retail Services, Delray Beach, FL. E-Mail: info@prologicretail.com, Web Site: www.prologicretail.com (35)

Keller, Jack, JAK Productions, Atlanta, GA. Tel: (404) 883-2450, FAX: (404) 883-2672, E-Mail: info@jak-productions.com (29)

Keller, James, JJ Keller & Associates Inc, Neenah, WI. Tel: (920) 722-2848, (800) 327-6868, FAX: (800) 727-7516, E-Mail: thines@jjkeller.com, Web Site: www.jjkeller.com/jjk (16)

Keller, Joel, San Francisco Bay Area Rapid Transit District (BART), Oakland, CA. Tel: (510) 464-6000, FAX: (510) 464-7103, Web Site: www.bart.gov (16)

Keller, Kevin Lane, Marketing Science Institute Review, Cambridge, MA. Tel: (617) 491-2060, FAX: (617) 491-2065, E-Mail: msi@msi.org, Web Site: www.msi.org (43)

Keller, Kimberly, National Audubon Society, New York, NY. Tel: (212) 979-3000, FAX: (212) 979-3188, Web Site: www.audubon.org (17)

Keller, Robert, JJ Keller & Associates Inc, Neenah, WI. Tel: (920) 722-2848, (800) 327-6868, FAX: (800) 727-7516, E-Mail: thines@jjkeller.com, Web Site: www.jjkeller.com/jjk (16)

Keller, Scott, Solar Components Corp, Manchester, NH. Tel: (603) 668-8186, FAX: (603) 668-1783, Web Site: www.solar-components.com (9)

Keller, Steven, Assurant Health, Milwaukee, WI. Tel: (414) 244-0658, (800) 800-1212, FAX: (414) 224-0472, Web Site: www.assuranthealth.com (15)

Kelley Swofford Roy Inc, Miami, FL. Tel: (305) 444-0004, (800) 537-5565, FAX: (305) 444-9057, E-Mail: info@ksrteam.com, Web Site: www. ksrteam.com (35)

Kelley, Barbara M., Bausch & Lomb Inc, Rochester, NY. Tel: (585) 338-6000, (800) 344-8815, FAX: (585) 338-6007, Web Site: www.bausch.com (16)

Kelley, Brian, Cognitronics Corp, Danbury, CT. Tel: (203) 830-3400, (888) 228-5061, FAX: (508) 624-0289, E-Mail: info@thinkengine.com, Web Site: www.cognitronics.com (34)

Kelley, Brian P., Green Mountain Coffee Roasters, Inc, Waterbury, VT. Tel: (802) 244-5621, (800) 545-2326, FAX: (802) 244-5436, Web Site: www.gmcr. com (4)

Kelley, Dana, CMI Direct, Pasadena, CA. Tel: (951) 300-1700, FAX: (866) 723-5433, Web Site: www. cmidirect.net (15)

Kelley, Don, Hanover Direct Inc, Weehawken, NJ. Tel: (201) 863-7300, FAX: (201) 272-3465, Web Site: www.hanoverdirect.com (16)

Kelley, Paul, Black Dot Group, Crystal Lake, IL. Tel: (815) 893-8799, E-Mail: pkelley@blackdot.com, Web Site: www.blackdot.com (35)

Kelley, Susan, Kelley Swofford Roy Inc, Miami, FL. Tel: (305) 444-0004, (800) 537-5565, FAX: (305) 444-9057, E-Mail: info@ksrteam.com, Web Site: www.ksrteam.com (35)

Kelliher Samets Volk, Burlington, VT. Tel: (802) 862-8261, FAX: (802) 863-4724, E-Mail: info@ksvc. com, Web Site: www.ksvc.com (35)

Kelliher, Linda, Kelliher Samets Volk, Burlington, VT. Tel: (802) 862-8261, FAX: (802) 863-4724, E-Mail: info@ksvc.com, Web Site: www.ksvc.com (35)

Kellogg, Peter N., Merck & Co Inc, Whitehouse Station, NJ. Tel: (908) 423-1000, Web Site: www.merck. com (16)

Kelly, Scott & Madison Inc, Chicago, IL. Tel: (312) 977-0772, FAX: (312) 977-0874, E-Mail: info@ ksmmedia.com, Web Site: www.ksmmedia.com (32)

Kelly, Anne, Namebank, Baltimore, MD. Tel: (410) 864-0854, FAX: (410) 864-0837, E-Mail: lists@ namebank.com, Web Site: www.namebank.com (23)

Kelly, Darcy, The Financial Times Group, New York, NY. Tel: (212) 641-6500, Web Site: www.ft.com (17)

Kelly, David, AnalyticsIQ Inc, Atlanta, GA. Tel: (770) 407-8855, (888) 612-4309, Web Site: www. analytics-iq.com (30)

Kelly, Ed, American Express Publishing Corp, New York, NY. Tel: (212) 382-5600, (888) 461-6180, FAX: (212) 827-6496, E-Mail: aepc@custmersvc. com, Web Site: www.amexpub.com (17)

Kelly, Edmund F., Liberty Mutual Group, Inc, Boston, MA. Tel: (617) 357-9500, (800) 837-5274, Web Site: www.libertymutual.com (15)

Kelly, Gene, Executive Protection Products Inc, Napa, CA. Tel: (707) 253-7142, FAX: (707) 253-7149, E-Mail: services@epsecuritysolutions.com, Web Site: epsecuritysolutions.com (16)

Kelly, John, Recording for the Blind & Dyslexic Inc, Princeton, NJ. Tel: (609) 452-0606, (800) 221-4792, FAX: (609) 520-7996, E-Mail: info@rfbd.org, Web Site: www.rfbd.org (16)

Kelly, Judy, Alpha List Marketing Inc, Marietta, GA. Tel: (404) 995-7049, FAX: (404) 601-0826 (23)

Kelly, Kevin P., Farm Bureau Insurance, Lansing, MI. Tel: (517) 323-7000, (800) 292-2680, FAX: (517) 327-0208, Web Site: www.farmbureauinsurance-mi. com (15)

Kelly, Maureen C., The Suburban Chamber of Commerce, Summit, NJ. Tel: (908) 522-1700, FAX: (908) 522-9252, E-Mail: info@suburbanchambers. org, Web Site: www.suburbanchambers.org (14)

Kelly, Michael, Bankers Warranty Group, Saint Petersburg, FL. Tel: (800) 431-5843, E-Mail: info@ bankerswarrantygroup.com, Web Site: www. bankerswarrantygroup.com (16)

Kelly, Michael, Editors Press Inc, Hyattsville, MD. Tel: (301) 853-4900, (888) 853-4900, FAX: (301) 853-4961, Web Site: www.edpress.com (27)

Kelly, Patrick, The Company Store Inc, La Crosse, WI. Tel: (608) 785-1400, FAX: (608) 791-5790, Web Site: www.thecompanystore.com (16)

Kelly, Rob, Earthrise, Irvine, CA. Tel: (949) 623-0980, FAX: (949) 623-0990, E-Mail: info@earthrise.com, Web Site: www.earthrise.com (16)

Kelly, Robert F., New York-Presbyterian/Columbia University Medical Center, New York, NY. Tel: (212) 305-2500, FAX: (212) 305-8023, Web Site: www.nyp.org (16)

Kelly, Thomas, Hawthorne Direct Inc, Los Angeles, CA. Tel: (301) 248-3972, E-Mail: inquiries@ hawthornedirect.com, Web Site: www. hawthornedirect.com (35)

Kelly, Thomas, New York Life Insurance Co/AARP, Tampa, FL. Tel: (813) 288-5500, FAX: (813) 288-5256, Web Site: www.nylaarp.com (15)

Kelly, Torri, WL Gore & Associates Inc, Newark, DE. Tel: (410) 506-7787, (888) 914-4673, E-Mail: info@wlgore.com, Web Site: www.wlgore.com (2)

Kelly, William J., HCI Direct, Bensalem, PA. Tel: (215) 244-9600, (888) 765-0062, FAX: (215) 244-0328, Web Site: www.silkies.com (16)

Kelly, William M., Alloyd Brands, Dekalb, IL. Tel: (815) 756-8451, (800) 756-7639, FAX: (815) 756-5187/9192, Web Site: www.alloyd.com (16)

Kelly-Radford, Ph.D. Lily M., Center for Creative Leadership, Greensboro, NC. Tel: (336) 545-2810, FAX: (336) 282-3284, E-Mail: info@ccl.org, Web Site: www.ccl.org (16)

Kellyco Metal Detector Distributors, Winter Springs, FL. Tel: (407) 699-8700, (800) 327-9697, FAX: (407) 695-6671, E-Mail: customerservice@ kellycodetectors.com, Web Site: www. kellycodetectors.com (11)

Kelly's Kids, Natchez, MS. Tel: (601) 442-5332, (800) 837-2066, FAX: (601) 442-4399, E-Mail: hello@ kellyskids.com, Web Site: www.kellyskids.com (2)

Kelsey III, Van, Kelsey National Corp, Los Angeles, CA. Tel: (310) 390-1000, (800) 366-5656, FAX: (310) 390-3158, E-Mail: info@kelsey.com, Web Site: www.kelsey.com (15)

Kelsey National Corp, Los Angeles, CA. Tel: (310) 390-1000, (800) 366-5656, FAX: (310) 390-3158, E-Mail: info@kelsey.com, Web Site: www.kelsey. com (15)

Kelsey, Mark, Kelsey National Corp, Los Angeles, CA. Tel: (310) 390-1000, (800) 366-5656, FAX: (310) 390-3158, E-Mail: info@kelsey.com, Web Site: www.kelsey.com (15)

Kelsey, Mark, LexisNexis Matthew Bender, Albany, NY. Tel: (518) 487-3000, (800) 424-4200, E-Mail: lexisnexis@matthewbender, Web Site: www.bender. lexisnexis.com (17)

Kelsey, Mark, LexisNexis Risk Soulutions, Alpharetta, GA. Tel: (678) 694-6000, Web Site: www. lexisnexis.com/risk (30)

Kelsey, Mark, Martindale-Hubbell, New Providence, NJ. Tel: (908) 771-7777, (800) 526-4902, FAX: (908) 771-8704, Web Site: www.martindale.com (17)

Kelsey, Meg, City of LaGrange, LaGrange, GA. Tel: (706) 883-2010, FAX: (706) 883-2020, Web Site: www.lagrange-ga.org (1)

Kelsey, Van, Kelsey National Corp, Los Angeles, CA. Tel: (310) 390-1000, (800) 366-5656, FAX: (310) 390-3158, E-Mail: info@kelsey.com, Web Site: www.kelsey.com (15)

Kelty, Robert, Amref Health Africa in the USA, New York, NY. Tel: (212) 768-2440, FAX: (212) 768-4230, Web Site: www.amrefusa.org (1)

Kemmitz, Greg, Skypoint Communications Inc, Loretto, MN. Tel: (763) 548-2600, FAX: (763) 548-2610, E-Mail: info@skypoint.com, Web Site: www. skypoint.com (16)

Kemp, Gil, Home Decorators Collection Inc, Marietta, GA. Tel: (800) 245-2217, Web Site: www. homedecoratorscom (8)

Kemp, Jennifer, Bluestem Brands, Eden Prairie, MN. Tel: (952) 656-3700, Web Site: www.fingerhut.com (16)

Kemp, Jim, Collector's Armoury Ltd, McDonough, GA. Tel: (678) 593-2660, (877) 276-6879, FAX: (678) 593-2660, E-Mail: sales@collectorsarmoury.com, Web Site: www.collectorsarmoury.com (6)

Kemper Corp, Chicago, IL. Tel: (312) 661-4600, (800) 733-7366, FAX: (312) 494-6995, Web Site: www.kemper.com (15)

Kemper, David W., Washington University, Saint Louis, MO. Tel: (314) 935-5000, Web Site: www.wustl.edu (1)

Kemper, Jane, PESI LLC, Eau Claire, WI. Tel: (800) 844-8260, FAX: (800) 554-9775, E-Mail: info@pesi.com, Web Site: www.pesi.com (17)

Kemper, Kimberly, Texas Farm Bureau Insurance Cos, Waco, TX. Tel: (254) 751-2688, Web Site: www.txfb-ins.com (15)

Kemper, Mike, Associated Materials, Cuyahoga Falls, OH. Tel: (330) 922-2182, Web Site: www.alside.com (8)

Kempske, Kevin, GKV, Baltimore, MD. Tel: (410) 539-5400, FAX: (410) 234-2441, E-Mail: newbusiness@gkv.com, Web Site: gvk.com (35)

Kempski, Luke, JPL Integrated Communications Inc, Harrisburg, PA. Tel: (717) 558-8048, E-Mail: jpl@jplcreative.com, Web Site: www.jplcreative.com (35)

Ken Elo, Montreal, QC Canada. Tel: (514) 926-6945 (20)

Kendall Products/Dri-Dek, Naples, FL. Tel: (239) 643-2244, (800) 348-2398, FAX: (800) 828-4248, E-Mail: info@dri-dek.com, Web Site: www.dri-dek.com (16)

Kendall, Clint, Allied Integrated Marketing, Boston, MA. Tel: (617) 859-4800, E-Mail: alliedimsocial@alliedim.com, Web Site: alliedim.com (35)

Kendrick, Carl, Bass Pro Shops, Springfield, MO. Tel: (417) 887-7334, FAX: (417) 873-5882, Web Site: www.basspro.com (11)

Kendrick, David, Interior Concepts Corp, Spring Lake, MI. Tel: (616) 842-5550, (800) 678-5550, FAX: (616) 846-3925, Web Site: www.interiorconcepts.com (34)

Kening, Phillip, Beacon Marketing Group, Smithville, NJ. Tel: (609) 677-1776, FAX: (609) 677-1777, Web Site: www.beaconmktg.com (35)

Keniston, Kimberly, Alfa Aesar-A Johnson Matthey Co, Ward Hill, MA. Tel: (800) 343-0660, FAX: (800) 322-4757, E-Mail: info@alfa.com, Web Site: www.alfa.com (9)

Kenmore Stamp Co, Milford, NH. Tel: (603) 673-1745, (800) 225-5059, FAX: (603) 673-3222, Web Site: www.kenmorestamp.com (6)

Kenna, III Frank, The Marlin Company, Wallingford, CT. Tel: (877) 890-9116, Web Site: www.themarlincompany.com (35)

Kennametal Inc, Latrobe, PA. Tel: (800) 222-9327, FAX: (800) 521-3319, E-Mail: mcs-na.service@kennmetal.com, Web Site: www.kennametal.com (16)

Kennedy Inner Circle, Phoenix, AZ. Tel: (602) 269-3111, FAX: (602) 269-3113 (20)

Kennedy, Ben, Proven Prospects Inc, Santa Barbara, CA. Tel: (805) 448-6253, Web Site: www.provemprospects.com (20)

Kennedy, Boyd, Texas Parks & Wildlife Dept, Austin, TX. Tel: (512) 389-4800, (800) 792-1112, FAX: (512) 389-8029, Web Site: www.tpwd.state.tx.us (1)

Kennedy, Bryan, Conversant Inc, Chicago, IL. Tel: (312) 588-3671, Web Site: www.conversantmedia.com (32)

Kennedy, Bryan, Epsilon, Irving, TX. Tel: (469) 262-0600, Web Site: www.epsilon.com (35)

Kennedy, Chris, CUNA Mutual Group, Madison, WI. Tel: (608) 238-5851, (800) 356-2644, FAX: (608) 231-8839, Web Site: www.cunamutual.com (15)

Kennedy, Dan, Annie's Attic LLC, Big Sandy, TX. Tel: (903) 636-4303, (800) 282-6643, FAX: (903) 636-4088, Web Site: www.anniesattic.com (11)

Kennedy, Dan S., Kennedy Inner Circle, Phoenix, AZ. Tel: (602) 269-3111, FAX: (602) 269-3113 (20)

Kennedy, Daniel W., Whitehorse Gear, Center Conway, NH. Tel: (603) 356-6556, FAX: (603) 356-6590, E-Mail: customerservice@whitehorsepress.com, Web Site: www.whitehorsepress.com (11)

Kennedy, David W., Wells Lamont Corp, Niles, IL. Tel: (847) 647-8200, (800) 247-3295, FAX: (847) 647-6943, Web Site: www.wellslamont.com (34)

Kennedy, Deborah, Channel Neutral Marketing, Oyster Bay, NY. Tel: (516) 992-7777, E-Mail: deb_kennedy1127@yahoo.com (35)

Kennedy, Doug, Pearson VUE, Bloomington, MN. Tel: (952) 681-3000, Web Site: home.pearsonvue.com (17)

Kennedy, Edward, Bausch & Lomb Inc, Rochester, NY. Tel: (585) 338-6000, (800) 344-8815, FAX: (585) 338-6007, Web Site: www.bausch.com (16)

Kennedy, Farrah, MailChimp, Atlanta, GA. Tel: (678) 999-0141, Web Site: mailchimp.com (24)

Kennedy, Hank, Amacom Books, New York, NY. Tel: (212) 903-8376, FAX: (212) 903-8083, E-Mail: customerservice@amanet.org, Web Site: www.amacombooks.org (17)

Kennedy, James A.C., T Rowe Price Associates Inc, Baltimore, MD. Tel: (410) 345-2000, (800) 638-7890, FAX: (410) 986-3618, E-Mail: info@troweprice.com, Web Site: www.troweprice.com (14)

Kennedy, Judith M., Whitehorse Gear, Center Conway, NH. Tel: (603) 356-6556, FAX: (603) 356-6590, E-Mail: customerservice@whitehorsepress.com, Web Site: www.whitehorsepress.com (11)

Kennedy, Kelly, MBS, Central Islip, NY. Tel: (631) 851-5000, Web Site: www.mbsinsight.com (22)

Kennedy, Kolleen T, Varian Medical Systems, Palo Alto, CA. Tel: (650) 493-4000, FAX: (650) 842-5196, Web Site: www.varian.com (9)

Kennedy, Susan Petersen, Penguin Group USA Inc, New York, NY. Tel: (212) 366-2000, Web Site: www.us.penguingroup.com (17)

Kennedy, Tracy, Suntrust Banks Inc, Atlanta, GA. Tel: (404) 588-7914, (800) 786-8787, FAX: (404) 532-0550, E-Mail: emmett.harmon@suntrust.com, Web Site: www.suntrust.com (14)

Kennel Vet, Laurel, DE. Tel: (302) 875-7111, (800) 782-0627, FAX: (302) 269-3986, E-Mail: info@petmarket.com, Web Site: www.kennelvet.com (11)

Judith Kennerk, Princeton Junction, NJ. Tel: (609) 240-2876 (20)

Kennesaw State University, Kennesaw, GA. Tel: (770) 423-6060, FAX: (770) 499-3261, Web Site: www.kennesaw.edu (41)

Kenney Marketing & Advertising Inc, King of Prussia, PA. Tel: (610) 341-0430, FAX: (610) 341-0480, E-Mail: info@kenneymarketing.com, Web Site: www.kmaphl.com (35)

Kenney, John, Esquire Magazine, New York, NY. Tel: (212) 649-4020, FAX: (212) 649-4303, E-Mail: esquire@hearst.com, Web Site: www.esquire.com (17)

Kenney, Rick, ST&P Marketing Communications Inc, Fairlawn, OH. Tel: (330) 668-1932, FAX: (330) 668-2078, Web Site: stpinc.com (35)

Kenney, Robert, Kenney Marketing & Advertising Inc, King of Prussia, PA. Tel: (610) 341-0430, FAX: (610) 341-0480, E-Mail: info@kenneymarketing.com, Web Site: www.kmaphl.com (35)

Kennon, Tim, The Direct Marketing Club of New York Inc, Garden City, NY. Tel: (516) 746-6700, FAX: (516) 294-8141, E-Mail: info@dmcny.org, Web Site: www.dmcny.org (1)

Kenny, David, The Weather Channel, Atlanta, GA. Tel: (770) 226-0000, FAX: (770) 226-2390, Web Site: www.weather.com (32)

Kenoly, Bonnie, Decision Analyst Inc, Arlington, TX. Tel: (817) 640-6166, (800) 262-5974, FAX: (817) 640-6567, E-Mail: jthomas@decisionanalyst.com, Web Site: www.decisionanalyst.com (30)

Kensey, John, Vance Industries Inc, Niles, IL. Tel: (847) 375-8900, FAX: (847) 375-6818, E-Mail: vance@vanceind.com, Web Site: www.vanceind.com (16)

Kensington Computer Products Group, Redwood Shores, CA. Tel: (650) 572-2700, FAX: (650) 267-2800, Web Site: www.kensington.com (16)

Kensington Publishing Corp, New York, NY. Tel: (212) 407-1500, (800) 221-2647, FAX: (212) 407-1590, Web Site: www.kensingtonbooks.com (17)

Kent, Muhtar, The Coca-Cola Co, Atlanta, GA. Tel: (404) 676-2121, (800) 438-2653, FAX: (404) 676-6792, Web Site: www.cocacola.com (16)

Kent, Penny, Travel Planners Inc, New York, NY. Tel: (212) 532-1660, (800) 221-3531, FAX: (212) 532-1556, Web Site: www.tphousing.com (19)

Kent, Richard, Lakeside Publishing Co LLC, Evanston, IL. Tel: (847) 491-6440, FAX: (847) 491-0459, E-Mail: cs@centurysports.net, Web Site: www.centurysports.net (17)

Kent, Stephen J., New Track Media LLC, Cincinnati, OH. Tel: (513) 421-6500, FAX: (513) 421-1244, E-Mail: lriggs@newtrackmedia.com, Web Site: www.newtrackmedia.com (17)

Kent, Terry, Kantar Media, New York, NY. Tel: (212) 991-6000, (800) 497-8450, FAX: (212) 991-6100, Web Site: kantarmedia.us (32)

Kentucky Bankers Association, Louisville, KY. Tel: (502) 582-2453, FAX: (502) 584-6390, Web Site: www.kybanks.com (1)

Kenworthy, John, Storey Kenworthy, Des Moines, IA. Tel: (515) 288-3243, (800) 622-4536, FAX: (515) 288-9807, E-Mail: info@storeykenworthy.com, Web Site: www.storeykenworthy.com (35)

Kenzer Group, LLC, New York, NY. Tel: (212) 308-4300, FAX: (917) 534-6280, E-Mail: info@kenzergroup.com, Web Site: kenzergroup.com (20)

Kenzer, Mark, Pacific Spirit Corp, Forest Grove, OR. Tel: (503) 357-1566, (800) 634-9057, FAX: (503) 357-1699, Web Site: www.pacificspiritcatalogs.com (6)

Kenzer, Robert, Kenzer Group, LLC, New York, NY. Tel: (212) 308-4300, FAX: (917) 534-6280, E-Mail: info@kenzergroup.com, Web Site: kenzergroup.com (20)

Keon, PhD John, The Marketing Advantage Inc, Stamford, CT. Tel: (203) 968-8400, FAX: (501) 968-8301, E-Mail: info@marketingadvantage.com, Web Site: www.marketingadvantage.com (21)

Keough, Michael J., Caraustar, Austell, GA. Tel: (770) 948-3101, E-Mail: info@caraustar.com, Web Site: www.caraustar.com (16)

Kepler, II David E., The Dow Chemical Co, Midland, MI. Tel: (989) 636-1000, (800) 258-2436, FAX: (989) 832-1556, Web Site: www.dow.com (16)

Keplinger, Teresa, The Columbian, Vancouver, WA. Tel: (360) 694-3391, FAX: (360) 735-4503, Web Site: www.columbian.com (17)

Keran, Timothy R, Western Graphics, Saint Paul, MN. Tel: (651) 603-6400, FAX: (651) 603-6401, E-Mail: info@westerngx.com, Web Site: www.westerngx.com (27)

Kerber, Cheryl, New York Findings, New York, NY. Tel: (212) 925-5745, (888) 925-5745, FAX: (212) 925-5870, E-Mail: nyfindings@aol.com, Web Site: www.newyorkfindings.com (6)

Kerckhoff, Arthur, Gabriel Group, Earth City, MO. Tel: (314) 743-5700, FAX: (314) 743-5800, E-Mail: sales@gabrielgr.com, Web Site: gabrielgr.com (21)

Kerekes-Bruscato, Kaye, Bunker Hill Auctions, Millbrook, IL. Tel: (630) 553-8968, E-Mail: bunkerhillauctions@joimail.com, Web Site: www.bunkerhillauctions.com (6)

Kerger, Paula, PBS Distribution, Arlington, VA. Tel: (617) 208-0720, Web Site: shoppbs.org (3)

KERN, Los Angeles, CA. Tel: (818) 703-8775, FAX: (818) 703-8458, E-Mail: info@kernagency.com, Web Site: kernagency.com (35)

Kern, Dan, Main Street Direct, New York, NY. Tel: (212) 779-3000, FAX: (212) 779-3061, E-Mail: contact@mainstreetdirect.com, Web Site: www.mainstreetdirect.com (31)

Kern, Judy, Forest Envelope Co, Lisle, IL. Tel: (630) 515-1200, FAX: (630) 515-1212, Web Site: forestenvelope.com (26)

Kern, Louise, Global Business Information Services Inc (GLoBIS), Chicago, IL. Tel: (877) 456-2478, FAX: (877) 456-2478, E-Mail: info@glo-bis.com, Web Site: www.glo-bis.com (30)

Kern, Russ, ST&P Marketing Communications Inc, Fairlawn, OH. Tel: (330) 668-1932, FAX: (330) 668-2078, Web Site: stpinc.com (35)

Kern, Russell, KERN, Los Angeles, CA. Tel: (818) 703-8775, FAX: (818) 703-8458, E-Mail: info@kernagency.com, Web Site: kernagency.com (35)

Dorothy Kerr & Associates, Milwaukee, WI. Tel: (414) 228-0335, FAX: (414) 228-0337 (20)

Kerr-Hays Co, Ligonier, PA. Tel: (724) 238-6694, FAX: (724) 238-7440 (16)

Kerr, David, Sunlife of Canada, Wellesley Hills, MA. Tel: (781) 237-6030, (800) SUNLIFE, FAX: (781) 446-1779, Web Site: www.sunlife-usa.com (15)

Kerr, Derek J, American Airlines, Fort Worth, TX. Tel: (817) 963-1234 (12)

Kerr, Derek J., American Airlines Inc, Fort Worth, TX. Tel: (817) 963-1234, FAX: (817) 967-2841, Web Site: www.aa.com (19)

Kerr, Dorothy, Dorothy Kerr & Associates, Milwaukee, WI. Tel: (414) 228-0335, FAX: (414) 228-0337 (20)

Kerr, Mary Ann, TMP Direct, Budd Lake, NJ. Tel: (973) 347-9400, (800) 328-2439, FAX: (973) 347-8773, E-Mail: ron.pearl@tmpwdirect.com, Web Site: www.tmpwdirect.com (29)

Kerrane, Brian, Neuberger & Berman Management, New York, NY. Tel: (212) 476-9000, (800) 877-9700, FAX: (212) 476-8937, Web Site: www.nb.com (14)

Kerrick, DeAnna, Safeco Insurance Co, Seattle, WA. Tel: (206) 545-5000, (800) 332-3226, FAX: (206) 545-5767/5651, Web Site: www.safeco.com (15)

Kerry, Barbara L., Script to Screen Inc, Santa Ana, CA. Tel: (714) 558-3971, (800) 453-0003, FAX: (714) 558-1759, E-Mail: newbusiness@scripttoscreen.com, Web Site: www.scripttoscreen.com (32)

Kerry, Ken, Script to Screen Inc, Santa Ana, CA. Tel: (714) 558-3971, (800) 453-0003, FAX: (714) 558-1759, E-Mail: newbusiness@scripttoscreen.com, Web Site: www.scripttoscreen.com (32)

Kersten, Tim, RobbinsKersten Direct, Richardson, TX. Tel: (800) 222-6070, E-Mail: connect@robbinskersten.com, Web Site: www.robbinskersten.com (1)

Kerstetter, Bert, Calico Corners, Kennett Square, PA. Tel: (610) 444-9700, (800) 213-6366, FAX: (610) 444-1221, Web Site: www.calicocorners.com (16)

Kerstetter, Bert G., Everfast Inc, Kennett Square, PA. Tel: (800) 213-6366, Web Site: www.calicocorners.com (8)

Kersting, Christopher J., Specialty Equipment Market Association, Diamond Bar, CA. Tel: (909) 396-0289, Web Site: www.sema.org (1)

Jim Kerwin Freelance Copywriter, Naples, FL. Tel: (239) 597-4445, E-Mail: jwkerwin@mac.com (39)

Kerwin, Jim, Jim Kerwin Freelance Copywriter, Naples, FL. Tel: (239) 597-4445, E-Mail: jwkerwin@mac.com (39)

Keshner, Maurice, Cinema World Studios, Greenpoint, NY. Tel: (718) 389-9800, FAX: (718) 389-9897, E-Mail: cinemaworldfd@verizon.net, Web Site: www.cinemaworldstudios.com (32)

Kesser, Peter H., Verso Paper, Memphis, TN. Tel: (901) 369-4100, FAX: (901) 369-4174, Web Site: www.versopaper.com (25)

Kessler, Donna, Morris Communications Corp, Augusta, GA. Tel: (706) 724-0851, (800) 622-6358, Web Site: www.morris.com (31)

Kessler, John, International Filing Corp LLC, Hattiesburg, MS. Tel: (601) 554-0521, FAX: (601) 554-0522, E-Mail: pcoerper@intfiling.com, Web Site: www.intfiling.com (26)

Kessler, Murray S., Lorillard Tobacco Co, Greensboro, NC. Tel: (336) 335-7000, (877) 703-0386, FAX: (336) 373-6917, E-Mail: externalaffairs@lortobco.com, Web Site: www.lorillard.com (16)

Kessler, Steven, Bristol Associates Inc, Los Angeles, CA. Tel: (310) 670-0525, FAX: (310) 670-4075, E-Mail: lfarber@bristolassoc.com, Web Site: www.bristolassoc.com (20)

Kessler, Wayne, American Arbitration Association, New York, NY. Tel: (212) 716-5800, (800) 778-7879, FAX: (212) 716-5905, E-Mail: kesslerw@adr.org, Web Site: www.adr.org (1)

Kestenbaum, Jeff, AIG Accident & Health, New York, NY. Tel: (212) 770-7000, (877) 638-4244, FAX: (212) 509-9705, Web Site: www.aig.com (15)

Kester, Paul, Kester's Wild Game Food Nurseries Inc, Omro, WI. Tel: (920) 685-2929, (800) 558-8815, FAX: (920) 685-6727, E-Mail: pkester@vbe.com, Web Site: www.kestersnursery.com (8)

Kester's Wild Game Food Nurseries Inc, Omro, WI. Tel: (920) 685-2929, (800) 558-8815, FAX: (920) 685-6727, E-Mail: pkester@vbe.com, Web Site: www.kestersnursery.com (8)

Kestler, George, AmeriCall Group Inc, Oak Brook, IL. Tel: (630) 955-9100, (800) 688-0078, FAX: (630) 955-9955, E-Mail: sales@americallgroup.com, Web Site: www.americallgroup.com (29)

Kestnbaum, Kate, KesTry, Chicago, IL. Tel: (312) 664-6060, FAX: (312) 664-6059, E-Mail: kkestnbaum@earthlink.net (20)

Kestner, R Steven, Baker & Hostetler LLP, Washington, DC. Tel: (202) 861-1500, FAX: (202) 861-1783, E-Mail: wschweitzer@bakerlaw.com, Web Site: www.bakerlaw.com (20)

KesTry, Chicago, IL. Tel: (312) 664-6060, FAX: (312) 664-6059, E-Mail: kkestnbaum@earthlink.net (20)

Ketcham, Jenelle, Namebank, Baltimore, MD. Tel: (410) 864-0854, FAX: (410) 864-0837, E-Mail: lists@namebank.com, Web Site: www.namebank.com (23)

Ketchel, Kim, Jones International Ltd, Centennial, CO. Tel: (303) 792-3111, (800) 525-7002, FAX: (303) 784-8508, E-Mail: publicrelations@jones.com, Web Site: www.jones.com (16)

Ketchiff, David, Charles F Beardsley Advertising, Avon, CT. Tel: (860) 676-0256, FAX: (860) 674-1917 (35)

Ketchiff, Nancy, Charles F Beardsley Advertising, Avon, CT. Tel: (860) 676-0256, FAX: (860) 674-1917 (35)

Ketchum, New York, NY. Tel: (646) 935-3900, Web Site: www.ketchum.com (35)

Kett Tool Co, Cincinnati, OH. Tel: (513) 271-0333, FAX: (513) 271-5318, E-Mail: info@kett-tool.com, Web Site: www.kett-tool.com (9)

Ketterer, Robert, HDA Inc, Saint Louis, MO. Tel: (314) 770-2222, (800) 533-4350, FAX: (314) 770-1454, E-Mail: plans@hdainc.com, Web Site: www.designamerica.com (17)

Ketterman, Ken, Zimmerman Irrigation Inc, Biglerville, PA. Tel: (717) 337-2727, (800) 452-5699, FAX: (717) 337-1785, E-Mail: info@trikl-eez.com, Web Site: www.trickl-eez.com (16)

Kettwig, Kay A., Osmonics Inc, Minnetonka, MN. Tel: (952) 264-3937, (800) 605-6698, FAX: (952) 536-3301, Web Site: www.osmonics.com (16)

Keuler, Jean, Society of the Divine Savior, New Holstein, WI. Tel: (920) 898-4201, Web Site: www.salvatoriancenter.com (1)

Keverian, Kenneth M., IBM Corp, Armonk, NY. Tel: (914) 765-1900, FAX: (914) 765-6633, Web Site: www.ibm.com (16)

Kevin J Shea & Associates, Arlington Heights, IL. Tel: (847) 392-2713 (39)

Kevorkian, Christopher, Magazine Publishers of America, New York, NY. Tel: (212) 872-3700, FAX: (212) 888-4217, E-Mail: mpa@magazine.org, Web Site: www.magazine.org (17)

Kewin, Jeff, Lasermax Roll Systems, Billerica, MA. Tel: (978) 608-0500, FAX: (978) 608-0558, Web Site: www.lasermaxroll.com (27)

Key Bank, Cleveland, OH. Tel: (800) 539-2968, FAX: (216) 689-5115, Web Site: www.key.com (14)

Key Bank National Association, Albany, NY. Tel: (518) 434-4871, (800) 539-2968, Web Site: www.keybank.com (14)

Key Communications Inc, Garrisonville, VA. Tel: (540) 720-5584, FAX: (540) 720-5687, E-Mail: usglass@aol.com, Web Site: www.key-com.com (17)

Key Computer Service of Chelsea, New York, NY. Tel: (212) 206-8060, FAX: (212) 206-8398 (28)

Key Marketing Advantage LLC, Newtown, CT. Tel: (203) 491-2200, FAX: (203) 491-2201, E-Mail: info@keymarketingadvantage.com, Web Site: keymarketingcorp.com (23)

Key West Aloe Holdings LLC, Fort Lauderdale, FL. Tel: (305) 883-3166, FAX: (305) 883-3185, Web Site: www.keywestaloe.com (16)

Keyboard Workshop, Medford, OR. Tel: (541) 664-7052, FAX: (541) 664-7052, E-Mail: duane@playpiano.com, Web Site: www.playpiano.com (17)

Keyes, Greg, Coastal Living, Birmingham, AL. Tel: (205) 445-6000, FAX: (205) 445-7263, E-Mail: coastalliving@customersvc.com, Web Site: www.coastalliving.com (43)

Keyes, Norman, Grant's Mailing Services Inc, Mississauga, ON Canada. Tel: (905) 826-1411, FAX: (905) 826-1450, E-Mail: mstephens@innovativeresponse.ca, Web Site: www.grants-mailing.ca (27)

Keyes, Thomas D., Protective Life Corp, Deerfield, IL. Tel: (847) 948-8988, (800) 323-5771, FAX: (847) 948-1156, Web Site: www.protective.com (15)

Keylor, Randy, Integrated Alliance Limited Partnership, Denton, TX. Tel: (940) 565-9415, FAX: (940) 383-1876, E-Mail: ryoung@integratedalliance.com, Web Site: www.integratedalliance.com (29)

KeyPath Education, Lenexa, KS. Tel: (913) 254-6000, Web Site: keypathedu.com (35)

The Keystone Equities Group, Oaks, PA. Tel: (610) 415-6300, (800) 715-9905, FAX: (610) 415-6328, Web Site: www.keystoneequities.com (20)

Keystone Press Agency Inc, Montreal, QC Canada. Tel: (514) 482-5312, (877) 482-5312, FAX: (514) 483-9005, E-Mail: pictures@keystonepressagency.com, Web Site: www.ketstonepressagency.com (38)

Keystone Promotions Inc, Union, NJ. Tel: (908) 688-6713, FAX: (908) 688-6645, E-Mail: mgunther_kpi@msn.com, Web Site: www.keystonepromotionsinc.com (27)

Kforce Inc, Tampa, FL. Tel: (813) 552-2394, Web Site: www.kforce.com (20)

Khachoian, Ani, Soitenly Stooges, Glendale, CA. Tel: (818) 543-0778, (800) 543-0778, FAX: (818) 543-0779, E-Mail: custserv@threestooges.com, Web Site: www.soitenlystooges.com (6)

Khan, Shobi, General Growth Properties, Chicago, IL. Tel: (312) 960-5000, Web Site: www.generalgrowth.com (5)

Khanna, Amit, InfoUSA, Papillion, NE. Tel: (800) 835-5856, Web Site: www.infousa.com (23)

Khanna, Vinit, OKS-Ameridial Inc, Bala Cynwyd, PA. Tel: (610) 667-3000, FAX: (610) 667-3002, E-Mail: info@oksgroup.com, Web Site: www.oksameridial.com (29)

Khator, Renu, Conrad N Hilton College of Hotel & Restaurant Management University of Houston, Houston, TX. Tel: (713) 743-2255 (1)

Khosrowshahi, Dara, Expedia Inc, Bellevue, WA. Tel: (425) 679-7200, Web Site: www.expedia.com (19)

Khubani, A.J., Telebrands Corp, Fairfield, NJ. Tel: (973) 247-8777, Web Site: www.telebrands.com (21)

Kichler, Florrie Binford, Publishers Marketing Association (PMA), Manhattan Beach, CA. Tel: (310) 372-2732, FAX: (310) 374-3342, E-Mail: info@pma-online.org, Web Site: www.pma-online.org (40)

Kid Stuff Marketing, Inc, North Canton, OH. Tel: (800) 837-5437, FAX: (330) 244-9518, Web Site: www.kidsstuff.com (33)

Kidd, Carla, IPacesetters, Montvale, NJ. Tel: (201) 391-1500, FAX: (201) 391-8357, Web Site: www.ipacesetters.com (22)

The Kidney Foundation of Canada/Greater Ontario Branch, Hamilton, ON Canada. Tel: (800) 414-3484, FAX: (905) 318-8491, E-Mail: kidneyfoundation@bellnet.ca, Web Site: www.kidney.on.ca (1)

Kiecker, Pamela, Interactive Marketing Institute, Richmond, VA. Tel: (800) 925-5308, Web Site: www.imi.vcu.edu (41)

Kiely, Garrett P., University of Chicago Press, Chicago, IL. Tel: (773) 702-7700, FAX: (773) 702-9756, Web Site: www.press.uchicago.edu (17)

Kieran, David, First National Information Network, Burbank, CA. Tel: (855) 909-6800, (800) 562-1999, FAX: (818) 558-6663, E-Mail: info@fnin.com, Web Site: www.fnin.com (30)

Kieschnick, Michael, Working Assets, San Francisco, CA. Tel: (800) 668-9253, FAX: (415) 371-1046, Web Site: www.workingassets.com (16)

Kiggins, John, Eclipse Direct Marketing, Mineola, NY. Tel: (212) 931-8344, FAX: (516) 493-9122, E-Mail: jkaiser@eclipsedm.com, Web Site: www.eclipsedm.com (23)

Kihm, Carolyn, Guiding Eyes for the Blind, Yorktown Heights, NY. Tel: (914) 245-4042, (800) 942-0149, FAX: (914) 245-1609, Web Site: www.guidingeyes.org (16)

Kiick, Kim, American Numismatic Association, Colorado Springs, CO. Tel: (719) 632-2646, Web Site: www.money.org (1)

Kilawee, Barbara, Houston Direct Marketing Association, Houston, TX. Tel: (281) 931-8883, FAX: (281) 820-4023, Web Site: www.houstondma.org (40)

Kilberry, William, Tempco Electric Heater Corp, Wood Dale, IL. Tel: (630) 350-2252, (800) 323-6859, FAX: (630) 350-0232, E-Mail: dpadlo@tempco.com, Web Site: www.tempco.com (9)

Kilcullen, Patrick, The Gallery Shop, Buffalo, NY. Tel: (716) 882-8700 X258, FAX: (716) 882-1958, E-Mail: gallshop@albrightknox.org, Web Site: www.albrightknox.org (6)

Kileen, Kieran, Marketing Agencies Association Worldwide, Edina, MN. Tel: (952) 922-0130, FAX: (203) 969-1499, E-Mail: keith.mccracker@maaw.org, Web Site: www.maaw.org (40)

Kiley, Leslee, Hill Holliday, Boston, MA. Tel: (617) 366-4000, Web Site: www.hhcc.com (35)

Kilgore, Paul, Capitol Hill Lists LLC, Statham, GA. Tel: (770) 725-9596, E-Mail: grant@capitolhilllists.com, Web Site: capitolhilllists.com (23)

Killeen, Patrick, Progressive Energy Corp, San Marcos, CA. Tel: (760) 727-2906, (800) 525-8624, FAX: (760) 727-0947, E-Mail: patrickkilleen@cox.net (5)

Killen, John, Win Craft Inc, Winona, MN. Tel: (507) 454-5510, (800) 533-8100, FAX: (507) 454-6403, E-Mail: inquiries@wincraftschool.com, Web Site: www.wincraftschool.com (5)

Killian Branding, Chicago, IL. Tel: (312) 836-0050, E-Mail: info@killianbranding.com, Web Site: www.killianbranding.com (35)

Killian, Bob, Killian Branding, Chicago, IL. Tel: (312) 836-0050, E-Mail: info@killianbranding.com, Web Site: www.killianbranding.com (35)

Killian, Tammy, Micro Plastics Inc, Flippin, AR. Tel: (870) 453-2261, (800) 466-1467, FAX: (870) 453-8676, E-Mail: mpsales@microplastics.com, Web Site: www.microplastics.com (16)

Killinger, Elizabeth, Reliant Energy, Houston, TX. Tel: (713) 497-7794, (866) 222-7100, Web Site: www.reliant.com (16)

Killinger, Kerry, Washington Mutual Home Loan, Inc, Vernon Hills, IL. Tel: (847) 918-5549, FAX: (847) 549-2975 (14)

Killingstad, Chris, TENNANT Co, Minneapolis, MN. Tel: (763) 540-1200, (800) 553-8033, FAX: (763) 513-2142, E-Mail: info@tennantco.com, Web Site: www.tennantco.com (34)

Kilpin, Tim, Mattel Inc, El Segundo, CA. Tel: (310) 252-2000, FAX: (310) 252-2180, Web Site: www.mattel.com (16)

Kilroy, Thomas M., Intel Corp, Santa Clara, CA. Tel: (408) 765-8080, (800) 548-4725, FAX: (408) 765-6187, Web Site: www.intel.com (16)

Kim Field, Jennifer, United Nations Foundation, Washington, DC. Tel: (202) 887-9040, FAX: (202) 887-9021, Web Site: www.unfoundation.org (1)

Kim, Ik-suk, School of Business & Economics, Los Angeles, CA. Tel: (323) 343-2800, FAX: (323) 343-2813, Web Site: cbe.calstatela.edu (41)

Kim, Jim Yong, The World Bank, Washington, DC. Tel: (202) 473-1000, FAX: (202) 477-6391, Web Site: www.worldbank.org (17)

Kim, Megan, COSE, Cleveland, OH. Tel: (216) 592-2222, (866) 553-5427, E-Mail: memberservices@cose.org, Web Site: www.cose.org (1)

Kim, Nobbie, KERN, Los Angeles, CA. Tel: (818) 703-8775, FAX: (818) 703-8458, E-Mail: info@kernagency.com, Web Site: kernagency.com (35)

Kim, Yoan, Longevity Network Ltd, Henderson, NV. Tel: (702) 454-7000, (800) 242-1000, FAX: (702) 434-8259, E-Mail: info@longevity.com, Web Site: www.longevity.com (7)

Stephen Kimball DM Copywriting, Pleasant Grove, UT. Tel: (801) 796-7234, FAX: (801) 796-5799, E-Mail: stephen@skcopywriting.com, Web Site: www.skcopywriting.com (39)

Kimball, Stephen, Stephen Kimball DM Copywriting, Pleasant Grove, UT. Tel: (801) 796-7234, FAX: (801) 796-5799, E-Mail: stephen@skcopywriting.com, Web Site: www.skcopywriting.com (39)

Kimber, Burke, Richard Bauer & Co Inc, Teaneck, NJ. Tel: (201) 692-1005, (800) 995-7881, FAX: (201) 692-8626, E-Mail: info@richardbauer.com, Web Site: www.richardbauer.com (25)

Kimberly-Clark Corp, Neenah, WI. Tel: (920) 721-2000, (888) 525-8388, FAX: (920) 721-7722, Web Site: www.kimberly-clark.com (16)

Kimble, Gertrude, Kimbo Educational, Long Branch, NJ. Tel: (732) 229-4949, (800) 631-2187, FAX: (732) 870-3340, E-Mail: service@kimboed, Web Site: www.kimboed.com (17)

Kimble, James, Kimbo Educational, Long Branch, NJ. Tel: (732) 229-4949, (800) 631-2187, FAX: (732) 870-3340, E-Mail: service@kimboed. Web Site: www.kimboed.com (17)

Kimble, Jeffrey, Kimbo Educational, Long Branch, NJ. Tel: (732) 229-4949, (800) 631-2187, FAX: (732) 870-3340, E-Mail: service@kimboed, Web Site: www.kimboed.com (17)

Kimbo Educational, Long Branch, NJ. Tel: (732) 229-4949, (800) 631-2187, FAX: (732) 870-3340, E-Mail: service@kimboed, Web Site: www.kimboed.com (17)

Kimm, David, TD Ameritrade Holding Corp, Omaha, NE. Tel: (800) 237-8692, Web Site: www.amtd.com (16)

Kimmerling Hoveling, Pamela, RolaKimmerling Associates, New York, NY. Tel: (646) 367-4815, FAX: (646) 367-4901 (35)

Kincaid, Cliff, Accuracy in Media Inc, Bethesda, MD. Tel: (202) 364-4401, FAX: (202) 364-4098, E-Mail: info@aim.org, Web Site: www.aim.org (1)

Kincaid, Judith W., JK Associates LLC, Palo Alto, CA. Tel: (650) 838-9816, FAX: (650) 838-9867, Web Site: www.jk-associates.com (20)

Kincaid, Paul, Freestyle Solutions, Parsippany, NJ. Tel: (973) 237-9415, (800) 858-3666, FAX: (973) 237-9043, E-Mail: sales@dydacomp.com, Web Site: www.dydacomp.com (22)

Kincheloe, Mark, Karol Media, Wilkes-Barre, PA. Tel: (570) 822-8899, (800) 526-4773, FAX: (570) 822-8226, Web Site: www.karolmedia.com (28)

Kincheloe, Michael, Karol Media, Wilkes-Barre, PA. Tel: (570) 822-8899, (800) 526-4773, FAX: (570) 822-8226, Web Site: www.karolmedia.com (28)

Kind, John, Masterpiece Studios Inc, Mankato, MN. Tel: (507) 388-8788, (800) 447-0219, FAX: (507) 344-4606, E-Mail: masterpiecestudios@ masterpiecestudios.com, Web Site: www. masterpiecestudios.com (16)

Kindler, Lizanne, Talbots, Hingham, MA. Tel: (781) 749-7600, (800) 825-2687, FAX: (781) 741-4369, Web Site: www.talbots.com (2)

Kinerk, Niles, Gardens Alive! Inc, Lawrenceburg, IN. Tel: (513) 354-1483, FAX: (513) 354-1484, E-Mail: service@gardensalive.com, Web Site: www. gardensalive.com (8)

King Computer Services Inc, La Crescenta, CA. Tel: (818) 951-5240, E-Mail: kingsoftware@aol.com, Web Site: www.kingcomputerservices.com (22)

King Direct Marketing Inc, Daytona Beach, FL. Tel: (386) 788-8925 (33)

King Features, New York, NY. Tel: (212) 455-4000, FAX: (212) 682-8332 (17)

King Pharmaceuticals, Inc, Tenafly, NJ. Tel: (972) 885-0929, (888) 840-5370, E-Mail: igal@navehpharma. com, Web Site: www.kingpharma.com (7)

King Printing Solutions, New Tazewell, TN. Tel: (423) 626-7700, (800) 251-9236, FAX: (423) 526-5225, E-Mail: sales@kbfcorp.com, Web Site: www. kbfcorp.com (27)

King Ranch Saddle Shop, Kingsville, TX. Tel: (800) 282-KING, E-Mail: krsaddleshop@king-ranch.com, Web Site: www.krsaddleshop.com (8)

King Teleservices, New York, NY. Tel: (718) 361-4100, (800) 817-5468, E-Mail: info@king-teleservices.com, Web Site: www.king-teleservices. com (29)

King, Allen, Universal Corp, Richmond, VA. Tel: (804) 359-9311, FAX: (804) 254-3582, Web Site: www. universalcorp.com (16)

King, Allison, FDAnews, Falls Church, VA. Tel: (703) 538-7600, (888) 838-5578, FAX: (703) 538-7676, E-Mail: customerservice@fdanews.com, Web Site: www.fdanews.com (17)

King, Andy, American Family Insurance Group, Madison, WI. Tel: (608) 249-2111, FAX: (608) 243-6525, E-Mail: akin1@amfam.com, Web Site: www. amfam.com (15)

King, Cathy, King Direct Marketing Inc, Daytona Beach, FL. Tel: (386) 788-8925 (33)

King, Gregory D., Elcom International Inc, Norwood, MA. Tel: (781) 501-4000, FAX: (781) 762-1540, Web Site: www.elcominternational.com (22)

King, Gyr, McGaw Graphics, Manchester Center, VT. Tel: (845) 353-8600, (888) 4BMCGAW, FAX: (845) 353-3155, E-Mail: sales@bmcgaw.com, Web Site: www.bmcgaw.com (6)

King, Jaime, Camp + King, San Francisco, CA. Tel: (415) 345-6680, Web Site: www.camp-king.com (35)

King, Jeff, Barkley, Kansas City, MO. Tel: (816) 842-1500, E-Mail: 411@barkleyus.com, Web Site: www.barkleyus.com (35)

King, Jim, King Printing Solutions, New Tazewell, TN. Tel: (423) 626-7700, (800) 251-9236, FAX: (423) 526-5225, E-Mail: sales@kbfcorp.com, Web Site: www.kbfcorp.com (27)

King, John, Fallon, Minneapolis, MN. Tel: (612) 758-2345, FAX: (612) 758-2346, E-Mail: info@fallon. com, Web Site: www.fallon.com (35)

King, John J., Hebron Academy, Hebron, ME. Tel: (207) 966-2100, (888) 432-7664, Web Site: www. habronacademy.org (1)

King, Karen, Homesteaders Life Co, West Des Moines, IA. Tel: (515) 440-7777, (800) 477-3633, E-Mail: service@homesteaderslife.com, Web Site: www. homesteaderslife.com (15)

King, Kelly S., Branch Banking & Trust Co, Winston-Salem, NC. Tel: (336) 733-2000, FAX: (336) 733-2189, Web Site: www.bbt.com (14)

King, Kevin, Year One Inc, Braselton, GA. Tel: (706) 658-2140, FAX: (706) 654-5355, E-Mail: info@ yearone.com, Web Site: www.yearone.com (16)

King, Mark, Texwipe Co, Kernersville, NC. Tel: (201) 684-1800, (800) TEXWIPE, FAX: (201) 684-1801, E-Mail: info@texwipe.com, Web Site: www. texwipe.com (16)

King, Michael, Volunteers of America, Alexandria, VA. Tel: (703) 341-5000, (800) 899-0089, FAX: (703) 341-7000, E-Mail: info@voa.org, Web Site: www. voa.org (1)

King, Mike, Year One Inc, Braselton, GA. Tel: (706) 658-2140, FAX: (706) 654-5355, E-Mail: info@ yearone.com, Web Site: www.yearone.com (16)

King, William, Strategy Corps LLC, Brentwood, TN. Tel: (615) 221-8381, (888) 577-6933, FAX: (615) 221-8479, E-Mail: info@strategycorps.com, Web Site: www.strategycorps.com (16)

Kingery Printing Co, Effingham, IL. Tel: (217) 347-5151, FAX: (217) 540-5400, Web Site: www. kingeryprinting.com (27)

Kingery, Mike, Kingery Printing Co, Effingham, IL. Tel: (217) 347-5151, FAX: (217) 540-5400, Web Site: www.kingeryprinting.com (27)

King's Chandelier Co, Eden, NC. Tel: (336) 623-6188, FAX: (336) 627-9935, E-Mail: crystal@chandelier. com, Web Site: www.chandelier.com (6)

Kingsbury, Bridget Ann, Barker Specialty Co, Cheshire, CT. Tel: (203) 272-2222, (800) 227-5377, E-Mail: promo@barkerspecialty.com, Web Site: www. barkerspecialty.com (33)

Kingsbury, Thomas A., Burlington Coat Factory, Burlington, NJ. Tel: (609) 387-7800, FAX: (609) 387-7071, Web Site: www.burlingtoncoatfactory.com (16)

Kingsley North Inc, Norway, MI. Tel: (906) 563-9228, (800) 338-9280, FAX: (906) 563-7143, E-Mail: sales@kingsleynorth.com, Web Site: www. kingsleynorth.com (11)

Kingsmill, Stephanie E., Manulife Financial Inc, Toronto, ON Canada. Tel: (416) 229-4515, (800) 387-0990, FAX: (416) 229-3028, Web Site: www. manulife.com (15)

Kinman, Eric, Veridian Credit Union, Waterloo, IA. Tel: (319) 236-5692, (800) 235-3228, FAX: (319) 833-1185, E-Mail: sarahma@veridiancu.org. Web Site: www.veridiancu.org (1)

Kinnan, R. Douglas, Amerisure Insurance Cos, Farmington Hills, MI. Tel: (248) 615-9000, (800) 257-1900, FAX: (248) 615-8224, Web Site: www. amerisure.com (15)

Kinney, J.D., MediaGraphics, Eau Claire, WI. Tel: (751) 590-4488, (866) 324-1658, E-Mail: mediagraphics@devkinney.com, Web Site: www. devkinney.com (12)

Kinstler, Brad, See's Candies Inc, Carson, CA. Tel: (800) 347-7337, Web Site: www.sees.com (4)

Kintz, Bruce G., Concordia Publishing House, Saint Louis, MO. Tel: (314) 268-1000, (800) 325-3040, FAX: (314) 268-1329, E-Mail: order@cph.org, Web Site: www.cph.org (17)

Kinzer, Jr Chuck, Aradius Group, Omaha, NE. Tel: (402) 734-4400, (800) 369-0033, FAX: (402) 734-7492, E-Mail: info@aradiusgroup.com, Web Site: www.aradiusgroup.com (21)

Kionka, Michelle, Wisconsin Direct Marketing Association, Milwaukee, WI. Tel: (414) 760-9362, FAX: (414) 431-4195, E-Mail: info@wdma.org, Web Site: www.wdma.org (40)

Kiper, Kevin, Excelligence Learning Corp, Monterey, CA. Tel: (831) 333-2000, E-Mail: contactus@ excelligence.com, Web Site: www. excelligencelearning.com (5)

Kiphart, Richard P., Columbia College Chicago, Chicago, IL. Tel: (312) 663-1600, FAX: (312) 344-0869, Web Site: www.colum.edu (41)

The Kiplinger Washington Editors Inc, Washington, DC. Tel: (202) 887-6400, (800) 544-0155, FAX: (202) 496-1817, Web Site: www.kiplinger.com (17)

Kiplinger, Knight A., The Kiplinger Washington Editors Inc, Washington, DC. Tel: (202) 887-6400, (800) 544-0155, FAX: (202) 496-1817, Web Site: www. kiplinger.com (17)

Kipp Brothers Inc, Greenfield, IN. Tel: (800) 428-1153, E-Mail: support@kippbrothers.com, Web Site: kippbrothers.com (33)

Kipplinger, Todd L., The Kiplinger Washington Editors Inc, Washington, DC. Tel: (202) 887-6400, (800) 544-0155, FAX: (202) 496-1817, Web Site: www. kiplinger.com (17)

Kirbey, Kevin, Amsterdam Printing, Amsterdam, NY. Tel: (518) 842-6000, (800) 203-9917, FAX: (518) 843-5204, E-Mail: customerservice@ amsterdamprinting.com, Web Site: www. amsterdamprinting.com (16)

Kirby, J Scott, American Airlines, Fort Worth, TX. Tel: (817) 963-1234 (12)

Kirby, Kevin, Go Promos, Amsterdam, NY. Tel: (800) 523-9909, FAX: (800) 523-3292, E-Mail: customerservice@gopromos.com, Web Site: www. gopromos.com (5)

Kirby, Kevin, K-D Lamp Co, Andover, OH. Tel: (440) 293-4064, FAX: (440) 293-4591, E-Mail: admin@ atc-lighting-plastics.com, Web Site: www.k-dlamp. com (12)

Kirchwehm, Michael, HDA Inc, Saint Louis, MO. Tel: (314) 770-2222, (800) 533-4350, FAX: (314) 770-1454, E-Mail: plans@hdainc.com, Web Site: www. designamerica.com (17)

Kirk, Justin, Delta Upsilon International Fraternity, Indianapolis, IN. Tel: (317) 875-8900, FAX: (317) 876-1629, E-Mail: ihq@deltau.org, Web Site: www. deltau.org (16)

Kirkham, John A., Open Text Inc, Waterloo, ON Canada. Tel: (519) 888-9933, (800) 499-6544, FAX: (519) 888-0677, E-Mail: support@opentext.com, Web Site: www.opentext.com (16)

Kirkland, John, MLS Data Management Solutions, Fort Worth, TX. Tel: (817) 989-3800, FAX: (817) 989-3899, Web Site: www.mlsc.com (22)

Kirkman, Carrie, Sears Canada Inc, Toronto, ON Canada. Tel: (416) 362-1711, (888) 473-2772, FAX: (613) 391-3047, E-Mail: home@sears.ca, Web Site: www.sears.ca (5)

Will Kirkpatrick Shorebird Decoys Inc, Hudson, MA. Tel: (978) 562-7841, FAX: (978) 562-3514, E-Mail: wekdecoys@aol.com, Web Site: www. kirkpatrickdecoys.com (6)

Kirkpatrick, Brad, Rhythm Band Inc, Fort Worth, TX. Tel: (817) 335-2561, (800) 424-4724, FAX: (800) 784-9401, E-Mail: sales@rhythmband.com, Web Site: www.rhythmband.com (11)

Kirkpatrick, Douglas, Heldref Publications, Washington, DC. Tel: (202) 296-6267, (215) 625-8900, FAX: (202) 296-5149, Web Site: www.heldref.org (17)

Kirkpatrick, Will, Will Kirkpatrick Shorebird Decoys Inc, Hudson, MA. Tel: (978) 562-7841, FAX: (978) 562-3514, E-Mail: wekdecoys@aol.com, Web Site: www.kirkpatrickdecoys.com (6)

Kirsch, Herbert, Best Mailing Lists Inc, Tucson, AZ. Tel: (520) 885-0400, (800) 692-2378, FAX: (520) 885-3100, E-Mail: best@bestmailing.com, Web Site: www.bestmailing.com (23)

Kirsch, John E., Sportif Mail Order Inc, Sparks, NV. Tel: (888) 260-7676, FAX: (775) 356-3567, Web Site: www.sportif.com (2)

Kirsch, Karen J, Best Mailing Lists Inc, Tucson, AZ. Tel: (520) 885-0400, (800) 692-2378, FAX: (520) 885-3100, E-Mail: best@bestmailing.com, Web Site: www.bestmailing.com (23)

Kirscher, Elizabeth, Morningstar Inc, Chicago, IL. Tel: (312) 696-6000, Web Site: www.morningstar.com (14)

Kirschner, Mike, Office Depot, Boca Raton, FL. Tel: (561) 438-4800, (800) 463-3768, FAX: (561) 438-4001, Web Site: www.officedepot.com (16)

Kirschner, Mike. OfficeMax Inc, Boca Raton, FL. Tel: (877) 633-4236, Web Site: www.officemax.com (10)

Kirshenbaum Bond Senecal & Partners, New York, NY. Tel: (212) 633-0080, FAX: (212) 463-8643, E-Mail: press@kbsp.com, Web Site: www.kbsp.com (35)

Kirwan, Tom, Bruno & Ridgway Research Associates Inc, Lawrenceville, NJ. Tel: (609) 895-9889, FAX: (609) 895-6665, E-Mail: info@brunoandridgway.com, Web Site: www.brra.com (3)

Kiser, Anita, I/D/E/A Inc, Caldwell, ID. Tel: (208) 459-6357, (800) 635-9261, FAX: (208) 459-6484, Web Site: www.relyonidea.com (16)

Liz Kislik Associates LLC, Rockville Centre, NY. Tel: (516) 568-2932, FAX: (516) 568-2936, Web Site: www.lizkislik.com (20)

Kislik, Liz, Liz Kislik Associates LLC, Rockville Centre, NY. Tel: (516) 568-2932, FAX: (516) 568-2936, Web Site: www.lizkislik.com (20)

Kisling, Zeke, Backe Digital Brand Marketing, Radnor, PA. Tel: (610) 947-6901, E-Mail: jbacke@backemarketing.com, Web Site: www.backemarketing.com (35)

Kisons, Constantine, Bitstream Inc, Marlborough, MA. Tel: (617) 497-6222, FAX: (617) 868-0784, Web Site: www.bitstream.com (22)

Kissell, David, Zimmerman Advertising, Fort Lauderdale, FL. Tel: (954) 644-4000, E-Mail: contact@zadv.com, Web Site: www.zadv.com (35)

Kistler-Tiffany Companies LLC, Berwyn, PA. Tel: (610) 722-3300, (866) 250-5413, Web Site: www.ktadv.com (20)

Kitchen Kompact Inc, Jeffersonville, IN. Tel: (812) 282-6681, FAX: (812) 282-7880, E-Mail: webmaster@kitchenkompact.com, Web Site: www.kitchenkompact.com (20)

Kitchen, Michelle, DDB Canada, Vancouver, BC Canada. Tel: (604) 687-7911, FAX: (604) 640-4343, E-Mail: vancouver.info@ddbcanada.com, Web Site: www.ddbcanada.com (35)

Kitt, Lonnie, QC Supply LLC, Schuyler, NE. Tel: (402) 352-3167, Web Site: www.qcsupply.com (16)

Kittleson, Kyle, Speedeon Data Corp, Cleveland, OH. Tel: (866) 647-9219, Web Site: www.speedeondata.com (30)

Kives, Philip, K-tel International, Golden Valley, MN. Tel: (204) 889-5430, (800) 665-5021, FAX: (612) 559-6803, Web Site: www.ktel.com (16)

Kizer, John, Central States Indemnity, Omaha, NE. Tel: (402) 997-8000, (402) 397-1111, (800) 445-6500, Web Site: www.csi-omaha.com (15)

Kizer, Jr. William, Wellness Councils of America, Omaha, NE. Tel: (402) 827-3590, FAX: (402) 827-3594, E-Mail: wellworkplace@welcoa.org, Web Site: www.welcoa.org (1)

Kizer, Richard T.. Central States Health & Life Co of Omaha, Omaha, NE. Tel: (402) 397-1111, (800) 826-6587, FAX: (402) 391-3772, Web Site: www.cso.com (15)

Kizer, T. Edward, Central States Health & Life Co of Omaha, Omaha, NE. Tel: (402) 397-1111, (800) 826-6587, FAX: (402) 391-3772, Web Site: www.cso.com (15)

Klamfoth, Dale L, Communispond Inc, East Hampton, NY. Tel: (631) 907-8010, (800) 529-5925, FAX: (631) 907-8011, Web Site: www.communispond.com (20)

Klang, David, Customer Growth Inc, Fairfield, CT. Tel: (203) 226-8795, FAX: (203) 286-1049, E-Mail: info@customer-growth.com, Web Site: www.customer-growth.com (35)

Klapmeier, Jolie, Bluewater Yachts, Mora, MN. Tel: (320) 679-3811, FAX: (320) 679-3820, E-Mail: bluewater@ncis.com, Web Site: www.bluewateryacht.com (16)

Klapmeier, Steve, Bluewater Yachts, Mora, MN. Tel: (320) 679-3811, FAX: (320) 679-3820, E-Mail: bluewater@ncis.com, Web Site: www.bluewateryacht.com (16)

Klar, Rick, Equitable Life & Casualty Insurance Co, Salt Lake City, UT. Tel: (801) 579-3400, FAX: (801) 579-3789, Web Site: www.equilife.com (15)

Klauser, Rick, Nestle HealthCare Nutrition, Florham Park, NJ. Tel: (800) 422-2752, Web Site: www.nestle-nutrition.com (16)

Klebaur, Erin, Creative Marketing Alliance Inc, Princeton Junction, NJ. Tel: (609) 297-2235, FAX: (609) 799-7032, E-Mail: info@cmasolutions.com, Web Site: www.gotocma.com (35)

Klebe, Tim, K-Log, Zion, IL. Tel: (800) 872-6611, FAX: (847) 872-3728, E-Mail: info@k-log.com, Web Site: www.k-log.com (8)

Kleeger, Neil L., Gallery of Cats, Valencia, CA. Tel: (818) 782-6264, E-Mail: helpdesk@galleryofcats.com, Web Site: www.galleryofcats.com (6)

Kleeman, Alan, AS Kleeman & Associates, Duluth, GA. Tel: (770) 752-0500, FAX: (770) 752-0066 (20)

Kleen, Tom, Stratford Hall, North Mankato, MN. Tel: (708) 496-4908, (800) 628-9028, FAX: (708) 496-8058, E-Mail: stratfordhall@myprinter.com, Web Site: www.stratfordhall.com (10)

B Klein Publications, Boca Raton, FL. Tel: (561) 496-3316, FAX: (561) 496-5546, E-Mail: bkleinpub@aol.com (17)

Calvin Klein Cosmetics Co, New York, NY. Tel: (212) 719-2600, E-Mail: customerservice@calvinklein.com, Web Site: www.calvinklein.com (7)

Klein, Abraham M, M&M Health Care Apparel Co, Brooklyn, NY. E-Mail: info@fashionease.com (2)

Klein, Al, Louisville Direct Marketing Association, Louisville, KY. Tel: (888) 392-1941, E-Mail: ldmacontact@ldma.org, Web Site: www.ldma.org (40)

Klein, Andy, US Tax Shield, Encino, CA. Tel: (877) 929-3535, Web Site: www.ustaxshield.com (14)

Klein, Bernard, B Klein Publications, Boca Raton, FL. Tel: (561) 496-3316, FAX: (561) 496-5546, E-Mail: bkleinpub@aol.com (17)

Klein, Bernard, Guide to American & International Directories, Delray Beach, FL. Tel: (561) 496-3316, FAX: (561) 451-0803, E-Mail: bkleinpub@aol.com (43)

Klein, Bernard, Mail Order Business Directory, Delray Beach, FL. Tel: (561) 496-3316, E-Mail: bkleinpub@aol.com (43)

Klein, Betty, B Klein Publications, Boca Raton, FL. Tel: (561) 496-3316, FAX: (561) 496-5546, E-Mail: bkleinpub@aol.com (17)

Klein, Bob, Corinthian Media, New York, NY. Tel: (212) 279-5700, FAX: (212) 239-1772, E-Mail: info@mediabuying.com, Web Site: www.mediabuying.com (35)

Klein, David, Auto Anything, San Diego, CA. Tel: (858) 569-8111, (800) 874-8888, FAX: (858) 569-8503, E-Mail: customerservice@autoanything.com, Web Site: www.autoanything.com (34)

Klein, David, Macromark Inc, Danbury, CT. Tel: (845) 230-6300, FAX: (845) 278-0650, E-Mail: sales@macromark.com, Web Site: www.macromark.com (23)

Klein, Debbie, Arizona Highways Magazine, Phoenix, AZ. Tel: (602) 712-2200, FAX: (602) 254-4505, E-Mail: editor@arizonahighways.com, Web Site: www.arizonahighways.com (17)

Klein, Debra, American Association of Critical-Care Nurses, Aliso Viejo, CA. Tel: (949) 362-2000, (800) 809-CARE, FAX: (949) 362-2020, E-Mail: info@aacn.com, Web Site: www.aacn.org (1)

Klein, Gary, The Franklin Mint, Exton, PA. Tel: (610) 497-4800, (800) THE-MINT, FAX: (610) 497-4956, E-Mail: support@franklinmint.com, Web Site: www.franklinmint.com (16)

Klein, Hans, Hannecke Display Systems Inc, Boonton, NJ. Tel: (973) 335-0434, FAX: (973) 335-1274, E-Mail: info.usa@hannecke.com, Web Site: www.hannecke.com (27)

Klein, Howard, Lanmark360 Inc, West Long Branch, NJ. Tel: (732) 389-4500, Web Site: www.lanmark360.com (35)

Klein, Jonathan, Getty Images, Seattle, WA. Tel: (206) 925-5000, (888) 888-5889, Web Site: www.gettyimages.com (38)

Klein, Lawrence, Thought Technology Ltd, Montreal, QC Canada. Tel: (514) 489-8251, (800) 361-3651, FAX: (514) 489-8255, E-Mail: lawrence@thoughttechnology.com, Web Site: www.thoughttechnology.com (14)

Klein, Paul, Rich Products Corp, Buffalo, NY. Tel: (716) 878-8000, (800) 828-2021, FAX: (716) 878-8765, Web Site: www.richs.com (16)

Klein, Russ, AMA Annual Conference, Chicago, IL. Tel: (312) 542-9000, (800) 262-1150, Web Site: www.ama.org (42)

Klein, Sabine, NETC, Hamden, CT. Tel: (617) 851-8535, (203) 288-5938, E-Mail: mail@netconline.org (5)

Klein, Stephen, Encore Marketing International, Lanham, MD. Tel: (301) 459-8020, (800) 846-9398, FAX: (301) 731-0525, E-Mail: customerservice@encoremarketing.com, Web Site: www.encoremarketing.com (16)

Klein, Steve, Wolf Blumberg Krody Inc, Cincinnati, OH. Tel: (513) 784-0066, FAX: (513) 784-0986, E-Mail: sklein@wbk.com, Web Site: www.wbk.com (35)

Klein, Susan, Walt Klein Advertising, Denver, CO. Tel: (303) 298-8015, FAX: (303) 298-8194, Web Site: www.wka.com (35)

Klein, Thomas, Sabre Holdings Inc, Southlake, TX. Tel: (682) 605-1000, FAX: (682) 605-7239, Web Site: www.sabre.com (19)

Klein, Tim, BellTower Technologies LLC, Richardson, TX. Tel: (214) 220-8000, Web Site: www.belltowertech.com (18)

Klein, Tom, MailChimp, Atlanta, GA. Tel: (678) 999-0141, Web Site: mailchimp.com (24)

Klein, Walt, Walt Klein Advertising, Denver, CO. Tel: (303) 298-8015, FAX: (303) 298-8194, Web Site: www.wka.com (35)

Klein, Ward M., Energizer Holdings Inc, Saint Louis, MO. Tel: (314) 985-2000, (800) 383-7323, FAX: (636) 733-4001, Web Site: www.energizer.com (16)

Kleinfeld, Neil, Growth Platforms Institute, Wilton, CT. Tel: (203) 529-0500, E-Mail: info@growthplatforms.org, Web Site: www.growthplatforms.org (20)

Kleinrock, Margaret, Renaissance Greeting Cards Inc, Downers Grove, IL. Tel: (800) 736-3383, Web Site: www.ftd.com (5)

Kleinrock, Randy, Renaissance Greeting Cards Inc, Downers Grove, IL. Tel: (800) 736-3383, Web Site: www.ftd.com (5)

Kleinschmidt, Roxann, Vocational Biographies Inc, Sauk Centre, MN. Tel: (320) 352-6516, (800) 255-0752, FAX: (320) 352-5546, E-Mail: careers@vocbios.com, Web Site: www.vocbio.com (31)

Klibanoff, Daniel, Multimedia Lists Inc, Asheville, NC. Tel: (800) 239-5478, E-Mail: daniel@multimedialists.com, Web Site: multimedialists.com (23)

Kling, Jeff, Fallon, Minneapolis, MN. Tel: (612) 758-2345, FAX: (612) 758-2346, E-Mail: info@fallon.com, Web Site: www.fallon.com (35)

Kling, Matt, Direct Connect Group, Cleveland, OH. Tel: (216) 651-9500, Web Site: www.directconnectgroup.com (35)

Klingel, Stephen J., National Council on Compensation Insurance Inc, Boca Raton, FL. Tel: (561) 893-1000, (800) 622-4123, FAX: (561) 893-1191, Web Site: www.ncci.com (1)

Klingensmith, Michael J., Star Tribune Media Co, Minneapolis, MN. Tel: (612) 673-4000, FAX: (612) 673-4359, Web Site: www.startribunecompany.com (17)

Klinger, Scott, Allconnect Inc, Atlanta, GA. Tel: (404) 260-2200, Web Site: www.allconnect.com (32)

Klingspor, Christoph, Ambient Shapes Inc, Hickory, NC. Tel: (800) 438-2244, FAX: (800) 872-2005, E-Mail: sales@ambientshapes.com, Web Site: www.ambientshapes.com (7)

Klingspor, Christoph, Klingspor's Woodworking Shop, Hickory, NC. Tel: (828) 326-WOOD, (800) 228-0000, FAX: (828) 327-4634, E-Mail: sales@woodworkingshop.com, Web Site: www.woodworkingshop.com (9)

Klingspor, Rosemarie, Ambient Shapes Inc, Hickory, NC. Tel: (800) 438-2244, FAX: (800) 872-2005, E-Mail: sales@ambientshapes.com, Web Site: www.ambientshapes.com (7)

Klingspor's Woodworking Shop, Hickory, NC. Tel: (828) 326-WOOD, (800) 228-0000, FAX: (828) 327-4634, E-Mail: sales@woodworkingshop.com, Web Site: www.woodworkingshop.com (9)

Klinkenberg, R.B., Harrington's of Vermont Inc, Richmond, VT. Tel: (802) 434-4444, E-Mail: info@harringtonham.com, Web Site: www.harringtonham.com (4)

Klipper, Mitchell S., BarnesandNoble.com, New York, NY. Tel: (212) 414-6000, (800) THE-BOOK, FAX: (212) 414-6140, E-Mail: service@barnesandnoble.com, Web Site: www.barnesandnoble.com (16)

Klise, Molly, Thomas Klise/Crimson Multimedia, Mystic, CT. Tel: (800) 937-0092, FAX: (860) 536-5141, E-Mail: info@crimsoninc.com, Web Site: www.crimsoninc.com (16)

Klitzner Industries, Cranston, RI. Tel: (401) 751-7500, (800) 556-6860, FAX: (800) 556-3199, E-Mail: info@klitzner.com, Web Site: www.klitzner.com; www.providenceline.com (6)

Klitzner, Alan, Klitzner Industries, Cranston, RI. Tel: (401) 751-7500, (800) 556-6860, FAX: (800) 556-3199, E-Mail: info@klitzner.com, Web Site: www.klitzner.com; www.providenceline.com (6)

Klitzner, Dean, Klitzner Industries, Cranston, RI. Tel: (401) 751-7500, (800) 556-6860, FAX: (800) 556-3199, E-Mail: info@klitzner.com, Web Site: www.klitzner.com; www.providenceline.com (6)

Klockit, Lake Geneva, WI. Tel: (262) 248-7000, (800) 556-2548, FAX: (262) 248-9899, E-Mail: klockit@klockit.com, Web Site: www.klockit.com (6)

Klonowski, Len, American Recreation Products Inc, Saint Louis, MO. Tel: (314) 576-8000, FAX: (314) 576-8072 (11)

Klopman, William A., Burlington Industries Inc, Greensboro, NC. Tel: (336) 379-2000, FAX: (336) 379-2498, Web Site: www.burlington.com (16)

Klotzman, Bruce, Our Data Works Inc, Lewisville, TX. Tel: (469) 546-3000, (800) 268-2505, FAX: (469) 546-3013, E-Mail: info@ourdataworks.com, Web Site: www.ourdataworks.com (29)

Kluger, Joel, Sunbelt Media Service, Chapel Hill, NC. Tel: (919) 967-7174, FAX: (919) 967-6050, E-Mail: jkluger@sunbelt-media.com, Web Site: www.sunbelt-media.com (32)

Klumack, Barbara, Donnelley Marketing, Pearl River, NY. Tel: (201) 476-2300, FAX: (201) 476-2151, Web Site: www.infousa.com (23)

Klune, Andy, Syntellect, Phoenix, AZ. Tel: (602) 789-2800, (800) 788-9733, FAX: (602) 789-2899, Web Site: www.syntellect.com (16)

Knab, Michael, Gennera Knab & Co, Studio City, CA (35)

Knapp, Judith, Andrew Associates Inc, Enfield, CT. Tel: (860) 253-0000, FAX: (860) 253-0007, Web Site: www.andrewdm.com (23)

Knapp, Kathy, S&S Worldwide, Colchester, CT. Tel: (860) 537-3451, (800) 288-9941, FAX: (860) 537-2866, E-Mail: cservice@ssww.com, Web Site: www.ssww.com (11)

Knapp, Pamela, GfK Custom Research LLC, New York, NY. Tel: (212) 240-5300, (800) 274-3577, FAX: (212) 240-5353, E-Mail: info@gfkamerica.com, Web Site: www.gfkamerica.com (30)

Knarr, Dustin, Calloway House Inc, Lancaster, PA. Tel: (717) 299-5703, (800) 233-0290, FAX: (717) 299-6754, Web Site: www.callowayhouse.com (34)

Knarr, Monica, Calloway House Inc, Lancaster, PA. Tel: (717) 299-5703, (800) 233-0290, FAX: (717) 299-6754, Web Site: www.callowayhouse.com (34)

Knauss, Donald R., The Clorox Co, Oakland, CA. Tel: (510) 271-7000, FAX: (510) 832-1463, Web Site: www.thecloroxcompany.com (16)

Knecht, Will, Wendell August Forge Inc, Grove City, PA. Tel: (724) 458-8360, (800) 923-1390, FAX: (724) 458-0906, E-Mail: info@wendell.com, Web Site: www.wendellaugust.com (6)

Knechtal, Brad, Richardson Electronics Ltd, Lafox, IL. Tel: (630) 208-2200, FAX: (630) 208-2550, E-Mail: edg@rell.com, Web Site: www.rell.com (16)

Knee, Kevin, Guthy-Renker Corp, Santa Monica, CA. Tel: (310) 581-6250, FAX: (310) 581-3232, Web Site: www.guthy-renker.com (32)

Kneib, Gina, DMW Worldwide LLC, Chesterbrook, PA. Tel: (610) 407-0407, (877) 744-3699, FAX: (610) 407-9201, E-Mail: info@dmwdirect.com, Web Site: www.dmwdirect.com (35)

Kneip, Maggie, Harry N Abrams Inc, New York, NY. Tel: (212) 206-7715, FAX: (212) 645-8437, Web Site: www.hnabooks.com (17)

Knight, Darrell, Message Technologies Inc, Atlanta, GA. Tel: (770) 240-8000, (800) 868-3684, FAX: (770) 240-7474, E-Mail: info@messagetech.com, Web Site: www.messagetech.com (30)

Knight, David E., Hatton-Brown Publishers Inc, Montgomery, AL. Tel: (334) 834-1170, FAX: (334) 834-4525, E-Mail: webman@hattonbrown.com, Web Site: www.hattonbrown.com (17)

Knight, Fred, BCR Enterprises Inc, Downers Grove, IL. Tel: (630) 986-1432, (800) 227-1234, FAX: (630) 323-5324, Web Site: www.bcr.com (17)

Knight, Jeff, International Currency LLC, Beaumont, TX. Tel: (409) 866-0588 (11)

Knight, Phil, Nike Inc, Beaverton, OR. Tel: (503) 671-4565, (800) 344-6543, FAX: (503) 671-6300, Web Site: www.nike.com (2)

Knight, Susan E., MTS Systems Corp, Eden Prairie, MN. Tel: (952) 937-4000, (800) 328-2255, FAX: (952) 937-4515, E-Mail: info@mts.com, Web Site: www.mts.com (16)

Knight, Tim, Chicago Sun-Times, Chicago, IL. Tel: (312) 321-3000, FAX: (312) 321-9655, E-Mail: jmorawez@suntimes.com, Web Site: www.suntimes.com (31)

Knipp, Greg, Dieste, Dallas, TX. Tel: (214) 259-8000, FAX: (214) 259-8040, E-Mail: contact@dieste.com, Web Site: www.dieste.com (35)

Knoche, Douglas, Communications Corp of America, Boston, VA. Tel: (540) 547-1700, FAX: (540) 302-8015, E-Mail: contact@cca.net, Web Site: www.cca.net (21)

Knodel, Todd, Bull Dog Media Group Inc, Madison, SD. Tel: (605) 256-9103, Web Site: www.commissionsoup.com (20)

Knodel, Todd, Bulldog Media Group Inc, Madison, SD. Tel: (866) 309-7687, E-Mail: info@bulldogmediagroup.com, Web Site: www.bulldogmediagroup.com (32)

Knoebel, Chris, LS Direct Marketing, Suffern, NY. Tel: (845) 357-1238, E-Mail: info@lsdirect.com, Web Site: www.lsdirect.com (23)

Knoll Group, New York, NY. Tel: (212) 343-4000, FAX: (212) 343-4180 (16)

Knoop, Brian, Victory Corps, New Hope, MN. Tel: (763) 561-5600, (800) 328-6120, FAX: (763) 561-8523, E-Mail: cs@victorycorps.com, Web Site: www.victorycorps.com (16)

Knope, Matt, Prakken Publications Inc, Ann Arbor, MI. Tel: (734) 975-2800, (800) 530-9673, FAX: (734) 975-2787, Web Site: www.techdirections.com; www.eddigest.com (17)

Knoploh, Terry, CTA Inc, Fenton, MO. Tel: (636) 305-3100, (800) 999-1874, FAX: (800) 315-8713, Web Site: www.ctainc.com (5)

Knoplol, Terry, Upbeat Inc, Saint Louis, MO. Tel: (314) 535-5005, (800) 325-3047, FAX: (314) 535-4419, E-Mail: custservice@upbeat.com, Web Site: www.upbeat.com (9)

Knott's Berry Farm Foods, Orrville, OH. Tel: (714) 220-5200, (866) 828-5502, FAX: (714) 220-5148, Web Site: www.knottsberryfarmfoods.com (4)

Knowledge Networks/SRI, Cranford, NJ. Tel: (908) 497-8000, FAX: (908) 497-8001, E-Mail: mclancey@knowledgenetworks.com, Web Site: www.knowledgenetworks.com (30)

Knowles, Milana, Spa-Finder Inc, New York, NY. Tel: (305) 307-5852, (800) ALL-SPAS, Web Site: www.spafinder.com (7)

Knox, Doug, Tyndale House Publishers, Carol Stream, IL. Tel: (630) 668-8300, FAX: (630) 668-3245 (17)

Knox, Douglas D., Armento Inc, Buffalo, NY. Tel: (716) 875-2423, (866) 276-3686, FAX: (716) 875-8011, E-Mail: info@armento.com, Web Site: www. armento-columbarium.com (5)

Knudsen, Dan, The Lacek Group, Minneapolis, MN. Tel: (612) 359-3700, FAX: (612) 359-9395, E-Mail: info@lacek.com, Web Site: www.lacek.com (35)

Knuston, Jerry, Miracle Ear, Minneapolis, MN. Tel: (800) 464-8002, FAX: (763) 268-4365, Web Site: www.miracle-ear.com (16)

Knutson, Daniel E., Land O' Lakes Inc, Arden Hills, MN. Tel: (651) 481-2222, (800) 328-9680, FAX: (651) 481-2000, Web Site: www.landolakesinc.com (16)

Kobie Marketing Inc, Saint Petersburg, FL. Tel: (727) 822-5353, (800) 821-7892, FAX: (727) 822-5265, E-Mail: info@kobie.com, Web Site: www.kobie. com (35)

Kobs Strategic Consulting, Chicago, IL. Tel: (312) 938-4430, FAX: (847) 934-1194, E-Mail: kobs4ksc@aol. com (20)

Kobs, Jim, Kobs Strategic Consulting, Chicago, IL. Tel: (312) 938-4430, FAX: (847) 934-1194, E-Mail: kobs4ksc@aol.com (20)

Kocerha, Rob, Allconnect Inc, Atlanta, GA. Tel: (404) 260-2200, Web Site: www.allconnect.com (32)

Koch, Douglas, Brown Shoe Co, Saint Louis, MO. Tel: (314) 854-4000, FAX: (314) 854-4274, Web Site: www.brownshoe.com (16)

Kochar, Father Joseph, Pallottine Center for Apostolic Causes Inc/St Jude Shrine, Baltimore, MD. Tel: (410) 685-6026, (877) 278-5833, FAX: (410) 234-1459, E-Mail: info@stjudeshrine.org, Web Site: www.stjudeshrine.org (1)

Kochberg, Keith, Mercury Media, Santa Monica, CA. Tel: (310) 451-2900, FAX: (310) 451-0180, Web Site: www.mercurymedia.com (32)

Kochevar Research Associates, Charlestown, MA. Tel: (617) 242-4332, FAX: (617) 242-8009, E-Mail: kra@bigfoot.com, Web Site: www. kochevarresearch.com (20)

Kochevar, John J., Kochevar Research Associates, Charlestown, MA. Tel: (617) 242-4332, FAX: (617) 242-8009, E-Mail: kra@bigfoot.com, Web Site: www. kochevarresearch.com (20)

Kodak Graphic Communications, Rochester, NY. Tel: (585) 724-0251, (800) 944-6171, FAX: (585) 724-0268, Web Site: www.kpgraphics.com (27)

Kodak, Skip, Lego Direct Marketing, Enfield, CT. Tel: (860) 749-2291, (800) 838-4386, FAX: (860) FAX-LEGO, Web Site: www.lego.com (11)

William Koechling Photography, Wheaton, IL. Tel: (630) 665-4379, Web Site: www.koechlingphoto. com (37)

Koechling, William, William Koechling Photography, Wheaton, IL. Tel: (630) 665-4379, Web Site: www. koechlingphoto.com (37)

Koehl, Emmy, Skullduggery, Anaheim, CA. Tel: (714) 777-6425, (800) 3 FOSSIL, FAX: (714) 832-1215, Web Site: www.skullduggery.com (16)

Koehl, Peter, Skullduggery, Anaheim, CA. Tel: (714) 777-6425, (800) 3 FOSSIL, FAX: (714) 832-1215, Web Site: www.skullduggery.com (16)

Koehler, James, Micro Center, Hilliard, OH. Tel: (614) 850-3675, (800) 634-3478, FAX: (614) 777-2620, E-Mail: csrs@microcenterorder.com, Web Site: www.microcenter.com (3)

Koelmel, John R., New York Power Authority, White Plains, NY. Tel: (914) 681-6200, E-Mail: info@ nypa.gov, Web Site: www.nypa.gov (16)

Koenig, Joe, CARFAX Inc, Centreville, VA. Tel: (703) 934-2664, Web Site: www.carfax.com (12)

Koenig, Marcia, St Louis Post-Dispatch, Saint Louis, MO. Tel: (314) 340-8000, (800) 365-0820, FAX: (314) 340-3140, Web Site: www.stltoday.com (17)

Koenigs, Eric, Clear Visions Inc, San Antonio, TX. Tel: (210) 496-6006, FAX: (210) 496-9225, E-Mail: bidrequest@clearvisionsinc.com, Web Site: www. clearvisionsinc.com (27)

Koepele, Eric, Ziff Davis Media Inc, New York, NY. Tel: (212) 503-5100, FAX: (212) 503-5023, Web Site: www.ziffdavis.com (17)

Koepke, Dennis, LemmonTree Marketing Group, Scottsdale, AZ. Tel: (480) 967-1405, (888) 536-6243, FAX: (480) 967-1407, E-Mail: 7solutions@ lemmontree.com, Web Site: www.lemmontree.com (35)

Koeppel Direct, Dallas, TX. Tel: (972) 732-6110, FAX: (972) 248-2759, E-Mail: pkoeppel@koeppelinc. com, Web Site: www.koeppeldirect.com (32)

Koeppel, Peter, Koeppel Direct, Dallas, TX. Tel: (972) 732-6110, FAX: (972) 248-2759, E-Mail: pkoeppel@koeppelinc.com, Web Site: www. koeppeldirect.com (32)

Koeze Co, Grand Rapids, MI. Tel: (800) 555-9688, E-Mail: service@koezedirect.com, Web Site: www. koeze.com (16)

Koeze, Jeff, Koeze Co, Grand Rapids, MI. Tel: (800) 555-9688, E-Mail: service@koezedirect.com, Web Site: www.koeze.com (16)

Kofler, Joe, DSP Inc USA, Charlottesville, VA. Tel: (434) 202-7870, E-Mail: iorder@delfortgroup.com, Web Site: www.delfortgroup.com (10)

Kofoid, Andy, ExactTarget, Indianapolis, IN. Tel: (317) 423-3928, FAX: (317) 396-1592, Web Site: www. exacttarget.com (32)

Kogan, Lindsay, Media Directions Creative Group, Lincolnshire, IL. Tel: (847) 948-0099, E-Mail: info@ mdcreativegroup.com, Web Site: www. mdcreativegroup.com (35)

Kogan, Marv, Media Directions Creative Group, Lincolnshire, IL. Tel: (847) 948-0099, E-Mail: info@ mdcreativegroup.com, Web Site: www. mdcreativegroup.com (35)

Kogler, Clare, Jordan Whitney Inc, Tustin, CA. Tel: (714) 832-3353, FAX: (714) 832-4422, E-Mail: info@jwgreensheet.com, Web Site: www. jwgreensheet.com (32)

Kogler, John, Jordan Whitney Inc, Tustin, CA. Tel: (714) 832-3353, FAX: (714) 832-4422, E-Mail: info@jwgreensheet.com, Web Site: www. jwgreensheet.com (32)

Kogler, Kevin, Microbiz Corp, Menlo Park, CA. Tel: (702) 749-5353, (800) 726-3282, FAX: (650) 440-4870, E-Mail: info@microbiz.com, Web Site: www. microbiz.com (3)

Kohler Burrows, Kristin, G H Bass & Co, New York, NY. Tel: (212) 381-3900, FAX: (212) 381-3950, E-Mail: help@ghbass.com, Web Site: www.ghbass. com (16)

Kohler, C. Bart, Hubert Co, Harrison, OH. Tel: (513) 367-8767, (800) 543-7374, FAX: (513) 367-8823, Web Site: www.hubert.com (16)

Kohler, Martin, PartyLite Gifts Inc, Norwell, MA. Tel: (508) 830-3100, (888)999-5706, FAX: (508) 830-0026, E-Mail: infona@partylite.com, Web Site: www.partylite.com (8)

Kohler, Mary, H & H Graphics, Lancaster, PA. Tel: (717) 393-3941, (866) 338-7569, E-Mail: info@ thehandhgroup.com, Web Site: www. hhgraphicsgroup.com (31)

Kohler, Terry, Windway Capital Corp, Sheboygan, WI. Tel: (920) 457-8600, FAX: (920) 457-8599, Web Site: www.windway.com (34)

Kohli, Tej, Indros Group, Brooklyn, NY. Tel: (866) 463-7671, E-Mail: info@indrosgroup.com, Web Site: www.indrosgroup.com (35)

Kohn, Andrew, Hyatt Legal Plans Inc, Cleveland, OH. Tel: (216) 241-0022, FAX: (216) 694-4305, Web Site: www.legalplans.com (16)

Kohnstamm, Abbey F, Pitney Bowes, Stamford, CT. Tel: (203) 356-5000, (800) MR-BOWES, Web Site: www.pitneybowes.com (10)

Kohrherr, Kira, K Public Relations LLC, New York, NY. Tel: (646) 756-4217, FAX: (646) 688-3017, Web Site: www.kpr-nyc.com (35)

Kohut, Dr James, Youngstown State University, Youngstown, OH. Tel: (330) 742-3064, Web Site: www.ysu.edu (41)

Koivisto, Mark, Product to Market LLC, Cokato, MN. Tel: (320) 286-9997 (20)

Kolb, Suzanne, E! Entertainment Television, Los Angeles, CA. Tel: (323) 954-2400, FAX: (323) 954-2665, Web Site: www.eonline.com (32)

Kolbe Corp, Phoenix, AZ. Tel: (602) 840-9770, (800) 642-2822, FAX: (602) 952-2706, E-Mail: info@ kolbe.com, Web Site: www.kolbe.com (17)

Kolbe, David, Kolbe Corp, Phoenix, AZ. Tel: (602) 840-9770, (800) 642-2822, FAX: (602) 952-2706, E-Mail: info@kolbe.com, Web Site: www.kolbe. com (17)

Kolbe, Dr. Rick, Northern Kentucky University, Highland Heights, KY. Tel: (859) 572-5220, (800) 637-9948, FAX: (859) 572-6177, Web Site: www.nku. edu (41)

Kolbe, Kathryn, Kolbe Corp, Phoenix, AZ. Tel: (602) 840-9770, (800) 642-2822, FAX: (602) 952-2706, E-Mail: info@kolbe.com, Web Site: www.kolbe. com (17)

Kolbrener, Tom, St Louis Slot Machine Co, Saint Louis, MO. Tel: (314) 432-1699, E-Mail: stlslot@earthlink. net, Web Site: www.stlouisslot.com (6)

Kolding, Kitty, Infocore Inc, Carlsbad, CA. Tel: (760) 607-2500, FAX: (760) 607-2505, E-Mail: info@ infocore.com, Web Site: www.infocore.com (23)

Kolier, Mark, Moddern Marketing, New York, NY. Tel: (212) 334-9800, E-Mail: mark@moddern.com, Web Site: www.moddern.com (35)

Kolinsky, Jay, MALM Chemical Corp, Pound Ridge, NY. Tel: (914) 764-5775, FAX: (914) 764-5386, E-Mail: custserv1@malms.com, Web Site: www. malms.com (16)

Kolke, Cynthia A., Whitewing Labs, Granada Hills, CA. Tel: (800) 950-3030, FAX: (818) 240-2785, E-Mail: service@whitewing.com, Web Site: www. whitewing.com (20)

Kolkka, Connie, Kappa Publishing Group, Blue Bell, PA. Tel: (215) 643-6385, FAX: (215) 628-3571, Web Site: www.kappapublishing.com (17)

Koll, Thomas, Laplink Software Inc, Bellevue, WA. Tel: (425) 952-6000, (800) 527-5465, FAX: (425) 952-6002, E-Mail: marketing@laplink.com, Web Site: www.laplink.com (3)

Koller, Jr. Edward R., Howard-Sloan-Koller Group, New York, NY. Tel: (212) 661-5250, FAX: (212) 557-9178, E-Mail: ekoller@hsksearch.com, Web Site: www.hsksearch.com (20)

Kollias & Associates, Chicago, IL. Tel: (312) 857-7707 (35)

Kollias, George, Kollias & Associates, Chicago, IL. Tel: (312) 857-7707 (35)

Kolling, Amanda, American Foundation for the Blind Inc, New York, NY. Tel: (212) 502-7600, FAX: (212) 502-7777, E-Mail: afbinfo@afb.org, Web Site: www.afb.org (1)

Kollman, Amber, Denver Metro Convention & Visitors Bureau, Denver, CO. Tel: (303) 892-1112, (800) 233-6837, FAX: (303) 892-1636, Web Site: www.denver.org (1)

Kollman, Terry, Charter Direct Marketing, New York, NY. Tel: (212) 717-2770, FAX: (561) 750-2150, E-Mail: terrykollman@charterdirectmarketing.com, Web Site: www.charterdirectmarketing.com (35)

Kollmann, Carol, Mailing Lists Plus Inc, Bellevue, WA. Tel: (425) 451-3335, FAX: (425) 646-4485, E-Mail: info@mailinglistsplus.com, Web Site: www.mailinglistsplus.com (23)

Kollmeyer, Rick, Direxxis Inc, Needham, MA. Tel: (781) 444-7900, FAX: (781) 444-7909, Web Site: www.direxxismarketing.com (22)

Kolodzieski, Edward J., Archway Marketing Services, Rogers, MN. Tel: (763) 428-3300, (866) 779-9855 X1933, FAX: (763) 488-6803, E-Mail: info@archway.com, Web Site: www.archway.com (28)

Kolowsky, Donald, Christian Herald Association, New York, NY. Tel: (212) 684-2800, (800) BOWERY-1, FAX: (212) 684-3740, E-Mail: info@chaonline.org, Web Site: www.bowery.org (1)

Susan G Komen for the Cure, Dallas, TX. Tel: (877) 465-6636, Web Site: www.komen.org (1)

Komisar, Randy, FileMaker Inc, Santa Clara, CA. Tel: (408) 987-7000, FAX: (408) 987-3823, Web Site: www.filemaker.com (22)

Komola, Christine T, Staples Inc, Framingham, MA. Tel: (508) 253-5000, FAX: (508) 253-7803, Web Site: www.staples.com (10)

Komunik, Montreal, QC Canada. Tel: (514) 904-0710, Web Site: www.komunik.com (20)

Kondo, Olgerta, Zeppo Marketing Inc, Brooklyn, NY. Tel: (212) 308-5734, FAX: (646) 304-7364, Web Site: www.zeppomarketing.com (32)

William S Konecky Associates Inc, Old Saybrook, CT. Tel: (860) 388-0878, FAX: (860) 388-0273 (17)

Konecky, Sean, William S Konecky Associates Inc, Old Saybrook, CT. Tel: (860) 388-0878, FAX: (860) 388-0273 (17)

Konecky, William, William S Konecky Associates Inc, Old Saybrook, CT. Tel: (860) 388-0878, FAX: (860) 388-0273 (17)

Konecny, Buddy, Seashore Vacations, Hilton Head Island, SC. Tel: (843) 785-2191, (800) 845-0077, FAX: (843) 785-6450, E-Mail: seashorehhi@hargray.com, Web Site: www.seashorehhi.com (19)

Konezny, Ron, Digi International, Minnetonka, MN. Tel: (952) 912-3444, (877) 912-3444, FAX: (952) 912-4952, Web Site: www.digi.com (3)

Kong, David, Best Western International, Phoenix, AZ. Tel: (602) 957-4200, FAX: (623) 780-6199, Web Site: www.bestwestern.com (19)

Konik & Co Inc, Skokie, IL. Tel: (847) 933-1800, E-Mail: amy@konik.com, Web Site: www.konik.com (33)

Konik, Stan, Konik & Co Inc, Skokie, IL. Tel: (847) 933-1800, E-Mail: amy@konik.com, Web Site: www.konik.com (33)

Konkle, Glen, Equity Management Inc, San Diego, CA. Tel: (858) 558-2500, FAX: (858) 558-2547, Web Site: www.equitymanagementinc.com (20)

Konstantino, John, Fosdick Fulfillment Corp, Wallingford, CT. Tel: (203) 269-0211, (800) 759-5588, FAX: (203) 679-3290, E-Mail: sales@fosdickcorp.com, Web Site: www.fosdickfulfillment.com (28)

Koogle, Margaret, Lilypons Water Gardens, Adamstown, MD. Tel: (800) 999-5459, FAX: (800) 879-5459, E-Mail: info@lilypons.com, Web Site: www.lilypons.com (8)

Koolish, Ruth, Information Sources Inc, Walnut Creek, CA. Tel: (510) 525-6220, FAX: (510) 525-1568, Web Site: www.tectrends.com (22)

Koper, Jennifer, Anderson Niebuhr & Associates Inc, Arden Hills, MN. Tel: (651) 486-8712, (800) 678-5577, FAX: (651) 486-0536, E-Mail: info@ana-inc.com, Web Site: www.ana-inc.com (30)

Kopf, Ken, KZSW Advertising Inc, East Setauket, NY. Tel: (631) 348-1440, FAX: (631) 348-1449, E-Mail: contact@kzswadvertising.com, Web Site: kzsadvertising.com (35)

Kophamal, Frank, American General Co, Neptune, NJ. Tel: (732) 922-7000, FAX: (732) 922-7595 (15)

Kopinski, Jason, American Academy of Neurology, Minneapolis, MN. Tel: (651) 695-2793, 800 (879)-1960, FAX: (612) 454-2746, E-Mail: memberservices@aan.com, Web Site: www.aan.com (1)

Korab, Holly, University of Illinois College of LAS, Office of Advancement, Urbana, IL. Tel: (217) 333-1705, E-Mail: las-studentoffice@illinois.edu, Web Site: www.las.illinois.edu (1)

Koran, Bob, United Communications Group, Gaithersburg, MD. Tel: (301) 287-2700, FAX: (301) 816-8945, E-Mail: webmaster@ucg.com, Web Site: www.ucg.com (17)

Korbas, Tom, Samsonite International SA, Mansfield, MA. Tel: (508) 851-1400, (800) 547-BAGS, FAX: (303) 373-8715, Web Site: www.samsonite.com (16)

Kordestarni, Omid, Google Inc, Mountain View, CA. Tel: (650) 253-0000, FAX: (650) 253-0001, Web Site: www.google.com (31)

Koren, Daniella, ARCHES Technology, Hoboken, NJ. Tel: (973) 882-0900, E-Mail: info@archestechnology.com, Web Site: www.archestechnology.com (35)

Korgman, Max, TouchPoint Data Solutions Inc, Alpharetta, GA. Tel: (770) 886-8611, FAX: (678) 686-1835, Web Site: touchpointdata.com (23)

Korn, Gail, Garden Perennials, Wayne, NE. Tel: (402) 375-3615, (888) 375-3615, Web Site: www.gardenperennials.net (8)

Kornberg, David, Express LLC, Columbus, OH. Tel: (614) 474-7000, Web Site: www.expressfashion.com (2)

Korowitz, Bill, Magnet LLC, Washington, MO. Tel: (636) 239-5661, (800) 458-9457, FAX: (636) 239-4490, E-Mail: contactus@themagnetgroup.com, Web Site: www.magnetllc.com (16)

Korowitz, Bill, Magnets 4 Media, Washington, MO. Tel: (843) 216-6665, (800) 642-6384, FAX: (636) 390-5147, E-Mail: sales@magnets4media.com, Web Site: www.magnets4media.com (30)

Korsmeyer, Mark, Dairy Farmers of America Inc, Kansas City, MO. Tel: (816) 801-6455, (888) 332-6455, FAX: (816) 801-6456, E-Mail: webmail@dfamilk.com, Web Site: www.dfamilk.com (16)

Korwin, Richard M., Wideband by Kars, New Rochelle, NY. Tel: (212) 691-9000, FAX: (212) 691-9835, E-Mail: info@widebandjewelry.com, Web Site: www.widebandjewelry.com (16)

Korzak, Carrie, Mid-Central Printing & Mailing Inc, Wilmette, IL. Tel: (847) 251-4040, FAX: (847) 251-8615, E-Mail: mcpm1910@yahoo.com, Web Site: www.mcpm.com (28)

Kosloff, David, Roosevelt Paper Co, Mount Laurel, NJ. Tel: (856) 303-4100, (856) 303-4200, (800) 523-3470, FAX: (856) 642-1950, (856) 642-1949, Web Site: www.rooseveltpaper.com (25)

Kosloff, Irving S., Roosevelt Paper Co, Mount Laurel, NJ. Tel: (856) 303-4100, (856) 303-4200, (800) 523-3470, FAX: (856) 642-1950, (856) 642-1949, Web Site: www.rooseveltpaper.com (25)

Kosloff, Ted, Roosevelt Paper Co, Mount Laurel, NJ. Tel: (856) 303-4100, (856) 303-4200, (800) 523-3470, FAX: (856) 642-1950, (856) 642-1949, Web Site: www.rooseveltpaper.com (25)

Kossoff, Maxine, Beta Research Corp, Syosset, NY. Tel: (516) 935-3800, FAX: (516) 935-4092, E-Mail: beta@nybeta.com, Web Site: www.nybeta.com (30)

Kostelini, Charles, Bontex, Honolulu, HI. Tel: (540) 261-2181, FAX: (540) 261-3784, E-Mail: bontex@bontex.com, Web Site: www.bontex.com (16)

Kostelni, J.C., Bontex, Honolulu, HI. Tel: (540) 261-2181, FAX: (540) 261-3784, E-Mail: bontex@bontex.com, Web Site: www.bontex.com (16)

Koster, William Frank, Aegon USA Investment Management, Inc, Cedar Rapids, IA. Tel: (502) 560-2000, FAX: (502) 560-2030, Web Site: www.aegonins.com (14)

Koszuta, Jeff, Rainbow Graphics Inc, Mundelein, IL. Tel: (847) 824-9600, E-Mail: jkoszuta@rainbowgraphics.com, Web Site: www.rainbowgraphics.com (27)

Kotch, Michael, Quadrant Engineering Plastic Products, Reading, PA. Tel: (610) 320-6600, (800) 366-0300, FAX: (610) 320-6868, Web Site: www.quadrantepp.com (16)

Kottler, Anne, Sage Communications, Framingham, MA. Tel: (508) 309-6678, FAX: (508) 309-6372, E-Mail: info@sagecommunications.com, Web Site: www.sagecommunications.com (35)

Kottler, Josef, Sage Communications, Framingham, MA. Tel: (508) 309-6678, FAX: (508) 309-6372, E-Mail: info@sagecommunications.com, Web Site: www.sagecommunications.com (35)

Kotula, Donald L., Northern Tool & Equipment Inc, Burnsville, MN. Tel: (952) 894-9510, (800) 221-0516, FAX: (952) 894-1020, Web Site: www.northerntool.com (16)

Kouroupas, Steve, Quality Park Products, Minneapolis, MN. Tel: (800) 828-7323, (800) 547-4252, FAX: (800) 398-9835, E-Mail: mktg@qualitypark.com, Web Site: www.qualitypark.com (26)

Kourtis, Spyro, HackerAgency Inc, Seattle, WA. Tel: (206) 805-1500, Web Site: www.hal2l.com (35)

Koury, Conny, Baker & Taylor Inc, Charlotte, NC. Tel: (704) 998-3100, (800) 775-1800, FAX: (704) 998-3316, E-Mail: btinfo@btol.com, Web Site: www.btol.com (16)

Kouyoumjian, Charles H., Blue Raven Technology, Wilmington, MA. Tel: ((978) 658-4676, (800) 274-5343, (800) 20RAVEN, FAX: (781) 778-4848, E-Mail: sales@blueraven.com, Web Site: www.blueraven.com (3)

Kouzmanoff, Catherine, Inter7 Internet Technologies Inc, Galena, IL. Tel: (815) 776-9465, Web Site: www.inter7.com (3)

Kovach, Al, Paralyzed Veterans of America, Washington, DC. Tel: (212) 255-9078, (800) 424-8200, FAX: (202) 416-7643, E-Mail: info@pva.org, Web Site: www.pva.org (1)

Kovach, David, Kistler-Tiffany Companies LLC, Berwyn, PA. Tel: (610) 722-3300, (866) 250-5413, Web Site: www.ktadv.com (20)

Koval, Judy, Jantz Supply Koval Knives, Davis, OK. Tel: (580) 369-2316, (800) 351-8900, FAX: (580) 369-3082, Web Site: www.knifemaking.com (9)

Koval, Mick, Jantz Supply Koval Knives, Davis, OK. Tel: (580) 369-2316, (800) 351-8900, FAX: (580) 369-3082, Web Site: www.knifemaking.com (9)

Kovar, Joe, SECO-LARM USA Inc, Irvine, CA. Tel: (949) 261-2999, (800) 662-0800, FAX: (949) 261-7326, E-Mail: info@seco-larm.com, Web Site: www.seco-larm.com (16)

Kovatch, Michael, Contact Center Compliance, Santa Rosa, CA. Tel: (707) 303-4437, (800) 308-0258, Web Site: www.dnc.com (22)

Kovitch, Richard, MDF Systems, Bristol, CT. Tel: (860) 584-4750, (800) 426-3752, FAX: (860) 584-4759, Web Site: www.mdfsystems.com (22)

Kowal & Associates Inc, Cambridge, MA. Tel: (617) 577-0700, FAX: (617) 577-0500, E-Mail: pkowal@kowalassociates.com, Web Site: www.kowalassociates.com (20)

Kowal, G. Paul, Kowal & Associates Inc, Cambridge, MA. Tel: (617) 577-0700, FAX: (617) 577-0500, E-Mail: pkowal@kowalassociates.com, Web Site: www.kowalassociates.com (20)

Kowalczyk, Jim, Black Dot Group, Crystal Lake, IL. Tel: (815) 893-8799, E-Mail: pkelley@blackdot.com, Web Site: www.blackdot.com (35)

Kowalski, Anita, C&H Distributors LLC, Milwaukee, WI. Tel: (414) 443-1700, (888) 316-2223, FAX: (414) 443-9213, E-Mail: customerservice@chdist.com, Web Site: www.chdist.com (9)

Kowalski, Ed, The United Methodist Publishing House, Nashville, TN. Tel: (615) 749-6000, (800) 672-1789, FAX: (615) 749-6417, E-Mail: productsandservices@umpublishing.com, Web Site: www.umpublishing.com (17)

Kowalsky, George, Response Insurance, Scranton, PA. Tel: (203) 634-7255, (800) 518-2984, FAX: (203) 634-7319, E-Mail: webcs@response.com, Web Site: www.response.com (15)

Kowkabany, Bruce, Core Technologies, Boulder, CO. Tel: (614) 231-3031, (866) 624-5927, FAX: (303) 395-1474, E-Mail: support@core-tech.com, Web Site: www.mailware.com (22)

Kowolaski, Michael J, Tiffany & Co, New York, NY. Tel: (212) 755-8000, FAX: (212) 320-7550, Web Site: www.tiffany.com (6)

Koye, Dennis, Source Communications, Hackensack, NJ. Tel: (201) 343-5222, E-Mail: admin@sourcead.com, Web Site: sourcead.com (35)

Kozak Auto Drywash Inc, Batavia, NY. Tel: (716) 343-8111, (800) 237-9927, FAX: (585) 343-3732, E-Mail: info@kozak.com, Web Site: www.dryautowash.com (16)

Kozeliski, Jon, Star Silkscreen Design Inc, Decatur, IL. Tel: (217) 877-0804, FAX: (217) 877-0843, Web Site: www.starsilkscreendesign.com (2)

Koziara, Tanya, Con-Way Freight, Ann Arbor, MI. Tel: (734) 994-6600, FAX: (734) 757-1153 (12)

Kozlak, Jodeen, Target Corp, Minneapolis, MN. Tel: (612) 304-6073, Web Site: www.target.com (16)

Kozlowski, Don, The Metal Ware Corp, Two Rivers, WI. Tel: (920) 793-1368, (800) 288-4545, FAX: (920) 794-3161, Web Site: www.nesco.com (32)

Kozma, Alicia, Crohn's & Colitis Foundation of America, New York, NY. Tel: (212) 685-3440, (800) 932-2423, E-Mail: info@ccfa.org, Web Site: www.ccfa.org (1)

Kozoman, Robert L., DePaul University, Chicago, IL. Tel: (312) 362-8000, (800) 4-DEPAUL, FAX: (312) 362-6639, E-Mail: skelly@wppost.depaul.edu, Web Site: www.depaul.edu (41)

Kraemer, Suzette, Magazine Publishers of America, New York, NY. Tel: (212) 872-3700, FAX: (212) 888-4217, E-Mail: mpa@magazine.org, Web Site: www.magazine.org (17)

Kraetzer, Kenneth, CBSI, Harrison, NY. Tel: (914) 381-5353, Web Site: www.cbsiservices.com (30)

The Kraft Heinz Co, Pittsburgh, PA. Tel: (412) 456-5700, Web Site: www.kraftheinzcompany.com (4)

Kraft, Carolyn, Holsted Marketing Inc, New York, NY. Tel: (212) 686-8537, FAX: (212) 481-0415, E-Mail: preulbach@holstedmarketing.com, Web Site: www.holstedmarketing.com (35)

Kraft, Larry, Digi International, Minnetonka, MN. Tel: (952) 912-3444, (877) 912-3444, FAX: (952) 912-4952, Web Site: www.digi.com (3)

Kraft, Walter, Eastern Michigan University, Ypsilanti, MI. Tel: (734) 487-1849, FAX: (734) 484-1151, Web Site: www.emich.edu (16)

Kraftbilt, Tulsa, OK. Tel: (918) 628-1260, (800) 331-7290, FAX: (918) 632-7371, Web Site: www.kraftbilt.com (10)

Kragen & Co, Beverly Hills, CA. Tel: (310) 854-4400, (877) 808-0698, FAX: (310) 854-0238, E-Mail: info@kragenandcompany.com, Web Site: www.kenkragen.com (32)

Kragen, Ken, Kragen & Co, Beverly Hills, CA. Tel: (310) 854-4400, (877) 808-0698, FAX: (310) 854-0238, E-Mail: info@kragenandcompany.com, Web Site: www.kenkragen.com (32)

Krakower, Susan, CNBC, Englewood Cliffs, NJ. Tel: (201) 735-2622, FAX: (201) 735-3200, Web Site: www.cnbc.com (32)

Kramer & Associates, Cincinnati, OH. Tel: (513) 792-5700, (800) 281-1400, FAX: (513) 792-5709, E-Mail: eservice@kramerandassociates.com, Web Site: www.kramerandassociates.com (20)

Kramer, Carl, Gilson Co Inc, Lewis Center, OH. Tel: (740) 548-7298, (800) 444-1508, FAX: (740) 548-5314, E-Mail: sales@gilsonco.com, Web Site: www.globalgilson.com (9)

Kramer, Howard, Listrak, Lititz, PA. Tel: (717) 627-4528, (877) 362-4556, E-Mail: info@listrak.com, Web Site: www.listrak.com (32)

Kramer, Larry, Newhouse School of Public Communications, Syracuse, NY. Tel: (315) 443-3611, FAX: (315) 443-4426, Web Site: newhouse.syr.edu (41)

Kramer, Larry, USA TODAY, Mc Lean, VA. Tel: (703) 854-3400, (800) 872-0001, E-Mail: accuracy@usatoday.com, Web Site: www.usatoday.com (17)

Kramer, Lyn, Kramer & Associates, Cincinnati, OH. Tel: (513) 792-5700, (800) 281-1400, FAX: (513) 792-5709, E-Mail: eservice@kramerandassociates.com, Web Site: www.kramerandassociates.com (20)

Kramer, Nancy, Resource/Ammirati, Columbus, OH. Tel: (614) 621-2888, FAX: (614) 621-2873, E-Mail: businessdevelopment@resourceammirati.com, Web Site: www.resourceammirati.com (35)

Kramer, Richard J, Goodyear Tire & Rubber Co, Akron, OH. Tel: (330) 796-2121, (800) 321-2136, FAX: (330) 796-2222, Web Site: www.goodyear.com (16)

Kramer, Ross, Listrak, Lititz, PA. Tel: (717) 627-4528, (877) 362-4556, E-Mail: info@listrak.com, Web Site: www.listrak.com (32)

Kramer, Scott, NY Now, White Plains, NY. Tel: (800) 272-7469, Web Site: www.nynow.com (42)

Kramer, Spence, Crispin Porter + Bogusky, Miami, FL. Tel: (305) 859-2070, FAX: (305) 854-3419, E-Mail: info@cpbgroup.com, Web Site: www.cpbgroup.com (35)

Kraner, Matt, Cable Direct Marketing Inc, Montville, NJ. Tel: (973) 244-0010, FAX: (973) 244-0302, E-Mail: cabledm@aol.com (31)

Kranjac, Paulette, List Process Direct Inc, New York, NY. Tel: (212) 517-8550, FAX: (212) 517-9728, E-Mail: pkranjac@listprocessdirect.com, Web Site: www.listprocessdirect.com (31)

Kranzberg, Ken, Tricor Braun, Woodridge, IL. Tel: (708) 385-9333, FAX: (708) 385-3015, Web Site: www.tricorbraun.com (16)

Krapf, Eric, BCR Enterprises Inc, Downers Grove, IL. Tel: (630) 986-1432, (800) 227-1234, FAX: (630) 323-5324, Web Site: www.bcr.com (17)

Krapf, Wallace, Magnatag Visible Systems, Macedon, NY. Tel: (315) 986-3033, FAX: (315) 986-4000, Web Site: www.magnatag.com (16)

Krasney, Kevin, Cole's Appliance & Furniture Co, Chicago, IL. Tel: (773) 525-1797, Web Site: shopcoles.com (8)

Krass, Katherine, Custometrics Inc, Richmond Hill, ON Canada. Tel: (905) 886-9020, E-Mail: info@custometrics.ca, Web Site: www.custometrics.com (30)

Krassin, Ron, Zotos International, Darien, CT. Tel: (203) 655-8911, (800) 242-9283, (800) 242-WAVE, FAX: (203) 656-7890, E-Mail: HumanResources@zotosintl.com, Web Site: www.zotos.com (16)

Kratovil, Jonathan, The Pond-Ekberg Co, Chicopee, MA. Tel: (413) 594-7511, (800) 225-7511, FAX: (413) 594-2179, E-Mail: sales@pond-ekberg.com, Web Site: www.pond-ekberg.com (27)

EC Kraus Home Wine & Beer Making Supplies, Independence, MO. Tel: (816) 254-7448, (800) 353-1906, FAX: (816) 254-7051, E-Mail: customerservice@eckraus.com, Web Site: www.eckraus.com (4)

Kraus, Ed, EC Kraus Home Wine & Beer Making Supplies, Independence, MO. Tel: (816) 254-7448, (800) 353-1906, FAX: (816) 254-7051, E-Mail: customerservice@eckraus.com, Web Site: www.eckraus.com (4)

Kraus, Peter Steven, Alliance Bernstein, New York, NY. Tel: (212) 969-1000, (800) 962-2134, FAX: (212) 969-2293, Web Site: www.alliancebernstein.com (14)

Kraus, Steve, Olan Mills Inc, Chattanooga, TN. Tel: (423) 622-5141, (800) 251-6320, FAX: (423) 629-8128, Web Site: www.olanmills.com (16)

Krause Publications Inc, Iola, WI. Tel: (715) 445-2214, FAX: (715) 445-4087, Web Site: www.krausebooks.com (17)

Krause, Bill, Llewellyn Publications, Woodbury, MN. Tel: (651) 291-1970, (877) 639-9753, FAX: (651) 291-1908, Web Site: www.llewellyn.com (17)

Krause, Jeffrey, Society of Manufacturing Engineers, Dearborn, MI. Tel: (313) 425-3000, (800) 733-4763, FAX: (313) 425-3400, E-Mail: communications@sme.org, Web Site: www.sme.org (1)

Krauss, Julianne, The Hartz Mountain Corp, Secaucus, NJ. Tel: (201) 271-4800, (800) 275-1414, FAX: (201) 271-0068, Web Site: www.hartz.com (16)

Krauss, Michael, Authentic Designs, West Rupert, VT. Tel: (802) 394-7713, (800) 844-9416, E-Mail: lighting@authenticdesigns.com, Web Site: www.authenticdesigns.com (8)

Krausz, Keira, NutriSystem Inc, Fort Washington, PA. Tel: (215) 706-5300, (800) 435-4074, FAX: (215) 706-5388, E-Mail: customerservice@nutrisystem.com, Web Site: www.nutrisystem.com (7)

Kravetz, David, Fairytale Brownies, Phoenix, AZ. Tel: (800) 324-7982, FAX: (602) 489-5133, E-Mail: service@brownies.com, Web Site: www.brownies.com (4)

Kravis, Marie Josee, The Museum of Modern Art, New York, NY. Tel: (212) 708-9400, FAX: (212) 333-1123, E-Mail: info@moma.org, Web Site: www.moma.org (5)

Kravitsky, Charles, Fireman's Fund Insurance Co, Novato, CA. Tel: (415) 899-2000, FAX: (415) 899-3600, Web Site: www.firemansfund.com (14)

Krawchuk, Barry, America's Call Center, Jacksonville, FL. Tel: (904) 224-2000, (800) 598-2580, FAX: (904) 737-1107, E-Mail: info@webcallusa.com, Web Site: www.webcallusa.com (29)

Krawitz, Natalie R., University of Missouri, Columbia, MO. Tel: (573) 882-6333, (800) 856-2181, FAX: (573) 882-2721, E-Mail: visitus@missouri.edu, Web Site: www.missouri.edu (41)

Krear, J. David, National Committee to Preserve Social Security & Medicare, Washington, DC. Tel: (202) 216-0420, (800) 966-1935, FAX: (202) 216-0446, E-Mail: kreard@ncpssm.org, Web Site: www.ncpssm.org (1)

Kreber Graphics Inc, Columbus, OH. Tel: (614) 529-5701, (800) 777-3501, FAX: (614) 777-4890, E-Mail: info@kreber.com, Web Site: www.kreber.com (27)

Kreber, Frank, Kreber Graphics Inc, Columbus, OH. Tel: (614) 529-5701, (800) 777-3501, FAX: (614) 777-4890, E-Mail: info@kreber.com, Web Site: www.kreber.com (27)

Kreczko, Alan J., The Hartford Financial Services Inc, Southington, CT. Tel: (860) 547-5000, (860) 843-8070, FAX: (860) 547-2680, Web Site: www.thehartford.com (15)

Kreek, Eerik, Marketing Advents, Washington, DC. Tel: (202) 955-5030, FAX: (202) 955-0085, E-Mail: info@dmaw.org, Web Site: www.dmaw.org (43)

Kreg Tool Co, Huxley, IA. Tel: (515) 597-6400, Web Site: www.kregtool.com (16)

Kreichman, Harris, eTargetMedia.com Inc, Coconut Creek, FL. Tel: (954) 480-8470, (888) 805-3282, FAX: (954) 480-8489, E-Mail: info@etargetmedia.com, Web Site: www.etargetmedia.com (32)

Kreider, Russ, IBSDirect, King of Prussia, PA. Tel: (610) 265-8210, FAX: (610) 265-7997, Web Site: www.ibsdm.com (27)

Krein, Erick, Markertek Video Supply, Saugerties, NY. Tel: (845) 246-3036, (800) 522-2025, FAX: (845) 246-1757, E-Mail: sales@markertek.com, Web Site: www.markertek.com (3)

Kremer, Frank, Summit Racing Equipment, Tallmadge, OH. Tel: (330) 630-0250, (800) 230-3030, FAX: (330) 630-5571, Web Site: www.summitracing.com (12)

Kremer, John, 1001 Ways to Market Your Books, Taos, NM. Tel: (575) 751-3398, FAX: (575) 751-3100, E-Mail: info@bookmarket.com, Web Site: www.bookmarket.com (43)

Kremer, John, Open Horizons, Taos, NM. Tel: (575) 751-3398, FAX: (575) 751-3100, E-Mail: info@bookmarket.com, Web Site: www.bookmarket.com (39)

Kremp, Dave, ITW Vortec, Cincinnati, OH. Tel: (513) 891-7474, (800) 441-7475, FAX: (513) 891-4092, E-Mail: techsupport@vortec.com, Web Site: www.vortec.com (16)

Kress, Staci, American Customer Care Inc, Bristol, CT. Tel: (866) 400-6886, Web Site: www.americancustomercare.com (29)

Kresse, Bill, STIR LLC, Milwaukee, WI. Tel: (414) 278-0040, FAX: (414) 278-0390, E-Mail: info@stirstuff.com, Web Site: www.stirstuff.com (35)

Kresser, David, Gift Services Inc, Vancouver, WA. Tel: (800) 379-4065, FAX: (360) 699-0597, E-Mail: corpsales@gifttree.com, Web Site: www.gifttree.com (6)

Kretschmann, Fred, Kennel Vet, Laurel, DE. Tel: (302) 875-7111, (800) 782-0627, FAX: (302) 269-3986, E-Mail: info@petmarket.com, Web Site: www.kennelvet.com (11)

Kretschmann, Meryl, Kennel Vet, Laurel, DE. Tel: (302) 875-7111, (800) 782-0627, FAX: (302) 269-3986, E-Mail: info@petmarket.com, Web Site: www.kennelvet.com (11)

Kretschmer, Diane, Continuing Education of the Bar (CEB), Oakland, CA. Tel: (510) 302-2000, (800) 232-3444, FAX: (510) 302-2001, Web Site: www.ceb.com (1)

Kreuze, Calvin W., Haworth Inc, Holland, MI. Tel: (616) 393-3000, (800) 344-2600, FAX: (616) 393-1570, Web Site: www.haworth.com (34)

Krieger, Lisa, Winn Devon, Richmond, BC Canada. Tel: (206) 763-9544, (800) 875-4150, FAX: (206) 762-1389, Web Site: www.winndevon.com (17)

Krieger, Lou, Poker Player, Sherman Oaks, CA. Tel: (310) 674-3365, FAX: (310) 674-3205, E-Mail: ard@gamblingtimes.com, Web Site: www.gamblingtimes.com (17)

Krieger, Niki, Winn Devon, Richmond, BC Canada. Tel: (206) 763-9544, (800) 875-4150, FAX: (206) 762-1389, Web Site: www.winndevon.com (17)

Kriemelmeyer, Katie, Automated Graphic Systems LLC, White Plains, MD. Tel: (800) 678-8760, FAX: (240) 222-3419, E-Mail: info@ags.com, Web Site: www.ags.com (31)

Kriete, Edward, Hasbro Inc, Pawtucket, RI. Tel: (401) 431-8697, (800) 242-7276, FAX: (401) 727-5121, Web Site: www.hasbro.com (11)

Krisel, Ross, Prosodie Interactive, Plantation, FL. Tel: (954) 671-6500, (866) 776-7634, FAX: (954) 915-0567, E-Mail: info@prosodiemail.com, Web Site: www.ivrinc.com (29)

Kristel, Alan J., Commercial Envelope Manufacturing Co Inc, Deer Park, NY. Tel: (631) 242-2500, FAX: (631) 242-6935, Web Site: www.commercial-envelope.com (26)

Kristo, Bryce, INX International Ink Co, Schaumburg, IL. Tel: (800) 631-7956, FAX: (847) 969-9758, E-Mail: info@inxink.com, Web Site: www.inxinternational.com (16)

Kritzeck, Paul, Crest Healthcare Supply, Dassel, MN. Tel: (800) 328-8908, (800) 369-9207, Web Site: www.cresthealthcare.com (16)

Krivkovich, Peter, Cramer-Krasselt, Chicago, IL. Tel: (312) 616-9600, FAX: (312) 616-3839, E-Mail: pkrivkov@c-k.com, Web Site: c-k.com (35)

Krizek, Bryan, Christian Relief Services Charities Inc, Alexandria, VA. Tel: (703) 317-9086, E-Mail: info@christianrelief.org, Web Site: www.christianrelief.org (1)

Krizek, Paul, Christian Relief Services Charities Inc, Alexandria, VA. Tel: (703) 317-9086, E-Mail: info@christianrelief.org, Web Site: www.christianrelief.org (1)

Kroeger, Dan, Gold Medal Products Co, Cincinnati, OH. Tel: (513) 769-7676, (800) 543-0862, FAX: (800) 542-1496, E-Mail: info@gmpopcorn.com, Web Site: www.gmpopcorn.com (16)

Kroeker, Lelani, The Orange County Register, Santa Ana, CA. Tel: (877) 469-7344, E-Mail: customerservice@ocregister.com, Web Site: www.ocregister.com (17)

The Kroger Co, Cincinnati, OH. Tel: (513) 762-4000, (866) 221-4141, FAX: (513) 762-1575, Web Site: www.kroger.com (4)

Krohmer, Steve, Rockler Woodworking & Hardware, Medina, MN. Tel: (763) 478-8200, (800) 279-4441, FAX: (800) 865-1229, E-Mail: info@rockler.com, Web Site: www.rockler.com (8)

Kroll Direct Marketing Inc, Wellington, FL. Tel: (609) 275-2900, E-Mail: lee@krolldirect.com, Web Site: www.krolldirect.com (23)

Kroll, Dr. Arnie, Back to the Bible, Lincoln, NE. Tel: (402) 464-7200, (800) 759-2425, FAX: (402) 464-7474, E-Mail: info@backtothebible.org, Web Site: www.backtothebible.org (5)

Kroll, Gretchen, Tripar International Inc, Roselle, IL. Tel: (630) 980-5100, (800) 222-1142, FAX: (800) 648-9015, E-Mail: sales@tripar.com, Web Site: www.tripar.com (28)

Kroll, Leland, Kroll Direct Marketing Inc, Wellington, FL. Tel: (609) 275-2900, E-Mail: lee@krolldirect.com, Web Site: www.krolldirect.com (23)

Kromer, Bob, The New Piper Aircraft Inc, Vero Beach, FL. Tel: (772) 567-4361, FAX: (772) 978-6573, E-Mail: marketing@piper.com, Web Site: www.newpiper.com (16)

Krone, Philip, Productive Strategies Inc, Northfield, IL. Tel: (847) 446-0008, FAX: (847) 446-0211, E-Mail: pkrone@productivestrategies.com, Web Site: www.productivestrategies.com (20)

Kronrad, Robert, All Star Carts & Vehicles, Bay Shore, NY. Tel: (631) 666-5252, (800) 831-3166, FAX: (631) 666-1319, Web Site: www.allstarcarts.com (16)

Kronrad, Stephen, All Star Carts & Vehicles, Bay Shore, NY. Tel: (631) 666-5252, (800) 831-3166, FAX: (631) 666-1319, Web Site: www.allstarcarts.com (16)

Kroot, Irwin, Parsons School of Design Human Resource Dept, New York, NY. Tel: (212) 229-5671, FAX: (212) 229-8975, E-Mail: communications@newschool.edu, Web Site: www.newschool.edu/parsons/ (41)

Kross Inc, Santa Clarita, CA. Tel: (661) 284-3557, (800) 456-3699, FAX: (661) 257-1914, Web Site: www.krosskits.com (16)

Krosser, Stuart, Sherman Specialty Toy Co Inc, Jericho, NY. Tel: (516) 861-6420, (516) 546-7400, (800) 645-6513, FAX: (516) 861-1033, (800) 853-8697, E-Mail: orders@shermanspecialty.com, Web Site: www.shermanspecialty.com (16)

Kroupa, Ivan, Kadant Johnson Inc, Three Rivers, MI. Tel: (269) 278-1715, FAX: (269) 279-5980, Web Site: www.kadantjohnson.com (16)

Kruckeberg, Lloyd, Shopguide.com, Amarillo, TX. Tel: (806) 351-0005, FAX: (806) 351-0059, E-Mail: info@shopguide.com, Web Site: www.shopguide.com (27)

Krueger, Eugene C., National Fulfillment Services, Holmes, PA. Tel: (610) 532-4700, (800) NFS-1306, FAX: (610) 586-3232, E-Mail: tkrueger@nfsrv.com, Web Site: www.nfsrv.com (28)

Krueger, Jim, Figi's Inc, Marshfield, WI. Tel: (715) 387-1771, (800) 422-3444, FAX: (715) 384-1129, Web Site: www.figis.com (4)

Krueger, Thomas, National Fulfillment Services, Holmes, PA. Tel: (610) 532-4700, (800) NFS-1306, FAX: (610) 586-3232, E-Mail: tkrueger@nfsrv.com, Web Site: www.nfsrv.com (28)

Herbert Krug & Associates Inc, Evanston, IL. Tel: (847) 864-0550, FAX: (847) 864-0575 (20)

Krug, E Herbert, Herbert Krug & Associates Inc, Evanston, IL. Tel: (847) 864-0550, FAX: (847) 864-0575 (20)

Krug, E. Herbert, Catalog Marketing Group, Evanston, IL. Tel: (847) 864-8089 (20)

Krug, Kirsten, Kansas City Chiefs, Kansas City, MO. Tel: (816) 920-9300, (888) 99-CHIEFS, FAX: (816) 923-4719, Web Site: www.kcchiefs.com (16)

Krulik, Stephen, MRV Communications, Chatsworth, CA. Tel: (818) 773-0900, FAX: (818) 773-0906, Web Site: www.mrv.com (3)

Krull, Stewart, Atmosphere Proximity, New York, NY. Tel: (212) 827-2500, FAX: (212) 827-2525, E-Mail: andreas.combuechen@atmospherebbdo.com, Web Site: www.atmosphereproximity.com (35)

Krumholz, Margaret, Disc Graphics Inc, Hauppauge, NY. Tel: (631) 234-1400, FAX: (631) 234-1460, E-Mail: info@discgraphics.com, Web Site: www.discgraphics.com (27)

Krupp, Steven, J&H Berge/The Lab Mart, South Plainfield, NJ. Tel: (908) 561-3002, (800) 684-1234, FAX: (908) 561-3002, E-Mail: info@jhberge.com, Web Site: www.jhberge.com (7)

Krutzberg, Keith, Epson America, Long Beach, CA. Tel: (562) 981-3840, (800) 873-7766, FAX: (562) 290-5220, Web Site: www.epson.com (10)

Kruysman, Gretchen, Thomas Moser Cabinetmakers, Freeport, ME. Tel: (207) 865-4519, (800) 708-9041, FAX: (207) 865-6539, E-Mail: freeportshowroom@thosmoser.com, Web Site: www.thosmoser.com (16)

Kruythoff, Kees, Unilever Best Foods, Englewood Cliffs, NJ. Tel: (201) 567-8000, FAX: (201) 871-8257, E-Mail: comments@unilever.com, Web Site: www.unilever.com (16)

Kryl & Co Inc, Chicago, IL. Tel: (312) 961-0928, E-Mail: info@krylandco.com, Web Site: www.krylandco.com (35)

Kryl, Susan, Kryl & Co Inc, Chicago, IL. Tel: (312) 961-0928, E-Mail: info@krylandco.com, Web Site: www.krylandco.com (35)

Krzanich, Brian M., Intel Corp, Santa Clara, CA. Tel: (408) 765-8080, (800) 548-4725, FAX: (408) 765-6187, Web Site: www.intel.com (16)

Kuamoo, Misty, Micro Center, Hilliard, OH. Tel: (614) 850-3675, (800) 634-3478, FAX: (614) 777-2620, E-Mail: csrs@microcenterorder.com, Web Site: www.microcenter.com (3)

Kubic, Joe, The Adcom Group, Cleveland, OH. Tel: (216) 574-9100, FAX: (216) 574-6131, Web Site: www.theadcomgroup.com (35)

Kubicki, Robert J., CTRAC Information Solutions, Strongsville, OH. Tel: (440) 572-1000, FAX: (440) 572-3330, E-Mail: ctrac@ctrac.com, Web Site: www.ctrac.com (22)

Kubis, Thaddeus, NAK Marketing & Communications, New York, NY. Tel: (212) 505-9290, Web Site: www.nakcomm.com (20)

Kubly, Pat, The Swiss Colony Inc, Monroe, WI. Tel: (608) 324-4603, FAX: (608) 328-8735, Web Site: www.swisscolony.com (4)

Kuczer, Ronald, Maverick Ventures Product Line, Chesterfield, MO. Tel: (636) 537-4656, (800) 467-4656, FAX: (636) 537-4657, E-Mail: hang10cd@aol.com, Web Site: www.hang10cd.com (5)

Kudeba, Wendy, The Kidney Foundation of Canada/Greater Ontario Branch, Hamilton, ON Canada. Tel: (800) 414-3484, FAX: (905) 318-8491, E-Mail: kidneyfoundation@bellnet.ca, Web Site: www.kidney.on.ca (1)

Kudelski, Andre, NAGRA USA, San Francisco, CA. Tel: (415) 962-5000, FAX: (415) 962-5300, E-Mail: dtv@nagra.com, Web Site: www.nagra.com (32)

Kuehn, Dr Alfred A., Management Science Associates Inc, Pittsburgh, PA. Tel: (412) 362-2000, (800) MSA-INFO, FAX: (412) 363-5598, E-Mail: info@msa.com, Web Site: www.msa.com (20)

Kuehn, Mary, K-tel International, Golden Valley, MN. Tel: (204) 889-5430, (800) 665-5021, FAX: (612) 559-6803, Web Site: www.ktel.com (16)

Kufner, Robert, Stock Drive Products, New Hyde Park, NY. Tel: (516) 328-3300, (800) 819-8900, FAX: (516) 326-8827, E-Mail: sdp-sisupport@sdp-si.com, Web Site: www.sdp.si.com (5)

Kugel, Moshe, 3 Gen Co, Brooklyn, NY. Tel: (718) 484-4354 (23)

Kugler, Josh, Ifbyphone, Chicago, IL. Tel: (877) 295-5100, (877) 387-7192, Web Site: www.ifbyphone.com (30)

Kugler, Larry, The Millard Group, Lincolnwood, IL. Tel: (847) 674-4100, (800) 339-6876, FAX: (847) 677-0790, E-Mail: sales@millardgroup.com, Web Site: www.millardgroup.com (16)

Kuhlman, Paul, Acme Tools, Grand Forks, ND. Tel: (701) 746-6481, (800) 732-4287, FAX: (701) 746-2857, Web Site: www.acmetools.com (8)

Kuhn, Brent, BKV Inc, Atlanta, GA. Tel: (404) 233-0332, E-Mail: rina.cook@bkv.com, Web Site: www.bkv.com (35)

Kuhn, Paul, Wolters Kluwer Financial Services, Minneapolis, MN. Tel: (612) 656-7700, (800) 552-9408, Web Site: www.wolterskluwerfs.com (14)

Kula, Ken, Eleven Inc, San Francisco, CA. Tel: (415) 707-1111, Web Site: www.eleveninc.com (35)

Kula, Mike, Falcon Products Inc, Newport, TN. Tel: (314) 991-9200, (800) 873-3252, FAX: (314) 991-9227, E-Mail: info@falconproducts.com, Web Site: www.falconproducts.com (16)

Kulczycki, Bill, Patagonia Mail Order Inc, Reno, NV. Tel: (775) 747-1992, (800) 638-6464, FAX: (775) 747-6159, Web Site: www.patagonia.com (2)

Kulick, John, Eckankar, Minneapolis, MN. Tel: (612) 544-3001, (800) 327-5113, FAX: (612) 474-1127, Web Site: www.eckankar.org (17)

Kulikowski, Frederick R, Commercial Federal Bank, Omaha, NE. Tel: (402) 554-9200, FAX: (402) 390-3592 (14)

Kullman, Ellen, Dupont Color Proofing, Wilmington, DE. Tel: (800) 441-7515, FAX: (302) 892-8030, Web Site: www.dupont.com/proofing (27)

Kullman, Ellen, E I DuPont De Nemours & Co, Wilmington, DE. Tel: (302) 774-1000, (800) 441-7515, FAX: (302) 774-7321, Web Site: www.dupont.com (16)

Kulsrud, Zachary, Dental Economics, Tulsa, OK. Tel: (800) 331-4633, E-Mail: christopherp@pennwell.com, Web Site: www.dentaleconomics.com (17)

Kulzer, Tom, AWeber Communications, Chalfont, PA. Tel: (877) 293-2371, Web Site: www.aweber.com (24)

Kuman, Peg, Farm Market iD, Westmont, IL. Tel: (844) 487-6322, E-Mail: sales@farmmarketid.com, Web Site: www.farmmarketid.com (23)

Kuman, Peg, Phoenix Data Processing LLC, Westmont, IL. Tel: (630) 654-4400, FAX: (630) 654-4470, E-Mail: sales@phoenixdataprocessing.com, Web Site: www.phoenixdataprocessing.com (22)

Kumbholz, David J, American Identity, Overland Park, KS. Tel: (913) 319-3100, (800) 848-8028 (33)

Kumbier, Michelle, Harley-Davidson Inc, Milwaukee, WI. Tel: (414) 343-7286, FAX: (414) 343-4806, Web Site: www.harley-davidson.com (12)

Kummer, Lisa, Wilsons Leather, Brooklyn Park, MN. Tel: (763) 391-4000, (866) 305-4704, FAX: (763) 391-4906, E-Mail: customercare@wilsonsleather.com, Web Site: www.wilsonsleather.com (2)

Kump, Gail, Association of American Publishers, Washington, DC. Tel: (202) 347-3375, FAX: (202) 347-3690, E-Mail: info@publishers.org, Web Site: www.publishers.org (1)

Kundahl, Dr. Edward, BusinessCreator Inc, Allentown, PA. Tel: (610) 437-8822, (855) 943-8736, FAX: (484) 709-1851, E-Mail: marketing@businesscreatorplus.com, Web Site: www.businesscreatorplus.com (35)

Kunkel, Gregory. Diversified Investment Advisors, Harrison, NY. Tel: (914) 627-3000, FAX: (914) 627-3280, Web Site: www.divinvest.com (14)

Kuntz, Richard E., Medtronic Inc, Minneapolis, MN. Tel: (763) 514-4000, (800) 328-2518, FAX: (763) 514-4879, Web Site: www.medtronic.com (16)

Kunz, Heidi, Blue Shield Life, San Francisco, CA. Tel: (888) 800-2742, FAX: (800) 329-2742, Web Site: www.blueshieldca.com (15)

Kunze, Mary A., Advanced Concepts Inc, Milwaukee, WI. Tel: (414) 362-9640, FAX: (414) 362-9646, E-Mail: info@advanced-concepts.com, Web Site: www.advanced-concepts.com (22)

Kuo, John W., Varian Medical Systems, Palo Alto, CA. Tel: (650) 493-4000, FAX: (650) 842-5196, Web Site: www.varian.com (9)

Kupchak, Mitchell, The Los Angeles Lakers Inc, El Segundo, CA. Tel: (310) 426-6000, FAX: (310) 426-6110, E-Mail: vlawlor@la-lakers.com, Web Site: www.nba.com/lakers (11)

Kuppens, Robbert, The Boston Consulting Group, New York, NY. Tel: (212) 446-2800 (20)

Kupperman, Dennis, RB Toy Design Inc, Glenview, IL. Tel: (847) 577-5683, FAX: (847) 272-4034, E-Mail: info@rbtoydesign.com, Web Site: www.rbtoy.com (33)

Kurkow, Richard M, SpencerStuart, Chicago, IL. Tel: (312) 822-0088, FAX: (312) 822-0116, Web Site: www.spencerstuart.com (20)

Kurnett, Dierdre, DeLuxe Laboratories Inc, Hollywood, CA. Tel: (323) 462-6171, FAX: (323) 960-7016, E-Mail: steven.vananda@bydeluxe.com, Web Site: www.bydeluxe.com (16)

Kurokawa, Tatsuo, Drug Information Association, Horsham, PA. Tel: (215) 442-6100, FAX: (215) 442-6199, Web Site: www.diahome.org (1)

Kurpiel, Marty, Valid USA Inc, Lisle, IL. Tel: (630) 852-8200, (855) 825-4387, E-Mail: info@validusa.com, Web Site: www.validusa.com (22)

Kurth, Chuck, Art.com, Emeryville, CA. Tel: (510) 879-4700, (800) 952-5592, FAX: (510) 588-3915, E-Mail: support@art.com, Web Site: www.art.com (8)

Kurtz, Brian, Boardroom Inc, Stamford, CT. Tel: (203) 973-5900, FAX: (203) 967-3086, Web Site: www.bottomlinepublications.com (17)

Kurtz, Heidi, Alliance of Nonprofit Mailers, Washington, DC. Tel: (202) 462-5132, FAX: (202) 462-0423, E-Mail: alliance@nonprofitmailers.org, Web Site: www.nonprofitmailers.org (40)

Kurtz, Jill, Our Sunday Visitor Publishing, Huntington, IN. Tel: (260) 356-8400, (800) 348-2440, FAX: (260) 356-8472, E-Mail: athomas@osv.com, Web Site: www.osv.com (17)

Kurtz, Richard, LSSiData, Blue Bell, PA. Tel: (610) 276-4300, (800) 210-9021, FAX: (610) 567-5698, E-Mail: info@lssi.net, Web Site: www.lssidata.com (22)

Kurtzman, Warren, Coleman Research Inc, Morrisville, NC. Tel: (919) 571-0000, FAX: (919) 571-9999, E-Mail: callcoleman@colemaninsights.com, Web Site: www.colemaninsights.com (30)

Kurtzweil, Jerry, Publications International Ltd, Lincolnwood, IL. Tel: (847) 676-3470, (800) 595-8484, FAX: (847) 676-3671, Web Site: www.pubint.com (17)

Kurz, George J., The HoneyBaked Ham Co, Holland, OH. Tel: (419) 724-4267, (866) 492-4267, E-Mail: info@honeybaked.com, Web Site: www.honeybaked.com (4)

Kurzius, Dan, MailChimp, Atlanta, GA. Tel: (678) 999-0141, Web Site: mailchimp.com (24)

Kuse, Allan, RSC The Quality Measurement Co, Evansville, IN. Tel: (812) 425-4562, FAX: (812) 425-2844 (30)

Kushner, Aaron, The Orange County Register, Santa Ana, CA. Tel: (877) 469-7344, E-Mail: customerservice@ocregister.com, Web Site: www.ocregister.com (17)

Kushner, Adam B., National Journal Group, Washington, DC. Tel: (202) 739-8400, (800) 613-6701, FAX: (202) 833-8069, Web Site: www.nationaljournal.com (17)

Kushner, Alexander M., Jasek Enterprises, Westlake Village, CA. Tel: (805) 379-2871, FAX: (805) 379-9839 (20)

Kuster, Bradley S., Continental Western Group, Des Moines, IA. Tel: (515) 473-3000, (800) 533-0303, FAX: (515) 473-3015, Web Site: www.cwgins.com (15)

Kuster, Jeffrey, Cornerstone Brands Inc, West Chester, OH. Tel: (513) 603-1400, Web Site: www.cornerstonebrands.com (5)

Kutasovic, Paul, School of Management, Old Westbury, NY. Tel: (516) 686-1000, (800) 345-NYIT, (800) 345-6948, E-Mail: asknyit@nyit.edu, Web Site: www.nyit.edu (41)

Kutz, Tim, Unisource Worldwide, Inc, Norcross, GA. Tel: (770) 447-9000, (800) 864-7687, FAX: (770) 734-2000, Web Site: www.unisourcelink.com (25)

Kuwait Airways Corp, Fort Lee, NJ. Tel: (201) 582-9222, (800) 4-KUWAIT, FAX: (212) 947-8113, E-Mail: nyc@kuwait-airways.com, Web Site: www.kuwait-airways.com (19)

Kuzins, Matt, Matt & Kumpany Kuzins, Sacramento, CA. Tel: (916) 446-2008, FAX: (916) 446-5302, E-Mail: matt@kuzins.com (1)

Kwak, Soomi, Canadian Business, Toronto, ON Canada. Tel: (416) 596-5100, FAX: (416) 764-1200, Web Site: www.canadianbusiness.com (17)

Kwik-File, Sheboygan, WI. Tel: (763) 572-1980, (800) 822-8037, FAX: (763) 572-0168, Web Site: www.mayline.com (27)

Kwok, Herbert, Time Products International, Del Rio, TX. Tel: (847) 459-8885, FAX: (847) 459-8111, E-Mail: cttpi@aol.com, Web Site: www.tpi2000.com (16)

Kydes, George, CertainSource Inc, Fairfield, CT. Tel: (203) 254-0404, (888) 655-0464, FAX: (203) 254-0411, E-Mail: neil@certainsource.com, Web Site: www.certainsource.com (32)

L

L & E Meridian, Springfield, VA. Tel: (703) 913-0300, (800) 555-1556, FAX: (703) 913-7052, E-Mail: estimating@l-e.com, Web Site: www.l-e.com (21)

L&L Management, Pasadena, CA. Tel: (626) 568-0338, FAX: (626) 568-9165 (16)

L Brands Inc, Columbus, OH. Tel: (614) 415-7000, FAX: (614) 415-7440, Web Site: www.lb.com (16)

L-Com Inc, North Andover, MA. Tel: (978) 682-6936, FAX: (978) 689-9484, Web Site: www.L-com.com (22)

L6 Holdings Corp, Duluth, GA. Tel: (678) 957-0511, FAX: (678) 957-0551 (14)

L3 Virtual Solutions LLC, Marengo, OH. Tel: (740) 625-6535, Web Site: www.l3vs.com (20)

L & D Mail Masters, New Albany, IN. Tel: (812) 981-7161, FAX: (812) 981-7169, E-Mail: info@ldmailmasters.com, Web Site: www.ldmailmasters.com (21)

LCH Direct Inc, Waltham, MA. Tel: (978) 664-2900, FAX: (978) 664-4812, E-Mail: info@lchdirect.com, Web Site: www.lchdirect.com (35)

LGP GEM LTD, New York, NY. Tel: (212) 840-2510, FAX: (212) 302-6182, E-Mail: sales@lgpltd.com, Web Site: www.lgpltd.com (16)

LIM College, New York, NY. Tel: (212) 752-1530, Web Site: www.limcollege.edu (1)

LIMRA International, Windsor, CT. Tel: (860) 688-3358, Web Site: www.limra.com (1)

LKH&S Inc, Chicago, IL. Tel: (312) 595-0200, FAX: (312) 595-0300, E-Mail: lkhs@lkhs.com, Web Site: www.lkhs.com (35)

LLR/Research, Haverhill, MA. Tel: (978) 374-0931, FAX: (978) 374-1008 (38)

LMS Inc, Orlando, FL. Tel: (407) 876-5544, (800) 257-5902, Web Site: lmsonline.com (35)

LN Marketing Associates, Emerald Hills, CA. Tel: (650) 368-7181 (20)

LP Thebault Co, Parsippany, NJ. Tel: (973) 884-1300, FAX: (973) 952-8282, E-Mail: info@earthcolor.com, Web Site: www.earthcolor.com (27)

LS Direct Marketing, Suffern, NY. Tel: (845) 357-1238, E-Mail: info@lsdirect.com, Web Site: www.lsdirect.com (23)

LS Records, Madison, TN. Tel: (615) 868-7171, FAX: (615) 860-7665, E-Mail: ls654@home.com, Web Site: www.cristylane.com (16)

LSC Marketing, Little Rock, AR. Tel: (501) 374-2332, (866) LSC-MKGT, FAX: (501) 372-6570, E-Mail: sales@lscmarketing.com. Web Site: www.lscmarketing.com (28)

LSSiData, Blue Bell, PA. Tel: (610) 276-4300, (800) 210-9021, FAX: (610) 567-5698, E-Mail: info@lssi.net, Web Site: www.lssidata.com (22)

LTD Supply Chain, Downingtown, PA. Tel: (610) 458-3636, FAX: (610) 458-8039, E-Mail: tomc@ltdsupplychain.com, Web Site: www.ltdsupplychain.com (20)

La Penta, George, Weichert Co, Morris Plains, NJ. Tel: (973) 397-8516, Web Site: www.weichert.com (14)

La Bine, Ronald, Premier Print and Services Group Inc, Chicago, IL. Tel: (312) 648-2266, (800) 648-3677, FAX: (312) 648-1361, Web Site: www.premierprint.com (21)

La Forgia, John, Mayo Clinic, Rochester, MN. Tel: (507) 284-2511, Web Site: www.mayoclinic.org (17)

Lab Safety Supply Inc, Janesville, WI. Tel: (608) 754-2345, (800) 356-2855, FAX: (800) 543-9910, Web Site: www.labsafety.com (5)

Laba, Larry, SOAR Inflatables, Healdsburg, CA. Tel: (707) 433-5599, FAX: (707) 433-4499, E-Mail: sales@soar1.com, Web Site: www.soar1.com (11)

Laban, Rick, Gold Medal Hair Products Inc, Farmingdale, NY. Tel: (631) 465-0202, FAX: (631) 465-0207, E-Mail: customerservice@goldmedalhair.com, Web Site: www.goldmedalhair.com (7)

Labberton, Mark, The Fuller Theological Seminary, Pasadena, CA. Tel: (626) 584-5200, (800) 235-2222, FAX: (626) 584-5449, Web Site: www.fuller.edu (16)

Label Colors Inc, Sussex, WI. Tel: (262) 549-1730, (800) 558-2126, FAX: (800) 784-2591, Web Site: www.lauterbachgroup.com (25)

Labels West Inc, Woodinville, WA. Tel: (425) 486-8484, (800) 540-3009, FAX: (425) 486-8488, Web Site: www.labelswest.com (27)

LaBorde, Charles, Vector Marketing Corp, Olean, NY. Tel: (716) 373-6141, (267) 880-1750, FAX: (716) 373-6145, Web Site: www.cutco.com (5)

Labos, Pia, Academic Management Services, Swansea, MA. Tel: (508) 235-2870, (800) 891-4203, FAX: (508) 235-2991, E-Mail: info@amsweb.com, Web Site: www.amsweb.com (14)

Labra, Ana, Saunders Military Insignia, Naples, FL. Tel: (239) 298-8228, (800) 442-3133, FAX: (239) 774-3323, E-Mail: info@saundersinsignia.com, Web Site: www.saundersinsignia.com (6)

Labrake, Mike, Amigo Mobility International Inc, Bridgeport, MI. Tel: (989) 777-0910, (800) 692-6446, FAX: (989) 777-8184, E-Mail: info@myamigo.com, Web Site: www.myamigo.com (16)

LaBree, Lela, PhotoSource International, Osceola, WI. Tel: (715) 248-3800, X27, (800) 223-3860, FAX: (715) 248-3800, E-Mail: info@photosource.com, Web Site: www.photosource.com (38)

Labs, Rick, CL&B Capital Management, Fayetteville, NY. Tel: (315) 637-0915, FAX: (815) 642-9396, E-Mail: webinquiry@clbcm.com, Web Site: www.clbcm.com (35)

The Lacek Group, Minneapolis, MN. Tel: (612) 359-3700, FAX: (612) 359-9395, E-Mail: info@lacek.com, Web Site: www.lacek.com (35)

Lacey, James, MassMutual Financial Group, Springfield, MA. Tel: (413) 788-8411, FAX: (413) 744-8889, E-Mail: name@www.massmutual.com, Web Site: www.massmutual.com (15)

Lachance, Janice R, Special Libraries Association (SLA), Alexandria, VA. Tel: (703) 647-4900, FAX: (703) 647-4901, E-Mail: sla@sla.org, Web Site: www.sla.org (40)

Lachapelle, Sue, Catholic Digest, New London, CT. Tel: (800) 321-0411, E-Mail: catholicdigest@bayardinc.com, Web Site: www.catholicdigest.com (17)

Lachman, Deborah F., Anthem Blue Cross, Westlake Village, CA. Tel: (805) 557-6655, (800) 333-0912, FAX: (805) 557-6872, Web Site: www.bluecrossca.com (15)

Lachnicht, Cheslie, A Caldwell List Co Inc, Norcross, GA. Tel: (770) 662-0255, (800) 241-7425, FAX: (770) 662-0351, E-Mail: guidance@caldwell-list.com, Web Site: www.caldwell-list.com (23)

Lacina, Kim, American Lung Association, Chicago, IL. Tel: (212) 889-3370, (800) 548-8252, FAX: (212) 889-3375, E-Mail: info@alany.org, Web Site: www.lungusa.org (1)

LaCivita, Steven, University of Chicago GSB, Chicago, IL. Tel: (312) 464-8733, E-Mail: exec.ed@chicagobooth.edu, Web Site: www.chicagobooth.edu (1)

Lackey, Doug, Mail Enterprises LLC, Birmingham, AL. Tel: (205) 595-4945, (800) 595-4945, FAX: (205) 595-4943, E-Mail: sswedenburg@mailent.com, Web Site: www.mailent.com (21)

LaCour, John, DMN3, Houston, TX. Tel: (713) 893-4275, (888) 721-0377, E-Mail: sales@dmn3.com, Web Site: www.dmn3.com (35)

LaCrosse Footwear Inc, Portland, OR. Tel: (503) 262-0110, (800) 323-2668, FAX: (503) 262-0115, E-Mail: customerservice@lacrossefootwear.com, Web Site: www.lacrossefootwear.com (16)

Lacy, Stephen M., Meredith Corp, Des Moines, IA. Tel: (515) 284-3000, FAX: (515) 284-2700, Web Site: www.meredith.com (17)

Ladd Associates Inc, San Francisco, CA. Tel: (415) 921-1001, FAX: (415) 921-2311, E-Mail: info@laddassociates.com, Web Site: laddassociates.com (20)

Ladd, Jack W., Ladd Associates Inc, San Francisco, CA. Tel: (415) 921-1001, FAX: (415) 921-2311, E-Mail: info@laddassociates.com, Web Site: laddassociates.com (20)

Ladden, Bernice, Women in Direct Marketing International, New York, NY. Tel: (516) 746-6700, FAX: (516) 294-8141, Web Site: www.wdmi.org (40)

Ladner, Robert, Behavioral Science Research, Coral Gables, FL. Tel: (305) 443-2000, (800) 282-2771, FAX: (305) 448-6825 (30)

Ladouceur, Mark, Drawing Board Inc, Waynesboro, PA. Tel: (301) 739-4487, (800) 527-9530, FAX: (800) 253-1838, E-Mail: customerservice@drawingboard.com, Web Site: www.drawingboard.com (16)

Ladouceur, Mark, Medco Supply Co Inc, Tonawanda, NY. Tel: (716) 743-8400, (800) 556-3326, FAX: (800) 222-1934, E-Mail: sales@medcosupply.com, Web Site: www.medcosupply.com (7)

The LadyBug Co, Berry Creek, CA. Tel: (530) 589-5227 (8)

Laerdal Medical, Wappingers Falls, NY. Tel: (845) 297-7770, FAX: (800) 227-1143, Web Site: www.laerdal.com (34)

LaFemina, Peter, Coastal Hotel Group, Bellevue, WA. Tel: (206) 388-0400, FAX: (206) 388-0401, E-Mail: info@coastalhotel.com, Web Site: www.coastalhotels.com (1)

Laferriere, Leo, Zoom Information Inc, Waltham, MA. Tel: (781) 693-7500, FAX: (781) 693-7510, Web Site: www.zoominfo.com (22)

Lafferty Equipment Manufacturing Inc, North Little Rock, AR. Tel: (501) 851-2820, (800) 999-2820, FAX: (501) 851-3719, (800) 699-3719, E-Mail: webmaster@laffertyequipment.com, Web Site: www.laffertyequipment.com (9)

Lafferty, Alex, Lafferty Equipment Manufacturing Inc, North Little Rock, AR. Tel: (501) 851-2820, (800) 999-2820, FAX: (501) 851-3719, (800) 699-3719, E-Mail: webmaster@laffertyequipment.com, Web Site: www.laffertyequipment.com (9)

Lafferty, Drew, Lafferty Equipment Manufacturing Inc, North Little Rock, AR. Tel: (501) 851-2820, (800) 999-2820, FAX: (501) 851-3719, (800) 699-3719, E-Mail: webmaster@laffertyequipment.com, Web Site: www.laffertyequipment.com (9)

Laffin, Joyce, FLEXcon, Spencer, MA. Tel: (508) 885-8200, Web Site: www.flexcon.com (16)

Lafley, Alan G., The Procter & Gamble Co, Cincinnati, OH. Tel: (513) 983-1100, Web Site: www.pg.com (16)

LaForet, Lou, Spring Global Delivery Solutions, Mississauga, ON Canada. Tel: (905) 678-2770, E-Mail: spring.cs.ca@springglobalmail.com, Web Site: www.spring-gds.com (21)

LaFrance, Nina, Forbes Inc, New York, NY. Tel: (212) 620-1887, (800) 295-0893, Web Site: www.forbes.com (17)

LaFreniere, Edward, The Marlin Company, Wallingford, CT. Tel: (877) 890-9116, Web Site: www.themarlincompany.com (35)

Lage, MAS Paul, Norwood Promotional Products, Clearwater, FL. Tel: (317) 275-2500, (800) 959-9138, FAX: (317) 275-2570, Web Site: www.norwood.com (16)

Lageman, Malia, Cardinal Mailing Services Ltd, Honolulu, HI. Tel: (808) 538-3884, FAX: (808) 521-1419, E-Mail: mail@cardinalservicesltd.com, Web Site: www.cardinalservicesltd.com (28)

Lagerlof, John, Paasche Airbrush Co, Chicago, IL. Tel: (773) 867-9191, FAX: (773) 867-9198, E-Mail: info@paascheairbrush.com, Web Site: www.paascheairbrush.com (10)

Lagerlof, Patricia, Paasche Airbrush Co, Chicago, IL. Tel: (773) 867-9191, FAX: (773) 867-9198, E-Mail: info@paascheairbrush.com, Web Site: www.paascheairbrush.com (10)

Laher, Sahal, Casual Male Retail Group, Canton, MA. Tel: (781) 828-9300, (800) 767-0319, E-Mail: info@casualmale.com, Web Site: www.casualmale.com (2)

Lahey Clinic, Burlington, MA. Tel: (781) 744-5100, Web Site: www.lahey.org (1)

Lahey, John L., Quinnipiac College, Hamden, CT. Tel: (203) 582-8200, (203) 582-8600, (800) 462-1944, FAX: (203) 281-8664, Web Site: www.quinnipiac.edu (41)

Laichas, Nancy J, Direct Selling Education Foundation, Washington, DC. Tel: (202) 452-8866, FAX: (202) 452-9015, E-Mail: info@dsef.org, Web Site: www.dsef.org (40)

Laiken, Thomas, Hygienic Fabrics & Filters Inc, Sheboygan, WI. Tel: (920) 457-7383, (800) 876-2009, FAX: (920) 457-2558, Web Site: www.hyfab.com (16)

Lail, Robert, MarketMakers Group Inc, Wayne, PA. Tel: (610) 254-8924, FAX: (610) 254-9190, E-Mail: rlail@marketmakers.com, Web Site: www.marketmakersgroup.com (29)

Laine, Jimmy, Wakefield Peanut Co, Wakefield, VA. Tel: (757) 899-5481, (800) 803-1309, FAX: (757) 899-7604, Web Site: www.wakefieldpeanutco.com (4)

Lair, Robert G., Oil & Gas Journal, Tulsa, OK. Tel: (918) 835-3161, (800) 331-4463, FAX: (918) 832-9497, Web Site: www.pennwell.com; www.ogj.com (17)

Laird, Cal, Veriad, Brea, CA. Tel: (714) 990-2700, (800) 962-0658, (800) 962-0658, E-Mail: info@veriad.com, Web Site: www.veriad.com (16)

Laitram Machinery, Harahan, LA. Tel: (504) 733-6000, FAX: (504) 733-6111 (16)

LaJeunesse, Jr Raymond J., National Right to Work Legal Defense Foundation, Springfield, VA. Tel: (703) 321-8510, (800) 336-3600, FAX: (703) 321-9613, E-Mail: info@nrtw.org, Web Site: www.nrtw.org (1)

Lajo, Fr. Saturnino, Oblate Missions, San Antonio, TX. Tel: (210) 736-1685, FAX: (210) 736-1314, E-Mail: contact@oblatemissions.org, Web Site: www.oblatemissions.org (1)

Lake County Press Inc, Waukegan, IL. Tel: (847) 336-4333, FAX: (847) 336-5846, Web Site: www.lakecountypress.com (27)

Lake Group Media Inc, Armonk, NY. Tel: (914) 925-2400, FAX: (914) 925-2499, E-Mail: ryan.lake@lakegroupmedia.com, Web Site: www.lakegroupmedia.com (23)

Lake Shore Industries, Erie, PA. Tel: (800) 458-0463, FAX: (814) 453-4293, E-Mail: info@lsisigns.com, Web Site: www.lsisigns.com (16)

Lake, Anthony, UNICEF, New York, NY. Tel: (212) 326-7000, FAX: (212) 887-7465, Web Site: www.unicef.org (1)

Lake, Jeff, Duncan Aviation, Lincoln, NE. Tel: (402) 475-2611, (800) 228-4277, FAX: (402) 475-5541, Web Site: www.duncanaviation.com (16)

Lake, Leslie, Marshall & Swift, Los Angeles, CA. Tel: (213) 683-9000, FAX: (213) 683-9010, Web Site: www.marshallswift.com (17)

Lake, Maddison, Everest Direct Mail & Marketing, Asheville, NC. Tel: (866) 811-1553, E-Mail: info@everestdmm.com, Web Site: www.everestdmm.com (21)

Lake, Marianne, JP Morgan Chase & Co, New York, NY. Tel: (212) 270-6000, E-Mail: jpmcinvestorrelations@jpmchase.com, Web Site: www.jpmorgan.com (14)

Lake, Ryan, Lake Group Media Inc, Armonk, NY. Tel: (914) 925-2400, FAX: (914) 925-2499, E-Mail: ryan.lake@lakegroupmedia.com, Web Site: lakegroupmedia.com (23)

Lake, Steve R., Connecticut Marketing Associates, Wilton, CT. Tel: (203) 761-9556, FAX: (203) 761-9763 (20)

Lakely, Dedra, Dynamic Engineering, Santa Cruz, CA. Tel: (831) 457-8891, FAX: (831) 457-4793, E-Mail: sales@dyneng.com, Web Site: www.dyneng.com (3)

Lakeside Publishing Co LLC, Evanston, IL. Tel: (847) 491-6440, FAX: (847) 491-0459, E-Mail: cs@centurysports.net, Web Site: www.centurysports.net (17)

The Lakeville Journal LLC, Lakeville, CT. Tel: (860) 435-9873, FAX: (860) 435-4802 (37)

Lakewood Products LLC, Suamico, WI. Tel: (920) 361-7717, (800) 872-8458, FAX: (920) 361-7719, E-Mail: info@lakewoodproducts.com, Web Site: www.lakewoodproducts.com (11)

Lakos, Tom, Koeze Co, Grand Rapids, MI. Tel: (800) 555-9688, E-Mail: service@koezedirect.com, Web Site: www.koeze.com (16)

Lakshmanan, Al, COMPITSS Inc, Newbury Park, CA. Tel: (805) 823-2286, E-Mail: info@compitss.com, Web Site: www.compitss.com (22)

Lalji, Firoz, Zones Inc, Auburn, WA. Tel: (253) 205-3000, (800) 408-9663, FAX: (425) 430-3626, E-Mail: corpsales@zones.com, Web Site: www.zones.com (3)

Lalljie, Paul, Neustar Inc, Sterling, VA. Tel: (571) 434-5400, (877) 245-5277, E-Mail: billingsupport@neustar.biz, Web Site: www.neustar.biz (29)

Lally, Eugene F., Dynamic Development Co, Mission Viejo, CA. Tel: (949) 768-5798, E-Mail: antiwear@dynamicdevelopment.com, Web Site: www.dynamicdevelopment.com (12)

Lamar, Craig, Leslie Jordan, Portland, OR. Tel: (503) 295-1987, (800) 935-3343, FAX: (503) 295-0939, E-Mail: ljsales@lesliejordan.com, Web Site: www.lesliejordan.com (2)

Lamb, Anthony, Chem-Tainer Industries Inc, North Babylon, NY. Tel: (631) 661-8300, (800) 275-2436, (800) ASK-CHEM, FAX: (631) 661-8209, E-Mail: sales@chemtainer.com, Web Site: www.chemtainer.com (9)

Lamb, Jerry, CCI Solutions, Olympia, WA. Tel: (360) 943-5378, (800) 426-8664, FAX: (360) 754-1566, (800) 339-TAPE, E-Mail: info@ccisolutions.com, Web Site: www.ccisolutions.com (16)

Lamb, Regan, OTM Partners, Arlington, VA. Tel: (800) 759-2244, Web Site: otmpartners.com (35)

Lamb, Ron, Reynolds & Reynolds Co, Kettering, OH. Tel: (937) 485-2000, (800) 883-3031, FAX: (866) 268-5407, Web Site: www.reyrey.com (22)

Lambert, Alan, GENESYS Sampling Systems, Horsham, PA. Tel: (215) 653-7100, (800) 336-7674, FAX: (215) 653-7115, E-Mail: alambert@m-s-g.com, Web Site: www.m-s-g.com (30)

Lambert, Dean, Homesteaders Life Co, West Des Moines, IA. Tel: (515) 440-7777, (800) 477-3633, E-Mail: service@homesteaderslife.com, Web Site: www.homesteaderslife.com (15)

Lambert, Robert, Belmont University, Nashville, TN. Tel: (615) 460-6000, FAX: (615) 460-6455, Web Site: www.belmont.edu (41)

Lamel, Ira J., Jason Natural Personal Care Products, Boulder, CO. Tel: (88) 659-7730, Web Site: www.jason-natural.com (7)

Lamere, Eva, Austin & Williams, Hauppauge, NY. Tel: (631) 938-2279, FAX: (212) 434-7022, E-Mail: info@austin-williams.com, Web Site: www.austin-williams.com (35)

Laminex Inc, Fort Mill, SC. Tel: (704) 679-4170, (800) 438-8850, FAX: (704) 679-8453, Web Site: www.laminex.com (16)

Lamirand, Jim, NRS, Decatur, TX. Tel: (940) 627-3949, Web Site: www.nrsworld.com (11)

Lamkin Corp, San Diego, CA. Tel: (619) 661-7090, (800) 642-7755, FAX: (619) 661-0014, E-Mail: info@lamkingrips.com, Web Site: www.lamkingrips.com (11)

Lamkin, Bob, Lamkin Corp, San Diego, CA. Tel: (619) 661-7090, (800) 642-7755, FAX: (619) 661-0014, E-Mail: info@lamkingrips.com, Web Site: www.lamkingrips.com (11)

Lammers, Jennifer, RBC Funds, Milwaukee, WI. Tel: (800) 422-2766, Web Site: us.rbcgam.com (14)

Lamond, Eric, Soitenly Stooges, Glendale, CA. Tel: (818) 543-0778, (800) 543-0778, FAX: (818) 543-0779, E-Mail: custserv@threestooges.com, Web Site: www.soitenlystooges.com (6)

Lamontagne, Lark, L3 Virtual Solutions LLC, Marengo, OH. Tel: (740) 625-6535, Web Site: www.l3vs.com (20)

Lampariello, Vincent, Maison Glass Delicacies, Cold Spring, NY. Tel: (212) 755-3316, (800) 822-5564, E-Mail: info@maisonglass.com, Web Site: www.maisonglass.com (4)

Lamparter, William, PrintCom Consulting Group, Waxhaw, NC. Tel: (704) 843-5350, FAX: (704) 843-5352, E-Mail: printcom@aol.com (20)

Lampert, Edward J., Sears Home Improvement Products & Services, Hoffman Estates, IL. Tel: (800) 424-2047, Web Site: www.searshomeservices.com (16)

Lampert, Edward S., Sears, Roebuck & Co, Hoffman Estates, IL. Tel: (847) 286-2500, FAX: (847) 286-7829, Web Site: www.sears.com (16)

Lan, Erlene, Mountain West Supply Co, Scottsdale, AZ. Tel: (602) 971-1200, (800) 528-6169, FAX: (602) 996-5077 (3)

Lancaster, Ron, Pearson VUE, Bloomington, MN. Tel: (952) 681-3000, Web Site: home.pearsonvue.com (17)

Lancer Insurance Co, Long Beach, NY. Tel: (516) 431-4441, (800) 782-8902, FAX: (516) 889-5111, E-Mail: roneill@lancer-ins.com, Web Site: www.lancer-ins.com (15)

Lancer Label, Omaha, NE. Tel: (402) 390-9119, (800) 228-7074, FAX: (800) 344-9456, E-Mail: customerservice@lancerlabel.com, Web Site: www.lancerlabel.com (27)

Lancino, Kristin, Music Sales Corp, New York, NY. Tel: (212) 254-2100, FAX: (212) 254-2013, E-Mail: info@musicsales.com, Web Site: www.musicsales.com (17)

Land O' Lakes Inc, Arden Hills, MN. Tel: (651) 481-2222, (800) 328-9680, FAX: (651) 481-2000, Web Site: www.landolakesinc.com (16)

LandaJob, Kansas City, MO. Tel: (816) 523-1881, (800) 931-8806, FAX: (816) 523-1876, E-Mail: adstaff@landajobnow.com, Web Site: www.landajobnow.com (20)

Landauer Corp, Urbandale, IA. Tel: (515) 287-2144, (800) 557-2144, FAX: (515) 276-5102, E-Mail: info@landauercorp.com, Web Site: www.landauercorp.com (17)

Landauer, Jeramy, Landauer Corp, Urbandale, IA. Tel: (515) 287-2144, (800) 557-2144, FAX: (515) 276-5102, E-Mail: info@landauercorp.com, Web Site: www.landauercorp.com (17)

Landino, Anita, Health Alliance Plan, Detroit, MI. Tel: (248) 443-1075, FAX: (248) 443-8851, E-Mail: alandin1@hapcorp.org, Web Site: www.hapcorp.org (15)

Landis, Clint, Frontier Natural Products Co-op, Norway, IA. Tel: (800) 669-3275, FAX: (800) 717-4372, E-Mail: info@frontiercoop.com, Web Site: www.frontiercoop.com (7)

Landmark Communications Inc, Alpharetta, GA. Tel: (770) 813-1000, Web Site: www.landmarkcommunications.net (17)

Landmark Graphics Corp, Houston, TX. Tel: (713) 839-2000, FAX: (713) 839-2015, Web Site: www.landmarksoftware.com (16)

Landolt, Mark, The Marketing Store, Chicago, IL. Tel: (312) 614-1400, Web Site: www.tmsw.com (35)

Landreth, Ron, Bromley Communications, San Antonio, TX. Tel: (210) 244-2000, E-Mail: ernest.bromley@bromley.biz, Web Site: bromley.biz (35)

Landrum, Kyle, Exhibitrac Direct Marketing, Las Vegas, NV. Tel: (702) 824-9651, (866) 988-6601, FAX: (702) 824-9376, E-Mail: info@exhibitrac.com, Web Site: www.exhibitrac.com (23)

Landscape Forms Inc, Kalamazoo, MI. Tel: (616) 381-0490, (800) 430-6209, FAX: (616) 381-3455, E-Mail: specify@landscapeforms.com, Web Site: www.landscapeforms.com (16)

Lane, Jamie, Wpromote Inc, El Segundo, CA. Tel: (310) 421-4844, Web Site: www.wpromote.com (30)

Lane, Scott, Farrow Logistics, Windsor, ON Canada. Tel: (844) 532-7769, E-Mail: info@farrowlogistics.com, Web Site: www.farrowlogistics.com (28)

Lanese, Michael, ClearSaleing Inc, Columbus, OH. Tel: (614) 448-2688, (800) 592-0463, Web Site: www.clearsaleing.com (16)

Laney, Herbert, Spilsbury Puzzle Co, Chicago, IL. Tel: (800) 722-1760, FAX: (630) 575-0857, E-Mail: service@spilsbury.com, Web Site: www.spilsbury.com (11)

Lang, Holly, Insurance Publications Inc, Overland Park, KS. Tel: (913) 383-9191, (800) 762-3387, FAX: (913) 383-1247, E-Mail: brokerwrld@primary.net, Web Site: www.brokerworldmag.com (17)

Lang, Jim, Imagination Works, Trumbull, CT. Tel: (203) 377-1747, FAX: (203) 377-7401, E-Mail: jim@imaginationworks.net, Web Site: www.imaginationworks.net (20)

Lang, John, Epson America, Long Beach, CA. Tel: (562) 981-3840, (800) 873-7766, FAX: (562) 290-5220, Web Site: www.epson.com (10)

Lang, Laura, Time Inc, New York, NY. Tel: (212) 522-1212, Web Site: www.timeinc.com (17)

Lang, Sharon, Dharma Trading Co, Petaluma, CA. Tel: (415) 456-1211, (800) 542-5227, FAX: (415) 456-8747, E-Mail: service@dharmatrading.com, Web Site: www.dharmatrading.com (2)

Langdon, John J., Pfaelzer Brothers, Maumee, OH. Tel: (419) 893-7611, (800) 345-9290, FAX: (419) 893-0164, Web Site: www.phaelzerbrothers.com (16)

Lange, Don, Cornerstone Group of Companies, Toronto, ON Canada. Tel: (416) 932-9555, FAX: (416) 932-9566, E-Mail: info@cstonecanada.com, Web Site: www.cstonecanada.com (22)

Lange, Mark, CVT Production Inc, Granger, IN. Tel: (574) 247-0647, Web Site: www.destinationfitness.com (16)

Langel, Sharon, Gerber Life Insurance Co, White Plains, NY. Tel: (914) 272-4000, (800) 704-2180, FAX: (914) 272-4099, Web Site: www.gerberlife.com (15)

Langevin Learning Services, Ottawa, ON Canada. Tel: (613) 288-3064, (800) 223-2209, Web Site: www.langevin.com (40)

Langevin, Erin, Langevin Learning Services, Ottawa, ON Canada. Tel: (613) 288-3064, (800) 223-2209, Web Site: www.langevin.com (40)

Langhoff, Linda, Dex Direct Marketing, Lone Tree, CO. Tel: (800) 999-4630, Web Site: www.dexlist.com (31)

Langhorne, Andrew, iMarketing Solutions Group Inc, Milwaukee, WI. Tel: (414) 224-0701, (800) 879-0076, FAX: (414) 224-0943, Web Site: imarketingsolutionsgroup.com (29)

Langlois, Ken, Collegiate Cap & Gown, Champaign, IL. Tel: (217) 351-9500, FAX: (217) 351-9214, Web Site: www.herff-jones.com (16)

Langon, Tom, The Bil-Ray Aluminum Siding Corp of Queens Inc, New Hyde Park, NY. Tel: (516) 616-4200, (800) 474-4415, FAX: (516) 616-4030, Web Site: www.homeclub.com (16)

Langro, Maryanne, Hofstra University, Hempstead, NY. Tel: (516) 463-7200, FAX: (516) 463-4833, E-Mail: ce@hofstra.edu, Web Site: www.hofstra.edu/Academics/CE (41)

Langstaff, Amori, Invenda Corp, Bethesda, MD. Tel: (240) 333-6111, E-Mail: sales@invenda.com, Web Site: www.invenda.com (32)

Langston, Jen, American Name Services Inc, Orem, UT. Tel: (801) 235-8061, (800) 434-1851, FAX: (801) 764-0613, E-Mail: sales@americannameservices.com, Web Site: www.americannameservices.com (23)

LanguageLine Solutions, Monterey, CA. Tel: (800) 752-6096, E-Mail: customercare@languageline.com, Web Site: www.languageline.com (29)

Lanman, Mike, MCI Communications Services Inc, Basking Ridge, NJ. Tel: (877) 297-7816, Web Site: www.mci.com (16)

Lanmark360 Inc, West Long Branch, NJ. Tel: (732) 389-4500, Web Site: www.lanmark360.com (35)

Lanning, Rebecca, American Association of University Women, Washington, DC. Tel: (202) 785-7700, FAX: (202) 872-1425, E-Mail: connect@aauw.org, Web Site: www.aauw.org (1)

Lannon, Larry, Telephony, Chicago, IL. Tel: (312) 595-1080, (800) 458-0479, FAX: (312) 595-0295, Web Site: www.internettelephony.com (17)

Lansing, John, Scripps Networks Interactive Inc, Knoxville, TN. Tel: (865) 560-2700, Web Site: scrippsnetworksinteractive.com (17)

Lant, Jeffrey, Jeffrey Lant Associates Inc, Cambridge, MA. Tel: (617) 547-6372, FAX: (617) 547-0061, E-Mail: drjlant@worldprofit.com, Web Site: www.thejeffreylanttrust.org (5)

Lant, Jeffrey, Sure-Fire Business Success Catalog, Cambridge, MA. Tel: (617) 547-6372, FAX: (617) 547-0061, E-Mail: drjlant@worldprofit.com, Web Site: www.worldprofit.com (17)

Lant, Jim, Turtle Bay Management Co Inc, Virginia Beach, VA. Tel: (757) 422-2760, FAX: (757) 422-1434, E-Mail: jimlant@turtlebaymanagement.com, Web Site: www.turtlebaymanagement.com (20)

Lantos, Phyllis R. F., New York-Presbyterian/Columbia University Medical Center, New York, NY. Tel: (212) 305-2500, FAX: (212) 305-8023, Web Site: www.nyp.org (16)

Lanzi, Nickolas, Direct Choice Inc, Wayne, PA. Tel: (610) 995-8201, (866) 995-2111, E-Mail: hello@directchoice.com, Web Site: www.directchoiceinc.com (35)

Lapedes, Richard, Lion Apparel, Dayton, OH. Tel: (937) 898-1949, (800) 548-6614, FAX: (937) 913-5667, Web Site: www.lionprotects.com (2)

LaPierre, Jr. Wayne R., National Rifle Association of America, Fairfax, VA. Tel: (703) 267-1000, (800) 672-3888, FAX: (703) 267-3957, E-Mail: nra.contact@nra.org, Web Site: www.nra.org (1)

Lapin, Phil, Falcon Safety Products, Branchburg, NJ. Tel: (908) 707-4900, FAX: (908) 707-8855, Web Site: www.falconsafety.com (16)

Laplink Software Inc, Bellevue, WA. Tel: (425) 952-6000, (800) 527-5465, FAX: (425) 952-6002, E-Mail: marketing@laplink.com, Web Site: www.laplink.com (3)

LaPlume, Joseph, Domestic Bank, Providence, RI. Tel: (401) 943-1600, (800) 566-6600, FAX: (401) 943-6708, Web Site: www.domesticbank.com (14)

LaPointe, Bob, INC Magazine, New York, NY. Tel: (212) 389-5377, FAX: (617) 248-8090, E-Mail: mail@inc.com, Web Site: www.inc.com (17)

Lapointe, Bruce, Amateur Electronic Supply LLC, Milwaukee, WI. Tel: (414) 558-0333, (800) 558-0411, FAX: (414) 358-3337, Web Site: www.aesham.com (16)

LaPreferida Inc, Chicago, IL. Tel: (773) 254-7200, (800) 621-5422, FAX: (773) 254-8546, Web Site: www.lapreferida.com (4)

Laran Communications Inc, Winfield, IL. Tel: (630) 690-2141, FAX: (630) 690-2143, Web Site: www.web-ads.com (16)

Lardy, Gary, IntelliQuote Insurance Services, El Dorado Hills, CA. Tel: (800) 543-3467, Web Site: www.intelliquote.com (15)

Lareau, Brad, Color Film Media Group LLC, Norwalk, CT. Tel: (203) 202-2930, E-Mail: info@itownstore.com, Web Site: www.itownstore.com (32)

Largiader, Jeff, Lifeboat Distribution, Shrewsbury, NJ. Tel: (732) 389-8950, FAX: (732) 389-9227, Web Site: www.programmersparadise.com (16)

Lariviere, Richard, The Field Museum, Chicago, IL. Tel: (312) 665-7600, FAX: (312) 665-7601, E-Mail: events@fieldmuseum.org, Web Site: www.fieldmuseum.org (1)

Lark in the Morning, Mendocino, CA. Tel: (707) 964-5569, FAX: (707) 964-1979, E-Mail: info@larkinam.com, Web Site: www.larkinthemorning.com (5)

Larkin, Edward, Speakers Guild Inc, Sandwich, MA. Tel: (508) 888-6702, (800) 343-4530, FAX: (508) 888-6771, E-Mail: info@speakersguild.com, Web Site: www.speakersguild.com (16)

Larkwood Group LLC, Oakland, CA. Tel: (510) 444-7766 (1)

Larlee, Dan, Harland Financial Solutions Inc, Lake Mary, FL. Tel: (407) 804-6600, (800) 815-5592, FAX: (407) 829-6702, Web Site: www.harlandfinancialsolutions.com (16)

Larmon, Patrick, Bunzl Distribution USA, Inc, Saint Louis, MO. Tel: (314) 997-5959, (888) 997-5959, FAX: (314) 997-1405, Web Site: www.bunzldistribution.com (16)

Laroche, Emmanuel, Symrise, Teterboro, NJ. Tel: (201) 288-3200, FAX: (201) 462-2200, Web Site: www.symrise.com (7)

Larrauri, Nicole, The EGC Group, Melville, NY. Tel: (516) 935-4944, FAX: (516) 935-7030, E-Mail: contact@egcgroup.com, Web Site: www.egcgroup.com (35)

Larrick, Pam, Javelin Marketing Group, Irving, TX. Tel: (972) 443-7000, FAX: (972) 443-7194, E-Mail: info@javelin.mg, Web Site: www.javelin.mg (30)

Larrimore, Randall W., United Stationers, Deerfield, IL. Tel: (847) 627-7000, FAX: (847) 647-7001, Web Site: www.unitedstationers.com (25)

Larsen, Beth, Thrivent Financial for Lutherans, Appleton, WI. Tel: (920) 734-5721, (800) 847-4836, FAX: (920) 730-4781, E-Mail: mail@thrivent.com, Web Site: www.thrivent.com (14)

Larsen, Edward, Talbots, Hingham, MA. Tel: (781) 749-7600, (800) 825-2687, FAX: (781) 741-4369, Web Site: www.talbots.com (2)

Larson, Aaron M., Continental Western Group, Des Moines, IA. Tel: (515) 473-3000, (800) 533-0303, FAX: (515) 473-3015, Web Site: www.cwgins.com (15)

Larson, Andy, Boelter + Lincoln Marketing Communications, Milwaukee, WI. Tel: (414) 271-0101, FAX: (414) 271-1436, E-Mail: jbrzeski@boelterlincoln.com, Web Site: boelterlincoln.com (35)

Larson, Chris, Ligonier Ministries, Sanford, FL. Tel: (407) 333-4244, (800) 435-4343, FAX: (407) 333-4377, Web Site: www.ligonier.org (5)

Larson, Dave, Brooks Sports Inc, Seattle, WA. Tel: (425) 402-1632, (800) 227-6657, FAX: (425) 489-1975, Web Site: www.brooksrunning.com (16)

Larson, David C., Deere & Co, Moline, IL. Tel: (309) 765-8000, FAX: (309) 748-0114, Web Site: www.deere.com (16)

Larson, David, Taymark Inc, White Bear Lake, MN. Tel: (651) 426-1667, (800) 479-2043, FAX: (651) 426-0275, Web Site: www.taymarkinc.com (1)

Larson, Esq. Gloria Cordes, Bentley University, Waltham, MA. Tel: (781) 891-2473, E-Mail: execed@bentley.edu, Web Site: www.bentley.edu (13)

Larson, John, Escort Inc, West Chester, OH. Tel: (513) 870-8500, (800) 964-3138, FAX: (513) 870-8509, E-Mail: sales@escortradar.com, Web Site: www.escortradar.com (14)

Larson, John, NGL Insurance Group, Madison, WI. Tel: (608) 257-5611, (800) 548-2962, FAX: (608) 257-9340, Web Site: www.nglic.com (15)

Larson, Rich, United Air Specialists Inc, Cincinnati, OH. Tel: (513) 891-0400, (800) 992-4422, FAX: (513) 891-4882, E-Mail: uas@uasinc.com, Web Site: www.uasinc.com (16)

Larson, Scott, Strategic Marketing Services, Eagan, MN. Tel: (651) 456-0100, E-Mail: sms@fishnet.com (33)

Larson, Timothy M., Jostens, Inc, Minneapolis, MN. Tel: (952) 830-3300, FAX: (952) 830-3293, Web Site: www.jostens.com (16)

Larson, Todd, Dow Jones & Co, Princeton, NJ. Tel: (609) 520-4000, FAX: (212) 416-4348, Web Site: www.dowjones.com/corp/index.html (17)

Larsson, Stefan, Polo Ralph Lauren, New York, NY. Tel: (212) 813-7868, (800) 377-7656, Web Site: www.ralphlauren.com (2)

LaRue, Jack, Thomson Tax & Accounting, Dexter, MI. Tel: (800) 968-8900, FAX: (734) 426-3750, E-Mail: jack.larue@thomson.com, Web Site: www.cs.thomson.com (22)

LaRue, Keri, Catalyst Marketing Group, Rocklin, CA. Tel: (916) 218-6066, E-Mail: info@catalystmarketinggroup.com, Web Site: www.catalystmarketinggroup.com (35)

Las Vegas Review Journal, Las Vegas, NV. Tel: (702) 383-0211, FAX: (702) 383-4646, Web Site: www.lvrj.com (17)

Lascano, Gina, Naturmed, Camp Verde, AZ. Tel: (928) 567-5175, (800) 720-1245, Web Site: www.ivlproducts.com (7)

Laschinger, Mary, xpedx, Loveland, OH. Tel: (513) 965-2900, FAX: (513) 965-2849, Web Site: www.xpedx.com (25)

Laser Label Technologies Inc, Stow, OH. Tel: (800) 882-4050, FAX: (800) 395-4721, E-Mail: sales@lltproducts.com, Web Site: www.lltproducts.com (10)

Lasermax Roll Systems, Billerica, MA. Tel: (978) 608-0500, FAX: (978) 608-0558, Web Site: www.lasermaxroll.com (27)

Lasky, William J., JLG Industries Inc, McConnellsburg, PA. Tel: (717) 485-5161, (877) JLG-SELL, FAX: (717) 485-6417, E-Mail: comments@jlg.com, Web Site: www.jlg.com (16)

Lassin, Gary, Harriet Carter Gifts Inc, Montgomeryville, PA. Tel: (215) 361-5100, FAX: (215) 361-1127, Web Site: www.harrietcarter.com (6)

Lassin, Ronald P., Harriet Carter Gifts Inc, Montgomeryville, PA. Tel: (215) 361-5100, FAX: (215) 361-1127, Web Site: www.harrietcarter.com (6)

Lassus, Don, WorleyParsons, Reading, PA. Tel: (610) 855-2000, FAX: (610) 885-2001, Web Site: www.worleyparsons.com (16)

Last, Ray, At Last Naturals, North Salem, NY. Tel: (914) 747-3599, (800) 527-8123, FAX: (914) 747-3791, E-Mail: info@atlastnaturals.com, Web Site: www.atlastnaturals.com (7)

Last, Zane, At Last Naturals, North Salem, NY. Tel: (914) 747-3599, (800) 527-8123, FAX: (914) 747-3791, E-Mail: info@atlastnaturals.com, Web Site: www.atlastnaturals.com (7)

Laster, Larry J., Intergraph Corp, Madison, AL. Tel: (256) 730-2000, (800) 345-4856, FAX: (256) 730-2048, Web Site: www.intergraph.com (16)

Latella, George, Beacon Marketing Group, Smithville, NJ. Tel: (609) 677-1776, FAX: (609) 677-1777, Web Site: www.beaconmktg.com (35)

Latest Products Corp, Woodbury, NY. Tel: (516) 367-4700, (800) 288-3547, FAX: (516) 367-4714, E-Mail: lpcorp@aol.com, Web Site: www.latestproducts.net (7)

Lathem Time Corp, Atlanta, GA. Tel: (404) 691-0400, (800) 241-4990, FAX: (404) 696-6048, Web Site: www.lathem.com (16)

Lathem, William, Lathem Time Corp, Atlanta, GA. Tel: (404) 691-0400, (800) 241-4990, FAX: (404) 696-6048, Web Site: www.lathem.com (16)

Latimer, Lisa, Helman Group Ltd, Oxnard, CA. Tel: (805) 487-7772, FAX: (805) 487-9975, E-Mail: barryh@helmangroup.com, Web Site: www.helmangroup.com (16)

Latimer, Wallace, Edmund Optics Inc, Barrington, NJ. Tel: (856) 573-6250, (800) 363-1992, FAX: (856) 573-6295, E-Mail: sales@edmundoptic.com, Web Site: www.edmundoptics.com (9)

Latin Force Group LLC, Miami, FL. Tel: (305) 860-1460, FAX: (305) 860-6161, Web Site: www. latinforce.com (22)

Latin-Pak, Chesterfield, MO. Tel: (636) 536-5344, (800) 625-4283, FAX: (636) 536-9456, E-Mail: latinpak@latinpak.com, Web Site: www.latinpak. com (35)

Latko, Chris, Webb Designs Inc, El Cajon, CA. Tel: (619) 596-6400, (800) 262-9322, FAX: (619) 596-4511, E-Mail: awebb@webbshade.com, Web Site: www.webbshade.com (16)

LaToure, Jonna, Aviva USA Corp, Des Moines, IA. Tel: (515) 362-3600, FAX: (800) 531-0038, Web Site: www.avivausa.com (14)

Latzen, Lorrie, Dataline Inc, Princeton, NJ. Tel: (609) 452-6014, FAX: (609) 951-0025, E-Mail: psobel@ datalinedata.com, Web Site: datalinedata.com (23)

Lauder, Aerin, Estee Lauder Inc, New York, NY. Tel: (212) 572-4200, FAX: (212) 893-7782, Web Site: www.esteelauder.com (16)

Lauder, William, Estee Lauder Inc, New York, NY. Tel: (212) 572-4200, FAX: (212) 893-7782, Web Site: www.esteelauder.com (16)

Laughlin Associates Inc, Carson City, NV. Tel: (775) 883-8484, (888) 273-8152, FAX: (775) 883-4874 (16)

Laughlin Constable, Chicago, IL. Tel: (312) 422-5900, FAX: (312) 422-5901, Web Site: www.laughlin.com (35)

Laughlin, Lewis E., Laughlin Associates Inc, Carson City, NV. Tel: (775) 883-8484, (888) 273-8152, FAX: (775) 883-4874 (16)

Laughlin, Steve, Laughlin Constable, Chicago, IL. Tel: (312) 422-5900, FAX: (312) 422-5901, Web Site: www.laughlin.com (35)

Laumeister, Bruce, CTC Corp, Bennington, VT. Tel: (802) 442-6371, FAX: (802) 442-8526 (16)

Laura, Timothy, On-Demand Mail Services, Auburn Hills, MI. Tel: (888) 954-6245, Web Site: www. odmailservices.com (28)

Laurello, David J., Stratus Technologies, Maynard, MA. Tel: (978) 461-7000, (800) 787-2887, FAX: (978) 461-3670, Web Site: www.stratus.com (16)

Lauren, Ralph, Polo Ralph Lauren, New York, NY. Tel: (212) 813-7868, (800) 377-7656, Web Site: www. ralphlauren.com (2)

Laurent, Louie, ZLR Ignition, Des Moines, IA. Tel: (515) 244-4456, FAX: (515) 244-5749, Web Site: www.zlrignition.com (35)

Lauridsen, Jeff, Direct One Inc, Winter Park, FL. Tel: (407) 673-4500, FAX: (407) 673-4501, E-Mail: wariagno@directoneinc.com, Web Site: www. directoneinc.com (28)

Lautenbach, Marc B, Pitney Bowes, Stamford, CT. Tel: (203) 356-5000, (800) MR-BOWES, Web Site: www.pitneybowes.com (10)

Lautenschlager, DVM Craig, Pine Castle Animal Hospital, Orlando, FL. Tel: (407) 855-5010 (16)

Lauterbach, Shane, Label Colors Inc, Sussex, WI. Tel: (262) 549-1730, (800) 558-2126, FAX: (800) 784-2591, Web Site: www.lauterbachgroup.com (25)

Lautman Maska Neill & Co, Washington, DC. Tel: (202) 296-9660, Web Site: www.lautmandc.com (1)

Lautt, Larry, Crest Healthcare Supply, Dassel, MN. Tel: (800) 328-8908, (800) 369-9207, Web Site: www. cresthealthcare.com (16)

Lautzenhiser, Gary G., Aristokraft Inc, Jasper, IN. Tel: (812) 482-2527, FAX: (812) 482-9872, Web Site: www.aristokraft.com (16)

Laux, Don, Medco Supply Co Inc, Tonawanda, NY. Tel: (716) 743-8400, (800) 556-3326, FAX: (800) 222-1934, E-Mail: sales@medcosupply.com, Web Site: www.medcosupply.com (7)

Laux, Steven A., The Fort Group, Ridgefield Park, NJ. Tel: (201) 445-0202, FAX: (201) 445-0626, E-Mail: info@fortgroupinc.com, Web Site: www. fortgroupinc.com (35)

LaVangie, Keith, Infotrends Inc, Weymouth, MA. Tel: (781) 616-2100, FAX: (781) 616-2121, E-Mail: info@infotrends.com, Web Site: www.infotrends. com (35)

Lavelle, Patrick M., Audiovox, Hauppauge, NY. Tel: (631) 436-6550, FAX: (631) 273-5939, Web Site: www.voxxintl.com (16)

Laven & Loeb Inc, Beachwood, OH. Tel: (216) 291-3483, (623) 217-2101, E-Mail: alaven@ lavenandloeb.com; vtaylor@lavenandloeb.com, Web Site: www.lavenandloeb.com (20)

Laven, Ava, Laven & Loeb Inc, Beachwood, OH. Tel: (216) 291-3483, (623) 217-2101, E-Mail: alaven@ lavenandloeb.com; vtaylor@lavenandloeb.com, Web Site: www.lavenandloeb.com (20)

Laven, Marc, The Gymboree Corp, San Francisco, CA. Tel: (877) 449-6932, Web Site: www.gymboree. com (2)

Laver, Scott B., Xpressdocs, Fort Worth, TX. Tel: (817) 870-4601, (866) 977-3627, FAX: (817) 870-1205, Web Site: www.xpressdocs.com (27)

Lavey, John, Hammock Publishing Inc, Nashville, TN. Tel: (615) 690-3400, FAX: (615) 690-3401, E-Mail: info@hammock.com, Web Site: www.hammock. com (17)

Lavoie, Daniel, The Hartford Financial Services Inc, Southington, CT. Tel: (860) 547-5000, (860) 843-8070, FAX: (860) 547-2680, Web Site: www. thehartford.com (15)

The Law Offices of James Sokolove, Wellesley Hills, MA. Tel: (617) 742-0696, Web Site: www. jimsokolove.com (14)

Richard Law, Deer Park, NY. Tel: (917) 267-8293 (20)

Law, Howard W., Sporty's Preferred Living, Batavia, OH. Tel: (513) 735-9000, (800) 776-7897, FAX: (800) 543-8633, E-Mail: csmgr@sportys.com, Web Site: www.sportys.com (5)

Law, Merry, WorldVu LLC, Baltimore, MD. Tel: (410) 522-4223, FAX: (410) 522-4233, E-Mail: info@ worldvu.com, Web Site: www.worldvu.com (17)

Lawce, Rich, MSC Metalworking, Melville, NY. Tel: (516) 812-2000, (800) 521-9520, E-Mail: inquiry@ rutlandtool.com, Web Site: www.rutlandtool.com (34)

Lawhorn, Charlie, Stibo Systems, Kennesaw, GA. Tel: (770) 425-3282, FAX: (770) 425-3012, Web Site: www.stibocatalog.com (22)

Lawitzen, Bruce, First of Omaha Merchant Processing, Omaha, NE. Tel: (402) 341-0500, (800) 228-2443 (20)

Lawler, Bette, American Institute of Chemical Engineers, New York, NY. Tel: (203) 702-7660, (800) 242-4363, FAX: (203) 775-5177, E-Mail: xpress@ aiche.org, Web Site: www.aiche.org (1)

Lawler, Don, Thomas Printworks, Houston, TX. Tel: (832) 201-2000, (800) 656-8883, FAX: (832) 201-2001, E-Mail: info@seebridgemedia.com, Web Site: www.thomasprintworks.com (21)

Lawlor, Janet, Licensing Industry Merchandisers' Association (LIMA), New York, NY. Tel: (212) 244-1944, FAX: (212) 563-6552, E-Mail: info@ licensing.org, Web Site: www.licensing.org (40)

Lawlor, John, Vestcom International Inc, Little Rock, AR. Tel: (501) 663-0100, (800) 264-0965, E-Mail: sales@vestcom.com, Web Site: vestcom.com (31)

Lawn Doctor Inc, Holmdel, NJ. Tel: (732) 946-0029, (800) 631-5660, FAX: (732) 946-9089, Web Site: www.lawndoctor.com (16)

Lawrence Direct Marketing Inc, Warrenton, VA. Tel: (540) 349-9278, FAX: (540) 347-7885, E-Mail: james@lawrencedirect.com, Web Site: www. lawrencedirect.com (21)

Lawrence, Bill, BannerDirect, Westhampton Beach, NY. Tel: (212) 858-9883, E-Mail: info@ bannerdirect.com, Web Site: www.bannerdirect.com (35)

Lawrence, Daren, McFeely's Square Drive Screws, Madison, WI. Tel: (434) 846-2729, (800) 443-7937, FAX: (804) 847-7136, E-Mail: tech@mcfeelys.com, Web Site: www.mcfeelys.com (16)

Lawrence, David, National Pecan Co, Frisco, TX. Tel: (469) 353-2993, E-Mail: info@nationalpecan.com, Web Site: www.nationalpecan.com (4)

Lawrence, E. Michael, Lawrence Direct Marketing Inc, Warrenton, VA. Tel: (540) 349-9278, FAX: (540) 347-7885, E-Mail: james@lawrencedirect.com, Web Site: www.lawrencedirect.com (21)

Lawrence, Gary, Lift Outreach, Richland Hills, TX. Tel: (817) 658-2980 (1)

Lawrence, James, Lawrence Direct Marketing Inc, Warrenton, VA. Tel: (540) 349-9278, FAX: (540) 347-7885, E-Mail: james@lawrencedirect.com, Web Site: www.lawrencedirect.com (21)

Lawrence, Pat, Galloway Farms, Miami, FL. Tel: (305) 274-7472, FAX: (305) 274-3233, E-Mail: galloway_inc@bellsouth.net, Web Site: www. gallowayfarm.com (8)

Lawrence, Paula, Governing Magazine, Washington, DC. Tel: (202) 862-8802, Web Site: www. governing.com (17)

Lawrence, Robyn Griggs, Mother Earth News Magazine, Topeka, KS. Tel: (785) 274-4300, (800) 678-5779, FAX: (785) 274-4305, E-Mail: bwelch@ ogdenpubs.com, Web Site: www.cappers.com (17)

Lawrence-Longo, Sue, Stratus Technologies, Maynard, MA. Tel: (978) 461-7000, (800) 787-2887, FAX: (978) 461-3670, Web Site: www.stratus.com (16)

Lawson, Brian, The Market Builder Inc, Mesa, AZ. Tel: (480) 641-6200, FAX: (480) 641-6239, E-Mail: info@themarketbuilder.com, Web Site: www. themarketbuilder.com (21)

Lawson, Keith, The Market Builder Inc, Mesa, AZ. Tel: (480) 641-6200, FAX: (480) 641-6239, E-Mail: info@themarketbuilder.com, Web Site: www. themarketbuilder.com (21)

Lawson, Paul, The Market Builder Inc, Mesa, AZ. Tel: (480) 641-6200, FAX: (480) 641-6239, E-Mail: info@themarketbuilder.com, Web Site: www. themarketbuilder.com (21)

Lawson, Peggy, The Market Builder Inc, Mesa, AZ. Tel: (480) 641-6200, FAX: (480) 641-6239, E-Mail: info@themarketbuilder.com, Web Site: www. themarketbuilder.com (21)

Lawson, Roger Allan, Fidelity Investments, Boston, MA. Tel: (617) 563-7000, (800) 343-3548, FAX: (617) 476-6150, Web Site: www.fidelity.com (14)

Lawson, Ron, National Technical Information Service, Alexandria, VA. Tel: (703) 605-6000, FAX: (703) 605-6900, Web Site: www.ntis.gov (17)

Lawyer, Jeff, Huck Spaulding Enterprises, Voorhees-ville, NY. Tel: (518) 768-2070, (888) 982-8866, FAX: (518) 768-2240, E-Mail: orders@spaulding-rogers.com, Web Site: www.spaulding-rogers.com (16)

Lawyer, William, Huck Spaulding Enterprises, Voorheesville, NY. Tel: (518) 768-2070, (888) 982-8866, FAX: (518) 768-2240, E-Mail: orders@spaulding-rogers.com, Web Site: www.spaulding-rogers.com (16)

Lawyers & Judges Publishing Co Inc, Tucson, AZ. Tel: (520) 323-1500, FAX: (520) 323-0055, E-Mail: sales@lawyersandjudges.com, Web Site: www.lawyersandjudges.com (17)

Lawyer's Weekly Publications, Boston, MA. Tel: (617) 451-7300, FAX: (617) 451-0132, Web Site: www.lawyersweekly.com (17)

Lay, Randall R, Lazydays RV Center, Seffner, FL. Tel: (813) 246-4333, FAX: (813) 246-4408, Web Site: www.lazydays.com (12)

Lay, Terry L., School Specialty Inc, Greenville, WI. Tel: (920) 734-5712, (888) 388-3224, FAX: (920) 734-5112, E-Mail: info@schoolspecialty.com, Web Site: www.schoolspecialty.com (16)

Laya, Bonnie, Corpus Christi Museum of Science & History, Corpus Christi, TX. Tel: (361) 826-4667, FAX: (361) 884-7392, Web Site: www.ccmuseum.com (1)

Layock, Pamela, Harlequin Enterprises Ltd, Don Mills, ON Canada. Tel: (416) 445-5860, FAX: (416) 445-8655, E-Mail: customer_ecare@harlequin.ca, Web Site: www.eharlequin.com (17)

Layt, Steven R., DineEquity Inc, Glendale, CA. Tel: (866) 995-DINE, Web Site: dineequity.com (16)

Layton, Kevin, Data-Dynamix Inc, Denver, CO. Tel: (720) 855-9282, (888) 314-0078, FAX: (720) 855-9099, E-Mail: sales@data-dynamix.com, Web Site: www.data-dynamix.com (23)

Layton, Les, Whitney Worldwide Inc, Saint Paul, MN. Tel: (651) 748-5000, (800) 597-0227, FAX: (651) 748-4000, Web Site: www.whitneyworld.com (20)

Lazar Media Group Inc, Charleston, SC. Tel: (877) 579-0222, FAX: (843) 577-5542, E-Mail: email@lazarshopping.com, Web Site: www.lazarmedia.com (17)

Lazar, Chaim, Net 60 LLC, New York, NY. Tel: (201) 833-9003, FAX: (201) 301-8182, E-Mail: chaim@net60.com, Web Site: net60.com (23)

Lazar, Elysa, Lazar Media Group Inc, Charleston, SC. Tel: (877) 579-0222, FAX: (843) 577-5542, E-Mail: email@lazarshopping.com, Web Site: www.lazarmedia.com (17)

Lazard Middle Market LLC, Minneapolis, MN. Tel: (612) 339-0500, FAX: (612) 339-0507, Web Site: www.lazardmm.com (14)

Lazardi, Stephanie, Emailogics Inc/Emailbrain, Vancouver, WA. Tel: (866) 873-3019, Web Site: www.emailbrain.com (20)

Lazarini Niclosi, Tina, Oden, Memphis, TN. Tel: (901) 578-8055, (800) 371-6233, FAX: (901) 578-1911, Web Site: www.oden.com (35)

Lazarus Direct Inc, Uniondale, NY. Tel: (516) 880-7000, E-Mail: inquiries@lazarusdirect.com, Web Site: www.lazarusmarketing.com (21)

Lazarus, Edward P., Tribune Co, Chicago, IL. Tel: (312) 222-9100, FAX: (312) 222-1573, Web Site: www.tribune.com (17)

Lazkani, Nancy, Icon Media Direct Inc, Sherman Oaks, CA. Tel: (818) 995-6400, FAX: (818) 995-6405, E-Mail: info@iconmediadirect.com, Web Site: www.iconmediadirect.com (35)

Lazydays RV Center, Seffner, FL. Tel: (813) 246-4333, FAX: (813) 246-4408, Web Site: www.lazydays.com (12)

Le Blanc, Robert E, Carestream Health Inc, Rochester, NY. Tel: (585) 627-1800, (888) 777-2072, E-Mail: corporatesecurity@carestream.com, Web Site: www.carestreamhealth.com (7)

Le Jardin Du Gourmet, Saint Johnsbury Center, VT. Tel: (802) 748-1446, FAX: (802) 748-1446, E-Mail: orderdesk@artisticgardens.com, Web Site: www.artisticgardens.com (8)

Le Poin, Charles G., The Bil-Ray Aluminum Siding Corp of Queens Inc, New Hyde Park, NY. Tel: (516) 616-4200, (800) 474-4415, FAX: (516) 616-4030, Web Site: www.homeclub.com (16)

Le, Nhien, Unisfair, San Mateo, CA. Tel: (866) 354-4030, Web Site: www.unisfair.com (20)

Lea & Perrins Inc, Fair Lawn, NJ. Tel: (201) 791-1600, FAX: (201) 791-8945, Web Site: www.leaperrins.com (16)

Leach, Ron, Shutterbug, Titusville, FL. Tel: (321) 269-3212, FAX: (321) 255-3146, Web Site: www.shutterbug.net (17)

The Lead Connection Inc, Denison, TX. Tel: (903) 337-1636, (888) 267-3165, FAX: (903) 337-1640, E-Mail: chriswithtlc@gmail.com, Web Site: www.leadconnections.com (28)

Lead Me Media, Delray Beach, FL. Tel: (888) 445-3282, FAX: (561) 423-7890, E-Mail: info@leadmemedia.com, Web Site: www.leadmemedia.com (30)

Leadcreations.com LLC, Fort Lauderdale, FL. Tel: (305) 851-0999, FAX: (707) 281-0421, E-Mail: info@leadcreations.com, Web Site: www.leadcreations.com (23)

Leader, Charles C., White Electronic Designs, Phoenix, AZ. Tel: (614) (602) 437-1520, FAX: (602) 437-9120, Web Site: www.whiteedc.com (27)

Leadership Directories Inc, New York, NY. Tel: (212) 627-4140, FAX: (212) 645-0931, E-Mail: info@leadershipdirectories.com, Web Site: www.leadershipdirectories.com (17)

Leadership Software Corp, Nyack, NY. Tel: (845) 358-0406, (800) 872-0068, FAX: (845) 358-0359, E-Mail: info@leadersoft.com, Web Site: www.leadersoft.com (16)

LeadFlash, Boca Raton, FL. Tel: (561) 997-5759, Web Site: www.leadflash.com (14)

LeadGen Media Group LLC, Staten Island, NY. Tel: (888) 206-3738, FAX: (888) 206-3796, E-Mail: info@leadgenmediagroup.com, Web Site: www.leadgenmediagroup.com (23)

Leads-Plus Inc, Killarney, FL. Tel: (800) 548-4571, E-Mail: eurekaman43@hotmail.com, Web Site: www.salesprospectingexpert.com (20)

League of American Orchestras, New York, NY. Tel: (212) 262-5161, FAX: (212) 262-5198, Web Site: www.symphony.org; www.americanorchestras.org (1)

Leahy, Bob, SoundBite Communications, Bedford, MA. Tel: (877) SOUNDBITE, Web Site: www.soundbite.com (32)

Leahy, Christine A., CDW Corp, Vernon Hills, IL. Tel: (847) 465-6000, (847) 371-6090, Web Site: www.cdw.com (16)

Leahy, Dawn, Silo-Hunt Hill Farm, New Milford, CT. Tel: (860) 355-0300, Web Site: thesiloct.org (8)

Leahy, James, American Hotel Register Co, Vernon Hills, IL. Tel: (708) 743-4163, FAX: (708) 564-5797, Web Site: www.americanhotel.com (16)

Leahy, Joe, HughesLeahyKarlovic, Saint Louis, MO. Tel: (314) 571-6300, FAX: (314) 862-1616, E-Mail: hello@hlkagency.com, Web Site: hlkagency.com (35)

Leahy, Michael, BCR Enterprises Inc, Downers Grove, IL. Tel: (630) 986-1432, (800) 227-1234, FAX: (630) 323-5324, Web Site: www.bcr.com (17)

Leahy, Michael, Shepard's Inc, Bethel, CT. Tel: (203) 830-8300, (800) 243-0993, FAX: (203) 794-1296, E-Mail: mleahy@shepardsinc.com, Web Site: www.shepardsinc.com (22)

Leanin' Tree Inc, Boulder, CO. Tel: (303) 530-7768, (800) 525-0656, FAX: (303) 530-5124, E-Mail: info@leanintree.com, Web Site: www.leanintree.com (6)

Leapfrog Online, Evanston, IL. Tel: (847) 492-1968, Web Site: www.leapfrogonline.com (35)

Leaps & Bounds LLC, Fort Lee, NJ. Tel: (201) 947-5459 (20)

LearnCom HR Consulting & Training, Irvine, CA. Tel: (515) 440-0890, (800) 698-8263, FAX: (515) 221-3149, E-Mail: nhartline@learncom.com, Web Site: www.learncomhr.com (16)

Learning Care Group, Novi, MI. Tel: (248) 697-9115, Web Site: www.learningcaregroup.com (16)

Learning Communications LLC, Irvine, CA. Tel: (800) 622-3610, FAX: (949) 727-4323, E-Mail: sales@learncom.com, Web Site: www.learncom.com (16)

Learning Resources Institute, Downers Grove, IL. Tel: (630) 963-0398 (20)

Learning Seed, Chicago, IL. Tel: (847) 540-8855, (800) 634-4941, FAX: (800) 998-0854, E-Mail: info@learningseed.com, Web Site: www.learningseed.com (3)

Leasure, G. Mark, Ghent Manufacturing Inc, Lebanon, OH. Tel: (513) 932-3445, (800) 543-0550, FAX: (513) 932-9252, E-Mail: customer_service@ghent.com, Web Site: www.ghent.com (10)

Leasure, George, Ghent Manufacturing Inc, Lebanon, OH. Tel: (513) 932-3445, (800) 543-0550, FAX: (513) 932-9252, E-Mail: customer_service@ghent.com, Web Site: www.ghent.com (10)

Leather Unlimited Corp, Belgium, WI. Tel: (920) 994-9464, FAX: (920) 994-4099, E-Mail: leatherunltd@yahoo.com, Web Site: www.leatherunltd.com (2)

Leatherman, Barth, ITW Bee Leitzke, Iron Ridge, WI. Tel: (920) 625-2342, FAX: (920) 625-2643, Web Site: www.itwbeeleitzke.com (16)

Leathers, Tammi, The Union Labor Life Insurance Co, Silver Spring, MD. Tel: (202) 962-2945, FAX: (202) 962-8429, E-Mail: info@ullico.com, Web Site: www.unioncare.com (15)

Leavens, PhD Donald R., National Electrical Manufacturers Association (NEMA), Rosslyn, VA. Tel: (703) 841-3200, FAX: (703) 841-5900, E-Mail: communications@nema.org, Web Site: www.nema.org (34)

Leavitt, Russell, Timberline Total Solutions LLC, Omaha, NE. Tel: (402) 397-6945, (877) 575-2255, FAX: (402) 255-5045, E-Mail: rleavitt@timberlinesolutions.com (29)

Leavy, David C., Discovery Communications Inc, Silver Spring, MD. Tel: (240) 662-2000, FAX: (240) 662-1868, Web Site: corporate.discovery.com (16)

Lebedoff, Randy, Star Tribune Media Co, Minneapolis, MN. Tel: (612) 673-4000, FAX: (612) 673-4359, Web Site: www.startribunecompany.com (17)

Leber, Ward, Time Motion Tools, Poway, CA. Tel: (800) 779-8170, FAX: (800) 779-8171, Web Site: www.timemotion.com (9)

LeBrun, John, Circulation Specialists Inc, Shelton, CT. Tel: (888) 315-2472, FAX: (888) 315-2507 (20)

Lechner, Andrew, TWL Knowledge Group, Carrollton, TX. Tel: (972) 309-4000, (800) 624-2272, FAX: (972) 309-5105, Web Site: www.twlk.com (3)

Leck, Brian, Allen, Matkins, Leck, Gamble & Mallory, Los Angeles, CA. Tel: (213) 622-5555, FAX: (213) 620-8816, E-Mail: communications@allenmatkins. com, Web Site: www.allenmatkins.com (20)

Lecker, Barb, American Speech-Language-Hearing Association, Rockville, MD. Tel: (301) 897-5700, (800) 638-8255, FAX: (301) 296-8580, E-Mail: productsales@asha.org, Web Site: www.asha.org (1)

Leckey, Dave, National Enquirer, New York, NY. Tel: (212) 545-4800, Web Site: www.nationalenquirer. com (17)

Leder, Julie, Datamart Direct Inc, Bloomingdale, IL. Tel: (630) 307-7100, FAX: (630) 307-8059, E-Mail: info@datamartdirect.com, Web Site: www. datamartdirect.com (27)

Lederer, Melissa, Q Interactive, Chicago, IL. Tel: (312) 977-0390, (888) 729-6465, FAX: (312) 224-5001, E-Mail: solutions@qinteractive.com, Web Site: www.qinteractive.com (40)

Lederman, Mark, Virgin Mobile USA LP, Warren, NJ. Tel: (908) 607-4000, (888) 322-1122, E-Mail: vmugeneral@sprint.com, Web Site: www. virginmobileusa.com (32)

Ledford, Tony, Watts Radiant, Springfield, MO. Tel: (417) 864-6108, (800) 276-2419, FAX: (417) 864-8161, Web Site: www.wattsheatway.com (9)

LeDrew, Rod, Grimes Horticulture Inc, Concord, OH. Tel: (800) 241-7333, FAX: (440) 352-1800, E-Mail: sales@grimes-hort.com, Web Site: www. grimesseeds.com (8)

Leduc, Laura, Voicelogic, Toronto, ON Canada. Tel: (888) 552-8858, Web Site: www.voicelogic.com (29)

Lee, Albert, Marshall Cavendish Corp, Tarrytown, NY. Tel: (914) 332-8888, (800) 821-9881, FAX: (914) 332-1888, Web Site: www.marshallcavendish.com (17)

Lee, Andy, Alorica Inc, Irvine, CA. Tel: (909) 606-3600, (866) 256-7422, FAX: (909) 606-7708, E-Mail: info@alorica.com, Web Site: www.alorica. com (29)

Lee, Brad, National Mail Order Association (NMOA), Minneapolis, MN. Tel: (612) 788-1673, E-Mail: info@nmoa.org, Web Site: www.nmoa.org (40)

Lee, Bruce K., Fifth Third Bank, Cincinnati, OH. Tel: (800) 972-3030, FAX: (231) 922-4060, Web Site: www.53.com (14)

Lee, Candy, Financial Services International Corp, Seattle, WA. Tel: (206) 386-5475, FAX: (206) 654-0499 (14)

Lee, Cassandra, North American Mailing Technologies Inc, Lawrenceville, GA. Tel: (770) 962-5833 (22)

Lee, Chau, Regitar USA Inc, Montgomery, AL. Tel: (334) 244-1885, (877) 734-4827, FAX: (334) 244-1901, E-Mail: info@regitar.com, Web Site: www. regitar.com (9)

Lee, Debra, Black Entertainment Television Inc, Washington, DC. Tel: (202) 608-2000, Web Site: www. bet.com (16)

Lee, Debra, Viacom Media Networks, New York, NY. Tel: (212) 258-6000, Web Site: www.viacom.com (32)

Lee, Dr. Lois, Children of the Night, Van Nuys, CA. Tel: (818) 908-4474, (800) 551-1300, FAX: (818) 908-1468, E-Mail: llee@childrenofthenight.com, Web Site: www.childrenofthenight.org (1)

Lee, Freddy S., School of Business & Economics, Los Angeles, CA. Tel: (323) 343-2800, FAX: (323) 343-2813, Web Site: cbe.calstatela.edu (41)

Lee, Granville R., Brownell Holly Farms, Oregon City, OR. Tel: (503) 631-7475, FAX: (503) 631-7481, E-Mail: sales@brownellhollyfarms.com, Web Site: www.brownellhollyfarms.com (6)

Lee, Jack, Andrews Wharton Inc, Commack, NY. Tel: (631) 470-4546, (631) 470-5683, E-Mail: info@ andrewswharton.com, Web Site: andrewswharton. com (35)

Lee, Jane, Lillian Vernon Corp, Colorado Springs, CO. Tel: (757) 427-7923, (800) 545-5426, FAX: (757) 427-7819, E-Mail: publicrelations@lillianvernon. com, Web Site: www.lillianvernon.com (6)

Lee, Jeff, People's United Bank, Bridgeport, CT. Tel: (203) 338-7171, Web Site: www.peoples.com (14)

Lee, Jenny, Brownell Holly Farms, Oregon City, OR. Tel: (503) 631-7475, FAX: (503) 631-7481, E-Mail: sales@brownellhollyfarms.com, Web Site: www. brownellhollyfarms.com (6)

Lee, John, Army Times Publishing Co, Springfield, VA. Tel: (703) 750-9000, (800) 336-4590, FAX: (703) 750-8129, E-Mail: cust-svc@atpco.com, Web Site: www.armytimes.com (17)

Lee, Ken, Michael Wiese Productions, Studio City, CA. Tel: (818) 379-8799, (800) 833-5738, FAX: (818) 986-3408, Web Site: www.mwp.com (17)

Lee, Kevin, Didit, Mineola, NY. Tel: (212) 631-0157, Web Site: www.did-it.com (16)

Lee, Lauren, Brownell Holly Farms, Oregon City, OR. Tel: (503) 631-7475, FAX: (503) 631-7481, E-Mail: sales@brownellhollyfarms.com, Web Site: www. brownellhollyfarms.com (6)

Lee, Margaret B., Oakton Community College, Des Plaines, IL. Tel: (847) 635-1600, FAX: (847) 635-1706, Web Site: www.oakton.edu (41)

Lee, Michael, International Advertising Association, New York, NY. Tel: (646) 722-2612, FAX: (646) 722-2501, E-Mail: iaa@iaaglobal.com, Web Site: www.iaaglobal.org (1)

Lee, Paul, Gates Corp, Denver, CO. Tel: (303) 744-1911, FAX: (303) 744-4000, Web Site: www.gates. com (9)

Lee, Randy, GBH Communications, Monrovia, CA. Tel: (818) 246-9900, (800) 222-5424, FAX: (818) 246-5850, E-Mail: customerservice@gbh.com, Web Site: www.gbh.com (3)

Lee, Robert, Hill Mailing & Printing of Florida Inc, Brandon, FL. Tel: (813) 258-5220, (888) 662-6951, FAX: (813) 944-2882, E-Mail: mail@hillmailing. com, Web Site: hillmailing.com (21)

Lee, Terry, Decker Communications Inc, San Francisco, CA. Tel: (415) 543-8100, (877) 485-0700, FAX: (415) 543-8103, E-Mail: info@ deckercommunications.com, Web Site: www. deckercommunications.com (20)

Lee, Thomas P., Territorial Newspapers, Tucson, AZ. Tel: (520) 294-1200, FAX: (520) 294-4040, Web Site: www.azbiz.com (17)

Lee, Travis, 3D Mail Results, Kent, WA. Tel: (888) 250-1834, FAX: (253) 398-1551, E-Mail: info@ 3dmailresults.com, Web Site: www.3dmailresults. com (5)

Leech, Grant, US Cellular, Chicago, IL. Tel: (888) 944-9400, Web Site: www.uscellular.com (32)

Leeds, Bob, Global Equipment Co Inc, Port Washington, NY. Tel: (516) 484-3100, (888) 381-2861, FAX: (516) 608-7111, E-Mail: sales@ globalindustrial.com, Web Site: www. globalindustrial.com (9)

Leeds, Bruce, Global Equipment Co Inc, Port Washington, NY. Tel: (516) 484-3100, (888) 381-2861, FAX: (516) 608-7111, E-Mail: sales@ globalindustrial.com, Web Site: www. globalindustrial.com (9)

Leeds, Bruce, TigerDirect Inc, El Segundo, CA. Tel: (305) 415-2199, (800) 800-8300, FAX: (305) 415-2202, Web Site: biz.tigerdirect.com (3)

Leeds, Richard, Global Equipment Co Inc, Port Washington, NY. Tel: (516) 484-3100, (888) 381-2861, FAX: (516) 608-7111, E-Mail: sales@ globalindustrial.com, Web Site: www. globalindustrial.com (9)

Leeds, Richard, Systemax Inc, Port Washington, NY. Tel: (516) 608-7000, FAX: (516) 6208-7001, Web Site: www.systemax.com (16)

Leeds, Richard, TigerDirect Inc, El Segundo, CA. Tel: (305) 415-2199, (800) 800-8300, FAX: (305) 415-2202, Web Site: biz.tigerdirect.com (3)

Leeds, Robert, TigerDirect Inc, El Segundo, CA. Tel: (305) 415-2199, (800) 800-8300, FAX: (305) 415-2202, Web Site: biz.tigerdirect.com (3)

Leek, Joseph, JHL Mail Marketing Inc, Stevens Point, WI. Tel: (715) 341-0581, (800) 236-0581, FAX: (715) 341-9645, E-Mail: ren@jhl.com, Web Site: www.jhl.com (28)

Leerentueld, Rudi, Kadant Johnson Inc, Three Rivers, MI. Tel: (269) 278-1715, FAX: (269) 279-5980, Web Site: www.kadantjohnson.com (16)

Lee's Nursery, McMinnville, TN. Tel: (931) 668-4870 (8)

Leesi, John-Peter, Astro Air, LP, Jacksonville, TX. Tel: (903) 586-3691, FAX: (903) 589-8094, E-Mail: sales@astroair.com, Web Site: www.astroair.com (9)

Lefar, Marc, Vonage, Holmdel, NJ. Tel: (732) 528-2600, Web Site: www.vonage.com (32)

LeFauve, Bryan, FARM, Depew, NY. Tel: (716) 989-3200, FAX: (716) 989-3220, E-Mail: bizdev@ farmbuffalo.com, Web Site: www.growwiththefarm. com (35)

LeFebvre, Adam, Specialty Print Communications Inc, Niles, IL. Tel: (847) 588-2580, FAX: (847) 588-2146, Web Site: www.specialtyprintcomm.com (27)

LeFebvre, Paul, Specialty Print Communications Inc, Niles, IL. Tel: (847) 588-2580, FAX: (847) 588-2146, Web Site: www.specialtyprintcomm.com (27)

Lefevre, Marc, CityTwist, Boca Raton, FL. Tel: (866) 798-2489, FAX: (561) 314-2692, Web Site: www. citytwist.com (32)

Leffelman, Brittanie, Wellness Councils of America, Omaha, NE. Tel: (402) 827-3590, FAX: (402) 827-3594, E-Mail: wellworkplace@welcoa.org, Web Site: www.welcoa.org (1)

Lefferts, Coni, Creative Packaging Solutions, Keyport, NJ. Tel: (732) 335-3700, (888) 826-1646, FAX: (732) 264-9313, E-Mail: info@packaging-usa.com, Web Site: www.packaging-usa.com (35)

Lefkowitz, Herb, We Deliver America Inc, Englewood Cliffs, NJ. Tel: (201) 307-8888, FAX: (201) 307-1200, E-Mail: info@we-deliver-america.com, Web Site: www.we-deliver-america.com (31)

Lefkowitz, Mark, Furman Roth Advertising, New York, NY. Tel: (212) 687-2300, FAX: (212) 687-0858, E-Mail: eroth@furmanroth.com, Web Site: www. furmanroth.com (35)

Lefty's Corner, Clarks Summit, PA. Tel: (570) 586-5338, (570) 586-LEFT, FAX: (570) 585-2906, E-Mail: info@leftyscorner.com, Web Site: www. leftyscorner.com (6)

Legal Sea Foods Inc, Boston, MA. Tel: (617) 530-9000, (800) 343-5804, FAX: (617) 530-9649, Web Site: www.legalseafoods.com (4)

The Legal Studies Forum, Morgantown, WV. Tel: (304) 293-5301, FAX: (304) 293-6891, E-Mail: wvulaw@mail.wvu.edu (1)

LegaLists, New Providence, NJ. Tel: (973) 642-1440 ext.109, FAX: (973) 642-3731, E-Mail: jwenzel@lawdiary.com, Web Site: www.lawdiary.com (24)

Legg, Ben, Adknowledge, Kansas City, MO. Tel: (816) 931-1771, (866) 730-2109, Web Site: www.adknowledge.com (32)

Legge, Dorri, Partners Village Store, Westport, MA. Tel: (508) 636-2572, FAX: (508) 636-2529, E-Mail: info@partnersvillagestore.com, Web Site: www.partnersvillagestore.com (11)

Leggio, Mark, The Jackson Group, Indianapolis, IN. Tel: (317) 791-9000, (888) 522-5766, FAX: (317) 791-9800, Web Site: www.jacksongroup.com (35)

Lego Direct Marketing, Enfield, CT. Tel: (860) 749-2291, (800) 838-4386, FAX: (860) FAX-LEGO, Web Site: www.lego.com (11)

Legrand Hart, Denver, CO. Tel: (303) 298-8470, FAX: (303) 298-8570, Web Site: www.legrandhart.com (20)

Legrand-Hart, DeeDee, Legrand Hart, Denver, CO. Tel: (303) 298-8470, FAX: (303) 298-8570, Web Site: www.legrandhart.com (20)

Lehigh Direct, Broadview, IL. Tel: (708) 681-3612, FAX: (708) 681-4694, Web Site: www.lehighdirect.com (27)

Lehman, Jay, Lehman's, Dalton, OH. Tel: (800) 438-5346, Web Site: www.lehmans.com (8)

Lehman, Timothy J., Thrivent Financial for Lutherans, Appleton, WI. Tel: (920) 734-5721, (800) 847-4836, FAX: (920) 730-4781, E-Mail: mail@thrivent.com, Web Site: www.thrivent.com (14)

Lehmann, Bill, Jones & Thomas Inc, Decatur, IL. Tel: (217) 423-1889, FAX: (217) 425-0680, E-Mail: corp@jonesthomas.com, Web Site: www.jonesthomas.com (35)

Lehman's, Dalton, OH. Tel: (800) 438-5346, Web Site: www.lehmans.com (8)

Lehmen, Ted, Ted's Promotions Inc, Baldwin, GA. Tel: (770) 972-8081, FAX: (770) 573-3141, E-Mail: ted@tedspromotions.com, Web Site: www.tedspromotions.com (33)

Lehmkuhl, W Gregory, Con-Way Freight, Ann Arbor, MI. Tel: (734) 994-6600, FAX: (734) 757-1153 (12)

Leibfried, Joe, Los Angeles Kings, Los Angeles, CA. Tel: (213) 742-7100, (888) KINGS-LA, FAX: (213) 742-7296, Web Site: kings.nhl.com (16)

Leibowitz Market Research Associates Inc, Charlotte, NC. Tel: (704) 357-1961, FAX: (704) 357-1965, E-Mail: info@leibowitz-research.com, Web Site: www.leibowitz-research.com (30)

Leibowitz, Teri, Leibowitz Market Research Associates Inc, Charlotte, NC. Tel: (704) 357-1961, FAX: (704) 357-1965, E-Mail: info@leibowitz-research.com, Web Site: www.leibowitz-research.com (30)

Leide, Dominic, The Office Gurus, Seminole, FL. Tel: (727) 803-7114, Web Site: www.theofficegurus.com (29)

Leigh, Kevin M., The Keystone Equities Group, Oaks, PA. Tel: (610) 415-6300, (800) 715-9905, FAX: (610) 415-6328, Web Site: www.keystoneequities.com (20)

Lein, Chuck, Stuller Inc, Lafayette, LA. Tel: (800) 877-7777, FAX: (800) 444-4741, E-Mail: info@stuller.com, Web Site: www.stuller.com (2)

Leinweber, Tabetha, Susan G Komen for the Cure, Dallas, TX. Tel: (877) 465-6636, Web Site: www.komen.org (1)

Leiss, Daniel, Jenny Products Inc, Somerset, PA. Tel: (814) 445-3400, FAX: (814) 445-2280, Web Site: www.jennyproducts.com (16)

Leiss, Peter, Jenny Products Inc, Somerset, PA. Tel: (814) 445-3400, FAX: (814) 445-2280, Web Site: www.jennyproducts.com (16)

Leisure Arts Inc, Maumelle, AR. Tel: (501) 868-8800, Web Site: www.leisurearts.com (17)

Leitch, Danielle, MoreVisibility, Boca Raton, FL. Tel: (561) 620-9682, (800) 787-0497, FAX: (561) 620-9684, E-Mail: info@morevisibility.com, Web Site: www.morevisibility.com (32)

Leite, Sharon M., Sally Beauty Supply LLC, Denton, TX. Tel: (940) 898-7500, (866) 234-9442, Web Site: www.sallybeauty.com (7)

Leitzell, Melissa, Golden Key International Honour Society, Atlanta, GA. Tel: (678) 689-2200, (800) 377-2401, FAX: (678) 689-2297, E-Mail: memberservices@goldenkey.org, Web Site: www.goldenkey.org (1)

Lemasters, S Craig, Assurant Solutions Preneed Division, Atlanta, GA. Tel: (770) 763-1000, (800) PRE NEED, FAX: (770) 859-4325, Web Site: www.assurantpreneed.com (15)

Lemay, Frankye, Sunnyland Farms Inc, Albany, GA. Tel: (800) 999-2488, Web Site: www.sunnylandfarms.com (4)

Lemberg, Steven J., Entertainment Publications Inc, Troy, MI. Tel: (248) 404-1000, (888) 231-SAVE, FAX: (248) 404-1915, Web Site: www.entertainment.com (31)

Lemee's Inc, Hanson, MA. Tel: (781) 294-8209, E-Mail: slemeephot@aol.com, Web Site: www.lemeesfireplace.com (8)

LeMenager, Lois M., Marketing Innovators, Rosemont, IL. Tel: (847) 696-1111, (800) 543-7373, FAX: (847) 696-3194, E-Mail: info@marketinginnovators.com, Web Site: www.marketinginnovators.com (35)

Lemer, Troy, Booyah! Online Advertising, Denver, CO. Tel: (303) 345-6100, FAX: (303) 345-6700, E-Mail: info@booyahadvertising.ocm, Web Site: www.booyahadvertising.com (35)

Lemmon, Nicolette, LemmonTree Marketing Group, Scottsdale, AZ. Tel: (480) 967-1405, (888) 536-6243, FAX: (480) 967-1407, E-Mail: 7solutions@lemmontree.com, Web Site: www.lemmontree.com (35)

LemmonTree Marketing Group, Scottsdale, AZ. Tel: (480) 967-1405, (888) 536-6243, FAX: (480) 967-1407, E-Mail: 7solutions@lemmontree.com, Web Site: www.lemmontree.com (35)

Lemonis, Marcus, Camping World Inc, Bowling Green, KY. Tel: (270) 781-2718, (800) 626-6189, FAX: (270) 796-8991, Web Site: www.campingworld.com (11)

Lemonis, Marcus, Woodall Publishing Co LP, Ventura, CA. Tel: (805) 667-4100, (800) 323-9076, FAX: (805) 667-4468, Web Site: www.woodalls.com (17)

Lemsky, James R., Jason Natural Personal Care Products, Boulder, CO. Tel: (88) 659-7730, Web Site: www.jason-natural.com (7)

Len, Charles, NestFamily.com, Lewisville, TX. Tel: (800) 596-7386, FAX: (972) 629-7181, Web Site: www.nestfamily.com (3)

Lenard, Peter, Rajant Corp, Malvern, PA. Tel: (484) 595-0233, FAX: (484) 595-0244, E-Mail: support@rajant.com, Web Site: www.rajant.com (32)

Lendhart, Alfonso E., McGruff Specialty Products Office, Amsterdam, NY. Tel: (518) 842-4388, (888) 776-7763, FAX: (800) 995-5121, E-Mail: mcgruff@spocentral.com, Web Site: www.mcgruffspo.com (16)

Lending Tree/Home Loan Center, Charlotte, NC. Tel: (704) 541-5351, (800) 555-8733, FAX: (704) 541-1824, Web Site: www.lendingtree.com (14)

Lenhart, Larry, F P International, Fremont, CA. Tel: (650) 261-5300, (800) 866-9946, FAX: (650) 361-1713, Web Site: www.fpintl.com (16)

Lennertz, Carl, HarperCollins, New York, NY. Tel: (212) 207-7000, (800) 242-7737, FAX: (212) 207-7145, Web Site: www.harpercollins.com (17)

Lennon, Bob, PTI Pyramid Technologies LLC, Meriden, CT. Tel: (203) 238-0550, (888) 479-7264, FAX: (203) 634-1696, Web Site: www.pyramid-technologies.com (10)

Lenny, Richard H., Information Resources Inc, Chicago, IL. Tel: (312) 726-1221, FAX: (312(726-8214, Web Site: www.infores.com (30)

Lenovo, Morrisville, NC. Tel: (919) 257-6315, (855) 253-6686, Web Site: www.uslenovo.com (3)

Lenox Group Inc, Bristol, PA. Tel: (267) 525-7800, (800) 223-4311, Web Site: www.lenox.com (6)

Lensch, Deb, KV Vet Supply Co, Inc, David City, NE. Tel: (402) 367-6047, Web Site: www.kvvet.com (5)

Max Lent Communications, Webster, NY. Tel: (585) 670-9322, E-Mail: max@maxlent.com, Web Site: www.maxlent.com (39)

Lent, Max, Max Lent Communications, Webster, NY. Tel: (585) 670-9322, E-Mail: max@maxlent.com, Web Site: www.maxlent.com (39)

L'Entraide Assurance, Quebec, QC Canada. Tel: (418) 658-0663, FAX: (418) 658-5065, E-Mail: service@lentraide.com, Web Site: www.lentraide.com (15)

Lentz, Rebecca, Home-Sew Inc, Bethlehem, PA. Tel: (610) 867-3833, (800) 344-4739, FAX: (610) 867-9717, E-Mail: customerservice@homesew.com, Web Site: www.homesew.com (11)

Leon, Eduardo, Liberman Broadcasting Inc, Burbank, CA. Tel: (818) 729-5300, E-Mail: lbiinfo@lbimedia.com, Web Site: www.lbimedia.com (32)

Leon, Ricardo, Majestic Products Co, Paris, KY. Tel: (859) 987-0740, Web Site: majesticproducts.com (16)

AM Leonard Inc, Piqua, OH. Tel: (800) 543-8955, FAX: (800) 433-0633, E-Mail: info@amleo.com, Web Site: www.amleo.com (8)

Hal Leonard Corp, Milwaukee, WI. Tel: (414) 774-3630, FAX: (414) 774-3259, Web Site: www.halleonard.com (17)

Leonard, David, MacLaren McCann, Toronto, ON Canada. Tel: (416) 594-6000, FAX: (416) 643-7026, Web Site: www.maclaren.com (32)

Leonard, J. Wayne, Entergy, New Orleans, LA. Tel: (504) 576-4000, (800) ENTERGY, FAX: (504) 576-4428, Web Site: www.entergy.com (16)

Leonard, Sara E., Freddie Mac, McLean, VA. Tel: (703) 903-2000, (800) 424-5401, Web Site: www.freddiemac.com (14)

Leonards, Jr. Stew, Stew Leonard's, Norwalk, CT. Tel: (203) 847-7214, FAX: (203) 846-3472, Web Site: www.stewleonards.com (4)

Leone, Paul, Magnet LLC, Washington, MO. Tel: (636) 239-5661, (800) 458-9457, FAX: (636) 239-4490, E-Mail: contactus@themagnetgroup.com, Web Site: www.magnetllc.com (16)

Augie Leopold Advertising Specialties, Metairie, LA. Tel: (504) 836-0525, E-Mail: sales@augieleopold.com (33)

Leopold, Gary, CP Travel, Boston, MA. Tel: (617) 521-5400, Web Site: travel.connellypartners.com (35)

Leopold, Jr. Augie, Augie Leopold Advertising Specialties, Metairie, LA. Tel: (504) 836-0525, E-Mail: sales@augieleopold.com (33)

Lepore, Peter, Ferrara Bakery & Cafe Inc, New York, NY. Tel: (212) 226-6150, FAX: (212) 226-0667, E-Mail: information@ferraracafe.com, Web Site: www.ferraracafe.com (4)

Lepoutre, Richard, Statware, Centerbrook, CT. Tel: (860) 767-9000, FAX: (860) 767-3145, E-Mail: info@statware.net, Web Site: www.powerlist.com (16)

Leppert, Thomas C., Kaplan Inc, Fort Lauderdale, FL. Tel: (954) 515-3993, Web Site: www.kaplan.com (16)

Leppert, Thomas C., Kaplan Publishing, Chicago, IL. Tel: (312) 606-8905, (800) 245-2665, FAX: (312) 606-8985, Web Site: www.kaplanpublishing.com (17)

Lerendu, Michael, Neolane, Newton, MA. Tel: (617) 467-6760, FAX: (617) 467-6701, Web Site: www.neolane.com (22)

Lerner Publishing Group, Minneapolis, MN. Tel: (612) 332-3344, (800) 328-4929, FAX: (800) 332-1132, E-Mail: info@lernerbooks.com, Web Site: www.lernerbooks.com (17)

Lerner, Adam, Lerner Publishing Group, Minneapolis, MN. Tel: (612) 332-3344, (800) 328-4929, FAX: (800) 332-1132, E-Mail: info@lernerbooks.com, Web Site: www.lernerbooks.com (17)

Lerner, David, Janice's LLC, Hartford, CT. Tel: (860) 523-4479, (800) 526-4237, FAX: (860) 523-4178, E-Mail: dlerner@janices.com, Web Site: www.janices.com (8)

Lerner, Harry, Lerner Publishing Group, Minneapolis, MN. Tel: (612) 332-3344, (800) 328-4929, FAX: (800) 332-1132, E-Mail: info@lernerbooks.com, Web Site: www.lernerbooks.com (17)

Lerose Copywriting, Uniondale, NY. Tel: (516) 486-0472, FAX: (516) 486-0386, E-Mail: robertler@optonline.net, Web Site: www.robertlerose.com (39)

Robert Lerose, Uniondale, NY. Tel: (516) 486-0472, FAX: (516) 486-0386, E-Mail: robertler@optonline.net, Web Site: www.robertlerose.com (39)

Lerose, Robert, Lerose Copywriting, Uniondale, NY. Tel: (516) 486-0472, FAX: (516) 486-0386, E-Mail: robertler@optonline.net, Web Site: www.robertlerose.com (39)

Lerose, Robert, Robert Lerose, Uniondale, NY. Tel: (516) 486-0472, FAX: (516) 486-0386, E-Mail: robertler@optonline.net, Web Site: www.robertlerose.com (39)

Leroux, Monique, Desjardins Financial Securities, Levis, QC Canada. Tel: (418) 838-7870, FAX: (418) 833-5985, Web Site: www.desjardinsfinancialsecurity.com (15)

Lesch, Sigrid, Thieme Medical Publishers Inc, New York, NY. Tel: (212) 760-0888, (800) 782-3488, FAX: (212) 947-1112, E-Mail: info@thieme.com, Web Site: www.thieme.com (17)

Leshner, Dr. Alan I., AAAS/Science, Washington, DC. Tel: (202) 326-6400, FAX: (202) 371-9526, E-Mail: membership@aaas.org, Web Site: www.aaas.org (1)

Lesjak, Catherine A., Hewlett-Packard Co, Palo Alto, CA. Tel: (650) 857-1501, (800) 752-0900, FAX: (650) 857-5518, Web Site: www.hp.com (16)

Lesko, Edward, Reb Storage Systems International, Chicago, IL. Tel: (773) 252-0400, (800) 252-5955, FAX: (773) 252-0303, E-Mail: sales@rebsteel.com, Web Site: www.industrialebuy.com (9)

Lesko, Stephanie, BP Rice & Company Inc, El Segundo, CA. Tel: (310) 322-2210, FAX: (310) 322-0617, E-Mail: stephanie@bprco.com, Web Site: www.bprco.com (35)

Lesko, Tom, Reb Storage Systems International, Chicago, IL. Tel: (773) 252-0400, (800) 252-5955, FAX: (773) 252-0303, E-Mail: sales@rebsteel.com, Web Site: www.industrialebuy.com (9)

Leslie Jordan, Portland, OR. Tel: (503) 295-1987, (800) 935-3343, FAX: (503) 295-0939, E-Mail: ljsales@lesliejordan.com, Web Site: www.lesliejordan.com (2)

Leslie Shoe Co Inc, Rogers City, MI. Tel: (989) 734-4030, (800) 716-8617, E-Mail: info@sexyshoes.com, Web Site: www.sexyshoes.com (2)

Leslie, David, Medic Alert Foundation, Salida, CA. Tel: (209) 668-3333, (800) 432-5378, FAX: (209) 669-2495, Web Site: www.medicalert.org (1)

Lesman Instrument Co, Bensenville, IL. Tel: (630) 595-8400, (800) 953-7626, FAX: (630) 595-2386, E-Mail: sales@lesman.com, Web Site: www.lesman.com (9)

Lesniak, Sharie, Born Free USA, Washington, DC. Tel: (202) 450-3168, (800) 348-7387, FAX: (202) 450-3581, E-Mail: info@bornfreeusa.org, Web Site: www.bornfreeusa.org (1)

Lessin, Larry, Charmaster, Grand Rapids, MN. Tel: (218) 326-6786, FAX: (218) 326-1065, E-Mail: info@charmaster.com, Web Site: www.charmaster.com (8)

Lester Inc, Branford, CT. Tel: (203) 488-5265, (800) 999-5265, FAX: (203) 483-0408, Web Site: www.lesterusa.com (29)

Lester, Robert, Parlay International, Walnut Creek, CA. Tel: (510) 601-1000, FAX: (510) 601-1008, E-Mail: info@parlay.com, Web Site: www.parlay.com (17)

Lester, Victoria, Huntsinger & Jeffer, Richmond, VA. Tel: (804) 266-2499, FAX: (804) 266-8563, E-Mail: info@huntsinger-jeffer.com, Web Site: www.huntsinger-jeffer.com (21)

Lestz, Paul, D'Lights, South El Monte, CA. Tel: (626) 246-1094, (800) 414-5109, FAX: (626) 433-0267, E-Mail: lizzy@spjlighting.com, Web Site: www.dlights.com (8)

Lethers, Alan, America's Finest Pet Doors, San Luis Obispo, CA. Tel: (805) 781-7700 X201, (800) 826-2871, FAX: (805) 781-9734, E-Mail: alan@petdoors.com, Web Site: www.petdoors.com (16)

Lettig, Mary Lou, Ultradent Products Inc, South Jordan, UT. Tel: (801) 572-4200, FAX: (801) 553-4600, E-Mail: onlineordersupport@ultradent.com, Web Site: www.ultradent.com (7)

Leucadia National Corp, New York, NY. Tel: (212) 460-1900, FAX: (212) 598-4869, Web Site: www.leucadia.com (14)

The Leukemia & Lymphoma Society, Rye Brook, NY. Tel: (914) 949-5213, FAX: (914) 949-6691, Web Site: www.lls.org (1)

Leung, Ray, Direct Mail Center, San Francisco, CA. Tel: (415) 252-1600, FAX: (415) 252-9100, E-Mail: dmc@directmailctr.com, Web Site: www.directmailctr.com (21)

Leurquin, Scott, New York Landmarks Conservancy, New York, NY. Tel: (212) 995-5260, FAX: (212) 995-5268, Web Site: www.nylandmarks.org (1)

Lev & Berlin, Norwalk, CT. Tel: (203) 838-8500, (800) 377-4508, FAX: (203) 854-1652, E-Mail: info@levberlin.com, Web Site: www.levberlin.com (20)

Lev, Bruce, Lev & Berlin, Norwalk, CT. Tel: (203) 838-8500, (800) 377-4508, FAX: (203) 854-1652, E-Mail: info@levberlin.com, Web Site: www.levberlin.com (20)

Levant, Ronald, American Psychological Association, Washington, DC. Tel: (202) 336-5500, (800) 374-2721, FAX: (202) 336-5568, E-Mail: order@apa.org, Web Site: www.apa.org (1)

Levatich, Matthew S, Harley-Davidson Inc, Milwaukee, WI. Tel: (414) 343-7286, FAX: (414) 343-4806, Web Site: www.harley-davidson.com (12)

Level 5 Communications Inc, Dublin, NH. Tel: (603) 563-1631, FAX: (603) 563-8912, E-Mail: de-news@deskeng.com, Web Site: www.deskeng.com (32)

Levenger, Delray Beach, FL. Tel: (561) 276-2436, (800) 544-0880, FAX: (800) 544-6910, E-Mail: corpsales@levenger.com, Web Site: www.levenger.com (5)

The Levenson Group, Dallas, TX. Tel: (214) 932-6000, E-Mail: hello@levensongroup.com, Web Site: levensongroup.com (35)

Levenson, Bruce, United Communications Group, Gaithersburg, MD. Tel: (301) 287-2700, FAX: (301) 816-8945, E-Mail: webmaster@ucg.com, Web Site: www.ucg.com (17)

Leverage Marketing Group, Newtown, CT. Tel: (203) 270-6699, E-Mail: info@lev-mg.com, Web Site: www.leverage-marketing.com (35)

Levesque, Paul, World Wrestling Entertainment Inc, Stamford, CT. Tel: (203) 352-8600, FAX: (203) 359-5180, Web Site: www.wwe.com (16)

Levey, Hugh, Gruppo Levey & Co, New York, NY. Tel: (212) 867-, FAX: (212) 949-7294, E-Mail: info@glconline.com, Web Site: www.glconline.com (14)

Levi Strauss & Co, San Francisco, CA. Tel: (415) 501-6000, FAX: (415) 501-7112, Web Site: www.levistrauss.com (16)

Levi, Mary, Ion Exhibits, Itasca, IL. Tel: (877) 499-6197, FAX: (630) 235-9501, E-Mail: info@ionexhibits.com, Web Site: www.ionexhibits.com (36)

Levi, Michael, Ion Exhibits, Itasca, IL. Tel: (877) 499-6197, FAX: (630) 235-9501, E-Mail: info@ionexhibits.com, Web Site: www.ionexhibits.com (36)

Levigne, Patrick, National Rural Electric Cooperative Association, Arlington, VA. Tel: (703) 907-5500, FAX: (703) 907-5528, Web Site: www.nreca.org (1)

Levin, Cliff, The Healthy Back Store, Beltsville, MD. Tel: (703) 339-1700, (800) 4 MY BACK, FAX: (703) 339-0671, E-Mail: service@healthyback.com, Web Site: www.healthyback.com (16)

Levin, David A, Casual Male Retail Group, Canton, MA. Tel: (781) 828-9300, (800) 767-0319, E-Mail: info@casualmale.com, Web Site: www.casualmale.com (2)

Levin, Irwin, Social Studies School Service, Culver City, CA. Tel: (310) 839-2436, (800) 421-4246, FAX: (310) 839-2249, (800) 944-5432, E-Mail: access@socialstudies.com, Web Site: www.socialstudies.com (16)

Levin, Jonathan, Cable Car Clothiers/Robert Kirk Ltd, San Francisco, CA. Tel: (415) 397-4740, FAX: (415) 616-8998, E-Mail: info@cablecarclothiers.com, Web Site: www.cablecarclothiers.com (2)

Levin, Marc H., Harris Interactive, Rochester, NY. Tel: (585) 272-8400, (800) 866-7655, FAX: (585) 272-8680, E-Mail: info@harrisinteractive.com, Web Site: www.harrisinteractive.com (30)

Levin, Mitchell, Life Investors Insurance Co of America, Cedar Rapids, IA. Tel: (319) 398-8511, (800) 231-7220, FAX: (319) 369-2188, Web Site: www.lifeinvestors.com (14)

Levin, Per H., Check Point Systems, Thorofare, NJ. Tel: (856) 848-1800, (800) 257-5540, FAX: (856) 848-0937, Web Site: www.checkpointsystems.com (34)

Levin, Wayne, Lionsgate Entertainment Inc, New York, NY. Tel: (212) 577-2400, FAX: (212) 962-2872, Web Site: www.lionsgate.com (32)

Levin, Wayne, Lionsgate Television Corp, Santa Monica, CA. Tel: (310) 449-9200, FAX: (310) 255-3870, Web Site: www.lionsgate.com (16)

Levine, Bruce, Smart Marketing, Dix Hills, NY. Tel: (631) 254-5259, (631) 254-4814, E-Mail: info@smartmarketing.com, Web Site: www.smartmarketing.com (35)

Levine, Ed, Sussex Publishers Inc, New York, NY. Tel: (212) 260-7210, FAX: (212) 260-7445, Web Site: www.blues-buster.com (17)

Levine, Ellen, Hearst Magazines, New York, NY. Tel: (212) 649-2824, FAX: (212) 765-3528, Web Site: www.hearst.com/magazines (17)

Levine, Glenn, List Team, Calabasas, CA. Tel: (818) 887-1166, (800) 553-2123, E-Mail: info@listteam.com, Web Site: www.listteam.com (23)

Levine, James, The Metropolitan Opera, New York, NY. Tel: (212) 362-6000, (212) 799-3100, FAX: (212) 870-7695, Web Site: www.metoperafamily.org (1)

Levine, Jeff, Tele Business USA, Northbrook, IL. Tel: (847) 480-1560, FAX: (847) 897-4120, Web Site: www.tbiz.com (29)

Levine, Jordan, Strofina Inc, Bainbridge Island, WA. Tel: (206) 855-9681 (20)

Levine, Joshua H., Mentor Corp, Santa Barbara, CA. Tel: (805) 879-6000, (800) 525-0245, FAX: (805) 964-2712, Web Site: www.mentorcorp.com (16)

Levine, Marty, Webb Mason, Hunt Valley, MD. Tel: (410) 785-1111, Web Site: www.webbmason.com (20)

Levine, Matthew, Research To Prevent Blindness Inc, New York, NY. Tel: (212) 752-4333, (800) 621-0026, FAX: (212) 688-6231, E-Mail: inforequest@rpbusa.org, Web Site: www.rpbusa.org (1)

Levine, Ronn, Specialized Information Publishers Association, Vienna, VA. Tel: (781) 754-4771, FAX: (703) 992-7512, E-Mail: nbrand@sia.net, Web Site: www.siia.net (1)

Levine, Russell, Zoe Marketing, San Diego, CA. Tel: (858) 408-1700 (20)

Levinson, Janine, The Hyiad Group, Garden City, NY. Tel: (516) 433-3800, FAX: (516) 822-6670, Web Site: www.thehyaidgroup.com (22)

Levinson, Leo, GroupLevinson, Philadelphia, PA. Tel: (215) 627-3030, Web Site: grouplevinson.com (35)

Levinson, Richard, The Hyiad Group, Garden City, NY. Tel: (516) 433-3800, FAX: (516) 822-6670, Web Site: www.thehyaidgroup.com (22)

Levison, Michael, ReMark USA, Minnetonka, MN. Tel: (952) 938-4699, FAX: (952) 988-8500, E-Mail: jessica.sbragia@remarkgroup.com, Web Site: www.remarkamericas.com (15)

Levitan, Ben, IMN, Waltham, MA. Tel: (781) 672-7000, (866) 964-6397, FAX: (781) 890-4701, E-Mail: support@imninc.com, Web Site: www.imninc.com (32)

Levitt, Walter, Comedy Central, New York, NY. Tel: (212) 767-8600, Web Site: www.cc.com (32)

Levitz, Bill, Argent Trading LLC, New York, NY. Tel: (212) 697-8800, FAX: (212) 697-8606, Web Site: www.Argenttrading.com (16)

LevLane Advertising, Philadelphia, PA. Tel: (215) 825-9600, FAX: (215) 825-9601, Web Site: www.levlane.com (35)

Karen Levy Calligraphy, New York, NY. Tel: (212) 472-1669 (36)

Levy, Brad, Fragrance International Inc, Youngstown, OH. Tel: (330) 747-3341, (888) 547-8355, FAX: (330) 747-3343, E-Mail: comments@kisstell.com, Web Site: www.kisstell.com (16)

Levy, David, Turner Broadcasting System Inc, Atlanta, GA. Tel: (404) 827-1700, Web Site: www.turner.com (32)

Levy, Debra A., Key Communications Inc, Garrisonville, VA. Tel: (540) 720-5584, FAX: (540) 720-5687, E-Mail: usglass@aol.com, Web Site: www.key-com.com (17)

Levy, Hal, Hal Levy & Associates, High Falls, NY. Tel: (845) 687-4400 (20)

Levy, James P., Steck-Vaughn, Austin, TX. Tel: (512) 343-8227, (800) 531-5015, (877) 866-2586, FAX: (512) 795-3617, (877) 265-2730, E-Mail: info@steck-vaughn.com, Web Site: www.steck-vaughn.com (17)

Levy, Judy, Fragrance International Inc, Youngstown, OH. Tel: (330) 747-3341, (888) 547-8355, FAX: (330) 747-3343, E-Mail: comments@kisstell.com, Web Site: www.kisstell.com (16)

Levy, Karen, Karen Levy Calligraphy, New York, NY. Tel: (212) 472-1669 (36)

Levy, Lester A., NCH Corp, Irving, TX. Tel: (972) 438-0211, FAX: (972) 438-0707, Web Site: www.nch.com (34)

Levy, Mark, Federal Citizen Information Center, Pueblo, CO. Tel: (719) 295-2675, (888) 8-PUEBLO, FAX: (719) 948-9724, E-Mail: pueblo@gpo.gov, Web Site: www.pueblo.gsa.gov (5)

Levy, Michael R., Texas Monthly, Austin, TX. Tel: (512) 320-6900, (800) 759-2000, FAX: (512) 476-9007, E-Mail: info@texasmonthly.com, Web Site: www.texasmonthly.com (17)

Levy, Robert M., NCH Corp, Irving, TX. Tel: (972) 438-0211, FAX: (972) 438-0707, Web Site: www.nch.com (34)

Levy, Robert, Tele Business USA, Northbrook, IL. Tel: (847) 480-1560, FAX: (847) 897-4120, Web Site: www.tbiz.com (29)

Levy, Steve, NEA's Member Benefits Corp, Gaithersburg, MD. Tel: (301) 251-9600, FAX: (301) 527-8210, Web Site: www.neamb.com (1)

Levy, Yoav, Phototake/The Creative Link, New York, NY. Tel: (212) 736-2525, (800) 542-3686, FAX: (212) 736-1919, E-Mail: photoinfo@phototakeusa.com, Web Site: www.phototakeusa.com (38)

Lewallen, Brian, Muscle Dynamics Corp, Santa Fe Springs, CA. Tel: (562) 926-3232, (888) 629-4226, FAX: (562) 926-9191, E-Mail: info@muscledynamics.com, Web Site: www.muscledynamics.com (32)

Lewark, Larry A., Macy's Marketing, New York, NY. Tel: (212) 695-4400, FAX: (212) 494-1517, Web Site: www.macys.com (16)

Lewin, Bart, American Marketing Association/New York Chapter, New York, NY. Tel: (212) 687-3280, FAX: (212) 557-9242, E-Mail: mlkeane@nyama.org, Web Site: www.nyama.org (40)

Lewin, Stanton, LKH&S Inc, Chicago, IL. Tel: (312) 595-0200, FAX: (312) 595-0300, E-Mail: lkhs@lkhs.com, Web Site: www.lkhs.com (35)

Lewis Direct, Baltimore, MD. Tel: (410) 539-5100, FAX: (410) 539-4700 (22)

Lewis Enterprises, Pompano Beach, FL. Tel: (954) 782-1750, FAX: (954) 785-3391, E-Mail: hglewis1@aol.com; hgl@herschellgordonlewis.com, Web Site: www.herschellgordonlewis.com (39)

Lewis, Allan, Grand Circle Travel, Boston, MA. Tel: (617) 350-7500, (800) 959-0405, FAX: (617) 346-6030, Web Site: www.gct.com (19)

Lewis, Barbara, Women in Direct Marketing International, New York, NY. Tel: (516) 746-6700, FAX: (516) 294-8141, Web Site: www.wdmi.org (40)

Lewis, Brian, International Society for Technology in Education, Eugene, OR. Tel: (800) 336-5191, FAX: (541) 302-3778, Web Site: www.iste.org (1)

Lewis, Charles J., Creativity International, Ada, MI. Tel: (616) 956-0053, FAX: (616) 956-6957 (16)

Lewis, Charlotte, House of Onyx, Inc, Greenville, KY. Tel: (270) 338-2363, (800) 844-3100, FAX: (270) 338-9605, E-Mail: sales@houseofonyx.com, Web Site: www.houseofonyx.com (16)

Lewis, Dwight, Beemak Plastics Inc, La Mirada, CA. Tel: (310) 886-5880, (800) 421-4393, FAX: (310) 764-0330, E-Mail: info@beemak.com, Web Site: www.beemak.com (16)

Lewis, Edward, Essence Communications Inc, New York, NY. Tel: (212) 522-1212, FAX: (212) 921-5173, Web Site: www.essence.com (17)

Lewis, Francisco, Creative Commerce LLC, West Chester, PA. Tel: (610) 918-8800, FAX: (610) 918-1349, E-Mail: info@creativecommerce.com, Web Site: creativecommerce.com (35)

Lewis, Harriet, Grand Circle Travel, Boston, MA. Tel: (617) 350-7500, (800) 959-0405, FAX: (617) 346-6030, Web Site: www.gct.com (19)

Lewis, Herschell Gordon, Lewis Enterprises, Pompano Beach, FL. Tel: (954) 782-1750, FAX: (954) 785-3391, E-Mail: hglewis1@aol.com; hgl@herschellgordonlewis.com, Web Site: www.herschellgordonlewis.com (39)

Lewis, Jean, Think Ink, Bothell, WA. Tel: (425) 778-1935, (800) 778-1935, E-Mail: jean.lewis1@comcast.net, Web Site: www.thinkink.net (10)

Lewis, Jeff, The Directors Network, Encino, CA. Tel: (818) 906-0006, E-Mail: info@tdnartists.com, Web Site: www.tdnartists.com (35)

Lewis, Joan M., The Procter & Gamble Co, Cincinnati, OH. Tel: (513) 983-1100, Web Site: www.pg.com (16)

Lewis, Jr. Morgan, Medical Economics Magazine, North Olmsted, OH. Tel: (440) 243-8100, FAX: (440) 891-2735, Web Site: medicaleconomics.modernmedicine.com/about (17)

Lewis, Margo E, Lewis Enterprises, Pompano Beach, FL. Tel: (954) 782-1750, FAX: (954) 785-3391, E-Mail: hglewis1@aol.com; hgl@herschellgordonlewis.com, Web Site: www.herschellgordonlewis.com (39)

Lewis, MD Phillip J., Rohm & Haas Co, Philadelphia, PA. Tel: (215) 592-3000, (877) 288-5881, FAX: (215) 592-3377, Web Site: www.rohmhaas.com (16)

Lewis, Peter B., The Progressive Corp, Mayfield Village, OH. Tel: (440) 461-5000, (800) PROGRESSIVE, (800) 776-4737, FAX: (800) 456-6590, Web Site: www.progressive.com (15)

Lewis, Rev. Beth A., Augsburg Fortress Publishers, Minneapolis, MN. Tel: (612) 330-3300, (800) 426-0115, FAX: (612) 330-3455, E-Mail: info@augsburgfortress.org, Web Site: www.augsburgfortress.org (17)

Lewis, Scott, AliMed Inc, Dedham, MA. Tel: (781) 329-2900, (800) 225-2610, FAX: (800) 437-2966, (781) 329-8392, E-Mail: info@alimed.com, Web Site: www.alimed.com (7)

Lewis, Sheri, Creativity International, Ada, MI. Tel: (616) 956-0053, FAX: (616) 956-6957 (16)

Lewis, Steve, The Directors Network, Encino, CA. Tel: (818) 906-0006, E-Mail: info@tdnartists.com, Web Site: www.tdnartists.com (35)

Lewis, Travis, Inmar, Winston-Salem, NC. Tel: (336) 631-2500, FAX: (336) 631-2888, E-Mail: ibizdev@inmar.com, Web Site: www.promotionslogistics.com (14)

Lewis-Hall, Freda C., Pfizer Inc, New York, NY. Tel: (212) 733-2323, Web Site: www.pfizer.com (16)

Lewnes, Ann, Adobe Systems Inc, San Jose, CA. Tel: (408) 536-6000, (800) 833-6687, FAX: (408) 537-6000, Web Site: www.adobe.com (22)

Lexinet Corp, Council Grove, KS. Tel: (620) 767-7000, FAX: (620) 767-7100, E-Mail: tlc@lexinetcorporation.com (22)

Lexington Luggage Limited, New York, NY. Tel: (212) 223-0698, (800) 822-0404, FAX: (212) 753-3298, E-Mail: sales@lexingtonluggage.com, Web Site: www.lexingtonluggage.com (19)

LexisNexis, New York, NY. Tel: (212) 309-8100, FAX: (800) 437-8674, Web Site: www.lexisnexis.com (16)

LexisNexis Matthew Bender, Albany, NY. Tel: (518) 487-3000, (800) 424-4200, E-Mail: lexisnexis@matthewbender, Web Site: www.bender.lexisnexis.com (17)

LexisNexis Risk Soulutions, Alpharetta, GA. Tel: (678) 694-6000, Web Site: www.lexisnexis.com/risk (30)

Lexus Division of Toyota, Torrance, CA. Tel: (213) 328-2075 (12)

Leyden, David, Alert Marketing, Lyndhurst, NJ. Web Site: www.alertmarketing.com (28)

Peter Li Education Group, Dayton, OH. Tel: (937) 293-1415, (800) 523-4625, FAX: (937) 293-1310, Web Site: www.peterli.com (17)

Li, Peter, Peter Li Education Group, Dayton, OH. Tel: (937) 293-1415, (800) 523-4625, FAX: (937) 293-1310, Web Site: www.peterli.com (17)

Li, Richard P., Demographic Research Co, Denver, CO. Tel: (310) 766-5590, FAX: (303) 831-9181, Web Site: www.drcmodel.com (22)

Liantonio, Collette, Concepts TV Productions Inc, Boonton, NJ. Tel: (973) 331-1500, FAX: (973) 331-1550, E-Mail: info@conceptstv.com, Web Site: www.conceptstv.com (32)

Liao, Sheila, Air Power USA, Los Angeles, CA. Tel: (310) 641-0830, (888) 888-8231, FAX: (310) 641-8515, Web Site: www.airpowerusa.com (12)

Liberman Broadcasting Inc, Burbank, CA. Tel: (818) 729-5300, E-Mail: lbiinfo@lbimedia.com, Web Site: www.lbimedia.com (32)

Liberman, Jose, Liberman Broadcasting Inc, Burbank, CA. Tel: (818) 729-5300, E-Mail: lbiinfo@lbimedia.com, Web Site: www.lbimedia.com (32)

Liberman, Lenard, Liberman Broadcasting Inc, Burbank, CA. Tel: (818) 729-5300, E-Mail: lbiinfo@lbimedia.com, Web Site: www.lbimedia.com (32)

Liberman, Mark S., The Los Angeles Convention & Visitors Bureau, Los Angeles, CA. Tel: (213) 624-7300, (800) 366-6116, FAX: (213) 627-9746, Web Site: discoverlosangeles.com (19)

Liberty Creative Solutions, Tinley Park, IL. Tel: (708) 633-7450, FAX: (708) 633-7449, E-Mail: info@libertycreativesolutions.com, Web Site: www.libertycreativesolutions.com (21)

Liberty Fund Inc, Indianapolis, IN. Tel: (317) 842-0880, Web Site: www.libertyfund.org (1)

Liberty Life Insurance Co, Greenville, SC. Tel: (864) 609-8111, (800) 344-5834 (Mktg), FAX: (864) 609-4411, Web Site: www.libertycorp.com (15)

Liberty Mutual Group, Inc, Boston, MA. Tel: (617) 357-9500, (800) 837-5274, Web Site: www.libertymutual.com (15)

Liberty Orchards Co Inc, Cashmere, WA. Tel: (509) 782-2191, (800) 888-5696, FAX: (509) 782-1487, E-Mail: service@libertyorchards.com, Web Site: www.libertyorchards.com (16)

Liberty Tax Service, Virginia Beach, VA. Tel: (757) 493-8855 X8115, (800) 790-3863, FAX: (800) 880-6432 (14)

LibertyTree Press, Oakland, CA. Tel: (510) 632-1366, (800) 927-8733, FAX: (510) 568-6040, E-Mail: info@liberty-tree.com, Web Site: www.independent.org (5)

Libey-Concordia, Cherry Hill, NJ. Tel: (877) 903-9448, FAX: (856) 885-5068, E-Mail: libey@libey.com, Web Site: www.libey.com (20)

Libey, Donald R., Libey-Concordia, Cherry Hill, NJ. Tel: (877) 903-9448, FAX: (856) 885-5068, E-Mail: libey@libey.com, Web Site: www.libey.com (20)

The Library of America, New York, NY. Tel: (212) 308-3360, (800) 964-5778, FAX: (212) 750-8352, E-Mail: info@loa.org, Web Site: www.loa.org (13)

Licata, Bill, LCH Direct Inc, Waltham, MA. Tel: (978) 664-2900, FAX: (978) 664-4812, E-Mail: info@lchdirect.com, Web Site: www.lchdirect.com (35)

Licensing Industry Merchandisers' Association (LIMA), New York, NY. Tel: (212) 244-1944, FAX: (212) 563-6552, E-Mail: info@licensing.org, Web Site: www.licensing.org (40)

Lich, Brad A., Eastman Chemical Co, Kingsport, TN. Tel: (423) 229-2000, (800) 325-4330, E-Mail: eastman1@eastman.com, Web Site: www.eastman.com (16)

Lichter, Jonathan, Kelly, Scott & Madison Inc, Chicago, IL. Tel: (312) 977-0772, FAX: (312) 977-0874, E-Mail: info@ksmmedia.com, Web Site: www.ksmmedia.com (32)

Lichwalla, Ron, Fosina Marketing Group Inc, Danbury, CT. Tel: (203) 790-0013, E-Mail: info@fosinamarketing.com, Web Site: fosinamarketinggroup.com (35)

Liebenson, Sid, Marketing Highway, Deerfield, IL. Tel: (312) 502-3732, E-Mail: info@marketinghighway.com, Web Site: www.marketinghighway.com (20)

Lieber & Associates, Chicago, IL. Tel: (773) 325-9400, FAX: (773) 325-0621, E-Mail: info@lieberandassociates.com, Web Site: www.lieberandassociates.com (29)

Lieber, Mitchell A., Lieber & Associates, Chicago, IL. Tel: (773) 325-9400, FAX: (773) 325-0621, E-Mail: info@lieberandassociates.com, Web Site: www.lieberandassociates.com (29)

Lieberfarb, Richard, Scan Optics Inc, Manchester, CT. Tel: (860) 645-7878, (800) 745-6001, FAX: (860) 645-7995, E-Mail: info@scanoptics.com, Web Site: www.scanoptics.com (16)

Lieberman Productions, San Francisco, CA. Tel: (415) 955-0855, FAX: (415) 955-0822, E-Mail: lpinfo@lieberman.com, Web Site: www.lieberman.com (32)

Lieberman, Barry, Advantage Plus Marketing Group, Aliso Viejo, CA. Tel: (714) 573-7300, (800) 432-9466, FAX: (714) 573-7301, E-Mail: info@apmg.com, Web Site: www.apmg.com (30)

Lieberman, Gerald, B&G Lieberman Co Inc, Charlotte, NC. Tel: (704) 376-0717, (800) 438-0346, FAX: (800) 248-2696, E-Mail: bgl@bglieberman.com, Web Site: www.bglieberman.com (16)

Lieberman, Larry, B&G Lieberman Co Inc, Charlotte, NC. Tel: (704) 376-0717, (800) 438-0346, FAX: (800) 248-2696, E-Mail: bgl@bglieberman.com, Web Site: www.bglieberman.com (16)

Lieberman, Lenny, Guthy-Renker Corp, Santa Monica, CA. Tel: (310) 581-6250, FAX: (310) 581-3232, Web Site: www.guthy-renker.com (32)

Lieberman, Lenny, Lieberman Productions, San Francisco, CA. Tel: (415) 955-0855, FAX: (415) 955-0822, E-Mail: lpinfo@lieberman.com, Web Site: www.lieberman.com (32)

Lieberman, Robert Jay, All-Ways Advertising Co, Bloomfield, NJ. Tel: (973) 338-0700, (800) 255-9291, FAX: (973) 338-1410, Web Site: www.awadv.com (33)

Lieberman, Ron, Family Album, Kinzers, PA. Tel: (717) 442-0220, FAX: (717) 442-7904, E-Mail: rarebooks@pobox.com (6)

Liebert Corp, Columbus, OH. Tel: (614) 841-6700, (800) LIEBERT, FAX: (614) 841-6022, Web Site: www.liebert.com (16)

Liebert, Martin, Freedom Graphic Systems Inc, Milton, WI. Tel: (608) 868-7007, (800) 334-3540, FAX: (608) 868-7006, E-Mail: information@fgs.com, Web Site: www.freedomgraphicsystems.com (28)

Liebl, Lisa, MEGA MEDIA, Reeds Spring, MO. Tel: (405) 623-0023, E-Mail: lisa@mega-media.biz, Web Site: mega-media.biz (32)

Liebling, Donald, Brant Publications Inc, New York, NY. Tel: (212) 941-2800, FAX: (212) 941-2885, Web Site: www.interviewmagazine.com (17)

Liebman, Lisa, Austin & Williams, Hauppauge, NY. Tel: (631) 938-2279, FAX: (212) 434-7022, E-Mail: info@austin-williams.com, Web Site: www.austin-williams.com (35)

Liebowitz, Stuart, Physicians Planning Association Services, Deerfield Beach, FL. Tel: (954) 571-1877, (800) 221-2168, FAX: (954) 571-8582, E-Mail: insurance@assnservices.com, Web Site: www.physiciansplanning.com (16)

Liebson, Laurence, Walter Karl Inc, Pearl River, NY. Tel: (845) 620-0700, FAX: (845) 620-1885, E-Mail: info@walterkarl.infousa.com, Web Site: www.walterkarl.com (22)

Liedel, Christopher A., Smithsonian Enterprises, New York, NY. Tel: (212) 916-1300, (800) 766-2149, FAX: (212) 490-0058, Web Site: www.smithsonianmag.com (17)

Lien, Christopher G., BCC Software Inc, Rochester, NY. Tel: (585) 272-9130, (800) 453-3130, FAX: (585) 272-9141, Web Site: www.bccsoftware.com (22)

Liess, Michael T., Global Ware Solutions, Haverhill, MA. Tel: (800) 469-7500, FAX: (978) 469-7373, E-Mail: sales@gwsmail.com, Web Site: www.globalwaresolutions.com (22)

Lievois, Jim, Mazda Motor of America Inc, Irvine, CA. Tel: (949) 727-1990, (800) 222-6500, FAX: (949) 727-6101, Web Site: www.mazdausa.com (16)

Life Extension Foundation, Fort Lauderdale, FL. Tel: (954) 766-8144, (800) 678-8989, FAX: (954) 771-2827, E-Mail: info@lef.org, Web Site: www.lef.org (7)

Life Fitness, Schiller Park, IL. Tel: (847) 288-3300, (800) 735-3867, FAX: (847) 288-3703, E-Mail: webmaster@lifefitness.com, Web Site: www.lifefitness.com (11)

Life Investors Insurance Co of America, Cedar Rapids, IA. Tel: (319) 398-8511, (800) 231-7220, FAX: (319) 369-2188, Web Site: www.lifeinvestors.com (14)

Life Line Screening, Austin, TX. Tel: (216) 581-6556, (800) 449-2350, Web Site: www.lifelinescreening.com (7)

Life-Study Fellowship Foundation Inc, Darien, CT. Tel: (203) 655-1436, FAX: (203) 655-1392, Web Site: www.lifestudyfellowship.com (17)

Life Technologies, Grand Island, NY. Tel: (716) 774-6700, (800) 955-6288, FAX: (800) 331-2286, E-Mail: catalog@lifetech.com, Web Site: www.lifetechnologies.com (9)

Life Works Inc, Hollywood, FL. Tel: (954) 929-8428, (888) 780-9400, FAX: (954) 925-3365, Web Site: www.healthwagon.com (20)

Lifeboat Distribution, Shrewsbury, NJ. Tel: (732) 389-8950, FAX: (732) 389-9227, Web Site: www.programmersparadise.com (16)

LifeLock, Tempe, AZ. Tel: (480) 457-2007, Web Site: www.lifelock.com (16)

LifeScript, Newport Beach, CA. Tel: (949) 454-0422, (800) 637-9382, Web Site: www.lifescript.com (7)

The Lifestyle Marketing Corp, Glen Rock, NJ. Tel: (201) 670-7985, FAX: (201) 251-2443 (35)

Lifetime Brands Inc, Garden City, NY. Tel: (516) 683-6000, FAX: (516) 555-0101, E-Mail: questions@lifetimebrands.com, Web Site: www.lifetimebrands.com (8)

Lifetips, Boston, MA. Tel: (617) 886-9001, Web Site: www.lifetips.com (16)

LifeWay Christian Resources, Nashville, TN. Tel: (615) 251-5822, Web Site: www.lifeway.com (1)

Lifeway Christian Stores, Nashville, TN. Tel: (615) 251-2000, (800) 458-2772, FAX: (513) 728-6975, E-Mail: customerservice@berean.com. Web Site: www.berean.com (5)

Lift Outreach, Richland Hills, TX. Tel: (817) 658-2980 (1)

Lifynski, Maj Ernest, Centaur Forge LLC, Burlington, WI. Tel: (262) 763-9175, (800) 666-9175, FAX: (262) 763-8350, E-Mail: info@centaurforge.com, Web Site: www.centaurforge.com (9)

Light Sources Inc, Virginia Beach, VA. Tel: (757) 424-8636, (800) 882-8834, FAX: (757) 424-6186, E-Mail: lightsources@earthlink.net, Web Site: www.lightsourcesinc.com (16)

Light, Mark, Sterling Jewelers Inc, Akron, OH. Tel: (330) 668-5000, FAX: (330) 668-5052, E-Mail: webmaster@jewels.com, Web Site: www.sterlingjewelers.com (16)

Lighthizer, O. James, Civil War Preservation Trust, Washington, DC. Tel: (202) 367-1861, (800) 298-7878, E-Mail: info@civilwar.org, Web Site: www.civilwar.org (1)

Lighthouse List Co, Pompano Beach, FL. Tel: (954) 489-3008, (800) 684-2180, FAX: (954) 489-0850, E-Mail: mtlistdude@aol.com, Web Site: www.lighthouselist.com (24)

Lightman, Steve, Crosstown Traders Inc, Tucson, AZ. Tel: (520) 745-4500 (2)

Lightman, Steven, Harry & David Holdings Inc, Medford, OR. Tel: (541) 864-2362, (877) 322-1200, FAX: (800) 648-6640, Web Site: www.hndcorp.com (4)

Ligonier Ministries, Sanford, FL. Tel: (407) 333-4244, (800) 435-4343, FAX: (407) 333-4377, Web Site: www.ligonier.org (5)

Ligouri, Peter, Tribune Co, Chicago, IL. Tel: (312) 222-9100, FAX: (312) 222-1573, Web Site: www.tribune.com (17)

Liguori Publications, Liguori, MO. Tel: (636) 464-2500, (800) 325-9521, FAX: (800) 325-9526, E-Mail: liguori@liguori.org, Web Site: www.liguori.org (17)

Liguory, Tom, National Pen Corp, San Diego, CA. Tel: (858) 675-3000, FAX: (858) 675-3030, E-Mail: info@nationalpen.com, Web Site: www.pens.com (6)

Likoff, Laurie, Facts On File Inc, New York, NY. Tel: (212) 967-8800, (800) 322-8755, FAX: (212) 678-3633, Web Site: www.infobasepublishing.com (17)

Lile, Katie, Har Court Inc, Orlando, FL. Tel: (407) 345-2000, FAX: (407) 345-1052 (17)

Lilienthal, Brad, Kreg Tool Co, Huxley, IA. Tel: (515) 597-6400, Web Site: www.kregtool.com (16)

Lillian Vernon Corp, Colorado Springs, CO. Tel: (757) 427-7923, (800) 545-5426, FAX: (757) 427-7819, E-Mail: publicrelations@lillianvernon.com, Web Site: www.lillianvernon.com (6)

Lillie, James E., Jarden Corp, Boca Raton, FL. Tel: (561) 912-4395, Web Site: www.jarden.com (16)

Lillie, James E., Sunbeam Products Inc, Boca Raton, FL. Tel: (561) 912-4100, FAX: (561) 912-4567, Web Site: www.sunbeam.com (16)

Lilly, Sam, Learning Resources Institute, Downers Grove, IL. Tel: (630) 963-0398 (20)

Lilly, Scott, Kendall Products/Dri-Dek, Naples, FL. Tel: (239) 643-2244, (800) 348-2398, FAX: (800) 828-4248, E-Mail: info@dri-dek.com, Web Site: www.dri-dek.com (16)

Lilypons Water Gardens, Adamstown, MD. Tel: (800) 999-5459, FAX: (800) 879-5459, E-Mail: info@lilypons.com, Web Site: www.lilypons.com (8)

Lin Terry, Paterson, NJ. Tel: (973) 345-6677, FAX: (973) 345-5551, E-Mail: linterry@aol.com, Web Site: www.linterry.com (6)

Lin, John, Everex Computer Systems Inc, Fremont, CA. Tel: (800) 383-7391, (866) 850-8835, FAX: (510) 683-2186, E-Mail: customerservice@everex.com, Web Site: www.everex.com (1)

Joel Linchitz Consulting Services/Phone for Success, New York, NY. Tel: (212) 431-6700, FAX: (212) 865-2008, E-Mail: phoneforsuccess@compuserve.com, Web Site: www.callcenter-salestraining.com/index.php (29)

Linchitz, Joel, Joel Linchitz Consulting Services/Phone for Success, New York, NY. Tel: (212) 431-6700, FAX: (212) 865-2008, E-Mail: phoneforsuccess@compuserve.com, Web Site: www.callcenter-salestraining.com/index.php (29)

Lincoln Educational Services Corp, West Orange, NJ. Tel: (973) 736-9340, Web Site: www.lincolnedu.com (13)

Lincoln Financial Group, Radnor, PA. Tel: (215) 448-1400, (877) 275-5462, FAX: (215) 448-3962, Web Site: www.lfg.com (15)

Lincoln Park Zoo, Chicago, IL. Tel: (312) 742-2000, FAX: (312) 742-2137, E-Mail: webmaster@lpzoo.com, Web Site: www.lpzoo.com (1)

Lincoln Picture Studio, Dayton, OH. Tel: (937) 439-9633 (38)

Lind, Bonnie C., Neenah Paper FR LLC, Neenah, WI. Tel: (920) 733-7341, (800) 558-8327, FAX: (920) 733-2975, E-Mail: info@foxriverpaper.com, Web Site: www.foxriverpaper.com (27)

Lindauer, Jennifer, Citi Cards / Citicorp Credit Services, Long Island City, NY. Tel: (718) 248-5400 (14)

Lindberg, Greg, Business Publishers Inc, Durham, NC. Tel: (800) 223-8720, FAX: (800) 508-2592, E-Mail: custserv@bpinews.com, Web Site: www.bpinews.com (17)

Lindberg, Greg, Eli Journals, Durham, NC. Tel: (585) 203-5248, (800) 223-8720, FAX: (585) 292-4392, Web Site: www.elijournals.com (16)

Lindeke, Bruce F., Bolind Inc, Boulder, CO. Tel: (303) 443-3142, FAX: (303) 443-9889, Web Site: www.bolind.com (16)

Lindemann, Robert E., Stock Drive Products, New Hyde Park, NY. Tel: (516) 328-3300, (800) 819-8900, FAX: (516) 326-8827, E-Mail: sdp-sisupport@sdp-si.com, Web Site: www.sdp.si.com (5)

Linden, Carmelita, Divine Word Missionaries, Techny, IL. Tel: (847) 412-7233, (800) 275-0626, Web Site: www.svdmissions.org (1)

Linden, Shira, PromoWriting, Trumbull, CT. Tel: (203) 371-0654, E-Mail: shira@promowriting.com, Web Site: promowriting.com (35)

Lindner, Bill, Center for Professional Development, Tallahassee, FL. Tel: (850) 487-1691, (850) 644-8004, FAX: (850) 644-2589, Web Site: www.Learningforlife.fsu.com (13)

Lindner, James, Mitchell International, San Diego, CA. Tel: (858) 368-7000, FAX: (858) 238-9111, Web Site: www.mitchell.com (17)

Lindquist, Joyce, Weston Distance Learning Inc, Fort Collins, CO. Tel: (970) 282-6322, Web Site: www.westondistancelearning.com (13)

Lindsay, Ronald C., Eastman Chemical Co, Kingsport, TN. Tel: (423) 229-2000, (800) 325-4330, E-Mail: eastman1@eastman.com, Web Site: www.eastman.com (16)

Lindsay, Tillman, Shield Healthcare, Valencia, CA. Tel: (661) 294-4200, (800) 765-8775, FAX: (661) 294-1043, (800) 748-0713, Web Site: www.shieldhealthcare.com (7)

Lindsey, David, DEFENDER Direct Inc, Indianapolis, IN. Tel: (317) 810-4720, (800) 860-0303, FAX: (317) 810-4723, Web Site: www.defenderdirect.com (32)

Lindsey, Dennis, IPS - Sendero Corp, Norcross, GA. Tel: (480) 941-8112, (800) 879-1996, FAX: (770) 409-1735, E-Mail: sales@ips-sendero.com, Web Site: www.ips-sendero.com (14)

Lindwall, Jared, The Bender Group, Reno, NV. Tel: (775) 788-8800, (800) 621-9402, FAX: (775) 788-8811, E-Mail: salesinfo@benderwhs.com, Web Site: www.bendergroup.com (28)

Linen, Worth, WLA Inc, New York, NY. Tel: (212) 584-1810 (20)

Linett & Harrison, Montville, NJ. Tel: (908) 686-0606, FAX: (908) 686-0623, E-Mail: sharrison@linettandharrison.com, Web Site: www.linettandharrison.com (35)

Ling, Liu, Marshall Cavendish Corp, Tarrytown, NY. Tel: (914) 332-8888, (800) 821-9881, FAX: (914) 332-1888, Web Site: www.marshallcavendish.com (17)

Ling, Tom, Power Direct, Mission Viejo, CA. Tel: (877) 737-8977, FAX: (949) 253-3458, E-Mail: info@powerdirect.net, Web Site: www.powerdirect.net (35)

Lingafelter, David, Moen Inc, North Olmsted, OH. Tel: (440) 962-2000, Web Site: www.moen.com (16)

Linguistic Systems Inc, Cambridge, MA. Tel: (877) 654-5006, FAX: (617) 528-7491, E-Mail: info@linguist.com, Web Site: www.linguist.com (27)

LinguiSystems, East Moline, IL. Tel: (309) 755-2300, (800) 776-4332, FAX: (800) 577-4555, E-Mail: service@linguisystems.com, Web Site: www.linguisystems.com (17)

The Linick Group Inc, Middle Island, NY. Tel: (631) 924-3888, FAX: (631) 924-8555, E-Mail: andrew@linick.com, Web Site: www.andrewlinickdirectmarketing.com (35)

Linick, Ph.D. Andrew S., The Linick Group Inc, Middle Island, NY. Tel: (631) 924-3888, FAX: (631) 924-8555, E-Mail: andrew@linick.com, Web Site: www.andrewlinickdirectmarketing.com (35)

Lininger, Nicole, InventHelp's INPEX, Pittsburgh, PA. Tel: (412) 288-1343, (888) 544-6739, FAX: (412) 288-4546, E-Mail: info@inpex.com, Web Site: www.inpex.com (42)

LinkedIn Marketing Solutions, Mountain View, CA. Tel: (650) 687-3600, Web Site: business.linkedin.com/biz (35)

Links Magazine, Hilton Head Island, SC. Tel: (843) 842-6200, FAX: (843) 842-6233, Web Site: www.linksmagazine.com (17)

LinkShare Corp, New York, NY. Tel: (646) 943-8200, FAX: (646) 943-8204, Web Site: www.linkshare.com (32)

LinkWorth, Lewisville, TX. Tel: (214) 440-3900, (866) 565-9784, Web Site: www.linkworth.com (32)

Linn, Chris, truTV, New York, NY. Tel: (212) 973-2800, (800) 268-7856, FAX: (212) 973-3210, Web Site: www.trutv.com (17)

Linnehan, Ph.D. Frank, College of Business Administration, Philadelphia, PA. Tel: (215) 895-2145, Web Site: www.drexel.edu (41)

Linnell, Neil, Concinnity Marketing & Technology Inc, Winston-Salem, NC. Tel: (336) 245-4561, E-Mail: chris@concinnitymarketing.com, Web Site: www.concinnitymarketing.com (35)

Linnemann, Mavis, Inside Direct Mail, Philadelphia, PA. Tel: (215) 238-5300, (800) 777-8074, FAX: (215) 238-5412, E-Mail: customservice@napco.com, Web Site: www.insidedirectmail.com (43)

Linscott, J., CashNetUSA II LLC, Chicago, IL. Tel: (312) 568-4200, (888) 801-9075, FAX: (866) 326-5265, Web Site: www.cashnetusa.com (14)

Linse, Mark, MGM Mailing Lists, South Sandwich, MA. Tel: (508) 539-1300, (800) 660-5322, FAX: (508) 539-0700 (23)

Lintner, Connie, Delmmar Communications, Cameron, MO. Tel: (816) 632-1583, (800) 872-2627, FAX: (816) 632-5107, E-Mail: sales@eradiostore.com, Web Site: www.delmmar.com (16)

The Linton Co, Darien, GA. Tel: (912) 437-3193, (800) 841-0200, FAX: (912) 437-3195, E-Mail: cinfo@davientel.net, Web Site: www.lintonlabels.com (34)

Linton, D.B., The Linton Co, Darien, GA. Tel: (912) 437-3193, (800) 841-0200, FAX: (912) 437-3195, E-Mail: cinfo@davientel.net, Web Site: www.lintonlabels.com (34)

Linville, Larry, The United Methodist Publishing House, Nashville, TN. Tel: (615) 749-6000, (800) 672-1789, FAX: (615) 749-6417, E-Mail: productsandservices@umpublishing.com, Web Site: www.umpublishing.com (17)

Linzer, Daniel H., Northwestern University, Evanston, IL. Tel: (847) 491-5665, FAX: (847) 491-5925, E-Mail: jimc@northwestern.edu, Web Site: www.northwestern.edu (41)

Liodice, Robert, Association of National Advertisers Inc, New York, NY. Tel: (212) 697-5950, FAX: (212) 687-7310, Web Site: www.ana.net (40)

Lion Apparel, Dayton, OH. Tel: (937) 898-1949, (800) 548-6614, FAX: (937) 913-5667, Web Site: www.lionprotects.com (2)

Lion's Share Marketing Group, Inc, Houston, TX. Tel: (713) 686-4252, Web Site: www.lionsshare.com (20)

Lionsgate Entertainment Inc, New York, NY. Tel: (212) 577-2400, FAX: (212) 962-2872, Web Site: www.lionsgate.com (32)

Lionsgate Television Corp, Santa Monica, CA. Tel: (310) 449-9200, FAX: (310) 255-3870, Web Site: www.lionsgate.com (16)

Lioon, Douglas L., Advanced Medical Nutrition Inc, Pittsburgh, PA. Tel: (412) 494-0100, (800) 437-8888, (800) 879-2664, FAX: (888) 245-4440, Web Site: www.douglaslabs.com (7)

Liotine, Joseph T., Whirlpool Corp, Benton Harbor, MI. Tel: (269) 923-5000, E-Mail: info@whirlpool.com, Web Site: www.whirlpoolcorp.com (16)

Lipic, Steve, Lipic's Recognition, Saint Louis, MO. Tel: (314) 775-2500, (800) 771-4640, FAX: (314) 775-2501, E-Mail: lipic@lipic.com, Web Site: www.lipicsengagement.com (33)

Lipic's Recognition, Saint Louis, MO. Tel: (314) 775-2500, (800) 771-4640, FAX: (314) 775-2501, E-Mail: lipic@lipic.com, Web Site: www.lipicsengagement.com (33)

Lippert, Jerry, Nelson-Jameson Inc, Marshfield, WI. Tel: (715) 387-1151, (800) 826-8302, FAX: (715) 387-8746, (800) 472-0840, E-Mail: sales@nelsonjameson.com, Web Site: www.nelsonjameson.com (9)

Lippincott, Williams & Wilkins, Baltimore, MD. Tel: (410) 528-4000, (800) 638-0672, FAX: (410) 528-8597, E-Mail: customerservice@lww.com, Web Site: www.lww.com (17)

Lipscomb, Jeff, GS&F, Nashville, TN. Tel: (615) 385-1100, (800) 241-3325, FAX: (615) 783-0500, E-Mail: biz@gsandf.com, Web Site: www.gsandf.com (35)

Lipscombe, Trevor C., The Catholic University of America Press, Washington, DC. Tel: (202) 319-5052, FAX: (202) 319-4985, E-Mail: cua-press@cua.edu, Web Site: cuapress.cua.edu (17)

Lipsen, Linda, American Association for Justice, Washington, DC. Tel: (202) 965-3500, (800) 424-2725, FAX: (202) 625-7313, E-Mail: membership@justice.org, Web Site: www.justice.org (1)

Lipsky, Mark, The Radio Agency, Media, PA. Tel: (610) 892-7300, (800) 969-2636, FAX: (610) 892-1899, E-Mail: contact@theradioagency.com, Web Site: www.radiodirect.com (35)

Lipson, David, Peak Impact Inc, Ottawa, ON Canada. Tel: (613) 592-3100, E-Mail: customerservice@peakimpact.com, Web Site: www.peakimpact.com (14)

E Trina Lipton, New York, NY. Tel: (212) 674-5558, (917) 327-6886, FAX: (212) 674-3523, E-Mail: trinalipton@hotmail.com (37)

Lipton, E. Trina, E Trina Lipton, New York, NY. Tel: (212) 674-5558, (917) 327-6886, FAX: (212) 674-3523, E-Mail: trinalipton@hotmail.com (37)

Liquid Focus Direct LLC, Bridgeport, CT. Tel: (866) 892-0259, FAX: (203) 339-0066, Web Site: www.getliquidfocus.com (32)

Liquori, Dorothy, Women in Direct Marketing International, New York, NY. Tel: (516) 746-6700, FAX: (516) 294-8141, Web Site: www.wdmi.org (40)

Liska, Tommy, Clampitt Paper Co, Dallas, TX. Tel: (214) 638-3300, FAX: (214) 634-7837, E-Mail: dcrew@clampitt.com, Web Site: www.clampitt.com (16)

Lisner, Stephen, League of American Orchestras, New York, NY. Tel: (212) 262-5161, FAX: (212) 262-5198, Web Site: www.symphony.org; www.americanorchestras.org (1)

A Liss & Co Inc, Woodside, NY. Tel: (718) 728-0600, (800) 221-0938, FAX: (718) 728-1227, E-Mail: alissco@aol.com (16)

Nancy Liss, New York, NY. Tel: (646) 418-5000 (20)

Liss, Jeffrey, A Liss & Co Inc, Woodside, NY. Tel: (718) 728-0600, (800) 221-0938, FAX: (718) 728-1227, E-Mail: alissco@aol.com (16)

Liss, Jerold, A Liss & Co Inc, Woodside, NY. Tel: (718) 728-0600, (800) 221-0938, FAX: (718) 728-1227, E-Mail: alissco@aol.com (16)

Liss, Samantha, Voice Systems Engineering Inc, Langhorne, PA. Tel: (215) 953-8568, E-Mail: info@vseinc.com, Web Site: www.vseinc.com (32)

List Advisor Inc, Farmingdale, NY. Tel: (631) 777-2900, FAX: (631) 777-3050 (23)

List Alliance Inc, Alamo, CA. Tel: (925) 820-3151, E-Mail: info@listalliance.com, Web Site: www.listalliance.com (23)

List America, Washington, DC. Tel: (202) 298-9206, FAX: (202) 244-7294, Web Site: mdginc.org (23)

List Connection Inc, Simpsonville, SC. Tel: (864) 962-0761, FAX: (864) 962-0769, E-Mail: leads@listconnection.net, Web Site: www.listconnection.net (24)

List Marketing Group Inc, Cleveland, OH. Tel: (216) 990-2000, E-Mail: fran@listmarketinggroup.com, Web Site: www.listmarketinggroup.com (23)

List Media Inc, Aurora, OH. Tel: (330) 995-0864, FAX: (330) 995-0873, E-Mail: sales@admail.net, Web Site: www.admail.net (32)

List Partners Inc, Atlanta, GA. Tel: (404) 350-0600, (800) 941-6562, E-Mail: contact@thelistinc.com, Web Site: listpartnersinc.com (24)

List Pro of America, San Diego, CA. Tel: (858) 483-1410, E-Mail: listpro@swmall.com, Web Site: swmall.com/listpro (23)

List Process Direct Inc, New York, NY. Tel: (212) 517-8550, FAX: (212) 517-9728, E-Mail: pkranjac@listprocessdirect.com, Web Site: www.listprocessdirect.com (31)

List Service Direct Inc, Leonia, NJ. Tel: (201) 585-1447, (800) 371-5487, FAX: (201) 585-1732, E-Mail: info@listservicedirect.com, Web Site: www.listservicedirect.com (23)

List Services Corporation, Bethel, CT. Tel: (203) 743-2600, E-Mail: info@listservices.com, Web Site: www.listservices.com (24)

List Source Direct, Delray Beach, FL. Tel: (561) 570-1287, E-Mail: info@listsourcedirect.com, Web Site: www.listsourcedirect (23)

List Strategies Inc, New York, NY. Tel: (212) 767-1000, FAX: (212) 541-4408, E-Mail: info@liststrategies.com, Web Site: www.liststrategies.com (23)

List Team, Calabasas, CA. Tel: (818) 887-1166, (800) 553-2123, E-Mail: info@listteam.com, Web Site: www.listteam.com (23)

ListAbility Inc, Venice, FL. Tel: (866) 446-2055, E-Mail: info@listability.com, Web Site: www.listability.com (23)

Listening Library Inc, Random House Audio, New York, NY. Tel: (212) 782-8482, (800) 726-0600, FAX: (212) 940-7381, E-Mail: rhacademic@penguinrandomhouse.com, Web Site: www.randomhouse.com/audio (3)

Lister Butler Inc, New York, NY. Tel: (212) 951-6100, FAX: (212) 481-0230, Web Site: www.listerbutler.com (20)

ListGIANT, Westlake Village, CA. Tel: (800) 383-1381, E-Mail: contact@listgiant.com, Web Site: www.listgiant.com (23)

ListK, Atlanta, GA. Tel: (800) 600-3389, FAX: (770) 825-9188, E-Mail: questions@listk.com, Web Site: www.listk.com (32)

Listmasters Direct Mail Services, Philadelphia, PA. Tel: (215) 633-8200, E-Mail: sales@listmastersdirect.com, Web Site: www.listmastersdirect.com (23)

Listrak, Lititz, PA. Tel: (717) 627-4528, (877) 362-4556, E-Mail: info@listrak.com, Web Site: www.listrak.com (32)

LISTS Inc, Jacksonville, FL. Tel: (904) 733-6106, (800) 805-5478, FAX: (904) 730-7540, E-Mail: info@lists-inc.com, Web Site: www.lists-inc.com (23)

ListSource, Irvine, CA. Tel: (866) 774-3282, E-Mail: sales@corelogic.com, Web Site: www.listsource.com (23)

Lisy, Paul, eFootage, Pasadena, CA. Tel: (626) 395-9593, FAX: (626) 395-5394, E-Mail: info@efootage.com, Web Site: www.efootage.com (38)

Literary Market Place, Medford, NJ. Tel: (609) 654-6266, FAX: (609) 654-4309, E-Mail: custserv@infotoday.com, Web Site: www.literarymarketplace.com (43)

Lithia Motors Inc, Medford, OR. Tel: (541) 774-7602 (12)

Litho-Web Inc, Bolton, ON Canada. Tel: (905) 857-9111, (800) 490-6688, FAX: (905) 857-9112, E-Mail: sales@lithoweb.ca, Web Site: www.lithoweb.ca (27)

Litle & Co, Lowell, MA. Tel: (978) 275-6500, (800) 548-5326, FAX: (978) 937-7250, Web Site: www.litle.com (14)

Litle, Tim, Litle & Co, Lowell, MA. Tel: (978) 275-6500, (800) 548-5326, FAX: (978) 937-7250, Web Site: www.litle.com (14)

Litrides, Lindy, CoreMessagink, Lancaster, PA. Tel: (717) 207-0212, Web Site: www.cormessagink.com (39)

Litt, M.D. Andrew W., New York University Medical Center, New York, NY. Tel: (212) 263-7800, FAX: (212) 263-8426, Web Site: www.med.nyu.edu (1)

Arthur D Little Inc, Boston, MA. Tel: (617) 532-9550, FAX: (617) 261-6630, Web Site: www.adlittle-us.com (20)

Little, Chris, Successful Farming, Des Moines, IA. Tel: (515) 284-2143, (800) 678-2711, FAX: (515) 284-3127 (17)

Little, Gavin, Tupperware Brands Corp, Orlando, FL. Tel: (407) 826-5050, (800) 366-3800, FAX: (407) 826-8874, Web Site: www.tupperwarebrands.com (16)

Little, Ken, NCC Media, New York, NY. Tel: (212) 548-3300, FAX: (212) 519-0099, Web Site: nccmedia.com (32)

Little, Michael D., Christian Broadcasting Network Inc, Virginia Beach, VA. Tel: (757) 226-7000, FAX: (757) 226-2017, Web Site: www.cbn.com (1)

Little, Randy, PFI Western Stores Inc, Springfield, MO. Tel: (417) 889-2668, (800) 222-4734, FAX: (417) 889-7204, E-Mail: pfi.@pfiwestern.com, Web Site: www.pfiwestern.com (2)

Little, Rita, Bed Bath & Beyond, Union, NJ. Tel: (631) 420-7050, (800) 462-3966, Web Site: bedbathandbeyond.com (8)

Little, Tony, Health International Corp, Tampa, FL. Tel: (800) 780-6744, FAX: (727) 595-6456, E-Mail: info@tonylittle.com, Web Site: www.tonylittle.com (32)

Littlefield, Elizabeth, Overseas Private Investment Corp (OPIC), Washington, DC. Tel: (202) 336-8799, FAX: (202) 336-7949, E-Mail: info@opic.gov, Web Site: www.opic.gov (14)

Littlefield, Gretchen, Infogroup Media Solutions, Papillion, NE. Tel: (800) 223-2194, E-Mail: infogroupmediasolutions@infogroup.com, Web Site: www.infogroupmediasolutions.com (23)

Littleton Coin Co Inc, Littleton, NH. Tel: (603) 444-5386, (800) 645-3122, FAX: (603) 444-0121, E-Mail: jhennessey@littletoncoin.com, Web Site: www.littletoncoin.com (6)

Littleton, Jeff, Ashrae Learning Institute, Atlanta, GA. Tel: (404) 636-8400, (800) 527-4723, FAX: (404) 321-5478, E-Mail: ashrae@ashrae.org, Web Site: www.ashrae.org (31)

Litvack, Neal, American Red Cross, Washington, DC. Tel: (202) 303-5214, (800) RED-CROSS, FAX: (202) 303-6604, Web Site: www.redcross.org (1)

Liu, Ching-Tl, Scientific Computing Associates Corp, River Forest, IL. Tel: (708) 771-4567, FAX: (708) 771-4569, E-Mail: sca@scausa.com, Web Site: www.scausa.com (22)

Liu, David, The Wedding Pages, New York, NY. Tel: (212) 219-8555, (800) 843-4983, FAX: (212) 219-1929, Web Site: www.theknot.com (16)

Liu, Eric, Nixle LLC, San Francisco, CA. Tel: (877) 649-5362, E-Mail: support@nixle.com, Web Site: www.nixle.com (35)

Live Design, New York, NY. Tel: (212) 204-4268, FAX: (212) 204-4291, Web Site: livedesignonline.com (17)

Live Nation, Beverly Hills, CA. Tel: (310) 867-7000, Web Site: www.livenation.com (19)

Lively, Mike, Direct Sports Supply, Pearisburg, VA. Tel: (540) 921-1243, (800) 456-0072, FAX: (540) 921-1475, Web Site: www.directsports.com (11)

LiveOps Inc, Redwood City, CA. Tel: (408) 844-2400, Web Site: www.liveops.com (29)

Liveris, Andrew, The Dow Chemical Co, Midland, MI. Tel: (989) 636-1000, (800) 258-2436, FAX: (989) 832-1556, Web Site: www.dow.com (16)

Livermore, Arnold, Blue Cross Blue Shield of Florida, Jacksonville, FL. Tel: (904) 791-6111, (800) 477-3736, FAX: (904) 905-6638, E-Mail: katie.magee@bcbsfl.com, Web Site: www.bcbsfl.com (15)

Livingston, Doug, Patriot Communications LLC, West Hollywood, CA. Tel: (888) 833-4711, FAX: (310) 482-6701, E-Mail: dlivingston@patriotllc.com, Web Site: www.patriotllc.com (32)

Livingston, Howard, Finley Products Inc, Lancaster, PA. Tel: (717) 735-8200, (888) 626-5301, FAX: (717) 735-8210, E-Mail: fininfo@finleyproducts.com, Web Site: www.2X4basics.com (16)

Livingston, Jr. Fin, Finley Products Inc, Lancaster, PA. Tel: (717) 735-8200, (888) 626-5301, FAX: (717) 735-8210, E-Mail: fininfo@finleyproducts.com, Web Site: www.2X4basics.com (16)

Livingston, Phil, LexisNexis Matthew Bender, Albany, NY. Tel: (518) 487-3000, (800) 424-4200, E-Mail: lexisnexis@matthewbender, Web Site: www.bender.lexisnexis.com (17)

Livingston, Phil, Martindale-Hubbell, New Providence, NJ. Tel: (908) 771-7777, (800) 526-4902, FAX: (908) 771-8704, Web Site: www.martindale.com (17)

Lizama, George, Production Solutions, Vienna, VA. Tel: (703) 734-5700 (20)

Lizotte, Mike, American Meadows Inc & Vermont Wild Flowers Farm, Shelburne, VT. Tel: (877) 309-7333, FAX: (802) 951-9089, E-Mail: customerservice@americanmeadows.com, Web Site: www.americanmeadows.com (8)

Lizza, Fred, Freestyle Solutions, Parsippany, NJ. Tel: (973) 237-9415, (800) 858-3666, FAX: (973) 237-9043, E-Mail: sales@dydacomp.com, Web Site: www.dydacomp.com (22)

Lladro USA Inc, Moonachie, NJ. Tel: (201) 807-1177, (800) 634-9088, FAX: (201) 807-1293, E-Mail: customer-services@us.lladro.com, Web Site: www.lladro.com (16)

Lladro, Rosa, Lladro USA Inc, Moonachie, NJ. Tel: (201) 807-1177, (800) 634-9088, FAX: (201) 807-1293, E-Mail: customer-services@us.lladro.com, Web Site: www.lladro.com (16)

Llewelin, Charlie, Texas Monthly, Austin, TX. Tel: (512) 320-6900, (800) 759-2000, FAX: (512) 476-9007, E-Mail: info@texasmonthly.com, Web Site: www.texasmonthly.com (17)

Llewellyn Publications, Woodbury, MN. Tel: (651) 291-1970, (877) 639-9753, FAX: (651) 291-1908, Web Site: www.llewellyn.com (17)

Llorens, John, Arch Telecom Inc, Austin, TX. Tel: (512) 492-0735, (800) 890-7575, FAX: (512) 495-7101, Web Site: www.archtelecom.com (16)

Lloyd, Steve, Direct Marketing News, Markham, ON Canada. Tel: (905) 201-6600, (800) 668-1838, FAX: (905) 201-6601, E-Mail: home@dmn.ca, Web Site: www.dmn.ca (43)

Lloyd, Allison, Creating Results LLC, Woodbridge, VA. Tel: (703) 494-7888, (888) 205-8899, Web Site: www.creatingresults.com (17)

Lloyd, Dan, Frontier Natural Products Co-op, Norway, IA. Tel: (800) 669-3275, FAX: (800) 717-4372, E-Mail: info@frontiercoop.com, Web Site: www.frontiercoop.com (7)

Lloyd, Marie Sauve, Stephen Thomas, Toronto, ON Canada. Tel: (416) 690-8801, FAX: (416) 690-7256, E-Mail: mail@stephenthomas.ca, Web Site: www.stephenthomas.ca (1)

Lloyd, Nancy, Day Runner Direct, Sidney, NY. Tel: (800) 643-9923, FAX: (800) 643-9927, Web Site: www.dayrunner.com (10)

Lloyd, Tracie, KV Vet Supply Co, Inc, David City, NE. Tel: (402) 367-6047, Web Site: www.kvvet.com (5)

Lloyd-Martin, Heather, SuccessWorks Search Marketing Inc, Portland, OR. Tel: (503) 922-3627, Web Site: www.seocopywriting.com (32)

LO-AD Communications, Pasadena, CA. Tel: (626) 304-7750, FAX: (626) 304-2716, Web Site: www.lo-ad.com (16)

Lo Giudice, Carolyn, LinguiSystems, East Moline, IL. Tel: (309) 755-2300, (800) 776-4332, FAX: (800) 577-4555, E-Mail: service@linguisystems.com, Web Site: www.linguisystems.com (17)

Lo Ink Specialties, Kennebunkport, ME. Tel: (207) 967-9110, (800) 777-6471, FAX: (800) 895-6465, E-Mail: rwatson@loink.com, Web Site: www.loink.com (16)

Lo, Jeffrey, Unicom Electric Inc, Walnut, CA. Tel: (626) 964-7873, (800) 346-6668, FAX: (626) 964-7880, E-Mail: info@unicomlink.com, Web Site: www.unicomlink.com (16)

Lobascio, Frank, Herbach & Rademan Co, Moorestown, NJ. Tel: (856) 802-0422, (800) 848-8001, FAX: (856) 802-0465, E-Mail: sales@herbach.com, Web Site: www.herbach.com (9)

Lobisco, Nicole, ListK, Atlanta, GA. Tel: (800) 600-3389, FAX: (770) 825-9188, E-Mail: questions@listk.com, Web Site: www.listk.com (32)

Lobrano-Markham, Elizabeth, Focus Plus Inc, New York, NY. Tel: (212) 675-0142, (800) 340-8846, FAX: (212) 645-3171, E-Mail: info@focusplusny.com, Web Site: www.focusplusny.com (30)

Local Corp, Irvine, CA. Tel: (877) 784-0805, FAX: (949) 784-0880, Web Site: www.local.com (32)

Local Government Federal Credit Union, Raleigh, NC. Tel: (919) 755-0534, Web Site: www.lgfcu.org (14)

Local Search Association, Troy, MI. Tel: (248) 244-6200, FAX: (248) 244-0700, Web Site: www.localsearchassociation.org (1)

LoCastro, Steve, Business Development Solutions Inc, Cherry Hill, NJ. Tel: (856) 787-1500, E-Mail: info@hdsdatabase.com, Web Site: www.bdsdatabase.com (22)

Location Sound Corp, North Hollywood, CA. Tel: (818) 980-9891, (800) 228-4429, FAX: (818) 980-9911, E-Mail: information@locationsound.com, Web Site: www.locationsound.com (3)

Location3 Media, Denver, CO. Tel: (720) 881-8510, FAX: (303) 298-1986, E-Mail: info@location3.com, Web Site: www.location3.com (32)

Loch, Joe, Hickory Farms, Maumee, OH. Tel: (419) 893-7611, (800) 776-4111, (800) 442-5671, FAX: (419) 893-0164, Web Site: www.hickoryfarms.com (4)

Lock, William, Elcom International Inc, Norwood, MA. Tel: (781) 501-4000, FAX: (781) 762-1540, Web Site: www.elcominternational.com (22)

Lockard & Wechsler Direct, Irvington, NY. Tel: (914) 250-0241, E-Mail: info@lwdirect.com, Web Site: www.lwdirect.com (35)

Lockard, Pamela, DMN3, Houston, TX. Tel: (713) 893-4275, (888) 721-0377, E-Mail: sales@dmn3.com, Web Site: www.dmn3.com (35)

Lockhart Industries Inc, Dallas, TX. Tel: (214) 348-1422, Web Site: www.lockhartadvantage.com (9)

Lockhart, Doris L, Lockhart Industries Inc, Dallas, TX. Tel: (214) 348-1422, Web Site: www.lockhartadvantage.com (9)

Lockheed Martin Corp, Bethesda, MD. Tel: (301) 897-6000, Web Site: www.lockheedmartin.com (16)

Locklund, Jean, Johnson & Quin Inc, Niles, IL. Tel: (847) 588-4800, FAX: (847) 647-6949, E-Mail: jqinfo@j-quin.com, Web Site: www.j-quin.com (28)

Lockwood, Lisa, Marketing Research Association, Washington, DC. Tel: (860) 682-1000, (202) 800-2545, FAX: (860) 682-1010, (888) 512-1050, E-Mail: membership@marketingresearch.org, Web Site: www.mra-net.org (40)

Locreille, Daniela, Hobsons, Cincinnati, OH. Tel: (513) 985-4186, Web Site: www.hobsons.com (16)

Loctite Corp, Rocky Hill, CT. Tel: (860) 571-5100, (800) 562-8483, (800) LOCTITE, FAX: (860) 571-5465, Web Site: www.loctite.com (16)

Lodato, Michael, Good Directions Co Inc, Danbury, CT. Tel: (203) 743-3775, FAX: (203) 743-5226, E-Mail: contact@gooddirections.com, Web Site: www.gooddirections.com (8)

Loeb & Loeb Inc, New York, NY. Tel: (212) 407-4000, Web Site: www.loeb.com (20)

Ben Loeb Inc, Fairfield, NJ. Tel: (908) 788-0542, FAX: (908) 788-6861, E-Mail: tbecker@bsloeb.com, Web Site: www.bsloeb.com (33)

Loeb, Richard, Laven & Loeb Inc, Beachwood, OH. Tel: (216) 291-3483, (623) 217-2101, E-Mail: alaven@lavenandloeb.com; vtaylor@lavenandloeb.com, Web Site: www.lavenandloeb.com (20)

Loeding, Deborah V., The HW Wilson Co, Bronx, NY. Tel: (718) 588-8400, (800) 367-6770, FAX: (800) 590-1617, E-Mail: custserv@hwwilson.com, Web Site: www.hwwilson.com (17)

Loeffler, Bob, H E Butt Grocery Co, San Antonio, TX. Tel: (210) 938-8357, (800) 432-3113, FAX: (210) 938-7511, Web Site: www.heb.com (16)

Loehmann's, Bronx, NY. Tel: (718) 409-2000, Web Site: www.loehmanns.com (2)

Loews Hotels, Inc, New York, NY. Tel: (212) 521-2000, (866) 563-9792, FAX: (212) 521-2379, Web Site: www.loewshotels.com (19)

Lofgren, Kevin, Farstar Inc, Frisco, TX. Tel: (214) 649-0422, E-Mail: realhuman@wedontplay.com, Web Site: blog.wedontplayfair.com (35)

Loflin, Stephen, National Society of Collegiate Scholars, Washington, DC. Tel: (202) 265-9000, Web Site: www.nscs.org (1)

Lofquist, John J, Take 5 Solutions LLC, Boca Raton, FL. Tel: (561) 819-5555, (866) 861-8862, FAX: (561) 819-0245, E-Mail: sales@take5s.com, Web Site: www.take5solutions.com (30)

LOG-ON, New York, NY. Tel: (212) 279-4567, E-Mail: sales@log-on.org, Web Site: www.log-on.org (21)

Logan, Dan, Trinity Marketing Inc, Boston, MA. Tel: (617) 292-7399, E-Mail: info@trinitynet.com, Web Site: www.trinitynet.com (35)

Logan, Denise, White Mane Publishing Co Inc, Shippensburg, PA. Tel: (717) 532-2237, (888) 948-6263, FAX: (717) 532-6110, E-Mail: marketing@whitemane.com, Web Site: www.whitemane.com (17)

Loggia, Joe, Advanstar Communications Inc, North Olmstead, OH. Tel: (440) 243-8100, (800) 225-4569, FAX: (440) 891-2651, E-Mail: info@advanstar.com, Web Site: www.advanstarlists.com (17)

Logical Computer Selections, Short Hills, NJ. Tel: (212) 949-2290, (800) 949-2701, FAX: (212) 697-5786, E-Mail: info@logicomputer.com, Web Site: www.logicomputer.com (16)

Logicnology Inc, Sunrise, FL. Tel: (954) 851-1200, FAX: (954) 846-8552 (22)

Lohkemper, Mark, CAIG Laboratories Inc, Poway, CA. Tel: (858) 486-8388, FAX: (858) 486-8398, E-Mail: caig123@caig.com, Web Site: www.caig.com (9)

Lohner, Mike, Home Interiors & Gifts Inc, Carrollton, TX. Tel: (972) 695-1000, FAX: (972) 695-1112 (16)

Loizzo, Larry, Lab Safety Supply Inc, Janesville, WI. Tel: (608) 754-2345, (800) 356-2855, FAX: (800) 543-9910, Web Site: www.labsafety.com (5)

Lojacono, Joseph, Valmark Associates LLC, Buffalo, NY. Tel: (716) 836-3414, FAX: (716) 836-3415, E-Mail: joe@valmarkassociates.com, Web Site: www.valmarkassociates.com (35)

Loken, Ted, Sight Marketing, Minneapolis, MN. Tel: (651) 379-4059, Web Site: www.sightmarketing.com (30)

Lokis, Marianna, Adirondack Direct, Long Island City, NY. Tel: (718) 932-4003, (800) 221-2444, FAX: (800) 477-1330, E-Mail: info@adirondackdirect.com, Web Site: www.adirondackdirect.com (10)

Lombard, Gary, Woodcraft Supply Corp LLC, Parkersburg, WV. Tel: (304) 422-5412, (800) 344-3348, FAX: (304) 422-5417, Web Site: www.woodcraft.com (9)

Lombardi Publishing Corp, Vaughan, ON Canada. Tel: (866) 744-3579, FAX: (905) 856-9416, E-Mail: customerservice@lombardipublishing.com, Web Site: www.lombardipublishing.com (17)

Lombardi, Dean, Los Angeles Kings, Los Angeles, CA. Tel: (213) 742-7100, (888) KINGS-LA, FAX: (213) 742-7296, Web Site: kings.nhl.com (3)

Lombardo, Anthony A., E-Z-EM Inc, Lake Success, NY. Tel: (516) 333-8230, (800) 544-4624, FAX: (516) 333-8278, E-Mail: webmaster@ezem.com, Web Site: www.ezem.com (7)

Lombardo, Katherine, Kurt Salmon Associates Inc, Atlanta, GA. Tel: (404) 892-0321, FAX: (404) 898-9590, E-Mail: infoksaweb@kurtsalmon.com, Web Site: www.kurtsalmon.com (20)

London, Terry E., Pier 1 Imports Inc, Fort Worth, TX. Tel: (817) 252-6300, (800) 245-4595, E-Mail: customerservice@pier1.com, Web Site: www.pier1.com (8)

Lone Star Web Inc, Dallas, TX. Tel: (214) 638-4946, FAX: (214) 630-4364, E-Mail: jerry@lonestarweb.com, Web Site: www.lonestarweb.com (27)

Lonergan, Daniel, L6 Holdings Corp, Duluth, GA. Tel: (678) 957-0511, FAX: (678) 957-0551 (14)

Long & Foster Insurance, Chantilly, VA. Tel: (703) 653-8500 (15)

Long, David H., Liberty Mutual Group, Inc, Boston, MA. Tel: (617) 357-9500, (800) 837-5274, Web Site: www.libertymutual.com (15)

Long, Erik, Pfaelzer Brothers, Maumee, OH. Tel: (419) 893-7611, (800) 345-9290, FAX: (419) 893-0164, Web Site: www.phaelzerbrothers.com (16)

Long, Joffrey, Joffrey Long Consultants, Granada Hills, CA. Tel: (818) 635-1777, Web Site: www.southwestbancorp.com (20)

Long, Joffrey, Southwest Consultants, Granada Hills, CA. Tel: (818) 635-1777, Web Site: www.southwestbancorp.com (20)

Long, Larry, CPM Delta 1, Inc, Dallas, TX. Tel: (214) 349-6886, (800) 627-0252, FAX: (214) 503-1557, Web Site: www.cpmdelta1.com (11)

Long, Laurie, Creative Teaching Associates, Clovis, CA. Tel: (559) 291-6626, (800) 767-4282, FAX: (559) 291-2953, Web Site: www.mastercta.com (16)

Long, Michael J., Arrow Electronics Inc, Englewood, CO. Tel: (952) 828-5350, (800) 833-3557, FAX: (952) 828-5399, Web Site: www.arrow.com (3)

Long, Paul, Kappa Studios, Burbank, CA. Tel: (818) 843-3400, FAX: (818) 559-5684, E-Mail: info@kappastudios.com, Web Site: www.kappastudios.com (32)

Long, Peter, MCH Strategic Data, Sweet Springs, MO. Tel: (660) 335-6373, (800) 776-6373, FAX: (660) 335-4157, E-Mail: sales@mchdata.com, Web Site: mchdata.com (23)

Long, Richard, USG Corp, Chicago, IL. Tel: (312) 436-4000, (800) 621-9622, FAX: (312) 672-4093, Web Site: www.usg.com (34)

Long, Ron, Pinkerton Security & Investigation Services, Parsippany, NJ. Tel: (973) 397-2276, (800) 724-1616, FAX: (973) 397-2491, Web Site: www.ci-pinkerton.com (16)

Long, Roy, Long's Electronics Inc, Irondale, AL. Tel: (205) 956-6767, (800) 633-3410, FAX: (800) 633-2530, E-Mail: info@longselectronics.com, Web Site: www.longselectronics.com (3)

Long, Tim, Laminex Inc, Fort Mill, SC. Tel: (704) 679-4170, (800) 438-8850, FAX: (704) 679-8453, Web Site: www.laminex.com (16)

Long, Tom, MillerCoors LLC, Chicago, IL. Tel: (312) 496-2700, (800) 645-5376, Web Site: www.millercoors.com (4)

Long, Wendy, Da-Lite Screen Co Inc, Warsaw, IN. Tel: (574) 267-8101, (800) 622-3737, FAX: (574) 267-7804, E-Mail: info@da-lite.com, Web Site: www.da-lite.com (16)

Longevity Network Ltd, Henderson, NV. Tel: (702) 454-7000, (800) 242-1000, FAX: (702) 434-8259, E-Mail: info@longevity.com, Web Site: www.longevity.com (7)

Longevity Pure Medicine, Los Angeles, CA. Tel: (800) 919-2090, FAX: (760) 329-3651, E-Mail: info@longetivtypuremedicine.com, Web Site: www.longevitypuremedicine.com (7)

Longinotti, Jeremy, eBureau LLC, Saint Cloud, MN. Tel: (320) 534-5000, FAX: (320) 534-5020, Web Site: www.ebureau.com (22)

Longley, Steve, TPG Direct Inc, Philadelphia, PA. Tel: (215) 592-8381, FAX: (215) 574-8316, E-Mail: slongley@tpgdirect.com, Web Site: www.tpgdirect. com (35)

Longo, Al, Publicity Inc, Mansfield, MA. Tel: (617) 367-3555, FAX: (617) 367-3557 (35)

Longo, Anthony, Rainbow Art Glass, Wall, NJ. Tel: (732) 681-6003, (800) 526-2356, FAX: (732) 681-4984, E-Mail: info@rainbowartglass.com. Web Site: www.rainbowartglass.com (16)

Longo, Charles M., Rainbow Art Glass, Wall, NJ. Tel: (732) 681-6003, (800) 526-2356, FAX: (732) 681-4984, E-Mail: info@rainbowartglass.com, Web Site: www.rainbowartglass.com (16)

Longo, Debbie, Ability Commerce, Delray Beach, FL. Tel: (561) 330-3151, Web Site: www. abilitycommerce.com (20)

Longo, Martin, Revana Digital, San Dimas, CA. Tel: (909) 599-8885, (866) 922-4632, Web Site: www. revanadigital.com (35)

Long's Electronics Inc, Irondale, AL. Tel: (205) 956-6767, (800) 633-3410, FAX: (800) 633-2530, E-Mail: info@longselectronics.com, Web Site: www.longselectronics.com (3)

Longseth, Ann, Veridian Credit Union, Waterloo, IA. Tel: (319) 236-5692, (800) 235-3228, FAX: (319) 833-1185, E-Mail: sarahma@veridiancu.org, Web Site: www.veridiancu.org (1)

Longsworth, Kathy, Phoenix Learning Group Inc, Maryland Heights, MO. Tel: (314) 569-0211, (800) 221-1274, FAX: (314) 569-2834, E-Mail: dealersales@ phoenixlearninggroup.com, Web Site: www. phoenixlearninggroup.com (16)

Longview Fibre Co, Longview, WA. Tel: (360) 425-1550, FAX: (360) 230-5135, E-Mail: info@ longviewfibre.com, Web Site: www.longfibre.com (25)

Lonsdale, Marty, World Vision Inc, Federal Way, WA. Tel: (253) 815-1000, (888) 511-6548, FAX: (253) 815-3140, E-Mail: info@worldvision.org, Web Site: www.worldvision.org (1)

Loomis, Daniel, Crystek Corp, Fort Myers, FL. Tel: (239) 561-3311, (800) 237-3061, FAX: (239) 561-1025, E-Mail: sales@crystek.com, Web Site: www. crystek.com (9)

LoParco, Melissa A., Catalyst Marketing Communications Inc, Stamford, CT. Tel: (203) 348-7541, FAX: (203) 348-5688, E-Mail: b2b@catalystmc.com, Web Site: www.catalystmc.com (35)

Lopes, Philip, MPBS Industries, Los Angeles, CA. Tel: (323) 268-8514, (800) 421-6265, FAX: (323) 268-6305, Web Site: www.mpbs.com (16)

Lopez Huston, Mary T., Integrated Advertising Inc, Jacksonville, FL. Tel: (904) 296-2585, FAX: (904) 296-2586, E-Mail: mary@intadvertising.com, Web Site: www.intadvertising.com (35)

Lopez Negrete Communications, Houston, TX. Tel: (713) 877-8777, FAX: (713) 877-8796, Web Site: lopeznegrete.com (35)

Lopez Negrete, Alex, Lopez Negrete Communications, Houston, TX. Tel: (713) 877-8777, FAX: (713) 877-8796, Web Site: lopeznegrete.com (35)

Lopez Negrete, Cathy, Lopez Negrete Communications, Houston, TX. Tel: (713) 877-8777, FAX: (713) 877-8796, Web Site: lopeznegrete.com (35)

Lopez, Alexander, Open Systems Services, Miami, FL. Tel: (305) 541-1970 (20)

Lopez, Ivan C., Assurant Solutions Preneed Division, Atlanta, GA. Tel: (770) 763-1000, (800) PRE NEED, FAX: (770) 859-4325, Web Site: www. assurantpreneed.com (15)

Lopez, Miguel, Harris Corp, Melbourne, FL. Tel: (321) 727-9100, (800) 442-7747, E-Mail: webmaster@ harris.com, Web Site: harris.com (16)

Lopez, William, Xpectrum Marketing Group, San Diego, CA. Tel: (858) 277-0079, FAX: (858) 277-0076, E-Mail: info@xpectrummg.com, Web Site: www. xpectrummg.com (35)

Loporto, Santo, AXA Equitable, New York, NY. Tel: (212) 554-1234, (212) 314-2956, Web Site: www. axaonline.com (15)

LoPresti, Michael, TNF, Toronto, ON Canada. Tel: (416) 924-5751, FAX: (416) 923-7085, Web Site: www.tnf-cf.com (30)

Lord, Bob, AOL Corp, New York, NY. Tel: (212) 206-4400, Web Site: www.aol.com (32)

LoRe, Linda, Frederick's of Hollywood Group Inc, Los Angeles, CA. Tel: (323) 466-5151, (855) 655-2514, FAX: (323) 464-5149, E-Mail: support@fredericks. com, Web Site: www.fredericks.com (2)

Lore, Marc, Diapers.com, Jersey City, NJ. Tel: (800) 342-7377, E-Mail: customercare@diapers.com, Web Site: www.diapers.com (5)

Loree, James M., Stanley Black & Decker Inc, New Britain, CT. Tel: (860) 225-5111, Web Site: www. stanleyblackanddecker.com (16)

Lorel Marketing Group, Philadelphia, PA. Tel: (610) 337-2343, FAX: (610) 768-9511, E-Mail: info@ lorel.com, Web Site: www.lorel.com (35)

Lorenzen, Andreas, Stibo Systems, Kennesaw, GA. Tel: (770) 425-3282, FAX: (770) 425-3012, Web Site: www.stibocatalog.com (16)

Lorex Inc, Elk River, MN. Tel: (763) 441-0055, (800) 792-8812, E-Mail: customerservice@lorexinc.com, Web Site: www.lorexinc.com (35)

Lorillard Tobacco Co, Greensboro, NC. Tel: (336) 335-7000, (877) 703-0386, FAX: (336) 373-6917, E-Mail: externalaffairs@lortobco.com, Web Site: www.lorillard.com (16)

Lorimer, James, Data Communications Management Corp, Brampton, ON Canada. Tel: (905) 791-3151, (800) 268-0128, FAX: (905) 791-3277, E-Mail: info@datacm.com, Web Site: www.datacm.com (21)

Lorman Education Services, Eau Claire, WI. Tel: (715) 833-3940 (1)

Lorton Data Inc, Arden Hills, MN. Tel: (651) 203-8200, FAX: (651) 203-8299, Web Site: www.lortondata. com (22)

The Los Angeles Convention & Visitors Bureau, Los Angeles, CA. Tel: (213) 624-7300, (800) 366-6116, FAX: (213) 627-9746, Web Site: discoverlosangeles.com (19)

Los Angeles Kings, Los Angeles, CA. Tel: (213) 742-7100, (888) KINGS-LA, FAX: (213) 742-7296, Web Site: kings.nhl.com (16)

The Los Angeles Lakers Inc, El Segundo, CA. Tel: (310) 426-6000, FAX: (310) 426-6110, E-Mail: vlawlor@la-lakers.com, Web Site: www.nba.com/ lakers (11)

Los Angeles Times, Los Angeles, CA. Tel: (213) 237-5000, (800) 528-4637, FAX: (213) 237-7679, E-Mail: rob.barrett@latimes.com, Web Site: www. latimes.com (31)

Losee, Kendra, National University, La Jolla, CA. Tel: (800) 628-8648, Web Site: www.nu.edu (1)

Lospaluto, Dawn, National Association for Printing Leadership, Paramus, NJ. Tel: (201) 634-9600, (800) 642-6275, FAX: (201) 634-0324, E-Mail: webwaster@napl.org, Web Site: www.napl.org (1)

Lotame Solutions, Columbia, MD. Tel: (410) 379-2195, FAX: (410) 379-2198, Web Site: www.lotame.com (22)

Loth, Susan M., Disabled American Veterans, Cincinnati, OH. Tel: (859) 441-7300, FAX: (859) 442-2084, E-Mail: feedback@davmail.org, Web Site: www.dav.org (1)

Lothman, Martin, Four Corners Direct Inc, Sarasota, FL. Tel: (941) 364-8585 (16)

Lotions & Lace, Riverside, CA. Tel: (951) 686-5223, FAX: (951) 686-5765, E-Mail: linda@ez-access. com, Web Site: www.sexyvideos.com (2)

LOTSolutions, Jacksonville, FL. Tel: (888) 784-3539, Web Site: www.lotsolutions.com (14)

Lotti, Michael, Marketing News, Chicago, IL. Tel: (312) 542-9000, (800) 262-1150, FAX: (312) 542-9001, E-Mail: news@ama.org, Web Site: www.ama. org (43)

Loube, Paul "Jacky", American Breast Cancer Foundation, Columbia, MD. Tel: (410) 730-5105, E-Mail: info@abcf.org, Web Site: www.abcf.org (1)

Loucks, Grant, Alan Gordon Enterprises Inc, Hollywood, CA. Tel: (323) 466-3561, FAX: (323) 871-2193, E-Mail: contactus@alangordon.com, Web Site: www.alangordon.com (32)

Loucks, Wayne, Alan Gordon Enterprises Inc, Hollywood, CA. Tel: (323) 466-3561, FAX: (323) 871-2193, E-Mail: contactus@alangordon.com, Web Site: www.alangordon.com (32)

Loud, Jamie, Clayman Promotional Group, Kansas City, KS. Tel: (913) 384-3600, FAX: (913) 384-1227, E-Mail: jloud@claymanpromo.com, Web Site: www.claymanpromo.com (33)

Louderback, John, JLG Industries Inc, McConnellsburg, PA. Tel: (717) 485-5161, (877) JLG-SELL, FAX: (717) 485-6417, E-Mail: comments@jlg.com, Web Site: www.jlg.com (16)

Loughran, Judy, Da-Lite Screen Co Inc, Warsaw, IN. Tel: (574) 267-8101, (800) 622-3737, FAX: (574) 267-7804, E-Mail: info@da-lite.com, Web Site: www.da-lite.com (16)

Loughran, Rev. James, Franciscan Friars of the Atonement - Graymoor, Garrison, NY. Tel: (845) 424-3671, (800) 338-2620, FAX: (845) 424-2168, E-Mail: info@atonementfriars.org, Web Site: atonementfriars.org (1)

Louie, Kelsey, Gay Men's Health Crisis, New York, NY. Tel: (212) 367-1000, FAX: (212) 367-1220, E-Mail: webmaster@gmhc.org, Web Site: www. gmhc.org (1)

Louis, Victor, Coach, New York, NY. Tel: (212) 594-1850, (800) 444-3611, FAX: (212) 594-1682, Web Site: www.coach.com (2)

Louisiana State Museum, New Orleans, LA. Tel: (504) 568-6968, (800) 568-6968, FAX: (504) 568-4995, Web Site: www.lsm.crt.state.la.us (1)

Louisville Direct Marketing Association, Louisville, KY. Tel: (888) 392-1941, E-Mail: ldmacontact@ ldma.org, Web Site: www.ldma.org (40)

Loukota, Ingrid, Atlantic List Company Inc, Arlington, VA. Tel: (703) 528-7482, FAX: (703) 528-7492, E-Mail: ingridloukota@atlanticlist.com, Web Site: www.atlanticlist.com (23)

Love Envelopes Inc, Dallas, TX. Tel: (214) 637-5900, (800) 569-5683, FAX: (214) 951-0469, E-Mail: sales.dallas@loveenvelopes.com, Web Site: www. loveenvelopes.com (26)

Love To Learn Inc, Salem, UT. Tel: (801) 423-2009, (888) 771-1034, FAX: (801) 423-9188, E-Mail: customerservice@lovetolearn.net, Web Site: www. lovetolearn.net (5)

Love, Christopher, E&D Web Printing Inc, Rochelle, IL. Tel: (708) 656-6600, (815) 562-5800, FAX: (708) 656-4154, E-Mail: info@eanddweb.com, Web Site: www.eanddweb.com (27)

Love, Louise, Columbia College Chicago, Chicago, IL. Tel: (312) 663-1600, FAX: (312) 344-0869, Web Site: www.colum.edu (41)

Love, Michael, Love Envelopes Inc, Dallas, TX. Tel: (214) 637-5900, (800) 569-5683, FAX: (214) 951-0469, E-Mail: sales.dallas@loveenvelopes.com, Web Site: www.loveenvelopes.com (26)

Love, Robert, AARP, Washington, DC. Tel: (202) 434-2277, FAX: (202) 434-2525, Web Site: www.aarp.org (1)

Love, Sharon Liles, Greater Fort Worth Builders Association, Fort Worth, TX. Tel: (817) 284-3566, FAX: (817) 284-6465, E-Mail: info@fortworthbuilders.org, Web Site: www.forthworthbuilders.org (1)

Love, Todd, Compass Ventures, Lincoln, NE. Tel: (402) 438-3222, FAX: (402) 438-3439, E-Mail: info@compassventures.com, Web Site: www.compassventures.com (23)

Love, Tom, Loves Travel Stops & Country Stores, Oklahoma City, OK. Tel: (405) 242-2490, (800) 655-6837, E-Mail: comments@loves.com, Web Site: www.loves.com (5)

Lovegrove, Michael, TracyLocke, Dallas, TX. Tel: (214) 969-9000, FAX: (214) 259-3550, E-Mail: parker.harrison@tracylocke.com, Web Site: tracylocke.com (35)

Lovejoy, Scott, Renaissance Greeting Cards Inc, Downers Grove, IL. Tel: (800) 736-3383, Web Site: www.ftd.com (5)

John Lovell Communication Services, Portland, ME. Tel: (207) 774-0232, FAX: (207) 774-0232 (39)

Lovell, John, John Lovell Communication Services, Portland, ME. Tel: (207) 774-0232, FAX: (207) 774-0232 (39)

Lovely, Richard J., Rohm & Haas Co, Philadelphia, PA. Tel: (215) 592-3000, (877) 288-5881, FAX: (215) 592-3377, Web Site: www.rohmhaas.com (16)

Loveman, Gary, Caesars Entertainment Corp, Las Vegas, NV. Tel: (702) 407-6000, (800) 634-6001, FAX: (702) 407-6037, Web Site: www.caesars.com (16)

Loves Travel Stops & Country Stores, Oklahoma City, OK. Tel: (405) 242-2490, (800) 655-6837, E-Mail: comments@loves.com, Web Site: www.loves.com (5)

Lovett, Gary, California Mustang Parts & Accessories, City of Industry, CA. Tel: (909) 598-3383, (800) 775-0101, FAX: (909) 598-5611, E-Mail: csmustang@cal-mustang.com, Web Site: www.cal-mustang.com (16)

Lovett, Mike, Ingram Book Group, La Vergne, TN. Tel: (615) 793-5000, (800) 937-8000, FAX: (800) 876-0186, Web Site: www.ipage.ingrambook.com (16)

Loving Promises & More, Longview, WA. Tel: (360) 425-8466, (800) 999-6909 (16)

Lovins, David, Banker & Tradesman, Boston, MA. Tel: (617) 428-5100, FAX: (617) 428-5119, Web Site: www.bankerandtradesman.com (17)

Low, Gary M., Metro Speedgear, Livingston, NJ. Tel: (973) 251-2814, (800) 777-4453, FAX: (908) 286-0002, E-Mail: info@speedgear.com, Web Site: www.speedgear.com (11)

Low, Tanya, PointOne Graphics Inc, Toronto, ON Canada. Tel: (416) 255-8202, (866) 717-5722, FAX: (416) 255-6917, Web Site: www.point-one.com (27)

Lowe Campbell Ewald, Detroit, MI. Tel: (586) 574-3400, E-Mail: lowecampbellewald@lowe-ce.com, Web Site: www.lowecampbellewald.com (35)

Lowe, Carol, Sealed Air Corp, Elmwood Park, NJ. Tel: (201) 791-7600, FAX: (201) 703-4205, Web Site: www.sealedair.com (26)

Lowe, Carol, See's Candies Inc, Carson, CA. Tel: (800) 347-7337, Web Site: www.sees.com (4)

Lowe, Chris, Dial 800 LLC, Los Angeles, CA. Tel: (310) 273-9023, (800) 700-1987, E-Mail: sales@dial800.com, Web Site: www.dial800.com (32)

Lowe, Don F., PIP Postal Instant Press, Mission Viejo, CA. Tel: (949) 282-3800, FAX: (949) 282-3899, Web Site: www.pip.com (27)

Lowe, Jonathan, Los Angeles Kings, Los Angeles, CA. Tel: (213) 742-7100, (888) KINGS-LA, FAX: (213) 742-7296, Web Site: kings.nhl.com (16)

Lowe, Kenneth W., Scripps Networks Interactive Inc, Knoxville, TN. Tel: (865) 560-2700, Web Site: scrippsnetworksinteractive.com (17)

Lowe, Robert R, American Society on Aging, San Francisco, CA. Tel: (415) 974-9600, (800) 537-9728, FAX: (415) 974-0300, E-Mail: info@asaging.org, Web Site: www.asaging.org (1)

Lowen, Chuck, Wholesale Tool Co, Warren, MI. Tel: (800) 521-3420, FAX: (800) 521-3661, E-Mail: wtmich@aol.com, Web Site: www.wttool.com (9)

Lowenthol, Barbara, Leucadia National Corp, New York, NY. Tel: (212) 460-1900, FAX: (212) 598-4869, Web Site: www.leucadia.com (14)

Lowe's Companies Inc, Mooresville, NC. Tel: (704) 758-1000, (800) 445-6937, Web Site: www.lowes.com (8)

Lowitz, Jennifer, Frederick's of Hollywood Group Inc, Los Angeles, CA. Tel: (323) 466-5151, (855) 655-2514, FAX: (323) 464-5149, E-Mail: support@fredericks.com, Web Site: www.fredericks.com (2)

Lowman, Paul, Case Design Corp, Telford, PA. Tel: (215) 703-0130, (800) 847-4176, FAX: (215) 703-0139, E-Mail: sales@casedesigncorp.com, Web Site: www.casedesigncorp.com (34)

Lowman, Suzanne, Iowa Student Loan Liquidity Corp, West Des Moines, IA. Tel: (515) 243-5626, Web Site: www.studentloan.org (1)

Lowman, W.M., CYRO Industries, Parsippany, NJ. Tel: (973) 541-8000, (800) 631-5384, FAX: (973) 442-6117, (973) 442-6135, Web Site: www.cyro.com (16)

Lown, Chris, CRB, Chicago, IL. Tel: (312) 554-8456, (800) 621-5271, FAX: (312) 939-4135, E-Mail: info@crbtrader.com, Web Site: www.crbtrader.com (17)

Lownds, Don, Pacific Propeller Inc, Kent, WA. Tel: (253) 872-7767, (800) 722-7767, FAX: (253) 872-7221, E-Mail: jheikke@pacprop.com, Web Site: www.pacificpropeller.com (16)

Lownstein, Tim, Stress Market, Port Angeles, WA. Tel: (360) 457-9223, (800) 578-7377, FAX: (360) 457-9466, E-Mail: info@stressmarket.com, Web Site: www.stressmarket.com (17)

Lowrance Electronics, Tulsa, OK. Tel: (918) 437-6881, FAX: (918) 234-1707, Web Site: www.lowrance.com (11)

Lowrance, Darrell, Lowrance Electronics, Tulsa, OK. Tel: (918) 437-6881, FAX: (918) 234-1707, Web Site: www.lowrance.com (11)

Lowrie, Doug, Datum Timing, Test & Measurement, Beverly, MA. Tel: (978) 927-8220, FAX: (978) 927-4099, E-Mail: wriley@datum.com, Web Site: www.datum.com (9)

Lowry, Bruce, Pro CD Inc, Omaha, NE. Tel: (800) 992-3766, FAX: (402) 750-0020 (17)

Lowry, Glen D., The Museum of Modern Art, New York, NY. Tel: (212) 708-9400, FAX: (212) 333-1123, E-Mail: info@moma.org, Web Site: www.moma.org (5)

Lowry, Richard, National Review, New York, NY. Tel: (212) 679-7330, FAX: (212) 849-2852, Web Site: www.nationalreview.com (17)

Lowry, William, Country Sampler Group, Saint Charles, IL. Tel: (630) 377-8000, FAX: (630) 377-8194, Web Site: www.sampler.com (17)

Loyalogy, Asheville, NC. Tel: (828) 333-5860, Web Site: loyalogy.com (35)

LoyaltyOne, Toronto, ON Canada. Tel: (416) 228-6500, Web Site: www.loyalty.com; www.airmiles.ca (22)

LoyaltyOne, Marblehead, MA. Tel: (781) 990-8844, Web Site: www.speechrep.com (20)

Loyaltyworks Inc, Atlanta, GA. Tel: (678) 539-5000, (800) 844-5000, FAX: (678) 539-5173, Web Site: www.loyaltyworks.com (21)

Loyd, Rick, Collector Books & American Quilters Society, Paducah, KY. Tel: (270) 898-6211, (800) 626-5420, FAX: (270) 898-8890, E-Mail: info@collectorbooks.com, Web Site: www.collectorbooks.com (17)

Loyle, Harry D., Moto Franchise Corp, Dayton, OH. Tel: (937) 291-1900, (800) 733-6686, FAX: (937) 291-2005, E-Mail: expert@motophoto.com, Web Site: www.motophoto.com; www.portraitavenue.com (3)

Loyola University Chicago, Chicago, IL. Tel: (312) 915-8900, Web Site: www.luc.edu (1)

Lozano, Jose, The Company of Others, Houston, TX. Tel: (800) 994-1681, E-Mail: inquiry@thecompany.com, Web Site: www.thecompany.com (35)

Lubar, Ken, EMI Strategic Marketing Inc, Boston, MA. Tel: (617) 224-1101, E-Mail: info@emiboston.com, Web Site: emiboston.com (35)

Lubarsky, Gary, New England Direct Marketing Association, Wellesley Hills, MA. Tel: (781) 237-1366, FAX: (781) 431-8118, E-Mail: info@nedma.com, Web Site: www.nedma.com (40)

Lubell, Mark, Magnum Photos Inc, New York, NY. Tel: (212) 929-6000, FAX: (212) 929-9325, E-Mail: photography@magnumphotos.com, Web Site: www.magnumphotos.com (38)

Lubovitz, Arye, Tabline Data Services Inc, New York, NY. Tel: (212) 695-4873, FAX: (212) 629-4423 (30)

Lubrano, Sharon, R R Bowker, New Providence, NJ. Tel: (888) BOWKER-2 (269-5372), FAX: (908) 771-8699, Web Site: www.bowker.com (17)

Lubrant, Trisha, The Jewish Publication Society, Philadelphia, PA. Tel: (215) 832-0600, (800) 234-3151, FAX: (215) 568-2017, Web Site: www.jewishpub.org (17)

Lucanish, James, O'Neil Data Systems Inc, Los Angeles, CA. Tel: (310) 448-6400, FAX: (310) 577-7350, Web Site: www.oneildata.com (27)

Lucas & Associates, Montebello, CA. Tel: (323) 728-7899 (29)

Lucas, Brian, Gifts Corp, Barrie, ON Canada. Tel: (905) 670-1126, (800) 565-3130, FAX: (905) 670-1127, E-Mail: customerservice@regal.ca, Web Site: www.regalgreetings.com (6)

Lucas, David Vance, Intergraph Corp, Madison, AL. Tel: (256) 730-2000, (800) 345-4856, FAX: (256) 730-2048, Web Site: www.intergraph.com (16)

Lucas, Ned, Lucas & Associates, Montebello, CA. Tel: (323) 728-7899 (29)

Lucas, Rae, The Directors Network, Encino, CA. Tel: (818) 906-0006, E-Mail: info@tdnartists.com, Web Site: www.tdnartists.com (35)

Lucci, Marysue, ToonUp Coach, Wayne, PA. Tel: (610) 902-0430, (866) 866-6877, E-Mail: info@toonupcoach.com, Web Site: www.toonupcoach.com (13)

Luce Corp, Hamden, CT. Tel: (203) 787-0281, FAX: (203) 230-2753 (16)

Luce, Elizabeth, Sugarbush Farm Inc, Woodstock, VT. Tel: (802) 457-1757, (800) 281-1757, FAX: (802) 457-3269, E-Mail: contact@sugarbushfarm.com, Web Site: www.sugarbushfarm.com (4)

Luce, Linda, Quick Draw Clip Systems Inc, Ventura, CA. Tel: (805) 644-6888, (888) 254-7797, FAX: (805) 644-7320, E-Mail: ron@clipsystems.com, Web Site: www.clipsystems.com (9)

Jack Lucey Art & Illustration, San Rafael, CA. Tel: (415) 453-3172, E-Mail: clucey1@sbcglobal.net (36)

Lucey, Jack, Jack Lucey Art & Illustration, San Rafael, CA. Tel: (415) 453-3172, E-Mail: clucey1@sbcglobal.net (36)

Luchene, Annette, Sappi Fine Paper North America, Boston, MA. Tel: (617) 423-7300, FAX: (617) 423-5494, Web Site: www.sappi.com (25)

LucidView, Oak Ridge, TN. Tel: (888) 582-4384, Web Site: www.lucidview.com (20)

Luciono, Mark, MGI Management Institute, Hawthorne, NY. Tel: (914) 428-6500, (800) 932-0191, FAX: (914) 428-0773, E-Mail: mgiusa@aol.com, Web Site: www.mgi.org (16)

Luck, Joel, Wasserman Uniform Co, Fort Lauderdale, FL. Tel: (614) 279-7000, (614) 279-8888, (800) 848-3576, FAX: (614) 464-0416, (800) 204-0416, E-Mail: custserv@wassermanuniform.com, Web Site: www.wassermanuniform.com (2)

Lucke, Zazie, The Atlantic Monthly, Washington, DC. Tel: (202) 266-6000, (800) 234-2411, FAX: (202) 266-6001, Web Site: www.theatlantic.com (17)

Lucky Heart Cosmetics Inc, Memphis, TN. Tel: (901) 526-7658, (800) 283-1014, FAX: (901) 526-7660, Web Site: www.luckyheart.com (1)

Ludgey, John, Vidi Emi Inc, San Leandro, CA. Tel: (510) 667-9999, FAX: (510) 352-9999, E-Mail: info@vidiemi.com, Web Site: www.vidiemi.com (32)

Ludgin, Robert S., Coastal Tool & Supply, West Hartford, CT. Tel: (860) 233-8213, (877) 551-8665, FAX: (860) 233-6295, E-Mail: sales@coastaltool.com, Web Site: www.coastaltool.com (16)

Ludwick, Suzanne, BBS & Associates, Akron, OH. Tel: (330) 665-5227, E-Mail: contactus@servantheart.com, Web Site: www.servantheart.com (1)

Luebbehusen, Gene, Jofco Inc, Jasper, IN. Tel: (812) 482-5154, (800) 23-JOFCO, FAX: (812) 634-2392, E-Mail: furniture@jofco.com, Web Site: www.jofco.com (16)

Lueck, Andy, Direct Connect Group, Cleveland, OH. Tel: (216) 651-9500, Web Site: www.directconnectgroup.com (35)

Luedtke, Brian, Hollister Inc, Libertyville, IL. Tel: (847) 680-1000, (888) 740-8999, FAX: (847) 680-2123, Web Site: www.hollister.com (16)

Lufthansa German Airlines, East Meadow, NY. Tel: (516) 296-9200, FAX: (516) 296-9386, Web Site: www.lufthansa-usa.com (19)

Luggage Base, Nipomo, CA. Tel: (805) 929-8191, (888) 832-1201, FAX: (805) 929-8192, E-Mail: service@luggagebase.com, Web Site: www.luggagebase.com (16)

Luisi, Gerard, TaCito Direct, Dallas, TX. Tel: (800) 621-2225, FAX: (972) 490-6520, E-Mail: contact@tacito.com, Web Site: www.tacito.com (35)

Luisi, Michael, World Wrestling Entertainment Inc, Stamford, CT. Tel: (203) 352-8600, FAX: (203) 359-5180, Web Site: www.wwe.com (16)

Lukacs, Laszlo M., NewPage Corp, Miamisburg, OH. Tel: (937) 242-9345, (877) 855-7243, FAX: (937) 242-9327, Web Site: www.newpagecorp.com (25)

Lukas, Michael T., Fry Communications Inc, Mechanicsburg, PA. Tel: (717) 766-0211, (800) 334-1429, FAX: (717) 691-0341, Web Site: www.frycomm.com (21)

Luke, Jr John A, Mead Westvaco Consumer & Office Products, Richmond, VA. Tel: (937) 222-6323, (804) 444-1000, FAX: (937) 495-3192, Web Site: www.meadwestvaco.com (10)

Luke, Teresa, Card Technology Inc, Hopkins, MN. Tel: (201) 845-7373, FAX: (201) 845-3337, E-Mail: info@nbstech.com, Web Site: www.nbstech.com (16)

The Lukens Company, Alexandria, VA. Tel: (703) 845-8484, FAX: (703) 845-9655, Web Site: www.thelukenscompany.com (35)

Lukens, III Walter G., The Lukens Company, Alexandria, VA. Tel: (703) 845-8484, FAX: (703) 845-9655, Web Site: www.thelukenscompany.com (35)

Lukoskie, Katherine, Bolind Inc, Boulder, CO. Tel: (303) 443-3142, FAX: (303) 443-9889, Web Site: www.bolind.com (16)

Lumm, John, Eastern Michigan University, Ypsilanti, MI. Tel: (734) 487-1849, FAX: (734) 484-1151, Web Site: www.emich.edu (16)

Lumpkin, Richard A., Consolidated Market Response, Charleston, IL. Tel: (217) 348-7050, FAX: (217) 348-7060 (29)

Lunar Cow, Akron, OH. Tel: (330) 253-9000, (800) 594-9620, FAX: (330) 253-9001, E-Mail: info@lunarcow.com, Web Site: www.lunarcow.com (35)

Lunati, David, Monadnock Paper Mills Inc, Bennington, NH. Tel: (603) 588-3311, (800) 221-2159, FAX: (603) 588-3158, Web Site: www.monadnockpaper.com (25)

Lund, Barbara, Informal Education Products, Milwaukie, OR. Tel: (503) 794-7045, (888) 444-5500, FAX: (503) 794-7111, E-Mail: sales@museumtour.com, Web Site: www.museumtour.com (11)

Lund, Peder C., Paladin Press, Boulder, CO. Tel: (303) 443-7250, (800) 392-2400, FAX: (303) 442-8741, E-Mail: service@paladin-press.com, Web Site: www.paladin-press.com (17)

Lund, Sharon, R Falls Agency, Minneapolis, MN. Tel: (612) 872-6372, (800) 339-1119, FAX: (612) 872-1018, E-Mail: info@fallsagency.com, Web Site: fallsagency.com (16)

Lunday, Don, Aspen Imaging International Inc, Cleveland, OH. Tel: (216) 881-5300, (800) 955-5555, FAX: (216) 881-8380, (800) 756-0990 (34)

Lundberg Family Farms, Richvale, CA. Tel: (530) 882-4551, FAX: (530) 882-4500, E-Mail: info@lundberg.com, Web Site: www.lundberg.com (16)

Lundberg, Theodore E., Life-Study Fellowship Foundation Inc, Darien, CT. Tel: (203) 655-1436, FAX: (203) 655-1392, Web Site: www.lifestudyfellowship.com (17)

Lundberg, Wendell, Lundberg Family Farms, Richvale, CA. Tel: (530) 882-4551, FAX: (530) 882-4500, E-Mail: info@lundberg.com, Web Site: www.lundberg.com (16)

Lunden, Denise S., Software Marketing Associates Inc, Rocky Hill, CT. Tel: (860) 721-8929, FAX: (860) 257-9679, E-Mail: sma@sma-promail.com, Web Site: www.sma-promail.com (22)

Lunden, Susan, National Audubon Society, New York, NY. Tel: (212) 979-3000, FAX: (212) 979-3188, Web Site: www.audubon.org (17)

Lunderman, William H., Colgate-Palmolive Co, New York, NY. Tel: (212) 310-2000, (800) 468-6502, FAX: (212) 310-2475, Web Site: www.colgate.com (16)

Lundgren, John F., Stanley Black & Decker Inc, New Britain, CT. Tel: (860) 225-5111, Web Site: www.stanleyblackanddecker.com (16)

Lundgren, Terry J., Macy's Inc, Cincinnati, OH. Tel: (513) 579-7912, (800) 289-6229, Web Site: www.macysinc.com (5)

Lundgren, Terry J., Macy's Marketing, New York, NY. Tel: (212) 695-4400, FAX: (212) 494-1517, Web Site: www.macys.com (16)

Lundin, Richard, Da-Lite Screen Co Inc, Warsaw, IN. Tel: (574) 267-8101, (800) 622-3737, FAX: (574) 267-7804, E-Mail: info@da-lite.com, Web Site: www.da-lite.com (16)

Lundmark Advertising + Design Inc, Kansas City, MO. Tel: (816) 842-5236, Web Site: lundmarkadvertising.com (35)

Lundstrom, Stephen D., Rees Associates Inc, Des Moines, IA. Tel: (515) 243-2127, FAX: (515) 243-1026, Web Site: www.reesassociates.com (28)

Lunenschloss, John T., Air-Lec Industries Inc, Madison, WI. Tel: (608) 244-4754, FAX: (608) 246-7676, E-Mail: info@air-lec.com, Web Site: www.air-lec.com (16)

Lunick, Stuart, Thermal Product Solutions, White Deer, PA. Tel: (570) 538-7200, (800) 586-2473 (16)

Lunt, Jim, DataCal Enterprises, Gilbert, AZ. Tel: (480) 813-3100, (800) 223-0123, FAX: (480) 545-8090, E-Mail: info@datacal.com, Web Site: www.datacal.com (16)

Lupia, Mario, The Collegebound Network, Staten Island, NY. Tel: (718) 761-4800, (888) 338-6960, FAX: (718) 761-3300, E-Mail: info@collegebound.net, Web Site: www.collegebound.net (32)

Lupinetti, Jim, BFS Credit Services Co, Brook Park, OH. Tel: (216) 362-5094, FAX: (216) 362-5236, E-Mail: lupinettijim@bfsusa.com (16)

Luposello, Jennifer, Macromark Inc, Danbury, CT. Tel: (845) 230-6300, FAX: (845) 278-0650, E-Mail: sales@macromark.com, Web Site: www.macromark.com (23)

Luqmani, Dr. Mushtaq, Haworth College of Business, Kalamazoo, MI. Tel: (616) 387-5050, FAX: (616) 387-5710, E-Mail: jessica.pelkey@wmich.edu, Web Site: www.wmich.edu/business (41)

Lure Craft, Lagrange, IN. Tel: (260) 463-2687, (800) 925-9088, FAX: (260) 463-8383, E-Mail: lurcraft@clickanerd.com, Web Site: www.lurecraft.com (11)

Lurie, Robert F., New York Power Authority, White Plains, NY. Tel: (914) 681-6200, E-Mail: info@nypa.gov, Web Site: www.nypa.gov (16)

Lusko, Beth, The New Yorker Magazine, New York, NY. Tel: (212) 286-2860, FAX: (212) 286-4168, Web Site: www.newyorker.com (17)

Lussier, Gary, Christian Book Distributors Inc, Peabody, MA. Tel: (978) 532-5300, FAX: (978) 977-5010, E-Mail: javedisian@chrbook.com, Web Site: www.chrbook.com (17)

Lustbader, Todd, Winston Marketing Group, Elk Grove Village, IL. Tel: (620) 584-8000, FAX: (847) 350-5701, Web Site: www.collectionset.com (8)

Lustberg, Alex, Lyris Inc, Emeryville, CA. Tel: (510) 844-1551, (800) 768-2929, FAX: (510) 844-1598, E-Mail: sales@lyris.com, Web Site: www.lyris.com (32)

Luster Care Products, Saint Louis, MO. Tel: (636) 272-1885, (800) 291-5223, FAX: (636) 272-1869, Web Site: www.lusterlace.com (16)

Lutheran Church Extension Fund - Missouri Synod, Saint Louis, MO. Tel: (800) 843-5233, FAX: (314) 996-1131, Web Site: www.lcef.org (1)

Lutz, Laurent C., SLM Corp. Newark, DE. Web Site: www.salliemae.com (16)

Luu, Frederic, Digi International, Minnetonka, MN. Tel: (952) 912-3444, (877) 912-3444, FAX: (952) 912-4952, Web Site: www.digi.com (3)

Lux, David P., RBC Funds, Milwaukee, WI. Tel: (800) 422-2766, Web Site: us.rbcgam.com (14)

Lux, Robert, Freddie Mac, McLean, VA. Tel: (703) 903-2000, (800) 424-5401, Web Site: www.freddiemac.com (14)

Luxe Collective Group, New York, NY. Tel: (212) 627-3300, FAX: (212) 627-3388, E-Mail: info@luxecg.com, Web Site: luxecg.com (35)

Luxeder, Tom, The Taunton Press, Newtown, CT. Tel: (203) 426-8171, (800) 477-8727, FAX: (203) 426-3434, Web Site: www.taunton.com (17)

Luxottica Retail, Mason, OH. Tel: (513) 765-6956, Web Site: www.luxottica.com (2)

Luzi, Armin, Thetford Corp, Ann Arbor, MI. Tel: (734) 769-6000, (800) 543-1219, FAX: (734) 769-2023, Web Site: www.thetford.com (16)

Luzier Personalized Cosmetics, Grandview, MO. Tel: (816) 531-8338, (800) 821-6632, FAX: (816) 531-6979, E-Mail: customerservice@luzier.com, Web Site: www.luzier.com (7)

Lyke, Andy, Ripon Printers, Ripon, WI. Tel: (920) 748-3136, (800) 321-3136, FAX: (920) 748-3741, E-Mail: info@riponprinters.com, Web Site: www.riponprinters.com (27)

Lyle, Abbe, Catalyst Marketing Group, Rocklin, CA. Tel: (916) 218-6066, E-Mail: info@catalystmarketinggroup.com, Web Site: www.catalystmarketinggroup.com (35)

Lyman, David H., The Maine Photographic Workshops, Rockport, ME. Tel: (207) 236-8581, (877) 577-7700, FAX: (207) 236-2558, E-Mail: info@theworkshops.com, Web Site: www.theworkshops.com (16)

Lyman, Jim, Edward Don & Co, Woodridge, IL. Tel: (708) 442-9400, (800) 777-4366, FAX: (708) 442-0436, Web Site: www.don.com (16)

Lynam, Joe, Integretel Inc, San Jose, CA. Tel: (408) 362-4000, FAX: (408) 362-2795, Web Site: www.integretel.com (16)

Lynch, Bob, South-Western Publishing, Madison, OH. Tel: (513) 299-1000, FAX: (513) 527-6992 (17)

Lynch, Chris, New England Journal of Medicine, Waltham, MA. Tel: (781) 893-3800, FAX: (781) 893-7729, Web Site: www.nejm.org (17)

Lynch, Jr John J., Renaissance Learning, Wisconsin Rapids, WI. Tel: (715) 424-3636, (800) 338-4204, FAX: (877) 280-7642, E-Mail: electronicorders@renaissance.com, Web Site: www.renlearn.com (5)

Lynch, Kate, Eastern Mountain Sports, Peterborough, NH. Tel: (603) 924-9571, (888) 463-6367, FAX: (603) 924-4320, Web Site: www.ems.com (16)

Lynch, Kirsten A., Vail Resorts Inc, Broomfield, CO. Tel: (303) 404-1800, FAX: (303) 404-6415, Web Site: www.vailresorts.com (19)

Lynch, Linda, Gordon Management Inc, Somerset, NJ. Tel: (732) 846-4800, FAX: (732) 846-4709, E-Mail: keith@gmidistribution.com, Web Site: www.gmidistribution.com (28)

Lynch, Neil P., Aristokraft Inc, Jasper, IN. Tel: (812) 482-2527, FAX: (812) 482-9872, Web Site: www.aristokraft.com (16)

Lynch, Ph.D. William F., Drexel University Goodwin College of Professional Studies, Philadelphia, PA. Tel: (215) 895-2159, E-Mail: goodwin@drexel.edu, Web Site: goodwin.drexel.edu (16)

Lynch, Philip, Brown-Forman Corp, Louisville, KY. Tel: (502) 585-1100, FAX: (502) 774-7876, E-Mail: brown-forman@b-f.com, Web Site: www.brown-forman.com (16)

Lynch, Rick, MailChimp, Atlanta, GA. Tel: (678) 999-0141, Web Site: mailchimp.com (24)

Lynch, Tom, Tyco Electronics Corp, Berwyn, PA. Tel: (610) 893-9800, Web Site: www.te.com (16)

Lyne, Susan, AOL Corp, New York, NY. Tel: (212) 206-4400, Web Site: www.aol.com (32)

Lynn, Devera, North Shore Animal League America Inc, Port Washington, NY. Tel: (516) 883-7575, Web Site: www.animalleague.org (1)

Lynn, Don. State Farm Insurance Cos, Bloomington, IL. Tel: (309) 766-2311, FAX: (309) 766-3621, Web Site: www.statefarm.com (15)

Lynn, Jim, McCormick & Co Inc, Sparks, MD. Tel: (410) 771-7301, (800) 474-7742, FAX: (410) 527-6337, Web Site: www.mccormick.com (4)

Lynn, Nancy, Kennel Vet, Laurel, DE. Tel: (302) 875-7111, (800) 782-0627, FAX: (302) 269-3986, E-Mail: info@petmarket.com, Web Site: www.kennelvet.com (11)

Lynn, Scott, Adknowledge, Kansas City, MO. Tel: (816) 931-1771, (866) 730-2109, Web Site: www.adknowledge.com (32)

Lyon, Patty, Signature Styles LLC, Wilmington, DE. Tel: (302) 636-5401 (2)

Lyon, Sharon, Lion's Share Marketing Group, Inc, Houston, TX. Tel: (713) 686-4252, Web Site: www.lionsshare.com (20)

Lyons, Bob, Affinion Group, Stamford, CT. Tel: (203) 956-1000, (800) 282-3315, Web Site: www.affinion.com (35)

Lyons-Tarr, Kevin, 4Imprint Inc, Oshkosh, WI. Tel: (920) 236-7272, (877) 446-7746, (888) 298-8190, FAX: (800) 355-5043, E-Mail: administrator@4imprint.com, Web Site: www.4imprint.com (16)

Lyris Inc, Emeryville, CA. Tel: (510) 844-1551, (800) 768-2929, FAX: (510) 844-1598, E-Mail: sales@lyris.com, Web Site: www.lyris.com (32)

Lysyj, Lesya, Weight Watchers International, New York, NY. Tel: (516) 390-1400, FAX: (516) 390-1302, Web Site: www.weight-watchers.com (16)

Steve Lytle, Chicago, IL. Tel: (312) 894-7000 (20)

Lytle, Ken, Merastar Insurance Co, Chattanooga, TN. Tel: (800) 637-2782, FAX: (800) 369-1430, E-Mail: merastar.assist.team@unitrindirect.com, Web Site: www.merastar.com (15)

M

M&M Health Care Apparel Co, Brooklyn, NY. E-Mail: info@fashionease.com (2)

M'Guinness, Jim, Jim M'Guinness Design, Los Altos, CA. Tel: (650) 967-3811 (36)

M2Media 360, Park Ridge, IL. Tel: (760) 318-7000, E-Mail: cnaughton@m2media360.com, Web Site: www.m2media360.com (17)

MAR Graphics, Valmeyer, IL. Tel: (800) 851-4460, Web Site: www.margraphics.com (27)

MBI Direct Mail, Deland, FL. Tel: (386) 736-9998, (800) 359-4780, FAX: (386) 736-1100, E-Mail: sales@mbidirectmail.com, Web Site: www.directmail-mbi.com (28)

MBI Inc, Norwalk, CT. Tel: (203) 853-2000, E-Mail: webmail@mbi-inc.com, Web Site: www.mbi-inc.com (16)

MBS, Central Islip, NY. Tel: (631) 851-5000, Web Site: www.mbsinsight.com (22)

MCCS, Mason, OH. Tel: (513) 573-2284, FAX: (513) 573-2197, Web Site: www.federated.com (14)

MCDM Strategic Direct Marketing, Plainfield, IL. Tel: (815) 436-5194, FAX: (815) 439-5941 (20)

MCH Strategic Data, Sweet Springs, MO. Tel: (660) 335-6373, (800) 776-6373, FAX: (660) 335-4157, E-Mail: sales@mchdata.com, Web Site: mchdata.com (23)

MCI Communications Services Inc, Basking Ridge, NJ. Tel: (877) 297-7816, Web Site: www.mci.com (16)

MDE Marketing, Mahwah, NJ. Tel: (201) 891-7010, Web Site: www.wdemarketing.com (16)

MDF Systems, Bristol, CT. Tel: (860) 584-4750, (800) 426-3752, FAX: (860) 584-4759, Web Site: www.mdfsystems.com (22)

MDR, Sunrise, FL. Tel: (954) 845-9500, (800) 637-8227, FAX: (954) 845-9505, E-Mail: info@mdr.org, Web Site: www.mdr.org (7)

MESA Media & Entertainment Services Alliancce, Port Washington, NY. Tel: (516) 767-6720, Web Site: www.mesalliance.org/ (22)

MFE Instruments, Salem, NH. Tel: (603) 893-8778, (800) 843-8011, FAX: (603) 893-8851, Web Site: www.stockeryale.com (9)

MFS Investment Management, Boston, MA. Tel: (617) 954-5000, FAX: (617) 350-2163, Web Site: www.mfs.com (14)

MGI Management Institute, Hawthorne, NY. Tel: (914) 428-6500, (800) 932-0191, FAX: (914) 428-0773, E-Mail: mgiusa@aol.com, Web Site: www.mgi.org (16)

MGM Grand Detroit, Detroit, MI. Tel: (877) 888-2121, Web Site: www.mgmgrand.com/det (16)

MGM Mailing Lists, South Sandwich, MA. Tel: (508) 539-1300, (800) 660-5322, FAX: (508) 539-0700 (23)

MGMA-ACMPE, Englewood, CO. Tel: (303) 799-1111, (877) 275-6462, E-Mail: infocenter@mgma.com, Web Site: www.mgma.com (16)

MGP Direct Inc, Clarksville, MD. Tel: (410) 531-0383, FAX: (410) 531-8142, E-Mail: roberta@mgpdirect.com, Web Site: www.mgpdirect.com (35)

Mi-T-M Corp, Peosta, IA. Tel: (563) 556-7484, Web Site: www.mitm.com (9)

Milberg Penn International, Mount Kisco, NY. Tel: (914) 239-4300, (914) 241-0858, E-Mail: contact@mpioutsourcing.com, Web Site: www.mpioutsourcing.com (29)

Mirage Resorts, Inc., Las Vegas, NV. Tel: (702) 693-7111, FAX: (702) 791-7446, Web Site: www.mirageresorts.com (19)

MJA International, Dix Hills, NY. Tel: (516) 676-5990, FAX: (516) 674-3309 (7)

MJM Incentives Inc, Henrietta, NY. Tel: (585) 334-6720, (888) 633-9655, E-Mail: pmarchese@mjmincentives.com, Web Site: www.mjmincentives.com (33)

MKE Enterprises, North Reading, MA. Tel: (978) 664-3877, FAX: (978) 664-2835, E-Mail: e.marilyn@mke-enterprises.com, Web Site: www.mke-enterprises.com (35)

MKS Marketing Inc, Austin, TX. Tel: (512) 263-8017, (800) 544-8989, FAX: (402) 333-9610, E-Mail: info@telemarketingoutsource.com, Web Site: www.telemarketingoutsource.com (29)

MLB Associates, Lake Placid, NY. Tel: (518) 523-2371, FAX: (518) 523-9011, E-Mail: mlbassoc@aol.com, Web Site: www.mlbassociates.com (20)

MLS Data Management Solutions, Fort Worth, TX. Tel: (817) 989-3800, FAX: (817) 989-3899, Web Site: www.mlsc.com (22)

MMI Direct LLC, Columbia, MD. Tel: (410) 561-1500, FAX: (410) 561-0833, Web Site: www.mmidirect.com (22)

MMS Education, Newtown, PA. Tel: (215) 579-8590, (800) 523-5948, FAX: (215) 579-8589, Web Site: www.mmseducation.com (5)

MNI, Evanston, IL. Tel: (847) 864-7000, (888) 752-5200, FAX: (847) 332-1100, Web Site: mni.net (23)

MPBS Industries, Los Angeles, CA. Tel: (323) 268-8514, (800) 421-6265, FAX: (323) 268-6305, Web Site: www.mpbs.com (16)

MPC Louisville Promotions, Louisville, KY. Tel: (800) 331-0989, FAX: (888) 451-8475, E-Mail: sales@mpcpromotions.com, Web Site: www.mpcpromotions.com (33)

MPS Multimedia Inc, San Mateo, CA. Tel: (650) 872-7100, FAX: (650) 872-7133, E-Mail: sales@gospg.com, Web Site: www.selectmedia.com (16)

The MR Group Inc, Charleston, SC. Tel: (843) 402-0566, FAX: (843) 852-9051, E-Mail: mgm@themrgroup.com, Web Site: www.themrgroup.com (9)

MRC Marketing, Emerson, NJ. Tel: (201) 406-9471, FAX: (201) 986-0361, Web Site: www.mrcmarketing.net (21)

MRI Norwalk, Pompano Beach, FL. Tel: (203) 926-1200, FAX: (203) 926-1211, E-Mail: jbgurn@mricoastalgroup.com, Web Site: www.mricoastalgroup.com (20)

MRM//McCann, New York, NY. Tel: (646) 865-6230, E-Mail: gbc@mrm-mccann.com, Web Site: mrm-mccann.com (35)

MRV Communications, Chatsworth, CA. Tel: (818) 773-0900, FAX: (818) 773-0906, Web Site: www.mrv.com (3)

MRW Communications, Pembroke, MA. Tel: (781) 924-5282, FAX: (718) 926-0371, E-Mail: jim@mrwinc.com, Web Site: www.mrwinc.com (35)

MSC Industrial Supply Co, Melville, NY. Tel: (516) 812-2000, (800) 645-7270, FAX: (800) 255-5067, E-Mail: executive@mscdirect.com, Web Site: www.mscdirect.com (9)

MSI, Chicago, IL. Tel: (312) 565-0044, FAX: (312) 946-6100, E-Mail: info@agencymsi.com, Web Site: agencymsi.com (35)

MSI Direct Response Inc, Newport Beach, CA. Tel: (949) 722-2524, FAX: (949) 650-0989, E-Mail: sales@mailingteam.com, Web Site: mailingteam.com (24)

MSI List Marketing, Palatine, IL. Tel: (847) 934-1111, FAX: (847) 890-6700, E-Mail: jeff@msilist.com, Web Site: www.msilist.com (23)

MSNI Inc, Roswell, GA. Tel: (770) 777-4121, Web Site: www.msniinc.com (23)

MSP Inc, Freedom, PA. Tel: (724) 774-3244, (800) 876-3211, FAX: (724) 774-6996, E-Mail: info@msp-pgh.com, Web Site: www.msp-pgh.com (21)

The MSR Group, Omaha, NE. Tel: (402) 392-0755, (800) 737-0755, FAX: (402) 392-1068, E-Mail: info@theMSRgroup.com, Web Site: www.theMSRgroup.com (30)

MSU Federal Credit Union, East Lansing, MI. Tel: (517) 333-2254, Web Site: www.msufcu.org (1)

MT&L Card Products & Fulfillment Services, Nashville, TN. Tel: (615) 254-9471, FAX: (615) 244-6063, E-Mail: sales@magticket.com, Web Site: www.mtlcard.com (28)

MTI Information Technologies LLC, Langhorne, PA. Tel: (267) 569-2400, FAX: (215) 741-3898, Web Site: www.mtiadvantage.com (30)

MTS Publishing, Naperville, IL. Tel: (630) 955-9750, (800) 332-4655, FAX: (630) 955-9787, E-Mail: info@midwesttruckshopper.com, Web Site: www.midwesttruckshopper.com (17)

MTS Systems Corp, Eden Prairie, MN. Tel: (952) 937-4000, (800) 328-2255, FAX: (952) 937-4515, E-Mail: info@mts.com, Web Site: www.mts.com (16)

MundoFOX22, Los Angeles, CA. Tel: (213) 344-3700, E-Mail: info@canal22.tv, Web Site: www.mundofox22.com (32)

MVI Marketing Ltd, San Luis Obispo, CA. Tel: (805) 239-2994, (805) 459-4455, FAX: (805) 239-2947, E-Mail: info@mvimarketing.com, Web Site: www.mvimarketing.com (20)

MVNP, Honolulu, HI. Tel: (808) 536-0881, FAX: (808) 529-6208, E-Mail: ideas@mvnp.com, Web Site: www.mvnp.com (35)

MVS Mailers Inc, Bohemia, NY. Tel: (800) 641-7917, FAX: (631) 699-0101, E-Mail: sales@mvsmailers.com, Web Site: www.mvsmailers.com (28)

MWM Dexter Inc, Aurora, MO. Tel: (417) 841-1040, (888) 833-1242, FAX: (417) 841-1025, Web Site: www.mwmdexter.com (27)

MXT Card Services, LLC, New Castle, DE. Tel: (302) 323-6203, FAX: (302) 323-6219, Web Site: www.mxtcs.com (14)

Mylan NV, Canonsburg, PA. Tel: (724) 514-1800, (800) 231-3052, FAX: (281) 240-0002, E-Mail: communications@mylan.com, Web Site: www.mylan.com (7)

Ma, Lysi, Sussex Publishers Inc, New York, NY. Tel: (212) 260-7210, FAX: (212) 260-7445, Web Site: www.blues-buster.com (17)

Ma, Yale, Everex Computer Systems Inc, Fremont, CA. Tel: (800) 383-7391, (866) 850-8835, FAX: (510) 683-2186, E-Mail: customerservice@everex.com, Web Site: www.everex.com (16)

Maag, Al, Business Marketing Association, Naperville, IL. Tel: (630) 544-5054, FAX: (630) 544-5055, E-Mail: info@marketing.org, Web Site: www.marketing.org (40)

Mac Direct, Colmar, PA. Tel: (215) 822-5775, (800) 278-1154, FAX: (215) 822-7977, E-Mail: info@macdirect.com, Web Site: www.macdirect.com (22)

Mac McIntosh Inc, North Kingstown, RI. Tel: (401) 294-7730, (800) 944-5553, FAX: (401) 679-0176, E-Mail: info@sales-lead-experts.com, Web Site: www.sales-lead-experts.com (20)

Mac Murray Petersen & Shuster LLP, New Albany, OH. Tel: (614) 939-9955, FAX: (614) 939-9955, E-Mail: dbryson@mpslawyers.com, Web Site: www.mpslawyers.com (20)

Mac Murray, Helen, Mac Murray Petersen & Shuster LLP, New Albany, OH. Tel: (614) 939-9955, FAX: (614) 939-9955, E-Mail: dbryson@mpslawyers.com, Web Site: www.mpslawyers.com (20)

Mac Naughton, Duncan, WalMart Stores Inc, Bentonville, AR. Tel: (479) 273-4000, (800) 925-6278, FAX: (479) 277-1830, Web Site: www.walmart.com (16)

Mac Pac Inc, Pembroke, MA. Tel: (781) 826-6900, FAX: (781) 826-6880, E-Mail: jsargeant@macpacinc.com, Web Site: www.macpacinc.com (26)

MacArthur, John R., Harper's Magazine, New York, NY. Tel: (212) 420-5720, FAX: (212) 228-5889, Web Site: www.harpers.org (17)

Macartney, III William N., Indium Corp of America, Clinton, NY. Tel: (315) 853-4900, (800) 446-3486, FAX: (800) 221-5759, E-Mail: askus@indium.com, Web Site: www.indium.com (16)

MacCarthy, John L., Nuveen Investments, Chicago, IL. Tel: (312) 917-7700, (800) 257-8787, FAX: (312) 917-8049, Web Site: www.nuveen.com (14)

MacCleary, Randy, Liebert Corp, Columbus, OH. Tel: (614) 841-6700, (800) LIEBERT, FAX: (614) 841-6022, Web Site: www.liebert.com (16)

MacCourtney, Leo, Katz Media Group, New York, NY. Tel: (212) 424-6000, Web Site: www.katz-media.com (32)

MacCurrach, Augio, Customer Portfolios LLC, Boston, MA. Tel: (617) 224-9501, E-Mail: getstarted@customerportfolios.com, Web Site: www.customerportfolios.com (22)

MacDonald, Bill, Stewart-MacDonald, Athens, OH. Tel: (740) 592-3021, (800) 848-2273, FAX: (740) 593-7922, E-Mail: hostetler@stewmac.com, Web Site: www.stewmac.com (16)

MacDonald, John, Sony DADC, Terre Haute, IN. Tel: (812) 462-8100, Web Site: www.sonydadc.com (3)

Macdonald, Kathy, Massachusetts Horticultural Society, Wellesley, MA. Tel: (617) 933-4900, (617) 933-4929, FAX: (617) 933-4901, E-Mail: hort_line@masshort.org, Web Site: www.masshort.org (1)

MacDonald, Scott, Print Products International, Annapolis Junction, MD. Tel: (910) 695-7223, FAX: (910) 944-1724, Web Site: www.paceworldwide.com (9)

MacDonald, Walt, Educational Testing Service, Princeton, NJ. Tel: (609) 921-9000, FAX: (609) 734-5410, Web Site: www.ets.org (16)

MacDonnell, Kyle, Pappas MacDonnell Inc, Southport, CT. Tel: (203) 254-1944, FAX: (203) 256-8232, E-Mail: info@pappasmacdonnell.com, Web Site: www.pappasmacdonnell.com (35)

MacDowell, Richard, Mac Pac Inc, Pembroke, MA. Tel: (781) 826-6900, FAX: (781) 826-6880, E-Mail: jsargeant@macpacinc.com, Web Site: www.macpacinc.com (26)

Macfarlan, M. Reid, Arquest Inc, Millstone Twp, NJ. Tel: (609) 395-9500, (888) 270-8378, (888) AR-QUEST, FAX: (609) 395-9778, Web Site: www.arquest.com (16)

MacGillivray, Peter, Specialty Equipment Market Association, Diamond Bar, CA. Tel: (909) 396-0289, Web Site: www.sema.org (1)

Machalek Communications, Burnsville, MN. Tel: (952) 736-8000, (800) 846-5520, FAX: (886) 490-8834, E-Mail: publisher@machalek.com, Web Site: www.machalek.com (31)

Machalek, Andrea, Machalek Communications, Burnsville, MN. Tel: (952) 736-8000, (800) 846-5520, FAX: (886) 490-8834, E-Mail: publisher@machalek.com, Web Site: www.machalek.com (31)

Machleit, Ph.D. Karen A., College of Business, Cincinnati, OH. Tel: (513) 556-7002, FAX: (513) 556-4891, E-Mail: business@uc.edu, Web Site: www.business.uc.edu (41)

Macht, Joshua, Harvard Business Review, Boston, MA. Tel: (617) 783-7410, FAX: (617) 783-7493, Web Site: hbr.org (17)

Macias-Lewis, Kimberly Kimberly Macias-Lewis, Henry Wurst Inc, North Kansas City, MO. Tel: (816) 842-3113, FAX: (816) 472-6221, E-Mail: info@henrywurst.com, Web Site: www.henrywurst.com (27)

MacInnes, Glenn I, Webster Bank, Waterbury, CT. Tel: (203) 578-2230, FAX: (203) 578-2507, Web Site: www.websterbank.com (14)

MacIntosh Survey Center, East Providence, RI. Tel: (401) 438-8330, FAX: (401) 434-9219, E-Mail: macsurvey@aol.com (30)

MacIntosh, Ann, MacIntosh Survey Center, East Providence, RI. Tel: (401) 438-8330, FAX: (401) 434-9219, E-Mail: macsurvey@aol.com (30)

MacIntyre, Ron, Do-It Corp, South Haven, MI. Tel: (269) 637-1121, (800) 426-4822, FAX: (269) 637-7223, E-Mail: sales@do-it.com, Web Site: www.do-it.com (9)

Mack, Ed, Fine Architectural Metalsmiths, Chester, NY. Tel: (845) 651-7550, FAX: (845) 651-7857, Web Site: www.iceforge.com (16)

Mack, Melissa, Kaplan Inc, Fort Lauderdale, FL. Tel: (954) 515-3993, Web Site: www.kaplan.com (16)

Mack, Odell, PM Productions, Los Angeles, CA. Tel: (310) 559-3127, FAX: (310) 559-3168, E-Mail: odellmack@hotmail.com, Web Site: www.pmproductionsvideos.com (32)

Mack, Rhoda Weber, Fine Architectural Metalsmiths, Chester, NY. Tel: (845) 651-7550, FAX: (845) 651-7857, Web Site: www.iceforge.com (16)

Mack, Robin, Creative Health Products, Plymouth, MI. Tel: (734) 996-5900, (800) 742-4478, FAX: (734) 996-4650, Web Site: www.chponline.com (16)

Mack, Timothy C., World Future Society, Chicago, IL. Tel: (301) 656-8274, (800) 989-8274, FAX: (301) 951-0394, E-Mail: info@wfs.org, Web Site: www.wfs.org (1)

Mackay, Harvey B., MackayMitchell Envelope Co, Minneapolis, MN. Tel: (612) 331-9311, (800) 622-5299, FAX: (612) 331-3460, Web Site: www.mackayenvelope.com (26)

Mackay, Keith, Village Software Inc, Boston, MA. Tel: (617) 695-9332, (800) 724-9332, FAX: (617) 695-1935, E-Mail: requests@villagesoft.com, Web Site: www.villagesoft.com (3)

MackayMitchell Envelope Co, Minneapolis, MN. Tel: (612) 331-9311, (800) 622-5299, FAX: (612) 331-3460, Web Site: www.mackayenvelope.com (26)

Macke Bindery Inc, Cincinnati, OH. Tel: (513) 771-7500, FAX: (531) 771-3830, Web Site: www.mackebrothers.com (28)

Macke, Bill, Macke Bindery Inc, Cincinnati, OH. Tel: (513) 771-7500, FAX: (531) 771-3830, Web Site: www.mackebrothers.com (28)

Macke, Sr. Joseph D., Macke Bindery Inc, Cincinnati, OH. Tel: (513) 771-7500, FAX: (531) 771-3830, Web Site: www.mackebrothers.com (28)

Macke, Susan, Macke Bindery Inc, Cincinnati, OH. Tel: (513) 771-7500, FAX: (531) 771-3830, Web Site: www.mackebrothers.com (28)

MacKenzie, Dan, Blue Cross Blue Shield of Illinois, Chicago, IL. Tel: (312) 938-6000, FAX: (312) 938-5722, Web Site: www.bcbsil.com (15)

Mackenzie, Iain, ISA International Sign Expo, Alexandria, VA. Tel: (703) 836-4012, FAX: (703) 836-8353, Web Site: signexpo.org (42)

MacKenzie, Leslie, Directory of Mail Order Catalogs, Amenia, NY. Tel: (518) 789-8700, (800) 562-2139, FAX: (518) 789-0556, E-Mail: cstupak@greyhouse.com, Web Site: www.greyhouse.com (43)

MacKenzie, Leslie, Grey House Publishing, Amenia, NY. Tel: (518) 789-8700, (800) 562-2139, FAX: (518) 789-0556, E-Mail: books@greyhouse.com, Web Site: www.greyhouse.com (43)

MacKenzie, Leslie, The Directory of Business Information Resources, Amenia, NY. Tel: (845) 373-8263, E-Mail: cstupak@greyhouse.com, Web Site: www.greyhouse.com (43)

Macko, Deb, Raybuck Autobody Parts, Punxsutawney, PA. Tel: (814) 938-5248, FAX: (814) 938-4250, E-Mail: service@raybuck.com, Web Site: www.raybuck.com (12)

Macko, Terry, World Wildlife Fund, Washington, DC. Tel: (202) 293-4800, Web Site: www.worldwildlife.org (1)

MacLaren McCann, Toronto, ON Canada. Tel: (416) 594-6000, FAX: (416) 643-7026, Web Site: www.maclaren.com (35)

MacLeod, Charles, SMM Advertising, Smithtown, NY. Tel: (631) 265-5160, FAX: (631) 265-5185, E-Mail: marketing@smmadvertising.com, Web Site: smmadvertising.com (35)

MacLeod, Jim, BBM Canada Inc, Don Mills, ON Canada. Tel: (416) 445-9800, FAX: (416) 445-8644, E-Mail: info@bbm.ca, Web Site: www.bbm.ca (30)

MacNeil, Dixie, University of Alabama, Tuscaloosa, AL. Tel: (205) 348-6330, (866) 307-3917, FAX: (205) 348-9246, Web Site: continuingstudies.ua.edu (13)

Macourek, Peter, Rose Electronics, Houston, TX. Tel: (281) 933-7673, (800) 333-9343, FAX: (281) 933-0044, E-Mail: sales@rose.com, Web Site: www.rose.com (3)

Macpherson, D.G., Grainger Industrial Supply, North Brook, IL. Tel: (847) 498-5900, FAX: (847) 498-3402, Web Site: www.grainger.com (16)

Macpherson, D.G., WW Grainger Inc, Lake Forest, IL. Tel: (847) 535-1000, (800) 472-4643, FAX: (847) 535-9122, Web Site: www.grainger.com (9)

Macromark Inc, Danbury, CT. Tel: (845) 230-6300, FAX: (845) 278-0650, E-Mail: sales@macromark.com, Web Site: www.macromark.com (23)

MacRostie, Don, Stewart-MacDonald, Athens, OH. Tel: (740) 592-3021, (800) 848-2273, FAX: (740) 593-7922, E-Mail: hostetler@stewmac.com, Web Site: www.stewmac.com (16)

MacSorley, Dominic, Concern Worldwide, New York, NY. Tel: (212) 557-8000, FAX: (212) 557-8004, Web Site: /www.concernusa.org (1)

Macy's Inc, Cincinnati, OH. Tel: (513) 579-7912, (800) 289-6229, Web Site: www.macysinc.com (5)

Macy's Marketing, New York, NY. Tel: (212) 695-4400, FAX: (212) 494-1517, Web Site: www.macys.com (16)

Mad Mimi, Scottsdale, AZ. Tel: (480) 505-8800, FAX: (480) 505-8844, E-Mail: support@madmimi.com, Web Site: madmimi.com (24)

Madara, James L., American Medical Association, Chicago, IL. Tel: (312) 464-5000, (800) 621-8335, FAX: (312) 464-4184, Web Site: www.ama-assn.org (1)

Madara, Steve, Liebert Corp, Columbus, OH. Tel: (614) 841-6700, (800) LIEBERT, FAX: (614) 841-6022, Web Site: www.liebert.com (16)

Maddocks, Andy, In Touch Ministries, Atlanta, GA. Tel: (800) 789-1473, Web Site: www.intouch.org (1)

Maddox, Jeff, Jobscope Corp, Greenville, SC. Tel: (864) 458-3143, (800) 443-5794, FAX: (864) 234-4852, E-Mail: marketing@jobscope.com, Web Site: www.jobscope.com (16)

Maddox, Melissa, Ashworth College, Norcross, GA. Tel: (770) 729-8400, (800) 957-5412, FAX: (770) 729-9294, Web Site: www.ashworthcollege.edu (13)

Mader, Don, Southeastern Printing, Hialeah, FL. Tel: (305) 855-8707, (800) 226-8221, FAX: (305) 888-9903, E-Mail: info@seprint.com, Web Site: www.seprint.com (27)

Madhany, Nasreen, Neo@Ogilvy, New York, NY. Tel: (212) 259-5200, Web Site: www.neoogilvy.com (35)

Madison Direct Marketing Ltd, Stamford, CT. Tel: (203) 653-3200, FAX: (203) 316-0518, Web Site: www.madisondm.com (31)

Madison Executive Search, Ridgefield, CT. Tel: (203) 431-6565, FAX: (203) 431-6060, E-Mail: mimi@directexec.com, Web Site: www.directexec.com (20)

Madison Sales Group, Northbrook, IL. Tel: (847) 480-2370, FAX: (847) 480-7437, E-Mail: sales@madisonsalesgroup.com, Web Site: madisonsalesgroup.com (33)

Madison, Paula, National Medical Fellowships, New York, NY. Tel: (212) 483-8880, FAX: (212) 483-8897, E-Mail: info@nmf-online.org, Web Site: www.nmf-online.org (1)

Madisonavegifts.com, Watertown, NY. Tel: (315) 779-9228, (866) 421-1744, E-Mail: magsales@madisonavegifts.com, Web Site: www.madisonavegifts.com (6)

Madonna, Wendy A., Penn Mutual, Horsham, PA. Tel: (215) 956-8083, FAX: (215) 956-8368, Web Site: www.pennmutual.com (15)

Madorin, Harry, American Association of Individual Investors, Chicago, IL. Tel: (312) 280-0170, FAX: (312) 280-9883, E-Mail: adam@aaii.com, Web Site: www.aaii.com (1)

Madorsky, Michelle, University of California Irvine Extension, Irvine, CA. Tel: (949) 824-5414, E-Mail: unex-services@uci.edu, Web Site: extension.uci.edu (1)

Madyda, Stan, Estee Marketing Group Inc, Rye Brook, NY. Tel: (914) 235-7080, FAX: (914) 235-6518, E-Mail: info@esteemarketing.com, Web Site: www.esteemarketing.com (24)

Mael, Michael L., Washington National Opera, Washington, DC. Tel: (202) 467-4600, (800) 444-1324, Web Site: www.kennedy-center.org/wno (16)

Maffucci, Tally, RMI Direct Marketing Inc, Danbury, CT. Tel: (203) 798-0448, FAX: (203) 778-6130, E-Mail: info@rmidirect.com, Web Site: www.rmidirect.com (23)

Magazine Publishers of America, New York, NY. Tel: (212) 872-3700, FAX: (212) 888-4217, E-Mail: mpa@magazine.org, Web Site: www.magazine.org (17)

Magee, Jennifer Keating, Keating Magee, Metairie, LA. Tel: (504) 299-8000, FAX: (504) 525-6647, E-Mail: info@keatingmagee.com, Web Site: www.keatingmagee.com (35)

Magee, Kathleen S., Operation Smile Inc, Virginia Beach, VA. Tel: (757) 321-7645, Web Site: www.operationsmile.org (1)

Magee, Monique Darnay, Editorial Code & Data Inc, Walled Lake, MI. Tel: (248) 926-5187, FAX: (248) 926-6047, E-Mail: Monique@marketsize.com, Web Site: www.marketsize.com (30)

Magee, William P., Operation Smile Inc, Virginia Beach, VA. Tel: (757) 321-7645, Web Site: www.operationsmile.org (1)

Magellan's Catalog, Chelmsford, MA. Tel: (800) 450-7115, FAX: (800) 866-3235, E-Mail: sales@magellans.com, Web Site: www.magellans.com (5)

Magento, Culver City, CA. Tel: (310) 954-8012, Web Site: www.magento.com (22)

Mager, Danny, Affirm Agency, Pewaukee, WI. Tel: (262) 650-9900, E-Mail: info@affirmagency.com, Web Site: affirmagency.com (35)

Maggio, Steven J., DaVinci Direct, Plymouth, MA. Tel: (508) 746-2555, FAX: (815) 301-9884, E-Mail: steve@davinci-direct.com, Web Site: www.davinci-direct.com (1)

Maggiore, Dick, Innis Maggiore Group Inc, Canton, OH. Tel: (330) 492-5500, (800) 460-4111, FAX: (330) 492-5568, E-Mail: dick@innismaggiore.com, Web Site: www.innismaggiore.com (35)

Magiathlin, Peter, MBI Inc, Norwalk, CT. Tel: (203) 853-2000, E-Mail: webmail@mbi-inc.com, Web Site: www.mbi-inc.com (16)

Frank N Magid Associates Inc, Marion, IA. Tel: (319) 377-7345, FAX: (319) 377-5861, E-Mail: iowa@magid.com, Web Site: www.magid.com (30)

Magid, Brent, Frank N Magid Associates Inc, Marion, IA. Tel: (319) 377-7345, FAX: (319) 377-5861, E-Mail: iowa@magid.com, Web Site: www.magid.com (30)

Magidson, Jay, Statistical Innovations Inc, Belmont, MA. Tel: (617) 489-4490, FAX: (617) 489-4499, E-Mail: statisticalinnovations@gmail.com, Web Site: www.statisticalinnovations.com (20)

Magill, Lenny, Gun Video Catalog/LMP, San Diego, CA. Tel: (858) 569-4000, (800) 942-8273, FAX: (858) 569-0505, Web Site: www.gunvideo.com; www.glockstore.com (11)

Magill, Michael D., Ennis Inc, Midlothian, TX. Tel: (972) 775-9801, (800) 962-0944, FAX: (800) 645-8339, Web Site: www.ennis.com (16)

Maginnis, John, Blue Cross Blue Shield of Louisiana, Baton Rouge, LA. Tel: (225) 295-3307, (800) 599-2583, FAX: (225) 295-2054, E-Mail: help@bcbsla.com, Web Site: www.bcbsla.com (15)

Magjak Printing Corp, Port Chester, NY. Tel: (914) 939-8800, Web Site: www.magjak.com (27)

Magna Publications Inc, Madison, WI. Tel: (608) 246-3590, FAX: (608) 246-3597, Web Site: www.magnapubs.com (17)

Magna-Tel Inc, Cape Girardeau, MO. Tel: (573) 334-3096, (800) 467-2537, FAX: (573) 335-1715, Web Site: www.magna.tel.com (5)

Magna Visual Inc, Saint Louis, MO. Tel: (314) 843-9000, (800) 843-3399, FAX: (314) 843-0000, E-Mail: magna@magnavisual.com, Web Site: www.magnavisual.com (9)

Magnaflux, Glenview, IL. Tel: (847) 657-5300, FAX: (847) 657-5388, Web Site: www.magnaflux.com (16)

Magnani, Greg, Sales Service/America Inc, Alexandria, VA. Tel: (703) 813-2400 (16)

Magnaplan Corp, Champlain, NY. Tel: (518) 298-8404, (800) 361-1192, FAX: (518) 298-2368, E-Mail: info@visualplanning.com, Web Site: www.visualplanning.com (10)

Magnatag Visible Systems, Macedon, NY. Tel: (315) 986-3033, FAX: (315) 986-4000, Web Site: www.magnatag.com (16)

Magnet LLC, Washington, MO. Tel: (636) 239-5661, (800) 458-9457, FAX: (636) 239-4490, E-Mail: contactus@themagnetgroup.com, Web Site: www.magnetllc.com (16)

Magnets 4 Media, Washington, MO. Tel: (843) 216-6665, (800) 642-6384, FAX: (636) 390-5147, E-Mail: sales@magnets4media.com, Web Site: www.magnets4media.com (30)

Magnets USA, Roanoke, VA. Tel: (540) 857-3045, (800) 869-7562, FAX: (800) 788-6872, Web Site: www.magnetsusa.com (30)

The Magni Co Inc, McKinney, TX. Tel: (972) 540-2050, (800) 645-9199, FAX: (972) 540-1057, E-Mail: sales@magnico.com, Web Site: www.magnico.com; www.magnilife.com (16)

Magnolia Hall, Jasper, GA. Tel: (404) 351-1910, (866) 410-2755, FAX: (404) 692-4068, E-Mail: belvedere@magnoliahall.com, Web Site: www.magnoliahall.com (8)

Magnum Photos Inc, New York, NY. Tel: (212) 929-6000, FAX: (212) 929-9325, E-Mail: photography@magnumphotos.com, Web Site: www.magnumphotos.com (38)

Maguire, Kelly, ISA International Sign Expo, Alexandria, VA. Tel: (703) 836-4012, FAX: (703) 836-8353, Web Site: signexpo.org (42)

Maguire, Michael, Structural Graphics, Essex, CT. Tel: (860) 767-2661, FAX: (860) 767-2451, Web Site: www.structuralgraphics.com (27)

Maguire, William, Peninsular Printing of Daytona Beach Inc, Daytona Beach, FL. Tel: (386) 274-4837, FAX: (386) 274-5023, E-Mail: penprint@bellsouth.net, Web Site: www.peninsularprinting.com (27)

Mahaffey, Lisa, AXA Equitable, New York, NY. Tel: (212) 554-1234, (212) 314-2956, Web Site: www.axaonline.com (15)

Mahan, Bart, Buggies Unlimited, Jacksonville, FL. Tel: (888) 444-6364, E-Mail: support@buggiesunlimited.com, Web Site: www.buggiesunlimited.com (12)

Mahan, Kathryn, Brooks Equipment Co, Charlotte, NC. Tel: (704) 596-9438, (800) 826-3473, FAX: (704) 596-1096, Web Site: www.brooksequipment.com (9)

Mahar, Brendan, PacNet Services Ltd, Vancouver, BC Canada. Tel: (604) 689-0399, FAX: (604) 689-0313, E-Mail: info@pacnetservices.com, Web Site: www.pacnetservices.com (14)

Maher, Chris, House Party Inc, Irvington, NY. Tel: (720) 496-2503, (888) 591-1678, FAX: (914) 591-4561, E-Mail: help@houseparty.com, Web Site: www.houseparty.com (30)

Maher, Frank, Integer Group, Des Moines, IA. Tel: (515) 288-7910, FAX: (515) 288-8439, E-Mail: fmaher@integermidwest.com, Web Site: www.integer.com (35)

Mahfood, Robin, Food for the Poor Inc, Coconut Creek, FL. Tel: (954) 427-2222, Web Site: www.foodforthepoor.com (1)

Mahler, Andy, The Mx Group, Burr Ridge, IL. Tel: (800) 827-0170, FAX: (630) 654-0302, Web Site: www.themxgroup.com (35)

Mahler, Hugh F., Wolf Envelope Co, Birmingham, MI. Tel: (248) 687-2745, (800) 258-5700, FAX: (248) 687-2751, Web Site: www.wolfenvelope.com (26)

Mahmood, Kal, Old World Ind, Northbrook, IL. Tel: (847) 559-2000, FAX: (847) 559-2266, Web Site: www.oldworldind.com (34)

Mahon, Jerry, Market Share Development Inc, Dunmore, PA. Tel: (570) 961-3762, FAX: (570) 941-0508, E-Mail: jmahon@market-shareinc.com, Web Site: www.market-shareinc.com (35)

Mahoney, Erin, Washington Lists Inc, McLean, VA. Tel: (703) 749-3110, FAX: (703) 749-0960, E-Mail: emahoney@washingtonlists.com, Web Site: www.washingtonlists.com (23)

Mahoney, Joanne M., New York Power Authority, White Plains, NY. Tel: (914) 681-6200, E-Mail: info@nypa.gov, Web Site: www.nypa.gov (16)

Mahoney, Kevin F., A T Cross Co, Lincoln, RI. Tel: (401) 333-1200, (800) 282-7677, FAX: (401) 334-2861, Web Site: www.cross.com (16)

Mahoney, Shaun, Higher Power Marketing, Phoenix, AZ. Tel: (480) 837-3580, (888) 501-5544, FAX: (480) 837-3589, E-Mail: info@hpowermarketing.com, Web Site: www.hpowermarketing.com (30)

Mahoney, Tom, ITAGroup, West Des Moines, IA. Tel: (800) 257-1985, E-Mail: drivenbyloyalty@itagroup.com, Web Site: www.itagroup.com (33)

Maiden, James, Long & Foster Insurance, Chantilly, VA. Tel: (703) 653-8500 (15)

Maier, Bruno, Pacific Cycle Inc, Madison, WI. Tel: (608) 268-2468, (800) 724-9466, FAX: (847) 236-3692, (847) 573-0602, E-Mail: info@pacificcycle.com, Web Site: www.pacificcycle.com (16)

Maier, Henry J., FedEx Ground, Coraopolis, PA. Tel: (412) 269-1000, (800) 762-3725, FAX: (412) 747-4295, Web Site: www.fedex.com/us/ground/main (28)

Maier, Jim, Baron/Barclay Bridge Supplies, Louisville, KY. Tel: (502) 426-0410, (800) 274-2221, FAX: (502) 426-2044, E-Mail: baronbarclay@baronbarclay.com, Web Site: www.baronbarclay.com (11)

Maier, Kelley, Ingram Book Group, La Vergne, TN. Tel: (615) 793-5000, (800) 937-8000, FAX: (800) 876-0186, Web Site: www.ipage.ingrambook.com (16)

Maier, Steven, Direct Mail Strategy Group (DMSG), Cresskill, NJ. Tel: (201) 567-3200, FAX: (201) 567-1530, E-Mail: listinfo@conraddirect.com, Web Site: www.conraddirect.com (31)

Mail Advertising Services Inc, Darnestown, MD. Tel: (301) 762-9015 (28)

Mail America Inc, Wheeling, WV. Tel: (304) 242-8081, (800) 421-2150, FAX: (304) 242-8082, E-Mail: sales@mailamerica.com, Web Site: www.mailamerica.com (35)

Mail Computer Service, West Bridgewater, MA. Tel: (508) 584-6490, (800) 640-8530, FAX: (508) 584-2890 (21)

Mail Enterprises LLC, Birmingham, AL. Tel: (205) 595-4945, (800) 595-4945, FAX: (205) 595-4943, E-Mail: sswedenburg@mailent.com, Web Site: www.mailent.com (21)

Mail Handling Services, Eden Prairie, MN. Tel: (952) 975-5000, FAX: (952) 975-5030, Web Site: www.mailhandling.com (28)

Mail Management Enterprises, Seaford, DE. Tel: (410) 883-3224, FAX: (410) 883-3392, E-Mail: mailmgt@aol.com, Web Site: www.mailmanagemententerprises.com (20)

Mail Movers & Mailing Services, Upper Darby, PA. Tel: (610) 888-6969, (610) 734-1220, FAX: (610) 734-1200, E-Mail: mailmovers@rcn.com, Web Site: www.mailmoversandmore.com (22)

Mail Order Business, Dubuque, IA. Tel: (319) 589-1000 X1076, (800) 228-0810, FAX: (319) 589-1046, Web Site: www.kendallhunt.com (43)

Mail Order Business Directory, Delray Beach, FL. Tel: (561) 496-3316, E-Mail: bkleinpub@aol.com (43)

MailBlazer, Santa Ana, CA. Tel: (714) 662-5396, Web Site: www.mailblazer.com (27)

The Mailbox of Ithaca Inc, Ithaca, NY. Tel: (607) 257-3865, (800) 382-6348, FAX: (607) 266-0508, E-Mail: mailbox@lightlink.com, Web Site: www.mailboxofithaca.com (28)

MailChimp, Atlanta, GA. Tel: (678) 999-0141, Web Site: mailchimp.com (24)

Mailer's Software, Rancho Santa Margarita, CA. Tel: (949) 858-3000, (800) 635-4772, FAX: (949) 589-5211, E-Mail: info@melissadata.com, Web Site: www.mailerssoftware.com (22)

MailGraphics Inc, Boulder, CO. Tel: (303) 449-4053, E-Mail: questions@mailgraphics.com, Web Site: www.mailgraphics.com (23)

Mailing and Fulfillment Service Association of New York, New York, NY. Tel: (212) 217-6824, (800) 394-5106, FAX: (212) 217-6824, E-Mail: info@ mfsany.com, Web Site: www.mfsany.com (34)

Mailing Lists Plus Inc, Bellevue, WA. Tel: (425) 451-3335, FAX: (425) 646-4485, E-Mail: info@ mailinglistsplus.com, Web Site: www. mailinglistsplus.com (23)

Mailing Source, Costa Mesa, CA. Tel: (949) 722-9391 (28)

Mailing Specialists Inc, Greensburg, PA. Tel: (724) 832-3840, (888) 216-1056, FAX: (724) 832-8419, E-Mail: sales@mailmsi.com, Web Site: www. mailmsi.com (28)

Mailmaster Corp, Jonesboro, AR. Tel: (870) 972-8845, (800) 551-7018, FAX: (870) 972-0877, E-Mail: info@mail-master.com, Web Site: www.mail-master.com (28)

Mailmen Inc, Hauppauge, NY. Tel: (631) 582-6900, FAX: (631) 582-6948, E-Mail: getresults@ mailmeninc.com, Web Site: www.mailmeninc.com (28)

MailNow Inc, Nashville, TN. Tel: (615) 844-4244, FAX: (615) 208-9757, E-Mail: randall@ xdatemarketing.com, Web Site: www. xdatemarketing.com (21)

Mailways Enterprises Inc, Crystal Lake, IL. Tel: (815) 455-4850, FAX: (815) 455-7327, E-Mail: dave@ mailways.com, Web Site: www.mailways.com (28)

Maiman, Dana, FCB Health, New York, NY. Tel: (212) 672-2300, FAX: (212) 672-2301, E-Mail: hello@ fcbhealthcare.com, Web Site: fcbhealthcare.com (35)

Maiman, Janice, American Institute of CPAs, New York, NY. Tel: (212) 596-6200, (888) 777-7077, FAX: (212) 596-6213, Web Site: www.aicpa.org (1)

Main Street Direct, New York, NY. Tel: (212) 779-3000, FAX: (212) 779-3061, E-Mail: contact@ mainstreetdirect.com, Web Site: www. mainstreetdirect.com (31)

Main, Barbara, Texas Refinery Corp, Fort Worth, TX. Tel: (817) 332-1161, FAX: (817) 336-8441, E-Mail: jhopkins@texasrefinery.com, Web Site: www. texasrefinery.com (9)

Main, Bill, Landscape Forms Inc, Kalamazoo, MI. Tel: (616) 381-0490, (800) 430-6209, FAX: (616) 381-3455, E-Mail: specify@landscapeforms.com, Web Site: www.landscapeforms.com (16)

The Maine Connection, Portland, ME. Tel: (207) 780-4355, FAX: (207) 780-4239, E-Mail: mainelaw@ maine.edu (27)

The Maine Photographic Workshops, Rockport, ME. Tel: (207) 236-8581, (877) 577-7700, FAX: (207) 236-2558, E-Mail: info@theworkshops.com, Web Site: www.theworkshops.com (16)

Maine Potato Board, Presque Isle, ME. Tel: (207) 769-5061, FAX: (207) 764-4148, E-Mail: mainepotatoes@mainepotatoes.com, Web Site: www.mainepotatoes.com (1)

Maine, James T., Automated Equipment Service Inc, Poughkeepsie, NY. Tel: (607) 733-2108, (800) 468-4068, FAX: (845) 485-8221, E-Mail: info@ aesmailpro.com, Web Site: www.aesmailpro.com (34)

Maingi, Shailesh, Supelco Inc, Bellefonte, PA. Tel: (814) 359-3441, (800) 359-3041, FAX: (814) 359-3044, E-Mail: supelco@sial.com, Web Site: www. sigma-aldrich.com (16)

Maison Glass Delicacies, Cold Spring, NY. Tel: (212) 755-3316, (800) 822-5564, E-Mail: info@ maisonglass.com, Web Site: www.maisonglass.com (4)

Maites, Alan, Radiant 1, Chicago, IL. Tel: (312) 933-7764, E-Mail: amaites@radiant-1.com, Web Site: www.radiant-1.com (35)

Maitino, Phil, Mailer's Software, Rancho Santa Margarita, CA. Tel: (949) 858-3000, (800) 635-4772, FAX: (949) 589-5211, E-Mail: info@melissadata.com, Web Site: www.mailerssoftware.com (22)

Maits, Boyd, Backe Digital Brand Marketing, Radnor, PA. Tel: (610) 947-6901, E-Mail: jbacke@ backemarketing.com, Web Site: www. backemarketing.com (35)

Majestic Marketing Inc, Corona, CA. Tel: (951) 280-2400, (800) 843-2247, FAX: (951) 280-2410, E-Mail: sales@bagmasters.com, Web Site: www. bagmasters.com (35)

Majestic Products Co, Paris, KY. Tel: (859) 987-0740, Web Site: majesticproducts.com (16)

Major Brands Group, Minneapolis, MN. Tel: (763) 767-6800, FAX: (763) 767-1264, E-Mail: mbgcustomerservice@mrgmn.com, Web Site: www. mrgrp.com (33)

Majorium, Stevens Point, WI. Tel: (715) 342-1018, (800) 654-4935, FAX: (715) 342-1118, E-Mail: sales@majorium.com, Web Site: www. letstalkselling.com (17)

Maka, Ted, Shape LLC, Addison, IL. Tel: (630) 620-8394, (800) 367-5811, FAX: (630) 620-0784, E-Mail: sales@shapellc.com, Web Site: www. shapellc.com (3)

Make-A-Wish Foundation of America, Phoenix, AZ. Tel: (602) 279-9474, FAX: (602) 279-0855, Web Site: www.wish.org (1)

Making It Big, Cotati, CA. Tel: (707) 795-1997, (877) 644-1995, FAX: (707) 795-4874, E-Mail: mib@ makingitbig.com, Web Site: www.makingitbig.com (2)

Makinson, John, Penguin Group USA Inc, New York, NY. Tel: (212) 366-2000, Web Site: www.us. penguingroup.com (17)

Makofsky, Bob, Conformer Expansion Products Inc, Great Neck, NY. Tel: (516) 504-6300, E-Mail: support@conformerinc.com, Web Site: www. conformerinc.com (26)

Makofsky, Marvin, Conformer Expansion Products Inc, Great Neck, NY. Tel: (516) 504-6300, E-Mail: support@conformerinc.com, Web Site: www. conformerinc.com (26)

Malak, Anthony Tony, FP Mailing Solutions, Addison, IL. Tel: (630) 827-5500, (800) 341-6052, FAX: (630) 693-0626, E-Mail: custserv@fp-usa.com, Web Site: www.fp-usa.com (34)

Malamed, David, Jamax Direct LLC, Englewood Cliffs, NJ. Tel: (201) 569-4540 (23)

Maland, Tim, Nevada Commission on Tourism, Carson City, NV. Tel: (775) 687-4322, (800) NEVADA 8, FAX: (775) 687-6779, Web Site: www. travelnevada.com (1)

Malco Products Inc, Barberton, OH. Tel: (330) 753-0361, (800) 253-2526, FAX: (330) 753-2025, Web Site: www.malcopro.com (16)

Malcolm, Phil, AAA Auto Club South, Tampa, FL. Tel: (813) 289-5800, FAX: (813) 289-1475, Web Site: www.aaa.com (1)

Malcolm, Richard (Rick), Acurian, Horsham, PA. Tel: (215) 323-9000, (866) 566-5966, FAX: (215) 323-9001, Web Site: www.acurian.com (7)

Maldonado, Louis, Dexposito & Partners, New York, NY. Tel: (646) 747-8800, Web Site: newamericanagency.com (35)

Male, Jane, Kansas City Direct Marketing Association, Kansas City, MO. Tel: (816) 561-5323, FAX: (816) 561-1991, E-Mail: info@kcdma.org, Web Site: www.kcdma.org (40)

Ken Malek Associates Inc, Yardley, PA. Tel: (215) 579-2070, FAX: (215) 860-3498, Web Site: www. kenmalek.com (20)

Malek, Kenneth, Ken Malek Associates Inc, Yardley, PA. Tel: (215) 579-2070, FAX: (215) 860-3498, Web Site: www.kenmalek.com (20)

Maliekel, V. George, Hollister Inc, Libertyville, IL. Tel: (847) 680-1000, (888) 740-8999, FAX: (847) 680-2123, Web Site: www.hollister.com (16)

Malin, Ira, Travel Planners Inc, New York, NY. Tel: (212) 532-1660, (800) 221-3531, FAX: (212) 532-1556, Web Site: www.tphousing.com (19)

Malin, Linda, Barton & Cooney, Burlington, NJ. Tel: (609) 747-9300, FAX: (609) 747-9700, E-Mail: pmdoyle@bartoncooney.com, Web Site: www. bartoncooney.com (28)

Malina, Marianne, GSD&M, Austin, TX. Tel: (512) 242-4736, Web Site: www.gsdm.com (35)

Maliska, Kelly, Arthritis Foundation, Atlanta, GA. Tel: (404) 872-7100, FAX: (404) 872-0457, Web Site: www.arthritis.org (1)

Malkmus, Paul, Hallelujah Acres, Gastonia, NC. Tel: (704) 481-1700, (800) 915-9355, Web Site: www. myhdiet.com (5)

Mallardi, Mark J., Educational Insights, Inc, Gardena, CA. Tel: (310) 884-2000, (888) 591-9334, FAX: (310) 886-8850, E-Mail: service@edin.com, Web Site: www.educationalinsights.com (16)

Mallette, Ken, Oxfam America, Boston, MA. Tel: (617) 482-1211, (800) 776-9326, FAX: (617) 728-2594, E-Mail: info@oxfamamerica.org, Web Site: www. oxfamamerica.org (1)

Malley, Kenneth, Medco Health Solutions Inc, Franklin Lakes, NJ. Tel: (201) 269-3400, (800) 556-3326, FAX: (800) 222-1934, E-Mail: customersupport@ medcosupply.com, Web Site: www.medco-athletics. com (7)

Mallie, Tina, Zurich, Schaumburg, IL. Tel: (847) 605-3712, (800) 382-2150, FAX: (847) 605-6403, Web Site: www.zurichna.com (15)

Mallin, Ed, Donnelley Marketing, Pearl River, NY. Tel: (201) 476-2300, FAX: (201) 476-2151, Web Site: www.infousa.com (23)

Mallof, Joseph T., World Kitchen Inc, Corning, NY. Tel: (607) 377-8000, (800) 999-3436, FAX: (607) 377-8946, Web Site: www.worldkitchen.com (16)

Mallon, Jim, AIG Accident & Health, New York, NY. Tel: (212) 770-7000, (877) 638-4244, FAX: (212) 509-9705, Web Site: www.aig.com (15)

Mallon, Jim, American General Life & Accident Insurance, Nashville, TN. Tel: (615) 749-1000, (800) 888-2452, Web Site: www.agla.com (15)

Mallory, Jackie, Petra Industries, Edmond, OK. Tel: (405) 216-2100, FAX: (405) 216-2102, Web Site: www.patra.com (3)

Mallory, Linda, Harriet Carter Gifts Inc, Montgomeryville, PA. Tel: (215) 361-5100, FAX: (215) 361-1127, Web Site: www.harrietcarter.com (6)

Mallory, Lisa, The Metropolitan Opera, New York, NY. Tel: (212) 362-6000, (212) 799-3100, FAX: (212) 870-7695, Web Site: www.metoperafamily.org (1)

Malloy, Mark, EMI Strategic Marketing Inc, Boston, MA. Tel: (617) 224-1101, E-Mail: info@emiboston. com, Web Site: emiboston.com (35)

MALM Chemical Corp, Pound Ridge, NY. Tel: (914) 764-5775, FAX: (914) 764-5386. E-Mail: custserv1@malms.com, Web Site: www.malms.com (16)

Malone, Donna, Affina, Peoria, IL. Tel: (309) 685-5901, (877) 4 AFFINA, FAX: (309) 679-4199, Web Site: www.affina.com (30)

Malone, Gayle, TALX Corp, Dallas, TX. Tel: (972) 755-2100, FAX: (972) 755-2080, E-Mail: consulting@managementinsights.com, Web Site: www.managementinsights.com (20)

Malone, John, Thousand Trails LP, Chicago, IL. Tel: (214) 618-7200, (800) 205-0606, FAX: (214) 618-7324, Web Site: www.1000trails.com (16)

Malone, Joseph J., Horace Mann Educators Corp, Springfield, IL. Tel: (217) 789-2500, FAX: (217) 788-5161, Web Site: www.horacemann.com (15)

Malone, Mary, Orient Expressed Imports Inc, New Orleans, LA. Tel: (888) 856-3948, FAX: (504) 899-5566, E-Mail: orient@orientexpressed.com, Web Site: www.orientexpressed.com (2)

Malone, Tim, Mohawk Lifts, Amsterdam, NY. Tel: (518) 842-1431, (800) 833-2006, FAX: (518) 842-1289, E-Mail: rwells@mohawklifts.com, Web Site: www.mohawklifts.com (9)

EF Maloney Inc, Mamaroneck, NY. Tel: (718) 549-7000, FAX: (718) 549-6320, E-Mail: efmaloney@aol.com, Web Site: www.efmaloney.com (16)

The Maloney Group, New York, NY. Tel: (212) 777-6655, FAX: (212) 777-6600 (16)

Maloney, Antoinette, The Maloney Group, New York, NY. Tel: (212) 777-6655, FAX: (212) 777-6600 (16)

Maloney, E. F., EF Maloney Inc, Mamaroneck, NY. Tel: (718) 549-7000, FAX: (718) 549-6320, E-Mail: efmaloney@aol.com, Web Site: www.efmaloney. com (16)

Maloney, Jim, GM Customer Relationship Management, Detroit, MI. Tel: (313) 665-6605, Web Site: www.gm.com (35)

Maloney, Martin J., Broadford & Maloney Inc, New York, NY. Tel: (212) 836-4710, FAX: (917) 322-2105, E-Mail: m.maloney@bmcorp.com, Web Site: bmcorp.com (35)

Maloney, Peter, Potpourri Group Inc, North Billerica, MA. Tel: (978) 256-4100, FAX: (978) 256-1961/0344, Web Site: www.potpourrigroup.com (6)

Maloney, Scott, Smart Practice, Phoenix, AZ. Tel: (800) 522-0800, FAX: (800) 522-8329, E-Mail: info@smartpractice.com, Web Site: www.smartpractice.com (17)

Maloof, George, New England Life Insurance Co, Boston, MA. Tel: (617) 578-2000, FAX: (617) 536-2393, Web Site: www.nefn.metlife.com (15)

Malordy, Jody, Metropolitan Museum of Art, New York, NY. Tel: (212) 570-3894, (800) 468-7386, FAX: (718) 628-5485, Web Site: www.metmuseum.org/store (8)

Maloy, Judith, Polaris Direct, Hooksett, NH. Tel: (603) 626-5800, E-Mail: info@polarisdirect.net, Web Site: www.polarisdirect.net (28)

Malpass, Greg, Traction On Demand, Burnaby, BC Canada. Tel: (604) 620-6040, Web Site: www.tractionondemand.com (35)

Malys, Marcia, MediaWorks Advertising & Marketing Inc, Ormond Beach, FL. Tel: (386) 676-4608, E-Mail: scott@mediaworksusa.com, Web Site: www.mediaworksusa.com (21)

Mammel, Kevin, Quark Inc, Denver, CO. Tel: (303) 894-8888, Web Site: www.quark.com (34)

Management Science Associates Inc, Pittsburgh, PA. Tel: (412) 362-2000, (800) MSA-INFO, FAX: (412) 363-5598, E-Mail: info@msa.com, Web Site: www. msa.com (20)

Manchester Farms Inc, Columbia, SC. Tel: (803) 845-0421, FAX: (803) 227-3103, E-Mail: customerservice@manchesterfarms.com, Web Site: www.manchesterfarms.com (4)

Mancinelli, Ozzie, Paradise Galleries, Laguna Hills, CA. Tel: (858) 793-4050, (800) 67-DOLLS, FAX: (949) 743-8974, E-Mail: omancinelli@paradisegalleries.com, Web Site: www.paradisegalleries.com (6)

Mancini, John F., AIIM International, Silver Spring, MD. Tel: (301) 587-8202, (800) 477-2446, FAX: (301) 587-2711, E-Mail: aiim@aiim.org, Web Site: www.aiim.org (1)

Mancomm Inc, Davenport, IA. Tel: (563) 323-6245, (877) 626-2666, FAX: (563) 323-0804, E-Mail: 411@mancomm.com, Web Site: mancomm.com (17)

Mancuso, Leslie, Chase Media Group, Yorktown Heights, NY. Tel: (914) 962-3871, FAX: (914) 962-2040, Web Site: www.chasemultimedia.com (27)

Mancuso, Paulanne, Calvin Klein Cosmetics Co, New York, NY. Tel: (212) 719-2600, E-Mail: customerservice@calvinklein.com, Web Site: www.calvinklein.com (7)

Mancuso, Steve, DMC Corp, Kearny, NJ. Tel: (973) 589-0606, (800) 275-4117, FAX: (973) 589-8931, Web Site: www.dmc-usa.com (16)

Mandel Co, Milwaukee, WI. Tel: (414) 271-6970, (800) 888-6970, FAX: (414) 271-1254, E-Mail: rick. mandel@mandelcompany.com, Web Site: www. mandelcompany.com (27)

Mandel, Leonard, PostLink Corp, Ottawa, ON Canada. Tel: (613) 741-4538, Web Site: www. ottawamailingservices.com (28)

Mandel, Leslie, The Rich List Co, Wainscott, NY. Tel: (212) 737-8917, FAX: (212) 861-5384, E-Mail: richlistco@aol.com, Web Site: www.richlist.com (24)

Mandel, Lon L., Specialists Marketing Services Inc, Hasbrouck Heights, NJ. Tel: (201) 865-5800, FAX: (201) 288-4295, E-Mail: info@sms-inc.com, Web Site: www.sms-inc.com (23)

Mandel, Rick, Mandel Co, Milwaukee, WI. Tel: (414) 271-6970, (800) 888-6970, FAX: (414) 271-1254, E-Mail: rick.mandel@mandelcompany.com, Web Site: www.mandelcompany.com (27)

Mandelbaum, Howard, Photofest, New York, NY. Tel: (212) 633-6330, FAX: (212) 366-9062, E-Mail: requests@photofestnyc.com (38)

Mandell, Andrew J., Data-Mail Inc, Newington, CT. Tel: (860) 666-0399, FAX: (860) 665-1226, E-Mail: aliceh@data-mail.com, Web Site: www.data-mail. com (28)

Mandell, Mark, Data-Mail Inc, Newington, CT. Tel: (860) 666-0399, FAX: (860) 665-1226, E-Mail: aliceh@data-mail.com, Web Site: www.data-mail. com (28)

Mandia, Mark, DMW Worldwide LLC, Chesterbrook, PA. Tel: (610) 407-0407, (877) 744-3699, FAX: (610) 407-9201, E-Mail: info@dmwdirect.com, Web Site: www.dmwdirect.com (35)

Mane Solutions, New York, NY. Tel: (212) 736-0306, FAX: (212) 239-2039 (16)

Maneto, Jim, Hemmings Motor News, Bennington, VT. Tel: (800) 227-4373, FAX: (802) 447-9631, Web Site: www.hmn.com (17)

Manetti, Louis, Polyair Packaging, Chicago, IL. Tel: (773) 995-1818, (888) POLYAIR X444, FAX: (773) 995-7725, E-Mail: marketing@polyair.com, Web Site: www.polyair.com (9)

Maneval, Judy, Sanky Communications Inc, New York, NY. Tel: (212) 868-4300, Web Site: www.sankyinc. com (1)

Mangan, Benjamin, Mancomm Inc, Davenport, IA. Tel: (563) 323-6245, (877) 626-2666, FAX: (563) 323-0804, E-Mail: 411@mancomm.com, Web Site: mancomm.com (17)

Mangano, Domenic J., Village Coin Shop, Plaistow, NH. Tel: (603) 382-5492/7151, FAX: (603) 382-5682, E-Mail: don@villagecoin.com, Web Site: www.villagecoin.com (6)

Mangieri/Hull Solutions LLC, Sandy Hook, CT. Tel: (203) 270-4800, FAX: (203) 270-4815, E-Mail: chris@mhrecruiters.com, Web Site: www. mhrecruiters.com (20)

Mangieri, Christopher J., Mangieri/Hull Solutions LLC, Sandy Hook, CT. Tel: (203) 270-4800, FAX: (203) 270-4815, E-Mail: chris@mhrecruiters.com, Web Site: www.mhrecruiters.com (20)

Mangrich, Gerry, Universal Engineering Corp, Cedar Rapids, IA. Tel: (319) 365-0441, (800) 366-2051, FAX: (319) 369-5440, E-Mail: info@universalcrusher.com, Web Site: www. universalcrusher.com (16)

Manhart, Lisa, Ventura Associates International LLC, New York, NY. Tel: (212) 302-8277, FAX: (212) 302-2587, E-Mail: info@sweepspros.com, Web Site: www.sweepspros.com (35)

Manhattan College, Bronx, NY. Tel: (718) 862-7285, Web Site: www.manhattan.edu (1)

Manhattan Media Services Inc, New York, NY. Tel: (212) 808-4077, FAX: (212) 808-4080, E-Mail: mmorello@manhmedia.com, Web Site: www. manhmedia.com (21)

Maniatis, Amy, National Geographic Society, Washington, DC. Tel: (202) 862-8638, (800) 373-1717, Web Site: www.nationalgeographic.com (17)

Maniscalco, Lee, DM News, New York, NY. Tel: (646) 638-6000, (800) 558-1703, FAX: (212) 925-8752, E-Mail: dmnewssubs@haymarketmedia.com, Web Site: www.dmnews.com (43)

Manistique Papers Inc, Manistique, MI. Tel: (906) 341-2175, FAX: (906) 341-5635 (25)

Manko, Janet, The Lakeville Journal LLC, Lakeville, CT. Tel: (860) 435-9873, FAX: (860) 435-4802 (37)

Manley, Michael A., Hess Print Solutions, Kent, OH. Tel: (800) 678-1222, E-Mail: info@hessprintsolutions.com, Web Site: www. thepressofohio.com (27)

Manly, IV Robert W., Smithfield Foods, Smithfield, VA. Tel: (800) 276-6158, Web Site: www. smithfieldfoods.com (16)

Mann, David, Professional Marketing Associates, Mount Pleasant, SC. Tel: (843) 971-8150, FAX: (843) 971-8159 (33)

Mann, Erica L., Bayer Corp Consumer Care Division, Whippany, NJ. Tel: (862) 404-3000, Web Site: www.consumercare.bayer.com (16)

Mann, Jim, BCC Software Inc, Rochester, NY. Tel: (585) 272-9130, (800) 453-3130, FAX: (585) 272-9141, Web Site: www.bccsoftware.com (22)

Mann, John, Datamann Inc, Wilder, VT. Tel: (802) 295-6600, (800) 451-4263, FAX: (802) 296-3623, Web Site: www.datamann.com (22)

Mann, Jr. Robert, Accenture, Boston, MA. Tel: (617) 488-4000, FAX: (617) 488-4001, Web Site: www. accenture.com (20)

Mann, Judith S., Capital Design, Providence, RI. Tel: (401) 270-6777, E-Mail: info@freemiums.com, Web Site: www.freemiums.com (33)

Manna, Christina, Association of National Advertisers Inc, New York, NY. Tel: (212) 697-5950, FAX: (212) 687-7310, Web Site: www.ana.net (40)

Mannatt, Wendy, Paladin Press, Boulder, CO. Tel: (303) 443-7250, (800) 392-2400, FAX: (303) 442-8741, E-Mail: service@paladin-press.com, Web Site: www.paladin-press.com (17)

Manning Materials, Birdsboro, PA. Tel: (610) 385-6797, (800) 445-1719, FAX: (610) 385-7524, E-Mail: mmsupport@manningmaterials.com, Web Site: www.manningmaterials.com (16)

Manning Media International, McKinney, TX. Tel: (972) 562-6960, FAX: (972) 542-3336, E-Mail: info@manningmedia.com, Web Site: www.manningmedia.com (23)

Manning, Frederick J., Celtic Life Insurance Co, Chicago, IL. Tel: (312) 332-5401, FAX: (312) 441-0341, E-Mail: info@celtic-net.com, Web Site: www.celtic-net.com (15)

Manning, Gay, Datasystem Solutions Inc, Overland Park, KS. Tel: (913) 362-6969, FAX: (913) 362-6383, E-Mail: sales@mutipub.com, Web Site: www.datasystem.com (22)

Manning, Jennifer, Country Financial, Bloomington, IL. Tel: (309) 821-3000 (15)

Manning, Kenneth P., Sensient Technologies, Saint Louis, MO. Tel: (314) 889-7600, (800) 325-8110, FAX: (314) 658-7318, Web Site: www.sensient-tech.com (16)

Manning, Kimberly, Cronin & Co, Glastonbury, CT. Tel: (860) 659-0514, Web Site: www.cronin-co.com (16)

Manning, Mike, Manning Media International, McKinney, TX. Tel: (972) 562-6960, FAX: (972) 542-3336, E-Mail: info@manningmedia.com, Web Site: www.manningmedia.com (23)

Manning, Mona, Golden Trophy, Chicago, IL. Tel: (773) 282-2900, (800) 821-3882, FAX: (800) 835-6601, E-Mail: goldentrophy@bruss.com, Web Site: www.giftsteaksonline.com (4)

Manning, Rob, Tennessee Valley Authority, Knoxville, TN. Tel: (865) 632-2101, Web Site: www.tva.gov (16)

Manning, Robert James, MFS Investment Management, Boston, MA. Tel: (617) 954-5000, FAX: (617) 350-2163, Web Site: www.mfs.com (14)

Mannion, Michael P, FedEx Ground, Coraopolis, PA. Tel: (412) 269-1000, (800) 762-3725, FAX: (412) 747-4295, Web Site: www.fedex.com/us/ground/main (28)

Mano, Barry, Referee Enterprises, Racine, WI. Tel: (800) 733-6100, FAX: (262) 632-5460, E-Mail: questions@referee.com, Web Site: www.referee.com (1)

Manoogian, Richard A., Masco Corp, Taylor, MI. Tel: (313) 274-7400, FAX: (313) 792-6135, E-Mail: webmaster@mascohq.com, Web Site: www.masco.com (16)

Manos, Joseph, MindFireInc, Irvine, CA. Tel: (949) 474-4418, Web Site: www.mindfireinc.com (22)

Manos, Steve, Kadant Johnson Inc, Three Rivers, MI. Tel: (269) 278-1715, FAX: (269) 279-5980, Web Site: www.kadantjohnson.com (16)

Manos, Wayne, Cold Spring Harbor Lab Press, Woodbury, NY. Tel: (516) 422-4100, (800) 843-4388, FAX: (516) 422-4097, E-Mail: cshpress@cshl.edu, Web Site: www.cshlpress.com (17)

Mansfield, Edward, The Washingtonian, Washington, DC. Tel: (202) 296-3600, E-Mail: editorial@washingtonian.com, Web Site: www.washingtonian.com (17)

Mansfield, John, The Durham Manufacturing Co, Durham, CT. Tel: (860) 349-3427, (800) 243-3774, FAX: (860) 349-8572, (800) 782-5499, E-Mail: info@durhammfg.com, Web Site: www.durhammfg.com (16)

Manson, Jeffrey, Western Psychological Services, Torrance, CA. Tel: (310) 478-2061, (800) 648-8857, FAX: (310)) 478-7838, E-Mail: marketing@wpspublish.com, Web Site: www.wpspublish.com (16)

Mansueto, Joe, Morningstar Inc, Chicago, IL. Tel: (312) 696-6000, Web Site: www.morningstar.com (14)

Mantica, Karen, Local Government Federal Credit Union, Raleigh, NC. Tel: (919) 755-0534, Web Site: www.lgfcu.org (14)

Mantz, Macia, Informal Education Products, Milwaukie, OR. Tel: (503) 794-7045, (888) 444-5500, FAX: (503) 794-7111, E-Mail: sales@museumtour.com, Web Site: www.museumtour.com (11)

Mantz, Marcia, McIntyre Direct Group LLC, Portland, OR. Tel: (503) 516-4592, FAX: (503) 286-7622, E-Mail: marcia@mcintyredirectgroup.com, Web Site: mcintyredirectgroup.com (21)

Manulife Financial Inc, Toronto, ON Canada. Tel: (416) 229-4515, (800) 387-0990, FAX: (416) 229-3028, Web Site: www.manulife.com (15)

Manus, Morty, Alfred Publishing Co Inc, Van Nuys, CA. Tel: (818) 891-5999, (800) 292-6122, FAX: (818) 893-5560, E-Mail: sales@alfred.com, Web Site: www.alfred.com (17)

Manus, Ron, Alfred Publishing Co Inc, Van Nuys, CA. Tel: (818) 891-5999, (800) 292-6122, FAX: (818) 893-5560, E-Mail: sales@alfred.com, Web Site: www.alfred.com (17)

Manville, Sheryl, American Family Life Assurance Co of Columbus (AFLAC), Columbus, GA. Tel: (706) 323-3431, (800) 992-3522, FAX: (706) 660-7446, Web Site: www.aflac.com (15)

Manzee, William, Eastern Mountain Sports, Peterborough, NH. Tel: (603) 924-9571, (888) 463-6367, FAX: (603) 924-4320, Web Site: www.ems.com (16)

Manzi, Jim P., Thermo Fisher Scientific Inc, Waltham, MA. Tel: (781) 622-1000, (800) 678-5599, FAX: (781) 622-1207, Web Site: www.thermofisher.com (9)

MAP International, Brunswick, GA. Tel: (912) 265-6010, (800) 225-8550, FAX: (912) 265-6170, Web Site: www.map.org (1)

Mapes, Ann, Drs Foster & Smith Inc, Rhinelander, WI. Tel: (715) 369-3305, Web Site: www.drsfostersmith.com (2)

Mapes, Christopher L., AO Smith Corp, Milwaukee, WI. Tel: (414) 359-4000, FAX: (414) 359-4064, Web Site: www.aosmith.com (16)

Maple Grove Farms of Vermont Inc, Saint Johnsbury, VT. Tel: (802) 748-5141, FAX: (802) 748-9647, E-Mail: maple@maplegrove.com, Web Site: www.maplegrove.com (4)

Mapping Analytics, Rochester, NY. Tel: (585) 271-6490, (877) 893-6490, FAX: (585) 271-1132, E-Mail: sales@mappinganalytics.com, Web Site: www.mappinganalytics.com (20)

Mar, Sandy, LiveOps Inc, Redwood City, CA. Tel: (408) 844-2400, Web Site: www.liveops.com (29)

Mara, Thomas, Leucadia National Corp, New York, NY. Tel: (212) 460-1900, FAX: (212) 598-4869, Web Site: www.leucadia.com (14)

Maracle, Russell, Challenge Industries Inc, Ithaca, NY. Tel: (607) 272-8990, FAX: (607) 277-7865, E-Mail: info@aboutchallenge.org, Web Site: www.aboutchallenge.org (28)

Maradonna, Bonnie, Winterthur Museum & Country Estate, Wilmington, DE. Tel: (302) 888-4600, (800) 448-3883, FAX: (302) 888-4730, E-Mail: tourinfo@winterthur.org, Web Site: www.winterthur.org (6)

Marathon Norco Aerospace Inc, Waco, TX. Tel: (254) 776-0650, FAX: (254) 776-6558, Web Site: www.mptc.com (16)

Marbert, Jeanette E., Interval International, South Miami, FL. Tel: (305) 666-1884, (800) 468-3782, FAX: (305) 667-5321, Web Site: www.intervalworld.com (35)

Marc G Gault Consulting, Stone Mountain, GA. Tel: (770) 938-0781 (35)

Marc USA, Pittsburgh, PA. Tel: (412) 562-2000, FAX: (412) 562-2022, E-Mail: pittsburgh@marcusa.com, Web Site: www.marcusa.com (35)

Marcado, Erik, KXEN Inc, San Francisco, CA. Tel: (415) 904-4160, FAX: (415) 904-9041, Web Site: www.kxen.com (22)

Marcantonio, Mike, Allegra Network, LLC, Plymouth, MI. Tel: (248) 596-8600, FAX: (248) 596-8601, Web Site: www2.allegranetwork.com (27)

Marcario, Rose, Patagonia, Ventura, CA. Tel: (805) 643-8616, (800) 638-6464, E-Mail: customer_service@patagonia.com, Web Site: www.patagonia.com (2)

Marcario, Rose, Patagonia Mail Order Inc, Reno, NV. Tel: (775) 747-1992, (800) 638-6464, FAX: (775) 747-6159, Web Site: www.patagonia.com (2)

Marcek, Steven, FileMaker Inc, Santa Clara, CA. Tel: (408) 987-7000, FAX: (408) 987-3823, Web Site: www.filemaker.com (22)

March of Dimes Foundation, White Plains, NY. Tel: (914) 997-4488, Web Site: www.marchofdimes.org (1)

March, David, Erdos & Morgan Inc, Syosset, NY. Tel: (516) 935-6959, FAX: (516) 935-4040, E-Mail: info@erdosmorgan.com, Web Site: www.erdosmorgan.com (30)

March, Todd, LoyaltyOne, Toronto, ON Canada. Tel: (416) 228-6500, Web Site: www.loyalty.com; www.airmiles.ca (22)

Marchak, Ed, Parker Boiler Co, Los Angeles, CA. Tel: (323) 727-9800, FAX: (323) 722-2848, E-Mail: mleeming@parkerboiler.com, Web Site: www.parkerboiler.com (34)

Marchand, Brett, Cossette, Quebec, QC Canada. Tel: (418) 647-2727, FAX: (418) 647-2564, E-Mail: info@cossette.com, Web Site: www.cossette.com (35)

Marchese Communications Inc, Marina Del Rey, CA. Tel: (866) 441-8086, E-Mail: david@marchesecommunications.com, Web Site: www.marchesecommunications.com (35)

Marchese, David, Marchese Communications Inc, Marina Del Rey, CA. Tel: (866) 441-8086, E-Mail: david@marchesecommunications.com, Web Site: www.marchesecommunications.com (35)

Marchese, Joseph, WS Ponton Inc, Pittsburgh, PA. Tel: (412) 782-2360, (800) 628-7806, FAX: (412) 782-1109, E-Mail: info@wsponton.com, Web Site: www.wsponton.com (23)

Marchetti, Karen J, Response FX, Carlsbad, CA. Tel: (760) 479-0012, E-Mail: services@responsefx.com, Web Site: www.responsefx.com (35)

Marchiscotta, Jodi, Better Homes & Gardens, New York, NY. Tel: (212) 551-7097, FAX: (212) 551-7114, E-Mail: support@bhg.com, Web Site: www.bhg.com (31)

Marcille, Esq. Douglas, US Gas & Electric, White Plains, NY. Tel: (888) 947-7880, FAX: (888) 400-1230, E-Mail: salesinfo@usgande.com, Web Site: www.usgande.com (16)

Marco Data Service, De Soto, MO. Tel: (636) 337-3109, FAX: (636) 586-1938 (22)

Marco Sales & Incentives Ltd, Brantford, ON Canada. Tel: (519) 751-2227, (888) 636-6161, FAX: (519) 751-0561, E-Mail: sales@themarcocorporation.com, Web Site: www.themarcocorporation.com (28)

Marco, Barbara, Marco Data Service, De Soto, MO. Tel: (636) 337-3109, FAX: (636) 586-1938 (22)

MarCom Technologies, Kelowna, BC Canada. Tel: (250) 868-9352, FAX: (250) 868-9362 (29)

Marconi, Luis G., Hormel Foods Corp, Austin, MN. Tel: (507) 437-5611, (800) 523-4635, FAX: (507) 437-5158, Web Site: www.hormelfoods.com (16)

MARCOR Remediation Inc, Halethorpe, MD. Tel: (410) 785-0001, (800) 547-0128, FAX: (410) 771-0348, E-Mail: info@marcor.com, Web Site: www.marcor.com (16)

Marcoux, Remi, Telemedia Communications US, North York, ON Canada. Tel: (416) 733-7600, (800) 461-3773 U.S., (888) 290-1466 Can., FAX: (416) 733-3563, E-Mail: info@transcontinental.ca, Web Site: www.transcontinental.com (17)

Marcoux, Remi, Trans Continental Inc, Montreal, QC Canada. Tel: (514) 954-4000, FAX: (514) 954-4016, Web Site: www.transcontinental-gtc.com (31)

Marcus Productions Inc, Fort Lauderdale, FL. Tel: (954) 965-5295, E-Mail: steve@marcusproductions.com, Web Site: www.marcusproductions.com (32)

Marcus, Barbara, Random House Children's Books, New York, NY. Tel: (212) 782-9000, (800) 726-0600, E-Mail: rhkidspublicity@randomhouse.com, Web Site: www.randomhousekids.com (13)

Marcus, Bruce D., The McGraw-Hill Financial, New York, NY. Tel: (212) 904-2000, Web Site: www.mhfi.com (17)

Marcus, Steven, Marcus Productions Inc, Fort Lauderdale, FL. Tel: (954) 965-5295, E-Mail: steve@marcusproductions.com, Web Site: www.marcusproductions.com (32)

Mardak, Keith, Hal Leonard Corp, Milwaukee, WI. Tel: (414) 774-3630, FAX: (414) 774-3259, Web Site: www.halleonard.com (17)

Marden-Kane Inc, Woodbury, NY. Tel: (516) 365-3999, FAX: (516) 365-5250, E-Mail: expert@mardenkane.com, Web Site: www.mardenkane.com (35)

Mardevdm2, Oak Brook, IL. Tel: (800) 323-4958, FAX: (303) 265-5457, E-Mail: info@mardevdm2.com, Web Site: www.mardevdm2.com (24)

Mardiron Optics, Stoneham, MA. Tel: (781) 938-8339, FAX: (781) 938-8339, Web Site: www.mardironooptics.com (11)

Mardirosian, K. Greg, Mardiron Optics, Stoneham, MA. Tel: (781) 938-8339, FAX: (781) 938-8339, Web Site: www.mardironooptics.com (11)

Marecek, Douglas, Integrated Print & Graphics, South Elgin, IL. Tel: (847) 695-6777, FAX: (847) 741-4090, E-Mail: info@ipandginc.com, Web Site: www.ipandginc.com (27)

The Marek Group, Waukesha, WI. Tel: (262) 549-8900, FAX: (262) 49-8910, E-Mail: info@marekgroup.com, Web Site: www.marekgroup.com (21)

Marek-Loper, Tami, The Marek Group, Waukesha, WI. Tel: (262) 549-8900, FAX: (262) 49-8910, E-Mail: info@marekgroup.com, Web Site: www.marekgroup.com (21)

Maresca, Bob, Bose Corp, Framingham, MA. Tel: (508) 879-7330, (800) 379-2703, FAX: (508) 766-7543, Web Site: www.bose.com (3)

Margro, Thomas E., San Francisco Bay Area Rapid Transit District (BART), Oakland, CA. Tel: (510) 464-6000, FAX: (510) 464-7103, Web Site: www.bart.gov (16)

Margulies, Jacob, Continental Envelope Corp, Geneva, IL. Tel: (630) 262-8080, (800) 621-8155, FAX: (630) 262-1450, E-Mail: sales@continentalenvelope.com, Web Site: www.continentalenvelope.com (26)

Marian Helpers Center, Stockbridge, MA. Tel: (413) 298-3691, (800) 462-7426, FAX: (413) 298-3583, Web Site: www.marian.org (1)

Marianacci, Thomas, ConvergeDirect, New York, NY. Tel: (212) 213-0111, E-Mail: info@convergedirect.com, Web Site: www.convergedirect.com (35)

Mariano, Joseph, Direct Selling Association, Washington, DC. Tel: (202) 452-8866, FAX: (202) 452-9010, E-Mail: info@dsa.org, Web Site: www.dsa.org (40)

Marie, Ruth, Association of Energy Engineers, Atlanta, GA. Tel: (770) 447-5083 x210, FAX: (770) 446-3969, E-Mail: info@aeecenter.org, Web Site: www.aeecenter.org (40)

Marimac Inc, Montreal, QC Canada. Tel: (514) 376-7882, FAX: (514) 376-0801, E-Mail: sales@marimacgroup.com, Web Site: www.marimac.com (8)

Marinelli, Janice, Buena Vista Home Entertainment, Burbank, CA. Tel: (818) 560-1000, FAX: (818) 845-8728, Web Site: www.bvhe.com (3)

Marini, Marco, ClickMail Marketing Inc, San Mateo, CA. Tel: (650) 653-8055, Web Site: clickmail.com (32)

Marino, Anne, Shiseido Cosmetics America, East Windsor, NJ. Tel: (212) 805-2300, FAX: (212) 688-0109, Web Site: www.sca.shiseido.com (7)

Marino, Felicia, Instructor's Choice Dancewear, Massapequa Park, NY. Tel: (516) 799-6000, FAX: (516) 799-7993, E-Mail: customerservice@instructorschoice.com, Web Site: www.instructorschoice.net (2)

Marino, Glenn, Premier Packaging Corp, Victor, NY. Tel: (877) 924-8460, FAX: (585) 924-8753, E-Mail: info@premiercustompkg.com, Web Site: www.premiercustompkg.com (16)

Marino, Michael, Wyse Advertising, Cleveland, OH. Tel: (216) 696-2424, E-Mail: info@wyseadv.com, Web Site: www.wyseadv.com (35)

Marino, Pamela, Choice Magazine, Middletown, CT. Tel: (860) 347-6933, (860) 347-1387, FAX: (860) 346-8586, E-Mail: adsales@ala-choice.org, Web Site: www.ala.org/ala/acrl/acrlpubs/choice/home.cfm (31)

Marion, Ed, The EZ-Forms Co, Kerrville, TX. Tel: (281) 667-4414, FAX: (281) 667-4415, E-Mail: ezformscontactus@gmail.com, Web Site: www.ez-forms.com (21)

Maris West & Baker, Jackson, MS. Tel: (601) 977-9200, FAX: (601) 977-9257, Web Site: www.mwb.com (35)

Maritz, Fenton, MO. Tel: (636) 827-4000, Web Site: www.maritz.com (35)

Maritz, Steve, Maritz, Fenton, MO. Tel: (636) 827-4000, Web Site: www.maritz.com (35)

Marjon, Steven, Shutterfly, Redwood City, CA. Tel: (650) 610-5200, Web Site: www.shutterfly.com (27)

The Mark Group, Boca Raton, FL. Tel: (561) 241-1700, (800) 637-0152, FAX: (561) 241-1055, Web Site: www.bostonproper.com (2)

Mark James & Associates Inc, Oswego, IL. Tel: (630) 548-8100, FAX: (630) 548-6107, E-Mail: info@markjamesassociates.com, Web Site: www.markjamesassociates.com/contact.html (16)

Marke Communications Inc, New York, NY. Tel: (212) 201-0600, (800) 716-2753, FAX: (212) 213-0785, Web Site: www.marke.com (35)

Markertek Video Supply, Saugerties, NY. Tel: (845) 246-3036, (800) 522-2025, FAX: (845) 246-1757, E-Mail: sales@markertek.com, Web Site: www.markertek.com (3)

Markese, John D., American Association of Individual Investors, Chicago, IL. Tel: (312) 280-0170, FAX: (312) 280-9883, E-Mail: adam@aaii.com, Web Site: www.aaii.com (1)

Market Approach Consulting Services LP, Lorena, TX. Tel: (254) 857-1100, FAX: (254) 857-1000, E-Mail: wmclean@marketapproach.net, Web Site: www.marketapproach.net (23)

The Market Builder Inc, Mesa, AZ. Tel: (480) 641-6200, FAX: (480) 641-6239, E-Mail: info@themarketbuilder.com, Web Site: www.themarketbuilder.com (21)

Market Data Retrieval, Shelton, CT. Tel: (203) 926-4800, (800) 333-8802, FAX: (203) 929-5253, E-Mail: mdrinfo@dnb.com, Web Site: schooldata.com (23)

Market Development Group Inc, Washington, DC. Tel: (202) 298-8030, FAX: (202) 244-4999, Web Site: www.mdginc.org (1)

Market Discovery Group, Roslyn, NY. Tel: (516) 365-8555, E-Mail: schiffmanl@aol.com (30)

Market Focus Direct, Markham, ON Canada. Tel: (905) 477-0801, FAX: (905) 477-4473, E-Mail: info@market-focus.com, Web Site: www.market-focus.com (28)

Market Focus Inc, Evanston, IL. Tel: (847) 328-2900, FAX: (847) 328-8121 (30)

Market Incentives Corp, Frazer, PA. Tel: (800) 486-8881, E-Mail: sales@marketincentives.com, Web Site: www.marketincentives.com (33)

Market Probe International Inc, New York, NY. Tel: (212) 725-7676, FAX: (212) 725-7529, E-Mail: info@marketprobeint.com, Web Site: www.marketprobeint.com (30)

Market Recognition, Boxborough, MA. Tel: (978) 314-0127, Web Site: www.marketrecognition.com (20)

Market Response International, Orleans, MA. Tel: (508) 240-1877, FAX: (508) 945-4010, E-Mail: rmiller@capecod.net, Web Site: www.millerinternational.com (30)

Market Share Development Inc, Dunmore, PA. Tel: (570) 961-3762, FAX: (570) 941-0508, E-Mail: jmahon@market-shareinc.com, Web Site: www.market-shareinc.com (35)

Market Square Communications Inc, Stevens Point, WI. Tel: (715) 344-4609, FAX: (715) 344-6885 (20)

Market Street Lists Inc, Exeter, NH. Tel: (603) 772-6666, (888) 675-5478, FAX: (603) 772-0184, E-Mail: info@market-street.com, Web Site: www.market-street.com (23)

Marketability Inc, Houston, TX. Tel: (713) 462-6000, FAX: (713) 481-8465, E-Mail: mickey@marketabilityinc.com, Web Site: www.marketabilityinc.com (35)

MarketAide Services Inc, Hutchinson, KS. Tel: (785) 825-7161, (800) 204-2433, FAX: (785) 825-4697, E-Mail: creative@marketaide.com, Web Site: www. marketaide.com (21)

Marketeers, Mission Viejo, CA. Tel: (949) 364-1669, FAX: (949) 582-0829, E-Mail: wbower@apc.net (29)

MarketerNet LLC, Chicago, IL. Tel: (312) 775-9320, (888) 443-3684, FAX: (312) 775-9328, E-Mail: info@marketernet.com, Web Site: www. marketernet.com (22)

MarketForce Corp, Havertown, PA. Tel: (610) 356-5220, FAX: (610) 356-5110, E-Mail: davethomas@ marketforcecorp.com, Web Site: www. marketforcecorp.com (23)

Marketing 1by1 Inc, Fairfax, VA. Tel: (703) 934-6020, FAX: (703) 591-3049, Web Site: marketing1by1. com (22)

The Marketing Advantage Inc, Stamford, CT. Tel: (203) 968-8400, FAX: (501) 968-8301, E-Mail: info@ marketingadvantage.com, Web Site: www. marketingadvantage.com (21)

Marketing Advents, Washington, DC. Tel: (202) 955-5030, FAX: (202) 955-0085, E-Mail: info@dmaw. org, Web Site: www.dmaw.org (43)

Marketing Agencies Association Worldwide, Edina, MN. Tel: (952) 922-0130, FAX: (203) 969-1499, E-Mail: keith.mccracker@maaw.org, Web Site: www.maaw.org (40)

The Marketing Agency LLC, Fort Lauderdale, FL. Tel: (954) 771-1177, FAX: (866) 379-5788, E-Mail: marketing@themarketingagency.com, Web Site: www.themarketingagency.com (35)

The Marketing Alliance, Fairfield, CT. Tel: (203) 254-0474 (20)

Marketing & Media Services LLC, Warwick, RI. Tel: (401) 737-7730, FAX: (401) 737-6465, Web Site: www.mmsipitv.com (30)

Marketing and Product Strategy, Peabody, MA. Tel: (978) 977-2000, (800) 825-5897, FAX: (781) 238-0986, Web Site: www.lhsl.com (16)

Marketing & Promotions Group, Ridgewood, NJ. Tel: (201) 251-8339, FAX: (201) 251-8340, E-Mail: michael@promowaves.com, Web Site: www. promowaves.com (35)

Marketing Communication Resource Inc, Willoughby, OH. Tel: (440) 484-3010, FAX: (440) 484-3020 (28)

Marketing Connections Corp, Manchester, NH. Tel: (603) 472-8989, (800) 472-1818, FAX: (603) 472-9881, E-Mail: lcasey@mccnh.com, Web Site: www. mcciq.com (29)

Marketing Consulting Services, Kingsport, TN. Tel: (423) 288-5866, FAX: (423) 288-5576 (20)

Marketing Economics Inc, Chicago, IL. Tel: (312) 642-2188, FAX: (312) 642-3091, E-Mail: codyh@ meimedia.com, Web Site: www.meimedia.com (23)

Marketing General Inc, Alexandria, VA. Tel: (703) 739-1000, (800) 644-6646, FAX: (703) 549-6057, Web Site: www.marketinggeneral.com (35)

Marketing Highway, Deerfield, IL. Tel: (312) 502-3732, E-Mail: info@marketinghighway.com, Web Site: www.marketinghighway.com (20)

Marketing Horizons Inc, Saint Louis, MO. Tel: (314) 432-1957, (800) 669-0839, FAX: (314) 432-7014, E-Mail: jkramer@mhorizons.com (30)

Marketing Incentives International Inc, Chicago, IL. Tel: (312) 440-3700, FAX: (312) 943-5813, E-Mail: info@mktgincentiveintl.com, Web Site: www. mktgincentiveintl.com (33)

Marketing Information Network, Edmond, OK. Tel: (405) 516-1215, FAX: (405) 516-1230, Web Site: www.minokc.com (22)

Marketing Innovators, Rosemont, IL. Tel: (847) 696-1111, (800) 543-7373, FAX: (847) 696-3194, E-Mail: info@marketinginnovators.com, Web Site: www.marketinginnovators.com (35)

The Marketing Machine, Irvine, CA. Tel: (949) 733-1778, (949) 733-3778, FAX: (949) 559-6993, E-Mail: request@the-marketing-machine.com, Web Site: www.mktgmach.com (39)

Marketing/Media Dynamics Inc, Harpers Ferry, WV. Tel: (304) 725-1119 (20)

Marketing News, Chicago, IL. Tel: (312) 542-9000, (800) 262-1150, FAX: (312) 542-9001, E-Mail: news@ama.org, Web Site: www.ama.org (43)

Marketing Research Association, Washington, DC. Tel: (860) 682-1000, (202) 800-2545, FAX: (860) 682-1010, (888) 512-1050, E-Mail: membership@ marketingresearch.org, Web Site: www.mra-net.org (40)

Marketing Results Inc, Sicklerville, NJ. Tel: (856) 740-3334, FAX: (856) 740-3335, Web Site: www. marketingresults.net (16)

Marketing Science Institute Review, Cambridge, MA. Tel: (617) 491-2060, FAX: (617) 491-2065, E-Mail: msi@msi.org, Web Site: www.msi.org (43)

Marketing Solutions, Lathrup Village, MI. Tel: (248) 443-5252, FAX: (248) 443-5252 (20)

Marketing Solutions Group Inc, Pleasanton, CA. Tel: (510) 331-7625, E-Mail: info@ marketingsolutionsgroup.biz, Web Site: marketingsolutionsgroup.biz (32)

Marketing Solutions Unlimited LLC, West Hartford, CT. Tel: (860) 523-0670, FAX: (860) 523-0675, E-Mail: info@msuprint.com, Web Site: msuprint. com (21)

The Marketing Store, Chicago, IL. Tel: (312) 614-1400, Web Site: www.tmsw.com (35)

Marketing Strategies Inc, North Myrtle Beach, SC. Tel: (843) 692-9662, FAX: (843) 692-0558, E-Mail: pr@ marketingstrategiesinc.com, Web Site: marketingstrategiesinc.com (35)

Marketing Synergy Inc, Naperville, IL. Tel: (630) 328-9550, FAX: (630) 328-9552, E-Mail: info@ MSINetwork.com, Web Site: www.msinetwork.com (30)

Marketing Systems Analysis, Ventnor, NJ. Tel: (609) 487-9340, FAX: (866) 214-3208, E-Mail: ernie@ schell.com, Web Site: www.schell.com (20)

Marketing Visions Inc, Tarrytown, NY. Tel: (914) 631-3900, FAX: (914) 693-8338, E-Mail: jsloofman@ marketingvisions.com, Web Site: www. marketingvisions.com (35)

MarketingWorks Inc, Los Angeles, CA. Tel: (323) 436-2000, E-Mail: chas@mwks.net, Web Site: www. marketingworksagency.com (32)

MarketLeverage, Lake Mary, FL. Tel: (407) 268-7700, FAX: (407) 268-7654, Web Site: www. precisionplaymedia.com (22)

Marketlinc, Saskatoon, SK Canada. Tel: (306) 956-7000, FAX: (306) 668-5812, E-Mail: info@ marketlinc.com, Web Site: www.marketlinc.com (29)

MarketMakers Group Inc, Wayne, PA. Tel: (610) 254-8924, FAX: (610) 254-9190, E-Mail: rlail@ marketmakers.com, Web Site: www. marketmakersgroup.com (29)

MarketNet Services LLC, Spring Lake, MI. Tel: (616) 847-7992, FAX: (616) 847-7994, Web Site: www. marketnetservices.com (22)

The MarketPlace Group Inc, Norwood, MA. Tel: (781) 762-6600, FAX: (781) 762-1300 (31)

MarketPower Direct Marketing, Atlanta, GA. Tel: (435) 565-1889, E-Mail: joelalpert123@gmail.com, Web Site: www.marketpoweronline.com (35)

Marketrac Inc, Westbury, NY. Tel: (516) 365-4330, FAX: (516) 365-5789 (20)

Marketry Inc, Bellevue, WA. Tel: (425) 451-1262, FAX: (425) 953-2957, E-Mail: greg@marketry.com, Web Site: www.marketry.com (23)

Marketshare Publications Inc, Overland Park, KS. Tel: (877) 880-8068, FAX: (913) 217-2895, Web Site: www.marketsharegroup.com (17)

Marketsmith Inc, Parsippany, NJ. Tel: (973) 889-0006, Web Site: www.marketsmithinc.com (20)

MarketVision Research Inc, Cincinnati, OH. Tel: (513) 791-3100, (800) 232-4250, FAX: (513) 794-3500, E-Mail: jpinnell@mv-research.com, Web Site: www.marketvisionresearch.com (30)

Markezin, Elaine, Partners Health, Philadelphia, PA. Tel: (215) 849-9600, (800) 553-0784, E-Mail: sroberts@healthpart.com, Web Site: www. healthpart.com (15)

Markgraf & Wells Marketing, Minneapolis, MN. Tel: (612) 870-8550 (35)

Markgraf, Richard J., Markgraf & Wells Marketing, Minneapolis, MN. Tel: (612) 870-8550 (35)

Markham, Ann, Communication Creativity, Buena Vista, CO. Tel: (720) 344-4388, (800) 331-8355, FAX: (866) 685-0307, E-Mail: steve@steveheimberg.com, Web Site: www.communicationcreativity.com (17)

Markham, John, Focus Plus Inc, New York, NY. Tel: (212) 675-0142, (800) 340-8846, FAX: (212) 645-3171, E-Mail: info@focusplusny.com, Web Site: www.focusplusny.com (30)

Marking Specialists Group, Buffalo Grove, IL. Tel: (847) 793-8100, (800) 678-8073, FAX: (847) 793-8109, E-Mail: info@marking-specialists.com, Web Site: www.marking-specialists.com (27)

Markinson, Brian A., King Pharmaceuticals, Inc, Tenafly, NJ. Tel: (972) 885-0929, (888) 840-5370, E-Mail: igal@navehpharma.com, Web Site: www. kingpharma.com (7)

MARKOTS, Brentwood, CA. Tel: (925) 240-0093, (877) 946-7253, FAX: (925) 240-0097, E-Mail: info@markots.com, Web Site: www.markots.com (35)

Markovich, Paul, Blue Shield Life, San Francisco, CA. Tel: (888) 800-2742, FAX: (800) 329-2742, Web Site: www.blueshieldca.com (15)

Markovich, Paul, Blue Shield of California, San Francisco, CA. Tel: (415) 229-5000, FAX: (415) 229-5056, Web Site: www.blueshieldca.com (15)

Markowitz, Eugene, The Goldmark Group Inc, Clifton, NJ. Tel: (973) 777-5720, (800) 632-9632, FAX: (973) 777-2390, E-Mail: info@goldmarkgroup.com, Web Site: www.goldmarkgroup.com (35)

Markowitz, Paula, Net 60 LLC, New York, NY. Tel: (201) 833-9003, FAX: (201) 301-8182, E-Mail: chaim@net60.com, Web Site: net60.com (23)

Markowitz, Scott, Blue Hill Marketing Solutions Inc, Pearl River, NY. Tel: (845) 627-6600, FAX: (845) 735-3985, E-Mail: sales@liftengine.com, Web Site: www.liftengine.com (22)

Marks, Dan, ServiceMaster Co, Memphis, TN. Tel: (901) 766-1400, (866) 782-6787, Web Site: www. servicemaster.com (8)

Marks, Fred, Marquis Who's Who Ventures LLC, Berkeley Heights, NJ. Tel: (908) 279-0100, (844) 394-6946, E-Mail: info@marquisww.com, Web Site: www.marquiswhoswho.com (17)

Marks, Gregg I., Anne Klein, New York, NY. Web Site: www.anneklein.com (16)

Marks, Peter, Maris West & Baker, Jackson, MS. Tel: (601) 977-9200, FAX: (601) 977-9257, Web Site: www.mwb.com (35)

Marks, Suzanne, Pasadena Advertising Marketing & Design, Pasadena, CA. Tel: (626) 584-0011, FAX: (626) 584-0907, Web Site: www.pasadenaadv.com (35)

Marks, Ted, Fowler's Chocolates Inc, Buffalo, NY. Tel: (716) 877-9983, (800) 824-2263, FAX: (716) 877-9959, E-Mail: customerservice@fowlerschocolates.com, Web Site: www.fowlerschocolates.com (4)

Marks, Tom, Leverage Marketing Group, Newtown, CT. Tel: (203) 270-6699, E-Mail: info@lev-mg.com, Web Site: www.leverage-marketing.com (35)

Markson Scientific LLC, Henderson, NC. Tel: (808) 791-0490, (800) 528-5114, FAX: (800) 858-2243, E-Mail: sales@markson.com, Web Site: www.markson.com (9)

Markson, Mitch, Edelman Direct Marketing Inc, Great Neck, NY. Tel: (516) 829-9398 (20)

Markwins International Corp, City of Industry, CA. Tel: (909) 595-8898, FAX: (909) 595-8820, Web Site: www.markwins.com (16)

The Marlin Company, Wallingford, CT. Tel: (877) 890-9116, Web Site: www.themarlincompany.com (35)

Marlow, Bruce W., 21st Century Insurance, Woodland Hills, CA. Tel: (818) 704-3700, FAX: (818) 226-1198, E-Mail: executiveoffice@21st.com, Web Site: www.21st.com (15)

Marlowe, Anthony, TMone LLC, Iowa City, IA. Tel: (868) 577-2461, E-Mail: info@massmarkets.com, Web Site: www.massmarkets.com (29)

Marlowe, John W., Markson Scientific LLC, Henderson, NC. Tel: (808) 791-0490, (800) 528-5114, FAX: (800) 858-2243, E-Mail: sales@markson.com, Web Site: www.markson.com (9)

Marmelstein Inc, Philadelphia, PA. Tel: (215) 925-9862, FAX: (215) 925-3889 (16)

Marmion, Sally, Leadership Software Corp, Nyack, NY. Tel: (845) 358-0406, (800) 872-0068, FAX: (845) 358-0359, E-Mail: info@leadersoft.com, Web Site: www.leadersoft.com (16)

Marmitt, Sandy, Burtch Works LLC, Evanston, IL. Tel: (847) 440-8550, FAX: (847) 440-8556, Web Site: www.burtchworks.com (20)

The Marmon Group LLC, Chicago, IL. Tel: (312) 372-9500, FAX: (312) 845-5305, Web Site: www.marmon.com (16)

Marnell Database Marketing, Chicago, IL. Tel: (312) 944-3511 (20)

Marnell, Thomas J., Marnell Database Marketing, Chicago, IL. Tel: (312) 944-3511 (20)

Maron, Esq. Lawrence, New Jersey Institute for Continuing Legal Education, New Brunswick, NJ. Tel: (732) 249-5100, Web Site: www.njicle.com (1)

Marquardt, Kent, Premera Blue Cross, Spokane, WA. Tel: (425) 670-4000, (800) 422-0032, FAX: (425) 670-5853, Web Site: www.premera.com (15)

Marquis Awards & Specialties Inc, Powell, WY. Tel: (307) 754-2272, (800) 327-2446, FAX: (307) 754-9577, E-Mail: marquisawards@bresnan.net, Web Site: www.rushawards.com (35)

Marquis Who's Who Ventures LLC, Berkeley Heights, NJ. Tel: (908) 279-0100, (844) 394-6946, E-Mail: info@marquisww.com, Web Site: www.marquiswhoswho.com (17)

Marra, Thomas M., Symetra Financial, Bellevue, WA. Tel: (425) 256-8000, (800) 426-7355, FAX: (425) 256-5737, Web Site: www.symetra.com (15)

Marra, Thomas M., The Hartford Financial Services Inc, Southington, CT. Tel: (860) 547-5000, (860) 843-8070, FAX: (860) 547-2680, Web Site: www.thehartford.com (15)

Marrachi, Tom, Aircraft Spruce & Specialty Co, Corona, CA. Tel: (909) 372-9555, (877) 4-Spruce, FAX: (909) 372-0555, E-Mail: info@aircraft-spruce.com, Web Site: www.aircraft-spruce.com (12)

Marrah, John, Profit Center Software Inc, Uniondale, NY. Tel: (516) 414-6300, (888) 446-6240, FAX: (516) 414-6304, E-Mail: jmarrah@profitcenter.com, Web Site: www.profitcenter.com (22)

Marriott International Inc, Bethesda, MD. Tel: (301) 380-3000, (301) 380-1791, E-Mail: internet.customer.care@marriott.com, Web Site: www.marriott.com (19)

Marriott Ownership Resorts Sales & Marketing, Orlando, FL. Tel: (407) 206-6000, (800) 850-6674, FAX: (407) 206-6097, Web Site: www.marriottvacationclub.com (19)

Marrocco, Tracy, Penn Mutual, Horsham, PA. Tel: (215) 956-8083, FAX: (215) 956-8368, Web Site: www.pennmutual.com (15)

Mars Research, Fort Lauderdale, FL. Tel: (954) 771-7725, (877) 755-2805, FAX: (954) 703-4377, E-Mail: ron@marsresearch.com, Web Site: www.marsresearch.com (30)

Marsh Affinity Group Services, Chicago, IL. Tel: (800) 621-3008, Web Site: www.seaburychicago.com (15)

Marsh US Consumer, Urbandale, IA. Tel: (515) 365-6102 (15)

Marsh, Jeffrey, Littleton Coin Co Inc, Littleton, NH. Tel: (603) 444-5386, (800) 645-3122, FAX: (603) 444-0121, E-Mail: jhennessey@littletoncoin.com, Web Site: www.littletoncoin.com (6)

Marsh, Paul, Teachers Credit Union, South Bend, IN. Tel: (574) 284-6247, (800) 552-4745, Web Site: www.tcunet.com (1)

Marsh, Ronald K., Audience Identification Inc, Lisle, IL. Tel: (630) 435-0460, FAX: (630) 435-0470, E-Mail: rmarsh@audienceid.com (22)

Marshall & Swift, Los Angeles, CA. Tel: (213) 683-9000, FAX: (213) 683-9010, Web Site: www.marshallswift.com (17)

Marshall Fields Dept Stores, Minneapolis, MN. Tel: (612) 375-3004, Web Site: www.fields.com (5)

Marshall Marketing & Communications Inc, Pittsburgh, PA. Tel: (412) 914-0970, FAX: (412) 914-0971, Web Site: www.mm-c.com (30)

Marshall, Beth, HighScope Educational Research Foundation, Ypsilanti, MI. Tel: (800) 587-5639, FAX: (734) 485-0704, E-Mail: info@highscope.org, Web Site: www.highscope.org (17)

Marshall, Cathy, D2: Direct, Denville, NJ. Tel: (973) 627-4410, FAX: (973) 627-3703, E-Mail: info@d2direct.com, Web Site: www.d2direct.com (35)

Marshall, Cindy, Pace Communications Inc, Greensboro, NC. Tel: (336) 378-6065, FAX: (336) 275-2864, Web Site: www.pacecommunications.com (17)

Marshall, Craig A., Marshall Marketing & Communications Inc, Pittsburgh, PA. Tel: (412) 914-0970, FAX: (412) 914-0971, Web Site: www.mm-c.com (30)

Marshall, Kathy, Chain Store Guide, Tampa, FL. Tel: (800) 927-9292, FAX: (813) 627-6882, E-Mail: info@csgis.com, Web Site: www.csgis.com (17)

Marshall, Peter, D2: Direct, Denville, NJ. Tel: (973) 627-4410, FAX: (973) 627-3703, E-Mail: info@d2direct.com, Web Site: www.d2direct.com (35)

Marshall, Sr. James, Epson America, Long Beach, CA. Tel: (562) 981-3840, (800) 873-7766, FAX: (562) 290-5220, Web Site: www.epson.com (10)

Marshall, Tom, Bowers Envelope Co, Indianapolis, IN. Tel: (317) 253-4321, FAX: (317) 254-2231, Web Site: www.bowersenvelope.com (26)

Marsicano, Denise, Frederick's of Hollywood Group Inc, Los Angeles, CA. Tel: (323) 466-5151, (855) 655-2514, FAX: (323) 464-5149, E-Mail: support@fredericks.com, Web Site: www.fredericks.com (2)

Marszalek, Lewis R., Celtic Life Insurance Co, Chicago, IL. Tel: (312) 332-5401, FAX: (312) 441-0341, E-Mail: info@celtic-net.com, Web Site: www.celtic-net.com (15)

Marte, Lorelis, National Enquirer, New York, NY. Tel: (212) 545-4800, Web Site: www.nationalenquirer.com (17)

Martel, David, Cable Direct Marketing Inc, Montville, NJ. Tel: (973) 244-0010, FAX: (973) 244-0302, E-Mail: cabledm@aol.com (31)

Martel, David, Harbor Freight Tools, Camarillo, CA. Tel: (805) 445-4791, (800) 423-2567, FAX: (800) 445-4925, Web Site: www.harborfreight.com (9)

Martell, Frank, CoreLogic Inc, Irvine, CA. Tel: (949) 214-1000, (800) 426-1466, Web Site: www.corelogic.com (22)

Martell, Robert, Volkswagen Group of America Inc, Herndon, VA. Tel: (248) 754-5000, Web Site: www.volkswagengroupamerica.com (16)

Martens, Chris, NextScreen LLC, Austin, TX. Tel: (512) 892-8682, Web Site: www.avguide.com (17)

Martens, Lisa, Everyday Media, Garrison, NY. Tel: (845) 788-3900, FAX: (212) 481-7800, Web Site: www.everydaymedia.com (31)

Martensen, Buddy, Ivie & Associates Inc, Flower Mound, TX. Tel: (972) 899-5000, FAX: (972) 899-5050, Web Site: www.ivieinc.com (35)

Martha, Geoffrey, Medtronic Inc, Minneapolis, MN. Tel: (763) 514-4000, (800) 328-2518, FAX: (763) 514-4879, Web Site: www.medtronic.com (16)

The Martin Agency, Richmond, VA. Tel: (804) 698-8000, FAX: (804) 698-8001, Web Site: www.martinagency.com (35)

Martin Gross & Friends, New York, NY. Tel: (212) 689-0772, FAX: (212) 481-0552, E-Mail: grossdirect@aol.com (39)

Martin Thomas International, Sterling, VA. Tel: (401) 225-3905, E-Mail: mpottle@martinthomas.com, Web Site: www.martinthomas.com (35)

Martin Williams Advertising, Minneapolis, MN. Tel: (612) 342-9739, FAX: (612) 342-9700, Web Site: www.martinwilliams.com (35)

Martin Worldwide Inc, Oak Park, CA. Tel: (888) 694-5478, Web Site: www.martinworldwide.net (23)

Martin, Bill, Century Photo, Newtown, CT. Tel: (800) 767-0777, FAX: (714) 441-4550, Web Site: www.centuryphoto.com (10)

Martin, Bob, Bike Nashbar, Crab Orchard, WV. Tel: (800) NAS-HBAR, FAX: (877) 778-9456, E-Mail: custserv@nashbar.com, Web Site: www.bikenashbar.com (11)

Martin, Chris, Cramer, Norwood, MA. Tel: (781) 278-2387, Web Site: www.crameronline.com (20)

Martin, Don, Bloomin Promotions, Boulder, CO. Tel: (303) 443-3591, E-Mail: flowers@bloomin.com, Web Site: www.bloominpromotions.com (25)

Martin, Greg, Cramer, Norwood, MA. Tel: (781) 278-2387, Web Site: www.crameronline.com (20)

Martin, Jean, Center for Professional Development, Tallahassee, FL. Tel: (850) 487-1691, (850) 644-8004, FAX: (850) 644-2589, Web Site: www.Learningforlife.fsu.com (16)

Martin, Joan, Brahmin Leather Works, Fairhaven, MA. Tel: (508) 994-4000, (800) 229-2428, FAX: (508) 994-4153, Web Site: www.brahminusa.com (16)

Martin, Joe, Monster Magnet, Louisville, KY. Tel: (866) 259-6554, E-Mail: joe@monstermagnet.com, Web Site: www.monstermagnet.com (35)

Martin, John, Turner Broadcasting System Inc, Atlanta, GA. Tel: (404) 827-1700, Web Site: www.turner. com (32)

Martin, Jonathan, Telecom Inc, Oakland, CA. Tel: (510) 873-8283, (800) 243-3101, FAX: (510) 873-8293, Web Site: www.telecominc.com (29)

Martin, Josh, ZenithOptimedia Direct, New York, NY. Tel: (212) 859-5100, FAX: (212) 757-9495, Web Site: www.zenithoptimedia.com (35)

Martin, Jr. Dumas, TheIdeaClub.com & Dumas Martin Consulting, Pomona, CA. Tel: (909) 620-4772, FAX: (909) 629-4739, Web Site: www.theideaclub. com (18)

Martin, Kristina M., West Virginia University, Morgantown, WV. Tel: (304) 293-3505, FAX: (304) 293-3072, E-Mail: wvuwebmaster@mail.wvu.edu, Web Site: www.wvu.edu (41)

Martin, Linda, Mary Elizabeth Granger & Associates Inc, Baltimore, MD. Tel: (410) 842-1170, FAX: (410) 842-1185, E-Mail: info@maryegranger.com, Web Site: www.maryegranger.com (23)

Martin, Lori, Saint Gregory Group, Cincinnati, OH. Tel: (513) 769-8440, FAX: (513) 769-1640, E-Mail: info@stgregory.com, Web Site: www.stgregory.com (35)

Martin, Louise, Psion Teklogix Inc, Mississauga, ON Canada. Tel: (905) 813-9900, (800) 322-3437, E-Mail: ptinfo@psion.com, Web Site: www. psionteklogix.com (3)

Martin, Michael, BellTower Technologies LLC, Richardson, TX. Tel: (214) 220-8000, Web Site: www. belltowertech.com (18)

Martin, Michael, Time Out New York, New York, NY. Tel: (646) 432-3000, FAX: (212) 677-9665, E-Mail: tnew@kable.com, Web Site: www.timeout.com/ newyork/ (18)

Martin, Patrick C., Saint Gregory Group, Cincinnati, OH. Tel: (513) 769-8440, FAX: (513) 769-1640, E-Mail: info@stgregory.com, Web Site: www. stgregory.com (35)

Martin, Paul, MSC Metalworking, Melville, NY. Tel: (516) 812-2000, (800) 521-9520, E-Mail: inquiry@ rutlandtool.com, Web Site: www.rutlandtool.com (34)

Martin, PhD Susan W., Eastern Michigan University, Ypsilanti, MI. Tel: (734) 487-1849, FAX: (734) 484-1151, Web Site: www.emich.edu (16)

Martin, Robert, Marco Sales & Incentives Ltd, Brantford, ON Canada. Tel: (519) 751-2227, (888) 636-6161, FAX: (519) 751-0561. E-Mail: sales@ themarcocorporation.com, Web Site: www. themarcocorporation.com (28)

Martin, Robert, WorleyParsons, Reading, PA. Tel: (610) 855-2000, FAX: (610) 885-2001, Web Site: www. worleyparsons.com (16)

Martin, Steve J., TruGreen/ChemLawn, Lewis Center, OH. Tel: (614) 846-1800, (800) TRUE-GREEN, FAX: (614) 431-0155, Web Site: www.trugreen.com (16)

Martin, Steve, Paymentech, Salem, NH. Tel: (603) 896-6000, FAX: (603) 896-8717, Web Site: www. paymentech.com (14)

Martin, Tad, Collective[i], New York, NY. Tel: (888) 890-0020, Web Site: www.collectivei.com (35)

Martin, Thomas P., Rutland Products, Rutland, VT. Tel: (800) 544-1307, FAX: (802) 775-5262, E-Mail: sales@rutland.com, Web Site: www.rutland.com (16)

Martin, Tim, Cramer, Norwood, MA. Tel: (781) 278-2387, Web Site: www.crameronline.com (20)

Martin, Tom, Cramer, Norwood, MA. Tel: (781) 278-2387, Web Site: www.crameronline.com (20)

Martin, Wayne, American Solutions for Business, Glenwood, MN. Tel: (320) 634-5471, FAX: (320) 634-5265, Web Site: www.americanbus.com (25)

Martin, William E., Charles Schwab & Co Inc, San Francisco, CA. Tel: (415) 627-7000, (800) 648-5300, FAX: (415) 627-8538, Web Site: www. schwab.com (14)

Martin, William R., Brahmin Leather Works, Fairhaven, MA. Tel: (508) 994-4000, (800) 229-2428, FAX: (508) 994-4153, Web Site: www.brahminusa.com (16)

Martin-Vachon, Anne, Home Shopping Network, Saint Petersburg, FL. Tel: (727) 872-1000, FAX: (727) 872-7292, Web Site: www.hsn.com (32)

Martindale-Hubbell, New Providence, NJ. Tel: (908) 771-7777, (800) 526-4902, FAX: (908) 771-8704, Web Site: www.martindale.com (17)

Martineau & Associates, Menlo Park, CA. Tel: (650) 326-5030, FAX: (650) 329-0883 (20)

Martineau, Catherine, Martineau & Associates, Menlo Park, CA. Tel: (650) 326-5030, FAX: (650) 329-0883 (20)

Martineau, Christian, Standard Life, Montreal, QC Canada. Tel: (514) 499-8855, (877) 499-9555, FAX: (514) 499-4908, Web Site: www.standardlife.ca (15)

Martinek, Paul J., Lawyer's Weekly Publications, Boston, MA. Tel: (617) 451-7300, FAX: (617) 451-0132, Web Site: www.lawyersweekly.com (17)

Martinez, Felipe, Cosmo International, Deerfield Beach, FL. Tel: (954) 798-4500, FAX: (954) 798-4514 (16)

Martinez, Mereille, Native American Rights Fund, Boulder, CO. Tel: (303) 447-8760, FAX: (303) 443-7776, Web Site: www.narf.org (1)

Martinez, Nubia, International Advertising Association, New York, NY. Tel: (646) 722-2612, FAX: (646) 722-2501, E-Mail: iaa@iaaglobal.com, Web Site: www.iaaglobal.org (1)

Martinez, Yemil, Institute for International Research Inc, New York, NY. Tel: (212) 661-3500, (800) 345-8016, FAX: (212) 599-2192, E-Mail: register@ iirusa.com, Web Site: www.iir-ny.com (16)

Martino, David, Bluespire Senior Living, West Hartford, CT. Tel: (888) 818-4715, Web Site: www. bluespireseniorliving.com (35)

Martino, Rocco, Guideposts, Danbury, CT. Tel: (800) 932-2154, Web Site: www.guideposts.org (1)

Martins, Tim, Barbour Publishing Inc, Uhrichsville, OH. Tel: (740) 922-6045, FAX: (740) 922-5948, (800) 220-5948, E-Mail: info@barbourbooks.com, Web Site: www.barbourbooks.com (17)

Martire, Frank R., NuEdge Systems, Brown Deer, WI. Tel: (800) 236-3282, Web Site: www. nuedgesystems.com (20)

Martore, Gracia C., Gannett Co Inc, Mc Lean, VA. Tel: (703) 854-6000, FAX: (703) 854-2046, Web Site: www.gannett.com (16)

Martucci, James, American Association of Advertising Agencies, New York, NY. Tel: (212) 682-2500, FAX: (212) 682-8391, Web Site: www.aaaa.org (40)

Marvel Associates, Old Greenwich, CT. Tel: (203) 637-4777 (20)

Marvel Entertainment Inc, New York, NY. Tel: (212) 576-4000, FAX: (212) 576-8506, Web Site: www. marvel.com (31)

Marvel, Hunter M., Marvel Associates, Old Greenwich. CT. Tel: (203) 637-4777 (20)

Marvin Envelope & Paper Co, Chicago, IL. Tel: (773) 489-3300, (800) 227-0011, FAX: (773) 489-4783, E-Mail: marvinenvelope@aol.com (27)

The Marx Group, San Rafael, CA. Tel: (415) 453-0844, FAX: (415) 451-0166, E-Mail: info@themarxgrp. com, Web Site: www.themarxgrp.com (35)

Marx, Tom, The Marx Group, San Rafael, CA. Tel: (415) 453-0844, FAX: (415) 451-0166, E-Mail: info@themarxgrp.com, Web Site: www.themarxgrp. com (35)

Mary Kay Cosmetics Inc, Addison, TX. Tel: (972) 687-6300, (800) MARY KAY, FAX: (972) 687-1611, Web Site: www.marykay.com (16)

Mary of Puddin Hill Inc, Duncanville, TX. Tel: (903) 455-2651, (800) 545-8889, FAX: (903) 455-4522, E-Mail: customerservice@puddinhill.com, Web Site: www.puddinhill.com (16)

Maryknoll Fathers & Brothers, Ossining, NY. Tel: (914) 941-7590, (888) 627-9566, FAX: (914) 944-3613, E-Mail: mkweb@maryknoll.org, Web Site: www. maryknoll.org (1)

Maryland Pennysaver, Hanover, MD. Tel: (888) 899-8992, Web Site: www.mdpennysaver.com (17)

The Maryland Saddlery Inc, Butler, MD. Tel: (410) 771-4135, (800) 428-5077, FAX: (410) 472-9722, E-Mail: mdsaddle@aol.com, Web Site: www. marylandsaddlery.com (11)

Mary's Plant Farm & Landscaping, Hamilton, OH. Tel: (513) 894-0022, FAX: (513) 892-2053, E-Mail: marysplantfarm@zoomtown.com, Web Site: www. marysplantfarm.com (8)

T Marzetti Co Inc, Columbus, OH. Tel: (614) 846-2232, FAX: (614) 848-8330, Web Site: www.marzetti.com (4)

Mas, Greg, Falcon Safety Products, Branchburg, NJ. Tel: (908) 707-4900, FAX: (908) 707-8855, Web Site: www.falconsafety.com (16)

Masaaoy, Lori, Links Magazine, Hilton Head Island, SC. Tel: (843) 842-6200, FAX: (843) 842-6233, Web Site: www.linksmagazine.com (17)

Mascari, Tom, Reliance Electric, Fort Smith, AR. Tel: (479) 646-4711, FAX: (479) 648-5792, E-Mail: smtraylor@powersystems.rockwell.com, Web Site: www.reliance.com (9)

Masco Corp, Taylor, MI. Tel: (313) 274-7400, FAX: (313) 792-6135, E-Mail: webmaster@mascohq.com, Web Site: www.masco.com (16)

Maska, Lisa, Lautman Maska Neill & Co, Washington, DC. Tel: (202) 296-9660, Web Site: www. lautmandc.com (1)

Maskalunas, Scott A., Thoma Cressey Bravo, Chicago, IL. Tel: (312) 777-4444, FAX: (312) 777-4445, Web Site: www.tcb.com (14)

Mason Companies Inc, Chippewa Falls, WI. Tel: (715) 723-1871, (800) 826-7030, FAX: (715) 720-4247, Web Site: www.masoncompaniesinc.com (2)

George Mason University School of Management, Fairfax, VA. Tel: (703) 993-1871 (1)

Mason Inc, Bethany, CT. Tel: (203) 393-1101, Web Site: mason23.com (35)

WB Mason Co, Brockton, MA. Tel: (800) 773-4488, Web Site: www.wbmason.com (16)

Mason, Caleb, DeLorme Mapping, Yarmouth, ME. Tel: (207) 846-7100, (800) 642-0970, FAX: (207) 846-7051, E-Mail: caleb.mason@delorme.com, Web Site: www.delorme.com (3)

Mason, Charlie, Mason Inc, Bethany, CT. Tel: (203) 393-1101, Web Site: mason23.com (35)

Mason, Claiborne, Virginia Home For Boys & Girls, Richmond, VA. Tel: (804) 270-6566, FAX: (804) 270-6574, E-Mail: info@vhbg.org, Web Site: www. vhbg.org (1)

Mason, Jeffery "Jeff", American Trucking Association, Arlington, VA. Tel: (703) 838-1700, FAX: (800) 254-2571, E-Mail: atamembership@trucking.org, Web Site: www.trucking.org (1)

Mason, Marvin D., C&H Distributors LLC, Milwaukee, WI. Tel: (414) 443-1700, (888) 316-2223, FAX: (414) 443-9213, E-Mail: customerservice@chdist. com, Web Site: www.chdist.com (9)

Mason, Neil, Direct Access Marketing Services Inc, Syosset, NY. Tel: (516) 364-2777, FAX: (516) 364-0644, E-Mail: info@daxcess.com, Web Site: www. daxcess.com (22)

Mason, Robert, Heinrich, Denver, CO. Tel: (303) 233-8660, (800) 356-5036, FAX: (303) 239-5352, E-Mail: info@heinrich.com, Web Site: www. heinrich.com (35)

Mason, Robert, Intelligencer Printing Co, Lancaster, PA. Tel: (717) 291-3100, (800) 233-0107, FAX: (717) 569-2643, Web Site: www.intellprinting.com (27)

Mason, Rodney, Blackhawk Engagement Solutions Inc, Fenton, MO. Tel: (636) 226-2000, Web Site: www. bhengagement.com (35)

Mason, Shari, The Smile Train, New York, NY. Tel: (212) 689-9199, (800) 932-9541, E-Mail: info@ smiletrain.org, Web Site: www.smiletrain.org (1)

Mason, Steve, Direct Advantage Partners, Rowayton, CT. Tel: (203) 286-7100 (20)

Mason, Thomas P., Sunoco Inc, Philadelphia, PA. Tel: (215) 977-3000, FAX: (215) 977-3409, Web Site: www.sunocoinc.com (16)

Masood, Faheem, ESL Federal Credit Union, Rochester, NY. Tel: (585) 336-1000, (800) 848-2265, FAX: (585) 336-1138, Web Site: www.esl.org (14)

Mass Transmit, New York, NY. Tel: (646) 797-4349, E-Mail: info@masstransmit.com, Web Site: www. masstransmit.com (32)

Mass, Otis, The Artists Co, New York, NY. Tel: (212) 679-7199, Web Site: blog.theartistscompany.com (32)

Massa, Gerald L., GLM Communications, New York, NY. Tel: (212) 929-1300, FAX: (212) 929-9574, E-Mail: info@glmcommunications.com, Web Site: www.glmcommunications.com (31)

Massa, Ronald E., AO Smith Corp, Milwaukee, WI. Tel: (414) 359-4000, FAX: (414) 359-4064, Web Site: www.aosmith.com (16)

Massachusetts Horticultural Society, Wellesley, MA. Tel: (617) 933-4900, (617) 933-4929, FAX: (617) 933-4901, E-Mail: hort_line@masshort.org, Web Site: www.masshort.org (1)

Massague, Joan, Memorial Sloan Kettering Cancer Center, New York, NY. Tel: (212) 639-2000, Web Site: www.mskcc.org (1)

Massari, Wayne, CTC Corp, Bennington, VT. Tel: (802) 442-6371, FAX: (802) 442-8526 (16)

Massaro, Joan, Panzano + Partners LLC, Moorestown, NJ. Tel: (856) 866-5500, E-Mail: info@p2site.com, Web Site: panzanoandpartners.com (35)

Masscot Internet Inc, West Yarmouth, MA. Tel: (508) 778-4500, FAX: (888) 884-9960, E-Mail: admin@ masscot.net, Web Site: masscothosting.com (32)

Massey, Michael J., PetSmart Inc, Phoenix, AZ. Tel: (623) 587-2009, (888) 839-9638, FAX: (623) 580-6183, Web Site: www.petsmart.com (1)

Massey, Ron, Mary of Puddin Hill Inc, Duncanville, TX. Tel: (903) 455-2651, (800) 545-8889, FAX: (903) 455-4522, E-Mail: customerservice@ puddinhill.com, Web Site: www.puddinhill.com (16)

MassMutual Financial Group, Springfield, MA. Tel: (413) 788-8411, FAX: (413) 744-8889, E-Mail: name@www.massmutual.com, Web Site: www. massmutual.com (15)

Masten Publishing Systems, Chesterfield, MO. Tel: (636) 527-1810, (800) 616-9476, E-Mail: steve@ mastensystems.com, Web Site: www. mastensystems.com (20)

Masten, Steve, Masten Publishing Systems, Chesterfield, MO. Tel: (636) 527-1810, (800) 616-9476, E-Mail: steve@mastensystems.com, Web Site: www.mastensystems.com (20)

MasterCard Worldwide, Purchase, NY. Tel: (914) 249-2000, (800) 622-7747, FAX: (914) 249-4220, Web Site: www.mastercard.com (14)

Mastergrip Inc, Irving, TX. Tel: (972) 554-4450, (800) 275-1100, FAX: (972) 554-1109, Web Site: www. mastergrip.com (11)

Mastermailer Inc, Hollywood, FL. Tel: (954) 921-0000, (800) 771-5478, FAX: (954) 925-7900, Web Site: www.mastermailer.com (23)

Masterpiece Studios Inc, Mankato, MN. Tel: (507) 388-8788, (800) 447-0219, FAX: (507) 344-4606, E-Mail: masterpiecestudios@masterpiecestudios. com, Web Site: www.masterpiecestudios.com (16)

Masters, Betsy, Insurance Publications Inc, Overland Park, KS. Tel: (913) 383-9191, (800) 762-3387, FAX: (913) 383-1247, E-Mail: brokerwrld@ primary.net, Web Site: www.brokerworldmag.com (17)

Mastervision Inc, New York, NY. Tel: (212) 879-0448, (800) 876-0091, FAX: (212) 744-3560, E-Mail: stadin1@aol.com, Web Site: www.mastervision.com (16)

Masterworks, Poulsbo, WA. Tel: (360) 394-4300, Web Site: www.masterworks.com (1)

Mastery Marketing Group, Columbus, OH. Tel: (203) 544-8997, (703) 938-0101, (800) MKT-0121, FAX: (203) 544-8397, (703) 938-0144, E-Mail: info@ masterymg.com, Web Site: www.masterymktgrp. com (20)

Mastropole, Anthony, Crystek Corp, Fort Myers, FL. Tel: (239) 561-3311, (800) 237-3061, FAX: (239) 561-1025, E-Mail: sales@crystek.com, Web Site: www.crystek.com (9)

Masucci, Richard, Prompt Direct, Staten Island, NY. Tel: (718) 447-6206, FAX: (718) 981-7333, E-Mail: info@promptmailers.com, Web Site: www. promptmailers.com (28)

Masuda, Noboru, Sunstar, Chicago, IL. Tel: (773) 777-4000, FAX: (773) 777-1417, E-Mail: dominico@ sunstar.com, Web Site: www.sunstar.com (16)

Masyr, Evan, Salem Media Group, Camarillo, CA. Tel: (804) 987-0400, E-Mail: info@salem.cc, Web Site: salemmedia.com (17)

Mathai, Suresh, Continuum Global, San Francisco, CA. Tel: (415) 685-3301, Web Site: www. continuumglobal.com (30)

Matherly, Jeana, The Herald & Review, Decatur, IL. Tel: (217) 429-5151, FAX: (217) 421-6913, E-Mail: hrdirect@herald-review.com, Web Site: www. herald-review.com (17)

Mathers, James T. Ames Taping Tool System Inc, Stone Mountain, GA. Tel: (770) 243-2647, (800) 303-1827, FAX: (770) 243-2658, Web Site: www. amestools.com (9)

Matheson, Brenda, Anchor Computer Inc, Farmingdale, NY. Tel: (631) 293-6100, FAX: (631) 293-0891, Web Site: www.anchorcomputer.com (22)

Mathews, Suresh, Unisys, Blue Bell, PA. Tel: (215) 986-4011, (800) 874-8647, FAX: (215) 986-2312, Web Site: www.unisys.com (16)

Mathias, Burl, Blue Vidalia, Toronto, ON Canada. Tel: (416) 572-5222, FAX: (416) 609-0670, E-Mail: info@bluevidalia.ca, Web Site: www.bluevidalia.ca (35)

Mathias, Rebecca, Destination Maternity Corp, Philadelphia, PA. Tel: (215) 873-2200, Web Site: www. motherswork.com (2)

Mathieson, David, Brady Corp, Milwaukee, WI. Tel: (414) 358-6600, (800) 541-1686, FAX: (800) 292-2289, Web Site: www.bradycorp.com (16)

Mathis, Catherine J., Standard & Poor's Corp, New York, NY. Tel: (212) 438-2000, FAX: (212) 438-7375, Web Site: www.standardandpoors.com (17)

Mathisen, Egil, Laerdal Medical, Wappingers Falls, NY. Tel: (845) 297-7770, FAX: (800) 227-1143, Web Site: www.laerdal.com (34)

Mathrani, Sandeep, General Growth Properties, Chicago, IL. Tel: (312) 960-5000, Web Site: www. generalgrowth.com (5)

Matkins, Gary W., University of California Irvine Extension, Irvine, CA. Tel: (949) 824-5414, E-Mail: unex-services@uci.edu, Web Site: extension.uci.edu (1)

Matloff, Robert. Guilford Publications Inc, New York, NY. Tel: (212) 431-9800, (800) 365-7006, FAX: (212) 966-6708, E-Mail: info@guilford.com, Web Site: www.guilford.com (17)

Matrix Manager, Roseville, CA. Tel: (916) 783-1536, (877)-258-9037, E-Mail: info@mymatrixmanager. com, Web Site: www.mymatrixmanager.com (28)

Matt & Kumpany Kuzins, Sacramento, CA. Tel: (916) 446-2008, FAX: (916) 446-5302, E-Mail: matt@ kuzins.com (1)

Matt Industries Inc, Syracuse, NY. Tel: (315) 472-1316, (800) 724-2477, FAX: (315) 422-3637, Web Site: www.duplionline.com (26)

Matt, Nicolas O., The FX Matt Brewing Co, Utica, NY. Tel: (315) 624-2400, (800) 765-6288, FAX: (315) 624-2401, E-Mail: info@saranac.com, Web Site: www.saranac.com (4)

Matt, Sr. J. Kemper, Matt Industries Inc, Syracuse, NY. Tel: (315) 472-1316, (800) 724-2477, FAX: (315) 422-3637, Web Site: www.duplionline.com (26)

Mattaliano, David M., Mail Order Business, Dubuque, IA. Tel: (319) 589-1000 X1076, (800) 228-0810, FAX: (319) 589-1046, Web Site: www.kendallhunt. com (43)

Mattel Inc, El Segundo, CA. Tel: (310) 252-2000, FAX: (310) 252-2180, Web Site: www.mattel.com (16)

Mattern, Bill, American Business Directories, Omaha, NE. Tel: (402) 593-4600, (800) 555-6124, FAX: (402) 596-0475, Web Site: www.infousa.com (43)

Mattes, Andy W., Diebold Inc, North Canton, OH. Tel: (330) 490-4000, (800) DIEBOLD, Web Site: www. diebold.com (16)

Matthes, Hans, GBH Communications, Monrovia, CA. Tel: (818) 246-9900, (800) 222-5424, FAX: (818) 246-5850, E-Mail: customerservice@gbh.com, Web Site: www.gbh.com (3)

Matthes, Mark, Duncan Aviation, Lincoln, NE. Tel: (402) 475-2611, (800) 228-4277, FAX: (402) 475-5541, Web Site: www.duncanaviation.com (16)

Matthew, Abe, Custom Accessories, Richmond, IL. Tel: (847) 966-6900, (800) 962-6676, FAX: (847) 966-9650, Web Site: www.causa.com (11)

Matthew, Ken, Custom Accessories, Richmond, IL. Tel: (847) 966-6900, (800) 962-6676, FAX: (847) 966-9650, Web Site: www.causa.com (11)

Matthew, Norman, Custom Accessories, Richmond, IL. Tel: (847) 966-6900, (800) 962-6676, FAX: (847) 966-9650, Web Site: www.causa.com (11)

Matthews 1812 House Inc, Cornwall Bridge, CT. Tel: (860) 672-0230, (800) 662-1812, FAX: (860) 672-1812, E-Mail: info@matthews1812house.com, Web Site: www.matthews1812house.com (4)

Robert J Matthews Co, Massillon, OH. Tel: (330) 834-3000, (800) 578-9234, FAX: (330) 830-2762, E-Mail: email@rjmatthews.com, Web Site: www.pbsanimalhealth.com (7)

Matthews, Blaine, Matthews 1812 House Inc, Cornwall Bridge, CT. Tel: (860) 672-0230, (800) 662-1812, FAX: (860) 672-1812, E-Mail: info@matthews1812house.com, Web Site: www.matthews1812house.com (4)

Matthews, Carl, Gould Paper Corp, New York, NY. Tel: (212) 301-0001, (800) 221-3043, FAX: (212) 481-0392, Web Site: www.gouldpaper.com (25)

Matthews, Deanna, Matthews 1812 House Inc, Cornwall Bridge, CT. Tel: (860) 672-0230, (800) 662-1812, FAX: (860) 672-1812, E-Mail: info@matthews1812house.com, Web Site: www.matthews1812house.com (4)

Matthews, J. Daniel, Robert J Matthews Co, Massillon, OH. Tel: (330) 834-3000, (800) 578-9234, FAX: (330) 830-2762, E-Mail: email@rjmatthews.com, Web Site: www.pbsanimalhealth.com (7)

Matthews, Kris, Mary Elizabeth Granger & Associates Inc, Baltimore, MD. Tel: (410) 842-1170, FAX: (410) 842-1185, E-Mail: info@maryegranger.com, Web Site: www.maryegranger.com (23)

Matthews, Nancy, American College of Physicians, Philadelphia, PA. Tel: (215) 351-2600, (800) 523-1546, FAX: (215) 351-2686, Web Site: www.acponline.org (17)

Mattingly, Brian, Welcomemat Services Inc, Atlanta, GA. Tel: (404) 841-2226, E-Mail: info@welcomematservices.com, Web Site: www.welcomematservices.com (9)

Mattox, Darryl, Gragg Advertising, Kansas City, MO. Tel: (877) GRAGGADV, FAX: (816) 931-2227, E-Mail: contact@graggadv.com, Web Site: www.graggadv.com (35)

Mattson, Robert, SMM Advertising, Smithtown, NY. Tel: (631) 265-5160, FAX: (631) 265-5185, E-Mail: marketing@smmadvertising.com, Web Site: smmadvertising.com (35)

Mattys, Gerry, Timm Medical Technologies, Inc, Lake Forest, IL. Tel: (952) 947-9410, (800) 438-8592, FAX: (952) 947-9411, Web Site: www.timmmedical.com (16)

Matuch, Andrew, LexisNexis, New York, NY. Tel: (212) 309-8100, FAX: (800) 437-8674, Web Site: www.lexisnexis.com (16)

Matzell, Tom, MRW Communications, Pembroke, MA. Tel: (781) 924-5282, FAX: (718) 926-0371, E-Mail: jim@mrwinc.com, Web Site: www.mrwinc.com (35)

Mauch, Dan, Goodway Group, Jenkintown, PA. Tel: (626) 355-7800, E-Mail: info@goodwaygroup.com, Web Site: goodwaygroup.com (35)

Mauer, Austin, LeadGen Media Group LLC, Staten Island, NY. Tel: (888) 206-3738, FAX: (888) 206-3796, E-Mail: info@leadgenmediagroup.com, Web Site: www.leadgenmediagroup.com (23)

Mauer, John, Gems Sensors & Controls, Plainville, CT. Tel: (860) 747-3000, (800) 378-1600, FAX: (860) 747-4244, E-Mail: info@gemssensors.com, Web Site: www.gemssensors.com (9)

Mauer, Scott, LeadGen Media Group LLC, Staten Island, NY. Tel: (888) 206-3738, FAX: (888) 206-3796, E-Mail: info@leadgenmediagroup.com, Web Site: www.leadgenmediagroup.com (23)

Maui Jim Inc, Peoria, IL. Tel: (309) 691-3700, FAX: (309) 683-2202, Web Site: www.mauijim.com (16)

Maul, Terry, Wimmer's Meat Products Inc, West Point, NE. Tel: (800) 762-9865, E-Mail: consumer.affairs@landofrost.com, Web Site: www.wimmersmeats.com (4)

Maull, Howard, Rose Resnick Lighthouse for the Blind & Visually Impaired, San Francisco, CA. Tel: (415) 431-1481, FAX: (415) 863-7568, E-Mail: executive@lighthouse-sf.org, Web Site: www.lighthouse-sf.org (1)

Maumee, George, Lesman Instrument Co, Bensenville, IL. Tel: (630) 595-8400, (800) 953-7626, FAX: (630) 595-2386, E-Mail: sales@lesman.com, Web Site: www.lesman.com (9)

Maunder, Jackie, The Missoulian, Missoula, MT. Tel: (406) 523-5200, (800) 366-7102, FAX: (406) 523-5221, Web Site: www.missoulian.com (31)

Maurer, Karmen, McKnight's Long-Term Care News, Northfield, IL. Tel: (847) 784-8706, (800) 558-1703, FAX: (847) 784-9346, E-Mail: mltcn-webmaster@mltcn.com, Web Site: www.mcknightsonline.com (17)

Maurer, Myron, The Merchandise Mart, Chicago, IL. Tel: (800) 677-6278, Web Site: www.merchandisemart.com (42)

Maurer, Ron, Falcon Safety Products, Branchburg, NJ. Tel: (908) 707-4900, FAX: (908) 707-8855, Web Site: www.falconsafety.com (16)

Maurice, Carl, Magnaplan Corp, Champlain, NY. Tel: (518) 298-8404, (800) 361-1192, FAX: (518) 298-2368, E-Mail: info@visualplanning.com, Web Site: www.visualplanning.com (10)

Maurin, Denise, Music Sales Corp, New York, NY. Tel: (212) 254-2100, FAX: (212) 254-2013, E-Mail: info@musicsales.com, Web Site: www.musicsales.com (17)

Mauro, Grace, BOC Gases, Murray Hill, NJ. Tel: (908) 464-8100, (800) 262-4273, FAX: (410) 749-4073, E-Mail: info@linde.com, Web Site: www.boc-gases.com (17)

Maus & Hoffman Inc, Fort Lauderdale, FL. Tel: (800) 628-6287, FAX: (954) 463-8735, E-Mail: info@mausandhoffman.com, Web Site: www.mausandhoffman.com (2)

Maus, Jr. William H., Maus & Hoffman Inc, Fort Lauderdale, FL. Tel: (800) 628-6287, FAX: (954) 463-8735, E-Mail: info@mausandhoffman.com, Web Site: www.mausandhoffman.com (2)

Mauss, James, Estes Industries, Penrose, CO. Tel: (719) 372-6565, FAX: (719) 372-3419, Web Site: www.estesrockets.com (11)

Mavel, James C., Scan Optics Inc, Manchester, CT. Tel: (860) 645-7878, (800) 745-6001, FAX: (860) 645-7995, E-Mail: info@scanoptics.com, Web Site: www.scanoptics.com (16)

Maverick Ventures Product Line, Chesterfield, MO. Tel: (636) 537-4656, (800) 467-4656, FAX: (636) 537-4657, E-Mail: hang10cd@aol.com, Web Site: www.hang10cd.com (5)

Mavis, Todd, Mitchell International, San Diego, CA. Tel: (858) 368-7000, FAX: (858) 238-9111, Web Site: www.mitchell.com (17)

MAX Federal Credit Union, Montgomery, AL. Tel: (334) 260-2600, (800) 776-6776, FAX: (334) 270-0921, Web Site: www.mymax.com (14)

Maxfield, Larry, Access Development, Salt Lake City, UT. Tel: (801) 656-1529, (800) 840-0032, Web Site: www.accessdevelopment.com (35)

Mary Maxim Inc, Port Huron, MI. Tel: (810) 987-2000, (800) 962-9504, FAX: (810) 987-5056, E-Mail: info@marymaxim.com, Web Site: www.marymaxim.com (11)

Maxon Furniture Inc, Muscatine, IA. Tel: (253) 395-4139, (800) 876-4274, FAX: (800) 257-2635, Web Site: www.maxonfurniture.com (10)

Maxson, Derek, Front Porch Inc, Sonora, CA. Tel: (209) 288-5500, (800) 728-1464, Web Site: www.frontporch.com (35)

Maxwell + Miller, Kalamazoo, MI. Tel: (269) 382-4060, FAX: (269) 382-0504, E-Mail: info@maxwellandmiller.com, Web Site: www.maxwellandmiller.com (35)

May, Alison, RedEnvelope Inc, San Diego, CA. Tel: (619) 528-4888, (877) 733-3683, Web Site: www.redenvelope.com (6)

May, Carl W., Biological Photo Service & Terraphotographics, Pacifica, CA. Tel: (650) 359-6219, FAX: (650) 359-6219, E-Mail: bpsterra@pacbell.net, Web Site: www.agpix.com/biologicalphoto (38)

May, Christy, DM Communications Inc, Sarasota, FL. Tel: (617) 482-5900, E-Mail: cmay@dmcommunications.com, Web Site: www.dmcommunications.com (35)

May, Craig G., American Health Information Management Association, Chicago, IL. Tel: (312) 233-1100, (800) 335-5535, FAX: (312) 233-1090, E-Mail: info@ahima.org, Web Site: www.ahima.org (1)

May, Linda, The Vestal Press Ltd, Lanham, MD. Tel: (301) 459-3366, (800) 462-6420, FAX: (301) 429-5746, E-Mail: sburnett@rowman.com, Web Site: www.nbnbooks.com (17)

May, Mark, Shopsmith Inc, Dayton, OH. Tel: (937) 898-6070, (800) 543-7586, FAX: (937) 890-5197, Web Site: www.shopsmith.com (16)

May, Michael C., Freddie Mac, McLean, VA. Tel: (703) 903-2000, (800) 424-5401, Web Site: www.freddiemac.com (14)

Frank Mayer & Associates Inc, Grafton, WI. Tel: (855) 294-2875, FAX: (262) 377-3449, E-Mail: info@frankmayer.com, Web Site: www.frankmayer.com (35)

Peter A Mayer Advertising Inc, New Orleans, LA. Tel: (504) 581-7191, FAX: (504) 581-3009, E-Mail: contact@petermayer.com, Web Site: www.peteramayer.com (35)

Mayer, Barry D., Harvard Square Records, Austin, TX. Tel: (877) 465-7669, E-Mail: LPnow@yahoo.com, Web Site: www.lpnow.com (3)

Mayer, Christopher M., The Boston Globe, Boston, MA. Tel: (617) 929-2000, (888) MY-GLOBE, FAX: (617) 929-2606, Web Site: www.bostonglobe.com (17)

Mayer, James, Viking Pump Inc, Cedar Falls, IA. Tel: (319) 266-1741, FAX: (319) 273-8157, E-Mail: info@vikingpump.com, Web Site: www.vikingpump.com (16)

Mayer, Jonathan, Cedar Fresh Products, Coral Gables, FL. Tel: (305) 870-9390, Web Site: www.cedarfresh.com (16)

Mayer, Josh, Peter A Mayer Advertising Inc, New Orleans, LA. Tel: (504) 581-7191, FAX: (504) 581-3009, E-Mail: contact@petermayer.com, Web Site: www.peteramayer.com (35)

Mayer, Margery W, Scholastic Inc, New York, NY. Tel: (212) 343-6100, (800) SCHOLASTIC, FAX: (212) 343-6484, Web Site: www.scholastic.com (17)

Mayer, Marissa, Yahoo! Inc, Sunnyvale, CA. Tel: (408) 349-3300, Web Site: www.yahoo.com (32)

Mayer, Mark, Peter A Mayer Advertising Inc, New Orleans, LA. Tel: (504) 581-7191, FAX: (504) 581-3009, E-Mail: contact@petermayer.com, Web Site: www.peteramayer.com (35)

Mayer, Mike, Frank Mayer & Associates Inc, Grafton, WI. Tel: (855) 294-2875, FAX: (262) 377-3449, E-Mail: info@frankmayer.com, Web Site: www.frankmayer.com (35)

Mayer, Robert, IMSI/Design LLC, Novato, CA. Tel: (415) 483-8000, (800) 833-4674, FAX: (415) 884-9023, Web Site: www.imsidesign.com (34)

Mayer, Russel P., Biosciences-Amersham, Piscataway, NJ. Tel: (732) 457-8000, FAX: (732) 457-0557, Web Site: www.amersham.com (16)

Mayfield, Ken, National Mailroom Service Inc, Knoxville, TN. Tel: (865) 862-4141, (866) 862-4141, FAX: (865) 862-4145, E-Mail: info@nationalmailroom.com, Web Site: nationalmailroom.com (27)

Mayfield, Mark, DMXENGAGE, Centennial, CO. Tel: (303) 339-9300, FAX: (303) 388-6363, E-Mail: workwithus@dmxengage.com, Web Site: dmxengage.com (21)

Mayhew, Karen, Infogroup Media Solutions, Papillion, NE. Tel: (800) 223-2194, E-Mail: infogroupmediasolutions@infogroup.com, Web Site: www.infogroupmediasolutions.com (23)

Maykoski, Jack, Graduate School USA, Washington, DC. Tel: (202) 314-3300, FAX: (202) 690-6577, E-Mail: pubaffairs@grad.usda.gov, Web Site: www.grad.usda.gov (1)

Maynard, Amy, Highlights For Children, Columbus, OH. Tel: (614) 487-2601, (800) 848-8922, FAX: (614) 487-2700, Web Site: www.highlights.com (17)

Maynard, Bruce, Amica Insurance, Lincoln, RI. Tel: (401) 334-6000, (800) 652-6422, FAX: (401) 334-4241, Web Site: www.amica.com (15)

Maynard, Mark, Crutchfield Corp, Charlottesville, VA. Tel: (434) 817-1000, (800) 955-9091, FAX: (804) 817-1010, E-Mail: administration@crutchfield.com, Web Site: www.crutchfield.com (3)

Mayne Associates, Lafayette, CA. Tel: (925) 284-8500, FAX: (925) 284-8502 (39)

Mayne, Clifton P., Mayne Associates, Lafayette, CA. Tel: (925) 284-8500, FAX: (925) 284-8502 (39)

Mayo Clinic, Rochester, MN. Tel: (507) 284-2511, Web Site: www.mayoclinic.org (17)

Mayor, Michael, Aptimus, San Francisco, CA. Tel: (415) 896-2123, FAX: (415) 896-2561 (22)

Mays Mission for the Handicapped Inc, Heber Springs, AR. Tel: (501) 362-7526, (888) 503-7955, FAX: (501) 362-7529, E-Mail: info@maysmission.org, Web Site: www.maysmission.org (27)

Mays, Crystal, Computer Business Services Inc, Americus, GA. Tel: (229) 924-4408, (866) 924-4408, FAX: (229) 924-3644, E-Mail: nelson@combusser.com, Web Site: www.combusser.com (22)

Mays, Greg, A&P, Montvale, NJ. Tel: (201) 573-9700, (866) 44 FRESH, FAX: (201) 505-3054, E-Mail: apcustomerrel@aptea.com, Web Site: www.aptea.com (16)

Mayton, Jr. James L., United Investors Life Insurance Co, Birmingham, AL. Tel: (205) 325-4300, (800) 288-2722, FAX: (205) 325-4157, Web Site: www.uilic.com (15)

Mazda Motor of America Inc, Irvine, CA. Tel: (949) 727-1990, (800) 222-6500, FAX: (949) 727-6101, Web Site: www.mazdausa.com (16)

Mazlish, Tony, The Healthy Back Store, Beltsville, MD. Tel: (703) 339-1700, (800) 4 MY BACK, FAX: (703) 339-0671, E-Mail: service@healthyback.com, Web Site: www.healthyback.com (16)

Mazzaschi, Michael, Stock Boston Inc, Brookline, MA. Tel: (617) 266-2300, FAX: (617) 277-0502, E-Mail: info@stockboston.com, Web Site: www.stockboston.com (38)

Mazzer, Ellen S., Norman Rockwell Museum, Stockbridge, MA. Tel: (413) 298-4100, (800) 742-9450, FAX: (413) 298-4144, E-Mail: emazzer@nrm.org, Web Site: www.nrm.org (16)

Mazzone Marketing Group LLC, Brooklyn, NY. Tel: (718) 369-0001, (866) 928-5478, FAX: (718) 369-0099, E-Mail: info@mazzonemarketinggroup.com, Web Site: www.mazzonemarketinggroup.com (23)

Mazzone, Jr Michael R., Mazzone Marketing Group LLC, Brooklyn, NY. Tel: (718) 369-0001, (866) 928-5478, FAX: (718) 369-0099, E-Mail: info@mazzonemarketinggroup.com, Web Site: www.mazzonemarketinggroup.com (23)

Mazzone, Marc, Cartera Commerce Inc, Lexington, MA. Tel: (781) 541-6800, (888) 456-6255, FAX: (781) 541-6801, E-Mail: info@cartera.com, Web Site: www.cartera.com (35)

Mc Abee, Ronald G., Vulcan Materials Co, Birmingham, AL. Tel: (205) 298-3000, FAX: (205) 298-2960, Web Site: www.vulcanmaterials.com (16)

Mc Hugh, Robert W., Champs Corp, Bradenton, FL. Tel: (941) 748-0577, (800) 991-6813, E-Mail: customer_service@champssports.com, Web Site: www.champssports.com (11)

McAdam, Lowell C., Verizon Communications Inc, New York, NY. Tel: (212) 395-1000, (800) 621-9900, FAX: (212) 571-1897, Web Site: www.verizon.com (3)

McAdams, Joe, TL Enterprises Inc, Ventura, CA. Tel: (805) 667-4100, FAX: (805) 667-4419 (17)

McAdams, Sharon, HB Distributors, Chatsworth, CA. Tel: (818) 882-0000, (800) 266-3478, FAX: (818) 700-1808, E-Mail: info@hbdistributors.com, Web Site: www.hddistributors.com (34)

McAfee, Rob, Sani Serv, Mooresville, IN. Tel: (317) 831-7030, FAX: (317) 381-7036, Web Site: www.saniserv.com (16)

McAlister, James, The Marketing Alliance, Fairfield, CT. Tel: (203) 254-0474 (20)

McAllister, Lisa, Conclusive Analytics, Inc, Huntersville, NC. Tel: (704) 887-5600, FAX: (704) 887-5601, E-Mail: info@conclusivemarketing.com, Web Site: www.conclusiveanalytics.com (22)

McAllister, Stephen, Design Matters Inc!, New York, NY. Tel: (212) 560-0681, FAX: (646) 478-9149, E-Mail: stephen@designmattersinc.com, Web Site: www.designmattersinc.com (35)

McAlmont, Shaun E., Lincoln Educational Services Corp, West Orange, NJ. Tel: (973) 736-9340, Web Site: www.lincolnedu.com (13)

McAlpine, Charles M., CM Consulting Services, Marshfield, MA. Tel: (781) 749-5000, FAX: (801) 749-5009, E-Mail: cmcalpine3@gmail.com (27)

McArdle Printing Co Inc, Upper Marlboro, MD. Tel: (301) 390-8500, FAX: (301) 390-8052, Web Site: www.mcardleprinting.com (27)

McAtee, Angie, Southwest Publishing & Mailing Corp, Topeka, KS. Tel: (785) 233-5662, Web Site: www.swpks.com (28)

McAuliffe, John, Sylvan Learning Inc, Baltimore, MD. Tel: (410) 843-8000, (800) 31-SUCCESS, FAX: (410) 843-8057, E-Mail: pr@sylvanlearning.com, Web Site: www.sylvanlearning.com (16)

McBee Associates Inc, Wayne, PA. Tel: (610) 964-9680, Web Site: www.mcbeeassociates.com (20)

McBee, Richard, Tektronix Inc, Beaverton, OR. Tel: (503) 627-7111, (800) 833-9200, FAX: (503) 627-3247, Web Site: www.tektronix.com (16)

McBride, Daniel G, Cooper Vision, Fairport, NY. Tel: (855) 526-6737, (800) 341-2020, Web Site: www.coopervision.com (7)

McBride, Ken, PhotoStamps.com, El Segundo, CA. Tel: (310) 482-5800, Web Site: www.photostamps.com (5)

McBride, Kenneth, Mane Solutions, New York, NY. Tel: (212) 736-0306, FAX: (212) 239-2039 (16)

McBride, R. Perley, Frontier Communications Corp, Stamford, CT. Tel: (203) 614-5600, Web Site: www.frontier.com (29)

McBurney, Susan, Wake Forest University Baptist Medical Center, Winston Salem, NC. Tel: (336) 716-2011, Web Site: www.wakehealth.edu (1)

McCabe Duval + Associates, Portland, ME. Tel: (207) 347-8614, FAX: (207) 773-7245, E-Mail: cduval@mccabe-duval.com, Web Site: www.mccabe-duval.com (35)

McCabe, Bill, A Eicoff & Co, Chicago, IL. Tel: (312) 527-7183, (800) 333-6605, FAX: (312) 527-7192, E-Mail: bill.mccabe@eicoff.com, Web Site: www.eicoff.com (35)

McCabe, Daniel C., John Deere Financial, Johnston, IA. Tel: (515) 267-3000, (800) 275-5322, FAX: (515) 267-3292, Web Site: www.deere.com (14)

McCabe, Edward, Gruppo Levey & Co, New York, NY. Tel: (212) 867-, FAX: (212) 949-7294, E-Mail: info@glconline.com, Web Site: www.glconline.com (14)

McCabe, Leslie, Orange Leap, Dallas, TX. Tel: (972) 220-0341, Web Site: www.orangeleap.com (1)

McCabe, Lisa, Bulletin of the Atomic Scientists, Chicago, IL. Tel: (773) 702-6301, FAX: (773) 980-6932, E-Mail: admin@thebulletin.org, Web Site: www.thebulletin.org (1)

McCabe, Randy, Orange Leap, Dallas, TX. Tel: (972) 220-0341, Web Site: www.orangeleap.com (1)

McCabe, Tom, KMA Direct Communications, Dallas, TX. Tel: (214) 866-7700, E-Mail: info@pursuant.com, Web Site: www.pursuant.com/kma (1)

McCaffrey, Mary Ann, Mullen & McCaffrey Communications, East Hampton, NY. Tel: (631) 324-4265, FAX: (631) 324-2135, E-Mail: mullenmccaffrey@aol.com, Web Site: www.mullenandmccaffrey.com (35)

McCaleb, Billy, ABS Graphics, Addison, IL. Tel: (630) 495-2400, FAX: (630) 495-0728, E-Mail: info@absinet.com, Web Site: www.absinet.com (27)

McCall, Bruce, Guaranty Bank, Brown Deer, WI. Tel: (414) 362-4000, (800) 235-4636, Web Site: www.guarantybank.com (14)

McCall, Jeff, Catholic Digest, New London, CT. Tel: (800) 321-0411, E-Mail: catholicdigest@bayardinc.com, Web Site: www.catholicdigest.com (17)

McCall, Josh, Jack Morton Worldwide, New York, NY. Tel: (212) 401-7000, (212) 401-7121, E-Mail: experience@jackmorton.com, Web Site: www.jackmorton.com (35)

McCall, Susan, The Peter A Tobin College of Business, Jamaica, NY. Tel: (718) 990-2600, FAX: (718) 990-1868, Web Site: www.stjohns.edu (41)

McCall, Tom, Gartner Inc, San Jose, CA. Tel: (408) 468-8000, (800) 419-3282, FAX: (408) 954-1780, E-Mail: tom.mccall@gartner.com, Web Site: www.gartner.com (20)

McCallen, Joan, ICMA Retirement Corp, Washington, DC. Tel: (202) 962-4600, (800) 669-7400, FAX: (202) 962-4601, E-Mail: investorservices@icmarc.org, Web Site: www.icmarc.org (14)

McCane, George, Richards Partners, Dallas, TX. Tel: (214) 891-5700, FAX: (214) 891-3515, E-Mail: ruth_fitzgibbons@richards.com, Web Site: richardspartners.com (35)

McCardell, John, Marketing 1by1 Inc, Fairfax, VA. Tel: (703) 934-6020, FAX: (703) 591-3049, Web Site: marketing1by1.com (22)

McCarney, Laurie, Bank of Hawaii, Honolulu, HI. Tel: (808) 537-8398, FAX: (808) 536-9433, Web Site: www.boh.com (1)

McCartan, Ann, DBMCatalyst, Holliston, MA. Tel: (339) 227-7591 (20)

McCarthy & King Marketing Inc, Milford, MA. Tel: (508) 473-8643, FAX: (508) 473-7294, E-Mail: bob@mccarthyandking.com, Web Site: www. mccarthyandking.com (35)

McCarthy Media Group Inc, Sun Prairie, WI. Tel: (608) 329-6097, E-Mail: mmg.greenlinks@charter.net, Web Site: www.mccarthymediagroup.com (23)

McCarthy, Daniel, Frontier Communications Corp, Stamford, CT. Tel: (203) 614-5600, Web Site: www.frontier.com (20)

McCarthy, Dr. Kevin, Tangent Media LLC, Atlanta, GA. Tel: (404) 444-2357, Web Site: www. tangentmedia.us (30)

McCarthy, Francis X., Resorts Casino Hotel, Atlantic City, NJ. Tel: (609) 334-6000, (800) 336-6378, FAX: (609) 340-6349, Web Site: www.resortsac. com (19)

McCarthy, Kari, Learning Seed, Chicago, IL. Tel: (847) 540-8855, (800) 634-4941, FAX: (800) 998-0854, E-Mail: info@learningseed.com, Web Site: www. learningseed.com (3)

McCarthy, Kathryn, Biosciences-Amersham, Piscataway, NJ. Tel: (732) 457-8000, FAX: (732) 457-0557, Web Site: www.amersham.com (16)

McCarthy, Kevin P., Unum Corp, Portland, ME. Tel: (207) 770-2211, (800) 421-0344, FAX: (207) 770-4510, Web Site: www.unum.com (15)

McCarthy, Margaret, AETNA - Marketing Product & Communication, Hartford, CT. Tel: (860) 273-0123, (800) 872-3862, FAX: (860) 273-3971, Web Site: www.aetna.com (14)

McCarthy, Mary, Andrew Associates Inc, Enfield, CT. Tel: (860) 253-0000, FAX: (860) 253-0007, Web Site: www.andrewdm.com (23)

McCarthy, Michael, McCarthy Media Group Inc, Sun Prairie, WI. Tel: (608) 329-6097, E-Mail: mmg. greenlinks@charter.net, Web Site: www. mccarthymediagroup.com (23)

McCarthy, Peter, Duplication Factory Inc, Chaska, MN. Tel: (952) 448-9912, (800) 279-2009, FAX: (952) 448-3983, E-Mail: info@duplicationfactory.com, Web Site: www.duplicationfactory.com (31)

McCarthy, Robert, McCarthy & King Marketing Inc, Milford, MA. Tel: (508) 473-8643, FAX: (508) 473-7294, E-Mail: bob@mccarthyandking.com, Web Site: www.mccarthyandking.com (35)

McCarthy, Terrance M., First Banks Inc, Clayton, MO. Tel: (314) 854-4600, FAX: (314) 592-6840, Web Site: www.firstbanks.com (14)

McCarthy, Terrence E., The Allant Group, Naperville, IL. Tel: (800) 367-7311, FAX: (630) 355-3090, E-Mail: dirwin@allantgroup.com, Web Site: www. allantgroup.com (22)

McCarthy, Thomas, International Marine, Camden, ME. Tel: (207) 236-4837, FAX: (207) 236-6314, Web Site: www.internationalmarine.com (17)

McCartin, Mike, Javelin Marketing Group, Irving, TX. Tel: (972) 443-7000, FAX: (972) 443-7194, E-Mail: info@javelin.mg, Web Site: www.javelin.mg (30)

McCartney, Barbara, Nestle HealthCare Nutrition, Florham Park, NJ. Tel: (800) 422-2752, Web Site: www. nestle-nutrition.com (16)

McCartney, John, Blast! Marketing & PR, Chicago, IL. Web Site: blastmarketing.net (35)

McCarty, Diane, Things Remembered, Highland Heights, OH. Tel: (440) 473-2000, (866) 902-4438, FAX: (440) 473-2018, E-Mail: customerservice@ thingsremembered.com, Web Site: www. thingsremembered.com (6)

McCarty, Joyce, American Stationery Co Inc, Peru, IN. Tel: (765) 473-4438, (800) 822-2577, FAX: (800) 253-9054, Web Site: www.americanstationery.com (10)

McCaslin, James A, Harley-Davidson Inc, Milwaukee, WI. Tel: (414) 343-7286, FAX: (414) 343-4806, Web Site: www.harley-davidson.com (12)

McCassney, Jim, The Wig Co, Pittsburgh, PA. Tel: (800) 568-3499, E-Mail: custserv@twcwigs.com, Web Site: www.thewigcompany.com (2)

McCauley, Andrew, BT Americas, Irving, TX. Tel: (972) 830-8169, FAX: (703) 755-6740, Web Site: www.btglobalservices.com (22)

McCauley, Frank, AETNA - Marketing Product & Communication, Hartford, CT. Tel: (860) 273-0123, (800) 872-3862, FAX: (860) 273-3971, Web Site: www.aetna.com (14)

McCaully, Josh, GrayHair Software, Mount Laurel, NJ. Tel: (856) 727-9372, FAX: (856) 727-1315, Web Site: www.grayhairsoftware.com (22)

McClanahan, David M., Centerpoint Energy, Minneapolis, MN. Tel: (612) 372-4664, FAX: (612) 321-4873, E-Mail: mgc-businessinformation@ centerpointenergy.com, Web Site: www. minnegasco.centerpointenergy.com (16)

McClanan, Martin, Norm Thompson Outfitters Inc, Hillsboro, OR. Tel: (800) 547-1160, (877) 718-7899, FAX: (503) 614-4599, Web Site: www. normthompson.com (2)

McClarin, Robert, Protection One Inc, Lawrence, KS. Tel: (785) 856-5500, (800) GET-HELP, Web Site: www.protectionone.com (16)

McClatchy Co, Sacramento, CA. Tel: (916) 321-1855, FAX: (916) 321-1869, Web Site: www.mcclatchy. com (17)

McClellan, Cyndi, E! Entertainment Television, Los Angeles, CA. Tel: (323) 954-2400, FAX: (323) 954-2665, Web Site: www.eonline.com (32)

McClellan, Michael, Plexus Marketing Group Inc, Atlanta, GA. Tel: (770) 390-9692, (800) 9-PLEXUS, FAX: (770) 390-9693, Web Site: www. plexusmarketing.com (20)

McClendon, Charles, Casablanca Express, Woodland Hills, CA. Tel: (818) 992-5100, (800) 315-2065, Web Site: www.casablancaexpress.com (33)

McClendon, Laura, AllMedia Inc, Plano, TX. Tel: (469) 467-9100, FAX: (214) 291-5431, E-Mail: brokerage@allmediainc.com, Web Site: www. allmediainc.com (22)

McClendon, Mark, Do-It Corp, South Haven, MI. Tel: (269) 637-1121, (800) 426-4822, FAX: (269) 637-7223, E-Mail: sales@do-it.com, Web Site: www.do-it.com (17)

McCloud, Lisa, Bunn-O-Matic Corp, Springfield, IL. Tel: (217) 529-6601, FAX: (217) 529-6622, E-Mail: bunn@bunn.com, Web Site: www.bunn.com (16)

McClunn, Jack, DoubleVerify, New York, NY. Tel: (212) 631-2111, Web Site: www.doubleverify.com (9)

McClure & Zimmerman, Randolph, WI. Tel: (800) 883-6998, FAX: (800) 374-6120, Web Site: www. mzbulb.com (8)

McClure, Brian, Echotouch Corp, Austin, TX. Tel: (512) 327-5638, Web Site: www.echotouch.com (20)

McClure, Charles, CCIM Institute, Chicago, IL. Tel: (312) 321-4460, (800) 621-7027, FAX: (312) 321-4530, Web Site: www.ccim.com (1)

McClure, Donald, American Mathematical Society, Providence, RI. Tel: (401) 455-4000, (800) 321-4267, FAX: (401) 331-3842, E-Mail: ams@ams.org, Web Site: www.ams.org (17)

McClure, Kenneth A., USAA, San Antonio, TX. Tel: (512) 498-6524, FAX: (512) 498-8000 (15)

McCluskey, Joseph, List Services Corporation, Bethel, CT. Tel: (203) 743-2600, E-Mail: info@listservices. com, Web Site: www.listservices.com (24)

McClymont, Patrick, Sotheby's, New York, NY. Tel: (212) 606-7000, FAX: (212) 606-7107, Web Site: www.sothebys.com (6)

McColgan, Elizabeth, New York Philharmonic, New York, NY. Tel: (212) 875-5691, Web Site: www. nyphil.org (1)

McConkey, Mike, Edible Landscaping, Afton, VA. Tel: (434) 361-9134, (800) 524-4156, FAX: (434) 361-1916, E-Mail: info@ediblelandscaping.com, Web Site: www.eat-it.com (8)

McConnell, Bringier, Bart's Watersports, North Webster, IN. Tel: (574) 834-7666, (800) 348-5016, FAX: (574) 834-4246, E-Mail: info@barts.com, Web Site: www.bartswatersports.com (11)

McConnell, John D., Wake Forest University Baptist Medical Center, Winston Salem, NC. Tel: (336) 716-2011, Web Site: www.wakehealth.edu (1)

McConnell, John, Journal Star, Peoria, IL. Tel: (309) 686-3026, FAX: (309) 686-3265, Web Site: www. pjstar.com (17)

McConnell, Marilyn R., AIDC (American International Distribution Corp), Williston, VT. Tel: (800) 678-2432, FAX: (802) 864-7749, E-Mail: jmacon@ aidcvt.com, Web Site: www.aidcvt.com (22)

McConnell, Patrick, Daily Commercial News & Construction Record, Markham, ON Canada. Tel: (905) 752-5408, (800) 465-6475, FAX: (905) 752-5450, (888) 396-9413, E-Mail: dcnonl@reedbusiness.com, Web Site: www.dcnonl.com (17)

McConnell, Sari, Conformer Expansion Products Inc, Great Neck, NY. Tel: (516) 504-6300, E-Mail: support@conformerinc.com, Web Site: www. conformerinc.com (26)

McCord, Ted, Wasserman Uniform Co, Fort Lauderdale, FL. Tel: (614) 279-7000, (614) 279-8888, (800) 848-3576, FAX: (614) 464-0416, (800) 204-0416, E-Mail: custserv@wassermanuniform.com, Web Site: www.wassermanuniform.com (2)

McCorkle, Scott, ExactTarget, Indianapolis, IN. Tel: (317) 423-3928, FAX: (317) 396-1592, Web Site: www.exacttarget.com (32)

McCormack, Robert, Gall's Inc, Lexington, KY. Tel: (859) 266-7227, (800) 477-7766, FAX: (859) 268-5954, E-Mail: help-desk@galls.com, Web Site: www.galls.com (16)

McCormack, Roger, Buick, Detroit, MI. Tel: (313) 556-5000, (800) 521-7300, FAX: (313) 556-5108, Web Site: www.buick.com (16)

McCormick & Co Inc, Sparks, MD. Tel: (410) 771-7301, (800) 474-7742, FAX: (410) 527-6337, Web Site: www.mccormick.com (4)

McCormick-Armstrong Co Inc, Wichita, KS. Tel: (316) 264-1363, (800) 733-1363, FAX: (316) 263-4511, E-Mail: sales@mccormickarmstrong.com, Web Site: www.mccormickarmstrong.com (27)

McCormick, Chris, Starkey Laboratories, Eden Prairie, MN. Tel: (952) 941-6401, Web Site: www.starkey.com (16)

McCormick, Christopher, LL Bean Inc, Freeport, ME. Tel: (207) 865-4761, (800) 441-5713, FAX: (207) 552-3080, Web Site: www.llbean.com (2)

McCormick, Ed, Infogroup, Papillion, NE. Tel: (402) 836-5290, E-Mail: contentfeedback@infogroup.com, Web Site: www.infogroup.com (32)

McCormick, Jim, SilverPop, Atlanta, GA. Tel: (678) 247-0500, (866) 745-8767, FAX: (678) 247-0501, E-Mail: contactsales@silverpop.com, Web Site: www.silverpop.com (32)

McCormick, Mike, Lois Geller Marketing Group, Aventura, FL. Tel: (646) 723-3231, E-Mail: info2@loisgellermarketinggroup.com, Web Site: www.loisgellermarketinggroup.com (35)

McCormick, Rachel, BBC Direct Mktg Svcs, Shamong, NJ. Tel: (609) 268-9919, (877) 786-4389, FAX: (609) 268-9939, E-Mail: csr@bbcglobal.com, Web Site: www.bbcglobal.com (20)

McCormick, Scott, VML Inc, Kansas City, MO. Tel: (816) 283-0700, FAX: (816) 283-0954, E-Mail: dl-vmlcommarketing@vml.com, Web Site: www.vml.com (35)

McCormick, Todd, SilverPop, Atlanta, GA. Tel: (678) 247-0500, (866) 745-8767, FAX: (678) 247-0501, E-Mail: contactsales@silverpop.com, Web Site: www.silverpop.com (32)

McCourt Label Co, Lewis Run, PA. Tel: (800) 458-2390, FAX: (814) 362-4156, Web Site: www.mccourtlabel.com (27)

McCoy, Jane, Chilcutt Direct Marketing, Edmond, OK. Tel: (405) 726-8780, FAX: (405) 726-8799, E-Mail: info@cdmlist.com, Web Site: www.cdmlist.com (24)

McCoy, Sheri, Avon Products Inc, New York, NY. Tel: (212) 282-7000, (800) 367-2866, FAX: (212) 282-6225, Web Site: www.avon.com (7)

McCrea, Marshall, Sunoco Inc, Philadelphia, PA. Tel: (215) 977-3000, FAX: (215) 977-3409, Web Site: www.sunocoinc.com (16)

McCrum, David, Thousand Trails LP, Chicago, IL. Tel: (214) 618-7200, (800) 205-0606, FAX: (214) 618-7324, Web Site: www.1000trails.com (16)

McCubbin, Gene, Pop Labs Inc, Houston, TX. Tel: (877) 500-1399, FAX: (877) 850-2420, Web Site: www.poplabs.com (35)

McCue, Michael, Sales & Marketing Management Magazine, New York, NY. Tel: (800) 821-6897, FAX: (905) 470-8561, E-Mail: joyce.cooney@nielsen.com, Web Site: www.salesandmarketing.com (16)

McCullough, Alan J., Homecraft Veneer & Woodworker Supply, Latrobe, PA. Tel: (724) 537-8435, (800) 796-6348, FAX: (724) 537-0543, E-Mail: woodman@homecraftveneer.com, Web Site: www.homecraftveneer.com (8)

McCumber, Chris, USA Network, New York, NY. Tel: (212) 664-4444, FAX: (212) 664-6365, Web Site: www.usanetwork.com (32)

McCune, Craig, Teraco Inc, Midland, TX. Tel: (888) 837-2261, Web Site: www.teraco.com (27)

McCune, Thomas, Navitar Inc, Rochester, NY. Tel: (585) 359-4000, (800) 828-6778, FAX: (585) 359-4999, E-Mail: info@navitar.com, Web Site: www.navitar.com (16)

McCurry, Kristin, MINDset Direct, Arlington, VA. Tel: (703) 538-6463, Web Site: www.mindsetdirect.com (1)

McCurry, Steve, V3, Oxnard, CA. Tel: (805) 981-2600, (800) 882-1844, FAX: (805) 981-1180, E-Mail: sales@printv3.com, Web Site: www.printv3.com (27)

McCutcheon, Ray, San Antonio Express-News, San Antonio, TX. Tel: (210) 250-2000, E-Mail: feedabck@express-news.net, Web Site: www.expressnews.com (17)

McDaneld, Brent, Lladro USA Inc, Moonachie, NJ. Tel: (201) 807-1177, (800) 634-9088, FAX: (201) 807-1293, E-Mail: customer-services@us.lladro.com, Web Site: www.lladro.com (14)

McDaniels, Deborah, Lead Me Media, Delray Beach, FL. Tel: (888) 445-3282, FAX: (561) 423-7890, E-Mail: info@leadmemedia.com, Web Site: www.leadmemedia.com (30)

McDermott, Glen, Red Rock Branding, New Haven, CT. Tel: (203) 295-4882, E-Mail: glen@redrockbranding.com, Web Site: www.redrockbranding.com (35)

McDermott, Jr. James E., Amica Insurance, Lincoln, RI. Tel: (401) 334-6000, (800) 652-6422, FAX: (401) 334-4241, Web Site: www.amica.com (15)

McDermott, Peter, PCI Paper Conversions Inc, Syracuse, NY. Tel: (315) 437-1641, FAX: (315) 437-3634, E-Mail: sales@padmaker.com, Web Site: www.padmaker.com (27)

McDonagh, Brendan Paul, HSBC Bank USA, NA, New York, NY. Tel: (716) 841-2424, FAX: (716) 841-5391, Web Site: www.banking.us.hsbc.com (14)

McDonald Obsolete Parts Co, Rockport, IN. Tel: (812) 359-4965, FAX: (812) 359-5555, E-Mail: parts@mcdonaldparts.com, Web Site: www.mcdonaldparts.com (16)

McDonald Paulson, Megan, INCOMPAS Show, Washington, DC. Tel: (202) 296-6650, FAX: (202) 296-7585, Web Site: show.incompas.org (42)

Shannon McDonald, New York, NY. Tel: (917) 838-2057 (20)

McDonald, Chris, Delicious Orchards, Colts Neck, NJ. Tel: (732) 462-1989, FAX: (732) 409-4993, E-Mail: info@deliciousorchardsnj.com, Web Site: www.deliciousorchardsnjonline.com (4)

McDonald, Dan, MSNI Inc, Roswell, GA. Tel: (770) 777-4121, Web Site: www.msniinc.com (23)

McDonald, Debbie, Bowers & Merena Auctions, Irvine, CA. Tel: (949) 253-0916, (800) 458-4646, FAX: (949) 253-4091, E-Mail: auction@bowersandmerena.com, Web Site: www.bowersandmerena.com (16)

McDonald, J. T., MarketNet Services LLC, Spring Lake, MI. Tel: (616) 847-7992, FAX: (616) 847-7994, Web Site: www.marketnetservices.com (22)

McDonald, John, Masscot Internet Inc, West Yarmouth, MA. Tel: (508) 778-4500, FAX: (888) 884-9960, E-Mail: admin@masscot.net, Web Site: masscothosting.com (32)

McDonald, Joseph, The Field Companies Fulfillment Center Inc, Watertown, MA. Tel: (617) 926-5550, (800) 346-6552, FAX: (617) 924-9011, E-Mail: info@fieldcompanies.com, Web Site: www.fieldcompanies.com (21)

McDonald, Marjorie, McDonald Obsolete Parts Co, Rockport, IN. Tel: (812) 359-4965, FAX: (812) 359-5555, E-Mail: parts@mcdonaldparts.com, Web Site: www.mcdonaldparts.com (16)

McDonald, Michael, Community Food Bank, Tucson, AZ. Tel: (520) 622-0525, FAX: (520) 624-6349, Web Site: www.communityfoodbank.org (1)

McDonald, Robert, McDonald Obsolete Parts Co, Rockport, IN. Tel: (812) 359-4965, FAX: (812) 359-5555, E-Mail: parts@mcdonaldparts.com, Web Site: www.mcdonaldparts.com (16)

McDonald, Scott, Oliver Wyman, New York, NY. Tel: (212) 345-8000, (212) 541-8100, Web Site: www.oliverwyman.com (14)

McDonald, Will, McDonald Obsolete Parts Co, Rockport, IN. Tel: (812) 359-4965, FAX: (812) 359-5555, E-Mail: parts@mcdonaldparts.com, Web Site: www.mcdonaldparts.com (16)

McDonald, William, Delicious Orchards, Colts Neck, NJ. Tel: (732) 462-1989, FAX: (732) 409-4993, E-Mail: info@deliciousorchardsnj.com, Web Site: www.deliciousorchardsnjonline.com (4)

McDonnell, George T, Allen, Matkins, Leck, Gamble & Mallory, Los Angeles, CA. Tel: (213) 622-5555, FAX: (213) 620-8816, E-Mail: communications@allenmatkins.com, Web Site: www.allenmatkins.com (20)

McDonnell, Mark, Facts On File Inc, New York, NY. Tel: (212) 967-8800, (800) 322-8755, FAX: (212) 678-3633, Web Site: www.infobasepublishing.com (17)

McDonnell, Mark, Films Media Group, New York, NY. Tel: (800) 322-8755, FAX: (800) 678- 3633, E-Mail: custserv@films.com, Web Site: www.films.com (3)

McDonough, Bill, Telephony, Chicago, IL. Tel: (312) 595-1080, (800) 458-0479, FAX: (312) 595-0295, Web Site: www.internettelephony.com (17)

McDonough, Tim, Moen Inc, North Olmsted, OH. Tel: (440) 962-2000, Web Site: www.moen.com (16)

McDougal Littell, Evanston, IL. Tel: (847) 869-2300, FAX: (847) 869-0841, Web Site: www.mcdougallittell.com (17)

McDowell, Amanda ., Children's Better Health Institute, Indianapolis, IN. Tel: (317) 634-1100, FAX: (317) 684-8094, E-Mail: a.mcdowell@cbhi.org, Web Site: www.cbhi.org (1)

McDowell, Anthony T., Finch Paper, Glens Falls, NY. Tel: (518) 793-2541, (800) 833-9983, FAX: (518) 793-7364, E-Mail: info@finchpaper.com, Web Site: www.finchpaper.com (25)

McDowell, Mary, CitiFinancial Credit Co, Baltimore, MD. Tel: (410) 332-3000, (800) 922-6235, (800) 995-2274, FAX: (410) 332-3489, Web Site: www.citifinancial.com (14)

McDowell, Matt, ETR Associates, Scotts Valley, CA. Tel: (800) 321-4407, E-Mail: customerservice@etr.org, Web Site: www.etr.org (7)

McDowell, Robert L., Olan Mills Inc, Chattanooga, TN. Tel: (423) 622-5141, (800) 251-6320, FAX: (423) 629-8128, Web Site: www.olanmills.com (16)

McDowell, T. J., Neutron Industries, Phoenix, AZ. Tel: (602) 864-0090, (888) 712-7127, FAX: (602) 357-3996, (877) 646-7337, E-Mail: questions@neutronindustries.com, Web Site: www.neutronindustries.com (16)

McDowell, Violet, SP Express, Tempe, AZ. Tel: (866) 773-7363, E-Mail: info@spexpress.com, Web Site: www.spexpress.com (28)

McEachern, Father Chad, Fathers of St Edmund Southern Missions Inc, Selma, AL. Tel: (334) 872-2359, FAX: (334) 875-8189, E-Mail: jm1428@aol.com, Web Site: www.edmunditemissions.org (1)

McElheney, J. Ronald, North Carolina Electric Membership Corp, Raleigh, NC. Tel: (919) 872-0800, (800) 662-8835, FAX: (919) 645-3410, E-Mail: info@ncemcs.com, Web Site: www.ncemcs.com (30)

McElroy, Evan, Boys & Girls Clubs of America National Headquarters, Atlanta, GA. Tel: (404) 487-5700, FAX: (404) 815-5757, (404) 487-5757, E-Mail: info@bgca.org, Web Site: www.bgca.org (1)

McElroy, I.D., Psion Teklogix Inc, Mississauga, ON Canada. Tel: (905) 813-9900, (800) 322-3437, E-Mail: ptinfo@psion.com, Web Site: www.psionteklogix.com (3)

McElroy, Kevin, Marketing Results Inc, Sicklerville, NJ. Tel: (856) 740-3334, FAX: (856) 740-3335, Web Site: www.marketingresults.net (16)

McElveen-Hunter, Bonnie, Pace Communications Inc, Greensboro, NC. Tel: (336) 378-6065, FAX: (336) 275-2864, Web Site: www.pacecommunications.com (17)

McEnany, Robert, The Levenson Group, Dallas, TX. Tel: (214) 932-6000, E-Mail: hello@levensongroup.com, Web Site: levensongroup.com (35)

McEntee, Elliott C., National Automated Clearing House Association, Herndon, VA. Tel: (703) 561-1100, FAX: (703) 787-0996, Web Site: www.nacha.org (1)

McEntee-Rome, Beth, Travel Planners Inc, New York, NY. Tel: (212) 532-1660, (800) 221-3531, FAX: (212) 532-1556, Web Site: www.tphousing.com (19)

McFadden, James E., American Telecast Products LLC, Exton, PA. Tel: (610) 430-7800, FAX: (484) 879-4046, E-Mail: info@americantelecast.com, Web Site: www.americantelecast.com (32)

McFadden, Ronald, Zones Inc, Auburn, WA. Tel: (253) 205-3000, (800) 408-9663, FAX: (425) 430-3626, E-Mail: corpsales@zones.com, Web Site: www.zones.com (3)

McFarland & Co Inc Publishers, Jefferson, NC. Tel: (336) 246-4460, (800) 253-2187, FAX: (336) 246-5018, E-Mail: info@mcfarlandpub.com, Web Site: www.mcfarlandpub.com (17)

McFarlend, Dave, Tax Management Inc, Bethesda, MD. Tel: (202) 452-4200, FAX: (202) 496-6013 (17)

McFeely's Square Drive Screws, Madison, WI. Tel: (434) 846-2729, (800) 443-7937, FAX: (804) 847-7136, E-Mail: tech@mcfeelys.com, Web Site: www.mcfeelys.com (16)

McFeeters, Paul J., Open Text Inc, Waterloo, ON Canada. Tel: (519) 888-9933, (800) 499-6544, FAX: (519) 888-0677, E-Mail: support@opentext.com, Web Site: www.opentext.com (16)

McGahey, Thomas S., High Cotton, Birmingham, AL. Tel: (877) 838-2345, FAX: (205) 836-5587, E-Mail: sales@highscottonusa.com, Web Site: www.highcottonusa.com (28)

McGarry, Andrew, ULTA Salon Cosmetics Fragrance, Bolingbrook, IL. Tel: (630) 410-4800, (866) 983-8582 (7)

McGarry, Steven J., SLM Corp, Newark, DE. Web Site: www.salliemae.com (16)

McGaw Graphics, Manchester Center, VT. Tel: (845) 353-8600, (888) 4BMCGAW, FAX: (845) 353-3155, E-Mail: sales@bmcgaw.com, Web Site: www.bmcgaw.com (6)

McGaw, Nancy, McGaw Graphics, Manchester Center, VT. Tel: (845) 353-8600, (888) 4BMCGAW, FAX: (845) 353-3155, E-Mail: sales@bmcgaw.com, Web Site: www.bmcgaw.com (6)

McGee, Bridget, ASM Press, Washington, DC. Tel: (202) 737-3600, (800) 546-2416, FAX: (202) 942-9342, E-Mail: books@asmusa.org, Web Site: www.asmpress.org (17)

McGee, Donald, Ultimate Office, Farmingdale, NJ. Tel: (732) 780-6911, (800) 631-2233, FAX: (732) 780-9833, Web Site: www.ultoffice.com (16)

McGee, Nancy, Starz Entertainment LLC, Englewood, CO. Tel: (855) 807-2929, Web Site: www.starz.com (16)

McGee, Vickie, Where 2 Get It Inc, Anaheim, CA. Tel: (888) 377-2767, Web Site: www.where2getit.com (30)

McGeehon, Priscilla, Fairchild Books, New York, NY. Tel: (212) 419-5292, Web Site: www.fairchildbooks.com (17)

McGill, Kim, BAM! Direct Inc, Suwanee, GA. Tel: (678) 947-1943, FAX: (678) 947-3562, Web Site: www.bamdirect.com (35)

McGill, Lee, Eagle Claw Fishing Tackle, Denver, CO. Tel: (720) 941-8700, FAX: (303) 321-4750, E-Mail: info@eagleclaw.com, Web Site: www.eagleclaw.com (11)

McGinley, James W., Methode Electronics Inc, Chicago, IL. Tel: (708) 867-6777, FAX: (708) 867-6999, E-Mail: info@methode.com, Web Site: www.methode.com (9)

McGinley, Patty, Arrowhead Mountain Spring Water, Wilkes Barre, PA. Tel: (800) 873-7775, Web Site: www.arrowheadwater.com (16)

McGinley, Paul A., Rodale Inc, Emmaus, PA. Tel: (610) 967-5171, FAX: (610) 967-8963, Web Site: www.rodaleinc.com (17)

McGinnis, Jr. Arthur J., Simmons-Boardman Publishing Corp, New York, NY. Tel: (212) 620-7200, (800) 257-5091, Web Site: www.simmonsboardman.com (17)

McGinnis, Ms Kim, Simmons-Boardman Publishing Corp, New York, NY. Tel: (212) 620-7200, (800) 257-5091, Web Site: www.simmonsboardman.com (17)

McGinnis, Ms Pat, Simmons-Boardman Publishing Corp, New York, NY. Tel: (212) 620-7200, (800) 257-5091, Web Site: www.simmonsboardman.com (17)

McGoey, Michael, Blanchard & Co Inc, New Orleans, LA. Tel: (504) 837-3010, (800) 880-4653, FAX: (504) 837-4884, Web Site: www.blanchardonline.com (16)

McGoldrick, Bill, Syfy, New York, NY. Tel: (212) 664-4444, Web Site: www.syfy.com (32)

McGonagle, Michael, ClickSquared, Boston, MA. Tel: (781) 622-1611, (866) 402-5425, FAX: (857) 246-7645, E-Mail: info@clicksquared.com, Web Site: www.clicksquared.com (20)

McGougall, Clif, Riverside Acquisition Group LLC, Moorestown, NJ. Tel: (856) 802-1900, Web Site: www.com-pak.com (28)

McGovern, Chris, Emerging Marketing, Columbus, OH. Tel: (614) 923-6000, FAX: (614) 424-6200, E-Mail: info@emergingmarketing.com, Web Site: www.emergingmarketing.com (35)

McGovern, Gail J., American Red Cross, Washington, DC. Tel: (202) 303-5214, (800) RED-CROSS, FAX: (202) 303-6604, Web Site: www.redcross.org (1)

McGovern, John C., Progressive Distribution Services Inc, Grand Rapids, MI. Tel: (616) 957-5900, (800) 304-3699, FAX: (616) 957-2990, E-Mail: sales@progressive-commerce.com, Web Site: www.prodist.com (28)

McGovern, Lisa, InfoSource Inc, Oviedo, FL. Tel: (407) 796-5200, (800) 393-4636, FAX: (407) 796-5190, E-Mail: isisale@howtomaster.com, Web Site: www.infosourcelearning.com (17)

McGowan, Jim, The Missoulian, Missoula, MT. Tel: (406) 523-5200, (800) 366-7102, FAX: (406) 523-5221, Web Site: www.missoulian.com (31)

McGowan, Mark, Online Print Solutions, San Francisco, CA. Tel: (415) 651-4157, (800) 875-7117, E-Mail: info@onlineprintsolutions.com, Web Site: www.onlineprintsolutions.com (32)

McGrady, Laura, Cafe Lango, Sharon Springs, NY. Tel: (203) 453-1456, (800) 243-1234, FAX: (203) 453-5110, E-Mail: mail@cafelango.com, Web Site: www.audioforum.com (16)

McGrath, Christopher, Bliss World LLC, New York, NY. Tel: (212) 931-6383, (888) 243-8825, Web Site: www.blissworld.com (5)

McGrath, Jack, Brigar Xpress Solutions, Inc, Albany, NY. Tel: (518) 438-7817, (877) 437-7817, FAX: (518) 438-0224, E-Mail: general@brigarxpress.com, Web Site: www.brigarxpress.com (28)

McGrath, John, The Offset House Inc, Essex Junction, VT. Tel: (317) 849-5155, FAX: (317) 842-3324, Web Site: www.offsethouse.com (27)

McGrath, John W., New York Easter Seal Society, New York, NY. Tel: (212) 220-2290, FAX: (212) 695-4807, Web Site: ny.easterseals.com (1)

McGrath, Kevin, The Offset House Inc, Essex Junction, VT. Tel: (317) 849-5155, FAX: (317) 842-3324, Web Site: www.offsethouse.com (27)

McGrath, Monica, Ultimate Products Inc, Chula Vista, CA. Tel: (813) 881-1575, (800) 477-4287, FAX: (813) 881-1831, E-Mail: office@ultimatehat.com, Web Site: www.ultimatehat.com (16)

McGrath, Timothy, PC Connection, Merrimack, NH. Tel: (603) 683-2167, (800) 800-0014, FAX: (603) 683-5773, E-Mail: pr@pcconnection.com, Web Site: www.pcconnection.com, macconnection.com (22)

McGrath, William J., ValueVision Media Inc, Eden Prairie, MN. Tel: (952) 943-6000, Web Site: www.shophq.com (32)

The McGraw-Hill Financial, New York, NY. Tel: (212) 904-2000, Web Site: www.mhfi.com (17)

McGraw, III Harold W., The McGraw-Hill Financial, New York, NY. Tel: (212) 904-2000, Web Site: www.mhfi.com (17)

McGregor, Danny, Amnesty International USA, New York, NY. Tel: (212) 807-8400, FAX: (212) 627-1451, Web Site: www.amnestyusa.org (1)

McGrory, Brian, The Boston Globe, Boston, MA. Tel: (617) 929-2000, (888) MY-GLOBE, FAX: (617) 929-2606, Web Site: www.bostonglobe.com (17)

McGruff Specialty Products Office, Amsterdam, NY. Tel: (518) 842-4388, (888) 776-7763, FAX: (800) 995-5121, E-Mail: mcgruff@spocentral.com, Web Site: www.mcgruffspo.com (16)

McGuigan, Charles C., L Brands Inc, Columbus, OH. Tel: (614) 415-7000, FAX: (614) 415-7440, Web Site: www.lb.com (16)

McGuiness, Anna, Hagemeyer - North America, Charleston, SC. Tel: (843) 745-2400, FAX: (843) 745-6942, E-Mail: info@hagemeyerna.com, Web Site: www.hagemeyerna.com (16)

McGuire, Deb, Bay Manufacturing, Milan, OH. Tel: (419) 499-4602, FAX: (419) 499-4603, Web Site: www.baymfg.com (16)

McGuire, Ingrid, Ernst & Young LLP, New York, NY. Tel: (212) 773-6146, FAX: (312) 879-4000, Web Site: www.ey.com (20)

McGuire, M.J., Bay Manufacturing, Milan, OH. Tel: (419) 499-4602, FAX: (419) 499-4603, Web Site: www.baymfg.com (16)

McGuire, Marilyn, Networking Alternatives for Publishers, Retailers & Artists, Inc, Eastsound, WA. Tel: (360) 376-2702, (800) 367-1907, FAX: (360) 376-2704, E-Mail: futureweb@rockisland.com (40)

McGuire, Michael, Corona-Lotus Inc, San Francisco, CA. Tel: (415) 956-8956, (800) 422-2924, FAX: (415) 956-4922, E-Mail: customerservice@biscoff. com, Web Site: www.biscoff.com (4)

McGuire, Mike, LSSiData, Blue Bell, PA. Tel: (610) 276-4300, (800) 210-9021, FAX: (610) 567-5698, E-Mail: info@lssi.net, Web Site: www.lssidata.com (22)

McGuire, Nicole, New Track Media LLC, Cincinnati, OH. Tel: (513) 421-6500, FAX: (513) 421-1244, E-Mail: lriggs@newtrackmedia.com, Web Site: www.newtrackmedia.com (17)

McGuire, Suzie, Names in the News, Oakland, CA. Tel: (415) 989-3350, FAX: (415) 433-7796, E-Mail: susananstrand@nincal.com, Web Site: www.nincal. com (23)

McGuire, Terry, Halo Branded Solutions, Sterling, IL. Tel: (815) 625-0980, (866) 840-6401, Web Site: www.halo.com (33)

McHie, Jessica, Tenet Partners, New York, NY. Tel: (212) 329-3030, FAX: (212) 329-3031, Web Site: tenetpartners.com (35)

McHugh, Daniel, National Institute for Trial Advocacy, Boulder, CO. Tel: (800) 225-6482, Web Site: www. nita.org (1)

McHugh, Mark, Valassis Canada, Toronto, ON Canada. Tel: (416) 259-3600, (866) 333-2386, Web Site: www.valassis.com (35)

McHugh, Mike, KeyPath Education, Lenexa, KS. Tel: (913) 254-6000, Web Site: keypathedu.com (35)

McHugh, Pam, Mintel International, Chicago, IL. Tel: (312) 932-0500, Web Site: www.comperemedia. com (30)

McIlquham, John, The NonProfit Times, Morris Plains, NJ. Tel: (973) 401-0202, FAX: (973) 401-0404, Web Site: www.nptimes.com (17)

The McIlvaine Co, Northfield, IL. Tel: (847) 784-0012, FAX: (847) 784-0061, E-Mail: editor@ mcilvainecompany.com, Web Site: www. mcilvainecompany.com (30)

McIlvaine, Marilyn, The McIlvaine Co, Northfield, IL. Tel: (847) 784-0012, FAX: (847) 784-0061, E-Mail: editor@mcilvainecompany.com, Web Site: www. mcilvainecompany.com (30)

Mcilvaine, Robert, Fifth Gear LLC, Indianapolis, IN. Tel: (317) 631-0907, FAX: (317) 631-6585, Web Site: www.infifthgear.com (22)

McIlvaine, Robert, The McIlvaine Co, Northfield, IL. Tel: (847) 784-0012, FAX: (847) 784-0061, E-Mail: editor@mcilvainecompany.com, Web Site: www. mcilvainecompany.com (30)

McIntosh, Damian, Thoma Cressey Bravo, Chicago, IL. Tel: (312) 777-4444, FAX: (312) 777-4445, Web Site: www.tcb.com (14)

McIntosh, M.H., Mac McIntosh Inc, North Kingstown, RI. Tel: (401) 294-7730, (800) 944-5553, FAX: (401) 679-0176, E-Mail: info@sales-lead-experts. com, Web Site: www.sales-lead-experts.com (20)

McIntosh, Robert, Creative Learning Systems Inc, Longmont, CO. Tel: (303) 772-6400, (800) 458-2880, FAX: (303) 772-6422, Web Site: www.clsinc. com (9)

McIntyre Direct Group LLC, Portland, OR. Tel: (503) 516-4592, FAX: (503) 286-7622, E-Mail: marcia@ mcintyredirectgroup.com, Web Site: mcintyredirectgroup.com (21)

McIntyre, Susan, McIntyre Direct Group LLC, Portland, OR. Tel: (503) 516-4592, FAX: (503) 286-7622, E-Mail: marcia@mcintyredirectgroup.com, Web Site: mcintyredirectgroup.com (21)

McIntyre, Suzanne Ostiguy, IRPP, Montreal, QC Canada. Tel: (514) 985-2461, FAX: (514) 985-2559, E-Mail: irpp@irpp.org, Web Site: www.irpp.org (30)

McIsaac, Susan, United Way Toronto & York Region, Toronto, ON Canada. Tel: (416) 777-2001, (866) 620-2993, FAX: (416) 777-0962, Web Site: www. unitedwaytyr.com (1)

McKay, Pat, Cole & Weber United, Seattle, WA. Tel: (206) 447-9595, FAX: (206) 233-0178, E-Mail: info@cwunited.com, Web Site: www.cwunited.com (35)

McKay, Scott J., Genworth Financial Inc, Richmond, VA. Tel: (804) 281-6000, (888) 436-9678, FAX: (804) 662-2414, Web Site: www.genworth.com (14)

McKean, Brian, Tom Snyder Productions, Watertown, MA. Tel: (617) 926-6000, (800) 342-0236, FAX: (800) 304-1254, E-Mail: ask@tomsnyder.com, Web Site: www.tomsnyder.com (16)

McKean, Lauri, Uncharted Country Publishing, Madison, WI. Tel: (575) 776-3470, E-Mail: ucp@ taichihealth.com, Web Site: www.taichihealth.com (17)

McKee Consulting LLC, Escondido, CA. Tel: (760) 738-8200, Web Site: www.trainyourcallcenter.com (20)

McKee, David, Annie's Attic LLC, Big Sandy, TX. Tel: (903) 636-4303, (800) 282-6643, FAX: (903) 636-4088, Web Site: www.anniesattic.com (11)

McKee, David, DRG, Berne, IN. Tel: (260) 589-4000, FAX: (260) 589-8093, Web Site: www.drgnetwork. com (17)

McKee, Marigay, Saks Fifth Avenue, New York, NY. Tel: (212) 940-5195, FAX: (212) 940-5339, Web Site: www.saksfifthavenue.com (16)

McKee, Patrick, Challenge Industries Inc, Ithaca, NY. Tel: (607) 272-8990, FAX: (607) 277-7865, E-Mail: info@aboutchallenge.org, Web Site: www. aboutchallenge.org (28)

McKeever, Jayme, Baber Direct Marketing, Memphis, TN. Tel: (901) 332-6300, (800) 847-7040, FAX: (901) 332-6441, E-Mail: info@baberweb.com, Web Site: www.baberweb.com (21)

McKelvey, Ryan, Ballard Designs, Atlanta, GA. Tel: (404) 603-7033, (800) 536-7551, FAX: (800) 989-4510, Web Site: www.ballarddesigns.com (8)

McKenna, Elizabeth, Westlake Plastics Co, Lenni, PA. Tel: (610) 459-1000, (800) 999-1700, FAX: (610) 459-1084, Web Site: www.westlakeplastics.com (16)

McKenna, Gwen, Mountain Press Publishing Co, Missoula, MT. Tel: (406) 728-1900, (800) 234-5308, FAX: (406) 728-1635, E-Mail: info@mountainpress.com, Web Site: mountain-press.com (17)

McKenna, Lore, Baker Corp, Seal Beach, CA. Tel: (562) 430-6262 (16)

McKenna, Michael, Editorial Projects in Education Inc, Bethesda, MD. Tel: (301) 280-3100, (800) 346-1834, FAX: (301) 280-3250, Web Site: www. edweek.org (17)

Mckenney, Sandra, Shape Global Technology, Sanford, ME. Tel: (207) 324-5200, (800) 627-5836, FAX: (207) 324-0875, E-Mail: info@shapeglobal.com, Web Site: www.shapenet.com (34)

McKensie, Lynn, PC Connection, Merrimack, NH. Tel: (603) 683-2167, (800) 800-0014, FAX: (603) 683-5773, E-Mail: pr@pcconnection.com, Web Site: www.pcconnection.com, macconnection.com (22)

McKenzie Taxidermy Supply, Granite Quarry, NC. Tel: (704) 279-7985, (800) 279-7985, Web Site: www. mckenziesp.com (16)

McKenzie, Barry, McKenzie Taxidermy Supply, Granite Quarry, NC. Tel: (704) 279-7985, (800) 279-7985, Web Site: www.mckenziesp.com (16)

McKenzie, David, Sun Harvest Citrus, Fort Myers, FL. Tel: (239) 768-2686, (800) 743-1480, FAX: (239) 768-9255, E-Mail: info@sunharvestcitrus.com, Web Site: www.SunHarvestCitrus.com (6)

McKenzie, Don, Innovairre Communications LLC, Cherry Hill, NJ. Tel: (856) 663-2500, E-Mail: info@ innovairre.com, Web Site: www.innovairre.com (35)

McKenzie, Don, SourceLink, Itasca, IL. Tel: (866) 947-6872, Web Site: www.sourcelink.com (20)

McKenzie, Jean, American Girl Brands LLC, Middleton, WI. Tel: (608) 836-4848, Web Site: www. americangirl.com (6)

McKenzie, Jean, Pleasant Company, Middleton, WI. Tel: (608) 831-4116, (800) 845-0005, FAX: (608) 836-1999, Web Site: www.americangirl.com (11)

McKenzie, Kevin, McKenzie Taxidermy Supply, Granite Quarry, NC. Tel: (704) 279-7985, (800) 279-7985, Web Site: www.mckenziesp.com (16)

McKenzie, Sandy, Sun Harvest Citrus, Fort Myers, FL. Tel: (239) 768-2686, (800) 743-1480, FAX: (239) 768-9255, E-Mail: info@sunharvestcitrus.com, Web Site: www.SunHarvestCitrus.com (6)

McKeon, David, C&H Distributors LLC, Milwaukee, WI. Tel: (414) 443-1700, (888) 316-2223, FAX: (414) 443-9213, E-Mail: customerservice@chdist. com, Web Site: www.chdist.com (9)

McKernan, Rob, APC by Schneider Electric, West Kingston, RI. Tel: (800) 555-7927, FAX: (401) 789-3710, E-Mail: public.relations@apcc.com, Web Site: www.apcc.com (3)

McKesson Corp, San Francisco, CA. Tel: (415) 983-8300, FAX: (415) 983-7160, Web Site: www. mckesson.com (7)

McKewen, Darren P., The Bureau of National Affairs, Inc, Arlington, VA. Tel: (703) 341-3000, (800) 372-1033, FAX: (703) 341-1688, Web Site: www.bna. com (17)

McKiernan, Terry, E3 Local Marketing Solutions, Cincinnati, OH. Tel: (513) 699-3300, (888) 878-2768, FAX: (513) 699-3310, Web Site: e3local.com (35)

McKinley, Bill, Benchmark Imaging & Display, Elk Grove Village, IL. Tel: (847) 290-0002, FAX: (847) 290-8608, Web Site: www.benchmarkimaging.com (27)

McKinley, Tracey, Rogers Publishing Ltd, Toronto, ON Canada. Tel: (416) 935-7777, FAX: (416) 935-3597, Web Site: www.rogerspublishing.ca (17)

McKinney, William E., Customer Marketing Group LLC, Weston, CT. Tel: (203) 226-9845, FAX: (203) 226-9837, E-Mail: bill@4cmg.com, Web Site: www.4cmg.com (35)

McKinnie, Pam, Concepts Unlimited, Frederick, CO. Tel: (303) 918-9416, E-Mail: conceptsunlimited@ estreet.com, Web Site: www.conceptsunlimitedinc. com (35)

McKinsey & Co, New York, NY. Tel: (212) 446-7000, FAX: (212) 446-8575, Web Site: www.mckinsey. com (20)

McKinstry, Nancy, Anatomical Chart Co, Riverwoods, IL. Tel: (847) 580-5000, (800) 621-7500, FAX: (847) 674-0211, E-Mail: service@anatomical.com, Web Site: www.anatomical.com (7)

McKnight, Andy, Tri-Chem Inc, Belleville, NJ. Tel: (973) 751-9200, FAX: (973) 450-1260, (973) 450-1057, E-Mail: paints@trichem.com, Web Site: www.trichem.com (16)

McKnight's Long-Term Care News, Northfield, IL. Tel: (847) 784-8706, (800) 558-1703, FAX: (847) 784-9346, E-Mail: mltcn-webmaster@mltcn.com, Web Site: www.mcknightsonline.com (17)

McLain, Craig, American Solutions for Business, Glenwood, MN. Tel: (320) 634-5471, FAX: (320) 634-5265, Web Site: www.americanbus.com (25)

McLain, Debbie, RMI Direct Marketing Inc, Danbury, CT. Tel: (203) 798-0448, FAX: (203) 778-6130, E-Mail: info@rmidirect.com, Web Site: www.rmidirect.com (23)

McLaren, Michael, MRM//McCann, New York, NY. Tel: (646) 865-6230, E-Mail: gbc@mrm-mccann.com, Web Site: mrm-mccann.com (35)

McLauchlin, Jay, HealthPlan Services, Tampa, FL. Tel: (813) 289-1000, (800) 545-6441, Web Site: www.healthplan.com (15)

McLaughlin, Jennifer, Pinnacle List Co, Arlington, VA. Tel: (703) 379-4394, FAX: (703) 379-5312, E-Mail: holly@pinnlistco.com, Web Site: www.pinnlistco.com (23)

McLaughlin, Joe, John Alden Life Insurance Co/North Star Marketing, Duluth, GA. Tel: (678) 473-1211, (800) 768-6288, FAX: (678) 473-9573, Web Site: www.nstarmarketing.com (15)

McLaughlin, Matt, DoubleVerify, New York, NY. Tel: (212) 631-2111, Web Site: www.doubleverify.com (9)

McLaughlin, Todd, Association of Fundraising Professionals, Arlington, VA. Tel: (703) 684-0410, (800) 666-3863, FAX: (703) 684-0540, Web Site: www.afpnet.org (1)

McLaughlin, Tom, E-Z-EM Inc, Lake Success, NY. Tel: (516) 333-8230, (800) 544-4624, FAX: (516) 333-8278, E-Mail: webmaster@ezem.com, Web Site: www.ezem.com (7)

McLaughlin, William, Select Comfort Corp, Minneapolis, MN. Tel: (763) 551-7000, (888) 411-2188, FAX: (763) 551-7826, Web Site: www.selectcomfort.com (16)

McLaurin, Mac, Fifteen Degrees, New York, NY. Tel: (212) 545-7400, FAX: (212) 545-7433, E-Mail: hello@fifteendegrees.com, Web Site: fifteendegrees.com (35)

McLean, Bob, Promotional Products Association International, Irving, TX. Tel: (972) 252-0404, FAX: (972) 258-3004, (800) I-AM-PPAI, E-Mail: membership@ppa.org, Web Site: www.ppa.org (40)

McLean, Mark, Market Approach Consulting Services LP, Lorena, TX. Tel: (254) 857-1100, FAX: (254) 857-1000, E-Mail: wmclean@marketapproach.net, Web Site: www.marketapproach.net (23)

McLean, Wade, Market Approach Consulting Services LP, Lorena, TX. Tel: (254) 857-1100, FAX: (254) 857-1000, E-Mail: wmclean@marketapproach.net, Web Site: www.marketapproach.net (23)

McLeod, Denise, Drexel University Goodwin College of Professional Studies, Philadelphia, PA. Tel: (215) 895-2159, E-Mail: goodwin@drexel.edu, Web Site: goodwin.drexel.edu (16)

McLoughlin, Jacqueline, Advertising Research Foundation, New York, NY. Tel: (212) 751-5656, FAX: (212) 319-5265, E-Mail: info@thearf.org, Web Site: www.thearf.org (40)

McLuster, Linda, Recognition Systems (Dot Works), Port Washington, NY. Tel: (516) 625-5000, FAX: (516) 625-1507, E-Mail: wade@dotworks.com, Web Site: www.dotworks.com (16)

McMahen, Nancy, National Rural Electric Cooperative Association, Arlington, VA. Tel: (703) 907-5500, FAX: (703) 907-5528, Web Site: www.nreca.org (1)

McMahon, Bill, K-tel International, Golden Valley, MN. Tel: (204) 889-5430, (800) 665-5021, FAX: (612) 559-6803, Web Site: www.ktel.com (16)

McMahon, Bill, Nautilus Inc, Vancouver, WA. Tel: (360) 859-2900, (800) 675-0171, FAX: (360) 694-2755, Web Site: www.nautilus.com (11)

McMahon, Pat, One Point, Scranton, PA. Tel: (570) 342-0737, (800) 526-4460, FAX: (570) 343-6361, Web Site: www.opoffice.com (10)

McMahon, Stephanie, World Wrestling Entertainment Inc, Stamford, CT. Tel: (203) 352-8600, FAX: (203) 359-5180, Web Site: www.wwe.com (16)

McMahon, Vincent K., World Wrestling Entertainment Inc, Stamford, CT. Tel: (203) 352-8600, FAX: (203) 359-5180, Web Site: www.wwe.com (16)

McManis, James, NetHawk Interactive, Emeryville, CA. Tel: (510) 595-2220, E-Mail: info@nethawk.net, Web Site: www.nethawk.net (23)

McManus, Donna, NestFamily.com, Lewisville, TX. Tel: (800) 596-7386, FAX: (972) 629-7181, Web Site: www.nestfamily.com (3)

McMaster-Carr Supply Co (HQ), Elmhurst, IL. Tel: (630) 834-9600, FAX: (630) 834-9427, E-Mail: chi.sales@mcmaster.com, Web Site: www.mcmaster.com (9)

McMaster, J. A, LSSiData, Blue Bell, PA. Tel: (610) 276-4300, (800) 210-9021, FAX: (610) 567-5698, E-Mail: info@lssi.net, Web Site: www.lssidata.com (22)

McMenamin, John, Princeton Book Co Publishers, Hightstown, NJ. Tel: (609) 426-0602, (800) 220-7149, FAX: (609) 426-1344, E-Mail: pbc@dancehorizons.com, Web Site: www.dancehorizons.com (17)

McMillan, Sheri, Microbiz Corp, Menlo Park, CA. Tel: (702) 749-5353, (800) 726-3282, FAX: (650) 440-4870, E-Mail: info@microbiz.com, Web Site: www.microbiz.com (3)

McMillen, Jim, Arends, Batavia, IL. Tel: (630) 990-0220, FAX: (630) 990-2556, Web Site: www.arends-inc.com (35)

McMillon, Doug, WalMart Stores Inc, Bentonville, AR. Tel: (479) 273-4000, (800) 925-6278, FAX: (479) 277-1830, Web Site: www.walmart.com (16)

McMorrow, Patrick J., Tuttle Printing & Engraving, Rutland, VT. Tel: (802) 773-9171, (800) 776-7682, FAX: (802) 773-5785, E-Mail: info@tuttleprinting.com, Web Site: www.tuttleprinting.com (10)

McMullen, John, Eastman Kodak Co, Rochester, NY. Tel: (585) 724-4000, (800) 698-3324, FAX: (585) 724-1089, Web Site: www.kodak.com (27)

McMullen, Ned, Equifax Database Marketing, Wakefield, MA. Tel: (781) 876-2000, (800) 660-5125, FAX: (781) 246-3720, E-Mail: monica.baker@equifax.com, Web Site: www.equifax.com/databaseservices (22)

McMullen, W. Rodney, The Kroger Co, Cincinnati, OH. Tel: (513) 762-4000, (866) 221-4141, FAX: (513) 762-1575, Web Site: www.kroger.com (4)

McMurry Inc, Phoenix, AZ. Tel: (602) 395-5850, Web Site: www.mcmurry.com (17)

McNabb, Amy, Infocore Inc, Carlsbad, CA. Tel: (760) 607-5000, FAX: (760) 607-2505, E-Mail: info@infocore.com, Web Site: www.infocore.com (23)

McNabb, Mark, Volkswagen Group of America Inc, Herndon, VA. Tel: (248) 754-5000, Web Site: www.volkswagengroupamerica.com (16)

McNair lll, James D., Garlinghouse Co, Beaufort, SC. Tel: (703) 547-4115, (800) 235-5700, FAX: (703) 222-9705, Web Site: www.familyhomeplans.com (17)

McNally, Edward M., Morris James Hitchens & Williams, Wilmington, DE. Tel: (302) 888-6800, FAX: (302) 571-1750, Web Site: www.morrisjames.com (20)

McNally, Tom, Taradel LLC, Glen Allen, VA. Tel: (804) 364-8444, (800) 481-1656, FAX: (888) 241-3023, E-Mail: info@taradel.com, Web Site: www.taradel.com (21)

McNamara & Associates, Van Nuys, CA. Tel: (818) 907-6212, E-Mail: jim@mcdrtv.com, Web Site: www.mcdrtv.com (39)

McNamara, Jim, McNamara & Associates, Van Nuys, CA. Tel: (818) 907-6212, E-Mail: jim@mcdrtv.com, Web Site: www.mcdrtv.com (39)

McNamara, John, One Call Systems Inc, Baden, PA. Tel: (412) 415-5000, (800) 845-9945, FAX: (412) 415-5023, E-Mail: jmcnamara@1-call.com, Web Site: www.1-call.com (29)

McNamara, Keith, Fujitsu Transaction Solutions Inc, Richardson, TX. Tel: (972) 963-2300, (800) 340-4425, Web Site: www.fujitsu.com (16)

McNamara, Michael, Key Bank, Cleveland, OH. Tel: (800) 539-2968, FAX: (216) 689-5115, Web Site: www.key.com (14)

McNamara, Shawn, DigDev Direct, Deerfield Beach, FL. Tel: (954) 949-9500, (800) 873-5137, FAX: (954) 337-0251, E-Mail: info@digdev.com, Web Site: www.digdevdirect.com (35)

McNamara, Tim C., Boyden Global Executive Search, Purchase, NY. Tel: (914) 747-0093, E-Mail: inquiry@boyden.com, Web Site: www.boyden.com (20)

McNamara, Tom, Quattro Direct LLC, Berwyn, PA. Tel: (610) 993-0070, Web Site: www.quattrodirect.com (35)

McNaughton, David M., Mediacom Communications Corp, Chester, NY. Tel: (855) 633-4226, FAX: (845) 698-4100, Web Site: www.mediacomcable.com (32)

McNaughton, Stanley W., PEMCO Insurance Cos, Seattle, WA. Tel: (206) 628-4000, (800) 467-3626, FAX: (206) 628-5886, Web Site: www.pemco.com (15)

McNeff, John, Nova DM Agency Inc, Dunmore, PA. Tel: (570) 342-8668, FAX: (570) 342-8666, E-Mail: info@novadmagency.com, Web Site: www.novadmagency.com (35)

McNeil, Keith, Catch The Wind Kite Shop, Lincoln City, OR. Tel: (541) 994-9500, (800) 227-7878, FAX: (541) 994-4766, E-Mail: catchthewindkites@yahoo.com, Web Site: www.catchthewind.com (11)

McNeil, Thomas, DineWise, Farmingdale, NY. Tel: (631) 694-1111, (800) 749-1170, FAX: (631) 694-4064, E-Mail: info@dinewise.com, Web Site: www.dinewise.com (4)

PJ McNerney & Associates Inc, Cincinnati, OH. Tel: (513) 825-5547, FAX: (513) 825-5601, E-Mail: tim@pjmcnerney.com, Web Site: www.pjmcnerney.com (28)

McNerney, Jr. W. James, Boeing Co, Chicago, IL. Tel: (312) 544-2000, FAX: (312) 544-2082, Web Site: www.boeing.com (16)

McNerney, Patrick, PJ McNerney & Associates Inc, Cincinnati, OH. Tel: (513) 825-5547, FAX: (513) 825-5601, E-Mail: tim@pjmcnerney.com, Web Site: www.pjmcnerney.com (28)

McNicholas, Christine, Q Interactive, Chicago, IL. Tel: (312) 977-0390, (888) 729-6465, FAX: (312) 224-5001, E-Mail: solutions@qinteractive.com, Web Site: www.qinteractive.com (40)

McNichols Co, Tampa, FL. Tel: (813) 282-3828, FAX: (813) 288-9342, E-Mail: sales@mcnichols.com, Web Site: www.mcnichols.com (16)

McNitt, Peter B., Harris Bancorp Inc, Chicago, IL. Tel: (312) 461-2121, (888) 340-BANK, FAX: (312) 461-7869, E-Mail: onlineservices@harrisbank.com, Web Site: www.harrisbank.com (14)

McNulty, Despina, Kappa Publishing Group, Blue Bell, PA. Tel: (215) 643-6385, FAX: (215) 628-3571, Web Site: www.kappapublishing.com (17)

McNutt, Bob, Collin Street Bakery, Corsicana, TX. Tel: (800) 292-7400, Web Site: www.collinstreetbakery.com (4)

McNutt, III William, International Direct Marketing Consultants Inc, Dallas, TX. Tel: (214) 443-9494, FAX: (214) 443-9512, E-Mail: billmcnutt@charter.net, Web Site: www.dmtrademissions.com (20)

McPeak, Jacquelyn, Mail Management Enterprises, Seaford, DE. Tel: (410) 883-3224, FAX: (410) 883-3392, E-Mail: mailmgt@aol.com, Web Site: www.mailmanagemententerprises.com (20)

McPhedrain, Rusty, Mary Maxim Inc, Port Huron, MI. Tel: (810) 987-2000, (800) 962-9504, FAX: (810) 987-5056, E-Mail: info@marymaxim.com, Web Site: www.marymaxim.com (11)

McPherson Associates Inc, Berwyn, PA. Tel: (610) 640-1555, Web Site: www.mcphersonassociates.com (1)

McPherson, Richard, McPherson Associates Inc, Berwyn, PA. Tel: (610) 640-1555, Web Site: www.mcphersonassociates.com (1)

McQuade, Eugene M., Freddie Mac, McLean, VA. Tel: (703) 903-2000, (800) 424-5401, Web Site: www.freddiemac.com (14)

McQuagge, Cassie, ARE Press, Virginia Beach, VA. Tel: (757) 428-3588, (800) 333-4499, FAX: (757) 491-0689, Web Site: www.arepress.com (1)

McQueen, Rob, Jack Morton Worldwide, New York, NY. Tel: (212) 401-7000, (212) 401-7121, E-Mail: experience@jackmorton.com, Web Site: www.jackmorton.com (35)

McQuillan, Karen, American Association of Critical-Care Nurses, Aliso Viejo, CA. Tel: (949) 362-2000, (800) 809-CARE, FAX: (949) 362-2020, E-Mail: info@aacn.com, Web Site: www.aacn.org (1)

McReynolds, Graham, National Multiple Sclerosis Society, Denver, CO. Tel: (303) 813-1052, Web Site: www.nmss.org (1)

McRuer, Jerry, Direct Partners, Marina Del Rey, CA. Tel: (310) 482-4200, FAX: (310) 482-4201, Web Site: www.directpartners.com (35)

McShane, Kevin, Equifax Database Marketing, Wakefield, MA. Tel: (781) 876-2000, (800) 660-5125, FAX: (781) 246-3720, E-Mail: monica.baker@equifax.com, Web Site: www.equifax.com/databaseservices (22)

McSlasrow, Kyle, National Cable & Telecommunications Association, Washington, DC. Tel: (202) 222-2300, FAX: (202) 775-3675, Web Site: www.ncta.com (40)

McStocker, Kim, Smith Hanley Associates, Southport, CT. Tel: (203) 319-4300, (888) 221-2900, FAX: (203) 319-4320, Web Site: www.smithhanley.com (20)

McSwain, Pam, Parker Systems Inc, Chesapeake, VA. Tel: (757) 485-2955, (866) 472-7537, FAX: (757) 487-5872, E-Mail: info@parkersystemsinc.com, Web Site: www.parkersystemsinc.com (16)

McSweeney, David, DM Info, Naperville, IL. Tel: (630) 357-0732, FAX: (630) 527-8136, E-Mail: dminfo@dmcsweeney.com (20)

McTaggart, Tanya, McBee Associates Inc, Wayne, PA. Tel: (610) 964-9680, Web Site: www.mcbeeassociates.com (20)

McTurk, Jennifer, Sedona Labs, Cottonwood, AZ. Tel: (928) 340-5400, (888) 816-8804, FAX: (928) 634-0657, E-Mail: info@sedonalabs.com, Web Site: www.sedonalabs.com (7)

McVay, Barry, Panoptic Enterprises, Burke, VA. Tel: (703) 451-5953, (800) 594-4766, FAX: (703) 451-5953, E-Mail: panoptic@fedgovcontracts.com, Web Site: www.fedgovcontracts.com (17)

McVay, Vivina, Panoptic Enterprises, Burke, VA. Tel: (703) 451-5953, (800) 594-4766, FAX: (703) 451-5953, E-Mail: panoptic@fedgovcontracts.com, Web Site: www.fedgovcontracts.com (17)

McVey, Alicia, UPMC Health Plan, Pittsburgh, PA. Tel: (888) 876-2756, (800) 361-2629, Web Site: www.upmchealthplan.com (1)

McVicker, Scott, NTL Institute, Silver Spring, MD. Tel: (301) 565-3200, E-Mail: info@ntl.org, Web Site: www.ntl.org (1)

McVoy, Marilyn, Stickers 'N' Stuff Inc, Louisville, CO. Tel: (303) 661-0200, E-Mail: sales@stickersnstuff.com, Web Site: www.stickersnstuff.biz (6)

McWeeney Marketing, Orange, CT. Tel: (800) 272-3440, E-Mail: gmcweeney@geiger.com, Web Site: www.mcweeneymarketing.geiger.com (33)

McWeeney, George, McWeeney Marketing, Orange, CT. Tel: (800) 272-3440, E-Mail: gmcweeney@geiger.com, Web Site: www.mcweeneymarketing.geiger.com (33)

McWhorter, Anthony, United Investors Life Insurance Co, Birmingham, AL. Tel: (205) 325-4300, (800) 288-2722, FAX: (205) 325-4157, Web Site: www.uilic.com (15)

McWilliams, Beth, Happy Trails Resort, Surprise, AZ. Tel: (623) 584-0066, (800) 872-4579, FAX: (623) 546-6293, E-Mail: happytrails@uccinc.net, Web Site: www.htresort.com (19)

McWilliams, Bruce, Teachers' Discovery, Auburn Hills, MI. Tel: (800) 832-2437, FAX: (800) 287-4509, E-Mail: orders@teachersdiscovery.com, Web Site: teachersdiscovery.com (5)

Meacham, Laurie, Broadmoor Hotel Inc, Colorado Springs, CO. Tel: (719) 623-5112, (866) 837-9520, FAX: (719) 577-5738, Web Site: www.broadmoor.com (19)

Mead Fine Paper Division, Sidney, NY. Tel: (800) 936-9811, Web Site: www.mead.com (25)

Mead Johnson Co, Evansville, IN. Tel: (812) 429-5204, Web Site: www.MeadJohnson.com (7)

Mead, Robert M, AETNA - Marketing Product & Communication, Hartford, CT. Tel: (860) 273-0123, (800) 872-3862, FAX: (860) 273-3971, Web Site: www.aetna.com (14)

Meadors, Alyce, The United Methodist Publishing House, Nashville, TN. Tel: (615) 749-6000, (800) 672-1789, FAX: (615) 749-6417, E-Mail: productsandservices@umpublishing.com, Web Site: www.umpublishing.com (17)

Meadowcroft, William D., Nautilus Inc, Vancouver, WA. Tel: (360) 859-2900, (800) 675-0171, FAX: (360) 694-2755, Web Site: www.nautilus.com (11)

Meadows Design Office Inc, Washington, DC. Tel: (202) 966-6007, FAX: (202) 966-6733, E-Mail: postmaster@mdomedia.com, Web Site: www.mdomedia.com (35)

Meadows, Marc, Meadows Design Office Inc, Washington, DC. Tel: (202) 966-6007, FAX: (202) 966-6733, E-Mail: postmaster@mdomedia.com, Web Site: www.mdomedia.com (35)

Mead Westvaco Consumer & Office Products, Richmond, VA. Tel: (937) 222-6323, (804) 444-1000, FAX: (937) 495-3192, Web Site: www.meadwestvaco.com (10)

Meakem, Glen, Surplus Record, Chicago, IL. Tel: (312) 372-9077, (800) 622-5449, FAX: (312) 372-6537, E-Mail: surplus@surplusrecord.com, Web Site: www.surplusrecord.com (17)

Means, Chris, Chattanooga Shooting Supplies Inc, Chattanooga, TN. Tel: (423) 894-3007, (800) 251-4808, FAX: (423) 855-5513, Web Site: www.chattanoogashooting.com (16)

Mearns, Geoffrey S., Northern Kentucky University, Highland Heights, KY. Tel: (859) 572-5220, (800) 637-9948, FAX: (859) 572-6177, Web Site: www.nku.edu (41)

Mears, Peter, Initiative, New York, NY. Tel: (212) 605-7000, FAX: (212) 605-7200, Web Site: www.initiative.com (32)

Mechanical Breakdown Administrators Inc, Scottsdale, AZ. Tel: (480) 860-2288, FAX: (480) 860-0867, E-Mail: gaylenb@mbadirect.com, Web Site: www.mbadirect.com (14)

Meckley, David, Wilton Armetale, Mount Joy, PA. Tel: (717) 653-4444, (800) 553-2048, FAX: (717) 653-6573, E-Mail: cservice@armetale.com, Web Site: www.armetale.com (16)

Medals of America, Fountain Inn, SC. Tel: (864) 862-0635, (800) 308-0849, FAX: (800) 407-8640, E-Mail: medals@usmedals.com, Web Site: www.usmedals.com (6)

Medavante, Hamilton, NJ. Tel: (609) 528-9413, Web Site: www.metavante.com (20)

Medco Health Solutions Inc, Franklin Lakes, NJ. Tel: (201) 269-3400, (800) 556-3326, FAX: (800) 222-1934, E-Mail: customersupport@medcosupply.com, Web Site: www.medco-athletics.com (7)

Medco Insurance Co, Omaha, NE. Tel: (800) 228-6080, E-Mail: clientservices@gomedico.com, Web Site: www.gomedico.com (15)

Medco Supply Co Inc, Tonawanda, NY. Tel: (716) 743-8400, (800) 556-3326, FAX: (800) 222-1934, E-Mail: sales@medcosupply.com, Web Site: www.medcosupply.com (7)

Medcom Inc, Cypress, CA. Tel: (800) 877-1443, FAX: (714) 891-3140, E-Mail: lhammonds@medcominc.com, Web Site: www.medcominc.com (14)

Meder, Mary, Harmelin Media, Bala Cynwyd, PA. Tel: (610) 668-7900, FAX: (610) 668-9257, E-Mail: info@harmelin.com, Web Site: www.harmelin.com (32)

Media Consultants, Lyndhurst, NJ. Tel: (201) 933-2015, FAX: (201) 933-6314, E-Mail: info@mediaconsultants.net, Web Site: mediaconsultants.net (35)

Media Consultants Inc, Bayside, NY. Tel: (718) 423-6300, FAX: (718) 428-7482, E-Mail: mediaconsults@aol.com (32)

The Media Crew, Largo, FL. Tel: (813) 551-0902, E-Mail: marketing@themediacrew.com, Web Site: www.themediacrew.com (35)

Media Directions Creative Group, Lincolnshire, IL. Tel: (847) 948-0099, E-Mail: info@mdcreativegroup.com, Web Site: www.mdcreativegroup.com (35)

Media Dynamics LLC, Greenwich, CT. Tel: (203) 531-6600, FAX: (203) 531-6661, E-Mail: bjann@mediadynamx.com, Web Site: www.Media-Dynamics.com (31)

Media Funding Corp, Malibu, CA. Tel: (310) 457-4140, FAX: (310) 774-1234, E-Mail: info@mediafunding.com, Web Site: mediafunding.com (32)

Media Horizons Inc, Norwalk, CT. Tel: (203) 857-0770, FAX: (203) 857-0296, E-Mail: info@mediahorizons.com, Web Site: www.mediahorizons.com (21)

Media Horizons Management LLC, Norwalk, CT. Tel: (203) 857-0770, FAX: (203) 857-0296, E-Mail: info@mediahorizons.com, Web Site: www.mediahorizons.com (31)

Media Link Communications, New York, NY. Tel: (212) 674-8843, FAX: (212) 260-8489, E-Mail: mlinkcom@aol.com, Web Site: www.getprinted.com (27)

Media Management Services Inc, Newton, PA. Tel: (215) 579-8590, (800) 523-5948, FAX: (215) 579-8589, Web Site: www.mmseducation.com (20)

Media Monitors Inc, White Plains, NY. Tel: (914) 428-5971, FAX: (914) 428-4541, E-Mail: jselig@mediamonitors.com, Web Site: www.mediamonitors.com (30)

Media People Inc, New York, NY. Tel: (212) 779-7172, FAX: (212) 779-7248, E-Mail: info@mediapeople.com, Web Site: www.mediapeople.com (31)

Media Printing Corp, Pompano Beach, FL. Tel: (954) 984-7300, FAX: (954) 984-7303 (27)

Media Recruiting Group Inc, Irvington, NY. Tel: (914) 591-5511, FAX: (914) 591-8911, E-Mail: resume@mediarecruiting.com, Web Site: www.mediarecruiting.com (20)

Media Resource Group Inc, Mount Kisco, NY. Tel: (914) 244-4250, FAX: (914) 244-4458, Web Site: www.mrginc.com (31)

Media Response Inc, Hollywood, FL. Tel: (954) 967-9899, E-Mail: info@media-response.com, Web Site: www.media-response.com (35)

Media Source Solutions, Pompano Beach, FL. Tel: (954) 788-0213, FAX: (954) 788-0215, Web Site: www.mediasourcesolutions.com (24)

Media Two, Baltimore, MD. Tel: (410) 828-0120, FAX: (410) 825-1002, Web Site: www.mediatwo.com (17)

Mediacom Communications Corp, Chester, NY. Tel: (855) 633-4226, FAX: (845) 698-4100, Web Site: www.mediacomcable.com (32)

MediaConcepts Corp, Assonet, MA. Tel: (508) 644-3131, FAX: (508) 644-5201, E-Mail: at3@mediaconceptscorp.com, Web Site: www.mediaconceptscorp.com (35)

MediaGraphics, Eau Claire, WI. Tel: (751) 590-4488, (866) 324-1658, E-Mail: mediagraphics@devkinney.com, Web Site: www.devkinney.com (35)

Mediamark Research Inc, New York, NY. Tel: (212) 884-9200, (800) 310-3305, FAX: (212) 884-9339, Web Site: www.mediamark.com (30)

Mediaspace Solutions, Hopkins, MN. Tel: (612) 253-3900, (888) 672-2100, FAX: (612) 454-2848, E-Mail: bstcy@mediaspace.com, Web Site: www.mediaspacesolutions.com (31)

MediaTree, Parsippany, NJ. Tel: (973) 781-1070, (800) 475-8703, FAX: (973) 781-1071, E-Mail: sales@mediatreegroup.com, Web Site: www.mediatreegroup.com (27)

MediaWorks Advertising & Marketing Inc, Ormond Beach, FL. Tel: (386) 676-4608, E-Mail: scott@mediaworksusa.com, Web Site: www.mediaworksusa.com (21)

Medibadge Inc, Omaha, NE. Tel: (402) 571-1800, (800) 228-0040, FAX: (800) 546-1072, E-Mail: stan@medibadge.com, Web Site: www.medibadge.com (5)

Medic Alert Foundation, Salida, CA. Tel: (209) 668-3333, (800) 432-5378, FAX: (209) 669-2495, Web Site: www.medicalert.org (1)

Medical Economics Magazine, North Olmsted, OH. Tel: (440) 243-8100, FAX: (440) 891-2735, Web Site: medicaleconomics.modernmedicine.com/about (17)

Medical Letter Inc, New Rochelle, NY. Tel: (914) 235-0500, Web Site: www.medicalletter.org (1)

Medical Marketing Service Inc, Schaumburg, IL. Tel: (630) 350-1717, (800) 633-5478, E-Mail: sales@mmslists.com, Web Site: www.mmslists.com (24)

Medico, Anthony, E+M Advertising Inc, New York, NY. Tel: (212) 981-5900, E-Mail: jtarsitano@emadv.com, Web Site: www.emadv.com (35)

Medico, Michael L., E+M Advertising Inc, New York, NY. Tel: (212) 981-5900, E-Mail: jtarsitano@emadv.com, Web Site: www.emadv.com (35)

Medifast Inc, Owings Mills, MD. Tel: (410) 581-8042, (800) 209-0878, FAX: 410 581-8070, Web Site: www.medifastdiet.com (4)

Medill IMC/Northwestern University, Evanston, IL. Tel: (847) 467-3433 (1)

Medina Associates, Rose Valley, PA. Tel: (610) 565-8836, FAX: (610) 565-8184, E-Mail: kurtmedina@aol.com, Web Site: www.medinaassociates.com (20)

Medina, John, CYRO Industries, Parsippany, NJ. Tel: (973) 541-8000, (800) 631-5384, FAX: (973) 442-6117, (973) 442-6135, Web Site: www.cyro.com (16)

Medina, Kurt, Medina Associates, Rose Valley, PA. Tel: (610) 565-8836, FAX: (610) 565-8184, E-Mail: kurtmedina@aol.com, Web Site: www.medinaassociates.com (20)

Medina, Luis, TechBA - Fumec, San Jose, CA. Tel: (408) 821-6297, Web Site: www.techba.com (1)

Medina, Melody, The Direct Channels Group, New York, NY. Tel: (212) 208-1479, FAX: (631) 514-8716, E-Mail: info@directchannelsgroup.com, Web Site: www.directchannelsgroup.com (35)

Medina-Warren, Billin, Billin Medina-Warren, Scottsdale, AZ. Tel: (972) 951-7291 (20)

Medlin, Connie, Babyshoe.com, Hendersonville, NC. Tel: (828) 697-5811, (800) 543-8566, FAX: (828) 697-5815, E-Mail: info@babyshoe.com, Web Site: www.babyshoe.com (6)

Medtronic, Minneapolis, MN. Tel: (763) 514-4000, (800) 633-8766, Web Site: www.covidien.com (7)

Medtronic Inc, Minneapolis, MN. Tel: (763) 514-4000, (800) 328-2518, FAX: (763) 514-4879, Web Site: www.medtronic.com (16)

Medved, Rob, Cannella Response Television Inc, Burlington, WI. Tel: (262) 763-4810, FAX: (262) 763-2875, Web Site: www.drtv.com (32)

Meehan, Jr. Leo J., WB Mason Co, Brockton, MA. Tel: (800) 773-4488, Web Site: www.wbmason.com (16)

Meeker, Bob, Preferred Communications, Butner, NC. Tel: (919) 575-4600, (877) 589-9800, E-Mail: bob.meeker@satstar.com, Web Site: www.satstar.com (3)

Meeker, Guy, Teraco Inc, Midland, TX. Tel: (888) 837-2261, Web Site: www.teraco.com (27)

Meeks, Matt, GameTime Inc, Fort Payne, AL. Tel: (256) 845-5610, (800) 235-2440, FAX: (256) 845-9361/2649, Web Site: www.gametime.com (11)

Meeks, Stephanie K., National Trust for Historic Preservation, Washington, DC. Tel: (202) 588-6000, (800) 944-6847, E-Mail: info@savingplaces.org, Web Site: www.preservationnation.org (1)

Meell, Susan, MMS Education, Newtown, PA. Tel: (215) 579-8590, (800) 523-5948, FAX: (215) 579-8589, Web Site: www.mmseducation.com (5)

Meemic Insurance Co, Auburn Hills, MI. Tel: (888) 463-3642, Web Site: www.meemic.com (15)

MEGA MEDIA, Reeds Spring, MO. Tel: (405) 623-0023, E-Mail: lisa@mega-media.biz, Web Site: mega-media.biz (32)

Megger, Dallas, TX. Tel: (214) 330-3539, Web Site: www.megger.com (16)

Megna, Jay, Life Fitness, Schiller Park, IL. Tel: (847) 288-3300, (800) 735-3867, FAX: (847) 288-3703, E-Mail: webmaster@lifefitness.com, Web Site: www.lifefitness.com (11)

Megna, Richard, Fundamental Photographs, New York, NY. Tel: (212) 473-5770, FAX: (212) 228-5059, E-Mail: mail@fphoto.com, Web Site: www.fphoto.com (38)

Meguiar, Barry, Meguiar's Inc, Irvine, CA. Tel: (949) 752-8000, (800) 347-5700, FAX: (949) 752-6659, Web Site: www.meguiars.com (16)

Meguiar's Inc, Irvine, CA. Tel: (949) 752-8000, (800) 347-5700, FAX: (949) 752-6659, Web Site: www.meguiars.com (16)

Mehta, Krishna, EXL, Jersey City, NJ. Tel: (201) 748-4729 (16)

Mei, John P, Modern Postcard, Carlsbad, CA. Tel: (800) 959-8365, Web Site: www.modernpostcard.com (10)

Meier, Bob, Nasco, Fort Atkinson, WI. Tel: (920) 563-2446, (800) 558-9595, FAX: (920) 563-8296, E-Mail: info@nasco.com, Web Site: www.enasco.com (5)

Meier, Manuela, Cobblestone Publishing, Peterborough, NH. Tel: (603) 924-7209, (800) 821-0115, FAX: (603) 924-7380, E-Mail: customerservice@caruspub.com, Web Site: www.cobblestonepub.com (17)

Meier, Rich, O'Connell Meier LLC, Alexandria, VA. Tel: (703) 635-2893, (866) 391-1415, FAX: (703) 739-0478, E-Mail: info@omdirect.com, Web Site: www.omdirect.com (21)

Meinen, Mary, Wag/Aero Group, Lyons, WI. Tel: (262) 763-9586, (800) 558-6868, FAX: (262) 763-7595, E-Mail: wagaero-sales@wagaero.com, Web Site: www.wagaero.com (16)

Meinert, Mark, Quality Park Products, Minneapolis, MN. Tel: (800) 828-7323, (800) 547-4252, FAX: (800) 398-9835, E-Mail: mktg@qualitypark.com, Web Site: www.qualitypark.com (26)

Meinhardt, Jim, Hal Leonard Corp, Milwaukee, WI. Tel: (414) 774-3630, FAX: (414) 774-3259, Web Site: www.halleonard.com (17)

Meisel, Eric, Turncraft Clocks Inc, Spring Park, MN. Tel: (952) 471-9573, (800) 544-1711, FAX: (952) 471-8579, E-Mail: office@meiselwoodhobby.com, Web Site: www.meiselwoodhobby.com (6)

Meisel, Greg, Turncraft Clocks Inc, Spring Park, MN. Tel: (952) 471-9573, (800) 544-1711, FAX: (952) 471-8579, E-Mail: office@meiselwoodhobby.com, Web Site: www.meiselwoodhobby.com (6)

Meisel, Paul, Turncraft Clocks Inc, Spring Park, MN. Tel: (952) 471-9573, (800) 544-1711, FAX: (952) 471-8579, E-Mail: office@meiselwoodhobby.com, Web Site: www.meiselwoodhobby.com (6)

Meisner, Thomas, DigitasLBi, Boston, MA. Tel: (617) 867-1000, E-Mail: newbusiness@digitas.com, Web Site: www.digitaslbi.com (23)

Meister Media Worldwide, Willoughby, OH. Tel: (440) 942-2000, (800) 572-7740, FAX: (440) 975-3447, E-Mail: info@meistermedia.com, Web Site: www.meistermedia.com (17)

Meister, Eileen, Sporting Clays Ltd, Titusville, FL. Tel: (321) 268-5010, FAX: (321) 267-7216, E-Mail: sales@sportingclays.net, Web Site: www.sportingclays.net (17)

Meredith, Rick, Premier Direct Marketing Inc, Louisville, KY. Tel: (502) 367-6441, (800) 737-0205, FAX: (502) 361-2961, E-Mail: rmeredith@premierdm.net, Web Site: www.premierdm.net (28)

Mergent Inc, Fort Mill, SC. Tel: (800) 342-5647, Web Site: www.mergent.com (14)

The Merging Technologies Group LLC, Hauppauge, NY. Tel: (631) 435-2955, FAX: (631) 952-0664, E-Mail: info@mt-group.com, Web Site: www.mt-group.com (22)

Mergner, Lee, JazzTimes Magazine Inc, Quincy, MA. Tel: (617) 706-9110, FAX: (617) 536-0102, E-Mail: info@jazztimes.com, Web Site: www.jazztimes.com (17)

Merisel, New York, NY. Tel: (212) 594-4800, FAX: (212) 594-4488, E-Mail: corp@merisel.com, Web Site: www.merisel.com (16)

MeritDirect, Rye Brook, NY. Tel: (914) 368-1000, FAX: (914) 368-1150, E-Mail: hq@meritdirect.com, Web Site: www.meritdirect.com (23)

Merkel-Sobotta, Eric, Springer Science & Business Media LLC, New York, NY. Tel: (212) 460-1500, FAX: (212) 460-1575, Web Site: www.springer.com (17)

Merkle Inc, Columbia, MD. Tel: (443) 542-4000, (877) 9MERKLE, FAX: (443) 542-4758, Web Site: www.merkleinc.com (22)

Merkur, Lawrence, Winslow Publishing, Toronto, ON Canada. Tel: (416) 789-4733, E-Mail: winslow@interlog.com, Web Site: www.winslowpublishing.com (17)

Merlo, Larry J., CVS Caremark, Woonsocket, RI. Tel: (401) 765-1500, FAX: (401) 769-4488, Web Site: www.cvs.com (2)

Meros, Meghan, Franciscan Mission Associates, Mount Vernon, NY. Tel: (914) 664-5604, FAX: (914) 664-3017, E-Mail: admin@franciscanmissionassoc.org, Web Site: www.franciscanmissionassoc.org (1)

Merrell Remington & Associates, Salt Lake City, UT. Tel: (801) 975-0109, FAX: (801) 975-0107, E-Mail: kent@mrdirect.com, Web Site: www.merrellremington.com (35)

Merrell, A. Kent, Merrell Remington & Associates, Salt Lake City, UT. Tel: (801) 975-0109, FAX: (801) 975-0107, E-Mail: kent@mrdirect.com, Web Site: www.merrellremington.com (35)

Merriam, Lloyd, Colinear Systems, Alpharetta, GA. Tel: (770) 643-0000, (800) COLINEAR, FAX: (770) 643-0265, E-Mail: sales@colinear.com, Web Site: www.colinear.com (22)

Merrick Bank, South Jordan, UT. Tel: (801) 545-6647, Web Site: www.merrickbank.com (14)

Merrick, Phillip, Message Systems, Columbia, MD. Tel: (410) 872-4910, (877) 887-3031, FAX: (410) 872-4912, E-Mail: information@messagesystems.com, Web Site: www.messagesystems.com (32)

Merrifield, Robin, Foundation for Chiropractic Education & Research, Norwalk, IA. Tel: (515) 981-9888 (1)

Merril, Richard, Golden Rule Insurance Co, Indianapolis, IN. Tel: (317) 297-4123, FAX: (317) 297-0908, Web Site: www.goldenrule.com (15)

Merrill Corp, Saint Cloud, MN. Tel: (320) 656-5000, FAX: (320) 656-5163 (18)

Merrill Lynch International Inc, New York, NY. Tel: (212) 449-1000, (800) 637-7455, FAX: (212) 449-9418, Web Site: www.ml.com (14)

Merrill, April, ProSource, Houston, TX. Tel: (713) 667-3690, FAX: (713) 660-9629, Web Site: www.prosourcedev.com (20)

Merrill, Brian, Western River Expeditions, Salt Lake City, UT. Tel: (801) 942-6669, (866) 904-1160, FAX: (801) 942-8514, Web Site: www.westernriver.com (19)

Merrill, Lee Ann, Spalding Laboratories Inc, Reno, NV. Tel: (888) 562-5696, (888) 880-1579, FAX: (866) 738-9632, Web Site: www.spalding-labs.com (7)

Merrill, Rick, Promotional Products Association International, Irving, TX. Tel: (972) 252-0404, FAX: (972) 258-3004, (800) I-AM-PPAI, E-Mail: membership@ppa.org, Web Site: www.ppa.org (40)

Merrimack College, North Andover, MA. Tel: (978) 837-5000, E-Mail: denise.tuccelli@merrimack.edu, Web Site: www.merrimack.edu (41)

Merrimade Stationery Co LLC, Chelmsford, MA. Tel: (800) 344-4256, FAX: (800) 883-6515, E-Mail: custserv@merrimadestationery.com, Web Site: www.merrimade.com (10)

Merritt, Chuck, White Post Media Group, Nashville, TN. Tel: (615) 469-4409, Web Site: whitepostmedia.com (35)

Merritt, Mark, Pharmaceutical Care Management Association, Washington, DC. Tel: (202) 756-7210, FAX: (202) 207-3623, E-Mail: info@pcmanet.org, Web Site: www.pcmanet.org (1)

Merryman, James, Oregon Freeze Dry Inc, Albany, OR. Tel: (541) 926-6001, FAX: (541) 967-6527, Web Site: www.ofd.com (4)

Mersco Medical, Pierre, SD. Tel: (605) 224-6687, (800) 234-1881, FAX: (605) 322-1801 (16)

Jim Mersfelder & Associates Inc, Cleveland, OH. Tel: (216) 574-9009, (800) 431-1101, FAX: (216) 574-9721, Web Site: www.jmapromotions.com (33)

Mershad, Richard M., Micro Center, Hilliard, OH. Tel: (614) 850-3675, (800) 634-3478, FAX: (614) 777-2620, E-Mail: csrs@microcenterorder.com, Web Site: www.microcenter.com (3)

Merti, Betty, Walch Publishing, Portland, ME. Tel: (207) 772-2846, (800) 558-2846, FAX: (207) 772-3105, E-Mail: customerservice@walch.com, Web Site: www.walch.com (17)

Mertz, Howard W., Relationship1, Pearl River, NY. Tel: (845) 732-8300, E-Mail: inforequest@relationship1.com, Web Site: www.relationship1.com (21)

Mertz, Tom, TradeNet Publishing Inc, Gardner, KS. Tel: (800) 884-7301, Web Site: www.tradenetonline.com (35)

Mertzel, Kenneth, Balboa Life & Casualty, Irvine, CA. Tel: (949) 222-8000, (800) 854-6115, FAX: (949) 222-8777, Web Site: www.balboainsurance.com (15)

Merz, Stefan E., Diebold Inc, North Canton, OH. Tel: (330) 490-4000, (800) DIEBOLD, Web Site: www.diebold.com (16)

Mesher, Page, Off the Wall Magnetics LLC, Portland, OR. Tel: (800) 337-2637, Web Site: www.4thefridge.com (16)

Message Systems, Columbia, MD. Tel: (410) 872-4910, (877) 887-3031, FAX: (410) 872-4912, E-Mail: information@messagesystems.com, Web Site: www.messagesystems.com (32)

Message Technologies Inc, Atlanta, GA. Tel: (770) 240-8000, (800) 868-3684, FAX: (770) 240-7474, E-Mail: info@messagetech.com, Web Site: www.messagetech.com (30)

Messelt, Jen, Bushnell Outdoor Products, Overland Park, KS. Tel: (913) 752-3400, (800) 423-3537, FAX: (913) 752-3550, Web Site: www.bushnell.com (16)

Messenger, Ed, Spectrum Data, Oregon, IL. Tel: (815) 732-6567, FAX: (815) 732-7035 (22)

Messenger, Michael, World Vision Canada, Mississauga, ON Canada. Tel: (905) 565-6100, (866) 595-5550, FAX: (866) 219-8620, Web Site: www.worldvision.ca (1)

Messer, Heidi, Collective[i], New York, NY. Tel: (888) 890-0020, Web Site: www.collectivei.com (35)

Messer, Jerry, Data Services Inc, Salisbury, MD. Tel: (410) 546-2206, (800) 432-4066, FAX: (410) 546-2274, Web Site: www.dataservicesinc.com (22)

Messer, Stephen, Collective[i], New York, NY. Tel: (888) 890-0020, Web Site: www.collectivei.com (35)

Messier, Earle Thomas, Southern Flavoring Co Inc, Bedford, VA. Tel: (540) 586-8565, (800) 765-8565, FAX: (540) 586-8568, E-Mail: tom@southernflavoring.com, Web Site: www.southernflavoring.com (16)

Messier, John P., Southern Flavoring Co Inc, Bedford, VA. Tel: (540) 586-8565, (800) 765-8565, FAX: (540) 586-8568, E-Mail: tom@southernflavoring.com, Web Site: www.southernflavoring.com (16)

Messina, Lori, Access Direct Systems Inc, Farmingdale, NY. Tel: (631) 420-0700, Web Site: www.accessdirect.com (28)

Messinger, William, Hillside Wire Cloth Co, Belleville, NJ. Tel: (973) 751-3131, (800) 826-7395, FAX: (973) 470-8183, E-Mail: info@hillsidewirecloth.com, Web Site: www.hillsidewirecloth.com (9)

Messmer, Jr Harold M., Robert Half International Inc, Menlo Park, CA. Tel: (650) 234-6000, FAX: (650) 234-6930, E-Mail: webmaster@rhi.com, Web Site: www.rhii.com (20)

Messmer, Jr. Harold M., Accountemps, Menlo Park, CA. Tel: (650) 234-6000, (800) 803-8367, FAX: (650) 234-6998, Web Site: www.accountemps.com (16)

Messner, Joe, Bushnell Outdoor Products, Overland Park, KS. Tel: (913) 752-3400, (800) 423-3537, FAX: (913) 752-3550, Web Site: www.bushnell.com (16)

Mestas, Richard, Datahouse Inc, Colorado Springs, CO. Tel: (866) 640-3282, E-Mail: data@datahouseinc.com, Web Site: www.datahouseinc.com (23)

The Metal Ware Corp, Two Rivers, WI. Tel: (920) 793-1368, (800) 288-4545, FAX: (920) 794-3161, Web Site: www.nesco.com (32)

MetaResponse Group Inc, Deerfield Beach, FL. Tel: (954) 360-0644, FAX: (954) 360-7712, E-Mail: info@metaresponse.com, Web Site: www.metaresponse.com (23)

Metcalf, James S., USG Corp, Chicago, IL. Tel: (312) 436-4000, (800) 621-9622, FAX: (312) 672-4093, Web Site: www.usg.com (34)

Metcalf, Paul, Burlington Coat Factory, Burlington, NJ. Tel: (609) 387-7800, FAX: (609) 387-7071, Web Site: www.burlingtoncoatfactory.com (16)

Metcalfe, Mark, Overton's Inc, Greenville, NC. Tel: (252) 355-5783, (800) 334-6541, FAX: (252) 355-2923, E-Mail: service@overtons.com, Web Site: www.overtons.com (11)

Metcalfe, Susan, Dr Leonard's Healthcare Corp, Edison, NJ. Tel: (732) 225-0100, (800) 455-1918, FAX: (732) 225-0302, Web Site: www.doctorleonard.com (7)

Methode Electronics Inc, Chicago, IL. Tel: (708) 867-6777, FAX: (708) 867-6999, E-Mail: info@methode.com, Web Site: www.methode.com (9)

MetLife International, Long Island City, NY. Tel: (212) 578-3128 (15)

Metro Speedgear, Livingston, NJ. Tel: (973) 251-2814, (800) 777-4453, FAX: (908) 286-0002, E-Mail: info@speedgear.com, Web Site: www.speedgear.com (11)

Metropolis Magazine, New York, NY. Tel: (212) 627-9977, (800) 334-3046, FAX: (212) 627-9988, E-Mail: edit@metropolismag.com, Web Site: www.metropolismag.com (2)

Metropolitan Graphic Arts, Mundelein, IL. Tel: (847) 566-9502, (800) 755-5936, FAX: (847) 566-9584, E-Mail: gregs@mgaprinting.com, Web Site: www.mgaprinting.com (27)

Metropolitan Museum of Art, New York, NY. Tel: (212) 570-3894, (800) 468-7386, FAX: (718) 628-5485, Web Site: www.metmuseum.org/store (8)

Metropolitan Newspaper Advertising Services Inc, Yonkers, NY. Tel: (212) 689-8200, FAX: (212) 779-9795, E-Mail: info@metrosn.com, Web Site: www.metrosn.com (31)

The Metropolitan Opera, New York, NY. Tel: (212) 362-6000, (212) 799-3100, FAX: (212) 870-7695, Web Site: www.metoperafamily.org (1)

Metropolitan Property & Casualty Ins, Warwick, RI. Tel: (401) 827-2104 (15)

Metropolitan Window Fashions at Fabricland, North Plainfield, NJ. Tel: (908) 755-4700, (877) 722-1100, FAX: (908) 755-6368 (8)

Metscher, Jim, Blair Corp, Warren, PA. Tel: (814) 723-3600, (800) 458-6057, FAX: (814) 726-6123, E-Mail: blair@blair.com, Web Site: www.blair.com (2)

Metso Minerals/WS Tyler, Waukesha, WI. Tel: (803) 699-4200, (262) 717-2500, FAX: (262) 717-2501, E-Mail: minerals.info.csr@metso.com, Web Site: www.metsominerals.com (16)

Metz, Don, Health Affairs, Bethesda, MD. Tel: (301) 656-7401, FAX: (301) 654-2845, Web Site: www.healthaffairs.org (17)

Metzger, Dave, Pacific Botanicals LLC, Grants Pass, OR. Tel: (541) 479-7777, FAX: (541) 479-7780, E-Mail: pacbot1@earthlink.net, Web Site: www.pacificbotanicals.com (7)

Metzler, Paul, The Professional Golfers' Association of America, Palm Beach Gardens, FL. Tel: (561) 624-8400, Web Site: www.pga.com (1)

Metzner, Raymond, KV Vet Supply Co, Inc, David City, NE. Tel: (402) 367-6047, Web Site: www.kvvet.com (5)

Meudt, Mark, West Corp, Omaha, NE. Tel: (800) 841-9000, FAX: (402) 963-1602, E-Mail: sales@west.com, Web Site: www.west.com (20)

Meyer Associates Teleservices, Saint Cloud, MN. Tel: (320) 259-4000, (800) 676-9233, FAX: (320) 259-4044, E-Mail: info@callmeyer.com, Web Site: www.callmeyer.com (29)

Fred Meyer Jewelers Inc, Portland, OR. Tel: (503) 232-8844, (800) 457-5977, FAX: (503) 797-7616, Web Site: www.fredmeyerjewelers.com (1)

Meyer Fulfillment, Stratford, CT. Tel: (203) 375-5801, (800) 873-6393, E-Mail: vdarish@meyerfulfillment.com, Web Site: www.meyerfulfillment.com (28)

Joyce Meyer Ministries, Fenton, MO. Tel: (636) 349-0303, Web Site: www.joycemeyer.org (1)

Meyer Partners, Schaumburg, IL. Tel: (630) 339-3930, (800) 676-4176, FAX: (630) 339-3939, E-Mail: info@meyerpartners.com, Web Site: www.meyerpartners.com (1)

Meyer, Bill, Adpress Inc, New York, NY. Tel: (212) 679-1710, FAX: (212) 532-9508, E-Mail: adpressinc@aol.com, Web Site: www.adpressinc.com (23)

Meyer, Bill, UAA Clearinghouse, Omaha, NE. Tel: (402) 991-2810, Web Site: www.uaaclearinghouse.com (22)

Meyer, Chris, Consumers Union, Yonkers, NY. Tel: (914) 378-2000, FAX: (914) 378-2906, Web Site: www.consumersunion.org (17)

Meyer, David, Dairy Farmers of America Inc, Kansas City, MO. Tel: (816) 801-6455, (888) 332-6455, FAX: (816) 801-6456, E-Mail: webmail@dfamilk.com, Web Site: www.dfamilk.com (16)

Meyer, Dennis L., Meyer Partners, Schaumburg, IL. Tel: (630) 339-3930, (800) 676-4176, FAX: (630) 339-3939, E-Mail: info@meyerpartners.com, Web Site: www.meyerpartners.com (1)

Meyer, Dr. Stan, Grand Canyon University, Phoenix, AZ. Tel: (602) 639-7500, (877) 860-3951, Web Site: www.gcu.edu (13)

Meyer, Gordon, eBureau LLC, Saint Cloud, MN. Tel: (320) 534-5000, FAX: (320) 534-5020, Web Site: www.ebureau.com (22)

Meyer, James E., SiriusXM Radio Inc, New York, NY. Tel: (212) 584-5100, Web Site: www.siriusxm.com (16)

Meyer, Jeff, Parker Steel Co, Toledo, OH. Tel: (419) 473-2481, (800) 333-4140, FAX: (419) 471-2655, Web Site: www.metricmetal.com (16)

Meyer, John, Angler's Catalog Co, Eagle, ID. Tel: (208) 378-9536, (800) 657-8040, FAX: (208) 735-8758, E-Mail: sales@anglers-catalog.com, Web Site: www.anglers-catalog.com (11)

Meyer, John, The B&F System Inc, Dallas, TX. Tel: (214) 333-2111, FAX: (214) 333-2137, Web Site: www.maxam.com (33)

Meyer, Kirk, Stonwurks, Eden Prairie, MN. Tel: (785) 526-7847, (888) 884-7881, FAX: (785) 526-7841, E-Mail: stonwurks@stonwurks.com, Web Site: www.stonwurks.com (16)

Meyer, Lawrence R, Meyer Associates Teleservices, Saint Cloud, MN. Tel: (320) 259-4000, (800) 676-9233, FAX: (320) 259-4044, E-Mail: info@callmeyer.com, Web Site: www.callmeyer.com (29)

Meyer, Marcia, BarterNews, Laguna Niguel, CA. Tel: (949) 831-0607, FAX: (949) 831-9378, E-Mail: bmeyer@barternews.com, Web Site: www.barternews.com (17)

Meyer, Mark, Domino Amjet Inc, Gurnee, IL. Tel: (847) 244-2501. FAX: (847) 244-1421, Web Site: www.dominoamjet.com (27)

Meyer, Robert B., BarterNews, Laguna Niguel, CA. Tel: (949) 831-0607, FAX: (949) 831-9378, E-Mail: bmeyer@barternews.com, Web Site: www.barternews.com (17)

Meyer, Robert, Journal of Marketing Research, Chicago, IL. Tel: (312) 542-9000, (800) AMA-1150, FAX: (312) 542-9001, E-Mail: info@ama.org, Web Site: www.marketingpower.org (43)

Meyer, Stephen F, Welch Allyn, Inc, Skaneateles Falls, NY. Tel: (315) 685-4100. Web Site: www.welchallyn.com (9)

Meyering, Kelly, The Blue Book Building & Construction Network, Jefferson Valley, NY. Tel: (800) 431-2584, FAX: (914) 243-0287, E-Mail: info@thebluebook.com, Web Site: www.thebluebook.com (17)

Meyerle, Susan, American Counseling Association, Broken Arrow, OK. Tel: (918) 994-4413, FAX: (918) 663-7058, E-Mail: webmaster@counseling.org, Web Site: www.counseling.org (1)

Meyers, David G., Native American Heritage Association, Black Hawk, SD. Tel: (605) 341-9110, FAX: (605) 341-91413, E-Mail: info@naha-inc.org, Web Site: www.naha-inc.org (1)

Meyers, Edwin W., Cadie Products Corp, Paterson, NJ. Tel: (973) 278-8300, FAX: (973) 278-0303, E-Mail: emeyers@cadie.com, Web Site: www.cadieproducts.com (16)

Meyers, Jr. George S., Diebold Inc, North Canton, OH. Tel: (330) 490-4000, (800) DIEBOLD, Web Site: www.diebold.com (16)

Meyers, Kenneth, Cadie Products Corp, Paterson, NJ. Tel: (973) 278-8300, FAX: (973) 278-0303, E-Mail: emeyers@cadie.com, Web Site: www.cadieproducts.com (16)

Meyers, Kenneth R., US Cellular, Chicago, IL. Tel: (888) 944-9400, Web Site: www.uscellular.com (32)

Meyers, Rich, Vitamin Specialties Co, Freehold, NJ. Tel: (732) 308-3000, FAX: (855) 482-3291, Web Site: www.ivcinc.com (7)

Meylan Corp, Montclair, NJ. Tel: (973) 744-6400, (888) 769-9667, FAX: (973) 744-1011, E-Mail: meylan1@aol.com, Web Site: www.meylan.com/home.html (9)

Meyn, Betty, BMI Home Decorating, Spring Grove, IL. Tel: (815) 675-3703, FAX: (815) 675-3703, E-Mail: bmigroup@aol.com (16)

Meyn, George, BMI Home Decorating, Spring Grove, IL. Tel: (815) 675-3703, FAX: (815) 675-3703, E-Mail: bmigroup@aol.com (16)

Meyocks, West Des Moines, IA. Tel: (515) 225-1200, FAX: (515) 225-6400, E-Mail: meanmore@meyocks.com, Web Site: www.meyocks.com (35)

Meza, Fernando, Oneupweb, Traverse City, MI. Tel: (231) 922-9977, (877) 568-7477, E-Mail: info@oneupweb.com, Web Site: www.oneupweb.com (35)

Jim M'Guinness Design, Los Altos, CA. Tel: (650) 967-3811 (36)

The Miami Herald Media Co, Miami, FL. Tel: (305) 350-2111 (17)

Miami Valley Marketing Group Inc, Dayton, OH. Tel: (937) 299-1825, FAX: (937) 299-9967, E-Mail: tomnorwalk@aol.com (35)

Micca, Father Louis, Pallottine Center for Apostolic Causes Inc/St Jude Shrine, Baltimore, MD. Tel: (410) 685-6026, (877) 278-5833, FAX: (410) 234-1459, E-Mail: info@stjudeshrine.org, Web Site: www.stjudeshrine.org (1)

Michael, Julie, Team One Advertising, Los Angeles, CA. Tel: (310) 437-2500, Web Site: www.teamone-usa.com (35)

Michael's, Irving, TX. Tel: (972) 409-1300, FAX: (972) 409-1551, Web Site: www.michaels.com (11)

John Michaels Associates Inc, Newington, CT. Tel: (860) 666-1414, (800) 499-2606, FAX: (860) 666-1515, E-Mail: info@jmalogos.com, Web Site: www.jmalogos.com (33)

Michaelson, Michael, Rainwater Associates Inc, New York, NY. Tel: (212) 861-2856, FAX: (212) 861-1729, E-Mail: rainwine@aol.com (20)

Michalski, Jim, Edmund Optics Inc, Barrington, NJ. Tel: (856) 573-6250, (800) 363-1992, FAX: (856) 573-6295, E-Mail: sales@edmundoptic.com, Web Site: www.edmundoptics.com (9)

Michaud, Jay, Brown & Jenkins Trading Co, Jeffersonville, VT. Tel: (802) 644-8300, (800) 456-JAVA, Web Site: www.brownjenkins.com (4)

Michaud, Joe, Blethen Maine Newspapers Inc, Portland, ME. Tel: (207) 791-6650, FAX: (207) 791-6925, Web Site: www.mainetoday.com (17)

Michaud, Lynn, Troy Biologicals Inc, Troy, MI. Tel: (248) 585-9720, (800) 521-0445, FAX: (248) 585-2490, E-Mail: info@troybio.com, Web Site: www.troybio.com (7)

Michaud, Maria, TD Bank NA, Falmouth, ME. Tel: (207) 770-2196, Web Site: www.tdbanknorth.com (14)

Michel Consulting, Bend, OR. Tel: (541) 633-7838 (20)

Michel, Bill, Michel Consulting, Bend, OR. Tel: (541) 633-7838 (20)

Michel, Lane, Quaero Corp, Charlotte, NC. Tel: (704) 414-0200, FAX: (704) 414-2195, Web Site: www.quaero.com (22)

Michels, Bart, Cheskin, Redwood Shores, CA. Tel: (650) 802-2100, FAX: (650) 593-1125, E-Mail: info@cheskin.com, Web Site: www.cheskin.com (30)

Michelson, Jaime, SMZ Advertising, Troy, MI. Tel: (248) 362-4242, FAX: (248) 362-2014, E-Mail: info@smz.com, Web Site: www.smz.com (35)

Michelson, James A., SMZ Advertising, Troy, MI. Tel: (248) 362-4242, FAX: (248) 362-2014, E-Mail: info@smz.com, Web Site: www.smz.com (35)

Michigan Apple Committee, Lansing, MI. Tel: (517) 669-8353, (800) 456-2753, FAX: (517) 669-9506, E-Mail: staff@michiganapples.com, Web Site: www.michiganapples.com (1)

Mickey, Bill, Audience Development, Norwalk, CT. Tel: (203) 854-6730, FAX: (203) 854-6735, E-Mail: inolan@red7media.com, Web Site: www.audiencedevelopment.com (43)

Mickwee Group Inc, Newark, CA. Tel: (510) 651-6522, FAX: (510) 770-9682, E-Mail: info@generatemarketing.com, Web Site: www.generatemarketing.com (16)

Mickwee, Ann, Mickwee Group Inc, Newark, CA. Tel: (510) 651-6522, FAX: (510) 770-9682, E-Mail: info@generatemarketing.com, Web Site: www.generatemarketing.com (16)

Mickwee, Ron, Mickwee Group Inc, Newark, CA. Tel: (510) 651-6522, FAX: (510) 770-9682, E-Mail: info@generatemarketing.com, Web Site: www.generatemarketing.com (16)

Micro Center, Hilliard, OH. Tel: (614) 850-3675, (800) 634-3478, FAX: (614) 777-2620, E-Mail: csrs@microcenterorder.com, Web Site: www.microcenter.com (3)

Micro Plastics Inc, Flippin, AR. Tel: (870) 453-2261, (800) 466-1467, FAX: (870) 453-8676, E-Mail: mpsales@microplastics.com, Web Site: www.microplastics.com (16)

Microbiz Corp, Menlo Park, CA. Tel: (702) 749-5353, (800) 726-3282, FAX: (650) 440-4870, E-Mail: info@microbiz.com, Web Site: www.microbiz.com (3)

Microfluidics Corp, Westwood, MA. Tel: (617) 969-5452, (800) 370-5452, FAX: (617) 965-1213, E-Mail: info@mfics.com, Web Site: www.microfluidicscorp.com (16)

Micron Corp, Norwood, MA. Tel: (781) 769-5771, (800) 456-0734, FAX: (781) 762-3531, E-Mail: info@microncorp.com, Web Site: www.microncorp.com (16)

Microsoft Corp, Redmond, WA. Tel: (425) 882-8080, FAX: (425) 936-8000, Web Site: www.microsoft.com/msft (22)

Mid America Designs Inc, Effingham, IL. Tel: (217) 540-4200, (800) 350-4543, FAX: (217) 540-4800, E-Mail: mail@mamotorworks.com, Web Site: www.mamotorworks.com (12)

Mid America Direct Marketing Association, Omaha, NE. Tel: (402) 965-4318, FAX: (402) 964-8484, Web Site: www.madma.org (40)

Mid America Motorworks, Effingham, IL. Tel: (217) 347-5591, (800) 500-1500, FAX: (217) 347-2952, E-Mail: mail@mamotorworks.com, Web Site: www.mamotorworks.com (12)

Mid-Central Printing & Mailing Inc, Wilmette, IL. Tel: (847) 251-4040, FAX: (847) 251-8615, E-Mail: mcpm1910@yahoo.com, Web Site: www.mcpm.com (28)

Mid West Floor Co Inc, Saint Louis, MO. Tel: (314) 647-6060, FAX: (314) 647-9189, E-Mail: sales@mid-westfloor.com, Web Site: www.mid-westfloor.com (16)

Midco Call Center Services, Sioux Falls, SD. Tel: (605) 330-4125, (800) 843-8800, FAX: (605) 357-5414, Web Site: www.midcocall.com (29)

Midcontinent Financial Center Inc, Columbia, MO. Tel: (573) 443-6002, Web Site: www.americanmutualloans.com (14)

Middendorf, Sandra, Augsburg Fortress Publishers, Minneapolis, MN. Tel: (612) 330-3300, (800) 426-0115, FAX: (612) 330-3455, E-Mail: info@augsburgfortress.org, Web Site: www.augsburgfortress.org (17)

The Middleby Corp, Elgin, IL. Tel: (847) 741-3300, FAX: (847) 741-0015, E-Mail: sales@middleby.com, Web Site: www.middleby.com (16)

Middleton, Kevin, FirstGroup America, Cincinnati, OH. Tel: (513) 241-2200, FAX: (513) 419-3242, Web Site: www.firstgroup.com/north_america (12)

The Midland Co, Amelia, OH. Tel: (513) 943-7200 (15)

Midland Marketing Group, Saint Joseph, MO. Tel: (816) 261-9007, FAX: (816) 233-0859, E-Mail: info@midlandmarketinggroup.com, Web Site: www.midlandmarketinggroup.com (16)

Midland Paper, Wheeling, IL. Tel: (847) 777-2700, (800) 323-8522, FAX: (847) 777-2552, E-Mail: whl@midlandpaper.com, Web Site: www.midlandpaper.com (25)

Midolo, John, Viahealth, Rochester, NY. Tel: (585) 922-4000, (585) 922-3677, FAX: (585) 922-3929, Web Site: www.viahealth.org (16)

Midpoint National Inc, Kansas City, KS. Tel: (913) 362-7400, (800) 228-4321, FAX: (913) 362-7401, E-Mail: info@midpt.com, Web Site: www.midpointorderfulfillment.com (28)

Midwest Center for Stress & Anxiety Inc, Oak Harbor, OH. Tel: (419) 898-4357, (877) 989-8229, FAX: (419) 898-0669, Web Site: www.stresscenter.com (7)

Midwest Direct Marketing Association Inc, Saint Paul, MN. Tel: (651) 999-5351, FAX: (651) 917-1835, E-Mail: mdma@mdma.org, Web Site: www.mdma.org (40)

Midwest Direct Marketing Inc, Spring Hill, KS. Tel: (913) 686-2220, FAX: (913) 686-2320, E-Mail: info@midwestdm.com, Web Site: www.midwestdm.com (23)

Midwest Lists & Media Ltd, Niles, IL. Tel: (847) 966-2770, FAX: (847) 966-8630, Web Site: www.thebradfordgroup.com (23)

Midwest Publishing Inc, Phoenix, AZ. Tel: (602) 943-1244, FAX: (602) 331-0702 (17)

Midwest Technology Products & Services, Sioux City, IA. Tel: (712) 252-3601, (800) 831-5904, FAX: (800) 258-7054, E-Mail: web@midwesttechnology.com, Web Site: www.midwesttechnology.com (9)

Mielke, Thomas J., Kimberly-Clark Corp, Neenah, WI. Tel: (920) 721-2000, (888) 525-8388, FAX: (920) 721-7722, Web Site: www.kimberly-clark.com (16)

Miers, Charles, Rizzoli International Publications Inc, New York, NY. Tel: (212) 387-3400, FAX: (212) 387-3535 (17)

Miglautsch Marketing Inc, Hartland, WI. Tel: (262) 369-3900, FAX: (262) 369-3915, E-Mail: info@migmar.com, Web Site: www.migmar.com (20)

Miglautsch, John, Miglautsch Marketing Inc, Hartland, WI. Tel: (262) 369-3900, FAX: (262) 369-3915, E-Mail: info@migmar.com, Web Site: www.migmar.com (20)

Miglino, Chris, Social Reality Inc, Los Angeles, CA. Tel: (323) 694-9800, Web Site: www.socialreality.com (35)

Mihalek, Ron, Zimmerman Irrigation Inc, Biglerville, PA. Tel: (717) 337-2727, (800) 452-5699, FAX: (717) 337-1785, E-Mail: info@trikl-eez.com, Web Site: www.trickl-eez.com (16)

Mihalko, Kristin, School of Business Administration, Portland, OR. Tel: (503) 725-3712, FAX: (503) 725-5850, E-Mail: info@sba.pdx.edu, Web Site: www.sba.pdx.edu (41)

Mikells, Kathryn, Xerox Corp, Norwalk, CT. Tel: (800) 275-9376, Web Site: www.xerox.com (16)

Mikhael, Kamel, Padulo Integrated, Toronto, ON Canada. Tel: (416) 966-4000, (800) 454-5321, FAX: (416) 966-4012, E-Mail: info@padulo.ca, Web Site: www.padulo.ca (35)

Miklosko, L. A., CTRAC Information Solutions, Strongsville, OH. Tel: (440) 572-1000, FAX: (440) 572-3330, E-Mail: ctrac@ctrac.com, Web Site: www.ctrac.com (22)

Mikola, Gary, Society of Manufacturing Engineers, Dearborn, MI. Tel: (313) 425-3000, (800) 733-4763, FAX: (313) 425-3400, E-Mail: communications@sme.org, Web Site: www.sme.org (1)

Mikos, Wayne, Courage Cards & Gifts, Golden Valley, MN. Tel: (800) 992-6872, Web Site: www.couragecards.org (1)

Milanesi, Perry, Enco Manufacturing Co, Fernley, NV. Tel: (775) 788-7175, (800) 873-3626, FAX: (800) 965-5857, E-Mail: milanesp@use-enco.com, Web Site: www.use-enco.com (9)

Milano, Denise, Veriad, Brea, CA. Tel: (714) 990-2700, (800) 962-0658, FAX: (800) 962-0658, E-Mail: info@veriad.com, Web Site: www.veriad.com (16)

Milberg, Fran, FJ Associates LLC, Wilmington, NC. Tel: (910) 452-2643, FAX: (630) 982-1056 (23)

Milberg, Jeffrey A., Milberg Penn International, Mount Kisco, NY. Tel: (914) 239-4300, (914) 241-0858, E-Mail: contact@mpioutsourcing.com, Web Site: www.mpioutsourcing.com (29)

Milberg, Jeffrey, FJ Associates LLC, Wilmington, NC. Tel: (910) 452-2643, FAX: (630) 982-1056 (23)

Miles, Carolyn, Save the Children Federation Inc, Fairfield, CT. Tel: (203) 221-4000, (800) 728-3843, FAX: (203) 222-1067, E-Mail: majorgivng@savethechildren.org, Web Site: www.savethechildren.org (1)

Miles, Gary, Detroit Newspapers, Detroit, MI. Tel: (313) 222-2300, FAX: (313) 496-5400, E-Mail: newsroom@detnews.com, Web Site: www.freep.com (18)

Miles, Jay, MacLaren McCann, Toronto, ON Canada. Tel: (416) 594-6000, FAX: (416) 643-7026, Web Site: www.maclaren.com (35)

Military Direct Marketing Inc, Poughkeepsie, NY. Tel: (845) 454-7900, FAX: (845) 454-7987, E-Mail: info@militarymedia.com (31)

Military Officers Association of America, Alexandria, VA. Tel: (703) 549-2311, (800) 234-6622, E-Mail: msc@moaa.org, Web Site: www.moaa.org (1)

Military Order of the Purple Heart Svc, Annandale, VA. Tel: (703) 256-6139 (1)

The Millard Group, Lincolnwood, IL. Tel: (847) 674-4100, (800) 339-6876, FAX: (847) 677-0790, E-Mail: sales@millardgroup.com, Web Site: www.millardgroup.com (16)

Millard, Steve, COSE, Cleveland, OH. Tel: (216) 592-2222, (866) 553-5427, E-Mail: memberservices@cose.org, Web Site: www.cose.org (1)

Millcraft of Michigan, Livonia, MI. Tel: (734) 266-3710, (800) 482-0556, FAX: (734) 266-3705, Web Site: www.millcraft.com (25)

Adrian Miller Direct Marketing, Port Washington, NY. Tel: (516) 767-9288, E-Mail: amiller@adrianmiller.com, Web Site: www.adrianmiller.com (20)

Miller Advertising Inc, Edison, NJ. Tel: (732) 494-5611, FAX: (732) 494-6075 (36)

Miller Direct Inc, Fort Mill, SC. Tel: (803) 548-6900, FAX: (803) 548-8701 (31)

The Miller Group, Los Angeles, CA. Tel: (310) 442-0101, FAX: (310) 442-0107, E-Mail: info@millergroupmarketing.com, Web Site: www.millergroupmarketing.com (35)

The Miller Group, Dupo, IL. Tel: (800) 325-3350, FAX: (618) 286-6202, E-Mail: info@miller-group.com, Web Site: www.multiplexdisplays.com (5)

Miller Rollman, Jane, Development Dimensions International, Bridgeville, PA. Tel: (412) 257-0600, (800) 933-4463, FAX: (412) 220-2942, E-Mail: info@ddiworld.com, Web Site: www.ddiworld.com (16)

Miller Stockman, Denver, CO. Tel: (303) 428-5696, FAX: (303) 430-1130 (2)

Miller, Adam, O'Currance Inc, Draper, UT. Tel: (801) 736-0500, (888) 628-7726, FAX: (801) 736-0510, E-Mail: sales@ocurrance.com, Web Site: www.ocurance.com (18)

Miller, Adrian, Adrian Miller Direct Marketing, Port Washington, NY. Tel: (516) 767-9288, E-Mail: amiller@adrianmiller.com, Web Site: www.adrianmiller.com (20)

Miller, Alex R., Svoboda Collins LLC, Chicago, IL. Tel: (312) 267-8750, FAX: (312) 267-6025, E-Mail: info@svoco.com, Web Site: www.svoco.com (5)

Miller, Anne, Peter Pan Bus Lines Inc, Springfield, MA. Tel: (413) 781-3320, (800) 343-9999, FAX: (413) 747-7626, E-Mail: info@peterpanbus.com, Web Site: www.peterpanbus.com (19)

Miller, Bill, Eagle Claw Fishing Tackle, Denver, CO. Tel: (720) 941-8700, FAX: (303) 321-4750, E-Mail: info@eagleclaw.com, Web Site: www.eagleclaw.com (11)

Miller, Bill, Portland Rescue Mission, Portland, OR. Tel: (503) 906-7605, Web Site: www.portlandrescuemission.org (1)

Miller, Bruce, World Publications Inc, Winter Park, FL. Tel: (407) 628-4802, FAX: (407) 628-7061, Web Site: www.worldpub.net (17)

Miller, Chandra, Lucky Heart Cosmetics Inc, Memphis, TN. Tel: (901) 526-7658, (800) 283-1014, FAX: (901) 526-7660, Web Site: www.luckyheart.com (7)

Miller, Charles, Key Bank National Association, Albany, NY. Tel: (518) 434-4871, (800) 539-2968, Web Site: www.keybank.com (14)

Miller, Chris, Canada Brokerlink Insurance, Edmonton, AB Canada. Tel: (780) 474-8911, FAX: (780) 479-0573, Web Site: www.brokerlink.ca (15)

Miller, Dan, North American Co for Life & Health Insurance, Chicago, IL. Tel: (312) 648-7600, (800) 800-3656, FAX: (312) 648-7796, Web Site: www.nacolah.com (15)

Miller, Dan, Transit Treasure Inc, New York, NY. Tel: (646) 706-1001, Web Site: www.transittreasure.com (12)

Miller, David, Safeguard Business Systems Inc, Dallas, TX. Tel: (214) 905-3935, (800) 523-2422, FAX: (800) 439-8423, Web Site: www.gosafeguard.com (16)

Miller, Doug, Boston Gift Show, Kennesaw, GA. Tel: (678) 285-3976, FAX: (678) 285-7469, Web Site: www.bostongiftshow.com (42)

Miller, Ed, Grafica Group, Morristown, NJ. Tel: (973) 309-7500, FAX: (973) 309-7501, E-Mail: information@grafica.com, Web Site: www.grafica.com (35)

Miller, Garth, Rexcraft Wedding Invitations, Rexburg, ID. Tel: (208) 359-1000, (800) 635-3898, FAX: (800) 826-2712, E-Mail: cs@rexcraft.com, Web Site: www.rexcraft.com (16)

Miller, Greg, Affinion Group, Stamford, CT. Tel: (203) 956-1000, (800) 282-3315, Web Site: www.affinion.com (35)

Miller, Greg, Maxwell + Miller, Kalamazoo, MI. Tel: (269) 382-4060, FAX: (269) 382-0504, E-Mail: info@maxwellandmiller.com, Web Site: www.maxwellandmiller.com (35)

Miller, III Henry L., Key Bank National Association, Albany, NY. Tel: (518) 434-4871, (800) 539-2968, Web Site: www.keybank.com (14)

Miller, III William M., US Naval Institute, Annapolis, MD. Tel: (410) 268-6110, (800) 233-8764, FAX: (410) 571-1703, E-Mail: customer@usni.org, Web Site: www.usni.org (38)

Miller, John, Clario Analytics, Eden Prairie, MN. Tel: (952) 653-0980, (866) 849-3341, FAX: (952) 653-5900, E-Mail: sales@clarioanalytics.com, Web Site: www.clarioanalytics.com (20)

Miller, John, West Farm Foods (Branch), Caldwell, ID. Tel: (208) 459-3687, FAX: (208) 459-9135, Web Site: www.westfarm.com (16)

Miller, Joy, Beach List Direct Inc, Nashville, TN. Tel: (615) 356-1100, E-Mail: cbeach@beachlistdirect.com, Web Site: www.beachlistdirect.com (23)

Miller, Justin, American Family Insurance Group, Madison, WI. Tel: (608) 249-2111, FAX: (608) 243-6525, E-Mail: akin1@amfam.com, Web Site: www.amfam.com (15)

Miller, Kenneth, Global Marketing Group Ltd, New York, NY. Tel: (212) 247-6060, FAX: (212) 586-5446, E-Mail: kimglobal@aol.com, Web Site: www.gmgsolution.com (20)

Miller, Larry, Corinthian Media, New York, NY. Tel: (212) 279-5700, FAX: (212) 239-1772, E-Mail: info@mediabuying.com, Web Site: www.mediabuying.com (35)

Miller, Linda, Condolink, Omaha, NE. Tel: (402) 592-3525, (800) 877-9600, FAX: (402) 592-4122, E-Mail: info@condolink.com, Web Site: www.condolink.com (16)

Miller, Lisa, Colle+McVoy, Minneapolis, MN. Tel: (612) 305-6000, FAX: (612) 305-6500, E-Mail: info@collemcvoy.com, Web Site: www.collemcvoy.com (35)

Miller, Mark, Allconnect Inc, Atlanta, GA. Tel: (404) 260-2200, Web Site: www.allconnect.com (32)

Miller, Mark, Children's Hospital Foundation, Silver Spring, MD. Tel: (202) 476-3000, (800) 884-LIFE, FAX: (202) 884-5999, Web Site: www.dcchildrens.com (1)

Miller, Mark, Ecolab Professional Products, Saint Paul, MN. Tel: (651) 293-4248, FAX: (651) 225-3025, E-Mail: ecolabs@ecolabs.com, Web Site: www.ecolab.com (16)

Miller, Marty, Melitta USA, Clearwater, FL. Tel: (727) 535-2111, Web Site: www.melitta.com (4)

Miller, Mary, Edison Electric Institute, Washington, DC. Tel: (202) 508-5000, FAX: (202) 508-5096, Web Site: www.eei.org (1)

Miller, Matt, Manchester Farms Inc, Columbia, SC. Tel: (803) 845-0421, FAX: (803) 227-3103, E-Mail: customerservice@manchesterfarms.com, Web Site: www.manchesterfarms.com (4)

Miller, Matt, Playworld Systems, Lewisburg, PA. Tel: (570) 522-9800, FAX: (570) 522-3030, Web Site: www.playworldsystems.com (34)

Miller, Meredith, Natural History Magazine, Durham, NC. Tel: (646) 356-6500, FAX: (646) 356-6511, E-Mail: nhmag@naturalhistorymag.com, Web Site: www.naturalhistorymag.com (17)

Miller, Nancy, Woodcraft Supply Corp LLC, Parkersburg, WV. Tel: (304) 422-5412, (800) 344-3348, FAX: (304) 422-5417, Web Site: www.woodcraft.com (19)

Miller, Nikki, GTM Sportswear, Manhattan, KS. Tel: (877) 569-3095, Web Site: www.gtmsportswear.com (2)

Miller, Pamela, Sunset Magazine, Menlo Park, CA. Tel: (650) 321-3600, FAX: (650) 328-6215 (17)

Miller, Paul, American Catalog Mailers Association, Providence, RI. Tel: (800) 509-9514, E-Mail: info@catalogmailers.org, Web Site: www.catalogmailers.org (1)

Miller, Philip D., Alternate Marketing Networks Inc, Hudsonville, MI. Tel: (616) 662-6420, FAX: (616) 662-6422, Web Site: www.altmarknet.com (28)

Miller, Renee, The Miller Group, Los Angeles, CA. Tel: (310) 442-0101, FAX: (310) 442-0107, E-Mail: info@millergroupmarketing.com, Web Site: www.millergroupmarketing.com (35)

Miller, Richard N., Market Response International, Orleans, MA. Tel: (508) 240-1877, FAX: (508) 945-4010, E-Mail: rmiller@capecod.net, Web Site: www.millerinternational.com (30)

Miller, Robert, Precise Media Services Inc, Ontario, CA. Tel: (908) 481-3305, (800) 444-4217, FAX: (908) 481-3405, Web Site: www.precisemedia.com (27)

Miller, Roger, Osmonics Inc, Minnetonka, MN. Tel: (952) 264-3937, (800) 605-6698, FAX: (952) 536-3301, Web Site: www.osmonics.com (16)

Miller, Ron, US Cavalry, Radcliff, KY. Tel: (270) 351-1164, (800) 777-7172, FAX: (270) 352-0266, E-Mail: hq@uscavalry.com, Web Site: www.uscavalry.com (6)

Miller, Roseann, Miller Advertising Inc, Edison, NJ. Tel: (732) 494-5611, FAX: (732) 494-6075 (36)

Miller, Scott, Heller Financial, Chicago, IL. Tel: (312) 441-7000, FAX: (312) 441-7499, Web Site: www.hellerfin.com (14)

Miller, Scott, The Innovation Machine, Chicago, IL. Tel: (312) 238-9362, E-Mail: contact@theinnovationmachine.com, Web Site: www.theinnovationmachine.com (1)

Miller, Sharon, Arbill Safety Products, Philadelphia, PA. Tel: (215) 632-2000, (800) 523-5367, FAX: (800) 426-5808, E-Mail: orders@arbill.com, Web Site: www.arbill.com (9)

Miller, Stephanie, Raycom Sports, Charlotte, NC. Tel: (704) 378-4456/4400, FAX: (704) 378-4465, E-Mail: whicks@raycomsports.com, Web Site: raycomsports.com (16)

Miller, Steve, Miller Direct Inc, Fort Mill, SC. Tel: (803) 548-6900, FAX: (803) 548-8701 (31)

Miller, Steve, PEMCO Insurance Cos, Seattle, WA. Tel: (206) 628-4000, (800) 467-3626, FAX: (206) 628-5886, Web Site: www.pemco.com (15)

Miller, Terry, Penske Logistics, Reading, PA. Tel: (800) 529-6531, FAX: (610) 775-2449, E-Mail: info.penskelogistics@penske.com, Web Site: www.penskelogistics.com (16)

Miller, Thomas, Vanguard Direct, New York, NY. Tel: (212) 736-0770, FAX: (212) 736-8305, Web Site: www.vanguarddirect.com (35)

Miller, Wendy, US Fund for UNICEF, New York, NY. Tel: (212) 686-5522, FAX: (212) 779-1679, Web Site: www.unicefusa.org (6)

Miller, William L., Kid Stuff Marketing, Inc, North Canton, OH. Tel: (800) 837-5437, FAX: (330) 244-9518, Web Site: www.kidsstuff.com (33)

Miller, William, Meister Media Worldwide, Willoughby, OH. Tel: (440) 942-2000, (800) 572-7740, FAX: (440) 975-3447, E-Mail: info@meistermedia.com, Web Site: www.meistermedia.com (17)

Miller, William, Naval Institute Press, Annapolis, MD. Tel: (410) 268-6110, (800) 233-8764, FAX: (410) 571-1703, E-Mail: webmaster@usni.org, Web Site: www.usni.org/navalinstitutepress (17)

MillerCoors LLC, Chicago, IL. Tel: (312) 496-2700, (800) 645-5376, Web Site: www.millercoors.com (4)

Miller's First Insurance Companies, Alton, IL. Tel: (618) 463-3636, (800) 558-0500, FAX: (618) 463-3614, Web Site: www.millersfirst.com (15)

Milligen, Stephen "Steve" D., Western Digital Corp, Irvine, CA. Tel: (949) 672-7000, FAX: (949) 672-7837, Web Site: www.westerndigital.com (22)

Millions By Marketing Inc, Mendham, NJ. Tel: (973) 222-0011, Web Site: www.millionsbymarketing.com (22)

Milliorn, Mike, Daydots, Fort Worth, TX. Tel: (817) 590-4500, (800) 321-3687, FAX: (800) 438-7002, E-Mail: customercare@daydots.com, Web Site: www.daydots.com (16)

Millipore Corp, Bedford, MA. Tel: (781) 869-5141, FAX: (781) 533-3110, Web Site: www.millipore.com (9)

Millman, Jeff, GKV, Baltimore, MD. Tel: (410) 539-5400, FAX: (410) 234-2441, E-Mail: newbusiness@gkv.com, Web Site: gvk.com (35)

Millner, Tommy, Cabela's Inc, Sidney, NE. Tel: (308) 254-5505, (800) 237-4444, FAX: (308) 254-4800, Web Site: www.cabelas.com (11)

Mills, John, AmMed Direct, Parsons, TN. Tel: (615) 941-3900, (800) 282-3524, Web Site: www.arrivamedical.com (7)

Mills, Mark, Progressive Communications, Lake Mary, FL. Tel: (407) 333-9500, (800) 571-9407, FAX: (407) 333-7979, E-Mail: info@progressivecommunications.com, Web Site: progressivecommunications.com (21)

Mills, Nancy, Upbeat Inc, Saint Louis, MO. Tel: (314) 535-5005, (800) 325-3047, FAX: (314) 535-4419, E-Mail: custservice@upbeat.com, Web Site: www.upbeat.com (9)

Mills, Rebecca, Combined Insurance Co of America, Glenview, IL. Tel: (847) 953-8116, (800) 490-1322, FAX: (847) 953-8070, Web Site: www.combinedinsurance.com (15)

Mills, Scott M., Viacom Inc, New York, NY. Tel: (212) 258-6000, FAX: (212) 258-6464, Web Site: www.viacom.com (16)

Fred Milman Associates, Glen Cove, NY. Tel: (516) 625-8075, FAX: (516) 625-5927, E-Mail: fmilman@compuserve.com (20)

Milman, Fred, Fred Milman Associates, Glen Cove, NY. Tel: (516) 625-8075, FAX: (516) 625-5927, E-Mail: fmilman@compuserve.com (20)

Milne, Tibby, McGruff Specialty Products Office, Amsterdam, NY. Tel: (518) 842-4388, (888) 776-7763, FAX: (800) 995-5121, E-Mail: mcgruff@spocentral.com, Web Site: www.mcgruffspo.com (16)

Milnor, George, Miller's First Insurance Companies, Alton, IL. Tel: (618) 463-3636, (800) 558-0500, FAX: (618) 463-3614, Web Site: www.millersfirst.com (15)

Milrod Executive Search, Princeton, NJ. Tel: (609) 683-8787, FAX: (609) 683-8221 (20)

Milrod, Jane, Milrod Executive Search, Princeton, NJ. Tel: (609) 683-8787, FAX: (609) 683-8221 (20)

Milstein, Howard P., Emigrant Savings Bank, New York, NY. Tel: (212) 850-4521, (800) EMIGRANT, FAX: (212) 850-4372, Web Site: www.emigrant.com (14)

Milstein, Ronald S., Lorillard Tobacco Co, Greensboro, NC. Tel: (336) 335-7000, (877) 703-0386, FAX: (336) 373-6917, E-Mail: externalaffairs@lortobco.com, Web Site: www.lorillard.com (16)

Milton, Jim, SoundBite Communications, Bedford, MA. Tel: (877) SOUNDBITE, Web Site: www.soundbite.com (32)

Milwaukee Direct Marketing Inc, Brookfield, WI. Tel: (262) 789-2240, FAX: (262) 789-2250, E-Mail: info@milwaukeedirect.com, Web Site: milwaukeedirect.com (35)

Milwaukee Electric Tool Corp, Brookfield, WI. Tel: (262) 781-3600, (800) 729-3878, FAX: (800) 638-9582, Web Site: www.milwaukeetool.com (16)

MIMAARTS LLC, New York, NY. Tel: (212) 584-1810 (20)

Minac, Elaine, Minacs Worldwide, Farmington Hills, MI. Tel: (416) 380-3800, FAX: (416) 380-3830, E-Mail: info@minacs.com, Web Site: www.minacs.com (29)

Minacs Worldwide, Farmington Hills, MI. Tel: (416) 380-3800, FAX: (416) 380-3830, E-Mail: info@minacs.com, Web Site: www.minacs.com (29)

Minardi, Eduardo, Bridgestone Americas Inc, Nashville, TN. Tel: (615) 937-1000, (800) 543-7522, FAX: (615) 937-3721, Web Site: www.bridgestonetire.com (16)

Minasian, Stanley, Animal Fund, San Francisco, CA. Tel: (415) 775-4636, E-Mail: delphinus@aol.com, Web Site: www.animalfund.org (38)

Minchak Jr, Robert J., JB Dollar Stretcher Magazine, Richfield, OH. Tel: (330) 659-3590, (800) 673-2531, FAX: (330) 659-6741, Web Site: www.jbdollar.com (31)

Minden Pictures, Watsonville, CA. Tel: (831) 761-3600, (888) 825-0641, FAX: (831) 761-3233, E-Mail: info@mindenpictures.com, Web Site: www.mindenpictures.com (38)

Minden, Larry, Minden Pictures, Watsonville, CA. Tel: (831) 761-3600, (888) 825-0641, FAX: (831) 761-3233, E-Mail: info@mindenpictures.com, Web Site: www.mindenpictures.com (38)

MindFireInc, Irvine, CA. Tel: (949) 474-4418, Web Site: www.mindfireinc.com (22)

MINDset Direct, Arlington, VA. Tel: (703) 538-6463, Web Site: www.mindsetdirect.com (1)

Miner, Gary, StatSoft Inc, Tulsa, OK. Tel: (918) 749-1119, FAX: (918) 749-2217, E-Mail: info@statsoft.com, Web Site: www.statsoft.com (9)

Minetto, Neil, Laplink Software Inc, Bellevue, WA. Tel: (425) 952-6000, (800) 527-5465, FAX: (425) 952-6002, E-Mail: marketing@laplink.com, Web Site: www.laplink.com (3)

Mini City Ltd, Webster, NY. Tel: (585) 872-6560, FAX: (716) 872-4094, E-Mail: minicityus@aol.com, Web Site: www.minicityltd.com (12)

Minitab Inc, State College, PA. Tel: (814) 238-3280, (800) 448-3555, FAX: (814) 238-4383, E-Mail: sales@minitab.com, Web Site: www.minitab.com (16)

Minix, Phil, Reiman Publications, Greendale, WI. Tel: (414) 423-0100, (800) 344-6913, FAX: (414) 423-3840, Web Site: www.reimanpub.com (17)

Minnesota Life, Saint Paul, MN. Tel: (651) 665-3500, (888) 237-1838, FAX: (651) 665-4488, Web Site: www.minnesotalife.com; www.securian.com (15)

Minnesota Multi Housing Association, Bloomington, MN. Tel: (952) 854-8500, FAX: (952) 854-3810, E-Mail: mha@mmha.com, Web Site: www.mmha.com (1)

Minnesota Public Radio, Saint Paul, MN. Tel: (651) 290-1500, (800) 228-7123, FAX: (651) 290-1260, E-Mail: mail@mpr.org, Web Site: www.mpr.org (1)

Minnick, Jill M., ITT Educational Services Inc, Carmel, IN. Tel: (317) 706-9200, Web Site: www.ittesi.com (16)

Minor, Marion, M2Media 360, Park Ridge, IL. Tel: (760) 318-7000, E-Mail: cnaughton@m2media360.com, Web Site: www.m2media360.com (17)

Mintel International, Chicago, IL. Tel: (312) 932-0500, Web Site: www.comperemedia.com (30)

Minto, Jennifer, BuyFilters.com LLC, Silverhill, AL. Tel: (866) 863-1262, E-Mail: customerservice@buyfilters.com, Web Site: www.buyfilters.com (5)

Mintz, Paul, Porta-Bote International, Mountain View, CA. Tel: (650) 961-5334, (800) 227-8882, Web Site: www.porta-bote.com (11)

Mirabal, Alisa, Marketing Results Inc, Sicklerville, NJ. Tel: (856) 740-3334, FAX: (856) 740-3335, Web Site: www.marketingresults.net (16)

Mirabello, Rhianna, US Games Systems Inc, Stamford, CT. Tel: (203) 353-8400, (800) 544-2637, FAX: (203) 353-8431, Web Site: www.usgamesinc.com (11)

Mirabille, Peter, TSI, Albany, NY. Tel: (518) 463-5555, FAX: (518) 463-4504, E-Mail: tsi@capital.net, Web Site: www.tsidrivers.com (20)

Miracle Ear, Minneapolis, MN. Tel: (800) 464-8002, FAX: (763) 268-4365, Web Site: www.miracle-ear.com (16)

Miracle of Aloe, Dallas, TX. Tel: (800) 966-2563, FAX: (800) 859-9881, E-Mail: LJohnson@miracleofaloe.com, Web Site: www.miracleofaloe.com (7)

Miranda, Amy, Academic Management Services, Swansea, MA. Tel: (508) 235-2870, (800) 891-4203, FAX: (508) 235-2991, E-Mail: info@amsweb.com, Web Site: www.amsweb.com (14)

Miranda, Karen, APC by Schneider Electric, West Kingston, RI. Tel: (800) 555-7927, FAX: (401) 789-3710, E-Mail: public.relations@apcc.com, Web Site: www.apcc.com (3)

Mirbach, H.W., Crossbow Group, Westport, CT. Tel: (203) 222-2244, FAX: (203) 226-7838, E-Mail: info@crossbowgroup.com, Web Site: www.crossbowgroup.com (40)

Mirchandani, Keith, Tristar Products, Fairfield, NJ. Tel: (973) 575-5400, FAX: (973) 683-6708, E-Mail: infotp@tristarproductsinc.com, Web Site: www.tristarproductsinc.com (16)

Mircroulis, Peter, Advanced Financial Services, Middletown, RI. Tel: (401) 849-0892, (800) 620-6292, FAX: (401) 851-5621, Web Site: www.embracehomeloans.com (14)

Mirels, Linda, United Jewish Appeal Federation of New York, New York, NY. Tel: (212) 980-1000, FAX: (212) 785-9321, E-Mail: contact@ujafedny.org, Web Site: www.ujafedny.org (1)

Misa, Donna, Dataprint Corp, San Mateo, CA. Tel: (650) 340-0550, (800) 227-6191, FAX: (650) 340-7028, Web Site: www.dataprint.com (34)

Mishek, Mark, Hazelden, Center City, MN. Tel: (651) 213-4200, (800) 257-7810, FAX: (651) 213-4411, E-Mail: info@hazeldenbettyford.org, Web Site: www.hazelden.org (7)

Mishica, Alice, Specialized Mailing Services Inc, Huntington Beach, CA. Tel: (714) 274-2284, E-Mail: info@specializedmailing.com, Web Site: www.specializedmailing.com (28)

Misischia, Frank L., FLM Graphics Corp, Fairfield, NJ. Tel: (973) 575-9450, E-Mail: info@flmgraphics.com, Web Site: www.flmgraphics.com (16)

Miskelley, Ricky, Mail Enterprises LLC, Birmingham, AL. Tel: (205) 595-4945, (800) 595-4945, FAX: (205) 595-4943, E-Mail: sswedenburg@mailent.com, Web Site: www.mailent.com (21)

MISSCO Corp, Flowood, MS. Tel: (601) 948-8600, (800) 647-5333, FAX: (601) 987-3038 (16)

Missett, Judi Shepphard, Jazzercise Inc, Carlsbad, CA. Tel: (760) 476-1750, FAX: (760) 602-7180, E-Mail: customercare@jazzercise.com, Web Site: www.jazzercise.com (2)

Missett, Kathy, Jazzercise Inc, Carlsbad, CA. Tel: (760) 476-1750, FAX: (760) 602-7180, E-Mail: customercare@jazzercise.com, Web Site: www.jazzercise.com (2)

Mission: A Consulting Group, Westport, CT. Tel: (203) 227-9475, FAX: (203) 227-6512, E-Mail: info@mission-consulting.com, Web Site: www.mission-consulting.com (20)

Missionary Society of St Columban, Saint Columbans, NE. Tel: (402) 291-1920, Web Site: www.columban.org (1)

The Missoulian, Missoula, MT. Tel: (406) 523-5200, (800) 366-7102, FAX: (406) 523-5221, Web Site: www.missoulian.com (31)

Missouri Landscape & Nursery Association, Bowling Green, MO. Tel: (636) 542-1234, E-Mail: admin@mlng.org, Web Site: www.mlna.org (1)

Missouri Life Inc, Boonville, MO. Tel: (660) 882-9898, (800) 492-2593, FAX: (660) 882-9899, E-Mail: info@missourilife.com, Web Site: www.missourilife.com (17)

Mr Fantastic LLC, Astor, FL. Tel: (407) 719-2020, E-Mail: sbillue@usa2net.net, Web Site: www.stanbillue.com (20)

Mr G's Enterprises, Fort Worth, TX. Tel: (817) 831-3501, FAX: (817) 831-0638, E-Mail: mrgs@mrgusa.com, Web Site: www.mrgusa.com (16)

Mr Wash Car Wash, Kensington, MD. Tel: (301) 933-4858, Web Site: www.mrwash.com (16)

Mistri, Deirdre J., Sculptz, Feasterville Trevose, PA. Tel: (215) 494-2900, E-Mail: sdudek@sculptz.com, Web Site: www.silkies.com (2)

Mitchel, Thomas, Las Vegas Review Journal, Las Vegas, NV. Tel: (702) 383-0211, FAX: (702) 383-4646, Web Site: www.lvrj.com (17)

Mitchell Graphics Inc, Petoskey, MI. Tel: (231) 347-5650, (800) 583-9401, FAX: (231) 347-9255, E-Mail: mgi@mitchellgraphics.com, Web Site: www.mitchellgraphics.com (27)

Mitchell International, San Diego, CA. Tel: (858) 368-7000, FAX: (858) 238-9111, Web Site: www.mitchell.com (17)

Mitchell, Bob, Replogle Globes Inc, Broadview, IL. Tel: (708) 343-0900, FAX: (708) 343-0923, E-Mail: info@replogleglobes.com, Web Site: www.replogleglobes.com (16)

Mitchell, Brad, Babcox Publications LLC, Akron, OH. Tel: (330) 670-1234, FAX: (330) 670-0874, E-Mail: bbabcox@babcox.com, Web Site: www.babcox.com (17)

Mitchell, Fenton, CX&B United Corp, Harbor City, CA. Tel: (310) 530-2102, (800) 292-8258, FAX: (310) 530-2513, E-Mail: sales@cxbunited.com, Web Site: www.cxbunited.com (33)

Mitchell, Joette, CUES Events, Training & Education, Madison, WI. Tel: (608) 271-2664, (800) 252-2664, FAX: (608) 271-2303, E-Mail: cues@cues.org, Web Site: www.cues.org (42)

Mitchell, Lee, Thoma Cressey Bravo, Chicago, IL. Tel: (312) 777-4444, FAX: (312) 777-4445, Web Site: www.tcb.com (14)

Mitchell, Lisa A., Hagemeyer - North America, Charleston, SC. Tel: (843) 745-2400, FAX: (843) 745-6942, E-Mail: info@hagemeyerna.com, Web Site: www.hagemeyerna.com (16)

Mitchell, Mark, INWAVE Internet, Janesville, WI. Tel: (888) 469-2831, FAX: (608) 752-8981, Web Site: www.inwave.com (16)

Mitchell, Patricia J., Americraft - The Gift Brokers Inc, Wendell, MA. Tel: (978) 544-7330, (800) 866-2723, FAX: (978) 544-2771, E-Mail: info@americraft.us, Web Site: www.americraft.us (16)

Mitchell, Patty, Pennsylvania State University Press, University Park, PA. Tel: (814) 865-1327, (800) 326-9180, FAX: (814) 863-1408, Web Site: www.psupress.org (17)

Mithun Agency, Minneapolis, MN. Tel: (612) 347-1000, FAX: (612) 347-1515, Web Site: www.everythingtalks.com (35)

Mitrani, Amy, Food Chemical News, Arlington, VA. Tel: (202) 887-6320, (888) 732-7070, FAX: (202) 887-6335, E-Mail: cs@foodregulation.com, Web Site: www.foodchemicalnews.com (17)

Mitson, Les W., Nilodor Inc, Bolivar, OH. Tel: (330) 874-1017, (800) 443-4321, FAX: (330) 874-3366, E-Mail: info@nilodor.com, Web Site: www.nilodor.com (16)

Mitsubishi Digital Electronics America Inc, Cypress, CA. Tel: (949) 465-6000, FAX: (949) 859-4770, Web Site: www.mitsubishi-tv.com (3)

Mitsubishi Motors North America Inc, Cypress, CA. Tel: (714) 372-6000, (888) 648-7820, Web Site: www.mitsubishicars.com (1)

Mitsui, Ken, Methode Electronics Inc, Chicago, IL. Tel: (708) 867-6777, FAX: (708) 867-6999, E-Mail: info@methode.com, Web Site: www.methode.com (9)

Frank Mittermeier Inc, Bronx, NY. Tel: (718) 828-3843, (800) 360-3843, FAX: (718) 518-7233, E-Mail: info@dastrausa.com, Web Site: www.dastrausa.com (11)

Mittlestadt, Mitchell, Imperial Supplies, Green Bay, WI. Tel: (920) 494-5403, (800) 558-2808, FAX: (800) 553-8769, Web Site: www.imperialsupplies.com (16)

Mitton Rivas, Kersten, Source, Norwalk, CT. Tel: (203) 291-4000, FAX: (203) 291-4010, E-Mail: info@sourcecxm.com, Web Site: www.sourcecxm.com (35)

Miville, Mark, Solar Components Corp, Manchester, NH. Tel: (603) 668-8186, FAX: (603) 668-1783, Web Site: www.solar-components.com (9)

Miyazaki, Go, Fujifilm Holdings America Corp, Valhalla, NY. Tel: (914) 789-8100, (800) 755-3854, FAX: (914) 789-8295, Web Site: www.fujifilmusa.com (16)

Mlotek, Mark E., Henry Schein Inc, Melville, NY. Tel: (631) 843-5500, (800) 472-4346, FAX: (631) 843-5658, E-Mail: custserv@henryschein.com, Web Site: www.henryschein.com (16)

Moat, Jeff, Canadian Blood Services, Ottawa, ON Canada. Tel: (613) 739-2300, Web Site: www.blood.ca (1)

Mobed, Ron, Elsevier, New York, NY. Tel: (212) 633-3805, FAX: (212) 633-3880, Web Site: www.elsevier.com (17)

Mobile Fusion, Lakewood, CO. Tel: (720) 963-8000, (800) 431-8556, Web Site: www.mobile-fusion.com (16)

Moby Wrap Inc, Chico, CA. Tel: (530) 898-8201, E-Mail: info@mobywrap.com (2)

Mochalski, Cynthia, American Family Insurance Group, Madison, WI. Tel: (608) 249-2111, FAX: (608) 243-6525, E-Mail: akin1@amfam.com, Web Site: www.amfam.com (15)

Mockler, Peter, Bearingpoint Inc, Dallas, TX. Tel: (703) 747-3000, FAX: (703) 747-3215, Web Site: www.bearingpoint.com (14)

Modaffari, Mary Kay, Brunner, Pittsburgh, PA. Tel: (412) 995-9500, FAX: (412) 995-9501, Web Site: www.brunnerworks.com (35)

Modany, Kevin M., ITT Educational Services Inc, Carmel, IN. Tel: (317) 706-9200, Web Site: www.ittesi.com (16)

MODCo Media, New York, NY. Tel: (212) 686-0006, FAX: (212) 686-6991, Web Site: modcomedia.com (35)

Moddern Marketing, New York, NY. Tel: (212) 334-9800, E-Mail: mark@moddern.com, Web Site: www.moddern.com (35)

Modek, Matt, Cotta Transmission Co, Beloit, WI. Tel: (608) 368-5600, FAX: (608) 368-5605, E-Mail: sales@cotta.com, Web Site: www.cotta.com (16)

Modern Graphic Arts, Saint Petersburg, FL. Tel: (727) 579-1527, FAX: (727) 579-1528, Web Site: www.sandyinc.com (27)

Modern Mail, Bear, DE. Tel: (302) 391-1200, Web Site: www.triggermarketing.com (20)

Modern Postcard, Carlsbad, CA. Tel: (800) 959-8365, Web Site: www.modernpostcard.com (10)

ModernAd Media LLC, Deerfield Beach, FL. Tel: (954) 312-4900, FAX: (954) 312-4853, Web Site: www.modernad.com (40)

Modernage Custom Digital Imaging Labs, New York, NY. Tel: (212) 997-1800, (800) 997-2510, FAX: (212) 869-4796, E-Mail: info@modernage.com, Web Site: www.modernage.com (16)

Modica, Wayne, AKA Direct, Portland, OR. Tel: (503) 467-2200, (800) 647-8587, FAX: (503) 445-0064, Web Site: www.akadirect.com (27)

Modlin, Cliff, Marking Specialists Group, Buffalo Grove, IL. Tel: (847) 793-8100, (800) 678-8073, FAX: (847) 793-8109, E-Mail: info@marking-specialists.com, Web Site: www.marking-specialists.com (27)

Modular Mailing Systems, Tampa, FL. Tel: (305) 826-9077, (800) 881-MAIL, E-Mail: sales@modularmailing.com, Web Site: www.modularmailing.com (34)

Mody, Parin, Mardevdm2, Oak Brook, IL. Tel: (800) 323-4958, FAX: (303) 265-5457, E-Mail: info@mardevdm2.com, Web Site: www.mardevdm2.com (24)

Moeller, Jim, Serenity, Maria Stein, OH. Tel: (419) 925-1215, (800) 869-1684, FAX: (419) 925-1216, E-Mail: serenity@bright.net, Web Site: www.serenitymusic.com (17)

Moeller, Jon R., The Procter & Gamble Co, Cincinnati, OH. Tel: (513) 983-1100, Web Site: www.pg.com (16)

Moen Inc, North Olmsted, OH. Tel: (440) 962-2000, Web Site: www.moen.com (16)

Mogck, Tim, 3M Post-It Custom Printed Products, Saint Paul, MN. Tel: (800) 328-2407, Web Site: www.3m.com (16)

Mogensen, Lisa A., Return Path Inc, New York, NY. Tel: (212) 905-5500, FAX: (212) 905-5501, Web Site: www.returnpath.biz (22)

Mogren, Todd, Coastal Tool & Supply, West Hartford, CT. Tel: (860) 233-8213, (877) 551-8665, FAX: (860) 233-6295, E-Mail: sales@coastaltool.com, Web Site: www.coastaltool.com (16)

Mohan-Neill, Sumaria, Walter E Heller College of Business Administration, Chicago, IL. Tel: (312) 281-3293, FAX: (312) 281-3290, Web Site: www.roosevelt.edu (41)

Mohawk Fine Papers Inc, Cohoes, NY. Tel: (518) 237-1740, (800) 843-6455, FAX: (518) 237-7394, E-Mail: info@mohawkpaper.com, Web Site: www.mohawkconnects.com (25)

Mohawk Lifts, Amsterdam, NY. Tel: (518) 842-1431, (800) 833-2006, FAX: (518) 842-1289, E-Mail: rwells@mohawklifts.com, Web Site: www.mohawklifts.com (9)

Mohindroo, Rohinee, LinkShare Corp, New York, NY. Tel: (646) 943-8200, FAX: (646) 943-8204, Web Site: www.linkshare.com (32)

Mohney, Ron A., Moto Franchise Corp, Dayton, OH. Tel: (937) 291-1900, (800) 733-6686, FAX: (937) 291-2005, E-Mail: expert@motophoto.com, Web Site: www.motophoto.com; www.portraitavenue.com (3)

Mohr, Eric, EBM Direct Marketing Services LLC, Port Washington, NY. Tel: (516) 874-7839, Web Site: www.ebmdirectmarketing.com (20)

Mohr, Randi, NY Now, White Plains, NY. Tel: (800) 272-7469, Web Site: www.nynow.com (42)

Mohr, Richard, Intermap Technologies, Englewood, CO. Tel: (303) 708-0955, FAX: (303) 708-0952, E-Mail: info@intermap.com, Web Site: www.intermap.com (32)

Moir, Doug, Sportif Mail Order Inc, Sparks, NV. Tel: (888) 260-7676, FAX: (775) 356-3567, Web Site: www.sportif.com (2)

Mokover, Peter, Spectrum Research, Ventnor City, NJ. Tel: (609) 822-0056, E-Mail: peter@spectrumresearch.com (30)

Moldenhauer, Walter, Texas Parks & Wildlife Dept, Austin, TX. Tel: (512) 389-4800, (800) 792-1112, FAX: (512) 389-8029, Web Site: www.tpwd.state.tx.us (1)

Molfetas, Jason, National Railroad Passenger Corp, Washington, DC. Tel: (202) 906-3000, (800) USA-RAIL, FAX: (202) 906-3306, Web Site: www.amtrak.com (16)

Molinari, Alfred, Data Translation Inc, Marlborough, MA. Tel: (508) 481-3700, (800) 525-8528, FAX: (508) 481-8620, E-Mail: info@datatranslation.com, Web Site: www.datatranslation.com (34)

Molson Coors Brewing Co, Denver, CO. Tel: (303) 927-2337, (800) 665-7661, Web Site: www.molsoncoors.com (16)

Molson, Andrew T., Molson Coors Brewing Co, Denver, CO. Tel: (303) 927-2337, (800) 665-7661, Web Site: www.molsoncoors.com (16)

Molter, Ted, Zoological Society of San Diego, San Diego, CA. Tel: (619) 231-1515, FAX: (619) 557-3937, Web Site: www.sandiegozoo.org (1)

Mom365, Saint Charles, MO. Tel: (636) 946-5136, Web Site: www.growingfamily.com (37)

Mona, Steve, Golf Card International, Englewood, CO. Tel: (303) 792-7284, (800) 321-8269, Web Site: www.golfcard.com (1)

Monaco, Rosemarie, Group M Inc, Nyack, NY. Tel: (845) 535-3453, E-Mail: gmi.prm@gmail.com, Web Site: www.groupm.org (35)

Monadnock Paper Mills Inc, Bennington, NH. Tel: (603) 588-3311, (800) 221-2159, FAX: (603) 588-3158, Web Site: www.monadnockpaper.com (25)

Monagle, Laura, Affirm Agency, Pewaukee, WI. Tel: (262) 650-9900, E-Mail: info@affirmagency.com, Web Site: affirmagency.com (35)

Monahan, Michael, Pitney Bowes, Stamford, CT. Tel: (203) 356-5000, (800) MR-BOWES, Web Site: www.pitneybowes.com (10)

Monarch Direct Response, Sherman Oaks, CA. Tel: (818) 817-8000, Web Site: www.monarchdr.com (35)

Monastra, Jim, Wrisco Industries Inc. Palm Beach Gardens, FL. Tel: (561) 626-5700, (800) 627-2646, FAX: (561) 627-3574, Web Site: www.wrisco.com (8)

Mondello, Mike, Sea Bear, Anacortes, WA. Tel: (360) 293-4661, (800) 645-3474, FAX: (888) 487-6427, Web Site: www.seabear.com (16)

Monestero, Andrew, Zim-American Israeli Shipping Co Inc, Staten Island, NY. Tel: (718) 313-1950, Web Site: www.zim.com (16)

Monetti, Kathy, Pleasant Company, Middleton, WI. Tel: (608) 831-4116, (800) 845-0005, FAX: (608) 836-1999, Web Site: www.americangirl.com (11)

Monex Deposit Co, Newport Beach, CA. Tel: (949) 752-1400, (800) 444-8317, FAX: (949) 752-7214, E-Mail: info@monex.com, Web Site: www.monex.com (14)

Money Mailer LLC, Garden Grove, CA. Tel: (800) 624-5371, Web Site: www.moneymailer.net (31)

MoneyGram International, Dallas, TX. Tel: (800) 666-3947, Web Site: www.moneygram.com (14)

Monfradi Dunn, JoAnne, Alliant, Brewster, NY. Tel: (845) 276-2600, FAX: (845) 276-2605, Web Site: www.alliantdata.com (22)

Monfried, Andrew, Lotame Solutions, Columbia, MD. Tel: (410) 379-2195, FAX: (410) 379-2198, Web Site: www.lotame.com (22)

Mongin, Bob, Web Graphics, Glens Falls, NY. Tel: (518) 792-6501, (800) 833-8863, FAX: (518) 792-9353, (800) 833-8861, E-Mail: proofs&pos@printatweb.com, Web Site: www.printatweb.com (27)

Monk, Mike, Alpha Dog Marketing Inc, Lincoln, NE. Tel: (402) 486-0668, Web Site: www.alphadogmktg.com (1)

Monkeyshines Publishers, Greensboro, NC. Tel: (336) 292-6999, FAX: (336) 292-6999, E-Mail: mkshines@nr.infi.net, Web Site: www.monkeyshinespublishers.com (17)

Monks, Tom, The Hyiad Group, Garden City, NY. Tel: (516) 433-3800, FAX: (516) 822-6670, Web Site: www.thehyaidgroup.com (22)

Monnett, Lori J., Customer Marketing Group LLC, Weston, CT. Tel: (203) 226-9845, FAX: (203) 226-9837, E-Mail: bill@4cmg.com, Web Site: www.4cmg.com (35)

Monroe, Bill, Customized Newspaper Advertising, Des Moines, IA. Tel: (515) 244-2145, (800) 227-7636, FAX: (515) 244-4855, Web Site: www.cnaads.com (18)

Monroe, Kipp, White64, Vienna, VA. Tel: (703) 793-3000, E-Mail: info@white64.com, Web Site: white64.com (35)

Monroy, Gerardo, Bankers Life & Casualty Co, Chicago, IL. Tel: (312) 396-6000, (800) 231-9150, Web Site: www.bankerslife.com (15)

Monsees, Gregg Peters, Putnam Rolling Ladder Co Inc, New York, NY. Tel: (212) 226-5147, FAX: (212) 941-1836, E-Mail: putnam1905@aol.com, Web Site: www.putnamrollingladder.com (5)

Monson, Craig, Schmidt, Byron, MN. Tel: (507) 775-6400, FAX: (507) 775-6655, E-Mail: sls@schmidt.com, Web Site: www.schmidt.com (27)

Monster Magnet, Louisville, KY. Tel: (866) 259-6554, E-Mail: joe@monstermagnet.com, Web Site: www.monstermagnet.com (35)

Monster Worldwide, Weston, MA. Tel: (888) MON-STER, Web Site: www.monster.com (20)

Montag & Caldwell Inc, Atlanta, GA. Tel: (404) 836-7100, (800) 458-5868, FAX: (404) 836-7168, Web Site: www.montag.com (14)

Montague, Larry N., Technical Association of the Pulp & Paper Industry, Norcross, GA. Tel: (770) 446-1400, (800) 332-8686, FAX: (770) 446-6947, E-Mail: memberconnection@tappi.org, Web Site: www.tappi.org (1)

Montalao, Debbie, The Hamilton Group Ltd Inc, Jacksonville, FL. Tel: (904) 279-1300, FAX: (904) 279-1414, Web Site: www.collectibletoday.com (16)

Montalvo, David, Active Web Group, Hauppauge, NY. Tel: (800) 978-3417, FAX: (800) 719-4402, E-Mail: info@activewebgroup.com, Web Site: www.activewebgroup.com (9)

Montano, Pete, Con-Way Truckload, Joplin, MO. Tel: (417) 623-5229, (800) CFI-DRIVE, FAX: (417) 623-8939, E-Mail: gnichols@cfi-us.com, Web Site: www.cfi-us.com (12)

MontBleu Resort Casino and Spa, Stateline, NV. Tel: (775) 586-2126, (888) 829-7630, FAX: (775) 588-3515, Web Site: www.montbleuresort.com (19)

Montegrande, Antoinette, Phoenix Learning Group Inc, Maryland Heights, MO. Tel: (314) 569-0211, (800) 221-1274, FAX: (314) 569-2834, E-Mail: dealersales@phoenixlearninggroup.com, Web Site: www.phoenixlearninggroup.com (16)

Monteith, Timothy J., Masco Corp, Taylor, MI. Tel: (313) 274-7400, FAX: (313) 792-6135, E-Mail: webmaster@mascohq.com, Web Site: www.masco.com (16)

Montes, Nisley, Torqmaster International, Stamford, CT. Tel: (203) 326-5945, (888) 414-4643, FAX: (203) 326-5944, E-Mail: info@torqmaster.com, Web Site: www.torqmaster.com (9)

Montgomery, Clifford, Vivitar Corp, Tempe, AZ. Tel: (800) 592-9541, FAX: (909) 348-6390, Web Site: www.vivitar.com (16)

Montgomery, Keith, Kaiser Foundation Health Plan of the Mid-Atlantic States Inc, Rockville, MD. Tel: (301) 816-5641, Web Site: kp.org (1)

Montgomery, Linda, Speedeon Data Corp, Cleveland, OH. Tel: (866) 647-9219, Web Site: www.speedeondata.com (30)

Montreal Envelope Inc, Quebec, QC Canada. Tel: (514) 331-7110, (800) 655-2709, FAX: (514) 748-7322, E-Mail: ybrochu@enveloppe-montreal.com, Web Site: www.enveloppe-montreal.com (26)

Montross, David, UGL Equis Corp, Chicago, IL. Tel: (312) 424-8000, FAX: (312) 424-8080, Web Site: www.equiscorp.com (16)

Montross, Steve, CPI Card Group, Littleton, CO. Tel: (303) 973-9311, FAX: (303) 973-8420, E-Mail: mbarber@cpicardgroup.com, Web Site: www. cpicardgroup.com (27)

Moody, J. Ward, Astronomical Society of the Pacific, San Francisco, CA. Tel: (415) 337-1100, (800) 335-2624, FAX: (415) 337-5205, E-Mail: service@ astrosociety.org, Web Site: www.astrosociety.org (1)

Moody, Jessica, Directory of Mail Order Catalogs, Amenia, NY. Tel: (518) 789-8700, (800) 562-2139, FAX: (518) 789-0556, E-Mail: cstupak@greyhouse. com, Web Site: www.greyhouse.com (43)

Moody, Jessica, Grey House Publishing, Amenia, NY. Tel: (518) 789-8700, (800) 562-2139, FAX: (518) 789-0556, E-Mail: books@greyhouse.com, Web Site: www.greyhouse.com (43)

Moody, Jessica, The Directory of Business Information Resources, Amenia, NY. Tel: (845) 373-8263, E-Mail: cstupak@greyhouse.com, Web Site: www. greyhouse.com (43)

Moody, Robin, Daedalus Books Inc, Columbia, MD. Tel: (410) 309-2706, (800) 944-8879, E-Mail: custserv@daedalusbooks.com, Web Site: www. salebooks.com (5)

Moog, Matthew, Q Interactive, Chicago, IL. Tel: (312) 977-0390, (888) 729-6465, FAX: (312) 224-5001, E-Mail: solutions@qinteractive.com, Web Site: www.qinteractive.com (40)

Moomau, Bud, Vet Vax, Tonganoxie, KS. Tel: (913) 845-3760, (800) 369-8297, FAX: (913) 845-9472, E-Mail: sales@vetvax.com (11)

Moon Shine Trading Co, Woodland, CA. Tel: (530) 668-0660, (800) 678-1226, FAX: (530) 668-6061, E-Mail: store@moonshinetrading.com, Web Site: www.moonshinetrading.com (4)

Moon, Samuel, Air Power USA, Los Angeles, CA. Tel: (310) 641-0830, (888) 888-8231, FAX: (310) 641-8515, Web Site: www.airpowerusa.com (12)

Moonan, Thomas J, The Hibbert Group, Trenton, NJ. Tel: (609) 394-7500, (800) 545-4747, FAX: (609) 695-6553, Web Site: www.hibbertco.com (28)

Moonan, Timothy J, The Hibbert Group, Trenton, NJ. Tel: (609) 394-7500, (800) 545-4747, FAX: (609) 695-6553, Web Site: www.hibbertco.com (28)

Mooney, Beth E., Key Bank National Association, Albany, NY. Tel: (518) 434-4871, (800) 539-2968, Web Site: www.keybank.com (14)

Mooney, Kevin W., Blackbaud Inc, Charleston, SC. Tel: (843) 216-6200, (800) 443-9441, FAX: (843) 216-6100, Web Site: www.blackbaud.com (22)

Mooney, Patricia, New & Unique Videos, San Diego, CA. Tel: (619) 644-3000, FAX: (619) 644-3001, E-Mail: info@newuniquevideos.com, Web Site: www.newuniquevideos.com (3)

Moore Medical LLC, Farmington, CT. Tel: (860) 826-3600, FAX: (860) 223-2382, E-Mail: e-support@ mooremedical.com, Web Site: www.mooremedical. com (7)

Thurston Moore Country Ltd, Madison, TN. Tel: (615) 868-7448, FAX: (615) 868-3738 (16)

Moore, Allie, Newport Creative Communications, Duxbury, MA. Tel: (781) 934-1414, Web Site: www. newportcreative.com (1)

Moore, Barry, The Press & Standard, Walterboro, SC. Tel: (843) 549-2586, Web Site: colletontoday.com (31)

Moore, Chris, Direct Mail Solutions, Richmond, VA. Tel: (804) 254-8300, (877) 367-0800, Web Site: www.directmailsolutions.com (28)

Moore, Christopher, International Data Management - a Dmh Marketing Partners Co, Akron, OH. Tel: (330) 869-8500, FAX: (330) 869-4027, Web Site: www. idmi.com (22)

Moore, Declan, National Geographic Society, Washington, DC. Tel: (202) 862-8638, (800) 373-1717, Web Site: www.nationalgeographic.com (17)

Moore, Delia, American Family Life Assurance Co of Columbus (AFLAC), Columbus, GA. Tel: (706) 323-3431, (800) 992-3522, FAX: (706) 660-7446, Web Site: www.aflac.com (15)

Moore, Gary B., Cisco Systems Inc, San Jose, CA. Tel: (408) 526-4000, (800) 553-NETS, FAX: (408) 526-4100, Web Site: www.cisco.com (22)

Moore, Gary, Jungle Consulting, Colorado Springs, CO. Tel: (702) 596-4366 (20)

Moore, Jan S., Direct Options, West Chester, OH. Tel: (513) 779-4416, (800) 749-3678, FAX: (513) 779-4426, E-Mail: info@directoptions.com, Web Site: www.directoptions.com (35)

Moore, Janet, Biomerica Inc, Irvine, CA. Tel: (949) 645-2111, (800) 854-3002, FAX: (949) 553-1231, E-Mail: info@biomerica.com, Web Site: www. biomerica.com (7)

Moore, Jim, University of Illinois Foundation, Urbana, IL. Tel: (217) 333-0810, FAX: (217) 333-5577, E-Mail: uif@uillinois.edu, Web Site: www.uif. uillinois.edu (1)

Moore, John, Collegiate Cap & Gown, Champaign, IL. Tel: (217) 351-9500, FAX: (217) 351-9214, Web Site: www.herff-jones.com (16)

Moore, Kevin, Indium Corp of America, Clinton, NY. Tel: (315) 853-4900, (800) 446-3486, FAX: (800) 221-5759, E-Mail: askus@indium.com, Web Site: www.indium.com (16)

Moore, Lester W.B., Polynesian Cultural Center, Honolulu, HI. Tel: (808) 293-3333, (800) 367-7060, FAX: (888) 722-7339, E-Mail: internetrez@polynesia. com, Web Site: www.polynesia.com (16)

Moore, Marc, Blue Cross Blue Shield of North Carolina, Durham, NC. Tel: (800) 250-3630, Web Site: www. bcbsnc.com (15)

Moore, Margot Murphy, New England Mail Order Association, Scarborough, ME. Tel: (207) 885-0090, (860) 691-1260, FAX: (207) 885-0097, Web Site: www.nemoa.org (40)

Moore, Mark, e-Pipeconnection, Evansville, IN. Tel: (812) 474-4529, (800) 262-4300, FAX: (812) 474-4531, E-Mail: sales@e-pipeconnection.com, Web Site: www.e-pipeconnection.com (9)

Moore, Mark, TeleDirect International Inc, Scottsdale, AZ. Tel: (480) 585-6464, (800) 531-6440, FAX: (480) 585-3373, Web Site: www.tdirect.com (29)

Moore, Pamela, Prakken Publications Inc, Ann Arbor, MI. Tel: (734) 975-2800, (800) 530-9673, FAX: (734) 975-2787, Web Site: www.techdirections. com; www.eddigest.com (17)

Moore, Robert J., Bausch & Lomb Inc, Rochester, NY. Tel: (585) 338-6000, (800) 344-8815, FAX: (585) 338-6007, Web Site: www.bausch.com (16)

Moore, Robert, The Dingley Press, Lisbon, ME. Tel: (207) 353-4151, (800) 317-4574, FAX: (207) 353-9886, E-Mail: webrequest@dingley.com, Web Site: www.dingley.com (27)

Moore, Sandra, Buick, Detroit, MI. Tel: (313) 556-5000, (800) 521-7300, FAX: (313) 556-5108, Web Site: www.buick.com (16)

Moore, Scott, SC Direct, West Bridgewater, MA. Tel: (800) 343-9695, Web Site: www.scdirect.com (2)

Moore, Steven D.R., Stream International, Wellesley, MA. Tel: (781) 304-1800, (888) 264-5834, FAX: (781) 575-6999, Web Site: www.stream.com (16)

Moore, Thurston, Thurston Moore Country Ltd, Madison, TN. Tel: (615) 868-7448, FAX: (615) 868-3738 (16)

Moorhead, Douglas P., Presque Isle Wine Cellars Inc, North East, PA. Tel: (814) 725-1314, (800) 488-7492, FAX: (814) 725-2092, E-Mail: info@piwine. com, Web Site: www.piwine.com (4)

Moorhead, Erik, Presque Isle Wine Cellars Inc, North East, PA. Tel: (814) 725-1314, (800) 488-7492, FAX: (814) 725-2092, E-Mail: info@piwine.com, Web Site: www.piwine.com (4)

Moosmann, Art, Fireman's Fund Insurance Co, Novato, CA. Tel: (415) 899-2000, FAX: (415) 899-3600, Web Site: www.firemansfund.com (14)

Mopsik, Eugene, American Society of Media Photographers (ASMP), Philadelphia, PA. Tel: (215) 451-ASMP, FAX: (215) 451-0880, Web Site: www. asmp.org (40)

Mora, John M., Creative Copywriting, Plainfield, IL. Tel: (815) 439-9160, FAX: (815) 439-9158 (39)

Mora, Michaela, Relevant Insights LLC, Euless, TX. Tel: (817) 545-8017 (30)

Morales, Angelo, Frank Mittermeier Inc, Bronx, NY. Tel: (718) 828-3843, (800) 360-3843, FAX: (718) 518-7233, E-Mail: info@dastrausa.com, Web Site: www.dastrausa.com (11)

Morales, Rose, King Ranch Saddle Shop, Kingsville, TX. Tel: (800) 282-KING, E-Mail: krsaddleshop@ king-ranch.com, Web Site: www.krsaddleshop.com (8)

Morales, Sylvia, Williams Worldwide Television, Santa Monica, CA. Tel: (310) 449-4506, FAX: (310) 449-4556, E-Mail: curious@williamsworldwidetv.com, Web Site: www.williamsworldwidetv.com (35)

Moran Direct Inc, Houston, TX. Tel: (713) 880-3725, FAX: (713) 263-7647, E-Mail: rmoran@ morandirect.com, Web Site: www.morandirect.com (20)

Moran, Adam, Macromark Inc, Danbury, CT. Tel: (845) 230-6300, FAX: (845) 278-0650, E-Mail: sales@ macromark.com, Web Site: www.macromark.com (23)

Moran, Corey, Hunt Marketing Group, Seattle, WA. Tel: (206) 447-5665, FAX: (206) 447-5789, E-Mail: info@hmgseattle.com, Web Site: www.hmgseattle. com (35)

Moran, Dan, Rock-Tred Corp, Waukegan, IL. Tel: (847) 673-8200, (800) 762-8733, FAX: (847) 679-6665, Web Site: www.rocktred.com (9)

Moran, Dori, Pacific Botanicals LLC, Grants Pass, OR. Tel: (541) 479-7777, FAX: (541) 479-7780, E-Mail: pacbot1@earthlink.net, Web Site: www. pacificbotanicals.com (7)

Moran, Jackie, Trophyland USA Inc, Hialeah, FL. Tel: (305) 823-4830, (800) 327-5820, FAX: (305) 823-4836, E-Mail: info@trophyland.com, Web Site: www.trophyland.com (5)

Moran, Jr Rock P., Gaw-O'Hara Envelope Co, Chicago, IL. Tel: (773) 638-1200 (26)

Moran, Kevin, Central States Indemnity, Omaha, NE. Tel: (402) 997-8000, (402) 397-1111, (800) 445-6500, Web Site: www.csi-omaha.com (15)

Moran, Lynn, Savitz, Dallas, TX. Tel: (310) 642-4799, FAX: (310) 642-7795, E-Mail: lmoran@ savitzfieldandfocus.com, Web Site: www. savitzfieldandfocus.com (20)

Moran, Ron, Moran Direct Inc, Houston, TX. Tel: (713) 880-3725, FAX: (713) 263-7647, E-Mail: rmoran@ morandirect.com, Web Site: www.morandirect.com (20)

Moran, Thomas J., Mutual of America Life Insurance Co, New York, NY. Tel: (212) 224-1600, (800) 468-3785, FAX: (212) 207-3001, Web Site: www. mutualofamerica.com (14)

Moran, Thomas, West Marine Inc, Watsonville, CA. Tel: (831) 728-2700, (800) 262-8464, (800) BOAT-ING, FAX: (831) 768-5000, E-Mail: customercare@ westmarine.com, Web Site: www.westmarine.com (11)

Moran, Tom, Thomson West, Eagan, MN. Tel: (651) 687-7000, (800) 328-9378, FAX: (651) 687-7849, E-Mail: jeff.patrios@thomsonreuters.com, Web Site: www.thomson.com (17)

Morandini, Kathy, ListK, Atlanta, GA. Tel: (800) 600-3389, FAX: (770) 825-9188, E-Mail: questions@ listk.com, Web Site: www.listk.com (32)

Morano, Vince, Markertek Video Supply, Saugerties, NY. Tel: (845) 246-3036, (800) 522-2025, FAX: (845) 246-1757, E-Mail: sales@markertek.com, Web Site: www.markertek.com (3)

S Morantz Inc, Philadelphia, PA. Tel: (215) 969-0266, (800) 695-4522, FAX: (215) 969-0566, E-Mail: info@morantz.com, Web Site: www.morantz.com (34)

Morantz, Heather, S Morantz Inc, Philadelphia, PA. Tel: (215) 969-0266, (800) 695-4522, FAX: (215) 969-0566, E-Mail: info@morantz.com, Web Site: www. morantz.com (34)

Morantz, Lisa, S Morantz Inc, Philadelphia, PA. Tel: (215) 969-0266, (800) 695-4522, FAX: (215) 969-0566, E-Mail: info@morantz.com, Web Site: www. morantz.com (34)

Morantz, Stan, S Morantz Inc, Philadelphia, PA. Tel: (215) 969-0266, (800) 695-4522, FAX: (215) 969-0566, E-Mail: info@morantz.com, Web Site: www. morantz.com (34)

Morcon Industrial Specialty Inc, Mesquite, NV. Tel: (702) 346-3447, (888) 842-7953, Web Site: www. morcon-ind.com (9)

More Media Direct Inc, Marina Del Rey, CA. Tel: (310) 577-2025, E-Mail: info@moremediadirect.com, Web Site: www.moremediadirect.com (3)

Morehead, Catherine, Outsource America Inc, Braden-ton, FL. Tel: (941) 746-4555, (800) 729-5694, FAX: (441) 746-3595, E-Mail: sales@oaiworld.com, Web Site: www.oaiworld.com (24)

Morehouse, Ted, Emigrant Savings Bank, New York, NY. Tel: (212) 850-4521, (800) EMIGRANT, FAX: (212) 850-4372, Web Site: www.emigrant.com (14)

Morelli, Michael, Littleton Coin Co Inc, Littleton, NH. Tel: (603) 444-5386, (800) 645-3122, FAX: (603) 444-0121, E-Mail: jhennessey@littletoncoin.com, Web Site: www.littletoncoin.com (6)

Morelli, Stephen, Ruud Lighting Inc, Racine, WI. Tel: (262) 886-1900, (800) 236-7000, FAX: (800) 236-7500, E-Mail: sales@ruudlighting.com, Web Site: www.ruudlighting.com (9)

Morello, Marcello, Manhattan Media Services Inc, New York, NY. Tel: (212) 808-4077, FAX: (212) 808-4080, E-Mail: mmorello@manhmedia.com, Web Site: www.manhmedia.com (21)

Morello, Marianna, Manhattan Media Services Inc, New York, NY. Tel: (212) 808-4077, FAX: (212) 808-4080, E-Mail: mmorello@manhmedia.com, Web Site: www.manhmedia.com (21)

Moreno, Victoria, Blue Coral Slick 50, Houston, TX. Tel: (713) 241-6161, (800) 416-1600, FAX: (713) 241-4044, E-Mail: SCD-ConsumerSolutions@Shell. com, Web Site: www.bluecoral.com (17)

Moresi, John, Impressions Direct, Saint Louis, MO. Tel: (314) 951-2100, Web Site: www.impressions-direct. com (28)

Jacques Moret Inc, New York, NY. Tel: (212) 354-2400, FAX: (212) 354-5544, E-Mail: info@moret. com, Web Site: www.moret.com (16)

Moret, Pam, Thrivent Financial for Lutherans, Apple-ton, WI. Tel: (920) 734-5721, (800) 847-4836, FAX: (920) 730-4781, E-Mail: mail@thrivent.com, Web Site: www.thrivent.com (14)

MoreVisibility, Boca Raton, FL. Tel: (561) 620-9682, (800) 787-0497, FAX: (561) 620-9684, E-Mail: info@morevisibility.com, Web Site: www. morevisibility.com (32)

Morey, John, The Lukens Company, Alexandria, VA. Tel: (703) 845-8484, FAX: (703) 845-9655, Web Site: www.thelukenscompany.com (35)

Alan Morgan & Associates Inc, Jacksonville, FL. Tel: (904) 262-1316, FAX: (904) 880-6182, E-Mail: amorgan@alanmorgan.com, Web Site: www. alanmorgan.com (29)

Morgan Kaufmann Publishers Inc, Burlington, MA. Tel: (781) 313-4700, E-Mail: order@mkp.com, Web Site: www.mkp.com (17)

Morgan Stanley, New York, NY. Tel: (212) 761-4000, FAX: (212) 761-0096 (14)

Morgan, Alan, Alan Morgan & Associates Inc, Jackson-ville, FL. Tel: (904) 262-1316, FAX: (904) 880-6182, E-Mail: amorgan@alanmorgan.com, Web Site: www.alanmorgan.com (29)

Morgan, Bob, Veneer Factory Outlet, Westport, KY. E-Mail: bob@veneerfactoryoutlet.com, Web Site: veneer-factory-outlet.com (8)

Morgan, Doug, Nexxlinx (HQ), Atlanta, GA. Tel: (770) 250-0349, (877) 747-0658, Web Site: www. nexxlinx.com (22)

Morgan, Edward H., Christian Herald Association, New York, NY. Tel: (212) 684-2800, (800) BOWERY-1, FAX: (212) 684-3740, E-Mail: info@chaonline.org, Web Site: www.bowery.org (1)

Morgan, John, Association of Coupon Professionals, Drexel Hill, PA. Tel: (610) 789-1478, FAX: (610) 789-5309, E-Mail: john.morgan@acp-hq.org, Web Site: www.couponpros.org (40)

Morgan, Katherine E., ASTM International, West Con-shohocken, PA. Tel: (610) 832-9500, FAX: (610) 832-9555, E-Mail: service@astm.org, Web Site: www.astm.org (1)

Morgan, Paul, PRM Media Group, Hackettstown, NJ. Tel: (973) 765-9600, (877) 588-9552, FAX: (973) 765-0004, E-Mail: paul.morgan@prmmediagroup. com, Web Site: www.prmmediagroup.com (35)

Morgan, Rick, Trone Brand Energy Inc, High Point, NC. Tel: (336) 886-1622, E-Mail: info@trone.com, Web Site: www.tronebrandenergy.com (35)

Morgan, Robert, ASTM International, West Consho-hocken, PA. Tel: (610) 832-9500, FAX: (610) 832-9555, E-Mail: service@astm.org, Web Site: www. astm.org (1)

Morgan, Scott, Brunner, Pittsburgh, PA. Tel: (412) 995-9500, FAX: (412) 995-9501, Web Site: www. brunnerworks.com (35)

Morgan, Tate, Petra Industries, Edmond, OK. Tel: (405) 216-2100, FAX: (405) 216-2102, Web Site: www. patra.com (34)

Morgan, Tim H., United America Advertising Inc, Enid, OK. Tel: (580) 233-7200, FAX: (580) 548-8432 (29)

Morgan, Willy, The NonProfit Times, Morris Plains, NJ. Tel: (973) 401-0202, FAX: (973) 401-0404, Web Site: www.nptimes.com (17)

Morgan-Prager, Karole, McClatchy Co, Sacramento, CA. Tel: (916) 321-1855, FAX: (916) 321-1869, Web Site: www.mcclatchy.com (17)

Morgano, Anthony, American Express Publishing Corp, New York, NY. Tel: (212) 382-5600, (888) 461-6180, FAX: (212) 827-6496, E-Mail: aepc@ custmersvc.com, Web Site: www.amexpub.com (17)

Mori, John, National Luggage Dealers Association, Glenview, IL. Tel: (847) 998-6869, FAX: (847) 998-6884, E-Mail: inquiry@nlda.com, Web Site: www. nlda.com (1)

Moriarty, Kerry, Bayard Inc, New London, CT. Tel: (860) 437-3012, (800) 321-0411, FAX: (800) 572-0788, Web Site: www.bayard-inc.com (31)

Morin, Dr. Geof, American Bible Society, New York, NY. Tel: (212) 408-1200, FAX: (212) 408-1264, Web Site: www.americanbible.org (1)

Morin, Matt, Reliable Technologies Inc, Manchester, NH. Tel: (603) 644-2528, (800) 346-7890, FAX: (603) 627-5553, Web Site: www.tei-imaging.com (16)

Moritt, Hock, Hamroff & Horowitz, Garden City, NY. Tel: (516) 873-2000, FAX: (516) 873-2010, E-Mail: lhauser@morritthock.com, Web Site: www. morritthock.com (16)

Moritt, Neil J., Moritt, Hock, Hamroff & Horowitz, Gar-den City, NY. Tel: (516) 873-2000, FAX: (516) 873-2010, E-Mail: lhauser@morritthock.com, Web Site: www.morritthock.com (16)

Moritz, Joshua, Customer Growth Inc, Fairfield, CT. Tel: (203) 226-8795, FAX: (203) 286-1049, E-Mail: info@customer-growth.com, Web Site: www. customer-growth.com (35)

Moritz, Robert E., PricewaterhouseCoopers LLP, New York, NY. Tel: (646) 471-4000, FAX: (813) 286-6000, Web Site: www.pwc.com (14)

Morkes Chocolates, Palatine, IL. Tel: (847) 359-3454, FAX: (847) 359-3553, E-Mail: yummy@ morkeschocolates.com, Web Site: www. morkeschocolates.com (4)

Morkes, Rhonda, Morkes Chocolates, Palatine, IL. Tel: (847) 359-3454, FAX: (847) 359-3553, E-Mail: yummy@morkeschocolates.com, Web Site: www. morkeschocolates.com (4)

Morley Companies, Saginaw, MI. Tel: (989) 791-2550, (800) 336-5554, FAX: (800) 426-6753, Web Site: www.morleynet.com (33)

Morley, David, UNICEF Canada, Toronto, ON Canada. Tel: (416) 482-4444, (800) 567-4483, FAX: (416) 487-8875, E-Mail: on.secretary@unicef.ca, Web Site: www.unicef.ca (1)

Morley, Kathryn, Penny Wise Office Products, Bowie, MD. Tel: (301) 805-7733, (800) 942-3311, FAX: (800) 622-4411, Web Site: www.penny-wise.com (10)

Morneau, Doug, Rhino Marketing Inc, Los Angeles, CA. Tel: (604) 472-3240, (877) 605-7022, FAX: (604) 637-5619, Web Site: www.rhino.ca (20)

Morningstar Inc, Chicago, IL. Tel: (312) 696-6000, Web Site: www.morningstar.com (14)

Morningstar, Renee, Campbell Tools Co, Springfield, OH. Tel: (937) 882-6716, FAX: (937) 882-6648, E-Mail: campbell@campbelltools.com, Web Site: www.campbelltools.com (9)

Moroney, Richard, Dow Theory Forecasts, Hammond, IN. Tel: (219) 931-6480, (800) 233-5922, FAX: (219) 931-6487, E-Mail: custserv@ horizonpublishing.com, Web Site: www.dowtheory. com (17)

Morpace Inc, Farmington Hills, MI. Tel: (248) 737-5300, FAX: (248) 737-5326, E-Mail: information@ morpace.com, Web Site: www.morpace.com (30)

Morra, Vincent, Whitaker National, Huntington, WV. Tel: (304) 525-0852, (800) 377-8721, FAX: (304) 525-0874, Web Site: www.neshold.com (16)

Morrell, Allen, Simmons-Boardman Publishing Corp, New York, NY. Tel: (212) 620-7200, (800) 257-5091, Web Site: www.simmonsboardman.com (17)

Morris & Fellows, Atlanta, GA. Tel: (404) 250-0225 (20)

Morris Communications Corp, Augusta, GA. Tel: (706) 724-0851, (800) 622-6358, Web Site: www.morris.com (31)

Morris James Hitchens & Williams, Wilmington, DE. Tel: (302) 888-6800, FAX: (302) 571-1750, Web Site: www.morrisjames.com (20)

Morris Visitors Publications LLC, Augusta, GA. Tel: (305) 892-6644, FAX: (305) 892-1005, E-Mail: mvpcustomerservice@morris.com, Web Site: www.morrisvisitorpublications.com (17)

Morris, Angela, Quality Contact Solutions Inc, Aurora, NE. Tel: (402) 210-2692, (866) 963-2889, FAX: (402) 210-2692, E-Mail: info@qualitycontactsolutions.com, Web Site: www.qualitycontactsolutions.com (29)

Morris, Bill, American Teleservices Association, Indianapolis, IN. Tel: (317) 816-9336, (877) 779-3974, FAX: (317) 218-0323, Web Site: www.ataconnect.org (40)

Morris, Cheri, Morris & Fellows, Atlanta, GA. Tel: (404) 250-0225 (20)

Morris, Dawn, Bankers Warranty Group, Saint Petersburg, FL. Tel: (800) 431-5843, E-Mail: info@bankerswarrantygroup.com, Web Site: www.bankerswarrantygroup.com (16)

Morris, Dianne, The Sperry & Hutchinson Co Inc, Delray Beach, FL. Tel: (561) 454-7621, FAX: (561) 265-2493, E-Mail: mediarelations@shsolutions.com, Web Site: www.greenpoints.com (6)

Morris, Donna, Adobe Systems Inc, San Jose, CA. Tel: (408) 536-6000, (800) 833-6687, FAX: (408) 537-6000, Web Site: www.adobe.com (22)

Morris, Dwight A., Carrot-Top Industries Inc, Hillsborough, NC. Tel: (919) 732-6200, (800) 628-3524, FAX: (919) 732-5526, E-Mail: service@carrot-top.com, Web Site: www.carrot-top.com (16)

Morris, Greg, Millions By Marketing Inc, Mendham, NJ. Tel: (973) 222-0011, Web Site: www.millionsbymarketing.com (22)

Morris, Harvey, Chicago Convention & Tourism Bureau, Chicago, IL. Tel: (312) 791-7000, FAX: (312) 567-8599, Web Site: www.choosechicago.com (1)

Morris, James, Direct Marketing Designs Inc, Greenwood Village, CO. Tel: (303) 649-9888, FAX: (303) 649-1917, E-Mail: info@directmarketingdesigns.com, Web Site: www.directmarketingdesigns.com (35)

Morris, Jeff, New Hampshire Public Television, Durham, NH. Tel: (603) 868-1100, E-Mail: themailbox@nhptv.org, Web Site: www.nhptv.org (32)

Morris, Jennifer, Conservation International, Arlington, VA. Tel: (703) 341-2400, E-Mail: community@conservation.org (1)

Morris, John, Bass Pro Shops, Springfield, MO. Tel: (417) 887-7334, FAX: (417) 873-5882, Web Site: www.basspro.com (11)

Morris, Kevin, The Pond-Ekberg Co, Chicopee, MA. Tel: (413) 594-7511, (800) 225-7511, FAX: (413) 594-2179, E-Mail: sales@pond-ekberg.com, Web Site: www.pond-ekberg.com (27)

Morris, Larry, Bontex, Honolulu, HI. Tel: (540) 261-2181, FAX: (540) 261-3784, E-Mail: bontex@bontex.com, Web Site: www.bontex.com (16)

Morris, Rick, CCI Digital, Burbank, CA. Tel: (818) 562-6300, FAX: (818) 562-8222, E-Mail: info@ccidigital.com, Web Site: www.ccidigital.com (32)

Morris, Shawn, National Auto Warranty, Wentzville, MO. Tel: (800) 649-1620 (16)

Morris, Shawn, RPM Direct LLC, Lambertville, NJ. Tel: (609) 566-7150, FAX: (609) 566-7155, E-Mail: jimarslan@rpmdirectllc.com, Web Site: www.rpmdirectllc.com (35)

Morris, Steve, WordCom Inc, Ellington, CT. Tel: (860) 875-7373, (800) 822-0622, FAX: (860) 872-2713, E-Mail: sales@wordcom-inc.com, Web Site: www.wordcom-inc.com (21)

Morris, Thomas E., TWL Knowledge Group, Carrollton, TX. Tel: (972) 309-4000, (800) 624-2272, FAX: (972) 309-5105, Web Site: www.twlk.com (3)

Morris, Todd, Catalina Marketing Corp, Saint Petersburg, FL. Tel: (727) 579-5000, FAX: (727) 556-2700, Web Site: www.catalinamarketing.com (31)

Morris, Tom, Stile-Tile Like Metal Roofing, Sellersburg, IN. Tel: (812) 246-1866, (800) 999-7777, FAX: (800) 477-9318, (800) 944-6884, Web Site: www.mtsales.com (9)

Morrison Printing Co, Morristown, TN. Tel: (423) 586-4812, (800) 251-0975, FAX: (423) 586-0322, E-Mail: info@morrcom.com, Web Site: www.morrcom.com (27)

Morrison, Denise M., Campbell Soup Co, Camden, NJ. Tel: (856) 342-4800, (800) 257-8443, FAX: (856) 342-3878, Web Site: www.campbellsoupcompany.com (16)

Morrison, Don, ForeSee Results Inc, Ann Arbor, MI. Tel: (734) 205-2600, (800) 621-2850, FAX: (734) 205-2601, Web Site: www.foreseeresults.com (30)

Morrison, James G., Association of Marian Helpers, Stockbridge, MA. Tel: (413) 298-3931, (800) 462-7426, Web Site: www.marian.org (1)

Morrison, Ken P., Doane, Saint Louis, MO. Tel: (314) 569-2700, (866) 647-0918, FAX: (314) 569-1083, Web Site: www.doane.com (17)

Morrison, Lindsay H, SRDS, Des Plaines, IL. Tel: (800) 851-7737, FAX: (847) 375-5001, Web Site: www.srds.com (17)

Morrison, Rick, Bartash Media Group, Philadelphia, PA. Tel: (215) 724-1700, (800) 599-9792, FAX: (215) 724-3313, Web Site: www.bartash.com (27)

Christopher Morrow Photography, Port Saint Lucie, FL. Tel: (845) 325-1233, E-Mail: chris@chrismorrow.com, Web Site: www.chrismorrow.com (37)

Morrow, Bill, Crain Communications Inc, Detroit, MI. Tel: (313) 446-6000, FAX: (313) 446-1616, Web Site: www.crain.com (17)

Morrow, Christopher, Christopher Morrow Photography, Port Saint Lucie, FL. Tel: (845) 325-1233, E-Mail: chris@chrismorrow.com, Web Site: www.chrismorrow.com (37)

Morrow, Joel, Mobile Fusion, Lakewood, CO. Tel: (720) 963-8000, (800) 431-8556, Web Site: www.mobile-fusion.com (16)

Morrows, Bruce, Skypoint Communications Inc, Loretto, MN. Tel: (763) 548-2600, FAX: (763) 548-2610, E-Mail: info@skypoint.com, Web Site: www.skypoint.com (16)

Morse, David, New American Dimensions, Los Angeles, CA. Tel: (310) 670-6800 (20)

Morten, James E., Interprint Web & Sheetfed, Clearwater, FL. Tel: (727) 531-8957, (800) 749-5152, FAX: (727) 536-0647, E-Mail: customerservice@printerusa.com, Web Site: www.printerusa.com (27)

Morter, Robert, NTP Distribution, Wilsonville, OR. Tel: (503) 570-0171, FAX: (888) 570-0342, Web Site: www.ntpdistribution.com (34)

Mortine, Neil, Fahlgren Mortine, Columbus, OH. Tel: (800) 731-8927, E-Mail: info@fahlgren.com, Web Site: www.fahlgrenmortine.com (35)

Mortland, Shirley A., Hitchcock Shoes Inc, Hingham, MA. Tel: (781) 749-3571, (888) 599-9433, FAX: (781) 749-3576, E-Mail: hitchcock@wideshoes.com, Web Site: www.wideshoes.com (2)

Morton Advertising Inc, New York, NY. Tel: (212) 465-2250, FAX: (212) 465-1575, E-Mail: info@mortonad.com, Web Site: www.mortonad.com (35)

The Morton Arboretum, Lisle, IL. Tel: (630) 968-0074, Web Site: www.mortonarb.org (1)

Morton, John E., Overseas Private Investment Corp (OPIC), Washington, DC. Tel: (202) 336-8799, FAX: (202) 336-7949, E-Mail: info@opic.gov, Web Site: www.opic.gov (14)

Morton, Larry, Hal Leonard Corp, Milwaukee, WI. Tel: (414) 774-3630, FAX: (414) 774-3259, Web Site: www.halleonard.com (17)

Morton, Mark, The Newman Group Computer Services Corp, Ann Arbor, MI. Tel: (734) 426-3200, FAX: (734) 426-0777, E-Mail: anewman@newman.com (3)

Morton, Sue, Data Dash Inc, Saint Louis, MO. Tel: (314) 832-5788, (800) 211-5988, FAX: (314) 832-5775, E-Mail: info@datadash.com, Web Site: www.datadash.com (22)

Morvay, Steven, Acquirgy Inc, Saint Petersburg, FL. Tel: (727) 576-6630, FAX: (727) 576-4864, Web Site: www.sendtec.com (35)

Mos, Martin, Springer Science & Business Media LLC, New York, NY. Tel: (212) 460-1500, FAX: (212) 460-1575, Web Site: www.springer.com (17)

Thomas Moser Cabinetmakers, Freeport, ME. Tel: (207) 865-4519, (800) 708-9041, FAX: (207) 865-6539, E-Mail: freeportshowroom@thosmoser.com, Web Site: www.thosmoser.com (16)

Moses, Andy, Penske Logistics, Reading, PA. Tel: (800) 529-6531, FAX: (610) 775-2449, E-Mail: info.penskelogistics@penske.com, Web Site: www.penskelogistics.com (16)

Moses, James, Elderhostel Inc, Lowell, MA. Tel: (978) 323-4291, (800) 454-5678, FAX: (617) 426-2166, Web Site: www.elderhostel.org (1)

Mosher, Adam, Tuttle, Wallingford, CT. Tel: (203) 949-4290, (800) 882-7511, FAX: (203) 949-4288, Web Site: www.tuttlecatalog.com (2)

Mosher, Fred, Associated Photo, Erlanger, KY. Tel: (859) 344-1460, (800) 727-2580, FAX: (859) 282-0032 (16)

Mosher, George A, National Business Furniture Inc, Milwaukee, WI. Tel: (414) 276-8511, (800) 558-1010, FAX: (414) 276-8371, Web Site: www.nationalbusinessfurniture.com (10)

Mosholder, Mark, ClickSquared, Boston, MA. Tel: (781) 622-1611, (866) 402-5425, FAX: (857) 246-7645, E-Mail: info@clicksquared.com, Web Site: www.clicksquared.com (20)

Mosier, Andrew, Mead Johnson Co, Evansville, IN. Tel: (812) 429-5204, Web Site: www.MeadJohnson.com (7)

Moskowitz, Aaron, MarketingWorks Inc, Los Angeles, CA. Tel: (323) 436-2000, E-Mail: chas@mwks.net, Web Site: www.marketingworksagency.com (32)

Mosley, Troy, Sportsmith LLC, Tulsa, OK. Tel: (918) 307-2446, (800) 713-2880, Web Site: www.sportsmith.net (11)

Moss, Carl, Four Star Marketing Inc, Lincolnwood, IL. Tel: (800) 888-2991, FAX: (847) 679-6449, E-Mail: cari@fourstarmarketing.com, Web Site: www.conventionbags.com (33)

Moss, Daniel, Inquiry Intelligence Systems, O'Fallon, MO. Tel: (636) 240-1800, (800) 467-2329, FAX: (636) 281-1517, E-Mail: sales@iqsalespro.com, Web Site: www.inquiry-tracking.com (22)

Moss, Mike, Inquiry Intelligence Systems, O'Fallon, MO. Tel: (636) 240-1800, (800) 467-2329, FAX: (636) 281-1517, E-Mail: sales@iqsalespro.com, Web Site: www.inquiry-tracking.com (22)

Mossotti, Ron, Hammond Communications Group Inc, Lexington, KY. Tel: (859) 254-1878, (888) 424-1878, FAX: (859) 254-4290, E-Mail: info@hammondcg.com, Web Site: www.hammondcg.com (35)

Mostad & Christensen, Oak Harbor, WA. Tel: (360) 679-4164, (800) 654-1654, FAX: (360) 679-4167, E-Mail: marketing@mostad.com, Web Site: www.mostad.com (16)

Mostad, Arvid, Mostad & Christensen, Oak Harbor, WA. Tel: (360) 679-4164, (800) 654-1654, FAX: (360) 679-4167, E-Mail: marketing@mostad.com, Web Site: www.mostad.com (16)

Mosterion, Kiki, Argent Trading LLC, New York, NY. Tel: (212) 697-8800, FAX: (212) 697-8606, Web Site: www.Argenttrading.com (16)

Motamed, Thomas F., CNA, Chicago, IL. Tel: (312) 822-5000, (800) 262-2000, E-Mail: cna_help@cna.com, Web Site: www.cna.com (15)

Motameni, Dr. Reza, California State University at Fresno, Fresno, CA. Tel: (559) 278-7830, FAX: (559) 278-8577, Web Site: www.csufresno.edu (41)

Mother Earth News Magazine, Topeka, KS. Tel: (785) 274-4300, (800) 678-5779, FAX: (785) 274-4305, E-Mail: bwelch@ogdenpubs.com, Web Site: www.cappers.com (17)

Mother Jones Magazine, San Francisco, CA. Tel: (415) 321-1700, Web Site: www.motherjones.com (17)

Motherhead, Ivan, UMI Publications Inc, Charlotte, NC. Tel: (800) 747-9287, FAX: (704) 374-0729, E-Mail: info@umipub.com, Web Site: www.umipub.com (17)

Motient Communications, Reston, VA. Tel: (847) 478-4330, (800) 752-2672, FAX: (703) 758-6111 (16)

Motion Picture & Television Fund, Woodland Hills, CA. Tel: (855) 760-6783, E-Mail: info@mptf.com, Web Site: www.mptf.com (1)

The Motley Fool, Alexandria, VA. Tel: (703) 838-3665, FAX: (703) 254-1999, E-Mail: cs@fool.com, Web Site: www.Fool.com (14)

Motley, Randy, Farrow Group, Windsor, ON Canada. Tel: (519) 966-3003, E-Mail: info@farrow.com, Web Site: www.farrow.com (16)

Moto Franchise Corp, Dayton, OH. Tel: (937) 291-1900, (800) 733-6686, FAX: (937) 291-2005, E-Mail: expert@motophoto.com, Web Site: www.motophoto.com; www.portraitavenue.com (3)

Moto, Nick, Hazelden, Center City, MN. Tel: (651) 213-4200, (800) 257-7810, FAX: (651) 213-4411, E-Mail: info@hazeldenbettyford.org, Web Site: www.hazelden.org (7)

Motor Coach Industries International Inc, Schaumburg, IL. Tel: (847) 285-2000, (800) 624-2622, Web Site: www.mcicoach.com (16)

Mott Media LLC, Fenton, MI. Tel: (810) 714-4280, FAX: (810) 714-2077, E-Mail: info@mottmedia.com, Web Site: www.mottmedia.com (17)

Motta, Sharon, Management Science Associates Inc, Pittsburgh, PA. Tel: (412) 362-2000, (800) MSA-INFO, FAX: (412) 363-5598, E-Mail: info@msa.com, Web Site: www.msa.com (20)

Moultrie Manufacturing Co, Moultrie, GA. Tel: (229) 985-1312, (800) 841-8674, FAX: (229) 890-7245, Web Site: www.moultriemanufacturing.com (8)

Moultrie, Armida, Ross Metals, New York, NY. Tel: (212) 869-1407, (800) 654-ROSS (16)

Mount, Clyde, 3PL Worldwide Inc, Milford, CT. Tel: (203) 567-1099, Web Site: www.3plworldwide.com (28)

Mount, Portia, Center for Creative Leadership, Greensboro, NC. Tel: (336) 545-2810, FAX: (336) 282-3284, E-Mail: info@ccl.org, Web Site: www.ccl.org (16)

Mount, Tenny, Eagle Claw Fishing Tackle, Denver, CO. Tel: (720) 941-8700, FAX: (303) 321-4750, E-Mail: info@eagleclaw.com, Web Site: www.eagleclaw.com (11)

Mountain Craft Shop Co, Proctor, WV. Tel: (877) 365-5869, FAX: (304) 455-1740, E-Mail: info@folktoys.com, Web Site: www.folktoys.com (11)

Mountain Media Enterprises, Fort Collins, CO. Tel: (970) 493-2499, FAX: (970) 493-3598, E-Mail: info@mountain-media.com, Web Site: fortcollinsdigitalprinting.com (21)

Mountain Press Publishing Co, Missoula, MT. Tel: (406) 728-1900, (800) 234-5308, FAX: (406) 728-1635, E-Mail: info@mountain-press.com, Web Site: mountain-press.com (17)

Mountain West Communications Inc, Hotchkiss, CO. Tel: (970) 872-2500, (800) 642-9378, FAX: (970) 872-3862, E-Mail: sales@mountainwest.com, Web Site: www.mountainwest.com (29)

Mountain West Supply Co, Scottsdale, AZ. Tel: (602) 971-1200, (800) 528-6169, FAX: (602) 996-5077 (3)

Mounts, L. David, Inmar, Winston-Salem, NC. Tel: (336) 631-2500, FAX: (336) 631-2888, E-Mail: ibizdev@inmar.com, Web Site: www.promotionslogistics.com (14)

Mouring, Veronica, Aegon Direct Marketing Services Inc, Baltimore, MD. Tel: (410) 209-5617, FAX: (410) 209-5932, Web Site: www.aegondms.com (15)

Mousseau, Bradley, PC Connection, Merrimack, NH. Tel: (603) 683-2167, (800) 800-0014, FAX: (603) 683-5773, E-Mail: pr@pcconnection.com, Web Site: www.pcconnection.com, macconnection.com (22)

Mousseau, Heather, Winnipeg Art Gallery, Winnipeg, MB Canada. Tel: (204) 786-6641, FAX: (204) 788-4998, E-Mail: inquiries@wag.mb.ca, Web Site: www.wag.ca (1)

Mouzakis, Andrea, Reed Smith Hall Dickler Advertising & Law Marketing Group, New York, NY. Tel: (212) 549-0377, FAX: (212) 521-5450, Web Site: www.reedsmith.com (20)

Movie Central, Toronto, ON Canada. Tel: (416) 479-6784, E-Mail: info@moviecentral.ca, Web Site: www.moviecentral.ca (32)

Mowell, Larry, Cotta Transmission Co, Beloit, WI. Tel: (608) 368-5600, FAX: (608) 368-5605, E-Mail: sales@cotta.com, Web Site: www.cotta.com (16)

Mowen, Ginny, Red Hill Corp, Gettysburg, PA. Tel: (717) 337-3038, (800) 822-4003, FAX: (717) 337-0732, E-Mail: custserv@supergrit.com, Web Site: www.supergrit.com (34)

Mower, Eric, Eric Mower + Associates, Syracuse, NY. Tel: (315) 466-1000, Web Site: www.mower.com (35)

Moxie, Atlanta, GA. Tel: (678) 916-4500, E-Mail: info@moxieusa.com, Web Site: moxieusa.com (35)

Moyer, Barry, Litho-Web Inc, Bolton, ON Canada. Tel: (905) 857-9111, (800) 490-6688, FAX: (905) 857-9112, E-Mail: sales@lithoweb.ca, Web Site: www.lithoweb.ca (27)

Moyer, Bruce, Direct Marketing Association of Detroit, Royal Oak, MI. Tel: (248) 478-4888, FAX: (248) 478-6437, E-Mail: dmad@ameritech.net, Web Site: www.dmad.org (40)

Moyer, Bruce S., Directions Marketing, Ann Arbor, MI. Tel: (734) 930-2820, FAX: (734) 930-9189, E-Mail: directions@directions.com.eg, Web Site: www.directions.com.eg (20)

Moyer, Chuck, Conney Safety Products LLC, Madison, WI. Tel: (888) 356-9100, FAX: (800) 845-9095, E-Mail: safety@conney.com, Web Site: www.conney.com (7)

Moylan, John J., Golden Gate Transportation District, San Rafael, CA. Tel: (415) 921-5858, FAX: (415) 923-2014, Web Site: www.goldengate.org (16)

Moyle, Shep, Shindigz, South Whitley, IN. Tel: (219) 723-5171, (800) 314-8736, FAX: (219) 723-6976, E-Mail: csr@shindigz.com, Web Site: www.shindigz.com (27)

Moyle, Wendy, Shindigz, South Whitley, IN. Tel: (219) 723-5171, (800) 314-8736, FAX: (219) 723-6976, E-Mail: csr@shindigz.com, Web Site: www.shindigz.com (27)

Moynier, Bob, Keystone Press Agency Inc, Montreal, QC Canada. Tel: (514) 482-5312, (877) 482-5312, FAX: (514) 483-9005, E-Mail: pictures@keystonepressagency.com, Web Site: www.ketstonepressagency.com (38)

Mozillo, Angelo R., Countrywide Financial Corp, Calabasas, CA. Tel: (818) 225-3000, FAX: (818) 225-4051, Web Site: www.countrywide.com (14)

MSC Metalworking, Melville, NY. Tel: (516) 812-2000, (800) 521-9520, E-Mail: inquiry@rutlandtool.com, Web Site: www.rutlandtool.com (34)

MSW Research, Lake Success, NY. Tel: (516) 394-6000, FAX: (516) 394-6001, E-Mail: mail@mswresearch.com, Web Site: www.mswresearch.com (30)

Mucci, Robert A., NGL Insurance Group, Madison, WI. Tel: (608) 257-5611, (800) 548-2962, FAX: (608) 257-9340, Web Site: www.nglic.com (15)

Muckler, Jeff, Direct Logic Solutions, Peoria, IL. Tel: (309) 688-5500, FAX: (309) 688-5502, E-Mail: nedbarrett@direct-logic.com, Web Site: www.direct-logic.com (22)

Mudd, Jason, Axia Public Relations, Jacksonville, FL. Tel: (904) 425-1500, (866) 773-4768, Web Site: www.axiapr.com (35)

Mudge, Chris, Customized Newspaper Advertising, Des Moines, IA. Tel: (515) 244-2145, (800) 227-7636, FAX: (515) 244-4855, Web Site: www.cnaads.com (18)

Mueke, Diane, Seastrom Manufacturing Co Inc, Twin Falls, ID. Tel: (208) 737-4300, (800) 634-2356, FAX: (208) 734-7222, E-Mail: info@seastrom-mfg.com, Web Site: www.seastrom-mfg.com (3)

Mueller, Brian, Grand Canyon University, Phoenix, AZ. Tel: (602) 639-7500, (877) 860-3951, Web Site: www.gcu.edu (13)

Mueller, Eduard R., Qwest, Denver, CO. Tel: (303) 992-1400, (800) 603-6000, FAX: (303) 896-8515, Web Site: www.qwest.com (20)

Mueller, Greg, CRC Public Relations, Alexandria, VA. Tel: (703) 683-5004, FAX: (703) 683-1703, E-Mail: crc@crcpublicrelations.com, Web Site: www.crcpublicrelations.com (35)

Mueller, Joan, Brushfire Inc, Cedar Knolls, NJ. Tel: (973) 871-1700, FAX: (973) 871-1717, E-Mail: vwarner@brushfireinc.com, Web Site: www.brushfireinc.com (35)

Mueller, Lee, Coyne American Institute, Chicago, IL. Tel: (773) 935-2520, (800) 999-5220, FAX: (773) 935-2920, Web Site: www.coyneamerican.edu (16)

Mueller, Roger P., RPM Industries Inc, Auburn, NY. Tel: (315) 255-1105, (800) 669-3676, FAX: (315) 252-1167, Web Site: www.rpmdisplays.com (33)

Mueller, Soren, Direct Link Worldwide, Elizabeth, NJ. Tel: (908) 289-0703, (800) 223-7967, FAX: (908) 289-0705, E-Mail: infousa@directlink.com, Web Site: www.directlink.com (28)

Mueller, Stephanie, Demco Inc, Madison, WI. Tel: (608) 241-1201, (800) 356-1200, FAX: (608) 241-1799, E-Mail: custserv@demco.com, Web Site: www.demco.com (10)

Mueller, Trish, The Home Depot Inc, Atlanta, GA. Tel: (770) 433-8211, (800) 466-3337, FAX: (770) 384-2356, Web Site: www.homedepot.com (16)

Mui, Philip ("Phil") L., Acxiom Corp, Little Rock, AR. Tel: (501) 342-1000, FAX: (501) 342-3913, Web Site: www.acxiom.com (22)

Muilenburg, Dennis A., Boeing Co, Chicago, IL. Tel: (312) 544-2000, FAX: (312) 544-2082, Web Site: www.boeing.com (16)

Muir, Bob, Chase Industries, Inc, Cincinnati, OH. Tel: (513) 860-5565, (800) 543-4455, FAX: (800) 245-7045, Web Site: www.chasedoors.com (16)

Muir, Stan, Harland Financial Solutions Inc, Lake Mary, FL. Tel: (407) 804-6600, (800) 815-5592, FAX: (407) 829-6702, Web Site: www.harlandfinancialsolutions.com (16)

Muirheid, Willard, Tower Hobbies/Hobbico, Champaign, IL. Tel: (217) 398-3636, (800) 637-6050, FAX: (217) 398-1104, Web Site: www.towerhobbies.com (11)

Mukherjee, Dr Debabrata, Finch Paper, Glens Falls, NY. Tel: (518) 793-2541, (800) 833-9983, FAX: (518) 793-7364, E-Mail: info@finchpaper.com, Web Site: www.finchpaper.com (25)

Mulally, Alan, Ford Motor Co, Dearborn, MI. Tel: (313) 845-8540, (800) 555-5259, FAX: (313) 845-6073, Web Site: www.ford.com (16)

Mulder, Don, Anritsu Co, Morgan Hill, CA. Tel: (408) 778-2000, (800) 267-4878, FAX: (408) 776-1744, Web Site: www.us.anritsu.com (16)

Muldoon & Baer Inc, Palm Beach Gardens, FL. Tel: (561) 630-0999, FAX: (561) 630-9466, Web Site: www.muldoonandbaer.com (20)

Muldoon, Katie, Muldoon & Baer Inc, Palm Beach Gardens, FL. Tel: (561) 630-0999, FAX: (561) 630-9466, Web Site: www.muldoonandbaer.com (20)

Mulhern, Pat, KEH.com, Smyrna, GA. Tel: (770) 333-4200, (800) 342-5534, FAX: (770) 333-4242, E-Mail: sales@keh.com, Web Site: www.keh.com (16)

Mulhern, Francis, Northwestern University, Evanston, IL. Tel: (847) 491-5665, FAX: (847) 491-5925, E-Mail: jimc@northwestern.edu, Web Site: www.northwestern.edu (41)

Mulinix, Rick, iDfour, Houston, TX. Tel: (281) 497-7606, FAX: (281) 497-7616, E-Mail: scotthaney@interdirectusa.com, Web Site: www.idfour.com (21)

Mullaney, Amber, Jefferson National, Louisville, KY. Tel: (502) 587-3853, Web Site: www.jeffnat.com (14)

Mullen & McCaffrey Communications, East Hampton, NY. Tel: (631) 324-4265, FAX: (631) 324-2135, E-Mail: mullenmccaffrey@aol.com, Web Site: www.mullenandmccaffrey.com (35)

Mullen, John J., Mullen & McCaffrey Communications, East Hampton, NY. Tel: (631) 324-4265, FAX: (631) 324-2135, E-Mail: mullenmccaffrey@aol.com, Web Site: www.mullenandmccaffrey.com (35)

Mullen, Micah, Jerry's Artarama, Raleigh, NC. Tel: (919) 878-8478, (800) U-ARTIST, FAX: (919) 873-9565, E-Mail: micah@jerrysartarama.com, Web Site: www.jerrysartarama.com (10)

Mullen, Rob, SmartFocus Inc, New York, NY. Tel: (425) 460-1000, (646) 356-1169, Web Site: www.smartfocus.com (22)

Mullen, Sean, The Hiebing Group, Madison, WI. Tel: (608) 256-6357, FAX: (608) 256-0693, E-Mail: ideas@hiebing.com, Web Site: www.hiebing.com (35)

MullenLowe US, Boston, MA. Tel: (617) 226-9000, FAX: (617) 226-9100, Web Site: us.mullenlowe.com (35)

Muller, Fred, Card Technology Inc, Hopkins, MN. Tel: (201) 845-7373, FAX: (201) 845-3337, E-Mail: info@nbstech.com, Web Site: www.nbstech.com (16)

Mullican, Mike, Altair Customer Intelligence, Franklin, TN. Tel: (615) 468-6800, (800) 241-6631, FAX: (615) 468-6878, E-Mail: asales@altairci.com, Web Site: www.altairci.com (23)

Mulligan, John, Target Corp, Minneapolis, MN. Tel: (612) 304-6073, Web Site: www.target.com (16)

Mullis, Rick, Aristokraft Inc, Jasper, IN. Tel: (812) 482-2527, FAX: (812) 482-9872, Web Site: www.aristokraft.com (16)

Mulloy, Garry, Money Mailer LLC, Garden Grove, CA. Tel: (800) 624-5371, Web Site: www.moneymailer.net (31)

Multi-Level Marketing International Association (MLMIA), Irvine, CA. Tel: (949) 257-0931, FAX: (949) 281-2114, E-Mail: info@mlmia.com, Web Site: www.mlmia.com (1)

Multi-Media Publishing & Packaging Inc, Panorama City, CA. Tel: (818) 341-7484, (800) 982-8138, FAX: (818) 341-2807, E-Mail: sales@mmppinc.com, Web Site: www.mmppinc.com (27)

Multichannel Merchant Magazine, Stamford, CT. Tel: (203) 358-4386, FAX: (203) 358-5823, E-Mail: melissa.dowling@penton.com, Web Site: www.multichannelmerchant.com (31)

Multimedia Lists Inc, Asheville, NC. Tel: (800) 239-5478, E-Mail: daniel@multimedialists.com, Web Site: multimedialists.com (23)

Multiple Sclerosis Association of America, Cherry Hill, NJ. Tel: (856) 488-4500, (800) 532-7667, FAX: (856) 661-9797, Web Site: www.mymsaa.com (1)

MultiView, Irving, TX. Tel: (972) 402-7056 (1)

Mulvaney, Kevin, American Society of Interior Designers, Washington, DC. Tel: (202) 546-3480, FAX: (202) 546-3240, E-Mail: membership@asid.org, Web Site: www.asid.org (1)

Mummert, Hallie, Inside Direct Mail, Philadelphia, PA. Tel: (215) 238-5300, (800) 777-8074, FAX: (215) 238-5412, E-Mail: customservice@napco.com, Web Site: www.insidedirectmail.com (43)

Mummert, Michele, Dentsply International, York, PA. Tel: (844) 848-0137, (800) 877-0020, E-Mail: contact@dentsplysirona.com, Web Site: www.dentsply.com (7)

Mumper, Melanie, Taylor Nelson Sofres Intersearch, Horsham, PA. Tel: (419) 725-8560, E-Mail: info@intersearch.tnsofres.com, Web Site: www.intersearch.tnsofres.com (30)

Munce, Don, National Research Center for College & University Admissions, Lees Summit, MO. Tel: (816) 525-2201, Web Site: www.nrccua.org (1)

Munch, Dr. James, Wright State University, Dayton, OH. Tel: (937) 775-3047, FAX: (513) 775-3952, E-Mail: teresa.stelmat@wright.edu, Web Site: www.wright.edu/business/acad/marketing (41)

Mundy, Robert P., Verso Paper, Memphis, TN. Tel: (901) 369-4100, FAX: (901) 369-4174, Web Site: www.versopaper.com (25)

Muniz, Sean, Patterson Dental, Saint Paul, MN. Tel: (651) 686-1600, (800) 328-5536, FAX: (651) 686-9331, Web Site: www.pattersondental.com (10)

Munoz, Jose, Nissan North America Inc, Franklin, TN. Tel: (615) 725-1000, Web Site: www.nissanusa.com (16)

Munoz, Julio, ADRA International, Silver Spring, MD. Tel: (301) 680-6373, (800) 424-2372, Web Site: www.adra.org (1)

Munroe, Dwight, Theodore Presser Co, King Of Prussia, PA. Tel: (610) 592-1222, FAX: (610) 592-1229, E-Mail: webmaster@presser.com, Web Site: www.presser.com (17)

Munson, Brenda, Rose Electronics, Houston, TX. Tel: (281) 933-7673, (800) 333-9343, FAX: (281) 933-0044, E-Mail: sales@rose.com, Web Site: www.rose.com (3)

Munson, Diane L., Oakstone Publishing LLC, Birmingham, AL. Tel: (205) 991-5188, (800) 952-0690, FAX: (205) 995-4656, E-Mail: info@oakstonepublishing.com, Web Site: www.oakstonepublishing.com (17)

Muoio, Michael, Lillian Vernon Corp, Colorado Springs, CO. Tel: (757) 427-7923, (800) 545-5426, FAX: (757) 427-7819, E-Mail: publicrelations@lillianvernon.com, Web Site: www.lillianvernon.com (6)

Murabito, John M., CIGNA International, Philadelphia, PA. Tel: (215) 761-1741, FAX: (215) 761-5515, Web Site: www.cigna.com (15)

Mike Murach & Associates Inc, Fresno, CA. Tel: (559) 440-9071, (800) 221-5528, FAX: (559) 440-0963, E-Mail: murachbooks@murach.com, Web Site: www.murach.com (17)

Murach, Mike, Mike Murach & Associates Inc, Fresno, CA. Tel: (559) 440-9071, (800) 221-5528, FAX: (559) 440-0963, E-Mail: murachbooks@murach.com, Web Site: www.murach.com (17)

Muraco, Steven, MVS Mailers Inc, Bohemia, NY. Tel: (800) 641-7917, FAX: (631) 699-0101, E-Mail: sales@mvsmailers.com, Web Site: www.mvsmailers.com (28)

Murad Inc, El Segundo, CA. Tel: (310) 726-0600, (888) 996-8723, Web Site: www.murad.com (7)

Murder by Mail, West Tisbury, MA. Tel: (508) 693-5205, (617) 670-9400, FAX: (508) 693-7997, E-Mail: info@murderbymail.com, Web Site: www.murderbymail.com (1)

Murdoch, Gina Ross, Multiple Sclerosis Association of America, Cherry Hill, NJ. Tel: (856) 488-4500, (800) 532-7667, FAX: (856) 661-9797, Web Site: www.mymsaa.com (1)

Murdoch, K. Rupert, News America Marketing, New York, NY. Tel: (212) 852-8000, (800) 462-0852, FAX: (212) 575-5845, Web Site: www.newsamerica.com (31)

Murdock, Shawn, Icon Marketing Communications, Fort Mitchell, KY. Tel: (859) 647-7271, FAX: (859) 647-0615, E-Mail: shawn@iconmc.com, Web Site: iconmc.com (21)

Murdy, Bruce, Rawle Murdy, Charleston, SC. Tel: (843) 577-7327, E-Mail: contact@rawlemurdy.com, Web Site: www.rawlemurdy.com (35)

Murph, Eleanora O., TheIdeaClub.com & Dumas Martin Consulting, Pomona, CA. Tel: (909) 620-4772, FAX: (909) 629-4739, Web Site: www.theideaclub.com (16)

Murphy, C. Joe, Scott's Dog Supply Inc, Indianapolis, IN. Tel: (317) 222-5382, (800) 966-3647, FAX: (317) 298-7284, E-Mail: cmurphy154@aol.com, Web Site: www.scottsdog.com (11)

Murphy, David P., Novus Media Inc, Plymouth, MN. Tel: (612) 758-8600, FAX: (612) 336-8600, Web Site: www.npmnetwork.com (31)

Murphy, David, Super Coups, Norwell, MA. Tel: (508) 977-2000, (800) 626-2620, FAX: (508) 977-0644, Web Site: www.supercoups.com (26)

Murphy, Dennis, Cooper Vision, Fairport, NY. Tel: (855) 526-6737, (800) 341-2020, Web Site: www.coopervision.com (7)

Murphy, Don, Paragon Printing & Mailing, Austin, TX. Tel: (512) 821-0222, FAX: (512) 821-0200, E-Mail: contact@paragonprinting.com, Web Site: www.paragonprinting.com (27)

Murphy, Eileen, The New York Times Co, New York, NY. Tel: (212) 556-1234, Web Site: www.nytimes.com (17)

Murphy, Gerry, Enterprise Ireland, New York, NY. Tel: (212) 371-3600, FAX: (212) 371-6398, Web Site: www.enterprise-ireland.com (16)

Murphy, James, Viking Pump Inc, Cedar Falls, IA. Tel: (319) 266-1741, FAX: (319) 273-8157, E-Mail: info@vikingpump.com, Web Site: www.vikingpump.com (16)

Murphy, John J., Craft-Diston Industries, Wichita, KS. Tel: (316) 838-4291, (800) 835-0028, FAX: (316) 838-8502, Web Site: www.craftdiston.com (16)

Murphy, John J., Home Loan Investment Bank, Warwick, RI. Tel: (401) 739-8800, (800) 223-1700 X278, FAX: (401) 739-9675, E-Mail: contactus@homeloanbank.com, Web Site: www.homeloanbankfsb.com (14)

Murphy, Lisa, Live Design, New York, NY. Tel: (212) 204-4268, FAX: (212) 204-4291, Web Site: livedesignonline.com (17)

Murphy, Liz, RedEngine Digital, Mc Lean, VA. Tel: (703) 556-6951, Web Site: www.redenginedigital.com (20)

Murphy, Margaret, ICF Olson, Minneapolis, MN. Tel: (612) 215-9800, FAX: (612) 215-9801, E-Mail: info@olson.com, Web Site: www.olson.com (35)

Murphy, Marion, GroupM Direct, New York, NY. Tel: (212) 474-0830, Web Site: www.groupm.com (35)

Murphy, Mark J., Advantage List Marketing Inc, Holliston, MA. Tel: (508) 429-4400, FAX: (508) 429-7117, E-Mail: markm@advantagelist.com, Web Site: www.advantagelist.com (23)

Murphy, Michael, Event 360 Inc, Chicago, IL. Tel: (773) 247-5360, Web Site: www.event360.com (1)

Murphy, Michael, Pearl Insurance Group LLC, Peoria Heights, IL. Tel: (309) 688-9000, Web Site: www.pearlinsurance.com (15)

Murphy, Michael R., Japs-Olson Co, Saint Louis Park, MN. Tel: (952) 932-9393, (800) 548-2897, FAX: (612) 912-1900, Web Site: www.japsolson.com (27)

Murphy, Patrick, Gems Sensors & Controls, Plainville, CT. Tel: (860) 747-3000, (800) 378-1600, FAX: (860) 747-4244, E-Mail: info@gemssensors.com, Web Site: www.gemssensors.com (9)

Murphy, Robert E., California Pacific Research & New Generation, Reno, NV. Tel: (775) 829-5600, (800) 745-5642, FAX: (775) 829-5619, E-Mail: sales@newgen2000.com, Web Site: www.newgen2000.com (7)

Murphy, Robert E., Japs-Olson Co, Saint Louis Park, MN. Tel: (952) 932-9393, (800) 548-2897, FAX: (612) 912-1900, Web Site: www.japsolson.com (27)

Murphy, Sean, MJM Incentives Inc, Henrietta, NY. Tel: (585) 334-6720, (888) 633-9655, E-Mail: pmarchese@mjmincentives.com, Web Site: www.mjmincentives.com (33)

Murphy, Shannon, Chapman Cubine Adams & Hussey, Arlington, VA. Tel: (703) 248-0025, Web Site: www.ahadirect.com (20)

Murphy, Terry M., AO Smith Corp, Milwaukee, WI. Tel: (414) 359-4000, FAX: (414) 359-4064, Web Site: www.aosmith.com (16)

Murray, Brian, HarperCollins, New York, NY. Tel: (212) 207-7000, (800) 242-7737, FAX: (212) 207-7145, Web Site: www.harpercollins.com (17)

Murray, Charles F., CMI Direct, Pasadena, CA. Tel: (951) 300-1700, FAX: (866) 723-5433, Web Site: www.cmidirect.net (15)

Murray, David, Spectrum Data, Oregon, IL. Tel: (815) 732-6567, FAX: (815) 732-7035 (22)

Murray, Gail, San Francisco Bay Area Rapid Transit District (BART), Oakland, CA. Tel: (510) 464-6000, FAX: (510) 464-7103, Web Site: www.bart.gov (16)

Murray, George, Sterling Jewelers Inc, Akron, OH. Tel: (330) 668-5000, FAX: (330) 668-5052, E-Mail: webmaster@jewels.com, Web Site: www.sterlingjewelers.com (16)

Murray, Jeffrey, Sencore Inc, Sioux Falls, SD. Tel: (605) 339-0100, (800) SEN-CORE, FAX: (605) 339-0317, E-Mail: sales@sencore.com, Web Site: www.sencore.com (16)

Murray, Johann, Hilton Grand Vacations Co, Orlando, FL. Tel: (407) 722-3100, FAX: (407) 521-3112, Web Site: www.hiltongrandvacations.com (19)

Murray, Michael, FirstGroup America, Cincinnati, OH. Tel: (513) 241-2200, FAX: (513) 419-3242, Web Site: www.firstgroup.com/north_america (12)

Murray, Mike, The MR Group Inc, Charleston, SC. Tel: (843) 402-0566, FAX: (843) 852-9051, E-Mail: mgm@themrgroup.com, Web Site: www.themrgroup.com (9)

Murray, Mike, TMA Direct Inc, Reston, VA. Tel: (703) 547-4940, (877) TMA-5566, FAX: (703) 547-4979, E-Mail: info@tmadirect.com, Web Site: www.tmadirect.com (23)

Murray, Shannon, MD Anderson Cancer Center - Children's Art Project, Houston, TX. Tel: (713) 745-2575, (800) 231-1580, FAX: (713) 794-1950, E-Mail: krenner@mdanderson.org, Web Site: www.childrensart.org (1)

Murray, Thomas, RPM Direct LLC, Lambertville, NJ. Tel: (609) 566-7150, FAX: (609) 566-7155, E-Mail: jimarslan@rpmdirectllc.com, Web Site: www.rpmdirectllc.com (35)

Murray, Virginia, Active Parenting, Marietta, GA. Tel: (770) 429-0565, (800) 825-0060, (800) 235-7755, FAX: (770) 429-0334, E-Mail: cservice@activeparenting.com, Web Site: www.activeparenting.com (17)

Murren, James J., Mirage Resorts, Inc., Las Vegas, NV. Tel: (702) 693-7111, FAX: (702) 791-7446, Web Site: www.mirageresorts.com (19)

Murrett, James L., Appraisal Institute, Chicago, IL. Tel: (312) 335-4100, (888) 756-4624, FAX: (312) 335-4400, E-Mail: aiservice@appraisalinstitute.org, Web Site: www.appraisalinstitute.org (1)

Murtha, Bill, Roberts Communications Inc, Rochester, NY. Tel: (716) 325-6000, FAX: (716) 325-6001, Web Site: www.robertscomm.com (35)

Muscle Dynamics Corp, Santa Fe Springs, CA. Tel: (562) 926-3232, (888) 629-4226, FAX: (562) 926-9191, E-Mail: info@muscledynamics.com, Web Site: www.muscledynamics.com (32)

Muscular Dystrophy Association, Chicago, IL. Tel: (800) 572-1717, Web Site: www.mda.org (1)

Muselman, Arthur K., Annie's Attic LLC, Big Sandy, TX. Tel: (903) 636-4303, (800) 282-6643, FAX: (903) 636-4088, Web Site: www.anniesattic.com (11)

Museum Masters Inc, New York, NY. Tel: (212) 360-7100, (917) 273-8710, FAX: (212) 360-7102, E-Mail: MMIMarilyn@aol.com, Web Site: www.museummasters.com (16)

The Museum of Modern Art, New York, NY. Tel: (212) 708-9400, FAX: (212) 333-1123, E-Mail: info@moma.org, Web Site: www.moma.org (5)

Musgrave, Michael K., Western Printing Machinery (WPM), Schiller Park, IL. Tel: (847) 678-1740, FAX: (847) 678-6176, E-Mail: info@wpm.com, Web Site: www.wpm.com (34)

Musgrove, Linda, Tri-Chem Inc, Belleville, NJ. Tel: (973) 751-9200, FAX: (973) 450-1260, (973) 450-1057, E-Mail: paints@trichem.com, Web Site: www.trichem.com (16)

Music Barn Inc, Niagara Falls, NY. Tel: (800) 984-0047, FAX: (905) 513-6918, E-Mail: info@themusicbarn.com, Web Site: www.themusicbarn.com (6)

Music Choice, Horsham, PA. Tel: (215) 784-5840, Web Site: www.musicchoice.com (16)

Music Sales Corp, New York, NY. Tel: (212) 254-2100, FAX: (212) 254-2013, E-Mail: info@musicsales.com, Web Site: www.musicsales.com (17)

Music Treasures Co, Richmond, VA. Tel: (804) 730-8800, (800) 666-7565, FAX: (888) MUSIC-TC, E-Mail: musict@musictreasures.com, Web Site: www.musictreasures.com (6)

Musician's Friend, Westlake Village, CA. Tel: (541) 772-5173, (800) 449-9128, Web Site: www.musiciansfriend.com (5)

Musilova, Dagner, Ethel M Chocolates Inc, Henderson, NV. Tel: (702) 435-2655, (800) 471-0352, FAX: (702) 451-8379, E-Mail: chocolatier@ethelm.com, Web Site: www.ethelm.com (4)

Muskegon Power Tool Corp, North Muskegon, MI. Tel: (231) 766-2194, (800) 635-5465, FAX: (231) 766-3846 (16)

Mussa, Joan, World Vision Inc, Federal Way, WA. Tel: (253) 815-1000, (888) 511-6548, FAX: (253) 815-3140, E-Mail: info@worldvision.org, Web Site: www.worldvision.org (1)

Mustafa, Frank, Get Seen Media Group, Los Angeles, CA. Tel: (323) 424-4669, Web Site: www.getseenmedia.com (1)

Mustek Inc, Tustin, CA. Tel: (949) 790-3800, FAX: (949) 788-3670, Web Site: www.mustek.com (3)

Mustich Jr, James, The Akadine Press Inc, White Plains, NY. Tel: (914) 747-0777, FAX: (914) 747-0778, Web Site: www.commonreader.com (16)

Muto, Gary, Ann Inc, New York, NY. Tel: (212) 541-3300, (800) 342-5266, FAX: (866) 232-9266, Web Site: www.anninc.com (2)

Mutual of America Life Insurance Co, New York, NY. Tel: (212) 224-1600, (800) 468-3785, FAX: (212) 207-3001, Web Site: www.mutualofamerica.com (14)

Mutual of Omaha, Omaha, NE. Tel: (402) 342-7600, (800) 775-6000, FAX: (402) 351-2775, Web Site: www.mutualofomaha.com (15)

Muyskens, James L., Queens College/CUNY Professional and Continuing Studies (PCS), Flushing, NY. Tel: (718) 997-5700, FAX: (718) 997-5723, E-Mail: pcs@qc.cuny.edu, Web Site: www.qc.cuny.edu/pcs (41)

Muzzy, Peter, QED Marketing Inc, Central Islip, NY. Tel: (631) 851-4254 (22)

Muzzy, Sean, Neo@Ogilvy, New York, NY. Tel: (212) 259-5200, Web Site: www.neoogilvy.com (35)

The Mx Group, Burr Ridge, IL. Tel: (800) 827-0170, FAX: (630) 654-0302, Web Site: www.themxgroup.com (35)

MxEnergy Inc, Stamford, CT. Tel: (203) 356-1318, Web Site: www.mxenergy.com (16)

Myers, Myers & Adams Advertising LLC, Fort Lauderdale, FL. Tel: (954) 523-6262, FAX: (954) 523-3517, E-Mail: pete@mmanda.com, Web Site: www.mmanda.com (35)

Myers, Bill, Diagraph Corp, Saint Charles, MO. Tel: (636) 300-2000, (800) 722-1125, FAX: (636) 300-2004, E-Mail: info@diagraph.com, Web Site: www.diagraph.com (16)

Myers, Brandon, Lundmark Advertising + Design Inc, Kansas City, MO. Tel: (816) 842-5236, Web Site: lundmarkadvertising.com (35)

Myers, Diana, Save the Children Federation Inc, Fairfield, CT. Tel: (203) 221-4000, (800) 728-3843, FAX: (203) 222-1067, E-Mail: majorgivng@savethechildren.org, Web Site: www.savethechildren.org (1)

Myers, Douglas G., Zoological Society of San Diego, San Diego, CA. Tel: (619) 231-1515, FAX: (619) 557-3937, Web Site: www.sandiegozoo.org (1)

Myers, Hal K., Thought Technology Ltd, Montreal, QC Canada. Tel: (514) 489-8251, (800) 361-3651, FAX: (514) 489-8255, E-Mail: lawrence@thoughttechnology.com, Web Site: www.thoughttechnology.com (16)

Myers, James M., Petco Animal Supplies, San Diego, CA. Tel: (858) 453-7845, (877) 738-6742, FAX: (858) 453-6585, Web Site: www.petco.com (5)

Myers, Jay, Trends International LLC, Indianapolis, IN. Tel: (317) 388-1212, (800) 354-4639, FAX: (317) 388-1414, E-Mail: info@trendsinternational.com, Web Site: www.trendsinternational.com (38)

Myers, John, A-Mark Inc, Dresher, PA. Tel: (215) 886-4740, FAX: (215) 886-4749 (15)

Myers, Martha, Northeast Hinge Distributors Inc, Hollis, NH. Tel: (603) 465-3244, (800) 882-0120, FAX: (603) 465-3313, E-Mail: nehinge@nehinge.com, Web Site: www.nehinge.com (5)

Myers, Mary, Wag/Aero Group, Lyons, WI. Tel: (262) 763-9586, (800) 558-6868, FAX: (262) 763-7595, E-Mail: wagaero-sales@wagaero.com, Web Site: www.wagaero.com (16)

Myers, Pamela J., Native American Heritage Association, Black Hawk, SD. Tel: (605) 341-9110, FAX: (605) 341-91413, E-Mail: info@naha-inc.org, Web Site: www.naha-inc.org (1)

Myers, Paul, Valley Forge Tape & Label Co Inc, Exton, PA. Tel: (610) 524-8900, (800) 345-1323, FAX: (610) 524-8906, E-Mail: vfsales@vftl.com, Web Site: www.vftl.com (27)

Myers, Peter, Myers, Myers & Adams Advertising LLC, Fort Lauderdale, FL. Tel: (954) 523-6262, FAX: (954) 523-3517, E-Mail: pete@mmanda.com, Web Site: www.mmanda.com (35)

Mylan Enterprises, Tarzana, CA. Tel: (818) 538-8080, (888) 528-3928, FAX: (818) 538-7646, E-Mail: calcos@silkskin.com, Web Site: www.silkskin.com (7)

Myllykoski North America, Westmont, IL. Tel: (203) 229-7400, Web Site: www.myllykoski.com (25)

MyPoints.com Inc, San Francisco, CA. Tel: (415) 856-0877, FAX: (415) 615-1122, E-Mail: memberservices@mypoints.com, Web Site: www.mypoints.com (35)

Myriad Systems Inc, Oklahoma City, OK. Tel: (405) 478-9000, (866) 505-1730, FAX: (405) 478-8315, E-Mail: sales@myriadsystems.com, Web Site: www.myriadsystems.com (22)

Myrland, Brian, Rainbow Group LLC, Middleton, WI. Tel: (608) 824-0068, Web Site: www.beaconathletics.com (11)

Myron Corp, Maywood, NJ. Tel: (201) 843-6464, (877) 803-3358, FAX: (201) 843-8390. Web Site: www.myron.com (16)

Myroniak, Tom, Specialty Equipment Market Association, Diamond Bar, CA. Tel: (909) 396-0289, Web Site: www.sema.org (1)

Myrvold, Steve, IWCO Direct, Chanhassen, MN. Tel: (952) 474-0961, FAX: (952) 474-6467, Web Site: www.iwco.com (21)

Mystic Logistics Inc, South Glastonbury, CT. Tel: (860) 659-1566, (800) 969-1566, FAX: (860) 659-1420, Web Site: www.mysticlogistics.com (28)

Mystic Seaport Museum Stores, Mystic, CT. Tel: (860) 572-5315, (860) 572-0711, FAX: (860) 572-5324, Web Site: www.mysticseaport.org (6)

Mystic Stamp Co Inc, Camden, NY. Tel: (866) 660-7147, FAX: (800) 385-4919, E-Mail: info@mysticstamp.com, Web Site: www.mysticstamp.com (16)

N

NAACP, Baltimore, MD. Tel: (410) 580-5777, Web Site: www.naacp.org (1)

NAB Show, Washington, DC. Tel: (202) 429-5300, (800) 622-3976, FAX: (202) 429-4199, E-Mail: nab@nab.org, Web Site: www.nabshow.com (42)

NADA Appraisal Guides, Costa Mesa, CA. Tel: (714) 556-8511, (800) 966-6232, FAX: (714) 957-0302, E-Mail: info@nadaguides.com, Web Site: www.nadaguides.com (17)

NAGRA USA, San Francisco, CA. Tel: (415) 962-5000, FAX: (415) 962-5300, E-Mail: dtv@nagra.com, Web Site: www.nagra.com (32)

NAMA Agri-Marketing Conference, Overland Park, KS. Tel: (913) 491-6500, FAX: (913) 491-6502, E-Mail: agrimktg@nama.org, Web Site: www.nama.org (42)

NAPCO Media, Philadelphia, PA. Tel: (215) 238-5300, FAX: (215) 238-5412, Web Site: www.napco.com (32)

NARAL Pro-Choice America, Washington, DC. Tel: (202) 973-3000, FAX: (202) 973-3096, Web Site: www.naral.com (1)

NASA Federal Credit Union, Upper Marlboro, MD. Tel: (301) 249-1800, Web Site: www.nasafcu.com (1)

NASW Assurance Services Inc, Frederick, MD. Tel: (800) 668-4274, E-Mail: zxi@naswasi.org, Web Site: www.naswinsurancetrust.org (1)

National General Insurance, Winston-Salem, NC. Tel: (888) 293-5108, Web Site: www.nationalgeneral.com (15)

NBI Inc, Eau Claire, WI. Tel: (715) 835-8525, Web Site: www.nbi-sems.com (1)

NBTY Inc, Ronkonkoma, NY. Tel: (631) 200-2000, FAX: (631) 567-7148, Web Site: www.nbty.com (7)

NCC Media, New York, NY. Tel: (212) 548-3300, FAX: (212) 519-0099, Web Site: nccmedia.com (32)

NCH Corp, Irving, TX. Tel: (972) 438-0211, FAX: (972) 438-0707, Web Site: www.nch.com (34)

NCO Financial Systems, Horsham, PA. Tel: (215) 441-3000, (800) 220-2274, FAX: (215) 441-3923, E-Mail: marketing@ncogroup.com, Web Site: www.ncogroup.com (29)

NCP Solutions, Reston, VA. Tel: (703) 438-6000, (800) 822-9919, FAX: (703) 438-3570, Web Site: www.nwf.org (17)

NCP Solutions, Birmingham, AL. Tel: (250) 849-5200, Web Site: www.ncprint.com (21)

NCR Corp, Duluth, GA. Tel: (937) 445-1936, (800) CALL-NCR, FAX: (937) 445-1682, Web Site: www.ncr.com (16)

NCRI List Management, Englewood Cliffs, NJ. Tel: (201) 541-9500, FAX: (201) 541-1944, E-Mail: info@ncrilists.com, Web Site: www.ncrilists.com (23)

NEA's Member Benefits Corp, Gaithersburg, MD. Tel: (301) 251-9600, FAX: (301) 527-8210, Web Site: www.neamb.com (1)

NEBS, Groton, MA. Tel: (978) 448-6111, (800) 225-6380, (888) 823-6327, FAX: (978) 448-3653, (800) 234-4324, E-Mail: customerservice@nebs.com, Web Site: www.nebs.com (10)

NETC, Hamden, CT. Tel: (617) 851-8535, (203) 288-5938, E-Mail: mail@netconline.org (5)

NGL Insurance Group, Madison, WI. Tel: (608) 257-5611, (800) 548-2962, FAX: (608) 257-9340, Web Site: www.nglic.com (15)

The NH Broadcaster, Lowell, MA. Tel: (978) 458-7100, Web Site: www.nhbroadcaster.com (31)

NNE Marketing, Concord, MA. Tel: (617) 429-7999, Web Site: www.nnemarketing.com (1)

The NPD Group Inc, Port Washington, NY. Tel: (516) 625-0700, FAX: (516) 625-2444, Web Site: www.npd.com (30)

NPI, Fort Worth, TX. Tel: (214) 634-2288, FAX: (682) 503-8214, E-Mail: sales@npisorters.com, Web Site: www.npisorters.com (16)

NPN360 Inc, Wheeling, IL. Tel: (847) 215-7300, FAX: (847) 215-7314, E-Mail: sales@npn360.com, Web Site: www.npn360.com (21)

NRS, Decatur, TX. Tel: (940) 627-3949, Web Site: www.nrsworld.com (11)

NTL Institute, Silver Spring, MD. Tel: (301) 565-3200, E-Mail: info@ntl.org, Web Site: www.ntl.org (1)

NTN Buzztime Inc, Carlsbad, CA. Tel: (760) 438-7400, (877) 963-9200, FAX: (760) 438-3505, Web Site: www.buzztimebusiness.com (32)

NTP Distribution, Wilsonville, OR. Tel: (503) 570-0171, FAX: (888) 570-0342, Web Site: www.ntpdistribution.com (34)

NY Now, White Plains, NY. Tel: (800) 272-7469, Web Site: www.nynow.com (42)

NYK Rapp Enterprises LLC, Hallandale, FL. Tel: (954) 457-9100, FAX: (954) 457-9015, Web Site: nykrapp.com (35)

NYSARC, Inc, Delmar, NY. Tel: (518) 439-8311, FAX: (518) 439-1893, E-Mail: info@nysarc.org, Web Site: www.nysarc.org (1)

Nabel, MD Elizabeth, ACP Medicine, Hamilton, ON Canada. Tel: (905) 522-8526, (855) 647-6511, FAX: (905) 522-9273, E-Mail: acpmedicine@deckerpublishing.com, Web Site: acpmedicine.com (17)

Nabipoor, Omid, Interface Engineering, Portland, OR. Tel: (503) 382-2266, FAX: (503) 382-2262, E-Mail: solutions@interfaceengineering.com, Web Site: www.ieice.com (20)

Naccarato, Vincent, Wilton Industries Inc. Woodridge, IL. Tel: (630) 963-1818, (800) 794-5866, FAX: (630) 963-7196, E-Mail: info@wilton.com, Web Site: www.wilton.com (16)

Nachemin, Farley, Gump's By Mail Inc, San Francisco, CA. Tel: (415) 982-1616, (800) 882-8055, FAX: (800) 984-9361, Web Site: www.gumpsbymail.com (6)

Nadella, Satya, Microsoft Corp, Redmond, WA. Tel: (425) 882-8080, FAX: (425) 936-8000, Web Site: www.microsoft.com/msft (22)

Nadelmann, Ethan, Drug Policy Alliance, New York, NY. Tel: (212) 613-8020, FAX: (212) 613-8021, E-Mail: nyc@drugpolicy.org, Web Site: www.drugpolicy.org (1)

Nadler, John, ProPhase Marketing Inc, Eden Prairie, MN. Tel: (952) 974-1100, (800) 969-6400, FAX: (952) 974-7874, E-Mail: sales@ppmi.com, Web Site: prophasemarketing.com (21)

Nadler, Pegg, Pegg Nadler Associates Inc, New York, NY. Tel: (212) 861-0846, E-Mail: pegg@peggnadler.com (22)

Naergaard, Leif, Chris Hansen, New Berlin, WI. Tel: (414) 607-5700, FAX: (414) 607-5704, Web Site: www.chr-hansen.com (16)

Nagamine, Kirk, NTN Buzztime Inc, Carlsbad, CA. Tel: (760) 438-7400, (877) 963-9200, FAX: (760) 438-3505, Web Site: www.buzztimebusiness.com (32)

Nagel, Jan, Christian Herald Association, New York, NY. Tel: (212) 684-2800, (800) BOWERY-1, FAX: (212) 684-3740, E-Mail: info@chaonline.org, Web Site: www.bowery.org (1)

Naggiar, Caroline, Tiffany & Co, New York, NY. Tel: (212) 755-8000, FAX: (212) 320-7550, Web Site: www.tiffany.com (6)

Nagourney, Donald, School of Management, Old Westbury, NY. Tel: (516) 686-1000, (800) 345-NYIT, (800) 345-6948, E-Mail: asknyit@nyit.edu, Web Site: www.nyit.edu (41)

Nagourney, Marvin, D&D Associates Inc, Garden City, NY. Tel: (516) 326-8800, (800) 554-0347 (22)

Nagy, Sandor, CTB/McGraw-Hill LLC, Monterey, CA. Tel: (800) 538-9547, FAX: (800) 282-0266, E-Mail: customer_service_ind@ctb.com, Web Site: www.ctb.com (16)

Nahan Printing Inc, Saint Cloud, MN. Tel: (320) 251-7611, E-Mail: info@nahan.com, Web Site: www.nahan.com (27)

Nahan, Mike, Nahan Printing Inc, Saint Cloud, MN. Tel: (320) 251-7611, E-Mail: info@nahan.com, Web Site: www.nahan.com (27)

Nahuz, Sergio, The Kraft Heinz Co, Pittsburgh, PA. Tel: (412) 456-5700, Web Site: www.kraftheinzcompany.com (4)

Najarian, John, E! Entertainment Television, Los Angeles, CA. Tel: (323) 954-2400, FAX: (323) 954-2665, Web Site: www.eonline.com (32)

Najarian, Richard A, Bruce Medical Supply, Waltham, MA. Tel: (781) 894-6262, (800) 225-8446, FAX: (781) 894-9519, E-Mail: sales@brucemedial.com, Web Site: www.brucemedical.com (7)

NAK Marketing & Communications, New York, NY. Tel: (212) 505-9290, Web Site: www.nakcomm.com (20)

Nakaguro, Kunio, Nissan North America Inc, Franklin, TN. Tel: (615) 725-1000, Web Site: www.nissanusa.com (16)

Nakashima, Alison, Schoolwise Press, San Francisco, CA. Tel: (415) 337-7971, (800) 247-8443 x 202, FAX: (415) 337-1146, E-Mail: info@schoolwisepress.com, Web Site: www.schoolwisepress.com (17)

Name Exchange, Frederick, MD. Tel: (301) 695-6140, FAX: (301) 695-5572, E-Mail: chris@nameexchange.us, Web Site: nameexchange.us (24)

Namebank, Baltimore, MD. Tel: (410) 864-0854, FAX: (410) 864-0837, E-Mail: lists@namebank.com, Web Site: www.namebank.com (23)

Names in the Mail Inc, Dallas, TX. Tel: (972) 681-5701, (800) 688-5701, FAX: (972) 681-5786, E-Mail: nimnames@att.net (23)

Names in the News, Oakland, CA. Tel: (415) 989-3350, FAX: (415) 433-7796, E-Mail: susananstrand@nincal.com, Web Site: www.nincal.com (23)

Namken, Darin, Bull Dog Media Group Inc, Madison, SD. Tel: (605) 256-9103, Web Site: www.commissionsoup.com (20)

Namken, Darin, Bulldog Media Group Inc, Madison, SD. Tel: (866) 309-7687, E-Mail: info@bulldogmediagroup.com, Web Site: www.bulldogmediagroup.com (32)

Nance, Amy, KCET, Burbank, CA. Tel: (747) 201-5000, FAX: (747) 201-5877, E-Mail: contact@kcet.org, Web Site: www.kcet.org (1)

Nancy's Notions LLC, Beaver Dam, WI. Tel: (920) 887-0321, (800) 833-0690, FAX: (800) 255-8119, E-Mail: comments@nancysnotions.com, Web Site: www.nancysnotions.com (11)

Nangle, Kevin, Reiman Publications, Greendale, WI. Tel: (414) 423-0100, (800) 344-6913, FAX: (414) 423-3840, Web Site: www.reimanpub.com (17)

Nanus, Jeff, AAA Umbrella Co Inc, Northvale, NJ. Tel: (201) 784-3242, (800) 426-7446, FAX: (201) 226-0041, E-Mail: sales@aaaumbrella.com, Web Site: www.aaaumbrella.com (16)

Napier, Elizabeth, Tully & Holland Inc, Wellesley, MA. Tel: (781) 239-2900, FAX: (781) 239-2901, E-Mail: info@tullyandholland.com, Web Site: www.tullyandholland.com (14)

Napior, David, Mediamark Research Inc, New York, NY. Tel: (212) 884-9200, (800) 310-3305, FAX: (212) 884-9339, Web Site: www.mediamark.com (30)

Naples, Mary Ann, Rodale Inc, Emmaus, PA. Tel: (610) 967-5171, FAX: (610) 967-8963, Web Site: www.rodaleinc.com (17)

Napoli, Michele, Women in Direct Marketing International, New York, NY. Tel: (516) 746-6700, FAX: (516) 294-8141, Web Site: www.wdmi.org (40)

Napolillo, Lissa, MBS, Central Islip, NY. Tel: (631) 851-5000, Web Site: www.mbsinsight.com (22)

Napolitano, Robert, St Joseph's College, Brooklyn, NY. Tel: (718) 399-1223, Web Site: www.sjcny.edu (1)

Napolitano, Russ, Tenet Partners, New York, NY. Tel: (212) 329-3030, FAX: (212) 329-3031, Web Site: tenetpartners.com (35)

Napolitano, Val, Petry Television Inc, New York, NY. Tel: (212) 230-5600, E-Mail: info@petrymedia.com, Web Site: www.petrymedia.com (32)

NAR Productions, Barryville, NY. Tel: (845) 557-8713, FAX: (845) 557-6770, E-Mail: info@aodceus.com, Web Site: www.aodceus.com (17)

Narayen, Shantanu, Adobe Systems Inc, San Jose, CA. Tel: (408) 536-6000, (800) 833-6687, FAX: (408) 537-6000, Web Site: www.adobe.com (22)

Nardo, Martino, Hanna Instruments Inc, Woonsocket, RI. Tel: (401) 765-7500, (800) 426-6287, FAX: (401) 765-7575, E-Mail: custsvc@hannainst.com, Web Site: www.hannainst.com (16)

Nardo, Pamela, Hanna Instruments, Woonsocket, RI. Tel: (401) 765-7500, (800) 426-6287, FAX: (401) 765-7575, E-Mail: custsvc@hannainst.com, Web Site: www.hannainst.com (16)

Narowski, Eric W., Harris Interactive, Rochester, NY. Tel: (585) 272-8400, (800) 866-7655, FAX: (585) 272-8680, E-Mail: info@harrisinteractive.com, Web Site: www.harrisinteractive.com (30)

Narrow Way, Lafayette, CA. Tel: (925) 283-4074 (6)

Nasco, Fort Atkinson, WI. Tel: (920) 563-2446, (800) 558-9595, FAX: (920) 563-8296, E-Mail: info@nasco.com, Web Site: www.enasco.com (5)

Nash, Cathy, Citizens Republic Bank, Flint, MI. Tel: (810) 766-7500, Web Site: www.citizensbanking.com (14)

Nash, Craig M., Interval International, South Miami, FL. Tel: (305) 666-1884, (800) 468-3782, FAX: (305) 667-5321, Web Site: www.intervalworld.com (35)

Nash, Edward, Direct Marketing Strategy, Planning & Execution, Blacklick, OH. Tel: (614) 755-4152, (800) 722-4726, Web Site: www.mcgraw-hill.com (43)

Nash, Lisa, LN Marketing Associates, Emerald Hills, CA. Tel: (650) 368-7181 (20)

Nasif, Teresa S., Federal Citizen Information Center, Pueblo, CO. Tel: (719) 295-2675, (888) 8-PUEBLO, FAX: (719) 948-9724, E-Mail: pueblo@gpo.gov, Web Site: www.pueblo.gsa.gov (5)

Nassar, Paul, Marimac Inc, Montreal, QC Canada. Tel: (514) 376-7882, FAX: (514) 376-0801, E-Mail: sales@marimacgroup.com, Web Site: www.marimac.com (8)

Nassau Community College, Garden City, NY. Tel: (516) 572-7501, FAX: (516) 572-7497, E-Mail: marketing-communications@ncc.edu, Web Site: www.ncc.edu (41)

Nassetta, Christopher, Hilton Hotels Corp, Mc Lean, VA. Tel: (703) 883-1000, (800) HILTONS, FAX: (310) 205-3670, Web Site: www.hilton.com (19)

Nasta, Frank A., Applied Info Group, Kenilworth, NJ. Tel: (908) 241-7007, FAX: (9080 241-7088, Web Site: www.appliedinfogroup.com (22)

Nastri, Kathleen, American Association for Justice, Washington, DC. Tel: (202) 965-3500, (800) 424-2725, FAX: (202) 625-7313, E-Mail: membership@justice.org, Web Site: www.justice.org (1)

Nat Com Marketing, Miami, FL. Tel: (305) 756-8600, FAX: (786) 425-0067, E-Mail: info@natcom-marketing.com, Web Site: www.natcom-marketing.com (33)

Natale, Roxanne, National Association for Female Executives, New York, NY. Tel: (800) 927-6233, E-Mail: info@nafe.com, Web Site: www.nafe.com (1)

Nate, Kent, Bonneville International, Salt Lake City, UT. Tel: (801) 575-7500, FAX: (801) 575-5820, E-Mail: bonneville@bonneville.com, Web Site: www.bonneville.com (35)

Nathan Associates Inc, Arlington, VA. Tel: (703) 516-7700, FAX: (703) 351-6162, Web Site: www.nathaninc.com (30)

Nathan, Elise, PlusMedia LLC, Danbury, CT. Tel: (203) 748-6500, FAX: (203) 748-6600, E-Mail: contact@plusme.com, Web Site: www.plusme.com (35)

Nathan, Tal, StrongView Systems Inc, Redwood City, CA. Tel: (650) 421-4200, (800) 971-0380, FAX: (650) 421-4201, E-Mail: info@strongview.com, Web Site: www.strongview.com (32)

Nathans, Aaron, American Institute for Economic Research, Great Barrington, MA. Tel: (413) 528-1216, (888) 528-1216, FAX: (413) 528-0103, E-Mail: info@aier.org, Web Site: www.aier.org (1)

Nathanson, David, Zimmerman Advertising, Fort Lauderdale, FL. Tel: (954) 644-4000, E-Mail: contact@zadv.com, Web Site: www.zadv.com (35)

National Active & Retired Federal Employees Association, Alexandria, VA. Tel: (703) 838-7760, (800) 456-8410, FAX: (703) 838-7785, Web Site: www.narfe.org (1)

National Administrative Service Co LLC, Dublin, OH. Tel: (614) 358-1500 (29)

National Archives & Records Administration, Washington, DC. Tel: (202) 357-5000, (866) 325-7208, Web Site: www.archives.gov (17)

National Association for Female Executives, New York, NY. Tel: (800) 927-6233, E-Mail: info@nafe.com, Web Site: www.nafe.com (1)

National Association for Printing Leadership, Paramus, NJ. Tel: (201) 634-9600, (800) 642-6275, FAX: (201) 634-0324, E-Mail: webwaster@napl.org, Web Site: www.napl.org (1)

National Association of Federal Credit Unions, Arlington, VA. Tel: (800) 336-4644, Web Site: www.nafcu.org (14)

National Association of Home Builders, Washington, DC. Tel: (202) 266-8200, (800) 368-5242, FAX: (202) 266-8400, Web Site: www.nahb.org (1)

National Association of Professional Insurance Agents, Alexandria, VA. Tel: (703) 836-9340, FAX: (703) 836-1279, E-Mail: web@pianet.org, Web Site: www.pianet.com (1)

National Association of Publishers Representatives, Hoffman Estates, IL. Tel: (877) 263-9640, FAX: (847) 885-8393, E-Mail: info@napronline.com, Web Site: www.napronline.com (1)

National Association of Realtors, Chicago, IL. Tel: (312) 329-8526, (800) 874-6500, Web Site: www.realtors.org (1)

National Audubon Society, New York, NY. Tel: (212) 979-3000, FAX: (212) 979-3188, Web Site: www.audubon.org (17)

National Auto Warranty, Wentzville, MO. Tel: (800) 649-1620 (16)

National Automated Clearing House Association, Herndon, VA. Tel: (703) 561-1100, FAX: (703) 787-0996, Web Site: www.nacha.org (1)

National Basketball Association, New York, NY. Tel: (212) 407-8000, FAX: (212) 826-0579, Web Site: www.nba.com (1)

National Bulk Equipment Inc, Holland, MI. Tel: (616) 399-2220, FAX: (616) 399-7365, E-Mail: sales@nbe-inc.com, Web Site: www.nbe-inc.com (16)

National Business Furniture Inc, Milwaukee, WI. Tel: (414) 276-8511, (800) 558-1010, FAX: (414) 276-8371, Web Site: www.nationalbusinessfurniture.com (10)

National Cable & Telecommunications Association, Washington, DC. Tel: (202) 222-2300, FAX: (202) 775-3675, Web Site: www.ncta.com (40)

National Catholic Reporter Publishing Co Inc, Kansas City, MO. Tel: (816) 531-0538, (800) 444-8910, FAX: (816) 968-2268, Web Site: www.ncronline.org (17)

National City Bank, Cleveland, OH. Tel: (216) 222-2000, (800) 622-8100, FAX: (216) 575-, Web Site: www.nationalcity.com (14)

National Committee to Preserve Social Security & Medicare, Washington, DC. Tel: (202) 216-0420, (800) 966-1935, FAX: (202) 216-0446, E-Mail: kreard@ncpssm.org, Web Site: www.ncpssm.org (1)

National Community Pharmacists Association, Alexandria, VA. Tel: (703) 683-8200, (800) 544-7447, FAX: (703) 683-3619, E-Mail: info@ncpanet.org, Web Site: www.ncpanet.org (1)

National Contract Management Association, Ashburn, VA. Tel: (571) 382-0082, (800) 344-8096, FAX: (703) 448-0939, E-Mail: memberservices@ncmghq.org, Web Site: www.ncmahq.org (1)

National Council on Compensation Insurance Inc, Boca Raton, FL. Tel: (561) 893-1000, (800) 622-4123, FAX: (561) 893-1191, Web Site: www.ncci.com (1)

National Court Reporters Association, Reston, VA. Tel: (703) 556-6272, (800) 272-6272, FAX: (703) 391-0629, E-Mail: msic@ncrahg.org, Web Site: www.ncraonline.org (1)

National Crime Prevention Council, Amsterdam, NY. Tel: (518) 842-4388, (888) 776-7763, FAX: (800) 995-5121, E-Mail: mcgruff@spocentral.com, Web Site: www.mcgruffspo.com (17)

National Defense Industrial Association, Arlington, VA. Tel: (703) 522-1820, FAX: (703) 522-1885, Web Site: www.ndia.org (1)

National Economic Research Associates Inc, Washington, DC. Tel: (202) 466-3510, FAX: (202) 466-3605, E-Mail: andrew.carron@nera.com, Web Site: www.nera.com (20)

National Electrical Manufacturers Association (NEMA), Rosslyn, VA. Tel: (703) 841-3200, FAX: (703) 841-5900, E-Mail: communications@nema.org, Web Site: www.nema.org (34)

National Emblem Sales, Indianapolis, IN. Tel: (317) 630-1247, (888) 453-4466, FAX: (317) 630-1381, E-Mail: emblem@legion.org, Web Site: www.emblem.legion.org (16)

National Enquirer, New York, NY. Tel: (212) 545-4800, Web Site: www.nationalenquirer.com (17)

National Federation of Independent Business, Nashville, TN. Tel: (615) 872-5800, Web Site: www.nfib.com (1)

National Fire Protection Association, Quincy, MA. Tel: (617) 770-3000, FAX: (617) 770-0700, Web Site: www.nfpa.org (1)

National Foundation for Cancer Research, Bethesda, MD. Tel: (301) 654-1250, (800) 321-CURE, FAX: (301) 654-5824, E-Mail: info@nfcr.org, Web Site: www.nfcr.org (1)

National 4-H Supply Service, Chevy Chase, MD. Tel: (301) 961-2959, FAX: (301) 961-2937, E-Mail: 4hsupply@fourhcouncil.edu, Web Site: www.fourhcouncil.edu (16)

National Fulfillment Services, Holmes, PA. Tel: (610) 532-4700, (800) NFS-1306, FAX: (610) 586-3232, E-Mail: tkrueger@nfsrv.com, Web Site: www.nfsrv.com (28)

National Fundraising Lists, Bowie, MD. Tel: (410) 721-5700, FAX: (410) 721-5795, E-Mail: info@nflists.com, Web Site: www.nflists.com (23)

National Gallery of Art Gift Shop, Washington, DC. Tel: (202) 842-6466, (800) 697-9350, FAX: (202) 842-4043, Web Site: www.nga.gov (16)

National Geographic Society, Washington, DC. Tel: (202) 862-8638, (800) 373-1717, Web Site: www.nationalgeographic.com (17)

National Golf Foundation, Jupiter, FL. Tel: (561) 744-6006, FAX: (561) 744-6107, E-Mail: ngf@ngf.org, Web Site: www.ngf.org (1)

National Graphics Inc, North Branford, CT. Tel: (203) 481-2351, FAX: (203) 483-0256, E-Mail: inquiries@natgraphics.com, Web Site: www.natgraphics.com (27)

National Hardware Show, Norwalk, CT. Tel: (203) 840-5622, (888) 425-9377, FAX: (203) 840-9622, E-Mail: inquiry@hardware.reedexpo.com, Web Site: www.nationalhardwareshow.com (42)

National Humane Education Society, Charles Town, WV. Tel: (304) 725-0506, FAX: (304) 725-1523, E-Mail: information@nhes.org, Web Site: www.nhes.org (1)

National Institute for Trial Advocacy, Boulder, CO. Tel: (800) 225-6482. Web Site: www.nita.org (1)

National Jewish Health, Denver, CO. Tel: (303) 398-1070, (800) 222-LUNG, (800) 423, FAX: (303) 398-1663, E-Mail: trubeyp@njhealth.org, Web Site: www.njhealth.org (1)

National Journal Group, Washington, DC. Tel: (202) 739-8400, (800) 613-6701, FAX: (202) 833-8069, Web Site: www.nationaljournal.com (17)

National Law Enforcement Officers Memorial Fund, Washington, DC. Tel: (202) 737-3400, Web Site: www.nleomf.com (1)

National League for Nursing, Washington, DC. Tel: (212) 363-5555, (800) 669-1656, FAX: (212) 812-0391, E-Mail: generalinfo@nln.org, Web Site: www.nln.org (1)

National Luggage Dealers Association, Glenview, IL. Tel: (847) 998-6869, FAX: (847) 998-6884, E-Mail: inquiry@nlda.com, Web Site: www.nlda.com (1)

National Mail Graphics Corp, Exton, PA. Tel: (610) 524-1600, FAX: (610) 524-7638, E-Mail: jsikorski@nmgcorp.com, Web Site: www.nmgcorp.com (27)

National Mail-It Inc, Shreveport, LA. Tel: (318) 683-0093, Web Site: www.nationalmailit.com (27)

National Mail/Marketing Corp, Broomall, PA. Tel: (610) 544-8200, FAX: (610) 544-1819, Web Site: www.natlmail.com (20)

National Mail Order Association (NMOA), Minneapolis, MN. Tel: (612) 788-1673, E-Mail: info@nmoa.org, Web Site: www.nmoa.org (40)

National Mailroom Service Inc, Knoxville, TN. Tel: (865) 862-4141, (866) 862-4141, FAX: (865) 862-4145, E-Mail: info@nationalmailroom.com, Web Site: nationalmailroom.com (27)

National Medical Fellowships, New York, NY. Tel: (212) 483-8880, FAX: (212) 483-8897, E-Mail: info@nmf-online.org, Web Site: www.nmf-online.org (1)

National Motor Club of America Inc, Irving, TX. Tel: (972) 999-4400, (800) 523-4582, FAX: (972) 999-4405, Web Site: www.nmca.com (1)

National Multiple Sclerosis Society, Denver, CO. Tel: (303) 813-1052, Web Site: www.nmss.org (1)

National Osteoporosis Foundation, Washington, DC. Tel: (202) 721-6346, Web Site: www.nof.org (1)

National Parkinson Foundation, Miami, FL. Tel: (305) 243-6666, (800) 937-4545, FAX: (305) 243-6073, E-Mail: contact@parkinson.org, Web Site: www.parkinson.org (1)

National Pecan Co, Frisco, TX. Tel: (469) 353-2993, E-Mail: info@nationalpecan.com, Web Site: www.nationalpecan.com (4)

National Pen Corp, San Diego, CA. Tel: (858) 675-3000, FAX: (858) 675-3030, E-Mail: info@nationalpen.com, Web Site: www.pens.com (6)

National Pension Service Inc, Burlington, VT. Tel: (802) 862-3994, FAX: (802) 865-2861, E-Mail: retirementservices@people.com, Web Site: www.peoples.com/retirementservices/ (14)

National Postal Forum, Fairfax, VA. Tel: (703) 218-5015, FAX: (703) 218-5020, E-Mail: info@npf.org, Web Site: www.npf.org (42)

National Railroad Passenger Corp, Washington, DC. Tel: (202) 906-3000, (800) USA-RAIL, FAX: (202) 906-3306, Web Site: www.amtrak.com (16)

National Relief Charities, Elkwood, VA. Tel: (540) 825-5950 (1)

National Research Center for College & University Admissions, Lees Summit, MO. Tel: (816) 525-2201, Web Site: www.nrccua.org (1)

National Research LLC, Washington, DC. Tel: (202) 686-9350, FAX: (202) 686-7163, E-Mail: survey@ nationalres.com, Web Site: www.nationalres.com (30)

The National Restaurant Association Educational Foundation, Washington, DC. Tel: (800) 424-5156 (1)

National Retail Federation Inc, Washington, DC. Tel: (202) 783-7971, (800) 673-4692, FAX: (202) 737-2849, E-Mail: webmaster@nrf.com, Web Site: www.nrf.com (1)

National Review, New York, NY. Tel: (212) 679-7330, FAX: (212) 849-2852, Web Site: www. nationalreview.com (17)

National Rifle Association of America, Fairfax, VA. Tel: (703) 267-1000, (800) 672-3888, FAX: (703) 267-3957, E-Mail: nra.contact@nra.org, Web Site: www.nra.org (1)

National Right to Work Legal Defense Foundation, Springfield, VA. Tel: (703) 321-8510, (800) 336-3600, FAX: (703) 321-9613, E-Mail: info@nrtw. org, Web Site: www.nrtw.org (1)

National Rural Electric Cooperative Association, Arlington, VA. Tel: (703) 907-5500, FAX: (703) 907-5528, Web Site: www.nreca.org (1)

National School Boards Association Inc, Alexandria, VA. Tel: (703) 838-6722, FAX: (703) 683-7590, E-Mail: info@nsba.org, Web Site: www.nsba.org (1)

National Seminars Group, Shawnee Mission, KS. Tel: (913) 432-7755, (800) 258-7246, FAX: (913) 432-0824, E-Mail: cstserv@natsem.com, Web Site: www.natsem.com (16)

National Society of Collegiate Scholars, Washington, DC. Tel: (202) 265-9000, Web Site: www.nscs.org (1)

National Stationery Show, White Plains, NY. Tel: (914) 421-3394, Web Site: www.nationalstationeryshow. com (42)

National Systems Corp, Chicago, IL. Tel: (312) 855-1000, FAX: (312) 222-1605, E-Mail: support@ nationalsystems.com, Web Site: www. nationalsystems.com (29)

National Technical Information Service, Alexandria, VA. Tel: (703) 605-6000, FAX: (703) 605-6900, Web Site: www.ntis.gov (17)

National Trust for Historic Preservation, Washington, DC. Tel: (202) 588-6000, (800) 944-6847, E-Mail: info@savingplaces.org, Web Site: www. preservationnation.org (1)

The National Underwriter Co, Erlanger, KY. Tel: (800) 543-0874, FAX: (856) 692-2246, E-Mail: customerservice@nuco.com, Web Site: www.nuco. com (17)

National University, La Jolla, CA. Tel: (800) 628-8648, Web Site: www.nu.edu (1)

National Wholesale Co Inc, Lexington, NC. Tel: (336) 248-5904, (800) 480-4673, FAX: (336) 248-2880, E-Mail: customerservice@shopnational.com, Web Site: www.shopnational.com (2)

National Wildlife Federation, Reston, VA. Tel: (703) 438-6000, Web Site: www.nwf.org (1)

Nationwide Argosy Solutions LLC, Houston, TX. Tel: (713) 961-4700, FAX: (713) 961-4701, Web Site: www.nationwidegraphics.com (27)

Nationwide Beauty & Barber Supply, Syracuse, NY. Tel: (315) 446-9026, FAX: (315) 446-8943, E-Mail: sales@nationwidebeauty.com, Web Site: www. nationwidebeauty.com (16)

Nationwide Displays Inc, Ronkonkoma, NY. Tel: (631) 467-2034, FAX: (631) 467-2079, E-Mail: info@ nationwidedisplays.com, Web Site: www. nationwidedisplays.com (16)

Nationwide Mutual Insurance Co, Columbus, OH. Tel: (614) 249-7111, (800) 882-2822, FAX: (614) 854-3676, Web Site: www.nationwide.com (15)

Native American Heritage Association, Black Hawk, SD. Tel: (605) 341-9110, FAX: (605) 341-91413, E-Mail: info@naha-inc.org, Web Site: www.naha-inc.org (1)

Native American Rights Fund, Boulder, CO. Tel: (303) 447-8760, FAX: (303) 443-7776, Web Site: www. narf.org (1)

Natural Essentials Inc, Streetsboro, OH. Tel: (330) 562-8022, (888) 968-7220, FAX: (330) 562-8022, E-Mail: questions@naturalessentials.com, Web Site: www.naturalessentials.com (5)

Natural History Magazine, Durham, NC. Tel: (646) 356-6500, FAX: (646) 356-6511, E-Mail: nhmag@ naturalhistorymag.com, Web Site: www. naturalhistorymag.com (17)

The Nature Conservancy, Arlington, VA. Tel: (703) 841-5300, (800) 628-6860, FAX: (703) 841-1283, Web Site: www.nature.org (1)

Nature Publishing Group, New York, NY. Tel: (212) 726-9200, FAX: (212) 696-9006, Web Site: www. nature.com (17)

Naturmed, Camp Verde, AZ. Tel: (928) 567-5175, (800) 720-1245, Web Site: www.ivlproducts.com (7)

Naughton, Cheryl, M2Media 360, Park Ridge, IL. Tel: (760) 318-7000, E-Mail: cnaughton@m2media360. com, Web Site: www.m2media360.com (17)

Nauman, Barbara, Providence Journal Telemarketing, Providence, RI. Tel: (401) 277-7000, FAX: (401) 277-8046, E-Mail: bnauman@projo.com, Web Site: www.projo.com (29)

Naumann, Michael, Theatre Development Fund Inc, New York, NY. Tel: (212) 912-9770, E-Mail: info@ tdf.org, Web Site: www.tdf.org (1)

Nauss, Donald W, Detroit Newspapers, Detroit, MI. Tel: (313) 222-2300, FAX: (313) 496-5400, E-Mail: newsroom@detnews.com, Web Site: www.freep. com (18)

Nautilus Inc, Vancouver, WA. Tel: (360) 859-2900, (800) 675-0171, FAX: (360) 694-2755, Web Site: www.nautilus.com (11)

Naval Institute Press, Annapolis, MD. Tel: (410) 268-6110, (800) 233-8764, FAX: (410) 571-1703, E-Mail: webmaster@usni.org, Web Site: www.usni. org/navalinstitutepress (17)

Navario, Peter, HealthRight International, New York, NY. Tel: (212) 226-9890, Web Site: www. healthright.org (1)

Navarra, Carlotta, NetHawk Interactive, Emeryville, CA. Tel: (510) 595-2220, E-Mail: info@nethawk. net, Web Site: www.nethawk.net (23)

Nave, Steve, Johnny Appleseed's Inc, Middleton, MA. Tel: (978) 922-2040, (800) 546-4554, FAX: (978) 922-7001, Web Site: www.appleseeds.blair.com (2)

Naveen Jindal School of Management, Richardson, TX. Tel: (972) 883-2705, (972) 883-2750, (972) 883-2275, Web Site: www.utdallas.edu (1)

Navistar, Lisle, IL. Tel: (331) 332-5000, Web Site: www.navistar.com (16)

Navitar Inc, Rochester, NY. Tel: (585) 359-4000, (800) 828-6778, FAX: (585) 359-4999, E-Mail: info@ navitar.com, Web Site: www.navitar.com (16)

Navy Federal Credit Union, Vienna, VA. Tel: (703) 206-4245, Web Site: www.navyfederal.org (14)

Naylor Inc, Atlanta, GA. Tel: (404) 739-7280, FAX: (404) 739-7284, Web Site: www.naylorinc.com (27)

Naylor, Aleia, Women's Sports Foundation, East Meadow, NY. Tel: (516) 542-4700, (800) 227-3988, FAX: (516) 542-0095, Web Site: www. womenssportsfoundation.org (1)

Naylor, Laura, CommercialWare Inc, Natick, MA. Tel: (508) 655-7500, FAX: (508) 647-9495, Web Site: www.commercialware.com (22)

Naylor, Steve, Naylor Inc, Atlanta, GA. Tel: (404) 739-7280, FAX: (404) 739-7284, Web Site: www. naylorinc.com (27)

Nazaruk, Dave, PlusNetMarketing Inc, Exton, PA. Tel: (610) 458-0707, E-Mail: info@pnmarketing.com, Web Site: www.plusnetmarketing.com (21)

Nazzaro, Khrysti, MoreVisibility, Boca Raton, FL. Tel: (561) 620-9682, (800) 787-0497, FAX: (561) 620-9684, E-Mail: info@morevisibility.com, Web Site: www.morevisibility.com (32)

Neagoe, Dan, CRK Computer Services, Bloomfield Hills, MI. Tel: (248) 569-3050, FAX: (248) 569-5259, E-Mail: information@crkusa.com, Web Site: www.crkusa.com (22)

Neal, Carl R., Amica Insurance, Lincoln, RI. Tel: (401) 334-6000, (800) 652-6422, FAX: (401) 334-4241, Web Site: www.amica.com (15)

Neal, Diane L, Sur La Table, Brownsburg, IN. Tel: (800) 243-0852, FAX: (317) 858-5521, E-Mail: customerservice@surlatable.com (8)

Neal, Michael A., GE Partnership Marketing Group, Schaumburg, IL. Tel: (847) 605-3000, FAX: (847) 605-3044, Web Site: www.gepmg.com (14)

Neal, Robin, Specialists Marketing Services Inc, Hasbrouck Heights, NJ. Tel: (201) 865-5800, FAX: (201) 288-4295, E-Mail: info@sms-inc.com, Web Site: www.sms-inc.com (23)

Neal, Scott, Gulfstream Aerospace Corp, Savannah, GA. Tel: (912) 965-3000, E-Mail: info@gulfstream. com, Web Site: www.gulfstream.com (16)

Neal, Stephen C., Levi Strauss & Co, San Francisco, CA. Tel: (415) 501-6000, FAX: (415) 501-7112, Web Site: www.levistrauss.com (16)

Nealis, Nora, Neighborhood Cleaners Association International, New York, NY. Tel: (212) 967-3002, (800) 888-1622, FAX: (212) 967-2240, E-Mail: info@nca-i.com, Web Site: www.nca-i.com (1)

Neanth, Greg, Gifts Corp, Barrie, ON Canada. Tel: (905) 670-1126, (800) 565-3130, FAX: (905) 670-1127, E-Mail: customerservice@regal.ca, Web Site: www.regalgreetings.com (6)

Neary, Amy, John Alden Life Insurance Co/North Star Marketing, Duluth, GA. Tel: (678) 473-1211, (800) 768-6288, FAX: (678) 473-9573, Web Site: www. nstarmarketing.com (15)

Neary, Daniel P., Mutual of Omaha, Omaha, NE. Tel: (402) 342-7600, (800) 775-6000, FAX: (402) 351-2775, Web Site: www.mutualofomaha.com (15)

Neary, Kevin, Prime Media Equine Group, Gaithersburg, MD. Tel: (301) 977-3900, FAX: (301) 990-9015, Web Site: www.equisearch.com (17)

Neat Co, Philadelphia, PA. Tel: (215) 382-3300, (866) 632-8732, FAX: (215) 386-2536, Web Site: neatco. com (22)

Neaves, David, CitiFinancial Credit Co, Baltimore, MD. Tel: (410) 332-3000, (800) 922-6235, (800) 995-2274, FAX: (410) 332-3489, Web Site: www. citifinancial.com (14)

Nebbia, Eric, National Business Furniture Inc, Milwaukee, WI. Tel: (414) 276-8511, (800) 558-1010, FAX: (414) 276-8371, Web Site: www. nationalbusinessfurniture.com (10)

Nebel, Randy, Longview Fibre Co, Longview, WA. Tel: (360) 425-1550, FAX: (360) 230-5135, E-Mail: info@longviewfibre.com, Web Site: www.longfibre.com (25)

Neejer, Kevin, CNY Awards & Apparel Inc, New Hartford, NY. Tel: (315) 733-0931, FAX: (800) 732-3617, Web Site: www.cnyapprel.com (5)

Neely, Daniel, Bosom Buddy Breast Forms, Boise, ID. Tel: (208) 343-9696, (800) 262-2789, FAX: (208) 343-9266, E-Mail: custserv@bosombuddy.com, Web Site: www.bosombuddy.com (7)

Neely, Stacie, Bosom Buddy Breast Forms, Boise, ID. Tel: (208) 343-9696, (800) 262-2789, FAX: (208) 343-9266, E-Mail: custserv@bosombuddy.com, Web Site: www.bosombuddy.com (7)

Neenah Paper FR LLC, Neenah, WI. Tel: (920) 733-7341, (800) 558-8327, FAX: (920) 733-2975, E-Mail: info@foxriverpaper.com, Web Site: www.foxriverpaper.com (27)

Neff, R.L., International Irrigation Systems, St. Catherines, ON Canada. Tel: (905) 688-4090, (877) 477-4476, FAX: (905) 688-4093, Web Site: www.irrigro.com (8)

Nehmer, David, Noble Communications Co, Springfield, MO. Tel: (417) 875-5015, Web Site: www.noble.net (35)

Nehmer, Kathy, Educators Progress Service Inc, Randolph, WI. Tel: (920) 326-3126, (888) 951-4469, Web Site: www.freeteachingaids.com (17)

Neibauer Press, Warminster, PA. Tel: (215) 322-6200, (800) 322-6203, FAX: (215) 322-2495, E-Mail: info@neibauer.com, Web Site: www.neibauer.com (27)

Neibauer, Nathan, Neibauer Press, Warminster, PA. Tel: (215) 322-6200, (800) 322-6203, FAX: (215) 322-2495, E-Mail: info@neibauer.com, Web Site: www.neibauer.com (27)

Neibauer, Ruth, Neibauer Press, Warminster, PA. Tel: (215) 322-6200, (800) 322-6203, FAX: (215) 322-2495, E-Mail: info@neibauer.com, Web Site: www.neibauer.com (27)

Neighborhood Cleaners Association International, New York, NY. Tel: (212) 967-3002, (800) 888-1622, FAX: (212) 967-2240, E-Mail: info@nca-i.com, Web Site: www.nca-i.com (1)

Neighborhood Greetings, Harrisburg, PA. Tel: (717) 839-6390, (800) 332-9200, Web Site: ngp.allegraharrisburg.com (23)

Neil, Sylvia, Columbia College Chicago, Chicago, IL. Tel: (312) 663-1600, FAX: (312) 344-0869, Web Site: www.colum.edu (41)

Neill, Tiffany, Lautman Maska Neill & Co, Washington, DC. Tel: (202) 296-9660, Web Site: www.lautmandc.com (1)

Neiman-Marcus Group, Dallas, TX. Tel: (214) 339-0396, (888) 888-4757, Web Site: www.neimanmarcus.com (8)

Neiman, Shirley, Stock Montage Inc, Chicago, IL. Tel: (773) 637-9790, (800) 404-0425, FAX: (773) 637-9794, E-Mail: mail@stockmontage.com, Web Site: www.stockmontage.com (38)

Neimer, Dave, VF Imagewear, Greensboro, NC. Tel: (336) 424-6000, (800) 733-5271, Web Site: www.vfimagewear.com (2)

Neiner, Jean, StayWell/Krames, San Bruno, CA. Tel: (650) 742-0400, FAX: (650) 244-4568, Web Site: www.staywell.com (17)

Nelis, Angie, Roche Diagnostics Corp, Indianapolis, IN. Tel: (317) 521-2000, Web Site: www.usdiagnostics.roche.com (7)

Nelles, William A., Monex Deposit Co, Newport Beach, CA. Tel: (949) 752-1400, (800) 444-8317, FAX: (949) 752-7214, E-Mail: info@monex.com, Web Site: www.monex.com (14)

Nelson Crab Inc, Tokeland, WA. Tel: (360) 267-2911, (800) 262-0069, FAX: (360) 267-2921, E-Mail: seatreats@techline.com, Web Site: www.nelsoncrab.com (4)

Nelson-Jameson Inc, Marshfield, WI. Tel: (715) 387-1151, (800) 826-8302, FAX: (715) 387-8746, (800) 472-0840, E-Mail: sales@nelsonjameson.com, Web Site: www.nelsonjameson.com (9)

Paul Nelson Direct Marketing, Santa Monica, CA. Tel: (310) 392-9533 (20)

Nelson Printing Corp - Direct Marketers of Charleston, Charleston, SC. Tel: (843) 723-7233, FAX: (843) 723-8098, E-Mail: info@nelsonprint.com, Web Site: nelsonprint.com (21)

Nelson Schmidt Inc, Milwaukee, WI. Tel: (414) 224-0210, FAX: (414) 224-9463, Web Site: nelsonschmidt.com (35)

Nelson, Andy, TRANZACT, Fort Lee, NJ. Tel: (201) 461-5665, E-Mail: info@tranzact.net, Web Site: www.tranzact.net (35)

Nelson, Brian, Trancos Inc, Pleasanton, CA. Tel: (650) 364-3110, Web Site: www.trancos.com (16)

Nelson, Carl A., Pastime Publications Inc, Denver, CO. Tel: (303) 534-7867, (888) 650-8665, FAX: (630) 214-7600, E-Mail: post@pastimecompany.com, Web Site: www.pastimecompany.com (17)

Nelson, Danielle, Anderson Direct & Digital, Poway, CA. Tel: (888) 694-5094, Web Site: www.andersondd.com (35)

Nelson, Dean, Prime Media Equine Group, Gaithersburg, MD. Tel: (301) 977-3900, FAX: (301) 990-9015, Web Site: www.equisearch.com (17)

Nelson, Dean, RentPath LLc, Norcross, GA. Tel: (678) 421-3000, (800) 216-1423, Web Site: www.primedia.com (31)

Nelson, Donna J., American Chemical Society, Washington, DC. Tel: (202) 872-4600, (800) 227-5558, FAX: (202) 452-8913, E-Mail: service@acs.org, Web Site: www.acs.org (1)

Nelson, Erik, PackStream LLC, Louisville, KY. Tel: (502) 552-9624, Web Site: www.packstream.com (20)

Nelson, Isio, IXI Services, McLean, VA. Tel: (703) 848-3800, FAX: (703) 848-3868, E-Mail: info.ixiservices@equifax.com, Web Site: www.ixicorp.com (35)

Nelson, John, Nelson-Jameson Inc, Marshfield, WI. Tel: (715) 387-1151, (800) 826-8302, FAX: (715) 387-8746, (800) 472-0840, E-Mail: sales@nelsonjameson.com, Web Site: www.nelsonjameson.com (9)

Nelson, Jr Daniel H., Nelson Schmidt Inc, Milwaukee, WI. Tel: (414) 224-0210, FAX: (414) 224-9463, Web Site: nelsonschmidt.com (35)

Nelson, Judy, Creative Catalogs Corp, Lemont, IL. Tel: (630) 783-2400, Web Site: www.personalcreations.com (6)

Nelson, Judy, Personal Creations, Lemont, IL. Tel: (630) 783-2400, (866) 834-7695, Web Site: www.personalcreations.com (6)

Nelson, Kristi, Nelson Crab Inc, Tokeland, WA. Tel: (360) 267-2911, (800) 262-0069, FAX: (360) 267-2921, E-Mail: seatreats@techline.com, Web Site: www.nelsoncrab.com (4)

Nelson, Lance J., Aptimus, San Francisco, CA. Tel: (415) 896-2123, FAX: (415) 896-2561 (22)

Nelson, Martha, Time Inc, New York, NY. Tel: (212) 522-1212, Web Site: www.timeinc.com (17)

Nelson, Michael S., National Court Reporters Association, Reston, VA. Tel: (703) 556-6272, (800) 272-6272, FAX: (703) 391-0629, E-Mail: msic@ncrahg.org, Web Site: www.ncraonline.org (1)

Nelson, Monique, UniWorld Group, Brooklyn, NY. Tel: (212) 219-1600, FAX: (212) 219-6395, E-Mail: newbiz@uwqny.com, Web Site: www.uwg.is (21)

Nelson, Paul, Paul Nelson Direct Marketing, Santa Monica, CA. Tel: (310) 392-9533 (20)

Nelson, Scott, Collector's Armoury Ltd, McDonough, GA. Tel: (678) 593-2660, (877) 276-6879, FAX: (678) 593-2660, E-Mail: sales@collectorsarmoury.com, Web Site: www.collectorsarmoury.com (6)

Nelson, Scott, Educational Testing Service, Princeton, NJ. Tel: (609) 921-9000, FAX: (609) 734-5410, Web Site: www.ets.org (16)

Nelson, Scott G., Gould & Goodrich, Lillington, NC. Tel: (910) 893-2071, (800) 277-0732, FAX: (910) 893-4742, E-Mail: service@gouldusa.com, Web Site: www.gouldusa.com (2)

Nelson, Shanna Missett, Jazzercise Inc, Carlsbad, CA. Tel: (760) 476-1750, FAX: (760) 602-7180, E-Mail: customercare@jazzercise.com, Web Site: www.jazzercise.com (2)

Nelson, Todd, Career Education Corp, Schaumburg, IL. Tel: (847) 781-3600, E-Mail: inquiries@careered.com, Web Site: www.careered.com (1)

Nelson, Todd, Kwik-File, Sheboygan, WI. Tel: (763) 572-1980, (800) 822-8037, FAX: (763) 572-0168, Web Site: www.mayline.com (27)

Nelson, Todd, The Herald & Review, Decatur, IL. Tel: (217) 429-5151, FAX: (217) 421-6913, E-Mail: hrdirect@herald-review.com, Web Site: www.herald-review.com (17)

Nelson, Tom, Collector's Armoury Ltd, McDonough, GA. Tel: (678) 593-2660, (877) 276-6879, FAX: (678) 593-2660, E-Mail: sales@collectorsarmoury.com, Web Site: www.collectorsarmoury.com (6)

Neo@Ogilvy, New York, NY. Tel: (212) 259-5200, Web Site: www.neoogilvy.com (35)

Neo-Tech Publishing Co, Henderson, NV. Tel: (702) 891-0303, FAX: (702) 795-8393 (17)

Neolane, Newton, MA. Tel: (617) 467-6760, FAX: (617) 467-6701, Web Site: www.neolane.com (22)

Neopost USA, Milford, CT. Tel: (203) 301-3400, Web Site: www.neopostusa.com (34)

Nerli, Barry, Magnolia Hall, Jasper, GA. Tel: (404) 351-1910, (866) 410-2755, FAX: (404) 692-4068. E-Mail: belvedere@magnoliahall.com, Web Site: www.magnoliahall.com (8)

Nesbitt, Kenneth, MAX Federal Credit Union, Montgomery, AL. Tel: (334) 260-2600, (800) 776-6776, FAX: (334) 270-0921, Web Site: www.mymax.com (14)

Ness, Antonia, Gruppo Levey & Co, New York, NY. Tel: (212) 867-, FAX: (212) 949-7294, E-Mail: info@glconline.com, Web Site: www.glconline.com (14)

NestFamily.com, Lewisville, TX. Tel: (800) 596-7386, FAX: (972) 629-7181, Web Site: www.nestfamily.com (3)

Nestle HealthCare Nutrition, Florham Park, NJ. Tel: (800) 422-2752, Web Site: www.nestle-nutrition.com (16)

Nestle USA, Glendale, CA. Tel: (818) 549-6000, (800) 225-2270, FAX: (818) 553-3547, Web Site: www.nestleusa.com (4)

Nestler, Eric, Society for Neuroscience, Washington, DC. Tel: (202) 962-4000, Web Site: www.sfn.org (1)

Net-Results, Golden, CO. Tel: (303) 771-2552, E-Mail: info@net-results.com, Web Site: www.net-results.com (32)

Net 60 LLC, New York, NY. Tel: (201) 833-9003, FAX: (201) 301-8182, E-Mail: chaim@net60.com, Web Site: net60.com (23)

NetHawk Interactive, Emeryville, CA. Tel: (510) 595-2220, E-Mail: info@nethawk.net, Web Site: www.nethawk.net (23)

NetProspex Inc, Waltham, MA. Tel: (888) 826-4877, E-Mail: sales@netprospex.com, Web Site: www.netprospex.com (22)

NetSpend, San Mateo, CA. Tel: (866) 387-7363, Web Site: www.netspend.com (14)

Nettesheim, Matt, Emergency Essentials Inc, Orem, UT. Tel: (801) 222-9596, FAX: (801) 222-9598, E-Mail: webmaster@beprepared.com, Web Site: www.beprepared.com (16)

Netweb/Omni LLC, Ellicott City, MD. Tel: (410) 591-1900, E-Mail: barry@netwebomni.com, Web Site: www.netwebomni.com (40)

Network for Good, Washington, DC. Tel: (240) 482-3211, Web Site: www.networkforgood.org (1)

Network Solutions LLC, Herndon, VA. Tel: (877) 628-8686, Web Site: www.networksolutions.com (32)

Network Telephone Services Inc, Woodland Hills, CA. Tel: (818) 992-4300, (800) 727-6874, FAX: (818) 992-8415, Web Site: www.nts.net (16)

Networking Alternatives for Publishers, Retailers & Artists, Inc, Eastsound, WA. Tel: (360) 376-2702, (800) 367-1907, FAX: (360) 376-2704, E-Mail: futureweb@rockisland.com (40)

Netzer, Oren, DoubleVerify, New York, NY. Tel: (212) 631-2111, Web Site: www.doubleverify.com (9)

Neuberger & Berman Management, New York, NY. Tel: (212) 476-9000, (800) 877-9700, FAX: (212) 476-8937, Web Site: www.nb.com (14)

Neufeld, Dan, Lin Terry, Paterson, NJ. Tel: (973) 345-6677, FAX: (973) 345-5551, E-Mail: linterry@aol.com, Web Site: www.linterry.com (6)

Neufeld, Heidi, Lin Terry, Paterson, NJ. Tel: (973) 345-6677, FAX: (973) 345-5551, E-Mail: linterry@aol.com, Web Site: www.linterry.com (6)

Richard K Neukranz Associates, Jacksonville, FL. Tel: (904) 998-1201, FAX: (904) 998-1579, E-Mail: rneukranz@bellsouth.net (39)

Neukranz, Richard K., Richard K Neukranz Associates, Jacksonville, FL. Tel: (904) 998-1201, FAX: (904) 998-1579, E-Mail: rneukranz@bellsouth.net (39)

Neuman, Debra, National Trust for Historic Preservation, Washington, DC. Tel: (202) 588-6000, (800) 944-6847, E-Mail: info@savingplaces.org, Web Site: www.preservationnation.org (1)

Neuman, Morris, SpeechSoft Inc, Armonk, NY. Tel: (914) 273-5560, (800) 878-8117, E-Mail: sales@speechsoft.com, Web Site: www.speechsoft.com (29)

Neustar Inc, Sterling, VA. Tel: (571) 434-5400, (877) 245-5277, E-Mail: billingsupport@neustar.biz, Web Site: www.neustar.biz (29)

Neustein, Barry, Poly-Flex Corp, Edgewood, NY. Tel: (631) 586-9500, FAX: (631) 586-6631, E-Mail: info@poly-flexcorp.com, Web Site: www.poly-flexcorp.com (26)

Neutron Industries, Phoenix, AZ. Tel: (602) 864-0090, (888) 712-7127, FAX: (602) 357-3996, (877) 646-7337, E-Mail: questions@neutronindustries.com, Web Site: www.neutronindustries.com (16)

Nevada Commission on Tourism, Carson City, NV. Tel: (775) 687-4322, (800) NEVADA 8, FAX: (775) 687-6779, Web Site: www.travelnevada.com (1)

Nevada Magazine, Carson City, NV. Tel: (775) 687-5416, FAX: (775) 687-6159, E-Mail: editor@nevadamagazine.com, Web Site: www.nevadamagazine.com (17)

Nevard, Stephen, One On One Advertising Inc, New Haven, CT. Tel: (203) 562-6259, (203) 671-2339, E-Mail: snevard@comcast.net, Web Site: snevard.wix.com/portfolio (35)

Nevco Scoreboard Co, Greenville, IL. Tel: (618) 664-0360, (800) 851-4040, FAX: (618) 664-0398, E-Mail: sales@nevcoscoreboards.com, Web Site: www.nevcoscoreboards.com (16)

Nevels, James E., Hershey Park, Hershey, PA. Tel: (717) 534-3149, (800) HERSHEY, E-Mail: info@hersheypa.com, Web Site: www.hersheypark.com (19)

Nevels, James, The Hershey Co, Hershey, PA. Tel: (717) 534-4200, (800) 454-7737, FAX: (717) 534-5204, Web Site: www.hersheygifts.com (4)

Neville, Vickie, Cole Information Services, Omaha, NE. Tel: (800) 403-5894, E-Mail: info@coleinformation.com, Web Site: www.coleinformation.com (23)

Nevin, Darius G., Protection One Inc, Lawrence, KS. Tel: (785) 856-5500, (800) GET-HELP, Web Site: www.protectionone.com (16)

Nevinger, MG, Nevco Scoreboard Co, Greenville, IL. Tel: (618) 664-0360, (800) 851-4040, FAX: (618) 664-0398, E-Mail: sales@nevcoscoreboards.com, Web Site: www.nevcoscoreboards.com (16)

Nevins, David, Showtime Networks Inc, New York, NY. Tel: (212) 708-1600, FAX: (212) 708-1450, Web Site: www.sho.com (16)

Nevitt, Toni, E Media Advantage, Livingston, NJ. Tel: (917) 994-3685, FAX: (973) 455-1312, E-Mail: tnevitt@emediaadvantage.com, Web Site: emediaadvantage.com (20)

New American Dimensions, Los Angeles, CA. Tel: (310) 670-6800 (20)

New & Unique Videos, San Diego, CA. Tel: (619) 644-3000, FAX: (619) 644-3001, E-Mail: info@newuniquevideos.com, Web Site: www.newuniquevideos.com (3)

New Customer Acquisition, Medford, OR. Tel: (541) 779-9999, FAX: (541) 779-1935, E-Mail: bobk@postage-exempt.com (31)

NEW Customer Service Companies Inc, Sterling, VA. Tel: (703) 707-1582, Web Site: www.newcorp.com (20)

New Day Marketing Ltd, Santa Barbara, CA. Tel: (805) 965-7833, FAX: (805) 965-1284, E-Mail: robert@ndm.tv, Web Site: www.newdaymarketing.com (35)

New Directions Publishing Corp, New York, NY. Tel: (212) 255-0230, FAX: (212) 255-0231, E-Mail: editorial@ndbooks.com, Web Site: www.ndbooks.com (17)

New England Cheesemaking Supply Co, South Deerfield, MA. Tel: (413) 397-2012, FAX: (413) 397-2014, E-Mail: info@cheesemaking.com, Web Site: www.cheesemaking.com (4)

New England Direct Marketing Association, Wellesley Hills, MA. Tel: (781) 237-1366, FAX: (781) 431-8118, E-Mail: info@nedma.com, Web Site: www.nedma.com (40)

New England Journal of Medicine, Waltham, MA. Tel: (781) 893-3800, FAX: (781) 893-7729, Web Site: www.nejm.org (17)

New England Life Insurance Co, Boston, MA. Tel: (617) 578-2000, FAX: (617) 536-2393, Web Site: www.nefn.metlife.com (15)

New England List Services Inc, Danville, VT. Tel: (802) 684-1179, (877) 252-2100, FAX: (802) 684-2113, E-Mail: dave@nelists.com, Web Site: www.nelists.com (23)

New England Mail Order Association, Scarborough, ME. Tel: (207) 885-0090, (860) 691-1260, FAX: (207) 885-0097, Web Site: www.nemoa.org (40)

New England Stock Photo, Glastonbury, CT. Tel: (860) 659-4949, FAX: (860) 659-3235 (38)

New Hampshire Public Television, Durham, NH. Tel: (603) 868-1100, E-Mail: themailbox@nhptv.org, Web Site: www.nhptv.org (32)

New Hermes Inc, Duluth, GA. Tel: (770) 623-0331, (800) 843-7637, FAX: (800) 533-7637, E-Mail: sales@gravograph-newhermes.com, Web Site: www.gravograph.com/usa/government/index.php (34)

New Jersey Institute for Continuing Legal Education, New Brunswick, NJ. Tel: (732) 249-5100, Web Site: www.njicle.com (1)

New Jersey Monthly, Morristown, NJ. Tel: (973) 539-8230, FAX: (973) 538-2953, E-Mail: research@njmonthly.com, Web Site: www.njmonthly.com (17)

New Mexico State University, Las Cruces, NM. Tel: (505) 646-3341, (575) 646-0111, FAX: (505) 646-1498, Web Site: www.nmsu.edu (41)

New Pig Corp, Tipton, PA. Tel: (814) 684-0101, (800) 468-4647, FAX: (814) 684-0961, E-Mail: hothogs@newpig.com, Web Site: www.newpig.com (9)

The New Piper Aircraft Inc, Vero Beach, FL. Tel: (772) 567-4361, FAX: (772) 978-6573, E-Mail: marketing@piper.com, Web Site: www.newpiper.com (16)

New Track Media LLC, Cincinnati, OH. Tel: (513) 421-6500, FAX: (513) 421-1244, E-Mail: lriggs@newtrackmedia.com, Web Site: www.newtrackmedia.com (17)

New Village Media Inc, Columbia, MD. Tel: (443) 832-4007, E-Mail: jskillington@newvillagemedia.com, Web Site: www.newvillagemedia.com (35)

New Wave Media Inc, Emeryville, CA. Tel: (510) 250-5500, FAX: (510) 250-5700, Web Site: www.exponential.com (5)

New Win Publishing Inc, El Monte, CA. Tel: (626) 448-3448, FAX: (626) 602-3817, E-Mail: info@AcademicLearningCompany.com, Web Site: www.newwinpublishing.com (17)

New York & Co, New York, NY. Tel: (212) 884-2169, (800) 961-9906, Web Site: www.nyandcompany.com (2)

New York Blood Center Inc, New York, NY. Tel: (212) 570-3000, (800) 933-2566, FAX: (212) 570-3195, Web Site: www.nybloodcenter.org (1)

New York Daily News, New York, NY. Tel: (212) 210-2100, FAX: (212) 643-7844, Web Site: www.nydailynews.com (31)

New York Easter Seal Society, New York, NY. Tel: (212) 220-2290, FAX: (212) 695-4807, Web Site: ny.easterseals.com (1)

New York Findings, New York, NY. Tel: (212) 925-5745, (888) 925-5745, FAX: (212) 925-5870, E-Mail: nyfindings@aol.com, Web Site: www.newyorkfindings.com (6)

New York Foundation For The Arts, Brooklyn, NY. Tel: (212) 366-6900, FAX: (212) 366-1778, Web Site: www.nyfa.org (1)

New York Landmarks Conservancy, New York, NY. Tel: (212) 995-5260, FAX: (212) 995-5268, Web Site: www.nylandmarks.org (1)

New York Life Insurance Co/AARP, Tampa, FL. Tel: (813) 288-5500, FAX: (813) 288-5256, Web Site: www.nylaarp.com (15)

New York Philharmonic, New York, NY. Tel: (212) 875-5691, Web Site: www.nyphil.org (1)

New York Power Authority, White Plains, NY. Tel: (914) 681-6200, E-Mail: info@nypa.gov, Web Site: www.nypa.gov (16)

New York-Presbyterian/Columbia University Medical Center, New York, NY. Tel: (212) 305-2500, FAX: (212) 305-8023, Web Site: www.nyp.org (16)

New York Road Runners, New York, NY. Tel: (855) 5MY-NYRR, E-Mail: mynyrr@nyrr.org, Web Site: www.nyrr.org (13)

The New York Times Agency - Photo, New York, NY. Tel: (212) 556-4939, (888) NYT-PHOTO, FAX: (212) 556-5257, E-Mail: photosales@nytimes.com, Web Site: www.nytimesagency.com (38)

The New York Times Co, New York, NY. Tel: (212) 556-1234, Web Site: www.nytimes.com (17)

New York University, New York, NY. Tel: (212) 992-3221, Web Site: www.scps.nyu.edu (1)

New York University/Center for Marketing, New York, NY. Tel: (212) 998-0100, FAX: (212) 995-4006, E-Mail: mkt@stern.nyu.edu, Web Site: www.stern.nyu.edu/marketing (41)

New York University Medical Center, New York, NY. Tel: (212) 263-7800, FAX: (212) 263-8426, Web Site: www.med.nyu.edu (1)

The New Yorker Magazine, New York, NY. Tel: (212) 286-2860, FAX: (212) 286-4168, Web Site: www.newyorker.com (17)

New Zealand Tourism Board, Santa Monica, CA. Tel: (310) 395-7480, (310) 395-5453, FAX: (310) 395-5453, E-Mail: nzinfo@nztb.govt.nz, Web Site: www.purenz.com (19)

New, David, AmerisourceBergen, Chesterbrook, PA. Tel: (610) 727-7000, (800) 829-3132, E-Mail: solutions@amerisourcebergan.com, Web Site: www.amerisourcebergan.com (7)

Newborn, Andrea, The Reader's Digest Association Inc, New York, NY. Tel: (800) 310-6261, Web Site: www.rda.com (17)

Newby, Lisa, Agri Drain Corp, Adair, IA. Tel: (641) 742-5211, (800) 232-4742, FAX: (800) 282-3353, (641) 742-5222, E-Mail: info@agridrain.com, Web Site: www.agridrain.com (9)

Newcomb Marketing Solutions, Michigan City, IN. Tel: (219) 874-3201, (800) 921-1221, FAX: (219) 874-8156, Web Site: www.newcombsolutions.com (27)

Newcomb, Doug, Special Libraries Association (SLA), Alexandria, VA. Tel: (703) 647-4900, FAX: (703) 647-4901, E-Mail: sla@sla.org, Web Site: www.sla.org (40)

Newcomb, Gloria, Newcomb Marketing Solutions, Michigan City, IN. Tel: (219) 874-3201, (800) 921-1221, FAX: (219) 874-8156, Web Site: www.newcombsolutions.com (27)

Newell Rubbermaid, Inc, Atlanta, GA. Tel: (770) 418-7000, Web Site: www.newellrubbermaid.com (16)

Newell, Bruce, GBE Plus, Hartford, CT. Tel: (860) 727-9100, (800) 842-0139, FAX: (860) 527-6041, Web Site: www.gbeplus.com (2)

Newhouse School of Public Communications, Syracuse, NY. Tel: (315) 443-3611, FAX: (315) 443-4426, Web Site: newhouse.syr.edu (41)

Newhouse, Jr. S.I., Conde Nast, New York, NY. Tel: (212) 286-2860, FAX: (212) 880-8289, Web Site: www.condenast.com (17)

Newlin, Steve, Poly One Corp, Avon Lake, OH. Tel: (440) 930-1000, (866) POLY-ONE, FAX: (440) 930-1428, Web Site: www.polyone.com (16)

Geraldine Newman Communications, New York, NY. Tel: (212) 988-3395, FAX: (212) 988-3407, E-Mail: ger@newthynk.com, Web Site: www.newthynk.com (39)

The Newman Group Computer Services Corp, Ann Arbor, MI. Tel: (734) 426-3200, FAX: (734) 426-0777, E-Mail: anewman@newman.com (3)

Newman, Adrian, Lombardi Publishing Corp, Vaughan, ON Canada. Tel: (866) 744-3579, FAX: (905) 856-9416, E-Mail: customerservice@lombardipublishing.com, Web Site: www.lombardipublishing.com (17)

Newman, Allan, The Newman Group Computer Services Corp, Ann Arbor, MI. Tel: (734) 426-3200, FAX: (734) 426-0777, E-Mail: anewman@newman.com (3)

Newman, Gary, 20th Century Fox Television, Los Angeles, CA. Tel: (310) 369-4636, FAX: (310) 969-0468, Web Site: www.foxstudios.com (16)

Newman, Geraldine, Geraldine Newman Communications, New York, NY. Tel: (212) 988-3395, FAX: (212) 988-3407, E-Mail: ger@newthynk.com, Web Site: www.newthynk.com (39)

Newman, Judith A, Scholastic Inc, New York, NY. Tel: (212) 343-6100, (800) SCHOLASTIC, FAX: (212) 343-6484, Web Site: www.scholastic.com (17)

Newman, Lee, MullenLowe US, Boston, MA. Tel: (617) 226-9000, FAX: (617) 226-9100, Web Site: us.mullenlowe.com (35)

Newman, Randy Louis, Alerus Financial National Assoc, Grand Forks, ND. Tel: (701) 795-3200, (800) 279-3200, Web Site: www2.alerusfinancial.com (14)

Newman, Steven M., Loehmann's, Bronx, NY. Tel: (718) 409-2000, Web Site: www.loehmanns.com (2)

NewPage Corp, Miamisburg, OH. Tel: (937) 242-9345, (877) 855-7243, FAX: (937) 242-9327, Web Site: www.newpagecorp.com (25)

Newport Creative Communications, Duxbury, MA. Tel: (781) 934-1414, Web Site: www.newportcreative.com (1)

News America Marketing, New York, NY. Tel: (212) 852-8000, (800) 462-0852, FAX: (212) 575-5845, Web Site: www.newsamerica.com (31)

News & Observer Direct Marketing, Raleigh, NC. Tel: (919) 836-5658, (800) 522-4205 (40)

News & Record, Greensboro, NC. Tel: (336) 373-7000, (800) 553-6880 (31)

News Marketing Canada, Toronto, ON Canada. Tel: (416) 775-3000, FAX: (416) 775-3055, E-Mail: spetkovich@newsmarketing.ca, Web Site: www.newsmarketing.ca (20)

The News Tribune, Tacoma, WA. Tel: (253) 597-8742, E-Mail: customerservice@thenewstribune.com, Web Site: www.thenewstribune.com (17)

Newsday, Melville, NY. Tel: (800) 639-7329, Web Site: www.newsday.com (17)

Newsmax List Management, West Palm Beach, FL. Tel: (561) 674-0726, (800) 485-4350, FAX: (561) 494-0922, E-Mail: matthewd@newsmax.com, Web Site: www.newsmax.com/advertise/list-management (24)

NewsNotes LLC, Middleton, WI. Tel: (608) 831-9600, (800) 676-9665, FAX: (608) 831-9665, E-Mail: sales@nastar-inc.com, Web Site: www.news-notes.com (27)

Newspaper Association of America, Arlington, VA. Tel: (571) 366-1000, FAX: (571) 366-1195, Web Site: www.naa.org (1)

Newstedt, George, Excalibur Enterprises Inc, Winston Salem, NC. Tel: (336) 744-5000, (800) 441-4193, FAX: (336) 767-8257, E-Mail: info@excaliburmail.com, Web Site: www.excaliburmail.com (28)

Newton, Grant, Firebrand Group, New York, NY. Tel: (866) 757-3362, E-Mail: info@firebrandgroup.com, Web Site: www.firebrandgroup.com (32)

Newton, Leslie, Evergreen Enterprises Inc, Richmond, VA. Tel: (800) 774-3837, E-Mail: customerservice@myevergreen.com, Web Site: www.myevergreen.com (8)

Newton, Michael, Dirmark Group Inc, Roswell, GA. Tel: (678) 245-1831, (888) 221-4968, E-Mail: dirmarkonline@dirmark.com, Web Site: dirmark.com (23)

Newton, Ronne, Demand Telemarketing Inc, Grosse Pointe, MI. Tel: (313) 823-8598, (888) 977-2256, FAX: (313) 823-8598, E-Mail: info@create-demand.com, Web Site: www.create-demand.com (29)

NextMark Inc, Hanover, NH. Tel: (603) 643-1307, FAX: (603) 643-1662, Web Site: www.nextmark.com (22)

NextScreen LLC, Austin, TX. Tel: (512) 892-8682, Web Site: www.avguide.com (17)

Nexus Direct, Norfolk, VA. Tel: (757) 340-5960, (800) 965-0577, FAX: (757) 340-5980, E-Mail: hello@nexusdirect.com, Web Site: www.nexusdirect.com (35)

Nexxa Group Inc, Fort Myers, FL. Tel: (239) 225-1516, (800) 566-1217, E-Mail: info@nexxagroup.com, Web Site: www.nexxagroup.com (23)

Nexxlinx (HQ), Atlanta, GA. Tel: (770) 250-0349, (877) 747-0658, Web Site: www.nexxlinx.com (22)

Nezwek, Joe, F P International, Fremont, CA. Tel: (650) 261-5300, (800) 866-9946, FAX: (650) 361-1713, Web Site: www.fpintl.com (16)

NFocus Consulting Inc, Lancaster, OH. Tel: (740) 654-5809, (800) 675-5809, FAX: 740 654-0934, Web Site: www.nfocusconsulting.com (22)

nFusion Group LLC, Austin, TX. Tel: (512) 716-7000, FAX: (512) 716-7001, E-Mail: info@nfusion.com, Web Site: nfusion.com (35)

Ng, Pamela, Teleflora, Los Angeles, CA. Tel: (310) 966-3586, Web Site: www.teleflora.com (16)

Ng, Ronald, DigitasLBi, Boston, MA. Tel: (617) 867-1000, E-Mail: newbusiness@digitas.com, Web Site: www.digitaslbi.com (35)

Nguyen, Jennifer, Colarelli Meyer & Associates Inc, Saint Louis, MO. Tel: (314) 721-1860, (800) 459-4548, FAX: (314) 721-1992, E-Mail: cmaconsult@cmaconsult.com, Web Site: www.cmaconsult.com (20)

Niaura, Matt, Engineering Services & Products Co, South Windsor, CT. Tel: (860) 528-1119, (800) 835-7877, FAX: (800) 457-8887, Web Site: www.teksupply.com (9)

Niblock, Robert A., Lowe's Companies Inc, Mooresville, NC. Tel: (704) 758-1000, (800) 445-6937, Web Site: www.lowes.com (8)

Nicely, Olza M., GEICO Direct, Washington, DC. Tel: (301) 986-2842, (800) 841-3000, FAX: (301) 986-2068, Web Site: www.geico.com (15)

Nicholas, J. K., Chelsea Clock Co Inc, Chelsea, MA. Tel: (617) 884-0250, (866) 899-2805, FAX: (617) 830-0599, Web Site: www.chelseaclock.com (6)

Nichols, Gaylord, California Institute of Technology, Pasadena, CA. Tel: (626) 395-3746, FAX: (626) 795-7174, E-Mail: execedu@caltech.edu, Web Site: www.irc.caltech.edu (16)

Nichols, John Paul, RCI LLC, Carmel, IN. Tel: (317) 805-9000, FAX: (317) 805-9335, Web Site: www.rci.com (19)

Nichols, Richard, Goss International, Durham, NH. Tel: (603) 749-6600, FAX: (603) 750-6860, Web Site: www.gossinternational.com (27)

Nichols, Rob, American Bankers Association, Washington, DC. Tel: (202) 663-5000, (800) 226-5377, FAX: (202) 663-7543, Web Site: www.aba.com (1)

Nichols, Sallianne, Austin & Williams, Hauppauge, NY. Tel: (631) 938-2279, FAX: (212) 434-7022, E-Mail: info@austin-williams.com, Web Site: www.austin-williams.com (35)

Nichols, Victor K., Experian, Costa Mesa, CA. Tel: (714) 830-7000, (888) EXPERIAN, FAX: (949) 242-2938, Web Site: www.experian.com (30)

Nicholson, James B., Amerisure Insurance Cos, Farmington Hills, MI. Tel: (248) 615-9000, (800) 257-1900, FAX: (248) 615-8224, Web Site: www.amerisure.com (15)

Nicholson, Nick, Keeneland Association Inc, Lexington, KY. Tel: (859) 254-3412, (800) 456-3412, FAX: (859) 255-2484, Web Site: www.keeneland.com (16)

Nicholson, Pamela, Alamo Rent A Car, Saint Louis, MO. Tel: (314) 512-2880, Web Site: www.alamo.com (16)

Nicholson, Pamela M., Enterprise Rent-A-Car, Saint Louis, MO. Tel: (314) 512-5000, FAX: (314) 512-4706, Web Site: www.enterprise.com (19)

Nicholson, Peter, Periscope Inc, Minneapolis, MN. Tel: (612) 339-0500, FAX: (612) 339-0600, E-Mail: info@periscope.com, Web Site: www.periscope.com (35)

Nichtawitz, Anthony, Caswell-Massey Co Ltd, Edison, NJ. Tel: (732) 225-2181, (800) 326-0500, FAX: (800) 868-4407, E-Mail: info@caswellmasseyltd.com, Web Site: www.caswellmassey.com (7)

Nickel, Jeff, TrueSense Marketing, Freedom, PA. Tel: (877) 878-6584, Web Site: www.truesense.com (35)

Nickerson, Mike, Price Weber Marketing Communications Inc, Louisville, KY. Tel: (502) 499-9220, FAX: (502) 491-5593, E-Mail: info@priceweber.com, Web Site: www.priceweber.com (35)

Nicklaus Companies LLC, North Palm Beach, FL. Tel: (561) 227-0300, FAX: (561) 227-0548, Web Site: www.nicklaus.com (16)

Nicklaus, Jack, Nicklaus Companies LLC, North Palm Beach, FL. Tel: (561) 227-0300, FAX: (561) 227-0548, Web Site: www.nicklaus.com (16)

John Nicksic, Santa Fe, NM. Tel: (505) 983-7656, FAX: (505) 983-7159, E-Mail: nicksic@mindspring.com (39)

Nicksic, John, John Nicksic, Santa Fe, NM. Tel: (505) 983-7656, FAX: (505) 983-7159, E-Mail: nicksic@mindspring.com (39)

Nicol, James, Gates Corp, Denver, CO. Tel: (303) 744-1911, FAX: (303) 744-4000, Web Site: www.gates.com (9)

Nicolichuk, Michael, Arrowhead Mountain Spring Water. Wilkes Barre, PA. Tel: (800) 873-7775, Web Site: www.arrowheadwater.com (16)

Nicolin, Magnus, Esselte Americas, Melville, NY. Tel: (631) 675-5700, (800) 645-6051, FAX: (631) 622-1970, Web Site: www.curtis.com (16)

Nicolosi, Tony, Volvo Cars of North America LLC, Northvale, NJ. Tel: (201) 768-7300, (800) 458-1552, E-Mail: customercare@volvocars.com, Web Site: www.volvocars.com (16)

Nicols, Virginia, The Marketing Machine, Irvine, CA. Tel: (949) 733-1778, (949) 733-3778, FAX: (949) 559-6993, E-Mail: request@the-marketing-machine.com, Web Site: www.mktgmach.com (39)

Nieberding, Paul, Lexus Division of Toyota, Torrance, CA. Tel: (213) 328-2075 (12)

Niehaus, Sherry, Mays Mission for the Handicapped Inc, Heber Springs, AR. Tel: (501) 362-7526, (888) 503-7955, FAX: (501) 362-7529, E-Mail: info@maysmission.org, Web Site: www.maysmission.org (27)

The Nielsen Co, New York, NY. Tel: (800) 864-1224, Web Site: www.nielsen.com (17)

Nielsen SiteReports, San Diego, CA. Tel: (800) 866-6520, FAX: (858) 550-5800, Web Site: www.claritas.com (30)

Nielsen Trade Dimensions, Wilton, CT. Tel: (203) 222-5750, (800) 291-0410, FAX: (203) 222-5701, E-Mail: tradedimensions.info@nielsen.com, Web Site: www.tradedimensions.com (17)

Niemeyer, W. Phil, Nasco, Fort Atkinson, WI. Tel: (920) 563-2446, (800) 558-9595, FAX: (920) 563-8296, E-Mail: info@nasco.com, Web Site: www.enasco.com (5)

Niemir, Chris, InfoSource Inc, Oviedo, FL. Tel: (407) 796-5200, (800) 393-4636, FAX: (407) 796-5190, E-Mail: isisale@howtomaster.com, Web Site: www.infosourcelearning.com (3)

Nierenberg, Roy A., Experience In Software Inc, Berkeley, CA. Tel: (510) 644-0694, (800) 678-7008, FAX: (510) 644-3823, Web Site: www.projectkickstart.com (16)

Niesen, Bob, Gummed Papers of America, Mc Cook, IL. Tel: (773) 650-2020, (800) 395-9000, FAX: (708) 485-8603, (800) 395-3581, E-Mail: info@labelexperts.com, Web Site: www.labelexperts.com (34)

Niggemeyer, W.F., Decko Products Inc, Sandusky, OH. Tel: (419) 626-5757, FAX: (419) 626-3135, Web Site: www.decko.com (4)

Nightingale-Conant Corp, Niles, IL. Tel: (847) 647-0300, (800) 557-1660, FAX: (847) 647-7145, Web Site: www.nightingale.com (17)

Nightingale Resources, Cold Spring, NY. Tel: (718) 338-3976, (212) 753-5383, (800) 953-9929 (17)

Nigrelli, Amy, CUNA - Trade Association, Madison, WI. Tel: (608) 231-4215, (800) 356-9655, FAX: (608) 231-4333, Web Site: www.cuna.org (1)

Nigro, Judy, Penn Mutual, Horsham, PA. Tel: (215) 956-8083, FAX: (215) 956-8368, Web Site: www.pennmutual.com (15)

Nigro, Lynne, Direct Marketing Consultant, Sharon, PA. Tel: (724) 699-0230 (20)

Nigro, Stephen, HP Indigo & Inkjet Press Solutions, Vancouver, WA. Tel: (360) 975-5000, Web Site: www.hp.com (16)

NigroNewMedia, Hermitage, PA. Tel: (724) 699-0230 (20)

Nihon Keizai Shimbun America Inc, New York, NY. Tel: (212) 261-6230, FAX: (212) 261-6239, Web Site: www.nikkeius.com (17)

Nike Inc, Beaverton, OR. Tel: (503) 671-4565, (800) 344-6543, FAX: (503) 671-6300, Web Site: www.nike.com (2)

Nikitas, Steve, Berkshire Record Outlet Inc, Lee, MA. Tel: (413) 243-4080, FAX: (413) 243-4340, E-Mail: broinc@berkshirerecordoutlet.com, Web Site: www2.broinc.com (3)

Niles, Matt, Starchtech, Golden Valley, MN. Tel: (763) 545-5400, (800) 597-7225, FAX: (763) 545-9450, Web Site: www.starchtech.com (16)

Nilodor Inc, Bolivar, OH. Tel: (330) 874-1017, (800) 443-4321, FAX: (330) 874-3366, E-Mail: info@nilodor.com, Web Site: www.nilodor.com (16)

Nimblefish Technologies, San Francisco, CA. Tel: (415) 247-7000, Web Site: www.nimblefish.com (30)

Nimeroff, Dr. Jeffry, Zeta Interactive, New York, NY. Tel: (212) 660-2500, FAX: (212) 967-1028, E-Mail: info@zetainteractive.com, Web Site: www.zetainteractive.com (32)

Nimlok, Niles, IL. Tel: (847) 647-1012, (800) 233-8870, FAX: (847) 647-2044, E-Mail: info@nimlok.com, Web Site: www.nimlok.com (16)

Nimmo, Andrew C., The MarketPlace Group Inc, Norwood, MA. Tel: (781) 762-6600, FAX: (781) 762-1300 (31)

925 Business Furniture, Kensington, MD. Tel: (301) 946-7288, (800) 525-0302, FAX: (302) 349-4587, E-Mail: bjfreed@erols.com, Web Site: www.natcofurniture.com (34)

Nino, Tony, Pasadena Advertising Marketing & Design, Pasadena, CA. Tel: (626) 584-0011, FAX: (626) 584-0907, Web Site: www.pasadenaadv.com (35)

Nishimori, Seiji, Shiseido Cosmetics America, East Windsor, NJ. Tel: (212) 805-2300, FAX: (212) 688-0109, Web Site: www.sca.shiseido.com (7)

Nissan Motor Acceptance Corp, Irving, TX. Tel: (972) 929-7214, (800) 647-7261, Web Site: www.nissanusa.com (14)

Nissan North America Inc, Franklin, TN. Tel: (615) 725-1000, Web Site: www.nissanusa.com (16)

Nissim, Donald, Heritage Direct, Oakhurst, NJ. Tel: (732) 531-2212, FAX: (732) 531-4798, Web Site: www.actionmarkets.com (22)

Nissim, Donald, The Data Base Inc, Oakhurst, NJ. Tel: (732) 531-4600, FAX: (732) 531-4798, E-Mail: don.nissim@heritagedirectdm.com, Web Site: www.heritagedirectdm.com (22)

Nittoli, Rocco, Leucadia National Corp, New York, NY. Tel: (212) 460-1900, FAX: (212) 598-4869, Web Site: www.leucadia.com (14)

Nixle LLC, San Francisco, CA. Tel: (877) 649-5362, E-Mail: support@nixle.com, Web Site: www.nixle.com (35)

Nixon, Gordon M., Royal Bank of Canada, Toronto, ON Canada. Tel: (416) 974-5151, FAX: (416) 955-7800, Web Site: www.royalbank.com (14)

Nixon, Richard R., Quadra Graphics Inc, Cherry Hill, NJ. Tel: (856) 665-4060, FAX: (856) 665-7324, E-Mail: richard.nixon@qgi.com (27)

Niyazov, Solomon, Profit Center Software Inc, Uniondale, NY. Tel: (516) 414-6300, (888) 446-6240, FAX: (516) 414-6304, E-Mail: jmarrah@profitcenter.com, Web Site: www.profitcenter.com (22)

No Fault Sports Products, Houston, TX. Tel: (713) 683-7101, (800) 462-7766, FAX: (713) 683-7103, E-Mail: nofaultsports@comcast.net, Web Site: www.nofaultsports.com (11)

No Load Fund Investor, Brentwood, TN. Tel: (800) 706-6364, FAX: (800) 785-9212, E-Mail: NoLoad@mleesmith.com, Web Site: www.noloadfundinvestor.com (14)

No Load FundX, San Francisco, CA. Tel: (415) 986-7979, (800) 763-8639, FAX: (415) 986-1595, Web Site: www.noloadfundx.com (14)

Noah, David M., Shipping Solutions, Eagan, MN. Tel: (651) 905-1727, (888) 890-7447, FAX: (651) 905-1827, E-Mail: info@shipsolutions.com, Web Site: www.shipsolutions.com (16)

Nober, Roger, Burlington Northern & Santa Fe LLC, Fort Worth, TX. Tel: (817) 878-2000, (800) 795-2673, FAX: (817) 333-7593, Web Site: www.bnsf.com (16)

Nobile, Lou, CityTwist, Boca Raton, FL. Tel: (866) 798-2489, FAX: (561) 314-2692, Web Site: www.citytwist.com (32)

Noble Communications Co, Springfield, MO. Tel: (417) 875-5015, Web Site: www.noble.net (35)

Noble, Bob, Noble Communications Co, Springfield, MO. Tel: (417) 875-5015, Web Site: www.noble.net (35)

Noble, Rebecca, DigDev Direct, Deerfield Beach, FL. Tel: (954) 949-9500, (800) 873-5137, FAX: (954) 337-0251, E-Mail: info@digdev.com, Web Site: www.digdevdirect.com (35)

Noce Kanarek, Monica, Purohit Navigation Inc, Chicago, IL. Tel: (312) 341-8100, FAX: (312) 341-8119, E-Mail: purohit@purohitnavigation.com, Web Site: www.purohitnavigation.com (35)

Nodine, Ronald, Nodine's Smokehouse, Torrington, CT. Tel: (860) 489-3213, (800) 222-2059, FAX: (860) 496-9787, E-Mail: nodinesmoke@optonline.net, Web Site: www.nodinesmokehouse.com (4)

Nodine's Smokehouse, Torrington, CT. Tel: (860) 489-3213, (800) 222-2059, FAX: (860) 496-9787, E-Mail: nodinesmoke@optonline.net, Web Site: www.nodinesmokehouse.com (4)

Noe, Diane, BT Americas, Irving, TX. Tel: (972) 830-8169, FAX: (703) 755-6740, Web Site: www.btglobalservices.com (22)

Noe, Dorothy C., Dorothy's Ruffled Originals Inc, Wilmington, NC. Tel: (800) 367-6849, FAX: (910) 791-0729, E-Mail: curtains@dorothysoriginals.com, Web Site: www.dorothysoriginals.com (8)

Nojowitz, Rabbi Dovid, Torah Umesorah Publications, Brooklyn, NY. Tel: (212) 227-1000, FAX: (212) 406-6934, E-Mail: umesorah@aol.com, Web Site: torahumesorah.com (5)

Nokes, Jon, Smart Inventions Inc, Paramount, CA. Tel: (562) 272-1416, (800) 275-7494, FAX: (562) 272-1423, E-Mail: customerservice@smartinventions.com, Web Site: www.smartinventions.com (32)

Nolan, Fiona, CommScope Inc, Hickory, NC. Tel: (828) 324-2200, (800) 982-1708, Web Site: www.commscope.com (16)

Nolan, Irene, Audience Development, Norwalk, CT. Tel: (203) 854-6730, FAX: (203) 854-6735, E-Mail: inolan@red7media.com, Web Site: www.audiencedevelopment.com (43)

Nolan, Kevin, Aegis Communications, Irving, TX. Tel: (972) 830-1800, (800) 332-0266, FAX: (972) 830-1801, E-Mail: info@aegisglobal.com, Web Site: www.aegiscomgroup.com (29)

Noland, Terrance, Chicago Magazine, Chicago, IL. Tel: (312) 222-8999, FAX: (312) 222-0287, Web Site: www.chicagomag.com (17)

Noll, Richard, Hanesbrands Inc, Winston Salem, NC. Tel: (336) 519-8080, Web Site: www.hanesbrands.com (2)

Nolte, David, The Garvey Group, Niles, IL. Tel: (847) 647-1900, FAX: (847) 647-6550, E-Mail: info@thegarveygroup.com, Web Site: www.thegarveygroup.com (27)

Nomadics Tipi Makers, Bend, OR. Tel: (541) 389-3980, FAX: (541) 389-3980, Web Site: www.tipi.com (11)

Non-Profit Management Program/Milano - The New School of Management & Urban Policy, New York, NY. Tel: (212) 229-5400, E-Mail: milanocommunications@newschool.edu, Web Site: www.newschool.edu/milano (41)

The NonProfit Times, Morris Plains, NJ. Tel: (973) 401-0202, FAX: (973) 401-0404, Web Site: www.nptimes.com (17)

Noonan, Charles, Boston Color Graphics, Billerica, MA. Tel: (978) 528-7999, (800) 767-0067, FAX: (978) 528-7609, E-Mail: sales@bostoncolorgraphics.com, Web Site: www.bostoncolorgraphics.com (27)

Noonan, Jim, The Computer Supply People, Menomonee Falls, WI. Tel: (262) 251-5511, (800) 242-2090, FAX: (262) 251-4737, E-Mail: medmgt@computersupplypeople.com, Web Site: www.computersupplypeople.com (3)

Noonan, Laura, 800 Response, Burlington, VT. Tel: (802) 860-0378, (800) 639-7253, FAX: (800) 639-6733, E-Mail: sales@800response.com, Web Site: www.800response.com (32)

Nor1, Santa Clara, CA. Tel: (408) 850-9937, FAX: (408) 608-0443, E-Mail: sales@nor1.com, Web Site: www.nor1.com (32)

Nordby, Matthew A., Playboy Enterprises Inc, Beverly Hills, CA. Tel: (310) 860-1215, Web Site: www.playboyenterprises.com (17)

Norderhaug, Mike, Assurant Health, Milwaukee, WI. Tel: (414) 244-0658, (800) 800-1212, FAX: (414) 224-0472, Web Site: www.assuranthealth.com (15)

Nordis Technologies Inc, Coral Springs, FL. Tel: (954) 323-5500, (800) 208-1169, FAX: (954) 323-0100, E-Mail: help@nordistechnologies.com, Web Site: www.nordistechnologies.com (21)

Nordloh, Christopher L., Lt Moses Willard Inc, Amelia, OH. Tel: (513) 248-5500, (800) 621-8956, FAX: (513) 831-0548, E-Mail: info@ltmoses.com, Web Site: www.ltmoses.com (16)

Nordskog Publishing Co, Ventura, CA. Tel: (805) 642-2070, FAX: (805) 642-1862, Web Site: www.nordskogpublishing.com (17)

Nordskog, Jerry, Nordskog Publishing Co, Ventura, CA. Tel: (805) 642-2070, FAX: (805) 642-1862, Web Site: www.nordskogpublishing.com (17)

Nordstrand, Barry J., Solutran, Plymouth, MN. Tel: (763) 559-2225, (888) 765-8872, FAX: (763) 559-8872, E-Mail: solutions@solutran.com, Web Site: www.solutran.com (20)

Nordstrom Inc, Seattle, WA. Tel: (888) 282-6060, FAX: (206) 373-3198 (2)

Nordstrom, Blake, Nordstrom Inc, Seattle, WA. Tel: (888) 282-6060, FAX: (206) 373-3198 (2)

Nordstrom, Daniel J., Outdoor Research, Seattle, WA. Tel: (206) 467-1496, (888) 467-4327, FAX: (206) 467-0374, Web Site: www.outdoorresearch.com (11)

Nordstrom, Eric, Nordstrom Inc, Seattle, WA. Tel: (888) 282-6060, FAX: (206) 373-3198 (2)

Nordstrom, Peter, Nordstrom Inc, Seattle, WA. Tel: (888) 282-6060, FAX: (206) 373-3198 (2)

Nordstrom, Scott, Eagle:xm, Denver, CO. Tel: (303) 320-5411, (800) 426-5376, FAX: (303) 393-6584, E-Mail: extendedmedia@eaglexm.com, Web Site: www.eaglexm.com (21)

Noren, Leif E., CRC Public Relations, Alexandria, VA. Tel: (703) 683-5004, FAX: (703) 683-1703, E-Mail: crc@crcpublicrelations.com, Web Site: www.crcpublicrelations.com (35)

Norheim, Oddvar, American Crane & Equipment Corp, Douglassville, PA. Tel: (610) 385-4876, (877) 877-6778, FAX: (610) 385-3191, E-Mail: info@americancrane.com, Web Site: www.americancrane.com (16)

Norin, Miles, AGORA Inc, Baltimore, MD. Tel: (410) 783-8499, FAX: (410) 783-8414, E-Mail: csteam@agorapublishinggroup.com, Web Site: www.agora-inc.com (17)

Norins, Art, Nor1, Santa Clara, CA. Tel: (408) 850-9937, FAX: (408) 608-0443, E-Mail: sales@nor1.com, Web Site: www.nor1.com (32)

Norinski, Dave, American Color, Irving, TX. Tel: (602) 333-1000, FAX: (602) 333-1099, Web Site: www.amcolor.com (27)

Norman Control Co, Cary, IL. Tel: (847) 639-5721, FAX: (847) 639-5755, E-Mail: susan@coffmanmfg.com, Web Site: www.coffmanmfg.com (16)

Norman Rockwell Museum, Stockbridge, MA. Tel: (413) 298-4100, (800) 742-9450, FAX: (413) 298-4144, E-Mail: emazzer@nrm.org, Web Site: www.nrm.org (16)

Norman, Bob, Delta Market Research Inc, Hatboro, PA. Tel: (215) 674-1180, (267) 960-1033, FAX: (215) 674-1271, E-Mail: information@deltamarketresearch.com, Web Site: www.deltamarketresearch.com (30)

Norman, Jr. John C., Personnel Policy Service Inc, Louisville, KY. Tel: (502) 899-5102, (800) 437-3735, FAX: (800) 755-7011, E-Mail: info@ppspublishers.com, Web Site: www.ppspublishers.com (17)

Norman, Larry M., Transamerica Life Insurance Co, Cedar Rapids, IA. Tel: (319) 398-8511, (800) 558-9011, FAX: (319) 369-2825, Web Site: www.transamerica.com (15)

Norman, Linda, UCEA, New York, NY. FAX: (212) 781-6500, Web Site: www.revike.org (1)

Norman, Roberta, Dick Davis Digest, Salem, MA. Tel: (978) 745-5532, FAX: (978) 745-1283, E-Mail: marketing@dickdavis.com, Web Site: www.dickdavis.com (17)

Norman, Vickie L., Robertson Mailing List Co, Leesburg, VA. Tel: (703) 509-8441, FAX: (888) 308-2572, E-Mail: vnorman@rmlc.net, Web Site: www.rmlc.net (23)

Norquist, Tom, GameTime Inc, Fort Payne, AL. Tel: (256) 845-5610, (800) 235-2440, FAX: (256) 845-9361/2649, Web Site: www.gametime.com (11)

Norrell, Brandon, cbsi, Fort Worth, TX. Tel: (817) 332-3681, FAX: (817) 332-3686, Web Site: www.buxtonco.com (30)

Norris, Gerri, 3D Mail Results, Kent, WA. Tel: (888) 250-1834, (253) 398-1551, E-Mail: info@3dmailresults.com, Web Site: www.3dmailresults.com (5)

Norris, Gwen, Danker Laboratories Inc, Sarasota, FL. Tel: (800) 237-9641, FAX: (800) 665-5086, E-Mail: sales@dankerlabs.com, Web Site: www.dankerlabs.com (14)

Norris, John, New Hermes Inc, Duluth, GA. Tel: (770) 623-0331, (800) 843-7637, FAX: (800) 533-7637, E-Mail: sales@gravograph-newhermes.com, Web Site: www.gravograph.com/usa/government/index.php (34)

Norris, Lauren, Liz Kislik Associates LLC, Rockville Centre, NY. Tel: (516) 568-2932, FAX: (516) 568-2936, Web Site: www.lizkislik.com (20)

Norris, Patsy, Village Interiors Carpet One, Newton, NC. Tel: (704) 325-2304, E-Mail: sales@carpet-one.net, Web Site: villlageinteriorshickory.com (8)

Norscot Group, Mequon, WI. Tel: (262) 241-3313, (800) 653-3313, FAX: (262) 241-4904, Web Site: www.norscot.com (5)

Norseng, Michael, Esquire Magazine, New York, NY. Tel: (212) 649-4020, FAX: (212) 649-4303, E-Mail: esquire@hearst.com, Web Site: www.esquire.com (17)

North America Life Insurance Co, Lakeway, TX. Tel: (512) 347-1835, Web Site: www.nagrp.com (15)

North American Communications Inc (East), Duncansville, PA. Tel: (814) 696-3553, (800) 624-1533, FAX: (814) 696-1180, E-Mail: marketing@nacmail.com, Web Site: www.nacmail.com (26)

North American Communications Inc, Katonah, NY. Tel: (914) 273-8620, E-Mail: info@nacmail.com, Web Site: www.nacmail.com (21)

North American Co for Life & Health Insurance, Chicago, IL. Tel: (312) 648-7600, (800) 800-3656, FAX: (312) 648-7796, Web Site: www.nacolah.com (15)

North American Mailing Technologies Inc, Lawrenceville, GA. Tel: (770) 962-5833 (22)

North Carolina Electric Membership Corp, Raleigh, NC. Tel: (919) 872-0800, (800) 662-8835, FAX: (919) 645-3410, E-Mail: info@ncemcs.com, Web Site: www.ncemcs.com (30)

North Point Resources, Alpharetta, GA. Tel: (678) 892-5000, Web Site: www.northpointstore.org (1)

North Shore Animal League America Inc, Port Washington, NY. Tel: (516) 883-7575, Web Site: www.animalleague.org (1)

North Wind Picture Archives, Alfred, ME. Tel: (207) 490-1940, (800) 952-0703, FAX: (207) 490-3627, E-Mail: mail@northwindpictures.com, Web Site: www.northwindpictures.com (38)

North, Adam, News Marketing Canada, Toronto, ON Canada. Tel: (416) 775-3000, FAX: (416) 775-3055, E-Mail: spetkovich@newsmarketing.ca, Web Site: www.newsmarketing.ca (20)

North, Jack W., State Farm Insurance Cos, Bloomington, IL. Tel: (309) 766-2311, FAX: (309) 766-3621, Web Site: www.statefarm.com (15)

North, Patricia, Union Federal Savings Bank, North Providence, RI. Tel: (401) 353-8900, (800) 992-0278, FAX: (401) 353-8938, Web Site: www.unionfsb.com (14)

Northeast Hinge Distributors Inc, Hollis, NH. Tel: (603) 465-3244, (800) 882-0120, FAX: (603) 465-3313, E-Mail: nehinge@nehinge.com, Web Site: www.nehinge.com (9)

Northeimer, John, Universal Vintage Tire Co, Hershey, PA. Tel: (717) 534-0175, (800) 233-3827, FAX: (717) 534-0719, E-Mail: sales@universaltire.com, Web Site: www.universaltire.com (11)

Northern Cross, Lecompton, KS. Tel: (785) 887-6010, (800) 625-7233, FAX: (785) 887-6263 (16)

Northern Greenhouse Sales, Neche, ND. Tel: (204) 327-5540, FAX: (204) 327-5527, E-Mail: info@northerngreenhouse.com, Web Site: www.northerngreenhouse.com (8)

Northern Illinois Consulting Inc, Libertyville, IL. Tel: (847) 828-1999, Web Site: www.cmsbusiness.com (20)

Northern Kentucky University, Highland Heights, KY. Tel: (859) 572-5220, (800) 637-9948, FAX: (859) 572-6177, Web Site: www.nku.edu (41)

Northern Lights Direct, Chicago, IL. Tel: (312) 263-8686, FAX: (312) 600-9050, E-Mail: contact@northernlightsdirect.com, Web Site: www.northernlightsdirect.com (32)

Northern Response International, Toronto, ON Canada. Tel: (905) 737-6698, (866) 584-1694, FAX: (905) 737-0099, E-Mail: general@nresponse.com, Web Site: northernresponse.com (8)

Northern Response (International) Ltd, Toronto, ON Canada. Tel: (905) 737-6698, (866) 584-1694, FAX: (905) 737-0099, E-Mail: general@nresponse.com, Web Site: www.shopnorthern.com (22)

Northern Safety Co Inc, Utica, NY. Tel: (315) 793-4900, Web Site: www.northernsafety.com (16)

Northern Tool & Equipment Inc, Burnsville, MN. Tel: (952) 894-9510, (800) 221-0516, FAX: (952) 894-1020, Web Site: www.northerntool.com (16)

The Northern Trust Co, Chicago, IL. Tel: (312) 630-6000, (888) 289-6542, FAX: (312) 444-5244, Web Site: www.ntrs.com (14)

Northlich, Cincinnati, OH. Tel: (513) 762-1717, FAX: (513) 421-8840, E-Mail: northlich@northlich.com, Web Site: www.northlich.com (35)

Northrop, Edward S., Mentor Corp, Santa Barbara, CA. Tel: (805) 879-6000, (800) 525-0245, FAX: (805) 964-2712, Web Site: www.mentorcorp.com (16)

Northrop, James, Princess House Inc, Taunton, MA. Tel: (508) 823-0711, (508) 832-6800, (800) 622-0039, FAX: (508) 823-5182, Web Site: www.princesshouse.com (16)

Northwest Laboratories, Seattle, WA. Tel: (206) 763-6252, FAX: (206) 763-3949, Web Site: www.nwlabs.net (9)

Northwest Mailing Service Inc, Chicago, IL. Tel: (773) 237-2264, Web Site: www.nwmail.com (28)

Northwestern Mutual, Milwaukee, WI. Tel: (414) 271-1444, FAX: (414) 299-7022, Web Site: www.northwesternmutual.com (14)

Northwestern University, Evanston, IL. Tel: (847) 491-5665, FAX: (847) 491-5925, E-Mail: jimc@northwestern.edu, Web Site: www.northwestern.edu (41)

Norton Moffatt, Laurie, Norman Rockwell Museum, Stockbridge, MA. Tel: (413) 298-4100, (800) 742-9450, FAX: (413) 298-4144, E-Mail: emazzer@nrm.org, Web Site: www.nrm.org (16)

Norton, Carl L., Nationwide Argosy Solutions LLC, Houston, TX. Tel: (713) 961-4700, FAX: (713) 961-4701, Web Site: www.nationwidegraphics.com (27)

Norton, Jeff, Missionary Society of St Columban, Saint Columbans, NE. Tel: (402) 291-1920, Web Site: www.columban.org (1)

Norton, Jeffrey, Cafe Lango, Sharon Springs, NY. Tel: (203) 453-1456, (800) 243-1234, FAX: (203) 453-5110, E-Mail: mail@cafelango.com, Web Site: www.audioforum.com (16)

Norton, Jennifer, Brant Publications Inc, New York, NY. Tel: (212) 941-2800, FAX: (212) 941-2885, Web Site: www.interviewmagazine.com (17)

Norton, Jim, AOL Corp, New York, NY. Tel: (212) 206-4400, Web Site: www.aol.com (32)

Norton, Negley, Local Search Association, Troy, MI. Tel: (248) 244-6200, FAX: (248) 244-0700, Web Site: www.localsearchassociation.org (1)

Norton, Pat, Active Web Group, Hauppauge, NY. Tel: (800) 978-3417, FAX: (800) 719-4402, E-Mail: info@activewebgroup.com, Web Site: www.activewebgroup.com (9)

Norton, Robert W., Scientific Marketing Services Inc, Landisville, NJ. Tel: (856) 697-1257, FAX: (856) 697-9639, E-Mail: info@smsmktg.com, Web Site: www.smsmktg.com (16)

Norton, Ronnie, Ventyx, Atlanta, GA. Tel: (770) 952-8444, (800) 868-0497, FAX: (770) 955-2977, E-Mail: support@ventyx.com, Web Site: www.ventyx.com (16)

Norwalk, Thomas S., Miami Valley Marketing Group Inc, Dayton, OH. Tel: (937) 299-1825, FAX: (937) 299-9967, E-Mail: tomnorwalk@aol.com (35)

Norwood Promotional Products, Clearwater, FL. Tel: (317) 275-2500, (800) 959-9138, FAX: (317) 275-2570, Web Site: www.norwood.com (16)

Nosbusch, Keith, Rockwell Automation, Milwaukee, WI. Tel: (414) 382-2000, FAX: (414) 382-4444, Web Site: www.rockwellautomation.com (16)

Noseworthy, John H., Mayo Clinic, Rochester, MN. Tel: (507) 284-2511, Web Site: www.mayoclinic.org (17)

Nostradamus Advertising, New York, NY. Tel: (212) 581-1362, E-Mail: nos@nostradamus.net, Web Site: www.nostradamus.net (36)

Nostrum Inc, Long Beach, CA. Tel: (562) 437-2200, Web Site: www.nostruminc.com (35)

Nourse Farms, South Deerfield, MA. Tel: (413) 665-2658, FAX: (413) 665-7888, E-Mail: info@noursefarms.com, Web Site: www.noursefarms.com (8)

Nourse, Tim, Nourse Farms, South Deerfield, MA. Tel: (413) 665-2658, FAX: (413) 665-7888, E-Mail: info@noursefarms.com, Web Site: www.noursefarms.com (8)

Nova Communications Inc, Geneva, IL. Tel: (630) 377-1889, (800) 816-6682, FAX: (630) 377-1899, E-Mail: jim@novacominc.com, Web Site: www.novacominc.com (35)

Nova DM Agency Inc, Dunmore, PA. Tel: (570) 342-8668, FAX: (570) 342-8666, E-Mail: info@novadmagency.com, Web Site: www.novadmagency.com (35)

Nova Marketing Services, Avon, CT. Tel: (800) 879-0288, Web Site: www.nova-marketing.com (35)

Nova Southeastern University Fischler College of Education, North Miami Beach, FL. Tel: (954) 262-8651, Web Site: www.schooloffed.nova.edu (1)

Novack, Janette, National Seminars Group, Shawnee Mission, KS. Tel: (913) 432-7755, (800) 258-7246, FAX: (913) 432-0824, E-Mail: cstserv@natsem.com, Web Site: www.natsem.com (16)

Novak, Jr Joseph, BFC, Batavia, IL. Tel: (630) 879-9240, Web Site: www.bfcprint.com (28)

Novak, Matt, BFC, Batavia, IL. Tel: (630) 879-9240, Web Site: www.bfcprint.com (28)

Novak, Patty, Battery Pros Inc, Horseshoe Beach, FL. Tel: (352) 498-2662, (800) 451-7171, FAX: (352) 498-2482, E-Mail: sales@probattery.com, Web Site: www.probattery.com (9)

Novak, Rocky, Fallon, Minneapolis, MN. Tel: (612) 758-2345, FAX: (612) 758-2346, E-Mail: info@fallon.com, Web Site: www.fallon.com (35)

Novartis Pharmaceuticals Corp, East Hanover, NJ. Tel: (862) 778-2100, (800) 669-6682, FAX: (973) 781-8119, Web Site: www.novartis.com (7)

Novelli, Bob, Anthem Blue Cross, Westlake Village, CA. Tel: (805) 557-6655, (800) 333-0912, FAX: (800) 557-6872, Web Site: www.bluecrossca.com (15)

Novelli, Bob, Blue Shield Life, San Francisco, CA. Tel: (888) 800-2742, FAX: (800) 329-2742, Web Site: www.blueshieldca.com (15)

Novick, Robert, Rodale Inc, Emmaus, PA. Tel: (610) 967-5171, FAX: (610) 967-8963, Web Site: www.rodaleinc.com (17)

Novik, Steve, Edward Jones, Des Peres, MO. Tel: (314) 515-2000, FAX: (314) 515-3269, Web Site: www.edwardjones.com (14)

Novus Media Inc, Plymouth, MN. Tel: (612) 758-8600, FAX: (612) 336-8600, Web Site: www.npmnetwork.com (31)

Nowakowski, James A., Interline Creative Group Inc, Palatine, IL. Tel: (847) 358-4848, FAX: (847) 358-8089, E-Mail: info@interlinegroup.com, Web Site: www.interlinegroup.com (35)

Nowell's Inc, San Rafael, CA. Tel: (415) 332-4933, E-Mail: contact@nowellslighting.com, Web Site: www.nowellslighting.com (8)

Nowels, K. Elliot, Meister Media Worldwide, Willoughby, OH. Tel: (440) 942-2000, (800) 572-7740, FAX: (440) 975-3447, E-Mail: info@meistermedia.com, Web Site: www.meistermedia.com (17)

Nowers, Suzanne Cole, Nexus Direct, Norfolk, VA. Tel: (757) 340-5960, (800) 965-0577, FAX: (757) 340-5980, E-Mail: hello@nexusdirect.com, Web Site: www.nexusdirect.com (35)

Nowetah's American Indian Store & Museum, New Portland, ME. Tel: (207) 628-4981, Web Site: www.nowetahs.webs.com (6)

Nowicki, Stefan, Domtar Inc, Fort Mill, SC. Tel: (270) 927-7204, (803) 802-7500, FAX: (270) 927-8714, Web Site: www.domtar.com (25)

Noyce, Kurt, Advanced Financial Services, Middletown, RI. Tel: (401) 849-0892, (800) 620-6292, FAX: (401) 851-5621, Web Site: www.embracehomeloans.com (14)

Noyes, Al, Walch Publishing, Portland, ME. Tel: (207) 772-2846, (800) 558-2846, FAX: (207) 772-3105, E-Mail: customerservice@walch.com, Web Site: www.walch.com (17)

Noyes, Erik, China Books & Periodicals Inc, South San Francisco, CA. Tel: (650) 872-7076, (800) 818-2017, FAX: (650) 872-7808, E-Mail: info@chinabooks.com, Web Site: www.chinabooks.com (17)

Nu-Parr Swimwear, Phoenix, AZ. Tel: (602) 279-4044, (800) 230-7277, FAX: (602) 212-2636, E-Mail: info@nu-parr.com. Web Site: www.nu-parr.com (2)

Nuance Speech Solutions, Burlington, MA. Tel: (781) 565-5000, FAX: (781) 565-5001, E-Mail: sales@speechworks.com, Web Site: www.nuance.com (16)

Nuclear Plant Journal, Downers Grove, IL. Tel: (630) 858-6161, FAX: (630) 852-8787, Web Site: www.nuclearplantjournal.com (17)

Nucor Corp, Charlotte, NC. Tel: (704) 366-7000, FAX: (704) 362-4208, E-Mail: info@nucor.com, Web Site: nucor.com (16)

NuEdge Systems, Brown Deer, WI. Tel: (800) 236-3282, Web Site: www.nuedgesystems.com (20)

The Nulman Group, Flemington, NJ. Tel: (908) 751-5299, (888) 440-3367, FAX: (908) 751-5621, E-Mail: info@nulmangroup.com, Web Site: www.nulmangroup.com (35)

Nulman, Philip R., The Nulman Group, Flemington, NJ. Tel: (908) 751-5299, (888) 440-3367, FAX: (908) 751-5621, E-Mail: info@nulmangroup.com, Web Site: www.nulmangroup.com (35)

Numark Brands, Edison, NJ. Tel: (732) 417-1870, (800) 338-8079, FAX: (732) 225-0066, E-Mail: newmark@injersey.com (7)

NuNaturals, Eugene, OR. Tel: (541) 344-9785, (800) 753-4372, FAX: (541) 343-0915, E-Mail: info@nunaturals.com, Web Site: www.nunaturals.com (16)

Nunes, Luis, PPI Benefit Solutions, Wallingford, CT. Tel: (888) 674-0046, FAX: (203) 468-9886, E-Mail: clientservices@ppibenefits.com, Web Site: www.ppibenefits.com (15)

Nunn, Michelle, CARE USA, Atlanta, GA. Tel: (404) 681-2552, (800) 422-7385, FAX: (404) 589-2600, E-Mail: info@care.org, Web Site: www.careusa.org (1)

Nuss, Mark, The Adcom Group, Cleveland, OH. Tel: (216) 574-9100, FAX: (216) 574-6131, Web Site: www.theadcomgroup.com (35)

Nuss, Robert L., Drumbeat Indian Arts Inc, Phoenix, AZ. Tel: (602) 266-4823, (800) 895-4859, FAX: (602) 265-2402, E-Mail: info@drumbeatindianarts.com, Web Site: www.drumbeatindianarts.com (6)

Nat Nussbaum & Associates Inc, Coral Springs, FL. Tel: (954) 345-9131, FAX: (954) 345-0786, E-Mail: nlnmktg@aol.com (16)

Nussbaum, Becky, Sa-So, Arlington, TX. Tel: (972) 641-4911, (800) 752-4294, FAX: (972) 660-3684, E-Mail: info@sa-so.com, Web Site: www.sa-so.com (16)

Nussbaum, Becky, SA-SO/Time Wise, Arlington, TX. Tel: (972) 641-4911, (800) 523-8060. FAX: (972) 660-5684, E-Mail: info@sa-so.com, Web Site: www.sa-so.com (33)

Nussbaum, David, F&W Media Inc, Blue Ash, OH. Tel: (513) 531-2690, FAX: (513) 531-0293, Web Site: www.fwmedia.com (17)

Nussbaum, Joe, Sa-So, Arlington, TX. Tel: (972) 641-4911, (800) 752-4294, FAX: (972) 660-3684, E-Mail: info@sa-so.com, Web Site: www.sa-so.com (16)

Nussbaum, Nathan, Nat Nussbaum & Associates Inc, Coral Springs, FL. Tel: (954) 345-9131, FAX: (954) 345-0786, E-Mail: nlnmktg@aol.com (16)

Nussbaum, Sharon, Net 60 LLC, New York, NY. Tel: (201) 833-9003, FAX: (201) 301-8182, E-Mail: chaim@net60.com, Web Site: net60.com (23)

Nussbaum, Stephen, Cold Spring Harbor Lab Press, Woodbury, NY. Tel: (516) 422-4100, (800) 843-4388, FAX: (516) 422-4097, E-Mail: cshpress@cshl.edu, Web Site: www.cshlpress.com (17)

Nussey, Bill, SilverPop, Atlanta, GA. Tel: (678) 247-0500, (866) 745-8767, FAX: (678) 247-0501, E-Mail: contactsales@silverpop.com, Web Site: www.silverpop.com (32)

NuStats Inc, Austin, TX. Tel: (512) 306-9065, (800) 44-STATS, FAX: (512) 306-9065, Web Site: www.nustats.com (30)

Nuti, Bill, NCR Corp, Duluth, GA. Tel: (937) 445-1936, (800) CALL-NCR, FAX: (937) 445-1682, Web Site: www.ncr.com (16)

NutriSystem Inc, Fort Washington, PA. Tel: (215) 706-5300, (800) 435-4074, FAX: (215) 706-5388, E-Mail: customerservice@nutrisystem.com, Web Site: www.nutrisystem.com (7)

Nutritional Research Associates Inc, South Whitley, IN. Tel: (260) 723-4931, (800) 456-4931, FAX: (260) 723-6297, E-Mail: info@nrfeeds.com, Web Site: www.nrfeeds.com (16)

Nutt, Bob, Zachry Associates Inc, Abilene, TX. Tel: (325) 677-1342, E-Mail: bnutt@zachryinc.com, Web Site: www.zachryinc.com (28)

Nuttall, Jeff, Alliance of Area Business Publications, Redondo Beach, CA. Tel: (310) 379-8261, FAX: (310) 379-8283, E-Mail: info@bizpubs.org, Web Site: www.bizpubs.org (1)

Nutting, Lori J., Military Direct Marketing Inc, Poughkeepsie, NY. Tel: (845) 454-7900, FAX: (845) 454-7987, E-Mail: info@militarymedia.com (31)

Nuveen Investments, Chicago, IL. Tel: (312) 917-7700, (800) 257-8787. FAX: (312) 917-8049, Web Site: www.nuveen.com (14)

Nye, John, Zimmerman Irrigation Inc, Biglerville, PA. Tel: (717) 337-2727, (800) 452-5699, FAX: (717) 337-1785, E-Mail: info@trikl-eez.com, Web Site: www.trickl-eez.com (16)

Nye, Sandra, Zimmerman Irrigation Inc, Biglerville, PA. Tel: (717) 337-2727, (800) 452-5699, FAX: (717) 337-1785, E-Mail: info@trikl-eez.com, Web Site: www.trickl-eez.com (16)

Nyenauis, Michael, MAP International, Brunswick, GA. Tel: (912) 265-6010, (800) 225-8550, FAX: (912) 265-6170, Web Site: www.map.org (1)

Nygren, Anthony, EMI Strategic Marketing Inc, Boston, MA. Tel: (617) 224-1101, E-Mail: info@emiboston.com, Web Site: emiboston.com (35)

Nylon Net Co, Memphis, TN. Tel: (901) 526-6500, (800) 238-7529, (877) 893-6535, FAX: (901) 526-6538, E-Mail: nylonnet@nylonnet.com, Web Site: www.nylonnet.com (11)

Nyrev Inc, New York, NY. Tel: (212) 757-8070, FAX: (212) 333-5374, E-Mail: mail@nybooks.com, Web Site: www.nybooks.com (17)

Nyugen, Tuong, Gero Vita, Costa Mesa, CA. Tel: (888) 382-9175, Web Site: www.gvi.com (16)

O

O'Bleness, Lance, The Woodlands Marketing Agency LLC, The Woodlands, TX. Tel: (281) 318-1601, Web Site: thewoodlandsagency.com (35)

O'Brien, Andrew, Nicklaus Companies LLC, North Palm Beach, FL. Tel: (561) 227-0300, FAX: (561) 227-0548, Web Site: www.nicklaus.com (16)

O'Brien, Chris, Go Ahead Vacations, Cambridge, MA. Tel: (617) 619-1000, (800) 242-4686, FAX: (617) 619-1001, E-Mail: goahead@et.com, Web Site: www.goaheadvacations.com (16)

O'Brien, Dan, Tech Image, Chicago, IL. Tel: (847) 279-0022, (888) 483-2477, FAX: (847) 279-8922, E-Mail: info@techimage.com, Web Site: www.techimage.com (35)

O'Brien, Declan, Destinations Ireland & Beyond, Kingston, NY. Tel: (800) 832-1848, FAX: (845) 810-7678, E-Mail: info@digbtravel.com, Web Site: www.allgolftravel.com/tours (19)

O'Brien, Diane, List Pro of America, San Diego, CA. Tel: (858) 483-1410, E-Mail: listpro@swmall.com, Web Site: swmall.com/listpro (23)

O'Brien, Eric, Sir Speedy Grand Rapids, Grand Rapids, MI. Tel: (616) 554-7777, Web Site: www.sirspeedy.com (27)

O'Brien, Geoffrey, The Library of America, New York, NY. Tel: (212) 308-3360, (800) 964-5778, FAX: (212) 750-8352, E-Mail: info@loa.org, Web Site: www.loa.org (13)

O'Brien, J. Brice, RJ Reynolds Tobacco Co, Winston Salem, NC. Tel: (336) 741-5111, (800) 341-5211, Web Site: www.rjrt.com (16)

O'Brien, James J., Ashland Inc, Covington, KY. Tel: (859) 815-3333, Web Site: www.ashland.com (16)

O'Brien, James, Print Management Partners, Des Plaines, IL. Tel: (847) 699-2999, FAX: (847) 699-2935, Web Site: www.ourpartners.com (27)

O'Brien, Jennel, Coastal Living, Birmingham, AL. Tel: (205) 445-6000, FAX: (205) 445-7263, E-Mail: coastalliving@customersvc.com, Web Site: www.coastalliving.com (43)

O'Brien, Jim, The Kidney Foundation of Canada/Greater Ontario Branch, Hamilton, ON Canada. Tel: (800) 414-3484, FAX: (905) 318-8491, E-Mail: kidneyfoundation@bellnet.ca, Web Site: www.kidney.on.ca (1)

O'Brien, Jim, Think Shapes Mail, Tampa, FL. Tel: (813) 885-2225, (800) 889-4406, Web Site: www.jigsawprinting.com (27)

O'Brien, Kerri, American Council on Exercise, San Diego, CA. Tel: (858) 576-6500, (888) 825-3636, FAX: (858) 576-6564, Web Site: www.acefitness.org (1)

O'Brien, Kevin, O'Brien Document Solutions, Bartlett, IL. Tel: (630) 830-0990, (800) 232-9595, FAX: (630) 830-0062, E-Mail: obrien_info@obinc.com, Web Site: www.obinc.com (27)

O'Brien, Linsay, AmeriCares, Stamford, CT. Tel: (203) 658-9500, (800) 486-4357, E-Mail: info@americares.org, Web Site: www.americares.org (1)

O'Brien, Mark, DDB North America, New York, NY. Tel: (212) 415-2000, FAX: (212) 415-3550, Web Site: ddbnorthamerica.com (35)

O'Brien, Morgan, Native American Rights Fund, Boulder, CO. Tel: (303) 447-8760, FAX: (303) 443-7776, Web Site: www.narf.org (1)

O'Brien, Patricia M., Effective Promotions Inc, Fort Johnson, NY. Tel: (518) 274-0291, (888) 467-3514, FAX: (518) 274-0290, Web Site: www.efpromotions.com (16)

O'Brien, Patrick M., Allstate Motor Club Inc, Arlington Heights, IL. Tel: (847) 551-2300, (800) 998-8697 (13)

O'Brien, Patrick, Paris Presents Inc, Gurnee, IL. Tel: (847) 263-5500, (800) 431-5723, FAX: (847) 263-5191, E-Mail: support@parispresents.com, Web Site: www.parispresents.com (7)

O'Brien, Sally, Badger Press Inc, Grayslake, IL. Tel: (847) 996-1190, E-Mail: info@badgerpressinc.com, Web Site: www.badgerpressinc.com (27)

O'Brien, Thomas E., AAA Auto Club South, Tampa, FL. Tel: (813) 289-5800, FAX: (813) 289-1475, Web Site: www.aaa.com (1)

O'Brien, Tom, PNC Bank Corp, Pittsburgh, PA. Tel: (412) 762-2000/3514, (800) 422-6537, FAX: (412) 762-4482 (14)

O'Bryan, Lisa, New Track Media LLC, Cincinnati, OH. Tel: (513) 421-6500, FAX: (513) 421-1244, E-Mail: lriggs@newtrackmedia.com, Web Site: www.newtrackmedia.com (17)

O'Connell, Joseph M., Leather Unlimited Corp, Belgium, WI. Tel: (920) 994-9464, FAX: (920) 994-4099, E-Mail: leatherunltd@yahoo.com, Web Site: www.leaterunltd.com (2)

O'Connell, Lynn, O'Connell Meier LLC, Alexandria, VA. Tel: (703) 635-2893, (866) 391-1415, FAX: (703) 739-0478, E-Mail: info@omdirect.com, Web Site: www.omdirect.com (21)

O'Connell, Maureen, Scholastic Inc, New York, NY. Tel: (212) 343-6100, (800) SCHOLASTIC, FAX: (212) 343-6484, Web Site: www.scholastic.com (17)

O'Connell, Patricia C., Leather Unlimited Corp, Belgium, WI. Tel: (920) 994-9464, FAX: (920) 994-4099, E-Mail: leatherunltd@yahoo.com, Web Site: www.leaterunltd.com (2)

O'Connell, Robert, Vanguard Direct, New York, NY. Tel: (212) 736-0770, FAX: (212) 736-8305, Web Site: www.vanguarddirect.com (35)

O'Connell, Susan, Compass Media, Gulf Shores, AL. Tel: (251) 968-4600, (800) 239-9880, E-Mail: info@compassmedia.com, Web Site: www.compassmedia.com (30)

O'Connor, Diane, Creative Irish Gifts, Little Rock, AR. Tel: (330) 954-1200, FAX: (330) 650-8888, E-Mail: gifts@shopirish.com, Web Site: www.shopirish.com (6)

O'Connor, Donald, Tully & Holland Inc, Wellesley, MA. Tel: (781) 239-2900, FAX: (781) 239-2901, E-Mail: info@tullyandholland.com, Web Site: www.tullyandholland.com (14)

O'Connor, Elizabeth, Multichannel Merchant Magazine, Stamford, CT. Tel: (203) 358-4386, FAX: (203) 358-5823, E-Mail: melissa.dowling@penton.com, Web Site: www.multichannelmerchant.com (31)

O'Connor, Jerry, Diversified Healthcare Services, Richardson, TX. Tel: (972) 238-1492, FAX: (972) 907-8283, Web Site: www.dhscorp.com (15)

O'Connor, John C., JVW Direct, Pittsburgh, PA. Tel: (412) 241-5920, FAX: (412) 241-5850, E-Mail: john@jvwdirect.com (35)

O'Connor, John, McKnight's Long-Term Care News, Northfield, IL. Tel: (847) 784-8706, (800) 558-1703, FAX: (847) 784-9346, E-Mail: mltcn-webmaster@mltcn.com, Web Site: www.mcknightsonline.com (17)

O'Connor, Jr. Thomas D., Mohawk Fine Papers Inc, Cohoes, NY. Tel: (518) 237-1740, (800) 843-6455, FAX: (518) 237-7394, E-Mail: info@mohawkpaper.com, Web Site: www.mohawkconnects.com (25)

O'Connor, Karne, Blethen Maine Newspapers Inc, Portland, ME. Tel: (207) 791-6650, FAX: (207) 791-6925, Web Site: www.mainetoday.com (17)

O'Connor, Kevin, Neopost USA, Milford, CT. Tel: (203) 301-3400, Web Site: www.neopostusa.com (34)

O'Connor, Robert, Creative Irish Gifts, Little Rock, AR. Tel: (330) 954-1200, FAX: (330) 650-8888, E-Mail: gifts@shopirish.com, Web Site: www.shopirish.com (6)

O'Connor, Tom, Springs Global Inc, New York, NY. Tel: (888) 926-7888, Web Site: www.springs.com (16)

O'Connor-Vos, Lynn, Grey Healthcare Group, New York, NY. Tel: (212) 886-3000, FAX: (212) 886-3297, E-Mail: info@ghgroup.com, Web Site: www.ghgroup.com (35)

O'Dell, Bob, Agile Education Marketing LLC, Denver, CO. Tel: (866) 783-0241, E-Mail: info@agile-ed.com, Web Site: www.agile-ed.com (24)

O'Donnell, John P., Neenah Paper FR LLC, Neenah, WI. Tel: (920) 733-7341, (800) 558-8327, FAX: (920) 733-2975, E-Mail: info@foxriverpaper.com, Web Site: www.foxriverpaper.com (27)

O'Donnell, Tim, Lundberg Family Farms, Richvale, CA. Tel: (530) 882-4551, FAX: (530) 882-4500, E-Mail: info@lundberg.com, Web Site: www.lundberg.com (16)

O'Donoghue, Patricia, DePaul University, Chicago, IL. Tel: (312) 362-8000, (800) 4-DEPAUL, FAX: (312) 362-6639, E-Mail: skelly@wppost.depaul.edu, Web Site: www.depaul.edu (41)

O'Drobinak, Larry, UGL Equis Corp, Chicago, IL. Tel: (312) 424-8000, FAX: (312) 424-8080, Web Site: www.equiscorp.com (16)

O'Dwyer, Jack, O'Dwyers Directory of Public Relations Firms New York, NY. Tel: (212) 683-2750, (866) 395-7710, FAX: (212) 683-2750, E-Mail: john@odwyerpr.com, Web Site: www.odwyerpr.com (43)

O'Grady, Matt, Nielsen SiteReports, San Diego, CA. Tel: (800) 866-6520, FAX: (858) 550-5800, Web Site: www.claritas.com (30)

O'Grady, Shawn P., The Pillsbury Co, Minneapolis, MN. Tel: (763) 764-7600, (800) 248-7310, FAX: (763) 764-8330, Web Site: www.pillsbury.com (16)

O'Halleran, Michael, AON Center, Chicago, IL. Tel: (312) 381-1000, FAX: (312) 381-6032, Web Site: www.aon.com (15)

O'Halloran, James, O'Halloran Advertising, Westport, CT. Tel: (203) 341-9400 (39)

O'Halloran, Kevin, O'Halloran Advertising, Westport, CT. Tel: (203) 341-9400 (39)

O'Halloran, Kevin, Tiffany & Co, New York, NY. Tel: (212) 755-8000, FAX: (212) 320-7550, Web Site: www.tiffany.com (6)

O'Handy III, Edward, Charter One Bank, Cleveland, OH. Tel: (216) 566-5300, (877) CHARTER, (877) 242-7837, FAX: (216) 664-1481, Web Site: www.charterone.com (14)

O'Hara, Arthur, Olympia Sales Inc, Enfield, CT. Tel: (860) 749-0751, (800) 338-9992, FAX: (860) 814-4451, E-Mail: info@olympiasales.net, Web Site: www.olympiasales.us (16)

O'Hara, Brian, Gaw-O'Hara Envelope Co, Chicago, IL. Tel: (773) 638-1200 (26)

O'Hara, Joseph M., Moto Franchise Corp, Dayton, OH. Tel: (937) 291-1900, (800) 733-6686, FAX: (937) 291-2005, E-Mail: expert@motophoto.com, Web Site: www.motophoto.com; www.portraitavenue.com (3)

O'Hara, Stephen M., Angelica Image Apparel, Saint Louis, MO. Tel: (314) 854-3800, (800) 235-8410, Web Site: www.angelica.com (16)

O'Hara, Thomas A., Olympia Sales Inc, Enfield, CT. Tel: (860) 749-0751, (800) 338-9992, FAX: (860) 814-4451, E-Mail: info@olympiasales.net, Web Site: www.olympiasales.us (16)

O'Keefe, Gianna, Ruud Lighting Inc, Racine, WI. Tel: (262) 886-1900, (800) 236-7000, FAX: (800) 236-7500, E-Mail: sales@ruudlighting.com, Web Site: www.ruudlighting.com (9)

O'Keefe, Kelly, Centerpoint Energy, Minneapolis, MN. Tel: (612) 372-4664, FAX: (612) 321-4873, E-Mail: mgc-businessinformation@centerpointenergy.com, Web Site: www.minnegasco.centerpointenergy.com (16)

O'Keefe, Matt, Infotrends Inc, Weymouth, MA. Tel: (781) 616-2100, FAX: (781) 616-2121, E-Mail: info@infotrends.com, Web Site: www.infotrends.com (35)

O'Keefe, Neil, The Direct Marketing Association, New York, NY. Tel: (212) 768-7277, E-Mail: info@the-dma.org, Web Site: thedma.org (1)

O'Keefe, William, Safti First, Brisbane, CA. Tel: (415) 824-4900, (888) 653-3333, FAX: (415) 824-5900, (888) 653-4444, E-Mail: info@safti.com, Web Site: www.safti.com (16)

O'Keeffe, Jr. William, Safti First, Brisbane, CA. Tel: (415) 824-4900, (888) 653-3333, FAX: (415) 824-5900, (888) 653-4444, E-Mail: info@safti.com, Web Site: www.safti.com (16)

O'Keeffe, Kathryn, Safti First, Brisbane, CA. Tel: (415) 824-4900, (888) 653-3333, FAX: (415) 824-5900, (888) 653-4444, E-Mail: info@safti.com, Web Site: www.safti.com (16)

O'Leary, Christopher D., The Pillsbury Co, Minneapolis, MN. Tel: (763) 764-7600, (800) 248-7310, FAX: (763) 764-8330, Web Site: www.pillsbury.com (16)

O'Leary, Ryan, Institute of Reading Development, Novato, CA. Tel: (415) 884-8100, (800) 964-2030, FAX: (415) 382-0760, E-Mail: contactus@readingprograms.org, Web Site: www.readingprograms.org (1)

O'Leary, Tim, R2C Group, Portland, OR. Tel: (866) 402-1124, E-Mail: getintouch@r2cgroup.com, Web Site: www.r2cgroup.com (35)

O'Leyne, Eithne, Book News Inc, Portland, OR. Tel: (503) 281-9230, FAX: (503) 287-4485, E-Mail: info@booknews.com (43)

O'Loughlin, John T., The Houston Chronicle, Houston, TX. Tel: (713) 362-7171, FAX: (713) 362-3575, Web Site: www.houstonchronicle.com (31)

O'Malley, Donna, Infotrends Inc, Weymouth, MA. Tel: (781) 616-2100, FAX: (781) 616-2121, E-Mail: info@infotrends.com, Web Site: www.infotrends. com (35)

O'Malley, John, Harland Financial Solutions Inc, Lake Mary, FL. Tel: (407) 804-6600, (800) 815-5592, FAX: (407) 829-6702, Web Site: www. harlandfinancialsolutions.com (16)

O'Malley, John P., Westcon, Tarrytown, NY. Tel: (914) 829-7000, FAX: (914) 829-7137, Web Site: www. westcon.com (16)

O'Malley, Thomas, American Dermatological Corp, Miami, FL. Tel: (305) 573-0763, (888) 573-0763, FAX: (305) 573-1704, E-Mail: info@dermatique. com, Web Site: www.dermatique.com (16)

O'Malley, Thomas, Winmill & Co, New York, NY. Tel: (212) 785-0900, (800) 400-MIDAS 6432, FAX: (212) 363-1100, E-Mail: info@midasfunds.com, Web Site: www.midasfunds.com (14)

O'Malley, William J., American Dermatological Corp, Miami, FL. Tel: (305) 573-0763, (888) 573-0763, FAX: (305) 573-1704, E-Mail: info@dermatique. com, Web Site: www.dermatique.com (16)

O'Mara, Rob, CRN International Inc, Hamden, CT. Tel: (203) 288-2002, FAX: (203) 281-3291, E-Mail: info@crnradio.com, Web Site: www.crnradio.com (32)

O'Neil, George F., Homeowner Data Services Inc, Lawrenceville, GA. Tel: (770) 925-9000, FAX: (770) 925-8977, E-Mail: hdsi@newhomedata.net, Web Site: www.newhomedata.net (23)

O'Neil, Mark, DealerTrack, New Hyde Park, NY. Tel: (516) 734-3600, Web Site: www.dealertract.com (14)

O'Neil, Mark, The NH Broadcaster, Lowell, MA. Tel: (978) 458-7100, Web Site: www.nhbroadcaster.com (31)

O'Neil, Michael, Bank of Hawaii, Honolulu, HI. Tel: (808) 537-8398, FAX: (808) 536-9433, Web Site: www.boh.com (14)

O'Neil, Michael, Mentor Corp, Santa Barbara, CA. Tel: (805) 879-6000, (800) 525-0245, FAX: (805) 964-2712, Web Site: www.mentorcorp.com (16)

O'Neil, Robert J., International City/County Management Association, Washington, DC. Tel: (202) 289-4262, FAX: (202) 962-3500, E-Mail: customerservice@icma.org, Web Site: www.icma. org (1)

O'Neil, Susan, Bamboo Cricket, West Palm Beach, FL. Tel: (561) 515-4546, (800) 260-8050, FAX: (561) 653-3990, E-Mail: info@bamboocricket.com, Web Site: www.bamboocricket.com (32)

O'Neil, William J., O'Neil Data Systems Inc, Los Angeles, CA. Tel: (310) 448-6400, FAX: (310) 577-7350, Web Site: www.oneildata.com (27)

O'Neill, James, Hickory Farms, Maumee, OH. Tel: (419) 893-7611, (800) 776-4111, (800) 442-5671, FAX: (419) 893-0164, Web Site: www. hickoryfarms.com (4)

O'Neill, Katie, Fulcrum Publishing, Golden, CO. Tel: (303) 277-1623, (800) 992-2908, FAX: (303) 279-7111, Web Site: www.fulcrum-books.com (17)

O'Neill, Michael, BMI, Nashville, TN. Tel: (615) 401-2000, (800) 925-8451, FAX: (615) 401-2812, E-Mail: nashville@bmi.com, Web Site: www.bmi. com (1)

O'Neill, Michael, Citigroup Inc, New York, NY. Tel: (212) 559-1000, (800) 285-3000, FAX: (212) 793-3946, Web Site: www.citigroup.com (14)

O'Neill, Paul, Direct Channel Inc, West Bridgewater, MA. Tel: (508) 588-4448, FAX: (508) 588-4644, E-Mail: sales@directchannel.com, Web Site: www. directchannel.com (23)

O'Neill, Randy, Lancer Insurance Co, Long Beach, NY. Tel: (516) 431-4441, (800) 782-8902, FAX: (516) 889-5111, E-Mail: roneill@lancer-ins.com, Web Site: www.lancer-ins.com (15)

O'Neill, Rita, O'Neill Marketing Co, Fairfax, VA. Tel: (703) 934-0272, FAX: (703) 934-0273, E-Mail: info@oneillmarketing.com, Web Site: www. oneillmarketing.com (21)

O'Neill, Rob, The Angler's Den, Pawling, NY. Tel: (845) 855-5182, E-Mail: flyfish@anglersden.net, Web Site: www.anglersden.net (11)

O'Neill, Sheila M., Standard & Poor's Corp, New York, NY. Tel: (212) 438-2000, FAX: (212) 438-7375, Web Site: www.standardandpoors.com (17)

O'Neill, Thomas, Harry Winston Inc, New York, NY. Tel: (212) 245-2000, FAX: (212) 489-0016, E-Mail: hw@harrywinston.com, Web Site: www.harry-winston.com (16)

O'Quinn-Humphries, Shelly, Jones School Supply Co Inc, Irmo, SC. Tel: (803) 772-3796, FAX: (800) 942-5921, Web Site: www.jonesawards.com (6)

O'Rahilly, Patrick J., Aspen Marketing Services, West Chicago, IL. Tel: (800) 848-0212, FAX: (630) 293-7584, Web Site: www.aspenms.com (35)

O'Reilly, Kathleen, CSPI/Nutrition Action Health Letter, Washington, DC. Tel: (202) 332-9110, FAX: (202) 265-4954, E-Mail: cspi@cspinet.org, Web Site: www.cspinet.org (17)

O'Reilly, Priscilla, Grand Circle Travel, Boston, MA. Tel: (617) 350-7500, (800) 959-0405, FAX: (617) 346-6030, Web Site: www.gct.com (19)

O'Rourke, Jeanne, Massachusetts Horticultural Society, Wellesley, MA. Tel: (617) 933-4900, (617) 933-4929, FAX: (617) 933-4901, E-Mail: hort_line@ masshort.org, Web Site: www.masshort.org (1)

O'Rourke, Paul, BolchalkFReY Marketing, Tucson, AZ. Tel: (520) 745-8221, FAX: (520) 745-5540, E-Mail: info-mb@adwiz.com, Web Site: www.adwiz.com (35)

O'Rourke, Richard, Nordis Technologies Inc, Coral Springs, FL. Tel: (954) 323-5500, (800) 208-1169, FAX: (954) 323-0100, E-Mail: help@ nordistechnologies.com, Web Site: www. nordistechnologies.com (21)

O'Rourke, Susan, O'Rourke Hospitality Marketing LLC, Newburyport, MA. Tel: (978) 465-5955, E-Mail: hello@orourkehospitality.com, Web Site: www. orourkehospitality.com (35)

O'Rourke, Tom, O'Rourke Hospitality Marketing LLC, Newburyport, MA. Tel: (978) 465-5955, E-Mail: hello@orourkehospitality.com, Web Site: www. orourkehospitality.com (35)

O'Sullivan, James J., Mazda Motor of America Inc, Irvine, CA. Tel: (949) 727-1990, (800) 222-6500, FAX: (949) 727-6101, Web Site: www.mazdausa. com (16)

O'Sullivan, Joan, Marsh Affinity Group Services, Chicago, IL. Tel: (800) 621-3008, Web Site: www. seaburychicago.com (15)

O'Toole, Brian, Crane Pumps & Systems Inc, Piqua, OH. Tel: (937) 773-2442, FAX: (937) 773-2238, E-Mail: cranepumps@cranepumps.com, Web Site: www.cranepumps.com (16)

O'Toole, David, Thomson Reuters, New York, NY. Tel: (212) 367-6300, (800) 950-1216, FAX: (212) 367-6301, Web Site: www.riahome.com (17)

O'Toole, Matthew, Reebok International Ltd, Canton, MA. Tel: (781) 401-5000, (800) 843-4444, FAX: (781) 401-4402, Web Site: www.reebok.com (2)

O2 Agency Inc, New York, NY. Tel: (212) 675-7334, E-Mail: newbiz@o2agency.com, Web Site: o2agency.strikingly.com (35)

O2 Consulting Inc, Atlanta, GA. Tel: (404) 384-3990 (22)

o2kl Advertising, New York, NY. Tel: (646) 839-6236, E-Mail: towens@o2kl.com, Web Site: www.o2kl. com (35)

OAG Worldwide, Downers Grove, IL. Tel: (630) 515-5300, FAX: (630) 515-5301, E-Mail: custsvc@oag. com, Web Site: www.oag.com (17)

OKS-Ameridial Inc, Bala Cynwyd, PA. Tel: (610) 667-3000, FAX: (610) 667-3002, E-Mail: info@ oksgroup.com, Web Site: www.oksameridial.com (29)

OMP, Washington, DC. Tel: (202) 467-0048, Web Site: www.ompdirect.com (1)

OMSI Inc, Belleville, IL. Tel: (618) 398-7640, Web Site: www.oblatesusa.org (1)

ORC Macro International, New York, NY. Tel: (212) 941-5555, FAX: (212) 941-7031, E-Mail: info@icfi. com, Web Site: www.icfi.com (30)

ORC ProTel LLC, Lansing, IL. Tel: (708) 418-7413, FAX: (708) 418-7457, Web Site: www.orcprotel. com (29)

OSG Billing, Englewood, NJ. Tel: (201) 871-1100, Web Site: www.osgbilling.com (20)

OSRAM Sylvania, Danvers, MA. Tel: (978) 777-1900, (800) LIGHTBULB, FAX: (978) 750-2152, Web Site: www.sylvania.com (16)

OTM Partners, Arlington, VA. Tel: (800) 759-2244, Web Site: otmpartners.com (35)

Oak Knoll Limited Liability Co, South Salem, NY. Tel: (914) 533-0208 (20)

Oakes, Katie, SCA Direct, Fairfax, VA. Tel: (703) 293-6339, Web Site: www.scadirect.com (1)

Oakes, Marvin, Wilton Industries Inc, Woodridge, IL. Tel: (630) 963-1818, (800) 794-5866, FAX: (630) 963-7196, E-Mail: info@wilton.com, Web Site: www.wilton.com (16)

Oakley Inc, Foothill Ranch, CA. Tel: (800) 403-7449, Web Site: www.oakley.com (2)

Oakley, Jr G David, Strongwell, Bristol, VA. Tel: (276) 645-8000, FAX: (276) 645-8132, E-Mail: gbarefoot@strongwell.com, Web Site: www. strongwell.com (9)

Oakley, Michele, Vector Marketing Corp, Olean, NY. Tel: (716) 373-6141, (267) 880-1750, FAX: (716) 373-6145, Web Site: www.cutco.com (5)

Oakstone Publishing LLC, Birmingham, AL. Tel: (205) 991-5188, (800) 952-0690, FAX: (205) 995-4656, E-Mail: info@oakstonepublishing.com, Web Site: www.oakstonepublishing.com (17)

Oakton Community College, Des Plaines, IL. Tel: (847) 635-1600, FAX: (847) 635-1706, Web Site: www. oakton.edu (41)

Oakwood Homes Corp, Greensboro, NC. Tel: (336) 664-2400, (800) 822-0633, FAX: (336) 315-3249, Web Site: www.oakwoodhomes.com (16)

Oates, Richard, Zig Ziglar Corp, Plano, TX. Tel: (972) 233-9191, (800) 527-0306, FAX: (469) 321-7556, E-Mail: info@ziglar.com, Web Site: www.zigziglar. com (16)

Oba, Koya, LaCrosse Footwear Inc, Portland, OR. Tel: (503) 262-0110, (800) 323-2668, FAX: (503) 262-0115, E-Mail: customerservice@lacrossefootwear. com, Web Site: www.lacrossefootwear.com (16)

Oberdorf, Joyce, National Parkinson Foundation, Miami, FL. Tel: (305) 243-6666, (800) 937-4545, FAX: (305) 243-6073, E-Mail: contact@parkinson.org, Web Site: www.parkinson.org (1)

Oberhelman, Doug, Caterpillar Inc, Peoria, IL. Tel: (309) 675-0545, Web Site: www.cat.com (16)

Oberman, Aaron, Omeda, Northbrook, IL. Tel: (847) 564-8900, FAX: (847) 564-1203, Web Site: www.omeda.com (22)

Obermier, Beanie, William-Neil Associates, Sidney, NE. Tel: (800) 216-2214, FAX: (308) 254-6102, E-Mail: bobermier@william-neil.com, Web Site: www.william-neil.com (24)

Obernier, Robert B., Horizon Paper Co Inc, Stamford, CT. Tel: (203) 358-0855, (866) 358-0855, FAX: (203) 358-0828, Web Site: www.horizonpaper.com (25)

Oberski, Mark, FlarePath LLC, Canaan, NY. Tel: (212) 927-1296 (20)

Oberthur Card Systems, Chantilly, VA. Tel: (703) 263-0100, FAX: (703) 263-0503, E-Mail: info@oberthurcs.com, Web Site: www.oberthurcs.com (28)

Oblate Missions, San Antonio, TX. Tel: (210) 736-1685, FAX: (210) 736-1314, E-Mail: contact@oblatemissions.org, Web Site: www.oblatemissions.org (1)

O'Brien Document Solutions, Bartlett, IL. Tel: (630) 830-0990, (800) 232-9595, FAX: (630) 830-0062, E-Mail: obrien_info@obinc.com, Web Site: www.obinc.com (27)

O'Brien Manufacturing, Marietta, OH. Tel: (740) 374-2306, (800) 638-1901, FAX: (740) 374-5447, Web Site: www.obrienmfg.com (9)

Ocat, Charles, AccountMate Software Corp, Petaluma, CA. Tel: (707) 774-7500, FAX: (707) 774-7590, E-Mail: information@accountmate.com, Web Site: www.accountmate.com (22)

The Occasions Group, North Mankato, MN. Tel: (507) 625-6464 (16)

Occhiuto, Tommaso, Progressive Direct Marketing, Depew, NY. Tel: (716) 681-6848, (800) 344-7593, FAX: (716) 681-9173, E-Mail: info@pdmny.com, Web Site: www.pdmny.com (35)

OccuNomix, Port Jefferson Station, NY. Tel: (631) 791-1955, (800) 466-0071, FAX: (631) 474-0073, Web Site: www.occunomix.com (34)

OCE North America Inc, Trumbull, CT. Tel: (773) 714-8500, (800) 523-5444, FAX: (773) 714-4056, Web Site: www.oceusa.com (34)

Ocean Conservancy, Washington, DC. Tel: (202) 429-5609, Web Site: www.oceanconservancy.org (1)

Ocello, Carmen, Direct Mail Depot Inc, Piscataway, NJ. Tel: (732) 469-5900, FAX: (732) 469-8414, E-Mail: sales@directmaildepot.com, Web Site: www.directmaildepot.com (28)

Ochsenbein, Roland, Greenwood Publishing Group Inc, Portsmouth, NH. Tel: (203) 226-3571, FAX: (203) 222-1502, E-Mail: sales@greenwood.com, Web Site: www.greenwood.com (17)

O'Connell Meier LLC, Alexandria, VA. Tel: (703) 635-2893, (866) 391-1415, FAX: (703) 739-0478, E-Mail: info@omdirect.com, Web Site: www.omdirect.com (21)

O'Currance Inc, Draper, UT. Tel: (801) 736-0500, (888) 628-7726, FAX: (801) 736-0510, E-Mail: sales@ocurrance.com, Web Site: www.ocurance.com (18)

Odden, Lee, TopRank Online Marketing, Spring Park, MN. Tel: (952) 400-0194, (877) 872-6628, E-Mail: winning@toprankmarketing.com, Web Site: www.toprankmarketing.com (32)

Odell, Simms & Lynch Inc, Tysons Corner, VA. Tel: (703) 903-9797, FAX: (703) 903-8850, Web Site: odellsimms.com (35)

Odell, Brian, Catalyst Inc, Providence, RI. Tel: (401) 732-1886, FAX: (401) 732-5528, Web Site: www.catalystb2b.com (35)

Odell, Patricia, Promo Magazine, New York, NY. Tel: (203) 358-9900, (800) 927-5007, FAX: (203) 358-5816, E-Mail: larry.jaffee@penton.com, Web Site: www.promomagazine.com (17)

Oden, Memphis, TN. Tel: (901) 578-8055, (800) 371-6233, FAX: (901) 578-1911, Web Site: www.oden.com (35)

Odenza Marketing Group, San Diego, CA. Tel: (866) 883-2968, Web Site: www.odenza.com (20)

Odenza Marketing Group Inc, Burnaby, BC Canada. Tel: (800) 515-5371, Web Site: www.odenza.com (35)

Odle, David, Hyman's, Hanahan, SC. Tel: (843) 571-7870, (800) 354-9626, FAX: (843) 571-7575, E-Mail: support@hymans.com, Web Site: www.hymans.com (22)

Odum, Marvin, Shell Oil Co, Houston, TX. Tel: (713) 241-6161, Web Site: www.shell.us (16)

O'Dwyers Directory of Public Relations Firms, New York, NY. Tel: (212) 683-2750, (866) 395-7710, FAX: (212) 683-2750, E-Mail: john@odwyerpr.com, Web Site: www.odwyerpr.com (43)

Oerthing, Laurie, Laitram Machinery, Harahan, LA. Tel: (504) 733-6000, FAX: (504) 733-6111 (16)

Off the Wall Magnetics LLC, Portland, OR. Tel: (800) 337-2637, Web Site: www.4thefridge.com (16)

Office Depot, Boca Raton, FL. Tel: (561) 438-4800, (800) 463-3768, FAX: (561) 438-4001, Web Site: www.officedepot.com (16)

Office Express Inc, Evanston, IL. Tel: (888) 526-8438, FAX: (773) 341-7322, E-Mail: sales@envelopesexpress.com, Web Site: www.envelopesexpress.com (26)

The Office Gurus, Seminole, FL. Tel: (727) 803-7114, Web Site: www.theofficegurus.com (29)

OfficeFurniture.com, West Allis, WI. Tel: (414) 272-6080, (800) 933-0053, FAX: (800) 468-1526, Web Site: www.officefurniture.com (8)

OfficeMax Inc, Boca Raton, FL. Tel: (877) 633-4236, Web Site: www.officemax.com (10)

Officer, John David, The Dreyfus Corp, New York, NY. Tel: (212) 922-6000, FAX: (212) 922-6880, Web Site: www.dreyfus.com (14)

Official Offset Corp, Amityville, NY. Tel: (631) 957-8500, Web Site: www.officialoffset.com (27)

The Offset House Inc, Essex Junction, VT. Tel: (317) 849-5155, FAX: (317) 842-3324, Web Site: www.offsethouse.com (27)

Ogarrio, Andrea, Rose Resnick Lighthouse for the Blind & Visually Impaired, San Francisco, CA. Tel: (415) 431-1481, FAX: (415) 863-7568, E-Mail: executive@lighthouse-sf.org, Web Site: www.lighthouse-sf.org (1)

Ogden, Nick, Lundmark Advertising + Design Inc, Kansas City, MO. Tel: (816) 842-5236, Web Site: lundmarkadvertising.com (35)

OgilvyOne Worldwide, New York, NY. Tel: (212) 237-4000, Web Site: www.ogilvy.com (35)

Oglander, Allen H., Dispensa-Matic Label Dispensers, Saint Louis, MO. Tel: (314) 231-6006, (800) 325-7303, FAX: (314) 621-1602, E-Mail: info@dispensamatic.com, Web Site: www.dispensa-matic.com (34)

Ogle, Jim, F&W Media Inc, Blue Ash, OH. Tel: (513) 531-2690, FAX: (513) 531-0293, Web Site: www.fwmedia.com (17)

Ogren, Rhonda, Llewellyn Publications, Woodbury, MN. Tel: (651) 291-1970, (877) 639-9753, FAX: (651) 291-1908, Web Site: www.llewellyn.com (17)

O'Halloran Advertising, Westport, CT. Tel: (203) 341-9400 (39)

Ohara, Kazuo, Toyota Motor Sales USA Inc, Torrance, CA. Tel: (310) 468-4000, (800) 331-4331, FAX: (310) 468-7841, Web Site: www.toyota.com (16)

Ohio Envelope Manufacturing Co, Cleveland, OH. Tel: (216) 267-2920, (800) 989-0336, FAX: (216) 267-1765, E-Mail: mgmt@ohioenvelope.com, Web Site: www.ohioenvelope.com (26)

The Ohlmann Group, Dayton, OH. Tel: (937) 278-0681, FAX: (937) 277-1723, E-Mail: info@ohlmanngroup.com, Web Site: ohlmanngroup.com (35)

Oil & Gas Journal, Tulsa, OK. Tel: (918) 835-3161, (800) 331-4463, FAX: (918) 832-9497, Web Site: www.pennwell.com; www.ogj.com (17)

O'Keefe Henry Direct Inc, Deerfield, IL. Tel: (847) 681-9200, FAX: (847) 681-9299, Web Site: www.okeefehenrydirect.com (20)

Okerstrom, Mark D., Expedia Inc, Bellevue, WA. Tel: (425) 679-7200, Web Site: www.expedia.com (19)

Oklahoma Dept of Commerce, Oklahoma City, OK. Tel: (405) 815-6552, (800) 879-6552, FAX: (405) 815-5344, Web Site: www.okcommerce.com (1)

Okun Brothers Shoes Inc, Kalamazoo, MI. Tel: (269) 342-1536, (800) 433-6344, FAX: (269) 383-3401 (2)

Okun, Marvin, Okun Brothers Shoes Inc, Kalamazoo, MI. Tel: (269) 342-1536, (800) 433-6344, FAX: (269) 383-3401 (2)

Olafsson, Olaf, Time Warner Inc, New York, NY. Tel: (212) 484-8000, Web Site: www.timewarner.com (16)

Olan Mills Inc, Chattanooga, TN. Tel: (423) 622-5141, (800) 251-6320, FAX: (423) 629-8128, Web Site: www.olanmills.com (16)

Olavarrieta, Paco, Dieste, Dallas, TX. Tel: (214) 259-8000, FAX: (214) 259-8040, E-Mail: contact@dieste.com, Web Site: www.dieste.com (35)

Olbres, Tamara C., Interex, Amesbury, MA. Tel: (978) 388-8755, (800) INTEREX, FAX: (978) 388-8747, Web Site: www.interexexhibits.com (17)

Old Vine Marketing, Napa, CA. Tel: (707) 694-9647, E-Mail: info@oldvinemarketing.com, Web Site: www.oldvinemarketing.com (22)

Old World Ind, Northbrook, IL. Tel: (847) 559-2000, FAX: (847) 559-2266, Web Site: www.oldworldind.com (34)

Old World Mouldings Inc, Bohemia, NY. Tel: (631) 563-8660, FAX: (631) 563-8815, E-Mail: mouldings@optonline.com, Web Site: www.oldworldmouldings.com (9)

Olden, Angela, Girl Scouts of the USA, New York, NY. Tel: (212) 852-8000, (800) 478-7248, Web Site: www.girlscouts.org (1)

Oldenkamp, Rick, Midwest Technology Products & Services, Sioux City, IA. Tel: (712) 252-3601, (800) 831-5904, FAX: (800) 258-7054, E-Mail: web@midwesttechnology.com, Web Site: www.midwesttechnology.com (1)

Oldham, Lisa, Specialized Products Co, Southlake, TX. Tel: (817) 329-6647, (800) 866-5353, FAX: (800) 234-8286, E-Mail: spc@specialized.net, Web Site: www.specialized.net (16)

Olding, Robert, Damilic Corp, Rockville, MD. Tel: (301) 251-2960, (800) 276-7749, FAX: (301) 251-8591, E-Mail: info@realsig.com, Web Site: www.realsig.com (16)

Oleda & Co Inc, Fort Worth, TX. Tel: (817) 731-1147, (800) 731-4247, FAX: (817) 731-1149, E-Mail: oleda@oleda.com, Web Site: www.oleda.com (16)

Oles Envelope Corp, Baltimore, MD. Tel: (410) 243-1520, (800) 822-6537, FAX: (410) 366-7022, Web Site: www.olesenvelope.com (26)

Olesuk Financial Services, McHenry, IL. Tel: (815) 363-0808, FAX: (815) 363-0843, E-Mail: folesuk@sagepointadvisor.com, Web Site: www.olesukfinancialservices.com (14)

Olesuk, Frank D., Olesuk Financial Services, McHenry, IL. Tel: (815) 363-0808, FAX: (815) 363-0843, E-Mail: folesuk@sagepointadvisor.com, Web Site: www.olesukfinancialservices.com (14)

Olesuk, Karlene M., Olesuk Financial Services, Mc-Henry, IL. Tel: (815) 363-0808, FAX: (815) 363-0843, E-Mail: folesuk@sagepointadvisor.com, Web Site: www.olesukfinancialservices.com (14)

Olesuk, Patricia S., Olesuk Financial Services, Mc-Henry, IL. Tel: (815) 363-0808, FAX: (815) 363-0843, E-Mail: folesuk@sagepointadvisor.com, Web Site: www.olesukfinancialservices.com (14)

Olin, John, DHL Express, Plantation, FL. Tel: (954) 888-7000, (800) 225-5345, FAX: (954) 888-7310, Web Site: www.dhl.com (28)

Oliva, Paulette, The Direct Marketing Club of New York Inc, Garden City, NY. Tel: (516) 746-6700, FAX: (516) 294-8141, E-Mail: info@dmcny.org, Web Site: www.dmcny.org (1)

Oliver of Adrian Inc, Adrian, MI. Tel: (517) 263-2132, (877) 668-0885, FAX: (517) 265-8698, E-Mail: info@oliverinstrument.com, Web Site: www.oliverofadrian.com (16)

Oliver Russell & Associates, Boise, ID. Tel: (208) 344-1734, E-Mail: info@oliverrussell.com, Web Site: www.oliverrussell.com (35)

Oliver Wyman, New York, NY. Tel: (212) 345-8000, (212) 541-8100, Web Site: www.oliverwyman.com (14)

Oliver, Deborah, International Marine, Camden, ME. Tel: (207) 236-4837, FAX: (207) 236-6314, Web Site: www.internationalmarine.com (17)

Oliver, Francois, Telemedia Communications US, North York, ON Canada. Tel: (416) 733-7600, (800) 461-3773 U.S., (888) 290-1466 Can., FAX: (416) 733-3563, E-Mail: info@transcontinental.ca, Web Site: www.transcontinental.com (17)

Oliver, Julia A., American Bible Society, New York, NY. Tel: (212) 408-1200, FAX: (212) 408-1264, Web Site: www.americanbible.org (1)

Oliver, Michael O., Brady Corp, Milwaukee, WI. Tel: (414) 358-6600, (800) 541-1686, FAX: (800) 292-2289, Web Site: www.bradycorp.com (16)

Oliver, Ray, Cablexpress Technologies, Syracuse, NY. Tel: (315) 476-3000, (800) 913-9467, FAX: (315) 455-1800, E-Mail: info@cablexpress.com, Web Site: www.CXTec.com (10)

Oliver, Tim, Tensar International Corporation, Alpharetta, GA. Tel: (404) 250-1290, Web Site: www.tensarcorp.com (16)

Olivier, Francois, TC Transcontinental, Montreal, QC Canada. Tel: (514) 954-4000, FAX: (514) 954-4016, Web Site: tctranscontinental.com (35)

Olmstead, C. Elvan, David C Cook, Colorado Springs, CO. Tel: (719) 536-0100, (800) 323-7543, FAX: (719) 536-3232, Web Site: www.davidccook.com (17)

Olmsted-Kirk Paper Co, Dallas, TX. Tel: (214) 637-2220, (800) 367-6526, FAX: (214) 637-2131, E-Mail: sales@okpaper.com, Web Site: www.okpaper.com (25)

Olmsted, Robert, Olmsted-Kirk Paper Co, Dallas, TX. Tel: (214) 637-2220, (800) 367-6526, FAX: (214) 637-2131, E-Mail: sales@okpaper.com, Web Site: www.okpaper.com (25)

Olper, Leo, Dexposito & Partners, New York, NY. Tel: (646) 747-8800, Web Site: newamericanagency.com (35)

Olrich, Scott, Responsys, San Bruno, CA. Tel: (650) 745-1700, Web Site: www.responsys.com (20)

Olsan, Mary Alice, American Counseling Association, Broken Arrow, OK. Tel: (918) 994-4413, FAX: (918) 663-7058, E-Mail: webmaster@counseling.org, Web Site: www.counseling.org (1)

Olsen, Christina, Sunset Magazine, Menlo Park, CA. Tel: (650) 321-3600, FAX: (650) 328-6215 (17)

Olsen, Kelsey, Quality Contact Solutions Inc, Aurora, NE. Tel: (402) 210-2692, (866) 963-2889, FAX: (402) 210-2692, E-Mail: info@qualitycontactsolutions.com, Web Site: www.qualitycontactsolutions.com (29)

Olsen, Michael, Ignition Network, Chicago, IL. Tel: (312) 893-5000, E-Mail: inquiries@ignitionnetwork.com, Web Site: www.ignitionnetwork.com (35)

Olsen, Peg R., National Audubon Society, New York, NY. Tel: (212) 979-3000, FAX: (212) 979-3188, Web Site: www.audubon.org (1)

Olsen, Peter, Listening Library Inc, Random House Audio, New York, NY. Tel: (212) 782-8482, (800) 726-0600, FAX: (212) 940-7381, E-Mail: rhacademic@penguinrandomhouse.com, Web Site: www.randomhouse.com/audio (3)

Olsen, Richard J., RJ Olsen Inc, Natick, MA. Tel: (508) 647-3777, FAX: (508) 647-6777, E-Mail: dickolsen@aol.com (30)

Olshefsky, Jim, ASTM International, West Conshohocken, PA. Tel: (610) 832-9500, FAX: (610) 832-9555, E-Mail: service@astm.org. Web Site: www.astm.org (1)

Olson, Karen, California Chamber of Commerce, Sacramento, CA. Tel: (800) 649-4921, FAX: (916) 325-1272, E-Mail: techsupport@calchamber.com, Web Site: www.calbizcentral.com (1)

Olson, Karol, Union Privilege, AFL-CIO, Washington, DC. Tel: (202) 293-5311, (800) 472-2005, FAX: (202) 293-5311, E-Mail: info@unionprivilege.org, Web Site: www.unionplus.org (1)

Olson, Kathryn, Women's Sports Foundation, East Meadow, NY. Tel: (516) 542-4700, (800) 227-3988, FAX: (516) 542-0095, Web Site: www.womenssportsfoundation.org (1)

Olson, Laurie, Pfizer Inc, New York, NY. Tel: (212) 733-2323, Web Site: www.pfizer.com (16)

Olson, Rick, PESI LLC, Eau Claire, WI. Tel: (800) 844-8260, FAX: (800) 554-9775, E-Mail: info@pesi.com, Web Site: www.pesi.com (17)

Olson, Sande, Rose Electronics, Houston, TX. Tel: (281) 933-7673, (800) 333-9343, FAX: (281) 933-0044, E-Mail: sales@rose.com, Web Site: www.rose.com (3)

Olson, Sandra S., TeleRep, Glen Burnie, MD. Tel: (800) 638-2000, FAX: (410) 761-3357, Web Site: www.telerep.com (29)

Olson, Sue, City of LaGrange, LaGrange, GA. Tel: (706) 883-2010, FAX: (706) 883-2020, Web Site: www.lagrange-ga.org (1)

OlymPak, Minneapolis, MN. Tel: (763) 504-5400, (800) 967-1705, FAX: (763) 504-5401, E-Mail: jgibas@olympak.com, Web Site: www.olympak.com (27)

Olympia Sales Inc, Enfield, CT. Tel: (860) 749-0751, (800) 338-9992, FAX: (860) 814-4451, E-Mail: info@olympiasales.net, Web Site: www.olympiasales.us (16)

Olzer, Timothy, O2 Consulting Inc, Atlanta, GA. Tel: (404) 384-3990 (22)

Omaha Creative Group Inc, Omaha, NE. Tel: (402) 597-3000, (800) 228-9872, FAX: (800) 428-1593, Web Site: www.omahasteaks.com (4)

Omaha Fixture International, Omaha, NE. Tel: (402) 592-3720, (800) 637-2257, FAX: (402) 593-5716, (800) 531-6627, E-Mail: sales@omahafixture.com, Web Site: www.omahafixture.com (8)

Omaha Steaks Inc, Omaha, NE. Tel: (402) 597-8370, FAX: (402) 597-8125, E-Mail: info@omahasteaks.com, Web Site: www.omahasteaks.com (4)

Omaha Vaccine Co, Omaha, NE. Tel: (402) 731-9600, (800) 367-4444, FAX: (800) 242-9447, E-Mail: customerservice@OmahaVaccine.com, Web Site: www.omahavaccine.com (16)

Oman, Peter, Meyer Fulfillment, Stratford, CT. Tel: (203) 375-5801, (800) 873-6393, E-Mail: vdarish@meyerfulfillment.com, Web Site: www.meyerfulfillment.com (28)

Omeda, Northbrook, IL. Tel: (847) 564-8900, FAX: (847) 564-1203, Web Site: www.omeda.com (22)

Omega Direct Response Inc, Richmond Hill, ON Canada. Tel: (905) 482-2340, FAX: (905) 482-9721, E-Mail: odrsales@omegadirect.com, Web Site: www.omegadirect.com (29)

Omega List Co, McLean, VA. Tel: (703) 821-1890, FAX: (703) 821-8794, E-Mail: listmanager@omegalist.com, Web Site: omegalist.com (23)

Omega Mobile, San Francisco, CA. Tel: (415) 596-6342, Web Site: www.omegamobile.com (29)

Omega Research & Development, Douglasville, GA. Tel: (770) 942-9876, (800) 554-4053, Web Site: www.caralarm.com (12)

Omega Studios, Elgin, IL. Tel: (972) 444-8556, FAX: (972) 444-8559, E-Mail: omegastudios@rrd.com, Web Site: www.omega-studios.com (37)

Omni Direct Inc, Miami, FL. Tel: (800) 459-4034, Web Site: www.omnidirect.tv (35)

Omni Farm, West Jefferson, NC. Tel: (336) 982-3475, (800) TREE-FARM, FAX: (336) 982-4163, E-Mail: omnifarm@omnifarm.com, Web Site: www.omnifarm.com (16)

Omni Print Inc, Lanham, MD. Tel: (301) 731-7000, FAX: (301) 731-7001, E-Mail: info@omniprint.net, Web Site: www.omniprint.net (27)

Omnicom Media Group, New York, NY. Tel: (212) 590-7020, E-Mail: info@omnicommediagroup.com, Web Site: www.omnicommediagroup.com (35)

Omnigraphics Inc, Aston, PA. Tel: (610) 461-3548, (800) 234-1340, FAX: (800) 875-1340, E-Mail: info@omnigraphics.com, Web Site: www.omnigraphics.com (17)

On-Demand Mail Services, Auburn Hills, MI. Tel: (888) 954-6245, Web Site: www.odmailservices.com (28)

On-Hand Adhesives Inc, Lake Zurich, IL. Tel: (847) 437-7773, (800) 323-5158, FAX: (847) 437-8006, E-Mail: help@on-hand.com, Web Site: www.on-hand.com (16)

OnBrand24, Beverly, MA. Tel: (855) 662-7263 (29)

One Call Systems Inc, Baden, PA. Tel: (412) 415-5000, (800) 845-9945, FAX: (412) 415-5023, E-Mail: jmcnamara@1-call.com, Web Site: www.1-call.com (29)

1-800-Contacts, Draper, UT. Tel: (800) 266-8228, FAX: (801) 924-9000, Web Site: www.1800contacts.com (7)

1-800-DialWord.com, Boone, NC. Tel: (800) DIAL-WORD, FAX: (877) 329-3627, Web Site: www.1800dialword.com (29)

1-800-Flowers.com, Carle Place, NY. Tel: (516) 237-6000, Web Site: www.1800flowers.com (16)

1-800-Mattress.com, Hicksville, NY. Tel: (800) 327-7720, Web Site: www.1800mattress.com (16)

One Hanes Place Catalog, Winston Salem, NC. Tel: (336) 519-8080, (800) 300-2600, FAX: (336) 519-0655, Web Site: www.onehanesplace.com (2)

100% Real Estate Inc, Orlando, FL. Tel: (800) 454-3422, E-Mail: rcs@100percentflorida.com, Web Site: www.100percentflorida.com (16)

One On One Advertising Inc, New Haven, CT. Tel: (203) 562-6259, (203) 671-2339, E-Mail: snevard@comcast.net, Web Site: snevard.wix.com/portfolio (35)

One Point, Scranton, PA. Tel: (570) 342-0737, (800) 526-4460, FAX: (570) 343-6361, Web Site: www.opoffice.com (10)

1000 Islands International Tourism Council, Alexandria Bay, NY. Tel: (315) 482-2520, (800) 847-5263, (800) 456-2267, FAX: (315) 482-5906, E-Mail: info@visit1000islands.com, Web Site: www.visit1000islands.com/visitorinfo/ (19)

1to1 Media, Stamford, CT. Tel: (203) 989-2200, Web Site: www.1to1media.com (35)

One World Projects, Batavia, NY. Tel: (585) 343-4490, FAX: (585) 344-3551, E-Mail: sales@oneworldprojects.com, Web Site: www.oneworldprojects.com (6)

One World Telecom, Miami, FL. Tel: (786) 664-6100 x6672, Web Site: www.nopin.us (29)

1001 Ways to Market Your Books, Taos, NM. Tel: (575) 751-3398, FAX: (575) 751-3100, E-Mail: info@bookmarket.com, Web Site: www.bookmarket.com (43)

Oneida Ltd, Oneida, NY. Tel: (315) 361-3000, (888) 263-7195, FAX: (315) 361-3700, Web Site: www.oneida.com (16)

O'Neil Data Systems Inc, Los Angeles, CA. Tel: (310) 448-6400, FAX: (310) 577-7350, Web Site: www.oneildata.com (27)

O'Neill Marketing Co, Fairfax, VA. Tel: (703) 934-0272, FAX: (703) 934-0273, E-Mail: info@oneillmarketing.com, Web Site: www.oneillmarketing.com (21)

Oneupweb, Traverse City, MI. Tel: (231) 922-9977, (877) 568-7477, E-Mail: info@oneupweb.com, Web Site: www.oneupweb.com (35)

Online Print Solutions, San Francisco, CA. Tel: (415) 651-4157, (800) 875-7117, E-Mail: info@onlineprintsolutions.com, Web Site: www.onlineprintsolutions.com (32)

OnTime Companies, Chelsea, MA. Tel: (617) 884-8488, Web Site: www.ontimecompanies.com (28)

Ontiveros, Gregg, Group O Inc, Milan, IL. Tel: (309) 736-8300, FAX: (309) 736-8301, Web Site: www.groupo.com (30)

Ontiveros, Robert, Group O Inc, Milan, IL. Tel: (309) 736-8300, FAX: (309) 736-8301, Web Site: www.groupo.com (30)

OnTrac, Chandler, AZ. Tel: (602) 333-4417, (800) 334-5000 (28)

Onyx Productions Direct Inc, Los Angeles, CA. Tel: (323) 692-9830, FAX: (323) 692-9832, E-Mail: joan@onyxprod.com, Web Site: www.onyxprod.com (32)

Oomingmak Musk Ox Producers Cooperative, Anchorage, AK. Tel: (907) 272-9225, (888) 360-9665, FAX: (907) 258-4225, E-Mail: oomingmak@qiviut.com, Web Site: www.qiviut.com (6)

Oommen, Sherry, McKnight's Long-Term Care News, Northfield, IL. Tel: (847) 784-8706, (800) 558-1703, FAX: (847) 784-9346, E-Mail: mltcn-webmaster@mltcn.com, Web Site: www.mcknightsonline.com (17)

Open Horizons, Taos, NM. Tel: (575) 751-3398, FAX: (575) 751-3100, E-Mail: info@bookmarket.com, Web Site: www.bookmarket.com (39)

Open Systems Services, Miami, FL. Tel: (305) 541-1970 (20)

Open Text Inc, Waterloo, ON Canada. Tel: (519) 888-9933, (800) 499-6544, FAX: (519) 888-0677, E-Mail: support@opentext.com, Web Site: www.opentext.com (16)

Operation Smile Inc, Virginia Beach, VA. Tel: (757) 321-7645, Web Site: www.operationsmile.org (1)

Opex Corp, Moorestown, NJ. Tel: (856) 727-1100, FAX: (856) 727-1955, Web Site: www.opex.com (34)

Opiela, Paul, International Auto Parts, Charlottesville, VA. Tel: (434) 973-0550, (800) 953-0813, FAX: (434) 973-2368, E-Mail: iap1@international-auto.com, Web Site: www.international-auto.com (12)

OPIN Systems Inc, Minneapolis, MN. Tel: (952) 567-2444, (800) 888-1804, FAX: (651) 994-7828, E-Mail: judywy@opin.com, Web Site: www.opin.com (22)

Oppenheimer Funds, New York, NY. Tel: (212) 323-0200, FAX: (212) 323-4070, Web Site: www.oppenheimerfunds.com (14)

Oppito, Gary, Escort Inc, West Chester, OH. Tel: (513) 870-8500, (800) 964-3138, FAX: (513) 870-8509, E-Mail: sales@escortradar.com, Web Site: www.escortradar.com (16)

Oprison, Rich, General Nutrition Corp, Pittsburgh, PA. Tel: (412) 288-4600, (877) 462-4700, FAX: (412) 402-7218, Web Site: www.gnc.com (7)

Opryland, Nashville, TN. Tel: (615) 889-1000, FAX: (615) 871-7741, E-Mail: info@gaylordhotels.com, Web Site: www.oprylandhotels.com (16)

Optronics Inc, Muskogee, OK. Tel: (918) 683-9514, (800) 364-5483, FAX: (918) 683-9517, E-Mail: sales@optronicsinc.com, Web Site: www.optronicsinc.com (11)

Opuszynski, Kyle, Vermont Ski Areas Association, Montpelier, VT. Tel: (802) 223-2439, FAX: (802) 229-6917, E-Mail: info@skivermont.com, Web Site: www.skivermont.com (1)

Opyd, Brian, Ignition Network, Chicago, IL. Tel: (312) 893-5000, E-Mail: inquiries@ignitionnetwork.com, Web Site: www.ignitionnetwork.com (35)

Oracle Corp, Redwood Shores, CA. Tel: (650) 506-7000, (800) 633-0738, FAX: (650) 506-7200, Web Site: www.oracle.com (16)

Oracle Data Cloud, Broomfield, CO. Tel: (800) 633-0738, E-Mail: thedatahotline@oracle.com, Web Site: cloud.oracle.com (22)

Oral Roberts University, Tulsa, OK. Tel: (918) 495-6161, FAX: (918) 495-6222, E-Mail: admissions@oru.edu, Web Site: www.oru.edu (1)

Oral, Ray, CNA, Chicago, IL. Tel: (312) 822-5000, (800) 262-2000, E-Mail: cna_help@cna.com, Web Site: www.cna.com (15)

The Orange County Register, Santa Ana, CA. Tel: (877) 469-7344, E-Mail: customerservice@ocregister.com, Web Site: www.ocregister.com (17)

Orange Leap, Dallas, TX. Tel: (972) 220-0341, Web Site: www.orangeleap.com (1)

Orbis Books, Maryknoll, NY. Tel: (914) 941-7636 X2576, (800) 258-5838, FAX: (914) 941-7005, E-Mail: orbisbooks@maryknoll.org, Web Site: www.orbisbooks.com (17)

Orbit Manufacturing Co, Perkasie, PA. Tel: (215) 257-0727, (888) 895-0958, FAX: (215) 257-7399, Web Site: www.orbitmfg.com (9)

Orchard Supply Hardware, San Jose, CA. Tel: (408) 281-3500, FAX: (408) 225-0388, Web Site: www.osh.com (16)

The Order Fulfillment Group, Zionsville, IN. Tel: (317) 733-7755, FAX: (317) 733-8799, E-Mail: thughes@tofg.com, Web Site: www.tofg.com (28)

Ordway, Paddy, iVisionMobile Inc, Chatsworth, CA. Tel: (866) 655-5302, FAX: (818) 812-6126, E-Mail: sales@ivisionmobile.com, Web Site: www.ivisionmobile.com (35)

Oregon Freeze Dry Inc, Albany, OR. Tel: (541) 926-6001, FAX: (541) 967-6527, Web Site: www.ofd.com (4)

Glen Orenstein, Merrick, NY. Tel: (516) 359-8785 (20)

Orenstein, Robert, International Wine Accessories Inc, Petaluma, CA. Tel: (214) 349-6097, (800) 527-4072, FAX: (214) 349-8712, E-Mail: customerservice@iwawine.com, Web Site: www.iwawine.com (7)

Oreskovich, Eva, Paris Presents Inc, Gurnee, IL. Tel: (847) 263-5500, (800) 431-5723, FAX: (847) 263-5191, E-Mail: support@parispresents.com, Web Site: www.parispresents.com (7)

Organ, Denise, DNE Nutraceuticals Inc, Farmingdale, NJ. Tel: (212) 235-5200, (800) 221-1833, FAX: (212) 235-5243, E-Mail: info@dnenutra.com, Web Site: www.dnenutra.com (7)

Organ, Eric, DNE Nutraceuticals Inc, Farmingdale, NJ. Tel: (212) 235-5200, (800) 221-1833, FAX: (212) 235-5243, E-Mail: info@dnenutra.com, Web Site: www.dnenutra.com (7)

Orgler, Joel, Tri-State Envelope Corp, Ashland, PA. Tel: (570) 875-0433, (800) 233-3102, FAX: (570) 875-0125, E-Mail: tsecny@attglobal.net, Web Site: www.tristateenvelope.com (26)

Orgler, Thomas, Northwest Mailing Service Inc, Chicago, IL. Tel: (773) 237-2264, Web Site: www.nwmail.com (28)

Orient Expressed Imports Inc, New Orleans, LA. Tel: (888) 856-3948, FAX: (504) 899-5566, E-Mail: orient@orientexpressed.com, Web Site: www.orientexpressed.com (2)

Oriental Trading Co Inc, Omaha, NE. Tel: (800) 348-6483, FAX: (800) 327-8904, Web Site: www.oriental.com (5)

Orina, Nann, CheckVantage, Austin, TX. Tel: (512) 970-4958, (877) 243-2501, FAX: (512) 442-5515, E-Mail: marya@checkvantage.com, Web Site: www.checkvantage.com (14)

Orion, Federal Way, WA. Tel: (253) 661-7805, Web Site: www.orionworks.org (1)

Orion Telescopes & Binoculars, Watsonville, CA. Tel: (831) 763-7000, (800) 447-1001, FAX: (408) 763-7017, E-Mail: sales@telescope.com, Web Site: www.telescope.com (11)

Orisek, Martin, Concept Communications Co, Romeoville, IL. Tel: (630) 829-8450, (800) 323-3524, FAX: (630) 629-8415, E-Mail: info@cstore1.com, Web Site: www.cstore1.com (16)

Orisek, Rudolf, Concept Communications Co, Romeoville, IL. Tel: (630) 829-8450, (800) 323-3524, FAX: (630) 629-8415, E-Mail: info@cstore1.com, Web Site: www.cstore1.com (16)

Orisek, Tim, Concept Communications Co, Romeoville, IL. Tel: (630) 829-8450, (800) 323-3524, FAX: (630) 629-8415, E-Mail: info@cstore1.com, Web Site: www.cstore1.com (16)

Orkin, Kenneth, ACNielsen Corp, New York, NY. Tel: (646) 654-5000, FAX: (646) 654-5002, E-Mail: globalc@nielsen.com, Web Site: www.acnielsen.com/us (30)

Orlando/ Orange County Convention & Visitor's Bureau, Orlando, FL. Tel: (407) 354-5568, Web Site: visitorlando.com (19)

Orlando, John, Millcraft of Michigan, Livonia, MI. Tel: (734) 266-3710, (800) 482-0556, FAX: (734) 266-3705, Web Site: www.millcraft.com (25)

Orloff, Brad, United Retail Inc, Rochelle Park, NJ. Tel: (201) 845-0880, Web Site: www.avenue.com (2)

Orlov, Alexei, Rapp, New York, NY. Tel: (212) 817-6800, FAX: (212) 686-7047, E-Mail: rick.doerr@rapp.com, Web Site: www.rapp.com (35)

Orme, Tom, Alpha Supply Inc, Bremerton, WA. Tel: (360) 373-3302, (800) 257-4211, FAX: (360) 377-9235 (16)

Orner, Lita, The Vestal Press Ltd, Lanham, MD. Tel: (301) 459-3366, (800) 462-6420, FAX: (301) 429-5746, E-Mail: sburnett@rowman.com, Web Site: www.nbnbooks.com (17)

Orons, Andy, Priority Systems Inc, Middletown, PA. Tel: (717) 939-2700, (800) 479-2208, FAX: (717) 939-6180, E-Mail: contactus@prioritysystems.com, Web Site: www.prioritysystems.com (34)

O'Rourke Hospitality Marketing LLC, Newburyport, MA. Tel: (978) 465-5955, E-Mail: hello@orourkehospitality.com, Web Site: www.orourkehospitality.com (35)

Orr, Charles L, Direct Selling Education Foundation, Washington, DC. Tel: (202) 452-8866, FAX: (202) 452-9015, E-Mail: info@dsef.org, Web Site: www.dsef.org (40)

Orr, Dwight W, Creative Marketing Programs of Kansas City, Kansas City, MO. Tel: (816) 472-6843, (800) 373-6843, FAX: (816) 472-8184, E-Mail: getresults@cmpkc.com, Web Site: www.cmpkc.com (21)

Orr, Ken, ICS Marketing Services, Lansing, MI. Tel: (517) 394-1890, (888) 394-1890, FAX: (517) 394-7408, E-Mail: sales@icshq.com, Web Site: icshq.com (21)

Ort-Mabry, Catherine, American College of Cardiology, Washington, DC. Tel: (202) 375-6000, FAX: (202) 375-7000, E-Mail: resource@acc.org, Web Site: www.acc.org (1)

Ortman, Ross, Dakota Digital, Sioux Falls, SD. Tel: (605) 332-6513, (800) 593-4160, FAX: (605) 339-4106, E-Mail: sales@dakotadigital.com, Web Site: www.dakotadigital.com (12)

The Orvis Co Inc, Manchester, VT. Tel: (802) 362-3622, FAX: (802) 362-3525, Web Site: www.orvis.com (11)

Osborn, Kenneth, Liquid Focus Direct LLC, Bridgeport, CT. Tel: (866) 892-0259, FAX: (203) 339-0066, Web Site: www.getliquidfocus.com (32)

Osborn, Michael, Catalyst, Rochester, NY. Tel: (585) 453-8300, (800) 836-7720, FAX: (585) 453-8360, E-Mail: info@catalystinc.com, Web Site: www.catalystinc.com (35)

Osborne, W. Jeffrey, WorleyParsons, Reading, PA. Tel: (610) 855-2000, FAX: (610) 885-2001, Web Site: www.worleyparsons.com (16)

Oseth, Todd, Intermap Technologies, Englewood, CO. Tel: (303) 708-0955, FAX: (303) 708-0952, E-Mail: info@intermap.com, Web Site: www.intermap.com (32)

Osmon, Roy, Spectrum Communication Services Inc, Brookfield, WI. Tel: (262) 821-8400, (800) 701-3559, FAX: (262) 821-1492, E-Mail: sales@spectrumcomm.com, Web Site: www.spectrumcomm.com (29)

Osmonics Inc, Minnetonka, MN. Tel: (952) 264-3937, (800) 605-6698, FAX: (952) 536-3301, Web Site: www.osmonics.com (16)

Ossa, Pamela, Anda Inc, Parsippany, NJ. Tel: (954) 217-4500, (800) 331-2632, FAX: (866) 600-3860, Web Site: www.andanet.com (7)

Osso, Michael, Crohn's & Colitis Foundation of America, New York, NY. Tel: (212) 685-3440, (800) 932-2423, E-Mail: info@ccfa.org, Web Site: www.ccfa.org (1)

Ostendorf, Dan, Lincoln Picture Studio, Dayton, OH. Tel: (937) 439-9633 (38)

Ostenso, Brian, Direct Marketing Group, Eden Prairie, MN. Tel: (952) 975-5060, (888) 397-5060, FAX: (952) 906-0608, Web Site: www.directmg.com (35)

Ostenso, Brian, Mail Handling Services, Eden Prairie, MN. Tel: (952) 975-5000, FAX: (952) 975-5030, Web Site: www.mailhandling.com (28)

Oster, Gary, US Travel Association, Washington, DC. Tel: (202) 408-8422, FAX: (202) 408-1255, E-Mail: feedback@ustravel.org, Web Site: www.ustravel.org (1)

Oster, Michelle, Cattle Kate, Boise, ID. Tel: (208) 377-5283, (800) 332-5283, FAX: (208) 375-3827, E-Mail: cattlekate@rmisp.com, Web Site: www.cattlekate.com (2)

Osterberg, Jon, PEMCO Insurance Cos, Seattle, WA. Tel: (206) 628-4000, (800) 467-3626, FAX: (206) 628-5886, Web Site: www.pemco.com (15)

Osterloh, Don, Grizzly Industrial Inc, Bellingham, WA. Tel: (360) 647-0801, (800) 523-4777, FAX: (360) 671-8375, E-Mail: csr@grizzly.com, Web Site: www.grizzly.com (9)

Ostertag, Robert, BJT Management Group, Ada, MI. Tel: (616) 682-0369, Web Site: www.bjtmgt.com (20)

Ostrom, Rachael, Aveda Corp, Blaine, MN. Tel: (763) 951-4201, (800) 644-4831, Web Site: www.aveda.com (7)

Ostrov, Gerald M., Bausch & Lomb Inc, Rochester, NY. Tel: (585) 338-6000, (800) 344-8815, FAX: (585) 338-6007, Web Site: www.bausch.com (16)

Ostrove, Michael, Paul Stuart, New York, NY. Tel: (800) 678-8278, E-Mail: info@paulstuart.com, Web Site: www.paulstuart.com (2)

Ostroy, Andy, Belardi/Ostroy, New York, NY. Tel: (212) 924-1300, FAX: (212) 381-1745, E-Mail: katel@belardiostroy.com, Web Site: belardiostroy.com (23)

Ostrusina, Edward, Flight Form Cases Inc, Bedford Park, IL. Tel: (708) 458-8989, (800) 657-1199, FAX: (708) 458-9023, E-Mail: info@caseguys.net, Web Site: www.flightform.com (9)

Otani, Noboru, Esprit Line Co Ltd USA, Greenwich, CT. Tel: (203) 629-5124 (16)

OTOlabs LLC, Charlestown, MA. Tel: (617) 236-8400, Web Site: www.otolabs.com (30)

Ott, Jeffrey, DB Alex Brown Inc, Baltimore, MD. Tel: (410) 727-1700, (800) 638-2956, Web Site: www.dbalexbrown.com (14)

Ott, Paul, Penske Logistics, Reading, PA. Tel: (800) 529-6531, FAX: (610) 775-2449, E-Mail: info.penskelogistics@penske.com, Web Site: www.penskelogistics.com (16)

Otting, Joseph M., US Bancorp, Minneapolis, MN. Tel: (651) 466-3000, (800) 872-2657, FAX: (612) 303-0782, Web Site: www.usbank.com (14)

Ottmar, Peter H., Mercury Print & Mail Co Inc, Pawtucket, RI. Tel: (401) 724-7600, FAX: (401) 724-9920, Web Site: www.mpmri.com (28)

Otto Environmental Systems of North America, Charlotte, NC. Tel: (704) 588-9191, (800) 227-5885, FAX: (704) 588-5250, E-Mail: info@otto-usa.com, Web Site: www.otto-usa.com (16)

Otto, Eddie, TXU Energy, Irving, TX. Tel: (972) 868-8345, Web Site: www.txu.com (16)

Otto, John, Visions Inc, Brooklyn Park, MN. Tel: (763) 425-4251, FAX: (763) 425-4614, E-Mail: general@visionsfirst.com, Web Site: www.visionsfirst.com (35)

Ottolenghi, Arturo M., Red Hill Corp, Gettysburg, PA. Tel: (717) 337-3038, (800) 822-4003, FAX: (717) 337-0732, E-Mail: custserv@supergrit.com, Web Site: www.supergrit.com (34)

Oubre, Linda, San Francisco State University, San Francisco, CA. Tel: (415) 338-1111, FAX: (415) 338-0501, Web Site: www.sfsu.edu (41)

Our Data Works Inc, Lewisville, TX. Tel: (469) 546-3000, (800) 268-2505, FAX: (469) 546-3013, E-Mail: info@ourdataworks.com, Web Site: www.ourdataworks.com (29)

Our Designs Inc, Vancouver, WA. Tel: (859) 282-5500, (800) 382-5252, FAX: (859) 282-5508, E-Mail: sales@ourdesigns.com, Web Site: www.ourdesigns.com (16)

Our Lady of Victory Homes of Charity, Lackawanna, NY. Tel: (716) 828-9648, FAX: (716) 828-9643, E-Mail: rheist@olv-bvs.org, Web Site: www.ourladyofvictory.org (1)

Our Sunday Visitor Publishing, Huntington, IN. Tel: (260) 356-8400, (800) 348-2440, FAX: (260) 356-8472, E-Mail: athomas@osv.com, Web Site: www.osv.com (17)

Outdoor Research, Seattle, WA. Tel: (206) 467-1496, (888) 467-4327, FAX: (206) 467-0374, Web Site: www.outdoorresearch.com (11)

Outlook Group Corp, Neenah, WI. Tel: (920) 727-7999, FAX: (920) 727-8529, E-Mail: info@outlookgroup.com, Web Site: www.outlookgroup.com (27)

Outrider North America, Saint Louis, MO. Tel: (314) 209-1005, FAX: (314) 209-1126, Web Site: www.outrider.com (30)

Outsource America Inc, Bradenton, FL. Tel: (941) 746-4555, (800) 729-5694, FAX: (441) 746-3595, E-Mail: sales@oaiworld.com, Web Site: www.oaiworld.com (24)

Outsourcing Solutions Inc, Wentzville, MO. Tel: (847) 419-1790, FAX: (847) 419-1818 (20)

Outtan, Keith, Woodcraft Supply Corp LLC, Parkersburg, WV. Tel: (304) 422-5412, (800) 344-3348, FAX: (304) 422-5417, Web Site: www.woodcraft.com (9)

Ovative/Group LLC, Minneapolis, MN. Tel: (612) 886-1010, Web Site: www.ovative.com (20)

Overmyer, David, Bunchball, Redwood City, CA. Tel: (408) 985-2034, Web Site: www.bunchball.com (32)

Overnight Prints, Las Vegas, NV. Tel: (888) 677-2000, E-Mail: service@overnightprints.com, Web Site: www.overnightprints.com (27)

Overseas Private Investment Corp (OPIC), Washington, DC. Tel: (202) 336-8799, FAX: (202) 336-7949, E-Mail: info@opic.gov, Web Site: www.opic.gov (14)

Overton's Inc, Greenville, NC. Tel: (252) 355-5783, (800) 334-6541, FAX: (252) 355-2923, E-Mail: service@overtons.com, Web Site: www.overtons.com (11)

Owen Beyer, Andrea, Adtron Inc, Bloomington, IL. Tel: (309) 662-1221, FAX: (309) 663-6691 (35)

Owen, Ford, Ames Taping Tool System Inc, Stone Mountain, GA. Tel: (770) 243-2647, (800) 303-1827, FAX: (770) 243-2658, Web Site: www.amestools.com (9)

Owen, J.D., Boys' Life & Scouting Magazines, Irving, TX. Tel: (972) 580-2000, (866) 584-6589, FAX: (972) 580-2079, Web Site: www.boyslife.org (17)

Buck Owens' Crystal Palace, Bakersfield, CA. Tel: (661) 328-7560, FAX: (805) 328-7565, E-Mail: mhufford@buckowens.com, Web Site: www.buckowens.com (19)

Owens, Alexandra, American Society of Journalists & Authors Directory, New York, NY. Tel: (212) 997-0947, FAX: (212) 768-7414, E-Mail: asjany@ibm.net (43)

Owens, Andy, 1-800-DialWord.com, Boone, NC. Tel: (800) DIALWORD, FAX: (877) 329-3627, Web Site: www.1800dialword.com (29)

Owens, Beth, Townsend Communications LLC, Kansas City, MO. Tel: (816) 361-0616, (800) 274-8867, FAX: (816) 361-6164, Web Site: www.townsendprint.com (17)

Owens, Michael, Coverdell & Co Inc, Chicago, IL. Tel: (404) 881-2227, (800) 992-2196, FAX: (404) 881-2222, Web Site: www.coverdell.com (15)

Owens, Tracey, o2kl Advertising, New York, NY. Tel: (646) 839-6236, E-Mail: towens@o2kl.com, Web Site: www.o2k1.com (35)

Oxbridge Communications Inc, New York, NY. Tel: (212) 741-0231, (800) 955-0231, FAX: (212) 633-2938, E-Mail: custserv@oxbridge.com, Web Site: www.mediafinder.com; www.oxbridge.com (30)

Oxfam America, Boston, MA. Tel: (617) 482-1211, (800) 776-9326, FAX: (617) 728-2594, E-Mail: info@oxfamamerica.org, Web Site: www.oxfamamerica.org (1)

Oxford Health Plans, Inc, Trumbull, CT. Tel: (800) 889-7658, FAX: (203) 459-6464, E-Mail: info@speedmat.com, Web Site: www.oxhp.com (15)

Oxford University Press Inc, New York, NY. Tel: (212) 726-6000, FAX: (212) 726-6455, Web Site: global.oup.com (17)

Oxford, Dave, Activision Value, Eden Prairie, MN. Tel: (952) 918-9400, FAX: (952) 918-9560 (16)

The Oyster Group, Dartmouth, NS Canada. Tel: (877) 405-4858, E-Mail: fdrinnan@theoystergroup.ca, Web Site: www.theoystergroup.ca (22)

Ozmina, Tracey A., Academy of Marketing Science Journal, Thousand Oaks, CA. Tel: (800) 818-7243, FAX: (800) 583-2665, E-Mail: journals@sagepub.com, Web Site: www.sagepub.com (43)

P

P & H Mining Equipment, Milwaukee, WI. Tel: (414) 671-4400, FAX: (414) 671-7618, Web Site: www.phmining.com (16)

PAC Worldwide, Redmond, WA. Tel: (425) 202-4000, (800) 535-0039, FAX: (425) 885-2934, Web Site: www.pac.com (26)

PBD Worldwide Fulfillment Services, Alpharetta, GA. Tel: (770) 442-8633, FAX: (770) 442-9742, E-Mail: sales.marketing@pbd.com, Web Site: www.pbd.com (28)

PBM Graphics, Greensboro, NC. Tel: (336) 664-5800, (800) 849-8200, FAX: (336) 931-0965, Web Site: www.pbmgraphics.com (28)

PBS Distribution, Arlington, VA. Tel: (617) 208-0720, Web Site: shoppbs.org (3)

PC Connection, Merrimack, NH. Tel: (603) 683-2167, (800) 800-0014, FAX: (603) 683-5773, E-Mail: pr@pcconnection.com, Web Site: www.pcconnection.com, macconnection.com (22)

PC/Nametag Inc, Verona, WI. Tel: (608) 845-1850, (800) 233-9767, E-Mail: sales@pcnametag.com, Web Site: www.pcnametag.com (16)

PC Ontario Fund, Toronto, ON Canada. Tel: (416) 861-0020, (416) 861-3085, (800) 903-6453, FAX: (416) 861-9593, (416) 861-1760, E-Mail: comments@ontariopc.net, Web Site: www.ontariopc.com (1)

PC World, San Francisco, CA. Tel: (415) 243-0500, FAX: (415) 442-1891, Web Site: www.pcworld.com (17)

PCCW Teleservices, Dublin, OH. Tel: (614) 280-1600, Web Site: www.influentinc.com (29)

PCG, Inc, Batavia, IL. Tel: (630) 482-9300, FAX: (630) 454-3750, E-Mail: sasmith@pcgnow.com, Web Site: www.pcgnow.com (20)

PCI Paper Conversions Inc, Syracuse, NY. Tel: (315) 437-1641, FAX: (315) 437-3634, E-Mail: sales@padmaker.com, Web Site: www.padmaker.com (27)

PDQ Post Group, Surrey, BC Canada. Tel: (604) 888-0676, (888) 998-9878, FAX: (604) 888-4467, E-Mail: sales@pdqpostgroup.com, Web Site: www.pdqpostgroup.com (21)

PDS International Mail Service, Hauppauge, NY. Tel: (631) 815-1750, Web Site: www.pdsmail.com; www.internationalmail.com (28)

PESI LLC, Eau Claire, WI. Tel: (800) 844-8260, FAX: (800) 554-9775, E-Mail: info@pesi.com, Web Site: www.pesi.com (17)

PFE Inc, Irvine, CA. Tel: (949) 417-0330, FAX: (949) 417-0331, Web Site: www.pfeinc.com (34)

PFI Western Stores Inc, Springfield, MO. Tel: (417) 889-2668, (800) 222-4734, FAX: (417) 889-7204, E-Mail: pfi@pfiwestern.com, Web Site: www.pfiwestern.com (2)

PGI Companies Inc, Minnetonka, MN. Tel: (952) 933-5745, FAX: (952) 933-5864, E-Mail: ddallum@pgicompanies.com, Web Site: www.pgicompanies.com (27)

PGS Printing & Graphics Services, Roslyn, NY. Tel: (917) 880-5397, FAX: (866) 361-2957, E-Mail: sales@pollack.com, Web Site: www.pollack.com (27)

PHE Inc, Hillsborough, NC. Tel: (919) 644-8100, (800) 293-4654, FAX: (919) 644-8150, E-Mail: custserv@adameve.com (5)

PI Inc, Athens, TN. Tel: (423) 745-6213, FAX: (423) 745-7039, Web Site: www.pi-inc.com (16)

pii, Bloomington, IL. Tel: (800) 664-0444, FAX: (309) 662-2055, E-Mail: sales@whateverittakes.com, Web Site: www.whateverittakes.com (35)

PIP Postal Instant Press, Mission Viejo, CA. Tel: (949) 282-3800, FAX: (949) 282-3899, Web Site: www.pip.com (27)

PM Productions, Los Angeles, CA. Tel: (310) 559-3127, FAX: (310) 559-3168, E-Mail: odellmack@hotmail.com, Web Site: www.pmproductionsvideos.com (32)

PMG, Columbia, MD. Tel: (410) 290-0667, Web Site: www.pmgdirect.net (20)

PMIC, Los Angeles, CA. Tel: (323) 954-0224, (800) 633-4215, FAX: (323) 954-0253, Web Site: pmiconline.stores.yahoo.net (17)

PMX Agency, New York, NY. Tel: (212) 387-0300, (888) 960-0177, FAX: (212) 387-7647, E-Mail: info@pmxagency.com, Web Site: www.pmxagency.com (23)

PNC Bank Corp, Pittsburgh, PA. Tel: (412) 762-2000/3514, (800) 422-6537, FAX: (412) 762-4482 (14)

PNC Global Investment Servicing, Lynnfield, MA. Tel: (781) 477-4124, Web Site: www.pnc.com (14)

PNT Marketing Services, Inc, Long Island City, NY. Tel: (718) 433-4063, (888) 768-2210, FAX: (914) 428-0504, E-Mail: tony@pntmarketingservices.com, Web Site: www.pntmarketingservices.com (22)

POPAI-The Global Association for Marketing at Retail, Chicago, IL. Tel: (312) 863-2900, FAX: (312) 229-1152, Web Site: www.popai.com (40)

PPAI Expo, Irving, TX. Tel: (972) 252-0404, (888) 426-7724, FAX: (972) 258-3004, E-Mail: expo@ppai.org, Web Site: expo.ppai.org (42)

PPC, Johnston, IA. Tel: (515) 986-5070, E-Mail: sales@ppcbest.com, Web Site: www.ppcbest.com (9)

PPI Benefit Solutions, Wallingford, CT. Tel: (888) 674-0046, FAX: (203) 468-9886, E-Mail: clientservices@ppibenefits.com, Web Site: www.ppibenefits.com (15)

PPS - Packaging Printing Specialists, Saint Charles, IL. Tel: (630) 513-8060, (877) 573-8060, FAX: (630) 513-8062, E-Mail: pps@ppsofil.com, Web Site: www.PPSofIL.com (27)

Precise Media Services Inc, Ontario, CA. Tel: (908) 481-3305, (800) 444-4217, FAX: (908) 481-3405, Web Site: www.precisemedia.com (27)

PRM Media Group, Hackettstown, NJ. Tel: (973) 765-9600, (877) 588-9552, FAX: (973) 765-0004, E-Mail: paul.morgan@prmmediagroup.com, Web Site: www.prmmediagroup.com (35)

Professional Education Institute, Chicago, IL. Tel: (312) 521-8002, (800) 320-7517, Web Site: www.thepei.com (13)

PSI Marketing Consultants Inc, Rolling Meadows, IL. Tel: (773) 878-0800, (800) 933-4774, FAX: (773) 878-4219 (29)

PTC, Needham, MA. Tel: (781) 370-5000, (877) 275-4782, Web Site: www.ptc.com (22)

PTI Pyramid Technologies LLC, Meriden, CT. Tel: (203) 238-0550, (888) 479-7264, FAX: (203) 634-1696, Web Site: www.pyramid-technologies.com (10)

PVC Plastics Co, Evansville, IN. Tel: (812) 476-3592, (800) 782-7527, FAX: (812) 474-4531 (16)

Paardercamp Hackney, Susan, The Christian Science Monitor, Boston, MA. Tel: (617) 450-2300, FAX: (617) 450-2031, Web Site: www.csmonitor.com (31)

Paasche Airbrush Co, Chicago, IL. Tel: (773) 867-9191, FAX: (773) 867-9198, E-Mail: info@paascheairbrush.com, Web Site: www.paascheairbrush.com (10)

Paasche, Carl, Woodcrafters Lumber Sales Inc, Portland, OR. Tel: (503) 231-0226, (800) 777-3709, FAX: (503) 232-0511, E-Mail: spen@worldnet.att.net, Web Site: www.woodcrafters.us (9)

PACCAR Inc, Bellevue, WA. Tel: (425) 468-7400, FAX: (425) 468-8216, Web Site: www.paccar.com (16)

Pace Communications Inc, Greensboro, NC. Tel: (336) 378-6065, FAX: (336) 275-2864, Web Site: www.pacecommunications.com (17)

Pace Inc, Southern Pines, NC. Tel: (910) 695-7223, FAX: (910) 695-1594, E-Mail: support@paceworldwide.com, Web Site: www.paceworldwide.com/index.asp (16)

Pace University, New York, NY. Tel: (212) 346-1781, (866) 722-3338, FAX: (212) 346-1821, Web Site: www.pace.edu (16)

Pace, Barry, Cortz Inc, West Chicago, IL. Tel: (630) 876-1080, (800) 288-7946, Web Site: www.intheswim.com (5)

Pace, Thomas, William Blair & Co LLC, Chicago, IL. Tel: (312) 236-1600, (800) 621-0687, FAX: (312) 368-9418, E-Mail: info@williamblair.com, Web Site: www.williamblair.com (14)

Pacelle, Wayne, The Humane Society of the US, Washington, DC. Tel: (202) 452-1100, (866) 720-2676, Web Site: www.hsus.org (1)

Pacer, Leonard A., Central States Health & Life Co of Omaha, Omaha, NE. Tel: (402) 397-1111, (800) 826-6587, FAX: (402) 391-3772, Web Site: www.cso.com (15)

Pachler, Christopher, Playboy Enterprises Inc, Beverly Hills, CA. Tel: (310) 860-1215, Web Site: www.playboyenterprises.com (17)

Pachmayr Ltd, Middletown, CT. Tel: (800) 225-9626, FAX: (860) 632-1699, Web Site: www.lymanproducts.com (11)

Pacific Botanicals LLC, Grants Pass, OR. Tel: (541) 479-7777, FAX: (541) 479-7780, E-Mail: pacbot1@earthlink.net, Web Site: www.pacificbotanicals.com (7)

Pacific Cycle Inc, Madison, WI. Tel: (608) 268-2468, (800) 724-9466, FAX: (847) 236-3692, (847) 573-0602, E-Mail: info@pacificcycle.com, Web Site: www.pacificcycle.com (16)

Pacific Propeller Inc, Kent, WA. Tel: (253) 872-7767, (800) 722-7767, FAX: (253) 872-7221, E-Mail: jheikke@pacprop.com, Web Site: www.pacificpropeller.com (16)

Pacific Spirit Corp, Forest Grove, OR. Tel: (503) 357-1566, (800) 634-9057, FAX: (503) 357-1699, Web Site: www.pacificspiritcatalogs.com (6)

Pacific Sportswear Co Inc, San Diego, CA. Tel: (619) 281-6688, (800) USA-8778, FAX: (619) 281-6687, E-Mail: info@pacsport.com, Web Site: www.pacsport.com (5)

PacificEast, Beaverton, OR. Tel: (800) 665-8400, Web Site: www.pacificeast.com (22)

Pacione, Frank, TigerDirect.ca, Richmond Hill, ON Canada. Tel: (800) 800-8300, (888) 771-9999, FAX: (905) 482-3134, Web Site: www.tigerdirect.ca (3)

Pacious, Patrick, Choice Hotels International, Rockville, MD. Tel: (301) 592-5000, Web Site: www.choicehotels.com (16)

Pacitti, Peter, DeLuxe Laboratories Inc, Hollywood, CA. Tel: (323) 462-6171, FAX: (323) 960-7016, E-Mail: steven.vananda@bydeluxe.com, Web Site: www.bydeluxe.com (16)

Pack, Jamie, Gillespie Magazine Marketing & Publishing, Lawrenceville, NJ. Tel: (609) 895-0200, FAX: (609) 895-0222, Web Site: www.gillespie.com (20)

Packer List Inc, Washington, DC. Tel: (202) 546-1889, FAX: (202) 546-1897, E-Mail: dpacker@packerlist.com, Web Site: www.packerlist.com (23)

Packer, Donna, Packer List Inc, Washington, DC. Tel: (202) 546-1889, FAX: (202) 546-1897, E-Mail: dpacker@packerlist.com, Web Site: www.packerlist.com (23)

Packer, Sharon, American Civil Defense Association, Draper, UT. Tel: (801) 501-0077, (800) 425-5397, FAX: (888) 425-5339, E-Mail: info@tacda.org, Web Site: www.tacda.org (16)

PackStream LLC, Louisville, KY. Tel: (502) 552-9624, Web Site: www.packstream.com (20)

PacNet Services Ltd, Vancouver, BC Canada. Tel: (604) 689-0399, FAX: (604) 689-0313, E-Mail: info@pacnetservices.com, Web Site: www.pacnetservices.com (14)

Pactiv Corp, Lake Forest, IL. Tel: (847) 482-2000, (800) 828-2850, FAX: (847) 482-4738, Web Site: www.pactiv.com (26)

Paczkowski, Walter, Data Analytics Corp, Plainsboro, NJ. Tel: (609) 936-8999, Web Site: www.dataanalyticscorp.com (30)

Paddon, Sherry, Team Cheer, Geneseo, NY. Tel: (800) 350-1562, (877) 243-5268, E-Mail: custserv@teamcheer.com, Web Site: www.teamcheer.com (2)

Padgett, Larry, Concordia Publishing House, Saint Louis, MO. Tel: (314) 268-1000, (800) 325-3040, FAX: (314) 268-1329, E-Mail: order@cph.org, Web Site: www.cph.org (17)

Padgitt, James L., Direct Marketing Insights Inc, Goodyear, AZ. Tel: (843) 817-7488, E-Mail: jimp@dminsights.com, Web Site: www.dminsights.com (20)

Padlo, Dennis C., Tempco Electric Heater Corp, Wood Dale, IL. Tel: (630) 350-2252, (800) 323-6859, FAX: (630) 350-0232, E-Mail: dpadlo@tempco.com, Web Site: www.tempco.com (9)

Padron, Otto, MundoFOX22, Los Angeles, CA. Tel: (213) 344-3700, E-Mail: info@canal22.tv, Web Site: www.mundofox22.com (32)

Padulo Integrated, Toronto, ON Canada. Tel: (416) 966-4000, (800) 454-5321, FAX: (416) 966-4012, E-Mail: info@padulo.ca, Web Site: www.padulo.ca (35)

Padulo, Richard, Padulo Integrated, Toronto, ON Canada. Tel: (416) 966-4000, (800) 454-5321, FAX: (416) 966-4012, E-Mail: info@padulo.ca, Web Site: www.padulo.ca (35)

Page Boettner, Tammy, Broadmoor Hotel Inc, Colorado Springs, CO. Tel: (719) 623-5112, (866) 837-9520, FAX: (719) 577-5738, Web Site: www.broadmoor.com (19)

Page, Bob, Replacements Ltd, Greensboro, NC. Tel: (800) REPLACE, E-Mail: inquire@replacements.com, Web Site: www.replacements.com (8)

Page, Graeme, Alzheimer Society of Canada, Toronto, ON Canada. Tel: (416) 488-8772, (800) 616-8816, FAX: (416) 488-3778, E-Mail: gpage@alzheimer.ca, Web Site: www.alzheimer.ca (1)

Page, John, Comcast Spectacor LP, Philadelphia, PA. Tel: (215) 336-3600, (800) 298-4200, FAX: (215) 389-9518, E-Mail: info@comcast-spectacor.com, Web Site: www.comcast-spectacor.com (16)

Page, Jr Henry C., Ethyl Corp, Richmond, VA. Tel: (804) 788-5000, FAX: (804) 788-5688, Web Site: www.ethyl.com (16)

Page, Larry, Google Inc, Mountain View, CA. Tel: (650) 253-0000, FAX: (650) 253-0001, Web Site: www.google.com (31)

Pageau, Mark, Darwill, Hillside, IL. Tel: (708) 236-4900, FAX: (708) 236-5820, Web Site: www.darwill.com (27)

Pagnam, Julia, Luce Corp, Hamden, CT. Tel: (203) 787-0281, FAX: (203) 230-2753 (16)

Pagnam, Mary, Luce Corp, Hamden, CT. Tel: (203) 787-0281, FAX: (203) 230-2753 (16)

Pagnam, Timothy F., Luce Corp, Hamden, CT. Tel: (203) 787-0281, FAX: (203) 230-2753 (16)

Pagos Haller, Stacy, BrightFocus Foundation, Clarksburg, MD. Tel: (301) 948-3224, (800) 437-2423, FAX: (301) 358-9454, E-Mail: info@brightfocus.org, Web Site: www.brightfocus.org (1)

Paharia, Rajat, Bunchball, Redwood City, CA. Tel: (408) 985-2034, Web Site: www.bunchball.com (32)

Paige, Jacqueline, Smith Hanley Associates, Southport, CT. Tel: (203) 319-4300, (888) 221-2900, FAX: (203) 319-4320, Web Site: www.smithhanley.com (20)

Paige, William H., New England Journal of Medicine, Waltham, MA. Tel: (781) 893-3800, FAX: (781) 893-7729, Web Site: www.nejm.org (17)

Paine, Kathy, Liberty Orchards Co Inc, Cashmere, WA. Tel: (509) 782-2191, (800) 888-5696, FAX: (509) 782-1487, E-Mail: service@libertyorchards.com, Web Site: www.libertyorchards.com (16)

Paine, Mike, Dukky Inc, Mandeville, LA. Tel: (888) 662-9096, E-Mail: info@dukky.com, Web Site: www.dukky.com (32)

Paine, Susan, Share Group Inc, Newton, MA. Tel: (617) 629-4500, FAX: (617) 629-4510, E-Mail: info@sharegroup.com, Web Site: www.sharegroup.com (29)

PAL Health Technologies, Pekin, IL. Tel: (309) 347-8785, (800) 223-2957, FAX: (309) 477-4456, Web Site: www.palhealth.com (16)

Paladin Press, Boulder, CO. Tel: (303) 443-7250, (800) 392-2400, FAX: (303) 442-8741, E-Mail: service@paladin-press.com, Web Site: www.paladin-press.com (17)

Palan, Dr. Kay, Haworth College of Business, Kalamazoo, MI. Tel: (616) 387-5050, FAX: (616) 387-5710, E-Mail: jessica.pelkey@wmich.edu, Web Site: www.wmich.edu/business (41)

Palange, Caitlin, Potpourri Group Inc, North Billerica, MA. Tel: (978) 256-4100, FAX: (978) 256-1961/0344, Web Site: www.potpourrigroup.com (6)

Palermo, Nicole, Harvard Business Review, Boston, MA. Tel: (617) 783-7410, FAX: (617) 783-7493, Web Site: hbr.org (17)

Palerno, Theresa, Vera Bradley, Roanoke, IN. Tel: (800) 823-8372, Web Site: www.verabradley.com (2)

Paley, William, Texwipe Co, Kernersville, NC. Tel: (201) 684-1800, (800) TEXWIPE, FAX: (201) 684-1801, E-Mail: info@texwipe.com, Web Site: www.texwipe.com (16)

Pallis, Justin, DS Graphics Inc, Lowell, MA. Tel: (978) 970-1359, E-Mail: sales@dsgraphics.com, Web Site: www.dsgraphics.com (21)

Pallottine Center for Apostolic Causes Inc/St Jude Shrine, Baltimore, MD. Tel: (410) 685-6026, (877) 278-5833, FAX: (410) 234-1459, E-Mail: info@stjudeshrine.org, Web Site: www.stjudeshrine.org (1)

Palm Coast Data LLC, Palm Coast, FL. Tel: (386) 445-4662, FAX: (386) 445-2728, Web Site: www.palmcoastd.com (28)

Palm, Joan, The Travelers Insurance Cos, Hartford, CT. Tel: (860) 277-8252, (651) 317-2685, FAX: (860) 954-7691, Web Site: www.travelers.com (15)

Palma, Roberto, American Appraisal Associates, Milwaukee, WI. Tel: (414) 271-7240, (800) 558-8650, FAX: (414) 221-7065, Web Site: www.american-appraisal.com (14)

Palmer, Andy, Nissan North America Inc, Franklin, TN. Tel: (615) 725-1000, Web Site: www.nissanusa.com (16)

Palmer, Anthony J., Kimberly-Clark Corp, Neenah, WI. Tel: (920) 721-2000, (888) 525-8388, FAX: (920) 721-7722, Web Site: www.kimberly-clark.com (16)

Palmer, Duncan, Reed Elsevier, New York, NY. Tel: (212) 309-8100, FAX: (212) 309-8187, Web Site: www.reedelsevier.com (17)

Palmer, Frank, DDB Canada, Vancouver, BC Canada. Tel: (604) 687-7911, FAX: (604) 640-4343, E-Mail: vancouver.info@ddbcanada.com, Web Site: www.ddbcanada.com (35)

Palmer, Graham, Telcordia Technologies, Piscataway, NJ. Tel: (732) 699-2000, FAX: (973) 829-2458, Web Site: www.telcordia.com (16)

Palmer, Greg, Reid Supply Co, Muskegon, MI. Tel: (231) 777-3951, (800) 253-0421, FAX: (231) 767-3882, E-Mail: mail@reidsupply.com, Web Site: www.reidsupply.com (16)

Palmer, Jim, Lowe Campbell Ewald, Detroit, MI. Tel: (586) 574-3400, E-Mail: lowecampbellewald@lowe-ce.com, Web Site: www.lowecampbellewald.com (35)

Palmer, Kate, Media Horizons Management LLC, Norwalk, CT. Tel: (203) 857-0770, FAX: (203) 857-0296, E-Mail: info@mediahorizons.com, Web Site: www.mediahorizons.com (31)

Palmer, Melissa, Butler Till Media Services, Rochester, NY. Tel: (855) 472-5100, FAX: (855) 274-5199, Web Site: www.butlertill.com (31)

Palmer, Michael, ANA/BMA National Conferences, New York, NY. Tel: (212) 697-5950, FAX: (212) 687-7310, E-Mail: info@marketing.net, Web Site: www.marketing.org (42)

Palmer, Rona, Woodwind & Brasswind Inc, Westlake Village, CA. Tel: (574) 251-3500, (800) 348-5003, FAX: (800) 266-5962, Web Site: www.wwbw.com (5)

Palmer, Shannon, Vestcom International Inc, Little Rock, AR. Tel: (501) 663-0100, (800) 264-0965, E-Mail: sales@vestcom.com, Web Site: vestcom.com (31)

Palmeri, Michael, Loews Hotels, Inc, New York, NY. Tel: (212) 521-2000, (866) 563-9792, FAX: (212) 521-2379, Web Site: www.loewshotels.com (19)

Palmore, Roderick A., The Pillsbury Co, Minneapolis, MN. Tel: (763) 764-7600, (800) 248-7310, FAX: (763) 764-8330, Web Site: www.pillsbury.com (16)

Palombo, Joe, Ventriloquist Voice Solutions International Inc, Mississauga, ON Canada. Tel: (866) 446-0860, E-Mail: info@ventriloquistsolutions.com, Web Site: www.ventriloquistsolutions.com (29)

Palozola, Nancy, Tailwinds Inc, Mill Valley, CA. Tel: (415) 380-8181, (800) TAILWIND, FAX: (415) 927-0199, E-Mail: service@tailwinds.com, Web Site: www.tailwinds.com (6)

Palzer, Tom, Wells Lamont Corp, Niles, IL. Tel: (847) 647-8200, (800) 247-3295, FAX: (847) 647-6943, Web Site: www.wellslamont.com (34)

Palzkil, Joe, Direct Tech Inc, Omaha, NE. Tel: (402) 895-2100, Web Site: www.direct-tech.com (34)

Pamperin, Theodore, American Catalog Partnerships LLC, Summit, NJ. Tel: (908) 598-1947 (20)

Pan Pacific Hotel & Resorts America, Seattle, WA. Tel: (206) 264-8111, (877) 324-4856, FAX: (206) 654-5049, Web Site: www.panpacific.com (19)

Pandit, Vikram, Citibank, New York, NY. Tel: (212) 559-9425, (800) 285-3000, FAX: (212) 527-2318, Web Site: www.citibank.com (14)

Panfili, David, Location Sound Corp, North Hollywood, CA. Tel: (818) 980-9891, (800) 228-4429, FAX: (818) 980-9911, E-Mail: information@locationsound.com, Web Site: www.locationsound.com (3)

Pang, David, Johnson Wilshire Distributors Service Corp, Santa Fe Springs, CA. Tel: (562) 777-0088, (800) 922-2456, FAX: (562) 777-0099, (800) 993-9699, E-Mail: jwigloves@aol.com, Web Site: www.johnsonwilshire.com (34)

Pangborn Design Ltd, Detroit, MI. Tel: (313) 259-3400, FAX: (313) 259-5690, E-Mail: info@pangborndesign.com, Web Site: www.pangborndesign.com (36)

Pangborn, Dominic, Pangborn Design Ltd, Detroit, MI. Tel: (313) 259-3400, FAX: (313) 259-5690, E-Mail: info@pangborndesign.com, Web Site: www.pangborndesign.com (36)

Pango Pango Swimwear Corp, Pompano Beach, FL. Tel: (954) 786-0255, (800) 858-9431, FAX: (954) 786-7745, E-Mail: pango_swimwear@bellsouth.net, Web Site: www.pango-pangoswimwear.com (2)

Panho, Jim, American Locker Security Systems Inc, Coppell, TX. Tel: (817) 329-1600, (800) 828-9118, E-Mail: info@americanlocker.com, Web Site: www.americanlocker.com (16)

Panico, Alyce, Luxe Collective Group, New York, NY. Tel: (212) 627-3300, FAX: (212) 627-3388, E-Mail: info@luxecg.com, Web Site: luxecg.com (35)

Panke, M.D.; Ph.D. Elizabeth, Genetica DNA Laboratories Inc, Cincinnati, OH. Tel: (513) 985-9777, (800) 433-6848, FAX: (513) 985-9983, Web Site: www.genetica.com (16)

Panoptic Enterprises, Burke, VA. Tel: (703) 451-5953, (800) 594-4766, FAX: (703) 451-5953, E-Mail: panoptic@fedgovcontracts.com, Web Site: www.fedgovcontracts.com (17)

Panos, Tassos, Volvo Cars of North America LLC, Northvale, NJ. Tel: (201) 768-7300, (800) 458-1552, E-Mail: customercare@volvocars.com, Web Site: www.volvocars.com (16)

Pantoja, Alberta, Armbrust Paper Tubes Inc, Chicago, IL. Tel: (773) 586-3232, FAX: (773) 586-8997, E-Mail: tubesrus@corecomm.net, Web Site: www.tubesrus.com (10)

Panzano + Partners LLC, Moorestown, NJ. Tel: (856) 866-5500, E-Mail: info@p2site.com, Web Site: panzanoandpartners.com (23)

Panzano, Michael, Panzano + Partners LLC, Moorestown, NJ. Tel: (856) 866-5500, E-Mail: info@p2site.com, Web Site: panzanoandpartners.com (35)

Paolucci, Joanne, Jacques Moret Inc, New York, NY. Tel: (212) 354-2400, FAX: (212) 354-5544, E-Mail: info@moret.com, Web Site: www.moret.com (16)

Papa John's International, Louisville, KY. Tel: (502) 261-7272, Web Site: www.papajohns.com (4)

Papa, John J., John Michaels Associates Inc, Newington, CT. Tel: (860) 666-1414, (800) 499-2606, FAX: (860) 666-1515, E-Mail: info@jmalogos.com, Web Site: www.jmalogos.com (3)

Papa, Sara, John Michaels Associates Inc, Newington, CT. Tel: (860) 666-1414, (800) 499-2606, FAX: (860) 666-1515, E-Mail: info@jmalogos.com, Web Site: www.jmalogos.com (33)

Papalia, John, Statlistics, Danbury, CT. Tel: (203) 778-8700, FAX: (203) 778-4839, E-Mail: info@statlistics.com, Web Site: www.statlistics.com (23)

Papamarcos, Ph.D. Steven D., The Peter A Tobin College of Business, Jamaica, NY. Tel: (718) 990-2600, FAX: (718) 990-1868, Web Site: www.stjohns.edu (41)

Paperweight Development Corp, Appleton, WI. Tel: (920) 734-9841, FAX: (920) 991-8796, Web Site: www.appletonideas.com (25)

Papillion Times Group, Bellevue, NE. Tel: (402) 733-7300, (877) 476-4237, FAX: (402) 537-2997, E-Mail: advertising@papilliontimes.com, Web Site: www.papilliontimes.com (31)

Pappas MacDonnell Inc, Southport, CT. Tel: (203) 254-1944, FAX: (203) 256-8232, E-Mail: info@pappasmacdonnell.com, Web Site: www.pappasmacdonnell.com (35)

Pappas, Milton, Redcats USA, New York, NY. Tel: (212) 613-9500, Web Site: www.brylane.com (2)

Pappas, William, Fosdick Fulfillment Corp, Wallingford, CT. Tel: (203) 269-0211, (800) 759-5588, FAX: (203) 679-3290, E-Mail: sales@fosdickcorp.com, Web Site: www.fosdickfulfillment.com (28)

Papsadore, Polly, LW Robbins Associates, Holliston, MA. Tel: (508) 893-0210, (800) 229-5972, FAX: (508) 893-0212, E-Mail: ppapsador@lwra.com, Web Site: www.lwra.com (31)

Papsadore, Polly, RobbinsKersten Direct, Richardson, TX. Tel: (800) 222-6070, E-Mail: connect@robbinskersten.com, Web Site: www.robbinskersten.com (1)

PAPYRUS, Fairfield, CA. Tel: (707) 428-0200, Web Site: www.papyrusonline.com (5)

Para Publishing, Santa Barbara, CA. Tel: (805) 968-7277, (800) PARAPUB, FAX: (805) 986-1379, E-Mail: danpoynter@parapublishing.com, Web Site: www.parapublishing.com (17)

Parade Publications, New York, NY. Tel: (212) 450-7000, FAX: (212) 450-7287, Web Site: www.parade.com (31)

Paradigm Promotions LLC, San Francisco, CA. Tel: (415) 387-2158, FAX: (415) 387-2185, E-Mail: brian@brianharris.com, Web Site: www.paradigmpromotions.com (35)

Paradis, Dany, Montreal Envelope Inc, Quebec, QC Canada. Tel: (514) 331-7110, (800) 655-2709, FAX: (514) 748-7322, E-Mail: ybrochu@enveloppe-montreal.com, Web Site: www.enveloppe-montreal.com (26)

Paradis, Francois, DXP Postexperts, Saint-Laurent, QC Canada. Tel: (514) 934-4545, E-Mail: info@dxp-postexperts.com, Web Site: www.postdestination.com (28)

Paradis, Judy, Crestline Specialties, Inc, Lewiston, ME. Tel: (207) 777-7075, (866) 488-4975, FAX: (207) 784-5038, E-Mail: info@crestline.com, Web Site: www.crestline.com (16)

Paradise Galleries, Laguna Hills, CA. Tel: (858) 793-4050, (800) 67-DOLLS, FAX: (949) 743-8974, E-Mail: omancinelli@paradisegalleries.com, Web Site: www.paradisegalleries.com (6)

Paradysz, Chris, PMX Agency, New York, NY. Tel: (212) 387-0300, (888) 960-0177, FAX: (212) 387-7647, E-Mail: info@pmxagency.com, Web Site: www.pmxagency.com (23)

Paragon Laboratories, Torrance, CA. Tel: (310) 370-1563, (800) 231-3670, FAX: (310) 370-7354, E-Mail: sales@paragonlabsusa.com, Web Site: www.paragonlabsusa.com (16)

Paragon Media Strategies, Denver, CO. Tel: (303) 922-5600, FAX: (303) 922-1589, E-Mail: info@paragonmediastrategies.com, Web Site: www.paragonmediastrategies.com (30)

Paragon Printing & Mailing, Austin, TX. Tel: (512) 821-0222, FAX: (512) 821-0200, E-Mail: contact@paragonprinting.com, Web Site: www.paragonprinting.com (27)

Paralyzed Veterans of America, Washington, DC. Tel: (212) 255-9078, (800) 424-8200, FAX: (202) 416-7643, E-Mail: info@pva.org, Web Site: www.pva.org (1)

Paramount Lists Inc, Erie, PA. Tel: (814) 459-8787, (800) 723-5478, FAX: (814) 459-1398, E-Mail: info@paramountlists.com, Web Site: www.paramountdirectmarketing.com (23)

Parasco, Barbara, Balducci Enterprises Inc, Germantown, MD. Tel: (240) 403-2440, FAX: (240) 403-2520 (16)

Paravano, Jeffrey H, Baker & Hostetler LLP, Washington, DC. Tel: (202) 861-1500, FAX: (202) 861-1783, E-Mail: wschweitzer@bakerlaw.com, Web Site: www.bakerlaw.com (20)

Parcel Insurance Plan Inc, Saint Louis, MO. Tel: (314) 692-0300, (800) 325-7390, FAX: (314) 692-7598, E-Mail: office@pipinsure.com, Web Site: www.pipinsure.com (15)

Pardee, Chip, Tennessee Valley Authority, Knoxville, TN. Tel: (865) 632-2101, Web Site: www.tva.gov (16)

Pardini, Kara, Crawford & Co, Atlanta, GA. Tel: (404) 300-1000, (800) 241-2541, FAX: (404) 300-1905, E-Mail: info@us.crawco.com, Web Site: us. crawfordandcompany.com (35)

Paresky, Susan S., Dana-Farber Cancer Institute, Boston, MA. Tel: (617) 632-3000, (866) 408-3324, FAX: (617) 632-4070, E-Mail: suzanne_fountain@ dfci.harvard.edu, Web Site: www.dana-farber.org (1)

Parham, John, J&P Cycles, Anamosa, IA. Tel: (319) 462-4819, (800) 318-4817, Web Site: www.j-pcycles.com (12)

Parikh, Sachin, Suntel Inc, Hamden, CT. Tel: (203) 287-9114, FAX: (203) 248-3883, E-Mail: info@ suntelinc.com, Web Site: www.suntelinc.com (22)

Paris Presents Inc, Gurnee, IL. Tel: (847) 263-5500, (800) 431-5723, FAX: (847) 263-5191, E-Mail: support@parispresents.com, Web Site: www. parispresents.com (7)

Parise Marketing Group, Millwood, NY. Tel: (914) 941-7467, FAX: (914) 941-7931, Web Site: www.parise. com (35)

James Robert Parish Consulting, Studio City, CA. Tel: (818) 753-9455, FAX: (818) 505-6509, E-Mail: jrparish@sbcglobal.net, Web Site: www. jamesrobertparish.com (20)

Parish, Danielle, James J Hill Reference Library, Saint Paul, MN. Tel: (651) 265-5500, Web Site: www. jjhill.org (1)

Parish, Glen, Virco Manufacturing Corp, Conway, AR. Tel: (501) 329-2901, (800) 448-4726, FAX: (800) 258-7367, E-Mail: info@virco.com, Web Site: www.virco.com (16)

Parish, James Robert, James Robert Parish Consulting, Studio City, CA. Tel: (818) 753-9455, FAX: (818) 505-6509, E-Mail: jrparish@sbcglobal.net, Web Site: www.jamesrobertparish.com (20)

Parisien, Maurice R., Direct Marketing Association of Saint Louis, Washington, MO. Tel: (866) 516-0121, FAX: (636) 239-2324, E-Mail: mparisien@mac. com, Web Site: www.dmastl.org (40)

George W Park Seed Co Inc, Hodges, SC. Tel: (864) 330-2003, (800) 845-3369, E-Mail: info@parkseed. com, Web Site: www.parkseed.com (8)

Park, Ernest, Select Comfort Corp, Minneapolis, MN. Tel: (763) 551-7000, (888) 411-2188, FAX: (763) 551-7826, Web Site: www.selectcomfort.com (16)

Park, Hunter, Jobscope Corp, Greenville, SC. Tel: (864) 458-3143, (800) 443-5794, FAX: (864) 234-4852, E-Mail: marketing@jobscope.com, Web Site: www. jobscope.com (16)

Parke, Sean, List Source Direct, Delray Beach, FL. Tel: (561) 570-1287, E-Mail: info@listsourcedirect.com, Web Site: www.listsourcedirect.com (23)

Parke-Bell, Carla, Touch of Class Catalog, Huntingburg, IN. Tel: (800) 457-7456, FAX: (812) 683-5921, E-Mail: customerservice@touchofclass.com, Web Site: www.touchofclass.com (8)

Parker Boiler Co, Los Angeles, CA. Tel: (323) 727-9800, FAX: (323) 722-2848, E-Mail: mleeming@ parkerboiler.com, Web Site: www.parkerboiler.com (34)

Parker Hannifin Corp, Cleveland, OH. Tel: (216) 896-2490, Web Site: www.parker.com (9)

Parker Software, Orlando, FL. Tel: (800) 680-7712, Web Site: www.parker-software.com (22)

Parker Steel Co, Toledo, OH. Tel: (419) 473-2481, (800) 333-4140, FAX: (419) 471-2655, Web Site: www.metricmetal.com (16)

Parker Systems Inc, Chesapeake, VA. Tel: (757) 485-2955, (866) 472-7537, FAX: (757) 487-5872, E-Mail: info@parkersystemsinc.com, Web Site: www.parkersystemsinc.com (16)

Parker, Cyrus, Power & Telephone Supply, Randolph, VT. Tel: (800) 451-4381, FAX: (802) 234-5006, E-Mail: cablesales@ptsupply.com, Web Site: www. ptsupply.com/enterprise (16)

Parker, Elissa, Environmental Law Institute, Washington, DC. Tel: (202) 939-3800, FAX: (202) 939-3868, E-Mail: law@eli.org, Web Site: www.eli.org (17)

Parker, Elizabeth, Caribe Direct Inc, San Juan, PR. Tel: (787) 722-5188, FAX: (787) 723-6165, E-Mail: islaonline@prw.net, Web Site: www.islaonline.com (6)

Parker, Ellen, Parker Systems Inc, Chesapeake, VA. Tel: (757) 485-2955, (866) 472-7537, FAX: (757) 487-5872, E-Mail: info@parkersystemsinc.com, Web Site: www.parkersystemsinc.com (16)

Parker, Guy, USA/DIRECT Inc, Stockholm, NJ. Tel: (973) 222-3800, FAX: (973) 823-8223, E-Mail: gparker@usadirectinc.com, Web Site: www. usadirectinc.com (30)

Parker, J. Scotty, Xpressdocs, Fort Worth, TX. Tel: (817) 870-4601, (866) 977-3627, FAX: (817) 870-1205, Web Site: www.xpressdocs.com (27)

Parker, Jamie, WGBH Educational Foundation, Brighton, MA. Tel: (617) 300-2000, FAX: (617) 300-1026, Web Site: www.wgbh.org (1)

Parker, John, Parker Systems Inc, Chesapeake, VA. Tel: (757) 485-2955, (866) 472-7537, FAX: (757) 487-5872, E-Mail: info@parkersystemsinc.com, Web Site: www.parkersystemsinc.com (16)

Parker, Julia, Parker Software, Orlando, FL. Tel: (800) 680-7712, Web Site: www.parker-software.com (22)

Parker, Mark, Nike Inc, Beaverton, OR. Tel: (503) 671-4565, (800) 344-6543, FAX: (503) 671-6300, Web Site: www.nike.com (2)

Parker, Michael, ITW Vortec, Cincinnati, OH. Tel: (513) 891-7474, (800) 441-7475, FAX: (513) 891-4092, E-Mail: techsupport@vortec.com, Web Site: www.vortec.com (16)

Parker, Raymond, Scan Optics Inc, Manchester, CT. Tel: (860) 645-7878, (800) 745-6001, FAX: (860) 645-7995, E-Mail: info@scanoptics.com, Web Site: www.scanoptics.com (16)

Parker, Rebecca. The Honey Agency, Sacramento, CA. Tel: (916) 444-0203, E-Mail: buzz@honeyagency. com, Web Site: honeyagency.com (35)

Parker, Stephen, Parker Software, Orlando, FL. Tel: (800) 680-7712, Web Site: www.parker-software. com (22)

Parker, Tim, American Tourister, Mansfield, MA. Tel: (800) 765-2247, Web Site: www.americantourister. com (12)

Parker, Tim, Classic Motorbooks Inc, Minneapolis, MN. Tel: (715) 294-3345, (800) 826-6600, FAX: (715) 294-4448, Web Site: www.motorbooks.com (17)

Parker, Timothy Charles, Samsonite International SA, Mansfield, MA. Tel: (508) 851-1400, (800) 547-BAGS, FAX: (303) 373-8715, Web Site: www. samsonite.com (16)

Parker, W Douglas, American Airlines, Fort Worth, TX. Tel: (817) 963-1234 (12)

Parker, William Douglas, American Airlines Inc, Fort Worth, TX. Tel: (817) 963-1234, FAX: (817) 967-2841, Web Site: www.aa.com (19)

Parkhill, Karen L., Comerica Inc, Dallas, TX. Tel: (800) 521-1190, FAX: (925) 941-1999, Web Site: www. comerica.com (14)

Parkinson, Carol, Naval Institute Press, Annapolis, MD. Tel: (410) 268-6110, (800) 233-8764, FAX: (410) 571-1703, E-Mail: webmaster@usni.org, Web Site: www.usni.org/navalinstitutepress (17)

Parkinson, Ron, JLS Mailing Services Inc, Brockton, MA. Tel: (508) 313-1050, (866) JLS-MAIL, FAX: (508) 313-1093, E-Mail: rparkinson@jlsms.com, Web Site: www.jlsms.com (28)

Parkinson's Disease Foundation, New York, NY. Tel: (212) 923-4700, (800) 457-6676, FAX: (212) 923-4778, E-Mail: info@pdf.org, Web Site: www.pdf. org (1)

Parks, Ben, General Physics Corp, Elkridge, MD. Tel: (410) 379-3600, (800) 727-6677, FAX: (410) 540-5302, E-Mail: info@gpworldwide.com, Web Site: www.gpworldwide.com (16)

Parks, Bob, Sport Supply Group, Dallas, TX. Tel: (972) 484-9484, FAX: (972) 247-0650, Web Site: www. sportsupplygroup.com (11)

Parks, David, Camellia Forest Nursery, Chapel Hill, NC. Tel: (919) 968-0504, FAX: (919) 929-8971, E-Mail: camelliaforest@gmail.com, Web Site: www.camforest.com (8)

Parks, Dennis, Texas Refinery Corp, Fort Worth, TX. Tel: (817) 332-1161, FAX: (817) 336-8441, E-Mail: jhopkins@texasrefinery.com, Web Site: www. texasrefinery.com (9)

Parks, Jason, Barkley, Kansas City, MO. Tel: (816) 842-1500, E-Mail: 411@barkleyus.com, Web Site: www.barkleyus.com (35)

Parks, Jim, Crain Communications Inc, Detroit, MI. Tel: (313) 446-6000, FAX: (313) 446-1616, Web Site: www.crain.com (17)

Parks, Kai-Mei, Camellia Forest Nursery, Chapel Hill, NC. Tel: (919) 968-0504, FAX: (919) 929-8971, E-Mail: camelliaforest@gmail.com, Web Site: www.camforest.com (8)

Parks, Kathy, IHFRA, High Point, NC. Tel: (336) 889-3920, FAX: (336) 464-2125, E-Mail: ihfra@ihfra. org, Web Site: www.ihfra.org (1)

Parks, Ken, Gates Corp, Denver, CO. Tel: (303) 744-1911, FAX: (303) 744-4000, Web Site: www.gates. com (9)

Parks, Kenneth, DigitasLBi, Boston, MA. Tel: (617) 867-1000, E-Mail: newbusiness@digitas.com, Web Site: www.digitaslbi.com (35)

Parks, Kent, Nasco, Fort Atkinson, WI. Tel: (920) 563-2446, (800) 558-9595, FAX: (920) 563-8296, E-Mail: info@nasco.com, Web Site: www.enasco. com (5)

Parlay International, Walnut Creek, CA. Tel: (510) 601-1000, FAX: (510) 601-1008, E-Mail: info@parlay. com, Web Site: www.parlay.com (17)

Parmelee Associates, Arlington, VA. Tel: (703) 502-0161, E-Mail: jtparmlee@aol.com (35)

Parmelee, James, Parmelee Associates, Arlington, VA. Tel: (703) 502-0161, E-Mail: jtparmlee@aol.com (35)

Parmer Books, San Diego, CA. Tel: (619) 287-0693, E-Mail: parmerbook@aol.com, Web Site: www. parmerbook.com (6)

Parmer, Jean Marie, Parmer Books, San Diego, CA. Tel: (619) 287-0693, E-Mail: parmerbook@aol.com, Web Site: www.parmerbook.com (6)

Parnell, Bill, Datalogic Scanning, Eugene, OR. Tel: (800) 695-5700, FAX: (541) 345-7140, Web Site: www.scanning.datalogic.com (34)

Parr, Steve, Prime Media Equine Group, Gaithersburg, MD. Tel: (301) 977-3900, FAX: (301) 990-9015, Web Site: www.equisearch.com (17)

Parrett, William G., Deloitte & Touche, Boston, MA. Tel: (617) 437-2000, FAX: (617) 437-2111, Web Site: www.deloitte.com (14)

Parrini, Dante C., Glatfelter, York, PA. Tel: (717) 225-4711, (866) 744-7380, FAX: (717) 225-6834, E-Mail: info@glatfelter.com, Web Site: www.glatfelter.com (25)

Parrish, J., Perfection Tip Co/Camping Products Co, Long Beach, CA. Tel: (562) 491-0076, (800) 525-4835, FAX: (562) 435-7599 (16)

Parrish, Selina, Kentucky Bankers Association, Louisville, KY. Tel: (502) 582-2453, FAX: (502) 584-6390, Web Site: www.kybanks.com (1)

Parrott, Bob, Jobscope Corp, Greenville, SC. Tel: (864) 458-3143, (800) 443-5794, FAX: (864) 234-4852, E-Mail: marketing@jobscope.com, Web Site: www.jobscope.com (16)

Parrott, Christina, American Family Insurance Group, Madison, WI. Tel: (608) 249-2111, FAX: (608) 243-6525, E-Mail: akin1@amfam.com, Web Site: www.amfam.com (15)

Parry, David T., Academic Travel Abroad Inc, Washington, DC. Tel: (202) 785-9000, (800) 556-7896, FAX: (202) 342-0317, Web Site: www.academictravel.com (19)

Parry, Jim, Stephan Partners Inc, New York, NY. Tel: (212) 524-8583, E-Mail: george@stephenpartners.com, Web Site: www.stephanpartners.com (35)

Parry, Tim, Multichannel Merchant Magazine, Stamford, CT. Tel: (203) 358-4386, FAX: (203) 358-5823, E-Mail: melissa.dowling@penton.com, Web Site: www.multichannelmerchant.com (31)

Mary Anne Parshall Consulting Inc, Camarillo, CA. Tel: (805) 445-7522, FAX: (805) 445-8876 (20)

Parshall, Mary Ann, Mary Anne Parshall Consulting Inc, Camarillo, CA. Tel: (805) 445-7522, FAX: (805) 445-8876 (20)

Parsons School of Design Human Resource Dept, New York, NY. Tel: (212) 229-5671, FAX: (212) 229-8975, E-Mail: communications@newschool.edu, Web Site: www.newschool.edu/parsons/ (41)

Parsons, Joe, The Economist Newspaper NA Inc, New York, NY. Tel: (212) 554-0600, FAX: (212) 586-1191, Web Site: www.economist.com (17)

Partain, Kathy, Military Officers Association of America, Alexandria, VA. Tel: (703) 549-2311, (800) 234-6622, E-Mail: msc@moaa.org, Web Site: www.moaa.org (1)

PartnerData LLC, Evanston, IL. Tel: (847) 733-0819 (30)

Partners for Incentives, Cleveland, OH. Tel: (800) 292-7371, Web Site: www.pfi-awards.com (33)

Partners Health, Philadelphia, PA. Tel: (215) 849-9600, (800) 553-0784, E-Mail: sroberts@healthpart.com, Web Site: www.healthpart.com (15)

Partners Marketing Inc, Saint Charles, IL. Tel: (630) 524-9901, FAX: (630) 524-9909, E-Mail: georgeb@partnersmarketing.com, Web Site: www.partnersmarketing.com (22)

Partners Village Store, Westport, MA. Tel: (508) 636-2572, FAX: (508) 636-2529, E-Mail: info@partnersvillagestore.com, Web Site: www.partnersvillagestore.com (11)

Parts Express, Springboro, OH. Tel: (937) 743-3000, (800) 338-0531, FAX: (937) 743-1677, E-Mail: sales@parts-express.com, Web Site: www.partsexpress.com (3)

Parts Place Inc, Warren, MI. Tel: (248) 373-2300, (888) 432-3548, FAX: (248) 373-5950, Web Site: www.partsplaceinc.com (12)

Party Kits & Equestrian Gifts, Louisville, KY. Tel: (502) 425-2126, (800) 99-DERBY, FAX: (502) 425-5230, E-Mail: info@partykits.com, Web Site: www.derbygifts.com (6)

PartyLite Gifts Inc, Norwell, MA. Tel: (508) 830-3100, (888)999-5706, FAX: (508) 830-0026, E-Mail: infona@partylite.com, Web Site: www.partylite.com (8)

Paruzynski, Dan, C&H Distributors LLC, Milwaukee, WI. Tel: (414) 443-1700, (888) 316-2223, FAX: (414) 443-9213, E-Mail: customerservice@chdist.com, Web Site: www.chdist.com (9)

Parvin, Pat, Wells Mailing, Montgomery, AL. Tel: (334) 286-4667, FAX: (334) 286-6008, E-Mail: info@wellsprinting.com, Web Site: www.wellsprinting.com (28)

Pasadena Advertising Marketing & Design, Pasadena, CA. Tel: (626) 584-0011, FAX: (626) 584-0907, Web Site: www.pasadenaadv.com (35)

Pascarelli, John G., Mediacom Communications Corp, Chester, NY. Tel: (855) 633-4226, FAX: (845) 698-4100, Web Site: www.mediacomcable.com (32)

Pasckvale, Alexandria, OSG Billing, Englewood, NJ. Tel: (201) 871-1100, Web Site: www.osgbilling.com (20)

Pascoe, Eric, Bell & Howell Ltd, North York, ON Canada. Tel: (416) 746-2200, FAX: (416) 228-2439, Web Site: www.bellhowell.com (9)

Pascoe, Michelle, Warnaco Swimwear Inc, Los Angeles, CA. Tel: (323) 726-1262, FAX: (323) 724-6931, Web Site: www.speedo.com (16)

Pashia, Gale, The Service Center LTD, Houston, TX. Tel: (713) 690-8175, FAX: (713) 690-6844, Web Site: www.calltsc.com (28)

Pashko, Sue, Envision, Newport, RI. Tel: (401) 619-1500, (800) 524-8238, FAX: (401) 619-0130, E-Mail: envision@att.net, Web Site: www.envisionstock.com (38)

Paslode, Vernon Hills, IL. Tel: (847) 634-1900, (800) 222-6990, FAX: (847) 634-6602, E-Mail: tech@paslode.com, Web Site: www.paslode.com (16)

Paslov, Eugene T., Harcourt Educational Measurement, San Antonio, TX. Tel: (210) 299-1061, (800) 211-8378, FAX: (800) 232-1223, Web Site: www.harcourtassessment.com (17)

Passoff, Alissa, McGaw Graphics, Manchester Center, VT. Tel: (845) 353-8600, (888) 4BMCGAW, FAX: (845) 353-3155, E-Mail: sales@bmcgaw.com, Web Site: www.bmcgaw.com (6)

Passon, Gary, Network Telephone Services Inc, Woodland Hills, CA. Tel: (818) 992-4300, (800) 727-6874, FAX: (818) 992-8415, Web Site: www.nts.net (16)

Pasternack Enterprises Inc, Irvine, CA. Tel: (949) 261-1920, Web Site: www.pasternack.com (16)

Pastime Publications Inc, Denver, CO. Tel: (303) 534-7867, (888) 650-8665, FAX: (630) 214-7600, E-Mail: post@pastimecompany.com, Web Site: www.pastimecompany.com (17)

Paszkiewic, Elizabeth, StatSoft Inc, Tulsa, OK. Tel: (918) 749-1119, FAX: (918) 749-2217, E-Mail: info@statsoft.com, Web Site: www.statsoft.com (9)

Patagonia, Ventura, CA. Tel: (805) 643-8616, (800) 638-6464, E-Mail: customer_service@patagonia.com, Web Site: www.patagonia.com (2)

Patagonia Mail Order Inc, Reno, NV. Tel: (775) 747-1992, (800) 638-6464, FAX: (775) 747-6159, Web Site: www.patagonia.com (2)

Pate Sr, Ronald O., VF Imagewear, Greensboro. NC. Tel: (336) 424-6000, (800) 733-5271, Web Site: www.vfimagewear.com (2)

Pate, A Mac, Texas Refinery Corp, Fort Worth, TX. Tel: (817) 332-1161, FAX: (817) 336-8441, E-Mail: jhopkins@texasrefinery.com, Web Site: www.texasrefinery.com (9)

Pate, Chris, Texas Refinery Corp, Fort Worth, TX. Tel: (817) 332-1161, FAX: (817) 336-8441, E-Mail: jhopkins@texasrefinery.com, Web Site: www.texasrefinery.com (9)

Patel, Nalin, Key West Aloe Holdings LLC, Fort Lauderdale, FL. Tel: (305) 883-3166, FAX: (305) 883-3185, Web Site: www.keywestaloe.com (16)

Patel, Nihar, Toyota Motor Sales USA Inc, Torrance, CA. Tel: (310) 468-4000, (800) 331-4331, FAX: (310) 468-7841, Web Site: www.toyota.com (16)

Patella, Tony, Prudent Publishing Co, Ridgefield Park, NJ. Tel: (201) 641-7900, FAX: (800) 772-1144 (16)

Patenaude, Jason, The Cricket Magazine Group, Chicago, IL. Tel: (603) 924-7209, (800) 821-0115, FAX: (815) 224-6615, E-Mail: customerservice@caruspub.com, Web Site: www.cricketmag.com (17)

Paternoster, Scott J., Chief Media LLC, New York, NY. Tel: (212) 300-8487, FAX: (212) 629-9505, E-Mail: info@chiefmedia.com, Web Site: www.chiefmedia.com (35)

Paterson, David J., Bowater America Inc, Greenville, SC. Tel: (864) 271-7733, (800) 921-3244, FAX: (864) 282-9320, E-Mail: hrsc@abitibibowater.com, Web Site: www.bowater.com (25)

Paterson, David J., Verso Paper, Memphis, TN. Tel: (901) 369-4100, FAX: (901) 369-4174, Web Site: www.versopaper.com (25)

Paterson, Jill, Allianz Life Insurance Co of North America, Minneapolis, MN. Tel: (763) 765-6500, (800) 950-5872, Web Site: www.allianzlife.com (15)

Path to Purchase Institute, Chicago, IL. Tel: (847) 675-7400, Web Site: www.p2pi.org (17)

Patient News, Niagara Falls, NY. Tel: (705) 457-4030, (800) 667-0268, FAX: (705) 457-4067, E-Mail: jbishop@patientnews.com, Web Site: www.patientnews.com (17)

Patmore, Kimberly S., First Data Merchant Services, Atlanta, GA. Tel: (404) 890-2000, FAX: (303) 967-5188, Web Site: www.firstdata.com (14)

Patneau, John, Graphic Communications Holdings Inc, Hudson, OH. Tel: (330) 650-5522, FAX: (330) 650-8998, E-Mail: info@graphiccommunications.com, Web Site: www.graphiccommunications.com (25)

Patota, Anne, Guilford Publications Inc, New York, NY. Tel: (212) 431-9800, (800) 365-7006, FAX: (212) 966-6708, E-Mail: info@guilford.com, Web Site: www.guilford.com (17)

Patrick, Barbara, Tax Management Inc, Bethesda, MD. Tel: (202) 452-4200, FAX: (202) 496-6013 (17)

Patrick, Kevin, Array Marketing Group Inc, Toronto, ON Canada. Tel: (416) 299-4865, FAX: (416) 292-9759, E-Mail: inquiry@arraymarketing.com, Web Site: arraymarketing.com (35)

Patrick, Kristin, Playboy Enterprises Inc, Beverly Hills, CA. Tel: (310) 860-1215, Web Site: www.playboyenterprises.com (17)

Patrickson, Clive. Laerdal Medical, Wappingers Falls, NY. Tel: (845) 297-7770, FAX: (800) 227-1143, Web Site: www.laerdal.com (34)

Patrios, Jeff, Thomson West, Eagan, MN. Tel: (651) 687-7000, (800) 328-9378, FAX: (651) 687-7849, E-Mail: jeff.patrios@thomsonreuters.com, Web Site: www.thomson.com (17)

Patriot Communications LLC, West Hollywood, CA. Tel: (888) 833-4711, FAX: (310) 482-6701, E-Mail: dlivingston@patriotllc.com, Web Site: patriotllc.com (32)

Patsuno, Paul, Invacare Supply Group, Milford, MA. Tel: (508) 429-1000, (800) 225-4792, FAX: (508) 429-1581, E-Mail: service.isg@invacare.com, Web Site: www.invacaresupplygroup.com (16)

Pattern, Kathleen, American Target Advertising Inc, Manassas, VA. Tel: (703) 392-7676, FAX: (703) 392-7654, E-Mail: info@americantarget.com, Web Site: americantarget.com (35)

Patterson Dental, Saint Paul, MN. Tel: (651) 686-1600, (800) 328-5536, FAX: (651) 686-9331, Web Site: www.pattersondental.com (10)

Patterson, Herbert, The Durham Manufacturing Co, Durham, CT. Tel: (860) 349-3427, (800) 243-3774, FAX: (860) 349-8572, (800) 782-5499, E-Mail: info@durhammfg.com, Web Site: www.durhammfg.com (16)

Patterson, James F., Nationwide Mutual Insurance Co, Columbus, OH. Tel: (614) 249-7111, (800) 882-2822, FAX: (614) 854-3676, Web Site: www.nationwide.com (15)

Patterson, Judith, TABcom, Hazleton, PA. Tel: (570) 384-5555, (800) 738-7877, FAX: (570) 384-2500, E-Mail: customerservice@petsupplies.com, Web Site: www.petsupplies.com (5)

Patterson, Pat, ColorTree of Virginia Inc, Richmond, VA. Tel: (804) 358-4245, FAX: (804) 358-0488, Web Site: www.colortree.com (26)

Patterson, R., Thomas Scientific, Swedesboro, NJ. Tel: (856) 467-2000, (800) 345-2100, FAX: (856) 467-3087, E-Mail: value@thomassci.com, Web Site: www.thomassci.com (9)

Patterson, Richard, The Durham Manufacturing Co, Durham, CT. Tel: (860) 349-3427, (800) 243-3774, FAX: (860) 349-8572, (800) 782-5499, E-Mail: info@durhammfg.com, Web Site: www.durhammfg.com (16)

Patterson, Steve, Trends International LLC, Indianapolis, IN. Tel: (317) 388-1212, (800) 354-4639, FAX: (317) 388-1414, E-Mail: info@trendsinternational.com, Web Site: www.trendsinternational.com (38)

Patterson, Stuart, Nuance Speech Solutions, Burlington, MA. Tel: (781) 565-5000, FAX: (781) 565-5001, E-Mail: sales@speechworks.com, Web Site: www.nuance.com (16)

Patterson, William, Demand Telemarketing Inc, Grosse Pointe, MI. Tel: (313) 823-8598, (888) 977-2256, FAX: (313) 823-8598, E-Mail: info@create-demand.com, Web Site: www.create-demand.com (29)

Patton, David, Brahmin Leather Works, Fairhaven, MA. Tel: (508) 994-4000, (800) 229-2428, FAX: (508) 994-4153, Web Site: www.brahminusa.com (16)

Patton, Lewis, UMI Publications Inc, Charlotte, NC. Tel: (800) 747-9287, FAX: (704) 374-0729, E-Mail: info@umipub.com, Web Site: www.umipub.com (17)

Patzer, Dave, The Scan Group Inc, Waukesha, WI. Tel: (262) 521-1365, FAX: (262) 521-3265, Web Site: www.scangroup.net (35)

Patzer, Gordon, Walter E Heller College of Business Administration, Chicago, IL. Tel: (312) 281-3293, FAX: (312) 281-3290, Web Site: www.roosevelt.edu (41)

Paul Chevannes, Brooklyn, NY. Tel: (718) 788-3550 (36)

Paul, Hastings, Janofsky & Walker LLP, New York, NY. Tel: (212) 318-6037, FAX: (212) 319-4090, E-Mail: robertsherman@paulhastings.com, Web Site: www.paulhastings.com (20)

Paul, Amy, HSP Direct, Ashburn, VA. Tel: (703) 793-3220, FAX: (703) 723-5405, E-Mail: info@hspdirect.com, Web Site: www.hspdirect.com (1)

Paul, Carl F., Golfsmith International Inc, Austin, TX. Tel: (512) 821-4050, (800) 813-6897, FAX: (512) 837-9347, E-Mail: comments@golfsmith.com, Web Site: www.golfsmith.com (11)

Paul, Christopher S., Fiddler's Rock Communications Inc, McLean, VA. Tel: (703) 406-1500, E-Mail: customerservice@frcmktg.com, Web Site: www.frcmarketing.com (33)

Paul, Frank C., Golfsmith International Inc, Austin, TX. Tel: (512) 821-4050, (800) 813-6897, FAX: (512) 837-9347, E-Mail: comments@golfsmith.com, Web Site: www.golfsmith.com (11)

Paul, John, AAA Southern New England, Providence, RI. Tel: (401) 868-2045, FAX: (401) 868-2088, Web Site: www.aaa.com (1)

Pauley, Dana, Trumble Greetings, Boulder, CO. Tel: (800) 525-0656, FAX: (303) 530-5124, E-Mail: info@leanintree.com, Web Site: www.leanintree.com (6)

Pauley, Jim, National Fire Protection Association, Quincy, MA. Tel: (617) 770-3000, FAX: (617) 770-0700, Web Site: www.nfpa.org (1)

Paulino, Frank, Official Offset Corp, Amityville, NY. Tel: (631) 957-8500, Web Site: www.officialoffset.com (27)

Paullin, James, Selling Solutions Inc, Atlanta, GA. Tel: (404) 261-4966, FAX: (404) 264-1767, E-Mail: information@selsol.com, Web Site: www.selsol.com (35)

Paullin, William, Selling Solutions Inc, Atlanta, GA. Tel: (404) 261-4966, FAX: (404) 264-1767, E-Mail: information@selsol.com, Web Site: www.selsol.com (35)

Paulson, Tim, Augsburg Fortress Publishers, Minneapolis, MN. Tel: (612) 330-3300, (800) 426-0115, FAX: (612) 330-3455, E-Mail: info@augsburgfortress.org, Web Site: www.augsburgfortress.org (17)

Paulus, Alan, Global Computer Corp, Port Jefferson, NY. Tel: (516) 625-4300, (888) 845-6225, FAX: (516) 625-4072, Web Site: www.globalcomputer.com (3)

Paulus, Holly, Nexxa Group Inc, Fort Myers, FL. Tel: (239) 225-1516, (800) 566-1217, E-Mail: info@nexxagroup.com, Web Site: www.nexxagroup.com (23)

Paupore, Daniel, Kingsley North Inc, Norway, MI. Tel: (906) 563-9228, (800) 338-9280, FAX: (906) 563-7143, E-Mail: sales@kingsleynorth.com, Web Site: www.kingsleynorth.com (11)

Paupore, Mark, Kingsley North Inc, Norway, MI. Tel: (906) 563-9228, (800) 338-9280, FAX: (906) 563-7143, E-Mail: sales@kingsleynorth.com, Web Site: www.kingsleynorth.com (11)

Pavely, Richard W., CMMC Market Research, Mount Freedom, NJ. Tel: (973) 989-0229, FAX: (973) 366-1185, E-Mail: dmmp@cmmcinc.com, Web Site: www.cmmcinc.com (30)

Pavlish, Michael, Profit Boosters Copywriting, Aurora, OH. Tel: (330) 963-0330, FAX: (330) 562-2446, E-Mail: mikepavlish@profitboosterscopy.com, Web Site: www.profitboosterscopy.com (39)

Pavloff, Susan, Coverdell & Co Inc, Chicago, IL. Tel: (404) 881-2227, (800) 992-2196, FAX: (404) 881-2222, Web Site: www.coverdell.com (15)

Pavona, Jason, Litle & Co, Lowell, MA. Tel: (978) 275-6500, (800) 548-5326, FAX: (978) 937-7250, Web Site: www.litle.com (14)

Paxton, Valerie, Insight Direct Inc, Tempe, AZ. Tel: (480) 333-3001, (800) 467-4448, FAX: (480) 902-1180, Web Site: www.insight.com (16)

Payless ShoeSource Inc, Topeka, KS. Tel: (785) 233-5171, (877) 474-6379, E-Mail: customerservice@csr.payless.com, Web Site: www.payless.com (2)

Paylor, Craig, JLG Industries Inc, McConnellsburg, PA. Tel: (717) 485-5161, (877) JLG-SELL, FAX: (717) 485-6417, E-Mail: comments@jlg.com, Web Site: www.jlg.com (16)

Paymentech, Salem, NH. Tel: (603) 896-6000, FAX: (603) 896-8717, Web Site: www.paymentech.com (14)

Payne, Howard L., Marketshare Publications Inc, Overland Park, KS. Tel: (877) 880-8068, FAX: (913) 217-2895, Web Site: www.marketsharegroup.com (17)

Payne, Jillian, Media Resource Group Inc, Mount Kisco, NY. Tel: (914) 244-4250, FAX: (914) 244-4458, Web Site: www.mrginc.com (31)

Payne, Kim, RentPath LLC, Norcross, GA. Tel: (678) 421-3000, (800) 216-1423, Web Site: www.primedia.com (31)

Payne, Stuart, Saatchi & Saatchi Canada, Toronto, ON Canada. Tel: (416) 359-9595, FAX: (416) 866-4111, Web Site: saatchi.ca (21)

PayPal Inc, San Jose, CA. Tel: (402) 935-2050, Web Site: www.paypal.com (14)

Payton, Billy, Brierley & Partners, Dallas, TX. Tel: (214) 760-8700, FAX: (214) 743-5511, E-Mail: bpayton@brierley.com, Web Site: www.brierley.com (35)

Pazderski, Richard, Bland Farms, Glennville, GA. Tel: (912) 654-1300, Web Site: www.blandfarms.com (4)

Peace, Sir John, Burberry, New York, NY. Tel: (877) 217-4085, E-Mail: us.customerservice@burberry.com, Web Site: www.burberry.com (2)

Peachtree Data Inc, Duluth, GA. Tel: (678) 987-4600, Web Site: www.peachtreedata.com (22)

Peacock, III William M., Cleveland Clinic Foundation, Cleveland, OH. Tel: (216) 444-2200, Web Site: www.clevelandclinic.org (1)

Peacock, Ken, Forestry Suppliers Inc, Jackson, MS. Tel: (601) 354-3565, (800) 647-5368, FAX: (601) 292-0165, E-Mail: fsi@forestry-suppliers.com, Web Site: www.forestry-suppliers.com (9)

Peak Computer Systems, Belleville, IL. Tel: (618) 398-5612, E-Mail: info@peaknet.net, Web Site: www.peaknet.net (22)

Peak Impact Inc, Ottawa, ON Canada. Tel: (613) 592-3100, E-Mail: customerservice@peakimpact.com, Web Site: www.peakimpact.com (14)

Pearce, Cody, Nelson Schmidt Inc, Milwaukee, WI. Tel: (414) 224-0210, FAX: (414) 224-9463, Web Site: nelsonschmidt.com (35)

Pearce, Walter, KCI Communications Inc, Falls Church, VA. Tel: (703) 394-4931, FAX: (703) 905-8100, Web Site: www.kci-com.com (17)

Pearl Insurance Group LLC, Peoria Heights, IL. Tel: (309) 688-9000, Web Site: www.pearlinsurance.com (15)

Pearl River Graphics Printing, Choctaw, MS. Tel: (601) 656-3636, FAX: (601) 650-3961, E-Mail: prgp@pearlriverprinting.com, Web Site: pearlriverprinting.com (27)

Pearl, Leilani, National Parkinson Foundation, Miami, FL. Tel: (305) 243-6666, (800) 937-4545, FAX: (305) 243-6073, E-Mail: contact@parkinson.org, Web Site: www.parkinson.org (1)

Pearl, Ron, TMP Direct, Budd Lake, NJ. Tel: (973) 347-9400, (800) 328-2439, FAX: (973) 347-8773, E-Mail: ron.pearl@tmpwdirect.com, Web Site: www.tmpwdirect.com (29)

Pearlman, Deborah E., DKP & Associates, Inc, Skokie, IL. Tel: (847) 933-9808, FAX: (847) 933-9821, E-Mail: dpearlman@dkpassociates.com, Web Site: www.dkpassociates.com (22)

Pearlstein, Mark, DoubleVerify, New York, NY. Tel: (212) 631-2111, Web Site: www.doubleverify.com (9)

Pearson Education, Upper Saddle River, NJ. Tel: (201) 236-7000, FAX: (201) 236-3290, Web Site: www.pearsoned.com (17)

Pearson VUE, Bloomington, MN. Tel: (952) 681-3000, Web Site: home.pearsonvue.com (17)

Pearson, Anita, OMP, Washington, DC. Tel: (202) 467-0048, Web Site: www.ompdirect.com (1)

Pearson, Bryan A., LoyaltyOne, Toronto, ON Canada. Tel: (416) 228-6500, Web Site: www.loyalty.com; www.airmiles.ca (22)

Pearson, David, Lahey Clinic, Burlington, MA. Tel: (781) 744-5100, Web Site: www.lahey.org (1)

Pearson, David, Vonage, Holmdel, NJ. Tel: (732) 528-2600, Web Site: www.vonage.com (32)

Pearson, Harry, NextScreen LLC, Austin, TX. Tel: (512) 892-8682, Web Site: www.avguide.com (17)

Pearson, Sylvia, L & E Meridian, Springfield, VA. Tel: (703) 913-0300, (800) 555-1556, FAX: (703) 913-7052, E-Mail: estimating@l-e.com, Web Site: www.l-e.com (21)

Pease, Alan, The Country Bed Shop, Ashby, MA. Tel: (978) 386-7550, FAX: (978) 386-7263, E-Mail: alan@countrybed.com, Web Site: www.countrybed.com (16)

Pease, John, Global Specialties, Wallingford, CT. Tel: (203) 272-3285, FAX: (203) 272-4330, Web Site: www.globalspecialties.com (16)

Pecan Producers International, Corsicana, TX. Tel: (903) 872-1337, (800) 732-2648, FAX: (903) 874-7143 (4)

Peck Rock Associates, Warren, RI. Tel: (401) 289-3757, FAX: (401) 289-3759, E-Mail: pra@aol.com, Web Site: www.peckrock.com (33)

Peck, James M., Trans Union Corp, Chicago, IL. Tel: (312) 985-2000, Web Site: www.transunion.com (14)

Peck, Thomas H., US News & World Report, Washington, DC. Tel: (202) 955-2000, Web Site: www.usnews.com (17)

Pecker, David, National Enquirer, New York, NY. Tel: (212) 545-4800, Web Site: www.nationalenquirer.com (17)

Peckham, Suzanne, Prakken Publications Inc, Ann Arbor, MI. Tel: (734) 975-2800, (800) 530-9673, FAX: (734) 975-2787, Web Site: www.techdirections.com; www.eddigest.com (17)

Pectol, Don, Emergency Essentials Inc, Orem, UT. Tel: (801) 222-9596, FAX: (801) 222-9598, E-Mail: webmaster@beprepared.com, Web Site: www.beprepared.com (16)

Peczeli, Mary, Clients & Profits Worldwide, Oceanside, CA. Tel: (760) 945-4334, Web Site: www.clientsandprofits.com (14)

Peddicord, Kathleen, AGORA Inc, Baltimore, MD. Tel: (410) 783-8499, FAX: (410) 783-8414, E-Mail: csteam@agorapublishinggroup.com, Web Site: www.agora-inc.com (17)

Pedersen, Amy, Morgan Kaufmann Publishers Inc, Burlington, MA. Tel: (781) 313-4700, E-Mail: order@mkp.com, Web Site: www.mkp.com (17)

Pederson, Jeffrey, TAB Boards International Inc, Westminster, CO. Tel: (303) 839-1200, FAX: (303) 839-0012, Web Site: www.tabboards.com (14)

Pedreiro, Anna, AC Pedreiro, Morganville, NJ. Tel: (732) 598-6766 (27)

Pedrick, Ray, Mohawk Lifts, Amsterdam, NY. Tel: (518) 842-1431, (800) 833-2006, FAX: (518) 842-1289, E-Mail: rwells@mohawklifts.com, Web Site: www.mohawklifts.com (9)

Peel, Jim, Texas Refinery Corp, Fort Worth, TX. Tel: (817) 332-1161, FAX: (817) 336-8441, E-Mail: jhopkins@texasrefinery.com, Web Site: www.texasrefinery.com (9)

Peerless Rattan, Plainwell, MI. Tel: (269) 685-1858, (877) 611-2263, E-Mail: sales@peerlessrattan.com, Web Site: www.peerlessrattan.com (16)

Peeters, Geert, Suez Energy North America, Houston, TX. Tel: (713) 636-0000, FAX: (713) 636-1364, Web Site: www.tractebelpowerinc.com (16)

Peet's Coffee & Tea Inc, Berkeley, CA. Tel: (510) 525-3207, (800) 999-2132, FAX: (510) 594-2180, E-Mail: mailorder@peets.com, Web Site: www.peets.com (4)

Pefanis, Peter J., Protection One Inc, Lawrence, KS. Tel: (785) 856-5500, (800) GET-HELP, Web Site: www.protectionone.com (16)

Peffers, Kathryn, Penny Wise Office Products, Bowie, MD. Tel: (301) 805-7733, (800) 942-3311, FAX: (800) 622-4411, Web Site: www.penny-wise.com (10)

Pegasus Auto Racing Supplies Inc, New Berlin, WI. Tel: (262) 317-1234, (800) 688-6946, FAX: (262) 317-1201, E-Mail: info@pegasusautoracing.com, Web Site: www.pegasusautoracing.com (12)

Pegg Nadler Associates Inc, New York, NY. Tel: (212) 861-0846, E-Mail: pegg@peggnadler.com (22)

Pegram, Norm, PremierIMS Inc, Houston, TX. Tel: (832) 608-6400, FAX: (832) 608-6420, E-Mail: contact@mailplex.com, Web Site: www.premiercompany.com (21)

Pegran, Ron, McFeely's Square Drive Screws, Madison, WI. Tel: (434) 846-2729, (800) 443-7937, FAX: (804) 847-7136, E-Mail: tech@mcfeelys.com, Web Site: www.mcfeelys.com (16)

Peha, Jamie, Seattle Magazine, Seattle, WA. Tel: (206) 284-1750, (800) 637-0334, FAX: (206) 284-2550, E-Mail: customerservice@seattlemag.com, Web Site: www.seattlemag.com (17)

Peirce, Jean-Marie, Trumble Greetings, Boulder, CO. Tel: (800) 525-0656, FAX: (303) 530-5124, E-Mail: info@leanintree.com, Web Site: www.leanintree.com (6)

Pekarek, Jim, Cornerstone Brands Inc, West Chester, OH. Tel: (513) 603-1400, Web Site: www.cornerstonebrands.com (5)

Pelfrey, Jody, Data Partners Inc, Fort Myers, FL. Tel: (239) 267-8762, (866) 423-1818, FAX: (239) 267-9043, E-Mail: info@data-partners.com, Web Site: www.datapartners.com (22)

Pelland, Michael, AIDC (American International Distribution Corp), Williston, VT. Tel: (800) 678-2432, FAX: (802) 864-7749, E-Mail: jmacon@aidcvt.com, Web Site: www.aidcvt.com (22)

Pellas, Jr F. Alfredo, American Nicaraguan Foundation, Miami, FL. Tel: (305) 374-3391, FAX: (305) 374-5993, Web Site: www.aidnicaragua.com (1)

Pellegrino, Gary, Natural Essentials Inc, Streetsboro, OH. Tel: (330) 562-8022, (888) 968-7220, FAX: (330) 562-8022, E-Mail: questions@naturalessentials.com, Web Site: www.naturalessentials.com (5)

Pellegrino, Louis, Profile Coverage Corp, Melville, NY. Tel: (631) 981-7600, FAX: (631) 981-7681, E-Mail: info@profileinsure.com, Web Site: www.profileinsure.com (15)

Tom Pelletier, Patchogue, NY. Tel: (631) 569-5552, FAX: (413) 825-7968, E-Mail: tom@tompelletier.com, Web Site: www.tompelletier.com (39)

Pelletier, Tom, Tom Pelletier, Patchogue, NY. Tel: (631) 569-5552, FAX: (413) 825-7968, E-Mail: tom@tompelletier.com, Web Site: www.tompelletier.com (39)

Pellett, Christina, AMC Publishing/Agent Media Corp, Clearwater, FL. Tel: (727) 446-1100, (800) 933-9449, FAX: (727) 446-1166, E-Mail: sales@agentmediacorp.com, Web Site: www.agentmediacorp.com (31)

Pelletuer, Mark, AAA Southern New England, Providence, RI. Tel: (401) 868-2045, FAX: (401) 868-2088, Web Site: www.aaa.com (1)

Pelligrini, Charles, William Charles Printing, Plainview, NY. Tel: (516) 349-0900, FAX: (516) 349-0935, Web Site: www.williamcharlesprinting.com (27)

Pelligrini, Joseph, William Charles Printing, Plainview, NY. Tel: (516) 349-0900, FAX: (516) 349-0935, Web Site: www.williamcharlesprinting.com (27)

Peloquin, Mike, Charity Dynamics, Austin, TX. Tel: (512) 241-0561, FAX: (512) 532-6037, Web Site: www.charitydynamics.com (1)

Peltz, Michael, Institutional Investor Inc, New York, NY. Tel: (212) 224-3300, FAX: (212) 224-3592, Web Site: www.institutionalinvestor.com (17)

Pembroke, John, CUES Events, Training & Education, Madison, WI. Tel: (608) 271-2664, (800) 252-2664, FAX: (608) 271-2303, E-Mail: cues@cues.org, Web Site: www.cues.org (42)

PEMCO Insurance Cos, Seattle, WA. Tel: (206) 628-4000, (800) 467-3626, FAX: (206) 628-5886, Web Site: www.pemco.com (15)

Penberthy, Stephen, Woodcrafters Lumber Sales Inc, Portland, OR. Tel: (503) 231-0226, (800) 777-3709, FAX: (503) 232-0511, E-Mail: spen@worldnet.att.net, Web Site: www.woodcrafters.us (9)

Pencek, Mary, Cuvaison Inc, Napa, CA. Tel: (707) 942-2455, E-Mail: info@cuvaison.com, Web Site: www.cuvaison.com (4)

Don Pendell & Associates, Dayton, OH. Tel: (937) 254-4210 (39)

Pendell, Donald, Don Pendell & Associates, Dayton, OH. Tel: (937) 254-4210 (39)

Pendergast, Jane, The Tog Shop Inc, Beverly, MA. Tel: (800) 262-8888, FAX: (800) 755-7557, Web Site: www.togshop.com (2)

Penders, Jim, Command Financial, New York, NY. Tel: (212) 274-0070, FAX: (212) 274-8262, E-Mail: csd@commandfinancial.com, Web Site: www.commandfinancial.com (35)

Penders, William P., Aptara, Inc, Falls Church, VA. Tel: (703) 352-0001, FAX: (703) 352-8862, E-Mail: info@aptaracorp.com, Web Site: www.aptaracorp.com (27)

Penguin Group USA Inc, New York, NY. Tel: (212) 366-2000, Web Site: www.us.penguingroup.com (17)

Peninsular Printing of Daytona Beach Inc, Daytona Beach, FL. Tel: (386) 274-4837, FAX: (386) 274-5023, E-Mail: penprint@bellsouth.net, Web Site: www.peninsularprinting.com (27)

Penn Herb Co Ltd, Philadelphia, PA. Tel: (215) 632-6100, (800) 523-9971, FAX: (215) 632-7945, E-Mail: information@pennherb.com, Web Site: www.pennherb.com (7)

Penn Mutual, Horsham, PA. Tel: (215) 956-8083, FAX: (215) 956-8368, Web Site: www.pennmutual.com (15)

Penn State Hazleton, Hazleton, PA. Tel: (570) 450-3175, Web Site: www.hn.psu.edu (1)

Penn, Yael, Imagine 360 Marketing, New York, NY. Tel: (212) 313-9616, Web Site: www.i360m.com (20)

Pennell, Dave, Malco Products Inc, Barberton, OH. Tel: (330) 753-0361, (800) 253-2526, FAX: (330) 753-2025, Web Site: www.malcopro.com (16)

Pennington, Eric, Carrot-Top Industries Inc, Hillsborough, NC. Tel: (919) 732-6200, (800) 628-3524, FAX: (919) 732-5526, E-Mail: service@carrot-top.com, Web Site: www.carrot-top.com (16)

Pennington, Roger, Direct Mail Systems, Clearwater, FL. Tel: (727) 573-1985, (800) 683-6245, FAX: (727) 573-1747, E-Mail: info@direct-mail-systems.com, Web Site: www.direct-mail-systems.com (20)

Pennington, Roger, Direct Response Marketing, Clearwater, FL. Tel: (727) 573-1985, (800) 683-6245, FAX: (727) 573-1747, E-Mail: drmclwr@tampabay.rr.com, Web Site: www.dmsmails.com (28)

Pennington, Sandy, Kansas City Direct Marketing Association, Kansas City, MO. Tel: (816) 561-5323, FAX: (816) 561-1991, E-Mail: info@kcdma.org, Web Site: www.kcdma.org (40)

Pennington, Terry, Ennis Inc, Midlothian, TX. Tel: (972) 775-9801, (800) 962-0944, FAX: (800) 645-8339, Web Site: www.ennis.com (16)

Pennstreet Bakery, Grand Rapids, MI. Tel: (616) 241-2583, (800) 84-CAKES, FAX: (616) 241-6332, Web Site: www.pennstreet.com (16)

Pennsylvania Firebacks, Philadelphia, PA. Tel: (215) 722-1221, E-Mail: info@fireback.com, Web Site: www.fireback.com (8)

Pennsylvania State University Press, University Park, PA. Tel: (814) 865-1327, (800) 326-9180, FAX: (814) 863-1408, Web Site: www.psupress.org (17)

PennWell Corp, Tulsa, OK. Tel: (918) 831-9782, (800) 944-0937, E-Mail: kellib@pennwell.com, Web Site: www.pennwell.com (24)

PennWell Publishing, Tulsa, OK. Tel: (918) 835-3161, (800) 331-4463, E-Mail: headquarters@pennwell.com, Web Site: www.pennwell.com (17)

Penny Wise Office Products, Bowie, MD. Tel: (301) 805-7733, (800) 942-3311, FAX: (800) 622-4411, Web Site: www.penny-wise.com (10)

Penny, Phil, Belvoir Media Group LLC, Norwalk, CT. Tel: (203) 857-3100, FAX: (203) 857-3103, E-Mail: customer_service@belvoir.com, Web Site: www.belvoir.com (17)

Pennypacker, Barry L., Champion, Quincy, IL. Tel: (217) 222-5400, FAX: (217) 228-8260, Web Site: www.championpneumatic.com (16)

Pensions & Investments, New York, NY. Tel: (212) 210-0100, FAX: (212) 210-0117, Web Site: www.pionline.com (17)

Penske Logistics, Reading, PA. Tel: (800) 529-6531, FAX: (610) 775-2449, E-Mail: info.penskelogistics@penske.com, Web Site: www.penskelogistics.com (16)

Pensotti, Fred, Radial Inc, King of Prussia, PA. Tel: (610) 491-7000, Web Site: www.radial.com (28)

Penta Edd, Frank B., Health Sciences Consortium, Chapel Hill, NC. Tel: (919) 942-8731, FAX: (919) 942-3689, E-Mail: tony.penta@edtsi.com, Web Site: www.healthsciencesconsortium.org (17)

Penta, Tony, Health Sciences Consortium, Chapel Hill, NC. Tel: (919) 942-8731, FAX: (919) 942-3689, E-Mail: tony.penta@edtsi.com, Web Site: www.healthsciencesconsortium.org (17)

Pente, Bob, WiredPente Inc, Markham, ON Canada. Tel: (416) 399-8458, Web Site: wiredpente.com (35)

Pentera Inc, Indianapolis, IN. Tel: (617) 277-5033, Web Site: www.pentera.com (28)

Penton Learning Systems Inc, New York, NY. Tel: (212) 885-2700, FAX: (212) 885-2703, E-Mail: info@iqpc.com, Web Site: www.iqpc.com (16)

Penzer, Michael, Hyatt Legal Plans Inc, Cleveland, OH. Tel: (216) 241-0022, FAX: (216) 694-4305, Web Site: www.legalplans.com (16)

People for the American Way, Washington, DC. Tel: (202) 467-4999, Web Site: www.pfaw.org (1)

Peoples Benefit Life Insurance Co, Exton, PA. Tel: (610) 648-5000, FAX: (610) 648-5348 (15)

People's United Bank, Bridgeport, CT. Tel: (203) 338-7171, Web Site: www.peoples.com (14)

Peoples, Jeffrey, Window Book Inc, Cambridge, MA. Tel: (617) 395-4500, (800) 524-0380, FAX: (617) 395-5900, E-Mail: sales@windowboo.com, Web Site: www.windowbook.com (22)

Pepe, Greg, Media People Inc, New York, NY. Tel: (212) 779-7172, FAX: (212) 779-7248, E-Mail: info@mediapeople.com, Web Site: www.mediapeople.com (31)

Pepicello, Dr. William J., University of Phoenix, Tempe, AZ. Tel: (480) 557-1662, (866) 766-0766, Web Site: www.phoenix.edu (13)

Pepper, Charlie, Tinsley Tool Supply Inc, Powell, TN. Tel: (865) 681-9633, FAX: (865) 982-1655, E-Mail: gene@tinsleytool.com, Web Site: www.tinsleytool.com (9)

Pepper, Ginger, Morris & Fellows, Atlanta, GA. Tel: (404) 250-0225 (20)

Pepper, Jeff, Foremost Insurance Group, Grand Rapids, MI. Tel: (616) 956-8241, (800) 527-3905, FAX: (800) 325-1507, Web Site: www.foremost.com (15)

Peppermill Marketing Inc, Los Angeles, CA. Tel: (866) 737-5478, E-Mail: inquiry@peppermillmarketing.com, Web Site: peppermillmarketing.com (23)

Percipio Media, LLC, Cambridge, MA. Tel: (617) 995-7855 (20)

James R Perdiew & Co, Inverness, IL. Tel: (847) 842-8525, FAX: (847) 842-8518, E-Mail: jrpco@perdiew.com, Web Site: www.perdiew.com (20)

Perdiew, James R., James R Perdiew & Co, Inverness, IL. Tel: (847) 842-8525, FAX: (847) 842-8518, E-Mail: jrpco@perdiew.com, Web Site: www.perdiew.com (20)

Perea, Lawrence, UGL Equis Corp, Chicago, IL. Tel: (312) 424-8000, FAX: (312) 424-8080, Web Site: www.equiscorp.com (16)

Pereira, Sergio, Quill Corp, Lincolnshire, IL. Tel: (847) 876-3535, (800) 789-1331, Web Site: www.quill.com (16)

Pereira, Sergio, Quill Lincolnshire Inc, Lincolnshire, IL. Tel: (800) 982-3400, FAX: (800) 789-8955, Web Site: www.quill.com (10)

Perell, Kim, Amobee, Foster City, CA. Tel: (650) 802-8871, Web Site: www.amobee.com (32)

Perennial Pleasures Nursery, East Hardwick, VT. Tel: (802) 472-5104, FAX: (802) 472-6572, E-Mail: annex@perennialpleasures.net, Web Site: perennialpleasures.net (8)

Peres, Elia, ABCO Inc, Dallas, TX. Tel: (214) 565-1191, Web Site: www.abcoinc.com (20)

Pereyra, April, Connex International Inc, Danbury, CT. Tel: (203) 731-5400, (800) 426-6639, FAX: (203) 730-9060, E-Mail: marketing@connexintl.com, Web Site: www.connexintl.com (22)

Perez, David B., Gambro Inc, Lakewood, CO. Tel: (303) 232-6800, (800) 525-2623, FAX: (303) 222-6810, Web Site: www.gambro.com (16)

Perez, David, Geoscape, Miami, FL. Tel: (305) 860-1460, FAX: (305) 860-6161, Web Site: www.geoscape.com (22)

Perez, Marcelo F., Merchant E-Solutions, Redwood City, CA. Tel: (509) 232-5639, (866) 663-6132, FAX: (509) 232-5625, E-Mail: help@merchante-solutions.com, Web Site: www.merchante-solutions.com (14)

Perez, Paul, American Appraisal Associates, Milwaukee, WI. Tel: (414) 271-7240, (800) 558-8650, FAX: (414) 221-7065, Web Site: www.american-appraisal.com (14)

Perez-Ayala, Patricia, Avon Products Inc, New York, NY. Tel: (212) 282-7000, (800) 367-2866, FAX: (212) 282-6225, Web Site: www.avon.com (7)

Perfect Plastic Printing Corp, Saint Charles, IL. Tel: (630) 584-1600, FAX: (630) 584-0648, E-Mail: ppp@perfectplastic.com, Web Site: www.perfectplastic.com (27)

Perfection Tip Co/Camping Products Co, Long Beach, CA. Tel: (562) 491-0076, (800) 525-4835, FAX: (562) 435-7599 (16)

Perfit, Stephen, CCIM Institute, Chicago, IL. Tel: (312) 321-4460, (800) 621-7027, FAX: (312) 321-4530, Web Site: www.ccim.com (1)

Performance Direct Inc, Atlanta, GA. Tel: (678) 608-2820, (800) 869-2300, FAX: (404) 869-2547, E-Mail: info@performancede.com (22)

Performance Media Solutions Inc & TrueWorx Inc, Las Vegas, NV. Tel: (866) 827-7077 (16)

Performance Printing/ Optigraphics, Dallas, TX. Tel: (214) 665-1038, (800) 727-27335, FAX: (214) 665-1090, Web Site: www.performancecompanies.com (27)

Perger, Rebecca, Marketing Results Inc, Sicklerville, NJ. Tel: (856) 740-3334, FAX: (856) 740-3335, Web Site: www.marketingresults.net (16)

Peribere, Jeroe, Sealed Air Corp, Elmwood Park, NJ. Tel: (201) 791-7600, FAX: (201) 703-4205, Web Site: www.sealedair.com (26)

Perimeter Technology Inc, Manchester, NH. Tel: (603) 645-1616, (800) 645-1650, FAX: (603) 645-1424, Web Site: www.perimetertechnology.com (34)

Perina, Kaja, Sussex Publishers Inc, New York, NY. Tel: (212) 260-7210, FAX: (212) 260-7445, Web Site: www.blues-buster.com (17)

Periodical Publisher's Service Bureau Inc, Fresno, CA. Tel: (419) 626-0623, (888) 206-0350, FAX: (419) 626-4576, Web Site: www.ppsb.com (17)

Periscope Inc, Minneapolis, MN. Tel: (612) 339-0500, FAX: (612) 339-0600, E-Mail: info@periscope.com, Web Site: www.periscope.com (35)

Perkins, John, Datapoint USA Inc, San Antonio, TX. Tel: (210) 614-9977, FAX: (210) 614-2297, E-Mail: info@datapointusa.com, Web Site: www.datapointusa.com (16)

Perkins, Leigh H., The Orvis Co Inc, Manchester, VT. Tel: (802) 362-3622, FAX: (802) 362-3525, Web Site: www.orvis.com (11)

Perkins, Patty, Directory of Major Mailers & What They Mail, Philadelphia, PA. Tel: (215) 238-5300, (800) 777-8074, FAX: (215) 238-5412, E-Mail: customerservice@napco.com, Web Site: www.majormailers.com (43)

Perkins, Patty, Inside Direct Mail, Philadelphia, PA. Tel: (215) 238-5300, (800) 777-8074, FAX: (215) 238-5412, E-Mail: customerservice@napco.com, Web Site: www.insidedirectmail.com (43)

Perkins, Perk, The Orvis Co Inc, Manchester, VT. Tel: (802) 362-3622, FAX: (802) 362-3525, Web Site: www.orvis.com (11)

Perkins, Terry, Peter Li Education Group, Dayton, OH. Tel: (937) 293-1415, (800) 523-4625, FAX: (937) 293-1310, Web Site: www.peterli.com (17)

Perl, Liz, Simon & Schuster Inc, New York, NY. Tel: (212) 698-7000, (800) 223-2348, Web Site: www. simonandschuster.com (17)

Perlman, Victor, American Society of Media Photographers (ASMP), Philadelphia, PA. Tel: (215) 451-ASMP, FAX: (215) 451-0880, Web Site: www. asmp.org (40)

Perlmutter, Isaac, Marvel Entertainment Inc, New York, NY. Tel: (212) 576-4000, FAX: (212) 576-8506, Web Site: www.marvel.com (31)

Perlstein, Joshua, Response Media, Norcross, GA. Tel: (770) 451-5478, FAX: (770) 451-4929, E-Mail: postmaster@responsemedia.com, Web Site: www. responsemedia.com (32)

Perlstein, Keith, Response Media, Norcross, GA. Tel: (770) 451-5478, FAX: (770) 451-4929, E-Mail: postmaster@responsemedia.com, Web Site: www. responsemedia.com (32)

Perlstein, Steve, Mohawk Lifts, Amsterdam, NY. Tel: (518) 842-1431, (800) 833-2006, FAX: (518) 842-1289, E-Mail: rwells@mohawklifts.com, Web Site: www.mohawklifts.com (9)

S Pernick & Associates, Wilmette, IL. Tel: (847) 256-0115 (20)

Pernod Ricard USA, Purchase, NY. Tel: (914) 848-4800, Web Site: www.pernod-ricard-usa.com (16)

Perrella, Ronald, Ron Perrella DRS, Laguna Niguel, CA. Tel: (949) 495-7661, FAX: (949) 495-7660, E-Mail: rperrdrs@aol.com, Web Site: www. ronperrelladrs.com (35)

Perret, Jan, Technology Marketing Corp/TMC, Norwalk, CT. Tel: (203) 852-6800, (800) 243-6002, FAX: (203) 953-2845, E-Mail: tmc@tmcnet.com, Web Site: www.tmcnet.com (29)

Perro, Perry R., The Northern Trust Co, Chicago, IL. Tel: (312) 630-6000, (888) 289-6542, FAX: (312) 444-5244, Web Site: www.ntrs.com (14)

Perrott, M. Ward, Madison Executive Search, Ridgefield, CT. Tel: (203) 431-6565, FAX: (203) 431-6060, E-Mail: mimi@directexec.com, Web Site: www.directexec.com (20)

Perruzza, Albert L., The Reader's Digest Association Inc, New York, NY. Tel: (800) 310-6261, Web Site: www.rda.com (17)

Perry, Joel, Tuttle Printing & Engraving, Rutland, VT. Tel: (802) 773-9171, (800) 776-7682, FAX: (802) 773-5785, E-Mail: info@tuttleprinting.com, Web Site: www.tuttleprinting.com (10)

Perry, Les, Seiko Corp of America, Mahwah, NJ. Tel: (201) 529-3316, E-Mail: custserv@seikousa.com, Web Site: www.seikousa.com (16)

Perry, Rick, Lippincott, Williams & Wilkins, Baltimore, MD. Tel: (410) 528-4000, (800) 638-0672, FAX: (410) 528-8597, E-Mail: customerservice@lww. com, Web Site: www.lww.com (17)

Perry, Scott, Bankers Life & Casualty Co, Chicago, IL. Tel: (312) 396-6000, (800) 231-9150, Web Site: www.bankerslife.com (15)

Perry, Scott, The Herald & Review, Decatur, IL. Tel: (217) 429-5151, FAX: (217) 421-6913, E-Mail: hrdirect@herald-review.com, Web Site: www. herald-review.com (17)

Perrygraf, Carol Stream, IL. Tel: (630) 665-3333, (800) 323-4433, FAX: (630) 665-3491, E-Mail: info2@ americanperrygraf.com, Web Site: www.perrygraf. com (16)

Person to Person Marketing LLC, Riverdale, NJ. Tel: (973) 835-8112, FAX: (973) 835-8525, E-Mail: sales@persontopersondirect.com, Web Site: www. persontopersondirect.com (29)

Personal Achievement Institute, Kingman, AZ. Tel: (928) 753-7546, (800) 321-1225, FAX: (928) 753-7554, E-Mail: burt@burtdubin.com, Web Site: www.speakingbizsuccess.com (17)

Personal Creations, Lemont, IL. Tel: (630) 783-2400, (866) 834-7695, Web Site: www.personalcreations. com (6)

Personnel Policy Service Inc, Louisville, KY. Tel: (502) 899-5102, (800) 437-3735, FAX: (800) 755-7011, E-Mail: info@ppspublishers.com, Web Site: www. ppspublishers.com (17)

RJ Persson Enterprises Inc, Montrose, CO. Tel: (303) 249-6000, FAX: (303) 249-0800 (16)

Persson, Richard, RJ Persson Enterprises Inc, Montrose, CO. Tel: (303) 249-6000, FAX: (303) 249-0800 (16)

Perusse, Edward, Home-Sew Inc, Bethlehem, PA. Tel: (610) 867-3833, (800) 344-4739, FAX: (610) 867-9717, E-Mail: customerservice@homesew.com, Web Site: www.homesew.com (11)

Perusse, Lucy, Home-Sew Inc, Bethlehem, PA. Tel: (610) 867-3833, (800) 344-4739, FAX: (610) 867-9717, E-Mail: customerservice@homesew.com, Web Site: www.homesew.com (11)

Perutz, Simon, Nimlok, Niles, IL. Tel: (847) 647-1012, (800) 233-8870, FAX: (847) 647-2044, E-Mail: info@nimlok.com, Web Site: www.nimlok.com (16)

Peruvian Connection Ltd, Tonganoxie, KS. Tel: (913) 845-2450, (800) 221-8520, E-Mail: sales@ peruvianconnection.com, Web Site: www. peruvianconnection.com (6)

Pesce, Greg, World Innovators Inc, Roxbury, CT. Tel: (860) 210-8088, FAX: (860) 210-7829, E-Mail: inquiry@worldinnovators.com, Web Site: www. worldinnovators.com (24)

Pesce, William J., John Wiley & Sons Inc, Hoboken, NJ. Tel: (201) 748-6000, FAX: (201) 748-6088, E-Mail: info@wiley.com, Web Site: www.wiley. com (17)

Peschke, Donald, August Home Publishing Co, Des Moines, IA. Tel: (515) 875-7000, FAX: (515) 333-5441, Web Site: www.augusthome.com (17)

Pesci, Greg, Propay USA Inc, Lehi, UT. Tel: (801) 766-3758, Web Site: www.propay.com (14)

Peskowitz, Ed, United Communications Group, Gaithersburg, MD. Tel: (301) 287-2700, FAX: (301) 816-8945, E-Mail: webmaster@ucg.com, Web Site: www.ucg.com (17)

Pessina, Stefano, Walgreens Co, Deerfield, IL. Tel: (800) 925-4733, Web Site: www.walgreens.com (7)

Pestarino, Bart, Sentinel Peak LLC, Redmond, WA. Tel: (360) 293-7271, Web Site: www.sentinel-peak. com (20)

Pestka, John, Bunzl Distribution USA, Inc, Saint Louis, MO. Tel: (314) 997-5959, (888) 997-5959, FAX: (314) 997-1405, Web Site: www.bunzldistribution. com (16)

Petco Animal Supplies, San Diego, CA. Tel: (858) 453-7845, (877) 738-6742, FAX: (858) 453-6585, Web Site: www.petco.com (5)

PetEdge, Beverly, MA. Tel: (978) 998-8100, (800) 738-3343, FAX: (978) 887-8499, E-Mail: support@ petedge.com, Web Site: www.petedge.com (16)

Petel, Nate, AccuData Integrated Marketing, Fort Myers, FL. Tel: (239) 425-4400, (800) 732-3440, FAX: (239) 425-4401, E-Mail: info@accudata.com, Web Site: www.accudata.com (23)

Peter Pan Bus Lines Inc, Springfield, MA. Tel: (413) 781-3320, (800) 343-9999, FAX: (413) 747-7626, E-Mail: info@peterpanbus.com, Web Site: www. peterpanbus.com (19)

Peter, Eugene W., Interstate Printing Co, Omaha, NE. Tel: (402) 341-8028, (800) 788-4177, FAX: (402) 341-6168, E-Mail: printer@interstateprinting.com, Web Site: www.interstateprinting.com (27)

J Peterman Co, Lexington, KY. Tel: (888) 647-2555, FAX: (859) 254-0869, Web Site: www.jpeterman. com (5)

Peters, Charles M., Gazette Communications Inc, Cedar Rapids, IA. Tel: (319) 398-8211, (800) 397-8211, FAX: (319) 368-8834, Web Site: www. gazettecommunications.com (17)

Peters, Craig, Getty Images, Seattle, WA. Tel: (206) 925-5000, (888) 888-5889, Web Site: www. gettyimages.com (38)

Peters, David, Sellstrom Manufacturing Co, Schaumburg, IL. Tel: (847) 358-2000, (800) 323-7402, FAX: (847) 358-8564, E-Mail: sellstrom@sellstrom. com, Web Site: www.sellstrom.com (16)

Peters, Geoffrey, CDR Fundraising Group, Bowie, MD. Tel: (301) 858-1500, FAX: (301) 858-0107, Web Site: www.cdr-nfl.com (1)

Peters, Jenny, Premier Farnell Corp, Richfield, OH. Tel: (216) 525-4300, (800) 458-3222, FAX: (216) 525-4509, E-Mail: information@premierfarnell.com, Web Site: www.premierfarnell.com (16)

Peters, Kristen, DWS Investments Service Co, Kansas City, MO. Tel: (800) 543-5776, Web Site: www. dws-investments.com (14)

Peters, Lauren B., Champs Corp, Bradenton, FL. Tel: (941) 748-0577, (800) 991-6813, E-Mail: customer_service@champssports.com, Web Site: www.champssports.com (11)

Peters, Mark A., RJ Reynolds Tobacco Co, Winston Salem, NC. Tel: (336) 741-5111, (800) 341-5211, Web Site: www.rjrt.com (16)

Peters, Pam, Airomat Corp, Fort Wayne, IN. Tel: (260) 747-7408, (800) 348-4905, FAX: (260) 747-7409, E-Mail: airomat@airomat.com, Web Site: www. mymatting.com (16)

Petersen, Kenneth, Direct Response Services, Glen Carbon, IL. Tel: (618) 288-8811, (800) 795-5478, FAX: (618) 288-3005, E-Mail: drs@drslist.com, Web Site: www.drslist.com (23)

Petersen, Kerri, The Marx Group, San Rafael, CA. Tel: (415) 453-0844, FAX: (415) 451-0166, E-Mail: info@themarxgrp.com, Web Site: www.themarxgrp. com (35)

Petersen, Matt, Jafra Cosmetics International Inc, Westlake Village, CA. Tel: (260) 423-9571, (888) 848-4077, FAX: (960) 423-6742, Web Site: www.jafra. com (7)

Peterson, Anne M, World Innovators Inc, Roxbury, CT. Tel: (860) 210-8088, FAX: (860) 210-7829, E-Mail: inquiry@worldinnovators.com, Web Site: www. worldinnovators.com (24)

Peterson, Chris, Integrated Marketing Solutions (IMS), Ashland, NE. Tel: (402) 486-3151, FAX: (402) 486-3161 (20)

Peterson, Deborah, Motient Communications, Reston, VA. Tel: (847) 478-4330, (800) 752-2672, FAX: (703) 758-6111 (16)

Peterson, Donna A, World Innovators Inc, Roxbury, CT. Tel: (860) 210-8088, FAX: (860) 210-7829, E-Mail: inquiry@worldinnovators.com, Web Site: www.worldinnovators.com (24)

Peterson, Douglas L., Standard & Poor's Corp, New York, NY. Tel: (212) 438-2000, FAX: (212) 438-7375, Web Site: www.standardandpoors.com (17)

Peterson, Gary, Western Web Printing, Sioux Falls, SD. Tel: (605) 339-2383, (800) 843-6805, FAX: (605) 339-8323, E-Mail: info@westernwebprinting.com, Web Site: www.westernwebprinting.com (27)

Peterson, George C., AutoPacific Inc, Tustin, CA. Tel: (714) 838-4234, FAX: (714) 838-4260, Web Site: www.autopacific.com (30)

Peterson, Jason, Interactive Search Group, Cleveland, OH. Tel: (216) 255-3388, Web Site: www.isgstaffingnow.com (20)

Peterson, John, Ligonier Ministries, Sanford, FL. Tel: (407) 333-4244, (800) 435-4343, FAX: (407) 333-4377, Web Site: www.ligonier.org (5)

Peterson, John, TransFirst Holdings Inc, Dallas, TX. Tel: (214) 453-7700, (888) 254-4137, FAX: (214) 453-7739, Web Site: www.transfirst.com (14)

Peterson, Jr. Chester, Sunshine Unlimited Inc, Lindsborg, KS. Tel: (785) 227-3880, FAX: (785) 227-3880, E-Mail: cpeterjr@aol.com, Web Site: www.sunshine-unlimited.com (9)

Peterson, Karen, The News Tribune, Tacoma, WA. Tel: (253) 597-8742, E-Mail: customerservice@thenewstribune.com, Web Site: www.thenewstribune.com (17)

Peterson, Kurt, Nilodor Inc, Bolivar, OH. Tel: (330) 874-1017, (800) 443-4321, FAX: (330) 874-3366, E-Mail: info@nilodor.com, Web Site: www.nilodor.com (16)

Peterson, Lisa, American Kennel Club, New York, NY. Tel: (212) 696-8200, FAX: (212) 696-8217, (212) 696-8299, Web Site: www.akc.org (17)

Peterson, Mark, Diamond Marketing Solutions, Carol Stream, IL. Tel: (630) 597-9100, E-Mail: info@dmsolutions.com, Web Site: www.dmsolutions.com (35)

Peterson, Renee J., The Toro Co, Bloomington, MN. Tel: (952) 888-8801, (800) 348-2424, FAX: (952) 887-8258, E-Mail: companyinfo@thetorocompany.com, Web Site: www.thetorocompany.com (16)

Peterson, Robin, Midwest Technology Products & Services, Sioux City, IA. Tel: (712) 252-3601, (800) 831-5904, FAX: (800) 258-7054, E-Mail: web@midwesttechnology.com, Web Site: www.midwesttechnology.com (9)

Peterson, Roy L., American Bible Society, New York, NY. Tel: (212) 408-1200, FAX: (212) 408-1264, Web Site: www.americanbible.org (1)

Peterson, Sandra E., Johnson & Johnson, New Brunswick, NJ. Tel: (732) 524-0400, FAX: (732) 214-0332, Web Site: www.jnj.com (1)

Peterson, Scott, Summit Racing Equipment, Tallmadge, OH. Tel: (330) 630-0250, (800) 230-3030, FAX: (330) 630-5571, Web Site: www.summitracing.com (12)

Peterson, Terry D., Deluxe Corp, Shoreview, MN. Tel: (651) 483-7111, FAX: (651) 481-4477, Web Site: www.deluxe.com (27)

Peterson, Vera, Miracle Ear, Minneapolis, MN. Tel: (800) 464-8002, FAX: (763) 268-4365, Web Site: www.miracle-ear.com (16)

Peterson's, Lawrenceville, NJ. Tel: (609) 896-1800, FAX: (609) 896-1811, E-Mail: custsvc@petersons.com, Web Site: www.petersons.com (17)

Petisi, Bob, Katalyst Partners Inc, New York, NY. Tel: (203) 257-4277, E-Mail: bpetisi@katalystresponse.com, Web Site: www.katalystresponse.com (21)

Petitt, Anthony B., Lorillard Tobacco Co, Greensboro, NC. Tel: (336) 335-7000, (877) 703-0386, FAX: (336) 373-6917, E-Mail: externalaffairs@lortobco.com, Web Site: www.lorillard.com (16)

Petra Industries, Edmond, OK. Tel: (405) 216-2100, FAX: (405) 216-2102, Web Site: www.patra.com (34)

Petrangelo, Gary, Japs-Olson Co, Saint Louis Park, MN. Tel: (952) 932-9393, (800) 548-2897, FAX: (612) 912-1900, Web Site: www.japsolson.com (27)

Petren, Carol Ann, CIGNA International, Philadelphia, PA. Tel: (215) 761-1741, FAX: (215) 761-5515, Web Site: www.cigna.com (15)

Petro, Eric, iN DEMAND LLC, New York, NY. Tel: (646) 638-8200, FAX: (646) 486-0855, Web Site: www.indemand.com (32)

Petro, Tom, JD Power Associates, Westlake Village, CA. Tel: (805) 418-8000, (888) 537-6937, FAX: (805) 418-8900, E-Mail: information@jdpa.com, Web Site: www.jdpower.com (30)

Petrocelli, Elaine, Book Passage Cafe, Corte Madera, CA. Tel: (415) 927-0960, (800) 999-7909, FAX: (415) 924-3838, Web Site: www.BookPassage.com (17)

Petroff, Chris, Gold Medal Products Co, Cincinnati, OH. Tel: (513) 769-7676, (800) 543-0862, FAX: (800) 542-1496, E-Mail: info@gmpopcorn.com, Web Site: www.gmpopcorn.com (16)

Petrosky, Mark, Duffey Petrosky, Farmington Hills, MI. Tel: (248) 489-8300, FAX: (248) 994-1600, Web Site: www.duffeypetrosky.com (35)

Petruzzelli, Diane, Fosina Marketing Group Inc, Danbury, CT. Tel: (203) 790-0013, E-Mail: info@fosinamarketing.com, Web Site: fosinamarketinggroup.com (35)

Petry Television Inc, New York, NY. Tel: (212) 230-5600, E-Mail: info@petrymedia.com, Web Site: www.petrymedia.com (32)

Petsky Prunier LLC, New York, NY. Tel: (212) 842-6001, FAX: (212) 842-6039, Web Site: www.petskyprunier.com (14)

Petsky, Michael, Petsky Prunier LLC, New York, NY. Tel: (212) 842-6001, FAX: (212) 842-6039, Web Site: www.petskyprunier.com (14)

PetSmart Inc, Phoenix, AZ. Tel: (623) 587-2009, (888) 839-9638, FAX: (623) 580-6183, Web Site: www.petsmart.com (5)

Pettersen, Brian, Paasche Airbrush Co, Chicago, IL. Tel: (773) 867-9191, FAX: (773) 867-9198, E-Mail: info@paascheairbrush.com, Web Site: www.paascheairbrush.com (10)

Petterson, Steven, Paasche Airbrush Co, Chicago, IL. Tel: (773) 867-9191, FAX: (773) 867-9198, E-Mail: info@paascheairbrush.com, Web Site: www.paascheairbrush.com (10)

Pettid, Joy, Crosslists Cross & Co, Lone Jack, MO. Tel: (816) 697-3306, FAX: (816) 697-3317, E-Mail: info@crosscompany.com, Web Site: www.crosscompany.com (23)

Petty, Richard, Power Music, Salt Lake City, UT. Tel: (801) 292-2418, (800) 777-BEAT, FAX: (801) 292-2462, Web Site: www.powermusic.com (16)

Pettygrove, Marshall J., Catalogs America, Gordonsville, VA. Tel: (540) 832-2253, (800) 283-4666, FAX: (540) 832-7253, E-Mail: dsayin@catalogsamerica.com, Web Site: www.catalogsamerica.com (27)

Pew, III Robert C., Steelcase Inc, Grand Rapids, MI. Tel: (616) 247-2710, FAX: (616) 475-2270, Web Site: www.steelcase.com (16)

Pfaelzer Brothers, Maumee, OH. Tel: (419) 893-7611, (800) 345-9290, FAX: (419) 893-0164, Web Site: www.phaelzerbrothers.com (16)

Pfaltzgraff Co, York, PA. Tel: (800) 999-2811, FAX: (800) 757-6872, E-Mail: service@pfaltzgraff.com, Web Site: www.pfaltzgraff.com (8)

Pfeffer, Adam B., American Association of Individual Investors, Chicago, IL. Tel: (312) 280-0170, FAX: (312) 280-9883, E-Mail: adam@aaii.com, Web Site: www.aaii.com (1)

Pfeffer, David Matthew, Oppenheimer Funds, New York, NY. Tel: (212) 323-0200, FAX: (212) 323-4070, Web Site: www.oppenheimerfunds.com (14)

Pfeifer, Rick, American Trim, Lima, OH. Tel: (419) 228-1145, FAX: (419) 996-4850, E-Mail: sales@amtrim.com, Web Site: www.amtrim.com (9)

Pfeiffer, Sr. Bill, Commercial Lithographing Co Inc, Kansas City, MO. Tel: (816) 241-2218, FAX: (816) 241-6901, E-Mail: sjohnson@commercial-lithographing.com, Web Site: www.clitho.com (31)

Pfiefer, Marty, Light Sources Inc, Virginia Beach, VA. Tel: (757) 424-8636, (800) 882-8834, FAX: (757) 424-6186, E-Mail: lightsources@earthlink.net, Web Site: www.lightsourcesinc.com (16)

Pfizer Inc, New York, NY. Tel: (212) 733-2323, Web Site: www.pfizer.com (16)

Pflanzer, Carl, EWA & Miniature Cars USA Inc, Berkeley Heights, NJ. Tel: (732) 424-7811, (800) 392-4454, FAX: (732) 424-7814, E-Mail: ewa@ewacars.com (11)

Pfund, Katie, Heldref Publications, Washington, DC. Tel: (202) 296-6267, (215) 625-8900, FAX: (202) 296-5149, Web Site: www.heldref.org (17)

Pfund, Niko, Oxford University Press Inc, New York, NY. Tel: (212) 726-6000, FAX: (212) 726-6455, Web Site: global.oup.com (17)

Pharmaceutical Care Management Association, Washington, DC. Tel: (202) 756-7210, FAX: (202) 207-3623, E-Mail: info@pcmanet.org, Web Site: www.pcmanet.org (1)

PharmArt, Circleville, OH. Tel: (860) 932-8588, (800) 848-1633, FAX: (800) 477-2923, Web Site: www.healthcarelogistics.com/Pharmart (6)

Pharmavite Corp LLC (HQ), Northridge, CA. Tel: (818) 221-6200, (800) 423-2405, FAX: (818) 221-6618, Web Site: www.pharmavite.com (16)

Pharris, Walt, Fairfield Industries Inc, Sugar Land, TX. Tel: (281) 275-7500, (800) 231-9809, FAX: (281) 275-7550, E-Mail: jblattman@fairfield.com, Web Site: www.fairfield.com (16)

Phelan, Mike, TransFirst ePayment Services, Omaha, NE. Tel: (888) 541-9800, Web Site: epay.transfirst.com (14)

Phelps, Craig, Amica Insurance, Lincoln, RI. Tel: (401) 334-6000, (800) 652-6422, FAX: (401) 334-4241, Web Site: www.amica.com (15)

Phelps, Dale, The News Tribune, Tacoma, WA. Tel: (253) 597-8742, E-Mail: customerservice@thenewstribune.com, Web Site: www.thenewstribune.com (17)

Phelps, Steven M., NGL Insurance Group, Madison, WI. Tel: (608) 257-5611, (800) 548-2962, FAX: (608) 257-9340, Web Site: www.nglic.com (15)

The Philadelphia Contributorship Insurance Co, Philadelphia, PA. Tel: (215) 627-1752, (800) 346-9229, E-Mail: info@contributorship.com, Web Site: www.contributorship.com (15)

The Philadelphia Inquirer & Daily News, Philadelphia, PA. Tel: (215) 854-2000, FAX: (215) 854-4788, Web Site: www.phil.com/inquirer (31)

Philadelphia Museum of Art, Philadelphia, PA. Tel: (215) 684-7840, FAX: (215) 235-0042, E-Mail: memberservices@philamuseum.org, Web Site: www.philamuseum.org (1)

Philip Morris USA Inc, Richmond, VA. Tel: (804) 274-2000, FAX: (804) 484-8231, Web Site: www.philipmorrisusa.com (16)

Philip, Bradford M., VisiPak Inc, Arnold, MO. Tel: (636) 282-6800, (800) 922-9391, FAX: (636) 282-6888, E-Mail: visipak@sinclair-rush.com, Web Site: www.visipak.com (34)

Philippe, Herve, Vivendi SA, New York, NY. Tel: (212) 572-7000, FAX: (212) 572-1080, Web Site: www. vivendi.com (16)

Philips Lifeline, Framingham, MA. Tel: (855) 332-7799, (800) 635-6156, Web Site: www.lifeline. philips.com (7)

Phillips Kiln Service LTD, South Sioux City, NE. Tel: (402) 494-6837, (800) 831-0876, FAX: (402) 494-6858, E-Mail: info@kilm.com, Web Site: www.kiln. com (16)

Phillips-Van Heusen Corp, New York, NY. Tel: (212) 381-3500, (800) 388-9122, FAX: (212) 381-3950, Web Site: www.pvh.com (2)

Phillips, Andy, Cardflex Financial Services, Costa Mesa, CA. Tel: (714) 361-1900, E-Mail: aphillips@ cliq.com, Web Site: www.flex1.com (14)

Phillips, Carol, Promotional Product Professionals of Canada, Dorval, QC Canada. Tel: (514) 489-5359, FAX: (800) 489-8741, (514) 489-7760, E-Mail: gladys@pppc.ca, Web Site: www.pppc.ca (1)

Phillips, Charles, Infor, Alpharetta, GA. Tel: (678) 319-8000, Web Site: www.infor.com (22)

Phillips, Dale W., Methode Electronics Inc, Chicago, IL. Tel: (708) 867-6777, FAX: (708) 867-6999, E-Mail: info@methode.com, Web Site: www. methode.com (9)

Phillips, Dennis, Hamilton Watch, Weehawken, NJ. Tel: (201) 271-1400, (800) 243-8463, Web Site: www.hamiltonwatches.com (16)

Phillips, Don, Morningstar Inc, Chicago, IL. Tel: (312) 696-6000, Web Site: www.morningstar.com (14)

Phillips, Glenna, Direct Marketing Association of Saint Louis, Washington, MO. Tel: (866) 516-0121, FAX: (636) 239-2324, E-Mail: mparisien@mac.com, Web Site: www.dmastl.org (40)

Phillips, Jack J., Roche Diagnostics Corp, Indianapolis, IN. Tel: (317) 521-2000, Web Site: www. usdiagnostics.roche.com (7)

Phillips, John, Sisk Fulfillment Service Inc, Federalsburg, MD. Tel: (410) 754-8141, FAX: (410) 754-8223, Web Site: www.siskfulfillment.com (22)

Phillips, Larry, Foremost Industrial Exchange, Van Nuys, CA. Tel: (818) 988-6900, FAX: (818) 787-0293 (16)

Phillips, Lisa Faith, Random House Direct Marketing, New York, NY. Tel: (212) 572-4985, (800) 678-5681, FAX: (212) 572-6018, Web Site: www. randomhousedirect.com (17)

Phillips, Marc C., Promotional Product Professionals of Canada, Dorval, QC Canada. Tel: (514) 489-5359, FAX: (800) 489-8741, (514) 489-7760, E-Mail: gladys@pppc.ca, Web Site: www.pppc.ca (1)

Phillips, Mark, Reputation.com, Redwood City, CA. Tel: (877) 425-5792, E-Mail: info@reputation.com, Web Site: www.reputation.com (32)

Phillips, Meghan, The Honey Agency, Sacramento, CA. Tel: (916) 444-0203, E-Mail: buzz@honeyagency. com, Web Site: honeyagency.com (35)

Phillips, Patrick L., The Urban Land Institute, Washington, DC. Tel: (202) 624-7000, FAX: (202) 624-7140, E-Mail: customerservice@uli.org, Web Site: www.uli.org (1)

Phillips, Thomas L., Eagle Publishing, Washington, DC. Tel: (202) 216-0600, FAX: (202) 216-0612, Web Site: www.eaglepub.com (17)

Philpin, John, Lyris Inc, Emeryville, CA. Tel: (510) 844-1551, (800) 768-2929, FAX: (510) 844-1598, E-Mail: sales@lyris.com, Web Site: www.lyris.com (32)

Philpott, Robert Allan, Harte-Hanks, San Antonio, TX. Tel: (210) 829-9000, FAX: (210) 829-9403, Web Site: www.hartehanks.com (22)

Phinney, Scott, Infotrends Inc, Weymouth, MA. Tel: (781) 616-2100, FAX: (781) 616-2121, E-Mail: info@infotrends.com, Web Site: www.infotrends. com (35)

Phipps, Cynthia, The Animal Medical Center, New York, NY. Tel: (212) 838-8100, FAX: (212) 832-9630, Web Site: www.amcny.org (16)

Phoenix Data Processing LLC, Westmont, IL. Tel: (630) 654-4400, FAX: (630) 654-4470, E-Mail: sales@phoenixdataprocessing.com, Web Site: www. phoenixdataprocessing.com (22)

Phoenix Learning Group Inc, Maryland Heights, MO. Tel: (314) 569-0211, (800) 221-1274, FAX: (314) 569-2834, E-Mail: dealersales@ phoenixlearninggroup.com, Web Site: www. phoenixlearninggroup.com (16)

Phoenix Marketing Group LLC, Redding, CT. Tel: (203) 544-7033, E-Mail: bseide@phoenix-marketing.com, Web Site: www.phoenix-marketing. com (21)

Phoenix Marketing International, Warrington, PA. Tel: (215) 392-0264, Web Site: www.phoenixmi.com (30)

Phoenix Poke Boats Inc, McKee, KY. Tel: (606) 965-2803, E-Mail: pokeboat@pokeboat.com, Web Site: www.pokeboat.com (16)

Phoenix Technologies Ltd, Campbell, CA. Tel: (408) 570-1000, (800) 677-7305, FAX: (408) 570-1001, Web Site: www.phoenix.com (22)

Phone Bank Systems Inc, East Lansing, MI. Tel: (517) 332-1500, FAX: (517) 332-1514, E-Mail: rusha@ phonebanks.com, Web Site: www.phonebanks.com (1)

Photo Researchers Inc, New York, NY. Tel: (212) 758-3420, (800) 833-9033, FAX: (212) 355-0731, E-Mail: info@photoresearchers.com, Web Site: www.photoresearchers.com (38)

Photo Shuttle Japan, Chapel Hill, NC. Tel: (919) 967-1585, E-Mail: sonia@photoshuttle.com, Web Site: www.photoshuttle.com (37)

PhotoEdit Inc, Costa Mesa, CA. Tel: (800) 860-2098, FAX: (800) 804-3707, E-Mail: sales@photoeditinc. com, Web Site: www.photoeditinc.com (38)

Photofest, New York, NY. Tel: (212) 633-6330, FAX: (212) 366-9062, E-Mail: requests@photofestnyc. com (38)

Photographer's Formulary Inc, Condon, MT. Tel: (406) 754-2891, (800) 922-5255, FAX: (406) 754-2896, E-Mail: formulary@blackfoot.net, Web Site: www. photoformulary.com (9)

Photographer's Market, Blue Ash, OH. Tel: (513) 531-2690, FAX: (513) 531-2686, E-Mail: photomarket@ fwpubs.com, Web Site: www.photographersmarket. com (43)

Photographic Society of America Inc (PSA), Oklahoma City, OK. Tel: (405) 843-1437, (855) 772-4636, FAX: (405) 843-1438, E-Mail: HQ@psa-photo.org, Web Site: www.psa-photo.org (40)

Photographix, Ann Arbor, MI. Tel: (734) 769-6756, FAX: (734) 476-2068, E-Mail: lkburghardt@ comcast.net (37)

PhotoSource International, Osceola, WI. Tel: (715) 248-3800, X27, (800) 223-3860, FAX: (715) 248-3800, E-Mail: info@photosource.com, Web Site: www. photosource.com (38)

PhotoStamps.com, El Segundo, CA. Tel: (310) 482-5800, Web Site: www.photostamps.com (5)

Phototake/The Creative Link, New York, NY. Tel: (212) 736-2525, (800) 542-3686, FAX: (212) 736-1919, E-Mail: photoinfo@phototakeusa.com, Web Site: www.phototakeusa.com (38)

Photoworks, Cleveland, OH. Tel: (206) 281-1390, (800) PHOTOWORKS, FAX: (206) 284-5357, E-Mail: info@photoworks.com, Web Site: www. photoworks.com (16)

Photri Images LLC, Fairfax, VA. Tel: (703) 978-0129, E-Mail: info@photriimages.com, Web Site: www. photriimages.com (38)

Physical Therapy Institute Inc, Poway, CA. Tel: (858) 485-7103 (16)

Physicians Mutual Insurance Co, Omaha, NE. Tel: (402) 633-1604, (888) 932-7642, FAX: (402) 633-1604, Web Site: www.physiciansmutual.com (15)

Physicians Planning Association Services, Deerfield Beach, FL. Tel: (954) 571-1877, (800) 221-2168, FAX: (954) 571-8582, E-Mail: insurance@ assnservices.com, Web Site: www. physiciansplanning.com (16)

Piantadosi, Joan, Titan List & Mailing Services Inc, Deerfield Beach, FL. Tel: (888) 345-7179, E-Mail: titanlms@bellsouth.net, Web Site: www.titanlists. com (24)

Piarowski, Pamela C., Harris Bancorp Inc, Chicago, IL. Tel: (312) 461-2121, (888) 340-BANK, FAX: (312) 461-7869, E-Mail: onlineservices@harrisbank.com, Web Site: www.harrisbank.com (14)

Picard, Lindsay, WB Mason Co, Brockton, MA. Tel: (800) 773-4488, Web Site: www.wbmason.com (16)

Picarella, Ryan, Wellness Councils of America, Omaha, NE. Tel: (402) 827-3590, FAX: (402) 827-3594, E-Mail: wellworkplace@welcoa.org, Web Site: www.welcoa.org (1)

Picchi, Mike, Allconnect Inc, Atlanta, GA. Tel: (404) 260-2200, Web Site: www.allconnect.com (32)

Pichette, Patrick, Google Inc, Mountain View, CA. Tel: (650) 253-0000, FAX: (650) 253-0001, Web Site: www.google.com (31)

Pickering, Chip, INCOMPAS Show, Washington, DC. Tel: (202) 296-6650, FAX: (202) 296-7585, Web Site: show.incompas.org (42)

Pickering, Christopher, MeritDirect, Rye Brook, NY. Tel: (914) 368-1000, FAX: (914) 368-1150, E-Mail: hq@meritdirect.com, Web Site: www.meritdirect. com (23)

Picket, Jenny, NAMA Agri-Marketing Conference, Overland Park, KS. Tel: (913) 491-6500, FAX: (913) 491-6502, E-Mail: agrimktg@nama.org, Web Site: www.nama.org (42)

Pickett, David, Interface Engineering, Portland, OR. Tel: (503) 382-2266, FAX: (503) 382-2262, E-Mail: solutions@interfaceengineering.com, Web Site: www.ieice.com (20)

Pickett, Mike, Moen Inc, North Olmsted, OH. Tel: (440) 962-2000, Web Site: www.moen.com (16)

Picknally, Thomas, Peter Pan Bus Lines Inc, Springfield, MA. Tel: (413) 781-3320, (800) 343-9999, FAX: (413) 747-7626, E-Mail: info@peterpanbus. com, Web Site: www.peterpanbus.com (19)

Picknelly, Peter A., Peter Pan Bus Lines Inc, Springfield, MA. Tel: (413) 781-3320, (800) 343-9999, FAX: (413) 747-7626, E-Mail: info@peterpanbus. com, Web Site: www.peterpanbus.com (19)

Pickwoad, Lauren, Safeguard Business Systems Inc, Dallas, TX. Tel: (214) 905-3935, (800) 523-2422, FAX: (800) 439-8423, Web Site: www.gosafeguard. com (16)

Picone, Terrence, Etchworld, Hawthorne, NJ. Tel: (973) 423-4002, (800) 872-3458, FAX: (973) 427-8823, Web Site: www.etchworld.com (11)

Picozzi, Alan, Petry Television Inc, New York, NY. Tel: (212) 230-5600, E-Mail: info@petrymedia.com, Web Site: www.petrymedia.com (32)

Pier 1 Imports Inc, Fort Worth, TX. Tel: (817) 252-6300, (800) 245-4595, E-Mail: customerservice@pier1.com, Web Site: www.pier1.com (8)

Lea Pierce Direct Response Strategy & Execution, Santa Rosa, CA. Tel: (707) 571-1586, (800) 932-4748, E-Mail: info@leapierce.com, Web Site: www.leapierce.com (39)

Pierce, Christopher A., The Dingley Press, Lisbon, ME. Tel: (207) 353-4151, (800) 317-4574, FAX: (207) 353-9886, E-Mail: webrequest@dingley.com, Web Site: www.dingley.com (27)

Pierce, Larry, Colorlith Corp, Providence, RI. Tel: (508) 837-6100, (800) 556-7171, FAX: (508) 677-4466, E-Mail: lep@colorlith.net, Web Site: www.colorlith.net (27)

Pierce, Lea, Lea Pierce Direct Response Strategy & Execution, Santa Rosa, CA. Tel: (707) 571-1586, (800) 932-4748, E-Mail: info@leapierce.com, Web Site: www.leapierce.com (39)

Pierce, Tracey, Rodale Inc, Emmaus, PA. Tel: (610) 967-5171, FAX: (610) 967-8963, Web Site: www.rodaleinc.com (16)

Pierce-Marutz, Laura, Allegra Network, LLC, Plymouth, MI. Tel: (248) 596-8600, FAX: (248) 596-8601, Web Site: www2.allegranetwork.com (27)

Pierer, Stefan, KTM Sportmotorcycle USA Inc, Amherst, OH. Tel: (440) 985-3553, FAX: (440) 985-3060, Web Site: www.ktmusa.com (16)

Piervincenzi, Ronald T., US Pharmacopeia, Rockville, MD. Tel: (301) 881-0666, (800) 227-8772, FAX: (301) 816-8236, Web Site: www.usp.org (1)

Pierzynski, Ed, Thomas Scientific, Swedesboro, NJ. Tel: (856) 467-2000, (800) 345-2100, FAX: (856) 467-3087, E-Mail: value@thomassci.com, Web Site: www.thomassci.com (9)

Pietranton, Arlene, American Speech-Language-Hearing Association, Rockville, MD. Tel: (301) 897-5700, (800) 638-8255, FAX: (301) 296-8580, E-Mail: productsales@asha.org, Web Site: www.asha.org (1)

Pietrantoni, Anthony, Alfa Aesar-A Johnson Matthey Co, Ward Hill, MA. Tel: (800) 343-0660, FAX: (800) 322-4757, E-Mail: info@alfa.com, Web Site: www.alfa.com (9)

Pietras, Kevin, FP Mailing Solutions, Addison, IL. Tel: (630) 827-5500, (800) 341-6052, FAX: (630) 693-0626, E-Mail: custserv@fp-usa.com, Web Site: www.fp-usa.com (34)

Pietrini, Mike, ProPhase Marketing Inc, Eden Prairie, MN. Tel: (952) 974-1100, (800) 969-6400, FAX: (952) 974-7874, E-Mail: sales@ppmi.com, Web Site: prophasemarketing.com (21)

Pietrzak, Sejal, ACTIVE Network LLC, Dallas, TX. Tel: (858) 964-6064, (877) 228-4808, Web Site: www.activenetwork.com (22)

Piggott, Julie A., Burlington Northern & Santa Fe LLC, Fort Worth, TX. Tel: (817) 878-2000, (800) 795-2673, FAX: (817) 333-7593, Web Site: www.bnsf.com (16)

Piggott, Mark C., PACCAR Inc, Bellevue, WA. Tel: (425) 468-7400, FAX: (425) 468-8216, Web Site: www.paccar.com (16)

Pikat, Eero, CRB, Chicago, IL. Tel: (312) 554-8456, (800) 621-5271, FAX: (312) 939-4135, E-Mail: info@crbtrader.com, Web Site: www.crbtrader.com (17)

Pike, Debbie, AFA Service Corp, Atlanta, GA. Tel: (404) 237-2964, (404) 262-2729, Web Site: www.arbys.com (16)

Pike, Gerry, DMSA Inc, Newfoundland, PA. Tel: (570) 676-6000 (40)

Pilani's Live in Style, Egg Harbor Township, NJ. Tel: (609) 927-4686, (800) 537-1832, FAX: (609) 927-5686, E-Mail: sihart@aol.com (2)

Pilgrim Printed Promotional Plastics, Brockton, MA. Tel: (508) 436-6300, (800) 343-7810, FAX: (508) 580-3542, E-Mail: pilgrimsales@pilgrimplastics.com, Web Site: www.pilgrimplastics.com (27)

Pilling, Leslie Ann, Presence II Productions, Bloomfield Hills, MI. Tel: (248) 723-9770, E-Mail: leslie@presenceiiproductiions.com, Web Site: www.presenceiiproductions.com (36)

The Pillsbury Co, Minneapolis, MN. Tel: (763) 764-7600, (800) 248-7310, FAX: (763) 764-8330, Web Site: www.pillsbury.com (16)

Pillsbury Winthrop Shaw Pittman LLP, Los Angeles, CA. Tel: (213) 488-7100, Web Site: www.pillsburywinthrop.com (20)

Pilot Interactive Inc, Toronto, ON Canada. Tel: (416) 840-6438, E-Mail: hello@pilotinteractive.ca, Web Site: pilotinteractive.ca (35)

The Pin Man, Tulsa, OK. Tel: (918) 587-2405, FAX: (918) 745-2162, Web Site: www.positivepin.com (16)

Pinand-Dumpert, Kristy, Concepts TV Productions Inc, Boonton, NJ. Tel: (973) 331-1500, FAX: (973) 331-1550, E-Mail: info@conceptstv.com, Web Site: www.conceptstv.com (32)

Pinchuk, Nicholas T., Snap-on Inc, Kenosha, WI. Tel: (262) 656-5200, (800) 866-5748, (800) 786-6600, FAX: (262) 656-5577, Web Site: www.snapon.com (9)

Pine Castle Animal Hospital, Orlando, FL. Tel: (407) 855-5010 (16)

Pine, Asieya, Lockard & Wechsler Direct, Irvington, NY. Tel: (914) 250-0241, E-Mail: info@lwdirect.com, Web Site: www.lwdirect.com (35)

Pinelli, Marc C., Accountants Education Group, Dallas, TX. Tel: (214) 373-3486, (800) 627-7310, FAX: (800) 627-7310, E-Mail: customerservice@accountantsed.com, Web Site: www.accountantsed.com (10)

Pines, Robert, Volt Delta, Blue Bell, PA. Tel: (610) 825-7720, FAX: (610) 567-5698, Web Site: www.voltdelta.com (22)

Pingry, Pat, Ideals Publications Inc, Nashville, TN. Tel: (615) 333-0478, FAX: (615) 781-1447, Web Site: www.idealspublications.com (17)

Pinkerton III, Henry, Fluid Metering Inc, Syosset, NY. Tel: (516) 922-6050, (800) 223-3388, FAX: (516) 624-8261, E-Mail: pumps@fmipump.com, Web Site: www.fmipump.com (16)

Pinkerton Security & Investigation Services, Parsippany, NJ. Tel: (973) 397-2276, (800) 724-1616, FAX: (973) 397-2491, Web Site: www.ci-pinkerton.com (16)

Pinkerton, Debbie, Promotional Product Professionals of Canada, Dorval, QC Canada. Tel: (514) 489-5359, FAX: (800) 489-8741, (514) 489-7760, E-Mail: gladys@pppc.ca, Web Site: www.pppc.ca (1)

Pinkin, James, CCG Marketing Solutions, West Caldwell, NJ. Tel: (973) 808-0009, (866) 902-2807, FAX: (973) 808-9740, E-Mail: info@corpcomm.com, Web Site: home.corpcomm.com (21)

Pinkston, Susan, Stonebridge Press Ltd, Henderson, KY. Tel: (270) 826-0341, FAX: (270) 826-8325 (33)

Pinnacle Direct Marketing LLC, Columbus, OH. Tel: (800) 716-0173, FAX: (888) 754-4511, Web Site: www.pinnacledirectonline.com (35)

Pinnacle List Co, Arlington, VA. Tel: (703) 379-4394, FAX: (703) 379-5312, E-Mail: holly@pinnlistco.com, Web Site: www.pinnlistco.com (23)

Pinnell, Jonathan M., MarketVision Research Inc, Cincinnati, OH. Tel: (513) 791-3100, (800) 232-4250, FAX: (513) 794-3500, E-Mail: jpinnell@mv-research.com, Web Site: www.marketvisionresearch.com (30)

Pinson, Ray, OPIN Systems Inc, Minneapolis, MN. Tel: (952) 567-2444, (800) 888-1804, FAX: (651) 994-7828, E-Mail: judywy@opin.com, Web Site: www.opin.com (22)

Pinter, Jason V, Ifbyphone, Chicago, IL. Tel: (877) 295-5100, (877) 387-7192, Web Site: www.ifbyphone.com (30)

The Pioneer Group, Waterloo, IA. Tel: (319) 234-8969, FAX: (319) 234-8518, E-Mail: jslife@thepioneergroup.com, Web Site: www.pioneergroup.com (28)

Pioneer Hi-Bred International Inc, Johnston, IA. Tel: (515) 535-3200, FAX: (515) 535-4415, E-Mail: web.editor@pioneer.com, Web Site: www.pioneer.com (16)

PIP Printing and Marketing Services, Indianapolis, IN. Tel: (317) 849-6244, Web Site: www.pip.com/pipindy (27)

Piper Jaffray, Minneapolis, MN. Tel: (612) 303-0000, Web Site: www.pjc.com (14)

Piper, Chris, Direxxis Inc, Needham, MA. Tel: (781) 444-7900, FAX: (781) 444-7909, Web Site: www.direxxismarketing.com (22)

Pippen, Carole, Lippincott, Williams & Wilkins, Baltimore, MD. Tel: (410) 528-4000, (800) 638-0672, FAX: (410) 528-8597, E-Mail: customerservice@lww.com, Web Site: www.lww.com (1)

Piretra, Judy, Cornwell Data Services Inc, Paramus, NJ. Tel: (201) 261-1050, FAX: (201) 261-7569, E-Mail: info@cornwelldata.com, Web Site: www.cornwelldata.com (22)

Pirkul, Dr. Hasan, Naveen Jindal School of Management, Richardson, TX. Tel: (972) 883-2705, (972) 883-2750, (972) 883-2275, Web Site: www.utdallas.edu (1)

Pirroni, John, Target Direct Marketing Inc, Kansas City, MO. Tel: (815) 558-0919, Web Site: www.targetdirectmarketing.com (35)

Pisano, Joseph, CCI Direct Mail, Carlstadt, NJ. Tel: (201) 507-5200, E-Mail: sales@ccidirectmail.com, Web Site: ccidirectmail.com (21)

Pisano, Kim, IDG List Services, Framingham, MA. Tel: (508) 766-5633, E-Mail: stozeski@idglist.com, Web Site: www.idglist.com (24)

Pistritto, Sebastian, Lorel Marketing Group, Philadelphia, PA. Tel: (610) 337-2343, FAX: (610) 768-9511, E-Mail: info@lorel.com, Web Site: www.lorel.com (35)

Piszel, Anthony S., Freddie Mac, McLean, VA. Tel: (703) 903-2000, (800) 424-5401, Web Site: www.freddiemac.com (14)

Pitcher, Craig, National Association of Publishers Representatives, Hoffman Estates, IL. Tel: (877) 263-9640, FAX: (847) 885-8393, E-Mail: info@napronline.com, Web Site: www.napronline.com (1)

Pitcherella, Tom, Quattro Direct LLC, Berwyn, PA. Tel: (610) 993-0070, Web Site: www.quattrodirect.com (35)

Pitney Bowes, Stamford, CT. Tel: (203) 356-5000, (800) MR-BOWES, Web Site: www.pitneybowes.com (10)

Pitney Bowes International Mail Services, Newark, NJ. Tel: (800) 521-0080, FAX: (973) 368-6301, E-Mail: marketing@pb.com, Web Site: www.intmail.com (28)

Pitney Bowes Software Systems, Stamford, CT. Tel: (203) 356-5000, (800) 624-5377, FAX: (203) 351-7336, Web Site: www.pitneybowes.com (22)

Pittenger, Karen, Black Olive Co, Chicago, IL. Tel: (312) 893-5454, FAX: (312) 276-8636, E-Mail: info@blackoliveco.com, Web Site: www.blackoliveco.com (35)

Pittman & Davis Inc, Harlingen, TX. Tel: (956) 423-2154, (800) 289-7829, FAX: (866) 329-7829, E-Mail: fruit@pittmandavis.com, Web Site: www.pittmandavis.com (4)

Pittsburgh Mailing, Pittsburgh, PA. Tel: (412) 922-8181, FAX: (412) 937-1730, E-Mail: ksmallhoover@pittsburghmailing.com, Web Site: www.pittsburghmailing.com (28)

Pittsburgh Parks Conservancy, Pittsburgh, PA. Tel: (412) 682-7275, Web Site: www.pittsburghparks.org (1)

Piunno, Dominic, Marketing Communication Resource Inc, Willoughby, OH. Tel: (440) 484-3010, FAX: (440) 484-3020 (28)

Piunno, Frank, Marketing Communication Resource Inc, Willoughby, OH. Tel: (440) 484-3010, FAX: (440) 484-3020 (28)

Piusz, Peter, Beckmann Converting Inc, Amsterdam, NY. Tel: (518) 842-0073, FAX: (518) 842-0282, E-Mail: ppiusz@beckmannconverting.com, Web Site: www.beckmannconverting.com (16)

Pizza Hut Inc, Plano, TX. Tel: (972) 338-7700, (866) 298-6986, FAX: (972) 338-6869, Web Site: www.pizzahut.com (16)

Pizzano, Susan, Dr Leonard's Healthcare Corp, Edison, NJ. Tel: (732) 225-0100, (800) 455-1918, FAX: (732) 225-0302, Web Site: www.doctorleonard.com (7)

The Plain Dealer, Cleveland, OH. Tel: (216) 999-5000, (800) 362-0727, FAX: (216) 999-6356, Web Site: www.plaindealer.com (18)

Plamieniak, Mary, Crossbow Group, Westport, CT. Tel: (203) 222-2244, FAX: (203) 226-7838, E-Mail: info@crossbowgroup.com, Web Site: www.crossbowgroup.com (40)

Plan International USA, Warwick, RI. Tel: (401) 562-8400, (800) 556-7918, FAX: (401) 738-5608, Web Site: www.planusa.org (1)

Planet Cotton, Gaithersburg, MD. Tel: (301) 948-0400, FAX: (301) 948-9031, Web Site: www.planetcotton.com (2)

Plank, Susan Patterson, Customized Newspaper Advertising, Des Moines, IA. Tel: (515) 244-2145, (800) 227-7636, FAX: (515) 244-4855, Web Site: www.cnaads.com (18)

Planned Parenthood Federation of America, New York, NY. Tel: (212) 541-7800, FAX: (212) 245-1845, Web Site: www.plannedparenthood.org (1)

Planned Parenthood Mar Monte, San Jose, CA. Tel: (408) 287-7532, FAX: (408) 971-6935, Web Site: www.plannedparenthood.org (1)

Bud Plant Illustrated Books, Palo Alto, CA. Tel: (650) 493-1191, FAX: (650) 493-1145, E-Mail: jim@bpib.com, Web Site: www.bpib.com (6)

Plant, Randy. AlphaGraphics World Headquarters, Salt Lake City, UT. Tel: (801) 595-7270, (800) 955-6246, FAX: (801) 595-7271, E-Mail: contactus@alphagraphics.com, Web Site: www.alphagraphics.com (27)

Plant, Roger, Truitt Brothers Inc, Salem, OR. Tel: (503) 362-3674, (800) 547-8712, FAX: (503) 588-2868, E-Mail: truittbrothers@truittbros.com, Web Site: www.truittbros.com (16)

Plas-Tanks Industries Inc, Hamilton, OH. Tel: (513) 942-3800, FAX: (513) 942-3993, E-Mail: info@plastanks.com, Web Site: www.plastanks.com (9)

Plasterer, Donald, Grower's Supply Co, Dexter, MI. Tel: (734) 426-5852, FAX: (734) 426-5750, E-Mail: growers@grower-supply.com, Web Site: www.growerssupplycompany.com (8)

Plastic Graphic, Wauconda, IL. Tel: (847) 487-2030, FAX: (847) 487-2050, E-Mail: bgrimespgc@sbcglobal.net, Web Site: www.plasticgraphic.com (27)

Plastic View ATC, Simi Valley, CA. Tel: (805) 520-9390, (800) 468-6301, FAX: (805) 520-0260, E-Mail: info@pvatc.com, Web Site: www.pvatc.com (9)

Plate, John P., The CPW Group, Ronkonkoma, NY. Tel: (888) 641-7901 (28)

Platinum Press, Killingworth, CT. Tel: (860) 663-3882, FAX: (718) 825-5065, E-Mail: herbertjcohen@aol.com (20)

Platt, Ethan, American Meadows Inc & Vermont Wild Flowers Farm, Shelburne, VT. Tel: (877) 309-7333, FAX: (802) 951-9089, E-Mail: customerservice@americanmeadows.com, Web Site: www.americanmeadows.com (8)

Platt, George R., Harty Integrated Solutions, New Haven, CT. Tel: (203) 562-5112, (800) 654-0562, FAX: (203) 782-9168, E-Mail: gplatt@hartynet.com, Web Site: www.hartynet.com (21)

Platt, Joel, The Bradford Group, Niles, IL. Tel: (847) 966-2770, FAX: (847) 581-8630, Web Site: www.collectiblestoday.com (16)

Platt, Mark, Heartland America, Chaska, MN. Tel: (952) 361-3640, (800) 229-2901, FAX: (952) 368-3452, E-Mail: info@heartlandamerica.com, Web Site: www.heartlandamerica.com (3)

Platt, Rick, The Franklin Mint, Exton, PA. Tel: (610) 497-4800, (800) THE-MINT, FAX: (610) 497-4956, E-Mail: support@franklinmint.com, Web Site: www.franklinmint.com (16)

Plawsky, Lawrence B., FTD Companies Inc, Downers Grove, IL. Tel: (630) 719-7800, Web Site: www.ftdcompanies.com (16)

Playboy Enterprises Inc, Beverly Hills, CA. Tel: (310) 860-1215, Web Site: www.playboyenterprises.com (17)

Player Piano Co Inc, Wichita, KS. Tel: (316) 263-3241, FAX: (316) 263-5480, Web Site: www.playerpianocompany.com (11)

Playworld Systems, Lewisburg, PA. Tel: (570) 522-9800, FAX: (570) 522-3030, Web Site: www.playworldsystems.com (34)

Pleasant Company, Middleton, WI. Tel: (608) 831-4116, (800) 845-0005, FAX: (608) 836-1999, Web Site: www.americangirl.com (11)

Pletch, Evelyn, North American Co for Life & Health Insurance, Chicago, IL. Tel: (312) 648-7600, (800) 800-3656, FAX: (312) 648-7796, Web Site: www.nacolah.com (15)

Pleva, Lavena, Princess House Inc, Taunton, MA. Tel: (508) 823-0711, (508) 832-6800, (800) 622-0039, FAX: (508) 823-5182, Web Site: www.princesshouse.com (16)

Plewa, Christine, Pro Media Marketing Group, Menomonee Falls, WI. Tel: (800) 328-0439, FAX: (262) 532-4147, E-Mail: sales@promediaus.com, Web Site: www.promediaus.com (35)

Plewa, Roman, A&R Mailing Machine Inc, East Hartford, CT. Tel: (860) 290-6640, FAX: (860) 290-6644, E-Mail: info@a-r-machine.com, Web Site: a-r-machine.com (34)

Plexus Marketing Group Inc, Atlanta, GA. Tel: (770) 390-9692, (800) 9-PLEXUS, FAX: (770) 390-9693, Web Site: www.plexusmarketing.com (20)

Plimpton, Thomas, PACCAR Inc, Bellevue, WA. Tel: (425) 468-7400, FAX: (425) 468-8216, Web Site: www.paccar.com (16)

Plisco, Drew, Infutor Data Solutions, Oakbrook Terrace, IL. Tel: (312) 348-7900, E-Mail: sales@infutor.com, Web Site: www.infutor.com (23)

Plockinger, Harald, KTM Sportmotorcycle USA Inc, Amherst, OH. Tel: (440) 985-3553, FAX: (440) 985-3060, Web Site: www.ktmusa.com (16)

Plotnick, Stanley, Encore Marketing International, Lanham, MD. Tel: (301) 459-8020, (800) 846-9398, FAX: (301) 731-0525, E-Mail: customerservice@encoremarketing.com, Web Site: www.encoremarketing.com (16)

The Plow & Hearth Inc, Madison, VA. Tel: (800) 494-7544, Web Site: www.plowhearth.com (8)

Plunkett, Dan, TFC Inc, Napa, CA. Tel: (707) 224-6161, Web Site: www.tfcinc.com (27)

Pluris Inc, Framingham, MA. Tel: (508) 663-1100, FAX: (508) 663-1060, E-Mail: info@plurismarketing.com, Web Site: www.plurismarketing.com (22)

PlusMedia LLC, Danbury, CT. Tel: (203) 748-6500, FAX: (203) 748-6600, E-Mail: contact@plusme.com, Web Site: www.plusme.com (35)

PlusNetMarketing Inc, Exton, PA. Tel: (610) 458-0707, E-Mail: info@pnmarketing.com, Web Site: www.plusnetmarketing.com (21)

Pluzynski & Associates Inc, Boulder, CO. Tel: (646) 434-8785, E-Mail: info@pluzynski.com, Web Site: www.pluzynski.com (35)

Pluzynski, Scott, CorCreative Group LLC, Boulder, CO. Tel: (917) 971-4847, E-Mail: ccginfo@corcreativegroup.com, Web Site: corcreativegroup.com (35)

Pluzynski, Scott, Pluzynski & Associates Inc, Boulder, CO. Tel: (646) 434-8785, E-Mail: info@pluzynski.com, Web Site: www.pluzynski.com (35)

Plymouth Rock Assurance, Lincroft, NJ. Tel: (732) 978-6255, Web Site: www.highpointins.com (15)

Pneuma Books, Elkton, MD. Tel: (410) 441-8200, FAX: (410) 441-8201, E-Mail: gettingstarted@pneumabooks.com, Web Site: www.pneumabooks.com (17)

Pocket Nurse Enterprises Inc, Monaca, PA. Tel: (720) 480-3777, (800) 225-1600, FAX: (720) 480-3778, E-Mail: sales@pocketnurse.com, Web Site: www.pocketnurse.com (17)

Podolec, Anna, National Crime Prevention Council, Amsterdam, NY. Tel: (518) 842-4388, (888) 776-7763, FAX: (800) 995-5121, E-Mail: mcgruff@spocentral.com, Web Site: www.mcgruffspo.com (17)

Poehling, John, Torcom Inbound Telemarketing, Madison, WI. Tel: (800) 832-4939, FAX: (608) 275-6557, E-Mail: torcom@torcom.com, Web Site: www.torcom.com (29)

Poffenberger, Chase, Academic Travel Abroad Inc, Washington, DC. Tel: (202) 785-9000, (800) 556-7896, FAX: (202) 342-0317, Web Site: www.academictravel.com (19)

Pogash, Thomas A., Rodale Inc, Emmaus, PA. Tel: (610) 967-5171, FAX: (610) 967-8963, Web Site: www.rodaleinc.com (17)

Pogell, Suzanne, Womanship, Annapolis, MD. Tel: (410) 267-6661, FAX: (410) 263-2036, E-Mail: sail@womanship.com, Web Site: www.womanship.com (16)

Pogwizd, Laura, BFC, Batavia, IL. Tel: (630) 879-9240, Web Site: www.bfcprint.com (28)

Pohaku Inc, Kaneohe, HI. Tel: (319) 653-2569, Web Site: www.gopohaku.com (20)

The Pohly Co, Boston, MA. Tel: (617) 451-1700, (800) 383-0888, FAX: (617) 338-7767, E-Mail: info@pohlyco.com, Web Site: www.pohlyco.com (17)

Pohly, Diana, The Pohly Co, Boston, MA. Tel: (617) 451-1700, (800) 383-0888, FAX: (617) 338-7767, E-Mail: info@pohlyco.com, Web Site: www.pohlyco.com (17)

Point To Point Marketing Inc, Fort Collins, CO. Tel: (513) 231-0344, E-Mail: info@ptpmarketing.com, Web Site: ptpmarketing.com (35)

PointOne Graphics Inc, Toronto, ON Canada. Tel: (416) 255-8202, (866) 717-5722, FAX: (416) 255-6917, Web Site: www.point-one.com (27)

Poitras, Steve, Group 236, Oakland, CA. Tel: (510) 874-0141, Web Site: group236.com (32)

Poker Player, Sherman Oaks, CA. Tel: (310) 674-3365, FAX: (310) 674-3205, E-Mail: ard@gamblingtimes.com, Web Site: www.gamblingtimes.com (17)

Pokrzyk, Steve, Vector Marketing Corp, Olean, NY. Tel: (716) 373-6141, (267) 880-1750, FAX: (716) 373-6145, Web Site: www.cutco.com (5)

Pola, Prasad, Diapers.com, Jersey City, NJ. Tel: (800) 342-7377, E-Mail: customercare@diapers.com, Web Site: www.diapers.com (5)

Polaris Direct, Hooksett, NH. Tel: (603) 626-5800, E-Mail: info@polarisdirect.net, Web Site: www.polarisdirect.net (28)

Polaroid Corp, Minnetonka, MN. Tel: (781) 386-2000, (800) 765-2764, FAX: (781) 386-3263, E-Mail: marketing@polaroid.com, Web Site: www.polaroid.com (16)

Polatseck, David, DPC Computers, Monsey, NY. Tel: (845) 426-3790, (866) 513-CORP, FAX: (845) 426-6275, E-Mail: learnmore@salestax.com, Web Site: www.salestax.com (16)

Polcha, Jon, Blue Cross Blue Shield of Oklahoma, Tulsa, OK. Tel: (918) 560-3500, (800) 942-5837, E-Mail: info@bcbsok.com, Web Site: www.bcbsok.com (15)

Polec, Laura, Brigar Xpress Solutions, Inc, Albany, NY. Tel: (518) 438-7817, (877) 437-7817, FAX: (518) 438-0224, E-Mail: general@brigarxpress.com, Web Site: www.brigarxpress.com (28)

Polestar Group, West Simsbury, CT. Tel: (860) 658-4992 (20)

Policay, Barbara, Claritas Express, Ithaca, NY. Tel: (607) 257-5757, (866) 737-7429, FAX: (607) 266-0425, E-Mail: info@claritas.com, Web Site: www.claritas.com/express (30)

Policinski, Chris, Land O' Lakes Inc, Arden Hills, MN. Tel: (651) 481-2222, (800) 328-9680, FAX: (651) 481-2000, Web Site: www.landolakesinc.com (16)

Politano, Tommy, Prestone Printing Co Inc, Long Island City, NY. Tel: (347) 468-7900, FAX: (347) 468-7885, E-Mail: info@prestoneprint.com, Web Site: www.prestoneprinting.com (25)

Political Resources Inc, Lake Worth, FL. Tel: (800) 423-2677, FAX: (561) 533-0104, E-Mail: chess@politicalresources.com, Web Site: www.politicalresources.com (23)

Polizzi, Suzanne, Remedy Magazine, New York, NY. Tel: (212) 695-2223, FAX: (212) 695-2936, E-Mail: info@rmedizine.com, Web Site: www.medizine.com (17)

Polkosky, Douglas, Thomas Computer Corp, Orlando, FL. Tel: (407) 855-2020, (800) 621-3906, FAX: (407) 426-2805, E-Mail: hildap@thomascompute.com, Web Site: www.thomascomputer.com (16)

Polkosky, Hilda, Thomas Computer Corp, Orlando, FL. Tel: (407) 855-2020, (800) 621-3906, FAX: (407) 426-2805, E-Mail: hildap@thomascompute.com, Web Site: www.thomascomputer.com (16)

Pollack, Daniel, Stock Yards Packing Co Inc, Medford, OR. Tel: (312) 733-6050, (888) 842-6111, FAX: (888) 700-9919, E-Mail: customerservice@stockyards.com, Web Site: www.stockyards.com (4)

Pollack, Kathy, Christian Broadcasting Network Inc, Virginia Beach, VA. Tel: (757) 226-7000, FAX: (757) 226-2017, Web Site: www.cbn.com (1)

Pollak, Isaac, LGP GEM LTD, New York, NY. Tel: (212) 840-2510, FAX: (212) 302-6182, E-Mail: sales@lgpltd.com, Web Site: www.lgpltd.com (16)

Pollitt, Ken, Woodworker's Supply Inc, Casper, WY. Tel: (307) 237-5528, (800) 321-9841, FAX: (307) 57-5272, E-Mail: kenp@woodworker.com, Web Site: www.woodworker.com (11)

Pollock, Brenda, School Annual Publishing Co, State College, PA. Tel: (800) 436-6030, E-Mail: yearbook@schoolannual.com, Web Site: www.schoolannual.com (17)

Pollock, Rob, Assurant Group, New York, NY. Tel: (305) 253-2244, FAX: (305) 252-6987, Web Site: www.assurant.com (15)

Polo Ralph Lauren, New York, NY. Tel: (212) 813-7868, (800) 377-7656, Web Site: www.ralphlauren.com (2)

Polomo, Nino, Blue Coral Slick 50, Houston, TX. Tel: (713) 241-6161, (800) 416-1600, FAX: (713) 241-4044, E-Mail: SCD-ConsumerSolutions@Shell.com, Web Site: www.bluecoral.com (16)

Polstein, John, Kaplan Test Prep, New York, NY. Tel: (212) 997-5800, Web Site: www.kaptest.com (1)

Poltrack, David, ARF Events, New York, NY. Tel: (212) 751-5656, FAX: (212) 319-5265, E-Mail: info@theARF.org, Web Site: theARF.org (42)

Poltrone, Kristi, Vita-Mix Corp, Cleveland, OH. Tel: (440) 235-4840, (800) VITA-MIX, FAX: (440) 235-3726, E-Mail: service@vitamix.com, Web Site: www.vitamix.com (16)

Polus, Paul, CDS Global, Des Moines, IA. Tel: (515) 246-6837, FAX: (515) 246-6687, E-Mail: dluther@cdsfulfillment.com, Web Site: www.cdsglobal.com (22)

Poly-Flex Corp, Edgewood, NY. Tel: (631) 586-9500, FAX: (631) 586-6631, E-Mail: info@poly-flexcorp.com, Web Site: www.poly-flexcorp.com (26)

Poly One Corp, Avon Lake, OH. Tel: (440) 930-1000, (866) POLY-ONE, FAX: (440) 930-1428, Web Site: www.polyone.com (16)

Polyair Packaging, Chicago, IL. Tel: (773) 995-1818, (888) POLYAIR X444, FAX: (773) 995-7725, E-Mail: marketing@polyair.com, Web Site: www.polyair.com (9)

Polyline LLC, Elmhurst, IL. Tel: (800) 701-7689, FAX: (630) 834-6800, E-Mail: customerservice@polylinecorp.com, Web Site: www.polylinecorp.com (3)

Polynesian Cultural Center, Honolulu, HI. Tel: (808) 293-3333, (800) 367-7060, FAX: (888) 722-7339, E-Mail: internetrez@polynesia.com, Web Site: www.polynesia.com (16)

Pomerantz, Michael H., FlrstMark Inc, Campton, NH. Tel: (603) 726-4800, (800) 729-2600, FAX: (603) 726-4840, E-Mail: sales@firstmark.com, Web Site: www.firstmark.com (23)

Pomeroy, William G., Cablexpress Technologies, Syracuse, NY. Tel: (315) 476-3000, (800) 913-9467, FAX: (315) 455-1800, E-Mail: info@cablexpress.com, Web Site: www.CXTec.com (10)

The Pond-Ekberg Co, Chicopee, MA. Tel: (413) 594-7511, (800) 225-7511, FAX: (413) 594-2179, E-Mail: sales@pond-ekberg.com, Web Site: www.pond-ekberg.com (27)

Pond, Eldon, Worcester Envelope, Auburn, MA. Tel: (508) 832-5394, (800) 343-1398, FAX: (508) 832-3796, E-Mail: sales@worcesterenvelope.com, Web Site: www.worcester-envelope.com (26)

Pond, Sara, Nightingale-Conant Corp, Niles, IL. Tel: (847) 647-0300, (800) 557-1660, FAX: (847) 647-7145, Web Site: www.nightingale.com (17)

Ponder, Dave, James Medical Rents & Sales Inc, Fort Wayne, IN. Tel: (260) 739-0874, E-Mail: sales@jamesmedical.com, Web Site: www.jamesmedical.net (7)

Pont Media Direct, Norwalk, CT. Tel: (203) 354-8074, FAX: (203) 956-9227, E-Mail: stefanie@listgoddess.com (23)

Pont, Stefanie, Pont Media Direct, Norwalk, CT. Tel: (203) 354-8074, FAX: (203) 956-9227, E-Mail: stefanie@listgoddess.com (23)

Pontifical Mission Societies in the US, New York, NY. Tel: (212) 563-8700, Web Site: www.onefamilyinmission.org (1)

WS Ponton Inc, Pittsburgh, PA. Tel: (412) 782-2360, (800) 628-7806, FAX: (412) 782-1109, E-Mail: info@wsponton.com, Web Site: www.wsponton.com (23)

Pontual, Romulo C., DIRECTV LLC, El Segundo, CA. Tel: (310) 535-5000, FAX: (310) 535-5225, Web Site: www.directv.com (16)

Ponze, Iwona, Arends, Batavia, IL. Tel: (630) 990-0220, FAX: (630) 990-2556, Web Site: www.arends-inc.com (35)

Ponzoni, Jaci, Pace Communications Inc, Greensboro, NC. Tel: (336) 378-6065, FAX: (336) 275-2864, Web Site: www.pacecommunications.com (17)

Pook, Barbara, Nutritional Research Associates Inc, South Whitley, IN. Tel: (260) 723-4931, (800) 456-4931, FAX: (260) 723-6297, E-Mail: info@nrfeeds.com, Web Site: www.nrfeeds.com (16)

Poole, Bob, Dome Printing, Sacramento, CA. Tel: (800) 343-3139 (27)

Poole, Mark M., Marsh US Consumer, Urbandale, IA. Tel: (515) 365-6102 (15)

Poole, Tim, Dome Printing, Sacramento, CA. Tel: (800) 343-3139 (27)

Pop Labs Inc, Houston, TX. Tel: (877) 500-1399, FAX: (877) 850-2420, Web Site: www.poplabs.com (35)

The Popcorn Factory, Lake Forest, IL. Tel: (847) 247-3342, (888) 238-8107, (888) 833-4595, E-Mail: service@thepopcornfactory.com, Web Site: www.thepopcornfactory.com (4)

Pope, Alice, Photographer's Market, Blue Ash, OH. Tel: (513) 531-2690, FAX: (513) 531-2686, E-Mail: photomarket@fwpubs.com, Web Site: www.photographersmarket.com (43)

Pope, C. Larry, Smithfield Foods, Smithfield, VA. Tel: (800) 276-6158, Web Site: www.smithfieldfoods.com (16)

Pope, John R., Williams Printing Co, Atlanta, GA. Tel: (404) 875-6611, (800) 950-7588, FAX: (404) 872-4025, Web Site: www.rrdonnelley.com (27)

Pope, Richard, Win Craft Inc, Winona, MN. Tel: (507) 454-5510, (800) 533-8100, FAX: (507) 454-6403, E-Mail: inquiries@wincraftschool.com, Web Site: www.wincraftschool.com (5)

Popkin, Ph.D. Michael H., Active Parenting, Marietta, GA. Tel: (770) 429-0565, (800) 825-0060, (800) 235-7755, FAX: (770) 429-0334, E-Mail: cservice@activeparenting.com, Web Site: www.activeparenting.com (17)

Popovich, Deidre, National Federation of Independent Business, Nashville, TN. Tel: (615) 872-5800, Web Site: www.nfib.com (1)

Population Connection, Washington, DC. Tel: (202) 332-2200, Web Site: www.populationconnection.net (1)

Popwell, David T., First Tennessee Bank, Memphis, TN. Tel: (901) 523-4883, FAX: (901) 523-4030, Web Site: www.firsttennessee.com (14)

Richard M Pordes LLC, Stamford, CT. Tel: (203) 316-9190 (1)

Pordes, Richard, Richard M Pordes LLC, Stamford, CT. Tel: (203) 316-9190 (1)

Porepp, Cathy, Successful Farming, Des Moines, IA. Tel: (515) 284-2143, (800) 678-2711, FAX: (515) 284-3127 (17)

Porray, Dale, Amateur Electronic Supply LLC, Milwaukee, WI. Tel: (414) 558-0333, (800) 558-0411, FAX: (414) 358-3337, Web Site: www.aesham.com (16)

Porta-Bote International, Mountain View, CA. Tel: (650) 961-5334, (800) 227-8882, Web Site: www.porta-bote.com (11)

Porter Wallace Corp, Brick, NJ. Tel: (732) 920-1405, FAX: (732) 920-1406, Web Site: www.porterwallace.com (33)

Porter, Alex, Location3 Media, Denver, CO. Tel: (720) 881-8510, FAX: (303) 298-1986, E-Mail: info@location3.com, Web Site: www.location3.com (32)

Porter, Amy, National Osteoporosis Foundation, Washington, DC. Tel: (202) 721-6346, Web Site: www.nof.org (1)

Porter, Chuck, Crispin Porter + Bogusky, Miami, FL. Tel: (305) 859-2070, FAX: (305) 854-3419, E-Mail: info@cpbgroup.com, Web Site: www.cpbgroup.com (35)

Porter, Martin, MESA Media & Entertainment Services Alliancce, Port Washington, NY. Tel: (516) 767-6720, Web Site: www.mesalliance.org/ (22)

Porteus, Anna, Startec Global Communications, Rockville, MD. Tel: (301) 610-4300, FAX: (301) 610-4301, Web Site: www.startec.com (32)

Portillo, Rhina, Liguori Publications, Liguori, MO. Tel: (636) 464-2500, (800) 325-9521, FAX: (800) 325-9526, E-Mail: liguori@liguori.org, Web Site: www.liguori.org (17)

Portland Cement Association, Washington, DC. Tel: (202) 408-9494, Web Site: www.cement.org (1)

Portland Rescue Mission, Portland, OR. Tel: (503) 906-7605, Web Site: www.portlandrescuemission.org (1)

Portman, Jeff, AMC Inc, Atlanta, GA. Tel: (404) 220-2000, FAX: (404) 220-3030 (2)

Portman, Jr John. AmericasMart Atlanta, Atlanta, GA. Tel: (404) 220-3000, FAX: (404) 220-3030, Web Site: www.americasmart.com (42)

Porto-Lenza, Gia, CIT, Livingston, NJ. Tel: (973) 740-5000, FAX: (973) 740-5383, Web Site: www.cit.com (14)

Portrait International Inc, Boston, MA. Tel: (617) 457-5200, Web Site: www.portraitsoftware.com (22)

Posacki, Roger, Elmers Products Inc, Westerville, OH. Tel: (614) 985-2600, (800) 848-9400, FAX: (614) 985-2605, E-Mail: comments@elmers.com, Web Site: www.elmers.com (25)

Posh Papers, Riverside, RI. Tel: (401) 331-9873, FAX: (401) 331-2229, E-Mail: info@poshpapersonline.com, Web Site: www.poshpapersonline.com (6)

Position Technologies Inc, Geneva, IL. Tel: (630) 262-5300, FAX: (630) 232-2998, Web Site: www.positiontech.com (16)

PossibleNOW Inc, Duluth, GA. Tel: (770) 255-1020, FAX: (770) 255-1025, Web Site: www.dncsolution.com (22)

Post Linx Corp, Scarborough, ON Canada. Tel: (416) 752-8100, FAX: (416) 752-8239, Web Site: www.postlinx.com (28)

Post University, Waterbury, CT. Tel: (203) 596-4520, (800) 345-2562, E-Mail: admissions@post.edu, Web Site: www.post.edu (41)

Post, Jeff, CUNA Mutual Group, Madison, WI. Tel: (608) 238-5851, (800) 356-2644, FAX: (608) 231-8839, Web Site: www.cunamutual.com (15)

Post, Jerry, Orchard Supply Hardware, San Jose, CA. Tel: (408) 281-3500, FAX: (408) 225-0388, Web Site: www.osh.com (16)

Post, Jim, Chattanooga Shooting Supplies Inc, Chattanooga, TN. Tel: (423) 894-3007, (800) 251-4808, FAX: (423) 855-5513, Web Site: www.chattanoogashooting.com (16)

Postal En Espanol Inc, Tampa, FL. Tel: (813) 885-8888, Web Site: www.postalenespanol.com (20)

PostLink Corp, Ottawa, ON Canada. Tel: (613) 741-4538, Web Site: www.ottawamailingservices.com (28)

Postmatic Inc, Minneapolis, MN. Tel: (763) 784-6046, (888) 784-6046, FAX: (763) 784-9433, E-Mail: info@postmatic.net, Web Site: www.postmatic.com (34)

Posty Cards Inc, Kansas City, MO. Tel: (816) 231-2323, (800) 554-5018, FAX: (888) 577-3800, E-Mail: customerservice@postycards.com, Web Site: www.postycards.com (16)

Potawatomi Bingo Casino, Milwaukee, WI. Tel: (414) 645-6888, (800) PAYS-BIG, FAX: (414) 847-7727, Web Site: www.paysbig.com (19)

Potente, Ralph, CyberData, Hicksville, NY. Tel: (516) 942-8000, FAX: (516) 942-0800, E-Mail: info@cyberdata.com, Web Site: www.cyberdata.com (22)

Potier, Bernard, Christian Dior Perfumes, New York, NY. Tel: (877) 903-4671, (800) 929-3467, FAX: (212) 931-2954, Web Site: www.dior.com (7)

Potiker, Lowell, Entertainment Publications Inc, Troy, MI. Tel: (248) 404-1000, (888) 231-SAVE, FAX: (248) 404-1915, Web Site: www.entertainment.com (31)

Potpourri Group Inc, North Billerica, MA. Tel: (978) 256-4100, FAX: (978) 256-1961/0344, Web Site: www.potpourrigroup.com (6)

Potrock, Ken, Disney Vacation Club, Kissimmee, FL. Tel: (407) 566-3000, (800) 500-3990, FAX: (407) 566-3393 (19)

Potrykus, Kristina, Potawatomi Bingo Casino, Milwaukee, WI. Tel: (414) 645-6888, (800) PAYS-BIG, FAX: (414) 847-7727, Web Site: www.paysbig.com (19)

Potter, Duncan, Westcon, Tarrytown, NY. Tel: (914) 829-7000, FAX: (914) 829-7137, Web Site: www.westcon.com (14)

Pottle, Martin K., Martin Thomas International, Sterling, VA. Tel: (401) 225-3905, E-Mail: mpottle@martinthomas.com, Web Site: www.martinthomas.com (35)

Potts, Cheryl, Alexian Brothers Bonaventure House, Chicago, IL. Tel: (773) 327-9921, FAX: (773) 327-9113, E-Mail: info@abam.org, Web Site: www.bonaventurehouse.org (1)

Potts, Jeffrey C., The Company Store Inc, La Crosse, WI. Tel: (608) 785-1400, FAX: (608) 791-5790, Web Site: www.thecompanystore.com (16)

Poulin, Pamela, Alfa Aesar-A Johnson Matthey Co, Ward Hill, MA. Tel: (800) 343-0660, FAX: (800) 322-4757, E-Mail: info@alfa.com, Web Site: www.alfa.com (9)

Poulose, Joseph, InterMedia Advertising, Woodland Hills, CA. Tel: (818) 995-1455, (800) 846-3289, FAX: (818) 719-9977, E-Mail: sales@intermedia-advertising.com, Web Site: www.intermedia-advertising.com (35)

Poulsen, Susan, Papa John's International, Louisville, KY. Tel: (502) 261-7272, Web Site: www.papajohns.com (4)

Pound, Sr. Alan, Epson America, Long Beach, CA. Tel: (562) 981-3840, (800) 873-7766, FAX: (562) 290-5220, Web Site: www.epson.com (10)

Pow, Gordon, DeLorme Mapping, Yarmouth, ME. Tel: (207) 846-7100, (800) 642-0970, FAX: (207) 846-7051, E-Mail: caleb.mason@delorme.com, Web Site: www.delorme.com (3)

Pow, Rebecca, University of Alabama, Tuscaloosa, AL. Tel: (205) 348-6330, (866) 307-3917, FAX: (205) 348-9246, Web Site: continuingstudies.ua.edu (13)

Powell, Bonnie P., Telenational Marketing, Omaha, NE. Tel: (800) 333-6106 X132, FAX: (402) 391-2044, Web Site: www.telenational.com (29)

Powell, III Earl A., National Gallery of Art Gift Shop, Washington, DC. Tel: (202) 842-6466, (800) 697-9350, FAX: (202) 842-4043, Web Site: www.nga.gov (16)

Powell, Jenny, US Bancorp, Minneapolis, MN. Tel: (651) 466-3000, (800) 872-2657, FAX: (612) 303-0782, Web Site: www.usbank.com (14)

Powell, Ken, Landmark Graphics Corp, Houston, TX. Tel: (713) 839-2000, FAX: (713) 839-2015, Web Site: www.landmarksoftware.com (16)

Powell, Kendall J., General Mills Inc, Minneapolis, MN. Tel: (800) 248-7310, FAX: (763) 764-8330, Web Site: www.generalmills.com (8)

Powell, Kendall J., The Pillsbury Co, Minneapolis, MN. Tel: (763) 764-7600, (800) 248-7310, FAX: (763) 764-8330, Web Site: www.pillsbury.com (16)

Powell, Michael, INTX - The Internet & Televison Expo, Washington, DC. Tel: (202) 222-2430, FAX: (202) 222-2431, E-Mail: infointx@ncta.com, Web Site: www.intxshow.com (42)

Powell, Mike, A Eicoff & Co, Chicago, IL. Tel: (312) 527-7183, (800) 333-6605, FAX: (312) 527-7192, E-Mail: bill.mccabe@eicoff.com, Web Site: www.eicoff.com (35)

Powell, Rick, PMG, Columbia, MD. Tel: (410) 290-0667, Web Site: www.pmgdirect.net (20)

Powell, Robert, The Total Mailing System, West Deptford, NJ. Tel: (856) 628-8800, FAX: (856) 628-8810, Web Site: www.ttms.com (22)

Powell, Shirley, The Weather Channel, Atlanta, GA. Tel: (770) 226-0000, FAX: (770) 226-2390, Web Site: www.weather.com (32)

Power & Telephone Supply, Randolph, VT. Tel: (800) 451-4381, FAX: (802) 234-5006, E-Mail: cablesales@ptsupply.com, Web Site: www.ptsupply.com/enterprise (16)

Power Direct, Mission Viejo, CA. Tel: (877) 737-8977, FAX: (949) 253-3458, E-Mail: info@powerdirect.net, Web Site: www.powerdirect.net (35)

JD Power Associates, Westlake Village, CA. Tel: (805) 418-8000, (888) 537-6937, FAX: (805) 418-8900, E-Mail: information@jdpa.com, Web Site: www.jdpower.com (30)

Power Music, Salt Lake City, UT. Tel: (801) 292-2418, (800) 777-BEAT, FAX: (801) 292-2462, Web Site: www.powermusic.com (16)

Press, Jeff, JWT Inside, Los Angeles, CA. Tel: (310) 309-8282, (877) 665-8768, FAX: (310) 309-8283, E-Mail: conversations@jwtinside.com, Web Site: www.jwtinside.com (35)

Press, Marvin S., CPI Card Group, Littleton, CO. Tel: (303) 973-9311, FAX: (303) 973-8420, E-Mail: mbarber@cpicardgroup.com, Web Site: www. cpicardgroup.com (27)

Theodore Presser Co, King Of Prussia, PA. Tel: (610) 592-1222, FAX: (610) 592-1229, E-Mail: webmaster@presser.com, Web Site: www.presser. com (17)

Presskits, East Walpole, MA. Tel: (781) 762-3003, (800) 472-3497, FAX: (781) 255-7791, Web Site: www.presskits.com (27)

ST Preston & Son Inc, Greenport, NY. Tel: (631) 477-1990, E-Mail: catalog@prestons.com, Web Site: www.prestons.com (8)

Preston, Joseph, Network Telephone Services Inc, Woodland Hills, CA. Tel: (818) 992-4300, (800) 727-6874, FAX: (818) 992-8415, Web Site: www. nts.net (16)

Preston, Leslie, Fashion Institute of Technology Library, New York, NY. Tel: (212) 217-7999, FAX: (212) 217-4371, Web Site: www.fitnyc.edu (1)

Prestone Printing Co Inc, Long Island City, NY. Tel: (347) 468-7900, FAX: (347) 468-7885, E-Mail: info@prestoneprint.com, Web Site: www. prestoneprinting.com (25)

Prestwick House Inc, Clayton, DE. Tel: (302) 659-2070, Web Site: www.prestwickhouse.com (17)

Prettyman, Tony, Datasystem Solutions Inc, Overland Park, KS. Tel: (913) 362-6969, FAX: (913) 362-6383, E-Mail: sales@mutipub.com, Web Site: www. datasystem.com (22)

Prevent Blindness America, Chicago, IL. Tel: (800) 331-2020, Web Site: www.preventblindness.org (1)

Price Target Media, Carson City, NV. Tel: (775) 434-4451, Fax: (206) 888-2403, E-Mail: info@ pricetargetmedia.com, Web Site: pricetargetmedia. com (32)

Price Weber Marketing Communications Inc, Louisville, KY. Tel: (502) 499-9220, FAX: (502) 491-5593, E-Mail: info@priceweber.com, Web Site: www.priceweber.com (35)

Price, Andrew Simon, Artemis International Solutions Corp, Austin, TX. Tel: (512) 201-8222, FAX: (512) 874-8900, Web Site: www.aisc.com (22)

Price, Bernadette, Orbis Books, Maryknoll, NY. Tel: (914) 941-7636 X2576, (800) 258-5838, FAX: (914) 941-7005, E-Mail: orbisbooks@maryknoll.org, Web Site: www.orbisbooks.com (17)

Price, Jan, Playworld Systems, Lewisburg, PA. Tel: (570) 522-9800, FAX: (570) 522-3030, Web Site: www.playworldsystems.com (34)

Price, Jeff, The Sporting News, Charlotte, NC. Tel: (704) 973-1546, (800) 443-1886, FAX: (704) 973-1552, Web Site: www.sportingnews.com (17)

Price, Michael, Post Linx Corp, Scarborough, ON Canada. Tel: (416) 752-8100, FAX: (416) 752-8239, Web Site: www.postlinx.com (28)

Price, Richard W., Crane Duplicating Service Inc, Naples, FL. Tel: (305) 280-6742, FAX: (239) 732-8415, Web Site: www.craneduplicating.com (28)

Price, William, Your Man Tours, El Segundo, CA. Tel: (310) 649-3820, FAX: (310) 649-2118, E-Mail: ymt@earthlink.net, Web Site: www.ymtvacations. com (19)

PricewaterhouseCoopers LLP, New York, NY. Tel: (646) 471-4000, FAX: (813) 286-6000, Web Site: www.pwc.com (14)

Priester Pecan Co Inc, Fort Deposit, AL. Tel: (334) 227-4301, (800) 277-3226, FAX: (334) 227-4294, E-Mail: customerservice@priester.com, Web Site: www.priesters.com (4)

Priester, Rick, Tower Hobbies/Hobbico, Champaign, IL. Tel: (217) 398-3636, (800) 637-6050, FAX: (217) 398-1104, Web Site: www.towerhobbies.com (11)

Priests of the Sacred Heart, Hales Corners, WI. Tel: (414) 425-3383, FAX: (414) 425-5719, Web Site: www.poshusa.org (1)

Prifitera, Aurelio, The Psychological Corp, San Antonio, TX. Tel: (800) 211-8378, FAX: (800) 232-1223, Web Site: www.psychcorp.com (17)

Primalani, Varsha, Marshall Cavendish Corp, Tarrytown, NY. Tel: (914) 332-8888, (800) 821-9881, FAX: (914) 332-1888, Web Site: www. marshallcavendish.com (17)

Prime, Bridgeport, CT. Tel: (203) 331-9100, (800) 873-7746, FAX: (203) 330-0123, Web Site: www. primeline.com (16)

Prime Graphics Inc, Wood Dale, IL. Tel: (630) 227-1300, FAX: (630) 227-1823, E-Mail: moreinfo@ primegraphicsinc.com, Web Site: www. primegraphicsinc.com (27)

Prime Media Equine Group, Gaithersburg, MD. Tel: (301) 977-3900, FAX: (301) 990-9015, Web Site: www.equisearch.com (17)

PrimeNet, Clearwater, FL. Tel: (651) 405-4000, FAX: (651) 405-4100, Web Site: www.pnms.com (22)

Primola, Nick, Association of National Advertisers Inc, New York, NY. Tel: (212) 697-5950, FAX: (212) 687-7310, Web Site: www.ana.net (40)

Prinaris, Alex, Meylan Corp, Montclair, NJ. Tel: (973) 744-6400, (888) 769-9667, FAX: (973) 744-1011, E-Mail: meylan1@aol.com, Web Site: www. meylan.com/home.html (9)

Prinaris, Celia, Meylan Corp, Montclair, NJ. Tel: (973) 744-6400, (888) 769-9667, FAX: (973) 744-1011, E-Mail: meylan1@aol.com, Web Site: www. meylan.com/home.html (9)

Prince, Robert, Richardson Electronics Ltd, Lafox, IL. Tel: (630) 208-2200, FAX: (630) 208-2550, E-Mail: edg@rell.com, Web Site: www.rell.com (16)

Princess Cruises (HQ), Santa Clarita, CA. Tel: (661) 753-0000, (800) (774)-6237, FAX: (661) 284-4747, Web Site: www.princesscruises.com (19)

Princess House Inc, Taunton, MA. Tel: (508) 823-0711, (508) 832-6800, (800) 622-0039, FAX: (508) 823-5182, Web Site: www.princesshouse.com (16)

Princeton Book Co Publishers, Hightstown, NJ. Tel: (609) 426-0602, (800) 220-7149, FAX: (609) 426-1344, E-Mail: pbc@dancehorizons.com, Web Site: www.dancehorizons.com (17)

Princeton Marketech, Princeton Junction, NJ. Tel: (609) 936-0021, FAX: (609) 936-0015, E-Mail: bzyontz@ princetonmarketech.com, Web Site: www. princetonmarketech.com (35)

Princeton Partners Inc, Princeton, NJ. Tel: (609) 452-8500, FAX: (609) 452-7212, E-Mail: moreinfo@ princetonpartners.com, Web Site: www. princetonpartners.com (35)

The Princeton Review, Natick, MA. Tel: (800) 273-8439, E-Mail: prep@review.com, Web Site: www. princetonreview.com (16)

Princing, Janet, Amigo Mobility International Inc, Bridgeport, MI. Tel: (989) 777-0910, (800) 692-6446, FAX: (989) 777-8184, E-Mail: info@ myamigo.com, Web Site: www.myamigo.com (16)

The Principal Financial Group, Des Moines, IA. Tel: (515) 247-5111, (800) 986-3343, FAX: (515) 246-5475, Web Site: www.principal.com (15)

The Print Box Inc, Brooklyn, NY. Tel: (212) 741-1381, (800) 546-4011, FAX: (212) 463-9071, E-Mail: info@promobrands.com, Web Site: www. promobrands.com (33)

Print Management Partners, Des Plaines, IL. Tel: (847) 699-2999, FAX: (847) 699-2935, Web Site: www. ourpartners.com (27)

Print Products International, Annapolis Junction, MD. Tel: (910) 695-7223, FAX: (910) 944-1724, Web Site: www.paceworldwide.com (9)

Print Services Distribution Association, Chicago, IL. Tel: (800) 230-0175, FAX: (312) 673-6880, Web Site: www.psda.org (1)

PrintCom Consulting Group, Waxhaw, NC. Tel: (704) 843-5350, FAX: (704) 843-5352, E-Mail: printcom@aol.com (20)

The Printer Inc, Des Moines, IA. Tel: (515) 288-7241, FAX: (515) 288-9234, E-Mail: info@the-printer. com, Web Site: www.the-printer.com (27)

Printing + Quick Copy, Philadelphia, PA. Tel: (215) 331-5999, FAX: (215) 333-2577, E-Mail: copyman@aolcom (27)

Printing Arts, Broadview, IL. Tel: (708) 938-1600, FAX: (708) 938-1717, E-Mail: webcontact@ printarts.com, Web Site: printarts.com (21)

Printing Corp of the Americas Inc (PCA), Fort Lauderdale, FL. Tel: (954) 781-8100, (866) 721-1722, FAX: (954) 781-8421, Web Site: www.pcaprinting. com (27)

Printing Spectrum, East Setauket, NY. Tel: (631) 689-1010, Web Site: www.printingspectrum.com (27)

Printmark, East Montpelier, VT. Tel: (802) 229-9743, FAX: (802) 229-9746, E-Mail: alex@printmark.net, Web Site: www.printmark.net (20)

PrintWest Communications Ltd, Regina, SK Canada. Tel: (306) 525-2304, (800) 236-6438, FAX: (306) 757-2439, E-Mail: general@printwest.com, Web Site: www.printwest.com (27)

PRIORITY Data Systems Inc, Omaha, NE. Tel: (402) 592-2550, (877) 273-7774, FAX: (402) 592-5052, E-Mail: sales@pdomaha.com, Web Site: www. priority-data.com (22)

Priority Systems Inc, Middletown, PA. Tel: (717) 939-2700, (800) 479-2208, FAX: (717) 939-6180, E-Mail: contactus@prioritysystems.com, Web Site: www.prioritysystems.com (34)

Prism Data Services Ltd, Mississauga, ON Canada. Tel: (905) 278-5556, FAX: (905) 278-6603, E-Mail: sales@prism-data.com, Web Site: www.prism-data. com (21)

Prism Marketing Group, Schaller, IA. Tel: (800) 862-4827, FAX: (712) 275-4855, E-Mail: cjgrothe@ schallertel.net, Web Site: www.prismktg.com (29)

Pritchard, Marc S., The Procter & Gamble Co, Cincinnati, OH. Tel: (513) 983-1100, Web Site: www.pg. com (16)

Pritchett & Hull Associates Inc, Atlanta, GA. Tel: (770) 451-0602, (800) 241-4925, FAX: (770) 454-7130, E-Mail: phsales@p-h.com, Web Site: www.p-h.com (17)

Pritzker, Penny, US Department of Commerce, Washington, DC. Tel: (202) 482-2000, E-Mail: thesec@ doc.gov, Web Site: www.commerce.gov (1)

Pritzker, Thomas J., Hyatt Hotels Corp, Chicago, IL. Tel: (312) 750-1234, FAX: (312) 780-5289, Web Site: www.hyatt.com (16)

Privacy & Information Practices Advisory, Saddle River, NJ. Tel: (201) 887-2157 (20)

Privacy Journal, Providence, RI. Tel: (401) 274-7861, FAX: (401) 274-4747, E-Mail: orders@ privacyjournal.net, Web Site: www.privacyjournal. net (17)

Prizer, Joshua, American Historic Inns Inc, Dana Point, CA. Tel: (949) 497-2232, (800) 397-4667, FAX: (949) 497-9228, E-Mail: comments@iloveinns.com, Web Site: www.iloveinns.com (17)

Pro CD Inc, Omaha, NE. Tel: (800) 992-3766, FAX: (402) 750-0020 (17)

PRO Chemical & Dye Inc, Fall River, MA. Tel: (508) 676-3838, FAX: (508) 676-3980, Web Site: www. prochemicalanddye.com (10)

Pro Media Marketing Group, Menomonee Falls, WI. Tel: (800) 328-0439, FAX: (262) 532-4147, E-Mail: sales@promedius.com, Web Site: www. promedius.com (35)

ProPhase Marketing Inc, Eden Prairie, MN. Tel: (952) 974-1100, (800) 969-6400, FAX: (952) 974-7874, E-Mail: sales@ppmi.com, Web Site: prophasemarketing.com (21)

Probert, Gregory, Herbalife International of America Inc, Los Angeles, CA. Tel: (310) 216-9661, (866) 866-4744, FAX: (310) 258-7019, Web Site: www. herbalife.com (7)

Prochaska, Gail, IMV, Des Plaines, IL. Tel: (847) 297-1404, FAX: (847) 297-5010, E-Mail: sales@ imvinfo.com, Web Site: www.imvlimited.com (20)

Prockow, Eric, Solarcom, Norcross, GA. Tel: (770) 449-6116, (888) SUN-DATA, FAX: (770) 448-7726, Web Site: www.solarcom.net (16)

The Procter & Gamble Co, Cincinnati, OH. Tel: (513) 983-1100, Web Site: www.pg.com (16)

Proctor, Deborah, WCPE-FM, Wake Forest, NC. Tel: (800) 556-5178, FAX: (919) 556-9273, Web Site: theclassicalstation.org (32)

Proctzer, Abram, School of Management, Old Westbury, NY. Tel: (516) 686-1000, (800) 345-NYIT, (800) 345-6948, E-Mail: asknyit@nyit.edu, Web Site: www.nyit.edu (41)

Prodigy Mailing Services, Bolingbrook, IL. Tel: (630) 783-9070, Web Site: www.prodigymailing.com (28)

Product Marketplace, Stratford, CT. Tel: (203) 375-8371, (800) 286-4768, FAX: (203) 386-1203, E-Mail: rita@sabinc.com (33)

Product to Market LLC, Cokato, MN. Tel: (320) 286-9997 (20)

Production Solutions, Vienna, VA. Tel: (703) 734-5700 (20)

Productive Strategies Inc, Northfield, IL. Tel: (847) 446-0008, FAX: (847) 446-0211, E-Mail: pkrone@ productivestrategies.com, Web Site: www. productivestrategies.com (20)

Productivity Development Group Inc, Westford, MA. Tel: (978) 692-1818, FAX: (978) 692-5080, E-Mail: info@martinstankard.com (20)

ProFaiser, Linda L., Woodall Publishing Co LP, Ventura, CA. Tel: (805) 667-4100, (800) 323-9076, FAX: (805) 667-4468, Web Site: www.woodalls. com (17)

Professional Advertising Systems Inc, Armonk, NY. Tel: (914) 765-0500, FAX: (914) 765-0503, E-Mail: info@paslists.com, Web Site: www.paslists.com (22)

Professional Binding Products Inc, Thousand Oaks, CA. Tel: (800) 443-7557, (800) 545-9413, E-Mail: sales@probinding.com, Web Site: www.probinding. com (16)

Professional Creations, New Castle, IN. Tel: (765) 529-1590, (800) 428-8855, E-Mail: sales@ professionaldesignllc.com, Web Site: www. professionaldesignllc.com (5)

The Professional Golfers' Association of America, Palm Beach Gardens, FL. Tel: (561) 624-8400, Web Site: www.pga.com (1)

Professional Mailing Services Inc, Springfield, NJ. Tel: (973) 376-0607, (800) 238-1316, FAX: (973) 376-0949, E-Mail: jschobel@profmail.com, Web Site: www.profmail.com (28)

Professional Marketing Associates, Mount Pleasant, SC. Tel: (843) 971-8150, FAX: (843) 971-8159 (33)

Professional Marketing Associates, Tempe, AZ. Tel: (480) 829-0131, FAX: (480) 829-9202, Web Site: www.pmafulfillment.com (22)

Professional Photographer Magazine, Atlanta, GA. Tel: (404) 522-8600, (800) 786-6277, FAX: (404) 614-6405, E-Mail: csc@ppa.com, Web Site: www.ppa. com (17)

Professional Print & Mail Inc, Fresno, CA. Tel: (559) 237-7468, (800) 654-7468, FAX: (559) 237-4929, E-Mail: info@printfresno.com, Web Site: www. printfresno.com (21)

The Professional Putters Association, Winston Salem, NC. Tel: (866) 788-8788, Web Site: www. proputters.com (1)

Professional Training Associates Inc, Duquesne, PA. Tel: (412) 460-0266, FAX: (412) 460-0269, E-Mail: info@ptainc.com, Web Site: www.ptainc.com (17)

Profile America List Co Inc, Englewood Cliffs, NJ. Tel: (201) 569-7272, FAX: (201) 569-5552, E-Mail: listmanager@profileamerica.com, Web Site: www. profileamerica.com (24)

Profile Coverage Corp, Melville, NY. Tel: (631) 981-7600, FAX: (631) 981-7681, E-Mail: info@ profileinsure.com, Web Site: www.profileinsure. com (15)

Profile Mailing Service Inc, Syosset, NY. Tel: (516) 802-3974 (16)

Profit Boosters Copywriting. Aurora, OH. Tel: (330) 963-0330, FAX: (330) 562-2446, E-Mail: mikepavlish@profitboosterscopy.com, Web Site: www.profitboosterscopy.com (39)

Profit Center Software Inc, Uniondale, NY. Tel: (516) 414-6300, (888) 446-6240, FAX: (516) 414-6304, E-Mail: jmarrah@profitcenter.com, Web Site: www. profitcenter.com (22)

Profit Potentials Inc, Hull, IA. Tel: (712) 439-1496, (800) 543-5480, FAX: (712) 439-1434, Web Site: www.profitpotentials.com (1)

Programmers Investment Corp, Arlington Heights, IL. Tel: (224) 265-6000, FAX: (224) 265-6142, E-Mail: pic@pic-online.com, Web Site: www.pic-online. com (21)

Progress Printing Co, Lynchburg, VA. Tel: (434) 239-9213, (800) 527-7804, FAX: (434) 237-1618, Web Site: www.progressprinting.net (27)

Progress Software Corp, Bedford, MA. Tel: (781) 280-4000, (800) 477-6473, FAX: (781) 280-4095, Web Site: www.progress.com (16)

Progressive Business Publications, Malvern, PA. Tel: (610) 695-8600, (800) 220-5000, FAX: (610) 647-8089, E-Mail: customer_service@pbp.com, Web Site: www.pbp.com (17)

Progressive Communications, Lake Mary, FL. Tel: (407) 333-9500, (800) 571-9407, FAX: (407) 333-7979, E-Mail: info@progressivecommunications. com, Web Site: progressivecommunications.com (21)

The Progressive Corp, Mayfield Village, OH. Tel: (440) 461-5000, (800) PROGRESSIVE, (800) 776-4737, FAX: (800) 456-6590, Web Site: www.progressive. com (15)

Progressive Direct Marketing, Depew, NY. Tel: (716) 681-6848, (800) 344-7593, FAX: (716) 681-9173, E-Mail: info@pdmny.com, Web Site: www.pdmny. com (35)

Progressive Distribution Services Inc, Grand Rapids, MI. Tel: (616) 957-5900, (800) 304-3699, FAX: (616) 957-2990, E-Mail: sales@progressive-commerce.com, Web Site: www.prodist.com (28)

Progressive Energy Corp, San Marcos, CA. Tel: (760) 727-2906, (800) 525-8624, FAX: (760) 727-0947, E-Mail: patrickkilleen@cox.net (5)

Project HOPE, Millwood, VA. Tel: (540) 837-2100, Web Site: www.projecthope.org (1)

Projection Video Services, Springfield, VA. Tel: (703) 912-1334, (800) 377-7650, FAX: (703) 912-1350, Web Site: www.projection.com (16)

ProjectSense, Gaithersburg, MD. Tel: (240) 476-1677, Web Site: www.projectsense.net (20)

ProLogic Retail Services, Delray Beach, FL. E-Mail: info@prologicretail.com, Web Site: www. prologicretail.com (35)

PromarkDirect Inc, Ramsey, NJ. Tel: (201) 489-0532, (800) 776-6275, FAX: (201) 489-2680, E-Mail: solutions@promarkdirect.com, Web Site: www. promarkdirect.com (21)

Promo Magazine, New York, NY. Tel: (203) 358-9900, (800) 927-5007, FAX: (203) 358-5816, E-Mail: larry.jaffee@penton.com, Web Site: www. promomagazine.com (17)

Promotion Fulfillment Ctr, Camanche, IA. Tel: (563) 259-0105, (800) 493-7063, FAX: (563) 259-0110, E-Mail: info@pfcfulfills.com, Web Site: www. pfcfulfills.com (28)

Promotion Marketing Association (PMA) Inc, New York, NY. Tel: (212) 420-1100, FAX: (212) 533-7622, E-Mail: pma@pmalink.org, Web Site: www. pmalink.org (1)

Promotion Support Services Inc, Rock Island, IL. Tel: (309) 788-4400, FAX: (309) 788-4465, E-Mail: dbender@pss-inc.net, Web Site: www.pss-inc.net (28)

Promotional Media Inc, Orange, CA. Tel: (714) 639-6590, (800) 346-5348, FAX: (714) 639-6270, E-Mail: contactus@promotionalmedia.com, Web Site: www.promotionalmedia.com (33)

Promotional Product Professionals of Canada, Dorval, QC Canada. Tel: (514) 489-5359, FAX: (800) 489-8741, (514) 489-7760, E-Mail: gladys@pppc.ca, Web Site: www.pppc.ca (1)

Promotional Products Association International, Irving, TX. Tel: (972) 252-0404, FAX: (972) 258-3004, (800) I-AM-PPAI, E-Mail: membership@ppa.org, Web Site: www.ppa.org (40)

Promotional Products Fulfillment & Distribution Ltd, Whitby, ON Canada. Tel: (905) 668-5060, (800) 263-4678, FAX: (905) 668-1195, E-Mail: sales@ ppfd.com, Web Site: www.ppfd.com (22)

The Promotional Resources Group of Companies, Inc, Topeka, KS. Tel: (785) 862-3707, (800) 467-4712, FAX: (785) 862-1424, E-Mail: info@kidstuff.com, Web Site: www.kidstuffnet.com (33)

PromoWriting, Trumbull, CT. Tel: (203) 371-0654, E-Mail: shira@promowriting.com, Web Site: promowriting.com (35)

Prompt Direct, Staten Island, NY. Tel: (718) 447-6206, FAX: (718) 981-7333, E-Mail: info@ promptmailers.com, Web Site: www.promptmailers. com (28)

Prondzinski, Laurie, Vemma Nutrition Co, Tempe, AZ. Tel: (480) 927-8999, (800) 577-0777, FAX: (888) 314-9827, E-Mail: ms@vemma.com, Web Site: www.vemma.com (7)

Proni, Barbara, AmerisourceBergen, Chesterbrook, PA. Tel: (610) 727-7000, (800) 829-3132, E-Mail: solutions@amerisourcebergan.com, Web Site: www.amerisourcebergan.com (7)

Propay USA Inc, Lehi, UT. Tel: (801) 766-3758, Web Site: www.propay.com (14)

Propco Incentives, Chicago, IL. Tel: (773) 463-9193, FAX: (773) 463-6673, E-Mail: sales@propco.com, Web Site: www.propco.com (35)

Propp, Dennis, Propco Incentives, Chicago, IL. Tel: (773) 463-9193, FAX: (773) 463-6673, E-Mail: sales@propco.com, Web Site: www.propco.com (35)

Prosodie Interactive, Plantation, FL. Tel: (954) 671-6500, (866) 776-7634, FAX: (954) 915-0567, E-Mail: info@prosodiemail.com, Web Site: www.ivrinc.com (29)

ProSource, Houston, TX. Tel: (713) 667-3690, FAX: (713) 660-9629, Web Site: www.prosourcedv.com (20)

Prospect Direct Inc, Milwaukee, WI. Tel: (414) 271-3313, FAX: (414) 271-4244, E-Mail: info@prospect-direct.com, Web Site: www.prospect-direct.com (21)

Prosper Inc, Provo, UT. Tel: (801) 371-0755, (800) 748-5799, FAX: (801) 374-2358, E-Mail: support@prospering.com, Web Site: www.prospering.com (32)

Prosser, Buz, Consolidated Mailing Corp, Shawnee Mission, KS. Tel: (913) 262-4400, (800) 706-6245, FAX: (913) 262-7801, E-Mail: cmcmail@swbell.net, Web Site: www.consolidatedmailing.com (28)

Prossick, Nancy, Thermo Pro, Duluth, GA. Tel: (678) 475-1647, (800) 523-5542, FAX: (678) 475-1747, Web Site: www.thermopro.com (16)

Protano, Mario, Ross-Simons, Cranston, RI. Tel: (401) 463-3100, (800) 835-0919, FAX: (401) 463-8599, Web Site: www.ross-simons.com (6)

Protection One Inc, Lawrence, KS. Tel: (785) 856-5500, (800) GET-HELP, Web Site: www.protectionone.com (16)

Protective Life Corp, Deerfield, IL. Tel: (847) 948-8988, (800) 323-5771, FAX: (847) 948-1156, Web Site: www.protective.com (15)

Protective Life Insurance Co, Birmingham, AL. Tel: (205) 268-1000, (800) 866-3555, FAX: (205) 868-3086, Web Site: www.protective.com (15)

Protheroe, Wesley, Gerber Life Insurance Co, White Plains, NY. Tel: (914) 272-4000, (800) 704-2180, FAX: (914) 272-4099, Web Site: www.gerberlife.com (14)

Protus, Ottawa, ON Canada. Tel: (613) 733-0000, (888) 733-0000, E-Mail: info@protus.com, Web Site: www.protus.com (32)

Proven Prospects Inc, Santa Barbara, CA. Tel: (805) 448-6253, Web Site: www.provemprospects.com (20)

Provenza, Salvatore, EOS International Inc, Carlsbad, CA. Tel: (760) 431-8400, (800) 876-5484, FAX: (760) 431-8448, Web Site: www.eosintl.com (5)

Provenzano, Tony, ModernAd Media LLC, Deerfield Beach, FL. Tel: (954) 312-4700, FAX: (954) 312-4853, Web Site: www.modernad.com (40)

Providence Journal Telemarketing, Providence, RI. Tel: (401) 277-7000, FAX: (401) 277-8046, E-Mail: bnauman@projo.com, Web Site: www.projo.com (29)

Prudent Publishing Co, Ridgefield Park, NJ. Tel: (201) 641-7900, FAX: (800) 772-1144 (16)

Prudential Financial, Newark, NJ. Tel: (973) 802-2195, Web Site: www.prudential.com (14)

Prugger, Patrick, KTM Sportmotorcycle USA Inc, Amherst, OH. Tel: (440) 985-3553, FAX: (440) 985-3060, Web Site: www.ktmusa.com (16)

Pruiniks, Robert H., University of Minnesota Alumni Association, Minneapolis, MN. Tel: (612) 624-2323, (800) 862-5867, FAX: (612) 626-8167, E-Mail: umalumni@umn.edu, Web Site: www.minnesotaalumni.org (1)

Pruitt, Charles, AB Data Ltd, Milwaukee, WI. Tel: (414) 963-7800, FAX: (414) 963-7899, E-Mail: dmservices@abdata.com, Web Site: dms.abdata.com (21)

Prunier, John, Petsky Prunier LLC, New York, NY. Tel: (212) 842-6001, FAX: (212) 842-6039, Web Site: www.petskyprunier.com (14)

Prvitt, David, Bike Nashbar, Crab Orchard, WV. Tel: (800) NAS-HBAR, FAX: (877) 778-9456, E-Mail: custserv@nashbar.com, Web Site: www.bikenashbar.com (11)

Fred Pryor Seminars, Mission, KS. Tel: (913) 967-8518, (800) 780-8476, FAX: (913) 967-8849, E-Mail: customerservice@pryor.com, Web Site: www.pryor.com (16)

Pryor, Douglas, Sport Supply Group, Dallas, TX. Tel: (972) 484-9484, FAX: (972) 247-0650, Web Site: www.sportsupplygroup.com (11)

Pryor, Ray, Gamma Photo Labs LLC, Chicago, IL. Tel: (312) 337-0022, FAX: (312) 337-3753, Web Site: www.photobition.com (16)

Psion Teklogix Inc, Mississauga, ON Canada. Tel: (905) 813-9900, (800) 322-3437, E-Mail: ptinfo@psion.com, Web Site: www.psionteklogix.com (3)

The Psychological Corp, San Antonio, TX. Tel: (800) 211-8378, FAX: (800) 232-1223, Web Site: www.psychcorp.com (17)

Ptak, Frank S., The Marmon Group LLC, Chicago, IL. Tel: (312) 372-9500, FAX: (312) 845-5305, Web Site: www.marmon.com (16)

PTM Communications, New York, NY. Tel: (212) 643-5458, FAX: (212) 643-5486, E-Mail: info@ptmcomm.com, Web Site: www.ptmcomm.com (29)

Public Interest Communications Inc, Falls Church, VA. Tel: (703) 847-8300, FAX: (703) 734-9620, Web Site: www.pubintcom.com (29)

Public Issues Management, Piedmont, CA. Tel: (510) 654-9114, FAX: (510) 654-0196 (20)

Publication Fulfillment Svcs, Cypress, CA. Tel: (714) 226-9785, FAX: (714) 226-9733, E-Mail: janpullin@pfsmag.com, Web Site: www.pfsmag.com (20)

Publications Groupe RR International Inc, Montreal, QC Canada. Tel: (514) 521-8148 (20)

Publications International Ltd, Lincolnwood, IL. Tel: (847) 676-3470, (800) 595-8484, FAX: (847) 676-3671, Web Site: www.pubint.com (17)

Publicis Worldwide North America, New York, NY. Tel: (212) 279-5550, E-Mail: andrew.bruce@publicisna.com, Web Site: publicisna.com (35)

Publicity Inc, Mansfield, MA. Tel: (617) 367-3555, FAX: (617) 367-3557 (35)

Publishers Circulation Fulfillment Inc, Towson, MD. Tel: (410) 821-8614, E-Mail: sales@pcfcorp.com, Web Site: www.pcfcorp.com (32)

Publishers Clearing House, Port Washington, NY. Tel: (516) 883-5432, FAX: (516) 767-4567, E-Mail: cirving@pch.com, Web Site: www.pch.com (18)

Publishers Computer Corp, New Milford, NJ. Tel: (201) 261-3700, FAX: (201) 261-9110, E-Mail: mail@publisherscomputer.com, Web Site: www.publisherscomputer.com (22)

Publishers Marketing Association (PMA), Manhattan Beach, CA. Tel: (310) 372-2732, FAX: (310) 374-3342, E-Mail: info@pma-online.org, Web Site: www.pma-online.org (40)

Publishers Press Inc, Shepherdsville, KY. Tel: (502) 955-6526, FAX: (502) 955-5586, E-Mail: info@pubpress.com, Web Site: www.pubpress.com (27)

Publishing Fulfillment Consulting LLC, Brewster, NY. Tel: (845) 278-2800, Web Site: www.fulfillmentconsulting.com (20)

Pucci, John, Hawthorne Direct Inc, Los Angeles, CA. Tel: (301) 248-3972, E-Mail: inquiries@hawthornedirect.com, Web Site: www.hawthornedirect.com (35)

Puccio, Dina, Microbiz Corp, Menlo Park, CA. Tel: (702) 749-5353, (800) 726-3282, FAX: (650) 440-4870, E-Mail: info@microbiz.com, Web Site: www.microbiz.com (3)

Puckett, Betsy, Droll Yankees Inc, Plainfield, CT. Tel: (860) 799-8980, (800) 352-9164, FAX: (860) 564-8031, E-Mail: drollbird@drollyankees.com, Web Site: www.drollyankees.com (8)

Puckett, Duane, Sportime International, Norcross, GA. Tel: (770) 449-5700, (800) 283-5700, FAX: (770) 510-7290, E-Mail: orders@sportime.com, Web Site: www.sportime.com (11)

Puckett-Dunn, Nancy, The Davis Center, Succasunna, NJ. Tel: (862) 251-4637, FAX: (862) 251-4642, E-Mail: info@thedaviscenter.com, Web Site: www.thedaviscenter.com (16)

Pudles, Gary, AnswerNet Network, Willow Grove, PA. Tel: (800) 411-5777, FAX: (215) 659-6486, Web Site: www.answernetnetwork.com (29)

Puga, Rafaeo, Ducktrap River Fish Farm, Belfast, ME. Tel: (207) 338-6280, (800) 828-3825, FAX: (207) 338-6288, E-Mail: smoked@ducktrap.com, Web Site: www.ducktrap.com (4)

Pugh, Mike, Protus, Ottawa, ON Canada. Tel: (613) 733-0000, (888) 733-0000, E-Mail: info@protus.com, Web Site: www.protus.com (32)

Pugliese Dean, Carla, Block & DeCorso, Verona, NJ. Tel: (973) 857-3900, FAX: (973) 857-4041, E-Mail: bdecorso@blockdecorso.com, Web Site: www.blockdecorso.com (35)

Pugliese, David, Cox Communications Inc, Atlanta, GA. Tel: (404) 843-5000, (888) 566-7751, FAX: (404) 269-2243, Web Site: www.cox.com (16)

Pugliese, Stephanie, Duluth Trading Co Inc, Belleville, WI. Tel: (800) 300-9719, FAX: (888) 950-3199, E-Mail: customerservice@duluthtrading.com, Web Site: www.duluthtrading.com (8)

Puglionisi, John, Grafica Group, Morristown, NJ. Tel: (973) 309-7500, FAX: (973) 309-7501, E-Mail: information@grafica.com, Web Site: www.grafica.com (35)

Puisis, Frank, Finishing Plus, Inc, Chicago, IL. Tel: (773) 523-5510, FAX: (773) 523-9155, E-Mail: info@finishingplus.com, Web Site: www.finishingplus.com (28)

Puleo, Bob, Globe Ticket & Label Co, Carol Stream, IL. Tel: (404) 762-9711, (800) 523-5968, FAX: (404) 762-7019, Web Site: www.globeticket.com (16)

Puleo, Steve, Bull HN Information Systems, Chelmsford, MA. Tel: (978) 294-6000, FAX: (978) 294-7999, Web Site: www.bull.com/us (16)

Pulite, William J., Del Webb, Bloomfield Hills, MI. Tel: (248) 644-7300, (888) 717-9777, FAX: (248) 433-4598, Web Site: www.delwebb.com (16)

Pullano, Paul, Omega Direct Response Inc, Richmond Hill, ON Canada. Tel: (905) 482-2340, FAX: (905) 482-9721, E-Mail: odrsales@omegadirect.com, Web Site: www.omegadirect.com (29)

Pulliam, Gary, AGCO Inc, Norcross, GA. Tel: (770) 447-6990, FAX: (770) 446-2102, Web Site: www.agcomarble.com (9)

Pulliam, Larry, AGCO Inc, Norcross, GA. Tel: (770) 447-6990, FAX: (770) 446-2102, Web Site: www. agcomarble.com (9)

Pullin, Ericka, Frost Bank, San Antonio, TX. Tel: (210) 220-4011, Web Site: www.frostbank.com (14)

PulseCX, Montgomeryville, PA. Tel: (215) 699-9200, FAX: (215) 699-9240, Web Site: www.pulsecx.com (35)

Pulsifer, Jason, HubCast Inc, Wakefield, MA. Tel: (781) 221-7200, FAX: (781) 221-7223, Web Site: www. hubeast.com (27)

Pumphrey, Kristen, Pharmaceutical Care Management Association, Washington, DC. Tel: (202) 756-7210, FAX: (202) 207-3623, E-Mail: info@pcmanet.org, Web Site: www.pcmanet.org (1)

Punter, Dylan, InfoSource Inc, Oviedo, FL. Tel: (407) 796-5200, (800) 393-4636, FAX: (407) 796-5190, E-Mail: isisale@howtomaster.com, Web Site: www. infosourcelearning.com (3)

Puopolo, Ernest S., ESP Printing & Mailing Inc, Boise, ID. Tel: (208) 345-4644, (888) 845-7665, FAX: (208) 345-4765, E-Mail: info@espdirectmail.com (28)

Purcell, Jack, Links Magazine, Hilton Head Island, SC. Tel: (843) 842-6200, FAX: (843) 842-6233, Web Site: www.linksmagazine.com (17)

Purcell, Nancy, Links Magazine, Hilton Head Island, SC. Tel: (843) 842-6200, FAX: (843) 842-6233, Web Site: www.linksmagazine.com (17)

Puritan's Pride, Ronkonkoma, NY. Tel: (631) 567-9500, (800) 645-1030, FAX: (631) 471-5693, E-Mail: info@puritan.com, Web Site: www.puritan.com (7)

Purohit Navigation Inc, Chicago, IL. Tel: (312) 341-8100, FAX: (312) 341-8119, E-Mail: purohit@ purohitnavigation.com, Web Site: www. purohitnavigation.com (35)

Purohit, Ahnal, Purohit Navigation Inc, Chicago, IL. Tel: (312) 341-8100, FAX: (312) 341-8119, E-Mail: purohit@purohitnavigation.com, Web Site: www. purohitnavigation.com (35)

Purohit, Anshal, Purohit Navigation Inc, Chicago, IL. Tel: (312) 341-8100, FAX: (312) 341-8119, E-Mail: purohit@purohitnavigation.com, Web Site: www. purohitnavigation.com (35)

Purse, Craig B., Video Jet Technologies Inc, Wood Dale, IL. Tel: (630) 860-7300, (800) 654-4663, FAX: (630) 616-3623, E-Mail: info@videojet.com, Web Site: www.videojet.com (34)

Pursuant Group, Dallas, TX. Tel: (214) 866-7700, E-Mail: info@pursuant.com, Web Site: www. pursuant.com (20)

Puryear, Paul, Heller Financial, Chicago, IL. Tel: (312) 441-7000, FAX: (312) 441-7499, Web Site: www. hellerfin.com (14)

Pusatera, John, Royal Envelope Corp, Chicago, IL. Tel: (773) 376-1212, (800) 279-0142, FAX: (773) 376-0011, E-Mail: info@royalenv.com, Web Site: www. royalenv.com (26)

Pusatera, Matt, Royal Envelope Corp, Chicago, IL. Tel: (773) 376-1212, (800) 279-0142, FAX: (773) 376-0011, E-Mail: info@royalenv.com, Web Site: www. royalenv.com (26)

Pusatera, Mike, Royal Envelope Corp, Chicago, IL. Tel: (773) 376-1212, (800) 279-0142, FAX: (773) 376-0011, E-Mail: info@royalenv.com, Web Site: www. royalenv.com (26)

Pushkin, Dennis, MoreVisibility, Boca Raton, FL. Tel: (561) 620-9682, (800) 787-0497, FAX: (561) 620-9684, E-Mail: info@morevisibility.com, Web Site: www.morevisibility.com (32)

Putala, Randall, MailNow Inc, Nashville, TN. Tel: (615) 844-4244, FAX: (615) 208-9757, E-Mail: randall@ xdatemarketing.com, Web Site: www. xdatemarketing.com (21)

Putman, Maureen M., Celestial Seasonings, Boulder, CO. Tel: (303) 530-5300, (800) 351-8175, FAX: (303) 581-1249, Web Site: www.celestialseasonings. com (16)

Putman, Maureen M., Hain Celestial Group Inc, Boulder, CO. Tel: (800) 434-4246, Web Site: www.hain-celestial.com (16)

Putnam Group Ltd, Trumbull, CT. Tel: (203) 452-7270, FAX: (203) 268-8071, E-Mail: info@putnamgroup. net, Web Site: putnamgroup.net (33)

Putnam Investments, Boston, MA. Tel: (617) 292-1400, (800) 225-1581, FAX: (617) 292-1683, Web Site: www.putnam.com (14)

Putnam Rolling Ladder Co Inc, New York, NY. Tel: (212) 226-5147, FAX: (212) 941-1836, E-Mail: putnam1905@aol.com, Web Site: www. putnamrollingladder.com (5)

Putnam, Chris, Collective - The Audience Engine, New York, NY. Tel: (646) 722-8550, FAX: (646) 442-6529, Web Site: www.collective.com (22)

Putnam, Sarah, Sarah Putnam, Cambridge, MA. Tel: (617) 547-3758, E-Mail: sarah@sarahputnam.com, Web Site: www.sarahputnam.com (37)

Putt Putt Fun Centers, Winston-Salem, NC. Tel: (336) 714-3950, (866) PUTT-PUTT, FAX: (336) 714-3955, Web Site: www.puttputt.com (16)

Pych, Joseph, NextMark Inc, Hanover, NH. Tel: (603) 643-1307, FAX: (603) 643-1662, Web Site: www. nextmark.com (22)

Pyhrr, Peter A, MT&L Card Products & Fulfillment Services, Nashville, TN. Tel: (615) 254-9471, FAX: (615) 244-6063, E-Mail: sales@magticket.com, Web Site: www.mtlcard.com (28)

Pyle, Charlie, Starchtech, Golden Valley, MN. Tel: (763) 545-5400, (800) 597-7225, FAX: (763) 545-9450, Web Site: www.starchtech.com (16)

Pyne, Elaine, The Gallery Shop, Buffalo, NY. Tel: (716) 882-8700 X258, FAX: (716) 882-1958, E-Mail: gallshop@albrightknox.org, Web Site: www.albrightknox.org (6)

Pyott, David E.I., Allergan Inc, Irvine, CA. Tel: (714) 246-4500, (800) 347-4500, FAX: (714) 246-6987, Web Site: www.allergan.com (16)

Q

Q Fact Marketing Research Inc & Videoconferencing Center, Cincinnati, OH. Tel: (513) 891-2271, FAX: (513) 984-7464, E-Mail: info@qfact.com, Web Site: www.qfact.com (30)

Q Interactive, Chicago, IL. Tel: (312) 977-0390, (888) 729-6465, FAX: (312) 224-5001, E-Mail: solutions@qinteractive.com, Web Site: www. qinteractive.com (40)

QC Supply LLC, Schuyler, NE. Tel: (402) 352-3167, Web Site: www.qcsupply.com (16)

QED Marketing Inc, Central Islip, NY. Tel: (631) 851-4254 (22)

QMSI, Montague, CA. Tel: (530) 459-0910, Web Site: www.quintmail.com (22)

QVC Inc, West Chester, PA. Tel: (484) 701-1000, FAX: (484) 701-8500, Web Site: www.qvc.com (32)

Qiu, Frank, Evergreen Enterprises Inc, Richmond, VA. Tel: (800) 774-3837, E-Mail: customerservice@ myevergreen.com, Web Site: www.myevergreen. com (8)

Quad/Graphics, Sussex, WI. Tel: (414) 566-6000, E-Mail: qgraphics@qg.com, Web Site: www.QG. com (28)

Quade, Nathan, Heaven & Earth, Virginia Beach, VA. Tel: (757) 420-3576, E-Mail: heavenandearthkr8@ gmail.com, Web Site: www.heavenandearth.com (5)

Quadra Graphics Inc, Cherry Hill, NJ. Tel: (856) 665-4060, FAX: (856) 665-7324, E-Mail: richard. nixon@qgi.com (27)

Quadracci, Joel, Quad/Graphics, Sussex, WI. Tel: (414) 566-6000, E-Mail: qgraphics@qg.com, Web Site: www.QG.com (28)

Quadrant Engineering Plastic Products, Reading, PA. Tel: (610) 320-6600, (800) 366-0300, FAX: (610) 320-6868, Web Site: www.quadrantepp.com (16)

Quaero Corp, Charlotte, NC. Tel: (704) 414-0200, FAX: (704) 414-2195, Web Site: www.quaero.com (22)

The Quaker Oats Co, Chicago, IL. Tel: (312) 821-1000, (800) 367-6287, FAX: (312) 222-8323, Web Site: www.quakeroats.com (16)

Qualco, Inc, Passaic, NJ. Tel: (973) 473-1222 (8)

Qualey, Thomas, Maine Potato Board, Presque Isle, ME. Tel: (207) 769-5061, FAX: (207) 764-4148, E-Mail: mainepotatoes@mainepotatoes.com, Web Site: www.mainepotatoes.com (1)

Quality Contact Solutions Inc, Aurora, NE. Tel: (402) 210-2692, (866) 963-2889, FAX: (402) 210-2692, E-Mail: info@qualitycontactsolutions.com, Web Site: www.qualitycontactsolutions.com (29)

Quality Letter Service Inc, New York, NY. Tel: (212) 268-3400, FAX: (212) 268-3401, E-Mail: info@ qletter.com, Web Site: www.qletter.com (21)

Quality Park Products, Minneapolis, MN. Tel: (800) 828-7323, (800) 547-4252, FAX: (800) 398-9835, E-Mail: mktg@qualitypark.com, Web Site: www. qualitypark.com (26)

Quality Products Inc, Columbus, MS. Tel: (662) 328-1477, (800) 647-1057, FAX: (800) 824-8510, E-Mail: kshep@classroomsupply.com, Web Site: www.classroomsupply.com (10)

Qualkenbush, Eric, Veritas Analytics Inc, Sterling, VA. Tel: (703) 707-5620, Web Site: www.veritas-analytics.com (30)

Quantum Color, Morton Grove, IL. Tel: (847) 967-3600, FAX: (847) 967-3610, Web Site: www. cpipress.com (27)

Quantum Group, Morton Grove, IL. Tel: (847) 967-3600, FAX: (847) 967-3610, Web Site: www. quantumgroup.com (35)

QuantumDigital, Austin, TX. Tel: (800) 637-7373, Web Site: www.quantumdigital.com (28)

Quark Inc, Denver, CO. Tel: (303) 894-8888, Web Site: www.quark.com (34)

Quartermaster Uniform & Equipment Co, Cerritos, CA. Tel: (866) 673-7645, FAX: (562) 304-7335, E-Mail: help@qmuniforms.com, Web Site: www. qmuniforms.com (2)

Quast, Bob, Life Fitness, Schiller Park, IL. Tel: (847) 288-3300, (800) 735-3867, FAX: (847) 288-3703, E-Mail: webmaster@lifefitness.com, Web Site: www.lifefitness.com (11)

Quattro Direct LLC, Berwyn, PA. Tel: (610) 993-0070, Web Site: www.quattrodirect.com (35)

Quaxar, Miami, FL. Tel: (305) 350-9520, Web Site: www.quaxar.com (35)

Quayside Publishing Group, Minneapolis, MN. Tel: (612) 344-8100, FAX: (612) 344-8691, Web Site: www.quaysidepub.com (17)

Queen Bee Gardens, Lovell, WY. Tel: (307) 548-2818, (800) 225-7553, FAX: (307) 548-7994, E-Mail: queenbee@queenbeegardens.com, Web Site: queenbeegardens.com (4)

Queens College/CUNY Professional and Continuing Studies (PCS), Flushing, NY. Tel: (718) 997-5700, FAX: (718) 997-5723, E-Mail: pcs@qc.cuny.edu, Web Site: www.qc.cuny.edu/pcs (41)

Queru, Gilles, Neolane, Newton, MA. Tel: (617) 467-6760, FAX: (617) 467-6701, Web Site: www. neolane.com (22)

Queue Inc, Stratford, CT. Tel: (203) 335-0906, (800) 232-2224, FAX: (800) 775-2729, E-Mail: jdk@queueinc.com, Web Site: www.qworkbooks.com (17)

Quick Draw Clip Systems Inc, Ventura, CA. Tel: (805) 644-6888, (888) 254-7797, FAX: (805) 644-7320, E-Mail: ron@clipsystems.com, Web Site: www. clipsystems.com (9)

Quick, Brad, Hamilton Sorter Co, Fairfield, OH. Tel: (513) 870-4400, (800) 503-9966, FAX: (800) 503-9963, E-Mail: sstreight@hamiltonsorter.com, Web Site: www.hamiltonsorter.com (34)

Quigley Consulting Group, Lake Forest, IL. Tel: (847) 604-6773 (20)

Quigley Simpson, Los Angeles, CA. Tel: (310) 996-5800, E-Mail: info@quigleysimpson.com, Web Site: www.quigleysimpson.com (35)

Quigley, James B., Merrill Lynch International Inc, New York, NY. Tel: (212) 449-1000, (800) 637-7455, FAX: (212) 449-9418, Web Site: www.ml. com (14)

Quigley, James H., Deloitte & Touche, Boston, MA. Tel: (617) 437-2000, FAX: (617) 437-2111, Web Site: www.deloitte.com (14)

Quigley, Robert, MTS Publishing, Naperville, IL. Tel: (630) 955-9750, (800) 332-4655, FAX: (630) 955-9787, E-Mail: info@midwesttruckshopper.com, Web Site: www.midwesttruckshopper.com (17)

Quigley, Robert, Quigley Consulting Group, Lake Forest, IL. Tel: (847) 604-6773 (20)

Quill Corp, Lincolnshire, IL. Tel: (847) 876-3535, (800) 789-1331, Web Site: www.quill.com (16)

Quill Healthcare, Minneapolis, MN. Tel: (763) 493-7300, (800) 328-2179, FAX: (800) 328-0023, Web Site: www.medicalartspress.com (27)

Quill Lincolnshire Inc, Lincolnshire, IL. Tel: (800) 982-3400, FAX: (800) 789-8955, Web Site: www.quill. com (10)

Quill, John A., Ecological Fibers Inc, Lunenburg, MA. Tel: (978) 537-0003, FAX: (978) 537-2238, E-Mail: jquill@ecofibers.com (25)

Quill, Stephen F., Ecological Fibers Inc, Lunenburg, MA. Tel: (978) 537-0003, FAX: (978) 537-2238, E-Mail: jquill@ecofibers.com (25)

Quin, Tony, IQ Agency, Atlanta, GA. Tel: (404) 255-3550, E-Mail: newbiz@iqagency.com, Web Site: iqagency.com (35)

Quine. Richard, DNE Nutraceuticals Inc, Farmingdale, NJ. Tel: (212) 235-5200, (800) 221-1833, FAX: (212) 235-5243, E-Mail: info@dnenutra.com, Web Site: www.dnenutra.com (16)

Quiniones, Gil C., New York Power Authority, White Plains, NY. Tel: (914) 681-6200, E-Mail: info@nypa.gov, Web Site: www.nypa.gov (16)

Quinlan, Bob, UniGraphic Inc, Woburn, MA. Tel: (781) 231-7200, FAX: (781) 938-7727, E-Mail: info@uni-graphic.com, Web Site: www.uni-graphic.com (27)

Quinlan, D.L., CYRO Industries, Parsippany, NJ. Tel: (973) 541-8000, (800) 631-5384, FAX: (973) 442-6117, (973) 442-6135, Web Site: www.cyro.com (16)

Quinlan, III Thomas J., RR Donnelley & Sons Co, Chicago, IL. Tel: (312) 326-8000, (800) 742-4455, FAX: (312) 326-7156, Web Site: www.rrdonnelly. com (31)

Quinlan, Jack, UniGraphic Inc, Woburn, MA. Tel: (781) 231-7200, FAX: (781) 938-7727, E-Mail: info@uni-graphic.com, Web Site: www.uni-graphic.com (27)

Quinlan, Michael, UniGraphic Inc, Woburn, MA. Tel: (781) 231-7200, FAX: (781) 938-7727, E-Mail: info@uni-graphic.com, Web Site: www.uni-graphic. com (27)

Quinlan, Raymond J., SLM Corp, Newark, DE. Web Site: www.salliemae.com (16)

Quinlan, Thomas J., BBS Chicago, Chicago, IL. Tel: (312) 326-8000, (800) 742-4455, Web Site: www. rrdonnelley.com (31)

Quinn, Christine, Meyer Fulfillment, Stratford, CT. Tel: (203) 375-5801, (800) 873-6393, E-Mail: vdarish@meyerfulfillment.com, Web Site: www. meyerfulfillment.com (28)

Quinn, Dave, Prism Data Services Ltd, Mississauga, ON Canada. Tel: (905) 278-5556, FAX: (905) 278-6603, E-Mail: sales@prism-data.com, Web Site: www. prism-data.com (21)

Quinn, Jane, Replogle Globes Inc, Broadview, IL. Tel: (708) 343-0900, FAX: (708) 343-0923, E-Mail: info@replogleglobes.com, Web Site: www. replogleglobes.com (16)

Quinn, Jesse, Solitron Devices Inc, West Palm Beach, FL. Tel: (561) 848-4311, FAX: (561) 863-5946, E-Mail: sales@solitrondevices.com, Web Site: www.solitrondevices.com (16)

Quinn, Kate, Anthem Blue Cross, Westlake Village, CA. Tel: (805) 557-6655, (800) 333-0912, FAX: (800) 557-6872, Web Site: www.bluecrossca.com (15)

Quinn, Pat, TWL Knowledge Group, Carrollton, TX. Tel: (972) 309-4000, (800) 624-2272, FAX: (972) 309-5105, Web Site: www.twlk.com (3)

Quinn, Stephen F., WalMart Stores Inc, Bentonville, AR. Tel: (479) 273-4000, (800) 925-6278, FAX: (479) 277-1830, Web Site: www.walmart.com (16)

Quinn, Tom, Academic Management Services, Swansea, MA. Tel: (508) 235-2870, (800) 891-4203, FAX: (508) 235-2991, E-Mail: info@amsweb.com, Web Site: www.amsweb.com (14)

Quinnipiac College, Hamden, CT. Tel: (203) 582-8200, (203) 582-8600, (800) 462-1944, FAX: (203) 281-8664, Web Site: www.quinnipiac.edu (41)

Quintero, Monica, Wexler Consulting Group LLC, Alexandria, VA. Tel: (202) 573-9355, E-Mail: welcome@wexlerllc.com, Web Site: wexlerconsultinggroup.com (35)

Quintos, Karen H., Dell Computer Corp, Round Rock, TX. Tel: (512) 338-4400, FAX: (512) 283-6161, Web Site: www.dell.com (16)

Quirk, Terrence, JJ Keller & Associates Inc, Neenah, WI. Tel: (920) 722-2848, (800) 327-6868, FAX: (800) 727-7516, E-Mail: thines@jjkeller.com, Web Site: www.jjkeller.com/jjk (16)

Quist, Nikki, Smith Hanley Associates, Southport, CT. Tel: (203) 319-4300, (888) 221-2900, FAX: (203) 319-4320, Web Site: www.smithhanley.com (20)

Qwest, Denver, CO. Tel: (303) 992-1400, (800) 603-6000, FAX: (303) 896-8515, Web Site: www.qwest. com (20)

R

R&S Industries Corp, Chesterfield, MO. Tel: (314) 781-5400, FAX: (314) 781-5169, E-Mail: sendeverything@miraclepolishingcloth.com, Web Site: www.miraclepolishingcloth.com (16)

R2C Group, Portland, OR. Tel: (866) 402-1124, E-Mail: getintouch@r2cgroup.com, Web Site: www. r2cgroup.com (35)

RB Toy Design Inc, Glenview, IL. Tel: (847) 577-5683, FAX: (847) 272-4034, E-Mail: info@rbtoydesign. com, Web Site: www.rbtoy.com (33)

RBC Dain Rauscher Inc, Minneapolis, MN. Tel: (612) 371-2711, FAX: (612) 373-1627, Web Site: www. rbcdain.com (14)

RBC Funds, Milwaukee, WI. Tel: (800) 422-2766, Web Site: us.rbcgam.com (14)

RBS Citizens Financial Group Inc, Dedham, MA. Tel: (781) 471-1565, Web Site: www.citizensbank.com (14)

RCS Response Technologies Inc, Charlotte, NC. Tel: (704) 522-1919, FAX: (704) 522-9092, E-Mail: results@rcsdirect.com, Web Site: www.rcsdirect. com (21)

RDO Marketing LLC, Minneapolis, MN. Tel: (952) 746-7585 (20)

REI-Recreational Equipment Inc, Kent, WA. Tel: (253) 891-2500, (800) 426-4840, FAX: (253) 891-2523, Web Site: www.rei.com (11)

RI Direct + Digital, Toronto, ON Canada. Tel: (416) 368-6211, E-Mail: info@responseinnovations.com, Web Site: www.responseinnovations.com (35)

RJ Olsen Inc, Natick, MA. Tel: (508) 647-3777, FAX: (508) 647-6777, E-Mail: dickolsen@aol.com (30)

RMA-The Risk Management Association, Philadelphia, PA. Tel: (215) 446-4000, FAX: (215) 446-4101, E-Mail: customers@rmahq.org, Web Site: www. rmahq.org (1)

RMI Direct Marketing Inc, Danbury, CT. Tel: (203) 798-0448, FAX: (203) 778-6130, E-Mail: info@rmidirect.com, Web Site: www.rmidirect.com (23)

RPM Direct LLC, Lambertville, NJ. Tel: (609) 566-7150, FAX: (609) 566-7155, E-Mail: jimarslan@rpmdirectllc.com, Web Site: www.rpmdirectllc.com (35)

RPM Industries Inc, Auburn, NY. Tel: (315) 255-1105, (800) 669-3676, FAX: (315) 252-1167, Web Site: www.rpmdisplays.com (33)

RR Donnelley Response Marketing Services, Warrenville, IL. Tel: (630) 963-9494, (800) 722-9001, FAX: (630) 322-6270, Web Site: www.rms.rrd.com (31)

RSC The Quality Measurement Co, Evansville, IN. Tel: (812) 425-4562, FAX: (812) 425-2844 (30)

RSM McGladrey Inc, Charlotte, NC. Tel: (980) 233-4700, Web Site: www.rsmmcgladrey.com (20)

RSVP Publications, Tampa, FL. Tel: (813) 960-7787, FAX: (866) 554-3003, Web Site: www. MailToTheAffluent.com (31)

RW Consulting, Asheville, NC. Tel: (828) 299-3645, Web Site: www.rwconsulting.net (20)

Raab Associates, Swarthmore, PA. Tel: (914) 241-2117, FAX: (914) 241-0080, E-Mail: info@raabassociates. com, Web Site: www.raabassociates.com (20)

Raab, David M., Raab Associates, Swarthmore, PA. Tel: (914) 241-2117, FAX: (914) 241-0080, E-Mail: info@raabassociates.com, Web Site: www. raabassociates.com (20)

Rabbu, Christopher, AdvanceMe Inc, Kennesaw, GA. Tel: (888) 700-8181, Web Site: www.advanceme. com (14)

Rabinowitz, Marianne, WS Ponton Inc, Pittsburgh, PA. Tel: (412) 782-2360, (800) 628-7806, FAX: (412) 782-1109, E-Mail: info@wsponton.com, Web Site: www.wsponton.com (23)

Raccah, Dominique, Sourcebooks Inc, Naperville, IL. Tel: (630) 961-3900, (800) 432-7444, FAX: (630) 961-2168, Web Site: www.sourcebooks.com (17)

Racer Walsh Co, Jacksonville, FL. Tel: (904) 721-2289, FAX: (904) 721-2935, Web Site: www.racerwalsh. com (12)

Racer's Equipment Warehouse, Warwick, RI. Tel: (401) 348-6010, (800) 556-2864, FAX: (401) 348-6023, E-Mail: scott@racers-eq.com, Web Site: www. racers-eq.com (16)

Rackley, Monica, Market Approach Consulting Services LP, Lorena, TX. Tel: (254) 857-1100, FAX: (254) 857-1000, E-Mail: wmclean@marketapproach.net, Web Site: www.marketapproach.net (23)

RAD Marketing, Mount Vernon, NY. Tel: (914) 668-3563, FAX: (914) 668-4247, E-Mail: cabletowns@ verizon.net (24)

Rademacher, Johnathon, Sundog, Fargo, ND. Tel: (701) 235-5525, (888) 9-SUNDOG, FAX: (701) 235-8941, E-Mail: info@sundoginteractive.com, Web Site: www.sundoginteractive.com (35)

Radetich, Alex, Take 5 Solutions LLC, Boca Raton, FL. Tel: (561) 819-5555, (866) 861-8862, FAX: (561) 819-0245, E-Mail: sales@take5s.com, Web Site: www.take5solutions.com (30)

Radial Inc, King of Prussia, PA. Tel: (610) 491-7000, Web Site: www.radial.com (28)

Radiant 1, Chicago, IL. Tel: (312) 933-7764, E-Mail: amaites@radiant-1.com, Web Site: www.radiant-1. com (35)

The Radio Agency, Media, PA. Tel: (610) 892-7300, (800) 969-2636, FAX: (610) 892-1899, E-Mail: contact@theradioagency.com, Web Site: www. radiodirect.com (35)

Radock, Leslie, Music Treasures Co, Richmond, VA. Tel: (804) 730-8800, (800) 666-7565, FAX: (888) MUSIC-TC, E-Mail: musict@musictreasures.com, Web Site: www.musictreasures.com (6)

Radzik, Kim, Sportif Mail Order Inc, Sparks, NV. Tel: (888) 260-7676, FAX: (775) 356-3567, Web Site: www.sportif.com (2)

Raether, Kandy, Enerpac, Menomonee Falls, WI. Tel: (262) 781-6600, (800) 433-2766, FAX: (262) 781-1028, Web Site: www.enerpac.com (16)

Raff, Beryl, Helzberg Diamonds, North Kansas City, MO. Tel: (816) 842-7780, (800) HELZBERG, FAX: (816) 480-0294, Web Site: www.helzberg.com (16)

Rafferty, Mark. FreshAddress Inc, Newton, MA. Tel: (617) 965-4500, (800) 321-3009, FAX: (617) 965-4551, Web Site: www.freshaddress.com (22)

Rafipour, Mary, Fairfield Industries Inc, Sugar Land, TX. Tel: (281) 275-7500, (800) 231-9809, FAX: (281) 275-7550, E-Mail: jblattman@fairfield.com, Web Site: www.fairfield.com (23)

Raftice, Jim, PowerPay, Portland, ME. Tel: (207) 775-6900, (877) 877-3737, FAX: (888) 204-4040, Web Site: www.powerpay.biz (14)

Raftus, J.B., GSD&M, Austin, TX. Tel: (512) 242-4736, Web Site: www.gsdm.com (35)

Ragen, Tom, Precision Dialogue Marketing LLC, Chicago, IL. Tel: (440) 471-6001, Web Site: www. precisiondialogue.com (35)

Raghubir, Priya, New York University/Center for Marketing, New York, NY. Tel: (212) 998-0100, FAX: (212) 995-4006, E-Mail: mkt@stern.nyu.edu, Web Site: www.stern.nyu.edu/marketing (23)

Ragland, Matt, Sunbeam Products Inc, Boca Raton, FL. Tel: (561) 912-4100, FAX: (561) 912-4567, Web Site: www.sunbeam.com (16)

Ragsdale, John, Williamson-Dickie Manufacturing Co, Fort Worth, TX. Tel: (800) 336-7201, FAX: (817) 877-5027, E-Mail: customerservice@dickies.com, Web Site: www.dickies.com (2)

Ragusa, Chris, Estee Marketing Group Inc, Rye Brook, NY. Tel: (914) 235-7080, FAX: (914) 235-6518, E-Mail: info@esteemarketing.com, Web Site: www. esteemarketing.com (24)

Raguso, John, Driscoll Label Co Inc, East Hanover, NJ. Tel: (973) 585-7291, FAX: (800) 342-1195, (973) 585-7295, E-Mail: info@driscolllabel.com, Web Site: www.driscolllabel.com (27)

Rahja, John, Augsburg Fortress Publishers, Minneapolis, MN. Tel: (612) 330-3300, (800) 426-0115, FAX: (612) 330-3455, E-Mail: info@augsburgfortress.org, Web Site: www.augsburgfortress.org (17)

Rahr, Tim, The Taunton Press, Newtown, CT. Tel: (203) 426-8171, (800) 477-8727, FAX: (203) 426-3434, Web Site: www.taunton.com (17)

Rahvar, David, Rose Electronics, Houston, TX. Tel: (281) 933-7673, (800) 333-9343, FAX: (281) 933-0044, E-Mail: sales@rose.com, Web Site: www. rose.com (3)

Lynda Raihofer & Associates LLC, Pelham, NY. Tel: (914) 738-8282 (20)

Raihofer, Lynda, Lynda Raihofer & Associates LLC, Pelham, NY. Tel: (914) 738-8282 (20)

Raim, Garry, GKV, Baltimore, MD. Tel: (410) 539-5400, FAX: (410) 234-2441, E-Mail: newbusiness@ gkv.com, Web Site: gvk.com (35)

Raimondo, Tony F., Behlen Manufacturing Co, Columbus, NE. Tel: (402) 564-3111, FAX: (402) 563-7405, E-Mail: behlen@megavision.com, Web Site: www.behlenmfg.com (16)

Rainbow Art Glass, Wall, NJ. Tel: (732) 681-6003, (800) 526-2356, FAX: (732) 681-4984, E-Mail: info@rainbowartglass.com, Web Site: www. rainbowartglass.com (16)

Rainbow Graphics Inc, Mundelein, IL. Tel: (847) 824-9600, E-Mail: jkoszuta@rainbowgraphics.com, Web Site: www.rainbowgraphics.com (27)

Rainbow Group LLC, Middleton, WI. Tel: (608) 824-0068, Web Site: www.beaconathletics.com (11)

Raine, Ed, AdPlex, Houston, TX. Tel: (281) 821-5522, FAX: (281) 443-1040, Web Site: www.adplex.com (35)

Rainer, Gebhard F., Hyatt Hotels Corp, Chicago, IL. Tel: (312) 750-1234, FAX: (312) 780-5289, Web Site: www.hyatt.com (16)

Raines, Ph.D. J. Patrick, Belmont University, Nashville, TN. Tel: (615) 460-6000, FAX: (615) 460-6455, Web Site: www.belmont.edu (41)

Raines, Philip, Globe Ticket & Label Co, Carol Stream, IL. Tel: (404) 762-9711, (800) 523-5968, FAX: (404) 762-7019, Web Site: www.globeticket.com (16)

Raines, Richard, CARFAX Inc, Centreville, VA. Tel: (703) 934-2664, Web Site: www.carfax.com (12)

Rainey, Brad, Golden Key International Honour Society, Atlanta, GA. Tel: (678) 689-2200, (800) 377-2401, FAX: (678) 689-2297, E-Mail: memberservices@goldenkey.org, Web Site: www. goldenkey.org (1)

Rainey, J. Mike, Liberty Orchards Co Inc, Cashmere, WA. Tel: (509) 782-2191, (800) 888-5696, FAX: (509) 782-1487, E-Mail: service@libertyorchards. com, Web Site: www.libertyorchards.com (16)

Rainwater Associates Inc, New York, NY. Tel: (212) 861-2856, FAX: (212) 861-1729, E-Mail: rainwine@aol.com (20)

Raitt, Eugene, AIG Marketing, New York, NY. Tel: (212) 770-7000, (212) 770-2237, Web Site: www. agac.com (14)

Rajant Corp, Malvern, PA. Tel: (484) 595-0233, FAX: (484) 595-0244, E-Mail: support@rajant.com, Web Site: www.rajant.com (32)

Rajczak, Daniel S., The Iams Co, Mason, OH. Tel: (800) 675-3849, Web Site: www.iams.com (16)

Rajee, Karen, Star Silkscreen Design Inc, Decatur, IL. Tel: (217) 877-0804, FAX: (217) 877-0843, Web Site: www.starsilkscreendesign.com (2)

Raley's Bel Air Markets, West Sacramento, CA. Tel: (916) 373-3333, FAX: (916) 373-6351, Web Site: www.raleys.com (16)

Ralph, Bill, Journal of Commerce Group, Newark, NJ. Tel: (973) 848-7000, FAX: (973) 848-7004, Web Site: www.joc.com (17)

Ralston, Jamie, Wyandotte West Communications Inc, Kansas City, KS. Tel: (913) 788-5565, FAX: (913) 788-9812, E-Mail: news@wyandottewest.com, Web Site: www.wyandottewest.com (17)

Ralston, Kate, Mapping Analytics, Rochester, NY. Tel: (585) 271-6490, (877) 893-6490, FAX: (585) 271-1132, E-Mail: sales@mappinganalytics.com, Web Site: www.mappinganalytics.com (20)

Ramirez, Edith, Bromley Communications, San Antonio, TX. Tel: (210) 244-2000, E-Mail: ernest. bromley@bromley.biz, Web Site: bromley.biz (35)

Ramirez, George, O'Halloran Advertising, Westport, CT. Tel: (203) 341-9400 (39)

Ramirez, Luisa, Indus-Tool, Chicago, IL. Tel: (312) 226-2473, (800) 662-5021, FAX: (312) 226-2480, E-Mail: sales@indus-tool.com, Web Site: www. indus-tool.com (12)

Ramirez, Michelle, NPI, Fort Worth, TX. Tel: (214) 634-2288, FAX: (682) 503-8214, E-Mail: sales@ npisorters.com, Web Site: www.npisorters.com (16)

Ramirez, Robert A., Answerthink, Miami, FL. Tel: (305) 375-8005. (866) 844-6514, FAX: (305) 379-8810, Web Site: www.answerthink.com (35)

Rammairone, Luciano, The Collegebound Network, Staten Island, NY. Tel: (718) 761-4800, (888) 338-6960, FAX: (718) 761-3300, E-Mail: info@ collegebound.net, Web Site: www.collegebound.net (32)

Ramos, Anthony, Children's Aid Society, New York, NY. Tel: (212) 949-4800, Web Site: www. childrensaidsociety.org (1)

Ramoutar, Ken, Advanced Software Applications Corp, Morgan, PA. Tel: (412) 220-9300, FAX: (412) 220-3878, E-Mail: asa@asacorp.com, Web Site: www. asacorp.com (22)

Ramstad, Peter M., The Toro Co, Bloomington, MN. Tel: (952) 888-8801, (800) 348-2424, FAX: (952) 887-8258, E-Mail: companyinfo@thetorocompany. com, Web Site: www.thetorocompany.com (16)

Ranaldi, Robert A., Far West Media Services, Long Beach, CA. Tel: (562) 496-3342, FAX: (562) 496-4329, E-Mail: info@farwestmedia.com, Web Site: www.farwestmedia.com (32)

Ranch House Meat Co, Billings, MT. Tel: (800) 749-6329, FAX: (888) 917-6328, E-Mail: sales@brisket. net, Web Site: www.brisket.net (4)

Rand Material Handling Equipment Co Inc, Janesville, WI. Tel: (401) 751-7657, (800) 366-2300, FAX: (800) 755-7263, E-Mail: cs@randmh.com, Web Site: www.randmh.com (16)

Randag, Bill, Datamark Inc, El Paso, TX. Tel: (800) 477-1944, E-Mail: info@datamark.net, Web Site: www.datamark.net (35)

Randall, Bernadette L., Choice Point, Alpharetta, GA. Tel: (770) 752-6000, (800) 342-5339, FAX: (770) 752-6005, Web Site: www.choicepoint.com (16)

Randall, Roger, Farm Journal Inc, Philadelphia, PA. Tel: (215) 557-8937, FAX: (215) 568-4238 (17)

Randall, William, Hatchholdings LLC, Plano, TX. Tel: (214) 505-4697 (20)

Randazzo, Peter, iCrossing, New York, NY. Tel: (212) 649-3900, FAX: (646) 280-1091, Web Site: www. icrossing.com (32)

Randolph, Timothy, Americana Sales Ventures Inc, Altamonte Springs, FL. Tel: (407) 862-8388, (800) 445-4302, FAX: (407) 862-6535, Web Site: www. americanashopper.com (35)

Random House Children's Books, New York, NY. Tel: (212) 782-9000, (800) 726-0600, E-Mail: rhkidspublicity@randomhouse.com, Web Site: www.randomhousekids.com (13)

Random House Direct Marketing, New York, NY. Tel: (212) 572-4985, (800) 678-5681, FAX: (212) 572-6018, Web Site: www.randomhousedirect.com (17)

Random Lengths Publications Inc, Eugene, OR. Tel: (541) 686-9925, (888) 686-9925, FAX: (541) 686-9629, (800) 874-7979, E-Mail: rlmail@rlpi.com, Web Site: www.randomlengths.com (17)

Rangel, Lynn, Finck Cigar Co, San Antonio, TX. Tel: (210) 341-8888, (800) 221-0638, FAX: (210) 341-8890, E-Mail: custser@finckcigarcompany.com, Web Site: www.finckcigar.com (5)

Ranger Joe's International Military Supply, Columbus, GA. Tel: (706) 689-0082, (800) 247-4541, FAX: (706) 682-8840, E-Mail: customerservice@ rangerjoes.com, Web Site: www.rangerjoes.com (2)

Rankers, Angie, Nevco Scoreboard Co, Greenville, IL. Tel: (618) 664-0360, (800) 851-4040, FAX: (618) 664-0398, E-Mail: sales@nevcoscoreboards.com, Web Site: www.nevcoscoreboards.com (16)

Rankin, Aaron, AD-Vantage Marketing, Santa Rosa, CA. Tel: (707) 578-8700, FAX: (707) 578-0258, E-Mail: info@ad-vantagemarketing.com, Web Site: ad-vantagemarketing.com (28)

Rankin, Charles E., University of Oklahoma Press, Norman, OK. Tel: (800) 627-7377, FAX: (405) 364-5798, Web Site: www.oupress.com (17)

Rankin, Dave, AD-Vantage Marketing, Santa Rosa, CA. Tel: (707) 578-8700, FAX: (707) 578-0258, E-Mail: info@ad-vantagemarketing.com, Web Site: ad-vantagemarketing.com (28)

Rankin, Glen, AD-Vantage Marketing, Santa Rosa, CA. Tel: (707) 578-8700, FAX: (707) 578-0258, E-Mail: info@ad-vantagemarketing.com, Web Site: ad-vantagemarketing.com (28)

Neil Ransick Marketing, San Francisco, CA. Tel: (415) 664-6728 (20)

Ransick, Neil, Neil Ransick Marketing, San Francisco, CA. Tel: (415) 664-6728 (20)

Rao, Steven, Relevate Group Inc, Springfield, VA. Tel: (703) 658-8300, (800) 523-7346, FAX: (703) 658-8301, E-Mail: sales@relevategroup.com, Web Site: www.relevategroup.com (22)

Rapa, Edward J., Central National-Gottesman Inc, Purchase, NY. Tel: (914) 696-9000, FAX: (914) 696-1066, E-Mail: purchase@cng-inc.com, Web Site: www.cng-inc.com (25)

Rapella, Steve, Neo-Tech Publishing Co, Henderson, NV. Tel: (702) 891-0303, FAX: (702) 795-8393 (17)

Raphel Marketing, Saint Johnsbury, VT. Tel: (802) 751-8802, FAX: (802) 751-8804, E-Mail: neil@raphel. com, Web Site: www.raphel.com (20)

Raphel, Neil, Raphel Marketing, Saint Johnsbury, VT. Tel: (802) 751-8802, FAX: (802) 751-8804, E-Mail: neil@raphel.com, Web Site: www.raphel.com (20)

Rapid City Journal, Rapid City, SD. Tel: (605) 394-8300, FAX: (605) 394-8462, E-Mail: classifieds@ rapidcityjournal.com, Web Site: www. rapidcityjournal.com (18)

Rapid Color Printing, Las Vegas, NV. Tel: (702) 792-6055, FAX: (702) 792-1437, Web Site: www. rapidcolor.com (27)

Rapid Insight Inc, Conway, NH. Tel: (603) 447-0240, Web Site: www.rapidinsightinc.com (20)

A Rapid Mailing Inc, Jessup, MD. Tel: (410) 792-4000, (800) US-RAPID, FAX: (301) 776-3690, E-Mail: info@rairapid.com, Web Site: www.rairapid.com (28)

Rapid Progress Marketing & Modeling LLC, Saint Petersburg, FL. Tel: (727) 528-8578, Web Site: www. rpmsquared.com (22)

Rapid Response Marketing, Las Vegas, NV. Tel: (702) 475-5235, Web Site: www.rapidresponseonline.com (32)

Rapids Wholesale Equipment, Marion, IA. Tel: (319) 447-1670, (800) 472-7431, FAX: (319) 447-1680, (800) 858-0327, E-Mail: judys@rapidswholesale. com, Web Site: www.rapidswholesale.com (16)

Rapino, Mike, Live Nation, Beverly Hills, CA. Tel: (310) 867-7000, Web Site: www.livenation.com (19)

Rapkin, Jon, USADATA Inc, New York, NY. Tel: (800) 395-7707, E-Mail: info@usadata.com, Web Site: www.usadata.com (23)

Raponi, Thomas, KICU-TV36, Oakland, CA. Tel: (510) 834-1212, E-Mail: kicu.public@coxmg.com, Web Site: www.ktvu.com/kicu/index (32)

Rapp, New York, NY. Tel: (212) 817-6800, FAX: (212) 686-7047, E-Mail: rick.doerr@rapp.com, Web Site: www.rapp.com (35)

Rapp, Howard, NYK Rapp Enterprises LLC, Hallandale, FL. Tel: (954) 457-9100, FAX: (954) 457-9015, Web Site: nykrapp.com (35)

Rapp, Rod, Conclusive Analytics, Inc, Huntersville, NC. Tel: (704) 887-5600, FAX: (704) 887-5601, E-Mail: info@conclusivemarketing.com, Web Site: www.conclusiveanalytics.com (22)

Rapp, William K., Kolbe Corp, Phoenix, AZ. Tel: (602) 840-9770, (800) 642-2822, FAX: (602) 952-2706, E-Mail: info@kolbe.com, Web Site: www.kolbe. com (17)

Rapp, William, Vance Industries Inc, Niles, IL. Tel: (847) 375-8900, FAX: (847) 375-6818, E-Mail: vance@vanceind.com, Web Site: www.vanceind. com (16)

Rappahannock Electric Cooperative, Fredericksburg, VA. Tel: (540) 898-8500, (800) 552-3904, E-Mail: office@myrec.coop, Web Site: www.myrec.coop (1)

Rappaport, Donn, ALC Inc, Princeton, NJ. Tel: (609) 580-2800, (800) 252-5478, FAX: (609) 580-2888, E-Mail: info@alc.com, Web Site: www.alc.com (23)

Rappaport, Susan, ALC Inc, Princeton, NJ. Tel: (609) 580-2800, (800) 252-5478, FAX: (609) 580-2888, E-Mail: info@alc.com, Web Site: www.alc.com (23)

Rardin, Eric, Care2, Washington, DC. Tel: (650) 622-0860, Web Site: www.care2.com (1)

Raritan Inc, Somerset, NJ. Tel: (732) 764-8886, FAX: (732) 764-8887, Web Site: www.raritan.com (22)

Rasch, Reginald, LinkShare Corp, New York, NY. Tel: (646) 943-8200, FAX: (646) 943-8204, Web Site: www.linkshare.com (32)

Raskin, Eric, Professional Advertising Systems Inc, Armonk, NY. Tel: (914) 765-0500, FAX: (914) 765-0503, E-Mail: info@paslists.com, Web Site: www. paslists.com (22)

Raskin, Micah, List Service Direct Inc, Leonia, NJ. Tel: (201) 585-1447, (800) 371-5487, FAX: (201) 585-1732, E-Mail: info@listservicedirect.com, Web Site: www.listservicedirect.com (23)

Rasmussen, Stephen S, Nationwide Mutual Insurance Co, Columbus, OH. Tel: (614) 249-7111, (800) 882-2822, FAX: (614) 854-3676, Web Site: www. nationwide.com (15)

Raspe, Bill, Office Express Inc, Evanston, IL. Tel: (888) 526-8438, FAX: (773) 341-7322, E-Mail: sales@ envelopesexpress.com, Web Site: www. envelopesexpress.com (26)

Rast, Bob, TT Publishing, Arlington, VA. Tel: (703) 838-1770, FAX: (703) 838-0285, Web Site: www. ttnews.com (17)

Ratcliff, Chris, MarketVision Research Inc, Cincinnati, OH. Tel: (513) 791-3100, (800) 232-4250, FAX: (513) 794-3500, E-Mail: jpinnell@mv-research. com, Web Site: www.marketvisionresearch.com (30)

Rath, Sam, Group Mojo, Portland, OR. Tel: (503) 493-2242, FAX: (503) 493-2246, E-Mail: sam@ groupmojo.com, Web Site: www.groupmojo.com (32)

Ratner, Dave, Dave's Soda & Pet City, Agawam, MA. Tel: (413) 786-3339, Web Site: www.daveratner. com (5)

Ratner, Howard, Nature Publishing Group, New York, NY. Tel: (212) 726-9200, FAX: (212) 696-9006, Web Site: www.nature.com (17)

Ratner, Irina, New York Daily News, New York, NY. Tel: (212) 210-2100, FAX: (212) 643-7844, Web Site: www.nydailynews.com (31)

Rattmann, Thomas E., Columbian Mutual Life Insurance Co, Binghamton, NY. Tel: (607) 724-2472, (800) 423-9765 (15)

Raube, James C., Select Comfort Corp, Minneapolis, MN. Tel: (763) 551-7000, (888) 411-2188, FAX: (763) 551-7826, Web Site: www.selectcomfort.com (16)

Rauch, Carolyn, IDG World Expo, Framingham, MA. Tel: (508) 879-0700, E-Mail: info@idgworldexpo. com, Web Site: www.idgworldexpo.com (42)

Rauff, Bill, Stimpson Co Inc, Pompano Beach, FL. Tel: (954) 946-3500, (877) 765-0748, FAX: (954) 941-1921, E-Mail: customerservice@stimpson.com, Web Site: www.stimpson.com (16)

Rauker, Thomas "Tom" C, NetProspex Inc, Waltham, MA. Tel: (888) 826-4877, E-Mail: sales@ netprospex.com, Web Site: www.netprospex.com (22)

Rausch, Erwin, Didactic Systems, Cranford, NJ. Tel: (908) 276-5413, FAX: (908) 276-7174, E-Mail: didacticra@aol.com (20)

Rauxa, Costa Mesa, CA. Tel: (714) 427-1271, E-Mail: newbiz@rauxa.com, Web Site: www.rauxa.com (35)

Raven, Abbe, A+E Television Networks LLC, New York, NY. Tel: (212) 210-1400, FAX: (212) 210-1326, E-Mail: aefeedback@aenetworks.com, Web Site: www.aenetworks.com (16)

Raven's Nest Herbals, LLC, Duluth, GA. Tel: (678) 642-6691, (678) 584-0830, E-Mail: info@ ravensnestherbals.com, Web Site: www. ravensnestherbals.com (7)

Ravich, Robert, ThorLo Inc, Statesville, NC. Tel: (704) 872-6522, (888) 846-7567, FAX: (704) 838-7005, Web Site: www.thorlo.com (16)

Rawle Murdy, Charleston, SC. Tel: (843) 577-7327, E-Mail: contact@rawlemurdy.com, Web Site: www. rawlemurdy.com (35)

Rawlings, Penny, Arctic Trading Co Inc, Churchill, MB Canada. Tel: (204) 675-8804, (800) 665-0431, FAX: (204) 675-2164, E-Mail: atcpenny@mts.net, Web Site: www.arctictradingco.com (6)

Rawson, Maureen, US Pharmacopeia, Rockville, MD. Tel: (301) 881-0666, (800) 227-8772, FAX: (301) 816-8236, Web Site: www.usp.org (1)

Ray, Gregory H., Philip Morris USA Inc, Richmond, VA. Tel: (804) 274-2000, FAX: (804) 484-8231, Web Site: www.philipmorrisusa.com (16)

Ray, James C., McFeely's Square Drive Screws, Madison, WI. Tel: (434) 846-2729, (800) 443-7937, FAX: (804) 847-7136, E-Mail: tech@mcfeelys.com, Web Site: www.mcfeelys.com (16)

Ray, Ronnie, Ipswitch Inc, Lexington, MA. Tel: (781) 676-5700, FAX: (781) 676-5710, Web Site: www. whatsupgold.com (22)

Raybuck Autobody Parts, Punxsutawney, PA. Tel: (814) 938-5248, FAX: (814) 938-4250, E-Mail: service@ raybuck.com, Web Site: www.raybuck.com (12)

Raybuck, Lisa, Raybuck Autobody Parts, Punxsutawney, PA. Tel: (814) 938-5248, FAX: (814) 938-4250, E-Mail: service@raybuck.com, Web Site: www.raybuck.com (12)

Raybuck, Randy, Raybuck Autobody Parts, Punxsutawney, PA. Tel: (814) 938-5248, FAX: (814) 938-4250, E-Mail: service@raybuck.com, Web Site: www.raybuck.com (12)

Rayburn, Todd, Fresno Oxygen, Fresno, CA. Tel: (559) 233-6684, (800) 404-9353, FAX: (559) 233-4206, E-Mail: info@fresnooxygen.com, Web Site: www. fresnooxygen.com (9)

Rayburn, William, FNC INC, Oxford, MS. Tel: (662) 236-8254, Web Site: www.fncinc.com (14)

Raycom Sports, Charlotte, NC. Tel: (704) 378-4456/ 4400, FAX: (704) 378-4465, E-Mail: whicks@ raycomsports.com, Web Site: raycomsports.com (16)

Rayher, Jack, Enco Manufacturing Co, Fernley, NV. Tel: (775) 788-7175, (800) 873-3626, FAX: (800) 965-5857, E-Mail: milanesp@use-enco.com, Web Site: www.use-enco.com (9)

Raymond, Kevin, Metropolitan Property & Casualty Ins, Warwick, RI. Tel: (401) 827-2104 (15)

Raymond, Leo, Association of Marketing Service Providers, Alexandria, VA. Tel: (703) 836-9200, (800) 333-6272, FAX: (703) 548-8204, E-Mail: mfsa-mail@mfsanet.org, Web Site: www.mfsanet.org (40)

Raymone, Michelle, Association of Marketing Service Providers, Alexandria, VA. Tel: (703) 836-9200, (800) 333-6272, FAX: (703) 548-8204, E-Mail: mfsa-mail@mfsanet.org, Web Site: www.mfsanet. org (40)

RayPress Corp, Birmingham, AL. Tel: (205) 989-3731, FAX: (205) 989-7203, Web Site: www.raypress.com (27)

Raz, Rita, Analytic Recruiting Inc, New York, NY. Tel: (212) 545-8511, FAX: (212) 545-8520, E-Mail: rita@analyticrecruiting.com, Web Site: www. analyticrecruiting.com (20)

RCI LLC, Carmel, IN. Tel: (317) 805-9000, FAX: (317) 805-9335, Web Site: www.rci.com (19)

Rea, Tim, Office Depot, Boca Raton, FL. Tel: (561) 438-4800, (800) 463-3768, FAX: (561) 438-4001, Web Site: www.officedepot.com (16)

Rea, Tim, OfficeMax Inc, Boca Raton, FL. Tel: (877) 633-4236, Web Site: www.officemax.com (10)

Reaburn, Paul, Transamerica Occidental Life Co, Los Angeles, CA. Tel: (213) 742-3111, FAX: (213) 741-6623, Web Site: www.transamerica.com (15)

ReachForce, Austin, TX. Tel: (844) 254-5405, E-Mail: info@reachforce.com, Web Site: www.reachforce. com (22)

Read, Erin, Creating Results LLC, Woodbridge, VA. Tel: (703) 494-7888, (888) 205-8899, Web Site: www.creatingresults.com (35)

Read, Ian C., Pfizer Inc, New York, NY. Tel: (212) 733-2323, Web Site: www.pfizer.com (16)

Read, Mark, Wunderman, New York, NY. Tel: (212) 941-3000, Web Site: www.wunderman.com (35)

Read, Phillip, Lillian Vernon Corp, Colorado Springs, CO. Tel: (757) 427-7923, (800) 545-5426, FAX: (757) 427-7819, E-Mail: publicrelations@ lillianvernon.com, Web Site: www.lillianvernon. com (6)

The Reader's Digest Association Inc, New York, NY. Tel: (800) 310-6261, Web Site: www.rda.com (17)

Reading for Education, Murfreesboro, TN. Tel: (615) 896-3800 (16)

Reading for Education, Murfreesboro, TN. Tel: (615) 494-4000, FAX: (615) 895-9041, Web Site: www. readingforeducation.com (1)

Readinger, Mark E., P & H Mining Equipment, Milwaukee, WI. Tel: (414) 671-4400, FAX: (414) 671-7618, Web Site: www.phmining.com (16)

Reagan, Kathy, Datamann Inc, Wilder, VT. Tel: (802) 295-6600, (800) 451-4263, FAX: (802) 296-3623, Web Site: www.datamann.com (22)

Reaka, Margie, Marketing Horizons Inc, Saint Louis, MO. Tel: (314) 432-1957, (800) 669-0839, FAX: (314) 432-7014, E-Mail: jkramer@mhorizons.com (30)

Real Goods Trading Corp, Hopland, CA. Tel: (707) 472-2403, (888) 919-2400, FAX: (707) 472-2430, Web Site: www.realgoods.com (5)

Real Media Solutions, Wayne, NJ. Tel: (973) 835-7060, Web Site: www.get-realmedia.com (27)

RealData Services Inc, Glenwood Springs, CO. Tel: (970) 945-2456, FAX: (970) 945-5356, E-Mail: rick@realdataservices.com, Web Site: www. realdataservices.com (22)

Reall, Gus, Stolle Machinery LLC, Centennial, CO. Tel: (303) 708-9044, (800) 228-4593, FAX: (303) 708-9045, E-Mail: cmd.info@stollemachinery.com, Web Site: www.stollemachinery.com (34)

Reardon, Martine, Macy's Marketing, New York, NY. Tel: (212) 695-4400, FAX: (212) 494-1517, Web Site: www.macys.com (16)

Reassure America Life Insurance Co, Jacksonville, IL. Tel: (800) 637-4475, FAX: (217) 291-2398, Web Site: www.swissre.com (15)

Reavis, Vicki, Accutrend Data Corp, Greenwood Village, CO. Tel: (303) 488-0011, FAX: (303) 488-0133, E-Mail: info@accutrend.com, Web Site: www.accutrend.com (24)

Reb Storage Systems International, Chicago, IL. Tel: (773) 252-0400, (800) 252-5955, FAX: (773) 252-0303, E-Mail: sales@rebsteel.com, Web Site: www. industrialebuy.com (9)

Recinos, Diane, Berkeley College, West Paterson, NJ. Tel: (973) 278-5400, (800) 446-5400, FAX: (973) 278-6243, E-Mail: info@berkeleycollege.edu, Web Site: www.berkeleycollege.edu (13)

Reckford, Jonathan, Habitat For Humanity International, Americus, GA. Tel: (229) 924-6935, (800) HABI-TAT, FAX: (229) 924-6541, Web Site: www. habitat.org (1)

Recko, Bob, Sentry Life Insurance Co, Stevens Point, WI. Tel: (715) 346-6000, FAX: (715) 346-7028, E-Mail: infoctr@coredcs.com, Web Site: www. sentry.com (15)

Recognition Products International, Easton, MD. Tel: (410) 820-0022, (800) 292-7354, FAX: (410) 820-5044, E-Mail: info@recognitionproducts.com, Web Site: www.shoprecognitionproducts.com (16)

Recognition Systems (Dot Works), Port Washington, NY. Tel: (516) 625-5000, FAX: (516) 625-1507, E-Mail: wade@dotworks.com, Web Site: www. dotworks.com (16)

Recording for the Blind & Dyslexic Inc, Princeton, NJ. Tel: (609) 452-0606, (800) 221-4792, FAX: (609) 520-7996, E-Mail: info@rfbd.org, Web Site: www. rfbd.org (16)

Recreational Equipment Inc, Kent, WA. Tel: (253) 395-4803, Web Site: www.rei.com (11)

Rector, Dave, MRC Marketing, Emerson, NJ. Tel: (201) 406-9471, FAX: (201) 986-0361, Web Site: www. mrcmarketing.net (21)

Rector, Susan, MRC Marketing, Emerson, NJ. Tel: (201) 406-9471, FAX: (201) 986-0361, Web Site: www.mrcmarketing.net (21)

Recycled Software Inc, Palm Springs, CA. Tel: (760) 655-5666, (760) 534-5338, FAX: (702) 323-5333, E-Mail: support@recycledsoftware.com, Web Site: www.recycledsoftware.com (3)

Red Clay Interactive, Buford, GA. Tel: (770) 297-2430, (866) 251-2800, E-Mail: hello@redclayinteractive. com, Web Site: www.redclayinteractive.com (35)

Red Hill Corp, Gettysburg, PA. Tel: (717) 337-3038, (800) 822-4003, FAX: (717) 337-0732, E-Mail: custserv@supergrit.com, Web Site: www.supergrit. com (34)

Red Rock Branding, New Haven, CT. Tel: (203) 295-4882, E-Mail: glen@redrockbranding.com, Web Site: www.redrockbranding.com (35)

Redbook Magazine, New York, NY. Tel: (212) 649-2000, (800) 888-0008, FAX: (212) 581-7605, Web Site: www.redbookmag.com (17)

Redcats USA, New York, NY. Tel: (212) 613-9500, Web Site: www.brylane.com (2)

Reddick, J. Rex, Crazy Crow Trading Post, Pottsboro, TX. Tel: (903) 786-2287, (800) 786-6210, FAX: (903) 786-9059, E-Mail: info@crazycrow.com, Web Site: www.crazycrow.com (11)

Reddick, Jessica, Crazy Crow Trading Post, Pottsboro, TX. Tel: (903) 786-2287, (800) 786-6210, FAX: (903) 786-9059, E-Mail: info@crazycrow.com, Web Site: www.crazycrow.com (11)

RedEngine Digital, Mc Lean, VA. Tel: (703) 556-6951, Web Site: www.redenginedigital.com (20)

RedEnvelope Inc, San Diego, CA. Tel: (619) 528-4888, (877) 733-3683, Web Site: www.redenvelope.com (6)

Redfern, Ronald, Press-Enterprise Co, Riverside, CA. Tel: (951) 684-1200, FAX: (951) 368-9022, Web Site: www.pe.com (17)

Redfield & Co Inc, Omaha, NE. Tel: (402) 341-0364, FAX: (402) 341-1454, Web Site: www. redfieldandcompany.com (17)

Redger, Jackie, Manhattan Media Services Inc, New York, NY. Tel: (212) 808-4077, FAX: (212) 808-4080, E-Mail: mmorello@manhmedia.com, Web Site: www.manhmedia.com (21)

Redi-Data Inc, Fairfield, NJ. Tel: (973) 227-4380, (800) 635-5833, FAX: (973) 808-5511, E-Mail: sales@ redidata.com, Web Site: www.redidata.com (23)

Redi-Direct Marketing Inc, Fairfield, NJ. Tel: (973) 808-4500, E-Mail: sales@redidirect.com, Web Site: www.redidirect.com (21)

Redi-Mail Direct Marketing Inc, Fairfield, NJ. Tel: (973) 808-4500, FAX: (973) 808-5511, E-Mail: sales@redimail.com, Web Site: www.redimail.com (28)

JP Redington & Co, Huntington, NY. Tel: (631) 754-0111, FAX: (631) 757-0878 (16)

Redington, Sue, Foote, Cone & Belding, Chicago, IL. Tel: (312) 425-5000, FAX: (312) 425-5010, E-Mail: chicago@fcb.com, Web Site: www.fcb.com (35)

Redirect, Salt Lake City, UT. Tel: (801) 453-0100, E-Mail: hello@redirectdigital.com, Web Site: redirectdigital.com (35)

Redleaf Press, Saint Paul, MN. Tel: (651) 641-6621, (800) 423-8309, FAX: (800) 641-0115, E-Mail: jvoltz@redleafpress.org, Web Site: www. redleafpress.org (17)

Redlin, Kim, Jacobs & Clevenger Inc, Chicago, IL. Tel: (312) 894-3000, FAX: (312) 645-9825, E-Mail: mail2350@jacobsclevenger.com, Web Site: www. jacobsclevenger.com (35)

Redling, Joseph, Vonage, Holmdel, NJ. Tel: (732) 528-2600, Web Site: www.vonage.com (32)

Redlon, Matt, Clario Analytics, Eden Prairie, MN. Tel: (952) 653-0980, (866) 849-3341, FAX: (952) 653-5900, E-Mail: sales@clarioanalytics.com, Web Site: www.clarioanalytics.com (20)

Redman, Arthur, Airlines Reporting Corp, Arlington, VA. Tel: (703) 816-8135, FAX: (703) 816-8104, E-Mail: corpcom@arccorp.com, Web Site: www. arccorp.com (16)

Redmon, David, dmh Marketing Partners - Louisville, Louisville, KY. Tel: (502) 339-6442, E-Mail: data@ dmhmarketingpartners.com, Web Site: www. dmhmarketingpartners.com (28)

Redmond, Bob, Aradius Group, Omaha, NE. Tel: (402) 734-4400, (800) 369-0033, FAX: (402) 734-7492, E-Mail: info@aradiusgroup.com, Web Site: www. aradiusgroup.com (21)

Redstone Federal Credit Union, Huntsville, AL. Tel: (256) 837-6110, Web Site: www.redfcu.org (1)

Redstone, Sumner E., Viacom Inc, New York, NY. Tel: (212) 258-6000, FAX: (212) 258-6464, Web Site: www.viacom.com (16)

Redwood City Seed Co, Redwood City, CA. Tel: (650) 325-7333, FAX: (650) 325-4056, Web Site: www. ecoseeds.com (8)

Redwood Partners Ltd, New York, NY. Tel: (212) 843-8585, FAX: (212) 843-9093, E-Mail: info@ redwoodpartners.com, Web Site: www. redwoodpartners.com (20)

Reebok International Ltd, Canton, MA. Tel: (781) 401-5000, (800) 843-4444, FAX: (781) 401-4402, Web Site: www.reebok.com (2)

Reed Elsevier, New York, NY. Tel: (212) 309-8100, FAX: (212) 309-8187, Web Site: www.reedelsevier. com (17)

Reed Exhibitions, Norwalk, CT. Tel: (203) 840-4800, (888) 745-7644, FAX: (203) 840-5805, E-Mail: inquiry@reedexpo.com, Web Site: www.reedexpo. com (16)

Reed Smith Hall Dickler Advertising & Law Marketing Group, New York, NY. Tel: (212) 549-0377, FAX: (212) 521-5450, Web Site: www.reedsmith.com (20)

VG Reed & Sons, Louisville, KY. Tel: (502) 560-0100, (800) 635-9788, FAX: (502) 560-0197, E-Mail: info@vgreed.com, Web Site: www.vgreed.com (27)

Reed, Bryan D., Thousand Trails LP, Chicago, IL. Tel: (214) 618-7200, (800) 205-0606, FAX: (214) 618-7324, Web Site: www.1000trails.com (16)

Reed, Bud, Timberline Interactive, Middlebury, VT. Tel: (802) 388-8377, Web Site: www. timberlineinteractive.com (20)

Reed, Dennis, Balfour, Austin, TX. Tel: (512) 444-0571, FAX: (512) 440-1138, Web Site: www. artcarved.com (16)

Reed, George, North American Communications Inc (East), Duncansville, PA. Tel: (814) 696-3553, (800) 624-1533, FAX: (814) 696-1180, E-Mail: marketing@nacmail.com, Web Site: www.nacmail. com (26)

Reed, Howard, VG Reed & Sons, Louisville, KY. Tel: (502) 560-0100, (800) 635-9788, FAX: (502) 560-0197, E-Mail: info@vgreed.com, Web Site: www. vgreed.com (27)

Reed, Joe, National Bulk Equipment Inc, Holland, MI. Tel: (616) 399-2220, FAX: (616) 399-7365, E-Mail: sales@nbe-inc.com, Web Site: www.nbe-inc.com (16)

Reed, Mike, Bob Barker Co Inc, Fuquay Varina, NC. Tel: (800) 334-9880, FAX: (800) 322-7537, Web Site: www.bobbarker.com (5)

Reed, Phil, The Staplex Co, Brooklyn, NY. Tel: (718) 768-3333, (800) 221-0822, FAX: (718) 965-0750, E-Mail: info@staplex.com, Web Site: www.staplex. com (34)

Reed, Robert A., Physicians Mutual Insurance Co, Omaha, NE. Tel: (402) 633-1604, (888) 932-7642, FAX: (402) 633-1604, Web Site: www.physiciansmutual. com (15)

Reed, Skip, Direct Partners, Marina Del Rey, CA. Tel: (310) 482-4200, FAX: (310) 482-4201, Web Site: www.directpartners.com (35)

Reed, Todd, National Bulk Equipment Inc, Holland, MI. Tel: (616) 399-2220, FAX: (616) 399-7365, E-Mail: sales@nbe-inc.com, Web Site: www.nbe-inc.com (16)

Reeder, Robin, National Automated Clearing House Association, Herndon, VA. Tel: (703) 561-1100, FAX: (703) 787-0996, Web Site: www.nacha.org (1)

Reedy, Gary M., American Cancer Society, Atlanta, GA. Tel: (404) 320-3333, (800) ACS-2345, FAX: (404) 329-5787, Web Site: www.cancer.org (1)

Rees Associates Inc, Des Moines, IA. Tel: (515) 243-2127, FAX: (515) 243-1026, Web Site: www. reesassociates.com (28)

Rees, Chris, Reed Exhibitions, Norwalk, CT. Tel: (203) 840-4800, (888) 745-7644, FAX: (203) 840-5805, E-Mail: inquiry@reedexpo.com, Web Site: www. reedexpo.com (16)

Rees, Hywel ap, Telecom Inc, Oakland, CA. Tel: (510) 873-8283, (800) 243-3101, FAX: (510) 873-8293, Web Site: www.telecominc.com (29)

Rees, Mark, Conclusive Analytics, Inc, Huntersville, NC. Tel: (704) 887-5600, FAX: (704) 887-5601, E-Mail: info@conclusivemarketing.com, Web Site: www.conclusiveanalytics.com (22)

Rees, Steve, Schoolwise Press, San Francisco, CA. Tel: (415) 337-7971, (800) 247-8443 x 202, FAX: (415) 337-1146, E-Mail: info@schoolwisepress.com, Web Site: www.schoolwisepress.com (17)

Reese, C. Richard, Iron Mountain Fulfillment Services, Milpitas, CA. Tel: (408) 945-1600, FAX: (408) 946-1135, E-Mail: info@comac.com, Web Site: www. ironmountain.com (28)

Reese, Jacqueline D., Yahoo! Inc, Sunnyvale, CA. Tel: (408) 349-3300, Web Site: www.yahoo.com (32)

Reese, Joyce, Schnuck Markets Inc, Saint Louis, MO. Tel: (314) 994-9900, FAX: (314) 994-4465, Web Site: www.schnucks.com (16)

Reese, Stuart, MassMutual Financial Group, Springfield, MA. Tel: (413) 788-8411, FAX: (413) 744-8889, E-Mail: name@www.massmutual.com, Web Site: www.massmutual.com (15)

Reese, Thomas, MBI Inc, Norwalk, CT. Tel: (203) 853-2000, E-Mail: webmail@mbi-inc.com, Web Site: www.mbi-inc.com (16)

Reeves, Anthony, Moxie, Atlanta, GA. Tel: (678) 916-4500, E-Mail: info@moxieusa.com, Web Site: moxieusa.com (35)

Reeves, Bonnie, Hansen Corp, Princeton, IN. Tel: (812) 385-3415, FAX: (812) 385-3013, E-Mail: sales@ hansen-motor.com, Web Site: www.hansen-motor. com (16)

Reeves, Rita S., Insurance Publications Inc, Overland Park, KS. Tel: (913) 383-9191, (800) 762-3387, FAX: (913) 383-1247, E-Mail: brokerwrld@ primary.net, Web Site: www.brokerworldmag.com (17)

Reeves, Toby, Rescott LLC Marketing & Technology, Noblesville, IN. Tel: (317) 816-0700, Web Site: www.rescott.com (20)

Referee Enterprises, Racine, WI. Tel: (800) 733-6100, FAX: (262) 632-5460, E-Mail: questions@referee. com, Web Site: www.referee.com (1)

Refkin, David, GreenPath Sustainability Consultants, New City, NY. Tel: (914) 980-8346 (20)

Regal Ware Inc, Kewaskum, WI. Tel: (262) 626-2121, E-Mail: pseitz@regalware.com, Web Site: www. regalware.com (16)

Regan, Harold, The HW Wilson Co, Bronx, NY. Tel: (718) 588-8400, (800) 367-6770, FAX: (800) 590-1617, E-Mail: custserv@hwwilson.com, Web Site: www.hwwilson.com (17)

Regan, Kathleen, The HoneyBaked Ham Co, Holland, OH. Tel: (419) 724-4267, (866) 492-4267, E-Mail: info@honeybaked.com, Web Site: www. honeybaked.com (4)

Regan, Tim, JLS Mailing Services Inc, Brockton, MA. Tel: (508) 313-1050, (866) JLS-MAIL, FAX: (508) 313-1093, E-Mail: rparkinson@jlsms.com, Web Site: www.jlsms.com (28)

The Reggio Register Co Inc, Leominster, MA. Tel: (978) 870-1020, (800) 880-3090, FAX: (978) 870-1030, E-Mail: reggio@reggioregister.com, Web Site: www.reggioregister.com (8)

Reggio, Michael, The Reggio Register Co Inc, Leominster, MA. Tel: (978) 870-1020, (800) 880-3090, FAX: (978) 870-1030, E-Mail: reggio@ reggioregister.com, Web Site: www.reggioregister. com (8)

Regions, Birmingham, AL. Tel: (205) 944-1300, FAX: (205) 326-4072, Web Site: www.regions.com (14)

REGIT Inc, Glen Ellyn, IL. Tel: (630) 495-1500, (800) 537-9786, FAX: (630) 495-1611, E-Mail: regit@ regitinc.com, Web Site: www.regitinc.com (15)

Regitar USA Inc, Montgomery, AL. Tel: (334) 244-1885, (877) 734-4827, FAX: (334) 244-1901, E-Mail: info@regitar.com, Web Site: www.regitar. com (9)

Reglero, Angel, Compass Bank, Birmingham, AL. Tel: (205) 297-4900, (800) 239-4357, FAX: (205) 933-3702, Web Site: www.compassbank.com (14)

Regnery Publishing, Washington, DC. Tel: (202) 216-0600, FAX: (202) 216-0612, Web Site: www. regnery.com (17)

Regul, Lisa, Ten Speed Press, Emeryville, CA. Tel: (510) 559-1600, (800) 841-BOOK, FAX: (510) 559-1629, E-Mail: order@tenspeed.com, Web Site: www.tenspeed.com (17)

Reich, Cathy, National Wholesale Co Inc, Lexington, NC. Tel: (336) 248-5904, (800) 480-4673, FAX: (336) 248-2880, E-Mail: customerservice@ shopnational.com, Web Site: www.shopnational. com (2)

Reichard, Sandy M., DL Blair Inc, Westbury, NY. Tel: (516) 746-3700, FAX: (516) 746-3889, Web Site: www.dlblair.com (35)

Reichenbach, C. Stephen, BBC Direct Mktg Svcs, Shamong, NJ. Tel: (609) 268-9919, (877) 786-4389, FAX: (609) 268-9939, E-Mail: csr@bbcglobal.com, Web Site: www.bbcglobal.com (20)

Reichenbach, Jr. Clarence, BBC Direct Mktg Svcs, Shamong, NJ. Tel: (609) 268-9919, (877) 786-4389, FAX: (609) 268-9939, E-Mail: csr@bbcglobal.com, Web Site: www.bbcglobal.com (20)

Reicher, Jerome, ARRCO Medical Advertising, Walpole, MA. Tel: (508) 404-1105, FAX: (508) 404-1106, E-Mail: info@arrco.com, Web Site: www.arrco.com (35)

Reichert & Associates Inc, Grand Marais, MN. Tel: (218) 387-1095, E-Mail: reichertln@aol.com (20)

Reichert, Leo N., Reichert & Associates Inc, Grand Marais, MN. Tel: (218) 387-1095, E-Mail: reichertln@aol.com (20)

Reid Supply Co, Muskegon, MI. Tel: (231) 777-3951, (800) 253-0421, FAX: (231) 767-3882, E-Mail: mail@reidsupply.com, Web Site: www.reidsupply.com (16)

Reid, Bethany, PharmArt, Circleville, OH. Tel: (860) 932-8588, (800) 848-1633, FAX: (800) 477-2923, Web Site: www.healthcarelogistics.com/Pharmart (6)

Reid, Brian, TC Transcontinental, Montreal, QC Canada. Tel: (514) 954-4000, FAX: (514) 954-4016, Web Site: tctranscontinental.com (35)

Reid, Keith A., Air Force Sergeants Association, Suitland, MD. Tel: (301) 899-3500, (800) 638-0594, FAX: (301) 899-8136, E-Mail: staff@hqafsa.org, Web Site: www.hqafsa.org (1)

Reid, Scott, MediaWorks Advertising & Marketing Inc, Ormond Beach, FL. Tel: (386) 676-4608, E-Mail: scott@mediaworksusa.com, Web Site: www.mediaworksusa.com (21)

Reidy, Carolyn, Simon & Schuster Inc, New York, NY. Tel: (212) 698-7000, (800) 223-2348, Web Site: www.simonandschuster.com (17)

Reidy, Martin, Ansira, Saint Louis, MO. Tel: (314) 783-2300, FAX: (314) 783-2301, E-Mail: dl-newbusiness@ansira.com, Web Site: ansira.com (35)

Reierson, Roger, Flint Communications, Fargo, ND. Tel: (701) 237-4850, FAX: (701) 234-9680, Web Site: www.flintcom.com (35)

Reighard, Tricia, Ampac Holdings LLC, Cincinnati, OH. Tel: (513) 671-1777, (800) 543-7030, FAX: (513) 671-2920, Web Site: www.ampaconline.com (27)

Reigle, Douglas J., Regal Ware Inc, Kewaskum, WI. Tel: (262) 626-2121, E-Mail: pseitz@regalware.com, Web Site: www.regalware.com (16)

Reigle, Jeffrey A., Regal Ware Inc, Kewaskum, WI. Tel: (262) 626-2121, E-Mail: pseitz@regalware.com, Web Site: www.regalware.com (16)

Reihl, Jeff, LexisNexis, New York, NY. Tel: (212) 309-8100, FAX: (800) 437-8674, Web Site: www.lexisnexis.com (16)

Reilly, Edward T., American Management Association, New York, NY. Tel: (212) 586-8100, FAX: (212) 903-8186, Web Site: www.amanet.org (1)

Reilly, Edward T., American Management Association International, New York, NY. Tel: (212) 586-8100, (877) 566-9441, FAX: (212) 903-8168, Web Site: www.amanet.org (41)

Reilly, John, OCE North America Inc, Trumbull, CT. Tel: (773) 714-8500, (800) 523-5444, FAX: (773) 714-4056, Web Site: www.oceusa.com (34)

Reilly, Michael, Award Co of America, Tuscaloosa, AL. Tel: (205) 349-2990, (800) 633-5953, FAX: (205) 752-0930, Web Site: www.randallpub.com (6)

Reiman Publications, Greendale, WI. Tel: (414) 423-0100, (800) 344-6913, FAX: (414) 423-3840, Web Site: www.reimanpub.com (17)

Reiman, Roy, Reiman Publications, Greendale, WI. Tel: (414) 423-0100, (800) 344-6913, FAX: (414) 423-3840, Web Site: www.reimanpub.com (17)

Rein Associates LLC, Conway, SC. Tel: (843) 234-0422, (888) 734-6462, FAX: (843) 234-0428, E-Mail: info@reinassociates.com, Web Site: reinassociates.com (23)

Rein, Jack, Rein Associates LLC, Conway, SC. Tel: (843) 234-0422, (888) 734-6462, FAX: (843) 234-0428, E-Mail: info@reinassociates.com, Web Site: reinassociates.com (23)

Reineke, Patrick, Ability Commerce, Delray Beach, FL. Tel: (561) 330-3151, Web Site: www.abilitycommerce.com (20)

Reinholtz, Michael, Comphealth, Salt Lake City, UT. Tel: (801) 930-3000, (800) 453-3030, FAX: (801) 930-4517, E-Mail: info@comphealth.com, Web Site: www.comphealth.com (16)

Reinke, Scott, Local Corp, Irvine, CA. Tel: (877) 784-0805, FAX: (949) 784-0880, Web Site: www.local.com (32)

Reinmuth, Chris, ERA D2C Convention, Washington, DC. Tel: (703) 841-1751, (800) 987-6462, FAX: (425) 977-1036, E-Mail: webadmin@retailing.org, Web Site: retailing.org/d2c (42)

Reinsfelder, Eric, American Recreation Products Inc, Saint Louis, MO. Tel: (314) 576-8000, FAX: (314) 576-8072 (11)

Reis, George, Friday Report, Garden City, NY. Tel: (516) 746-6700, FAX: (516) 294-8141 (43)

Reis, George, FRM Weekly, Garden City, NY. Tel: (516) 746-6700, FAX: (516) 294-8141 (43)

Reis, Timothy C., EMS Technologies, Norcross, GA. Tel: (770) 263-9200, FAX: (770) 447-4405, Web Site: www.ems-t.com (16)

Reisberg, Jerry, Leaps & Bounds LLC, Fort Lee, NJ. Tel: (201) 947-5459 (20)

Reisfeld, Donald, Morton Advertising Inc, New York, NY. Tel: (212) 465-2250, FAX: (212) 465-1575, E-Mail: info@mortonad.com, Web Site: www.mortonad.com (35)

Reiss, Michael B., The Colonial Williamsburg Foundation, Williamsburg, VA. Tel: (757) 229-1000, (757) 220-7275, (800) 761-8331, Web Site: www.williamsburgmarketplace.com (1)

Rekus, Allison, Wilen Group, Farmingdale, NY. Tel: (631) 439-5000, FAX: (631) 439-4536, Web Site: www.wilengroup.com (27)

Relationship1, Pearl River, NY. Tel: (845) 732-8300, E-Mail: inforequest@relationship1.com, Web Site: www.relationship1.com (21)

Relaxo-Bak Inc, Anderson, IN. Tel: (765) 643-2934, (866) 369-6914, FAX: (765) 641-7448, Web Site: www.relaxobak.com (7)

Relevant Insights LLC, Euless, TX. Tel: (817) 545-8017 (30)

Relevate Group Inc, Springfield, VA. Tel: (703) 658-8300, (800) 523-7346, FAX: (703) 658-8301, E-Mail: sales@relevategroup.com, Web Site: www.relevategroup.com (22)

Reliable Mail Service Inc, Edison, NJ. Tel: (732) 346-9779, (800) 773-6338, FAX: (732) 346-9799, E-Mail: bdobin@reliablemailservice.com, Web Site: www.reliablemailservice.com (20)

Reliable Racing Supply, Queensbury, NY. Tel: (518) 793-5677, FAX: (518) 793-6491, Web Site: www.reliableracing.com (11)

Reliable Technologies Inc, Manchester, NH. Tel: (603) 644-2528, (800) 346-7890, FAX: (603) 627-5553, Web Site: www.tei-imaging.com (16)

Reliance Electric, Fort Smith, AR. Tel: (479) 646-4711, FAX: (479) 648-5792, E-Mail: smtraylor@powersystems.rockwell.com, Web Site: www.reliance.com (9)

Reliant Data Processing, North Aurora, IL. Tel: (630) 844-4210, FAX: (630) 844-9530, E-Mail: rdpmail@aol.com (28)

Reliant Energy, Houston, TX. Tel: (713) 497-7794, (866) 222-7100, Web Site: www.reliant.com (16)

Relyco, Dover, NH. Tel: (603) 742-0999, (800) 777-7359, FAX: (603) 742-9993, E-Mail: info@relyco.com, Web Site: www.relyco.com (27)

ReMark USA, Minnetonka, MN. Tel: (952) 938-4699, FAX: (952) 988-8500, E-Mail: jessica.sbragia@remarkgroup.com, Web Site: www.remarkamericas.com (15)

Remedy Magazine, New York, NY. Tel: (212) 695-2223, FAX: (212) 695-2936, E-Mail: info@rmedizine.com, Web Site: www.medizine.com (17)

Remick, Rick, Integrated Merchandising Systems LLC, Morton Grove, IL. Tel: (877) 467-1200, E-Mail: doug.carlson@imsfastpak.com, Web Site: www.imsfastpak.com (21)

Remilon LLC, Mountain View, CA. Tel: (650) 425-7511, Web Site: www.remilon.com (17)

Remington College, Heathrow, FL. Tel: (407) 562-5691, (800) 560-6192, Web Site: www.remingtoncollege.edu (13)

Remington, Dr Steven J., Harold Walter Siebens School of Business, Storm Lake, IA. Tel: (712) 749-2410, (800) 383-2821, FAX: (712) 749-2037, Web Site: www2.bvu.edu/academics/business (41)

Remington, Scott, Omaha Vaccine Co, Omaha, NE. Tel: (402) 731-9600, (800) 367-4444, FAX: (800) 242-9447, E-Mail: customerservice@OmahaVaccine.com, Web Site: www.omahavaccine.com (16)

Remnick, Dave, The New Yorker Magazine, New York, NY. Tel: (212) 286-2860, FAX: (212) 286-4168, Web Site: www.newyorker.com (17)

Remsberg, Charles, Calibre Press Inc, San Francisco, CA. Tel: (214) 545-3060, (800) 323-0037, FAX: (866) 225-4273, Web Site: www.calibrepress.com (17)

Remy, Scott, DineEquity Inc, Glendale, CA. Tel: (866) 995-DINE, Web Site: dineequity.com (16)

Renaissance Greeting Cards Inc, Downers Grove, IL. Tel: (800) 736-3383, Web Site: www.ftd.com (5)

Renaissance Learning, Wisconsin Rapids, WI. Tel: (715) 424-3636, (800) 338-4204, FAX: (877) 280-7642, E-Mail: electronicorders@renaissance.com, Web Site: www.renlearn.com (5)

Render, David, AccountMate Software Corp, Petaluma, CA. Tel: (707) 774-7500, FAX: (707) 774-7590, E-Mail: information@accountmate.com, Web Site: www.accountmate.com (22)

Renfrow, Joan, Onyx Productions Direct Inc, Los Angeles, CA. Tel: (323) 692-9830, FAX: (323) 692-9832, E-Mail: joan@onyxprod.com, Web Site: www.onyxprod.com (22)

Renk, Karen, Incentive Manufacturers Representatives Association (IMRA), Naperville, IL. Tel: (630) 369-7786, FAX: (630) 369-3773, E-Mail: nicole@incentivemarketing.org, Web Site: www.imraonline.org (40)

Renker, Greg, Guthy-Renker Corp, Santa Monica, CA. Tel: (310) 581-6250, FAX: (310) 581-3232, Web Site: www.guthy-renker.com (32)

Renkim Corp, Southgate, MI. Tel: (734) 374-8300, FAX: (734) 374-9165, E-Mail: info@renkim.com, Web Site: www.renkim.com (22)

Renner, Debbie, Rapid City Journal, Rapid City, SD. Tel: (605) 394-8300, FAX: (605) 394-8462, E-Mail: classifieds@rapidcityjournal.com, Web Site: www.rapidcityjournal.com (18)

Renner, Jon, Brushfire Inc, Cedar Knolls, NJ. Tel: (973) 871-1700, FAX: (973) 871-1717, E-Mail: vwarner@brushfireinc.com, Web Site: www.brushfireinc.com (35)

Renner, Kelly, MD Anderson Cancer Center - Children's Art Project, Houston, TX. Tel: (713) 745-2575, (800) 231-1580, FAX: (713) 794-1950, E-Mail: krenner@mdanderson.org, Web Site: www.childrensart.org (1)

Reno Gazette Journal, Reno, NV. Tel: (775) 788-6200, FAX: (775) 788-6563 (17)

The Renovator's Supply Inc, Millers Falls, MA. Tel: (413) 423-3300, (800) 659-2211, FAX: (413) 423-3800, E-Mail: customercare@rensup.com, Web Site: www.rensup.com (9)

Rent-A-Center Inc, Plano, TX. Tel: (972) 801-1100, (800) 275-2996, FAX: (972) 943-0113, Web Site: www.rentacenter.com (16)

Rent Mother Nature, Cambridge, MA. Tel: (617) 868-5059, (800) 232-4048, FAX: (617) 868-5861, Web Site: www.rentmothernature.com (4)

Renton's Inc, Parker, CO. Tel: (303) 865-7025, (800) 365-6644, E-Mail: info@rentons.com, Web Site: www.rentons.com (10)

RentPath LLc, Norcross, GA. Tel: (678) 421-3000, (800) 216-1423, Web Site: www.primedia.com (31)

Renwick, Glen M., The Progressive Corp, Mayfield Village, OH. Tel: (440) 461-5000, (800) PROGRESSIVE, (800) 776-4737, FAX: (800) 456-6590, Web Site: www.progressive.com (15)

Renwick, Scott, Kemper Corp, Chicago, IL. Tel: (312) 661-4600, (800) 733-7366, FAX: (312) 494-6995, Web Site: www.kemper.com (15)

Renwick, Terry, Potpourri Group Inc, North Billerica, MA. Tel: (978) 256-4100, FAX: (978) 256-1961/0344, Web Site: www.potpourrigroup.com (6)

Renz, Daniel, Summit Marketing, Saint Louis, MO. Tel: (844) 792-2013, (800) 843-7347, E-Mail: info@summitmarketing.com, Web Site: www.summitmarketing.com (35)

Renzi, Jeff, Unisys, Blue Bell, PA. Tel: (215) 986-4011, (800) 874-8647, FAX: (215) 986-2312, Web Site: www.unisys.com (16)

Repasch, Annette, ValueVision Media Inc, Eden Prairie, MN. Tel: (952) 943-6000, Web Site: www.shophq.com (32)

Replacements Ltd, Greensboro, NC. Tel: (800) RE-PLACE, E-Mail: inquire@replacements.com, Web Site: www.replacements.com (8)

Replogle Globes Inc, Broadview, IL. Tel: (708) 343-0900, FAX: (708) 343-0923, E-Mail: info@replogleglobes.com, Web Site: www.replogleglobes.com (16)

Reputation.com, Redwood City, CA. Tel: (877) 425-5792, E-Mail: info@reputation.com, Web Site: www.reputation.com (32)

Rescott LLC Marketing & Technology, Noblesville, IN. Tel: (317) 816-0700, Web Site: www.rescott.com (20)

Research & Response International Inc, New York, NY. Tel: (212) 489-8610, FAX: (212) 262-3474 (23)

Research Boston Corp, Lafayette, CA. Tel: (978) 225-8030, FAX: (267) 295-8704, Web Site: www.researchboston.com (20)

Research Communications Ltd, Canton, MA. Tel: (781) 341-1190, FAX: (781) 341-1191, E-Mail: info@researchcommunications.com (30)

Research To Prevent Blindness Inc, New York, NY. Tel: (212) 752-4333, (800) 621-0026, FAX: (212) 688-6231, E-Mail: inforequest@rpbusa.org, Web Site: www.rpbusa.org (1)

Reserve National Insurance Co, Oklahoma City, OK. Tel: (405) 848-7931, Web Site: www.reservenational.com (15)

Rose Resnick Lighthouse for the Blind & Visually Impaired, San Francisco, CA. Tel: (415) 431-1481, FAX: (415) 863-7568, E-Mail: executive@lighthouse-sf.org, Web Site: www.lighthouse-sf.org (1)

Resnick, Lynda R., Roll International Corp, Los Angeles, CA. Tel: (310) 966-5700, FAX: (310) 914-4747, Web Site: www.roll.com (16)

Resnick, Richard, Intromark Inc, Pittsburgh, PA. Tel: (412) 288-1300, (800) 851-6030 X1368, FAX: (412) 338-0497, E-Mail: licensing@intromark.com (16)

Resnick, Stewart, Roll International Corp, Los Angeles, CA. Tel: (310) 966-5700, FAX: (310) 914-4747, Web Site: www.roll.com (16)

Resnik, David A., Emblem & Badge Inc, Johnston, RI. Tel: (401) 365-1265, (800) 875-5444, FAX: (401) 365-1263, E-Mail: sales@recognition.com, Web Site: www.recognition.com (6)

Resorts Casino Hotel, Atlantic City, NJ. Tel: (609) 334-6000, (800) 336-6378, FAX: (609) 340-6349, Web Site: www.resortsac.com (19)

Resource/Ammirati, Columbus, OH. Tel: (614) 621-2888, FAX: (614) 621-2873, E-Mail: businessdevelopment@resourceammirati.com, Web Site: www.resourceammirati.com (35)

Resource Publications Inc, San Jose, CA. Tel: (408) 286-8505, (888) 273-7782, FAX: (408) 287-8748, E-Mail: info@rpinet.com, Web Site: www.rpinet.com (17)

Response ADvantage, Playa Del Rey, CA. Tel: (310) 577-0389, Web Site: www.responseadvantage.com (20)

Response Agency Inc, Sandy, UT. Tel: (801) 352-9100, E-Mail: info@responseagency.com, Web Site: www.responseagency.com (35)

Response Design Corp, Ocean City, NJ. Tel: (609) 601-5866, (800) 366-4732, FAX: (609) 788-3619, E-Mail: rdc@responsedesign.com, Web Site: www.responsedesign.com (20)

Response Dynamics Inc, Vienna, VA. Tel: (703) 442-7595, FAX: (703) 442-4565, E-Mail: info@responsedynamicsinc.com, Web Site: www.responsedynamicsinc.com (35)

Response FX, Carlsbad, CA. Tel: (760) 479-0012, E-Mail: services@responsefx.com, Web Site: www.responsefx.com (35)

Response Insurance, Scranton, PA. Tel: (203) 634-7255, (800) 518-2984, FAX: (203) 634-7319, E-Mail: webcs@response.com, Web Site: www.response.com (15)

Response Magazine, Santa Ana, CA. Tel: (714) 513-8624, (800) 371-6897, FAX: (714) 338-6710, Web Site: www.responsemagazine.com (43)

Response Management Technologies Inc, Berkeley, CA. Tel: (510) 843-8180, FAX: (510) 843-8020, E-Mail: info@respmgt.com, Web Site: www.respmgt.com (22)

Response Marketing Group, Richmond, VA. Tel: (866) 574-7665, E-Mail: info@rmg-info.com, Web Site: rmg-usa.com (35)

Response Marketing Inc, Eden Prairie, MN. Tel: (952) 949-4913 (35)

Response Media, Norcross, GA. Tel: (770) 451-5478, FAX: (770) 451-4929, E-Mail: postmaster@responsemedia.com, Web Site: www.responsemedia.com (32)

Response Mine Interactive Inc, Atlanta, GA. Tel: (404) 233-0370, Web Site: www.responsemine.com (35)

The Response Shop Inc, Palm Desert, CA. Tel: (858) 735-7646, FAX: (858) 777-5418, E-Mail: marla@responseshop.com, Web Site: www.responseshop.com (35)

Response Unlimited, Waynesboro, VA. Tel: (540) 943-6721, FAX: (540) 943-0841, E-Mail: info@responseunlimited.com, Web Site: www.responseunlimited.com (23)

Responsys, San Bruno, CA. Tel: (650) 745-1700, Web Site: www.responsys.com (20)

Resteghini, Matthew, Monster Worldwide, Weston, MA. Tel: (888) MONSTER, Web Site: www.monster.com (20)

Results Advertising Inc, Hasbrouck Heights, NJ. Tel: (201) 288-7888, FAX: (201) 288-5112, E-Mail: info@resultsinc.com, Web Site: www.resultsinc.com (35)

The Results Group, Boston, MA. Tel: (617) 227-0229, Web Site: www.verdant-results-group.com (20)

Results Producers, Los Angeles, CA. Tel: (818) 985-9200, E-Mail: info@resultsproducers.com, Web Site: resultsproducers.com (32)

Resumate Inc, Ann Arbor, MI. Tel: (734) 429-8510, E-Mail: info@resumate.com, Web Site: www.resumate.com (3)

Retawmatic Corp, Flushing, NY. Tel: (718) 886-0502 (9)

Retrieval Masters Creditors Bureau Inc, Elmsford, NY. Tel: (914) 592-0055, (800) 666-8097, FAX: (914) 345-5023, E-Mail: info@retrievalmasters.com, Web Site: www.retrievalmasters.com (20)

Rettew, Robin, Targetbase, Irving, TX. Tel: (972) 506-3400, E-Mail: info@targetbase.com, Web Site: targetbase.com (35)

Return Path Inc, New York, NY. Tel: (212) 905-5500, FAX: (212) 905-5501, Web Site: www.returnpath.biz (22)

Reulbach, Paul, Holsted Marketing Inc, New York, NY. Tel: (212) 686-8537, FAX: (212) 481-0415, E-Mail: preulbach@holstedmarketing.com, Web Site: www.holstedmarketing.com (35)

Reummell, Paul L., Cooper Surgical Inc, Trumbull, CT. Tel: (203) 601-5202, (800) 243-2974, FAX: (203) 601-1007, E-Mail: orders@coopersurgical.com, Web Site: www.coopersurgical.com (7)

Reuning, Karl, Datum Timing, Test & Measurement, Beverly, MA. Tel: (978) 927-8220, FAX: (978) 927-4099, E-Mail: wriley@datum.com, Web Site: www.datum.com (9)

Reuter Lloyd, Heidi, Reiman Publications, Greendale, WI. Tel: (414) 423-0100, (800) 344-6913, FAX: (414) 423-3840, Web Site: www.reimanpub.com (17)

Revana Digital, San Dimas, CA. Tel: (909) 599-8885, (866) 922-4632, Web Site: www.revanadigital.com (35)

Revana Inc, Tempe, AZ. Tel: (408) 902-5900, (800) 535-0343, Web Site: www.revana.com (35)

Revelli, Vanessa, Prakken Publications Inc, Ann Arbor, MI. Tel: (734) 975-2800, (800) 530-9673, FAX: (734) 975-2787, Web Site: www.techdirections.com; www.eddigest.com (17)

Rex Three Inc, Sunrise, FL. Tel: (954) 452-8301, (800) 782-6509, FAX: (954) 452-0569, E-Mail: info@rex3.com, Web Site: www.rexthree.com (27)

Rexcraft Wedding Invitations, Rexburg, ID. Tel: (208) 359-1000, (800) 635-3898, FAX: (800) 826-2712, E-Mail: cs@rexcraft.com, Web Site: www.rexcraft.com (16)

Reynes, Anthony, Tesar Reynes Inc, Chicago, IL. Tel: (312) 726-1900, E-Mail: tony@tesar-reynes.com, Web Site: www.tesar-reynes.com (20)

Reynolds & Reynolds Co, Kettering, OH. Tel: (937) 485-2000, (800) 883-3031, FAX: (866) 268-5407, Web Site: www.reyrey.com (22)

Reynolds, Craig, The Family Handyman, Eagan, MN. Tel: (651) 454-9200, FAX: (651) 994-2250 (17)

Reynolds, Darlene, The Magni Co Inc, McKinney, TX. Tel: (972) 540-2050, (800) 645-9199, FAX: (972) 540-1057, E-Mail: sales@magnico.com, Web Site: www.magnico.com; www.magnilife.com (16)

Reynolds, Douglas W., Horace Mann Educators Corp, Springfield, IL. Tel: (217) 789-2500, FAX: (217) 788-5161, Web Site: www.horacemann.com (15)

Reynolds, Eugene, Greystone Graphics, Kansas City, MO. Tel: (913) 342-1393, (800) 458-7407, FAX: (913) 621-4856, E-Mail: info@greystonegraphics. com, Web Site: www.greystonegraphics.com (27)

Reynolds, Evan, The Magni Co Inc, McKinney, TX. Tel: (972) 540-2050, (800) 645-9199, FAX: (972) 540-1057, E-Mail: sales@magnico.com, Web Site: www.magnico.com; www.magnilife.com (16)

Reynolds, Harry, F P International, Fremont, CA. Tel: (650) 261-5300, (800) 866-9946, FAX: (650) 361-1713, Web Site: www.fpintl.com (16)

Reynolds, Julian, Reliable Technologies Inc, Manchester, NH. Tel: (603) 644-2528, (800) 346-7890, FAX: (603) 627-5553, Web Site: www.tei-imaging.com (16)

Reynolds, Paula Rosput, Safeco Insurance Co, Seattle, WA. Tel: (206) 545-5000, (800) 332-3226, FAX: (206) 545-5767/5651, Web Site: www.safeco.com (15)

Reynolds, Sidney, The Signature Agency, Wake Forest, NC. Tel: (919) 878-8989, (800) 870-8700, FAX: (919) 878-3939, E-Mail: info@signatureagency. com, Web Site: www.signatureagency.com (35)

Reynolds, Tom, Media Horizons Inc, Norwalk, CT. Tel: (203) 857-0770, FAX: (203) 857-0296, E-Mail: info@mediahorizons.com, Web Site: www. mediahorizons.com (21)

Reynolds, Vicki, KCET, Burbank, CA. Tel: (747) 201-5000, FAX: (747) 201-5877, E-Mail: contact@kcet. org, Web Site: www.kcet.org (1)

Reznyk, Christopher, Assurant Solutions Preneed Division, Atlanta, GA. Tel: (770) 763-1000, (800) PRE NEED, FAX: (770) 859-4325, Web Site: www. assurantpreneed.com (15)

Rhino Marketing Inc, Los Angeles, CA. Tel: (604) 472-3240, (877) 605-7022, FAX: (604) 637-5619, Web Site: www.rhino.ca (20)

Rhode Island Novelty, Cumberland, RI. Tel: (401) 335-3300, (800) 528-5599, FAX: (800) 448-1775, E-Mail: info@rinovelty.com, Web Site: www. rinovelty.com (16)

Rhode, Naomi, Smart Practice, Phoenix, AZ. Tel: (800) 522-0800, FAX: (800) 522-8329, E-Mail: info@ smartpractice.com, Web Site: www.smartpractice. com (17)

Bruce Rhodes, Sudbury, MA. Tel: (978) 443-8389 (20)

Rhodes, Bruce, Bruce Rhodes, Sudbury, MA. Tel: (978) 443-8389 (20)

Rhodes, Kevin, Viking Pump Inc, Cedar Falls, IA. Tel: (319) 266-1741, FAX: (319) 273-8157, E-Mail: info@vikingpump.com, Web Site: www. vikingpump.com (16)

Rhodes, Tom, Direct Mail Solutions, Richmond, VA. Tel: (804) 254-8300, (877) 367-0800, Web Site: www.directmailsolutions.com (28)

Rhum, Andrea, ValCom Inc, Boonton, NJ. Tel: (973) 588-7084, FAX: (973) 257-7216, E-Mail: info@ valcom.tv, Web Site: www.valcom.tv (32)

Rhyan, Tracy, Frederick's of Hollywood Group Inc, Los Angeles, CA. Tel: (323) 466-5151, (855) 655-2514, FAX: (323) 464-5149, E-Mail: support@fredericks. com, Web Site: www.fredericks.com (2)

Rhythm Band Inc, Fort Worth, TX. Tel: (817) 335-2561, (800) 424-4724, FAX: (800) 784-9401, E-Mail: sales@rhythmband.com, Web Site: www. rhythmband.com (11)

Riazzi, Bob, ReachForce, Austin, TX. Tel: (844) 254-5405, E-Mail: info@reachforce.com, Web Site: www.reachforce.com (22)

Ribeiro, Cesar, Lincoln Educational Services Corp, West Orange, NJ. Tel: (973) 736-9340, Web Site: www.lincolnedu.com (13)

Riccelli, Richard, Richard Riccelli Inc, Charleston, SC. Tel: (843) 727-0183, FAX: (843) 727-0184, E-Mail: richard@riccelli.com, Web Site: riccelli.com (35)

Ricci Lee Hubbart Associates Inc, Cupertino, CA. Tel: (408) 725-1242, FAX: (408) 716-2704, E-Mail: susan@riccilee.com, Web Site: www.riccilee.com (16)

Ricci, Paul, Nuance Speech Solutions, Burlington, MA. Tel: (781) 565-5000, FAX: (781) 565-5001, E-Mail: sales@speechworks.com, Web Site: www.nuance. com (16)

Ricciardi, Marie, JP Redington & Co, Huntington, NY. Tel: (631) 754-0111, FAX: (631) 757-0878 (16)

Riccitelli, Hank, Klitzner Industries, Cranston, RI. Tel: (401) 751-7500, (800) 556-6860, FAX: (800) 556-3199, E-Mail: info@klitzner.com, Web Site: www. klitzner.com; www.providenceline.com (6)

Rice, Denis, Eagle:xm, Denver, CO. Tel: (303) 320-5411, (800) 426-5376, FAX: (303) 393-6584, E-Mail: extendedmedia@eaglexm.com, Web Site: www.eaglexm.com (21)

Rice, John G., GE Partnership Marketing Group, Schaumburg, IL. Tel: (847) 605-3000, FAX: (847) 605-3044, Web Site: www.gepmg.com (14)

Rice, Keith, Print Products International, Annapolis Junction, MD. Tel: (910) 695-7223, FAX: (910) 944-1724, Web Site: www.paceworldwide.com (9)

Rice, Randy, Arch Telecom Inc, Austin, TX. Tel: (512) 492-0735, (800) 890-7575, FAX: (512) 495-7101, Web Site: www.archtelecom.com (16)

Rice, Steve, Tetley USA Inc, Montvale, NJ. Tel: (201) 571-0300, Web Site: www.tetleyusa.com (16)

Rich Brands, Phoenix, AZ. Tel: (602) 889-4800, (877) 856-1753, FAX: (602) 889-4830, E-Mail: sales@ esscentualbrands.com, Web Site: esscentualbrands. com (16)

Rich Jr, Robert E., Rich Products Corp, Buffalo, NY. Tel: (716) 878-8000, (800) 828-2021, FAX: (716) 878-8765, Web Site: www.richs.com (16)

The Rich List Co, Wainscott, NY. Tel: (212) 737-8917, FAX: (212) 861-5384, E-Mail: richlistco@aol.com, Web Site: www.richlist.com (24)

Rich Products Corp, Buffalo, NY. Tel: (716) 878-8000, (800) 828-2021, FAX: (716) 878-8765, Web Site: www.richs.com (16)

Rich, Melinda R., Rich Products Corp, Buffalo, NY. Tel: (716) 878-8000, (800) 828-2021, FAX: (716) 878-8765, Web Site: www.richs.com (16)

Rich, Susan, InventHelp's INPEX, Pittsburgh, PA. Tel: (412) 288-1343, (888) 544-6739, FAX: (412) 288-4546, E-Mail: info@inpex.com, Web Site: www. inpex.com (42)

Rich-Duval, Catherin, Merrimack College, North Andover, MA. Tel: (978) 837-5000, E-Mail: denise. tuccelli@merrimack.edu, Web Site: www. merrimack.edu (41)

Richard Riccelli Inc, Charleston, SC. Tel: (843) 727-0183, FAX: (843) 727-0184, E-Mail: richard@ riccelli.com, Web Site: riccelli.com (35)

Richard, Kevin P., Mohawk Fine Papers Inc, Cohoes, NY. Tel: (518) 237-1740, (800) 843-6455, FAX: (518) 237-7394, E-Mail: info@mohawkpaper.com, Web Site: www.mohawkconnects.com (25)

Richards Communications, Russell, OH. Tel: (216) 514-7800, FAX: (216) 514-7801, E-Mail: jrichards@ richardsgo.com, Web Site: www.richardsgo.com (35)

Richards Partners, Dallas, TX. Tel: (214) 891-5700, FAX: (214) 891-3515, E-Mail: ruth_fitzgibbons@ richards.com, Web Site: richardspartners.com (35)

Richards Tulley, Elizabeth, Tully & Holland Inc, Wellesley, MA. Tel: (781) 239-2900, FAX: (781) 239-2901, E-Mail: info@tullyandholland.com, Web Site: www.tullyandholland.com (14)

Richards, Alison Miller, International City/County Management Association, Washington, DC. Tel: (202) 289-4262, FAX: (202) 962-3500, E-Mail: customerservice@icma.org, Web Site: www.icma. org (1)

Richards, Cheryl S., Kenneth Hollander Associates Inc, Mendocino, CA. Tel: (707) 962-1648, FAX: (707) 962-1635, Web Site: www.kharesearch.com (30)

Richards, Jared, Richards Communications, Russell, OH. Tel: (216) 514-7800, FAX: (216) 514-7801, E-Mail: jrichards@richardsgo.com, Web Site: www. richardsgo.com (35)

Richards, Jim, Houston Direct Marketing Association, Houston, TX. Tel: (281) 931-8883, FAX: (281) 820-4023, Web Site: www.houstondma.org (40)

Richards, John, Richards Communications, Russell, OH. Tel: (216) 514-7800, FAX: (216) 514-7801, E-Mail: jrichards@richardsgo.com, Web Site: www. richardsgo.com (35)

Richards, Karen M., Data Intelligence Group, Franklin, TN. Tel: (615) 861-3301, Web Site: www. wedigdata.com (22)

Richards, Laura, Veriad, Brea, CA. Tel: (714) 990-2700, (800) 962-0658, FAX: (800) 962-0658, E-Mail: info@veriad.com, Web Site: www.veriad. com (16)

Richards, Mark R., Paperweight Development Corp, Appleton, WI. Tel: (920) 734-9841, FAX: (920) 991-8796, Web Site: www.appletonideas.com (25)

Richards, Perrie, Mid America Designs Inc, Effingham, IL. Tel: (217) 540-4200, (800) 350-4543, FAX: (217) 540-4800, E-Mail: mail@mamotorworks.com, Web Site: www.mamotorworks.com (12)

Richards, Scott, Dial 800 LLC, Los Angeles, CA. Tel: (310) 273-9023, (800) 700-1987, E-Mail: sales@ dial800.com, Web Site: www.dial800.com (32)

Richards, Steven K., Outsourcing Solutions Inc, Wentzville, MO. Tel: (847) 419-1790, FAX: (847) 419-1818 (20)

Richards, Thomas E., CDW Corp, Vernon Hills, IL. Tel: (847) 465-6000, (847) 371-6090, Web Site: www.cdw.com (16)

Richardson Electronics Ltd, Lafox, IL. Tel: (630) 208-2200, FAX: (630) 208-2550, E-Mail: edg@rell.com, Web Site: www.rell.com (16)

Richardson, E.J., Richardson Electronics Ltd, Lafox, IL. Tel: (630) 208-2200, FAX: (630) 208-2550, E-Mail: edg@rell.com, Web Site: www.rell.com (16)

Richardson, Kathleen, Communispond Inc, East Hampton, NY. Tel: (631) 907-8010, (800) 529-5925, FAX: (631) 907-8011, Web Site: www. communispond.com (20)

Richardson, Keith, Sierra Trading Post, Cheyenne, WY. Tel: (800) 713-4534, FAX: (800) 378-8946, E-Mail: customerservice@sierratradingpost.com, Web Site: www.sierratradingpost.com (2)

Richardson, Rev. John T., DePaul University, Chicago, IL. Tel: (312) 362-8000, (800) 4-DEPAUL, FAX: (312) 362-6639, E-Mail: skelly@wppost.depaul.edu, Web Site: www.depaul.edu (41)

Richardson-Heron, Dara, YWCA of the USA, Washington, DC. Tel: (202) 467-0801, FAX: (202) 467-0802, E-Mail: info@ywca.org, Web Site: www.ywca.org (1)

Richer, Claire S., Fidelity Investments, Boston, MA. Tel: (617) 563-7000, (800) 343-3548, FAX: (617) 476-6150, Web Site: www.fidelity.com (14)

Richey, Terry, National Trust for Historic Preservation, Washington, DC. Tel: (202) 588-6000, (800) 944-6847, E-Mail: info@savingplaces.org, Web Site: www.preservationnation.org (1)

Richieri, Kenneth, The New York Times Co, New York, NY. Tel: (212) 556-1234, Web Site: www.nytimes.com (17)

Richman, Joshua, Straw Hat Cooperative Corp, San Ramon, CA. Tel: (925) 837-3400, FAX: (925) 820-1080, E-Mail: info@strawhatpizza.com, Web Site: www.strawhatpizza.com (16)

Richman, Keith, Defy Media Inc, New York, NY. E-Mail: info@defymedia.com, Web Site: www.defymedia.com (35)

Richman, Steven P., Milwaukee Electric Tool Corp, Brookfield, WI. Tel: (262) 781-3600, (800) 729-3878, FAX: (800) 638-9582, Web Site: www.milwaukeetool.com (16)

Richmond, Michael, DigDev Direct, Deerfield Beach, FL. Tel: (954) 949-9500, (800) 873-5137, FAX: (954) 337-0251, E-Mail: info@digdev.com, Web Site: www.digdevdirect.com (35)

Richmond, Russell, SCI Management, Houston, TX. Tel: (713) 525-7783, Web Site: www.sci-corp.com (16)

Richter, Alan, Marden-Kane Inc, Woodbury, NY. Tel: (516) 365-3999, FAX: (516) 365-5250, E-Mail: expert@mardenkane.com, Web Site: www.mardenkane.com (35)

Richter, George H., Smithfield Foods, Smithfield, VA. Tel: (800) 276-6158, Web Site: www.smithfieldfoods.com (16)

Richter, Glenn R., Nuveen Investments, Chicago, IL. Tel: (312) 917-7700, (800) 257-8787, FAX: (312) 917-8049, Web Site: www.nuveen.com (14)

Richtman, Max, National Committee to Preserve Social Security & Medicare, Washington, DC. Tel: (202) 216-0420, (800) 966-1935, FAX: (202) 216-0446, E-Mail: kreard@ncpssm.org, Web Site: www.ncpssm.org (1)

Riciutti, Jack, Bartash Media Group, Philadelphia, PA. Tel: (215) 724-1700, (800) 599-9792, FAX: (215) 724-3313, Web Site: www.bartash.com (27)

Pete Rickard Inc, Cobleskill, NY. Tel: (518) 234-2731, (800) 282-5663, FAX: (518) 234-2454, E-Mail: info@peterickard.com, Web Site: www.peterickard.com (11)

Rickard Squared, Hauppauge, NY. Tel: (631) 249-8710, FAX: (631) 382-8248, E-Mail: mrickard@rickard2.com, Web Site: rickard2.com (23)

Rickard, Jennifer, Rickard Squared, Hauppauge, NY. Tel: (631) 249-8710, FAX: (631) 382-8248, E-Mail: mrickard@rickard2.com, Web Site: rickard2.com (23)

Rickard, Lisa A, US Chamber Institute for Legal Reform, Washington, DC. Tel: (202) 463-5724, Web Site: www.uschamber.com (40)

Rickard, Mark, Rickard Squared, Hauppauge, NY. Tel: (631) 249-8710, FAX: (631) 382-8248, E-Mail: mrickard@rickard2.com, Web Site: rickard2.com (23)

Ricker, Trent, Pursuant Group, Dallas, TX. Tel: (214) 866-7700, E-Mail: info@pursuant.com, Web Site: www.pursuant.com (20)

Ricketts, Robert, Troy Biologicals Inc, Troy, MI. Tel: (248) 585-9720, (800) 521-0445, FAX: (248) 585-2490, E-Mail: info@troybio.com, Web Site: www.troybio.com (7)

Ricketts, Tom, Troy Biologicals Inc, Troy, MI. Tel: (248) 585-9720, (800) 521-0445, FAX: (248) 585-2490, E-Mail: info@troybio.com, Web Site: www.troybio.com (7)

Rickless, Edward B., Sterling Business Services, Cary, NC. Tel: (919) 467-5062 (14)

Ricks, Franklin K., King's Chandelier Co, Eden, NC. Tel: (336) 623-6188, FAX: (336) 627-9935, E-Mail: crystal@chandelier.com, Web Site: www.chandelier.com (6)

Ridart, Rick, Insight Direct Inc, Tempe, AZ. Tel: (480) 333-3001, (800) 467-4448, FAX: (480) 902-1180, Web Site: www.insight.com (16)

Riddick, Jeff, OfficeFurniture.com, West Allis, WI. Tel: (414) 272-6080, (800) 933-0053, FAX: (800) 468-1526, Web Site: www.officefurniture.com (8)

Ridding, John, The Financial Times Group, New York, NY. Tel: (212) 641-6500, Web Site: www.ft.com (17)

Riddle, Tom, Centaur Forge LLC, Burlington, WI. Tel: (262) 763-9175, (800) 666-9175, FAX: (262) 763-8350, E-Mail: info@centaurforge.com, Web Site: www.centaurforge.com (9)

Ridenour & Associates, Sarasota, FL. Tel: (312) 787-8228, FAX: (312) 787-8528, E-Mail: ssridenour@aol.com, Web Site: www.ridenourassociates.com (20)

Ridenour, Suzanne S., Ridenour & Associates, Sarasota, FL. Tel: (312) 787-8228, FAX: (312) 787-8528, E-Mail: ssridenour@aol.com, Web Site: www.ridenourassociates.com (20)

Ridenour, Tony, Communication Solutions LLC, Springfield, MO. Tel: (417) 862-4567, Web Site: www.comsollc.com (29)

Rideout, Michelle, Capitol Advantage/Roll Call Group, Washington, DC. Tel: (202) 6550-6500, (800) 432-2250, E-Mail: sales@cq.com, Web Site: www.corporate.cqrollcall.com (31)

Ridge, Mike, Recognition Products International, Easton, MD. Tel: (410) 820-0022, (800) 292-7354, FAX: (410) 820-5044, E-Mail: info@recognitionproducts.com, Web Site: www.shoprecognitionproducts.com (16)

Ridge, Susan, Save the Children Federation Inc, Fairfield, CT. Tel: (203) 221-4000, (800) 728-3843, FAX: (203) 222-1067, E-Mail: majorgivng@savethechildren.org, Web Site: www.savethechildren.org (1)

Ridgway, Joseph, Bruno & Ridgway Research Associates Inc, Lawrenceville, NJ. Tel: (609) 895-9889, FAX: (609) 895-6665, E-Mail: info@brunoandridgway.com, Web Site: www.brra.com (30)

Ridinger, JR, Shop.com, Miami, FL. Tel: (866) 420-1709, E-Mail: customerservice@shop.com, Web Site: www.shop.com (16)

Ridner, Adrian, Remilon LLC, Mountain View, CA. Tel: (650) 425-7511, Web Site: www.remilon.com (17)

Rieck, Dean, Direct Creative, Westerville, OH. Tel: (614) 882-8823, E-Mail: dean@directcreative.com, Web Site: www.directcreative.com (39)

Riehle, Parker, Vermont Ski Areas Association, Montpelier, VT. Tel: (802) 223-2439, FAX: (802) 229-6917, E-Mail: info@skivermont.com, Web Site: www.skivermont.com (1)

Riehle, Thomas, Ipsos America Inc, New York, NY. Tel: (212) 265-3200, FAX: (212) 265-3790, E-Mail: info@ipsos-asi.com, Web Site: www.ipsos-asi.com (30)

Rielly, Mike, The Family Handyman, Eagan, MN. Tel: (651) 454-9200, FAX: (651) 994-2250 (17)

Rigano, Frank, Interactive Marketing Solutions, Stamford, CT. Tel: (203) 653-2762, FAX: (203) 653-2767, E-Mail: solutions@ims-dm.com (22)

Rigden Inc, Boulder, CO. Tel: (303) 442-8190, FAX: (303) 442-8686, E-Mail: rigden@rigden.com, Web Site: www.rigden.com (22)

Riggio, Leonard S., BarnesandNoble.com, New York, NY. Tel: (212) 414-6000, (800) THE-BOOK, FAX: (212) 414-6140, E-Mail: service@barnesandnoble.com, Web Site: www.barnesandnoble.com (16)

Riggs, Russ, Integrative Logic LLC, Lawrenceville, GA. Tel: (678) 638-2600, FAX: (678) 638-2601, Web Site: www.integrativelogic.com (30)

The Right Lists Ltd, Gaithersburg, MD. Tel: (301) 869-2020, E-Mail: bfletch@rightlists.com, Web Site: www.rightlists.com (23)

The Right Start Inc, Denver, CO. Tel: (303) 320-8312, (888) 856-8004, E-Mail: customerservice@rightstart.org, Web Site: www.rightstart.com (5)

Riglian, Walter, Vitasoy USA Inc, Ayer, MA. Tel: (978) 772-6880, (800) VITA-SOY, FAX: (978) 772-6881, E-Mail: info@vitasoy-usa.com, Web Site: www.vitasoy-usa.com (16)

Rigoni, Doug, Coast Hotels Limited, Seattle, WA. Tel: (206) 826-2700, FAX: (206) 826-2701, Web Site: www.coasthotels.com (19)

Rilee-Kelley, Beth, The Martin Agency, Richmond, VA. Tel: (804) 698-8000, FAX: (804) 698-8001, Web Site: www.martinagency.com (35)

Riley, Kevin, Dayton Daily News, Dayton, OH. Tel: (937) 222-5700, (888) 397-6397, FAX: (937) 225-2153, E-Mail: daytondaily@coxohio.com, Web Site: www.daytondailynews.com (18)

Riley, Kevin, Digi International, Minnetonka, MN. Tel: (952) 912-3444, (877) 912-3444, FAX: (952) 912-4952, Web Site: www.digi.com (13)

Riley, P Daniel, The Aldrich Group, Woodbury, CT. Tel: (860) 274-7693, (203) 263-5505, FAX: (203) 263-5572, E-Mail: jeff.aldrich@aldrichsearch.com, Web Site: www.aldrichsearch.com (20)

Riley, Patricia, MDR, Sunrise, FL. Tel: (954) 845-9500, (800) 637-8227, FAX: (954) 845-9505, E-Mail: info@mdr.org, Web Site: www.mdr.org (7)

Riley, Peter Booth, John Wiley & Sons Inc, Hoboken, NJ. Tel: (201) 748-6000, FAX: (201) 748-6088, E-Mail: info@wiley.com, Web Site: www.wiley.com (17)

Rill, Linda L., LLR/Research, Haverhill, MA. Tel: (978) 374-0931, FAX: (978) 374-1008 (38)

Rimel, John A., Mountain Press Publishing Co, Missoula, MT. Tel: (406) 728-1900, (800) 234-5308, FAX: (406) 728-1635, E-Mail: info@mountain-press.com, Web Site: mountain-press.com (17)

Rinaldi, Matthew J., Arquest Inc, Millstone Twp, NJ. Tel: (609) 395-9500, (888) 270-8378, (888) AR-QUEST, FAX: (609) 395-9778, Web Site: www.arquest.com (16)

Rinaldi, Molly, Robertson Mailing List Co, Leesburg, VA. Tel: (703) 509-8441, FAX: (888) 308-2572, E-Mail: vnorman@rmlc.net, Web Site: www.rmlc. net (23)

Riney, Charles, Myriad Systems Inc, Oklahoma City, OK. Tel: (405) 478-9000, (866) 505-1730, FAX: (405) 478-8315, E-Mail: sales@myriadsystems.com, Web Site: www.myriadsystems.com (22)

Rinfret Ltd, Greenwich, CT. Tel: (203) 622-0000, E-Mail: jmz@rinfretltd.com, Web Site: www. rinfretltd.com (8)

Rinfret, Cindy, Rinfret Ltd, Greenwich, CT. Tel: (203) 622-0000, E-Mail: jmz@rinfretltd.com, Web Site: www.rinfretltd.com (8)

Ring, Julie, SWBC, San Antonio, TX. Tel: (210) 525-1241, Web Site: www.swbc.com (14)

Rink, Joe, Biomerica Inc, Irvine, CA. Tel: (949) 645-2111, (800) 854-3002, FAX: (949) 553-1231, E-Mail: info@biomerica.com, Web Site: www. biomerica.com (7)

Rinke, Barry, Golfsmith International Inc, Austin, TX. Tel: (512) 821-4050, (800) 813-6897, FAX: (512) 837-9347, E-Mail: comments@golfsmith.com, Web Site: www.golfsmith.com (11)

Rio Brands, Philadelphia, PA. Tel: (215) 632-2800, FAX: (215) 824-1172 (16)

Rio Grande, Albuquerque, NM. Tel: (505) 839-3000, (800) 545-6566, FAX: (800) 965-2329, E-Mail: info@riogrande.com, Web Site: www.riogrande. com (16)

Riordan, Michael, National Mail-It Inc, Shreveport, LA. Tel: (318) 683-0093, Web Site: www.nationalmailit. com (27)

Rios, Al, Time Motion Tools, Poway, CA. Tel: (800) 779-8170, FAX: (800) 779-8171, Web Site: www. timemotion.com (9)

Rios, Manuel Z., American Modern Insurance Group, Amelia, OH. Tel: (513) 943-7200, (800) 759-9008, FAX: (513) 947-4779, (800) 217-5150, E-Mail: customer_care@amig.com, Web Site: www.amig. com (15)

Riotto, Charles M., Licensing Industry Merchandisers' Association (LIMA), New York, NY. Tel: (212) 244-1944, FAX: (212) 563-6552, E-Mail: info@ licensing.org, Web Site: www.licensing.org (40)

Ripon Printers, Ripon, WI. Tel: (920) 748-3136, (800) 321-3136, FAX: (920) 748-3741, E-Mail: info@ riponprinters.com, Web Site: www.riponprinters. com (27)

Rippe, Mary, Minnesota Multi Housing Association, Bloomington, MN. Tel: (952) 854-8500, FAX: (952) 854-3810, E-Mail: mha@mmha.com, Web Site: www.mmha.com (1)

Ripple, Laura, Red Hill Corp, Gettysburg, PA. Tel: (717) 337-3038, (800) 822-4003, FAX: (717) 337-0732, E-Mail: custserv@supergrit.com, Web Site: www.supergrit.com (34)

Risch, Deborah, Nordis Technologies Inc, Coral Springs, FL. Tel: (954) 323-5500, (800) 208-1169, FAX: (954) 323-0100, E-Mail: help@ nordistechnologies.com, Web Site: www. nordistechnologies.com (21)

Risch, Joe, JC Whitney, Chicago, IL. Tel: (312) 431-6000, FAX: (312) 431-5650, (800) 537-2700, Web Site: www.jcwhitney.com (12)

Risdall Marketing Group, New Brighton, MN. Tel: (651) 286-6700, (888) 747-3255, FAX: (651) 631-2561, E-Mail: info@risdall.com, Web Site: www. risdall.com (35)

Risdall, Jennifer, Risdall Marketing Group, New Brighton, MN. Tel: (651) 286-6700, (888) 747-3255, FAX: (651) 631-2561, E-Mail: info@risdall.com, Web Site: www.risdall.com (35)

Risdall, John, Risdall Marketing Group, New Brighton, MN. Tel: (651) 286-6700, (888) 747-3255, FAX: (651) 631-2561, E-Mail: info@risdall.com, Web Site: www.risdall.com (35)

Risdall, Ted, Risdall Marketing Group, New Brighton, MN. Tel: (651) 286-6700, (888) 747-3255, FAX: (651) 631-2561, E-Mail: info@risdall.com, Web Site: www.risdall.com (35)

Riser, John, Ashworth College, Norcross, GA. Tel: (770) 729-8400, (800) 957-5412, FAX: (770) 729-9294, Web Site: www.ashworthcollege.edu (13)

Rishagen, Nancy, KCET, Burbank, CA. Tel: (747) 201-5000, FAX: (747) 201-5877, E-Mail: contact@kcet. org, Web Site: www.kcet.org (1)

Riske, Kris Brandt, American Federation of Astrologers, Tempe, AZ. Tel: (480) 838-1751, (888) 301-7630, FAX: (480) 838-8293, E-Mail: afa@msn.com, Web Site: www.astrologers.com (1)

Riss, Suzanne, Working Mother, New York, NY. Tel: (212) 221-9595, FAX: (212) 219-7448, Web Site: www.workingmother.com (31)

Rist, Larry, The Marmon Group LLC, Chicago, IL. Tel: (312) 372-9500, FAX: (312) 845-5305, Web Site: www.marmon.com (16)

Ritchey, Mary, JC Direct Mail Inc, Groveport, OH. Tel: (614) 836-4848, FAX: (614) 836-4847 (28)

Ritchie, Chester, CAM Commerce Solutions, Fountain Valley, CA. Tel: (714) 241-9241, FAX: (714) 241-9893, Web Site: www.camcommerce.com (22)

Ritchie, Joe, Cenveo Commercial Envelope Group, Seattle, WA. Tel: (206) 682-7171, (800) 347-6989, FAX: (206) 329-2017, E-Mail: info@cenveo.com, Web Site: www.cenveo.com (26)

Ritchie, Mac, Markwins International Corp, City of Industry, CA. Tel: (909) 595-8898, FAX: (909) 595-8820, Web Site: www.markwins.com (16)

Ritt, Juliane, Springer Science & Business Media LLC, New York, NY. Tel: (212) 460-1500, FAX: (212) 460-1575, Web Site: www.springer.com (17)

Rittenhouse, Josh, H & H Graphics, Lancaster, PA. Tel: (717) 393-3941, (866) 338-7569, E-Mail: info@ thehandhgroup.com, Web Site: www. hhgraphicsgroup.com (31)

Ritter, Cathy, Denver Metro Convention & Visitors Bureau, Denver, CO. Tel: (303) 892-1112, (800) 233-6837, FAX: (303) 892-1636, Web Site: www. denver.org (1)

Ritter, Fred, Metro Speedgear, Livingston, NJ. Tel: (973) 251-2814, (800) 777-4453, FAX: (908) 286-0002, E-Mail: info@speedgear.com, Web Site: www.speedgear.com (11)

Ritter, Kurt, Team One Advertising, Los Angeles, CA. Tel: (310) 437-2500, Web Site: www.teamone-usa. com (35)

Ritter, Robert, First Direct Corp, Hopewell Junction, NY. Tel: (845) 221-3800, (800) 935-4386, E-Mail: info@1stdirect.com, Web Site: www.1stdirect.com (35)

Ritts, Carol Anne, MTI Information Technologies LLC, Langhorne, PA. Tel: (267) 569-2400, FAX: (215) 741-3898, Web Site: www.mtiadvantage.com (30)

Rittwage, William, California Offset Printers, Glendale, CA. Tel: (818) 291-1100, (800) 280-6446, FAX: (818) 291-1190, E-Mail: info@copprints.com, Web Site: www.copprints.com (27)

River Street Sweets, Savannah, GA. Tel: (912) 234-4608, (800) 793-3876, Web Site: www. riverstreetsweets.com (4)

Rivera, Jose, USI Affinity, Philadelphia, PA. Tel: (610) 833-2876, (800) 625-2876, FAX: (610) 265-2876, E-Mail: info@usiaffinity.com, Web Site: www. brcorp.com (15)

Riverside Acquisition Group LLC, Moorestown, NJ. Tel: (856) 802-1900, Web Site: www.com-pak.com (28)

Rivkin, Harry W., The IDT Group, Philadelphia, PA. Tel: (215) 487-4420, FAX: (215) 487-3110, Web Site: www.idthospitality.com (22)

Rizzoli International Publications Inc, New York, NY. Tel: (212) 387-3400, FAX: (212) 387-3535 (17)

Rizzuto, Jr. Leandro, Cuisinart, Stamford, CT. Tel: (203) 975-4600, FAX: (203) 975-4660, E-Mail: marketing@cuisinart.com, Web Site: www.cuisinart. com (16)

RJ Reynolds Tobacco Co, Winston Salem, NC. Tel: (336) 741-5111, (800) 341-5211, Web Site: www. rjrt.com (16)

Ro, Frances, Roland Products Inc, Los Angeles, CA. Tel: (323) 731-1111, (800) 321-2226, FAX: (323) 731-9585, E-Mail: salesinfo@rolandinc.com, Web Site: www.rolandinc.com (16)

Roach, Brian, The Catholic University of America Press, Washington, DC. Tel: (202) 319-5052, FAX: (202) 319-4985, E-Mail: cua-press@cua.edu, Web Site: cuapress.cua.edu (17)

Road Runner Sports Inc, San Diego, CA. Tel: (858) 974-4455, (800) 636-3560, FAX: (800) 453-5443, Web Site: www.roadrunnersports.com (11)

Roark, Ed, Graham Field Health Products Inc, Atlanta, GA. Tel: (770) 368-4700, (800) 347-5678, FAX: (800) 726-0601, E-Mail: cs@grahamfield.com, Web Site: www.grahamfield.com (7)

Roath, Tammy, Klockit, Lake Geneva, WI. Tel: (262) 248-7000, (800) 556-2548, FAX: (262) 248-9899, E-Mail: klockit@klockit.com, Web Site: www. klockit.com (6)

Robb, IV Walter E., Whole Foods Market Inc, Austin, TX. Tel: (512) 477-4455, FAX: (512) 482-7000, Web Site: www.wholefoodsmarket.com (4)

Robb, Larry, FARM, Depew, NY. Tel: (716) 989-3200, FAX: (716) 989-3220, E-Mail: bizdev@ farmbuffalo.com, Web Site: www.growwiththefarm. com (35)

Robb, Russ, Tully & Holland Inc, Wellesley, MA. Tel: (781) 239-2900, FAX: (781) 239-2901, E-Mail: info@tullyandholland.com, Web Site: www. tullyandholland.com (14)

Robbins Doctoroff, Alisa, United Jewish Appeal Federation of New York, New York, NY. Tel: (212) 980-1000, FAX: (212) 785-9321, E-Mail: contact@ ujafedny.org, Web Site: www.ujafedny.org (1)

LW Robbins Associates, Holliston, MA. Tel: (508) 893-0210, (800) 229-5972, FAX: (508) 893-0212, E-Mail: ppapsador@lwra.com, Web Site: www. lwra.com (1)

Robbins, Ken, Response Mine Interactive Inc, Atlanta, GA. Tel: (404) 233-0370, Web Site: www. responsemine.com (35)

Robbins, Miriam, Grand Canyon Association, Grand Canyon, AZ. Tel: (928) 638-2481, (800) 858-2808, FAX: (928-638-2484, E-Mail: gcassociation@ grandcanyon.org, Web Site: www.grandcanyon.org (1)

Robbins, Scott, Midwest Direct Marketing Inc, Spring Hill, KS. Tel: (913) 686-2220, FAX: (913) 686-2320, E-Mail: info@midwestdm.com, Web Site: www.midwestdm.com (23)

Robbins, Steve, Level 5 Communications Inc, Dublin, NH. Tel: (603) 563-1631, FAX: (603) 563-8912, E-Mail: de-news@deskeng.com, Web Site: www.deskeng.com (32)

RobbinsKersten Direct, Richardson, TX. Tel: (800) 222-6070, E-Mail: connect@robbinskersten.com, Web Site: www.robbinskersten.com (1)

Roberge, Tom, New Directions Publishing Corp, New York, NY. Tel: (212) 255-0230, FAX: (212) 255-0231, E-Mail: editorial@ndbooks.com, Web Site: www.ndbooks.com (17)

Robert Burger Illustration, Stockton, NJ. Tel: (609) 397-3737, E-Mail: burgerbobz@aol.com (36)

Robert Marketing Inc, Northbrook, IL. Tel: (847) 564-3550, FAX: (847) 564-3551 (5)

Robert, Elisabeth, Vermont Teddy Bear Co, Shelburne, VT. Tel: (802) 985-3001, (800) 829-BEAR, (800) 282-3131, FAX: (802) 985-1304, E-Mail: info@vtbear.com, Web Site: www.vermontteddybear.com (6)

Robert, Jeff, Robert Marketing Inc, Northbrook, IL. Tel: (847) 564-3550, FAX: (847) 564-3551 (5)

Robert, Lewis, Robert Marketing Inc, Northbrook, IL. Tel: (847) 564-3550, FAX: (847) 564-3551 (5)

Roberts & Buchanan Inc, Concordia, MO. Tel: (660) 463-2192, E-Mail: kmroberts@centurytel.net (31)

Roberts Communications Inc, Rochester, NY. Tel: (716) 325-6000, FAX: (716) 325-6001, Web Site: www.robertscomm.com (35)

H Armstrong Roberts Inc, Philadelphia, PA. Tel: (212) 685-3870, (800) 786-6300, FAX: (800) 786-1920, E-Mail: info@robertstock.com, Web Site: www.robertstock.com (38)

The John Roberts Co, Minneapolis, MN. Tel: (763) 755-5500, (800) 551-1534, FAX: (763) 755-0394, E-Mail: jfoster@johnroberts.com, Web Site: www.johnroberts.com (28)

Roberts Stock/Classic Stock, Philadelphia, PA. Tel: (213) 386-4600, (800) 786-6300, FAX: (213) 365-7171, E-Mail: aspstockpix@earthlink.net, Web Site: www.americanstockphotos.com (38)

Roberts, Adam, Born Free USA, Washington, DC. Tel: (202) 450-3168, (800) 348-7387, FAX: (202) 450-3581, E-Mail: info@bornfreeusa.org, Web Site: www.bornfreeusa.org (1)

Roberts, Bob, H Armstrong Roberts Inc, Philadelphia, PA. Tel: (212) 685-3870, (800) 786-6300, FAX: (800) 786-1920, E-Mail: info@robertstock.com, Web Site: www.robertstock.com (38)

Roberts, Brian L., Comcast Corp, Philadelphia, PA. Tel: (215) 665-1700, Web Site: www.comcast.com (32)

Roberts, Carol L., International Paper, Memphis, TN. Tel: (901) 419-9000, (800) 207-4003, E-Mail: internationalpaper.comm@ipaper.com, Web Site: www.internationalpaper.com (16)

Roberts, Carter, World Wildlife Fund, Washington, DC. Tel: (202) 293-4800, Web Site: www.worldwildlife.org (1)

Roberts, James, Redirect, Salt Lake City, UT. Tel: (801) 453-0100, E-Mail: hello@redirectdigital.com, Web Site: redirectdigital.com (35)

Roberts, Jonathan, Echo Data Group, New Holland, PA. Tel: (800) 511-3870, E-Mail: sroberts@echodata.com, Web Site: www.echodata.com (22)

Roberts, Karen, WalMart Stores Inc, Bentonville, AR. Tel: (479) 273-4000, (800) 925-6278, FAX: (479) 277-1830, Web Site: www.walmart.com (16)

Roberts, Margaret Rose, Roberts & Buchanan Inc, Concordia, MO. Tel: (660) 463-2192, E-Mail: kmroberts@centurytel.net (31)

Roberts, Martin, Linguistic Systems Inc, Cambridge, MA. Tel: (877) 654-5006, FAX: (617) 528-7491, E-Mail: info@linguist.com, Web Site: www.linguist.com (27)

Roberts, Richard, Oral Roberts University, Tulsa, OK. Tel: (918) 495-6161, FAX: (918) 495-6222, E-Mail: admissions@oru.edu, Web Site: www.oru.edu (1)

Roberts, Stephen H., Echo Data Group, New Holland, PA. Tel: (800) 511-3870, E-Mail: sroberts@echodata.com, Web Site: www.echodata.com (22)

Roberts, Tom, National Catholic Reporter Publishing Co Inc, Kansas City, MO. Tel: (816) 531-0538, (800) 444-8910, FAX: (816) 968-2268, Web Site: www.ncronline.org (17)

Roberts, Wayne, Blue Cross Blue Shield of South Carolina, Columbia, SC. Tel: (803) 788-0222, (800) 288-2227, FAX: (803) 736-4516, Web Site: www.bcbssc.com (15)

Robertson Mailing List Co, Leesburg, VA. Tel: (703) 509-8441, FAX: (888) 308-2572, E-Mail: vnorman@rmlc.net, Web Site: www.rmlc.net (23)

Robertson, Ben, Game Show Placements Ltd, Hollywood, CA. Tel: (323) 874-7818, E-Mail: gsp@ix.netcom.com, Web Site: www.gameshowplacements.com (35)

Robertson, Dale, JLG Industries Inc, McConnellsburg, PA. Tel: (717) 485-5161, (877) JLG-SELL, FAX: (717) 485-6417, E-Mail: comments@jlg.com, Web Site: www.jlg.com (16)

Robertson, Geoff, JC Whitney, Chicago, IL. Tel: (312) 431-6000, FAX: (312) 431-5650, (800) 537-2700, Web Site: www.jcwhitney.com (12)

Robertson, Gloria, Student Union at SJSU, San Jose, CA. Tel: (408) 924-5950, FAX: (408) 924-5953, E-Mail: getinvolved@sjsu.edu, Web Site: www.union.sjsu.edu (1)

Robertson, M. G., Christian Broadcasting Network Inc, Virginia Beach, VA. Tel: (757) 226-7000, FAX: (757) 226-2017, Web Site: www.cbn.com (1)

Robertson, Ms. Sigrun C., Oomingmak Musk Ox Producers Cooperative, Anchorage, AK. Tel: (907) 272-9225, (888) 360-9665, FAX: (907) 258-4225, E-Mail: oomingmak@qiviut.com, Web Site: www.qiviut.com (6)

Robertson, Randy, List Alliance Inc, Alamo, CA. Tel: (925) 820-3151, E-Mail: info@listalliance.com, Web Site: www.listalliance.com (23)

Robertson, Rev. Robert C., Lutheran Church Extension Fund - Missouri Synod, Saint Louis, MO. Tel: (800) 843-5233, FAX: (314) 996-1131, Web Site: www.lcef.org (1)

Robertson, Sharon, McNichols Co, Tampa, FL. Tel: (813) 282-3828, FAX: (813) 288-9342, E-Mail: sales@mcnichols.com, Web Site: www.mcnichols.com (16)

Robidoux, David, PIP Postal Instant Press, Mission Viejo, CA. Tel: (949) 282-3800, FAX: (949) 282-3899, Web Site: www.pip.com (27)

Robidoux, David, PIP Printing and Marketing Services, Indianapolis, IN. Tel: (317) 849-6244, Web Site: www.pip.com/pipindy (27)

Robillard, Mark, Clients & Profits Worldwide, Oceanside, CA. Tel: (760) 945-4334, Web Site: www.clientsandprofits.com (14)

Robins, Christine M, Char-Broil Grill Lover's Catalog, Columbus, GA. Tel: (866) 241-7548, Web Site: charbroil.com (8)

C H Robinson Worldwide Inc, Eden Prairie, MN. Tel: (952) 937-8500, FAX: (952) 937-6740, E-Mail: info@chrobinson.com, Web Site: www.chrobinson.com (16)

Robinson Direct, Center Valley, PA. Tel: (610) 838-5589, FAX: (610) 838-5589, E-Mail: carole@robinson-direct.com, Web Site: www.robinson-direct.com (35)

Robinson Home Products, Buffalo, NY. Tel: (716) 685-6300, FAX: (716) 685-4916 (16)

Robinson, Amy, Direct Selling Association, Washington, DC. Tel: (202) 452-8866, FAX: (202) 452-9010, E-Mail: info@dsa.org, Web Site: www.dsa.org (40)

Robinson, Anne E., Caswell-Massey Co Ltd, Edison, NJ. Tel: (732) 225-2181, (800) 326-0500, FAX: (800) 868-4407, E-Mail: info@caswellmasseyltd.com, Web Site: www.caswellmassey.com (7)

Robinson, Carole, Robinson Direct, Center Valley, PA. Tel: (610) 838-5589, FAX: (610) 838-5589, E-Mail: carole@robinson-direct.com, Web Site: www.robinson-direct.com (35)

Robinson, Dale, PetEdge, Beverly, MA. Tel: (978) 998-8100, (800) 738-3343, FAX: (978) 887-8499, E-Mail: support@petedge.com, Web Site: www.petedge.com (16)

Robinson, Jim, Farm Bureau Insurance, Lansing, MI. Tel: (517) 323-7000, (800) 292-2680, FAX: (517) 327-0208, Web Site: www.farmbureauinsurance-mi.com (15)

Robinson, Jo Ann, Golden Rule Insurance Co, Indianapolis, IN. Tel: (317) 297-4123, FAX: (317) 297-0908, Web Site: www.goldenrule.com (15)

Robinson, Joe, Lake Group Media Inc, Armonk, NY. Tel: (914) 925-2400, FAX: (914) 925-2499, E-Mail: ryan.lake@lakegroupmedia.com, Web Site: www.lakegroupmedia.com (23)

Robinson, Marian, Guilford Publications Inc, New York, NY. Tel: (212) 431-9800, (800) 365-7006, FAX: (212) 966-6708, E-Mail: info@guilford.com, Web Site: www.guilford.com (17)

Robinson, Nick, North American Communications Inc (East), Duncansville, PA. Tel: (814) 696-3553, (800) 624-1533, FAX: (814) 696-1180, E-Mail: marketing@nacmail.com, Web Site: www.nacmail.com (26)

Robinson, Richard, Scholastic Inc, New York, NY. Tel: (212) 343-6100, (800) SCHOLASTIC, FAX: (212) 343-6484, Web Site: www.scholastic.com (17)

Robinson, Rick, AcuSport Corp, Bellefontaine, OH. Tel: (937) 593-7010, FAX: (937) 592-5625, E-Mail: mwsales@acusport.com, Web Site: www.acusport.com (11)

Robinson, Robert, SGD Golf LLC, Hudson, OH. Tel: (234) 380-5037, (800) 321-3411, E-Mail: sales@sgdgolf.com, Web Site: www.sgdgolf.com (34)

Robinson, Steve, Jossey-Bass Inc Publishers, San Francisco, CA. Tel: (415) 433-1740, FAX: (415) 433-0499, Web Site: www.josseybass.com (17)

Robinson, Susan, Homespun Tapes Music Instruction, Woodstock, NY. Tel: (845) 246-2550, (800) 338-2737, FAX: (845) 246-5282, E-Mail: info@homespuntapes.com, Web Site: www.homespuntapes.com (3)

Robinson, Tony, Thomas Printworks, Houston, TX. Tel: (832) 201-2000, (800) 656-8883, FAX: (832) 201-2001, E-Mail: info@seebridgemedia.com, Web Site: www.thomasprintworks.com (21)

Robinson, Whitney, Clampitt Paper Co, Dallas, TX. Tel: (214) 638-3300, FAX: (214) 634-7837, E-Mail: dcrew@clampitt.com, Web Site: www.clampitt.com (16)

Robison, Ted, MailBlazer, Santa Ana, CA. Tel: (714) 662-5396, Web Site: www.mailblazer.com (27)

Robitaille, Luc, Los Angeles Kings, Los Angeles, CA. Tel: (213) 742-7100, (888) KINGS-LA, FAX: (213) 742-7296, Web Site: kings.nhl.com (16)

The Roblin Group Inc, White Plains, NY. Tel: (914) 686-7221, FAX: (914) 372-1028, E-Mail: freethingsusa@yahoo.com, Web Site: www. freethingsusa.com (17)

Robo, James L., Florida Power & Light Co, Juno Beach, FL. Tel: (305) 552-3552, (800) 468-8243, FAX: (305) 552-2487, Web Site: www.fpl.com (16)

Robustelli Merchandise, Stamford, CT. Tel: (203) 965-0200, FAX: (203) 965-0387, Web Site: www. robustelli.com (33)

Robustelli, Richard, Robustelli Merchandise, Stamford, CT. Tel: (203) 965-0200, FAX: (203) 965-0387, Web Site: www.robustelli.com (33)

Rocco, Frank, CCMR Global Marketing, Mill Valley, CA. Tel: (415) 847-1239, E-Mail: globalmarketing1@aol.com, Web Site: www. gotoccmr.com (35)

Rocco, Leo, Merchant E-Solutions, Redwood City, CA. Tel: (509) 232-5639, (866) 663-6132, FAX: (509) 232-5625, E-Mail: help@merchante-solutions.com, Web Site: www.merchante-solutions.com (14)

Rocco, Mark, Old World Ind, Northbrook, IL. Tel: (847) 559-2000, FAX: (847) 559-2266, Web Site: www.oldworldind.com (34)

Rocco, Matt, Etech Inc, Lufkin, TX. Tel: (936) 633-9333, Web Site: www.effectiveteleservices.com (29)

Roche Diagnostics Corp, Indianapolis, IN. Tel: (317) 521-2000, Web Site: www.usdiagnostics.roche.com (7)

Roche, Dorothy, Herrmann Global LLC, Lake Lure, NC. Tel: (828) 625-9153, (800) 432-4234, E-Mail: info@hbdi.com, Web Site: www.herrmannsolutions. com (35)

Roche, Kevin, Getronics, Tewksbury, MA. Tel: (978) 625-5000, Web Site: www.getronics.com (16)

Rochefort, Lauren, Ivy Tech Community College of Indiana, Indianapolis, IN. Tel: (317) 921-4800, (888) IVY-LINE, FAX: (317) 921-4753, Web Site: www. ivytech.edu (13)

Rochester Institute of Technology, Rochester, NY. Tel: (585) 475-7436, Web Site: www.rit.edu (1)

Rochester, Geof, The Nature Conservancy, Arlington, VA. Tel: (703) 841-5300, (800) 628-6860, FAX: (703) 841-1283, Web Site: www.nature.org (1)

Rochester, Shelley, Accoona Corp, Jersey City, NJ. Tel: (201) 557-9388, Web Site: www.accoona.com (16)

Rochling Engineered Plastics, Dallas, NC. Tel: (704) 922-7814, (800) 541-4419, FAX: (704) 922-7651, E-Mail: rep@roechling-plastics.us, Web Site: www. roechling-plastics.us (34)

Rock-Tred Corp, Waukegan, IL. Tel: (847) 673-8200, (800) 762-8733, FAX: (847) 679-6665, Web Site: www.rocktred.com (9)

Rocket Direct Marketing Inc, New York, NY. Tel: (212) 689-5800, FAX: (212) 689-0635, E-Mail: info@rocketdirect.com, Web Site: www. rocketdirect.com (32)

Rockett Communications Inc, Danvers, MA. Tel: (978) 774-1780, E-Mail: rockett.comm@verizon.net, Web Site: www.rockett.us (35)

Rockett, Brian, Rockett Communications Inc, Danvers, MA. Tel: (978) 774-1780, E-Mail: rockett.comm@ verizon.net, Web Site: www.rockett.us (35)

RocketWear, New York, NY. Tel: (212) 977-9227, E-Mail: info@rocketwear.com, Web Site: www. rocketwear.net (2)

Rockler Woodworking & Hardware, Medina, MN. Tel: (763) 478-8200, (800) 279-4441, FAX: (800) 865-1229, E-Mail: info@rockler.com, Web Site: www. rockler.com (8)

Rockwell Automation, Milwaukee, WI. Tel: (414) 382-2000, FAX: (414) 382-4444, Web Site: www. rockwellautomation.com (16)

Rocky Mountain Chocolate Factory, Durango, CO. Tel: (970) 259-0554, (888) 525-2462, FAX: (970) 259-5895, E-Mail: customerservice@rmcfusa.com, Web Site: www.rmcf.com (4)

Rocque, Greg, Farrington Transportation, Bolingbrook, IL. Tel: (630) 783-9200 (12)

Rodale Inc, Emmaus, PA. Tel: (610) 967-5171, FAX: (610) 967-8963, Web Site: www.rodaleinc.com (17)

Rodale, Maria, Rodale Inc, Emmaus, PA. Tel: (610) 967-5171, FAX: (610) 967-8963, Web Site: www. rodaleinc.com (17)

Rode, Cid, Ameriprise Financial Services Inc, Minneapolis, MN. Tel: (612) 671-3131, (651) 671-3434, (800) 386-2042, FAX: (612) 547-2736, Web Site: www.ameriprise.com (14)

Rodelinde Graphic Design, Lenox Dale, MA. Tel: (413) 243-4350, FAX: (413) 243-3066, E-Mail: rodelinde@earthlink.net (36)

Rodgers, Mary, Cuisinart, Stamford, CT. Tel: (203) 975-4600, FAX: (203) 975-4660, E-Mail: marketing@cuisinart.com, Web Site: www.cuisinart. com (16)

Rodgers, Michael, Women's Sports Foundation, East Meadow, NY. Tel: (516) 542-4700, (800) 227-3988, FAX: (516) 542-0095, Web Site: www. womenssportsfoundation.org (1)

Rodgers, Ralph, Tennessee Valley Authority, Knoxville, TN. Tel: (865) 632-2101, Web Site: www.tva.gov (16)

Rodgers, Will, SHR Perceptual Branding, Phoenix, AZ. Tel: (480) 483-3700, FAX: (480) 483-9675, E-Mail: info@shrbranding.com, Web Site: www. shrbranding.com (35)

Rodriguez, Al, Marathon Norco Aerospace Inc, Waco, TX. Tel: (254) 776-0650, FAX: (254) 776-6558, Web Site: www.mptc.com (16)

Rodriguez, Arturo, United Farm Workers of America, AFL-CIO, Keene, CA. Tel: (661) 823-6151, FAX: (661) 823-6177, E-Mail: execoffice@ufw.org, Web Site: www.ufw.org (1)

Rodriguez, Carlos, ADP Inc, Roseland, NJ. Tel: (973) 974-5000, (800) 225-5237, FAX: (973) 974-3334, Web Site: www.adp.com (14)

Rodriguez, David, TMC Internet Telephony & Expo, Norwalk, CT. Tel: (203) 852-6800, (800) 243-6002, FAX: (203) 866-3326, E-Mail: tmc@tmcnet.com, Web Site: www.tmcnet.com (42)

Rodriguez, Don, Utretch Art Supplies, Cranbury, NJ. Tel: (609) 409-8001, (800) 223-9132, FAX: (800) 382-1979, Web Site: www.utrechtart.com (10)

Rodriguez, Lawrence D., Central Pacific Bank, Honolulu, HI. Tel: (808) 544-0500, (800) 544-0500, (800) 342-8422, FAX: (808) 531-2875, Web Site: www. centralpacificbank.com (14)

Rodriguez, Mark, Hickory Farms, Maumee, OH. Tel: (419) 893-7611, (800) 776-4111, (800) 442-5671, FAX: (419) 893-0164, Web Site: www. hickoryfarms.com (4)

Rodriguez, Nancy, SCA Promotions Inc, Dallas, TX. Tel: (214) 860-3700, (888) 860-3700, FAX: (214) 860-3723, E-Mail: scainfo@scapromo.com, Web Site: www.scapromo.com (15)

Rodriguez, Rebecca, Icon Media Direct Inc, Sherman Oaks, CA. Tel: (818) 995-6400, FAX: (818) 995-6405, E-Mail: info@iconmediadirect.com, Web Site: www.iconmediadirect.com (35)

Rodriguez, Robert, Nat Com Marketing, Miami, FL. Tel: (305) 756-8600, FAX: (786) 425-0067, E-Mail: info@natcom-marketing.com, Web Site: www. natcom-marketing.com (33)

Rodriquez, Manon, Society of American Magicians Inc, Littleton, CO. Tel: (303) 362-0575, E-Mail: samadministrator@magicsam.com, Web Site: www. magicsam.com (1)

Rod's Western Palace, Columbus, OH. Tel: (614) 268-8200, (800) 325-8508, FAX: (800) 330-7637, E-Mail: rods@rods.com, Web Site: www.rods.com (2)

Rodstein, Rich, Shakespeare Co, Columbia, SC. Tel: (803) 754-7000, (800) 347-3759, FAX: (803) 754-7342, Web Site: www.shakespeare-fishing.com (11)

Rodwell, Diane, Col Voce Consulting, Exton, PA. Tel: (215) 266-2992, Web Site: www.colvoce.com (20)

Roe, Susan, AGIA Insurance Services, Carpinteria, CA. Tel: (805) 566-9191, FAX: (805) 566-1887, Web Site: www.agia.com (15)

Roeber, Brad, AAA-Chicago Motor Club, Aurora, IL. Tel: (630) 328-7000, FAX: (630) 499-8200, Web Site: www.aaa.com (1)

Roebuck, Malcolm, Badge-A-Minit, Oglesby, IL. Tel: (815) 883-8822, (800) 223-4103, FAX: (815) 883-9696, Web Site: www.badgeaminit.com (16)

Roedel, Jeff, American Insurance Administrators Inc, Columbus, OH. Tel: (614) 486-5388, FAX: (614) 486-2728 (15)

Roedel, Jeff, USI Affinity Collegiate Insurance Resources, Columbus, OH. Tel: (614) 486-5388, Web Site: www.collegiateinsuranceresources.com (15)

Roehlke, Katherine H., Howell Marketing Services, Elmira, NY. Tel: (607) 734-6291, FAX: (607) 734-6759, E-Mail: jjs@howellmarketingservices.com, Web Site: www.howellmarketingservices.com (28)

Roelandts, William, Xilinx Inc, San Jose, CA. Tel: (408) 559-7778, FAX: (408) 559-7114, Web Site: www.xilinx.com (16)

Roels, Jan, Deloitte & Touche, Boston, MA. Tel: (617) 437-2000, FAX: (617) 437-2111, Web Site: www. deloitte.com (14)

Roeseler, Armin, DirectBuy Inc, Merrillville, IN. Tel: (219) 736-1100, FAX: (219) 755-6279, Web Site: www.ucctotalhome.com (11)

Roeser, Prugh, The Devereux Group, Marblehead, MA. Tel: (781) 631-9213, FAX: (781) 639-3044, E-Mail: roeser@devereuxgroup.com, Web Site: www. devereuxgroup.com (20)

Roeske, Richard, Kemper Corp, Chicago, IL. Tel: (312) 661-4600, (800) 733-7366, FAX: (312) 494-6995, Web Site: www.kemper.com (15)

Roessner, Barbara T., The Hartford Courant, Hartford, CT. Tel: (860) 241-6200, FAX: (860) 293-0178, Web Site: www.courant.com (31)

Roeth, George, The Clorox Co, Oakland, CA. Tel: (510) 271-7000, FAX: (510) 832-1463, Web Site: www. thecloroxcompany.com (16)

Roever, Rick, MAR Graphics, Valmeyer, IL. Tel: (800) 851-4460, Web Site: www.margraphics.com (27)

Rogalski, David, Benchmark Brands Inc, Norcross, GA. Tel: (770) 242-1254, FAX: (770) 242-1962, Web Site: www.footsmart.com (5)

Roger, Roy, SDI Marketing, Toronto, ON Canada. Tel: (416) 674-9010, (877) SDI-TEAM, FAX: (416) 674-9011, E-Mail: info@sdicapital.com, Web Site: www.sdimarketing.com (14)

Rogers Publishing Ltd, Toronto, ON Canada. Tel: (416) 935-7777, FAX: (416) 935-3597, Web Site: www. rogerspublishing.ca (17)

Rogers, Bob, Development Dimensions International, Bridgeville, PA. Tel: (412) 257-0600, (800) 933-4463, FAX: (412) 220-2942, E-Mail: info@ ddiworld.com, Web Site: www.ddiworld.com (16)

Rogers, Bradley, Neo@Ogilvy, New York, NY. Tel: (212) 259-5200, Web Site: www.neoogilvy.com (35)

Rogers, Donald, Demco Inc, Madison, WI. Tel: (608) 241-1201, (800) 356-1200, FAX: (608) 241-1799, E-Mail: custserv@demco.com, Web Site: www. demco.com (10)

Rogers, Doug, News & Observer Direct Marketing, Raleigh, NC. Tel: (919) 836-5658, (800) 522-4205 (40)

Rogers, Earl, Automod, Atlanta, GA. Tel: (770) 457-9663, (800) 241-1832, FAX: (770) 457-6089, E-Mail: info@automod.fdn.com, Web Site: www. automod.net (12)

Rogers, Floyd D., Steck-Vaughn, Austin, TX. Tel: (512) 343-8227, (800) 531-5015, (877) 866-2586, FAX: (512) 795-3617, (877) 265-2730, E-Mail: info@ steck-vaughn.com, Web Site: www.steck-vaughn. com (17)

Rogers, James E., Caraustar, Austell, GA. Tel: (770) 948-3101, E-Mail: info@caraustar.com, Web Site: www.caraustar.com (16)

Rogers, Mike, StrategicOne, Overland Park, KS. Tel: (913) 342-9100 x102, Web Site: www.strategic-one. com (20)

Rogers, Richard R., Mary Kay Cosmetics Inc, Addison, TX. Tel: (972) 687-6300, (800) MARY KAY, FAX: (972) 687-1611, Web Site: www.marykay.com (16)

Rogers, Robert D., Texas Industries Inc, Dallas, TX. Tel: (972) 647-6700, FAX: (972) 647-3878, Web Site: www.txi.com (16)

Rogers, Robin, Wendover Associates Inc, Greensboro, NC. Tel: (336) 299-6611, FAX: (336) 292-4261, E-Mail: wendover@wendoverassociates.com, Web Site: www.wendoverassociates.com (35)

Rogers, Ron, Tri Tech Laboratories Inc, Lynchburg, VA. Tel: (434) 845-7073, FAX: (434) 847-4360, Web Site: www.tritechlabs.com (16)

Rogers, Russel, Arrowhead Mountain Spring Water, Wilkes Barre, PA. Tel: (800) 873-7775, Web Site: www.arrowheadwater.com (16)

Rogers, Thomas J., ESL Federal Credit Union, Rochester, NY. Tel: (585) 336-1000, (800) 848-2265, FAX: (585) 336-1138, Web Site: www.esl.org (14)

Roggenkamp, Mark, Safeguard Business Systems Inc, Dallas, TX. Tel: (214) 905-3935, (800) 523-2422, FAX: (800) 439-8423, Web Site: www.gosafeguard. com (16)

Rogin, Robert, The Sound Direct Marketing Group, Austin, TX. Tel: (512) 306-0879 (20)

Roglin, Dan, Dorn Marketing, Geneva, IL. Tel: (630) 232-2010, FAX: (630) 232-2033, E-Mail: info@ dornmarketing.com, Web Site: www.dornmarketing. com (35)

Rogosin, Don, Channel 13 WNET Catalog Division, New York, NY. Tel: (212) 560-1313, FAX: (212) 560-1314, E-Mail: programming@thirteen.org, Web Site: www.thirteen.org (5)

Rogovy, Hugh, Satori Software Inc, Seattle, WA. Tel: (206) 357-2900, (800) 553-6477, FAX: (206) 357-2901, E-Mail: sales@satorisoftware.com, Web Site: www.satorisoftware.com (16)

Rohlik Specialties Co, Bloomfield Hills, MI. Tel: (248) 858-8880, FAX: (248) 858-7323 (33)

Rohm & Haas Co, Philadelphia, PA. Tel: (215) 592-3000, (877) 288-5881, FAX: (215) 592-3377, Web Site: www.rohmhaas.com (16)

Rohman, Ken, Archer Malmo Inc, Memphis, TN. Tel: (901) 523-2000, FAX: (901) 524-5578, Web Site: www.archermalmo.com (35)

Rohr, Ann, Weston Distance Learning Inc, Fort Collins, CO. Tel: (970) 282-6322, Web Site: www. westondistancelearning.com (13)

Rola, Fernando E., RolaKimmerling Associates, New York, NY. Tel: (646) 367-4815, FAX: (646) 367-4901 (35)

RolaKimmerling Associates, New York, NY. Tel: (646) 367-4815, FAX: (646) 367-4901 (35)

Roland Advisors, Annapolis, MD. Tel: (410) 268-3648 (20)

Roland Products Inc, Los Angeles, CA. Tel: (323) 731-1111, (800) 321-2226, FAX: (323) 731-9585, E-Mail: salesinfo@rolandinc.com, Web Site: www. rolandinc.com (16)

Roland, Donald, Roland Advisors, Annapolis, MD. Tel: (410) 268-3648 (20)

Roldan, Sergio, Shell Oil Co, Houston, TX. Tel: (713) 241-6161, Web Site: www.shell.us (16)

Roll International Corp, Los Angeles, CA. Tel: (310) 966-5700, FAX: (310) 914-4747, Web Site: www. roll.com (16)

Roll, Nancy, Protection One Inc, Lawrence, KS. Tel: (785) 856-5500, (800) GET-HELP, Web Site: www. protectionone.com (16)

Roller, Ruth, Friedman Marketing Svcs, Harrison, NY. Tel: (914) 698-0800, FAX: (914) 698-0485, E-Mail: paula.wynne@gfk.com, Web Site: www. friedmanmktg.com (30)

Rollins, Lyn, The Burris Agency Inc, Greensboro, NC. Tel: (336) 378-1221, FAX: (336) 378-1221, E-Mail: info@burris.com, Web Site: www.burris.com (35)

Rollins, Meredith, Redbook Magazine, New York, NY. Tel: (212) 649-2000, (800) 888-0008, FAX: (212) 581-7605, Web Site: www.redbookmag.com (17)

Rollins, Stacy, SLR Associates, Portland, OR. Tel: (503) 645-0675 (20)

Rollins, Thomas, The Teaching Co, Chantilly, VA. Tel: (703) 502-7300, (800) 832-2412, FAX: (703) 378-3819, Web Site: www.teach12.com (17)

Rollyson Financial Group, Pasadena, MD. Tel: (410) 437-5596 (14)

Rollyson, Richard V., Rollyson Financial Group, Pasadena, MD. Tel: (410) 437-5596 (14)

Roman Research Inc/Simply Whispers Earring, Hanson, MA. Tel: (800) 225-8652, FAX: (781) 447-0995, E-Mail: earpiercingstore@romanresearch.com, Web Site: www.simplywhispers.com (2)

Roman, Alison, Bon Appetit Magazine, New York, NY. Tel: (212) 286-2860, FAX: (212) 286-2536, E-Mail: paul_jowdy@bonappetit.com, Web Site: www. bonappetit.com (31)

Roman, Ernan, Ernan Roman Direct Marketing Corp, Little Neck, NY. Tel: (718) 225-4151, FAX: (718) 225-4889, E-Mail: ernan@erdm.com, Web Site: www.erdm.com (20)

Roman, Paul, DineWise, Farmingdale, NY. Tel: (631) 694-1111, (800) 749-1170, FAX: (631) 694-4064, E-Mail: info@dinewise.com, Web Site: www. dinewise.com (4)

Roman, Suzanne, The Taunton Press, Newtown, CT. Tel: (203) 426-8171, (800) 477-8727, FAX: (203) 426-3434, Web Site: www.taunton.com (17)

Romanello, Richard J., Holiday Travel of America, Carlsbad, CA. Tel: (760) 431-8600, (888) 732-2479, FAX: (760) 431-3131, E-Mail: sales@htoa.com, Web Site: www.htoa.com (19)

Romberg, Harry, Houston Direct Marketing Association, Houston, TX. Tel: (281) 931-8883, FAX: (281) 820-4023, Web Site: www.houstondma.org (40)

Romero, Anthony, American Civil Liberties Union Foundation, New York, NY. Tel: (212) 549-2500, Web Site: www.aclu.org (1)

Romero, Rick, MVS Mailers Inc, Bohemia, NY. Tel: (800) 641-7917, FAX: (631) 699-0101, E-Mail: sales@mvsmailers.com, Web Site: www. mvsmailers.com (28)

Rometty, Virginia M., IBM Corp, Armonk, NY. Tel: (914) 765-1900, FAX: (914) 765-6633, Web Site: www.ibm.com (16)

Romm, Preston, Iomega Corp, Roy, UT. Tel: (801) 332-1000, (888) 446-6342, FAX: (801) 332-3158, Web Site: www.iomega.com (16)

Ron Perrella DRS, Laguna Niguel, CA. Tel: (949) 495-7661, FAX: (949) 495-7660, E-Mail: rperrdrs@aol. com, Web Site: www.ronperrelladrs.com (35)

Ronald Erkes & Associates Inc, Palm Harbor, FL (35)

Ronan, Brian, Hello Direct, Nashua, NH. Tel: (408) 972-1990, (800) 435-5634, FAX: (408) 972-8155, Web Site: www.hello-direct.com (16)

Ronco Corp, Austin, TX. Tel: (800) 486-1806, E-Mail: customerservice@ronco.com, Web Site: www. ronco.com (16)

Rondeau, William B., Priests of the Sacred Heart, Hales Corners, WI. Tel: (414) 425-3383, FAX: (414) 425-5719, Web Site: www.poshusa.org (1)

The RONED Group, East Hanover, NJ. Tel: (973) 386-1848, FAX: (973) 386-0969, E-Mail: info@roned. com, Web Site: www.roned.com (27)

Ronell Clock Co, Grants Pass, OR. Tel: (800) 334-0135, FAX: (541) 471-0099, E-Mail: info@ronellclock. com, Web Site: www.ronellclock.com (5)

Roney, Patrick, Windsor Vineyards, Santa Rosa, CA. Tel: (800) 289-9463, (800) 741-6070, E-Mail: webmaster@windsorvineyards.com, Web Site: www.windsorvineyards.com (16)

Ronk, Bret, Gulf Publishing Co, Houston, TX. Tel: (713) 529-4301, FAX: (713) 520-4433, E-Mail: publications@gulfpub.com, Web Site: www. gulfpub.com (17)

Ronon, Lynne, HSN Inc, Saint Petersburg, FL. Tel: (727) 872-1000, (800) 284-5757, Web Site: www. hsn.com (5)

Roome, Hugh, Scholastic Inc, New York, NY. Tel: (212) 343-6100, (800) SCHOLASTIC, FAX: (212) 343-6484, Web Site: www.scholastic.com (17)

Rooney, Joseph J., Cox Communications Inc, Atlanta, GA. Tel: (404) 843-5000, (888) 566-7751, FAX: (404) 269-2243, Web Site: www.cox.com (16)

Roos, Andy, National Audubon Society, New York, NY. Tel: (212) 979-3000, FAX: (212) 979-3188, Web Site: www.audubon.org (17)

Roosevelt Paper Co, Mount Laurel, NJ. Tel: (856) 303-4100, (856) 303-4200, (800) 523-3470, FAX: (856) 642-1950, (856) 642-1949, Web Site: www. rooseveltpaper.com (25)

Root, Gary, San Francisco Victoriana Inc, San Francisco, CA. Tel: (415) 648-0313, FAX: (415) 648-2812, Web Site: www.sfvictoriana.com (9)

Root, Marlene, Crispin Porter + Bogusky, Miami, FL. Tel: (305) 859-2070, FAX: (305) 854-3419, E-Mail: info@cpbgroup.com, Web Site: www.cpbgroup.com (35)

Roovers Inc, Hazleton, PA. Tel: (570) 455-7548, FAX: (570) 454-1477 (34)

Rosa, Bill, Mailing Specialists Inc, Greensburg, PA. Tel: (724) 832-3840, (888) 216-1056, FAX: (724) 832-8419, E-Mail: sales@mailmsi.com, Web Site: www.mailmsi.com (28)

Rosane, Edwin L., USAA, San Antonio, TX. Tel: (512) 498-6524, FAX: (512) 498-8000 (15)

Rosanswank, Donna, Magna-Tel Inc, Cape Girardeau, MO. Tel: (573) 334-3096, (800) 467-2537, FAX: (573) 335-1715, Web Site: www.magna.tel.com (5)

Rosanvallon, John, Dassault Falcon Jet Corp, Little Ferry, NJ. Tel: (201) 440-6700, FAX: (201) 541-4515, Web Site: www.dassaultfalcon.com (16)

Rose Displays Ltd, Salem, MA. Tel: (978) 219-8100, Web Site: www.rosedisplays.com (16)

Rose Electronics, Houston, TX. Tel: (281) 933-7673, (800) 333-9343, FAX: (281) 933-0044, E-Mail: sales@rose.com, Web Site: www.rose.com (3)

Rose Printing Co Inc, Tallahassee, FL. Tel: (850) 576-4151, (800) 227-3725, FAX: (850) 576-4153, E-Mail: roseprt@roseprinting.com, Web Site: www.roseprinting.com (27)

Rose, Beth, Lesman Instrument Co, Bensenville, IL. Tel: (630) 595-8400, (800) 953-7626, FAX: (630) 595-2386, E-Mail: sales@lesman.com, Web Site: www.lesman.com (9)

Rose, Bob, St Louis Post-Dispatch, Saint Louis, MO. Tel: (314) 340-8000, (800) 365-0820, FAX: (314) 340-3140, Web Site: www.stltoday.com (17)

Rose, Brian, Archaeology Magazine, Long Island City, NY. Tel: (718) 472-3050, FAX: (718) 472-3051, E-Mail: production@archaeology.org, Web Site: www.archaeology.org (17)

Rose, Brian, US Gas & Electric, White Plains, NY. Tel: (888) 947-7880, FAX: (888) 400-1230, E-Mail: salesinfo@usgande.com, Web Site: www.usgande.com (16)

Rose, Eric B., Home Loan Investment Bank, Warwick, RI. Tel: (401) 739-8800, (800) 223-1700 X278, FAX: (401) 739-9675, E-Mail: contactus@homeloanbank.com, Web Site: www.homeloanbankfsb.com (14)

Rose, Gideon, Council on Foreign Relations Inc, New York, NY. Tel: (212) 434-9400, FAX: (212) 861-2759, E-Mail: editor@foreignaffairs.com, Web Site: www.foreignaffairs.org (17)

Rose, Henry A., Unicol Inc, Pembroke Pines, FL. Tel: (954) 431-7871, FAX: (954) 430-7227, E-Mail: customerservice@unicol-publishing.com, Web Site: www.unicol-publishing.com (17)

Rose, Jeffrey D., JDR Microdevices, Dublin, CA. Tel: (650) 625-1400, (800) 538-5000, FAX: (800) 538-5005, E-Mail: sales@jdr.com, Web Site: www.jdr.com (3)

Rose, R. Michael, Dominion Retail Inc, Richmond, VA. Tel: (804) 819-2268, Web Site: www.dom.com (16)

Rose, Robert, Media Link Communications, New York, NY. Tel: (212) 674-8843, FAX: (212) 260-8489, E-Mail: mlinkcom@aol.com, Web Site: www.getprinted.com (27)

Rose, Russ, Watts Radiant, Springfield, MO. Tel: (417) 864-6108, (800) 276-2419, FAX: (417) 864-8161, Web Site: www.wattsheatway.com (9)

Rose, Stuart, Tully & Holland Inc, Wellesley, MA. Tel: (781) 239-2900, FAX: (781) 239-2901, E-Mail: info@tullyandholland.com, Web Site: www.tullyandholland.com (14)

Roseberry Direct List Management & Brokerage, Elon, NC. Tel: (336) 532-1000, FAX: (336) 532-1003, E-Mail: churteau@roseberrydirect.com, Web Site: roseberrydirect.com (23)

Roseman, Karl-Heinz, McFarland & Co Inc Publishers, Jefferson, NC. Tel: (336) 246-4460, (800) 253-2187, FAX: (336) 246-5018, E-Mail: info@mcfarlandpub.com, Web Site: www.mcfarlandpub.com (17)

Rosen Inc, Portland, OR. Tel: (503) 224-9811, Web Site: rosenconvergence.com (35)

Rosen, Alan, Junior's Cheesecake, Brooklyn, NY. Tel: (718) 852-5257, (800) 458-6467, FAX: (718) 260-9849, E-Mail: info@juniorscheesecake.com, Web Site: www.juniorscheesecake.com (16)

Rosen, Andrew S., Kaplan Inc, Fort Lauderdale, FL. Tel: (954) 515-3993, Web Site: www.kaplan.com (16)

Rosen, Andrew S., Kaplan Publishing, Chicago, IL. Tel: (312) 606-8905, (800) 245-2665, FAX: (312) 606-8985, Web Site: www.kaplanpublishing.com (17)

Rosen, Arlene, ARA Media Solutions Inc, New York, NY. Tel: (212) 245-6691, Web Site: www.aramediasolutions.com (31)

Rosen, David, Island Pacific Inc, Irvine, CA. Tel: (949) 476-2212, (800) 569-1122, FAX: (949) 476-0177, Web Site: www.islandpacific.com (22)

Rosen, Jane C., Rosen Inc, Portland, OR. Tel: (503) 224-9811, Web Site: rosenconvergence.com (35)

Rosen, Jesse, League of American Orchestras, New York, NY. Tel: (212) 262-5161, FAX: (212) 262-5198, Web Site: www.symphony.org; www.americanorchestras.org (1)

Rosen, Marvin, Junior's Cheesecake, Brooklyn, NY. Tel: (718) 852-5257, (800) 458-6467, FAX: (718) 260-9849, E-Mail: info@juniorscheesecake.com, Web Site: www.juniorscheesecake.com (16)

Rosen, Neil, CertainSource Inc, Fairfield, CT. Tel: (203) 254-0404, (888) 655-0464, FAX: (203) 254-0411, E-Mail: neil@certainsource.com, Web Site: www.certainsource.com (32)

Rosen, Richard G., Rosen Inc, Portland, OR. Tel: (503) 224-9811, Web Site: rosenconvergence.com (35)

Rosen, Stacey M, At Last Naturals, North Salem, NY. Tel: (914) 747-3599, (800) 527-8123, FAX: (914) 747-3791, E-Mail: info@atlastnaturals.com, Web Site: www.atlastnaturals.com (7)

Rosen, Walter, Junior's Cheesecake, Brooklyn, NY. Tel: (718) 852-5257, (800) 458-6467, FAX: (718) 260-9849, E-Mail: info@juniorscheesecake.com, Web Site: www.juniorscheesecake.com (16)

Rosenbauer, Tom, The Orvis Co Inc, Manchester, VT. Tel: (802) 362-3622, FAX: (802) 362-3525, Web Site: www.orvis.com (11)

Rosenbaum, Davey, Marketsmith Inc, Parsippany, NJ. Tel: (973) 889-0006, Web Site: www.marketsmithinc.com (20)

Rosenbaum, Jan, MCCS, Mason, OH. Tel: (513) 573-2284, FAX: (513) 573-2197, Web Site: www.federated.com (14)

Rosenberg, Allen G., Marke Communications Inc, New York, NY. Tel: (212) 201-0600, (800) 716-2753, FAX: (212) 213-0785, Web Site: www.marke.com (35)

Rosenberg, Bill, Barterbing.com, Cranston, RI. Tel: (800) 345-6733, FAX: (401) 679-0326, Web Site: www.barterbing.com (29)

Rosenberg, Charles, Rose Printing Co Inc, Tallahassee, FL. Tel: (850) 576-4151, (800) 227-3725, FAX: (850) 576-4153, E-Mail: roseprt@roseprinting.com, Web Site: www.roseprinting.com (27)

Rosenberg, Jay, JSR Advertising Corp, New York, NY. Tel: (212) 995-1661, E-Mail: jay@tqm1.com, Web Site: www.quantmethod.com (17)

Rosenberg, Robert, Springboard Brand & Creative Strategy Ltd, Arlington Heights, IL. Tel: (847) 398-4920, FAX: (847) 398-4921, E-Mail: springboard@springboardbrand.com, Web Site: www.springboardbrand.com (20)

Rosenberg, Roberta, MGP Direct Inc, Clarksville, MD. Tel: (410) 531-0383, FAX: (410) 531-8142, E-Mail: roberta@mgpdirect.com, Web Site: www.mgpdirect.com (35)

Rosenblatt, MD Michael, Merck & Co Inc, Whitehouse Station, NJ. Tel: (908) 423-1000, Web Site: www.merck.com (16)

Rosenfeld, Theodore, Walker Publishing Co Inc, New York, NY. Tel: (212) 727-8300, (800) 289-2553, FAX: (212) 727-0984 (17)

Rosengarten, Troy, Ruud Lighting Inc, Racine, WI. Tel: (262) 886-1900, (800) 236-7000. FAX: (800) 236-7500, E-Mail: sales@ruudlighting.com, Web Site: www.ruudlighting.com (9)

Rosenhaus, Janice, Harris Marketing Group, Birmingham, MI. Tel: (248) 723-6300, FAX: (248) 723-6301, E-Mail: info@harris-hmg.com, Web Site: www.harris-hmg.com (35)

Robert Rosenheim Associates, Sharon, CT. Tel: (860) 364-0050, FAX: (860) 364-5577, Web Site: rrallc.com (32)

Rosenheim, Robert, Robert Rosenheim Associates, Sharon, CT. Tel: (860) 364-0050, FAX: (860) 364-5577, Web Site: rrallc.com (32)

Alan Rosenspan & Associates, Sharon, MA. Tel: (781) 784-2228, Web Site: www.alanrosenspan.com (20)

Rosenspan, Alan, Alan Rosenspan & Associates, Sharon, MA. Tel: (781) 784-2228, Web Site: www.alanrosenspan.com (20)

Rosenthal, Jim, Morgan Stanley, New York, NY. Tel: (212) 761-4000, FAX: (212) 761-0096 (14)

Rosenthal, Larry, Teva Pharmaceuticals USA, North Wales, PA. Tel: (215) 591-3000, (888) 838-2872, FAX: (215) 591-8600, Web Site: www.tevausa.com (7)

Rosenthal, Paul, TT Publishing, Arlington, VA. Tel: (703) 838-1770, FAX: (703) 838-0285, Web Site: www.ttnews.com (17)

Rosenthal, William, Communispond Inc, East Hampton, NY. Tel: (631) 907-8010, (800) 529-5925, FAX: (631) 907-8011, Web Site: www.communispond.com (20)

Rosenzweig, Charles, National Basketball Association, New York, NY. Tel: (212) 407-8000, FAX: (212) 826-0579, Web Site: www.nba.com (1)

Rosicrucian Order AMORC, San Jose, CA. Tel: (408) 947-3600, FAX: (408) 947-3677, E-Mail: membership@rosicrucian.org, Web Site: www.rosicrucian.org (1)

Roski, Jr. Edward P., Los Angeles Kings, Los Angeles, CA. Tel: (213) 742-7100, (888) KINGS-LA, FAX: (213) 742-7296, Web Site: kings.nhl.com (16)

Roskos, Bob, Virco Manufacturing Corp, Conway, AR. Tel: (501) 329-2901, (800) 448-4726, FAX: (800) 258-7367, E-Mail: info@virco.com, Web Site: www.virco.com (16)

Rosland Capital LLC, Santa Monica, CA. Tel: (800) 891-2341, Web Site: www.roslandcapital.com (14)

Rosmarin, John, Saunders Manufacturing Co Inc, Readfield, ME. Tel: (207) 685-3385, (800) 341-4674, FAX: (207) 685-9918, E-Mail: jsherwood@saunders-usa.com, Web Site: www.saunders-usa.com (16)

Ross Culbert & Lavery, New York, NY. Tel: (212) 206-0044, Web Site: www.rclnyc.com (20)

Ross Metals, New York, NY. Tel: (212) 869-1407, (800) 654-ROSS (16)

Ross-Simons, Cranston, RI. Tel: (401) 463-3100, (800) 835-0919, FAX: (401) 463-8599, Web Site: www.ross-simons.com (6)

Ross, Darrell S., Ross-Simons, Cranston, RI. Tel: (401) 463-3100, (800) 835-0919, FAX: (401) 463-8599, Web Site: www.ross-simons.com (6)

Ross, Donald, Vanderbilt Advertising, New York, NY. Tel: (212) 907-1500, FAX: (212) 907-1914, Web Site: www.valueline.com (14)

Ross, E. Rod, Equitable Life & Casualty Insurance Co, Salt Lake City, UT. Tel: (801) 579-3400, FAX: (801) 579-3789, Web Site: www.equilife.com (15)

Ross, Elizabeth, Periscope Inc, Minneapolis, MN. Tel: (612) 339-0500, FAX: (612) 339-0600, E-Mail: info@periscope.com, Web Site: www.periscope.com (35)

Ross, Jack Angel, Ross Metals, New York, NY. Tel: (212) 869-1407, (800) 654-ROSS (16)

Ross, Jack J., Dominion Enterprises, Norfolk, VA. Tel: (757) 351-7000, Web Site: www.dominionenterprises.com (32)

Ross, Jeffrey, Wunderman DC, Washington, DC. Tel: (202) 625-2111, FAX: (202) 424-7900, E-Mail: anne.wolek@wundermandc.com, Web Site: wundermandc.com (35)

Ross, John, Dexposito & Partners, New York, NY. Tel: (646) 747-8800, Web Site: newamericanagency.com (35)

Ross, John, Torcom Inbound Telemarketing, Madison, WI. Tel: (800) 832-4939, FAX: (608) 275-6557, E-Mail: torcom@torcom.com, Web Site: www.torcom.com (29)

Ross, Kimberly A., Avon Products Inc, New York, NY. Tel: (212) 282-7000, (800) 367-2866, FAX: (212) 282-6225, Web Site: www.avon.com (7)

Ross, Maribeth, NetProspex Inc, Waltham, MA. Tel: (888) 826-4877, E-Mail: sales@netprospex.com, Web Site: www.netprospex.com (22)

Ross, Marilyn, Communication Creativity, Buena Vista, CO. Tel: (720) 344-4388, (800) 331-8355, FAX: (866) 685-0307, E-Mail: steve@steveheimberg.com, Web Site: www.communicationcreativity.com (17)

Ross, Marji, Regnery Publishing, Washington, DC. Tel: (202) 216-0600, FAX: (202) 216-0612, Web Site: www.regnery.com (17)

Ross, Marshall, Cramer-Krasselt, Chicago, IL. Tel: (312) 616-9600, FAX: (312) 616-3839, E-Mail: pkrivkov@c-k.com, Web Site: c-k.com (35)

Ross, Michael, CIGNA International, Philadelphia, PA. Tel: (215) 761-1741, FAX: (215) 761-5515, Web Site: www.cigna.com (15)

Ross, Peter, Ross Culbert & Lavery, New York, NY. Tel: (212) 206-0044, Web Site: www.rclnyc.com (20)

Ross, Rhianna, Rapid Response Marketing, Las Vegas, NV. Tel: (702) 475-5235, Web Site: www.rapidresponseonline.com (32)

Ross, Robert, CCG Marketing Solutions, West Caldwell, NJ. Tel: (973) 808-0009, (866) 902-2807, FAX: (973) 808-9740, E-Mail: info@corpcomm.com, Web Site: home.corpcomm.com (21)

Ross, Robert, Schoolwise Press, San Francisco, CA. Tel: (415) 337-7971, (800) 247-8443 x 202, FAX: (415) 337-1146, E-Mail: info@schoolwisepress.com, Web Site: www.schoolwisepress.com (17)

Ross, Tom, About Books Inc, Colorado Springs, CO. Tel: (719) 632-8226, FAX: (719) 471-2182, E-Mail: infoabi2@about-books.com, Web Site: www.about-books.com (20)

Ross, Tom, Communication Creativity, Buena Vista, CO. Tel: (720) 344-4388, (800) 331-8355, FAX: (866) 685-0307, E-Mail: steve@steveheimberg.com, Web Site: www.communicationcreativity.com (17)

Rossell, Tony, Marketing General Inc, Alexandria, VA. Tel: (703) 739-1000, (800) 644-6646, FAX: (703) 549-6057, E-Mail: info@marketinggeneral.com, Web Site: www.marketinggeneral.com (35)

Rossi, Arleen, Eastern Collection Corp, Sag Harbor, NY. Tel: (631) 563-2112, (800) 243-1204, FAX: (631) 563-2471, E-Mail: ecc1626@aol.com (20)

Rossi, Richard, Eagle Asset Management Inc, Saint Petersburg, FL. Tel: (727) 573-2453, FAX: (727) 573-8655, Web Site: www.eagleasset.com (14)

Rossi, Steve, San Jose Mercury News, San Jose, CA. Tel: (408) 920-5000, FAX: (408) 288-8060, Web Site: www.mercurynews.com (17)

Rossier, Mark, New York Foundation For The Arts, Brooklyn, NY. Tel: (212) 366-6900, FAX: (212) 366-1778, Web Site: www.nyfa.org (1)

Rossnagel, Thomas, Sunrise Medical Inc, Boulder, CO. Tel: (303) 218-4500, (800) 333-4000, FAX: (303) 218-4949, Web Site: www.sunrisemedical.com (16)

Rossner, Kathy, 800 Response, Burlington, VT. Tel: (802) 860-0378, (800) 639-7253, FAX: (800) 639-6733, E-Mail: sales@800response.com, Web Site: www.800response.com (32)

Rosson, Mark, O'Neil Data Systems Inc, Los Angeles, CA. Tel: (310) 448-6400, FAX: (310) 577-7350, Web Site: www.oneildata.com (27)

Rossou, Alfred, Tully & Holland Inc, Wellesley, MA. Tel: (781) 239-2900, FAX: (781) 239-2901, E-Mail: info@tullyandholland.com, Web Site: www.tullyandholland.com (14)

Rostick, Gary, Comcast Spectacor LP, Philadelphia, PA. Tel: (215) 336-3600, (800) 298-4200, FAX: (215) 389-9518, E-Mail: info@comcast-spectacor.com, Web Site: www.comcast-spectacor.com (16)

Rosyn, Chris, China Books & Periodicals Inc, South San Francisco, CA. Tel: (650) 872-7076, (800) 818-2017, FAX: (650) 872-7808, E-Mail: info@chinabooks.com, Web Site: www.chinabooks.com (17)

Roth Advertising Inc, Glen Cove, NY. Tel: (516) 674-8603, FAX: (516) 368-3885, E-Mail: charles@rothadvertising.com, Web Site: www.rothadvertising.com (35)

Roth, Andy, Norwood Promotional Products, Clearwater, FL. Tel: (317) 275-2500, (800) 959-9138, FAX: (317) 275-2570, Web Site: www.norwood.com (16)

Roth, Charles A., Roth Advertising Inc, Glen Cove, NY. Tel: (516) 674-8603, FAX: (516) 368-3885, E-Mail: charles@rothadvertising.com, Web Site: www.rothadvertising.com (35)

Roth, Chris, Professional Marketing Associates, Tempe, AZ. Tel: (480) 829-0131, FAX: (480) 829-9202, Web Site: www.pmafulfillment.com (22)

Roth, Daniel J., Roth Advertising Inc, Glen Cove, NY. Tel: (516) 674-8603, FAX: (516) 368-3885, E-Mail: charles@rothadvertising.com, Web Site: www.rothadvertising.com (35)

Roth, Ernie M., Furman Roth Advertising, New York, NY. Tel: (212) 687-2300, FAX: (212) 687-0858, E-Mail: eroth@furmanroth.com, Web Site: www.furmanroth.com (35)

Roth, Lawrence H., American Society of Civil Engineers, Reston, VA. Tel: (703) 295-6000, (800) 548-2723, FAX: (703) 295-6343, Web Site: www.asce.org (1)

Roth, Melanie, Fulcrum Publishing, Golden, CO. Tel: (303) 277-1623, (800) 992-2908, FAX: (303) 279-7111, Web Site: www.fulcrum-books.com (17)

Roth, Michael, Tools for Wellness, Austin, TX. Tel: (800) 456-9887, FAX: (818) 532-1775, E-Mail: info@toolsforwellness.com, Web Site: www.toolsforwellness.com (7)

Roth, Steve, Ventyx, Atlanta, GA. Tel: (770) 952-8444, (800) 868-0497, FAX: (770) 955-2977, E-Mail: support@ventyx.com, Web Site: www.ventyx.com (16)

Rothering, Larry, Enerpac, Menomonee Falls, WI. Tel: (262) 781-6600, (800) 433-2766, FAX: (262) 781-1028, Web Site: www.enerpac.com (16)

Rothfelder, Ralph, Mapping Analytics, Rochester, NY. Tel: (585) 271-6490, (877) 893-6490, FAX: (585) 271-1132, E-Mail: sales@mappinganalytics.com, Web Site: www.mappinganalytics.com (20)

Rothman, Jeanne, Media Funding Corp, Malibu, CA. Tel: (310) 457-4140, FAX: (310) 774-1234, E-Mail: info@mediafunding.com, Web Site: mediafunding.com (32)

Rothman, LaVonda, JR Cigar, Burlington, NC. Tel: (800) 572-4427, FAX: (800) 457-3299, E-Mail: manager@jrburlington.com, Web Site: www.jrcigars.com (5)

Rothman, Lew, JR Cigar, Burlington, NC. Tel: (800) 572-4427, FAX: (800) 457-3299, E-Mail: manager@jrburlington.com, Web Site: www.jrcigars.com (5)

Rothschild, David, Sunshine Discount Crafts, Largo, FL. Tel: (727) 538-2878, (800) 729-2878, FAX: (727) 531-2739, E-Mail: webmaster@sunshinecrafts.com, Web Site: www.sunshinecrafts.com (11)

Rothstein, Larry, Source Communications, Hackensack, NJ. Tel: (201) 343-5222, E-Mail: admin@sourcead.com, Web Site: sourcead.com (35)

Roto-Rooter Services Co, Cincinnati, OH. Tel: (513) 762-6690, FAX: (513) 762-6590, Web Site: www.rotorooter.com (16)

Rottman, Jill, Covenant House International Headquarters, New York, NY. Tel: (212) 613-0300, (800) 388-3888, FAX: (212) 727-4992, Web Site: www.covenanthouse.org (1)

Roundtree, Mark, Landmark Communications Inc, Alpharetta, GA. Tel: (770) 813-1000, Web Site: www.landmarkcommunications.net (17)

Roundtree, Patricia K., Dundee Internet Services Inc, Dundee, MI. Tel: (734) 529-5331, FAX: (734) 529-5085, E-Mail: pat@dundee.net, Web Site: mailing-list-services.com/dundee.net (22)

Roundtree, Richard, Dundee Internet Services Inc, Dundee, MI. Tel: (734) 529-5331, FAX: (734) 529-5085, E-Mail: pat@dundee.net, Web Site: mailing-list-services.com/dundee.net (22)

Rouse, John, Ghent Manufacturing Inc, Lebanon, OH. Tel: (513) 932-3445, (800) 543-0550, FAX: (513) 932-9252, E-Mail: customer_service@ghent.com, Web Site: www.ghent.com (10)

Rouse, Paul, Dex Media, Dallas-Fort Worth Airport, TX. Tel: (972) 453-7000, Web Site: www.dexmedia.com (31)

Roush, Tim, 1-800-Contacts, Draper, UT. Tel: (800) 266-8228, FAX: (801) 924-9000, Web Site: www.1800contacts.com (7)

Rousseau, David, Salt River Project, Tempe, AZ. Tel: (602) 236-5900, FAX: (602) 236-8640, Web Site: www.srpnet.com (34)

Rousseau, Rita, Diakon Lutheran Social Ministries, Allentown, PA. Tel: (877) 342-5667, FAX: (610) 682-1559, E-Mail: swangerb@diakon.org, Web Site: www.diakon.org (1)

Roussel, Carrie, Nevada Magazine, Carson City, NV. Tel: (775) 687-5416, FAX: (775) 687-6159, E-Mail: editor@nevadamagazine.com, Web Site: www.nevadamagazine.com (17)

Roussel, Daniel, Desjardins Financial Securities, Levis, QC Canada. Tel: (418) 838-7870, FAX: (418) 833-5985, Web Site: www.desjardinsfinancialsecurity.com (15)

Rovit, Hugh R, Sure Fit Inc, Alburtis, PA. Tel: (888) 796-0500, FAX: (610) 336-8995, Web Site: www. surefit.net (8)

Row Resources Inc, Northport, NY. Tel: (631) 261-0525 (16)

Rowe Pottery Works Inc, Cambridge, WI. Tel: (608) 423-3363, (800) 356-5003, FAX: (608) 423-4273, E-Mail: sales@rowepottery.com, Web Site: www. rowepottery.com (16)

Rowe, Adam, Vermont Ski Areas Association, Montpelier, VT. Tel: (802) 223-2439, FAX: (802) 229-6917, E-Mail: info@skivermont.com, Web Site: www.skivermont.com (1)

Rowe, James, Rowe Pottery Works Inc, Cambridge, WI. Tel: (608) 423-3363, (800) 356-5003, FAX: (608) 423-4273, E-Mail: sales@rowepottery.com, Web Site: www.rowepottery.com (16)

Rowe, Shirley, House of Onyx, Inc, Greenville, KY. Tel: (270) 338-2363, (800) 844-3100, FAX: (270) 338-9605, E-Mail: sales@houseofonyx.com, Web Site: www.houseofonyx.com (6)

Rowell, Fred, Blue Cross Blue Shield of South Carolina, Columbia, SC. Tel: (803) 788-0222, (800) 288-2227, FAX: (803) 736-4516, Web Site: www. bcbssc.com (15)

Rowell, Joseph A, RCS Response Technologies Inc, Charlotte, NC. Tel: (704) 522-1919, FAX: (704) 522-9092, E-Mail: results@rcsdirect.com, Web Site: www.rcsdirect.com (21)

Rowell, Steve, Audio Classics Ltd, Vestal, NY. Tel: (607) 766-3501, FAX: (607) 766-3502, E-Mail: steve@audioclassics.com, Web Site: www. audioclassics.com (3)

Rowland, Kenneth, Row Resources Inc, Northport, NY. Tel: (631) 261-0525 (16)

Rowny, Elizabeth, Cole & Weber United, Seattle, WA. Tel: (206) 447-9595, FAX: (206) 233-0178, E-Mail: info@cwunited.com, Web Site: www.cwunited.com (35)

Rowsom, Andrew, ST Preston & Son Inc, Greenport, NY. Tel: (631) 477-1990, E-Mail: catalog@ prestons.com, Web Site: www.prestons.com (8)

Roxanis, Dean, University Press of America Inc, Lanham, MD. Tel: (301) 459-3366, (800) 462-6420, FAX: (301) 429-5748, E-Mail: custserv@rowman. com, Web Site: www.univpress.com (17)

Roy, PhD William R, Kelley Swofford Roy Inc, Miami, FL. Tel: (305) 444-0004, (800) 537-5565, FAX: (305) 444-9057, E-Mail: info@ksrteam.com, Web Site: www.ksrteam.com (35)

Roy, Robert, CBT Direct, Tarpon Springs, FL. Tel: (727) 724-8994, (877) 872-4646, FAX: (727) 797-9143, Web Site: www.cbtdirect.com (16)

Royal Bank of Canada, Toronto, ON Canada. Tel: (416) 974-5151, FAX: (416) 955-7800, Web Site: www. royalbank.com (14)

Royal Canadian Mint, Ottawa, ON Canada. Tel: (613) 993-1912 (16)

Royal Canin, Saint Charles, MO. Tel: (636) 926-0003, Web Site: www.royalcanin.us (16)

Royal Caribbean International Ltd, Miami, FL. Tel: (305) 539-6000, FAX: (305) 374-7354, Web Site: www.royalcaribbean.com (16)

Royal Envelope Corp, Chicago, IL. Tel: (773) 376-1212, (800) 279-0142, FAX: (773) 376-0011, E-Mail: info@royalenv.com, Web Site: www. royalenv.com (26)

Royal Performance Group, Lisle, IL. Tel: (630) 353-7900, (888) 774-0125, FAX: (630) 353-7902, E-Mail: info@rpgglobal.com, Web Site: www. rpggiftcards.com (34)

Royall, John T., Gulf Publishing Co, Houston, TX. Tel: (713) 529-4301, FAX: (713) 520-4433, E-Mail: publications@gulfpub.com, Web Site: www. gulfpub.com (17)

Royall, Ro, Business Extension Bureau, Houston, TX. Tel: (713) 528-5568, (800) 969-5568, FAX: (713) 528-1648, E-Mail: ronr@bebtexas.com, Web Site: bebtexas.com (23)

Royall, Ron, Business Extension Bureau, Houston, TX. Tel: (713) 528-5568, (800) 969-5568, FAX: (713) 528-1648, E-Mail: ronr@bebtexas.com, Web Site: bebtexas.com (23)

Royce, Michael L., New York Foundation For The Arts, Brooklyn, NY. Tel: (212) 366-6900, FAX: (212) 366-1778, Web Site: www.nyfa.org (1)

Royle, Cyndee, The Journal News, White Plains, NY. Tel: (914) 694-9300, FAX: (914) 696-8152, Web Site: www.nyjournalnews.com (17)

Royse, Alvin L., American Heart Association, Dallas, TX. Tel: (214) 373-6300, (800) AHA-USA-1, FAX: (214) 373-3406, Web Site: www.americanheart.org (1)

Royse, Connie, Plas-Tanks Industries Inc, Hamilton, OH. Tel: (513) 942-3800, FAX: (513) 942-3993, E-Mail: info@plastanks.com, Web Site: www. plastanks.com (9)

Roza, Eric, Oracle Data Cloud, Broomfield, CO. Tel: (800) 633-0738, E-Mail: thedatahotline@oracle. com, Web Site: cloud.oracle.com (22)

Rozansky, Phil, Tower Media Advertising Inc, Chicago, IL. Tel: (312) 856-9200, FAX: (312) 856-1300, E-Mail: info@towermedia.com, Web Site: www. towermedia.com (35)

Rozelle, Peggy, Sport Supply Group, Dallas, TX. Tel: (972) 484-9484, FAX: (972) 247-0650, Web Site: www.sportsupplygroup.com (11)

Rozzell, Scott, Centerpoint Energy, Minneapolis, MN. Tel: (612) 372-4664, FAX: (612) 321-4873, E-Mail: mgc-businessinformation@centerpointenergy.com, Web Site: www.minnegasco.centerpointenergy.com (16)

Rubber Stamps of America, Dublin, NH. Tel: (800) 553-5031, FAX: (603) 563-8102, E-Mail: stampusa@verizon.net, Web Site: www.stampusa. com (6)

Ruben, Peter, Home Shopping Network, Saint Petersburg, FL. Tel: (727) 872-1000, FAX: (727) 872-7292, Web Site: www.hsn.com (32)

Rubenstein, Herb, Associated Bag Co, Milwaukee, WI. Tel: (414) 769-1000, (800) 926-6100, FAX: (800) 926-4610, E-Mail: customerservice@associatedbag. com, Web Site: www.associatedbag.com (10)

Rubenzer, Bill, Storage Battery Systems Inc, Menomonee Falls, WI. Tel: (262) 703-5800, (800) 554-2243, FAX: (262) 703-3073, E-Mail: sbs@sbsbattery.com, Web Site: www.sbsbattery.com (12)

Rubenzer, Robert, Storage Battery Systems Inc, Menomonee Falls, WI. Tel: (262) 703-5800, (800) 554-2243, FAX: (262) 703-3073, E-Mail: sbs@ sbsbattery.com, Web Site: www.sbsbattery.com (12)

Rubenzer, Scott, Storage Battery Systems Inc, Menomonee Falls, WI. Tel: (262) 703-5800, (800) 554-2243, FAX: (262) 703-3073, E-Mail: sbs@sbsbattery.com, Web Site: www.sbsbattery.com (12)

Rubin, Adrea, Adrea Rubin Marketing Inc, New York, NY. Tel: (212) 983-0020, FAX: (212) 983-1057, E-Mail: info@adrearubin.com, Web Site: www. adrearubin.com (21)

Rubin, Arlene, LGP GEM LTD, New York, NY. Tel: (212) 840-2510, FAX: (212) 302-6182, E-Mail: sales@lgpltd.com, Web Site: www.lgpltd.com (16)

Rubin, Evan, New York & Co, New York, NY. Tel: (212) 884-2169, (800) 961-9906, Web Site: www. nyandcompany.com (2)

Rubin, Frank, The Contest Center, Wappingers Falls, NY. Tel: (845) 297-4833, E-Mail: contestcen@aol. com, Web Site: www.contestcen.com (19)

Rubin, Gary K., Society for Human Resource Management, Alexandria, VA. Tel: (703) 548-3440, (800) 283-7476, FAX: (703) 535-6490, E-Mail: shrmstore@shrm.org, Web Site: www.shrm.org (1)

Rubin, Jeff, Results Advertising Inc, Hasbrouck Heights, NJ. Tel: (201) 288-7888, FAX: (201) 288-5112, E-Mail: info@resultsinc.com, Web Site: www.resultsinc.com (35)

Rubin, Mark A., Society of Petroleum Engineers, Richardson, TX. Tel: (972) 952-9393, (800) 456-6863, FAX: (972) 952-9435, E-Mail: spedal@spe.org, Web Site: www.spe.org (1)

Rubin, Mitchell, Applied Info Group, Kenilworth, NJ. Tel: (908) 241-7007, FAX: (9080 241-7088, Web Site: www.appliedinfogroup.com (22)

Rubin, Roy, Magento, Culver City, CA. Tel: (310) 954-8012, Web Site: www.magento.com (22)

Rubin, Scott, Great Ideas Inc/CSP, Highland Park, IL. Tel: (800) 611-5515, FAX: (847) 432-8557, E-Mail: art@greatideasinc.com, Web Site: www. greatideasinc.com (33)

Rubin, Steven, General Binding Corp, Northbrook, IL. Tel: (800) 723-4000, FAX: (847) 272-1389, (800) 952-1166, Web Site: www.gbc.com (13)

Rubin, Steven, R&S Industries Corp, Chesterfield, MO. Tel: (314) 781-5400, FAX: (314) 781-5169, E-Mail: sendeverything@miraclepolishingcloth.com, Web Site: www.miraclepolishingcloth.com (16)

Rubin, Steven, Torqmaster International, Stamford, CT. Tel: (203) 326-5945, (888) 414-4643, FAX: (203) 326-5944, E-Mail: info@torqmaster.com, Web Site: www.torqmaster.com (9)

Rubino, Bill, Jofco Inc, Jasper, IN. Tel: (812) 482-5154, (800) 23-JOFCO, FAX: (812) 634-2392, E-Mail: furniture@jofco.com, Web Site: www.jofco.com (16)

Rubino, Robert C., Citizens Bank, Boston, MA. Tel: (617) 725-5900, FAX: (617) 725-5921, Web Site: www.citizensbank.com (14)

Rubino, Victor J., Practicing Law Institute, New York, NY. Tel: (212) 824-5700, (800) 260 4PLI, FAX: (800) 321-0093, E-Mail: info@pli.edu, Web Site: www.pli.edu (16)

Rubinstein, Helene F., Esquire Magazine, New York, NY. Tel: (212) 649-4020, FAX: (212) 649-4303, E-Mail: esquire@hearst.com, Web Site: www. esquire.com (17)

Rubinstein, Joel, Dentino Marketing, Princeton, NJ. Tel: (609) 454-3202, FAX: (609) 454-3239, E-Mail: karl@dentinomarketing.com, Web Site: www. dentinomarketing.com (35)

Ruble, Bill, Naturmed, Camp Verde, AZ. Tel: (928) 567-5175, (800) 720-1245, Web Site: www. ivlproducts.com (7)

Ruble, Holly, Pinnacle List Co, Arlington, VA. Tel: (703) 379-4394, FAX: (703) 379-5312, E-Mail: holly@pinnlistco.com, Web Site: www.pinnlistco. com (23)

Ruch, Heinz, Miracle Ear, Minneapolis, MN. Tel: (800) 464-8002, FAX: (763) 268-4365, Web Site: www. miracle-ear.com (16)

Ruchman, Neal H., A Rapid Mailing Inc, Jessup, MD. Tel: (410) 792-4000, (800) US-RAPID, FAX: (301) 776-3690, E-Mail: info@rairapid.com, Web Site: www.rairapid.com (28)

Rucker, Michael, Time Out New York, New York, NY. Tel: (646) 432-3000, FAX: (212) 677-9665, E-Mail: tnew@kable.com, Web Site: www.timeout.com/newyork/ (18)

Rudasill, Susann, Center for Professional Development, Tallahassee, FL. Tel: (850) 487-1691, (850) 644-8004, FAX: (850) 644-2589, Web Site: www.Learningforlife.fsu.com (16)

Rudd, Leslie, Windsor Vineyards, Santa Rosa, CA. Tel: (800) 289-9463, (800) 741-6070, E-Mail: webmaster@windsorvineyards.com, Web Site: www.windsorvineyards.com (16)

Rudd, Michael, Boscobel Marketing Communications Inc, Silver Spring, MD. Tel: (301) 588-2900, E-Mail: info@boscobel.com, Web Site: www.boscobel.com (35)

Rudder, Michael, Smart Dog Products, Winchester, TN. Tel: (931) 967-7482, (800) 264-3647, FAX: (931) 967-7483, E-Mail: sales@shopsmartdog.com (11)

Ruder Finn Inc, New York, NY. Tel: (212) 593-6400, FAX: (212) 715-1556, E-Mail: rfnewyork@ruderfinn.com, Web Site: www.ruderfinn.com (30)

Rudin, Max, The Library of America, New York, NY. Tel: (212) 308-3360, (800) 964-5778, FAX: (212) 750-8352, E-Mail: info@loa.org, Web Site: www.loa.org (13)

Rudnick, Bryan, Best ROI Lists, Boca Raton, FL. Tel: (877) 301-5478, E-Mail: info@bestroilists.com, Web Site: www.bestroilists.com (24)

Rudnick, Bryan G, Alliance Strategies Group Inc, Boca Raton, FL. Tel: (561) 499-3201, E-Mail: info@asgroupinc.com, Web Site: www.asgroupinc.com (23)

Rue, Mark, Major Brands Group, Minneapolis, MN. Tel: (763) 767-6800, FAX: (763) 767-1264, E-Mail: mbgcustomerservice@mrgmn.com, Web Site: www.mrgrp.com (33)

Rue, Sally, Caswell-Massey Co Ltd, Edison, NJ. Tel: (732) 225-2181, (800) 326-0500, FAX: (800) 868-4407, E-Mail: info@caswellmasseyltd.com, Web Site: www.caswellmassey.com (7)

Rueff, Andrew, TransFirst Holdings Inc, Dallas, TX. Tel: (214) 453-7700, (888) 254-4137, FAX: (214) 453-7739, Web Site: www.transfirst.com (14)

Ruf Corp, Olathe, KS. Tel: (913) 782-8544, (800) 829-8544, FAX: (913) 782-0150, E-Mail: solutions@ruf.com, Web Site: www.ruf.com (30)

Ruf Strategic Solutions, Olathe, KS. Tel: (913) 782-8544, (800) 829-8544, FAX: (913) 782-0150, Web Site: www.ruf.com (22)

Ruf, Jacob F., Ruf Strategic Solutions, Olathe, KS. Tel: (913) 782-8544, (800) 829-8544, FAX: (913) 782-0150, Web Site: www.ruf.com (22)

Ruf, Kurtis M., Ruf Corp, Olathe, KS. Tel: (913) 782-8544, (800) 829-8544, FAX: (913) 782-0150, E-Mail: solutions@ruf.com, Web Site: www.ruf.com (30)

Ruffner, Jr. Frederick G., Omnigraphics Inc, Aston, PA. Tel: (610) 461-3548, (800) 234-1340, FAX: (800) 875-1340, E-Mail: info@omnigraphics.com, Web Site: www.omnigraphics.com (17)

Ruffner, Peter E., Omnigraphics Inc, Aston, PA. Tel: (610) 461-3548, (800) 234-1340, FAX: (800) 875-1340, E-Mail: info@omnigraphics.com, Web Site: www.omnigraphics.com (17)

Rufus, Gregory, Marathon Norco Aerospace Inc, Waco, TX. Tel: (254) 776-0650, FAX: (254) 776-6558, Web Site: www.mptc.com (16)

Rugeiro, Carol, Investors Marketing Services, Danvers, MA. Tel: (978) 774-2990, (800) 462-2551, FAX: (978) 774-4249, Web Site: www.investorsmarketing.com (14)

Ruggiero, Carl, Universal Training, Lake Forest, IL. Tel: (847) 235-2170, E-Mail: information@universaltraining.com, Web Site: www.universaltraining.com (16)

Ruggiero, Tamara, American Kidney Fund, Rockville, MD. Tel: (301) 881-3052, (800) 638-8299, FAX: (301) 881-0898, Web Site: www.kidneyfund.org (1)

Ruhanen, Troy, TBWA Worldwide, New York, NY. Tel: (212) 804-1300, E-Mail: info@tbwa.com, Web Site: www.tbwa.com (35)

Ruhl, Christopher, Ivy Tech Community College of Indiana, Indianapolis, IN. Tel: (317) 921-4800, (888) IVY-LINE, FAX: (317) 921-4753. Web Site: www.ivytech.edu (13)

Rukstales, Bradley, Cogensia, Schaumburg, IL. Tel: (847) 805-9800, FAX: (847) 805-9313, E-Mail: info@cac-group.com, Web Site: www.cogensia.com (22)

Rulle, Gail, Integrated Mail Industries Ltd, Milwaukee, WI. Tel: (414) 908-3500, FAX: (414) 449-2906, E-Mail: sales@integratedmail.com, Web Site: www.integratedmail.com (28)

Rullo, Jim, Skies America International Publishing & Communications, Beaverton, OR. Tel: (503) 520-1955, FAX: (503) 520-1275, E-Mail: skies@skies.com, Web Site: www.skies.com (36)

Runberg, John, BCF, Virginia Beach, VA. Tel: (757) 497-4811, FAX: (757) 497-3684, Web Site: www.bcfagency.com (35)

Runice, Paul, MTS Systems Corp, Eden Prairie, MN. Tel: (952) 937-4000, (800) 328-2255, FAX: (952) 937-4515, E-Mail: info@mts.com, Web Site: www.mts.com (16)

Runnette, Brooke, National Geographic Society, Washington, DC. Tel: (202) 862-8638, (800) 373-1717, Web Site: www.nationalgeographic.com (17)

Runstrom, Erik, BCC Software Inc, Rochester, NY. Tel: (585) 272-9130, (800) 453-3130, FAX: (585) 272-9141, Web Site: www.bccsoftware.com (22)

Runstrom, K. Jon, BCC Software Inc, Rochester, NY. Tel: (585) 272-9130, (800) 453-3130, FAX: (585) 272-9141, Web Site: www.bccsoftware.com (22)

Runyan, W. Tim, Oneida Ltd, Oneida, NY. Tel: (315) 361-3000, (888) 263-7195, FAX: (315) 361-3700, Web Site: www.oneida.com (16)

Runyon, Thomas E., Seedburo Equipment Co, Des Plaines, IL. Tel: (312) 738-3700, (800) 284-5779, E-Mail: sales@seedburo.com, Web Site: www.seedburo.com (8)

Runzheimer, L. Lee, Osmonics Inc, Minnetonka, MN. Tel: (952) 264-3937, (800) 605-6698, FAX: (952) 536-3301, Web Site: www.osmonics.com (16)

Rupricht, William F., Sotheby's, New York, NY. Tel: (212) 606-7000, FAX: (212) 606-7107, Web Site: www.sothebys.com (6)

Rural Alaska Community Action Program Inc, Anchorage, AK. Tel: (907) 279-2511, FAX: (907) 278-2309, Web Site: www.ruralcap.com (1)

Rusbridge, Mike, Reed Exhibitions, Norwalk, CT. Tel: (203) 840-4800, (888) 745-7644, FAX: (203) 840-5805, E-Mail: inquiry@reedexpo.com, Web Site: www.reedexpo.com (16)

Rush Industries, Inc, Mineola, NY. Tel: (516) 741-0346, FAX: (516) 741-0348, Web Site: www.rushindustries.com (16)

The Rusin Group, LLC, Wilton, CT. Tel: (203) 529-3257 (20)

Rusin, Paul, Dexta Corp, Napa, CA. Tel: (707) 255-2454, (800) 733-3982, FAX: (707) 255-8520, Web Site: www.dexta.com (16)

Ruskin, Moscou, Faltischek, PC, Uniondale, NY. Tel: (516) 663-6600, FAX: (516) 663-6601, E-Mail: info@rmfpc.com, Web Site: www.rmfpc.com (16)

Rusnak, Anton, Abbey of Gethsemani, Trappist, KY. Tel: (502) 549-4133, FAX: (502) 549-4124, E-Mail: reservations@monks.org, Web Site: www.monks.org (1)

Russ, August & Kabat, Los Angeles, CA. Tel: (310) 826-7474, FAX: (310) 826-6991, E-Mail: info@raklaw.com, Web Site: www.raklaw.com (20)

Russ Reid Co, Pasadena, CA. Tel: (626) 449-6100, FAX: (626) 449-6190, E-Mail: info@russreid.com, Web Site: www.russreid.com (35)

Russ, Larry C., Russ, August & Kabat, Los Angeles, CA. Tel: (310) 826-7474, FAX: (310) 826-6991, E-Mail: info@raklaw.com, Web Site: www.raklaw.com (20)

Russ, Susan Fraysse, The Reader's Digest Association Inc, New York, NY. Tel: (800) 310-6261, Web Site: www.rda.com (17)

Russak, Donald A., New York Power Authority, White Plains, NY. Tel: (914) 681-6200, E-Mail: info@nypa.gov, Web Site: www.nypa.gov (16)

AG Russell Knives Inc, Rogers, AR. Tel: (479) 631-0055, (800) 255-9034, FAX: (479) 631-8493, E-Mail: ag@agrussell.com, Web Site: www.agrussell.com (11)

Russell Investments, Seattle, WA. Tel: (206) 505-7877, (800) 426-7969, Web Site: www.russell.com (14)

Russell, A.G., AG Russell Knives Inc, Rogers, AR. Tel: (479) 631-0055, (800) 255-9034, FAX: (479) 631-8493, E-Mail: ag@agrussell.com, Web Site: www.agrussell.com (11)

Russell, Bill, Roman Research Inc/Simply Whispers Earring, Hanson, MA. Tel: (800) 225-8652, FAX: (781) 447-0995, E-Mail: earpiercingstore@romanresearch.com, Web Site: www.simplywhispers.com (2)

Russell, Goldie, AG Russell Knives Inc, Rogers, AR. Tel: (479) 631-0055, (800) 255-9034, FAX: (479) 631-8493, E-Mail: ag@agrussell.com, Web Site: www.agrussell.com (11)

Russell, Jay, GSD&M, Austin, TX. Tel: (512) 242-4736, Web Site: www.gsdm.com (35)

Russell, Liz, Media Horizons Inc, Norwalk, CT. Tel: (203) 857-0770, FAX: (203) 857-0296, E-Mail: info@mediahorizons.com, Web Site: www.mediahorizons.com (21)

Russell, Melanie, Association for Audience Marketing Professionals (AAMP), North Hollywood, CA. Tel: (310) 323-7220, FAX: (310) 323-7231, E-Mail: mjordan@espcomp.com, Web Site: www.wfma.org (40)

Russell, Richard F., Amerisure Insurance Cos, Farmington Hills, MI. Tel: (248) 615-9000, (800) 257-1900, FAX: (248) 615-8224, Web Site: www.amerisure.com (15)

Russell, Rick, Naval Institute Press, Annapolis, MD. Tel: (410) 268-6110, (800) 233-8764, FAX: (410) 571-1703, E-Mail: webmaster@usni.org, Web Site: www.usni.org/navalinstitutepress (17)

Russell, Robert, Washington Products Inc, Massillon, OH. Tel: (330) 837-5101, FAX: (330) 837-5401 (34)

Russell, Samuel, Davidoff of Geneva Inc, Pinellas Park, FL. Tel: (727) 828-5400, (800) 328-4365, FAX: (203) 975-0090 (6)

Russo, Charles, Arch Telecom Inc, Austin, TX. Tel: (512) 492-0735, (800) 890-7575, FAX: (512) 495-7101, Web Site: www.archtelecom.com (16)

Russo, Edward, Vaxserve, Moosic, PA. Tel: (800) 752-9338, FAX: (800) 553-9908, Web Site: www.vaxserve.com (7)

Russo, Ken, PPS - Packaging Printing Specialists, Saint Charles, IL. Tel: (630) 513-8060, (877) 573-8060, FAX: (630) 513-8062, E-Mail: pps@ppsofil.com, Web Site: www.PPSofIL.com (27)

Russo, Paul W., OccuNomix, Port Jefferson Station, NY. Tel: (631) 791-1955, (800) 466-0071, FAX: (631) 474-0073, Web Site: www.occunomix.com (34)

Russo, Ronald N., The RONED Group, East Hanover, NJ. Tel: (973) 386-1848, FAX: (973) 386-0969, E-Mail: info@roned.com, Web Site: www.roned.com (27)

Russo, Tony, Demandbase Inc, San Francisco, CA. Tel: (415) 683-2660, E-Mail: info@demandbase.com, Web Site: www.demandbase.com (22)

Rust, Jr. Edward B., State Farm Insurance Cos, Bloomington, IL. Tel: (309) 766-2311, FAX: (309) 766-3621, Web Site: www.statefarm.com (15)

Shelly Rusten, Hankins, NY. Tel: (917) 421-0980, (845) 887-5662, E-Mail: srusten@msn.com, Web Site: www.shellyrusten.com (37)

Rusten, Shelly, Shelly Rusten, Hankins, NY. Tel: (917) 421-0980, (845) 887-5662, E-Mail: srusten@msn.com, Web Site: www.shellyrusten.com (37)

Rutenberg, Lorraine, DHL Express, Plantation, FL. Tel: (954) 888-7000, (800) 225-5345, FAX: (954) 888-7310, Web Site: www.dhl.com (28)

Anne Ruth, Bronxville, NY. Tel: (914) 337-7931 (20)

Ruth, Anne, Anne Ruth, Bronxville, NY. Tel: (914) 337-7931 (20)

Rutherford, James P., Veronis Suhler Stevenson LLC, New York, NY. Tel: (212) 935-4990, FAX: (212) 381-8168, E-Mail: stevensonj@vss.com, Web Site: www.vss.com (14)

Rutiedge, Michael A., The Houston Chronicle, Houston, TX. Tel: (713) 362-7171, FAX: (713) 362-3575, Web Site: www.houstonchronicle.com (31)

Rutkowski, Donna, Joint Commission, Oakbrook Terrace, IL. Tel: (630) 792-5000, Web Site: www.jcaho.org (1)

Rutland Products, Rutland, VT. Tel: (800) 544-1307, FAX: (802) 775-5262, E-Mail: sales@rutland.com, Web Site: www.rutland.com (16)

Rutledge, Thomas M., Charter Communications, Stamford, CT. Tel: (203) 905-7801, Web Site: www.charter.com (16)

Rutrough, James E., State Farm Insurance Cos, Bloomington, IL. Tel: (309) 766-2311, FAX: (309) 766-3621, Web Site: www.statefarm.com (15)

Ruttan, Sandra, Leslie Shoe Co Inc, Rogers City, MI. Tel: (989) 734-4030, (800) 716-8617, E-Mail: info@sexyshoes.com, Web Site: www.sexyshoes.com (2)

Ruttenberg, Jonathan M., American Locker Security Systems Inc, Coppell, TX. Tel: (817) 329-1600, (800) 828-9118, E-Mail: info@americanlocker.com, Web Site: www.americanlocker.com (16)

Rutter, David, Brooke Distributors Inc, Miami, FL. Tel: (305) 624-9752, (800) 275-8792, FAX: (305) 620-3988, E-Mail: sales@brookedms.com, Web Site: www.brookedist.com (3)

Ruud Lighting Inc, Racine, WI. Tel: (262) 886-1900, (800) 236-7000, FAX: (800) 236-7500, E-Mail: sales@ruudlighting.com, Web Site: www.ruudlighting.com (9)

Ruud, Alan, Ruud Lighting Inc, Racine, WI. Tel: (262) 886-1900, (800) 236-7000, FAX: (800) 236-7500, E-Mail: sales@ruudlighting.com, Web Site: www.ruudlighting.com (9)

Ruvolo, Larry, Texwipe Co, Kernersville, NC. Tel: (201) 684-1800, (800) TEXWIPE, FAX: (201) 684-1801, E-Mail: info@texwipe.com, Web Site: www.texwipe.com (16)

Ruzzamenti, LeAnne, Dairy Council of California, Irvine, CA. Tel: (949) 756-7892, Web Site: www.dairycouncilofca.org (1)

Ryall, Debbie, Arnaud's, New Orleans, LA. Tel: (504) 523-0611, (866) 230-8895, FAX: (504) 581-7908, Web Site: www.arnauds.com (16)

Ryall, Eric, Ashworth College, Norcross, GA. Tel: (770) 729-8400, (800) 957-5412, FAX: (770) 729-9294, Web Site: www.ashworthcollege.edu (13)

Ryan, Barbara, Minitab Inc, State College, PA. Tel: (814) 238-3280, (800) 448-3555, FAX: (814) 238-4383, E-Mail: sales@minitab.com, Web Site: www.minitab.com (16)

Ryan, Dick, Publishers Press Inc, Shepherdsville, KY. Tel: (502) 955-6526, FAX: (502) 955-5586, E-Mail: info@pubpress.com, Web Site: www.pubpress.com (27)

Ryan, Donald, Jenny Products Inc, Somerset, PA. Tel: (814) 445-3400, FAX: (814) 445-2280, Web Site: www.jennyproducts.com (16)

Ryan, Frank, Enterprise Ireland, New York, NY. Tel: (212) 371-3600, FAX: (212) 371-6398, Web Site: www.enterprise-ireland.com (16)

Ryan, J. Patrick, Skystone Ryan, Cincinnati, OH. Tel: (513) 241-6778, FAX: (513) 241-0551, E-Mail: cincinnati@skystoneryan.com, Web Site: www.skystoneryan.com (20)

Ryan, James T., Grainger Industrial Supply, North Brook, IL. Tel: (847) 498-5900, FAX: (847) 498-3402, Web Site: www.grainger.com (16)

Ryan, James T., W W Grainger Inc, Bradenton, FL. Tel: (941) 747-5566, (800) 472-4643, E-Mail: info@grainger.com, Web Site: www.grainger.com (5)

Ryan, James T., WW Grainger Inc, Lake Forest, IL. Tel: (847) 535-1000, (800) 472-4643, FAX: (847) 535-9122, Web Site: www.grainger.com (9)

Ryan, John, Center for Creative Leadership, Greensboro, NC. Tel: (336) 545-2810, FAX: (336) 282-3284, E-Mail: info@ccl.org, Web Site: www.ccl.org (16)

Ryan, Jr T. Timothy, SIFMA, New York, NY. Tel: (212) 313-1200, FAX: (212) 313-1301, E-Mail: inquiry@sifma.org, Web Site: www.sifma.org (1)

Ryan, Kevin M., Covenant House International Headquarters, New York, NY. Tel: (212) 613-0300, (800) 388-3888, FAX: (212) 727-4992, Web Site: www.covenanthouse.org (1)

Ryan, Michael, Cactus Mailing Company, Scottsdale, AZ. Tel: (480) 443-1442, (888) 632-5282, FAX: (866) 828-7794, E-Mail: info@cactusmailing.com, Web Site: www.cactusmailing.com (21)

Ryan, Michael, Techni-Tool Inc, Worcester, PA. Tel: (610) 941-2400, (800) 832-4866, FAX: (800) 854-8665, E-Mail: sales@techni-tool.com, Web Site: www.techni-tool.com (16)

Ryan, Paula, Communication Industries Corp, Grafton, VT. Tel: (802) 869-6500, FAX: (802) 869-6565, E-Mail: info@cicmail.com, Web Site: www.careersatcic.com (10)

Ryan, Tim, 89 Degrees, Burlington, MA. Tel: (781) 221-5400, Web Site: www.89degrees.com (9)

Rybolt, Terry, Teleperformance Canada, Toronto, ON Canada. Tel: (416) 922-8240, E-Mail: canada@teleperformance.com, Web Site: www.teleperformance.com (35)

Rydell, Catherine M., American Academy of Neurology, Minneapolis, MN. Tel: (651) 695-2793, 800 (879)-1960, FAX: (612) 454-2746, E-Mail: memberservices@aan.com, Web Site: www.aan.com (1)

Ryder, Fred, Blue Cross Blue Shield of Florida, Jacksonville, FL. Tel: (904) 791-6111, (800) 477-3736, FAX: (904) 905-6638, E-Mail: katie.magee@bcbsfl.com, Web Site: www.bcbsfl.com (15)

Rygiel, JoAnne, Recording for the Blind & Dyslexic Inc, Princeton, NJ. Tel: (609) 452-0606, (800) 221-4792, FAX: (609) 520-7996, E-Mail: info@rfbd.org, Web Site: www.rfbd.org (16)

Rymer, William, MTI Information Technologies LLC, Langhorne, PA. Tel: (267) 569-2400, FAX: (215) 741-3898, Web Site: www.mtiadvantage.com (30)

Ryskamp, Bruce, Zondervan Corp, Grand Rapids, MI. Tel: (616) 698-6900, (800) 727-3060, FAX: (616) 698-3235, Web Site: www.zondervan.com (17)

The RYTEX Co, Peru, IN. Tel: (317) 872-8553, (800) 277-5458, FAX: (317) 872-8535, (800) 329-1669, Web Site: www.rytex.com (10)

S

S&S Worldwide, Colchester, CT. Tel: (860) 537-3451, (800) 288-9941, FAX: (860) 537-2866, E-Mail: cservice@ssww.com, Web Site: www.ssww.com (11)

S Group Inc, Akron, OH. Tel: (330) 535-2103, (800) 686-7435, FAX: (330) 535-1723, E-Mail: info@s-groupinc.com, Web Site: www.s-groupinc.com (33)

SAE International, Warrendale, PA. Tel: (724) 776-4841, Web Site: www.sae.org (6)

SAS Group, Tarrytown, NY. Tel: (914) 332-7878, FAX: (914) 332-7859, Web Site: www.sasgroup.com (32)

SAS Institute, Cary, NC. Tel: (919) 677-8000, FAX: (919) 677-4444, Web Site: www.sas.com (22)

SBC Advertising, Columbus, OH. Tel: (614) 255-2333, Web Site: www.sbcadvertising.com (35)

SBDP Corp, Cincinnati, OH. Tel: (513) 871-7019, FAX: (513) 871-0134, E-Mail: info@sbdp.com, Web Site: www.sbdp.com (22)

SC Direct, West Bridgewater, MA. Tel: (800) 343-9695, Web Site: www.scdirect.com (2)

SCA Direct, Fairfax, VA. Tel: (703) 293-6339, Web Site: www.scadirect.com (1)

SCA Promotions Inc, Dallas, TX. Tel: (214) 860-3700, (888) 860-3700, FAX: (214) 860-3723, E-Mail: scainfo@scapromo.com, Web Site: www.scapromo.com (15)

SCI Management, Houston, TX. Tel: (713) 525-7783, Web Site: www.sci-corp.com (16)

SDI Marketing, Toronto, ON Canada. Tel: (416) 674-9010, (877) SDI-TEAM, FAX: (416) 674-9011, E-Mail: info@sdicapital.com, Web Site: www.sdimarketing.com (14)

SEI, Oaks, PA. Tel: (610) 676-1000, FAX: (610) 676-1406, E-Mail: webmaster@seic.com, Web Site: www.seic.com (14)

SEOinhouse, Saint Charles, MO. Tel: (888) 899-0195, FAX: (888) 899-0195, Web Site: www.seoinhouse.com (32)

SF Global Sourcing Inc, San Francisco, CA. Tel: (415) 288-9400, (800) 545-5865, FAX: (415) 288-9410, E-Mail: selfservice@sfvideo.com, Web Site: www.sfvideo.com (3)

SGD Golf LLC, Hudson, OH. Tel: (234) 380-5037, (800) 321-3411, E-Mail: sales@sgdgolf.com, Web Site: www.sgdgolf.com (34)

SHR Capital Partners, Greenwich, CT. Tel: (203) 618-1110 (30)

SHR Perceptual Branding, Phoenix, AZ. Tel: (480) 483-3700, FAX: (480) 483-9675, E-Mail: info@shrbranding.com, Web Site: www.shrbranding.com (35)

SHSMD Annual Conference, Chicago, IL. Tel: (312) 422-3888, FAX: (312) 278-0883, E-Mail: shsmd@aha.org, Web Site: www.shsmd.org (42)

SIE (Select Information Exchange), New York, NY. Tel: (212) 496-6435, FAX: (212) 787-4269, Web Site: www.siecom.com (23)

SIFMA, New York, NY. Tel: (212) 313-1200, FAX: (212) 313-1301, E-Mail: inquiry@sifma.org, Web Site: www.sifma.org (1)

SIGMA Marketing Group LLC, Rochester, NY. Tel: (585) 473-7300, (888) 277-9837, FAX: (585) 473-0332, E-Mail: mbush@sigmamarketing.com, Web Site: www.sigmamarketing.com; www.jthgearanalytics.com (Blog) (20)

SK&A, Irvine, CA. Tel: (800) 752-5478, FAX: (949) 476-9131, E-Mail: skasales@skainfo.com, Web Site: www.skainfo.com (23)

SKO-Brenner-American, Baldwin, NY. Tel: (516) 771-4400, (800) 645-3390, FAX: (516) 771-7810, E-Mail: collect@skobrenner.com, Web Site: www.skobrenner.com (20)

SLM Corp, Newark, DE. Web Site: www.salliemae.com (16)

SLR Associates, Portland, OR. Tel: (503) 645-0675 (20)

SMM Advertising, Smithtown, NY. Tel: (631) 265-5160, FAX: (631) 265-5185, E-Mail: marketing@smmadvertising.com, Web Site: smmadvertising.com (35)

SMY Media Inc, Chicago, IL. Tel: (312) 621-9600, FAX: (312) 621-0924, E-Mail: info@smymedia.com, Web Site: www.smymedia.com (32)

SNL Financial, Charlottesville, VA. Tel: (434) 977-1600, FAX: (434) 977-4466, E-Mail: support@sni.com, Web Site: www.snl.com (17)

SOS Children's Villages - USA, Washington, DC. Tel: (202) 347-7920, Web Site: www.sos-usa.org (1)

SP Express, Tempe, AZ. Tel: (866) 773-7363, E-Mail: info@spexpress.com, Web Site: www.spexpress.com (28)

SPSS Inc, Chicago, IL. Tel: (312) 651-3000, (800) 543-2185, FAX: (312) 651-3668, E-Mail: sales@spss.com, Web Site: www.spss.com (22)

SRB Marketing Inc, New Paltz, NY. Tel: (866) 210-1183, Web Site: www.srbmarketing.com (30)

SRDS, Des Plaines, IL. Tel: (800) 851-7737, FAX: (847) 375-5001, Web Site: www.srds.com (17)

SSHC Inc/Radiant Heating Commercial Applications, Old Saybrook, CT. Tel: (860) 399-5434, (800) 544-5182, FAX: (860) 399-6460, (877) 675-4968, E-Mail: info@sshcinc.com, Web Site: www.sshcinc.com (9)

ST&P Marketing Communications Inc, Fairlawn, OH. Tel: (330) 668-1932, FAX: (330) 668-2078, Web Site: stpinc.com (35)

ST Media Group International, Cincinnati, OH. Tel: (513) 421-2050, (800) 925-1110, FAX: (513) 421-5144, E-Mail: customer@stmediagroup.com, Web Site: www.signweb.com (17)

SW Caging Corp, Topeka, KS. Tel: (785) 232-0061, Web Site: www.swcaging.com (14)

SWAT Marketing Team, Grove City, PA. Tel: (412) 851-9700, FAX: (412) 291-1155, E-Mail: cdbloch@swatmarketingteam.com, Web Site: swatmarketingteam.com (23)

SWB&R Inc, Bethlehem, PA. Tel: (610) 866-0611, (877) 377-9286, FAX: (610) 866-8650, E-Mail: swbr@swbrinc.com, Web Site: www.swbrinc.com (35)

SWBC, San Antonio, TX. Tel: (210) 525-1241, Web Site: www.swbc.com (14)

Sa-So, Arlington, TX. Tel: (972) 641-4911, (800) 752-4294, FAX: (972) 660-3684, E-Mail: info@sa-so.com, Web Site: www.sa-so.com (16)

Saatchi & Saatchi Canada, Toronto, ON Canada. Tel: (416) 359-9595, FAX: (416) 866-4111, Web Site: saatchi.ca (21)

Saatchi & Saatchi New York, New York, NY. Tel: (212) 463-2000, FAX: (212) 463-9856, Web Site: www.saatchiny.com (32)

Saati, Laura, 89 Degrees, Burlington, MA. Tel: (781) 221-5400, Web Site: www.89degrees.com (9)

Sabater, Julio, Workforce Advantage USA, Elizabeth, NJ. Tel: (908) 355-2299, FAX: (908) 352-2931, Web Site: www.workforceadvantageusa.com (13)

Sabin, David, Stanley Home Products, Great Bend, KS. Tel: (800) 732-1118, E-Mail: customer@fuller.com, Web Site: www.fullerdirect.com (8)

Sabin, David, The Fuller Brush Co, Great Bend, KS. Tel: (800) 522-0499, FAX: (620) 792-1906, E-Mail: custom@fuller.com, Web Site: www.fuller.com (5)

Sablosky, Warren, NuNaturals, Eugene, OR. Tel: (541) 344-9785, (800) 753-4372, FAX: (541) 343-0915, E-Mail: info@nunaturals.com, Web Site: www.nunaturals.com (16)

Sabo, Bill, Apollo Technologies Inc, Smyrna, GA. Tel: (770) 433-0210, (800) 533-3548, FAX: (770) 433-0132, E-Mail: customerservice@apolloind.com, Web Site: www.apolloind.com (34)

Sabre Holdings Inc, Southlake, TX. Tel: (682) 605-1000, FAX: (682) 605-7239, Web Site: www.sabre.com (19)

Sacher, Kevin, American Mint LLC, Mechanicsburg, PA. Tel: (717) 458-9200, (877) 807-MINT, FAX: (717) 458-9211, E-Mail: contact@americanmint.com, Web Site: www.americanmint.com (6)

Sacher, Marc, Auriemma Consulting Group, New York, NY. Tel: (516) 333-4800, FAX: (516) 333-4815, E-Mail: info@acg.net, Web Site: www.acg.net (20)

Sacher, Paul, Paul Fredrick Menstyle, Fleetwood, PA. Tel: (610) 944-0909, (800) 247-1417, FAX: (610) 944-6452, E-Mail: custserv@menstyle.com, Web Site: www.paulfredricks.com (2)

Sachs, Patty, Neo@Ogilvy, New York, NY. Tel: (212) 259-5200, Web Site: www.neoogilvy.com (35)

Sacred Heart League, Walls, MS. Tel: (662) 781-1360, (800) 232-9079, FAX: (662) 781-3340, E-Mail: comments@shl.org, Web Site: www.shl.org (28)

Sadh, Devyani, Data Square LLC, Stamford, CT. Tel: (203) 964-9733, FAX: (203) 964-0783, E-Mail: info@datasquare.com, Web Site: www.datasquare.com (22)

Sadler, Linda, Dataline Inc, Princeton, NJ. Tel: (609) 452-6014, FAX: (609) 951-0025, E-Mail: psobel@datalinedata.com, Web Site: datalinedata.com (23)

Sadorf, Nedra, Hunter Business Group LLC, Milwaukee, WI. Tel: (414) 203-8060, (800) 423-4010, FAX: (414) 203-8225, E-Mail: hunter@hunterbusiness.com, Web Site: www.hunterbusiness.com (20)

Sadowski, Bart, Bluberries Advertising Agency, Garfield, NJ. Tel: (973) 478-2200, FAX: (973) 478-9662, E-Mail: mail@bluberries.com, Web Site: www.bluberries.com (35)

Sadowski, Chris, Bluberries Advertising Agency, Garfield, NJ. Tel: (973) 478-2200, FAX: (973) 478-9662, E-Mail: mail@bluberries.com, Web Site: www.bluberries.com (35)

Sadowski, Nick, Bluberries Advertising Agency, Garfield, NJ. Tel: (973) 478-2200, FAX: (973) 478-9662, E-Mail: mail@bluberries.com, Web Site: www.bluberries.com (35)

Sadun, Raffaele, Adknowledge, Kansas City, MO. Tel: (816) 931-1771, (866) 730-2109, Web Site: www.adknowledge.com (32)

Saef, David, Exhibitgroup/Giltspur, Roselle, IL. Tel: (972) 538-3031, (800) 843-3944, Web Site: www.e-g.com (30)

Saenz, Dave, AlarmingYou.com, Boca Raton, FL. Tel: (714) 981-2900, Web Site: www.alarmingyou.com (16)

Safe Publications Inc, Doylestown, PA. Tel: (215) 357-9049, FAX: (215) 357-5202, E-Mail: sales@safepub.com, Web Site: www.safepub.com (11)

Safe Specialties, Kingston, TN. Tel: (865) 675-2815, (800) 695-2815, FAX: (865) 717-8249, E-Mail: black223@aol.com, Web Site: www.safespec.com (33)

Safeco Insurance Co, Seattle, WA. Tel: (206) 545-5000, (800) 332-3226, FAX: (206) 545-5767/5651, Web Site: www.safeco.com (15)

Safeguard Business Systems Inc, Dallas, TX. Tel: (214) 905-3935, (800) 523-2422, FAX: (800) 439-8423, Web Site: www.gosafeguard.com (16)

Safeware, The Insurance Agency Inc, Columbus, OH. Tel: (614) 781-1492, (800) 800-1492, FAX: (614) 781-0559, E-Mail: service@safeware.com, Web Site: www.safeware.com (15)

Safian Communications Inc, Maplewood, NJ. Tel: (973) 378-3672, FAX: (973) 378-2456, E-Mail: gail.safian@safianhealth.com, Web Site: safianhealth.com (35)

Safon, Scot, The Weather Channel, Atlanta, GA. Tel: (770) 226-0000, FAX: (770) 226-2390, Web Site: www.weather.com (32)

Saftchick, Jay, WinterSilks LLC, Warren, PA. Tel: (904) 645-6000, Web Site: www.wintersilks.com (2)

Safti First, Brisbane, CA. Tel: (415) 824-4900, (888) 653-3333, FAX: (415) 824-5900, (888) 653-4444, E-Mail: info@safti.com, Web Site: www.safti.com (16)

Sagan, Rachel, Playboy Enterprises Inc, Beverly Hills, CA. Tel: (310) 860-1215, Web Site: www.playboyenterprises.com (17)

Sage Communications, Framingham, MA. Tel: (508) 309-6678, FAX: (508) 309-6372, E-Mail: info@sagecommunications.com, Web Site: www.sagecommunications.com (35)

Sage Direct Inc, Grand Rapids, MI. Tel: (616) 940-8311, (800) 729-8310, FAX: (616) 940-3383, E-Mail: sageinc@sagedirect.com, Web Site: www.sagedirect.com (22)

Sage Financial Group, West Conshohocken, PA. Tel: (484) 342-4400, FAX: (484) 537-0550, E-Mail: sage@sagefinancial.com, Web Site: www.sagefinancial.com (14)

Sage Software Inc, Irvine, CA. Tel: (949) 753-1222, (800) 854-3415, FAX: (949) 753-0374, Web Site: www.sagesoftware.com (16)

Sage, Gary, Sage Direct Inc, Grand Rapids, MI. Tel: (616) 940-8311, (800) 729-8310, FAX: (616) 940-3383, E-Mail: sageinc@sagedirect.com, Web Site: www.sagedirect.com (22)

Sage, Pamela, Sage Direct Inc, Grand Rapids, MI. Tel: (616) 940-8311, (800) 729-8310, FAX: (616) 940-3383, E-Mail: sageinc@sagedirect.com, Web Site: www.sagedirect.com (22)

Sagen, Warren, AllBrands.com Sewing Machine Superstore, Baton Rouge, LA. Tel: (225) 923-1285, (866) 255-2726, FAX: (225) 923-1261, E-Mail: info@allbrands.com, Web Site: www.allbrands.com (11)

Sager, Dan, Insight Direct Inc, Tempe, AZ. Tel: (480) 333-3001, (800) 467-4448, FAX: (480) 902-1180, Web Site: www.insight.com (16)

Saggio, Joseph, PDS International Mail Service, Hauppauge, NY. Tel: (631) 815-1750, Web Site: www.pdsmail.com; www.internationalmail.com (28)

Sahadeo, Meere, Pango Pango Swimwear Corp, Pompano Beach, FL. Tel: (954) 786-0255, (800) 858-9431, FAX: (954) 786-7745, E-Mail: pango_swimwear@bellsouth.net, Web Site: www.pango-pangoswimwear.com (2)

Sahlberg, John, Boise Cascade Holdings LLC, Boise, ID. Tel: (208) 384-6451, FAX: (208) 384-7189, E-Mail: mediarelations@bc.com, Web Site: www.bc.com (16)

Sahlein, Don, Alan Gordon Enterprises Inc, Hollywood, CA. Tel: (323) 466-3561, FAX: (323) 871-2193, E-Mail: contactus@alangordon.com, Web Site: www.alangordon.com (32)

Sahlein, Stacey, Alan Gordon Enterprises Inc, Hollywood, CA. Tel: (323) 466-3561, FAX: (323) 871-2193, E-Mail: contactus@alangordon.com, Web Site: www.alangordon.com (32)

Saide, Barry, United Staffing Systems, New York, NY. Tel: (800) 972-9725, FAX: (646) 224-8393, Web Site: www.unitedstaffing.com (16)

Saiia, Donna, Potpourri Group Inc, North Billerica, MA. Tel: (978) 256-4100, FAX: (978) 256-1961/0344, Web Site: www.potpourrigroup.com (6)

The Sailing Co, Palm Coast, FL. Tel: (866) 436-2460, FAX: (401) 848-5048, Web Site: www.sailingworld.com (17)

Sailrite Enterprises, Inc, Columbia City, IN. Tel: (260) 693-2242, (800) 348-2769, FAX: (260) 693-2246, E-Mail: sailrite@sailrite.com, Web Site: www.sailrite.com (11)

The Saint Francis Community Services, Salina, KS. Tel: (785) 825-0541, (800) 423-1342, FAX: (785) 825-2940, Web Site: www.st-francis.org (1)

Saint Gregory Group, Cincinnati, OH. Tel: (513) 769-8440, FAX: (513) 769-1640, E-Mail: info@stgregory.com, Web Site: www.stgregory.com (35)

St Joseph's College, Brooklyn, NY. Tel: (718) 399-1223, Web Site: www.sjcny.edu (1)

St Joseph's Indian School, Chamberlain, SD. Tel: (605) 734-3300, Web Site: www.stjo.org (1)

St Labre Indian School, Ashland, MT. Tel: (406) 784-4500, Web Site: www.stlabre.org (1)

St Lawrence Island Original Ivory Cooperative, Gambell, AK. Tel: (907) 985-5707, FAX: (907) 985-5927 (6)

St Louis Post-Dispatch, Saint Louis, MO. Tel: (314) 340-8000, (800) 365-0820, FAX: (314) 340-3140, Web Site: www.stltoday.com (17)

St Louis Slot Machine Co, Saint Louis, MO. Tel: (314) 432-1699, E-Mail: stlslot@earthlink.net, Web Site: www.stlouisslot.com (6)

Saint Mary's Paper Corp, Wheaton, IL. Tel: (630) 668-6279, FAX: (630) 668-6292, Web Site: www.stmarys-paper.com (25)

St Petersburg/Clearwater Area CVB, Clearwater, FL. Tel: (727) 464-7200, Web Site: www.floridasbeach.com (1)

Saint Thomas, Robert, Children International, Kansas City, MO. Tel: (816) 942-2000, (800) 888-3089, FAX: (816) 942-3714, E-Mail: RobS@cikc.org, Web Site: www.children.org (1)

Sakach, Stephen, American Historic Inns Inc, Dana Point, CA. Tel: (949) 497-2232, (800) 397-4667, FAX: (949) 497-9228, E-Mail: comments@iloveinns.com, Web Site: www.iloveinns.com (17)

Sakach, Tim, American Historic Inns Inc, Dana Point, CA. Tel: (949) 497-2232, (800) 397-4667, FAX: (949) 497-9228, E-Mail: comments@iloveinns.com, Web Site: www.iloveinns.com (17)

Saks Fifth Avenue, New York, NY. Tel: (212) 940-5195, FAX: (212) 940-5339, Web Site: www.saksfifthavenue.com (16)

Saladini, Mauro, NAGRA USA, San Francisco, CA. Tel: (415) 962-5000, FAX: (415) 962-5300, E-Mail: dtv@nagra.com, Web Site: www.nagra.com (32)

Salatino, Joseph, Great Western Supply, Dallas, TX. Tel: (972) 481-6100, (800) 527-2782, FAX: (972) 481-6215, Web Site: www.proforma.com/greatwesternsupply (16)

Salaway, Kevin, Penn State Hazleton, Hazleton, PA. Tel: (570) 450-3175, Web Site: www.hn.psu.edu (1)

Salbi, Zainab, Women for Women International, Washington, DC. Tel: (202) 737-7705, Web Site: www.womenforwomen.org (40)

Saleh, Sarah, Academic Travel Abroad Inc, Washington, DC. Tel: (202) 785-9000, (800) 556-7896, FAX: (202) 342-0317, Web Site: www.academictravel.com (19)

Salem Media Group, Camarillo, CA. Tel: (804) 987-0400, E-Mail: info@salem.cc, Web Site: salemmedia.com (17)

Salem, Michael, National Jewish Health, Denver, CO. Tel: (303) 398-1070, (800) 222-LUNG, (800) 423, FAX: (303) 398-1663, E-Mail: trubeyp@njhealth.org, Web Site: www.njhealth.org (1)

Salem, Richard M., WearGuard Corp, Norwell, MA. Tel: (781) 871-4100, (800) 388-3300, FAX: (781) 871-2639, Web Site: www.wearguard.com (2)

Salerno, James, DigDev Direct, Deerfield Beach, FL. Tel: (954) 949-9500, (800) 873-5137, FAX: (954) 337-0251, E-Mail: info@digdev.com, Web Site: www.digdevdirect.com (35)

Sales & Marketing Management Magazine, New York, NY. Tel: (800) 821-6897, FAX: (905) 470-8561, E-Mail: joyce.cooney@nielsen.com, Web Site: www.salesandmarketing.com (16)

Sales by Dees, Montgomery, AL. Tel: (334) 333-1567, E-Mail: dees@sbdees.com, Web Site: www.sbdees.com (35)

Sales Development Associates Inc, Saint Louis, MO. Tel: (314) 862-8828, FAX: (314) 862-8829, E-Mail: patb@sdastl.com, Web Site: www.sdastl.com (21)

Sales Leads, Jupiter, FL. Tel: (866) 725-3753, FAX: (866) 702-5558, E-Mail: info@salesleadsinc.com, Web Site: www.salesleadsinc.com (17)

Sales Magic Inc, Boynton Beach, FL. Tel: (561) 732-5263, (800) 985-9956, FAX: (561) 375-9413, E-Mail: custsvc@names.com, Web Site: www.names.com (32)

Sales Portal, Mountain View, CA. Tel: (800) 634-3474, Web Site: www.salesportal.com (30)

Sales Service/America Inc, Alexandria, VA. Tel: (703) 813-2400 (16)

Salesian Missions, New Rochelle, NY. Tel: (914) 633-8344, FAX: (914) 633-7404, E-Mail: info@salesianmissions.org, Web Site: www.salesianmissions.org. (1)

SalesLeads.tv Inc, Boca Raton, FL. Tel: (561) 239-0364, (800) 590-5323, FAX: (561) 981-8786, E-Mail: bear@salesleads.tv, Web Site: www.salesleads.tv (23)

Salford Systems, San Diego, CA. Tel: (619) 543-8880, FAX: (619) 543-8888, Web Site: www.salford-systems.com (22)

Salguero, Jeff, Colgate-Palmolive Co, New York, NY. Tel: (212) 310-2000, (800) 468-6502, FAX: (212) 310-2475, Web Site: www.colgate.com (16)

Salic, Jacob, Talas, Brooklyn, NY. Tel: (212) 219-0770, FAX: (212) 219-0735, E-Mail: info@talasonline.com, Web Site: www.talasonline.com (10)

Salinas, Martin. Sunoco Inc, Philadelphia, PA. Tel: (215) 977-3000, FAX: (215) 977-3409, Web Site: www.sunocoinc.com (16)

Salisbury, Franklin C., National Foundation for Cancer Research, Bethesda, MD. Tel: (301) 654-1250, (800) 321-CURE, FAX: (301) 654-5824, E-Mail: info@nfcr.org, Web Site: www.nfcr.org (1)

Salk, Jonathan, CCIM Institute, Chicago, IL. Tel: (312) 321-4460, (800) 621-7027, FAX: (312) 321-4530, Web Site: www.ccim.com (1)

Salkin, Jonathan, Rocket Direct Marketing Inc, New York, NY. Tel: (212) 689-5800, FAX: (212) 689-0635, E-Mail: info@rocketdirect.com, Web Site: www.rocketdirect.com (32)

Salkind, Sussanne J, Human Rights Campaign, Washington, DC. Tel: (202) 216-1500, (800) 777-4723, Web Site: www.hrc.org (40)

Salley, Sr. Tom, WTS Media, Chattanooga, TN. Tel: (423) 894-9427, (800) 251-7228, FAX: (423) 894-7281, E-Mail: customerservice@wtsmedia.com, Web Site: www.wts-tape.com (16)

Sallorenzo, Gaetano, Calvin Klein Cosmetics Co, New York, NY. Tel: (212) 719-2600, E-Mail: customerservice@calvinklein.com, Web Site: www.calvinklein.com (7)

Sally Beauty Supply LLC, Denton, TX. Tel: (940) 898-7500, (866) 234-9442, Web Site: www.sallybeauty.com (7)

Salmans, Scott J., WRS Group Ltd, Waco, TX. Tel: (254) 776-6461, (800) 299-3366, FAX: (888) 977-7653, E-Mail: custom@wrsgroup.com, Web Site: www.wrsgroup.com (7)

Kurt Salmon Associates Inc, Atlanta, GA. Tel: (404) 892-0321, FAX: (404) 898-9590, E-Mail: infoksaweb@kurtsalmon.com, Web Site: www.kurtsalmon.com (20)

Salmon, Melissa, John Hancock Financial Services Inc, Boston, MA. Tel: (617) 572-6000, (800) 732-5543, FAX: (617) 572-6451, Web Site: www.johnhancock.com (15)

Salmore, Charles, MarketingWorks Inc, Los Angeles, CA. Tel: (323) 436-2000, E-Mail: chas@mwks.net, Web Site: www.marketingworksagency.com (32)

Salt River Project, Tempe, AZ. Tel: (602) 236-5900, FAX: (602) 236-8640, Web Site: www.srpnet.com (34)

Salt, Matt, FDAnews, Falls Church, VA. Tel: (703) 538-7600, (888) 838-5578, FAX: (703) 538-7676, E-Mail: customerservice@fdanews.com, Web Site: www.fdanews.com (17)

Salta, Robert, All American List Corp, Upper Marlboro, MD. Tel: (301) 420-5760, (888) 690-2252, FAX: (301) 420-5765, E-Mail: info@allamericanlist.com, Web Site: www.allamericanlist.com (23)

Salta, Robert, DirectMail.com, Prince Frederick, MD. Tel: (888) 690-2252, FAX: (301) 855-9810, Web Site: www.directmail.com (28)

Salta, Shawn, DirectMail.com, Prince Frederick, MD. Tel: (888) 690-2252, FAX: (301) 855-9810, Web Site: www.directmail.com (28)

Saltzman, David, Triangle Printers Inc, Skokie, IL. Tel: (847) 675-3700, FAX: (847) 674-1230, E-Mail: blevin@triangleprinters.com, Web Site: www.triangleprinters.com (27)

Saltzman, Gary P., B'nai B'rith International, Washington, DC. Tel: (202) 857-6600, (888) 388-4224, FAX: (202) 857-6609, E-Mail: info@bnaibrith.org, Web Site: www.bnaibrith.org (1)

Saltzman, Jeffrey, Entertainment Music Marketing Corp, Baldwin, NY. Tel: (631) 243-0600, FAX: (631) 243-0605, E-Mail: emmcmusic@aol.com, Web Site: www.emmcmusic.com (16)

Salu, Eran, Direct List Technology Inc, Orange, CA. Tel: (714) 772-3282, (888) 341-1117, FAX: (714) 772-6947, E-Mail: info@directlist.com, Web Site: www.directlist.com (23)

Saluto, Christine, Direct Mail of NY-PostHaste, Buchanan, NY. Tel: (914) 736-2239 (28)

The Salvation Army National Headquarters, Alexandria, VA. Tel: (703) 684-5500, Web Site: www.salvationarmyusa.org (1)

Salyers, Ms. Donna, Donna Salyers' Fabulous-Bridal Inc, Covington, KY. Tel: (859) 291-3300, (800) 848-4650, E-Mail: abell@fabulousfurs.com, Web Site: fabulousfurs.com (2)

Salzinger, Mark, No Load Fund Investor, Brentwood, TN. Tel: (800) 706-6364, FAX: (800) 785-9212, E-Mail: NoLoad@mleesmith.com, Web Site: www.noloadfundinvestor.com (14)

Salzman, Russ, Institute of Real Estate Management, Chicago, IL. Tel: (312) 329-6000, (800) 837-0706, FAX: (312) 338-4736, E-Mail: custserv@irem.org, Web Site: www.irem.org (1)

Sam Ash Music Direct, Hicksville, NY. Tel: (800) 472-6274, E-Mail: sales@samash.com, Web Site: www.samash.com (5)

Samant, Rajiv, Lester Inc, Branford, CT. Tel: (203) 488-5265, (800) 999-5265, FAX: (203) 483-0408, Web Site: www.lesterusa.com (29)

Samaro, Stephanie, Allegra Marketing Services, Louisville, KY. Tel: (502) 895-1530, FAX: (502) 895-1624, Web Site: www.allegra-east.com (27)

Samet, Marcy, MRM//McCann, New York, NY. Tel: (646) 865-6230, E-Mail: gbc@mrm-mccann.com, Web Site: mrm-mccann.com (35)

Samets, Yoram, Kelliher Samets Volk, Burlington, VT. Tel: (802) 862-8261, FAX: (802) 863-4724, E-Mail: info@ksvc.com, Web Site: www.ksvc.com (35)

Samford University, Birmingham, AL. Tel: (205) 726-2011, Web Site: www.samford.edu (41)

Samiri, Omer, iVisionMobile Inc, Chatsworth, CA. Tel: (866) 655-5302, FAX: (818) 812-6126, E-Mail: sales@ivisionmobile.com, Web Site: www.ivisionmobile.com (35)

Samph, Tom, Post University, Waterbury, CT. Tel: (203) 596-4520, (800) 345-2562, E-Mail: admissions@post.edu, Web Site: www.post.edu (41)

Sampson, Clinton, Citizens Republic Bank, Flint, MI. Tel: (810) 766-7500, Web Site: www.citizensbanking.com (14)

Sampson, Dave, All Star Directories, Seattle, WA. Tel: (888) 404-8043, FAX: (707) 667-1524, Web Site: www.allstardirectories.com (17)

Sams, Pam King, Children's Hospital Foundation, Silver Spring, MD. Tel: (202) 476-3000, (800) 884-LIFE, FAX: (202) 884-5999, Web Site: www.dcchildrens.com (1)

Sams, Russell, Audience Identification Inc, Lisle, IL. Tel: (630) 435-0460, FAX: (630) 435-0470, E-Mail: rmarsh@audienceid.com (22)

Samsonite International SA, Mansfield, MA. Tel: (508) 851-1400, (800) 547-BAGS, FAX: (303) 373-8715, Web Site: www.samsonite.com (16)

Samuelson, Mark, PAC Worldwide, Redmond. WA. Tel: (425) 202-4000, (800) 535-0039, FAX: (425) 885-2934, Web Site: www.pac.com (26)

San Antonio Express-News, San Antonio, TX. Tel: (210) 250-2000, E-Mail: feedabck@express-news.net, Web Site: www.expressnews.com (17)

San Antonio, Randall, Warrantech Direct Inc, Bedford, TX. Tel: (817) 786-1000, (800) 833-8801, FAX: (817) 786-1020, Web Site: www.warrantech.com (29)

San Francisco Bay Area Rapid Transit District (BART), Oakland, CA. Tel: (510) 464-6000, FAX: (510) 464-7103, Web Site: www.bart.gov (16)

San Francisco Chronicle, San Francisco, CA. Tel: (415) 777-1111, FAX: (415) 536-5178, Web Site: www.sfgate.com (17)

San Francisco Herb & Natural Food Co, San Francisco, CA. Tel: (510) 770-1215, (800) 227-2830, FAX: (510) 770-9021, E-Mail: customerservice@herbspicetea.com, Web Site: www.herbspicetea.com (4)

San Francisco State University, San Francisco, CA. Tel: (415) 338-1111, FAX: (415) 338-0501, Web Site: www.sfsu.edu (41)

San Francisco Victoriana Inc, San Francisco, CA. Tel: (415) 648-0313, FAX: (415) 648-2812, Web Site: www.sfvictoriana.com (9)

San Jose Mercury News, San Jose, CA. Tel: (408) 920-5000, FAX: (408) 288-8060, Web Site: www.mercurynews.com (17)

San Julian, Robert, Neutron Industries, Phoenix, AZ. Tel: (602) 864-0090, (888) 712-7127, FAX: (602) 357-3996, (877) 646-7337, E-Mail: questions@neutronindustries.com, Web Site: www.neutronindustries.com (16)

Sanborn, Liz, James J Hill Reference Library, Saint Paul, MN. Tel: (651) 265-5500, Web Site: www.jjhill.org (1)

Sanches, Jr Enrique, Aerovox Inc, New Bedford, MA. Tel: (508) 994-9661, (888) AEROVOX, FAX: (508) 995-3000, E-Mail: sales1@aerovox.com, Web Site: www.aerovox.com (16)

Sanchez, Jaime, SIGMA Marketing Group LLC, Rochester, NY. Tel: (585) 473-7300, (888) 277-9837, FAX: (585) 473-0332, E-Mail: mbush@sigmamarketing.com, Web Site: www.sigmamarketing.com; www.jthgearanalytics.com (Blog) (20)

Sanchez, Joseph, Protection One Inc, Lawrence, KS. Tel: (785) 856-5500, (800) GET-HELP, Web Site: www.protectionone.com (16)

Sanchez, Manuel, Compass Bank, Birmingham, AL. Tel: (205) 297-4900, (800) 239-4357, FAX: (205) 933-3702, Web Site: www.compassbank.com (14)

Sanchez, Miguel, Christian Herald Association, New York, NY. Tel: (212) 684-2800, (800) BOWERY-1, FAX: (212) 684-3740, E-Mail: info@chaonline.org, Web Site: www.bowery.org (1)

Sanchez, Rafael, American Nicaraguan Foundation, Miami, FL. Tel: (305) 374-3391, FAX: (305) 374-5993, Web Site: www.aidnicaragua.org (1)

Sanchez, Rob, MeritDirect, Rye Brook, NY. Tel: (914) 368-1000, FAX: (914) 368-1150, E-Mail: hq@meritdirect.com, Web Site: www.meritdirect.com (23)

Sancoa International LP, Lumberton, NJ. Tel: (856) 273-0700, FAX: (856) 273-2710, E-Mail: sancoa@sancoa.com, Web Site: sancoa.com (31)

Sand, Matthew, BUYSEASONS Inc, New Berlin, WI. Tel: (262) 901-2000, FAX: (262) 901-2315, Web Site: www.buyseasons.com (5)

Sandberg, Sheryl, Facebook Inc, Menlo Park, CA. Tel: (650) 543-4800, Web Site: www.facebook.com (31)

Sanders, Bruce, Micro Plastics Inc, Flippin, AR. Tel: (870) 453-2261, (800) 466-1467, FAX: (870) 453-8676, E-Mail: mpsales@microplastics.com, Web Site: www.microplastics.com (16)

Sanders, Gina, Fairchild Fashion Media, New York, NY. Tel: (212) 286-2860, Web Site: www.condenast.com/fairchild (17)

Sanders, Greg, Rowe Pottery Works Inc, Cambridge, WI. Tel: (608) 423-3363, (800) 356-5003, FAX: (608) 423-4273, E-Mail: sales@rowepottery.com, Web Site: www.rowepottery.com (16)

Sanderson, Dean, Nature Publishing Group, New York, NY. Tel: (212) 726-9200, FAX: (212) 696-9006, Web Site: www.nature.com (17)

Sanderson, Matt, Print Services Distribution Association, Chicago, IL. Tel: (800) 230-0175, FAX: (312) 673-6880, Web Site: www.psda.org (1)

Sandfort, Gregory A., Tractor Supply Co, Brentwood, TN. Tel: (615) 366-4600, (877) 718-6750, FAX: (615) 227-4608, Web Site: www.mytscstore.com (5)

Sandgeroth, Mike, Baldwin Filters, Kearney, NE. Tel: (308) 234-1951, (800) 822-5394, FAX: (800) 828-4453, E-Mail: info@baldwinfilter.com, Web Site: www.baldwinfilter.com (16)

Sandhu, Kevin, Sales Portal, Mountain View, CA. Tel: (800) 634-3474, Web Site: www.salesportal.com (30)

Sandi Brown Marketing, Saint Petersburg, FL. Tel: (727) 528-6980, FAX: (703) 960-4492 (35)

Sandin, Lennart, Nowell's Inc, San Rafael, CA. Tel: (415) 332-4933, E-Mail: contact@nowellslighting.com, Web Site: www.nowellslighting.com (8)

Sandler Techworks, New York, NY. Tel: (917) 697-9678, Web Site: www.sandlertechworks.com (20)

Sandler, David, MSC Industrial Supply Co, Melville, NY. Tel: (516) 812-2000, (800) 645-7270, FAX: (800) 255-5067, E-Mail: executive@mscdirect.com, Web Site: www.mscdirect.com (9)

Sandler, Marvin, Independent Living Aids, Buffalo, NY. Tel: (516) 450-3829, (800) 537-2118, FAX: (516) 937-3906, E-Mail: techsupport@independentliving.com, Web Site: www.independentliving.com (7)

Sandler, Robert M., 21st Century Insurance, Woodland Hills, CA. Tel: (818) 704-3700, FAX: (818) 226-1198, E-Mail: executiveoffice@21st.com, Web Site: www.21st.com (15)

Sandman, Elizabeth, Tristar Products, Fairfield, NJ. Tel: (973) 575-5400, FAX: (973) 683-6708, E-Mail: infotp@tristarproductsinc.com, Web Site: www.tristarproductsinc.com (16)

Sando, Barry, CoreLogic Inc, Irvine, CA. Tel: (949) 214-1000, (800) 426-1466, Web Site: www.corelogic.com (22)

Sandonato, Dan, JLG Industries Inc, McConnellsburg, PA. Tel: (717) 485-5161, (877) JLG-SELL, FAX: (717) 485-6417, E-Mail: comments@jlg.com, Web Site: www.jlg.com (16)

Sands, David T., Toland Home and Garden Inc, Port Townsend, WA. Tel: (504) 893-9503, (800) 989-6287, E-Mail: info@tolandhomeandgarden.com, Web Site: www.tolandhomeandgarden.com (16)

Sands, Jill, Toland Home and Garden Inc, Port Town-send, WA. Tel: (504) 893-9503, (800) 989-6287, E-Mail: info@tolandhomeandgarden.com, Web Site: www.tolandhomeandgarden.com (16)

Sandy Alexander Inc, Clifton, NJ. Tel: (973) 470-8100, FAX: (973) 470-9269, E-Mail: sandy@sandyinc. com, Web Site: www.sandyinc.com (32)

Sandy Corp, Troy, MI. Tel: (800) 733-4739, FAX: (248) 729-4701, E-Mail: info@sandycorp.com, Web Site: www.sandycorp.com (16)

Sandy Goldshein Associates Inc, New York, NY. Tel: (212) 366-5105, E-Mail: info@sgany.com, Web Site: www.sgany.com (35)

Sandy Mush Herb Nursery, Leicester, NC. Tel: (828) 683-2014, E-Mail: info@sandymushherbs.com, Web Site: www.sandymushherbs.com (8)

Sanek, Larry, Agile Education Marketing LLC, Denver, CO. Tel: (866) 783-0241, E-Mail: info@agile-ed. com, Web Site: www.agile-ed.com (24)

Sanfilippo, Tony, Pennsylvania State University Press, University Park, PA. Tel: (814) 865-1327, (800) 326-9180, FAX: (814) 863-1408, Web Site: www. psupress.org (17)

Sanford, W. Scott, KCET, Burbank, CA. Tel: (747) 201-5000, FAX: (747) 201-5877, E-Mail: contact@ kcet.org, Web Site: www.kcet.org (1)

Sanford, William, JA Sexauer, Elmsford, NY. Tel: (914) 472-7501, (800) 431-1872, FAX: (914) 472-5834, Web Site: www.jasmro.com (16)

Sangerman, Richard, More Media Direct Inc, Marina Del Rey, CA. Tel: (310) 577-2025, E-Mail: info@ moremediadirect.com, Web Site: www. moremediadirect.com (35)

Sangha, Pav, Odenza Marketing Group, San Diego, CA. Tel: (866) 883-2968, Web Site: www.odenza.com (20)

Sangha, Pav, Odenza Marketing Group Inc, Burnaby, BC Canada. Tel: (800) 515-5371, Web Site: www. odenza.com (35)

Sanheim, John, Wm K Walthers Inc, Milwaukee, WI. Tel: (414) 527-0770, (800) 487-2467, FAX: (414) 527-4423, Web Site: www.walthers.com (11)

Sani Serv, Mooresville, IN. Tel: (317) 831-7030, FAX: (317) 381-7036, Web Site: www.saniserv.com (16)

Sank, David, Oneida Ltd, Oneida, NY. Tel: (315) 361-3000, (888) 263-7195, FAX: (315) 361-3700, Web Site: www.oneida.com (16)

Sanky Communications Inc, New York, NY. Tel: (212) 868-4300, Web Site: www.sankyinc.com (1)

Sano, Shigeru, Fujifilm Holdings America Corp, Valhal-la, NY. Tel: (914) 789-8100, (800) 755-3854, FAX: (914) 789-8295, Web Site: www.fujifilmusa.com (16)

Sansone, Daniel F., Vulcan Materials Co, Birmingham, AL. Tel: (205) 298-3000, FAX: (205) 298-2960, Web Site: www.vulcanmaterials.com (16)

Sant, Victoria P., National Gallery of Art Gift Shop, Washington, DC. Tel: (202) 842-6466, (800) 697-9350, FAX: (202) 842-4043, Web Site: www.nga. gov (16)

Santa Barbara Greenhouses, Oxnard, CA. Tel: (800) 544-5276, E-Mail: robsbg@aol.com, Web Site: www.sbgreenhouse.com (8)

Santa Fe Natural Tobacco Co, Santa Fe, NM. Tel: (505) 982-4257, Web Site: www.nascigs.com (16)

Santa Fe School of Cooking, Santa Fe, NM. Tel: (505) 983-4511, (800) 982-4688, FAX: (505) 983-7540, Web Site: www.santafeschoolofcooking.com (4)

Santaniello, Becky, Infinite Media Concepts Inc, White Plains, NY. Tel: (914) 948-8300, FAX: (914) 949-1605, Web Site: mailinglists.com (23)

Santiago, Estela, ProLogic Retail Services, Delray Beach, FL. E-Mail: info@prologicretail.com, Web Site: www.prologicretail.com (35)

Santiago, Noel, Herbert L Jamison & Co LLC, West Or-ange, NJ. Tel: (973) 731-0806, (800) 526-4766, (800) JAMISON, FAX: (973) 731-3035, Web Site: www.jamisongroup.com (15)

Santini, Joe, Barcoding Inc, Baltimore, MD. Tel: (410) 385-8532, (888) 860-SCAN, (888) 860-7226, FAX: (410) 385-8559, E-Mail: info@barcoding.com, Web Site: www.barcoding.com (22)

Santoli, Joseph, Physicians Planning Association Serv-ices, Deerfield Beach, FL. Tel: (954) 571-1877, (800) 221-2168, FAX: (954) 571-8582, E-Mail: insurance@assnservices.com, Web Site: www. physiciansplanning.com (16)

Santomassimo, Adele, Parise Marketing Group, Mill-wood, NY. Tel: (914) 941-7467, FAX: (914) 941-7931, Web Site: www.parise.com (35)

Santoro, P.J., Nike Inc, Beaverton, OR. Tel: (503) 671-4565, (800) 344-6543, FAX: (503) 671-6300, Web Site: www.nike.com (2)

Santos, Begona Vazquez, The Nature Conservancy, Ar-lington, VA. Tel: (703) 841-5300, (800) 628-6860, FAX: (703) 841-1283, Web Site: www.nature.org (1)

Santos, Melissa, Rose Displays Ltd, Salem, MA. Tel: (978) 219-8100, Web Site: www.rosedisplays.com (16)

Santrella, Dave, Salem Media Group, Camarillo, CA. Tel: (804) 987-0400, E-Mail: info@salem.cc, Web Site: salemmedia.com (17)

Santucci, Anthony P., Weingeroff Enterprises Inc, Cran-ston, RI. Tel: (401) 467-2200, FAX: (401) 785-1320, Web Site: www.weingeroff.com (16)

Sapp, Dien, Aegon Direct Marketing Services Inc, Balti-more, MD. Tel: (410) 209-5617, FAX: (410) 209-5932, Web Site: www.aegondms.com (15)

Sapp, Ellen, Tinsley Tool Supply Inc, Powell, TN. Tel: (865) 681-9633, FAX: (865) 982-1655, E-Mail: gene@tinsleytool.com, Web Site: www.tinsleytool. com (9)

Sapp, Gene, Tinsley Tool Supply Inc, Powell, TN. Tel: (865) 681-9633, FAX: (865) 982-1655, E-Mail: gene@tinsleytool.com, Web Site: www.tinsleytool. com (9)

Sapp, Michael, Tinsley Tool Supply Inc, Powell, TN. Tel: (865) 681-9633, FAX: (865) 982-1655, E-Mail: gene@tinsleytool.com, Web Site: www.tinsleytool. com (9)

Sappi Fine Paper North America, Boston, MA. Tel: (617) 423-7300, FAX: (617) 423-5494, Web Site: www.sappi.com (25)

Sara Lee Direct Home Shopping, Winston-Salem, NC. Tel: (336) 519-4400, (800) 671-5056, E-Mail: ohp. manager@onehanesplace.com, Web Site: www. onehanesplace.com (2)

Saracco, Thomas, Direct Access Marketing Services Inc, Syosset, NY. Tel: (516) 364-2777, FAX: (516) 364-0644, E-Mail: info@daxcess.com, Web Site: www.daxcess.com (22)

Saracino, Joan, The Philadelphia Contributorship Insur-ance Co, Philadelphia, PA. Tel: (215) 627-1752, (800) 346-9229, E-Mail: info@contributorship.com, Web Site: www.contributorship.com (15)

Saraf, Shevach, Solitron Devices Inc, West Palm Beach, FL. Tel: (561) 848-4311, FAX: (561) 863-5946, E-Mail: sales@solitrondevices.com, Web Site: www.solitrondevices.com (16)

Sarah Putnam, Cambridge, MA. Tel: (617) 547-3758, E-Mail: sarah@sarahputnam.com, Web Site: www. sarahputnam.com (37)

Sargeant House Design Studio, Westchester, PA. Tel: (610) 399-1983, E-Mail: sargeant house @verizon. net, Web Site: www.sargeanthouse.com (36)

Sargeant, Julie, Mac Pac Inc, Pembroke, MA. Tel: (781) 826-6900, FAX: (781) 826-6880, E-Mail: jsargeant@macpacinc.com, Web Site: www. macpacinc.com (26)

Sargent, Grant, Publications International Ltd, Lincoln-wood, IL. Tel: (847) 676-3470, (800) 595-8484, FAX: (847) 676-3671, Web Site: www.pubint.com (17)

Sargent, Ronald L, Staples Inc, Framingham, MA. Tel: (508) 253-5000, FAX: (508) 253-7803, Web Site: www.staples.com (10)

Sargent, Ronald L., Staples Business Advantage, Atlan-ta, GA. Tel: (770) 997-2512, (877) 826-7754, FAX: (888) 387-9592, Web Site: www.staples.com (34)

Sarka, Pat, Educational Insights, Inc, Gardena, CA. Tel: (310) 884-2000, (888) 591-9334, FAX: (310) 886-8850, E-Mail: service@edin.com, Web Site: www. educationalinsights.com (16)

Sarkis, Gustavo, Crispin Porter + Bogusky, Miami, FL. Tel: (305) 859-2070, FAX: (305) 854-3419, E-Mail: info@cpbgroup.com, Web Site: www.cpbgroup.com (35)

Sarli, Rick, Macromark Inc, Danbury, CT. Tel: (845) 230-6300, FAX: (845) 278-0650, E-Mail: sales@ macromark.com, Web Site: www.macromark.com (23)

Sarma, Pat, American Megatrends Inc, Norcross, GA. Tel: (770) 246-8600, (800) 828-9264, FAX: (770) 246-8790, Web Site: www.ami.com (3)

Sarnaaik, Annand, Decision One, Devon, PA. Tel: (610) 296-6000, (800) 767-2876, FAX: (610) 296-2910, Web Site: www.decisionone.com (34)

Sarne, Chris, CommercialWare Inc, Natick, MA. Tel: (508) 655-7500, FAX: (508) 647-9495, Web Site: www.commercialware.com (22)

Sarnoff, Ann, BBC Worldwide Americas Inc, New York, NY. Tel: (212) 705-9300, (800) 898-4921, FAX: (212) 888-0576, Web Site: www.bbcamerica. com (3)

Sarnow, Greg, Direct Response Academy, Austin, TX. Tel: (512) 301-5900, FAX: (512) 301-7900, Web Site: www.directresponseacademy.com (41)

Sartorius, Rick, Fisher Group Inc, Hiawatha, IA. Tel: (319) 393-5405, FAX: (319) 393-2738, E-Mail: info@fishergroup.com, Web Site: www.fishergroup. com (27)

Sasinski, Karen, Interstate Printing Co, Omaha, NE. Tel: (402) 341-8028, (800) 788-4177, FAX: (402) 341-6168, E-Mail: printer@interstateprinting.com, Web Site: www.interstateprinting.com (27)

Saski, Joseph, Sancoa International LP, Lumberton, NJ. Tel: (856) 273-0700, FAX: (856) 273-2710, E-Mail: sancoa@sancoa.com, Web Site: sancoa.com (31)

SA-SO/Time Wise, Arlington, TX. Tel: (972) 641-4911, (800) 523-8060, FAX: (972) 660-5684, E-Mail: info@sa-so.com, Web Site: www.sa-so.com (33)

Sass, Anita, US Monitor, New City, NY. Tel: (845) 634-1331, (800) 767-7967, FAX: (845) 634-9618, E-Mail: info@usmonitor.com, Web Site: www. usmonitor.com (28)

Sass, Brian, Champion Printing Inc, Cincinnati, OH. Tel: (513) 541-1100, (800) 543-1957, FAX: (513) 541-9398, E-Mail: cpi@championprintinginc.com, Web Site: www.championprintinginc.com (27)

Sass, Brian, Double Envelope, Gainesville, FL. Tel: (800) 543-5275, Web Site: www.double-envelope. com (26)

Sassano, Carl E., Transcat, Rochester, NY. Tel: (585) 352-9460, (800) 800-5001, FAX: (585) 352-1486, Web Site: www.transcat.com (16)

Sastra, Mike, Audio Classics Ltd, Vestal, NY. Tel: (607) 766-3501, FAX: (607) 766-3502, E-Mail: steve@audioclassics.com, Web Site: www.audioclassics.com (3)

Satell, Ed, Progressive Business Publications, Malvern, PA. Tel: (610) 695-8600, (800) 220-5000, FAX: (610) 647-8089, E-Mail: customer_service@pbp.com, Web Site: www.pbp.com (17)

Satisfaction Software Inc, Jamaica, NY. Tel: (732) 382-8736, FAX: (732) 382-8736, E-Mail: db@biink.com (20)

Satori Software Inc, Seattle, WA. Tel: (206) 357-2900, (800) 553-6477, FAX: (206) 357-2901, E-Mail: sales@satorisoftware.com, Web Site: www.satorisoftware.com (16)

Satran, Fritz, AESU Inc, Baltimore, MD. Tel: (410) 366-5494, (800) 638-7640, FAX: (410) 366-6999, E-Mail: res@aesu.com, Web Site: www.aesu.com (19)

Satran, Lisabeth, AESU Inc, Baltimore, MD. Tel: (410) 366-5494, (800) 638-7640, FAX: (410) 366-6999, E-Mail: res@aesu.com, Web Site: www.aesu.com (19)

Satren, Beth. AESU Inc, Baltimore, MD. Tel: (410) 366-5494, (800) 638-7640, FAX: (410) 366-6999, E-Mail: res@aesu.com, Web Site: www.aesu.com (19)

Satriano, Pietro, US Foodservice, Rosemont, IL. Tel: (847) 720-8000, FAX: (847) 720-8099, Web Site: www.usfoodservice.com (4)

Saturn Corp, Hyattsville, MD. Tel: (301) 772-7000, (800) USA-0090, FAX: (301) 386-4538, E-Mail: sales@saturncorp.com, Web Site: www.saturncorp.com (22)

Sauerberg, Robert, Conde Nast, New York, NY. Tel: (212) 286-2860, FAX: (212) 880-8289, Web Site: www.condenast.com (17)

Sauers Group, Inc, Stone Mountain, GA. Tel: (770) 621-8888, (866) 458-5212, FAX: (770) 621-8866, E-Mail: info@sauersgroup.com, Web Site: www.sauersgroup.com (27)

Sauers, Richard S., Sauers Group, Inc, Stone Mountain, GA. Tel: (770) 621-8888, (866) 458-5212, FAX: (770) 621-8866, E-Mail: info@sauersgroup.com, Web Site: www.sauersgroup.com (27)

Saul, George, Fosina Marketing Group Inc, Danbury, CT. Tel: (203) 790-0013, E-Mail: info@fosinamarketing.com, Web Site: fosinamarketinggroup.com (35)

Saul, George, Scholastic Direct Mktg, Danbury, CT. Tel: (203) 797-3500, FAX: (203) 797-3667 (29)

Saulsberry, Vanessa, 1to1 Media, Stamford, CT. Tel: (203) 989-2200, Web Site: www.1to1media.com (35)

Saunders Manufacturing Co Inc, Readfield, ME. Tel: (207) 685-3385, (800) 341-4674, FAX: (207) 685-9918, E-Mail: jsherwood@saunders-usa.com, Web Site: www.saunders-usa.com (16)

Saunders Military Insignia, Naples, FL. Tel: (239) 298-8228, (800) 442-3133, FAX: (239) 774-3323, E-Mail: info@saundersinsignia.com, Web Site: www.saundersinsignia.com (6)

Richard Saunders International, Cincinnati, OH. Tel: (513) 271-9911, FAX: (513) 271-9966, E-Mail: doug@eurekaranch.com, Web Site: www.eurekaranch.com (20)

Saunders, Dr. Kenneth, Nassau Community College, Garden City, NY. Tel: (516) 572-7501, FAX: (516) 572-7497, E-Mail: marketing-communications@ncc.edu, Web Site: www.ncc.edu (41)

Saunders, Rick, Orchard Supply Hardware, San Jose, CA. Tel: (408) 281-3500, FAX: (408) 225-0388, Web Site: www.osh.com (16)

Saunders, Thomas, Western Pennsylvania Conservancy, Pittsburgh, PA. Tel: (412) 288-2777, (866) 564-6972, FAX: (412) 231-1414, E-Mail: info@paconserve.org, Web Site: www.paconserve.org (1)

The Sausage Maker Inc, Buffalo, NY. Tel: (716) 824-5814, (888) 490-8525, FAX: (716) 824-6465, E-Mail: customerservice@sausagemaker.com, Web Site: www.sausagemaker.com (4)

The Sausalito Group, Sausalito, CA. Tel: (415) 332-3333, FAX: (415) 332-6571, Web Site: www.sausolitogroup.com (30)

Sauser, Todd, Nilodor Inc, Bolivar, OH. Tel: (330) 874-1017, (800) 443-4321, FAX: (330) 874-3366, E-Mail: info@nilodor.com, Web Site: www.nilodor.com (16)

Sausto, Joanne, David Geller Associates, New York, NY. Tel: (212) 455-0100, FAX: (212) 455-0164 (31)

Sauter, Richard, IPacesetters, Montvale, NJ. Tel: (201) 391-1500, FAX: (201) 391-8357, Web Site: www.ipacesetters.com (22)

Sautter, Elise, New Mexico State University, Las Cruces, NM. Tel: (505) 646-3341, (575) 646-0111, FAX: (505) 646-1498, Web Site: www.nmsu.edu (41)

Savage, Ed, Sacred Heart League, Walls, MS. Tel: (662) 781-1360, (800) 232-9079, FAX: (662) 781-3340, E-Mail: comments@shl.org, Web Site: www.shl.org (28)

Savasta, Bob, Spectronics Corp, Westbury, NY. Tel: (516) 333-4840, (800) 274-8888, FAX: (800) 491-6868, E-Mail: vscherer@spectroline.com, Web Site: www.spectroline.com (9)

Save the Children Federation Inc, Fairfield, CT. Tel: (203) 221-4000, (800) 728-3843, FAX: (203) 222-1067, E-Mail: majorgivng@savethechildren.org, Web Site: www.savethechildren.org (1)

Savein, R, Ventriloquist Voice Solutions International Inc, Mississauga, ON Canada. Tel: (866) 446-0860, E-Mail: info@ventriloquistsolutions.com, Web Site: www.ventriloquistsolutions.com (29)

Savicom, San Francisco, CA. Tel: (415) 983-0990, FAX: (415) 445-9999, E-Mail: sales@savicom.net, Web Site: www.savicom.net (22)

Savig, Patricia, Taylor Corp, North Mankato, MN. Tel: (507) 625-2828, FAX: (507) 625-3388 (16)

Savignano, Fae, Marden-Kane Inc, Woodbury, NY. Tel: (516) 365-3999, FAX: (516) 365-5250, E-Mail: expert@mardenkane.com, Web Site: www.mardenkane.com (35)

Savings Bank Life Insurance Co of MA (SBLI), Woburn, MA. Tel: (781) 938-3500, Web Site: www.sbli.com (15)

Savio, Tom, CSE Inc, New Berlin, WI. Tel: (262) 786-8400, (800) 999-0001, FAX: (262) 796-2089, E-Mail: info@csepromo.com, Web Site: www.topideas.cseideas.com (33)

Saviski, Mark, Stock Yards Packing Co Inc, Medford, OR. Tel: (312) 733-6050, (888) 842-6111, FAX: (888) 700-9919, E-Mail: customerservice@stockyards.com, Web Site: www.stockyards.com (4)

Savitt, Kathy, Yahoo! Inc, Sunnyvale, CA. Tel: (408) 349-3300, Web Site: www.yahoo.com (32)

Savitz, Dallas, TX. Tel: (310) 642-4799, FAX: (310) 642-7795, E-Mail: lmoran@savitzfieldandfocus.com, Web Site: www.savitzfieldandfocus.com (20)

Savoff, Mark T., Entergy, New Orleans, LA. Tel: (504) 576-4000, (800) ENTERGY, FAX: (504) 576-4428, Web Site: www.entergy.com (16)

Savoni, Charles F., Artemis International Solutions Corp, Austin, TX. Tel: (512) 201-8222, FAX: (512) 874-8900, Web Site: www.aisc.com (22)

Savoy, Mark, First National Information Network, Burbank, CA. Tel: (855) 909-6800, (800) 562-1999, FAX: (818) 558-6663, E-Mail: info@fnin.com, Web Site: www.fnin.com (30)

Savvis Inc, Town and Country, MO. Tel: (314) 628-7000, (800) 728-8471, FAX: (703) 667-6298 (22)

Sawchuck, Arthur R., John Hancock Financial Services Inc, Boston, MA. Tel: (617) 572-6000, (800) 732-5543, FAX: (617) 572-6451, Web Site: www.johnhancock.com (15)

Sawicki, Craig, Tricor Braun, Woodridge, IL. Tel: (708) 385-9333, FAX: (708) 385-3015, Web Site: www.tricorbraun.com (16)

Sawtooth Group, Red Bank, NJ. Tel: (732) 945-1004, Web Site: www.sawtoothgroup.com (35)

Sawyer-Lueck, Jessica, Silliker Inc, Chicago, IL. Tel: (708) 957-7878, FAX: (708) 957-3798, E-Mail: cjx@netcom.com, Web Site: www.silliker.com (20)

Sax Arts & Crafts, Appleton, WI. Tel: (800) 558-6696, FAX: (800) 328-4729, E-Mail: info@saxarts.com, Web Site: www.saxarts.com (10)

Sax, Pearl, Checks by Phone/Checks by Web, Boynton Beach, FL. Tel: (561) 737-8700, FAX: (561) 737-5800, E-Mail: LarrySchwartz@checksbyphone.com, Web Site: www.checksbyphone.com (14)

Sax, Pearl, Fraud & Theft Information Bureau, Boynton Beach, FL. Tel: (561) 737-8700, FAX: (561) 737-5800, E-Mail: sales@fraudandtheft.com, Web Site: www.fraudandtheftinfo.com (43)

Saxberg, Bror, Kaplan Inc, Fort Lauderdale, FL. Tel: (954) 515-3993, Web Site: www.kaplan.com (16)

Saya, Sr. Wayne P., Association for Facilities Engineering, McLean, VA. Tel: (571) 203-7171, FAX: (571) 766-2142, E-Mail: info@afe.org, Web Site: www.afe.org (1)

Sayre, Bill, Merkle Inc, Columbia, MD. Tel: (443) 542-4000, (877) 9MERKLE, FAX: (443) 542-4758, Web Site: www.merkleinc.com (22)

Sbragia. Jessica, ReMark USA, Minnetonka, MN. Tel: (952) 938-4699, FAX: (952) 988-8500, E-Mail: jessica.sbragia@remarkgroup.com, Web Site: www.remarkamericas.com (15)

Scalercio, Alaina, ASM Press, Washington, DC. Tel: (202) 737-3600, (800) 546-2416, FAX: (202) 942-9342, E-Mail: books@asmusa.org, Web Site: www.asmpress.org (17)

The Scan Group Inc, Waukesha, WI. Tel: (262) 521-1365, FAX: (262) 521-3265, Web Site: www.scangroup.net (35)

Scan Optics Inc, Manchester, CT. Tel: (860) 645-7878, (800) 745-6001, FAX: (860) 645-7995, E-Mail: info@scanoptics.com, Web Site: www.scanoptics.com (16)

Scanlan, T.C., Surplus Record, Chicago, IL. Tel: (312) 372-9077, (800) 622-5449, FAX: (312) 372-6537, E-Mail: surplus@surplusrecord.com, Web Site: www.surplusrecord.com (17)

Scanlon, Brian, Thieme Medical Publishers Inc, New York, NY. Tel: (212) 760-0888, (800) 782-3488, FAX: (212) 947-1112, E-Mail: info@thieme.com, Web Site: www.thieme.com (17)

Scanlon, Richard, Pensions & Investments, New York, NY. Tel: (212) 210-0100, FAX: (212) 210-0117, Web Site: www.pionline.com (17)

Scannell, Herb, BBC Worldwide Americas Inc, New York, NY. Tel: (212) 705-9300, (800) 898-4921, FAX: (212) 888-0576, Web Site: www.bbcamerica. com (3)

Scapperotti, Sherry, PlusMedia LLC, Danbury, CT. Tel: (203) 748-6500, FAX: (203) 748-6600, E-Mail: contact@plusme.com, Web Site: www.plusme.com (35)

Scarafile, Andrew J., Clemente Novelties Inc, Utica, NY. Tel: (315) 732-4145, FAX: (315) 732-2251, E-Mail: clemente@6org.com (16)

Scarborough, Dean A., Avery Dennison Corp, Brea, CA. Tel: (714) 674-8500, (800) 462-8379, FAX: (714) 674-6929, Web Site: www.avery.com (10)

Scarborough, Scott L., University of Akron, Akron, OH. Tel: (330) 972-7111 (1)

Scardino, Janet, The Wedding Pages, New York, NY. Tel: (212) 219-8555, (800) 843-4983, FAX: (212) 219-1929, Web Site: www.theknot.com (16)

Scarpelli, Guy J., CTC Teleservices, De Kalb, IL. Tel: (815) 748-4200, FAX: (630) 773-4765, Web Site: www.ctcteleservices.com (29)

Scartz, Don T., EMS Technologies, Norcross, GA. Tel: (770) 263-9200, FAX: (770) 447-4405, Web Site: www.ems-t.com (16)

Scenic Photo!, Minneapolis, MN. Tel: (612) 810-0797, E-Mail: manager@scenicphoto.com, Web Site: www.scenicphoto.com (38)

Schachte, Bob, Mitchell International, San Diego, CA. Tel: (858) 368-7000, FAX: (858) 238-9111, Web Site: www.mitchell.com (17)

Schaefer, Deborah, ABR Employment Services, Madison, WI. Tel: (608) 244-3526, FAX: (608) 244-8279, E-Mail: info@abrjobs.com, Web Site: www.abrjobs.com (22)

Schaefer, Greg, NCC Media, New York, NY. Tel: (212) 548-3300, FAX: (212) 519-0099, Web Site: nccmedia.com (32)

Schaefer, Jr George A., Fifth Third Bank, Cincinnati, OH. Tel: (800) 972-3030, FAX: (231) 922-4060, Web Site: www.53.com (14)

Schaefer, Rita, McDougal Littell, Evanston, IL. Tel: (847) 869-2300, FAX: (847) 869-0841, Web Site: www.mcdougallittell.com (17)

Schaefer, Tracy, Abbey Press, Saint Meinrad, IN. Tel: (812) 357-8368, FAX: (812) 357-8388, Web Site: www.abbeypress.com (6)

Schaeffer, Anne A., Interactive Marketing Institute, Richmond, VA. Tel: (800) 925-5308, Web Site: www.imi.vcu.edu (41)

Schaeffer, Anne, Grey Birch Group LLC, Irvington, NY. Tel: (914) 479-5088, Web Site: www.greybirch.com (20)

Schaeffer, John, Gaiam Inc, Boulder, CO. Tel: (877) 989-6321, Web Site: life.gaiam.com (9)

Schaeffer, John, Real Goods Trading Corp, Hopland, CA. Tel: (707) 472-2403, (888) 919-2400, FAX: (707) 472-2430, Web Site: www.realgoods.com (5)

Schaeffer, Sandor, Andell Packaging Corp, Manhasset, NY. Tel: (718) 937-6500, FAX: (718) 482-9416 (27)

Schaeffer, Susannah, The Smile Train, New York, NY. Tel: (212) 689-9199, (800) 932-9541, E-Mail: info@smiletrain.org, Web Site: www.smiletrain.org (1)

Schaenzer, Chris, Wm K Walthers Inc, Milwaukee, WI. Tel: (414) 527-0770, (800) 487-2467, FAX: (414) 527-4423, Web Site: www.walthers.com (11)

Schafer, Bernard J., DirecTech Holding Company Inc, Maysville, KY. Tel: (866) 550-5030, E-Mail: ceo@directech.com, Web Site: www.directech.com (22)

Schafer, Charlie, Agri Drain Corp, Adair, IA. Tel: (641) 742-5211, (800) 232-4742, FAX: (800) 282-3353, (641) 742-5222, E-Mail: info@agridrain.com, Web Site: www.agridrain.com (9)

Schaffer, Eric, CCL Label, Cold Spring, KY. Tel: (859) 781-6161, (800) 422-6633, FAX: (859) 781-6339 (27)

Schaffer, John, American Automobile Association, Heathrow, FL. Tel: (407) 444-8000, Web Site: www.aaa.com (16)

Schaffer, Russell, Kaplan Test Prep, New York, NY. Tel: (212) 997-5800, Web Site: www.kaptest.com (1)

Schaffer, Stewart, Lazydays RV Center, Seffner, FL. Tel: (813) 246-4333, FAX: (813) 246-4408, Web Site: www.lazydays.com (12)

Schaffrath, Susan, McDougal Littell, Evanston, IL. Tel: (847) 869-2300, FAX: (847) 869-0841, Web Site: www.mcdougallittell.com (17)

Schaldenbrand, C.L., Resumate Inc, Ann Arbor, MI. Tel: (734) 429-8510, E-Mail: info@resumate.com, Web Site: www.resumate.com (21)

Schalle, Bonnie, E&M Media Group Inc, New York, NY. Tel: (212) 455-0177, FAX: (212) 455-0176, Web Site: www.emtvsales.com (35)

Schanen, III William F., Wind in the Rigging, Port Washington, WI. Tel: (262) 284-3494, (800) 236-7444, FAX: (262) 284-0067, E-Mail: info@windintherigging.com, Web Site: www.windintherigging.com (11)

Schanen, Jean, Wind in the Rigging, Port Washington, WI. Tel: (262) 284-3494, (800) 236-7444, FAX: (262) 284-0067, E-Mail: info@windintherigging.com, Web Site: www.windintherigging.com (11)

Schang, Scott, Environmental Law Institute, Washington, DC. Tel: (202) 939-3800, FAX: (202) 939-3868, E-Mail: law@eli.org, Web Site: www.eli.org (17)

Schapiro, Jeff, CSI, Conklin, NY. Tel: (607) 775-7905, Web Site: www.cleanersupply.com (16)

Schapiro, Morton, Northwestern University, Evanston, IL. Tel: (847) 491-5665, FAX: (847) 491-5925, E-Mail: jimc@northwestern.edu, Web Site: www.northwestern.edu (41)

Schatz, Thomas A., Citizens Against Government Waste, Washington, DC. Tel: (202) 467-5300, (800) USA-DEBT, FAX: (202) 467-4253, E-Mail: membership@cagw.org, Web Site: www.cagw.org (1)

Schatzel, Kim, Eastern Michigan University, Ypsilanti, MI. Tel: (734) 487-1849, FAX: (734) 484-1151, Web Site: www.emich.edu (16)

Schauble, Julie, KPBS FM/TV, San Diego, CA. Tel: (619) 594-1515, Web Site: www.kpbs.org (1)

Schaus, Cynthia M., ING USA Annuity & Life Ins Co, Des Moines, IA. Tel: (515) 698-7100, FAX: (515) 698-2001, Web Site: www.ing-usa.com (15)

Schaus, Sonny, Mountain Media Enterprises, Fort Collins, CO. Tel: (970) 493-2499, FAX: (970) 493-3598, E-Mail: info@mountain-media.com, Web Site: fortcollinsdigitalprinting.com (21)

Schawk Inc, Des Plaines, IL. Tel: (847) 827-8424, Web Site: www.schawk.com (27)

Schawk, David A., Schawk Inc, Des Plaines, IL. Tel: (847) 827-8424, Web Site: www.schawk.com (27)

Schecter, Dan, ER Carpenter, Taylor, TX. Tel: (512) 365-5833, (800) 234-9105, FAX: (512) 352-6025, Web Site: www.carpenter.com (16)

Schecterson, Jack, Jack Schecterson visualmarketing Consultants, Little Neck, NY. Tel: (718) 225-3536 (20)

Scheevel, Michael, MultiView, Irving, TX. Tel: (972) 402-7056 (1)

Scheffer, Sarah, Reliable Technologies Inc, Manchester, NH. Tel: (603) 644-2528, (800) 346-7890, FAX: (603) 627-5553, Web Site: www.tei-imaging.com (16)

Scheffers, Todd, Goodheart-Willcox Publisher, Tinley Park, IL. Tel: (708) 687-5000, (800) 323-0440, FAX: (708) 687-0315, E-Mail: custserv@g-w.com, Web Site: www.g-w.com (17)

Scheibemantel, Peter, Issues & Answers Network Inc, Virginia Beach, VA. Tel: (757) 456-1100, FAX: (757) 456-0377, E-Mail: info@issans.com, Web Site: www.issans.com (30)

Scheider, Mark, Edward Don & Co, Woodridge, IL. Tel: (708) 442-9400, (800) 777-4366, FAX: (708) 442-0436, Web Site: www.don.com (16)

Henry Schein Inc, Melville, NY. Tel: (631) 843-5500, (800) 472-4346, FAX: (631) 843-5658, E-Mail: custserv@henryschein.com, Web Site: www.henryschein.com (16)

Schell, Ernest H., Marketing Systems Analysis, Ventnor, NJ. Tel: (609) 487-9340, FAX: (866) 214-3208, E-Mail: ernie@schell.com, Web Site: www.schell.com (20)

Schell, John, Easthill Group Inc, Pottstown, PA. Tel: (610) 323-9063, (610) 323-9099, (610) 323-2200, (800) 345-1178, (888) 869-4433, FAX: (610) 323-6268, Web Site: www.eastwoodcompany.com (12)

Schell, Mark, Valdawn Watch Co, Long Island City, NY. Tel: (201) 807-1110, FAX: (201) 807-0228 (16)

Scheller, Tom, Bathroom Machineries, Murphys, CA. Tel: (209) 728-2031, (800) 255-4426, FAX: (209) 728-2320, Web Site: www.deabath.com (8)

Schember, Jack, SK&A, Irvine, CA. Tel: (800) 752-5478, FAX: (949) 476-9131, E-Mail: skasales@skainfo.com, Web Site: www.skainfo.com (23)

Schena, Robert, Rajant Corp, Malvern, PA. Tel: (484) 595-0233, FAX: (484) 595-0244, E-Mail: support@rajant.com, Web Site: www.rajant.com (32)

Schencker, Sylvia, The Miami Herald Media Co, Miami, FL. Tel: (305) 350-2111 (17)

Schenk, Matthew, HSP Direct, Ashburn, VA. Tel: (703) 793-3220, FAX: (703) 723-5405, E-Mail: info@hspdirect.com, Web Site: www.hspdirect.com (1)

Schenk, Theresa, HighScope Educational Research Foundation, Ypsilanti, MI. Tel: (800) 587-5639, FAX: (734) 485-0704, E-Mail: info@highscope.org, Web Site: www.highscope.org (17)

Schenk, Walter D., CDI Network Inc, Naperville, IL. Tel: (708) 409-8585, FAX: (708) 409-8589, Web Site: www.cdinet.biz (27)

Schenkel, Scott, eBay Inc, San Jose, CA. Tel: (408) 376-7400, (800) 322-7400, Web Site: www.ebayinc.com (16)

Schenker, Debra, Anchor Computer Inc, Farmingdale, NY. Tel: (631) 293-6100, FAX: (631) 293-0891, Web Site: www.anchorcomputer.com (22)

Schenker, Len, Anchor Computer Inc, Farmingdale, NY. Tel: (631) 293-6100, FAX: (631) 293-0891, Web Site: www.anchorcomputer.com (22)

Schenker, Mark, Anchor Computer Inc, Farmingdale, NY. Tel: (631) 293-6100, FAX: (631) 293-0891, Web Site: www.anchorcomputer.com (22)

Schepp, Robina, Pace University, New York, NY. Tel: (212) 346-1781, (866) 722-3338, FAX: (212) 346-1821, Web Site: www.pace.edu (16)

Scher, Laura, Working Assets, San Francisco, CA. Tel: (800) 668-9253, FAX: (415) 371-1046, Web Site: www.workingassets.com (16)

Scherer, Bruce, Pinkerton Security & Investigation Services, Parsippany, NJ. Tel: (973) 397-2276, (800) 724-1616, FAX: (973) 397-2491, Web Site: www.ci-pinkerton.com (16)

Scherer, Gary W., Programmers Investment Corp, Arlington Heights, IL. Tel: (224) 265-6000, FAX: (224) 265-6142, E-Mail: pic@pic-online.com, Web Site: www.pic-online.com (21)

Scherer, Jerry D., Blue Cross Blue Shield of Oklahoma, Tulsa, OK. Tel: (918) 560-3500, (800) 942-5837, E-Mail: info@bcbsok.com, Web Site: www.bcbsok.com (15)

Scherer, Valerie, Spectronics Corp, Westbury, NY. Tel: (516) 333-4840, (800) 274-8888, FAX: (800) 491-6868, E-Mail: vscherer@spectroline.com, Web Site: www.spectroline.com (9)

Schermer Pecans, Glennville, GA. Tel: (912) 654-2230, (800) 841-3403, E-Mail: information@schermerpecans.com, Web Site: www.pecantreats.com (4)

Schern, Gregory, Tamrac Inc, Ogden, UT. Tel: (385) 405-2700, E-Mail: info@tamrac.com, Web Site: www.tamrac.com (2)

Scherschel, Dave, Exhibitrac Direct Marketing, Las Vegas, NV. Tel: (702) 824-9651, (866) 988-6601, FAX: (702) 824-9376, E-Mail: sales@exhibitrac.com, Web Site: www.exhibitrac.com (23)

Schiavone, Raymond, Quark Inc, Denver, CO. Tel: (303) 894-8888, Web Site: www.quark.com (34)

Schiel, Tina, Target Corp, Minneapolis, MN. Tel: (612) 304-6073, Web Site: www.target.com (16)

Schiela, John, Phoenix Marketing International, Warrington, PA. Tel: (215) 392-0264, Web Site: www.phoenixmi.com (30)

Jacques C Schiff Jr Inc, Ridgefield Park, NJ. Tel: (201) 641-5566, FAX: (201) 641-5705 (5)

Schiff Jr, Jacques C., Jacques C Schiff Jr Inc, Ridgefield Park, NJ. Tel: (201) 641-5566, FAX: (201) 641-5705 (5)

Schiffman, Leon, Market Discovery Group, Roslyn, NY. Tel: (516) 365-8555, E-Mail: schiffmanl@aol.com (30)

Schiller, Howard, Hollywood Film Archive, Los Angeles, CA. Tel: (323) 655-4968, Web Site: www.hfarchive.com (17)

Schiller, Philip W., Apple Inc, Cupertino, CA. Tel: (408) 996-1010, FAX: (408) 996-0275, Web Site: www.apple.com (16)

Schimberg, John, The Computer Supply People, Menomonee Falls, WI. Tel: (262) 251-5511, (800) 242-2090, FAX: (262) 251-4737, E-Mail: medmgt@computersupplypeople.com, Web Site: www.computersupplypeople.com (3)

Schimke, David, Mother Earth News Magazine, Topeka, KS. Tel: (785) 274-4300, (800) 678-5779, FAX: (785) 274-4305, E-Mail: bwelch@ogdenpubs.com, Web Site: www.cappers.com (17)

Schimmel, Kurt, West Virginia University, Morgantown, WV. Tel: (304) 293-3505, FAX: (304) 293-3072, E-Mail: wvuwebmaster@mail.wvu.edu, Web Site: www.wvu.edu (41)

Schinco, Jim, Affinitas Corp, Boys Town, NE. Tel: (402) 397-7077, (800) 369-6495, FAX: (402) 397-7576, Web Site: www.affinitas.net (29)

Schipp, Norma, Abbey Press, Saint Meinrad, IN. Tel: (812) 357-8368, FAX: (812) 357-8388, Web Site: www.abbeypress.com (6)

Schlachter, Chris, Touch of Class Catalog, Huntingburg, IN. Tel: (800) 457-7456, FAX: (812) 683-5921, E-Mail: customerservice@touchofclass.com, Web Site: www.touchofclass.com (8)

Schlager, Ken, New Jersey Monthly, Morristown, NJ. Tel: (973) 539-8230, FAX: (973) 538-2953, E-Mail: research@njmonthly.com, Web Site: www.njmonthly.com (17)

Schlegel, Beth, Anheuser-Busch Inc Promotional Products Group, Shelton, CT. Tel: (800) 742-5283, Web Site: www.budshop.com (6)

Schleich, Paul, Taylor Corp, North Mankato, MN. Tel: (507) 625-2828, FAX: (507) 625-3388 (16)

Schleider, Ernie, Audio Classics Ltd, Vestal, NY. Tel: (607) 766-3501, FAX: (607) 766-3502, E-Mail: steve@audioclassics.com, Web Site: www.audioclassics.com (3)

Schleiter, Jim, Vance Industries Inc, Niles, IL. Tel: (847) 375-8900, FAX: (847) 375-6818, E-Mail: vance@vanceind.com, Web Site: www.vanceind.com (16)

Schlerf, Steven G, NEBS, Groton, MA. Tel: (978) 448-6111, (800) 225-6380, (888) 823-6327, FAX: (978) 448-3653, (800) 234-4324, E-Mail: customerservice@nebs.com, Web Site: www.nebs.com (10)

Schlig, Joseph, Solitron Devices Inc, West Palm Beach, FL. Tel: (561) 848-4311, FAX: (561) 863-5946, E-Mail: sales@solitrondevices.com, Web Site: www.solitrondevices.com (16)

Schlig, Sabine, SPSS Inc, Chicago, IL. Tel: (312) 651-3000, (800) 543-2185, FAX: (312) 651-3668, E-Mail: sales@spss.com, Web Site: www.spss.com (22)

Schlossnagle, George, Message Systems, Columbia, MD. Tel: (410) 872-4910, (877) 887-3031, FAX: (410) 872-4912, E-Mail: information@messagesystems.com, Web Site: www.messagesystems.com (32)

Schlumpf, Steve, Haband Co Inc, Oakland, NJ. Tel: (201) 651-1000, FAX: (201) 405-7777, Web Site: www.haband.blair.com (12)

J Schmid & Associates Inc, Mission, KS. Tel: (913) 236-8988, FAX: (913) 236-8987, E-Mail: info@jschmid.com, Web Site: www.jschmid.com (20)

Schmid, Barbara, Terumo Cardiovascular Systems Corp, Ann Arbor, MI. Tel: (734) 663-4145, (800) 521-2818, Web Site: www.terumo-cvs.com (5)

Schmidt, Byron, MN. Tel: (507) 775-6400, FAX: (507) 775-6655, E-Mail: sls@schmidt.com, Web Site: www.schmidt.com (27)

The Schmidt Group International Inc, Vero Beach, FL. Tel: (772) 492-0073, FAX: (772) 492-0293, E-Mail: catalogprofit@att.net, Web Site: www.the-schmidt-group.com (20)

Schmidt, Andreas, Hanley Wood LLC, Washington, DC. Tel: (202) 452-0800, FAX: (202) 785-1974, Web Site: www.hanleywood.com (16)

Schmidt, Bob, CCI Solutions, Olympia, WA. Tel: (360) 943-5378, (800) 426-8664, FAX: (360) 754-1566, (800) 339-TAPE, E-Mail: info@ccisolutions.com, Web Site: www.ccisolutions.com (16)

Schmidt, Darrell, Cuneo Advertising, Bloomington, MN. Tel: (952) 707-1212, FAX: (952) 707-1295, E-Mail: agency@cuneocom.com, Web Site: cuneocom.com (35)

Schmidt, Eric E., Google Inc, Mountain View, CA. Tel: (650) 253-0000, FAX: (650) 253-0001, Web Site: www.google.com (31)

Schmidt, Herbert, Con-Way Truckload, Joplin, MO. Tel: (417) 623-5229, (800) CFI-DRIVE, FAX: (417) 623-8939, E-Mail: gnichols@cfi-us.com, Web Site: www.cfi-us.com (12)

Schmidt, Jennifer, DunnData Co, Brewster, NY. Tel: (845) 278-1200, Web Site: www.dunndataco.com (23)

Schmidt, Jr. Alfred M., The Schmidt Group International Inc, Vero Beach, FL. Tel: (772) 492-0073, FAX: (772) 492-0293, E-Mail: catalogprofit@att.net, Web Site: www.the-schmidt-group.com (20)

Schmidt, Julie, KET, Lexington, KY. Tel: (859) 258-7000, (800) 432-0951, FAX: (606) 258-7396, E-Mail: rgriffin@ket.org, Web Site: www.ket.org (17)

Schmidt, Kim, Escort Inc, West Chester, OH. Tel: (513) 870-8500, (800) 964-3138, FAX: (513) 870-8509, E-Mail: sales@escortradar.com, Web Site: www.escortradar.com (16)

Schmidt, Kurt T., Gerber Products Co, Florham Park, NJ. Tel: (973) 593-7500, (800) 284-9488, Web Site: www.gerber.com (16)

Schmidt, Liz, Cosco Industries Inc, Chicago, IL. Tel: (708) 867-5800, (800) 323-0253, FAX: (800) 323-0275 (16)

Schmidt, Nathan, Communication Industries Corp, Grafton, VT. Tel: (802) 869-6500, FAX: (802) 869-6565, E-Mail: info@cicmail.com, Web Site: www.careersatcic.com (10)

Schmidt, Stephanie G., Direct Success Communications Inc, Chester Springs, PA. Tel: (610) 321-0321, FAX: (610) 321-0322 (35)

Schmidt, William T., Foundation Fighting Blindness, Columbia, MD. Tel: (410) 423-0600, (800) 683-5555, Web Site: www.fightblindness.org (1)

Schmitt, Geri, Rapids Wholesale Equipment, Marion, IA. Tel: (319) 447-1670, (800) 472-7431, FAX: (319) 447-1680, (800) 858-0327, E-Mail: judys@rapidswholesale.com, Web Site: www.rapidswholesale.com (16)

Schmitt, Jeff L., WS Live LLC, Dubuque, IA. Tel: (563) 582-9501, (800) 582-9501, FAX: (563) 582-2003, Web Site: www.wslive.com (29)

Schmitt, Joe, Rapids Wholesale Equipment, Marion, IA. Tel: (319) 447-1670, (800) 472-7431, FAX: (319) 447-1680, (800) 858-0327, E-Mail: judys@rapidswholesale.com, Web Site: www.rapidswholesale.com (16)

Schmittberger, R. Wayne, Kappa Publishing Group, Blue Bell, PA. Tel: (215) 643-6385, FAX: (215) 628-3571, Web Site: www.kappapublishing.com (17)

Schmitz, Darlene, The Metal Ware Corp, Two Rivers, WI. Tel: (920) 793-1368, (800) 288-4545, FAX: (920) 794-3161, Web Site: www.nesco.com (32)

Schmookler, Alexis, Wordright Enterprises Inc, Buffalo Grove, IL. Tel: (847) 215-5190, Web Site: www.globalsources.com (17)

Schnabel, Bobby, Association for Computing Machinery, New York, NY. Tel: (212) 626-0500, (800) 342-6626, FAX: (212) 944-1318, Web Site: www.acm.org (1)

Schnabel, Jr Robert R., Fitness Quest, Canton, OH. Tel: (330) 478-0755, (800) 321-9236, FAX: (330) 479-9213, E-Mail: customersupport@fitnessquest.com, Web Site: www.fitnessquest.com (16)

Schnabel, Will, SilverPop, Atlanta, GA. Tel: (678) 247-0500, (866) 745-8767, FAX: (678) 247-0501, E-Mail: contactsales@silverpop.com, Web Site: www.silverpop.com (3)

Schnaidman, Mauro, Jafra Cosmetics International Inc, Westlake Village, CA. Tel: (260) 423-9571, (888) 848-4077, FAX: (960) 423-6742, Web Site: www.jafra.com (7)

Schnatter, John H., Papa John's International, Louisville, KY. Tel: (502) 261-7272, Web Site: www.papajohns.com (4)

Schneeberger, Ray, The Direct Marketing Club of New York Inc, Garden City, NY. Tel: (516) 746-6700, FAX: (516) 294-8141, E-Mail: info@dmcny.org, Web Site: www.dmcny.org (1)

Schneider Saddlery, Chagrin Falls, OH. Tel: (440) 543-2700, (800) 365-1311, FAX: (440) 543-2710, Web Site: www.sstack.com (11)

Schneider, Anthony, Mass Transmit, New York, NY. Tel: (646) 797-4349, E-Mail: info@masstransmit.com, Web Site: www.masstransmit.com (32)

Schneider, Donald, Schneider Saddlery, Chagrin Falls, OH. Tel: (440) 543-2700, (800) 365-1311, FAX: (440) 543-2710, Web Site: www.sstack.com (11)

Schneider, Ellen, Active Voice, San Francisco, CA. Tel: (415) 487-2000, FAX: (415) 487-2260, E-Mail: info@activevoice.net, Web Site: www.activevoice.net (21)

Schneider, Mary Lee, Follett School Solutions Inc, McHenry, IL. Tel: (815) 759-1700, (888) 511-5114, FAX: (800) 852-5458, E-Mail: customerservice@follett.com, Web Site: www.flr.follett.com (16)

Schneider, Michael A., Coast to Coast Inc, Englewood, CO. Tel: (303) 728-2267, Web Site: www.coastresorts.com (1)

Schneider, Michael, Haymarket Group Ltd, New York, NY. Tel: (212) 239-0855, FAX: (212) 967-4184, Web Site: www.chocalatiermagazine.com (17)

Schneider, Paul, Warnaco Swimwear Inc, Los Angeles, CA. Tel: (323) 726-1262, FAX: (323) 724-6931, Web Site: www.speedo.com (16)

Schneider, Robert, Sweet Tooth Candies, Newport, KY. Tel: (859) 581-4663, (877) 581-5132, FAX: (859) 581-1979 (4)

Schneider, Stan, Schneider Saddlery, Chagrin Falls, OH. Tel: (440) 543-2700, (800) 365-1311, FAX: (440) 543-2710, Web Site: www.sstack.com (11)

Schneiderman, Larry, Corinthian Media, New York, NY. Tel: (212) 279-5700, FAX: (212) 239-1772, E-Mail: info@mediabuying.com, Web Site: www.mediabuying.com (35)

Schneweiss, Victor, Bear Woods Supply Co Inc, Cornwallis, NS Canada. Tel: (902) 638-8622, (800) 565-5066, FAX: (902) 638-8637, Web Site: www.bearwood.com, www.woodparts.ca (11)

Schnuck Markets Inc, Saint Louis, MO. Tel: (314) 994-9900, FAX: (314) 994-4465, Web Site: www.schnucks.com (16)

Schnuck, Scott C., Schnuck Markets Inc, Saint Louis, MO. Tel: (314) 994-9900, FAX: (314) 994-4465, Web Site: www.schnucks.com (16)

Schnuck, Todd, Schnuck Markets Inc, Saint Louis, MO. Tel: (314) 994-9900, FAX: (314) 994-4465, Web Site: www.schnucks.com (16)

Schnur, Barry, SilverPop, Atlanta, GA. Tel: (678) 247-0500, (866) 745-8767, FAX: (678) 247-0501, E-Mail: contactsales@silverpop.com, Web Site: www.silverpop.com (32)

Schnyder, George H., IBSDirect, King of Prussia, PA. Tel: (610) 265-8210, FAX: (610) 265-7997, Web Site: www.ibsdm.com (27)

Schoch, Bonnie Britton, Cuvaison Inc, Napa, CA. Tel: (707) 942-2455, E-Mail: info@cuvaison.com, Web Site: www.cuvaison.com (1)

Schoedler, Michael W., Telephone Look-Up Service Co, Yardley, PA. Tel: (215) 321-0706, (800) 366-0706, FAX: (215) 321-3229, E-Mail: computer@telephonelookup.com, Web Site: www.telephonelookup.com (22)

Schoeler, Larry, Unicover Corp, Cheyenne, WY. Tel: (307) 771-3000, (800) 443-3232, FAX: (307) 771-3134, E-Mail: qands@unicover.com, Web Site: www.unicover.com (6)

Schoemann, Jerry, MKS Marketing Inc, Austin, TX. Tel: (512) 263-8017, (800) 544-8989, FAX: (402) 333-9610, E-Mail: info@telemarketingoutsource.com, Web Site: www.telemarketingoutsource.com (29)

Schoenberg, Patricia, Spectra Merchandising International Inc, Chicago, IL. Tel: (773) 202-8408, FAX: (773) 202-8409 (16)

Schoenrock, Doug, Ducks Unlimited, Memphis, TN. Tel: (901) 758-3825, (800) 45DUCKS, FAX: (901) 758-3850, Web Site: www.ducks.org (1)

Schoenthaler, Emily Leonard, Campaigns & Elections Magazine, Arlington, VA. Tel: (703) 778-4028, (800) 771-8252, FAX: (703) 778-4024, Web Site: www.campaignsandelections.com (17)

Schoenwald, Mark, Thomas Nelson, Nashville, TN. Tel: (615) 889-9000, (800) 251-4000, FAX: (615) 889-5940, Web Site: www.thomasnelson.com (17)

Schofer, Connie, Media Management Services Inc, Newton, PA. Tel: (215) 579-8590, (800) 523-5948, FAX: (215) 579-8589, Web Site: www.mmseducation.com (20)

Scholastic Direct Mktg, Danbury, CT. Tel: (203) 797-3500, FAX: (203) 797-3667 (29)

Scholastic Inc, New York, NY. Tel: (212) 343-6100, (800) SCHOLASTIC, FAX: (212) 343-6484, Web Site: www.scholastic.com (17)

The Scholl Group, Bryn Mawr, PA. Tel: (610) 527-7310, FAX: (610) 527-7323, E-Mail: rscholl@thescholgroup.com, Web Site: www.thescholgroup.com (35)

School of Business & Economics, Los Angeles, CA. Tel: (323) 343-2800, FAX: (323) 343-2813, Web Site: cbe.calstatela.edu (41)

Scholl, Richard J., The Scholl Group, Bryn Mawr, PA. Tel: (610) 527-7310, FAX: (610) 527-7323, E-Mail: rscholl@thescholgroup.com, Web Site: www.thescholgroup.com (35)

Scholtens, Jim, MISSCO Corp, Flowood, MS. Tel: (601) 948-8600, (800) 647-5333, FAX: (601) 987-3038 (16)

Schonberger, Jr. M., Adams Manufacturing Co, Cleveland, OH. Tel: (216) 587-6801, FAX: (216) 587-6807, E-Mail: adamsx@att.net, Web Site: www.adamsmanufacturing.com (9)

Schonberger, Ruth, Adams Manufacturing Co, Cleveland, OH. Tel: (216) 587-6801, FAX: (216) 587-6807, E-Mail: adamsx@att.net, Web Site: www.adamsmanufacturing.com (9)

Schonberger, Sr. Marty, Adams Manufacturing Co, Cleveland, OH. Tel: (216) 587-6801, FAX: (216) 587-6807, E-Mail: adamsx@att.net, Web Site: www.adamsmanufacturing.com (9)

Schonfeld, Maxeen, D2: Direct, Denville, NJ. Tel: (973) 627-4410, FAX: (973) 627-3703, E-Mail: info@d2direct.com. Web Site: www.d2direct.com (35)

Schonwald, Barbara, Conrad Direct Inc, Cresskill, NJ. Tel: (201) 567-3200, FAX: (201) 567-1530, E-Mail: listinfo@conraddirect.com, Web Site: www.conraddirect.com (23)

Schonwald, Barbara, Direct Mail Strategy Group (DMSG), Cresskill, NJ. Tel: (201) 567-3200, FAX: (201) 567-1530, E-Mail: listinfo@conraddirect.com, Web Site: www.conraddirect.com (31)

Schoofield, Gail. Photri Images LLC, Fairfax, VA. Tel: (703) 978-0129, E-Mail: info@photriimages.com, Web Site: www.photriimages.com (38)

School Annual Publishing Co, State College, PA. Tel: (800) 436-6030, E-Mail: yearbook@schoolannual.com, Web Site: www.schoolannual.com (17)

School Market Research Institute Inc, Centerbrook, CT. Tel: (800) 838-3444, FAX: (860) 581-8549, E-Mail: info@smriinc.com, Web Site: www.smriinc.com (35)

School of Business Administration, Portland, OR. Tel: (503) 725-3712, FAX: (503) 725-5850, E-Mail: info@sba.pdx.edu, Web Site: www.sba.pdx.edu (41)

School of Management, Old Westbury, NY. Tel: (516) 686-1000, (800) 345-NYIT, (800) 345-6948, E-Mail: asknyit@nyit.edu, Web Site: www.nyit.edu (41)

School Specialty Inc, Greenville, WI. Tel: (920) 734-5712, (888) 388-3224, FAX: (920) 734-5112, E-Mail: info@schoolspecialty.com, Web Site: www.schoolspecialty.com (16)

Schoolcraft College, Livonia, MI. Tel: (734) 462-4400, Web Site: www.schoolcraft.edu (1)

Schooley, Debbie, Creative Health Products, Plymouth, MI. Tel: (734) 996-5900, (800) 742-4478, FAX: (734) 996-4650, Web Site: www.chponline.com (16)

Schooley, Kim, TechniServe Inc, Troy, MI. Tel: (248) 989-0100, FAX: (248) 989-0111, E-Mail: info@techni-serve.com, Web Site: www.techni-serve.com (22)

Schoolwise Press, San Francisco, CA. Tel: (415) 337-7971, (800) 247-8443 x 202, FAX: (415) 337-1146, E-Mail: info@schoolwisepress.com. Web Site: www.schoolwisepress.com (17)

Schorsch, Louis, ArcelorMittal, Chicago, IL. Tel: (312) 899-3440, FAX: (312) 899-3504, Web Site: www.mittalsteel.com (16)

Schottenstein, Jay L, American Eagle Outfitters, Pittsburgh, PA. Tel: (412) 432-3382, Web Site: www.ae.com (2)

Schrack, Dana, Mi-T-M Corp, Peosta, IA. Tel: (563) 556-7484, Web Site: www.mitm.com (9)

Schrafft, Theodore P., Premiere Global Services Inc, Atlanta, GA. Tel: (404) 262-8400, (800) 546-1541, FAX: (404) 262-8540, Web Site: www.pgi.com (22)

Schram, Lee J., Deluxe Corp, Shoreview, MN. Tel: (651) 483-7111, FAX: (651) 481-4477, Web Site: www.deluxe.com (27)

Schramm Marketing Group, New York, NY. Tel: (212) 983-0219, E-Mail: info@schrammnyc.com, Web Site: www.schrammnyc.com (35)

Schramm, Joseph F., Schramm Marketing Group, New York, NY. Tel: (212) 983-0219, E-Mail: info@schrammnyc.com, Web Site: www.schrammnyc.com (35)

Schreck, Brad S., E-Z-EM Inc, Lake Success, NY. Tel: (516) 333-8230, (800) 544-4624, FAX: (516) 333-8278, E-Mail: webmaster@ezem.com, Web Site: www.ezem.com (7)

Schreier, Bradley J., Taylor Corp, North Mankato, MN. Tel: (507) 625-2828, FAX: (507) 625-3388 (16)

Schrempp, Jurgen E, DaimlerChrysler Corp, Auburn Hills, MI. Tel: (248) 512-1879, Web Site: www.daimlerchrysler.com (12)

Schreurs, John, Strategic America, West Des Moines, IA. Tel: (515) 453-2000, (888) 898-6400, FAX: (515) 224-4181, Web Site: www.strategicamerica.com (35)

Schreurs, Mike, Strategic America, West Des Moines, IA. Tel: (515) 453-2000, (888) 898-6400, FAX: (515) 224-4181, Web Site: www.strategicamerica.com (35)

Schrier, Jack, The Copy Shoppe, Mendham, NJ. Tel: (973) 543-2679, FAX: (973) 543-2679, E-Mail: catalogistics@juno.com, Web Site: www.catalogistics.com (39)

Schriver, John, Viahealth, Rochester, NY. Tel: (585) 922-4000, (585) 922-3677, FAX: (585) 922-3929, Web Site: www.viahealth.org (16)

Schroeder, Clint, Hagadone Printing Co, Honolulu, HI. Tel: (808) 847-5310, (800) 491-4888, FAX: (808) 841-0094, E-Mail: sales@hagadoneprinting.com, Web Site: www.hagadoneprinting.com (27)

Schroeder, Jr. Bill, Collector Books & American Quilters Society, Paducah, KY. Tel: (270) 898-6211, (800) 626-5420, FAX: (270) 898-8890, E-Mail: info@collectorbooks.com, Web Site: www.collectorbooks.com (17)

Schroeder, Meredith, Collector Books & American Quilters Society, Paducah, KY. Tel: (270) 898-6211, (800) 626-5420, FAX: (270) 898-8890, E-Mail: info@collectorbooks.com, Web Site: www.collectorbooks.com (17)

Schroeder, Susan, Grand Canyon Association, Grand Canyon, AZ. Tel: (928) 638-2481, (800) 858-2808, FAX: (928-638-2484, E-Mail: gcassociation@grandcanyon.org, Web Site: www.grandcanyon.org (1)

W J Schroer Co, Battle Creek, MI. Tel: (269) 963-4874, FAX: (269) 963-5930, E-Mail: info@socialmarketing.org, Web Site: www.socialmarketing.org (30)

Schroer, William J., W J Schroer Co, Battle Creek, MI. Tel: (269) 963-4874, FAX: (269) 963-5930, E-Mail: info@socialmarketing.org, Web Site: www.socialmarketing.org (30)

Schroeter, Martin, IBM Corp, Armonk, NY. Tel: (914) 765-1900, FAX: (914) 765-6633, Web Site: www.ibm.com (16)

Schug, David, SEI, Oaks, PA. Tel: (610) 676-1000, FAX: (610) 676-1406, E-Mail: webmaster@seic.com, Web Site: www.seic.com (14)

Schuh, C. Scott, LSC Marketing, Little Rock, AR. Tel: (501) 374-2332, (866) LSC-MKGT, FAX: (501) 372-6570, E-Mail: sales@lscmarketing.com, Web Site: www.lscmarketing.com (28)

Schuh, Dale, Sentry Life Insurance Co, Stevens Point, WI. Tel: (715) 346-6000, FAX: (715) 346-7028, E-Mail: infoctr@coredcs.com, Web Site: www.sentry.com (15)

Schuler, Michael, Gragg Advertising, Kansas City, MO. Tel: (877) GRAGGADV, FAX: (816) 931-2227, E-Mail: contact@graggadv.com, Web Site: www.graggadv.com (35)

Schulhofer, Kelli, Civil Service Employees Insurance Group, Walnut Creek, CA. Tel: (415) 274-7803, (925) 817-6300, (800) 282-6848, Web Site: www.cseinsurance.com (15)

Schull, Tom, AAFES, Dallas, TX. Tel: (214) 312-2011, (800) 527-2345, FAX: (800) 446-0163, Web Site: www.aafes.com (5)

Schulman, Dan, PayPal Inc, San Jose, CA. Tel: (402) 935-2050, Web Site: www.paypal.com (14)

Schulman, John, Frederick's of Hollywood Group Inc, Los Angeles, CA. Tel: (323) 466-5151, (855) 655-2514, FAX: (323) 464-5149, E-Mail: support@fredericks.com, Web Site: www.fredericks.com (2)

Schulte Associates, Minneapolis, MN. Tel: (612) 788-1673, FAX: (612) 788-1147, E-Mail: schulte@nmoa.org, Web Site: www.nmoa.org/schulte (20)

Schulte, J., Midcontinent Financial Center Inc, Columbia, MO. Tel: (573) 443-6002, Web Site: www.americanmutualloans.com (14)

Schulte, John D., National Mail Order Association (NMOA), Minneapolis, MN. Tel: (612) 788-1673, E-Mail: info@nmoa.org, Web Site: www.nmoa.org (40)

Schulte, John D., Schulte Associates, Minneapolis, MN. Tel: (612) 788-1673, FAX: (612) 788-1147, E-Mail: schulte@nmoa.org, Web Site: www.nmoa.org/schulte (20)

Schulte, John, Direct Marketing Digest, Minneapolis, MN. Tel: (612) 788-1673, E-Mail: info@nmoa.org, Web Site: www.nmoa.org (43)

Schulte, John, Direct Marketing Tool Kit for Small Business, Minneapolis, MN. Tel: (612) 788-1673, E-Mail: info@nmoa.org, Web Site: www.nmoa.org/directmarketingtoolkit (43)

Schulte, John, Directory of Mail Order Catalogs, Minneapolis, MN. Tel: (612) 788-1673, E-Mail: info@nmoa.org, Web Site: www.nmoa.org (43)

Schultheis, Jack, KZSW Advertising Inc, East Setauket, NY. Tel: (631) 348-1440, FAX: (631) 348-1449, E-Mail: contact@kzswadvertising.com, Web Site: kzsadvertising.com (35)

Schults, Eric, HubCast Inc, Wakefield, MA. Tel: (781) 221-7200, FAX: (781) 221-7223, Web Site: www.hubeast.com (27)

Schultz & Williams Inc, Philadelphia, PA. Tel: (215) 625-9955, FAX: (215) 625-2701, E-Mail: mail@schultzwilliams.com, Web Site: www.sw-inc.com (1)

Schultz, Eric H., Harvard Pilgrim Health Care, Wellesley, MA. Tel: (617) 509-1000, (888) 888-4742, FAX: (617) 509-7590, Web Site: www.harvardpilgrim.org (7)

Schultz, James R., Great Lakes Integrated, Cleveland, OH. Tel: (216) 651-1500, (800) 745-4846, FAX: (216) 651-8311, E-Mail: bbemer@glintergrated.com, Web Site: www.gll.com (27)

Schultz, Joey, AT&T Inc, San Antonio, TX. Tel: (210) 821-4105, FAX: (210) 351-2071, Web Site: www.bellsouth.com (32)

Schultz, Jonathan D., Concordia Publishing House, Saint Louis, MO. Tel: (314) 268-1000, (800) 325-3040, FAX: (314) 268-1329, E-Mail: order@cph.org, Web Site: www.cph.org (17)

Schultz, L. Scott, Schultz & Williams Inc, Philadelphia, PA. Tel: (215) 625-9955, FAX: (215) 625-2701, E-Mail: mail@schultzwilliams.com, Web Site: www.sw-inc.com (1)

Schultz, Steven A., Protective Life Insurance Co, Birmingham, AL. Tel: (205) 268-1000, (800) 866-3555, FAX: (205) 868-3086, Web Site: www.protective.com (15)

Schultz, Trish, Uline, Pleasant Prairie, WI. Tel: (847) 473-3000, (800) 295-5510, FAX: (800) 295-5571, E-Mail: customer.service@uline.com, Web Site: www.uline.com (5)

Schulz, Jean, Canine Companions for Independence, Santa Rosa, CA. Tel: (707) 577-1700, (800) 572-2275, FAX: (707) 577-1711, E-Mail: info@cci.org, Web Site: www.caninecompanions.org (16)

Schulze, Cornelia, Thieme Medical Publishers Inc, New York, NY. Tel: (212) 760-0888, (800) 782-3488, FAX: (212) 947-1112, E-Mail: info@thieme.com, Web Site: www.thieme.com (17)

Schulze, Fred, AM Solutions, Edgerton, WI. Tel: (800) 410-6245, E-Mail: fschulze@amsolutionswi.com, Web Site: www.amsolutionswi.com (21)

Schulze, Mark, New & Unique Videos, San Diego, CA. Tel: (619) 644-3000, FAX: (619) 644-3001, E-Mail: info@newuniquevideos.com, Web Site: www.newuniquevideos.com (3)

Schumacher, Gunther, OgilvyOne Worldwide, New York, NY. Tel: (212) 237-4000, Web Site: www.ogilvy.com (35)

Schumacher, Jenny, Agile Education Marketing LLC, Denver, CO. Tel: (866) 783-0241, E-Mail: info@agile-ed.com, Web Site: www.agile-ed.com (24)

Schumacher, Mark S., Presentation Packaging, Minneapolis, MN. Tel: (763) 540-9544, (800) 818-2698, FAX: (763) 540-9522, E-Mail: customerservice@presentationpackaging.com, Web Site: www.presentationpackaging.com (35)

Schuman, Joan, CCMR Global Marketing, Mill Valley, CA. Tel: (415) 847-1239, E-Mail: globalmarketing1@aol.com, Web Site: www.gotoccmr.com (35)

Schupak Group Inc, New York, NY. Tel: (212) 582-4210 (20)

Schupak, Donald, Schupak Group Inc, New York, NY. Tel: (212) 582-4210 (20)

Schupp, Brad, Sportsmith LLC, Tulsa, OK. Tel: (918) 307-2446, (800) 713-2880, Web Site: www.sportsmith.net (11)

Schuppert, Jay, Cuvaison Inc, Napa, CA. Tel: (707) 942-2455, E-Mail: info@cuvaison.com, Web Site: www.cuvaison.com (4)

Schure, Teri, World Press Review, New York, NY. Tel: (212) 982-8880, Web Site: www.worldpressreview.com (18)

Schurenberg, Eric, INC Magazine, New York, NY. Tel: (212) 389-5377, FAX: (617) 248-8090, E-Mail: mail@inc.com, Web Site: www.inc.com (17)

Schurmann, Karen, Osmonics Inc, Minnetonka, MN. Tel: (952) 264-3937, (800) 605-6698, FAX: (952) 536-3301, Web Site: www.osmonics.com (16)

Schus & Co, Glendale, CA. Tel: (818) 550-8100, E-Mail: sschus@aol.com (20)

Schus, Stephanie, Schus & Co, Glendale, CA. Tel: (818) 550-8100, E-Mail: sschus@aol.com (20)

Schuster, Mike, Nancy's Notions LLC, Beaver Dam, WI. Tel: (920) 887-0321, (800) 833-0690, FAX: (800) 255-8119, E-Mail: comments@nancysnotions.com, Web Site: www.nancysnotions.com (11)

Schuster, Pauline, Imperial Supplies, Green Bay, WI. Tel: (920) 494-5403, (800) 558-2808, FAX: (800) 553-8769, Web Site: www.imperialsupplies.com (16)

Schutte, Ron, The Fort Group, Ridgefield Park, NJ. Tel: (201) 445-0202, FAX: (201) 445-0626, E-Mail: info@fortgroupinc.com, Web Site: www.fortgroupinc.com (35)

Schuyler, Henry, MarCom Technologies, Kelowna, BC Canada. Tel: (250) 868-9352, FAX: (250) 868-9362 (29)

Charles Schwab & Co Inc, San Francisco, CA. Tel: (415) 627-7000, (800) 648-5300, FAX: (415) 627-8538, Web Site: www.schwab.com (14)

Schwab, John, Citizens Republic Bank, Flint, MI. Tel: (810) 766-7500, Web Site: www.citizensbanking.com (14)

Schwalm, Kim Krause, Creative Synergy Inc, Germantown, MD. Tel: (301) 515-9397, Web Site: kimschwalm.com (20)

The Schwan Food Co, Marshall, MN. Tel: (507) 532-3274, Web Site: www.theschwanfoodcompany.com (5)

Schwandt, Kandy, Sunrise Greetings, Kansas City, MO. Tel: (812) 336-4045, (800) 457-4045, FAX: (812) 336-8712, E-Mail: info@interart.com, Web Site: www.interartdistribution.com (17)

Schwarcz, Ronald, Indus-Tool, Chicago, IL. Tel: (312) 226-2473, (800) 662-5021, FAX: (312) 226-2480, E-Mail: sales@indus-tool.com, Web Site: www.indus-tool.com (12)

Schwartz & Associates Creative, Clayton, MO. Tel: (314) 531-6810, FAX: (314) 531-1448, E-Mail: info@sacreative.com, Web Site: www.sacreative.com (32)

Schwartz & Co, Verona, NJ. Tel: (973) 571-2160, (800) 526-1440, FAX: (973) 571-2165, E-Mail: swartzandcompany@gmail.com, Web Site: www.natschwartz.com (6)

William W Schwartz Associates Inc, Sheboygan, WI. Tel: (920) 458-4661, FAX: (920) 458-6297, E-Mail: wws1503@excel.net, Web Site: www.wschwartz.com (33)

Schwartz, Adam, S&S Worldwide, Colchester, CT. Tel: (860) 537-3451, (800) 288-9941, FAX: (860) 537-2866, E-Mail: cservice@ssww.com, Web Site: www.ssww.com (11)

Schwartz, Barry L., The Jewish Publication Society, Philadelphia, PA. Tel: (215) 832-0600, (800) 234-3151, FAX: (215) 568-2017, Web Site: www.jewishpub.org (17)

Schwartz, David, Infomercial Solutions Inc, Agoura Hills, CA. Tel: (818) 879-1140, FAX: (818) 879-1148, E-Mail: david@infomercialsolutions.com, Web Site: www.infomercialsolutions.com (32)

Schwartz, Donald A., Recognition Products International, Easton, MD. Tel: (410) 820-0022, (800) 292-7354, FAX: (410) 820-5044, E-Mail: info@recognitionproducts.com, Web Site: www.shoprecognitionproducts.com (16)

Schwartz, Hy, S&S Worldwide, Colchester, CT. Tel: (860) 537-3451, (800) 288-9941, FAX: (860) 537-2866, E-Mail: cservice@ssww.com, Web Site: www.ssww.com (11)

Schwartz, Ilene, Response Magazine, Santa Ana, CA. Tel: (714) 513-8624, (800) 371-6897, FAX: (714) 338-6710, Web Site: www.responsemagazine.com (43)

Schwartz, Jacob, Emfluence, Kansas City, MO. Tel: (816) 472-4455, (877) 81-EMAIL, FAX: (816) 472-8855, E-Mail: expert@emfluence.com, Web Site: www.emfluence.com (21)

Schwartz, Jeff, William W Schwartz Associates Inc, Sheboygan, WI. Tel: (920) 458-4661, FAX: (920) 458-6297, E-Mail: wws1503@excel.net, Web Site: www.wschwartz.com (33)

Schwartz, Jeremy, The Body Shop Inc, New York, NY. Tel: (919) 554-4900, (800) 263-9746, FAX: (919) 554-4361, Web Site: www.thebodyshop.com (7)

Schwartz, Jim, KD Mailing & Fulfillment Service, Lincolnwood, IL. Tel: (847) 673-0186, (866) 330-6245, FAX: (874) 673-0188, E-Mail: dan@kdmailing.com, Web Site: www.kdmailing.com (28)

Schwartz, Kathy, Interex, Amesbury, MA. Tel: (978) 388-8755, (800) INTEREX, FAX: (978) 388-8747, Web Site: www.interexhibits.com (17)

Schwartz, Ken, CityTwist, Boca Raton, FL. Tel: (866) 798-2489, FAX: (561) 314-2692, Web Site: www.citytwist.com (32)

Schwartz, Larry, Checks by Phone/Checks by Web, Boynton Beach, FL. Tel: (561) 737-8700, FAX: (561) 737-5800, E-Mail: LarrySchwartz@checksbyphone.com, Web Site: www.checksbyphone.com (14)

Schwartz, Larry, Fraud & Theft Information Bureau, Boynton Beach, FL. Tel: (561) 737-8700, FAX: (561) 737-5800, E-Mail: sales@fraudandtheft.com, Web Site: www.fraudandtheftinfo.com (43)

Schwartz, Larry, Schwartz & Co, Verona, NJ. Tel: (973) 571-2160, (800) 526-1440, FAX: (973) 571-2165, E-Mail: swartzandcompany@gmail.com, Web Site: www.natschwartz.com (6)

Schwartz, Lisa, ICIS Inc, Upper Black Eddy, PA. Tel: (610) 982-0429, E-Mail: icis@ptdprolog.net, Web Site: www.icisjewelry.com (2)

Schwartz, Marc, Novartis Pharmaceuticals Corp, East Hanover, NJ. Tel: (862) 778-2100, (800) 669-6682, FAX: (973) 781-8119, Web Site: www.novartis.com (7)

Schwartz, Marilyn, Schwartz & Co, Verona, NJ. Tel: (973) 571-2160, (800) 526-1440, FAX: (973) 571-2165, E-Mail: swartzandcompany@gmail.com, Web Site: www.natschwartz.com (6)

Schwartz, Michael, Babyshoe.com, Hendersonville, NC. Tel: (828) 697-5811, (800) 543-8566, FAX: (828) 697-5815, E-Mail: info@babyshoe.com, Web Site: www.babyshoe.com (6)

Schwartz, PhD Elizabeth, Schwartz & Associates Creative, Clayton, MO. Tel: (314) 531-6810, FAX: (314) 531-1448, E-Mail: info@sacreative.com, Web Site: www.sacreative.com (32)

Schwartz, Rob, TBWA/Chiat/Day Inc, New York, NY. Tel: (212) 804-1000, FAX: (212) 804-1200, Web Site: www.tbwachiatdayny.com (35)

Schwartz, Ronald B., R&S Industries Corp, Chesterfield, MO. Tel: (314) 781-5400, FAX: (314) 781-5169, E-Mail: sendeverything@miraclepolishingcloth.com, Web Site: www.miraclepolishingcloth.com (16)

Schwartz, Steve, Lion Apparel, Dayton, OH. Tel: (937) 898-1949, (800) 548-6614, FAX: (937) 913-5667, Web Site: www.lionprotects.com (2)

Schwartz, Steven A., Your Move Chess & Games, North Massapequa, NY. Tel: (516) 882-9800, (800) 645-4710, FAX: (631) 424-3405, E-Mail: icd@icdchess.com, Web Site: www.icdchess.com (11)

Schwartz, Steven, Intersections, Chantilly, VA. Tel: (703) 488-6100, Web Site: www.charteredmarketing.com (14)

Schwartz, Susan, Agate Publishing, Evanston, IL. Tel: (847) 475-4457, (800) 326-4430, FAX: (312) 751-7334, Web Site: www.surreybooks.com (17)

Schwartz, Tyler, Schwartz & Associates Creative, Clayton, MO. Tel: (314) 531-6810, FAX: (314) 531-1448, E-Mail: info@sacreative.com, Web Site: www.sacreative.com (32)

Schwartzman, Michael, Lea & Perrins Inc, Fair Lawn, NJ. Tel: (201) 791-1600, FAX: (201) 791-8945, Web Site: www.leaperrins.com (16)

Schwarz, Earle J., Benchmark Brands Inc, Norcross, GA. Tel: (770) 242-1254, FAX: (770) 242-1962, Web Site: www.footsmart.com (5)

Schwedelson, Jay, Worldata, Boca Raton, FL. Tel: (561) 393-8200, (800) 331-8102, FAX: (561) 368-8345, E-Mail: hello@worldata.com, Web Site: www.worldata.com (23)

Schwedock, Eric, Economy Handicrafts, Brooklyn, NY. Tel: (718) 431-9300, (800) 216-1601, FAX: (718) 431-9309, Web Site: www.vanguardcrafts.com (16)

Schweinhart, Larry, HighScope Educational Research Foundation, Ypsilanti, MI. Tel: (800) 587-5639, FAX: (734) 485-0704, E-Mail: info@highscope.org, Web Site: www.highscope.org (17)

Schweitzer, William H., Baker & Hostetler LLP, Washington, DC. Tel: (202) 861-1500, FAX: (202) 861-1783, E-Mail: wschweitzer@bakerlaw.com, Web Site: www.bakerlaw.com (20)

Schwertley, Wayne, Service Net Warranty LLC, Jeffersonville, IN. Tel: (812) 258-4700, (812) 258-4722, FAX: (812) 258-4693, Web Site: www.servicenet.com (22)

Schwing, Rob, Char-Broil, Columbus, GA. Tel: (706) 571-7000, Web Site: www.charbroil.com (16)

Schwotka, Alex, VistaPrint USA Inc, Lexington, MA. Tel: (800) 961-2075, Web Site: www.vistaprint.com (27)

Scialfa, Chris, Carl Fischer Music, New York, NY. Tel: (212) 777-0900, (800) 762-2328, FAX: (212) 477-6996, E-Mail: cf-info@carlfischer.com, Web Site: www.carlfischer.com (17)

Sciarrotta, Art, Chain Store Guide, Tampa, FL. Tel: (800) 927-9292, FAX: (813) 627-6882, E-Mail: info@csgis.com, Web Site: www.csgis.com (17)

Scientific Computing Associates Corp, River Forest, IL. Tel: (708) 771-4567, FAX: (708) 771-4569, E-Mail: sca@scausa.com, Web Site: www.scausa.com (22)

Scientific Games Canada, Montreal, QC Canada. Tel: (514) 254-3000, FAX: (514) 254-1411, Web Site: www.scientificgames.com (27)

Scientific Marketing Services Inc, Landisville, NJ. Tel: (856) 697-1257, FAX: (856) 697-9639, E-Mail: info@smsmktg.com, Web Site: www.smsmktg.com (35)

Scime, Joe, Conney Safety Products LLC, Madison, WI. Tel: (888) 356-9100, FAX: (800) 845-9095, E-Mail: safety@conney.com, Web Site: www.conney.com (7)

Scinta, Sam, Fulcrum Publishing, Golden, CO. Tel: (303) 277-1623, (800) 992-2908, FAX: (303) 279-7111, Web Site: www.fulcrum-books.com (17)

Sciuto, Kenneth, Fosina Marketing Group Inc, Danbury, CT. Tel: (203) 790-0013, E-Mail: info@fosinamarketing.com, Web Site: fosinamarketinggroup.com (35)

Sclaventis, Wanda M., American Graphics Network Inc, Glenview, IL. Tel: (847) 729-7220, FAX: (847) 724-5080, E-Mail: info@agninc.com, Web Site: www.agninc.com (27)

Scoggin, Patrick B., Savicom, San Francisco, CA. Tel: (415) 983-0990, FAX: (415) 445-9999, E-Mail: sales@savicom.net, Web Site: www.savicom.net (22)

Scolpino, Janine, The Taunton Press, Newtown, CT. Tel: (203) 426-8171, (800) 477-8727, FAX: (203) 426-3434, Web Site: www.taunton.com (17)

Scope 1, Kalamazoo, MI. Tel: (269) 323-1333, (877) 7SCOPE1, Web Site: www.scope1.com (16)

Scorecards USA, North Kingstown, RI. Tel: (401) 294-4049, (800) 553-4154, FAX: (401) 294-4076, E-Mail: sales@scorecardsusa.com, Web Site: www.scorecardsusa.com (16)

Scott Benson, Lisa, Russ Reid Co, Pasadena, CA. Tel: (626) 449-6100, FAX: (626) 449-6190, E-Mail: info@russreid.com, Web Site: www.russreid.com (35)

Scott Publications, Inc, Muskegon, MI. Tel: (231) 755-2200, (866) 733-9382, FAX: (231) 755-1003, Web Site: www.scottpublications.com (17)

Scott Sign Systems Inc, Sarasota, FL. Tel: (941) 355-5171, (800) 237-9447, FAX: (941) 351-1787, E-Mail: mail@scottsigns.com, Web Site: www.scottsigns.com (16)

Scott, Alan, Aspen Publishers Inc, New York, NY. Tel: (212) 771-0600, (800) 638-8437, Web Site: www.aspenpublishers.com (17)

Scott, Allison, Broadmoor Hotel Inc, Colorado Springs, CO. Tel: (719) 623-5112, (866) 837-9520, FAX: (719) 577-5738, Web Site: www.broadmoor.com (19)

Scott, Beth, Hilton HHonors, McLean, VA. Tel: (703) 883-1000, Web Site: hhonors.hilton.com (16)

Scott, Daniel T., Unz & Co, Middlesex, NJ. Tel: (732) 667-1020, (800) 631-3098, FAX: (732) 868-0260, E-Mail: unzco@unzco.com, Web Site: www.unzco.com (27)

Scott, David A., Comcast Spectacor LP, Philadelphia, PA. Tel: (215) 336-3600, (800) 298-4200, FAX: (215) 389-9518, E-Mail: info@comcast-spectacor. com, Web Site: www.comcast-spectacor.com (16)

Scott, Debbie-Ann, DHL Express, Plantation, FL. Tel: (954) 888-7000, (800) 225-5345, FAX: (954) 888-7310, Web Site: www.dhl.com (28)

Scott, Deirdre, Bronx Council on the Arts, Bronx, NY. Tel: (718) 931-9500, FAX: (718) 409-6445, E-Mail: info@bronxarts.org, Web Site: www.bronxarts.org (1)

Scott, Gary, Cascade Outfitters, Boise, ID. Tel: (208) 322-4411, (800) 223-7328, FAX: (208) 322-5016, E-Mail: mail@cascadeoutfitters.com, Web Site: www.cascadeoutfitters.com (11)

Scott, Jeff. Duffey Petrosky, Farmington Hills, MI. Tel: (248) 489-8300, FAX: (248) 994-1600, Web Site: www.duffeypetrosky.com (35)

Scott, John, Toter Inc, Statesville, NC. Tel: (704) 872-8171, (800) 424-0422, FAX: (704) 878-0734, E-Mail: info@toter.com, Web Site: www.toter.com (16)

Scott, Julie, Rosicrucian Order AMORC, San Jose, CA. Tel: (408) 947-3600, FAX: (408) 947-3677, E-Mail: membership@rosicrucian.org, Web Site: www.rosicrucian.org (1)

Scott, Michele, Ultimate Office, Farmingdale, NJ. Tel: (732) 780-6911, (800) 631-2233, FAX: (732) 780-9833, Web Site: www.ultoffice.com (16)

Scott, Opal, Saturn Corp, Hyattsville, MD. Tel: (301) 772-7000, (800) USA-0090, FAX: (301) 386-4538, E-Mail: sales@saturncorp.com, Web Site: www.saturncorp.com (22)

Scott, Pam, Clement Communications, Buffalo, NY. Tel: (800) 253-6368, E-Mail: customerservice@clement.com, Web Site: www.clement.com (17)

Scott, Rekdal, National Defense Industrial Association, Arlington, VA. Tel: (703) 522-1820, FAX: (703) 522-1885, Web Site: www.ndia.org (1)

Scott, Richard, Edelmann Scott Inc, Richmond, VA. Tel: (804) 643-1931, FAX: (804) 643-1934 (35)

Scott, Timothy, Bass Pro Shops, Springfield, MO. Tel: (417) 887-7334, FAX: (417) 873-5882, Web Site: www.basspro.com (11)

Scotti, Marie, International Advertising Association, New York, NY. Tel: (646) 722-2612, FAX: (646) 722-2501, E-Mail: iaa@iaaglobal.com, Web Site: www.iaaglobal.org (1)

Scotti, Phil, Body by Jake Global LLC, Los Angeles, CA. Tel: (310) 571-7101, FAX: (310) 571-7107, E-Mail: info@bodybyjake.com, Web Site: www.bodybyjake.com (16)

The Scotts Co LLC, Marysville, OH. Tel: (888) 270-3714, Web Site: www.scotts.com (8)

Scott's Directories, Toronto, ON Canada. Tel: (416) 510-5131, FAX: (416) 510-5129, E-Mail: info@scottsinfo.com, Web Site: www.scottsinfo.com (31)

Scott's Dog Supply Inc, Indianapolis, IN. Tel: (317) 222-5382, (800) 966-3647, FAX: (317) 298-7284, E-Mail: cmurphy154@aol.com, Web Site: www.scottsdog.com (11)

Scotts-Sierra Horticultural, Marysville, OH. Tel: (888) 270-3714, Web Site: www.scottscompany.com (16)

Scripps Networks Interactive Inc, Knoxville, TN. Tel: (865) 560-2700, Web Site: scrippsnetworksinteractive.com (17)

Script to Screen Inc, Santa Ana, CA. Tel: (714) 558-3971, (800) 453-0003, FAX: (714) 558-1759, E-Mail: newbusiness@scripttoscreen.com, Web Site: www.scripttoscreen.com (32)

Scriven, Glen, Spalding Laboratories Inc, Reno, NV. Tel: (888) 562-5696, (888) 880-1579, FAX: (866) 738-9632, Web Site: www.spalding-labs.com (7)

Scruton, Steve, Direxxis Inc, Needham, MA. Tel: (781) 444-7900, FAX: (781) 444-7909, Web Site: www.direxxismarketing.com (22)

Scudder, David, American Telecast Products LLC, Exton, PA. Tel: (610) 430-7800, FAX: (484) 879-4046, E-Mail: info@americantelecast.com, Web Site: www.americantelecast.com (32)

Scudder, Mike, Precision Solutions, Owings Mills, MD. Tel: (443) 870-3079, FAX: (443) 548-2954, E-Mail: info@precisionsolutions.net, Web Site: www.precisionsolutions.net (21)

Scullion, Jim, Bunchball, Redwood City, CA. Tel: (408) 985-2034, Web Site: www.bunchball.com (32)

Sculpture House Inc, Skillman, NJ. Tel: (609) 466-2986, FAX: (888) 529-1980, E-Mail: customercare@sculpturehouse.com, Web Site: www.sculpturehouse.com (16)

Sculptz, Feasterville Trevose, PA. Tel: (215) 494-2900, E-Mail: sdudek@sculptz.com, Web Site: www.silkies.com (2)

Scundi, Mary, Independent Consultant, Saint Paul, MN. Tel: (612) 239-6572 (20)

Sea Bear, Anacortes, WA. Tel: (360) 293-4661, (800) 645-3474, FAX: (888) 487-6427, Web Site: www.seabear.com (16)

Seabach, Karen, Shopsmith Inc, Dayton, OH. Tel: (937) 898-6070, (800) 543-7586, FAX: (937) 890-5197, Web Site: www.shopsmith.com (16)

Seagle, Carole, Brooks Equipment Co, Charlotte, NC. Tel: (704) 596-9438, (800) 826-3473, FAX: (704) 596-1096, Web Site: www.brooksequipment.com (9)

Seal, Oney, Databazaar.com, Miramar, FL. Tel: (954) 843-0483, (888) 335-3282, FAX: (954) 843-0429, E-Mail: rudy@databazaar.com, Web Site: www.databazaar.com (10)

Sealed Air Corp, Elmwood Park, NJ. Tel: (201) 791-7600, FAX: (201) 703-4205, Web Site: www.sealedair.com (26)

Sealey, Ph.D. Peter, The Sausalito Group, Sausalito, CA. Tel: (415) 332-3333, FAX: (415) 332-6571, Web Site: www.sausolitogroup.com (30)

Seaman, Glen, Chase Media Group, Yorktown Heights, NY. Tel: (914) 962-3871, FAX: (914) 962-2040, Web Site: www.chasemultimedia.com (27)

Seaman, Karen, Cramer-Krasselt, Chicago, IL. Tel: (312) 616-9600, FAX: (312) 616-3839, E-Mail: pkrivkov@c-k.com, Web Site: c-k.com (35)

Seamens, Kim, Americana Sales Ventures Inc, Altamonte Springs, FL. Tel: (407) 862-8388, (800) 445-4302, FAX: (407) 862-6535, Web Site: www.americanashopper.com (35)

Searcy, Tim, IPacesetters, Montvale, NJ. Tel: (201) 391-1500, FAX: (201) 391-8357, Web Site: www.ipacesetters.com (22)

Searles, Michael M., Wilsons Leather, Brooklyn Park, MN. Tel: (763) 391-4000, (866) 305-4704, FAX: (763) 391-4906, E-Mail: customercare@wilsonsleather.com, Web Site: www.wilsonsleather.com (2)

Searles, Rey, Life Extension Foundation, Fort Lauderdale, FL. Tel: (954) 766-8144, (800) 678-8989, FAX: (954) 771-2827, E-Mail: info@lef.org, Web Site: www.lef.org (7)

Sears Canada Inc, Toronto, ON Canada. Tel: (416) 362-1711, (888) 473-2772, FAX: (613) 391-3047, E-Mail: home@sears.ca, Web Site: www.sears.ca (5)

Sears Home Improvement Products & Services, Hoffman Estates, IL. Tel: (800) 424-2047, Web Site: www.searshomeservices.com (16)

Sears, Roebuck & Co, Hoffman Estates, IL. Tel: (847) 286-2500, FAX: (847) 286-7829, Web Site: www.sears.com (16)

Sears, James M., James M Sears Associates, Bergenfield, NJ. Tel: (201) 501-9977, FAX: (201) 453-0833 (30)

Sears, William, Williams Direct Marketing Inc, Pickering, ON Canada. Tel: (416) 292-7459, FAX: (416) 292-4635, E-Mail: info@williamsdirectmarketing.com, Web Site: www.williamsdirectmarketing.com (33)

Seashore Vacations, Hilton Head Island, SC. Tel: (843) 785-2191, (800) 845-0077, FAX: (843) 785-6450, E-Mail: seashorehhi@hargray.com, Web Site: www.seashorehhi.com (19)

Seastrom Manufacturing Co Inc, Twin Falls, ID. Tel: (208) 737-4300, (800) 634-2356, FAX: (208) 734-7222, E-Mail: info@seastrom-mfg.com, Web Site: www.seastrom-mfg.com (3)

Seastrom, Robert A., Seastrom Manufacturing Co Inc, Twin Falls, ID. Tel: (208) 737-4300, (800) 634-2356, FAX: (208) 734-7222, E-Mail: info@seastrom-mfg.com, Web Site: www.seastrom-mfg.com (3)

Seaton, Flint, Accellos Inc, Colorado Springs, CO. Tel: (719) 433-7000, Web Site: www.accellos.com (12)

Seattle Magazine, Seattle, WA. Tel: (206) 284-1750, (800) 637-0334, FAX: (206) 284-2550, E-Mail: customerservice@seattlemag.com, Web Site: www.seattlemag.com (17)

Seavers, Dean S., Simplex Grinnell, Westminster, MA. Tel: (978) 731-2500, (800) SIMPLEX, FAX: (978) 731-7856, Web Site: www.simplexgrinnel.com (16)

Seavey, Ava, Avalanche Creative Services Inc, New York, NY. Tel: (212) 206-9335, FAX: (212) 206-1538, E-Mail: info@avalanchecreative.tv, Web Site: www.avalanchecreative.tv (35)

Seavy, Mark, Warren Communications News, Washington, DC. Tel: (202) 872-9200, (800) 771-9202, FAX: (202) 318-8350, E-Mail: info@warren-news.com, Web Site: www.warren-news.com (17)

Sebastian, Bob, JC Whitney, Chicago, IL. Tel: (312) 431-6000, FAX: (312) 431-5650, (800) 537-2700, Web Site: www.jcwhitney.com (12)

Seberg, Randy, AlanizMetroGroup, Mount Pleasant, IA. Tel: (319) 385-7259, FAX: (319) 385-2825, E-Mail: info@alanizdirect.com, Web Site: www.alanizdirect.com (28)

Secker, Karen, National Contract Management Association, Ashburn, VA. Tel: (571) 382-0082, (800) 344-8096, FAX: (703) 448-0939, E-Mail: memberservices@ncmghq.org, Web Site: www.ncmahq.org (1)

SECO-LARM USA Inc, Irvine, CA. Tel: (949) 261-2999, (800) 662-0800, FAX: (949) 261-7326, E-Mail: info@seco-larm.com, Web Site: www.seco-larm.com (16)

Second Renaissance Books, Irvine, CA. Tel: (860) 354-5448, (800) 729-6149, FAX: (860) 355-7161, Web Site: www.aynrandbookstore.com (17)

Sedgwick Moran Detert & Arnold LLP, Chicago, IL. Tel: (312) 849-1985, Web Site: www.michaelbest.com (9)

Sedlak, Highland Hills, OH. Tel: (216) 206-4700, FAX: (216) 206-4840, E-Mail: info@jasedlak.com, Web Site: www.jasedlak.com (20)

Sedona Labs, Cottonwood, AZ. Tel: (928) 340-5400, (888) 816-8804, FAX: (928) 634-0657, E-Mail: info@sedonalabs.com, Web Site: www.sedonalabs.com (7)

Sedonaen, Maureen, Goodwill Industries of San Francisco, San Francisco, CA. Tel: (415) 575-2240, FAX: (415) 575-2170, Web Site: www.sfgoodwill.org (1)

Seeber, Bruce, Kurt Salmon Associates Inc, Atlanta, GA. Tel: (404) 892-0321, FAX: (404) 898-9590, E-Mail: infoksaweb@kurtsalmon.com, Web Site: www.kurtsalmon.com (20)

Seedburo Equipment Co, Des Plaines, IL. Tel: (312) 738-3700, (800) 284-5779, E-Mail: sales@seedburo.com, Web Site: www.seedburo.com (8)

Seelye, Matthew, Kaplan Inc, Fort Lauderdale, FL. Tel: (954) 515-3993, Web Site: www.kaplan.com (16)

Seelye, Matthew, Kaplan Publishing, Chicago, IL. Tel: (312) 606-8905, (800) 245-2665, FAX: (312) 606-8985, Web Site: www.kaplanpublishing.com (17)

Seemann, Luke, Chicago Magazine, Chicago, IL. Tel: (312) 222-8999, FAX: (312) 222-0287, Web Site: www.chicagomag.com (17)

See's Candies Inc, Carson, CA. Tel: (800) 347-7337, Web Site: www.sees.com (4)

Segal, Alan, Bits & Pieces Inc, Lawrenceburg, IN. Tel: (866) 503-6395, FAX: (513) 354-1290, Web Site: www.bitsandpieces.com (11)

Segal, Brian, Rogers Publishing Ltd, Toronto, ON Canada. Tel: (416) 935-7777, FAX: (416) 935-3597, Web Site: www.rogerspublishing.ca (17)

Segal, Ronald, Spectrum Systems Inc, Reston, VA. Tel: (703) 591-7400 X217, (800) 929-3781, FAX: (703) 591-9780, E-Mail: spectrum@spectrum-systems.com, Web Site: www.spectrum-systems.com (34)

Segal, Sarah Kroloff, The Jewish Publication Society, Philadelphia, PA. Tel: (215) 832-0600, (800) 234-3151, FAX: (215) 568-2017, Web Site: www.jewishpub.org (17)

Segal, Stu, Voice Systems Engineering Inc, Langhorne, PA. Tel: (215) 953-8568, E-Mail: info@vseinc.com, Web Site: www.vseinc.com (32)

Segall, Leigh, InnerWorkings Inc, Chicago, IL. Tel: (317) 642-3700, (866) 766-5176, E-Mail: info@inwk.com, Web Site: www.inwk.com (35)

Segall, Tim, SoundBite Communications, Bedford, MA. Tel: (877) SOUNDBITE, Web Site: www.soundbite.com (32)

Segerdahl Graphics Inc, Wheeling, IL. Tel: (847) 850-8800, FAX: (847) 850-8801, Web Site: www.segerdahlgraphics.com (27)

Segermark, Howard, International Prepaid Communications Association, Washington, DC. Tel: (202) 544-4448, (800) 333-3513, FAX: (202) 547-7417 (40)

Segert, Robert E E., GXS Corp, Gaithersburg, MD. Tel: (301) 340-4000, (800) 560-4347, FAX: (301) 340-5299, Web Site: www.gxs.com (37)

Segovia, Cheri, America's Finest Pet Doors, San Luis Obispo, CA. Tel: (805) 781-7700 X201, (800) 826-2871, FAX: (805) 781-9734, E-Mail: alan@petdoors.com, Web Site: www.petdoors.com (16)

Seibert, Drew, Manning Materials, Birdsboro, PA. Tel: (610) 385-6797, (800) 445-1719, FAX: (610) 385-7524, E-Mail: mmsupport@manningmaterials.com, Web Site: www.manningmaterials.com (16)

Seibert, Gregg G., Cablevision Systems Corp, Bethpage, NY. Tel: (516) 803-2300, FAX: (516) 803-3134, Web Site: www.cablevision.com (1)

Seide, Bruce, Phoenix Marketing Group LLC, Redding, CT. Tel: (203) 544-7033, E-Mail: bseide@phoenix-marketing.com, Web Site: www.phoenix-marketing.com (21)

Seiden, Lee Smith, Schoolwise Press, San Francisco, CA. Tel: (415) 337-7971, (800) 247-8443 x 202, FAX: (415) 337-1146, E-Mail: info@schoolwisepress.com, Web Site: www.schoolwisepress.com (17)

Seider, Regina, American Healthways, Franklin, TN. Tel: (615) 665-7716, FAX: (615) 665-7697, Web Site: www.americanhealthways.com (16)

Seifert, Thomas, Symantec, Mountain View, CA. Tel: (408) 517-8000, FAX: (408) 517-8186, Web Site: www.symantec.com (16)

Seigle, Mike, Landmark Communications Inc, Alpharetta, GA. Tel: (770) 813-1000, Web Site: www.landmarkcommunications.net (17)

Seiko Corp of America, Mahwah, NJ. Tel: (201) 529-3316, E-Mail: custserv@seikousa.com, Web Site: www.seikousa.com (16)

Seiler, Roger W., Leadership Software Corp, Nyack, NY. Tel: (845) 358-0406, (800) 872-0068, FAX: (845) 358-0359, E-Mail: info@leadersoft.com, Web Site: www.leadersoft.com (16)

Seits, Gary, CTRAC Information Solutions, Strongsville, OH. Tel: (440) 572-1000, FAX: (440) 572-3330, E-Mail: ctrac@ctrac.com, Web Site: www.ctrac.com (22)

Seitter, David, CTB/McGraw-Hill LLC, Monterey, CA. Tel: (800) 538-9547, FAX: (800) 282-0266, E-Mail: customer_service_ind@ctb.com, Web Site: www.ctb.com (16)

Seitz, Pat, Regal Ware Inc, Kewaskum, WI. Tel: (262) 626-2121, E-Mail: pseitz@regalware.com, Web Site: www.regalware.com (16)

Sekaran, Sharda, Drug Policy Alliance, New York, NY. Tel: (212) 613-8020, FAX: (212) 613-8021, E-Mail: nyc@drugpolicy.org, Web Site: www.drugpolicy.org (1)

Seki, Mamoru, ITOCHU International Inc, New York, NY. Tel: (212) 818-8000, FAX: (212) 818-8282, Web Site: www.adpackusa.com (25)

Seklemian Newell Inc (CRMC), Miami Beach, FL. Tel: (310) 622-5405, FAX: (520) 842-7344, Web Site: www.thecrmc.com (20)

Selan, Bruce, Zotos International, Darien, CT. Tel: (203) 655-8911, (800) 242-9283, (800) 242-WAVE, FAX: (203) 656-7890, E-Mail: HumanResources@zotosintl.com, Web Site: www.zotos.com (16)

Selcke, Jim, Rock-Tred Corp, Waukegan, IL. Tel: (847) 673-8200, (800) 762-8733, FAX: (847) 679-6665, Web Site: www.rocktred.com (9)

Select Comfort Corp, Minneapolis, MN. Tel: (763) 551-7000, (888) 411-2188, FAX: (763) 551-7826, Web Site: www.selectcomfort.com (16)

Select Press, Novato, CA. Tel: (415) 209-9838, E-Mail: selectpr@aol.com (17)

Selig, Bob, Davis Instruments Corp, Hayward, CA. Tel: (510) 732-9229, (510) 670-0589, (800) 678-3669, FAX: (510) 732-9188, E-Mail: info@davisnet.com, Web Site: www.davisnet.com (8)

Seligman, Robert, Laughlin Associates Inc, Carson City, NV. Tel: (775) 883-8484, (888) 273-8152, FAX: (775) 883-4874 (16)

Seligmann, Peter, Conservation International, Arlington, VA. Tel: (703) 341-2400, E-Mail: community@conservation.org (1)

Selimic, Nermin, Americatel Corp, Rockville, MD. Tel: (800) 221-3020, E-Mail: customerservice@americatel.com, Web Site: www.americatel.com (32)

Selinger, Ronnie, Nordis Technologies Inc, Coral Springs, FL. Tel: (954) 323-5500, (800) 208-1169, FAX: (954) 323-0100, E-Mail: help@nordistechnologies.com, Web Site: www.nordistechnologies.com (21)

Selker, Kathy, Northlich, Cincinnati, OH. Tel: (513) 762-1717, FAX: (513) 421-8840, E-Mail: northlich@northlich.com, Web Site: www.northlich.com (35)

Selkirk Press, Sandpoint, ID. Tel: (208) 263-7523, FAX: (208) 263-2229, E-Mail: weprint@selkirkpress.com (27)

Selland, Mark, Diamond Marketing Solutions, Carol Stream, IL. Tel: (630) 597-9100, E-Mail: info@dmsolutions.com, Web Site: www.dmsolutions.com (35)

Selldorff, John, C2G, Moraine, OH. Tel: (937) 224-8646, (800) 506-9607, FAX: (937) 496-2666, (800) 331-2841, Web Site: www.cablestogo.com (3)

Selleck, Michael, Simon & Schuster Inc, New York, NY. Tel: (212) 698-7000, (800) 223-2348, Web Site: www.simonandschuster.com (17)

Selling Solutions Inc, Atlanta, GA. Tel: (404) 261-4966, FAX: (404) 264-1767, E-Mail: information@selsol.com, Web Site: www.selsol.com (35)

Sellstrom Manufacturing Co, Schaumburg, IL. Tel: (847) 358-2000, (800) 323-7402, FAX: (847) 358-8564, E-Mail: sellstrom@sellstrom.com, Web Site: www.sellstrom.com (16)

Selltel Inc, Brick, NJ. Tel: (732) 920-8700, (888) 840-9481, FAX: (732) 903-0836, E-Mail: info@nationalprotection.com (29)

Selman & Co, Cleveland, OH. Tel: (440) 646-9336, (800) 735-6262, FAX: (440) 646-9339, E-Mail: ldenning@selmaninsurance.com, Web Site: www.sel-co.com (15)

LH Selman Ltd, Chicago, IL. Tel: (831) 427-1177, (800) 538-0766, FAX: (831) 427-0111 (6)

Selman, David L., Selman & Co, Cleveland, OH. Tel: (440) 646-9336, (800) 735-6262, FAX: (440) 646-9339, E-Mail: ldenning@selmaninsurance.com, Web Site: www.sel-co.com (15)

Selman, John L., Selman & Co, Cleveland, OH. Tel: (440) 646-9336, (800) 735-6262, FAX: (440) 646-9339, E-Mail: ldenning@selmaninsurance.com, Web Site: www.sel-co.com (15)

Selman, L.H., LH Selman Ltd, Chicago, IL. Tel: (831) 427-1177, (800) 538-0766, FAX: (831) 427-0111 (6)

Selover, John, The Christian Science Publishing Society, Boston, MA. Tel: (617) 450-2000, E-Mail: info@christianscience.com, Web Site: jsh.christianscience.com (17)

Seltz, Ann, Hanley Wood LLC, Washington, DC. Tel: (202) 452-0800, FAX: (202) 785-1974, Web Site: www.hanleywood.com (16)

Seltzer, Harriet, Things Deco, New York, NY. Tel: (212) 362-8961, E-Mail: thingsdeco@hotmail.com, Web Site: www.thingsdeco.com (16)

Sembos, Al, Aerovox Inc, New Bedford, MA. Tel: (508) 994-9661, (888) AEROVOX, FAX: (508) 995-3000, E-Mail: sales1@aerovox.com, Web Site: www.aerovox.com (16)

Semeta, Mary, The Interfaith Alliance, Washington, DC. Tel: (202) 466-0567, Web Site: www.interfaithalliance.org (1)

Semler, David, United Jewish Communities, New York, NY. Tel: (212) 284-6500, E-Mail: info@jewishfederations.org, Web Site: www.jewishfederations.org (1)

Semmelhack, John, Creative Catalogs Corp, Lemont, IL. Tel: (630) 783-2400, Web Site: www. personalcreations.com (6)

Semmelhack, John, Personal Creations, Lemont, IL. Tel: (630) 783-2400, (866) 834-7695, Web Site: www.personalcreations.com (6)

Sen, Laura, BJ's Wholesale Club Inc, Westborough, MA. Tel: (508) 651-7400, FAX: (508) 651-6167, Web Site: www.bjs.com (13)

Sena, Dan, Democratic Congressional Campaign Committee, Washington, DC. Tel: (202) 863-1500, FAX: (202) 485-3436, Web Site: www.dccc.com (1)

Senackerib, Michael P., Campbell Soup Co, Camden, NJ. Tel: (856) 342-4800, (800) 257-8443, FAX: (856) 342-3878, Web Site: www.campbellsoupcompany.com (16)

Sencore Inc, Sioux Falls, SD. Tel: (605) 339-0100, (800) SEN-CORE, FAX: (605) 339-0317, E-Mail: sales@sencore.com, Web Site: www.sencore.com (16)

Sene, Jamie, CBT Direct, Tarpon Springs, FL. Tel: (727) 724-8994, (877) 872-4646, FAX: (727) 797-9143, Web Site: www.cbtdirect.com (16)

Senecal, Lori, Kirshenbaum Bond Senecal & Partners, New York, NY. Tel: (212) 633-0080, FAX: (212) 463-8643, E-Mail: press@kbsp.com, Web Site: www.kbsp.com (35)

Senft, Anne, National Wildlife Federation, Reston, VA. Tel: (703) 438-6000, Web Site: www.nwf.org (1)

Sengupta, Kalyan, Government of India Tourist Office, New York, NY. Tel: (212) 586-4901, (800) 953-9399, FAX: (212) 582-3274, Web Site: www.incredibleindia.org (1)

Senio, Michael, Dimmock Hill Golf Course Pro Shop, Binghamton, NY. Tel: (607) 729-5511, (800) 727-5511, FAX: (607) 797-7434, Web Site: www.dimmockhill.com (11)

Senior Publishers Media Group, San Diego, CA. Tel: (858) 272-9023, (800) 727-3646, FAX: (858) 272-7275, E-Mail: info@spmg.com, Web Site: www.spmg.com (31)

Senkler, Robert L., Minnesota Life, Saint Paul, MN. Tel: (651) 665-3500, (888) 237-1838, FAX: (651) 665-4488, Web Site: www.minnesotalife.com; www.securian.com (15)

Senn, Martin, Zurich, Schaumburg, IL. Tel: (847) 605-3712, (800) 382-2150, FAX: (847) 605-6403, Web Site: www.zurichna.com (15)

Sensient Technologies, Saint Louis, MO. Tel: (314) 889-7600, (800) 325-8110, FAX: (314) 658-7318, Web Site: www.sensient-tech.com (16)

Sensory Effects Powder System, Bridgeton, MO. Tel: (314) 291-5444, (800) 422-5444, FAX: (314) 291-3289, E-Mail: info@sensoryeffects.com (16)

Sentinel Peak LLC, Redmond, WA. Tel: (360) 293-7271, Web Site: www.sentinel-peak.com (20)

Sentry Life Insurance Co, Stevens Point, WI. Tel: (715) 346-6000, FAX: (715) 346-7028, E-Mail: infoctr@coredcs.com, Web Site: www.sentry.com (15)

Sepanski, Tom, Spire Creative Group, New York, NY. Tel: (212) 391-0200, Web Site: www.spirecreativegroup.com (27)

Sepate, Patrick, SummitQwest, Dayton, OH. Tel: (937) 291-4333, Web Site: www.sqinteractive.com (30)

September Productions, Nantucket, MA. Tel: (508) 332-3577, FAX: (508) 228-3853, E-Mail: info@september.com, Web Site: www.september.com (32)

Serenity, Maria Stein, OH. Tel: (419) 925-1215, (800) 869-1684, FAX: (419) 925-1216, E-Mail: serenity@bright.net, Web Site: www.serenitymusic.com (17)

Sergent, Kim, Fiserv, Norcross, GA. Tel: (678) 375-3000, Web Site: www.checkfreecorp.com (14)

Sernovitz, Andy, GasPedal, Chicago, IL. Tel: (312) 932-9000, Web Site: www.gaspedal.net (20)

Seroka, Brookfield, WI. Tel: (866) 379-0400, E-Mail: information@seroka.com, Web Site: www.seroka.com (35)

Seroka, Patrick H., Seroka, Brookfield, WI. Tel: (866) 379-0400, E-Mail: information@seroka.com, Web Site: www.seroka.com (35)

Serota, Gary, Affinity Marketing Services Corp, McLean, VA. Tel: (703) 917-9822, FAX: (703) 917-9804, E-Mail: serota@affinitymarketingservicescorp.com, Web Site: www.affinitymarketingservicescorp.com (35)

Serra, Matthew D., Champs Corp, Bradenton, FL. Tel: (941) 748-0577, (800) 991-6813, E-Mail: customer_service@champssports.com, Web Site: www.champssports.com (11)

Serrano, Rafael, Strang Communications Co, Lake Mary, FL. Tel: (407) 333-0600, FAX: (407) 333-7100, E-Mail: magcustsvc@strang.com, Web Site: www.strang.com (17)

Serreino, Christopher J., Herbert L Jamison & Co LLC, West Orange, NJ. Tel: (973) 731-0806, (800) 526-4766, (800) JAMISON, FAX: (973) 731-3035, Web Site: www.jamisongroup.com (15)

Servaas, Joan, Children's Better Health Institute, Indianapolis, IN. Tel: (317) 634-1100, FAX: (317) 684-8094, E-Mail: a.mcdowell@cbhi.org, Web Site: www.cbhi.org (1)

The Service Center LTD, Houston, TX. Tel: (713) 690-8175, FAX: (713) 690-6844, Web Site: www.calltsc.com (28)

Service Litho Print Inc, Oshkosh, WI. Tel: (920) 231-3060, (800) 544-1493, FAX: (920) 231-1272, E-Mail: slp@service-litho.com (27)

Service Mailers & Fulfillment Inc, Vernon, CA. Tel: (323) 292-0133, FAX: (323) 292-1038, E-Mail: dgsteinhart@gmail.com, Web Site: servicemailersandfulfillment.com (28)

Service Net Warranty LLC, Jeffersonville, IN. Tel: (812) 258-4700, (812) 258-4722, FAX: (812) 258-4693, Web Site: www.servicenet.com (22)

ServiceMaster Co, Memphis, TN. Tel: (901) 766-1400, (866) 782-6787, Web Site: www.servicemaster.com (8)

The Services Group (TSG), Arlington, VA. Tel: (703) 528-7444, FAX: (703) 522-2329, E-Mail: tsq@tsginc.com, Web Site: www.tsginc.com (20)

Servin, Carlos, Nissan North America Inc, Franklin, TN. Tel: (615) 725-1000, Web Site: www.nissanusa.com (16)

Servison, Roger T., Fidelity Investments, Boston, MA. Tel: (617) 563-7000, (800) 343-3548, FAX: (617) 476-6150, Web Site: www.fidelity.com (14)

Servon, Lisa J., Non-Profit Management Program/Milano - The New School of Management & Urban Policy, New York, NY. Tel: (212) 229-5400, E-Mail: milanocommunications@newschool.edu, Web Site: www.newschool.edu/milano (41)

Sesame Workshop, New York, NY. Tel: (212) 875-6677, Web Site: www.sesameworkshop.org (1)

Sescleifer, Daniel J., Energizer Holdings Inc, Saint Louis, MO. Tel: (314) 985-2000, (800) 383-7323, FAX: (636) 733-4001, Web Site: www.energizer.com (16)

Sesook, Ebraham, Data Direct Group Inc, Mississauga, ON Canada. Tel: (905) 564-0150, FAX: (905) 564-7246, E-Mail: info@datadirect.ca, Web Site: datadirect.ca (21)

Sessions, John, Bellomy Research Inc, Winston Salem, NC. Tel: (336) 721-1140, (800) 443-7344, FAX: (336) 721-1597, E-Mail: bellomy@interpath.com, Web Site: www.bellomyresearch.com (30)

Sessler, Scott, LexisNexis Risk Soulutions, Alpharetta, GA. Tel: (678) 694-6000, Web Site: www.lexisnexis.com/risk (30)

Sessoms, Vicki, Partners Health, Philadelphia, PA. Tel: (215) 849-9600, (800) 553-0784, E-Mail: sroberts@healthpart.com, Web Site: www.healthpart.com (15)

Seta Corp of Boca Inc, Boca Raton, FL. Tel: (561) 994-2660, (800) 497-7209, FAX: (561) 994-2660, Web Site: www.setacorporatin.com (5)

Seta, Angie, Seta Corp of Boca Inc, Boca Raton, FL. Tel: (561) 994-2660, (800) 497-7209, FAX: (561) 994-2660, Web Site: www.setacorporatin.com (5)

Seta, Joe D., Seta Corp of Boca Inc, Boca Raton, FL. Tel: (561) 994-2660, (800) 497-7209, FAX: (561) 994-2660, Web Site: www.setacorporatin.com (5)

Seton Hall University, South Orange, NJ. Tel: (973) 761-9000, Web Site: www.shu.edu (1)

Settle, William E., Husky Envelope Products, Walled Lake, MI. Tel: (248) 624-7070, FAX: (248) 624-5990, E-Mail: bmuehl@huskyenvelope.com, Web Site: www.huskyenvelope.com (26)

Settles, Art, USAA, San Antonio, TX. Tel: (512) 498-6524, FAX: (512) 498-8000 (15)

Severens, Pete, Strategic Alliance Group, Atlanta, GA. Tel: (404) 275-1077, E-Mail: pete@sagpromo.com, Web Site: www.sagpromo.com (35)

Severini Communications LLC, New York, NY. Tel: (917) 734-3991, E-Mail: mark@severinicommunications.com, Web Site: www.severinicommunications.com (20)

Severini, Mark, Severini Communications LLC, New York, NY. Tel: (917) 734-3991, E-Mail: mark@severinicommunications.com, Web Site: www.severinicommunications.com (20)

Severson, Andy, Compu-Mail Direct Marketing, Grand Island, NY. Tel: (716) 775-8001, (800) 255-0607, FAX: (716) 775-5681, E-Mail: marketing@compu-mail.com, Web Site: compu-mail.com (21)

Sevigny, Jerry, Opryland, Nashville, TN. Tel: (615) 889-1000, FAX: (615) 871-7741, E-Mail: info@gaylordhotels.com, Web Site: www.oprylandhotels.com (16)

Sewell, Kenneth, Database Marketing Services, Guaynabo, PR. Tel: (787) 792-7005 (22)

Sewell, Nancy, The Wexner Companies Inc, Memphis, TN. Tel: (901) 763-3925, (800) 890-5470, FAX: (901) 763-3736, E-Mail: info@JosephStores.com, Web Site: www.josephstores.com (2)

Sewell, Yolanda, Gaco Western Inc, Seattle, WA. Tel: (206) 575-0450, (800) 456-4226, FAX: (206) 575-0587, E-Mail: info@gaco.com, Web Site: www.gaco.com (16)

JA Sexauer, Elmsford, NY. Tel: (914) 472-7501, (800) 431-1872, FAX: (914) 472-5834, Web Site: www.jasmro.com (16)

Sexton, Neil, Northern Safety Co Inc, Utica, NY. Tel: (315) 793-4900, Web Site: www.northernsafety.com (16)

Seybold Publications, Gilbertsville, PA. Tel: (610) 327-3958, (888) 544-7104, FAX: (888) 463-4814, E-Mail: molly@thejossgroup.com, Web Site: www.seyboldreports.com (17)

Seyferth, William A., Muskegon Power Tool Corp, North Muskegon, MI. Tel: (231) 766-2194, (800) 635-5465, FAX: (231) 766-3846 (16)

Seymour, Jane, Deck the Walls Inc, Saint Peters, MO. Tel: (314) 719-8200, (866) 719-8200, FAX: (314) 719-8290, E-Mail: dtwcontact@fcibiz.com, Web Site: www.deckthewalls.com (5)

Seymour, Peter, Disney/ABC Television Group, Burbank, CA. Tel: (818) 460-7477, Web Site: www. disneyabctv.com (32)

Seymour, Sloan, PMX Agency, New York, NY. Tel: (212) 387-0300, (888) 960-0177, FAX: (212) 387-7647, E-Mail: info@pmxagency.com, Web Site: www.pmxagency.com (23)

SG360, Wheeling, IL. Tel: (847) 541-1080, FAX: (847) 541-5237, Web Site: www.sg360.com, (27)

Shackleton, John, Open Text Inc, Waterloo, ON Canada. Tel: (519) 888-9933, (800) 499-6544, FAX: (519) 888-0677, E-Mail: support@opentext.com, Web Site: www.opentext.com (16)

B Shackman & Co Inc, Galesburg, MI. Tel: (269) 484-1000, (800) 221-7656, FAX: (269) 484-1010, Web Site: www.shackman.com (6)

Shada, Mark, UAA Clearinghouse, Omaha, NE. Tel: (402) 991-2810, Web Site: www.uaaclearinghouse. com (22)

Shadding, Fred, Cyber City Teleservices Marketing Inc, Hackensack, NJ. Tel: (201) 487-1616, (800) 213-4144, E-Mail: info@cctll.com, Web Site: www.cctll. com (22)

Shaddock, Rob, Tyco Electronics Corp, Berwyn, PA. Tel: (610) 893-9800, Web Site: www.te.com (16)

Shadduck, Dave, True Value Co, Chicago, IL. Tel: (773) 695-5000, Web Site: www.truevaluecompany. com (16)

Shadek, Ed, Wildlife Education Ltd, Park Hills, KY. Tel: (858) 513-7600, FAX: (858) 513-7660, E-Mail: animals@zoobooks.com, Web Site: www.zoobooks. com (17)

Shades of Light, Richmond, VA. Tel: (804) 288-6515, (877) 288-5029, E-Mail: customercare@ shadesoflight.com, Web Site: www.shadesoflight. com (8)

Shadyac, Richard C., ALSAC - St Jude, Memphis, TN. Tel: (901) 495-3300, (800) 278-5833, FAX: (901) 495-3966, Web Site: www.stjude.org (1)

Shafer, Jay, A La Mode Inc, Oklahoma City, OK. Tel: (405) 359-6587, (800) ALAMODE, FAX: (405) 359-8612, Web Site: www.alamode.com (22)

Shaffer, Jacob W., McCormick-Armstrong Co Inc, Wichita, KS. Tel: (316) 264-1363, (800) 733-1363, FAX: (316) 263-4511, E-Mail: sales@ mccormickarmstrong.com, Web Site: www. mccormickarmstrong.com (27)

Shaffer, James W., Angelica Image Apparel, Saint Louis, MO. Tel: (314) 854-3800, (800) 235-8410, Web Site: www.angelica.com (16)

Shaffer, Michael, Phillips-Van Heusen Corp, New York, NY. Tel: (212) 381-3500, (800) 388-9122, FAX: (212) 381-3950, Web Site: www.pvh.com (2)

Shah, Amy, Tyco Electronics Corp, Berwyn, PA. Tel: (610) 893-9800, Web Site: www.te.com (16)

Shah, Vivek, Ziff Davis Media Inc, New York, NY. Tel: (212) 503-5100, FAX: (212) 503-5023, Web Site: www.ziffdavis.com (17)

Shahani, Vinay, Volkswagen Group of America Inc, Herndon, VA. Tel: (248) 754-5000, Web Site: www. volkswagengroupamerica.com (16)

Shaker Workshops, Ashburnham, MA. Tel: (978) 827-9900, (800) 849-9121, FAX: (978) 827-6554, E-Mail: shakerworkshops.customerservice@gmail. com, Web Site: www.shakerworkshops.com (8)

Shaker, William, Washington Marketing Group, Arlington, VA. Tel: (703) 534-9331, FAX: (703) 534-0242, E-Mail: william.shaker@twmg.com, Web Site: www.twmg.com (1)

Shakespeare Co, Columbia, SC. Tel: (803) 754-7000, (800) 347-3759, FAX: (803) 754-7342, Web Site: www.shakespeare-fishing.com (11)

Shakespeare Mailing Service, Union City, NJ. Tel: (212) 560-8958, E-Mail: support@ shakespearemailing.com, Web Site: www. shakespearemailing.com (28)

Shale, Joshua, Speedeon Data Corp, Cleveland, OH. Tel: (866) 647-9219, Web Site: www.speedeondata. com (30)

Shankar, Subromanian, American Megatrends Inc, Norcross, GA. Tel: (770) 246-8600, (800) 828-9264, FAX: (770) 246-8790, Web Site: www.ami.com (3)

Shanks, David, Penguin Group USA Inc, New York, NY. Tel: (212) 366-2000, Web Site: www.us. penguingroup.com (17)

Shanks, Robert L., Ford Motor Co, Dearborn, MI. Tel: (313) 845-8540, (800) 555-5259, FAX: (313) 845-6073, Web Site: www.ford.com (16)

Shanley, Mary, TTC Marketing Solutions, Chicago, IL. Tel: (773) 545-0407, (800) 777-6348, FAX: (773) 545-4034, E-Mail: sales@ttcmarketingsolutions. com, Web Site: www.ttcmarketingsolutions.com (29)

Shannon, Patty, The Wordstation, Avon By The Sea, NJ. Tel: (732) 774-4831, FAX: (732) 869-1822, E-Mail: pattyshannone@optonline.net (39)

Shape Global Technology, Sanford, ME. Tel: (207) 324-5200, (800) 627-5836, FAX: (207) 324-0875, E-Mail: info@shapeglobal.com, Web Site: www. shapenet.com (34)

Shape LLC, Addison, IL. Tel: (630) 620-8394, (800) 367-5811, FAX: (630) 620-0784, E-Mail: sales@ shapellc.com, Web Site: www.shapellc.com (3)

Shapes Marketing Inc, Highland Park, IL. Tel: (847) 291-1110, FAX: (847) 291-1308, Web Site: www. shapesmarket.com (20)

Shapin, John L., Shapes Marketing Inc, Highland Park, IL. Tel: (847) 291-1110, FAX: (847) 291-1308, Web Site: www.shapesmarket.com (20)

Shapin, Margaret, Shapes Marketing Inc, Highland Park, IL. Tel: (847) 291-1110, FAX: (847) 291-1308, Web Site: www.shapesmarket.com (20)

Shapiro, Alexandra, USA Network, New York, NY. Tel: (212) 664-4444, FAX: (212) 664-6365, Web Site: www.usanetwork.com (32)

Shapiro, David, Barcoding Inc, Baltimore, MD. Tel: (410) 385-8532, (888) 860-SCAN, (888) 860-7226, FAX: (410) 385-8559, E-Mail: info@barcoding. com, Web Site: www.barcoding.com (22)

Shapiro, Glenn, Executive Enterprises Inc, Hawthorne, NY. Tel: (860) 701-5900, (800) 831-8333, FAX: (860) 701-5909, (800) 250-3861, E-Mail: info@ eeiconferences.com, Web Site: www. eeiconferences.com (16)

Shapiro, Neal B., Channel 13 WNET Catalog Division, New York, NY. Tel: (212) 560-1313, FAX: (212) 560-1314, E-Mail: programming@thirteen.org, Web Site: www.thirteen.org (5)

Shapiro, Neal, Thirteen/WNET, New York, NY. Tel: (212) 560-1313, FAX: (212) 560-1314, E-Mail: programming@thirteen.org, Web Site: www. thirteen.org (1)

Shapiro, Peter, Puritan's Pride, Ronkonkoma, NY. Tel: (631) 567-9500, (800) 645-1030, FAX: (631) 471-5693, E-Mail: info@puritan.com, Web Site: www. puritan.com (7)

Shapiro, Sally, LIM College, New York, NY. Tel: (212) 752-1530, Web Site: www.limcollege.edu (1)

Shapley, Rick, Cade & Associates Advertising Inc, Tallahassee, FL. Tel: (850) 385-0300, (800) 715-CADE, FAX: (850) 385-1165, E-Mail: webmaster@ cade1.com, Web Site: www.cade1.com (35)

Share Group Inc, Newton, MA. Tel: (617) 629-4500, FAX: (617) 629-4510, E-Mail: info@sharegroup. com, Web Site: www.sharegroup.com (29)

Sharf Woodward & Associates Inc, Sherman Oaks, CA. Tel: (818) 988-2200, (877) 482-6687, Web Site: www.swjobs.com (20)

Sharf, Bernie, Sharf Woodward & Associates Inc, Sherman Oaks, CA. Tel: (818) 988-2200, (877) 482-6687, Web Site: www.swjobs.com (20)

Sharif, Tariq, D&B, Parsippany, NJ. Tel: (973) 605-6000, FAX: (973) 605-6920, Web Site: www.dnb. com (22)

Sharman, James A., World Kitchen Inc, Corning, NY. Tel: (607) 377-8000, (800) 999-3436, FAX: (607) 377-8946, Web Site: www.worldkitchen.com (16)

Sharp, Dolph, Dental Products Report, New York, NY. Tel: (847) 441-3700, FAX: (847) 441-3702, Web Site: www.dentalproducts.net (17)

Sharp, Gary, PharmArt, Circleville, OH. Tel: (860) 932-8588, (800) 848-1633, FAX: (800) 477-2923, Web Site: www.healthcarelogistics.com/Pharmart (6)

Sharp, Phillip A., AAAS/Science, Washington, DC. Tel: (202) 326-6400, FAX: (202) 371-9526, E-Mail: membership@aaas.org, Web Site: www.aaas.org (1)

Sharp, Robert "Bob" R., AAA Auto Club South, Tampa, FL. Tel: (813) 289-5800, FAX: (813) 289-1475, Web Site: www.aaa.com (1)

Sharp, Vickie, Recognition Products International, Easton, MD. Tel: (410) 820-0022, (800) 292-7354, FAX: (410) 820-5044, E-Mail: info@recognitionproducts. com, Web Site: www.shoprecognitionproducts.com (16)

Sharpe, Bill, Arnold Worldwide Toronto, Toronto, ON Canada. Tel: (416) 355-5009, E-Mail: bsharp@ arnoldworldwide.ca, Web Site: arn.com (35)

Sharpe, David, CertainTeed Corp, Valley Forge, PA. Tel: (610) 341-7000/7739, (800) 233-8990, FAX: (610) 341-7777, Web Site: www.certainteed.com (16)

Shasho Jones Direct Inc, New York, NY. Tel: (212) 929-2300, E-Mail: glenda@sjdirect.com, Web Site: www.sjdirect.com (20)

Shasho Jones, Glenda, Shasho Jones Direct Inc, New York, NY. Tel: (212) 929-2300, E-Mail: glenda@ sjdirect.com, Web Site: www.sjdirect.com (20)

Shaub, Yuko, The IEI Corp, Princeton, NJ. Tel: (609) 987-2700, FAX: (609) 987-2703 (6)

Shaukat, Tariq M., Caesars Entertainment Corp, Las Vegas, NV. Tel: (702) 407-6000, (800) 634-6001, FAX: (702) 407-6037, Web Site: www.caesars.com (16)

Shaver Direct Inc, Phoenix, AZ. Tel: (623) 594-3076, (857) 498-1853, E-Mail: dshaver934@aol.com (35)

Shaw, Carl, Fisher Scientific, Pittsburgh, PA. Tel: (800) 766-7000, FAX: (800) 772-7702, Web Site: www. fishersci.com (16)

Shaw, David Evans, AAAS/Science, Washington, DC. Tel: (202) 326-6400, FAX: (202) 371-9526, E-Mail: membership@aaas.org, Web Site: www.aaas.org (1)

Shaw, Douglas, Douglas Shaw & Associates, Naperville, IL. Tel: (630) 562-1321, Web Site: www. douglasshaw.com (1)

Shaw, Gary, Dex Media, Dallas-Fort Worth Airport, TX. Tel: (972) 453-7000, Web Site: www. dexmedia.com (31)

Shaw, Lisa, Raycom Sports, Charlotte, NC. Tel: (704) 378-4456/4400, FAX: (704) 378-4465, E-Mail: whicks@raycomsports.com, Web Site: raycomsports.com (16)

Shaw, Mark A., AAA Southern New England, Providence, RI. Tel: (401) 868-2045, FAX: (401) 868-2088, Web Site: www.aaa.com (1)

Shaw, Michael, Federal Envelope Co, Bensenville, IL. Tel: (630) 595-2000, FAX: (630) 595-1212, E-Mail: postmaster@federalenvelope.com, Web Site: www.federalenvelope.com (26)

Shaw, Ray, Watering Inc/Hemmings Motor News, Bennington, VT. Tel: (802) 442-3101, (800) 227-4373, FAX: (802) 447-1561, E-Mail: hmnmail@hemmings.com, Web Site: www.hemmings.com (17)

Shaw, Richard, Catalyst Computer Services Inc, Los Angeles, CA. Tel: (310) 441-4300, (800) 659-2267, FAX: (310) 441-4332, E-Mail: sales@catalystsoftware.com, Web Site: www.catalystsoftware.com (32)

Shaw, Richard, Union Federal Savings Bank, North Providence, RI. Tel: (401) 353-8900, (800) 992-0278, FAX: (401) 353-8938, Web Site: www.unionfsb.com (14)

Shaw, Sarah, Phone Bank Systems Inc, East Lansing, MI. Tel: (517) 332-1500, FAX: (517) 332-1514, E-Mail: rusha@phonebanks.com, Web Site: www.phonebanks.com (1)

Shaw, Scott M., Lincoln Educational Services Corp, West Orange, NJ. Tel: (973) 736-9340, Web Site: www.lincolnedu.com (13)

Shaw, Whitney, The Book of Lists, Charlotte, NC. Tel: (800) 433-4565, Web Site: www.bizjournals.com/bizbooks (23)

Shawyer, Kyla, Operation Smile Inc, Virginia Beach, VA. Tel: (757) 321-7645, Web Site: www.operationsmile.org (1)

Shay, Matthew, National Retail Federation Inc, Washington, DC. Tel: (202) 783-7971, (800) 673-4692, FAX: (202) 737-2849, E-Mail: webmaster@nrf.com, Web Site: www.nrf.com (1)

Shaytin, Paul, Empire Coffee & Tea Co, New York, NY. Tel: (212) 268-1220, (800) 262-5908, E-Mail: owners@empirecoffeetea.com, Web Site: www.empirecoffeetea.com (1)

Shea Zillner, Ronda, Zillner, Lenexa, KS. Tel: (913) 599-3230, Web Site: zillner.com (35)

Shea, Kevin J., Kevin J Shea & Associates, Arlington Heights, IL. Tel: (847) 392-2713 (39)

Shea, Mindy, 3M Post-It Custom Printed Products, Saint Paul, MN. Tel: (800) 328-2407, Web Site: www.3m.com (16)

Shea, Peter, Entrepreneur Media Inc, Irvine, CA. Tel: (949) 261-2325, (800) 274-6229, FAX: (949) 261-0234, Web Site: www.entrepreneur.com (17)

Shea, Stefani, Princess House Inc, Taunton, MA. Tel: (508) 823-0711, (508) 832-6800, (800) 622-0039, FAX: (508) 823-5182, Web Site: www.princesshouse.com (16)

Sheadoker, Carl, American Megatrends Inc, Norcross, GA. Tel: (770) 246-8600, (800) 828-9264, FAX: (770) 246-8790, Web Site: www.ami.com (3)

Shear, Debra, Liberty Mutual Group, Inc, Boston, MA. Tel: (617) 357-9500, (800) 837-5274, Web Site: www.libertymutual.com (15)

Sheats, Phillip F., CDMI Inc, Huntington Beach, CA. Tel: (714) 969-4064 (1)

Shebesta, Sarah, HY-KO Products Co, Northfield, OH. Tel: (330) 467-7446, Web Site: www.hy-ko.com (16)

Sheck, Steven, Infinite Media Concepts Inc, White Plains, NY. Tel: (914) 948-8300, FAX: (914) 949-1605, Web Site: mailinglists.com (23)

Sheckler, Julie, Baldwin Filters, Kearney, NE. Tel: (308) 234-1951, (800) 822-5394, FAX: (800) 828-4453, E-Mail: info@baldwinfilter.com, Web Site: www.baldwinfilter.com (16)

Sheehan, Becky A., FTD Companies Inc, Downers Grove, IL. Tel: (630) 719-7800, Web Site: www.ftdcompanies.com (16)

Sheehan, Timothy R, Lazydays RV Center, Seffner, FL. Tel: (813) 246-4333, FAX: (813) 246-4408, Web Site: www.lazydays.com (12)

Sheehan, Tom, tomsheehan worldwide, Reading, PA. Tel: (610) 478-8448, FAX: (610) 478-8449, E-Mail: tomsheehan@tomsheehan.com, Web Site: www.tomsheehan.com (35)

Sheehey, Mike, Comcast Spectacor LP, Philadelphia, PA. Tel: (215) 336-3600, (800) 298-4200, FAX: (215) 389-9518, E-Mail: info@comcast-spectacor.com, Web Site: www.comcast-spectacor.com (16)

Sheeks, Jeff, S Group Inc, Akron, OH. Tel: (330) 535-2103, (800) 686-7435, FAX: (330) 535-1723, E-Mail: info@s-groupinc.com, Web Site: www.s-groupinc.com (33)

Sheena, Esra, Rush Industries, Inc, Mineola, NY. Tel: (516) 741-0346, FAX: (516) 741-0348, Web Site: www.rushindustries.com (16)

Sheeran Direct Marketing, New Castle, DE. Tel: (302) 324-0200, (888) 325-2101, FAX: (302) 324-0213, E-Mail: jjs@jjsheeran.com, Web Site: www.jjsheeran.com (28)

Sheeran, Joseph J., Sheeran Direct Marketing, New Castle, DE. Tel: (302) 324-0200, (888) 325-2101, FAX: (302) 324-0213, E-Mail: jjs@jjsheeran.com, Web Site: www.jjsheeran.com (28)

Sheets, David, Emergency Essentials Inc, Orem, UT. Tel: (801) 222-9596, FAX: (801) 222-9598, E-Mail: webmaster@beprepared.com, Web Site: www.beprepared.com (16)

Sheets, J. Donald, Dow Corning Corp, Midland, MI. Tel: (989) 496-4400, (800) 248-2481, FAX: (989) 496-4572, Web Site: www.dowcorning.com (16)

Sheffield, Michael L., Multi-Level Marketing International Association (MLMIA), Irvine, CA. Tel: (949) 257-0931, FAX: (949) 281-2114, E-Mail: info@mlmia.com, Web Site: www.mlmia.com (1)

Sheffield, Sally, Executive Enterprises Inc, Hawthorne, NY. Tel: (860) 701-5900, (800) 831-8333, FAX: (860) 701-5909, (800) 250-3861, E-Mail: info@eeiconferences.com, Web Site: www.eeiconferences.com (16)

Shelby Insurance Companies, Birmingham, AL. Tel: (800) 443-1573, FAX: (877) 837-8203, Web Site: www.vesta.com (15)

Sheldon, Ricky, House of Eyes, Greensboro, NC. Tel: (336) 852-7107, FAX: (336) 854-0311 (2)

Sheldon, Robin, Soft Surroundings, Saint Louis, MO. Tel: (314) 812-5200, Web Site: www.softsurroundings.com (2)

Shell Oil Co, Houston, TX. Tel: (713) 241-6161, Web Site: www.shell.us (16)

Shell, Gary, EMS Technologies, Norcross, GA. Tel: (770) 263-9200, FAX: (770) 447-4405, Web Site: www.ems-t.com (16)

Shelton, Brent, FatWallet, Beloit, WI. Tel: (888) 634-0098, Web Site: www.fatwallet.com (14)

Shelton, Dave, Graphik Dimensions Ltd, High Point, NC. Tel: (336) 887-3500, (800) 221-0262, FAX: (336) 887-3773, E-Mail: customercare@pictureframes.com, Web Site: www.pictureframes.com (16)

Shelton, Todd A., United Stationers, Deerfield, IL. Tel: (847) 627-7000, FAX: (847) 647-7001, Web Site: www.unitedstationers.com (25)

Shen, Zhengda, Merkle Inc, Columbia, MD. Tel: (443) 542-4000, (877) 9MERKLE, FAX: (443) 542-4758, Web Site: www.merkleinc.com (22)

Shenkute, Sossina, DFS Group Limited, San Francisco, CA. Tel: (415) 977-2700, FAX: (415) 977-2970, Web Site: www.dfsgalleria.com (5)

David Shepard Associates Inc, Melville, NY. Tel: (516) 271-5567, FAX: (516) 271-5589, E-Mail: davidshepard@dsadirect.com, Web Site: www.dsadirect.com (20)

Shepard, David B., David Shepard Associates Inc, Melville, NY. Tel: (516) 271-5567, FAX: (516) 271-5589, E-Mail: davidshepard@dsadirect.com, Web Site: www.dsadirect.com (20)

Shepard, Douglas "Doug" C., Harte-Hanks, San Antonio, TX. Tel: (210) 829-9000, FAX: (210) 829-9403, Web Site: www.hartehanks.com (22)

Shepard, III T.R., King Features, New York, NY. Tel: (212) 455-4000, FAX: (212) 682-8332 (17)

Shepard's Inc, Bethel, CT. Tel: (203) 830-8300, (800) 243-0993, FAX: (203) 794-1296, E-Mail: mleahy@shepardsinc.com, Web Site: www.shepardsinc.com (22)

Shepherd, Danny R., Vulcan Materials Co, Birmingham, AL. Tel: (205) 298-3000, FAX: (205) 298-2960, Web Site: www.vulcanmaterials.com (16)

Shepley, Bob, Standard Tools & Equipment Co, Greensboro, NC. Tel: (336) 697-7177, (800) 336-2776, Web Site: www.toolsusa.com (9)

Sheppard Envelope Co, Auburn, MA. Tel: (508) 791-5588, (800) 325-6622, FAX: (508) 754-3108, E-Mail: sales@sheppardenvelope.com, Web Site: www.sheppardenvelope.com (26)

Sheppard, David, Swords Music Co Inc, Fort Worth, TX. Tel: (817) 53-MUSIC, (800) 522-3028, FAX: (817) 536-4293, E-Mail: daveshep4300@sbcglobal.net, Web Site: www.swordsmusicinc.com (34)

Sher, Barry, Nostradamus Advertising, New York, NY. Tel: (212) 581-1362, E-Mail: nos@nostradamus.net, Web Site: www.nostradamus.net (36)

Sher, Debra, American College of Physician Executives, Tampa, FL. Tel: (813) 287-2000, (800) 562-8088, FAX: (813) 287-8993, E-Mail: acpe@acpe.org, Web Site: www.acpe.org (1)

Sher, Robert, Alvion LLC, Cape Coral, FL. Tel: (239) 574-8600, (877) 528-7800, FAX: (239) 574-8551, Web Site: www.alvion.com (22)

Sheridan Books Inc, Chelsea, MI. Tel: (734) 475-9145, (800) 999-BOOK, FAX: (734) 475-7337, E-Mail: info@sheridanbooks.com, Web Site: www.sheridanbooks.com (27)

Sheridan Labarge, Joan, Working Mother, New York, NY. Tel: (212) 221-9595, FAX: (212) 219-7448, Web Site: www.workingmother.com (31)

Sheridan, Karen P., SMY Media Inc, Chicago, IL. Tel: (312) 621-9600, FAX: (312) 621-0924, E-Mail: info@smymedia.com, Web Site: www.smymedia.com (32)

Sherk, Kyle, Gaco Western Inc, Seattle, WA. Tel: (206) 575-0450, (800) 456-4226, FAX: (206) 575-0587, E-Mail: info@gaco.com, Web Site: www.gaco.com (16)

Sherman & Associates Inc, Warren, OH. Tel: (330) 399-4500, FAX: (330) 399-6747, E-Mail: info@shermanexperience.com, Web Site: www.shermanexperience.com (35)

Sherman Specialty Toy Co Inc, Jericho, NY. Tel: (516) 861-6420, (516) 546-7400, (800) 645-6513, FAX: (516) 861-1033, (800) 853-8697, E-Mail: orders@ shermanspecialty.com, Web Site: www. shermanspecialty.com (16)

Sherman, Bethany, Dow Jones & Co, Princeton, NJ. Tel: (609) 520-4000, FAX: (212) 416-4348, Web Site: www.dowjones.com/corp/index.html (17)

Sherman, Esq. Robert, Paul, Hastings, Janofsky & Walker LLP, New York, NY. Tel: (212) 318-6037, FAX: (212) 319-4090, E-Mail: robertsherman@ paulhastings.com, Web Site: www.paulhastings.com (20)

Sherman, Howard, Doremus & Co, New York, NY. Tel: (212) 366-3000, FAX: (212) 366-3060, E-Mail: mbroom@doremus.com, Web Site: www.doremus. com (35)

Sherman, Jonathan, Sherman & Associates Inc, Warren, OH. Tel: (330) 399-4500, FAX: (330) 399-6747, E-Mail: info@shermanexperience.com, Web Site: www.shermanexperience.com (35)

Sherman, Lisa, The Advertising Council Inc, New York, NY. Tel: (212) 922-1500, FAX: (212) 922-1676, E-Mail: info@adcouncil.org, Web Site: www. adcouncil.org (1)

Sherman, Marc, AtlantaPrintAndMail.com Inc, Atlanta, GA. Tel: (404) 321-6222, E-Mail: info@ mymailingservice.com, Web Site: www. mymailingservice.com (21)

Sherman, Mike, Direct Marketing Solutions Inc, Portland, OR. Tel: (503) 281-1400, FAX: (503) 249-5120, Web Site: www.teamdms.com (35)

Sherman, Steve, Direct Marketing Solutions Inc, Portland, OR. Tel: (503) 281-1400, FAX: (503) 249-5120, Web Site: www.teamdms.com (35)

Shertzer, Chris, Maryland Pennysaver, Hanover, MD. Tel: (888) 899-8992, Web Site: www. mdpennysaver.com (17)

Sherwin, Theodore D., IBSDirect, King of Prussia, PA. Tel: (610) 265-8210, FAX: (610) 265-7997, Web Site: www.ibsdm.com (27)

Sherwood Design & Development Center, Carlstadt, NJ. Tel: (201) 372-3900, FAX: (201) 372-0917 (27)

Sherwood, Cindy, Glens Falls Hospital Foundation, Glens Falls, NY. Tel: (518) 926-5960, FAX: (518) 926-7012, Web Site: www.glensfallshospital.org (1)

Sherwood, Hank, GS&F, Nashville, TN. Tel: (615) 385-1100, (800) 241-3325, FAX: (615) 783-0500, E-Mail: biz@gsandf.com, Web Site: www.gsandf. com (35)

Sherwood, Jennifer, Saunders Manufacturing Co Inc, Readfield, ME. Tel: (207) 685-3385, (800) 341-4674, FAX: (207) 685-9918, E-Mail: jsherwood@ saunders-usa.com, Web Site: www.saunders-usa. com (16)

Sherwood, Juliana, National Hardware Show, Norwalk, CT. Tel: (203) 840-5622, (888) 425-9377, FAX: (203) 840-9622, E-Mail: inquiry@hardware. reedexpo.com, Web Site: www. nationalhardwareshow.com (42)

Sheshunoff Management Services, Austin, TX. Tel: (512) 472-4000, (800) 477-1772, FAX: (512) 479-8189, E-Mail: info@smslp.com, Web Site: www. ashesh.com (20)

Sheshunoff, Alex, Sheshunoff Management Services, Austin, TX. Tel: (512) 472-4000, (800) 477-1772, FAX: (512) 479-8189, E-Mail: info@smslp.com, Web Site: www.ashesh.com (20)

Shevers, Jr. Hal, Sporty's Preferred Living, Batavia, OH. Tel: (513) 735-9000, (800) 776-7897, FAX: (800) 543-8633, E-Mail: csmgr@sportys.com, Web Site: www.sportys.com (5)

Shibuya, Shiro, Teikoku Databank America Inc, New York, NY. Tel: (212) 421-9805, FAX: (212) 421-9806, E-Mail: info@teikoku.com, Web Site: www. teikoku.com (24)

Shield Healthcare, Valencia, CA. Tel: (661) 294-4200, (800) 765-8775, FAX: (661) 294-1043, (800) 748-0713, Web Site: www.shieldhealthcare.com (7)

Shields, Barbara, USAA, San Antonio, TX. Tel: (512) 498-6524, FAX: (512) 498-8000 (15)

Shields, Viola, American Target Advertising Inc, Manassas, VA. Tel: (703) 392-7676, FAX: (703) 392-7654, E-Mail: info@americantarget.com, Web Site: americantarget.com (35)

Kate Shifman Consulting, Brooklyn, NY. Tel: (917) 710-0219 (20)

Shiftan, Ronald, Lifetime Brands Inc, Garden City, NY. Tel: (516) 683-6000, FAX: (516) 555-0101, E-Mail: questions@lifetimebrands.com, Web Site: www. lifetimebrands.com (8)

Shilcock, Nick, Fairfield Industries Inc, Sugar Land, TX. Tel: (281) 275-7500, (800) 231-9809, FAX: (281) 275-7550, E-Mail: jblattman@fairfield.com, Web Site: www.fairfield.com (16)

Shillcraft Inc, Annapolis, MD. Tel: (410) 682-3060, (800) 638-1542, FAX: (410) 682-3130, Web Site: www.shillcraft.com (16)

Shimatani, Yoichi, Shiseido Cosmetics America, East Windsor, NJ. Tel: (212) 805-2300, FAX: (212) 688-0109, Web Site: www.sca.shiseido.com (7)

Shindigz, South Whitley, IN. Tel: (219) 723-5171, (800) 314-8736, FAX: (219) 723-6976, E-Mail: csr@ shindigz.com, Web Site: www.shindigz.com (27)

Shinn, Duane, Keyboard Workshop, Medford, OR. Tel: (541) 664-7052, FAX: (541) 664-7052, E-Mail: duane@playpiano.com, Web Site: www.playpiano. com (17)

Shinn, Meghan, Horticulture Magazine, Cincinnati, OH. Tel: (513) 531-2690, FAX: (513) 891-7153, Web Site: www.hortmag.com (17)

Shipley, Bob, The Hartz Mountain Corp, Secaucus, NJ. Tel: (201) 271-4800, (800) 275-1414, FAX: (201) 271-0068, Web Site: www.hartz.com (16)

Shipping Solutions, Eagan, MN. Tel: (651) 905-1727, (888) 890-7447, FAX: (651) 905-1827, E-Mail: info@shipsolutions.com, Web Site: www. shipsolutions.com (16)

Shirer, Joyce, Rodale Inc, Emmaus, PA. Tel: (610) 967-5171, FAX: (610) 967-8963, Web Site: www. rodaleinc.com (17)

Shirley, John, Alfa Aesar-A Johnson Matthey Co, Ward Hill, MA. Tel: (800) 343-0660, FAX: (800) 322-4757, E-Mail: info@alfa.com, Web Site: www.alfa. com (9)

Shiseido Cosmetics America, East Windsor, NJ. Tel: (212) 805-2300, FAX: (212) 688-0109, Web Site: www.sca.shiseido.com (7)

Shisler and Associates, Dallas, TX. Tel: (972) 387-8656 (20)

Shisler, Arden L., Nationwide Mutual Insurance Co, Columbus, OH. Tel: (614) 249-7111, (800) 882-2822, FAX: (614) 854-3676, Web Site: www.nationwide. com (15)

Shisler, Jack, Shisler and Associates, Dallas, TX. Tel: (972) 387-8656 (20)

Shiunko, Jean, The Psychological Corp, San Antonio, TX. Tel: (800) 211-8378, FAX: (800) 232-1223, Web Site: www.psychcorp.com (17)

Shkordoff, Nick, Ideal Industries (Canada) Corp, Ajax, ON Canada. Tel: (905) 683-3400, (800) 824-3325, FAX: (905) 683-0209, E-Mail: nick.shkordoff@ idealindustries.com, Web Site: www.idealindustries. com (9)

Shmidman, Yehuda, The Franklin Mint, Exton, PA. Tel: (610) 497-4800, (800) THE-MINT, FAX: (610) 497-4956, E-Mail: support@franklinmint.com, Web Site: www.franklinmint.com (16)

Shneider, Michael A., Woodall Publishing Co LP, Ventura, CA. Tel: (805) 667-4100, (800) 323-9076, FAX: (805) 667-4468, Web Site: www.woodalls. com (17)

Shocker, Mark W, AdSell Companies, Saint Louis, MO. Tel: (314) 773-0500, FAX: (314) 773-0555, E-Mail: marks@adsell.com, Web Site: www.adsell.com (21)

Shoen, James P., U-Haul International, Phoenix, AZ. Tel: (602) 263-6011, (800) GO-UHAUL, FAX: (602) 263-6598, Web Site: www.uhaul.com (16)

Shoen, Joe, U-Haul International, Phoenix, AZ. Tel: (602) 263-6011, (800) GO-UHAUL, FAX: (602) 263-6598, Web Site: www.uhaul.com (16)

Shoff, Patricia, Florida Today, Melbourne, FL. Tel: (321) 242-3500, (877) 424-0156, FAX: (321) 242-3729, Web Site: www.floridatoday.com (17)

Shoffner, Harry L., Carolina Biological Supply Co, Burlington, NC. Tel: (800) 334-5551, (800) 222-7112, E-Mail: carolina@carolina.com, Web Site: www. carolina.com (9)

Shoham, Mark, A-T Surgical Manufacturing Co, Holyoke, MA. Tel: (413) 532-4551, (800) 225-2023, FAX: (413) 532-0826, Web Site: www.atsurgical. com (2)

Iris Shokoff Associates, New York, NY. Tel: (212) 295-9191, FAX: (212) 293-3779 (31)

Shokoff, Iris, Iris Shokoff Associates, New York, NY. Tel: (212) 295-9191, FAX: (212) 293-3779 (31)

Sholes, Greg, All-n-One List Marketing Inc, Fishersville, VA. Tel: (703) 717-5621, FAX: (703) 286-5418, E-Mail: info@allinonelistmarketing.com, Web Site: www.allinonelistmarketing.com (23)

Sholley, Craig, African Wildlife Foundation, Washington, DC. Tel: (202) 939-3333, (888) 494-5354, FAX: (202) 939-3332, Web Site: www.awf.org (1)

Shonebarger, Steven, Harry Winston Inc, New York, NY. Tel: (212) 245-2000, FAX: (212) 489-0016, E-Mail: hw@harrywinston.com, Web Site: www. harry-winston.com (16)

Shooster, Frank, Global Response Corp, Margate, FL. Tel: (954) 973-7300, (800) 537-8000, FAX: (954) 968-9862, E-Mail: wendys@globalresponse.com, Web Site: www.globalresponse.com (29)

Shooster, Herman, Global Response Corp, Margate, FL. Tel: (954) 973-7300, (800) 537-8000, FAX: (954) 968-9862, E-Mail: wendys@globalresponse.com, Web Site: www.globalresponse.com (29)

Shooting Star International, Hollywood, CA. Tel: (323) 469-2020, FAX: (323) 464-0880, Web Site: www. shootingstaragency.com (38)

Shop.com, Miami, FL. Tel: (866) 420-1709. E-Mail: customerservice@shop.com, Web Site: www.shop. com (16)

Shopguide.com, Amarillo, TX. Tel: (806) 351-0005, FAX: (806) 351-0059, E-Mail: info@shopguide. com, Web Site: www.shopguide.com (27)

Shopsmith Inc, Dayton, OH. Tel: (937) 898-6070, (800) 543-7586, FAX: (937) 890-5197, Web Site: www. shopsmith.com (16)

Shor, Tama J., Directory of Major Malls Inc, Nyack, NY. Tel: (845) 348-7000, (800) 898-6255, Web Site: shoppingcenters.com (23)

Shore, Linda, Astronomical Society of the Pacific, San Francisco, CA. Tel: (415) 337-1100, (800) 335-2624, FAX: (415) 337-5205, E-Mail: service@ astrosociety.org, Web Site: www.astrosociety.org (1)

Shoreham, Lee, Privacy Journal, Providence, RI. Tel: (401) 274-7861, FAX: (401) 274-4747, E-Mail: orders@privacyjournal.net, Web Site: www. privacyjournal.net (17)

Shorette, Ken, Time Logistics Inc, Columbia, TN. Tel: (866) 293-8463, FAX: (866) 591-5697, E-Mail: quote@timelogisticsinc.com, Web Site: www. timelogisticsinc.com (12)

Shorette, Laura, Time Logistics Inc, Columbia, TN. Tel: (866) 293-8463, FAX: (866) 591-5697, E-Mail: quote@timelogisticsinc.com, Web Site: www. timelogisticsinc.com (12)

Shorette, Michael, Time Logistics Inc, Columbia, TN. Tel: (866) 293-8463, FAX: (866) 591-5697, E-Mail: quote@timelogisticsinc.com, Web Site: www. timelogisticsinc.com (12)

Short, Diane, Easthill Group Inc, Pottstown, PA. Tel: (610) 323-9063, (610) 323-9099, (610) 323-2200, (800) 345-1178, (888) 869-4433, FAX: (610) 323-6268, Web Site: www.eastwoodcompany.com (12)

Short, John, NewsNotes LLC, Middleton, WI. Tel: (608) 831-9600, (800) 676-9665, FAX: (608) 831-9665, E-Mail: sales@nastar-inc.com, Web Site: www.news-notes.com (27)

Shortage Control Inc & SC Video, Strongsville, OH. Tel: (440) 238-5432, (800) 332-2288, FAX: (440) 238-8687, E-Mail: sales@shortagecontrol.com, Web Site: www.shortagecontrol.com (5)

Shortt, Kriya, Cessna Aircraft Co, Wichita, KS. Tel: (316) 517-6000, (800) 4-CESSNA, FAX: (316) 517-6640, Web Site: www.cessna.com (16)

Shortt, Tom, Unisource Worldwide, Inc, Norcross, GA. Tel: (770) 447-9000, (800) 864-7687, FAX: (770) 734-2000, Web Site: www.unisourcelink.com (25)

Shostak, Nick, Connecticut Color Inc, Meriden, CT. Tel: (203) 237-1400, FAX: (203) 440-3678, Web Site: www.connecticutcolor.com (27)

Shoup, John, Great Chefs Television Publishing, New Orleans, LA. Tel: (504) 581-5000, (800) 321-1499, FAX: (504) 581-1188, E-Mail: info@greatchefs. com, Web Site: www.greatchefs.com (6)

Shoup, Mike, Antique Rose Emporium, Brenham, TX. Tel: (979) 836-9051, (800) 441-0002, FAX: (979) 836-0928, E-Mail: roses@weareroses.com, Web Site: antiqueroseemporium.com (8)

Showerman, Sandy, Hess Print Solutions, Kent, OH. Tel: (800) 678-1222, E-Mail: info@ hessprintsolutions.com, Web Site: www. thepressofohio.com (27)

Showtime Networks Inc, New York, NY. Tel: (212) 708-1600, FAX: (212) 708-1450, Web Site: www. sho.com (16)

Shrimp, Robert, Oracle Corp, Redwood Shores, CA. Tel: (650) 506-7000, (800) 633-0738, FAX: (650) 506-7200, Web Site: www.oracle.com (16)

Shriver, Norman, Orbit Manufacturing Co, Perkasie, PA. Tel: (215) 257-0727, (888) 895-0958, FAX: (215) 257-7399, Web Site: www.orbitmfg.com (9)

Shrivers, Timothy, Special Olympics International, Washington, DC. Tel: (202) 628-3630, (800) 700-8585, FAX: (202) 824-0200, E-Mail: info@ specialolympics.org, Web Site: www. specialolympics.org (1)

Shroeder, Sr. Bill, Collector Books & American Quilters Society, Paducah, KY. Tel: (270) 898-6211, (800) 626-5420, FAX: (270) 898-8890, E-Mail: info@ collectorbooks.com, Web Site: www.collectorbooks. com (17)

Shroyer, Bart, DEFENDER Direct Inc, Indianapolis, IN. Tel: (317) 810-4720, (800) 860-0303, FAX: (317) 810-4723, Web Site: www.defenderdirect.com (32)

Shtulman, Jill, JSA Creative Services LLC, Chicago, IL. Tel: (773) 772-3445, FAX: (773) 772-3446, E-Mail: jsacreative@comcast.net, Web Site: www. jsacreative.com (39)

Shuchman, Salem, Entrepreneur Partners, Philadelphia, PA. Tel: (267) 322-7000, FAX: (267) 322-7001, E-Mail: info@epfunds.com, Web Site: www. epfunds.com (14)

Shukla, Abhinav, True Value Co, Chicago, IL. Tel: (773) 695-5000, Web Site: www.truevaluecompany. com (16)

Shuler, Elizabeth, AFL-CIO, Washington, DC. Tel: (202) 637-5000, FAX: (202) 637-5323, (202) 637-5058, Web Site: www.aflcio.org (1)

Shulkin, Mike, A La Carte, Chicago, IL. Tel: (773) 745-5900, (800) 723-2370, FAX: (773) 237-3075, E-Mail: service@alacarteline.com, Web Site: www. alacarteline.com (16)

Shull, Cecily, Pritchett & Hull Associates Inc, Atlanta, GA. Tel: (770) 451-0602, (800) 241-4925, FAX: (770) 454-7130, E-Mail: phsales@p-h.com, Web Site: www.p-h.com (17)

Shull, Craig, Campaign Monitor, San Francisco, CA. Tel: (888) 533-8098, E-Mail: info@ campaignmonitor.com, Web Site: www. campaignmonitor.com (24)

Shulman, Joshua, Bergdorf Goodman, New York, NY. Tel: (646) 735-5200, (800) 967-3788, (800) 218-4918, FAX: (212) 872-8677, E-Mail: clientservices@bergdorfgoodman.com, Web Site: www.bergdorfgoodman.com (2)

Shultz, Dakota, Agency 360 LLC, Naperville, IL. Tel: (312) 316-7070, (312) 371-4104, E-Mail: mail@ agencythreesixty.com, Web Site: agencythreesixty. com (35)

Shultz, Sasha, Sylvan Learning Inc, Baltimore, MD. Tel: (410) 843-8000, (800) 31-SUCCESS, FAX: (410) 843-8057, E-Mail: pr@sylvanlearning.com, Web Site: www.sylvanlearning.com (16)

Shumate, Stephen, MTS Publishing, Naperville, IL. Tel: (630) 955-9750, (800) 332-4655, FAX: (630) 955-9787, E-Mail: info@midwesttruckshopper.com, Web Site: www.midwesttruckshopper.com (17)

Gloria Shurn Creative Services, Chicago, IL. Tel: (312) 337-0032, FAX: (312) 337-3958 (35)

Shurn, Gloria J., Gloria Shurn Creative Services, Chicago, IL. Tel: (312) 337-0032, FAX: (312) 337-3958 (35)

Shurtleff, Jane, Market Recognition, Boxborough, MA. Tel: (978) 314-0127, Web Site: www. marketrecognition.com (20)

Shusterman, Howard, Rex Three Inc, Sunrise, FL. Tel: (954) 452-8301, (800) 782-6509, FAX: (954) 452-0569, E-Mail: info@rex3.com, Web Site: www. rexthree.com (27)

Shute, Dave, TransAmerica Retirement Services, Los Angeles, CA. Tel: (213) 742-3363, Web Site: www. ta-retirement.com (15)

Shutterbug, Titusville, FL. Tel: (321) 269-3212, FAX: (321) 255-3146, Web Site: www.shutterbug.net (17)

Shutterfly, Redwood City, CA. Tel: (650) 610-5200, Web Site: www.shutterfly.com (27)

Shutts, Anthony, Charisma Brands LLC, Laguna Hills, CA. Tel: (949) 788-8803, (800) 779-5335, Web Site: www.charismabrands.com (6)

Siadak, Amy, House of Marketing Research, Pasadena, CA. Tel: (626) 486-1400, FAX: (626) 486-1404, Web Site: www.hmr-research.com (30)

Sichel, Bart, Burlington Coat Factory, Burlington, NJ. Tel: (609) 387-7800, FAX: (609) 387-7071, Web Site: www.burlingtoncoatfactory.com (16)

Sickafus Sheepskins, Strausstown, PA. Tel: (610) 488-1782, (888) 751-1300, FAX: (610) 488-1576, E-Mail: pat@patgarrett.com, Web Site: www. sheepcoat.com (2)

SickKids Foundation, Toronto, ON Canada. Tel: (800) 661-1083, FAX: (416) 813-5024, Web Site: www. sickkidsfoundation.com (1)

Sidell, Bob, Mylan Enterprises, Tarzana, CA. Tel: (818) 538-8080, (888) 528-3928, FAX: (818) 538-7646, E-Mail: calcos@silkskin.com, Web Site: www. silkskin.com (7)

Sideroff, Barry, Direct Ventures Inc, Rye, NY. Tel: (914) 939-9842, FAX: (914) 834-3883, E-Mail: bsideroff@directventuresmcinc.wm (20)

Sidwell, Lawrence W., John Deere Financial, Johnston, IA. Tel: (515) 267-3000, (800) 275-5322, FAX: (515) 267-3292, Web Site: www.deere.com (14)

Sieber, Kayrle, Quill Corp, Lincolnshire, IL. Tel: (847) 876-3535, (800) 789-1331, Web Site: www.quill. com (16)

Sieber, Kayrle, Quill Lincolnshire Inc, Lincolnshire, IL. Tel: (800) 982-3400, FAX: (800) 789-8955, Web Site: www.quill.com (10)

Siegel, Daniel, Lifetime Brands Inc, Garden City, NY. Tel: (516) 683-6000, FAX: (516) 555-0101, E-Mail: questions@lifetimebrands.com, Web Site: www. lifetimebrands.com (8)

Siegel, Jeffrey, Lifetime Brands Inc, Garden City, NY. Tel: (516) 683-6000, FAX: (516) 555-0101, E-Mail: questions@lifetimebrands.com, Web Site: www. lifetimebrands.com (8)

Siegel, Kenneth S., Starwood Hotels & Resorts Worldwide Inc, Stamford, CT. Tel: (203) 964-6000, FAX: (914) 640-8310, Web Site: www.starwoodhotels. com (19)

Siegel, Neal, Tri-Media Marketing Services Inc, Wilmette, IL. Tel: (800) 874-0338, E-Mail: neals@ trimediaonline.com, Web Site: www.trimediaonline. com (23)

Siegel, Peri, Potpourri Group Inc, North Billerica, MA. Tel: (978) 256-4100, FAX: (978) 256-1961/0344, Web Site: www.potpourrigroup.com (6)

Siegel, Stephen, UV Process Supply, Chicago, IL. Tel: (773) 248-0099, (800) 621-1296, FAX: (773) 880-6647, E-Mail: info@uvps.com, Web Site: www. uvprocess.com (34)

Siegel, Todd H., Affinion Group, Stamford, CT. Tel: (203) 956-1000, (800) 282-3315, Web Site: www. affinion.com (35)

Siegel, Todd H., Affinion Group, Stamford, CT. Tel: (203) 956-1000, (800) 251-2148, Web Site: www. affiniongroup.com (16)

Siegenthaler, Michael, Initiative, New York, NY. Tel: (212) 605-7000, FAX: (212) 605-7200, Web Site: www.initiative.com (32)

Siegfried, Bradford, BLS Inc, Wilmington, DE. Tel: (302) 631-1616, (800) 545-7766, FAX: (302) 631-1619, E-Mail: bls@tutorsystems.com, Web Site: www.tutorsystems.com (17)

Siemens, Mike, Camping World Inc, Bowling Green, KY. Tel: (270) 781-2718, (800) 626-6189, FAX: (270) 796-8991, Web Site: www.campingworld.com (11)

Siemers, Scott, Morcon Industrial Specialty Inc, Mesquite, NV. Tel: (702) 346-3447, (888) 842-7953, Web Site: www.morcon-ind.com (9)

Sieracki, Eric P., Countrywide Financial Corp, Calabasas, CA. Tel: (818) 225-3000, FAX: (818) 225-4051, Web Site: www.countrywide.com (14)

Sierke, William H., Gothic Arch Greenhouses Inc, Mobile, AL. Tel: (251) 471-5238, (800) 531-4769, FAX: (251) 471-5465, E-Mail: info@gothicarchgreenhouses.net, Web Site: www.GothicArchGreenhouses.com (8)

Sierra Scientific Inc, Phoenix, AZ. Tel: (602) 256-0540, FAX: (602) 252-1972, Web Site: www.value-tek.com (9)

Sierra Trading Post, Cheyenne, WY. Tel: (800) 713-4534, FAX: (800) 378-8946, E-Mail: customerservice@sierratradingpost.com, Web Site: www.sierratradingpost.com (2)

Sierra, Rodrigo A., American Medical Association, Chicago, IL. Tel: (312) 464-5000, (800) 621-8335, FAX: (312) 464-4184, Web Site: www.ama-assn.org (1)

Sifton, Michael, Data Communications Management Corp, Brampton, ON Canada. Tel: (905) 791-3151, (800) 268-0128, FAX: (905) 791-3277, E-Mail: info@datacm.com, Web Site: www.datacm.com (21)

Sight Marketing, Minneapolis, MN. Tel: (651) 379-4059, Web Site: www.sightmarketing.com (30)

The Signature Agency, Wake Forest, NC. Tel: (919) 878-8989, (800) 870-8700, FAX: (919) 878-3939, E-Mail: info@signatureagency.com, Web Site: www.signatureagency.com (35)

Signature Communications Inc, Philadelphia, PA. Tel: (215) 922-3022, FAX: (215) 922-3033, Web Site: www.signatureteam.com (21)

Signature Inc, Ann Arbor, MI. Tel: (734) 426-2000, FAX: (734) 426-2109, E-Mail: johnagno@signatureseries.com, Web Site: www.mentoringandcoaching.com (20)

Signature Styles LLC, Wilmington, DE. Tel: (302) 636-5401 (2)

Sikanas, Debra, Baudville Inc, Grand Rapids, MI. Tel: (616) 698-0889, (800) 728-0888, FAX: (616) 698-0554, E-Mail: service@baudville.com, Web Site: www.baudville.com (16)

Sikorski, John, National Mail Graphics Corp, Exton, PA. Tel: (610) 524-1600, FAX: (610) 524-7638, E-Mail: jsikorski@nmgcorp.com, Web Site: www.nmgcorp.com (27)

Silagy, Eric, Florida Power & Light Co, Juno Beach, FL. Tel: (305) 552-3552, (800) 468-8243, FAX: (305) 552-2487, Web Site: www.fpl.com (16)

Silber, Tony, Audience Development, Norwalk, CT. Tel: (203) 854-6730, FAX: (203) 854-6735, E-Mail: inolan@red7media.com, Web Site: www.audiencedevelopment.com (43)

Silberman, S., American Thermoplastic Co, Pittsburgh, PA. Tel: (412) 967-0900, (800) 245-6600, FAX: (412) 967-9990, E-Mail: atc@binders.com, Web Site: www.binders.com (27)

Siler, Steve J., Hurletron Inc, Libertyville, IL. Tel: (847) 680-7022, FAX: (847) 680-7338, E-Mail: sales@hurletron.com, Web Site: www.hurletron.com (34)

Silicato, Steve, MARCOR Remediation Inc, Halethorpe, MD. Tel: (410) 785-0001, (800) 547-0128, FAX: (410) 771-0348, E-Mail: info@marcor.com, Web Site: www.marcor.com (16)

Silicon Graphics Inc, Fremont, CA. Tel: (510) 933-8300, Web Site: www.sgi.com (16)

Silk, Tom, CorporateRewards.com, New York, NY. Tel: (212) 689-1200, Web Site: www.corporaterewards.com (35)

Silliker Inc, Chicago, IL. Tel: (708) 957-7878, FAX: (708) 957-3798, E-Mail: cjx@netcom.com, Web Site: www.silliker.com (20)

Silo-Hunt Hill Farm, New Milford, CT. Tel: (860) 355-0300, Web Site: thesiloct.org (8)

Silva, Joseph, DS Services of North America LP, Lakeland, FL. Tel: (770) 933-1400, (800) 669-3402, FAX: (770) 956-9495, E-Mail: customerservice@water.com, Web Site: www.water.com (4)

Silver Marketing Inc, Bethesda, MD. Tel: (301) 951-3505, FAX: (301) 652-3691, E-Mail: psilver@silvermktg.com, Web Site: www.silvermarketing.com (35)

Silver Star Brands, Oshkosh, WI. Tel: (920) 231-3800, FAX: (920) 231-1247, Web Site: www.silverstarbrands.com (6)

Silver, Adam, National Basketball Association, New York, NY. Tel: (212) 407-8000, FAX: (212) 826-0579, Web Site: www.nba.com (1)

Silver, Patricia, Silver Marketing Inc, Bethesda, MD. Tel: (301) 951-3505, FAX: (301) 652-3691, E-Mail: psilver@silvermktg.com, Web Site: www.silvermarketing.com (35)

Silverdides, Ian, National Wholesale Co Inc, Lexington, NC. Tel: (336) 248-5904, (800) 480-4673, FAX: (336) 248-2880, E-Mail: customerservice@shopnational.com, Web Site: www.shopnational.com (2)

Richard Silverman, Kew Gardens, NY. Tel: (718) 441-5358, FAX: (718) 441-5358, E-Mail: vze268ci@verizon.net (39)

Silverman, George, The Teleconference Network, Nanuet, NY. Tel: (845) 624-0633, FAX: (845) 623-9394, E-Mail: nospam@mnav.com, Web Site: www.market-navigation.com (30)

Silverman, Ivan, TelAmerica Media Inc, Philadelphia, PA. Tel: (215) 568-7066, FAX: (215) 564-5388, Web Site: www.telamericamedia.com (31)

Silverman, Mickey, More Media Direct Inc, Marina Del Rey, CA. Tel: (310) 577-2025, E-Mail: info@moremediadirect.com, Web Site: www.moremediadirect.com (35)

Silverman, Richard, Richard Silverman, Kew Gardens, NY. Tel: (718) 441-5358, FAX: (718) 441-5358, E-Mail: vze268ci@verizon.net (39)

Silverman, Robert, The Bil-Ray Aluminum Siding Corp of Queens Inc, New Hyde Park, NY. Tel: (516) 616-4200, (800) 474-4415, FAX: (516) 616-4030, Web Site: www.homeclub.com (2)

SilverPop, Atlanta, GA. Tel: (678) 247-0500, (866) 745-8767, FAX: (678) 247-0501, E-Mail: contactsales@silverpop.com, Web Site: www.silverpop.com (32)

Silvers, Robert, Nyrev Inc, New York, NY. Tel: (212) 757-8070, FAX: (212) 333-5374, E-Mail: mail@nybooks.com, Web Site: www.nybooks.com (17)

SilverState Marketing Solutions, Las Vegas, NV. Tel: (702) 489-2124, Web Site: www.silverstateprintmail.com (28)

Silverstein, Amy, Kantar Media, New York, NY. Tel: (212) 991-6000, (800) 497-8450, FAX: (212) 991-6100, Web Site: www.kantarmedia.us (32)

Silverstone, Bruce T., Product Marketplace, Stratford, CT. Tel: (203) 375-8371, (800) 286-4768, FAX: (203) 386-1203, E-Mail: rita@sabinc.com (33)

Sim, Judith, Oracle Corp, Redwood Shores, CA. Tel: (650) 506-7000, (800) 633-0738, FAX: (650) 506-7200, Web Site: www.oracle.com (16)

Simcic, Christian, Fasson Roll Div, Mentor, OH. Tel: (440) 354-7900, FAX: (440) 358-4712, (440) 358-6025, Web Site: www.fasson.com (16)

Simmonds, David, Foremost Insurance Group, Grand Rapids, MI. Tel: (616) 956-8241, (800) 527-3905, FAX: (800) 325-1507, Web Site: www.foremost.com (15)

Simmons-Boardman Publishing Corp, New York, NY. Tel: (212) 620-7200, (800) 257-5091, Web Site: www.simmonsboardman.com (17)

Simmons College, Boston, MA. Tel: (617) 521-2000, Web Site: www.simmons.edu (1)

Simmons, Debra Adams, The Plain Dealer, Cleveland, OH. Tel: (216) 999-5000, (800) 362-0727, FAX: (216) 999-6356, Web Site: www.plaindealer.com (18)

Simmons, Jean, Catholic Relief Services, Baltimore, MD. Tel: (877) 435-7277, (888) 277-7575, Web Site: www.catholicrelief.org (1)

Simmons, Mark, ITW Bee Leitzke, Iron Ridge, WI. Tel: (920) 625-2342, FAX: (920) 625-2643, Web Site: www.itwbeeleitzke.com (16)

Simmons, Patricia S., University of Minnesota Alumni Association, Minneapolis, MN. Tel: (612) 624-2323, (800) 862-5867, FAX: (612) 626-8167, E-Mail: umalumni@umn.edu, Web Site: www.minnesotaalumni.org (1)

Simmons, Ron, Viatech Publishing Solutions Inc, Bay Shore, NY. Tel: (631) 968-8500, (800) 645-8558, FAX: (631) 968-0830, Web Site: www.viatechpub.com (16)

Simmons, Steve, ACCUSPLIT Inc, Livermore, CA. Tel: (925) 226-0888, (800) 935-1996, FAX: (925) 463-0147, E-Mail: sales@accusplit.com, Web Site: www.accusplit.com (16)

Simms, Daryl, Omnicom Media Group, New York, NY. Tel: (212) 590-7020, E-Mail: info@omnicommediagroup.com, Web Site: www.omnicommediagroup.com (35)

Simms, Derek, iVisionMobile Inc, Chatsworth, CA. Tel: (866) 655-5302, FAX: (818) 812-6126, E-Mail: sales@ivisionmobile.com, Web Site: www.ivisionmobile.com (35)

Simms, John M., Odell, Simms & Lynch Inc, Tysons Corner, VA. Tel: (703) 903-9797, FAX: (703) 903-8850, Web Site: odellsimms.com (35)

Simon & Schuster Inc, New York, NY. Tel: (212) 698-7000, (800) 223-2348, Web Site: simonandschuster.com (17)

Simon Property Group, Indianapolis, IN. Tel: (317) 636-1600, FAX: (317) 263-7925, Web Site: www.shopsimon.com (16)

Simon, Alan D., Omaha Steaks Inc, Omaha, NE. Tel: (402) 597-8370, FAX: (402) 597-8125, E-Mail: info@omahasteaks.com, Web Site: www.omahasteaks.com (4)

Simon, Bruce A., Omaha Steaks Inc, Omaha, NE. Tel: (402) 597-8370, FAX: (402) 597-8125, E-Mail: info@omahasteaks.com, Web Site: www.omahasteaks.com (4)

Simon, Frederick J., Omaha Steaks Inc, Omaha, NE. Tel: (402) 597-8370, FAX: (402) 597-8125, E-Mail: info@omahasteaks.com, Web Site: www.omahasteaks.com (4)

Simon, Irwin David, Celestial Seasonings, Boulder, CO. Tel: (303) 530-5300, (800) 351-8175, FAX: (303) 581-1249, Web Site: www.celestialseasonings.com (16)

Simon, Irwin David, Hain Celestial Group Inc, Boulder, CO. Tel: (800) 434-4246, Web Site: www.hain-celestial.com (16)

Simon, Irwin David, Jason Natural Personal Care Products, Boulder, CO. Tel: (88) 659-7730, Web Site: www.jason-natural.com (7)

Simon, Keith, MediaTree. Parsippany, NJ. Tel: (973) 781-1070, (800) 475-8703, FAX: (973) 781-1071, E-Mail: sales@mediatreegroup.com, Web Site: www.mediatreegroup.com (27)

Simon, Marc S., Halo Branded Solutions, Sterling, IL. Tel: (815) 625-0980, (866) 840-6401, Web Site: www.halo.com (33)

Simon, Mark, Federal Citizen Information Center, Pueblo, CO. Tel: (719) 295-2675, (888) 8-PUEBLO, FAX: (719) 948-9724, E-Mail: pueblo@gpo.gov, Web Site: www.pueblo.gsa.gov (5)

Simon, Mark, Lowe Campbell Ewald, Detroit, MI. Tel: (586) 574-3400, E-Mail: lowecampbellewald@lowe-ce.com, Web Site: www.lowecampbellewald.com (35)

Simon, Matt, Cherry Tree Toys Inc, Beloit, WI. Tel: (608) 314-3090, (800) 848-4363, FAX: (608) 314-3097, E-Mail: sales@cherrytreetoys.com, Web Site: www.cherrytreetoys.com (11)

Simon, Michael J., Publishers Press Inc, Shepherdsville, KY. Tel: (502) 955-6526, FAX: (502) 955-5586, E-Mail: info@pubpress.com, Web Site: www.pubpress.com (27)

Simon, Nicholas X., Publishers Press Inc, Shepherdsville, KY. Tel: (502) 955-6526, FAX: (502) 955-5586, E-Mail: info@pubpress.com, Web Site: www.pubpress.com (27)

Simon, Shari, Simon Property Group, Indianapolis, IN. Tel: (317) 636-1600, FAX: (317) 263-7925, Web Site: www.shopsimon.com (16)

Simon, Todd D., Omaha Steaks Inc, Omaha, NE. Tel: (402) 597-8370, FAX: (402) 597-8125, E-Mail: info@omahasteaks.com, Web Site: www.omahasteaks.com (4)

Simonds, Terry, Universal Fidelity Corp, Houston, TX. Tel: (281) 647-4100, (800) 580-8887, FAX: (281) 647-4207, Web Site: www.ufccorp.com (14)

Simone, Jim, Norwood Promotional Products, Clearwater, FL. Tel: (317) 275-2500, (800) 959-9138, FAX: (317) 275-2570, Web Site: www.norwood.com (16)

Simone, Robert, Ross-Simons, Cranston, RI. Tel: (401) 463-3100, (800) 835-0919, FAX: (401) 463-8599, Web Site: www.ross-simons.com (6)

Simonich, Melissa, Alliance of Nonprofit Mailers, Washington, DC. Tel: (202) 462-5132, FAX: (202) 462-0423, E-Mail: alliance@nonprofitmailers.org, Web Site: www.nonprofitmailers.org (40)

Simons, Adam, Crest Healthcare Supply, Dassel, MN. Tel: (800) 328-8908, (800) 369-9207, Web Site: www.cresthealthcare.com (16)

Simonson, Richard A., Sabre Holdings Inc, Southlake, TX. Tel: (682) 605-1000, FAX: (682) 605-7239, Web Site: www.sabre.com (19)

Simplex Grinnell, Westminster, MA. Tel: (978) 731-2500, (800) SIMPLEX, FAX: (978) 731-7856, Web Site: www.simplexgrinnel.com (16)

Simplicity Pattern Co Inc/Style Patterns Ltd/New Look English Pattern Co Ltd, New York, NY. Tel: (212) 372-0500, (800) 653-7301, Web Site: www.simplicitypatt.com (8)

Simply Batteries Inc, De Kalb, IL. Tel: (815) 758-8332, Web Site: www.simplybatteries.com (7)

Simpson Electric Co, Lac Du Flambeau, WI. Tel: (715) 588-3311, FAX: (715) 588-3327, E-Mail: cservice@simpsonelectric.com, Web Site: www.simpsonelectric.com (16)

Simpson, Art, EU Services, Rockville, MD. Tel: (301) 424-3300, (800) 230-3362, FAX: (301) 424-3696, E-Mail: marketing@euservices.com, Web Site: www.euservices.com (21)

Simpson, Bill, Periscope Inc, Minneapolis, MN. Tel: (612) 339-0500, FAX: (612) 339-0600, E-Mail: info@periscope.com, Web Site: www.periscope.com (35)

Simpson, Donald, Directory of American Business & Insurance Attorneys, New York, NY. Tel: (732) 458-7788, (800) 445-7995, FAX: (732) 458-7710, E-Mail: staff@abialaw.com, Web Site: www.abialaw.com (15)

Simpson, Gerry, Vesey's Seeds Ltd, Charlottetown, PE Canada. Tel: (902) 368-7333, (800) 363-7333, FAX: (800) 686-0329, E-Mail: customerservice@veseys.com, Web Site: www.veseys.com (8)

Simpson, John, Dermac Labs Inc, Salem, OR. Tel: (503) 399-8181, (800) 547-9164, FAX: (503) 581-7439, Web Site: www.touchofmink.com (16)

Simpson, Kate, Academic Travel Abroad Inc, Washington, DC. Tel: (202) 785-9000, (800) 556-7896, FAX: (202) 342-0317, Web Site: www.academictravel.com (19)

Simqu, Blaise R., Academy of Marketing Science Journal, Thousand Oaks, CA. Tel: (800) 818-7243, FAX: (800) 583-2665, E-Mail: journals@sagepub.com, Web Site: www.sagepub.com (43)

Sims Stoves, Billings, MT. Tel: (406) 259-5644, (800) 736-5259, Web Site: www.simsstoves.com (11)

Sims, Barbara, Carol Enters List Co Inc, Fairfax, VA. Tel: (703) 425-0052, FAX: (703) 425-0056, E-Mail: listmanagement@carolenters.com, Web Site: www.carolenters.com (23)

Sims, Camelyn, Bull Dog Media Group Inc, Madison, SD. Tel: (605) 256-9103, Web Site: www.commissionsoup.com (20)

Sims, J. R., American Society of Mechanical Engineers, New York, NY. Tel: (973) 882-1167, (800) 843-2763, FAX: (973) 882-1717, E-Mail: infocentral@asme.org, Web Site: www.asme.org (20)

Sims, Jesse, Martin Worldwide Inc, Oak Park, CA. Tel: (888) 694-5478, Web Site: www.martinworldwide.net (23)

Sims, Lenny, NADA Appraisal Guides, Costa Mesa, CA. Tel: (714) 556-8511, (800) 966-6232, FAX: (714) 957-0302, E-Mail: info@nadaguides.com, Web Site: www.nadaguides.com (17)

Sims, Susie, EBSCO Reception Room Subscription Services, Birmingham, AL. Tel: (205) 991-1409, (800) 527-5901, FAX: (205) 995-1621, Web Site: www.ebsco.com/errss (18)

Sims, Wyatt, Sims Stoves, Billings, MT. Tel: (406) 259-5644, (800) 736-5259, Web Site: www.simsstoves.com (11)

Sinacori, Matt, Innovyx Inc, Seattle, WA. Tel: (206) 674-8720, Web Site: www.innovyx.com (32)

Sinclair, Colby, 100% Real Estate Inc, Orlando, FL. Tel: (800) 454-3422, E-Mail: rcs@100percentflorida.com, Web Site: www.100percentflorida.com (16)

Sinclair, Robert C., 100% Real Estate Inc, Orlando, FL. Tel: (800) 454-3422, E-Mail: rcs@100percentflorida.com, Web Site: www.100percentflorida.com (16)

Sindlinger & Co Inc, Wallingford, PA. Tel: (610) 565-0247, E-Mail: nelSind@aol.com (30)

Sindlinger, Nellie H., Sindlinger & Co Inc, Wallingford, PA. Tel: (610) 565-0247, E-Mail: nelSind@aol.com (30)

Sinfield, Leslie, Merisel, New York, NY. Tel: (212) 594-4800, FAX: (212) 594-4488, E-Mail: corp@merisel.com, Web Site: www.merisel.com (16)

Singelais, Barry, Alfa Aesar-A Johnson Matthey Co, Ward Hill, MA. Tel: (800) 343-0660, FAX: (800) 322-4757, E-Mail: info@alfa.com, Web Site: www.alfa.com (9)

Singer, Andrew, iThink Direct LLC, West Harrison, NY. Tel: (914) 984-2109, E-Mail: info@ithinkdirect.com, Web Site: www.ithinkdirect.com (31)

Singer, Dan, Houston Direct Marketing Association, Houston, TX. Tel: (281) 931-8883, FAX: (281) 820-4023, Web Site: www.houstondma.org (40)

Singer, David, TVGuide.com, New York, NY. Tel: (212) 626-2500, Web Site: www.tvguide.com (31)

Singer, Fred, iThink Direct LLC, West Harrison, NY. Tel: (914) 984-2109, E-Mail: info@ithinkdirect.com, Web Site: www.ithinkdirect.com (31)

Singer, Jon, Freedom Graphic Systems Inc, Milton, WI. Tel: (608) 868-7007, (800) 334-3540, FAX: (608) 868-7006, E-Mail: information@fgs.com, Web Site: www.freedomgraphicsystems.com (28)

Singer, Leslie, The NPD Group Inc, Port Washington, NY. Tel: (516) 625-0700, FAX: (516) 625-2444, Web Site: www.npd.com (31)

Singer, Lloyd, Learning Communications LLC, Irvine, CA. Tel: (800) 622-3610, FAX: (949) 727-4323, E-Mail: sales@learncom.com, Web Site: www.learncom.com (16)

Singer, Lori, Calvin Klein Cosmetics Co, New York, NY. Tel: (212) 719-2600, E-Mail: customerservice@calvinklein.com, Web Site: www.calvinklein.com (7)

Singer, Robert M., Timberline Geodesics, Berkeley, CA. Tel: (510) 849-4481, (800) 366-3466, FAX: (510) 849-3265, E-Mail: info@domehome.com, Web Site: www.domehome.com (8)

Singer, Steve, G-Neil Direct Mail, Sunrise, FL. Tel: (800) 999-9111, FAX: (954) 851-1264, E-Mail: tcs@gneil.com, Web Site: www.gneil.com (10)

Singh, Harmit, Levi Strauss & Co, San Francisco, CA. Tel: (415) 501-6000, FAX: (415) 501-7112, Web Site: www.levistrauss.com (16)

Singh, Livleen, The Fidelis Group Inc, Little Ferry, NJ. Tel: (410) 721-3450, Web Site: www.thefidelisgroup.net (22)

Singh, Man Jit, Sony Pictures Home Entertainment, Culver City, CA. Tel: (310) 244-4000, FAX: (310) 244-1544, Web Site: www.cthe.com (16)

Singh, Ranjit, Diamond Essence, Edison, NJ. Tel: (800) 909-2525, E-Mail: info@diamondessence.com, Web Site: www.diamond-essence.com (2)

Singh, Sally, Ross Metals, New York, NY. Tel: (212) 869-1407, (800) 654-ROSS (16)

Singh, Shri, Diamond Essence, Edison, NJ. Tel: (800) 909-2525, E-Mail: info@diamondessence.com, Web Site: www.diamond-essence.com (2)

Single Scene News, Tempe, AZ. Tel: (480) 945-6746, FAX: (480) 945-6746, E-Mail: publisher@azsinglescene.com, Web Site: www.azsinglescene.com (17)

Singleton, Bob, Communication Industries Corp, Grafton, VT. Tel: (802) 869-6500, FAX: (802) 869-6565, E-Mail: info@cicmail.com, Web Site: www.careersatcic.com (10)

Singleton, Mark E., The Union Labor Life Insurance Co, Silver Spring, MD. Tel: (202) 962-2945, FAX: (202) 962-8429, E-Mail: info@ullico.com, Web Site: www.unioncare.com (15)

Sinish Marketing Communications, Stratford, CT. Tel: (203) 375-1919, E-Mail: jon@sinishmarketing.com, Web Site: www.sinishmarketing.com (35)

Sinish, Jon, Sinish Marketing Communications, Stratford, CT. Tel: (203) 375-1919, E-Mail: jon@sinishmarketing.com, Web Site: www.sinishmarketing.com (35)

Sinisi, Karen, Ethnic Technologies LLC, South Hackensack, NJ. Tel: (201) 440-8923, (866) 333-8324, FAX: (201) 440-2168, E-Mail: karens@ethnictechnologies.com, Web Site: www.ethnictechnologies.com (23)

Sinkin, Don, Disc Graphics Inc, Hauppauge, NY. Tel: (631) 234-1400, FAX: (631) 234-1460, E-Mail: info@discgraphics.com, Web Site: www.discgraphics.com (27)

Sinn, Melinda, Kansas State University Division of Continuing Education, Manhattan, KS. Tel: (785) 532-5888, Web Site: www.dce.ksu.edu (1)

Sins, Lisa, Arnaud's, New Orleans, LA. Tel: (504) 523-0611, (866) 230-8895, FAX: (504) 581-7908, Web Site: www.arnauds.com (16)

Sion, John J., Sage Financial Group, West Conshohocken, PA. Tel: (484) 342-4400, FAX: (484) 537-0550, E-Mail: sage@sagefinancial.com, Web Site: www.sagefinancial.com (14)

Sipa Press, New York, NY. Tel: (212) 463-0150, FAX: (212) 463-0160, E-Mail: sipa@usa.com, Web Site: www.sipa.com (38)

SipcamAdvan, Durham, NC. Tel: (800) 295-0733, FAX: (919) 226-1196, Web Site: www.sipcamadvan.com (5)

Siquis Ltd, Baltimore, MD. Tel: (410) 323-4800, FAX: (410) 323-4113, Web Site: www.siquis.com (35)

Sir Speedy Grand Rapids, Grand Rapids, MI. Tel: (616) 554-7777, Web Site: www.sirspeedy.com (27)

Sir Speedy Green Bay, Green Bay, WI. Tel: (920) 494-4236, FAX: (920) 494-4075, E-Mail: office@sirspeedygb.com, Web Site: www.sirspeedygb.com (27)

Sir Speedy Newtown, Newtown, PA. Tel: (215) 968-2080, Web Site: www.sirspeedynewtown.com (27)

Sir Speedy Printing and Marketing Services, Tacoma, WA. Tel: (253) 473-0765), FAX: (253) 475-3012, Web Site: www.sirspeedy0905.com (27)

Sir Speedy Westbury, Westbury, NY. Tel: (516) 334-7400, Web Site: www.sirspeedyny.net (27)

SiriusXM Radio Inc, New York, NY. Tel: (212) 584-5100, Web Site: www.siriusxm.com (16)

Sisco, Julie, Teachers Credit Union, South Bend, IN. Tel: (574) 284-6247, (800) 552-4745, Web Site: www.tcunet.com (1)

Sisk Fulfillment Service Inc, Federalsburg, MD. Tel: (410) 754-8141, FAX: (410) 754-8223, Web Site: www.siskfulfillment.com (22)

Sisk, Clyde, EU Services, Stevensville, MD. Tel: (410) 643-7900, FAX: (410) 643-7933, E-Mail: clyde_sisk@siskmail.com, Web Site: www.siskmail.com (28)

Sitel, Nashville, TN. Tel: (615) 301-7100, (866) 95-SITEL, Web Site: www.sitel.com (29)

Siteman, Frank, Frank Siteman Photography, Winchester, MA. Tel: (781) 729-3747, E-Mail: frank@franksiteman.com, Web Site: www.franksiteman.com (37)

Sjolander, Peter, Helly-Hansen, Auburn, WA. Tel: (800) 435-5901, FAX: (425) 649-3740, Web Site: www.hellyhansen.com (16)

Skaar, Cynthia, Group f/64, Winston-Salem, NC. Tel: (336) 748-8272, FAX: (336) 748-8780 (20)

Skaggs, John, Aegon USA Investment Management, Inc, Cedar Rapids, IA. Tel: (502) 560-2000, FAX: (502) 560-2030, Web Site: www.aegonins.com (14)

Skalski, Steve, Graphic Converting Inc, Elmhurst, IL. Tel: (630) 758-4100, (800) 447-1935, FAX: (630) 833-1058, E-Mail: sales@graphicconverting.com, Web Site: www.graphicconverting.com (36)

Skar Advertising, Omaha, NE. Tel: (402) 330-0110, (866) 330-0112, FAX: (402) 330-8791, E-Mail: skar@skar.com, Web Site: skar.com (35)

Skelley, Christie, Strategy Corps LLC, Brentwood, TN. Tel: (615) 221-8381, (888) 577-6933, FAX: (615) 221-8479, E-Mail: info@strategycorps.com, Web Site: www.strategycorps.com (16)

Skerker, Joan, Robinson Home Products, Buffalo, NY. Tel: (716) 685-6300, FAX: (716) 685-4916 (16)

Skerker, Larry, Robinson Home Products, Buffalo, NY. Tel: (716) 685-6300, FAX: (716) 685-4916 (16)

Skerker, Robert, Robinson Home Products, Buffalo, NY. Tel: (716) 685-6300, FAX: (716) 685-4916 (16)

Skies America International Publishing & Communications, Beaverton, OR. Tel: (503) 520-1955, FAX: (503) 520-1275, E-Mail: skies@skies.com, Web Site: www.skies.com (36)

Skillings, Jim, DeLorme Mapping, Yarmouth, ME. Tel: (207) 846-7100, (800) 642-0970, FAX: (207) 846-7051, E-Mail: caleb.mason@delorme.com, Web Site: www.delorme.com (3)

Skillington, James, New Village Media Inc, Columbia, MD. Tel: (443) 832-4007, E-Mail: jskillington@newvillagemedia.com, Web Site: www.newvillagemedia.com (35)

Skinder-Strauss Associates, New Providence, NJ. Tel: (973) 642-1440, FAX: (973) 242-1905, Web Site: www.elaw.com (14)

Skinner, James, Walgreens Co, Deerfield, IL. Tel: (800) 925-4733, Web Site: www.walgreens.com (7)

Skinner, Vayia, Iris Marketing, Bel Air, MD. Tel: (443) 742-1232 (20)

Skipper, John, ESPN, Bristol, CT. Tel: (212) 456-4995 (5)

Skjekkeland, Atle, AIIM International, Silver Spring, MD. Tel: (301) 587-8202, (800) 477-2446, FAX: (301) 587-2711, E-Mail: aiim@aiim.org, Web Site: www.aiim.org (1)

Sklorenko, Michael, Alesco Data Group LLC, Fort Myers, FL. Tel: (239) 275-5006, (800) 701-6531, FAX: (239) 275-7737, E-Mail: lists@alescodata.com, Web Site: www.alescodata.com (23)

Skogerson, Dirk, JT International, Teaneck, NJ. Tel: (201) 871-1210, Web Site: www.jti.com (16)

Skolits, Richard, Dentino Marketing, Princeton, NJ. Tel: (609) 454-3202, FAX: (609) 454-3239, E-Mail: karl@dentinomarketing.com, Web Site: www.dentinomarketing.com (35)

Skolnick, Robert, Synovate, New York, NY. Tel: (212) 293-6100, FAX: (212) 293-6666 (30)

Skop, Joe, Satori Software Inc, Seattle, WA. Tel: (206) 357-2900, (800) 553-6477, FAX: (206) 357-2901, E-Mail: sales@satorisoftware.com, Web Site: www.satorisoftware.com (16)

Skow, Kathi, Anderson/Skow, San Francisco, CA. Tel: (888) 983-0880, Web Site: www.andersonskow.com (20)

Skredsvig, Janice, PACCAR Inc, Bellevue, WA. Tel: (425) 468-7400, FAX: (425) 468-8216, Web Site: www.paccar.com (16)

Skullduggery, Anaheim, CA. Tel: (714) 777-6425, (800) 3 FOSSIL, FAX: (714) 832-1215, Web Site: www.skullduggery.com (16)

SkyMall Inc, Phoenix, AZ. Tel: (602) 254-9777, (800) SKY-MALL, FAX: (602) 254-6075, Web Site: www.skymall.com (16)

Skypoint Communications Inc, Loretto, MN. Tel: (763) 548-2600, FAX: (763) 548-2610, E-Mail: info@skypoint.com, Web Site: www.skypoint.com (16)

Skystone Ryan, Cincinnati, OH. Tel: (513) 241-6778, FAX: (513) 241-0551, E-Mail: cincinnati@skystoneryan.com, Web Site: www.skystoneryan.com (20)

Skytel Communications Inc, Lewisville, TX. Tel: (800) 759-8737, Web Site: www.skytel.com (29)

Slade, Colin L., Tektronix Inc, Beaverton, OR. Tel: (503) 627-7111, (800) 833-9200, FAX: (503) 627-3247, Web Site: www.tektronix.com (16)

Slagle, Dennis, Volvo Cars of North America LLC, Northvale, NJ. Tel: (201) 768-7300, (800) 458-1552, E-Mail: customercare@volvocars.com, Web Site: www.volvocars.com (16)

Slamkowski, Peter, Collegiate Cap & Gown, Champaign, IL. Tel: (217) 351-9500, FAX: (217) 351-9214, Web Site: www.herff-jones.com (16)

Slater, Chad, IDM Inc, Reston, VA. Tel: (703) 547-4961, E-Mail: info@integrated-dm.com, Web Site: www.idm.us.com (23)

Slater, George, Innovation Printing Inc, Philadelphia, PA. Tel: (215) 969-4600, FAX: (215) 464-7664, Web Site: www.innovationprinting.com (27)

Slattery, Colleen, Hofstra University, Hempstead, NY. Tel: (516) 463-7200, FAX: (516) 463-4833, E-Mail: ce@hofstra.edu, Web Site: www.hofstra.edu/Academics/CE (41)

Slattery, Jack, Armbrust Paper Tubes Inc, Chicago, IL. Tel: (773) 586-3232, FAX: (773) 586-8997, E-Mail: tubesrus@corecomm.net, Web Site: www.tubesrus.com (10)

Slattery, Jim, Farrington Transportation, Bolingbrook, IL. Tel: (630) 783-9200 (12)

Slattery, Kevin, E3 Local Marketing Solutions, Cincinnati, OH. Tel: (513) 699-3300, (888) 878-2768, FAX: (513) 699-3310, Web Site: e3local.com (35)

Slaughter, Ken, Gazette Communications Inc, Cedar Rapids, IA. Tel: (319) 398-8211, (800) 397-8211, FAX: (319) 368-8834, Web Site: www.gazettecommunications.com (17)

Slavin, Tracy, Invenda Corp, Bethesda, MD. Tel: (240) 333-6111, E-Mail: sales@invenda.com, Web Site: www.invenda.com (32)

Slavonic, Gary, Promotional Products Association International, Irving, TX. Tel: (972) 252-0404, FAX: (972) 258-3004, (800) I-AM-PPAI, E-Mail: membership@ppa.org, Web Site: www.ppa.org (40)

Slayton, Derek, NetProspex Inc, Waltham, MA. Tel: (888) 826-4877, E-Mail: sales@netprospex.com, Web Site: www.netprospex.com (22)

Slayton, Karalee, Trilithic, Indianapolis, IN. Tel: (317) 423-6604, Web Site: www.trilithic.com (16)

Sleepy's Inc, Hicksville, NY. Tel: (516) 844-8800, (800) sleepys, FAX: (516) 844-8847, Web Site: www.sleepys.com (16)

Slife, James H., The Pioneer Group, Waterloo, IA. Tel: (319) 234-8969, FAX: (319) 234-8518, E-Mail: jslife@thepioneergroup.com, Web Site: www.pioneergroup.com (28)

Slifter, New York, NY. Tel: (212) 488-2222, Web Site: www.slifter.com (16)

Slight, Jim, JS Direct Address Ltd, North Vancouver, BC Canada. Tel: (604) 987-1282, FAX: (604) 987-1283, E-Mail: jim.slight@jsdirect.com, Web Site: www.jsdirect.com (23)

Brent Slinkard Consultant, Bloomington, IN. Tel: (812) 336-1111 (20)

Slinkard, Brent, Brent Slinkard Consultant, Bloomington, IN. Tel: (812) 336-1111 (20)

Slipko, Spencer, Empire Scientific, Deer Park, NY. Tel: (631) 595-9206, (800) 645-7220, FAX: (631) 595-9384, (800) 343-5733, E-Mail: sales@empirescientific.com, Web Site: www.empirescientific.com (16)

Sloan, Timothy J, Wells Fargo, San Francisco, CA. Tel: (800) 869-3557, (866) 249-3302, FAX: (626) 312-3015, Web Site: www.wellsfargo.com (14)

Sloane, Mark, Kelly, Scott & Madison Inc, Chicago, IL. Tel: (312) 977-0772, FAX: (312) 977-0874, E-Mail: info@ksmmedia.com, Web Site: www.ksmmedia.com (32)

Sloofman, Jay, Marketing Visions Inc, Tarrytown, NY. Tel: (914) 631-3900, FAX: (914) 693-8338, E-Mail: jsloofman@marketingvisions.com, Web Site: www.marketingvisions.com (35)

Slotten, Randy, Foremost Insurance Group, Grand Rapids, MI. Tel: (616) 956-8241, (800) 527-3905, FAX: (800) 325-1507, Web Site: www.foremost.com (15)

Slovin, Jeffrey T., Dentsply International, York, PA. Tel: (844) 848-0137, (800) 877-0020, E-Mail: contact@dentsplysirona.com, Web Site: www.dentsply.com (7)

Sludikoff, Stanley R., Poker Player, Sherman Oaks, CA. Tel: (310) 674-3365, FAX: (310) 674-3205, E-Mail: ard@gamblingtimes.com, Web Site: www.gamblingtimes.com (17)

Ray Slyper Associates, New York, NY. Tel: (212) 439-0710 (20)

Slyper, Ray, Ray Slyper Associates, New York, NY. Tel: (212) 439-0710 (20)

Small Business Service Bureau Inc, Worcester, MA. Tel: (508) 756-3513, (800) 343-0939, FAX: (508) 770-0528, E-Mail: info@sbsb.com, Web Site: www.sbsb.com (1)

Smallhoover, Kurt, Pittsburgh Mailing, Pittsburgh, PA. Tel: (412) 922-8181, FAX: (412) 937-1730, E-Mail: ksmallhoover@pittsburghmailing.com, Web Site: www.pittsburghmailing.com (28)

Smaron, Marilyn, REGIT Inc, Glen Ellyn, IL. Tel: (630) 495-1500, (800) 537-9786, FAX: (630) 495-1611, E-Mail: regit@regitinc.com, Web Site: www.regitinc.com (15)

Smart Dog Products, Winchester, TN. Tel: (931) 967-7482, (800) 264-3647, FAX: (931) 967-7483, E-Mail: sales@shopsmartdog.com (11)

Smart Inventions Inc, Paramount, CA. Tel: (562) 272-1416, (800) 275-7494, FAX: (562) 272-1423, E-Mail: customerservice@smartinventions.com, Web Site: www.smartinventions.com (32)

Smart Marketing, Dix Hills, NY. Tel: (631) 254-5259, FAX: (631) 254-4814, E-Mail: info@smartmarketing.com, Web Site: www.smartmarketing.com (35)

Smart Practice, Phoenix, AZ. Tel: (800) 522-0800, FAX: (800) 522-8329, E-Mail: info@smartpractice.com, Web Site: www.smartpractice.com (17)

Smart Source Direct, New York, NY. Tel: (617) 375-0404, FAX: (617) 420-0115, Web Site: www.newsamerica.com (20)

Smart, Brent, Saatchi & Saatchi New York, New York, NY. Tel: (212) 463-2000, FAX: (212) 463-9856, Web Site: www.saatchiny.com (32)

SmartFocus Inc, New York, NY. Tel: (425) 460-1000, (646) 356-1169, Web Site: www.smartfocus.com (22)

Smarthome/INSTEON, Irvine, CA. Tel: (949) 221-0037, (800) 762-7846, FAX: (949) 221-9240, E-Mail: feedback@smarthome.com, Web Site: www.smarthome.com (32)

SmartReply Inc, Irvine, CA. Tel: (949) 340-0700, Web Site: www.smartreply.com (29)

SmartSource Corp, Bedford, MA. Tel: (781) 785-3375, (800) 239-0239, Web Site: www.smartsourceonline.com (32)

Smati, Zin, Suez Energy North America, Houston, TX. Tel: (713) 636-0000, FAX: (713) 636-1364, Web Site: www.tractebelpowerinc.com (16)

Smedley, Howard, Perimeter Technology Inc, Manchester, NH. Tel: (603) 645-1616, (800) 645-1650, FAX: (603) 645-1424, Web Site: www.perimetertechnology.com (34)

Smidt, Alan, Harbor Freight Tools, Camarillo, CA. Tel: (805) 445-4791, (800) 423-2567, FAX: (800) 445-4925, Web Site: www.harborfreight.com (9)

Smidt, Eric, Harbor Freight Tools, Camarillo, CA. Tel: (805) 445-4791, (800) 423-2567, FAX: (800) 445-4925, Web Site: www.harborfreight.com (9)

Smigel, Jason, The Teaching Co, Chantilly, VA. Tel: (703) 502-7300, (800) 832-2412, FAX: (703) 378-3819, Web Site: www.teach12.com (17)

The Smile Train, New York, NY. Tel: (212) 689-9199, (800) 932-9541, E-Mail: info@smiletrain.org, Web Site: www.smiletrain.org (1)

Smit, Neil, Comcast Corp, Philadelphia, PA. Tel: (215) 665-1700, Web Site: www.comcast.com (32)

Smit, Pierre, Direct Mail Center, San Francisco, CA. Tel: (415) 252-1600, FAX: (415) 252-9100, E-Mail: dmc@directmailctr.com, Web Site: www.directmailctr.com (21)

AO Smith Corp, Milwaukee, WI. Tel: (414) 359-4000, FAX: (414) 359-4064, Web Site: www.aosmith.com (16)

Smith & Noble, Corona, CA. Tel: (888) 241-2134, E-Mail: contactus@smithnoble.com, Web Site: www.smithandnoble.com (8)

Arleen Smith Marketing Inc, Stoughton, MA. Tel: (781) 341-0882, FAX: (781) 344-0710, Web Site: www.arleensmithmarketing.com (28)

Smith-Browning Direct Inc, Sedona, AZ. Tel: (928) 203-9420 (20)

Daniel Smith Inc, Seattle, WA. Tel: (206) 223-9599, (800) 426-6740, FAX: (800) 238-4065, E-Mail: sales@danielsmith.com, Web Site: www.danielsmith.com (10)

Smith Hanley Associates, Southport, CT. Tel: (203) 319-4300, (888) 221-2900, FAX: (203) 319-4320, Web Site: www.smithhanley.com (20)

Smith O'Keefe & Associates, Egg Harbor Township, NJ. Tel: (609) 653-0400, (800) 222-0461, FAX: (609) 653-6483, E-Mail: info@smithokeefe.com, Web Site: www.smithokeefe.com (20)

Smith Swann, Lynda, National Wholesale Co Inc, Lexington, NC. Tel: (336) 248-5904, (800) 480-4673, FAX: (336) 248-2880, E-Mail: customerservice@shopnational.com, Web Site: www.shopnational.com (2)

Smith, Al, ProLogic Retail Services, Delray Beach, FL. E-Mail: info@prologicretail.com, Web Site: www.prologicretail.com (35)

Smith, Alex, Kaye-Smith, Renton, WA. Tel: (425) 228-8600, (800) 822-9987, FAX: (425) 291-3167, E-Mail: info@kayesmith.com, Web Site: www.kayesmith.com (21)

Smith, Alex, Vertex Inc, Berwyn, PA. Tel: (610) 640-4200, (800) 355-3500, FAX: (610) 640-5892, Web Site: www.vertexinc.com (16)

Smith, Allen, Four Seasons Hotels & Resorts, Toronto, ON Canada. Tel: (416) 449-1750, (800) 819-5053, FAX: (416) 441-4437, Web Site: www.fourseasons.com (19)

Smith, Angie, Beach List Direct Inc, Nashville, TN. Tel: (615) 356-1100, E-Mail: cbeach@beachlistdirect.com, Web Site: www.beachlistdirect.com (23)

Smith, Arleen, Arleen Smith Marketing Inc, Stoughton, MA. Tel: (781) 341-0882, FAX: (781) 344-0710, Web Site: www.arleensmithmarketing.com (28)

Smith, Barry S., ITT Educational Services Inc, Carmel, IN. Tel: (317) 706-9200, Web Site: www.ittesi.com (16)

Smith, Ben, Channel 13 WNET Catalog Division, New York, NY. Tel: (212) 560-1313, FAX: (212) 560-1314, E-Mail: programming@thirteen.org, Web Site: www.thirteen.org (5)

Smith, Ben, Listrak, Lititz, PA. Tel: (717) 627-4528, (877) 362-4556, E-Mail: info@listrak.com, Web Site: www.listrak.com (32)

Smith, Bowen, John Alden Life Insurance Co/North Star Marketing, Duluth, GA. Tel: (678) 473-1211, (800) 768-6288, FAX: (678) 473-9573, Web Site: www.nstarmarketing.com (15)

Smith, Brad, Hal Leonard Corp, Milwaukee, WI. Tel: (414) 774-3630, FAX: (414) 774-3259, Web Site: www.halleonard.com (17)

Smith, Brad, Intuit, Mountain View, CA. Tel: (650) 944-6000, Web Site: www.inuit.com (10)

Smith, Brad, ReMark USA, Minnetonka, MN. Tel: (952) 938-4699, FAX: (952) 988-8500, E-Mail: jessica.sbragia@remarkgroup.com, Web Site: www.remarkamericas.com (15)

Smith, Brian, Audio Classics Ltd, Vestal, NY. Tel: (607) 766-3501, FAX: (607) 766-3502, E-Mail: steve@audioclassics.com, Web Site: www.audioclassics.com (3)

Smith, Cathie, Perrygraf, Carol Stream, IL. Tel: (630) 665-3333, (800) 323-4433, FAX: (630) 665-3491, E-Mail: info2@americanperrygraf.com, Web Site: www.perrygraf.com (16)

Smith, Christopher, Artemis International Solutions Corp, Austin, TX. Tel: (512) 201-8222, FAX: (512) 874-8900, Web Site: www.aisc.com (22)

Smith, Christopher, Jockey International Global Inc, Kenosha, WI. Tel: (262) 658-8111 (2)

Smith, Chuck, National Relief Charities, Elkwood, VA. Tel: (540) 825-5950 (1)

Smith, Clay, Speedway, Lincoln, NE. Tel: (402) 323-3100, FAX: (402) 477-7476 (12)

Smith, Clint, Emma, Nashville, TN. Tel: (800) 595-4401, E-Mail: hi@myemma.com, Web Site: myemma.com (24)

Smith, Dan, San Jose Mercury News, San Jose, CA. Tel: (408) 920-5000, FAX: (408) 288-8060, Web Site: www.mercurynews.com (17)

Smith, Daniel, Daniel Smith Inc, Seattle, WA. Tel: (206) 223-9599, (800) 426-6740, FAX: (800) 238-4065, E-Mail: sales@danielsmith.com, Web Site: www.danielsmith.com (10)

Smith, Daniel, DeHart & Darr Associates, McLean, VA. Tel: (703) 448-1000, FAX: (703) 790-3460 (20)

Smith, Dave, Calibre Press Inc, San Francisco, CA. Tel: (214) 545-3060, (800) 323-0037, FAX: (866) 225-4273, Web Site: www.calibrepress.com (17)

Smith, David Cloyce, The Library of America, New York, NY. Tel: (212) 308-3360, (800) 964-5778, FAX: (212) 750-8352, E-Mail: info@loa.org, Web Site: www.loa.org (13)

Smith, David, Fidelity Security Life Insurance Co, Kansas City, MO. Tel: (816) 756-1060, (800) 648-8624, FAX: (816) 968-0580, E-Mail: info@fslins.com, Web Site: www.fslins.com (15)

Smith, David G., Veriad, Brea, CA. Tel: (714) 990-2700, (800) 962-0658, FAX: (800) 962-0658, E-Mail: info@veriad.com, Web Site: www.veriad.com (16)

Smith, Derek V., Choice Point, Alpharetta, GA. Tel: (770) 752-6000, (800) 342-5339, FAX: (770) 752-6005, Web Site: www.choicepoint.com (16)

Smith, Diane, Michigan Apple Committee, Lansing, MI. Tel: (517) 669-8353, (800) 456-2753, FAX: (517) 669-9506, E-Mail: staff@michiganapples.com, Web Site: www.michiganapples.com (1)

Smith, Don, Merastar Insurance Co, Chattanooga, TN. Tel: (800) 637-2782, FAX: (800) 369-1430, E-Mail: merastar.assist.team@unitrindirect.com, Web Site: www.merastar.com (15)

Smith, Ed, American Direct Marketing Resources Inc, Chesterfield, MO. Tel: (636) 532-7703, FAX: (636) 532-2427, E-Mail: admr@admr.com, Web Site: www.americandirectmarketing.com (21)

Smith, Edward, CityTwist, Boca Raton, FL. Tel: (866) 798-2489, FAX: (561) 314-2692, Web Site: www.citytwist.com (32)

Smith, Elizabeth, Smith-Browning Direct Inc, Sedona, AZ. Tel: (928) 203-9420 (20)

Smith, Ernie, Computer Solutions Inc, Miami, FL. Tel: (305) 558-7000, FAX: (305) 557-0003, E-Mail: info@csiflorida.com, Web Site: www.csiflorida.com (22)

Smith, Fedor, Atlantic-ACM, Boston, MA. Tel: (617) 720-3700, FAX: (617) 720-1077, E-Mail: atlantic@atlantic-acm.com, Web Site: www.atlantic-acm.com (20)

Smith, Frederick W., FedEx Corp, Memphis, TN. Tel: (901) 369-3600, FAX: (901) 395-5082, Web Site: www.fedex.com (16)

Smith, Gem, Houston Direct Marketing Association, Houston, TX. Tel: (281) 931-8883, FAX: (281) 820-4023, Web Site: www.houstondma.org (40)

Smith, Gordon, NAB Show, Washington, DC. Tel: (202) 429-5300, (800) 622-3976, FAX: (202) 429-4199, E-Mail: nab@nab.org, Web Site: www.nabshow.com (42)

Smith, Gordon, United States Tennis Association, White Plains, NY. Tel: (914) 696-7000, (800) 990-8782, E-Mail: memberservices@usta.com, Web Site: www.usta.com (1)

Smith, Greg, Boeing Co, Chicago, IL. Tel: (312) 544-2000, FAX: (312) 544-2082, Web Site: www.boeing.com (16)

Smith, Greg, Schoolwise Press, San Francisco, CA. Tel: (415) 337-7971, (800) 247-8443 x 202, FAX: (415) 337-1146, E-Mail: info@schoolwisepress.com, Web Site: www.schoolwisepress.com (17)

Smith, Greg, Tomahawk Live Trap Co, Tomahawk, WI. Tel: (715) 453-3550, (800) 272-8727, FAX: (715) 453-4326, E-Mail: trapem@livetrap.com, Web Site: www.livetrap.com (16)

Smith, Gregg, Direct Marketing Group, Eden Prairie, MN. Tel: (952) 975-5060, (888) 397-5060, FAX: (952) 906-0608, Web Site: www.directmg.com (35)

Smith, Gregory J., University of Texas School of Law, Austin, TX. Tel: (512) 475-6700, FAX: (512) 475-6876, E-Mail: services@utcle.org, Web Site: www.utcle.org (1)

Smith, Harold B., Christianity Today Inc, Carol Stream, IL. Tel: (630) 260-6200, FAX: (630) 260-0114, Web Site: www.christianitytoday.com (17)

Smith, Harold B., Today's Christian Woman, Carol Stream, IL. Tel: (630) 260-6200, FAX: (630) 260-0114, E-Mail: tcwedit@christianitytoday.com, Web Site: www.todayschristianwoman.net (31)

Smith, III L. Lyne, Fry Consultants Inc, Atlanta, GA. Tel: (770) 226-8888, FAX: (770) 226-8899, E-Mail: lynesmith@fryconsultants.com, Web Site: www.fryconsultants.com (30)

Smith, Jack, Empire Blue Cross & Blue Shield, New York, NY. Tel: (212) 476-1000, (877) 476-7111, FAX: (212) 476-1281, Web Site: www.empireblue.com (15)

Smith, James C., Webster Bank, Waterbury, CT. Tel: (203) 578-2230, FAX: (203) 578-2507, Web Site: www.websterbank.com (14)

Smith, James, Hello Direct, Nashua, NH. Tel: (408) 972-1990, (800) 435-5634, FAX: (408) 972-8155, Web Site: www.hello-direct.com (16)

Smith, James T., Ipsos America Inc, New York, NY. Tel: (212) 265-3200, FAX: (212) 265-3790, E-Mail: info@ipsos-asi.com, Web Site: www.ipsos-asi.com (30)

Smith, Jill L., Infomercial Sales Inc, Las Vegas, NV. Tel: (702) 253-0433, FAX: (702) 871-0759, Web Site: www.infomercialsalesinc.com (32)

Smith, Jim, AmMed Direct, Parsons, TN. Tel: (615) 941-3900, (800) 282-3524, Web Site: www.arrivamedical.com (7)

Smith, Jimmy T., AMVETS National Service Foundation, Lanham, MD. Tel: (301) 459-6181, (800) 810-7148, FAX: (301) 459-5578, Web Site: www.amvetsnsf.org (1)

Smith, Joan A., Madisonavegifts.com, Watertown, NY. Tel: (315) 779-9228, (866) 421-1744, E-Mail: magsales@madisonavegifts.com, Web Site: www.madisonavegifts.com (6)

Smith, John, Software Assistance International Ltd, Morris Plains, NJ. Tel: (973) 285-1400, FAX: (201) 539-3253 (3)

Smith, Joy, Partners for Incentives, Cleveland, OH. Tel: (800) 292-7371, Web Site: www.pfi-awards.com (33)

Smith, Jr. Charles, Parcel Insurance Plan Inc, Saint Louis, MO. Tel: (314) 692-0300, (800) 325-7390, FAX: (314) 692-7598, E-Mail: office@pipinsure.com, Web Site: www.pipinsure.com (15)

Smith, Judy Reed, Atlantic-ACM, Boston, MA. Tel: (617) 720-3700, FAX: (617) 720-1077, E-Mail: atlantic@atlantic-acm.com, Web Site: www.atlantic-acm.com (20)

Smith, Keith E., Boyd Gaming Corp, Las Vegas, NV. Tel: (702) 792-7200, FAX: (702) 792-7313, Web Site: www.boydgaming.com (16)

Smith, Kenneth M., Poly One Corp, Avon Lake, OH. Tel: (440) 930-1000, (866) POLY-ONE, FAX: (440) 930-1428, Web Site: www.polyone.com (16)

Smith, Kenneth P., Smith O'Keefe & Associates, Egg Harbor Township, NJ. Tel: (609) 653-0400, (800) 222-0461, FAX: (609) 653-6483, E-Mail: info@smithokeefe.com, Web Site: www.smithokeefe.com (20)

Smith, Kristin, People for the American Way, Washington, DC. Tel: (202) 467-4999, Web Site: www.pfaw.org (1)

Smith, Leslie S., American Preferred Reader's Service Inc, Fort Lauderdale, FL. Tel: (954) 767-6022, (888) 482-2443, FAX: (954) 767-6065, E-Mail: jfarrell@amerpref.com, Web Site: www.amerpref.com (18)

Smith, Lisa, Woolrich Inc, Woolrich, PA. Tel: (570) 769-6464, (800) 966-5372, Web Site: www.woolrich.com (6)

Smith, Lowndes A., Symetra Financial, Bellevue, WA. Tel: (425) 256-8000, (800) 426-7355, FAX: (425) 256-5737, Web Site: www.symetra.com (15)

Smith, Mark, ColorTree of Virginia Inc, Richmond, VA. Tel: (804) 358-4245, FAX: (804) 358-0488, Web Site: www.colortree.com (26)

Smith, Mark, Navitar Inc, Rochester, NY. Tel: (585) 359-4000, (800) 828-6778, FAX: (585) 359-4999, E-Mail: info@navitar.com, Web Site: www.navitar.com (16)

Smith, Mark, Opex Corp, Moorestown, NJ. Tel: (856) 727-1100, FAX: (856) 727-1955, Web Site: www.opex.com (34)

Smith, Mark, Portrait International Inc, Boston, MA. Tel: (617) 457-5200, Web Site: www.portraitsoftware.com (22)

Smith, Mary, Oliver of Adrian Inc, Adrian, MI. Tel: (517) 263-2132, (877) 668-0885, FAX: (517) 265-8698, E-Mail: info@oliverinstrument.com, Web Site: www.oliverofadrian.com (16)

Smith, Mary S., Tomahawk Live Trap Co, Tomahawk, WI. Tel: (715) 453-3550, (800) 272-8727, FAX: (715) 453-4326, E-Mail: trapem@livetrap.com, Web Site: www.livetrap.com (16)

Smith, Matthew, JDR Microdevices, Dublin, CA. Tel: (650) 625-1400, (800) 538-5000, FAX: (800) 538-5005, E-Mail: sales@jdr.com, Web Site: www.jdr.com (3)

Smith, Michelle, Daily Commercial News & Construction Record, Markham, ON Canada. Tel: (905) 752-5408, (800) 465-6475, FAX: (905) 752-5450, (888) 396-9413, E-Mail: dcnonl@reedbusiness.com, Web Site: www.dcnonl.com (17)

Smith, Mickey, MGMA-ACMPE, Englewood, CO. Tel: (303) 799-1111, (877) 275-6462, E-Mail: infocenter@mgma.com, Web Site: www.mgma.com (1)

Smith, Monica C., Brushfire Inc, Cedar Knolls, NJ. Tel: (973) 871-1700, FAX: (973) 871-1717, E-Mail: vwarner@brushfireinc.com, Web Site: www.brushfireinc.com (35)

Smith, Murray, Nelson-Jameson Inc, Marshfield, WI. Tel: (715) 387-1151, (800) 826-8302, FAX: (715) 387-8746, (800) 472-0840, E-Mail: sales@nelsonjameson.com, Web Site: www.nelsonjameson.com (9)

Smith, Nick, Group 1 Software Inc, Lanham, MD. Tel: (301) 731-2300, (888) 413-6763, FAX: (301) 731-0360, E-Mail: info@g1.com, Web Site: www.g1.com (22)

Smith, Pete, Specialized Products Co, Southlake, TX. Tel: (817) 329-6647, (800) 866-5353, FAX: (800) 234-8286, E-Mail: spc@specialized.net, Web Site: www.specialized.net (16)

Smith, Phil, One World Projects, Batavia, NY. Tel: (585) 343-4490, FAX: (585) 344-3551, E-Mail: sales@oneworldprojects.com, Web Site: www.oneworldprojects.com (6)

Smith, Rachelle, University of Southern California, Los Angeles, CA. Tel: (213) 821-2366, FAX: (213) 740-2343, E-Mail: taube@usc.edu, Web Site: www.usc.edu (38)

Smith, Randal, Virco Manufacturing Corp, Conway, AR. Tel: (501) 329-2901, (800) 448-4726, FAX: (800) 258-7367, E-Mail: info@virco.com, Web Site: www.virco.com (16)

Smith, Rex, Times Union, Albany, NY. Tel: (518) 454-5694, FAX: (518) 454-5628, Web Site: www.timesunion.com (18)

Smith, Richard, Amrigon, Bloomfield Hills, MI. Tel: (248) 332-2300, FAX: (248) 333-9710 (29)

Smith, Richard, Entergy, New Orleans, LA. Tel: (504) 576-4000, (800) ENTERGY, FAX: (504) 576-4428, Web Site: www.entergy.com (16)

Smith, Richard F., Equifax Credit Information Services Inc, Atlanta, GA. Tel: (404) 885-8000, (800) 685-5000, FAX: (404) 885-8988, Web Site: www. equifax.com (20)

Smith, Richard P., Dairy Farmers of America Inc, Kansas City, MO. Tel: (816) 801-6455, (888) 332-6455, FAX: (816) 801-6456, E-Mail: webmail@dfamilk. com, Web Site: www.dfamilk.com (16)

Smith, Richard, Telcordia Technologies, Piscataway, NJ. Tel: (732) 699-2000, FAX: (973) 829-2458, Web Site: www.telcordia.com (16)

Smith, Robert, All Star Carts & Vehicles, Bay Shore, NY. Tel: (631) 666-5252, (800) 831-3166, FAX: (631) 666-1319, Web Site: www.allstarcarts.com (16)

Smith, Robert, American Management Association, New York, NY. Tel: (212) 586-8100, FAX: (212) 903-8186, Web Site: www.amanet.org (1)

Smith, Robert Ellis, Privacy Journal, Providence, RI. Tel: (401) 274-7861, FAX: (401) 274-4747, E-Mail: orders@privacyjournal.net, Web Site: www. privacyjournal.net (17)

Smith, Robin B., Publishers Clearing House, Port Washington, NY. Tel: (516) 883-5432, FAX: (516) 767-4567, E-Mail: cirving@pch.com, Web Site: www. pch.com (18)

Smith, Roland C., Office Depot, Boca Raton, FL. Tel: (561) 438-4800, (800) 463-3768, FAX: (561) 438-4001, Web Site: www.officedepot.com (16)

Smith, Roland C., OfficeMax Inc, Boca Raton, FL. Tel: (877) 633-4236, Web Site: www.officemax.com (10)

Smith, Roscoe, AMC Publishing/Agent Media Corp, Clearwater, FL. Tel: (727) 446-1100, (800) 933-9449, FAX: (727) 446-1166, E-Mail: sales@ agentmediacorp.com, Web Site: www. agentmediacorp.com (31)

Smith, Stacy J., Intel Corp, Santa Clara, CA. Tel: (408) 765-8080, (800) 548-4725, FAX: (408) 765-6187, Web Site: www.intel.com (16)

Smith, Stephen, Eilenberger's Bakery Inc, Palestine, TX. Tel: (903) 729-2176, (800) 831-2544, FAX: (903) 723-2915, Web Site: www.eilenbergerbakery.com (4)

Smith, Stephen J., Hain Celestial Group Inc, Boulder, CO. Tel: (800) 434-4246, Web Site: www.hain-celestial.com (16)

Smith, Stephen M., Do It Yourself Direct Marketing, Hoboken, NJ. Tel: (201) 748-6000, FAX: (201) 748-6088, E-Mail: info@wiley.com, Web Site: www. wiley.com (43)

Smith, Steve, BJU Press, Greenville, SC. Tel: (864) 242-5100, (800) 845-5731, FAX: (864) 271-8151, (800) 525-8398, E-Mail: bjupinfo@bjupress.com, Web Site: www.bjupress.com (17)

Smith, Steve, Mailmaster Corp, Jonesboro, AR. Tel: (870) 972-8845, (800) 551-7018, FAX: (870) 972-0877, E-Mail: info@mail-master.com, Web Site: www.mail-master.com (28)

Smith, Terresa, Eilenberger's Bakery Inc, Palestine, TX. Tel: (903) 729-2176, (800) 831-2544, FAX: (903) 723-2915, Web Site: www.eilenbergerbakery.com (4)

Smith, Terry, Norman Rockwell Museum, Stockbridge, MA. Tel: (413) 298-4100, (800) 742-9450, FAX: (413) 298-4144, E-Mail: emazzer@nrm.org, Web Site: www.nrm.org (16)

Smith, Timothy C., Smith-Browning Direct Inc, Sedona, AZ. Tel: (928) 203-9420 (20)

Smith, Todd, Shield Healthcare, Valencia, CA. Tel: (661) 294-4200, (800) 765-8775, FAX: (661) 294-1043, (800) 748-0713, Web Site: www. shieldhealthcare.com (7)

Smith, Wayne, Greenwood Publishing Group Inc, Portsmouth, NH. Tel: (203) 226-3571, FAX: (203) 222-1502, E-Mail: sales@greenwood.com, Web Site: www.greenwood.com (17)

Smith, William D., e-Pipeconnection, Evansville, IN. Tel: (812) 474-4529, (800) 262-4300, FAX: (812) 474-4531, E-Mail: sales@e-pipeconnection.com, Web Site: www.e-pipeconnection.com (9)

Smith, William D., PVC Plastics Co, Evansville, IN. Tel: (812) 476-3592, (800) 782-7527, FAX: (812) 474-4531 (16)

Smith, William M, Telecom Inc, Oakland, CA. Tel: (510) 873-8283, (800) 243-3101, FAX: (510) 873-8293, Web Site: www.telecominc.com (29)

Smith, William, Moultrie Manufacturing Co, Moultrie, GA. Tel: (229) 985-1312, (800) 841-8674, FAX: (229) 890-7245, Web Site: www. moultriemanufacturing.com (8)

Smith-McKee, Maureen, Universal Training, Lake Forest, IL. Tel: (847) 235-2170, E-Mail: information@ universaltraining.com, Web Site: www. universaltraining.com (16)

Smith-Miller, April, Coin Laundry Association, Oakbrook Terrace, IL. Tel: (630) 963-7920, (800) 570-5629, FAX: (630) 963-7925, Web Site: www. coinlaundry.org (1)

FL Smithe Machine Co Inc, Duncansville, PA. Tel: (814) 695-5521, FAX: (814) 695-0860, E-Mail: info@flsmithe.com, Web Site: www.flsmithe.com (34)

Smithe, Jr Edgar, FL Smithe Machine Co Inc, Duncansville, PA. Tel: (814) 695-5521, FAX: (814) 695-0860, E-Mail: info@flsmithe.com, Web Site: www. flsmithe.com (34)

Smithfield Foods, Smithfield, VA. Tel: (800) 276-6158, Web Site: www.smithfieldfoods.com (16)

Smithsonian Enterprises, New York, NY. Tel: (212) 916-1300, (800) 766-2149, FAX: (212) 490-0058, Web Site: www.smithsonianmag.com (17)

Smithwick, Gary, Turner Greenhouses, Goldsboro, NC. Tel: (800) 672-4770, E-Mail: customerservice@ turnergreenhouses.com, Web Site: www. turnergreenhouses.com (8)

Smoczynski, Matt, Perfect Plastic Printing Corp. Saint Charles, IL. Tel: (630) 584-1600, FAX: (630) 584-0648, E-Mail: ppp@perfectplastic.com, Web Site: www.perfectplastic.com (27)

Smolen, Daniel T., Dan Smolen Direct Search LLC, Stafford, VA. Tel: (703) 835-9900, FAX: (703) 835-9966, E-Mail: dsmolen@dansmolen.com, Web Site: www.dansmolen.com (20)

Smolen, Meggie, Path to Purchase Institute, Chicago, IL. Tel: (847) 675-7400, Web Site: www.p2pi.org (17)

Smolik, Kim, Franciscan Mission Associates, Mount Vernon, NY. Tel: (914) 664-5604, FAX: (914) 664-3017, E-Mail: admin@franciscanmissionassoc.org, Web Site: www.franciscanmissionassoc.org (1)

Smolsky, Matt, Mid America Direct Marketing Association, Omaha, NE. Tel: (402) 965-4318, FAX: (402) 964-8484, Web Site: www.madma.org (40)

The JM Smucker Co, Orrville, OH. Tel: (888) 550-9555, Web Site: www.smucker.com (4)

Smucker, Richard K., The JM Smucker Co, Orrville, OH. Tel: (888) 550-9555, Web Site: www.smucker. com (4)

Smuda, Joan, Freedom Graphic Systems Inc, Milton, WI. Tel: (608) 868-7007, (800) 334-3540, FAX: (608) 868-7006, E-Mail: information@fgs.com, Web Site: www.freedomgraphicsystems.com (28)

Smyrnios, Dimitrios, The Schwan Food Co, Marshall, MN. Tel: (507) 532-3274, Web Site: www. theschwanfoodcompany.com (5)

Albert S Smyth Co Inc, Timonium, MD. Tel: (410) 252-6666, (800) 638-3333, FAX: (410) 252-2355, E-Mail: smyth@albertsmyth.com, Web Site: www. albertsmyth.com (6)

Smyth Dengler, Joan H., Covenant House International Headquarters, New York, NY. Tel: (212) 613-0300, (800) 388-3888, FAX: (212) 727-4992, Web Site: www.covenanthouse.org (1)

Smyth, D. Edward, The McGraw-Hill Financial, New York, NY. Tel: (212) 904-2000, Web Site: www. mhfi.com (17)

Smyth, Robert E., Citizens Bank, Boston, MA. Tel: (617) 725-5900, FAX: (617) 725-5921, Web Site: www.citizensbank.com (14)

Smyth, Tom, Albert S Smyth Co Inc, Timonium, MD. Tel: (410) 252-6666, (800) 638-3333, FAX: (410) 252-2355, E-Mail: smyth@albertsmyth.com, Web Site: www.albertsmyth.com (6)

Brody Smythe Direct Inc, Beverly Hills, CA. Tel: (310) 779-9682, FAX: (310) 550-1659, E-Mail: rsollish@ brodysmythe.com, Web Site: www.brodysmythe. com (35)

SMZ Advertising, Troy, MI. Tel: (248) 362-4242, FAX: (248) 362-2014, E-Mail: info@smz.com, Web Site: www.smz.com (35)

Snap-on Inc, Kenosha, WI. Tel: (262) 656-5200, (800) 866-5748, (800) 786-6600, FAX: (262) 656-5577, Web Site: www.snapon.com (9)

Snapper, Michael, Demco Inc, Madison, WI. Tel: (608) 241-1201, (800) 356-1200, FAX: (608) 241-1799, E-Mail: custserv@demco.com, Web Site: www. demco.com (10)

Snavely, Katharene, Chesapeake Bay Foundation, Annapolis, MD. Tel: (410) 268-8816, Web Site: www. savethebay.cbf.org (1)

Snead, David, New York Philharmonic, New York, NY. Tel: (212) 875-5691, Web Site: www.nyphil.org (1)

Snead, Tom, Trigon Blue Cross/Blue Shield, Roanoke, VA. Tel: (540) 853-5000, (800) 553-3164, FAX: (540) 853-3053, Web Site: www.trigon.com (15)

Snell, Jim, Shield Healthcare, Valencia, CA. Tel: (661) 294-4200, (800) 765-8775, FAX: (661) 294-1043, (800) 748-0713, Web Site: www.shieldhealthcare. com (7)

Snelson, Nate, Katalyst Partners Inc, New York, NY. Tel: (203) 257-4277, E-Mail: bpetisi@ katalystresponse.com, Web Site: www. katalystresponse.com (21)

Sniado, Joseph D., Standard & Poor's Corp, New York, NY. Tel: (212) 438-2000, FAX: (212) 438-7375, Web Site: www.standardandpoors.com (17)

Snider, Brian S., The GRI Marketing Group Inc, Trumbull, CT. Tel: (203) 261-3337, FAX: (203) 261-1113, E-Mail: bsnider@gridirect.com, Web Site: www.gridirect.com (35)

Snider, Edward M., Comcast Spectacor LP, Philadelphia, PA. Tel: (215) 336-3600, (800) 298-4200, FAX: (215) 389-9518, E-Mail: info@comcast-spectacor.com, Web Site: www.comcast-spectacor. com (16)

Snitzer, Tina, Corinthian Media, New York, NY. Tel: (212) 279-5700, FAX: (212) 239-1772, E-Mail: info@mediabuying.com, Web Site: www. mediabuying.com (35)

Snook, Gary, Bike Nashbar, Crab Orchard, WV. Tel: (800) NAS-HBAR, FAX: (877) 778-9456, E-Mail: custserv@nashbar.com, Web Site: www. bikenashbar.com (11)

Snow, Chuck, University of Pennsylvania, Philadelphia, PA. Tel: (215) 898-5000, FAX: (215) 898-9659, Web Site: www.upenn.edu (1)

Snow, David, Medco Health Solutions Inc, Franklin Lakes, NJ. Tel: (201) 269-3400, (800) 556-3326, FAX: (800) 222-1934, E-Mail: customersupport@ medcosupply.com, Web Site: www.medco-athletics. com (7)

Snow, Jeff, PAC Worldwide, Redmond, WA. Tel: (425) 202-4000, (800) 535-0039, FAX: (425) 885-2934, Web Site: www.pac.com (26)

Snow, Keith, B2E Direct Marketing Inc, Grimes, IA. Tel: (515) 986-1992, Web Site: www. bwbmarketing.com (22)

Snow, Keith, BWB Marketing Services, Ankeny, IA. Tel: (515) 986-1992, Web Site: www. bwbmarketing.com (22)

Snow, Terry, World Publications Inc, Winter Park, FL. Tel: (407) 628-4802, FAX: (407) 628-7061, Web Site: www.worldpub.net (17)

Snow, Therese, J&L Industrial Supply, Southfield, MI. Tel: (734) 458-7000, (800) 521-9520, FAX: (734) 261-0352, Web Site: www.jlindustrial.com (9)

The Snyder Agency, Missouri City, TX. Tel: (281) 437-9200, FAX: (832) 460-3022, E-Mail: info@ snyderagency.com, Web Site: snyderagency.com (35)

Snyder Glenn J & Assocs, Jacksonville Beach, FL. Tel: (904) 246-6223, FAX: (904) 246-6229 (20)

Tom Snyder Productions, Watertown, MA. Tel: (617) 926-6000, (800) 342-0236, FAX: (800) 304-1254, E-Mail: ask@tomsnyder.com, Web Site: www. tomsnyder.com (16)

Snyder, Becky, ABC Clio, Santa Barbara, CA. Tel: (805) 968-1911, FAX: (805) 685-9685, E-Mail: elott@abc-clio.com, Web Site: www.abc-clio.com (17)

Snyder, Diane, NCP Solutions, Reston, VA. Tel: (703) 438-6000, (800) 822-9919, FAX: (703) 438-3570, Web Site: www.nwf.org (17)

Snyder, Gail G., Nationwide Mutual Insurance Co, Columbus, OH. Tel: (614) 249-7111, (800) 882-2822, FAX: (614) 854-3676, Web Site: www.nationwide. com (15)

Snyder, George, Direct Impact Inc, Saint Louis, MO. Tel: (314) 336-1300, FAX: (314) 336-0013, E-Mail: info@directimpactinc.com, Web Site: www. directimpactinc.com (35)

Snyder, George, Direct Marketing Association of Saint Louis, Washington, MO. Tel: (866) 516-0121, FAX: (636) 239-2324, E-Mail: mparisien@mac.com, Web Site: www.dmastl.org (40)

Snyder, Glenn J., Snyder Glenn J & Assocs, Jacksonville Beach, FL. Tel: (904) 246-6223, FAX: (904) 246-6229 (20)

Snyder, Kim, Cherry Brothers LLC/Cherrydale, Lansdale, PA. Tel: (800) 333-4525, Web Site: www. cherrydale.com (1)

Snyder, Paula, Tinsley Tool Supply Inc, Powell, TN. Tel: (865) 681-9633, FAX: (865) 982-1655, E-Mail: gene@tinsleytool.com, Web Site: www.tinsleytool. com (9)

Snyder, Philip R., The Snyder Agency, Missouri City, TX. Tel: (281) 437-9200, FAX: (832) 460-3022, E-Mail: info@snyderagency.com, Web Site: snyderagency.com (35)

Snyder, Richard D., Gateway Inc, Irvine, CA. Tel: (949) 471-7000, (800) 369-1409, FAX: (949) 471-7041, Web Site: www.gateway.com (3)

Snyder, Shane, Barcoding Inc, Baltimore, MD. Tel: (410) 385-8532, (888) 860-SCAN, (888) 860-7226, FAX: (410) 385-8559, E-Mail: info@barcoding. com, Web Site: www.barcoding.com (22)

Snyder, Steve, Digi International, Minnetonka, MN. Tel: (952) 912-3444, (877) 912-3444, FAX: (952) 912-4952, Web Site: www.digi.com (3)

Snyder, Thomas J., Ivy Tech Community College of Indiana, Indianapolis, IN. Tel: (317) 921-4800, (888) IVY-LINE, FAX: (317) 921-4753, Web Site: www. ivytech.edu (13)

Snyder, USAF (Ret) Col Robin A., Uniformed Services Benefit Association, Overland Park, KS. Tel: (800) 368-7021, Web Site: www.usba.com (15)

SOAR Inflatables, Healdsburg, CA. Tel: (707) 433-5599, FAX: (707) 433-4499, E-Mail: sales@soar1. com, Web Site: www.soar1.com (11)

Sobczak, Art, Telephone Selling Report, Scottsdale, AZ. Tel: (402) 895-9399, FAX: (402) 896-3353, E-Mail: arts@businessbyphone.com, Web Site: www. businessbyphone.com (43)

Sobel, Paul, Dataline Inc, Princeton, NJ. Tel: (609) 452-6014, FAX: (609) 951-0025, E-Mail: psobel@ datalinedata.com, Web Site: datalinedata.com (23)

Sobieraj, Cindy, Team Cheer, Geneseo, NY. Tel: (800) 350-1562, (877) 243-5268, E-Mail: custserv@ teamcheer.com, Web Site: www.teamcheer.com (2)

Sobo, Scott, SAS Group, Tarrytown, NY. Tel: (914) 332-7878, FAX: (914) 332-7859, Web Site: www. sasgroup.com (32)

Social Reality Inc, Los Angeles, CA. Tel: (323) 694-9800, Web Site: www.socialreality.com (35)

Social Studies School Service, Culver City, CA. Tel: (310) 839-2436, (800) 421-4246, FAX: (310) 839-2249, (800) 944-5432, E-Mail: access@ socialstudies.com, Web Site: www.socialstudies. com (16)

Society for Human Resource Management, Alexandria, VA. Tel: (703) 548-3440, (800) 283-7476, FAX: (703) 535-6490, E-Mail: shrmstore@shrm.org, Web Site: www.shrm.org (1)

Society for Neuroscience, Washington, DC. Tel: (202) 962-4000, Web Site: www.sfn.org (1)

Society of American Magicians Inc, Littleton, CO. Tel: (303) 362-0575, E-Mail: samadministrator@ magicsam.com, Web Site: www.magicsam.com (1)

Society of Financial Service Professionals, Newtown Square, PA. Tel: (610) 526-2500, FAX: (610) 359-8115, E-Mail: info@financialpro.org, Web Site: www.financialpro.org (1)

Society of Manufacturing Engineers, Dearborn, MI. Tel: (313) 425-3000, (800) 733-4763, FAX: (313) 425-3400, E-Mail: communications@sme.org, Web Site: www.sme.org (1)

Society of Petroleum Engineers, Richardson, TX. Tel: (972) 952-9393, (800) 456-6863, FAX: (972) 952-9435, E-Mail: spedal@spe.org, Web Site: www.spe. org (1)

Society of the Divine Savior, New Holstein, WI. Tel: (920) 898-4201, Web Site: www.salvatoriancenter. com (1)

Soderberg, Marcia, Trumble Greetings, Boulder, CO. Tel: (800) 525-0656, FAX: (303) 530-5124, E-Mail: info@leanintree.com, Web Site: www.leanintree. com (6)

Soderlin, Barbara, Rapid City Journal, Rapid City, SD. Tel: (605) 394-8300, FAX: (605) 394-8462, E-Mail: classifieds@rapidcityjournal.com, Web Site: www. rapidcityjournal.com (18)

Sodi, Marco, Veronis Suhler Stevenson LLC, New York, NY. Tel: (212) 935-4990, FAX: (212) 381-8168, E-Mail: stevensonj@vss.com, Web Site: www.vss.com (14)

Soergel, Rich C., Pacific Sportswear Co Inc, San Diego, CA. Tel: (619) 281-6688, (800) USA-8778, FAX: (619) 281-6687, E-Mail: info@pacsport.com, Web Site: www.pacsport.com (5)

Soft Surroundings, Saint Louis, MO. Tel: (314) 812-5200, Web Site: www.softsurroundings.com (2)

Softic, Dzenis, Clickbooth.com LLC, Sarasota, FL. Tel: (941) 483-4188, Web Site: www.clickbooth.com (35)

SofTrek Corp, Amherst, NY. Tel: (716) 691-2800, (800) 442-9211, FAX: (716) 691-2828, Web Site: www. softrek.com (22)

Software AG USA, Reston, VA. Tel: (703) 860-5050, (877) 724-4965, FAX: (703) 391-6975, E-Mail: sales@softwareagusa.com, Web Site: www. softwareagusa.com (3)

Software Assistance International Ltd, Morris Plains, NJ. Tel: (973) 285-1400, FAX: (201) 539-3253 (3)

Software Marketing Associates Inc, Rocky Hill, CT. Tel: (860) 721-8929, FAX: (860) 257-9679, E-Mail: sma@sma-promail.com, Web Site: www.sma-promail.com (22)

Soitenly Stooges, Glendale, CA. Tel: (818) 543-0778, (800) 543-0778, FAX: (818) 543-0779, E-Mail: custserv@threestooges.com, Web Site: www. soitenlystooges.com (6)

Soja, Joe, The Durham Manufacturing Co, Durham, CT. Tel: (860) 349-3427, (800) 243-3774, FAX: (860) 349-8572, (800) 782-5499, E-Mail: info@ durhammfg.com, Web Site: www.durhammfg.com (16)

Sok, Ming, Bridge City Tool Works Inc, Portland, OR. Tel: (503) 282-6997, (800) 253-3332, FAX: (503) 287-1085, E-Mail: jjeconomaki@comcast.net, Web Site: www.bridgecitytools.com (9)

Soken, Susan, First Hawaiian Bank, Honolulu, HI. Tel: (808) 525-6273, (888) 844-4444, FAX: (808) 525-5798, E-Mail: bfarias@fhb.com, Web Site: www. fhb.com (14)

Sokol, Jr. Gerald, National Railroad Passenger Corp, Washington, DC. Tel: (202) 906-3000, (800) USA-RAIL, FAX: (202) 906-3306, Web Site: www. amtrak.com (16)

Sokolowski, Michael, Coin Laundry Association, Oakbrook Terrace, IL. Tel: (630) 963-7920, (800) 570-5629, FAX: (630) 963-7925, Web Site: www. coinlaundry.org (1)

Sokolski, Andrew, Whirley Drink Works, Warren, PA. Tel: (814) 723-7600, (800) 825-5575, FAX: (814) 723-3245, E-Mail: info@whirleydrinkworks.com, Web Site: www.whirleydrinkworks.com (5)

Sokolski, Lincoln, Whirley Drink Works, Warren, PA. Tel: (814) 723-7600, (800) 825-5575, FAX: (814) 723-3245, E-Mail: info@whirleydrinkworks.com, Web Site: www.whirleydrinkworks.com (5)

Soladay, Ed, Fujitsu Transaction Solutions Inc, Richardson, TX. Tel: (972) 963-2300, (800) 340-4425, Web Site: www.fujitsu.com (16)

Solar Cine Products Inc, Chicago, IL. Tel: (773) 254-8310, (800) 621-8796, FAX: (773) 254-4124 (5)

Solar Communications, Naperville, IL. Tel: (630) 983-1400, (800) 890-6906, FAX: (630) 983-6125, Web Site: www.solarcommunications.com (31)

Solar Components Corp, Manchester, NH. Tel: (603) 668-8186, FAX: (603) 668-1783, Web Site: www. solar-components.com (9)

Solarcom, Norcross, GA. Tel: (770) 449-6116, (888) SUN-DATA, FAX: (770) 448-7726, Web Site: www.solarcom.net (16)

Solitron Devices Inc, West Palm Beach, FL. Tel: (561) 848-4311, FAX: (561) 863-5946, E-Mail: sales@ solitrondevices.com, Web Site: www. solitrondevices.com (16)

Soliven, Vince, MVNP, Honolulu, HI. Tel: (808) 536-0881, FAX: (808) 529-6208, E-Mail: ideas@mvnp. com, Web Site: www.mvnp.com (35)

Sollish, Rochelle, Brody Smythe Direct Inc, Beverly Hills, CA. Tel: (310) 779-9682, FAX: (310) 550-1659, E-Mail: rsollish@brodysmythe.com, Web Site: www.brodysmythe.com (35)

Solly, Bruce, Toland Home and Garden Inc, Port Townsend, WA. Tel: (504) 893-9503, (800) 989-6287, E-Mail: info@tolandhomeandgarden.com, Web Site: www.tolandhomeandgarden.com (16)

Solo Printing, Miami, FL. Tel: (305) 594-8699, FAX: (305) 599-5245, Web Site: www.soloprinting.com (27)

Peter J Solomon Co, New York, NY. Tel: (212) 508-1600, FAX: (212) 508-1633, Web Site: www.pjsc. com (14)

Solomon, David, Gall's Inc, Lexington, KY. Tel: (859) 266-7227, (800) 477-7766, FAX: (859) 268-5954, E-Mail: help-desk@galls.com, Web Site: www. galls.com (16)

Solomon, Peter J., Peter J Solomon Co, New York, NY. Tel: (212) 508-1600, FAX: (212) 508-1633, Web Site: www.pjsc.com (14)

Solomon, Romeo, KICU-TV36, Oakland, CA. Tel: (510) 834-1212, E-Mail: kicu.public@coxmg.com, Web Site: www.ktvu.com/kicu/index (32)

Solomons, Richard, InterContinental Hotels Group, Atlanta, GA. Tel: (800) 621-0555, FAX: (801) 975-1846, Web Site: www.ichotelsgroup.com (19)

Solomons, Seth, Wunderman, New York, NY. Tel: (212) 941-3000, Web Site: www.wunderman.com (35)

Solow, Alan, Prudent Publishing Co, Ridgefield Park, NJ. Tel: (201) 641-7900, FAX: (800) 772-1144 (16)

Soltoff, Paul, Acquirgy Inc, Saint Petersburg, FL. Tel: (727) 576-6630, FAX: (727) 576-4864, Web Site: www.sendtec.com (35)

Solutran, Plymouth, MN. Tel: (763) 559-2225, (888) 765-8872, FAX: (763) 559-8872, E-Mail: solutions@solutran.com, Web Site: www.solutran. com (20)

Solverud, Mark L., NGL Insurance Group, Madison, WI. Tel: (608) 257-5611, (800) 548-2962, FAX: (608) 257-9340, Web Site: www.nglic.com (15)

Somanoff, Harris, Neat Co, Philadelphia, PA. Tel: (215) 382-3300, (866) 632-8732, FAX: (215) 386-2536, Web Site: neatco.com (22)

Somer, Norman, Blakar Inc, Englewood, CO. Tel: (201) 672-0705, FAX: (201) 673-0725, Web Site: www. blakar.com (33)

Somers, Jr. Bruce, TVA Media Group, Studio City, CA. Tel: (818) 505-8300, (888) 322-4296, FAX: (818) 505-8370, E-Mail: info@tvamediagroup.com, Web Site: www.tvamediagroup.com (35)

Somers, Kristin, Eaton Corp, Raleigh, NC. Tel: (216) 523-4400, (800) 356-5794, FAX: (216) 523-4787, Web Site: www.eaton.com (16)

Sommer, Joerg, Volkswagen Group of America Inc, Herndon, VA. Tel: (248) 754-5000, Web Site: www. volkswagengroupamerica.com (16)

Sommers, John G., Allied Printing Services Inc, Manchester, CT. Tel: (860) 643-1101, (800) 225-8777, (800) 224-8894, FAX: (860) 646-7954, E-Mail: allied@alliedprinting.com, Web Site: www. alliedprinting.com (27)

Song, Adi, Longevity Network Ltd, Henderson, NV. Tel: (702) 454-7000, (800) 242-1000, FAX: (702) 434-8259, E-Mail: info@longevity.com, Web Site: www.longevity.com (7)

Song, Delong, Boundless Corp, Phelps, NY. Tel: (631) 962-1500, (800) 231-5445, FAX: (631) 962-1505, E-Mail: sales@boundless.com, Web Site: www. boundless.com (16)

Song, Jim, Longevity Network Ltd, Henderson, NV. Tel: (702) 454-7000, (800) 242-1000, FAX: (702) 434-8259, E-Mail: info@longevity.com, Web Site: www.longevity.com (7)

Songbird Hearing Inc, North Brunswick, NJ. Tel: (732) 422-7203, (800) 647-5560, Web Site: www. songbirdhearing.com (7)

Songer, Jim, Esco Corp, Portland, OR. Tel: (503) 228-2141, FAX: (503) 778-6682, Web Site: www. escocorp.com (16)

Sony Creative Software, Middleton, WI. Tel: (608) 256-3133 (3)

Sony DADC, Terre Haute, IN. Tel: (812) 462-8100, Web Site: www.sonydadc.com (3)

Sony Electronics Inc, San Diego, CA. Tel: (858) 942-2400, Web Site: www.sony.com (16)

Sony Pictures Home Entertainment, Culver City, CA. Tel: (310) 244-4000, FAX: (310) 244-1544, Web Site: www.cthe.com (16)

Soonagrook, Jr. William, St Lawrence Island Original Ivory Cooperative, Gambell, AK. Tel: (907) 985-5707, FAX: (907) 985-5927 (6)

Debbie Sorace, Valley Stream, NY. Tel: (516) 659-5614 (20)

Sorenson, Jr. Arne M., Marriott International Inc, Bethesda, MD. Tel: (301) 380-3000, (301) 380-1791, E-Mail: internet.customer.care@marriott.com, Web Site: www.marriott.com (19)

Sorenson, Mike, Cuneo Advertising, Bloomington, MN. Tel: (952) 707-1212, FAX: (952) 707-1295, E-Mail: agency@cuneocom.com, Web Site: cuneocom.com (35)

Sorge, Anjee M., Fire Light Group, Madison, WI. Tel: (608) 441-3473, E-Mail: info@firelightgroup.com, Web Site: firelightgroup.com (33)

Sorin, Andrei, Andsor Research Inc, Etobicoke, ON Canada. Tel: (416) 245-8073, FAX: (416) 240-8473 (22)

Soriot, Pascal, AstraZeneca, Wilmington, DE. Tel: (302) 866-1482, Web Site: www.astrazeneca-us.com (7)

Sorkin, Murray L., Sorkins Inc, Saint Louis, MO. Tel: (314) 373-3975, E-Mail: sales@sorkins.com, Web Site: www.sorkins.com (23)

Sorkins Inc, Saint Louis, MO. Tel: (314) 373-3975, E-Mail: sales@sorkins.com, Web Site: www. sorkins.com (23)

Sorrells, III Tom, Motor Coach Industries International Inc, Schaumburg, IL. Tel: (847) 285-2000, (800) 624-2622, Web Site: www.mcicoach.com (16)

Sotheby's, New York, NY. Tel: (212) 606-7000, FAX: (212) 606-7107, Web Site: www.sothebys.com (6)

Soucy, Mike, Kadant Johnson Inc, Three Rivers, MI. Tel: (269) 278-1715, FAX: (269) 279-5980, Web Site: www.kadantjohnson.com (16)

Souers, Steve, Tristar Products, Fairfield, NJ. Tel: (973) 575-5400, FAX: (973) 683-6708, E-Mail: infotp@ tristarproductsinc.com, Web Site: www. tristarproductsinc.com (16)

Soulliard, Eric, Gemalto Inc, Montgomeryville, PA. Tel: (215) 390-2000, E-Mail: us.sales@gemalto. com, Web Site: www.gemalto.com (16)

Sound Beach Marketing Partners LLC, Old Greenwich, CT. Tel: (203) 698-0708, FAX: (203) 698-0712, E-Mail: thudock@soundbeachmarketing.com, Web Site: www.soundbeachmarketing.com (23)

The Sound Direct Marketing Group, Austin, TX. Tel: (512) 306-0879 (20)

SoundBite Communications, Bedford, MA. Tel: (877) SOUNDBITE, Web Site: www.soundbite.com (32)

Sounder, Rick, Crutchfield Corp, Charlottesville, VA. Tel: (434) 817-1000, (800) 955-9091, FAX: (804) 817-1010, E-Mail: administration@crutchfield.com, Web Site: www.crutchfield.com (3)

Soundprints, Norwalk, CT. Tel: (203) 846-2274, (800) 228-7839, FAX: (203) 846-1776, E-Mail: soundprints@soundprints.com, Web Site: www. soundprints.com (6)

The Source, Huntsville, AL. Tel: (256) 536-7305, (800) 433-2375, FAX: (256) 539-8547, Web Site: www. thesource-wti.com (33)

Source, Norwalk, CT. Tel: (203) 291-4000, FAX: (203) 291-4010, E-Mail: info@sourcecxm.com, Web Site: www.sourcecxm.com (35)

Source Communications, Hackensack, NJ. Tel: (201) 343-5222, E-Mail: admin@sourcead.com, Web Site: sourcead.com (35)

Source 4 Inc, Huntersville, NC. Tel: (704) 602-0110, (800) 541-5400, FAX: (704) 602-0119, E-Mail: source4newyork@source4.com, Web Site: www. source4.com (27)

Source Link, Itasca, IL. Tel: (866) 947-6872, FAX: (937) 885-8010, E-Mail: info@sourcelink.com, Web Site: www.sourcelink.com (28)

The Source Stock Footage Library Inc, Tucson, AZ. Tel: (520) 298-4810, FAX: (520) 290-8831, E-Mail: requests@sourcefootage.com, Web Site: www. sourcefootage.com (38)

Sourcebooks Inc, Naperville, IL. Tel: (630) 961-3900, (800) 432-7444, FAX: (630) 961-2168, Web Site: www.sourcebooks.com (17)

SourceLink, Itasca, IL. Tel: (866) 947-6872, Web Site: www.sourcelink.com (20)

South Seas Island Resort, Captiva Island, FL. Tel: (866) 565-5089, FAX: (941) 482-2470, Web Site: www. southseas.com (19)

South-Western Publishing, Madison, OH. Tel: (513) 299-1000, FAX: (513) 527-6992 (17)

Southeast Toyota Distributors LLC, Deerfield Beach, FL. Tel: (954) 429-2000, Web Site: www.jmfamily. com (16)

Southeastern Printing, Hialeah, FL. Tel: (305) 855-8707, (800) 226-8221, FAX: (305) 888-9903, E-Mail: info@seprint.com, Web Site: www.seprint. com (27)

Southern California Gas Co, Anaheim, CA. Tel: (714) 634-3054, (877) 238-0092, FAX: (714) 937-7712, E-Mail: Tjavid@socalgas.com, Web Site: www. socalgas.com (1)

Southern Flavoring Co Inc, Bedford, VA. Tel: (540) 586-8565, (800) 765-8565, FAX: (540) 586-8568, E-Mail: tom@southernflavoring.com, Web Site: www.southernflavoring.com (16)

Southern Fulfillment Services, Vero Beach, FL. Tel: (772) 226-3321 (28)

Southern Poverty Law Center, Montgomery, AL. Tel: (334) 956-8200, (888) 414-7752, FAX: (334) 956-8483, Web Site: www.splcenter.org (1)

Southern Progress Corp, Birmingham, AL. Tel: (205) 877-6000, FAX: (205) 877-6283, Web Site: www. southernprogress.com (17)

Southwell, Donald G., Kemper Corp, Chicago, IL. Tel: (312) 661-4600, (800) 733-7366, FAX: (312) 494-6995, Web Site: www.kemper.com (15)

Southwest Consultants, Granada Hills, CA. Tel: (818) 635-1777, Web Site: www.southwestbancorp.com (20)

Southwest Publishing & Mailing Corp, Topeka, KS. Tel: (785) 233-5662, Web Site: www.swpks.com (28)

Southworth, Dale, Roman Research Inc/Simply Whispers Earring, Hanson, MA. Tel: (800) 225-8652, FAX: (781) 447-0995, E-Mail: earpiercingstore@romanresearch.com, Web Site: www.simplywhispers.com (2)

Sovereign Bank New England, Glastonbury, CT. Tel: (860) 633-3688, FAX: (860) 727-6517 (14)

Sovern, Michael I., Sotheby's, New York, NY. Tel: (212) 606-7000, FAX: (212) 606-7107, Web Site: www.sothebys.com (6)

Sowell, Dr. Debbie, Oral Roberts University, Tulsa, OK. Tel: (918) 495-6161, FAX: (918) 495-6222, E-Mail: admissions@oru.edu, Web Site: www.oru.edu (1)

Sowers, Lee, Audio & Video Labs Inc, Pennsauken, NJ. Tel: (856) 663-9030, (800) 468-9353, FAX: (856) 661-3450, E-Mail: info@discmakers.com, Web Site: www.discmakers.com (16)

Spa-Finder Inc, New York, NY. Tel: (305) 307-5852, (800) ALL-SPAS, Web Site: www.spafinder.com (7)

Spack, Mark, Central States Indemnity, Omaha, NE. Tel: (402) 997-8000, (402) 397-1111, (800) 445-6500, Web Site: www.csi-omaha.com (15)

Spadet, New York, NY. Tel: (781) 275-8363, E-Mail: soapfac@verizon.net, Web Site: www.alcasoft.com/soapfact/ (7)

Spaeth, Steven E., Latest Products Corp, Woodbury, NY. Tel: (516) 367-4700, (800) 288-3547, FAX: (516) 367-4714, E-Mail: lpcorp@aol.com, Web Site: www.latestproducts.net (7)

Spagnola, Ed, A Marketing Resource, South St Paul, MN. Tel: (651) 451-1765, Web Site: www.amr-advantage.com (29)

Spaide, Kuipers & Co, Newport, RI. Tel: (610) 668-8296, FAX: (610) 579-3844, E-Mail: spaide@spaidekuipers.com, Web Site: www.spaidekuipers.com (20)

Spaide, William J., Spaide, Kuipers & Co, Newport, RI. Tel: (610) 668-8296, FAX: (610) 579-3844, E-Mail: spaide@spaidekuipers.com, Web Site: www.spaidekuipers.com (20)

Spaight, Terry, Hoffman Mint, Fort Lauderdale, FL. Tel: (954) 971-5451, (800) 227-5813, (800) 441-0292, FAX: (954) 917-3079, E-Mail: sales@hoffmanmint.com, Web Site: www.hoffmanmint.com (6)

Spalding Laboratories Inc, Reno, NV. Tel: (888) 562-5696, (888) 880-1579, FAX: (866) 738-9632, Web Site: www.spalding-labs.com (7)

Spalding, Denise, Allegra Marketing Services, Louisville, KY. Tel: (502) 895-1530, FAX: (502) 895-1624, Web Site: www.allegra-east.com (27)

Spalding, Tom, Spalding Laboratories Inc, Reno, NV. Tel: (888) 562-5696, (888) 880-1579, FAX: (866) 738-9632, Web Site: www.spalding-labs.com (7)

Spangler, Karl, Data Communications Management Corp, Brampton, ON Canada. Tel: (905) 791-3151, (800) 268-0128, FAX: (905) 791-3277, E-Mail: info@datacm.com, Web Site: www.datacm.com (21)

Spano, Michael, Todaro Brothers Mail Order Co, New York, NY. Tel: (212) 679-7766, (877) 472-2767, FAX: (212) 689-1679, E-Mail: eat@todarobros.com, Web Site: www.todarobros.com (4)

Sparkman, Wesley, Association of the Miraculous Medal, Perryville, MO. Tel: (573) 547-8343, (800) 264-6279, FAX: (573) 547-1389, E-Mail: amm1@amm.org, Web Site: www.amm.org (1)

Sparks, Janice, Murder by Mail, West Tisbury, MA. Tel: (508) 693-5205, (617) 670-9400, FAX: (508) 693-7997, E-Mail: info@murderbymail.com, Web Site: www.murderbymail.com (1)

Spates The Florist, Newport, VT. Tel: (802) 334-8330, (800) 473-3688, E-Mail: sales@spatestheflorist.com, Web Site: www.spatestheflorist.com (8)

Spates, Douglas, Spates The Florist, Newport, VT. Tel: (802) 334-8330, (800) 473-3688, E-Mail: sales@spatestheflorist.com, Web Site: www.spatestheflorist.com (8)

Spatz, D. Dean, Osmonics Inc, Minnetonka, MN. Tel: (952) 264-3937, (800) 605-6698. FAX: (952) 536-3301, Web Site: www.osmonics.com (16)

Huck Spaulding Enterprises, Voorheesville, NY. Tel: (518) 768-2070, (888) 982-8866, FAX: (518) 768-2240, E-Mail: orders@spaulding-rogers.com, Web Site: www.spaulding-rogers.com (16)

Spaulding, Huck, Huck Spaulding Enterprises, Voorheesville, NY. Tel: (518) 768-2070, (888) 982-8866, FAX: (518) 768-2240, E-Mail: orders@spaulding-rogers.com, Web Site: www.spaulding-rogers.com (16)

Spaulding, J Lincoln, Sheppard Envelope Co, Auburn, MA. Tel: (508) 791-5588, (800) 325-6622, FAX: (508) 754-3108, E-Mail: sales@sheppardenvelope.com, Web Site: www.sheppardenvelope.com (26)

Spaulding, Josephine, Huck Spaulding Enterprises, Voorheesville, NY. Tel: (518) 768-2070, (888) 982-8866, FAX: (518) 768-2240, E-Mail: orders@spaulding-rogers.com, Web Site: www.spaulding-rogers.com (16)

Spaulding, Karen Lee, The Gallery Shop, Buffalo, NY. Tel: (716) 882-8700 X258, FAX: (716) 882-1958, E-Mail: gallshop@albrightknox.org, Web Site: www.albrightknox.org (14)

Spaulding, Scott, Reliable Technologies Inc, Manchester, NH. Tel: (603) 644-2528, (800) 346-7890, FAX: (603) 627-5553, Web Site: www.tei-imaging.com (16)

Speakers Guild Inc, Sandwich, MA. Tel: (508) 888-6702, (800) 343-4530, FAX: (508) 888-6771, E-Mail: info@speakersguild.com, Web Site: www.speakersguild.com (16)

Spear Engineering Co, Colorado Springs, CO. Tel: (719) 471-9850 (16)

Spear, Nancy, Datasystem Solutions Inc, Overland Park, KS. Tel: (913) 362-6969, FAX: (913) 362-6383, E-Mail: sales@mutipub.com, Web Site: www.datasystem.com (22)

Special Libraries Association (SLA), Alexandria, VA. Tel: (703) 647-4900, FAX: (703) 647-4901, E-Mail: sla@sla.org, Web Site: www.sla.org (40)

Special Markets Sales Co, Indianapolis, IN. Tel: (317) 595-6587, FAX: (317) 595-9853, E-Mail: info@specialmkts.com, Web Site: www.specialmkts.com (33)

Special Olympics International, Washington, DC. Tel: (202) 628-3630, (800) 700-8585, FAX: (202) 824-0200, E-Mail: info@specialolympics.org, Web Site: www.specialolympics.org (1)

Specialists Marketing Services Inc, Hasbrouck Heights, NJ. Tel: (201) 865-5800, FAX: (201) 288-4295, E-Mail: info@sms-inc.com, Web Site: www.sms-inc.com (23)

Specialized Association Services, Irving, TX. Tel: (469) 524-5000, E-Mail: hvincent@1sas.com, Web Site: www.1sas.com (1)

Specialized Information Publishers Association, Vienna, VA. Tel: (781) 754-4771, FAX: (703) 992-7512, E-Mail: nbrand@sia.net, Web Site: www.siia.net (1)

Specialized Mailing Services Inc, Huntington Beach, CA. Tel: (714) 274-2284, E-Mail: info@specializedmailing.com, Web Site: www.specializedmailing.com (28)

Specialized Marketing Inc, Brewster, NY. Tel: (845) 278-6100, FAX: (845) 278-6150, Web Site: www.specialized-mktg.com (31)

Specialized Products Co, Southlake, TX. Tel: (817) 329-6647, (800) 866-5353, FAX: (800) 234-8286, E-Mail: spc@specialized.net, Web Site: www.specialized.net (16)

Specialty Envelope Inc, Cincinnati, OH. Tel: (513) 542-4700, (800) 288-8884, FAX: (513) 542-5260, E-Mail: info@specialtyenevelope.com, Web Site: www.specialtyenevelope.com (26)

Specialty Equipment Market Association, Diamond Bar, CA. Tel: (909) 396-0289, Web Site: www.sema.org (1)

Specialty Print Communications Inc, Niles, IL. Tel: (847) 588-2580, FAX: (847) 588-2146, Web Site: www.specialtyprintcomm.com (27)

Specialty Store Services Inc, Des Plaines, IL. Tel: (847) 470-7000, (888) 441-4440, FAX: (847) 470-5355, Web Site: www.specialtystoreservices.com (16)

The Spector Agency, Fair Oaks, CA. Tel: (916) 966-1605, FAX: (916) 966-1609, Web Site: www.spectoragency.com (35)

Spector, Jonathan, The Conference Board Inc, New York, NY. Tel: (212) 759-0900, FAX: (212) 980-7014, Web Site: www.conference-board.org (16)

Spector, Paul, The Spector Agency, Fair Oaks, CA. Tel: (916) 966-1605, FAX: (916) 966-1609, Web Site: www.spectoragency.com (35)

Spector, Rick, Consolidated Technologies Group LLC, Cleveland, OH. Tel: (866) 742-0109, E-Mail: info@ctgconvergence.com, Web Site: www.ctgadvisor.com (32)

Spectra Merchandising International Inc, Chicago, IL. Tel: (773) 202-8408, FAX: (773) 202-8409 (16)

Spectra Products LLC, Johnson City, NY. Tel: (607) 770-1985, FAX: (607) 798-7771, E-Mail: info@spectraproducts.com, Web Site: www.spectraproducts.com (31)

Spectronics Corp, Westbury, NY. Tel: (516) 333-4840, (800) 274-8888, FAX: (800) 491-6868, E-Mail: vscherer@spectroline.com, Web Site: www.spectroline.com (9)

Spectrum Chemicals & Laboratory Products, Gardena, CA. Tel: (310) 516-8000, Web Site: www.spectrumchemical.com (16)

Spectrum Communication Services Inc, Brookfield, WI. Tel: (262) 821-8400, (800) 701-3559, FAX: (262) 821-1492, E-Mail: sales@spectrumcomm.com, Web Site: www.spectrumcomm.com (29)

Spectrum Data, Oregon, IL. Tel: (815) 732-6567, FAX: (815) 732-7035 (22)

Spectrum eCommerce, Mission Viejo, CA. Tel: (949) 600-7900, Web Site: elifemarketers.com (15)

Spectrum Research, Ventnor City, NJ. Tel: (609) 822-0056, E-Mail: peter@spectrumresearch.com (30)

Spectrum Retail Associates, Ardmore, PA. Tel: (610) 645-9520, (800) 570-6565, FAX: (610) 645-9524 (20)

Spectrum Systems Inc, Reston, VA. Tel: (703) 591-7400 X217, (800) 929-3781, FAX: (703) 591-9780, E-Mail: spectrum@spectrum-systems.com, Web Site: www.spectrum-systems.com (34)

Spedding, Dave, UNICEF Canada, Toronto, ON Canada. Tel: (416) 482-4444, (800) 567-4483, FAX: (416) 487-8875, E-Mail: on.secretary@unicef.ca, Web Site: www.unicef.ca (1)

Spedding, Michelle, The Hibbert Group, Trenton, NJ. Tel: (609) 394-7500, (800) 545-4747, FAX: (609) 695-6553, Web Site: www.hibbertco.com (28)

SpeechSoft Inc, Armonk, NY. Tel: (914) 273-5560, (800) 878-8117, E-Mail: sales@speechsoft.com, Web Site: www.speechsoft.com (29)

Speed-Mat, Biddeford, ME. Tel: (207) 294-4358, (800) 882-7017, FAX: (207) 882-9279, E-Mail: info@speed-mat.com, Web Site: www.speed-mat.com (16)

Speedeon Data Corp, Cleveland, OH. Tel: (866) 647-9219, Web Site: www.speedeondata.com (30)

Speedway, Lincoln, NE. Tel: (402) 323-3100, FAX: (402) 477-7476 (12)

Speers, J. Alvin, Aardvark Enterprises, Calgary, AB Canada. Tel: (360) 779-5374 (17)

Speinhour, J. Patrick, TruGreen/ChemLawn, Lewis Center, OH. Tel: (614) 846-1800, (800) TRUE-GREEN, FAX: (614) 431-0155, Web Site: www.trugreen.com (16)

Spell, Randy B., Lorillard Tobacco Co, Greensboro, NC. Tel: (336) 335-7000, (877) 703-0386, FAX: (336) 373-6917, E-Mail: externalaffairs@lortobco.com, Web Site: www.lorillard.com (16)

Spellman, Cindy Kerber, Outrider North America, Saint Louis, MO. Tel: (314) 209-1005, FAX: (314) 209-1126, Web Site: www.outrider.com (30)

Spellman, Kate, United Business Media, Manhasset, NY. Tel: (516) 562-5000, Web Site: www.ubmtechnology.com (17)

Speltz, Christopher J, Creditcards.com, Austin, TX. Tel: (512) 996-8663, Web Site: www.creditcards.com (20)

Spence, Betty, National Association for Female Executives, New York, NY. Tel: (800) 927-6233, E-Mail: info@nafe.com, Web Site: www.nafe.com (1)

Spencer Zahn & Associates, Philadelphia, PA. Tel: (215) 564-5979, FAX: (215) 564-6285, E-Mail: szahn@erols.com, Web Site: www.spencerzahn.com (35)

Spencer, Carole, Children International, Kansas City, MO. Tel: (816) 942-2000, (800) 888-3089, FAX: (816) 942-3714, E-Mail: RobS@cikc.org, Web Site: www.children.org (1)

Spencer, Elaine, Harvard Business Review, Boston, MA. Tel: (617) 783-7410, FAX: (617) 783-7493, Web Site: hbr.org (17)

Spencer, Elaine, Harvard Business School Publishing, Boston, MA. Tel: (617) 783-7400, Web Site: www.harvardbusiness.org (17)

Spencer, Gunnar, Foxfire Printing & Packaging Inc, Newark, DE. Tel: (302) 368-9466, (800) 497-0516, FAX: (302) 368-5164, E-Mail: info@foxfiresigns.com, Web Site: www.foxfiresigns.com (27)

Spencer, Jameel, The Franklin Mint, Exton, PA. Tel: (610) 497-4800, (800) THE-MINT, FAX: (610) 497-4956, E-Mail: support@franklinmint.com, Web Site: www.franklinmint.com (16)

Spencer, Kevin, MGMA-ACMPE, Englewood, CO. Tel: (303) 799-1111, (877) 275-6462, E-Mail: infocenter@mgma.com, Web Site: www.mgma.com (1)

Spencer, Nelson, Heartland Boating Magazine, Saint Louis, MO. Tel: (314) 241-4310, (800) 366-9630, FAX: (314) 241-4207, E-Mail: info@heartlandboating.com, Web Site: www.heartlandboating.com (17)

Spencer, Scott, Clario Analytics, Eden Prairie, MN. Tel: (952) 653-0980, (866) 849-3341, FAX: (952) 653-5900, E-Mail: sales@clarioanalytics.com, Web Site: www.clarioanalytics.com (20)

Spencer, Vicki, Zale Corp, Irving, TX. Tel: (972) 580-4376, (800) 311-5393, Web Site: www.zalecorp.com (6)

SpencerStuart, Chicago, IL. Tel: (312) 822-0088, FAX: (312) 822-0116, Web Site: www.spencerstuart.com (20)

Speranza, Ernest V., Toys "R" Us, Wayne, NJ. Tel: (973) 617-5879, FAX: (973) 617-4006, Web Site: www.toysrus.com (11)

The Sperry & Hutchinson Co Inc, Delray Beach, FL. Tel: (561) 454-7621, FAX: (561) 265-2493, E-Mail: mediarelations@shsolutions.com, Web Site: www.greenpoints.com (6)

Spethman, Martin, Globalization Partners International, Mc Lean, VA. Tel: (703) 268-2193, (866) 272-5874, FAX: (202) 478-0956, E-Mail: info@globalizationpartners.com, Web Site: www.globalizationpartners.com (35)

Spett, Kenneth, Graham Field Health Products Inc, Atlanta, GA. Tel: (770) 368-4700, (800) 347-5678, FAX: (800) 726-0601, E-Mail: cs@grahamfield.com, Web Site: www.grahamfield.com (7)

Speyer, Jerry I., The Museum of Modern Art, New York, NY. Tel: (212) 708-9400, FAX: (212) 333-1123, E-Mail: info@moma.org, Web Site: www.moma.org (5)

Spicer, Vickee, The Saint Francis Community Services, Salina, KS. Tel: (785) 825-0541, (800) 423-1342, FAX: (785) 825-2940, Web Site: www.st-francis.org (1)

Spiegel Brands Inc, New York, NY. Tel: (800) 222-5680, E-Mail: customerservice@spiegel.com, Web Site: www.spiegel.com (2)

Spiegel, AJ, Mi-T-M Corp, Peosta, IA. Tel: (563) 556-7484, Web Site: www.mitm.com (9)

Spiegel, Lawrence E., Laran Communications Inc, Winfield, IL. Tel: (630) 690-2141, FAX: (630) 690-2143, Web Site: www.web-ads.com (17)

Spiegel, Tom, Presskits, East Walpole, MA. Tel: (781) 762-3003, (800) 472-3497, FAX: (781) 255-7791, Web Site: www.presskits.com (27)

Spiegel, Wendy, Pearson Education, Upper Saddle River, NJ. Tel: (201) 236-7000, FAX: (201) 236-3290, Web Site: www.pearsoned.com (17)

Spielman, Harold, MSW Research, Lake Success, NY. Tel: (516) 394-6000, FAX: (516) 394-6001, E-Mail: mail@mswresearch.com, Web Site: www.mswresearch.com (30)

Spilos, Jim, Society of Manufacturing Engineers, Dearborn, MI. Tel: (313) 425-3000, (800) 733-4763, FAX: (313) 425-3400, E-Mail: communications@sme.org, Web Site: www.sme.org (1)

Spilsbury Puzzle Co, Chicago, IL. Tel: (800) 722-1760, FAX: (630) 575-0857, E-Mail: service@spilsbury.com, Web Site: www.spilsbury.com (11)

Spinali, Rosanne, Chelsea Clock Co Inc, Chelsea, MA. Tel: (617) 884-0250, (866) 899-2805, FAX: (617) 830-0599, Web Site: www.chelseaclock.com (6)

Spindell, Lynn, Phillips-Van Heusen Corp, New York, NY. Tel: (212) 381-3500, (800) 388-9122, FAX: (212) 381-3950, Web Site: www.pvh.com (2)

Spinelli, Ozzie, Barely Nothings Lingerie, Nipomo, CA. Tel: (805) 489-5591, (800) 422-7359, FAX: (888) 489-5987, E-Mail: lingerie@barelynothings.com, Web Site: www.getpassionhere.com (2)

Spinelli, Sandi, Barely Nothings Lingerie, Nipomo, CA. Tel: (805) 489-5591, (800) 422-7359, FAX: (888) 489-5987, E-Mail: lingerie@barelynothings.com, Web Site: www.getpassionhere.com (2)

Spink, Bill, DMW Worldwide LLC, Chesterbrook, PA. Tel: (610) 407-0407, (877) 744-3699, FAX: (610) 407-9201, E-Mail: info@dmwdirect.com, Web Site: www.dmwdirect.com (35)

Spinneybeck Enterprises, Getzville, NY. Tel: (716) 446-2380, (800) 482-7777, FAX: (716) 446-2396, E-Mail: sales@spinneybeck.com, Web Site: www.spinneybeck.com (16)

Spire Creative Group, New York, NY. Tel: (212) 391-0200, Web Site: www.spirecreativegroup.com (27)

SPIRE Printing & Packaging LLC, New York, NY. Tel: (212) 661-1157, E-Mail: bweiser@spireprintingandpackaging.com, Web Site: www.spireprintingandpackaging.com (27)

Spiro, Diane, Olympia Sales Inc, Enfield, CT. Tel: (860) 749-0751, (800) 338-9992, FAX: (860) 814-4451, E-Mail: info@olympiasales.net, Web Site: www.olympiasales.us (16)

Spitalny, Eileen, Fairytale Brownies, Phoenix, AZ. Tel: (800) 324-7982, FAX: (602) 489-5133, E-Mail: service@brownies.com, Web Site: www.brownies.com (4)

Spitz, Eric, The Orange County Register, Santa Ana, CA. Tel: (877) 469-7344, E-Mail: customerservice@ocregister.com, Web Site: www.ocregister.com (17)

Splashnet Inc, Fairfield, NJ. Tel: (877) 244-9362, E-Mail: contactus@splashnet.com, Web Site: www.splashnet.com (23)

Splithoff, Darrell, Kaplan Inc, Fort Lauderdale, FL. Tel: (954) 515-3993, Web Site: www.kaplan.com (16)

Splithoff, Darrell, Kaplan Publishing, Chicago, IL. Tel: (312) 606-8905, (800) 245-2665, FAX: (312) 606-8985, Web Site: www.kaplanpublishing.com (17)

Spofford, Claire, Garnet Hill Inc, Franconia, NH. Tel: (603) 823-5545, (800) 870-3513, FAX: (888) 842-9696, Web Site: www.garnethill.com (2)

Spohn, Beth, Creating Results LLC, Woodbridge, VA. Tel: (703) 494-7888, (888) 205-8899, Web Site: www.creatingresults.com (35)

Spohr, Carsten, Lufthansa German Airlines, East Meadow, NY. Tel: (516) 296-9200, FAX: (516) 296-9386, Web Site: www.lufthansa-usa.com (19)

Spokane Teachers Credit Union, Liberty Lake, WA. Tel: (509) 326-1954, Web Site: www.stcu.org (14)

Spoken Arts, Holmes, NY. Tel: (845) 878-9600, (800) 326-4090, FAX: (845) 878-9009, E-Mail: sales@spokenartsmedia.com, Web Site: www.spokenartsmedia.com (17)

The Spokesman-Review, Spokane, WA. Tel: (509) 459-5060, FAX: (509) 459-5083, E-Mail: shaunh@spokesman.com, Web Site: www.spokane.net (17)

Spooren, Ellen, Marketing and Product Strategy, Peabody, MA. Tel: (978) 977-2000, (800) 825-5897, FAX: (781) 238-0986, Web Site: www.lhsl.com (16)

Sport Supply Group, Dallas, TX. Tel: (972) 484-9484, FAX: (972) 247-0650, Web Site: www.sportsupplygroup.com (11)

Sportif Mail Order Inc, Sparks, NV. Tel: (888) 260-7676, FAX: (775) 356-3567, Web Site: www.sportif.com (2)

Sportime International, Norcross, GA. Tel: (770) 449-5700, (800) 283-5700, FAX: (770) 510-7290, E-Mail: orders@sportime.com, Web Site: www.sportime.com (11)

Sporting Clays Ltd, Titusville, FL. Tel: (321) 268-5010, FAX: (321) 267-7216, E-Mail: sales@sportingclays.net, Web Site: www.sportingclays.net (17)

The Sporting News, Charlotte, NC. Tel: (704) 973-1546, (800) 443-1886, FAX: (704) 973-1552, Web Site: www.sportingnews.com (17)

The Sportsman's Guide Inc, South Saint Paul, MN. Tel: (651) 451-3030, (800) 882-2962, FAX: (651) 450-6130, E-Mail: custserv@sportsmansguide.com, Web Site: www.sportsmansguide.com (11)

Sportsmith LLC, Tulsa, OK. Tel: (918) 307-2446, (800) 713-2880, Web Site: www.sportsmith.net (11)

Sporty's Preferred Living, Batavia, OH. Tel: (513) 735-9000, (800) 776-7897, FAX: (800) 543-8633, E-Mail: csmgr@sportys.com, Web Site: www.sportys.com (5)

Spottiswood, Juli, Blackhawk Engagement Solutions Inc, Fenton, MO. Tel: (636) 226-2000, Web Site: www.bhengagement.com (35)

Sprague, Lori, American Mathematical Society, Providence, RI. Tel: (401) 455-4000, (800) 321-4267, FAX: (401) 331-3842, E-Mail: ams@ams.org, Web Site: www.ams.org (17)

Spring Global Delivery Solutions, Mississauga, ON Canada. Tel: (905) 678-2770, E-Mail: spring.cs.ca@springglobalmail.com, Web Site: www.spring-gds.com (21)

Spring-Green Lawn Care Corp, Plainfield, IL. Tel: (815) 436-8777, FAX: (815) 436-9056, Web Site: www.spring-green.com (16)

Spring Hill Laser Services, Sterling, PA. Tel: (570) 689-0970, FAX: (570) 689-7915, E-Mail: kkshls@icontech.com, Web Site: www.springhilllaser.com (27)

Spring O'Brien & Co, New York, NY. Tel: (212) 620-7100, FAX: (212) 620-7166, E-Mail: info@spring-obrien.com, Web Site: www.spring-obrien.com (35)

Spring, Chris, Zeta Interactive, New York, NY. Tel: (212) 660-2500, FAX: (212) 967-1028, E-Mail: info@zetainteractive.com, Web Site: www.zetainteractive.com (32)

Spring, Christopher, Spring O'Brien & Co, New York, NY. Tel: (212) 620-7100, FAX: (212) 620-7166, E-Mail: info@spring-obrien.com, Web Site: www.spring-obrien.com (35)

Spring, Declan, New Directions Publishing Corp, New York, NY. Tel: (212) 255-0230, FAX: (212) 255-0231, E-Mail: editorial@ndbooks.com, Web Site: www.ndbooks.com (17)

Spring, Tony, Bloomingdale's Direct, New York, NY. Tel: (212) 705-2000, (800) 777-0000, FAX: (212) 705-2805, Web Site: www.bloomingdales.com (16)

Springboard Brand & Creative Strategy Ltd, Arlington Heights, IL. Tel: (847) 398-4920, FAX: (847) 398-4921, E-Mail: springboard@springboardbrand.com, Web Site: www.springboardbrand.com (35)

Springer Science & Business Media LLC, New York, NY. Tel: (212) 460-1500, FAX: (212) 460-1575, Web Site: www.springer.com (17)

Springman, Paul J., Equifax Credit Information Services Inc, Atlanta, GA. Tel: (404) 885-8000, (800) 685-5000, FAX: (404) 885-8988, Web Site: www.equifax.com (20)

Springs Global Inc, New York, NY. Tel: (888) 926-7888, Web Site: www.springs.com (16)

Springstead, Candace, Outdoor Research, Seattle, WA. Tel: (206) 467-1496, (888) 467-4327, FAX: (206) 467-0374, Web Site: www.outdoorresearch.com (11)

Sprint Corp, Overland Park, KS. Tel: (703) 433-4000, Web Site: www.sprint.com (3)

Sproul, Brandon, RCS Response Technologies Inc, Charlotte, NC. Tel: (704) 522-1919, FAX: (704) 522-9092, E-Mail: results@rcsdirect.com, Web Site: www.rcsdirect.com (21)

Sproul, Dr. R. C., Ligonier Ministries, Sanford, FL. Tel: (407) 333-4244, (800) 435-4343, FAX: (407) 333-4377, Web Site: www.ligonier.org (5)

Sproul, Vesta, Ligonier Ministries, Sanford, FL. Tel: (407) 333-4244, (800) 435-4343, FAX: (407) 333-4377, Web Site: www.ligonier.org (5)

Sproull, Joanne V., Mystic Logistics Inc, South Glastonbury, CT. Tel: (860) 659-1566, (800) 969-1566, FAX: (860) 659-1420, Web Site: www.mysticlogistics.com (28)

Sprumont, Joseph, American Thermoplastic Co, Pittsburgh, PA. Tel: (412) 967-0900, (800) 245-6600, FAX: (412) 967-9990, E-Mail: atc@binders.com, Web Site: www.binders.com (27)

Sprung, Dennis B., American Kennel Club, New York, NY. Tel: (212) 696-8200, FAX: (212) 696-8217, (212) 696-8299, Web Site: www.akc.org (17)

Sprunger, Steve, MarketNet Services LLC, Spring Lake, MI. Tel: (616) 847-7992, FAX: (616) 847-7994, Web Site: www.marketnetservices.com (22)

Spuller, Peter, Klingspor's Woodworking Shop, Hickory, NC. Tel: (828) 326-WOOD, (800) 228-0000, FAX: (828) 327-4634, E-Mail: sales@woodworkingshop.com, Web Site: www.woodworkingshop.com (9)

Spyke, Pete, G&S Fruit Packers LLC, Weirsdale, FL. Tel: (352) 821-2251, (800) 949-9074, FAX: (352) 821-0278, E-Mail: info@gsfruitpackers.com, Web Site: www.gsfruitpackers.com (16)

Squadron Mail Order, Carrollton, TX. Tel: (972) 242-8663, (877) 414-0434, FAX: (972) 242-3775, E-Mail: mailorder@squadron.com, Web Site: www.squadron.com (16)

Squibb, Dennis, Foremost Insurance Group, Grand Rapids, MI. Tel: (616) 956-8241, (800) 527-3905, FAX: (800) 325-1507, Web Site: www.foremost.com (15)

Squicciarino, Joseph, King Pharmaceuticals, Inc, Tenafly, NJ. Tel: (972) 885-0929, (888) 840-5370, E-Mail: igal@navehpharma.com, Web Site: www.kingpharma.com (7)

Squires, Charles, Haymarket Group Ltd, New York, NY. Tel: (212) 239-0855, FAX: (212) 967-4184, Web Site: www.chocalatiermagazine.com (17)

Squires, Christine, US Fund for UNICEF, New York, NY. Tel: (212) 686-5522, FAX: (212) 779-1679, Web Site: www.unicefusa.org (6)

Srdjevic, Milos, ActiveCampaign Inc, Chicago, IL. Tel: (800) 357-0402, E-Mail: help@activecampaign.com, Web Site: www.activecampaign.com (24)

Srinivasan, Krishna, Frost & Sullivan Inc, Mountain View, CA. Tel: (877) 463-7678, (877) 690-3329, FAX: (877) 690-3329, E-Mail: myfrost@frost.com, Web Site: www.frost.com (30)

Srinivasan, Nagaraj, Landmark Graphics Corp, Houston, TX. Tel: (713) 839-2000, FAX: (713) 839-2015, Web Site: www.landmarksoftware.com (16)

St Cyr, Brian, Mediaspace Solutions, Hopkins, MN. Tel: (612) 253-3900, (888) 672-2100, FAX: (612) 454-2848, E-Mail: bstcy@mediaspace.com, Web Site: www.mediaspacesolutions.com (31)

St James, Sydney, Etchworld, Hawthorne, NJ. Tel: (973) 423-4002, (800) 872-3458, FAX: (973) 427-8823, Web Site: www.etchworld.com (11)

St Joseph Communications, Concord, ON Canada. Tel: (905) 660-3111, FAX: (905) 669-1972, Web Site: www.stjoseph.com (27)

St Louis, Diane, Digital Vision Resources Group - DVRG, Lenexa, KS. Tel: (913) 402-5900, E-Mail: info@dvrg.com, Web Site: www.dvrg.com (27)

Staaterman, Stacy, American Express Publishing Corp, New York, NY. Tel: (212) 382-5600, (888) 461-6180, FAX: (212) 827-6496, E-Mail: aepc@custmersvc.com, Web Site: www.amexpub.com (17)

Stabel, Marsha, Ranch House Meat Co, Billings, MT. Tel: (800) 749-6329, FAX: (888) 917-6328, E-Mail: sales@brisket.net, Web Site: www.brisket.net (4)

Stabel, Max, Ranch House Meat Co, Billings, MT. Tel: (800) 749-6329, FAX: (888) 917-6328, E-Mail: sales@brisket.net, Web Site: www.brisket.net (4)

Stacey, Richard, Northern Response (International) Ltd, Toronto, ON Canada. Tel: (905) 737-6698, (866) 584-1694, FAX: (905) 737-0099, E-Mail: general@nresponse.com, Web Site: www.shopnorthern.com (4)

Stachura, Cheryl T., Elks Magazine, Chicago, IL. Tel: (773) 755-4700, FAX: (773) 775-4792, E-Mail: elksmag@elks.org, Web Site: www.elks.org (17)

J Stack & Associates, Baltimore, MD. Tel: (410) 889-3327, FAX: (410) 889-9039 (39)

Tom Stack & Associates Inc, Tavernier, FL. Tel: (305) 852-5520, E-Mail: tomstack@earthlink.net, Web Site: www.tomstackassociatesphotoshelter.com (38)

Stack, John, Edmund Optics Inc, Barrington, NJ. Tel: (856) 573-6250, (800) 363-1992, FAX: (856) 573-6295, E-Mail: sales@edmundoptic.com, Web Site: www.edmundoptics.com (9)

Stack, John, J Stack & Associates, Baltimore, MD. Tel: (410) 889-3327, FAX: (410) 889-9039 (39)

Stack, Louis, Fitter International Inc, Calgary, AB Canada. Tel: (403) 243-6830, (800) 348-8371, FAX: (403) 229-1230, E-Mail: sales2@filler1.com, Web Site: www.fitter1.com (1)

Stack, Margaret, Fitter International Inc, Calgary, AB Canada. Tel: (403) 243-6830, (800) 348-8371, FAX: (403) 229-1230, E-Mail: sales2@filler1.com, Web Site: www.fitter1.com (1)

Stack, Sandy, Lithia Motors Inc, Medford, OR. Tel: (541) 774-7602 (12)

Stack, Thomas, Tom Stack & Associates Inc, Tavernier, FL. Tel: (305) 852-5520, E-Mail: tomstack@earthlink.net, Web Site: www.tomstackassociatesphotoshelter.com (38)

Stacks, Ed, Airs Inc, Douglasville, GA. Tel: (770) 949-0133, FAX: (770) 949-2773, E-Mail: estacks@aol.com (22)

Stacy, Steven, Sundancer Jewelry Co Inc, Albuquerque, NM. Tel: (505) 345-7475, FAX: (505) 345-7561, E-Mail: sales@sundancer.net, Web Site: www.sundancer.net (16)

Stadin, Richard N., Mastervision Inc, New York, NY. Tel: (212) 879-0448, (800) 876-0091, FAX: (212) 744-3560, E-Mail: stadin1@aol.com, Web Site: www.mastervision.com (16)

Stadtler, DJ, National Railroad Passenger Corp, Washington, DC. Tel: (202) 906-3000, (800) USA-RAIL, FAX: (202) 906-3306, Web Site: www.amtrak.com (16)

Staff, Scott, TSE Services, Raleigh, NC. Tel: (919) 875-3037, Web Site: www.ncemcs.com (30)

Staffieri, Jr Joe A., Business Direct Marketing Associates Inc, Cumming, GA. Tel: (770) 888-8300, FAX: (770) 888-6482, E-Mail: joes@bdmainc.com, Web Site: www.bdmainc.com (35)

Stagestep Inc, Philadelphia, PA. Tel: (215) 636-9000, (800) 523-0960, FAX: (267) 672-2912, E-Mail: stagestep@stagestep.com, Web Site: www. stagestep.com (5)

Stagg Direct Marketing Inc, Scarsdale, NY. Tel: (914) 725-3990, FAX: (914) 472-7298 (20)

Stagg, Phyllis C., Stagg Direct Marketing Inc, Scarsdale, NY. Tel: (914) 725-3990, FAX: (914) 472-7298 (20)

Stagner, Ross, United Investors Life Insurance Co, Birmingham, AL. Tel: (205) 325-4300, (800) 288-2722, FAX: (205) 325-4157, Web Site: www.uilic.com (15)

Stahl, Jeffrey, Parts Express, Springboro, OH. Tel: (937) 743-3000, (800) 338-0531, FAX: (937) 743-1677, E-Mail: sales@parts-express.com, Web Site: www. partsexpress.com (3)

Staib, Markus, MVNP, Honolulu, HI. Tel: (808) 536-0881, FAX: (808) 529-6208, E-Mail: ideas@mvnp. com, Web Site: www.mvnp.com (35)

Stalam, Vic, Kodak Graphic Communications, Rochester, NY. Tel: (585) 724-0251, (800) 944-6171, FAX: (585) 724-0268, Web Site: www.kpgraphics.com (27)

Staley, Jay, Colarelli Meyer & Associates Inc, Saint Louis, MO. Tel: (314) 721-1860, (800) 459-4548, FAX: (314) 721-1992, E-Mail: cmaconsult@ cmaconsult.com, Web Site: www.cmaconsult.com (20)

Stallings, Tom, EasyLink Services International Corp, Piscataway, NJ. Tel: (800) 828-7115, FAX: (732) 652-3810, E-Mail: sales@easylink.com, Web Site: www.easylink.com (16)

Stalnaker, Harry, CyberData, Hicksville, NY. Tel: (516) 942-8000, FAX: (516) 942-0800, E-Mail: info@ cyberdata.com, Web Site: www.cyberdata.com (22)

Stam, Chris, Nancy's Notions LLC, Beaver Dam, WI. Tel: (920) 887-0321, (800) 833-0690, FAX: (800) 255-8119, E-Mail: comments@nancysnotions.com, Web Site: www.nancysnotions.com (11)

Stamey, Allen, Audio-Digest Foundation, Glendale, CA. Tel: (818) 240-7500, (800) 423-2308, FAX: (818) 240-7379, Web Site: www.audio-digest.org (1)

Standard & Poor's Corp, New York, NY. Tel: (212) 438-2000, FAX: (212) 438-7375, Web Site: www. standardandpoors.com (17)

Standard Buying Service Ltd, New York, NY. Tel: (212) 686-6800, FAX: (212) 532-4102, E-Mail: info@sbspromo.com, Web Site: www. standardbuying.com (33)

Standard Communications Corp, San Diego, CA. Tel: (858) 546-5300, (800) 745-2445, FAX: (858) 546-5301, E-Mail: satcommsales@stdcom.com, Web Site: www.standardcomm.com (16)

Standard Directory of Advertising Agencies, Summit, NJ. Tel: (800) 908-5395 (43)

Standard Life, Montreal, QC Canada. Tel: (514) 499-8855, (877) 499-9555, FAX: (514) 499-4908, Web Site: www.standardlife.ca (15)

Standard Publishing, Cincinnati, OH. Tel: (513) 931-4050, (800) 543-1301, FAX: (877) 867-5751, Web Site: www.standardpub.com (17)

Standard Tools & Equipment Co, Greensboro, NC. Tel: (336) 697-7177, (800) 336-2776, Web Site: www. toolsusa.com (9)

Standing, Mark, Deseret Book, Salt Lake City, UT. Tel: (801) 534-1515, (800) 453-4532, FAX: (801) 517-3392, Web Site: www.deseretbook.com (16)

Standish, Thomas R., Centerpoint Energy, Minneapolis, MN. Tel: (612) 372-4664, FAX: (612) 321-4873, E-Mail: mgc-businessinformation@ centerpointenergy.com, Web Site: www. minnegasco.centerpointenergy.com (16)

Staneff, Lynn, Magellan's Catalog, Chelmsford, MA. Tel: (800) 450-7715, (800) 866-3235, E-Mail: sales@magellans.com, Web Site: www.magellans. com (5)

The Stanford Group, New York, NY. Tel: (212) 333-5514, E-Mail: info@stanfordgroupinc.com, Web Site: www.stanfordgroupinc.com (35)

Stanford, Sheila, The Stanford Group, New York, NY. Tel: (212) 333-5514, E-Mail: info@ stanfordgroupinc.com, Web Site: www. stanfordgroupinc.com (35)

Stanga, Michael, Saunders Manufacturing Co Inc, Readfield, ME. Tel: (207) 685-3385, (800) 341-4674, FAX: (207) 685-9918, E-Mail: jsherwood@ saunders-usa.com, Web Site: www.saunders-usa. com (16)

Robert A Stanger & Co Inc, Shrewsbury, NJ. Tel: (732) 389-3600, FAX: (732) 389-1751, E-Mail: info@ rastanger.com, Web Site: www.rastranger.com (14)

Stanich, Mark, American Express Publishing Corp, New York, NY. Tel: (212) 382-5600, (888) 461-6180, FAX: (212) 827-6496, E-Mail: aepc@custmrsvc. com, Web Site: www.amexpub.com (17)

Stankard, Martin F., Productivity Development Group Inc, Westford, MA. Tel: (978) 692-1818, FAX: (978) 692-5080, E-Mail: info@martinstankard.com (20)

Stanley Home Products, Great Bend, KS. Tel: (800) 732-1118, E-Mail: customer@fuller.com, Web Site: www.fullerdirect.com (8)

Stanley Supply & Services, North Andover, MA. Tel: (978) 682-9844, (800) 225-5370, FAX: (800) 743-8141, Web Site: www.stanleysupplyservices.com (16)

Stanley, Clive, Performance Media Solutions Inc & TrueWorx Inc, Las Vegas, NV. Tel: (866) 827-7077 (16)

Stanley, Debra, DS Direct Response, Torrance, CA. Tel: (310) 251-1830, E-Mail: info@dsdirectresponse. com, Web Site: dsdirectresponse.com (23)

Stanley, Jr George F., Vagabond Creations Inc, Dayton, OH. Tel: (937) 298-1124, (800) 738-7237, FAX: (937) 298-1124, E-Mail: sales@vagabondcreations. net, Web Site: www.vagabondcreations.net (10)

Stanley, Lori, Coastal Training Technologies Corp, Virginia Beach, VA. Tel: (877) 262-7825, FAX: (757) 498-3657, E-Mail: info@training.dupont.com, Web Site: www.coastalhealth.com (7)

Stanley, Tracey, Print Products International, Annapolis Junction, MD. Tel: (910) 695-7223, FAX: (910) 944-1724, Web Site: www.paceworldwide.com (9)

Stansbury, H Tayloe, Intuit, Mountain View, CA. Tel: (650) 944-6000, Web Site: www.inuit.com (10)

Stanton Direct Marketing Inc, Horseheads, NY. Tel: (607) 734-1665, (877) 734-1665, FAX: (607) 734-3708, Web Site: www.stantondirect.com (31)

Stanton, Aloysius F., Stanton Direct Marketing Inc, Horseheads, NY. Tel: (607) 734-1665, (877) 734-1665, FAX: (607) 734-3708, Web Site: www. stantondirect.com (31)

Stanton, Scott, Nancy's Notions LLC, Beaver Dam, WI. Tel: (920) 887-0321, (800) 833-0690, FAX: (800) 255-8119, E-Mail: comments@nancysnotions.com, Web Site: www.nancysnotions.com (11)

Stanuscek, Kris, The Sausage Maker Inc, Buffalo, NY. Tel: (716) 824-5814, (888) 490-8525, FAX: (716) 824-6465, E-Mail: customerservice@sausagemaker. com, Web Site: www.sausagemaker.com (4)

Stapelfeld, Ben, New Pig Corp, Tipton, PA. Tel: (814) 684-0101, (800) 468-4647, FAX: (814) 684-0961, E-Mail: hothogs@newpig.com, Web Site: www. newpig.com (9)

Staples Business Advantage, Atlanta, GA. Tel: (770) 997-2512, (877) 826-7754, FAX: (888) 387-9592, Web Site: www.staples.com (34)

Staples Inc, Framingham, MA. Tel: (508) 253-5000, FAX: (508) 253-7803, Web Site: www.staples.com (10)

Staples Industrial, Framingham, MA. Tel: (978) 443-9592, (800) 638-9899, FAX: (978) 443-2678 (28)

Stapleton, Amy, Missouri Life Inc, Boonville, MO. Tel: (660) 882-9898, (800) 492-2593, FAX: (660) 882-9899, E-Mail: info@missourilife.com, Web Site: www.missourilife.com (17)

Stapleton, John, 22squared Inc, Atlanta, GA. Tel: (404) 347-8700, FAX: (404) 347-8800, Web Site: www. 22squared.com (35)

The Staplex Co, Brooklyn, NY. Tel: (718) 768-3333, (800) 221-0822, FAX: (718) 965-0750, E-Mail: info@staplex.com, Web Site: www.staplex.com (34)

Star Direct Mail, Brooklyn, NY. Tel: (718) 257-3500, (877) 978-2762, FAX: (718) 649-5470, Web Site: www.stardirectmail.com (21)

Star Silkscreen Design Inc, Decatur, IL. Tel: (217) 877-0804, FAX: (217) 877-0843, Web Site: www. starsilkscreendesign.com (2)

Star Sprinkler Inc, Lansdale, PA. Tel: (414) 570-5000, (800) 558-5236, FAX: (414) 570-5010, Web Site: www.starsprinkler.com (9)

Star Tribune Media Co, Minneapolis, MN. Tel: (612) 673-4000, FAX: (612) 673-4359, Web Site: www. startribunecompany.com (17)

Star, Doug, Potpourri Group Inc, North Billerica, MA. Tel: (978) 256-4100, FAX: (978) 256-1961/0344, Web Site: www.potpourrigroup.com (6)

Starbird Creative, Sebastopol, CA. Tel: (707) 829-0277, E-Mail: susan@starbirdcreative.com, Web Site: www.starbirdcreative.com (35)

Starbird, Susan, Starbird Creative, Sebastopol, CA. Tel: (707) 829-0277, E-Mail: susan@starbirdcreative. com, Web Site: www.starbirdcreative.com (35)

Starbucks Corp, Seattle, WA. Tel: (206) 447-1575, (800) 344-1575, FAX: (206) 447-0828, Web Site: www.starbucks.com (4)

Starchtech, Golden Valley, MN. Tel: (763) 545-5400, (800) 597-7225, FAX: (763) 545-9450, Web Site: www.starchtech.com (16)

Starck, Paul, Blexrud Direct, Spartanburg, SC. Tel: (864) 583-7399, FAX: (864) 583-7399, E-Mail: blexrud@bellsouth.net (20)

Starcom MediaVest Group, Chicago, IL. Tel: (312) 220-3535, Web Site: smvgroup.com (35)

Starcrest Products of California Inc, Perris, CA. Tel: (909) 943-2011, FAX: (909) 943-2971, E-Mail: tmc@tstonramp.com (16)

Stark Brothers Nurseries & Orchards, Louisiana, MO. Tel: (573) 754-8800, (800) 325-4180, E-Mail: info@starkbros.com, Web Site: www.starkbros.com (8)

Stark, Ben, Faultless Starch/Bon Ami Co, Kansas City, MO. Tel: (816) 842-1230, FAX: (816) 842-3417, E-Mail: info@faultless.com, Web Site: www. faultless.com (16)

Stark, David, Dozier Equipment International, Milwaukee, WI. Tel: (800) 251-1234, FAX: (800) 336-6608, Web Site: www.dozierequip.com (9)

Starkey Laboratories, Eden Prairie, MN. Tel: (952) 941-6401, Web Site: www.starkey.com (16)

Starmount Life Insurance Co, Baton Rouge, LA. Tel: (225) 926-2888, (888) 729-5433, (888) 729-7827, E-Mail: info@starmountlife.com, Web Site: www.starmountlife.com (15)

Staron, Carley, Nielsen Trade Dimensions, Wilton, CT. Tel: (203) 222-5750, (800) 291-0410, FAX: (203) 222-5701, E-Mail: tradedimensions.info@nielsen.com, Web Site: www.tradedimensions.com (17)

Starr, Marlon, RentPath LLc, Norcross, GA. Tel: (678) 421-3000, (800) 216-1423, Web Site: www.primedia.com (31)

START International, Addison, TX. Tel: (972) 248-1999, (800) 259-1986, FAX: (972) 248-1991, E-Mail: info@startinternational.com, Web Site: www.startinternational.com (9)

Startec Global Communications, Rockville, MD. Tel: (301) 610-4300, FAX: (301) 610-4301, Web Site: www.startec.com (32)

Starwood Hotels & Resorts Worldwide Inc, Stamford, CT. Tel: (203) 964-6000, FAX: (914) 640-8310, Web Site: www.starwoodhotels.com (19)

Starz Entertainment LLC, Englewood, CO. Tel: (855) 807-2929, Web Site: www.starz.com (16)

Stasiak, Denise, Stolle Machinery LLC, Centennial, CO. Tel: (303) 708-9044, (800) 228-4593, FAX: (303) 708-9045, E-Mail: cmd.info@stollemachinery.com, Web Site: www.stollemachinery.com (34)

State Farm Insurance Cos, Bloomington, IL. Tel: (309) 766-2311, FAX: (309) 766-3621, Web Site: www.statefarm.com (15)

State Mutual Insurance Co, Rome, GA. Tel: (706) 291-1054, FAX: (706) 291-9459 (15)

State Street Global Advisors, Boston, MA. Tel: (617) 786-3000, FAX: (617) 664-2950, Web Site: www.ssga.com (14)

State University of New York-College of Plattsburgh, Plattsburgh, NY. Tel: (518) 564-2000, FAX: (518) 564-3183, E-Mail: nancy.church@plattsburgh.edu, Web Site: www.plattsburgh.edu (41)

Stateside Associates, Arlington, VA. Tel: (703) 525-7466 X228 (20)

Statile, Robert, CertainTeed Corp, Valley Forge, PA. Tel: (610) 341-7000/7739, (800) 233-8990, FAX: (610) 341-7777, Web Site: www.certainteed.com (16)

Statistical Innovations Inc, Belmont, MA. Tel: (617) 489-4490, FAX: (617) 489-4499, E-Mail: statisticalinnovations@gmail.com, Web Site: www.statisticalinnovations.com (20)

Statlistics, Danbury, CT. Tel: (203) 778-8700, FAX: (203) 778-4839, E-Mail: info@statlistics.com, Web Site: www.statlistics.com (23)

StatSoft Inc, Tulsa, OK. Tel: (918) 749-1119, FAX: (918) 749-2217, E-Mail: info@statsoft.com, Web Site: www.statsoft.com (9)

Statware, Centerbrook, CT. Tel: (860) 767-9000, FAX: (860) 767-3145, E-Mail: info@statware.net, Web Site: www.powerlist.com (16)

Statz, Steve, Mersco Medical, Pierre, SD. Tel: (605) 224-6687, (800) 234-1881, FAX: (605) 322-1801 (16)

Stauffer, Rick, PossibleNOW Inc, Duluth, GA. Tel: (770) 255-1020, FAX: (770) 255-1025, Web Site: www.dncsolution.com (22)

Stavarz, Alexander, Synergy Direct Marketing Solutions LLC, Barberton, OH. Tel: (330) 869-5886, Web Site: www.synmar.biz (29)

Stavenjord, Chris, Padulo Integrated, Toronto, ON Canada. Tel: (416) 966-4000, (800) 454-5321, FAX: (416) 966-4012, E-Mail: info@padulo.ca, Web Site: www.padulo.ca (35)

Stavitski, Richard L., Crutchfield Corp, Charlottesville, VA. Tel: (434) 817-1000, (800) 955-9091, FAX: (804) 817-1010, E-Mail: administration@crutchfield.com, Web Site: www.crutchfield.com (3)

The StayWell Co, Yardley, PA. Tel: (267) 685-2800, Web Site: www.staywell.com (7)

StayWell/Krames, San Bruno, CA. Tel: (650) 742-0400, FAX: (650) 244-4568, Web Site: www.staywell.com (17)

Steacy, Brian, ClickMail Marketing Inc, San Mateo, CA. Tel: (650) 653-8055, Web Site: clickmail.com (32)

Stead, Bob, American Trim, Lima, OH. Tel: (419) 228-1145, FAX: (419) 996-4850, E-Mail: sales@amtrim.com, Web Site: www.amtrim.com (9)

Stead, Jerre L., IHS Markit, Englewood, CO. Tel: (303) 858-6187, (800) 447-2273, Web Site: www.ihs.com (17)

Steady, Glen, Quadrant Engineering Plastic Products, Reading, PA. Tel: (610) 320-6600, (800) 366-0300, FAX: (610) 320-6868, Web Site: www.quadrantepp.com (14)

Stearns, Gary, Aspen Packaging Corp, Cicero, IL. Tel: (708) 652-6444, (800) 367-5493, FAX: (708) 652-6444, E-Mail: sales@aspenpkg.com, Web Site: www.aspenpkg.com (27)

Stearns, Mark S., Crystek Corp, Fort Myers, FL. Tel: (239) 561-3311, (800) 237-3061, FAX: (239) 561-1025, E-Mail: sales@crystek.com, Web Site: www.crystek.com (9)

Stearns, Richard, World Vision Inc, Federal Way, WA. Tel: (253) 815-1000, (888) 511-6548, FAX: (253) 815-3140, E-Mail: info@worldvision.org, Web Site: www.worldvision.org (1)

Steck-Vaughn, Austin, TX. Tel: (512) 343-8227, (800) 531-5015, (877) 866-2586, FAX: (512) 795-3617, (877) 265-2730, E-Mail: info@steck-vaughn.com, Web Site: www.steck-vaughn.com (17)

Steedman, Donald, Taylor-Stiles Division, Florence, KY. Tel: (859) 525-7600, (800) 365-8555, FAX: (859) 525-1446, E-Mail: sales@littleford.com, Web Site: www.littleford.com (16)

Steel Media Inc, New York, NY. Tel: (212) 601-2840, E-Mail: info@steelmediainc.com, Web Site: www.steelmediainc.com (35)

Steel, Richard, Social Reality Inc, Los Angeles, CA. Tel: (323) 694-9800, Web Site: www.socialreality.com (35)

Steelcase Inc, Grand Rapids, MI. Tel: (616) 247-2710, FAX: (616) 475-2270, Web Site: www.steelcase.com (16)

Steele, Elinor, Tupperware Brands Corp, Orlando, FL. Tel: (407) 826-5050, (800) 366-3800, FAX: (407) 826-8874, Web Site: www.tupperwarebrands.com (16)

Steele, Jenine, Hampshire Pewter Co, Somersworth, NH. Tel: (603) 569-4944, (800) 639-7704, FAX: (603) 569-4524, E-Mail: gifts@hampshirepewter.com, Web Site: www.hampshirepewter.com (6)

Steele, Joey, Fauntleroy Supply Co/Wing Supply, Greenville, KY. Tel: (270) 338-5866, (800) 388-9464, FAX: (270) 338-0057, Web Site: www.wingsupply.com (11)

Steele, Julie, The LadyBug Co, Berry Creek, CA. Tel: (530) 589-5227 (8)

Steele, Patricia, Spa-Finder Inc, New York, NY. Tel: (305) 307-5852, (800) ALL-SPAS, Web Site: www.spafinder.com (7)

Steele, Robert S., Hampshire Pewter Co, Somersworth, NH. Tel: (603) 569-4944, (800) 639-7704, FAX: (603) 569-4524, E-Mail: gifts@hampshirepewter.com, Web Site: www.hampshirepewter.com (6)

Steen, Scott, American Forests, Washington, DC. Tel: (202) 737-1944, FAX: (202) 737-2457, E-Mail: info@amfor.org, Web Site: www.americanforests.org (1)

Stefanki, Luke, Multi-Media Publishing & Packaging Inc, Panorama City, CA. Tel: (818) 341-7484, (800) 982-8138, FAX: (818) 341-2807, E-Mail: sales@mmppinc.com, Web Site: www.mmppinc.com (27)

Stefano, Brian, Peter Pan Bus Lines Inc, Springfield, MA. Tel: (413) 781-3320, (800) 343-9999, FAX: (413) 747-7626, E-Mail: info@peterpanbus.com, Web Site: www.peterpanbus.com (19)

Steffen, Ed, Gundersen Partners LLC, New York, NY. Tel: (212) 677-7660, FAX: (212) 358-0275, Web Site: www.gundersenpartners.com (20)

Steig, Donald B., Practical Computer Solutions, South Orange, NJ. Tel: (973) 761-6099, FAX: (215) 243-8283, E-Mail: dbsteig@alum.mit.edu, Web Site: www.donsteig.com (20)

Steigler, Ernie, SWB&R Inc, Bethlehem, PA. Tel: (610) 866-0611, (877) 377-9286, FAX: (610) 866-8650, E-Mail: swbr@swbrinc.com, Web Site: www.swbrinc.com (35)

Stein IAS, New York, NY. Tel: (212) 213-1112, Web Site: www.steinias.com (35)

Stein, Eric, AM Solutions, Edgerton, WI. Tel: (800) 410-6245, E-Mail: fschulze@amsolutionswi.com, Web Site: www.amsolutionswi.com (21)

Stein, Johanna, Santa Fe Natural Tobacco Co, Santa Fe, NM. Tel: (505) 982-4257, Web Site: www.nascigs.com (16)

Stein, Kay, Recognition Products International, Easton, MD. Tel: (410) 820-0022, (800) 292-7354, FAX: (410) 820-5044, E-Mail: info@recognitionproducts.com, Web Site: www.shoprecognitionproducts.com (16)

Stein, Kevin, HAVE Inc, Hudson, NY. Tel: (518) 828-2000, (800) 999-HAVE (4283), FAX: (518) 828-2008, E-Mail: kstein@haveinc.com, Web Site: www.haveinc.com (3)

Stein, Lonny, Dictionary of Marketing Terms, Hauppauge, NY. Tel: (631) 434-3311, (800) 645-3476, FAX: (631) 434-3723, E-Mail: barrons@barronseduc.com, Web Site: www.barronseduc.com (43)

Stein, Robert G., American Society on Aging, San Francisco, CA. Tel: (415) 974-9600, (800) 537-9728, FAX: (415) 974-0300, E-Mail: info@asaging.org, Web Site: www.asaging.org (1)

Stein, Seymour S., K-D Lamp Co, Andover, OH. Tel: (440) 293-4064, FAX: (440) 293-4591, E-Mail: admin@atc-lighting-plastics.com, Web Site: www.k-dlamp.com (12)

Stein, Thomas, Stein IAS, New York, NY. Tel: (212) 213-1112, Web Site: www.steinias.com (35)

Steinbauer, Thomas M., Ameristar Casinos Inc, Las Vegas, NV. Tel: (702) 567-7000, FAX: (702) 369-8860, Web Site: www.ameristarcasinos.com (19)

Steinberg, Andrea, Gary's Perennials, LLC, Maple Glen, PA. Tel: (215) 628-4070, (800) 898-6653, FAX: (215) 628-0216, E-Mail: roots@garysperennials.com, Web Site: www.garysperennials.com; www.perennialmarket.com (8)

Steinberg, Carol, ValueVision Media Inc, Eden Prairie, MN. Tel: (952) 943-6000, Web Site: www.shophq.com (32)

Steinberg, David A., Zeta Interactive, New York, NY. Tel: (212) 660-2500, FAX: (212) 967-1028, E-Mail: info@zetainteractive.com, Web Site: www.zetainteractive.com (32)

Steinberg, Dr. Dan, Salford Systems, San Diego, CA. Tel: (619) 543-8880, FAX: (619) 543-8888, Web Site: www.salford-systems.com (22)

Steinberg, Gary, Gary's Perennials, LLC, Maple Glen, PA. Tel: (215) 628-4070, (800) 898-6653, FAX: (215) 628-0216, E-Mail: roots@garysperennials.com, Web Site: www.garysperennials.com; www.perennialmarket.com (8)

Steinberg, Joseph S., Leucadia National Corp, New York, NY. Tel: (212) 460-1900, FAX: (212) 598-4869, Web Site: www.leucadia.com (14)

Steinberg, Lisa, Diversified Investment Advisors, Harrison, NY. Tel: (914) 627-3000, FAX: (914) 627-3280, Web Site: www.divinvest.com (14)

Steinberg, Lori, Moore Medical LLC, Farmington, CT. Tel: (860) 826-3600, FAX: (860) 223-2382, E-Mail: e-support@mooremedical.com, Web Site: www.mooremedical.com (7)

Steinbrunner, Carla, Associated Photo, Erlanger, KY. Tel: (859) 344-1460, (800) 727-2580, FAX: (859) 282-0032 (16)

Steiner, Paula, Blue Cross Blue Shield of Illinois, Chicago, IL. Tel: (312) 938-6000, FAX: (312) 938-5722, Web Site: www.bcbsil.com (15)

Steinhardt, David J., Idealliance, Alexandria, VA. Tel: (703) 837-1070, FAX: (703) 837-1072 (40)

Steinhart, David, Service Mailers & Fulfillment Inc, Vernon, CA. Tel: (323) 292-0133, FAX: (323) 292-1038, E-Mail: dgsteinhart@gmail.com, Web Site: servicemailersandfulfillment.com (28)

Steinhour, Jeff, Crispin Porter + Bogusky, Miami, FL. Tel: (305) 859-2070, FAX: (305) 854-3419, E-Mail: info@cpbgroup.com, Web Site: www.cpbgroup.com (35)

Steinhouse, Eric, Commerce Bancshares Inc, Saint Louis, MO. Tel: (800) 453-2265, Web Site: www.commercebank.com (14)

Steinle, Peter, Profit Center Software Inc, Uniondale, NY. Tel: (516) 414-6300, (888) 446-6240, FAX: (516) 414-6304, E-Mail: jmarrah@profitcenter.com, Web Site: www.profitcenter.com (22)

Steinman, Andy, Falcon Safety Products, Branchburg, NJ. Tel: (908) 707-4900, FAX: (908) 707-8855, Web Site: www.falconsafety.com (16)

Steinmetz, Jay, Barcoding Inc, Baltimore, MD. Tel: (410) 385-8532, (888) 860-SCAN, (888) 860-7226, FAX: (410) 385-8559, E-Mail: info@barcoding.com, Web Site: www.barcoding.com (22)

Steinour, Stephen, Huntington Bancshares, Columbus, OH. Tel: (614) 480-5160, (800) 480-BANK, FAX: (614) 480-5284, Web Site: www.huntington.com (14)

Stella, Richard, Zotos International, Darien, CT. Tel: (203) 655-8911, (800) 242-9283, (800) 242-WAVE, FAX: (203) 656-7890, E-Mail: HumanResources@zotosintl.com, Web Site: www.zotos.com (16)

Stellar Technology Inc, Amherst, NY. Tel: (716) 250-1900, (800) 274-1846, FAX: (716) 250-1909, E-Mail: info@stellartech.com, Web Site: www.stellartech.com (9)

Stelmachowicz, John, Pharmaceutical Care Management Association, Washington, DC. Tel: (202) 756-7210, FAX: (202) 207-3623, E-Mail: info@pcmanet.org, Web Site: www.pcmanet.org (1)

The Stelter Co, Des Moines, IA. Tel: (800) 331-6881 (20)

Stenebring, Thomas, General Binding Corp, Northbrook, IL. Tel: (800) 723-4000, FAX: (847) 272-1389, (800) 952-1166, Web Site: www.gbc.com (10)

Stengel, Jim, Clairol Inc, Stamford, CT. Tel: (203) 357-5000, (800) 252-4765, FAX: (203) 357-5003, Web Site: www.clairol.com (7)

Stephan & Brady Inc, Madison, WI. Tel: (608) 241-4141, FAX: (608) 241-4246, E-Mail: gwhitely@stephanbrady.com, Web Site: www.stephanbrady.com (35)

Stephan Partners Inc, New York, NY. Tel: (212) 524-8583, E-Mail: george@stephenpartners.com, Web Site: www.stephanpartners.com (35)

Stephan, George N., Stephan Partners Inc, New York, NY. Tel: (212) 524-8583, E-Mail: george@stephanpartners.com, Web Site: www.stephanpartners.com (35)

Stephan, Mark E., Mediacom Communications Corp, Chester, NY. Tel: (855) 633-4226, FAX: (845) 698-4100, Web Site: www.mediacomcable.com (32)

Stephen-Bradford Search, New York, NY. Tel: (212) 221-6333, X346, (800) 720-0922, FAX: (212) 391-7826, E-Mail: info@stephenbradford.com, Web Site: www.stephenbradford.com (20)

Stephens Direct Inc, Dayton, OH. Tel: (937) 299-4993, E-Mail: info@stephensdirect.com, Web Site: www.stephensdirect.com (35)

Stephens Inc, New York, NY. Tel: (212) 891-1777, Web Site: www.stephens.com (20)

Stephens Publishing Co, Sandusky, OH. Tel: (419) 626-5592, (800) 236-5592, FAX: (419) 626-9333, Web Site: www.stephenspublishing.com (17)

Stephens, Craig S., Stephens Publishing Co, Sandusky, OH. Tel: (419) 626-5592, (800) 236-5592, FAX: (419) 626-9333, Web Site: www.stephenspublishing.com (17)

Stephens, Gregory, AM Leonard Inc, Piqua, OH. Tel: (800) 543-8955, FAX: (800) 433-0633, E-Mail: info@amleo.com, Web Site: www.amleo.com (8)

Stephens, J.T., EBSCO Reception Room Subscription Services, Birmingham, AL. Tel: (205) 991-1409, (800) 527-5901, FAX: (205) 995-1621, Web Site: www.ebsco.com/errss (18)

Stephens, J.T., Vulcan Information Packaging, Vincent, AL. Tel: (205) 672-2241, (800) 633-4526, FAX: (205) 672-1276, Web Site: www.vulcan-online.com (16)

Stephens, Jess, SmartFocus Inc, New York, NY. Tel: (425) 460-1000, (646) 356-1169, Web Site: www.smartfocus.com (22)

Stephens, Mike, Historical Replications Inc, Jackson, MS. Tel: (800) 426-5628, FAX: (601) 981-8185, E-Mail: info@historicaldesigns.com, Web Site: www.historicaldesigns.com (8)

Stephens, Pat, International Filing Corp LLC, Hattiesburg, MS. Tel: (601) 554-0521, FAX: (601) 554-0522, E-Mail: pcoerper@intfiling.com, Web Site: www.intfiling.com (26)

Stephens, Phil, Stephens Direct Inc, Dayton, OH. Tel: (937) 299-4993, E-Mail: info@stephensdirect.com, Web Site: www.stephensdirect.com (35)

Stephens, Tammy, Eichten's Hidden Acres, Center City, MN. Tel: (651) 257-4752, FAX: (651) 257-6286, E-Mail: eichtens@frontiernet.net, Web Site: www.specialtycheese.com (4)

Stephens, Verlan, Agile Education Marketing LLC, Denver, CO. Tel: (866) 783-0241, E-Mail: info@agile-ed.com, Web Site: www.agile-ed.com (24)

Stephens, William Thomas, Boise Cascade Holdings LLC, Boise, ID. Tel: (208) 384-6451, FAX: (208) 384-7189, E-Mail: mediarelations@bc.com, Web Site: www.bc.com (16)

Stephenson Printing Inc, Alexandria, VA. Tel: (703) 642-9000, (800) 336-4637, FAX: (703) 354-0384, E-Mail: gstephenson@stephensonprinting.com, Web Site: www.stephensonprinting.com (27)

Stephenson, APR Lucinda, Iowa Medical Society, Des Moines, IA. Tel: (515) 223-1401, (800) 747-3070, FAX: (515) 223-0590, Web Site: www.iowamedical.org (1)

Stephenson, Chad, Cyril-Scott Co, Lancaster, OH. Tel: (740) 654-2112, FAX: (740) 654-7712, E-Mail: mstephenson@cyrilscott.com, Web Site: www.cyrilscott.com (27)

Stephenson, Don, Volkswagen Group of America Inc, Herndon, VA. Tel: (248) 754-5000, Web Site: www.volkswagengroupamerica.com (16)

Stephenson, George W., Stephenson Printing Inc, Alexandria, VA. Tel: (703) 642-9000, (800) 336-4637, FAX: (703) 354-0384, E-Mail: gstephenson@stephensonprinting.com, Web Site: www.stephensonprinting.com (27)

Stephenson, Laura, Lifeway Christian Stores, Nashville, TN. Tel: (615) 251-2000, (800) 458-2772, FAX: (513) 728-6975, E-Mail: customerservice@berean.com, Web Site: www.berean.com (5)

Stephenson, Lena, Wisconsin Direct Marketing Association, Milwaukee, WI. Tel: (414) 760-9362, FAX: (414) 431-4195, E-Mail: info@wdma.org, Web Site: www.wdma.org (40)

Stephenson, Randall L., AT&T Inc, Dallas, TX. Tel: (210) 821-4105, Web Site: www.att.com (16)

Stephenson, Tim, Creative Lift Inc, San Francisco, CA. Tel: (415) 248-3170, E-Mail: hello@creativelift.net, Web Site: www.creativelift.net (35)

Steppin' Out & See America, Las Vegas, NV. Tel: (702) 798-6522, FAX: 702 798-6562, E-Mail: sales@see-america.net, Web Site: steppinoutseeamerica.com (19)

Steptoe & Wife Antiques Ltd, Scarborough, ON Canada. Tel: (416) 780-1707, (800) 461-0060, FAX: (416) 780-1814, E-Mail: info@steptoewife.com, Web Site: www.steptoewife.com (8)

Steputis, Mark, Eagle:xm, Denver, CO. Tel: (303) 320-5411, (800) 426-5376, FAX: (303) 393-6584, E-Mail: extendedmedia@eaglexm.com, Web Site: www.eaglexm.com (21)

Sterba-Miller, Karen, National Electrical Manufacturers Association (NEMA), Rosslyn, VA. Tel: (703) 841-3200, FAX: (703) 841-5900, E-Mail: communications@nema.org, Web Site: www.nema.org (34)

Sterk, Leo G., B2BMarketing.com, Scottsdale, AZ. Tel: (602) 402-6588, Web Site: www.b2bmarketing.com (35)

Sterk, Leo, Wheaton Group, Chapel Hill, NC. Tel: (919) 969-8859, FAX: (425) 675-6014, E-Mail: jim.wheaton@wheatongroup.com, Web Site: www.wheatongroup.com (22)

Sterling Business Services, Cary, NC. Tel: (919) 467-5062 (14)

Sterling Fluid Systems, Indianapolis, IN. Tel: (317) 925-9661, (800) 879-0182, FAX: (317) 924-7388, Web Site: www.peerlesspump.com (16)

Sterling Jewelers Inc, Akron, OH. Tel: (330) 668-5000, FAX: (330) 668-5052, E-Mail: webmaster@jewels.com, Web Site: www.sterlingjewelers.com (16)

Sterling Name Tape Inc, Winsted, CT. Tel: (860) 379-5142, (800) 654-5210, FAX: (860) 379-0394, E-Mail: postman@sterlingtape.com, Web Site: www.sterlingtape.com (16)

Sterling Print & Mail System, Peterborough, NH. Tel: (603) 924-9401, (800) 439-9401, FAX: (603) 924-9247, E-Mail: sbc@sbc.mv.com, Web Site: www.mv.com/ipusers/sbc (27)

Sterling Publishing Co Inc, New York, NY. Tel: (212) 532-7160, (800) 367-9692, FAX: (212) 213-2495, Web Site: www.sterlingpublishing.com (17)

Sterling, Gabriel, Landmark Communications Inc, Alpharetta, GA. Tel: (770) 813-1000, Web Site: www.landmarkcommunications.net (17)

Sterling, George A., Sterling Print & Mail System, Peterborough, NH. Tel: (603) 924-9401, (800) 439-9401, FAX: (603) 924-9247, E-Mail: sbc@sbc.mv.com, Web Site: www.mv.com/ipusers/sbc (27)

Sterling, Rhonda, Phoenix Learning Group Inc, Maryland Heights, MO. Tel: (314) 569-0211, (800) 221-1274, FAX: (314) 569-2834, E-Mail: dealersales@phoenixlearninggroup.com, Web Site: www.phoenixlearninggroup.com (16)

Stern, Bruce H., American Association for Justice, Washington, DC. Tel: (202) 965-3500, (800) 424-2725, FAX: (202) 625-7313, E-Mail: membership@justice.org, Web Site: www.justice.org (1)

Stern, Laurie, Bristol Associates Inc, Los Angeles, CA. Tel: (310) 670-0525, FAX: (310) 670-4075, E-Mail: lfarber@bristolassoc.com, Web Site: www.bristolassoc.com (20)

Stern, Leslie F., Central Lewmar, Clifton, NJ. Tel: (973) 622-6377, (800) 772-7301, FAX: (973) 623-4323, E-Mail: dan.watkoske@expedx.com, Web Site: www.centrallewmar.com (25)

Stern, Molly, Broadway Books, New York, NY. Tel: (212) 782-9644, FAX: (212) 782-8338, E-Mail: bwaypub@randomhouse.com, Web Site: www.randomhouse.com/broadway (17)

Stern, Norm, Norscot Group, Mequon, WI. Tel: (262) 241-3313, (800) 653-3313, FAX: (262) 241-4904, Web Site: www.norscot.com (5)

Stern, Patrick, iCrossing, New York, NY. Tel: (212) 649-3900, FAX: (646) 280-1091, Web Site: www.icrossing.com (32)

Stern, Scott, Norscot Group, Mequon, WI. Tel: (262) 241-3313, (800) 653-3313, FAX: (262) 241-4904, Web Site: www.norscot.com (5)

Stern, Yonatan, Zoom Information Inc, Waltham, MA. Tel: (781) 693-7500, FAX: (781) 693-7510, Web Site: www.zoominfo.com (22)

Sternberg, Deborah, Starmount Life Insurance Co, Baton Rouge, LA. Tel: (225) 926-2888, (888) 729-5433, (888) 729-7827, E-Mail: info@starmountlife.com, Web Site: www.starmountlife.com (15)

Sternberg, Donna, Starmount Life Insurance Co, Baton Rouge, LA. Tel: (225) 926-2888, (888) 729-5433, (888) 729-7827, E-Mail: info@starmountlife.com, Web Site: www.starmountlife.com (15)

Sternberg, Erich, Starmount Life Insurance Co, Baton Rouge, LA. Tel: (225) 926-2888, (888) 729-5433, (888) 729-7827, E-Mail: info@starmountlife.com, Web Site: www.starmountlife.com (15)

Sternberg, Hans J., Starmount Life Insurance Co, Baton Rouge, LA. Tel: (225) 926-2888, (888) 729-5433, (888) 729-7827, E-Mail: info@starmountlife.com, Web Site: www.starmountlife.com (15)

Sternbert, Todd, START International, Addison, TX. Tel: (972) 248-1999, (800) 259-1986, FAX: (972) 248-1991, E-Mail: info@startinternational.com, Web Site: www.startinternational.com (9)

George Sterne Agency Inc, Fallbrook, CA. Tel: (760) 432-6913, (800) 772-8174, FAX: (760) 432-9570, E-Mail: info@georgesterneagency.net, Web Site: georgesterneagency.net (23)

Sternkopf, Eric, iContact LLC, Morrisville, NC. Tel: (919) 820-7837, (877) 820-7837, E-Mail: sales@icontact.com, Web Site: www.icontact.com (32)

Sterns, Jeremy, StrongView Systems Inc, Redwood City, CA. Tel: (650) 421-4200, (800) 971-0380, FAX: (650) 421-4201, E-Mail: info@strongview.com, Web Site: www.strongview.com (32)

Stetson University, Deland, FL. Tel: (904) 822-7405/7406, FAX: (904) 822-7430, Web Site: www.stetson.edu (41)

Stettner, Ron, Mazda Motor of America Inc, Irvine, CA. Tel: (949) 727-1990, (800) 222-6500, FAX: (949) 727-6101, Web Site: www.mazdausa.com (16)

Stevens International Inc, Fort Worth, TX. Tel: (817) 831-3911, FAX: (817) 838-4344, E-Mail: main@stevensintl.com (34)

Stevens, David, Opex Corp, Moorestown, NJ. Tel: (856) 727-1100, FAX: (856) 727-1955, Web Site: www.opex.com (34)

Stevens, Harry, Datamatx Inc, Ashland, VA. Tel: (804) 365-1000, (800) 943-5240, FAX: (804) 550-2527, E-Mail: info@datamatx.com, Web Site: www.datamatx.com (27)

Stevens, John, Paragon Media Strategies, Denver, CO. Tel: (303) 922-5600, FAX: (303) 922-1589, E-Mail: info@paragonmediastrategies.com, Web Site: www.paragonmediastrategies.com (30)

Stevens, Jonathan J., CDW Corp, Vernon Hills, IL. Tel: (847) 465-6000, (847) 371-6090, Web Site: www.cdw.com (16)

Stevens, Linda, Mystic Stamp Co Inc, Camden, NY. Tel: (866) 660-7147, FAX: (800) 385-4919, E-Mail: info@mysticstamp.com, Web Site: www.mysticstamp.com (16)

Stevens, Mark, International Gamco Inc, Omaha, NE. Tel: (402) 571-2449, (800) 524-2626, FAX: (402) 571-7941, E-Mail: mark.stevens@intlgamco.com, Web Site: www.intlgamco.com (31)

Stevens, Mark, Opex Corp, Moorestown, NJ. Tel: (856) 727-1100, FAX: (856) 727-1955, Web Site: www.opex.com (34)

Stevens, Martin B., Forum Publishing Co, Centerport, NY. Tel: (631) 754-5000, (800) 635-7654, FAX: (631) 754-0630, E-Mail: forumpublishing@aol.com, Web Site: www.forum123.com (17)

Stevens, Richard I., Stevens International Inc, Fort Worth, TX. Tel: (817) 831-3911, FAX: (817) 838-4344, E-Mail: main@stevensintl.com (34)

Stevens, Ruth, eMarketing Strategy Group, New York, NY. Tel: (212) 679-6486, Web Site: www.ruthstevens.com (20)

Stevenson, Bill, Who's Who - The MFSA Buyers' Guide to Blue Ribbon Mailing Services, Alexandria, VA. Tel: (703) 836-9200, FAX: (703) 548-8204, E-Mail: masa-mail@masa.org, Web Site: www.mfsanet.org (43)

Stevenson, Christopher, Credit Union Executives Society, Fitchburg, WI. Tel: (608) 271-2664, FAX: (608) 271-2303, E-Mail: cues@cues.org, Web Site: www.cues.org (1)

Stevenson, Dudley, DWS Associates, Saint Paul, MN. Tel: (602) 321-6512, Web Site: www.dwstevenson.com (20)

Stevenson, Eric, Price Target Media, Carson City, NV. Tel: (775) 434-4451, FAX: (206) 888-2403, E-Mail: info@pricetargetmedia.com, Web Site: pricetargetmedia.com (32)

Stevenson, J. John, North Shore Animal League America Inc, Port Washington, NY. Tel: (516) 883-7575, Web Site: www.animalleague.org (1)

Stevenson, Jeffrey T., Veronis Suhler Stevenson LLC, New York, NY. Tel: (212) 935-4990, FAX: (212) 381-8168, E-Mail: stevensonj@vss.com, Web Site: www.vss.com (14)

Stevenson, Steve, Comdata Corp, Brentwood, TN. Tel: (615) 370-7000, (800) 266-3282, FAX: (615) 370-7614, Web Site: www.comdata.com (14)

Stever, Jeff, Booyah! Online Advertising, Denver, CO. Tel: (303) 345-6100, FAX: (303) 345-6700, E-Mail: info@booyahadvertising.ocm, Web Site: www.booyahadvertising.com (35)

Stevick, Tom, Eastern Michigan University, Ypsilanti, MI. Tel: (734) 487-1849, FAX: (734) 484-1151, Web Site: www.emich.edu (16)

Stew Leonard's, Norwalk, CT. Tel: (203) 847-7214, FAX: (203) 846-3472, Web Site: www.stewleonards.com (4)

Steward, R. Andrew, VW Credit, Herndon, VA. Tel: (248) 340-5000 (14)

Steward, Shawn, Associated Integrated Marketing, Wichita, KS. Tel: (316) 683-4691, E-Mail: info@meetassociated.com, Web Site: www.meetassociated.com (35)

Don Stewart Association, Tulsa, OK. Tel: (602) 326-2267, FAX: (602) 678-3288, Web Site: www.donstewartassociation.com (1)

Stewart Enterprises Inc, Jefferson, LA. Tel: (504) 729-1400, (800) 535-6017, FAX: (504) 729-1984, Web Site: www.stewartenterprises.com (16)

Stewart-MacDonald, Athens, OH. Tel: (740) 592-3021, (800) 848-2273, FAX: (740) 593-7922, E-Mail: hostetler@stewmac.com, Web Site: www.stewmac.com (16)

Martha Stewart Living Omnimedia, New York, NY. Tel: (212) 827-8000, Web Site: www.marthastewart.com (17)

Stewart, Barbara S., Conseco Inc, Carmel, IN. Tel: (317) 817-6100, FAX: (317) 817-2847, Web Site: www.conseco.com (15)

Stewart, Bill, National Mail Graphics Corp, Exton, PA. Tel: (610) 524-1600, FAX: (610) 524-7638, E-Mail: jsikorski@nmgcorp.com, Web Site: www.nmgcorp.com (27)

Stewart, Bill, Petra Industries, Edmond, OK. Tel: (405) 216-2100, FAX: (405) 216-2102, Web Site: www.patra.com (34)

Stewart, C.E., Stewart-MacDonald, Athens, OH. Tel: (740) 592-3021, (800) 848-2273, FAX: (740) 593-7922, E-Mail: hostetler@stewmac.com, Web Site: www.stewmac.com (16)

Stewart, Cynthia, Cherry Tree Toys Inc, Beloit, WI. Tel: (608) 314-3090, (800) 848-4363, FAX: (608) 314-3097, E-Mail: sales@cherrytreetoys.com, Web Site: www.cherrytreetoys.com (11)

Stewart, Dave, Associated Integrated Marketing, Wichita, KS. Tel: (316) 683-4691, E-Mail: info@meetassociated.com, Web Site: www.meetassociated.com (35)

Stewart, Don, Don Stewart Association, Tulsa, OK. Tel: (602) 326-2267, FAX: (602) 678-3288, Web Site: www.donstewartassociation.com (1)

Stewart, Donald A., Sunlife of Canada, Wellesley Hills, MA. Tel: (781) 237-6030, (800) SUNLIFE, FAX: (781) 446-1779, Web Site: www.sunlife-usa.com (15)

Stewart, Duff, GSD&M, Austin, TX. Tel: (512) 242-4736, Web Site: www.gsdm.com (35)

Stewart, J. Staley, Aegon USA Investment Management, Inc, Cedar Rapids, IA. Tel: (502) 560-2000, FAX: (502) 560-2030, Web Site: www.aegonins.com (14)

Stewart, Jim, ADS Media Group Inc, San Antonio, TX. Tel: (210) 655-6613, FAX: (210) 655-6269, Web Site: www.adsmediagroup.com (27)

Stewart, Jr. Frank B., Stewart Enterprises Inc, Jefferson, LA. Tel: (504) 729-1400, (800) 535-6017, FAX: (504) 729-1984, Web Site: www.stewartenterprises. com (16)

Stewart, Julia A., DineEquity Inc, Glendale, CA. Tel: (866) 995-DINE, Web Site: dineequity.com (16)

Stewart, Keith R., ValueVision Media Inc, Eden Prairie, MN. Tel: (952) 943-6000, Web Site: www.shophq. com (32)

Stewart, Marie, The Boston Co Asset Management LLC, Boston, MA. Tel: (617) 722-7029, FAX: (617) 722-3928, Web Site: www.thebostoncompany.com (14)

Stewart, Russ, EU Services, Rockville, MD. Tel: (301) 424-3300, (800) 230-3362, FAX: (301) 424-3696, E-Mail: marketing@euservices.com, Web Site: www.euservices.com (21)

Stewart, Russ, Riverside Acquisition Group LLC, Moorestown, NJ. Tel: (856) 802-1900, Web Site: www. com-pak.com (28)

Stewart, Sue, Consumer Focus, Plano, TX. Tel: (972) 378-9697, (214) 542-8787, E-Mail: sstewart@consumerfocusco.com, Web Site: www. consumerfocusco.com (30)

Stewart-Allen, Allyson, International Marketing Partners Ltd, Los Angeles, CA. Tel: (310) 665-1155, FAX: (310) 665-1155, E-Mail: info@ intermarketingonline.com, Web Site: www. intermarketingonline.com (35)

Steyer, Scott, Homespun Tapes Music Instruction, Woodstock, NY. Tel: (845) 246-2550, (800) 338-2737, FAX: (845) 246-5282, E-Mail: info@ homespuntapes.com, Web Site: www. homespuntapes.com (3)

Stezzi Direct Inc, Atlanta, GA. Tel: (770) 448-9900, (800) 954-5100, FAX: (770) 448-9480, E-Mail: info@stezzi.com, Web Site: www.stezzi.com (21)

Stezzi, Joseph, Stezzi Direct Inc, Atlanta, GA. Tel: (770) 448-9900, (800) 954-5100, FAX: (770) 448-9480, E-Mail: info@stezzi.com, Web Site: www. stezzi.com (21)

Stibo Systems, Kennesaw, GA. Tel: (770) 425-3282, FAX: (770) 425-3012, Web Site: www.stibocatalog. com (22)

Sticco, Father Peter, Pallottine Center for Apostolic Causes Inc/St Jude Shrine, Baltimore, MD. Tel: (410) 685-6026, (877) 278-5833, FAX: (410) 234-1459, E-Mail: info@stjudeshrine.org, Web Site: www.stjudeshrine.org (1)

Sticker, Pat, Sheridan Books Inc, Chelsea, MI. Tel: (734) 475-9145, (800) 999-BOOK, FAX: (734) 475-7337, E-Mail: info@sheridanbooks.com, Web Site: www.sheridanbooks.com (27)

Stickers 'N' Stuff Inc, Louisville, CO. Tel: (303) 661-0200, E-Mail: sales@stickersnstuff.com, Web Site: www.stickersnstuff.biz (6)

Kirk Stieff Co, Bristol, PA. Tel: (267) 525-7800, (800) 635-3669, Web Site: www.lenox.com (16)

Stieve, Robert, Arizona Highways Magazine, Phoenix, AZ. Tel: (602) 712-2200, FAX: (602) 254-4505, E-Mail: editor@arizonahighways.com, Web Site: www.arizonahighways.com (17)

Stiffa, Jane, Erdos & Morgan Inc, Syosset, NY. Tel: (516) 935-6959, FAX: (516) 935-4040, E-Mail: info@erdosmorgan.com, Web Site: www. erdosmorgan.com (30)

Stile-Tile Like Metal Roofing, Sellersburg, IN. Tel: (812) 246-1866, (800) 999-7777, FAX: (800) 477-9318, (800) 944-6884, Web Site: www.mtsales.com (9)

Stiles, Dawn J., Da-Lite Screen Co Inc, Warsaw, IN. Tel: (574) 267-8101, (800) 622-3737, FAX: (574) 267-7804, E-Mail: info@da-lite.com, Web Site: www.da-lite.com (16)

Stiles, Sandra, The Wedding Pages, New York, NY. Tel: (212) 219-8555, (800) 843-4983, FAX: (212) 219-1929, Web Site: www.theknot.com (16)

Galen Stilson Copywriter, Trinity, FL. Tel: (727) 372-2032, E-Mail: galen@galenstilson.com, Web Site: www.galenstilson.com (39)

Stilson, Galen, Galen Stilson Copywriter, Trinity, FL. Tel: (727) 372-2032, E-Mail: galen@galenstilson. com, Web Site: www.galenstilson.com (39)

Stiltz, Dick, Doane, Saint Louis, MO. Tel: (314) 569-2700, (866) 647-0918, FAX: (314) 569-1083, Web Site: www.doane.com (17)

Stilwell, Amy L., The World Bank, Washington, DC. Tel: (202) 473-1000, FAX: (202) 477-6391, Web Site: www.worldbank.org (17)

Stimolo, Bob, School Market Research Institute Inc, Centerbrook, CT. Tel: (800) 838-3444, FAX: (860) 581-8549, E-Mail: info@smriinc.com, Web Site: www.smriinc.com (35)

Stimolo, Lynn, School Market Research Institute Inc, Centerbrook, CT. Tel: (800) 838-3444, FAX: (860) 581-8549, E-Mail: info@smriinc.com, Web Site: www.smriinc.com (35)

Stimpson Co Inc, Pompano Beach, FL. Tel: (954) 946-3500, (877) 765-0748, FAX: (954) 941-1921, E-Mail: customerservice@stimpson.com, Web Site: www.stimpson.com (16)

Stineman, Shirley D, The Plain Dealer, Cleveland, OH. Tel: (216) 999-5000, (800) 362-0727, FAX: (216) 999-6356, Web Site: www.plaindealer.com (18)

Stinson, David, SOS Children's Villages - USA, Washington, DC. Tel: (202) 347-7920, Web Site: www. sos-usa.org (1)

STIR LLC, Milwaukee, WI. Tel: (414) 278-0040, FAX: (414) 278-0390, E-Mail: info@stirstuff.com, Web Site: www.stirstuff.com (35)

Stites, Robert, Numark Brands, Edison, NJ. Tel: (732) 417-1870, (800) 338-8079, FAX: (732) 225-0066, E-Mail: newmark@injersey.com (7)

Stobaugh, Clay, Do It Yourself Direct Marketing, Hoboken, NJ. Tel: (201) 748-6000, FAX: (201) 748-6088, E-Mail: info@wiley.com, Web Site: www.wiley. com (43)

Stober, Loretta, Country Dance and Song Society, Easthampton, MA. Tel: (413) 203-5467, FAX: (413) 203-5471. E-Mail: office@cdss.org, Web Site: www.cdss.org (1)

Stock Boston Inc, Brookline, MA. Tel: (617) 266-2300, FAX: (617) 277-0502, E-Mail: info@stockboston. com, Web Site: www.stockboston.com (38)

Stock Drive Products, New Hyde Park, NY. Tel: (516) 328-3300, (800) 819-8900, FAX: (516) 326-8827, E-Mail: sdp-sisupport@sdp-si.com, Web Site: www. sdp.si.com (5)

Stock Montage Inc, Chicago, IL. Tel: (773) 637-9790, (800) 404-0425, FAX: (773) 637-9794, E-Mail: mail@stockmontage.com, Web Site: www. stockmontage.com (38)

The Stock Solution Inc, West Jordan, UT. Tel: (801) 566-8684, (888) 366-0430, FAX: (801) 961-8030, E-Mail: info@tssphoto.com, Web Site: www. tssphoto.com (38)

Stock Yards Packing Co Inc, Medford, OR. Tel: (312) 733-6050, (888) 842-6111, FAX: (888) 700-9919, E-Mail: customerservice@stockyards.com, Web Site: www.stockyards.com (4)

Stock, Dennis, Ion Exhibits, Itasca, IL. Tel: (877) 499-6197, FAX: (630) 235-9501, E-Mail: info@ ionexhibits.com, Web Site: www.ionexhibits.com (36)

Stocker, Steve, Affirm Agency, Pewaukee, WI. Tel: (262) 650-9900, E-Mail: info@affirmagency.com, Web Site: affirmagency.com (35)

Stockham Consulting, Eden Prairie, MN. Tel: (952) 250-2206 (20)

Stockham, Maria, Stockham Consulting, Eden Prairie, MN. Tel: (952) 250-2206 (20)

Stockhausen, Jay, Great Lakes List Management, Erie, PA. Tel: (814) 456-2175, (800) 964-5478, FAX: (814) 455-1942, E-Mail: info@greatlakeslists.com, Web Site: www.greatlakeslists.com (24)

Stockton Inc, Gaithersburg, MD. Tel: (301) 527-1550, FAX: (301) 527-1503, E-Mail: info@stocktoninc. com, Web Site: www.stocktoninc.com (22)

Stockton, Bryan, Fisher-Price, East Aurora, NY. Tel: (716) 687-3000, FAX: (716) 687-3636, Web Site: www.fisherprice.com (16)

Stockton, Bryan, Mattel Inc, El Segundo, CA. Tel: (310) 252-2000, FAX: (310) 252-2180, Web Site: www.mattel.com (16)

Stoddard, Russ, Oliver Russell & Associates, Boise, ID. Tel: (208) 344-1734, E-Mail: info@oliverrussell. com, Web Site: www.oliverrussell.com (35)

Stoddart, Rich, Leo Burnett Worldwide, Chicago, IL. Tel: (312) 220-5959, Web Site: leoburnett.com (35)

Stoebe, Richard, Jostens, Inc, Minneapolis, MN. Tel: (952) 830-3300, FAX: (952) 830-3293, Web Site: www.jostens.com (16)

Stoebich, Cindy, Chris Hansen, New Berlin, WI. Tel: (414) 607-5700, FAX: (414) 607-5704, Web Site: www.chr-hansen.com (16)

Stoeckig, Tricia, United Community Bank, Blairsville, GA. Tel: (706) 745-0911, Web Site: www.ucbi.com (14)

Stoer, Dean, National Business Furniture Inc, Milwaukee, WI. Tel: (414) 276-8511, (800) 558-1010, FAX: (414) 276-8371, Web Site: www. nationalbusinessfurniture.com (10)

Stoffels, MD Paulus, Johnson & Johnson, New Brunswick, NJ. Tel: (732) 524-0400, FAX: (732) 214-0332, Web Site: www.jnj.com (16)

Stokes Seeds Inc, Buffalo, NY. Tel: (800) 396-9238, FAX: (800) 272-5560, E-Mail: stokes@stokeseeds. com, Web Site: www.stokeseeds.com (8)

Stokes, Linda, Marshall Fields Dept Stores, Minneapolis, MN. Tel: (612) 375-3004, Web Site: www. fields.com (5)

Stoll, Kevin, Liebert Corp, Columbus, OH. Tel: (614) 841-6700, (800) LIEBERT, FAX: (614) 841-6022, Web Site: www.liebert.com (16)

Stolle Machinery LLC, Centennial, CO. Tel: (303) 708-9044, (800) 228-4593, FAX: (303) 708-9045, E-Mail: cmd.info@stollemachinery.com, Web Site: www.stollemachinery.com (34)

Stoller, Erica, Esto Photographics Inc, Mamaroneck, NY. Tel: (914) 698-4060, FAX: (914) 698-1033, E-Mail: esto@esto.com, Web Site: www.esto.com (38)

Stoller, Kevin, LS Records, Madison, TN. Tel: (615) 868-7171, FAX: (615) 860-7665, E-Mail: ls654@ home.com, Web Site: www.cristylane.com (16)

Stoller, Lee, LS Records, Madison, TN. Tel: (615) 868-7171, FAX: (615) 860-7665, E-Mail: ls654@home. com, Web Site: www.cristylane.com (16)

Stolls, Steven, ASL Marketing Inc, Farmingdale, NY. Tel: (516) 248-6100, FAX: (516) 248-6364, E-Mail: info@aslmarketing.com, Web Site: www. aslmarketing.com (23)

Stolowski, Rick, Pro Media Marketing Group, Menomonee Falls, WI. Tel: (800) 328-0439, FAX: (262) 532-4147, E-Mail: sales@promediaus.com, Web Site: www.promediaus.com (35)

Stoltze, Steve, Edroy Products Co Inc, Nyack, NY. Tel: (845) 358-6600, (800) 233-8803, FAX: (845) 358-4098, E-Mail: sales@edroyproducts.com, Web Site: www.edroyproducts.com (16)

Stonaker, Daniel, North Point Resources, Alpharetta, GA. Tel: (678) 892-5000, Web Site: www. northpointstore.org (1)

The Stone Group Inc, Pleasanton, CA. Tel: (925) 846-4432, FAX: (925) 846-2767, E-Mail: kbutler@ stonegroupinc.com, Web Site: stonegroupinc.com (35)

Stone, Adam, Hanna Andersson Corp, Portland, OR. Tel: (503) 242-0920, (800) 222-0544, FAX: (503) 321-5289, Web Site: www.hannaandersson.com (2)

Stone, Davey L., Butler Schein Animal Health, Dublin, OH. Tel: (614) 761-9095, (888) 691-2724, FAX: (888) 329-3861, Web Site: www.butlerschein.com (16)

Stone, Gail, PTM Communications, New York, NY. Tel: (212) 643-5458, FAX: (212) 643-5486, E-Mail: info@ptmcomm.com, Web Site: www.ptmcomm. com (29)

Stone, Jay, Infomart, Dallas, TX. Tel: (214) 800-8000, FAX: (214) 800-8100, Web Site: www.infomartusa. com (16)

Stone, John W., Artech House, Norwood, MA. Tel: (781) 769-9750, FAX: (781) 769-6334, E-Mail: artech@artechhouse.com, Web Site: www. artechhouse.com (17)

Stone, Karin, National City Bank, Cleveland, OH. Tel: (216) 222-2000, (800) 622-8100, FAX: (216) 575-, Web Site: www.nationalcity.com (14)

Stone, Matthew, HealthInfo Direct, Schaumburg, IL. Tel: (630) 936-9465 (20)

Stone, Mike, Butler Schein Animal Health, Dublin, OH. Tel: (614) 761-9095, (888) 691-2724, FAX: (888) 329-3861, Web Site: www.butlerschein.com (16)

Stone, Nancy, School Annual Publishing Co, State College, PA. Tel: (800) 436-6030, E-Mail: yearbook@ schoolannual.com, Web Site: www.schoolannual. com (17)

Stone, Robert W., City of Hope National Medical Center, Duarte, CA. Tel: (626) 256-4673, FAX: (626) 301-8468, Web Site: www.cityofhope.org (1)

Stone, Will, Neighborhood Greetings, Harrisburg, PA. Tel: (717) 839-6390, (800) 332-9200, Web Site: ngp.allegraharrisburg.com (23)

Stonebridge Press Ltd, Henderson, KY. Tel: (270) 826-0341, FAX: (270) 826-8325 (33)

Stoner, Greg, Aristokraft Inc, Jasper, IN. Tel: (812) 482-2527, FAX: (812) 482-9872, Web Site: www. aristokraft.com (16)

Stonwurks, Eden Prairie, MN. Tel: (785) 526-7847, (888) 884-7881, FAX: (785) 526-7841, E-Mail: stonwurks@stonwurks.com, Web Site: www. stonwurks.com (1)

Stopka, Michael, Design Toscano, Inc, Elk Grove Village, IL. Tel: (847) 952-0100, (800) 525-5141, FAX: (847) 952-8992, Web Site: www.designtoscano.com (6)

Storage Battery Systems Inc, Menomonee Falls, WI. Tel: (262) 703-5800, (800) 554-2243, FAX: (262) 703-3073, E-Mail: sbs@sbsbattery.com, Web Site: www.sbsbattery.com (12)

Storch, Gerald L., Toys "R" Us, Wayne, NJ. Tel: (973) 617-5879, FAX: (973) 617-4006, Web Site: www. toysrus.com (11)

Stordahl, Derek, Fairchild Books, New York, NY. Tel: (212) 419-5292, Web Site: www.fairchildbooks.com (17)

Store Smart Express/Visual Horizons, Rochester, NY. Tel: (585) 424-5300, (800) 424-1011, FAX: (585) 424-1064, E-Mail: cs@storesmart.com, Web Site: www.storesmart.com (16)

Storey, Des Moines, IA. Tel: (515) 288-3243, (800) 622-4536, FAX: (515) 288-9807, E-Mail: info@storeykenworthy.com, Web Site: www.storeykenworthy.com (35)

Storm, K. J., Life Investors Insurance Co of America, Cedar Rapids, IA. Tel: (319) 398-8511, (800) 231-7220, FAX: (319) 369-2188, Web Site: www. lifeinvestors.com (14)

Storms, Byron, National General Insurance, Winston-Salem, NC. Tel: (888) 293-5108, Web Site: www. nationalgeneral.com (15)

Story, Mike, Physicians Mutual Insurance Co, Omaha, NE. Tel: (402) 633-1604, (888) 932-7642, FAX: (402) 633-1604, Web Site: www.physiciansmutual. com (15)

Stotz, Beverly, Illy Caffe North America, Rye Brook, NY. Tel: (914) 253-4500, (877) 469-4559, E-Mail: info@illyusa.com, Web Site: www.illyusa.com (4)

Stotzer, Shelly, Highlights For Children, Columbus, OH. Tel: (614) 487-2601, (800) 848-8922, FAX: (614) 487-2700, Web Site: www.highlights.com (17)

Stout, Tamara, Metropolis Magazine, New York, NY. Tel: (212) 627-9977, (800) 334-3046, FAX: (212) 627-9988, E-Mail: edit@metropolismag.com, Web Site: www.metropolismag.com (2)

Stover, Catherine, Magna Publications Inc, Madison, WI. Tel: (608) 246-3590, FAX: (608) 246-3597, Web Site: www.magnapubs.com (17)

Stowe, Robert D., RJ Reynolds Tobacco Co, Winston Salem, NC. Tel: (336) 741-5111, (800) 341-5211, Web Site: www.rjrt.com (16)

Stowers, III James Evans, American Century Investments, Kansas City, MO. Tel: (816) 531-5575, (800) 345-2021, FAX: (816) 340-4964, Web Site: www. americancentury.com (14)

Stracher, Patti, National Stationery Show, White Plains, NY. Tel: (914) 421-3394, Web Site: www. nationalstationeryshow.com (42)

Strack, Stephen, Stockton Inc, Gaithersburg, MD. Tel: (301) 527-1550, FAX: (301) 527-1503, E-Mail: info@stocktoninc.com, Web Site: www.stocktoninc. com (22)

Straczynski, Stacy, Sales & Marketing Management Magazine, New York, NY. Tel: (800) 821-6897, FAX: (905) 470-8561, E-Mail: joyce.cooney@ nielsen.com, Web Site: www.salesandmarketing. com (16)

Strader, Chuck, Kappler Protective Apparel & Fabrics, Guntersville, AL. Tel: (256) 505-4005, (800) 600-4019, FAX: (256) 505-4151, E-Mail: customerservice@kappler.com, Web Site: www. kappler.com (2)

Stradtman, Steve, Otto Environmental Systems of North America, Charlotte, NC. Tel: (704) 588-9191, (800) 227-5885, FAX: (704) 588-5250, E-Mail: info@ otto-usa.com, Web Site: www.otto-usa.com (14)

Strahl, Dr. Stuart D., Brookfield Zoo, Brookfield, IL. Tel: (708) 485-0263, (800) 201-0784, FAX: (708) 485-3532, Web Site: www.brookfieldzoo.org (1)

Straley, Kim, Lure Craft, Lagrange, IN. Tel: (260) 463-2687, (800) 925-9088, FAX: (260) 463-8383, E-Mail: lurcraft@clickanerd.com, Web Site: www. lurecraft.com (11)

Straley, Shawn, Lure Craft, Lagrange, IN. Tel: (260) 463-2687, (800) 925-9088, FAX: (260) 463-8383, E-Mail: lurcraft@clickanerd.com, Web Site: www. lurecraft.com (11)

Stranberg, Mark, PNC Global Investment Servicing, Lynnfield, MA. Tel: (781) 477-4124, Web Site: www.pnc.com (14)

Strand, Geoffrey, Harwil Corp, Oxnard, CA. Tel: (805) 988-6800, (800) 562-2447, FAX: (805) 988-6804, E-Mail: harwil@harwil.com, Web Site: www. harwil.com (9)

Strang Communications Co, Lake Mary, FL. Tel: (407) 333-0600, FAX: (407) 333-7100, E-Mail: magcustsvc@strang.com, Web Site: www.strang. com (17)

Strang, Stephen, Strang Communications Co, Lake Mary, FL. Tel: (407) 333-0600, FAX: (407) 333-7100, E-Mail: magcustsvc@strang.com, Web Site: www.strang.com (17)

Stransky, John E., Life Fitness, Schiller Park, IL. Tel: (847) 288-3300, (800) 735-3867, FAX: (847) 288-3703, E-Mail: webmaster@lifefitness.com, Web Site: www.lifefitness.com (11)

Stranzl, Brandon, Sears Canada Inc, Toronto, ON Canada. Tel: (416) 362-1711, (888) 473-2772, FAX: (613) 391-3047, E-Mail: home@sears.ca, Web Site: www.sears.ca (5)

Strasbourger, Jim, Data Management Inc, Mc Lean, VA. Tel: (703) 893-5627, (800) 334-8331, FAX: (703) 356-1698, E-Mail: info@data-management. com, Web Site: www.data-management.com (22)

Strata Marketing Inc, Chicago, IL. Tel: (312) 222-1555, FAX: (312) 222-2510, Web Site: www.stratag.com (30)

Strategic Alliance Group, Atlanta, GA. Tel: (404) 275-1077, E-Mail: pete@sagpromo.com, Web Site: www.sagpromo.com (35)

Strategic America, West Des Moines, IA. Tel: (515) 453-2000, (888) 898-6400, FAX: (515) 224-4181, Web Site: www.strategicamerica.com (35)

Strategic Data Intelligence LLC, Northbrook, IL. Tel: (847) 897-5707, FAX: (847) 897-5715, E-Mail: info@sdintelligence.com, Web Site: www. sdintelligence.com (22)

Strategic Marketing & Mailing, Champaign, IL. Tel: (217) 355-2600, (800) 871-4524, Web Site: www. strategicmail.com (28)

Strategic Marketing Services, Eagan, MN. Tel: (651) 456-0100, E-Mail: sms@fishnet.com (33)

Strategic Software Systems LLC, Richmond, VA. Tel: (804) 288-8827x110, Web Site: www.sss1.com (22)

StrategicOne, Overland Park, KS. Tel: (913) 342-9100 x102, Web Site: www.strategic-one.com (20)

Strategy Corps LLC, Brentwood, TN. Tel: (615) 221-8381, (888) 577-6933, FAX: (615) 221-8479, E-Mail: info@strategycorps.com, Web Site: www. strategycorps.com (16)

Stratford Hall, North Mankato, MN. Tel: (708) 496-4908, (800) 628-9028, FAX: (708) 496-8058, E-Mail: stratfordhall@myprinter.com, Web Site: www.stratfordhall.com (10)

Stratmar Systems Inc, Port Chester, NY. Tel: (914) 937-7171, (800) 866-2399, FAX: (914) 937-6045, E-Mail: info@stratmar.com, Web Site: www. stratmar.com (29)

The Stratosphere Las Vegas, Las Vegas, NV. Tel: (702) 380-7777, (800) 998-6937, FAX: (702) 383-4755, Web Site: www.stratospherehotel.com (19)

Stratus Technologies, Maynard, MA. Tel: (978) 461-7000, (800) 787-2887, FAX: (978) 461-3670, Web Site: www.stratus.com (16)

Straub, Sarah, Communication Logistics, Inc, Plover, WI. Tel: (715) 341-6180, FAX: (715) 341-7971, Web Site: www.comloginc.com (22)

Straus Tucker, Diane, The Washington Monthly Co, Washington, DC. Tel: (202) 955-9010, FAX: (202) 955-9011, E-Mail: editors@washingtonmonthly.com, Web Site: www.washingtonmonthly.com (17)

Strauser, Jack, Karaoke USA, Largo, FL. Tel: (727) 209-1313, (800) 776-7464, FAX: (702) 209-1312, Web Site: www.karaokeusa.com (5)

Strauss, Andrew W., Skinder-Strauss Associates, New Providence, NJ. Tel: (973) 642-1440, FAX: (973) 242-1905, Web Site: www.elaw.com (14)

Strauss, Herschel, Hamakor Judaica Inc, Skokie, IL. Tel: (847) 966-4040, (800) 677-4150, FAX: (847) 966-4033, E-Mail: service@ewishource.com, Web Site: www.jewishsource.com (5)

Strauss, Lane, Wyse Advertising, Cleveland, OH. Tel: (216) 696-2424, E-Mail: info@wyseadv.com, Web Site: www.wyseadv.com (35)

Strauss, M, Ventriloquist Voice Solutions International Inc, Mississauga, ON Canada. Tel: (866) 446-0860, E-Mail: info@ventriloquistsolutions.com, Web Site: www.ventriloquistsolutions.com (29)

Strauss, Naomi, Hamakor Judaica Inc, Skokie, IL. Tel: (847) 966-4040, (800) 677-4150, FAX: (847) 966-4033, E-Mail: service@ewishource.com, Web Site: www.jewishsource.com (5)

Straw Hat Cooperative Corp, San Ramon, CA. Tel: (925) 837-3400, FAX: (925) 820-1080, E-Mail: info@strawhatpizza.com, Web Site: www.strawhatpizza.com (16)

Stream International, Wellesley, MA. Tel: (781) 304-1800, (888) 264-5834, FAX: (781) 575-6999, Web Site: www.stream.com (16)

Streamfeeder, Minneapolis, MN. Tel: (763) 502-0000, FAX: (763) 502-0100, Web Site: www.streamfeeder.com (34)

Street, Tim, Tribune Direct LLC, Northlake, IL. Tel: (708) 836-2700, (800) 545-9657, FAX: (708) 836-0605, Web Site: tribunedirect.com (21)

Streibich, Karl-Heinz, Software AG USA, Reston, VA. Tel: (703) 860-5050, (877) 724-4965, FAX: (703) 391-6975, E-Mail: sales@softwareagusa.com, Web Site: www.softwareagusa.com (3)

Streight, Steve, Hamilton Sorter Co, Fairfield, OH. Tel: (513) 870-4400, (800) 503-9966, FAX: (800) 503-9963, E-Mail: sstreight@hamiltonsorter.com, Web Site: www.hamiltonsorter.com (34)

Elizabeth Streitz & Associates, New York, NY. Tel: (212) 749-3152 (20)

Streitz, Elizabeth, Elizabeth Streitz & Associates, New York, NY. Tel: (212) 749-3152 (20)

Stress Market, Port Angeles, WA. Tel: (360) 457-9223, (800) 578-7377, FAX: (360) 457-9466, E-Mail: info@stressmarket.com, Web Site: www.stressmarket.com (17)

Stretch Multimedia LLC, Dublin, OH. Tel: (614) 363-4444, FAX: (614) 363-3772, E-Mail: dougj@stretch-multimedia.com, Web Site: www.stretch-multimedia.com (35)

Stretch-Stephenson, Shirley M., School of Business & Economics, Los Angeles, CA. Tel: (323) 343-2800, FAX: (323) 343-2813, Web Site: cbe.calstatela.edu (41)

Strickland, Brantley, The Press & Standard, Walterboro, SC. Tel: (843) 549-2586, Web Site: colletontoday.com (31)

Strickland, Frederic, Sandy Corp, Troy, MI. Tel: (800) 733-4739, FAX: (248) 729-4701, E-Mail: info@sandycorp.com, Web Site: www.sandycorp.com (16)

Strickland, Heidi Lee, Scorecards USA, North Kingstown, RI. Tel: (401) 294-4049, (800) 553-4154, FAX: (401) 294-4076, E-Mail: sales@scorecardsusa.com, Web Site: www.scorecardsusa.com (16)

Strickland, Pamela, River Street Sweets, Savannah, GA. Tel: (912) 234-4608, (800) 793-3876, Web Site: www.riverstreetsweets.com (4)

Strickland, Ronnie, LSSiData, Blue Bell, PA. Tel: (610) 276-4300, (800) 210-9021, FAX: (610) 567-5698, E-Mail: info@lssi.net, Web Site: www.lssidata.com (22)

Strickland, Tim, River Street Sweets, Savannah, GA. Tel: (912) 234-4608, (800) 793-3876, Web Site: www.riverstreetsweets.com (4)

Striem, Barry, Essential Products Co Inc, New York, NY. Tel: (212) 344-4288 (7)

Stringer, Matt, Joseph A Bank Clothiers Inc, Hampstead, MD. Tel: (410) 239-2700, (800) 285-2265, FAX: (410) 239-5911, E-Mail: service@jos-a-bank.com, Web Site: www.josbank.com (2)

Striplin, Deborah, Oxbridge Communications Inc, New York, NY. Tel: (212) 741-0231, (800) 955-0231. FAX: (212) 633-2938, E-Mail: custserv@oxbridge.com, Web Site: www.mediafinder.com; www.oxbridge.com (30)

Strofina Inc, Bainbridge Island, WA. Tel: (206) 855-9681 (20)

Strohacker, Curt, Easthill Group Inc, Pottstown, PA. Tel: (610) 323-9063, (610) 323-9099, (610) 323-2200, (800) 345-1178, (888) 869-4433, FAX: (610) 323-6268, Web Site: www.eastwoodcompany.com (12)

Stroller, John R., Del Webb, Bloomfield Hills, MI. Tel: (248) 644-7300, (888) 717-9777, FAX: (248) 433-4598, Web Site: www.delwebb.com (16)

Stromberg Brand, Valley Cottage, NY. Tel: (914) 739-7410, (800) 724-0996, FAX: (914) 739-8642, E-Mail: info@stromberggroup.com, Web Site: www.strombergbrand.com (33)

Stromberg, Helen, Stromberg Brand, Valley Cottage, NY. Tel: (914) 739-7410, (800) 724-0996, FAX: (914) 739-8642, E-Mail: info@stromberggroup.com, Web Site: www.strombergbrand.com (33)

Strong Enterprises, Orlando, FL. Tel: (407) 859-9317, (800) 344-6319, FAX: (407) 850-6978, E-Mail: sales@strongparachutes.com, Web Site: www.strongparachutes.com (34)

Strong, Ted, Strong Enterprises, Orlando, FL. Tel: (407) 859-9317, (800) 344-6319, FAX: (407) 850-6978, E-Mail: sales@strongparachutes.com, Web Site: www.strongparachutes.com (34)

StrongView Systems Inc, Redwood City, CA. Tel: (650) 421-4200, (800) 971-0380, FAX: (650) 421-4201, E-Mail: info@strongview.com, Web Site: www.strongview.com (32)

Strongwell, Bristol, VA. Tel: (276) 645-8000, FAX: (276) 645-8132, E-Mail: gbarefoot@strongwell.com, Web Site: www.strongwell.com (9)

Strope, Keith, Tricor Braun, Woodridge, IL. Tel: (708) 385-9333, FAX: (708) 385-3015, Web Site: www.tricorbraun.com (16)

Strosin, Raphael, Biosciences-Amersham, Piscataway, NJ. Tel: (732) 457-8000, FAX: (732) 457-0557, Web Site: www.amersham.com (16)

Stroud, Roland, Mays Mission for the Handicapped Inc, Heber Springs, AR. Tel: (501) 362-7526, (888) 503-7955, FAX: (501) 362-7529, E-Mail: info@maysmission.org, Web Site: www.maysmission.org (27)

Stroup, Diana, New Jersey Monthly, Morristown, NJ. Tel: (973) 539-8230, FAX: (973) 538-2953, E-Mail: research@njmonthly.com, Web Site: www.njmonthly.com (17)

Stroup, Jr. Ray, Stuller Inc, Lafayette, LA. Tel: (800) 877-7777, FAX: (800) 444-4741, E-Mail: info@stuller.com, Web Site: www.stuller.com (2)

Structural Graphics, Essex, CT. Tel: (860) 767-2661, FAX: (860) 767-2451, Web Site: www.structuralgraphics.com (27)

Strum, Adam M., Wine Enthusiast Cos, Mount Kisco, NY. Tel: (914) 345-9463, (800) 356-8466, FAX: (914) 345-3129, Web Site: www.wineenthusiast.com (4)

Strum, Sybil N., Wine Enthusiast Cos, Mount Kisco, NY. Tel: (914) 345-9463, (800) 356-8466, FAX: (914) 345-3129, Web Site: www.wineenthusiast.com (4)

Strunk, Scott, Systemax Inc, Port Washington, NY. Tel: (516) 608-7000, FAX: (516) 6208-7001, Web Site: www.systemax.com (16)

Strutzel, Dan, Nightingale-Conant Corp, Niles, IL. Tel: (847) 647-0300, (800) 557-1660, FAX: (847) 647-7145, Web Site: www.nightingale.com (17)

Stryker, Richard, Corpus Christi Museum of Science & History, Corpus Christi, TX. Tel: (361) 826-4667, FAX: (361) 884-7392, Web Site: www.ccmuseum.com (1)

Stuart Karten Design, Marina Del Rey, CA. Tel: (310) 827-8722, FAX: (310) 821-4492, Web Site: www.kartendesign.com (36)

Paul Stuart, New York, NY. Tel: (800) 678-8278, E-Mail: info@paulstuart.com, Web Site: www.paulstuart.com (2)

Stuart, Mark, Zoological Society of San Diego, San Diego, CA. Tel: (619) 231-1515, FAX: (619) 557-3937, Web Site: www.sandiegozoo.org (1)

Stuart, Patrick, Art Instruction Schools, Minneapolis, MN. Tel: (612) 362-5075, (800) 801-6940, FAX: (612) 362-5260, Web Site: www.artinstructionschools.edu (13)

Stuart, Randall L., AvMed Health Plan Inc, Miami, FL. Tel: (305) 671-5437, FAX: (305) 671-4782, Web Site: www.avmed.org (1)

Stubblefield, Greg, Alamo Rent A Car, Saint Louis, MO. Tel: (314) 512-2880, Web Site: www.alamo.com (16)

Stubbs, Angela, Federal Direct, Clifton, NJ. Tel: (973) 667-9800, (800) 927-5123, Web Site: www.feddirect.com (27)

Stubbs, Barbara, Business Promotion Ideas Inc, Tenafly, NJ. Tel: (201) 569-9777, FAX: (201) 569-2642, E-Mail: bpi@buspromoideas.com, Web Site: www.buspromoideas.com (33)

Stubbs, Charles, RentPath LLc, Norcross, GA. Tel: (678) 421-3000, (800) 216-1423, Web Site: www.primedia.com (31)

Stuck, Bruce, The Lukens Company, Alexandria, VA. Tel: (703) 845-8484, FAX: (703) 845-9655, Web Site: www.thelukenscompany.com (35)

Student Union at SJSU, San Jose, CA. Tel: (408) 924-5950, FAX: (408) 924-5953, E-Mail: getinvolved@sjsu.edu, Web Site: www.union.sjsu.edu (1)

Stuebing, Laura, Simply Batteries Inc, De Kalb, IL. Tel: (815) 758-8332, Web Site: www.simplybatteries.com (7)

Stull, Elaine, Industrial Uniform Co Inc, Wichita, KS. Tel: (316) 264-2871, (800) 333-3666, FAX: (316) 264-2708, E-Mail: info@logodepotweb.com, Web Site: www.industrialuniform.com (2)

Stuller Inc, Lafayette, LA. Tel: (800) 877-7777, FAX: (800) 444-4741, E-Mail: info@stuller.com, Web Site: www.stuller.com (2)

Stuller, Matthew G., Stuller Inc, Lafayette, LA. Tel: (800) 877-7777, FAX: (800) 444-4741, E-Mail: info@stuller.com, Web Site: www.stuller.com (2)

Stullman, Steve, Direct Marketing Association of Southern California, Newbury Park, CA. Tel: (818) 541-1152, FAX: (818) 541-1959, Web Site: www.ladma.org (40)

Stumm, Matthew, BBK Worldwide, Needham Heights, MA. Tel: (617) 630-4477, FAX: (617) 630-5090, E-Mail: info@bbkworldwide.com, Web Site: www.bbkworldwide.com (35)

Stumpf, John, Wells Fargo, San Francisco, CA. Tel: (800) 869-3557, (866) 249-3302, FAX: (626) 312-3015, Web Site: www.wellsfargo.com (14)

Stupak, Caitlin, Directory of Mail Order Catalogs, Amenia, NY. Tel: (518) 789-8700, (800) 562-2139, FAX: (518) 789-0556, E-Mail: cstupak@greyhouse.com, Web Site: www.greyhouse.com (43)

Stupak, Caitlin, Grey House Publishing, Amenia, NY. Tel: (518) 789-8700, (800) 562-2139, FAX: (518) 789-0556, E-Mail: books@greyhouse.com, Web Site: www.greyhouse.com (43)

Sturbridge Yankee Workshop Inc, Portland, ME. Tel: (207) 774-9045, (800) 343-1144, FAX: (207) 774-2561, Web Site: www.sturbridgeyankee.com (4)

Sturchio, Richard, Cramer, Norwood, MA. Tel: (781) 278-2387, Web Site: www.cramandonline.com (20)

Sturgeon, Bryan, Indianapolis Newspapers Inc, Indianapolis, IN. Tel: (317) 444-4444, FAX: (317) 633-9414, Web Site: www.indystar.com (17)

Sturges Sportswear, Battleboro, NC. Tel: (252) 446-0096, (866) 532-6748, FAX: (252) 977-3932, E-Mail: estu73123@aol.com, Web Site: www.sturgessportswear.com (16)

Sturges, Eddie, Sturges Sportswear, Battleboro, NC. Tel: (252) 446-0096, (866) 532-6748, FAX: (252) 977-3932, E-Mail: estu73123@aol.com, Web Site: www.sturgessportswear.com (16)

Sturges, Johnny, Sturges Sportswear, Battleboro, NC. Tel: (252) 446-0096, (866) 532-6748, FAX: (252) 977-3932, E-Mail: estu73123@aol.com, Web Site: www.sturgessportswear.com (16)

Sturley, Wendy, Society for Neuroscience, Washington, DC. Tel: (202) 962-4000, Web Site: www.sfn.org (1)

Sturm, Jim, Brierley & Partners, Dallas, TX. Tel: (214) 760-8700, FAX: (214) 743-5511, E-Mail: bpayton@brierley.com, Web Site: www.brierley.com (35)

Sturner & Klein, Fort Worth, TX. Tel: (800) 678-4960, FAX: (301) 881-3745 (29)

Sturner, Jerry, Sturner & Klein, Fort Worth, TX. Tel: (800) 678-4960, FAX: (301) 881-3745 (29)

Stutes, Rhonda, Bell Performance Inc, Longwood, FL. Tel: (407) 834-3690, (800) 659-2355, FAX: (407) 767-8685, E-Mail: info@bellperformance.net, Web Site: www.bellperformance.net (9)

Stutz, Jeff, Herman Miller Inc, Zeeland, MI. Tel: (616) 654-3000, FAX: (616) 654-5234, E-Mail: investor@hermanmiller.com, Web Site: www.hermanmiller.com (16)

Stutz, Robert, Glengarry Marketing, Austin, TX. Tel: (800) 883-1924 (20)

Styes, Doug, Enco Manufacturing Co, Fernley, NV. Tel: (775) 788-7175, (800) 873-3626, FAX: (800) 965-5857, E-Mail: milanesp@use-enco.com, Web Site: www.use-enco.com (9)

Styled Packaging LLC, Philadelphia, PA. Tel: (610) 529-4122, FAX: (610) 520-9662, E-Mail: bill@styledpackaging.com, Web Site: www.styledpackaging.com (34)

Suarez, Evelio, Faneuil ISG, Hampton, VA. Tel: (757) 722-3235, FAX: 757-722-5293, Web Site: www.faneuil.com (30)

Subers, Mark, Grade Finders Inc, Philadelphia, PA. Tel: (800) 777-8074, E-Mail: info@gradefinders.com, Web Site: www.gradefinders.com (17)

Subers, William A., Grade Finders Inc, Philadelphia, PA. Tel: (800) 777-8074, E-Mail: info@gradefinders.com, Web Site: www.gradefinders.com (17)

Submit Express Inc, Burbank, CA. Tel: (818) 567-3030, (877) 737-3083, FAX: (818) 567-0202, E-Mail: feedbacks@submitexpress.com, Web Site: www.submitexpress.com (18)

Subrizi, Mike, Market Data Retrieval, Shelton, CT. Tel: (203) 926-4800, (800) 333-8802, FAX: (203) 929-5253, E-Mail: mdrinfo@dnb.com, Web Site: schooldata.com (23)

SubscriberMail LLC, Lisle, IL. Tel: (630) 303-5000, FAX: (630) 303-5100, Web Site: www.subscribermail.com (22)

SubscriptionAgency.com Inc, Winter Haven, FL. Tel: (863) 229-2557, (866) 590-6247, FAX: (866) 890-6247, E-Mail: info@subscriptionagency.com, Web Site: www.subscriptionagency.com (18)

The Suburban Chamber of Commerce, Summit, NJ. Tel: (908) 522-1700, FAX: (908) 522-9252, E-Mail: info@suburbanchambers.org, Web Site: www.suburbanchambers.org (14)

Success Magazine, Lake Dallas, TX. Tel: (877) 243-8383, E-Mail: editor@success.com, Web Site: www.successmagazine.com (43)

SUCCESS Partners Co, Lake Dallas, TX. Tel: (940) 497-9700, (800) 752-2030, FAX: (940) 497-9987, Web Site: successpartners.com (32)

Successful Farming, Des Moines, IA. Tel: (515) 284-2143, (800) 678-2711, FAX: (515) 284-3127 (17)

SuccessWorks Search Marketing Inc, Portland, OR. Tel: (503) 922-3627, Web Site: www.seocopywriting.com (32)

Sucharczuk, Guy, Aurora Marketing Inc, Princeton, NJ. Tel: (609) 520-8863, FAX: (908) 359-1108, E-Mail: aurora@voicenet.com, Web Site: www.auroramarketing.net (30)

Suchecki, Glen, UniServ Advertising Inc, Neptune City, NJ. Tel: (732) 774-1010, FAX: (732) 774-3311, Web Site: www.uniservinc.com (33)

Suesskind, Dan, Teva Pharmaceuticals USA, North Wales, PA. Tel: (215) 591-3000, (888) 838-2872, FAX: (215) 591-8600, Web Site: www.tevausa.com (7)

Suez Energy North America, Houston, TX. Tel: (713) 636-0000, FAX: (713) 636-1364, Web Site: www.tractebelpowerinc.com (16)

Sugarbush Farm Inc, Woodstock, VT. Tel: (802) 457-1757, (800) 281-1757, FAX: (802) 457-3269, E-Mail: contact@sugarbushfarm.com, Web Site: www.sugarbushfarm.com (4)

Sugarman, Joseph, BluBlocker Corp, Las Vegas, NV. Tel: (702) 597-2000, (800) BLUBLOCKER, FAX: (702) 597-2002, Web Site: www.blublocker.com (2)

Sugg, Ed, DataLever Corp, Boulder, CO. Tel: (303) 541-1515, Web Site: www.datalever.com (16)

Suhler, John S., Veronis Suhler Stevenson LLC, New York, NY. Tel: (212) 935-4990, FAX: (212) 381-8168, E-Mail: stevensonj@vss.com, Web Site: www.vss.com (14)

Sukol, Amy, Lautman Maska Neill & Co, Washington, DC. Tel: (202) 296-9660, Web Site: www.lautmandc.com (1)

Sukuyama, Masaki, Mitsubishi Digital Electronics America Inc, Cypress, CA. Tel: (949) 465-6000, FAX: (949) 859-4770, Web Site: www.mitsubishi-tv.com (3)

Sullivan-Victory Groves, Rockledge, FL. Tel: (800) 672-6431, (866) 676-4311, E-Mail: sales@sullivancitrus.com, Web Site: www.sullivancitrus.com (4)

Sullivan, Daniel J., Collette Vacations, Pawtucket, RI. Tel: (401) 728-3805, FAX: (401) 727-9014, E-Mail: czesk@collettetours.com, Web Site: www.collettevacations.com (19)

Sullivan, Daniel J., Direct Marketing Resources, Charlotte, NC. Tel: (704) 845-5890, (888) 644-4DMR, E-Mail: dan@dmresources.com, Web Site: www.dmresources.com (20)

Sullivan, Diane M., Brown Shoe Co, Saint Louis, MO. Tel: (314) 854-4000, FAX: (314) 854-4274, Web Site: www.brownshoe.com (16)

Sullivan, Dianne C., Hatton-Brown Publishers Inc, Montgomery, AL. Tel: (334) 834-1170, FAX: (334) 834-4525, E-Mail: webman@hattonbrown.com, Web Site: www.hattonbrown.com (17)

Sullivan, E. Thomas, University of Minnesota Alumni Association, Minneapolis, MN. Tel: (612) 624-2323, (800) 862-5867, FAX: (612) 626-8167, E-Mail: umalumni@umn.edu, Web Site: www.minnesotaalumni.org (1)

Sullivan, Greg, ByOwner.com Inc, Boca Raton, FL. Tel: (800) BY-OWNER, Web Site: www.byowner.com (35)

Sullivan, Jim, MFE Instruments, Salem, NH. Tel: (603) 893-8778, (800) 843-8011, FAX: (603) 893-8851, Web Site: www.stockeryale.com (9)

Sullivan, Jodi, Hilton HHonors, McLean, VA. Tel: (703) 883-1000, Web Site: hhonors.hilton.com (16)

Sullivan, John Fox, The Atlantic Monthly, Washington, DC. Tel: (202) 266-6000, (800) 234-2411, FAX: (202) 266-6001, Web Site: www.theatlantic.com (17)

Sullivan, Kenneth M., Smithfield Foods, Smithfield, VA. Tel: (800) 276-6158, Web Site: www.smithfieldfoods.com (16)

Sullivan, Lisa, Cox Target Media Inc, St. Petersburg, FL. Tel: (727) 399-3000, (800) 678-2743, FAX: (727) 399-3061, E-Mail: info@coxtarget.com, Web Site: www.coxtarget.com (21)

Sullivan, Michael, Aptimus, San Francisco, CA. Tel: (415) 896-2123, FAX: (415) 896-2561 (22)

Sullivan, Michael, Carefirst Blue Cross Blue Shield, Washington, DC. Tel: (202) 479-8000, FAX: (301) 470-8049, Web Site: www.carefirst.com (15)

Sullivan, Michael, Lotame Solutions, Columbia, MD. Tel: (410) 379-2195, FAX: (410) 379-2198, Web Site: www.lotame.com (22)

Sullivan, Mike, Electric Insurance Co, Beverly, MA. Tel: (978) 921-2080, (800) 227-2757, FAX: (978) 524-5583, E-Mail: sales@electricinsurance.com, Web Site: www.electricinsurance.com (15)

Sullivan, Myrna, Hogard Business Services Inc, Kankakee, IL. Tel: (815) 932-1835, FAX: (815) 932-4793, E-Mail: hogards@att.net, Web Site: www.hogardbusinessservices.com (28)

Sullivan, Nick, Esquire Magazine, New York, NY. Tel: (212) 649-4020, FAX: (212) 649-4303, E-Mail: esquire@hearst.com, Web Site: www.esquire.com (17)

Sullivan, Steve, Hammock Publishing Inc, Nashville, TN. Tel: (615) 690-3400, FAX: (615) 690-3401, E-Mail: info@hammock.com, Web Site: www.hammock.com (17)

Sullivan, Thomas, Princeton Partners Inc, Princeton, NJ. Tel: (609) 452-8500, FAX: (609) 452-7212, E-Mail: moreinfo@princetonpartners.com, Web Site: www.princetonpartners.com (35)

Sullivan, William F., Union Federal Savings Bank, North Providence, RI. Tel: (401) 353-8900, (800) 992-0278, FAX: (401) 353-8938, Web Site: www.unionfsb.com (14)

Sullo, David, Super Coups, Norwell, MA. Tel: (508) 977-2000, (800) 626-2620, FAX: (508) 977-0644, Web Site: www.supercoups.com (26)

Sultan, Greg, Customer Communications Group Inc, Lakewood, CO. Tel: (303) 525-0313, E-Mail: info@customer.com, Web Site: www.customer.com (35)

Sultz, Tara, Medical Economics Magazine, North Olmsted, OH. Tel: (440) 243-8100, FAX: (440) 891-2735, Web Site: medicaleconomics.modernmedicine.com/about (17)

Sulzberger, Jr. Arthur O., The New York Times Co, New York, NY. Tel: (212) 556-1234, Web Site: www.nytimes.com (17)

Suman Inc, Potomac, MD. Tel: (301) 461-7625, E-Mail: anil.chaturvedi@sumaninc.com, Web Site: www.sumaninc.com (21)

Sumi Printing, Carson, CA. Tel: (310) 769-1600, Web Site: www.getsumi.com (27)

Sumi, Michael, Sumi Printing, Carson, CA. Tel: (310) 769-1600, Web Site: www.getsumi.com (27)

Sumi, Roland, Sumi Printing, Carson, CA. Tel: (310) 769-1600, Web Site: www.getsumi.com (27)

Summers, Betsy, Herrmann Global LLC, Lake Lure, NC. Tel: (828) 625-9153, (800) 432-4234, E-Mail: info@hbdi.com, Web Site: www.herrmannsolutions.com (35)

Summit Direct Mail Inc, Dallas, TX. Tel: (469) 916-5170, (877) 247-0993, E-Mail: info@summitdm.com, Web Site: www.summitdm.com (28)

Summit Industries Inc, Marietta, GA. Tel: (770) 590-0600, (800) 241-6996, FAX: (770) 590-0714, E-Mail: info@summitinds.com, Web Site: www.summitinds.com (5)

Summit Marketing, Saint Louis, MO. Tel: (844) 792-2013, (800) 843-7347, E-Mail: info@summitmarketing.com, Web Site: www.summitmarketing.com (35)

Summit Racing Equipment, Tallmadge, OH. Tel: (330) 630-0250, (800) 230-3030, FAX: (330) 630-5571, Web Site: www.summitracing.com (12)

SummitQwest, Dayton, OH. Tel: (937) 291-4333, Web Site: www.sqinteractive.com (30)

Sumner, Jr Bryceon J., Exhibitgroup/Giltspur, Roselle, IL. Tel: (972) 538-3031, (800) 843-3944, Web Site: www.e-g.com (30)

Sumner, Tiffany, Carl Fischer Music, New York, NY. Tel: (212) 777-0900, (800) 762-2328, FAX: (212) 477-6996, E-Mail: cf-info@carlfischer.com, Web Site: www.carlfischer.com (17)

Sumotext, Inc, Little Rock, AR. Tel: (800) 480-1248, Web Site: www.sumotext.com (21)

Sun Harvest Citrus, Fort Myers, FL. Tel: (239) 768-2686, (800) 743-1480, FAX: (239) 768-9255, E-Mail: info@sunharvestcitrus.com, Web Site: www.SunHarvestCitrus.com (6)

Sunbeam Products Inc, Boca Raton, FL. Tel: (561) 912-4100, FAX: (561) 912-4567, Web Site: www.sunbeam.com (16)

Sunbelt Media Service, Chapel Hill, NC. Tel: (919) 967-7174, FAX: (919) 967-6050, E-Mail: jkluger@sunbelt-media.com, Web Site: www.sunbelt-media.com (32)

Sunbilt Solar Products, Jamaica, NY. Tel: (718) 297-0228, FAX: (718) 297-3090, E-Mail: robin@jsussmaninc.com, Web Site: jsussmaninc.com/sunbilt-solar-products (8)

Sunburst Digital Inc, Hoffman Estates, IL. Tel: (800) 321-7511, E-Mail: sales@sunburst.com, Web Site: www.sunburst.com (17)

Sunburst Farms Inc, Miami, FL. Tel: (305) 594-4300, (800) 333-1223, E-Mail: moreinfo@sunburstfarms.com, Web Site: www.sunburstfarms.com (8)

Sundance Catalog Co, Salt Lake City, UT. Tel: (801) 973-2711, (800) 422-2770, FAX: (801) 973-4989, E-Mail: jessica.bassin@sundance.net, Web Site: www.sundancecatalog.com (6)

Sundancer Jewelry Co Inc, Albuquerque, NM. Tel: (505) 345-7475, FAX: (505) 345-7561, E-Mail: sales@sundancer.net, Web Site: www.sundancer.net (16)

Sundman, David, Littleton Coin Co Inc, Littleton, NH. Tel: (603) 444-5386, (800) 645-3122, FAX: (603) 444-0121, E-Mail: jhennessey@littletoncoin.com, Web Site: www.littletoncoin.com (6)

Sundman, Donald J., Mystic Stamp Co Inc, Camden, NY. Tel: (866) 660-7147, FAX: (800) 385-4919, E-Mail: info@mysticstamp.com, Web Site: www.mysticstamp.com (16)

Sundog, Fargo, ND. Tel: (701) 235-5525, (888) 9-SUN-DOG, FAX: (701) 235-8941, E-Mail: info@sundoginteractive.com, Web Site: www.sundoginteractive.com (35)

Sungard Computer Services, Wayne, PA. Tel: (484) 582-5673, E-Mail: GetInfo@SunGard.com, Web Site: www.sungard.com (22)

Sunlife of Canada, Wellesley Hills, MA. Tel: (781) 237-6030, (800) SUNLIFE, FAX: (781) 446-1779, Web Site: www.sunlife-usa.com (15)

Sunnyland Farms Inc, Albany, GA. Tel: (800) 999-2488, Web Site: www.sunnylandfarms.com (4)

Sunoco Inc, Philadelphia, PA. Tel: (215) 977-3000, FAX: (215) 977-3409, Web Site: www.sunocoinc.com (16)

Sunrise Business Products, Mineola, NY. Tel: (800) 222-7367, FAX: (631) 588-3900 (10)

Sunrise Greetings, Kansas City, MO. Tel: (812) 336-4045, (800) 457-4045, FAX: (812) 336-8712, E-Mail: info@interart.com, Web Site: www.interartdistribution.com (17)

Sunrise Medical Inc, Boulder, CO. Tel: (303) 218-4500, (800) 333-4000, FAX: (303) 218-4949, Web Site: www.sunrisemedical.com (16)

Sunset Magazine, Menlo Park, CA. Tel: (650) 321-3600, FAX: (650) 328-6215 (17)

Sunshine Discount Crafts, Largo, FL. Tel: (727) 538-2878, (800) 729-2878, FAX: (727) 531-2739, E-Mail: webmaster@sunshinecrafts.com, Web Site: www.sunshinecrafts.com (11)

Sunshine Farm & Gardens, Renick, WV. Tel: (304) 497-2208, E-Mail: barry@sunfarm.com, Web Site: www.sunfarm.com (8)

Sunshine Glassworks Ltd, Buffalo, NY. Tel: (716) 668-2918, (800) 828-7159, FAX: (716) 668-2932, E-Mail: info23@sunshineglass.com, Web Site: www.sunshineglass.com (11)

Sunshine Minting Inc, Coeur D'Alene, ID. Tel: (208) 772-9592, (800) 274-5837, FAX: (208) 772-9739, E-Mail: sunshine@sunshinemint.com, Web Site: www.sunshinemint.com (14)

Sunshine Unlimited Inc, Lindsborg, KS. Tel: (785) 227-3880, FAX: (785) 227-3880, E-Mail: cpeterjr@aol.com, Web Site: www.sunshine-unlimited.com (9)

Sunstar, Chicago, IL. Tel: (773) 777-4000, FAX: (773) 777-1417, E-Mail: dominico@sunstar.com, Web Site: www.sunstar.com (16)

Suntel Inc, Hamden, CT. Tel: (203) 287-9114, FAX: (203) 248-3883, E-Mail: info@suntelinc.com, Web Site: www.suntelinc.com (22)

Suntrust Banks Inc, Atlanta, GA. Tel: (404) 588-7914, (800) 786-8787, FAX: (404) 532-0550, E-Mail: emmett.harmon@suntrust.com, Web Site: www.suntrust.com (14)

Supelco Inc, Bellefonte, PA. Tel: (814) 359-3441, (800) 359-3041, FAX: (814) 359-3044, E-Mail: supelco@sial.com, Web Site: www.sigma-aldrich.com (16)

Super Coups, Norwell, MA. Tel: (508) 977-2000, (800) 626-2620, FAX: (508) 977-0644, Web Site: www.supercoups.com (26)

Super 8 Hotels Worldwide, Parsippany, NJ. Tel: (800) 800-8000, FAX: (720) 535-2199, Web Site: www.super8.com (19)

Super, Philip, American Insurance Administrators Inc, Columbus, OH. Tel: (614) 486-5388, FAX: (614) 486-2728 (15)

Superstock Inc, Jacksonville, FL. Tel: (904) 565-0066, (800) 828-4545, FAX: (904) 641-4480, E-Mail: yourfriends@superstock.com, Web Site: www.superstockimages.com (38)

The Supplies Guys, Midland Park, NJ. Tel: (201) 493-8433, Web Site: www.suppliesguys.com (3)

Support Plus, Hudson, OH. Tel: (866) 553-8875, (800) 229-2910, FAX: (800) 950-9569, E-Mail: cs@supportplus.com, Web Site: www.supportplus.com (7)

Support Services Corp, Fort Myers, FL. Tel: (239) 332-5300, FAX: (239) 332-4555, E-Mail: s.ward@ss-corp.com, Web Site: www.ss-corp.com (22)

Supreme Specialty Advertising, Mount Arlington, NJ. Tel: (973) 770-8700, FAX: (973) 770-0808 (33)

Supremex Inc, Etobicoke, ON Canada. Tel: (416) 675-9370, (800) 465-7603, FAX: (416) 675-1952, (416) 848-8388, E-Mail: sales.central@supremex.com, Web Site: www.supremex.com (26)

Supremex Inc, La Salle, QC Canada. Tel: (514) 595-0555, FAX: (514) 595-1112, E-Mail: vente@supremex.com, Web Site: www.supremex.com (26)

Sur La Table, Brownsburg, IN. Tel: (800) 243-0852, FAX: (317) 858-5521, E-Mail: customerservice@surlatable.com (8)

Surane, John J., Ace Hardware Corp, Oak Brook, IL. Tel: (630) 990-6600, FAX: (630) 990-6838, Web Site: www.acehardware.com (16)

Surchin Advanced Mailing Technologies, Deer Park, NY. Tel: (631) 667-0200, (800) 645-5240, FAX: (631) 667-0242, E-Mail: info@surchin.com, Web Site: www.surchin.com (34)

Surchin, Hyman M., Surchin Advanced Mailing Technologies, Deer Park, NY. Tel: (631) 667-0200, (800) 645-5240, FAX: (631) 667-0242, E-Mail: info@surchin.com, Web Site: www.surchin.com (34)

Surdell & Partners, Omaha, NE. Tel: (402) 501-7400, (800) 733-7765, FAX: (402) 733-2083, E-Mail: info@surdellpartners.com, Web Site: www.surdellpartners.com (27)

Surdell, Daniel L., Surdell & Partners, Omaha, NE. Tel: (402) 501-7400, (800) 733-7765, FAX: (402) 733-2083, E-Mail: info@surdellpartners.com, Web Site: www.surdellpartners.com (27)

Sure-Fire Business Success Catalog, Cambridge, MA. Tel: (617) 547-6372, FAX: (617) 547-0061, E-Mail: drjlant@worldprofit.com, Web Site: www.worldprofit.com (17)

Sure Fit Inc, Alburtis, PA. Tel: (888) 796-0500, FAX: (610) 336-8995, Web Site: www.surefit.net (8)

Surfass, Ken, Equitable Life & Casualty Insurance Co, Salt Lake City, UT. Tel: (801) 579-3400, FAX: (801) 579-3789, Web Site: www.equilife.com (15)

Surmani, Andrew, Alfred Publishing Co Inc, Van Nuys, CA. Tel: (818) 891-5999, (800) 292-6122, FAX: (818) 893-5560, E-Mail: sales@alfred.com, Web Site: www.alfred.com (17)

Surplus Center, Lincoln, NE. Tel: (402) 474-4055, (800) 488-3407, FAX: (402) 474-5198, E-Mail: customerservice@surpluscenter.com, Web Site: www.surpluscenter.com (9)

Surplus Record, Chicago, IL. Tel: (312) 372-9077, (800) 622-5449, FAX: (312) 372-6537, E-Mail: surplus@surplusrecord.com, Web Site: www.surplusrecord.com (17)

Susel, Joel, Eagle:xm, Denver, CO. Tel: (303) 320-5411, (800) 426-5376, FAX: (303) 393-6584, E-Mail: extendedmedia@eaglexm.com, Web Site: www.eaglexm.com (21)

Suskavcevic, Andrej, Financial Executives International, Morristown, NJ. Tel: (973) 765-1000, FAX: (973) 765-1018, Web Site: www.financialexecutives.org (1)

Sussex Publishers Inc, New York, NY. Tel: (212) 260-7210, FAX: (212) 260-7445, Web Site: www.bluesbuster.com (17)

Sussman, David, Sunbilt Solar Products, Jamaica, NY. Tel: (718) 297-0228, FAX: (718) 297-3090, E-Mail: robin@jsussmaninc.com, Web Site: jsussmaninc.com/sunbilt-solar-products (8)

Sussman, Edward A., Easy Analytic Software Inc, Bellmawr, NJ. Tel: (856) 931-5780, FAX: (856) 931-4115, Web Site: www.easidemographics.com (22)

Sussman, Steve, Sunbilt Solar Products, Jamaica, NY. Tel: (718) 297-0228, FAX: (718) 297-3090, E-Mail: robin@jsussmaninc.com, Web Site: jsussmaninc.com/sunbilt-solar-products (8)

Sustainable Forestry Initiative Inc, Washington, DC. Tel: (202) 596-3450, FAX: (202) 596-3451, E-Mail: info@sfiprogram.org, Web Site: www.sfiprogram.org (1)

Sutherland Global Services, Pittsford, NY. Tel: (585) 586-5757, (800) 388-4557, Web Site: www.sutherlandglobal.com (35)

John Sutherland & Associates, San Diego, CA. Tel: (858) 535-1139, (800) 545-9591, FAX: (858) 535-9124 (15)

Sutherland, Alden, Jostens, Inc, Minneapolis, MN. Tel: (952) 830-3300, FAX: (952) 830-3293, Web Site: www.jostens.com (16)

Sutherland, Jason, Perimeter Technology Inc, Manchester, NH. Tel: (603) 645-1616, (800) 645-1650, FAX: (603) 645-1424, Web Site: www.perimetertechnology.com (34)

Sutherland, PhD John, UF College of Advertising, Journalism, & Communications, Gainesville, FL. Tel: (352) 392-4046, FAX: (352) 392-3919, Web Site: www.jou.ufl.edu (41)

Sutherland, Smokey, John Sutherland & Associates, San Diego, CA. Tel: (858) 535-1139, (800) 545-9591, FAX: (858) 535-9124 (15)

Sutherlin, Michael W., P & H Mining Equipment, Milwaukee, WI. Tel: (414) 671-4400, FAX: (414) 671-7618, Web Site: www.phmining.com (16)

Suto Seckler, Kirsten, Special Olympics International, Washington, DC. Tel: (202) 628-3630, (800) 700-8585, FAX: (202) 824-0200, E-Mail: info@specialolympics.org, Web Site: www.specialolympics.org (1)

Sutter Marketing Inc, Palatine, IL. Tel: (847) 358-3100, Web Site: www.suttermarketing.com (35)

Sutter, Conrad, Landscape Forms Inc, Kalamazoo, MI. Tel: (616) 381-0490, (800) 430-6209, FAX: (616) 381-3455, E-Mail: specify@landscapeforms.com, Web Site: www.landscapeforms.com (16)

Sutter, Lynn R., Sutter Marketing Inc, Palatine, IL. Tel: (847) 358-3100, Web Site: www.suttermarketing.com (35)

Sutter, Mark, Terumo Cardiovascular Systems Corp, Ann Arbor, MI. Tel: (734) 663-4145, (800) 521-2818, Web Site: www.terumo-cvs.com (5)

Sutton, Cindy, Sara Lee Direct Home Shopping, Winston-Salem, NC. Tel: (336) 519-4400, (800) 671-5056, E-Mail: ohp.manager@onehanesplace.com, Web Site: www.onehanesplace.com (2)

Sutton, Jeff, MSI List Marketing, Palatine, IL. Tel: (847) 934-1111, FAX: (847) 890-6700, E-Mail: jeff@msilist.com, Web Site: www.msilist.com (23)

Sutton, W. Ron, ACCUSPLIT Inc, Livermore, CA. Tel: (925) 226-0888, (800) 935-1996, FAX: (925) 463-0147, E-Mail: sales@accusplit.com, Web Site: www.accusplit.com (16)

Svetik, Steve, Aristokraft Inc, Jasper, IN. Tel: (812) 482-2527, FAX: (812) 482-9872, Web Site: www.aristokraft.com (16)

Svoboda Collins LLC, Chicago, IL. Tel: (312) 267-8750, FAX: (312) 267-6025, E-Mail: info@svoco.com, Web Site: www.svoco.com (5)

Svoboda, Jim, Mid America Direct Marketing Association, Omaha, NE. Tel: (402) 965-4318, FAX: (402) 964-8484, Web Site: www.madma.org (40)

Svoboda, John A., Svoboda Collins LLC, Chicago, IL. Tel: (312) 267-8750, FAX: (312) 267-6025, E-Mail: info@svoco.com, Web Site: www.svoco.com (5)

Swab, Mark, Con-Way Truckload, Joplin, MO. Tel: (417) 623-5229, (800) CFI-DRIVE, FAX: (417) 623-8939, E-Mail: gnichols@cfi-us.com, Web Site: www.cfi-us.com (12)

Swag Inc, Wichita, KS. Tel: (316) 685-3811, FAX: (316) 685-4422, E-Mail: swag@cox.net, Web Site: www.swagpromos.com (33)

Jimmy Swaggart Ministries, Baton Rouge, LA. Tel: (225) 768-8300, (800) 288-8350, FAX: (225) 769-2244, E-Mail: swaggart@cogeco.net, Web Site: www.jsm.org (1)

Swaggart, Rev Jimmy, Jimmy Swaggart Ministries, Baton Rouge, LA. Tel: (225) 768-8300, (800) 288-8350, FAX: (225) 769-2244, E-Mail: swaggart@cogeco.net, Web Site: www.jsm.org (1)

Swain, Kirk, All American List Corp, Upper Marlboro, MD. Tel: (301) 420-5760, (888) 690-2252, FAX: (301) 420-5765, E-Mail: info@allamericanlist.com, Web Site: www.allamericanlist.com (23)

Swain, Kirk L., DirectMail.com, Prince Frederick, MD. Tel: (888) 690-2252, FAX: (301) 855-9810, Web Site: www.directmail.com (28)

Swainson, John A., CA Inc, Islandia, NY. Tel: (800) 225-5224, FAX: (631) 342-3300, E-Mail: info@ca.com, Web Site: www.ca.com (16)

Swallow, G., Winn Technology Group Inc, Palm Harbor, FL. Tel: (727) 789-0006, (800) 444-5622, FAX: (727) 789-0638, E-Mail: winn@winntech.net, Web Site: www.winntech.net (29)

Swan Packaging Fulfillment, Wayne, NJ. Tel: (973) 790-8417, FAX: (973) 790-0216, E-Mail: info@swanpkg.com, Web Site: www.swanpackaging.com (28)

Swan, Craig, University of Minnesota Alumni Association, Minneapolis, MN. Tel: (612) 624-2323, (800) 862-5867, FAX: (612) 626-8167, E-Mail: umalumni@umn.edu, Web Site: www.minnesotaalumni.org (1)

Swann, Joseph, Reliance Electric, Fort Smith, AR. Tel: (479) 646-4711, FAX: (479) 648-5792, E-Mail: smtraylor@powersystems.rockwell.com, Web Site: www.reliance.com (9)

Swanson Health Products, Fargo, ND. Tel: (701) 356-2700, (800) 824-4491, FAX: (701) 356-2708, E-Mail: customercare@swansonvitamins.com, Web Site: www.swansonvitamins.com (4)

Swanson, Art, Health O Meter, Countryside, IL. Tel: (708) 377-0600, (800) 815-6615, FAX: (708) 377-0601, E-Mail: HomProCS@homscales.com, Web Site: www.homscales.com (16)

Swanson, Byron, Back to the Bible, Lincoln, NE. Tel: (402) 464-7200, (800) 759-2425, FAX: (402) 464-7474, E-Mail: info@backtothebible.org, Web Site: www.backtothebible.org (5)

Swanson, Mark, Tele Resources Inc, Duluth, MN. Tel: (888) 698-8787 X114, FAX: (218) 724-2466, E-Mail: mark.swanson@teleresources.net, Web Site: www.teleresources.net (29)

Swanson, Richard, Beltone Corp, Glenview, IL. Tel: (800) 235-8663, FAX: (847) 832-3300, E-Mail: info@beltone.com, Web Site: www.beltone.com (3)

Swanson, Scott, CAS Inc, Omaha, NE. Tel: (402) 964-9998, (866) 461-4693, FAX: (402) 963-2103, E-Mail: sales@cas-online.com, Web Site: www.cas-online.com (23)

Swart, David, Polyair Packaging, Chicago, IL. Tel: (773) 995-1818, (888) POLYAIR X444, FAX: (773) 995-7725, E-Mail: marketing@polyair.com, Web Site: www.polyair.com (9)

Swart, Mary, Q Fact Marketing Research Inc & Videoconferencing Center, Cincinnati, OH. Tel: (513) 891-2271, FAX: (513) 984-7464, E-Mail: info@qfact.com, Web Site: www.qfact.com (30)

Swartz, Elaine, Blaine Window Hardware Inc, Hagerstown, MD. Tel: (301) 797-6500, (800) 678-1919, FAX: (888) 250-3960, E-Mail: info@blainewindow.com, Web Site: www.blainewindow.com (12)

Swartz, Jan, Princess Cruises (HQ), Santa Clarita, CA. Tel: (661) 753-0000, (800) (774)-6237, FAX: (661) 284-4747, Web Site: www.princesscruises.com (19)

Swartz, Kress, Quadrant Engineering Plastic Products, Reading, PA. Tel: (610) 320-6600, (800) 366-0300, FAX: (610) 320-6868, Web Site: www.quadrantepp.com (16)

Swartz, Randy, Stagestep Inc, Philadelphia, PA. Tel: (215) 636-9000, (800) 523-0960, FAX: (267) 672-2912, E-Mail: stagestep@stagestep.com, Web Site: www.stagestep.com (5)

Swartz, Steven R., The Hearst Corp, New York, NY. Tel: (212) 649-2000, FAX: (212) 649-2108, Web Site: www.hearst.com/magazines/ (17)

Swartzentruber, John S., Gohn Brothers, Middlebury, IN. Tel: (574) 825-2400, (800) 595-0031, E-Mail: gohnbrothers@gmail.com, Web Site: www.gohnbrothers.com (5)

Swayne, Doug, Uncharted Country Publishing, Madison, WI. Tel: (575) 776-3470, E-Mail: ucp@taichihealth.com, Web Site: www.taichihealth.com (17)

Sweda, Stewart, Careington International, Frisco, TX. Tel: (972) 335-6970, (800) 441-0380, Web Site: www.careington.com (7)

Swedenburg, Scott, Mail Enterprises LLC, Birmingham, AL. Tel: (205) 595-4945, (800) 595-4945, FAX: (205) 595-4943, E-Mail: sswedenburg@mailent. com, Web Site: www.mailent.com (21)

Swedish, Joseph R., Anthem Inc, Indianapolis, IN. Tel: (317) 488-6000, Web Site: www.antheminc.com (7)

Sweeney, Anne, Disney/ABC Television Group, Burbank, CA. Tel: (818) 460-7477, Web Site: www. disneyabctv.com (32)

Sweeney, Ariane E., Citizens Against Government Waste, Washington, DC. Tel: (202) 467-5300, (800) USA-DEBT, FAX: (202) 467-4253, E-Mail: membership@cagw.org, Web Site: www.cagw.org (1)

Sweeney, Brian G., Cablevision Systems Corp, Bethpage, NY. Tel: (516) 803-2300, FAX: (516) 803-3134, Web Site: www.cablevision.com (16)

Sweeney, Daniel F., Ikon Communications Consultants Inc, Wellesley, MA. Tel: (781) 237-6060, FAX: (781) 235-3504, E-Mail: info@ ikoncommunications.com, Web Site: www. ikoncommunications.com (35)

Sweeney, Darlene, Level 5 Communications Inc, Dublin, NH. Tel: (603) 563-1631, FAX: (603) 563-8912, E-Mail: de-news@deskeng.com, Web Site: www. deskeng.com (32)

Sweeney, Dawn, The National Restaurant Association Educational Foundation, Washington, DC. Tel: (800) 424-5156 (1)

Sweeney, Gregg M., Ikon Communications Consultants Inc, Wellesley, MA. Tel: (781) 237-6060, FAX: (781) 235-3504, E-Mail: info@ ikoncommunications.com, Web Site: www. ikoncommunications.com (35)

Sweeney, Judy, Disabled American Veterans, Cincinnati, OH. Tel: (859) 441-7300, FAX: (859) 442-2084, E-Mail: feedback@davmail.org, Web Site: www.dav.org (1)

Sweeney, Kevin, Publicis Worldwide North America, New York, NY. Tel: (212) 279-5550, E-Mail: andrew.bruce@publicisna.com, Web Site: publicisna.com (35)

Sweeney, Matthew, Computerworld DataBase Div, Framingham, MA. Tel: (508) 879-0700, (800) 343-6474, FAX: (508) 875-4394, Web Site: www. computerworld.com (22)

Sweeney, Ric, College of Business, Cincinnati, OH. Tel: (513) 556-7002, FAX: (513) 556-4891, E-Mail: business@uc.edu, Web Site: www.business.uc.edu (41)

Sweepstakes Clearinghouse, Dallas, TX. Tel: (214) 915-7100, (800) 481-2631, FAX: (214) 915-7458, E-Mail: customersupport@ sweepstakesclearinghouse.com, Web Site: www. schstore.com (16)

Sweet Tooth Candies, Newport, KY. Tel: (859) 581-4663, (877) 581-5132, FAX: (859) 581-1979 (4)

Sweet, Bob, Dow Theory Forecasts, Hammond, IN. Tel: (219) 931-6480, (800) 233-5922, FAX: (219) 931-6487, E-Mail: custserv@horizonpublishing.com, Web Site: www.dowtheory.com (17)

Sweetgrass Marketing LLC, Charleston, SC. Tel: (843) 834-1884, Web Site: sweetgrassmarketing.net (35)

Sweeton, Mary Kent, The Great Books Foundation, Chicago, IL. Tel: (312) 332-5870, (800) 222-5870, FAX: (312) 407-0224, Web Site: www.greatbooks. org (1)

Sweigart, Nicole, Incentive Manufacturers Representatives Association (IMRA), Naperville, IL. Tel: (630) 369-7786, FAX: (630) 369-3773, E-Mail: nicole@ incentivemarketing.org, Web Site: www.imraonline. org (40)

Swenson, Judith J., Response Marketing Inc, Eden Prairie, MN. Tel: (952) 949-4913 (35)

Swent, Greg, Marketry Inc, Bellevue, WA. Tel: (425) 451-1262, FAX: (425) 953-2957, E-Mail: greg@ marketry.com, Web Site: www.marketry.com (23)

Swiatkowski, Kenneth J, The Hibbert Group, Trenton, NJ. Tel: (609) 394-7500, (800) 545-4747, FAX: (609) 695-6553, Web Site: www.hibbertco.com (28)

Swift, Amber, Vierk National Supply, North Chicago, IL. Tel: (847) 869-4318, (800) 428-7548, FAX: (847) 689-4412, Web Site: www.vierk.com (16)

Swimmer Design Associates, Prospect Heights, IL. Tel: (847) 215-0900, FAX: (847) 215-9821, E-Mail: mail@swimmerdesign.com, Web Site: www. swimmerdesign.com (36)

Swimmer, Mark, Swimmer Design Associates, Prospect Heights, IL. Tel: (847) 215-0900, FAX: (847) 215-9821, E-Mail: mail@swimmerdesign.com, Web Site: www.swimmerdesign.com (36)

Swinburn, Peter, Molson Coors Brewing Co, Denver, CO. Tel: (303) 927-2337, (800) 665-7661, Web Site: www.molsoncoors.com (16)

Swindell, John, NextMark Inc, Hanover, NH. Tel: (603) 643-1307, FAX: (603) 643-1662, Web Site: www. nextmark.com (22)

Swinwood, Craig, Harlequin Enterprises Ltd, Don Mills, ON Canada. Tel: (416) 445-5860, FAX: (416) 445-8655, E-Mail: customer_ecare@harlequin.ca, Web Site: www.eharlequin.com (17)

The Swiss Colony Inc, Monroe, WI. Tel: (608) 324-4603, FAX: (608) 328-8735, Web Site: www. swisscolony.com (4)

Swords Music Co Inc, Fort Worth, TX. Tel: (817) 53-MUSIC, (800) 522-3028, FAX: (817) 536-4293, E-Mail: daveshep4300@sbcglobal.net, Web Site: www.swordsmusicinc.com (34)

Swords, Logan, Swords Music Co Inc, Fort Worth, TX. Tel: (817) 53-MUSIC, (800) 522-3028, FAX: (817) 536-4293, E-Mail: daveshep4300@sbcglobal.net, Web Site: www.swordsmusicinc.com (34)

Swormstedt, Tedd, ST Media Group International, Cincinnati, OH. Tel: (513) 421-2050, (800) 925-1110, FAX: (513) 421-5144, E-Mail: customer@ stmediagroup.com, Web Site: www.signweb.com (17)

Swormstedt, Wade, ST Media Group International, Cincinnati, OH. Tel: (513) 421-2050, (800) 925-1110, FAX: (513) 421-5144, E-Mail: customer@ stmediagroup.com, Web Site: www.signweb.com (17)

Sybase Inc, Dublin, CA. Tel: (925) 236-5000, FAX: (925) 236-4321, Web Site: www.sybase.com/ product/datawarehousing (22)

Sycoff, Jerry, IC International, Hicksville, NY. Tel: (516) 479-2200, (800) 631-0209, FAX: (516) 479-2215, E-Mail: info@ic-mr.com, Web Site: www.ic-mr.com (30)

Syfy, New York, NY. Tel: (212) 664-4444, Web Site: www.syfy.com (32)

Sykes Acquisition, Newtown, PA. Tel: (800) 799-6880, Web Site: www.ictgroup.com (29)

Sykes, Chris, Miracle of Aloe, Dallas, TX. Tel: (800) 966-2563, FAX: (800) 859-9881, E-Mail: LJohnson@miracleofaloe.com, Web Site: www. miracleofaloe.com (7)

Sykes, E.C., Black Box Corp, Lawrence, PA. Tel: (724) 746-5500, (877) 877-2269, FAX: (800) 321-0746, E-Mail: brian.kutchma@blackbox.com, Web Site: www.blackbox.com (3)

Sylvan Learning Inc, Baltimore, MD. Tel: (410) 843-8000, (800) 31-SUCCESS, FAX: (410) 843-8057, E-Mail: pr@sylvanlearning.com, Web Site: www. sylvanlearning.com (16)

Sylvester, David C., Steelcase Inc, Grand Rapids, MI. Tel: (616) 247-2710, FAX: (616) 475-2270, Web Site: www.steelcase.com (16)

Sylvester, Marcia, Princeton Book Co Publishers, Hightstown, NJ. Tel: (609) 426-0602, (800) 220-7149, FAX: (609) 426-1344, E-Mail: pbc@dancehorizons. com, Web Site: www.dancehorizons.com (17)

Sylvester, Maryrose, GE Lighting North America, Cleveland, OH. Tel: (216) 266-2121, FAX: (216) 266-2930, Web Site: www.gelighting.com/na (16)

Sylvia, Mike, Reliable Racing Supply, Queensbury, NY. Tel: (518) 793-5677, FAX: (518) 793-6491, Web Site: www.reliableracing.com (11)

Symantec, Mountain View, CA. Tel: (408) 517-8000, FAX: (408) 517-8186, Web Site: www.symantec. com (16)

Symes, Dominic, Innovyx Inc, Seattle, WA. Tel: (206) 674-8720, Web Site: www.innovyx.com (32)

Symetra Financial, Bellevue, WA. Tel: (425) 256-8000, (800) 426-7355, FAX: (425) 256-5737, Web Site: www.symetra.com (15)

Symrise, Teterboro, NJ. Tel: (201) 288-3200, FAX: (201) 462-2200, Web Site: www.symrise.com (7)

Synapse Group Inc, Stamford, CT. Tel: (203) 595-8255, FAX: (203) 329-8237, E-Mail: webmaster@ synapsemail.com, Web Site: www.synapsegroupinc. com (18)

Synergy Arts Interactive, White Plains, NY. Tel: (914) 997-7222, FAX: (914) 997-8893, E-Mail: bgeorge@ synergyarts.com, Web Site: www.synergyarts.com (36)

Synergy Direct Marketing Solutions LLC, Barberton, OH. Tel: (330) 869-5886, Web Site: www.synmar. biz (29)

Syngenta, Greensboro, NC. Tel: (336) 632-6000, FAX: (336) 632-7065 (16)

Synovate, New York, NY. Tel: (212) 293-6100, FAX: (212) 293-6666 (30)

Syntellect, Phoenix, AZ. Tel: (602) 789-2800, (800) 788-9733, FAX: (602) 789-2899, Web Site: www. syntellect.com (16)

Syracuse University, Syracuse, NY. Tel: (315) 443-1870, (315) 443-4226, E-Mail: orange@syr.edu, Web Site: syr.edu (1)

Syracuse, Dennis, Datran Media, New York, NY. Tel: (212) 706-9781, FAX: (212) 706-9758, Web Site: www.datranmedia.com (22)

Syroka, Cynthia, Avaya Communication, Temecula, CA. Tel: (866) 462-8292, Web Site: www.avaya. com (34)

Syron, Richard F., Freddie Mac, McLean, VA. Tel: (703) 903-2000, (800) 424-5401, Web Site: www. freddiemac.com (14)

System Pavers, Newport Beach, CA. Tel: (949) 263-8300, Web Site: www.systempavers.com (16)

Systemax Inc, Port Washington, NY. Tel: (516) 608-7000, FAX: (516) 6208-7001, Web Site: www. systemax.com (16)

Systems Analytics Inc, Needham, MA. Tel: (781) 444-4837, E-Mail: info@systemsanalytics.com, Web Site: www.systemsanalytics.com (20)

Szanger, Michael, V3, Oxnard, CA. Tel: (805) 981-2600, (800) 882-1844, FAX: (805) 981-1180, E-Mail: sales@printv3.com, Web Site: www. printv3.com (27)

Szczupak, David, Whirlpool Corp, Benton Harbor, MI. Tel: (269) 923-5000, E-Mail: info@whirlpool.com, Web Site: www.whirlpoolcorp.com (16)

Szefc, Richard, The Wedding Pages, New York, NY. Tel: (212) 219-8555, (800) 843-4983, FAX: (212) 219-1929, Web Site: www.theknot.com (16)

Szenasy, Susan S., Metropolis Magazine, New York, NY. Tel: (212) 627-9977, (800) 334-3046, FAX: (212) 627-9988, E-Mail: edit@metropolismag.com, Web Site: www.metropolismag.com (2)

Szilagyi, Steve, Elderly Instruments, Lansing, MI. Tel: (517) 372-7890, (888) 473-5810, FAX: (517) 372-5155, E-Mail: web@elderly.com, Web Site: www. elderly.com (5)

Szkutak, Thomas J., Amazon.com, Seattle, WA. Tel: (206) 266-1000, Web Site: www.amazon.com (16)

Szlosek, Tom, Honeywell, Morristown, NJ. Tel: (973) 455-2000, FAX: (973) 455-4807, Web Site: www. honeywell.com (16)

Sznewajs, John G., Masco Corp, Taylor, MI. Tel: (313) 274-7400, FAX: (313) 792-6135, E-Mail: webmaster@mascohq.com, Web Site: www.masco. com (16)

Szot, Colleen, Wonderful Writer LLC, Minneapolis, MN. Tel: (763) 557-7116, (888) 557-7116, FAX: (763) 551-4831, E-Mail: colleen@wonderfulwriter. com, Web Site: www.wonderfulwriter.com (39)

Szymanski, Greg, Metropolitan Graphic Arts, Mundelein, IL. Tel: (847) 566-9502, (800) 755-5936, FAX: (847) 566-9584, E-Mail: gregs@mgaprinting.com, Web Site: www.mgaprinting.com (27)

Szymanski, Joseph, Metropolitan Graphic Arts, Mundelein, IL. Tel: (847) 566-9502, (800) 755-5936, FAX: (847) 566-9584, E-Mail: gregs@mgaprinting.com, Web Site: www.mgaprinting.com (27)

T

T-Mobile, Bellevue, WA. Tel: (425) 999-2084, Web Site: www.t-mobile.com (29)

T Rowe Price Associates Inc, Baltimore, MD. Tel: (410) 345-2000, (800) 638-7890, FAX: (410) 986-3618, E-Mail: info@troweprice.com, Web Site: www.troweprice.com (14)

TAB Boards International Inc, Westminster, CO. Tel: (303) 839-1200, FAX: (303) 839-0012, Web Site: www.tabboards.com (14)

TALX Corp, Dallas, TX. Tel: (972) 755-2100, FAX: (972) 755-2080, E-Mail: consulting@ managementinsights.com, Web Site: www. managementinsights.com (20)

TBC Inc, Baltimore, MD. Tel: (410) 347-7500, FAX: (410) 986-1299, E-Mail: info@tbc.us, Web Site: www.tbc.us (35)

TBWA/Chiat/Day Inc, New York, NY. Tel: (212) 804-1000, FAX: (212) 804-1200, Web Site: www. tbwachiatdayny.com (35)

TBWA Worldwide, New York, NY. Tel: (212) 804-1300, E-Mail: info@tbwa.com, Web Site: www. tbwa.com (35)

TC Transcontinental, Montreal, QC Canada. Tel: (514) 954-4000, FAX: (514) 954-4016, Web Site: tctranscontinental.com (35)

TD Ameritrade Holding Corp, Omaha, NE. Tel: (800) 237-8692, Web Site: www.amtd.com (14)

TD Bank NA, Falmouth, ME. Tel: (207) 770-2196, Web Site: www.tdbanknorth.com (14)

TDS Telecom, Madison, WI. Tel: (608) 664-4119, Web Site: www.tdstelecom.com (16)

TEC Mailing Solutions, LLC, Sun Prairie, WI. Tel: (608) 825-8525, (866) 379-9437, FAX: (608) 825-8526, E-Mail: info@tecmailing.com (22)

TechBA - Fumec, San Jose, CA. Tel: (408) 821-6297, Web Site: www.techba.com (1)

TFC Inc, Napa, CA. Tel: (707) 224-6161, Web Site: www.tfcinc.com (27)

THD Inc, Lexington, MA. Tel: (781) 859-1400, FAX: (781) 859-1500, E-Mail: info@thdinc.com, Web Site: www.thdinc.com (1)

Thomson Reuters, New York, NY. Tel: (212) 367-6300, (800) 950-1216, FAX: (212) 367-6301, Web Site: www.riahome.com (17)

TIAA-CREF, New York, NY. Tel: (212) 490-9000, FAX: (212) 916-6505, Web Site: www.tiaa-cref.org (15)

TKLi, The Colony, TX. Tel: (972) 370-7878, (800) 789-3893, FAX: (972) 370-7879, E-Mail: info@tkli.com, Web Site: www.tkli.com (23)

TL Enterprises Inc, Ventura, CA. Tel: (805) 667-4100, FAX: (805) 667-4419 (17)

TLC, Silver Spring, MD. Tel: (240) 662-2000, Web Site: www.tlc.com (32)

TMA Direct Inc, Reston, VA. Tel: (703) 547-4940, (877) TMA-5566, FAX: (703) 547-4979, E-Mail: info@tmadirect.com, Web Site: www.tmadirect.com (23)

TMP Direct, Budd Lake, NJ. Tel: (973) 347-9400, (800) 328-2439, FAX: (973) 347-8773, E-Mail: ron. pearl@tmpwdirect.com, Web Site: www. tmpwdirect.com (29)

TMP Directional Marketing, Boston, MA. Tel: (212) 351-7595, Web Site: www.tmpdm.com (30)

TMP Worldwide, New York, NY. Tel: (800) 867-2001, E-Mail: wecanhelp@tmp.com, Web Site: www.tmp. com (35)

TN Marketing, Wayzata, MN. Tel: (763) 577-1200, Web Site: www.tnmarketing.com (35)

TNF, Toronto, ON Canada. Tel: (416) 924-5751, FAX: (416) 923-7085, Web Site: www.tnf-cf.com (30)

TNS Intersearch, White Plains, NY. Tel: (914) 684-6100, FAX: (914) 684-6078, Web Site: www.tns-global.com (30)

TNT International Express, Melville, NY. Tel: (800) 558-5555 (28)

TNT Packaging Inc, Miami, FL. Tel: (305) 633-2556, (305) 769-0616, (800) 327-6085, FAX: (305) 769-0619, E-Mail: tntpackaging@bellsouth.net, Web Site: www.tntpackaging.com (16)

TPG Direct Inc, Philadelphia, PA. Tel: (215) 592-8381, FAX: (215) 574-8316, E-Mail: slongley@tpgdirect. com, Web Site: www.tpgdirect.com (35)

TRG World, Washington, DC. Tel: (202) 289-9898 (29)

TSE Services, Raleigh, NC. Tel: (919) 875-3037, Web Site: www.ncemcs.com (30)

TSI, Albany, NY. Tel: (518) 463-5555, FAX: (518) 463-4504, E-Mail: tsi@capital.net, Web Site: www. tsidrivers.com (20)

TT Publishing, Arlington, VA. Tel: (703) 838-1770, FAX: (703) 838-0285, Web Site: www.ttnews.com (17)

TTC Marketing Solutions, Chicago, IL. Tel: (773) 545-0407, (800) 777-6348, FAX: (773) 545-4034, E-Mail: sales@ttcmarketingsolutions.com, Web Site: www.ttcmarketingsolutions.com (29)

TVA Media Group, Studio City, CA. Tel: (818) 505-8300, (888) 322-4296, FAX: (818) 505-8370, E-Mail: info@tvamediagroup.com, Web Site: www. tvamediagroup.com (35)

TVC Enterprises and the TV Collector Magazine, Las Vegas, NV. Tel: (760) 495-7956, E-Mail: tvcinquiries@happyretrogirl.com, Web Site: www. angelfire.com/ma/tvcollector/home.html (6)

TVGuide.com, New York, NY. Tel: (212) 626-2500, Web Site: www.tvguide.com (31)

TWL Knowledge Group, Carrollton, TX. Tel: (972) 309-4000, (800) 624-2272, FAX: (972) 309-5105, Web Site: www.twlk.com (3)

TXU Energy, Irving, TX. Tel: (972) 868-8345, Web Site: www.txu.com (16)

Tabacinic, Jose, Arnet Pharmaceutical, Davie, FL. Tel: (954) 236-9053, (800) 968-6673, FAX: (954) 370-2508, E-Mail: arnet@arnetusa.com, Web Site: www.arnetusa.com (7)

Tabacinic, Manuel, Arnet Pharmaceutical, Davie, FL. Tel: (954) 236-9053, (800) 968-6673, FAX: (954) 370-2508, E-Mail: arnet@arnetusa.com, Web Site: www.arnetusa.com (7)

Tabacinic, Mark, Arnet Pharmaceutical, Davie, FL. Tel: (954) 236-9053, (800) 968-6673, FAX: (954) 370-2508, E-Mail: arnet@arnetusa.com, Web Site: www.arnetusa.com (7)

Tabaco, Alex, Itochu Chemicals America Inc, White Plains, NY. Tel: (914) 333-7800, (800) 423-6870, FAX: (914) 333-7848, Web Site: www.itochu-sc. com (16)

TABcom, Hazleton, PA. Tel: (570) 384-5555, (800) 738-7877, FAX: (570) 384-2500, E-Mail: customerservice@petsupplies.com, Web Site: www. petsupplies.com (5)

Tabel, Brian, Isuzu Motors America LLC, Anaheim, CA. Tel: (562) 229-5000, (800) 255-6727, FAX: (562) 229-5463, Web Site: www.isuzu.com (16)

Tableau Software, Seattle, WA. Tel: (206) 633-3400, FAX: (206) 633-3004, Web Site: www. tableausoftware.com (22)

Tabline Data Services Inc, New York, NY. Tel: (212) 695-4873, FAX: (212) 629-4423 (30)

TaCito Direct, Dallas, TX. Tel: (800) 621-2225, FAX: (972) 490-6520, E-Mail: contact@tacito.com, Web Site: www.tacito.com (35)

Tacito, Anthony J., TaCito Direct, Dallas, TX. Tel: (800) 621-2225, FAX: (972) 490-6520, E-Mail: contact@tacito.com, Web Site: www.tacito.com (35)

Tackle Craft, Ellsworth, WI. Tel: (715) 273-5300, FAX: (715) 273-5320, E-Mail: customer service@tackle-craft.com (11)

Taeschler, Debra, Grafica Group, Morristown, NJ. Tel: (973) 309-7500, FAX: (973) 309-7501, E-Mail: information@grafica.com, Web Site: www.grafica. com (35)

Taeusch, Ben, Amateur Electronic Supply LLC, Milwaukee, WI. Tel: (414) 558-0333, (800) 558-0411, FAX: (414) 358-3337, Web Site: www.aesham.com (16)

Tafarella, Jonathan, Institute of Business Forecasting, Great Neck, NY. Tel: (516) 504-7576, E-Mail: info@ibf.org, Web Site: www.ibf.org (1)

Tafford Uniforms, Charlotte, NC. Tel: (215) 643-9666, E-Mail: customerservice@tafford.com, Web Site: www.tafford.com (2)

Taft, John, RBC Dain Rauscher Inc, Minneapolis, MN. Tel: (612) 371-2711, FAX: (612) 373-1627, Web Site: www.rbcdain.com (14)

Tailwinds Inc, Mill Valley, CA. Tel: (415) 380-8181, (800) TAILWIND, FAX: (415) 927-0199, E-Mail: service@tailwinds.com, Web Site: www.tailwinds. com (6)

Takashima, Christine, Daily Commercial News & Construction Record, Markham, ON Canada. Tel: (905) 752-5408, (800) 465-6475, FAX: (905) 752-5450, (888) 396-9413, E-Mail: dcnonl@reedbusiness.com, Web Site: www.dcnonl.com (17)

Take 5 Solutions LLC, Boca Raton, FL. Tel: (561) 819-5555, (866) 861-8862, FAX: (561) 819-0245, E-Mail: sales@take5s.com, Web Site: www.take5solutions.com (30)

Talabisco, Barbara, Wakefield Talabisco International, New York, NY. Tel: (212) 661-8600, FAX: (212) 661-8832, Web Site: www.wtali.com (20)

Talamantes, Patrick J., McClatchy Co, Sacramento, CA. Tel: (916) 321-1855, FAX: (916) 321-1869, Web Site: www.mcclatchy.com (17)

Talas, Brooklyn, NY. Tel: (212) 219-0770, FAX: (212) 219-0735, E-Mail: info@talasonline.com, Web Site: www.talasonline.com (10)

Talbert, Nancy, King's Chandelier Co, Eden, NC. Tel: (336) 623-6188, FAX: (336) 627-9935, E-Mail: crystal@chandelier.com, Web Site: www.chandelier.com (6)

Talbot, Eric, Village Software Inc, Boston, MA. Tel: (617) 695-9332, (800) 724-9332, FAX: (617) 695-1935, E-Mail: requests@villagesoft.com, Web Site: www.villagesoft.com (3)

Talbot, John, Postmatic Inc, Minneapolis, MN. Tel: (763) 784-6046, (888) 784-6046, FAX: (763) 784-9433, E-Mail: info@postmatic.net, Web Site: www.postmatic.com (34)

Talbot, Keith, Form House Inc, Chicago, IL. Tel: (773) 577-8500, E-Mail: ktalbot@theformhouse.com, Web Site: www.theformhouse.com (28)

Talbots, Hingham, MA. Tel: (781) 749-7600, (800) 825-2687, FAX: (781) 741-4369, Web Site: www.talbots.com (2)

Taliaferro, Susan, Tolliver Inc, New York, NY. Tel: (212) 758-7344, FAX: (212) 750-8617, E-Mail: tolliver12@aol.com (20)

Talian, Elizabeth, Communication Managers, LLC, Brookfield, CT. Tel: (203) 775-4213, FAX: (203) 775-6413, E-Mail: etalian@communicationmanagers.com, Web Site: www.communicationmanagers.com (20)

Talin, Patricia A., Amica Insurance, Lincoln, RI. Tel: (401) 334-6000, (800) 652-6422, FAX: (401) 334-4241, Web Site: www.amica.com (15)

Tallal, Scott V., Advanced Research Services, Malibu, CA. Tel: (310) 589-0223, Web Site: www.tvsurveys.com (30)

Tallentire, Daniel, Parker Software, Orlando, FL. Tel: (800) 680-7712, Web Site: www.parker-software.com (22)

Talmage, Jayne, ARRCO Medical Advertising, Walpole, MA. Tel: (508) 404-1105, FAX: (508) 404-1106, E-Mail: info@arrco.com, Web Site: www.arrco.com (23)

Tamke, George W., TruGreen/ChemLawn, Lewis Center, OH. Tel: (614) 846-1800, (800) TRUE-GREEN, FAX: (614) 431-0155, Web Site: www.trugreen.com (16)

Tamney, Joseph, Boyd Tamney Cross Inc, Wayne, PA. Tel: (610) 293-0500, FAX: (610) 687-8199, E-Mail: info@btcmarketing.com, Web Site: www.boydtamneycross.com (35)

Tamrac Inc, Ogden, UT. Tel: (385) 405-2700, E-Mail: info@tamrac.com, Web Site: www.tamrac.com (2)

Tan, Tommy, AccountMate Software Corp, Petaluma, CA. Tel: (707) 774-7500, FAX: (707) 774-7590, E-Mail: information@accountmate.com, Web Site: www.accountmate.com (22)

Tancer, Bill, Experian Simmons, New York, NY. Tel: (212) 749-3162, FAX: (212) 471-2940, E-Mail: ellenr@smrb.com, Web Site: www.smrb.com (30)

Tancredi, Christina, Music Choice, Horsham, PA. Tel: (215) 784-5840, Web Site: www.musicchoice.com (16)

Tandy Leather Co, Fort Worth, TX. Tel: (817) 872-3200, FAX: (817) 496-7859, E-Mail: tlfhelp@tandyleather.com, Web Site: www.tandyleatherfactory.com (11)

Tanen Directed Advertising, Norwalk, CT. Tel: (203) 855-5855, FAX: (203) 855-5865, E-Mail: ilene@tanendirected.com, Web Site: www.tanendirected.com (35)

Tanen, Ilene, Tanen Directed Advertising, Norwalk, CT. Tel: (203) 855-5855, FAX: (203) 855-5865, E-Mail: ilene@tanendirected.com, Web Site: www.tanendirected.com (35)

Tangent Media LLC, Atlanta, GA. Tel: (404) 444-2357, Web Site: www.tangentmedia.us (30)

Tanguay, Diane, Publications Groupe RR International Inc, Montreal, QC Canada. Tel: (514) 521-8148 (20)

Tanner, Bruce L., Lockheed Martin Corp, Bethesda, MD. Tel: (301) 897-6000, Web Site: www.lockheedmartin.com (16)

Tanner, Christy, TVGuide.com, New York, NY. Tel: (212) 626-2500, Web Site: www.tvguide.com (31)

Tanner, Glen E., ITT Educational Services Inc, Carmel, IN. Tel: (317) 706-9200, Web Site: www.ittesi.com (16)

Tanner, Josephine, Dante University Press, Wellesley, MA. Tel: (781) 790-1059, FAX: (781) 790-1056, E-Mail: dante@danteuniversity.org, Web Site: www.danteuniversity.org (17)

Tanton, Tom, Collegiate Cap & Gown, Champaign, IL. Tel: (217) 351-9500, FAX: (217) 351-9214, Web Site: www.herff-jones.com (16)

Tapp, Lynell L., Ronell Clock Co, Grants Pass, OR. Tel: (800) 334-0135, FAX: (541) 471-0099, E-Mail: info@ronellclock.com, Web Site: www.ronellclock.com (5)

Tapp, Roland V., Ronell Clock Co, Grants Pass, OR. Tel: (800) 334-0135, FAX: (541) 471-0099, E-Mail: info@ronellclock.com, Web Site: www.ronellclock.com (5)

Tappan, Robert A., Arrow Mailing Services II Inc, Hawthorne, CA. Tel: (310) 219-7740, FAX: (310) 219-3335 (28)

Taradel LLC, Glen Allen, VA. Tel: (804) 364-8444, (800) 481-1656, FAX: (888) 241-3023, E-Mail: info@taradel.com, Web Site: www.taradel.com (21)

Taravella, Tony, Industrial Uniform Co Inc, Wichita, KS. Tel: (316) 264-2871, (800) 333-3666, FAX: (316) 264-2708, E-Mail: info@logodepotweb.com, Web Site: www.industrialuniform.com (2)

Tarde, Jery, Golf Digest Co, Wilton, CT. Tel: (203) 761-5100, FAX: (203) 371-2572, Web Site: www.golfdigest.com (17)

Tardugno. Anthony F., AvMed Health Plan Inc, Miami, FL. Tel: (305) 671-5437, FAX: (305) 671-4782, Web Site: www.avmed.org (1)

Target & Response Inc, Naperville, IL. Tel: (312) 321-0500, FAX: (312) 321-0051, Web Site: www.target-response.com (35)

Target Corp, Minneapolis, MN. Tel: (612) 304-6073, Web Site: www.target.com (16)

Target Direct Marketing Inc, Kansas City, MO. Tel: (815) 558-0919, Web Site: www.targetdirectmarketing.com (35)

Target MarkeTeam, Atlanta, GA. Tel: (770) 274-3700, FAX: (770) 274-3730, E-Mail: inquiries@tmtinc.com, Web Site: www.tmtinc.com (35)

Target Marketing Group, Philadelphia, PA. Tel: (215) 238-5300, Web Site: www.targetonline.com (31)

Target Marketing Magazine, Philadelphia, PA. Tel: (215) 238-5300, (800) 777-8074, FAX: (215) 238-5270, Web Site: www.targetmarketingmag.com (43)

Targetbase, Irving, TX. Tel: (972) 506-3400, E-Mail: info@targetbase.com, Web Site: targetbase.com (35)

Tarman, Dan, eBay Inc, San Jose, CA. Tel: (408) 376-7400, (800) 322-7400, Web Site: www.ebayinc.com (16)

Tarman, John, Decker Communications Inc, San Francisco, CA. Tel: (415) 543-8100, (877) 485-0700, FAX: (415) 543-8103, E-Mail: info@deckercommunications.com, Web Site: www.deckercommunications.com (20)

Tarr, Peter, Union Federal Savings Bank, North Providence, RI. Tel: (401) 353-8900, (800) 992-0278, FAX: (401) 353-8938, Web Site: www.unionfsb.com (14)

Tarsitano, Jennifer, E+M Advertising Inc, New York, NY. Tel: (212) 981-5900, E-Mail: jtarsitano@emadv.com, Web Site: www.emadv.com (35)

Tartamella, Samuel, Integrated Business Services Inc, Lake Forest, IL. Tel: (847) 735-1690, (800) 451-5478, Web Site: www.medbase200.com (22)

Tartarsky, Amy, Dozier Equipment International, Milwaukee, WI. Tel: (800) 251-1234, FAX: (800) 336-6608, Web Site: www.dozierequip.com (9)

Tarver, Kenny, Schermer Pecans, Glennville, GA. Tel: (912) 654-2230, (800) 841-3403, E-Mail: information@schermerpecans.com, Web Site: www.pecantreats.com (4)

Tarvin, Paul, Cinmar LP, West Chester, OH. Tel: (888) 263-9850, Web Site: www.frontgate.com (8)

Tarvin, Paul, Redcats USA, New York, NY. Tel: (212) 613-9500, Web Site: www.brylane.com (2)

Tastad, Carolyn M., The Procter & Gamble Co, Cincinnati, OH. Tel: (513) 983-1100, Web Site: www.pg.com (16)

Tate, Carolyn, Relevate Group Inc, Springfield, VA. Tel: (703) 658-8300, (800) 523-7346, FAX: (703) 658-8301, E-Mail: sales@relevategroup.com, Web Site: www.relevategroup.com (22)

Tate, Eric, Astro Air, LP, Jacksonville, TX. Tel: (903) 586-3691, FAX: (903) 589-8094, E-Mail: sales@astroair.com, Web Site: www.astroair.com (9)

Tate, Mike, National Wholesale Co Inc, Lexington, NC. Tel: (336) 248-5904, (800) 480-4673, FAX: (336) 248-2880, E-Mail: customerservice@shopnational.com, Web Site: www.shopnational.com (2)

Tatko, Raymond J., Summit Racing Equipment, Tallmadge, OH. Tel: (330) 630-0250, (800) 230-3030, FAX: (330) 630-5571, Web Site: www.summitracing.com (12)

Tatsch, Roland, Vintage Wood Works, Quinlan, TX. Tel: (903) 356-2158, FAX: (903) 356-3023, E-Mail: mail@vintagewoodworks.com, Web Site: www.vintagewoodworks.com (8)

Tatten, Laura, Father Flanagan's Boy's Home, Boys Town, NE. Tel: (402) 498-1111, FAX: (402) 498-1969, Web Site: www.boystown.org (1)

Tattum, Lyn, Chemical Week, New York, NY. Tel: (212) 621-4900, FAX: (212) 621-4800, E-Mail: clientservices@chemweek.com, Web Site: www.chemweek.com (17)

Tatum, Eric, Advantage Fulfillment Services, Marietta, GA. Tel: (678) 921-2134, FAX: (770) 592-0204, Web Site: www.atlantamailervices.com (35)

Taub, Brian, Unitron Ltd, Commack, NY. Tel: (631) 589-6666, FAX: (631) 589-6795, E-Mail: johnc@unitronusa.com, Web Site: www.unitronusa.com (9)

Taube, Dace, University of Southern California, Los Angeles, CA. Tel: (213) 821-2366, FAX: (213) 740-2343, E-Mail: taube@usc.edu, Web Site: www.usc.edu (38)

Taubenpost Inc, Lake Forest, CA. Tel: (949) 770-3233, FAX: (949) 380-3940, E-Mail: info@taubenpost. com, Web Site: www.taubenpost.com (28)

Taubes, Sheri, Bronson Nutritionals LLC, Hauppauge, NY. Tel: (631) 750-0000, Web Site: www. bronsonnutritionals.com (7)

Tauck World Discovery, Norwalk, CT. Tel: (203) 899-6760, Web Site: www.tauck.com (19)

The Taunton Press, Newtown, CT. Tel: (203) 426-8171, (800) 477-8727, FAX: (203) 426-3434, Web Site: www.taunton.com (17)

Tauscher, William Y., Vertical Communications Inc, Santa Clara, CA. Tel: (408) 404-1600, (800) COM-DIAL, FAX: (408) 969-9601, Web Site: www. comdial.com (34)

Tautz, Nicole, Tecra Tools Inc, Englewood, CO. Tel: (303) 338-9224, (800) 284-0808, FAX: (303) 338-9289, E-Mail: info@tecratools.com, Web Site: www.tecratools.com (9)

Tautz, Terry, Tecra Tools Inc, Englewood, CO. Tel: (303) 338-9224, (800) 284-0808, FAX: (303) 338-9289, E-Mail: info@tecratools.com, Web Site: www.tecratools.com (9)

Tavlin, Mike, Speedway, Lincoln, NE. Tel: (402) 323-3100, FAX: (402) 477-7476 (12)

Tawakol, Omar, Oracle Data Cloud, Broomfield, CO. Tel: (800) 633-0738, E-Mail: thedatahotline@ oracle.com, Web Site: cloud.oracle.com (22)

Tax Management Inc, Bethesda, MD. Tel: (202) 452-4200, FAX: (202) 496-6013 (17)

Tax Reduction Institute, Germantown, MD. Tel: (301) 972-3600, (800) TRI-0-TAX, FAX: (301) 972-0819, E-Mail: info@taxreductioninstitute.com, Web Site: www.taxreductioninstitute.com (14)

Taylor Capital Group, Inc, Rosemont, IL. Tel: (847) 653-7978, FAX: (847) 653-7890, E-Mail: investor. relations@coletaylor.com, Web Site: www. taylorcapitalgroup.com (14)

Taylor Communications, North Mankato, MN. Tel: (800) 755-6405, Web Site: www. taylorcommunications.com (21)

Taylor Corp, North Mankato, MN. Tel: (507) 625-2828, FAX: (507) 625-3388 (16)

Taylor Nelson Sofres Intersearch, Horsham, PA. Tel: (419) 725-8560, E-Mail: info@intersearch.tnsofres. com, Web Site: www.intersearch.tnsofres.com (30)

Taylor-Stiles Division, Florence, KY. Tel: (859) 525-7600, (800) 365-8555, FAX: (859) 525-1446, E-Mail: sales@littleford.com, Web Site: www. littleford.com (16)

Taylor, Andrew C., Enterprise Rent-A-Car, Saint Louis, MO. Tel: (314) 512-5000, FAX: (314) 512-4706, Web Site: www.enterprise.com (19)

Taylor, Audrey, Chabin Concepts, Chico, CA. Tel: (530) 345-0364, FAX: (530) 345-6417, E-Mail: chabininc@aol.com (16)

Taylor, Bill, Bunn-O-Matic Corp, Springfield, IL. Tel: (217) 529-6601, FAX: (217) 529-6622, E-Mail: bunn@bunn.com, Web Site: www.bunn.com (16)

Taylor, Blair, Rexcraft Wedding Invitations, Rexburg, ID. Tel: (208) 359-1000, (800) 635-3898, FAX: (800) 826-2712, E-Mail: cs@rexcraft.com, Web Site: www.rexcraft.com (16)

Taylor, Bruce W., Taylor Capital Group, Inc, Rosemont, IL. Tel: (847) 653-7978, FAX: (847) 653-7890, E-Mail: investor.relations@coletaylor.com, Web Site: www.taylorcapitalgroup.com (14)

Taylor, Cami, Crossroads Films Inc, Los Angeles, CA. Tel: (310) 659-6220, FAX: (310) 659-3105, Web Site: www.crossroadfilms.com (32)

Taylor, Carter S.D., Performance Direct Inc, Atlanta, GA. Tel: (678) 608-2820, (800) 869-2300, FAX: (404) 869-2547, E-Mail: info@performancede.com (22)

Taylor, Cynthia L., National Humane Education Society, Charles Town, WV. Tel: (304) 725-0506, FAX: (304) 725-1523, E-Mail: information@nhes.org, Web Site: www.nhes.org (1)

Taylor, Dale, AbelsonTaylor Inc, Chicago, IL. Tel: (312) 894-5500, FAX: (312) 894-5526, E-Mail: info@abelsontaylor.com, Web Site: www. abelsontaylor.com (35)

Taylor, David H., Lorillard Tobacco Co, Greensboro, NC. Tel: (336) 335-7000, (877) 703-0386, FAX: (336) 373-6917, E-Mail: externalaffairs@lortobco. com, Web Site: www.lorillard.com (16)

Taylor, Diane, American Bronzing Co, Columbus, OH. Tel: (614) 252-7388, (800) 423-5678, FAX: (6!4) 252-4602, E-Mail: bronzeinfo@bronshoe.com, Web Site: www.abcbronze.com (16)

Taylor, Diane, Health Care Logistics, Circleville, OH. Tel: (800) 848-1633, Web Site: www. healthcarelogistics.com (16)

Taylor, Don, DCA, West Chester, PA. Tel: (610) 344-7488, (800) 638-6684, FAX: (610) 431-6500, E-Mail: ortho@dentalcorp.com, Web Site: www. dentalcorp.com (16)

Taylor, Earl, Marketing Science Institute Review, Cambridge, MA. Tel: (617) 491-2060, FAX: (617) 491-2065, E-Mail: msi@msi.org, Web Site: www.msi. org (43)

Taylor, Frank, GC Services, Houston, TX. Tel: (713) 777-4441, FAX: (713) 776-6535, E-Mail: marketing.communications@gcserv.com, Web Site: www.gcserv.com (20)

Taylor, Gary, InfoCision Management Corp, Akron, OH. Tel: (330) 668-1400, FAX: (330) 668-1401, E-Mail: infocision@infocision.com, Web Site: www.infocision.com (29)

Taylor, Glenn, Amsterdam Printing, Amsterdam, NY. Tel: (518) 842-6000, (800) 203-9917, FAX: (518) 843-5204, E-Mail: customerservice@ amsterdamprinting.com, Web Site: www. amsterdamprinting.com (16)

Taylor, Greg, Liberty Orchards Co Inc, Cashmere, WA. Tel: (509) 782-2191, (800) 888-5696, FAX: (509) 782-1487, E-Mail: service@libertyorchards.com, Web Site: www.libertyorchards.com (16)

Taylor, James D., National Humane Education Society, Charles Town, WV. Tel: (304) 725-0506, FAX: (304) 725-1523, E-Mail: information@nhes.org, Web Site: www.nhes.org (1)

Taylor, James H., Hamilton Beach Brands Inc, Glen Allen, VA. Tel: (804) 273-9777, FAX: (804) 527-7142, Web Site: www.hamiltonbeach.com (16)

Taylor, James, Loeb & Loeb Inc, New York, NY. Tel: (212) 407-4000, Web Site: www.loeb.com (20)

Taylor, Jeff, Indianapolis Newspapers Inc, Indianapolis, IN. Tel: (317) 444-4444, FAX: (317) 633-9414, Web Site: www.indystar.com (17)

Taylor, Jeffrey W., Taylor Capital Group, Inc, Rosemont, IL. Tel: (847) 653-7978, FAX: (847) 653-7890, E-Mail: investor.relations@coletaylor.com, Web Site: www.taylorcapitalgroup.com (14)

Taylor, John C., U-Haul International, Phoenix, AZ. Tel: (602) 263-6011, (800) GO-UHAUL, FAX: (602) 263-6598, Web Site: www.uhaul.com (16)

Taylor, John, Olmsted-Kirk Paper Co, Dallas, TX. Tel: (214) 637-2220, (800) 367-6526, FAX: (214) 637-2131, E-Mail: sales@okpaper.com, Web Site: www. okpaper.com (25)

Taylor, Judy, Mike Murach & Associates Inc, Fresno, CA. Tel: (559) 440-9071, (800) 221-5528, FAX: (559) 440-0963, E-Mail: murachbooks@murach. com, Web Site: www.murach.com (17)

Taylor, Kevin, U-Bild, Oceanside, CA. Tel: (800) 828-2453, FAX: (760) 754-2356, Web Site: www.ubild. com (8)

Taylor, Leo J., Del Webb, Bloomfield Hills, MI. Tel: (248) 644-7300, (888) 717-9777, FAX: (248) 433-4598, Web Site: www.delwebb.com (16)

Taylor, Luke, DigitasLBi, Boston, MA. Tel: (617) 867-1000, E-Mail: newbusiness@digitas.com, Web Site: www.digitaslbi.com (35)

Taylor, Mark, Tyndale House Publishers, Carol Stream, IL. Tel: (630) 668-8300, FAX: (630) 668-3245 (17)

Taylor, MD Patrick A., Holy Cross Hospital, Fort Lauderdale, FL. Tel: (954) 771-8000, FAX: (954) 229-8597, Web Site: www.holy-cross.com (16)

Taylor, Michael, Continuing Education of the Bar (CEB), Oakland, CA. Tel: (510) 302-2000, (800) 232-3444, FAX: (510) 302-2001, Web Site: www. ceb.com (1)

Taylor, Paul, Le Jardin Du Gourmet, Saint Johnsbury Center, VT. Tel: (802) 748-1446, FAX: (802) 748-1446, E-Mail: orderdesk@artisticgardens.com, Web Site: www.artisticgardens.com (8)

Taylor, Peter, Road Runner Sports Inc, San Diego, CA. Tel: (858) 974-4455, (800) 636-3560, FAX: (800) 453-5443, Web Site: www.roadrunnersports.com (11)

Taylor, Sam, Oriental Trading Co Inc, Omaha, NE. Tel: (800) 348-6483, FAX: (800) 327-8904, Web Site: www.oriental.com (5)

Taylor, Scott, Symantec, Mountain View, CA. Tel: (408) 517-8000, FAX: (408) 517-8186, Web Site: www.symantec.com (16)

Taylor, T. Robert, The Creative Alliance Inc, Lafayette, CO. Tel: (303) 665-8101, FAX: (303) 665-3136, E-Mail: info@thecreativealliance.com, Web Site: www.thecreativealliance.com (35)

Taylor, Tim, True North Inc, New York, NY. Tel: (212) 557-4202, Web Site: truenorthinc.com (35)

Taylor, Victor, Laven & Loeb Inc, Beachwood, OH. Tel: (216) 291-3483, (623) 217-2101, E-Mail: alaven@lavenandloeb.com; vtaylor@lavenandloeb. com, Web Site: www.lavenandloeb.com (20)

Taymark Inc, White Bear Lake, MN. Tel: (651) 426-1667, (800) 479-2043, FAX: (651) 426-0275, Web Site: www.taymarkinc.com (1)

Teachers Credit Union, South Bend, IN. Tel: (574) 284-6247, (800) 552-4745, Web Site: www.tcunet.com (1)

Teachers' Discovery, Auburn Hills, MI. Tel: (800) 832-2437, FAX: (800) 287-4509, E-Mail: orders@ teachersdiscovery.com, Web Site: teachersdiscovery.com (5)

The Teaching Co, Chantilly, VA. Tel: (703) 502-7300, (800) 832-2412, FAX: (703) 378-3819, Web Site: www.teach12.com (17)

Teahon, Nathan, Quality Contact Solutions Inc, Aurora, NE. Tel: (402) 210-2692, (866) 963-2889, FAX: (402) 210-2692, E-Mail: info@ qualitycontactsolutions.com, Web Site: www. qualitycontactsolutions.com (29)

Team Cheer, Geneseo, NY. Tel: (800) 350-1562, (877) 243-5268, E-Mail: custserv@teamcheer.com, Web Site: www.teamcheer.com (2)

Team One Advertising, Los Angeles, CA. Tel: (310) 437-2500, Web Site: www.teamone-usa.com (35)

Teblum, Ron, Mars Research, Fort Lauderdale, FL. Tel: (954) 771-7725, (877) 755-2805, FAX: (954) 703-4377, E-Mail: ron@marsresearch.com, Web Site: www.marsresearch.com (30)

Teboul, Luke, MSP Inc, Freedom, PA. Tel: (724) 774-3244, (800) 876-3211, FAX: (724) 774-6996, E-Mail: info@msp-pgh.com, Web Site: www.msp-pgh.com (21)

Tech Image, Chicago, IL. Tel: (847) 279-0022, (888) 483-2477, FAX: (847) 279-8922, E-Mail: info@techimage.com, Web Site: www.techimage.com (35)

Tech, Eric, Navistar, Lisle, IL. Tel: (331) 332-5000, Web Site: www.navistar.com (16)

Techar, Franklin J., Harris Bancorp Inc, Chicago, IL. Tel: (312) 461-2121, (888) 340-BANK, FAX: (312) 461-7869, E-Mail: onlineservices@harrisbank.com, Web Site: www.harrisbank.com (14)

Techcom Inc, Indianapolis, IN. Tel: (317) 865-2530, FAX: (317) 865-2540, E-Mail: info@techcom.com, Web Site: www.techcom.com (35)

Technekes LLC, Charlotte, NC. Tel: (704) 342-2900, FAX: (704) 342-2975, Web Site: www.technekes.com (22)

Techni-Tool Inc, Worcester, PA. Tel: (610) 941-2400, (800) 832-4866, FAX: (800) 854-8665, E-Mail: sales@techni-tool.com, Web Site: www.techni-tool.com (16)

Technical Assistance Research Programs (TARP), Arlington, VA. Tel: (703) 524-1456, FAX: (703) 524-6374, Web Site: www.tarp.com (20)

Technical Association of the Pulp & Paper Industry, Norcross, GA. Tel: (770) 446-1400, (800) 332-8686, FAX: (770) 446-6947, E-Mail: memberconnection@tappi.org, Web Site: www.tappi.org (1)

Technical Marketing Group, Santa Clara, CA. Tel: (888) 554-0256, Web Site: www.technicalmarketing.org (35)

TechniServe Inc, Troy, MI. Tel: (248) 989-0100, FAX: (248) 989-0111, E-Mail: info@techni-serve.com, Web Site: www.techni-serve.com (22)

Technology Marketing Corp/TMC, Norwalk, CT. Tel: (203) 852-6800, (800) 243-6002, FAX: (203) 953-2845, E-Mail: tmc@tmcnet.com, Web Site: www.tmcnet.com (29)

Technology Review, Cambridge, MA. Tel: (617) 475-8000, FAX: (617) 258-5850, Web Site: www.technologyreview.com (17)

Tecra Tools Inc, Englewood, CO. Tel: (303) 338-9224, (800) 284-0808, FAX: (303) 338-9289, E-Mail: info@tecratools.com, Web Site: www.tecratools.com (9)

Tedeschi, Robert J., Citizens Against Government Waste, Washington, DC. Tel: (202) 467-5300, (800) USA-DEBT, FAX: (202) 467-4253, E-Mail: membership@cagw.org, Web Site: www.cagw.org (1)

Tedesco, Mike, Viahealth, Rochester, NY. Tel: (585) 922-4000, (585) 922-3677, FAX: (585) 922-3929, Web Site: www.viahealth.org (16)

Tedford, Thomas W., Day-Timer, East Texas, PA. Tel: (610) 398-1151, (800) 457-5702, (800) 225-5005, FAX: (800) 452-7398, E-Mail: connie@lomottastrategic.com, Web Site: www.daytimer.com (13)

Ted's Promotions Inc, Baldwin, GA. Tel: (770) 972-8081, FAX: (770) 573-3141, E-Mail: ted@tedspromotions.com, Web Site: www.tedspromotions.com (33)

Teets, Charles E., Wise, Alpharetta, GA. Tel: (770) 442-1060, (888) 815-9473, FAX: (770) 751-3599 (27)

Tehrani, Nadji, Technology Marketing Corp/TMC, Norwalk, CT. Tel: (203) 852-6800, (800) 243-6002, FAX: (203) 953-2845, E-Mail: tmc@tmcnet.com, Web Site: www.tmcnet.com (29)

Tehrani, Nadji, TMC Internet Telephony & Expo, Norwalk, CT. Tel: (203) 852-6800, (800) 243-6002, FAX: (203) 866-3326, E-Mail: tmc@tmcnet.com, Web Site: www.tmcnet.com (42)

Tehrani, Rich, TMC Internet Telephony & Expo, Norwalk, CT. Tel: (203) 852-6800, (800) 243-6002, FAX: (203) 866-3326, E-Mail: tmc@tmcnet.com, Web Site: www.tmcnet.com (42)

Teicher, Ben, Healthy Directions LLC, Bethesda, MD. Tel: (301) 340-2100, FAX: (301) 309-8516, Web Site: www.healthydirections.com (34)

Teichgraeber, Gretchen G., Leadership Directories Inc, New York, NY. Tel: (212) 627-4140, FAX: (212) 645-0931, E-Mail: info@leadershipdirectories.com, Web Site: www.leadershipdirectories.com (17)

Teiken, Brent, Sundog, Fargo, ND. Tel: (701) 235-5525, (888) 9-SUNDOG, FAX: (701) 235-8941, E-Mail: info@sundoginteractive.com, Web Site: www.sundoginteractive.com (35)

Teikoku Databank America Inc, New York, NY. Tel: (212) 421-9805, FAX: (212) 421-9806, E-Mail: info@teikoku.com, Web Site: www.teikoku.com (24)

Teissler, Scott, Turner Broadcasting System Inc, Atlanta, GA. Tel: (404) 827-1700, Web Site: www.turner.com (32)

Teitler, David, Guideposts, Danbury, CT. Tel: (800) 932-2154, Web Site: www.guideposts.org (1)

Tektronix Inc, Beaverton, OR. Tel: (503) 627-7111, (800) 833-9200, FAX: (503) 627-3247, Web Site: www.tektronix.com (16)

TelAmerica Media Inc, Philadelphia, PA. Tel: (215) 568-7066, FAX: (215) 564-5388, Web Site: www.telamericamedia.com (31)

Telcordia Technologies, Piscataway, NJ. Tel: (732) 699-2000, FAX: (973) 829-2458, Web Site: www.telcordia.com (16)

Tele Business USA, Northbrook, IL. Tel: (847) 480-1560, FAX: (847) 897-4120, Web Site: www.tbiz.com (29)

Tele Resources Inc, Duluth, MN. Tel: (888) 698-8787 X114, FAX: (218) 724-2466, E-Mail: mark.swanson@teleresources.net, Web Site: www.teleresources.net (29)

Telebrands Corp, Fairfield, NJ. Tel: (973) 247-8777, Web Site: www.telebrands.com (21)

Telecom Inc, Oakland, CA. Tel: (510) 873-8283, (800) 243-3101, FAX: (510) 873-8293, Web Site: www.telecominc.com (29)

Telecommunications Reports International Inc, Washington, DC. Tel: (202) 312-6060, (800) 234-1660, FAX: (202) 312-6111, E-Mail: bhammond@tr.com, Web Site: www.tr.com (17)

The Teleconference Network, Nanuet, NY. Tel: (845) 624-0633, FAX: (845) 623-9394, E-Mail: nospam@mnav.com, Web Site: www.market-navigation.com (30)

Telect Inc, Liberty Lake, WA. Tel: (509) 926-6000, FAX: (509) 926-8915, E-Mail: getinfo@telect.com, Web Site: www.telect.com (16)

TeleDevelopment Services Inc, Richfield, OH. Tel: (330) 659-4441, FAX: (330) 659-4442, E-Mail: jkaplan@teledevelopment.com, Web Site: www.teledevelopment.com (20)

TeleDirect International Inc, Scottsdale, AZ. Tel: (480) 585-6464, (800) 531-6440, FAX: (480) 585-3373, Web Site: www.tdirect.com (29)

Teleflora, Los Angeles, CA. Tel: (310) 966-3586, Web Site: www.teleflora.com (16)

Telefonix Inc, Waukegan, IL. Tel: (847) 244-4500, Web Site: www.telefonixinc.com (16)

TeleManagement Search, Port Washington, NY. Tel: (516) 767-6990, FAX: (516) 767-6980, E-Mail: connie@tmrecruiters.com, Web Site: www.tmrecruiters.com (20)

Telemedia Communications US, North York, ON Canada. Tel: (416) 733-7600, (800) 461-3773 U.S., (888) 290-1466 Can., FAX: (416) 733-3563, E-Mail: info@transcontinental.ca, Web Site: www.transcontinental.com (17)

Telenational Marketing, Omaha, NE. Tel: (800) 333-6106 X132, FAX: (402) 391-2044, Web Site: www.telenational.com (29)

Teleperformance Canada, Toronto, ON Canada. Tel: (416) 922-8240, E-Mail: canada@teleperformance.com, Web Site: www.teleperformance.com (35)

Teleperformance Interactive, Miami Beach, FL. Tel: (786) 437-3300, FAX: (786) 276-8452, Web Site: www.teleperformance.com (29)

Telephone Look-Up Service Co, Yardley, PA. Tel: (215) 321-0706, (800) 366-0706, FAX: (215) 321-3229, E-Mail: computer@telephonelookup.com, Web Site: www.telephonelookup.com (22)

Telephone Selling Report, Scottsdale, AZ. Tel: (402) 895-9399, FAX: (402) 896-3353, E-Mail: arts@businessbyphone.com, Web Site: www.businessbyphone.com (43)

Telephony, Chicago, IL. Tel: (312) 595-1080, (800) 458-0479, FAX: (312) 595-0295, Web Site: www.internettelephony.com (17)

TeleRep, Glen Burnie, MD. Tel: (800) 638-2000, FAX: (410) 761-3357, Web Site: www.telerep.com (29)

Telerx, Horsham, PA. Tel: (800) 2TELERX, Web Site: www.telerx.com (29)

TeleServices Direct, Indianapolis, IN. Tel: (888) 646-6626, Web Site: www.teleservicesdirect.com (29)

Telesystems Marketing Inc, Houston, TX. Tel: (713) 784-3439, (800) 622-0190, FAX: (713) 780-5974, E-Mail: kimberly@nwpros.com, Web Site: www.telesystemsmarketing.com (29)

TeleTech, Englewood, CO. Tel: (303) 397-8100, (800) TELETECH, FAX: (303) 397-8199, E-Mail: solutions@TeleTech.com, Web Site: www.teletech.com (22)

Teletrack Inc, Norcross, GA. Tel: (770) 449-8809 (29)

Tellinghuisen, Brian, Data-Dynamix Inc, Denver, CO. Tel: (720) 855-9282, (888) 314-0078, FAX: (720) 855-9099, E-Mail: sales@data-dynamix.com, Web Site: www.data-dynamix.com (23)

Telpro Inc, Grand Forks, ND. Tel: (701) 775-0551, FAX: (701) 775-0629 (9)

Temkin & Temkin, Highland Park, IL. Tel: (847) 831-0237, FAX: (847) 851-0409, E-Mail: t2@temkin.com, Web Site: temkin.com (35)

Temkin, Steve, Temkin & Temkin, Highland Park, IL. Tel: (847) 831-0237, FAX: (847) 851-0409, E-Mail: t2@temkin.com, Web Site: temkin.com (35)

Tempco Electric Heater Corp, Wood Dale, IL. Tel: (630) 350-2252, (800) 323-6859, FAX: (630) 350-0232, E-Mail: dpadlo@tempco.com, Web Site: www.tempco.com (9)

Temple University, Philadelphia, PA. Tel: (215) 204-7282, FAX: (215) 204-4554, Web Site: www.sbm.temple.edu (41)

Templeton, Mark B., Citrix Systems, Inc, Fort Lauderdale, FL. Tel: (954) 267-3000, FAX: (954) 267-3101, Web Site: www.citrix.com (22)

Templeton, Sheila, CMS Inc, Winston Salem, NC. Tel: (336) 631-2500, FAX: (336) 631-2903, Web Site: www.promotionslogistics.com (14)

TempoGraphics Inc, Carol Stream, IL. Tel: (630) 462-8200, FAX: (630) 462-0350, E-Mail: info@tempographics.com (27)

Ten Speed Press, Emeryville, CA. Tel: (510) 559-1600, (800) 841-BOOK, FAX: (510) 559-1629, E-Mail: order@tenspeed.com, Web Site: www.tenspeed.com (17)

Tenet Partners, New York, NY. Tel: (212) 329-3030, FAX: (212) 329-3031, Web Site: tenetpartners.com (35)

TENNANT Co, Minneapolis, MN. Tel: (763) 540-1200, (800) 553-8033, FAX: (763) 513-2142, E-Mail: info@tennantco.com, Web Site: www.tennantco.com (34)

Tennant, J. Keith, Intermap Technologies, Englewood, CO. Tel: (303) 708-0955, FAX: (303) 708-0952, E-Mail: info@intermap.com, Web Site: www.intermap.com (32)

Tennant, William, Tillamook County Creamery Association, Tillamook, OR. Tel: (503) 842-4481, Web Site: www.tillamook.com (4)

Tennessee Valley Authority, Knoxville, TN. Tel: (865) 632-2101, Web Site: www.tva.gov (16)

Tennille, Mary Craig, Excalibur Enterprises Inc, Winston Salem, NC. Tel: (336) 744-5000, (800) 441-4193, FAX: (336) 767-8257, E-Mail: info@excaliburmail.com, Web Site: www.excaliburmail.com (28)

Tensar International Corporation, Alpharetta, GA. Tel: (404) 250-1290, Web Site: www.tensarcorp.com (16)

Tension Corp, Kansas City, MO. Tel: (816) 471-3800, FAX: (816) 283-1498, E-Mail: info@tensioncorp.com, Web Site: www.tension.com (26)

Teplitz, Paul, Research Boston Corp, Lafayette, CA. Tel: (978) 225-8030, FAX: (267) 295-8704, Web Site: www.researchboston.com (20)

Teraco Inc, Midland, TX. Tel: (888) 837-2261, Web Site: www.teraco.com (27)

Teradata Corp, Miamisburg, OH. Tel: (937) 242-4800, Web Site: www.teradata.com (22)

Teramoto, Masao, Fujitsu Transaction Solutions Inc, Richardson, TX. Tel: (972) 963-2300, (800) 340-4425, Web Site: www.fujitsu.com (16)

Teran, Vivian, Alliance Direct Marketing Solutions LLC, Jersey City, NJ. Tel: (201) 863-1360, (888) 455-2367, FAX: (201) 863-3910, E-Mail: vteran@alliancedirectleads.com, Web Site: www.alliancedirectleads.com (20)

Tercek, Mark, The Nature Conservancy, Arlington, VA. Tel: (703) 841-5300, (800) 628-6860, FAX: (703) 841-1283, Web Site: www.nature.org (1)

Teres Consulting Inc, Framingham, MA. Tel: (508) 872-4922, FAX: (253) 595-6748, E-Mail: info@teresconsulting.com, Web Site: www.teresconsulting.com (20)

Teres, Wayne, Teres Consulting Inc, Framingham, MA. Tel: (508) 872-4922, FAX: (253) 595-6748, E-Mail: info@teresconsulting.com, Web Site: www.teresconsulting.com (20)

Terlizzi, Michael, Capezio Ballet Makers Inc, Totowa, NJ. Tel: (973) 595-9000, (800) 533-1887, FAX: (800) 595-9120, E-Mail: info@capezio.com, Web Site: www.capezio.com (16)

Terminix International, The Trugreen Companies, Memphis, TN. Tel: (901) 766-1105, Web Site: www.trugreenchemlawn.com (16)

Terner, Moni, Bijoux Terner, Miami, FL. Tel: (305) 500-7500, (800) 262-3614, FAX: (305) 262-9286, E-Mail: customerservice@bijouxterner.com, Web Site: www.bijouxterner.com (16)

Terner, Rosa, Bijoux Terner, Miami, FL. Tel: (305) 500-7500, (800) 262-3614, FAX: (305) 262-9286, E-Mail: customerservice@bijouxterner.com, Web Site: www.bijouxterner.com (16)

Ternes, Don, Thetford Corp, Ann Arbor, MI. Tel: (734) 769-6000, (800) 543-1219, FAX: (734) 769-2023, Web Site: www.thetford.com (16)

Terp, Jeff, Ivy Tech Community College of Indiana, Indianapolis, IN. Tel: (317) 921-4800, (888) IVY-LINE, FAX: (317) 921-4753, Web Site: www.ivytech.edu (13)

Terranova, Sandy, Institutional Real Estate Inc, San Ramon, CA. Tel: (925) 244-0500, FAX: (925) 244-0520, Web Site: www.irei.com (17)

Territorial Newspapers, Tucson, AZ. Tel: (520) 294-1200, FAX: (520) 294-4040, Web Site: www.azbiz.com (17)

Terrell, Bruce, Christian Herald Association, New York, NY. Tel: (212) 684-2800, (800) BOWERY-1, FAX: (212) 684-3740, E-Mail: info@chaonline.org, Web Site: www.bowery.org (1)

Terry, Maarten, ConvergeDirect, New York, NY. Tel: (212) 213-0111, E-Mail: info@convergedirect.com, Web Site: www.convergedirect.com (35)

Terry, Paul, Convertible Service, San Gabriel, CA. Tel: (626) 285-2255, (800) 333-1140, FAX: (626) 285-9004, Web Site: www.convertibleparts.com (16)

Terry, Scott, Rapid Progress Marketing & Modeling LLC, Saint Petersburg, FL. Tel: (727) 528-8578, Web Site: www.rpmsquared.com (22)

Terteryan, Marina, Alfred Publishing Co Inc, Van Nuys, CA. Tel: (818) 891-5999, (800) 292-6122, FAX: (818) 893-5560, E-Mail: sales@alfred.com, Web Site: www.alfred.com (17)

Terumo Cardiovascular Systems Corp, Ann Arbor, MI. Tel: (734) 663-4145, (800) 521-2818, Web Site: www.terumo-cvs.com (5)

Terwilleger, Bret, Oden, Memphis, TN. Tel: (901) 578-8055, (800) 371-6233, FAX: (901) 578-1911, Web Site: www.oden.com (35)

Terzariol, Giulio, Allianz Life Insurance Co of North America, Minneapolis, MN. Tel: (763) 765-6500, (800) 950-5872, Web Site: www.allianzlife.com (15)

Tesar Reynes Inc, Chicago, IL. Tel: (312) 726-1900, E-Mail: tony@tesar-reynes.com, Web Site: www.tesar-reynes.com (20)

Teschner, Jr. Charles L., The McGraw-Hill Financial, New York, NY. Tel: (212) 904-2000, Web Site: www.mhfi.com (17)

Tesija, Kathryn, Target Corp, Minneapolis, MN. Tel: (612) 304-6073, Web Site: www.target.com (16)

Tessco Inc, Hunt Valley, MD. Tel: (410) 229-1000, (800) 508-5444, FAX: (410) 527-0005, E-Mail: webhelp@tessco.com, Web Site: www.tessco.com (16)

Tessier, Christine, Omega List Co, McLean, VA. Tel: (703) 821-1890, FAX: (703) 821-8794, E-Mail: listmanager@omegalist.com, Web Site: omegalist.com (23)

Tessier, Patrick, Northwest Laboratories, Seattle, WA. Tel: (206) 763-6252, FAX: (206) 763-3949, Web Site: www.nwlabs.net (9)

The Testimonial Wrangler, La Jolla, CA. Tel: (858) 735-7646, FAX: (858) 777-5418 (35)

Tetley USA Inc, Montvale, NJ. Tel: (201) 571-0300, Web Site: www.tetleyusa.com (16)

Tetstone, Joseph, NCP Solutions, Birmingham, AL. Tel: (250) 849-5200, Web Site: www.ncprint.com (21)

Teutsch, Stanley, Medibadge Inc, Omaha, NE. Tel: (402) 571-1800, (800) 228-0040, FAX: (800) 546-1072, E-Mail: stan@medibadge.com, Web Site: www.medibadge.com (5)

Teutsch, Teri A., Medibadge Inc, Omaha, NE. Tel: (402) 571-1800, (800) 228-0040, FAX: (800) 546-1072, E-Mail: stan@medibadge.com, Web Site: www.medibadge.com (5)

Teva Pharmaceuticals USA, North Wales, PA. Tel: (215) 591-3000, (888) 838-2872, FAX: (215) 591-8600, Web Site: www.tevausa.com (7)

Tewes, Patty, Agilis Co, Albert Lea, MN. Tel: (507) 377-5028 (14)

Tewmey, Jim, VF Imagewear, Greensboro, NC. Tel: (336) 424-6000, (800) 733-5271, Web Site: www.vfimagewear.com (2)

Texada Capital Corp, Grasonville, MD. Tel: (866) 595-6224, Web Site: www.texada.com (14)

Texas Children's Hospital, Houston, TX. Tel: (832) 824-1000, Web Site: www.texaschildrenshospital.org (1)

Texas Farm Bureau Insurance Cos, Waco, TX. Tel: (254) 751-2688, Web Site: www.txfb-ins.com (15)

Texas Graphic Resource, Dallas, TX. Tel: (214) 630-2800, FAX: (214) 630-0713 (27)

Texas Industries Inc, Dallas, TX. Tel: (972) 647-6700, FAX: (972) 647-3878, Web Site: www.txi.com (16)

Texas Monthly, Austin, TX. Tel: (512) 320-6900, (800) 759-2000, FAX: (512) 476-9007, E-Mail: info@texasmonthly.com, Web Site: www.texasmonthly.com (17)

Texas Parks & Wildlife Dept, Austin, TX. Tel: (512) 389-4800, (800) 792-1112, FAX: (512) 389-8029, Web Site: www.tpwd.state.tx.us (1)

Texas Refinery Corp, Fort Worth, TX. Tel: (817) 332-1161, FAX: (817) 336-8441, E-Mail: jhopkins@texasrefinery.com, Web Site: www.texasrefinery.com (9)

Texwipe Co, Kernersville, NC. Tel: (201) 684-1800, (800) TEXWIPE, FAX: (201) 684-1801, E-Mail: info@texwipe.com, Web Site: www.texwipe.com (16)

Thamodaran, Dhamu, Smithfield Foods, Smithfield, VA. Tel: (800) 276-6158, Web Site: www.smithfieldfoods.com (16)

Thane International Inc, El Segundo, CA. Tel: (310) 531-1956, FAX: (310) 531-1957, E-Mail: info@thaneinc.com, Web Site: www.thaneinc.com (35)

THARLER DIRECTs, Wayland, MA. Tel: (508) 358-3554, FAX: (508) 358-5623, E-Mail: steve@tharlerdirects.com, Web Site: www.tharlerdirects.com (35)

Tharler, Steven R., THARLER DIRECTs, Wayland, MA. Tel: (508) 358-3554, FAX: (508) 358-5623, E-Mail: steve@tharlerdirects.com, Web Site: www.tharlerdirects.com (35)

Tharp, Michele, Paragon Media Strategies, Denver, CO. Tel: (303) 922-5600, FAX: (303) 922-1589, E-Mail: info@paragonmediastrategies.com, Web Site: www.paragonmediastrategies.com (30)

Thau, Paul, PlusMedia LLC, Danbury, CT. Tel: (203) 748-6500, FAX: (203) 748-6600, E-Mail: contact@plusme.com, Web Site: www.plusme.com (35)

Theatre Development Fund Inc, New York, NY. Tel: (212) 912-9770, E-Mail: info@tdf.org, Web Site: www.tdf.org (1)

Thebault, Brian, LP Thebault Co, Parsippany, NJ. Tel: (973) 884-1300, FAX: (973) 952-8282, E-Mail: info@earthcolor.com, Web Site: www.earthcolor.com (27)

TheIdeaClub.com & Dumas Martin Consulting, Pomona, CA. Tel: (909) 620-4772, FAX: (909) 629-4739, Web Site: www.theideaclub.com (16)

Theiler, Thomas, Lancer Insurance Co, Long Beach, NY. Tel: (516) 431-4441, (800) 782-8902, FAX: (516) 889-5111, E-Mail: roneill@lancer-ins.com, Web Site: www.lancer-ins.com (15)

Theis, Peter F., Conversational Voice Technologies Corp, Fox Lake, IL. Tel: (847) 265-4901, (800) 994-4400, FAX: (847) 265-4915, E-Mail: sales@conservit.com, Web Site: www.conservit.com (29)

Theisen, Henry J., Bemis Co Inc, Neenah, WI. Tel: (920) 727-4100, E-Mail: contact@beemis.com, Web Site: www.bemis.com (34)

TheLaw.net Corp, San Diego, CA. Tel: (858) 554-0583, Web Site: www.thelaw.net (22)

Thelen, Kris, Eclipse Direct Marketing, Mineola, NY. Tel: (212) 931-8344, FAX: (516) 493-9122, E-Mail: jkaiser@eclipsedm.com, Web Site: www.eclipsedm.com (23)

Theodore, Phil, John Harland Co, Decatur, GA. Tel: (770) 981-5580, (800) 723-3690, FAX: (770) 593-5367, E-Mail: jhhwebmaster@harland.net, Web Site: www.harland.net (16)

Theos, Charles W., Micron Corp, Norwood, MA. Tel: (781) 769-5771, (800) 456-0734, FAX: (781) 762-3531, E-Mail: info@microncorp.com, Web Site: www.microncorp.com (16)

Theos, John, Micron Corp, Norwood, MA. Tel: (781) 769-5771, (800) 456-0734, FAX: (781) 762-3531, E-Mail: info@microncorp.com, Web Site: www.microncorp.com (16)

Theos, William, Micron Corp, Norwood, MA. Tel: (781) 769-5771, (800) 456-0734, FAX: (781) 762-3531, E-Mail: info@microncorp.com, Web Site: www.microncorp.com (16)

ThePort Network, Atlanta, GA. Tel: (703) 431-2208 (32)

Theriot, Paul, Alesco Data Group LLC, Fort Myers, FL. Tel: (239) 275-5006, (800) 701-6531, FAX: (239) 275-7737, E-Mail: lists@alescodata.com, Web Site: www.alescodata.com (23)

Thermal Product Solutions, White Deer, PA. Tel: (570) 538-7200, (800) 586-2473 (16)

Thermo Fisher Scientific Inc, Waltham, MA. Tel: (781) 622-1000, (800) 678-5599, FAX: (781) 622-1207, Web Site: www.thermofisher.com (9)

Thermo Pro, Duluth, GA. Tel: (678) 475-1647, (800) 523-5542, FAX: (678) 475-1747, Web Site: www.thermopro.com (16)

Theroux, David J., LibertyTree Press, Oakland, CA. Tel: (510) 632-1366, (800) 927-8733, FAX: (510) 568-6040, E-Mail: info@liberty-tree.com, Web Site: www.independent.org (5)

Thetford Corp, Ann Arbor, MI. Tel: (734) 769-6000, (800) 543-1219, FAX: (734) 769-2023, Web Site: www.thetford.com (16)

Thibadeau, Patrick, AW Direct Inc, Madison, WI. Tel: (860) 828-7800, (800) 243-3194, FAX: (800) 828-9678, E-Mail: contactus@awdirect.com, Web Site: www.awdirect.com (12)

Thibadeau, Richard, AW Direct Inc, Madison, WI. Tel: (860) 828-7800, (800) 243-3194, FAX: (800) 828-9678, E-Mail: contactus@awdirect.com, Web Site: www.awdirect.com (12)

Thibault, David, The Marlin Company, Wallingford, CT. Tel: (877) 890-9116, Web Site: www.themarlincompany.com (35)

Thibeau, Matthew, Standard Publishing, Cincinnati, OH. Tel: (513) 931-4050, (800) 543-1301, FAX: (877) 867-5751, Web Site: www.standardpub.com (17)

Thiel, Fred, Local Corp, Irvine, CA. Tel: (877) 784-0805, FAX: (949) 784-0880, Web Site: www.local.com (32)

Thieme Medical Publishers Inc, New York, NY. Tel: (212) 760-0888, (800) 782-3488, FAX: (212) 947-1112, E-Mail: info@thieme.com, Web Site: www.thieme.com (17)

Thieme, Alan, Amigo Mobility International Inc, Bridgeport, MI. Tel: (989) 777-0910, (800) 692-6446, FAX: (989) 777-8184, E-Mail: info@myamigo.com, Web Site: www.myamigo.com (16)

Thieme, Beth, Amigo Mobility International Inc, Bridgeport, MI. Tel: (989) 777-0910, (800) 692-6446, FAX: (989) 777-8184, E-Mail: info@myamigo.com, Web Site: www.myamigo.com (16)

Things Deco, New York, NY. Tel: (212) 362-8961, E-Mail: thingsdeco@hotmail.com, Web Site: www.thingsdeco.com (6)

Things Remembered, Highland Heights, OH. Tel: (440) 473-2000, (866) 902-4438, FAX: (440) 473-2018, E-Mail: customerservice@thingsremembered.com, Web Site: www.thingsremembered.com (6)

Think Ink, Bothell, WA. Tel: (425) 778-1935, (800) 778-1935, E-Mail: jean.lewis1@comcast.net, Web Site: www.thinkink.net (10)

Think Shapes Mail, Tampa, FL. Tel: (813) 885-2225, (800) 889-4406, Web Site: www.jigsawprinting.com (27)

Thinkalytics, Millburn, NJ. Tel: (973) 671-1590, Web Site: www.thinkalytics.com (20)

ThinkDirect Marketing Group, Largo, FL. Tel: (727) 369-2700, E-Mail: info@tdmg.com, Web Site: www.tdmg.com (28)

Thirteen/WNET, New York, NY. Tel: (212) 560-1313, FAX: (212) 560-1314, E-Mail: programming@thirteen.org, Web Site: www.thirteen.org (1)

Thiry, Robert, Array Marketing Group Inc, Toronto, ON Canada. Tel: (416) 299-4865, FAX: (416) 292-9759, E-Mail: inquiry@arraymarketing.com, Web Site: arraymarketing.com (35)

Thissen, Richard, National Active & Retired Federal Employees Association, Alexandria, VA. Tel: (703) 838-7760, (800) 456-8410, FAX: (703) 838-7785, Web Site: www.narfe.org (1)

Thoma Cressey Bravo, Chicago, IL. Tel: (312) 777-4444, FAX: (312) 777-4445, Web Site: www.tcb.com (14)

Thoma, Carl, Thoma Cressey Bravo, Chicago, IL. Tel: (312) 777-4444, FAX: (312) 777-4445, Web Site: www.tcb.com (14)

Thomas Computer Corp, Orlando, FL. Tel: (407) 855-2020, (800) 621-3906, FAX: (407) 426-2805, E-Mail: hildap@thomascompute.com, Web Site: www.thomascomputer.com (16)

Thomas Klise/Crimson Multimedia, Mystic, CT. Tel: (800) 937-0092, FAX: (860) 536-5141, E-Mail: info@crimsoninc.com, Web Site: www.crimsoninc.com (16)

Thomas Nelson, Nashville, TN. Tel: (615) 889-9000, (800) 251-4000, FAX: (615) 889-5940, Web Site: www.thomasnelson.com (17)

Thomas Printworks, Houston, TX. Tel: (832) 201-2000, (800) 656-8883, FAX: (832) 201-2001, E-Mail: info@seebridgemedia.com, Web Site: www.thomasprintworks.com (21)

Thomas Scientific, Swedesboro, NJ. Tel: (856) 467-2000, (800) 345-2100, FAX: (856) 467-3087, E-Mail: value@thomassci.com, Web Site: www.thomassci.com (9)

Stephen Thomas, Toronto, ON Canada. Tel: (416) 690-8801, FAX: (416) 690-7256, E-Mail: mail@stephenthomas.ca, Web Site: www.stephenthomas.ca (1)

Thomas, Albert, Vaxserve, Moosic, PA. Tel: (800) 752-9338, FAX: (800) 553-9908, Web Site: www.vaxserve.com (7)

Thomas, Amy, Our Sunday Visitor Publishing, Huntington, IN. Tel: (260) 356-8400, (800) 348-2440, FAX: (260) 356-8472, E-Mail: athomas@osv.com, Web Site: www.osv.com (17)

Thomas, Arleen R., American Institute of CPAs, New York, NY. Tel: (212) 596-6200, (888) 777-7077, FAX: (212) 596-6213, Web Site: www.aicpa.org (1)

Thomas, Brad, Liberty Orchards Co Inc, Cashmere, WA. Tel: (509) 782-2191, (800) 888-5696, FAX: (509) 782-1487, E-Mail: service@libertyorchards.com, Web Site: www.libertyorchards.com (16)

Thomas, Brad, The Guardian Life Insurance Co, New York, NY. Tel: (212) 598-8000, Web Site: www.guardianlife.com (15)

Thomas, Bret, Peter Li Education Group, Dayton, OH. Tel: (937) 293-1415, (800) 523-4625, FAX: (937) 293-1310, Web Site: www.peterli.com (17)

Thomas, Brian, Western Psychological Services, Torrance, CA. Tel: (310) 478-2061, (800) 648-8857, FAX: (310)) 478-7838, E-Mail: marketing@wpspublish.com, Web Site: www.wpspublish.com (16)

Thomas, Caroline, Resource Publications Inc, San Jose, CA. Tel: (408) 286-8505, (888) 273-7782, FAX: (408) 287-8748, E-Mail: info@rpinet.com, Web Site: www.rpinet.com (17)

Thomas, Cindy, Bank of Hawaii, Honolulu, HI. Tel: (808) 537-8398, FAX: (808) 536-9433, Web Site: www.boh.com (14)

Thomas, Darryl K., Nautilus Inc, Vancouver, WA. Tel: (360) 859-2900, (800) 675-0171, FAX: (360) 694-2755, Web Site: www.nautilus.com (11)

Thomas, Daryl, Herr Foods Inc, Nottingham, PA. Tel: (610) 932-9330, (800) 344-3777, FAX: (610) 932-2137, E-Mail: info@herrs.com, Web Site: www.herrs.com (16)

Thomas, Dave, MarketForce Corp, Havertown, PA. Tel: (610) 356-5220, FAX: (610) 356-5110, E-Mail: davethomas@marketforcecorp.com, Web Site: www.marketforcecorp.com (23)

Thomas, Dave, ThomasARTS, Farmington, UT. Tel: (801) 451-5365, E-Mail: welcome@thomasarts.com, Web Site: thomasarts.com (35)

Thomas, David A., Georgetown University McDonough School of Business, Washington, DC. Tel: (202) 687-3883, Web Site: www.msb.edu (1)

Thomas, Elbert L., First Tennessee Bank, Memphis, TN. Tel: (901) 523-4883, FAX: (901) 523-4030, Web Site: www.firsttennessee.com (14)

Thomas, James, ASTM International, West Conshohocken, PA. Tel: (610) 832-9500, FAX: (610) 832-9555, E-Mail: service@astm.org, Web Site: www.astm.org (1)

Thomas, Jay, The Marek Group, Waukesha, WI. Tel: (262) 549-8900, FAX: (262) 49-8910, E-Mail: info@marekgroup.com, Web Site: www.marekgroup.com (21)

Thomas, Jerry W., Decision Analyst Inc, Arlington, TX. Tel: (817) 640-6166, (800) 262-5974, FAX: (817) 640-6567, E-Mail: jthomas@decisionanalyst.com, Web Site: www.decisionanalyst.com (30)

Thomas, John, Tennessee Valley Authority, Knoxville, TN. Tel: (865) 632-2101, Web Site: www.tva.gov (16)

Thomas, John, Wildseed Farms, Fredericksburg, TX. Tel: (800) 848-0078, FAX: (830) 990-8090, E-Mail: orders1@wildseedfarms.com, Web Site: www.wildseedfarms.com (8)

Thomas, Jonathan Stuart, American Century Investments, Kansas City, MO. Tel: (816) 531-5575, (800) 345-2021, FAX: (816) 340-4964, Web Site: www.americancentury.com (14)

Thomas, Larry, Equitable Life & Casualty Insurance Co, Salt Lake City, UT. Tel: (801) 579-3400, FAX: (801) 579-3789, Web Site: www.equilife.com (15)

Thomas, Linda, PennWell Publishing, Tulsa, OK. Tel: (918) 835-3161, (800) 331-4463, E-Mail: headquarters@pennwell.com, Web Site: www.pennwell.com (17)

Thomas, Lisa, Bacompt Systems Inc, Carmel, IN. Tel: (317) 574-7474, (800) 533-7109, FAX: (317) 574-7475, E-Mail: customer.service@bacompt.com, Web Site: www.bacompt.com (21)

Thomas, Lisa, Chase Media Group, Yorktown Heights, NY. Tel: (914) 962-3871, FAX: (914) 962-2040, Web Site: www.chasemultimedia.com (27)

Thomas, Matthew, Manning Materials, Birdsboro, PA. Tel: (610) 385-6797, (800) 445-1719, FAX: (610) 385-7524, E-Mail: mmsupport@manningmaterials.com, Web Site: www.manningmaterials.com (16)

Thomas, Michelle, Zappos.com, Las Vegas, NV. Tel: (800) 927-7671, Web Site: www.zappos.com (2)

Thomas, Noreen, Relevate Group Inc, Springfield, VA. Tel: (703) 658-8300, (800) 523-7346, FAX: (703) 658-8301, E-Mail: sales@relevategroup.com, Web Site: www.relevategroup.com (22)

Thomas, Norma, Sullivan-Victory Groves, Rockledge, FL. Tel: (800) 672-6431, (866) 676-4311, E-Mail: sales@sullivancitrus.com, Web Site: www.sullivancitrus.com (4)

Thomas, Tony, Windstream Communications Inc, Little Rock, AR. Tel: (501) 748-7000, Web Site: www.windstream.com (32)

ThomasARTS, Farmington, UT. Tel: (801) 451-5365, E-Mail: welcome@thomasarts.com, Web Site: thomasarts.com (35)

ThomasNet RPM, New York, NY. Tel: (844) 851-8715, Web Site: rpm.thomasnet.com (24)

Thompsen, Ken, ER Carpenter, Taylor, TX. Tel: (512) 365-5833, (800) 234-9105, FAX: (512) 352-6025, Web Site: www.carpenter.com (16)

Thompson Cigar Co, Tampa, FL. Tel: (813) 884-6344, (800) 216-7107, FAX: (813) 882-4605, Web Site: www.thompsoncigar.com (6)

David J Thompson Mailing Corp, Bloomsburg, PA. Tel: (570) 759-6690, FAX: (570) 759-7160, E-Mail: sales@thompsonmailing.com, Web Site: www.thompsonmailing.com (28)

Norm Thompson Outfitters Inc, Hillsboro, OR. Tel: (800) 547-1160, (877) 718-7899, FAX: (503) 614-4599, Web Site: www.normthompson.com (2)

Thompson Publishing Group Inc, Washington, DC. Tel: (202) 872-4000, (800) 677-3789, FAX: (800) 999-5661, E-Mail: service@thompson.com, Web Site: www.thompson.com (17)

Thompson, Barbara, International Crystal Manufacturing Co, Oklahoma City, OK. Tel: (405) 236-3741, (800) 252-6780, FAX: (405) 235-1904, E-Mail: info@icmfg.com, Web Site: www.icmfg.com (16)

Thompson, Bradley L., Inland Press, Detroit, MI. Tel: (313) 961-6000, FAX: (313) 961-7817, Web Site: www.inlandpress.com (27)

Thompson, Cale, Oakley Inc, Foothill Ranch, CA. Tel: (800) 403-7449, Web Site: www.oakley.com (2)

Thompson, Carol, Christianity Today Inc, Carol Stream, IL. Tel: (630) 260-6200, FAX: (630) 260-0114, Web Site: www.christianitytoday.com (17)

Thompson, David J, Alliance Strategies Group Inc, Boca Raton, FL. Tel: (561) 499-3201, E-Mail: info@asgroupinc.com, Web Site: www.asgroupinc.com (23)

Thompson, David J., David J Thompson Mailing Corp, Bloomsburg, PA. Tel: (570) 759-6690, FAX: (570) 759-7160, E-Mail: sales@thompsonmailing.com, Web Site: www.thompsonmailing.com (28)

Thompson, Everton, Omega Direct Response Inc, Richmond Hill, ON Canada. Tel: (905) 482-2340, FAX: (905) 482-9721, E-Mail: odrsales@omegadirect.com, Web Site: www.omegadirect.com (29)

Thompson, Hubert O, Brothers & Thompson PC, Chicago, IL. Tel: (312) 372-2909, FAX: (312) 704-6693, E-Mail: hthompson@brothersthompson.net, Web Site: www.brothersthompson.net (20)

Thompson, Jim, Ipsos America Inc, New York, NY. Tel: (212) 265-3200, FAX: (212) 265-3790, E-Mail: info@ipsos-asi.com, Web Site: www.ipsos-asi.com (30)

Thompson, Joan E., David J Thompson Mailing Corp, Bloomsburg, PA. Tel: (570) 759-6690, FAX: (570) 759-7160, E-Mail: sales@thompsonmailing.com, Web Site: www.thompsonmailing.com (28)

Thompson, John, Solar Communications, Naperville, IL. Tel: (630) 983-1400, (800) 890-6906, FAX: (630) 983-6125, Web Site: www.solarcommunications.com (31)

Thompson, Larry, ColorTree of Virginia Inc, Richmond, VA. Tel: (804) 358-4245, FAX: (804) 358-0488, Web Site: www.colortree.com (26)

Thompson, Laura, Goodyear Tire & Rubber Co, Akron, OH. Tel: (330) 796-2121, (800) 321-2136, FAX: (330) 796-2222, Web Site: www.goodyear.com (16)

Thompson, Lee, The Wexner Companies Inc, Memphis, TN. Tel: (901) 763-3925, (800) 890-5470, FAX: (901) 763-3736, E-Mail: info@JosephStores.com, Web Site: www.josephstores.com (2)

Thompson, Linda, JR Cigar, Burlington, NC. Tel: (800) 572-4427, FAX: (800) 457-3299, E-Mail: manager@jrburlington.com, Web Site: www.jrcigars.com (5)

Thompson, Mace, Pachmayr Ltd, Middletown, CT. Tel: (800) 225-9626, FAX: (860) 632-1699, Web Site: www.lymanproducts.com (11)

Thompson, Mark, Quinnipiac College, Hamden, CT. Tel: (203) 582-8200, (203) 582-8600, (800) 462-1944, FAX: (203) 281-8664, Web Site: www.quinnipiac.edu (41)

Thompson, Mark, The New York Times Co, New York, NY. Tel: (212) 556-1234, Web Site: www.nytimes.com (17)

Thompson, Martha, Ventyx, Atlanta, GA. Tel: (770) 952-8444, (800) 868-0497, FAX: (770) 955-2977, E-Mail: support@ventyx.com, Web Site: www.ventyx.com (16)

Thompson, Martin E., Ghirardelli Chocolate Co, San Leandro, CA. Tel: (510) 483-6970, (800) 877-9338, FAX: (510) 297-2649, Web Site: www.ghirardelli.com (16)

Thompson, Mike, Suez Energy North America, Houston, TX. Tel: (713) 636-0000, FAX: (713) 636-1364, Web Site: www.tractebelpowerinc.com (16)

Thompson, Page, Omnicom Media Group, New York, NY. Tel: (212) 590-7020, E-Mail: info@omnicommediagroup.com, Web Site: www.omnicommediagroup.com (35)

Thompson, Patti, American Name Services Inc, Orem, UT. Tel: (801) 235-8061, (800) 434-1851, FAX: (801) 764-0613, E-Mail: sales@americannameservices.com, Web Site: www.americannameservices.com (23)

Thompson, Robert, Dwyer Instruments Inc, Michigan City, IN. Tel: (219) 879-8868, Web Site: www.dwyer-inst.com (16)

Thompson, Roger, Group Mojo, Portland, OR. Tel: (503) 493-2242, FAX: (503) 493-2246, E-Mail: sam@groupmojo.com, Web Site: www.groupmojo.com (32)

Thompson, Simon, ESRI, Redlands, CA. Tel: (909) 793-2853, Web Site: www.esri.com (22)

Thompson, Theresa, Sterling Publishing Co Inc, New York, NY. Tel: (212) 532-7160, (800) 367-9692, FAX: (212) 213-2495, Web Site: www.sterlingpublishing.com (17)

Thompson-Hass, Ann, Larkwood Group LLC, Oakland, CA. Tel: (510) 444-7766 (1)

Thomsom, Joe, Sheridan Books Inc, Chelsea, MI. Tel: (734) 475-9145, (800) 999-BOOK, FAX: (734) 475-7337, E-Mail: info@sheridanbooks.com, Web Site: www.sheridanbooks.com (27)

Thomson Research, Boston, MA. Tel: (617) 856-2000, Web Site: research.thomsonib.com (14)

Thomson Reuters, New York, NY. Tel: (646) 223-4000, Web Site: www.thomsonreuters.com (34)

Thomson Reuters LPC, New York, NY. Tel: (646) 223-6890, E-Mail: lpc.americas@reuters.com, Web Site: www.loanpricing.com (14)

Thomson Tax & Accounting, Dexter, MI. Tel: (800) 968-8900, FAX: (734) 426-3750, E-Mail: jack.larue@thomson.com, Web Site: www.cs.thomson.com (22)

Thomson West, Eagan, MN. Tel: (651) 687-7000, (800) 328-9378, FAX: (651) 687-7849, E-Mail: jeff.patrios@thomsonreuters.com, Web Site: www.thomson.com (17)

Thomson, David, List Partners Inc, Atlanta, GA. Tel: (404) 350-0600, (800) 941-6562, E-Mail: contact@thelistinc.com, Web Site: listpartnersinc.com (24)

Thomson, James, J&H Berge/The Lab Mart, South Plainfield, NJ. Tel: (908) 561-3002, (800) 684-1234, FAX: (908) 561-3002, E-Mail: info@jhberge.com, Web Site: www.jhberge.com (7)

Thomson, Jeff, New Day Marketing Ltd, Santa Barbara, CA. Tel: (805) 965-7833, FAX: (805) 965-1284, E-Mail: robert@ndm.tv, Web Site: www.newdaymarketing.com (35)

Thomson, Jeffrey C., Institute of Management Accountants Inc, Montvale, NJ. Tel: (201) 573-9000, (800) 638-4427, FAX: (201) 474-1600, E-Mail: ima@imanet.org, Web Site: www.imanet.org (1)

Thoren-Peden, Deborah, Pillsbury Winthrop Shaw Pittman LLP, Los Angeles, CA. Tel: (213) 488-7100, Web Site: www.pillsburywinthrop.com (20)

Thoreson, John, Sax Arts & Crafts, Appleton, WI. Tel: (800) 558-6696, FAX: (800) 328-4729, E-Mail: info@saxarts.com, Web Site: www.saxarts.com (10)

Thoreson, John, Walch Publishing, Portland, ME. Tel: (207) 772-2846, (800) 558-2846, FAX: (207) 772-3105, E-Mail: customerservice@walch.com, Web Site: www.walch.com (17)

ThorLo Inc, Statesville, NC. Tel: (704) 872-6522, (888) 846-7567, FAX: (704) 838-7005, Web Site: www.thorlo.com (16)

Thorndike Press, Waterville, ME. Tel: (207) 859-1000, (800) 223-1244, E-Mail: gale.salesassistance@cengage.com, Web Site: www.galegroup.com (17)

Thorne, Philip, Goolara LLC, Alameda, CA. Tel: (510) 522-8000, (888) 362-4575, FAX: (510) 522-2457, E-Mail: info@goolara.com, Web Site: www. goolara.com (32)

Thornsbury, Mike, DM Data Solutions LLC, Alexandria, VA. Tel: (703) 415-6222, Web Site: www. dmdatasolutions.com (22)

Grant Thornton LLP, Philadelphia, PA. Tel: (215) 561-4200, FAX: (215) 561-1066, Web Site: www. grantthornton.com (20)

Thornton, Michael A., Progress Printing Co, Lynchburg, VA. Tel: (434) 239-9213, (800) 527-7804, FAX: (434) 237-1618, Web Site: www.progressprinting. net (27)

Thought Technology Ltd, Montreal, QC Canada. Tel: (514) 489-8251, (800) 361-3651, FAX: (514) 489-8255, E-Mail: lawrence@thoughttechnology.com, Web Site: www.thoughttechnology.com (16)

Thousand Trails LP, Chicago, IL. Tel: (214) 618-7200, (800) 205-0606, FAX: (214) 618-7324, Web Site: www.1000trails.com (16)

3Com Corp, Marlborough, MA. Tel: (508) 323-5000, FAX: (508) 323-1111 (22)

3D Mail Results, Kent, WA. Tel: (888) 250-1834, FAX: (253) 398-1551, E-Mail: info@3dmailresults.com, Web Site: www.3dmailresults.com (5)

3 Gen Co, Brooklyn, NY. Tel: (718) 484-4354 (23)

Three Georges and the Nuthouse, Mobile, AL. Tel: (334) 433-1689, FAX: (334) 433-3364, E-Mail: sales@threegeorges.com, Web Site: www. threegeorges.com (16)

3M Post-It Custom Printed Products, Saint Paul, MN. Tel: (800) 328-2407, Web Site: www.3m.com (16)

3PL Worldwide Inc, Milford, CT. Tel: (203) 567-1099, Web Site: www.3plworldwide.com (28)

Threefold, Indianapolis, IN. Tel: (317) 607-1995, Web Site: www.certaindy.com (16)

ThreeSource Fulfillment, Manteno, IL. Tel: (815) 936-1094 x4179, (888) 673-4650, FAX: (815) 936-9743, Web Site: www.threesource.tv (28)

Thrivent Financial for Lutherans, Appleton, WI. Tel: (920) 734-5721, (800) 847-4836, FAX: (920) 730-4781, E-Mail: mail@thrivent.com, Web Site: www. thrivent.com (14)

Thumann, Albert, Association of Energy Engineers, Atlanta, GA. Tel: (770) 447-5083 x210, FAX: (770) 446-3969, E-Mail: info@aeecenter.org, Web Site: www.aeecenter.org (40)

Thurston, Chris, BrandCommand LLC, Richmond, VA. Tel: (804) 708-7100, E-Mail: cthurston@ brandcommand.com, Web Site: www. brandcommand.com (35)

Thurston, Jack, BAI, Chicago, IL. Tel: (312) 683-2464, FAX: (312) 683-2373, E-Mail: info@bai.org, Web Site: www.bai.org (17)

Tian, Shawn, Thought Technology Ltd, Montreal, QC Canada. Tel: (514) 489-8251, (800) 361-3651, FAX: (514) 489-8255, E-Mail: lawrence@ thoughttechnology.com, Web Site: www. thoughttechnology.com (16)

Tidbits Media, Montgomery, AL. Tel: (334) 290-0225, (800) 523-3096, FAX: (334) 386-0302, E-Mail: editors@tidbitsweekly.com, Web Site: www. tidbitsweekly.com (17)

Tidewater Direct LLC, Centreville, MD. Tel: (410) 758-1500, FAX: (410) 758-2478, Web Site: www. tidewaterdirect.com (27)

Tidewater Workshop, Galloway, NJ. Tel: (800) 666-8433, E-Mail: help@tidewaterworkshop.com, Web Site: www.tidewaterworkshop.net (8)

Tidey, R. Scott, Hamilton Beach Brands Inc, Glen Allen, VA. Tel: (804) 273-9777, FAX: (804) 527-7142, Web Site: www.hamiltonbeach.com (16)

Tiedeken, Robert, GrayHair Software, Mount Laurel, NJ. Tel: (856) 727-9372, FAX: (856) 727-1315, Web Site: www.grayhairsoftware.com (22)

Tiernan, Frank, Anritsu Co, Morgan Hill, CA. Tel: (408) 778-2000, (800) 267-4878, FAX: (408) 776-1744, Web Site: www.us.anritsu.com (16)

Tiernan, James S., Brokers/Consultants Inc, Flossmoor, IL. Tel: (708) 957-2900, FAX: (708) 957-4155 (15)

Tiernan, Michael W., The Mark Group, Boca Raton, FL. Tel: (561) 241-1700, (800) 637-0152, FAX: (561) 241-1055, Web Site: www.bostonproper.com (2)

Tierney Communications, Philadelphia, PA. Tel: (215) 790-4100, FAX: (215) 790-4363, Web Site: www. tierneyagency.com (35)

Tiesling, Karen, Global Turnkey Systems Inc, Parsippany, NJ. Tel: (973) 331-1010, FAX: (973) 331-0042, E-Mail: sales@gtsystems.com, Web Site: www.gtsystems.com (22)

Tietge, Ted, Anderson Direct & Digital, Poway, CA. Tel: (888) 694-5094, Web Site: www.andersondd. com (35)

Tiffany & Co, New York, NY. Tel: (212) 755-8000, FAX: (212) 320-7550, Web Site: www.tiffany.com (6)

TigerDirect.ca, Richmond Hill, ON Canada. Tel: (800) 800-8300, (888) 771-9999, FAX: (905) 482-3134, Web Site: www.tigerdirect.ca (3)

TigerDirect Inc, El Segundo, CA. Tel: (305) 415-2199, (800) 800-8300, FAX: (305) 415-2202, Web Site: biz.tigerdirect.com (3)

Tigert Communications, Nashville, TN. Tel: (615) 298-9957 (35)

Tigert, Bob, Tigert Communications, Nashville, TN. Tel: (615) 298-9957 (35)

Tignanelli, Bill, Admore Inc, Macomb, MI. Tel: (810) 949-8200, (800) 523-6673, FAX: (800) 215-2664, Web Site: www.admoreonline.com (10)

Tigner, Robert S., ADRFCO, Washington, DC. Tel: (202) 293-9640, FAX: (202) 463-7980, E-Mail: adrfco@msn.com, Web Site: www.adrfco.org (1)

Tigner, Terry, Ronco Corp, Austin, TX. Tel: (800) 486-1806, E-Mail: customerservice@ronco.com, Web Site: www.ronco.com (16)

Tilford, Todd, Foote, Cone & Belding, Chicago, IL. Tel: (312) 425-5000, FAX: (312) 425-5010, E-Mail: chicago@fcb.com, Web Site: www.fcb.com (35)

Tillamook County Creamery Association, Tillamook, OR. Tel: (503) 842-4481, Web Site: www.tillamook. com (4)

Tiller, Caleb, United Nations Foundation, Washington, DC. Tel: (202) 887-9040, FAX: (202) 887-9021, Web Site: www.unfoundation.org (1)

Tilley, Matthew, CMS Inc, Winston Salem, NC. Tel: (336) 631-2500, FAX: (336) 631-2903, Web Site: www.promotionslogistics.com (14)

Tillinghast, Richard, DIA - Nielsen USA Inc, Moorestown, NJ. Tel: (856) 642-9700, (800) 893-6361, FAX: (856) 642-9709, Web Site: www.dianielsen. com (16)

Timber Crest Farms, Healdsburg, CA. Tel: (707) 433-8251, FAX: (707) 433-8255, E-Mail: tcf@sonic.net, Web Site: www.sonic.net/tcf (16)

Timberland LLC, Stratham, NH. Tel: (603) 772-9500, (888) 802-9947, Web Site: www.timberland.com (16)

Timberline Geodesics, Berkeley, CA. Tel: (510) 849-4481, (800) 366-3466, FAX: (510) 849-3265, E-Mail: info@domehome.com, Web Site: www. domehome.com (8)

Timberline Interactive, Middlebury, VT. Tel: (802) 388-8377, Web Site: www.timberlineinteractive.com (20)

Timberline Total Solutions LLC, Omaha, NE. Tel: (402) 397-6945, (877) 575-2255, FAX: (402) 255-5045, E-Mail: rleavitt@timberlinesolutions.com (29)

Time Communications, Saint Paul, MN. Tel: (800) 486-8581, FAX: (612) 298-1945, E-Mail: info@ timecommunications.biz, Web Site: www. timecommunications.biz (29)

Time Customer Service Inc, Tampa, FL. Tel: (813) 878-6100, (800) 723-NCOA, FAX: (813) 878-6452, Web Site: www.timecustomerservice.com (22)

Time Inc, New York, NY. Tel: (212) 522-1212, Web Site: www.timeinc.com (17)

Time Logistics Inc, Columbia, TN. Tel: (866) 293-8463, FAX: (866) 591-5697, E-Mail: quote@ timelogisticsinc, Web Site: www. timelogisticsinc.com (12)

Time Motion Tools, Poway, CA. Tel: (800) 779-8170, FAX: (800) 779-8171, Web Site: www.timemotion. com (9)

Time Out New York, New York, NY. Tel: (646) 432-3000, FAX: (212) 677-9665, E-Mail: tnew@kable. com, Web Site: www.timeout.com/newyork/ (18)

Time Products International, Del Rio, TX. Tel: (847) 459-8885, FAX: (847) 459-8111, E-Mail: cttpi@aol. com, Web Site: www.tpi2000.com (16)

Time/System, Chicopee, MA. Tel: (800) 637-9942, FAX: (800) 269-3075, E-Mail: customerservice@ timesystem.us, Web Site: www.timesystem.us (16)

Time Warner Inc, New York, NY. Tel: (212) 484-8000, Web Site: www.timewarner.com (16)

Times Publishing Co, Erie, PA. Tel: (814) 870-1600, FAX: (814) 870-1808, E-Mail: terry.cascioli@ timesnews.com (18)

Times Union, Albany, NY. Tel: (518) 454-5694, FAX: (518) 454-5628, Web Site: www.timesunion.com (18)

Timm Medical Technologies, Inc, Lake Forest, IL. Tel: (952) 947-9410, (800) 438-8592, FAX: (952) 947-9411, Web Site: www.timmmedical.com (16)

Timm, Bryan L., Columbia Sportswear, Portland, OR. Tel: (503) 985-4203, (800) 622-6953, Web Site: www.columbia.com (2)

Timm, Gerry, Timm Medical Technologies, Inc, Lake Forest, IL. Tel: (952) 947-9410, (800) 438-8592, FAX: (952) 947-9411, Web Site: www. timmmedical.com (16)

Timm-Brock, Barbara, Sylvan Learning Inc, Baltimore, MD. Tel: (410) 843-8000, (800) 31-SUCCESS, FAX: (410) 843-8057, E-Mail: pr@sylvanlearning. com, Web Site: www.sylvanlearning.com (16)

Tinberg, Rich, The Bradford Group, Niles, IL. Tel: (847) 966-2770, FAX: (847) 581-8630, Web Site: www.collectiblestoday.com (16)

Tinberg, Richard W., Collectibles Today Network, Ltd, Niles, IL. Tel: (800) 323-5577 #6, Web Site: www. collectiblestoday.com (16)

Tinberg, Richard W., Hammacher Schlemmer & Co Inc, Niles, IL. Tel: (847) 581-8600, (800) 233-4800, FAX: (847) 581-8616, Web Site: www.hammacher. com (16)

Tinkham, Wes, Hometown Mailing Lists & Direct Mail, Dallas, TX. Tel: (800) 798-4811, E-Mail: tinkham@ hometownlists.com, Web Site: www.hometownlists. com (23)

Tinnon, John, Graphic Converting Inc, Elmhurst, IL. Tel: (630) 758-4100, (800) 447-1935, FAX: (630) 833-1058, E-Mail: sales@graphicconverting.com, Web Site: www.graphicconverting.com (36)

Tino, Jill, Connex International Inc, Danbury, CT. Tel: (203) 731-5400, (800) 426-6639, FAX: (203) 730-9060, E-Mail: marketing@connexintl.com, Web Site: www.connexintl.com (22)

Tinsley Tool Supply Inc, Powell, TN. Tel: (865) 681-9633, FAX: (865) 982-1655, E-Mail: gene@tinsleytool.com, Web Site: www.tinsleytool.com (9)

Tinsley, III Tuck, American Printing House for the Blind, Louisville, KY. Tel: (502) 895-2405, (800) 223-1839, FAX: (502) 899-2274, E-Mail: info@aph.org, Web Site: www.aph.org (7)

Tinton, Lynn, Spiegel Brands Inc, New York, NY. Tel: (800) 222-5680, E-Mail: customerservice@spiegel.com, Web Site: www.spiegel.com (2)

Tipsord, Michael L., State Farm Insurance Cos, Bloomington, IL. Tel: (309) 766-2311, FAX: (309) 766-3621, Web Site: www.statefarm.com (15)

Tipton, Gary, FATHOM Works, Saint Joseph, MI. Tel: (269) 932-3623, (800) 800-9547, Web Site: fathom-works.com (35)

Tipton, Virgil, Liguori Publications, Liguori, MO. Tel: (636) 464-2500, (800) 325-9521, FAX: (800) 325-9526, E-Mail: liguori@liguori.org, Web Site: www.liguori.org (17)

Tira, Peter, McClatchy Co, Sacramento, CA. Tel: (916) 321-1855, FAX: (916) 321-1869, Web Site: www.mcclatchy.com (17)

Tirocchi, Bob, Bizzaro Rubber Stamps, Greenville, RI. Tel: (401) 231-8777, FAX: (401) 231-4770, E-Mail: bizzaroinc@earthlink.net, Web Site: www.bizzaro.com (6)

Tirocchi, Doreen, Bizzaro Rubber Stamps, Greenville, RI. Tel: (401) 231-8777, FAX: (401) 231-4770, E-Mail: bizzaroinc@earthlink.net, Web Site: www.bizzaro.com (6)

Tisi, Sal, List Strategies Inc, New York, NY. Tel: (212) 767-1000, FAX: (212) 541-4408, E-Mail: info@liststrategies.com, Web Site: www.liststrategies.com (23)

Titan List & Mailing Services Inc, Deerfield Beach, FL. Tel: (888) 345-7179, E-Mail: titanlms@bellsouth.net, Web Site: www.titanlists.com (24)

Titan Manufacturing, Holbrook, MA. Tel: (781) 767-1963, Web Site: www.americantitan.com (34)

TitanTV Media, Cedar Rapids, IA. Tel: (319) 365-5597, (800) 365-7629, FAX: (319) 365-5694, E-Mail: mktg@titantv.com, Web Site: www.titantv.com (20)

Tittsworth, Barry, The Source, Huntsville, AL. Tel: (256) 536-7305, (800) 433-2375, FAX: (256) 539-8547, Web Site: www.thesource-wti.com (33)

Tiziani Whitmyre Inc, Sharon, MA. Tel: (781) 793-9380, FAX: (781) 793-9395, E-Mail: info@tizinc.com, Web Site: www.tizinc.com (21)

Tiziani, Robert, Tiziani Whitmyre Inc, Sharon, MA. Tel: (781) 793-9380, FAX: (781) 793-9395, E-Mail: info@tizinc.com, Web Site: www.tizinc.com (21)

TMC Internet Telephony & Expo, Norwalk, CT. Tel: (203) 852-6800, (800) 243-6002, FAX: (203) 866-3326, E-Mail: tmc@tmcnet.com, Web Site: www.tmcnet.com (42)

TMone LLC, Iowa City, IA. Tel: (868) 577-2461, E-Mail: info@massmarkets.com, Web Site: www.massmarkets.com (29)

Toal, Jennifer, Driasi, Chanhassen, MN. Tel: (952) 556-5600, (800) 688-0760, FAX: (952) 556-8200, E-Mail: tpa@driasi.com, Web Site: www.driasi.com (21)

Tobe Direct, Bolingbrook, IL. Tel: (630) 910-7080, FAX: (630) 910-3670, E-Mail: sales@tobedirect.com, Web Site: www.tobedirect.com (35)

Tobe, John, Tobe Direct, Bolingbrook, IL. Tel: (630) 910-7080, FAX: (630) 910-3670, E-Mail: sales@tobedirect.com, Web Site: www.tobedirect.com (35)

Tobey, John, ICMA Retirement Corp, Washington, DC. Tel: (202) 962-4600, (800) 669-7400, FAX: (202) 962-4601, E-Mail: investorservices@icmarc.org, Web Site: www.icmarc.org (14)

Tobias, PhD Christopher, Dudnyk, Horsham, PA. Tel: (215) 443-9406, (800) 438-3695, E-Mail: fpowers@dudnyk.com, Web Site: dudnyk.com (35)

The Peter A Tobin College of Business, Jamaica, NY. Tel: (718) 990-2600, FAX: (718) 990-1868, Web Site: www.stjohns.edu (41)

Tobin, Paul, United Spinal Association, Kew Gardens, NY. Tel: (718) 803-3782, (800) 404-2898, FAX: (718) 803-0414, E-Mail: info@unitedspinal.org, Web Site: www.unitedspinal.org (1)

Tobin, Timothy N., Bank of America, Charlotte, NC. Tel: (704) 386-5681, (800) 841-4000, FAX: (704) 386-6699, Web Site: www.bankofamerica.com (14)

Tobol, Mitch, CGT Marketing LLC, Amityville, NY. Tel: (631) 842-4600, E-Mail: info@cgtmarketing.com, Web Site: www.cgtmarketing.com (35)

Tocquigny, Yvonne, Archer Malmo Inc, Memphis, TN. Tel: (901) 523-2000, FAX: (901) 524-5578, Web Site: www.archermalmo.com (35)

Todaro Brothers Mail Order Co, New York, NY. Tel: (212) 679-7766, (877) 472-2767, FAX: (212) 689-1679, E-Mail: eat@todarobros.com, Web Site: www.todarobros.com (4)

Todaro, Linda, Magna Visual Inc, Saint Louis, MO. Tel: (314) 843-9000, (800) 843-3399, FAX: (314) 843-0000, E-Mail: magna@magnavisual.com, Web Site: www.magnavisual.com (9)

Todaro, Luciano, Todaro Brothers Mail Order Co, New York, NY. Tel: (212) 679-7766, (877) 472-2767, FAX: (212) 689-1679, E-Mail: eat@todarobros.com, Web Site: www.todarobros.com (4)

Today's Christian Woman, Carol Stream, IL. Tel: (630) 260-6200, FAX: (630) 260-0114, E-Mail: tcwedit@christianitytoday.com, Web Site: www.todayschristianwoman.net (31)

Todd, Michael, Mustek Inc, Tustin, CA. Tel: (949) 790-3800, FAX: (949) 788-3670, Web Site: www.mustek.com (3)

Todd, Patrick, The Travelers Insurance Cos, Hartford, CT. Tel: (860) 277-8252, (651) 317-2685, FAX: (860) 954-7691, Web Site: www.travelers.com (15)

Toennies, Melissa, Anheuser-Busch Inc Promotional Products Group, Shelton, CT. Tel: (800) 742-5283, Web Site: www.budshop.com (6)

Toepfer, Andy, Rubber Stamps of America, Dublin, NH. Tel: (800) 553-5031, FAX: (603) 563-8102, E-Mail: stampusa@verizon.net, Web Site: www.stampusa.com (6)

Toepfer, Phil, Fort Hays State University, Hays, KS. Tel: (785) 628-FHSU, FAX: (785) 628-4046, Web Site: www.fhsu.edu (41)

Toffler, Van, Viacom Media Networks, New York, NY. Tel: (212) 258-6000, Web Site: www.viacom.com (32)

The Tog Shop Inc, Beverly, MA. Tel: (800) 262-8888, FAX: (800) 755-7557, Web Site: www.togshop.com (2)

Tognoli, Dawn, SF Global Sourcing Inc, San Francisco, CA. Tel: (415) 288-9400, (800) 545-5865, FAX: (415) 288-9410, E-Mail: selfservice@sfvideo.com, Web Site: www.sfvideo.com (3)

Tokar, Bob, Wolverine Solutions Group, Detroit, MI. Tel: (313) 873-6800, FAX: (313) 873-8730, Web Site: www.wolverinemail.com (28)

Tokayer, Barry, TNT Packaging Inc, Miami, FL. Tel: (305) 633-2556, (305) 769-0616, (800) 327-6085, FAX: (305) 769-0619, E-Mail: tntpackaging@bellsouth.net, Web Site: www.tntpackaging.com (16)

Tokayer, Jeffrey, TNT Packaging Inc, Miami, FL. Tel: (305) 633-2556, (305) 769-0616, (800) 327-6085, FAX: (305) 769-0619, E-Mail: tntpackaging@bellsouth.net, Web Site: www.tntpackaging.com (16)

Tokheim, Sara, Brokers International Ltd, Panora, IA. Tel: (641) 755-2775, FAX: (641) 755-4201 (20)

Toland Home and Garden Inc, Port Townsend, WA. Tel: (504) 893-9503, (800) 989-6287, E-Mail: info@tolandhomeandgarden.com, Web Site: www.tolandhomeandgarden.com (16)

Toledano, Sidney, Christian Dior Perfumes, New York, NY. Tel: (877) 903-4671, (800) 929-3467, FAX: (212) 931-2954, Web Site: www.dior.com (7)

Toler, John, Evergreen Enterprises Inc, Richmond, VA. Tel: (800) 774-3837, E-Mail: customerservice@myevergreen.com, Web Site: www.myevergreen.com (8)

Tolia, Sam, Triton College, River Grove, IL. Tel: (708) 456-0300, FAX: (708) 583-3121, Web Site: www.triton.edu (16)

TollFreeForwarding.com, Los Angeles, CA. Tel: (213) 452-1505, Web Site: www.tollfreeforwarding.com (29)

Tolliver Inc, New York, NY. Tel: (212) 758-7344, FAX: (212) 750-8617, E-Mail: tolliver12@aol.com (20)

Tomahawk Live Trap Co, Tomahawk, WI. Tel: (715) 453-3550, (800) 272-8727, FAX: (715) 453-4326, E-Mail: trapem@livetrap.com, Web Site: www.livetrap.com (16)

Tomasone, Marina, Toronto Hydro-Electric System, Toronto, ON Canada. Tel: (416) 542-8000, Web Site: www.torontohydro.com (1)

Tomczyk, Fred, TD Ameritrade Holding Corp, Omaha, NE. Tel: (800) 237-8692, Web Site: www.amtd.com (16)

Tome, Carol B., The Home Depot Inc, Atlanta, GA. Tel: (770) 433-8211, (800) 466-3337, FAX: (770) 384-2356, Web Site: www.homedepot.com (16)

Tomkins, Mark E, ServiceMaster Co, Memphis, TN. Tel: (901) 766-1400, (866) 782-6787, Web Site: www.servicemaster.com (8)

Tomkins, Paul, The Reader's Digest Association Inc, New York, NY. Tel: (800) 310-6261, Web Site: www.rda.com (17)

Tomlinson, Mark C., Society of Manufacturing Engineers, Dearborn, MI. Tel: (313) 425-3000, (800) 733-4763, FAX: (313) 425-3400, E-Mail: communications@sme.org, Web Site: www.sme.org (1)

Tomlinson, William, Professional Training Associates Inc, Duquesne, PA. Tel: (412) 460-0266, FAX: (412) 460-0269, E-Mail: info@ptainc.com, Web Site: www.ptainc.com (17)

Tompkins, Hope, Bedford/St Martin's, Boston, MA. Tel: (617) 426-7440, FAX: (617) 426-8582, Web Site: www.bedfordstmartins.com (17)

tomsheehan worldwide, Reading, PA. Tel: (610) 478-8448, FAX: (610) 478-8449, E-Mail: tomsheehan@tomsheehan.com, Web Site: www.tomsheehan.com (35)

TomTom North American, Lebanon, NH. Tel: (603) 643-0330, (800) 331-7881, FAX: (603) 653-0249, Web Site: www.tomtom.com (22)

Tonchuk, Robert, Datasystem Solutions Inc, Overland Park, KS. Tel: (913) 362-6969, FAX: (913) 362-6383, E-Mail: sales@mutipub.com, Web Site: www.datasystem.com (22)

Toner, Mark, R2C Group, Portland, OR. Tel: (866) 402-1124, E-Mail: getintouch@r2cgroup.com, Web Site: www.r2cgroup.com (35)

Tong, Peter, Abbey of Gethsemani, Trappist, KY. Tel: (502) 549-4133, FAX: (502) 549-4124, E-Mail: reservations@monks.org, Web Site: www.monks.org (1)

Tony Stone Images, Chicago, IL. Tel: (800) 234-7880, FAX: (312) 922-9075, Web Site: www.getty-images.com (38)

Tools for Wellness, Austin, TX. Tel: (800) 456-9887, FAX: (818) 532-1775, E-Mail: info@toolsforwellness.com, Web Site: www.toolsforwellness.com (7)

ToonUp Coach, Wayne, PA. Tel: (610) 902-0430, (866) 866-6877, E-Mail: info@toonupcoach.com, Web Site: www.toonupcoach.com (13)

Top USA Corp, Worthington, OH. Tel: (614) 431-1601, (800) 843-3381, FAX: (614) 431-1239, E-Mail: info@topusa.com, Web Site: www.topusa.com (27)

Top Year International Inc, Yorba Linda, CA. Tel: (714) 692-6688, (800) 942-8722, FAX: (714) 692-8691, E-Mail: sales@akirausa.com, Web Site: www.akirausa.com (33)

Topec, Marsha, Cytec Industries Inc, Olean, NY. Tel: (716) 372-9650, FAX: (716) 372-1594, Web Site: www.conap.com (16)

Topitzes, Nick, PC/Nametag Inc, Verona, WI. Tel: (608) 845-1850, (800) 233-9767, E-Mail: sales@pcnametag.com, Web Site: www.pcnametag.com (16)

Topol, Bruce, Eyeglass Service Industries, Lynbrook, NY. Tel: (516) 599-1135, FAX: (516) 599-4825 (2)

Topp Direct Marketing, Harlingen, TX. Tel: (956) 421-5750, FAX: (956) 421-5721, E-Mail: info@toppmarketing.com, Web Site: www.toppmarketing.com (21)

Topp, John W., Topp Direct Marketing, Harlingen, TX. Tel: (956) 421-5750, FAX: (956) 421-5721, E-Mail: info@toppmarketing.com, Web Site: www.toppmarketing.com (21)

TopRank Online Marketing, Spring Park, MN. Tel: (952) 400-0194, (877) 872-6628, E-Mail: winning@toprankmarketing.com, Web Site: www.toprankmarketing.com (32)

Torah Umesorah Publications, Brooklyn, NY. Tel: (212) 227-1000, FAX: (212) 406-6934, E-Mail: umesorah@aol.com, Web Site: torahumesorah.com (5)

Toran, Daniel J., Penn Mutual, Horsham, PA. Tel: (215) 956-8083, FAX: (215) 956-8368, Web Site: www.pennmutual.com (15)

Torbeck, Theodore H., Cincinnati Bell Inc, Cincinnati, OH. Tel: (888) CIN-BELL, Web Site: www.cincinnatibell.com (19)

Torcom Inbound Telemarketing, Madison, WI. Tel: (800) 832-4939, FAX: (608) 275-6557, E-Mail: torcom@torcom.com, Web Site: www.torcom.com (29)

Tordella, Stephen J, Decision Demographics, Arlington, VA. Tel: (703) 931-9200, FAX: (703) 527-1448, E-Mail: tordella@decision-demographics.com, Web Site: www.decision-demographics.com (30)

Torgerson, Dell, Replogle Globes Inc, Broadview, IL. Tel: (708) 343-0900, FAX: (708) 343-0923, E-Mail: info@replogleglobes.com, Web Site: www.replogleglobes.com (16)

Tornabene, Patrick, Newsday, Melville, NY. Tel: (800) 639-7329, Web Site: www.newsday.com (17)

The Toro Co, Bloomington, MN. Tel: (952) 888-8801, (800) 348-2424, FAX: (952) 887-8258, E-Mail: companyinfo@thetorocompany.com, Web Site: www.thetorocompany.com (16)

Toronto Hydro-Electric System, Toronto, ON Canada. Tel: (416) 542-8000, Web Site: www.torontohydro.com (1)

Torqmaster International, Stamford, CT. Tel: (203) 326-5945, (888) 414-4643, FAX: (203) 326-5944, E-Mail: info@torqmaster.com, Web Site: www.torqmaster.com (9)

Tortorella, Bernadette, Gerber Products Co, Florham Park, NJ. Tel: (973) 593-7500, (800) 284-9488, Web Site: www.gerber.com (16)

Torvik, Elin, Torcom Inbound Telemarketing, Madison, WI. Tel: (800) 832-4939, FAX: (608) 275-6557, E-Mail: torcom@torcom.com, Web Site: www.torcom.com (29)

Toscas, James G., Portland Cement Association, Washington, DC. Tel: (202) 408-9494, Web Site: www.cement.org (1)

Toschak, Barb, GlaserDirect Inc, Glen Ellyn, IL. Tel: (630) 469-2075, (888) 380-1356, FAX: (630) 790-5244, E-Mail: info@glaserdirect.com, Web Site: www.glaserdirect.com (23)

The Total Mailing System, West Deptford, NJ. Tel: (856) 628-8800, FAX: (856) 628-8810, Web Site: www.ttms.com (22)

Total Training Solutions LLC, Waunakee, WI. Tel: (608) 849-5563, (800) 831-0678, FAX: (608) 849-5605, (800) 831-3776, E-Mail: khennett@ttstrain.com, Web Site: www.ttstrain.com (5)

Toter Inc, Statesville, NC. Tel: (704) 872-8171, (800) 424-0422, FAX: (704) 878-0734, E-Mail: info@toter.com, Web Site: www.toter.com (16)

Totton, Patricia, TeleServices Direct, Indianapolis, IN. Tel: (888) 646-6626, Web Site: www.teleservicesdirect.com (29)

Touch-Base Computing, Silver Creek, GA. Tel: (706) 378-0964, E-Mail: sales@touchbase.com, Web Site: www.touchbase.com (22)

Touch of Class Catalog, Huntingburg, IN. Tel: (800) 457-7456, FAX: (812) 683-5921, E-Mail: customerservice@touchofclass.com, Web Site: www.touchofclass.com (8)

TouchPoint Data Solutions Inc, Alpharetta, GA. Tel: (770) 886-8611, FAX: (678) 686-1835, Web Site: touchpointdata.com (23)

Tova Corp, West Chester, PA. Tel: (800) 852-9999, Web Site: www.beautybytova.com (7)

Towell, Leonor, Amanet, Canoga Park, CA. Tel: (818) 786-1113, FAX: (818) 786-5736, E-Mail: info@amanet-usa.com, Web Site: www.amanet.com (16)

Tower Hobbies/Hobbico, Champaign, IL. Tel: (217) 398-3636, (800) 637-6050, FAX: (217) 398-1104, Web Site: www.towerhobbies.com (11)

Tower Media Advertising Inc, Chicago, IL. Tel: (312) 856-9200, FAX: (312) 856-1300, E-Mail: info@towermedia.com, Web Site: www.towermedia.com (35)

TowerData, New York, NY. Tel: (646) 742-1771, FAX: (646) 365-3060, Web Site: www.towerdata.com (32)

Towers Watson, New York, NY. Tel: (212) 725-7550, FAX: (212) 644-7432, Web Site: www.towerswatson.com (20)

Town Money Saver, Lucas, OH. Tel: (419) 892-1913, Web Site: www.townmoneysaver.com (31)

Towne AllPoints, Santa Ana, CA. Tel: (714) 540-3095, (800) 243-8099, FAX: (714) 540-4192, E-Mail: info@towne.com, Web Site: www.towne.com (21)

TownNews.com, Moline, IL. Tel: (309) 743-0800, (800) 293-9576, FAX: (309) 743-0830, E-Mail: info@townnews.com, Web Site: www.townnews365.com (32)

Towns, Faye, Mountain West Supply Co, Scottsdale, AZ. Tel: (602) 971-1200, (800) 528-6169, FAX: (602) 996-5077 (3)

Townsend Communications LLC, Kansas City, MO. Tel: (816) 361-0616, (800) 274-8867, FAX: (816) 361-6164, Web Site: www.townsendprint.com (17)

Townsend, III H. Guyon, Townsend Communications LLC, Kansas City, MO. Tel: (816) 361-0616, (800) 274-8867, FAX: (816) 361-6164, Web Site: www.townsendprint.com (17)

Townsend, Jr. H.G., Townsend Communications LLC, Kansas City, MO. Tel: (816) 361-0616, (800) 274-8867, FAX: (816) 361-6164, Web Site: www.townsendprint.com (17)

Townsend, Julia, Kayser-Roth Corp Inc, Greensboro, NC. Tel: (800) 575-3497, Web Site: www.nononsense.com (2)

Toyota Motor Sales USA Inc, Torrance, CA. Tel: (310) 468-4000, (800) 331-4331, FAX: (310) 468-7841, Web Site: www.toyota.com (16)

Toyota Racing Development USA Inc, Costa Mesa, CA. Tel: (714) 444-1188, FAX: (714) 444-0339, Web Site: www.trdusa.com (34)

Toys "R" Us, Wayne, NJ. Tel: (973) 617-5879, FAX: (973) 617-4006, Web Site: www.toysrus.com (11)

Toys To Grow On, Carson, CA. Tel: (310) 537-8600, (800) 874-4242, FAX: (800) 537-5403, E-Mail: toyinfo@toystogrowon.com, Web Site: www.ttgo.com (11)

Tozeski, Stephen, IDG List Services, Framingham, MA. Tel: (508) 766-5633, E-Mail: stozeski@idglist.com, Web Site: www.idglist.com (24)

Tozier, Scott, Direct Mail Solutions, Richmond, VA. Tel: (804) 254-8300, (877) 367-0800, Web Site: www.directmailsolutions.com (28)

Trabucco, Robert, Sterling Jewelers Inc, Akron, OH. Tel: (330) 668-5000, FAX: (330) 668-5052, E-Mail: webmaster@jewels.com, Web Site: www.sterlingjewelers.com (16)

Traction On Demand, Burnaby, BC Canada. Tel: (604) 620-6040, Web Site: www.tractionondemand.com (35)

Tractor Supply Co, Brentwood, TN. Tel: (615) 366-4600, (877) 718-6750, FAX: (615) 227-4608, Web Site: www.mytscstore.com (5)

Tracy, John J., Boeing Co, Chicago, IL. Tel: (312) 544-2000, FAX: (312) 544-2082, Web Site: www.boeing.com (16)

Tracy, Richard, Optronics Inc, Muskogee, OK. Tel: (918) 683-9514, (800) 364-5483, FAX: (918) 683-9517, E-Mail: sales@optronicsinc.com, Web Site: www.optronicsinc.com (11)

TracyLocke, Dallas, TX. Tel: (214) 969-9000, FAX: (214) 259-3550, E-Mail: parker.harrison@tracylocke.com, Web Site: tracylocke.com (35)

TradeNet Publishing Inc, Gardner, KS. Tel: (800) 884-7301, Web Site: www.tradenetonline.com (35)

Trahan, Connie, Biomerica Inc, Irvine, CA. Tel: (949) 645-2111, (800) 854-3002, FAX: (949) 553-1231, E-Mail: info@biomerica.com, Web Site: www.biomerica.com (7)

Traina, Sharon, Conrad Direct Inc, Cresskill, NJ. Tel: (201) 567-3200, FAX: (201) 567-1530, E-Mail: listinfo@conraddirect.com, Web Site: www.conraddirect.com (23)

Trainer, William, Wells Lamont Corp, Niles, IL. Tel: (847) 647-8200, (800) 247-3295, FAX: (847) 647-6943, Web Site: www.wellslamont.com (34)

Training Consultants Inc, Highland Park, IL. Tel: (847) 432-9428, FAX: (847) 432-9318, E-Mail: wetrain2@home.com (20)

Traister, Scott, Arquest Inc, Millstone Twp, NJ. Tel: (609) 395-9500, (888) 270-8378, (888) ARQUEST, FAX: (609) 395-9778, Web Site: www.arquest.com (16)

Tram, Michael, Arthur D Little Inc, Boston, MA. Tel: (617) 532-9550, FAX: (617) 261-6630, Web Site: www.adlittle-us.com (20)

Trancos Inc, Pleasanton, CA. Tel: (650) 364-3110, Web Site: www.trancos.com (16)

Trandem, Don, Win Craft Inc, Winona, MN. Tel: (507) 454-5510, (800) 533-8100, FAX: (507) 454-6403, E-Mail: inquiries@wincraftschool.com, Web Site: www.wincraftschool.com (5)

Trani, Louis, Equitable Life & Casualty Insurance Co, Salt Lake City, UT. Tel: (801) 579-3400, FAX: (801) 579-3789, Web Site: www.equilife.com (15)

Trans Continental Inc, Montreal, QC Canada. Tel: (514) 954-4000, FAX: (514) 954-4016, Web Site: www.transcontinental-gtc.com (31)

Trans Union Corp, Chicago, IL. Tel: (312) 985-2000, Web Site: www.transunion.com (14)

Transaction Publishers, Piscataway, NJ. Tel: (732) 445-1245, FAX: (732) 748-9801, E-Mail: trans@transactionpub.com, Web Site: www.transactionpub.com (17)

Transamerica Life & Protection, Baltimore, MD. Tel: (410) 209-5617, Web Site: www.aegondms.com (15)

Transamerica Life Insurance Co, Cedar Rapids, IA. Tel: (319) 398-8511, (800) 558-9011, FAX: (319) 369-2825, Web Site: www.transamerica.com (15)

Transamerica Occidental Life Co, Los Angeles, CA. Tel: (213) 742-3111, FAX: (213) 741-6623, Web Site: www.transamerica.com (15)

TransAmerica Retirement Services, Los Angeles, CA. Tel: (213) 742-3363, Web Site: www.ta-retirement.com (14)

Transamerican Mailing, Escondido, CA. Tel: (760) 745-5343, Web Site: www.transdirect.com (20)

Transcat, Rochester, NY. Tel: (585) 352-9460, (800) 800-5001, FAX: (585) 352-1486, Web Site: www.transcat.com (16)

TransContinental Yorkville - O'Keefe, Etobicoke, ON Canada. Tel: (416) 741-1900, (800) 361-9690, FAX: (416) 401-2220, Web Site: www.transcontinentalprinting.com (27)

Transemantics Inc, Washington, DC. Tel: (202) 362-2505, FAX: (202) 686-5603, E-Mail: ili@transemantics.com, Web Site: www.transemantics.com (16)

TransFirst ePayment Services, Omaha, NE. Tel: (888) 541-9800, Web Site: epay.transfirst.com (14)

TransFirst Holdings Inc, Dallas, TX. Tel: (214) 453-7700, (888) 254-4137, FAX: (214) 453-7739, Web Site: www.transfirst.com (14)

Transglobal Consultants Inc, Canton, OH. Tel: (330) 477-6450, E-Mail: transglobal@earthlink.net (20)

Transit Treasure Inc, New York, NY. Tel: (646) 706-1001, Web Site: www.transittreasure.com (12)

TransitCenter Inc, New York, NY. Tel: (646) 395-9555, E-Mail: info@transitcenter.org, Web Site: www.transitcenter.org (1)

TRANZACT, Fort Lee, NJ. Tel: (201) 461-5665, E-Mail: info@tranzact.net, Web Site: www.tranzact.net (35)

Traola, John, Bobley-Harmann Corp, Ronkonkoma, NY. Tel: (516) 364-1800, (800) 323-1692, FAX: (516) 364-1899, E-Mail: info.giftvalues@gmail.com, Web Site: www.giftvalues.com (5)

Trapanese, Mark, McCormick-Armstrong Co Inc, Wichita, KS. Tel: (316) 264-1363, (800) 733-1363, FAX: (316) 263-4511, E-Mail: sales@mccormickarmstrong.com, Web Site: www.mccormickarmstrong.com (27)

Trask, Linda, 802 Creative Partners Inc, Montpelier, VT. Tel: (802) 234-9755, FAX: (802) 732-9056, E-Mail: info@802creative.com, Web Site: www.802creative.com (35)

Traub, Ken, MRV Communications, Chatsworth, CA. Tel: (818) 773-0900, FAX: (818) 773-0906, Web Site: www.mrv.com (3)

Traum, Harry, Homespun Tapes Music Instruction, Woodstock, NY. Tel: (845) 246-2550, (800) 338-2737, FAX: (845) 246-5282, E-Mail: info@homespuntapes.com, Web Site: www.homespuntapes.com (3)

Traum, Jane, Homespun Tapes Music Instruction, Woodstock, NY. Tel: (845) 246-2550, (800) 338-2737, FAX: (845) 246-5282, E-Mail: info@homespuntapes.com, Web Site: www.homespuntapes.com (3)

Trautmann, Kathleen, Zurich, Schaumburg, IL. Tel: (847) 605-3712, (800) 382-2150, FAX: (847) 605-6403, Web Site: www.zurichna.com (15)

Trautwein, Joanne, Creative Marketing Alliance Inc, Princeton Junction, NJ. Tel: (609) 297-2235, FAX: (609) 799-7032, E-Mail: info@cmasolutions.com, Web Site: www.gotocma.com (35)

Travel Planners Inc, New York, NY. Tel: (212) 532-1660, (800) 221-3531, FAX: (212) 532-1556, Web Site: www.tphousing.com (19)

Travelclick, Schaumburg, IL. Tel: (847) 585-5016 (19)

The Travelers Insurance Cos, Hartford, CT. Tel: (860) 277-8252, (651) 317-2685, FAX: (860) 954-7691, Web Site: www.travelers.com (15)

Travelex America Inc, Washington, DC. Tel: (202) 408-1200, FAX: (202) 513-5215, Web Site: business.travelex.com/us (14)

Traverso, Mark, Lighthouse List Co, Pompano Beach, FL. Tel: (954) 489-3008, (800) 684-2180, FAX: (954) 489-0850, E-Mail: mtlistdude@aol.com, Web Site: www.lighthouselist.com (24)

Travis, Jr. Richard L., Ennis Inc, Midlothian, TX. Tel: (972) 775-9801, (800) 962-0944, FAX: (800) 645-8339, Web Site: www.ennis.com (16)

Travis, Mark, TransFirst Holdings Inc, Dallas, TX. Tel: (214) 453-7700, (888) 254-4137, FAX: (214) 453-7739, Web Site: www.transfirst.com (14)

Travis, Tracey T., Estee Lauder Inc, New York, NY. Tel: (212) 572-4200, FAX: (212) 893-7782, Web Site: www.esteelauder.com (16)

Traylor, Mark H., Ames-Tru-Temper, Camp Hill, PA. Tel: (800) 393-1846, Web Site: ames.com (8)

Traylor, Shawn, Reliance Electric, Fort Smith, AR. Tel: (479) 646-4711. FAX: (479) 648-5792, E-Mail: smtraylor@powersystems.rockwell.com, Web Site: www.reliance.com (9)

Treacy, Dennis H., Smithfield Foods, Smithfield, VA. Tel: (800) 276-6158, Web Site: www.smithfieldfoods.com (16)

Treasure Chest, New York, NY. Tel: (212) 590-2332, Web Site: treasurechestonline.com (19)

Treis, James, Arandell Corp, Menomonee Falls, WI. Tel: (262) 255-4400, (800) 558-8724, FAX: (262) 253-3162, E-Mail: jft@arandell.com, Web Site: www.arandell.com (27)

Treizman, Eddie, Dial 800 LLC, Los Angeles, CA. Tel: (310) 273-9023, (800) 700-1987, E-Mail: sales@dial800.com, Web Site: www.dial800.com (32)

Trellist Marketing and Technology, Wilmington, DE. Tel: (302) 778-1300, Web Site: www.trellist.com (30)

Tremblay, Lorene, Amanet, Canoga Park, CA. Tel: (818) 786-1113, FAX: (818) 786-5736, E-Mail: info@amanet-usa.com, Web Site: www.amanet.com (16)

Trend Magazines Inc, Saint Petersburg, FL. Tel: (727) 821-5800, (800) 821-5800, FAX: (727) 822-5083, E-Mail: feedback@fltrend.com, Web Site: www.floridatrend.com (17)

Trends International LLC, Indianapolis, IN. Tel: (317) 388-1212, (800) 354-4639, FAX: (317) 388-1414, E-Mail: info@trendsinternational.com, Web Site: www.trendsinternational.com (38)

Trepoint, New York, NY. Tel: (646) 867-2252, E-Mail: challengeus@trepoint.com, Web Site: www.trepoint.com (35)

Trepp, Gregory H., Hamilton Beach Brands Inc, Glen Allen, VA. Tel: (804) 273-9777, FAX: (804) 527-7142, Web Site: www.hamiltonbeach.com (16)

Tretton, Timothy, MontBleu Resort Casino and Spa, Stateline, NV. Tel: (775) 586-2126, (888) 829-7630, FAX: (775) 588-3515, Web Site: www.montbleuresort.com (19)

Treul, Nancy, Foremost Insurance Group, Grand Rapids, MI. Tel: (616) 956-8241, (800) 527-3905, FAX: (800) 325-1507, Web Site: www.foremost.com (15)

Trevalyan, Jan A., Direct Data Capture Ltd, Evergreen, CO. Tel: (631) 547-5500, FAX: (631) 547-6800, E-Mail: jan@datacapture.com, Web Site: www.datacapture.com (22)

Trevaskis, Judith, Progressive Energy Corp, San Marcos, CA. Tel: (760) 727-2906, (800) 525-8624, FAX: (760) 727-0947, E-Mail: patrickkilleen@cox.net (5)

Trevvett, Paul H., Commercial Travelers Mutual Insurance Co, Utica, NY. Tel: (315) 797-5200, (800) 422-6200, FAX: (315) 797-3198, E-Mail: comtravl@commercialtravelers.com, Web Site: www.commercialtravelers.com (15)

Tri-Chem Inc, Belleville, NJ. Tel: (973) 751-9200, FAX: (973) 450-1260, (973) 450-1057, E-Mail: paints@trichem.com, Web Site: www.trichem.com (16)

Tri-Media Marketing Services Inc, Wilmette, IL. Tel: (800) 874-0338, E-Mail: neals@trimediaonline.com, Web Site: www.trimediaonline.com (23)

Tri-State Envelope Corp, Ashland, PA. Tel: (570) 875-0433, (800) 233-3102, FAX: (570) 875-0125, E-Mail: tsecny@attglobal.net, Web Site: tristateenvelope.com (26)

Tri Tech Laboratories Inc, Lynchburg, VA. Tel: (434) 845-7073, FAX: (434) 847-4360, Web Site: www.tritechlabs.com (16)

Triangle Printers Inc, Skokie, IL. Tel: (847) 675-3700, FAX: (847) 674-1230, E-Mail: blevin@triangleprinters.com, Web Site: www.triangleprinters.com (27)

Triax Data Inc, Knoxville, TN. Tel: (865) 971-4333, (888) 241-9559, FAX: (865) 971-4333, E-Mail: info@triaxdata.com, Web Site: www.triaxdata.com (23)

Tribune Co, Chicago, IL. Tel: (312) 222-9100, FAX: (312) 222-1573, Web Site: www.tribune.com (17)

Tribune Direct LLC, Northlake, IL. Tel: (708) 836-2700, (800) 545-9657, FAX: (708) 836-0605, Web Site: tribunedirect.com (21)

Tribune Direct Orlando, Orlando, FL. Tel: (407) 420-5100, E-Mail: kkeenan@tribunedirect.com, Web Site: www.orlandosentinelmediagroup.com/DirectMail (21)

Trice, Eleanor, Union Privilege, AFL-CIO, Washington, DC. Tel: (202) 293-5311, (800) 472-2005, FAX: (202) 293-5311, E-Mail: info@unionprivilege.org, Web Site: www.unionplus.org (1)

Tricor Braun, Woodridge, IL. Tel: (708) 385-9333, FAX: (708) 385-3015, Web Site: www.tricorbraun.com (16)

Tricor Direct Inc, Branford, CT. Tel: (203) 488-8059, (800) 243-6624, FAX: (800) 571-2596, E-Mail: custsvc_setonus@seton.com, Web Site: www.seton.com (9)

Tridium Inc, Richmond, VA. Tel: (804) 525-1648, Web Site: www.tridium.com (9)

Triggerfish Marketing, San Francisco, CA. Tel: (415) 671-4699, Web Site: www.triggerfish.com (30)

Trigon Blue Cross/Blue Shield, Roanoke, VA. Tel: (540) 853-5000, (800) 553-3164, FAX: (540) 853-3053, Web Site: www.trigon.com (15)

Trilithic, Indianapolis, IN. Tel: (317) 423-6604, Web Site: www.trilithic.com (16)

Trimberger, John, Stephen Fossler Co Inc, Des Plaines, IL. Tel: (847) 635-7200, (800) 762-0030, FAX: (800) 424-9292, E-Mail: customerservice@fossler.com, Web Site: sfc.stephen-fossler.com (27)

Trimensions Inc, Englewood, NJ. Tel: (201) 816-8820, FAX: (201) 816-8870, E-Mail: jghossn@trimensionsinc.com, Web Site: www.trimensionsinc.com (21)

Trine, David E., Choice Point, Alpharetta, GA. Tel: (770) 752-6000, (800) 342-5339, FAX: (770) 752-6005, Web Site: www.choicepoint.com (16)

Trinity Direct LLC, Butler, NJ. Tel: (973) 283-3600, FAX: (973) 283-3606, E-Mail: trinity.info@trinitydirect.net, Web Site: www.trinitydirect.net (23)

Trinity Marketing Inc, Boston, MA. Tel: (617) 292-7399, E-Mail: info@trinitynet.com, Web Site: www.trinitynet.com (35)

Trinity Road LLC, Charlotte, NC. Tel: (704) 940-2240 (28)

Trinity Technical Group, Inc, Arlington, TX. Tel: (817) 879-7907, E-Mail: info@trinitytechnicalgroup.com, Web Site: www.trinitytechnicalgroup.com (22)

Tripar International Inc, Roselle, IL. Tel: (630) 980-5100, (800) 222-1142, FAX: (800) 648-9015, E-Mail: sales@tripar.com, Web Site: www.tripar.com (28)

Karen Tripi Associates, New York, NY. Tel: (212) 972-5258, FAX: (212) 599-3809, E-Mail: karen@karentripi.com, Web Site: www.karentripi.com (20)

Tripi, Karen, Karen Tripi Associates, New York, NY. Tel: (212) 972-5258, FAX: (212) 599-3809, E-Mail: karen@karentripi.com, Web Site: www.karentripi.com (20)

Tripodi, Joseph V., The Coca-Cola Co, Atlanta, GA. Tel: (404) 676-2121, (800) 438-2653, FAX: (404) 676-6792, Web Site: www.cocacola.com (16)

Tristar Products, Fairfield, NJ. Tel: (973) 575-5400, FAX: (973) 683-6708, E-Mail: infotp@tristarproductsinc.com, Web Site: www.tristarproductsinc.com (16)

Triton College, River Grove, IL. Tel: (708) 456-0300, FAX: (708) 583-3121, Web Site: www.triton.edu (16)

Triumph Learning, New York, NY. Tel: (212) 652-0200, Web Site: http://triumphlearning.com (17)

Trivino, Ezequiel, Wikreate, San Francisco, CA. Tel: (415) 362-0440, FAX: (415) 362-0430, E-Mail: ezequieltrivino@wikreate.com, Web Site: www.wikreate.com (35)

Troiano, Kenneth, Modernage Custom Digital Imaging Labs, New York, NY. Tel: (212) 997-1800, (800) 997-2510, FAX: (212) 869-4796, E-Mail: info@modernage.com, Web Site: www.modernage.com (16)

Troiano, Richard, Modernage Custom Digital Imaging Labs, New York, NY. Tel: (212) 997-1800, (800) 997-2510, FAX: (212) 869-4796, E-Mail: info@modernage.com, Web Site: www.modernage.com (16)

Trombley, Rich, Brigar Xpress Solutions, Inc, Albany, NY. Tel: (518) 438-7817, (877) 437-7817, FAX: (518) 438-0224, E-Mail: general@brigarxpress.com, Web Site: www.brigarxpress.com (28)

Trone Brand Energy Inc, High Point, NC. Tel: (336) 886-1622, E-Mail: info@trone.com, Web Site: www.tronebrandenergy.com (35)

Trophyland USA Inc, Hialeah, FL. Tel: (305) 823-4830, (800) 327-5820, FAX: (305) 823-4836, E-Mail: info@trophyland.com, Web Site: www.trophyland.com (5)

Trotta, Melissa, NCRI List Management, Englewood Cliffs, NJ. Tel: (201) 541-9500, FAX: (201) 541-1944, E-Mail: info@ncrilists.com, Web Site: www.ncrilists.com (23)

Troup, Wilson, Clarin by Hussey Seating, North Berwick, ME. Tel: (800) 341-0401, FAX: (207) 676-2222, Web Site: www.husseyseating.com (5)

Trout Unlimited, Arlington, VA. Tel: (703) 522-0200, (800) 834-2419, FAX: (703) 284-9400, E-Mail: trout@tu.org, Web Site: www.tu.org (1)

Trowbridge, C. Robertson, Yankee Publishing Inc, Dublin, NH. Tel: (603) 563-8111, FAX: (603) 563-8732, Web Site: www.yankeemagazine.com (17)

Trowbridge, Keith, ActivStyle, Minneapolis, MN. Tel: (612) 520-9333, (800) 651-6223, FAX: (612) 520-9300, Web Site: www.activstyle.com (16)

Troy Biologicals Inc, Troy, MI. Tel: (248) 585-9720, (800) 521-0445, FAX: (248) 585-2490, E-Mail: info@troybio.com, Web Site: www.troybio.com (7)

Troy, William, American Society for Quality, Milwaukee, WI. Tel: (414) 272-8575, (800) 248-1946, FAX: (414) 272-1734, E-Mail: help@asq.org, Web Site: www.asq.org (1)

The Troyanos Group Ltd, Irvington, NY. Tel: (914) 479-1801, FAX: (914) 993-9554, E-Mail: dennis@troyanosgroup.com, Web Site: www.troyanosgroup.com (20)

Troyanos, Dennis, The Troyanos Group Ltd, Irvington, NY. Tel: (914) 479-1801, FAX: (914) 993-9554, E-Mail: dennis@troyanosgroup.com, Web Site: www.troyanosgroup.com (20)

Trozzolo Communications Group, Kansas City, MO. Tel: (816) 842-8111, Web Site: www.trozzolo.com (35)

Trozzolo, Angelo, Trozzolo Communications Group, Kansas City, MO. Tel: (816) 842-8111, Web Site: www.trozzolo.com (35)

Trudell, Libby, The Dialog Corp, Morrisville, NC. Tel: (919) 804-6400, (800) 3 DIALOG, FAX: (919) 804-6410, E-Mail: customer@dialog.com, Web Site: www.dialog.com (30)

True North Inc, New York, NY. Tel: (212) 557-4202, Web Site: truenorthinc.com (35)

True Value Co, Chicago, IL. Tel: (773) 695-5000, Web Site: www.truevaluecompany.com (16)

Truesdell, Melanie, SubscriptionAgency.com Inc, Winter Haven, FL. Tel: (863) 229-2557, (866) 590-6247, FAX: (866) 890-6247, E-Mail: info@subscriptionagency.com, Web Site: www.subscriptionagency.com (18)

TrueSense Marketing, Freedom, PA. Tel: (877) 878-6584, Web Site: www.truesense.com (35)

TruGreen/ChemLawn, Lewis Center, OH. Tel: (614) 846-1800, (800) TRUE-GREEN, FAX: (614) 431-0155, Web Site: www.trugreen.com (16)

Truitt Brothers Inc, Salem, OR. Tel: (503) 362-3674, (800) 547-8712, FAX: (503) 588-2868, E-Mail: truittbrothers@truittbros.com, Web Site: www.truittbros.com (16)

Truitt, David, Truitt Brothers Inc, Salem, OR. Tel: (503) 362-3674, (800) 547-8712, FAX: (503) 588-2868, E-Mail: truittbrothers@truittbros.com, Web Site: www.truittbros.com (16)

Truitt, Mark, National Seminars Group, Shawnee Mission, KS. Tel: (913) 432-7755, (800) 258-7246, FAX: (913) 432-0824, E-Mail: cstserv@natsem.com, Web Site: www.natsem.com (16)

Truitt, Peter, Truitt Brothers Inc, Salem, OR. Tel: (503) 362-3674, (800) 547-8712, FAX: (503) 588-2868, E-Mail: truittbrothers@truittbros.com, Web Site: www.truittbros.com (16)

Trulby, Vera, Doremus & Co, New York, NY. Tel: (212) 366-3000, FAX: (212) 366-3060, E-Mail: mbroom@doremus.com, Web Site: www.doremus.com (35)

Trullenque, Alfredo, No Fault Sports Products, Houston, TX. Tel: (713) 683-7101, (800) 462-7766, FAX: (713) 683-7103, E-Mail: nofaultsports@comcast.net, Web Site: www.nofaultsports.com (11)

Trumble Greetings, Boulder, CO. Tel: (800) 525-0656, FAX: (303) 530-5124, E-Mail: info@leanintree.com, Web Site: www.leanintree.com (6)

Trumble, Ed, Leanin' Tree Inc, Boulder, CO. Tel: (303) 530-7768, (800) 525-0656, FAX: (303) 530-5124, E-Mail: info@leanintree.com, Web Site: www.leanintree.com (6)

Trumble, Jane, Leanin' Tree Inc, Boulder, CO. Tel: (303) 530-7768, (800) 525-0656, FAX: (303) 530-5124, E-Mail: info@leanintree.com, Web Site: www.leanintree.com (6)

Trumble, Tom, Leanin' Tree Inc, Boulder, CO. Tel: (303) 530-7768, (800) 525-0656, FAX: (303) 530-5124, E-Mail: info@leanintree.com, Web Site: www.leanintree.com (6)

Trumble, Tom, Trumble Greetings, Boulder, CO. Tel: (800) 525-0656, FAX: (303) 530-5124, E-Mail: info@leanintree.com, Web Site: www.leanintree.com (6)

Trumka, Richard, AFL-CIO, Washington, DC. Tel: (202) 637-5000, FAX: (202) 637-5323, (202) 637-5058, Web Site: www.aflcio.org (1)

The Trumpet Club, New York, NY. Tel: (212) 343-6100, FAX: (212) 343-7709, Web Site: www.scholastic.com (17)

Trust, David, Professional Photographer Magazine, Atlanta, GA. Tel: (404) 522-8600, (800) 786-6277, FAX: (404) 614-6405, E-Mail: csc@ppa.com, Web Site: www.ppa.com (17)

TRUSTe, San Francisco, CA. Tel: (415) 520-3490, FAX: (415) 520-3420, Web Site: www.truste.org (22)

truTV, New York, NY. Tel: (212) 973-2800, (800) 268-7856, FAX: (212) 973-3210, Web Site: www.trutv.com (17)

Tsai, Susan, Top Year International Inc, Yorba Linda, CA. Tel: (714) 692-6688, (800) 942-8722, FAX: (714) 692-8691, E-Mail: sales@akirausa.com, Web Site: www.akirausa.com (33)

Tsai, Y.T., Regitar USA Inc, Montgomery, AL. Tel: (334) 244-1885, (877) 734-4827, FAX: (334) 244-1901, E-Mail: info@regitar.com, Web Site: www.regitar.com (9)

Tschiffely, Donna, Direct Marketing Association of Washington, Reston, VA. Tel: (703) 689-DMAW, FAX: (703) 481-DMAW, E-Mail: info@dmaw.org, Web Site: www.dmaw.org (40)

Tschiffely, Donna, Marketing Advents, Washington, DC. Tel: (202) 955-5030, FAX: (202) 955-0085, E-Mail: info@dmaw.org, Web Site: www.dmaw.org (43)

Tshibangu, Judith, Liberty Life Insurance Co, Greenville, SC. Tel: (864) 609-8111, (800) 344-5834 (Mktg), FAX: (864) 609-4411, Web Site: www.libertycorp.com (15)

Tsourides, Holly, Stanley Supply & Services, North Andover, MA. Tel: (978) 682-9844, (800) 225-5370, FAX: (800) 743-8141, Web Site: www.stanleysupplyservices.com (16)

Tsujihara, Kevin, Warner Bros, Burbank, CA. Tel: (818) 954-6000, Web Site: www.warnerbros.com (3)

Tsukichi, Steven G., Digi-Key Corp, Thief River Falls, MN. Tel: (218) 681-6674, (800) 344-4539, FAX: (218) 681-3380, E-Mail: sales@digikey.com, Web Site: www.digikey.com (3)

Tu, Andy, Defy Media Inc, New York, NY. E-Mail: info@defymedia.com, Web Site: www.defymedia.com (35)

Tuan, Mia, University of Washington Educational Outreach, Seattle, WA. Tel: (206) 685-6566, E-Mail: edinfo@u.washington.edu, Web Site: www.pce.uw.edu (1)

Tuchman, Kenneth, TeleTech, Englewood, CO. Tel: (303) 397-8100, (800) TELETECH, FAX: (303) 397-8199, E-Mail: solutions@TeleTech.com, Web Site: www.teletech.com (22)

Tuchman, Murray, Printing Corp of the Americas Inc (PCA), Fort Lauderdale, FL. Tel: (954) 781-8100, (866) 721-1722, FAX: (954) 781-8421, Web Site: www.pcaprinting.com (27)

Tucker Capital Corp, Princeton, NJ. Tel: (609) 924-5710, FAX: (609) 924-5027, E-Mail: info@tuckercapital.com, Web Site: www.tuckercapital.com (20)

Tucker Electronics Co, Garland, TX. Tel: (214) 348-8800, (887) 667-6044, FAX: (214) 348-0367, E-Mail: sales@tucker.com, Web Site: www.tucker.com (3)

Tucker Printers, Henrietta, NY. Tel: (585) 359-3030, Web Site: www.tuckerprinters.com (27)

Tucker, James, Integrated Marketing Technology Inc, San Francisco, CA. Tel: (415) 699-2280, FAX: (917) 591-5333, E-Mail: information@imtnetwork.com, Web Site: www.imtnetwork.com (22)

Tucker, James, Tucker Electronics Co, Garland, TX. Tel: (214) 348-8800, (887) 667-6044, FAX: (214) 348-0367, E-Mail: sales@tucker.com, Web Site: www.tucker.com (3)

Tucker, Kathleen, Suntrust Banks Inc, Atlanta, GA. Tel: (404) 588-7914, (800) 786-8787, FAX: (404) 532-0550, E-Mail: emmett.harmon@suntrust.com, Web Site: www.suntrust.com (14)

Tucker, Larry, We Deliver America Inc, Englewood Cliffs, NJ. Tel: (201) 307-8888, FAX: (201) 307-1200, E-Mail: info@we-deliver-america.com, Web Site: www.we-deliver-america.com (31)

Tucker, Patrick, World Future Society, Chicago, IL. Tel: (301) 656-8274, (800) 989-8274, FAX: (301) 951-0394, E-Mail: info@wfs.org, Web Site: www.wfs.org (1)

Tucker, Robert, Beacon Shoe Co Inc, Maryland Heights, MO. Tel: (636) 488-5444, FAX: (636) 488-3103 (16)

Tucker, Ronnie, New York Road Runners, New York, NY. Tel: (855) 5MY-NYRR, E-Mail: mynyrr@nyrr.org, Web Site: www.nyrr.org (13)

Tucker, Sharon, Alcom, Harleysville, PA. Tel: (215) 513-1600, E-Mail: stucker@alcomprinting.com, Web Site: www.alcomprinting.com (21)

Tudor, Dr. Keith, Kennesaw State University, Kennesaw, GA. Tel: (770) 423-6060, FAX: (770) 499-3261, Web Site: www.kennesaw.edu (41)

Tuerberg, Janice, Bobley-Harmann Corp, Ronkonkoma, NY. Tel: (516) 364-1800, (800) 323-1692, FAX: (516) 364-1899, E-Mail: info.giftvalues@gmail.com, Web Site: www.giftvalues.com (5)

Tuff, Tim, John Harland Co, Decatur, GA. Tel: (770) 981-5580, (800) 723-3690, FAX: (770) 593-5367, E-Mail: jhhwebmaster@harland.net, Web Site: www.harland.net (16)

Tuggles, Alf, Boy Scouts of America/National Supply Group, Charlotte, NC. Tel: (800) 323-0736, FAX: (704) 588-5822, E-Mail: customerservice@scoutstuff.org, Web Site: www.scoutstuff.org (1)

Tukes, Terry, G-Neil Direct Mail, Sunrise, FL. Tel: (800) 999-9111, FAX: (954) 851-1264, E-Mail: tcs@gneil.com, Web Site: www.gneil.com (10)

Tukulj, Amir, Thane International Inc, El Segundo, CA. Tel: (310) 531-1956, FAX: (310) 531-1957, E-Mail: info@thaneinc.com, Web Site: www.thaneinc.com (35)

Tull, Susan, Convio Inc, Austin, TX. Tel: (512) 652-2600, (888) 528-9501, FAX: (512) 652-2699, Web Site: www.convio.com (22)

Tullos, Jr. Mark A., Louisiana State Museum, New Orleans, LA. Tel: (504) 568-6968, (800) 568-6968, FAX: (504) 568-4995, Web Site: www.lsm.crt.state.la.us (1)

Tully & Holland Inc, Wellesley, MA. Tel: (781) 239-2900, FAX: (781) 239-2901, E-Mail: info@tullyandholland.com, Web Site: www.tullyandholland.com (14)

Tully, Timothy, Tully & Holland Inc, Wellesley, MA. Tel: (781) 239-2900, FAX: (781) 239-2901, E-Mail: info@tullyandholland.com, Web Site: www.tullyandholland.com (14)

Tulp, Peter, SC Direct, West Bridgewater, MA. Tel: (800) 343-9695, Web Site: www.scdirect.com (2)

Tunick, Barry, Estes Industries, Penrose, CO. Tel: (719) 372-6565, FAX: (719) 372-3419, Web Site: www.estesrockets.com (11)

Tunioli, Carlo, Benetton USA, New York, NY. Tel: (212) 593-0290, (800) 274-7192, FAX: (212) 371-1438, E-Mail: mtaylor@bennettonusa.com, Web Site: www.benetton.com (2)

Tunney, Greg A., RG Barry Corp, Pickerington, OH. Tel: (614) 864-6400, (800) 848-7560, FAX: (614) 866-9787, E-Mail: sales@rgbarry.com, Web Site: www.rgbarry.com (2)

Tupperware Brands Corp, Orlando, FL. Tel: (407) 826-5050, (800) 366-3800, FAX: (407) 826-8874, Web Site: www.tupperwarebrands.com (16)

Turec, Lori, KeyPath Education, Lenexa, KS. Tel: (913) 254-6000, Web Site: keypathedu.com (35)

Turetzky, Julie, Home Planners, Tucson, AZ. Tel: (520) 297-8200, FAX: (520) 297-6219, E-Mail: sales@homeplanners.com, Web Site: www.homeplanners.com (17)

Turicchi, Scott, Protus, Ottawa, ON Canada. Tel: (613) 733-0000, (888) 733-0000, E-Mail: info@protus.com, Web Site: www.protus.com (32)

Turkel Brands, Miami, FL. Tel: (305) 445-9111, FAX: (305) 448-6691, E-Mail: speaking@turkelbrands.com, Web Site: turkelbrands.com (35)

Turkel, Bruce, Turkel Brands, Miami, FL. Tel: (305) 445-9111, FAX: (305) 448-6691, E-Mail: speaking@turkelbrands.com, Web Site: turkelbrands.com (35)

Brian Turley & Co, Melrose, MA. Tel: (781) 662-8538, FAX: (781) 662-5590, E-Mail: turley@shore.net (39)

Turley, Brian C., Brian Turley & Co, Melrose, MA. Tel: (781) 662-8538, FAX: (781) 662-5590, E-Mail: turley@shore.net (39)

Turnbull, Thomas, Volunteers of America, Alexandria, VA. Tel: (703) 341-5000, (800) 899-0089, FAX: (703) 341-7000, E-Mail: info@voa.org, Web Site: www.voa.org (1)

Turncraft Clocks Inc, Spring Park, MN. Tel: (952) 471-9573, (800) 544-1711, FAX: (952) 471-8579, E-Mail: office@meiselwoodhobby.com, Web Site: www.meiselwoodhobby.com (6)

Turner Broadcasting System Inc, Atlanta, GA. Tel: (404) 827-1700, Web Site: www.turner.com (32)

Turner Greenhouses, Goldsboro, NC. Tel: (800) 672-4770, E-Mail: customerservice@turnergreenhouses.com, Web Site: www.turnergreenhouses.com (8)

Turner Network Television (TNT), Atlanta, GA. Tel: (404) 827-1700, E-Mail: tnt@turner.com, Web Site: www.turner.com (32)

Turner, Alan, Magnets USA, Roanoke, VA. Tel: (540) 857-3045, (800) 869-7562, FAX: (800) 788-6872, Web Site: www.magnetsusa.com (30)

Turner, Alexandra, ACBL, Horn Lake, MS. Tel: (662) 253-3100, FAX: (662) 253-3187, E-Mail: service@acbl.org, Web Site: www.acbl.org (1)

Turner, Bill, Whirley Drink Works, Warren, PA. Tel: (814) 723-7600, (800) 825-5575, FAX: (814) 723-3245, E-Mail: info@whirleydrinkworks.com, Web Site: www.whirleydrinkworks.com (5)

Turner, Brant, American Database Marketing Inc, Jacksonville, FL. Tel: (888) 565-7724, FAX: (888) 270-4338, E-Mail: admdun@cs.com, Web Site: www.admlists.com (23)

Turner, Brent, Cramer, Norwood, MA. Tel: (781) 278-2387, Web Site: www.crameronline.com (20)

Turner, Janet, Fred Pryor Seminars, Mission, KS. Tel: (913) 967-8518, (800) 780-8476, FAX: (913) 967-8849, E-Mail: customerservice@pryor.com, Web Site: www.pryor.com (16)

Turner, Sherran, Hanover Direct Inc, Weehawken, NJ. Tel: (201) 863-7300, FAX: (201) 272-3465, Web Site: www.hanoverdirect.com (5)

Turner, Steven M., Creative Printing Services Inc, Saint Louis, MO. Tel: (314) 863-4550, (800) 886-4551, FAX: (314) 863-6036, E-Mail: steve@cpsstl.com, Web Site: www.cpsstl.com (27)

Turner, Will, Infolure, Phoenix, AZ. Tel: (602) 308-6700, FAX: (602) 308-6801, E-Mail: glenn.gottfried@infolure.com, Web Site: www.infolure.com (22)

Turner, Willis, Huntsinger & Jeffer, Richmond, VA. Tel: (804) 266-2499, FAX: (804) 266-8563, E-Mail: info@huntsinger-jeffer.com, Web Site: www.huntsinger-jeffer.com (21)

Turnmire, Margie, McFarland & Co Inc Publishers, Jefferson, NC. Tel: (336) 246-4460, (800) 253-2187, FAX: (336) 246-5018, E-Mail: info@mcfarlandpub.com, Web Site: www.mcfarlandpub.com (17)

Turtle Bay Management Co Inc, Virginia Beach, VA. Tel: (757) 422-2760, FAX: (757) 422-1434, E-Mail: jimlant@turtlebaymanagement.com, Web Site: www.turtlebaymanagement.com (20)

Tuszynski, Jr. Daniel J., Music Treasures Co, Richmond, VA. Tel: (804) 730-8800, (800) 666-7565, FAX: (888) MUSIC-TC, E-Mail: musict@musictreasures.com, Web Site: www.musictreasures.com (6)

Tutssel, Mark, Leo Burnett Worldwide, Chicago, IL. Tel: (312) 220-5959, Web Site: leoburnett.com (35)

Tuttle, Wallingford, CT. Tel: (203) 949-4290, (800) 882-7511, FAX: (203) 949-4288, Web Site: www.tuttlecatalog.com (2)

Tuttle Printing & Engraving, Rutland, VT. Tel: (802) 773-9171, (800) 776-7682, FAX: (802) 773-5785, E-Mail: info@tuttleprinting.com, Web Site: www.tuttleprinting.com (10)

Tuxhorn, William J., McNichols Co, Tampa, FL. Tel: (813) 282-3828, FAX: (813) 288-9342, E-Mail: sales@mcnichols.com, Web Site: www.mcnichols.com (16)

Tveit, Elizabeth, Seattle Magazine, Seattle, WA. Tel: (206) 284-1750, (800) 637-0334, FAX: (206) 284-2550, E-Mail: customerservice@seattlemag.com, Web Site: www.seattlemag.com (17)

Gilbert Tweed Associates, New York, NY. Tel: (212) 758-3000, FAX: (212) 832-1040, E-Mail: hrdptgt@gmail.com, Web Site: www.gilberttweed.com (20)

Tweed, Janet, Gilbert Tweed Associates, New York, NY. Tel: (212) 758-3000, FAX: (212) 832-1040, E-Mail: hrdptgt@gmail.com, Web Site: www.gilberttweed.com (20)

20th Century Fox Television, Los Angeles, CA. Tel: (310) 369-4636, FAX: (310) 969-0468, Web Site: www.foxstudios.com (16)

21st Century Insurance, Woodland Hills, CA. Tel: (818) 704-3700, FAX: (818) 226-1198, E-Mail: executiveoffice@21st.com, Web Site: www.21st.com (15)

21st Century Marketing, Altamonte Springs, FL. Tel: (321) 663-4640, E-Mail: tony@21stcenturymarketingonline.com, Web Site: 21stcenturymarketingonline.com (24)

Twin City Engraving/Premier Promotions, Saint Joseph, MI. Tel: (616) 983-0601, (800) 222-7752, FAX: (616) 983-3571, Web Site: www.premierpromos.com (33)

Twitchell, Kim, HF Direct, Birmingham, AL. Tel: (205) 458-8200, FAX: (205) 458-8206, E-Mail: info@hfdirect.com, Web Site: www.hfdirect.com (35)

2ergo, Arlington, VA. Tel: (703) 879-3400, Web Site: www.2ergo.com (30)

2-10 Home Buyers Warranty, Denver, CO. Tel: (720) 747-6000, Web Site: www.2-10.com (15)

22squared Inc, Atlanta, GA. Tel: (404) 347-8700, FAX: (404) 347-8800, Web Site: www.22squared.com (35)

Ty Pac, Baldwinsville, NY. Tel: (315) 638-9431, (800) 356-8964, FAX: (315) 638-9433, E-Mail: info@typac.com, Web Site: www.typack.com (34)

Tyco Electronics Corp, Berwyn, PA. Tel: (610) 893-9800, Web Site: www.te.com (16)

Tyco Valves & Controls, Houston, TX. Tel: (713) 986-4665, (800) 343-0990, FAX: (713) 937-5466, Web Site: www.tycovalves.com (16)

Tyler, Dave, Kappa Publishing Group, Blue Bell, PA. Tel: (215) 643-6385, FAX: (215) 628-3571, Web Site: www.kappapublishing.com (17)

Tyler, Tiffany, Sensory Effects Powder System, Bridgeton, MO. Tel: (314) 291-5444, (800) 422-5444, FAX: (314) 291-3289, E-Mail: info@sensoryeffects.com (16)

Tyndale House Publishers, Carol Stream, IL. Tel: (630) 668-8300, FAX: (630) 668-3245 (17)

Type-A-Scan Inc, New York, NY. Tel: (212) 367-8406, FAX: (212) 691-8134, E-Mail: info@typeascan.com, Web Site: www.typeascan.com (22)

Tyson Associates Inc, Brookfield, CT. Tel: (203) 775-9465, FAX: (203) 775-0563, E-Mail: elaine@tysonassociates.com, Web Site: www.tysonassociates.com (17)

Tyson, Elaine, Tyson Associates Inc, Brookfield, CT. Tel: (203) 775-9465, FAX: (203) 775-0563, E-Mail: elaine@tysonassociates.com, Web Site: www.tysonassociates.com (17)

Tyson, Gloria, Profit Center Software Inc, Uniondale, NY. Tel: (516) 414-6300, (888) 446-6240, FAX: (516) 414-6304, E-Mail: jmarrah@profitcenter.com, Web Site: www.profitcenter.com (22)

Tyson, Karen, National Association of Federal Credit Unions, Arlington, VA. Tel: (800) 336-4644, Web Site: www.nafcu.org (14)

Tyson, Karen, Trend Magazines Inc, Saint Petersburg, FL. Tel: (727) 821-5800, (800) 821-5800, FAX: (727) 822-5083, E-Mail: feedback@fltrend.com, Web Site: www.floridatrend.com (17)

Tzou, Dr. Shin-Yuan, BroadVision Inc, Redwood City, CA. Tel: (650) 295-0716, (866) 246-4887, FAX: (650) 364-3425, E-Mail: sales@broadvision.com, Web Site: www.broadvision.com (16)

U

U-Bild, Oceanside, CA. Tel: (800) 828-2453, FAX: (760) 754-2356, Web Site: www.ubild.com (8)

U-Haul International, Phoenix, AZ. Tel: (602) 263-6011, (800) GO-UHAUL, FAX: (602) 263-6598, Web Site: www.uhaul.com (16)

The UPS Store, Inc., San Diego, CA. Tel: (858) 455-8800, FAX: (858) 546-7488, Web Site: www.mbe.com (28)

UAA Clearinghouse, Omaha, NE. Tel: (402) 991-2810, Web Site: www.uaaclearinghouse.com (22)

UBS Wealth Management US, Weehawken, NJ. Tel: (201) 352-3000, (888) 279-3343, FAX: (201) 617-8589, Web Site: www.ubs.com/financialservicesinc (14)

UCEA, New York, NY. FAX: (212) 781-6500, Web Site: www.revike.org (1)

UCI/Dream Giveaways, Clearwater, FL. Tel: (727) 536-2777, Web Site: www.dreamgiveaways.com (20)

UF College of Advertising, Journalism, & Communications, Gainesville, FL. Tel: (352) 392-4046, FAX: (352) 392-3919, Web Site: www.jou.ufl.edu (41)

UGL Equis Corp, Chicago, IL. Tel: (312) 424-8000, FAX: (312) 424-8080, Web Site: www.equiscorp.com (16)

ULTA Salon Cosmetics Fragrance, Bolingbrook, IL. Tel: (630) 410-4800, (866) 983-8582 (7)

UMI Publications Inc, Charlotte, NC. Tel: (800) 747-9287, FAX: (704) 374-0729, E-Mail: info@umipub.com, Web Site: www.umipub.com (17)

UNICEF, New York, NY. Tel: (212) 326-7000, FAX: (212) 887-7465, Web Site: www.unicef.org (1)

UNICEF Canada, Toronto, ON Canada. Tel: (416) 482-4444, (800) 567-4483, FAX: (416) 487-8875, E-Mail: on.secretary@unicef.ca, Web Site: www.unicef.ca (1)

UPMC Health Plan, Pittsburgh, PA. Tel: (888) 876-2756, (800) 361-2629, Web Site: www.upmchealthplan.com (1)

USAA, San Antonio, TX. Tel: (512) 498-6524, FAX: (512) 498-8000 (15)

USAA Alliance Services Marketing, San Antonio, TX. Tel: (210) 456-9857, FAX: (210) 498-4542, Web Site: www.usaa.com (14)

USC Viterbi School of Engineering, Los Angeles, CA. Tel: (213) 740-7832, Web Site: viterbi.usc.edu (1)

USG Corp, Chicago, IL. Tel: (312) 436-4000, (800) 621-9622, FAX: (312) 672-4093, Web Site: www.usg.com (34)

USI Affinity, Philadelphia, PA. Tel: (610) 833-2876, (800) 625-2876, FAX: (610) 265-2876, E-Mail: info@usiaffinity.com, Web Site: www.brcorp.com (15)

USI Affinity Collegiate Insurance Resources, Columbus, OH. Tel: (614) 486-5388, Web Site: www.collegiateinsuranceresources.com (15)

USO Inc, Washington, DC. Tel: (703) 908-6400, (888) 484-3876, Web Site: www.uso.org (1)

USX, Pittsburgh, PA. Tel: (412) 433-1121, E-Mail: webmaster@usx.com, Web Site: www.usx.com (16)

USY Consulting Inc, Dumont, NJ. Tel: (201) 585-7402, FAX: (201) 585-2754, E-Mail: usyconsulting@hotmail.com (20)

UV Process Supply, Chicago, IL. Tel: (773) 248-0099, (800) 621-1296, FAX: (773) 880-6647, E-Mail: info@uvps.com, Web Site: www.uvprocess.com (34)

Uberti, Laurent, Sitel, Nashville, TN. Tel: (615) 301-7100, (866) 95-SITEL, Web Site: www.sitel.com (29)

Udell, Sandra, Winnipeg Art Gallery, Winnipeg, MB Canada. Tel: (204) 786-6641, FAX: (204) 788-4998, E-Mail: inquiries@wag.mb.ca, Web Site: www.wag.ca (1)

Uggla, Lance, IHS Markit, Englewood, CO. Tel: (303) 858-6187, (800) 447-2273, Web Site: www.ihs.com (17)

Uhrich, Marie A., Thrivent Financial for Lutherans, Appleton, WI. Tel: (920) 734-5721, (800) 847-4836, FAX: (920) 730-4781, E-Mail: mail@thrivent.com, Web Site: www.thrivent.com (14)

Uhrynowski, Peter, Queue Inc, Stratford, CT. Tel: (203) 335-0906, (800) 232-2224, FAX: (800) 775-2729, E-Mail: jdk@queueinc.com, Web Site: www.qworkbooks.com (17)

Uihlein, Elizabeth, Uline, Pleasant Prairie, WI. Tel: (847) 473-3000, (800) 295-5510, FAX: (800) 295-5571, E-Mail: customer.service@uline.com, Web Site: www.uline.com (5)

Uihlein, Richard, Uline, Pleasant Prairie, WI. Tel: (847) 473-3000, (800) 295-5510, FAX: (800) 295-5571, E-Mail: customer.service@uline.com, Web Site: www.uline.com (5)

Ulano Corp, Brooklyn, NY. Tel: (718) 237-4700, (800) 221-0616, FAX: (718) 802-1119, E-Mail: ulano@ulano.com, Web Site: www.ulano.com (34)

Ulbrich, Tom, University at Buffalo Center for Entrepreneurial Leadership, Buffalo, NY. Tel: (716) 885-5715, FAX: (716) 845-6999, E-Mail: mgt-cel@buffalo.edu, Web Site: http://mgt.buffalo.edu/entrepreneurship/cel (5)

Uline, Pleasant Prairie, WI. Tel: (847) 473-3000, (800) 295-5510, FAX: (800) 295-5571, E-Mail: customer.service@uline.com, Web Site: www.uline.com (5)

Ulla, Jorge, Dexposito & Partners, New York, NY. Tel: (646) 747-8800, Web Site: newamericanagency.com (35)

Ullery, Cathryn, Mentor Corp, Santa Barbara, CA. Tel: (805) 879-6000, (800) 525-0245, FAX: (805) 964-2712, Web Site: www.mentorcorp.com (16)

Ullman, Mike, JC Penney Inc, Plano, TX. Tel: (972) 431-1000, FAX: (972) 431-1977, Web Site: www.jcpenney.com (5)

Ullmann, Michael H., Johnson & Johnson, New Brunswick, NJ. Tel: (732) 524-0400, FAX: (732) 214-0332, Web Site: www.jnj.com (16)

Ulrich, Catherine, Weight Watchers International, New York, NY. Tel: (516) 390-1400, FAX: (516) 390-1302, Web Site: www.weight-watchers.com (16)

Ulrich, Dave, IPS - Sendero Corp, Norcross, GA. Tel: (480) 941-8112, (800) 879-1996, FAX: (770) 409-1735, E-Mail: sales@ips-sendero.com, Web Site: www.ips-sendero.com (14)

Ultimate Office, Farmingdale, NJ. Tel: (732) 780-6911, (800) 631-2233, FAX: (732) 780-9833, Web Site: www.ultoffice.com (16)

Ultimate Products Inc, Chula Vista, CA. Tel: (813) 881-1575, (800) 477-4287, FAX: (813) 881-1831, E-Mail: office@ultimatehat.com, Web Site: www.ultimatehat.com (16)

Ultra Direct Marketing Inc, Jackson, NJ. Tel: (732) 364-8337, (800) 365-8587, FAX: (732) 364-9598, E-Mail: contact@ultradirect.com, Web Site: www.ultradirect.com (16)

Ultradent Products Inc, South Jordan, UT. Tel: (801) 572-4200, FAX: (801) 553-4600, E-Mail: onlineordersupport@ultradent.com, Web Site: www.ultradent.com (7)

UMarketing LLC, Lombard, IL. Tel: (630) 916-1717, Web Site: www.umarketing.com (35)

UMass Dartmouth, North Dartmouth, MA. Tel: (508) 999-8000, (508) 999-9250, Web Site: www.umassd.edu (1)

Umbrell, Trish Wesley, Massachusetts Horticultural Society, Wellesley, MA. Tel: (617) 933-4900, (617) 933-4929, FAX: (617) 933-4901, E-Mail: hort_line@masshort.org, Web Site: www.masshort.org (1)

Unadilla Laminated Products, Unadilla, NY. Tel: (607) 369-9341, FAX: (607) 369-3608, E-Mail: info@unalam.com, Web Site: www.unalam.com (16)

Uncharted Country Publishing, Madison, WI. Tel: (575) 776-3470, E-Mail: ucp@taichihealth.com, Web Site: www.taichihealth.com (17)

Uncle Ben's Inc, Greenville, MS. Tel: (601) 335-8000, (800) 54-UNCLE, (800) 548-6253, FAX: (601) 378-4370, E-Mail: info@unclebens.com, Web Site: www.unclebens.com (4)

UndercoverWear Inc, Tewksbury, MA. Tel: (978) 851-8580, (800) 733-0007, FAX: (978) 640-2882, E-Mail: service@undercoverwear.com, Web Site: www.undercoverwear.com (2)

Underhill, Robert, Channing L Bete Co Inc, South Deerfield, MA. Tel: (800) 477-4776, FAX: (800) 499-6464, E-Mail: custscvs@channing.bete.com, Web Site: www.channing-bete.com (17)

Underline Communications LLC, New York, NY. Tel: (212) 994-4340, FAX: (212) 686-8234, E-Mail: inquiries@underline.com, Web Site: www.underlinecom.com (35)

Underwood Photo Archives Inc, Woodside, CA. Tel: (650) 851-5190, FAX: (650) 851-5193, E-Mail: ray@underwoodarchives.com, Web Site: www.underwoodarchives.com (38)

Underwood, John, Behlen Manufacturing Co, Columbus, NE. Tel: (402) 564-3111, FAX: (402) 563-7405, E-Mail: behlen@megavision.com, Web Site: www.behlenmfg.com (16)

Ungashick, Charlie, PTC, Needham, MA. Tel: (781) 370-5000, (877) 275-4782, Web Site: www.ptc.com (22)

Unger, Steven, Howard-Sloan-Koller Group, New York, NY. Tel: (212) 661-5250, FAX: (212) 557-9178, E-Mail: ekoller@hsksearch.com, Web Site: www.hsksearch.com (20)

Unicall International Inc, Fairlawn, OH. Tel: (330) 864-9364, FAX: (330) 864-9367, E-Mail: harrisb@unicallinc.com, Web Site: www.unicallinc.com (29)

Unicol Inc, Pembroke Pines, FL. Tel: (954) 431-7871, FAX: (954) 430-7227, E-Mail: customerservice@unicol-publishing.com, Web Site: www.unicol-publishing.com (17)

Unicom Electric Inc, Walnut, CA. Tel: (626) 964-7873, (800) 346-6668, FAX: (626) 964-7880, E-Mail: info@unicomlink.com, Web Site: www.unicomlink.com (16)

UNICOM Government Inc, Herndon, VA. Tel: (703) 502-2000, FAX: (703) 463-5011, Web Site: unicomgov.com (16)

Unicom Marketing Group Inc, Broadview, IL. Tel: (312) 738-1404, FAX: (312) 738-1405 (35)

UNICOR- Services Business Group, Washington, DC. Tel: (202) 305-3500, Web Site: www.unicor.gov/services (28)

Unicover Corp, Cheyenne, WY. Tel: (307) 771-3000, (800) 443-3232, FAX: (307) 771-3134, E-Mail: qands@unicover.com, Web Site: www.unicover.com (6)

UniFirst Corp, Wilmington, MA. Tel: (270) 683-5250 X523, Web Site: www.unifirst.com (2)

Uniformed Services Benefit Association, Overland Park, KS. Tel: (800) 368-7021, Web Site: www.usba.com (15)

Uniforms & Scrubs.com, Ballwin, MO. Tel: (636) 391-9200, (855) 391-9200, FAX: (636) 391-9205, E-Mail: questions@uniformsandscrubs.com, Web Site: www.uniformsandscrubs.com (7)

UniGraphic Inc, Woburn, MA. Tel: (781) 231-7200, FAX: (781) 938-7727, E-Mail: info@uni-graphic.com, Web Site: www.uni-graphic.com (27)

Unilever Best Foods, Englewood Cliffs, NJ. Tel: (201) 567-8000, FAX: (201) 871-8257, E-Mail: comments@unilever.com, Web Site: www.unilever.com (14)

Union Federal Savings Bank, North Providence, RI. Tel: (401) 353-8900, (800) 992-0278, FAX: (401) 353-8938, Web Site: www.unionfsb.com (14)

The Union Labor Life Insurance Co, Silver Spring, MD. Tel: (202) 962-2945, FAX: (202) 962-8429, E-Mail: info@ullico.com, Web Site: www.unioncare.com (15)

Union Privilege, AFL-CIO, Washington, DC. Tel: (202) 293-5311, (800) 472-2005, FAX: (202) 293-5311, E-Mail: info@unionprivilege.org, Web Site: www.unionplus.org (1)

Union Switch & Signal Inc, Pittsburgh, PA. Tel: (412) 688-2400, (800) 351-1520, FAX: (412) 688-2399, Web Site: www.switch.com (16)

UniServ Advertising Inc, Neptune City, NJ. Tel: (732) 774-1010, FAX: (732) 774-3311, Web Site: www.uniservinc.com (33)

Unisfair, San Mateo, CA. Tel: (866) 354-4030, Web Site: www.unisfair.com (20)

Unisource Worldwide, Inc, Norcross, GA. Tel: (770) 447-9000, (800) 864-7687, FAX: (770) 734-2000, Web Site: www.unisourcelink.com (25)

Unisys, Blue Bell, PA. Tel: (215) 986-4011, (800) 874-8647, FAX: (215) 986-2312, Web Site: www.unisys.com (16)

United Air Specialists Inc, Cincinnati, OH. Tel: (513) 891-0400, (800) 992-4422, FAX: (513) 891-4882, E-Mail: uas@uasinc.com, Web Site: www.uasinc.com (16)

United America Advertising Inc, Enid, OK. Tel: (580) 233-7200, FAX: (580) 548-8432 (29)

United Business Media, Manhasset, NY. Tel: (516) 562-5000, Web Site: www.ubmtechnology.com (17)

United Church Homes, Marion, OH. Tel: (740) 382-4885, (800) 837-2211, FAX: (740) 382-4884, Web Site: www.unitedchurchhomes.org (1)

United Communications Group, Gaithersburg, MD. Tel: (301) 287-2700, FAX: (301) 816-8945, E-Mail: webmaster@ucg.com, Web Site: www.ucg.com (17)

United Community Bank, Blairsville, GA. Tel: (706) 745-0911, Web Site: www.ucbi.com (14)

United Envelope, Ridgefield, NJ. Tel: (201) 699-5800, (800) 752-4012, FAX: (201) 313-7177, Web Site: www.unitedenvelope.com (26)

United Farm Workers of America, AFL-CIO, Keene, CA. Tel: (661) 823-6151, FAX: (661) 823-6177, E-Mail: execoffice@ufw.org, Web Site: www.ufw.org (1)

United Investors Life Insurance Co, Birmingham, AL. Tel: (205) 325-4300, (800) 288-2722, FAX: (205) 325-4157, Web Site: www.uilic.com (15)

United Jewish Appeal Federation of New York, New York, NY. Tel: (212) 980-1000. FAX: (212) 785-9321, E-Mail: contact@ujafedny.org, Web Site: www.ujafedny.org (1)

United Jewish Communities, New York, NY. Tel: (212) 284-6500, E-Mail: info@jewishfederations.org, Web Site: www.jewishfederations.org (1)

The United Methodist Publishing House, Nashville, TN. Tel: (615) 749-6000, (800) 672-1789, FAX: (615) 749-6417, E-Mail: productsandservices@umpublishing.com, Web Site: www.umpublishing.com (17)

United Nations Federal Credit Union, Long Island City, NY. Tel: (347) 686-6000, E-Mail: email@unfcu.org, Web Site: www.unfcu.org (1)

United Nations Foundation, Washington, DC. Tel: (202) 887-9040, FAX: (202) 887-9021, Web Site: www.unfoundation.org (1)

United Parcel Service, Atlanta, GA. Tel: (404) 828-6000, (800) 874-5877, FAX: (404) 828-6562, Web Site: www.ups.com (28)

United Retail Inc, Rochelle Park, NJ. Tel: (201) 845-0880, Web Site: www.avenue.com (2)

United Security Products Inc, Poway, CA. Tel: (858) 413-0149, (800) 227-1592, FAX: (858) 413-0124, E-Mail: usp@unitedsecurity.com, Web Site: www.unitedsecurity.com (16)

United Spinal Association, Kew Gardens, NY. Tel: (718) 803-3782, (800) 404-2898, FAX: (718) 803-0414, E-Mail: info@unitedspinal.org, Web Site: www.unitedspinal.org (1)

United Staffing Systems, New York, NY. Tel: (800) 972-9725, FAX: (646) 224-8393, Web Site: www.unitedstaffing.com (16)

US Bancorp, Minneapolis, MN. Tel: (651) 466-3000, (800) 872-2657, FAX: (612) 303-0782, Web Site: www.usbank.com (14)

US Bank, Minneapolis, MN. Tel: (612) 973-1111, Web Site: www.usbank.com (14)

US Branding Group LLC, Lake Worth, FL. Tel: (561) 966-8090 (16)

United States Bronze Sign Co Inc, New Hyde Park, NY. Tel: (516) 352-5155, (800) 872-5155, FAX: (516) 253-2328, E-Mail: peter@usbronze.com, Web Site: www.usbronze.com (1)

US Cavalry, Radcliff, KY. Tel: (270) 351-1164, (800) 777-7172, FAX: (270) 352-0266, E-Mail: hq@ uscavalry.com, Web Site: www.uscavalry.com (6)

US Cellular, Chicago, IL. Tel: (888) 944-9400, Web Site: www.uscellular.com (32)

US Chamber Institute for Legal Reform, Washington, DC. Tel: (202) 463-5724, Web Site: www. uschamber.com (40)

US Chamber of Commerce, Washington, DC. Tel: (202) 659-6000, (800) 638-6582, FAX: (202) 887-3430, Web Site: www.uschamber.com (1)

US Data Corp, Omaha, NE. Tel: (402) 502-5623, (888) 578-3282, FAX: (402) 502-5623, E-Mail: info@ usdatacorporation.com, Web Site: www. usdatacorporation.com (29)

US Data Corp, Omaha, NE. Tel: (402) 758-0290, (888) 578-3282, FAX: (402) 934-3885, E-Mail: info@ usdatacorporation.com, Web Site: www.usdatacorp. net (23)

US Department of Commerce, Washington, DC. Tel: (202) 482-2000, E-Mail: thesec@doc.gov, Web Site: www.commerce.gov (1)

US Digital Transactions Corporation, New York, NY. Tel: (800) 728-1190, FAX: (800) 729-6530, Web Site: www.usdtcorp.com (14)

US Foodservice, Rosemont, IL. Tel: (847) 720-8000, FAX: (847) 720-8099, Web Site: www. usfoodservice.com (4)

US Fund for UNICEF, New York, NY. Tel: (212) 686-5522, FAX: (212) 779-1679, Web Site: www. unicefusa.org (6)

US Games Systems Inc, Stamford, CT. Tel: (203) 353-8400, (800) 544-2637, FAX: (203) 353-8431, Web Site: www.usgamesinc.com (11)

US Gas & Electric, White Plains, NY. Tel: (888) 947-7880, FAX: (888) 400-1230, E-Mail: salesinfo@ usgande.com, Web Site: www.usgande.com (16)

US Monitor, New City, NY. Tel: (845) 634-1331, (800) 767-7967, FAX: (845) 634-9618, E-Mail: info@ usmonitor.com, Web Site: www.usmonitor.com (28)

US Naval Institute, Annapolis, MD. Tel: (410) 268-6110, (800) 233-8764, FAX: (410) 571-1703, E-Mail: customer@usni.org, Web Site: www.usni. org (38)

US News & World Report, Washington, DC. Tel: (202) 955-2000, Web Site: www.usnews.com (17)

USA/DIRECT Inc, Stockholm, NJ. Tel: (973) 222-3800, FAX: (973) 823-8223, E-Mail: gparker@ usadirectinc.com, Web Site: www.usadirectinc.com (30)

USA 800 Inc, Raytown, MO. Tel: (816) 358-1303, (800) 821-7539, FAX: (816) 358-8845, E-Mail: dlabatt@usa-800.com, Web Site: www.usa-800.com (29)

USA Hosts Ltd, New Orleans, LA. Tel: (504) 524-8687, FAX: (504) 524-8842, Web Site: www.usahosts. com (19)

USA Network, New York, NY. Tel: (212) 664-4444, FAX: (212) 664-6365, Web Site: www.usanetwork. com (32)

USA TODAY, Mc Lean, VA. Tel: (703) 854-3400, (800) 872-0001, E-Mail: accuracy@usatoday.com, Web Site: www.usatoday.com (17)

USA Weekend, New York, NY. Tel: (800) 487-4956, FAX: (703) 854-2122, Web Site: www.usaweekend. com (31)

US Pharmacopeia, Rockville, MD. Tel: (301) 881-0666, (800) 227-8772, FAX: (301) 816-8236, Web Site: www.usp.org (1)

US Playing Card Co, Erlanger, KY. Tel: (800) 543-2273, FAX: (859) 815-7566, E-Mail: sales@ usplayingcard.com, Web Site: www.usplayingcard. com (16)

US Postal Service-Library, Washington, DC. Tel: (202) 268-2904, FAX: (202) 268-6436, Web Site: www. usps.com (28)

US Tape & Label Corp, Saint Louis, MO. Tel: (314) 824-4444, (800) 569-1906, FAX: (314) 824-4400, E-Mail: harrisonc@ustl.com, Web Site: www.ustl. com (27)

US Tax Shield, Encino, CA. Tel: (877) 929-3535, Web Site: www.ustaxshield.com (14)

United States Tennis Association, White Plains, NY. Tel: (914) 696-7000, (800) 990-8782, E-Mail: memberservices@usta.com, Web Site: www.usta. com (1)

US Travel Association, Washington, DC. Tel: (202) 408-8422, FAX: (202) 408-1255, E-Mail: feedback@ustravel.org, Web Site: www.ustravel.org (1)

United Stationers, Deerfield, IL. Tel: (847) 627-7000, FAX: (847) 647-7001, Web Site: www. unitedstationers.com (25)

United Systems c/o Biomed, Concord, CA. Tel: (925) 609-2820 (7)

United Way Store, Alexandria, VA. Tel: (703) 212-6300, (800) 772-0008, FAX: (703) 212-6319, E-Mail: customerservice@unitedwaystore.com, Web Site: www.unitedwaystore.com (34)

United Way Toronto & York Region, Toronto, ON Canada. Tel: (416) 777-2001, (866) 620-2993, FAX: (416) 777-0962, Web Site: www.unitedwaytyr.com (1)

United Way Worldwide, Alexandria, VA. Tel: (703) 836-7112, Web Site: www.unitedway.org (1)

United Wire Service, Peoria, IL. Tel: (309) 689-6160, FAX: (309) 689-6488, Web Site: www.unitedwire. net (28)

Unitron Ltd, Commack, NY. Tel: (631) 589-6666, FAX: (631) 589-6795, E-Mail: johnc@unitronusa. com, Web Site: www.unitronusa.com (9)

Unity School of Christianity, Unity Village, MO. Tel: (816) 254-3550, FAX: (816) 251-3554, E-Mail: unity@unityonline.org, Web Site: www.unityonline. org (17)

Univenture Inc, Marysville, OH. Tel: (937) 645-4600, FAX: (937) 645-4700, Web Site: www.univenture. com (27)

Universal Corp, Richmond, VA. Tel: (804) 359-9311, FAX: (804) 254-3582, Web Site: www. universalcorp.com (16)

Universal Distribution Services, Reno, NV. Tel: (775) 332-5700, FAX: (775) 332-5715, E-Mail: sales@ udsi.com, Web Site: www.udsi.com (28)

Universal Engineering Corp, Cedar Rapids, IA. Tel: (319) 365-0441, (800) 366-2051, FAX: (319) 369-5440, E-Mail: info@universalcrusher.com, Web Site: www.universalcrusher.com (16)

Universal Fidelity Corp, Houston, TX. Tel: (281) 647-4100, (800) 580-8887, FAX: (281) 647-4207, Web Site: www.ufccorp.com (14)

Universal Hovercraft, Cordova, IL. Tel: (309) 654-2588, FAX: (309) 654-2588, Web Site: www. hovercraft.com (11)

Universal Media Syndicate Inc, Canton, OH. Tel: (330) 966-9000, E-Mail: lfish@uni-syn.com, Web Site: www.universalmediasyndicate.com (35)

Universal Printing, Saint Louis, MO. Tel: (314) 771-6900, FAX: (314) 771-7987, E-Mail: info@ universalprintingco.com, Web Site: www. universalprintingco.com (27)

Universal Security Instruments Inc, Owings Mills, MD. Tel: (410) 363-3000, FAX: (410) 363-2218, E-Mail: sales@universalsecurity.com, Web Site: www. universalsecurity.com (16)

Universal Studios Inc, Universal City, CA. Tel: (818) 777-1000, FAX: (818) 866-3330, Web Site: www. universalstudios.com (3)

Universal Tea Co Inc, Tigard, OR. Tel: (503) 684-4482, (800) 547-1514, FAX: (503) 684-4424, E-Mail: stash@stashtea.com, Web Site: www.stashtea.com (4)

Universal Training, Lake Forest, IL. Tel: (847) 235-2170, E-Mail: information@universaltraining.com, Web Site: www.universaltraining.com (16)

Universal Vintage Tire Co, Hershey, PA. Tel: (717) 534-0175, (800) 233-3827, FAX: (717) 534-0719, E-Mail: sales@universaltire.com, Web Site: www. universaltire.com (11)

Universal Wilde, Westwood, MA. Tel: (781) 251-2700, FAX: (781) 251-2613, E-Mail: marketing@ universalwilde.com, Web Site: www.universalwilde. com (21)

University at Buffalo Center for Entrepreneurial Leadership, Buffalo, NY. Tel: (716) 885-5715, FAX: (716) 845-6999, E-Mail: mgt-cel@buffalo.edu, Web Site: http://mgt.buffalo.edu/entrepreneurship/cel (5)

University Bank, Ann Arbor, MI. Tel: (734) 741-5858, FAX: (734) 741-5859, E-Mail: ranzini@university-bank.com, Web Site: www.university-bank.com (14)

University of Akron, Akron, OH. Tel: (330) 972-7111 (1)

University of Alabama, Tuscaloosa, AL. Tel: (205) 348-6330, (866) 307-3917, FAX: (205) 348-9246, Web Site: continuingstudies.ua.edu (13)

University of California Irvine Extension, Irvine, CA. Tel: (949) 824-5414, E-Mail: unex-services@uci. edu, Web Site: extension.uci.edu (1)

University of Chicago GSB, Chicago, IL. Tel: (312) 464-8733, E-Mail: exec.ed@chicagobooth.edu, Web Site: www.chicagobooth.edu (1)

University of Chicago Press, Chicago, IL. Tel: (773) 702-7700, FAX: (773) 702-9756, Web Site: www. press.uchicago.edu (17)

University of Illinois College of LAS, Office of Advancement, Urbana, IL. Tel: (217) 333-1705, E-Mail: las-studentoffice@illinois.edu, Web Site: www.las.illinois.edu (1)

University of Illinois Foundation, Urbana, IL. Tel: (217) 333-0810, FAX: (217) 333-5577, E-Mail: uif@ uillinois.edu, Web Site: www.uif.uillinois.edu (1)

University of Minnesota, Minneapolis, MN. Tel: (612) 625-0256, Web Site: www.twin-cities.umn.edu (1)

University of Minnesota Alumni Association, Minneapolis, MN. Tel: (612) 624-2323, (800) 862-5867, FAX: (612) 626-8167, E-Mail: umalumni@umn. edu, Web Site: www.minnesotaalumni.org (1)

University of Missouri, Columbia, MO. Tel: (573) 882-6333, (800) 856-2181, FAX: (573) 882-2721, E-Mail: visitus@missouri.edu, Web Site: missouri.edu (41)

University of Missouri/Kansas City, Kansas City, MO. Tel: (816) 235-2215, FAX: (816) 235-2312, Web Site: www.umkc.edu (41)

University of North Texas, Denton, TX. Tel: (940) 565-2000, Web Site: www.unt.edu (1)

University of Oklahoma Press, Norman, OK. Tel: (800) 627-7377, FAX: (405) 364-5798, Web Site: www. oupress.com (17)

University of Pennsylvania, Philadelphia, PA. Tel: (215) 898-5000, FAX: (215) 898-9659, Web Site: www. upenn.edu (1)

University of Pennsylvania - Veterinary Medicine (Development), Philadelphia, PA. Tel: (215) 898-8841, E-Mail: vetdean@vet.upenn.edu, Web Site: www.vet.upenn.edu (1)

University of Phoenix, Tempe, AZ. Tel: (480) 557-1662, (866) 766-0766, Web Site: www.phoenix.edu (13)

University of Pittsburgh at Bradford, Bradford, PA. Tel: (814) 362-7500, FAX: (814) 362-5150, E-Mail: admissions@www.upb.pitt.edu, Web Site: www.upd.pitt.edu (41)

University of Southern California, Los Angeles, CA. Tel: (213) 821-2366, FAX: (213) 740-2343, E-Mail: taube@usc.edu, Web Site: www.usc.edu (38)

University of Southern Mississippi, Hattiesburg, MS. Tel: (601) 266-1000, Web Site: www.usm.edu (1)

University of Texas School of Law, Austin, TX. Tel: (512) 475-6700, FAX: (512) 475-6876, E-Mail: services@utcle.org, Web Site: www.utcle.org (1)

University of Washington Educational Outreach, Seattle, WA. Tel: (206) 685-6566, E-Mail: edinfo@u.washington.edu, Web Site: www.pce.uw.edu (1)

University of Wisconsin-Madison School of Business, Madison, WI. Tel: (608) 262-1550, E-Mail: info@bus.wisc.edu, Web Site: bus.wisc.edu (1)

University Press of America Inc, Lanham, MD. Tel: (301) 459-3366, (800) 462-6420, FAX: (301) 429-5748, E-Mail: custserv@rowman.com, Web Site: www.univpress.com (17)

University Subscription Service, Downers Grove, IL. Tel: (630) 960-3233, (888) 877-1213, FAX: (630) 960-3246, Web Site: www.ussmag.com (18)

Uniway Management Corp, Forest Park, GA. Tel: (404) 363-6200, (888) 386-4929, FAX: (404) 363-8848, E-Mail: uniway@bellsouth.net, Web Site: www.uniway.com (16)

UniWorld Group, Brooklyn, NY. Tel: (212) 219-1600, FAX: (212) 219-6395, E-Mail: newbiz@uwqny.com, Web Site: www.uwg.is (21)

Unsur, Annette, Washington University, Saint Louis, MO. Tel: (314) 935-5000, Web Site: www.wustl.edu (1)

Unsworth, Lisa, Arnold Worldwide Boston, Boston, MA. Tel: (617) 587-8000, FAX: (617) 587-8004, Web Site: www.arn.com (35)

Untiedt, Allison Webb, Webb Designs Inc, El Cajon, CA. Tel: (619) 596-6400, (800) 262-9322, FAX: (619) 596-4511, E-Mail: awebb@webbshade.com, Web Site: www.webbshade.com (16)

Unum Corp, Portland, ME. Tel: (207) 770-2211, (800) 421-0344, FAX: (207) 770-4510, Web Site: www.unum.com (15)

Unz & Co, Middlesex, NJ. Tel: (732) 667-1020, (800) 631-3098, FAX: (732) 868-0260, E-Mail: unzco@unzco.com, Web Site: www.unzco.com (27)

Upbeat Inc, Saint Louis, MO. Tel: (314) 535-5005, (800) 325-3047, FAX: (314) 535-4419, E-Mail: custservice@upbeat.com, Web Site: www.upbeat.com (9)

Upbin, Hal, American Recreation Products Inc, Saint Louis, MO. Tel: (314) 576-8000, FAX: (314) 576-8072 (11)

Updike, Vicki, Silver Star Brands, Oshkosh, WI. Tel: (920) 231-3800, FAX: (920) 231-1247, Web Site: www.silverstarbrands.com (6)

Upstart, Madison, WI. Tel: (920) 563-9571, FAX: (800) 448-5828, Web Site: www.highsmith.com (16)

Upton, Suzie, American Heart Association, Dallas, TX. Tel: (214) 373-6300, (800) AHA-USA-1, FAX: (214) 373-3406, Web Site: www.americanheart.org (1)

Urbach, Ronald R., Davis & Gilbert, New York, NY. Tel: (212) 468-4800, FAX: (212) 468-4888, Web Site: www.dglaw.com (20)

The Urban Land Institute, Washington, DC. Tel: (202) 624-7000, FAX: (202) 624-7140, E-Mail: customerservice@uli.org, Web Site: www.uli.org (1)

Urban Mapping Inc, San Francisco, CA. Tel: (415) 946-8170, Web Site: www.urbanmapping.com (16)

Urban Response LLC, Hartville, OH. Tel: (330) 877-0800, (866) 550-3501, FAX: (330) 877-0802 (17)

Urban Science Applications Inc, Detroit, MI. Tel: (313) 259-9900, Web Site: www.urbanscience.com (20)

Urbani Truffles USA Corp, New York, NY. Tel: (212) 247-8800, FAX: (212) 247-8900, E-Mail: info@urbani.com, Web Site: www.urbani.com (4)

Urbani, Olga, Urbani Truffles USA Corp, New York, NY. Tel: (212) 247-8800, FAX: (212) 247-8900, E-Mail: info@urbani.com, Web Site: www.urbani.com (4)

Urbania, Carl, Cengage Learning, Independence, KY. Tel: (800) 354-9706, FAX: (800) 487-8488, Web Site: www.delmar.com (17)

Urbanski, Al, DM News, New York, NY. Tel: (646) 638-6000, (800) 558-1703, FAX: (212) 925-8752, E-Mail: dmnewssubs@haymarketmedia.com, Web Site: www.dmnews.com (43)

Urquhart, Wendy, Taradel LLC, Glen Allen, VA. Tel: (804) 364-8444, (800) 481-1656, FAX: (888) 241-3023, E-Mail: info@taradel.com, Web Site: www.taradel.com (21)

USADATA Inc, New York, NY. Tel: (800) 395-7707, E-Mail: info@usadata.com, Web Site: www.usadata.com (23)

USC Marshall School of Business Dept of Marketing, Los Angeles, CA. Tel: (213) 740-5033, FAX: (213) 740-7828, E-Mail: dennis.rook@marshall.usc.edu (41)

USDiscs, Duarte, CA. Tel: (626) 359-9955, Web Site: www.usdiscs.com (27)

Usher, Thomas J., USX, Pittsburgh, PA. Tel: (412) 433-1121, E-Mail: webmaster@usx.com, Web Site: www.usx.com (16)

Utilities Supply Corp, Woburn, MA. Tel: (781) 395-9023, (800) 343-7555, FAX: (800) 232-8726, (781) 395-2329, E-Mail: jge@fwwebb.com, Web Site: www.uscosupply.com (16)

Utley, Holland, Redbook Magazine, New York, NY. Tel: (212) 649-2000, (800) 888-0008, FAX: (212) 581-7605, Web Site: www.redbookmag.com (17)

Utley, Valerie, Morpace Inc, Farmington Hills, MI. Tel: (248) 737-5300, FAX: (248) 737-5326, E-Mail: information@morpace.com, Web Site: www.morpace.com (30)

Utretch Art Supplies, Cranbury, NJ. Tel: (609) 409-8001, (800) 223-9132, FAX: (800) 382-1979, Web Site: www.utrechtart.com (10)

Uwharrie Capital Corp, Albemarle, NC. Tel: (704) 991-1181, Web Site: www.uwharriecapitalcorp.com (14)

V

V3, Oxnard, CA. Tel: (805) 981-2600, (800) 882-1844, FAX: (805) 981-1180, E-Mail: sales@printv3.com, Web Site: www.printv3.com (27)

V12 Data, Wesley Chapel, FL. Tel: (813) 960-7800, FAX: (813) 960-7811, E-Mail: info@v12data.com, Web Site: www.v12data.com (22)

VF Imagewear, Greensboro, NC. Tel: (336) 424-6000, (800) 733-5271, Web Site: www.vfimagewear.com (2)

VMF Inc, Washington, DC. Tel: (202) 966-3361, FAX: (202) 362-8409, E-Mail: veflei@aol.com (20)

VML Inc, Kansas City, MO. Tel: (816) 283-0700, FAX: (816) 283-0954, E-Mail: dl-vmlcommarketing@vml.com, Web Site: www.vml.com (35)

VW Credit, Herndon, VA. Tel: (248) 340-5000 (14)

VWR International, Radnor, PA. Tel: (610) 386-1700, (800) 932-5000, FAX: (610) 431-9174, Web Site: www.vwrsp.com (34)

Vaccaro, Thomas, The Orvis Co Inc, Manchester, VT. Tel: (802) 362-3622, FAX: (802) 362-3525, Web Site: www.orvis.com (11)

Vache, Noel, Ward's Natural Science, Rochester, NY. Tel: (585) 359-2502, (800) 962-2660, FAX: (585) 334-6174, E-Mail: customer_service@wardsci.com, Web Site: www.wardsci.com (34)

Vadar, Umut, Leadcreations.com LLC, Fort Lauderdale, FL. Tel: (305) 851-0999, FAX: (707) 281-0421, E-Mail: info@leadcreations.com, Web Site: www.leadcreations.com (23)

Vadeboncoeur, Jr. Jim, Bud Plant Illustrated Books, Palo Alto, CA. Tel: (650) 493-1191, FAX: (650) 493-1145, E-Mail: jim@bpib.com, Web Site: www.bpib.com (6)

Vagabond Creations Inc, Dayton, OH. Tel: (937) 298-1124, (800) 738-7237, FAX: (937) 298-1124, E-Mail: sales@vagabondcreations.net, Web Site: www.vagabondcreations.net (10)

Vail Resorts Inc, Broomfield, CO. Tel: (303) 404-1800, FAX: (303) 404-6415, Web Site: www.vailresorts.com (19)

Vail, Walter, Saint Mary's Paper Corp, Wheaton, IL. Tel: (630) 668-6279, FAX: (630) 668-6292, Web Site: www.stmarys-paper.com (25)

Vakalis, Marianne, Berkeley College, West Paterson, NJ. Tel: (973) 278-5400, (800) 446-5400, FAX: (973) 278-6243, E-Mail: info@berkeleycollege.edu, Web Site: www.berkeleycollege.edu (13)

Valassis Canada, Toronto, ON Canada. Tel: (416) 259-3600, (866) 333-2386, Web Site: www.valassis.com (35)

Valassis Direct Mail Inc, Windsor, CT. Tel: (860) 285-6100, FAX: (203) 845-5338, Web Site: www.valassis.com (31)

ValCom Inc, Boonton, NJ. Tel: (973) 588-7084, FAX: (973) 257-7216, E-Mail: info@valcom.tv, Web Site: www.valcom.tv (32)

Valdawn Watch Co, Long Island City, NY. Tel: (201) 807-1110, FAX: (201) 807-0228 (16)

Valderrama, Leila, Air Power USA, Los Angeles, CA. Tel: (310) 641-0830, (888) 888-8231, FAX: (310) 641-8515, Web Site: www.airpowerusa.com (12)

Vale, Tom, DeLuxe Laboratories Inc, Hollywood, CA. Tel: (323) 462-6171, FAX: (323) 960-7016, E-Mail: steven.vananda@bydeluxe.com, Web Site: www.bydeluxe.com (16)

Valenta, Tommy A., Texas Industries Inc, Dallas, TX. Tel: (972) 647-6700, FAX: (972) 647-3878, Web Site: www.txi.com (16)

Valente, Dennis J., APSCO, Davenport Center, NY. Tel: (607) 278-6218, FAX: (607) 278-6218, E-Mail: webmaster@antiquephono.com, Web Site: www.antiquephono.com (11)

Valente, Patricia F., APSCO, Davenport Center, NY. Tel: (607) 278-6218, FAX: (607) 278-6218, E-Mail: webmaster@antiquephono.com, Web Site: www.antiquephono.com (11)

Valenti Classics, Franklin, WI. Tel: (262) 835-2070, FAX: (262) 835-2575, Web Site: www.valenticlassics.com (16)

Valenti, Steve, Valenti Classics, Franklin, WI. Tel: (262) 835-2070, FAX: (262) 835-2575. Web Site: www.valenticlassics.com (16)

Valentine Research Inc, Cincinnati, OH. Tel: (513) 984-8900, (800) 331-3030, FAX: (513) 984-8976, E-Mail: sales@valentine1.com, Web Site: www. valentine1.com (16)

Valentine, Michael D., Valentine Research Inc, Cincinnati, OH. Tel: (513) 984-8900, (800) 331-3030, FAX: (513) 984-8976, E-Mail: sales@valentine1. com, Web Site: www.valentine1.com (16)

Valentino, Claudia, Archaeology Magazine, Long Island City, NY. Tel: (718) 472-3050, FAX: (718) 472-3051, E-Mail: production@archaeology.org, Web Site: www.archaeology.org (17)

Valentino, Gina, Hemisphere Marketing, Kansas City, MO. Tel: (816) 444-5439, Web Site: www. hemispheremarketing.com (20)

Valentino, Joanne, Medical Letter Inc, New Rochelle, NY. Tel: (914) 235-0500, Web Site: www. medicalletter.org (1)

Valetta, John, Super 8 Hotels Worldwide, Parsippany, NJ. Tel: (800) 800-8000, FAX: (720) 535-2199, Web Site: www.super8.com (19)

Valid USA Inc, Lisle, IL. Tel: (630) 852-8200, (855) 825-4387, E-Mail: info@validusa.com, Web Site: www.validusa.com (22)

Valkenburgh, Van, Torqmaster International, Stamford, CT. Tel: (203) 326-5945, (888) 414-4643, FAX: (203) 326-5944, E-Mail: info@torqmaster.com, Web Site: www.torqmaster.com (9)

Valley Forge Tape & Label Co Inc, Exton, PA. Tel: (610) 524-8900, (800) 345-1323, FAX: (610) 524-8906, E-Mail: vfsales@vftl.com, Web Site: www. vftl.com (27)

Valley, Derek, DMB Financial, Beverly, MA. Tel: (866) 810-3210, FAX: (978) 338-2347, E-Mail: help@ dmbfinancial.com, Web Site: www.dmbfinancial. com (14)

Valli, Chris, Super Coups, Norwell, MA. Tel: (508) 977-2000, (800) 626-2620, FAX: (508) 977-0644, Web Site: www.supercoups.com (26)

Vallone-Raffaele, Helene, US Fund for UNICEF, New York, NY. Tel: (212) 686-5522, FAX: (212) 779-1679, Web Site: www.unicefusa.org (6)

Valmark Associates LLC, Buffalo, NY. Tel: (716) 836-3414, FAX: (716) 836-3415, E-Mail: joe@ valmarkassociates.com, Web Site: www. valmarkassociates.com (35)

Valore, Jason, Alairis Interactive, Medina, OH. Tel: (877) 770-0350, E-Mail: info@alairis.com, Web Site: www.alairis.com (35)

Valpak Direct Marketing Systems Inc, Largo, FL. Tel: (727) 399-3000, Web Site: www.valpak.com (31)

Valpak of New York, New York, NY. Tel: (212) 560-9400, Web Site: www.valpaknewyork.com (41)

Value Line Publishing Inc, New York, NY. Tel: (212) 907-1500, FAX: (212) 818-9747, Web Site: www. valueline.com (17)

ValueVision Media Inc, Eden Prairie, MN. Tel: (952) 943-6000, Web Site: www.shophq.com (32)

Van Arsdel, Heather, American Society of Journalists & Authors Directory, New York, NY. Tel: (212) 997-0947, FAX: (212) 768-7414, E-Mail: asjany@ibm. net (43)

K Van Bourgondien & Sons Inc, Tel: (800) 552-9916, E-Mail: blooms@dutchbulbs.com, Web Site: www. dutchbulbs.com (8)

Van Bourgondien, Fred, K Van Bourgondien & Sons Inc, Virginia Beach, VA. Tel: (800) 552-9916, E-Mail: blooms@dutchbulbs.com, Web Site: www. dutchbulbs.com (8)

Van Buren McNider, Anna, Faneuil ISG, Hampton, VA. Tel: (757) 722-3235, FAX: 757-722-5293, Web Site: www.faneuil.com (30)

Van Castle, Robin, Taylor Capital Group, Inc, Rosemont, IL. Tel: (847) 653-7978, FAX: (847) 653-7890, E-Mail: investor.relations@coletaylor.com, Web Site: www.taylorcapitalgroup.com (14)

Van Cott, Craig H., Unadilla Laminated Products, Unadilla, NY. Tel: (607) 369-9341, FAX: (607) 369-3608, E-Mail: info@unalam.com, Web Site: www. unalam.com (16)

Van Dam Inc, New York, NY. Tel: (212) 929-0416, (800) UNFOLDS, FAX: (212) 929-0426, E-Mail: info@vandam.com, Web Site: www.vandam.com (17)

Van de Bunt, Ben, Guthy-Renker Corp, Santa Monica, CA. Tel: (310) 581-6250, FAX: (310) 581-3232, Web Site: www.guthy-renker.com (32)

Van De Voorde, Mathew. Orion, Federal Way, WA. Tel: (253) 661-7805, Web Site: www.orionworks. org (1)

van der Horst, Carl, Upbeat Inc, Saint Louis, MO. Tel: (314) 535-5005, (800) 325-3047, FAX: (314) 535-4419, E-Mail: custservice@upbeat.com, Web Site: www.upbeat.com (9)

Van Der Veer, Gina, Dr Leonard's Healthcare Corp, Edison, NJ. Tel: (732) 225-0100, (800) 455-1918, FAX: (732) 225-0302, Web Site: www. doctorleonard.com (7)

van der Veldt, Ben, Breck's Bulbs, Guilford, IN. Tel: (513) 354-1512, FAX: (513) 354-1505, E-Mail: service@brecks.com, Web Site: brecks.com (8)

Van der Walt, Christina, Haymarket Group Ltd, New York, NY. Tel: (212) 239-0855, FAX: (212) 967-4184, Web Site: www.chocalatiermagazine.com (17)

Van Der Wiel, Donald J.B., Fifth Gear LLC, Indianapolis, IN. Tel: (317) 631-0907, FAX: (317) 631-6585, Web Site: www.infifthgear.com (22)

Van Dyke, Brandon, Darwill, Hillside, IL. Tel: (708) 236-4900, FAX: (708) 236-5820, Web Site: www. darwill.com (27)

Van Dyke, Tony, Darwill, Hillside, IL. Tel: (708) 236-4900, FAX: (708) 236-5820, Web Site: www. darwill.com (27)

Van Ert, Mark, FG Companies, Wayzata, MN. Tel: (952) 476-8900, E-Mail: mmelius@fgcompanies. com, Web Site: www.fgcompanies.com (22)

van Galen, Laura, Bleu Marketing Solutions Inc, San Francisco, CA. Tel: (415) 345-3300, FAX: (415) 353-0299, E-Mail: helpdesk@bleumarketing.com, Web Site: bleumarketing.com (35)

Van Gelder, Kim E., Eastman Kodak Co, Rochester, NY. Tel: (585) 724-4000, (800) 698-3324, FAX: (585) 724-1089, Web Site: www.kodak.com (27)

Van Gilse, Rob, Alloyd Brands, Dekalb, IL. Tel: (815) 756-8451, (800) 756-7639, FAX: (815) 756-5187/ 9192, Web Site: www.alloyd.com (16)

Van Groesbeck & Co, Richmond, VA. Tel: (804) 285-3176, FAX: (804) 359-7271, E-Mail: info@ vangroesbeckco.com, Web Site: www. vangroesbeckco.com (1)

Van Kirk, Phil, The Taunton Press, Newtown, CT. Tel: (203) 426-8171, (800) 477-8727, FAX: (203) 426-3434, Web Site: www.taunton.com (17)

Van Meter, Leila, Making It Big, Cotati, CA. Tel: (707) 795-1997, (877) 644-1995, FAX: (707) 795-4874, E-Mail: mib@makingitbig.com, Web Site: www. makingitbig.com (2)

Van Oss, Stephen A., WESCO, Pittsburgh, PA. Tel: (412) 454-2200, (800) 343-1201, E-Mail: info@ wesco.com, Web Site: www.wescodist.com (16)

Van Rees, Linda F., The HoneyBaked Ham Co, Holland, OH. Tel: (419) 724-4267, (866) 492-4267, E-Mail: info@honeybaked.com, Web Site: www. honeybaked.com (4)

Van Remmen, Roger, Brown, Van Remmen, Kanuit, Inc, El Segundo, CA. Tel: (310) 640-0777, FAX: (310) 640-0606, E-Mail: info@bvksearch.com, Web Site: www.bvksearch.com (20)

Van Rockel, Gary, Melissa Data Corp, Rancho Santa Margarita, CA. Tel: (949) 858-3000, (800) 800-6245, FAX: (949) 589-5211, E-Mail: sales@ melissadata.com, Web Site: www.melissadata.com (22)

Van Roekel, Gary, Mailer's Software, Rancho Santa Margarita, CA. Tel: (949) 858-3000, (800) 635-4772, FAX: (949) 589-5211, E-Mail: info@ melissadata.com, Web Site: www.mailerssoftware. com (22)

van Rooyen, Guy, Donna Salyers' Fabulous-Bridal Inc, Covington, KY. Tel: (859) 291-3300, (800) 848-4650, E-Mail: abell@fabulousfurs.com, Web Site: fabulousfurs.com (2)

Van Ryzin, Wade, Elemental Scientific LLC, Appleton, WI. Tel: (920) 882-1277, E-Mail: info@ elementalscientific.net, Web Site: www. elementalscientific.net (9)

Van Sickle, Fred, Columbia University, Annual Fund Programs, New York, NY. E-Mail: donorrelations@ columbia.edu, Web Site: http://giving.columbia.edu (5)

Van Straten, Tami L., Paperweight Development Corp, Appleton, WI. Tel: (920) 734-9841, FAX: (920) 991-8796, Web Site: www.appletonideas.com (25)

Van Tine, Mark, Jeppesen, Englewood, CO. Tel: (303) 799-9090, (800) 353-2107, Web Site: www. jeppesen.com (22)

Van Veen, Tony, Disc Makers, New York, NY. Tel: (800) 468-9353, Web Site: www.discmakers.com (3)

Van Vliet, Dave, Hasco First Photo, Saint Charles, MO. Tel: (636) 946-5115, FAX: (636) 946-7148, Web Site: www.growingfamily.com (16)

van Wagenen, Jay, JVW Direct, Pittsburgh, PA. Tel: (412) 241-5920, FAX: (412) 241-5850, E-Mail: john@jvwdirect.com (35)

Van Wyk, Chris, Village Weavers, San Antonio, TX. Tel: (210) 222-0776, E-Mail: shop@villageweavers. com, Web Site: www.villageweavers.com (16)

VanBesien, Matthew, New York Philharmonic, New York, NY. Tel: (212) 875-5691, Web Site: www. nyphil.org (1)

Vance Industries Inc, Niles, IL. Tel: (847) 375-8900, FAX: (847) 375-6818, E-Mail: vance@vanceind. com, Web Site: www.vanceind.com (16)

Vance, Adam, US Travel Association, Washington, DC. Tel: (202) 408-8422, FAX: (202) 408-1255, E-Mail: feedback@ustravel.org, Web Site: www.ustravel.org (1)

VanDam, Stephan C., Van Dam Inc, New York, NY. Tel: (212) 929-0416, (800) UNFOLDS, FAX: (212) 929-0426, E-Mail: info@vandam.com, Web Site: www.vandam.com (17)

Vande More, Dan, Net-Results, Golden, CO. Tel: (303) 771-2552, E-Mail: info@net-results.com, Web Site: www.net-results.com (32)

VandeBoom, Jason, ActiveCampaign Inc, Chicago, IL. Tel: (800) 357-0402, E-Mail: help@activecampaign. com, Web Site: www.activecampaign.com (24)

Vandegrift, Don, Consolidated Printing & Stationary Co Inc, Salina, KS. Tel: (785) 825-5426, (800) 432-0266, FAX: (785) 825-6536, Web Site: www. consolidatedprinting.com (35)

VandenBos, Gary R., American Psychological Association, Washington, DC. Tel: (202) 336-5500, (800) 374-2721, FAX: (202) 336-5568, E-Mail: order@apa.org, Web Site: www.apa.org (1)

Vander Horst, Paul, Compu-Mail Direct Marketing, Grand Island, NY. Tel: (716) 775-8001, (800) 255-0607, FAX: (716) 775-5681, E-Mail: marketing@compu-mail.com, Web Site: compu-mail.com (21)

Vander Ploeg, David, Direct Response Media Group, Oakville, ON Canada. Tel: (905) 465-1233, (866) 993-0600, FAX: (905) 465-1228, E-Mail: info@drmg.ca, Web Site: www.drmg.com (21)

Vander Ploeg, David, School Specialty Inc, Greenville, WI. Tel: (920) 734-5712, (888) 388-3224, FAX: (920) 734-5112, E-Mail: info@schoolspecialty.com, Web Site: www.schoolspecialty.com (16)

Vander Waal, Brent, ITAGroup, West Des Moines, IA. Tel: (800) 257-1985, E-Mail: drivenbyloyalty@itagroup.com, Web Site: www.itagroup.com (33)

Vander Zanden, David J., School Specialty Inc, Greenville, WI. Tel: (920) 734-5712, (888) 388-3224, FAX: (920) 734-5112, E-Mail: info@schoolspecialty.com, Web Site: www.schoolspecialty.com (16)

Vanderbilt Advertising, New York, NY. Tel: (212) 907-1500, FAX: (212) 907-1914, Web Site: www.valueline.com (14)

Vanderhook, Chris, Viant Technology LLC, Irvine, CA. Tel: (949) 861-8888, E-Mail: info@viantinc.com, Web Site: viantinc.com (35)

Vanderhook, Russ, Viant Technology LLC, Irvine, CA. Tel: (949) 861-8888, E-Mail: info@viantinc.com, Web Site: viantinc.com (35)

Vanderhook, Tim, Viant Technology LLC, Irvine, CA. Tel: (949) 861-8888, E-Mail: info@viantinc.com, Web Site: viantinc.com (35)

VanderVeen, Ken, ABS Graphics, Addison, IL. Tel: (630) 495-2400, FAX: (630) 495-0728, E-Mail: info@absinet.com, Web Site: www.absinet.com (27)

Vandervlugt, Leo, Dutch Gardens USA Inc, Bloomington, IL. Tel: (800) 944-2250, E-Mail: customerservice@dutchgardens.com, Web Site: www.dutchgardens.com (8)

vanDongen, Henk, Mid America Motorworks, Effingham, IL. Tel: (217) 347-5591, (800) 500-1500, FAX: (217) 347-2952, E-Mail: mail@mamotorworks.com, Web Site: www.mamotorworks.com (12)

The Vane Brothers Co, Baltimore, MD. Tel: (410) 631-5096, FAX: (410) 631-7781, E-Mail: webmaster@vanebros.com, Web Site: www.vanebros.com (16)

Vanguard, Malvern, PA. Tel: (610) 669-1000, FAX: (610) 669-6600, Web Site: www.vanguard.com (14)

Vanguard Direct, New York, NY. Tel: (212) 736-0770, FAX: (212) 736-8305, Web Site: www.vanguarddirect.com (35)

Vannett, Paul, Dovetail, Littleton, CO. Tel: (303) 904-4771, FAX: (303) 904-4776, E-Mail: welcome@dovetailnet.com, Web Site: www.dovetailnet.com (22)

VanPatten, Mark, NCP Solutions, Reston, VA. Tel: (703) 438-6000, (800) 822-9919, FAX: (703) 438-3570, Web Site: www.nwf.org (17)

Vansickle, Lisa K., First Banks Inc, Clayton, MO. Tel: (314) 854-4600, FAX: (314) 592-6840, Web Site: www.firstbanks.com (14)

The Vantage Group Inc, Boston, MA. Tel: (617) 878-6000, FAX: (617) 878-6154, Web Site: www.vantagetravel.com (14)

Varga, Paul C., Brown-Forman Corp, Louisville, KY. Tel: (502) 585-1100, FAX: (502) 774-7876, E-Mail: brown-forman@b-f.com, Web Site: www.brown-forman.com (16)

Vargas, Colette F., Diversified Investment Advisors, Harrison, NY. Tel: (914) 627-3000, FAX: (914) 627-3280, Web Site: www.divinvest.com (14)

Vargas, Jane, JR Cigar, Burlington, NC. Tel: (800) 572-4427, FAX: (800) 457-3299, E-Mail: manager@jrburlington.com, Web Site: www.jrcigars.com (5)

Varian Medical Systems, Palo Alto, CA. Tel: (650) 493-4000, FAX: (650) 842-5196, Web Site: www.varian.com (9)

Varner, Barbara, ACBL, Horn Lake, MS. Tel: (662) 253-3100, FAX: (662) 253-3187, E-Mail: service@acbl.org, Web Site: www.acbl.org (1)

Varner, Jean, Cuvaison Inc, Napa, CA. Tel: (707) 942-2455, E-Mail: info@cuvaison.com, Web Site: www.cuvaison.com (4)

Varner, Maribett, BKV Inc, Atlanta, GA. Tel: (404) 233-0332, E-Mail: rina.cook@bkv.com, Web Site: www.bkv.com (35)

Vartorella, William F., Craig/Vartorella International Marketing & Advertising Inc, Camden, SC. Tel: (803) 432-4353, FAX: (803) 432-4353, E-Mail: globebiz@juno.com, Web Site: www.colasc.com/Marketing_&_Fundraising (1)

Vas, Kevin, Media Resource Group Inc, Mount Kisco, NY. Tel: (914) 244-4250, FAX: (914) 244-4458, Web Site: www.mrginc.com (31)

Vasile, Joseph, Viahealth, Rochester, NY. Tel: (585) 922-4000, (585) 922-3677, FAX: (585) 922-3929, Web Site: www.viahealth.org (16)

Vasquez, Cyndi, Mike Murach & Associates Inc, Fresno, CA. Tel: (559) 440-9071, (800) 221-5528, FAX: (559) 440-0963, E-Mail: murachbooks@murach.com, Web Site: www.murach.com (17)

Vasquez, Kevin, Butler Schein Animal Health, Dublin, OH. Tel: (614) 761-9095, (888) 691-2724, FAX: (888) 329-3861, Web Site: www.butlerschein.com (16)

Vasquez-Perez, Carmen, Chain Store Guide, Tampa, FL. Tel: (800) 927-9292, FAX: (813) 627-6882, E-Mail: info@csgis.com, Web Site: www.csgis.com (17)

Vassallo, Vincent, The Results Group, Boston, MA. Tel: (617) 227-0229, Web Site: www.verdant-results-group.com (20)

VastCast Media Inc, Las Vegas, NV. Tel: (702) 221-8261, (800) 946-7112, FAX: (702) 666-8553, E-Mail: support@vastcast.com, Web Site: www.vastcastmedia.com (35)

Vastola, Ray, Travel Planners Inc, New York, NY. Tel: (212) 532-1660, (800) 221-3531, FAX: (212) 532-1556, Web Site: www.tphousing.com (19)

Vatuone, Timothy V., Syntellect, Phoenix, AZ. Tel: (602) 789-2800, (800) 788-9733, FAX: (602) 789-2899, Web Site: www.syntellect.com (16)

Vaughan, Scott, United Business Media, Manhasset, NY. Tel: (516) 562-5000, Web Site: www.ubmtechnology.com (17)

Vaughn, Blake, Fifth Gear LLC, Indianapolis, IN. Tel: (317) 631-0907, FAX: (317) 631-6585, Web Site: www.infifthgear.com (22)

Vavra, John, Hasler Inc, Milford, CT. Tel: (203) 301-3400, (800) 995-2035, FAX: (203) 301-2600, E-Mail: info@haslerinc.com, Web Site: www.haslerinc.com (34)

Vaxserve, Moosic, PA. Tel: (800) 752-9338, FAX: (800) 553-9908, Web Site: www.vaxserve.com (7)

Vazin, Scott, Volkswagen Group of America Inc, Herndon, VA. Tel: (248) 754-5000, Web Site: www.volkswagengroupamerica.com (16)

Vazquez, Carlos, Front Porch Inc, Sonora, CA. Tel: (209) 288-5500, (800) 728-1464, Web Site: www.frontporch.com (35)

Vcom International Multi-Media Corp, South Hackensack, NJ. Tel: (201) 229-9800, (800) 572-6373, FAX: (973) 439-1522, E-Mail: info@vcomimc.com, Web Site: www.vcomimc.com (3)

Veach, H. Duncan, Beau Graphics Ltd Inc, Lexington, KY. Tel: (859) 277-2328, (877) 279-2328, FAX: (859) 278-6193, Web Site: www.beaugraphics.com (36)

Veal, Greg, Grand Pacific Resorts, Carlsbad, CA. Tel: (760) 827-4100, (800) 374-7779, Web Site: www.grandpacificresorts.com (19)

Vector Marketing Corp, Olean, NY. Tel: (716) 373-6141, (267) 880-1750, FAX: (716) 373-6145, Web Site: www.cutco.com (5)

Vedder, Bret, Creative Learning Systems Inc, Longmont, CO. Tel: (303) 772-6400, (800) 458-2880, FAX: (303) 772-6422, Web Site: www.clsinc.com (9)

Veer, Calgary, AB Canada. Tel: (403) 234-7901, Web Site: www.veer.com (16)

Vega, David, Bankers Life & Casualty Co, Chicago, IL. Tel: (312) 396-6000, (800) 231-9150, Web Site: www.bankerslife.com (15)

Vega, Frank J., San Francisco Chronicle, San Francisco, CA. Tel: (415) 777-1111, FAX: (415) 536-5178, Web Site: www.sfgate.com (17)

Vegetarian Times, El Segundo, CA. Tel: (310) 356-4100, FAX: (310) 356-4110, Web Site: www.vegetariantimes.com (31)

Vehicle Assurance, Saint Charles, MO. Tel: (636) 925-7800, (866) 522-5581 (5)

Velamakanni, Srikanth, Fractal Analytics, Jersey City, NJ. Tel: (201) 469-0600, Web Site: www.fractalanalytics.com (35)

Vella, Nino, New Pig Corp, Tipton, PA. Tel: (814) 684-0101, (800) 468-4647, FAX: (814) 684-0961, E-Mail: hothogs@newpig.com, Web Site: www.newpig.com (9)

Vellante, Richard, Legal Sea Foods Inc, Boston, MA. Tel: (617) 530-9000, (800) 343-5804, FAX: (617) 530-9649, Web Site: www.legalseafoods.com (4)

Velletri, Christopher L., Market Street Lists Inc, Exeter, NH. Tel: (603) 772-6666, (888) 675-5478, FAX: (603) 772-0184, E-Mail: info@market-street.com, Web Site: www.market-street.com (23)

Vellodi, Dilip R., Sutherland Global Services, Pittsford, NY. Tel: (585) 586-5757, (800) 388-4557, Web Site: www.sutherlandglobal.com (35)

Vellucci, Bethany, Media Two, Baltimore, MD. Tel: (410) 828-0120, FAX: (410) 825-1002, Web Site: www.mediatwo.com (17)

Veltri, Eugene, A&E Promotions LLC, Atlantic Highlands, NJ. Tel: (732) 275-1520, FAX: (732) 275-1147, E-Mail: eveltri@aepromo.com, Web Site: www.promoplace.com (27)

Velu, Param, University Subscription Service, Downers Grove, IL. Tel: (630) 960-3233, (888) 877-1213, FAX: (630) 960-3246, Web Site: www.ussmag.com (18)

Velu, Pethi, University Subscription Service, Downers Grove, IL. Tel: (630) 960-3233, (888) 877-1213, FAX: (630) 960-3246, Web Site: www.ussmag.com (18)

Vemma Nutrition Co, Tempe, AZ. Tel: (480) 927-8999, (800) 577-0777, FAX: (888) 314-9827, E-Mail: ms@vemma.com, Web Site: www.vemma.com (7)

Venable LLP Conference Center, Washington, DC. Tel: (202) 344-4860, (202) 344-4000, (888) VENABLE, FAX: (202) 344-8300, E-Mail: info@venable.com, Web Site: www.venable.com (20)

Venables, Jeffrey, American Running Association, Bethesda, MD. Tel: (301) 913-9517, (800) 776-2732, FAX: (301) 913-9520, E-Mail: run@americanrunning.org, Web Site: www.americanrunning.org (1)

Vendice, Beth, Mercury Media, Santa Monica, CA. Tel: (310) 451-2900, FAX: (310) 451-0180, Web Site: www.mercurymedia.com (32)

Veneer Factory Outlet, Westport, KY. E-Mail: bob@veneerfactoryoutlet.com, Web Site: veneer-factory-outlet.com (8)

Venenga, Steven J., Hormel Foods Corp, Austin, MN. Tel: (507) 437-5611, (800) 523-4635, FAX: (507) 437-5158, Web Site: www.hormelfoods.com (16)

Venhuizen, John, Ace Hardware Corp, Oak Brook, IL. Tel: (630) 990-6600, FAX: (630) 990-6838, Web Site: www.acehardware.com (16)

Venskus, Joe, Inforonics Global Services LLC, Littleton, MA. Tel: (315) 261-7525, FAX: (978) 698-7500, E-Mail: info@inforonics.com, Web Site: www.inforonics.com (22)

Vente Inc, Omaha, NE. Tel: (402) 898-6800, (877) 899-9691, FAX: (402) 334-4829, Web Site: www.venteinc.com (30)

Ventresca, Jr. Benjamin J., Brandywine Consulting Group Inc, West Chester, PA. Tel: (610) 696-5872, FAX: (610) 429-1954, Web Site: www.brandywineconsulting.com (20)

Ventriloquist Voice Solutions International Inc, Mississauga, ON Canada. Tel: (866) 446-0860, E-Mail: info@ventriloquistsolutions.com, Web Site: www.ventriloquistsolutions.com (29)

Ventura Associates International LLC, New York, NY. Tel: (212) 302-8277, FAX: (212) 302-2587, E-Mail: info@sweepspros.com, Web Site: www.sweepspros.com (35)

Venture Encoding Service Inc, Fort Worth, TX. Tel: (817) 283-9500, FAX: (817) 540-6966, E-Mail: sales@venture-encoding.com, Web Site: www.venture-encoding.com (27)

Venturella, Frank J., Magna Visual Inc, Saint Louis, MO. Tel: (314) 843-9000, (800) 843-3399, FAX: (314) 843-0000, E-Mail: magna@magnavisual.com, Web Site: www.magnavisual.com (9)

Venturelli, Larry, Whirlpool Corp, Benton Harbor, MI. Tel: (269) 923-5000, E-Mail: info@whirlpool.com, Web Site: www.whirlpoolcorp.com (16)

Ventyx, Atlanta, GA. Tel: (770) 952-8444, (800) 868-0497, FAX: (770) 955-2977, E-Mail: support@ventyx.com, Web Site: www.ventyx.com (16)

Venus Fashion, Inc, Jacksonville, FL. Tel: (904) 645-6000, Web Site: www.venus.com (2)

Veratad Technologies LLC, Teaneck, NJ. Tel: (201) 510-6000, FAX: (201) 510-6036, Web Site: www.veratad.com (22)

Verbesselt, Ivan, NAGRA USA, San Francisco, CA. Tel: (415) 962-5000, FAX: (415) 962-5300, E-Mail: dtv@nagra.com, Web Site: www.nagra.com (32)

The Verdi Group Inc, Pittsford, NY. Tel: (585) 381-4275, FAX: (585) 381-4293, E-Mail: info@theverdigroup.com, Web Site: www.theverdigroup.com (35)

Verdy, Sonia, Scientific Games Canada, Montreal, QC Canada. Tel: (514) 254-3000, FAX: (514) 254-1411, Web Site: www.scientificgames.com (27)

Vere, Brenda, Philips Lifeline, Framingham, MA. Tel: (855) 332-7799, (800) 635-6156, Web Site: www.lifeline.philips.com (7)

Verey, Andrew, MSC Metalworking, Melville, NY. Tel: (516) 812-2000, (800) 521-9520, E-Mail: inquiry@rutlandtool.com, Web Site: www.rutlandtool.com (34)

Verheyen, Mark, CNA, Chicago, IL. Tel: (312) 822-5000, (800) 262-2000, E-Mail: cna_help@cna.com, Web Site: www.cna.com (15)

Verhulst, Candace, Inforonics Global Services LLC, Littleton, MA. Tel: (315) 261-7525, FAX: (978) 698-7500, E-Mail: info@inforonics.com, Web Site: www.inforonics.com (22)

Veriad, Brea, CA. Tel: (714) 990-2700, (800) 962-0658, FAX: (800) 962-0658, E-Mail: info@veriad.com, Web Site: www.veriad.com (16)

Veridian Credit Union, Waterloo, IA. Tel: (319) 236-5692, (800) 235-3228, FAX: (319) 833-1185, E-Mail: sarahma@veridiancu.org, Web Site: www.veridiancu.org (1)

Veritas Analytics Inc, Sterling, VA. Tel: (703) 707-5620, Web Site: www.veritas-analytics.com (30)

Verizon Communications Inc, New York, NY. Tel: (212) 395-1000, (800) 621-9900, FAX: (212) 571-1897, Web Site: www.verizon.com (3)

Verjee, Aman, Collective - The Audience Engine, New York, NY. Tel: (646) 722-8550, FAX: (646) 442-6529, Web Site: www.collective.com (22)

Vermette, David, MassMutual Financial Group, Springfield, MA. Tel: (413) 788-8411, FAX: (413) 744-8889, E-Mail: name@www.massmutual.com, Web Site: www.massmutual.com (15)

Vermie, Craig D., Transamerica Occidental Life Co, Los Angeles, CA. Tel: (213) 742-3111, FAX: (213) 741-6623, Web Site: www.transamerica.com (15)

Vermillion, Richard, Fulcrum, New York, NY. Tel: (212) 651-7000, (888) 245-9450 (22)

Vermilye, Robert, Commerce Register Inc, Midland Park, NJ. Tel: (201) 445-3000, FAX: (201) 445-5806, E-Mail: cri@comreginc.com, Web Site: www.comreginc.com (22)

The Vermont Country Store, Manchester Center, VT. Tel: (802) 362-8200, Web Site: www.vermontcountrystore.com (5)

Vermont Media Publishing Co, West Dover, VT. Tel: (802) 464-3388, FAX: (802) 464-7255, E-Mail: publisher@vermontmedia.com, Web Site: www.dvalnews.com (17)

Vermont/New Hampshire Direct Marketing Group, Woodstock, VT. Tel: (802) 457-2807, FAX: (802) 457-2807, E-Mail: vtnhmg@vtnhmg, Web Site: www.vtnhmg.org (40)

Vermont Ski Areas Association, Montpelier, VT. Tel: (802) 223-2439, FAX: (802) 229-6917, E-Mail: info@skivermont.com, Web Site: www.skivermont.com (1)

Vermont Teddy Bear Co, Shelburne, VT. Tel: (802) 985-3001, (800) 829-BEAR, (800) 282-3131, FAX: (802) 985-1304, E-Mail: info@vtbear.com, Web Site: www.vermontteddybear.com (6)

Vernerey, Laurent, APC by Schneider Electric, West Kingston, RI. Tel: (800) 555-7927, FAX: (401) 789-3710, E-Mail: public.relations@apcc.com, Web Site: www.apcc.com (22)

Verney, Geoff, Monadnock Paper Mills Inc, Bennington, NH. Tel: (603) 588-3311, (800) 221-2159, FAX: (603) 588-3158, Web Site: www.monadnockpaper.com (25)

Verney, Richard G., Monadnock Paper Mills Inc, Bennington, NH. Tel: (603) 588-3311, (800) 221-2159, FAX: (603) 588-3158, Web Site: www.monadnockpaper.com (25)

Veronesi, Danielle, Peter Pan Bus Lines Inc, Springfield, MA. Tel: (413) 781-3320, (800) 343-9999, FAX: (413) 747-7626, E-Mail: info@peterpanbus.com, Web Site: www.peterpanbus.com (19)

Veronis Suhler Stevenson LLC, New York, NY. Tel: (212) 935-4990, FAX: (212) 381-8168, E-Mail: stevensonj@vss.com, Web Site: www.vss.com (14)

Veronis, John J., Veronis Suhler Stevenson LLC, New York, NY. Tel: (212) 935-4990, FAX: (212) 381-8168, E-Mail: stevensonj@vss.com, Web Site: www.vss.com (14)

Verrecchia, Alfred, Hasbro Inc, Pawtucket, RI. Tel: (401) 431-8697, (800) 242-7276, FAX: (401) 727-5121, Web Site: www.hasbro.com (11)

Verso Paper, Memphis, TN. Tel: (901) 369-4100, FAX: (901) 369-4174, Web Site: www.versopaper.com (25)

Versoy, Jr. Irving R., Faire Harbour Limited, Scituate, MA. Tel: (781) 545-2465, FAX: (781) 545-2465 (5)

Versoy, Mary J., Faire Harbour Limited, Scituate, MA. Tel: (781) 545-2465, FAX: (781) 545-2465 (5)

Vertex Inc, Berwyn, PA. Tel: (610) 640-4200, (800) 355-3500, FAX: (610) 640-5892, Web Site: www.vertexinc.com (16)

Vertical Communications Inc, Santa Clara, CA. Tel: (408) 404-1600, (800) COMDIAL, FAX: (408) 969-9601, Web Site: www.comdial.com (34)

Vertical Media Group, Fort Lee, NJ. Tel: (201) 245-7935 (20)

VerticalResponse Inc, San Francisco, CA. Tel: (866) 683-7842, E-Mail: askus@verticalresponse.com, Web Site: www.verticalresponse.com (24)

Vesey's Seeds Ltd, Charlottetown, PE Canada. Tel: (902) 368-7333, (800) 363-7333, FAX: (800) 686-0329, E-Mail: customerservice@veseys.com, Web Site: www.veseys.com (8)

Vest, Ulrich, Springer Science & Business Media LLC, New York, NY. Tel: (212) 460-1500, FAX: (212) 460-1575, Web Site: www.springer.com (17)

The Vestal Press Ltd, Lanham, MD. Tel: (301) 459-3366, (800) 462-6420, FAX: (301) 429-5746, E-Mail: sburnett@rowman.com, Web Site: www.nbnbooks.com (17)

Vestcom International Inc, Little Rock, AR. Tel: (501) 663-0100, (800) 264-0965, E-Mail: sales@vestcom.com, Web Site: vestcom.com (31)

Vet Vax, Tonganoxie, KS. Tel: (913) 845-3760, (800) 369-8297, FAX: (913) 845-9472, E-Mail: sales@vetvax.com (11)

Veterans of Foreign Wars of the US, Kansas City, MO. Tel: (816) 756-3390, FAX: (816) 968-1149, E-Mail: info@vfw.org, Web Site: www.vfw.org (1)

Vetter, Johanna, FEEDING AMERICA, Chicago, IL. Tel: (312) 263-2303, FAX: (312) 263-5626, Web Site: www.secondharvest.org (1)

Via, Gerald, Source 4 Inc, Huntersville, NC. Tel: (704) 602-0110, (800) 541-5400, FAX: (704) 602-0119, E-Mail: source4newyork@source4.com, Web Site: www.source4.com (22)

Via, Thomas, Brookstone Co, Merrimack, NH. Tel: (603) 880-9500, (800) 846-3000, FAX: (603) 577-8005, E-Mail: customerservice@brookstone.com, Web Site: www.brookstone.com (3)

Viacom Inc, New York, NY. Tel: (212) 258-6000, FAX: (212) 258-6464, Web Site: www.viacom.com (16)

Viacom Media Networks, New York, NY. Tel: (212) 258-6000, Web Site: www.viacom.com (32)

Viahealth, Rochester, NY. Tel: (585) 922-4000, (585) 922-3677, FAX: (585) 922-3929, Web Site: www.viahealth.org (16)

VisiPak Inc, Arnold, MO. Tel: (636) 282-6800, (800) 922-9391, FAX: (636) 282-6888, E-Mail: visipak@sinclair-rush.com, Web Site: www.visipak.com (34)

VistaPrint USA Inc, Lexington, MA. Tel: (800) 961-2075, Web Site: www.vistaprint.com (27)

Visual Horizons, Rochester, NY. Tel: (585) 424-5300, (800) 424-1011, FAX: (800) 424-5411, E-Mail: cs@visualhorizons.com, Web Site: www.visualhorizons.com (16)

Visual Reference Publications, New York, NY. Tel: (212) 279-7000, (800) 251-4545, FAX: (212) 279-7014 (17)

Vita-Mix Corp, Cleveland, OH. Tel: (440) 235-4840, (800) VITA-MIX, FAX: (440) 235-3726, E-Mail: service@vitamix.com, Web Site: www.vitamix.com (16)

Vitale, Salvatore J., The Conference Board Inc, New York, NY. Tel: (212) 759-0900, FAX: (212) 980-7014, Web Site: www.conference-board.org (16)

Vitale, Thomas P., Syfy, New York, NY. Tel: (212) 664-4444, Web Site: www.syfy.com (32)

Vitamin Power Inc, Hauppauge, NY. Tel: (516) 378-0900, (800) 645-6567, FAX: (631) 273-4394, E-Mail: contactus@vitaminpower.com, Web Site: www.vitaminpower.com (7)

Vitamin Research Products, Cottonwood, AZ. Tel: (888) 362-1699, FAX: (775) 884-1331, E-Mail: customerservice@vrp.com, Web Site: www.vrp.com (7)

Vitamin Specialties Co, Freehold, NJ. Tel: (732) 308-3000, FAX: (855) 482-3291, Web Site: www.ivcinc.com (17)

Vitangcol, Alvin, Einhorn Associates Inc, Milwaukee, WI. Tel: (414) 453-4488, FAX: (414) 453-4831, Web Site: www.einhornassociates.com (20)

Vitasoy USA Inc, Ayer, MA. Tel: (978) 772-6880, (800) VITA-SOY, FAX: (978) 772-6881, E-Mail: info@vitasoy-usa.com, Web Site: www.vitasoy-usa.com (16)

Vitch, Michael, Compu-Mail Direct Marketing, Grand Island, NY. Tel: (716) 775-8001, (800) 255-0607, FAX: (716) 775-5681, E-Mail: marketing@compu-mail.com, Web Site: compu-mail.com (21)

Vitrano, Christopher, Nelson Schmidt Inc, Milwaukee, WI. Tel: (414) 224-0210, FAX: (414) 224-9463, Web Site: nelsonschmidt.com (35)

Vittor, Kenneth M., The McGraw-Hill Financial, New York, NY. Tel: (212) 904-2000, Web Site: www.mhfi.com (17)

Vivendi SA, New York, NY. Tel: (212) 572-7000, FAX: (212) 572-1080, Web Site: www.vivendi.com (16)

Vivio, Michael, Cox Target Media Inc, St. Petersburg, FL. Tel: (727) 399-3000, (800) 678-2743, FAX: (727) 399-3061, E-Mail: info@coxtarget.com, Web Site: www.coxtarget.com (21)

Vivitar Corp, Tempe, AZ. Tel: (800) 592-9541, FAX: (909) 348-6390, Web Site: www.vivitar.com (16)

Vlok, Nicolaas, Vision Solutions, Irvine, CA. Tel: (949) 253-6500, (800) 683-4667, FAX: (949) 253-6501, E-Mail: info@visionsolutions.com, Web Site: www.visionsolutions.com (22)

Vocational Biographies Inc, Sauk Centre, MN. Tel: (320) 352-6516, (800) 255-0752, FAX: (320) 352-5546, E-Mail: careers@vocbios.com, Web Site: www.vocbio.com (17)

Vodicka, Nancy, iContact LLC, Morrisville, NC. Tel: (919) 820-7837, (877) 820-7837, E-Mail: sales@icontact.com, Web Site: www.icontact.com (32)

Voelker, Raymond M., The Progressive Corp, Mayfield Village, OH. Tel: (440) 461-5000, (800) PROGRESSIVE, (800) 776-4737, FAX: (800) 456-6590, Web Site: www.progressive.com (15)

Vogel, Eileen, Spectrum Retail Associates, Ardmore, PA. Tel: (610) 645-9520, (800) 570-6565, FAX: (610) 645-9524 (20)

Vogel, Paul, Planned Parenthood Federation of America, New York, NY. Tel: (212) 541-7800, FAX: (212) 245-1845, Web Site: www.plannedparenthood.org (1)

Vogel, W., Viking Pump Inc, Cedar Falls, IA. Tel: (319) 266-1741, FAX: (319) 273-8157, E-Mail: info@vikingpump.com, Web Site: www.vikingpump.com (16)

Vogel, William Alan, Montag & Caldwell Inc, Atlanta, GA. Tel: (404) 836-7100, (800) 458-5868, FAX: (404) 836-7168, Web Site: www.montag.com (14)

Vogenson, Todd, Chico's FAS Inc, Fort Myers, FL. Tel: (239) 277-6200, Web Site: www.chicos.com (2)

Voges, Chris, Plastic View ATC, Simi Valley, CA. Tel: (805) 520-9390, (800) 468-6301, FAX: (805) 520-0260, E-Mail: info@pvatc.com, Web Site: www.pvatc.com (9)

Voges, Ryan, Plastic View ATC, Simi Valley, CA. Tel: (805) 520-9390, (800) 468-6301, FAX: (805) 520-0260, E-Mail: info@pvatc.com, Web Site: www.pvatc.com (9)

Voges, Sonny, Plastic View ATC, Simi Valley, CA. Tel: (805) 520-9390, (800) 468-6301, FAX: (805) 520-0260, E-Mail: info@pvatc.com, Web Site: www.pvatc.com (9)

Vogt, Ed, GM Customer Relationship Management, Detroit, MI. Tel: (313) 665-6605, Web Site: www.gm.com (35)

Voice Message Broadcasting Corp, Aliso Viejo, CA. Tel: (714) 437-0600, FAX: (714) 242-1989, Web Site: www.vmbc.com (32)

Voice Systems Engineering Inc, Langhorne, PA. Tel: (215) 953-8568, E-Mail: info@vseinc.com, Web Site: www.vseinc.com (32)

Voicelogic, Toronto, ON Canada. Tel: (888) 552-8858, Web Site: www.voicelogic.com (29)

Voit, Tim, Streamfeeder, Minneapolis, MN. Tel: (763) 502-0000, FAX: (763) 502-0100, Web Site: www.streamfeeder.com (34)

Volansky, Debora, Connex International Inc, Danbury, CT. Tel: (203) 731-5400, (800) 426-6639, FAX: (203) 730-9060, E-Mail: marketing@connexintl.com, Web Site: www.connexintl.com (22)

Volkema, Michael A., Herman Miller Inc, Zeeland, MI. Tel: (616) 654-3000, FAX: (616) 654-5234, E-Mail: investor@hermanmiller.com, Web Site: www.hermanmiller.com (16)

Volkert, Dr. Jo, San Francisco State University, San Francisco, CA. Tel: (415) 338-1111, FAX: (415) 338-0501, Web Site: www.sfsu.edu (41)

Volkswagen Group of America Inc, Herndon, VA. Tel: (248) 754-5000, Web Site: www.volkswagengroupamerica.com (16)

Vollowitz, Eileen, Back Designs Inc, Novato, CA. Tel: (415) 883-4683, (800) 466-1341, FAX: (707) 557-2225, E-Mail: info@backdesigns.com, Web Site: www.backdesigns.com (7)

Volner, Ian, Venable LLP Conference Center, Washington, DC. Tel: (202) 344-4860, (202) 344-4000, (888) VENABLE, FAX: (202) 344-8300, E-Mail: info@venable.com, Web Site: www.venable.com (20)

Volpe, Michele, Media Source Solutions, Pompano Beach, FL. Tel: (954) 788-0213, FAX: (954) 788-0215, Web Site: www.mediasourcesolutions.com (24)

Volt Delta, Blue Bell, PA. Tel: (610) 825-7720, FAX: (610) 567-5698, Web Site: www.voltdelta.com (22)

Voltz, Joanne, Redleaf Press, Saint Paul, MN. Tel: (651) 641-6621, (800) 423-8309, FAX: (800) 641-0115, E-Mail: jvoltz@redleafpress.org, Web Site: www.redleafpress.org (17)

Volunteers of America, Alexandria, VA. Tel: (703) 341-5000, (800) 899-0089, FAX: (703) 341-7000, E-Mail: info@voa.org, Web Site: www.voa.org (1)

Volvo Cars of North America LLC, Northvale, NJ. Tel: (201) 768-7300, (800) 458-1552, E-Mail: customercare@volvocars.com, Web Site: www.volvocars.com (16)

Von Birgelen, Catherine, Center for eBusiness & Advanced IT, Erie, PA. Tel: (814) 898-6500, FAX: (814) 898-6534, Web Site: www.ebizitpa.org (1)

Von Deylen, Larry, Oregon Freeze Dry Inc, Albany, OR. Tel: (541) 926-6001, FAX: (541) 967-6527, Web Site: www.ofd.com (4)

Von Gal, Timothy C, Boston Gift Show, Kennesaw, GA. Tel: (678) 285-3976, FAX: (678) 285-7469, Web Site: www.bostongiftshow.com (42)

Von Hertsenberg, Kurt, Wildlife Education Ltd, Park Hills, KY. Tel: (858) 513-7600, FAX: (858) 513-7660, E-Mail: animals@zoobooks.com, Web Site: www.zoobooks.com (17)

Vonage, Holmdel, NJ. Tel: (732) 528-2600, Web Site: www.vonage.com (32)

Vonderschmidt, Tom, BAM! Direct Inc, Suwanee, GA. Tel: (678) 947-1943, FAX: (678) 947-3562, Web Site: www.bamdirect.com (35)

Vook, Barbara, Health O Meter, Countryside, IL. Tel: (708) 377-0600, (800) 815-6615, FAX: (708) 377-0601, E-Mail: HomProCS@homscales.com, Web Site: www.homscales.com (16)

Voorhees, Janice, Ranger Joe's International Military Supply, Columbus, GA. Tel: (706) 689-0082, (800) 247-4541, FAX: (706) 682-8840, E-Mail: customerservice@rangerjoes.com, Web Site: www.rangerjoes.com (2)

Voorhees, Paul, Ranger Joe's International Military Supply, Columbus, GA. Tel: (706) 689-0082, (800) 247-4541, FAX: (706) 682-8840, E-Mail: customerservice@rangerjoes.com, Web Site: www.rangerjoes.com (2)

Voors, Jerry, Arrow Companies, LLC, Delavan, WI. Tel: (262) 724-8822, FAX: (262) 724-8824, Web Site: www.arrowcompanies.com (22)

Voris, Steve, Business Services Network, San Francisco, CA. Tel: (415) 282-8161, FAX: (415) 282-8176, E-Mail: sales@bsnc.com, Web Site: www.bsnc.com (28)

Vorthmann, Mary, Mid America Direct Marketing Association, Omaha, NE. Tel: (402) 965-4318, FAX: (402) 964-8484, Web Site: www.madma.org (40)

Vorwerck, Carol, Mary Elizabeth Granger & Associates Inc, Baltimore, MD. Tel: (410) 842-1170, FAX: (410) 842-1185, E-Mail: info@maryegranger.com, Web Site: www.maryegranger.com (23)

Voss, Mike, Applied Printing Technologies, Moonachie, NJ. Tel: (201) 896-6600, (888) 282-4141, FAX: (201) 896-6839, E-Mail: vpsales@appliedprinting.com, Web Site: www.appliedprinting.com (27)

Vouros, Peter, TempoGraphics Inc, Carol Stream, IL. Tel: (630) 462-8200, FAX: (630) 462-0350, E-Mail: info@tempographics.com (27)

Voxdata Telecom, Montreal, QC Canada. Tel: (514) 871-1920, (800) 861-9599, FAX: (514) 871-0445, E-Mail: fcouture@voxdata.com, Web Site: www.voxdata.com (29)

Voyageur Inc, Easley, SC. Tel: (802) 496-3127, (800) 311-7245, FAX: (802) 496-6247 (11)

Ed Voyles Hyundai Inc, Smyrna, GA. Tel: (770) 952-8881, (877) 579-0642, FAX: (770) 612-9396, Web Site: www.edvoyleshyundai.com (16)

Voyles, Charles Edwin, Ed Voyles Hyundai Inc, Smyrna, GA. Tel: (770) 952-8881, (877) 579-0642, FAX: (770) 612-9396, Web Site: www.edvoyleshyundai.com (16)

Vozzo, Thomas, Gall's Inc, Lexington, KY. Tel: (859) 266-7227, (800) 477-7766, FAX: (859) 268-5954, E-Mail: help-desk@galls.com, Web Site: www.galls.com (16)

Vross, Frank J., Jaff Marketing Group Inc, Spring, TX. Tel: (281) 353-0004, FAX: (281) 288-0970 (16)

Vukelich, Ty, EMPLOYERS Insurance, Reno, NV. Tel: (775) 327-2677, Web Site: www.employers.com (15)

Vulcan Information Packaging, Vincent, AL. Tel: (205) 672-2241, (800) 633-4526, FAX: (205) 672-1276, Web Site: www.vulcan-online.com (16)

Vulcan Materials Co, Birmingham, AL. Tel: (205) 298-3000, FAX: (205) 298-2960, Web Site: www.vulcanmaterials.com (16)

W

WCPE-FM, Wake Forest, NC. Tel: (800) 556-5178, FAX: (919) 556-9273, Web Site: theclassicalstation.org (32)

WDS Marketing & Public Relations, Overland Park, KS. Tel: (913) 362-4541, FAX: (913) 362-7342, E-Mail: bwilson@wdspr.com, Web Site: www.wdspr.com (20)

WGBH Educational Foundation, Brighton, MA. Tel: (617) 300-2000, FAX: (617) 300-1026, Web Site: www.wgbh.org (1)

WLA Inc, New York, NY. Tel: (212) 584-1810 (20)

WLNY-TV 10/55, Melville, NY. Tel: (631) 777-8855, Web Site: newyork.cbslocal.com/station/wlny (32)

WPG Americas Inc, San Jose, CA. Tel: (408) 392-8100, FAX: (408) 436-9551, E-Mail: notherncalifornia.sales@wpgamericas.com, Web Site: www.wpgamericas.com (20)

WRS Group Ltd, Waco, TX. Tel: (254) 776-6461, (800) 299-3366, FAX: (888) 977-7653, E-Mail: custom@wrsgroup.com, Web Site: www.wrsgroup.com (7)

WS Live LLC, Dubuque, IA. Tel: (563) 582-9501, (800) 582-9501, FAX: (563) 582-2003, Web Site: www.wslive.com (29)

WSI, Mississauga, ON Canada. Tel: (905) 678-7588, (888) 678-7588, FAX: (905) 678-7242, E-Mail: contact@wsiworld.com, Web Site: www.wsiworld.com (35)

WTB Associates Inc, Wilmette, IL. Tel: (847) 251-4188 (20)

WTS Media, Chattanooga, TN. Tel: (423) 894-9427, (800) 251-7228, FAX: (423) 894-7281, E-Mail: customerservice@wtsmedia.com, Web Site: www.wts-tape.com (16)

Wachob, George, Hearthside Quilts & Supplies, Hinesburg, VT. Tel: (802) 482-7800, (800) 451-3533, FAX: (802) 482-7803, E-Mail: hearthsidequilts@att.net, Web Site: www.hearthsidequilts.com (11)

Wachowiak, Rick, National Business Furniture Inc, Milwaukee, WI. Tel: (414) 276-8511, (800) 558-1010, FAX: (414) 276-8371, Web Site: www.nationalbusinessfurniture.com (10)

Wachowiak, Rodney, Replogle Globes Inc, Broadview, IL. Tel: (708) 343-0900, FAX: (708) 343-0923, E-Mail: info@reploggleglobes.com, Web Site: www.reploggleglobes.com (16)

Wachsstock, Mel, Sunbilt Solar Products, Jamaica, NY. Tel: (718) 297-0228, FAX: (718) 297-3090, E-Mail: robin@jsussmaninc.com, Web Site: jsussmaninc.com/sunbilt-solar-products (8)

Wachtel, Christopher, WordCom Inc, Ellington, CT. Tel: (860) 875-7373, (800) 822-0622, FAX: (860) 872-2713, E-Mail: sales@wordcom-inc.com, Web Site: www.wordcom-inc.com (21)

Wachtel, George, WordCom Inc, Ellington, CT. Tel: (860) 875-7373, (800) 822-0622, FAX: (860) 872-2713, E-Mail: sales@wordcom-inc.com, Web Site: www.wordcom-inc.com (21)

Waddell, Frederick H., The Northern Trust Co, Chicago, IL. Tel: (312) 630-6000, (888) 289-6542, FAX: (312) 444-5244, Web Site: www.ntrs.com (14)

Wade Paper Corp, Deerfield, IL. Tel: (847) 940-9777, (800) 828-8318, FAX: (847) 940-1077, E-Mail: info@wadepaper.com, Web Site: www.wadepaper.com (25)

Wade, Beth, VML Inc, Kansas City, MO. Tel: (816) 283-0700, FAX: (816) 283-0954, E-Mail: dl-vmlcommarketing@vml.com, Web Site: www.vml.com (35)

Wade, Dan, Sporting Clays Ltd, Titusville, FL. Tel: (321) 268-5010, FAX: (321) 267-7216, E-Mail: sales@sportingclays.net, Web Site: www.sportingclays.net (17)

Wade, Gordon, CheckMark Communications, Saint Louis, MO. Tel: (314) 982-1000, FAX: (314) 982-3580, Web Site: www.purina.com (4)

Wade, Kevin P., Wade Paper Corp, Deerfield, IL. Tel: (847) 940-9777, (800) 828-8318, FAX: (847) 940-1077, E-Mail: info@wadepaper.com, Web Site: www.wadepaper.com (25)

Wade, Wyatt, Davis Art Images, Worcester, MA. Tel: (508) 754-7201, (800) 533-2847, FAX: (508) 831-9260, (508) 753-3834, E-Mail: lkeenekendrick@davisart.com, Web Site: www.davisartimages.com (38)

Wade, Wyatt, Davis Publications Inc, Worcester, MA. Tel: (508) 754-7201, (800) 533-2847, FAX: (508) 753-3834, Web Site: www.davisart.com (17)

Wadhams, Timothy, Masco Corp, Taylor, MI. Tel: (313) 274-7400, FAX: (313) 792-6135, E-Mail: webmaster@mascohq.com, Web Site: www.masco.com (16)

Wadhwani, David, Adobe Systems Inc, San Jose, CA. Tel: (408) 536-6000, (800) 833-6687, FAX: (408) 537-6000, Web Site: www.adobe.com (22)

Wadleigh, Maya, MCCS, Mason, OH. Tel: (513) 573-2284, FAX: (513) 573-2197, Web Site: www.federated.com (14)

Wadler, Jason, Leapfrog Online, Evanston, IL. Tel: (847) 492-1968, Web Site: www.leapfrogonline.com (35)

Wadsworth II, Eliot, White Flower Farm, Litchfield, CT. Tel: (860) 496-9624, (800) 503-9624, FAX: (860) 496-1418, Web Site: www.whiteflowerfarm.com (8)

Waechter, Joseph W., Photoworks, Cleveland, OH. Tel: (206) 281-1390, (800) PHOTOWORKS, FAX: (206) 284-5357, E-Mail: info@photoworks.com, Web Site: www.photoworks.com (16)

Waechter, Thomas, JDS Uniphase Corp, Milpitas, CA. Tel: (408) 546-5000, FAX: (408) 546-4300, Web Site: www.jdsu.com (32)

Wag/Aero Group, Lyons, WI. Tel: (262) 763-9586, (800) 558-6868, FAX: (262) 763-7595, E-Mail: wagaero-sales@wagaero.com, Web Site: www.wagaero.com (16)

Wagaheim, Art, Modular Mailing Systems, Tampa, FL. Tel: (305) 826-9077, (800) 881-MAIL, E-Mail: sales@modularmailing.com, Web Site: www.modularmailing.com (34)

Wagenfeld, Sandra J., National Committee to Preserve Social Security & Medicare, Washington, DC. Tel: (202) 216-0420, (800) 966-1935, FAX: (202) 216-0446, E-Mail: kreard@ncpssm.org, Web Site: www.ncpssm.org (1)

Wager, Russell, Mazda Motor of America Inc, Irvine, CA. Tel: (949) 727-1990, (800) 222-6500, FAX: (949) 727-6101, Web Site: www.mazdausa.com (16)

Waghray, Ajay, MCI Communications Services Inc, Basking Ridge, NJ. Tel: (877) 297-7816, Web Site: www.mci.com (16)

Wagley, Ron, Transamerica Occidental Life Co, Los Angeles, CA. Tel: (213) 742-3111, FAX: (213) 741-6623, Web Site: www.transamerica.com (15)

Wagner Hines & Avary Inc, Alexandria, VA. Tel: (703) 684-7740, FAX: (703) 548-3721 (20)

Wagner, Andrew, American Craft Council, Minneapolis, MN. Tel: (212) 274-0630, FAX: (212) 274-0650, E-Mail: council@craftcouncil.org, Web Site: www.craftcouncil.org (17)

Wagner, Bill, StrongView Systems Inc, Redwood City, CA. Tel: (650) 421-4200, (800) 971-0380, FAX: (650) 421-4201, E-Mail: info@strongview.com, Web Site: www.strongview.com (32)

Wagner, Charlotte, Direct Sports Supply, Pearisburg, VA. Tel: (540) 921-1243, (800) 456-0072, FAX: (540) 921-1475, Web Site: www.directsports.com (11)

Wagner, Dan, Blue Cross Blue Shield of Louisiana, Baton Rouge, LA. Tel: (225) 295-3307, (800) 599-2583, FAX: (225) 295-2054, E-Mail: help@bcbsla.com, Web Site: www.bcbsla.com (15)

Wagner, Dean, The Burris Agency Inc, Greensboro, NC. Tel: (336) 378-1221, FAX: (336) 378-1221, E-Mail: info@burris.com, Web Site: www.burris.com (35)

Wagner, Don, Pearson VUE, Bloomington, MN. Tel: (952) 681-3000, Web Site: home.pearsonvue.com (17)

Wagner, Gerald, Discover Financial Services, Riverwoods, IL. Tel: (224) 405-0900 (14)

Wagner, Greg, Einhorn Associates Inc, Milwaukee, WI. Tel: (414) 453-4488, FAX: (414) 453-4831, Web Site: www.einhornassociates.com (20)

Wagner, Ira J., American Capital, Bethesda, MD. Tel: (301) 951-6122, FAX: (301) 654-6714, E-Mail: info@americancapital.com, Web Site: www.americancapital.com (15)

Wagner, Jack, Forest Envelope Co, Lisle, IL. Tel: (630) 515-1200, FAX: (630) 515-1212, Web Site: forestenvelope.com (26)

Wagner, Judy, Bart's Watersports, North Webster, IN. Tel: (574) 834-7666, (800) 348-5016, FAX: (574) 834-4246, E-Mail: bart@bart.com, Web Site: www.bartswatersports.com (11)

Wagner, Kae Groshong, John Alden Life Insurance Co/North Star Marketing, Duluth, GA. Tel: (678) 473-1211, (800) 768-6288, FAX: (678) 473-9573, Web Site: www.nstarmarketing.com (15)

Wagner, Lori, Talbots, Hingham, MA. Tel: (781) 749-7600, (800) 825-2687, FAX: (781) 741-4369, Web Site: www.talbots.com (2)

Wagner, Mark, Pfaelzer Brothers, Maumee, OH. Tel: (419) 893-7611, (800) 345-9290, FAX: (419) 893-0164, Web Site: www.phaelzerbrothers.com (16)

Wagner, Meredith, Magazine Publishers of America, New York, NY. Tel: (212) 872-3700, FAX: (212) 888-4217, E-Mail: mpa@magazine.org, Web Site: www.magazine.org (17)

Wagner, Paul V., Direct Sports Supply, Pearisburg, VA. Tel: (540) 921-1243, (800) 456-0072, FAX: (540) 921-1475, Web Site: www.directsports.com (11)

Wagner, Scott, Mad Mimi, Scottsdale, AZ. Tel: (480) 505-8800, FAX: (480) 505-8844, E-Mail: support@madmimi.com, Web Site: madmimi.com (24)

Wagnitz, Steve, Lakewood Products LLC, Suamico, WI. Tel: (920) 361-7717, (800) 872-8458, FAX: (920) 361-7719, E-Mail: info@lakewoodproducts.com, Web Site: www.lakewoodproducts.com (11)

Wait, Rick, CPM Delta 1, Inc, Dallas, TX. Tel: (214) 349-6886, (800) 627-0252, FAX: (214) 503-1557, Web Site: www.cpmdelta1.com (11)

Waite, Greg, Diamond Marketing Solutions, Carol Stream, IL. Tel: (630) 597-9100, E-Mail: info@dmsolutions.com, Web Site: www.dmsolutions.com (35)

Waite, Katherine, Peck Rock Associates, Warren, RI. Tel: (401) 289-3757, FAX: (401) 289-3759, E-Mail: pra@aol.com, Web Site: www.peckrock.com (33)

Waiter, Eric, EWA & Miniature Cars USA Inc, Berkeley Heights, NJ. Tel: (732) 424-7811, (800) 392-4454, FAX: (732) 424-7814, E-Mail: ewa@ewacars.com (11)

Waizer, Mindy, Transaction Publishers, Piscataway, NJ. Tel: (732) 445-1245, FAX: (732) 748-9801, E-Mail: trans@transactionpub.com, Web Site: www.transactionpub.com (17)

Wakabayashi, Tomoko, HighScope Educational Research Foundation, Ypsilanti, MI. Tel: (800) 587-5639, FAX: (734) 485-0704, E-Mail: info@highscope.org, Web Site: www.highscope.org (17)

Wakamatsu, Makoto, Fujisankei Communications International Inc, New York, NY. Tel: (212) 753-8100, FAX: (212) 702-0420, Web Site: www.fujisankei.com (32)

Wake Forest University Baptist Medical Center, Winston Salem, NC. Tel: (336) 716-2011, Web Site: www.wakehealth.edu (1)

Wakefield Peanut Co, Wakefield, VA. Tel: (757) 899-5481, (800) 803-1309, FAX: (757) 899-7604, Web Site: www.wakefieldpeanutco.com (4)

Wakefield Talabisco International, New York, NY. Tel: (212) 661-8600, FAX: (212) 661-8832, Web Site: www.wtali.com (20)

Walch Publishing, Portland, ME. Tel: (207) 772-2846, (800) 558-2846, FAX: (207) 772-3105, E-Mail: customerservice@walch.com, Web Site: www.walch.com (17)

Wald, Dan, Brunner, Pittsburgh, PA. Tel: (412) 995-9500, FAX: (412) 995-9501, Web Site: www.brunnerworks.com (35)

Wald, Frederica N., Pace University, New York, NY. Tel: (212) 346-1781, (866) 722-3338, FAX: (212) 346-1821, Web Site: www.pace.edu (16)

Walden, Dana, 20th Century Fox Television, Los Angeles, CA. Tel: (310) 369-4636, FAX: (310) 969-0468, Web Site: www.foxstudios.com (16)

Walden, John, FTD Group Inc, Downers Grove, IL. Tel: (630) 719-7800, (800) 788-9000, FAX: (630) 719-6170, E-Mail: ftdmemberservices@ftdi.com, Web Site: www.ftdi.com (29)

Waldie, Greg, Farm Bureau Insurance, Lansing, MI. Tel: (517) 323-7000, (800) 292-2680, FAX: (517) 327-0208, Web Site: www.farmbureauinsurance-mi.com (15)

Walding, Jim, Disabled American Veterans, Cincinnati, OH. Tel: (859) 441-7300, FAX: (859) 442-2084, E-Mail: feedback@davmail.org, Web Site: www.dav.org (1)

Waldmann, George, Odell, Simms & Lynch Inc, Tysons Corner, VA. Tel: (703) 903-9797, FAX: (703) 903-8850, Web Site: odellsimms.com (35)

Waldt, Medio, Corporate Express US Inc, Broomfield, CO. Tel: (303) 664-2000, (888) 238-6329, FAX: (303) 664-3474, Web Site: www.cexp.com (22)

Walgreens Co, Deerfield, IL. Tel: (800) 925-4733, Web Site: www.walgreens.com (7)

Walk Thru The Bible Ministries Inc, Norcross, GA. Tel: (770) 458-9300, (800) 361-6131, Web Site: www.walkthru.org (1)

Walk, Steve, Com-Pak, Berlin, CT. Tel: (856) 802-1900, (856) 802-3097, E-Mail: info@com-pak.com, Web Site: www.marketpointdirect.com (28)

Walker & Associates, Welcome, NC. Tel: (336) 731-6391, (800) WALKER-1, FAX: (336) 731-7253/6973, E-Mail: info@walkerfirst.com, Web Site: www.walkerfirst.com (29)

Walker/Fitzgibbon TV & Film Productions, Los Angeles, CA. Tel: (323) 469-6800, FAX: (323) 878-0600, E-Mail: mo@walkerfitzgibbon.com, Web Site: www.walkerfitzgibbon.com (32)

Walker Publishing Co Inc, New York, NY. Tel: (212) 727-8300, (800) 289-2553, FAX: (212) 727-0984 (17)

Walker, Bob, Jim Mersfelder & Associates Inc, Cleveland, OH. Tel: (216) 574-9009, (800) 431-1101, FAX: (216) 574-9721, Web Site: www.jmapromotions.com (33)

Walker, Bob, The Dwyer Group, Waco, TX. Tel: (254) 759-5850, Web Site: www.dwyergroup.com (16)

Walker, Bradley K., Coastal Hotel Group, Bellevue, WA. Tel: (206) 388-0400, FAX: (206) 388-0401, E-Mail: info@coastalhotel.com, Web Site: www.coastalhotels.com (1)

Walker, Brian C., Herman Miller Inc, Zeeland, MI. Tel: (616) 654-3000, FAX: (616) 654-5234, E-Mail: investor@hermanmiller.com, Web Site: www.hermanmiller.com (16)

Walker, Chris, Moxie, Atlanta, GA. Tel: (678) 916-4500, E-Mail: info@moxieusa.com, Web Site: moxieusa.com (35)

Walker, Clay, Forestry Suppliers Inc, Jackson, MS. Tel: (601) 354-3565, (800) 647-5368, FAX: (601) 292-0165, E-Mail: fsi@forestry-suppliers.com, Web Site: www.forestry-suppliers.com (9)

Walker, Darren, PC/Nametag Inc, Verona, WI. Tel: (608) 845-1850, (800) 233-9767, E-Mail: sales@pcnametag.com, Web Site: www.pcnametag.com (16)

Walker, Geoff, Fisher-Price, East Aurora, NY. Tel: (716) 687-3000, FAX: (716) 687-3636, Web Site: www.fisherprice.com (16)

Walker, Jim, Walch Publishing, Portland, ME. Tel: (207) 772-2846, (800) 558-2846, FAX: (207) 772-3105, E-Mail: customerservice@walch.com, Web Site: www.walch.com (17)

Walker, Joanne, EMS Technologies, Norcross, GA. Tel: (770) 263-9200, FAX: (770) 447-4405, Web Site: www.ems-t.com (16)

Walker, John, Sport Supply Group, Dallas, TX. Tel: (972) 484-9484, FAX: (972) 247-0650, Web Site: www.sportsupplygroup.com (11)

Walker, Ken, TKLi, The Colony, TX. Tel: (972) 370-7878, (800) 789-3893, FAX: (972) 370-7879, E-Mail: info@tkli.com, Web Site: www.tkli.com (23)

Walker, Kevin, Magnaflux, Glenview, IL. Tel: (847) 657-5300, FAX: (847) 657-5388, Web Site: www.magnaflux.com (16)

Walker, Lisa, Vance Industries Inc, Niles, IL. Tel: (847) 375-8900, FAX: (847) 375-6818, E-Mail: vance@vanceind.com, Web Site: www.vanceind.com (16)

Walker, Peggy, The National Underwriter Co, Erlanger, KY. Tel: (800) 543-0874, FAX: (856) 692-2246, E-Mail: customerservice@nuco.com, Web Site: www.nuco.com (17)

Walker, Renee, RC Bigelow Inc, Fairfield, CT. Tel: (203) 334-1212, Web Site: www.bigelowtea.com (4)

Walker, Robert, Walker/Fitzgibbon TV & Film Productions, Los Angeles, CA. Tel: (323) 469-6800, FAX: (323) 878-0600, E-Mail: mo@walkerfitzgibbon.com, Web Site: www.walkerfitzgibbon.com (32)

Walker, Rod, International Specialized Book Services Inc, Portland, OR. Tel: (503) 287-3093, (800) 944-6190, FAX: (503) 280-8832, E-Mail: isbs_sales@isbs.com, Web Site: www.isbscatalog.com (16)

Walker, Rosemary, Peter Li Education Group, Dayton, OH. Tel: (937) 293-1415, (800) 523-4625, FAX: (937) 293-1310, Web Site: www.peterli.com (17)

Walker, Samuel, Molson Coors Brewing Co, Denver, CO. Tel: (303) 927-2337, (800) 665-7661, Web Site: www.molsoncoors.com (16)

Walker, Theresa, The Catholic University of America Press, Washington, DC. Tel: (202) 319-5052, FAX: (202) 319-4985, E-Mail: cua-press@cua.edu, Web Site: cuapress.cua.edu (17)

Walker, Thomas "Tom", Tableau Software, Seattle, WA. Tel: (206) 633-3400, FAX: (206) 633-3004, Web Site: www.tableausoftware.com (22)

Walker, Virginia, Walker & Associates, Welcome, NC. Tel: (336) 731-6391, (800) WALKER-1, FAX: (336) 731-7253/6973, E-Mail: info@walkerfirst.com, Web Site: www.walkerfirst.com (29)

Walkes, Amy, Professional Photographer Magazine, Atlanta, GA. Tel: (404) 522-8600, (800) 786-6277, FAX: (404) 614-6405, E-Mail: csc@ppa.com, Web Site: www.ppa.com (17)

Wall, Debra Steidel, National Archives & Records Administration, Washington, DC. Tel: (202) 357-5000, (866) 325-7208, Web Site: www.archives.gov (17)

Wall, Joann, Spear Engineering Co, Colorado Springs, CO. Tel: (719) 471-9850 (16)

Wall, John, Demco Inc, Madison, WI. Tel: (608) 241-1201, (800) 356-1200, FAX: (608) 241-1799, E-Mail: custserv@demco.com, Web Site: www.demco.com (10)

Wall, Reverend John J., Catholic Church Extension Society, Chicago, IL. Tel: (312) 795-5109, (800) 842-7804, FAX: (312) 236-5276, E-Mail: info@catholicextension.org, Web Site: www.catholicextension.org (1)

Wall, Roger, Spinneybeck Enterprises, Getzville, NY. Tel: (716) 446-2380, (800) 482-7777, FAX: (716) 446-2396, E-Mail: sales@spinneybeck.com, Web Site: www.spinneybeck.com (16)

Wall, Steve, FGI Research Inc, Chapel Hill, NC. Tel: (919) 929-7759, FAX: (919) 932-8829, E-Mail: info@fgiresearch.com, Web Site: www.fgiresearch.com (35)

Wallace, Brian, Coin Laundry Association, Oakbrook Terrace, IL. Tel: (630) 963-7920, (800) 570-5629, FAX: (630) 963-7925, Web Site: www.coinlaundry.org (1)

Wallace, Bridgit, Novus Media Inc, Plymouth, MN. Tel: (612) 758-8600, FAX: (612) 336-8600, Web Site: www.npmnetwork.com (31)

Wallace, Jack, Intellidyn Corp, Hingham, MA. Tel: (781) 741-5503, (866) 773-5756, FAX: (781) 741-5545, E-Mail: kmf@intellidyn.com, Web Site: www.intellidyn.com (22)

Wallace, Jim, GuideOne Insurance, West Des Moines, IA. Tel: (877) 448-4331, Web Site: www.guideone.com (15)

Wallace, Kendall, The NH Broadcaster, Lowell, MA. Tel: (978) 458-7100, Web Site: www.nhbroadcaster.com (31)

Wallace, Mark A., Texas Children's Hospital, Houston, TX. Tel: (832) 824-1000, Web Site: www.texaschildrenshospital.org (1)

Wallace, Michael W., Elephant Group Inc, Fort Lauderdale, FL. Tel: (954) 657-9611, FAX: (866) 699-5786, Web Site: www.elephantgroup.com (30)

Wallace, Pat, Leanin' Tree Inc, Boulder, CO. Tel: (303) 530-7768, (800) 525-0656, FAX: (303) 530-5124, E-Mail: info@leanintree.com, Web Site: www.leanintree.com (4)

Wallace, Ray, Gold Medal Hair Products Inc, Farmingdale, NY. Tel: (631) 465-0202, FAX: (631) 465-0207, E-Mail: customerservice@goldmedalhair.com, Web Site: www.goldmedalhair.com (7)

Wallach, Andrew, Central National-Gottesman Inc, Purchase, NY. Tel: (914) 696-9000, FAX: (914) 696-1066, E-Mail: purchase@cng-inc.com, Web Site: www.cng-inc.com (25)

Wallach, Kenneth L., Central National-Gottesman Inc, Purchase, NY. Tel: (914) 696-9000, FAX: (914) 696-1066, E-Mail: purchase@cng-inc.com, Web Site: www.cng-inc.com (25)

Wallake, Randy F., Minnesota Life, Saint Paul, MN. Tel: (651) 665-3500, (888) 237-1838, FAX: (651) 665-4488, Web Site: www.minnesotalife.com; www.securian.com (15)

Waller, Craig, Pace Communications Inc, Greensboro, NC. Tel: (336) 378-6065, FAX: (336) 275-2864, Web Site: www.pacecommunications.com (17)

Waller, Mollie, Dairy Management Inc, Rosemont, IL. Tel: (847) 803-2000, FAX: (847) 803-2077, Web Site: www.nationaldairycouncil.org (1)

Wallin, Ian, TVGuide.com, New York, NY. Tel: (212) 626-2500, Web Site: www.tvguide.com (31)

Wallis, John, Hyatt Hotels Corp, Chicago, IL. Tel: (312) 750-1234, FAX: (312) 780-5289, Web Site: www.hyatt.com (16)

Wallis, William Budge, Writer's Digest Books, Blue Ash, OH. Tel: (513) 531-2690, (800) 666-0963, Web Site: www.fwpublications.com (17)

Wallrapp, Chris, Hill Holliday, Boston, MA. Tel: (617) 366-4000, Web Site: www.hhcc.com (35)

Wallstrom, Robert, Vera Bradley, Roanoke, IN. Tel: (800) 823-8372, Web Site: www.verabradley.com (2)

WalMart Stores Inc, Bentonville, AR. Tel: (479) 273-4000, (800) 925-6278, FAX: (479) 277-1830, Web Site: www.walmart.com (16)

Walpert Levy, Tara, Visible World, New York, NY. Tel: (212) 739-1900, E-Mail: info@visibleworld.com, Web Site: www.visibleworld.com (32)

Walsh, Carrie, Pizza Hut Inc, Plano, TX. Tel: (972) 338-7700, (866) 298-6986, FAX: (972) 338-6869, Web Site: www.pizzahut.com (16)

Walsh, Jerry, Decal Shop, Jacksonville, FL. Tel: (800) 634-1889, FAX: (253) 276-3467, E-Mail: decalshop@decalshop.com (10)

Walsh, Jerry, Racer Walsh Co, Jacksonville, FL. Tel: (904) 721-2289, FAX: (904) 721-2935, Web Site: www.racerwalsh.com (12)

Walsh, Jim, EasyLink Services International Corp, Piscataway, NJ. Tel: (800) 828-7115, FAX: (732) 652-3810, E-Mail: sales@easylink.com, Web Site: www.easylink.com (16)

Walsh, Joe, Dex Media, Dallas-Fort Worth Airport, TX. Tel: (972) 453-7000, Web Site: www.dexmedia.com (31)

Walsh, Joe, The Great Amarillo Directory, Amarillo, TX. Tel: (806) 353-5155, FAX: (806) 359-2974, Web Site: www.worldpages.com (17)

Walsh, Michael, National Archives & Records Administration, Washington, DC. Tel: (202) 357-5000, (866) 325-7208, Web Site: www.archives.gov (17)

Walsh, Mike, LexisNexis, New York, NY. Tel: (212) 309-8100, FAX: (800) 437-8674, Web Site: www.lexisnexis.com (16)

Walsh, Mike, LexisNexis Matthew Bender, Albany, NY. Tel: (518) 487-3000, (800) 424-4200, E-Mail: lexisnexis@matthewbender, Web Site: www.bender.lexisnexis.com (17)

Walsh, Mike, Martindale-Hubbell, New Providence, NJ. Tel: (908) 771-7777, (800) 526-4902, FAX: (908) 771-8704, Web Site: www.martindale.com (17)

Walsh, Mike, Standard Directory of Advertising Agencies, Summit, NJ. Tel: (800) 908-5395 (43)

Walsh, Patrick M, Texas Refinery Corp, Fort Worth, TX. Tel: (817) 332-1161, FAX: (817) 336-8441, E-Mail: jhopkins@texasrefinery.com, Web Site: www.texasrefinery.com (9)

Walsh, Peter, Harvard Business School Publishing, Boston, MA. Tel: (617) 783-7400, Web Site: www.harvardbusiness.org (17)

Walsh, Tim, Harvard Pilgrim Health Care, Wellesley, MA. Tel: (617) 509-1000, (888) 888-4742, FAX: (617) 509-7590, Web Site: www.harvardpilgrim.org (7)

Walshe, Michael, The Historical Research Center International Inc, Boynton Beach, FL. Tel: (561) 732-5263, (800) 985-9956, FAX: (561) 940-7991, E-Mail: custsvc@names.com, Web Site: www.historicalresearchcenter.net (16)

Walshe, Mick, Sales Magic Inc, Boynton Beach, FL. Tel: (561) 732-5263, (800) 985-9956, FAX: (561) 375-9413, E-Mail: custsvc@names.com, Web Site: www.names.com (32)

Walt Klein Advertising, Denver, CO. Tel: (303) 298-8015, FAX: (303) 298-8194, Web Site: www.wka.com (35)

Waltenspiel, Ronald E., Timber Crest Farms, Healdsburg, CA. Tel: (707) 433-8251, FAX: (707) 433-8255, E-Mail: tcf@sonic.net, Web Site: www.sonic.net/tcf (16)

Waltenspiel, Ruth, Timber Crest Farms, Healdsburg, CA. Tel: (707) 433-8251, FAX: (707) 433-8255, E-Mail: tcf@sonic.net, Web Site: www.sonic.net/tcf (16)

Walter Weissman Photo Studio, New York, NY. Tel: (212) 989-9694, FAX: (212) 989-9694, E-Mail: wweissmanphoto@nyc.rr.com, Web Site: www.weissmanphoto.com (37)

Walter, Beverly, The Adcentive Group Inc, San Diego, CA. Tel: (858) 278-9200, FAX: (858) 571-2832, Web Site: www.brownandbigelow.com (35)

Walter, Charles, Industrial Instruments & Supplies Inc, Southampton, PA. Tel: (215) 396-0822, (800) 523-6079, FAX: (215) 396-0833, E-Mail: customerservice@iisusa.com, Web Site: www.iisusa.com (9)

Walter, Christine, Industrial Instruments & Supplies Inc, Southampton, PA. Tel: (215) 396-0822, (800) 523-6079, FAX: (215) 396-0833, E-Mail: customerservice@iisusa.com, Web Site: www.iisusa.com (9)

Walter, Gary, Infutor Data Solutions, Oakbrook Terrace, IL. Tel: (312) 348-7900, E-Mail: sales@infutor.com, Web Site: www.infutor.com (23)

Walter, Kevin, Mother Jones Magazine, San Francisco, CA. Tel: (415) 321-1700, Web Site: www.motherjones.com (17)

Walter, W Todd, Elizabeth Arden Spas LLC, Stamford, CT. Tel: (203) 905-1700, FAX: (203) 905-1716, Web Site: www.reddoorspas.com (19)

Walter, William G., FMC Corp, Philadelphia, PA. Tel: (215) 299-6000, FAX: (215) 299-5998, Web Site: www.fmc.com (16)

Walters, Chris, The Weather Channel, Atlanta, GA. Tel: (770) 226-0000, FAX: (770) 226-2390, Web Site: www.weather.com (32)

Walters, Edward T., Pactiv Corp, Lake Forest, IL. Tel: (847) 482-2000, (800) 828-2850, FAX: (847) 482-4738, Web Site: www.pactiv.com (26)

Walters, Hazel, Jenco Productions Inc, San Bernardino, CA. Tel: (909) 381-9453, FAX: (909) 383-1106, Web Site: www.jencoproductions.com (28)

Walters, John C., John Harland Co, Decatur, GA. Tel: (770) 981-5580, (800) 723-3690, FAX: (770) 593-5367, E-Mail: jhhwebmaster@harland.net, Web Site: www.harland.net (16)

Walters, Keith S., Ennis Inc, Midlothian, TX. Tel: (972) 775-9801, (800) 962-0944, FAX: (800) 645-8339, Web Site: www.ennis.com (16)

Wm K Walthers Inc, Milwaukee, WI. Tel: (414) 527-0770, (800) 487-2467, FAX: (414) 527-4423, Web Site: www.walthers.com (11)

Walthers, Phil, Wm K Walthers Inc, Milwaukee, WI. Tel: (414) 527-0770, (800) 487-2467, FAX: (414) 527-4423, Web Site: www.walthers.com (11)

Walton, Resa, The Bureau Inc, Stuart, FL. Tel: (772) 283-8850, Web Site: www.bureauinc.com (28)

Walton, S. Robson, WalMart Stores Inc, Bentonville, AR. Tel: (479) 273-4000, (800) 925-6278, FAX: (479) 277-1830, Web Site: www.walmart.com (16)

Carl Waltzer Digital Service Bureau, New York, NY. Tel: (212) 475-7848, FAX: (212) 475-9359, E-Mail: cwdigital@aol.com, Web Site: www.waltzer.com (36)

Waltzer, Carl, Carl Waltzer Digital Service Bureau, New York, NY. Tel: (212) 475-7848, FAX: (212) 475-9359, E-Mail: cwdigital@aol.com, Web Site: www.waltzer.com (36)

Wambach, James S., Sybase Inc, Dublin, CA. Tel: (925) 236-5000, FAX: (925) 236-4321, Web Site: www.sybase.com/product/datawarehousing (22)

Wambold, Richard L., Pactiv Corp, Lake Forest, IL. Tel: (847) 482-2000, (800) 828-2850, FAX: (847) 482-4738, Web Site: www.pactiv.com (26)

Wampler, Kira, Art.com, Emeryville, CA. Tel: (510) 879-4700, (800) 952-5592, FAX: (510) 588-3915, E-Mail: support@art.com, Web Site: www.art.com (8)

Wanamaker, Mary Ellen, Christian Brands, Phoenix, AZ. Tel: (602) 243-5200, (800) 521-2914, FAX: (602) 232-1855, Web Site: www.christian-brands.com (16)

Wanda, John, Chapman Cubine Adams & Hussey, Arlington, VA. Tel: (703) 248-0025, Web Site: www.ahadirect.com (20)

Wang, Mark D., Hilton Grand Vacations Co, Orlando, FL. Tel: (407) 722-3100, FAX: (407) 521-3112, Web Site: www.hiltongrandvacations.com (19)

Wang, Xitian, Boundless Corp, Phelps, NY. Tel: (631) 962-1500, (800) 231-5445, FAX: (631) 962-1505, E-Mail: sales@boundless.com, Web Site: www.boundless.com (16)

Wank, Vincent, Innovative Marketing Solutions LLC, Bangor, ME. Tel: (207) 262-6233, Web Site: www.imsmaine.net (29)

Wanning, Jeffrey J., Central States Health & Life Co of Omaha, Omaha, NE. Tel: (402) 397-1111, (800) 826-6587, FAX: (402) 391-3772, Web Site: www.cso.com (15)

Bill Ward Inc, Wilmington, DE. Tel: (302) 762-6600, FAX: (302) 397-2153, E-Mail: billward@billwardinc.com (30)

Ward Jr, William F., Bill Ward Inc, Wilmington, DE. Tel: (302) 762-6600, FAX: (302) 397-2153, E-Mail: billward@billwardinc.com (30)

Ward, Anthony, DPC Computers, Monsey, NY. Tel: (845) 426-3790, (866) 513-CORP, FAX: (845) 426-6275, E-Mail: learnmore@salestax.com, Web Site: www.salestax.com (16)

Ward, Brad, TownNews.com, Moline, IL. Tel: (309) 743-0800, (800) 293-9576, FAX: (309) 743-0830, E-Mail: info@townnews.com, Web Site: www.townnews365.com (32)

Ward, Chris, Aircraft Owners & Pilots Association, Frederick, MD. Tel: (301) 695-2000, (800) 872-2672, FAX: (301) 695-2375, E-Mail: aopahq@aopa.org, Web Site: www.aopa.org (1)

Ward, Daniel, Foote-Jones/Illinois Gear, Aberdeen, SD. Tel: (605) 225-0360, FAX: (605) 225-0567, Web Site: www.footejones.com (16)

Ward, Deb, AcuSport Corp, Bellefontaine, OH. Tel: (937) 593-7010, FAX: (937) 592-5625, E-Mail: mwsales@acusport.com, Web Site: www.acusport.com (11)

Ward, Jerry, Successful Farming, Des Moines, IA. Tel: (515) 284-2143, (800) 678-2711, FAX: (515) 284-3127 (17)

Ward, Laysha L., Target Corp, Minneapolis, MN. Tel: (612) 304-6073, Web Site: www.target.com (16)

Ward, Michael, Net-Results, Golden, CO. Tel: (303) 771-2552, E-Mail: info@net-results.com, Web Site: www.net-results.com (32)

Ward, Richard, 22squared Inc, Atlanta, GA. Tel: (404) 347-8700, FAX: (404) 347-8800, Web Site: www.22squared.com (35)

Ward, Stephen, Support Services Corp, Fort Myers, FL. Tel: (239) 332-5300, FAX: (239) 332-4555, E-Mail: s.ward@ss-corp.com, Web Site: www.ss-corp.com (22)

Ward, Tamara, Camping World Inc, Bowling Green, KY. Tel: (270) 781-2718, (800) 626-6189, FAX: (270) 796-8991, Web Site: www.campingworld.com (11)

Ward, Ted, GEICO Direct, Washington, DC. Tel: (301) 986-2842, (800) 841-3000, FAX: (301) 986-2068, Web Site: www.geico.com (15)

Ward-Burns, J. Robert, Beauticontrol Cosmetics Inc, Carrollton, TX. Tel: (972) 458-0601, (800) BEAU-TI-1, FAX: (972) 458-6904, E-Mail: clientservices@beauticontrol.com, Web Site: www.beauticontrol.com (7)

Ward-Llewellyn, Terry, Quick Draw Clip Systems Inc, Ventura, CA. Tel: (805) 644-6888, (888) 254-7797, FAX: (805) 644-7320, E-Mail: ron@clipsystems.com, Web Site: www.clipsystems.com (9)

Wardell, Keith, Marketing 1by1 Inc, Fairfax, VA. Tel: (703) 934-6020, FAX: (703) 591-3049, Web Site: marketing1by1.com (22)

Warden, Cynthia K., AMA Insurance Agency Inc, Chicago, IL. Tel: (312) 464-2425, (800) 458-5736, FAX: (312) 419-5096, Web Site: www.amainsure.com (15)

Wardour, Scott, EMED Co Inc, Buffalo, NY. Tel: (716) 626-1616, (800) 442-3633, FAX: (716) 626-1630, E-Mail: customerservice@emedco.com, Web Site: www.emedco.com (16)

Ward's Natural Science, Rochester, NY. Tel: (585) 359-2502, (800) 962-2660, FAX: (585) 334-6174, E-Mail: customer_service@wardsci.com, Web Site: www.wardsci.com (34)

Ware, Lane, Customer Communications Group Inc, Lakewood, CO. Tel: (303) 525-0313, E-Mail: info@customer.com, Web Site: www.customer.com (35)

Warehall, Larissa, DataLab USA, Germantown, MD. Tel: (301) 972-1430, (800) 972-1430, E-Mail: information@datalabusa.com, Web Site: datalabusa.com (21)

Warehall, Ryder, DataLab USA, Germantown, MD. Tel: (301) 972-1430, (800) 972-1430, E-Mail: information@datalabusa.com, Web Site: datalabusa.com (21)

Warman, Ann Jensen, brandUNITY Inc, Rollingbay, WA. Tel: (206) 842-4948, FAX: (206) 842-4958, E-Mail: admin@brandunity.com, Web Site: www.brandunity.com (20)

Warman, David J, brandUNITY Inc, Rollingbay, WA. Tel: (206) 842-4948, FAX: (206) 842-4958, E-Mail: admin@brandunity.com, Web Site: www.brandunity.com (20)

Warnaco Swimwear Inc, Los Angeles, CA. Tel: (323) 726-1262, FAX: (323) 724-6931, Web Site: www.speedo.com (16)

Warner Bros, Burbank, CA. Tel: (818) 954-6000, Web Site: www.warnerbros.com (3)

Warner Press, Anderson, IN. Tel: (765) 644-7721, (800) 741-7721, FAX: (765) 640-8005, E-Mail: wporders@warnerpress.org, Web Site: www.warnerpress.com (17)

Warner, Herb, Fluid Metering Inc, Syosset, NY. Tel: (516) 922-6050, (800) 223-3388, FAX: (516) 624-8261, E-Mail: pumps@fmipump.com, Web Site: www.fmipump.com (16)

Warner, Nancy, Reliable Technologies Inc, Manchester, NH. Tel: (603) 644-2528, (800) 346-7890, FAX: (603) 627-5553, Web Site: www.tei-imaging.com (16)

Warner, Valerie, Brushfire Inc, Cedar Knolls, NJ. Tel: (973) 871-1700, FAX: (973) 871-1717, E-Mail: vwarner@brushfireinc.com, Web Site: www.brushfireinc.com (35)

Warrantech Direct Inc, Bedford, TX. Tel: (817) 786-1000, (800) 833-8801, FAX: (817) 786-1020, Web Site: www.warrantech.com (29)

Warren Communications News, Washington, DC. Tel: (202) 872-9200, (800) 771-9202, FAX: (202) 318-8350, E-Mail: info@warren-news.com, Web Site: www.warren-news.com (17)

Warren, Gorham & Lamont Inc, New York, NY. Tel: (617) 423-2020, Web Site: ria.thomsonreuters.com (17)

Warren, Albert, Warren Communications News, Washington, DC. Tel: (202) 872-9200, (800) 771-9202, FAX: (202) 318-8350, E-Mail: info@warren-news.com, Web Site: www.warren-news.com (17)

Warren, Dan, Warren Communications News, Washington, DC. Tel: (202) 872-9200, (800) 771-9202, FAX: (202) 318-8350, E-Mail: info@warren-news.com, Web Site: www.warren-news.com (17)

Warren, Denise, The New York Times Co, New York, NY. Tel: (212) 556-1234, Web Site: www.nytimes.com (17)

Warren, Erin, Cartera Commerce Inc, Lexington, MA. Tel: (781) 541-6800, (888) 456-6255, FAX: (781) 541-6801, E-Mail: info@cartera.com, Web Site: www.cartera.com (35)

Warren, Jr. Timothy M., Banker & Tradesman, Boston, MA. Tel: (617) 428-5100, FAX: (617) 428-5119, Web Site: www.bankerandtradesman.com (17)

Warren, Kelcy L., Sunoco Inc, Philadelphia, PA. Tel: (215) 977-3000, FAX: (215) 977-3409, Web Site: www.sunocoinc.com (16)

Warren, Paul, Warren Communications News, Washington, DC. Tel: (202) 872-9200, (800) 771-9202, FAX: (202) 318-8350, E-Mail: info@warren-news.com, Web Site: www.warren-news.com (17)

Warren, Phillip C, Farrington Transportation, Bolingbrook, IL. Tel: (630) 783-9200 (12)

Warren, Robert D, NEBS, Groton, MA. Tel: (978) 448-6111, (800) 225-6380, (888) 823-6327, FAX: (978) 448-3653, (800) 234-4324, E-Mail: customerservice@nebs.com, Web Site: www.nebs.com (10)

Warren, Victor, Farrington Transportation, Bolingbrook, IL. Tel: (630) 783-9200 (12)

Warrick, Ed, KEH.com, Smyrna, GA. Tel: (770) 333-4200, (800) 342-5534, FAX: (770) 333-4242, E-Mail: sales@keh.com, Web Site: www.keh.com (16)

Warrior Custom Golf Inc, Irvine, CA. Tel: (949) 699-2499, (800) 600-5113, Web Site: www.warriorcustomgolf.com (11)

Warner, Thomas, InfoSource Inc, Oviedo, FL. Tel: (407) 796-5200, (800) 393-4636, FAX: (407) 796-5190, E-Mail: isisale@howtomaster.com, Web Site: www.infosourcelearning.com (3)

Warsaw, Stephen R., CDMC/Carefree Direct Marketing Corp, Carefree, AZ. Tel: (480) 488-4227, FAX: (480) 488-2841 (20)

Mal Warwick Associates, Berkeley, CA. Tel: (510) 843-8888, FAX: (510) 843-0142, E-Mail: info@malwarwick.com, Web Site: www.malwarwick.com (1)

Warwick, Peter, Thomson West, Eagan, MN. Tel: (651) 687-7000, (800) 328-9378, FAX: (651) 687-7849, E-Mail: jeff.patrios@thomsonreuters.com, Web Site: www.thomson.com (17)

Wasco, Sonia Shaner, Grant Heilman Photography Inc, Lititz, PA. Tel: (717) 626-0296, (800) 622-2046, FAX: (717) 626-0971, E-Mail: info@heilmanphoto.com, Web Site: www.heilmanphoto.com (38)

Washburn, Sarah, Business Marketing Association, Naperville, IL. Tel: (630) 544-5054, FAX: (630) 544-5055, E-Mail: info@marketing.org, Web Site: www.marketing.org (40)

Washchilla, Jr. Edward, Fairfield Marketing Group Inc, Easton, CT. Tel: (203) 261-5585 X202, (203) 261-5568, FAX: (203) 261-0884, E-Mail: info@fairfieldmarketing.com, Web Site: www.fairfieldmarketing.com (22)

Washington Gas Energy Services, Herndon, VA. Tel: (703) 793-7500, Web Site: www.wges.com (16)

Washington Lists Inc, McLean, VA. Tel: (703) 749-3110, FAX: (703) 749-0960, E-Mail: emahoney@washingtonlists.com, Web Site: www.washingtonlists.com (23)

Washington Marketing Group, Arlington, VA. Tel: (703) 534-9331, FAX: (703) 534-0242, E-Mail: william.shaker@twmg.com, Web Site: www.twmg.com (1)

The Washington Monthly Co, Washington, DC. Tel: (202) 955-9010, FAX: (202) 955-9011, E-Mail: editors@washingtonmonthly.com, Web Site: www. washingtonmonthly.com (17)

Washington Mutual Home Loan, Inc, Vernon Hills, IL. Tel: (847) 918-5549, FAX: (847) 549-2975 (14)

Washington National Opera, Washington, DC. Tel: (202) 467-4600, (800) 444-1324, Web Site: www. kennedy-center.org/wno (16)

The Washington Post, Washington, DC. Tel: (202) 334-6000, (800) 627-1150, E-Mail: letters@washpost. com, Web Site: www.washingtonpost.com (17)

Washington Post Digital, Washington, DC. Tel: (202) 334-9900 (17)

Washington Products Inc, Massillon, OH. Tel: (330) 837-5101, FAX: (330) 837-5401 (34)

Washington University, Saint Louis, MO. Tel: (314) 935-5000, Web Site: www.wustl.edu (1)

The Washingtonian, Washington, DC. Tel: (202) 296-3600, E-Mail: editorial@washingtonian.com, Web Site: www.washingtonian.com (17)

Andrew D Washton Books On the Fine Arts, Port Chester, NY. Tel: (914) 933-0479, E-Mail: andrew@ washtonbooks.com, Web Site: www.washtonbooks. com (16)

Washton, Andrew, Andrew D Washton Books On the Fine Arts, Port Chester, NY. Tel: (914) 933-0479, E-Mail: andrew@washtonbooks.com, Web Site: www.washtonbooks.com (16)

Washton, Ruth, Andrew D Washton Books On the Fine Arts, Port Chester, NY. Tel: (914) 933-0479, E-Mail: andrew@washtonbooks.com, Web Site: www.washtonbooks.com (16)

Wasik, Ken, Stephens Inc, New York, NY. Tel: (212) 891-1777, Web Site: www.stephens.com (20)

Wasser, Marcia, Source Communications, Hackensack, NJ. Tel: (201) 343-5222, E-Mail: admin@sourcead. com, Web Site: sourcead.com (35)

Wasserberg, Edie, Christian Broadcasting Network Inc, Virginia Beach, VA. Tel: (757) 226-7000, FAX: (757) 226-2017, Web Site: www.cbn.com (1)

Wasserman Uniform Co, Fort Lauderdale, FL. Tel: (614) 279-7000, (614) 279-8888, (800) 848-3576, FAX: (614) 464-0416, (800) 204-0416, E-Mail: custserv@wassermanuniform.com, Web Site: www. wassermanuniform.com (2)

Watchorn, Ryan, Cabela's Inc, Sidney, NE. Tel: (308) 254-5505, (800) 237-4444, FAX: (308) 254-4800, Web Site: www.cabelas.com (11)

Waterhouse, Scott, Worcester Envelope, Auburn, MA. Tel: (508) 832-5394, (800) 343-1398, FAX: (508) 832-3796, E-Mail: sales@worcesterenvelope.com, Web Site: www.worcester-envelope.com (26)

Watering Inc/Hemmings Motor News, Bennington, VT. Tel: (802) 442-3101, (800) 227-4373, FAX: (802) 447-1561, E-Mail: hmnmail@hemmings.com, Web Site: www.hemmings.com (17)

Waterlow, Simon, Ideals Publications Inc, Nashville, TN. Tel: (615) 333-0478, FAX: (615) 781-1447, Web Site: www.idealspublications.com (17)

Waters Corp, Milford, MA. Tel: (508) 482-2000, (800) 252-4752, FAX: (508) 872-1990, Web Site: www. waters.com (16)

Water's Edge Resort & Spa, Westbrook, CT. Tel: (860) 399-5901, (800) 222-5901, FAX: (860) 399-8644, Web Site: www.watersedgeresort.com (19)

Waters, Craig, Fitness Quest, Canton, OH. Tel: (330) 478-0755, (800) 321-9236, FAX: (330) 479-9213, E-Mail: customersupport@fitnessquest.com, Web Site: www.fitnessquest.com (16)

Waterson, Sherry, Warnaco Swimwear Inc, Los Angeles, CA. Tel: (323) 726-1262, FAX: (323) 724-6931, Web Site: www.speedo.com (16)

Wathne Ltd, New York, NY. Tel: (212) 757-3001, FAX: (212) 757-2448 (2)

Wathne, Bergljot, Wathne Ltd, New York, NY. Tel: (212) 757-3001, FAX: (212) 757-2448 (2)

Watjen, Thomas R., Unum Corp, Portland, ME. Tel: (207) 770-2211, (800) 421-0344, FAX: (207) 770-4510, Web Site: www.unum.com (15)

Watkins, Richard, Frog Tool Co Ltd, Dixon, IL. Tel: (815) 288-3811, E-Mail: info@frogwoodtools.com, Web Site: www.frogwoodtools.com (11)

Watkins, Robert, A Dean Watkins, Okemos, MI. Tel: (517) 349-7700, FAX: (517) 349-7748, E-Mail: adeanwatkins@aol.com, Web Site: www. adeanwatkins.com (33)

Watkins, Ron, Fetter Printing Company Inc, Louisville, KY. Tel: (502) 634-4771, (800) 234-4771, FAX: (502) 634-3587, E-Mail: info@fettergroup.com (27)

Watkinson, Kevin, Gifts Corp, Barrie, ON Canada. Tel: (905) 670-1126, (800) 565-3130, FAX: (905) 670-1127, E-Mail: customerservice@regal.ca, Web Site: www.regalgreetings.com (6)

Watson, Alex, LexisNexis, New York, NY. Tel: (212) 309-8100, FAX: (800) 437-8674, Web Site: www. lexisnexis.com (16)

Watson, Duncan, Sherwood Design & Development Center, Carlstadt, NJ. Tel: (201) 372-3900, FAX: (201) 372-0917 (27)

Watson, Greg, Florida Today, Melbourne, FL. Tel: (321) 242-3500, (877) 424-0156, FAX: (321) 242-3729, Web Site: www.floridatoday.com (17)

Watson, III Robert C., Lo Ink Specialties, Kennebunkport, ME. Tel: (207) 967-9110, (800) 777-6471, FAX: (800) 895-6465, E-Mail: rwatson@loink.com, Web Site: www.loink.com (16)

Watson, Jerry, Direct Response Consulting, McLean, VA. Tel: (703) 749-3100, FAX: (703) 749-0962, E-Mail: info@drcs.com, Web Site: www.drcs.com (17)

Watson, John, Bear Computer Systems Inc, Dallas, TX. Tel: (818) 509-0459, (800) 252-1691, FAX: (818) 769-3055, E-Mail: info@bearcom.com, Web Site: www.bearcom.com (16)

Watson, Richard, SSHC Inc/Radiant Heating Commercial Applications, Old Saybrook, CT. Tel: (860) 399-5434, (800) 544-5182, FAX: (860) 399-6460, (877) 675-4968, E-Mail: info@sshcinc.com, Web Site: www.sshcinc.com (9)

Watt, Andrew, Association of Fundraising Professionals, Arlington, VA. Tel: (703) 684-0410, (800) 666-3863, FAX: (703) 684-0540, Web Site: www. afpnet.org (1)

Watt, David, American Running Association, Bethesda, MD. Tel: (301) 913-9517, (800) 776-2732, FAX: (301) 913-9520, E-Mail: run@americanrunning.org, Web Site: www.americanrunning.org (1)

Watts Radiant, Springfield, MO. Tel: (417) 864-6108, (800) 276-2419, FAX: (417) 864-8161, Web Site: www.wattsheatway.com (9)

Watts, Edwin, Edwin Watts Golf, Fort Walton Beach, FL. Tel: (850) 244-2066, (800) 874-0146, FAX: (850) 244-5217, Web Site: www.edwinwatts.com (11)

Watts, Jim, MRW Communications, Pembroke, MA. Tel: (781) 924-5282, FAX: (718) 926-0371, E-Mail: jim@mrwinc.com, Web Site: www.mrwinc.com (35)

Watts, John, Edwin Watts Golf, Fort Walton Beach, FL. Tel: (850) 244-2066, (800) 874-0146, FAX: (850) 244-5217, Web Site: www.edwinwatts.com (11)

Watts, Jr. J. C., Feed the Children, Oklahoma City, OK. Tel: (800) 627-4556, Web Site: www. feedthechildren.org (1)

Wax, Marie-Laurence, Transemantics Inc, Washington, DC. Tel: (202) 362-2505, FAX: (202) 686-5603, E-Mail: ili@transemantics.com, Web Site: www. transemantics.com (16)

Wax, Sherry, National Mail-It Inc, Shreveport, LA. Tel: (318) 683-0093, Web Site: www.nationalmailit.com (27)

Waxman, Armond, JA Sexauer, Elmsford, NY. Tel: (914) 472-7501, (800) 431-1872, FAX: (914) 472-5834, Web Site: www.jasmro.com (16)

Wayne, Arthur, Brooks Brothers, New York, NY. Tel: (212) 682-8800, (800) 274-1815, FAX: (212) 309-7273, Web Site: www.brooksbrothers.com (2)

Wayne, Jack, The American Vintage Library, Los Angeles, CA. Tel: (310) 552-3176, (800) 235-1919, Web Site: www.vintagelibrary.com (17)

Waytek, Chanhassen, MN. Tel: (952) 465-0431, Web Site: www.waytekwire.com (16)

We Deliver America Inc, Englewood Cliffs, NJ. Tel: (201) 307-8888, FAX: (201) 307-1200, E-Mail: info@we-deliver-america.com, Web Site: www.we-deliver-america.com (31)

We-No-Nah Canoe Inc, Winona, MN. Tel: (507) 454-5430, FAX: (507) 454-5448, E-Mail: info@ wenonah.com, Web Site: www.wenonah.com (11)

Wead, Dr. Ann, Florida A&M University, Tallahassee, FL. Tel: (850) 599-3379, E-Mail: sjgc@famu.edu, Web Site: sjgc.famu.edu (16)

Weaks, Allen, Marketing Solutions, Lathrup Village, MI. Tel: (248) 443-5252, FAX: (248) 443-5252 (20)

WearGuard Corp, Norwell, MA. Tel: (781) 871-4100, (800) 388-3300, FAX: (781) 871-2639, Web Site: www.wearguard.com (2)

The Weather Channel, Atlanta, GA. Tel: (770) 226-0000, FAX: (770) 226-2390, Web Site: www. weather.com (32)

Weaver, Jerry, Alltel Publishing Corp, Hudson, OH. Tel: (330) 650-7100, FAX: (330) 650-7883, Web Site: www.alltel.com (22)

Weaver, Michael, Networking Alternatives for Publishers, Retailers & Artists, Inc, Eastsound, WA. Tel: (360) 376-2702, (800) 367-1907, FAX: (360) 376-2704, E-Mail: futureweb@rockisland.com (40)

Weaver, Shanon, Doane, Saint Louis, MO. Tel: (314) 569-2700, (866) 647-0918, FAX: (314) 569-1083, Web Site: www.doane.com (17)

Web Decisions, Greensboro, NC. Tel: (336) 545-7817 x100 (22)

Web Graphics, Glens Falls, NY. Tel: (518) 792-6501, (800) 833-8863, FAX: (518) 792-9353, (800) 833-8861, E-Mail: proofs&pos@printatweb.com, Web Site: www.printatweb.com (27)

Webb Designs Inc, El Cajon, CA. Tel: (619) 596-6400, (800) 262-9322, FAX: (619) 596-4511, E-Mail: awebb@webbshade.com, Web Site: www. webbshade.com (16)

Webb Mason, Hunt Valley, MD. Tel: (410) 785-1111, Web Site: www.webbmason.com (20)

Webb, Art, BCF, Virginia Beach, VA. Tel: (757) 497-4811, FAX: (757) 497-3684, Web Site: www. bcfagency.com (35)

Webb, Bob, Potpourri Group Inc, North Billerica, MA. Tel: (978) 256-4100, FAX: (978) 256-1961/0344, Web Site: www.potpourrigroup.com (6)

Webb, Eric, RSM McGladrey Inc, Charlotte, NC. Tel: (980) 233-4700, Web Site: www.rsmmcgladrey.com (20)

Webb, Felecia, Gay Men's Health Crisis, New York, NY. Tel: (212) 367-1000, FAX: (212) 367-1220, E-Mail: webmaster@gmhc.org, Web Site: www.gmhc.org (1)

Webb, Justin, Cornerstone Group of Companies, Toronto, ON Canada. Tel: (416) 932-9555, FAX: (416) 932-9566, E-Mail: info@cstonecanada.com, Web Site: www.cstonecanada.com (22)

Webb, Robert W., The Marmon Group LLC, Chicago, IL. Tel: (312) 372-9500, FAX: (312) 845-5305, Web Site: www.marmon.com (16)

Webb, Steve, International Crystal Manufacturing Co, Oklahoma City, OK. Tel: (405) 236-3741, (800) 252-6780, FAX: (405) 235-1904, E-Mail: info@icmfg.com, Web Site: www.icmfg.com (16)

Webb, Thomas J., Consumer's Energy, Jackson, MI. Tel: (517) 788-0550, (800) 805-0490, FAX: (517) 788-1859, E-Mail: businesscenter@consumerenergy.com, Web Site: www.consumersenergy.com (16)

Webb, Tony, Webb Designs Inc, El Cajon, CA. Tel: (619) 596-6400, (800) 262-9322, FAX: (619) 596-4511, E-Mail: awebb@webbshade.com, Web Site: www.webbshade.com (16)

Weber, Beth, New York Easter Seal Society, New York, NY. Tel: (212) 220-2290, FAX: (212) 695-4807, Web Site: ny.easterseals.com (16)

Weber, Harley, Zeppo Marketing Inc, Brooklyn, NY. Tel: (212) 308-5734, FAX: (646) 304-7364, Web Site: www.zeppomarketing.com (32)

Weber, James M., Brooks Sports Inc, Seattle, WA. Tel: (425) 402-1632, (800) 227-6657, FAX: (425) 489-1975, Web Site: www.brooksrunning.com (16)

Weber, Kurt, The Flinchbaugh Co Inc, Manchester, PA. Tel: (717) 266-2202, FAX: (717) 266-7055, E-Mail: flinchbaugh@blazenet.net, Web Site: www.flinchbaugh.com (16)

Weber, Louis, Publications International Ltd, Lincolnwood, IL. Tel: (847) 676-3470, (800) 595-8484, FAX: (847) 676-3671, Web Site: www.pubint.com (17)

Weber, Mike, Fry Communications Inc, Mechanicsburg, PA. Tel: (717) 766-0211, (800) 334-1429, FAX: (717) 691-0341, Web Site: www.frycomm.com (27)

Weber, Nancy, Meredith Corp, Des Moines, IA. Tel: (515) 284-3000, FAX: (515) 284-2700, Web Site: www.meredith.com (17)

Weber, Randy, Consumers Digest Inc, Deerfield, IL. Tel: (847) 607-3000, FAX: (847) 763-0200, E-Mail: postmaster@consumersdigest.com, Web Site: www.consumersdigest.com (16)

Weber, Ronald, Lowrance Electronics, Tulsa, OK. Tel: (918) 437-6881, FAX: (918) 234-1707, Web Site: www.lowrance.com (11)

Weber, Wendy, Crandall Associates Inc, Port Washington, NY. Tel: (516) 767-6800, E-Mail: joyce@crandallassociates.com, Web Site: www.crandallassociates.com (20)

Weber, Wesley R., Wesley R Weber & Associates, West Chester, PA. Tel: (610) 909-8040, E-Mail: wesweber@aol.com (20)

Weberg, Inga, Redleaf Press. Saint Paul, MN. Tel: (651) 641-6621, (800) 423-8309, FAX: (800) 641-0115, E-Mail: jvoltz@redleafpress.org, Web Site: redleafpress.org (17)

Webloyalty.com, Stamford, CT. Tel: (203) 956-1000, E-Mail: info@webloyalty.com, Web Site: www.webloyalty.com (32)

WebReply Inc, Natick, MA. Tel: (508) 318-4600, E-Mail: info@webreply.com, Web Site: www.webreply.com (35)

Webster Bank, Waterbury, CT. Tel: (203) 578-2230, FAX: (203) 578-2507, Web Site: www.websterbank.com (14)

Webster, Kathy, The Miller Group, Dupo, IL. Tel: (800) 325-3350, FAX: (618) 286-6202, E-Mail: info@miller-group.com, Web Site: www.multiplexdisplays.com (5)

Wechsler, Ira, Prestone Printing Co Inc, Long Island City, NY. Tel: (347) 468-7900, FAX: (347) 468-7885, E-Mail: info@prestoneprint.com, Web Site: www.prestoneprinting.com (25)

Wechsler, Richard, Lockard & Wechsler Direct, Irvington, NY. Tel: (914) 250-0241, E-Mail: info@lwdirect.com, Web Site: www.lwdirect.com (35)

JM Wechter & Associates Inc, Monroe, CT. Tel: (203) 452-0063, FAX: (203) 452-0414, Web Site: www.wechter.com (33)

Wechter, Janet, JM Wechter & Associates Inc, Monroe, CT. Tel: (203) 452-0063, FAX: (203) 452-0414, Web Site: www.wechter.com (33)

The Wedding Pages, New York, NY. Tel: (212) 219-8555, (800) 843-4983, FAX: (212) 219-1929, Web Site: www.theknot.com (16)

Wedding, Paula, AGCO Inc, Norcross, GA. Tel: (770) 447-6990, FAX: (770) 446-2102, Web Site: www.agcomarble.com (9)

Weddle, Tiffini, Directory of Major Mailers & What They Mail, Philadelphia, PA. Tel: (215) 238-5300, (800) 777-8074, FAX: (215) 238-5412, E-Mail: customerservice@napco.com, Web Site: www.majormailers.com (43)

Wede, Thomas, Jeppesen, Englewood, CO. Tel: (303) 799-9090, (800) 353-2107, Web Site: www.jeppesen.com (22)

Wedel, Randy, Schnuck Markets Inc, Saint Louis, MO. Tel: (314) 994-9900, FAX: (314) 994-4465, Web Site: www.schnucks.com (16)

Weeden, Jeffrey B., Key Bank National Association, Albany, NY. Tel: (518) 434-4871, (800) 539-2968, Web Site: www.keybank.com (14)

Weeks, Doug, Magnatag Visible Systems, Macedon, NY. Tel: (315) 986-3033, FAX: (315) 986-4000, Web Site: www.magnatag.com (16)

Weeks, Sherri, Grand Pacific Resorts, Carlsbad, CA. Tel: (760) 827-4100, (800) 374-7779, Web Site: www.grandpacificresorts.com (19)

Wehberg, Joyce, Shillcraft Inc, Annapolis, MD. Tel: (410) 682-3060, (800) 638-1542, FAX: (410) 682-3130, Web Site: www.shillcraft.com (16)

Wehmann, George, Direct Marketing Resources Group Inc, Raleigh, NC. Tel: (919) 231-2728, (800) 517-5253, Web Site: www.improvedmarketingresults.com (20)

Wehner, Todd, Steck-Vaughn, Austin, TX. Tel: (512) 343-8227, (800) 531-5015, (877) 866-2586, FAX: (512) 795-3617, (877) 265-2730, E-Mail: info@steck-vaughn.com, Web Site: www.steck-vaughn.com (17)

Wehrley, Paul, TVGuide.com, New York, NY. Tel: (212) 626-2500, Web Site: www.tvguide.com (31)

Weichert Co, Morris Plains, NJ. Tel: (973) 397-8516, Web Site: www.weichert.com (14)

Weideman, Bill, The Dow Chemical Co, Midland, MI. Tel: (989) 636-1000, (800) 258-2436, FAX: (989) 832-1556, Web Site: www.dow.com (16)

Weideman, Robert, Marketing and Product Strategy, Peabody, MA. Tel: (978) 977-2000, (800) 825-5897, FAX: (781) 238-0986, Web Site: www.lhsl.com (16)

Weidenbach, Julie, Response Management Technologies Inc, Berkeley, CA. Tel: (510) 843-8180, FAX: (510) 843-8020, E-Mail: info@respmgt.com, Web Site: www.respmgt.com (22)

Weider History Group, Ridgefield, CT. Tel: (203) 273-1092 (43)

Weidman, Robert J., Nuance Speech Solutions, Burlington, MA. Tel: (781) 565-5000, FAX: (781) 565-5001, E-Mail: sales@speechworks.com, Web Site: www.nuance.com (16)

Weight Watchers International, New York, NY. Tel: (516) 390-1400, FAX: (516) 390-1302, Web Site: www.weight-watchers.com (16)

Wein, Alex, SIE (Select Information Exchange), New York, NY. Tel: (212) 496-6435, FAX: (212) 787-4269, Web Site: www.siecom.com (23)

Wein, George, SIE (Select Information Exchange), New York, NY. Tel: (212) 496-6435, FAX: (212) 787-4269, Web Site: www.siecom.com (23)

Weinand, Italia Commisso, Mediacom Communications Corp, Chester, NY. Tel: (855) 633-4226, FAX: (845) 698-4100, Web Site: www.mediacomcable.com (32)

Weinberg, Bob, RW Consulting, Asheville, NC. Tel: (828) 299-3645, Web Site: www.rwconsulting.net (20)

Weinberg, David, US Gas & Electric, White Plains, NY. Tel: (888) 947-7880, FAX: (888) 400-1230, E-Mail: salesinfo@usgande.com, Web Site: www.usgande.com (16)

Weinberg, Gary, National Seminars Group, Shawnee Mission, KS. Tel: (913) 432-7755, (800) 258-7246, FAX: (913) 432-0824, E-Mail: cstserv@natsem.com, Web Site: www.natsem.com (16)

Weinberg, Gary, Quality Letter Service Inc, New York, NY. Tel: (212) 268-3400, FAX: (212) 268-3401, E-Mail: info@qletter.com, Web Site: www.qletter.com (21)

Weinberg, Robert, Quality Letter Service Inc, New York, NY. Tel: (212) 268-3400, FAX: (212) 268-3401, E-Mail: info@qletter.com, Web Site: www.qletter.com (21)

Weinberger, MD Steven E, American College of Physicians, Philadelphia, PA. Tel: (215) 351-2600, (800) 523-1546, FAX: (215) 351-2686, Web Site: www.acponline.org (17)

Richard Weiner Consultant, North Miami Beach, FL. Tel: (305) 441-6470 (14)

Weiner, Barry, Homeowners Marketing Services Inc, North Hollywood, CA. Tel: (888) 743-3037, E-Mail: inquiry@homeownersmarketingservices.com, Web Site: www.homeownersmarketingservices.com (23)

Weiner, David, Social Studies School Service, Culver City, CA. Tel: (310) 839-2436, (800) 421-4246, FAX: (310) 839-2249, (800) 944-5432, E-Mail: access@socialstudies.com, Web Site: www.socialstudies.com (16)

Weiner, Earl D., Theatre Development Fund Inc, New York, NY. Tel: (212) 912-9770, E-Mail: info@tdf.org, Web Site: www.tdf.org (14)

Weiner, Janis, Kappa Publishing Group, Blue Bell, PA. Tel: (215) 643-6385, FAX: (215) 628-3571, Web Site: www.kappapublishing.com (17)

Weiner, Michael, National General Insurance, Winston-Salem, NC. Tel: (888) 293-5108, Web Site: www.nationalgeneral.com (15)

Weiner, Richard, Richard Weiner Consultant, North Miami Beach, FL. Tel: (305) 441-6470 (14)

Weiner, Sanford, Social Studies School Service, Culver City, CA. Tel: (310) 839-2436, (800) 421-4246, FAX: (310) 839-2249, (800) 944-5432, E-Mail: access@socialstudies.com, Web Site: www. socialstudies.com (16)

Weineski, Bob, Huck Spaulding Enterprises, Voorheesville, NY. Tel: (518) 768-2070, (888) 982-8866, FAX: (518) 768-2240, E-Mail: orders@spaulding-rogers.com, Web Site: www.spaulding-rogers.com (16)

Weingarten, Henry, Astrologer's Fund Inc, Brooklyn, NY. Tel: (212) 949-7275, FAX: (212) 608-6964, E-Mail: books@afund.com, Web Site: www.afund. com (16)

Weingeroff Enterprises Inc, Cranston, RI. Tel: (401) 467-2200, FAX: (401) 785-1320, Web Site: www. weingeroff.com (16)

Weingeroff, Frederick L., Weingeroff Enterprises Inc, Cranston, RI. Tel: (401) 467-2200, FAX: (401) 785-1320, Web Site: www.weingeroff.com (16)

Weingeroff, Gregg, Weingeroff Enterprises Inc, Cranston, RI. Tel: (401) 467-2200, FAX: (401) 785-1320, Web Site: www.weingeroff.com (16)

Weingeroff, Lisa, JJI International Inc, Cranston, RI. Tel: (401) 780-8668 (35)

Weingeroff, Lisa, Weingeroff Enterprises Inc, Cranston, RI. Tel: (401) 467-2200, FAX: (401) 785-1320, Web Site: www.weingeroff.com (16)

Weinik, Mary, American Horse Products, San Juan Capistrano, CA. Tel: (949) 248-5300, (800) 500-0799, FAX: (949) 248-5305, E-Mail: zjim@sbcglobal.net, Web Site: www.americanhorseproducts.com (11)

Weinisch, Kris, The New Yorker Magazine, New York, NY. Tel: (212) 286-2860, FAX: (212) 286-4168, Web Site: www.newyorker.com (17)

Weinstein, Eric, Specialty Store Services Inc, Des Plaines, IL. Tel: (847) 470-7000, (888) 441-4440, FAX: (847) 470-5355, Web Site: www. specialtystoreservices.com (16)

Weinstein, Erika, Stephen-Bradford Search, New York, NY. Tel: (212) 221-6333, X346, (800) 720-0922, FAX: (212) 391-7826, E-Mail: info@ stephenbradford.com, Web Site: www. stephenbradford.com (20)

Weinstein, James N., Dartmouth-Hitchcock, Lebanon, NH. Tel: (603) 650-5000, Web Site: www.dmsnet. org (1)

Weinstein, Jody, Mr Wash Car Wash, Kensington, MD. Tel: (301) 933-4858, Web Site: www.mrwash.com (16)

Weintraub, Eric, Advertising Gifts Inc, Port Washington, NY. Tel: (516) 767-3577, FAX: (516) 7673567, E-Mail: sales@adgiftsinc.com, Web Site: www. adgiftsinc.com (33)

Weintraub, Floyd, Conmio Inc, New York, NY. Tel: (917) 583-2651, Web Site: www.conmio.com (16)

Weintraub, Michael, Healthy Offers Inc, Scottsdale, AZ. Tel: (480) 614-0060, FAX: (480) 614-0160, E-Mail: info@medicxmedia.com, Web Site: www. medicxmedia.com (23)

Weintraub, Steve, Lawyers & Judges Publishing Co Inc, Tucson, AZ. Tel: (520) 323-1500, FAX: (520) 323-0055, E-Mail: sales@lawyersandjudges.com, Web Site: www.lawyersandjudges.com (17)

Weisenborn, Dr Gregory, Fort Hays State University, Hays, KS. Tel: (785) 628-FHSU, FAX: (785) 628-4046, Web Site: www.fhsu.edu (41)

Weisenseel, John C., Alliance Bernstein, New York, NY. Tel: (212) 969-1000, (800) 962-2134, FAX: (212) 969-2293, Web Site: www.alliancebernstein. com (14)

Weiser, Bruce, SPIRE Printing & Packaging LLC, New York, NY. Tel: (212) 661-1157, E-Mail: bweiser@ spireprintingandpackaging.com, Web Site: www. spireprintingandpackaging.com (27)

Weishar, Jr. Paul J., Accent Advertising Inc, North Kansas City, MO. Tel: (816) 842-1860, FAX: (816) 471-4836, E-Mail: lindaaccentadv@sbcglobal.net, Web Site: www.accentadv.com (33)

Weisman, James, United Spinal Association, Kew Gardens, NY. Tel: (718) 803-3782, (800) 404-2898, FAX: (718) 803-0414, E-Mail: info@unitedspinal. org, Web Site: www.unitedspinal.org (1)

Weisman, Tony, DigitasLBi, Boston, MA. Tel: (617) 867-1000, E-Mail: newbusiness@digitas.com, Web Site: www.digitaslbi.com (35)

Weiss Research Inc, Palm Beach Gardens, FL. Tel: (561) 627-3300, (800) 291-8545, FAX: (561) 625-6685, Web Site: www.weissinc.com (17)

Weiss, Harriet, CRW Graphics, Pennsauken, NJ. Tel: (856) 662-9111, (800) 820-3000, FAX: (856) 665-1789, E-Mail: service@crwgraphics.com, Web Site: www.crwgraphics.com (27)

Weiss, Jeffrey, AG Interactive, Cleveland, OH. Tel: (216) 252-7300, (800) 711-4474, FAX: (216) 252-6778, Web Site: www.americangreetings.com (32)

Weiss, Jeffrey, American Greetings Corp, Cleveland, OH. Tel: (216) 252-7300, FAX: (216) 252-6778, Web Site: www.americangreetings.com (16)

Weiss, Jordan P., Roll International Corp, Los Angeles, CA. Tel: (310) 966-5700, FAX: (310) 914-4747, Web Site: www.roll.com (16)

Weiss, Kathy, Blass Communications LLC, Old Chatham, NY. Tel: (518) 766-2222, FAX: (518) 766-2445, E-Mail: brandthink@blasscommunications. com, Web Site: www.blasscom.com (35)

Weiss, Kevin, SkyMall Inc, Phoenix, AZ. Tel: (602) 254-9777, (800) SKY-MALL, FAX: (602) 254-6075, Web Site: www.skymall.com (16)

Weiss, Larry, Atlantic Business Products, New York, NY. Tel: (212) 741-6400, FAX: (212) 645-1518, E-Mail: info@tomorrowsoffice.com, Web Site: www.tomorrowsoffice.com (29)

Weiss, Mark, CRW Graphics, Pennsauken, NJ. Tel: (856) 662-9111, (800) 820-3000, FAX: (856) 665-1789, E-Mail: service@crwgraphics.com, Web Site: www.crwgraphics.com (27)

Weiss, Matt, Havas Worldwide LLC, New York, NY. Tel: (212) 886-2000, FAX: (212) 886-5013, Web Site: www.havasworldwide.com (35)

Weiss, Morry, AG Interactive, Cleveland, OH. Tel: (216) 252-7300, (800) 711-4474, FAX: (216) 252-6778, Web Site: www.americangreetings.com (32)

Weiss, Morry, American Greetings Corp, Cleveland, OH. Tel: (216) 252-7300, FAX: (216) 252-6778, Web Site: www.americangreetings.com (16)

Weiss, Paul, Techni-Tool Inc, Worcester, PA. Tel: (610) 941-2400, (800) 832-4866, FAX: (800) 854-8665, E-Mail: sales@techni-tool.com, Web Site: www. techni-tool.com (16)

Weiss, Ph. D. Martin D., Weiss Research Inc, Palm Beach Gardens, FL. Tel: (561) 627-3300, (800) 291-8545, FAX: (561) 625-6685, Web Site: www. weissinc.com (17)

Weiss, Sr Tibor, ORC Macro International, New York, NY. Tel: (212) 941-5555, FAX: (212) 941-7031, E-Mail: info@icfi.com, Web Site: www.icfi.com (30)

Weiss, Steven, Techni-Tool Inc, Worcester, PA. Tel: (610) 941-2400, (800) 832-4866, FAX: (800) 854-8665, E-Mail: sales@techni-tool.com, Web Site: www.techni-tool.com (16)

Weiss, Stuart, Techni-Tool Inc, Worcester, PA. Tel: (610) 941-2400, (800) 832-4866, FAX: (800) 854-8665, E-Mail: sales@techni-tool.com, Web Site: www.techni-tool.com (16)

Weiss, Zev, AG Interactive, Cleveland, OH. Tel: (216) 252-7300, (800) 711-4474, FAX: (216) 252-6778, Web Site: www.americangreetings.com (32)

Weiss, Zev, American Greetings Corp, Cleveland, OH. Tel: (216) 252-7300, FAX: (216) 252-6778, Web Site: www.americangreetings.com (16)

Weissenborn, James, General Pencil Co Inc, Jersey City, NJ. Tel: (201) 653-5351, FAX: (201) 653-2298, E-Mail: info@generalpencil.com, Web Site: www.generalpencil.com (16)

Weissman, Walter, Walter Weissman Photo Studio, New York, NY. Tel: (212) 989-9694, FAX: (212) 989-9694, E-Mail: wweissmanphoto@nyc.rr.com, Web Site: www.weissmanphoto.com (37)

Weisz, Stephen P., Marriott Ownership Resorts Sales & Marketing, Orlando, FL. Tel: (407) 206-6000, (800) 850-6674, FAX: (407) 206-6097, Web Site: www. marriottvacationclub.com (19)

Weitman, Gary, Tribune Co, Chicago, IL. Tel: (312) 222-9100, FAX: (312) 222-1573, Web Site: www. tribune.com (17)

Weitner, David, Techni-Tool Inc, Worcester, PA. Tel: (610) 941-2400, (800) 832-4866, FAX: (800) 854-8665, E-Mail: sales@techni-tool.com, Web Site: www.techni-tool.com (16)

Weitzell, Kim, Mazzone Marketing Group LLC, Brooklyn, NY. Tel: (718) 369-0001, (866) 928-5478, FAX: (718) 369-0099, E-Mail: info@ mazzonemarketinggroup.com, Web Site: www. mazzonemarketinggroup.com (23)

Weitzner, Harriet, Amacom Books, New York, NY. Tel: (212) 903-8376, FAX: (212) 903-8083, E-Mail: customerservice@amanet.org, Web Site: www. amacombooks.org (17)

Welch Allyn, Inc, Skaneateles Falls, NY. Tel: (315) 685-4100, Web Site: www.welchallyn.com (9)

Welch, Bryan, Mother Earth News Magazine, Topeka, KS. Tel: (785) 274-4300, (800) 678-5779, FAX: (785) 274-4305, E-Mail: bwelch@ogdenpubs.com, Web Site: www.cappers.com (17)

Welch, Kimberly, Profile America List Co Inc, Englewood Cliffs, NJ. Tel: (201) 569-7272, FAX: (201) 569-5552, E-Mail: listmanager@profileamerica. com, Web Site: www.profileamerica.com (24)

Welch, Mark, Bushnell Corporation, Overland Park, KS. Tel: (913) 752-3400, (800) 423-3537, FAX: (913) 752-3561, Web Site: www.bushnell.com (11)

Welch, Steve, PBM Graphics, Greensboro, NC. Tel: (336) 664-5800, (800) 849-8200, FAX: (336) 931-0965, Web Site: www.pbmgraphics.com (28)

Welcomemat Services Inc, Atlanta, GA. Tel: (404) 841-2226, E-Mail: info@welcomematservices.com, Web Site: www.welcomematservices.com (9)

Wellen, Paul, Walter E Heller College of Business Administration, Chicago, IL. Tel: (312) 281-3293, FAX: (312) 281-3290, Web Site: www.roosevelt. edu (41)

Weller, Ann, Ancient Circles, Willits, CA. Tel: (800) 726-8032, FAX: (707) 459-0261, E-Mail: ancient@ pacific.net, Web Site: www.ancientcircles.com (6)

Weller, Gary, Ansira, Saint Louis, MO. Tel: (314) 783-2300, FAX: (314) 783-2301, E-Mail: dl-newbusiness@ansira.com, Web Site: ansira.com (35)

Weller, Ted, DNE Nutraceuticals Inc, Farmingdale, NJ. Tel: (212) 235-5200, (800) 221-1833, FAX: (212) 235-5243, E-Mail: info@dnenutra.com, Web Site: www.dnenutra.com (7)

Weller, Todd, DNE Nutraceuticals Inc, Farmingdale, NJ. Tel: (212) 235-5200, (800) 221-1833, FAX: (212) 235-5243, E-Mail: info@dnenutra.com, Web Site: www.dnenutra.com (7)

Wellmark Blue Cross & Blue Shield of Iowa, Des Moines, IA. Tel: (515) 376-4500, (800) 524-9242, FAX: (515) 323-7722, Web Site: www.wellmark.com (15)

Wellness Councils of America, Omaha, NE. Tel: (402) 827-3590, FAX: (402) 827-3594, E-Mail: wellworkplace@welcoa.org, Web Site: www.welcoa.org (1)

Wellott, Henry, Fidelity Investments, Boston, MA. Tel: (617) 563-7000, (800) 343-3548, FAX: (617) 476-6150, Web Site: www.fidelity.com (14)

Wells Fargo, San Francisco, CA. Tel: (800) 869-3557, (866) 249-3302, FAX: (626) 312-3015, Web Site: www.wellsfargo.com (14)

Wells Lamont Corp, Niles, IL. Tel: (847) 647-8200, (800) 247-3295, FAX: (847) 647-6943, Web Site: www.wellslamont.com (34)

Wells Mailing, Montgomery, AL. Tel: (334) 286-4667, FAX: (334) 286-6008, E-Mail: info@wellsprinting.com, Web Site: www.wellsprinting.com (28)

Wells, Dr. Gail W., Northern Kentucky University, Highland Heights, KY. Tel: (859) 572-5220, (800) 637-9948, FAX: (859) 572-6177, Web Site: www.nku.edu (41)

Wells, Jonathan, Sipa Press, New York, NY. Tel: (212) 463-0150, FAX: (212) 463-0160, E-Mail: sipa@usa.com, Web Site: www.sipa.com (38)

Wells, Jonathan, The Christian Science Monitor, Boston, MA. Tel: (617) 450-2300, FAX: (617) 450-2031, Web Site: www.csmonitor.com (31)

Wells, Rick, Mohawk Lifts, Amsterdam, NY. Tel: (518) 842-1431, (800) 833-2006, FAX: (518) 842-1289, E-Mail: rwells@mohawklifts.com, Web Site: www.mohawklifts.com (9)

Welsh, Daniel, Spoken Arts, Holmes, NY. Tel: (845) 878-9600, (800) 326-4090, FAX: (845) 878-9009, E-Mail: sales@spokenartsmedia.com, Web Site: www.spokenartsmedia.com (17)

Welsh, Edward, Council on Foreign Relations Inc, New York, NY. Tel: (212) 434-9400, FAX: (212) 861-2759, E-Mail: editor@foreignaffairs.com, Web Site: www.foreignaffairs.org (17)

Welsh, Susan, Spoken Arts, Holmes, NY. Tel: (845) 878-9600, (800) 326-4090, FAX: (845) 878-9009, E-Mail: sales@spokenartsmedia.com, Web Site: www.spokenartsmedia.com (17)

Welty, Dan, John Henry Packaging, Lansing, MI. Tel: (707) 778-1250, (800) 327-5997, FAX: (707) 762-1253, Web Site: www.jhpackaging.com (27)

Welty, John, California State University at Fresno, Fresno, CA. Tel: (559) 278-7830, FAX: (559) 278-8577, Web Site: www.csufresno.edu (41)

Welz, Ed, New York Power Authority, White Plains, NY. Tel: (914) 681-6200, E-Mail: info@nypa.gov, Web Site: www.nypa.gov (16)

Wenaas, Wendy, iMarketing Solutions Group Inc, Milwaukee, WI. Tel: (414) 224-0701, (800) 879-0076, FAX: (414) 224-0943, Web Site: imarketingsolutionsgroup.com (29)

Wenck, Eric, Sylvan Learning Inc, Baltimore, MD. Tel: (410) 843-8000, (800) 31-SUCCESS, FAX: (410) 843-8057, E-Mail: pr@sylvanlearning.com, Web Site: www.sylvanlearning.com (16)

Wendel, Pia, Top USA Corp, Worthington, OH. Tel: (614) 431-1601, (800) 843-3381, FAX: (614) 431-1239, E-Mail: info@topusa.com, Web Site: www.topusa.com (27)

Wendover Associates Inc, Greensboro, NC. Tel: (336) 299-6611, FAX: (336) 292-4261, E-Mail: wendover@wendoverassociates.com, Web Site: www.wendoverassociates.com (35)

Wendt, Doug, Combined Insurance Co of America, Glenview, IL. Tel: (847) 953-8116, (800) 490-1322, FAX: (847) 953-8070, Web Site: www.combinedinsurance.com (15)

Wenger, Bruce, IDC, Ltd, Henderson, NV. Tel: (702) 450-1000, FAX: (702) 450-1020, E-Mail: info@goidc.com, Web Site: www.goidc.com (1)

Wenig, Dave, eBay Inc, San Jose, CA. Tel: (408) 376-7400, (800) 322-7400, Web Site: www.ebayinc.com (16)

Wenitsky, Susan, Voice Systems Engineering Inc, Langhorne, PA. Tel: (215) 953-8568, E-Mail: info@vseinc.com, Web Site: www.vseinc.com (32)

Wenneker, Mark, MullenLowe US, Boston, MA. Tel: (617) 226-9000, FAX: (617) 226-9100, Web Site: us.mullenlowe.com (35)

Wenner Media LLC, New York, NY. Tel: (212) 484-1616, FAX: (212) 484-1713 (17)

Wenner, Dave, Maple Grove Farms of Vermont Inc, Saint Johnsbury, VT. Tel: (802) 748-5141, FAX: (802) 748-9647, E-Mail: maple@maplegrove.com, Web Site: www.maplegrove.com (4)

Wenner, Jann S., Wenner Media LLC, New York, NY. Tel: (212) 484-1616, FAX: (212) 484-1713 (17)

WennSoft, New Berlin, WI. Tel: (262) 821-4100, FAX: (262) 821-3838, Web Site: www.wennsoft.com (22)

Wentworth-Bete, Carol W., Channing L Bete Co Inc, South Deerfield, MA. Tel: (800) 477-4776, FAX: (800) 499-6464, E-Mail: custscvs@channing.bete.com, Web Site: www.channing-bete.com (17)

Wentz, Michael, Entertainment Music Marketing Corp, Baldwin, NY. Tel: (631) 243-0600, FAX: (631) 243-0605, E-Mail: emmcmusic@aol.com, Web Site: www.emmcmusic.com (16)

Wentz, S., Jaffe Brothers Natural Foods, Valley Center, CA. Tel: (760) 749-1133, (877) 975-2333, FAX: (760) 749-1282, E-Mail: jaffebros@att.net, Web Site: www.organicfruitsandnuts.com (4)

Wentzel, Robyn, MCCS, Mason, OH. Tel: (513) 573-2284, FAX: (513) 573-2197, Web Site: www.federated.com (14)

Wenzel, Jill, LegaLists, New Providence, NJ. Tel: (973) 642-1440 ext.109, FAX: (973) 642-3731, E-Mail: jwenzel@lawdiary.com, Web Site: www.lawdiary.com (24)

Weprin, Kim, Associated Integrated Marketing, Wichita, KS. Tel: (316) 683-4691, E-Mail: info@meetassociated.com, Web Site: www.meetassociated.com (35)

Werbalowsky, Jeffrey, Houlihan Lokey Howard & Zukin, Los Angeles, CA. Tel: (310) 553-8871, (800) 788-5300, FAX: (310) 553-2173, Web Site: www.hlhz.com (14)

WerBell, Geoffrey, Brigade Quartermasters Ltd, Providence, RI. Tel: (770) 428-1248, (800) 338-4327, FAX: (800) 892-2992, Web Site: www.actiongear.com (11)

WerBell, IV Mitchell L., Brigade Quartermasters Ltd, Providence, RI. Tel: (770) 428-1248, (800) 338-4327, FAX: (800) 892-2992, Web Site: www.actiongear.com (11)

Werbin, Stanley R., Elderly Instruments, Lansing, MI. Tel: (517) 372-7890, (888) 473-5810, FAX: (517) 372-5155, E-Mail: web@elderly.com, Web Site: www.elderly.com (5)

Werder, Claude, The Dartnell Corp, Naples, FL. Tel: (585) 240-7301, (800) 447-4030, FAX: (585) 292-4392, E-Mail: customerservice@dartnellcorp.com, Web Site: www.dartnellcorp.com (17)

Werkley, Timothy S., Swan Packaging Fulfillment, Wayne, NJ. Tel: (973) 790-8417, FAX: (973) 790-0216, E-Mail: info@swanpkg.com, Web Site: www.swanpackaging.com (28)

Werner, James, Territorial Newspapers, Tucson, AZ. Tel: (520) 294-1200, FAX: (520) 294-4040, Web Site: www.azbiz.com (17)

Werner, Michael, InfoSource Inc, Oviedo, FL. Tel: (407) 796-5200, (800) 393-4636, FAX: (407) 796-5190, E-Mail: isisale@howtomaster.com, Web Site: www.infosourcelearning.com (3)

Werner-Robinson, Gail, GWR Wealth Management, Omaha, NE. Tel: (402) 452-3737, FAX: (402) 452-3676, Web Site: www.gwrwealth.com (14)

Werning, Tom J., Universal Engineering Corp, Cedar Rapids, IA. Tel: (319) 365-0441, (800) 366-2051, FAX: (319) 369-5440, E-Mail: info@universalcrusher.com, Web Site: www.universalcrusher.com (16)

Frederick Wershaw Management Co, Stamford, CT. Tel: (203) 329-3000, FAX: (203) 329-3044 (20)

Wershaw, Frederick I., Frederick Wershaw Management Co, Stamford, CT. Tel: (203) 329-3000, FAX: (203) 329-3044 (20)

Wert, Larry, Tribune Co, Chicago, IL. Tel: (312) 222-9100, FAX: (312) 222-1573, Web Site: www.tribune.com (17)

Wertheim, A.J., Abbeon Cal Inc, Santa Barbara, CA. Tel: (805) 966-0810, (800) 922-0977, FAX: (805) 966-7659, E-Mail: abbeoncal@abbeon.com, Web Site: www.abbeon.com (9)

Weschcke, Carl L., Llewellyn Publications, Woodbury, MN. Tel: (651) 291-1970, (877) 639-9753, FAX: (651) 291-1908, Web Site: www.llewellyn.com (17)

Weschcke, Gabe, Llewellyn Publications, Woodbury, MN. Tel: (651) 291-1970, (877) 639-9753, FAX: (651) 291-1908, Web Site: www.llewellyn.com (17)

WESCO, Pittsburgh, PA. Tel: (412) 454-2200, (800) 343-1201, E-Mail: info@wesco.com, Web Site: www.wescodist.com (16)

Wesley R Weber & Associates, West Chester, PA. Tel: (610) 909-8040, E-Mail: wesweber@aol.com (20)

Wesloh, Kim, IMA Executive Summit, Minneapolis, MN. Tel: (952) 928-4649, E-Mail: info@incentivemarketing.com, Web Site: www.incentivemarketing.com (42)

Wesner, Gerald, Thomas Scientific, Swedesboro, NJ. Tel: (856) 467-2000, (800) 345-2100, FAX: (856) 467-3087, E-Mail: value@thomassci.com, Web Site: www.thomassci.com (9)

Wessan, Amy, McGaw Graphics, Manchester Center, VT. Tel: (845) 353-8600, (888) 4BMCGAW, FAX: (845) 353-3155, E-Mail: sales@bmcgaw.com, Web Site: www.bmcgaw.com (6)

Wessner, Mike, Conney Safety Products LLC, Madison, WI. Tel: (888) 356-9100, FAX: (800) 845-9095, E-Mail: safety@conney.com, Web Site: www.conney.com (7)

West Bend, West Bend, WI. Tel: (262) 334-5107, (866) 290-1851, FAX: (262) 334-6800, Web Site: www.focuselectrics.com (16)

West Cary Group, Richmond, VA. Tel: (804) 343-2029 (20)

West Companies Inc, Seminole, FL. Tel: (212) 319-7069 (20)

West Corp, Omaha, NE. Tel: (800) 841-9000, FAX: (402) 963-1602, E-Mail: sales@west.com, Web Site: www.west.com (20)

West End Diving Centers Inc, Bridgeton, MO. Tel: (314) 209-7200, (888) 843-3483, E-Mail: info@2dive.com, Web Site: www.westenddiving.com (19)

West Farm Foods (Branch), Caldwell, ID. Tel: (208) 459-3687, FAX: (208) 459-9135, Web Site: www.westfarm.com (16)

West Marine Inc, Watsonville, CA. Tel: (831) 728-2700, (800) 262-8464, (800) BOATING, FAX: (831) 768-5000, E-Mail: customercare@westmarine.com, Web Site: www.westmarine.com (11)

West Shore Distributors, Westlake, OH. Tel: (440) 835-5600, (800) 344-8141, FAX: (440) 835-8654, E-Mail: westshore@ameritech.net, Web Site: www.westshoreframes.com (8)

West Virginia University, Morgantown, WV. Tel: (304) 293-3505, FAX: (304) 293-3072, E-Mail: wvuwebmaster@mail.wvu.edu, Web Site: www.wvu.edu (41)

West, Alfred, SEI, Oaks, PA. Tel: (610) 676-1000, FAX: (610) 676-1406, E-Mail: webmaster@seic.com, Web Site: www.seic.com (14)

West, Doreen, Midco Call Center Services, Sioux Falls, SD. Tel: (605) 330-4125, (800) 843-8800, FAX: (605) 357-5414, Web Site: www.midcocall.com (29)

West, Elizabeth, Dunham & Co, Plano, TX. Tel: (469) 454-0100 (1)

West, Kim, Unity School of Christianity, Unity Village, MO. Tel: (816) 254-3550, FAX: (816) 251-3554, E-Mail: unity@unityonline.org, Web Site: www.unityonline.org (17)

West, Larry J., West Companies Inc, Seminole, FL. Tel: (212) 319-7069 (20)

West, Michelle, Winslow Publishing, Toronto, ON Canada. Tel: (416) 789-4733, E-Mail: winslow@interlog.com, Web Site: www.winslowpublishing.com (17)

West, Mitchell, Abbott, Abbott Park, IL. Tel: (224) 667-6100, FAX: (847) 937-9555, Web Site: www.abbott.com (7)

West, Nancy, Random Lengths Publications Inc, Eugene, OR. Tel: (541) 686-9925, (888) 686-9925, FAX: (541) 686-9629, (800) 874-7979, E-Mail: rlmail@rlpi.com, Web Site: www.randomlengths.com (17)

West, Richard, Peachtree Data Inc, Duluth, GA. Tel: (678) 987-4600, Web Site: www.peachtreedata.com (22)

West, Robert, Santa Barbara Greenhouses, Oxnard, CA. Tel: (800) 544-5276, E-Mail: robsbg@aol.com, Web Site: www.sbgreenhouse.com (8)

West, Shane, TDS Telecom, Madison, WI. Tel: (608) 664-4119, Web Site: www.tdstelecom.com (16)

West, Thomas M, JC Whitney, Chicago, IL. Tel: (312) 431-6000, FAX: (312) 431-5650, (800) 537-2700, Web Site: www.jcwhitney.com (17)

West, Todd, Malco Products Inc, Barberton, OH. Tel: (330) 753-0361, (800) 253-2526, FAX: (330) 753-2025, Web Site: www.malcopro.com (16)

Westbeth Gallery, New York, NY. Tel: (212) 989-4650 (36)

Westcon, Tarrytown, NY. Tel: (914) 829-7000, FAX: (914) 829-7137, Web Site: www.westcon.com (16)

Westcott, Bruce, Stanley Supply & Services, North Andover, MA. Tel: (978) 682-9844, (800) 225-5370, FAX: (800) 743-8141, Web Site: www.stanleysupplyservices.com (16)

Wester, Earl, Quadrant Engineering Plastic Products, Reading, PA. Tel: (610) 320-6600, (800) 366-0300, FAX: (610) 320-6868, Web Site: www.quadrantepp.com (16)

Wester, III Al B., Ventura Associates International LLC, New York, NY. Tel: (212) 302-8277, FAX: (212) 302-2587, E-Mail: info@sweepspros.com, Web Site: www.sweepspros.com (35)

Westerfield, Blake A., Celtic Life Insurance Co, Chicago, IL. Tel: (312) 332-5401, FAX: (312) 441-0341, E-Mail: info@celtic-net.com, Web Site: www.celtic-net.com (15)

Western Connecticut State University, Danbury, CT. Tel: (203) 837-8200, FAX: (203) 837-8527, E-Mail: hills@wcsu.edu, Web Site: www.wcsu.edu (41)

Western Data Services Inc, Carlsbad, NM. Tel: (575) 628-8318, (877) 870-5566, FAX: (575) 628-8917, E-Mail: directmail@wdsi.net, Web Site: www.wdsi.net (35)

Western Digital Corp, Irvine, CA. Tel: (949) 672-7000, FAX: (949) 672-7837, Web Site: www.westerndigital.com (22)

Western Graphics, Saint Paul, MN. Tel: (651) 603-6400, FAX: (651) 603-6401, E-Mail: info@westerngx.com, Web Site: www.westerngx.com (27)

Western Pennsylvania Conservancy, Pittsburgh, PA. Tel: (412) 288-2777, (866) 564-6972, FAX: (412) 231-1414, E-Mail: info@paconserve.org, Web Site: www.paconserve.org (1)

Western Printing Machinery (WPM), Schiller Park, IL. Tel: (847) 678-1740, FAX: (847) 678-6176, E-Mail: info@wpm.com, Web Site: www.wpm.com (34)

Western Psychological Services, Torrance, CA. Tel: (310) 478-2061, (800) 648-8857, FAX: (310) 478-7838, E-Mail: marketing@wpspublish.com, Web Site: www.wpspublish.com (16)

Western River Expeditions, Salt Lake City, UT. Tel: (801) 942-6669, (866) 904-1160, FAX: (801) 942-8514, Web Site: www.westernriver.com (19)

Western-Southern Life, Cincinnati, OH. Tel: (513) 629-1800, Web Site: www.westernsouthernlife.com (15)

Western Web Printing, Sioux Falls, SD. Tel: (605) 339-2383, (800) 843-6805, FAX: (605) 339-8323, E-Mail: info@westernwebprinting.com, Web Site: www.westernwebprinting.com (27)

Westfield, Brian, Westcon, Tarrytown, NY. Tel: (914) 829-7000, FAX: (914) 829-7137, Web Site: www.westcon.com (16)

Westgroup, Eagan, MN. Tel: (800) 344-5008, Web Site: www.westgroup.com (17)

Westhoff Machine Co, Saint Louis, MO. Tel: (314) 963-7130, (800) 364-0280, FAX: (800) 324-1942, E-Mail: mail@westhoffinc.com, Web Site: www.westhoffinc.com (9)

Westhorpe, Barbara, Bamboo Cricket, West Palm Beach, FL. Tel: (561) 515-4546, (800) 260-8050, FAX: (561) 653-3990, E-Mail: info@bamboocricket.com, Web Site: www.bamboocricket.com (32)

Westhorpe, Paul, Bamboo Cricket, West Palm Beach, FL. Tel: (561) 515-4546, (800) 260-8050, FAX: (561) 653-3990, E-Mail: info@bamboocricket.com, Web Site: www.bamboocricket.com (32)

Westlake Plastics Co, Lenni, PA. Tel: (610) 459-1000, (800) 999-1700, FAX: (610) 459-1084, Web Site: www.westlakeplastics.com (16)

Westlake, Larry, Sandy Alexander Inc, Clifton, NJ. Tel: (973) 470-8100, FAX: (973) 470-9269, E-Mail: sandy@sandyinc.com, Web Site: www.sandyinc.com (32)

Westland, Stewart, Bike Nashbar, Crab Orchard, WV. Tel: (800) NAS-HBAR, FAX: (877) 778-9456, E-Mail: custserv@nashbar.com, Web Site: www.bikenashbar.com (11)

Westman, Penny, Standard Life, Montreal, QC Canada. Tel: (514) 499-8855, (877) 499-9555, FAX: (514) 499-4908, Web Site: www.standardlife.ca (15)

Westminster International Inc, Markham, ON Canada. Tel: (416) 494-6245, (866) 635-8050, FAX: (905) 771-9349, E-Mail: info@westminster.ca, Web Site: www.westminster.ca (21)

Weston Distance Learning Inc, Fort Collins, CO. Tel: (970) 282-6322, Web Site: www.westondistancelearning.com (13)

Edward Weston Fine Art & Photography, Chatsworth, CA. Tel: (818) 885-1044, FAX: (818) 885-1021, E-Mail: edwardweston@westoncollection.com, Web Site: edward-weston.com (36)

Weston, Ann, Edward Weston Fine Art & Photography, Chatsworth, CA. Tel: (818) 885-1044, FAX: (818) 885-1021, E-Mail: edwardweston@westoncollection.com, Web Site: edward-weston.com (36)

Weston, Carolyn H., Massachusetts Horticultural Society, Wellesley, MA. Tel: (617) 933-4900, (617) 933-4929, FAX: (617) 933-4901, E-Mail: hort_line@masshort.org, Web Site: www.masshort.org (1)

Weston, Marla J., American Nurses' Association, Silver Spring, MD. Tel: (301) 628-5000, (800) 274-4262, (800) 284-2378, FAX: (301) 628-5001, Web Site: www.nursingworld.org (1)

Westphal, Jeff, Vertex Inc, Berwyn, PA. Tel: (610) 640-4200, (800) 355-3500, FAX: (610) 640-5892, Web Site: www.vertexinc.com (16)

Westpro Inc, Provo, UT. Tel: (801) 373-2525, (800) 533-3885, FAX: (801) 373-8778, E-Mail: sales@westpro.net, Web Site: www.westpro.net (27)

Westrate, Valerie, Catholic Digest, New London, CT. Tel: (800) 321-0411, E-Mail: catholicdigest@bayardinc.com, Web Site: www.catholicdigest.com (17)

Westwood Publishing Co, Glendale, CA. Tel: (818) 242-1159, FAX: (818) 247-9379 (17)

Wetli, Joe, Elmers Products Inc, Westerville, OH. Tel: (614) 985-2600, (800) 848-9400, FAX: (614) 985-2605, E-Mail: comments@elmers.com, Web Site: www.elmers.com (25)

Wetzel, Charles, Group O Inc, Milan, IL. Tel: (309) 736-8300, FAX: (309) 736-8301, Web Site: www.groupo.com (30)

Wetzel, Cheryl M., Anglicans United & Latimer Press, Cedar Hill, TX. Tel: (972) 293-7443, (800) 553-3645, FAX: (972) 293-7559, E-Mail: anglicansunited@sbcglobal.net, Web Site: www.anglicansunited.com, www.latimerpress.com (1)

Wetzel, Rev Todd H., Anglicans United & Latimer Press, Cedar Hill, TX. Tel: (972) 293-7443, (800) 553-3645, FAX: (972) 293-7559, E-Mail: anglicansunited@sbcglobal.net, Web Site: www.anglicansunited.com, www.latimerpress.com (1)

Wetzel, Tom, Marketing & Media Services LLC, Warwick, RI. Tel: (401) 737-7730, FAX: (401) 737-6465, Web Site: www.mmsipitv.com (30)

Wetzler, Andrew, MoreVisibility, Boca Raton, FL. Tel: (561) 620-9682, (800) 787-0497, FAX: (561) 620-9684, E-Mail: info@morevisibility.com, Web Site: www.morevisibility.com (35)

Wexler Consulting Group LLC, Alexandria, VA. Tel: (202) 573-9355, E-Mail: welcome@wexlerllc.com, Web Site: wexlerconsultinggroup.com (35)

Steve Wexler Creative Group, Farmingville, NY. Tel: (631) 736-6565, Web Site: www.wexdirect.com (20)

Wexler, Andrew, Herschend Family Entertainment, Norcross, GA. Tel: (417) 338-3810, FAX: (417) 338-8144, Web Site: www.hfecorp.com (5)

Wexler, David, Lerner Publishing Group, Minneapolis, MN. Tel: (612) 332-3344, (800) 328-4929, FAX: (800) 332-1132, E-Mail: info@lernerbooks.com, Web Site: www.lernerbooks.com (17)

Wexler, Mark, Quill Healthcare, Minneapolis, MN. Tel: (763) 493-7300, (800) 328-2179, FAX: (800) 328-0023, Web Site: www.medicalartspress.com (27)

Wexler, Steve, Steve Wexler Creative Group, Farmingville, NY. Tel: (631) 736-6565, Web Site: www.wexdirect.com (20)

Wexler, Zeev, Wexler Consulting Group LLC, Alexandria, VA. Tel: (202) 573-9355, E-Mail: welcome@wexlerllc.com, Web Site: wexlerconsultinggroup.com (35)

The Wexner Companies Inc, Memphis, TN. Tel: (901) 763-3925, (800) 890-5470, FAX: (901) 763-3736, E-Mail: info@JosephStores.com, Web Site: www.josephstores.com (2)

Wexner, Alfred B., The Wexner Companies Inc, Memphis, TN. Tel: (901) 763-3925, (800) 890-5470, FAX: (901) 763-3736, E-Mail: info@JosephStores.com, Web Site: www.josephstores.com (2)

Wexner, Leslie H., L Brands Inc, Columbus, OH. Tel: (614) 415-7000, FAX: (614) 415-7440, Web Site: www.lb.com (16)

Weyerhaeuser Co, Federal Way, WA. Tel: (253) 924-2345, (800) 525-5440, FAX: (253) 924-2685, Web Site: www.wy.com (25)

Weyers, Sheeri, Tower Media Advertising Inc, Chicago, IL. Tel: (312) 856-9200, FAX: (312) 856-1300, E-Mail: info@towermedia.com, Web Site: www.towermedia.com (35)

Weyhrich, Todd, Burlington Coat Factory, Burlington, NJ. Tel: (609) 387-7800, FAX: (609) 387-7071, Web Site: www.burlingtoncoatfactory.com (16)

GJ Whalen & Co Inc, Tarrytown, NY. Tel: (914) 333-0085, E-Mail: george@gjwhalen.com (39)

Whalen, Chris, Embassy Digital, Oakville, ON Canada. Tel: (905) 829-9969, (888) 477-8629, FAX: (905) 829-9429, E-Mail: info@embassydigital.com, Web Site: www.embassydigital.com (27)

Whalen, David, A T Cross Co, Lincoln, RI. Tel: (401) 333-1200, (800) 282-7677, FAX: (401) 334-2861, Web Site: www.cross.com (16)

Whalen, George J., GJ Whalen & Co Inc, Tarrytown, NY. Tel: (914) 333-0085, E-Mail: george@gjwhalen.com (39)

Whalen, Julie P, Williams-Sonoma Inc, San Francisco, CA. Tel: (415) 421-7900, (800) 840-2591, Web Site: www.williams-sonomainc.com (8)

Whalen, Kelly, ProPhase Marketing Inc, Eden Prairie, MN. Tel: (952) 974-1100, (800) 969-6400, FAX: (952) 974-7874, E-Mail: sales@ppmi.com, Web Site: prophasemarketing.com (21)

Whalen, Lou, Peoples Benefit Life Insurance Co, Exton, PA. Tel: (610) 648-5000, FAX: (610) 648-5348 (15)

Whaley, Craig, ProPhase Marketing Inc, Eden Prairie, MN. Tel: (952) 974-1100, (800) 969-6400, FAX: (952) 974-7874, E-Mail: sales@ppmi.com, Web Site: prophasemarketing.com (21)

Wharton, Dennis, NAB Show, Washington, DC. Tel: (202) 429-5300, (800) 622-3976, FAX: (202) 429-4199, E-Mail: nab@nab.org, Web Site: www.nabshow.com (42)

Wharton, Peter, Iomega Corp, Roy, UT. Tel: (801) 332-1000, (888) 446-6342, FAX: (801) 332-3158, Web Site: www.iomega.com (16)

What on Earth, Hudson, OH. Tel: (330) 963-6554, (800) 945-2552, FAX: (800) 950-9569, Web Site: www.whatonearthcatalog.com (5)

Whatley, Randall P., Cypress Media Group Inc, Atlanta, GA. Tel: (770) 640-9918, E-Mail: info@cypressmedia.net, Web Site: www.cypressmedia.net (35)

Whealy, Michael T., First Data Merchant Services, Atlanta, GA. Tel: (404) 890-2000, FAX: (303) 967-5188, Web Site: www.firstdata.com (14)

Wheaton Group, Chapel Hill, NC. Tel: (919) 969-8859, FAX: (425) 675-6014, E-Mail: jim.wheaton@wheatongroup.com, Web Site: www.wheatongroup.com (22)

Wheaton, Cynthia, Wheaton Group, Chapel Hill, NC. Tel: (919) 969-8859, FAX: (425) 675-6014. E-Mail: jim.wheaton@wheatongroup.com, Web Site: www.wheatongroup.com (22)

Wheaton, Jim, B2BMarketing.com, Scottsdale, AZ. Tel: (602) 402-6588, Web Site: www.b2bmarketing.com (35)

Wheaton, Jim, Wheaton Group, Chapel Hill, NC. Tel: (919) 969-8859, FAX: (425) 675-6014, E-Mail: jim.wheaton@wheatongroup.com, Web Site: www.wheatongroup.com (22)

Wheeler, Brent, Response Mine Interactive Inc, Atlanta, GA. Tel: (404) 233-0370, Web Site: www.responsemine.com (35)

Wheeler, Mark, Pacific Botanicals LLC, Grants Pass, OR. Tel: (541) 479-7777, FAX: (541) 479-7780, E-Mail: pacbotl@earthlink.net, Web Site: www.pacificbotanicals.com (7)

Whelan, Claire, Winnipeg Art Gallery, Winnipeg, MB Canada. Tel: (204) 786-6641, FAX: (204) 788-4998, E-Mail: inquiries@wag.mb.ca, Web Site: www.wag.ca (1)

Whelan, Raymond F., Globe Photos Inc, West Islip, NY. Tel: (631) 661-3131 (38)

Whelan, Rick, Marketing General Inc, Alexandria, VA. Tel: (703) 739-1000, (800) 644-6646, FAX: (703) 549-6057, E-Mail: info@marketinggeneral.com, Web Site: www.marketinggeneral.com (35)

Whelan, Robert, Pearson VUE, Bloomington, MN. Tel: (952) 681-3000, Web Site: home.pearsonvue.com (17)

Whelpley, John, Vector Marketing Corp, Olean, NY. Tel: (716) 373-6141, (267) 880-1750, FAX: (716) 373-6145, Web Site: www.cutco.com (5)

Where 2 Get It Inc, Anaheim, CA. Tel: (888) 377-2767, Web Site: www.where2getit.com (30)

Whetzel, Anthony, O2 Agency Inc, New York, NY. Tel: (212) 675-7334, E-Mail: newbiz@o2agency.com, Web Site: o2agency.strikingly.com (35)

Whipple, Lance, Lathem Time Corp, Atlanta, GA. Tel: (404) 691-0400, (800) 241-4990, FAX: (404) 696-6048, Web Site: www.lathem.com (16)

Whipple, Wayne, One Point, Scranton, PA. Tel: (570) 342-0737, (800) 526-4460, FAX: (570) 343-6361, Web Site: www.opoffice.com (10)

Whirley Drink Works, Warren, PA. Tel: (814) 723-7600, (800) 825-5575, FAX: (814) 723-3245, E-Mail: info@whirleydrinkworks.com, Web Site: www.whirleydrinkworks.com (5)

Whirlpool Corp, Benton Harbor, MI. Tel: (269) 923-5000, E-Mail: info@whirlpool.com, Web Site: www.whirlpoolcorp.com (16)

Whitaker National, Huntington, WV. Tel: (304) 525-0852, (800) 377-8721, FAX: (304) 525-0874, Web Site: www.neshold.com (16)

Whitaker, Kenneth, Public Interest Communications Inc, Falls Church, VA. Tel: (703) 847-8300, FAX: (703) 734-9620, Web Site: www.pubintcom.com (29)

Whitcomb, Paula, Recording for the Blind & Dyslexic Inc, Princeton, NJ. Tel: (609) 452-0606, (800) 221-4792, FAX: (609) 520-7996, E-Mail: info@rfbd.org, Web Site: www.rfbd.org (16)

White Cap Wholesale Contractors Supplies, Costa Mesa, CA. Tel: (800) 944-8322, FAX: (866) 791-8396, E-Mail: customerservice@whitecap.com, Web Site: www.whitecapdirect.com (16)

White Electronic Designs, Phoenix, AZ. Tel: (614) (602) 437-1520, FAX: (602) 437-9120, Web Site: www.whiteedc.com (27)

White Flower Farm, Litchfield, CT. Tel: (860) 496-9624, (800) 503-9624, FAX: (860) 496-1418, Web Site: www.whiteflowerfarm.com (8)

White Mane Publishing Co Inc, Shippensburg, PA. Tel: (717) 532-2237, (888) 948-6263, FAX: (717) 532-6110, E-Mail: marketing@whitemane.com, Web Site: www.whitemane.com (17)

White Point Leads Group LLC, Gulf Breeze, FL. Tel: (850) 934-5577, Web Site: www.whitepointleads.com (29)

White Post Media Group, Nashville, TN. Tel: (615) 469-4409, Web Site: whitepostmedia.com (35)

White, Bill, Quantum Group, Morton Grove, IL. Tel: (847) 967-3600, FAX: (847) 967-3610, Web Site: www.quantumgroup.com (35)

White, Byron, Lifetips, Boston, MA. Tel: (617) 886-9001, Web Site: www.lifetips.com (16)

White, Carole, Advertising Research Foundation, New York, NY. Tel: (212) 751-5656, FAX: (212) 319-5265, E-Mail: info@thearf.org, Web Site: www.thearf.org (40)

White, Celso, Molson Coors Brewing Co, Denver, CO. Tel: (303) 927-2337, (800) 665-7661, Web Site: www.molsoncoors.com (16)

White, Charlie, Chico's FAS Inc, Fort Myers, FL. Tel: (239) 277-6200, Web Site: www.chicos.com (2)

White, Colin, OlympPak, Minneapolis, MN. Tel: (763) 504-5400, (800) 967-1705, FAX: (763) 504-5401, E-Mail: jgibas@olympak.com, Web Site: www.olympak.com (27)

White, David, Choice Hotels International, Rockville, MD. Tel: (301) 592-5000, Web Site: www.choicehotels.com (16)

White, Ian, Urban Mapping Inc, San Francisco, CA. Tel: (415) 946-8170, Web Site: www.urbanmapping.com (16)

White, Jeff, Incept Corp, Canton, OH. Tel: (330) 649-8000, Web Site: www.inceptcorp.com (29)

White, Lorraine, Executive Connections LLC, Sarasota, FL. Tel: (941) 323-8300, Web Site: www.executiveconnectionsllc.com (20)

White, Matthew C., White64, Vienna, VA. Tel: (703) 793-3000, E-Mail: info@white64.com, Web Site: white64.com (35)

White, Michael, DIRECTV LLC, El Segundo, CA. Tel: (310) 535-5000, FAX: (310) 535-5225, Web Site: www.directv.com (16)

White, Miles, Abbott, Abbott Park, IL. Tel: (224) 667-6100, FAX: (847) 937-9555, Web Site: www.abbott.com (7)

White, Nanette, Academic Management Services, Swansea, MA. Tel: (508) 235-2870, (800) 891-4203, FAX: (508) 235-2991, E-Mail: info@amsweb.com, Web Site: www.amsweb.com (14)

White, Randall, EDC Publishing, Tulsa, OK. Tel: (918) 622-4522, (800) 475-4522, FAX: (800) 747-4509, Web Site: www.edcpub.com (17)

White, Richard, Herr Foods Inc, Nottingham, PA. Tel: (610) 932-9330, (800) 344-3777, FAX: (610) 932-2137, E-Mail: info@herrs.com, Web Site: www.herrs.com (16)

White, Sari, Vermont/New Hampshire Direct Marketing Group, Woodstock, VT. Tel: (802) 457-2807, FAX: (802) 457-2807, E-Mail: vtnhmg@vtnhmg, Web Site: www.vtnhmg.org (40)

Whitehat Inc, Tempe, AZ. Tel: (480) 858-9000, FAX: (480) 858-9001, E-Mail: sales@whitehat.com, Web Site: www.whitehat.com (32)

Whitehorse Gear, Center Conway, NH. Tel: (603) 356-6556, FAX: (603) 356-6590, E-Mail: customerservice@whitehorsepress.com, Web Site: www.whitehorsepress.com (11)

Whitely, George, Stephan & Brady Inc, Madison, WI. Tel: (608) 241-4141, FAX: (608) 241-4246, E-Mail: gwhitely@stephanbrady.com, Web Site: www.stephanbrady.com (35)

Whiteman, Doug, Penguin Group USA Inc, New York, NY. Tel: (212) 366-2000, Web Site: www.us.penguingroup.com (17)

Whiteman, Tim, Condolink, Omaha, NE. Tel: (402) 592-3525, (800) 877-9600, FAX: (402) 592-4122, E-Mail: info@condolink.com, Web Site: www.condolink.com (16)

White64, Vienna, VA. Tel: (703) 793-3000, E-Mail: info@white64.com, Web Site: white64.com (35)

Whiteway, Jerry, MetaResponse Group Inc, Deerfield Beach, FL. Tel: (954) 360-0644, FAX: (954) 360-7712, E-Mail: info@metaresponse.com, Web Site: www.metaresponse.com (23)

Whitewing Labs, Granada Hills, CA. Tel: (800) 950-3030, FAX: (818) 240-2785, E-Mail: service@whitewing.com, Web Site: www.whitewing.com (20)

Whiting & Davis, Attleboro Falls, MA. Tel: (508) 699-4412, (800) 876-MESH, FAX: (508) 695-7606, E-Mail: info@whitinganddavis.com, Web Site: www.whitinganddavis.com (16)

Whiting, Susan, The Nielsen Co, New York, NY. Tel: (800) 864-1224, Web Site: www.nielsen.com (17)

Whitlock, Gary L., Centerpoint Energy, Minneapolis, MN. Tel: (612) 372-4664, FAX: (612) 321-4873, E-Mail: mgc-businessinformation@centerpointenergy.com, Web Site: www.minnegasco.centerpointenergy.com (16)

Whitlock, Ruth, Association of Energy Engineers, Atlanta, GA. Tel: (770) 447-5083 x210, FAX: (770) 446-3969, E-Mail: info@aeecenter.org, Web Site: www.aeecenter.org (40)

Whitman Publishing LLC, Atlanta, GA. Tel: (800) 546-2995, FAX: (256) 246-1116, E-Mail: info@whitmanbooks.com, Web Site: www.whitmanbooks.com (16)

Whitman, Meg, Hewlett-Packard Co, Palo Alto, CA. Tel: (650) 857-1501, (800) 752-0900, FAX: (650) 857-5518, Web Site: www.hp.com (16)

Whitmyre, Rick, Tiziani Whitmyre Inc, Sharon, MA. Tel: (781) 793-9380, FAX: (781) 793-9395, E-Mail: info@tizinc.com, Web Site: www.tizinc.com (21)

Jordan Whitney Inc, Tustin, CA. Tel: (714) 832-3353, FAX: (714) 832-4422, E-Mail: info@jwgreensheet.com, Web Site: www.jwgreensheet.com (32)

Whitney Worldwide Inc, Saint Paul, MN. Tel: (651) 748-5000, (800) 597-0227, FAX: (651) 748-4000, Web Site: www.whitneyworld.com (20)

Whitney, Bill, Hooleon Corp, Melrose, NM. Tel: (575) 253-4503, (800) 937-1337, E-Mail: sales@hooleon.com, Web Site: www.hooleon.com (3)

Whitney, Jim, Educational Insights, Inc, Gardena, CA. Tel: (310) 884-2000, (888) 591-9334, FAX: (310) 886-8850, E-Mail: service@edin.com, Web Site: www.educationalinsights.com (16)

Whitney, Mark, TheLaw.net Corp, San Diego, CA. Tel: (858) 554-0583, Web Site: www.thelaw.net (22)

Whitrock, Steve, NTP Distribution, Wilsonville, OR. Tel: (503) 570-0171, FAX: (888) 570-0342, Web Site: www.ntpdistribution.com (34)

Whittaker, Cindy, The Mailbox of Ithaca Inc, Ithaca, NY. Tel: (607) 257-3865, (800) 382-6348, FAX: (607) 266-0508, E-Mail: mailbox@lightlink.com, Web Site: www.mailboxofithaca.com (28)

Whitters, Joseph E., Mentor Corp, Santa Barbara, CA. Tel: (805) 879-6000, (800) 525-0245, FAX: (805) 964-2712, Web Site: www.mentorcorp.com (16)

Whittier, Richard, Majestic Marketing Inc, Corona, CA. Tel: (951) 280-2400, (800) 843-2247, FAX: (951) 280-2410, E-Mail: sales@bagmasters.com, Web Site: www.bagmasters.com (35)

Whittington, Brent, Windstream Communications Inc, Little Rock, AR. Tel: (501) 748-7000, Web Site: www.windstream.com (32)

Whole Foods Market Inc, Austin, TX. Tel: (512) 477-4455, FAX: (512) 482-7000, Web Site: www.wholefoodsmarket.com (4)

Wholesale Tool Co, Warren, MI. Tel: (800) 521-3420, FAX: (800) 521-3661, E-Mail: wtmich@aol.com, Web Site: www.wttool.com (9)

Who's Calling, College Station, TX. Tel: (866) 688-9300, FAX: (888) 821-4260, E-Mail: contact@whoscalling.com, Web Site: www.whoscalling.com (30)

Who's Who - The MFSA Buyers' Guide to Blue Ribbon Mailing Services, Alexandria, VA. Tel: (703) 836-9200, FAX: (703) 548-8204, E-Mail: masa-mail@masa.org, Web Site: www.mfsanet.org (43)

Wicker, Gary, Zondervan Corp, Grand Rapids, MI. Tel: (616) 698-6900, (800) 727-3060, FAX: (616) 698-3235, Web Site: www.zondervan.com (17)

Wicker, Ron, LinkWorth, Lewisville, TX. Tel: (214) 440-3900, (866) 565-9784, Web Site: www.linkworth.com (32)

Wickizer, Chris, Premera Blue Cross, Spokane, WA. Tel: (425) 670-4000, (800) 422-0032, FAX: (425) 670-5853, Web Site: www.premera.com (15)

Wicklander, Phillip J., Carqueville Graphics Inc, Streamwood, IL. Tel: (630) 837-4500, FAX: (630) 837-4510, Web Site: www.carqueville.com (27)

Wideband by Kars, New Rochelle, NY. Tel: (212) 691-9000, FAX: (212) 691-9835, E-Mail: info@widebandjewelry.com, Web Site: www.widebandjewelry.com (16)

Widen, Susan, PlusNetMarketing Inc, Exton, PA. Tel: (610) 458-0707, E-Mail: info@pnmarketing.com, Web Site: www.plusnetmarketing.com (21)

Widess, Jim, The Caning Shop, Berkeley, CA. Tel: (510) 527-5010, (800) 544-3373, FAX: (510) 527-7718, Web Site: www.caning.com (11)

Widing, Laura, Kerr-Hays Co, Ligonier, PA. Tel: (724) 238-6944, FAX: (724) 238-7440 (16)

Wiebe, Richard, Creative Teaching Associates, Clovis, CA. Tel: (559) 291-6626, (800) 767-4282, FAX: (559) 291-2953, Web Site: www.mastercta.com (16)

Wiedemann, George, UMarketing LLC, Lombard, IL. Tel: (630) 916-1717, Web Site: www.umarketing.com (35)

Wiedman, Stephen, Mid America Designs Inc, Effingham, IL. Tel: (217) 540-4200, (800) 350-4543, FAX: (217) 540-4800, E-Mail: mail@mamotorworks.com, Web Site: www.mamotorworks.com (12)

Wiedman, Steve, Mid America Motorworks, Effingham, IL. Tel: (217) 347-5591, (800) 500-1500, FAX: (217) 347-2952, E-Mail: mail@mamotorworks.com, Web Site: www.mamotorworks.com (12)

Wiehoff, John P., C H Robinson Worldwide Inc, Eden Prairie, MN. Tel: (952) 937-8500, FAX: (952) 937-6740, E-Mail: info@chrobinson.com, Web Site: www.chrobinson.com (16)

Wiener, Adelle S., PRO Chemical & Dye Inc, Fall River, MA. Tel: (508) 676-3838, FAX: (508) 676-3980, Web Site: www.prochemicalanddye.com (10)

Wiener, Donald, PRO Chemical & Dye Inc, Fall River, MA. Tel: (508) 676-3838, FAX: (508) 676-3980, Web Site: www.prochemicalanddye.com (10)

Wier, Mark, American Civil Liberties Union Foundation, New York, NY. Tel: (212) 549-2500, Web Site: www.aclu.org (1)

Wiercinski, Sara, National Catholic Reporter Publishing Co Inc, Kansas City, MO. Tel: (816) 531-0538, (800) 444-8910, FAX: (816) 968-2268, Web Site: www.ncronline.org (17)

Michael Wiese Productions, Studio City, CA. Tel: (818) 379-8799, (800) 833-5738, FAX: (818) 986-3408, Web Site: www.mwp.com (17)

Wiese, Michael, Michael Wiese Productions, Studio City, CA. Tel: (818) 379-8799, (800) 833-5738, FAX: (818) 986-3408, Web Site: www.mwp.com (17)

Simon Wiesenthal Center, Los Angeles, CA. Tel: (310) 553-9036, (800) 900-9036, FAX: (310) 553-4521, E-Mail: information@wiesenthal.com, Web Site: wiesenthal.com (1)

Wietecha, Mark, Kurt Salmon Associates Inc, Atlanta, GA. Tel: (404) 892-0321, FAX: (404) 898-9590, E-Mail: infoksaweb@kurtsalmon.com, Web Site: www.kurtsalmon.com (16)

The Wig Co, Pittsburgh, PA. Tel: (800) 568-3499, E-Mail: custserv@twcwigs.com, Web Site: www.thewigcompany.com (2)

Wight, Don, Demandbase Inc, San Francisco, CA. Tel: (415) 683-2660, E-Mail: info@demandbase.com, Web Site: www.demandbase.com (22)

Wight, Katy, Edward Elgar Publishing Inc, Northampton, MA. Tel: (413) 584-5551, FAX: (413) 584-9933, E-Mail: sales@e-elgar.com, Web Site: www.e-elgar.com (17)

Wikreate, San Francisco, CA. Tel: (415) 362-0440, FAX: (415) 362-0430, E-Mail: ezequieltrivino@wikreate.com, Web Site: www.wikreate.com (35)

Wikstrom, Robert L., Jerden Records/SpeechWorks, Redmond, WA. Tel: (425) 882-3344, (888) 401-4487, FAX: (425) 882-3494, E-Mail: jerden@aol.com, Web Site: www.soundworks.net (16)

Wiland Direct, Longmont, CO. Tel: (303) 485-8686, Web Site: www.wilanddirect.com (22)

Wiland, Phillip, Wiland Direct, Longmont, CO. Tel: (303) 485-8686, Web Site: www.wilanddirect.com (22)

Wilber, Elaine, VF Imagewear, Greensboro, NC. Tel: (336) 424-6000, (800) 733-5271, Web Site: www.vfimagewear.com (2)

Wilbur, Dylan, Group 236, Oakland, CA. Tel: (510) 874-0141, Web Site: group236.com (32)

Wilbur, Michael, MBI Inc, Norwalk, CT. Tel: (203) 853-2000, E-Mail: webmail@mbi-inc.com, Web Site: www.mbi-inc.com (16)

Wilcher, Thomas, Soft Surroundings, Saint Louis, MO. Tel: (314) 812-5200, Web Site: www.softsurroundings.com (2)

Wilcox & Associates, Longwood, FL. Tel: (407) 830-4808, FAX: (407) 830-5265 (33)

Wilcox, Derek, Label Colors Inc, Sussex, WI. Tel: (262) 549-1730, (800) 558-2126, FAX: (800) 784-2591, Web Site: www.lauterbachgroup.com (25)

Wilcox, Jack, Wilcox & Associates, Longwood, FL. Tel: (407) 830-4808, FAX: (407) 830-5265 (33)

Wilcox, Mark, DB Consulting, Harrison, NY. Tel: (914) 698-2008, E-Mail: darcybev@yahoo.com (20)

Wilcox, Mark, Gianfagna Strategic Marketing Inc, Westlake, OH. Tel: (440) 808-4700, FAX: (440) 808-4707, E-Mail: tellmemore@gianfagnamarketing.com, Web Site: www.gianfagnamarketing.com (35)

WILD Flavors Inc, Erlanger, KY. Tel: (859) 342-3600, FAX: (859) 342-3610, Web Site: www.wildflavors.com (4)

Gilbert H Wild & Son Inc, Reeds, MO. Tel: (417) 548-3514, (888) 449-4537, FAX: (417) 548-6831, E-Mail: gregj@gilberthwild.com, Web Site: www.gilberthwild.com (8)

Wild, Bill, Jaypro Sports, Waterford, CT. Tel: (860) 447-3001, (800) 243-0533, FAX: (800) 988-3363, E-Mail: info@jaypro.com, Web Site: www.jaypro.com (11)

Wild, Valerie, Power & Telephone Supply, Randolph, VT. Tel: (800) 451-4381, FAX: (802) 234-5006, E-Mail: cablesales@ptsupply.com, Web Site: www.ptsupply.com/enterprise (16)

The Wilderness Society, Washington, DC. Tel: (202) 429-2609, Web Site: www.wilderness.org (40)

Wildlife Education Ltd, Park Hills, KY. Tel: (858) 513-7600, FAX: (858) 513-7660, E-Mail: animals@zoobooks.com, Web Site: www.zoobooks.com (17)

Wildseed Farms, Fredericksburg, TX. Tel: (800) 848-0078, FAX: (830) 990-8090, E-Mail: orders1@wildseedfarms.com, Web Site: www.wildseedfarms.com (8)

Wildt, Andrea, Campaign Monitor, San Francisco, CA. Tel: (888) 533-8098, E-Mail: info@campaignmonitor.com, Web Site: www.campaignmonitor.com (24)

Wilen Group, Farmingdale, NY. Tel: (631) 439-5000, FAX: (631) 439-4536, Web Site: www.wilengroup.com (24)

Wilen, Darrin, Wilen Group, Farmingdale, NY. Tel: (631) 439-5000, FAX: (631) 439-4536, Web Site: www.wilengroup.com (27)

Wiles, Susan, Leisure Arts Inc, Maumelle, AR. Tel: (501) 868-8800, Web Site: www.leisurearts.com (17)

John Wiley & Sons Canada Ltd, Etobicoke, ON Canada. Tel: (416) 236-4433, FAX: (416) 236-4448, Web Site: www.wiley.com (17)

John Wiley & Sons Inc, Hoboken, NJ. Tel: (201) 748-6000, FAX: (201) 748-6088, E-Mail: info@wiley.com, Web Site: www.wiley.com (17)

Wiley, Deborah E., John Wiley & Sons Inc, Hoboken, NJ. Tel: (201) 748-6000, FAX: (201) 748-6088, E-Mail: info@wiley.com, Web Site: www.wiley.com (17)

Wiley, II Bradford, John Wiley & Sons Inc, Hoboken, NJ. Tel: (201) 748-6000, FAX: (201) 748-6088, E-Mail: info@wiley.com, Web Site: www.wiley.com (17)

Wiley, Lori, Compact Information Systems, Redmond, WA. Tel: (425) 869-1379, (800) 632-1379, FAX: (425) 558-2638, E-Mail: pat@compactlists.com, Web Site: www.compactlists.com (23)

Wiley, Mason, Hydra Group LLC, Los Angeles, CA. Tel: (310) 526-6680, FAX: (310) 526-6682, Web Site: www.hydragroup.com (9)

Wiley, Pat, Compact Information Systems, Redmond, WA. Tel: (425) 869-1379, (800) 632-1379, FAX: (425) 558-2638, E-Mail: pat@compactlists.com, Web Site: www.compactlists.com (23)

Wiley, Peter B., Do It Yourself Direct Marketing, Hoboken, NJ. Tel: (201) 748-6000. FAX: (201) 748-6088, E-Mail: info@wiley.com, Web Site: www.wiley.com (43)

Wilgus, Dan, A+ Letter Service, Lakewood, NJ. Tel: (732) 905-2010, FAX: (732) 905-4662, E-Mail: aplus@aplusletter.com, Web Site: www.aplusletters.com (28)

Wilhelm, Markus, AKS Marketing & Media, Chapel Hill, NC. Tel: (919) 240-5496 (20)

Wilhite, Gerald, Abbey Press, Saint Meinrad, IN. Tel: (812) 357-8368, FAX: (812) 357-8388, Web Site: www.abbeypress.com (6)

Wilhoit, Zachary, Ethnic Technologies LLC, South Hackensack, NJ. Tel: (201) 440-8923, (866) 333-8324, FAX: (201) 440-2168, E-Mail: karens@ethnictechnologies.com, Web Site: www.ethnictechnologies.com (23)

Wilke, Jeffrey A., Amazon.com, Seattle, WA. Tel: (206) 266-1000, Web Site: www.amazon.com (16)

Wilke, Marty, St Louis Slot Machine Co, Saint Louis, MO. Tel: (314) 432-1699, E-Mail: stlslot@earthlink.net, Web Site: www.stlouisslot.com (6)

Wilkes, Corbin M., The Kiplinger Washington Editors Inc, Washington, DC. Tel: (202) 887-6400, (800) 544-0155, FAX: (202) 496-1817, Web Site: www.kiplinger.com (17)

Wilkes, Mark, Corporate Graphics Direct Marketing Solutions, Arden Hills, MN. Tel: (651) 494-1740, (800) 728-2615, FAX: (651) 494-1750, E-Mail: contact@cgdms.com, Web Site: www.cgids.com (22)

Wilkes, Mary Beth, Resorts Casino Hotel, Atlantic City, NJ. Tel: (609) 334-6000, (800) 336-6378, FAX: (609) 340-6349, Web Site: www.resortsac.com (19)

Wilkie, Michael, DoAll Co, Wheeling, IL. Tel: (847) 824-1122, (800) 92-DOALL, FAX: (847) 699-7524, E-Mail: info@doall.com, Web Site: www.doall.com (16)

Wilkin, Gene, Bunn-O-Matic Corp, Springfield, IL. Tel: (217) 529-6601, FAX: (217) 529-6622, E-Mail: bunn@bunn.com, Web Site: www.bunn.com (16)

Wilkins, Donna, Charity Dynamics, Austin, TX. Tel: (512) 241-0561, FAX: (512) 532-6037, Web Site: www.charitydynamics.com (1)

Wilkins, Jane, Mystic Seaport Museum Stores, Mystic, CT. Tel: (860) 572-5315, (860) 572-0711, FAX: (860) 572-5324, Web Site: www.mysticseaport.org (6)

Wilkins, Jesse, AIIM International, Silver Spring, MD. Tel: (301) 587-8202, (800) 477-2446, FAX: (301) 587-2711, E-Mail: aiim@aiim.org, Web Site: www.aiim.org (1)

Wilkinson, Harvie, Keeneland Association Inc, Lexington, KY. Tel: (859) 254-3412, (800) 456-3412, FAX: (859) 255-2484, Web Site: www.keeneland.com (16)

Wilkinson, Jane, Institutional Investor Inc, New York, NY. Tel: (212) 224-3300, FAX: (212) 224-3592, Web Site: www.institutionalinvestor.com (16)

Wilkinson, Todd G., Datacard Ga-Vehren Corp, Minnetonka, MN. Tel: (952) 933-1223, (800) 621-6972 x6930, FAX: (952) 931-0418, E-Mail: info@datacard.com, Web Site: www.gavehren.com (34)

Wilkus, Malon, American Capital, Bethesda, MD. Tel: (301) 951-6122, FAX: (301) 654-6714, E-Mail: info@americancapital.com, Web Site: www.americancapital.com (15)

Lt Moses Willard Inc, Amelia, OH. Tel: (513) 248-5500, (800) 621-8956, FAX: (513) 831-0548, E-Mail: info@ltmoses.com, Web Site: www.ltmoses.com (16)

Willard, Bruce, Sundance Catalog Co, Salt Lake City, UT. Tel: (801) 973-2711, (800) 422-2770, FAX: (801) 973-4989, E-Mail: jessica.bassin@sundance.net, Web Site: www.sundancecatalog.com (6)

Willard, Rev Donald, Liguori Publications, Liguori, MO. Tel: (636) 464-2500, (800) 325-9521, FAX: (800) 325-9526, E-Mail: liguori@liguori.org, Web Site: www.liguori.org (17)

Willet, Bill, Lifeboat Distribution, Shrewsbury, NJ. Tel: (732) 389-8950, FAX: (732) 389-9227, Web Site: www.programmersparadise.com (16)

Willi, Jim, Audience Research & Development, Fort Worth, TX. Tel: (817) 924-6922, FAX: (817) 924-7539, E-Mail: jgumbert@ar-d.com, Web Site: www.ar-d.com (20)

William Charles Printing, Plainview, NY. Tel: (516) 349-0900, FAX: (516) 349-0935, Web Site: www.williamcharlesprinting.com (27)

William-Neil Associates, Sidney, NE. Tel: (800) 216-2214, FAX: (308) 254-6102, E-Mail: bobermier@william-neil.com, Web Site: www.william-neil.com (24)

William, Bryan, Premier Packaging Corp, Victor, NY. Tel: (877) 924-8460, FAX: (585) 924-8753, E-Mail: info@premiercustompkg.com, Web Site: www.premiercustompkg.com (16)

Williams, Caliri, Miller & Otley, Wayne, NJ. Tel: (973) 694-0800, FAX: (973) 694-0302, Web Site: www.wcmolaw.com (20)

Williams Direct Marketing Inc, Pickering, ON Canada. Tel: (416) 292-7459, FAX: (416) 292-4635, E-Mail: info@williamsdirectmarketing.com, Web Site: www.williamsdirectmarketing.com (33)

Williams Printing Co, Atlanta, GA. Tel: (404) 875-6611, (800) 950-7588, FAX: (404) 872-4025, Web Site: www.rrdonnelley.com (27)

Williams-Sonoma Inc, San Francisco, CA. Tel: (415) 421-7900, (800) 840-2591, Web Site: www.williams-sonomainc.com (8)

Williams Worldwide Television, Santa Monica, CA. Tel: (310) 449-4506, FAX: (310) 449-4556, E-Mail: curious@williamsworldwidetv.com, Web Site: www.williamsworldwidetv.com (35)

Williams, Barbara, Careington International, Frisco, TX. Tel: (972) 335-6970, (800) 441-0380, Web Site: www.careington.com (7)

Williams, Bill, Medcom Inc, Cypress, CA. Tel: (800) 877-1443, FAX: (714) 891-3140, E-Mail: lhammonds@medcominc.com, Web Site: www.medcominc.com (17)

Williams, Chip, Parise Marketing Group, Millwood, NY. Tel: (914) 941-7467, FAX: (914) 941-7931, Web Site: www.parise.com (35)

Williams, Connie, Deck the Walls Inc, Saint Peters, MO. Tel: (314) 719-8200, (866) 719-8200, FAX: (314) 719-8290, E-Mail: dtwcontact@fcibiz.com, Web Site: www.deckthewalls.com (5)

Williams, Darrell, Group Mojo, Portland, OR. Tel: (503) 493-2242, FAX: (503) 493-2246, E-Mail: sam@groupmojo.com, Web Site: www.groupmojo.com (32)

Williams, David, FileMaker Inc, Santa Clara, CA. Tel: (408) 987-7000, FAX: (408) 987-3823, Web Site: www.filemaker.com (22)

Williams, David, Make-A-Wish Foundation of America, Phoenix, AZ. Tel: (602) 279-9474, FAX: (602) 279-0855, Web Site: www.wish.org (1)

Williams, David S., Merkle Inc, Columbia, MD. Tel: (443) 542-4000, (877) 9MERKLE, FAX: (443) 542-4758, Web Site: www.merkleinc.com (22)

Williams, Denise, Goodman Marketing Partners Inc, San Rafael, CA. Tel: (415) 507-9060, FAX: (415) 507-9067, E-Mail: info@goodmanmarketing.com, Web Site: www.goodmanmarketing.com (35)

Williams, Dustin, AccuData Integrated Marketing, Fort Myers, FL. Tel: (239) 425-4400, (800) 732-3440, FAX: (239) 425-4401, E-Mail: info@accudata.com, Web Site: www.accudata.com (23)

Williams, Galen, Galen Williams Landscaping & Garden Design, East Hampton, NY. Tel: (631) 324-6220, FAX: (631) 329-3684 (16)

Williams, Glenn, Bell Performance Inc, Longwood, FL. Tel: (407) 834-3690, (800) 659-2355, FAX: (407) 767-8685, E-Mail: info@bellperformance.net, Web Site: www.bellperformance.net (9)

Williams, James, Cluett Peabody, New York, NY. Tel: (212) 984-8900, FAX: (212) 984-8910, Web Site: www.arrowshirt.com (16)

Williams, Jamie, The Wilderness Society, Washington, DC. Tel: (202) 429-2609, Web Site: www.wilderness.org (40)

Williams, Jeff, Alderman Co, High Point, NC. Tel: (336) 889-6121, FAX: (336) 889-7717, E-Mail: sales@aldermancompany.com, Web Site: www.aldermancompany.com (37)

Williams, Jerry, American Name Services Inc, Orem, UT. Tel: (801) 235-8061, (800) 434-1851, FAX: (801) 764-0613, E-Mail: sales@americannameservices.com, Web Site: www.americannameservices.com (23)

Williams, Jim, Hagie Manufacturing Co, Clarion, IA. Tel: (515) 532-2861, (800) 247-4885, FAX: (515) 532-3553, E-Mail: info@hagie.com, Web Site: www.hagie.com (9)

Williams, Joe, Luggage Base, Nipomo, CA. Tel: (805) 929-8191, (888) 832-1201, FAX: (805) 929-8192, E-Mail: service@luggagebase.com, Web Site: www.luggagebase.com (16)

Williams, Joni, Kelly, Scott & Madison Inc, Chicago, IL. Tel: (312) 977-0772, FAX: (312) 977-0874, E-Mail: info@ksmmedia.com, Web Site: www.ksmmedia.com (32)

Williams, Jr. Bill, Telect Inc, Liberty Lake, WA. Tel: (509) 926-6000, FAX: (509) 926-8915, E-Mail: getinfo@telect.com, Web Site: www.telect.com (16)

Williams, Karen, Editorial Freelance Association, New York, NY. Tel: (212) 929-5400, (866) 929-5425, FAX: (212) 929-5439, E-Mail: office@the-efa.org, Web Site: www.the-efa.org (31)

Williams, Kim, College of Business Administration, Philadelphia, PA. Tel: (215) 895-2145, Web Site: www.drexel.edu (41)

Williams, Landa, LandaJob, Kansas City, MO. Tel: (816) 523-1881, (800) 931-8806, FAX: (816) 523-1876, E-Mail: adstaff@landajobnow.com, Web Site: www.landajobnow.com (20)

Williams, Linda, Planned Parenthood Mar Monte, San Jose, CA. Tel: (408) 287-7532, FAX: (408) 971-6935, Web Site: www.plannedparenthood.org (1)

Williams, M. Jane, Schultz & Williams Inc, Philadelphia, PA. Tel: (215) 625-9955, FAX: (215) 625-2701, E-Mail: mail@schultzwilliams.com, Web Site: www.sw-inc.com (1)

Williams, Matt, The Martin Agency, Richmond, VA. Tel: (804) 698-8000, FAX: (804) 698-8001, Web Site: www.martinagency.com (35)

Williams, Pete, Alderman Co, High Point, NC. Tel: (336) 889-6121, FAX: (336) 889-7717, E-Mail: sales@aldermancompany.com, Web Site: aldermancompany.com (37)

Williams, R. James, Keeneland Association Inc, Lexington, KY. Tel: (859) 254-3412, (800) 456-3412, FAX: (859) 255-2484, Web Site: www.keeneland.com (16)

Williams, Renee, KCET, Burbank, CA. Tel: (747) 201-5000, FAX: (747) 201-5877, E-Mail: contact@kcet.org, Web Site: www.kcet.org (1)

Williams, Richard B., American Indian College Fund, Denver, CO. Tel: (303) 426-8900, (800) 776-3863, FAX: (303) 426-1200, Web Site: www.collegefund.org (1)

Williams, Rob, Mountain Press Publishing Co, Missoula, MT. Tel: (406) 728-1900, (800) 234-5308, FAX: (406) 728-1635, E-Mail: info@mountain-press.com, Web Site: mountain-press.com (17)

Williams, Ronald A., AETNA - Marketing Product & Communication, Hartford, CT. Tel: (860) 273-0123, (800) 872-3862, FAX: (860) 273-3971, Web Site: www.aetna.com (14)

Williams, Russ, Archer Malmo Inc, Memphis, TN. Tel: (901) 523-2000, FAX: (901) 524-5578, Web Site: www.archermalmo.com (35)

Williams, Scott, Emisare Inc, Greensboro, NC. Tel: (336) 378-0510, E-Mail: info@emisare.com, Web Site: www.emisare.com (32)

Williams, Sheryl, Amplify Federal Credit Union, Austin, TX. Tel: (512) 836-5901, Web Site: www.goamplify.com (1)

Williams, Susan, Luggage Base, Nipomo, CA. Tel: (805) 929-8191, (888) 832-1201, FAX: (805) 929-8192, E-Mail: service@luggagebase.com, Web Site: www.luggagebase.com (16)

Williams, Tony, Sunshine Minting Inc, Coeur D'Alene, ID. Tel: (208) 772-9592, (800) 274-5837, FAX: (208) 772-9739, E-Mail: sunshine@sunshinemint.com, Web Site: www.sunshinemint.com (14)

Williams, Wayne E., Telect Inc, Liberty Lake, WA. Tel: (509) 926-6000, FAX: (509) 926-8915, E-Mail: getinfo@telect.com, Web Site: www.telect.com (16)

Williams-Milam, Ola, Bell Performance Inc, Longwood, FL. Tel: (407) 834-3690, (800) 659-2355, FAX: (407) 767-8685, E-Mail: info@bellperformance.net, Web Site: www.bellperformance.net (9)

Williamsburg Blacksmiths Inc, Williamsburg, MA. Tel: (413) 268-7341, (800) 248-1776, FAX: (413) 268-9317, E-Mail: williamsburgblacksmiths@gmail.com, Web Site: www.williamsburgblacksmiths.com (8)

Williamson-Dickie Manufacturing Co, Fort Worth, TX. Tel: (800) 336-7201, FAX: (817) 877-5027, E-Mail: customerservice@dickies.com, Web Site: www.dickies.com (2)

Williamson Printing, Dallas, TX. Tel: (214) 904-2100, (800) 843-5423, FAX: (214) 352-1842, E-Mail: jandagu@twpc.com, Web Site: www.wpcnet.com (27)

Williamson, Jerry, Williamson Printing, Dallas, TX. Tel: (214) 904-2100, (800) 843-5423, FAX: (214) 352-1842, E-Mail: jandagu@twpc.com, Web Site: www.wpcnet.com (27)

Williamson, Matt O., Brady Corp, Milwaukee, WI. Tel: (414) 358-6600, (800) 541-1686, FAX: (800) 292-2289, Web Site: www.bradycorp.com (16)

Williamson, Phillip C., Williamson-Dickie Manufacturing Co, Fort Worth, TX. Tel: (800) 336-7201, FAX: (817) 877-5027, E-Mail: customerservice@dickies.com, Web Site: www.dickies.com (2)

Williamson, Susan, CTRAC Information Solutions, Strongsville, OH. Tel: (440) 572-1000, FAX: (440) 572-3330, E-Mail: ctrac@ctrac.com, Web Site: www.ctrac.com (22)

Willingham, Teresa, Automated Graphic Systems LLC, White Plains, MD. Tel: (800) 678-8760, FAX: (240) 222-3419, E-Mail: info@ags.com, Web Site: www.ags.com (31)

Willins, Stanton, Covalent Marketing, Denver, CO. Tel: (303) 588-7754, Web Site: www.covalentmarketing.com (22)

Willis Music Co, Florence, KY. Tel: (859) 283-2050, (800) 354-9799, FAX: (859) 283-1784, E-Mail: ordpt@willis-music.com, Web Site: www.willismusic.com (17)

Willis, Aaron, Social Studies School Service, Culver City, CA. Tel: (310) 839-2436, (800) 421-4246, FAX: (310) 839-2249, (800) 944-5432, E-Mail: access@socialstudies.com, Web Site: www.socialstudies.com (16)

Willis, Bernice, Matt Brown & Associates Inc, Dayton, OH. Tel: (937) 434-3949, (800) 233-3949, FAX: (937) 434-6272, E-Mail: mba@mbalists.com, Web Site: www.mbalists.com (23)

Willis, Ethan, Prosper Inc, Provo, UT. Tel: (801) 371-0755, (800) 748-5799, FAX: (801) 374-2358, E-Mail: support@prospering.com, Web Site: www.prospering.com (32)

Willis, Mike, Kappler Protective Apparel & Fabrics, Guntersville, AL. Tel: (256) 505-4005, (800) 600-4019, FAX: (256) 505-4151, E-Mail: customerservice@kappler.com, Web Site: www.kappler.com (2)

Willits, Ed. D. Paula P., The Dartnell Corp, Naples, FL. Tel: (585) 240-7301, (800) 447-4030, FAX: (585) 292-4392, E-Mail: customerservice@dartnellcorp.com, Web Site: www.dartnellcorp.com (17)

Willms, James A., Unicover Corp, Cheyenne, WY. Tel: (307) 771-3000, (800) 443-3232, FAX: (307) 771-3134, E-Mail: qands@unicover.com, Web Site: www.unicover.com (6)

Willms, Jesse, JustThink Inc, Sherwood Park, AB Canada. Tel: (780) 416-0244 (16)

Wills, Richard, Baker & Taylor Inc, Charlotte, NC. Tel: (704) 998-3100. (800) 775-1800, FAX: (704) 998-3316, E-Mail: btinfo@btol.com, Web Site: www.btol.com (16)

Wills, Rick, Tektronix Inc, Beaverton, OR. Tel: (503) 627-7111, (800) 833-9200, FAX: (503) 627-3247, Web Site: www.tektronix.com (16)

Willson, Jane, Sunnyland Farms Inc, Albany, GA. Tel: (800) 999-2488, Web Site: www.sunnylandfarms.com (4)

Willson, Larry, Sunnyland Farms Inc, Albany, GA. Tel: (800) 999-2488, Web Site: www.sunnylandfarms.com (4)

Willumstad, Rob B., AIG Accident & Health, New York, NY. Tel: (212) 770-7000, (877) 638-4244, FAX: (212) 509-9705, Web Site: www.aig.com (15)

Wilmerding, John, National Gallery of Art Gift Shop, Washington, DC. Tel: (202) 842-6466, (800) 697-9350, FAX: (202) 842-4043, Web Site: www.nga.gov (16)

Wilmet, Michael, FMP Direct Inc, Libertyville, IL. Tel: (847) 816-1919, (800) 995-3343, FAX: (847) 816-1969, E-Mail: info@fmpdirect.com, Web Site: www.fmpdirect.com (21)

Wilmet, Rachel, FMP Direct Inc, Libertyville, IL. Tel: (847) 816-1919, (800) 995-3343, FAX: (847) 816-1969, E-Mail: info@fmpdirect.com, Web Site: www.fmpdirect.com (21)

Wilmonth, Mark C., PennWell Publishing, Tulsa, OK. Tel: (918) 835-3161, (800) 331-4463, E-Mail: headquarters@pennwell.com, Web Site: www.pennwell.com (17)

Wilmsen, Jamie, Garden Botanika Inc, Saint Louis, MO. Tel: (425) 881-9603, (800) 724-7227, FAX: (314) 633-4804, E-Mail: customercare@zidle.com, Web Site: www.zidle.com (7)

Wilschek, Art, New England Journal of Medicine, Waltham, MA. Tel: (781) 893-3800, FAX: (781) 893-7729, Web Site: www.nejm.org (17)

The HW Wilson Co, Bronx, NY. Tel: (718) 588-8400, (800) 367-6770, FAX: (800) 590-1617, E-Mail: custserv@hwwilson.com, Web Site: www. hwwilson.com (17)

Wilson, Hugh & Associate Consultants Ltd, Thornhill, ON Canada. Tel: (905) 764-5312 (22)

Wilson Jr, John F., Hygienic Fabrics & Filters Inc, Sheboygan, WI. Tel: (920) 457-7383, (800) 876-2009, FAX: (920) 457-2558, Web Site: www.hyfab.com (16)

LG Wilson & Associates, Larchmont, NY. Tel: (914) 649-5928, E-Mail: lisa@lgwilson.com, Web Site: www.lgwilson.com (22)

Michael Wilson Photographer, Cincinnati, OH. Tel: (513) 921-1749, E-Mail: michaelwilson@fuse.net, Web Site: www.michaelwilsonphotographer.com (37)

Wilson RMS, New York, NY. Tel: (212) 473-6900, Web Site: www.wilsonrms.com (35)

Wilson, Alan D., McCormick & Co Inc, Sparks, MD. Tel: (410) 771-7301, (800) 474-7742, FAX: (410) 527-6337, Web Site: www.mccormick.com (4)

Wilson, Andrew, Electronic Arts Inc, Redwood City, CA. Tel: (650) 628-1500, Web Site: www.ea.com (3)

Wilson, Angus Grover, Creative Commerce LLC, West Chester, PA. Tel: (610) 918-8800, FAX: (610) 918-1349, E-Mail: info@creativecommerce.com, Web Site: creativecommerce.com (35)

Wilson, Barbara, University of Illinois College of LAS, Office of Advancement, Urbana, IL. Tel: (217) 333-1705, E-Mail: las-studentoffice@illinois.edu, Web Site: www.las.illinois.edu (1)

Wilson, Becky S., WDS Marketing & Public Relations, Overland Park, KS. Tel: (913) 362-4541, FAX: (913) 362-7342, E-Mail: bwilson@wdspr.com, Web Site: www.wdspr.com (20)

Wilson, Bud, Photographer's Formulary Inc, Condon, MT. Tel: (406) 754-2891, (800) 922-5255, FAX: (406) 754-2896, E-Mail: formulary@blackfoot.net, Web Site: www.photoformulary.com (9)

Wilson, Cairine, Canadian Institute of Chartered Accountants, Toronto, ON Canada. Tel: (416) 977-3222, FAX: (416) 977-8585, Web Site: www.cica.ca (1)

Wilson, David, FGI Research Inc, Chapel Hill, NC. Tel: (919) 929-7759, FAX: (919) 932-8829, E-Mail: info@fgiresearch.com, Web Site: www.fgiresearch.com (35)

Wilson, David, Potpourri Group Inc, North Billerica, MA. Tel: (978) 256-4100, FAX: (978) 256-1961/0344, Web Site: www.potpourrigroup.com (6)

Wilson, David, Toyota Racing Development USA Inc, Costa Mesa, CA. Tel: (714) 444-1188, FAX: (714) 444-0339, Web Site: www.trdusa.com (34)

Wilson, David, Wilson RMS, New York, NY. Tel: (212) 473-6900, Web Site: www.wilsonrms.com (35)

Wilson, Dow R, Varian Medical Systems, Palo Alto, CA. Tel: (650) 493-4000, FAX: (650) 842-5196, Web Site: www.varian.com (9)

Wilson, George, Directory of American Business & Insurance Attorneys, New York, NY. Tel: (732) 458-7788, (800) 445-7995, FAX: (732) 458-7710, E-Mail: staff@abialaw.com, Web Site: www. abialaw.com (15)

Wilson, Gerry, Plymouth Rock Assurance, Lincroft, NJ. Tel: (732) 978-6255, Web Site: www.highpointins. com (15)

Wilson, Grant, Southeast Toyota Distributors LLC, Deerfield Beach, FL. Tel: (954) 429-2000, Web Site: www.jmfamily.com (16)

Wilson, Hugh, Wilson, Hugh & Associate Consultants Ltd, Thornhill, ON Canada. Tel: (905) 764-5312 (22)

Wilson, Jan, American Business Directories, Omaha, NE. Tel: (402) 593-4600, (800) 555-6124, FAX: (402) 596-0475, Web Site: www.infousa.com (43)

Wilson, John, Dairy Farmers of America Inc, Kansas City, MO. Tel: (816) 801-6455, (888) 332-6455, FAX: (816) 801-6456, E-Mail: webmail@dfamilk. com, Web Site: www.dfamilk.com (16)

Wilson, Jr Jackson D., Excalibur Enterprises Inc, Winston Salem, NC. Tel: (336) 744-5000, (800) 441-4193, FAX: (336) 767-8257, E-Mail: info@ excaliburmail.com, Web Site: www.excaliburmail. com (28)

Wilson, Kevin, Esrock Partners, Orland Park, IL. Tel: (708) 349-8400, (888) ESROCKS, FAX: (708) 349-8471, E-Mail: kwilson@esrock.com, Web Site: www.esrock.com (35)

Wilson, Lance, Labels West Inc, Woodinville, WA. Tel: (425) 486-8484, (800) 540-3009, FAX: (425) 486-8488, Web Site: www.labelswest.com (27)

Wilson, Lisa, LG Wilson & Associates, Larchmont, NY. Tel: (914) 649-5928, E-Mail: lisa@lgwilson. com, Web Site: www.lgwilson.com (22)

Wilson, Lynn, Photographer's Formulary Inc, Condon, MT. Tel: (406) 754-2891, (800) 922-5255, FAX: (406) 754-2896, E-Mail: formulary@blackfoot.net, Web Site: www.photoformulary.com (9)

Wilson, Marc, TownNews.com, Moline, IL. Tel: (309) 743-0800, (800) 293-9576, FAX: (309) 743-0830, E-Mail: info@townnews.com, Web Site: www. townnews365.com (32)

Wilson, Matt, SBC Advertising, Columbus, OH. Tel: (614) 255-2333, Web Site: www.sbcadvertising.com (35)

Wilson, Michael, Bart's Watersports, North Webster, IN. Tel: (574) 834-7666, (800) 348-5016, FAX: (574) 834-4246, E-Mail: info@barts.com, Web Site: www.bartswatersports.com (11)

Wilson, Michael, International Foundation of Employee Benefit Plans, Brookfield, WI. Tel: (262) 373-7758, FAX: (262) 786-8670, Web Site: www.ifebp.org (1)

Wilson, Michael, Michael Wilson Photographer, Cincinnati, OH. Tel: (513) 921-1749, E-Mail: michaelwilson@fuse.net, Web Site: www. michaelwilsonphotographer.com (37)

Wilson, Michelle D., World Wrestling Entertainment Inc, Stamford, CT. Tel: (203) 352-8600, FAX: (203) 359-5180, Web Site: www.wwe.com (16)

Wilson, Patricia, National Journal Group, Washington, DC. Tel: (202) 739-8400, (800) 613-6701, FAX: (202) 833-8069, Web Site: www.nationaljournal. com (17)

Wilson, Perry, Advanced Image Direct, Fullerton, CA. Tel: (714) 502-3900, (800) 540-3848, FAX: (714) 502-3901, Web Site: www.advancedimagedirect. com (28)

Wilson, Shirley, Gump's By Mail Inc, San Francisco, CA. Tel: (415) 982-1616, (800) 882-8055, FAX: (800) 984-9361, Web Site: www.gumpsbymail.com (6)

Wilson, Steve, McFarland & Co Inc Publishers, Jefferson, NC. Tel: (336) 246-4460, (800) 253-2187, FAX: (336) 246-5018, E-Mail: info@mcfarlandpub. com, Web Site: www.mcfarlandpub.com (17)

Wilson, Tom G., Phoenix Poke Boats Inc, McKee, KY. Tel: (606) 965-2803, E-Mail: pokeboat@pokeboat. com, Web Site: www.pokeboat.com (16)

Wilson, Tony, Micro Plastics Inc, Flippin, AR. Tel: (870) 453-2261, (800) 466-1467, FAX: (870) 453-8676, E-Mail: mpsales@microplastics.com, Web Site: www.microplastics.com (16)

Wilson, W. David, Poly One Corp, Avon Lake, OH. Tel: (440) 930-1000, (866) POLY-ONE, FAX: (440) 930-1428, Web Site: www.polyone.com (16)

Wilson, W. Weldon, Reassure America Life Insurance Co, Jacksonville, IL. Tel: (800) 637-4475, FAX: (217) 291-2398, Web Site: www.swissre.com (15)

Wilsons Leather, Brooklyn Park, MN. Tel: (763) 391-4000, (866) 305-4704, FAX: (763) 391-4906, E-Mail: customercare@wilsonsleather.com, Web Site: www.wilsonsleather.com (2)

Wilt, Kay, Johnson & Quin Inc, Niles, IL. Tel: (847) 588-4800, FAX: (847) 647-6949, E-Mail: jqinfo@j-quin.com, Web Site: www.j-quin.com (28)

Wilton Armetale, Mount Joy, PA. Tel: (717) 653-4444, (800) 553-2048, FAX: (717) 653-6573, E-Mail: cservice@armetale.com, Web Site: www.armetale. com (16)

Wilton Industries Inc, Woodridge, IL. Tel: (630) 963-1818, (800) 794-5866, FAX: (630) 963-7196, E-Mail: info@wilton.com, Web Site: www.wilton. com (16)

Wilton, Fred, Wilton Armetale, Mount Joy, PA. Tel: (717) 653-4444, (800) 553-2048, FAX: (717) 653-6573, E-Mail: cservice@armetale.com, Web Site: www.armetale.com (16)

Wilver, Peter M., Thermo Fisher Scientific Inc, Waltham, MA. Tel: (781) 622-1000, (800) 678-5599, FAX: (781) 622-1207, Web Site: www. thermofisher.com (9)

Wimbley, Ronald, Relyco, Dover, NH. Tel: (603) 742-0999, (800) 777-7359, FAX: (603) 742-9993, E-Mail: info@relyco.com, Web Site: www.relyco. com (27)

Wimmer, Dave, Wimmer's Meat Products Inc, West Point, NE. Tel: (800) 762-9865, E-Mail: consumer. affairs@landofrost.com, Web Site: www. wimmersmeats.com (4)

Wimmer, Harold P., American Lung Association, Chicago, IL. Tel: (212) 889-3370, (800) 548-8252, FAX: (212) 889-3375, E-Mail: info@alany.org, Web Site: www.lungusa.org (1)

Wimmer's Meat Products Inc, West Point, NE. Tel: (800) 762-9865, E-Mail: consumer.affairs@ landofrost.com, Web Site: www.wimmersmeats.com (4)

Win Craft Inc, Winona, MN. Tel: (507) 454-5510, (800) 533-8100, FAX: (507) 454-6403, E-Mail: inquiries@wincraftschool.com, Web Site: www. wincraftschool.com (5)

Winans, James, The Bowery Mission, New York, NY. Tel: (212) 684-2800, Web Site: www.bowery.org (1)

Winchell, Tom, SmartSource Corp, Bedford, MA. Tel: (781) 785-3375, (800) 239-0239, Web Site: www. smartsourceonline.com (32)

Winchester, Dawn, Publicis Worldwide North America, New York, NY. Tel: (212) 279-5550, E-Mail: andrew.bruce@publicisna.com, Web Site: publicisna.com (35)

Wind in the Rigging, Port Washington, WI. Tel: (262) 284-3494, (800) 236-7444, FAX: (262) 284-0067, E-Mail: info@windintherigging.com, Web Site: www.windintherigging.com (11)

Wind River Group, Akron, OH. Tel: (330) 644-7774, FAX: (330) 645-2045 (20)

Winders, Jett, Charity Dynamics, Austin, TX. Tel: (512) 241-0561, FAX: (512) 532-6037, Web Site: www.charitydynamics.com (1)

Windlass, Pradeep, Atlanta Cutlery Corp, Conyers, GA. Tel: (770) 922-3700, (800) 833-8838, FAX: (770) 760-8993, E-Mail: webmaster@atlantacutlery.com, Web Site: www.atlantacutlery.com (11)

Windlass, Sudhir, Atlanta Cutlery Corp, Conyers, GA. Tel: (770) 922-3700, (800) 833-8838, FAX: (770) 760-8993, E-Mail: webmaster@atlantacutlery.com, Web Site: www.atlantacutlery.com (11)

Windolph, John, JWT Inside, Los Angeles, CA. Tel: (310) 309-8282, (877) 665-8768, FAX: (310) 309-8283, E-Mail: conversations@jwtinside.com, Web Site: www.jwtinside.com (35)

Window Book Inc, Cambridge, MA. Tel: (617) 395-4500, (800) 524-0380, FAX: (617) 395-5900, E-Mail: sales@windowboo.com, Web Site: www.windowbook.com (22)

Windsor House, Windsor Locks, CT. Tel: (860) 627-5927, FAX: (860) 627-0252, E-Mail: ahalley@windsormarketing.com, Web Site: windsormarketing.com (20)

Windsor Vineyards, Santa Rosa, CA. Tel: (800) 289-9463, (800) 741-6070, E-Mail: webmaster@windsorvineyards.com, Web Site: www.windsorvineyards.com (16)

Windstar Cruises, Seattle, WA. Tel: (206) 292-9606, (800) 258-SAIL, FAX: (206) 340-0975, E-Mail: info@windstarcruises.com, Web Site: www.windstarcruises.com (19)

Windstream Communications Inc, Little Rock, AR. Tel: (501) 748-7000, Web Site: www.windstream.com (32)

Windt, R.J., Universal Hovercraft, Cordova, IL. Tel: (309) 654-2588, FAX: (309) 654-2588, Web Site: www.hovercraft.com (11)

Windward Group, Shelburne, VT. Tel: (802) 985-3631, Web Site: www.windwardgroup.us (20)

Windway Capital Corp, Sheboygan, WI. Tel: (920) 457-8600, FAX: (920) 457-8599, Web Site: www.windway.com (34)

Wine Enthusiast Cos, Mount Kisco, NY. Tel: (914) 345-9463, (800) 356-8466, FAX: (914) 345-3129, Web Site: www.wineenthusiast.com (4)

Wine, Randi, The Direct Marketing Specialists Inc, Chicago, IL. Tel: (312) 266-7906, FAX: (312) 266-9230, E-Mail: rwinedms@networkgci.com, Web Site: thedirectmarketingspecialists.com (35)

Winer, Cynthia, Texas Monthly, Austin, TX. Tel: (512) 320-6900, (800) 759-2000, FAX: (512) 476-9007, E-Mail: info@texasmonthly.com, Web Site: www.texasmonthly.com (17)

Winetasting.com, Napa, CA. Tel: (800) 435-2225, FAX: (707) 257-7470, Web Site: www.winetasting.com (4)

Winfield Marketing Corp, Chicago, IL. Tel: (773) 743-8784, FAX: (440) 764-4871 (31)

Winfrey, Christopher L., Charter Communications, Stamford, CT. Tel: (203) 905-7801, Web Site: www.charter.com (16)

Wingate, Paul J., BeaconFey LLC, Baltimore, MD. Tel: (410) 583-1203, FAX: (410) 583-1506, E-Mail: info@beaconfey.com, Web Site: www.beaconfey.com (35)

Winger, Amy, VML Inc, Kansas City, MO. Tel: (816) 283-0700, FAX: (816) 283-0954, E-Mail: dl-vmlcommarketing@vml.com, Web Site: www.vml.com (35)

Winger, Michael, Fitness USA Super Centers, West Bloomfield, MI. Tel: (248) 737-7200, (800) GET-FIT-1, FAX: (248) 932-3300, Web Site: www.fitnessusa.com (16)

Winites, Eleanor, National Cable & Telecommunications Association, Washington, DC. Tel: (202) 222-2300, FAX: (202) 775-3675, Web Site: www.ncta.com (40)

Winkenwerder, Jr William, Highmark Blue Cross Blue Shield, Pittsburgh, PA. Tel: (412) 544-7000, FAX: (412) 544-5350, Web Site: www.highmark.com (15)

Winkler, Wayne, WorldVu LLC, Baltimore, MD. Tel: (410) 522-4223, FAX: (410) 522-4233, E-Mail: info@worldvu.com, Web Site: www.worldvu.com (17)

Winmill & Co, New York, NY. Tel: (212) 785-0900, (800) 400-MIDAS 6432, FAX: (212) 363-1100, E-Mail: info@midasfunds.com, Web Site: www.midasfunds.com (14)

Winmill, Bassett S., Winmill & Co, New York, NY. Tel: (212) 785-0900, (800) 400-MIDAS 6432, FAX: (212) 363-1100, E-Mail: info@midasfunds.com, Web Site: www.midasfunds.com (14)

Winmill, Thomas, Winmill & Co, New York, NY. Tel: (212) 785-0900, (800) 400-MIDAS 6432, FAX: (212) 363-1100, E-Mail: info@midasfunds.com, Web Site: www.midasfunds.com (14)

Winn Devon, Richmond, BC Canada. Tel: (206) 763-9544, (800) 875-4150, FAX: (206) 762-1389, Web Site: www.winndevon.com (17)

Winn Technology Group Inc, Palm Harbor, FL. Tel: (727) 789-0006, (800) 444-5622, FAX: (727) 789-0638, E-Mail: winn@winntech.net, Web Site: www.winntech.net (29)

Winn, MD Daniel, Carefirst Blue Cross Blue Shield, Washington, DC. Tel: (202) 479-8000, FAX: (301) 470-8049, Web Site: www.carefirst.com (15)

Winnipeg Art Gallery, Winnipeg, MB Canada. Tel: (204) 786-6641, FAX: (204) 788-4998, E-Mail: inquiries@wag.mb.ca, Web Site: www.wag.ca (1)

Winslow Publishing, Toronto, ON Canada. Tel: (416) 789-4733, E-Mail: winslow@interlog.com, Web Site: www.winslowpublishing.com (17)

Winston & Winston PC, New York, NY. Tel: (212) 922-9483, FAX: (212) 532-2722, Web Site: www.winstonandwinston.com (20)

Harry Winston Inc, New York, NY. Tel: (212) 245-2000, FAX: (212) 489-0016, E-Mail: hw@harrywinston.com, Web Site: www.harry-winston.com (16)

Winston Marketing Group, Elk Grove Village, IL. Tel: (620) 584-8000, FAX: (847) 350-5701, Web Site: www.collectionset.com (8)

Winston, Arthur, Winston & Winston PC, New York, NY. Tel: (212) 922-9483, FAX: (212) 532-2722, Web Site: www.winstonandwinston.com (20)

Winter, Richard, POPAI-The Global Association for Marketing at Retail, Chicago, IL. Tel: (312) 863-2900, FAX: (312) 229-1152, Web Site: www.popai.com (40)

Winterberry Group, New York, NY. Tel: (212) 842-6000, FAX: (212) 842-6010, E-Mail: info@winterberrygroup.com, Web Site: www.winterberrygroup.com (20)

Winterfield, Mike, Traction On Demand, Burnaby, BC Canada. Tel: (604) 620-6040, Web Site: www.tractionondemand.com (35)

Wintermute, Eric, Amvac Chemical Corp, Los Angeles, CA. Tel: (323) 264-3910, (888) 462-6822, Web Site: www.amvac-chemical.com (8)

Winters, Jeff, Summit Racing Equipment, Tallmadge, OH. Tel: (330) 630-0250, (800) 230-3030, FAX: (330) 630-5571, Web Site: www.summitracing.com (12)

WinterSilks LLC, Warren, PA. Tel: (904) 645-6000, Web Site: www.wintersilks.com (2)

Winterthur Museum & Country Estate, Wilmington, DE. Tel: (302) 888-4600, (800) 448-3883, FAX: (302) 888-4730, E-Mail: tourinfo@winterthur.org, Web Site: www.winterthur.org (6)

Winthrop, Douglas A., Howard Rice Nemerovski Canady Falk & Rabkin, San Francisco, CA. Tel: (415) 464-1600, FAX: (415) 217-5910, Web Site: www.howardrice.com (14)

Wintrub, Charles, Catalyst Marketing Communications Inc, Stamford, CT. Tel: (203) 348-7541, FAX: (203) 348-5688, E-Mail: b2b@catalystmc.com, Web Site: www.catalystmc.com (35)

Wiputra, Herry, Campaign Monitor, San Francisco, CA. Tel: (888) 533-8098, E-Mail: info@campaignmonitor.com, Web Site: www.campaignmonitor.com (24)

Wire Works, Chester, PA. Tel: (610) 485-1981, (800) 292-1940, Web Site: www.wire-works.com (9)

Wired Assets Data Corp, Greenwich, CT. Tel: (203) 340-2316, Web Site: www.wiredassets.com (22)

WiredPente Inc, Markham, ON Canada. Tel: (416) 399-8458, Web Site: wiredpente.com (35)

Wirth, Gray, Rohm & Haas Co, Philadelphia, PA. Tel: (215) 592-3000, (877) 288-5881, FAX: (215) 592-3377, Web Site: www.rohmhaas.com (16)

Wirth, Jr John, Woodworker's Supply Inc, Casper, WY. Tel: (307) 237-5528, (800) 321-9841, FAX: (307) 57-5272, E-Mail: kenp@woodworker.com, Web Site: www.woodworker.com (11)

Wirth, Tom, NAGRA USA, San Francisco, CA. Tel: (415) 962-5000, FAX: (415) 962-5300, E-Mail: dtv@nagra.com, Web Site: www.nagra.com (32)

Wirthwein, Chris, 5MetaCom, Carmel, IN. Tel: (317) 580-7540, FAX: (317) 580-7550, E-Mail: mail@5metacom.com, Web Site: www.5metacom.com (35)

Wischnia, Janet, ATD American Co, Wyncote, PA. Tel: (215) 576-1380, (866) 283-9327, FAX: (215) 576-1827, E-Mail: janet@atd.com, Web Site: www.atdamerican.com (34)

Wisconsin Converting Inc, Green Bay, WI. Tel: (920) 437-6400, (800) 544-1935, FAX: (920) 436-4964, E-Mail: wci@wisconsinconverting.com, Web Site: www.wisconsinconverting.com (26)

Wisconsin Direct Marketing Association, Milwaukee, WI. Tel: (414) 760-9362, FAX: (414) 431-4195, E-Mail: info@wdma.org, Web Site: www.wdma.org (40)

Wisconsin Historical Foundation, Madison, WI. Tel: (608) 318-1044 (1)

Wisdom Marketing Group, San Antonio, TX. Tel: (210) 499-0777, (800) 952-1973, FAX: (210) 499-4217, E-Mail: sales@kruseasset.com, Web Site: www.kruseasset.com (35)

Wise, Alpharetta, GA. Tel: (770) 442-1060, (888) 815-9473, FAX: (770) 751-3599 (27)

Wise, Judy, OPIN Systems Inc, Minneapolis, MN. Tel: (952) 567-2444, (800) 888-1804, FAX: (651) 994-7828, E-Mail: judywy@opin.com, Web Site: www.opin.com (22)

Wise, Kathy, DME Holdings, Daytona Beach, FL. Tel: (877) 720-0082, E-Mail: info@dmedelivers.com, Web Site: dmedelivers.com (21)

Wise, Matt, Q Interactive, Chicago, IL. Tel: (312) 977-0390, (888) 729-6465, FAX: (312) 224-5001, E-Mail: solutions@qinteractive.com, Web Site: www.qinteractive.com (40)

Wise, R. Halsey, Intergraph Corp, Madison, AL. Tel: (256) 730-2000, (800) 345-4856, FAX: (256) 730-2048, Web Site: www.intergraph.com (16)

Wise, Terri, Coin World, Sidney, OH. Tel: (937) 498-0800, (800) 253-4555, FAX: (937) 498-0812, E-Mail: cwcustomerservice@coinworld.com, Web Site: www.coinworld.com (17)

Wise, Tomas, Music Sales Corp, New York, NY. Tel: (212) 254-2100, FAX: (212) 254-2013, E-Mail: info@musicsales.com, Web Site: www.musicsales.com (17)

Wiseman, Bob, Burkholder Flint Associates, Columbus, OH. Tel: (614) 228-2425, FAX: (614) 228-0631, E-Mail: easterday@burkholderflint.com, Web Site: www.burkholderflint.com (35)

Wiseman, Irwin, Mercury International Trading, North Attleboro, MA. Tel: (508) 699-9000, FAX: (508) 699-9088, Web Site: www.mercuryfootwear.com (2)

Wisemen, Howard, Mercury International Trading, North Attleboro, MA. Tel: (508) 699-9000, FAX: (508) 699-9088, Web Site: www.mercuryfootwear.com (2)

Wisley, Carol, Harrington's of Vermont Inc, Richmond, VT. Tel: (802) 434-4444, E-Mail: info@harringtonham.com, Web Site: www.harringtonham.com (4)

Wispelwey, June C., American Institute of Chemical Engineers, New York, NY. Tel: (203) 702-7660, (800) 242-4363, FAX: (203) 775-5177, E-Mail: xpress@aiche.org, Web Site: www.aiche.org (1)

Wit Postal Logistics LLC, Chicago, IL. Tel: (815) 215-5100, Web Site: www.witpostal.com (28)

Withers, Claudia, NAACP, Baltimore, MD. Tel: (410) 580-5777, Web Site: www.naacp.org (1)

Witmire, Jeff, Creditcards.com, Austin, TX. Tel: (512) 996-8663, Web Site: www.creditcards.com (20)

Witsell, Rick, Alliant, Brewster, NY. Tel: (845) 276-2600, FAX: (845) 276-2605, Web Site: www.alliantdata.com (22)

Witte, Bill, Fujitsu Transaction Solutions Inc, Richardson, TX. Tel: (972) 963-2300, (800) 340-4425, Web Site: www.fujitsu.com (16)

Witte, Carl, Walter E Heller College of Business Administration, Chicago, IL. Tel: (312) 281-3293, FAX: (312) 281-3290, Web Site: www.roosevelt.edu (41)

Wittenberg, Mary, New York Road Runners, New York, NY. Tel: (855) 5MY-NYRR, E-Mail: mynyrr@nyrr.org, Web Site: www.nyrr.org (13)

Wittenmeyer, Chuck, Valid USA Inc, Lisle, IL. Tel: (630) 852-8200, (855) 825-4387, E-Mail: info@validusa.com, Web Site: www.validusa.com (22)

Witter, Matt, HackerAgency Inc, Seattle, WA. Tel: (206) 805-1500, Web Site: www.hal2l.com (35)

Witty, David, Lazydays RV Center, Seffner, FL. Tel: (813) 246-4333, FAX: (813) 246-4408, Web Site: www.lazydays.com (12)

Witty, Jonathan, Media Two, Baltimore, MD. Tel: (410) 828-0120, FAX: (410) 825-1002, Web Site: www.mediatwo.com (17)

Witty, Sir Andrew, GlaxoSmithKline USA, Philadelphia, PA. Tel: (888) 825-5249, Web Site: us.gsk.com (16)

Wixom, Kam, Western River Expeditions, Salt Lake City, UT. Tel: (801) 942-6669, (866) 904-1160, FAX: (801) 942-8514, Web Site: www.westernriver.com (19)

Wnorowski, Doug, Surplus Record, Chicago, IL. Tel: (312) 372-9077, (800) 622-5449, FAX: (312) 372-6537, E-Mail: surplus@surplusrecord.com, Web Site: www.surplusrecord.com (17)

Woerner, Bill, Solarcom, Norcross, GA. Tel: (770) 449-6116, (888) SUN-DATA, FAX: (770) 448-7726, Web Site: www.solarcom.net (16)

Woertz, Patricia, WILD Flavors Inc, Erlanger, KY. Tel: (859) 342-3600, FAX: (859) 342-3610, Web Site: www.wildflavors.com (4)

Wogoman, Jeff, Patagonia Mail Order Inc, Reno, NV. Tel: (775) 747-1992, (800) 638-6464, FAX: (775) 747-6159, Web Site: www.patagonia.com (2)

Wohlfahrt, Jeff, Advanced Concepts Inc, Milwaukee, WI. Tel: (414) 362-9640, FAX: (414) 362-9646, E-Mail: info@advanced-concepts.com, Web Site: www.advanced-concepts.com (22)

Wojcik, Paul, The Bureau of National Affairs, Inc, Arlington, VA. Tel: (703) 341-3000, (800) 372-1033, FAX: (703) 341-1688, Web Site: www.bna.com (17)

Wojtkiewicz, George H., GHW Associates, Lake Suzy, FL. Tel: (941) 625-4293, E-Mail: info@ghw-associates.com, Web Site: www.ghw-associates.com (35)

Wold, Mary Kate, Church Pension Fund, New York, NY. Tel: (866) 802-6333, (800) 223-6602, Web Site: www.cpg.org (1)

Wolek, Anne, Wunderman DC, Washington, DC. Tel: (202) 625-2111, FAX: (202) 424-7900, E-Mail: anne.wolek@wundermandc.com, Web Site: wundermandc.com (35)

Wolf Blumberg Krody Inc, Cincinnati, OH. Tel: (513) 784-0066, FAX: (513) 784-0986, E-Mail: sklein@wbk.com, Web Site: www.wbk.com (35)

Wolf Envelope Co, Birmingham, MI. Tel: (248) 687-2745, (800) 258-5700, FAX: (248) 687-2751, Web Site: www.wolfenvelope.com (26)

Marty Wolf Game Co, Las Vegas, NV. Tel: (702) 385-2963, FAX: (702) 385-6963, E-Mail: info@gamblersjunkyard.com, Web Site: www.gamblersjunkyard.com (33)

Wolf, Alexander L., Association for Computing Machinery, New York, NY. Tel: (212) 626-0500, (800) 342-6626, FAX: (212) 944-1318, Web Site: www.acm.org (1)

Wolf, Allen E., ORC ProTel LLC, Lansing, IL. Tel: (708) 418-7413, FAX: (708) 418-7457, Web Site: www.orcprotel.com (29)

Wolf, Carol, Steck-Vaughn, Austin, TX. Tel: (512) 343-8227, (800) 531-5015, (877) 866-2586, FAX: (512) 795-3617, (877) 265-2730, E-Mail: info@steck-vaughn.com, Web Site: www.steck-vaughn.com (17)

Wolf, Jack, Spinneybeck Enterprises, Getzville, NY. Tel: (716) 446-2380, (800) 482-7777, FAX: (716) 446-2396, E-Mail: sales@spinneybeck.com, Web Site: www.spinneybeck.com (16)

Wolf, Marty, Marty Wolf Game Co, Las Vegas, NV. Tel: (702) 385-2963, FAX: (702) 385-6963, E-Mail: info@gamblersjunkyard.com, Web Site: www.gamblersjunkyard.com (33)

Wolf, Ruth R., ORC ProTel LLC, Lansing, IL. Tel: (708) 418-7413, FAX: (708) 418-7457, Web Site: www.orcprotel.com (29)

Brian Wolfe, New York, NY. Tel: (516) 840-3748 (20)

Wolfe Pereira, Steven, Neustar Inc, Sterling, VA. Tel: (571) 434-5400, (877) 245-5277, E-Mail: billingsupport@neustar.biz, Web Site: www.neustar.biz (29)

Wolfe Publishing Co Inc, Prescott, AZ. Tel: (928) 445-7810, (800) 899-7810, FAX: (928) 778-5124, E-Mail: wolfepub@riflemag.com, Web Site: www.riflemagazine.com (17)

Wolfe, Greg, Circulation Specialists Inc, Shelton, CT. Tel: (888) 315-2472, FAX: (888) 315-2507 (20)

Wolfe, Howard A., Crawford Advertising Associates Ltd, New City, NY. Tel: (914) 946-2444, FAX: (914) 946-9236, E-Mail: crawads@aol.com, Web Site: www.crawfordadv.com (35)

Wolfe, Jami, Colarelli Meyer & Associates Inc, Saint Louis, MO. Tel: (314) 721-1860, (800) 459-4548, FAX: (314) 721-1992, E-Mail: cmaconsult@cmaconsult.com, Web Site: www.cmaconsult.com (20)

Wolfe, John F., The Columbus Dispatch, Columbus, OH. Tel: (614) 461-5000, FAX: (614) 461-7551, E-Mail: csmith@the.dispatch.com, Web Site: www.dispatch.com (1)

Wolfe, Peggy, Micro Center, Hilliard, OH. Tel: (614) 850-3675, (800) 634-3478, FAX: (614) 777-2620, E-Mail: csrs@microcenterorder.com, Web Site: www.microcenter.com (3)

Wolfe, Scott, SBC Advertising, Columbus, OH. Tel: (614) 255-2333, Web Site: www.sbcadvertising.com (35)

Wolfe, Thomas F., Coast to Coast Inc, Englewood, CO. Tel: (303) 728-2267, Web Site: www.coastresorts.com (1)

Wolfe, Thomas F., Woodall Publishing Co LP, Ventura, CA. Tel: (805) 667-4100, (800) 323-9076, FAX: (805) 667-4468, Web Site: www.woodalls.com (17)

Wolfenson, Stewart, Ansafone Communications, Santa Ana, CA. Tel: (714) 560-1000, FAX: (714) 560-1035, Web Site: www.ansafone.com (29)

Wolfer, R., Dreis & Krump Manufacturing Co, Peotone, IL. Tel: (708) 258-1200, FAX: (708) 258-9682, E-Mail: chicago@dreis-krump.com, Web Site: www.dreis-krump.com (16)

Wolff/SMG, Macedon, NY. Tel: (315) 986-1155, FAX: (315) 986-1161, E-Mail: rdelmonte@wolff-smg.com, Web Site: www.wolff-smg.com (28)

Wolff, Brian, Edison Electric Institute, Washington, DC. Tel: (202) 508-5000, FAX: (202) 508-5096, Web Site: www.eei.org (1)

Wolfish, Barry, Land O' Lakes Inc, Arden Hills, MN. Tel: (651) 481-2222, (800) 328-9680, FAX: (651) 481-2000, Web Site: www.landolakesinc.com (16)

Wolfson, Jeff, The Fort Group, Ridgefield Park, NJ. Tel: (201) 445-0202, FAX: (201) 445-0626, E-Mail: info@fortgroupinc.com, Web Site: www.fortgroupinc.com (35)

Wolk, Beryl, IMC - Multi Media Marketing, Jenkintown, PA. Tel: (215) 887-5700 X107, FAX: (215) 887-7076, E-Mail: berylwolk@aol.com, Web Site: berylsworld.com (31)

Wolk, David, Goodway Group, Jenkintown, PA. Tel: (626) 355-7800, E-Mail: info@goodwaygroup.com, Web Site: goodwaygroup.com (35)

Wolk, Howard L., The Cross Country Group LLC, Medford, MA. Tel: (781) 396-3700, FAX: (781) 391-7504, E-Mail: info@crosscountrygroup.com, Web Site: www.ccgroup.com (13)

Wolk, Jeffrey, The Cross Country Group LLC, Medford, MA. Tel: (781) 396-3700, FAX: (781) 391-7504, E-Mail: info@crosscountrygroup.com, Web Site: www.ccgroup.com (13)

Wolk, Sidney D., The Cross Country Group LLC, Medford, MA. Tel: (781) 396-3700, FAX: (781) 391-7504, E-Mail: info@crosscountrygroup.com, Web Site: www.ccgroup.com (13)

Woll, Alan M., Tackle Craft, Ellsworth, WI. Tel: (715) 273-5300, FAX: (715) 273-5320, E-Mail: customer service@tackle-craft.com (11)

Woll, Linda J., Tackle Craft, Ellsworth, WI. Tel: (715) 273-5300, FAX: (715) 273-5320, E-Mail: customer service@tackle-craft.com (11)

Wolman, Jonathan, Detroit Newspapers, Detroit, MI. Tel: (313) 222-2300, FAX: (313) 496-5400, E-Mail: newsroom@detnews.com, Web Site: www.freep. com (18)

Wolter, Joel, Media Directions Creative Group, Lincolnshire, IL. Tel: (847) 948-0099, E-Mail: info@ mdcreativegroup.com, Web Site: www. mdcreativegroup.com (35)

Wolters Kluwer Financial Services, Minneapolis, MN. Tel: (612) 656-7700, (800) 552-9408, Web Site: www.wolterskluwerfs.com (14)

Woltz, William, WCPE-FM, Wake Forest, NC. Tel: (800) 556-5178, FAX: (919) 556-9273, Web Site: theclassicalstation.org (32)

Wolverine Solutions Group, Detroit, MI. Tel: (313) 873-6800, FAX: (313) 873-8730, Web Site: www. wolverinemail.com (28)

Woman's Missionary Union, Birmingham, AL. Tel: (205) 991-8100, FAX: (205) 991-4990, E-Mail: email@wmu.org, Web Site: www.wmu.org (17)

Womanship, Annapolis, MD. Tel: (410) 267-6661, FAX: (410) 263-2036, E-Mail: sail@womanship. com, Web Site: www.womanship.com (16)

Women for Women International, Washington, DC. Tel: (202) 737-7705, Web Site: www. womenforwomen.org (40)

Women in Direct Marketing International, New York, NY. Tel: (516) 746-6700, FAX: (516) 294-8141, Web Site: www.wdmi.org (40)

Woman's Day Special Interest Publications, New York, NY. Tel: (212) 767-6000, FAX: (212) 767-5612, Web Site: www.womensday.com (17)

Women's Sports Foundation, East Meadow, NY. Tel: (516) 542-4700, (800) 227-3988, FAX: (516) 542-0095, Web Site: www.womenssportsfoundation.org (1)

Wonderful Writer LLC, Minneapolis, MN. Tel: (763) 557-7116, (888) 557-7116, FAX: (763) 551-4831, E-Mail: colleen@wonderfulwriter.com, Web Site: www.wonderfulwriter.com (39)

Wong, Frederick K., Beauty Naturally, Burlingame, CA. Tel: (650) 596-5742, (800) 432-4323, FAX: (650) 596-5742, E-Mail: sales@beautynaturally. com, Web Site: www.beautynaturally.com (7)

Wong, Janet, Beauty Naturally, Burlingame, CA. Tel: (650) 596-5742, (800) 432-4323, FAX: (650) 596-5742, E-Mail: sales@beautynaturally.com, Web Site: www.beautynaturally.com (7)

Wong, Leader, Bell & Howell Ltd, North York, ON Canada. Tel: (416) 746-2200, FAX: (416) 228-2439, Web Site: www.bellhowell.com (9)

Wong, Leslie E., San Francisco State University, San Francisco, CA. Tel: (415) 338-1111, FAX: (415) 338-0501, Web Site: www.sfsu.edu (41)

Wood & Associates Direct Marketing Services Ltd, Pickering, ON Canada. Tel: (416) 293-2511, FAX: (416) 293-2594, E-Mail: clientservices@wood-and-associates.com, Web Site: www.wood-and-associates.com (28)

Wood Carvers Supply Inc, Englewood, FL. Tel: (941) 698-0123, (800) 284-6229, FAX: (941) 698-0329, E-Mail: info@woodcarverssupply.com, Web Site: www.woodcarverssupply.com (9)

Wood, Andy L., Photoworks, Cleveland, OH. Tel: (206) 281-1390, (800) PHOTOWORKS, FAX: (206) 284-5357, E-Mail: info@photoworks.com, Web Site: www.photoworks.com (16)

Wood, Annabelle, Wood & Associates Direct Marketing Services Ltd, Pickering, ON Canada. Tel: (416) 293-2511, FAX: (416) 293-2594, E-Mail: clientservices@wood-and-associates.com, Web Site: www.wood-and-associates.com (28)

Wood, Bill, Access International, Cambridge, MA. Tel: (617) 218-5000, (877) 433-9097, FAX: (617) 494-8404, E-Mail: info@accessint.com, Web Site: www. accessint.com (22)

Wood, Bob, Specialized Marketing Inc, Brewster, NY. Tel: (845) 278-6100, FAX: (845) 278-6150, Web Site: www.specialized-mktg.com (31)

Wood, Chris, Trout Unlimited, Arlington, VA. Tel: (703) 522-0200, (800) 834-2419, FAX: (703) 284-9400, E-Mail: trout@tu.org, Web Site: www.tu.org (1)

Wood, Craig, Clarity Group LLC, Chapel Hill, NC. Tel: (919) 932-6036, Web Site: www.claritygroupinc. com (20)

Wood, David, Network Telephone Services Inc, Woodland Hills, CA. Tel: (818) 992-4300, (800) 727-6874, FAX: (818) 992-8415, Web Site: www.nts.net (16)

Wood, Diane, John Wiley & Sons Canada Ltd, Etobicoke, ON Canada. Tel: (416) 236-4433, FAX: (416) 236-4448, Web Site: www.wiley.com (17)

Wood, Donald W., Arrowhead Mountain Spring Water, Wilkes Barre, PA. Tel: (800) 873-7775, Web Site: www.arrowheadwater.com (16)

Wood, Doris, Multi-Level Marketing International Association (MLMIA), Irvine, CA. Tel: (949) 257-0931, FAX: (949) 281-2114, E-Mail: info@mlmia. com, Web Site: www.mlmia.com (1)

Wood, Douglas, Reed Smith Hall Dickler Advertising & Law Marketing Group, New York, NY. Tel: (212) 549-0377, FAX: (212) 521-5450, Web Site: www. reedsmith.com (20)

Wood, Ed, Cygnus Business Media, Fort Atkinson, WI. Tel: (203) 227-4037, (800) 547-7377, FAX: (203) 227-4245, Web Site: www.cygnus.com (17)

Wood, Greg, Missouri Life Inc, Boonville, MO. Tel: (660) 882-9898, (800) 492-2593, FAX: (660) 882-9899, E-Mail: info@missourilife.com, Web Site: www.missourilife.com (17)

Wood, III David, Association of Bridal Consultants, New Milford, CT. Tel: (860) 355-0464, FAX: (860) 354-1404, E-Mail: office@bridalassn.com, Web Site: www.bridalassn.com (1)

Wood, Joseph, DB Alex Brown Inc, Baltimore, MD. Tel: (410) 727-1700, (800) 638-2956, Web Site: www.dbalexbrown.com (14)

Wood, Joy, PacNet Services Ltd, Vancouver, BC Canada. Tel: (604) 689-0399, FAX: (604) 689-0313, E-Mail: info@pacnetservices.com, Web Site: www. pacnetservices.com (14)

Wood, Ken, List Connection Inc, Simpsonville, SC. Tel: (864) 962-0761, FAX: (864) 962-0769, E-Mail: leads@listconnection.net, Web Site: www. listconnection.net (24)

Wood, Kevin, Quill Corp, Lincolnshire, IL. Tel: (847) 876-3535, (800) 789-1331, Web Site: www.quill. com (16)

Wood, Phillip R., Ten Speed Press, Emeryville, CA. Tel: (510) 559-1600, (800) 841-BOOK, FAX: (510) 559-1629, E-Mail: order@tenspeed.com, Web Site: www.tenspeed.com (17)

Wood, Scott, Shape LLC, Addison, IL. Tel: (630) 620-8394, (800) 367-5811, FAX: (630) 620-0784, E-Mail: sales@shapellc.com, Web Site: www. shapellc.com (3)

Wood, Wayne, Farm Bureau Insurance, Lansing, MI. Tel: (517) 323-7000, (800) 292-2680, FAX: (517) 327-0208, Web Site: www.farmbureauinsurance-mi. com (15)

Woodall Publishing Co LP, Ventura, CA. Tel: (805) 667-4100, (800) 323-9076, FAX: (805) 667-4468, Web Site: www.woodalls.com (17)

Woodbury, Ward, UMI Publications Inc, Charlotte, NC. Tel: (800) 747-9287, FAX: (704) 374-0729, E-Mail: info@umipub.com, Web Site: www.umipub.com (17)

Woodcock, Chris, Simplex Grinnell, Westminster, MA. Tel: (978) 731-2500, (800) SIMPLEX, FAX: (978) 731-7856, Web Site: www.simplexgrinnel.com (16)

Woodcraft Supply Corp LLC, Parkersburg, WV. Tel: (304) 422-5412, (800) 344-3348, FAX: (304) 422-5417, Web Site: www.woodcraft.com (9)

Woodcrafters Lumber Sales Inc, Portland, OR. Tel: (503) 231-0226, (800) 777-3709, FAX: (503) 232-0511, E-Mail: spen@worldnet.att.net, Web Site: www.woodcrafters.us (9)

Wooden Computer Services, Saint Louis, MO. Tel: (314) 576-1124 (22)

Wooden, Don, A&M Direct Mail Service Inc, San Dimas, CA. Tel: (909) 599-3905, (909) 579-0111, (800) 735-3905, FAX: (909) 599-3516, E-Mail: mail@amdirectmail.com (28)

Wooden, Roger, Wooden Computer Services, Saint Louis, MO. Tel: (314) 576-1124 (22)

Woodfolk, Michael, Darden School Foundation Executive Foundation, Charlottesville, VA. Tel: (434) 924-3900, Web Site: www.darden.virginia.edu/execed (1)

Woodford, Charles H., Princeton Book Co Publishers, Hightstown, NJ. Tel: (609) 426-0602, (800) 220-7149, FAX: (609) 426-1344, E-Mail: pbc@ dancehorizons.com, Web Site: www.dancehorizons. com (17)

Woodhead, Robin G., Sotheby's, New York, NY. Tel: (212) 606-7000, FAX: (212) 606-7107, Web Site: www.sothebys.com (6)

Woodis, Ginny, The Boston Consulting Group, New York, NY. Tel: (212) 446-2800 (20)

The Woodlands Marketing Agency LLC, The Woodlands, TX. Tel: (281) 318-1601, Web Site: thewoodlandsagency.com (35)

Woodrooffe, Allyson, Northern Response International, Toronto, ON Canada. Tel: (905) 737-6698, (866) 584-1694, FAX: (905) 737-0099, E-Mail: general@ nresponse.com, Web Site: northernresponse.com (8)

Woodrow, Mark, Hubert Co, Harrison, OH. Tel: (513) 367-8767, (800) 543-7374, FAX: (513) 367-8823, Web Site: www.hubert.com (16)

Sylvia Woods Harp Center, Montrose, CA. Tel: (800) 272-4277, FAX: (818) 247-5212, E-Mail: info@ harpcenter.com, Web Site: www.harpcenter.com (11)

Woods, Dana, American Association of Critical-Care Nurses, Aliso Viejo, CA. Tel: (949) 362-2000, (800) 809-CARE, FAX: (949) 362-2020, E-Mail: info@ aacn.com, Web Site: www.aacn.org (1)

Woods, Kimberly Winters, Nordskog Publishing Co, Ventura, CA. Tel: (805) 642-2070, FAX: (805) 642-1862, Web Site: www.nordskogpublishing.com (17)

Woods, Raylene, Marketing General Inc, Alexandria, VA. Tel: (703) 739-1000, (800) 644-6646, FAX: (703) 549-6057, E-Mail: info@marketinggeneral. com, Web Site: www.marketinggeneral.com (35)

Woods, Steven K., Eloqua Inc, Vienna, VA. Tel: (703) 584-2750, Web Site: www.eloqua.com (22)

Woods, Sylvia, Sylvia Woods Harp Center, Montrose, CA. Tel: (800) 272-4277, FAX: (818) 247-5212, E-Mail: info@harpcenter.com, Web Site: www. harpcenter.com (11)

Woodson, Mark W., American Society of Civil Engineers, Reston, VA. Tel: (703) 295-6000, (800) 548-2723, FAX: (703) 295-6343, Web Site: www.asce.org (1)

Woodward, Craig, Kappler Protective Apparel & Fabrics, Guntersville, AL. Tel: (256) 505-4005, (800) 600-4019, FAX: (256) 505-4151, E-Mail: customerservice@kappler.com, Web Site: www.kappler.com (2)

Woodward, Jr. James H., P & H Mining Equipment, Milwaukee, WI. Tel: (414) 671-4400, FAX: (414) 671-7618, Web Site: www.phmining.com (16)

Woodward, Judith, Winn Technology Group Inc, Palm Harbor, FL. Tel: (727) 789-0006, (800) 444-5622, FAX: (727) 789-0638, E-Mail: winn@winntech.net, Web Site: www.winntech.net (29)

Woodward, Kelly, Huntsinger & Jeffer, Richmond, VA. Tel: (804) 266-2499, FAX: (804) 266-8563, E-Mail: info@huntsinger-jeffer.com, Web Site: www. huntsinger-jeffer.com (21)

Woodward, Ken, Tidbits Media, Montgomery, AL. Tel: (334) 290-0225, (800) 523-3096, FAX: (334) 386-0302, E-Mail: editors@tidbitsweekly.com, Web Site: www.tidbitsweekly.com (17)

Woodward, Ted, GG Direct, Portland, ME. Tel: (207) 772-0414, FAX: (207) 871-1444, E-Mail: data@ggdirect.com, Web Site: www.ggdirect.com (21)

Woodwind & Brasswind Inc, Westlake Village, CA. Tel: (574) 251-3500, (800) 348-5003, FAX: (800) 266-5962, Web Site: www.wwbw.com (5)

Woodworker's Supply Inc, Casper, WY. Tel: (307) 237-5528, (800) 321-9841, FAX: (307) 57-5272, E-Mail: kenp@woodworker.com, Web Site: www. woodworker.com (11)

Woodworth, Lindsay, 2ergo, Arlington, VA. Tel: (703) 879-3400, Web Site: www.2ergo.com (30)

Woodworth, Stephen, Masterworks, Poulsbo, WA. Tel: (360) 394-4300, Web Site: www.masterworks.com (1)

Fred Woolf List Co Inc, Somers, NY. Tel: (914) 694-4466, (800) 431-1557, FAX: (914) 694-1710, E-Mail: info@woolflist.com, Web Site: www. woolflist.com (23)

Woolf, Fred, Fred Woolf List Co Inc, Somers, NY. Tel: (914) 694-4466, (800) 431-1557, FAX: (914) 694-1710, E-Mail: info@woolflist.com, Web Site: www. woolflist.com (23)

Woolf, Sheila, Fred Woolf List Co Inc, Somers, NY. Tel: (914) 694-4466, (800) 431-1557, FAX: (914) 694-1710, E-Mail: info@woolflist.com, Web Site: www.woolflist.com (23)

Woolley, Ryan, Response Mine Interactive Inc, Atlanta, GA. Tel: (404) 233-0370, Web Site: www. responsemine.com (35)

Woolrich Inc, Woolrich, PA. Tel: (570) 769-6464, (800) 966-5372, Web Site: www.woolrich.com (2)

Woolson, Tyler L., Georgia-Pacific Corp LLC, Atlanta, GA. Tel: (404) 652-4000, FAX: (404) 230-7052, Web Site: www.gp.com (25)

Worcester Envelope, Auburn, MA. Tel: (508) 832-5394, (800) 343-1398, FAX: (508) 832-3796, E-Mail: sales@worcesterenvelope.com, Web Site: www. worcester-envelope.com (26)

WordCom Inc, Ellington, CT. Tel: (860) 875-7373, (800) 822-0622, FAX: (860) 872-2713, E-Mail: sales@wordcom-inc.com, Web Site: www. wordcom-inc.com (21)

Worden, Maia, Atlantic List Company Inc, Arlington, VA. Tel: (703) 528-7482, FAX: (703) 528-7492, E-Mail: ingridloukota@atlanticlist.com, Web Site: www.atlanticlist.com (23)

Wordright Enterprises Inc, Buffalo Grove, IL. Tel: (847) 215-5190, Web Site: www.globalsources.com (17)

The Wordstation, Avon By The Sea, NJ. Tel: (732) 774-4831, FAX: (732) 869-1822, E-Mail: pattyshannone@optonline.net (39)

Worick, Dick, The MSR Group, Omaha, NE. Tel: (402) 392-0755, (800) 737-0755, FAX: (402) 392-1068, E-Mail: info@theMSRgroup.com, Web Site: www. theMSRgroup.com (30)

Work, Bill, Cytec Industries Inc, Olean, NY. Tel: (716) 372-9650, FAX: (716) 372-1594, Web Site: www. conap.com (16)

Workforce Advantage USA, Elizabeth, NJ. Tel: (908) 355-2299, FAX: (908) 352-2931, Web Site: www. workforceadvantageusa.com (13)

Working Assets, San Francisco, CA. Tel: (800) 668-9253, FAX: (415) 371-1046, Web Site: www. workingassets.com (16)

Working Mother, New York, NY. Tel: (212) 221-9595, FAX: (212) 219-7448, Web Site: www. workingmother.com (31)

Workman, Eric, Polynesian Cultural Center, Honolulu, HI. Tel: (808) 293-3333, (800) 367-7060, FAX: (888) 722-7339, E-Mail: internetrez@polynesia. com, Web Site: www.polynesia.com (16)

The World Bank, Washington, DC. Tel: (202) 473-1000, FAX: (202) 477-6391, Web Site: www. worldbank.org (17)

World Book Inc, Chicago, IL. Tel: (312) 729-5800, (800) 255-1750, FAX: (312) 729-5600, Web Site: www.worldbook.com (17)

World Future Society, Chicago, IL. Tel: (301) 656-8274, (800) 989-8274, FAX: (301) 951-0394, E-Mail: info@wfs.org, Web Site: www.wfs.org (1)

World Innovators Inc, Roxbury, CT. Tel: (860) 210-8088, FAX: (860) 210-7829, E-Mail: inquiry@ worldinnovators.com, Web Site: www. worldinnovators.com (24)

World Kitchen Inc, Corning, NY. Tel: (607) 377-8000, (800) 999-3436, FAX: (607) 377-8946, Web Site: www.worldkitchen.com (16)

World Press Review, New York, NY. Tel: (212) 982-8880, Web Site: www.worldpressreview.com (18)

World Publications Inc, Winter Park, FL. Tel: (407) 628-4802, FAX: (407) 628-7061, Web Site: www. worldpub.com (17)

World Vision Canada, Mississauga, ON Canada. Tel: (905) 565-6100, (866) 595-5550, FAX: (866) 219-8620, Web Site: www.worldvision.ca (1)

World Vision Inc, Federal Way. WA. Tel: (253) 815-1000, (888) 511-6548, FAX: (253) 815-3140, E-Mail: info@worldvision.org, Web Site: www. worldvision.org (1)

World Wildlife Fund, Washington, DC. Tel: (202) 293-4800, Web Site: www.worldwildlife.org (1)

World Wrestling Entertainment Inc, Stamford, CT. Tel: (203) 352-8600, FAX: (203) 359-5180, Web Site: www.wwe.com (16)

Worldata, Boca Raton, FL. Tel: (561) 393-8200, (800) 331-8102, FAX: (561) 368-8345, E-Mail: hello@ worldata.com, Web Site: www.worldata.com (23)

WorldVu LLC, Baltimore, MD. Tel: (410) 522-4223, FAX: (410) 522-4233, E-Mail: info@worldvu.com, Web Site: www.worldvu.com (17)

WorleyParsons, Reading, PA. Tel: (610) 855-2000, FAX: (610) 885-2001, Web Site: www. worleyparsons.com (16)

Worman, Lori, Mid America Designs Inc, Effingham, IL. Tel: (217) 540-4200, (800) 350-4543, FAX: (217) 540-4800, E-Mail: mail@mamotorworks.com, Web Site: www.mamotorworks.com (12)

Worman, Lori, Mid America Motorworks, Effingham, IL. Tel: (217) 347-5591, (800) 500-1500, FAX: (217) 347-2952, E-Mail: mail@mamotorworks.com, Web Site: www.mamotorworks.com (12)

Woronko, Zig, L-Com Inc, North Andover, MA. Tel: (978) 682-6936, FAX: (978) 689-9484, Web Site: www.L-com.com (22)

Worra, Jonathan, Mergent Inc, Fort Mill, SC. Tel: (800) 342-5647, Web Site: www.mergent.com (14)

Worrell, Greg, Scholastic Inc, New York, NY. Tel: (212) 343-6100, (800) SCHOLASTIC, FAX: (212) 343-6484, Web Site: www.scholastic.com (17)

Worrell, Lynnette, Sir Speedy Printing and Marketing Services, Tacoma, WA. Tel: (253) 473-0765), FAX: (253) 475-3012, Web Site: www.sirspeedy0905.com (27)

Worth, Ron, The Premium Connection, Las Vegas, NV. Tel: (800) 683-0933, Web Site: www. premiumconnection.net (33)

Woychick, Jay F., Transcat, Rochester, NY. Tel: (585) 352-9460, (800) 800-5001, FAX: (585) 352-1486, Web Site: www.transcat.com (16)

Woytcke, Linda, Informal Education Products, Milwaukie, OR. Tel: (503) 794-7045, (888) 444-5500, FAX: (503) 794-7111, E-Mail: sales@museumtour. com, Web Site: www.museumtour.com (11)

Wpromote Inc, El Segundo, CA. Tel: (310) 421-4844, Web Site: www.wpromote.com (30)

Wrenn, A.R., International Direct Media Co & Information Publishing Co, San Francisco, CA. Tel: (415) 661-4730, E-Mail: infopubsf@aol.com, Web Site: www.bookwormproductions.com (17)

Wright State University, Dayton, OH. Tel: (937) 775-3047, FAX: (513) 775-3952, E-Mail: teresa. stelmat@wright.edu, Web Site: www.wright.edu/business/acad/marketing (41)

Wright, David, Dow Theory Forecasts, Hammond, IN. Tel: (219) 931-6480, (800) 233-5922, FAX: (219) 931-6487, E-Mail: custserv@horizonpublishing. com, Web Site: www.dowtheory.com (17)

Wright, Doug, MSP Inc, Freedom, PA. Tel: (724) 774-3244, (800) 876-3211, FAX: (724) 774-6996, E-Mail: info@msp-pgh.com, Web Site: www.msp-pgh.com (21)

Wright, Emily, Pace Communications Inc, Greensboro, NC. Tel: (336) 378-6065, FAX: (336) 275-2864, Web Site: www.pacecommunications.com (17)

Wright, Gary A, GA Wright Sales Inc, Denver, CO. Tel: (303) 333-4453, FAX: (303) 393-5320, E-Mail: info@gawright.com, Web Site: www.gawrightsales. com (35)

Wright, Kasie, Mid West Floor Co Inc, Saint Louis, MO. Tel: (314) 647-6060, FAX: (314) 647-9189, E-Mail: sales@mid-westfloor.com, Web Site: www. mid-westfloor.com (16)

Wright, Lauren, Fred Pryor Seminars, Mission, KS. Tel: (913) 967-8518, (800) 780-8476, FAX: (913) 967-8849, E-Mail: customerservice@pryor.com, Web Site: www.pryor.com (16)

Yardis, Alan, Ligonier Ministries, Sanford, FL. Tel: (407) 333-4244, (800) 435-4343, FAX: (407) 333-4377, Web Site: www.ligonier.org (5)

Yares, Jim, CrownPeak Technology Inc, Los Angeles, CA. Tel: (310) 841-5920, FAX: (310) 841-5913, Web Site: www.crownpeak.com (22)

Yarnold, David, National Audubon Society, New York, NY. Tel: (212) 979-3000, FAX: (212) 979-3188, Web Site: www.audubon.org (17)

Yarrington, John, Response Magazine, Santa Ana, CA. Tel: (714) 513-8624, (800) 371-6897, FAX: (714) 338-6710, Web Site: www.responsemagazine.com (43)

Yasuoka, Shigeto, Sunstar, Chicago, IL. Tel: (773) 777-4000, FAX: (773) 777-1417, E-Mail: dominico@sunstar.com, Web Site: www.sunstar.com (16)

Yates Advertising, San Francisco, CA. Tel: (415) 887-9545, FAX: (415) 887-9549 (35)

Yates, Susan, Yates Advertising, San Francisco, CA. Tel: (415) 887-9545, FAX: (415) 887-9549 (35)

Yaverski, Aaron, Aspen Publishers Inc, New York, NY. Tel: (212) 771-0600, (800) 638-8437, Web Site: www.aspenpublishers.com (17)

Yeager, Douglas, Alcom, Harleysville, PA. Tel: (215) 513-1600, E-Mail: stucker@alcomprinting.com, Web Site: www.alcomprinting.com (21)

Yeakle, Kate, American Writers & Artists Inc, Delray Beach, FL. Tel: (561) 278-5557, Web Site: www.awaionline.com (36)

Year One Inc, Braselton, GA. Tel: (706) 658-2140, FAX: (706) 654-5355, E-Mail: info@yearone.com, Web Site: www.yearone.com (16)

Yearwood, Darryl, DHL Express, Plantation, FL. Tel: (954) 888-7000, (800) 225-5345, FAX: (954) 888-7310, Web Site: www.dhl.com (28)

Yeck Brothers Co, Dayton, OH. Tel: (937) 294-4000, (800) 417-2767, FAX: (937) 294-6985, E-Mail: byeck@yeck.com, Web Site: www.yeck.com (35)

Yeck, Robert, Yeck Brothers Co, Dayton, OH. Tel: (937) 294-4000, (800) 417-2767, FAX: (937) 294-6985, E-Mail: byeck@yeck.com, Web Site: www.yeck.com (35)

Yee, Amanda, Air Power USA, Los Angeles, CA. Tel: (310) 641-0830, (888) 888-8231, FAX: (310) 641-8515, Web Site: www.airpowerusa.com (12)

Yehle, Monica, Pontifical Mission Societies in the US, New York, NY. Tel: (212) 563-8700, Web Site: www.onefamilyinmission.org (1)

Yellow Book USA, Uniondale, NY. Tel: (516) 730-1900, (800) 666-8230, FAX: (845) 278-3299, Web Site: www.yellowbook.com (17)

Yellowbook, King of Prussia, PA. Tel: (610) 731-2335, Web Site: www.yellowbook.com (29)

Yenkin-Majestic, Columbus, OH. Tel: (614) 253-8511, FAX: (614) 253-6327 (16)

Andrew Yoelin & Co, Scottsdale, AZ. Tel: (602) 482-6214, E-Mail: corpdating@aol.com (20)

Yoelin, Andrew, Andrew Yoelin & Co, Scottsdale, AZ. Tel: (602) 482-6214, E-Mail: corpdating@aol.com (20)

Yoga Journal / Active Interest Media, San Francisco, CA. Tel: (415) 591-0555, Web Site: www.yogajournal.com (17)

Yohannan, Joanne, North Shore Animal League America Inc, Port Washington, NY. Tel: (516) 883-7575, Web Site: www.animalleague.org (1)

Yokogawa, Jon, interTrend Communications Inc, Long Beach, CA. Tel: (562) 733-1888, E-Mail: info@intertrend.com, Web Site: www.intertrend.com (35)

Yokozawa, Yoichi, Mitsubishi Motors North America Inc, Cypress, CA. Tel: (714) 372-6000, (888) 648-7820, Web Site: www.mitsubishicars.com (1)

Yonker, Michael E., Marriott Ownership Resorts Sales & Marketing, Orlando, FL. Tel: (407) 206-6000, (800) 850-6674, FAX: (407) 206-6097, Web Site: www.marriottvacationclub.com (19)

York Label, York, PA. Tel: (717) 266-9675, FAX: (717) 266-9834, Web Site: www.yorklabel.com (27)

York, Jennifer, Bamboo Sourcery, Sebastopol, CA. Tel: (707) 823-5866, FAX: (707) 829-8106, Web Site: www.bamboosourcery.com (8)

Yorke, Matt, IDG Enterprise, Framingham, MA. Tel: (508) 872-0080, Web Site: www.idgenterprise.com (17)

Yortsos, Yannis C, USC Viterbi School of Engineering, Los Angeles, CA. Tel: (213) 740-7832, Web Site: viterbi.usc.edu (1)

Yoshida, Reizo, USY Consulting Inc, Dumont, NJ. Tel: (201) 585-7402, FAX: (201) 585-2754, E-Mail: usyconsulting@hotmail.com (20)

Yost, Fielding, Saturn Corp, Hyattsville, MD. Tel: (301) 772-7000, (800) USA-0090, FAX: (301) 386-4538, E-Mail: sales@saturncorp.com, Web Site: www.saturncorp.com (22)

Young America's Foundation, Reston, VA. Tel: (800) USA-1776, FAX: (703) 318-9122, Web Site: www.yaf.org (1)

Young, Curt, Golfsmith International Inc, Austin, TX. Tel: (512) 821-4050, (800) 813-6897, FAX: (512) 837-9347, E-Mail: comments@golfsmith.com, Web Site: www.golfsmith.com (11)

Young. Dana, Telpro Inc, Grand Forks, ND. Tel: (701) 775-0551, FAX: (701) 775-0629 (9)

Young, David, Kansas City Chiefs, Kansas City, MO. Tel: (816) 920-9300, (888) 99-CHIEFS, FAX: (816) 923-4719, Web Site: www.kcchiefs.com (16)

Young, Dennis, Jenny Products Inc, Somerset, PA. Tel: (814) 445-3400, FAX: (814) 445-2280, Web Site: www.jennyproducts.com (16)

Young, Gregg, Argent Trading LLC, New York, NY. Tel: (212) 697-8800, FAX: (212) 697-8606, Web Site: www.Argenttrading.com (16)

Young, J. Morgan, Dassault Falcon Jet Corp, Little Ferry, NJ. Tel: (201) 440-6700, FAX: (201) 541-4515, Web Site: www.dassaultfalcon.com (16)

Young, James A., USI Affinity, Philadelphia, PA. Tel: (610) 833-2876, (800) 625-2876, FAX: (610) 265-2876, E-Mail: info@usiaffinity.com, Web Site: www.brcorp.com (15)

Young, Joanne, Baker & Taylor Inc, Charlotte, NC. Tel: (704) 998-3100, (800) 775-1800, FAX: (704) 998-3316, E-Mail: btinfo@btol.com, Web Site: www.btol.com (16)

Young, John R., Oles Envelope Corp, Baltimore, MD. Tel: (410) 243-1520, (800) 822-6537, FAX: (410) 366-7022, Web Site: www.olesenvelope.com (26)

Young, Joseph, Shortage Control Inc & SC Video, Strongsville, OH. Tel: (440) 238-5432, (800) 332-2288, FAX: (440) 238-8687, E-Mail: sales@shortagecontrol.com, Web Site: www.shortagecontrol.com (5)

Young, Mark, Shortage Control Inc & SC Video, Strongsville, OH. Tel: (440) 238-5432, (800) 332-2288, FAX: (440) 238-8687, E-Mail: sales@shortagecontrol.com, Web Site: www.shortagecontrol.com (5)

Young, Michael, Vision Marketing Inc. Englewood Cliffs, NJ. Tel: (201) 816-1560, FAX: (201) 816-1610, E-Mail: vminfo@visionmarketing.com, Web Site: www.visionmarketing.com (23)

Young, Rolland, Telpro Inc, Grand Forks, ND. Tel: (701) 775-0551, FAX: (701) 775-0629 (9)

Youngberg, Rebecca, Journal of Marketing Research, Chicago, IL. Tel: (312) 542-9000, (800) AMA-1150, FAX: (312) 542-9001, E-Mail: info@ama.org, Web Site: www.marketingpower.org (43)

Youngblood, Mike, Sportif Mail Order Inc, Sparks, NV. Tel: (888) 260-7676, FAX: (775) 356-3567, Web Site: www.sportif.com (2)

Youngerman, David, Whiting & Davis, Attleboro Falls, MA. Tel: (508) 699-4412, (800) 876-MESH, FAX: (508) 695-7606, E-Mail: info@whitinganddavis.com, Web Site: www.whitinganddavis.com (16)

Youngman, Michael L., Wisconsin Historical Foundation, Madison, WI. Tel: (608) 318-1044 (1)

Youngo, Leonard, Wendell August Forge Inc, Grove City, PA. Tel: (724) 458-8360, (800) 923-1390, FAX: (724) 458-0906, E-Mail: info@wendell.com, Web Site: www.wendellaugust.com (6)

Youngs, Ross O., Univenture Inc, Marysville, OH. Tel: (937) 645-4600, FAX: (937) 645-4700, Web Site: www.univenture.com (27)

Youngs, Tillie, 1000 Islands International Tourism Council, Alexandria Bay, NY. Tel: (315) 482-2520, (800) 847-5263, (800) 456-2267, FAX: (315) 482-5906, E-Mail: info@visit1000islands.com, Web Site: www.visit1000islands.com/visitorinfo/ (19)

Youngstown State University, Youngstown, OH. Tel: (330) 742-3064, Web Site: www.ysu.edu (41)

Younquist, Jon, Westwood Publishing Co, Glendale, CA. Tel: (818) 242-1159, FAX: (818) 247-9379 (17)

Your Choice Or Mine, San Mateo, CA. Tel: (650) 340-7959, FAX: (650) 340-0449 (16)

Your Man Tours, El Segundo, CA. Tel: (310) 649-3820, FAX: (310) 649-2118, E-Mail: ymt@earthlink.net, Web Site: www.ymtvacations.com (19)

Your Move Chess & Games, North Massapequa, NY. Tel: (516) 882-9800, (800) 645-4710, FAX: (631) 424-3405, E-Mail: icd@icdchess.com, Web Site: www.icdchess.com (11)

Yousendit Inc, Campbell, CA. Tel: (408) 879-9118, Web Site: www.yousendit.com (22)

Youtoo TV, Irving, TX. Web Site: www.youtoo.com (32)

Ysambart, Tish, Financial Executives International, Morristown, NJ. Tel: (973) 765-1000, FAX: (973) 765-1018, Web Site: www.financialexecutives.org (1)

Ysasi-Diaz, Gloria, Zoro Tools Inc, Buffalo Grove, IL. Tel: (855) 289-9676, E-Mail: askzoro@zorotools.com, Web Site: www.zorotools.com (9)

Yu, Tricia, Uncharted Country Publishing, Madison, WI. Tel: (575) 776-3470, E-Mail: ucp@taichihealth.com, Web Site: www.taichihealth.com (17)

Yuan, Walter, Enterprex International Corp, Arcadia, CA. Tel: (626) 256-1444, FAX: (626) 256-1404, E-Mail: premium@enterprex.com, Web Site: www.enterprex.com (16)

Yuanquing, Yang, Lenovo, Morrisville, NC. Tel: (919) 257-6315, (855) 253-6686, Web Site: www.uslenovo.com (3)

Yue, Cindy, Business Services Network, San Francisco, CA. Tel: (415) 282-8161, FAX: (415) 282-8176, E-Mail: sales@bsnc.com, Web Site: www.bsnc.com (28)

Yue, Harry, Business Services Network, San Francisco, CA. Tel: (415) 282-8161, FAX: (415) 282-8176, E-Mail: sales@bsnc.com, Web Site: www.bsnc.com (28)

Yuhn, Mark, Urban Science Applications Inc, Detroit, MI. Tel: (313) 259-9900, Web Site: www.urbanscience.com (20)

Yukevich, Stan, ER Carpenter, Taylor, TX. Tel: (512) 365-5833, (800) 234-9105, FAX: (512) 352-6025, Web Site: www.carpenter.com (16)

Yun, Michelle, Tucker Printers, Henrietta, NY. Tel: (585) 359-3030, Web Site: www.tuckerprinters.com (27)

David Yurman Enterprises LLC, New York, NY. Tel: (212) 896-1550, (888) 398-7626, Web Site: davidyurman.com (5)

Yurman, David, David Yurman Enterprises LLC, New York, NY. Tel: (212) 896-1550, (888) 398-7626, Web Site: davidyurman.com (5)

Yves Rocher North America Inc, Exton, PA. Tel: (450) 442-9555, (888) 909-0771, E-Mail: customer_services@yrnet.com, Web Site: www. yvesrocherusa.com (7)

Z

ZLR Ignition, Des Moines, IA. Tel: (515) 244-4456, FAX: (515) 244-5749, Web Site: www.zlrignition. com (35)

ZS Associates, Evanston, IL. Tel: (847) 492-3600, FAX: (847) 864-6280, E-Mail: inquiry@ zsassociates.com, Web Site: www.zsassociates.com (20)

Zabel, Cynthia, Brant Publications Inc, New York, NY. Tel: (212) 941-2800, FAX: (212) 941-2885, Web Site: www.interviewmagazine.com (17)

Zablocka-Peterson, Marta, GetResponse Services Inc, Wilmington, DE. Tel: (877) 362-4547, Web Site: www.getresponse.com (24)

Zacharius, Steven, Kensington Publishing Corp, New York, NY. Tel: (212) 407-1500, (800) 221-2647, FAX: (212) 407-1590, Web Site: www. kensingtonbooks.com (17)

Zachry Associates Inc, Abilene, TX. Tel: (325) 677-1342, E-Mail: bnutt@zachryinc.com, Web Site: www.zachryinc.com (28)

Zadins, Paul M., American Locker Security Systems Inc, Coppell, TX. Tel: (817) 329-1600, (800) 828-9118, E-Mail: info@americanlocker.com, Web Site: www.americanlocker.com (16)

Zagalo de Lima, Armando, Xerox Corp, Norwalk, CT. Tel: (800) 275-9376, Web Site: www.xerox.com (16)

Zagieboylo, Cyndi, National Multiple Sclerosis Society, Denver, CO. Tel: (303) 813-1052, Web Site: www. nmss.org (1)

Zahavich, Tim, St Joseph Communications, Concord, ON Canada. Tel: (905) 660-3111, FAX: (905) 669-1972, Web Site: www.stjoseph.com (27)

Zahn, Ron, Titan List & Mailing Services Inc, Deerfield Beach, FL. Tel: (888) 345-7179, E-Mail: titanlms@ bellsouth.net, Web Site: www.titanlists.com (24)

Zahn, Spencer, Spencer Zahn & Associates, Philadelphia, PA. Tel: (215) 564-5979, FAX: (215) 564-6285, E-Mail: szahn@erols.com, Web Site: www. spencerzahn.com (35)

Zajac, Raymond, CJ Hummul Co, Nescopeck, PA. Tel: (570) 752-0936, (800) 762-0235, FAX: (570) 752-0938, E-Mail: mail@hummul.com, Web Site: www. hummul.com (11)

Zakarian, Karin, Ross Metals, New York, NY. Tel: (212) 869-1407, (800) 654-ROSS (16)

Zale Corp, Irving, TX. Tel: (972) 580-4376, (800) 311-5393, Web Site: www.zalecorp.com (6)

Zales, Sam, ClickSquared, Boston, MA. Tel: (781) 622-1611, (866) 402-5425, FAX: (857) 246-7645, E-Mail: info@clicksquared.com, Web Site: clicksquared.com (20)

Zambello, Francesca, Washington National Opera, Washington, DC. Tel: (202) 467-4600, (800) 444-1324, Web Site: www.kennedy-center.org/wno (16)

Zammit, Kristin, Institutional Investor Inc, New York, NY. Tel: (212) 224-3300, FAX: (212) 224-3592, Web Site: www.institutionalinvestor.com (17)

Zampino, Nicole, ABI Inc, New York, NY. Tel: (212) 529-4500, FAX: (212) 529-4442, E-Mail: info@ abipr.com, Web Site: www.abipr.com (35)

Zang, Bill, Universal Hovercraft, Cordova, IL. Tel: (309) 654-2588, FAX: (309) 654-2588, Web Site: www.hovercraft.com (11)

Zank, Gregg A., Dow Corning Corp, Midland, MI. Tel: (989) 496-4400, (800) 248-2481, FAX: (989) 496-4572, Web Site: www.dowcorning.com (16)

Zapenski, David, Commercial Atlas & Marketing Guide, Skokie, IL. Tel: (847) 329-8100, (800) 678-7263, FAX: (800) 934-3479, E-Mail: store@ randmcnally.com, Web Site: www.randmcnally.com (43)

Zapfel, Robert, Xerox Corp, Norwalk, CT. Tel: (800) 275-9376, Web Site: www.xerox.com (16)

RL Zapin Associates Inc, New York, NY. Tel: (212) 297-6248, E-Mail: roni@rlzapinassociates.com, Web Site: www.rlzapinassociates.com (20)

Zapin, Roni L., RL Zapin Associates Inc, New York, NY. Tel: (212) 297-6248, E-Mail: roni@ rlzapinassociates.com, Web Site: www. rlzapinassociates.com (20)

Zappos.com, Las Vegas, NV. Tel: (800) 927-7671, Web Site: www.zappos.com (2)

Zardin, John, Mel Bay Publications Inc, Pacific, MO. Tel: (800) 8-MELBAY, FAX: (636) 257-5062, E-Mail: email@melbay.com, Web Site: www. melbay.com (17)

Zaretsky, Arthur, Famous Smoke Shop Inc, Easton, PA. Tel: (610) 559-7000, (800) 672-5544, FAX: (610) 559-7170, E-Mail: info@famous-smoke.com, Web Site: www.famous-smoke.com (16)

Zarghami, Cyma, Viacom Media Networks, New York, NY. Tel: (212) 258-6000, Web Site: www.viacom. com (32)

Zaritsky, David, PulseCX, Montgomeryville, PA. Tel: (215) 699-9200, FAX: (215) 699-9240, Web Site: www.pulsecx.com (35)

Zarokian, Pierre, Submit Express Inc, Burbank, CA. Tel: (818) 567-3030, (877) 737-3083, FAX: (818) 567-0202, E-Mail: feedbacks@submitexpress.com, Web Site: www.submitexpress.com (32)

Zaslav, David, Discovery Communications Inc, Silver Spring, MD. Tel: (240) 662-2000, FAX: (240) 662-1868, Web Site: corporate.discovery.com (16)

Zavistovich, Alex, Boscobel Marketing Communications Inc, Silver Spring, MD. Tel: (301) 588-2900, E-Mail: info@boscobel.com, Web Site: www. boscobel.com (35)

Zawaski, John K., Dependable Business Forms, Villa Park, IL. Tel: (630) 530-1734, FAX: (630) 530-1789, E-Mail: j.zawaski@comcast.net, Web Site: www.dependablebusinessforms.com (27)

ZCard North America, New York, NY. Tel: (212) 797-3450, Web Site: www.zcard.com (31)

Zdravecky, Robert G., Ames Taping Tool System Inc, Stone Mountain, GA. Tel: (770) 243-2647, (800) 303-1827, FAX: (770) 243-2658, Web Site: www. amestools.com (9)

Zeanah, Eric, American Accessories International, Knoxville, TN. Tel: (865) 525-9100, Web Site: www.americanaccessoriesintl.com (33)

Zed Marketing Group, Edmond, OK. Tel: (405) 348-8145, FAX: (405) 348-5541, E-Mail: zed@zedmktg. com, Web Site: www.zedmktg.com (27)

Zefkin, Daniel, Zephyr Media Group Inc, Evanston, IL. Tel: (847) 328-1519, FAX: (847) 328-3518, Web Site: www.zephyr-media.com (35)

Zeh, Tim, Fisher Scientific, Pittsburgh, PA. Tel: (800) 766-7000, FAX: (800) 772-7702, Web Site: www. fishersci.com (16)

Zeisler, Stacye, The Jewish Federation of Greater Washington, North Bethesda, MD. Tel: (301) 230-7200, Web Site: www.shalomdc.org (1)

Zeitz, Joshua, American Heritage Picture Library, New York, NY. Tel: (212) 206-5107, (800) 777-1222, FAX: (212) 367-3151, Web Site: www. americanheritage.com (38)

Zekiel, Gretchen, Tax Management Inc, Bethesda, MD. Tel: (202) 452-4200, FAX: (202) 496-6013 (17)

Zekley, Elizabeth, Lark in the Morning, Mendocino, CA. Tel: (707) 964-5569, FAX: (707) 964-1979, E-Mail: info@larkinam.com, Web Site: www. larkinthemorning.com (5)

Zekley, Mickie, Lark in the Morning, Mendocino, CA. Tel: (707) 964-5569, FAX: (707) 964-1979, E-Mail: info@larkinam.com, Web Site: www. larkinthemorning.com (5)

Zeldner, Ishai, Moon Shine Trading Co, Woodland, CA. Tel: (530) 668-0660, (800) 678-1226, FAX: (530) 668-6061, E-Mail: store@moonshinetrading.com, Web Site: www.moonshinetrading.com (4)

Neil Zelenetz & Associates, East Hampton, NY. Tel: (516) 746-2981, E-Mail: nzelenetz@aol.com (20)

Zelenetz, Neil, Neil Zelenetz & Associates, East Hampton, NY. Tel: (516) 746-2981, E-Mail: nzelenetz@ aol.com (20)

Zelinskas, Mike, Halsom Home Care Inc, Centerville, OH. Tel: (937) 438-6600, (800) 345-5438, FAX: (937) 438-6620, E-Mail: main@halsom.com, Web Site: www.halsom.com (16)

Zeller, Ben, Queen Bee Gardens, Lovell, WY. Tel: (307) 548-2818, (800) 225-7553, FAX: (307) 548-7994, E-Mail: queenbee@queenbeegardens.com, Web Site: queenbeegardens.com (4)

Zeller, Bessie, Queen Bee Gardens, Lovell, WY. Tel: (307) 548-2818, (800) 225-7553, FAX: (307) 548-7994, E-Mail: queenbee@queenbeegardens.com, Web Site: queenbeegardens.com (4)

Zeller, Gene, Queen Bee Gardens, Lovell, WY. Tel: (307) 548-2818, (800) 225-7553, FAX: (307) 548-7994, E-Mail: queenbee@queenbeegardens.com, Web Site: queenbeegardens.com (4)

Zeller, John H., University of Pennsylvania, Philadelphia, PA. Tel: (215) 898-5000, FAX: (215) 898-9659, Web Site: www.upenn.edu (1)

Zellmer, Gary, Taylor Corp, North Mankato, MN. Tel: (507) 625-2828, FAX: (507) 625-3388 (16)

Zelstar, Craig, NNE Marketing, Concord, MA. Tel: (617) 429-7999, Web Site: www.nnemarketing.com (1)

Zemrak, Gary, Blethen Maine Newspapers Inc, Portland, ME. Tel: (207) 791-6650, FAX: (207) 791-6925, Web Site: www.mainetoday.com (17)

Zemsky, Joann, GMI Distribution, Somerset, NJ. Tel: (732) 846-4800, FAX: (732) 846-4709, E-Mail: keith@gmidistribution.com, Web Site: www. gmidistribution.com (28)

ZenithOptimedia Direct, New York, NY. Tel: (212) 859-5100, FAX: (212) 757-9495, Web Site: www. zenithoptimedia.com (35)

Zenos, George, JDR Microdevices, Dublin, CA. Tel: (650) 625-1400, (800) 538-5000, FAX: (800) 538-5005, E-Mail: sales@jdr.com, Web Site: www.jdr. com (3)

Zentmaier, Robert L., Photo Researchers Inc, New York, NY. Tel: (212) 758-3420, (800) 833-9033, FAX: (212) 355-0731, E-Mail: info@photoresearchers.com, Web Site: www.photoresearchers.com (38)

Zeoli, Michael, PNT Marketing Services, Inc, Long Island City, NY. Tel: (718) 433-4063, (888) 768-2210, FAX: (914) 428-0504, E-Mail: tony@pntmarketingservices.com, Web Site: www.pntmarketingservices.com (22)

Zepeda, Angela, Lowe Campbell Ewald, Detroit, MI. Tel: (586) 574-3400, E-Mail: lowecampbellewald@lowe-ce.com, Web Site: www.lowecampbellewald.com (35)

Zepeda, Angela, Quigley Simpson, Los Angeles, CA. Tel: (310) 996-5800, E-Mail: info@quigleysimpson.com, Web Site: www.quigleysimpson.com (35)

Zephyr Media Group Inc, Evanston, IL. Tel: (847) 328-1519, FAX: (847) 328-3518, Web Site: www.zephyr-media.com (35)

Zeppo Marketing Inc, Brooklyn, NY. Tel: (212) 308-5734, Fax: (646) 304-7364, Web Site: www.zeppomarketing.com (32)

Greg Zerovnik, Upland, CA. Tel: (909) 982-3787, FAX: (909) 931-2402 (36)

Zerovnik, Greg, Greg Zerovnik, Upland, CA. Tel: (909) 982-3787, FAX: (909) 931-2402 (36)

Zeta Interactive, New York, NY. Tel: (212) 660-2500, FAX: (212) 967-1028, E-Mail: info@zetainteractive.com, Web Site: www.zetainteractive.com (32)

Zhang, John, Systems Analytics Inc, Needham, MA. Tel: (781) 444-4837, E-Mail: info@systemsanalytics.com, Web Site: www.systemsanalytics.com (20)

Zheng, Shusheng, 3Com Corp, Marlborough, MA. Tel: (508) 323-5000, FAX: (508) 323-1111 (22)

Ziegler, Ann E., CDW Corp, Vernon Hills, IL. Tel: (847) 465-6000, (847) 371-6090, Web Site: www.cdw.com (16)

Ziegler, David, Ace Hardware Corp, Oak Brook, IL. Tel: (630) 990-6600, FAX: (630) 990-6838, Web Site: www.acehardware.com (16)

Ziegler, Jennifer E., California Society of CPA's, San Mateo, CA. Tel: (800) 922-5272, FAX: (650) 522-3009, E-Mail: info@culcpa.org, Web Site: www.calcpa.org (1)

Zier, Dawn M., NutriSystem Inc, Fort Washington, PA. Tel: (215) 706-5300, (800) 435-4074, FAX: (215) 706-5388, E-Mail: customerservice@nutrisystem.com, Web Site: www.nutrisystem.com (7)

Zieser, John S., Meredith Corp, Des Moines, IA. Tel: (515) 284-3000, FAX: (515) 284-2700, Web Site: www.meredith.com (17)

Ziff Davis Media Inc, New York, NY. Tel: (212) 503-5100, FAX: (212) 503-5023, Web Site: www.ziffdavis.com (17)

Zig Ziglar Corp, Plano, TX. Tel: (972) 233-9191, (800) 527-0306, FAX: (469) 321-7556, E-Mail: info@ziglar.com, Web Site: www.zigziglar.com (16)

Ziglar, Tom, Zig Ziglar Corp, Plano, TX. Tel: (972) 233-9191, (800) 527-0306, FAX: (469) 321-7556, E-Mail: info@ziglar.com, Web Site: www.zigziglar.com (16)

Ziglar, Zig, Zig Ziglar Corp, Plano, TX. Tel: (972) 233-9191, (800) 527-0306, FAX: (469) 321-7556, E-Mail: info@ziglar.com, Web Site: www.zigziglar.com (16)

Zilling, Mark, MeritDirect, Rye Brook, NY. Tel: (914) 368-1000, FAX: (914) 368-1150, E-Mail: hq@meritdirect.com, Web Site: www.meritdirect.com (23)

Zillner, Lenexa, KS. Tel: (913) 599-3230, Web Site: zillner.com (35)

Zim-American Israeli Shipping Co Inc, Staten Island, NY. Tel: (718) 313-1950, Web Site: www.zim.com (16)

Zimbalist, Michael, The New York Times Co, New York, NY. Tel: (212) 556-1234, Web Site: www.nytimes.com (17)

Zimmer, John J., Transcat, Rochester, NY. Tel: (585) 352-9460, (800) 800-5001, FAX: (585) 352-1486, Web Site: www.transcat.com (16)

Zimmer, Mark A., The Keystone Equities Group, Oaks, PA. Tel: (610) 415-6300, (800) 715-9905, FAX: (610) 415-6328, Web Site: www.keystoneequities.com (20)

Zimmerling, Judy, Blue Valley Tele-Marketing Inc, Home, KS. Tel: (785) 799-3500, (800) 882-0803, FAX: (785) 799-3504, E-Mail: info@bluevalleytelemarketing.com (29)

Zimmerman Advertising, Fort Lauderdale, Fl.. Tel: (954) 644-4000, E-Mail: contact@zadv.com, Web Site: www.zadv.com (35)

Zimmerman Business Consulting Inc, New York, NY. Tel: (212) 860-3107, FAX: (212) 860-7730, E-Mail: ljzzbci@aol.com, Web Site: www.zbcinc.com (20)

Zimmerman Irrigation Inc, Biglerville, PA. Tel: (717) 337-2727, (800) 452-5699, FAX: (717) 337-1785, E-Mail: info@trikl-eez.com, Web Site: www.trickl-eez.com (16)

Zimmerman-McDonald Machinery Inc, Saint Louis, MO. Tel: (314) 291-9360, FAX: (314) 291-2981, E-Mail: zimsales@zimmermanmcdonald.com, Web Site: www.zimmermanmcdonald.com (16)

Zimmerman, Brad, Zimmerman-McDonald Machinery Inc, Saint Louis, MO. Tel: (314) 291-9360, FAX: (314) 291-2981, E-Mail: zimsales@zimmermanmcdonald.com, Web Site: www.zimmermanmcdonald.com (16)

Zimmerman, Clayton, Stratmar Systems Inc, Port Chester, NY. Tel: (914) 937-7171, (800) 866-2399, FAX: (914) 937-6045, E-Mail: info@stratmar.com, Web Site: www.stratmar.com (29)

Zimmerman, Dan, Photoworks, Cleveland, OH. Tel: (206) 281-1390, (800) PHOTOWORKS, FAX: (206) 284-5357, E-Mail: info@photoworks.com, Web Site: www.photoworks.com (16)

Zimmerman, Heidi, USA TODAY, Mc Lean, VA. Tel: (703) 854-3400, (800) 872-0001, E-Mail: accuracy@usatoday.com, Web Site: www.usatoday.com (17)

Zimmerman, John, Gates Corp, Denver, CO. Tel: (303) 744-1911, FAX: (303) 744-4000, Web Site: www.gates.com (9)

Zimmerman, Leonard J., Zimmerman Business Consulting Inc, New York, NY. Tel: (212) 860-3107, FAX: (212) 860-7730, E-Mail: ljzzbci@aol.com, Web Site: www.zbcinc.com (20)

Zimmerman, P.R., Kano Laboratories, Nashville, TN. Tel: (615) 833-4101, (800) 311-3374, FAX: (615) 833-5790, Web Site: www.kanolabs.com (16)

Zimmerman, Peter, Kano Laboratories, Nashville, TN. Tel: (615) 833-4101, (800) 311-3374, FAX: (615) 833-5790, Web Site: www.kanolabs.com (16)

Zimmerman, Stan, Zimmerman-McDonald Machinery Inc, Saint Louis, MO. Tel: (314) 291-9360, FAX: (314) 291-2981, E-Mail: zimsales@zimmermanmcdonald.com, Web Site: www.zimmermanmcdonald.com (16)

Zimmerman, Tom, Pharmavite Corp LLC (HQ), Northridge, CA. Tel: (818) 221-6200, (800) 423-2405, FAX: (818) 221-6618, Web Site: www.pharmavite.com (16)

Zimpleman, Larry D., The Principal Financial Group, Des Moines, IA. Tel: (515) 247-5111, (800) 986-3343, FAX: (515) 246-5475, Web Site: www.principal.com (15)

Zindel, Jon Walter, William Blair & Co LLC, Chicago, IL. Tel: (312) 236-1600, (800) 621-0687, FAX: (312) 368-9418, E-Mail: info@williamblair.com, Web Site: www.williamblair.com (14)

Zinio Systems Inc, San Francisco, CA. Tel: (415) 494-2700, FAX: (415) 494-2701, Web Site: www.zinio.com (31)

Zink, Alan, USI Affinity, Philadelphia, PA. Tel: (610) 833-2876, (800) 625-2876, FAX: (610) 265-2876, E-Mail: info@usiaffinity.com, Web Site: www.brcorp.com (15)

Zink, Mark, Gorham's Inc, Springfield, IL. Tel: (217) 544-1727, FAX: (217) 544-1623, E-Mail: gorhams@gorhams.com, Web Site: www.gorhams.com (33)

Zinkel, James R., Camelot Enterprises, Bristol, WI. Tel: (262) 857-2695 (9)

Zinkel, Sandra L., Camelot Enterprises, Bristol, WI. Tel: (262) 857-2695 (9)

ZIP Mailing Services Inc, Landover, MD. Tel: (301) 386-3633, FAX: (301) 386-3637, E-Mail: zipmail@zipmailing.com, Web Site: www.zipmailing.com (28)

Zircon Co Inc, Salem, MA. Tel: (978) 741-7000, FAX: (978) 532-0012 (22)

Zirzow, William, Town Money Saver, Lucas, OH. Tel: (419) 892-1913, Web Site: www.townmoneysaver.com (31)

Zitzow, Tish, Petra Industries, Edmond, OK. Tel: (405) 216-2100, FAX: (405) 216-2102, Web Site: www.patra.com (34)

Zlotnik, A., Air-Scent International, Pittsburgh, PA. Tel: (800) 247-0770, FAX: (412) 252-2000, E-Mail: laura@aromaresource.com, Web Site: www.airscent.com (16)

Zodhiates, Philip, Response Unlimited, Waynesboro, VA. Tel: (540) 943-6721, FAX: (540) 943-0841, E-Mail: info@responseunlimited.com, Web Site: www.responseunlimited.com (23)

Zoe Marketing, San Diego, CA. Tel: (858) 408-1700 (20)

Zoghbi, George, The Kraft Heinz Co, Pittsburgh, PA. Tel: (412) 456-5700, Web Site: www.kraftheinzcompany.com (4)

Zoltners, Andris, ZS Associates, Evanston, IL. Tel: (847) 492-3600, FAX: (847) 864-6280, E-Mail: inquiry@zsassociates.com, Web Site: www.zsassociates.com (20)

Zompa, Paul, Ecological Fibers Inc, Lunenburg, MA. Tel: (978) 537-0003, FAX: (978) 537-2238, E-Mail: jquill@ecofibers.com (25)

Zondag, Richard, JW Jung Seed Co, Randolph, WI. Tel: (800) 297-3123, Web Site: www.jungseed.com (8)

Zondag, Richard, McClure & Zimmerman, Randolph, WI. Tel: (800) 883-6998, FAX: (800) 374-6120, Web Site: www.mzbulb.com (8)

Zondervan Corp, Grand Rapids, MI. Tel: (616) 698-6900, (800) 727-3060, FAX: (616) 698-3235, Web Site: www.zondervan.com (17)

Zones Inc, Auburn, WA. Tel: (253) 205-3000, (800) 408-9663, FAX: (425) 430-3626, E-Mail: corpsales@zones.com, Web Site: www.zones.com (3)

Zonin, Richard, Simplicity Pattern Co Inc/Style Patterns Ltd/New Look English Pattern Co Ltd, New York, NY. Tel: (212) 372-0500, (800) 653-7301, Web Site: www.simplicitypatt.com (8)

Zoological Society of San Diego, San Diego, CA. Tel: (619) 231-1515, FAX: (619) 557-3937, Web Site: www.sandiegozoo.org (1)

Zoom Information Inc, Waltham, MA. Tel: (781) 693-7500, FAX: (781) 693-7510, Web Site: www.zoominfo.com (22)

Zoradi, Michael, Medcom Inc, Cypress, CA. Tel: (800) 877-1443, FAX: (714) 891-3140, E-Mail: lhammonds@medcominc.com, Web Site: www.medcominc.com (17)

Zoria, Jill, Communifx Corp, Cranberry, PA. Tel: (724) 935-8655, Web Site: www.communifax.com (27)

Zorn, Scott, Direct Resources Group Inc, Seattle, WA. Tel: (206) 455-6157, FAX: (206) 749-0005, E-Mail: results@drg.com, Web Site: www.drg.com (35)

Zoro Tools Inc, Buffalo Grove, IL. Tel: (855) 289-9676, E-Mail: askzoro@zorotools.com, Web Site: www.zorotools.com (9)

Zotos International, Darien, CT. Tel: (203) 655-8911, (800) 242-9283, (800) 242-WAVE, FAX: (203) 656-7890, E-Mail: HumanResources@zotosintl.com, Web Site: www.zotos.com (16)

Zouire, Leawood, KS. Tel: (913) 384-6888, (800) 346-8991, FAX: (913) 384-5757, E-Mail: info@zouire.com, Web Site: www.zouire.com (33)

Zuccarini, Deborah, Experian, Costa Mesa, CA. Tel: (714) 830-7000, (888) EXPERIAN, FAX: (949) 242-2938, Web Site: www.experian.com (30)

Zucker, Hemi, Protus, Ottawa, ON Canada. Tel: (613) 733-0000, (888) 733-0000, E-Mail: info@protus.com, Web Site: www.protus.com (32)

Zucker, Janice, Jaz Holdings LLC, Liberty Corner, NJ. Tel: (973) 574-7600, (800) 999-9554, FAX: (973) 944-5073, E-Mail: webmaster@regentbook.com, Web Site: www.regentbook.com (16)

Zucker, Joshua, Jaz Holdings LLC, Liberty Corner, NJ. Tel: (973) 574-7600, (800) 999-9554, FAX: (973) 944-5073, E-Mail: webmaster@regentbook.com, Web Site: www.regentbook.com (16)

Zuckerberg, Lloyd P., New York Landmarks Conservancy, New York, NY. Tel: (212) 995-5260, FAX: (212) 995-5268, Web Site: www.nylandmarks.org (1)

Zuckerberg, Mark, Facebook Inc, Menlo Park, CA. Tel: (650) 543-4800, Web Site: www.facebook.com (31)

Zuckerman, Mitchell, Sotheby's, New York, NY. Tel: (212) 606-7000, FAX: (212) 606-7107, Web Site: www.sothebys.com (6)

Zuckerman, Mortimer B., US News & World Report, Washington, DC. Tel: (202) 955-2000, Web Site: www.usnews.com (17)

Zuckerman, Steven, Clipper Magazine, Mountville, PA. Tel: (888) 569-5100, FAX: (717) 569-5101, Web Site: www.clippermagazine.com (31)

Zuckermandel, Jim, Zed Marketing Group, Edmond, OK. Tel: (405) 348-8145, FAX: (405) 348-5541, E-Mail: zed@zedmktg.com, Web Site: www.zedmktg.com (27)

Zukowski, Perry, General Binding Corp, Northbrook, IL. Tel: (800) 723-4000, FAX: (847) 272-1389, (800) 952-1166, Web Site: www.gbc.com (10)

Zullo, Eda, Smith Hanley Associates, Southport, CT. Tel: (203) 319-4300, (888) 221-2900, FAX: (203) 319-4320, Web Site: www.smithhanley.com (20)

Zuniga, Diana G., Investors Alliance Inc, Austin, TX. Tel: (512) 480-8100, FAX: (512) 480-9100, E-Mail: info@powerinvestor.com, Web Site: www.powerinvestor.com (1)

Zunker, Bob, Direct Mail Solutions LLC, Carol Stream, IL. Tel: (630) 653-6863, FAX: (630) 653-7144, E-Mail: support@dmspostal.com, Web Site: www.dmspostal.com (28)

Zupan, Leo, Discover Publications, Worthington, OH. Tel: (877) 872-3080, FAX: (614) 431-3324, E-Mail: info@discoverpubs.com, Web Site: www.discoverpubs.com (17)

Zuraitis, Marita, Horace Mann Educators Corp, Springfield, IL. Tel: (217) 789-2500, FAX: (217) 788-5161, Web Site: www.horacemann.com (15)

Zurich, Schaumburg, IL. Tel: (847) 605-3712, (800) 382-2150, FAX: (847) 605-6403, Web Site: www.zurichna.com (15)

Zvesper, Joseph, American Appraisal Associates, Milwaukee, WI. Tel: (414) 271-7240, (800) 558-8650, FAX: (414) 221-7065, Web Site: www.american-appraisal.com (14)

Zwart, Fred, Datum Timing, Test & Measurement, Beverly, MA. Tel: (978) 927-8220, FAX: (978) 927-4099, E-Mail: wriley@datum.com, Web Site: www.datum.com (9)

Zwiebel, Joe, Alliance of Area Business Publications, Redondo Beach, CA. Tel: (310) 379-8261, FAX: (310) 379-8283, E-Mail: info@bizpubs.org, Web Site: www.bizpubs.org (1)

Zwiefka, Wojciech, GetResponse Services Inc, Wilmington, DE. Tel: (877) 362-4547, Web Site: www.getresponse.com (24)

Zylkuski, Gene, SmartSource Corp, Bedford, MA. Tel: (781) 785-3375, (800) 239-0239, Web Site: www.smartsourceonline.com (32)

Zyontz, Robert, Princeton Marketech, Princeton Junction, NJ. Tel: (609) 936-0021, FAX: (609) 936-0015, E-Mail: bzyontz@princetonmarketech.com, Web Site: www.princetonmarketech.com (35)

Zysman, Dennis, The Du-Rite Group Inc, Englewood, NJ. Tel: (201) 387-7000, FAX: (201) 385-8513, E-Mail: information@duriteconstruction.com, Web Site: www.duriteconstruction.com (16)

Zysman, Gary, The Du-Rite Group Inc, Englewood, NJ. Tel: (201) 387-7000, FAX: (201) 385-8513, E-Mail: information@duriteconstruction.com, Web Site: www.duriteconstruction.com (16)